P9-CRK-372
AVON FREE PUBLIC LIBRARY
Louis Mitnick Trust

THE OXFORD ENGLISH DICTIONARY

SECOND EDITION

THE OXFORD ENGLISH DICTIONARY

First Edited by

JAMES A. H. MURRAY, HENRY BRADLEY, W. A. CRAIGIE
and C. T. ONIONS

COMBINED WITH

A SUPPLEMENT TO THE OXFORD ENGLISH DICTIONARY

Edited by

R. W. BURCHFIELD

AND RESET WITH CORRECTIONS, REVISIONS
AND ADDITIONAL VOCABULARY

THE OXFORD ENGLISH DICTIONARY

SECOND EDITION

Prepared by
J. A. SIMPSON *and* E. S. C. WEINER

VOLUME XIV
Rob–Sequyle

CLARENDON PRESS · OXFORD
1989

Oxford University Press, Walton Street, Oxford OX2 6DP
Oxford New York Toronto
Delhi Bombay Calcutta Madras Karachi
Petaling Jaya Singapore Hong Kong Tokyo
Nairobi Dar es Salaam Cape Town
Melbourne Auckland
and associated companies in
Berlin Ibadan

British Library Cataloguing in Publication Data
Oxford English dictionary.—2nd ed.
1. English language-Dictionaries
I. Simpson, J. A. (John Andrew), 1953-
II. Weiner, Edmund S. C., 1950-
423
ISBN 0-19-861226-5 (vol. XIV)
ISBN 0-19-861186-2 (set)

Library of Congress Cataloging-in-Publication Data
The Oxford English dictionary.—2nd ed.
prepared by J. A. Simpson and E. S. C. Weiner
Bibliography: p.
ISBN 0-19-861226-5 (vol. XIV)
ISBN 0-19-861186-2 (set)
1. English language—Dictionaries. I. Simpson, J. A.
II. Weiner, E. S. C. III. Oxford University Press.
PE1625.087 1989
423—dc19 88-5330

Data capture by ICC, Fort Washington, Pa.
Text-processing by Oxford University Press
Typesetting by Filmtype Services Ltd., Scarborough, N. Yorks.
Manufactured in the United States of America by
Rand McNally & Company, Taunton, Mass.

KEY TO THE PRONUNCIATION

THE pronunciations given are those in use in the educated speech of southern England (the so-called 'Received Standard'), and the keywords given are to be understood as pronounced in such speech.

I. *Consonants*

b, d, f, k, l, m, n, p, t, v, z *have their usual English values*

g as in *go* (gəʊ)
h ... *ho*! (həʊ)
r ... *r*un (rʌn), te*rr*ier ('tɛrɪə(r))
(r) ... he*r* (hɜː(r))
s ... *s*ee (siː), *success* (sək'sɛs)
w ... *w*ear (wɛə(r))
hw ... *wh*en (hwɛn)
j ... *y*es (jɛs)

θ as in *th*in (θɪn), ba*th* (bɑːθ)
ð ... *th*en (ðɛn), ba*the* (beɪð)
ʃ ... *sh*op (ʃɒp), di*sh* (dɪʃ)
tʃ ... *ch*op (tʃɒp), di*tch* (dɪtʃ)
ʒ ... vi*s*ion ('vɪʒən), dé*j*euner (deʒøne)
dʒ ... *j*u*dg*e (dʒʌdʒ)
ŋ ... si*ng*i*ng* ('sɪŋɪŋ), thi*n*k (θiŋk)
ŋg ... fi*ng*er ('fɪŋgə(r))

(FOREIGN AND NON-SOUTHERN)

ʎ as in It. serra*gl*io (ser'raʎo)
ɲ ... Fr. co*gn*ac (kɔɲak)
x ... Ger. a*ch* (ax), Sc. lo*ch* (lɒx), Sp. fri*j*oles (fri'xoles)
ç ... Ger. i*ch* (ɪç), Sc. ni*ch*t (nɪçt)
ɣ ... North Ger. sagen ('zaːɣən)
c ... Afrikaans baardmanne*tj*ie ('baːrtmanəci)
ɥ ... Fr. c*u*isine (kɥizin)

Symbols in parentheses are used to denote elements that may be omitted either by individual speakers or in particular phonetic contexts: e.g. *bottle* ('bɒt(ə)l), *Mercian* ('mɜːʃ(ɪ)ən), *suit* (s(j)uːt), *impromptu* (ɪm'prɒm(p)tjuː), *father* ('fɑːðə(r)).

II. *Vowels and Diphthongs*

SHORT

ɪ as in p*i*t (pɪt), -n*e*ss, (-nɪs)
ɛ ... p*e*t (pɛt), Fr. *sept* (sɛt)
æ ... p*a*t (pæt)
ʌ ... p*u*tt (pʌt)
ɒ ... p*o*t (pɒt)
ʊ ... p*u*t (pʊt)
ə ... *a*nother (ə'nʌðə(r))
(ə) ... beat*e*n ('biːt(ə)n)
i ... Fr. s*i* (si)
e ... Fr. b*é*b*é* (bebe)
a ... Fr. m*a*ri (mari)
ɑ ... Fr. b*â*timent (bɑtimɑ̃)
ɔ ... Fr. h*o*mme (ɔm)
o ... Fr. *eau* (o)
ø ... Fr. p*eu* (pø)
œ ... Fr. b*oe*uf (bœf) c*oeu*r (kœr)
u ... Fr. d*ou*ce (dus)
ʏ ... Ger. M*ü*ller ('mʏlər)
y ... Fr. d*u* (dy)

LONG

iː as in b*ea*n (biːn)
ɑː ... b*ar*n (bɑːn)
ɔː ... b*or*n (bɔːn)
uː ... b*oo*n (buːn)
ɜː ... b*ur*n (bɜːn)
eː ... Ger. Schn*ee* (ʃneː)
ɛː ... Ger. F*ä*hre ('fɛːrə)
aː ... Ger. T*a*g (taːk)
oː ... Ger. S*oh*n (zoːn)
øː ... Ger. G*oe*the ('gøːtə)
yː ... Ger. gr*ü*n (gryːn)

NASAL

ɛ̃, æ̃ as in Fr. f*in* (fɛ̃, fæ̃)
ɑ̃ ... Fr. fr*anc* (frɑ̃)
ɔ̃ ... Fr. b*on* (bɔ̃)
œ̃ ... Fr. *un* (œ̃)

DIPHTHONGS, etc.

eɪ as in b*ay* (beɪ)
aɪ ... b*uy* (baɪ)
ɔɪ ... b*oy* (bɔɪ)
əʊ ... n*o* (nəʊ)
aʊ ... n*ow* (naʊ)
ɪə ... p*ee*r (pɪə(r))
ɛə ... p*ai*r (pɛə(r))
ʊə ... t*ou*r (tʊə(r))
ɔə ... b*oa*r (bɔə(r))

aɪə as in f*ie*ry ('faɪərɪ)
aʊə ... s*ou*r (saʊə(r))

The incidence of main stress is shown by a superior stress mark (') preceding the stressed syllable, and a secondary stress by an inferior stress mark (ˌ), e.g. *pronunciation* (prəˌnʌnsɪ'eɪʃ(ə)n).

For further explanation of the transcription used, see *General Explanations*, Volume I.

LIST OF ABBREVIATIONS, SIGNS, ETC.

Some abbreviations listed here in italics are also in certain cases printed in roman type, and vice versa.

a. (in Etym.)	adoption of, adopted from
a (as *a* 1850)	*ante*, 'before', 'not later than'
a.	adjective
abbrev.	abbreviation (of)
abl.	ablative
absol.	absolute, -ly
Abstr.	(in titles) *Abstract, -s*
acc.	accusative
Acct.	(in titles) *Account*
A.D.	*Anno Domini*
ad. (in Etym.)	adaptation of
Add.	Addenda
adj.	adjective
Adv.	(in titles) *Advance, -d, -s*
adv.	adverb
advb.	adverbial, -ly
Advt.	advertisement
Aeronaut.	(as label) in Aeronautics; (in titles) *Aeronautic, -al, -s*
AF., AFr.	Anglo-French
Afr.	Africa, -n
Agric.	(as label) in Agriculture; (in titles) *Agriculture, -al*
Alb.	Albanian
Amer.	American
Amer. Ind.	American Indian
Anat.	(as label) in Anatomy; (in titles) *Anatomy, -ical*
Anc.	(in titles) *Ancient*
Anglo-Ind.	Anglo-Indian
Anglo-Ir.	Anglo-Irish
Ann.	Annals
Anthrop., Anthropol.	(as label) in Anthropology; (in titles) *Anthropology, -ical*
Antiq.	(as label) in Antiquities; (in titles) *Antiquity*
aphet.	aphetic, aphetized
app.	apparently
Appl.	(in titles) *Applied*
Applic.	(in titles) *Application, -s*
appos.	appositive, -ly
Arab.	Arabic
Aram.	Aramaic
Arch.	in Architecture
arch.	archaic
Archæol.	in Archæology
Archit.	(as label) in Architecture; (in titles) *Architecture, -al*
Arm.	Armenian
assoc.	association
Astr.	in Astronomy
Astrol.	in Astrology
Astron.	(in titles) *Astronomy, -ical*
Astronaut.	(in titles) *Astronautic, -s*
attrib.	attributive, -ly
Austral.	Australian
Autobiogr.	(in titles) *Autobiography, -ical*
A.V.	Authorized Version
B.C.	Before Christ
B.C.	(in titles) British Columbia
bef.	before
Bibliogr.	(as label) in Bibliography; (in titles) *Bibliography, -ical*
Biochem.	(as label) in Biochemistry; (in titles) *Biochemistry, -ical*
Biol.	(as label) in Biology; (in titles) *Biology, -ical*
Bk.	*Book*
Bot.	(as label) in Botany; (in titles) *Botany, -ical*
Bp.	Bishop
Brit.	(in titles) *Britain, British*
Bulg.	Bulgarian

Bull.	(in titles) *Bulletin*
c (as *c* 1700)	*circa*, 'about'
c. (as 19th c.)	century
Cal.	(in titles) *Calendar*
Cambr.	(in titles) *Cambridge*
Canad.	Canadian
Cat.	Catalan
catachr.	catachrestically
Catal.	(in titles) *Catalogue*
Celt.	Celtic
Cent.	(in titles) *Century, Central*
Cent. Dict.	*Century Dictionary*
Cf., cf.	*confer*, 'compare'
Ch.	Church
Chem.	(as label) in Chemistry; (in titles) *Chemistry, -ical*
Chr.	(in titles) *Christian*
Chron.	(in titles) *Chronicle*
Chronol.	(in titles) *Chronology, -ical*
Cinemat., Cinematogr.	in Cinematography
Clin.	(in titles) *Clinical*
cl. L.	classical Latin
cogn. w.	cognate with
Col.	(in titles) *Colonel, Colony*
Coll.	(in titles) *Collection*
collect.	collective, -ly
colloq.	colloquial, -ly
comb.	combined, -ing
Comb.	Combinations
Comm.	in Commercial usage
Communic.	in Communications
comp.	compound, composition
Compan.	(in titles) *Companion*
compar.	comparative
compl.	complement
Compl.	(in titles) *Complete*
Conc.	(in titles) *Concise*
Conch.	in Conchology
concr.	concrete, -ly
Conf.	(in titles) *Conference*
Congr.	(in titles) *Congress*
conj.	conjunction
cons.	consonant
const.	construction, construed with
contr.	contrast (with)
Contrib.	(in titles) *Contribution*
Corr.	(in titles) *Correspondence*
corresp.	corresponding (to)
Cotgr.	R. Cotgrave, *Dictionarie of the French and English Tongues*
cpd.	compound
Crit.	(in titles) *Criticism, Critical*
Cryst.	in Crystallography
Cycl.	(in titles) *Cyclopædia, -ic*
Cytol.	(in titles) *Cytology, -ical*
Da.	Danish
D.A.	*Dictionary of Americanisms*
D.A.E.	*Dictionary of American English*
dat.	dative
D.C.	District of Columbia
Deb.	(in titles) *Debate, -s*
def.	definite, -ition
dem.	demonstrative
deriv.	derivative, -ation
derog.	derogatory
Descr.	(in titles) *Description, -tive*
Devel.	(in titles) *Development, -al*
Diagn.	(in titles) *Diagnosis, Diagnostic*
dial.	dialect, -al

Dict.	Dictionary; *spec.*, the *Oxford English Dictionary*
dim.	diminutive
Dis.	(in titles) *Disease*
Diss.	(in titles) *Dissertation*
D.O.S.T.	*Dictionary of the Older Scottish Tongue*
Du.	Dutch
E.	East
Eccl.	(as label) in Ecclesiastical usage; (in titles) *Ecclesiastical*
Ecol.	in Ecology
Econ.	(as label) in Economics; (in titles) *Economy, -ics*
ed.	edition
E.D.D.	*English Dialect Dictionary*
Edin.	(in titles) *Edinburgh*
Educ.	(as label) in Education; (in titles) *Education, -al*
EE.	Early English
e.g.	*exempli gratia*, 'for example'
Electr.	(as label) in Electricity; (in titles) *Electricity, -ical*
Electron.	(in titles) *Electronic, -s*
Elem.	(in titles) *Element, -ary*
ellipt.	elliptical, -ly
Embryol.	in Embryology
e.midl.	east midland (dialect)
Encycl.	(in titles) *Encyclopædia, -ic*
Eng.	England, English
Engin.	in Engineering
Ent.	in Entomology
Entomol.	(in titles) *Entomology, -logical*
erron.	erroneous, -ly
esp.	especially
Ess.	(in titles) *Essay, -s*
et al.	*et alii*, 'and others'
etc.	et cetera
Ethnol.	in Ethnology
etym.	etymology
euphem.	euphemistically
Exam.	(in titles) *Examination*
exc.	except
Exerc.	(in titles) *Exercise, -s*
Exper.	(in titles) *Experiment, -al*
Explor.	(in titles) *Exploration, -s*
f.	feminine
f. (in Etym.)	formed on
f. (in subordinate entries)	form of
F.	French
fem. (*rarely* f.)	feminine
fig.	figurative, -ly
Finn.	Finnish
fl.	*floruit*, 'flourished'
Found.	(in titles) *Foundation, -s*
Fr.	French
freq.	frequent, -ly
Fris.	Frisian
Fund.	(in titles) *Fundamental, -s*
Funk or *Funk's Stand. Dict.*	*Funk and Wagnalls Standard Dictionary*
G.	German
Gael.	Gaelic
Gaz.	(in titles) *Gazette*
gen.	genitive
gen.	general, -ly
Geogr.	(as label) in Geography; (in titles) *Geography, -ical*

Geol.	(as label) in Geology; (in titles) *Geology, -ical*
Geom.	in Geometry
Geomorphol.	in Geomorphology
Ger.	German
Gloss.	Glossary
Gmc.	Germanic
Godef.	F. Godefroy, *Dictionnaire de l'ancienne langue française*
Goth.	Gothic
Govt.	(in titles) *Government*
Gr.	Greek
Gram.	(as label) in Grammar; (in titles) *Grammar, -tical*
Gt.	Great
Heb.	Hebrew
Her.	in Heraldry
Herb.	among herbalists
Hind.	Hindustani
Hist.	(as label) in History; (in titles) *History, -ical*
hist.	historical
Histol.	(in titles) *Histology, -ical*
Hort.	in Horticulture
Househ.	(in titles) *Household*
Housek.	(in titles) *Housekeeping*
Ibid.	*Ibidem*, 'in the same book or passage'
Icel.	Icelandic
Ichthyol.	in Ichthyology
id.	*idem*, 'the same'
i.e.	*id est*, 'that is'
IE.	Indo-European
Illustr.	(in titles) *Illustration, -ted*
imit.	imitative
Immunol.	in Immunology
imp.	imperative
impers.	impersonal
impf.	imperfect
ind.	indicative
indef.	indefinite
Industr.	(in titles) *Industry, -ial*
inf.	infinitive
infl.	influenced
Inorg.	(in titles) *Inorganic*
Ins.	(in titles) *Insurance*
Inst.	(in titles) *Institute, -tion*
int.	interjection
intr.	intransitive
Introd.	(in titles) *Introduction*
Ir.	Irish
irreg.	irregular, -ly
It.	Italian
J., (J.)	(quoted from) Johnson's *Dictionary*
(Jam.)	Jamieson, *Scottish Dict.*
Jap.	Japanese
joc.	jocular, -ly
Jrnl.	(in titles) *Journal*
Jun.	(in titles) *Junior*
Knowl.	(in titles) *Knowledge*
l.	line
L.	Latin
lang.	language
Lect.	(in titles) *Lecture, -s*
Less.	(in titles) *Lesson, -s*
Let., Lett.	letter, letters
LG.	Low German
lit.	literal, -ly
Lit.	Literary
Lith.	Lithuanian
LXX	Septuagint
m.	masculine
Mag.	(in titles) *Magazine*
Magn.	(in titles) *Magnetic, -ism*
Mal.	Malay, Malayan
Man.	(in titles) *Manual*
Managem.	(in titles) *Management*
Manch.	(in titles) *Manchester*
Manuf.	in Manufacture, -ing
Mar.	(in titles) *Marine*
masc. (*rarely* m.)	masculine
Math.	(as label) in Mathematics; (in titles) *Mathematics, -al*
MDu.	Middle Dutch
ME.	Middle English
Mech.	(as label) in Mechanics; (in titles) *Mechanics, -al*
Med.	(as label) in Medicine; (in titles) *Medicine, -ical*
med.L.	medieval Latin
Mem.	(in titles) *Memoir, -s*
Metaph.	in Metaphysics
Meteorol.	(as label) in Meteorology; (in titles) *Meteorology, -ical*
MHG.	Middle High German
midl.	midland (dialect)
Mil.	in military usage
Min.	(as label) in Mineralogy; (in titles) *Ministry*
Mineral.	(in titles) *Mineralogy, -ical*
MLG.	Middle Low German
Misc.	(in titles) *Miscellany, -eous*
mod.	modern
mod.L	modern Latin
(Morris),	(quoted from) E. E. Morris's *Austral English*
Mus.	(as label) in Music; (in titles) *Music, -al; Museum*
Myst.	(in titles) *Mystery*
Mythol.	in Mythology
N.	North
n.	neuter
N. Amer.	North America, -n
N. & Q.	*Notes and Queries*
Narr.	(in titles) *Narrative*
Nat.	(in titles) *Natural*
Nat. Hist.	in Natural History
Naut.	in nautical language
N.E.	North East
N.E.D.	*New English Dictionary*, original title of the *Oxford English Dictionary* (first edition)
Neurol.	in Neurology
neut. (*rarely* n.)	neuter
NF., NFr.	Northern French
No.	Number
nom.	nominative
north.	northern (dialect)
Norw.	Norwegian
n.q.	no quotations
N.T.	New Testament
Nucl.	Nuclear
Numism.	in Numismatics
N.W.	North West
N.Z.	New Zealand
obj.	object
obl.	oblique
Obs., obs.	obsolete
Obstetr.	(in titles) *Obstetrics*
occas.	occasionally
OE.	Old English (= Anglo-Saxon)
OF., OFr.	Old French
OFris.	Old Frisian
OHG.	Old High German
OIr.	Old Irish
ON.	Old Norse
ONF.	Old Northern French
Ophthalm.	in Ophthalmology
opp.	opposed (to), the opposite (of)
Opt.	in Optics
Org.	(in titles) *Organic*
orig.	origin, -al, -ally
Ornith.	(as label) in Ornithology; (in titles) *Ornithology, -ical*
OS.	Old Saxon
OSl.	Old (Church) Slavonic
O.T.	Old Testament
Outl.	(in titles) *Outline*
Oxf.	(in titles) *Oxford*
p.	page
Palæogr.	in Palæography
Palæont.	(as label) in Palæontology; (in titles) *Palæontology, -ical*
pa. pple.	passive participle, past participle
(Partridge),	(quoted from) E. Partridge's *Dictionary of Slang and Unconventional English*
pass.	passive, -ly
pa.t.	past tense
Path.	(as label) in Pathology; (in titles) *Pathology, -ical*
perh.	perhaps
Pers.	Persian
pers.	person, -al
Petrogr.	in Petrography
Petrol.	(as label) in Petrology; (in titles) *Petrology, -ical*
(Pettman),	(quoted from) C. Pettman's *Africanderisms*
pf.	perfect
Pg.	Portuguese
Pharm.	in Pharmacology
Philol.	(as label) in Philology; (in titles) *Philology, -ical*
Philos.	(as label) in Philosophy; (in titles) *Philosophy, -ic*
phonet.	phonetic, -ally
Photogr.	(as label) in Photography; (in titles) *Photography, -ical*
phr.	phrase
Phys.	physical; (*rarely*) in Physiology
Physiol.	(as label) in Physiology; (in titles) *Physiology, -ical*
Pict.	(in titles) *Picture, Pictorial*
pl., plur.	plural
poet.	poetic, -al
Pol.	Polish
Pol.	(as label) in Politics; (in titles) *Politics, -al*
Pol. Econ.	in Political Economy
Polit.	(in titles) *Politics, -al*
pop.	popular, -ly
Porc.	(in titles) *Porcelain*
poss.	possessive
Pott.	(in titles) *Pottery*
ppl. a., pple. adj.	participial adjective
pple.	participle
Pr.	Provençal
pr.	present
Pract.	(in titles) *Practice, -al*
prec.	preceding (word or article)
pred.	predicative
pref.	prefix
pref., Pref.	preface
prep.	preposition
pres.	present
Princ.	(in titles) *Principle, -s*
priv.	privative
prob.	probably
Probl.	(in titles) *Problem*
Proc.	(in titles) *Proceedings*
pron.	pronoun
pronunc.	pronunciation
prop.	properly
Pros.	in Prosody
Prov.	Provençal
pr. pple.	present participle
Psych.	in Psychology
Psychol.	(as label) in Psychology; (in titles) *Psychology, -ical*
Publ.	(in titles) *Publications*
Q.	(in titles) *Quarterly*
quot(s).	quotation(s)
q.v.	*quod vide*, 'which see'
R.	(in titles) *Royal*
Radiol.	in Radiology
R.C.Ch.	Roman Catholic Church
Rec.	(in titles) *Record*
redupl.	reduplicating
Ref.	(in titles) *Reference*
refash.	refashioned, -ing
refl.	reflexive
Reg.	(in titles) *Register*

reg.	regular
rel.	related to
Reminisc.	(in titles) *Reminiscence, -s*
Rep.	(in titles) *Report, -s*
repr.	representative, representing
Res.	(in titles) *Research*
Rev.	(in titles) *Review*
rev.	revised
Rhet.	in Rhetoric
Rom.	Roman, -ce, -ic
Rum.	Rumanian
Russ.	Russian
S.	South
S.Afr.	South Africa, -n
sb.	substantive
sc.	*scilicet*, 'understand' or 'supply'
Sc., Scot.	Scottish
Scand.	(in titles) *Scandinavia, -n*
Sch.	(in titles) *School*
Sc. Nat. Dict.	*Scottish National Dictionary*
Scotl.	(in titles) *Scotland*
Sel.	(in titles) *Selection, -s*
Ser.	Series
sing.	singular
Sk.	(in titles) *Sketch*
Skr.	Sanskrit
Slav.	Slavonic
S.N.D.	*Scottish National Dictionary*
Soc.	(in titles) *Society*
Sociol.	(as label) in Sociology; (in titles) *Sociology, -ical*
Sp.	Spanish
Sp.	(in titles) *Speech, -es*
sp.	spelling
spec.	specifically
Spec.	(in titles) *Specimen*
St.	Saint
Stand.	(in titles) *Standard*
Stanf.	(quoted from) *Stanford Dictionary of Anglicised Words & Phrases*
str.	strong
Struct.	(in titles) *Structure, -al*
Stud.	(in titles) *Studies*
subj.	subject
subord. cl.	subordinate clause
subseq.	subsequent, -ly
subst.	substantively
suff.	suffix
superl.	superlative
Suppl.	Supplement
Surg.	(as label) in Surgery; (in titles) *Surgery, Surgical*
s.v.	*sub voce*, 'under the word'
Sw.	Swedish
s.w.	south-western (dialect)
Syd. Soc. Lex.	Sydenham Society, *Lexicon of Medicine & Allied Sciences*
syll.	syllable
Syr.	Syrian
Syst.	(in titles) *System, -atic*
Taxon.	(in titles) *Taxonomy, -ical*
techn.	technical, -ly
Technol.	(in titles) *Technology, -ical*
Telegr.	in Telegraphy
Teleph.	in Telephony
(Th.),	(quoted from) Thornton's *American Glossary*
Theatr.	in the Theatre, theatrical
Theol.	(as label) in Theology; (in titles) *Theology, -ical*
Theoret.	(in titles) *Theoretical*
Tokh.	Tokharian
tr., transl.	translated, translation
Trans.	(in titles) *Transactions*
trans.	transitive
transf.	transferred sense
Trav.	(in titles) *Travel(s)*
Treas.	(in titles) *Treasury*
Treat.	(in titles) *Treatise*
Treatm.	(in titles) *Treatment*
Trig.	in Trigonometry
Trop.	(in titles) *Tropical*
Turk.	Turkish
Typog., Typogr.	in Typography
ult.	ultimately
Univ.	(in titles) *University*
unkn.	unknown
U.S.	United States
U.S.S.R.	Union of Soviet Socialist Republics
usu.	usually
v., vb.	verb
var(r)., vars.	variant(s) of
vbl. sb.	verbal substantive
Vertebr.	(in titles) *Vertebrate, -s*
Vet.	(as label) in Veterinary Science; (in titles) *Veterinary*
Vet. Sci.	in Veterinary Science
viz.	*videlicet*, 'namely'
Voy.	(in titles) *Voyage, -s*
v.str.	strong verb
vulg.	vulgar
v.w.	weak verb
W.	Welsh; West
wd.	word
Webster	*Webster's (New International) Dictionary*
Westm.	(in titles) *Westminster*
WGmc.	West Germanic
Wks.	(in titles) *Works*
w.midl.	west midland (dialect)
WS.	West Saxon
(Y.),	(quoted from) Yule & Burnell's *Hobson-Jobson*
Yrs.	(in titles) *Years*
Zoogeogr.	in Zoogeography
Zool.	(as label) in Zoology; (in titles) *Zoology, -ical*

Signs and Other Conventions

Before a word or sense

† = obsolete
|| = not naturalized, alien
¶ = catachrestic and erroneous uses

In the listing of Forms

1 = before 1100
2 = 12th c. (1100 to 1200)
3 = 13th c. (1200 to 1300), etc.
5–7 = 15th to 17th century
20 = 20th century

In the etymologies

* indicates a word or form not actually found, but of which the existence is inferred
:— = normal development of

The printing of a word in SMALL CAPITALS indicates that further information will be found under the word so referred to.

.. indicates an omitted part of a quotation.

- (in a quotation) indicates a hyphen doubtfully present in the original; (in other text) indicates a hyphen inserted only for the sake of a line-break.

PROPRIETARY NAMES

THIS Dictionary includes some words which are or are asserted to be proprietary names or trade marks. Their inclusion does not imply that they have acquired for legal purposes a non-proprietary or general significance nor any other judgement concerning their legal status. In cases where the editorial staff have established in the records of the Patent Offices of the United Kingdom and of the United States that a word is registered as a proprietary name or trade mark this is indicated, but no judgement concerning the legal status of such words is made or implied thereby.

rob (rɒb), *sb.* Now *rare.* Also 6 robbe, 8–9 robb. [a. mod.L. or F. *rob*, = Sp. *rob*, Pg. *robe*, *arrobe*, It. *rob*, *robbo*; also G. and older Da. *rob*. The ultimate source is Arab. *robb*, *rubb* or Pers. *rob*, *rub* fruit-syrup.] The juice of a fruit, reduced by boiling to the consistency of a syrup and preserved with sugar; a conserve of fruit.

1578 LYTE *Dodoens* 683 The Robbe or dried iuyce thereof. *Ibid.*, The rob made with the iuyce of common Ribes and Sugar, is very good for all the diseases aboue sayde. **1620** VENNER *Via Recta* vii. 124 The Rob, that is, the iuyce of the berries boyled with a third part..of sugar added vnto it,.. is preferred before the raw berries. **1656** W. COLES *Art of Simpling* xxv. 80 Continue boyling it..till it attaine unto the consistence of Honey, and then it is by Physitians called the Rob. **1694** WESTMACOTT *Script. Herb.* 203 These Robs,.. and Conserves, are not to be given to costive Bodies. **1747** WESLEY *Prim. Physick* (1765) 122 Take an ounce of Rob of Elder in Broth. **1796** WITHERING *Brit. Pl.* (ed. 3) II. 351 *note*, The berries are so very acid that birds will not eat them, but boiled with sugar they form a most agreeable rob or jelly. **1821** W. P. C. BARTON *Flora N. Amer.* I. 61 A rob might also be prepared..by evaporating the syrup obtained from them. **1864** *Chambers's Encycl.* VI. 603/1 A rob made of it [white mulberry] is useful in sore throat.

fig. **1790** H. WALPOLE *Let. to Miss Berry* 31 Oct., There is ..a quantity of calculations, and one is forced to..boil milliards of livres down to a rob of pounds sterling.

rob (rɒb), *v.* Forms: 3–5 robben, 5 robbyn; 4 robbi, robby, 4–6 robbe, 5 (6 *Sc.*) rub, 6– rob, 7 robb (*Sc.* robe). [ad. OF. *robber*, *rober*, *rouber*, etc., = Sp. *robar*, Pg. *roubar*, It. *rubare*, of Teutonic origin, the stem *roub-* being that represented in English by REAVE *v.*]

1. a. *trans.* To deprive (a person) of something by unlawful force or the exercise of superior power; to despoil by violence. Also *fig.* and *refl.*

a **1225** *Ancr. R.* 86 þe knihte þet robbeð his poure men. *Ibid.* 150 Him luste leosen hit & beon irobbed. *c* **1290** *St. Eustace* 57 in *S. Eng. Leg.* I. 394 þo comen þeoues and robbeden him. **1340** *Ayenb.* 39 þise greate prelates þet benimeþ and robbeþ hire onderlinges. **1362** LANGL. *P. Pl.* A. III. 188 Withouten pite, pilour! pore Men þou robbedest. **1387** TREVISA *Higden* (Rolls) IV. 443 þerfore anon the hous was i-broke; þe pore men were i-spoylled and i-robbed. **1422** tr. *Secreta Secret., Priv. Priv.* 183 The extorcioner rubbyth and Preyeth good men. **1535** COVERDALE *Prov.* xxii. 22 Se yᵗ thou robbe not yᵉ poore because he is weake. **1595** SHAKS. *John* IV. iii. 78 Must I rob the Law? **1604** —— *Oth.* I. iii. 209 He robs himselfe, that spends a bootlesse griefe. **1651** HOBBES *Leviath.* I. viii. 35 When a man robbs one to pay another. **1715** DE FOE *Fam. Instruct.* I. iv. (1841) I. 74 Oh, thieves, thieves, I am robbed. **1759** MILLS tr. *Duhamel's Husb.* I. iv. 10 To hinder weeds from robbing the cultivated plants. **1791** MRS. RADCLIFFE *Rom. Forest* i, Their intention was to rob and murder him. **1857** KINGSLEY *Two Y. Ago* I. 280 As usual; poor Nature is being robbed and murdered by rich grace. **1892** TENNYSON *Foresters* III, We never robb'd one friend of the true King. We robb'd the traitors that are leagued with John. **1926** *Publishers' Weekly* 19 June 1966/1 You may improve your golf game... Why not get rid of that disconcerting slice which robs your drive? **1948** R. M. AYRES *Missing Tide* i. 44 The food's quite good, and they don't rob you, anyway.

b. *to rob Peter to pay* (†*give to, clothe*) *Paul* (see PETER *sb.*[1] 2).

c **1380** WYCLIF *Sel. Wks.* III. 174 Lord, hou schulde God approve þat þou robbe Petur, and gif þis robbere to Poule in þe name of Crist? *c* **1440** *Jacob's Well* 305 þei robbyn seynt petyr & ȝeuyn it seynt Poule. **1515** [see PETER *sb.*[1] 2]. **1546** J. HEYWOOD *Prov. & Epigr.* (1867) 26 Lyke a pyckpurs pilgrim, ye prie and ye proule At rouers, to rob Peter and paie Poule. **1596** NASHE *Saffron Walden* Ep. Ded. Bij b, Thow shalt not find many powling pence about him neither, except he rob Peter to pay Powle. **1657–1692** [see PETER *sb.*[1] 2]. **1737** *Gentl. Mag.* VII. 172/1 This Scheme is..calculated ..to Rob Peter to pay Paul, or, to remove yᵉ Burthen from one Part of the Community, and lay it upon another. [**1855** MOTLEY *Dutch Rep.* III. v. (1866) 430 It was not desirable to rob Saint Peter's altar in order to build one to Saint Paul.]

c. *Mining.* (See quot.)

1797 *Encycl. Brit.* (ed. 3) II. 86/2 Sometimes it [antimony] is blended with the richer ores of silver, and renders the extraction of that metal difficult by volatilizing a part of the silver, or, in the language of the miners, *robbing the ore.*

d. *Association Football.* To deprive (an opposing player) of the ball.

1882 *Blackburn Times* 1 Apr. 6/3 Goodhart started the ball from the centre, but he was instantly robbed by Strachan. **1970** *Times* 30 Sept. 15/4 Novak held on too long in midfield and was robbed by Graham. **1976** *Morecambe Guardian* 7 Dec. 8/2 Towers and Thomas forced the defence into some confusion when a backpass went astray. Finch had to move quickly to rob Thomas who was charging through.

2. a. To plunder or strip (a person) feloniously *of* (something belonging to him); to deprive (one) *of* (something due). Also *transf.* or *fig.* (with a thing as object).

13.. *Coer de L.* 2286 In an evil tyme our emperour Robbed King Richard of his tresour. **1340–70** *Alex. & Dind.* 789 To robbe men of hure riht ful redy ben alle. *c* **1400** *Destr. Troy* 6419 Ector..Wold haue Robbit the Renke of his riche wede. *c* **1440** *Jacob's Well* 217 Myn eyȝe has robbyd my soule of his lyif with watyr of lustys. **1535** COVERDALE *2 Sam.* xvii. 8 As a Beer that is robbed of hir yonge ones in the felde. **1563** WINȜET *Wks.* (S.T.S.) I. 105 He hes..rubbit him of his geris or honouris. **1591** SPENSER *M. Hubberd* 16 My weake bodie..Was rob'd of rest and naturall reliefe. **1634** MILTON *Comus* 390 For who would rob a Hermit of his Weeds. **1665** BOYLE *Occas. Refl.* IV. xii. (1675) 240 A Cloud, which does no longer receive or transmit the Light, but robs the Earth of it. **1692** DRYDEN *St. Euremont's Ess.* 11 The Zeal of the Citizen robbed the Man of Himself. **1765** A. DICKSON *Treat. Agric.* (ed. 2) 92 By allowing them to grow, we allow the land..to be robbed of its vegetable food. **1784** COWPER *Task* IV. 458 His victims, robb'd of their defenceless all. **1807–8** IRVING *Salmagundi* (1824) 265 [It] long since ceased bearing,..every tempest robs it of a limb. **1867** TROLLOPE *Chron. Barset* lxiii, The troubles of life had almost robbed the elder lady of her beauty. **1878** HUXLEY *Physiogr.* 78 The air..which had been thus robbed of its oxygen.

†**b.** Similarly with double object. *Obs.* (Cf. 5.)

c **1330** *Arth. & Merl.* 4323 (Kölbing), Kepe we þe strait wais..& robben hem her sustenaunce. **1613** HEYWOOD *Silver Age* III. i, Ceres nor loue, nor all the Gods aboue, Shall rob me this rich purchase.

3. a. To plunder, pillage, rifle (a place, house, etc.).

c **1230** *Hali Meid.* 15 Wes helle irobbed, & heuene beð ifulled. *a* **1240** *Sawles Warde* in *O.E. Hom.* I. 247 Ah ne bihoueð hit nawt þat tis hus beo irobbet. **1338** R. BRUNNE *Chron.* (1810) 38 þe Danes vp aryued, Souhamptone þei brent, & robbed Cornwaille. *c* **1400** *Destr. Troy* 1912 He.. told furth of his tale,..How þe rewme was robbet. *c* **1465** in *Three 15th Cent. Chron.* (Camden) 23 The Kynge off Scottes ..robbed and revid the contre aboute Derham. **1513** DOUGLAS *Æneis* XII. v. 103 Ȝon ilk stranger..our marchis.. Invadis, rubbis, and spulȝeis. **1599** SHAKS. *Hen. V*, III. vi. 106 One that is like to be executed for robbing a Church. **1651** tr. *De-las-Coveras' Don Fenise* 198 Pirats who..rob upon the sea all the vessells they could render themselves masters of. *a* **1716** SOUTH *Serm.* (1744) IV. 153 Robbing the Spittle. **1816** J. WILSON *City of Plague* II. iii. 249 Wilt thou rob a church And share..The general spoil? **1855** MACAULAY *Hist. Eng.* xii. III. 221 In the country his house was robbed.

transf. **1877** RAYMOND *Statist. Mines & Mining* 316 Former operations were principally confined to robbing the rich pockets, while good milling-ore was left standing.

b. Const. *of* that which is taken.

c **1330** *Arth. & Merl.* 5105 (Kölbing), Mani cursed painem..hadden robbed þis cuntray Of al þis ich fair pray. *c* **1400** *Destr. Troy* 3209 To the tempull full tyte [he] turnyt agayne, To rob of þe Riches, and Renkes to helpe. *c* **1420** *Cont. Brut* ccxxvii. (1908) 298 þe toun..of al þing þat myȝte be bore & caryed out was robbid and despoyled. **1590** SPENSER *F.Q.* III. vi. 4 All the rest it seemd they robbed bare Of bounty, and of beautie. **1613** SHAKS. *Hen. VIII*, III. ii. 255 Thy Ambition..robb'd this bewailing Land Of Noble Buckingham.

4. a. *absol.* To commit depredations; to plunder; to take away property by force.

1297 R. GLOUC. (Rolls) 6041 Hii drowe hom toward kanterbury, to robbi þere al so. **1338** R. BRUNNE *Chron.* (1810) 38 Of Danmark dukes riche.. Men & women slouh, & robbed þorgh þe lond. **1390** GOWER *Conf.* II. 134 For every thief upon richesse Awaiteth forto robbe and stele. *c* **1400** *Rom. Rose* 5686 To swinke and traveile he not feynith, For for to robben he disdeynith. **1534** MORE *Comf. agst. Trib.* Wks. 1200, I mene not, to let euery malefactor passe furth vnpunished, and frely runne out and rob at rouers. **1596** SHAKS. *1 Hen. IV*, II. ii. 10, I am accurst to rob in that Theefe company. **1662** HIBBERT *Body Divinity* I. 165 A man may rob with a pair of ballances or metewand in his hand. **1682** *Lond. Gaz.* No. 1737/4 They Robbed the night before on Brainford-Road. **1831** *Insect Misc.* (L.E.K.) 330 Sometimes..small parties of three or four [bees] will unite to rob, as we may say, on the highway.

b. *Mining.* (See quots.)

1881 RAYMOND *Mining Gloss.*, *Rob*, to extract pillars previously left for support; or, in general, to take out ore or coal from a mine with a view to immediate product, and not to subsequent working. **1883** GRESLEY *Gloss. Coal-mining*, *Rob*, to cut away or reduce the size of pillars of coal, &c.

5. a. To carry off as plunder; to steal. Now *rare.*

1297 R. GLOUC. (Rolls) 381 þat strange men..asaileden is lond..& robbed is bestes & is game. **13..** *K. Alis.* 3450 (Laud MS.), Hij robbeden tresores & cloþes. **1390** GOWER *Conf.* II. 160 He anon hem wolde assaile And robbe what thing that thei ladden. **1426** LYDG. *De Guil. Pilgr.* 16014 Swych gostly goodys euerychon Ben yrobbyd And agon. **1456** SIR G. HAYE *Law Arms* (S.T.S.) 91 A man gais to the were for..to pele and rub gudis. **1530** PALSGR. 693/1, I robbe his treasour from hym. **1579** W. WILKINSON *Confut. Fam. of Love* Ep. Ded. *ij, Whiche Vine the Foxes sometimes spoyle and endamage by robbyng the fruite. **1646** R. BAILLIE *Anabapt.* (1647) 10 The Priests vestments, which he had robbed in the Cathedrall. **1697** DRYDEN *Virg. Georg.* IV. 312 They themselves contrive To Rob the Honey, and subvert the Hive. **1830** CAMPBELL *Farewell to Love* 7 But Passion robs my peace no more. **1850** THACKERAY *Pendennis* xxxvii[i], There was a sideboard robbed out of the carved work of a church in the Low Countries. **1887** MOLONEY *Forestry W. Africa* 176 The descendants of the Negroes who were robbed from Africa. **1919** G. B. SHAW *Heartbreak House* II. 77, I should rob all the money back from Mangan. **1939** JOYCE *Finnegans Wake* (1964) III. 453 Robbing leaves out of my taletold book. **1953** [see *robber trench* s.v. ROBBER 2 b]. **1977** *Irish Press* 29 Sept. 5/5 Vincent Walker..was found guilty of robbing the sum of £8,798.

†**b.** *fig.* To remove, take *away*, cut off *from* something; to ravish. *Obs. rare.*

1377 LANGL. *P. Pl.* B. XIV. 132 Allas! þat ricchesse shal reue and robbe mannes soule Fram þe loue of owre lorde. **1594** SHAKS. *Rich. II*, I. iii. 173 What is thy sentence then, but speechlesse death, Which robs my tongue from breathing natiue breath? **1596** SPENSER *F.Q.* IV. iv. 16 The which..to it drew The eyes of all,..And hearts quite robbed with so glorious sight. **1627** *Lisander & Cal.* Ded., By their conversation they may endeavour to rob away teadiousnes though but from one houre.

6. *Card playing.* (See quots.)

With quot. 1611 compare Littré s.v. *Piller* 6.

1611 COTGR., *Piller*,..also, to rub, or rob, at cards. **1897** FOSTER *Compl. Hoyle* 277 (Spoil Five), Robbing the trump card. If the trump card is an ace, the dealer may discard any card he pleases in exchange for it. *Ibid.* 299 (Cinch), He may search the remainder of the pack, and take from it any cards that he pleases. This is called robbing the deck.

rob-, the stem of ROB *v.*, used in a few combs. in the 17th cent., in the sense of 'one who robs (the person or thing specified)', as **rob-altar**, **-carrier**, **-God**, **-orchard**, **-thief**. Also ROB-POT.

1614 T. ADAMS *Devil's Banquet* II. 49 'Will a man rob God?'.. But, alas, what law can be giuen to *rob Altars? **1649** LEYCESTER *Civil Wars* 69 The strong Garrison of Basing the very receptacle of rogueing *Rob-Carriers. **1612** W. SCLATER *Ministers Portion* 47 Search records, divine, humane: where findest thou a *rob-God without his vengeance? **1623** R. CARPENTER *Conscionable Christian* 80 Sacrilegious rob-Gods, desperate mocke-Preachers. **1673** S. PARKER *Repr. Reh. Transp.* 517 Truants, loiterers, and *rob-orchards. **1600** *Look About You* xxx, Could I meet him, I'd play *rob-thief, at least part stakes with him. **1614** T. ADAMS *Devil's Banquet* II. 82 His extortion hath erst stolne from others, and now hee plays rob-thiefe, and steales from himselfe.

rob, obs. form of ROBE.

‖**roba.** *Obs.*⁻¹ = BONA-ROBA.

1602 MIDDLETON *Blurt Master-Constable* II. ii, Hah! fast, my roba fast, and but young night?

roband ('rəʊbænd). *Naut.* Also 8–9 roban. [Later var. of *robin* ROBBIN, app. more directly representing one or other of the forms cited under RABAND. Sometimes improved into *rope-band.*] A piece of small rope passed through an eyelet-hole in the head of a sail and used to secure it to the yard above.

1762 FALCONER *Shipwreck* II. 80 To each yard-arm, the head-rope they extend, And soon their earings and the robands bend. **1769** —— *Dict. Marine* (1780) s.v. *Sail*, The heads of all four-sided sails, and the fore-leeches of lateen sails, are attached to their respective yard or gaff by a number of small cords called robands. **1840** R. H. DANA *Bef. Mast* xiv, All hands were..picking old rope to pieces, or laying up gaskets and robands. **1860** H. STUART *Seaman's Catech.* 2 What is a roband or rolling hitch used for? For bending sails,..for reefing courses,..&c. **1899** F. T. BULLEN *Log of Sea-waif* 82 In a man-of-war, where they can send a man to every roband.

attrib. **1762** FALCONER *Shipwreck* 157 The reef-lines next ..Through eye-lid-holes and roband-legs are reev'd. **1769** —— *Dict. Marine* (1780) s.v. *Reefing*, Provided that the turns are inserted through the roband-legs.

Robardesmen, variant of ROBERDSMEN.

robbare, obs. form of ROBBER.

robbe, obs. form of ROB *sb.* and *v.*, ROBE.

robbed (rɒbd), *ppl. a.* [f. ROB *v.*]

1. Plundered, despoiled. Also *absol.*

c **1400** *Rom. Rose* 6823, I..Robbe bothe robbed and robbours. *c* **1450** *Mirour Saluacioun* (Roxb.) 18 A Samaritene..heled this robbed man of his woundes. **1604** SHAKS. *Oth.* I. iii. 208 The rob'd that smiles, steales something from the Thiefe. **1679** DRYDEN & LEE *Œdipus* V. i, As a robbed tigress bounding o'er the woods. **1700** DRYDEN *Ovid's Met.* XII. 342 Bold Amycus, from the robb'd vestry brings The chalices of heaven. **1874** WOOD *Nat. Hist.* 621 The cod thus hollowed are technically called 'robbed' fish. **1894** MRS. DYAN *Man's Keeping* (1899) 164 The sadness of the eyes with the look of robbed motherhood they often wore.

2. Carried off; taken away.

1590 SPENSER *F.Q.* II. viii. 40 A Lyon, which hath long time saught His robbed whelpes. **1870** *Standard* 5 Dec., They are all the more savage by reason of robbed repose.

robber ('rɒbə(r)). Forms: α. 2 rubbere, 3 robbare, 3–4 robbere, 5 robare, robbar, 6 *Sc.* rubber, 4– robber. β. 4 robeour, robbeo(u)r, -youre, 4–5 robour(e, robbour(e, -or(e, 5 robbowre, -eur. [The α- and β-forms are respectively a. AF. and OF. *robbere*, *robere*, and *robeour*, *robbour*, etc., nom. and acc. types of the agent-noun from *robber* to ROB. Cf. Sp. *robador*, Pg. *roubador*, It. *rubatore.*]

1. a. One who practises or commits robbery; a depredator, plunderer, despoiler.

α. *c* **1175** *Lamb. Hom.* 29 Rubberes, and þa reueres, and þa þeoues. *a* **1225** *Ancr. R.* 150 In one weie þet is al ful of þeoues & of robbares, & of reauares. *c* **1250** *Lutel soth Serm.* 27 in *O.E. Misc.* 186 Alle bac-biteres wendet to helle, Robberes, and reueres. **1340** *Ayenb.* 39 þe þridde is ine robberes and kueade herberȝeres þet berobbeþ þe pilgrimes. **1377** LANGL. *P. Pl.* B. XIV. 182 þus..Ihesu Cryst seyde, To robberes and to reueres. *c* **1425** LYDG. *Assembly of Gods* 688 Robbers, reuers, rauenous ryfelers. *c* **1440** *Promp. Parv.* 437/2 Robare, or robbar yn the see,..*pirata.* *a* **1533** LD. BERNERS *Huon* xlviii. 160 They were robbers of the see. **1535** COVERDALE *Ps.* xxxiv. 10 Who is like vnto the? which delyuerest..the poore and the nedy from his robbers. **1593** SHAKS. *Rich. II*, III. ii. 39 Then Theeues and Robbers raunge abroad vnseene. **1634** MILTON *Comus* 485 Som roaving Robber calling to his fellows. **1671** —— *Samson* 1188 Thou..like a Robber stripdst them of thir robes. **1727** GAY *Fables* I. i, Robbers invade their neighbour's right. **1794** MRS. RADCLIFFE *Myst. Udolpho* xxviii, Montoni was become a captain of robbers. **1838** DICKENS *Nich. Nick.* iv, Where desperate robbers congregate. **1878** STUBBS *Const. Hist.* III. xviii. 243 There is more spirit and a better heart in a robber than in a thief.

fig. *a* **1225** *Ancr. R.* 334 þus þeos two unðeawes beoð two grimme robbares.

β. **1297** R. GLOUC. (Rolls) 8006 William vr king.. robbeour he was. **1303** R. BRUNNE *Handl. Synne* 6127 Euery man he wened had be a robbour, For drede þat he had tresoure. *c* **1380** *Sir Ferumb.* 4113 Al ys lygnage in euery syde, For robbours þai were y-kud. *c* **1400** *Pilgr. Sowle* IV.

xxxv. (Caxton, 1483) 83 Vpon theues and morderers, Robbours and reuours,.. they shalle be fyers in jugement. *c***1440** *Promp. Parv.* 435/2 Robbowre, on the londe, *spoliator. Ibid.*, Robbowre, on the see, *pirata.* *c***1500** *Melusine* 245 Locher, whiche afterward delyuered the Countrey of Ardane fro thevys, murdrers, & robbeurs.

b. Const. *of* a place, etc.

1465 *Paston Lett.* II. 251 Slyford was the chyff robber of the cherch. **1526** TINDALE *Acts* xix. 37 Nether robbers off churches, nor yett despisers of youre goddes. **1557** R. EDGEWORTH *Serm.* 289 He putteth example of disers, and gameners, and robbers of dead mens graues. **1632** SHERWOOD, A robber of the Princes, and publicke treasure, *peculateur.*

c. *transf.* (See quots.)

1670 *Phil. Trans.* V. 1197 Therefore they term it a Robber, as a substance which spoyls, and takes away the richness of the Ore. **1725** *Family Dict.* s.v. *Bee*, To preserve Bees from Robbers, which very commonly infest them,.. the way is to cloom the Hives very close. **1816** KIRBY & SP. *Entomol.* xx. (1818) II. 207 These are called by Schirach *corsair* bees, and by English writers, *robbers.* **1831** *Insect Misc.* (L.E.K.) 329.

2. *attrib.* and *Comb.* **a.** Attrib. in various senses, as ***robber-book***, ***-gold***, ***-haunt***, ***-hold***, ***-inn***, ***-lair***, etc. Also objective, as ***robber-hunting***.

1884 'MARK TWAIN' *Huck. Finn* ii. 13 The rest [of the oath] was out of pirate books, and *robber books. **1850** MRS. BROWNING *Calls on the heart* ii, The world.. Has counted its *robber-gold. **1937** J. W. DAY *Sporting Adventure* 91 The magpies will go off to their *robber-haunts in lonely carrs of willows down on the marshes. **1876** GREEN *Stray Stud.* (1892) 319 The countless *robber-holds of the Angevin noblesse. **1890** 'R. BOLDREWOOD' *Miner's Right* (1899) 123/2, I had no great natural inclination to the trade of *robber-hunting. **1879** STEVENSON *Ess. Trav., Amateur Emigrant* (1905) 82 He had visited a *robber inn. **1866** CONINGTON *Æneid* 266 Grim Cacus in his *robber-lair. **1860** PUSEY *Min. Proph.* 243 Probably.. Edom.. continued his *robber-life along the Southern borders of Judah. **1856** VAUGHAN *Mystics* (1860) I. 142 At every turn have we to wrangle.. with these vultures about their *robber-toll. **1839** CARLYLE *Chartism* v. 139 Silesian *robber-wars.

b. Appositive, as ***robber-chief***, ***-company***, ***-crew***, etc.; **robber baron** [BARON 1], a feudal lord who engaged in plundering; also *transf.*, *spec.* [BARON 2b] in *U.S.*, a financial or industrial magnate of the late nineteenth century who behaved with ruthless and irresponsible acquisitiveness; also *attrib.*; **robber-council** or **-synod**, the ecclesiastical council held at Ephesus in 449, the decrees of which were subsequently rescinded; **robber trench** *Archæol.*, a trench representing the foundations of a wall, the stones of which have been partially or entirely removed.

1878 C. F. ADAMS *Railroads* 145 The commissioner has not hesitated to give his opinion of the foreign owner as a '*robber baron'. **1882** C. SCHURZ in *Boston Herald Suppl.* 30 June 1/3 It will not be surprising at all to see some day a movement set on foot to put an end to the operations of the modern robber barons, who, by corporate rascality, supplemented with tricks of the stock exchange, manage to plunder at will not only their fellow-gamblers, but the innocent bona fide investors in corporate enterprises. **1930** J. S. HUXLEY *Bird-Watching* ii. 32 Predaceous glaucous gulls, the robber barons of the Arctic bird-world. **1934** M. JOSEPHSON *(title)* The robber barons. **1949** *Jrnl. Econ. Hist.* Nov. 187 In studying the so-called 'robber barons', Destler was impelled to consider also a few early 'career men'. **1957** *Times Lit. Suppl.* 8 Nov. 670/3 Next she builds up an immensely lucrative cosmetic business, backed by a robber-baron tycoon named Jim Seymour. **1962** J. BRAINE *Life at Top* x. 131 A robber baron of the Middle Ages. **1976** M. J. LASKY *Utopia & Revolution* (1977) ii. 74 Bakunin joined the call for a crusade of destruction, and he, too, became a robber baron in a holy cause. **1979** *Time* 2 Apr. 45/1 For years psychiatrists have also been regarded as medicine's robber barons. **1816** BYRON *Ch. Har.* III. xlviii, In proud state Each *robber chief upheld his armed halls. **1899** *Q. Rev.* Jan. 11 *Robber-companies, and bishops in coats of mail. **1865** PUSEY *Truth Eng. Ch.* 90 Before the *robber-Council of Ephesus could be displaced by the Fourth General Council at Chalcedon. **1776** MICKLE tr. *Camoens' Lusiad* 346 Soon shall our powers the *robber-crew destroy. **1797** *The College* 38 Arm'd Justice forth the *robber-demons drove. **1869** TOZER *Highl. Turkey* II. 164 Mr. Curzon describes his *robber-guard. **1836–48** B. D. WALSH *Aristoph., Acharnians* I. v, I have pierced the *robber-horde Like a reed. **1865** RUSKIN *Sesame* I. (1907) 27/2 The Rust-kings.. lay up treasures for the rust; and the *Robber-kings, treasures for the robber. **1871** FREEMAN *Norm. Conq.* (1876) IV. 201 William Peverel reared his castle of Peak Forest, the true vulture's nest of a *robber-knight. **1862** DRAPER *Intell. Develop. Europe* ix. (1864) I. 287 Eutyches appealed to the emperor, who summoned.. a council to meet at Ephesus. This was the celebrated '*Robber Synod'. **1953** R. J. C. ATKINSON *Field Archaeol.* (ed. 2) ii. 72 On many Roman and later sites where ancient buildings have once stood, the stone will have been partially or completely robbed from the walls and foundations for re-use elsewhere. In such cases the walls can be traced only as '*robber-trenches'. **1967** *Antiquaries Jrnl.* XLVII. 196 The outer edge of the wall and robber trenches has been found along most of the edge of the north aisle and around the west end. **1978** *Ibid.* LVIII. 106 A late Roman beaded and corrugated pin similar to one found at Lydney was found in robber trenches of the medieval cloister. **1825** SCOTT *Talism.* ii, I have heard that the road is infested with *robber-tribes. **1853** KINGSTON *Manco* ii, The Spaniards attacked Peru with their small but determined band of *robber-warriors.

c. Appositive with names of insects, birds, etc., as ***robber-bee***, ***-fowl***, ***gull***; **robber-crab**, a large tropical crab which steals coco-nuts; **robber-fly**, a fly of the family *Asilidæ*, given to preying upon other insects.

1831 *Insect Misc.* (L.E.K.) 329 *Robber-bees. [Cf. 1 c.] **1864–5** WOOD *Homes without H.* (1868) 90 There is a very remarkable burrowing crustacean, called the *Robber-Crab (*Birgus latro*). **1871** *Amer. Naturalist* IV. 686 A *robber-fly.. burrows in the sand. **1899** D. SHARP *Insects* 491 Asilidae (Robber-flies)... The Asilidae is one of the largest families of flies. **1970** *Age* (Melbourne) 22 June, Another [family] comprising the predatory robber-flies. **1891** ATKINSON *Last of Giant-killers* 144 As soon as the *robber fowl had begun its steady flight. **1946** J. W. DAY *Harvest Adventure* vi. 86 The big *robber gull dropped like a sack of wheat, without a kick, at seventy yards.

Hence **robbe'raceously** *adv.*, in a manner suggestive of robbers; **'robberhood**, brigandage, robbery; **'robberish** [-ISH[1]], *a.*, suggestive of robbers; **'robberism** [-ISM], control by or the business of robbers; robbery; **'robberlet**, a petty robber; **'robberling** [-LING[1]], a little or puny robber.

1772 H. WALPOLE *Lett.* (1904) 128, I did not know that housebreaking might not be still improving... In less than another minute, the door rattled and shook still more robberaceously. **1855** SWINBURNE *Let.* 4 Aug. (1959) I. 6, I longed for you all to be there,.. for it [*sc.* a cave] was admirably robberish. **1863** MARY HOWITT *F. Bremer's Greece* II. 172 The sight of unburied corpses contributed more than anything else to put an end of the system of robberhood in this part of the country. **1865** KINGSLEY *Herew.* xxxiv, Latrunculi (*robberlets*), sicarii, cut-throats. **1884** J. PAYNE *Tales fr. Arabic* II. 83, I fear lest, if thou slay him in our dwelling-place and he savour not of robberhood, suspicion will revert upon ourselves. **1913** D. H. LAWRENCE *Love Poems & Others* 8 Under the glistening cherries... Three dead birds lie: Pale-breasted throstles and a blackbird, robberlings Stained with red dye. **1921** *Glasgow Herald* 18 Jan. 6 Communism in Russia is robberism.

robbery ('rɒbərɪ). Forms: α. 3–4 **roberie**, 4 **roborrye**, 5–6 **robery**, 7 *Sc.* **roborie**; 3–6 **robberye**, 3–7 **robberie** (4 **-eriȝe**), 6 *Sc.* **rubberie**, **-ery**, 4– **robbery**. β. 4–6 **robry(e, -rie**, 5 **roubry**, 6 **robri**; 5–6 *Sc.* **rubry**, **-rie**. [a. OF. *roberie* (AF. also *roberye*), f. *rober* to ROB: see -ERY.]

1. a. The action or practice of feloniously seizing, by violence or intimidation, property belonging to another; spoliation, depredation.

Prov. ***exchange is no robbery***: see EXCHANGE *sb.* 1.

α. *c***1200** *Trin. Coll. Hom.* 61 ȝif he binimeð us ure aȝte, oðer þurh fur, oðer þurh þiefes, oðer þurh roberie. *c***1250** *Old Kent. Serm.* in *O.E. Misc.* 30 Roberie, Manslechtes, Husberners,.. and.. oþre euele deden. *c***1290** *Beket* 2152 in *S. Eng. Leg.* I. 168 þis luþere kniȝtes.. duden gret robberie. **1303** R. BRUNNE *Handl. Synne* 2449 þat ys boþe thefte and robberye, And hyt ful dere shal he a-bye. **1387** TREVISA *Higden* (Rolls) I. 137 þei greiþeþ no þing þat þey dredeþ to lese, þey acounteþ no trespas gretter þan robberie. **1415** HOCCLEVE *Sir J. Oldcastle* 456 By violence or by maistrie, My good to take of me,.. þat is verray wrong & robberie. **1484** CAXTON *Fables of Æsop* III. vi, He that lyueth but of rauyn and robberye shal at the last be knowen and robbed. **1533** BELLENDEN *Livy* I. vii. (S.T.S.) I. 39 Invading þe samyn mare be rubbery þan ony ordoure of chevelrie. **1542** UDALL *Erasm. Apoph.* 140b, That persone committeth plaine robberie or spoyle, who denyeth an almes to any poore creature beeyng in extreme neede. **1605** SHAKS. *Meas. for M.* II. ii. 176 Theeues for their robbery haue authority, When Iudges steale themselues. *c***1670** HOBBES *Dial. Com. Laws* (1681) 117 Robbery is committed by Force, or Terror, of which neither is in Theft; for Theft is a secret Act. **1769** BLACKSTONE *Comm.* IV. 241 Larciny from the person is either by privately stealing, or by open and violent assault, which is usually called robbery. **1797–1805** S. & HT. LEE *Canterb. T.* I. 114 He was an easy mark for robbery. **1815** ELPHINSTONE *Acc. Caubul* (1842) II. 125, I think it probable that the people of those parts of the country which are out of sight of the government, are always addicted to robbery.

β. *c***1330** *Arth. & Merl.* 3501 (Kölbing), þo kniȝtes.. Were ywent in to desert, To libben bi her robrie. *c***1400** *Laud Troy Bk.* 8357 Ther was neuere theff.. That wayted better his a-vauntage, To do his stelthe and his robrye. *c***1470** HENRY *Wallace* IX. 222 Her I gyff our roubry for euirmar. **1531** ELYOT *Gov.* I. xxvi, Compacte of malice and robry. **1596** DALRYMPLE tr. *Leslie's Hist. Scot.* IX. II. 165 Tha war the only authoris of thift, rubrie, and rinning of forrayis.

b. An instance of this; a depredation.

1297 R. GLOUC. (Rolls) 7597 He broȝte vp moni oþer hous of religion also, To bete þulke robberie, þat him þoȝte he adde ydo. **1340** *Ayenb.* 39 þer byeþ zuo uele oþre maneres of roberies. **1390** GOWER *Conf.* II. 333 Ensample of suche Robberies I finde write. *c***1460** in *Three 15th Cent. Chron.* (Camden) 41 Of whiche robrye Syr Gylbert.. was atteynt. **1513** MORE in Grafton *Chron.* (1568) II. 770 There they deuise newe robberyes nightly. **1591** SPENSER *M. Hubberd* 1306 Each place.. fil'd with treasure rackt with robberies. **1612** ROWLANDS *More Knaues Yet* (Hunterian Cl.) 15 Many bolde robberies he did commit. **1657** G. THORNLEY *Daphnis & Chloe* 43 A young Rustick, yet un-skill'd in the Assassinations and Robberies of Love. **1780** BENTHAM *Princ. Legisl.* xii. §10 Where robberies are frequent and unpunished robberies are committed without shame. **1838** JAMES *Robber* i, Giving evidence about that robbery. **1877** RAYMOND *Statist. Mines & Mining* 316 The placer-mining of the gulch.. is really a still worse robbery of the gold-deposits.

†**2.** *concr.* Plunder, spoil, booty. *Obs.*

*c***1330** *Arth. & Merl.* 6684 (Kölbing), þe king.. come priueliche.. To binimen hem her robrie. **1450–1530** *Myrr. our Ladye* 255 Helle ys pryued of robry. **1465** *Paston Lett.* II. 251 Slyford.. hath most of the robbery next the Baylly of Ey. **1535** COVERDALE *Amos* iii. 10 They gather together euell gotten goodes, and laye vp robbery in their houses.

3. *fig.* An excessive financial demand; a proposal which wholly or chiefly benefits the proposer; an outrageous injustice; esp. in ***daylight robbery***, ***highway robbery*** (s.v. HIGHWAY 4).

*c***1863** T. TAYLOR *Ticket-of-Leave Man* I. 10 *Dalton*: I won't go higher than fifteen bob for a fiver. *Moss*... Only fifteen—it's robbery. **1874** E. P. ROE *Barriers burned Away* v. 38 'I want five dollars out of you before you take that trunk off.' 'Why, this is sheer robbery,' exclaimed Dennis. **1886**, etc. [see *highway robbery* s.v. HIGHWAY 4]. **1949** D. M. DAVIN *Roads from Home* I. i. 8 'I can never afford it,' said his sister. 'It's daylight robbery.' **1976** *Springfield* (Mass.) *Daily News* 23 Apr. 39/1 Though the Celtics are well known for their game-long verbal abuse of officials, Wednesday night they got away with robbery. **1977** *Times* 28 Feb. 8/5 It was, in fact, a bit of daylight robbery. As Jimmy Andrews, the disappointed Cardiff manager, said later: 'Everton had all the big names and the luck.'

'robbin. *Naut.* Now *rare* or *Obs.* Forms: 5 **robyn**, 7–8 **robin**, 7–9 **robbin**, 9 **-en**. [Var. of ROBAND; the form suggests that the immediate source may have been French, but mod.F. *raban* appears to be a later adoption of Du. *raband*.] = ROBAND.

1497 *Naval Accs. Hen. VII* (1896) 321, iiij Smale lynes for lachetes & Robyns to the seid Ship. **1626** CAPT. SMITH *Accid. Yng. Seamen* 15 The Robins, garnit, Clew garnits, tyes, martlits. **1627** —— *Seaman's Gram.* v. 22 The Robbins are little lines reeued into the eylet holes of the saile vnder the head ropes, to make fast the saile to the yard. **1729** WRIGLESWORTH *Jrnl. Lyell* 6 Dec., Keep the People at Work in making Points, Gaskets, Robins, Matts, Sinnet, &c. for Sea Store. **1867** SMYTH *Sailor's Word-bk.* 576.

Robbin, variant of ROBIN.

'robbing, *vbl. sb.* [f. ROB *v.*]

1. The action of ROB vb.; spoliation, robbery. Also *attrib.*

1377 LANGL. *P. Pl.* B. XIV. 301 ȝe, þorw þe pas of altoun Pouerte myȝte passe with-oute peril of robbynge. *c***1425** *Eng. Conq. Irel.* 26 All þe contreys about dyuelyn, wyth robynge & bernyng & sleyng, weren neght I-broght to noght. **1465** *Paston Lett.* II. 251 The chyff maysters of robbyng was the Baylly of Ey, [etc.]. **1512** *Act 4 Hen. VIII*, c. 20 Preamble, The same mysgoverned persons shall lyf in robbyng and mysgovernaunce duryng ther lyves. **1591** SPARRY tr. *Cattan's Geomancie* 119 It is very ill in all demandes, but such as concerne.. robbing, rifling, spoiling. **1665** PEPYS *Diary* 21 Sept., I rode in some fear of robbing. **1678** R. L'ESTRANGE *Seneca's Mor.* (1776) 62 There is no travelling upon the road for robbing. **1725** *Fam. Dict.* s.v *Bee*, This subject of the Bees robbing of one another. **1831** *Insect Misc.* (L.E.K.) 329 The robbing season.. occurs sooner or later as the summer has been more or less favourable.

b. With *a* and pl. = ROBBERY 1 b.

*c***1220** *Bestiary* 792 Ilc robbinge do we of bac. **1340** *Ayenb.* 39 Zuyche reuen, prouost, bedeles,.. þet makeþ þe greate robbynges. *c***1460** *Contin. Brut* (1908) 518 Also, At which robbyng diuerse men of London.. wer.., & toke part with him. **1560** J. DAUS tr. *Sleidane's Comm.* 405 Spoylynges and robbinges of townes. **1657** *Divine Lover* 300 The tediousnesse of the way, beatinges, robbings, and the like are but necessarie Mortifications. **1693** *Mem. Cnt. Teckely* II. 103 The War was more like a tumultuous Robbing than a War manag'd with prudence.

†**2.** *concr.* Plunder, booty. In quot. *pl. Obs.*

*c***1330** *Arth. & Merl.* 4730 (Kölbing), þis four heþen kinges Went, to loken þis robbeinges.

'robbing, *ppl. a.* [f. ROB *v.*] That robs; thieving, predatory.

1657 S. PURCHAS *Pol. Flying-Ins.* 334 The robbing Bee and the Waspe.. will without strife or difference concurre together to rob a hive of Bees. **1886** *Lett. Donegal* 54 There need then have been no fear that the robbing scoundrels.. would have escaped punishment.

robbing, obs. form of ROBING.

†**robble**: see ROUNCE-ROBBLE-HOBBLE.

1616 B. JONSON *Masque of Queenes* Wks. 954 Rouncy is ouer, Robble is vnder, A flash of light and a clap of thunder.

robbo ('rɒbəʊ). *Austral. local slang.* [f. the name *Rob(inson* (see quot. 1897) + -o[2].] A horse and trap; a sulky; a poor horse; the driver of a horse and trap. Also, anything or anyone not up to standard, and in other extended uses.

1897 *Bulletin* (Sydney) 23 Jan. 11/3 In answer to a correspondent's question as to the derivation of 'robbo' (Sydney slang for the vehicle ordinarily called a 'sulky') 'J.P.' writes as follows..:—'Four Bob Robbo'—four shillings Robinson. Robinson, who lived in the classic suburb of Waterloo, Sydney.., came into a bit of money and bought a horse and trap. The money was spent, and Robinson tired of feeding the horse, which got poor; so he then sometimes let out the horse and trap (both somewhat worse for wear) for 4s. per half-day. There was a run on the cheap hire, and Rob. bought two other horses and traps, which he let out at the same price. A neighbouring livery-stable keeper and his employés resented Rob's cutting-down prices; and, when any of the rival's equipages passed, used to cry out, in derision, 'Four Bob Robbo!' The cry was taken up by the kids, and has now become a Waterloo classic. *Ibid.*, 'Robbo' has in an extensive Sydney circle come to mean anything unsatisfactory. For instance, a girl enters a jeweller's shop with: 'Watcher been givin' us? Look at the clasp of this 'ere bracelet I bought of yer last week. It's gone bung already. It's a fair robbo.' *Ibid.*, Also 'robbo' has come to mean amateur. **1906** A. J. TOMPKINS *With Swag & Billy* 51 Right out of the haunts of the motor, the bike and the Robbo. **1939** K. TENNANT *Foveaux* IV. v. 430 There was old Bert Robinson... 'E kept a livery stable down at the Foot. I s'pose you've 'eard of the Four-bob Robbos, then? The chaps used to go an' hire a cart for four bob and take it round loaded with vegetables. The kids used to call after 'em, 'Four Bob Robbo, Four Bob Robbo.' Old Bob Noblett, 'e's an old man now, but I can remember when Bob Noblett was a four-bob robbo. **1956** *Collins New Eng. Dict.* (Austral. & N.Z. Suppl.) 1279/2 *Robbo, Four-Bob-Robbo*, a horse and sulky... Now used only for a decrepit horse.

robbyng, obs. form of RUBBING.

robe (rəʊb), *sb.*[1] Also 5 roob(e, 6 robbe, 6–7 roab(e; *Sc.* 5–7 rob, 5 rowb. [a. OF. *robe* (*robbe*, *roube*), = Prov. *rouba*, Catal. and It. *roba*, Sp. *ropa*, Pg. *roupa*; the stem is that of the verb ROB, the original sense being 'spoil, booty', as in OF.]

1. a. A long loose outer garment reaching to the feet or the ankles, worn by both sexes in the Middle Ages, and still by men of some Eastern nations; a gown. Now *rare*, except as in 2.

c **1275** *Passion Our Lord* 66 in *O.E. Misc.* 39 Ne hedde he none robe of fowe ne of gray. *a* **1300** *Cursor M.* 3676 His moder..cled him..Wit his broþer robe. **1340** *Ayenb.* 119 Yef me yefþ ine þe kinges cort ane robe to ane childe. **1377** LANGL. *P. Pl.* B. XIII. 227 And fewe robes I fonge or furred gounes. **1422** tr. *Secreta Secret.*, *Priv. Priv.* 151 Hym Suffysid a lytill graue..for his halle, and for his roob. **1474** CAXTON *Chesse* 4 Theym that ben clad in thy clothyng and robys. **1501** DOUGLAS *Pal. Hon.* II. iii, With lawreir crownit, in robbis side all new, Of a fassoun. **1582** STANYHURST *Æneis* II. (Arb.) 68 Theare [is] wardrob abundant Of roabs most pretiouse. **1601** HOLLAND *Pliny* XXXIV. v, In auncient time all the Images and Statues erected to the honour of any men, were in their gownes and robes. **1667** MILTON *P.L.* II. 543 As when Alcides..felt th' envenom'd robe. **1730–46** THOMSON *Autumn* 1240 The glittering robe Of every hue reflected light can give. **1796** HUNTER *St. Pierre's Stud. Nat.* II. 511 Turbans and flowing robes are adapted to hot countries. **1840** THIRLWALL *Greece* VII. 89 The looms of Ionia were kept in constant activity to supply purple robes for the courtiers. **1877** BRYANT *Odyss.* v. 278 The nymph too, in a robe of silver white,..Arrayed herself.

transf. **1595** SHAKS. *John* II. i. 141 O well did he become that Lyons robe, That did disrobe the Lion of that robe.

fig. **1611** BIBLE *Isaiah* lxi. 10 He hath couered me with the robe of righteousnes. **1628** MILTON *Vac. Exerc.* 21 Hail native Language,..cull those richest Robes, and gay'st attire Which deepest Spirits, and choicest Wits desire. **1667** —— *P.L.* x. 222.

b. A trade name for a special form of lady's dress; a piece of material, either plain or embroidered, partly shaped for a gown.

1878 *Sylvia's Home Jrnl.* Feb., Ball dress (robe Princess), of blue faille. **1892** *Fashions of To-day* May 13 Robe of old gold velvet, collar of passementerie. **1899** *World of Dress* Jan. 3 Handsome embroidered chenille robe. *Ibid.*, White and cream lace robes in enormous variety.

c. A dressing-gown. See also *bath robe* s.v. BATH *sb.*[1] VI.

1854 DICKENS *Hard T.* II. viii. 223 She arose, put on a loose robe, and went out of her room in the dark. **1931** J. B. FAGAN *Improper Duchess* I. 25, I puta on my silk robe, I go down to his rooms. **1938** M. ALLINGHAM *Fashion in Shrouds* vi. 73 'Robe's' the new name for dressing-gown. **1945** 'L. LEWIS' *Birthday Murder* (1951) x. 152 She..put on the white terry-cloth robe. **1955** T. STERLING *Evil of Day* xiii. 134 A man in a robe and slippers. **1957** F. & R. LOCKRIDGE *Practise to Deceive* (1959) xiii. 181 Susan wore a white towelling robe. **1966** *Wall St. Jrnl.* 7 Jan. 2/2 Penney officials noted heavy sales in women's robes and sleepwear. **1970** G. F. NEWMAN *Sir, You Bastard* viii. 246 Tying his robe, he stepped out and along to the kitchen. **1976** *New Yorker* 26 Jan. 50/3 At lunch, Mrs Fox, still in pajamas, slippers, and robe, nearly drops a tray on Mrs Tompkins' head.

2. a. A long outer garment of a special form and material worn in virtue of, and betokening, a particular rank, calling, condition, or office.

c **1290** *Beket* 324 in *S. Eng. Leg.* I. 116 þe Abite of Monek he nam, And a-boue al þan clerkene Robe. *a* **1300** *Cursor M.* 9072 Tas of..mi king rob..þat i wer. **1362** LANGL. *P. Pl.* A. III. 277 Schal no seriaunt for þat seruise were a selk houue, Ne no Ray Robe wiþ Riche pelure. **1484** CAXTON *Curiall* 4 Oftymes the peple make grete wondrynges of the ryche robe of the courtyour. **1537** STARKEY *Let.* in *England* (1878) p. lxv, Master Pole hathe gotten the Cardynallys hatte & robbe made. **1596** SHAKS. *1 Hen. IV*, III. ii. 56 Thus I did keepe my Person fresh and new, My Presence like a Robe Pontificall Ne're seene, but wondred at. **1603** —— *Meas. for M.* II. ii. 61 Nor the deputed sword, The Marshalls Truncheon, nor the Iudges Robe. **1778** POTTER *Æschylus, To Mrs. Montague* (1808) p. xxviii, My pontifical robe trailing on the pavement. **1841** LANE *Arab. Nts.* I. 85 He then bestowed upon him a robe of honour. **1855** MACAULAY *Hist. Eng.* xiv. III. 382 Johnson had therefore been stripped of his robe by persons who had no jurisdiction over him.

fig. **1837** J. H. NEWMAN *Par. Serm.* I. xxvi. 398 Surely these attainments are but our first manly robe.

b. *pl.* with the same connotation. Often with qualifying word prefixed, as ***coronation***, ***parliament robes***, etc. ***Master***, ***Mistress***, ***Yeoman, of the Robes***: see these words.

1445 tr. *Claudian* in *Anglia* XXVIII. 259 With whos preyers he lyst be mevid to clothe him in his roobys..as consulers vsid before. *c* **1450** *Merlin* vii. 110 But first hadde Arthur the kynge put on hym an habergon vndir his robes. **1526** *Pilgr. Perf.* (W. de W. 1531) 156 b, Though the kynge were before hym in his robes of golde. **1596** SHAKS. *1 Hen. IV*, v. i. 12 You haue..made vs doffe our easie Robes of Peace. *a* **1618** SYLVESTER *Wks.* (Grosart) II. 61 Their garments passe..The glorious Salomon's rich roabes of Parliament. **1671** MILTON *P.R.* IV. 64 Pretors, Proconsuls to thir Provinces Hasting or on return, in robes of State. *a* **1715** BURNET *Own Time* III. (1724) I. 499 He put on his robes in hast,..and called up the Commons. **1769** SIR W. JONES *Seven Sisters* Poems (1777) 35 Accept the robes and sceptre of the land. **1832** G. DOWNES *Lett. Cont. Countries* I. 248 The senators and magistrates of Rome appear clad in the ecclesiastical robes of the period, in which the manuscript was written. **1849** MACAULAY *Hist. Eng.* v. I. 592 The..aldermen came in their robes to welcome the Duke.

3. a. *pl.* Outer garments or clothes in general.

c **1575** GASCOIGNE *Flowers* Wks. (1575) 44 You shall knowe the cause, wherefore these roabes are worne, And why I goe outlandishe lyke, yet being Englishe borne. **1596** SHAKS. *Tam. Shr.* I. ii. 132 Now shal my friend Petruchio do me grace, And offer me disguis'd in sober robes, To old Baptista. *Ibid.* III. ii. 114 See not your Bride in these vnreuerent robes. **1770** GOLDSM. *Des. Vill.* 336 She left her wheel and robes of country brown.

b. *fig.* A covering or vesture compared to a long enveloping garment.

1623 DRUMM. OF HAWTH. *Poems* Wks. (1711) 25 The Moon..Impearling with her Tears her Rob of Night. **1633** *Ibid.* 39 Now, ancient Caledon, Thy Beauties heighten, richest Robs put on. **1697** DAMPIER *Voy.* (1729) I. 165 In a weeks time the Tree casts off her old Robes, and is cloathed in a new pleasant Garb. **1727–46** THOMSON *Summer* 92 Prime cheerer, Light!.. Nature's resplendent robe! **1849** ROBERTSON *Serm.* Ser. I. ii. (1866) 38 Before the world has put on its full robe of light. **1864** TENNYSON *Aylmer's Field* 158 Another [cottage] wore A close-set robe of jasmine.

4. a. ***the long robe***, (the dress of) the legal or clerical profession; ***the short robe***, (that of) 'all that profess arms, or usually wear swords' (Cotgr.). So ***both robes***, ***either robe***.

1601– [see LONG ROBE]. **1622** BACON *Hen. VII* (1876) 127 He sent..commissioners of both robes, the prior of Lanthony to be his chancellor..; and Sir Edward Poynings ..with a civil power of his lieutenant. *a* **1641** BP. MOUNTAGU *Acts & Mon.* (1642) 95 A Sanhedrim, or standing great Councell,..made up of both Robes, honourable persons amongst their brethren, Priests and Laicks both. **1642–3** in Rushw. *Hist. Coll.* (1721) II. III. 137 They have spared..no Orders of Men, the long Robe as well as the Short hath felt their Fury. **1672** MARVELL *Reh. Transp.* I. 282 There was a gentleman of your robe a Dignitary of Lincoln. **1711** STEELE *Spect.* No. 157 ⁋6 Our learned Men of either Robe. **1712–1875** [see LONG ROBE].

b. ***the Robe***, the legal profession.

1647 CLARENDON *Hist. Reb.* I. §96 He was a son of the Robe; his Father having been a Judge in the Court of the Common Pleas. **1671** *Buccleuch MSS.* (Hist. MSS. Comm.) I. 497 Mr. Commartin..is a man of the robe, but in very good esteem with everybody. **1707** *Refl. upon Ridicule* 109 The most eminent Persons of the Robe. **1770** FOOTE *Lame Lover* III, I was some years in the Temple; but the death of my brother robb'd the robe of my labours. **1850** THACKERAY *Pendennis* xxix, The cadets of many of our good families follow the robe as a profession. **1855** MOTLEY *Dutch Rep.* I. 377 Rich advocates, and other Gentlemen of the Robe.

5. *transf.* Persons of high estate. *rare*$^{-1}$.

1589 WARNER *Alb. Eng.* VI. xxxiii. (1602) 163 So plagueth ciuill Warre, and so from Robe to Rag doth scoure.

6. *U.S.* and *Canada.* The dressed skin of a buffalo (musk-ox, etc.) used as a garment or rug.

1836 *Backwoods of Canada* 55 A light waggon comfortably lined with buffalo robes. **1848** BARTLETT *Dict. Amer.* s.v., A pack of robes, is ten skins, tied in a pack, which is the manner in which they are brought from the far West to market. **1892** W. PIKE *Barren Ground N. Canada* 106 The robes were in splendid condition; the undergrowth, which resembles a sheep's fleece.., was now thick and firm.

7. *attrib.* and *Comb.*, as ***robe-cloak***, ***-coat***, ***-maker***, ***-spinning***, ***-tearing***; † **robe-chamber**, † **robes-room**, a robing-room; † **robe-goer**, one who has charge of the robes.

1598 SYLVESTER *Du Bartas* II. i. IV. *Handycrafts* 131 The shining wooll Whence the robe-spinning precious Worms are ful. **1665** PEPYS *Diary* 23 June, My Lord Sandwich did take me aside in the robe-chamber. **1679–88** *Secr. Serv. Money Chas. & Jas.* (Camden) 146 In consideracion of his services and extraordinary attendances at the robes-roome upon his said Majestie and the Privy Councill and Committees. **1701** *Cal. Treasury P.* (1871) 529 Robegoers and bedgoers. **1746** in R. Chambers *Traditions of Edinburgh* (1846) 47 No misses in skirts and jackets, robe-coats, nor stay-bodied gowns, to be allowed to dance in country-dances. **1831** J. MACDONALD in *Life* (1849) III. 174 A species of religious robe-tearing. **1836–7** DICKENS *Sk. Boz* (1850) 149/2 There were Mr. Harris the law-stationer, and Mr. Jennings the robemaker. **1902** *Q. Rev.* Apr. 533 His father and grandfather were both robe-makers. **1908** G. B. SHAW *Lett. to Granville Barker* (1956) 139, I have persuaded her to be discovered next time in a robe-cloak. **1911** C. MACKENZIE *Passionate Elopement* xviii. 170 Swansdown misses..put into corsets almost as soon as they were out of robe-coats. **1964** *New Shetlander* No. 70. 27 She wuir a hap, rob cott an bratt.

robe (rəʊb), *sb.*[2] Also 'robe. Abbrev. of WARDROBE.

1935 *Spectator* 7 June 972/1 Mr. Toop, a wholesale furniture-maker in the Curtain Road with whom I once had dealings, introduced me to some pretty examples of what grammarians, I believe, call aphaeresis. 'If you want a 'Board,' he would say, 'I'd choose wawnut every time: but when it comes to a 'Robe, there's nothing to touch m'yogany.' **1969** *Sydney Morning Herald* 24 May 43/9 (Advt.), Built-in robes. **1974** T. R. DENNIS in J. Burnett *Useful Toil* III. 354, I did a bedroom suite for £21; it had a six-foot robe..dressing-table and tall-boy and bed to match. **1977** *Evening Gaz.* (Middlesbrough) 11 Jan. 11/7 (Advt.), Two double bedrooms, one with fitted unit and 'robe.

robe (rəʊb), *v.* Also 7 roab. [f. ROBE *sb.*[1]]

1. *trans.* To clothe or invest in a robe or robes; to apparel; to dress. Also *refl.* Also, to apparel (oneself) in a dressing-gown.

1377 LANGL. *P. Pl.* B. XV. 333 ȝe robeth and fedeth Hem þat han as ȝe han. **1655** tr. *Sorel's Com. Hist. Francion* III. 60 A Piece of rich Satin, to new Robe him. **1711** G. HICKES *Two Treat. Chr. Priesth.* (1847) II. 290 He robed and unrobed himself in his throne. **1725** POPE *Odyss.* v. 294 Ulysses rob'd him in the cloak and vest. **1859** TENNYSON *Geraint & Enid* 691 Rise therefore; robe yourself in this. **1886** MABEL COLLINS *Prettiest Woman* v, She robed herself again in her national costume. **1969** *New Yorker* 31 May 32/1 If I am resolute, I will arise and robe myself.

fig. **1638** SIR T. HERBERT *Trav.* (ed. 2) 14 Nature roabing the fruitfull earth with her choisest Tapistry. **1803** FOSTER in *Life & Corr.* (1846) I. 223 He robes himself in moonlight. **1850** LYNCH *Theoph. Trinal* ix, Love robed her in a blush. **1892** TENNYSON *Foresters* IV, A thousand winters Will strip you bare as death, a thousand summers Robe you life-green again.

2. *intr.* To put on robes or vestments.

a **1626** BACON *Advt. touching Holy War* (1629) 96 Only to Roab, and Feast, and performe Rites, and Obseruances. **1829** SOUTHEY *All for Love* III. xxi, And there the Priests are robing now. **1869** *Daily News* 14 Dec., The Bishops were to meet at half-past 8 o'clock in a meeting hall, where they were to robe and form in procession.

robed (rəʊbd), *ppl. a.* [f. ROBE *v.* or *sb.*[1]]

1. Clad in robes; wearing robes. Also with *in.*

c **1325** *Metr. Hom.* 41 A man robed in wlank wede. **1362** LANGL. *P. Pl.* A. IX. 1 Thus i-robed in russet, romed I a-boute. *a* **1400** *Isumbras* 269 So semly als thay bothe ware, If thay were robed riche. **1608** SHAKS. *Lear* III. vi. 38 (Q.[1]), Thou robbed man of Iustice take thy place. **1634** SIR T. HERBERT *Trav.* 194 Roabed and laden with..Gemmes. **1757** GRAY *Bard* 17 Rob'd in the sable garb of Woe. **1784** COWPER *Task* II. 823 The cause..has been found..in the skirts Of the rob'd pedagogue! **1834** LYTTON *Pompeii* I. iv, In the centre of the steps appeared a priest robed in white from head to foot. **1885** *Law Times* LXXIX. 385/1 Judge Powell..intimated that he should sit robed.

fig. **1632** MILTON *L'Allegro* 61 Wher the great Sun begins his state, Rob'd in flames, and Amber light. **1712** ADDISON *Spect.* No. 265 ⁋9 Ovid..tells us..that Aurora..is robed in Saffron. **1881** TENNYSON *To Virgil* i, Roman Virgil, thou that singest Ilion's lofty temples robed in fire. *a* **1901** F. W. H. MYERS *Hum. Personality* (1903) II. 299 Minds still robed in flesh.

2. Wearing robes of a specified kind, as ***long-***, ***loose-robed***, etc. Also *fig.*

1777 ELIZ. RYVES *Poems* 60 Where loose-rob'd Pleasure careless roves. **1838** ELIZA COOK *Spring* i, Beauty shines forth in the blossom-robed trees. **1849** M. ARNOLD *Strayed Reveller* 269 Passing through the dark stems Flowing-robed. **1857** DUFFERIN *Lett. High Lat.* (ed. 3) 92 Silence and deep peace brooded over the fair grass-robed plain.

‖**robe de chambre** (rɔb də ʃɑ̃br). Also 8 -chamber. [F.; see ROBE *sb.*[1] and CHAMBER *sb.*] A dressing-gown or négligé robe.

1731 *Gentl. Mag.* I. 321 Instead of which [knowledge], we have brought home the French *Coifure*, the *Robe de Chambre* of the Women, and *Toupé* and *Solitaire* of the Men. **1732** *Lond. Mag.* Oct. 351/1 Her Lady Aunt was dress'd in a *Robe de chambre*. **1824** BYRON *Juan* XVI. xi, Our robe de chambre May sit like that of Nessus. **1848** THACKERAY *Van. Fair* xxiv, Pointing to the spot of his *robe de chambre* under which his heart was still feebly beating. **1893** *Pioneer of Fashion* I. IV, A particular study has been made of our robes de chambre.

attrib. **1746** FRANCIS tr. *Horace, Sat.* I. ii. 38 That Youth ..All but a robe-de-chamber Dame disdains.

‖**robe de nuit** (rɔb də nɥi). [Fr.] A nightdress.

1855 TROLLOPE *Warden* ii. 21 He has exchanged..those shining black habiliments for his accustomed *robe de nuit*. **1897** G. STEVENS *Let.* 2 Nov. in *Lett. W. Stevens* (1967) 16 Your Mother is making up some sort of..a Robe-de-Nuit something to cover your abused anatomy as you wander..to the toilet. **1911** E. M. CLOWES *On Wallaby* v. 119 A lady whose husband had seen another lady going to the bath in her *robe de nuit* alone. **1968** J. IRONSIDE *Fashion Alphabet* 71 *Robe de Nuit*, nightdress.

‖**robe de style** (rɔb də stil). [Fr., lit. 'robe of style'.] (See quot. 1969.) Also *fig.* and *attrib.*

1928 [see *eau-de-Nil* s.v. EAU]. **1931** *Times Lit. Suppl.* 25 June p. i/4 Dignincont's..etchings and Coulouma's clear setting in Baskerville lend an expensive *robe de style* to a novel which seems more at home in a yellow jacket. **1963** *Times* 24 Jan. 12/4 John Cavanagh's bridal model, a soft vision in white chiffon, cut on *robe de style* lines, with chiffon veil falling from a flowered chignon, has given rise to much speculation whether this studied simplicity will be reflected in the gown that Princess Alexandra will choose for her wedding. **1969** R. T. WILCOX *Dict. Costume* (1970) 293/1 *Robe de style*, the twentieth century infanta style, an evening fashion for which Lanvin of Paris became famous; its vogue was in the nineteen twenties and thirties. It had a tight bodice with a bouffant skirt, ankle or floor length.

ˈ**robeless**, *a.* [f. ROBE *sb.*[1] + -LESS.] Without robes; destitute or deprived of robes.

1652 BENLOWE *Theoph.* IX. xxviii, John, Joseph, Robelesse fly; Peter, thou stay'st, and stay'st but to deny! **1880** RUSKIN *Our Fathers have told Us* I. i. 26 Going, in his full robes, to say prayers in church,..he came across some un-happily robeless person by the wayside.

robell(e, obs. forms of RUBBLE.

rober (ˈrəʊbə(r)). [f. ROBE *sb.*[1] or *v.* + -ER[1].] One who has charge of, or who invests with, robes; a robe-maker.

1884 *Manch. Exam.* 28 June 7/1 He was steward and rober to the Connaught Bar on Circuit. **1887** *Eng. Hist. Rev.* II. 480 A *prepositus*..summoned the robers to place the diadem on the imperial head.

roberd, obs. form of ROBERT.

† **Roberdavy.** *Obs.* Also 6 Rob Dauie, 7 Rob-o-Dauy. [Of obscure origin.] A kind of wine used in the 16–17th centuries.

1542 BOORDE *Dyetary* x. (1870) 255 Also these hote wynes, as..caprycke, tynt, roberdauy. **1553** BALE *Vocation* 22 They went in heaps from tauerne to tauerne to seke after the best

Rob dauie and aqua vite, which are their speciall drinkes there. **1620** J. Taylor (Water-P.) *Praise Hempseed* Wks. (1630) II. 65 Sherry, nor Rob-o-Dauy here could flowe.

†**Roberdsmen.** *Obs.* Forms: 4 (7) **Roberdesmen** (7–8 **Roberdsmen**), 4 **Robertes men**, 6, 8–9 **Robertsmen**. [Probably from the proper name *Roberd* Robert, but the allusion is obscure.] A certain class of marauding vagabonds that infested the country in the 14th century.

All the instances later than the 14th century are merely historical.

1331 *Act 5 Edw. III*, c. 14 Diverses roberies, homicides, & felonies, ont este faitz einz ces heures par gentz qi sont appellez Roberdesmen, Wastours & Draghlacche. **1383** *Act 7 Rich. II*, c. 1 §5 Ordeignez est & assentuz que lestatutz.. de Roberdesmen & Drawlacches soient fermement tenus & gardez. *c* **1394** *P. Pl. Crede* 72 Ryȝt as Robertes men [they] raken aboute, At feires & at ful ales & fyllen þe cuppe. **1567** Harman *Caveat* (1869) 27 These were then the commen names of these leud leuterars, Faytores, Robardesmen, Drawlatches, and valyant beggares. **1581** Lambarde *Eiren.* II. vi. (1588) 196 Drawlatches, Wastours, or Robertsmen, that is to say, either miching or mightie theeues. *a* **1633** Coke *On Litt.* (1648) III. 197 What this Robin Hood was that hath raised a name to these kind of men called Roberdsmen, his followers. **1731** *Gentl. Mag.* I. 238/1 [He] instances in Robin Hood, and says that from him Thieves and Highwaymen are called Robertsmen. **1769** Blackstone *Comm.* IV. xvii. 244 Persons in disguise.. (who seem to have resembled the Roberdsmen, or followers of Robin Hood). **1796** *Sporting Mag.* VIII. 76 Men of his [Robin Hood's] lawless profession were from him called Roberdsmen.

roberie, obs. form of robbery.

Robert ('rɒbət). [A personal name, a. F. *Robert*, ultimately of Teutonic origin.]

†**1.** = Robin (redbreast). *Obs.*

14.. in Wr.-Wülcker 702 *Hec frigella*, a roberd. **14..** *Camb. MS. Gg. 4. 27* lf. 9b, Robert red brest and the wrenne.

2. = herb Robert. Also ***robert's-bill***.

1847 Halliwell, *Robert*, the herb stork-bill. **1856** Capern *Poems* 158 The foxglove, the robert, the gorse, and the thyme. **1859** —— *Ball. & Songs* 129 The yarrow and the robert's-bill.

3. A policeman. Cf. bobby 2.

1870 *Figaro* 18 Nov. (Farmer), The 'British Peeler'.. is, after all, a sensitive creature. The blood of the Roberts is at length aroused. **1899** 'J. Flynt' *Tramping with Tramps* II. 231 But look out for the Robert and the Dee (the policeman and the detective). **1929** T. L. Davidson *Murder in Laboratory* xiv. 108, I stopped and asked a Robert the time. **1968** J. Lock *Lady Policeman* iv. 34 Believe it or not PCs are still occasionally wished, 'Good morning, Robert!'

4. A waiter.

From a series of articles, professedly written by a waiter named Robert, which appeared in *Punch* in 1881–2.

1886 *Pall Mall G.* 10 Aug. 3/2 The Parisian Roberts now on strike. *Ibid.* 3 Sept. 3/1 The Swiss 'Robert' proposes that his new 'Union for Swiss Waiters' shall be called the 'Winkelriedverein'.

5. *Robert sauce, sauce Robert*: see sauce *sb.* 1

6. *Naut. slang.* A spell off duty; a sleep, a 'nap'.

1935 'L. Luard' *Conquering Seas* xii. 140 I'll get head down for a proper robert.

Robert(e)s-men, variants of Roberdsmen.

Robertian (rə'bɜːtɪən), *a.* [f. Robert + -ian.] Of or pertaining to Robert the Strong (*d.* 866), count of Anjou and of Blois, or his descendants, who became kings of France. Also as *sb.*, a follower or successor of Robert the Strong.

1903 D. C. Munro *Hist. Middle Ages* vii. 66 Charles the Simple.. had little power, and the kingdom was wrested from him in 923 by a member of the Robertian house. **1942** Strayer & Munro *Middle Ages* vi. 147 Otto had the advantage of being the brother-in-law both of the Carolingian king and of the head of the rival Robertian family. **1957** *Encycl. Brit.* IX. 589 Henceforth there ensued a long duel between the Robertians and the Carolingians in which three times the Robertians were chosen and might have taken the crown.

Robertine ('rɒbətiːn, -aɪn), *sb.* and *a.* [f. as prec. + -ine[1].] **A.** *sb.* A follower of Robert of Melun (d. 1167), English-born scholastic theologian.

1846 T. Wright *Biogr. Brit. Lit.: Anglo-Norman Period* IV. 201 His disciples formed a sect which was long known by the name of Robertines. **1906** W. H. Schofield *Eng. Lit. to Chaucer* ii. 52 At Mont St. Geneviève the 'Robertines' long continued to discuss their leader's great work.. the *Summa Theologiae*, which above all gave warrant for his repute as a metaphysician.

B. *adj.* = Robertian *a.*

1938 Z. N. Brooke *Hist. Europe* iv. 96 The ambition of the Robertine house dictated the fortunes of the French kingdom in the tenth century.

Hence **Rober'tinian** *sb.*, a follower or successor of Robert the Strong.

1910 *Encycl. Brit.* X. 813/1 The struggle against the Robertinians went on relentlessly. *Ibid.* 813/2 There was a kind of *entente cordiale* between the Carolingians and the Robertinians and Otto.

Robertonian (ˌrɒbə'təʊnɪən). [f. as prec. + *-onian* as in *Caledonian, Patagonian*, etc.] A follower of Robert the Strong (see Robertian *a.*).

1936 H. A. L. Fisher *Hist. Europe* I. xvii. 208 Robert the Strong, Count of Paris, fought for ten years against the Northmen... The Robertonians were as distinguished for caution as for courage.

Robertsonian (ˌrɒbət'səʊnɪən), *a.* *Cytology.* [f. the name of William R. B. *Robertson* (1881–1941), U.S. biologist, who first described such translocations in 1916 (*Jrnl. Morphol.* XXVII. 220) + -ian.] Applied to the formation of a metacentric chromosome from two heterologous acrocentric chromosomes by the fusion of their centromeres or by a translocation with the loss of a small fragment; and to karyotypic changes brought about by this process.

1954 M. J. D. White *Animal Cytol. & Evol.* (ed. 2) x. 192 In certain groups such as the Acrididae, 'Robertsonian' rearrangements or whole-arm transpositions account for a large part of the obvious differences in caryotypes. **1955** *Nature* 2 Apr. 601/1 The wide variation in the mitotic numbers must be attributed to Robertsonian changes. **1960** *Jrnl. Nat. Cancer Inst.* XXIV. 1187 A large mediocentric chromosome and a heterochromatic minute were formed, apparently at the expense of two acrocentric chromosomes, providing a classic example of a Robertsonian relationship, manifesting itself within the neoplastic cell population of a transplantable tumor. **1973** *Nature* 3 Aug. 262/1 The most common chromosomal changes seen in vertebrate evolution are Robertsonian fusions which create one metacentric from two acrocentrics and inversions which, if pericentric in nature, change the position of a centromere. **1974** *Ibid.* 10 May 164/1 These consisted of thirty-eight Robertsonian translocations, forty-seven reciprocal translocations and nine pericentric inversions.

Robertson's law ('rɒbətsənz). *Cytology.* [f. as prec. + law *sb.*[1]] The law that states that the number of chromosome arms of a population or species tends to remain constant, although the number of chromosomes may vary. Cf. prec.

1945 M. J. D. White *Animal Cytol. & Evol.* viii. 170 In certain groups 'Robertson's law' explains many of the more obvious changes in chromosome shape. **1956** *Jrnl. Morphol.* XCIX. 265 Well-documented instances of chromosomal phylogeny conforming to Robertson's law have been reported from several groups of animals.

Robespierrist ('rəʊbspɪɛərɪst), *sb.* and *a.* [f. the name of *Robespierre* (see below) + -ist.]

A. *sb.* A follower of Maximilien François Marie Isidore de Robespierre (1758–94), one of the leaders in the French revolution; a Jacobin (sense 2). **B.** *adj.* Associated with, or adhering to, Robespierre.

1834 [see Orleanist]. **1904** J. R. M. Macdonald in *Cambr. Mod. Hist.* (1907) VIII. xii. 338 The Commune, whose conception of the ultimate ends of the *coup d'état* differed *toto cœlo* from those of both Dantonists and Robespierrists. **1929** L. R. Gottschalk *Era of French Revol.* I. III. iii. 263 (*heading*) The Robespierrists destroyed. **1937** *Downside Rev.* Oct. 519 It is certain that the laws [of Ventôse] contributed to the fall of the Robespierrists. *Ibid.*, The majority of the Committee were unsympathetic and obstructive, which increased the tension between them and the Robespierrist minority. **1975** G. Rudé *Robespierre* 9 It marks a welcome addition to Robespierrist studies. *Ibid.* 43 While the Jacobins and the Convention—even the Robespierrists among them—were prepared to tolerate controls and State-direction of the nation's economy merely as exceptional and temporary measures, [etc.].

robeux, obs. f. rubbish.

robi, obs. f. ruby.

robiboo, var. rubbaboo.

†**ro'biginous**, *a.* *Obs.*—[0] [ad. L. *rōbīginōsus*, f. *rōbīgo* rust.] 'Much blasted, rusty' (Blount, 1656).

robiis, obs. form of rubbish.

robill, obs. form of rubble.

Robin[1] ('rɒbɪn). Except in sense 1, usu. with lower-case initial. Forms: 4–5 **Robyn**, 6 **Roben**, *Sc.* **Robene, Robeen**, 7 *Sc.* **Robein**, 7, 9 **Robbin**, 5– **Robin**. [a. OF. *Robin*, a dim. or familiar form of the personal name *Robert*.]

For several specific uses see round robin.

I. 1. The personal name, in more or less allusive or general application.

poor Robin: see poor *a.* 8. For dial. uses such as *Robin-round-cap, -run-rake*, etc., see the *Eng. Dial. Dict.*

c **1374** Chaucer *Troylus* v. 1174 From hasell wode there Ioly Robin pleyde. **1377** Langl. *P. Pl.* B. vi. 75 Saue Iakke þe iogeloure.. And Robyn þe Rybaudoure. *c* **1400** *Rom. Rose* 6337 Now am I Robert, now Robyn; Now frere Menour, now Iacobyn. *Ibid.* 7455 He, that whylom was so gay, And of the daunce Ioly Robin, Was tho become a Iacobin. **1555** Latimer in Foxe *A. & M.* (1570) III. 1919/2 Now that would I see, quoth long Roben, *ut dicitur vulgariter*. **1586** A. Day *Eng. Secretary* II. (1625) 23 Some Robin the divell, or I wot not what spirit of the Ayre. **1603** *Philotus* cxxxvi, Now grace and honour on that face, Quod Robein to the Haggies.

II. 2. = Robin redbreast 1 a. (Cf. Fris. *robyn(tsje, robynderke*, Du. dial. *robijntje*, the linnet.)

1549 *Compl. Scotl.* vi. 39 Robeen and the litil vran var hamely in vyntir. **1665** Sir T. Herbert *Trav.* (1677) 383 Here are also Ayeries of Hawks and sundry others Birds; as Goshawks,.. Robbins, Herons white and beautiful. **1802** Wordsw. *Redbreast chasing Butterfly* 3 The pious bird with the scarlet breast, Our little English Robin. **1864** Tennyson *Enoch Arden* 677 On the nigh-naked tree the robin piped Disconsolate.

b. Any bird of the genus *Erithacus*.

1855 *Orr's Circle Sci., Org. Nat.* III. 303 In the sub-family of the *Erythacinæ* or Robins, the bill is rather short, slender, tapering,.. and depressed at the base.

3. *N. Amer.* The red-breasted thrush, *Turdus migratorius*.

1703 S. Sewall *Diary* 16 Mar. (1879) II. 75 The Robbins cheerfully utter their Notes this morn. **1798** *Monthly Mag.* May 331/2 The American robin, larger than ours. **1808** Wilson *Amer. Ornith.* I. 37 The Robin is one of our earliest songsters. **1858** Longf. *M. Standish* III. 3 Into the tranquil woods, where blue-birds and robins were building. **1888** G. H. Kingsley *Sport & Trav.* vi. (1900) 182 In America I shoot robins and find them thrushes. **1944** S. Bellow *Dangling Man* 172 A few large birds, robins and grackles, appeared in the trees. **1966** *Vancouver Province* 19 Nov. 1/5 The robin had been sitting in a mountain ash tree in his front yard.

4. The name given to various birds (esp. in former colonies), as in New Zealand to those of the genus *Miro*, in Australia to species of *Petroica* and other genera, in Jamaica to the green tody, etc.

Recent American dicts. assign the name to the red-breasted snipe and merganser, and to the mouse-bird or coly.

a **1880** R. Davies *Poems & Lit. Rem.* (1884) 264 In the bush [of New Zealand].. the robin always comes about. **1880** Mrs. Meredith *Tasmanian Friends & Foes* 123 The Robin (*Petroica multicolor*) is.. certainly more brilliantly beautiful than his English namesake. **1894** Newton *Dict. Birds* 791 *Robin*, a well-known nickname of the Red-breast,.. has been transplanted.. to Jamaica in the case of the Green Tody.

b. With distinctive epithets (adj. or sb.) applied to many birds, esp. of the (former) colonies or India, as ***blue robin***, the bluebird, *Sialia sialis*; ***golden robin***, the Baltimore oriole; ***Indian robin*** (see quot. 1855); ***magpie robin*** (see magpie 8); ***yellow robin*** (see quot. 1855); etc.

For an enumeration of the various Australian birds thus named see Morris *Austral English* 390–1.

1827 *Trans. Linn. Soc.* XV. 242 'This bird,' Mr. Cayley says, 'is called yellow-robin by the colonists. It is an inhabitant of bushes'. **1844** J. E. DeKay *Zool. N.Y.* II. 65 The Bluebird, or Blue Robin as it is called in the western counties. **1855** *Orr's Circle Sci., Org. Nat.* III. 265 One of the commonest species, the Baltimore Oriole,.. has received the name of *fire-bird*... It is also called the Golden Robin. *Ibid.* 283 The *Eopsaltaria australis*, which is also an Australian species, is known to the colonists of New South Wales as the *Yellow Robin*. *Ibid.* 307 The *Thamnobia fulicata*, or Indian Robin, even exceeds his European representative in boldness and familiarity. **1884** *Harper's Mag.* Mar. 610/1 Our New England forefathers call him the 'blue robin'.

c. Used attributively or appositively in names of various birds.

robin accentor, a small red-breasted bird of the thrush family (*Tharraleus rubeculoides*), inhabiting the Himalayas; **robin breast**, = *robin snipe*; **robin breastie**, *Sc.*, = Robin redbreast; **robin-chat**, one of several African thrush-like birds belonging to the genus *Cossypha* of the family Turdidæ; **robin dipper**, *U.S.*, the buffle-headed duck; **robin** (†**rock**), **-rook, -ruck**, *dial.*, = sense 2; **robin sandpiper**, the knot; **robin snipe**, (*a*) = prec.; (*b*) the red-breasted snipe. See also Robin ruddock.

1555 Gesner *Hist. Anim.* III. 699 A robin.. *alibi* a robbyn rock. **1736** Pegge *Kenticisms* (E.D.S.), *Robin-rook*, a robin-redbreast. **1824** Mactaggart *Gallovid. Encycl.* 412 The tane o' them was the Robbin Breestie. **1872** Coues *N. Amer. Birds* 256 Robin-snipe... Bill equalling or rather exceeding the head. *Ibid.* 632 *Tringa*,.. Robin Sandpiper. Bill about as long as, or rather longer than, the head. **1890** Oates *Fauna Brit. India Birds* II. 169 *Tharrhaleus rubeculoides*, the Robin Accentor. **1901** A. C. Stark *Birds S. Afr.* II. 209 (*heading*) Noisy Robin-Chat. **1931** *Discovery* May 138/2 The robin chat.. is smart in appearance, with.. blue shoulder patches and bright orange-rufous underparts. **1960** *Times* 29 Sept. (Nigeria Suppl.) p. xxi/7 The colourful white-headed robin chat, that richest and most versatile of Nigerian songsters.

5. *attrib.* and *Comb.*, as ***robin-anthem, -song***; ***robin-red*** adj.; **robin dinner**, a Christmas dinner given to London waifs by subscription; **robin's egg**, *U.S.*, (of) a greenish-blue colour; usu., **robin's egg blue**; **robin-snow**, *U.S.*, a light snow coming before the departure or after the return of the American robin.

1853 Thoreau *Jrnl.* 11–12 Jan. in *Writings* (1906) x. 462 He says that the most snow we have had this winter (it has not been more than one inch deep) has been only a 'robin snow' as it is called, *i.e.* a snow which does not drive off the robins. *a* **1862** Thoreau *Early Spring in Mass.* (1881) 49 The slight robin snow of yesterday is already mostly dissipated. **1873** Eliz. Phelps *Trotty's Wedding Tour* 166 She saw her robin's egg sash and gloves. **1880** Lanier *Owl agst. Robin* Poems (1892), Nothing but robin-songs heard under heaven. **1881** Robin's-egg blue [see peacock *sb.* 5]. **1887** M. E. Wilkins *Humble Romance* 15 A dress-pattern of robin's-egg blue silk. **1892** *Daily News* 21 Jan. 3/1 A 'Robin' dinner took place last night at the headquarters of the Camberwell Mission. **1896** —— 17 Oct. 6/5 A robin-red velvet waistcoat. **1910** *Busy Man's Mag.* Dec. 65/1 On either side were swift hills mottled with green and gold, ahead a curdle of snow-capped mountains, above a sky of robin's-egg blue. **1933** N. Waln *House of Exile* I. iii. 43 Two lovely robin's-egg-blue bowls and two pairs of ivory chopsticks. **1951** E. Paul *Springtime in Paris* v. 91 Cloud battalions retreating, and stragglers streaked with red—geranium, salmon, vermilion, magenta. Between them, their complements of robin's egg, turquoise, and faint bottle green. **1951** Auden *Nones* (1952) 15 A robin with no

Christian name ran through The Robin-Anthem which was all it knew. **1970** R. Lowell *Notebk.* 27 The boys.. Crawling the swimming pool's robin's-egg sky. **1978** M. Puzo *Fools Die* xi. 118, I gave up all thoughts of buying a Cadillac and settled for the robin's-egg blue Dodge.

III. 6. A name given locally or dialectally to various plants, as red campion, ragged robin, herb Robert, etc. (See Britten & Holland.)

red robin: see RED *a.* 19 and RED RAG 2.

1694 Westmacott *Script. Herb.* 23 Altering the taste with a handful of.. Ground Ivy, or Robin leaves. **1906** *Academy* 5 May 425/2 Dewdropt daffodillies, With robin, medled in the thicket grass. **1913** D. H. Lawrence in *New Statesman* 16 Aug. 595/2 We called the purple primroses 'robins', for no reason, unless that they bloomed in winter.

b. The first element in several popular names of plants, esp. ***Robin in the hedge*** (see quot. 1828); ***Robin-run-(in-)the-hedge***, ground-ivy; goose-grass or cleavers; bindweed; Lady's bedstraw, etc.

See also Britten & Holland, and the *Eng. Dial. Dict.*

1796 Withering *Brit. Pl.* (ed. 3) III. 526 Ground Ivy... Robin run in the hedge. Groves, hedges, and shady places. **1824** Mactaggart *Gallovid. Encycl.*, *Robbin-rin-the-Hedge*, a trailing kind of weed, which runs along hedges, a robbin net. **1828** *Craven Gloss.*, *Robin-ith-hedge*, red flowered Campion. *Lychnis dioica.* **1834** *Tait's Mag.* I. 446/2 The wild-pink on the craggy ledge,.. And e'en the Robin-run-i'-the-hedge, Are precious in mine eyes. **1846** Keightley *Notes Virg.* Flora 385 Cleavers, Clivers, Goose-grass. In some places (particularly in Ireland) it is called Robin-run-the-hedge. **1847** Halliwell s.v. *Robin*, Robin in the hose, *lychnis silvestris.* **1883** Burne *Shropsh. Folk-Lore* xxiii, The old Ludlow custom of dining on a leg of pork stuffed with Robin-run-i'-the-hedge.

c. Used attributively in plant-names, as **robin-flower**, ragged robin; herb Robert (Britten & Holland); **robin-net** (see b, quot. 1824); **robin-wheat**, *U.S.*, = *robin's rye.*

robin-wake, = wake-robin, in Crabb's *Technol. Dict.* (1823), is prob. a mistake.

1886 *Pop. Sci. Monthly* XXIX. 368 The birds are not the only harvesters of the pretty moss known as robin-wheat.

d. In genitive combs. forming plant-names, as **robin's cushion**, = *robin's pincushion*; **robin's eye(s, flower**, herb Robert; rose campion, etc. (*Eng. Dial. Dict.*); **robin's pincushion** (see quot. 1850); **robin's plantain**, *U.S.*, a species of fleabane (*Erigeron bellidifolium*); **robin's rye** (see quot. 1897).

1846-50 A. Wood *Class-bk. Bot.* 326 Robin's Plantain. **1850** *Episodes Ins. Life* 67 The rose bedeguar wears the appearance of a mossy tuft... In some parts of England it is said to be known by the name of Robin's Pincushion. **1862** H. Marryat *Year in Sweden* II. 286 A stunted wild-rose, now covered with those feathery red excrescences.. called in England 'robin's-cushions'. **1897** *Syd. Soc. Lex.*, *Robin's rye*, a common name for the hair-cap moss, *Polytrichum juniperinum.*

IV. 7. The name of various fishes: **a.** *dial.* A small or an inferior codfish.

1618 *Naworth Househ. Bks.* (Surtees) 81, 2 robbins, 12 codds,.. 3 robbins. **1807** C. Waugh *Fisherman's Def.* 4 (Cumb. Gloss.), The small cod called Robins. **1892** H. A. Macpherson *Fauna Lakeland* 484 The 'Robbin' or 'Robin' is a deformed-looking fish, often taken at the end of the winter fishing.

b. *U.S.* (See quots.)

1853 J. Richardson *Let.* 24 May in N. E. Eliason *Tarheel Talk* (1956) 290 We caught 19 brim & robbins. **1876** Goode *Fishes Bermudas* 10 The Pilchard.., Shad.., and the Robin (*Decapterus punctatus*), are used as 'full-baits'. **1888** —— *Amer. Fishes* 99 The 'Sailor's Choice'.. bears several other names,.. as the 'Robin' and 'Pin-fish'. **1894** *Outing* XXIV. 263/2 'Here's a sea-robin!'.. The robin grunted vigorously as I relieved him of the hook.

c. *attrib.*, as **robin huss** (see quot. 1879).

1879 *N. & Q.* 5th Ser. XII. 193/2 The Sussex coast, where the small-spotted dog-fish (*Scyllium canicula*) is termed a robin huss. **1883** Day *Fishes Gt. Brit. & Irel.* II. 310.

†**robin**[2]. *Obs.* Also 8 robbin. [var. of ROBING *vbl. sb.*] = ROBING *vbl. sb.* 2.

1748 Richardson *Clarissa* (1811) III. 29 The cuffs and robins curiously embroidered by the fingers of this ever charming Arachne. **1777** Mme. D'Arblay *Early Diary* 7 Apr., Her green and grey [gown],.. trimmed with gauze, white ribbons, gauze apron, cuffs, robins, etc. **1789** Mrs. Piozzi *Journ. France* I. 306 With heavy lace robbins ending at the elbow.

'**robin**[3]. *Commerce.* Also robbin. [a. Fr. *robin.*] (See quot. 1858.)

1858 Simmonds *Dict. Trade*, *Robbin*, a package in which pepper and other dry goods are sometimes imported from Ceylon. The robbin of rice in Malabar weighs about 84 lbs. **1880** Whiteley *Diary & Alm.* 82 Robin of coffee = 1 to $1\frac{1}{2}$ cwt. **1887** *Daily News* 6 Oct. 2/8 Of 230 cases 240 bags and robins [of] Cochin ginger.

'**robin**[4]. *Chem.* [irreg. f. ROBINIA: see -IN[1].] The specific toxin of *Robinia pseudacacia.*

1901 *British Med. Jrnl.* 4 May 1070 The vegetable toxins of ricin, abrin, and robin.

robin, variant of ROBBIN.

‖**Robine.** *Obs.* Also **Robin.** [F.] An early variety of pear.

1706 London & Wise *Retired Gardener* I. 29 The Robine, or Summer-Pear-Royal, is.. of a strong perfum'd Taste, very sugary. **1725** *Family Dict.* s.v. *Pear*, Robin.. is in Shape and Size like a small Bergamot,.. sugar'd and perfum'd Juice [etc.]. *Ibid.*, Robine described before. **1786** [see MUSK *sb.* 4 d].

robinet ('rɒbɪnɛt). Forms: 4-5 **robynet**, 5-6 **-ett**, 6 **-ette**, **-att(e**; 5 **robenet**, 6- **robinet**, 9 *dial.* **robinut**, **robbinat**. [a. OF. *Robinet*, dim. of the personal name *Robin* ROBIN[1].]

In the following quot. probably the proper name of the single engine (but cf. sense 2): **13..** *Coer de L.* 1390 Another schyp was laden yet With an engyne hyghte Robynet: It was Rychardys o mangenel.

†**1.** App. some form or part of hoisting-tackle.

1497 *Naval Acc. Hen. VII* (1896) 89 Gynne with a robenet & other apparell, j. *Ibid.* 113 Crane rope, j, Robenet rope, j, Slyngrope, j. **1512** in Willis & Clark *Cambridge* (1886) I. 608 Gynnes, wheles, cables, robynettes, sawes.

†**2.** A kind of small cannon. *Obs.*

1547 in *Archaeologia* LI. 263 Skottishe Gounes of Brasse .. Fawcons oone. Fawconetts ix. Robynetts oone. **1587** Harrison *England* II. xvi, The names of our greatest ordinance are commonlie these. Robinet, whose weight is two hundred pounds, and it hath one inch and a quarter within the mouth. **1611** Florio, *Ribadochino*, a small piece of ordinance called of vs a Robinet.

3. = Robin[1] 2. Now *north. dial.*

c **1425** *Voc.* in Wr.-Wülcker 640 *Hec frigella*, robynet redbrest. **1483** *Cath. Angl.* 310/2 A Robynett, *frigella.* **1604** Drayton *Owl* 137 The Sparrow and the Robinet agen, to live neere to the Mansion place of Men. **1630** —— *Muses' Elys.* viii. 106 The Nightingale,.. To doe her best shall straine her voyce; And to this bird to make a Set, The Mauis, Merle, and Robinet. **1867-** in Lanc. and Yorks. glossaries.

4. A cock or faucet of a pipe (see quot.).

The ordinary sense of F. *robinet.*

1867 Smyth *Sailor's Word-bk.*, *Robinet*, the name of some useful cocks in the steam-engine, as for gauge, brine, trial, and steam-regulator.

'**robing**, *vbl. sb.* [f. ROBE *v.* + -ING[1].]

1. Apparel, array; a costume or gown.

c **1470** *Golagros & Gaw.* 1265 Yone riche cummis arait in riche robbing. **1760-72** H. Brooke *Fool of Qual.* (1809) IV. 143 He seized the hem of her robing, and glued it to his mouth. **1853** Kane *Grinnell Exp.* xxxiv. (1856) 302 The three under-shirts, the fur outer robing, and the seal-skin boots. **1867** Mrs. Whitney *L. Goldthwaite* ix, Her accumulating treasure of reserved robings. **1888** *Pall Mall G.* 20 Mar. 5/2 The woman whose graceful personality shines through her robing.

2. A trimming in the form of bands or stripes upon a gown or robe.

1727 Mrs. Delany *Life & Corr.* (1861) I. 143 Gold chains .. were tacked on the robings of their gowns in loose scollops in the manner of a galloon. **1741** Richardson *Pamela* I. 49, I made Robings and Facings of a pretty Bit of printed Calico, I had by me. **1747** Garrick *Miss in her Teens* I, I'd give the world I had put on my pink and silver robings to-day. **1814** *Hist. Univ. of Oxford* I. 111 The Doctors in Divinity being distinguished by robeings of black fur. **1886** *St. James's Gaz.* 25 Sept. 11/1 The most lovely trimmings are of large panels and stripes, or robings, composed partly of lace, partly of beaded passementerie.

3. The action of putting on robes.

1838 Dickens *Nich. Nick.* xxv, This pious reasoning supported the bride through the ceremony of robing.

4. *attrib.*, as ***robing-table***; **robing-room**, a room specially appropriated to the putting on the official robes; so ***robing accommodation.***

1711-2 Swift *Journal to Stella* 2 Jan., So I only went into the robing-room, to give my four brothers joy. **1830** Macaulay in *Trevelyan* 10 Feb., Brougham.. has blamed Lord Lansdowne in the robing-room of the Court of the King's Bench. **1859** Dickens *T. Two Cities* II. iv, Stryver shouldered his way back to the robing-room. **1897** *Daily News* 15 Oct. 5/1 Robing accommodation will be provided. **1927** T. Wilder *Bridge San Luis Rey* ii. 19, I slipped into the sacristy, climbed the robing-table.. and walked in.

Robin Goodfellow ('rɒbɪn 'gʊdfɛləʊ). [See Robin[1] and goodfellow. For the use of the adj. cf. good *a.* 2 d.]

1. A sportive and capricious elf or goblin believed to haunt the English country-side in the 16-17th centuries; also called Hobgoblin or Puck.

A full account of the popular beliefs concerning Robin Goodfellow is given by Shakspere in *Mids. N.* II. i. 33 ff. In R. Scot *Disc. Witchcraft* (1584) *Devils & Sp.* I. xxi. he is described as a helpful being, similar to the Scottish brownie.

1531 Tindale *Wks.* (Parker Soc. 1849) 139 The scripture .. is become a maze unto them, in which they wander as in a mist, or (as we say) led by Robin Goodfellow, that they cannot come to the right way, no, though they turn their caps. **1570** B. Googe *Pop. Kingd.* III. (1880) 33 Masse driues out Robyn good fellow, & bugs that walke by night. **1590** Shaks. *Mids. N.* II. i. 34 That shrew'd and knauish spirit, Cal'd Robin Good-fellow. **1601** Sir W. Cornwallis *Disc. Seneca* (1631) 84 But warres best use, is the same that nurses make of Robin-goodfellow, to terrifie. **1622** Breton *Strange News* Wks. (Grosart) II. 10/2 In the old time when Hobgoblin and Robin good Fellow made country wenches keepe their houses cleane ouernight. **1701** Farquhar *Sir H. Wildair* I. i, The English came in like Robin Good-fellow, cried Boh! and made 'em be quiet. [**1827** Hood *Mids. Fairies* ix, Robin Goodfellow, that merry swain.]

transf. **1600** E. Guilpin in *Eng. Parnassus* 223 Let us esteeme Opinion as she is;.. The Proteus Robin Goodfellow of change.

†**b.** In general sense: A fairy or goblin of this kind. *Obs.*

a **1593** Nashe *Terrors of Night* Wks. (Grosart) III. 222 The Robbin good-fellowes, Elfes, Fairies, Hobgoblins of our latter age,.. did most of their merry prankes in the Night. **1621** Burton *Anat. Mel.* I. ii. I. ii, A bigger kind there is of them called with vs Hobgoblins, and Robin good fellowes, that would in those superstitious times, grind Corne for a messe of milke. **1635** Heywood *Hierarch.* IX. 574 These.. Make fearefull noise in Buttries and in Dairies; Robin good-fellowes some, some call them Fairies.

c. With punning allusion to *robbing* ppl. a.

1686 W. de Britaine *Hum. Prud.* xii. 59 If not to practice the Law, yet to gain so much knowledge therein, as to defend your.. Estate from the Robbing-good-Fellows of it.

†**2.** ***Robin Goodfellow's louse***, the wood-louse.

1552 Huloet, Cheeselippe worme, otherwise called Robin-goodfellowe his lowse, *tylus.*

Robin Hog. ? A constable.

1705 Hickeringill *Priest-cr.* I. (1721) 56 Calling upon the Jailors, the Sumners, the Rascals, the *Robin Hogs*, and Bumbailiffs, to help you to smother a Book, and stop it in the Press.

Robin Hood ('rɒbɪn 'hʊd), *sb.* Forms: 4 **Robyn hood**, 4-6 **hode**; *Sc.* 5 **Robyne**, 6 **Robyn**, **Robene Hude**, 6 **Robeyn Hwde**; 6 **Robin Hoode**, **-hoode**, 6- **Robin Hood**, **-hood**, 8 **-Hood**. [A personal name, whether real or fictitious is uncertain: see Child's *Ballads* III. 40-56, and the prefatory matter to Ritson's *Robin Hood.*]

1. The name of a popular English outlaw traditionally famous from at least the fourteenth century; hence allusively, an outlaw or bandit, or leader of such persons. Also, more widely, any person who acts irregularly for the benefit of the poor. †***a tale*** (or ***gest***) ***of Robin Hood***, an extravagant story.

1377 Langl. *P. Pl.* B. v. 402, I can rymes of Robyn hood, and Randolf erle of Chestre. *c* **1425** Wyntoun *Cron.* VII. x. 3525 Lytill Ihon and Robyne Hude.. In Yngilwode and Barnysdale Thai oysyd all this tyme thare trawale. **1439** *Rolls of Parlt.* V. 16 The same Piers Venables.. with many other unknowyn,.. in manere of Insurrection, wente into the wodes in that Contre, like as it hadde be Robyn-hode and his meyne. **1471** Ripley *Comp. Alch.* in Ashm. (1652) 175 Many man spekyth.. Of Robyn Hode, and of his Bow, Whych never shot therin, I trow. **1509** Barclay *Shyp of Folys* (1874) II. 155 Fables and Iestis of Robyn hode, Or other tryfyls that skantly ar so gode. **1562** J. Heywood *Prov. & Epigr.* (1867) 77 Tales of Robin hood are good among fooles. *a* **1586** Sidney *Apol. Poetry* (Arb.) 51 Lastly,.. they cry out with an open mouth, as if they out shot Robin Hood. **1597** *Carew MSS.* (1869) 273 Sundry loose persons, as some of the McShees.. and others, became Robin Hoods, and slew some of the Undertakers. **1617** Moryson *Itin.* II. 181 Hugh MacGuyer Lord of Fermanagh, and the first Robinhood of this great rebellion. **1625** Hart *Anat. Ur.* I. iii. 36 Let vs proceed to a point.. which will seeme to many a strange Paradox, or a tale of Robin Hood. **1875** F. Hall in *Lippincott's Mag.* XV. 343/2 It was a notorious freebooter, a Hindu Robin Hood, that I had dropped upon. **1931** J. Buchan *Blanket of Dark* v. 96 This Catti.. robbed especially rich men.. but spared the Church and the poor —a shabby Robin Hood. **1948** G. V. Galwey *Lift & Drop* iv. 70 Strip cartoons relating the adventures of Hugh Stinton the Robin Hood of private enquiry agents. **1967** *Listener* 30 Mar. 421/2 The challenge of an Asian-style Robin Hood telling the poor that they will be fattened with good food for which the rich and corrupt.. will be forced to pay. **1973** P. B. Austin tr. *Sjöwall & Wahlöö's Locked Room* xxiv. 203 She thought of him as a Robin Hood who stole from the rich to give to the poor. **1976** *Oadby & Wigston* (Leics.) *Advertiser* 26 Nov. 2/4 The plot involves five main characters, all budding Robbin Hoods who realise there is money in fur coats. **1978** M. Puzo *Fools Die* xi. 119, I still had a little bit of the Robin Hood in me.

attrib. and *Comb.* **1653** Chisenhale *Cath. Hist.* 284 If any contemn the authority of the Romane Church, that he shall not be able to assure himself of Scripture, any more then of a Robinhood-tale. **1835** James *Gipsy* vi, 'This is a very Robin-Hood-like scene,' said Colonel Manners. **1851** Palgrave *Norm. & Eng.* I. 563 Prosecuting a Robinhood insurrectionary warfare in Lotharingia. **1951** Koestler *Age of Longing* II. iii. 235 Pierre.. practised a kind of Robin Hood democracy. **1963** A. Lubbock *Austral. Roundabout* 161 The bushrangers also had a number of allies.. for their Robin Hood attitude to their victims. **1975** *Times* 18 Apr. 4/7 A home loan fraud with a Robin Hood quality.. to obtain mortgages for Asian immigrant families. **1977** *It* May 29/3 Ideally these would be assessed on a Robin Hood basis.

†**2. a.** One who acted the part of Robin Hood in a mummer's play or yearly festival. Hence ***Robin Hood's days, men.*** *Obs.*

1473 *Paston Lett.* III. 89, I have kepyd hym thys iij yer to pleye Seynt Jorge and Robyn Hod and the Shryff off Notyngham. **1531** *Acc. Ld. High Treas. Scot.* V. 432 Item, vj quarteris gray taffatis of Jeynes to be ane parte of the Kingis Robene Hudis baner. **1549** Latimer *6th Serm. bef. Edw. VI*, X v b, Syr thys is a busye daye wyth vs,.. it is Robyn hoodes daye. *Ibid.*, It was faine to geue place to Robyn hoodes men. **1579** Tomson *Calvin's Serm. Tim.* 23/1 God will not haue us occupied like little children in puppets or hobbie-horses, as players and Robin hoodes. **1589** *Hay, any Work for a Cooper* 3 Hearing either the Sommer Lord with his Maie game, or Robin Hood with his Morrice daunce going by the Church. **1616** Niccolls *Londons Artillery* 87 This worthy practise,.. when her Robin Hood Had wont each yeare.. to lead his yong men out.

†**b.** The play or mummery in which Robin Hood was the leading character. *Obs.*

1578 *Gen. Assembly* in Child *Ballads* III. 45/1 All kynd of insolent playis, as King of May, Robin Hood, and sick others, in the moneth of May, played either be bairnes at the schools, or others. **1580** *Reg. Privy Council Scot.* III. 277 Dischargeing all and sindrie his Majesteis liegis of using of Robene Hude and uther vane and unlesum gammis.

3. As a plant-name: †**a.** (See quot.) *Obs.*

1665 Rea *Flora* 126 This common Anemone is by many Gentlewomen, and others as ignorant, called Robin Hood, Scarlet and John.

b. *dial.* = Robin[1] 6.

1844 W. BARNES *Poems Rural Life* 105 Theös bank wi' eltrot flow'r An Robinhoods drest. **1848-** in south-western dialect use (see Britten & Holland, and *Eng. Dial. Dict.*).

4. Used *fig.* with allusion to *hood.*

1611 BEAUM. & FL. *Philaster* v. iv, Let not.. Your Robinhoods, Scarlets and Johns, tie your affections In darkness to your shops.

5. In various genitive combs., as **Robin Hood's bargain, pennyworth**: see PENNYWORTH 3 d; **Robin Hood's barn**, used as the type of an out-of-the-way place; esp. in phr. *(a)round Robin Hood's barn*, by a circuitous route (lit. and fig.); **Robin Hood's feather, hatband** (see quots. 1820, 1828); **Robin Hood's mile**, one of several times the recognized length.

1559 W. CUNNINGHAM *Cosmogr. Glasse* 57 Those are Robin Hodes miles, as the prouerbe is. **1709** *Brit. Apollo* No. 58. 3/1 When.. a Purchace you reap, That is wondrous Cheap, They Robin-Hood Bargains are call'd. **1820** KNOWLSON *Cattle-Doctor* 47 Traveller's joy, (or Robin Hood's feather): it grows among ling, and runs to a great length. **1828** *Craven Gloss., Robin Hood's hat-band*, common club-moss. *Lycopodium clavatum.* *a* **1854** J. F. KELLEY *Humors of Falconbridge* (1856) 220 The way some folks have of going round 'Robin Hood's barn' to come at a thing. **1878** *N. & Q.* 22 June 486/2 'Where have you been today?' 'All round Robin Hood's barn! I have been all about the country, first here and then there.' **1913** E. M. WRIGHT *Rustic Speech* xi. 189 To go round by Robin Hood's barn (Cmb. w. Midl.) is to go a roundabout way, to go the farthest way. **1928** S. LEWIS *Man who knew Coolidge* 17 When it came to *talking*, why say, he wandered all round Robin Hood's barn! **1934** E. M. RHODES *Beyond Desert* 201 Wagon-road goes all around Robin Hood's barn to get to my place. **1951** H. WOUK *Caine Mutiny* xxxix. 464, I have gone all the way around Robin Hood's barn to arrive at the old platitudes, which I guess is the process of growing up. **1977** *Time* 31 Jan. 1/3 Your article on birth control goes around Robin Hood's barn for an answer to the birth control problem.

6. Used *attrib.* and *absol.* to designate a type of high-crowned hat with the brim turned up at the back and down at the front, trimmed with a feather.

1894 C. G. HARPER *Revolted Woman* ii. 43 Rational Dress .. is only Bloomerism with a difference... A 'Robin Hood' hat, even as in the bygone years, crowns this confection. **1939** R. CHANDLER *Big Sleep* xi. 79 Her black hair was glossy under a brown Robin Hood hat. **1944** A. THIRKELL *Headmistress* x. 220 What interested him was her hat; a kind of Robin Hood hat of green felt with a long quill stuck jauntily through the crown. **1960** *News Chron.* 11 Apr. 8/4 Gone are the heavy-looking trilbies... In their place have come the delta and the Robin Hood. **1966** 'A. YORK' *Eliminator* iv. 66 Wilde.. dressed in flannel bags and a sports coat, added an old Robin Hood. **1975** W. HILDICK *Bracknell's Law* 36, I was accosted by a little old woman in black: black coat, black stockings, black hat—and all a throwback to the forties, with the hat of the Robin Hood type.

Hence **Robin-Hood** *v.*, to live like Robin Hood; **Robin-'Hoodish** *a.*, characteristic of a Robin Hood; beneficent to or benefiting the poor; **Robin-Hoodism** (see quot.). *nonce-words.*

1856 KINGSLEY *Poems, The Invitation*, Once a year, like schoolboys, Robin-hooding go. **1887** *Ch. Times* 9 Dec. 1013/1 If the question were merely a matter of Robin-Hoodism—the robbing of the rich for the sake of the poor. **1974** *Listener* 18 July 86/3 The morally respectable, Robin-Hoodish bank robbery.

‖**Robinia** (rəʊˈbɪnɪə). *Bot.* [mod.L. (Linnæus), f. *Robin*, name of the royal gardener at Paris, who introduced these trees to Europe in 1635.] A genus of North American trees and shrubs of the bean family, chiefly represented by the locust-tree.

1759 B. STILLINGFL. *Misc. Tracts* (1762) 186 From that distant countrey we have the robinia's and a honey-suckle. **1786** ABERCROMBIE *Arr.* in *Gard. Assist.* 32 *Robinia*, or false acacia. **1841** *Penny Cycl.* XX. 45/2 The best known species of Robinia is the *R. pseudacacia*, the Bastard or False Acacia, or Locust-tree. *Ibid.* 46/1 There are two other species.. *R. viscosa*, Clammy Robinia, and *R. hispida*, Hairy Robinia, or Rose Acacia. **1882** *Garden* 15 July 41/1 The Robinias, except Pseudacacia, are a neglected class of low trees.

Robinocracy (rɒbɪˈnɒkrəsɪ). [f. the name *Robin* (ROBIN[1]) + -OCRACY.] The régime of Sir Robert Walpole (1676–1745), the predominant figure in British politics between 1721 and 1742; the clique led by Walpole; the period of Walpole's supremacy.

1727 *Craftsman* 22 July 71 This week was publish'd Robin's Panegyrick on Himself and his Friends at Westminster; modestly proving that they were all very honest Fellows and deserving Patriots; with a full Confutation of the charge of Bribery and Corruption Offered to the consideration of the Freeholders; Citizens, Burgesses and Freemen of Great-Britain. *Populus me sibilat, at mihi plaudo.* Hor. Printed for S.B. W.W. and T.W. Printers to the Robinocracy. *a* **1902** ACTON *Lect. Mod. Hist.* (1906) xvi. 274 After the fall of Walpole it was observed.. that the country felt itself superior to the government. This was the natural result of the time known as the Robinocracy; not because he devised liberal measures, but because he was careful to be neither wiser nor more liberal than the public. **1974** J. B. OWEN *Eighteenth Cent.* i. 23 On 19 April 1722 Sunderland died of pleurisy, and the way was open for Walpole to assert his supremacy. The Robinocracy had begun. **1977** W. A. SPECK *Stability & Strife* x. 222 Bolingbroke could be highly persuasive and his essays were the most substantial contemporary critiques of the Robinocracy.

'Robin 'redbreast. [Cf. ROBIN[1] and REDBREAST.]

1. a. The European redbreast or robin (*Erithacus rubecula*), usually as a proper name, but also with *a* and pl.

c **1450** HOLLAND *Howlat* 647 Robyn Redbrest nocht ran, Bot raid as a hensman. *a* **1529** SKELTON *P. Sparowe* 399 Robyn redbrest, He shall be the preest The requiem masse to synge. **1550** CROWLEY *Epigr.* 863 When the short dayes begyn to be colde, robinredbrest will come home to ye. **1612** WEBSTER *White Devil* v. (Routledge) 45/2 The robin-red-breast and the wren.. with leaves and flowers do cover The friendless bodies of unburied men. **1683** TRYON *Way to Health* 448 The Raven as unfit for food,.. and the pretty Robbin-Red-Breast for its Innocency, are very seldom killed. **1710** STEELE *Tatler* No. 134 ¶2 Hearing by Chance of your Worship's great Humanity towards Robin-Redbreasts and Tom Tits. **1774** GOLDSM. *Nat. Hist.* (1776) V. 314 Among slender billed birds, he enumerates the thrush,.. the red-start, the robin red-breast. **1826** SCOTT *Woodst.* xxviii, Robin-red-breast, whose chirruping song was heard among the bushes. **1862** *All Year Round* 13 Sept. 9 The infliction.. is hard upon the innocent traveller, who has been brought up to respect robin redbreasts.

b. *dial.* (See quots. and cf. ROBIN[1] 6 d.)

1878 *Folk-Lore Rec.* I. 38 The excrescence often found upon the briar-rose, and called here in Sussex by the name of Robin Redbreast's Cushion. **1886** *Cheshire Gloss., Robin red-breast*, the red, mossy gall which grows upon the branches of the wild rose.

c. *dial.* The red campion, *Lychnis diurna.*

1886 BRITTEN & HOLLAND *Plant-Names.*

d. *U.S.* = ROBIN *sb.*[1] 3.

1696 S. SEWALL *Diary* 4 Jan. (1878) I. 242 Some say they saw a Robin-Redbrest to-day. **1865** *Atlantic Monthly* May 517/1 Shortly after Robin-Redbreast .. [arrives] the Golden-Winged Woodpecker. **1949** *Hobbies* Oct. 155/1 Robin Redbreast—most familiar of North American birds—has thrived as man's close neighbor.

2. *slang.* A Bow Street runner. Cf. REDBREAST 2.

1841 J. T. HEWLETT *Parish Clerk* II. 173 The New Police Bill, by which raw lobsters were introduced in place of robin-red-breasts. **1885** WINGFIELD *Barb. Philpot* III. ii. 45 Vended by hawkers in the street under the noses of the robin-redbreasts.

robin'redbreasted, *a. nonce-wd.* [f. ROBIN REDBREAST + -ED[2].] Clad in a red waistcoat.

1922 JOYCE *Ulysses* 465 Tom Rochford, robinredbreasted, in cap and breeches.

'Robin 'ruddock. Now *dial.* Also 7, 9 reddock(e, 9 riddick. [See ROBIN[1] and RUDDOCK.] = prec. 1 a.

a **1566** R. EDWARDES *Damon & Pithias* in Dodsley (1744) I. 272 Did you ever see two such litle Robin ruddocks? **1620** SHELTON *Quix.* II. x. 61 Then sayd Sancho: By Saint Roque, our Mistres is as light as a Robin-ruddocke. **1639** in *Glouc. Gloss.* (1890) 201 Hee drew it as blith as a Robin reddocke: viz[t]. As a robin redbrest. **1825** JENNINGS *Obs. Dial. W. Eng.* 128 Wrans an robin-riddicks Tell all the cares o' God. **1873-** in *Eng. Dial. Dict.*

Robinsonade (ˌrɒbɪnsəˈneɪd, ‖-aːdə). Also Robinsonnade and with lower-case initial. Pl. Robinsonades, ‖-aden. [ad. G. *Robinsonade* (coined by J. G. Schnabel, *Die Insel Felsenburg* (1731), Preface): see next and -ADE.] A novel with a subject similar to that of *Robinson Crusoe*; a story about shipwreck on a desert island.

1847 *Blackw. Mag.* Sept. 330/2 These outcasts from civilisation, the adventures of most of whom would furnish abundant materials for a Robinsonade. **1941** P. B. GOVE *Imaginary Voy. Prose Fiction* p. ix, The late Hermann Ullrich, whose knowledge of the influence of *Robinson Crusoe* has probably never been equaled, put on the title page of his bibliography of robinsonades in 1898 'Teil I'. *Ibid.* I. v. 125 Imitations of *Robinson* have been known usually as *Robinsonaden* or *robinsonades* (only rarely as robinsoniads), and similar works published before 1719 as *prerobinsonades.* **1967** B. W. ALDERSON tr. *B. Hürlimann's Three Centuries Children's Bks. in Europe* xvii. 252 Robinsonnades, like history, geography, and travel books, have always had a big attraction for the Swiss. **1974** *Encycl. Brit. Micropædia* VIII. 618/3 *Robinsonade*, novel written in imitation of *Robinson Crusoe*.. dealing with the problem of the castaway's survival on a desert island. **1978** D. WAGGONER *Hills of Faraway* 16 The Robinsonade is, of course, named for *Robinson Crusoe*, and is the story of a castaway—a voyage cut short—in an isolated setting, which the author can use to describe his ideas of the basic elements separating man from beast.

Robinson Crusoe (ˈrɒbɪnsən ˈkruːsəʊ). The name of the eponymous hero of Daniel Defoe's fictional narrative (1719), who survives shipwreck on a desert island, used allusively. Also *attrib.* and (rare) *ellipt.* as ***Robinson.*** Cf. CRUSOE[2]. So **'Robinson 'Crusoe** *v. trans.*, to maroon on a desert island; **'Robinson 'Crusoic** *a.*

1768 *London Mag.* Oct. 543/1, I am of late from a sprightly fellow become a peevish mal-content; and am as unhappy among the people of England, as if some misadventure had Robinson-crusoed me, by throwing me into a desert-isle.. where I could have nothing but seals and wild goats for my companions. **1849** L. HUNT *Bk. for Corner* I. 14 There are Robinson Crusoes in the moral as well as physical world..; —men, cast on desert islands of thought and speculation; without companionship; without worldly resources; forced to arm and clothe themselves out of the remains of shipwrecked hopes, and to make a home for their solitary hearts in the nooks and corners of imagination and reading. **1856** E. K. KANE *Arctic Explorations* I. xxvi. 348 A host of expedients were to be resorted to, and much Robinson Crusoe labor ahead. **1878** TROLLOPE *How 'Mastiffs' went to Iceland* ii. 6 Though the life of a Robinson Crusoe or a few Robinson Crusoes may be very picturesque, humanity will always desire to restore a Robinson Crusoe back to the community of the world. **1919** G. B. SHAW *Matter with Ireland* (1962) 213 His Robinson Crusoic independence of his neighbors. **1930** R. CAMPBELL *Adamastor* 30 Of all the ocean-gods and mages The last surviving Robinson. **1941** L. MACNEICE *Poetry W. B. Yeats* x. 218 Eliot.. in *After Strange Gods* has grouped Lawrence and Yeats.. as writers who have suffered from the lack of an established religion and a traditional moral code and who have invented for these things Robinson Crusoe substitutes. **1974** H. MACINNES *Climb to Lost World* iv. 53 The army compound.. had a Robinson Crusoe atmosphere with the palm and pau pau trees. **1979** 'G. BLACK' *Night Run from Java* viii. 76 One [island] where I could Robinson Crusoe the marine accident victims.

robinsonite (ˈrɒbɪnsənaɪt). *Min.* [f. the name of S. C. *Robinson* (b. 1911), Canadian geologist + -ITE[1].] A bluish or grey lead antimony sulphide occurring as slender prismatic crystals and fibrous or compact masses.

1952 L. G. BERRY et al. in *Amer. Mineralogist* XXXVII. 438 The powder pattern obtained by Professor Peacock was found to be identical with one of several unidentified patterns obtained by Dr. S. C. Robinson at Queen's University during his investigation of the synthesis of lead antimony sulphides... The name robinsonite is given to this new mineral in honor of Dr. Robinson, whose synthesis made its identification possible. *Ibid.*, Robinsonite occurs as a primary mineral with pyrite, sphalerite, stibnite, and boulangerite in small pieces in oxidized ore bodies at the Red Bird mercury mine, Pershing County, Nevada. **1973** *Canad. Mineralogist* XII. 199/1 The Pb-Sb-S system.. has been examined.. between 300 and 700°C. Five phases have been synthesized: Phase I ($3PbS{:}Sb_2S_3$) stable between 642 and 605°C; boulangerite ($5PbS{:}2Sb_2S_3$) stable below 638°C; Phase II ($3PbS{:}Sb_2S_3$) stable between 603 and 405°C; robinsonite ($6PbS{:}5Sb_2S_3$) stable between 582° and 318°C; zinckenite ($PbS{:}Sb_2S_3$) stable below 545°C. *Ibid.* 205/2 Preservation of robinsonite, which appears to break down below 318°C, as a mineral is a perplexing problem; natural robinsonite may be stabilized by small amounts of impurities.

robishe, obs. form of RUBBISH *sb.*

‖**roble** (ˈroble). [Sp. and Pg. *roble*, = It. *rovere*, Prov. *roure*, F. *rouvre*:—L. *rōbor-, rōbur* oak-tree.] **a.** The Californian weeping oak (*Quercus lobata*). **b.** A timber tree (*Platymiscium platystachyum*) of the West Indies. **c.** A West-Indian species of catalpa (*C. longisiliqua* or *longissima*). **d.** A Chilean species of beech (*Fagus obliqua*).

1864 GRISEBACH *Flora W. Ind. Isl.* Col. Names, Roble, *Platymiscium platystachyum.* **1866** *Treas. Bot.* 987/1 *Roble*, a shipbuilding wood obtained from *Catalpa longissima.* **1871** KINGSLEY *At Last* vii, That.. is.. a Carapo, that a Cedar, that a Roble (oak). **1885** LADY BRASSEY *The Trades* 177 There were.. the roble (*Catalpa longissima*), a tree very like an elm [etc.].

roble, obs. form of ROUBLE.

roble, error for *romble*: see RUMBLE *v.*

†**'roblet,** *sb. Obs. rare.* In 8 roiblet. [Perh. for *Robinet* (cf. dial. *remlet* for *remnant*), which occurs as the name of a goblin in Wright's *Latin Stories* 38.] A goblin leading persons astray in the dark. In comb. ***roblet-led.***

1755 J. CLUBBE *Misc. Tracts* (1770) I. 52 From hence superstition has possessed the inhabitants, that.. it is impossible to find the way out of this field in the dark, but that every one that is so hardy as to make the experiment is *Roiblet-led*; by which they mean led by some ghost or phantom.

Hence †**'roblet** *v. trans.*, to lead astray. *Obs.*

1674 N. FAIRFAX *Bulk & Selv.* 65 One reason.. why the understanding has been robletted in to these wastes and wildnesses. *Ibid.* 173 If the man.. will needs be setting up a Will in the wisp, no wonder if the glare of it sometimes roblet him into bogs and marlpits.

robomb (ˈrəʊbɒm). *temporary.* [f. ROB(OT + BOMB *sb.*] = *robot bomb, flying bomb.*

1944 *Saturday Night* (Toronto) 22 July 17 (*heading*) Germany's robombs another case of 'too little and too late'. **1945** H. S. ZIM *Rockets & Jets* xix. 266 Like the V-1 robomb it must be given a high initial speed before the engine begins to operate.

roborant (ˈrəʊb-, ˈrɒbərənt), *sb.* and *a. Med.* [ad. L. *rōborant-, rōborans*, pres. pple. of *rōborāre*: see next.]

A. *sb.* An invigorating or strengthening medicine.

1661 R. LOVELL *Hist. Anim. & Min.* 403 The vertigo is helped by temporal repellers, discutients, roborants,.. and quinces. **1789** CULLEN *Mat. Med.* II. 6 Upon the same ground [astringents] are fitly enough named Strengtheners or Roborants. **1822-34** *Good's Study Med.* (ed. 4) IV. 97 In China, ginseng has for ages been in high esteem.. as a general restorative and roborant. **1875** H. C. WOOD *Therap.* (1879) 59 Prunus Virginiana.. is frequently useful in phthisis when a roborant is needed.

B. *adj.* Strengthening; restorative.

1836 in SMART. **1885** W. ROBERTS *Urin. & Renal Dis.* III. iv. 491 Medicinal agents of roborant character should be exhibited from time to time.

†'**roborate**, *pa. pple. Obs.* [ad. L. *rōborāt-us*, pa. pple. of *rōborāre*: see next.] Confirmed, ratified, strengthened.

1432-50 tr. *Higden* (Rolls) VIII. 245 The kynge made a chartoure roborate by auctorite of the pope. **1533** BELLENDEN *Livy* I. x. (S.T.S.) I. 54 Mony vthir bandis war roborate betuix þe two pepill. **1536** —— *Cron. Scot.* (1821) I. 21 The peace beand roborat in this maner, baith the kingis returnit hame. *c* **1550** ROLLAND *Crt. Venus* II. 251 His Fortoun was with strenth so roborait. *Ibid.* 585 With subtill wark it was sa roborat.

†'**roborate**, *v. Obs.* [ad. ppl. stem of L. *rōborāre* to strengthen, f. *rōbor-*, *rōbur* strength.]

1. *trans.* To ratify, confirm (a charter, league, etc.).

1432-50 tr. *Higden* (Rolls) VIII. 203 Gregorius..roborate the sentence of excommunicacion ageyne Frederyke the emperoure. **1513** BRADSHAW *St. Werburge* I. 2460 It to confyrme, and roborate specyall With charters and dedes, and seales patent. **1611** SPEED *Hist. Gt. Brit.* IX. iv. §20. 454/2 Euen now will I confirme..your ouer-worne and vndermined Charters, and will roborate them most firmely with a new oath. **1655** FULLER *Hist. Camb.* ii. §36 This Bull also relateth to ancient priviledges of Popes and Princes, bestowed upon her; which herein are roborated and confirmed.

2. To strengthen, invigorate; to fortify. Also *fig.*

1533 tr. *Erasm. Expos. Commune Crede* 118 b, Anone after as waxyng yonge men, they were roborated and made stronge vnto greate batayles. **1615** CROOKE *Body of Man* 163 He prescribeth stiptické..to roborate or strengthen the vertue of the guttes. **1675** BAXTER *Cath. Theol.* I. III. 74 By preventing Grace.., the Liberty of the Will..is wonderfully perfected and roborated. **1710** T. FULLER *Pharm. Extemp.* 85 It roborates the Parts that are hurt.

absol. **1590** BARROUGH *Med. Physick* v. v. (1639) 275 Those things which doe confirme and roborate. **1657** TOMLINSON *Renou's Disp.* Pref., Some Simples..to qualify, the rest to roborate.

3. To make obdurate; to harden. *rare*$^{-1}$.

1652 GAULE *Magastrom.* 217 To what end served those false mirables of the magicians, but to roborate or harden Pharaohs heart?

Hence †'**roborating** *ppl. a. Obs.*

1684 tr. *Bonet's Merc. Compit.* XIX. 680 Before all things roborating and comforting things should be given to the Sick.

†**robo'ration**. *Obs.* Also 5 roboracion, 6 -acioun, -acyone. [ad. med.L. *rōborātio*, noun of action f. *rōborāre*: see prec.] Confirmation; strengthening; support; invigoration.

1432-50 tr. *Higden* (Rolls) III. 193 Hit hade be sufficiaunte to the roboracion of a sentence if hit hade be seide 'Pictagoras seide so'. **1473** in *Sheriffdoms of Lanark & Renfrew* (Maitland Cl.) 194 In strenthnin and roboration of this present obligation. **1533** BELLENDEN *Livy* I. xii. (S.T.S.) I. 70 To þe strenth & Roboracioun of all religioun and ordoure afore divisit. **1536** *Exhort. to North* in Furniv. *Ballads* I. 306 The machabies beyng fewe in the comparason of ther enmys,..Zit, trustyng in gode, thai haid Roboracyone. **1657** TOMLINSON *Renou's Disp.* 54 This Lotion is commended, as of sufficient roboration to ballance the weakness of the Liver.

†**ro'borean**, *a. Obs.*$^{-0}$ [f. L. *rōbore-us* + -AN.] 'Made of Oak, or such like strong Timber.'

1656 BLOUNT *Glossogr.* Hence in some later Dicts.

ro'boreous, *a. Obs.*$^{-0}$ [f. as prec. + -OUS.] 'Of the nature of, or pertaining to oak.'

1727 BAILEY (vol. II.). Hence in some later Dicts.

robot ('rəʊbɒt). [Czech, f. *robota* forced labour; used by Karel Čapek (1890–1938) in his play *R.U.R.* ('Rossum's Universal Robots') (1920).]

1. a. One of the mechanical men and women in Čapek's play; hence, a machine (sometimes resembling a human being in appearance) designed to function in place of a living agent, esp. one which carries out a variety of tasks automatically or with a minimum of external impulse.

1923 P. SELVER tr. *Čapek's R.U.R.* 28 You see..the Robots have no interest in life. They have no enjoyments. **1923** *Times* 9 June 10/5 If Almighty God had populated the world with Robots, legislation of this sort might have been reasonable. **1928** *Daily News & Westm. Gaz.* 20 Apr. 11/4 The latest..Rotary Press, a veritable Robot in the complicated work it performs night after night without hitch. **1937** *Spectator* 23 Apr. 758/1 Men who will go to their doom with the unswerving directness of robots. **1942**, etc. [see ROBOTIC *sb.* 1]. **1945** *Sun* (Baltimore) 9 Feb. 6-O/2 A robot, which never forgets, will do the job. **1958** [see ANDROID]. **1969** I. & P. OPIE *Children's Games* xii. 340 'They pretend to be robots gone mad,' reports a headmaster. **1976** *Sci. Amer.* Feb. 77 (*caption*) Spot-welding robots..are used in assembling the under-bodies of Chevrolet Novas. **1979** *Daily Tel.* 7 Nov. 6/8 The British Robot Association believes between 6,000 and 7,000 robots were in use worldwide in industry last year. **1980** *Times* 1 July 19/5 A *real* robot is programmable; it can be programmed to perform different, and changing tasks. In 1978 Japan put 1,100 playback or programmable robots into its factories.

b. A person whose work or activities are entirely mechanical; an automaton.

1923 *Westm. Gaz.* 22 June 7/5 Mr. G. Bernard Shaw defined Robots as persons all of whose activities were imposed on them. **1926** C. E. M. JOAD *Babbitt Warren* 82 Robots live by standardization. **1929** C. CONNOLLY *Let.* in *Romantic Friendship* (1975) 325 America is..a great youthful boisterous robot. **1943** J. B. PRIESTLEY *Daylight on Saturday* ix. 55, I thought it would be better having a fairly intelligent..girl instead of one of these little office robots. **1977** G. W. H. LAMPE *God as Spirit* ii. 51 The person who is 'seized' by the Spirit is thought of as a passive object, temporarily reduced to the status of a robot.

c. Chiefly *S. Afr.* An automatic traffic-signal.

1931 *Even. Standard* 5 Aug. 2/1 (*heading*) Traffic 'Robots' in the City. **1939** *Forum* (Johannesburg) 4 Feb. 35/1 The Daily Dispatch, East London, is critical of a proposal to fix robots in the town's streets. **1948** H. V. MORTON *In Search of S. Afr.* 17 Another word used in South Africa, but long discontinued in England, is robot for traffic lights. **1958** *Johannesburg Star* 16 Dec. 6/7 Johannesburg drivers..want to turn right or left while pedestrians, with the robot in their favour, are crossing. **1969** A. FUGARD *Boesman & Lena* II. 38 When the robot said 'Go' there at Berry's Corner I was nearly *bang in my broek*. **1974** *Eastern Province Herald* 2 Oct. 9 Vandals removed the lamps from seven traffic robots and the flashing head from a warning pole.

d. A robot bomb. *temporary.*

1944 *Daily Tel.* 11 July 1/5 Many of the robots launched against England on Sunday night finished up in the sea. **1944** J. LEES-MILNE *Prophesying Peace* (1977) 86 From here Jamesy saw his first robot.

2. *attrib.* and *Comb.*, as ***robot army***, ***astronaut***, ***-brain***, ***clerk***, ***-land***, ***-maker***, ***masses***, (***petrol***) ***station***, ***-pilot***, ***satellite***, ***system***, ***type***, ***-worker***; ***robot-controlled***, ***-like*** (also *adv.*), ***-run*** adjs.; **robot bomb** = *flying bomb* s.v. FLYING *vbl. sb.* 3; **robot plane**, (*a*) = *queen bee* s.v. QUEEN *sb.* 14; (*b*) = *robot bomb*; **robot roost**, a place for the storage of robot bombs; **robot teacher**, an electronic teaching aid; **robot train**, a robot-controlled underground train.

1927 *Morning Post* 20 Aug. 9 (*heading*) Robot army 'gassed'. **1961** *Daily Tel.* 14 Sept. 1/4 Technicians at Cape Canaveral, Florida, successfully sent a Project Mercury space capsule carrying a robot astronaut and recovered it from the Atlantic. **1944** *Sun* (Baltimore) 20 June 9/1 Most military authorities here are generally agreed that the robot bomb or plane is of..little military value. **1944** *N.Y. Times* 25 June 4E/1 (*heading*) Germans' robot bomb is a potential menace. **1945** G. MILLAR *Maquis* xiv. 292 A false report that a certain factory there was making parts for the robot bombs that the Germans had begun to send to London. **1951** KOESTLER *Age of Longing* I. viii. 140 The ancient Neanderthaler with a modern robot-brain. **1954** *Britannica Bk. of Year* 637/2 *Radar-Brain*, a device used to guide supersonic missiles from the ground, and *Robot-Brain*, a similar apparatus built into the missile. **1928** *Daily Express* 8 June 3/2 A new automatic selling machine, described as the 'Robot clerk', which will say 'Thank you' and give change, will replace the present automatic machines. **1964** *Ann. Reg. 1963* 394 London transport had also developed a robot-controlled underground train. **1960** KOESTLER *Lotus & Robot* II. vi. 173 The robotland reflected in the mirror makes us shudder. **1927** *N.Y. Times* 7 Mar. 16 An iron Robotlike woman Rotwang had made previously. **1928** *Daily Express* 11 Aug. 3/7 The romance of past centuries and robot-like drama of modern times meet at Sandwich. **1972** T. MCHUGH *Time of Buffalo* xi. 132 Among the most widespread was the Pawnee myth of the robotlike buffalo skull that pursued and devoured people. *Ibid.* 133 Marching robotlike after the coyote, the skull eventually devoured him. **1976** B. BOVA *Multiple Man* (1977) xiv. 147 That same robot-like Oriental butler served us steaks. **1946** J. T. SHIPLEY in W. S. Knickerbocker *20th Cent. Eng.* 131 Despite robot-makers..human nature changes, if at all, but slowly. **1946** J. S. HUXLEY *Unesco* ii. 43 The robot masses and class-types of ancient Mesopotamia and Egypt. **1972** *Times* 9 Nov. 35/1 (*heading*) Robot petrol stations. *Ibid.*, The two trends now being combined to produce what BP..calls robot stations, namely self-service and automatic money acceptance. **1930** *Aberdeen Press & Jrnl.* 31 Mar. 7/3 One of these robot-pilots has been fitted to a big twin-engined Supermarine Napier flying boat. **1951** A. Y. BRAMBLE *Air-Plane Flight* xv. 247 Automatic control or 'robot-pilot' is really a piece of control mechanism rather than an instrument as generally understood. **1935** Robot plane [see *queen bee*]. **1944** J. LEES-MILNE *Prophesying Peace* (1977) 84 Dame Una made stately preparations to dive under the table at the first sound of a robot plane. **1944** *Sun* (Baltimore) 20 June 1/3 United States heavy bombers struck twice today at the robot roost around Pas de Calais. **1958** I. ASIMOV *Naked Sun* i. 11 Fear of open spaces that barred them from the robot-run farming and mining areas of their own planet. **1958** C. C. ADAMS *Space Flight* 142 A manned satellite will be a formidable project... Unlike the robot satellite, it cannot be built in the laboratory and then installed in or on a rocket for delivery to orbit. **1976** *Sci. Amer.* Feb. 77 (*heading*) Robot systems. **1961** *Daily Tel.* 5 Sept. 21/5 Two robot teachers were on show in the Psychology Section. One, like a portable television set, had nine black knobs and a red button on the front. The pupil presses the black knobs to give his answer and the red button to obtain the correct solution. **1963** *Ibid.* 9 Apr. 17/4 (*heading*) Robot train tested with passengers. **1959** H. BARNES *Oceanogr. & Marine Biol.* 177 It is convenient to mount a Robot-type camera in a water-tight case, usually fastened to a pole. **1935** H. G. WELLS *Things to Come* 13 All the balderdash..about 'robot workers' and ultra skyscrapers, etc., etc., should be cleared out of your minds.

Hence **robo'teer**, an expert in the making of robots; **robo'tesque** *a.*, resembling or suggestive of a robot; **ro'botian** *a.*, of or belonging to a robot or robots; '**robotism**, mechanical behaviour or character; **ro'botnik** [-NIK], a person behaving with mindless obedience to authority; '**robotry**, the condition or behaviour of robots; '**roboty** *a.*, robot-like.

1924 *Observer* 6 Jan. 12/2 When we reach the gloomy depths of 'commercial English'—..we are dealing with a mere thing of use, the very pith and genius of Robotry. **1927** *Daily Express* 30 Aug. 3/4 The Girl in the Lift must on some occasions drop her magnificent Robotry. *Ibid.* 5 Sept. 9/1 There are times when they seem to be purely robotesque, automata driven by impulses of destruction beyond their control. **1928** *Ibid.* 17 Mar. 4/2 A few have their wooden craniums transfixed by bodkins, and some have Robotian hooks instead of hands. **1928** *Observer* 29 Jan. 9/3 (*heading*) The robotism of architecture. **1933** E. E. CUMMINGS *eimi* 3 Horridly roboty child smothered by ferocious Blau, swinging a ditto balloon at end of wire. **1944** C. L. MOORE in *Astounding Sci. Fiction* Dec. 155/2 The impression of robotism was what she meant to convey. **1946** *Amer. Jrnl. Psychol.* LIX. 190, I wish to define the rôle of robotism in psychology, to show what sense there is in talking about robots. **1955** *Times* 27 July 9 It might be a pretty compliment to the brothers Capek..if we called this new way of life robotry. **1960** *Times Lit. Suppl.* 16 Sept. 593/2 Too much law, and too centralized authority in all things breeds a society of automata, robotniks and helots. **1970** A. TOFFLER *Future Shock* ix. 180 Despite setbacks and difficulties, the roboteers are moving forward.

robotic (rəʊ'bɒtɪk), *a.* and *sb.* [f. ROBOT + -IC.]

A. *adj.* Of or pertaining to robots; characteristic of or resembling a robot.

1941 I. ASIMOV in *Astounding Sci. Fiction* May 50 You'd cut your own nose off before you'd let me get the credit for solving robotic telepathy. **1946** *Amer. Jrnl. Psychol.* LIX. 192, I believe that robotic thinking helps precision of psychological thought. **1947** I. ASIMOV in 'E. Crispin' *Best SF Two* (1956) 111 The mathematical interpretation of verbal reactions of robots is one of the more intricate branches of robotic analysis. **1959** *Archit. Rev.* CXXV. 212/3 His line is bold, his colour is bright but lifeless, and his figuration is decoratively robotic. **1963** *New Worlds Sci. Fiction* Apr. 52 Johnston wouldn't have been..surprised to find out that more than half of the city's population was robotic, no matter how cleverly they were disguised. **1973** M. AMIS *Rachel Papers* 49, I said in a robotic voice: 'Christ I'm sorry about that I had no idea it was your party and I wondered whether you might possibly let me make it up to you.' **1976** L. DEIGHTON *Twinkle, Twinkle Little Spy* viii. 84 The kind of dispassionate robotic bastard that communism breeds.

B. *sb.* **1.** *pl.* The art or science of the design, construction, operation, and application of robots and the like; the study of robots; ***laws of robotics***, a set of rules devised to govern the actions of robots, enunciated in the science fiction stories of Isaac Asimov (see quot. 1968[1]).

At first a science-fiction term but now more generally used of automatic processes in industry.

1941 I. ASIMOV in *Astounding Sci. Fiction* May 53 There's irony in three of the greatest experts in robotics in the world falling into the same elementary trap, isn't there? **1942** —— in *Ibid.* Mar. 100/1 Let's start with the three fundamental rules of Robotics—the three rules that are built most deeply into a robot's positronic brain. **1957** —— *Naked Sun* (1958) i. 21 The robot showed no adverse response. It couldn't, of course. Its reponses were limited and controlled by the Laws of Robotics. **1968** —— in *Sci. Jrnl.* Oct. 116/2 Eventually, I formulated these safeguards in the shape of 'The Three Laws of Robotics'. 1. A robot may not injure a human being or, through inaction, allow a human being to come to harm. 2. A robot must obey the orders given it by human beings, except where such orders would conflict with the First Law. 3. A robot must protect its own existence, except where such protection would conflict with the First or Second Law. **1968** *Times* 1 Nov. 23/2 Significant technological advances in the field of 'robotics'—the use of robots in the field of industrial automation—were announced today. **1974** G. BUTLER *Coffin for Canary* viii. 100 Perhaps we are robots. Robots acting out the last Law of Robotics... To tend towards the human. **1978** *Observer* (Colour Suppl.) 22 Oct. 15/2 In dealing with the many aspects of robotics—historical, philosophical, mythical, actual and projected—Jasia Reichardt defends the machine against some of our more excessive fears about this artificial image of ourselves. **1979** *Topic* (Imperial Coll., London) 22 Jan. 9/1 Support is planned for..new computer applications (e.g. industrial robotics).

2. *sing.* A robot. *rare.*

1951 C. SIMAK *Time & Again* (1956) v. 20 The robotic clicked and chuckled. It moved a pawn... A human simply can't beat a robotic expert. **1981** *Times* 10 Mar. 4/1 Will he consider direct grants for the purchase of such robotics?

So **ro'botical** *a.*; **ro'botically** *adv.*; **ro'boticist**, an expert in making and operating robots; **ro'boticized** *a.*, robotized.

1940 I. ASIMOV in *Super Sci. Stories* Sept. 70/2 Johnson is an expert Roboticist. **1942** —— in *Amazing Stories* Feb. 227/1 Austin Wilde, Robotical Engineer, turned to Sam Tobe and said, 'Did you get anything out of the robot?' **1947** —— in 'E. Crispin' *Best SF Two* (1956) 127 The government cruiser was making ready to carry the two roboticists back to Earth. **1957** —— *Naked Sun* iii. 35 A thoroughly roboticized economy. **1960** M. SCRIVEN in S. Hook *Dimensions of Mind* xiii. 120 The roboticist in his task of duplicating the brain functions of higher vertebrates. **1972** *Internat. Jrnl. Man-Machine Stud.* IV. 444 The most obvious computer solution would be to simple search serially through each region to find which was the largest. For a roboticist using a serial computer, that may well be the best approach. **1976** K. BONFIGLIOLI *Something Nasty in Woodshed* v. 53 Sam got up in a robotical sort of way. **1979** C. THOMAS *Snow Falcon* 24 Asked to rehearse once more lines he knew by heart... Robotically, he began.

robotize ('rəʊbətaɪz), *v.* [f. ROBOT + -IZE.] *trans.* **a.** = AUTOMATE *v.* I. **b.** *fig.* To render mechanical or lifeless, to cause to act as if lacking will or consciousness. So '**robotized** *ppl. a.*; also **roboti'zation**.

1927 C. M. GRIEVE *Albyn* 46 Dostoevsky's mistake was to imagine that Russia alone could prevent the robotization of Europe. **1927** *Daily Express* 7 Nov. 10/2 Lacking a skilled class of artisans, it is only by Robotising industry that she can hope to fight her way back to prosperity. **1928** *Ibid.* 20 Apr. 13/3 Sir William Joynson-Hicks..protested that he had not seen any sign during the last few months that the House [of Commons] had become robotised. **1928** *Observer* 15 Jan. 11/2 These robotised people..are only employed and allowed to exist because no one has yet been sufficiently energetic to invent a machine to replace them. **1930** *Ibid.* 16 Feb. 17/6 He adds..that in machine mass production lies the foundation of the evil, saying: 'We must not robotise America.' **1952** B. WOLFE *Limbo* xv. 236 Even when I was a kid the big plants had been pretty completely robotized. **1967** L. VON BERTALANFFY *Robots, Men & Minds* II. 64 The robotization of the human individual. **1969** *N.Y. Rev. Bks.* 2 Jan. 13/4 The masses, through state victory chants, book burning,..robotized phalanxes of soldiers, devour their enemies. **1975** *New Yorker* 21 Apr. 24/2 Katharine Ross plays the young New Yorker who moves to Stepford and discovers that the wives have been robotized by their husbands. **1976** *Sci. Amer.* Feb. 77/1 During the 1930's and 1940's petroleum refineries and petrochemical plants were extensively 'robotized' by inserting rather simple analogue control instruments in the feedback loops that regulated the pressure, temperature and flow rates in distillation columns, catalytic crackers and other equipment designed to process continuously flowing materials.

robotology (rəʊbə'tɒlədʒɪ). [f. ROBOT + -OLOGY.] The study of robots; robotics. So **robo'tologist**.

1946 *Amer. Jrnl. Psychol.* LIX. 190 The second robot is beginning the progress in his world which, if generalized, would make him into a scientist,..or at least a robotologist. *Ibid.* 192 When the physiological picture is complete it will be found that physiology is not necessarily identical with robotology. **1970** A. TOFFLER *Future Shock* (1971) ix. 210 In a quite different field of robotology there is progress, too. Technicians at Disneyland have created extremely life-like computer-controlled humanoids capable of moving their arms and legs, grimacing, smiling, [etc.]. **1972** *Computers & Humanities* VI. 135 Such a theory will..be part of a general performance theory, certain aspects of which are..covered in what one might call 'general robotology'..such as questions pertaining to the interaction between robot and man.

robotomorphic (ˌrəʊbɒtəʊ'mɔːfɪk), *a.* [f. ROBOT + *-omorphic*, after ANTHROPOMORPHIC *a.*] Designating or pertaining to a view of man as a robot or an automaton.

1969 KOESTLER in Koestler & Smythies *Beyond Reductionism* 2 The common target of these 'holy discontents'..seems to be what von Bertalanffy called the robotomorphic view of man. **1970** *Times* 17 Dec. 15/4 You say I overestimate the dangers of the Robotomorphic or Ratomorphic view. **1974** *Nature* 30 Aug. 765/1 The 'robotomorphic' mechanistic view of man implied in behaviouristic psychology.

robous, -ows, -oys, obs. forms of RUBBISH.

†**rob-pot**. *Obs.* [f. ROB *v.* + POT *sb.*[1] I c.] A deep drinker, a toper.

1599 PORTER *Angry Wom. Abingd.* (Percy Soc.) 48 Ile challenge all the true rob-pots in Europe to leape vp to the chinne in a barrell of Beere. **1603** DEKKER *Wonderfull Yeare* Wks. (Grosart) I. 139 My puffing Host..blest himselfe, that a Londoner (who had wont to be the most valiant rob-pots) should now be strooke downe only with two hoopes. **1622** MASSINGER & DEKKER *Virg. Martyr* II. i, Bacchus,..grand Patron of rob-pots.

robrisshe, obs. form of RUBBISH, rubric.

Rob Roy (rɒb 'rɔɪ). [The name (meaning 'Red Robert') of a famous Highland freebooter (1671–1734).] **1.** *Rob Roy canoe*, a light canoe for a single person propelled by alternate strokes of a double-bladed paddle. Also *ellipt.*

[Name given by John Macgregor (1825–1892) to a canoe in which he made extensive voyages.]

[**1866** J. MACGREGOR (*title*), A thousand Miles in the Rob Roy Canoe.] **1876** *Encycl. Brit.* IV. 812/1 The general type of this 'Rob Roy' canoe is built of oak with a cedar deck. **1883** *Pall Mall G.* 28 Sept. 14/1 For Sale, a Rob Roy Canoe, ..with sail, mast and vane. **1938** J. BETJEMAN *Oxf. Univ. Chest* v. 97 At the ferry you board a punt or canoe or rob roy and paddle down the stream of the Cherwell. **1976** *Country Life* 8 Apr. 870 The Rob Roys were essentially all-purpose canoes.

2. A cocktail made of Scotch whisky and vermouth.

1960 'P. QUENTIN' *Green-Eyed Monster* i. 5 The two of them were..drinking Rob Roys. **1962** H. KANE *Killer's Kiss* xi. 75 'A drink, Mr. Chambers?' 'Double Rob Roy, not too sweet.' **1975** M. H. CLARK *Where are Children?* vi. 44 Jonathan's favorite drink—a Rob Roy with a twist.

robryk, obs. form of RUBRIC.

‖**robur** ('rəʊbə(r)). *rare.* [L. *rōbur* an oak.] A very hard-wooded variety of oak. Also *robur-oak*.

1601 HOLLAND *Pliny* I. 542 The same is the case of the mast-Holme, the wild Robur also, and the common Oke. **1611** FLORIO, *Essalbarnáto*, a kind of Robur or Oke tree. **1882** 'OUIDA' *Maremma* ii, It was again noon when she passed the last robur-oak and cork trees.

roburite ('rəʊbəraɪt). [f. L. *rōbur* strength + -ITE 4.] A flameless explosive of very high power. Also *attrib.*

1887 *Pall Mall G.* 24 Jan. 1/1 The German Army also possesses a new explosive agent, called Roburite. **1891** *Athenæum* 17 Jan. 91/1 Roburite..consists of chlorinated dinitrobenzene mixed with sufficient ammonium nitrate to completely oxidize it. **1897** *Allbutt's Syst. Med.* II. 956 The result of his [Bedson's] analyses shewed the absence of deleterious gases in roburite smoke.

†**ro'burnean**, *a.* *Obs.*$^{-0}$ [f. late L. *rōburneus.*] 'Of or belonging to Oak' (Blount, 1656).

robust (rəʊ'bʌst), *a.* Also 6–7 robuste. [ad. L. *rōbust-us*, f. *rōbur* strength.]

1. a. Of persons: Strong and hardy in body or constitution; possessed of rude strength; strongly and stoutly built; of a full and healthy habit.

1549 *Compl. Scot.* xvii. 146 The pepil chesit ane certan of gouuernours of the maist robust & maist prudent to be there deffendours. **1563** T. GALE *Enchirid.* 43 b (Stanf.), Stronge & robuste persons. *c* **1645** HOWELL *Lett.* III. xxi, He being newly awak'd,..and thinking to defend himself, a robust boysterous rogue knockt him down. **1660** R. COKE *Justice Vind.* 9 The most furious and robust man is not the best horse-breaker and pacer. **1736** CARTE *Ormonde* I. 576 To fall in with them sword and pike in hand, which would give the victory to the robuster men. **1789** W. BUCHAN *Dom. Med.* (1790) 31 Though grown people, who are hardy and robust, may live in such situations, yet they generally prove fatal to their offspring. **1832** MACGILLIVRAY *Trav. Humboldt* xviii. (1836) 258 On this journey she must have undergone hardships from which the most robust man would have shrunk. **1845** DAY tr. *Simon's Anim. Chem.* I. 264 The individual whose blood was analysed..was a robust young man, aged 29 years. **1895** SHAND *Gen. Hamley* I. 28 Although his constitution afterwards hardened.., at that time he was far from robust.

Comb. **1824** MISS FERRIER *Inherit.* ix, The portrait represents a considerably larger and more robust-looking person than Miss St. Clair.

absol. **1836** THIRLWALL *Greece* xx. III. 137 All other maladies terminated in this, which appeared to prey equally upon the robust and the infirm.

b. Similarly of the body or its parts, constitution or habit, health, etc.

1625 BACON *Ess., Anger* (Arb.) 566 Tender and Delicate Persons..haue so many Things to trouble them; Which more Robust Natures haue little Sense of. **1632** LITHGOW *Trav.* ii. 46 Dalmatians..of a robust nature, couragious and desperate. **1719** YOUNG *Par. Job* 260 Survey the warlike horse! didst thou invest With thunder his robust distended chest? **1784** COWPER *Task* IV. 360 Thy frame, robust and hardy, feels indeed The piercing cold, but feels it unimpair'd. **1834** LYTTON *Pompeii* II. i, His form was still so robust and athletic. **1860** W. COLLINS *Wom. in White* 134 How I envy you your robust nervous system. **1876** BRISTOWE *Th. & Pract. Med.* (1878) 452 The patient may seem in fair, if not in his ordinary robust, health.

Comb. **1884** *Pall Mall G.* 7 Apr. 3/1 The most robust-lunged must find the stifling atmosphere a severe drain on their vital force.

c. Of plants: Strong and healthy; sturdy.

1756 BURKE *Subl. & B.* III. xvi, It is not the oak..or any of the robust trees of the forest. **1769** E. BANCROFT *Guiana* 12 Canes,..even after this precaution, are usually too robust and luxuriant to make sugar with. **1796** C. MARSHALL *Gardening* xviii. (1813) 292 A robust and erect stature is the beauty of any plant. **1846** J. BAXTER *Libr. Pract. Agric.* (ed. 4) I. 141 It grows very robust, with large leaves, flat and narrow, with thick veins. **1881** *Encycl. Brit.* XII. 249/2 The Brompton Stock..is a robust plant, growing 3 feet high.

d. *Zool.* Of animal structures: Stout, thick-set, strongly made. Also *Anthrop.* Opp. *gracile.*

1828 STARK *Elem. Nat. Hist.* I. 281 Alectorides. Bill shorter than the head, or of the same length; strong, robust. **1841** *Penny Cycl.* XXI. 158/2 The zygomatic arches are more open and robust in the former. **1964** B. S. KRAUS *Basis Human Evol.* vii. 224 Those [individuals] of Swartkrans and Kromdraai were considerably taller and more robust, perhaps attaining the stature and weight of modern Man. **1977** *Times Educ. Suppl.* 21 Oct. 11/2 The first gracile australopithicene to be found was the skull that Dart found at Sterkfontein half a century ago, but more recently robust hominids have also been identified at the South African sites.

2. a. Coarse, rough, rude. Now *rare.*

c **1560** A. SCOTT *Poems* (S.T.S.) iv. 11 To hant that game robust, And beistly appetyte. **1665** HOOKE *Microgr.* Pref. C ij b, Feeling..being a sense that judges of the more gross and robust motions of the Particles of Bodies. **1667** *Decay Chr. Piety* 195 To consider our ways, to reflect not only on those robust gyant-like provocations which have thus bid defiance to Heaven. **1730–46** THOMSON *Autumn* 529 Romp-loving Miss Is, haul'd about, in gallantry robust. **1748** FOOTE *Knights* II, You are grown too headstrong and robust for me. **1872** HOWELLS *Wedding Journ.* (1892) 15 He..presently began a robust flirtation with one of them. He possessed himself, after a brief struggle, of her parasol.

b. Pertaining to, or requiring, bodily strength or hardiness; vigorous.

1683 TRYON *Way to Health* 271 Men ought not to put Women to such robust Imployments and hard Labours as many do, except pure Necessity compels them to it. *a* **1697** AUBREY *Lives* (1898) I. 107 He was an early riser and studyed well, but also took his robust pleasures of fishing, fowling, &c. **1707** MORTIMER *Husb.* (1721) II. 31 They [chestnuts] afford a good robust Diet, and are very nourishing. **1801** STRUTT *Sports & Past.* Introd. p. ii, Most of them consisted of robust exercises. **1871** LOWELL *My Study Windows, Good Word for Winter*, Cowper..preferred his..garden-walk to those robuster joys.

3. a. *fig.* Strong, vigorous, healthy.

1788 *New Lond. Mag.* 238 To prevent the robust title of occupancy from again taking place, the doctrine of escheats is adopted. **1836** *Penny Cycl.* V. 264 They exhibit a robust sense, a mind stored with classical erudition. **1888** *Glasgow Even. Times* 24 Aug. 2/5 English is a robust language.

Comb. **1898** *Westm. Gaz.* 11 July 3/2 Probably, as a robust-minded man, he may have agreed with Kinglake.

b. *Philol.* (See quots.)

1776 J. RICHARDSON *Arab. Gram.* 8 The three letters ى و ا are called weak... All the others are stiled robust. **1843** *Proc. Philol. Soc.* I. 138 It [Berber] has a distinction of letters..into robust and weak. The weak letters of course are W, Y, and A.

c. Vigorous in mind, voice, etc.

1852 H. ROGERS *Ess.* (1874) I. vii. 333 The beneficial influence he has exerted as a most robust thinker and a most admirable writer. **1870** LOWELL *Among my Bks.* Ser. I. (1873) 203 Can this be said of any other modern? of robust Corneille? **1897** *Daily News* 5 Feb. 8/7 Signor Ceppi, a robust tenor.

4. Applied to a statistical test that yields approximately correct results despite the falsity of certain of the assumptions on which it is based; also, to a calculation, process, or result if the result is largely independent of certain aspects of the input.

1955 BOX & ANDERSEN in *Jrnl. R. Statistical Soc.* B. XVII. 1 To fulfil the needs of the experimenter, statistical criteria should (1) be sensitive to change in the specific factors tested, (2) be insensitive to changes, of a magnitude likely to occur in practice, in extraneous factors. A test which satisfies the first requirement is said to be powerful and we shall typify a test which satisfies the second by calling it 'robust'. **1966** S. BEER *Decision & Control* x. 232 What is important is the recognition of common features in the set of outcomes; these are the inductive inferences which may be classed as forecasts. We say that the system is robust in respect to a particular set of outcomes. **1972** *Jrnl. Social Psychol.* LXXXVIII. 204 The tests are robust regarding the assumptions of normality and equality of variances, but only when sample sizes are equal. **1978** *Nature* 16 Nov. 264/1 The ANOVA assumes equality of variances, a condition not satisfied here, however the test is robust to small deviations in homoscedasticity. **1979** *Sci. Amer.* Apr. 69/2 This conclusion, they point out, 'is robust, in that we have derived it from the global geochemical distribution of uranium, and we have also derived it from the U.S. uranium-mining history and from a wide variety of subsets of the U.S. uranium-mining history'.

Hence **ro'bustful** *a.*; **ro'bustfulness**.

1802 COURTIER *Solitude* 38 Join with new ardour the robustful strife. **1879** MEREDITH *Egoist* III. xi. 241 He knew his breathing robustfulness to be as an east wind to weak nerves.

robusta (rəʊ'bʌstə). [fem. of L. *rōbusta* ROBUST, specific (now varietal) epithet (L. Linden *Catal. Plantes économiques de l'Horticole coloniale* (1900) 64).] An evergreen variety of coffee, *Coffea canephora* var. *robusta*, native to Africa and widely cultivated elsewhere for its heavy crops of small beans; also, the beans produced by a tree of this kind. Also *attrib.*

1909 *Philippine Agric. Rev.* II. 590 A new variety of coffee known as 'robusta'..was discovered some years ago growing wild on the estates in Africa. *Ibid.*, The robusta coffee planted in east Java yields after three years. **1922** [see ARABICA]. **1944** *Empire Jrnl. Exper. Agric.* XII. 191 Robusta coffee..grows wild in many of the wetter forests of Uganda. **1959** [see ARABICA]. **1961** F. L. WELLMAN *Coffee* v. 81 The most common variety is named Robusta, and this type has large, dark-green leaves... Trees of the Robusta variety tend to have a flattened top. **1796** *Times* 7 May 22/5 Fears of a shortage..sent robusta coffee prices to new all-time highs on the London markets. *Ibid.*, Shortages will increase the demand for African robustas.

†**ro'bustic**, *a.* *Obs.* Also 7–8 -ick. [f. ROBUST + -IC.] Robust, robustious.

1683 TRYON *Way to Health* 10 Such People are..fit for all robustick, dirty, killing Imployments. **1694** SALMON *Bate's Dispens.* (1713) 651/2 Unless you meet with a very hard and robustick Habit of Body. **1719** D'URFEY *Pills* (1872) III. 27 In fine it rules all, though ne'er so robustick.

Hence **ro'busticness**. *Obs.*

1676 HUBBARD *Happiness of a People* 3 By reason of the robusticness of their body.

robu'sticity. Chiefly *Anthrop.* and *Zool.* [f. as ROBUSTIC + -ITY.] Robustness.

1777 R. DONKIN *Milit. Coll.* 201 Robusticity is no valour, nor is debility always pusillanimity. **1874** JULIA WARD *Home in Sex & Educ.* 22 The stout sisters whose full outlines attest their own robusticity. **1946** F. E. ZEUNER *Dating Past* ix. 299 They show nothing of the robusticity and exuberance of bodily growth of Crô-Magnon Man, whose contemporaries they were. **1959** *Chambers's Encycl.* I. 460/2 Other features than size, e.g. shape and robusticity, are expressed in anthropometry by indices. **1971** *Nature* 5 Feb. 407/1 In overall size and robusticity the fossil closely resembles the pygmy chimpanzee.

ro'bustihood. *nonce-wd.* [f. ROBUST, after *hardihood*, etc.] Robustness.

1834 MEDWIN *Angler in Wales* II. 50 He was a Highlander, and his limbs showed the robustihood of the mountaineer.

ro'bustious, *a.* [f. ROBUST + -IOUS.]

In common use during the 17th century. In the 18th it becomes rare, and is described by Johnson (1755) as 'now only used in low language, and in a sense of contempt'. During the 19th it has been considerably revived, esp. by archaizing writers.

1. Of persons: Robust; stout and strong or healthy-looking.

a **1548** HALL *Chron., Rich. III*, 56 b, Let us..marche furth like stronge & robustious champions. **1615** DANIEL *Hymen's Triumph* II. i, Not degenerate From my robustious manly Ancestors. **1654** H. L'ESTRANGE *Chas. I* (1655) 72 This Gunner was a robustious Vulcan. **1727** SWIFT *On a Woman's Mind*, She gets a Cold as sure as Death;..Admires how modest Women can Be so robustious like a Man. **1822** IRVING *Bracebr. Hall* viii. (1845) 39 The number of robustious footmen and retainers of all kinds bustling about. **1863** A. SMITH *Dreamthorp* 24 The robustious fellow who sits at the head of the table. **1875** DOWDEN *Shaks.* 213 Carriers and drawers, and merchants, and pilgrims, and loud robustious women.

b. So of the body or its parts, constitution, appearance, etc.

1584 R. PARSONS *Leycester's Commonw.* (1641) 94 Her highnesse..well stricken in yeeres, and of no great good health or robustious and strong complexion. **1599** Nashe *Lenten Stuffe* Wks. (Grosart) V. 256 It will..harden his soft bleding vaines as stiffe and robustious, as branches of Corrall. **1620** Venner *Via Recta* vii. 128 The dry Walnuts are onely good for robustious bodies. **1671** Milton *Samson* 569 These redundant locks Robustious to no purpose clustring down. **1771** in Hone *Every-day Bk.* II. 207 It is by far too dainty for their robustious constitution. **1817** Byron *Let. to Murray* 9 May, I am..congratulated..on my robustious appearance. **1820** L. Hunt *Indicator* (1822) II. 88 Ladies who are shocked at that robustious indication of good health, a moist palm.

c. Of things: Big and strong; massive.

a **1548** Hall *Chron., Hen. VI*, 85 b, When the duke of Yorke had fastened his chaine betwene these twoo strong and robustious pillers [i.e. the Earls of Warwick and Salisbury]. **1612–8** Daniel *Life & Reign William I.* Wks. (Grosart) IV. 135 Roul, or Rou, a great Commander amongst them, furnished a robustious power,..and first landed in England. **1679** G. R. tr. *Boaistuau's Theat. World* 139 His Cloak..was likewise so very heavy and robustious. **1809** Irving *Knickerb.* (1861) 32 When erect he had not a little the appearance of a robustious beer barrel.

transf. **1654** Jer. Taylor *Real Pres.* 90 Against this Bellarmine brings..a most robustious argument. **1664** H. More *Myst. Iniq.* 437 Assertours and Abettours of Truth, then which nothing is more robustious and strong.

2. Violent, boisterous, noisy, strongly self-assertive: **a.** Of persons, their disposition, etc.

a **1548** Hall *Chron., Hen. VII*, 57 Men throughe aboundaunce of ryches waxe more insolent, hedstronge and robustius. **1602** Shaks. *Ham.* III. ii. 10 O it offends mee to the Soule, to see a robustious Pery-wig-pated Fellow, teare a Passion to tatters. **1681** H. More *Exp. Dan.* v. 155 Men of a more fierce, strong, robustious temper..are more inept to see any such Spectra. **1732–8** Swift *Polite Conv.* 109 You are so robustious, you are like to put out my Eye. **1839** Disraeli *Corr. w. Sister* (1886) 146 They had a roaring, robustious, romping party. **1881** *World* 28 Dec., He is a strong 'robustious' lecturer. **1881** A. Lang *Library* 47 The man who is defective as to the love of books..we may call..the Robustious Philistine.

b. Of actions, movements, etc.

1599 Shaks. *Hen. V*, III. vii. 159 The men doe sympathize with the Mastiffes, in robustious and rough coming on. **1612** Drayton *Poly-olb.* I. 250 This robustious play By which the toiles of warre most livelie are exprest. **1649** Milton *Eikon.* 37 In Scotland they had handl'd the Bishops in a more robustious manner. **1701** Wolley *Jrnl. N.Y.* (1860) 46 They [the Indians]..love extremes either to sit still or to be in robustious motions. **1839** *Blackw. Mag.* XLVI. 39 The laughter becomes louder and more robustious. **1897** Sprigge *Life Wakley* xxx. 276 The crude and robustious declamations of a demagogue.

c. Of storms or climate; Violent, severe.

1612 Drayton *Poly-olb.* x. 77 Meeting from the South Great Neptunes surlier tides, with their robustious shockes. **1632** Quarles *Div. Fancies* Wks. (Grosart) II. 213/2 If a robustious Storme should rise..they Harbour's safe enough. **1641** *Newsfr. Hell, Rome*, etc. in *Harl. Misc.* (Malh.) IV. 399 A robustious storm of wind out of the North.

1889 Stevenson *Edinb.* 144 Slunk from the robustious winter to an inn fire-side.

ro'bustiously, *adv.* Now *arch.* [f. robustious + -ly[2].] In a rough or boisterous manner; with noisy self-assertion.

1607 Middleton *Phœnix* I. iv, There's a kind of captain very robustiously inquires for you. **1624** Heywood *Gunaik.* II. 115 Tall and spreading trees amongst whose leaves the wind onely whispers, but never robustiously blowes. **1655** Bp. Richardson *Obs. O.T.* 287 Speaketh wickedly, roughly, and robustiously.

1893 Stevenson *Catriona* 322, 'I believe I have been quite plain from the beginning!' cries he robustiously.

ro'bustiousness. Now *rare.* [f. robustious + -ness.] Robustness; boisterousness.

1600 Abbot *Jonah* 388 For which..we are fit, by the stayedness of our Constitution and robustiousnesse of nature. **1650** Gentilis *Consid.* 10 The Philosopher from the robustiousnesse of the complexion, argues a weaknesse of the intellect.

1882 *St. James's Gaz.* 11 Oct. 6 There was a certain 'robustiousness' about the morals put together by the firm. **1894** Hall Caine *Manxman* 401 He threw Auntie Nan into tremors of nervousness by his noise and robustiousness.

ro'bustly, *adv.* [f. robust + -ly[2].] In a robust manner; strongly.

1708 Motteux *Rabelais* (1737) V. 230 Your Phrase, robustly propt. **1709** Mrs. Manley *Secr. Mem.* (1736) II. 46 Insensible, Hoydening, ungainly Brisk, robustly Gay. **1836** *Random Recoll. Ho. of Lords* ix. 190 He is of the ordinary height, rather stoutly, though not robustly made. **1878** Bayne *Purit. Rev.* xi. 458 Constituting a robustly Protestant and Liberal Church.

ro'bustness. [f. robust + -ness.] Robust character or quality.

1599 Sandys *Europæ Spec.* (1632) 187 That robustnesse of body, and puissance of person, which is the onely fruict of strength that those colder climes doe yeild. **1632** Lithgow *Trav.* vi. 253 They were in great danger of perishing, although the robustnesse of my body carried mee through on my feete. **1672** Boyle *Wks.* (1772) III. 620 Rather from the robustness of the bladder,..than from the non-gravitation of water. **1756** Burke *Subl. & B.* Wks. I. 56 An air of robustness and strength is very prejudicial to beauty. **1768–74** Tucker *Lt. Nat.* (1834) I. 236 It shows more robustness to carry a weight for miles, than to pull out a wedge at a jerk. **1817** Rickman *Gothic Arch.* (1862) 8 Strength and robustness are retained in the Doric. **1838** James *Robber* i, His arms were not such as would have called attention from their robustness. **1870** Hooker *Student's Flora* 391 Very variable in habit, size, robustness. **1953** G. E. P. Box in *Biometrika* XL. 318 This remarkable property of 'robustness' to non-normality which these tests for comparing means possess, and without which they would be much less appropriate to the needs of the experimenter, is not necessarily shared by other statistical tests. **1973** J. Buettner-Janusch *Physical Anthropol.* viii. 240 [Modern man] may walk bipedally. Among the specializations that permit this are the shape of the arch and the position and robustness of the big toe. **1974** Adby & Dempster *Introd. Optimization Methods* iv. 78 A concept both more vague and much more difficult to ensure is termed robustness. A robust algorithm is one which in practice usually yields the global minimum or a good local minimum of any function of even a large number of variables from a poor initial approximation.

†**ro'bustous**, *a. Obs.* [f. robust + -ous.] Robust, robustious.

1597 Gerarde *Herbal* II. lxxviii. 315 Vnto robustous or strong bodies twelue sponfuls may be giuen. **1655** Hartlib *Ref. Silk-worm* 23 She is not a nice curious kinde of Silk-worme; but stout and robustous, that will require little care or attendance. **1681** Rycaut tr. *Gracian's Critick* 185 The Bonds.., though but feeble, were yet the Chains of the most robustous Champions.

†**ro'bustuous**, *a. Obs.* [f. robust, after *tempestuous*.] = robustious.

1637 Heywood *Pleas. Dial.* Wks. 1874 VI. 258 Nymphs, not generated..from violent and robustuous seas. **1648** J. Beaumont *Psyche* xiv. xlv, No constraint Can..breed Robustuous Firmness in a broken Reed.

Hence †**ro'bustuousness.** *Obs.*$^{-1}$

1679 Dryden *Pref. Troil. & Cr.* Ess. (ed. Ker) I. 221 If he want the skill which is necessary to a wrestler, he shall make but small advantage of his natural robustuousness.

†**robwort**, ? variant of ribwort.

c **1475** *Pict. Voc.* in Wr.-Wülcker 786 *Hec lancea*, a robworte.

robyl, obs. f. rubble.

Robyn, obs. f. Robin.

robys, obs. f. rubbish.

roc (rɒk). Forms: α. 6 roche, 7 roque, 8 rock, 9 roc (rokh). β. 6–7 ruc, ruch, ruck(e, 9 rukh(kh. [ad. Arab. *rokh*, *rukh(kh*: hence also F. *rock*, It. †*roche*, Sp. †*rocho*, Pg. *roco*; Sp., It., Pg. *ruc* (*ruch*). The older source for the word is the account of Madagascar in Marco Polo III. clxxxv ('et l'appellent les genz de ces isles *ruc*'); in mod. use it is partly from the *Arabian Nights*.] A mythical bird of Eastern legend, imagined as being of enormous size and strength.

α *a* **1579** Twyne *Phis. agst. Fortune* II. Ep. Ded. 159 About the Indian sea there is a certeine birde of an incredible bignesse, whom our countriemen call a Roche, which is able and accustomed to take vp, not onelie a man, but also an whole shippe in her beake. **1631** Mabbe tr. *Celestina* Prol. (1894) 15 Of a bird called Roque, which is bred in the East Indian Sea, it is said to be of an incredible greatness. **1774** Goldsm. *Nat. Hist.* (1824) II. 251 It is supposed that the great bird called the Rock, described by Arabian writers,..is but a species of the condor. **1802** *Arab. Nts.* (1815) I. 242 The roc comes and seizes them both in its claws. **1839–52** Bailey *Festus* (1864) 418 Mild rokh, simorgh, wise sun-spirit. **1855** Thackeray *Newcomes* xlvii, I might wish for the roc's egg. **1865** Kingsley *Herew.* i, But beyond, things unspeakable—dragons, giants, rocs.

β. **1598** Bp. Hall *Sat.* iv. vi. 68 Of the bird Ruc that beares an elephant. **1621** Burton *Anat. Mel.* II. ii. II. i, As I goe by Madagascar I would see that great bird Rucke that can carry a man and horse, or an Elephant. *a* **1635** Corbet *Poems* (1807) 99 O that I ere might have the hap To get the bird which in the map Is called the Indian Ruck! **1691** T. Heyrick *Misc. Poems* 7 The Ruck, in Madagascar bred,..Whom greatest Beasts and armed Horsemen dread.

1841 Lane *Arab. Nts.* (1859) I. iii. 188 Wherupon a bird called the rukh' will come to thee, and..fly away with thee. **1924** *Nature* 19 Apr. 564/2 Purely fabulous species, such as the phœnix and the rukh, are likewise dealt with. **1974** *Encycl. Brit. Micropædia* VIII. 619/2 The Kublai Khan inquired..about the *rukh* and was brought what was claimed to be a *rukh*'s feather, which may really have been a frond of the *Raphia* palm.

roc, obs. form of rock, rook.

‖**rocaille** (rɔkɑj). Also rocail and with capital initial. [a. F. *rocaille* rock-work, rococo.] An artistic or architectural style of decoration characterized by ornate rock- and shell-work; a rococo style. Also *attrib.* or as *adj.*

1856 M. Digby Wyatt in O. Jones *Grammar of Ornament* I. xix. 109 The twisted and foliated scrolls and shells..grew into the 'rocaille' and grotto-work of [baroque]..; degenerating at last into..'Chinoiserie'. **1905** *Scribner's Mag.* July 47 Rocaille differs from our rockwork in that it does not attempt to imitate the natural formation of rocks, but rather seeks to create architectural forms by combinations of pebbles and shells, such as conventionalized figures of sea-gods, and dolphins. **1936** *Burlington Mag.* Oct. 187/1 Louis XVI, who did not care for the 'rocaille' style like his grandfather. **1944** J. Lees-Milne *Prophesying Peace* (1977) 69 A cliff-like structure hung with reliefs, and encrusted with shells, sea urchins and rocaille ornaments. **1958** *Listener* 2 Oct. 530/1 The staggering rocaille on Bena Lulua figures. **1960** *Times* 14 Jan. 14/5 Sauceboats of 1737 having shell shaped bowls or *rocaille* bases. **1975** J. Gores *Hammett* (1976) xi. 82 The ornate rocaille pier glass. **1979** E. H. Gombrich *Sense of Order* vii. 189 To what extent can Riegl's method be used for the explanation and analysis of the Rocaille? Are these playful shells..just another metamorphosis of the acanthus?

rocambole ('rɒkəmbəʊl). Forms: 7 roccombo, rockamboy (?); 8 rockenbole, rockanbowl; rocambol, rockam-, rocombole; 8–9 rocambole. [a. F. *rocambole*, of obscure origin: hence also G. dial. *rockenboll(e*, *-polle*, which has by some been regarded as the source of the F. word.]

1. A species of leek (*Allium Scorodoprasum*) indigenous to Northern Europe, used as a seasoning for dishes; Spanish garlic, sand-leek.

1698 M. Lister *Journ. Paris* (1699) 150 Also Leeks, Rockamboy, and Shallots are here in great use. **1699** Evelyn *Acetaria* 28 A light touch on the dish, much better supply'd by the gentler Roccombo. **1709** W. King *Cookery* 336 Where rocombole, shallot, and the rank garlic grow. **1786** Abercrombie *Arr.* in *Gard. Assist.* p. ix, Some [are raised] by small bulbs at top of the stalks, as rocambole and tree onion. *c* **1820** *Edin. Encycl.* XI. 264 The Rocambole..is a perennial plant, indigenous to Sweden and Denmark. **1855** Delamer *Kitch. Gard.* (1861) 48 Rocambole produces bulbs on the top of its stem, and in the axillæ of its leaves. **1882** *Garden* 11 Nov. 425/2 Rocambole..is a mild form of Garlic.

attrib. **1699** Evelyn *Acetaria* App. P. 4, Adding to the Spice some Roccombo-Seeds. **1766** Anstey *Bath Guide* (ed. 3) 91 Puffs his vile Rocambol Breath in her Face. **1793** Woodville *Med. Bot.* III. 459 Rocambole Garlick.

b. *fig.* That which gives flavour or piquancy.

1702 Vanbrugh *False Friend* I. i, Difficulties are the Rocombolle of Love; I never valu'd an easy conquest in my life.

2. A plant of this, or the edible portion of one. (See also quot. 1716.)

1707 Mortimer *Husb.* (1721) II. 163 Rocamboles are a sort of wild Garlick, otherwise called Spanish Garlick. **1716** M. Davies *Athen. Brit.* II. 349 Which Heads [of leeks] some call Rockenboles, tho' others say that the Cluster of the Cloves of Garlick is the proper Rockanbowl. **1863** *Life Normandy* II. 60 A very small quantity of herbs—..chives and rocamboles—were put into a flat plan.

‖**rocambolesque** (rɒˌkæmbɒ'lɛsk), *a.* [a. F. *rocambolesque* fantastic, f. *Rocambole* the name of a character in the novels of Ponson du Terrail (1829–71), French author, the subject of improbable and fantastic adventures + -esque.] Of or resembling Rocambole (see etym.); incredible, fantastic.

1949 Koestler *Promise & Fulfilment* I. viii. 91 It was the first anti-British terror act of the Irgun and it displayed already all the features of rocambolesque etiquette. **1960** B. Marshall *Divided Lady* I. xxi. 75 How amused the General would have been by this rocambolesque religiosity. **1976** *New Society* 13 May 370/3 An exemplary surrealistic life..which included a *rocambolesque* episode..in which he kidnapped his Bulgarian mistress from her husband.

rocate, obs. Sc. form of rocket.

roccellate (rɒk'sɛleɪt). *Chem.* [f. as next + -ate.] A salt formed by the action of roccellic acid upon a base.

1838 T. Thomson *Chem. Org. Bodies* 128 Dr. Heeren, from the analysis of several roccellates, has determined the atomic weight of the acid to be 18·82. **1845** *Penny Cycl.* Suppl. I. 350/1 The alkaline roccellates dissolve in water, and yield solutions which froth like soap.

roccellic (rɒk'sɛlɪk), *a. Chem.* (See quots.)

1838 T. Thomson *Chem. Org. Bodies* 128 Of roccellic acid. This acid was discovered by Dr. Heeren in the *Rocella tinctoria*. **1868** Watts *Dict. Chem.* s.v., Roccellic acid forms delicate, white, rectangular..plates, having a silvery lustre. *Ibid.*, *Roccellic anhydride*..is a colourless or faintly yellow neutral oil, having a fatty odour.

roc'cellin. *Chem.* Also -ine. [f. as prec. + -in[1], -ine[5].] A coal-tar colour used in dyeing, derived from the orchil lichen.

1852 Gregory *Org. Chem.* (ed. 3) 307 Rocelline..is neutral, yields no red colour with bleaching liquor.

roc'cellinin. *Chem.* Also -ine. [Cf. prec.] 'A crystalline substance obtained from *Roccella tinctoria*' (Watts).

1848 *Chem. Gaz.* VI. 126 Roccellinine.—Obtained by drying the gelatinous mass which is precipitated from the lime solution by muriatic acid, and boiling in strong spirit. **1863** *Fownes' Chem.* (ed. 9) 666 Hair-like crystals of a silvery lustre, of a substance called *roccellinin*.

roccelo, obs. variant of roquelaure.

roccombo, obs. var. rocambole.

†**rocester earth.** *Obs.*$^{-0}$ (See quot.)

1483 *Cath. Angl.* 310 Rocester erthe, *campanum*, *nitrum*.

roch, obs. f. ratch *sb.*[1]

roch, obs. f. roach *sb.*[1] and *sb.*[2]

rochate, obs. f. rochet[1].

roche (rəʊtʃ), *sb.*[1] Now *dial.* Forms: 3– roche (4 rooche), 4–7 roch, 5–6, 9 *dial.* rotch(e, 7 roach. [a. OF. *roche*, *rocche* (mod.F. *roche*), var. of *rocque*, *roke* rock *sb.*[1] Hence also MDu. *roche*, *rotche*, *rotse* (Du. and Fris. *rots*).]

1. A rock or cliff; a rocky height.

c **1250** *Gen. & Ex.* 256 Til ihesus was..biried in ðe roche cold. *c* **1290** *St. Agatha* 124 in *S. Eng. Leg.* I. 197 Strong fuyr..barnde þe hard roche of ston ase þei it Col were. *a* **1300** *Cursor M.* 6390 Moyses on þe roche kan stand, & smat it wit þis forsaid wand. *c* **1380** *Sir Ferumb.* 1108 By hilles & roches swyþe horrible on hur cors þay wente. *c* **1400** Maundev. (Roxb.) ii. 6 Vnder þe roche of mount Caluarie. **1470–85** Malory *Arthur* I. xxv. 73 Within that lake is a roche. **1515** *Scottish Field* 634 in *Chetham Misc.* (1856), All rang with that rowte, roches and other. **1589** *Golden Mirr.* (Chetham Soc.) 12, I durst not well approch,.. But closly kept me vnderneath a roch. **1631** BRATHWAIT *Whimzies, Jealous Neighbour* 115 His earth-reverting body..is to be buried in some cell, roach, or vault. [*c* **1700** KENNETT in *MS. Lansd. 1033* fol. 326 Several of the mountains in Staffordsh. are called Roches, bearing no grass, but running in bare ridges like stone walls.]

fig. *a* **1300** *Cursor M.* 9975 þat roche þat es polist sa slight, es maiden maria hert ful right. **1340** *Ayenb.* 142 þe ilke roche is Iesu crist him-zelf.

attrib. **1549** *Compl. Scotl.* vi. 38 The depe hou cauernis of cleuchis & rotche craggis ansuert vitht ane hie not. **1601** HOLLAND *Pliny* I. 331 The wild Goats called Roch-goats, haue their hornes turning backward.

†**b.** A huge mass of stone; a boulder. *Obs.*

1297 R. GLOUC. (Rolls) 4165 Anon riȝt he hom ssende Mid gleyue oþer mid roches, & vewe aliue he let. *c* **1330** R. BRUNNE *Chron. Wace* (Rolls) 12171 Grete roches at þem he cast, & þer schipes to-rof & brast. *a* **1585** MONTGOMERIE *Cherrie & Slae* 82, I saw an river rin..With tumbling and rumbling, Amang the rochis round.

2. In north and north-midland dial. use, applied to various kinds of rock, stone, or geological strata. Also *attrib.* Cf. ROACH *sb.*[2] 4.

1803 PLYMLEY *Agric. Shropsh.* 53 Rotch, dark-grey hard rock. **1820** WILBRAHAM *Gloss. Cheshire, Roche*, refuse stone. **1831** J. HODGSON in Raine *Mem.* (1858) II. 217 Perpendicular fissures too are formed in the roche. *Ibid.* 218 The roche pebbles are glazed. **1841** HARTSHORNE *Salop. Antiq.* Gloss., *Roche*, 1. The strata above a marshy deposit; 2. Earth mingled with stone; 3. Any strata which is superincumbent to the one about to be worked. **1883** GRESLEY *Gloss. Coal-mining, Rotche* or *Roche* (South Staff.), a softish and moderately friable sandstone.

†**3.** ? Alum or borax. (So F. *roche.*) *Obs.*

1494 in *Cov. Corpus Christi Plays* 88 It. paid for a strawen hate, ob; a leffe of roche clere, j d. **1510** in Willis and Clark *Cambridge* (1886) II. 199 Item to Paule Smyth for certen coloures as..mastyke vernysch yelowe moty orpment roch vermylyon vergres.

roche, *sb.*[2]: see ROCHE MOUTONNÉE.

†**roche**, *sb.*[3] *Obs.*$^{-1}$ A kind of wine.

Perhaps for *Rochel* ROCHELLE, but *Roche* is a common place-name in France, and sugar *de Roche* is freq. mentioned in the Durham Account Rolls along with that from Morocco and Cyprus.

a **1400** *Sir Degrevant* 1414 (Linc. MS.), Ever scho drewe thame the wyne, Bathe the Roche and the Ryne.

Roche (rəʊʃ), *sb.*[4] *Astron.* The name of Edouard Albert *Roche* (1820–83), French mathematician, used *attrib.* and in the possessive to denote concepts arising out of his work, as **Roche('s) limit**, (*a*) the closest distance to which a self-gravitating body (strictly a fluid body: see quot. 1900) can approach a more massive body without being pulled apart by the gravitational field of the latter body; (*b*) the smallest continuous equipotential surface (having the form of two lobes meeting at a point) which can exist around both members of a system of two gravitating bodies, *spec.* a binary star system; **Roche lobe**, either of the two volumes of space (meeting at a point) that are bounded by Roche's limit (*b*) in a binary system; **Roche zone**, the region of space within Roche's limit (sense (*a*)).

1889 G. H. DARWIN in *Harper's Mag.* June 73/1 The distance of..2·44 of a planet's radius I call Roche's limit for that planet. **1900** *Astrophysical Jrnl.* XI. 122 In the derivation of Roche's limit the assumption was made that the satellite was a perfectly homogeneous incompressible fluid, and that its rotation and revolution were performed in the same period. **1930** R. H. BAKER *Astron.* v. 212 All parts of Saturn's rings lie within Roche's limit. **1959** Z. KOPAL *Close Binary Syst.* iii. 133 Such configurations represent the largest closed equipotentials capable of containing the whole mass of the respective components, and will hereafter be referred to as their Roche limits. **1969** *Times* 10 July 12/8 If the moon had ever come within a critical distance of earth, known as the Roche limit, the tidal forces raised by the earth would have disrupted it. **1972** W. STROHMEIER *Variable Stars* vii. 182 Expansion of the components in close binaries towards their Roche limits, in a time scale of 10^6 years, can also give rise to an exchange between the rotational and orbital momenta. **1974** *Sci. Amer.* Feb. 53/1 Only a body with more than gravitational cohesion can withstand the tidal effects within Roche's limit. [**1960** *Astrophysical Jrnl.* CXXXII. 149 (*caption*) The radii of the Roche-limit lobes for a mass ratio of unity.] **1969** *Ibid.* CLVIII. 571 Morton concluded that on such a time scale the contact component would be stable, shrinking within the Roche lobe after initial mass loss. **1975** *Sci. Amer.* Mar. 30/3 In the evolution of a typical binary, as soon as one of the components expands to a volume larger than that of its Roche lobe the matter outside the lobe will begin to flow toward the companion star. **1971** I. G. GASS et al. *Understanding Earth* vii. 112/2 What would happen if the Moon were to enter the Roche zone? **1978** *New Scientist* 23 Nov. 607/2 One or more former moons of Uranus spiralled into the planet's Roche zone where they broke up because of tidal forces, producing the parent fragments of the rings.

roche (rəʊtʃ), *v.*[1] Also 7, 9 roach. [f. ROCHE *sb.*[1] Cf. ROCHE ALUM.]

†**1.** *trans.* To make hard like a rock. *Obs.*$^{-1}$

1582 STANYHURST *Æneis*, etc. (Arb.) 136 Thee winters coldnesse thee riuer hardlye roching.

2. †**a.** *intr.* To form crystals. *Obs.*

1631 [see ROCHING *vbl. sb.*]. **1673** RAY *Trav.* (1738) 403 When burnt it is turned into a white calx, which naturally roches into parellelipipedums of the figure of a lozenge.

b. *trans.* To recrystallize (alum) in lead-lined casks after previous dissolution by water or steam.

1678 *Phil. Trans.* XII. 1056 After which it [alum] is Roached, as followeth. Being washed, it is put into another Pan with a quantity of Water, where it melts and boils a little. Then is it scooped into a great Cask, where it commonly stands ten days, and is then fit to take down for the Market. **1853** URE *Dict. Arts* I. 58 The rough alum thus made is sometimes purified by a subsequent recrystallization, after which it is 'roched' for the market, —a process intended merely to give it the ordinary commercial aspect.

†**roche**, *v.*[2] *Obs.*$^{-1}$ [? var. of *ruche* RICH *v.*[2]] *trans.* To tug or tear (asunder).

c **1400** *Destr. Troy* 12511 The sea..cut down þere sailes, Ropis al-to rochit, rent vp the hacches.

roche, obs. form of ROACH *sb.*[1]; obs. var. ROOK *sb.*[2]; var. ROTCH *Obs.*; obs. f. ROUGH *a.*

rochea (ˈrəʊʃɪə). [mod.L. (A. P. de Candolle *Plantarum Historia Succulentarum* (1803 ?) 103), f. the name of François de la *Roche* (d. 1813), French botanist + -A 2.] A succulent plant of the genus so called, belonging to the family Crassulaceæ, native to South Africa, and bearing leathery leaves and clusters of white, pink, or red flowers.

1932 A. J. MACSELF *Amateur's Greenhouse* xi. 253 Hybrid Kalosanthes or Rocheas in white, rose, etc., are similar in habit. **1955** V. HIGGINS tr. *Bertrand's Indoor Plants* 84 Rochea... For some years now the florists have offered this attractive plant on Mother's Day. **1979** A. HUXLEY *Reader's Digest Success with House Plants* 340/3 Rocheas are small shrubs grown primarily for their clusters of flowers.

roche alum (rəʊtʃ ˈæləm). Also 5 rooch, 5–9 roch, 7–8 roach. [f. ROCHE *sb.*[1] + ALUM *sb.*, after F. *alun de roche* (cf. *alun en roque*, 1368), It. *allume di rocca*: cf. Du. *rotsaluin*, G. *rotsalaun*, and the synonymous Sp. *piedra alumbre*, Pg. *pedra (a)hume*.

The statement that the name is derived from Roccha, a Turkish province in N. Syria, is evidently quite unfounded.]

= Rock alum (see ALUM *sb.* 1).

α. **1436** *Libel Eng. Policy* in *Pol. Poems* (Rolls) II. 172 They bringe wyth hem..Coton, roche-alum, and gode golde of Jene. **1453** in Heath *Grocers' Comp.* (1869) 422 Alum, foyle or rooch, ye bale, iiijd. **1597** LOWE *Chirurg.* Y 4b, Betonie, worme-wood, roch allom. **1601** HOLLAND *Pliny* II. 165 Seeth the same..together with Safron, Roch-allom, Myrrh, and the best Attick hony. **1669** STURMY *Mariner's Mag.* VII. xxxiv. 50 Put in it the bigness of a Hens Egg of Roch Allom. **1747** WESLEY *Prim. Physick* (1762) 42 Make a Plaister of Roch Allum, Vinegar and Honey. **1753** J. BARTLET *Gentl. Farriery* (1754) 190 Giving drinks prepared with green vitriol, roch allum, Roman vitriol. **1853** URE *Dict. Arts* (ed. 4) I. 57 The mother liquor of the 'roch alum' is called 'tun liquor'. **1860** [see ROCK ALUM].

β. **1619** BERT *Hawkes* 84 Seeth some spring water, and.. put into it a peece of Roach-Allum. **1620** *Observ. Silkwormes* D j b, Roach Allum, called Romish Allum. **1704** *Lond. Gaz.* No. 4008/4 Roach-Allum, Coffee, Brimstone. **1753** CHAMBERS *Cycl. Suppl.* s.v. *Phosphorus fæcalis*, Mix it with the same quantity of roach alum grossly powdered. **1799** G. SMITH *Laboratory* II. 401 Together with..half a pound of roach alum, &c.

roched, *ppl. a. rare*$^{-1}$. [f. ROCHE *v.*[1]] Subjected to roching. †***roched petre***, = ROCHE PETRE.

1666 BOYLE *Formes & Qual.* 227 And yet these Christals, though sometimes they would shoot into Prisme-like Figures, as Roch'd Petre; and sometimes [etc.].

roche lime. Also 7–8 roach. [f. ROCHE *sb.*[1]] Unslaked lime; lime-shells.

1756 C. LUCAS *Ess. Waters* I. 41 Lime-water is prepared by infusing unslaked lime or roche-lime in water. **1776** G. SEMPLE *Building in Water* 49 We spread a plentiful Coat of Roach-lime and sharp Gravel over the Ground. **1800** *Hull Advertiser* 5 Apr. 1/3 Mortar composed of clean sand and Roche Lime. **1830–2** CARLETON *Traits* (1843) I. 118 Our plan was to bring a pocketful of roche lime with us, and put it into the pool.

Rochelle (rəʊˈʃɛl). *Obs.* Also 6, 8 Rochel, 6–7 Rochell. [The place-name (*La*) *Rochelle*, a seaport of western France.]

1. Used *attrib.* or *absol.* to designate the kind of wine exported from this place.

1391 *Earl of Derby's Exped.* (Camden) 10 Pro lxxvj stopis vini Rochelle ab ipsis emptis ibidem. ? *a* **1400** *Morte Arthure* 203 Rynisch wyne and Rochelle. ? *c* **1475** *Sqr. lowe Degre* 760 Wyne of Greke, and muscadell, Both clare, pyment, and Rochell. **1533** MORE *Answ. Poysoned Bk.* Wks. 1103/1 A little tast of holesome ynough, though some-what small and rough rochel wine. **1552** *Reg. Privy Counc. Scot.* I. 129, vi d. the pynt of Rochell wyne. **1592** GREENE *Upst. Courtier* Wks. (Grosart) XI. 278 If he hath a strong gascoigne wine,.. he can allay it with a small rochel wine. **1615** MARKHAM *Eng. Housew.* II. iv, There are Rochell wines, which are in pipes long and slender. **1731** MILLER *Gard. Dict.* s.v. *Wine*, They transform poor Rochel and Cogniac White-wines into Rhenish.

2. ***Rochelle salt***: (see quots.). ***Rochelle powder***, = Seidlitz powder.

1753 LEWIS *New Dispensatory* (1765) 475/2 *Sal Rupellensis*, Sel de Seignette, or Rochel salt. **1767** MONRO in *Phil. Trans.* LVII. 501 The Rochelle salt, made with the acid of tartar, and the fossil alkali, is so common a purging salt, that I shall not enter into any description of it. **1808** REECE *Dict. Dom. Med.* s.v. *Rheumatism*, Then strain, and add Rochelle, or Epsom Salt. **1854** *Pereira's Polarized Light* (ed. 2) 227 In Rochelle salt (tartrate of potash and soda), the optic axes of the..rays are considerably separated. **1888** *Encycl. Brit.* XXIII. 69/2 *Rochelle salt*..is prepared by not quite neutralizing hot solution of carbonate of soda with powdered cream of tartar.

‖**roche moutonnée** (rɔʃ mutɔne). *Physical Geogr.* [Fr., f. *roche* rock, ROCHE *sb.*[1] + *moutonnée* MOUTONNÉE.] A bare rock outcrop which has been shaped by glacial erosion, characteristically smoothed and rounded by abrasion but often also displaying one side (the 'downstream' side) which is rougher and steeper because of plucking. Hence ˌ**roche mouˈtonnéed** *a.*, abounding in *roches moutonnées*.

De Saussure (see quot. 1786), to whom the term is frequently attributed, applied the adj. *moutonnée* to small rounded hillocks (usu. covered with vegetation) which suggested, *en masse*, a fleece or a wig of a style termed *moutonnée*. These features do not correspond to the meaning of *roches moutonnées* which later became accepted, and were not associated by de Saussure with glaciers. (See also s.v. in *Gloss. Geol.* (Amer. Geol. Inst., 1972) 613.)

[**1786** H.-B. DE SAUSSURE *Voyages dans Alpes* II. xlviii. 512–3 Plus loin, derriere le village de *Juviana* ou *Envionne* on voit des rochers qui ont une forme que je nomme *moutonnée*. .. Les montagnes que je désigne par cette expression sont composées d'un assemblage de têtes arrondies, couvertes quelquefois de bois, mais plus souvent d'herbes, ou tout au plus de broussailles. Ces rondeurs contigues & répétées forment en grand l'effet d'une toison bien fournie, ou de ces perruques que l'on nomme aussi *moutonnées*.] **1843** J. D. FORBES *Trav. through Alps* iii. 53 The surface of rock..is even and rounded, often dome-shaped or spheroidal, showing the structure of the rock in section... Such surfaces were called Roches Moutonnées by De Saussure. **1862** *Q. Jrnl. Geol. Soc.* XVIII. 187 For many miles in the Alb Valley, both above and below St. Blasien, *roches moutonnées* stand like islands through the alluvium. **1865** tr. *Figuier's World Before Deluge* (1891) 443. **1872** C. KING *Sierra Nevada* 70 Here, sheltered among *roches moutonnées*, began to appear little fields of alpine grass. **1874** J. GEIKIE *Gt. Ice Age* vii. 90 *note*, Rocks which are so rounded, whether striated or not, are known as *roches moutonnées*. **1905** *Bull. Geol. Soc. Amer.* XVI. 51 The northern slopes..have been considerably smoothed by ice action... The whole surface is rochemoutonnéed, especially on the north, where nearly all rocks are absolutely fresh. **1935** *Discovery* Mar. 79/2 Dome-like rocks are exposed which in appearance recall the ice-formed *roches moutonnées*. **1957** J. K. CHARLESWORTH *Quaternary Era* I. xi. 251 De Saussure gave the name roche moutonnée to the distinctive, rounded forms which abound in glaciated terrain (he himself failed to associate them with ice) and give the effect of a thick fleece or the wavy wigs styled *moutonnées* in his day (they were slicked down with mutton tallow). **1977** A. HALLAM *Planet Earth* 86/3 Many valleys are very deeply incised, with U-shaped cross-profiles and floors composed of smoothed, striated and streamlined rock hummocks (called roches moutonnées).

†ˈ**rochen**, *a.* *Obs.*$^{-1}$ [f. ROCHE *sb.*[1] + -EN.] Having the nature of rock.

a **1300** *Cursor M.* 9915 þe grund neist þar es ful tru, Metand wit þat rochen stan.

†**roche petre.** *Obs.* In 7 rochpeter, rochpeeter, roch-peter. [f. ROCHE *sb.*[1] + PETRE.] Native saltpetre, occurring as an efflorescence on rocks.

1634 J. B[ATE] *Myst. Nature* 54 The ingredients likewise are chiefly these, Saltpeter, Rochpeter, Sulpher. **1665** *Phil. Trans.* I. 36 A fine white Salt, which..seemed to have Sides and Angles in the same number and figure as Rochpeeter. **1669** STURMY *Mariner's Mag.* V. xiii. 87 Roch-Peter.., Quick-Brimstone.., and fine Powder-dust.

rocher (ˈrɒtʃə(r)). *Obs.* exc. *dial.* [a. OF. *rochier* (mod.F. *rocher*) masc., or *rochere, -iere* fem., f. *roche* ROCHE *sb.*[1]] A rock; also *dial.* a stony or rocky bank.

13.. *K. Alis.* 7090 Ther he fond latimeris That ladde him to hyghe rocheris, To rocheris and wildernes. **13..** *Gaw. & Gr. Knt.* 1427 Such a glauerande glam..Ros, þat þe rocherez rungen aboute. *c* **1450** *Merlin* 342 These vj kynges com down the rocher sore hem diffendinge. **1637** in *Sheffield Gloss.* (1888), They grow out of such a rocher of stone that you would hardly thinke there were earth enough to nourish the rootes of the said trees. **1675** HOBBES *Odyssey* (1677) 65 A rocher with his arms he then imbrac't. **1676** —— *Iliad* 224 They the prey let go To save it self i' th' woods or rochers high. **1888** *Sheffield Gloss.*, *Rocher*, a rock.

rochet[1] (ˈrɒtʃɪt). Forms: α. 4– rochet, 5–6 rochett (5 -yt, -ytt, 6 -ate, rogett), 6, 8 rochette; 6–8 rotchet (6 -ette). β. 6 rechet, rachet, ratchet. [a. OF. *rochet* (also *roket, roquet*, whence ROCKET *sb.*[1]), = It. *roccetto, rocchetto*, Sp. *roqueta*, Pg. *rochete, roquete*, med.L. *rochetum, roquetum*, etc. (see Du Cange); a dimin. of the Teutonic word which appears as OHG. *(h)roch, roc, rokk* (MHG. *roc, rock-*, G. *rock*), OS. *hroc* (LG. *rock*, whence Sw. *rock*, Icel. *rokkr*), MDu. *roc, rock-* (Du. *rok*), OFris. *(h)rock*, OE. *rocc*, and in med.L. as *roccus* (808).]

1. An outer garment of the nature of a smock-frock, cloak, or mantle. Now *dial.*

c **1400** *Rom. Rose* 4754 For al-so wel wol love be set Under ragges as riche rochet. ? **14..** *MS. Bibl. Reg.* 12 B. i. f. 12 (Halliw.), *Superior vestis mulierum, Anglice* a rochet. **1547** *Test. Ebor.* (Surtees) VI. 257 To Edward Hungaite, my sone, my velvett rochett. **1662** J. DAVIES tr. *Olearius' Voy. Ambass.* 400 The Envoy help'd him to put it on, with a Rochet of cloath of Gold, a Girdle, and Turbant. **1755** SMOLLETT *Don Quix.* (1803) IV. 139 They threw down their staves, laid aside their rochets or mantles, so as to remain in their doublets. **1793** *Minstrel* I. 27 The young ladies attired in a kind of uniform, in fine white rochets. **1837-** in *Eng. Dial. Dict.* (Lanc. and Devon).

2. *Eccl.* A vestment of linen, of the nature of a surplice, usually worn by bishops and abbots.

α. *a* **1382** WYCLIF *Exod.* xxviii. 4 Coope, coote, and a rochet, and a streyt myter, and a girdil thei shulen make. *a* **1400** *Stac. Rome* 501 An Arm men seyn is þer Of seint Thomas.. And a Rochet þat is good, Al be-spreint with his blod. *c* **1425** *Voc.* in Wr.-Wülcker 649 *Hec poderis*, rochytt. **1506** in *Clerk's Bk.* (1903) 76 The said clerkis or one of theym shall daily intende in his Rogett at morowe masse. **1532** MORE *Confut. Barnes* VIII. Wks. 735/1 But yet he iesteth on theym ferther, because..yᵉ bishoppes wear white rochettes. **1581** J. BELL *Haddon's Answ. Osor.* 258 Having embrued your rotchets in so much Christian bloud, play the Butchers morelike then Byshops. **1628-9** LAUD *Diary* 31 Jan., I dreamed that I put off my rochet, all save one sleeve. **1653** GATAKER *Vind. Annot. Jer.* 9 The Puritans..would cut my rochet onely, but the Papists would cut my throat. **1730** SWIFT *Ballads* Wks. 1755 IV. I. 112 To give thee lawn sleeves, a mitre, and rotchet. **1790** BURKE *Fr. Rev.* Wks. V. 396 They will tell you that they see no difference between an idler with a hat and a national cockade, and an idler in a cowl or in a rochet. **1849** ROCK *Ch. of Fathers* II. 17 The rochet is only a modification of the surplice, as the surplice is of the alb. **1884** *Pall Mall G.* 1 Jan. 8/1 The sermon being ended, the Bishop-elect was conducted to the Islip Chapel to put on his rochet.

β. **1534** tr. *Lindewood's Const. Provinc.* 67, iii. surplyces, one rechet. **1552-3** *Inv. Ch. Goods, Stafford* 49 One surples and a rachet. **1559** AYLMER *Harborowe* N iv, To see the daye wherein they myght washe their goodly whyte ratchettes in her innocent bloude. **1570** LEVINS *Manip.* 88 A ratchet, *superpelliceum*.

b. *transf.* One who wears a rochet; a bishop.

1581 J. BELL *Haddon's Answ. Osor.* 216 Then follow in order the Roystyng route of Mytred Prelates, of the Scarlet crew of Rochettes, and shavelynges. *a* **1661** FULLER *Worthies* (1840) I. 270 For let not the cloaks carry away the credit from the gowns and rochet in that work. **1678** BUTLER *Hud.* III. ii. 544 When Zeal with aged Clubs and Gleaves Gave chase to Rochets and White Sleeves.

†**c.** *attrib.* as *adj.* Episcopal. *Obs.*

1554 BALE *Decl. Bonner's Art.* xxiv. (1561) 90 b, All the other fine Rochet men of Englande. **1641** MILTON *Reform.* II. Wks. 1851 III. 46 Our Prelatical Schism, and captivity to Rotchet Apothegmes.

3. (See quot.)

1728 CHAMBERS *Cycl.* s.v., Rochets are also the Mantles wore on Days of Ceremony, by the Peers sitting in the English Parliament... Those of Viscounts have two Bands or Borders and a half; those of Earls three; those of Marquisses three and a half; those of Dukes four.

rochet² (ˈrɒtʃɪt). Now *local.* Forms: α. 4 **ruget**, 5 **roget(t**. β. 5 **ruchet**, 6 **rochett(e**, 6-9 **rotchet**, 5- **rochet**. [a. OF. *rouget*, f. *rouge* red.] The Red Gurnard.

α. *a* **1377** *Abingdon Acc.* (1892) 38 In ruget, vj s. *c* **1450** *Contin. Brut* (1908) 447 Halybut, Gurnard rosted. Roget broyled. *c* **1481** CAXTON *Dialogues* 12 Whityng, sprotte, rogettis [F. *rouges*].

β. *c* **1430** *Two Cookery-bks.* 60 Codlyng, Ruchet, Rochys. **1465** *Mann. & Househ. Exp.* (Roxb.) 305 Item, for rochetes the same day, ob. **1508** W. DE WORDE *Bk. Keruynge* in *Babees Bk.* (1868) 280 Gornarde, rochet, breme, cheuene. **1528** PAYNELL *Salerne's Regim.* (1541) 54 b, Among all see fyshe, the forsayd condicions consydered, the rochet and gurnarde seme to be most holsome. **1605** B. JONSON *Volpone* III. vii, I will..rip up Thy mouth,..And slit thy nose, Lik a raw rotchet. **1655** MOUFET & BENNET *Health's Improv.* (1746) 258 Rochets, or rather Rougets, because they are so red, differ from Gournards and Curs, in that they are redder by a great deal, and also less. **1727** *Counter Scuffle* in *Dryden's Misc.* III. 336 Sitting quiet and at his ease, With butter'd Rochets thought to please his Palate. **1740** R. BROOKES *Art of Angling* II. xliii. 161 The Red-Gurnard or Rotchet..has a large Boney Head arm'd with Prickles. **1863** COUCH *Brit. Fishes* II. 19 Elleck.., Red Gurnard, Rotchet. **1888** GOODE *Amer. Fishes* 306 The Red Gurnard, or Rochet, *T. cuculus*, and the Piper, *T. lyra* reach three or four pounds.

†**rochet**³. *Obs.*⁻¹ [a. F. *rochet.*] A bobbin.

1728 CHAMBERS *Cycl.* s.v. *Cloth*, That for the Warp is wound on a kind of Rochets, or large wooden Bobbins, to dispose it for warping.

rochet, obs. form of RATCHET.

ˈ**rocheted**, *a.* [f. ROCHET *sb.*¹ 2.] Wearing a rochet.

1842 F. E. PAGET *M. Malvoisin* 32 That arch-traitor William Laud,—that rochetted viper. **1868** BROWNING *Ring & Bk.* VI. 1263 Still rocheted and mitred more or less.

†ˈ**rocheter**. *Obs.*⁻¹ In 6 **ratchetter**. [f. ROCHET¹.] One who wears a rochet; a prelate.

1559 AYLMER *Harborowe* N iv, Had not these ratchetters good cause to hoope, that this blessed woman should haue followed?

rochett, obs. form of RATCHET.

‖**rochetta**. *Obs.* [ad. It. *rocchetta.*] = POLVERINE. Also *attrib.*

1662 MERRETT tr. *Neri's Art of Glass* i, Polverine, or Rochetta, which comes from the Levant and Syria, is the ashes of a certain herb growing there in abundance. *Ibid.* xxii, For the said tubes, they take half Crystal Fritt, and half Rochetta Fritt. **1748** *Phil. Trans.* XLV. 563 There are some other Plants that are known to make a kind of Pot-ash, commonly called Rochetta, which is said to be even preferable to the Barrilha, especially for making Glass. **1765** *Ibid.* LV. 21 With metal that hath much salt, as crystal and rochetta have, you cannot make a fair green. **1799** G. SMITH *Laboratory* I. 174 Take of calcined lead 15 pounds; of rochetta, or pulverized crystal frit 12 pounds.

roching (ˈrəʊtʃɪŋ), *vbl. sb.* Also 7, 9 **roaching**. [f. ROCHE *v.* + -ING¹.] The action of the vb. ROCHE; chiefly *attrib.* in **roching cask, pan.**

1631 E. JORDAN *Nat. Bathes* vii. (1669) 45 The shooting or roching of concrete juyces, is worthy to be observed. **1670** W. SIMPSON *Hydrol. Ess.* 68 Their last decoction, which is performed in their roaching pan. **1839** URE *Dict. Arts* 38 Whenever..dissolved in a saturated state, it is run off into the crystallising vessels, which are called roching casks. **1854** *Pharmac. Jrnl.* XIII. 622 The formation of large masses of the alum,..by means of 'roaching' or 'rocking'. **1888** W. WHITE *Month in Yorks.* 120 When of the required density, the liquor is run off from the pan to the 'roching casks'—great butts rather, big as a sugar hogshead.

rocht, var. *raught*, obs. pa. t. of RECK *v.*

Rōchū, var. RŌJŪ.

ˈ**rochy**, *a. Obs.* exc. *dial.* [f. ROCHE *sb.*¹ + -Y.] †**1.** Full of rocks; rocky. *Obs.*⁻¹

1297 R. GLOUC. (Rolls) 2499 In an harde rochi stede is þuong aboute he drou.

2. *dial.* Having the character of roche.

1841-87 in Shropshire and Cheshire glossaries.

rock (rɒk), *sb.*¹ Forms: 4-6 **rokk(e**, 4-7 **rocke**, 5 **roc**, 5-6 **rok(e**, 6 **roocke**, **rough**, *Sc.* **roik**, **rolk**, **rouk**, *pl.* **rox**; 4- **rock**. [a. OF. *roke*, *roque*, *rocque* fem. (also *roche* ROCHE *sb.*¹, and in later F. *roc* masc.), = Prov. *roca*, *rocha*, Pg. *rocha*, Sp. *roca*, It. *rocca*, *roccia*, med.L. *rocca* (767), *rocha*, of unknown origin. OE. *stanrocc*, glossing L. *scopulus* and *obeliscus*, appears to imply an earlier adoption of the Romanic word.]

I. 1. a. A large rugged mass of stone forming a cliff, crag, or natural prominence on land or in the sea.

the Rock is freq. used ellipt. for the Rock of Gibraltar.

13.. *Gaw. & Gr. Knt.* 2198 He romez vp to þe rokke of þo roȝ wonez. *c* **1385** CHAUCER *L.G.W.* 2193 *Ariadne*, The holwe rokkis answerden hire a-gayn. *c* **1400** *Destr. Troy* 5699 His shippes..rut on a Rocke, & rent all to peses. *c* **1440** *Promp. Parv.* 436/1 Rokke, yn þe see, *idem quod* roche. **1486** *Bk. St. Albans* d iij b, Ther is a Fawken of the rock, And that is for a duke. **1538** STARKEY *England* I. ii. 65 Lyke as maryners..by neclygence run apon some roke. **1591** SHAKS. *Two Gent.* I. ii. 121 That, some whirle-winde beare Vnto a ragged, fearefull, hanging Rocke, And throw it thence into the raging Sea. **1606** G. W[OODCOCKE] *Hist. Ivstine* XII. 53 He came to a maruellous rough and huge rocke, into which many people were fled. **1687** A. LOVELL tr. *Thevenot's Trav.* I. 140 A pair of stairs cut out in the Rock. **1718** LADY M. W. MONTAGU *Lett.* II. xlix. 61 We..came safe to Malta... It is a whole rock covered with very little earth. *a* **1774** GOLDSM. *Nat. Hist.* (1776) I. 156 Splitting the most solid rocks, and thus shattering the summits of the mountain. **1843** RUSKIN *Mod. Painters* I. II. i. §4 Every minor rock comes out from the soil about it as an island out of the sea. **1860** TYNDALL *Glaciers* I. vii. 49 We diverged from the snow to the adjacent rocks.

fig. **1607** SHAKS. *Cor.* v. ii. 117 The worthy Fellow is our General. He's the Rock, The Oake not to be winde-shaken. *c* **1665** MRS. HUTCHINSON *Mem. Col. Hutchinson* (1846) 29 He that was a rock to all assaults of might and violence.

b. A large detached mass of stone; a boulder; also (orig. *U.S.*), a stone of any size. Also freq., a stone used as a projectile.

1709 POPE *Ess. Crit.* 370 When Ajax strives some rock's vast weight to throw. **1712** S. SEWALL *Diary* 14 Apr., I lay'd a Rock in the North-east corner of the Foundation of the Meetinghouse. It was a stone I got out of the Common. **1793** HELY tr. *O'Flaherty's Ogygia* II. 186 The sling.. directed rocks nearly with as much violence as the *onager*. *Ibid.* 187 Stones and rocks were thrown from the crosbow. **1838** S. PARKER *Explor. Tour* (1846) 51 It is one of the peculiarities of the dialect of..the western states, to call small stones, rocks. *a* **1862** THOREAU *Cape Cod* x. (1894) 269, I saw one man underpinning a new house in Eastham with some 'rocks', as he called them. **1890** BARRÈRE & LELAND *Dict. Slang* II. 183/2 *Rocks* (American), small stones or pebbles... The term is used in some parts of England. **1895** *Harper's Mag.* Apr. 713/2 A stone-pile near at hand where they filled their pockets full of rocks. **1939** J. STUART in *Esquire* May 55/1, I pull a round rock from my pocket. I let th' rock go. I holler: 'Rocks! Watch out!' **1968** *New Society* 29 Aug. 304/1 It is now frequent for British newspapers to record that during some riot or disturbance the crowd has thrown 'rocks' (= 'stones'). **1969** *West Australian* 5 July 1/1 Several policemen fell to the ground after they were hit with rocks. **1976** *Billings* (Montana) *Gaz.* 17 June 1-F/5 Ambulance services were suspended when mobs hurled rocks at the vehicles, injuring drivers. **1979** *Observer* 16 Sept. 1/1 The Belfast house of Mr Gerry Fitt, Social Democratic and Labour MP for East Belfast, was besieged by about 200 youths armed with rocks yesterday.

c. *transf.* A large mass or pile *of* something.

1766 STORK *Acc. E. Florida* 52 The oysters are so plentiful here, that nothing is more common, than at low water, to see whole rocks of them. **1779** PALLAS in *Lett. Lit. Men* (Camden) 407 They were stopt by insurmountable rocks of Ice, and obliged to return.

d. *Canad.* = CURLING-STONE.

1911 R. E. KNOWLES *Singer of Kootenay* 296 Every man of them held his breath as the flying rock came to the port. **1963** *Times* 25 Feb. (Canada Suppl.) p. xvi/1 The Scots melted cannon balls to fashion their 'rocks' and played the game on the frozen St. Lawrence river and ponds in the area. It is interesting that rocks made of iron were still being used in parts of Ontario and Quebec as late as 20 years ago. **1974** *Globe & Mail* (Toronto) 20 Feb. 33/7 Dr. Will McTavish of Winnipeg and Ralph Smith of Noranda excelled at getting their draws into the centre of the house and knocking out opposition rocks.

2. In figurative or allusive uses:

a. A source of danger or destruction, usually with allusion to shipwreck.

1526 *Pilgr. Perf.* (W. de W. 1531) 240 b, The meditacyon of deth maketh man to eschewe yᵉ rockes and perylles of damnacyon. **1560** DAUS tr. *Sleidane's Comm.* 376 It is not unknowen unto you, how they stroke upon these rocks. **1606** S. GARDINER *Bk. Angling* 8 If it dasheth against the rocke of sinne, it is in great ieopardie. **1651** HOBBES *Leviath.* II. xxxi. 186 To avoyd both these Rocks, it is necessary to know what are the Lawes Divine. **1683** TEMPLE *Mem.* Wks. 1720 I. 377 It would be a Rock upon which our firmest Alliances would be in danger to strike and to split. **1734** SWIFT *Reasons agst. Tythe of Hemp* Wks. 1745 VIII. 96 A rock that many Corporations have split upon, to their..utter undoing. **1857** TROLLOPE *Barchester T.* II. xv, [He] will not be so shortsighted as to run against such a rock. **1875** JOWETT *Plato* (ed. 2) II. 295 The rocks which lay concealed under the ambiguous terms, good, pleasure and the like.

b. Something which affords a sure foundation or support; something which gives shelter or protection; used *esp.* with reference to Christ.

1526 TINDALE *Matt.* xvi. 18, I saye..that thou arte Peter. And apon this roocke I wyll bylde my congregacion. **1535** COVERDALE *Deut.* xxxii. 37 Where are their goddes, their rocke wherin they trusted? **1571** *Satir. Poems Reform.* xxviii. 102 Swa of this lyfe the Lord was miscontent, Seand my faith not foundit on ane Roik. **1606** S. GARDINER *Bk. Angling* 8 So long as we cast our faith and hope vpon our rocke Christ Iesus. **1633** P. FLETCHER *Purple Isl.* XII. lii, Be thou my rock, though I poore changeling rove. **1738** WESLEY *Hymns*, '*Praise by all to Christ be given*' xiii, Hell in vain against us rages; Can it shock Christ the Rock Of eternal Ages? **1780** COWPER *Progr. Error* 143 Will not the sickliest sheep of every flock Resort to this example as a rock? **1809-10** COLERIDGE *Friend* (1865) 31 The rock which is both their quarry and their foundation, from which and on which they are built. **1872** O. W. HOLMES *Poet Breakf.-t.* v, It is the material image of the Christian; his heart resting on the Rock of Ages.

c. In allusion to Numbers xx. 11.

1526 TINDALE *1 Cor.* x. 4 They dronke off that spretuall rocke that folowed them, which rocke was Christ. **1850** TENNYSON *In Mem.* cxxxi, O living will.., Rise in the spiritual rock, Flow thro' our deeds and make them pure. **1880** N. SMYTH *Old Faiths in New Lt.* II. (1882) 45 The water of life will flow from the rock which the scholar strikes with his rod.

d. In various phrases. ***on the rocks***, quite destitute of means; also (esp. of marriage, etc.), on the point of dissolution; finished.

1760-72 H. BROOKE *Fool of Qual.* (1809) I. 78 His prayers and tears were cast to the winds and the rocks. **1829** LYTTON *Devereux* I. i, Six weeks after her confinement, she put this rock into motion—they eloped. **1889** A. G. MURDOCH *Scot. Readings* Ser. III. 101 Fork out, for I'm fair on the rocks. **1958** E. WILSON in *N.Y. Post* 1 June 2/3 [Roberto Rossellini's] headlined romance with Sonali Das Gupta is now reported on the rocks. **1975** *Globe & Mail* (Toronto) 12 Sept. 12/6 Simply adding more ice to a marriage that's already on the rocks won't save the partnership, the Law Reform Commission of Canada says in a paper on divorce.

e. *U.S. slang.* A piece of money, *spec.* a dollar. ***to pile up the rocks***, to make money. ***a pocketful of rocks***, a large amount of money.

1840 *Picayune* (New Orleans) 31 July 2/2 He was just on the eve of leaving town with his 'pockets full of rocks'. **1846** in D. Corcoran *Pickings from New Orleans Picayune* 143 Here I am in town without a rock in my pocket. **1847** J. S. ROBB *Streaks of Squatter Life* 165 If I had a 'pocket full of *rocks*', you should share them. *a* **1848** in Bartlett *Dict. Amer.* 277 Here I am in town without a rock in my pocket. **1849** SAXE *Poems, The Times* 365 When out of the heaps of auriferous ore We can fill up his pockets with 'rocks' of his own. **1858** J. R. LOWELL *Poet. Wks.* II. 284 A pocket-full of rocks 'twould take To build a house of free-stone. **1897** KIPLING *Capt. Courageous* i, Old man's piling up the rocks. Don't want to be disturbed I guess. **1905** *Dialect Notes* III. 17 *Rocks*, dollars. **1942** Z. N. HURSTON in A. Dundes *Mother Wit* (1973) 224/1, I don't bet, but I'll doubt you. Five rocks! **1949** *Cavalier Daily* (Univ. of Va.) 22 Oct. 4/1 They got a campaign goin' around here to try to stick us students six rocks just to go..and listen to some old bag yell her fool head off.

f. *slang* (orig. *U.S.*). A precious stone, *spec.* a diamond. Cf. *rock-diamond* (sense 6 d).

1908 H. GREEN *Maison de Shine* 83 'So that's his new wife, eh?' said Goldie later. 'Did you pipe the rocks she had on?' **1926** J. BLACK *You can't Win* xiii. 178 I'll unharness these 'rocks'. **1929** [see LOOGAN]. **1936** J. CURTIS *Gilt Kid* v. 57 Some of the women present, he saw, were wearing goodish rocks. **1953** 'S. RANSOME' *Drag Dark* (1954) vi. 60 Goodlee wrote his check..then walked out with the rock. **1968** A. DIMENT *Bang Bang Birds* vii. 106 He..listened to my vague replies like my advice was worth its weight in sparkling rocks. **1973** 'I. DRUMMOND' *Jaws of Watchdog* i. 12 'We will see some of the most beautiful jewellery in the world... The emeralds.'.. 'Personally,' said Jenny, 'I call it vulgar, having all those rocks on a yacht.'

g. In *U.S.* colloq. phr. ***between a rock and a hard place***: without a satisfactory alternative, in difficulty (see also quot. 1921).

1921 *Dialect Notes* V. 113 *To be between a rock and a hard place*,..to be bankrupt. Common in Arizona in recent panics; sporadic in California. **1959** L. ROBERTS *Up Cutshin & Down Greasy* v. 82 That was one time dad was between a rock and a hard place. **1963** D. OGILVY *Confessions Advertising Man* xi. 160 As a private person, I would gladly pay for the privilege of watching it without commercial interruptions. Morally, I find myself between the rock and the hard place. **1976** T. WOLFE *Mauve Gloves & Madmen* 37 The dive brings you down so low, you are now down into the skeet range of that insidiously well-aimed flak! This, as they say, puts you between a rock and a hard place.

h. Usu. *pl.* An ice-cube or crushed ice for use in a drink. In phr. ***on the rocks***, (of a spirituous liquor) served with ice. *slang* (orig. *U.S.*).

1946 *Amer. Speech* XXI. 35 *Rocks*, ice. **1948** F. Brown *Murder can be Fun* (1951) iii. 44 A slug or two of rock and rye won't hurt you. **1949** *Life* 14 Nov. 63 Ordering a Scotch on the rocks at the bar. **1952** N. Spain in C. Asquith *Second Ghost Bk.* 36, I..went in and fixed myself a Scotch on rocks, neat. **1955** J. B. Priestley *Journey down Rainbow* 220 They all drank a lot of whisky-on-the-rocks. **1959** 'J. Christopher' *Scent of White Poppies* vi. 82 Rocks in your Scotch, Cam? I can get some from the fridge. **1966** *Listener* 20 Oct. 573/2 For some reason, no one knows quite why, Americans insist on having ice, or 'rocks' as they call it, always in easy reach. **1978** R. Ludlum *Holcroft Covenant* iii. 39 That was scotch on the rocks, wasn't it?

i. pl. *slang*. The testicles; = stone *sb.* 11 a. In coarse phr. ***to get one's rocks off***, to achieve sexual satisfaction, to ejaculate; also, in weakened sense, to obtain enjoyment.

1948 *Amer. Speech* XXIII. 249/1 *Get your rocks off*, an expression used to denote extreme enjoyment. **1961** *Ibid.* XXXVI. 150 Expressions using *rocks* and *stones* to mean testes are at least as old as the Renaissance, but in the mouths of today's teen-agers, *hot rocks* seems to imply only a warm romantic interest by a teen-ager of either sex in one of the opposite gender. **1971** *Frendz* 5 Aug. 22/2 Get yer rocks off Seymour. OK. But there are limits. Surely. **1972** *Show* Sept. 55/2 Unrelenting sequences of unsympathetic characters getting their rocks off. **1975** J. Braine *Pious Agent* vi. 23 I'd get a swift kick in the rocks. **1975** G. V. Higgins *City on Hill* vii. 195 I've been reduced to dressing up in order to get my rocks off. **1978** *Chicago* June 90/3 This is a good film for getting your rocks off, but not the sort you will remember much about two weeks later. **1978** J. Irving *World according to Garp* xi. 205, I don't get my rocks off by humiliating myself, you know.

j. *U.S. Baseball slang*. An error. In phr. ***to pull a rock***, to make a mistake.

1939 E. J. Nichols *Hist. Dict. Baseball Terminol.* (thesis, Pa. State College) 57 *Pull a rock*, see 'boner'. *Ibid.* 9 *Boner*, an error in judgment. **1951** *Birmingham* (Alabama) *News* 31 July 16/3 How does a guy who has been labeled 'the perfect player' feel after pulling his first 'rock' in a long and brilliant baseball career? **1952** *Philadelphia Even. Bull.* 4 Oct. 13/2 Who deserved the rap for the 'rock' that cost the Yankees yesterday's World Series game? **1955** *Daily Progress* (Charlottesville, Va.) 5 May 10/7 'Luckily, it didn't hurt us but I pulled a rock.' Durocher then went on to explain his 'rock', which didn't prevent the Giants from winning... 'Good strategy, my foot,' mocked Durocher after the game. 'It was a real rock.' **1956** *Sun* (Baltimore) 26 Apr. B 25/3 Bill changed his mind and lifted Rhodes out of the lineup... The criticism was that he had 'pulled a rock'.

3. a. Without article, or in generalized use: Hard and massive stone. Also *fig.*

1590 Spenser *F.Q.* I. vii. 33 But all of Diamond..It framed was, one massy entire mould, Hewen out of Adamant rocke with engines keene. **1603** Shaks. *Hen. VIII*, I. i. 158 To th' King Ile say't, & make my vouch as strong As shore of Rocke. **1604** E. G[rimstone] tr. *D'Acosta's Hist. Indies* III. xvii. 173 In running, the water turnes to rocke. **1667** Milton *P.L.* XI. 491 Sight so deform what heart of Rock could long Drie-ey'd behold? **1784** Cowper *Task* v. 534 We build with what we deem eternal rock: A distant age asks where the fabric stood. **1842** Tennyson *Morte d'Arthur* 50 Stepping down By zig-zig paths, and juts of pointed rock. **1888** Fergus Hume *Mme. Midas* I. Prol., Their combined action had broken off great masses of rock.

†**b.** ***oil of the rock***, = rock-oil. *Obs.*

1653. Walton *Angler* viii. 172 Oyl of Peter, called by some, Oyl of the Rock.

c. ***of the old***, or ***new***, ***rock***, said of precious stones. Also *transf.*

An echo of French usage, *de la vieille*, or *nouvelle*, *roche*: see Littré s.v. *Roche*.

1698 Fryer *Acc. E. India & P.* 34 Diamonds of both Rocks, the Old and New. **1728** Chambers *Cycl.* s.v. *Turcoise*, There are Turcoises..of the new Rock and the old... Those of the old Rock are a deep blue, and those of the new Rock more whitish. **1763** H. Walpole *Let. to G. Montagu* 12 Nov., Sir Michael Foster is dead, a Whig of the old rock.

d. *spec.* Sandstone. (See also quot. 1712.) *local.*

1712 Morton *Nat. Hist. Northants* 265 Sand-stone, Lime-stone, and others Kind of Stone, that are usually dispos'd into Strata, a Pile, or Parcel of which is here called a Rock. **1863** J. Sleigh *Hist. Leek* 259 The 'Rough Rock', or upper beds of Millstone Grit are not very fossiliferous. **1883** Gresley *Gloss. Coal-mining*, *Rock* generally means sandstone. *Ibid.*, *Rock and Rig*,..a sandstone full of little patches and shreds of coal.

e. *Agric.* (See quot. 1844.)

1765 *Museum Rust.* IV. 307 The soil is light and stoney, with a rock of gravel about ten or twelve inches deep. **1844** *Civil Eng. & Arch. Jrnl.* VII. 72/1 The different strata give rise to what are usually called the different rocks, the term 'rock' being usually applied in agriculture to the base on which the sub-soil immediately lies.

f. *Geol.* One of the stratified or igneous mineral constituents of which the earth's crust is composed, including sands, clays, etc.

1789 John Williams *Nat. Hist. Min. Kingd.* I. 3 Lime-stone, whinstone, basaltes, and many other hard rocks, continue firm..quite up to the superficies of the strata. **1819** *Pantologia* s.v. *Sienite*, This rock is composed essentially of crystals of felspar and hornblende. **1834** J. Phillips *Geol.* in *Encycl. Metrop.* (1845) VI. 537 The series of stratified rocks in the North of England. **1878** Huxley *Physiogr.* 169 The rocks are comparatively soft, consisting for the most part of sands, clays and chalk.

g. Mineral ore. *U.S.*

1830 *Workingman's Gaz.* (Woodstock, Vermont) 28 Oct. 38/1 The surface is almost covered with rock, all which contains gold..which is obtained by breaking or pounding the rock. **1896** C. H. Shinn *Story of Mine* 78 The quartz prospector..only pans out a few ounces of powdered rock. **1902** O. Wister *Virginian* xv. 172 Are they taking much mineral out? Have yu' seen any of the rock? **1948** *Los Angeles Times* 12 Jan. II. 8/3 (*heading*) Ruby mine runs into rich rock.

4. *transf.* **a.** A hard confection of candied sugar variously flavoured; *dial.* sweetstuff. Also with qualifying words, as ***almond***, ***peppermint rock***.

App. ellipt. for *rock-candy* or *-sugar*: see 9 below.

1736 Bailey *Household Dict.* s.v. *Rock-Sugar*, All the rock will slip out, and fall most of it in small pieces. **1843** [see nonpareil 3]. **1857** Kingsley *Two Years Ago* xv, Promising them rock and bullseyes. **1878** Meredith *Teeth* 20 Biting into rock and other hard candies is certainly a very reprehensible practice. **1897** Mary Kingsley *W. Africa* 227 Its appearance is that of almond rock, and it is cut easily with a knife.

b. An insoluble soap formed by the blending of calcium stearate and oleate of tallow dissolved through lime.

1856 *Orr's Circle Sci., Pract. Chem.* 455 The soap thus formed is very hard, and is generally called rock. **1885** W. L. Carpenter *Soap & Candles* 254 These salts,..when mixed together, constitute an insoluble soap, technically called 'rock'.

c. *ellipt.* (See quot.)

1811 *Trans. Geol. Soc.* I. 53 The rock-salt obtained from it, being principally exported to the Baltic, obtains the name of Prussia Rock.

d. *ellipt.* A rock-cake.

1892 F. Davies *Cakes & Biscuits* 101 This quantity should make fifty rocks.

e. A crystallized form of cocaine which is smoked for its stimulating effect; = crack *sb.* 20. *slang* (orig. *U.S. West Coast*).

1973 Smith & Wesson *Uppers & Downers* 150 *Rock*, cocaine in rock form. **1985** *Los Angeles Times* 11 Jan. I. 2/6 An Inglewood 'rock house', where cocaine in hardened form was being sold. **1985** *Daily Tel.* 1 Mar. 15/4 The 'rock' is.. put in a pipe and smoked, with far more potent effects than inhaling the powder. **1986** *Observer* 17 Aug. 12/2 'Rock' or 'Crack' cocaine is a potent, purified, smokable form of the drug which can be lethal.

5. a. = rock-fish 1.

1698 G. Thomas *Pennsilvania* (1848) 14 There are.. Salmon, Trout, Sturgeon, Rock, Oysters. **1776** Carroll *Jrnl.* (1845) 52 Lake George abounds with perch, trout, rock, and eels. **1872** De Vere *Americanisms* 383 The Rock is beautifully marked with seven or eight black lines on a silver-bright ground. **1888** Goode *Amer. Fishes* 22 In the North it is called the 'Striped Bass', in the South the 'Rock Fish', or the 'Rock'. **1977** *Grimsby Even. Tel.* 5 May 18/2 Principal sorts were: Cod 1,712 kits, haddock 1,059,..rocks 23, skate 58,..monk 16.

b. The rock-dove or rock-pigeon (*Columba livia*). Usually ***blue rock***.

1863 [see blue *a.* 12]. **1882** 'Ouida' *Maremma* I. v. 116 The blue-rock was carrying dry twigs and grass to his home. **1885** *Field* 4 Apr. (Cassell), Being a bit slow in firing a fast rock escaped him.

c. *ellipt.* = Plymouth Rock.

1908 *Daily Chron.* 10 Jan. 3/4 The order of merit now stands as follows:—First, White Wyandottes; second, La Bresse; third, buff rocks.

II. *attrib.* and *Comb.*

6. Attrib. or appositive: **a.** With words denoting something which consists of, or is formed by, rock, as ***rock-abode***, ***-altar***, ***-arch***, ***-barrier***, ***-bluff***, ***-cavern***, ***-chamber***, ***-chimney***, ***-cliff***, ***-crust***, ***-drift***, ***-dwelling***, ***-flat***, ***-floor***, ***-fortress***, ***-hill***, ***ledge***, ***-point***, ***-pool***, ***-rampart***, ***-shelter***, ***-shrine***, ***-stack***, ***-terrace***, ***-wall***, etc.

The number of these is practically unlimited; many examples occur in recent geological works.

1887 Morris *Odyssey* XII. 255 So they were lifted gasping into that *rock-abode. **1832** in *Archaeologia* (1834) XXV. 204 A *Rock Altar on the heights on the eastern side of the lake of La Trinité. **1936** H. Nicolson *Let.* 28 Sept. (1966) 274 The precipices,..the *rock-arches..roared back at us. **1940** C. Day Lewis tr. *Virgil's Georgics* IV. 90 Proteus shelters within behind a huge *rock-barrier. **1886** A. Winchell *Walks & Talks in Geol. Field* 53 We have seen.. the *rock-bluffs bounding..the basins of the great lakes. **1847** Singer *Wayland Smith* p. xxix, The Swedes..show a *rock-cavern..as having been his workshop. **1954** J. R. R. Tolkien *Fellowship of Ring* 217 There was a cave or *rock-chamber behind. *Ibid.* 401 There were many birds about the cliffs and the *rock-chimneys. **1972** *Shooting Times & Country Mag.* 1 July 17/3 A rock 'chimney' up which I was none too happy in ascending. **1856** W. L. Lindsay *Brit. Lichens* 13 The *rock-clefts and gullies of our Highland mountains. **1952** S. Spender *Learning Laughter* 9 From the ship we saw houses on a green shelf above a *rock-cliff. *a* **1963** C. S. Lewis *Poems* (1964) 45 Down far under his *rock-crust. **1951** W. de la Mare *Winged Chariot* 16 Sweet salt-tanged air, birds, *rock-drift. **1959** Blunden *Hong Kong House* 2 It was no garden—so adust, red-dry the rock-drift soil was. **1860** Pusey *Min. Proph.* 145 Edom.., its ancient capital, its *rock-dwellings, have been..anew revealed. **1855** Leifchild *Cornwall* 87 A fissure filled by basaltic or other rocks, would be called a *rock dyke. **1883** Gresley *Gloss. Coal-mining*, **Rock Fault*, a replacement of a coal seam over a greater or less area, by some other rock, usually sandstone. **1967** *Oceanogr. & Marine Biol.* V. 483 In the most subtropical areas,..the fauna living between the algae covering these *rock-flats may be greatly impoverished. **1905** *Jrnl. Geol.* XIII. 393 The desert plain may be reduced to a lower level than that of the deepest initial basin; and then a *rock-floor,..unrelated to normal baselevel, will prevail throughout. **1946** F. E. Zeuner *Dating Past* vii. 223 Resting on an irregular rock-floor at about 7·5 metres above low sea-level, a beach conglomerate is found. **1831** M. Russell *Egypt* xi. §1 The relative positions of the great *rock-formations. **1934** W. S. Churchill *Marlborough* II. xv. 331 Coblenz..stands opposite the majestic *rock-fortress of Ehrenbreitstein. **1946** R. Campbell *Talking Bronco* 41 Rock-fortress of your sex and gender! *a* **1862** Thoreau *Maine Woods* (1864) 262 Being struck with the perfect parallelism of these singular *rock-hills,..I took out my compass. **1754** Borlase *Antiq. Cornwall* 161 Of *Rock Idols. **1763** J. Hutchins in *Mem. W. Stukeley* (Surtees) II. 128, I am apt to think it was a rock idol. **1963** D. W. & E. E. Humphries tr. *Termier's Erosion & Sedimentation* xiii. 260 This type of coastal cornice, or *rock ledge, is thus a phenomenon of marine abrasion. *a* **1700** Evelyn *Diary* (1644) 7 Oct., An high and steepe mountainous ground consisting all of *rock marble. **1863** A. C. Ramsay *Phys. Geogr.* 15 The whole *rock-masses of the outer world. **1849** D. G. Rossetti *Let.* 18 Oct. (1965) I. 74 One *rock-point standing buffeted alone, vexed at its base with a foul beast unknown. **1948** L. MacNeice *Holes in Sky* 31 Foam-quoits on rock-points. **1853** *Zoologist* II. 4059 Its own selected hole in the *rock-pool. **1907** E. Gosse *Father & Son* vi. 156 The antiquity of these rock-pools..used to occupy my Father's fancy. **1955** V. Palmer in B. James *Austral. Short Stories* (1963) 32 He stared into rock-pools. **1924** R. Campbell *Flaming Terrapin* vi. 94 The brink of the abyss, Where into space the sharp *rock-rampart drops. **1886** Kipling *Departm. Ditties, Overland Mail*, From rice-field to *rock-ridge, from rock-ridge to spur. **1821** Scott *Pirate* xxvii, A native of Zetland familiar..with every variety of *rock-scenery. **1865** Lubbock *Preh. Times* 245 A number of small caves and *rock-shelters in the Dordogne. **1927** Peake & Fleure *Hunters & Artists* 40 A small rock-shelter, now quarried away. **1971** *World Archaeol.* III. 147 Puntutjarpa is a minor sacred site about 150 ft west of the rockshelter. **1933** *Burlington Mag.* June 290/2 A small seated Buddha-image,..cut out of a *rock-shrine at Yiin-Kang. **1969** *Tanzania Notes & Rec.* July 3 The great rock-shrine of Tita, in southern Turu near Puma, is in the eyes of the Turu themselves less powerful than similar shrines in the mountains of Sandawe country and in Isanzu. **1586** W. Webbe *Eng. Poetrie* (Arb.) 75 Vnder a *Rock side here will proyner chaunt merrie ditties. **1877** Squier *Peru* (1878) 493 These *rockslips are frequent among the Andes. **1969** G. M. Brown *Orkney Tapestry* i. 17 There among them, standing out to sea a little, is the *rock-stack called The Old Man of Hoy. **1877** Raymond *Statist. Mines & Mining* 126 The great changes..wrought in the underlying *rock-strata. **1850** Sir G. Wilkinson *Archit. Anc. Egypt* 92 *Rock Temples may be classified under three heads. **1892** *Bull. Geol. Soc. Amer.* III. 65 Raised marine deposits with an arctic fauna occur over the latest moraines in Scandinavia... Bravais, half a century ago came to the conclusion that two elevated *rock-terraces in northern Norway examined by him are not horizontal but descend toward the north. **1968** R. W. Fairbridge *Encycl. Geomorphol.* 1184/2 [River] terraces may be cut into the solid rock or consist of a rock bench veneered with a comparatively small thickness of alluvium (rock terrace). **1850** Sir G. Wilkinson *Archit. Anc. Egypt* 109 The *rock tombs at Thebes. **1904** W. M. Ramsay *Lett. Seven Churches* xxv. 360 At times an oblique crack develops in the *rock-wall. **1954** J. R. R. Tolkien *Two Towers* 73 At the far end the rock-wall was sheer.

b. With sbs. denoting markings upon rocks, as ***rock art***, ***-carving***, ***drawing***, ***-engraving***, ***-inscription***, ***-painting***, ***-picture***, etc.

1959 J. D. Clark *Prehist. S. Afr.* ix. 248 The *rock art tells us little for certain about marriage customs. **1974** B. & R. Hill *Spirit in Stone* 11 With very few exceptions most rock art sites are located near villages. **1907** H. M. Chadwick *Origin Eng. Nation* xii. 306 The *rock-carvings at Tegneby. **1950** H. L. Lorimer *Homes & Monuments* vi. 354 The well-known rock-carving of Ivriz on which a King appears before the god of vegetation. **1938** H. A. Winkler *Rock-Drawings of Southern Upper Egypt* I. 26 The discovery of *rock-drawings showing boats of a type foreign to Egypt. **1977** H. Innes *Big Footprints* I. i. 33 The location of the rock drawings. **1920** H. G. Wells *Outl. Hist.* I. xvii. 126/1 From *rock engravings we may deduce the theory that the desert was crossed from oasis to oasis. **1959** J. D. Clark *Prehist. S. Afr.* ii. 29 The first European in Rhodesia to see rock engravings was probably Thomas Leask who saw those near Wankie in 1869 when on a hunting trip to the Zambezi. **1874** Deutsch *Rem.* 177 The long *rock-inscription of Hamamât. **1908** *Encycl. Relig. & Ethics* I. 822/2 The *rock-paintings.. are either stencilled..or painted in outline. **1977** *Times* 23 Apr. 14/1, I read of a Bushman woman wearing a circle of beads..'exactly like that of her ancient prototype' in an early rock painting. **1939** *Man* No. 119. 178/2 On one of the stalactite pillars..was found a big round stone with..traces of red paint on its surface, as used in the *rock-pictures. **1952** V. G. Childe *New Light Most Anc. East* (ed. 4) ii. 17 The rock-pictures..demonstrate the survival of the 'Rhodesian fauna'. **1861** G. Moore (*title-p.*), The Lost Tribes and the Saxons of the East,..with..translations of *Rock-Records in India. **1865** Tylor *Early Hist. Man.* v. 88 *Rock-sculptures may often be..symbolic boundary marks.

c. With abstract sbs., as ***rock-accumulation***, ***-arrangement***, ***-disintegration***, ***-movement***, ***porosity***, ***-type***, etc.

1874 Geikie *Gt. Ice Age* (1894) 220 The direction of the streams never being in any degree influenced by the rock-dislocations. **1881** Judd *Volcanoes* 283 This work of rock-disintegration. **1886** A. Winchell *Walks Geol. Field* 71 During the long history of rock-accumulation. *Ibid.* 78 We catch sight of a general method in rock-arrangements. **1907** *Bull. Geol. Survey N.Z.* No. 3. 95 Differential rock-movement is recorded by the well-slickensided faces and the plastic finely comminuted rock-material occurring in the plane of contact. **1946** *Nature* 6 July 31/1 G. A. Maximovich.., after making a compilation of several thousands of determination[s] of rock-porosity,..has calculated the average porosities of different types of rocks. *Ibid.* 3 Aug. 172/1 The commonest rock-type [on Heard Island] is trachybasalt.

d. In miscellaneous uses, as ***rock-cut***, ***-cutting***, ***-demon***, ***-diamond***, ***-fishing***, ***-flower***, ***-herb***, ***-land***, ***-spring***, ***-tackle***, ***-top***, ***-vine***, ***-wilderness***.

1873 J. H. Beadle *Undevel. West* 139 A long *rock-cut. **1965** G. McInnes *Road to Gundagai* ix. 134 Each rattling rock-cut, each looping embankment and low trestle bridge carried us further into an unbelievable land. **1873** 'Mark Twain' & Warner *Gilded Age* 420 There is Newark,..then marshes, then long *rock cuttings, devoted to the advertisements of patent medicines. **1871** Tylor *Prim. Cult.* II. 189 An early missionary account of a *rock-demon worshipped by the Huron Indians. **1836** Furness *Astrologer* I. 66 Jacinth, *rock-diamond, crystal, sapphires blue. **1740**

R. Brookes (*title*), The Art of Angling, *Rock and Sea-Fishing. *c* **1820** S. Rogers *Italy* (1839) 32 Every where gathering *rock-flowers. **1626** Bacon *Sylva* §570 There be likewise *Rock-Herbs; But I suppose those are where there is some Mould or Earth. **1891** M. E. Ryan *Pagan of Alleghanies* 96 The rest of that *rock-land is going to break away sometime. **1946** W. de la Mare *Traveller* 17 He.. had wakened to the rock-land. **1960** *Wall St. Jrnl.* 30 Nov. 7/3 The technique of 'rockland' farming was developed a few years ago in south Florida... Growers use the rockland in preference to more fertile soil partly because.. rocklands are on higher ground and are less subject to flooding. **1712** Morton *Nat. Hist. Northants* 265 This County.. abounds with those called *Rock-Springs, that is, the lasting or perennial ones, whose Ducts or Chanels are in the Fissures or Intervalls of those Rocks. **1884** *19th Cent.* Feb. 325 The pure outflow of a rock-spring. **1793** Smeaton *Edystone L.* §261 The shears, the windlass, and all the *rock tackle. **1927** D. H. Lawrence *Mornings in Mexico* 135 High on a narrow *rock-top. **1927** Joyce *Pomes Penyeach*, Gold-brown upon the sated flood The *rockvine clusters lift and sway. **1927** D. H. Lawrence *Mornings in Mexico* 162 The great, hollow, *rock-wilderness space of that part of Arizona.

e. Placed after the words qualified. *rare.*

1562 Legh *Armory* A j, The fourth is a Iugge and cuppe of Ruby rocke, in a field siluer. **1575** Laneham *Let.* (1871) 51 Great Diamons, Emerauds, Rubyes, and Saphyres: poynted, tabld, rok, and roound.

7. Objective or objective genitive: **a.** With pres. pples., as ***rock-battering***, ***-boring***, ***-crushing***, ***-forming***, ***-infesting***, ***-loving***, ***-rolling***, etc.

1605 Sylvester *Du Bartas* II. iii. *Lawe* 13 *Rock-batt'ring Bumbards, Valour-murdering Guns. **1875** *Encycl. Brit.* III. 808 A good *rock-boring machine.. ensures considerable economy in time and labour. **1966** A. Battersby *Math. in Managem.* i. 16 This *rock-crushing argument may well be used to suppress a bright boy. **1893** J. W. Gregory (*title*), Tables for the determination of the *Rock-Forming Minerals, compiled by F. Lawinson-Lessing. **1850** R. G. Cumming *Hunter's Life S. Afr.* (1902) 38/1 Even the *rock-frequenting koodoos themselves made bad weather of it. **1940** A. H. Gardiner *Theory of Proper Names* i. 7 The *rock-infesting monsters. **1847** Emerson *Poems* 230 A wild-rose, or *rock-loving columbine, Salve my worst wounds. **1850** R. G. Cumming *Hunter's Life S. Afr.* (1902) 37/2 It was just the country to suit the taste of the rock-loving koodoos. **1886** Winchell *Walks Geol. Field* 99 A *rock-melting temperature. **1876** L. Stephen *Eng. Th. 18th C.* I. v. 281 Like some mass of *rockpiercing strata of a different formation. **1608** Sylvester *Du Bartas* II. iv. *Decay* 656 O Arm that Kings dis-thrones: O Army-shaving Sword! *Rock-razing Hands! **1957** R. Campbell *Coll. Poems* II. 106 But now the longed-for sound, As of *rock-rolling torrents underground, Approaches.

b. With vbl. sbs., as ***rock-blasting***, ***-boring***, ***-climbing***, ***-folding***, ***-painting***, etc.

1838 Darwin in *Life & Lett.* (1887) I. 292 The good science of rock-breaking. **1877** Raymond *Statist. Mines & Mining* 366 The great improvements in mining machinery, in rock-drilling, in explosives. **1886** Winchell *Walks Geol. Field* 64 A similar process to rock-making. **1892** *Pall Mall G.* 25 Feb. 2/1 Putting to an end rock-climbing for some.. time. **1923** G. D. Abraham *First Steps to Climbing* iv. 45 It is a well-considered opinion that rock climbing is the most important branch of mountaineering. **1965** G. J. Williams *Econ. Geol. N.Z.* iii. 20/1 It is very clear that there is a general parallelism between rock-folding and the trend of the lodes. **1965** R. & D. Morris *Men & Snakes* i. 17 Australia is the only continent where rock painting is still practised regularly today. **1977** *Times* 19 Jan. 14/1 Wasdale Head proclaims itself as the birth-place of rock climbing.

c. With agent-nouns (also forming names of machines), as ***rock beater***, ***-breaker***, ***-builder***, ***climber***, ***-hopper***, ***-hunter***, ***-painter***, etc.

1935 *Discovery* July 203/2 The rock is.. crushed in *rock beaters. **1874** Raymond *Statist. Mines & Mining* 409 The fine ore and clay,.. without sending them through the *rock-breakers, which the clay tends to choke up. **1881** —— *Mining Gloss., Rock-breaker*, usually applied to a class of machines.. in which the rock is crushed between two jaws. **1876** Page *Adv. Text-bk. Geol.* iii. 67 The principal *rock-builders among these microscopic organisms. **1896** *Westm. Gaz.* 13 Nov. 2/1 Accustomed to the *rock-climbers of the Tyrol, we found our guides slow. **1940** F. Smythe *Adventures of Mountaineer* vii. 75, I knew my companion to be a magnificent rock climber, as agile and as active as a cat. **1977** *R.A.F. News* 27 Apr.-10 May 20/6 St Athan's mountain rescue team.. were asked to help rescue a rock climber who had fallen in the Brecon Beacons. **1959** S. J. Baker *Drum* 140 **Rock-hopper*, a person who fishes from rocks on a sea-coast. **1969** *Man* (Austral.) Mar. 12/2 Many rock-hoppers are experienced rock climbers, of a breed who, for sport, crawl like flies over the granite. **1971** R. Purvis *Treasure Hunting in Brit. Columbia* ii. 47 The first *rockhunter to emerge in the early stone age wasn't interested in the beauty or gem quality of stones. **1919** H. G. Wells *Outl. Hist.* xii. 77/2 The simplicity, directness, and detachment of a later Palæolithic *rock-painter appeal more to modern sympathies than does the state of mind of these Neolithic men. **1961** L. van der Post *Heart of Hunter* 9, I gave a brief account of the tragic extermination of this little hunter and rock-painter by the Black and the White invaders of his ancient country. **1875** Knight *Dict. Mech.* 1960/2 **Rock-pulverizer*, a machine or mill for breaking stone. **1887** *Pall Mall G.* 12 Feb. 11/1 Receiving a few bruises from vagrant *rock-throwers.

8. a. Instrumental and locative, as ***rock-begirdled***, ***-bestudded***, ***-born***, ***-bound***, ***-bred***, ***-bristled***, ***-cut***, ***-girt***, ***-guarded***, ***-living***, ***-nurtured***, ***-perched***, ***-rooted***, ***-staked***, etc.

1813 Scott *Rokeby* II. i, *Rock-begirdled Gilmanscar. **1828** Wordsw. *Power of Sound* iii, From rocky steep and *rock-bestudded meadows. **1635** Quarles *Embl.* III. xi. 28 O shall my *Rock-bethreatned Soul be drown'd? **1849** J. R. Lowell in *National Anti-Slavery Standard* 23 Aug. 50/6 Taghkanic's *rockborn child Dares gloriously the dangerous leap. **1913** W. B. Yeats in *Brit. Rev.* Apr. 89, I have kept my faith though faith was tried To that rock-born, rock-wandering foot. **1840** Longf. *Wreck Hesperus* x, 'Tis a fog-bell on a *rock-bound coast! **1937** De la Mare & Jones *This year: Next Year* 12/2 The lovely sirens sing.. in their rock-bound solitude. **1978** *Amer. Poetry Rev.* Nov./Dec. 20/3 Along the stormy, rockbound Ligurian coast. **1830** Scott *Auchindrane* I. i, As the *rock-bred eaglet soars Up to her nest. **1920** W. B. Yeats in *Dial* Nov. 462 She seemed to have grown clean and sweet Like any rock-bred, sea borne bird. **1941** L. B. Lyon *Tomorrow is Revealing* 22 Encounter The rock-bred wolf or risk the valley road. **1847** J. R. Lowell *Summer Storm* in *Poems* 2nd Ser. 66 Like the toothless sea mumbling A *rock-bristled shore. **1856** Kane *Arctic Expl.* I. xviii. 220 The glaciers descend.. from an interior of lofty *rock-clad hills. *Ibid.* ix. 96 The same frowning cliffs and *rock-covered ice-belt. **1834** *Penny Cycl.* II. 283/1 The *rock-cut tombs or temples in Nubia. **1933** *Burlington Mag.* Nov. 237/1 The paintings in the rock-cut Chapels of Cappadocia. **1979** *London Rev. Bks.* 25 Oct. 14/2 (Advt.), Two hundred years ago.. Buddhist rock-cut shrines, the mosques of Moslems,.. were all but unknown to Europeans. **1820** Shelley *Prometh. Unb.* I. 120 Oh, *rock-embosomed lawns, and snow-fed streams. **1807** Wordsw. *White Doe* VII. 253 The grassy *rock-encircled Pound. **1770** Hodson *Dedic. Temple of Solomon* 12 Down whose *Rock-encumber'd Side.. roll'd the chrystal Stream. **1839** Talfourd *Glencoe* III. ii, With grief For *rock-enthroned Scotland. **1598** Sylvester *Du Bartas* I. *Eden* 548 *Rock-fal'n spowts, congealed by colder air. **1649** Daniel *Trinarch., Hen. V*, clv, They cleave *Rocke-firmed Towers. *a* **1847** Eliza Cook *There would I be* ii, The *rock-girded ocean. **1845** E. A. Poe in *Graham's Mag.* Dec. 251/1 No billow breaking into foam Upon the *rock-girt shore of Time. **1860** Pusey *Min. Proph.* 236 The rock-girt Petra.., a gem in its mountain-setting. **1929** C. E. Robinson *Hist. Greece* vi. 63 One great advantage indeed the Attic folk possessed in the admirable *rock-guarded harbours adjacent to their capital. **1923** D. H. Lawrence *Birds, Beasts & Flowers* 41 A *rock-living, sweet-fleshed sea-anemone. **1913** W. B. Yeats in *Brit. Rev.* Apr. 87 *Rock-nurtured Aoife took a pin. **1913** W. de la Mare *Peacock Pie* 64, I long to watch the sea-mew wheel Back to her *rock-perched mate. **1627** Drayton *Agincourt*, etc. 110 Comming next to *Rocke-reard Nottingham. **1815** Shelley *Alastor* 562 A pine, *Rock-rooted, stretched athwart the vacancy Its swinging boughs. **1890** *Congress. Rec.* 7 June 5802/1, Every rock-rooted advocate of the gold standard is in favor of [this provision]. **1930** W. B. Yeats *Wild Apples* I Unsheltered by steading, Rock-rooted and grown, A great tree of Erin, It stands up alone. **1860** G. H. K. *Vac. Tour* 165 The little *rock-set basin not ten yards across. **1894** Kipling *Seven Seas* (1896) 131 Thou hast not toiled at the fishing.. Nor worked the war-boats outward through the rush of the *rock-staked seas. **1891** Kipling *Light that Failed* ii. (1900) 24 The *rock-strewn ridges were alive with armed men. **1842** A. de Vere *Song of Faith* 253 High in her cloudy court The *rock-throned osprey. **1833** Tennyson *Palace of Art* 71 You seem'd to hear them [*sc.* waves].. roar *rock-thwarted under bellowing caves. *a* **1847** Eliza Cook *Stanzas* vi, The *rock-torn plank and shattered spar.

b. Parasynthetic, as ***rock-arched***, ***-based***, ***-browed***, ***-chested***, ***-crested***, ***-faced***, ***-floored***, ***-roofed***, ***-scarped***, ***-walled***, ***-wombed***.

1833 J. G. Whittier *Poet. Wks.* (1898) 559/2 Through *rock-arched Winooski the salmon leaps free. **1877** L. Morris *Epic of Hades* II. 100 To a wild headland, *rockbased in the sea. **1944** Blunden *Shells by Stream* 19 Above the *rock-browed shag-haired weir. **1939** Dylan Thomas *Map of Love* 4 If the dead starve, their stomachs turn to tumble An upright man in the antipodes Or spray-based and *rock-chested sea. **1837** A. Tennent *Vis. Glencoe* 10 The *rock-crested Ailsa begirt with the wave. **1840** *Civil Eng. & Arch. Jrnl.* III. 84/1 The substructure is a stylobate, or continuous pedestal, resting upon a deep *rock-faced plinth. **1889** *Cath. Househ.* 30 Nov. 3 It is faced with coursed rock-faced ashlar. **1905** W. M. Davis in *Jrnl. Geol.* XIII. 388 The initial relief will be extinguished even under the slow processes of desert erosion, and there will appear instead large, *rock-floored plains sloping toward large waste-floored plains. **1777** Potter *Æschylus, Prometheus* 22 Thy *rock-roof'd grottos arch'd by nature's hand. **1819** Shelley *Cyclops* 74 The gathered flocks into the rock-roofed cave. **1852** Mundy *Antipodes* (1857) 2 A *rock-scarped table-land covered with a stunted shrub-like gorse. **1879** J. G. Whittier *Poet. Wks.* (1898) 257/1 Church that.. Saw within the *rock-walled bay Treville's lilied pennons play. **1798** W. Taylor in *Monthly Mag.* V. 208 For gain to dig the *rock-womb'd gold. **1954** W. Faulkner *Fable* 260 The rock-wombed powder magazines under the Gates of Hercules.

c. Similative, as ***rock-fast***, ***-firm***, ***-footed***, ***-hard***, ***-hearted***, ***-solid***, ***-steady***, ***-still***, ***-white***; also ***rock-blackness***, ***-heart***.

1968 R. P. Warren *Incarnations* (1970) 11 The moon, eastward and over The ridge and *rock-blackness, rears. **1898** Meredith *Odes Fr. Hist.* 23 What he constructed held *rock-fast. **1891** Hardy *Tess* (1900) 38/1 When.. malignant possibilities stand *rock-firm as facts. **1911** Beerbohm *Zuleika D.* xxii. 317 Sole and splendid survivor he stood, *rock-footed, before her. **1935** 'L. Luard' *Conquering Seas* v. 69 Plenty of *rock-hard, shelf cod. **1978** S. Sheldon *Bloodline* xxii. 250 The man was fully aroused now, rock-hard. **1647** Wm. Fenner *Wks.* (1658) 225 Can any *rock-heart hold out and not be broken with the blowes of it? **1647** Cowley *Mistr., Innocent Ill* iii, Though savage, and *rock-hearted those Appear, that weep not ev'n Romances woes. **1972** *Ulster* (Sunday Times Insight Team) xvi. 273 They had seen their support in the area—once *rock-solid—steadily and severely eroded. **1976** A. Price *War Game* I. ix. 175 He'll never sit for this seat... It's rock-solid Conservative. **1928** *Outlook* 26 May 650/1 Consols were *rock-steady at 112. **1976** J. Wainwright *Who goes Next?* 151 The killer held the rifle rock-steady. **1976** J. B. Hilton *Gamekeeper's Gallows* ii. 20 He cocked his eye up to the pressure-dial. The needle was *rock still, not even trembling. **1916** Blunden *Pastorals* 21 Through the bindweed's *rock-white mesh.

d. Misc., as ***rock-free***, ***-rushing*** adjs.

1605 Sylvester *Du Bartas* II. iii. *Captains* 623 Rock-rushing Tempests do retreat, or charge. **1615** Chapman *Odyssey* VII. 391 A flood, Whose shores.. on good aduantage stood, For my receit, rock-free, and fenc't from wind.

9. a. Special combs., as **rock-apostle**, St. Peter (in allusion to Matt. xvi. 18); **rock bar** *Physical Geogr.* = riegel; **rock-berg**, a mass of rock resembling an iceberg; **rock-bind(ers)**, sandy shale (Gresley, 1883); **rock biscuit**, a hard variety of fancy biscuit; **rock bit** *Oil Industry*, a drilling bit for use in hard formations; **rock bolt** *Mining*, a tensioned rod passing through a bed of rock and anchoring it to the body of rock behind; so **rock bolting**, the practice or technique of using rock bolts; **rock-bone** (see quots.); **rock-bottom**, bed-rock; also *fig.*, the fundamental or lowest possible level, nadir (see also quot. 1866); also *attrib.* or as *adj.*, lowest possible, unbeatable (of prices, etc.); fundamental, firmly grounded, honest, sound; **rock-bun**, = *rock-cake*; **rock butter** (see butter *sb.*[1] 3); **rock cake**, a small cake or bun with a rugged surface; **rock candy** (see sense 4 a); also in ***Big Rock Candy Mountain***(*s*), a song about a mythical earthly paradise, used allusively in sense 'utopia'; **rock climb**, the ascent of a rock-face; also as *v. intr.*; **rock coal** *U.S.*, anthracite; **rock cocoa** (see quot.); **rock coral**, ? coral of a massive form; **rock cork**, a light variety of asbestos; pilolite; **rock cotton**, ? mineral cotton (see cotton *sb.*[1] 7); **rock-craft**, skill in climbing, or moving among, rocks; **rock creep**, the creep (creep *sb.* 7 a) of rock, boulders, etc.; **rock-crusher**, (*a*) a machine used to break down rocks; (*b*) *fig.* in *Bridge*, a superlative hand; also *attrib.*; **rock-drill**, a rock-boring instrument or machine; **rock-dust** *N. Amer.*, pulverized stone used to prevent explosions in coal mines; so **rock-dusting** *vbl. sb.*; hence **rock-dust** *v. trans.*, to treat (a mine) with pulverized stone; **rock-duster** (see quot. 1975); **rock English**, the mixed English of Gibraltar; **rock-face**, a vertical expanse of natural rock; also *transf.* and *fig.*; also **rock-faced** *a.*; **rockfall**, the descent of loose rocks; a mass of fallen rock; **rock fan** *Physical Geogr.*, an eroded rock surface similar in shape to an alluvial fan, with a convex profile in transverse section; **rock fence** chiefly *Southern U.S.*, a stone wall; **rock fever**, an enteric fever common at Gibraltar; Malta or Mediterranean fever; **rock-fill** *Engin.*, large rock fragments used to form the bulk of the material of a dam; freq. *attrib.*; **rock-fire** (see quot.); **rock-flesh**, a spongy variety of asbestos; **rock-flint**, impure flint; chert; **rock-flour**, finely powdered rock, esp. that formed as a result of glacial erosion; **rock-froth**, fused lava much inflated by bubbles of steam or gas; **rock-garden**, a garden consisting of rocks and rock-plants; so **rock-gardener**, **-gardening**; **rock gas**, natural gas obtained by boring through rock; **rock glacier**, a large mass of rock debris, in some cases mingled with ice, which moves gradually downhill in the manner of a glacier; **rock gong** *Archæol.* (see quots.); **rock-hammer**, a hammer used for rock-breaking; **rock happy** *U.S. Mil. slang*, mentally disturbed through serving too long on a (Pacific) island; **rock harmonicon**, **-head**, (see quots.); **rock-hog**, a labourer engaged in tunnelling through rock; **rock hole**, (*a*) a tunnel; (*b*) *Austral.*, a natural depression in a rock that catches water; **rock-honey**, **hopping** (see quots.); **rock hound** *colloq.* (orig. *U.S.*), (*a*) a geologist; (*b*) an amateur mineralogist; hence **rock-hounding** *vbl. sb.*, the hobby or activity of an amateur mineralogist; **rock-house**, (*a*) a house built of stone or quarried rock; (*b*) a shady place under over-hanging rocks providing a suitable habitat for ferns; **rock-isinglass** (see gypsine *a.*); **rock leather**, a variety of asbestos, mountain leather; **rock lizard**, **-marl**, **-marrow**, **-meal**, **-milk**, **-mine**, **-nosing** (see quots.); **rock mechanics**, the branch of science and engineering concerned with the mechanical properties and behaviour of rock; **rock of ages** *Rhyming slang*, wages; **rock-paper**, a very thin and flexible variety of asbestos; **rock-peg** *Mountaineering*, a nail-like device hammered into rock to assist climbing; **rock phosphate**, a sedimentary rock containing phosphates in high proportion; phosphorite; **rock pile** *U.S. slang*, (*a*) a heap of stones; (*b*) a jail or prison, in allusion to the convict's task of breaking stones; also *transf.* and *fig.*; **rock pitch** *Mountaineering*, an expanse of rock between belay points; **rock piton** *Mountaineering*, a piton used to assist climbing of rock; † **rock-ray**, a line or reef of rocks; **rock river** = *rock glacier* above; **rock scorpion**, = *rock lizard*; **rock silk**, a silky variety of asbestos; **rock-slide** orig. *U.S.*, a slippage of rock; a rough mass of rock that has subsided thus; also *fig.*; **rocksman** *Sc.* = ROCKMAN 1; **rock-soap**, a kind of bole; mountain soap; **rock stream** = *rock glacier* above; **rock sugar** (see sense 4a); **rock tar**, petroleum; **rock waste**, fragments of rock produced by weathering; **rock well**, an oil well drilled through superficial deposits of clay, sand, or the like into underlying rock; **rock-wood**, a compact variety of asbestos; **rock wool**, a material such as limestone, slag, or the like, made into the form of a fine, matted fibre, esp. for use in thermal insulation or soundproofing.

1865 RUSKIN Sesame I. §24 The strong angels of whom the *rock-apostle is the image. 1912 W. H. HOBBS Earth Features xxvi. 377 When the backward grades upon the valley floor are especially steep, the rock step becomes a *rock bar, or riegel, of which nearly every Alpine valley has its example. 1954, 1957 [see RIEGEL]. 1963 D. W. & E. E. HUMPHRIES tr. Termier's Erosion & Sedimentation v. 121 Special characteristics such as cirques.. and rock bars can always be recognized. 1865 BURRITT Walk Land's End 242 The tors looked like *rockbergs, once floating on the great revolving drift. 1862 RAMSAY Rock Spec. 71 Argillaceous sandstones.. which pass under the name of 'rock' or '*rock binds'. 1861 MRS. BEETON Bk. Househ. Managem. 852 (heading) *Rock biscuits. 1893 EMILE HÉRISSÉ Pastry Making 84 Raspberry Rock Biscuits. Proceed as in making Almond Rock Biscuits. 1920 Engin. & Mining Jrnl. 7 Feb. 404/1 The invention and development of rotary *rock bits lagged behind the introduction and successful application of the rotary method of drilling. 1974 R. D. GRACE in P. L. Moore et al. Drilling Practices Man. iv. 66 Rock bits should be economical in the shale. 1955 L. A. PANEK in Rep. Investigations U.S. Bureau of Mines (1956) No. 5154. 1 The practice of roof bolting or *rock bolting to stabilize rock surrounding underground excavations has increased.. within a few years. 1957 Q. Colorado School of Mines July 235 Because of their increasingly extensive use in non-coal mines, we prefer to call these devices '*rock' rather than 'roof' *bolts and will refer to them as such. 1973 L. J. THOMAS Introd. Mining viii. 310 Rock bolts, sometimes called roof bolts, are the first line of defence in many mining and civil engineering applications. 1701 GREW Cosm. Sacra I. v. §6 Among many varieties both in the Inner and the Outer Ear, those which appear in the Passage into the *Rock-bone, are remarkable. 1768-74 TUCKER Lt. Nat. (1834) I. 390 In.. the os petrosum or rock-bone of the ear, they grow into a substance hard as steel. [1856 'OLD COLONIST' How to Farm & Settle in Austral. 56 This lowest bottom, 'the rock' as it is emphatically termed, in reference to its character as a bar to further digging for gold.] 1866 Oregon State Jrnl. 24 Nov. 2/2 A sound democrat, or '*rock bottom', never shrinks from the requirements of his master. 1884 Lisbon (Dakota) Star 10 Oct., Boots, shoes and rubbers in great variety and at rock-bottom prices. 1890 in Barrère & Leland Dict. Slang II. 183/1 Other freight wars, covering much less territory than the present, have gone to rock bottom before any attempt has been made to restore rates. 1902 W. N. HARBEN Abner Daniel 273 See here, I've got a rock-bottom proposal to make to your people. 1904 —— Georgians 200 Now cool off, an' let's git down to rock-bottom. 1923 D. L. SAYERS Whose Body? vii. 167 There aren't many men who wouldn't be nice—to her, and even then, if they aren't rock-bottom she can see through them. 1930 Sat. Even. Post 26 July 14/1 'Pay you?.. How much, Angelo?' 'The rock bottom is half a million.' 1935 H. EDIB Clown & his Daughter xlv. 258 By the time she had touched the rock-bottom of misery she had also reached a decision. 1955 D. DAVIE Articulate Energy vii. 69 We are sobered and shocked when the mood reaches rock-bottom. 1977 Belfast Tel. 19 Jan. 7/8 Builders engaged in this work were rapidly reaching 'rock bottom'. 1980 Daily Tel. 16 Jan. 23/4 In this way, the service can be offered at rock-bottom prices. 1889 J. WHITEHEAD Steward's Handbk. IV. 420/2 *Rock buns, rough rocky looking cakes made of ¾ lb. each butter, sugar and currants, [etc.]. 1893 EMILE HÉRISSÉ Pastry Making 140 Finish as in making the preceding Rock Buns. 1805 JAMESON Syst. Min. II. 30 *Rock Butter.. appears to have nearly the same constituent parts as alum. 1868 M. JEWRY Warne's Model Cookery 613/1 *Rock cakes,.. butter.. flour.. sugar.. lemon.. eggs.. brandy. 1883 MRS. CLARKE Plain Cookery 71 Rock Cakes. 1886 Confectioner's Receipt Bk. 26 Rock Cakes.. when baked.. will have a rough, irregular surface. 1723 J. NOTT Cook's & Confectioner's Dict. sig. U6, To candy Nutmegs... Pour your Candy to them,.. set them in a warm Place for about three Weeks, and they will be of a *Rock Candy. 1769 MRS. RAFFALD Eng. Housekeeper (1778) 203 Garnish with rock candy sweetmeats. 1815 MAR. EDGEWORTH Love & Law. III. xliii, A knot of rock-candy. 1906 M. P. W. LOCKE (song-title) Big Rock Candy Mountains. Ibid., Come to the Big Rock Candy Mountains, And I'll show you the bees and the cigarette trees And the soda water fountains. 1930 G. MILBURN Hobo's Hornbk. 61 To homeguards 'The Big Rock Candy Mountains' may appear a nonsense song, but to all pied pipers in on the know it is an amusing exaggeration of the ghost stories used [by jockers] in recruiting kids. Ibid., Said the bum to the son, 'O, will you come To the Big Rock Candy Mountains.' 1949 C. HIMES Black on Black (1973) 278 He set up all the boys in the neighbourhood to peanut brittle and icecream and rock candy. 1961 Life Treas. Amer. Folklore 294 The Hobo Special climbs Big Rock Candy Mountain. 1975 Daily Colonist (Victoria, B.C.) 16 Apr. 4/4 The goal is their 20th century version of the big rock candy mountain. 1895 W. M. CONWAY Alps from End to End 402/2 (Index), *Rock Climbs, Where to find. 1929 F. S. SMYTHE Climbs & Ski Runs iii. 14 My first rock climb was the Little Gully. 1934 WEBSTER, Rock climb v. 1960 Guardian 11 July 1/4 He had intended to rock-climb with a companion. 1976 G. MOFFAT Over Sea to Death v. 52 She would be even happier were she to reach the top by way of a rock climb. 1858 Southern Lit. Messenger XXVI. 189/2 Ef thar had bin.. a fier-plais instid uv a great to burn *rock cole, the thing would uv bin kumpleat. 1913 O. A. ROTHERT Hist. Muhlenberg County 389 The early blacksmiths called this fuel 'rock coal', thus distinguishing it from charcoal. 1891 Daily News 24 Dec. 7/2 That *rock cocoa was a recognised article of commerce, manufactured of cocoa, starch, and sugar in such quantities as to be easily soluble in water. 1705 Phil. Trans. XXV. 2217 It very much resembles a piece of white unpolished *Rock Coral. 1804 JAMESON Syst. Min. I. 439 *Rock Cork.. occurs some-times massive, sometimes in plates and with impressions. 1855 Orr's Circ. Sci., Elem. Chem. 174 Asbestos, rock cork, and other minerals. 1875 DAWSON Dawn of Life ii. 21 A vein of fibrous serpentine, yielding '*rock cotton', for packing steam pistons. 1892 Pall Mall G. 19 July 3/1 The difference between snowcraft and *rockcraft. 1938 C. F. S. SHARPE Landslides iii. 31 *Rock-creep.—It is sometimes observed that although creeping masses of rock have moved many feet their original relation to the bedrock can still be recognized. 1960 [see CREEP sb. 7a]. 1968 R. W. FAIRBRIDGE Encycl. Geomorphol. 275/2 Such movement of rock debris induced by gravity as talus creep, rock creep, and debris slides all transport rock fragments to lower elevations. 1897 Outing XXX. 136/1 The men do their own work without the use of a *rock crusher, but they seem to like the life. 1952 I. MACLEOD Bridge iv. 39 The Two Club bid.. has the double advantage of freeing the other bids of Two of a suit for specialized use, and coping with the rockcrusher hands which do not qualify for a Strong Two opening. 1965 Times 9 Jan. 9/7 Her bidding was cautious to a degree, requiring a positive rock crusher for anything above the level of one. 1973 Country Life 24 May 1503/1 A first-class collection of hands... 5 [Clubs].. shows a rock-crusher, asking partner to choose the suit. 1877 RAYMOND Statist. Mines & Mining 37 Had it not been for the Burleigh *rock-drill the work would have been abandoned long since. 1938 Richmond (Va.) Times-Dispatch 7 Nov. 6/2 Sprinkling of the *rock-dust through the mines allays the highly explosive coal dust. Ibid., The Bureau of Mines has a new argument in support of its plea that all coal mines be rock-dusted to prevent explosions. 1947 Sun (Baltimore) 27 Mar. 1/2 Reports of the State Inspection said the mine was 'not adequately rock-dusted'. 1977 Transatlantic Rev. LX. 80 Inside, [there is] the rockdust rumble of grinding teeth, molar on molar. 1975 Publ. Amer. Dial. Soc. 1973 LIX. 48 *Rock duster,.. 1, a mechanical blower, often caterpillar track or train wheel mounted, which forces rock dust against the dangerously dusty areas of the mine... 2, a worker in charge of distributing rock dust throughout the mine, by hand or machine. 1926 Daily Colonist (Victoria, B.C.) 20 July 12/4 By *rock dusting is meant the spreading of incombustible dust throughout a mine in sufficient amount to cool and extinguish the flame of an incipient explosion. 1932 Durant (Okla.) Daily Democrat 10 Mar. 4/5 By rock dusting, a practice made mandatory by the 1929 legislature, this coal dust is mixed with an equal amount of rock dust, the latter lowering the ignition point of the mixture. 1938 Richmond (Va.) Times-Dispatch 7 Nov. 6/2 Rock-dusting also is advocated as a means of increasing visibility in the mines and preventing minor accidents. 1842 BORROW Bible in Spain (1843) III. xiv. 272 They were.. conversing in the rock Spanish, or *rock English, as the fit took them. 1855 KINGSLEY Glaucus (1878) 16 It was the crawling of a glacier which polished that *rock-face. 1931 C. DAY LEWIS Coll. Poems (1935) 76 As one who wanders into old workings Dazed by the noonday, desiring coolness, Has found retreat barred by fall of rockface. 1940 Chambers's Techn. Dict. 728/2 Rockface, (Masonry) the form of face given to a building-stone which has been quarry-faced. 1968 Amer. Speech 1967 XLII. 295 Rock-face stone,.. slabs of stone sawed on the top and bottom surface (up to five surfaces), which are then placed in a machine exerting pressure and cracking the stone. This leaves a pleasing rough surface toward the outside. 1972 Times 29 Nov. 28/8 (Advt.), The.. appeal is to the younger person who really wants a vital and interesting job as a change agent at the 'rock face'. 1944 K. LEVIS in Murdoch & Drake-Brockman Austral. Short Stories (1951) 427 The men were separated in bunches cut off by *rock-faced water-beds. 1970 H. BRAUN Parish Churches xviii. 216 The face of the stone is left 'rock-faced' and not worked at all except along its margins. 1930 Times Educ. Suppl. 24 May p. i/2 Crossing the débris of a huge *rockfall which apparently came down recently. 1967 M. J. COE Ecol. Alpine Zone Mt. Kenya 87 The Tarn.. is enclosed at its lower edge by the rock fall. 1971 World Archaeol. III. 150 The rockfall layers at Puntutjarpa were of considerable archaeological interest. 1900 W. M. DAVIS in Bull. Geol. Soc. Amer. XI. 210 Near the base of the mountain front nearly all of the ravines broaden and their floors become distinctly convex, thus imitating the form well known in alluvial fans, though rarely matched in an eroded surface of solid rock. These convex floors will be called *rock fans. 1932 Amer. Jrnl. Sci. CCXXIII. 392 The alluvial fan is the expression of that form where deposition alone has occurred, or where considerable deposition has accompanied erosion of bedrock. The 'rock fan'.. is the same form.. where erosion has exceeded deposition. Ibid. 393 Rock fans must be carved by streams, and cannot be produced by simple weathering back of the mountain front. 1968 R. W. FAIRBRIDGE Encycl. Geomorphol. 965/1 The rock fans described range in area from several acres when steep, 20–26°, to one or more square miles when gentle, ½–7°. 1970 R. J. SMALL Study of Landforms ix. 310 The existence of rock fans.. has been disputed by many geomorphologists, who have claimed that such fans are in reality no more than the alluvial fans that they are supposed to resemble so closely. 1896 Dial. Notes I. 423 *Rock fence, a stone wall. 1949 H. KURATH Word Geogr. Eastern U.S. 31/2 For a fence built of loose stone the North Midland uses stone fence as against the Northern stone wall and the Southern rock fence. 1974 Amer. Speech 1971 XLVI. 60 Rock fence appears in southern Illinois (a South Midland settlement area) as expected. 1897 HUGHES Mediterranean Fever 21 The idea of a specifically distinct '*Rock Fever' cannot be entertained. 1911 Sci. Amer. 17 June 592 (caption) Characteristic *rockfill across a creek. 1960 Times 7 Mar. 8/3 It is hoped.. to save the Temples from inundation by means of an earth and rock-fill dam. 1969 E. W. MORSE Fur Trade Canoe Routes II. v. 55 The dam and its rockfill now obscure the upper portion of the portage. 1976 National Observer (U.S.) 19 June 4/1 The Interior Department's Bureau of Reclamation has been building dams, including 250 out of rock-fill and earth. 1875 KNIGHT Dict. Mech. 1960/1 *Rock-fire, an incendiary composition which burns slowly and is difficult to extinguish. 1804 JAMESON Syst. Min. I. 439 note, *Rock flesh. 1822 P. CLEAVELAND Min. & Geol. (ed. 2) I. 407 When in thick, spongy plates, it has been called rock or fossil flesh. 1883 Science I. 404/1 Much *rock-flour, washed away by the sub-glacial streams. 1937 Geogr. Jrnl. LXXXIX. 43 Great angular blocks of rock are embedded in a jumble of fragments from the size of dust upwards, it is, in fact, a loose breccia of large pieces associated with smaller ones grading down to the finest rock-flour. 1963 G. L. PICKARD Descriptive Physical Oceanogr. iii. 23 In fjords fed by rivers from glaciers, the surface low-salinity layer may be a milky white from the finely divided 'rock flour'. 1975 J. G. EVANS Environment Early Man Brit. Isles ii. 44 A prerequisite of the formation of wind-blown deposits is a dry land surface from which frost-shattered rock flour can be whipped up and transported. 1878 LE CONTE Elem. Geol. iii. 84 The whole liquid mass may swell into a *rock-froth, which rises to the lip of the crater. 1836 FURNESS Astrologer I. note, Poet. Wks. (1858) 132 The grotto, *rock-gardens, and fossils of the late Thomas Birds. 1962 R. PAGE Education of Gardener viii. 231 By the end of the nineteenth century rock-gardens had become a lasting feature of British gardens. 1942 E. WAUGH Put out More Flags iii. 172 The word 'Colonel' for Basil had connoted an elderly *rock-gardener. 1849 Florist 229 A more appropriate ornament for *rock-gardening could hardly be met with. 1905 W. CROSS Silverton Folio (U.S. Geol. Survey. Geol. Atlas of U.S. No. 120) 25/2 All the accumulations.. just described impress one with the sense of motion.. So noticeable was this that in the field they were spoken of as '*rock-glaciers' and upon the map receive the name 'rock streams'. 1910 S. R. CAPPS in Jrnl. Geol. XVIII. 360 The special agents of degradation with which I wish to deal at present.. I have called rock glaciers... In material the rock glaciers are composed of angular talus. 1954 W. D. THORNBURY Princ. Geomorphol. iv. 85 Kesseli concluded that the rock glaciers of the Sierra Nevada were essentially fossil glaciers. 1968 R. W. FAIRBRIDGE Encycl. Geomorphol. 711/1 If the surface of the ice is densely covered with blocks, one may speak of a rock glacier, but, in North America, 'rock glacier' does not necessarily involve ice. 1955 B. E. B. FAGG in 3rd Pan-Afr. Congr. Prehist. (1957) xlvii. 310 Very extensive exploration of the granite hills revealed the existence of large numbers of these hammered rocks, which I think can best be described as *rock gongs. They consist of huge natural spalls or exfoliations of rock which happen to rest or be wedged in a position favourable to the production of musical notes. 1959 S. Afr. Archaeol. Bull. XIV. 112/2 Rock gongs should be described as 'ringing rocks' or 'sounding stones'. 1961 K. P. WACHSMANN in A. Baines Mus. Instruments through Ages i. 30 Recent studies have revealed many instances of slabs of rock being used as if they were drums. These 'rock gongs', as their discoverers called them, occur in Africa north of the equator, in Europe, and in Asia. 1874 RAYMOND Statist. Mines & Mining 408 In preparing ore for the stamps,.. I used merely *rock-hammers. 1945 Yank 15 June 2/2 The set routine can drive a man nuts wherever he is... Out here [sc. the Marianas] the expression is *rock happy... In the Pacific there is no escape from places like Kwajalein. 1946 Richmond (Va.) Times-Dispatch 9 May 12/1 GI's.. were growing rock happy from too long internment on a coral island. 1876 STAINER & BARRETT Dict. Mus. Terms, *Rock harmonicon, an instrument, the sounds of which are produced by striking graduated lengths of rock-crystal with a hammer. 1885 [see HARMONICON]. 1839 URE Dict. Arts 960 The outcrop or basset edge of the strata, called by miners the *rock-head. 1875 CROLL Climate & T. xxix. 467 It is seldom that the geologist has an opportunity of seeing a complete section down to the rock-head in such a place. 1909 Chambers's Jrnl. Dec. 828/2 The *rock-hogs had not proceeded far before they pierced a large pocket. 1954 V. LYSENKO Yellow Boots 190 They spoke of dynamite and flying rock responsible for the death of many a 'rock-hog'. 1895 M. PEMBERTON Impregnable City II. xiv. 285 Darkness of the *rock-hole. 1936 I. L. IDRIESS Cattle King iv. 30 He learned probabilities and signs by means of which waterholes may be located in apparently dry creeks, and in rock-holes in valley or gorge. 1944 Living off Land iii. 50 Locating water in the form of soaks, springs and rock-holes. 1815 KIRBY & SP. Entomol. x. (1818) I. 332 What is called *rock honey in some parts of America,.. is the produce of wild bees, which suspend their clusters.. to a rock. 1887 GOODE Fisheries & Fish. Indust. U.S. II. 437 The end of the rope is thrown to a boat just outside the breakers, and the raft of blubber is towed to the tender or vessel. This rafting process is called by the sealers '*rock-hopping'. 1922 Daily Ardmoreite (Ardmore, Okla.) 10 Jan. 6/2 (heading) Interesting tale of work in Africa told by Texas *rock hound. 1940 Fortune Mar. 83 Drillers consider themselves a superior breed, look with scorn upon 'rockhounds' (geologists), 'chemicos,' pipemen, roughnecks, etc. 1949 Natural Hist. LVIII. 220/1 There are numerous semiprecious stones to interest the 'rock hound'. 1962 E. LUCIA Klondike Kate viii. 175 Kate was central Oregon's first serious rock hound, of which there are thousands today. 1970 Nature 4 Apr. 45/2 Its bias is naturally towards the United States, where 'rock hounds' and geological societies are much more common than in the United Kingdom. 1979 N.Y. Times Mag. 30 Sept. 88/2 (Advt.), Exclusive metal ratchet device permits shovel to be locked into any position... A necessity, too, for sportsmen,.. fishermen, hikers, rockhounds. 1949 Desert Mag. June 31/1 In all my *rockhounding I have never seen sand fly so fast. 1973 Daily Tel. 25 Aug. 16/1 The objects of his search might be coins, lost jewellery, Victorian ceramics, or if he feels like a change a spot of rockhounding—searching for semi-precious stones—or gold-panning in Scotland. 1976 Globe & Mail (Toronto) 3 July 35 (heading) Go rock-hounding or trail riding, for everything goes in Ontario. 1818 E. P. FORDHAM Jrnl. 26 Jan. in Personal Narr. Trav. (1906) 154 They had a strong *rock house among the hills. 1883 E. A. SMITH Rep. Geol. Survey Alabama 1881–82 438 Underneath the overhanging cliffs, or 'rock houses', as they are termed, grow abundantly some of our rarest and most beautiful ferns. 1889 Harper's Mag. Dec. 120/1 Thet thar rock house o' his'n, which he hev quayried the rock an' put up hisse'f, I 'low it's the beatenes' house in creation. 1901 C. MOHR Plant Life Alabama 17 The.. fern, Trichomanes petersii,.. with others like it hidden in the dark recesses of rocky defiles and the so-called 'rock houses'. 1948 E. N. DICK Dixie Frontier 26 Along the rivers in certain places the rocks projected out over the banks. Hunters and early settlers sometimes lived in the shelter of these for months. They were known as rock houses. 1695 Phil. Trans. XIX. 151 Built of Gypsine Stone, or *Rock-Ising-glass, resembling

Alabaster, but not so hard. **1804** JAMESON *Syst. Min.* I. 439 *note*, The plate-shaped variety is named *rock leather. **1822** P. CLEAVELAND *Min. & Geol.* (ed. 2) I. 407 Its plates have also received the trivial names of rock or mountain leather, rock paper, &c., according to the.. thickness and flexibility, which they possess. **1842** BORROW *Bible in Spain* (1843) III. xiv. 269 He was..what is called a *rock lizard, that is, a person born at Gibraltar of English parents. **1832** DE LA BECHE *Geol. Man.* (ed. 2) 147 Shell-marl, containing in parts tufaceous limestone, provincially termed '*rock-marl'. **1876** PAGE *Adv. Text-bk. Geol.* xx. 411 Where solidified by the subsequent percolation of calcareous waters, it is known as rock-marl. **1837** *Proc. Berw. Nat. Club* I. 158 It..answers to the description of Lithomarge or *rock-marrow. **1887** *Cassell's Dict.*, **Rock-meal*, a white cotton-like variety of carbonate of lime, occurring as an efflorescence, falling into a powder when touched. **1956** *Q. Colorado School of Mines* LI. III. (*title-page*) Symposium on rock mechanics. Papers and discussion from the first annual symposium on *rock mechanics. **1966** *McGraw-Hill Encycl. Sci. & Technol.* XI. 599/2 An understanding of rock mechanics is essential to elucidate the processes which mold the face of the earth. **1977** A. HALLAM *Planet Earth* 104/2 The engineering geologist works with experts in the related fields of soil mechanics and rock mechanics. **1804** JAMESON *Syst. Min.* I. 471 *Rock Milk. Its colour is yellowish white. **1845** *Encycl. Metrop.* VI. 503/1 Rock milk is an absurd name for a variety of carbonate of lime which occurs in the form of a fine white powder in the crevices of calcareous rocks. *a* **1650** BOATE *Ireland's Nat. Hist.* (1652) 126 Of the second sort of Iron-mine, called *Rock-mine. **1886** *Cheshire Gloss.*, *Rock mine*, salt-mining term; the local name for a rock salt mine. **1888** *Encycl. Brit.* XXIV. 527/1 Only the larger individuals, however,..come close down along the land of the west side. These the ships send their boats out to intercept, and this forms the inshore fishing or '*rock-nosing'. **1937** PARTRIDGE *Dict. Slang* 702/2 **Rock of ages*, wages. **1974** P. WRIGHT *Lang. Brit. Industry* x. 89 If there's no *rock of ages* (wages), there may well be a *bull an' cow* (row). **1822** *Rock-paper [see *rock-leather* above]. **1971** C. BONINGTON *Annapurna South Face* x. 118 He put in a couple of ice-screws, then, having run out of these, hammered in ordinary *rock-pegs, which are much shorter than ice-screws and not nearly as secure. **1868** *Chem. News* 13 Nov. 238/2 (*heading*) *Rock phosphates. **1900** [see *phosphatizing* vbl. sb. s.v. PHOSPHATIZE *v.*]. **1936** [see PHOSPHATE 1 b]. **1949** *Thorpe's Dict. Appl. Chem.* (ed. 4) IX. 482 Sedimentary rock phosphate, or phosphorite, occurs in two forms: in thick beds, usually of high phosphatic content; and in layers of nodules, commonly of lower phosphatic grade. **1965** G. J. WILLIAMS *Econ. Geol. N.Z.* xvi. 250/2 Free went on to suggest the possibility of fusing rock-phosphate with greensands and dolomite to give a mixed fertilizer. **1888** *Congress. Rec.* 1 May 3571/1 If this were a police court, the Senator from Indiana would be sent to the *rock-pile for being drunk and disorderly. **1927** K. EUBANK *Horse & Buggy Days* 127 We were..given 30 days on the rock pile or the privilege of leaving town on the first rattler out, which took us into Memphis. **1945** *Seafarers' Log* 13 Apr. 6/3 Had one of the Bull Line rock piles [*i.e.* a ship on board which work is hard] in. **1945** L. SHELLY *Jive Talk Dict.* 16/2 *Rockpile*, a very tall building. **1947** *Sat. Even. Post* 23 Oct. 132/3 Everybody was dead-pan and silent. But disciplined—like convicts on a rock pile. **1949** W. STEVENS *Let.* 12 Dec. (1967) 659 We call the office the rockpile, yet so large a rockpile is a good deal more than that. **1970** C. MAJOR *Dict. Afro-Amer. Slang* 98 *Rock pile*, any tall building. **1929** *Rock pitch [see *ice-ridge* s.v. ICE *sb.* 7 b]. **1955** [see ETRIER]. **1934** *Canad. Alpine Jrnl.* XXII. 128 These analogs of *rock pitons..have now definitely passed their test for usefulness. **1972** D. HASTON *In High Places* i. 12 It should be noted that ice overhangs can be tackled on ice-pitons in the same way as rock overhangs on rock-pitons. **1582** STANYHURST *Æneis* III. (Arb.) 93 Then we grate on *rockrayes [L. *cautes*], and bancks of stoanye Pachynus. **1920** *Natural Hist.* XX. 172/1 In rate of flow these *rock rivers are probably slower than the ice rivers, or glaciers. **1954** W. D. THORNBURY *Princ. Geomorphol.* iv. 85 Striking examples of rock glaciers, rock streams, or rock rivers have been described..in the Sierra Nevada of California. **1818** 'A. BURTON' *Adventures J. Newcome* IV. 239 Fagged he was in every limb, And the *Rock Scorpions laughed at him. **1867** SMYTH *Sailor's Word-bk.*, *Rock-Scorpion*, a name applied to persons born at Gibraltar. **1916** 'TAFFRAIL' *Pincher Martin* viii. 145 They arrived at Gibraltar, where the ships went alongside the Mole..to take in coal. But here..the fuel was carried on board in small baskets on the backs of nondescript, garlic-scented aliens known as 'rock scorpions'. **1976** *Daily Colonist* (Victoria, B.C.) 10 June 4/1 The 29,000 Gibraltarians—affectionately known to generations of British seafarers as Rockscorpions—have been eyeing Madrid hopefully. **1878** HEDDLE in *Mineral. Mag.* II. 215 One side of these veins is sheathed with a variety of this mineral [*i.e.* pilolite], which may be well described under the name of *rock silk. **1851** H. MELVILLE *Moby Dick* II. xiv. 123 Some mossy *rock-slide from the Patagonian cliffs. **1921** *Daily Colonist* (Victoria, B.C.) 29 Mar. 13/5 Owing to a big rockslide west of Terrace, B.C., the G.T.P. passenger train from Prince Rupert is now twenty-four hours late. **1959** R. CAMPBELL *I would do It Again* xviii. 127 We took saddle horses across the flat as far as the mountain slope, which was covered by a rockslide. **1970** R. LOWELL *Notebk.* 203 Is it my imagination or..Pound's Cantos lost in the rockslide of history? **1971** *Islander* (Victoria, B.C.) 13 June 2/4 The pica and ground squirrel may be seen around the rock slides on the edge of the meadow. **1980** *Beautiful Brit. Columbia* Summer 33 The main trail to Eva Lake..across rock slides. **1852** W. MACGILLIVRAY *Hist. Brit. Birds* V. 434 The dexterity of these *rocksmen is truly astonishing. **1804** JAMESON *Syst. Min.* I. 395 *Rock Soap..is massive and disseminated. **1856** *Orr's Circ. Sci., Pract. Chem.* 456 The ground rock-soap is placed in wooden vats. **1905** *Rock stream [see *rock glacier* above]. **1909** *Prof. Papers U.S. Geol. Survey* No. 67. 31 The name 'rock stream', which has been found a convenient descriptive term, was suggested by the peculiar streamlike appearance of the deposits, which look as if they had moved down the cirques or valleys after the manner of glaciers. **1964** W. C. PUTNAM *Geol.* x. 238/1 (*caption*) A rock steam or rock glacier is composed of frost- and ice-shattered rock filled with interstitial ice which slowly moves downslope. **1970** R. J. SMALL *Study of Landforms* x. 333 Fossil rock streams exist in many temperate lands today. **1736** BAILEY *Household Dict.* s.v., To make *Rock-sugar. **1889** J. WHITEHEAD *Steward's Handbk.* IV. 420/2 *Rock sugar*,..candy rock work used to build up ornamental pieces of confectionery and to sell as sponge candy. **1854** R. D. THOMSON *Cycl. Chem.* 441 *Rock..Tar, or Mineral Naphtha. **1907** *Bull. Geol. Soc. Amer.* XVIII. 358 If the moist epoch last long, the mountains of arid countries, such as Persia,..must lose their naked character and become well shrouded with *rock waste. **1946** F. E. ZEUNER *Dating Past* vii. 220 This cave, the Grotta Gualtari ..was completely sealed by rock-waste. **1865** A. GESNER *Pract. Treat. Coal, Petroleum, & Other Distilled Oils* (ed. 2) ii. 40 The *rock wells, as they are termed, are those deeper borings which resemble those of Pennsylvania. **1867** *Ure's Dict. Arts* (ed. 6) III. 404 The rock-wells are of two characters, namely, 'pumping' and 'flowing'. **1804** JAMESON *Syst. Min.* I. 449 *Rock Wood. **1821** URE *Dict. Chem.*, *Rock-wood*: see Asbestus. **1928** E. R. POWELL *U.S. Pat. 1,656,828* 2/1 It is to be understood that so-called *rock wool is made directly from the rock which contains only the slight trace of sulphur; while so-called mineral wool is made from the slag which contains the higher percentages of sulphur. **1936** [see PLASTERBOARD]. **1959** *House & Garden* Dec.–Jan. 57 The outer walls of the house are constructed of two brick skins with a cavity between filled with rock wool for insulation. **1975** G. J. KING *Audio Handbk.* vi. 136 A material..which possesses a high value of acoustical absorbitivity; some commonly used materials being rockwool..and polyurethane foam.

b. In names of animals, as **rock badger**, the Cape hyrax (see BADGER *sb.*^{2} 1 c); **rock barnacle**, a cirriped of the genus *Balanus*; **rock borer**, a bivalve mollusc of the superfamily Saxicavacea; †**rock buck**, the ibex; **rock cavy**, a Brazilian species of cavy (*Cavia rupestris*); **rock chuck**, the North American yellow-bellied marmot, *Marmota flaviventris*; **rock crab**, a crab frequenting rocky coasts, esp. the American *Cancer irroratus*; †**rock doe**, the female ibex; **rock goat**, the ibex; **rock hare**, a variety of hare native to the Cape; **rock hyrax** = *rock rabbit* (*a*), DASSIE 1; **rock kangaroo** (see KANGAROO *sb.* 2); **rock limpet**, the common limpet; **rock lizard**, an African or Australian dragon lizard belonging to the family Agamidæ; (see also sense 9 a); **rock lobster**, a crustacean of the family *Palinuridæ*, to which the crayfish belongs; esp. the marine crayfish, *Palinurus vulgaris*; †**rock marder**, the stone-marten (G. *steinmarder*); **rock mouse** (see quot.); **rock-noser**, the right whale; **rock oyster** (see quot. *a* 1774); **rock-piercer**, a worm of the genus *Terebella*; **rock python**, one of several large snakes of the family Boidæ, esp. the African *Python sebæ*; **rock rabbit**, (*a*) a hyrax belonging to the genus *Procavia* or *Dendrohyrax*, esp. the African *P. capensis*; (*b*) = PIKA; **rock rat**, (*a*) = *rock mouse*; (*b*) a South African rodent (*Petromys typicus*); (*c*) a South American rodent, *Aconæmys fuscus*; (*d*) an Australian thick-tailed rat belonging to the genus *Zyzomys*; **rock scorpion**, a southern African scorpion, *Hadogenes lawrencei*; (see also sense 9 a); **rock seal**, the common seal (*Phoca vitulina*); **rock serpent**, (*a*) = *rock snake*; (*b*) a poisonous Indian snake of the genus *Bungarus*; **rock shell** (see quot. 1848); **rock slater**, a wood-louse of the genus *Ligia*; **rock snail** (see quots.); **rock snake**, a python, esp. *P. reticulatus* or *molurus*; **rock squid** (see quot.); **rock squirrel**, a variety of squirrel native to Sri Lanka (Ceylon); **rock wallaby**, = *rock kangaroo*; **rock whelk** (see quot.); **rock whistler**, the Alpine marmot; **rock worm**, a marine polychæte worm belonging to the family Eunicidæ.

1792 KERR *Anim. Kingd.* 285 Bastard African Marmot, or *Rock Badger. **1824** [see BADGER *sb.*^{2} 1 c]. **1884** GOODE, etc. *Nat. Hist. Aquatic Anim.* 828 The *Rock Barnacle inhabits the entire North Atlantic coasts of both continents. **1854** A. ADAMS, etc. *Man. Nat. Hist.* 149 *Rock-Borers. **1928** RUSSELL & YONGE *Seas* vi. 148 The largest and most efficient rock borers are bivalve Molluscs. **1971** *Oxf. Bk. Invertebr.* 86/1 *Hiatella* is a rock-borer (if the rock is soft enough). **1681** GREW *Musæum* I. ii. ii. 25 A very great Horn of the *Rock-Buck, or of the *Ibex mas.* **1771** PENNANT *Synops. Quadrup.* 244 *Rock Cavy. **1801** SHAW *Gen. Zool.* II. 29 The Rock Cavy is considered as an excellent article of food, and is even superior to the rabbet. **1876** *Encycl. Brit.* V. 277/2 The Rock Cavy, distinguished by its short, blunt nails, is found in rocky situations throughout Brazil. **1913** *Outing* Jan. 451 (*caption*) Not a woodchuck, but a '*rockchuck'. **1947** B. A. DE VOTO *Across Wide Missouri* 162 Robes..were made from..beaver,..wolf, or even rockchuck. **1968** *National Observer* (U.S.) 22 July 6/5 Bones of such small mammals as the rock chuck, rock squirrel, northern pocket gopher, and pygmy rabbit, were found in the Altithermal strata. **1837** J. L. WILLIAMS *Territory of FLorida* 105 The *Rock Crab is common on the Atlantic coast. **1871–2** in Goode *Nat. Hist. Aquat. Anim.* 766 The common 'Rock Crab', *Cancer irroratus*, is generally common under the large rocks near low-water mark. **1887** in Goode *Fisheries & Fish. Indust. U.S.* II. 658 The large red rock crab (*Echidnoceros setimanus*) of the Farallone Islands. **1681** GREW *Musæum* I. ii. ii. 24 The *Rock-Doe, *Ibex fæmina*, a kind of wild Goat. **1607** TOPSELL *Foure-f. Beasts* 244 (*heading*) The Helvetian Alpian wilde or *Rocke-Goat. **1635** SWAN *Spec. M.* (1643) 475 There is another Goat called the Rock-goat, differing from the rest. **1731** MEDLEY *Kolben's Cape G. Hope* II. 116 The Rock-goat is as well known in the Cape countries as he is in Europe. **1811** PINKERTON *Mod. Geogr.* Switzerland 282 Among the animals peculiar to the Alps may be first named the ibex, or rock goat. **1820** J. CAMPBELL *Trav. S. Afr.* I. ii. 29 The rock-goat..had found its way to a place, which no human foot had ever yet trod. **1848** G. R. WATERHOUSE *Nat. Hist. Mamm.* II. 93 The *Rock Hare..is about equal in size to the Common Hare. **1954** G. DURRELL *Bafut Beagles* iii. 59 '*Rock hyrax.'.. 'Yes. How you de call um for Bafut?' 'Here we call um N'eer.' **1966** C. SWEENEY *Scurrying Bush* iii. 36 Although the rock hyrax is only about sixteen inches long and weighs little more than eight pounds when adult, it is not an animal to trifle with. **1835** *Penny Cycl.* III. 127/2 The *rock kangaroo (*Macropus rupestris*), remarkable for its bushy fox-like tail. **1846**, **1863** [see KANGAROO 2]. **1884** *Cassell's Fam. Mag.* Apr. 272/1 The rock-wallabies, or rock-kangaroos belong to these mountains. **1859–62** RICHARDSON, etc. *Mus. Nat. Hist.* II. 346/2 These shells are usually found fixed upon rocks on the shore, hence their name of *Rock limpets. **1937** *Discovery* May 137/2 The *Rock Lizard can be met with all over the [Nullarbor] plains. **1947** J. STEVENSON-HAMILTON *Wild Life S. Afr.* xxxv. 318 There are nine species of so-called Rock Lizards (*Agama*) known as koggelmannetjies in South Africa. **1884** GOODE, etc. *Nat. Hist. Aquatic Anim.* 780 The Spiny Lobster or *Rock Lobster—*Palinurus interruptus.* **1928** RUSSELL & YONGE *Seas* xiv. 316 The handsome Spiny or Rock Lobster or Crawfish..differs from the lobster in its larger size. **1953** *Sun* (Baltimore) 9 Sept. 10/7 The name of the South African crawfish was changed by law to 'rock lobster'. **1961** [see CRAWFISH *sb.* 1 b]. **1969** *N.Z. News* 17 Dec. 5/3 Under the [new] regulations crayfish are referred to as rock lobster. The change is necessary to promote the labelling of crayfish as rock lobster in marketing in overseas countries. **1974** *Times* 9 Dec. 12/4 A notice outside advertised baby rock lobster tails with two veg. **1607** TOPSELL *Four-footed Beasts* 386 They come sometimes to houses and to rocks; for which..it is called a House-marder and *Rock-marder. **1792** KERR *Anim. Kingd.* 234 *Rock Mouse,..*Mus saxatilis*... Inhabits the eastern parts of Siberia. **1898** *Nat. Sci.* June 411 From their habit of hugging the shore..these whales are known as '*rock-nosers'. **1716** *Petiveriana* I. 130 This resembles the Virginia *Rock-Oyster. *a* **1774** GOLDSM. *Nat. Hist.* (1776) VII. 51 The oysters..found sticking to rocks at the bottom of the sea, and usually called rock-oysters. **1852** MUNDY *Antipodes* (1857) 17 The small rock-oyster of New South Wales is excellent in its way, although inferior to the Carlingford. **1783** BARBUT *Vermes* 63, 10th Genus. The *Rock Piercer... The body is filiform. **1910** R. L. DITMARS *Reptiles of World* IV. 227 Another big serpent is the African *Rock Python. **1934** A. RUSSELL *Tramp-Royal in Wild Austral.* xxxviii. 251 We rode almost on top of a rock python one day... He was ten feet long. **1965** R. & D. MORRIS *Men & Snakes* i. 16 Bushmen will eat snakes when available and especially prize the large rock python. **1840** B. SHAW *Memorials S. Afr.* xii. 147 There were numerous traces of *rock rabbits. **1846** [see DASSY]. **1849** CRAIG s.v. *Rock*, *Rock-rabbit*, the Hyrax syriacus,..is a small rabbit-like animal, both in point of colour and size, but has no tail. **1878** J. H. BEADLE *Western Wilds* 457 The rock rabbits..ran from covert to covert with a peculiar low moaning cry. **1892** HAGGARD *Nada* 211 The sides of it were sheer, offering no foothold except to the rock-rabbits and the lizards. **1927** A. PHILIP *Painted Cliff* 69 Rock-rabbits shrilled, darting amongst the rubble. **1931**, **1952** [see DASSIE 1]. **1962** *Field, Horse & Rodeo* (Calgary) Nov. 15/3 THe Pika (or Rock Rabbit) spends most of the daylight hours cutting and gathering vegetation. **1972** J. McCLURE *Caterpillar Cop* iv. 46 Danny was going up and down those stairs like a rock rabbit. **1976** T. WALKER *Spatsizi* vii. 68 A rock rabbit had been busy storing dried leaves and grasses for winter. **1781** PENNANT *Hist. Quadrup.* II. 450 *Rock Rat, *Mus Saxatilis.* **1801** SHAW *Gen. Zool.* II. 72 The Mus Saxatilis or Rock Rat was first described by Dr. Pallas. **1964** E. P. WALKER et al. *Mammals of World* II. 1045/2 Rock rats are active beneath the snow in winter. **1970** W. D. L. RIDE *Guide Native Mammals Austral.* ix. 148 Adults of these rock-rats are easily recognized because they have thick tails. **1971** L. H. MATTHEWS *Life Mammals* II. vii. 216 The rock rat, *Aconæmys fuscus*, the only species of the genus, with short, hairy, but untufted tail is about the size of a common rat. **1976** *Nature* 24 June 639/2 Many surveys produce novelties; animals considered very rare or extinct are discovered in some numbers (for example..the rock rat, *Zyzomys woodwardi*). **1789** W. PATERSON *Narr. Four Journeys Country of Hottentots* 165 The Black, or *Rock Scorpion, is nearly as venomous as any of the serpent tribe. **1973** *Stand. Encycl. S. Afr.* IX. 544/2 The rock-scorpion, *Hadogenes*, is extraordinarily flattened, being adapted for living in narrow fissures between rocks. **1884** GOODE, etc. *Nat. Hist. Aquatic Anim.* 62 The Harbor Seal.. is also often termed Bay Seal,..and also *Rock Seal (*Steen-Kobbe*). *a* **1801** PULTENEY *View Writ. Linnæus* (1805) 229 *Rock-shell. Aperture terminating in a straight spout. **1819** TURTON *Conchol. Dict.* 87 The fishermen of the northern coasts of Ireland occasionally saw, what they called the great rock-shell. **1849** CRAIG s.v. *Rock*, In Conchology, *Rock-shells*, the common name of certain univalves, characterized by the long straight canal which terminates the mouths of their shells. **1877** *Encycl. Brit.* VI. 646/2 In the '*rock-slater', *Ligia*.., the embryo is bent upwards within the egg. **1777** PENNANT *Brit. Zool.* IV. 115 *Helix Lapicida*, *Rock Snail..: a land shell. Inhabits clefts of rocks. **1819** TURTON *Conchol. Dict.* 44 *Helix lapicida*, Rock Snail-shell. **1850** R. G. CUMMING *Hunter's Life S. Afr.* (1902) 119/1, I suddenly detected an enormous old *rock-snake stealing in beneath a mass of rock beside me. **1859** TENNENT *Ceylon* II. 127 A rock-snake, *python reticulatus*,..a beautiful specimen at least ten feet long. **1839** BEALE *Nat. Hist. Sperm Whale* 68 It was that species of sepia, which is called by whalers '*rock-squid'. **1852** E. F. KELAART *Prodr. Faunæ Zeylanicæ* 49 The common *Rock Squirrel. **1841** J. GOULD *Monograph Macropodidæ* I. pl. 5 The Great *Rock Wallaby..inhabits summits of sterile and rocky mountains. **1884** 'R. BOLDREWOOD' *Melb. Mem.* viii. 58 A light active chap, spinning over the stones like a rock-wallaby. **1819** WM. TURTON *Conchol. Dict.* 14 *Buccinum Lapillus*, *Rock Whelk. **1865** *Intellect. Obs.* 113 The *Rock-whistler (*Arctomys*). **1883** *Fish. Exhib. Catal.* 289 Baits, natural... These include ..*rockworms, prawns, 'red bait', small fish. **1963** R. P. DALES *Annelids* 14 Some relatives of the eunicid rockworms ..are surprisingly like earthworms. **1971** *Oxf. Bk. Invertebr.* 98 The eunicids (rock worms and palolos) form a large and varied family of rock-dwellers and mud-burrowers.

c. In names of birds, as **rock babbler**, a South African bird of the genus *Chætops*; **rock bunting** (see quot.); **rock-cock**, a bird of the genus *Rupicola*, a 'cock of the rock'; † **rock cormorant**, ? the shag; **rock crow**, = ROCK-THRUSH; **rock duck**, the harlequin duck, *Histrionicus histrionicus*; **rock fowl**, a bird that haunts rocks; **rock goose**, the kelp goose (KELP[1] 4); **rock grouse**, (*a*) = *rock ptarmigan*; (*b*) the ptarmigan (*Lagopus mutus*); **rock-hawk**, the merlin; **rock-hopper (penguin)**, a species of crested penguin (*Eudyptes chrysocome*); **rock lark**, = *rock pipit*; **rock manakin**, the crested manakin (see quots. and MANIKIN 3); **rock martin** (see quots.); † **rock martinet** (see MARTINET[1] 1, quot. 1544); **rock parakeet**, an Australian grass-parakeet (*Euphema petrophila*); **rock partridge**, (*a*) the white grouse or ptarmigan; (*b*) the Greek or Barbary partridge (PARTRIDGE B. 2); **rock pebbler** (see quot.); **rock pipit**, the sea-lark (*Anthus obscurus*) of the British Islands; **rock plover**, *local U.S.*, the purple sandpiper; **rock ptarmigan**, the American species, *Lagopus rupestris*; **rock sandpiper**, the purple sandpiper, *Erolia maritima*, or a similar bird, *E. ptilocnemis*, of the Pacific coast of North America; **rock shrike** (see quot.); **rock snipe**, = *rock sandpiper*; **rock sparrow**, a bird of the genus *Petronia*; **rock swallow**, a swallow that builds its nest upon a cliff, esp. *Cotile* or *Hirundo rupestris*; **rock swift**, the white-throated swift of N.W. America (*Panyptila saxatilis*); **rock warbler** (see quot. 1848); **rock wren**, (*a*) one of several wrens belonging to the genus *Salpinctes*, found in parts of western North America; (*b*) a New Zealand wren, *Xenicus gilviventris*.

1875-84 SHARPE *Layard's Birds S. Afr.* 217 *Chætops Aurantius*, Orange-breasted *Rock-Babbler. *Ibid.* 218 *Chætops Pycnopygius*, Damara Rock-Babbler. *Ibid.* 490 *Fringillaria Tahapisi*, *Rock Bunting. **1838** *Encycl. Metrop.* (1845) XXIV. 192/2 Guianan, or Orange *Rockcock. Rather larger than a Wood Pigeon. *a* **1682** SIR T. BROWNE *Norf. Birds* Wks. (Bohn) III. 315 The *rock cormorant.. breedeth in the rocks, in northern counties. **1785** PENNANT *Arct. Zool.* II. 252 *Rock crow... Breeds in crevices of rocks. **1704** *Churchill's Voy.* II. 185/2 This Country [the Cape]..abounds in..*Rock-ducks with yellow necks, Teal [etc.]. **1965** E. RICHARDSON *Living Island* 185 The handsomest duck I have seen..the male harlequin or rock-duck. **1902** CORNISH *Naturalist Thames* 150 Of the *rock-fowl, the puffins fly away to the Mediterranean. **1876** *Proc. Zool. Soc.* 369 It [*Bernicla antarctica*] lives exclusively on rocky parts of the sea-coast; hence the name '*Rock-Goose', given to it by sailors. **1785** PENNANT *Arct. Zool.* II. 312 *Rock Gr[ouse]... Never takes shelter in the woods, but sits on the rocks, or burrows in the snow. **1831** RICHARDSON in *Wilson's Amer. Ornith.* IV. 330 The rock grouse, in its manners and mode of living, resembles the willow grouse. **1862** C. A. JOHNS *Brit. Birds* Index, *Rock-Grouse*, the Ptarmigan. **1840** MACGILLIVRAY *Brit. Birds* III. 317 *Falco Æsalon*, the Merlin Falcon. Stone Falcon. *Rock Hawk. **1875** KIDDER *Nat. Hist. Kerguelen Isl.* I. 46 The whaler's epithet '*rock-hopper' is in this case particularly well applied, since they are the most agile of all penguins, skipping from rock to rock. *Ibid.* 9, I discovered a lot of nests, near a rookery of 'rock-hopper' penguins. **1802** MONTAGU *Ornith. Dict.* (1831) 427 We discovered these birds in great plenty on the coast of South Wales, where it was known by some of the natives by the name of *rock lark. **1888** SAXBY *Lads of Lunda* 259 I'll never kill a rock-lark while I live. **1783** LATHAM *Gen. Synop. Birds* II. II. 518 *Rock Manakin, *Pipra rupicola*,..inhabits various parts of Surinam, Cayenne, & Guiana, in rocky situations. **1852** TH. ROSS tr. *Humboldt's Trav.* II. xix. 210 The rock-manakin with gilded plumage (Pipra rupicola), one of the most beautiful birds of the tropics. **1842** *Penny Cycl.* XXIII. 363/1 The European species of this family are the Swift..; the *Rock-Martin [etc.]. **1883** NEWTON in *Encycl. Brit.* XV. 581/2 The Rock-Martin of Europe, *Hirundo* or *Biblis rupestris*. **1888** SCLATER & HUDSON *Argentine Ornith.* I. 30 *Petrochelidon pyrrhonota*, Red-backed Rock-martin. **1865** GOULD *Handbk. Birds Austral.* II. 76 *Rock-Parraket. **1787** LATHAM *Gen. Synop. Birds* Suppl. I. 217 This is called by the natives *Uscathachish*, by the English, *Rock-Partridge. **1893** E. H. BARKER *Wand. S. Waters* 267 The rock-partridge, or *bartavelle*, is also found, but is rare. **1898** MORRIS *Austral Engl.*, **Rock-Pebbler*, another name for the black-tailed Parrakeet. **1831** RENNIE *Montagu's Ornith. Dict.* 427 *Rock Pipit (*Anthus rupestris*). **1862** C. A. JOHNS *Brit. Birds* 175 The Rock Pipit is very similar in form and colour to the last species [i.e. the Meadow Pipit]. **1888** TRUMBULL *Names Birds* 182 It is the Rock-bird, *Rock-Plover, and Rock Snipe at Rowley and Salem, Mass. **1819** *Shaw's Gen. Zool.* XI. 290 *Rock Ptarmigan (*Lagopus rupestris*). **1872** COUES *N. Amer. Birds* 235 Rock Ptarmigan. Tail black,..with a black transocular stripe. **1862** C. A. JOHNS *Brit. Birds* Index, **Rock Sandpiper*, the Purple Sandpiper. **1903** E. COUES *Key to N. Amer. Birds* (ed. 5) II. 817 Feather-leg Sandpipers. Rock Sandpipers. **1961** R. T. PETERSON *Field Guide Western Birds* (ed. 2) 112 Rock Sandpiper... In winter, very similar to Purple Sandpiper of Atlantic. **1809** SHAW *Gen. Zool.* VII. 302 *Rock shrike, *Lanius infaustus*. **1888** *Rock snipe [see *rock-plover* above]. **1835** J. J. AUDUBON *Ornith. Biogr.* III. 558 Their marked predilection for rocky shores has caused them to be named 'Rock Snipes' by the gunners of our eastern coast. **1917** T. G. PEARSON *Birds Amer.* I. 232 Purple Sandpiper... Other Names.—Rock Sandpiper; Rock Snipe. **1879** NEWTON in *Encycl. Brit.* IX. 192 The Mountain-Finches..may be regarded as pointing first to the *Rock Sparrows (*Petronia*) and then to the true Sparrows (*Passer*). **1783** LATHAM *Gen. Synop. Birds* II. II. 569 *Hirundo rupestris*,..*Rock Sw[allow]. **1880** L. WALLACE *Ben-Hur* 7 Lark and chat and rock-swallow leaped to wing. **1874** COUES *Birds N.W.* 265 White-throated or *Rock Swift. **1848** GOULD *Birds Austr.* III. pl. 69 *Origma Rubricata*, *Rock-Warbler. **1864-5** WOOD *Homes without H.* xii. (1868) 215 The bird..is called indifferently the Rock Warbler, or the Cataract Bird. **1858** S. F. BAIRD *Birds Pacific Railway Routes* 357 *Rock Wren. .. High central plains through the Rocky mountains. **1869** [see *cactus wren*]. **1872** COUES *N. Amer. Birds* 85 Rock Wren. Brownish gray,..everywhere speckled with black and white dots. **1882** BULLER *Man. Birds N. Zeal.* 15 *Xenicus Gilviventris*, Rock-wren. **1946** D. C. PEATTIE *Road of Naturalist* iii. 39 The rock wrens and the canyon wrens.. watered the air with rapture. **1966** R. A. FALLA et al. *Field Guide Birds N.Z.* 194 Rock Wren... Habitat is distinctive, mainly open screes, moraines and fell-fields of mountains above the bushline. **1973** R. D. SYMONS *Where Wagon Led* I. v. 77 All around us rose the bubbling songs of the rock wrens.

d. In names of fishes, as **rock bass**, a name given to several American fishes, as the red-eye or goggle-eye (*Amboplites rupestris*), the striped bass, and black sea-bass; † **rock-beard**, some American fish; **rock beauty**, a small, dark brown and yellow, Caribbean reef fish, *Holacanthus tricolor*; **rock blackfish** (see quot.); **rock codling**, a North American species of cod; **rock cook**, a species of wrasse; **rock eel**, (*a*) (see quot. 1876); (*b*) = *rock salmon* (*c*); **rock flounder** (see quot. 1867); **rock goby**, the black goby; **rock grenadier** (see quot.); **rock gurnard**, (*a*) the French gurnard; (*b*) an Australian fish of the genus *Centropogon*; **rock hind** (see quot. 1867); **rock ling**, an Australian sea-fish (see quot.); **rock native** (see NATIVE *sb.* 8 b); **rock perch**, † (*a*) some American fish; (*b*) an Australian coral-fish; **rock podler**, the whiting pollack; **rock pouter**, = POUTER *sb.*[1] 3; † **rock ray**, the thornback; **rock salmon**, (*a*) the coalfish; (*b*) an American fish of the genus *Seriola*; (*c*) a commercial name for the catfish, *Anarhichas lupus*, or a dogfish, *Scyliorhinus stellaris* or *S. caniculus*; cf. HUSS; **rock shark**, **sparus** (see quots.); **rock skipper**, a small marine fish belonging to the family Gobiidæ, able to survive out of water for a limited time; **rock sole**, a flatfish, *Lepidopsetta bilineata*, found in the Pacific Ocean off the western coast of North America; **rock sturgeon**, the American lake-sturgeon, *Acipenser fulvescens*; **rock-sucker**, the sea-lamprey; **rock toadfish**, **trout**, **whiting** (see quots.).

? **1811** LESUEUR *Hist. Poissons* III. 88 Le centrarchus..sous le nom anglais de '*rock basse'. **1892** *Daily News* 14 July 5/5 Rock and strawberry bass abound in the Delaware and Schuykill Rivers after the successful planting of four years ago. *c* **1702** in *Dampier's Voy.* (1729) III. 411 The *Rock-beard. Tis fat and good Meat, easily skinn'd. **1892** T. D. A. COCKERELL in *Bull. Inst. Jamaica* I. 9/1 *Rock Beauty. Head, anterior part of the trunk, caudal and margins of the soft dorsal and anal fins yellow: the remainder brownish-black. **1959** R. P. L. STRAUGHAN *Salt-Water Aquarium in Home* iv. 85 Rock Beauties..need plenty of aeration. **1965** MRS. L. B. JOHNSON *White House Diary* 3 June (1970) 281 Rock beauties, yellow about half-way back and yellow tails, and the rest of them brown. **1977** D. J. COFFEY *Encycl. Aquarium Fish* 141/1 Rock Beauty... From the Caribbean, this yellow fish has a black patch that expands with age. **1884** GOODE, etc. *Nat. Hist. Aquatic Anim.* 410 There is a small species (*Serranus trifurcus*) resembling the Sea Bass which has been found only in the vicinity of Charleston.., where it is called the *Rock Black fish. **1836** J. RICHARDSON *Fauna Bor. Amer.* III. Fishes 246 The *rock codling.., which they take near Cape Isabella. **1859-62** RICHARDSON, etc. *Mus. Nat. Hist.* II. 118/2 The British species are..the Sea-wife (*Acantholabrus yarrellii*); the *Rock-cook (*Acantholabrus exoletus*). **1876** GOODE *Fishes Bermudas* 29 Their habits closely resembling those of the '*Rock-eel' (*Murænoides mucronatus*). **1969** A. WHEELER *Fishes Brit. Isles & N.-W. Europe* 46/1 The dogfish..is sold as rock eel and rock salmon. **1867** SMYTH *Sailor's Word-bk.*, *Craig-flook*, the smear-dab, or *rock-flounder. **1863** COUCH *Brit. Fishes* II. 153 An example..which differed..greatly in appearance from what is usual with the *Rock Goby. **1836** RICHARDSON *Fauna Bor. Amer.* III. 254 *Macrourus rupestris*, *Rock Grenadier. **1836** YARRELL *Brit. Fishes* I. 41 French Gurnard, and *Rock gurnard. **1859-62** RICHARDSON, etc. *Mus. Nat. Hist.* II. 121/1 The British species are—the Red Gurnard,..or Gaverick (*Trigla cuculus*); the Rock Gurnard (*Tr. lineata*). **1867** SMYTH *Sailor's Word-bk.*, **Rock-Hind*, a large fish of tropical regions, *Serranus catus*. **1883** *Fish. Exhib. Catal.* (ed. 4) 179 Flying Fish and Jack Fish are good eating, and likewise the Rock Hind. **1898** MORRIS *Austral Engl.* 392/1 The Australian *Rock-Ling is *Genypterus australis*,..family *Ophidiidæ*. *c* **1702** in *Dampier's Voy.* (1729) III. 415 The *Rock-Pearch. **1898** MORRIS *Austral Engl.*, *Rock-Perch*, the name given in Melbourne to the.. Coral-fishes. It is not a true Perch. **1769** J. WALLIS *Nat. Hist. Northumb.* I. 384 Whiting-Pollack.., *Rock Podler. **1889** *Pall Mall G.* 16 Nov. 6/3 Small haddocks and *rock pouters—cheap, common fish—are often..sold at a high price for whiting. **1611** COTGR., *Raye bouclée*, the *Rock-Ray; the Ray whose backe is set thicke with little knurles, not vnlike vnto buckles. **1881** DAY *Fishes Gt. Brit.* I. 295 *Gadus virens*,..locally..*rock-salmon, saithe. **1882** *Bulletin U.S. Fish Commission* I. 42 The 'Rock Salmon' of Pensacola. **1931** J. R. NORMAN *Hist. Fishes* xix. 385 It has been found convenient to market this perfectly wholesome fish [*sc.* cat-fish] under a more pleasing name, and..it is sold as 'Rock Salmon'. **1957** R. CAMPBELL *Portugal* iv. 65 In the [London] fried-fish shops..'rock salmon'..is the trade name for shark. **1958** *Times* 18 July 7/1 Rock salmon is in fact usually catfish. **1963** [see HUSS *sb.*]. **1969** A. WHEELER *Fishes Brit. Isles & N.-W. Europe* 452/2 It [*sc.* the catfish] is sold with the related species under the names rock salmon and rockfish. **1977** *Times* 8 Feb. 9/4 Rock salmon has had its name changed..by the trades description act, and is now called Huss. **1804** SHAW *Gen. Zool.* V. 336 *Rock shark, *Squalus stellaris*... Native of the European seas. **1905** D. S. JORDAN *Guide to Study of Fishes* II. xxix. 510 The *rock-skippers..are herbivorous, with serrated teeth set loosely in their jaws. These live in rock-pools of the tropics and leap from rock to rock. **1966** C. SWEENEY *Scurrying Bush* xi. 154 There are perhaps a hundred or more kinds of rock skippers in tropical oceans, all able to shuffle and wriggle along on spray-soaked rocks. The kind that I found was as goggle-eyed as any and..resembled a small seal with a frog's head, the flipper-like pectoral fins supporting the front of the body. **1965** A. J. MCCLANE *Stand. Fishing Encycl.* 730/2 *Rock sole are only occasionally taken by hook and line. **1971** *Islander* (Victoria, B.C.) 21 Mar. 2/3, I have taken in recent years..rock sole and sand sole. **1803** SHAW *Gen. Zool.* IV. 448 *Rock Sparus, *Sparus Rupestris*... Native of the Northern seas, frequenting the shores. **1877** C. HALLOCK *Sportsman's Gazetteer* I. 329 *Rock Sturgeon.—*Acipenser rubicundus*. This is the sturgeon of the great lakes. **1961** E. S. HERALD *Living Fishes of World* 67/2 The eastern American lake or rock sturgeon has been known to reach a weight of 300 pounds. **1884** GOODE, etc. *Nat. Hist. Aquatic Anim.* 258 There is also..a large, brilliantly colored form [of sculpin], known as the 'Sea raven', '*Rock Toad-fish', or 'Deep-water Sculpin'. **1844-8** RICHARDSON *Ichthyol.* 77/1 *Galaxias alepidotus*... New Zealand. Named..'*Rock-trout' by Cook's sailors. **1876** GOODE *Anim. Res. U.S.* 65 Rock trout (*Chirus constellatus*). **1883** E. P. RAMSAY *Food Fishes N.S.W.* 25 *Odax semifasciatus*, known locally as the '*rock-whiting', 'stranger,' &c.

e. In names of plants, as **rock alyssum**, the gold-dust (*Alyssum saxatile*); **rock beauty**, an Alpine and Pyrenæan plant (*Draba* or *Petrocallis pyrenaica*) with lilac flowers; **rock brake(s)**, the parsley fern; **rock button-flower**, a tropical flower of the genus *Gomphia*; **rock candytuft** (see quot.); **rock cantaloup**, a species of melon; **rock chestnut-oak**, a North American species of oak-tree (*Quercus prinus*); **rock cist**, **cistus**, = ROCK-ROSE; **rock club-moss** (see quot.); **rock elm**, one of several North American elms, esp. *Ulmus thomasii* or its timber; † **rock germander**, a species of veronica; **rock hair** (see quot. 1861); † **rock herb** (?); **rock kelp**, = ROCK-WEED; **rock knotweed**, various species of *Polygonum*; **rock lily**, (*a*) a cryptogamous plant of tropical America; (*b*) an Australian orchid (*Dendrobium speciosum*); **rock lychnis**, a lychnis of the sub-genus *Viscaria*; **rock madwort**, = *rock alyssum*; **rock maple**, the sugar maple, *Acer saccharum*, or its timber; **rock melon** = CANTALOUP; **rock mint** (see MINT *sb.*[2] 2); **rock moss**, (*a*) the orchil lichen; (*b*) cudbear; **rock oak**, = *rock chestnut-oak*; **rock onion** (see ONION *sb.* 2); **rock parsley** (see quots. and PARSLEY 2); **rock pine** (see quot.); † **rock rampion**, a species of campanula, *Campanula pyramidalis*; † **rock sage** (see quot.); **rock samphire**, (*a*) common samphire or sea-fennel; (*b*) marsh samphire or glasswort; **rock savory** (see quot.); **rock scorpion-grass**, **sedge**, **silk**, **speedwell**, **stone-crop** (see quots. and these names); **rock tripe** (see quot.).

1870 W. ROBINSON *Alpine Flowers for Eng. Gardens* II. 272 *Petrocallis Pyrenaica*—Beauty of the Rocks... A '*rock beauty!' as everybody must confess who sees its fresh light-green tufts, not more than an inch high, and cushioned snugly amidst the broken rocks. **1930** H. CORREVON *Rock Garden & Alpine Plants* xii. 249 *D*[*raba*] (*Petrocallis*) *pyrenaica*. Rock Beauty. **1964** A. N. GRIFFITH *Collins Guide to Alpines* 205 This very small genus [sc. *Petrocallis*] provides us with one charming little plant which well deserves its name of Rock Beauty. **1846-50** A. WOOD *Class-bk. Bot.* 632 *Pteris atropurpurea*, *Rock Brake. **1859** T. MOORE *Brit. Ferns* (1864) 33 The Rock Brakes is a mountain Fern, choosing to grow in stony situations. It is comparatively rare and local. *c* **1711** PETIVER *Gazophyl.* IX. §90 *Rock Button-Flower..growing luxuriently wild, about that Fertile Promontory the Cape of Good Hope. **1822** *Hortus Anglicus* II. 149 *Iberis Saxatilis*, *Rock Candy Tuft. **1786** ABERCROMBIE *Arr.* in *Gard. Assist.* p. vii, *Melons*, ..*Rock Cantaleupe, Black rock Cantaleupe. **1813** VANCOUVER *Agric. Devon* 7 From two of these hills, which were occupied by three plants each, 6½ brace..of the rock-cantelope melon, were cut. **1810** F. A. MICHAUX *Hist. Arbres Forestiers de l'Amérique Septentrionale* I. 23 *Rock chestnut oak..seul nom donné à cette espèce dans les Etats de New-York et de Vermont. **1832** D. J. BROWNE *Sylva Amer.* 285 The rock chestnut oak is sometimes 3 feet in diameter, and more than 60 feet high. **1897** G. B. SUDWORTH *Nomencl. Arborescent Flora U.S.* 156 Chestnut Oak..[also called] Rock Chestnut Oak. **1866** *Treas. Bot.* 987/2 *Rockcist, *Helianthemum*. **1872** OLIVER *Elem. Bot.* II. 141 Many species of Rockcist are commonly cultivated in shrubberies and on rock-work. **1836** FURNESS *Astrologer* I. 14 Where the *rock-cistus scents the vernal morn. **1873** [see CISTUS]. **1771** J. R. FORSTER *Flora Amer. Septentr.* 48 *Lycopodium rupestre*, *rock Club-moss. **1830** *Trans. Lit. & Hist. Soc. Quebec* III. 84 The timber of this variety..is known by the name of *Rock Elm. **1843** HOLTZAPFFEL *Turning* I. 85 Rock Elm..is extensively used for boat-building. **1853** MOODIE *Life Clearings* 26 Its rocky banks.. are fringed with..rock-elm, that queen of the Canadian forest. **1955** *Bush News* (Port Arthur, Ontario) Feb. 3/5 Southern Ontario..is sending..rock elm timbers to Britain. **1972** *Handbk. Hardwoods* (Forest Prod. Res. Lab.) (ed. 2) 73 Rock elm may be distinguished from other commercial elms by the small size and sparse distribution of its early wood pores. **1760** J. LEE *Introd. Bot.* App. 324 *Rock Germander, *Veronica*. **1756** *Phil. Trans.* XLIX. 858 *Muscus corallinus* *saxatilis*,..*Rock Hair. **1759** B. STILLINGFL. *Misc. Tracts* (1791) 180 The *lichen jubatus*, or rock-hair in exulcerations of the skin. **1861** H. MACMILLAN *Footnotes fr. Nature* 94 A very curious lichen called rock-hair (*Alectoria jubata*), which covers with its beard-like tufts the trunks of almost every tree. **1694** *Acc. Sev. Late Voy.* (1711) 73 The Leaves of the great *Rock Herb, are very like unto a Man's Tongue. **1846** LINDLEY *Veget. Kingd.* 70 So also the *rock-lily, a name sometimes given to *Selaginella convoluta*. **1879** H. N. MOSELEY *Naturalist on Challenger* 270 (N.S.W.), A luxuriant vegetation, with huge masses of Stagshorn Fern (*Platycerium*) and 'rock-lilies' (orchids). **1753** CHAMBERS *Cycl. Suppl.* s.v. *Lychnis*, The dwarf juniper leaved *rock lychnis. **1822** *Hortus Anglicus* II. 150, 2. *Alyssum Saxatile*, *Rock Mad Wort, or Yellow Alyssum. **1775** S. THAYER *Jrnl.* 30 Sept. in *Rhode Island Hist. Soc. Coll.* (1867) VI. 4 The timber [is] large and of various kinds, such as Pine, Oak, Hemlock and *Rock Maple. **1809** A. HENRY *Trav.* 68 A ridge..covered with the rock or sugar maple, or sugar-wood. **1866** WHITTIER *Prose Wks.* (1889) I. 206 Two noble rock-maples arched over with their dense foliage the little red gate. **1949** 'J. NELSON' *Backwoods Teacher* xxvi. 265 Hi Slocum..had tapped a few rock maples he knew about—though this is not really maple syrup country. **1977** *New Yorker* 27 June 30/3, I..fell over a rock-maple chair and skinned my knee. **1980** *Early Music Gaz.* July 12/1 (Advt.), Made of impregnated rock maple and finished in dark color. **1871** V. LUSH *Jrnl.* 16 Mar. (1975) 105 Blanche bought 8 fine *rock melons for 4/0... Blanche has reduced 6 of them into jam. **1882** [see *pie-melon*]. **1929** [see CANTALOUP]. **1972** J. S. GUNN in G. W. Turner *Good Austral. Eng.* iii. 60 Is there any difference at all between..rock melon/cantaloup and many other pairs? **1793–8** NEMNICH *Polygl.-Lex.* v. 957 *Rock moss, *Lichen roccella*. **1839** URE *Dict. Arts* 377 Most of which lichens are imported from Sweden and Norway, under the name of rock moss. **1887** MOLONEY *Forestry W. Afr.* 527 Orchella weed, dyer's weed, rock moss. **1699** *Public Rec. Colony Connecticut* (1868) IV. 304 Running eastward three hundred rod to a *rock-oak tree markt. **1773** *Connect. Col. Rec.* (1887) XIV. 172 Resolved..that the rock-oak aforesaid with stones about it is the southwest corner of Midletown. **1852** C. MORFIT *Tanning & Currying* (1853) 99 It is known as the rock oak, from the situations in which it is found. **1949** COLLINGWOOD & BRUSH *Knowing your Trees* 224 Sometimes this tree is called rock oak or mountain oak because it grows on high, rocky slopes. **1611** COTGR., *Persil de Roc*,..*Rocke Parseley, stone Parseley. **1744** J. WILSON *Synop. Brit. Pl.* 72 *Peucedanum*, Rock Parsley. **1859** MISS PRATT *Brit. Grasses* 168 Curled Rock-brake, Mountain Parsley, or Rock Parsley. **1889** MAIDEN *Useful Native Pl.* 546 *Frenela robusta*..is known as '*Rock Pine' in Western New South Wales. **1688** HOLME *Armoury* II. 67/2 The *Rock Rampions, or the Steeple Bell-flower, the leaves grow in a bunch like Primroses, the Bells by multitudes hanging ..one above another Pyramidically to the top..and a pointel in the middle. **1562** TURNER *Herbal* II. 135 Thys kinde [of sideritis]..may be called in English Yronwurt or *Rock Sage. **1597** GERARDE *Herbal* 427 *Rocke Sampier hath many fat and thicke leaues. **1744** J. WILSON *Synop. Brit. Pl.* 13 Salt-wort is used for a pickle at Newcastle upon Tyne, where they call it Rock-sampire. **1802–3** tr. *Pallas' Trav.* II. 449 *Crithmum*, the genuine rock-samphire of the English. **1877** *Holderness Gloss.*, *Rock-semper*,..rock samphire. A favourite dish with those living on the banks of the Humber. **1822** *Hortus Anglicus* II. 96 *Satureia Rupestris*, *Rock Savory. **1855** MISS PRATT *Flower. Pl.* IV. 47 *Rock Scorpion-grass... This beautiful species is a mountain plant. **1859** —— *Brit. Grasses* 25 *Rock Sedge,..a very rare plant, from 3–6 inches high. **1694** *Acc. Sev. Late Voy.* IV. 74 The Herb was like Dodder, Wherefore it may be call'd Water or *Rock Silk. **1855** MISS PRATT *Flower. Pl.* IV. 91 Blue *Rock Speedwell..is a mountain flower. **1882** *Garden* 22 July 60/1 All the Rock Speedwells with which I am acquainted are beautiful. **1802** WILLICH *Domest. Encycl.* IV. 143 The *rupestre*, or *Rock Stone-crop,..differs from the preceding species [i.e. yellow stone-crop] only in its smaller flowers. **1854** MAYNE REID *Young Voyageurs* 384 *Rock-tripe..was a black, hard crumply substance that nearly covered the surface of the rock, and was evidently of a vegetable nature. **1866** *Treas. Bot.* 1172/2 *Tripe de Roche*. This name, or that of Rock Tripe, is given in North America, in consequence of the blistered thallus, to several species of lichens belonging to *Gyrophora* and *Umbilicaria*, but especially to the latter. **1907** *St. Nicholas* July 847/1 'Rock-tripe', another lichen, has been eaten in the arctic regions in times of famine. **1952** F. MOWAT *People of Deer* 37 Sometimes she scrabbled through the drifts on hilltops and found..a handfull of rock-tripe, a kind of moss.

rock (rɒk), *sb.*[2] Forms: 4, 6 roc, 5–6 rok(k, 6– rock; 4–5 rokke, 4–7 rocke. [Corresponds to MDu. *rocke* (Du. *rok*), also later *rocken* (Du. *rokken*), MLG. *rocken*, OHG. *rocco*, *ro(c)cho* (MHG. *rocke*, *roche*, G. *rocken*), ON. *rokkr* (Icel. *rokkur*, Norw. *rokk*, Sw. *rock*, Da. *rok*). It is not clear whether the word is native English, or a later adoption from the Continent. The Ital. *rocca*, Sp. *rueca*, Pg. *roca* are supposed to be of Teutonic origin.]

1. A distaff. Now *arch.* or *Hist.*

c **1310** *Northern Poem* in *Rel. Ant.* VII. 146 Hic am an ald quyne and a lam;..Wit my roc y me fede. *c* **1340** *Nominale* (Skeat) 535 *Conoil, trahul, et ramoun*, Rokke, reel, and besme. **1387** TREVISA *Higden* (Rolls) III. 33 Sardanapallus ..was founde..drawenge purpulle of a rocke. *c* **1425** WYNTOUN *Cron.* III. v. 721 His oysse was mare wiþe rok to spyn þan landis to þe crowne to wyn. *c* **1440** *Alph. Tales* 290 He made his doghters to be clothe-makers, & for to lere at spyn on þe rokk. **1519** HORMAN *Vulg.* 237 b, A rocke or a distaffe lade with flexe or wolle. **1553** T. WILSON *Rhet.* 80 b, When wilt thou come to my house, swete wenche, with thy rocke and thy spindle? **1607** BEN JONSON *Entertainm. at Theobalds* 32 The three Parcæ,..the one holding the rock, the other the spindle, and the third the sheeres. *a* **1687** H. MORE *Cont. Remark. Stories* (1689) 424 Once as Alice sat spinning, the Rock or Distaff leapt several times out of the wheel. **1725** RAMSAY *Gentle Sheph.* IV. i, Speak that again, and trembling dread my rock. **1776** ADAM SMITH *W.N.* I. xi. (1869) I. 260 The exchange of the rock and spindle for the spinning-wheel was the first capital improvement. **1825** J. NICHOLSON *Operat. Mechanic* 405 The flax, rendered straight and smooth by hackling, is wrapped loosely round the rock, from which it is gradually drawn by the left hand. **1851** *Art Jrnl. Illustr. Catal.* I **/2 The operation of spinning is carried on by drawing out the fibre from the rock, and supplying it regularly to the fly. **1870** MORRIS *Earthly Par.* III. IV. 41 Coarse and brown The thread was that her rock gave forth.

fig. **1737** E. ERSKINE *Serm.* Wks. 1871 II. 241 It is easy for God to give wicked men another tow in their rock than to molest the Lord's people. **1826** SCOTT *Jrnl.* 9 Feb., Perhaps she has no tow on her rock.

2. A distaff together with the wool or flax attached to it; the quantity of wool or flax placed on a distaff for spinning.

15.. *Wyfe of Auchtermuchty* viii, Than hame he ran to an rok of tow, And he satt doun to say the spynning. **1615** CHAPMAN *Odyssey* VI. 77 Her mother..at [the] fire, who had to spin A rock, whose tincture with sea-purple shin'd. **1648** HEXHAM II, *Een Rocke, ofte rocksel*, a Rock of yarne, or the yarne hanging on the Rock. **1735** in Heslop *Northumbld. Gloss.* s.v., Now it will be twelve o'clock And more; for I've spun off my rock. **1768** A. ROSS *Songs, Rock & Wee Pickle Tow* i, She louted her down, an' her rock took a low. **1827** CARLYLE *Germ. Rom.* I. 100 She had just spun off a rock of flax. **1856** [see 3]. **1894** HESLOP *Northumbld. Gloss.* s.v., To 'spin off a rock'—to finish off the quantity of material on the rock.

†**b.** *fig.* (See quot. and ROCKING *sb.*) *Obs.*

1793 *Stat. Acc. Scotland, Muirkirk* VII. 613 When one neighbour says to another,..'I am coming over with my rock,' he means no more than to tell him that he intends soon to spend an evening with him.

3. *attrib.* and *Comb.*, as ***rock-spun*** adj.; **rock-guards**, *dial.*, young men escorting girls to or from a rocking; **rock-stick**, *dial.*, = sense 1.

1769 *Dubl. Mercury* 16–19 Sept. 2/2 Superfine rockspun and common poplins. **1807** J. STAGG *Poems* 64 Frae house to house the rock gairds went. **1856** P. THOMPSON *Hist. Boston* 721 *Rock*, a portion of flax wrapped round a stick called the rock-stick, attached to a spinning-wheel.

b. Rock Day, Monday (see quots. 1841).

1589 WARNER *Alb. Eng.* V. xxiv. 108 Rock, & plow Mondaies gams sal gang, with Saint-feast & Kirk-sights. **1602–13** [see HOCKEY[1] 2]. **1838** SIR H. NICOLAS *Chronol.* (ed. 2) 169 Rock Day, or St. Distaff's day, the day after Twelfth day, *i.e.* Jan. 7. **1841** HAMPSON *Medii Aevi Cal.* I. 138 The day after Twelfth Day, was called Rock Day,..because women on that day resumed their spinning, which had been interrupted by the sports of Christmas. *Ibid.* 139 The Monday following Twelfth day, was for the same reason, denominated Rock Monday.

rock (rɒk), *sb.*[3] [f. ROCK *v.*[1]] **1. a.** The action of the vb. ROCK[1]; a movement or swaying to and fro, or a spell of this.

1823 CHALMERS *Mem.* (1851) III. 4, I dislike the idea of him getting such a rock upon the occasion [of a voyage]. **1876** SMILES *Sc. Natur.* iv. 61 Giving the cradle a final and heavy rock, he left the house. **1891** KIPLING *Light that Failed* xv. (1900) 284 Dick adjusted himself comfortably to the rock and pitch of the [camel's] pace.

b. Phr. ***rock of eye*** = *rack of (the) eye* s.v. RACK *sb.*[1] 4 f.

1890 BARRÈRE & LELAND *Dict. Slang* II. 183/2 *Rock of eye and rule of thumb* (tailors), refers to doing anything which requires scientific treatment by guesswork. **1957** N. SQUIRE *Theory of Bidding* xlii. 216 Honour-tricks will be counted at their normal value as in the Table of Honour-tricks, but with additions found by rock-of-eye.

2. orig. *U.S.* **a.** Musical rhythm characterized by a strong beat.

1946 MEZZROW & WOLFE *Really Blues* vii. 90 The Cotton Pickers..came on with a steady rock that was really groovy. **1952** H. SINCLAIR *Music out of Dixie* vi. 245 He played eight bars of a new introduction he had thought up and..[said] 'I want that steady rock.' **1952** R. A. WATERMAN in S. Tax *Acculturation in Americas* 217 Musical terms like 'rock' and 'swing' express ideas of rhythm foreign to European folk tradition, and stem from African concepts. **1970** P. OLIVER *Savannah Syncopators* 36 Jazz developed a different kind of rhythmic feeling with a lifting movement between adjacent beats which the jazz musician identifies as 'rock' or 'swing'.

b. = ROCK AND ROLL. Now freq. used to encompass most modern popular music with a rocking or swinging beat. Also the last element in *Combs.*, as ***acid rock***, ***folk rock***, etc.; see *hard rock* (*c*) s.v. HARD *a.* 23 a, PUNK ROCK, *raga rock* s.v. RAGA 2.

1957 *Beat* Sept. 7/1 'It's the answer to Rock,' said one and all... But a new sound package of diluted Rock, Hill-Billy tunes and ersatz Blues assails our ears. **1959** *Daily Mail* 17 Feb. 4/4 *Yellow Dog Blues* played in basic style by Joe Darensbourg's band..unexpectedly popped up among the rock. **1960** M. SPARK *Ballad of Peckham Rye* (1964) iv. 58 Findlater's rooms were not given to rowdy rock but concentrated instead upon a more cultivated jive, cha-cha, and variants. **1963** J. T. STORY *Something for Nothing* v. 166 'It's only folk singing,' Albert told him. 'Well, it makes a change from all this old rock,' said Sid. **1965** *Time* 17 Sept. 102/2 Folk rock owes its origins to Bob Dylan, 24, folk music's most celebrated contemporary composer. **1968** *National Observer* (U.S.) 3 Nov. 24 It has been clear for some time that 'rock' is getting longer, more sophisticated, more ambitious, restless with chordal limitations and the three-minute format. **1969** *Britannica Bk. of Year* (U.S.) 799/1 *Acid rock*, rock 'n' roll songs whose titles or lyrics make cryptic reference to drugs. **1969** *Rolling Stone* 28 June 38/4 (Advt.), Two guitarists needed immediately... Booked for TV show in a few mos. Have material, underground & acidrock. **1972** *Saturday Night* (Toronto) Sept. 42/2 Like light shows, psychedelic posters and acid rock, it seems to have emerged first in California. **1976** *New Statesman* 17 Dec. 884/1 The whole of rock..had grown away from its roots, absorbing the influences of poetry, folk and protest music, and in the Sixties becoming central to the internal communications of a whole generation.

c. *attrib.* and *Comb.*, as ***rock album***, ***artist***, ***band***, ***beat***, ***club***, ***critic***, ***criticism***, ***culture***, ***fan***, ***festival***, ***group***, ***guitarist***, ***history***, ***idiom***, ***lyric***, ***movement***, ***movie***, ***music***, ***musical***, ***musician***, ***number***, ***opera***, ***press***, ***record***, ***show***, ***singer***, ***singing***, ***song***, ***star***, ***thing***; also ***rock-dominated***, ***-tinged*** adjs.

1979 *Yale Alumni Mag.* Apr. 30/3 Many sociable Soviets turned out to be dealers on the thriving Soviet black market ..interested primarily in acquiring American blue jeans.., *rock albums, dollars, or chewing gum. **1973** *Black World* Nov. 45/2 Many *rock and soul *artists have retained their interest in..gospel music. **1968** *Listener* 13 June 774/1 There was a *rock band that whooped it up all the louder, to drown the inevitable news. **1978** G. VIDAL *Kalki* vi. 154 A rock band deafened us. **1969** *Listener* 20 Feb. 251/1 They.. claim to have brought 'the *rock beat, the *now* sound, to the American Musical Theatre'. **1972** *Jazz & Blues* Sept. 4/2 A slashing rock beat. **1965** M. MORSE *Unattached* v. 177 A '*rock' club was started for younger teenagers. **1977** *Rolling Stone* 13 Jan. 8/3 If *rock critics recognize and understand this as a problem, why don't they do something about it? **1977** *N.Y. Rev. Bks.* 14 Apr. 40/4 Mark Miller's 'review'.. of recent *rock criticism seriously distorts its subject. **1967** *Economist* 8 Apr. 144/1 This is politics fashioned for the young: 'the *rock culture', it is being called. **1977** *Rolling Stone* 24 Mar., His full-blown, upper-register style is ingeniously contrasted with Walden's simple, melodic, *rock-dominated charts. **1961** *Times* 12 Aug. 7/6 More intelligent than the majority of '*rock' fans. **1968** *Rolling Stone* 12 Oct. 1/3 'The best freaking scene ever,' said one musician. The Sky River *Rock Festival and Lighter Than Air Show was not dampened by the rain that fell over Labor Day weekend. **1971** M. SMITH *Gypsy in Amber* xix. 144 I've never seen a rock festival. **1967** *Listener* 14 Sept. 350/2 *Rock groups..concentrated on achieving the authentic and personal expression. **1977** *It* May 10/1 Perhaps there are also rock groups who would be prepared to perform at benefit concerts. **1977** *Gay News* 24 Mar. 28/2 His cohorts perform well too especially Ray Russell, even if he is inclined to go in for circular solos, just like a *rock guitarist. **1976** *New Statesman* 17 Dec. 884/2 It is this concern with *rock history which distinguishes them from others who have called for a return to the basic virtues of good ole rock-'n'roll. **1976** *Gramophone* Dec. 952/2 The Amazing Rhythm Aces, a band from Tennessee..successfully combine country, rockabilly, swing and nostalgia into the *rock idiom. **1976** *Listener* 18 Nov. 645/2 Most *rock lyrics are straight melodramas. **1975** *Ibid.* 18 Sept. 370/2 The *rock movement saw our present crisis coming and died of shock. **1971** *It* 4–18 Nov. 19/1 The financial success of cheap *rock movies. **1967** *Listener* 23 Nov. 681/3 Is there an analogy between films and *rock music? **1978** *Hi-Fi News* Sept. 7 Popular and rock music benefit from this performance. **1969** L. ROXON *Rock Encycl.* 420 By the end of 1968, in spite of all the talk about rock and the new music, the big *rock musical had still to be done. **1977** F. WELDON in *Winter's Tales 23* 192 Brian offers..Hugo a part in a new rock musical going on in the West End. **1968** *Listener* 4 July 18/1 *Rock musicians can now sing anything that can be said by traditional forms of creative expression, and more besides. **1969** L. ROXON *Rock Encycl.* 42 There is not a rock musician working today who has not consciously or unconsciously borrowed from his [*sc.* Chuck Berry's] sound. **1957** *Sat. Rev.* (U.S.) 5 Oct. 6 You feel it in a beat—in jazz—real cool jazz or a good gutty *rock number. **1969** *Newsweek* 9 June 95 It was almost inevitable that the British group The Who should write the first *rock opera. **1979** *Newsday* 31 Dec. 26 Francis Coppola's dazzlingly beautiful, nightmarish Vietnam combat adventure, staged like a psychedelic rock opera, is a provocative drama flawed by a murky ending. **1977** *Zigzag* Aug. 6/2 He's one of the only *rock press geezers worth reading. **1977** *Chainsaw* Sept./Oct. 7/1 The national weekly rock press do have articles on new-wave groups. **1971** B. MALAMUD *Tenants* 45 They danced to some *rock records Willie had brought along in a paper bag. **1960** *New Left Rev.* May–June 33/1 He met Mr. Parnes at a Liverpool *rock show. **1959** *Punch* 10 June 788/2 Richard, like most *rock singers, dances from the knees in a style borrowed from African warriors. **1973** J. JONES *Touch of Danger* xxvii. 164, I met this boy and dropped out with him. He wanted to be a rock singer. **1977** *Rolling Stone* 30 June 25/1 One good reason Elliman wants to remain with Clapton is that his band serves as a fine outlet for her *rock singing. **1960** *Times* 26 Feb. 16/4 This song conforms to the pattern of the teenagers' acceptance to-day. It is a *rock song with a rock gimmick. **1976** *New Yorker* 17 May 125/2 A *rock star with a limp feather boa draped around her shoulders. **1978** G. VIDAL *Kalki* vi. 153 Deafening was what H.V.W. would call the din from the rock stars' dressing rooms where electric guitars whined. **1959** C. MACINNES *Absolute Beginners* 56 The days when the *Rock thing first broke. **1977** *Rolling Stone* 7 Apr. 26/2 His first solo album, *Solid*, a fine mixture of love ballads with jazz- and *rock-tinged soul, has been selling short of hit status.

†**rock**, *sb.*[4] *Obs.*[−1] Some species of dog.

1719 D'URFEY *Pills* (1872) II. 330 With deep mouth'd Jowlers too, and Rocks.

rock, obs. form of ROC, ROKE *sb.*[1]

rock (rɒk), *v.*[1] Forms: 1 roccian, 3, 5 rocken, 5 rokken; 4 rocky, rokky, 4–5 rokk(e, 4–7 rocke, 5 roke, 5–6 *Sc.* rok, 6– rock. [Late OE. *roccian*, app. f. the Teutonic stem *rukk-*, derivatives of which are cited under RICH *v.*[2] It is not clear whether MDu. and MHG. *rocken* (Da. *rokke*) are to be equated with OE. *roccian*, or are mere variants of the usual *rucken*.]

1. a. *trans.* To move (a child) gently to and fro in a cradle, in order to soothe or send it to sleep. Also in fig. contexts.

a **1100** in Kluge *Ags. Lesebuch* (ed. 2) 89 Heo hine baðede & beðede & smerede & bær & frefrede & swaðede & roccode. *a* **1225** *Ancr. R.* 82 Heo makeð of hire tunge cradel to þes deofles bearn, & rockeð hit ȝeorneliche ase nurice. *c* **1340** *Nominale* (Skeat) 402 *Femme bercelet berce*, Woman childe in cradul rokkith. 1387 TREVISA *Higden* (Rolls) II. 159 Gentil men children beeþ i-tauȝt to speke Frensche from þe tyme þat þey beeþ i-rokked in here cradel. 14.. W. PARIS *Cristine* 318 (Horstm. 1878), Ther she laye als innocente In credylle rokkede. c1440 *Promp. Parv.* 436/1 Rokke chylder, yn a cradyle, *cunagito, motito.* 1530 PALSGR. 693/1 Go rocke the chylde, here you nat howe he cryeth. 1592 SHAKS. *Ven. & Ad.* 1186 Lo, in this hollow cradle take thy rest, My throbbing heart shall rock thee day and night. 1602 MARSTON *Antonio's Rev.* II. ii, That's not my native place, where I was rockt. 1656 COWLEY *Pindar. Odes, 1st Nem. Ode* vi, The big-limm'd Babe in his huge Cradle lay, Too weighty to be rockt by Nurses hands, Wrapt in purple swadling bands. 1796 *Grose's Vulgar T.* (ed. 3) s.v., He was rocked in a stone kitchen; a saying meant to convey the idea that the person spoken of is a fool, his brains having been disordered by the jumbling of his cradle. 1820 SHELLEY *Vision of Sea* 81 This pale bosom, thy cradle and bed, Will it rock thee not, infant? 1866 G. MACDONALD *Ann. Q. Neighb.* xxv. (1878) 437, I remember rocking you in your cradle.

b. *transf.* and *fig.* of the wind, sea, earth, sleep, etc.

1597 SHAKS. *2 Hen. IV*, III. i. 19 Wilt thou.. Seale vp the Ship-boyes Eyes, and rock his Braines In Cradle of the rude imperious Surge? 1602 —— *Ham.* III. ii. 237 Sleepe rocke thy Braine. 1602 MARSTON *Antonio's Rev.* III. iv, To rock your baby thoughts in the cradle of sleepe. a1656 BP. HALL *Serm.* Wks. 1837 V. 433 Surely, he were a bold man, that could sleep, while the earth rocks him. 1673 [R. LEIGH] *Transp. Reh.* 141 A geographer born and bred,.. rockt from his child-hood on the seas. 1784 COWPER *Tiroc.* 44 Spring hangs her infant blossoms on the trees, Rock'd in the cradle of the western breeze. 1877 TALMAGE *Serm.* 256 It was rocked in the cradle of the wind.

2. a. To bring into a state of slumber, rest, or peace by gentle motion to and fro. Const. *to, into*, or *asleep*. Also *fig.*

a1400 *Seven Sages* in *MS. Cott. Galba E. ix.* fol. 26b, Ye third wasshes ye shetes oft, And rokkes it on slepe soft. 1377 LANGL. *P. Pl.* B. xv. 11 Resoun hadde reuthe on me, and rokked me aslepe. c1489 CAXTON *Sonnes of Aymon* xvi. 376 We ben noo children for to be rokked a slepe. 1584 LYLY *Sappho* III. iv, I shoulde bee quickly rocked into a deepe rest. 1607 HIERON *Wks.* I. 317 It is one of Sathans principall businesses to rocke men asleepe in it. 1635 QUARLES *Embl.* I. xiv. 5 Blow Ignorance; O thou, whose idle knee Rocks earth into a Lethargie. 1681–6 J. SCOTT *Chr. Life* (1747) III. 87 To chase them from our Minds, and rock ourselves into a deep Security. 1784 COWPER *Task* VI. 739 As the working of a sea Before a calm, that rocks itself to rest. 1819 SHELLEY *Cenci* IV. ii. 39 Ye conscience-stricken cravens, rock to rest Your baby hearts.

b. To maintain *in* a lulling state of security, plenty, hope, etc.

1581 MULCASTER *Positions* xxxvii. (1887) 149 While he was rockt in ease, and his state vnassailed by any miscontentment. 1583 BABINGTON *Commandm.* (1590) 66 Sometimes Sathan hath rocked this soule of mine in the chayer of securitie. 1633 FORD *Broken H.* IV. iii, The favour of a princess Rock thee, brave man, in ever-crowned plenty. 1880 MCCARTHY *Own Times* xliv. III. 333 Up to the last he had been rocked in the vainest hopes.

3. To move or sway (one) to and fro, esp. in a gentle or soothing manner. Also *fig.*

14.. W. PARIS *Cristine* 313 (Horstm. 1878), Foure mene rokede hire to & froo, To make hire payne more violente. a1586 SIDNEY *Arcadia* III. (1605) 343 He tooke her in his armes, and rocking her to and fro [etc.]. 1680 DRYDEN *Ovid's Ep.* XI. 75 High in his hall, rock'd in a chair of state, The king with his tempestuous council sate. 1847 DE QUINCEY *Sp. Mil. Nun* v. Wks. 1853 III. 7 Our poor Kate, that had for fifteen years been so tenderly rocked in the arms of St. Sebastian and his daughters. 1891 KIPLING *Light that Failed* xi. (1900) 187 Torpenhow put his arm round Dick and began to rock him gently to and fro.

refl. 1859 GEO. ELIOT *A. Bede* x, After Lisbeth had been rocking herself and moaning for some minutes, she suddenly paused. 1865 DICKENS *Mut. Fr.* III. xv, She rocked herself upon her breast, and cried, and sobbed.

4. a. To make (a cradle) swing to and fro, in order to put a child to sleep. Also *transf.* and *fig.*

c1386 CHAUCER *Reeve's T.* 237 The Cradel at hir beddes feet is set, To rokken, and to yeue the child to sowke. 1393 LANGL. *P. Pl.* C. x. 79 To ryse to þe ruel to rocke þe cradel. c1532 DU WES *Introd. Fr.* in *Palsgr.* 939 To rocke the cradel, *berchér.* 1590 SPENSER *F.Q.* III. vi. 2 All the Graces rockt her cradle being borne. 1601 HOLLAND *Pliny* XXVIII. iv. II. 303 To procure sleepe, by lying in some pretie bed that may be rocked too and fro. 1604 SHAKS. *Oth.* II. iii. 136 He'le watch the Horologe a double set, If Drinke rocke not his Cradle. 1781 COWPER *Expost.* 470 This island,.. The cradle that receiv'd thee at thy birth, Was rock'd by many a rough Norwegian blast. 1864 TENNYSON *En. Ard.* 194 Lightly rocking baby's cradle. 1898 *Westm. Gaz.* 20 Sept. 4/1 He has rocked the cradles of more than one fresh world.

b. *transf.* in gold-washing (see CRADLE *sb.* 14). Hence *absol.*, to use a rocker in gold-digging. Also *trans.*, to work *out* with a rocker.

1849 *Illustr. Lond. News* 17 Nov. 325/1 The one digging and carrying the earth in a bucket, and the other washing and rocking the cradle. 1884 'R. BOLDREWOOD' *Melb. Mem.* 168 Each man dug, or rocked, or bore, As if salvation with the ore Of the mine monarch lay. 1898 *Daily News* 15 Aug. 7/2 Their efforts were confined to rocking out bars in the river-bed.

5. a. To cause to sway to and fro or from side to side; to move backwards and forwards. Also *refl.*

1297 R. GLOUC. (Rolls) 2179 þe romeins.. nolde.. hor poer so sende Ne to rokky hom so in þe se. 1340 *Ayenb.* 116 þeruore bit sainte pawel his deciples þet hi by yzet ase tours, yroted ase trawes, in loue, zuo þet non uondinge him ne moȝe resye ne rocky. c1460 *Towneley Myst.* xxi. 330 We shall so rok hym, and with buffettys knok hym. 1567 *Gude & Godlie B.* (S.T.S.) 153, I was.. as ane fule mockit, Euill tocheit and rockit. 1590 SHAKS. *Mids. N.* IV. i. 91 Come, my Queen, take hands with me, And rocke the ground whereon these sleepers be. 1598 CHAPMAN *Iliad* VI. 111 The blacke Buls hide.. was with his gate so rockt, That (being large) it (both at once) his necke and ankles knockt. 1718 POPE *Iliad* XIII. 68 The god whose earth-quakes rock the solid ground. 1786 tr. *Beckford's Vathek* (1868) 52 A sudden hurricane blew out our lights and rocked our habitation. 1853 URE *Dict. Arts* (ed. 4) II. 5 This frame.. is furnished with a handle, whereby it is rocked to bring down the types and discs upon the card. 1874 J. W. LONG *Amer. Wild-fowl* xii. 174 The boat should then be 'rocked' continually to break the ice as it goes.

†**b.** ? To clean by shaking. *Obs. rare*$^{-1}$.

See the note on the word in the glossary to the poem. But the form *ruokeden* in Laȝamon 22287 makes it doubtful whether this is the true explanation.

13.. *Gaw. & Gr. Knt.* 2018 þe ryngez rokked of þe roust, of his riche bruny.

c. *colloq.* (orig. *U.S.*). To cause to move with musical rhythm, esp. with the beat of ROCK *sb.*^{3} 2b. Occas. (esp. in early use) with sexual connotations (see also sense 7b).

1922 T. SMITH in Godrich & Dixon *Blues & Gospel Records 1902–1942* (1969) 648 (*song-title*) My man rocks me (with one steady roll). 1938 C. CALLOWAY *Hi de Ho* in R. S. Gold *Jazz Lexicon* (1964) 256 *Rock me*, send me, kill me, move me with rhythm. 1939 W. HOBSON *Amer. Jazz Music* (1940) iii. 54 Albert Ammon's *Boogie Woogie Stomp*.., in jazz slang, might be said to 'rock the joint'. *Ibid.* iv. 87 Simple jazz-rhythmic phrases.. may be blasted out by players with enough lip and lung strength in a way that will 'rock' the crowd. 1951 DAVIS & HUNTER *Rock Little Baby* (song) 3 Some girls like men who are big and strong, You'll be my man, Just as long as you Rock little daddy, Work little daddy, Rock little daddy, Rock me all night long. 1956 B. HOLIDAY *Lady sings Blues* (1973) xi. 103 We used to rock that joint. 1961 *Jazz Notes* Feb.–Mar. 39, I don't remember anyone who could 'rock' a Kenilworth audience before! 1972 *Even. Telegram* (St. John's, Newfoundland) 24 June 10/4 Joan Morrissey and a group known as The Commanders Showband were 'really rockin' 'er' at the Staff Club. 1977 *Rolling Stone* 7 Apr. 3/2 (Advt.), Boston, man. They really rock and roll. They rocked the place apart.

d. *fig.* To distress, perturb, upset; to surprise, startle, dumbfound. ***to rock the boat***: see BOAT *sb.* 1d. *colloq.*

1940 E. POUND *Cantos* lii. 11 Gold brokers made profit Rocked the exchange against gold. 1941 *Argus Weekend Mag.* (Melbourne) 15 Nov. 1/3 Another universal favourite [in Australia] is still the famous 'Wouldn't it ——!' Never given the final words (the completed sentence has several variants on 'Wouldn't it rock you!' or 'Wouldn't it rip you!'), the exclamation depends upon inflexion as to whether it conveys disgust, amazement, or pleasure. 1947 N. MARSH *Final Curtain* ix. 139 Has Troy seen about the Will?... It'll rock them considerably. 1951 *Sun* (Baltimore) 9 June B1/1 His diplomatic phrasing wrapped the punch in polite words, but Grady was nonetheless rocked. 1955 'N. SHUTE' *Requiem for Wren* vii. 197 It turned out you were a Rhodes scholar, which rocked her a bit. 1960 *Sunday Express* 24 July 1/3 It is not only from the Opposition that Mr. Macmillan can expect criticism. His decision will rock the Tory Party too. 1966 [see OFF-BROADWAY *sb.*]. 1981 *Observer* 22 Mar. 7 (*heading*) New sex scandals rock Washington.

6. a. *intr.* To sway to and fro under some impact or stress; to move or swing from side to side; to oscillate. Also *dial.*, to stagger or reel in walking.

1398 TREVISA *Barth. De P.R.* v. xx. (Bodl. MS.), Somtyme teeþ rokkeþ and waggeþ. a1460 *Lybeaus Disc.* 1621 Syr Lambard.. rokkede yn his sadell, As chyld doth yn a kradell. 1530 PALSGR. 693/1, I love nat to lye in his house, for if there be any wynde styrryng, one shall rocke to and fro in his bedde. 1593 SHAKS. *Lucrece* 262 And how her hand, in my hand being lock'd, Forced it to tremble.. and then it faster rock'd. 1600 HEYWOOD *1st Pt. Edw. IV*, IV. iv, Thou hast two ploughs going, and ne'er a cradle rocking. 1695 BLACKMORE *Pr. Arth.* IV. 224 He rocks with every Wind. 1718 RAMSAY *Christ's Kirk Gr.* III. xiv, Some fell, and some gaed rockin. 1797–1805 S. & HT. LEE *Cant. T.* II. 145 The earth rocked beneath his feet. 1820 SHELLEY *Prometh. Unb.* I. i. 68 As thunder, louder than your own, made rock The orbed world! 1850 TENNYSON *In Mem.* Concl. 63 The blind wall rocks, and on the trees The dead leaf trembles to the bells. 1898 *Daily News* 24 Nov. 7/3 Sharkey.. sent his right straight in Corbett's face, making his head rock.

fig. 1861 *Sat. Rev.* 23 Nov. 534 The rapid fluctuations of prevalent belief which this generation has witnessed, have necessarily set many minds rocking more or less. 1898 *Allbutt's Syst. Med.* V. 824 Not only does it.. pacify the organ rocking under the tumult of its unbalanced parts [etc.].

b. Of vessels under the effect of waves.

1513 DOUGLAS *Æneis* v. xiv. 77 Prince Enee persauit, by his rais, Quhow that the schip did rok and tailȝevey. 1807 P. GASS *Jrnl.* 49 The waves ran very high and the boat rocked a great deal. 1873 BLACK *Pr. Thule* xxiv. 406 The.. vessel that scarcely rocked in the water below.

transf. 1836 KINGSLEY *Lett.* (1878) I. 35 The sea-birds played about over the sea, or sat rocking on its bosom.

c. To swing oneself to and fro, esp. while sitting in a rocking-chair.

1795 SOUTHEY *Joan of Arc* I, Elves love to lie and rock upon its leaves, And bask in moonshine. 1844 DICKENS *Mart. Chuz.* xliv, During the whole dialogue, Jonas had been rocking on his chair. 1898 *Nat. Rev.* Aug. 898 He is more likely to spend his summer holiday fishing with a male friend than rocking beside his wife on a hotel piazza.

d. Const. with preps. or advs.

1858 CARLYLE *Fredk. Gt.* II. vii. (1872) I. 92 Germany was rocking down towards one saw not what. 1862 *Catal. Internat. Exhib., Brit.* II. No. 5993 This lever has teeth.., which when the bolt is shot by the key, rock upwards and fit into corresponding recesses. 1863 JEAN INGELOW *Songs of Seven, Seven times seven* i, Lightly she rocked to her port remote. 1937 I. BAIRD *John* ix. 103 Tiber rocked back on his heels.

e. ***to rock along***, to continue in typical fashion. *U.S. colloq.*

1906 J. W. CARR in *Dial. Notes* III. 153 *Rock along*, to continue unsettled... 'So the matter rocked along and nothing was done.' 1946 *Sun* (Baltimore) 10 Oct. 2/1 The creation of a new board or administrator.. would permit the program to rock along much as it is now. 1972 J. S. HALL *Sayings from Old Smoky* 115 *Rockin' along*, going along as usual. 'Everything is rockin' along just like when Lena was here.'

f. In Mountaineering: to work one's way *up* a chimney by a rocking movement.

1920 G. W. YOUNG *Mountain Craft* 168 The body is kept upright in the middle on the spring of the bent knees and supported by the pressure of the hands, placed like the feet one against each wall. In this fashion we can 'rock' up satisfactorily.

7. a. Of popular music: to possess a rocking rhythm (see ROCKING *ppl. a.* 1c); to exhibit the characteristics of rock music.

1938 *Metronome* July 21 *Harry James' Lullaby in Rhythm* really rocks. 1946 R. BLESH *Shining Trumpets* xiii. 309 The music.. jumps rather than rocks. 1977 *Rolling Stone* 24 Mar., Waters has written six new tunes for the album, marking the end of a long dry spell, but his standards and one old Willie Dixon tune rock the hardest.

b. To perform, or dance vigorously and in an improvised way to, popular music with a strong beat (ROCK *sb.*^{3} 2a); hence, to play or dance to rock music (ROCK *sb.*^{3} 2b), to rock and roll. Occas. (esp. in early use) with sexual connotations (see sense 5c).

[1934: see ROCK AND ROLL.] 1948 MOORE & REIG (*song-title*) We're gonna rock. 1951 DAVIS & HUNTER (*song-title*) Rock little baby. 1953 FREEDMAN & DE KNIGHT (*song-title*) We're gonna rock around the clock. 1956 *Look* 26 June 45 Elvis Presley. The hottest thing rockin', sings throbbing lyrics that sound almost unintelligible. c1956 'L. SLIM' *Rooster Blues* in P. Oliver *Screening Blues* (1968) vi. 193 We got to rock tonight baby, yes, we got to rock tonight. 1974 *Down Beat* 18 July 38/2 The band now isn't together enough to play all that... I mean they try to rock and they don't. 1977 *Time* 1 Aug. 16/2 In a Salisbury discothèque last week.. 'troopies' (soldiers) and their birds were rocking to a song about the country's bad news.

c. ***to rock out***, to enjoy oneself enthusiastically, *esp.* by playing or dancing to rock music. Also as *attrib. phr. colloq.* (chiefly *U.S.*).

1968 *Surfer Mag.* Jan. 47/3 Maria likes rock-out dancing and surfing. 1972 B. RODGERS *Queens' Vernacular* 173 *Rock out*,.. to enjoy oneself to the fullest. 1977 *Rolling Stone* 5 May 74/3 Even on the Stones' 'Happy', Lofgren changes the rock-out showpiece of hero Keith into a more subdued and funky shuffle. 1977 C. MCFADDEN *Serial* (1978) lii. 110/2 Kate.. went to find the Reverend Thurston on the dance floor, where he was rocking out with Marlene.

rock, *v.*^{2} [f. ROCK *sb.*^{1}]

†**1.** *trans.* To encompass or wall with or as with rocks. *Obs. rare.*

1600 E. BLOUNT tr. *Conestaggio* 309 Rocked rounde about, and seated in the most inconstant sea that is. 1634 ROWLANDS *Noble Soldier* IV. i, The mother Stands rock'd so strong with friends ten thousand billowes Cannot.. shake her.

2. *U.S. slang.* To throw stones at; to stone.

1836 *Public Ledger* (Philadelphia) 30 Aug. 1/4 Rock him! rock him! cried the boys, rock him round the corner... The wearer was 'rocked' till he turned his cloak inside out. a1848 in Bartlett *Dict. Amer.* 277 They commenced rocking the Clay Club House in June. 1872 O. W. HOLMES *Poet Breakf.-t.* xii, The boys would follow after him, crying, 'Rock him! Rock him! He's got a long-tailed coat on!' 1885 *Where Chineses Drive* 127 On the whole it is simpler to rock him.

3. *W. Country dial.* To remove the calcareous deposit or 'fur' from the inside of (a kettle).

1880 HARDY *Trumpet-Major* II. i. 4 The broken clock-line was mended, the kettles rocked, the creeper nailed up, and a new handle put to the warming-pan. 1905 in *Eng. Dial. Dict.* V. 138/1 Kettle wants rocking.

'rocka,billy. orig. *U.S.* Also **rock-a-billy.** [Blend of ROCK (AND ROLL and HILL)-BILLY.]

1. A type of popular music, originating in the southeastern U.S., combining elements of rock and roll and hill-billy music. Also *attrib.*

1956 *Billboard* 8 Dec. 22/3 Johnny Burnette is on hand to inject a touch of rockabilly in 'Lonesome Train'. 1957 *Variety* 23 Oct. 18/1 [The film] 'Rockabilly Baby' will hit a responsive chord among teenagers. 1959 *Times* 9 Nov. 9/6 Rockabilly and hula hoops came and went. 1962 *Globe & Mail* (Toronto) 19 Nov. 6/6, I suggest that as a public service the rock-a-billy radio stations join together to present an informative, unsponsored, prime time, two-hour program. 1971 R. A. CARTER *Manhattan Primitive* (1972) xx. 190 A drummer, a guitarist, and a trumpet player pounded out rockabilly. 1976 *Time* 27 Sept. 90/3 Honky-tonk songs.. came out of Texas in the late 1930s and early '40s. Elvis and Jerry Lee Lewis adapted the style to rock 'n' roll in the '50s. Sometimes called rockabilly, it celebrates booze, gambling, fighting, steppin' out, temptation and, like all country music, love. 1980 *Daily Mirror* 10 Apr. 12/2 Rockabilly is Eighties style. Special shops are opening to cater for the revived demand.

2. A person who performs this music.

1958 *Britannica Bk. of Year* 519/2 *Rockabilly*, a word ingeniously compounded from the expressions *Rock 'n' roll* and *Hillbilly*, and meaning a country singer. 1968 *Rolling Stone* 25 May 1/3 They called Elvis the 'rockabilly'. 1969 B. C. MALONE *Country Music U.S.A.* 246 A hybrid specimen developed: an individual who possessed characteristics of both the rock-and-roll and country singer, the rockabilly.

'rocka,boogie. Also **rock-a-boogie.** [Blend of ROCK (AND ROLL and BOOGIE(-WOOGIE.] A type of popular music, combining elements of rock and roll and boogie-woogie. Also *attrib.*

1956 B. DARNELL et al. (*song-title*) Rock-a-boogie baby. *Ibid.*, He's got a little rattle He shakes around, I don't know where that rhythm he ever found, Oh he's a Rock-a-boogie Baby, Rock-a-boogie Baby of mine. **1956** BENSON & JONES (*song-title*) Rock-a-boogie swing. *Ibid.*, You can see the kids a-dancin', Hear the music ring, It's a brand new beat, It's the rock-a-boogie swing... You got-ta rock. You got-ta roll. **1975** *Listener* 25 Dec. 889/2 That noted rockaboogie guide, the *Daily Express*. **1977** *Zigzag* Apr. 14/2 We were more refined, tasteful if you like, as opposed to the old good time rock-a-boogie.

rock-a-bye ('rɒkəbaɪ), *v.* Also **rock-a-by.** [f. ROCK *v.*[1] + *bye* (see BYE-BYE[1]).] *imp. phr. rock-a-bye, baby*: a traditional phrase (esp. in a nursery rhyme) to induce an infant to fall asleep, used as an accompaniment to the rocking of a cradle. Also with joc. var. (see quot. 1954). Cf. HUSHABY *int.*

1805 *Songs for Nursery* 36 Rock-a-bye, baby, thy cradle is green, Father's a nobleman, mother's a queen. **1812** *Mother's Gift* 5 Rocka-by baby bunting, My father's gone a hunting. *c* **1820** in I. & P. Opie *Oxf. Dict. Nursery Rhymes* (1951) 58 Rock a bye baby—puss is a lady.. So hush a bye babe lie still. **1954** DYLAN THOMAS *Under Milk Wood* 81 Rockabye, grandpa, in the tree top.. When the bough breaks the cradle will fall, Down will come grandpa, whiskers and all. **1975** *101 Favourite Nursery Rhymes* 58 Rock-a-bye, baby, on the tree top, When the wind blows the cradle will rock; When the bough breaks the cradle will fall, Down will come baby, cradle and all.

rocka'hominy. *U.S.* Also 8 **roccahomony, rockahomonie, -homine.** [Algonquin Indian, f. *rok* corn, + *oham* to grind, with the termination *min.* See *Notes & Queries* (1906) 28 Apr. 326.] = HOMINY.

1705 BEVERLY *Virginia* III. §19 Sometimes also in their Travels, each Man takes with him a Pint or Quart of Rockahomonie, that is, the finest Indian Corn, parched and beaten to Powder. **1737** BRICKELL *Nat. Hist. Carolina* 288 Rockahomine meal which is made of their maize or Indian corn. **1743** M. CATESBY *Nat. Hist.* I. p. x, They thicken their broth with roccahomony. **1901** MARY JOHNSTON *Audrey* i, Platters of smoking venison and turkey, flanked by rockahominy and sea biscuit.

rockalow, variant of ROQUELAURE.

rock alum. [ROCK *sb.*[1]] (See ALUM *sb.* 1 and ROCHE ALUM.)

1671 PHILLIPS s.v. *Allum*, Called Roch or Rock Allum. **1678** R. RUSSELL tr. *Geber* IV. iv. 246 Glassy or Rock Allom hath a two fold way of Preparation. *a* **1756** MRS. HEYWOOD *New Present* (1771) 263 A pound of rock-allum, burnt and beat to powder. **1806** TURTON *Linnæus' Syst. Nat.* VII. 221 *Alumen romanum*, Rock alum. **1860** PIESSE *Lab. Chem. Wonders* 107 The name rock or roche alum indicative of good quality. **1875** *Encycl. Brit.* I. 644/2 The term *rock alum*, commonly employed in Europe.

rockamboy, rockanbowl: see ROCAMBOLE.

rock and roll. Also rock-and-roll, rock 'n' roll. [f. vbl. phr. *to rock and roll*: see ROCK *v.*[1] and ROLL *v.*[2]] **1.** A type of popular dance-music characterized by a heavy beat and simple melodies, often with elements of the 'blues'. Cf. *rhythm and blues* s.v. RHYTHM *sb.* 9 a.

[**1934** S. CLARE (*song-title*) Rock and roll. **1951** DAVIS & HUNTER *Rock Little Baby* (song) 1 Rock little daddy, Work little daddy, Rock little daddy, Send me with a rock and roll. **1954** *Billboard* 27 Nov. 29 (Advt.), Rockin' rollin' rhythmic! Ella Mae Morse with Big Dave and his orchestra.] *Ibid.* 25 Dec. 18/4 Alan Freed.. will sponsor his first 'Rock and Roll Jubilee Ball' at the St. Nicolas Arena here on January 14 and 15. **1955** *N.Y. Times* 26 Mar. 17 According to William E. Kelsey Jr., a business man who has organized such parties, 'Rock 'n Roll' is less to blame for the situation than are the alcoholic beverages taken straight by boys and girls from 16 to 19 years old. **1956** *Observer* 30 Dec. 8/8 What else happened in 1956? Elvis Presley happened. So did Rock 'n' Roll. **1957** D. HAGUE in S. Traill *Concerning Jazz* 113 The only blot on the ledger of good productive jazz is that monstrosity at first referred to as 'Rhythm and Blues' and now more popularly called 'Rock and Roll'. **1959** *Times* 27 June 7/3 'Rock 'n' Roll' was so closely followed by Skiffle that the uninitiated were apt to confuse the two. **1962** *Listener* 1 Nov. 703/2 The bulletins last night kept breaking into the rock-'n'-roll. **1968** A. LIPSON *Russian Course* I Hooliganism is defined [in the Soviet Union] as 'behavior exhibiting disrespect for the social order'. Includes: scoffing at authority, playing rock and roll, wearing loud clothes, as well as rowdyism and petty criminal acts. **1969** N. COHN *A Wop Bopa Loo Bop* (1970) i. 15 In 1951, a DJ called Alan Freed launched a series of rhythm reviews at the Cleveland Arena... These shows featured coloured acts but were aimed at predominantly white audiences and, to avoid what he called 'the racial stigma of the old classification', Freed dropped the term R&B and invented the phrase Rock'n'Roll instead. **1974** A. SHAW *Rockin' '50s* xii. 106 In a liner note for an End album *Alan Freed's Top 15*, Freed claimed that he began using the term 'rock and roll' in 1951. **1977** *Rolling Stone* 21 Apr. 74/1 You know her life was saved by rock and roll. **1977** *Zigzag* Aug. 5/1 Y'see I write about punk and you just want to read about something that'll scare your mum, I'm sure that elsewhere someone will let ya know it IS only rock'n'roll.

2. A dance to this music.

1958 [see CHARLESTON]. **1958** *Times Lit. Suppl.* 21 Nov. p. xxxii/5 Alex Moore leads beginners of any age through the mysteries of ballroom dancing, from the waltz.. to the Mambo and 'Rock 'n' Roll (Jive)'. **1960** *Master Detective* July 83/2 Rock and Roll, that's what I'm good at. I got a terrific collection of platters.

3. *attrib.*, as **rock and roll ball, band, craze, dance, dancer, group, lyric, music, number, party, record, revivalism, revivalist, riot, road show, singer, song, star, station, stuff, tune.**

1954 *Billboard* 25 Dec. 18 (*heading*) Freed to sponsor 'Rock & Roll' ball. **1972** *Guardian* 28 June 16/1 It [*sc.* the Rolling Stones] is the raunchiest, flashiest, most exciting rock 'n' roll band in existence. **1980** *Oxford Times* 1 Feb. 23/3 On tracks like 'Rock Music' they seem to want to be a hard rock 'n' roll band. **1977** *Times* 18 Apr. (Gramophone Suppl.) p. iv/3 By the 1950s.. popular music was to make another revolution for the record business... The rock'n'roll craze symbolized in the figure of Elvis Presley. **1955** *Life* 2 May 19, I am a teen-ager and I see no future in the rock 'n roll dance craze. **1966** A. YOUNG in *Spero* I. II. 21 New things he'd worked out on drums for a Rock & Roll dance. **1957** E. PAUL *That Crazy Amer. Music* 243 The contemporary crop of rock and roll dancers include the young folks near the head or toward the foot of each class. **1968** *Crescendo* Feb. 16/3 This is a rock and roll group! **1955** *Life* 2 May 19, I think you need a teenager's view on rock 'n roll lyrics. **1956** *Look* 26 June 47 A record spins, and the boys and girls react to rock 'n' roll lyrics with laughter, not involvement. **1956** *Newsweek* 23 Apr. 32 Rock-and-roll music, he [*sc.* Asa Carter] said, 'is the basic, heavy-beat music of Negroes. It appeals to the base in man, brings out animalism and vulgarity.' **1958** *Publ. Amer. Dial. Soc.* xxx. 39 Now that that age group [*sc.* teenagers] is concerned with 'rock and roll' music, the jazz audience still remains composed.. of young people of college age. **1955** *Life* 18 Apr. 168/2 *Cash Box*.. challenged anybody to find smut in the top rock 'n roll numbers. **1969** *Listener* 3 Apr. 470/3 He can get them swinging with a rock-and-roll number. **1955** *N.Y. Times* 26 Mar. 17/3 A month ago Mr. Kelsey organized a 'Rock'n Roll' party for 2,000 at an armory here. **1957** *Gramophone Popular Record Catal.* III. 157 Rock and roll party. **1955** *Life* 18 Apr. 168 But parents and police were startled by other rock 'n roll records' words which were frequently suggestive and occasionally lewd. **1974** *Guardian* 27 Mar. 12/6 Bill Haley's return to London for yet another bout of rock and roll revivalism. **1972** *Jazz & Blues* Sept. 5/1 The Rock 'N' Roll revivalists. **1958** *Punch* 19 Nov. 665/1 If in the fullness of time it sparks off a rock-'n'-roll riot in Hamburg or Tokyo they receive the news with a grunt. **1977** *Sounds* 1 Jan. 2/4 The Glitter Band will no longer back him up and the old rock 'n' roll road show has been wound up. **1956** *Look* 26 June 42 Lillian Briggs is a rock 'n' roll singer who also plays at the trombone. **1964** *Amer. Folk Music Occasional* I. 16, I think a lot of Rock and Roll singers and blue singers, they really have the feeling exactly as we about gospel. **1955** *Life* 18 Apr. 168 *Variety*.. cranked out indignant stories about 'leerics' in the rock 'n roll or rhythm and blues songs. *Ibid.* (*caption*) Contingent of bounding dance fans at Easter show in Brooklyn's Paramount Theater greet roster of rock 'n roll stars performing latest songs on stage. **1972** J. L. DILLARD *Black English* vi. 261 A title from one of the rock and roll star's songs. **1973** E. BULLINS *Theme is Blackness* 46 Steve fumbles with the radio dial and finds a rock 'n' roll station. **1957** *New Yorker* 26 Oct. 35/2, I do enjoy a good opera production... I don't enjoy this rock-'n'-roll stuff. **1972** D. HASTON *In High Places* iii. 45 Robin.. was whistling a rock-'n-roll tune.

Hence as *v. intr.* (freq. considered as comprising two separate verbal units for the purpose of forming derivatives, etc.: see also ROCKING *vbl. sb.*[1] 4), to play or dance to rock-and-roll music; **rock and roller; rock and rolling** *vbl. sb.* and *ppl. a.*

[**1951** DAVIS & HUNTER *Rock Little Baby* (song) 1 Rock little baby, Rock and roll, Rock me in rhythm, Satisfy my soul.] **1956** *Time* (Overseas/Atlantic ed.) 18 June 37 Pop Record Maker Mitch Miller, no rock 'n' roller, sums up for the defense: 'You can't call any music immoral.' **1956** *Time* 24 Sept. 48 *My Boy Elvis*.. is a real rock 'n' roller. **1956** *N.Y. Times Mag.* 4 Nov. 44/3 (*heading*) Europe rocks 'n' rolls. **1957** *Economist* 21 Sept. 946 (Advt.), Fibreglass.. baffles the chatter of rock-'n-rollers—and keeps the place warm as neatly as it keeps the peace. **1957** *Observer* 15 Dec. 7/4 Gay shirts for the boys who skiffle and rock 'n' roll are equally hard to discover. **1958** H. MAXWELL *Railway Mag. Miscellany* 6 We can.. for an hour or so Rock and Roll to a more thunderous and more significant beat than that which passes for Music with us today. **1959** A. WESKER *Roots* I. 19 There's nothing wrong with rock 'n rolling, only God preserve me from the girl that can do nothing else! **1960** *News Chron.* 29 Mar. 3/2 Rock 'n' roller Cliff Richard. **1960** P. HASTINGS *Sandals for my Feet* I. vi. 61 Those rock and rolling Romeos. **1966** *Listener* 20 Oct. 568/1 There were already a dozen or so young people rocking and rolling wildly to some vintage discs of Elvis Presley. **1976** *Weekend Echo* (Liverpool) 4/5 Dec. 1/2 A concert by veteran rock-and-roller Bill Haley. **1977** [see ROCK *v.*[1] 5 c]. **1977** *Sounds* 9 July 18/1 Silly really that the American rock 'n' rolling public.. should take Starz to its heart so readily.

rockat, obs. form of ROCKET.

Rockaway ('rɒkəweɪ). *U.S.* [f. the place name of *Rockaway*, New Jersey.] A four-wheeled carriage, open at the sides, with two or three seats and a standing top, used in the United States. Also *attrib.*

1845 M. M. NOAH *Gleanings from Gathered Harvest* 174, I keep a little Rockaway wagon. **1846** *Spirit of Times* 9 May 121/1 The price of a 'Rockaway' carriage which will carry eight persons depends very much on its finish. **1846** LOWELL *Lett.* (1894) I. 121 Dr. Liddon Pennock has driven by me in his rockaway. **1863** MISS HOPLEY *Life in South* I. 58 Those not possessing carriages and 'rockaways' availing themselves of waggons. **1884** *Harper's Mag.* June 86/2 With the aid of the family rockaway the.. party were at the boat-house. **1944** T. D. CLARK *Pills, Petticoats & Plows* 292 Everywhere carriage makers turned out fancy.. 'cutunders', 'rockaways',.. and 'heavy duties'. **1948** J. D. RITTENHOUSE *Amer. Horse-Drawn Vehicles* 19 Rockaway or depot wagon.

rock-basin. [ROCK *sb.*[1]] A basin-shaped hollow in a rock, esp. one of natural origin; *spec.* in *Geol.* a large depression in a rocky area, attributed to the action of ice-masses.

1754 BORLASE *Antiq. Cornwall* 164 The Rock-basons shew that it was usual to get upon the top of this Karn. **1763** J. HUTCHINS in *Mem. W. Stukeley* (Surtees Soc.) II. 128, I am apt to think it was a rock idol and the rock-basons on it seem to favour such a conjecture. **1839** DE LA BECHE *Rep. Geol. Cornw.*, etc. xiv. 451 The highest block is decomposed on the upper surface, so that one of those cavities, commonly termed rock basins,.. is produced. **1853** *Zoologist* II. 4081, I took another look at my pretty little rock-basin at Oddicombe. **1882** GEIKIE *Text-bk. Geol.* VI. i. 888 The abundant ice-ground and lake-filled rock-basins of glaciated regions.

'rock-bed. [ROCK *sb.*[1]] A floor or base of rock; a rocky bottom or under-stratum; often *fig.* (Cf. *bed-rock*, s.v. BED *sb.* 18.)

1839–52 BAILEY *Festus* 305 Ocean's depths He clove unto their rock-bed. **1849** ROBERTSON *Serm.* Ser. I. ii. (1866) 27 Frivolity has turned the heart into a rockbed of selfishness. **1862** A. C. RAMSAY *Rock Spec.* (ed. 3) 126 In some localities in Oxfordshire.. the 'Rock bed' of the Marlstone becomes highly ferruginous. **1883** E. P. RAMSAY *Food-Fishes N.S.W.* 42 A hard rock-bed with large loose stones.

attrib. **1883** *Home Missionary* Sept. 201 The religious conceptions which are the rockbed ideas of Christianity.

'rock-bird. [ROCK *sb.*[1]] **a.** A bird that haunts rocks; *esp.* a puffin. **b.** A bird of the genus *Rupicola*; a 'cock of the rock'. **c.** *U.S.* The spotted, or the purple, sandpiper (*Tringa maculata*, or *maritima*).

1766 *Chron.* in *Ann. Reg.* 129/1 The place of resort.. of.. numbers of rock birds or puffins. **1796** MORSE *Amer. Geogr.* I. 212 Spotted Tring. Rock bird. *Tringa Maculata*. **1810** in *Risdon's Surv. Devon* 414 Rockbirds are very plentiful. **1859** ATKINSON *Walks & Talks* (1892) 328 Mr. Spencer made some inquiries about rockbird's eggs. **1862** JOHNS *Brit. Birds* Index, Rock-birds, the Auk, Puffin, and Guillemot. **1888** [see *rock-plover*, s.v. ROCK *sb.*[1] 9 c].

rockbridgeite ('rɒkbrɪdʒaɪt). *Min.* [f. the name of *Rockbridge* County, Virginia, where the first specimens were recognized + -ITE[1].] A basic phosphate of iron and manganese which is found as dark green or black masses and crusts (turning brown in air owing to oxidation) in limonite and pegmatite deposits.

1949 C. FRONDEL in *Amer. Mineralogist* XXXIV. 513 The specific name dufrenite is here re-defined to apply to a particular member of the dufrenite-complex, and the new name rockbridgeite is proposed for another common member of this complex. **1951** C. PALACHE et al. *Dana's Syst. Min.* (ed. 7) II. 868 Rockbridgeite occurs in the United States in a limonite deposit on South Mountain near Midvale, Rockbridge County, Virginia. **1970** *Amer. Mineralogist* LV. 166 A remarkable occurrence at Fodderstack Mountain, Montgomery Co., Arkansas, shows fibrous masses of rockbridgeite with mammillary surfaces and color banding.

'rock-built, *a.* [ROCK *sb.*[1]] Constructed of, built with or upon, rocks.

1777 POTTER *Æschylus, Prometheus* 28 Arabia's martial race.. Thro' all their rock-built cities moan. **1797** *The College* 11 And rears her rock-built Tuscan piles on high. **1818** BYRON *Ch. Har.* IV. clxxxi, The armaments which thunderstrike the walls Of rock-built cities. **1840** CARLYLE *Heroes* i. 11 This green, flowery, rock-built earth.

rockburst ('rɒkbɜːst). Also **rock burst.** [f. ROCK *sb.*[1] + BURST *sb.*] A sudden, violent rupture or collapse of highly stressed rock in a mine.

1928 *Daily Mail* 3 Aug. 18/1 The rockburst at a depth of nearly 5,000ft. in the City Deep mine that has.. caused the deaths of two Europeans and eleven natives, is described as one of the biggest pressure bursts experienced on the Rand goldfield. **1942** *Mine & Quarry Engin.* VII. 233/1 One of the major problems of mining at depth lies in the occurrence of rockbursts. **1946** C. B. JEPPE *Gold Mining on Witwatersrand* I. x. 790 'Pressure bursts' or 'rock bursts'.. major effects of excessive differential stresses. **1967** *New Scientist* 14 Dec. 678/1 The success of US and Soviet workers in predicting rockbursts underground. **1978** *Mining Equipment Internat.* June 17/1 Rockbursts currently account for about 80% of South African underground mine fatalities.

rock cod. [ROCK *sb.*[1]]

1. A cod found on rocky sea-bottoms or ledges. Chiefly *Sc.* and *north.*

The first quot. may belong to sense 2.

1634 W. WOOD *New Eng. Prosp.* (1865) 45 Besides here is a great deale of Rock-cod and Macrill. *a* **1705–1758** [see RED *a.* 17 c]. **1821** SCOTT *Pirate* ii, In an overcharge of about one hundred per cent on a bargain of rock-cod. **1838** *Proc. Berw. Nat. Club* I. 173 The young are called Codlings; and when the fish is of a red colour, which it assumes after lying some time among weedy rocks, it is then called Rock Cod, or Codling. **1854** H. MILLER *Sch. & Schm.* (1858) 533 We.. caught, ere our return, a basket of rock-cod or coal-fish for supper.

2. Applied to various fishes of other genera, as the Californian yellow-tailed rock-fish, the red garrupa, the rock-trout of Puget Sound, several South African serranoid fishes, the New Zealand blue cod, etc.

1796 STEDMAN *Surinam* II. 46 The other is that fine large fish called by the English rock-cod. **1837** *Penny Cycl.* VII. 76/1 Of edible sea fish, the best kinds near Canton are a sort of rock-cod. **1840** F. D. BENNETT *Whaling Voy.* II. 16 The most valuable fish in the waters around the coast is the rock-cod. **1859** *All Year Round* No. 4. 82 The deep sea fish—the 'schnapper', the 'king fish', the 'grounder', and the rock cod—were beyond their reach. **1880** *R. Comm. Fish. N.S.W.* 10 The genus *Serranus* comprises most of the fishes known as

'Rock Cod'... One only is sufficiently useful as an article of food to merit notice, and that is the 'Black Rock-Cod' (*Serranus damelii*, Günther).

So **rock codfish**.

1821 SCOTT *Pirate* ii, Erickson had gone too far in.. charging the rock codfish at a penny instead of a halfpenny a-pound. **1845** COULTER *Adv. Pacific* xi, A number of rock cod-fish.

rock cress. [ROCK *sb.*[1]] **a.** A plant of the genus *Arabis*. †**b.** Samphire.

c **1710** PETIVER *Catal. Ray's Eng. Herbal* L, Welsh Rock Cress. **1756** *Phil. Trans.* XLIX. 839 The lesser Shepherd's Purse or Rock-Cress. **1796** WITHERING *Brit. Plants* (ed. 3) III. 576 *Iberis nudicaulis*,.. Rock cress. Naked Candytuft. **1863** BARING-GOULD *Iceland* 355 A trembling Alpine Rock-cress (*Arabis petræa*) was nestled within the lip [of the slag chimney]. **1882** *Garden* 10 June 405/2 The common White Rock Cress (*Arabis albida*) is very effective.

rock 'crystal. [ROCK *sb.*[1]]

1. Pure silica or quartz in a transparent and colourless form, most usually occurring in hexagonal prisms with hexagonal pyramid ends.

1666 *Phil. Trans.* I. 362 Rock-Crystal is not fit for Optick-Glasses. **1716** LADY MONTAGU *Let. to C'tess Mar* 8 Sept., In almost every room [are] large lustres of rock crystal. **1786** tr. *Beckford's Vathek* (1883) 79 Beneath a vast dome, illuminated by a thousand lamps of rock crystal. **1854** *Pereira's Polarized Light* (ed. 2) 19 Quartz or rock crystal is used, under the name of Brazil pebble, as a refracting medium for spectacles. **1878** HUXLEY *Physiogr.* 59 Rock-crystal is sometimes found in crystals of gigantic size; at other times in excessively small specimens.

2. A piece of this.

1839 DE LA BECHE *Rep. Geol. Cornw.*, etc. xv. 496 Rock-crystals are, as might be expected, somewhat frequent among the quartziferous veins in the granite. **1867** A. BILLING *Science of Gems* 54 It has just been shown that quartz (rock) crystals are stalagmitic in their nature.

rock-dove. [ROCK *sb.*[1]] = ROCK-PIGEON I.

1655 MOUFET & BENNET *Health's Improv.* 96 Rock-doves breed upon Rocks by the Sea-side.

1802 MONTAGU *Ornith. Dict.* s.v., The Rock Dove is considered to be the origin of our tame Pigeons. **1844** H. STEPHENS *Bk. Farm* II. 247 The white-backed or rock dove, which was long confounded with the blue-backed dove. **1889** F. A. KNIGHT *By Leafy Ways* 132 A party of rockdoves .. settle down in a corner by themselves.

rocke, obs. form of ROCK, ROOK.

rocked (rɒkt), *ppl. a.* Also rockt. [f. ROCK *v.*[1] + -ED[2].]

1. Of a child: Swung to and fro in a cradle.

?*a* **1500** *Chester Pl.* (E.E.T.S.) viii. 396 That rocked Ribald, and I may raigne, rufully shalbe his reade! *Ibid.* x. 31. **1905** HOLMAN HUNT *Pre-Raphaelitism* II. 46 The sweet composure of rocked babyhood came back to me.

2. Subjected to rocking or swaying.

1892 LD. LYTTON *King Poppy* Prol. 693 Down from the rockt mast's windy rigging. **1894** *Daily News* 19 June 6/6 This sets in motion a couple of cog wheels, which work in a rocked quadrant at the back of the bascule.

†**rocked,** *a. Obs.* [f. ROCK *sb.*[1] + -ED[1].] Hard as a rock; stony.

1609 BIBLE (Douay) *Wisd.* v. 23 And from rocked wrath [L. *petrosa ira*] shal thicke hailе stones be cast.

Rockefeller ('rɒkəfelə(r)). The name of John D. *Rockefeller* (1839–1937), Amer. financier and philanthropist, used as the type of an immensely rich man. Also *attrib.* Hence ,**Rockefe'llerian** *a.*, designating that which only a rich man could afford.

1938 I. GOLDBERG *Wonder of Words* vii. 136 Anciently, men looked up to Crœsus.. as a man of immense wealth... Thousands of years later men still say, 'He is a Rockefeller,' or 'He is a Rothschild.' **1939** 'F. O'BRIEN' *At Swim-Two-Birds* i. 63, I rejoined.. that I.. was no Rockefeller, thus utilizing a figure of speech to convey the poverty of my circumstances. **1941** B. SCHULBERG *What makes Sammy Run?* i. 14 I'm not exactly Rockefeller, but I'm always good for a little touch. **1975** P. LORRAINE *Ask Rattlesnake* I. v. 88 'You don't remember anything?.. But, James, you could be —' 'A Rockefeller?' **1976** *National Observer* (U.S.) 24 Apr. 14/2 The daily rates are Rockefellerian,.. beginning at about $183 for two in high season from Dec. 20 through April 21. **1976** R. CONDON *Whisper of Axe* I. xiii. 77 Nobody, not even the Rockefeller boys, can shake up the cash for a hunnert keyes [of heroin]. **1979** *N.Y. Times Mag.* 30 Sept. 14/4 That uncle, whom I still think of as a Mellon, a Rockefeller,.. would collapse in awe of my annual grocery bill today.

rockelow, variant of ROQUELAURE.

rockenbole, obs. variant of ROCAMBOLE.

rocker[1] ('rɒkə(r)). Also 5–6 **rokker(e**, 6 **rok(k)ar**. [f. ROCK *v.*[1] + -ER[1].]

1. a. A nurse or attendant charged with the duty of rocking a child in the cradle. Now *arch.* or *Obs.* Also generally, one who rocks a cradle.

14.. *Lat. Eng. Voc.* in Wr.-Wülcker 576 *Crepundarius*, a rokkere. *Ibid.* 577 *Cunabulator*,.. a rokkere. **1491** HEN. VII in Ellis *Orig. Lett.* Ser. II. I. 170 Agnes Butler and Emlyn Hobbes rokkers of oure said son. **1539** in Nichols *Lit. Rem. Edw. VI* (Roxb.) I. p. xxviii, The lady Maistres, the Nurice, the Rocker, and such as be appointed contynually to be in the Prince's grace privie chambre. **1577–87** HOLINSHED *Chron.* III. 1130/2 Midwiues, rockers, nurses, with the cradle and all were prepared and in a readinesse. **1660** FULLER *Mixt Contempl.* (1841) 261 It happened that an aged rocker, which waited on him, took the steel boots from his legs. **1678** VAUGHAN *Thalia Rediv.*, *Nativity* 229 No rockers waited on thy birth, No cradles stirred, nor songs of mirth. **1707** tr. *Wks. C'tess D'Anois* (1715) 481 Her Nurse, her Foster-Sister, her Dresser, and Rocker. **1762** *Chron.* in *Ann. Reg.* 98 Attendants on.. the prince of Wales... Wet nurse, .. Dry nurse,.. Necessary women,.. Rockers. **1813** *Ibid.* 35 She was originally engaged as a rocker to the princesses. **1876** SMILES *Sc. Natur.* i, Sometimes he was set to rock the cradle. But on his mother's arrival at home, she found the rocker had disappeared.

fig. **1804** *Spirit Public Jrnls.* VIII. 166 The cradle of science; to which cradle.. some of our own countrymen have had the honour to be appointed rockers.

b. One who sends others to sleep.

1762 FOOTE *Orators* I. (1780) 29 The astonishing abilities of the Rockers, (for by that appellation I choose to distinguish this order of Orators).

c. A popular song that rocks (see ROCK *v.*[1] 5 c and 7 a); a rock song.

1954 *Billboard* 6 Nov. 52/4 The deep-voiced chanter hands the rocker a good performance... The boys bow on the label with a so-so reading of a new rocker here. **1970** *New Yorker* 12 Dec. 187/1 'One More Weekend', a honky-tonk rocker.. is about getting away. **1974** *Guardian* 22 Mar. 14/5 'Raised on Robbery' is a successful all-out rocker (with witty but still bleak lyrics). **1977** *Sounds* 1 Jan. 4/2 The songs they write alternate between brittle rockers, melodramatic movies and clever pop songs.

d. One who performs, dances to, or enjoys rock music (see ROCK *sb.*[3] 2 b); *spec.* a teenager or young adult of a type characterized by liking rock and roll, typically wearing long hair and a leather jacket, and riding a motor-cycle (freq. contrasted with MOD *sb.*[3]). Also *transf.*

1963 [see MOD *sb.*[3] and *a.*]. **1963** *Economist* 28 Dec. 1332/2 Teenagers want.. motor bikes and leather jackets to show that they are 'rockers'. **1964** *Spectator* 17 Apr. 503/1 Brighton cancelled its proposed 'beat festival' next month on hearing that the Mods and Rockers were coming in force. **1965** *New Statesman* 19 Nov. 801/1 A couple of literary Rockers rang up anonymously: 'We'll bomb the gallery if [Ezra] Pound turns up.' **1966** C. MACKENZIE *Paper Lives* iv. 54, I cannot think that *Romeo and Juliet* is made more accessible to the imagination of young people by making the Capulets what I believe are called Mods and the Montagues what I believe are called Rockers. **1972** *Listener* 10 Aug. 187/2 Chuck Berry is the rocker's rocker and the real man. **1973** J. WAINWRIGHT *Pride of Pigs* 82 He was.. a nineteen-year-old who had once identified himself as a greaser and, before that, as a Rocker, but who now led a provincial chapter of Hell's Angels. **1977** *Time* 3 Jan. 56/2 The debuting Barbra brings a hostile rocker audience to their feet with the wonder of her funkiness.

2. †**a.** *pl.* A cradle. *Sc. Obs.*

1566 in Hay Fleming *Mary Q. of Scots* (1897) 499 Fyftein elne of blew plading for to mak ane cannabie to the rokaris. *Ibid.* 500 Linnyng.. to be schetis to the rokaris.

b. One of the pieces of wood with a convex under-surface fixed to each end of a cradle, to the legs of a chair, or any other thing, in order to enable it to rock.

For some technical uses see Knight *Dict. Mech.*

1787 M. CUTLER in *Life*, etc. (1888) I. 269 He also showed us.. his great arm chair, with rockers. **1793** SMEATON *Edystone L.* §80 In some degree rounding, like the Rockers of a cradle. **1865** DICKENS *Mut. Fr.* I. i, The very basket that you slept in:.. the very rockers that I put it upon to make a cradle of it. **1883** *Harper's Mag.* Mar. 577/2 His child should not have its brains addled on a pair of rockers. **1892** *Photogr. Ann.* II. 478 A light frame on rockers, upon which the developing dish rests.

c. *off one's rocker*, crazy. *slang.*

1897 *Daily News* 29 June 3/5 When asked if he had swallowed the liniment, he said, 'Yes, I was off my rocker'. **1923** WODEHOUSE *Inimitable Jeeves* viii. 78 The Duke is off his rocker. **1932** E. WAUGH *Black Mischief* v. 195 It's going to be awkward for us if the Emperor goes off his rocker. **1943** 'C. DICKSON' *She died a Lady* vii. 58 We're wondering if there was anybody who cared enough about Mrs. Wainright to go off his rocker and kill both of 'em when she fell for somebody else. **1953** 'M. INNES' *Christmas at Candleshoe* xxi. 221 'His behaviour is certainly very aberrant. Would it, one wonders, be occasioned by a sudden abnegation of the ratiocinative faculty?' 'Off his rocker—eh?' **1961** [see FLIP *sb.*[2] 5]. **1976** T. SHARPE *Wilt* xiv. 144 'To put the record straight, what I said was that some of them were...' 'Off their rockers?' suggested the reporter.

3. †**a.** The device by which a smith's bellows is worked. *Obs.*

1677 MOXON *Mech. Exer.* i. 2 At the ear of the upper Bellows-board is fastned a Rope.. which reaches up to the Rocker, and is fastned.. to the farther end of the Handle.

b. (See quot. 1837.)

1794 W. FELTON *Carriages* (1801) I. 10 The bottom boards are confined thereto, by the assistance of a rocker, which is firmly fixed in the inside. **1837** W. B. ADAMS *Carriages* 221 The rocker or false bottom beneath the bottom framing, intended to give greater height, scarcely shows at all in perspective. **1877** THRUPP *Hist. Coaches* 136 At one time the fashion of the day is for deep quarters, deep rockers, and very shallow panels. **1880** *Coach Builders' Jrnl.* II. 134/1 After the inside bottom edge has been boxed out for the footboard, and the recess boxed out on the outside to show a sham rocker.

4. Something which rocks or is rocked after the manner of a cradle; in various special senses:

a. A rocking-horse. *nonce-use.*

1846 DICKENS *Cricket on Hearth* ii, Horses.. of every breed; from the spotted barrel on four pegs.. to the thoroughbred rocker on his highest mettle.

b. orig. *U.S.* A rocking-chair.

1852 in Mrs. Stowe *Key to Uncle Tom's Cabin* (1853) 136/1 Will be sold,.. Hairseat Chairs, Sofas and Rockers. **1855** S. ROBINSON *Jrnl.* 18 Nov. in *Kansas* (1856) viii. 98 [He was] seated in the nice large rocker drawn up before [the fire]. **1857** OLMSTED *Journ. Texas* 49 She sat down in the rocker at one end of the table. **1895** SARAH M. H. GARDNER *Quaker Idyls* i, The half dozen rockers and lounging chairs. **1905** *Delineator* May 829/1 The Windsor rockers are not so common as the side chairs. **1911** *Daily Colonist* (Victoria, B.C.) 30 Apr. 4/5 (Advt.), Bedroom suites in white enamel .. rockers, in white enamel to match. **1978** *Lancashire Life* Apr. 42/3 Ah sit theer i' mi rocker, Just startin' to nod off.

c. A gold-miner's cradle; = CRADLE *sb.* 14.

1830 *Boston Transcript* 15 Dec. 2/3 The surface mines, which are of very inferior importance, require no other labour than that necessary in washing the earth in *rockers*, or large inclined troughs with mercury. **1833** H. BARNARD *Let.* 18 Apr. in *Maryland Hist. Mag.* (1918) XIII. 346 The top soil is removed—then the gravel is washed, by being thrown into what is called a rocker, or cradle, which is in fact a little more than a large cradle. **1852** [see LONG TOM 2]. **1858** *Times* 1 Dec. 9/3 The only mode of 'washing' here, is with the rocker, an inefficient, laborious, and slow, implement. **1882** *U.S. Rep. Prec. Met.* 196 A great extent of ground has been worked along Salmon River, principally by rockers and other primitive appliances.

d. A scientific instrument illustrating the effect of heat in producing vibration.

1863 TYNDALL *Heat* iv. §113 (1870) 99 He determined the best form to be given to the 'rocker', as the vibrating mass is now called, and throughout Europe this instrument is known as Trevelyan's Instrument. **1882** J. MAIER tr. *Hospitalier's Electr.* 170 The armatures of the two electro-magnets were placed at the two extremities of a rocker.

e. *Engraving.* = CRADLE *sb.* 13.

1875 KNIGHT *Dict. Mech.* 1430/1 The instruments used are the cradle or rocker, scraper, burnisher, roulettes. **1885** *Harper's Mag.* Jan. 233/2 A 'rocker' or 'cradle' with which to lay the ground.

f. A tanning vat in which hides are rocked to and fro on a pivoted frame. Freq. *attrib.*

1885 C. T. DAVIS *Manuf. Leather* xviii. 353 Another form of handler in use is known as the rocker handler, and it consists of a frame constructed of wood, and hung by pivots in the centre of the top of the vat so as to give a dipping movement of 7 or 8 in. to each end of the frame. **1897** *Ibid* (ed. 2) xxiv. 382 The hides are next suspended in 'rockers'. .. They remain in the 'rockers' from seven to ten days. **1969** T. C. THORSTENSEN *Pract. Leather Technol.* v. 69 The hides are tied and hung in rocker racks and tanned by the vegetable tanning process. Prior to vegetable tanning, the hides in the lime condition are put in rockers containing deliming and bating materials.

g. A rock-shaft, rocker arm, or any similar rocking device forming part of a mechanism; *esp.* (*a*) a device for controlling the positions of brushes in a dynamo, and (*b*) a rocker arm in an internal-combustion engine.

1888 S. P. THOMPSON *Dynamo-Electric Machinery* (ed. 3) iii. 63 The rockers which support the brush-holders should admit of sufficient angular displacement being given to the brushes. **1893** R. GRIMSHAW *Locomotive Catechism* 178 Lengthen the rocker, so as to lower the entire motion. **1915** G. A. BURLS *Aero Engines* vi. 108 When the 'plus' part of the cam comes into contact with the roller the upper end of the rocker U is pushed upwards and the lower-end depressed, thus opening the valve. **1921** *Motor Electr. Manual* iii. 50 A magneto that has been standing out of use.. is very liable to have a sticking rocker. **1928** *Evening News* 18 Aug. 1/3 Gallop then had to go into the pits with rocker trouble. **1935** T. E. LAWRENCE *Lett.* (1938) 855 The front rocker ran dry. .. So we pulled down the rocker assembly, and found more bits of Harry M's. string in the rocker-fulcrum pipe! **1961** *Carbon Brushes & Electr. Machines* xiv. 221 The correct location of the brush rocker is usually indicated by the machine constructor by a pair of marks, one on the rocker and one on the frame of the machine. **1970** K. BALL *Fiat 600, 600D Autobk.* i. 9/1 The design is conventional, incorporating.. overhead valves operated by pushrods through rockers. **1975** F. PORGES *Design of Electr. Services for Buildings* i. 3 The switch opens when the bottom of the rocker is pressed and shuts when the top is pressed.

5. Chiefly *U.S.* **a.** A keel having a marked upward curve; a curve on a keel; a boat, etc., having a keel of this type.

1876 *Encycl. Brit.* IV. 812/2 Other canoes are built chiefly for sailing, and these carry 'drop keels', 'rockers', and heavy ballast. *a* **1890** *Tribune Bk. of Sports* 251 (Cent.), When a fast sloop of the straight-keel type came out, the rockers were beaten. **1895** *Outing* XXVI. 382/1 Two thirds of the keel is almost flat, with a very slight rocker at the heel and a more pronounced curve under the fore-foot.

b. A skate with a curving sole.

1854 B. F. TAYLOR *Jan. & June* II. 155 The boys sha'n't skate? Who grudges them the 'rockers'? **1869** VANDERVELL & WITHAM *Figure-Skating* iii. 81 The American and Canadian 'rockers'.. are much too highly curved. **1875** KNIGHT *Dict. Mech.* 2192/2 A machine for grinding skates, straight-edged or rockers.

c. *Ice-skating.* = *rocking turn* s.v. ROCKING *vbl. sb.*[1] 3.

1892, 1902 [see COUNTER *sb.*[4] 6]. **1936** *Sun* (Baltimore) 15 Feb. 13/2 There are 72 different school figures the skater must learn... Counters, rockers, brackets, loops, threes. **1973** *Times* 7 Feb. 15/8 He looked ill at ease on the first figure, the forward outside rocker.

d. 'One of the curved stripes under the three chevrons that indicate the grade of a sergeant (as in the U.S. Army and Marine Corps)' (Webster 1961). Also *transf.*, any similar badge bearing a slogan or device.

1944 *Yank* 6 Oct. 15/1 'Woddya want, fellah?' said the sergeant. He was thin for a top kick and his blouse was much too big. The bottom rocker reached down to his elbow. **1948** *Christian Sci. Monitor* (Mag. Sect.) 6 Nov. 8/1 Sergeant second class—three stripes, two 'rockers'—has been changed to sergeant first class. **1967** E. E. KERRIGAN *Amer. Badges & Insignia* i. 27 Next come first, second, and third grade sergeants, which were separated into both line and staff grades. The arcs, or 'rockers', indicated line grade, and straight lines below indicated grade. **1971** J. MANDELKAU

Buttons vii. 81 The patch consisted of the top rocker—three inches wide, red on white—*Hell's Angels.* The bottom rocker said, *England* and between them I carried the small death's head. **1976** *New Yorker* 15 Mar. 102/2 Wetsel, a staff sergeant (E-6) with three stripes and one rocker, arrived in the company.

e. The upward curve on a surfboard.

1963 *Surfing Yearbk.* 43/1 *Rocker*, the slight upward slope in a surfboard. **1968** W. WARWICK *Surfriding in N.Z.* 3/2 The nose, was rounded with a slight uplift or rocker. **1970** *Studies in Eng.* (Univ. of Cape Town) I. 27 Less familiar words include *rocker*, or *banana*, which indicates the curvature of the surfboard along its length.

6. *attrib.* and *Comb.* (in senses 2 b, 4, and 5), as ***rocker bearing, box, -cam, gear, pump, -shaft, sieve, -sleeve, tailing, type; rocker-less*** adj.; **rocker arm**, a rocking lever in an engine; *esp.* one in an internal-combustion engine which serves to work a valve and is operated by a push-rod from the camshaft; **rocker(-bottom) foot** *Med.*, a foot with the sole curved downwards; **rocker panel**, in a motor vehicle, a panel forming part of the bodywork below the level of the passenger door; **rocker switch**, an electrical switch having a mechanism incorporating a spring-loaded rocker.

1860 CLARK & COLBURN *Rec. Pract. Locomotive Engine* 67/1 The block..is carried upon the upper end of an arm, attached to, and vibrating upon the lower end of the *rocker-arm. **1874** *Railroad Gaz.* 9 May 170/2 This block is attached to the lower rocker-arm by a pin, *c*, which works freely in the block. **1928** *Evening News* 18 Aug. 1/3 Baron d'Erlanger's Lagonda broke a valve rocker arm, and had to retire. **1970** K. BALL *Fiat 600, 600D Autobk.* i. 12/2 Take off cylinder head cover, rocker arm and shaft assembly. **1930** *Engineering* 30 May 696/3 The Aintree end [of the bridge] was treated..by means of four 100-ton jacks, and fixed *rocker bearings weighing 5 tons each were placed in position. **1975** *New Yorker* 17 Feb. 26/2 He [*sc.* a robot] has rocker bearings for hands, shock absorbers for forearms,.. hubcaps for shoulders. **1950** *Jrnl. Bone & Joint Surg.* XXXII A. 344 Sonnenburg saw 688 cases of congenital club-foot, 42 cases of flat-foot, and 15 cases of congenital convex pes valgus or '*rocker-bottom' foot... In two of the cases club-foot was present originally; due to mistreatment, rocker-foot developed. **1956** *Clin. Orthopaedics* VIII. 94/2 If applied properly to give pressure under the cuboid, the packed felt will prevent the disastrous deformity of rocker foot. **1977** N. E. SHAW in *Bone & Joint Dis.* (Brit. Med. Assoc.) 114 (*caption*) Calcaneus is in equinus and is tucked up behind ankle joint. Rocker-bottom deformity has developed. **1892** J. G. A. MEYER *Mod. Locomotive Constr.* 199 The lifting-shaft bearing and *rocker-box..are bolted to the front splice. **1965** *Motor* 17 July 3/2 Condensation in the rocker box of his B.M.C. 1100. **1875** KNIGHT *Dict. Mech.*, **Rocker-cam*, a vibrating cam. **1902** F. J. A. MATTHEWS *Electr. Motor Installations* iii. 51 No *rocker-gear is fitted to the machine, so that it is impossible..to alter the position of the brushes. **1950** NEWTON & STEEDS *Motor Vehicle* (ed. 4) vi. 118 (*caption*) Rocker gear of refined design for overhead camshaft. **1922** D. H. LAWRENCE *Aaron's Rod* i. 9 A baby was cooing in a *rocker-less wicker cradle. **1921** C. W. TERRY *Pract. Motor Body Building* xxxviii. 255 A standard pattern taxi-cab with recessed *rocker panels at the back. **1952** T. A. WOHLFEIL et al. *Automobile Body Reconditioning* vii. 88/1 Rocker panels are boxlike sections consisting of inner and outer panels welded to the edge of the floor pan. **1978** *N.Y. Times* 29 Mar. A25/4 (Advt.), Porsche '77... Sport wheel, fogs, alloys, rocker panel. **1892** *Daily News* 11 July 12/5 *Rocker pumps, pair of 8in. lift pumps. **1842** R. & G. L. SCHUYLER in *Q. Papers Engin.* (1844) I. IV. 2 The valves..are of our own contrivance, and peculiar to this ship; they are worked by a separate eccentric and *rocker shaft, which is set as to follow the motion of the steam valve. **1939** *Automobile Engineer* XXIX. 300/2 Rubber gland packing effectively seals the rocker shaft against leakage. **1950** *Engineering* 4 Aug. 104/1 A number of parts such as valves and valve gear..rocker shaft components, and bearings, are interchangeable with the six- and eight-cylinder engines. **1869** *Overland Monthly* III. 301/2 The united crash of pebbles on hundreds of quickly agitated *rocker sieves, sounded in his ear like the roar of a cotton factory. **1884** *Bull. U.S. Nat. Museum* No. 27. 575 Cradle or Rocker Sieve, for washing the contents of the dredges. **1890** *Cent. Dict.*, **Rocker-sleeve*, a part of the breech-action of a magazine-gun. **1964** *Electr. Engineer's Ref. Bk.* (ed. 11) xxx. 79 (*heading*) *Rocker switch. **1971** *Daily Tel.* 24 Nov. 11/4 The facia has been tidied up and rocker switches provided. **1975** F. PORGES *Design of Electr. Services for Buildings* i. 3 The advantages of the rocker switch are that it is easier to operate and that it is almost impossible to hold half open, even deliberately. **1906** C. DE L. CANFIELD *Diary of Forty-Niner* ii. 18 Worked out the claim and before I moved the Tom, tried some of the *rocker tailings. **1899** *Westm. Gaz.* 28 Sept. 3/3 A bulb fin keel of the *rocker type.

'rocker². [f. ROCK *sb.*¹ + -ER¹.] = ROCKIER.

1862 [see ROCKIER]. **1895** P. H. EMERSON *Birds Norf. Broadland* 239 The Stock-Dove, miscalled the 'blue rocker', is a smaller bird than the old 'ring-dow'.

'rocker³. *Sc. rare*⁻¹. [f. ROCK *sb.*²] One who takes part in a rocking.

1818 *Edinb. Mag.* Aug. 153 He was esteemed the most acceptable rocker, whose memory was most plentifully stored with such thrilling narratives.

rockered ('rɒkəd), *a.* [f. ROCKER *sb.*¹ + -ED².] Curved like a rocker.

1880 KEMP *Neison's Pract. Boat-Building* 67 The rockered keel curves downwards, or the reverse way to the cambered keel. **1895** *Outing* XXVII. 200/2 A twelve-inch skate, rockered.

rockeried ('rɒkərɪd), *a.* [f. ROCKERY + -ED².] Furnished with a rockery or rockeries.

1966 J. BETJEMAN *High & Low* 67 But strew the roads with tin signs 'Keep Left', 'M4', 'Keep Out!' Command, instruction, warning, Repetitive adorning The rockeried roundabout.

rockery ('rɒkərɪ). [f. ROCK *sb.*¹ + -ERY.]

1. An artificial heap or pile of rough stones and soil used for the ornamental growing of ferns and other plants. Also *transf.*

1845 *Florist Jrnl.* 224 On the top and sides of the rockery, ..many others of a similar nature may be placed. **1878** WILLIAMS *Midl. Railw.* 406 These quarries form natural rockeries of vast size. **1880** J. FOTHERGILL *Probation* II. xii, A kind of rockery which ran along one side of the terrace. *attrib.* **1892** *Garden* 27 Aug. 190/1 *C. decumbens*..is a pretty and desirable rockery plant.

2. Natural rockwork.

1856 STANLEY *Sinai & Pal.* Introd. (1858) p. xlv, The two ranges, here of red sandstone, closed in upon the Nile..; fantastic rockery, deep sand-drifts, tombs and temples hewn out of the stone.

rocket ('rɒkɪt), *sb.*¹ Now *rare.* Forms: 3–5 **roket** (5 **-ete, -ett, -ytte,** 6 **-it**), 5 **rocat,** 6 **rokkat, -et;** 4– **rocket** (9 **-at**), 5–6 **rockett,** 8–9 **rocquet.** [a. OF. *roket, ro(c)quet*, northern variant of *rochet* ROCHET¹. Hence also Flem. *rokket.*]

1. = ROCHET¹ 1. Now *dial.* Also *attrib.*

c **1290** *St. Agnes* 73 in *S. Eng. Leg.* I. 183 A Roket he brouȝte on is hond to hire, ȝwittore nas neuere non. Þat [maide] dude on þis Roket. ? *a* **1366** CHAUCER *Rom. Rose* 1240 Ther is no cloth sitteth bet On damiselle, than doth roket. A womman wel more fetys is In roket than in cote, y-wis. **1382** WYCLIF *Gen.* xxxviii. 14 The which [Thamar], the clothis of widewhed don down, toke to a roket [L. *theristrum*]. *c* **1400** *Destr. Troy* 13525 Þan Pirrus full prestly put of his clothes; Toke a Roket full rent,..couert hym þerwith. *a* **1529** SKELTON *E. Rummyng* 54 In her furred flocket, And gray russet rocket. **1650** *Rel. Execution Montrose* in *Harl. Misc.* (1745) V. 319 He came..into the Parliament-house with a Scarlet Rocket, and a Suit of pure Cloth. **1662** J. DAVIES tr. *Olearius' Voy. Ambass.* 316 Persons of quality..wear, over this Coat, a kind of Rocket, without sleeves. **1688** HOLME *Armoury* IV. vi. (Roxb.) 322/1 There is an other kinde of Mantle called a Rockett Mantle. .. A Rockett is a scant cloak without a cape. *c* **1710** CELIA FIENNES *Diary* (1888) 205 You meete all sorts of Country women wrappd up in the mantles Called West Country Rockets, a Large Mantle doubled together of a sort of serge. **1823** SCOTT *Quentin D.* Note D, Their only clothes a large old duffle garment,..and under it a miserable rocket. **1901** F. E. TAYLOR *Folk-Speech S. Lanc.*, *Rocket*, an outer garment worn by country-women.

2. *Eccl.* = ROCHET¹ 2. Chiefly *Sc.*

1382 WYCLIF *Exod.* xxix. 5 Thow shalt clothe Aaron with his clothes, that is to seie, with rocket, and coote, and coope. *c* **1450** HOLLAND *Howlat* 172 In quhyte rocatis arrayd;.. That thai war bischopis blist, I was the blythar. **1500–20** DUNBAR *Poems* lx. 33 Sum ramyis ane rokkat fra the roy. *a* **1578** LINDESAY (Pitscottie) *Chron. Scot.* (S.T.S.) I. 283 James Bettone..was taine out behind the hie allter and his rokit revin off him. **1647** WARD *Simp. Cobler* 56 Hath Episcopacy beene such a religious Jewell..that you will sell all or most of your Coronets, Caps of honour, and blue Garters..for so many Rockets? **1686** J. S[ERGEANT] *Hist. Monast. Convent.* 157 The Judge of Confidence, is attired in Purple, in the Habit of a Prelate, wearing a Rocket. **1808** SCOTT *Marm.* VI. xi, With mitre sheen, and rocquet white. **1828–43** TYTLER *Hist. Scot.* (1864) I. 326 The palls, copes, rocquets, crosiers, censers, and church plate, were.. sumptuous.

rocket ('rɒkɪt), *sb.*² Also 6 **rokat, rockat, rok(k)et, rocked,** 8 **rockett, roquet.** [a. F. *roquette*, ad. It. *ruchetta*, dim. of *ruca*:—L. *ērūca* a kind of cabbage. Hence also older Du. *rocket(te.*]

1. A cruciferous annual (*Eruca sativa*) having purple-veined white flowers and acrid leaves, used in Southern Europe as a salad. (Classed by Linnæus as *Brassica eruca.*) †Also, wild rocket, hedge mustard.

1530 PALSGR. 263/2 Rocket an herbe, *rocquette.* **1548** TURNER *Names Herbs* (E.D.S.) 36 The other kynde called in latin Eruca syluestris is communely called in englishe Rokket, it hath a yealowe floure. **1578** LYTE *Dodoens* 622 Rockat flowreth cheefely in Iune and Iuly. **1605** TIMME *Quersit.* Pref. p. vi, Like bad and unskilful herborists, to sowe rocket and to weede endive. **1693** EVELYN *De la Quint. Compl. Gard.* II. 200 Rocket is one of our Sallet Furnitures, which is sown in the Spring as most of the others are. Its Leaf is pretty like that of Radishes. **1718** QUINCY *Compl. Disp.* 115 Rocket.—This is not often met with either in Composition or Prescription. **1731** MILLER *Gard. Dict.* s.v. *Erucago*, It may be propagated in like manner as the Rocket; but..is hardly worth cultivating. **1746** P. FRANCIS tr. *Hor. Sat.* II. viii. 68 I first..knew Roquets and herbs in cockle brine to stew.

b. With specific epithets, esp. ***garden rocket, Roman rocket,*** and ***rocket gentle.***

For an enumeration of the varieties see Miller *Gard. Dict.* (1731) and Chambers *Cycl. Suppl.* (1753), s.v. *Eruca.*

1548 TURNER *Names Herbes* (E.D.S.) 36 After Dioscorides and Plinie there are two kyndes of rokket. The one is gardine Rokket, whiche is much greater then the other, and it hath a white leafe, some abuse thys for whyte mustarde. *c* **1550** H. LLOYD *Treas. Health* Y v, 3 i. of Nettels sede roket royal. **1578** LYTE *Dodoens* 629 Erysimon hath long leaves not muche unlyke the leaves of Rockat gentle. **1597** GERARDE *Herbal* 191 Garden Rocket or Rocket gentle, hath broade leaues like those of Turneps. *Ibid.* 192 Romaine Rocket is cherished in gardens. **1629** PARKINSON *Parad.* II. xxxiv. 502 Our Garden Rocket is but a wilde kinde brought into Gardens. **1731** MILLER *Gard. Dict.* s.v. *Eruca*, Great Garden Rocket, with a white strip'd Flower,..was formerly very much cultivated in Gardens as a Sallad-Herb, but at present is very little us'd. **1753** CHAMBERS *Cycl. Suppl.* s.v. *Eruca*, The broad-leav'd, narrow-podded Rockett, called the Rockett gentle, or Roman Rockett. **1830** *Edin. Encycl.* XI. 283/2 Garden Rocket..is an annual plant, a native of Switzerland. **1855** DELAMER *Kitch. Gard.* (1861) 113 *Garden Rocket*... Not unusually eaten in France, where it comes up in gardens like a weed.

2. A cruciferous plant of the genus *Hesperis*, esp. *H. matronalis*, a garden-flower which is sweet-scented after dark.

[**1629** PARKINSON *Parad.* 264 Dodonæus accounteth the ordinary sort [of *Hesperis*] to be a kinde of Rocket.]

1731 MILLER *Gard. Dict.* s.v. *Hesperis*, The double white Rocket is by far the most beautiful plant of all the Kinds. **1785** MARTYN *Rousseau's Bot.* xxiii. (1794) 323 Rocket has the petals obliquely bent. **1829** *Encycl. Metrop.* (1845) XX. 244 *H. matronalis*, the Rocket, of which there are several cultivated varieties, is a native of England. **1856** DELAMER *Fl. Gard.* (1861) 102 The Garden Rocket varies in colour from light blush or French white, to light purple or violet. **1882** *Garden* 27 May 358/2 A pure white single Rocket, with dense-set, small flowers.

3. With qualifying word prefixed, applied to various plants:

base rocket, the wild mignonette (*Reseda luteola*). **bastard rocket**, †(*a*) = prec.; (*b*) one of the mustard plants (*Brassica erucastrum*). **blue rocket**, (*a*) one of several kinds of wolf's-bane or aconite, esp. *Aconitum Napellus*; (*b*) applied to various kinds of larkspur (*Delphinium*); (*c*) the blue-bell (*Scilla nutans*). **corn rocket**, a salad plant, *Bunias* or *Crambe orientalis*. †**crambling rocket**, = *scrambling rocket.* **cress rocket** (see CRESS 3). **dame's rocket**, dame's violet (see sense 2). **dyer's rocket** (see DYER 2). **false rocket**, *U.S.*, a cruciferous perennial (*Iodanthus pinnatifida*). **golden rocket**, = *London rocket.* **Italian rocket**, = *base rocket.* **London rocket** (see LONDON). **marsh rocket** (see MARSH¹ 4 c). **native, scrambling, sea rocket** (see quots.). **square-codded** or **-podded, Turkish rocket**, = *corn-rocket.* **wall rocket**, = *wild rocket.* **water rocket** (see quot. 1796). **white rocket**, = sense 2. **wild rocket**, hedge mustard. **winter rocket** (see quots.). †**wound rocket**, Turner's name for Herb Barbara. **yellow rocket**, the winter-cress (CRESS 1 b).

1775 JENKINSON *Brit. Plants* 102 *Reseda Lutea.* *Base Rocket with all the leaves trifid. **1828** J. E. SMITH *Eng. Flora* II. 348 *R. lutea.* Base Rocket. Wild Mignonette. **1863** [see BASE *a.* 1 b]. **1760** J. LEE *Introd. Bot.* App. 324 Rocket, *Bastard, *Reseda.* **1866** *Treas. Bot.* 987/2 Rocket, Bastard, *Brassica Erucastrum.* **1827** T. FORSTER *Encycl. Nat. Phenomena* 290 Monkshood and several sorts of Wolfsbane, and Larkspur now are in full flower, the long blue spikes of some of these flowers in our cottage gardens are called *blue rockets. **1848** A. S. TAYLOR *Poisons* 763 Monkshood.. which is also known under the name of Wolfs-bane and Blue-Rocket. **1882** *Hardwicke's Science Gossip* 43 Wild Hyacinth (*Agraphis nutans*), 'Blue rocket'. **1731** MILLER *Gard. Dict.* s.v. *Erucago*, We have but one Species of this Plant, which is..*Corn-Rocket. **1753** CHAMBERS *Cycl. Suppl.* App., Corn-Rocket, or square-podded Rocket, a distinct genus of plants, called by botanists Erucago. **1760** J. LEE *Introd. Bot.* App. 324 Rocket, Corn, *Bunias.* **1597** GERARDE *Herbal* 215 *Crambling Rocket hath many large leaues cut into sundry sections. **1775** JENKINSON *Brit. Plants* 147 *Vella annua.* *Cresse Rocket with pinnatifid leaves. **1822** *Hortus Anglicus* II. 146 *Vella Pseudo Cytisus*, Shrubby Cress Rocket. **1866** *Treas. Bot.* 987/2 Rocket, *Dame's, *Hesperis matronalis.* **1828** J. E. SMITH *Eng. Flora* II. 347 *Reseda luteola.* *Dyer's Rocket. **1856** A. GRAY *Man. Bot.* 31 *Iodanthus*, *False Rocket. **1597** GERARDE *Herbal* 278 Reseda is called..in English *Italian Rocket. **1898** MORRIS *Austral Eng.* 392/1 *Rocket*, **Native*, a Tasmanian name for *Epacris lanuginosa.* **1796** WITHERING *Brit. Plants* (ed. 3) III. 584 *Erysimum officinale*..Hedge Mustard, or Wormseed. Bank Cresses. *Scrambling Rocket. **1611** COTGR., *Cachile*, *Sea-rocket. **1796** WITHERING *Brit. Plants* (ed. 3) III. 563 *Bunias Cakile*, Sea Rocket. **1846–50** A. WOOD *Class-bk. Bot.* 171 *Cakile Maritima*,..Sea Rocket... Native of the sea-coast! and of the lake-shores of N.Y. **1760** J. LEE *Introd. Bot.* App. 324 Rocket, *Square-codded, of Montpelier, *Bunias.* **1753** CHAMBERS *Cycl. Suppl.* s.v. *Erucago*, This plant has been called, by other authors, the *square podded rockett, and the echinated mustard. **1887** *Amer. Naturalist* XXI. 442 It is called in England *Turkish Rocket. **1611** COTGR., *Roquette sauvage*, wild Rocket, *wall Rocket. *c* **1710** PETIVER *Catal. Ray's Eng. Herbal* xlvi, *Water Rocket. **1753** CHAMBERS *Cycl. Suppl.* s.v. *Sisymbrium*, The creeping water-sisymbrium with leaves like those of the nasturtiums. This is called by some water-rocket. **1796** WITHERING *Brit. Plants* (ed. 3) III. 581 *Sisymbrium sylvestre.* Creeping Water Cress. Water Rocket. **1866** *Treas. Bot.* II. 987/2 Rocket, *white, *Hesperis matronalis.* **1578** LYTE *Dodoens* 621 *Eruca sylvestris.* *Wild Rockat. **1830** *Edin. Encycl.* XI. 283/2 Wild-rocket, or Hedge-mustard.., has been sometimes sown and used as a spring pot-herb. **1753** CHAMBERS *Cycl. Suppl.* App., Water-Rocket, or *Winter-Rocket, the name of a species of *Sisymbrium.* **1796** WITHERING *Brit. Plants* (ed. 3) III. 584 *Erysimum Barbarea.* Winter Cresses. Winter Rocket. Rocket Wormseed. **1548** TURNER *Names Herbes* (E.D.S.) 82 Barbare herba..hath leaues lyke Rocket, wherefore it maye be called in englishe *wound-rocket, for it is good for a wounde. **1826–7** *Encycl. Metrop.* (1845) XVIII. 616/1 *Erysimum officinale*, *Barbareum*, a double variety is cultivated in gardens, and is called the Double *Yellow Rocket. **1863** PRIOR *Plant-n.* 191 Rocket, winter-, or Yellow-, *Barbarea vulgaris.*

4. *attrib.* and *Comb.*, as ***rocket-seed; rocket-like, -leaved*** adjs.; **rocket larkspur** (see quots.); †**rocket watercress**, the meadow cress (CRESS 1 b); **rocket wormseed**, = *winter rocket* (see 3); **rocket yellow-weed**, = *base rocket* (see 3).

1548 TURNER *Names Herbes* (E.D.S.) 74 Sisymbrium alterum is called also Cardamine, and in english water cresses, or rocket water cresses. **1580** BLUNDEVIL *Horsemanship* III. 34 Some would giue him Onions and Roket seede to drinke with wine. **1661** CULPEPPER *Lond. Disp.* 18/1 Roket seed, provokes urine. **1753** CHAMBERS *Cycl. Suppl.* s.v. *Crambe*, The broad rocket-leav'd sea crambe. *Ibid.*, The narrower-leav'd, rocket-like sea crambe.

1796 WITHERING *Brit. Plants* (ed. 3) II. 446 *Reseda lutea.* Rocket Yellow-weed. **1852** G. W. JOHNSON *Cottage Gard. Dict.* 782/1 Rocket Larkspur, *Delphinium ajacis.* **1866** *Treas. Bot.* 325/1 *Delphinium orientale* and *D. Ajacis*, the rocket larkspurs, are often cultivated.

5. A butterfly of the genus *Mancipium*.

1832 J. RENNIE *Consp. Butterfl. & M.* 4 The Rocket (*M. Daplidice*, Hubner) appears April, May and August.

rocket (ˈrɒkɪt), *sb.*³ Also 7 racket, rocquet. [a. F. *roquet* (16th c.), or ad. It. *rocchetta*, in med.L. *roccheta*, *rocheta* (1379), app. a dim. of It. *rocca* ROCK *sb.*², with reference to the form of the thing. With the form *racket* cf. F. *raquette*, G. *rakete* (earlier *rackete*, *rachete*, and *racket*), Du., Da., and Sw. *raket*.]

1. a. An apparatus consisting of a cylindrical case of paper or metal containing an inflammable composition, by the ignition of which it may be projected to a height or distance.

Pyrotechnic rockets are usually constructed so as to burst in the air and scatter a shower of sparks. *Congreve rocket*: see CONGREVE 1.

1611 FLORIO, *Rocchello*,..any kind of rocket or squib of wilde fire... *Rocchetti*, rockets, or squibs of wilde-fire. **1624** CAPT. SMITH *Virginia* III. 60 In the evening we fired a few rackets, which flying in the ayre..terrified the poore Salvages. **1669** STURMY *Mariner's Mag.* v. xiii. 87 To make the Composition for Rockets of any size. *Ibid.* 88 Rockets that will run upon a Line. **1714** *Lond. Gaz.* No. 5258/1 Any Squibs, Rockets, Serpents or other Fireworks. **1766** R. JONES *Fireworks* II. 57 All rockets under one pound are made chiefly of gun-powder and charcoal. **1816** BYRON *Siege Corinth* xxxiii, Up to the sky like rockets go All that mingled there below. **1858** GREENER *Gunnery* 123 My experience with rockets goes to justify me in asserting that rockets discharged from a gun..can be..effectually controlled. **1889** *Infantry Drill* 425 Rockets with fireballs of different colours are best for signalling during night attacks.

fig. **1716** GAY *Trivia* III. 414 When..Tragedies, turn'd Rockets, bounce in Air. **1751** EARL ORRERY *Remarks Swift* (1752) 53 His friend Dr. Sheridan, who..was continually letting off squibs, rockets, and all sorts of little fireworks from the press.

b. In proverbial phr. ***to rise like a rocket and fall like a stick*** (cf. STICK *sb.*¹ 4 h) and varr., describing a sudden, meteoric rise and subsequent fall, as of fortune, etc.

1792 T. PAINE *Let. to Addressers* 4 As he [*sc.* Burke] rose like a rocket, he fell like the stick. **1838** R. H. BARHAM *Let.* 7 Mar. (1870) II. vii. 48 Poor man, he has gone up like a rocket and is coming down like the stick. **1909** *Brit. Weekly* 7 Jan. 405/3 We know the talk about a man going up like a rocket and coming down like a stick... It is generally the man's own fault. **1922** JOYCE *Ulysses* 364 My fireworks. Up like a rocket, down like a stick. **1950** G. B. SHAW *Farfetched Fables* 83 Political adventurers and 'tin Jesuses' rose like rockets to dictatorships and fell to earth like sticks.

c. Any elongated device or craft (as a flying bomb, a missile, a spacecraft) in which a rocket engine is the means of propulsion.

1919 R. H. GODDARD *Method of reaching Extreme Altitudes* (Smithsonian Misc. Coll. LXXI. (No. 2) 1 The problem was to determine the minimum initial mass of an ideal rocket necessary, in order that on continuous loss of mass, a final mass of one pound would remain, at any desired altitude. **1920** *Photo Play* 7 Sept. 1/1 The theory of a Professor Goddard that a rocket could be sent to the moon. *Ibid.*, The propulsive power of the rocket..is derived from a series of multiple charges. **1929** *Amazing Stories* May 151 In the meantime, Dr. Mueller busied himself with making the rocket shipshape, for in spite of every precaution the supplies were in chaos. **1944** *Times* 11 Nov. 2/1 For the last few weeks the enemy has been using his new weapon, the long-range rocket, and a number have landed at widely scattered points in this country. **1949** W. LEY *Conquest of Space* (1950) i. 21 The rocket is a mile high and the spectators realize that there is still a deafening sound beating upon their ears. **1964** *Yearbk. Astron. 1965* 160 The rocket plummeted down near Guericke in the Mare Nubium, within a few miles of its intended position. **1970** N. ARMSTRONG et al. *First on Moon* iv. 76 At the time of Apollo II there was no doubt that the Saturn V was the most powerful operational rocket on earth. **1977** *Whitaker's Almanack 1978* 595/1 Mozambique troops fired rockets into the centre of Rhodesia's border city of Umtali but damage was stated to be minimal.

d. In full ***rocket engine*** or ***motor***. An engine operating on the principle of the pyrotechnic rocket, providing thrust by the same method as a jet engine but without depending on the surrounding air for combustion (see also quot. 1971).

1919 R. H. GODDARD *Method of reaching Extreme Altitudes* (Smithsonian Misc. Coll. LXXI. No. 2) 6 By application of the above principles, it is possible to convert the rocket from a very inefficient heat engine into the most efficient heat engine that ever has been devised. **1929** *Sci. Wonder Q.* Fall 7 Prof. Hermann Oberth, a German of Mediarch, and Prof. Robert H. Goddard, an American of Worcester, Massachusetts..have solved it, though..only theoretically, by means of the rocket motor. **1931** *Jrnl. R. Aeronaut. Soc.* XXXV. 34 The fuel loading for rocket engines is a different matter from that of an engine of the explosion type. **1939** *Astounding Sci. Fiction* May 61/1 Each man in the crew tensed himself, gathering his abdominal muscles to resist the enormous acceleration developed by the launching catapult and the ship's own rockets acting in conjunction. **1960** C. H. GIBBS-SMITH *Aeroplane* xv. 122 The Messerschmitt Me 163 *Komet* fighter..had swept-back wings, a Walter liquid-fuel rocket motor, and a speed of 590 m.p.h. **1965** W. R. CORLISS *Space Probes & Planetary Exploration* x. 204 Because they will be used for delicate maneuvers, the on-board rockets have to be precisely controlled not only in thrust level but also in thrust duration and direction. **1971** P. J. MCMAHON *Aircraft Propulsion* x. 294 The convention of speaking of liquid fuel rocket *engines* but of solid fuel rocket *motors* is established in Britain. **1972** *Guinness Bk. Records* 128/2 The car was powered by a liquid natural gas/hydrogen peroxide rocket engine delivering 22,000 lb. s.t. maximum and thus theoretically capable of 900 m.p.h. **1977** *Engin. Materials & Design* Aug. 25/1 In rocket motors extremely high temperatures are developed (up to 3500°C). **1977** I. RIDPATH *Signs of Life* viii. 153 In its simplest form, the nuclear rocket uses as a propellant liquid hydrogen, which is heated to a gas by the reactor and expelled at high speed.

e. ***off one's rocket***, mad. Cf. ROCKER¹ 2 c. *slang.*

1925 FRASER & GIBBONS *Soldier & Sailor Words* 244 *Rocket, off one's*, mad. **1959** I. & P. OPIE *Lore & Lang. Schoolch.* x. 179 He is cracked, he's cuckoo... He's off his rocket ('Off your rocket' is a development of 'off your rocker').

f. A severe reprimand. Freq. ***to give*** (or ***get***) ***a rocket***. *slang* (orig. *Mil.*).

1941 *New Statesman* 30 Aug. 218/3 [War-time slang.] *To stop a rocket*, receive a reprimand. **1942** E. WAUGH *Put out More Flags* ii. 153 The C.O. led Captain Brown away. 'He's getting a rocket,' said the anti-tank man. *a* **1944** K. DOUGLAS *Alamein to Zem Zem* (1946) xii. 77, I contended [*sic*] myself with giving him a rocket, and told them to hurry up and mend the tank. **1949** 'N. BLAKE' *Head of Traveller* III. xiv. 231 Your Superintendent gave me a rocket yesterday about 'harbouring her', as he put it. **1957** I. MURDOCH *Sandcastle* vii. 104 Demoyte had pondered the outrage..made a mental note to give Mor a rocket when he next saw him,..and felt immensely better. **1961** A. WILSON *Old Men at Zoo* i. 36 If Beard's to blame, then he should get the rocket. **1975** J. I. M. STEWART *Young Pattullo* vii. 155 Fish was sent to the Provost and given a rocket.

2. *transf.* **a.** *U.S.* A form of cheering used in certain American universities.

1868 in *Westm. Gaz.* (1901) 26 Sept. 3/1 Three cheers.. were given with a will, followed by the usual tiger and 'rocket'. **1879** *Princeton Bk.* 387 The twofold tradition in regard to the origin of the college cheer, or Nassau rocket.

b. A rapid rise to a high note. *nonce-use.*

1894 DU MAURIER *Trilby* III. 138 The little soft ascending rocket, up to E in alt.

3. *attrib.* and *Comb.*, as ***rocket aeroplane***, ***age***, ***airplane***, ***apparatus***, ***base***, ***battalion***, ***boat***, ***boy***, ***brigade***, ***engineer***, ***flight***, ***flyer***, ***flying***, ***frame***, ***fuel***, ***installation***, ***jet***, ***-maker***, ***pilot***, ***projectile***, ***propellant***, ***propulsion***, ***research***, ***scientist***, etc.; also ***rocket-launching*** vbl. sb. and ppl. adj., ***-shooting*** vbl. sb.; ***rocket-assisted***, ***-boosted***, ***-borne***, ***-carrying***, ***-driven***, ***-firing***, ***-powered***, ***-propelled***, ***-tracking*** adjs.; ***rocket-like*** adv.; **rocket astronomy**, the branch of astronomy in which measurements are made by instruments carried by rockets above the atmosphere; **rocket-bird**, an Indian bird (see quot.); **rocket-bomb**, (*a*) (see quot. 1895); (*b*) = *flying bomb* s.v. FLYING *vbl. sb.* 3; (see also quot. 1973); **rocket car**, a car powered by a rocket engine; **rocket chamber**, the combustion chamber of a rocket engine; **rocket gun**, a gun firing rockets; **rocket launcher**, a device or structure for launching rockets; **rocket-man**, (*a*) a soldier responsible for firing rockets (? *obs.*); (*b*) *colloq.* an astronaut; **rocket net** *sb.*, a net having small rockets attached, which is laid on the ground and then propelled so as to envelope a group of feeding birds for ringing; hence **rocket-net** *v. trans.*, to trap in this way; **rocket netting** *vbl. sb.*; **rocket pad**, a launching pad for a rocket; **rocket plane**, (*a*) an aircraft powered by a rocket motor; (*b*) an aeroplane armed with rockets; **rocket projector** = *rocket launcher* above; **rocket range**, (*a*) a rocket-launching range (cf. RANGE *sb.*¹ 11 c); (*b*) the area within range of a rocket; **rocket-rattling** *vbl. sb.* and *ppl. a. colloq.*, threatening with the military use of rockets or nuclear weapons (after *sabre-rattling* s.v. SABRE *sb.* 4 a); **rocket ship**, (*a*) a spaceship powered by rockets; (*b*) a warship armed with rockets; **rocket sled**: see SLED *sb.*¹ 2 b; **rocket tube**, (*a*) a tube out of which a rocket is fired; † (*b*) a rocket motor.

1932 H. NICOLSON *Public Faces* I. 16 With this explosion chamber the problem of the *rocket aeroplane was finally solved. **1959** *Globe & Mail* (Toronto) 15 July 1/3 Scout laws created in the horse and buggy days don't always fit into today's *rocket age. **1959** *Listener* 10 Dec. 1024/1 The strange and striking contrasts that must exist between the buildings of the Victorian and Edwardian periods and those that will be put up in the Rocket Age. **1928** *Sci. Amer.* Sept. 260/1 (heading) Can there be a *Rocket Airplane? **1929** *Amazing Stories* May 148 The series of experiments were given their first impetus by the German rocket airplanes, successfully designed for the Berlin-to-New York air service. **1880** *Daily News* 26 Nov. 2/2 The lifeboat being of no avail, the *rocket apparatus was got into action. **1941** *Flight* 23 Jan. p. b/1 It may be expected that *rocket-assisted take-off can be made more effective if not very efficient. **1950** *Sci. News* XV. 82 Rocket assisted take-offs by heavy bombers are quite common. **1959** *Economist* 17 Jan. 221/1 The RAT (rocket-assisted torpedo), a complicated but highly praised anti-submarine device. **1960** *McGraw-Hill Encycl. Sci. & Technol.* XI. 600/2 *Rocket astronomy, first used in 1945 in the United States with German V-2 rockets, has been especially fruitful in studies of solar phenomena. **1971** *New Scientist* 18 Mar. 636/2 The emphasis is on the more modern approach which has grown up over the past 10 years as balloon and rocket astronomy have aided observations. **1954** M. CAIDIN *Worlds in Space* 177 In the opinion of many, the combination of the moon-launched rocket with an atomic bomb war head merited a thorough investigation of the value of the lunar *rocket base. **1958** *New Statesman* 4 Jan. 1/1 The government seems determined to go ahead and establish American rocket-bases in Britain. **1976** *New Yorker* 15 Mar. 79/1 He explained that Intelligence had come to suspect that a North Vietnamese Army *rocket-battalion command group had moved into the Song Quan Valley. **1885** *Field* 4 Apr. 454/1 The Paradise flycatcher (*Tchitræa paradisi*), generally yclept the *rocket bird by our countrymen. *c* **1829** D. JERROLD in M. R. Booth *Eng. Plays of 19th Cent.* (1969) I. 168 I'd fight yard-arm to yard-arm for you.., or fight in a *rocket boat. *c* **1860** J. STUART *Seaman's Catech.* 9 They can..be fitted as rocket boats. **1948** W. LEY *Rockets & Space Travel* 197 They..were massed on the decks of special 'rocketboats', rack after rack of self-propelled projectiles, fired electrically from below deck... One such rocket boat could, in the space of a few minutes, throw as much steel and high explosive as the turrets of three battleships. **1883** *Fisheries Exhib. Catal.* 199 The bomb-lance, dasting-bomb, and *rocket-bomb. **1895** *Funk's Stand. Dict.*, *Rocket-bomb*, a harpoon-rocket. **1943** MRS. BELLOC LOWNDES *Let.* 20 Dec. (1971) 247 A good many people believe the rocket-bomb is coming, but a famous airman laughed at the idea of its being a real danger to London. **1949** 'G. ORWELL' *Nineteen Eighty-Four* I. viii. 85 'Steamer' was a nickname which..the proles applied to rocket bombs. **1973** J. QUICK *Dict. Weapons & Mil. Terms* 375/3 *Rocket bomb*, an aerial bomb equipped with a rocket to give it added velocity and penetrating power after being dropped from an aircraft. **1958** *Technology* Mar. 25/1 Scientists and the services have hurried into print with space plans.., among them *rocket-boosted..engines to fire a payload to the moon. **1962** W. B. THOMPSON *Introd. Plasma Physics* i. 4 Recently, *rocket- and satellite-*borne counters have detected belts of energetic radiation..high above the earth's atmosphere. **1971** *Sci. Amer.* July 74/2 X-ray observations with rocket-borne instruments have shown that the remnant of Tycho's nova is also a strong source of X rays. **1782** in *Gentl. Mag.* (1818) LXXXVIII. II. 123 Their infantry and *rocket-boys gained the back of the hill. **1813** WELLINGTON in Gurw. *Desp.* (1838) XI. 314 I have received your letter of the 11th regarding the *Rocket brigade. **1930** *Times Educ. Suppl.* 25 Oct. p. iv/1 The *rocket-car experiments of the late Herr Max Valier. **1976** *Star* (Sheffield) 30 Nov. 12/9 Gabelich strapped himself into a rocket car named Blue Flame and covered two measured miles..at an average speed of 630 mph. **1961** *Guardian* 25 Oct. 11/2 *Rocket-carrying submarines. **1936** *Smithsonian Misc. Coll.* XCV. No. 3. 2 In these experiments it was shown that a *rocket chamber and nozzle, since termed a 'rocket motor', could use liquid oxygen together with a liquid fuel, and could exert a lifting force without danger of explosion. **1939** *Astounding Sci. Fiction* May 59/1 Injecting excess charges of fuel into the rocket chambers. **1875** KNIGHT *Dict. Mech.* 1960/1 **Rocket-drift*, a cylinder of wood tipped with copper, employed for driving rockets. **1928** *Rocket-driven [see *rocket-propelled* below]. **1978** R. V. JONES *Most Secret War* viii. 68 The German Navy was said to have developed remote-controlled rocket-driven gliders of about three metres span and three metres long. **1951** *Jrnl. R. Aeronaut. Soc.* LV. 92/1 Rocket propellants must have certain undesirable features, and it is the task of the *rocket engineer to minimise the consequences of these. **1834** *Penny Cycl.* II. 420/1 A *rocket establishment now forms a regular branch of the British military service. *a* **1854** H. REED *Lect. Brit. Poets* xiv. (1857) 171 A *rocket fire will leap up into the heavens, outshining and outstripping the stars. **1970** H. TREVELYAN *Middle East in Revolution* 149 The Iraqi Air Force..attacked the rebel headquarters with *rocket-firing aircraft. **1978** R. V. JONES *Most Secret War* xliii. 403 The attack took place on 16th March with rocket-firing Typhoons of No. 198 Squadron. **1930** H. CHATLEY *Princ. Rocket Propulsion* 3 This is the basis of the dreams of *rocket flight to the moon. **1934** H. G. WELLS *Exper. Autobiogr.* I. vi. 328 They did not so much climb to success; they were rather caught by success and blown sky high... Only one item in this rocket flight is significant here. **1959** *Times Lit. Suppl.* 20 Mar. 167/2 The book is, in the main, a really excellent elementary account of rocket flight and space travel. **1799** G. SMITH *Laboratory* I. 26 Of *rocket-flyers, and the manner of charging them. **1927** *Amazing Stories* Nov. 725 Many schemes have been proposed for space flying, and some of the more recent ones, notably the Goddard Rocket Flyer, seem to come closest toward a strictly scientific solution of the problem. **1939** *Ibid.* Sept. 112 She had attached herself to him, demanding that he teach her how to pilot a rocket flier. **1929** *Sci. Wonder Q.* Fall 7 While writing the story, the author has had the collaboration of practically all the German scientists who have of late come into prominence in their researches into not only *rocket flying, but space flying and astro-physics. **1931** *Wonder Stories* Jan. 900 We have succeeded in securing near Berlin a suitable rocket flying field, a large field on which the starting supports for the different rockets were set up. **1835** J. E. ALEXANDER *Sketches in Portugal* v. 126 Saldanha's artillery consisted of four 5½-inch howitzers, six 9-pounders, six of 6, two of 3, and three *rocket frames. **1867** SMYTH *Sailor's Word-bk.*, *Rocket-Frame*, the stand from which Congreve rockets are fired. **1931** *Amazing Stories* Dec. 804 A battleship has destroyed Albertville, Ontario, site of the Canadian *rocketfuel factory and magazine. **1937** *Discovery* Sept. 277/2 Equipping this type of aeroplane with rocket engines, complete with rocket fuel. **1977** *Time* 18 July 35/3 It is known as phencyclidine hydrochloride, but youngsters on this latest and fastest-spreading high know it as 'angel dust', 'rocket fuel' and 'goon'. **1884** *Bull. U.S. Nat. Museum* No. 27. 281 The *rocket-gun..throws a large rocket and explosive lance weighing eighteen or twenty pounds, which acts in the capacity of a harpoon and bomb, and is used mainly in coast whaling. **1935** *Jrnl. R. Aeronaut. Soc.* XXXIX. 410 The main characteristic of..rocket guns..is the increase of their efficiency when the ratio of weight of the rocket..to the weight of the charge decreases. **1944** *Jane's All World's Aircraft* p. iii/2 The rocket-guns with which some..fighters were equipped..enabled them to attack. **1875** KNIGHT *Dict. Mech.* 1960/1, **Rocket-harpoon*, a device for killing whales. It consists of a rocket having a pointed shell at its front. **1959** E. H. CLEMENTS *High Tension* ii. 33 The Hebridean *rocket-installations. **1944** *Aviation* Jan. 149/3 The mass of a *rocket jet can be readily varied by feeding more or less fuel ..into the rocket motor. **1944** *Rocket launcher [see LAUNCHER 2]. **1977** *N.Y. Rev. Bks.* 23 June 3/2 He learned to slaughter people with rifles and knives and explosives or to blast them to pieces with rocket launchers. **1956** A. H. COMPTON *Atomic Quest* 223 The great installations along the coast..turned out to be *rocket launching platforms. **1968** *Times* 16 Dec. 7/3 The systematic recording of disturbances like these could be used to provide remote observers with information about rocket launchings. **1973** D. KYLE *Raft of Swords* (1974) iii. 19 Our force of rocket-launching submarines came into service. **1832** SCOTT *Redgauntlet* Note P, The Scots people assembled in numbers by signal of *rocket lights. **1856** R. A. VAUGHAN *Mystics* (1860) I. 96 Up mounts speculation, *rocket-like. **1952** S. SPENDER *Learning Laughter* 38 There was a screen of cypress trees with the column of one palm tree in their midst, bursting rocket-like at the apex. **1882** *Encycl. Brit.* XIV. 572/2 The tail-block, having been detached from the *rocket-line, is fastened to a mast, or other portion of the wreck, high above the water. **1799** C. BUTLER *Hor. Bibl.* 126 They had been sold to a *rocket-maker. **1821** G. R. GLEIG *Narr. Campaigns Brit. Army* XIX. 270 Attached to this corps of infantry, were a party of *rocket-men, and two light three-pounder guns. **1938** *Sci. Amer.* May 270 (*heading*) Number one rocket man. **1964** *Galaxy Mag.* Oct. 181/1, I was a Rocketman 3/c on the Moon, guarding the Aristarchus base against invaders from outer space. **1972** *Melody Maker* 20 May 16/2 Elton John remains..a writer (with Bernie Taupin) of songs of lasting merit... The success of his beautiful 'Rocket Man' single proves that he has survived all the flack. **1858** HOMANS *Cycl. Comm.* 1215/2 The establishment of life-boats and *rocket-mortars at all the dangerous parts of the coast. **1948** *Severn Wildfowl Trust Ann. Rep.* 43 Although this report is primarily concerned with the activities of the Trust during the year 1947, it seems that such an important development as the first attempt with the Trust's new *rocket nets for ringing the wild geese should be included although it took place early in 1948. **1952** *Blackw. Mag.* Feb. 106/1 When they want to tell t'other from which, they rocket-net them and paint their sterns. **1954** *Brit. Birds* XLVII. 316 By rocket nets, it has been possible to make an intensive study of the population of the Pinkfoot. **1973** *Wildfowl* XXIV. 164/2 A lot of effort went into attempting to rocket net Barnacle Geese. **1979** *Ibid.* XXX. 165/2 A single catch of 372 Barnacle Geese at Caerlaverock in October (one of the largest catches made with rocket nets) provided much valuable data. **1953** *Severn Wildfowl Trust 5th Ann. Rep.* 22 The *rocket-netting technique has undergone considerable modification during the four years since the first experiments were made. **1969** *Wildfowl* XX. 86/1 The Wildfowl Trust's rocket-netting programme had concentrated on the Pink-footed Goose since this proved the easiest to trap in the large numbers needed. **1965** *Time* 23 July 36 For those pictures, JPL's boss ..and his crew had sweated out Mariner's launch from a Cape Kennedy *rocket pad. **1977** *Jersey Even. Post* 26 July 14/3 It was vandalized by the German rocket-pad crews. **1949** R. A. HEINLEIN *Red Planet* i. 6, I still think I'd like to be a *rocket pilot. **1958** C. C. ADAMS *Space Flight* p. vii, There have been space books for children—our present space cadets and future rocket pilots. **1928** *Pop. Mechanics* Nov. 718/2 Valier has calculated that a *rocket plane could be shot from Berlin to New York in ninety-three minutes. **1929** *Mech. Engin.* Nov. 865/1 The rocket plane with its possibility of moving at speeds..would seem to be the answer to the problem of quick transportation. **1932** A. HUXLEY *Brave New World* iv. 70 The deeper drone of the rocket-planes hastening, invisible, through the bright sky five or six miles overhead. **1945** *Daily Tel.* 7 Aug. 1/6 R.A.F. shattered panzer counter-attack in Normandy. Rocket planes knocked out 35 tanks. **1949** *Ann. Reg. 1948* IV. 416 Earlier in the year (in May) it was reported from America that the rocket-plane Bell XS-1 had been flown faster than sound. **1965** W. R. CORLISS *Space Probes & Planetary Exploration* x. 209 Rocket planes and helicopters are possible prime movers for unmanned landers, but surface locomotion is much more likely. **1799** G. SMITH *Laboratory* I. 16 How to proportion the *rocket-poles. **1936** *Pop. Science* May 16/2 An experimental *rocket-powered glider ..carried the cargo to its intended destination. **1948** *Electronics* June 93/1 Rocket-powered engines of one particular type employ two kinds of fuel. **1959** *Daily Tel.* 23 Feb. 11/6 This year two test pilots are expected to make the first flights in the rocket-powered North American X-15. **1943** *Fortune* June 92/2 A strange gun called the bazooka that fires a *rocket projectile. **1944** T. N. DALTON *Jet Propulsion* 44 The Encyclopaedia Britannica says that rocket projectiles were used by the Chinese. **1945** L. E. O. CHARLTON *R.A.F. & U.S.A.A.F. July 1943–Sept. 1944* 292 (*caption*) Thunderbolt showing *rocket projectors fitted to one of its wings. **1961** B. FERGUSSON *Watery Maze* ix. 235 The mass of rocket projectors pointing into the air from an LCT 2. **1932** *Bull. Amer. Interplanetary Soc.* Feb. 8 How best can we utilize each of these as a *rocket propellent? **1944** C. P. LENT *Rocket Res.* 67/1 After using the rocket propellants the flying weight is only 1780 Kg and during the period of ascent the total weight averages less than 2000 Kg. **1928** *Sci. Amer.* Sept. 260/1 The recent German experiments with *rocket propelled cars and gliders have attracted much attention, and it is now asked whether rocket-driven airplanes are not possible, navigating at fantastic speeds. **1951** *Mind* LX. 119 We have the idea now of a rocket-propelled missile capable of flying from Moscow to New York. **1978** R. V. JONES *Most Secret War* xxxix. 371, I already knew of two liquids used by the Germans in the rocket-propelled glider bombs they had been using against our ships. **1928** *Explosives Engineer* VI. 457 (*heading*) Motoring by *rocket propulsion. **1929** *Sci. Wonder Stories* Aug. 265 Aeronautical authorities have stated recently that the future development of the airplane will be along the lines of rocket-propulsion. **1942** *Aeronautics* Aug. 49/2 The greatest reason against rocket propulsion of aeroplanes is the question of oxygen, its weight and storage in an aeroplane. **1963** *Listener* 23 May 866/1 Even before Verne's death the idea of using rocket propulsion for space-travel had been put forward by..Konstantin Eduardovich Tsiolkovskii. **1948** *Hansard Commons* 15 Mar. 1805 We have joint research stations; for instance, the one about which there has been considerable publicity, the *rocket range in Australia. **1971** 'D. HALLIDAY' *Dolly & Doctor Bird* ii. 24 The tracking of moonshots and other missiles from the American rocket range is done by the electronic brains in these stations. **1976** *New Yorker* 15 Mar. 79/1 A..command group had moved into the Song Quan Valley, ten miles to the west and almost within rocket range of the division headquarters. **1960** *News Chron.* 21 July 4/5 The..retaliation threats, the *rocket-rattling over Cuba. **1961** *Sunday Express* 29 Jan. 1/4 President Kennedy has put a sharp curb on rocket-rattling, anti-Russian speeches. **1969** *Guardian* 31 Mar. 10/1 Rocket-rattling by any large Power over a weaker neighbour is deplorable. **1937** *Discovery* Sept. 269/1 Fundamental problems of *rocket research. **1977** *Whitaker's Almanack 1978* 165/1 The progress of rocket research during the last war led to the development by the Germans in 1944 of the V.2 rocket. **1952** *Sun* (Baltimore) 5 Sept. 2/6 Take it from the *rocket scientists who expect to fly to Mars some day —flying saucers are not space ships from another planet. **1959** *Listener* 5 Mar. 410/1 Rocket-scientists are not unaware of this. **1927** *Literary Digest* 25 June 20/1 He [*sc.* Max Valier] is even now building a *rocket-ship. **1928** *Amazing Stories* Aug. 427 Not to mention the rocketships that might be in the air. **1936** *Forum & Century* July 38/2 But the question of whether rocket ships will ever reach the planets can be even approximately answered only when intensive research has been carried on over many years. **1951** W. LEY *Rockets, Missiles & Space Travel* p. viii (*caption*) One of the Navy's 'rocket ships' bombarding Peleliu Island on the same morning that was D-Day in Europe. **1969** *New Yorker* 12 Apr. 53/1 Anybody on earth with a pair of binoculars can see that setting a rocket ship down there would be a tricky operation. **1981** *Daily Tel.* 15 Apr. 1 The American space shuttle landed on a dry lake bed in California's Mojave Desert yesterday to complete the maiden flight of the first re-usable rocketship. **1925** R. GRAVES *Welchman's Hose* 35 And watched the nightly *rocket-shooting, varied With red and green, and livened with gun-fire. **1882** *Encycl. Brit.* XIV. 572/2 The *rocket stations on the coast at the 30th June 1881 numbered 288. **1799** G. SMITH *Laboratory* I. 16 How to proportion the *rocket sticks. **1884** FROUDE *Carlyle Life Lond.* II. 273 He had just discovered that he could not end with 'Frederick' like a rocket-stick. **1971** 'D. HALLIDAY' *Dolly & Doctor Bird* ii. 24 There are four main *rocket-tracking stations in the Bahamas. **1841** *Penny Cycl.* XX. 55/1 In 1813 the British *rocket-troop rendered considerable service at the battle of Leipzig. **1881** W. D. HAY *300 Years Hence* iv. 70 The largest [projectiles] requiring apparatus like the old *rocket-tubes and howitzers, and dealing certain death to every living thing within a mile of the place of explosion. **1898** D. BEATTY *Diary* 8 Apr. in W. S. Chalmers *Life & Lett. David, Earl Beatty* (1951) ii. 33, I with the Rocket tube first occupied a position on the left of the Artillery. **1932** *Flight* XXIV. 1023/1 The rocket tube or rocket motor, as it is called in Germany..is filled with powder of special composition.

† '**rocket**, *sb.*^{4} *Obs.* Also 5 **roket**, 5–6 **-ette**. [a. OF. *roquet*, northern form of *rochet*, = It. *rocchetto*: see RATCHET *sb.*]

1. A bobbin. = ROCHET^{3}. *rare*$^{-0}$.

c **1440** *Promp. Parv.* 436/1 Roket, of the rokke (*P.* roket of spynnynge), *librum, pensum.* **1611** FLORIO, *Rocchello*, a rocket or bobbin to winde silke vpon.

2. A blunt-headed lance.

1525 LD. BERNERS *Froiss.* II. clxii. [clviii.] 448 All maner of knyghtes and squyers..that wyll come thyder for the breakynge of fyue speares, outher sharpe or rokettes at their pleasure. *Ibid.* clxxiii. [clxix.] 511 Suche as wolde iust with rokettes.

† '**rocket**, *sb.*^{5} *Obs. rare.* In 6 **rokket**, pl. **rokettes**. [f. ROCK *sb.*^{1} + -ET^{1}, or a. OF. *roquette* (Picard *rokette*).] A small rock.

1538 LELAND *Itin.* (1769) VII. 115 In the Mouth of the Ryver..ys the Rokket Godryve wheryn bredeth Se Fowle. *Ibid.* 116 Ther be of the Isles of Scylley cxlvii. that bere Gresse (besyde blynd Rokettes).

† **rocket**, *sb.*^{6}, var. of, or error for, ROCHET *sb.*^{2}

a **1655** SIR T. MAYERNE *Archimag. Anglo-Gall.* No. 40 (1658) 35 To make a sauce for fryed Gurnet or Rocket.

rocket ('rɒkɪt), *v.* [f. ROCKET *sb.*^{3}]

1. a. *trans.* To discharge rockets at; to bombard with rockets.

1803 WELLINGTON in Gurw. *Desp.* (1835) II. 467 They continued to rocket us till dark. **1810** *Ibid.* (1836) VI. 624 You must..rocket Santarem if you believe that the boats and materials are still there. **1967** [see NAPALM *v.*]. **1973** *Houston* (Texas) *Chron.* 21 Oct. 1/1 The 22-year-old officer, whose tank had been rocketed, said the Egyptian soldiers.. threw what they apparently thought was his body out of the ditch. **1978** *Guardian Weekly* 12 Feb. 6/1 Six vessels..are rocketing besieging guerrilla forces around the port of Massawa.

b. To propel (someone) at speed, as by a rocket; to send by rocket. Also *fig.*

1837 J. COTTLE *Killcrop* in *Early Recoll.* II. 316 From yon tall rock I'll hurl him to perdition... I'll rocket him. **1958** *Listener* 16 Oct. 603/2 Probably he [*sc.* an astronaut] will come down in a large sphere..because the retardation he will experience in this way will expose him to no worse strains than those he suffers in any case as he is rocketed upwards. **1959** *Times* 11 June 3/6 A boundary rocketed his score to a dozen. **1966** I. ASIMOV *Fantastic Voyage* i. 10 We would pile him into an X-52 and rocket him through inner space.

c. To reprimand severely. Cf. ROCKET *sb.*^{3} 1 f. *slang* (orig. *Mil.*).

1948 PARTRIDGE *Dict. Forces' Slang* 156 He rocketed me like hell. **1971** J. WAINWRIGHT *Dig Grave* 96 The assistant chief constable was still rocketing Sergeant Sykes.

2. *intr.* **a.** Of a horse (or rider). To spring or bound up like a rocket; to dart like a rocket.

1883 E. PENNELL-ELMHIRST *Cream Leicestersh.* 296 [His] small mare rockets over without touching a twig. **1891** KIPLING *Light that Failed* xiii. (1900) 224 If you'd seen me rocketing about on a half-trained French troop-horse under a blazing sun you'd have laughed. **1898** HEWLETT *Forest Lovers* xxv, The man swerved at the onset; Prosper rocketed into him; horse and man went over in a heap.

b. Of game-birds: To fly up almost vertically when flushed; to fly fast and high overhead.

1860 RUSSELL *Diary India* II. 169 Nothing was shot, though some pheasants 'rocketed' over our guns. **1879** JEFFERIES *Amateur Poacher* ii. (1889) 24 Up rose a large bird out of the water with a bustling of wings and splashing, compelled to 'rocket' by the thick bushes and willow poles.

c. In general use: to move like a rocket, to speed; (of prices, etc.) to increase substantially, to soar. Also const. with advbs.

1881 *Baily's Mag.* Oct. 37 He played too forward and a little too quick to a very quick, straight ball, and she 'rocketted' between the wickets. **1924** W. J. LOCKE *Coming of Amos* xxiv. 312 A flash of lightning rocketed across the black gap of the open window. **1924** H. G. WELLS *Exper. Autobiogr.* I. v. 219 The more brilliant investigators rocket off into mathematical pyrotechnics and return to common speech with statements that are..nonsensical. **1937** J. BETJEMAN *Coll. Poems* (1958) 44 The heart of Thomas Hardy flew out of Stinsford churchyard... It rocketed over the elm trees. **1947** *Evening News* 5 Nov. 1/5 A hectic day's trading..sent the shares rocketing on Monday from 13s. 3d. to 23s. 9d. **1952** DYLAN THOMAS *Coll. Poems* 132 Up through the lubber crust of Wales I rocketed to astonish The flashing needle rock of squatters. **1957** *Economist* 2 Nov. 375 Manufacturer's exports rocket 23 times in 7 years! **1972** D. HASTON *In High Places* ii. 29 The rope rocketed out. This was really high-quality ice climbing in action. **1976** *Times* 17 Mar. 2/8 Mr Benn rocketed to prominence as a potential future party leader..in the early 1970s. **1979** *Jrnl. R. Soc. Arts* CXXVII. 431/2 It goes along relatively steadily till 1972, then rockets up and comes back down and has just rocketed up again.

rocke'teer. [f. ROCKET *sb.*^{3} + -EER^{1}.]

1. A discharger of rockets.

1832 SOUTHEY *Hist. Penins. War* III. 837 With this force there were..forty rocketeers, and an officer with a few artillerymen. **1945** F. H. M. LLOYD *Hurricane* i. 12 Fighter, night-fighter, fighter-bomber, tank-buster, 'rocketeer', ship-fighter, merchant-ship protector..in thirty different forms and on thirty-seven different fronts, the Hurricane went into action. **1974** D. SEAMAN *Bomb that could Lip-Read* ix. 70 The flash..won't affect the man firing the rocket-launcher... I want every rocketeer to fire his two rounds.

2. One who experiments or works with rockets; a rocket expert or enthusiast.

1929 *Review of Reviews* Sept. 91 (*heading*) The new race of rocketeers. **1935** *Jrnl. Brit. Interplanetary Soc.* Oct. 13 *Rocketeer*, one who experiments with rockets. **1953** J. N. LEONARD *Flight into Space* 25 One philosophical rocketeer pointed to the fact that man's body stands mid-way in size between the atoms it contains and the great galaxies that float beyond the stars. **1957** P. MOORE *Sci. & Fiction* 18 Lucian's seamen are the logical ancestors of the rocketeers and space-cadets of to-day. **1960** *New Statesman* 2 Jan. 7/3 While the rocketeers burst into space, the advances that touched the man in the street were mostly of the kind of wide-screen movies and stereophonic records. **1971** *Nature* 23 Apr. 494/2 The group of astronomers at the University of Leicester, who have been among the most successful X-ray rocketeers, are still producing valuable data. **1972** *Sci. Amer.* Dec. 118/3 Model rocketeers fly light reflyable rockets they make themselves or from kits.

rocke'teering, *vbl. sb.* [f. prec. + -ING^{1}.] = ROCKETRY.

1932 D. LASSER *Conquest of Space* vii. 116 The support of a financier of world-wide experience, and of men of science ..comes as a revelation to those who viewed the field of 'rocketeering' as a visionary dream. **1938** *Forum* Feb. 96/2 Rocketeering may, in some distant future, take us to the moon or elsewhere in space. **1962** *Times Lit. Suppl.* 2 Feb. 68/5 The race is therefore on, for a greater prize..than any that can be won by rocketeering.

rocketer ('rɒkɪtə(r)). Also 9 **rocketter**. [f. ROCKET *v.* 2 b + -ER.] **a.** A game-bird that 'rockets'.

1863 'OUIDA' *Held in Bondage* (1870) 93 Isn't it beautiful to see Sabretasche knock down the rocketers? **1883** *19th Cent.* Dec. 1090 The 'rocketer', which I may at once define as a bird flying fast and high in the air towards the shooter.

† **b.** *Cricket.* = SKYER. *Obs.*

1886 *Cricket* 25 Feb. 18/1 A good man..is the man to go for a 'pocketer' [*sic*] between the wickets. *Ibid.* 25 Mar. 35/2 In my last letter of course 'Pocketer' ought to read 'Rocketer'. **1887** F. GALE *Game of Cricket* iv. 70 He hit [the ball] too quick, and instead of going out of the field, as it might have done, it went up a tremendous rocketer. **1900** *Badminton Mag.* Oct. 380 The great smiter..hit a ball very high straight to the young blacksmith... But for some reason—whether he was thinking too much of the style of the thing, or was unused to rocketers— ..the ball fell with a hollow clank on the top of his head.

'**rocketing**, *ppl. a.* [f. ROCKET *v.* + -ING^{2}.] That rockets, in the senses of the verb.

1869 *Pall Mall G.* 24 Sept. 5 There is more knack and greater coolness required to kill..partridges driven over his head, or rocketing pheasants. **1883** E. PENNELL-ELMHIRST *Cream Leicestersh.* 275 To the rocketting bound of a good free horse you catch your breath, thankfully, happily. **1897** W. H. THORNTON *Reminis. Clergym.* xii. 339, I shot a rocketing cock pheasant..with a single bullet. **1952** DYLAN THOMAS *Coll. Poems* 172 He..prays, Who knows the rocketing wind will blow The bones out of the hills. **1959** *Economist* 25 Apr. 318/2 Behind the increase in imports there is cited a 'rocketing' increase in Dutch production. **1964** M. ARGYLE *Psychol. & Social Probl.* xvi. 199 We are astounded however by the rocketing crime rate, [etc.]. **1970** *Daily Tel.* 8 May 17 Doctors, headmasters and health educationists are disturbed by the rocketing numbers of young smokers.

'rocketing, *vbl. sb.* [f. ROCKET *v.* + -ING[1].] The action or practice of the vb. in various senses.
1928 P. F. NOWLAN in *Amazing Stories* Aug. 427 The favorite American method of propulsion was known as 'rocketing'. **1972** *Guardian* 4 May 15/8 Rocketing of Saigon, plus ground probes near the capital, could shake the politicians..out of their current isolation. **1975** *Church Times* 14 Mar. 1/5 Rocketing and shelling of the airfield was going on as the plane left.

rocketry ('rɒkɪtrɪ). [f. ROCKET *sb.*[3] + -RY.] The science or use of rockets and rocket propulsion. Also *fig.*
1930 G. E. PENDRAY in *Bull. Amer. Interplanetary Soc.* Nov.–Dec. 4 The practical work of getting a liquid-fuel rocket actually into the air was a contribution of America's, as were the three most fundamental achievements of modern rocketry. **1934** *Jrnl. Brit. Interplanetary Soc.* I. I. 3 There you have the nucleus of the British movement in rocketry. **1934** *Astronautics* Mar. 7 'Rocketry' itself is a coined word, first suggested at a meeting of the American Interplanetary Society in 1930 and since widely adopted. **1943** C. S. LEWIS *Perelandra* vi. 91 He was a man obsessed with the idea which is..circulating all over our planet in obscure works of 'scientifiction', in little Interplanetary Societies and Rocketry Clubs. **1951** 'J. WYNDHAM' *Day of Triffids* ii. 30 Sustained research in rocketry had at last succeeded in attaining one of its objectives. It had sent up a missile which stayed up. **1957** *Times* 10 Oct. 10/1 The American programme..called for the launching of small test spheres this year..to check rocketry instrumentation. **1958** *Sunday Times* 14 Sept. 7/4 His [*sc.* Thomas Wolfe's] absurd rocketry about great America, decadent Europe and so on. **1962** F. I. ORDWAY et al. *Basic Astronautics* ii. 21 A scientific analysis of rocketry applied to high altitude meteorological research. **1968** A. DIMENT *Bang Bang Birds* v. 70 A collection of scientists..who weren't quite bright enough to get into the rocketry racket. **1977** *Daily Tel.* 28 July 1/6 The small spaceport at Kagoshima..looked more like a station for amateur rocketry than a serious rival to Cape Canaveral.

rocketsonde ('rɒkɪtsɒnd). Also **rocket-sonde, rocket sonde.** [f. ROCKET *sb.*[3] + *-sonde*, after RADIOSONDE.] A package of meteorological or other scientific instruments which is carried aloft by a rocket, released in the upper atmosphere, and floats down by parachute, transmitting measurements automatically by radio.
1949 E. DURAND in G. P. Kuiper *Atmospheres Earth & Planets* iv. 134 (*heading*) Rocket sonde research at the Naval Research Laboratory. **1951** *Jrnl. Brit. Interplanetary Soc.* X. 18 Direct measurements have been made by means of rocket-sondes to altitudes of over 100 miles. **1963** *Proc. 1st Internat. Symp. Rocket & Satellite Meteorol.* 23 The rocketsonde, at the present time, measures the temperature only; the wind is determined by radar tracking of the metallized parachute. **1969** MCINTOSH & THOM *Essent. Meteorol.* vii. 112 Above the ceiling of balloons, information is provided by rocket sonde or by satellite. **1976** *Nature* 13 May 124/1 The phase of the annual oscillation in the zonal winds at 82 km is consistent with the phase of this oscillation in the lower mesosphere determined from rocketsonde data.

'rockety, *a.* [f. ROCKET *sb.*[3] + -Y[1].] Acting like a rocket; flighty.
1881 *Nation* XXXII. 289 We complained in February of the fact that Mr. Blaine had no legal training, no diplomatic experience,..and a rockety mind.

'rock-fish. [ROCK *sb.*[1]]
1. A fish frequenting rocks or rocky bottoms, *spec.* as the name of many unrelated fishes, such as the black goby or sea-gudgeon, the striped bass, the wrasse, etc. Also = *rock salmon* (*c*) s.v. ROCK *sb.*[1] 9 d.
Also with defining terms, as *bearded, black, grass, green*, etc., applied to a number of American fishes, chiefly of the genera *Sebastichthys* and *Sebastomus*.
1598 FLORIO *Worlde of Wordes* 279/1 Piota,..a kind of rock fish. **1611** COTGR., *Canadelle*, the smallest of rock-fishes, beautified with spots of sundry colours. **1613** PURCHAS *Pilgrimage* IX. xiv. (1614) 912 Mullets, Breames, Lobstars, and angel-like Hog-fish, Rock-fish, &c. **1666** J. DAVIES *Hist. Caribby Isles* 100 Also Rock-fishes, which are red intermixt with several other colours. **1697** DAMPIER *Voy.* (1729) I. 91 The Rock-fish is called by Sea-men a Grooper. **1712** E. COOKE *Voy. S. Sea* 115 Pollock, Cavallos, Rock-Fish, Silver-Fish. **1740** R. BROOKES *Art of Angling* 135 The Sea-Gudgeon or Rock-Fish..is a slender roundish Fish, about six Inches long. **1775** A. BURNABY *Trav.* 9 These waters are stored with incredible quantities of fish, such as sheeps-heads, rock-fish, drums, white pearch. ?**1835** *Encycl. Metrop.* (1845) XXIII. 223/1 The Striped Basse, or Rock-fish, as it is called, is very common along the coast of New York. **1862** ANSTED *Channel Isl.* II. ix. 211 The fishes most commonly brought into market in Guernsey are the rock-fish (wrasse or *vraic*-fish,..) and the conger. **1888** GOODE *Amer. Fishes* 21 Closely allied to the Pike-Perches is the log-perch, *P. caprodes*, also known as the 'Rock-fish', and 'Hog-fish'. **1969** [see *rock-salmon* s.v. ROCK *sb.*[1] 9 d].
2. 'A codfish split, washed, and dried on the rocks' (*Cent. Dict.* 1890).
3. = KLIPFISH I.
1731, 1806 [see KLIPFISH I].

rockfoil ('rɒkfɔɪl). [f. ROCK *sb.*[1] + FOIL *sb.*[1]] = SAXIFRAGE.
1879 RUSKIN *Proserpina* I. viii. 160 Their names..can be pleasantly said..in this order..Roof-foil, Rock-foil, Primrose. **1887** G. NICHOLSON *Illustr. Dict. Gardening* III. 311/1 Rockfoil. A name, suggested by Ruskin, for the genus *Saxifraga*. **1914** IRVING & MALBY *Saxifrages* i. 1 There is no other genus of rock plants that is so extensive as that of the Rockfoils. **1963** R. D. MEIKLE *Garden Flowers* 159 (*heading*) Saxifrage, Rockfoil.

'rock-hewn, *a.* [ROCK *sb.*[1]] Cut out of the rock.
1804 J. GRAHAME *Sabbath* 674 Winding adown the rock-hewn paths. **1853** ROCK *Church of Our Fathers* III. I. 154 That angel-trumpet blast which will crack the rock-hewn sepulchre. **1890** A. J. C. HARE *S.-E. France* 577 A rock-hewn staircase winding round the steep.

rockie, var. ROCKY *sb.*

'rockier. *dial.* [f. ROCK *sb.*[1] + -IER[1].] The rock-dove (*Columba livia*).
1780 G. WHITE *Selborne* xciv, There were among them little parties of small blue doves, which he calls rockiers. **1802** MONTAGU *Ornith. Dict.* s.v., Rock Dove... *Provincial.* Rockier. **1859** ATKINSON *Walks & Talks* (1892) 350 The first proved to be only a domestic pigeon. The other, however, was a genuine wild rockier. **1862** JOHNS *Brit. Birds* Index, Rocker and Rockier, the Rock Dove.

rockilo, obs. variant of ROQUELAURE.

'rockiness. Also 7 rockienes, rockinesse, 9 rockyness. [f. ROCKY *a.*[1] + -NESS.] The quality of being rocky; rocky character.
1611 COTGR., *Rochaille*, rockes; rockinesse. **1640** *Boston Rec.* (1877) II. 55 Brother Robert Scott hath the like 200 acres graunted him there,..without alowance for rockienes or swampe. **1661** CHILDREY *Brit. Bacon.* 3 The rockiness and dryness of the Countrey. **1775** ADAIR *Amer. Ind.* 228 The Alps of Italy are much inferior to several of the Cheerake Mountains, both in height and rockiness. **1805** SAUNDERS *Min. Waters* 153 The New Town,..from the great inequality of its site, and the rockyness of its soil, is very soon dry after the severest showers.

'rocking, *sb. Sc.* [f. ROCK *sb.*[2]] A social gathering (originally a spinning party) of a kind formerly held on winter evenings in the country districts of Scotland.
1785 BURNS *1st Ep. to Lapraik* ii, On Fasteneen we had a rockin, To ca' the crack and weave our stockin. **1798** G. BURNS in Currie *Wks. Burns* (1809) III. 377 It was at one of these rockings at our house..that Lapraik's song..was sung. **1825** J. WILSON *Noct. Ambr.* Wks. 1855 I. 62 A' sorts o' deivelry amang lads and lasses at rockins and kirns.

'rocking, *vbl. sb.*[1] [f. ROCK *v.*[1] + -ING[1].]
1. The action of swinging or swaying to and fro, or of causing such motion.
1398 TREVISA *Barth. De P.R.* v. xx. (Bodl. MS.), þe passions of teeþ is diuers.., as..breking and brusing.., rocking, wagging and falling.., and oþer suche. **1586** B. YOUNG *Guazzo's Civ. Conv.* IV. 223 b, It hath wrought euen so with you, as the rocking of yᵉ cradil to little children. **1647** HEXHAM I, A rocking of a child, *een wieginghe*. **1756** BURKE *Subl. & B.* Wks. 1842 I. 67 Rocking sets children to sleep better than absolute rest. **1774** GOLDSM. *Nat. Hist.* (1824) II. 299 Some branches..may not be sufficiently strong, and still others may be too much exposed to the rockings of the wind. **1814** SCOTT *Diary* 21 Aug. in *Lockhart*, Go to bed and sleep soundly, notwithstanding the rough rocking. **1902** BANKS *Newspaper Girl* 26, I was awakened..by so violent a rocking of my bed that I was tumbled out upon the floor.
2. a. The operation of using the rocker or cradle in engraving. Also *attrib.*
1883 J. C. SMITH *Brit. Mezzotinto Portr.* IV. ii. p. xxiii, The cradle, or rocking-tool, the scraper, etc. **1896** *Daily News* 16 Jan. 8/6 Those preliminaries of biting, rocking and other technicalities which have for so long deterred the painter from taking to etching or mezzotint-engraving.
b. The action of using a rocker (ROCKER[1] 4 c) in gold-mining.
1850 J. W. AUDUBON *Western Jrnl.* (1906) 202 The men began 'rocking' yesterday, one cradle, and get about a dollar an hour. **1859** *Brit. Colonist* (Victoria, B.C.) 3 Apr. 2/1 The lowest sum named by any miner as the product of a day's rocking is three to five dollars. **1896** C. H. SHINN *Story of Mine* 42 We started to rocking with my water.
3. rocking-turn, a movement or figure in skating (see quot.). Cf. ROCKER[1] 5 c.
1869 VANDERVELL & WITHAM *Syst. Figure-Skating* 219 After having exhausted the Q, I began to consider the feasibility of making the change direct from the inside forwards to inside backwards and *vice versâ*..by the employment of a kind of turn, for which..I can find no more simple..name than the 'Rocking Turn'.
4. The action or practice of playing or dancing to popular music with a strong beat and rocking rhythm, *esp.* rock and roll.
1948 R. BROWN (*song-title*) Good rockin' tonight. **1956** *Newsweek* 18 June 42/3 (*heading*) Rocking and rolling. **1974** *Down Beat* 18 July 38/2 The lyricism is as fervent as ever, but the rocking isn't... I don't mean..that the band ought to be rocking.

'rocking, *vbl. sb.*[2], variant of, or error for, ROCHING *vbl. sb.*
In quot. 1839 prob. after F. *rocher* (see Littré).
1674 RAY *Coll. Words, Allom-Work* 141 Thence it is taken and cast into a pan, which they call the rocking pan; and there melted. **1839** URE *Dict. Arts* 121 Bismuth has the advantage of boiling up, as well as of rocking or vegetating, with the silver, when the cupellation requires a high heat. **1854** *Pharmac. Jrnl.* XIII. 622 The formation of large masses of the alum..by..'roaching' or 'rocking'.

'rocking, *vbl. sb.*[3] [f. ROCK *sb.*[1]] A rough mode of dressing stone.
1856 MORTON *Cycl. Agric.* II. 395/1 *Rockwork*, or *rocking*, ..is that mode in which the stone has an artificial roughness given to it to imitate the natural face of a rock.

rocking ('rɒkɪŋ), *ppl. a.* [ROCK *v.*[1]]
1. a. That rocks; swaying, oscillating; also, causing to rock.
1398 TREVISA *Barth. De P.R.* XVI. xlviii. (Bodl. MS.), Poudre þereof to feble teeþe and rokkinge strengþeþ and fasteþ ham. *Ibid.* XVII. xc. (1495) 658 Mastyck..fastnyth waggynge and rockynge teeth. **1632** MILTON *Penseroso* 126 While rocking Winds are Piping loud. **1708** J. PHILIPS *Cyder* I. 225 The rocking Town Supplants their Footsteps. **1812** J. WILSON *Isle of Palms* I. 109 The quiet voice of the rocking sea To cheer the gliding vision sings. **1817** SHELLEY *Rev. Islam* II. xiv, And who shall stand Amid the rocking earthquake steadfast still? **1899** MACKAIL *W. Morris* I. 217 A stranger might well, from his rocking walk and ruddy complexion, have taken him for a Baltic sea-captain.
b. *Prosody.* Designating a metre in which each foot consists of a stressed syllable standing between two unstressed syllables.
c **1883** G. M. HOPKINS *Poems* (1918) Pref. 1 If the stress is between two slacks there will be Rocking Feet and Rhythms. **1932** F. R. LEAVIS *New Bearings in Engl. Poetry* v. 167 Rocking Feet and Outriders will help no one to read his [*sc.* Hopkins's] verse. **1957** B. DEUTSCH *Poetry Handbk.* (1958) 130 When the stress falls between two unstressed syllables, as in this line of Swinburne's 'Far oút to the shállows and stráits of the fúture, by róugh ways or pleásant', the rhythm is a rocking one. **1965** A. F. SCOTT *Current Lit. Terms* 249 When the metrical stress falls between two unstressed syllables, the rhythm is called rocking.
c. Of popular music: characterized by a strong beat and rocking rhythm (cf. ROCK *sb.*[3] 2); that is performed in the style of rock music.
1949 *Billboard* 3 Dec. 108/2 Combo drives thru a rocking riffer, with a punching bary sax leading the way. **1954** *Ibid.* 13 Nov. 98 Another spirited rhythmic side in which the lead singer soars out wild and free over the rocking beat provided by the rest of the group. **1959** G. AVAKIAN in M. T. Williams *Art of Jazz* (1960) ix. 88 One of the fastest rocking blues ever made. **1968** *Melody Maker* 30 Nov. 6/6 A rocking version of B. B. King's 'Sweet Sixteen'. **1976** *Leicester Trader* 24 Nov. 4/7 One rocking track called Winnebago even reminds me of ..the opening track from Argent's second album.
2. In various technical terms, as ***rocking bar, beam, lever, rod, shaft, tree,*** etc.
1805 R. W. DICKSON *Pract. Agric.* I. Pl. 10 A cylinder or segment of wood,..called a *rocking tree*, which goes across the frame, and moves on the pivots fixed into it. **1841** *Civil Eng. & Arch. Jrnl.* IV. 187/2 A double lever on the rocking-shaft for working the valve. **1844** *Ibid.* VII. 192/2 The rocking rods..enabled the water to open and close them. **1876** PREECE & SIVEWRIGHT *Telegraphy* 121 Let the ends of two rocking levers, by the tension of the springs *s* and *s'*, rest on these pins. *Ibid.* 125 The vibrations of the rocking-beam must be slower for long lines than for short ones. **1884** F. J. BRITTEN *Watch & Clockm.* 131 Three wheels gearing together are planted on the rocking bar.

'rocking-chair. [ROCKING *ppl. a.*] **1.** A chair mounted on rockers; also, a chair having a rocking seat attached to the base by springs.
1766 in *Hobbies* (1949) Sept. 50/2 1st Mo. 1766, to a rocking Chair for andrew hunter 3/. **1832** MRS. TROLLOPE *Manners Amer.* (1901) II. 109 They..sit in a rocking-chair, and sew a great deal. **1855** BAIN *Senses & Int.* II. i. §19 The rocking chair, introduced by the Americans,..is another mode of gaining pleasure from movement. **1897** 'MERRIMAN' *In Kedar's Tents* xxx, She was asleep in a rocking-chair, with a newspaper on her lap.
2. Used *attrib.* to designate something considered as being conducted or obtained at home, without first-hand experience of normal difficulties; spec. ***rocking-chair money***, unemployment benefit. Cf. ARM-CHAIR, ARMCHAIR. Chiefly *U.S.*
1933 *Sun* (Baltimore) 27 Feb. 6/3 A question which delights every sewing circle and rocking-chair parade in the country. **1944** *Amer. Speech* XIX. 156/2 *Rockin' chair money*, unemployment compensation. **1946** *Richmond* (Va.) *Times-Dispatch* 16 Jan. 5/2 An increase in 'rocking chair money' for the State's unemployed. **1959** *Globe & Mail* (Toronto) 22 Apr. 7/1 The somewhat less sophisticated people of the Maritimes have a happier name for Unemployment Insurance... 'Rockin' Chair Money'. **1962** *Daily Tel.* 10 Sept. 10/2 A third U2 incident over Communist territory..will renew groans at the President's rocking-chair diplomacy.

Rockingham ('rɒkɪŋəm). The title of Charles Watson-Wentworth, second Marquis of *Rockingham* (1730–82), applied *attrib.* to earthenware, china, a variety of glaze, etc., produced on his estate at the Old Works, Swinton, Yorks., from *c* 1745 to 1842. Also applied loosely to similar products. Now usu. designating pieces of a tea-service. Also *ellipt.*
[**1832** G. RICHARDSON in *Cabinet Cycl.* No. 26. 22 At the Rockingham works, which have been so named in compliment to their early patron, the celebrated marquess of Rockingham, porcelain is now produced which vies successfully in every kind of excellence with that of older English establishments.] **1857** J. MARRYAT *Hist. Pott. & Porc.* (ed. 2) xii. 291 They [*sc.* the works] also manufactured the brown or chocolate-coloured ware, which obtained the name of 'Rockingham ware'. **1863** W. CHAFFERS *Marks Pott. & Porc.* 134 A sort of brown or chocolate-coloured ware, made in the beginning of the present Century, obtained the name of Rockingham ware. **1869** C. SCHREIBER *Jrnl.* 4 Nov. (1911) I. 60, 3 Rockingham cups and saucers and 3 plates. **1870** *Ibid.* 11 Feb. (1911) I. 66 A few good bits of Chelsea,..one of Rockingham (very good). **1881** C. C. HARRISON *Woman's Handiwork* II. 110 The temperature at which Rockingham ware is fired is suitable for this [underglaze] work. **1900** F. LITCHFIELD *Pott. & Porc.* vii. 94 The ware is highly glazed, some of it being not unlike the

brown Rockingham ware. **1935** G. GREENE *England made Me* ii. 57 The Minister stood above his Rockingham china. **1957** MANKOWITZ & HAGGAR *Conc. Encycl. Eng. Pott. & Porc.* 194/1 '*Rockingham' glaze*, a lustrous, purple-brown lead glaze (stained with manganese) made at the Rockingham factory, Swinton, early nineteenth century, and in Staffordshire. **1960** R. COLLIER *House called Memory* xii. 171 Croquet on the lawn at four o'clock with the Rockingham tea-service as background. **1963** *Times* 23 Feb. 11/7 There were many bone china potters in Staffordshire making cottages: their productions, without any justification, are classed arbitrarily as Rockingham and thus acquire the market value of that establishment's brilliant reputation. The flowers on Rockingham cottages are usually less disproportionately large than those ornamenting cottages made elsewhere. **1965** [see DAVENPORT[2]]. **1973** L. COOPER *Tea on Sunday* 11 The dark blue and gold Rockingham cup.

'rocking-horse. [ROCKING *ppl. a.*] A wooden horse mounted on rockers for children to ride upon with a rocking motion. Also *fig.*

1724 in *N. & Q.* (1942) 7 Feb. 76/1 Rocking Horse. William Bird, turner, just without Newgate. *c* **1804** H. KNAPP in *Etoniana* 225 Who.. Makes Pegasus a rocking-horse. **1826** HONE *Every-day Bk.* I. 292 Before I had ridden anything but my rocking horse. **1869** TROLLOPE *He knew,* etc. lxxviii. (1878) 433 The boy is here, you may be sure..; the rocking-horse makes that certain.

attrib. **1834** *West India Sk. Bk.* I. 48 Porpoises.. pursued their course with a sort of rocking-horse motion on the surface. **1871** LOWELL *Wks.* (1890) IV. 23 Common-place set to this rocking-horse jig irritates the nerves. **1922** JOYCE *Ulysses* 495 Result of the rockinghorse races. **1936** F. R. LEAVIS *Revaluation* iv. 112 Prior takes happily to those anapaestic, rocking-horse rhythms. **1964** D. VARADAY *Gara-Yaka* vii. 64 Then she bounded back in rocking-horse cheetah gait.

'rocking-stone. [ROCKING *ppl. a.*] A large stone or boulder so poised on a limited base as to be easily swayed to and fro; a logan-stone.

1740 STUKELEY *Stonehenge* xi. 49, I have seen one of these rocking stones, as call'd commonly, in Derbyshire. **1799** J. ROBERTSON *Agric. Perth* 573 The rocking stone of Dron is 10 feet long and 7 broad, standing in an inclined position. **1802** PLAYFAIR *Huttonian Theory* 395 What are called rocking-stones or in Cornwall, Logan-stones. **1855** J. R. LEIFCHILD *Cornwall* 2 Picturesque coast views,.. rocking-stones and stones innumerable. **1871** L. STEPHEN *Playgr. Eur.* (1894) iv. 96 A mass of huge loose rocks, which I can only compare to a continuous series of.. rocking-stones.

'rockish, *a.* Also 6 **rockishe.** [f. ROCK *sb.*[1] + -ISH.] †Growing upon, composed of, rocks.

1562 TURNER *Herbal* II. (1568) 71 The rockishe ashe is of a yelow color. **1570** DEE *Math. Pref.* A iiij b, Consider the rockish huge mountaines, and the perilous vnbeaten wayes. **1582** STANYHURST *Æneis* III. (Arb.) 78 On the typ of rockish turret stood gastlye Celæno.

Rockite ('rɒkaɪt). Now only *Hist.* [f. the assumed name Captain *Rock.*] A member of an Irish organization associated with agrarian disorders in the earlier part of the nineteenth century. Also **'Rockism.**

1828 *Blackw. Mag.* Dec. 757/1 Every night he could see houses in the distance burning round about him, the work of the incendiary Rockites. **1830** *Times* 6 Nov. 3/6 There is little doubt that distress and desperation form the mystery, and that a kind of English *Rockism* is in operation. **1831** *Lincoln Herald* 27 May, A band of Rockites attacked the residence of a magistrate in the county of Clare. **1848** MILL *Pol. Econ.* I. II. ix. 375 Rockism and Whiteboyism are the determination of a people, who have nothing that can be called theirs but a daily meal.., not to submit to being deprived of that for other people's convenience. **1880** W. J. FITZPATRICK *Life Doyle* II. 333 He urged.. the 'Rockites' and the Ribbonmen to cast their evil combinations to the winds. **1949** C. GRAVES *Ireland Revisited* viii. 101 The Rockites, hidden among the cliffs and intending to trap the Bantry party, revealed their presence.

attrib. **1832** *Lincoln Herald* 14 Feb. 2/6 A Rockite notice.. was served in the most populous part of the town of Longford.. on Saturday evening.

rocklay, obs. form of ROKELAY.

rockless ('rɒklɪs), *a.* [f. ROCK *sb.*[1] + -LESS.] Devoid of rocks; without rocks.

c **1640** WALLER *Of Loving at First Sight* ii, 'Tis so rockless and so clear That the rich bottom does appear. **1670** DRYDEN *Conq. Granada* IV. i, My Heart's so plain,.. 'Tis weedless all above, and rockless all below. **1682** —— *Duke of Guise* III. i, I'm clear by nature, as a rockless stream. **1883** *Harper's Mag.* Feb. 328 The coast.. is flat and rockless. **1977** *Lancashire Life* Nov. 82/1 What, on its almost rockless coast, has the County Palatine got?

'rocklet ('rɒklɪt). [-LET.] A small rock.

1845 HIRST *Poems* 65 From every rocklet running, flow a myriad murmuring springs. **1868** W. CORY *Lett. & Jrnls.* (1897) 230 Up to the heights, almost up to the protruding rocklets. **1880** SENIOR *Trav. & Trout in Antip.* 109 A reef of black-headed, slippery rocklets.

'rock-like, *a.* [f. ROCK *sb.*[1]] Resembling a rock; possessing the qualities of rock; hard or firm as rock. Also *fig.*

1595 MARKHAM *Sir R. Grinvile* cii, Well might we crush his keele with rocklike powers. **1819** SHELLEY *Lett.* Pr. Wks. 1880 IV. 85 We entered by the ancient gate, which is now no more than a chasm in the rock-like wall. **1824** MISS MITFORD *Village* Ser. I. (1863) 146 Wriggling the gig round the rock-like stones. **1896** BADEN-POWELL *Matabele Campaign* xiii, A nugget of rock-like bread. **1959** P. BULL *I know Face* ii. 29 This line had to be delivered in a steady rock-like voice. **1963** *Times* 5 June 16/3 His endearing character with its rocklike qualities won him innumerable friends from many generations. **1975** R. BARCLAY *Ernest Bevin & Foreign Office* iv. 79 Just as he himself had always been rock-like in his loyalty to Churchill, so from now on he remained absolutely firm in his support of Attlee.

rockling ('rɒklɪŋ). [ROCK *sb.*[1] + -LING.] A small gadoid fish of the genera *Onos* or *Rhinonemus* (formerly *Motella*), esp. the sea-loach or whistle-fish (*R. cimbrius*).

1602 CAREW *Cornwall* 32 Of flat [fish there are] Brets, Turbets, Dories,.. Cunna, Rockling, Cod, &c. *a* **1705** RAY *Syn. Pisc.* (1713) 164 *Mustela marina vulgaris,*.. Rockling,.. Whistle Fish. **1769** PENNANT *Brit. Zool.* III. 164 Three bearded Cod, Rockling. **1836** YARRELL *Brit. Fishes* II. 186 Three-Bearded Rockling, *Motella vulgaris. Ibid.* 190 The Five-Bearded Rockling, *Motella quinquecirrata.* **1863** COUCH *Brit. Fishes* III. 111 Four Bearded Rockling, *Motella cimbria.* **1883** *Fisheries Exhib. Catal.* (ed. 4) 107 Collection of Stuffed.. Rockling, Broad-nosed Eel, &c.

'rockman. [ROCK *sb.*[1]]

1. *Sc.* One who takes birds on rocks or cliffs.

1825 JAMIESON *Suppl.*, *Rockman*, a bird catcher, Orkn.; so named from the hazardous nature of his employment, being often suspended from the top of a perpendicular rock.

2. In slate quarries, a skilled workman who gets out the slate rock.

1865 J. BOWER *Slate Quarries* 20 The rockman.. gets the blocks in the quarry, and splits them.. ready to be carried out to the sawing machinery. **1884** *Christian World* 11 Sept. 678/5 As to rockmen and labourers, they are wanted by the hundred. **1892** *Min. Evid. Labour Comm.* Group A. II. 2 He [*sc.* a rubbisher] is the man who carries away all the material from the rock-men to the place where the slates are made.

rock 'n' roll: see ROCK AND ROLL.

rock-oil. [ROCK *sb.*[1]] Native naphtha.

1668 CHARLETON *Onomast.* 236 Rock oil, or Petroleum. **1802–3** tr. *Pallas's Trav.* (1812) II. 282 In the same country are springs, having inspissated rock-oil on their surface. **1839** URE *Dict. Arts* 879 Rock-oil is very inflammable. **1856** *Orr's Circle Sci., Pract. Chem.* 482 An oil matter called rock-oil oozes out of the ground.

rockoon (rɒ'ku:n). [Blend of ROCK(ET *sb.*[3] and BALL)OON *sb.*[1]] A rocket fired from a balloon; a balloon carrying a rocket to be fired in the upper atmosphere.

1953 *Sci. News Let.* 8 Aug. 89/2 The balloon-rocket technique, commonly referred to as Balloon Assisted Take-Off or Rockoon, was developed by Dr. James A. Van Allen, head of the State University of Iowa physics department. **1955** *Sun* (Baltimore) (B ed.) 23 Nov. 14/6 The release of rockoons will be synchronized with similar releases in the Northern Hemisphere. **1959** *New Scientist* 20 Aug. 244/2 Analysis of magnetic measurements by balloon-borne rockets (rockoons).. has revealed a second 'electrojet' current.. around the Earth. **1963** A. MACLEAN *Ice Station Zebra* iv. 59 Drift Stations habitually carried rockets.. and radio-sondes and rockoons. The sondes were radio-carrying balloons..: the rockoons, radio rockets fired from balloons.

rockoon, obs. form of RACOON.

rock-ouzel. [ROCK *sb.*[1]] The ring-ouzel.

1678 RAY *Willughby's Ornith.* 195 This.. was shot.. not far from a Village called Hathers-edge in the Mountains of the Peak of Derbyshire, where the Inhabitants call it Rock-Ouzel. *Ibid.* 197 The greater Redstart of Olina, called by Aldrovand, *Merula Saxatilis* [*marg.* i.e. The Rock Ouzel]. **1772** *Phil. Trans.* LXII. 266 The Royston Crow, and Rock Ouzel, furnish instances of such a regular migration. **1802** MONTAGU *Ornith. Dict.* s.v. *Ring-ouzel,* The young birds, before the white on the breast appears, have been considered as a different species, under the name of Rock-Ouzel. **1862** JOHNS *Brit. Birds* Index, Rock Ouzel, the Ring Ouzel.

†rock-petre. *Obs.*[−1] = ROCHE-PETRE.

1736 BAILEY *Househ. Dict.* E 6 Take five handfuls of common salt, three handfuls of bay salt, and rock petre and petre salt of each one handful.

rock-pigeon. [ROCK *sb.*[1]]

1. A species of dove (*Columba livia*) inhabiting rocks and believed to be the source of the domestic pigeon; the rock-dove.

1611 COTGR., *Colombe rocheraye,* a rocke Pigeon. **1668** CHARLETON *Onomast.* 77 *Palumbus Rupicola*.., the Rock-Pidgeon. **1704** *Dict. Rust.* (1726) II. N n 4, Pigeons or doves are of various kinds.., as Wood-pigeons, Rock-pigeons [etc.]. **1780** G. WHITE *Selborne* xciv, I readily concur with you in supposing that house-doves are derived from the small blue rock-pigeon. **1802** MONTAGU *Ornith. Dict.* s.v. *Rock-dove,* Ornithologists seem to differ in opinion concerning the Rock and Stock Pigeon. **1859** DARWIN *Orig. Spec.* i. (ed. 2) 25 The rock-pigeon is of a slaty-blue. **1892** AGNES CLERKE *Fam. Stud. Homer* 130 The rock-pigeon, called from its slate-coloured plumage *peleia.*

2. *Anglo-Indian.* A sand-grouse.

1885 NEWTON in *Encycl. Brit.* XIX. 84/2 It may be observed that the 'Rock-Pigeons' of Anglo-Indians are *Sand-Grouse.* **1886** *Ibid.* XXI. 259/1 The expression is decidedly Dove-like,.. so that among Anglo-Indians these birds are commonly known as 'Rock-Pigeons'.

rock-pipit. [ROCK *sb.*[1]] The rock-lark or shore-lark (*Anthus obscurus*).

1831 RENNIE *Montagu's Ornith. Dict.* 427 Rock pipit... This species appears to have remained long either unnoticed, or confounded with others, by the early ornithologists. **1871** NEWTON *Yarrell's Brit. Birds* I. 588 The Rock-Pipit is a constant inhabitant of nearly all the shores of the United Kingdom. **1896** DIXON *Brit. Sea Birds* 269 The Rock Pipit.. is an olive-brown little bird.

rock-plant. [ROCK *sb.*[1]]

†**1.** A petrified plant. *Obs.*

1691 RAY *Creation* I. (1692) 82 Our ordinary Star-stones and Trochites, which I look upon as a sort of Rock-Plants. **1753** CHAMBERS *Cycl. Suppl.* s.v. *Saint Cuthbert's Beads,* They.. have been so far mistaken, by authors, as to be supposed a sort of rock plants.

2. A plant that grows upon or among rocks.

1694 tr. *Marten's Voy. Spitzbergen* 58 The Rock-plant, with but one leaf. *Ibid.* 72 The Root groweth out of the Rocks, wherefore I call it a Rock plant.

1824 LOUDON *Encycl. Gard.* 884 Mountain or rock plants only should be introduced on artificial rock-work. **1841** *Penny Cycl.* XX. 53/1 *Rock-plants* are those plants which are distinguished by growing on or among naked rocks, and are confined to no particular region or latitude. **1884** *Gardening Illustr.* 8 Nov. 426/1 Rock Plants.. have suffered considerably from the long-continued drought.

3. *spec.* The biting stonecrop. *dial.*

1882 *Devon Plant-names* (E.D.S.).

rock-ribbed, *a.* [ROCK *sb.*[1]] **1.** Having ribs of rock.

1776 MICKLE tr. *Camoens' Lusiad* v. 212 And Me the rock-ribb'd mother gave to fame. **1841** BRYANT *Thanatopsis* 38 The hills Rock-ribb'd and ancient as the sun. **1900** *Scribner's Mag.* Sept. 293/2 Nearer and nearer we drew to the rock-ribbed, ice-encompassed shore.

2. *fig.* Resolute, uncompromising, staunch; esp. of political allegiance. orig. *U.S.*

1887 *Courier-Jrnl.* (Louisville, Kentucky) 3 May 414 Mr. Straus is a rock-ribbed Democrat. **1911** H. S. HARRISON *Queed* 292 Various feelings had gradually stiffened an early general approval into a rock-ribbed resolve. **1925** T. DREISER *Amer. Trag.* (1926) I. I. xvi. 122 Clyde always struck her as one who was not any too.. rock-ribbed morally or mentally. **1950** *Manch. Guardian* 20 Feb. 6/6 The dyed-in-the-wool Democrat can be fanatical in devotion to his party's creed and traditions. So can the rock-ribbed Republican. **1961** *Economist* 28 Oct. 341/2 He is a man of such rock-ribbed integrity. **1969** *Daily Tel.* 11 Oct. 12 A Massachusetts seat that has always been held by rockribbed Republicans. **1976** *Publishers Weekly* 16 Apr. 88/1 Goldwater, rockribbed in his sincerity, speaks for many Americans currently disenchanted with Washington's government-by-bureaucracy.

rock-rose. [ROCK *sb.*[1]]

†**1.** ? A variety of *Daphne Cneorum. Obs.*

1629 PARKINSON *Parad.* 397 *Cneorum Matthioli,* Small Rocke Roses.

2. A plant of the genus *Helianthemum* or *Cistus* (formerly united in the Linnæan genus *Cistus*), esp. *H. vulgare.* (See also CISTUS.)

1731 MILLER *Gard. Dict.* s.v. *Cistus,* The Male Cistus or Rock Rose, with oblong hoary Leaves. **1753** CHAMBERS *Cycl. Suppl.* App., *Rock-rose,* a name sometimes given to the Cistus of botanists. **1825** HOGG *Queen Hynde* 14 The day-breeze play'd in eddies weak, And waved the rock-rose to her cheek. **1846** LINDLEY *Veget. Kingd.* 350 South Europe and the north of Africa are the countries that Rock Roses chiefly inhabit. **1882** *Garden* 10 June 405/2 Rock Roses (Helianthemum) give also striking masses of various colours —golden yellow, rose, and salmon-coloured.

attrib. **1841** *Penny Cycl.* XX. 53/2 Almost all the Rock-rose tribe (Cistaceæ) may be grown with success on rock-work. **1861** BENTLEY *Man. Bot.* 455 *Cistaceæ.*—The Rock-Rose Order.

3. ***Australian rock-rose,*** a plant of the genus *Hibbertia.*

1889 in *Cent. Dict.* s.v. *Hibbertia.*

4. *N. Amer.* The bitter root, *Lewisia rediviva,* a small perennial herb belonging to the family Portulacaceæ, native to western North America, and bearing solitary pink or white flowers.

1906 *Contrib. U.S. Nat. Herbarium* XI. 49 The rock-rose or bitterroot.. occurs abundantly in crevices of 'scab', making a brave show with its beautiful rose-colored flowers. **1963** *Beaver* Autumn 53/1 The rolling hills, cactus and rock roses.. flooded the dry land with character and colour. **1973** R. D. SYMONS *Where Wagon Led* I. v. 77 We should find some rock roses here.

5. An aggregate of tabular crystals of a mineral suggestive of the petals of a rose; = ROSE *sb.* 16 e, ROSETTE *sb.* 5 e.

1933 *Amer. Mineralogist* XVIII. 261 The barite occurs as sand barites or barite rosettes (locally called 'rock roses') and barite accretions. **1962** W. A. DEER et al. *Rock-Forming Minerals* V. 193 Concretions of barytes in sandstone sometimes take the form of rosettes known as 'sand barites', 'rock roses' or 'desert roses'. **1977** A. HALLAM *Planet Earth* 85 (*caption*) Desert roses (or rock roses) display one of the more unusual modes of occurrence of evaporitic minerals... Found.. only in arid areas, these clusters of platy crystals are typically of barite or gypsum.

†rock-ruby. *Obs.* [Cf. ROCK *sb.*[1] 6 e.] A species of garnet or amethyst (see quot. 1748).

1544 *Will of Cornwaleys* (Somerset Ho.), Rocke ruby. **1572–3** in Nichols *Progr. Eliz.* (1823) I. 323 One tablet of mother-of-perle.. set with 2 rock rubyes and 2 emeraldes. **1626** BACON *Sylva* §1 In like manner, Cornish Diamonds, and Rock Rubies,.. are the fine Exudations of Stone. **1748** J. HILL *Hist. Fossils* 591 The Rock-Ruby. This is the name they very improperly give to the Garnet, when it is of a very strong but not deep red, and has a fairer cast of the blue. *Ibid.*, The bluer Amethysts being by some [jewellers] call'd Rock Rubies.

rock-salt. [ROCK *sb.*[1]] Salt found in a free state disposed in strata, and capable of being extracted in large lumps.

1707 *Lond. Gaz.* No. 4385/3 The Antelope of.. Leverpole, with Rock-Salt, taken the 12th Instant by two Privateers. **1748** *Anson's Voy.* II. viii. 309 Some oakum, about a tun of rock salt, and between 30 and 40*l.* in specie. **1802** PLAYFAIR *Huttonian Theory* 364 The district.. in Cheshire, which contains rock-salt, extends over a tract of fourteen or fifteen miles. **1853** GREGORY *Inorg. Chem.* 98 Chlorine..occurs in prodigious quantity in the well-known substance, sea or rock-salt, in which it is combined with sodium. **1886** WINCHELL *Walks Geol. Field* 131 The sediments..would be deposited upon the bed of rock-salt.

b. *attrib.* and *Comb.*

1708 *Lond. Gaz.* No. 4453/3 A Survey will be held at Topsham,..on Thursday the 5th of August, for a Rock Salt-house, with three Iron Pans. **1811** *Trans. Geol. Soc.* I. 38 The Cheshire Rock-Salt District. **1834-6** *Encycl. Metrop.* (1845) VIII. 430/2 Rock salt-pits are sunk at great expense. **1839** URE *Dict. Arts* 1086 The great rock-salt formation of England occurs within the red marl. **1883** *Science* I. 518/2 Magnus found that rock-salt plates absorbed heat [etc.].

ˈrock-shaft. [ROCK *v.*[1]] A shaft which merely rocks or oscillates about its axis in place of making complete revolutions; *esp.* one working the levers connected with certain valves in some forms of engines.

1875 KNIGHT *Dict. Mech.* 1960/2. **1896** *Cosmopolitan* XX. 421/1 On the bottom of the vehicle, in front of the operator is a rock shaft, upon which the operator places his foot to manage the vehicle.

ˈrockship. [f. ROCK *sb.*[1]] The fact of being a rock (with allusion to Matt. xvi. 18).

1840 G. S. FABER *Christ's Disc. Capernaum* Introd. p. lxii. *note*, Demonstrating..that the Roman Bishop must needs be the inheritor of Peter's imaginary Rockship.

ˈrock-staff[1]. [ROCK *v.*[1]] Part of the apparatus for working a smith's bellows.

1677 MOXON *Mech. Exercises* i. 2 This Handle is fastened a cross a Rock-staff, which moves between two Cheeks upon two Center-pins, in two Sockets. **1831** J. HOLLAND *Manuf. in Metal* I. 177 The bellows occupying the inside, and being worked by a rockstaff from without. **1894** HESLOP *Northumbld. Gloss.*, *Rock-staff*, the lever or long handle by which a blacksmith works his bellows.

rock-staff[2]. *E. Anglian dial.* [ROCK *sb.*[2]] A distaff. Also *fig.*, a superstition; a fancy, crotchet; esp. in phr. ***an old woman's rock-staff.***

1765 *Compl. Maltster & Brewer* p. xxiii, The notion of pease bloom, and weeds being up in the water, is but a meer old woman's rockstaff. *a* **1825** R. FORBY *Vocab. E. Anglia* (1830) II. 279 *Rock-staff*,..a distaff; from which..the wool *was* spun 'by twirling a ball below'... 'An old woman's *rockstaff*,' is a contemptuous expression for a silly superstitious fancy. **1867** *N. & Q.* 3rd Ser. XI. 215 She is so full of her old woman's rock-staffs. **1895** P. H. EMERSON *Birds, Beasts, & Fishes Norfolk Broad-land* II. xix. 396 There is a curious rockstaff in the marshlands that a viper's slough will draw thorns from your flesh.

rocksteady (ˈrɒkˌstɛdɪ). Also **rock-steady, rock steady.** [f. ROCK *sb.*[3] 2 + STEADY *a.* 4.] A style of popular music, originating in Jamaica, characterized by slow tempo and stressed off-beat. Also, a dance to such music. Also *attrib.* Cf. REGGAE.

1969 *Observer* 12 Jan. 3/8 West Indian teenagers.. nowadays..danced to music called 'rocksteady'. *Ibid.* 23 Nov. 25/8 Aspiring Kingston..dancing the Reggae, Jamaica's successor to the Ska and the Rocksteady. **1971** A. SALKEY in *One Love* 7 We have been quick to recognise the excellence and the appeal in the musical alternative of the ..*Rock Steady* and *Reggae*. **1971** *Daily Tel.* (Colour Suppl.) 30 July 7/4 As ska, rocksteady or blue-beat, music like this has been around in Britain for more than a decade, hidden amidst the West Indian subculture in London, Birmingham and elsewhere. **1973** *Telegraph-Jrnl.* (St. John, New Brunswick) 28 July 5/2 A West Indian rock-steady band was playing. **1977** MCKNIGHT & TOBLER *Bob Marley* iii. 41 Ska mutated into 'rock steady'... Rock steady was slower in tempo than ska—again to assist the singers in their unenviable task of shouting louder than the volcanic eruptions produced by a bass player with..amplification... Rock steady is further distinguished from ska by the extra syncopation involved. *Ibid.* vi. 72 It was 1968 and Johnny Nash, a black American singer..had achieved several hits with rock steady type songs. **1980** *Melody Maker* 19 Jan. 25/4 Saxa played with some of the early rock-steady acts that toured Britain, like Desmond Dekker and Laurel Aitken.

†**ˈrockster.** *Obs.* Forms: 4 rokster, 5 rokkestere. [f. ROCK *v.*[1] + -STER.] = ROCKER[1] I.

1377-80 *Accs.*, etc. *Exch. Q.R.* (Bundle 400 No. 4 m. 20), Mundine, nutrici domini nostri regis, et Raimunde oberd, rokster. **14..** *Lat. Eng. Voc.* in Wr.-Wülcker 576 *Crepundaria*, a rokkestere. *Ibid.* 577 *Cunabulatrix*,..a rokkestere.

rock-stone. [ROCK *sb.*[1]] A stone of the nature of a rock; stone obtained by quarrying or cutting from the rock.

1545 BALE *Image Both Ch.* I. xv. (1550) h vj, These stande euermore on the glassy sea, they set sure fotyng vpon the rocke stone. **1668** CHARLETON *Onomast.* 241 *Saxum*,.. Rock-stone. **1748** J. HILL *Hist. Fossils* 447 White or whitish Rock Stone, *Sympexium albidum*. **1765** *Museum Rust.* IV. 146 In one of which [kilns] I burn chalk cut in pieces, and the other small rock-stones. **1795** J. PHILLIPS *Treat. Inland Nav.* Add. 172 Coals, coak, iron, iron-stone, lime-stone, rock-stone, bricks, tiles, and other minerals. **1808** FORSYTH *Beauties Scotl.* V. 517 Rock-stone, formed of mica and quartz [is found in Colonsay].

rock-thrush. [ROCK *sb.*[1]] A thrush of the genus *Monticola* (formerly *Petrocincla*).

1783 LATHAM *Gen. Synop. Birds* II. I. 54 Rock Thrush, *Merula saxatilis*. Size of a Thrush. Bill pale brown. **1826** *Shaw's Gen. Zool.* XIV. 349 *Petrocincla*,..Rock-thrush. **1835** *Penny Cycl.* IV. 479/1 There are other European species of the tribe, such as *Turdus saxatilis*, the rock thrush. **1859** DARWIN *Orig. Spec.* iv. (ed. 2) 89 The rock-thrush of Guiana, birds of Paradise, and some others, congregate. **1875-84** SHARPE *Layard's Birds S. Africa* 219 Cape Rock-Thrush. This is the largest of the three South African Rock-Thrushes.

ˈrockward, *adv.* [ROCK *sb.*[1] + -WARD.] Towards a rock.

1823 BYRON *Island* II. xvii, The tropic bird wheel'd rockward to his nest.

rock-water. [ROCK *sb.*[1]] Water issuing from a rock, naturally clear and cold.

1605 SYLVESTER *Du Bartas* II. iii. *Lawe* 9 Christ-Typing Manna, Quails, Rock-waters fall. **1650** TRAPP *Comm. Deut.* xxviii. 2 As the rock-water followed the Israelites in the wilderness. **1705** ADDISON *Italy* 461 It was extreamly muddy at its Entrance..though as clear as Rock Water at its going out. **1772** GRAVES *Spir. Quix.* (1820) I. 190, I don't pretend to live upon roots and rock-water. **1838** MISS PARDOE *River & Desert* I. 159 A delicious fountain, into whose basin the sparkling rock-water is poured. **1948** F. BLAKE *Johnny Christmas* I. 40 Yet in this utter lack of sound, except for the sputter of flames and the musical seep of rock-water, Johnny came alert, strangely, as if awakened by a thin cry of warning.

attrib. **1748** RICHARDSON *Clarissa* (1811) VII. 239 Her invitation most certainly runs all in the rock-water style.

rock-weed. [ROCK *sb.*[1]] A seaweed, esp. one of the genera *Fucus* and *Sargassum*, growing on tide-washed rocks.

1626 CAPT. SMITH *Accid. Yng. Seamen* 29 Rocke-weede, adrift, or flotes. **1627** —— *Seaman's Gram.* ix. 43 Rockweed doth grow by the shore, and is a signe of land. **1664** *Phil. Trans.* I. 13 Upon which..Rock-weed or Sea-tangle did grow a hand long. **1777** G. FORSTER *Voy. round World* I. 113 A great bed of floating rock-weeds. **1819** WARDEN *United States* I. 366 The coast [of Maine] furnishes a marine vegetable called rock-weed. **1888** GOODE *Amer. Fishes* 171 He took the sprays of rock-weed in his hands and pulled them slowly to him.

Rockwell (ˈrɒkwɛl). The name of Stanley P. *Rockwell*, 20th-cent. U.S. metallurgist, used *attrib.* with reference to a hardness test which he introduced, in which the depth of penetration of the material (usu. a metal) by a steel ball or a diamond cone is measured under specified conditions; hence also used to denote values of relative hardness determined by such methods.

1920 *Foundry Trade Jrnl.* XXII. 778/2 A new hardness testing apparatus, called the Rockwell hardness tester, is now available. **1922** S. P. ROCKWELL in *Trans. Amer. Soc. Steel Treating* II. 1013 The Rockwell hardness tester is at present made in three sizes. **1922** *Chem. Abstr.* XVI. 3296 Formulas..are given for conversion from the Rockwell value to the Brinell value. **1930** *Engineering* 19 Sept. 358/1 Rockwell hardness measurements and X-ray diffraction patterns had shown that lattice distortion could be accompanied by appreciable softening. **1945** A. T. BIRKBY *Phenolic Plastics* v. 56 The V.P.N. and Rockwell 'C' test equivalents of this are 700–750 and 58–60 respectively. **1976** *Islander* (Victoria, B.C.) 16 May 15/3 Get a blade with a Rockwell hardness factor of 57 to 59... Steel less than Rockwell 57–59 is too soft and won't hold a cutting edge.

ˈrock-work. [f. ROCK *sb.*[1]]

1. A natural mass or group of rocks or stones.

1706 *Phil. Trans.* XXV. 1954 These are pretty Shells, and frequently found in Rock-work. **1713** STEELE *Guard.* No. 101 The garden..is fenced on the lower end by a natural mound of rock-work. **1781** COWPER *Charity* 96 This genial intercourse..softens human rock-work into men. **1841** *Penny Cycl.* XX. 53/2 Hints should be taken from the natural rock-work that often meets us by the mountain side. **1890** *Cent. Mag.* Aug. 490/2 We come within a few miles to the Vernal and Nevada falls..set in the midst of most novel and sublime rock-work.

transf. **1761** *Chron.* in *Ann. Reg.* 233/2 Their majesties' desert, in which the confectioner had lavished all his ingenuity in rock work and emblematical figures.

2. Stones piled together with soil interspersed for growing Alpine and other plants in a garden; a rockery; also, grotto-work, rough stone-work resembling or imitating natural rocks.

1790 W. WRIGHTE *Grotesque Archit.* 9 A cascade.. decorated with rock-work. **1833** LOUDON *Encycl. Archit.* §1979 Rockwork is one of the most common ornaments of gardens. **1845** *Florist* 225 Maritime plants can be planted appropriately at intervals round the pond at the base of the rock-work. **1880** JESSIE FOTHERGILL *Probation* II. xii, A bench situated in a kind of rockery..; the seat was a little retired in a hollow of the rockwork.

attrib. **1824** LOUDON *Encycl. Gard.* (ed. 2) Gloss. s.v. *Mitella*, N[orth] Amer[ican] rockwork plants, which prefer light rich soil. **1882** *Garden* 1 Apr. 211/2, I wish to warn all rockwork planters against this evening Primrose.

3. *Arch.* Masonry very rudely or roughly faced.

1842 GWILT *Archit.* §2670 Rustics and rockwork on columns are rarely justifiable except for the purpose of some particular picturesque effect.

4. Skill in climbing rocks; 'rock-craft'.

1898 *Westm. Gaz.* 30 Mar. 3/2 Though the climbs are short they afford excellent practice for learning rock work of the most difficult kind.

Hence **ˈrock-worked** *a.*, very rudely faced.

1859 GWILT *Archit.* §2666 Many [basement stories] are capriciously rock-worked on their surface. *Ibid.* §2669 We now return to the subject of the rock-worked rustic.

rocky (ˈrɒkɪ), *a.*[1] Also 5-6 **rokky**, 6 **rokki**, 6-7 **rockie**, 7-8 **rockey**. [f. ROCK *sb.*[1] + -Y.]

1. a. Full of, abounding in, rocks; consisting or formed of rock; having the character of rock.

14.. *Sailing Directions* (Hakl. Soc., 1889) 21 And in xiiij. or xvj. fadome there is rokky grounde. **1538** LELAND *Itin.* (1768) I. 106 The Castelle of Nottingham stondith on a rokky Hille on the west side of the Towne. **1593** SHAKS. *Rich. II*, II. i. 62 England.., Whose rocky shore beates backe the enuious siedge Of watery Neptune. **1614** RALEIGH *Hist. World* v. ii. (1634) 338 The Citadell, called Acrocorinthus, stood upon a steepe rockie hill on the North side of the towne. **1659** PEARSON *Creed* (1839) 315 In a vault made by the excavation of the rocky firm part of the earth. **1710** ADDISON *Tatler* No. 120 ¶2 Rocky Paths and pleasing Grotto's. **1787** WINTER *Syst. Husb.* 347 Where the ground is free from springs, stoney or rockey. **1853** SIR H. DOUGLAS *Milit. Bridges* 244 The left bank was rocky, and nearly level with the water. **1860** TYNDALL *Glac.* I. xx. 139 The Trifti glacier, embraced on all sides by the rocky arms of the Breithorn.

Comb. **1610** SHAKS. *Temp.* IV. i. 69 Thy Sea-marge stirrile, and rockey-hard. **1728-46** THOMSON *Spring* 398 The next pursue their rocky-channel'd maze Down to the river. **1764** GOLDSM. *Trav.* 85 Though the rocky-crested summits frown. **1768-74** TUCKER *Lt. Nat.* (1834) I. 634 The rocky-pointed causey of punishment.

b. ***Rocky Mountains***, the great mountain-range lying towards the western coast of N. America. Also *attrib.*, as ***Rocky Mountain Indian***.

1802 in *Med. Repository 1803* 238 In the fall of 1800 I was on an excursion, on horseback, through the plains that are situated between the Sascatchievan and Mississourie Rivers, along the rocky mountains. **1805** LEWIS & CLARK *Exped. Missouri* (1815) I. 320 A tribe on this side of the Rocky mountains [*Ibid.* 311–9 the Rock mountains]. **1806** P. WAKEFIELD *Excursions N. Amer.* xliii. 380 We saw some straggling parties of Rocky Mountain Indians. **1818-22** *Encycl. Metrop.* (1845) XIV. 395/2 To these are joined the Rocky or Stony Mountains, which extend as far as N. lat. 55°. **1842** PRICHARD *Nat. Hist. Man* 407 Rocky Mountains Indians are said to have a complexion of a swarthy yellow. **1850** B. TAYLOR *Eldorado* II. 22 Fort Laramie, at the foot of the Rocky Mountains.

c. Special collocations. **Rocky Mountain bee plant**, an annual herb, *Cleome serrulata*, belonging to the family Capparidaceæ and bearing racemes of pink flowers; **Rocky Mountain canary**, a burro or jack-ass; **Rocky Mountain feathers**, wood shavings; **Rocky Mountain (spotted) fever**, a sometimes fatal rickettsial disease transmitted by ticks; **Rocky Mountain goat**, the North American mountain goat, *Oreamnos americanus*; = MAZAME 2, *mountain goat* s.v. MOUNTAIN 9c; **Rocky Mountain grasshopper** = *Rocky Mountain locust*; **Rocky Mountain iris**, a blue-flowered iris, *Iris missouriensis*, found in south-western North America; **Rocky Mountain juniper**, a small conifer, *Juniperus scopulorum*, found in the south-western United States; **Rocky Mountain locust**, a migratory North American grasshopper, *Melanoplus spretus*; **Rocky Mountain oyster**, lamb's fry; **Rocky Mountain sheep**, the bighorn sheep, *Ovis canadensis*; = *big-horn* s.v. BIG *a.* B. 2; **Rocky Mountain spotted fever** = *Rocky Mountain fever*; **Rocky Mountain spotted (fever) tick**, a brown or grey tick, *Dermacentor andersoni*, found in parts of western North America, where it is the vector of Rocky Mountain fever; **Rocky Mountain wood tick** = prec.

1900 B. B. SMYTH *Plants & Flowers of Kansas* i. 14 Such temperatures..are generally supposed to be destructive to plant life; but the following plants live through them and continue to thrive: Pincushion cactus, prickly pear, ..*Rocky Mountain bee plant. **1939** *Nat. Geogr. Mag.* Aug. 227/2 Bees are attracted in such great numbers to the nectar secreted abundantly by these dainty blossoms..that the species is often called 'Rocky Mountain bee plant'. **1963** J. J. CRAIGHEAD et al. *Field Guide Rocky Mt. Wildflowers* 69 Rocky Mountain Bee-plant..is a much-branched annual 2–5 ft. tall. **1905** *Outing* Apr. 47/2 His varied outfit he packs on the back of the '*Rocky Mountain canary'. **1929** *Amer. Speech* V. 147 The burro or jackass of the early days is still called a *Rocky Mountain canary*, because of its tuneful voice. **1828** RICHARDSON in *Zool. Jrnl.* III. 517 *Rocky Mountain Dormouse. **1962** *Maclean's Mag.* 18 July 44/2, I started a fire with a handful of '*Rocky Mountain feathers'—dry shavings—made that morning before we left our previous camp. **1886** *Buck's Handbk. Med. Sci.* III. 85/2 The '*Rocky Mountain Fever', so called by practitioners on the slope of that great mountain chain, exhibits frequent divergences from the true clinical features of typhoid fever, and may show a continued remittent type, but the pathology observed in not a few of these cases links them to typhoid fever. **1917** *Indian Med. Gaz.* LII. 16/1 Most observers place the incubation of the Rocky Mountain fever at three to seven days. **1939** *Brit. Encycl. Med. Pract.* XII. 340 The other types [of tick-borne typhus] can be most easily understood by considering the respects in which they differ from Rocky Mountain fever. **1828** RICHARDSON in *Zool. Jrnl.* III 520 *Rocky Mountain Flying Squirrel. **1842** J. E. DEKAY *Zool. N.Y.* I. 112 *Rocky Mountain Goat..larger than the common goat. **1884-5** [see GOAT 1 b]. **1901** *Daily Colonist* (Victoria, B.C.) 11 Oct. 1/6 The Rocky Mountain goat captured..last spring..is to be sent to the London Zoo this week. **1949** *Canad. Alpine Jrnl.* May 55 We had seen elk, moose, Rocky Mountain goats, and bighorn. **1909** WEBSTER 944/1 The allied migratory *Rocky Mountain grasshopper..sometimes travels in vast hordes in the region west of the Mississippi. **1966** DAVIDSON & PEAIRS *Insect Pests* (ed. 6) viii. 129 The Rocky Mountain grasshopper is considered the most important migratory species in the United States and Canada. **1880** T. MEEHAN *Native Flowers & Ferns U.S.* 2nd Ser. I. 103 As it is the only species of *Iris* found there the common name of '*Rocky Mountain Iris' has suggested itself to us. **1963** J. J. Craighead *Field Guide Rocky Mt. Wildflowers* 34 Rocky Mountain Iris..usually bears from 1 to 4 variegated violet-blue flowers. **1898** G. B. Sudworth *Check List Forest Trees U.S.* 35 *Juniperus scopulorum* Sargent. *Rocky Mountain Juniper. **1949** Collingwood & Brush *Knowing your Trees* 135 The twigs of the Rocky Mountain juniper..are four-sided, with leaves arranged alternately in pairs. **1972** L. Hancock *There's a Seal in my Sleeping Bag* viii. 182 Old dried whitened Rocky Mountain juniper trees sprout the artistic bulky stick nests of the double-crested cormorants. **1878** *Rep. Comm. Agric. 1877* (U.S. Dept. Agric.) 264 The *Rocky Mountain Locust, or Grasshopper of the West. **1930** S. Henry *Conquering our Great Amer. Plains* 319 Coming home late one afternoon for supper I stepped back surprised to see what became known as Rocky Mountain locusts covering the side of the house. **1972** V. A. Little *Gen. & Applied Entomol.* (ed. 3) vii. 94 Although the Rocky Mountain locust is found throughout most of the United States, it is considered a pest of importance only in the Great Plains region. **1889** J. Whitehead *Steward's Handbk.* iv. 420/2 **Rocky Mountain oysters*, Lambs' fries. **1940** C. L. Brown et al. *Amer. Cooks* 71 (*heading*) Fried lamb's fries, or Rocky Mountain oysters. **1859** Baird *Mammals N. Amer.* 499 *Rocky Mountain Rat. **1872** Coues *N. Amer. Birds* 153 *Rocky Mountain region, U.S. and southward, northeast to Kansas. [**1804** Lewis & Clark *Exped. Missouri* (1815) I. 197 Two horns of the animal called by the French, the *Rock mountain sheep.] **1818** T. Laurie in *Mem. Wernerian Nat. Hist. Soc.* (1821) III. 308 Remarks..on the Skin of the Rocky Mountain Sheep. **1904** [see argal]. **1936** D. McCowan *Animals Canad. Rockies* v. 45 Rocky Mountain sheep..are almost entirely guided by what we call instinct. **1977** D. Anthony *Stud Game* xxviii. 188 They hunted Rocky Mountain sheep with bow-and-arrow. You have to be good to do that. [**1903** Rocky Mountain spotted fever: see *spotted fever* s.v. spotted *a.* and *ppl. a.* 3 a.] **1905** *U.S. Hygienic Lab. Bull.* XX. 8 *Rocky Mountain 'spotted fever' is reported for Idaho, Montana, Nevada, Oregon, Wyoming, ?Washington State, and possibly Utah and Alaska. **1906** *Jrnl. Amer. Med. Assoc.* 7 July 33/1, I arrived in Missoula, Montana, April 21, 1906, equipped for the bacteriologic and hematologic study of the so-called Rocky Mountain spotted fever. **1947** *Ann. Rev. Microbiol.* I. 346 The fatality rate in Rocky Mountain spotted fever is greatly influenced by age. **1974** *Greenville* (S. Carolina) *News* 23 Apr. 3/2 The little ticks that carry Rocky Mountain spotted fever didn't have to find a warm spot under a log this winter. **1937** *Jrnl. Econ. Entomol.* XXX. 52 The first, known popularly as the *Rocky Mountain spotted fever tick, or Rocky Mountain wood tick, is our most versatile species as a disease vector. **1976** *Islander* (Victoria, B.C.) 7 June 14/2 The most serious type of infection, called tick fever, is transmitted by the Rocky Mountain spotted tick. **1937** *Rocky Mountain wood tick [see *Rocky Mountain spotted fever tick*]. **1951** Metcalf & Flint *Destructive & Useful Insects* (ed. 3) xxiii. 983 The Rocky Mountain wood tick is the most important tick in the United States. **1976** *National Observer* (U.S.) 21 Aug. 8/4 The Rocky Mountain wood tick carries the illness in the West.

d. quasi-*sb.* ***the Rockies***, the Rocky Mountains.

1827 J. Smith *Let.* 12 July in *Dict. Americanisms* (1951) II. 1409/2, I allude to the country of the Great Salt Lake, West of the Rockies. *a* **1861** T. Winthrop *John Brent* (1862) vi. 60 At the foot of those bare, bulky mounds of mountain by which the Wasatch range tones off into the great plains between it and the Rockys, we overtook the Salt Lake mail. **1882** W. A. B. Grohmann (*title*), Camp in the Rockies. **1892** *Month* Apr. 88 The solitude of the snow-capped Rockies.

2. *fig.* **a.** Of the heart or disposition: Flinty, stony, hard, unfeeling, unyielding.

a **1586** Sidney *Arcadia* iii. (1605) 327 The grace wherewith Anaxius spake it, to perswade rockie minds to their owne harm. **1596** R. Linche *Diella* (1877) 20, I know ..all will not remoue flynt-harted rigour from your rocky breast. **1650** Howell *Lett.* III. 7 May He also move My mind, and rockie heart so strike and rend. **1690** Norris *Beatitudes* (1692) 46 Some men of Rocky Hearts..that would see the whole World in Flames without any concern. **1839–52** Bailey *Festus* 27 Like God's voice Upon the worldling's proud, cold, rocky heart.

Comb. *c* **1602** F. Davison in Farr *S.P. Eliz.* (1845) II. 331 Whose rocks and rocky-hearted foes My flight on euery side enclose. *a* **1849** Mangan *Poems* (1859) 238 This rocky-bosomed beauty.

b. Firm as a rock; unflinching, steadfast.

1622 Massinger & Dekker *Virgin Martyr* ii. iii, I'll send my daughters to her, And they shall turn her rocky faith to wax. **1692** Hickeringill *Good Old Cause* Wks. 1716 II. 518 Let [such effeminate constitutions] leave the rugged and boysterous Wars to rugged and rocky Complexions and Constitutions. **1856** Ruskin *Mod. Paint.* IV. v. xv. §23 Written in larger and rockier characters upon the sky.

c. Resembling a rock in solidity.

1825 J. Neal *Bro. Jonathan* I. 274 A smile of barbarous exultation..brightened his..rocky, square forehead.

†**3. a.** ***rocky bone***, one of the bones of the ear. (Cf. *rock-bone*, s.v. rock *sb.*[1] 9). *Obs.*

1615 Crooke *Body of Man* 440 Aboue the eares..aboue the bones called *petrosa* or the rockie bones. **1683** Snape *Anat. Horse* iii. xiv. (1686) 139 Which Cavities are wrought by Nature in the Rocky-bone, and contain in them the in-bred Air.

†**b.** ***rocky ruby***, = rock-ruby. *Obs.*

a **1728** Woodward *Fossils* i. 29 The Rocky-Ruby, ..*Rubinus rupium*. This is of a Red deep, and the hardest of all the kinds.

4. Growing upon or among rocks. *rare.*

1640 Parkinson *Theatr. Bot.* 707 The rockie Cranes bill [*Geranium saxatile*] is a lesser plant then the ordinary Doves foot. **1731** Miller *Gard. Dict.* s.v. *Lychnis*, Maritime Rocky Campion, with an Orpine Leaf. **1805** Lambert tr. *Michaux' Trav. Allegany Mts.* 301 The remainder of this tract.. produces only the white, red,..and rocky oaks, &c. intermixed with pines.

5. *Brewing.* (See quots.)

Connected with *rock* as a variant of *roche*: see rocking *vbl. sb.*[2] (quot. 1839) and cf. F. *rocher* in Littré.

1835 W. Black *Brewing* 52 The third change is the cauliflower or curling top, rising to a fine rocky or light yeasty head. **1836** *Penny Cycl.* V. 405/1 The stages of a healthy fermentation are, first, a creamy scum rising on the surface: this, after a time, begins to curl and becomes frosted in appearance; it then becomes rocky, and the air vesicles which appeared frosted enlarge.

Hence **'rockily** *adv.*

1972 D. Haston *In High Places* ix. 100 Almost an ideal mountain panorama. Fitzroy, Poincenot and satellites rockily bounding the right, rounding off towards Pere Giorgio at the head of the valley. **1981** *Times Lit. Suppl.* 6 Feb. 147/5 The difficulties of absorbing women into a group so rockily traditional as the police.

rocky ('rɒkɪ), *a.*[2] [f. rock *v.*[1]]

a. Unsteady, tottering, unstable; tipsy, drunken.

1737 *Pennsylvania Gaz.* 6–13 Jan. 2 He's Rocky, Raddled, ..Lost his Rudder. **1770** *Gentl. Mag.* XL. 559 To express the condition of an Honest fellow and no Flincher under the Effects of good Fellowship it is said that he is..Rocky. **1791–3** in *Spirit Public Jrnls.* I. 3 Our Rulers too are—rocky. **1828** *Craven Gloss.*, *Rocky*, drunken, tottering in his gait. **1895** J. G. Millais *Breath fr. Veldt* (1899) 253 The vision of these splendid horns..made me a bit 'rocky', as the big beast swung round to stare at us. **1897** *Westm. Gaz.* 14 Apr. 7/2 He understood that the society in which his money was invested was in a 'rocky' condition. **1912** A. Bennett *Matador of Five Towns* 157 'What's up with that wheel?' 'It's rocky, that's what that wheel is.' **1938** 'N. Shute' *Ruined City* x. 204 The whole thing was a pretty rocky deal. **1941** *Direction* IV. v. 15/2 Stack had been..gettin leapin drunk... One morning in April, 1906, after he had had a rocky night and had a headache built for a hippopotamus he was out..to cool the burnin thirst in his throat. **1947** *Partisan Rev.* XIV. 493, I was drinking scotch on an empty stomach, and beginning to feel a trifle rocky myself. **1951** A. Baron *Rosie Hogarth* i. vi. 62 A chap always felt a bit rocky after he'd shown what he was made of. **1977** D. Beaty *Excellency* vii. 90 The régime's rocky. The future of the country's uncertain.

b. *colloq.*, in vaguely depreciative use. Now usu. in sense 'difficult, hard'.

Some cases may be equally well interpreted as examples of a *fig.* use of rocky *a.*[1] 1 a.

1873 J. Miller *Life amongst Modocs* 71 We may have a rocky time down there, my boy. **1883** *Bicycling News* 28 Dec. 830 A very jolly day having been spent, notwithstanding the rocky weather. **1890** L. C. D'Oyle *Notches* 12 It'll be a little bit rocky on some of us. **1960** B. Keaton *My Wonderful World of Slapstick* 13, I am by no means overlooking the rough and rocky years I've lived through. **1976** E. Dunphy *Only a Game?* iii. 90, I had played well in the first half at Swindon when things were rocky.

c. *colloq.* In poor health; ill, unwell.

The sense in quot. 1792 is unclear; it may be rocky *a.*[1] 2 b.

1792 F. Burney *Let.* 28 Jan. (1972) I. 106 A former Patient is often alarmed..but she is very *Rocky*..& she will be glad when the alarm passes over. **1926** E. Hemingway *Sun also Rises* i. vii. 56 What's the matter, darling? Do you feel rocky? **1929** M. de la Roche *Whiteoaks* iii. 56 Is Wake feeling rocky to-night? **1932** G. Greene *Stamboul Train* ii. i. 62, I guess you're a bit rocky. You haven't escaped from anywhere, have you? **1954** G. Durrell *Bafut Beagles* viii. 151 'Made you feel a bit rocky?' inquired the doctor cheerfully, feeling my pulse.

'rocky, *sb. Naval slang.* Also rockie. [f. rocky *a.*[2]] (See quots.) Also *attrib.* or as *adj.*

1919 W. Lang *Sea Lawyer's Log* 29, I have seen an officer who presides directly over our naval destinies fix the eye of a basilisk upon a luckless 'rockie' who incautiously spoke of a parade. **1927** 'Giraldus' *Musings of Merry Matloe* (ed. 2) 186 *Rocky*, a Royal Naval or Fleet Reserve man. Also a R.N. Reserve officer who once was more commonly known as a 'Cargo Shifter'. **1929** F. C. Bowen *Sea Slang* 112 *Rockies*, R.N.V.R. ratings training in H.M. ships in peace time and very highly valued as worked ratings. Before the War it was also applied to R.N.R. ratings, seldom since. **1948** Partridge *Dict. Forces' Slang* 156 *Rockies*, officers of the Naval Reserves. **1957** Kerr & Granville *Royal Naval Volunteer Reserve* vi. 91 The active-service men labelled them [*sc.* RNVR ratings] a 'rocky' lot—'rocky' being an oblique reference to unstable sea-legs and the waved tapes in their blue jean collars.

rocky, obs. form of rock *v.*[1]

roco'cesque, *a. rare*[−1]. [f. next + -esque.] Of rococo character or style; suggesting rococo.

1885 Freeman in *Times* 20 Jan. 10/6 Not to imitate the rococesque lantern arches.

rococo (rəʊ'kəʊkəʊ), *a.* and *sb.* Also roccoco. [a. F. *rococo*, supposed to be a fanciful formation on the stem of *rocaille* pebble- or shell-work.

1836 *Fraser's Mag.* XIII. 214 There are two especial new *mots d'argot*, *rococo* and *décousu*.]

A. *adj.* **1.** Old-fashioned, antiquated.

1836 *Foreign Q. Rev.* XVII. 432 This species of delicacy seems now to be so thoroughly *perruque*, and *rococo*, or whatever be the newest and most approved term for old-fashioned, that [etc.]. **1839** Lady Lytton *Cheveley* (ed. 2) I. xii. 278 [He] had even been sufficiently 'rococo' to assert boldly that he did not think Victor Hugo so great a genius as Racine. **1859** Sala *Tw. Round Clock* (1861) 300, I do not even know the names of the fashionable dances of the day, and very probably those to which I have alluded are by this time old fashioned, out of date, *rococo*, and pigtaily. **1870** M. Arnold in *Pall Mall Gaz.* 29 Nov. 3/2 We heard the honest German soldiers *Hoch-ing*, hurrahing, and God-blessing in their true-hearted but somewhat *rococo* manner. **1902** H. L. Wilson *Spenders* ix. 92 She is rather a beauty, you'll find;.. a bit rococo in manner, I suspect.

2. a. Of furniture or architecture: Having the characteristics of Louis Quatorze or Louis Quinze workmanship, such as conventional shell- and scroll-work and meaningless decoration; excessively or tastelessly florid or ornate. Also of interior decoration.

1841 C'tess Blessington *Idler in France* I. i. 21 The whole [of the terraces near La Tour-Magne at Nîmes] offering a curious mixture of military and *rococo* taste. **1844** Thackeray *Little Trav.* Wks. 1900 VI. 27 The rococo architects have introduced their ornaments. **1851** Mogford *Preserv. Pict.* (ed. 3) i. 10 The poverty of invention, and rococo design of most of the picture-frames now made. **1876** Hardy *Ethelberta* I. 24 An oval mirror of rococo workmanship. **1887** Pater *Imag. Portraits* 150 That *rococo* seventeenth-century French imitation of the true Renaissance. **1918** *Heal & Son Catal.: Cottage Furnit.* 1 The 'new art' overmantel smothered in rococo photograph frames. **1967** N. Freeling *Strike Out* 40 Presentation silver ..in every conceivable pattern from curliest rococo to bleakest Swedish. **1972** *Country Life* 7 Dec. 1574/1 All these rooms have delicate rococo plaster ceilings picked out in pale pastel shades. **1980** *Early Music* Apr. 173/2 The organ sonatas of C. P. E. Bach from the 1750s are a good match for the rococo organ in Midwolda (1772).

transf. **1878** E. Jenkins *Haverholme* 65 The florid and rococo notions of Imperial glory flourished by his political chief. **1881** *Daily Telegr.* 27 Dec., That stately rococo dance, the Minuet de la Cour. **1931** *N. & Q.* 15 Aug. 109/2 It is further planned to give Goethe plays and rococo concerts on an open-air stage. **1938** W. S. Maugham *Summing Up* 28 Dryden flourished at a happy moment... He was the first of the rococo artists. **1941** *Jazz Information* Nov. 21/2 James P. [Johnson] made his first player piano rolls..as a 'race' feature alongside the rococo but immensely popular efforts of Phil Ohman. **1955** *Times* 21 July 7/7 Stravinsky's choice of a more or less definite rococo pastiche is a highly appropriate musical idiom. **1959** *Listener* 26 Nov. 952/1 Haydn's symphonic music began as rococo entertainment. **1967** G. Steiner *Lang. & Silence* 28 This would..lead one to ask whether..the rococo virtuosity of Salinger is arguing an absurdly diminished and enervating view of human existence. **1970** *Oxf. Compan. Art* 987/1 The painter to whom the epithet 'Rococo' has most often been loosely applied is, perhaps, Watteau, and in his rejection of the *grand sujet* and his fanciful and curvacious rhythms he does ..fit into the movement.

b. *Embroidery.* (See quots.)

1882 Caulfield & Saward *Dict. Needlework* 426/1 Rococo Embroidery is used for table borders, fire screens, and cushion covers, and is made with écru linen foundations, ornamented with filoselles. **1934** M. Thomas *Dict. Embroidery Stitches* 171 *Rococo stitch*,..must be worked on a very wide-meshed canvas of even weave and the little groups or bundles of stitches are set in alternate squares, leaving the others open and rather 'pulled' in effect. **1960** G. Lewis *Handbk. Crafts* 38 Frequently these two are the only stitches used to the neglect of the many others which would greatly enrich many pieces of work, such as.. French stitch..and Rococo stitch. **1960** B. Snook *Eng. Hist. Embroidery* 82 Rococo stitch is particularly effective. *Ibid.* 98 Designs of flowers, bouquets, ferns, ribbons and tassels..were either in varied silk stitchery on satin, or in tent stitch on canvas if enclosed in a rococo border.

B. *sb.* **1.** The style of architecture, art, etc., having rococo characteristics.

1840 *Civil Eng. & Arch. Jrnl.* III. 94/1 The type of the ancient church was replaced by the absurdities of the rococo. **1881** H. James *Portrait of a Lady* xxxv, Miss Osmond, indeed, in the bloom of her juvenility, had a touch of the rococo. **1884** Symonds *Shaks. Predec.* xiv. 563 The whole passage illustrates the rococo of the English Renaissance which Marlowe made fashionable. **1935** W. S. Maugham *Don Fernando* x. 224 Decoration..degenerated with time to the frivolous ornament of rococo. **1947** A. Einstein *Mus. Romantic Era* iii. 20 The 18th-century stylistic period that preceded the Empire, the Rococo, had been a last tremulous echo of the grandeur of the Baroque. **1954** [see baroque *a.* (*sb.*)]. **1965** *Listener* 3 June 830/1 The drawing in nearly all Monticelli's pictures is reminiscent of the rococo.

2. A piece of work in this style.

1876 *Academy* 30 Dec. 623 These *Scenes* are rococoes sufficiently out of the common track to be worthy of notice.

Hence **roco'cocity**. *nonce-wd.*

1844 E. FitzGerald *Lett.* (1889) I. 125 Think of the rococicity of a gentleman studying Seneca in the middle of February..in a remarkably damp cottage. **1916** A. Huxley *Let.* 29 Dec. (1969) 118 My monocle is very grandiose, but gives me rather a Greco-Roman air of rococicity.

rocolo, obs. variant of roquelaure.

rocou, variant of roucou.

†**rocquet.** *Obs. rare.* Also roquet. [? Adaptation of a native name.] (See quots.)

The original source for the name and description is Rochefort *Hist. Antilles* (1658) i. xiii. 131.

1666 J. Davies *Hist. Caribby Isles* 75 Besides these greater sorts of lizzards, there are in these islands..others which are much less; and these are called..Roquets. **1685** R. Burton *Eng. Emp. Amer.* 196 The rocquet is a pretty animal in this isle. **1708** Oldmixon *Brit. Emp.* II. 227 The Rocquet, an animal whose skin is like a wither'd leaf. **1753** *Chambers's Cycl.* Suppl. s.v. *Roquet.*

rocquet, obs. form of rocket *sb.*[1]

rod (rɒd), *sb.*[1] Also 1–6 rodd-, 4–5 rodd, 5–7 rodde. [OE. *rodd*, corresponding in sense to the continental forms cited under rood *sb.*, but in form quite distinct. Prob. related to ON. *rudda* 'club', Norw. dial. *rudda*, *rydda* 'a large pliant twig or stick used as a whip', *rodda* 'a stake set upright to hang things on' (Ross).]

I. 1. a. A straight, slender shoot or wand, growing upon or cut from a tree, bush, etc.

a **1150** [see sense 2]. *a* **1250** *Owl & Night.* 1123 Vor me þe hoþ in one rodde, An þu, mid þine fule codde,.. Biwerest manne corn urom dore. *c* **1400** MAUNDEV. (Roxb.) xi. 41 Hingand apon a spere or apon a rodd. *c* **1430** *Two Cookery-bks.* 52 Pryke þe cofyn with a pynne y-stekyd on a roddys ende. **1526** *Pilgr. Perf.* (W. de W. 1531) 139 The aungell sate downe & knyt roddes & wrought on yᵉ basket. **1572** in Feuillerat *Revels Q. Eliz.* (1908) 166 For wicker Roddes to make frettes. **1611** BIBLE *Gen.* xxx. 37 Iacob tooke him rods of greene poplar, and of the hasel and chestnut tree. **1688** HOLME *Armoury* III. 107/2 To put two rods through the cross thrids that were crossed at the Warping. **1766** *Compl. Farmer* s.v. *Surveying* 7 F 2/1 It is good that he.. carry in his hand a bundle of rods, to stick down one at the end of the chain. **1784** COWPER *Task* VI. 166 So thick a swarm Of flow'rs, like flies clothing her slender rods, That scarce a leaf appears. **1802** JAMES *Milit. Dict.* s.v., Rods, or sticks, fastened to sky-rockets, to make them rise in a straight line. **1867** JEAN INGELOW *Laurance* ii. 130 The hazel rods Were nodding with their catkins. **1885** C. G. W. LOCK *Workshop Rec.* Ser. IV. 276/1 'Osiers',.. under the technical name of 'rods' and willows, are a merchantable commodity.

b. *fig.* An offshoot, a scion; a tribe. (Biblical.)

1460 *Pol., Rel., & L. Poems* (1866) 81 To the all synners do go,.. As thou art parfyte rodde of Iesse. **1535** COVERDALE *Isaiah* xi. 1 After this there shal come a rod forth of yᵉ Kynrede of Iesse, and a blossome out of his rote. **1611** BIBLE *Ps.* lxxiv. 2 Remember.. the rod [*marg.* Or, tribe] of thine inheritance which thou hast redeemed. **1780** [E. PERRONET] *Occas. Verses* (1785) 22 Extol the stem of Jesse's rod, And crown Him Lord of All. *c* **1850** NEALE *Hymns East. Ch.* (1866) 73 Rod of the Root of Jesse, Thou, Flower of Mary born.

c. In phr. *by the rod*, descriptive of an old form of taking or surrendering land.

Cf. Cotgrave (1611), s.v. *Verge*.

1736 *Brasenose Coll. Doc.* C² 88 Came and surrendered by the rod into the hands of the Lords of the fee, a cottage [etc.]. **1818** CRUISE *Digest* (ed. 2) V. 560 An attorney who makes a surrender ought to pursue the usual form, as by the rod, &c., according to the custom of the manor.

2. a. An instrument of punishment, either one straight stick, or a bundle of twigs bound together. *to spare the rod*, etc.: see SPARE *v.*

a **1150** *Ags. Hom.* (ed. Assmann) xv. 119 Ða het se ȝerefa hi niman.. & mid greatum roddum beaton. **1390**, *c* **1450** [see b]. *c* **1491** *Chast. Goddes Chyld.* 14 Yf the childe wexe wanton the moder beteth him fyrst with a litell rodde and the strenger he wexeth the gretter rodde she takyth. **1551** T. WILSON *Logike* (1580) 36 The rodde as an instrument.. helpeth forward to bryng the boye to some goodnesse. **1580** in Boys *Coll. Hist. Sandwich* (1792) 231 Punished.. with rodd, shame, restraint of plaie, or otherwyse. **1603** SHAKS. *Meas. for M.* I. iii. 26 As fond Fathers, Hauing bound vp the threatning twigs of birch..: in time the rod [is] More mock'd, then fear'd. **1636** COWLEY *Poetical Blossoms, Vote* iii, I would not be a School-master, though he His Rods no lesse than *Fasces* deemes to be. **1733** FIELDING *Intriguing Chambermaid* Epil., 'Tis hard to pay them who our faults reveal, As boys are forced to buy the rods they feel. **1780** COWPER *Boadicea* 2 The British warrior queen, Bleeding from the Roman rods. **1824** W. IRVING *T. Trav.* I. 270 It makes a vast difference in opinion about the utility of the rod, which end happens to fall to one's share. **1865** KINGSLEY *Herew.* xxxix, To fast all the year on bread and water; and to be disciplined with rods or otherwise.

b. *fig.* A means or instrument of punishment; also, punishment, chastisement. Formerly common in phr. ***to make a rod for oneself, one's own back***, etc. ***to kiss the rod***: see KISS *v.* 6.

1390 GOWER *Conf.* II. 44 Cupide, which of love is godd, In chastisinge hath mad a rodd To dryve awei hir wantounesse. *c* **1450** tr. *De Imitatione* III. lv. 132 Thy discipline is upon me, & þy rodde she shal teche me... I encline me under þe rodde of þy correccion. **1470–85** MALORY *Arthur* V. ii. 162, I fere me ye haue made a rodde for your self. **1535** COVERDALE *Lam.* iii. 1, I am the man, that thorow the rodd of his wrath haue experience of misery. **1546** HEYWOOD *Prov.* (1867) 5 Whan haste proueth a rod made for his owne tayle. **1596** SHAKS. *1 Hen. IV*, III. ii. 10 Thou do'st.. Make me beleeue, that thou art.. the Rod of heauen To punish my Mistreadings. *c* **1611** CHAPMAN *Iliad* v. 606 And therefore.. never strive, but gently take your rod. **1655** FULLER *Ch. Hist.* v. 234 It hapned that this Lord first felt the smart of this rod which he made for others. **1677** W. HUGHES *Man of Sin* I. ix. 39 Oh how the good man smiles to see what a Rod we have made for our own Back! **1697** DRYDEN *Virg. Georg.* IV. 654 No vulgar God Pursues thy Crimes, nor with a common Rod. **1734** E. ERSKINE *Serm.* Wks. 1871 II. 284 How little fruit is there of rods, whether public or personal. **1771** *Junius Lett.* lxix. (1788) 368 Shortening the duration of parliaments.. is keeping the representative under the rod of the constituent. **1801** I. MILNER in *Life* xiii. (1842) 249, I have long seen it very plain that mild methods will not do for me. Nothing but the rod answers at all. **1860** MOTLEY *Netherl.* iii. I. 67 It was the policy of both.. governments.. to make use of him as a rod over the head of Philip.

c. ***a rod in pickle***, † ***lye***, † ***piss***, usually *fig.*, a punishment in store. (Cf. PICKLE *sb.*¹ 1 b.)

1553 *Respublica* III. v. 820 Some would in no wyse to owre desyres applye. But we have Roddes in pysse for them. **1593** G. HARVEY *Pierce's Super.* Wks. (Grosart) II. 327, I know One, that experimentally prooued what a rod in lye could do with the curstest boy in a Citty. **1648** J. DILLINGHAM in *Ld. Montagu of Beaulieu's P.* (Hist. MSS. Comm.) 163 No doubt there are many rods in pickle against many great ones. **1714** MANDEVILLE *Fab. Bees* (1733) I. 331, I see a thousand rods in piss, and the whole posse of diminutive pedants against me. **1798** *Anti-Jacobin* 5 Mar. (1852) 77 He keeps for Pitt a rod in pickle. **1848** MRS. JAMESON *Sacr. & Leg. Art* (1850) 267 He has as certainly a rod in pickle for the idle and unruly. **1886** A. J. C. HARE *Story Life* (1900) VI. 5 The incarnation of a rod in pickle, but with very fine qualities.

†**d.** ***a rod under*** or ***at one's girdle***, implying a whipping or the fact of having been whipped. *Obs.*

1579 LYLY *Euphues* (Arb.) 34 They put gold into the hands of youth, where they should put a rod vnder their gyrdle. **1591** —— *Endym.* II. ii, Away peeuish boy, a rodde were better vnder thy girdle than loue in thy mouth. **1598** B. JONSON *Ev. Man in Hum.* V. i. (Q.¹), You signior shall be carried to the market crosse, and be there bound: and so shall you sir, in a large motlie coate, with a rodde at your girdle.

3. a. A wand or stick carried in the hand, such as a walking-stick, shepherd's or herdsman's stick, enchanter's wand, etc.

c **1290** *S. Eng. Leg.* I. 274/123 His rodde he piȝte in þe grounde: and heo bi-gan a-non To leui and blowe and bere fruyt. **1474** CAXTON *Chess* III. (1883) 76 A man holdynge.. a rodde in the lifte hand. *Ibid.*, The rodde is for to dryue and conduyte wyth all the bestes vnto her pasture. **1511** *Guylforde's Pilgr.* (Camden) 45 Yᵉ relyques yᵗ Titus caryed to Rome, that is to say,.. Aarons rodde, Moyses rod. **1526** TINDALE *Matt.* x. 10 Possess nott golde, nor silver.., Nether shues, nor yet a rod [so Cranmer (1539) and Rheims (1582)]. **1611** BIBLE *Ps.* xxiii. 4 Thy rod and thy staffe, they comfort me. **1634** MILTON *Comus* 816 Without his rod revers't, And backward mutters of dissevering power, We cannot free the Lady. **1667** —— *P.L.* XI. 133 Charm'd with Arcadian Pipe, the Pastoral Reed Of Hermes, or his opiate Rod. **1756–7** tr. *Keysler's Trav.* (1760) II. 192 Here also they pretend to shew the rods of Moses and Aaron, &c. **1781** COWPER *Expost.* 85 He that rul'd them with a shepherd's rod, In form a man, in dignity a God. **1819** SHELLEY *Œd. Tyr.* I. 149, I struck the crust o' the earth With this enchanted rod, and Hell lay bare! **1885** J. PAYN *Luck of Darrells* xxxi, Her later life, with its far more important incidents, had swallowed it up like Aaron's rod.

b. A stick or switch carried in the hand when riding. See also RIDING-ROD.

1432–50 tr. *Higden* (Rolls) I. 353 Thei haue a wonde, other a rodde,.. to cause the horses to move. **1614** MARKHAM *Cheap Husb.* I. ii, Carry your rod without offence to his eye in your right hand. **1633** G. HERBERT *Temple, Charms & Knots* 3 A poore mans rod, when thou dost ride, Is both a weapon and a guide. *a* **1648** LD. HERBERT *Autobiogr.* (1886) 73 The rule for graceful riding is, that a man hold.. his rod over the left ear of his horse. **1753** *Chambers's Cycl.* Suppl. s.v.

c. A divining-rod: see DIVINING-, DOWSING-ROD, and cf. MOSAICAL 2.

1617 MORYSON *Itin.* I. 12 When they goe over silver, they say the Rod bends or breakes, if it be straightly held. **1641** THORNDIKE *Govt. Churches* I. i. § 1 Those that seek for mines have.. a rod which they hold even-balanced over the place where they hope for a vein. **1778** PRYCE *Min. Cornub.* 114 The corpuscles, it was said, that rise from the Minerals, entering the rod, determine it to bow down. **1836** R. FURNESS *Astrologer* 1, To cut the wondrous rod, and thence define The place and bearing of the hidden mine. **1865** KINGSLEY *Herew.* xxv, There might be iron-ore in the wolds; and if you could find it by the rod, we might get it up and smelt it.

transf. **1649** G. DANIEL *Trinarch., Hen. V*, clv, Soe great a faith have Princes, when the Sword (Their Rod of Prophecie) leads on.

4. a. A wand or staff (of wood, ivory, or metal) carried as a symbol of office, authority, or dignity. (See also BLACK ROD.)

c **1440** *Sir Gowther* 314 There come the steward with a rod in his honde, To do him thens thus he wold fonde. *c* **1450** *Brut* 545 Sir Thomas Percy,.. stuard of the Kynges howsold, come into the hall amonges the pepill, and there he brak the rodde of his office. *a* **1548** HALL *Chron., Hen. VIII*, 215 The erle of Arrondel whiche bare the rod of Yvery with the Dove both together. **1557** N.T. (Genev.) *Mark* xiv. 65 The sergeantes smote him with their rods of office. **1613** SHAKS. *Hen. VIII*, IV. i. 89 Holy Oyle,.. The Rod, and Bird of Peace, and all such Emblemes. **1641** BAKER *Chron.* (1653) 211 Receiving at the Kings hands the Rod and the Cap, as investitures of that Dutchy. **1677** F. SANDFORD *Geneal. Hist. Eng.* 75 Delivering Him the Scepter to hold in His Right Hand, and the Rod Royal in his Left Hand. **1728** CHAMBERS *Cycl.* s.v. *Vergers*, Inferior Officers, who go before the Bishop, Dean, &c., with a Verge, or Rod tip'd with Silver. **1777** BRAND *Observ. Pop. Antiq.* xxv. 261 The Staff or Rod of Authority in the Civil and in the Military.. are both derived from hence. **1822** SCOTT *Nigel* ix, Maxwell, still keeping his rod across the door, said,.. 'My lord, this gentleman is not known'.

b. As a symbol of power or tyrannical sway.

1526 TINDALE *Rev.* ii. 27 He shall rule them with a rodde of yeron. **1667** MILTON *P.L.* v. 884 That Golden Scepter.. Is now an Iron Rod to bruise and breake Thy disobedience. **1748** GRAY *Alliance* 58 Proud of the yoke, and pliant to the rod. **1750** —— *Elegy* 47 Hands that the rod of empire might have sway'd. **1786** BURNS *Address to Edinburgh* 14 Here Justice.. High wields her balance and her rod. **1813** SHELLEY *Q. Mab* v. 127 The iron rod of Penury still compels Her wretched slave to bow the knee to wealth. *Ibid.* IX. 187 Tamely crouching to the tyrant's rod. **1879** FROUDE *Cæsar* xxvi. 437 They would fall only under the rod of less scrupulous conquerors.

5. a. An angling-rod; a fishing-rod.

a **1450** *Fysshynge w. Angle* (1883) 6 Ye muste furst lurne to mak.. your rod, your lynys.. & your hokes. *Ibid.* 7 How ȝe schall make your Rodde craftely. **1523–98** [see ANGLE-ROD; ANGLING 3]. **1630** DRAYTON *Muses' Elys.* Nymphal vi, The lusty Samon.. wresting at my Rod doth make my Boat turne round. **1653** WALTON *Angler* 120 This kind of fishing with a dead rod, and laying night-hooks, are like putting money to use. **1711** GAY *Rural Sports* I. 134 Let the fisherman.. Encrease his tackle, and his rod retye. **1753** *Scots Mag.* Mar. 134/1 He got a rod, and went a-fishing. **1856** 'STONEHENGE' *Brit. Rural Sports* 252/2 The short rod is then to be held over the stream, and the bait gently dropped into the water.

b. *transf.* An angler.

1867 F. FRANCIS *Angling* xii. (1880) 441 One of the keenest and best rods on the river. **1894** *Outing* XXIV. 257/2 He lands more big fish and throws back more small ones than any other rod in his district. **1935** B. PERRY *And gladly Teach* viii. 181 After showing me how often he had been 'high rod' on his stretch of the river, he would 'O.K.' all of my estimates with a smile. **1975** *Oxf. Univ. Gaz.* 16 Jan. 428/1 (Advt.), Prospective rods may apply for descriptive booklet.

c. Used in association with GUN *sb.* to designate the twin pursuits of fishing and shooting.

1840 J. WILSON (*title*) The rod and the gun, being two treatises on angling and shooting. *c* **1860** in A. Adburgham *Shops & Shopping* (1964) vii. 74 Their [*sc.* the fabrics'] close imitation of the colour of the natural objects surrounding the *Sportsman* have rendered them an absolute necessity for the pursuits of the rod or gun. **1912** E. D. CUMING (*title*) With rod and gun. **1966** *Times* 28 Feb. (Canada Suppl.) p. ii, Canada is a.. catch-your-limit rod-and-gun of a country.

d. *transf.* The right to fish a length of river.

1932 G. CORNWALLIS-WEST *Edwardians go Fishing* v. 60 A friend of mine was invited to fish.. on one of the upper reaches of the Test owned by Colonel Sneyd, who had kept a rod himself but had let two other rods to men who had little if any knowledge of the art of dry fly fishing. **1958** *Angling Times* 28 Feb. 11/3 The Board offers 14 rods to let during the 1958 season for its fishery on the River Piddle. **1970** *Daily Tel.* 9 Nov. 8/6 Fishing fees range from £250 to £400 a rod annually.

II. 6. a. A stick used for measuring with. Also ***measuring rod***.

1495 *Trevisa's Barth. De P.R.* XVII. clxxv. 716 He that meetyth, kepyth and departyth feldes.. and meedys vsyth a rodde. **1502**, **1599** [see GAD *sb.*¹ 6]. **1648** HEXHAM, *Een Roede*, .. a Rod of ten foot long, to measure grounds or fields. **1656** [see MEASURING *vbl. sb.* 4]. **1705** ARBUTHNOT *Coins*, etc. viii. (1727) 58 Decempeda was a sort of measuring Rod for taking the dimensions of Buildings. **1728** CHAMBERS *Cycl.*, *Ezechiel's Reed*, or *Rod*, a Scripture Measure [etc.]. **1823** P. NICHOLSON *Pract. Build.* 386 The Rod is from five to ten feet in length, and is used for measuring lengths, heights and breadths. **1844** H. STEPHENS *Bk. Farm* I. 509 The rod, divided into feet and inches, is put down to ascertain the depth of the drain.

b. A small piece of wood, bone, etc., marked with figures and used in calculating.

1619 T. BRETNOR *A Prognost.* To Mathem., There is.. an excellent treatise of Rabdologia, or Arithmeticall Rods, invented and published by the learned Lord of Merchiston. **1667** [see RHABDOLOGY]. **1678** PHILLIPS s.v. *Nepiers Bones* or *Rods*, Which Rods being rightly.. disposed one with another, represent the true product of any two sums. **1825** [see RHABDOLOGICAL].

7. a. A measure of length, equal to 5½ yards or 16½ feet; a PERCH or POLE.

c **1450** LOVELICH *Merlin* 1940 Whanne this werk was thus begonne, & the heythe of fowre roddis vpe was j-ronne aboven the erthe. *c* **1450** *Godstow Reg.* 375 The which acre holdeth in lengthe xxxij. roddis and iiij. fote of the kyngis standard. **1474** *Cov. Leet Book* II. 397 Out of the seid yard growith a Rodde to mesure lond by, the wich Rod conteyneth in lengthe v yardes & halfe. **1570–6** LAMBARDE *Peramb. Kent* (1826) 352 This auncient bridge.. conteined in length, about twenty and sixe roddes. **1657** S. PURCHAS *Pol. Flying-Ins.* 90 Those that were seeking for her abroad (although some rods distant) are instantly sensible of their felicity. **1678** MOXON *Math. Dict.* App. 166 Eight Furlongs, *viz.* 320 Rods, make a Mile. **1706** [see POLE *sb.*¹ 3]. **1769** E. BANCROFT *Guiana* 362 Extending a thousand or fifteen hundred rods in front of the River. **1865** E. BURRITT *Walk to Land's End* (1868) 191 Then at every rod you have a sea-view of peculiar interest. **1884** *Law Times Rep.* LI. 230/2 That A.B. do back and cope a hundred rods of their wall.. on penalty, by the rod, sixteen shillings.

Comb. **1778** [W. MARSHALL] *Minutes Agric.* 25 Oct. 1775, To harrow-in the wheat on the rod-wide beds of Barnfield.

b. A measure of area: A square perch or pole; †also, a ROOD.

c **1477** CAXTON *Jason* 81 Thou shalte yoke hem and make hem to tourne foure rodd of londe. **1542** RECORDE *Gr. Artes* (1575) 208, 1 Perche in bredth, and 40 in length, doe make a Rod of lande, whiche some call a roode. **1571** DIGGES *Pantom.* II. xvi. O ij, Now bycause I would cut off from that figure one acre, and an acre conteineth 160 rods: I multiply 160 in 50. **1660** SHARROCK *Vegetables* 19 A rod or pole of ground, which is the square of sixteen feet and a half. **1725** *Fam. Dict.* s.v. *Surveying*, Which you multiply by 40, because there are 40 Perches in a Rod. **1766** *Compl. Farmer* s.v. *Surveying* 7 F 1/1 Example. 19 rods the diagonal. 5 rods the perpendicular. 95 square rods the content. **1846** J. BAXTER *Libr. Pract. Agric.* (ed. 4) I. 188 Half an acre, or eighty rods, of land.., is sufficient to keep a cow during a year. **1868** *Rep. U.S. Commissioner Agric.* (1869) 405 Five and a half square rods of ground, which had not been manured.

c. A measure of brickwork: (see quots.).

1663 GERBIER *Counsel* 56 Bricklayers do work at twenty seaven shillings the Rod. *Ibid.* 63 A Rod 16½ Foot square, 1½ Bricks. **1667** PRIMATT *City & C. Build.* 53 The Bricklayer .. doth for the most part agree by the Rod, which is sixteen Foot and a half square every way, and two hundred seventy two foot in all. **1825** J. NICHOLSON *Operat. Mech.* 550 A rod of standard brick-work, making the necessary allowance for mortar and waste, will require 4500 bricks. **1842** GWILT *Encycl. Arch.* §2300 Consequently 272 feet is universally taken as the superficial standard content of a rod. *Ibid.*, A cubic rod of brickwork would be.. 306 feet cube.

†**d.** (See quot.) *Obs.*⁻¹

1630 in Binnell *Descr. Thames* (1758) 81 No Fisherman.. shall lay any more or greater Quantity [of lampern-leaps] than only one Rod of forty Fathom, containing seven Dozen of Leaps.

III. 8. †**a.** The shaft of a spear. *Obs. rare.*

c **1400** *Destr. Troy* 1234 The king share thrugh his shild with þe sharpe ende, And the rod all to roofe right to his honde. *Ibid.* 11094 The roddis all to Roofe right to þaire hond.

b. *dial.* The shafts of a cart or waggon.

1695 KENNETT *Par. Antiq.* Gloss. s.v. *Pullanus*, In a team, the horse which goes in the rods is commonly call'd the Fillar. **1736** PEGGE *Kenticisms* (E.D.S.), *Rods*, of a cart or waggon; in Derb. the sills. **1855** J. C. MORTON *Cycl. Agric.* II. 725 *Rods* (Sussex), cart and waggon shafts.

attrib. **1736** AINSWORTH, A rode, or roddle horse (filler), *equus carro proxime subjectus.* **1887** *Kentish Gloss.*, *Rod-horse*, a horse in the shafts or rods.

9. a. A straight slender bar of metal; a connecting part or shaft which is slender in proportion to its length. *spec.* = *control rod* s.v. CONTROL *sb.* 5; also (in full *fuel rod*), a long, slender piece of fuel for a nuclear reactor. See also CONNECTING-ROD, *guiding-*, *lightning-*, *piston-rod*.

1728 CHAMBERS *Cycl.* s.v. *Pendulum Clock*, The Iron Rod or Wiar which bears the Bob at Bottom. **1750** FRANKLIN *Opinions & Conject.* Wks. 1887 II. 183 Would not these pointed rods probably draw the electrical fire silently out of a cloud? *a* **1774** GOLDSM. *Surv. Exp. Philos.* (1776) I. 155 As the rod of the pendulum, like all other bodies, contracts with cold. **1815** J. SMITH *Panorama Sci. & Art* I. 4 A rod of good steel, in its hardest state.., may be broken almost as easily as a rod of glass. **1858** LARDNER *Hand-bk. Nat. Phil.* 30 This plunger hangs from a rod..which passes through the cover of the cylinder. **1883** *Encycl. Brit.* XVI. 458/2 The rod in the shaft, known as the main rod or spear rod, is usually made of strong balks of timber butted together. **1956** *Ann. Rev. Nucl. Sci.* VI. 329 The fuel loading consists of roughly five tons of natural UO_2 or uranium metal as round rods clad with Zircaloy. *Ibid.* 334 Two automatic regulating rods ordinarily hold the power level within 3 per cent of the desired value. **1959** C. HODDER-WILLIAMS *Chain Reaction* ix. 113 Did he leave it so late that the 'X holes' had warped out of alignment and the rods wouldn't drop? **1964** *Jrnl. Brit. Nucl. Energy Soc.* III. 298/1 By utilizing a high energy, high strain rate deformation process, the fuel rod is not only completely encapsulated but..the can wall is pressurized into the anti-rachetting grooves. **1975** J. R. LAMARSH *Introd. Nucl. Engin.* vii. 262 The ordinary movement of the rods in most power reactors is controlled..by an on-line computer. **1979** K. FOLLETT *Triple* iv. 77 The reactor has three thousand fuel channels, each channel containing eight fuel rods.

b. In scientific use: An animal or vegetable structure having an elongated slender form.

1864 LUBBOCK in *Nat. Hist. Rev.* IV. 269 In the younger females..the eggs did not descend in the uterus as far as the 'rod'. **1878** BELL tr. *Gegenbaur's Comp. Anat.* 264 The rods ..become united, and form a special structure, the 'rhabdom'. **1884** BOWER & SCOTT *De Bary's Phaner.* 85 Examples of the aggregated rods are found on the white Eucalypti.

c. Something resembling a rod in shape.

c **1860** FARADAY *Forces Nat.* iii. 50 A continuous rod of fluid mercury. **1905** *Athenæum* 22 Apr. 487/2 In the cry of the wind, in the grey rods of rain, and in all the shifting shows of the universe.

d. One of the elongated light-sensitive cells in the retina responsible primarily for vision in poor light. Cf. CONE *sb.*[1] 10.

1866 HUXLEY *Physiol.* ix. 223 This is the layer of rods and cones, and occupies about a quarter of the whole thickness [of the retina]. **1905** A. FLINT *Handbk. Physiol.* xxvi. 658 The rods are regular cylinders, their length corresponding to the thickness of the layer, terminating above in truncated extremities, and below in points which probably are continuous with the filaments of connection with the nerve-cells. **1937** CARLSON & JOHNSON *Machinery of Body* xi. 447 At the point where the optic nerve enters the retina there are no rods and cones. **1958** BROCKLEHURST & WARD *Gen. School Biol.* xiv. 185 Rods are more numerous near the periphery of the retina, and cones..near its centre.

e. *slang.* The penis; the erect member.

1902 in FARMER & HENLEY *Slang* s.v. Penis. **1934** E. POUND *Eleven New Cantos* xxxix. 46 His rod hath made god in my belly. **1960** A. WEST *Trend is Up* x. 454 'I want you to love me and cherish me all the days of my life.' 'You want the rod, you silly bitch, you fouled-up boarding-house bitch,' he said, 'that's what you want.' **1975** B. MEGGS *Matter of Paradise* VI. iii. 142 He was seventeen..rod cocked and aimed at every passing female object.

f. *slang* (chiefly *U.S.*). A gun; a pistol or revolver.

1903 H. HAPGOOD *Autobiogr. of Thief* xii. 289 The dago dropped the smoke-wagon and the bartender threatened to put him in prison for pulling a rod on respectable people. **1926** J. BLACK *You can't Win* xi. 145, I think I shall put a small 'rod' in my coat pocket hereafter. **1929** D. RUNYON in *Hearst's Internat.* Oct. 201/1 Dave the Dude takes personal charge of Wild William and removes a rod from his pants pocket. **1934** A. MERRITT *Burn Witch Burn!* v. 65 'Pass your rods, Paul.' Without a word the chauffeur dipped into his pockets and handed him a pair of automatics. **1942** WODEHOUSE *Money in Bank* (1946) xxv. 224 If I've got to stick up an eat-'em-alive baby like her with nothing but a finger in my pocket, I want an extra cut... Either I have a rod, or it's seventy-five-twenty-five. **1953** K. TENNANT *Joyful Condemned* iv. 34 What's wrong with *you*, waving that rod about like a bloody half-wit. **1965** [see BETSY]. **1978** J. CARROLL *Mortal Friends* II. iv. 179, I ain't getting my ass blown off because you're stupid. You won't get near Zorelli with a rod anyways.

g. *N. Amer. slang.* The draw-rod of a railway carriage or truck. Cf. RIDE *v.* 18 d.

1904 *Outing* July 486/2 Thousands of miles in the United States and Canada he has wandered on rods and blind baggages. **1924** J. TULLY *Beggars of Life* 56, I beat it through De Kalb last night on the rods of a mannerfest meat train. **1931** 'D. STIFF' *Milk & Honey Route* 192 We beat it on the run... Some rode the rods on passengers, While some blew out on freights. **1959** *Punch* 17 June 799/2 One does not picture train-robbers lurking at the top of the bank, nor even hoboes riding the rods.

h. *slang* (chiefly *U.S.*). = HOT ROD.

1945 [see HOT ROD]. **1948** *Hot Rod Mag.* July 4/3 With Carson upholstery And all the fine gear Of a more beautiful rod You never will hear. **1957** J. KEROUAC *On Road* I. xii. 79 A burly blond kid in a souped-up rod. **1972** J. GORES *Dead Skip* vii. 45 A two-bit Mission District auto and accessory dealer who specialized in old cars for conversion to dune buggies, drag cars, rods, and the like. **1978** *Hot Car* June 91/1 With just a beach buggy to his credit at that stage, Brian saw some US rods in Chicago and planned to build himself a C Cab on his return to this country.

IV. 10. *attrib.*, in sense 'having the form of a rod': **a.** Of metal, etc., as ***rod-bolt***, ***-iron***, ***-lead***.

1690 *Act 2 Will. & Mary* c. 4, Every Hundred Weight of Iron slit or hammered into Rods, commonly known by the Name of Rod Iron. **1805** R. W. DICKSON *Pract. Agric.* I. Pl. 48 The rod screw for the auger, four feet. **1833** LOUDON *Encycl. Archit.* §84 To have Norfolk thumb latches..and eight-inch rod bolts. **1868** JOYNSON *Metals* 58 Hammered and rolled into the various sections known in commerce as bar, rod iron, and the like. **1876** VOYLE & STEVENSON *Milit. Dict.* 220/2 *Rod Lead*... In this form it is used in the manufacture of compressed bullets. **1897** *Outing* XXX. 371/1, I..unfolded my patent rod-lock, and left my wheel supported by this device.

b. Of organic structures, as ***rod-body***, ***-cell***.

1877 *Q. Jrnl. Microsc. Sci.* XVII. 276 Numerous rod-bodies were observed to be shot out of a fresh section just as in Geoplana, but the rod-cells were not isolated successfully. **1888** ROLLESTON & JACKSON *Anim. Life* 332 In the *Turbellaria* very similar structures are met with in the rhabdocysts or rod-cells.

11. *attrib.* and *Comb.* **a.** General, as ***rod divination***, ***-grower***, ***-merchant***; ***rod-shaped*** adj.

1777 BRAND *Pop. Antiq.* 96 *note*, Our vulgar Notion of the Hazel's Tendency to a Vein of Lead Ore..seems to be a Vestige of this Rod Divination. **1851** *Census Gt. Brit.* (1854), Rod grower, dealer 12. **1858** SIMMONDS *Dict. Trade*, *Rod-merchant*, a dealer in osiers or birch and alder rods for basket-making, etc. **1876** *Nature* 30 Nov. 108/1 Very minute rod-shaped spicules.

b. In sense 5, as ***rod-bearer***, ***-bender***, ***-holder***; ***rod-case***, ***-hand***, ***licence***, ***-ring***, ***-stand***; ***rod-fishing***, ***-season***; ***rod-caught*** adj.

1852 C. M. YONGE *Two Guardians* i. 2 His numerous equipments, consisting of a long rod-case, a fishing-basket and landing-net. **1864** ATKINSON *Stanton Grange* 13 The glancing trout made the rod-bearers' fingers itch to try their art. **1879** *Cassell's Techn. Educ.* II. 356 They..thus decrease the rental of waters either from net or rodholders. **1883** *Century Mag.* July 376/1 The Professor climbed up..with the rod-cases. *Ibid.* 382/1 By a simple turning over of the rod-hand while drawing firmly on the line. **1885** J. W. MARTIN *Float Fishing & Spinning* (ed. 2) 181/2 Rod-rings. **1885** *Globe* 2 Sept. (Cassell), Rod-fishing is permissible until the end of October. **1898** *Westm. Gaz.* 5 May 4/2 The spring rod season for salmon is nearly over. **1901** *Scotsman* 4 Mar. 10/1 He landed his record rod-caught fish—a salmon of sixty-seven pounds. **1902** *Chambers's Jrnl.* July 425/1 Any trout-rod, even after a brief life spent in such a manner, might have accepted its pensioner peg on the rod-stand. **1918** KIPLING in *Story-Teller* Dec. 221/2 'Did you? Good!' he replied heartily over the rod-case on his shoulders. **1956** *People* 13 May 12/6 He reckons that morning and evening are the best times for rod-benders, using bread flake and paste, on a 16- or 18-hook, for roach. **1969** *Sears, Roebuck & Co. Catal.* Spring–Summer 713/1 Ted Williams Rod Case. .. Foam-lined compartments at both ends for reels, accessories. **1972** *Shooting Times & Country Mag.* 1 July 12/1 Take care to ensure that the line can still run through the rod rings. **1976** *Eastern Daily Press* (Norwich) 19 Nov. 21/4 The proposed new charges..will be in addition to, and completely separate from, the rod licence charge. **1976** *S. Wales Echo* 26 Nov., Steve..thought he had hooked a good cod when he struck into a real rod-bender at The Leys.

c. In sense 9 d as ***rod cell***, ***pigment***, ***vision***; ***rod-free*** adj.

1940 *Chambers's Techn. Dict.* 728/2 Rod-cell. **1970** AMBROSE & EASTY *Cell Biol.* i. 26 In the complex light-sensitive rod cells of the vertebrate retina the membrane and fibre structure of cilia have been modified to receive light and convert it into an electrochemical stimulus. **1915** J. H. PARSONS *Introd. Study of Colour Vision* III. 204 Beyond the rod-free central area the cones diminish continuously in number. **1921** E. B. TITCHENER *Text-bk. Psychol.* xxii. 89 Animals whose eyes lack this rod-pigment —fowls, pigeons—are strictly diurnal in their habits. *Ibid.*, Whether the visual purple is essentially concerned in rod-vision. **1921** R. S. WOODWORTH *Psychol.* (1922) x. 226 Dim-light vision, or twilight vision as it is sometimes called, is rod vision and not cone vision.

12. Special combs., as **rod-bat** (see quot. 1842); **rod-chisel** (see quot.); **rod-fall** (see quot. 1887); **rod-ham**, a piece of meadow-land on which osiers grow; **rod-machine** (see quot.); **rod-mill**, a workshop where iron is rolled into rods; **rod-planer** (see quot.); **rod puppet**, a puppet operated and supported by rods; **rod-rider** *U.S.*, one who rides the rods (see sense 9 g above); hence **rod-riding** *ppl. a.*; **rod-roller**, a workman engaged in rolling iron into rods; **rod-rope**, the rope by which boring-rods are worked; †**rod-woman**, a seller of twigs.

1842 C. W. JOHNSON *Farmer's Encycl.* s.v. *Plough* 981/1 The ploughman next changes the position of the coulter to the opposite side, by what is called the '*rod bat', that is, a wood-set stick with a crook in it. **1855** J. C. MORTON *Cycl. Agric.* s.v. *Plough*, The..sheath, coulter, road bat [*sic*]. **1875** KNIGHT *Dict. Mech.* 1961/1 **Rod-chisel*, a chisel on the end of a withe or rod, used by the smith in cutting hot metal. **1664** *MS. Agreement, Maldon, Essex* Bdl. 97 fol. 3 Parcell of land called Withers, with ye *rodfall and other appurtenances. **1887** *Kentish Gloss.*, *Rodfall*,..a belt of wood about a rod..deep, not belonging to the same owner as the bulk of the wood, and felled at a different time. **1883** TAUNT *Thames* (ed. 5) 44 From here a quarter of a mile of crooked stream, bordered with *rodhams, brings us to Shillingford Bridge. **1884** KNIGHT *Dict. Mech.* Suppl. 762/2 **Rod Machine*, a machine for making round sticks, such as dowels, pins, stretchers, broom-handles, etc. **1885** *Census Instruct.* Index, *Rod Mill Roller. **1901** *Westm. Gaz.* 10 Dec. 10/2 A man having charge of a rod mill. **1875** KNIGHT *Dict. Mech.* 1961/2 **Rod-planer*, a special machine-tool for planing locomotive connecting-rods, guide-bars, and similar work. **1930** *Puppetry* I. 64 Stick or *Rod Puppets. **1949** P. MCPHARLIN *Puppet Theatre in Amer.* xx. 347 Rod-puppets have stirred up interest for their novelty and adaptability. **1960** *Guardian* 19 Oct. 9/5 The Chinese theatre, with its impressive traditional rod puppets. **1976** *Jrnl. R. Soc. Arts* Apr. 254/1 A larger form of glove puppet can be produced by placing the figure on a rod; this is called a rod puppet. **1952** L. HUGHES *Laughing to keep from Crying* 60 The *rod-riders got off nowhere near the station. **1967** B. J. BANFILL *Pioneer Nurse* iv. 43 Many readers may not have heard about the Rod Riders, who formed a part of history in opening the west. During the 'Awful Thirties', this name was given to wandering embittered men. *Ibid.* 44 Rod Riders..planned to steal rides on trains. **1953** W. BURROUGHS *Junkie* x. 95 This type cop could just as well be an oldtime *rod-riding thug. **1901** *Westm. Gaz.* 10 Dec. 10/2 Upon the basis on which *rod rollers are paid to-day. **1839** URE *Dict. Arts* 966 Substituting for the wheel and axle, a number of ropes attached to the *rod-rope. **1602** MIDDLETON *Blurt, Master-Constable* II. ii, My mistress cries like the *rod-woman,—quick, quick, quick, buy any rosemary and bays?

†**rod**, *sb.*[2] *Sc. Obs.* Also 6 roid, rode. [Of obscure origin; perh. due to a wrong analysis of an early **fóttrod*: see TROD.

Fute rode occurs in Kennedy's *Passion of Christ* 11, and is probably still represented by Sc. *fit-rŏd*. The quality and quantity of *o* in Sc. are so variable, that it is now impossible to say whether *rōd*, *rŏd* represents this word or the Eng. *road*. Cf. however the dim. form *roddin(g.)*]

A path, a way or road.

1375 BARBOUR *Bruce* VI. 237 A litill rod he fan Vp toward the crag strikand. *Ibid.* x. 379 Thai..on range in ane rod can ga On handis and feit. **1513** DOUGLAS *Æneis* VI. vii. 43 The hiddillis held thai and the roddis darn. **1567** *Gude & Godlie B.* (S.T.S.) 197 Preistis, wirschip God, And put away ȝour Imagerie,..To hell the way and rod. **1581** BURNE in *Cath. Tract.* (S.T.S.) 160 Ane edder in the hie vay, and serpent in the rod. **1600** *Reg. Privy Counc. Scot.* VI. 125 Making of roidis, gaittis and passageis throw the landis, and taking of.. wair furth thairof.

rod, obs. form of ROAD, ROOD, RUD *sbs.*

†**rod**, erroneous variant of RAD *a.*, afraid.

1535 STEWART *Cron. Scot.* II. 210 Germanus bad thame tha sould nocht be rod, Bot haif gude hoip and put thair help in God.

rod (rɒd), *v.* [f. ROD *sb.*[1]]

†**1.** *trans.* To furnish with rods or laths. *Obs.*[−0]

1591 PERCIVALL *Sp. Dict.*, *Ripiar pared*, to lath, to rod a wall.

2. *U.S.* To fit with lightning-conductors.

a **1890** *Sci. Amer.* LVIII. 358 (Cent.), Several other houses in the town were rodded in the same way. **1891** *Boston* (Mass.) *Jrnl.* 11 Feb. 2/3 An old man down the country refused to have me rod his dwelling.

3. *intr.* To cut and peel osiers. *dial.*

1886 *S.W. Linc. Gloss.* 121 They kep' the childer away rodding.

4. *trans.* To push a rod through (a drain or pipe) in order to clear it. Hence **'roddable** *a.*, capable of being rodded.

1924 E. G. BLAKE *Plumbing* I. xvii. 149 A manhole should be provided at each alteration of the direction of the drain, and at intervals of not more than from 80 yds. to 100 yds. in all straight runs. This will enable any obstruction to be cleared by rodding the drain. **1949** ESCRITT & RICH *Work of Sanitary Engineer* (ed. 2) xxii. 275 The disconnecting trap ..is provided with a rodding arm which permits the outgoing line of pipe to be rodded. *Ibid.* xxiv. 283 The outlet should..be arranged so that it is easily roddable. **1971** B. LINDEN *Home Owner's Maintenance Guide* ii. 28 The drain pipes will probably have to be rodded to clear the blockage.

5. *intr.* Const. *up.* To arm oneself with a gun or guns. Cf. ROD *sb.*[1] 9 f. *U.S. slang.*

1929 [implied in RODDED *ppl. a.* 4]. **1935** N. ERSINE *Underworld & Prison Slang* 63 *Rod up* and we'll blow. **1950** *Harper's Mag.* Feb. 75/2 They do not rod up, or arm themselves.

6. *trans.* To 'soup *up*' or convert (a car) into a hot rod. Cf. ROD *sb.*[1] 9 h. *U.S. slang.*

1972 J. GORES *Dead Skip* v. 32 A young man with an old car (hence, probably rodding it up, hence, probably, a car-lover).

rod, *v.* (to rub): see RUD *v.*[2]

rod, obs. or dial. pa. t. or pa. pple. of RIDE *v.*

rodde, obs. pa. t. of RIDE *v.*

'rodded, *ppl. a.* [f. ROD *sb.*[1] or *v.* + -ED.]

†**1.** Formed into rounded pleats. *Obs.*[−1]

1562 PHAER *Æneid* VIII. L iv, In garded frocks they shine with roddid welts about theyr necks [L. *virgatis lucent sagulis*].

2. Made or furnished with rods.

1750 ELLIS *Mod. Husb.* IV. iv. 64 (E.D.S.), Rodded hurdles. **1805** R. W. DICKSON *Pract. Agric.* II. 674 The hurdles employed for this purpose are generally of two kinds, either flatted or rodded. **1844** H. STEPHENS *Bk. Farm* I. 148 A rack made of malleable iron,..not sparred but rodded, in the sides, to keep in the straw.

3. Shaped like a rod.

1842 H. MILLER *O.R. Sandst.* v. (ed. 2) 122 Its [the Glyptolepis] rodded, obelisk-like spires. **1899** tr. *Jaksch's Clin. Diagnosis* vii. (ed. 4) 295 Certain histological changes ..especially affecting the 'rodded' lining cells.

4. Const. *up.* Armed with a gun or guns. Cf. ROD *v.* 5. *U.S. slang.*

1929 D. RUNYON in *Hearst's Internat.* Oct. 201/1 None of the guests are supposed to come rodded up, this being strictly a social matter. **1930** *Flynn's* 12 Apr. 402/2, I was rodded up an' I could 'a' give him the works..but it wasn't worth it. **1938** D. RUNYON *Furthermore* ix. 171 It is very much against the law for guys to go around rodded up this way in New York City.

rodden ('rɒd(ə)n), *sb. Sc.* Also 6 **roddyne**, 8–9 **roddin**, 9 **roddan**, **r(h)oddon**. [Of obscure formation, but prob. related to RED *a.*, from the same grade as OE. *rudiȝ*, *rudu*, and ON. *roð*, *roði*, etc.] A berry of the rowan or mountain ash. Also *attrib.*, as ***rodden-tree***.

15.. in *Bannatyne MS.* (1879) 775 Quhen..gud reid wyne growis on the roddyne treis. *a* **1694** SIR A. BALFOUR *Lett.* (1700) 31 The Fruit whereof hangs in Clusters like our Roddens. *a* **1783** *Willy o Douglass-dale* xix, O had I a bunch o yon red roddins, That grows in yonder wood. **1850** W. JAMIE *Stray Effusions* 58 Twa wimpling burnies meet Beside the rodden glen. **1853** CADENHEAD *Bon-Accord* 200 (E.D.D.), The roddens hangin' ripe and red.

rodden, *a. rare.* [f. ROD *sb.*[1]] Made of rods.

1796 W. H. MARSHALL *W. England* II. 209 Round rodden cow cribs.

rodden: see RODHAM.

'rodden-fluke. *Sc.* Also **roddan-**. [Perh. f. RODDING *vbl. sb.*[2]: cf. the synonymous *rawn-fluke*. In Northumb. called *roddams*.] The turbot.

1795 J. DONALDSON *Agric. Kincardine* 415 Scate, turbot, (called here rodden fluke, and bannock fluke) and flounders. **1802** PINKERTON *Mod. Geogr.* I. 192 The Turbot..in Scotland is called Rodden-fleuk; the last word being a general denomination for flounders and other flat fish. **1882** DAY *Fishes Gr. Brit.* II. 12 Turbot,..Roddan or roan fleuk, ..east coast of Scotland.

rodder ('rɒdə(r)). *slang* (chiefly *U.S.*). [f. ROD *sb.*[1]] = *hot rodder* s.v. HOT ROD; one who converts cars into hot rods. Cf. ROD *sb.*[1] 9 h.

1949 *Hot Rod Mag.* Feb. 18/2 The rod news is rather short this month. I guess the California rodders now know why we keep our cars parked in the winter months. **1953** BERREY & VAN DEN BARK *Amer. Thes. Slang* (1954) §81a/2 '*Hot rod*' *owner*,..hot rodder, rod jockey, rodder. **1972** *World of Wild Wheels* (Custom Car) 58/1 When the British rodder glances through American Street Rod magazines he is faced with 99 per cent American cars. **1977** *Hot Car* Oct. 15/2 Brighter news for the rodder is another kit available from G. A. Stanley Palmer Ltd.

'roddikin. *Sc.* Also 6 **rodekein**, 8 **-ikin**, **roddickin**, 9 **ruddiken**. [Perh. ad. Du. or Flem. **roodeken*, dim. of *roode* (Kilian), = READ *sb.*[1]] The fourth stomach of a ruminant animal.

1599 in *Stirling Nat. Hist. Soc. Trans.* (1902) 28 Item xij rodekeins. **1796** *Young's Annals Agric.* XXVII. 69 An obstruction takes place, and..the stomach, called the Rodikin, is greatly inflamed. *c* **1805** MACNEILL *Poems* (1844) 88 Roasted hen, and collops plenty; And roddickins, and penches too. **1817** *Blackw. Mag.* Dec. 302 Pray, sir, allow me to help you—I shall send you a nice piece of ruddiken.

roddin(g, *Sc.*, a path: see *sheep-rodding*.

'rodding, (*vbl.*) *sb.*[1] [f. ROD *sb.*[1] or *v.*]

1. The action of beating with a rod; caning.

1630 *R. Johnson's Kingd. & Commw.* 478 Their capitall punishments are hanging, rodding, knocking on the heads, drowning. **1906** H. S. SALT *Consolat. Faddist* 30 The less they did attend, The more he brayed of rodding.

2. *techn.* **a.** (See quot.)

1883 GRESLEY *Gloss. Coal-mining*, *Rodding*, the operation of fixing or repairing wooden cage guides in shafts.

b. The action of ROD *v.* 4.

a **1890** *Electr. Rev.* XVI. 14 (Cent.), In most of the systems the cable is inserted by a process technically called rodding—that is, pushing rods through the duct from one manhole to the next. **1945** W. J. WOOLGAR *Pract. Plumber & Sanitary Engin.* 313/1 Rodding eyes are useful at changes of direction and at the top end of a long branch drain. **1953** L. B. ESCRITT *Building Sanitation* (ed. 3) viii. 94 A light manhole cover is provided in a central position to facilitate rodding. **1973** *BSI News* Apr. 5 (*caption*) Members of the code drafting committee..watch a demonstration of rodding to remove blockages in drainage pipes.

3. *concr.* Metal in the form of rods; an arrangement of rods.

1889 G. FINLAY *Eng. Railway* 80 It has been found that a steel channel section of rodding is far superior for the purpose. **1899** *Daily News* 1 July 4/5 Electro pneumatic signalling does away with rodding and wires.

4. *Geol.* A linear structure in metamorphic rocks characterized by the arrangement of grains of a constituent mineral, esp. quartz, in parallel rods. Also ***rodding structure***.

1907 B. N. PEACH et al. *Geol. Structure of N.-W. Highlands of Scotland* (Mem. Geol. Survey) xii. 211 In the exposures of these dykes, which happen to cross the direction of rodding almost at right angles, no plane-foliation is observable. **1923** *Q. Jrnl. Geol. Soc.* LXXIX. 439 In the hornblende-schists there is actual rodding or elongation of the crystals. **1953** *Proc. Geologists' Assoc.* LXIV. 119 Rodding is developed from quartz that has been introduced into, or has segregated in, the rocks. **1970** K. C. JACKSON *Textbk. Lithology* vii. 426 Associated with the larger-scale folding may be the segregation of more mobile constituents such as quartz, resulting in a small-scale rodding structure.

'rodding, *vbl. sb.*[2] *Sc. rare.* [f. *rodd*, var. of *rudd* spawn: see REDD *sb.*] The spawning of fish. Hence ***rodding-time***.

1795 *Statist. Acc. Scotl., Campsie* XV. 321 *note*, It is said that the raising of the Damhead..is the sole cause why the fish come not up in rodding time to the Glazert.

roddle, variant of RADDLE *sb.*[1]

roddon: see RODHAM.

'roddy, *a. rare*⁻⁰. [f. ROD *sb.*[1]] (See quot.)

1611 COTGR., *Vergeux*, roddie, full of rods.

roddy, obs. form of RUDDY *a.*

roddy, obs. var. RHODY.

†**rode**, *sb.*[1] *Obs. rare.* [Prob. a. Du. *roede* measuring-rod (ten feet long): see ROOD *sb.*] A certain length of dyke.

1662 DUGDALE *Imbanking & Draining* 242 That the sewer ..should be dyked..before Michaelmasse following, upon pain of every rode not done 3[s]. 4[d]. *Ibid.*, Upon pain also of iij[s]. iiij[d]. for every rode unfinished at Michaelmasse.

rode (rəʊd), *sb.*[2] *N. Amer.* Also 7–8 **road(e**, 9 **rhode**. [Of obscure origin.] A rope, esp. one attached to a boat-anchor or trawl. (Cf. RODING.)

1679 *Boston Rec.* (1881) VII. 135 A roade taken out of his Boate in the time of ye fire, & made vse of to pull downe houses. **1726** PENHALLOW *Indian Wars* (1859) 53 They fired ..with such resolution, as made them quit one of their boats by cutting their roads and lashings. **1792** G. CARTWRIGHT *Jrnl.* I. p. xiii, *Rode*, a small tow-line, of four inches and an half; made use of by shallops, by way of a cable. **1883** *Fisheries Exhib. Catal.* 12 Manilla Trawl Rhode, large yarn. *a* **1890** *Cent. Dict.*, *Rode*,..a rope attached to a boat-anchor or killock. *Perley.* [Bay of Fundy.] **1950** R. MOORE *Candlemas Bay* I. 45 His anchor and rode were stowed down under the stern. **1963** J. T. ROWLAND *North to Adventure* x. 147 With both hooks down and a long scope of rode she should be able to ride out anything.

rode, *sb.*[3] *dial.* (See quot. and RODE *v.*[2])

1838 HOLLOWAY *Prov. Dict.* s.v., 'To go to Rode,' means to go late at night, or early in the morning, to shoot wild fowl, which pass over-head on the wing.

rode, *v.*[1] Also 7 **road**. [Prob. ad. older Du. *roden*, *roeden* (Kilian), = LG. *roden*, *raden* (see Grimm), OFris. *rotha* to root out, extirpate.] *trans.* To clear (a stream, dyke, etc.) from weeds. Hence **'roding** *vbl. sb.*[1]

1616 in W. H. Wheeler *Hist. Fens* (1897) App. IV. 11 The Welland to be roaded, rooked, hooked, haffed, scowered and cleansed. **1662** DUGDALE *Hist. Imbanking & Draining* 242 The sewer called the Beche..should be dyked, roded, and scoured. **1664–5** *Act 16–17 Chas. II*, c. 11 §2 [They] shall.. maintaine and keepe the Rivers of Gleane and Welland with sufficient Dyking, Roading, Scowering and Bancking. **1858** W. H. WHEELER *Drainage Fens & Low Lands* 17 The cost of this work in the fen district, where it is termed 'roding', is about 20*s.* a mile. [Descr. precedes.]

rode, *v.*[2] Also 8 **rod**, 9 **road**. [Of obscure origin. Sense 2 is evidently related in some way to *cock-rode*, *-road*.]

1. *intr.* Of wild-fowl: To fly landward in the evening.

1768 PENNANT *Brit. Zool.* II. 464 As soon as the evening sets in, the decoy rises (as they term it)... This rising of the decoy in the evening, is in Somersetshire called rodding. **1885** *N. & Q.* 6th Ser. XI. 188 Gunners..wait in the marshes in the Bristol Channel, in the evening, to shoot wild fowl 'roding in' half an hour after sunset.

2. Of woodcock: To perform a regular evening flight during the breeding season.

1865 J. SLEIGH *Derbyshire Gloss.* (E.D.D.). **1907** BENSUSAN *Wild-Life Stories* 208 When a woodcock is roding, he must not vary his pace, his flight, or his song.

Hence **'roding** *vbl. sb.*[2] (freq. *attrib.*) and *ppl. a.*

1888, **1898** [see ROADING *vbl. sb.*[2]]. **1927** E. SANDARS *Bird Bk. for Pocket* 156 Cock's nuptial display ('Roding'),.. plumage fluffed out and uttering call. **1955** *Times* 10 May 12/5 These two sounds, so useful as an aid to seeing woodcock, are constantly uttered during its 'roding' flights, which start at sunset, are continued for perhaps an hour, and are resumed at dawn. **1973** *Ibis* CXV. 135 Many workers have described the roding behaviour of the Woodcock and speculated on its biological meaning.

rode, obs. f. REED, ROAD, ROID *a.*, ROOD, RUD, RUDE; pa. t. or pa. pple. of RIDE *v.*

-rode (f. RIDE *v.*): see *tide-*, *wind-rode*.

'roded, *a.* Also **roaded**. [Of obscure origin: cf. RODY *a.*] Streaky. (Generally used of bacon.)

1848- in dialect glossaries. **1893** *Natal Times* 30 Sept., They..make splendid roded bacon and good hams.

rode-horse, obs. f. ROAD-HORSE.

rode-lofte, obs. f. ROOD-LOFT.

rodely, var. of ROIDLY *Obs.*; obs. f. RUDELY.

rodent ('rəʊdənt), *a.* and *sb.* [ad. L. *rōdent-*, *rōdens*, pr. pple. of *rōdĕre* to gnaw.]

A. *adj.* **1.** *Zool.* Gnawing; belonging to the order *Rodentia*.

1833 *Penny Cycl.* I. 184/2 Of the Rodent mammals (*Rodentia*) of Africa..we have no very extensive knowledge. **1840** tr. *Cuvier's Anim. Kingd.* 108 In this we may discern a slight approach to the rodent character of *Cheiromys*. **1877** W. MATTHEWS *Ethn. & Phil. Hidatsa Ind.* 50 The rodent teeth of the beaver are regarded as potent charms. **1883** *Encycl. Brit.* XV. 419/2 Rodent Moles, with very small or rudimentary eyes and ear-conchs.

2. *Path.* (See quots.)

1853 PAGET *Lect. Surg. Path.* II. 452 The Rodent Ulcer is the disease which has been described under various names: such as cancerous ulcer of the face, cancroid ulcer [etc.]. **1878** T. BRYANT *Pract. Surg.* I. 125 Rodent ulcers are closely allied to the cancers. **1893** *St. Bartholomew's Hosp. Rep.* XXIX. 191 Rodent cancer most commonly occurs on the face.

3. Of waves: Wearing away the shore.

1875 G. MACDONALD *Malcolm* III. x. 148 Out came the lovely carving of the rodent waves.

B. *sb. Zool.* **1.** An animal of the order *Rodentia*, characterized by having no canine teeth and strong incisors.

1835 KIRBY *Hab. & Inst. Anim.* II. xxiv. 503 The animals included in the Order of *Rodents*, or gnawers and nibblers. **1859** DARWIN *Orig. Spec.* v. (1860) 137 The eyes of moles and of some burrowing rodents are rudimentary in size. **1880** HAUGHTON *Phys. Geogr.* vi. 287 The peculiar families of South American Rodents—cavies, spiny-rats, and chinchillas.

transf. **1885** LD. R. CHURCHILL *Sp.* (1889) I. 235 Lord Derby belongs to a tribe of political rodents.

2. *attrib.* and *Comb.*, as ***rodent controller***, ***officer***, ***operative***, ***operator***; ***rodent-carried***, ***infested***, ***-like***, ***proof*** adjs.; **rodent-run** *Ornith.*, a run made by some birds when disturbed in which they resemble a running rodent.

1959 *New Biol.* XXIX. 96 A *rodent-carried bacterium caused the Black Death. **1970** *Daily Tel.* 14 May 2/8 A senior *rodent controller..was yesterday presented with the British Empire Medal for his 18 years' work destroying rats. **1979** *Dædalus* Summer 137 They all confirm that the chapel was *rodent infested. **1978** P. PORTER *Cost of Seriousness* 3 Just as at seven the teeth stick out which Later slope in, *rodent-like. **1944** *Liverpool Echo* 31 Jan. 2/2 Westminster City Council's rat-catcher is in future to be called *Rodent Officer. **1973** in *Fremdsprachen* (1976) XX. 212/1 Fourteen visits from a rodent officer..had not stemmed the infestation. **1944** *Sunday Times* 5 Nov. 6/2 When it comes to official jargon, can you beat turning our old friend the rat-catcher into a '*Rodent Operative'? **1972** *Daily Tel.* 1 May 3/4 The Ministry also advises people to consult their local authority's rodent operative on the best way of applying whatever measures they decide on. **1979** J. GARDNER *Nostradamus Traitor* li. 248 'Are you a rat-catcher, Mr. Kruger?'..'They are called rodent operatives nowadays.' **1946** *Word Study* May 2/2 Euphemisms..**rodent operator* for *rat-catcher*. **1972** C. DRUMMOND *Death at Bar* vii. 179 The lunatic..is now a traveller for a firm of rodent operators. **1977** *Field* 13 Jan. 68/1 (Advt.), It's horse sense to buy your food storage bins direct from the manufacturer. A quality product. *Rodent proof. **1950** *Ibis* XCII. 28 We observed that a husky dog would immediately chase the Purple Sandpiper that made a '*rodent-run' and would be completely fooled. **1961** D. A. BANNERMAN *Birds Brit. Isles* X. 197 Birds of this northern race [of golden plover] will sit until almost trodden upon, and then shuffle away looking much like a teal in the process, though some would prefer —without too much regard for the truth—to speak of its 'rodent-run'. **1976** VAN TYNE & BERGER *Fund. Ornith.* (ed. 2) iv. 209 The 'rodent-run' display..has been reported for a number of shorebirds.., for some tundra species, and for the Green-Tailed Towhee.

rodential (rəʊ'dɛnʃəl), *a.* [f. prec. + -IAL.] Of or pertaining to the *Rodentia* or rodent animals. Hence **ro'dentially** *adv.*

1890 *Nature* XLII. 193/1 The dingo and several other, chiefly rodential, placental mammals. **1892** *Pall Mall G.* 2 Aug. 2/2 A nose rodentially keen.

rodentian (rəʊ'dɛnʃən), *a. rare.* [f. as prec. + -IAN.] Of, pertaining to, or consisting of rodents.

1854 BADHAM *Halieut.* 157 A little string of raw rodentian delicacies, dangling by their tails in a bunch. **1974** *Amer. N. & Q.* XIII. 25/1 The latent comedy in Chaucer's further gathering of words with obvious rodentian associations.

rodenticide (rəʊ'dɛntɪsaɪd). [f. RODENT *sb.* + -CIDE 1, after *insecticide*, etc.] A poison used to kill rodents.

1938 *Bull. Calif. Dept. Agric.* XXVII. 172 This material ..might serve both as a rodenticide and an insecticide. **1961** *Times* 18 July 6/6 The use of toxic chemicals is governed by a voluntary notification scheme agreed between the Government departments and the industrial association concerned, covering insecticides, fungicides, herbicides and rodenticides. **1975** *Nature* 24 Jan. 275/2 Field populations of common rats..resistant to anti-coagulant rodenticides.. have appeared in Scotland, Denmark, [etc.].

Hence **rodenti'cidal** *a.*, of or pertaining to a rodenticide; poisonous to rodents.

1939 *Jrnl. Amer. Vet. Med. Assoc.* XCV. 486/1 Human poisoning has resulted from..accidental ingestion of the metal used for entomological and rodenticidal purposes. **1979** P. L. G. BATEMAN *Household Pests* I. 25 Pest control chemicals are selected for their insecticidal or rodenticidal efficiency.

rodeo (rəʊ'deɪəʊ, 'rəʊdiːəʊ). orig. *U.S.* [Sp. *rodeo* a going round, a cattle-ring, etc., f. *rodear* to go round.]

1. A driving together of cattle in order to separate, count, inspect, or mark them; a round-up.

1834 DARWIN *Jrnl.* 16 Aug. in *Voy. Beagle* (1839) III. 311 Once every year there is a grand 'rodeo' when all the cattle are driven down, counted, and marked. **1851** *Laws*

California xcii, Every owner of a stock farm shall be obliged to give yearly one general rodeo. **1891** B. HARTE *First Fam. Tasajara* vii, Her native-bred animal fondly believed that he was participating in a *rodeo*.

2. A place or enclosure where cattle are brought together for any purpose.

1847 W. C. L. MARTIN *The Ox* 24/1 To collect the herd once a week, driving them from all quarters to a rodéo, or circuit, where an account is taken of their numbers. **1866** *Athenæum* 24 Nov. 672/3 In fine weather they are left on the 'rodeo', a bare piece of ground near the house, to which they are driven to pass the night.

3. a. A public exhibition of skill, often in the form of a competition, in the riding of unbroken horses, the roping of calves, wrestling with steers, etc.

1914 B. M. BOWER *Flying U Ranch* 16 They have them rodeos on a Sunday, mostly, and they invite everybody to it, like it was a picnic. **1925** *Annual Rodeo Program* (Tucson, Arizona) 3 We extend a cordial invitation to you to come to Tucson for our Annual Rodeo. **1938** D. COOLIDGE *Arizona Cowboys* ii. 27 The round-up had just begun. They call it *rodéo*, in Spanish, but the cactus cowboys pronounced it rodér. The contest riders of today have given it another twist and call it ró-deo. **1940** *Arizona* (Arizona Work Projects Administration Writers' Project) 72 That distinctively western entertainment, the rodeo, was originally an exhibition of cowboy skill in the regular activities of cattle ranch and range. But today it is largely commercialized and many of its features are of the circus type, remote from the cowpuncher's everyday life. **1950** *Manch. Guardian Weekly* 5 Oct. 6/2 Madison Square Garden is presently dedicated to Gene Autry and the annual rodeo. **1976** *Columbus* (Montana) *News* 27 May 1/4 One of those injured was a prime mover and instigator of this rodeo, Ed Miller, who is currently in St. Vincent's with a broken leg.

b. *transf.* A similar exhibition of competitive skill in the riding of motor-cycles, fishing, etc.; also used more generally of other types of competition. Also *fig.* Cf. ROADEO.

1927 *My Oklahoma* July 23/1 Oklahoma is going to have a state-wide baby rodeo next year. **1928** *Daily Express* 7 May 15/3 On Wednesday .. a motor-cycle rodeo in the afternoon will be followed by a carnival procession through the town. **1940** *Sun* (Baltimore) 11 Sept. 1/7 Nazi bombers smashed at London with increasing violence early today in their fourth consecutive dusk-to-dawn rodeo of destruction. **1949** *Daily Progress* (Charlottesville, Va.) 22 Aug. 9/1 Entries for the fishing rodeo for youngsters here must be in by Thursday.

4. *attrib.* and *Comb.*, as ***rodeo circuit, clown, cowboy, ground, parade, queen, rider, riding*** (*sb.* and *a.*).

1961 M. S. ROBERTSON *Rodeo* 101/1 The California Rodeo .. is one of the Big Four, the rodeos whose pioneering and consistent greatness bridged the years from the inception of the 'cowboy tournaments' to the modern *rodeo circuit. **1980** *Country Life* 13 Nov. 1819/1 He .. started bronc riding in the rodeos... Demobbed, he returned to the rodeo circuit. **1927** *Progressive Arizona* IV. ii. 7 The arena presents a scene of animation with the judges, time-keepers, contestants, performers, event clerks, and Jolly, 'the funniest *rodeo clown of them all' milling about. **1941** L. B. CHAFFIN *Sons of West* xv. 222 This trick, in almost every identical move, is practiced by modern rodeo clowns of today. **1958** E. H. PEPLOW *Hist. Arizona* II. xx. 405 The competitive life of a *rodeo cowboy is shorter than that of an athlete in almost any other sport. **1892** GERTRUDE ATHERTON *Doomswoman* xxiv, The platform on one side of the circular *rodeo-ground. **1979** *Tucson Mag.* Apr. 68/3 Admission is charged for this event at the rodeo grounds. **1941** *La Fiesta de los Vaqueros Program* (Tucson, Arizona) 9 Tucson and its guests spend two hours .. standing on each other's toes in order to see the *rodeo parade. **1976** *Billings* (Montana) *Gaz.* 10 June 1-A/5 In Hardin, activities include a week-long carnival beginning Monday followed by a rodeo Friday and a rodeo parade at noon Sunday. **1945** *Pueblo* (Colorado) *Star-Jrnl.* 3 June 7/3 Nine girls at the Pueblo ordnance depot will don cowboy hats, bright shirts, and jeans to vie for the honor of *rodeo queen. **1975** R. HOBAN *Turtle Diary* xxv. 115 She'd .. been a *rodeo rider, done roller derbies, wrestled, had three husbands and all kinds of troubles. **1979** 'G. BLACK' *Night Run from Java* i. 7 A rodeo rider thrown by a bronco. **1974** *Times* 7 Jan. 8/3 We did hunter trials, show jumping, *rodeo riding, and so on. **1976** *Evening Standard* 29 Dec., The Hard Breed. Rodeo-riding Cain slain by younger brother.

Hence **ro'deo** *v. intr.*, to compete in a rodeo. Also **ro'deoer**; **ro'deoing** *vbl. sb.* (All also with stress on first syllable.)

1959 *Rodeo Sports News* 1 Nov. 2/1 I've wondered .. what the contestants do when they quit rodeoing. *Ibid.* 15 Nov. 2/4 A cowboy who would rather hunt than rodeo—we've got everything in the northwest! **1970** *Ibid.* 15 Nov. 2/2 A top bull rider who rodeoed up through the mid-sixties stopped by and said hello the other day. **1976** *Oregonian* (Portland, Oregon) 14 June C3/2 Because it is not a sport sanctioned by the National Collegiate Athletic Association, rodeoers are free to compete in professional rodeo while they are still on the college circuit. **1977** *New Yorker* 6 June 74/2 They loved making cowhands of their frisky little girls—they took them riding and roping and rodeoing.

roder, obs. form of ROADER[1].

† **roderigo.** *Obs.*$^{-1}$ [A Spanish personal name.] Some kind of snuff.

a **1704** T. BROWN *Dial. Dead* Wks. 1711 IV. 34 As long as I could .. have my Diamond Snuff-box full of *Orangeree* or *Roderigo*.

rodetreo, obs. variant of ROOD-TREE.

† **rodewort.** *Obs. rare.* [f. *rode* RUD *sb.* + WORT.] The marigold.

14.. *MS. Sloane* 5, lf. 46 a/2 *Solsequium*, Rodewort oþer marygoldys. *c* **1450** *Alphita* (Anecd. Oxon.) 86 *Incuba, sponsa solis, kalendula*, .. goldwort *uel* rodeuurt.

† **rodge**, variant of (or error for) RADGE.

1678 PHILLIPS, *Rodge*, a sort of Water-foul, somewhat like a Duck, but lesser. [Hence in some later Dicts.]

rodgersia (rɒˈdʒɜːzɪə). Also **Rodgersia**. [mod.L. (A. Gray 1859, in *Mem. Amer. Acad.* New Ser. VI. 389), f. the name of John *Rodgers* (1812–82), American admiral + -IA[1].] A large perennial herb of the genus so called, belonging to the family Saxifragaceæ, native to eastern Asia, and bearing compound leaves and terminal panicles of small white flowers.

[**1902** *Gardeners' Chron.* 23 Aug. 131/2 At present in the rock garden at Kew there is in flower, for the first time in Europe, a new species of Rodgersia.] **1908** R. FARRER *Alpines & Bog-Plants* ix. 185 Of foliage plants for the lake-side .. there is nothing to surpass the Rodgersias. **1962** *Amateur Gardening* 24 Mar. 4/2 Among foliage plants for the waterside there are none to surpass the rodgersias. **1976** *Country Life* 6 May 1172/3 There is a wealth of plants .. including hardy plants such as gunneras, rodgersias, hostas and hellebores.

rodges-blast, variant of ROGER'S BLAST.

1883 G. C. DAVIES *Norfolk Broads* iv. (1884) 28 Occasionally a 'rodges-blast' sweeps like a whirlwind over the marsh, lifting the reed-stacks, wrecking windmills, and dis-masting the wherries. *Ibid.* xxxiv. 266 You may see .. the trees uprooted for a space where a rodges-blast has descended. **1890** 'D. DALE' *Noah's Ark* i, A sudden squall came up, as these rodges-blasts do spring up on the Broads.

rodham (ˈrɒdəm). *E. Anglia.* Also **rodden, roddon**. [Of obscure formation (see note below).] A raised bank in the Fen district of East Anglia, consisting of the bed and levees of a dry river-course which have been raised above the level of the adjacent land by deposition of silt, usu. by the incoming tide, and by compaction and lowering of the adjacent peat soil; occas. used to signify only a levee bounding such a river-course.

The spelling *roddon* was adopted and popularized by G. Fowler (see quot. 1932), whilst the older form in -(*h*)*am* remains dominant in local use. Any connection with *roddin* (cf. E.D.D. and ROD *sb.*[2]) is unlikely.

[**1857** T. WRIGHT *Dict. Obsolete & Provincial Engl.* II. 806 *Roddam*, a bed of sand resting on the clay beneath the peat, in the fens of Cambridgeshire.] **1932** G. FOWLER in *Geogr. Jrnl.* LXXIX. 210 There are numerous raised banks of laminated silt or shell maul meandering through the Fens. Neither historians nor geologists appear to have noticed them... Fen dwellers however have noted these banks but generally without realizing their origin. They call them *roddons*. This word appears to be allied to *roddin* or *rodden*, which Wright in his 'English Dialect Dictionary' .. gives as meaning a narrow road, path or sheep track. I spell the word *roddon* as it sounds; and I prefer it as a spelling to *rodham*, as used in the name Rodham Farm, as the latter appears corrupted in the second syllable. **1945** B. E. DORMAN *Story of Ely* i. 3 These raised river beds are known as roddens... One fine example .. can be seen .. alongside .. the road from Littleport to Shippea Hill. The few houses along this road are nearly all built on the rodden, for it provides a firmer foundation than peat. **1957** A. K. ASTBURY *Black Fens* v. 26 Levees formed as parallel ridges one on either side of the main channel... Where subsequent cultivation has been long and constant the two levees may tend to merge into one general bank of silt... But all such levees, whether separate or merged, are in the black fens known as rodhams. *Ibid.* 27 Fowler .. used the form roddon—influenced by the fact that in the north of England the word roddin or rodden means a narrow road... But although later writers have adopted Fowler's spelling, the fact remains that fenmen themselves call these things rodhams. **1957** G. E. HUTCHINSON *Treat. Limnol.* I. i. 119 The tidal water from this shallow arm of the sea, the southward continuation of the modern Wash, was evidently very turbid and deposited levees at the sides of the channels, known as roddons, along which it ran. **1963** E. S. WOOD *Collins Field Guide to Archaeol.* II. 199 Silt Banks, otherwise known as roddons, or rodhams, are caused by tidal action depositing silt up slow rivers. **1971** *Norfolk Fair* Feb. 36/3 Old extinct watercourses can be traced by the rodhams of silt and the slades of chalky material. **1974** J. R. RAVENSDALE *Liable to Floods* i. 21 Gordon Fowler .. noticed a roddon in the north-east corner of Cottenham parish.

rodi(e, obs. forms of RUDDY.

rodiane, obs. form of RHODIAN.

rodinal (ˈrɒdɪnəl). [Trade name.] A preparation of salts of paramidophenol together with sodium sulphite, used as a developer in photography.

1892 *Photogr. Ann.* II. 90 Rodinal .. has a developing power equal to that of the rapid quinol developer. **1893** *Ibid.* III. 91 Longer development than with rodinal is required in order to obtain sufficient opacity.

Rodinesque (rəʊdæˈnɛsk), *a.* [f. the name of Auguste *Rodin* (1840–1917), French Romantic School sculptor + -ESQUE.] Of, pertaining to, or reminiscent of Rodin or his work, marked by masterly realism and love of movement.

1905 G. B. SHAW *Let.* 13 Mar. (1972) II. 521 It is a bad case of helpless genius in the first blaze of youth; and the drawings are queer and Rodinesque enough to be presentable at this particular moment. **1934** *Sunday Times* 11 Feb. 6/1 Mr. O'Casey's eye-appeal is the old business of Rodinesque, Volga-Boatmannish stage-grouping. **1934** F. SCOTT FITZGERALD *Tender is Night* I. iv, As if the features .. had been molded with a Rodinesque intention. **1962** *Times* 14 Feb. 15/1 Little Rodinesque bronze figures .. are on show in the front gallery.

'roding. [Cf. RODE *sb.*[2]] An anchor rope.

1897 KIPLING *Captains Courageous* iii. 57 Dan .. twitched once or twice on the roding, and .. the anchor drew up at once. *Ibid.* viii. 153 Three boats found their rodings fouled.

rodingite (ˈrəʊdɪŋaɪt). *Petrogr.* [f. the name of the River *Roding*, S. of Nelson, New Zealand + -ITE[1].] A crystalline rock consisting of diallage and grossularite (or hydrogrossularite), often with prehnite and chlorite, and typically found in or adjacent to serpentinite masses, having been formed by the calcium metasomatism of basic or ultrabasic igneous rocks.

1911 J. M. BELL et al. in *Bull. N.Z. Geol. Survey* No. 12. 31 Dykes of a coarse-grained gabbro-like rock penetrate the serpentines in many places... The writers have applied to the rock the name 'rodingite', owing to the typical exposure occurring on the River Roding. **1954** *Mineral. Mag.* XXX. 525 (*heading*) Rodingite from the Girvan-Ballantrae complex, Ayrshire. **1976** *Neues Jahrb. für Mineral.* (*Monatshefte*) 188 The rodingites described here show an absolute prevalence of garnet, which has a variable composition ranging from an almost pure grossularite .. to an intermediate member of the grossularite-andradite series.

Hence **rodin'gitic** *a.*; also **'rodingitized** *ppl. a.*, converted into rodingite; **'rodingi,tizing** *ppl. a.*, **,rodingiti'zation**.

1953 *Jrnl. Faculty of Sci., Hokkaido Univ.* 4th Ser. VIII. 419 (*heading*) On the rodingitic rocks within the serpentinite masses of Hokkaido. **1971** *Canad. Jrnl. Earth Sci.* VIII. 642/2 This subdivision .. improved the permeability for rodingitizing fluids. *Ibid.* 643/1 (*caption*) Serpentinized and partially rodingitized peridotite. *Ibid.* 644/1 Development of garnets, hydrogarnets (hibschite), in a process somewhat similar to rodingitization. **1975** *Contrib. Mineral. & Petrol.* XLIX. 233 The latter described rodingitic material in their study of serpentinized ultramafic rocks dredged from the Mid-Atlantic Ridge at 45°N. *Ibid.*, Partially rodingitized olivine gabbros were also found. *Ibid.* 253 The rodingitization of the gabbroids and the serpentinization of the ultramafics appear to be two concomitant and complementary metasomatic processes.

† **rodion.** *Obs.*$^{-1}$ (See quot.)

Apparently = *rodjon*, and now represented by ROGER[2] 5, with its variants RODGES- or ROGER'S BLAST.

1430–40 LYDG. *Bochas* II. xv. (MS. Bodl. 263) lf. 240, I haue herd seid of ful yore agon A whirle wynd blowing nothing softe Was in old Englissh callid a Rodion, That reiseth duste & strauh ful hih alofte.

† **rod-knight.** *Obs.* [Later form of OE. *rádcniht*.] = RAD-KNIGHT.

c **1280** BRACTON II. xxxv. §6 Ut si quis debeat equitare cum domino suo de manerio in manerium, & tales dicuntur Rodknights. *c* **1290** *Fleta* III. xiv. §7 Per servitium equitandi mecum, vel cum uxore mea, qui Rodknyghts vocabantur. [**1614** SELDEN *Titles Honor* 334 Our old word Rodknights (that is, Riding Knights, or Knight-riders). **1617** MINSHEU *Ductor* 422 *Rodknights*, or *Radknights*, are certaine seruitours, which hold their lands by seruing their Lord on horsebacke. **1682** WARBURTON *Hist. Guernsey* (1822) 69 Bracton calls such tenants as held by the service of riding with the lords from one manor to another, Rod Knights. **1778** PENNANT *Tour Wales* (1883) I. 56 This last [the Radman] seems to have been the same with the Rod or Rad-knights.]

'rodless, *a.* [f. ROD *sb.*[1] + -LESS.] Having no (fishing-) rod.

1834 *Blackw. Mag.* XXXV. 783 Angler .. walking rodless along the banks. **1859** HOLE *Tour Irel.* 83 Away went Frank to his boat; and I, rodless, to wander .. among the great mountains.

'rodlet. [f. ROD *sb.*[1] + -LET.] A little rod or rod-shaped object.

1877 ROSENTHAL *Muscles & Nerves* 21 Assuming that the rod or thread consists of a number of smaller rodlets or tiny threads. **1883** *Science* I. 370/2 An envelope composed of little rodlets, standing perpendicular to the surface.

'rod-like, *a.* [f. ROD *sb.*[1] + -LIKE.] Resembling a rod; shaped like a rod.

1611 COTGR., *Vergé*, made of rods, or twigs; also, streaked with long, and rod-like rayes. **1796** WITHERING *Brit. Plants* (ed. 3) III. 553 Stem spreading, rod-like. **1830** LINDLEY *Nat. Syst. Bot.* 158 Shrubs or herbs, with rod-like branches. **1877** HUXLEY & MARTIN *Elem. Biol.* 214 An elongated rod-like bone, rather thicker towards its anterior end.

rod lofte, obs. form of ROOD-LOFT.

'rodman. Also **rodsman**. [f. ROD *sb.*[1]]

1. An angler; a rodster.

1888 *Pall Mall G.* 19 May 6 [He] is not only a penman, but a gunman, a rodman, and a horseman. **1894** *Daily News* 20 Feb. 5/3 The complaints by the rodsmen .. against over-netting are louder than ever.

2. One who holds up the rod in surveying. Chiefly *U.S.*

1853 A. W. WHIPPLE in *Rep. Explorations for Railroad to Pacific Ocean* (U.S. War Dept.) (1856) I. i. 5 The chainmen and rodmen being ignorant of their duties, little more than teaching them could this day be accomplished. **1891** *Anthony's Photogr. Bulletin* IV. 177 The rodman, with his rod held vertically, appearing in the center of each picture, or near the center. **1972** *Publishers' Weekly* 7 Aug. 48/2 In Chicago in 1925, when he was a rodman with a Cook County surveying crew.

3. *slang.* One who handles a gun; a gunman. Cf. ROD *sb.*[1] 9 f.

1924 G. C. HENDERSON *Keys to Crookdom* 396 Assaulter, rough guy, hard bird, rod man, rod toter. **1931** *Amer. Speech* VII. 113 He used to be a rodman on the convoy, but he didn't have the guts for that job. **1940** W. R. BURNETT *High Sierra* i. 12 We need a rodman.. You're it. *a* **1953** DYLAN THOMAS *Quite Early one Morning* (1954) 39 A raid by the vice-squad on a clip-joint for retired rod-men. **1962** *John o' London's* 4 Oct. 325/2 Robert is victim number two of this assassination, the only witness who could identify the rod-man.

† **rod-net**, var. of *road-net*: see ROAD *sb.* 12.

1617 MINSHEU *Ductor* 422 Rodnet, a net to catch blackbirds, or woodcockes in. [Hence in some later Dicts.]

rodney ('rɒdnɪ). [Of obscure origin.]

1. *Coal-mining.* (See quot.)

1860 *Eng. & Foreign Mining Gloss.* 77 *Rodney*, a roughly constructed platform, with old rails, near the pit's mouth, upon which a large fire is made during the winter nights, to light the bank.

2. An idler or loafer; a casual worker; a disreputable character. Also *attrib.*, hulking, rough.

In extensive dialect use: see *Eng. Dial. Dict.*

1866 in *N. & Q.* 3rd Ser. XI. (1867) 494/1 There was Devil Lees.., a great big rodney fellow, as hard as a grounsell toad. **1892** *Daily News* 14 Mar. 6/1 The 'Rodney' has no home; he sleeps with his back against his coke oven, or in it when it is cleared out.

3. [Perh. a different word.] A small fishing boat or punt. *Canad.*

1895 *Christmas Rev.* (Newfoundland) 18 Jim Leary, whose handiwork, whether displayed in the construction of baitskiff, smack, skiff, punt or rodney, was always superior to what any other man in the settlement could turn out. *c* **1900** in *Regional Lang. Stud.—Newfoundland* (1978) VIII. 24 *Rodney*, small, single crosshand[ed] punt. **1908** N. DUNCAN *Every Man for Himself* ix. 260 'Launch that rodney,' Wull directed, 'an' put me on shore.' **1923** *Sunday at Home* Dec. 153/1 The punt.. was one of the small, light type of boat called a 'rodney', and it was used mainly for shooting about the harbour, or on sealing trips. **1931** J. R. SMALLWOOD *New Newfoundland* 266 Often he'd take us to sail in his rodney, Out over the water. **1966** A. R. SCAMMELL *My Newfoundland* 36 Sid, go over to Blanchard's and keep an eye on what they're doing. Take the rodney.

rodochrome, var. RHODOCHROME.

rodok, obs. f. RUDDOCK.

rodomel(le: see RHODOMEL.

rodomont ('rɒdəmɒnt). Also 7 rodomond, 7–9 rodomonte, 6–7 rhodomonte. [a. F. *rodomont* or It. *rodomonte*, from the name of the boastful Saracen leader in Ariosto's *Orlando Furioso*.] A great bragger or boaster. Now *arch.*

1598 DALLINGTON *Meth. Trav.* X. 4, The fourth of Tullies Rhetorickes, where he speaketh of a bragging Rhodomonte. **1600** O. E. (M. SUTCLIFFE) *Repl. Libel* I. viii. 207 As if there were more terrible Rodomontes among the Spaniardes, then otherwhere. **1661** BOYLE *Style of Script.* 69 St. Jude argues with the Rodomonts of his Time. **1770** BARETTI *Journ. Lond. to Genoa* II. 11 Of such rodomonts I am told that Portugal has even a larger number than of idlers. [**1893** STEVENSON *Catriona* 362, I can never think how I avoided being stabbed myself or stabbing one of these two Rodomonts.]

attrib. and *Comb.* **1611** COTGR., *À pied de plomb*,.. Rodomont-like. **1626** B. JONSON *Masques* Wks. (1692) 646 Who had thought to have.. triumpht our whole Nation, In his Rodomont Fashion.

rodomontade (rɒdəʊmɒn'teɪd), *sb.* and *a.* Also 7 rodomantade. *β.* 7–9 rhodomontade (7 rhado-, rhada-), 7–8 rhodomantade. [a. F. *rodomontade*, It. *rodomontata*, †-*ada* (Florio): see prec. and -ADE.]

A. *sb.* **1. a.** A vainglorious brag or boast; an extravagantly boastful or arrogant saying or speech; †an arrogant act.

α. **1612** DONNE *Lett.* (1651) 128, 5 Challengers cartells, full of Rodomontades. **1646** BUCK *Rich. III*, I. 12 Then they might have acted their Rodomontades and injuries in a higher Straine. **1672** DRYDEN *Heroic Plays* Ess. (Ker) I. 157, I could easily show you, that the rodomontades of Almanzor are neither so irrational as his, nor so impossible to be put in execution. **1782** WESLEY *Wks.* (1872) XI. 163 We need not care for all the *fervida dicta*, all the rodomontades, of France and Spain. **1849** MACAULAY *Hist. Eng.* vi. II. 50 Wherever he came he pressed horses in defiance of law,.. and almost raised mobs by his insolent rodomontades. **1862** THACKERAY *Philip* viii, Poor Phil used to bore me after dinner with endless rodomontades about his passion and his charmer. **1874** MOTLEY *John of Barneveld* I. i. 74 Spain laughed at these rodomontades.

β. **1653** H. COGAN tr. *Pinto's Trav.* ii. 4 At the first view of so many Rhodomontades and bravings, we were in some doubt and amaze. **1670** G. H. *Hist. Cardinals* I. I. 29 The Theologist should be forbidden to write such Rhodomontads. **1748** SMOLLETT *Rod. Rand.* xliv, The rhodomontades they uttered on the subject of their generosity and courage. **1784** MME. D'ARBLAY *Lett.* 7 Dec., I was called away in the midst of my rhodomontade, and have lost all zest for pursuing it. **1815** W. H. IRELAND *Scribbleomania* 136 *note*, A species of conversation.. which consisted of the most improbable rhodomontades. **1881** *Littell's Living Age* 482 This disloyal rhodomontade was freely circulated throughout England.

b. Boastful or inflated language; extravagant boasting or bragging.

α. **1668** WILKINS *Real Char.* 209 Arrogance,.. Rodomontade, affectation of Empire. **1734** tr. *Rollins' Anc. Hist.* III. VII. 449 Supplying his want of courage with rodomontade. **1829** MACAULAY *Misc. Writ.* (1860) I. 392 We could discern its meaning through a cloud of rodomontade. **1877** MORLEY *Crit. Misc.* Ser. II. 9 A detestable compound of vulgarity and rodomontade.

β. *a* **1648** LD. HERBERT *Autobiogr.* (1764) 160 The Duke de Crouy.. said by way of Rhodomontade,.. he saw all the rest of the World must bow under the Spaniard. **1711** SHAFTESB. *Charac.* (1737) III. 276 To see.. their rhodomontade and poetical bravado, we need only turn to our famous poet-laureat. **1796** SOUTHEY *Lett. fr. Spain* (1799) 194 The Spaniards are not inferior in rhodomontade and national prejudices. **1822** HAZLITT *Table-t.* II. viii. 194 A profusion of barbarous epithets and wilful rhodomontade. **1892** *Nation* 25 Aug. 150/2 Tricoupis.. has no sympathy with bluster and rhodomontade.

†**2.** *transf.* A braggart. = RODOMONT. *Obs.*

1692 HICKERINGILL *Good Old Cause* Wks. 1716 II. 530, I can scarce pity that Rhodomantade, that dy'd upon the point of that Sword. *a* **1697** AUBREY *Lives* (1898) I. 90 There was a Rhadamontade that would fight with any man and bragged of his valour.

B. *adj.* Bragging; boastful; ranting.

α. *a* **1754** CARTE *Hist. Eng.* (1755) IV. 661 There happened some rodomontad discourses in which he conceived himself affronted. **1803** MARY CHARLTON *Wife & Mistress* II. 175 Listening to the flighty and rodomontade ideas that passed his lips. **1822** SCOTT *Nigel* xi, He again ran on in a grotesque and rodomontade account of the host.

β. **1767** S. PATERSON *Anoth. Trav.* II. 36 All this rhodomontade popish stuff. **1768** GOLDSM. *Goodn. Man* II. i, He has got into such a rhodomontade manner. **1818** HAZLITT *Shaks. Plays* (1838) 111 He is too hot and choleric, and somewhat rhodomontade. **1832** S. R. MAITLAND *Albigenses & Wald.* 13 The same rhodomontade style of special pleading.

rodomon'tade, *v.* Also rhod-. [f. prec.] *intr.* To boast, brag, talk big, rant.

1681 W. ROBERTSON *Phraseol. Gen.* (1693) 1083 To Rodomontade, *inaniter.. gloriari.* **1755** in JOHNSON. **1840** H. AINSWORTH *Tower of London* (1864) 7 You have learnt to rhodomontade at the court of Madrid, I perceive. **1855** *Woman's Devotion* III. 49 How long she would have rhodomontaded in this way, Nest could not tell.

Hence **rodomon'tading** *vbl. sb.* and *ppl. a.*

1698 COLLIER *Immor. Stage* ii. (1738) 59 *Rhodomontading*.., bombastic. **1782** MISS BURNEY *Cecilia* x. vi, He soon finds there's nothing to be got by rhodomontading. **1787** —— *Diary* 16 Feb., I think his rhodomontading as innocent as that of our cousin. **1831** W. IRVING *Life & Lett.* (1864) II. 449 His hero a rodomontading Congressman from the Western States. **1859** *Athenæum* 7 May 610 The careless or rhodomontading statements of earlier writers.

rodomon'tader. Also rhodo-. [f. prec.] A boaster, braggart.

a **1853** W. JAY *Autobiogr. & Rem.* (1854) 413 This fanatical rodomontader. **1869** TOZER *Highl. Turkey* II. 264 Among the characters.. are clever Tom Thumbs, half-witted simpletons, bold rhodomontaders.

So **rodomon'tadist**.

1655 TERRY *Voy. E. India* 167 When this Rhadomantadist had ended his perillous story, it was dinner.

†**rodomon'tado**, *sb.* and *a.* *Obs.* Also 6–7 rodomantada, 7 roda-, 8 rhodomantado, rhodomontado. [See RODOMONTADE *sb.* and -ADO.]

A. *sb.* **1.** = RODOMONTADE *sb.* 1.

α. **1598** FLORIO *Dict.* To Rdr. a 6 b, [Men whose] valour [is] bragardrie, *Astolpheidas*, or *Rodomontadas*, or if it come to action crueltie. **1603** —— *Montaigne* II. xxxi. (1632) 403 These Rodomontados must be employed on such as feare them. **1631** WEEVER *Anc. Funeral Mon.* 23 Rodamantadoes, or thundring declamations. **1715** LEONI *Palladio's Archit.* (1742) II. 91 This must be either a Mistake, or a Rodomontado.

β. **1652** *Plea for Free State* 31 The Roman Religion.. being replenished with the high Rhodomontadoes of Saints and miraculous Stories. **1673** H. STUBBE *Further Vind. Dutch War* 65 It was a Rhodomontado of Philip II.. that He had rather have no Subjects at all, then those He had to be Hereticks. **1700** DE FOE *Two Grt. Quest. considered* 4 It does not use to be the Temper of the English to run on such Rhodomantado's.

2. = RODOMONTADE *sb.* 2.

1600 B. JONSON *Cynth. Rev.* v. iv. Wks. (1616) 245 Most terribly he comes off; like your Rodomantada. **1657** TOMLINSON *Renou's Disp.* Pref., As for those flashy Rhodomantadoes that go about to adulterate the best Exoticks. **1779** SWINBURNE *Trav. Spain* 269 The Andalusians seem to me the great talkers and rodomontadoes of Spain.

B. *adj.* = RODOMONTADE *a.*

c **1645** HOWELL *Lett.* II. xxiv, The Duke of Espernon in a kind of Rodomontado way, desired leave of the King to block up Rochel. **1658** OSBORN *Mem. Q. Eliz.* 100 He sought peace in a posture far below the usuall pride and Rhodomontado-gallantry of that Nation. **1698** T. RYMER *Short View* 159 This ratling Rodomontado speech.

Hence †**rodomon'tado** *v. Obs. rare.*

1693 W. FREKE *Sel. Ess.* xxxii. 200 If they deal in History they sophisticate it; or if in morality they Rhodomontado it.

Rodriguan (rɒ'driːgən), *a.* and *sb.* [f. *Rodrigues* (see below) + -AN.] **A.** *adj.* Of, pertaining to, or characteristic of the island of Rodrigues, a dependency of Mauritius in the western Indian Ocean, or its people. **B.** *sb.* A native or inhabitant of Rodrigues.

1973 *Times* 5 Mar. (Mauritius Suppl.) p. v/1 The islanders are very Rodriguan-minded. *Ibid.*, An elected island council.. would give Rodriguans a chance to put their views. **1974** *Islander* (Victoria, B.C.) 25 Aug. 2/4 We found the Rodriguans interesting. **1977** G. DURRELL *Golden Bats & Pink Pigeons* iv. 86 A large, chocolate-coloured Rodriguan in a handsome, khaki uniform.

rodsman: see RODMAN.

'**rodster.** [f. ROD *sb.*[1]] An angler.

1879 *Leeds Mercury* 8 July 8 (Davies), There were close upon 500 competitors, who included in their ranks rodsters from all parts of the three kingdoms. **1883** *Sportsman* 1 Sept. 4 Old rodsters and young rodsters can find plenty of occupation on the river banks.

'**rod-wood.** [ROD *sb.*[1]] One of several West Indian trees or shrubs belonging to the genera *Lætia*, *Eugenia*, and *Calyptranthes.*

1716 *Petiveriana* I. §258 Rodwood, *Myrtis Barbadensis viminalibus virgis.* **1756** P. BROWNE *Jamaica* 240 It [*Eugenia virgata*] is now commonly called Rod-wood by the negroes. *Ibid.* 249 Rod-wood. The tree grows to a considerable size, and is esteemed a fine timber wood. **1864** GRISEBACH *Flora W. Ind. Isl.* Col. Names, Black, broad-leaved, red, small-leaved, white Rod-wood.

'**rody**, *a. dial.* Also **roady**. = RODED *a.*

1864 *Reader* 19 Nov. 642/1 *Rody.*—Streaked alternately with lean and fat. This very common word seems to be exclusively applied to bacon which presents this appearance. **1878-** in *Eng. Dial. Dict.*

rody, obs. form of RUDDY *a.*

rodyr, obs. form of RUDDER.

roe[1] (rəʊ). Forms: *α.* 1 raha, 1, 5–6 raa, 1, 4–6 ra, 6 ray, 7 rey, 6– rae, 6 re. *β.* 3 roa, 4–6 ro, roo, 6 rhoo, row(e, 6– roe. [Common Teut.: OE. *râha*, *râa*, *râ*, = MDu. *rē*, *ree* (Du. *ree*), OS. *rêho* (LG. *rê*), OHG. *rêho* (also *rêh* neut., G. *reh*), ON. *rá* (Da. *raa*, Sw. *rå*), of uncertain etym. OE. had also a fem. *rǣȝe* corresponding to OHG. *reia*. After 1300 the *α*-forms are only northern and Sc.]

1. A small species of deer (*Capreolus capræa*, formerly *Cervus capreolus*) inhabiting various parts of Europe and Asia; a deer belonging to this species.

α. *c* **725** *Corpus Gloss.* 403 *Capria*, raha. *c* **875** *Erfurt Gloss.* 1161 *Capriolus*, raa. *c* **900** tr. *Baeda's Hist.* I. i. (1890) 30 Hit is fiscwylle & fuȝolwylle, & mære on huntunge heorta & rana. *c* **1000** *Sax. Leechd.* I. 166 Ðyf man on huntuþe ran oððe rægean mid flane.. ȝewæceþ. *a* **1300** *Cursor M.* 19080 Þe propheci was þan fild sua þat said þat halt suld scep as ra. *c* **1386** CHAUCER *Reeve's T.* 4097, I is ful wight, god waat, as is a raa. *c* **1400** MAUNDEV. (Roxb.) xxxi. 143 In þat cuntree also er many camelieouns, þe whilk es a lytill beste of þe mykilnes of a raa. *c* **1480** HENRYSON *Mor. Fables* (*Wolf & Wether*) 2511 Went neuer Hound mair haistelie fra the hand, Quhen he wes rynnand maist raklie at the ra. **1513** DOUGLAS *Æneis* IV. iv. 55 Lo! ther the rais, rynning swyft as fyre. *Ibid.* XII. Prol. 182 Kyddis skippand throw ronnis eftir rayis. *a* **1585** MONTGOMERIE *Cherrie & Slae* 21 The hart, the hynd, the dae, the rae,.. War skowping all frae brae to brae. **1612** *Naworth Househ. Bks.* (Surtees) 28 H. Geldart's son bringing a rey. **17..** RAMSAY *To Starrat* 32 Blythly wald I ..stend o'er burns as light as ony rae. **1881** *Berwick Nat. Club Proc.* IX. 454 'As wild as the rae' is a well-known Border phrase.

β. *a* **1200** in *Fragm. Ælfric's Gram.* etc. (1838) 3 *Caprea*, roa. *a* **1225** *St. Marher.* 3 As fisch ahon on hoke, as þe roa inumen iþe net. *c* **1275** *Serving Christ* 71 in *O.E. Misc.* 92 Ne geyneþ vs.. þe ronke racches þat ruskit þe ron. *c* **1330** R. BRUNNE *Chron. Wace* (Rolls) 15750 Fond þey neuere.. bukke ne do,.. cony, fowen, no ro. **1387** TREVISA *Higden* (Rolls) I. 311 In þat londe beeþ many scheep.. and fewe roos and hertes. *c* **1407** LYDG. *Reson & Sens.* 3728 Hert, and hynde, buk, and doo,.. reyndere and the dredful roo. **1481** CAXTON *Reynard* (Arb.) 99 Moche mete of hertes and hyndes, roes,.. and moche other venyson. **1535** COVERDALE *1 Chron.* xiii. 8 Men of armes, which.. were as swifte as the Roes vpon yᵉ mountaynes. **1575** TURBERV. *Venerie* 241 The tayle of Harte, Bucke, Rowe, or any other Deare, is to be called the Syngle. **1600** J. PORY tr. *Leo's Africa* IV. 216 Here are great store of roes, deere, and ostriches. **1735** SOMERVILLE *Chase* II. 160 Their Coursers, than the Mountain Roe More fleet. **1799** J. ROBERTSON *Agric. Perth* 329 The roes travel in single families, seldom more than four together. **1802** BINGLEY *Anim. Biog.* (1813) I. 446 The height of the Roe at the shoulders is about two feet and a half. **1865** KINGSLEY *Herew.* i, The yellow roes stood and stared at him.

2. *attrib.* and *Comb.*, as **roe-doe**, **-drive** (cf. DRIVE *sb.* 1 c and 2 b), **-head**, **-hunt**, **-kid**, **-leather**, etc.; **roe-hunter**, **-hunting**, **-shooting**; **roe-footed**; **roe ring**, a track worn by roe deer running in circles prior to mating; **roe-stalking**, the hunting of roe-deer on foot; so **roe-stalker**.

1570 LEVINS *Manip.* 154/13 A *Roe doe, *capræa.* **1575** TURBERV. *Venerie* 142 They neuer part vntil the Row-doe haue fawned. **1897** *Daily News* 17 Nov. 9/6 There are *roe-drives in the woods. **1631** CHETTLE *Hoffman* C ij, I, my good Lord, being *roefooted, outstript him in running. **1577** in H. Hall *Eliz. Soc.* (1886) 154, 18 *roeheads, £4. **1840** COLQUHOUN *Moor & Loch* 34 The generality of *roe-hunts are nothing but blunders from beginning to end. *Ibid.* 35 One or two experienced *roe-hunters had the whole sport to themselves. **1728** CHAMBERS *Cycl.* s.v. *Hunting*, *Roe Hunting. **1840** COLQUHOUN *Moor & Loch* 39, I had not then much knowledge of roe-hunting. **1618** in Macpherson *Fauna Lakeland* (1892) 73 Making a pannell.. for carrying iij *rey kidds to London, xxᵈ. **1634** *Ibid.* 72 Goinge with a roe kidd to Judge Cawlye, xijᵈ. **1347** in Riley *Mem. Lond.* (1868) 234 The hundred of *rolether, 16s. **1398** *Ibid.* 547 That no manner of shepeslether or calveslether.. be dyed after the manner of rolether. **1354-5** *Durh. Acc. Rolls* (Surtees) 555 Pro *Ranettes et cordulis pro eisdem. **1383-4** *Ibid.* 593 In cordis emp. pro le Raanet. **1840** COLQUHOUN

Moor & Loch 35 Their love of a *roe-pasty prevailing over their love of the chase. **1620** in Macpherson *Fauna Lakeland* (1892) 72 For careing *roe pyes to my Lord Chancler's, xviij[d]. **1951** H. TEGNER *Roe Deer* iii. 27 (*caption*) Shape of *roe rings: small circles denote small trees or bushes as axes around which roe form these runs. **1960** M. BURTON *Wild Animals* 128 A feature of the rutting season [of roe deer] which has attracted a good deal of attention in recent years has to do with the use of 'roe rings', in which a form of courtship takes place. **1974** F. HOLMES *Following Roe* i. 10 Roe rings, well-trodden runs in the shape of a circle or a figure-of-eight, are evidence of roe residence if they have been recently used. **1840** COLQUHOUN *Moor & Loch* 38 Recommending the above manner of *roe-shooting. **1571** *Wills & Inv. N.C.* (Surtees, 1835) 352 Item I gyue to Edward Archibald iij *Roye [? *read* raye] skinnes. **1927** EDWARDS & WALLACE *Hunting & Stalking Deer* xlii. 237, I have never yet met a *roe-stalker who did not love the roe. **1906** J. G. MILLAIS *Mammals Gt. Brit. & Ireland* III. 178 There are of course hundreds of estates in the North where *Roe-stalking is not possible. **1973** *Country Life* 26 July 254/3 A week's roe-stalking in Britain is..one of the most sought-after privileges among European devotees. *c* **1400** *Rom. Rose* 7048 *Roo-venisoun y-bake in paste. **1814** SCOTT *Wav.* xii. *note*, The learned in cookery..hold the roe-venison dry and indifferent food, unless [etc.].

roe[2] (rəʊ). Forms: *α.* 5–6 **roughe**, 6–7 **rough;** 5 roof, 7 roff(e; 6–7 rowe, 7–8 row. *β.* 7– roe. [ME. type *roȝ(e, row(e, = MDu. *roch, roge* (Kilian *roghe*), Flem. *rog*, MLG. *roge, rogge*, MHG. *roge*, OHG. *rogo*. It is not clear whether the word is native in English or of later adoption. For forms with final *n* see ROWN.]

1. The mass of eggs contained in the ovarian membrane of a fish. ***hard roe***, the spawn of a female fish; ***soft roe***, the milt or sperm of a male fish. Also ***in roe***.

α. **14..** *Voc.* in Wr.-Wülcker 591 *Lactes*, roof of fyshe, or mylke of fyshe. *c* **1430** *Two Cookery Bks.* 114 Tak ye rowys of fissh & ye liuere. *c* **1460** J. RUSSELL *Bk. Nurture* in *Babees Bk.* (1868) 161 White herynge in a dische,..looke he be white by þe boon, þe roughe white & nesche. **1530** PALSGR. 177 *Oeue*, the roughe of a fysshe. *Ibid.* 264/1 Rowe in a fysshes belly, *oevue*. **1617** MINSHEU *Ductor* 422 Roffes or Roughes of fish that spawne. **1653** H. COGAN tr. *Pinto's Trav.* x. 31 He got his Merchandise aboard, which..was nothing but the rows of shads. **1696** *Phil. Trans.* XIX. 256 Composed of Globules, so like the Rowes or Spawn of Fishes. **1773** P. LINDSAY *Interest Scotl.* 201 The..Herrings that have little or no Milt or Row. **1774** GOLDSM. *Nat. Hist.* (1776) VI. 340 That small kind of mackarel that have neither melts nor rows. **1832** [see SALMON *sb.*[1] 4].

β. **1595** SHAKS. *Rom. & Jul.* II. iv. 39 Here comes Romeo. *Mer.* Without his Roe, like a dryed Hering. **1606** —— *Troil. & Cr.* v. i. 68 To be..a Herring without a Roe, I would not care. **1653** WALTON *Angler* viii. 162 You shall scarce..take a Male Carp without a Melt, or a Female without a Roe or Spawn. **1714** MANDEVILLE *Fab. Bees* (1733) II. 287 You mean the prodigious quantity of roe they spawn. **1769** PENNANT *Brit. Zool.* III. 141 [Cod] begin to spawn in January... Some continue in roe till the beginning of April. **1800** *Phil. Trans.* XC. 169 It is remarkable that the hard roe, in general, does not emit so much light as the soft-roe. **1848** LYTTON *Harold* VI. i, A Moorish compound, made of eggs and roes of carp. **1875** NICHOLSON *Man. Zool.* (ed. 4) 412 Fishes are, for the most part, truly oviparous, the ovaries being familiarly known as the 'roe'.

2. *attrib.* and *Comb.*, as ***roe-fish, -laden, -like, mullet, sauce, -shad, -sick***; **roe corn**, a single egg from a roe.

1868 *Rep. U.S. Commissioner Agric.* (1869) 321 These boxes contain each two thousand *roe 'corns'. **1894** *Outing* XXIV. 54/2 The killing of a *roe-laden fish on her way to spawn. **1898** P. MANSON *Trop. Diseases* xxxvii. 573 A white or yellowish *roe-like substance. **1888** GOODE *Amer. Fishes* 368 Between the seasons of 'Fat Mullet' and '*Roe Mullet' there is an intermission of two or three weeks in the fishing. **1883** *Cent. Mag.* Aug. 549/2 Another cook will prepare the *roe sauce to accompany the shad. **1884** *Harper's Mag.* June 88/2 There was a great *roe-shad hanging by his gills. **1641** S. SMITH *Herring Buss Trade* 24 For what sort he will sell them [*sc.* herrings]..*roe-sicke, cleere or pure ware.

roe[3]. [Perh. a transf. use of ROE[2].] (See quots.)

1850 CHALONER & FLEMING *Mahogany Tree* 57 Roe is that alternate streak or flake of light and shade running in the grain. **1920** A. L. HOWARD *Man. Timbers of World* 144 *Mahogany, Cuba*... Many of the logs are beautifully figured or marked with wavy and curly grain, which is variously termed splash mottle, roe and mottle, fiddle-back, plum, snail, blister and cross-bar. **1938** B. J. RENDLE *Commerc. Mahoganies* 5 Mahogany is remarkably stable and does not shrink and swell so much as most woods. Irregularities of the grain produce a variety of figure—fiddleback, blister, stripe or roe, curl, mottle, etc. **1952** J. GLOAG *Short Dict. Furnit.* 396 *Roe*, a name given to the regular appearance of dark figures and spots in figured mahogany, which give a mottled effect, like a fish roe. A form of roe figure occurs in flowered, or East Indian, satinwood. **1968** *Canad. Antiques Coll.* Aug. 24/2 *Roe figure*, this is alternate bands of twisted grain which produce stripes parallel to the length of the tree. When viewed in certain lights from either end the light and dark stripes are reversed.

roebin, obs. form of ROBBIN.

rœblingite (ˈrɜːblɪŋaɪt). *Min.* [f. the name of W. A. *Rœbling* (1837–1926), U.S. civil engineer + -ITE[1].] A rare, monoclinic, basic sulphate-silicate of lead, calcium, and other elements, occurring as compact white masses of minute crystals.

1897 PENFIELD & FOOTE in *Amer. Jrnl. Sci.* CLIII. 415 At the request of Mr. Nason the authors take pleasure in naming this mineral roeblingite in honor of the celebrated engineer, Mr. W. A. Rœbling of Trenton, N.J. **1966** *Amer. Mineralogist* LI. 507 Only a tentative formula, $(Pb_4S_4O_{16})R_{16}Si_{12}O_{44}H_{20}$, where R = Ca, Mn, Sr, Na, and K,..can be assigned to roeblingite.

roebuck (ˈrəʊbʌk). Forms: *α.* 5 **ra(a)buke, rabukk**, 6 **raybuck**, *Sc.* **rebuke**. *β.* 4–6 **ro-**, 5 **roo-**, 6 **rho-**, **rowe-**, 5, 7 **roebucke**, 6– **roebuck**. [f. ROE[1] + BUCK. Cf. MDu. *reebuck* (Du. *-bok*), OHG. *rêhbock* (G. *rehbock*), ON. *rábukkr* (MSw. *robuk*, Sw. *råbock*).] The buck or male of the roe-deer; a male roe.

α. **14..** *Nom.* in Wr.-Wülcker 700 *Hec capra*, a rabuke. **1471** *Exch. Rolls Scotl.* VIII. 36 De ij capitibus de rabukkis. **1483** *Cath. Angl.* 298/1 Raa buke, *capreus, caprea*. *a* **1578** LINDESAY (Pitscottie) *Chron. Scot.* (S.T.S.) I. 338 Wther small beistis as re and rebuke.

β. **1398** TREVISA *Barth. De P.R.* XVIII. xxxi. (Bodl. MS.), Ceruus is þe name of þe herte of þe bucke and of þe Robucke. *c* **1410** *Master of Game* (MS. Digby 182) iii, He is more lasse þen an hert and he is more þenn a Roo bucke. **1486** *Bk. St. Albans* e ij b, A fayre Roobucke and a fayre doo. **1530** PALSGR. 263/1 Rho bucke, a beest. **1575** TURBERV. *Venerie* 143 He is not called a greate Rowebucke, but a fayre Rowbucke. **1590** SPENSER *F.Q.* I. vi. 24 He would him make .. the Robuckes in flight to overtake. **1608** TOPSELL *Serpents* (1658) 739 They took them to be Serpents, being in quantity as big as Roe-bucks. **1661** LOVELL *Hist. Anim. & Min.* 106 Roe-buck. The flesh is better than that of other wild creatures. **1732** LEDIARD *Sethos* II. IX. 296 This natural wall along which..a Roe-buck would hardly have clamber'd. **1774** GOLDSM. *Nat. Hist.* (1776) III. 71 They resemble the roe-buck in the colour and nature of their hair. **1801** SHAW *Gen. Zool.* II. 288 It is about the size of the common or European Roebuck. **1881** GREENER *Gun* 513 Roe bucks are occasionally stalked with the ·360 Express rifle.

attrib. *c* **1410** *Master of Game* (MS. Digby 182) iv, þe Roo bucke flessh is most holsome to eete of eny. **1551** *Records of Elgin* (New Spald. Cl.) I. 107 Tua raybuck skynnis. **1801** SHAW *Gen. Zool.* II. 289 A pair of horns of some animal of the Roebuck kind. **1892** MACPHERSON *Fauna Lakeland* 72 A coat of arms which included three Roebuck heads.

ˈroebuck-berry. [f. prec.] The fruit of a herbaceous species of *Rubus* (see quots.), or the plant producing this.

1771 PENNANT *Tour in Scotland* (1774) 94 They..are remarkably fond of the *Rubus Saxatilis*, called in the Highlands on that account the Roebuck Berry. **1795** *Statist. Acc. Scotl., Lanark* XV. 25 Wild fruits are here in great abundance, such as..Roebuck-berries, and strawberries. **1845** *New Statist. Acc. Scotl., Ross* XIV. 191 The native fruits of the parish are brambles, roebuck-berries, raspberries. **1882** *Garden* 28 Jan. 57/3 Of the British species not hitherto mentioned..the Roebuck-berry is Rubus saxatilis.

roed (rəʊd), *a.* [f. ROE[2].] Having roe; full of spawn. Also in combs. ***full-, hard-, soft-roed***.

1611 COTGR. s.v. *Oeuf*, *Harenc aux œufs*, a full-rowed, or hard-rowed Herring. *Ibid.*, *Ouvé*, full rowed, as a fish. **1769** PENNANT *Brit. Zool.* III. 161 The fishermen take great numbers [of ling] without ever finding any of the female or roed fish among them. **1799** *Spirit Publ. Jrnls.* II. 221 There are also hard-roed mackarel. **1819** *Chron.* in *Ann. Reg.* 7 Scotch herrings.., being roed, and very luscious, do not keep so sound.

Roedean (ˈrəʊdiːn). The name of an independent public school for girls (founded 1885) in the borough of Brighton, applied (usu. *attrib.*) to refined speech or behaviour in (young) women, such as is popularly associated with the girls of this school. (Freq. in derogatory use.)

1948 C. DAY LEWIS *Otterbury Incident* 83 Now don't go all Roedean with me, beautiful. **1958** J. CANNAN *And be a Villain* iv. 94 Dropping the high clear Roedean voice she affected and speaking naturally. **1963** M. FRAYN in Sissons & French *Age of Austerity* 336 The orange-girls.. articulating 'Come, gentle people, buy', in sub-Roedean accents. **1969** S. HYLAND *Top Bloody Secret* ii. 114 The switchboard girl spoke English in the best Roedean manner. **1972** J. ROSSITER *Rope for General Dietz* iii. 31 Her accent was a creamy 1969-vintage Roedean. **1977** F. BRANSTON *Up & Coming Man* x. 95 A Roedean accent which could have flayed the skin off a waiter.

ˈroe-deer. Forms: 1 **rah-**, 2 **roadeor;** 6 **rowdeare**, 7 **roe deere**, 8– **roe-deer** (9 *Sc.* **rae-**). [f. ROE[1] + DEER. Cf. MDa. and MSw. *raadiur* (Da. *raadyr*, Sw. *rådjur*).] Deer, or a deer, of the roe kind; a roe.

c **1000** *Sax. Leechd.* III. 2 Nim..foxes smero & rahdeores mearh. *c* **1000** ÆLFRIC *Gram.* (Z.) 309 *Capreolus*, rahdeor [*a* **1200** roadeor].

1575 TURBERV. *Venerie* 142 They are sweeter of Sent vnto the houndes than the Harte or the Rowdeare. **1688** HOLME *Armoury* II. 134/2 A Roe Deere..when Lodged..Beddeth. **1728** CHAMBERS *Cycl.* s.v. *Hunting*, We have no Roe Deer in England; but they abound in Scotland, Germany, Africa, &c. **1797** *Encycl. Brit.* (ed. 3) IV. 306/1 The roe-deer differs from the stag and fallow-deer. **1853** JAMES *Agnes Sorel* (1860) I. 130 The foot-prints of the hare and the roe-deer could be seen. **1876** SMILES *Sc. Nat.* vii, The horse-like bark of the Roe-deer..puzzled him very much.

Roederer (ˈrøːdərə(r)). Also **Rœderer**. The proprietary name of a champagne produced by the firm of Roederer in Rheims.

1872 B. JERROLD *London* vii. 68 The would-be aristocrat flashing his silver mug of foaming Rœderer in the eyes of the Vulgar. **1876** *Trade Marks Jrnl.* 15 Nov. 803/1 Theophile Roederer & Co. Reims. Maison fondée en 1864... Gustave Bousigues, dit Bley, of and on behalf of the firm of Theophile Roederer and Co., Reims, France; champagne wine merchants... Champagne wine. **1907** [see MUMM]. **1920** G. SAINTSBURY *Notes on Cellar-bk.* v. 74, I had some good wines of it—Pommery and Krug and Roederer among them. **1974** H. R. F. KEATING *Underside* xvi. 156 There was Roederer to drink, a small case of it packed in ice.

roelme, obs. form of REALM.

‖**roemer** (ˈrøːmə(r)). [a. Du. *roemer*, G. *römer*; cf. RUMMER.] A type of decorated German or Dutch wine-glass with a knobbed or 'prunted' stem.

1897 A. HARTSHORNE *Old Eng. Glasses* 47 Germans were making roemers in the Low Countries before the middle of the seventeenth century, and there also the quaint vessel had a long course, being the glass *par excellence*, with its delicate shades of blue, yellow, or green, that the painters never tired of painting. **1926** W. BUCKLEY *European Glass* 55 Particular mention should be made of the 'roemer', a form that is usually acknowledged not only to be the most beautiful product of the German industry but one of the most beautiful forms that has been made in glass in any country. **1942** [see PASSGLAS]. **1972** *Country Life* 23 Mar. 700/2 No one who is familiar with German and Dutch glass..can fail to notice..the prunts on the stems of the popular wine glass of those days—the roemer.

roemerite (ˈrɜːməraɪt). *Min.* Also **römerite**. [ad. G. *römerit* (J. Grailich 1858, in *Sitzungsber. d. K. Akad. d. Wissensch. in Wien* XXVIII. 272), f. the name of Friedrich Adolph *Römer* (1809–69), German geologist: see -ITE[1].] A hydrated sulphate of ferrous and ferric iron, often containing zinc, which occurs as rust-brown to yellow triclinic crystals, usu. as an oxidation product of pyrite.

1877 E. S. DANA *Text-bk. Mineral.* III. 373 Alum and Halotrichite Groups. Here belong: Tschermigite, ammonium alum. Kalinite, potassium alum... Also Roemerite, and Voltaite. **1903** *Jrnl. Chem. Soc.* LXXXIV. II. 555 Römerite was prepared by allowing a mixture of powdered ferrous sulphate and acid ferric sulphate to remain in contact with moist air for several months. **1927** *Amer. Mineralogist* XII. 282 Chemically, roemerite is a double sulphate of ferrous and ferric iron, the ferrous iron of which may sometimes be replaced by zinc and magnesium, and the ferric iron by aluminum. **1970** *Ibid.* LV. 78 Roemerite is generally the result of an oxidation of iron sulfides.

Roentgen, roentgen (ˈrœntyən, ˈrœntçən; now usu. anglicized, as ˈrʌntjən; also ˈrɜːnt-, ˈrɒnt-; -gən, -ʒən), Also **Röntgen, röntgen**. [The name of Wilhelm Conrad *Röntgen* (1845–1923), German physicist, who discovered X-rays in 1895 (*Sitzungsber. d. Phys.-Med. Ges. z. Würzburg* 132).]

1. *attrib.* (†or in the possessive), as ***Roentgen rays***, X-rays. Hence ***Roentgen photograph, therapy***, etc. Occas. written as a prefix (cf. ROENTGEN-, ROENTGENO-). Now chiefly *U.S.*

1896 THOMSON in *Proc. Royal Soc.* LIX. 274 The Röntgen rays, when they fall upon electrified bodies, rapidly discharge the electrification. **1896** —— in *Nature* 27 Feb. 391 The methods of producing Röntgen photographs. **1896** *McClure's Mag.* Apr. 405 The Röntgen rays are certain invisible rays resembling, in many respects, rays of light, which are set free when a high pressure electric current is discharged through a vacuum tube. **1896** *Lancet* 1 Feb. 326/2 Do Roentgen's rays possess germicidal properties? *Ibid.* 22 Feb. 477/1 Two preliminary short exposures to Roentgen rays indicated that the metal..was probably embedded among the bones of the wrist. **1898** SIR W. CROOKES *Addr. Brit. Assoc.* 24 No other source for Röntgen rays but the Crookes tube has yet been discovered, but rays of kindred sorts are recognized. **1910** *Arch. Roentgen Ray* XV. 85 In Roentgentherapy the filter has brought the treatment of hypertrichosis once more into the domain of practical politics. **1911** *Encycl. Brit.* XXIII. 695/1 The radiation..from tin is as penetrating as that given out by a fairly efficient Röntgen tube. *Ibid.*, The incidence of Röntgen rays on matter causes the matter to emit cathodic rays. **1933** U. V. PORTMANN in O. Glasser *Sci. of Radiol.* xii. 221 In the beginning of roentgen therapy only skin diseases and some superficial malignant conditions were treated. **1940** H. K. PANCOAST et al. (*title*) The head and neck in roentgen diagnosis. *Ibid.* xi. 773 The chest should always be included as a part of any roentgen examination of the neck, particularly in infants and young children. **1953** A. J. DELARIO *Roentgen, Radium & Radioisotope Therapy* iii. 17 Because roentgen rays have such short wave-lengths, they cannot be diffracted by various diffraction gratings, as can visible light. **1956** L. A. HADLEY *Spine* iv. 95 By this method it is possible to furnish roentgen evidence of ligamentous or soft tissue injury. **1959** W. T. MOSS *Therapeutic Radiol.* ii. 35 With few exceptions all roentgentherapy techniques, by necessity, entail skin irradiation. **1959** W. T. MURPHY *Radiation Therapy* xxxvi. 770 Roentgen sickness is not frequently seen after pelvic irradiation. **1972** H. L. KUNDEL in E. J. Potchen *Current Concepts in Radiol.* I. i. 1 (*heading*) Factors limiting roentgen interpretation—physical and psychologic. **1978** S. SHELDON *Bloodline* ii. 33 A Roentgen desk in the library.

2. (Usu. in the form **roentgen**.) In full **roentgen unit**. The unit of exposure to X or gamma radiation, equal to the quantity of radiation that gives rise to ions carrying a total charge of 2·58 coulombs (regardless of sign) per kilogramme of air. Abbrev. *r.* [Proposed (in Fr.) by I. Solomon 1921, in *Arch. d' Électr. méd. expér. & clin.* XXIX. 362.]

The precise definition of this unit has been altered several times. Cf. REM *sb.*[1], REP[7].

1922 [see R II. 4]. **1932** *Radiology* XVIII. 95/2 At the second International Congress of Radiology in 1928..the measurement of air ionization was accepted as the basis of international dosage measurement and a definition was given of the unit of dosage designating a roentgen unit and written in abbreviated form as 'r'. **1938** R. W. LAWSON tr. *Hevesy & Paneth's Man. Radioactivity* (ed. 2) xxiv. 258 The maximum daily dosage of γ-rays that a human being can tolerate without apparent harm is 0·1 röntgen unit. **1950** *Radiology* LV. 744/1 As our exciting energies increased, we were placed in a position of having continually to modify the definition of the roentgen in order to cope with the new properties of the higher-energy radiations. Because of this situation, minor modifications in the definition of the roentgen were made in 1931, 1934 and 1937. **1955** *Bull. Atomic Scientists* Sept. 257/2 It is known that radiation dosages in the levels of 400 roentgen units..are lethal to about half the individuals exposed. **1956** *Brit. Jrnl. Radiol.* XXIX. 355/2 The radiation dose in röntgens within any volume element is determined by the number and energy of the photons passing through that element during the exposure, irrespective of the local distribution of matter. *Ibid.* 356/1 Difficulties have only arisen when we have tried to make the röntgen do service for a unit of absorbed dose. **1959** *Listener* 26 Nov. 929/2 The fall-out from testing bombs gives a thirty-year dose of ·1 roentgen... The dose from natural radiation is about 3-5 roentgens. **1970** PASSMORE & ROBSON *Compan. Med. Stud.* II. xxxiii. 4/2 The same exposure (in roentgens) may result in different absorbed doses (in rads) in different tissues. **1977** [see PROTOCOL *sb.* 3].

Hence †'**Roentgenism**; †'**Roentgenized** *ppl. a.*, subjected to the action of X-rays; also †'**Roentgenize** *v. trans.* (*rare*: in quot. *fig.*); †,**Roentgeni'zation**.

1897 *Phil. Mag.* XLIII. 243 The effect can in no way be due to conduction through the Röntgenized air. **1899** *Proc. Royal Soc.* LXV. 120 The analogy between the conductivity of salt vapours and that of Röntgenised gases. **1900** *Dunglison's Med. Dict.* App., *Roentgenism*, morbid condition induced by X-rays. **1907** *Med. Rec.* (N.Y.) 9 Nov. 760/2 In the use of radium, if enclosed in aluminium or mica receptacles, we utilize the beta or cathode ray. This we cannot do in Roentgenisation. **1909** E. REICH *Nights with Gods* 17 It [*sc.* jealousy] has Röntgenised the most hidden interiors. **1920** *Arch. Radiol. & Electrotherapy* XXIV. 270/1 Röntgenisation of the lymphatic glands should always supplement radium therapy.

roentgen-, roentgeno-. Chiefly *U.S.* Also röntgen(o)-. Comb. forms of ROENTGEN, as in **roentgen'kymogram** [ad. G. *röntgenkymogramm* (Gött & Rosenthal 1912, in *München med. Wochenschr.* 17 Sept. 2033)], a recording made with a kymograph (sense 2); **roentgen'kymograph** = KYMOGRAPH 2; ,**roentgenkymo'graphic** *a.*, of, pertaining to, or involving the roentgenkymograph; hence ,**roentgenkymo'graphically** *adv.*; ,**roentgenky'mography** [ad. G. *röntgenkymographie* (Gött & Rosenthal 1912, loc. cit.)], the process or technique of using a kymograph (sense 2); kymography; '**roentgenogram**, an X-ray photograph; cf. RADIOGRAPH *sb.* 2; '**roentgenograph** *sb.* = prec.; also as *v. trans.*, to take an X-ray picture of (an organ, etc.); = RADIOGRAPH *v.*; **roentgeno'graphic** *a.*, pertaining to or involving roentgenography; hence **roentgeno'graphically** *adv.*; **roentge'nography**, radiography carried out by means of X-rays; **roentgeno'logic, -'logical** *adjs.*, of, pertaining to, or involving roentgenology; hence **roentgeno'logically** *adv.*; **roentge'nologist**, one who practises roentgenology; **roentge'nology**, †(*a*) (see quot. 1905); (*b*) (the field of science concerned with) the medical use of X-rays, esp. as a diagnostic tool; cf. RADIOLOGY; '**roentgenoscope** *sb.* = FLUOROSCOPE; hence as *v. trans.*, to examine by means of a fluoroscope; **roentgeno'scopic** *a.*, fluoroscopic; hence **roentgeno'scopically** *adv.*; **roentge'noscopy**, fluoroscopy; **roentgeno'therapy**, radiotherapy carried out by means of X-rays.

1913 *Arch. Roentgen Ray* XVII. 379 (*caption*) Roentgenkymogram of the left ventricle. **1930** *Arch. Internal Med.* XLV. 63 The slit in the lead sheet was placed over this point and the roentgen-kymogram taken. **1942** A. M. MASTER *Electrocardiogram* (ed. 2) 226 The character of the ventricular pulsations, as seen..in the roentgenkymogram, may..lead to the suspicion of cardiac aneurysm. **1913** *Jrnl. Amer. Med. Assoc.* 4 Apr. 1127/2 (*heading*) Analysis of electrocardiogram by means of the Roentgen-kymograph. **1968** LUISADA & SAINANI *Primer of Cardiac Diagnosis* xviii. 117 The waves revealed by the electrokymograph are similar to those of the roentgenkymograph. **1930** *Arch. Internal Med.* XLV. 71 Variability of stroke volume was surmised because of..the different shape of the roentgenkymographic curves produced by ventricular systole. **1970** G. H. ALEXANDER *Heart* i. 10/2 The roentgenkymographic studies of the heart which have been done at St. Francis by the author since 1957. **1940** *Amer. Heart Jrnl.* XIX. 462 Characteristic abnormalities in left ventricular pulsation as recorded roentgenkymographically in 200 cases of myocardial infarction. **1913** *Arch. Roentgen Ray* XVII. 378 (*heading*) Roentgenkymography: a roentgenographic method of demonstrating the movement of the heart. **1971** *Amer. Jrnl. Roentgenol.* CXI. 868/1 The authors have studied by analytic roentgen kymography the pulsations of the thoracic aorta in 5 patients. **1904** F. P. FOSTER *Appleton's Med. Dict.* 1707/1 *Röntgenogram*, a Röntgen ray picture. **1907** *Med. Rec.* (N.Y.) 10 Aug. 246/1 He remembered a case where a Roentgenogram demonstrated an object in the right ureter, and a diagnosis of a stone was made; but on incision no stone was found. **1977** *Jrnl. Bone & Joint Surg.* LIX. 575/1 The fracture was demonstrated..by a roentgenogram of the carpal tunnel. **1905** *Jrnl. Amer. Med. Assoc.* 23 Dec. 1971/1 The film is then inserted, held in place by an assistant or the patient himself, the point of pressure being..on the particular tooth to be Roentgenographed. **1909** *Cent. Dict.* Suppl., *Roentgenograph*,..a radiograph; a Röntgenogram. **1940** *Amer. Jrnl. Roentgenol.* XLIV. 944/1 The side of a bone cavity opposite the focus is to be roentgenographed. **1965** *Ibid.* XCV. 135/1 When roentgenographed, the involved areas show widened diploic space and radial striation of bone spicules. **1977** *Environmental Res.* XIII. 47 Serial roentgenographs of histologically confirmed massive fibrotic lesions in 14 deceased gold miners were retrospectively studied. **1909** *Amer. Jrnl. Med. Sci.* CXXXVII. 377 (*heading*) A Röntgenographic study of peristalsis. **1961** R. D. BAKER *Essent. Path.* ix. 169 It is the calcification in the primary tuberculous complex which makes possible the recognition of the condition by roentgenographic study. **1977** *Amer. Jrnl. Med.* LXII. 366/2 Eight of the 14 atypical cases were diagnostic problems because of atypical roentgenographic and clinical features. **1909** *Amer. Jrnl. Med. Sci.* CXXXVII. 420 The width of the apices of the lungs has not yet been sufficiently studied roentgenographically to find employment diagnostically. **1965** *Arch. Internal Med.* CXV. 580/2 Her hands were normal and roentgenographically both hands and feet were normal. **1905** *Nature* 27 July 301/1 Among the results of the recent Röntgen congress at Berlin has been the authoritative adoption by a special committee of the following terminology:—Röntgenology = the study of Röntgen rays, Röntgenoscopy = observation by Röntgen rays, Röntgenography = photography by the rays... Röntgenotherapy and the verb to Röntgenise in their obvious meanings. **1958** *Optima* Sept. 130/2 The double platinum salts, such as platinum lithium cyanide or platinum thorium cyanide, are brilliantly fluoroscopic, and are used in roentgenography and fluoroscopy. **1912** *Amer. Jrnl. Med. Sci.* CXLIII. 754 (*heading*) A Röntgenologic study of spastic obstipation. **1967** *Amer. Jrnl. Roentgenol.* CI. 457/2 (*caption*) Roentogenologic signs of hypertrophic pyloric muscle in a 66 year old man. **1911** *Arch. Roentgen Ray* XV. 328, I propose to give my impressions from the Roentgenological point of view. **1925** S. LEWIS *Martin Arrowsmith* xxv. 292 The clinic did, perhaps, give overmany roentgenological examinations to socially dislocated women who needed children and floor-scrubbing more than pretty little skiagraphs. **1977** *Surgery* LXXXII. 848 (*heading*) An aggressive roentgenological and surgical approach to acute mesenteric ischemia. **1915** *Amer. Jrnl. Roentgenol.* II. 795/1 The cases to be examined roentgenologically are selected from those which have gastric symptoms. **1968** JACKMAN & BEAHRS *Tumors of Large Bowel* iv. 50 This method enabled them to find additional polyps, other than those detected roentgenologically. **1905** *Jrnl. Amer. Med. Assoc.* 23 Dec. 1971/2 Permit me to make a few remarks about the technic employed, which, I think, will be of value to every Roentgenologist. **1961** R. D. BAKER *Essent. Path.* xix. 533 Granules of calcium often form in the pineal after puberty and are helpful in locating the midline of the brain for the roentgenologist. **1905** Roentgenology [see *roentgenography* above]. **1914** *Jrnl. Amer. Med. Assoc.* 22 Aug. 651/2 The utility of some insight into Roentgen procedures on the part of the general practitioner does not nullify the advantages of specialization in roentgenology. **1977** *Surg., Gynecol. & Obstetr.* CXLIV. 563/2 Conventional roentgenology confirmed the presence of a tumor at the gastroesophageal junction. **1923** *Amer. Jrnl. Roentgenol.* X. 722 (*heading*) A plea for the use of the roentgenoscope in the diagnosis of urinary calculi. **1924** *Ibid.* XI. 93/2 With most..types of the tilt-table roentgenoscope, it will be necessary to remove the screen ordinarily used. **1926** *Jrnl. Amer. Med. Assoc.* 19 June 1904/2 An arrangement should be made by which the patient can be roentgenoscoped at right angles without change of position. **1955** *Amer. Jrnl. Roentgenol.* LXXIV. 812/1 Anyone who has roentgenoscoped an infant's chest realizes that an infant can squeeze virtually all the macroscopic air out of his lungs..with crying. **1909** *Amer. Jrnl. Med. Sci.* CXXXVII. 418 When both apices are equally or only slightly darkened, I have grown cautious with röntgenoscopic diagnosis. **1965** *Biol. Abstr.* XLVI. 8241/2 (*heading*) Roentgenoscopic investigation of oil-bearing seeds. **1909** *Amer. Jrnl. Med. Sci.* CXXXVII. 420 The process, röntgenoscopically at least, slowly advances, and after weeks is recognized as tuberculosis. **1945** *Amer. Jrnl. Roentgenol.* LIII. 608/1 The alimentary canal as observed roentgenoscopically. **1904** F. P. FOSTER *Appleton's Med. Dict.* 1707/1 *Röntgenoscopy*, examination with the aid of the Röntgen rays. **1914** *Jrnl. Amer. Med. Assoc.* 21 Nov. 1828/1 Roentgenoscopy has proved that ossification may..occur in the epiglottis. **1971** *Biol. Abstr.* LII. 5081/1 The essential methods of roentgenological examination..are roentgenoscopy and roentgenography. **1903** *Med. Rec.* (N.Y.) 31 Jan. 168/2 Extravagant promises will discredit the new and delicate field of Röntgenotherapy. **1925** *Jrnl. Amer. Med. Assoc.* 28 Feb. 671/1 Roentgenotherapy effects a complete disappearance of palpable lymph nodes and reduces the spleen to its normal size. **1960** *Biol. Abstr.* XXXV. 4048/1 Giving 2-3 drops each of validol..on sugar to patients with carcinoma of various sites (50) after a session of roentgenotherapy..usually eased the general reaction to the irradiation.

'**roentgenite.** *Min.* Also röntgenite. [f. ROENTGEN, ROENTGEN + -ITE[1].] A rhombohedral fluorocarbonate of cerium, lanthanum, and calcium, $Ca_2(Ce,La)_3(CO_3)_5F_3$, found as small yellow or brown crystals in association with other rare-earth minerals at Narsarsuk, Greenland.

1953 G. DONNAY in *Amer. Mineralogist* XXXVIII. 868 (*heading*) Roentgenite, $3CeFCO_3.2CaCO_3$, a new mineral from Greenland. **1966** Z. LERMAN tr. *K. A. Vlasow's Geochem. & Mineral. of Rare Elements* II. VIII. 272 Röntgenite $Ce_3Ca_2(CO_3)_5F_3$. Identity established by Donnay in 1953 during X-ray analysis of rare-earth fluocarbonate specimens from Greenland. **1975** *Amer. Mineralogist* LX. 351 Intimate syntaxy between parisite, synchisite, roentgenite, and bastnaesite was..observed even on a very fine scale.

roepperite ('rɜːpəraɪt). *Min.* [f. the name of William T. *Roepper* (1810-80), German-born U.S. mineralogist + -ITE[1].] A black mineral of the olivine group containing iron, manganese, and zinc.

The name *röpperit* (G.) was also proposed in 1872 by A. Kenngott (in *Neues Jahrb. f. Mineral.* 188) for a species of manganiferous dolomite described by Roepper.

1872 G. J. BRUSH in *Dana's Syst. Min.* (ed. 5) App. I. 13 Roepperite. Iron, manganese, zinc, chrysolite... Roepperite, *G. J. Brush.* **1875** E. S. DANA *Ibid.* App. II. 49 Kenngott..has proposed to give the name rœpperite to the manganese dolomite, analysed by Rœpper... Almost simultaneously..Brush gave the name rœpperite to the new chrysolite of Rœpper, and there is no question but that this name should be received. **1961** *Amer. Mineralogist* XLVI. 549 Roepperite is black... It has been described as a variety of tephroite containing notably high amounts of FeO and ZnO. **1972** *Ibid.* LVII. 977 The infrared spectrum of the zincian olivine roepperite..is comparable to those of Fe-Mn olivines and bears no resemblances to the spectrum of willemite containing tetrahedral Zn^{2+}.

‖**roer** (rʊə(r)). [Du. *roer*, ad. G. *rohr* (OHG. *rôr*), gun-barrel, pipe, reed. So Da. *rør*, Sw. *rör*.] A long-barrelled gun used by the Boers of S. Africa in hunting large game.

1834 PRINGLE *Afr. Sk.* 88 Bold Arend! come help with your long-barrelled roer. **1850** R. G. CUMMING *Hunter's Life S. Afr.* (1902) 17/1 He was a keen hunter, and himself and household subsisted, in a great measure, by the proceeds of his long single-barrelled 'roer'. **1899** RIDER HAGGARD *Swallow* xvi, All were well armed with 'roers' or other guns.

roesslerite ('rɜːslərаɪt). *Min.* Also rösslerite. [ad. G. *rösslerit* (R. Blum 1861, in *Jahresber. der Wetterauischen Ges. für die ges. Naturkunde* 33), f. the name of Carl *Rössler*, 19th-c. German scientist: see -ITE[1].] A hydrated acid arsenate of magnesium, $MgHAsO_4.7H_2O$, which occurs as small colourless plates forming an oxidized crust on some arsenical deposits, and has been prepared artificially.

1868 J. D. DANA *Syst. Min.* (ed. 5) 556 A mineral in monoclinic crystals occurs at Joachimsthal and Kremnitz... which is probably rœsslerite. **1903** *Jrnl. Chem. Soc.* LXXXIV. II. 656 Crystals..of the arsenic compound, $(NH_4)MgAsO_4,6H_2O$, isomorphous with struvite were obtained, and at the same time crystals of rösslerite $(MgHAsO_4,7H_2O)$. **1951** C. PALACHE et al. *Dana's Syst. Min.* (ed. 7) II. 712 Artificial roesslerite is precipitated together with $MgNH_4AsO_4.6H_2O$..from an acid solution of disodium arsenate and ammonium sulfate by a solution of magnesium sulfate. **1973** *Acta Crystallographica* B. XXIX. 287/1 Roesslerite is biaxial negative.

‖**roesti** ('rœsti). Also rosti, rösti. [Swiss Ger.] A Swiss style of fried potatoes. (Variously taken as *sing.* and *pl.*)

1952 H. SUTTON *Footloose in Switzerland* ii. 55 The most typical dish of Zurich is something known as *g'schnetzeltes*... It comes served with noodles or roesti, which are home fries. **1953** *New Horizons* (Pan Amer. World Airways) (new ed.) 122/1 Each region [of Switzerland] has its specialties: *Fondue* and *Raclette*..in the French section..sausages, roasts and fried potatoes (*Rösti*) in the German section. **1961** P. CANNON *Eating European* 223 The Swiss *Rosti*, which is close to being their national home dish, is made with cooked potatoes. **1961** N. S. HAZELTON *Continental Flavor* 304 *Roesti* is really a version of home-fried potatoes, and certainly the best. **1973** M. WALDO *Compl. Round-World Cookbk.* 145 Fried Potatoes... Rösti.

'**roestone.** [f. ROE[1].] = OOLITE.

1804 R. JAMESON *Syst. Min.* I. 480 Roestone... Its colour is hair brown and chestnut brown. **1839** URE *Dict. Arts* 772 Oolite or roe-stone.—It consists of spherical grains of various size, from a millet seed, to a pea, or even an egg. **1876** PAGE *Adv. Text-bk. Geol.* xvii. 332 The true oolites or roestones seem to be more of chemical than of mechanical origin.

roet, variant of ROWET.

'**roey,** *a.* [f. ROE[3].] Streaky.

1850 CHALONER & FLEMING *Mahogany Tree* 49 The Mahogany, which is the best adapted for Shipbuilding, is that which is firm, tough and roey.

rof(e, obs. pa. t. of RIVE *v.*[1]; obs. ff. ROOF.

†**rofe.** *Obs.*[−0] [Perh. the same as E. Anglian *rove* scurf, scab.] ? Rind, skin.

1530 PALSGR. 263/2 Rofe of baken or befe.

rofe, obs. f. ROVE *sb.*

rofel, obs. f. RUFFLE.

roff(e, obs. pa. t. RIVE *v.*[1]; obs. ff. ROE[2], ROOF, ROVE.

rofia (ruː'fiːə). Also 8 rofeer, 9 roffia. [Malagasy.] A kind of palm: see RAFFIA and RAPHIA.

1729 DRURY *Madagascar* (1890) 172 Where the cattle are kept is a tree called rofeer. **1878** *Antananarivo Annual* 113 Of the Palmae there is but one species found in Imerina, the Rofia. **1880** J. SIBREE *Grt. African Isl.* iv. 75 The rofia has a trunk of from thirty to fifty feet in height, and at the end divides into seven or eight immensely long leaves.

attrib. **1883** *Encycl. Brit.* XV. 170/1 The rôfia palm (*Sagus Ruffia*), from whose pinnate leaves a valuable fibre used for cloth is obtained.

rofling, obs. form of RUFFLING.

roftile, obs. form of ROOF-TILE.

†**rog**, *sb. Obs.* Also **roge**. (Meaning obscure: perh. not the same word in the two quots.)

? *a* **1400** *Morte Arth.* 3273 That euer I regnede one þir rog, me rewes it euer! ? *a* **1500** *Chester Pl.* (Shaks. Soc.) II. 94 What! laye thou still in that stonde And let that losinger go on the roge [*rime* dogge].

rog (rɒg), *v. Obs.* exc. *dial.* Also 4–6 **rogge**, 5 **roggyn**. [Of obscure origin; perhaps related to RUG *v.* Cf. also Norw. dial. *rogga* to set in motion, drive on; *rogg* energy.]

1. *trans.* To shake (a person or thing). Also *absol.* with *on*, *at*.

1377 LANGL. *P. Pl.* B. XVI. 78 It [the tree] made a foule noyse, þat I had reuth whan Piers rogged, it gradde so reufulliche. *c* **1385** CHAUCER *L.G.W.* 2708 *Hypermnestra*, In hyre armys [she] gan hym to enbrace And hym she roggith & a-wakyth softe. *c* **1422** HOCCLEVE *Jereslaus' Wife* 355 Shee ..rogged on hir lord and him awook. *c* **1430** LYDG. *Minor Poems* (Percy Soc.) 41 She rogged on hym,..And badde hym turne hym. *c* **1440** *Promp. Parv.* 435/2 Roggyn, or mevyn (or schoggyn, *K.* rokkyn), *agito*. **1811** WILLAN in *Archæologia* (E.D.S.), *Roggle*, or *Rogge*, to shake, to jumble. **1867** WAUGH *Owd Blanket* i. 7 Then he 'rogged' at the door, and shouted 'Hello'!

2. *intr.* To shake; to move to and fro.

? *a* **1400** *Morte Arth.* 784 He romede, he rarede, that roggede alle þe erthe! *c* **1440** *Promp. Parv.* 435/2 Roggyn, or waveryn (or schakyn), *vacillo*. **1600** SURFLET *Countrie Farme* II. lxii. 404 The hiues shall be so set, as that..there may not any occasion be giuen to shake or rogge vpon the other. **1886** CUNLIFFE *Rochdale Gloss.*, *Rog*, to shake with a dull sound, as a door or a window when the wind is high. **1886** HOLLAND *Cheshire Gloss.* s.v., A window or door *rogs* with the wind.

Hence **'rogging** *vbl. sb.*

c **1440** *Promp. Parv.* 435/2 Roggynge, or schakynge, *vacillacio*. **1626** COSIN *Corr.* (Surtees) I. 87, I came home,.. having clered my self by the way, through rogging of the coatch, of 2 stones.

rog (rɒdʒ), *int.* Abbrev. of ROGER[2] 6.

1955 R. J. SCHWARTZ *Compl. Dict. Abbrev.* 155/3 *Rog*, roger. **1969** *Guardian* 21 July 1/3 Back came the single syllable answer from the spacecraft... 'Rog.' **1970** N. ARMSTRONG et al. *First on Moon* xiv. 354 'You're cleared for landing.'.. 'Rog. Gear is down and locked.'

'rogal, ro'galian, *adjs. rare*$^{-0}$. [f. L. *rogālis*, f. *rogus* pyre.] 'Of or pertaining to a great fire.'

1656 BLOUNT *Glossogr.*

Rogallo (rəʊ'gæləʊ). Also **rogallo**. The name of Francis M. *Rogallo*, 20th-c. U.S. engineer, used *attrib.* and *absol.* to designate a light, flexible, triangular wing deployed by means of tension lines or rigid tubes and used on spacecraft and for hang-gliding.

1961 Rogallo wing [see PARAGLIDER]. **1968** *McGraw-Hill Encycl. Space* i. 127 The tanks..are specially arranged to accommodate the housing of the recovery wing. The latter, known by the names of Paraglider, Flex-wing or Rogallo Wing (from the name of its inventor, Francis M. Rogallo, director of the large wind-tunnel at NASA's Langley Research Center) is a flexible wing which is deployed in flight and enables the rocket to glide. **1974** *Observer* (Colour Suppl.) 7 Apr. 68/1 The rogallo, a triangular kite-shape wing made of aluminium tubing with a nylon sail. **1974** *Sci. Amer.* Dec. 138/1 Most sky surfers first learn to fly on a Rogallo kite. **1978** A. WELCH *Bk. of Airsports* i. 9/2 They come in an increasing variety of shapes and sizes, ranging from the basic rogallo for club and school use to almost aerodynamic planform hang gliders.

'rogament. *rare*$^{-0}$. [ad. L. *rogāmentum*, f. *rogāre* to ask.] 'A Proposition to be granted.'

1727 BAILEY (vol. II.).

rogan ('rəʊgən). *Canad.* Also 8 **roggan**, 9 **roggin**. [ad. Canad. Fr. (*h*)*ouragan*, f. Algonkian (see W. S. Avis *Dict. Canadianisms*).] A water-tight container made of birch-bark.

1743 J. ISHAM in *Publ. Hudson's Bay Rec. Soc.* (1949) XII. 188 A Roggan. Slawee. **1791** P. FIDLER *Jrnl.* 10 Nov. in *Publ. Champlain Soc.* (1934) XXI. 523 We are obliged to roast all & make water by immersing red hot stones into a roggan of Snow. **1820** J. CLOUSTON *Jrnl.* 10 July in K. G. Davies *Northern Quebec & Labrador Jrnls. & Corr. 1819–35* (1963) 57 He had a wooden roggin which would hold about five gallons. **1894** *Outing* Nov. 127/1, I saw..the 'rogans', or water-tight vessels of birch-bark, beautifully stitched with roots, and trimmed around the opening with colored porcupine-quills. **1922** *Beaver* June 7/1 Ornamented work baskets, plain baskets or 'rogans', for holding fish, game, berries, or canoe pitch are also made of the bark. **1968** E. S. RUSSENHOLT *Heart of Continent* I. i. 1 These hunters heat stones in their open fires; and drop them into birch bark rogans filled with water and meat—until the water boils and cooks the meat.

Rogatian (rəʊ'geɪʃən). [f. *Rogatus*, the leader of the sect, who flourished in the 4th century.] = ROGATIST.

1564 *Brief Exam.* 4* b, You shall reade of the Donatistes, Rogatians,..and Papistes. **1781** GIBBON *Decl. & F.* xxi. (1787) II. 237 Even the imperceptible sect of the Rogatians could affirm, without a blush, that when Christ should descend [etc.]. **1845** *Encycl. Metrop.* XI. 325/2 A fourth part of the Donatist Prelates followed the standard of Maximin, and a large Body was distinguished by the name of Rogatians.

So **Ro'gatianist**. *rare*$^{-1}$.

1608 T. MORTON *Preamble to Incounter* Pref. 2, Heretikes, called Rogationists (*sic*).

rogation (rəʊ'geɪʃən). Forms: 4–6 **rogacioun**, 5–6 **rogacion**, 5 **-cyon** (**ragacyoun**), 6 **-tioun**, 6– **rogation**. [ad. L. *rogātio*, *-iōnis* (f. *rogāre* to ask), whence also F. *rogation* (14th c.), Sp. *rogacion*, Pg. *rogação*, It. *rogazione*. The pl. form used in sense 1 corresponds to med.L. *Rogationes*, *Rogaciones*, F. *Rogations*, Sp. *Rogaciones*, Pg. *Rogações*, It. *Rogazioni*.]

1. *Eccl.* (Usually *pl.*) Solemn supplications consisting of the litany of the saints, chanted during procession on the three days before Ascension Day; hence freq., the days upon which this is done, the Rogation days. (Cf. ROVEISON.)

1387 TREVISA *Higden* (Rolls) V. 299 Seint Mammertus.. ordeyned solempne letanyes þat beeþ i-cleped þe Rogaciouns, aȝenst erþe schakynge. **1430** in Halliw. *Rara Mathem.* (1841) 92 Þis table tellyȝt qwen lentyn fallyth,.. qwen þe Rogacyons and qwen qwytesoneday. *c* **1440** *Astron. Cal.* (MS. Ashm. 391), And so in like forme Estre, Rogacion, and Wytsonday. **1483** CAXTON *Gold. Leg.* 22 a/1 [The second litany] is said the letanye the lasse, the rogacions, and processions. **1547** *Bk. of Marchauntes* b j b, Pardons, indulgences, remissions,..rogacions,..and holy workes of God. **1597** HOOKER *Eccl. Pol.* v. xli. §2 Supplications with this solemnitie for the appeasing of Gods wrath.. were of the Greeke Church termed Litanies, Rogations, of the Latine. **1604** *Bk. Com. Prayer, Tables*, etc., Rogations, after Easter v weekes. **1660** JER. TAYLOR *Ductor Dubit.* III. iv. (1676) 643 The solemn days of Rogation which we observe in the Church of England were not of an immemorial beginning. **1704** NELSON *Fest. & Fasts* II. vi. (1739) 516 The Curate..in the Days of Rogations..shall admonish the People. **1782** PRIESTLEY *Corrupt. Chr.* II. VIII. 134 Mamert..first instituted the fast of Rogation. **1872** SHIPLEY *Eccl. Terms* 315 The inner narthex was the place for rogations, watches, funeral rites, and sometimes baptisms. **1884** *Cath. Dict.* (1897) 794/1 The Rogations began in the kingdom of Burgundy.

attrib. **1660** JER. TAYLOR *Duct. Dubit.* III. iv. xiii. §23 The Rogation fast (all the World knows) was instituted by Mammercus Bishop of Vienna. **1812** J. BRADY *Clavis Cal.* I. 338 Leaving..the object of Mumertus's alteration in the Rogation ceremony undecided. **1872** SHIPLEY *Eccl. Terms* s.v. *Rogational*, Antiphons used at Rogation-tide, or in connexion with litanies.

b. ***Rogation days***, the Monday, Tuesday, and Wednesday preceding Ascension Day. (Cf. GANG-DAYS.) ***Rogation week***, the week in which Ascension Day falls. (Cf. GANG-WEEK.) ***Rogation Sunday***, the fifth Sunday after Easter, being the Sunday before Ascension Day.

(*a*) *c* **1400** *Harl. MS. 2247* lf. 105 b, Euery man..shulde faste Monday, Tewsday & Wednesday, and go in procession; for þei be called Rogacion dayes of prayer. **1480** CAXTON *Chron. Eng.* (1520) v. 58 b/1 In his tyme were the Rogacyon dayes ordeyned. **1503** in *Trans. Roy. Hist. Soc.* (1902) 152 So was it..ether yn the Rogacion dayes or a litill befor. **1563** FOXE *A. & M.* 476 b, I wold..that you would but once search and set out the first origin of these Rogation days. **1611** COTGR., *Rogations*, Rogation dayes, the Rogation weeke. **1728** CHAMBERS *Cycl.* s.v., The Monday, Tuesday, and Wednesday, call'd Rogations, or Rogation Days. **1812** J. BRADY *Clavis Cal.* I. 335 So early as the year 550, Claudius Mumertus..extended the object of the Rogation days. **1882** *Encycl. Brit.* XIV. 696/1 The three days before Ascension.. are still known in the English Church as Rogation Days.

(*b*) **1530** PALSGR. 263/2 Rogation weke, *la sepmaine des rouaisons*. **1535** WRIOTHESLEY *Chron.* (Camden) I. 27 The 4th day of May followinge, being Tewsday in the Rogation week. **1599** NASHE *Lenten Stuffe* 30 Lent might be cleane spung'd out of the Kalender, with Rogation weeks. **1634** CANNE *Necess. Separ.* (1849) 123 The observation of Gangdays, or rogation week, is wholly popish. **1672** MARVELL *Reh. Transp.* II. 186 You that do, as if it were in Rogation week, perambulate the Bounds of government. **1725** BOURNE in Brand *Pop. Antiq.* (1777) xxvi. 264 The Litanies or Rogations, which..gave Name to the Time of Rogation-Week. **1812** J. BRADY *Clavis Cal.* I. 336 The whole week in which these days happen is styled Rogation week. **1826** DIGBY *Broadstone Hon.* (1846) II. 364 Cross-flower, or rogation-flower,..was carried in the processions of rogation week.

(*c*) **1662** *Bk. Com. Prayer, Tables*, etc., Rogation-Sunday is five weeks after Easter. **1681** WHARTON *Facts & Fest.* Wks. (1683) 20 This is also called Rogation Sunday and the week following Rogation Week. **1725** BOURNE in Brand *Pop. Antiq.* (1777) xxvi. 267 The particular Office order'd by our Church for Rogation-Sunday. **1841** HAMPSON *Medii Ævi Cal.* II. 339 The 1st of the Rogations, April 26, is the first day on which Rogation Sunday can fall. **1872** SHIPLEY *Eccl. Terms*, Rogation Sunday, the Sunday before Ascension day.

c. ***rogation flower***, the milkwort (*Polygala vulgaris*), formerly made into garlands and carried in processions on Rogation days.

1597 GERARDE *Herbal* 450 Milke woort..in English we may cal it Crosse flower, Gang flower, Rogation flower. **1826** DIGBY *Broadstone Hon.* (1846) II. 364 Cross-flower, or rogation-flower, [blooms] about the 3rd of May. **1890** *Sarum Dioc. Gaz.* Jan. 6/1 To make 'Good Friday' and 'Rogation Flower' fit guides to the search for early blossoms of Tuberous Moschatel and Milkwort.

†**d.** *transf.* Supplication for alms; begging. Also punningly, with allusion to 'rogue'. *Obs.*

c **1540** COPLAND *Hye Way to Spyttel Ho.* 425 And so they lewter in suche rogacyons Seven or eyght yeres, walkyng theyr stacyons, And do but gull, and folow beggery. **1607** MIDDLETON *Fam. Love* I. iii, *Gud.* How is't? methinks thou hast been a long vagrant. *Lip.* The rogation hath been long indeed.

2. *Rom. Antiq.* The act, on the part of a consul or tribune, of submitting a proposed law to the people for their acceptance; also, a law so submitted and accepted.

1432–50 tr. *Higden* (Rolls) IV. 155 Graccus desirede those possessiones to be restorede to the peple in a day of Rogacion, when thynges to be restorede awede to be askede. **1533** BELLENDEN *Livy* III. xviii. (S.T.S.) II. 21 Be þis law wes gevin ane scharp brod to þe rogatioun of tribunis. *a* **1577** SIR T. SMITH *Commw. Eng.* I. vii. (1609) 7 The Emperors claime this tyrannical power by pretence of that Rogation or *Plebiscitum* which Caius Caesar or Octauius obtained. **1653** [F. PHILLIPS] *Consid. Crt. Chancery* 2 The Romans..in the Rogation and promulgation of their Laws. **1728** CHAMBERS *Cycl.* s.v. *Rogatio*, Frequently, also, Rogation is used in the same Sense with Law; because there never was any Law established among the Romans, but what was done by this kind of Rogation. **1774** DE LOLME *Constit. Eng.* II. xv. 325 The Tribunes..insisting that the Tribes should vote on their three rogations. **1853** MERIVALE *Fall Rom. Rep.* I. i. 28 Still more were they alarmed when he proposed and carried a rogation for the foundation of ample colonies. **1872** E. W. ROBERTSON *Hist. Ess.* 261 The era before the Rogations of Licinius became law.

†**3.** A formal request. *Obs.*

1603 JAS. I *True Law Free Mon.* Wks. (1616) 202 In the Parliament..the lawes are but craued by his subiects, and onely made by him at their rogation. **1647** DIGGES *Unlawf. taking up Arms* 140 Their rogation must precede His ratification. **1680** FILMER *Patriarcha* iii. §15 In Parliament all Statutes or Laws are made properly by the King alone, at the Rogation of the people.

Hence **ro'gational** *a.* (See quot.)

1872 SHIPLEY *Eccl. Terms*, *Rogational Antiphons*, antiphons used at Rogation-tide, or in connexion with litanies.

Rogatist ('rəʊgətɪst). [See ROGATIAN.] A member or adherent of a certain Donatist sect.

1565 T. STAPLETON *Fort. Faith* 26* Then we shoulde passe to the Rogatistes for the Church. **1656** BLOUNT *Glossogr.*, *Circumcelians*, the rigid sort of Donatists, as the Rogatists were the moderate. **1874** BLOUNT *Dict. Sects* 133/1 The party of Rogatists inclined to moderation. **1893** *Dubl. Rev.* Apr. 399 [St. Augustine] writing to Vincent the Rogatist.

'rogative. *rare*$^{-1}$. [ad. Sp. *rogativa*.] A prayer or supplication.

1882 *Christian World* Sept. 266 Sermons preached against the evangelicals during the rogatives for rain.

'rogatory, *a. rare.* [ad. F. *rogatoire*, ad. med.L. *rogatorius*: cf. *interrogatory*.] (See quots.)

1843–56 BOUVIER *Law Dict. U.S.*, *Rogatory, Letters*, a kind of commission from a judge authorizing and requesting a judge of another jurisdiction to examine a witness. **1874** WOOLSEY *Introd. Intern. Law* (ed. 4) §76 Many countries aid one another's judicial proceedings by consenting that their judges may accept rogatory commissions, or act as agents of foreign courts, for the purpose of examining witnesses or otherwise ascertaining facts.

†**roge**. *Obs.*$^{-1}$ [ad. L. *rogus*.] A pyre.

1661 HICKERINGILL *Jamaica* 76 Then if he have a Slave, he then must die; And the same Roge burn both.

roge, see ROG *sb.*; obs. form of ROGUE.

†**'roger**, *sb.*[1] *Obs. rare.* [An early canting word. The *g* was probably hard (cf. *rogacyons* s.v. ROGATION 1 d), so that *roger* may be connected with *rogue*.]

A begging vagabond who pretended to be a poor scholar from Oxford or Cambridge.

c **1540** COPLAND *Hye Way to Spyttel Ho.* 391 Cometh not this way Of these rogers, that dayly syng and pray, With *Ave Regina*, or *de profundis*? *Ibid.* 413 There is another company Of the same sect,..To whom these rogers obey as capytayns.

Roger ('rɒdʒə(r)), *sb.*[2] [A personal name of men, a. OF. *Roger*, *Rogier*, of Teut. origin, = OHG. *Ruodegêr*, *Hrôdgêr*.]

1. Used as a generic or special name for persons.

1631 WEEVER *Anc. Funeral Mon.* 75 The seruant obeyed, and (like a good trustie Roger) performed his Masters commandement. **1725** *New Cant. Dict.*, *Roger*,..likewise a Thief-taker. *Ibid.*, *Old Roger*, the Devil. **1885** *Pudsey Olm.* 19 (E.D.D.), T' next customer wor a roger.

2. †**a.** *Cant.* A goose. *Obs.*

1567 HARMAN *Caveat* (1869) 83 A Roger, or tyb of the buttery, a Goose. **1622** FLETCHER *Beggar's Bush* v. i, Surprizing a Boors ken, for grunting cheats! *Prig.* Or cackling Cheats? *Hig.* Or Mergery-praters, Rogers, and Tibs o' th' Buttery?

b. A ram. *rare*$^{-1}$.

1762 E. COLLINS *Misc.* 116 The Ram first wore that very Coat of thine. Shou'd Roger's Cast-off make thee proud or fine? [*note.* The Ram is by the Shepherd so call'd.]

3. *slang.* **a.** (See quot. *a* 1700.)

Quot. 1653 seems to be a ghost.

1653 URQUHART *Rabelais* I. xi. *a* **1700** B. E. *Dict. Cant. Crew*, *Roger*,..a Man's Yard. **1719** D'URFEY *Pills* VI. 201. **1720** D'URFEY *Pills* VI. 201 Here's a Health to the Queen, let's Bumpers take in hand, And may Prince G——'s Roger grow stiff again and stand. *c* **1800** BURNS in *Merry Muses of Caledonia* (1959) 147 Bonie lassie, braw lassie, Will ye hae a soger? Then she took up her duddie sark, An' he shot in his Roger. *c* **1863** 'PHILO CUNNUS' *Festival of Passions* II. 25 With my right hand, I grasped my flaming Roger.

†**b.** A portmanteau. *Obs.*

a **1700** B. E. *Dict. Cant. Crew.*

4. ***the Jolly Roger***, the pirate's flag.

1785 GROSE *Dict. Vulgar T.* s.v. *Roger, Jolly roger*, a flag hoisted by pirates. **1867** SMYTH *Sailor's Word-bk., Jolly Roger*, a pirate's flag; a white skull in a black field. **1883** STEVENSON *Treas. Isl.* IV. xix, There was the Jolly Roger—the black flag of piracy—flying from her peak. **1892** *Daily News* 16 June 5/1 It was also pirated at once..by an American publishing company. The author was popular enough to be worth flying the Jolly Roger for.

5. *E. Anglia.* = ROGER'S BLAST.

1893 in Cozens-Hardy *Broad Norf.* 12 Whenever I have heard the Broadland sirocco spoken of it has always been as 'Sir Rodger'. **1895** PATTERSON *Man & Nat.* 67 A sudden squall, a regular 'Roger',..strikes us; and heavy rain drops down from an overcast sky. **1899** *East Anglian* Ser. III. VIII. 127 'Roger's Blast.'.. At and around Hadleigh, Suff., it is called 'a Roger'.

6. Also with small initial. As *int.* Used to represent the letter *r* (= received) in radio transmission (see quot. 1947). Also *transf.* in general use, an expression of affirmation.

1941 *Amer. Speech* XVI. 168/1 *Roger!* Expression used instead of *okay* or *right.* (Air Corps). **1943** *Signal Training (All Arms): Signal Procedure* I. 9 *Roger*, used to mean 'message received'. **1945** *Sun* (Baltimore) 25 Jan. 9 Sometimes a voice called, 'Flak.' Once I heard one pilot say, 'Are you hit?' The reply was, 'Roger, I am hit. Going home.' **1947** *Amer. Speech* XXII. 110 In radio procedure the letter R, or *roger*, possesses the code designations 'received', or 'I have received your message', when signalled by the station addressed... Nevertheless, since radio operators or pilots signalling *roger* are receipting for a message, it has also come to mean unofficially 'O.K.' or 'I understand'. **1954** J. MASTERS *Bhowani Junction* xix. 170, I heard the duty officer on the R/T: 'Dogfish Six speaking... Roger, over.' **1960** *Sunday Express* 18 Sept. 1/3 If he wanted to speak to you he would ask you to go in. Roger? **1963** D. IRVING *Destruction of Dresden* III. ii. 132 'Tell the aircraft in top height band to come down below the medium cloud.' 'Roger.' **1971** D. HASTON in C. Bonington *Annapurna South Face* xvii. 210 At first it had been a chore to use them [*sc.* radios] and the jargon of Roger, Over, etcetera, had seemed artificial, but sitting in the specific loneliness of Camp VI it was a good feeling to communicate with others.

roger (ˈrɒdʒə(r)), *v.*[1] *slang.* Also **rodger.** [f. ROGER[2].] *trans.* To copulate with (a woman); to have sexual intercourse with. Also *absol.* Hence ˈ**rogering** *vbl. sb.* and *ppl. a.*

1711 W. BYRD *Secret Diary* 26 Dec. (1941) 459, I rogered my wife. *c* **1750** A. ROBERTSON *Poems* 98 Dear sweet Mr. Wright..Go rodger to-night Your Wife, for ye want her. **1763** BOSWELL *Jrnl.* 4 June in *London Jrnl.* (1950) 273, I picked up a little profligate wretch and gave her sixpence... 'Should not a half-pay officer r-g-r for sixpence?' **1771** [see RAGMATICAL *a.*]. **1870** *Cythera's Hymnal* 81 He rogered the National School. **1884** tr. *Abishag* in *Old Man Young Again* (1898) I. 36, I gave Mrs. P—— a really good rogering, and sent her to sleep perfectly contented. **1919** E. POUND *Sel. Lett.* (1971) 150 If I were, however, a professor of Latin in Chicago, I should probably have to resign on divulging the fact that Propertius occasionally copulavit, i.e. rogered the lady to whom he was not legally wedded. **1931** E. WAUGH *Diary* 14 Jan. (1976) 347 He got very drunk and brought a sluttish girl back to the house. He woke me up later in night to tell me he had rogered her and her mama too. **1942** E. PAUL *Narrow St.* xvi. 116 When Rudolph Valentino died... 'Hey, American,' yelled Madame Absalom... 'What did that *type* have that other men have not? He must have rogered half the women in your country?' **1953** *Landfall* Sept. 179 You black-mouth, you night bird, you rogering swine. **1953** DYLAN THOMAS *Let.* 22 June (1966) 409, I..sulked all morning over my warm beer as they..rolled rodgering down. **1961** A. WILSON *Old Men at Zoo* i. 54 I'm not at all sure about the Empress Theodora. I fancy she was rogered by an ape more than once in her circus acts. **1967** D. PINNER *Ritual* xvii. 167 He singed the rogering labourers... It took minutes before fornication subsided. **1972** 'R. GORDON' *Doctor on Brain* xxiii. 168 'Who is the father of the child?' 'The man who rodgered her, of course.' **1976** K. BONFIGLIOLI *Something Nasty in Woodshed* iii. 32 You won't catch him... The bloke who rogered Mrs Breakspear.

roger (ˈrɒdʒə(r)), *v.*[2] *U.S.* [f. ROGER[2] 6.] *trans.* To acknowledge (a message, etc.) as received.

1962 J. GLENN in *Into Orbit* 195 Both of these readings were within limits and I rogered the message. **1977** J. WAMBAUGH *Black Marble* (1978) vi. 83 'We just got a call,' he said. 'Roger it, please.'

Roger de Coverley (ˈrɒdʒə diː ˈkʌvəlɪ). [In early use *Roger of Coverly*: the later form is due to Addison's introduction of Sir Roger de Coverly (afterwards Coverley) in the *Spectator*.

Acc. to Ralph Thoresby the place-name is the same as Calverley in Yorkshire (see *Notes & Queries* I. 369), a statement which is perhaps supported by the occurrence of 'O brave Roger of Cauverly' as the refrain of a song in D'Urfey's *Pills* (1719) VI. 31.]

An English country-dance (and tune). Also used with the prefix *Sir*, and abbreviated as *Sir Roger.*

1685 PLAYFORD *Division Violin* C, Roger of Coverly [name of tune]. **1696** *Dancing Master* (1716) 167 Roger of Coverly. **1698** FRYER *Acc. E. India & P.* 111 [They] dance so many hours to a Tune called the Patamars Tune, when they labour as much as a Lancashire Man does at Roger of Coverly. *c* **1700** in W. Chappell *Pop. Music Olden Time* 534 Old Roger of Coverlay for evermore, a Lancashire Hornpipe. **1804** H. WYNNE *Diary* 19 Dec. (1940) III. v. 147 We danced Sir Roger de Coverly. **1811** T. WILSON *Country Dances* (ed. 2) 88 Sir Roger de Coverley, or the Finishing Dance. **1860** MOTLEY *Let. to Mother* 28 Oct., Reels and flings, and strathspeys and Roger de Coverleys. **1874** *Ball-Room Guide* 80 Any *contre danse*..answers this purpose; but the prime favourite is Sir Roger de Coverley. **1875** L. TROUBRIDGE *Life amongst Troubridges* (1966) x. 101, I danced every dance except Sir Roger, at the end. **1894** *19th Cent.* XXXVI. 430 The performers ranged themselves in two rows, as in Sir Roger.

Rogerene (ˈrɒdʒəriːn). *U.S.* [f. the name *Rogers* (see below) + *-ene* as in NAZARENE *a.* and *sb.*] A member of a small religious sect founded by John *Rogers* (1648–1721) in Connecticut, opposed to some of the formal practices of churches and participation in military service. Also *attrib.* in ***Rogerene Quaker.***

1754 J. HEMPSTEAD *Diary* 17 Mar. in *Coll. New London Co. Hist. Soc.* (1901) I, A Company of the Rogerens..held their meeting after our meeting was over. **1820** *Niles' Reg.* 22 July 366/1 A contagious disorder is now raging among the sect known by the name of Rogereen Quakers in Grotan. **1865** *Harper's Mag.* May 812/2 In the year 1720 a sect arose in New London, Connecticut, called, from their leader, 'Rogerenes'. **1865** *Massachusetts Hist. Soc. Coll.* VII. 584 John, the third son of James Rogers, of New London, and the founder of the sect of Rogerenes, of whom a small number still remain in that vicinity. **1931** *Times Lit. Suppl.* 6 Aug. 602/3 The Shakers, the Christadelphians and the Rogerenes are other sects. **1943** *New England Q.* Mar. 3 On a wooded hill above Mystic, Connecticut, live the remnants of a little-known religious sect called the Rogerenes, or sometimes Rogerene Quakers.

†**Roˈgerian.** *Obs.*$^{-1}$ [? f. the name *Roger.*] Some form of wig.

1597 HALL *Sat.* III. v, The sportfull winde, to mocke the headlesse man, Tosses apace his pitch'd Rogerian.

Roger's blast. *E. Anglian.* [Evidently a survival of Lydgate's RODION, with assimilation to the personal name.] (See quot. *a* 1825, and cf. RODGES-BLAST and ROGER[2] 5.)

a **1825** FORBY *Voc. E. Anglia, Roger's-blast*, a sudden and local motion of the air,..whirling up the dust..somewhat in the manner of a water-spout. It is reckoned a sign of approaching rain. **1866** *East Anglian* II. 64 When the fresh-waterman sees the waving of the reeds and sedges by the river-side, he knows a 'Roger's blast' is coming, which may hurl himself and his craft to the bottom. **1893** COZENS-HARDY *Broad Norf.* 95 These heavy gusts of wind were called Sir Roger's blasts.

Roget (ˈrɒʒeɪ). The name of Peter Mark *Roget* (1779–1869), English physician and philologist, used *absol.* with reference to his *Thesaurus of English Words and Phrases*, a catalogue of synonyms first published in 1852. Also in *Comb.*

1940 *Times* 19 Apr. 7/4 To journalists and other writers, weary of racking their brains or raking the well-thumbed pages of Roget in search of alternatives, the word 'Quisling' is a gift from the gods. **1955** E. BLISHEN *Roaring Boys* III. 152 Charles was like some oral Roget, uttering long lists of horrid synonyms. **1962** L. DEIGHTON *Ipcress File* xiii. 75 A few books remained on the shelves, a *Roget*, a business directory..and a *Chambers's Dictionary.* **1970** D. L. EMBLEN *P. M. Roget* xv. 276 Again and again, letters to *The Times* and other papers call upon other writers..to consult their 'Roget' before making such execrable use of the language. **1973** M. AMIS *Rachel Papers* 113 So ended my short, derivative, *Roget*-roughaged essay, complete with stage-directions.

roget(t, obs. ff. ROCHET *sb.*[2]

rogg(e, obs. variants of RUG *v.*

rogged, obs. f. RUGGED *a.*

roggery, obs. f. ROGUERY.

ˈ**roggle,** *v.* Now *dial.* [f. ROG *v.* + -LE.] To shake, or cause to shake.

1398 TREVISA *Barth. De P.R.* XI. xiii. (Bodl. MS.), þat makeþ and sowneþ somdele, as it were in þe manere of roggeling and hurlinge. **1811** [see ROG *v.* 1]. **1829–** in northern dial. glossaries.

rogh(e, roghlich, obs. ff. ROUGH *a.*, ROUGHLY *adv.*

roght, obs. pa. t. RECK *v.*; obs. form of ROUGH *a.*

roghtless, obs. f. RUTHLESS *a.*

roging, obs. f. ROGUING.

†ˈ**rogitate,** *v.*; **rogiˈtation.** *Obs.*$^{-0}$ [ad. L. *rogitāre, rogitātio.*] (See quots.)

1656 BLOUNT *Glossogr., Rogitate*,..to bid, to intreat, to require often, to beg. **1658** PHILLIPS, *Rogitation*, an asking often, an intreating earnestly.

‖**rognon** (rɔɲɔ̃). [Fr.] **1.** Chiefly *pl.* In Gastronomy, (a dish of) kidneys. Also *attrib.* and *Comb.*

1828 LYTTON *Pelham* I. xii. 79 What cook *can* possibly respect men who..eat *rognons* at dinner instead of at breakfast. *c* **1864** S. O. BEETON in N. Spain *Mrs. Beeton* (1948) II. vi. 212 Everybody had just well breakfasted upon cotelletes, omelettes, Rognons. **1877** C. READE *Woman-Hater* I. v. 97 After the *rognons à la brochette*, and a bottle of champagne, he let out. **1923** A. HUXLEY *Antic Hay* iv. 61 'And where are my *rognons sautés*?' he shouted at the waiter. **1967** A. WILSON *No Laughing Matter* iii. 337 She..cooked specially for him as she had not done for ages, rognons Bercy and omelette confiture. **1972** *Guardian* 11 Mar. 15/3 [The] Brasserie du Nord..is noted..for its *saucisson* and *rognon* dishes. **1979** *Times* 15 Dec. 6/6 My mother followed the sun. .. She lay down..darkening like *rognons* on a spit.

2. *Mountaineering.* A rounded outcrop of rock or stones surrounded by a glacier or an ice-field.

1935 S. SPENCER *Mountaineering* 364 *Rognon*, rounded rock in the centre of a glacier. **1957** R. G. COLLOMB *Dict. Mountaineering* 127 In Victorian days some *rognons* were used as sleeping places.., e.g. the Stöckje on the Scheonbuhl [*sic*] glacier near Zermatt. **1958** *Jrnl. Glaciology* III. 264 On the upper parts of the Glaciar Universidad there had been little change. After 1945 the surface sank slightly around a *rognon* (rounded nunatak) at 3930 m. **1963** *Oxford Mountaineering* 11 At the top of the rognon the snow steepened and we had to traverse up and round to the foot of the..couloir which leads on to the face. **1973** C. BONINGTON *Next Horizon* xxi. 279 Our way lay across the glacier and up a rognon, a sort of island of rocks round which the glacier flowed on either side.

†**rogorous,** *a.* *Obs.*$^{-1}$? Roguish.

1609 *Ev. Wom. in Hum.* D iv b, Alas good hearts, what rogorous villaine would commit with him?

rogue (rəʊg), *sb.* Also 6 rog, rogge, rooge, 6–7 roog, roge, roag(e, roague. [One of the numerous canting words introduced about the middle of the 16th cent. to designate the various kinds of beggars and vagabonds, and perhaps in some way related to ROGER *sb.*[1] There is no evidence of connexion with F. *rogue* arrogant.]

1. a. One belonging to a class of idle vagrants or vagabonds. Now *arch.* as a legal term.

For the legal definition, see the Act 14 Eliz. c. 5 §5.

α. **1561** [see b]. **1567** HARMAN *Caveat* (1869) 36 A Roge is neither so stoute or hardy as the vpright man. **1570** GOOGE *Pop. Kingd.* 56 Both jeasters, Roges and Minstrels with their instruments are heare. **1590** SIR J. SMYTH *Disc. Weapons* Ded. 8 Some of them bare legged, or bare footed like roges. *Ibid.* 11 b, The very scomme, theeues, and roges of England.

β. **1577** *Bullinger's Decades* (1592) 129 The sturdie roag vnworthie of an almes. **1587** *Mirr. Mag., Sabrina* x, The rascall rude, the roag, the clubfist griepte My sclender arme. **1600** J. PORY tr. *Leo's Africa* III. 153 These lewd miscreants run like roagues naked and sauage throughout all Africa. **1600** BRETON *Pasquil's Madcappe* Wks. (Grosart) I. 6/1 He shall..in a iacket and a paire of broages Goe passe among the company of roages.

γ. **1591** SPENSER *M. Hubberd* 187 Wildly to wander.. Withouten pasport or good warrantye, For feare least we like rogues should be reputed. **1605** SHAKS. *Lear* IV. vii. 39 And was't thou faine..To houell thee with Swine and Rogues forlorne, In short, and musty straw? *a* **1661** FULLER *Worthies* (1840) III. 335 The anti-friarists maintaining, that such [begging friars] were rogues by the laws of God and man. **1731–8** SWIFT *Pol. Conv.* 62 Ay, a rich Rogue, two Shirts and a Rag. **1764** BURN *Poor Laws* 125 The vagrant acts of late years have distinguished the offenders into three kinds; 'idle and disorderly persons, rogues and vagabonds, and incorrigible rogues'. **1824** *Act 5 Geo. IV*, c. 83 §8. **1838** *Act 1 & 2 Vict.* c. 38 (*title*), An Act to amend an Act for punishing idle and disorderly Persons and Rogues and Vagabonds.

†**b.** ***wild rogue***: (see quots.). *Obs.*

1561 AWDELAY *Frat. Vacab.* (1869) 5 A wilde Roge is he that hath no abiding place.., and all that be of hys corporation be properly called Roges. **1567** HARMAN *Caveat* (1869) 41 A wilde Roge is he that is borne a Roge: he is more subtil and more geuen by nature to all kinde of knauery than the other. **1608** DEKKER *Belman of London* Wks. (Grosart) III. 97 The Tame Rogue begets a Wilde-Rogue. **1673** R. HEAD *Canting Acad.* 70 *Wild Rogues* were formerly such who were begotten by very Rogues, such who had been burnt in the hand or shoulder, or..whipt at the Carts arse.

2. a. A dishonest, unprincipled person; a rascal.

1578 LYTE *Dodoens* 143 Certayne deceytfull and naughtie rogues that would be taken for cunning physitions. **1592** *Arden of Feversham* II. i. 5 Such a slaue, so vile a roge as he, Lyues not againe vppon the earth. **1605** *First Pt. Jeronimo* I. vi. 49 My Lord, he is the most notorious rogue That euer breathed. **1680** PRIDEAUX *Lett.* (Camden) 81 Those rogues have designes goeing on, but if the King will but put on a little rigour he may easyly quel them. **1768–74** TUCKER *Lt. Nat.* (1834) II. 53 It is a common saying, that you must set a rogue to catch a rogue. **1792** ALMON *Aneсd. W. Pitt* II. xxii. 28 The Duke of Newcastle said: Fox was rogue enough to do any thing, but..not fool enough to do this. **1814** EARL DUDLEY *Lett.* (1840) 34 Talleyrand, to be sure, is a rogue; but he is a rogue of long experience. **1858** O. W. HOLMES *Aut. Breakf.-t.* xii, He who is carried by horses must deal with rogues. **1888** BRYCE *Amer. Commw.* li. (1889) I. 619 The newer frames of government are an improvement upon the older. Rogues are less audacious.

transf. **1904** MAX PEMBERTON *Red Morn* xi, A rogue of a ship and a drunken man in charge of her.

†**b.** Applied abusively to servants. *Obs.*

1596 SHAKS. *Tam. Shr.* IV. i. 150 Off with my boots, you rogues: you villaines, when?.. Out you rogue, you plucke my foot awrie. **1701** CIBBER *Love Makes Man* II. i, What, will none of my Rogues come near me now? O! here they are. [*Enter several Servants.*] **1713** STEELE *Englishm.* No. 1. 8 My Lord, your Rogue has me safe here. **1781** COWPER *Conversat.* 415 Yet ev'n the rogue that serves him..Prefers his fellow-grooms.

†**c.** (See quot.) *Obs.*

1688 HOLME *Armoury* III. xiv. (Roxb.) 2/1 He beareth sable, a chamber pot... There is nothing neuer so vsefull, but it may be abused, so is this when it is called..a Rogue with one eare.

d. ***rogue and villain***: rhyming slang for 'shilling'.

1859 HOTTEN *Dict. Slang* 145 *Rogue and villain*, a shillin, —common pronunciation of shilling. **1877** J. W. HORSLEY *Jottings from Jail* i. 3 Come, cows and kisses, put the battle of the Nile on your Barnet Fair, and a rogue and villain in your sky-rocket. **1965** *Australasian Post* 4 Mar. 46 *Shilling.* .. Sometimes known in rhyming slang as a 'rogue and villain'. **1973** B. AYLWIN *Load of Cockney Cobblers* xiv. 62 *Rogue & villain*, shilling.

3. One who is of a mischievous disposition.

Common as a playful term of reproof or reproach, and freq. used as a term of endearment by 17th c. dramatists.

1597 SHAKS. *2 Hen. IV*, II. iv. 233 Ah, you sweet little Rogue, you: alas, poore Ape. *Ibid.* 235 Ah Rogue, I loue thee. **1602** *2nd Pt. Return fr. Parnass.* II. vi. 1025, I shall be his little rogue, and his white villaine for a whole week after. **1672** VILLIERS (Dk. Buckhm.) *Rehearsal* I. i, I, it's a pretty little rogue; she is my Mistress. I knew her face would set off Armor extreamly. *a* **1744** POPE *Hor. Sat.* I. vii. 27 What? rob your Boys? those pretty rogues! **1784** J. POTTER *Virtuous Villagers* I. 161 It is evident, that sly rogue Cupid has pierced your heart with one of his keenest arrows. **1807–8** W. IRVING *Salmagundi* (1824) 369 The very negroes, those holiday-loving rogues, gorgeously arrayed in cast off finery. **1832** L. HUNT *Poems* 185 Fondled by the ladies, With 'What a young rogue this is!'

4. *Hort.* An inferior plant among seedlings.

1859 DARWIN *Orig. Spec.* i. (1860) 32 The seed-raisers.. go over their seed-beds, and pull up the 'rogues', as they call the plants that deviate from the proper standard. **1868** —— *Anim. & Pl.* II. 31 If gardeners did not generally.. pull up the false plants or 'rogues' as they are called.

5. a. An elephant driven away, or living apart, from the herd, and of a savage or destructive disposition. Also *fig.*

A rendering of Cingalese *hora, sora* = Skr. *chōra* thief.

1859 TENNENT *Ceylon* II. VIII. iii. 327 The outcasts from the herd, the 'Rogues' or *hora allia*;.. there is not probably one rogue to be found for every five hundred of those in herds. **1885** H. O. FORBES *E. Archipel.* 164 We had at length the satisfaction of feeling that.. no elephant, unless a rogue, would trample us down. **1886** P. ROBINSON *Teetotum Trees* 55 Killing a rogue.. now falls into the same category as any other act of public justice.

attrib. **1859** *All Year Round* No. 32. 131 The rogue elephants haunt and destroy plantations. **1885** G. S. FORBES *Wild Life in Canara* 167 A friend of mine travelling.. along this road had a very hazardous meeting with a rogue elephant. **1963** *Times Lit. Suppl.* 18 Jan. 44/3 His role is that of the *advocatus diaboli* rather than the rogue elephant. **1978** K. GREGORY *First Cuckoo* 21 The nation's rogue elephants rampage, shattering complacency and compelling many to an agonizing reappraisal.

b. Any large wild animal of a similar character. Also *attrib.* Also *fig.*

1872 R. F. BURTON *Zanzibar* II. 244 The 'rogue'.. is found amongst hippopotami, elk, deer and other gramnivors as well as amongst elephants, lions, tigers, and the larger carnivors. *Ibid.*, The 'rogue' hippopotamus is an old male no longer able to hold his own against the young adults. **1892** *Spectator* 10 Sept. 349 The ferocity of the 'rogue' buffalo and 'rogue' hippopotamus. **1926** J. MASEFIELD *Odtaa* x. 171 He roused up as a big, elderly rogue-bull of a man.. came in. **1939** G. HOUSEHOLD (*title*) Rogue male. **1977** N. ADAM *Triplehip Cracksman* v. 56 I wasn't sure I liked myself.. rogue male acting instinctively, obeying the territorial imperative.

6. A horse which is inclined to shirk its work on the race-course or in the hunting field. ***rogue's badge***, a hood or blinkers put on a race-horse of this description.

1881 *Standard* 29 Aug. 5/3 Gentle breaking, on the other hand, may.. prevent a racehorse from becoming a 'rogue' or a 'savage'. **1884** *Pall Mall G.* 7 June 4/1 A description of a 'rogue' thoroughbred. *Ibid.*, The ordinary 'rogue' has become fainthearted through punishment of whip and spur in race or trial. **1891** *Lic. Vict. Gaz.* (Farmer), He wore the rogue's badge, but is built on racing lines.

7. *attrib.* or as *adj.* in general use, denoting: **a.** An inexplicably aberrant result or phenomenon; an extra or misplaced item in a list, table, etc.

1952 *Analyst* LXXVII. 171 With the exception of one rogue result, the present estimates are as concordant as can reasonably be expected. **1964** C. DENT *Quantity Surveying by Computer* iii. 30 A device enabling you to switch the machine to manual and continue using it as an ordinary typewriter is very useful if, for instance, you wish to insert a 'spot' item, or other 'rogue' item in the bill of quantities, at the last moment. **1972** *Physics Bull.* Oct. 611/1 The tables have been well produced and very few errors were detected. In the body of the table, only one rogue point was noticed. **1979** *Personal Computer World* Nov. 73/2 When the program detects the rogue value, this is an indication that the input list is complete and further processing can continue.

b. Something that is inexplicably faulty or defective.

1962 *Daily Tel.* 18 Jan. 12/7 Manufacturers are aware that 'rogue' and sub-standard cars are sold to the public. **1965** *New Statesman* 30 Apr. 665/2 A group of American bombers .. go rogue through a mechanical foul-up. **1971** *Atom* Apr. 99/1 Such differences are readily detectable and allow experimental fuel elements to be checked for rogue fuel pellets. **1974** *Guardian* 14 Mar. 9/2 His counsel.. told Mr Justice Phillips... 'You are familiar with the expression 'rogue car'. Well, this was rather like a rogue house.'

c. That which lacks appropriate control; something which is irresponsible or undisciplined.

1964 *Daily Tel.* 22 Feb. 14/6 Frequent complaints were made about a very small number of 'rogue' firms which belonged to neither the Association of British Travel Agents nor the Travel Trade Association. **1972** *Accountant* 19 Oct. 496/1 How is the ordinary man in the street to tell whether it has been calculated on the 'fair' basis as laid down by the legislation, or the unfair basis which will no doubt be perpetrated by a considerable number of rogue traders? **1979** *Daily Tel.* 4 Apr. 3 A housewife's game of patience came to an abrupt end when a 20-ton 'rogue' mechanical shovel begun crunching its way through the walls of her semi-detached home. **1981** *New Scientist* 29 Jan. 278/3 (*caption*) Gamma-ray bursts may come from collisions between rogue asteroids and neutron stars.

8. *attrib.* and *Comb.*, as ***rogue-catcher, -face, -hero, -land, -lawyer, -priest, Radical, -word***; ***rogue-eyed, -like*** *adjs.*; †**rogue-house** (see quot.); **rogue-pease** (?); **rogue-sapling**, a sapling of an inferior kind.

For *rogue elephant*, etc., see 5 and 5 b.

1630 DEKKER *2nd Pt. Honest Whore* I. i. Wks. 1873 II. 179 Hold, you *Rogue-Catcher, hold. **1869** R. WALTON *Midland Circuit* 142 The Bow Street Runners were never excelled as rogue-catchers by any other body of men. **1867** MEREDITH *Vittoria* I. ix. 133 She had, in tripping down the Piazza with her *rogue-eyed cousin from Milan, looked away [etc.]. **1697** VANBRUGH *Prov. Wife* v. iii, Stand off, *rogue-face. **1790** GROSE *Prov. Gloss.* (ed. 2) Suppl., **Rogue-House*, the house of correction. **1898** BESANT *Orange Girl* II. xx, This man had for years exercised absolute sway over *Rogueland. **1824** SCOTT *St. Ronan's* xviii, But the *rogue-lawyers.. have at length roundly told me the clause must be complied with. **1707** *Lond. Gaz.* No. 4357/4 At Ham.. are to be sold, Garden Beans, Gosport-Beans, *Rogue-Pease, and Hotspur-Pease. **1679** DRYDEN *Troil. & Cress.* III. ii, Thou must be gone, to the fugitive *rogue-priest, thy father. **1824** SCOTT in *Lockhart* (1839) V. 357 The *rogue Radicals had nearly set me on horseback again. **1889** PASK *Eyes Thames* 146 Apple standards laden with the light silky-skinned Manx codlins, sometimes broken by the rosy-red of an intruding '*rogue' sapling. **1922** JOYCE *Ulysses* 48 *Roguewords, tough nuggets patter in their pockets.

9. Special combs. with genitive, as **rogue's gallery**, a collection of the portraits of criminals; also *transf.* and *fig.*; **rogue's gilliflower**, the rocket (*Hesperis matronalis*); **rogue's Latin**, thieves' Latin (cf. LATIN B. 1 c); **rogue's march, tattoo, walk, yarn** (see quots.). Also ***rogue's badge*** (see 6).

1859 *Amer. Jrnl. Photogr.* II. 75 The *Rogues' Gallery is located at the police head quarters... The photographer is a regularly appointed policeman. **1889** *Boston* (Mass.) *Jrnl.* 24 Apr. 1/8 Their features adorn the rogues' galleries in the cities of the Union. **1904** [see PINK *sb.*[5]]. **1945** 'E. QUEEN' (*title*) Rogues' gallery. **1955** *Publ. Amer. Dial. Soc.* XXIV. 41 His [*sc.* a pickpocket's] face appears more frequently than any other type of criminal in 'rogue's galleries' and police files. **1959** *Listener* 26 Nov. 946/1 Mr. Klein's second collection of arch-deceivers, his new rogues' gallery, is fascinating. **1973** 'I. DRUMMOND' *Jaws of Watchdog* x. 133 His face was not recognised in the rogues' gallery, nor did his description tally with any known criminal. **1977** MCKNIGHT & TOBLER *Bob Marley* 10 Bob Dylan, Arthur Lee, Keith Richard, Bob Marley—the rogue's gallery of rebel input that forms the hard stuff at the centre of rock. **1578** LYTE *Dodoens* 153 These floures be now called.. in English Damaske violets.. and *Rogues gillofers. **1818** SCOTT *Hrt. Midl.* xxv, He knows my gybe as well as the jark of e'er a queer cuffin in England—and there's *rogue's Latin for you. **1802** JAMES *Milit. Dict.* s.v. *March*, **Rogue's March*, a tune which is played by trumpeters or fifers of a regiment ..for the purpose of drumming out any person who has behaved disorderly..in a camp or garrison. **1894** BLACKMORE *Perlycross* 81 To have him drummed out of the parish to the *rogue's tattoo. **1882** *Daily News* 11 Jan. 2/1 The *Rogues'-walk—that broad ribbon of pavement stretching from Piccadilly-circus past the Criterion Theatre and Restaurant to the top of the Haymarket. **1769** FALCONER *Dict. Marine* (1780), **Rogues-yarn*,.. a rope-yarn, of a particular construction,.. placed in the middle of every strand, in all cables and cordage in the king's service... The use of this contrivance is to examine whether any cordage, supposed to be stolen.., has been formed for the king's service. **1846** A. YOUNG *Naut. Dict.*, *Rogue's Yarn*, a thread of worsted in the strands of rope manufactured for the Royal Navy, introduced for the purpose of detecting theft or embezzlement:.. it serves also to trace any bad rope to the precise yard where it was made. **1867** SMYTH *Sailor's Word-bk.* 577 Lately the rogue's yarn has been superseded by a thread of worsted.

rogue (rəʊg), *v.* Also 6 ro(a)ge, 6–7 roague. [f. ROGUE *sb.*]

1. a. *intr.* To wander idly about after the manner of rogues; to live like a rogue or vagrant; also, in later use, to play the rogue or rascal.

Very common *c* 1575–1650; now *rare*.

α. **1570** LEVINS *Manip.* 157/47 To Roge, *vagari*. **1583** STUBBES *Anat. Abus.* II. (1882) 53 A sort of vagarants, who run stragling (I wil not saie roging) ouer the countries. **1589** ? LYLY *Pappe w. Hatchet* E ij b, Trusse vp thy packet of flim flams, & roage to some Countrey Faire. **1610** G. FLETCHER *Christ's Vict.* xiv, And in the midst, Strife still would roaguing be.

β. **1600** HOLLAND *Livy* VIII. xxxiv. 306 Without pasport, the souldiors may wander and rogue. **1656** *Burton's Diary* (1828) I. 21 You give them sixty miles compass to rogue in, which is more privilege than ever beggars enjoyed. **1667** PEPYS *Diary* 1 June, Which will be becoming him much more than to live wenching and roguing, as he now do. **1680** SHADWELL *Woman-Capt.* II, Where have you been roguing, Sirrah, that you did not wait on me home? **1702** *Burlesque R. L'Estrange's Vis. Quev.* 250 He's at the Playhouse roguing bin. **1755** JOHNSON *Rogue*, To play knavish tricks. **1896** KIPLING *Seven Seas* 190, I've rogued an' I've ranged in my time.

†**b.** So *to rogue it*. *Obs.*

1615 J. TAYLOR (Water-P.) *Fennor's Defence* Wks. (1630) II. 149 Although I cannot Rogue it, as he can, Yet will I shew myselfe an honest man. **1632** SHERWOOD, To rogue it vp and downe the countrie, *roder le pais*.

†**2. a.** *trans.* To denounce as a rogue, to call (one) a rogue; to accuse of roguery. *Obs.*

1630 J. TAYLOR (Water-P.) *Wks.* (Nares), It may bee thou wast put in office lately, Which makes thee rogue me so, and rayle so stately. **1683** T. HUNT *Def. Charter Lond.* 25 The Poet hath undertaken for their being kicked..about the Stage to the Gallows, infamously rogued and rascalled.

†**b.** To cast discredit on (something). *Obs.*

1678 CUDWORTH *Intell. Syst.* I. v. §32. 778 Though the Atheists may endeavour to rogue and ridicule all incorporeal substance in that manner. **1685** H. MORE *Refl. Baxter* 15 More like prophane Buffonry, to rogue and abuse so Sacred a Writing.

3. To practise roguery upon; to swindle.

1841 SUSANNA HAWKINS *Poems* V. 45 An' likewise rogue and cheat the poor, Who for their meat do labour sore. **1869** BLACKMORE *Lorna D.* lv, We have rogues to deal with: but try we not to rogue them. **1889** W. WESTALL *Birch Dene* II. xii. 201 If he helps me to rogue other folks, he'll help other folks to rogue me.

4. To free from inferior plants or seedlings. Also, to take *out* (inferior plants) from a crop.

1766 *Compl. Farmer* s.v. *Pease* 5 Z 1/1 The only way to prevent this, is to rogue them, as the gardeners term it, that is to say,.. to draw out all the bad plants from among the good ones. **1905** *Dundee Advertiser* 25 July 6 Of late agriculturists have had excellent opportunities for 'rogueing' their drills. **1965** *Sunday Mail Mag.* (Brisbane) 26 Sept. 15 Sometimes we speak of 'rogueing' a crop, which means taking out the plants which aren't typical of the variety or which have become diseased. **1967** *Sunday Times* 19 Feb. 31/4 Small flowered plants should be rogued out or not allowed to seed. **1978** *Country Life* 20 July 184/3 White foxgloves.. once established will seed themselves. If you keep roguing out any coloured throwbacks they could become a permanent feature.

'roguedom. [f. ROGUE *sb.*] The world of rogues; rogues collectively.

1889 EARL OF DESART *Little Chatelaine* II. xx, When you trust one rogue, you trust all roguedom.

'rogueling. [f. ROGUE *sb.*] A minor rogue.

1790 *Political Misc.* 32 Take notice, roguelings, I prohibit Your walking underneath yon gibbet.

†**rogue money.** *Sc.* and *north. Obs.* [ROGUE *sb.*] A tax formerly levied on a parish or county to provide a fund for the expenses of the apprehension, prosecution, and maintenance in gaol of rogues. Also *attrib.*

1585 *Vestry Bks.* (Surtees) 19 For our charges.. when we wer at the Querter Sessions concerninge the Rogge mony. **1640** *Ibid.* 102 Item for Roog mony, 1l. 4s. **1658** *Ibid.* 19 *note*, The Rogue money is a yearely payment due by this Parish at Midsommer, payable to the High Constable for prisoners in goale, correction, &c. **1750** in Lang *Highl. Scot.* (1898) 150 That to Answer the Expence of such prosecutions Rogue money be imposed upon the Respective Shires as usual. **1757** in *Stat. Law Scot. Abridg.* 335 Rogue-Money: see Delinquency. **1838** W. BELL *Dict. Law Scot.* 613 The sums so received form part of the rogue money of the county. **1862** *Act 25 & 26 Vict.* c. 35 §20 The proceeds of such sale shall be paid into the rogue money funds of the county.

roguer ('rəʊgə(r)). [f. ROGUE *v.* + -ER[1].] A person employed to identify and eliminate inferior plants in a crop, esp. of potatoes.

1945 T. WHITEHEAD et al. *Potato in Health & Dis.* (ed. 2) vii. 77 The roguer should remove or mark all plants which in any character differ substantially from the variety under consideration. **1960** *Times* 29 July 12/6 The roguer's job is to sample the crop for wrong varieties or disease. **1967** A. E. COX *Potato* vii. 157 The roguers working in pairs—one marking plants and the other lifting and carrying them off —should deal with only two drills at a time.

roguery ('rəʊgərɪ). [f. ROGUE *sb.* + -ERY.]

1. Conduct or practices characteristic of rogues; knavishness, rascality; †idle vagrancy.

1596 SHAKS. *1 Hen. IV*, II. iv. 138 Heere's Lime in this Sacke too: there is nothing but Roguery to be found in Villanous man. **1611** COTGR., *Maraudise*, beggerie, roguerie, idle knauerie,.. vagabondrie. **1660** F. BROOKE tr. *Le Blanc's Trav.* 97 Thus was discovered the roguerie of those Magitians. **1745** in Ellis *Orig. Lett.* Ser. II. IV. 356, I should have succeeded better, but for the folly and roguery of mankind. **1792** A. YOUNG *Trav. France* 225 There is a known and curious piece of roguery, against which much of this caution is bent. **1838** LYTTON *Alice* II. vii, My neglect of my own duties tempted you to roguery. **1875** JOWETT *Plato* (ed. 2) IV. 326 The unrighteous man.. had far better not yield to the illusion that his roguery is clever.

personif. **1794** SOUTHEY *Botany-Bay Ecl.* III, When Roguery rules all the rest of the earth, God be thank'd, in this corner I've got a good berth.

2. A practice, procedure, or action characteristic of rogues; a knavish or rascally act.

c **1620** DONNE *Poems* (1633) 48 To live in one land, is captivitie, To run all countries, a wild roguery. **1667–8** PEPYS *Diary* 8 Feb., The ripping up of so many notorious rogueries and cheats of my Lord's. **1722** DE FOE *Col. Jack* i, A constable and his watch, crying out for one Wry-neck, who it seems had done some roguery. **1797–1805** S. & HT. LEE *Canterb. T.* I. 212 He has been in more rogueries than battles, I believe. **1850** THACKERAY *Pendennis* v, There are worse men.. who have never committed half so many rogueries as he. **1879** BROWNING *Ned Bratts* 91 Not a single roguery, from the cutting of a purse to the cutting of a throat, but paid us toll.

3. Playful mischief; waggishness; fun.

1664 COTTON *Scarron.* I. Wks. (1715) 47 Cupid.. prepares him for his Roguery. **1681** WOOD *Life* 11 June, The other *Terræ Filius* made up what was wanting..; full of Waggery and Roguery, but little Wit. **1711** SWIFT *Lett.* (1767) III. 165 Lady Berkeley after dinner clapt my hat on another lady's head, and she in roguery put it upon the rails. **1755** JOHNSON, *Roguery*, waggery; arch tricks. *a* **1834** COLERIDGE *Shaks. Notes* (1875) 91 As a father speaks of the rogueries of a child. **1840** DICKENS *Barn. Rudge* ii, The smile of one expecting to detect in this unpromising stranger some latent roguery of eye or lip.

4. *collect.* Weeds. *rare.*

1763 *Museum Rust.* I. 33 Keep the land plowing the whole following summer,.. to keep down the roguery. **1764** *Ibid.* II. 8 A most excellent plant to sow where land is rich, and inclined to breed roguery.

5. A place in which persons are trained to become rogues.

1822 GALT *Sir A. Wylie* I. xxiii. 208 I kept a roguery for the supply of the London Market.

6. Rogues collectively; rascaldom.

1898 BESANT *Orange Girl* II. xxii, A thing at which all Roguery rejoiced.

rogueship ('rəʊgʃɪp). Also 7 **roagushipp.** [f. ROGUE *sb.*] The state of being a rogue, used as a mock title in 'your rogueship', etc.

?*c* **1600** *Distr. Emperor* II. i. in Bullen *Old Pl.* (1884) III. 194 It had beene better for your perjurd roagushipp, Your harte had gorgd a hauke. **1625** FLETCHER *Night-Walker* III. v, I would lose a limb to see their rogueships totter. **1709** MRS. CENTLIVRE *Gamester* v, What makes you look so, Sirrah? Ha! I suspect your rogueship has done something with it. **1797** BRYDGES *Hom. Trav.* I. 144 His rogueship from the flowers and trees Would call the very birds and bees.

roguing ('rəʊgɪŋ), *vbl. sb.* [f. ROGUE *v.*]

†**1.** The action of wandering about the country; tramping from one place to another as a rogue or vagrant; also, an instance of this. *Obs.*

1577 HARRISON *Descr. Brit.* III. v, For their idle roging about the countrie, the law ordeineth this maner of correction. *c* **1585** R. BROWNE *Answ. Cartwright* 3 Beyng children of Death, euen for smaller Theftes, Felonyes, Roginges, and Wanderinges. **1631** HEYLIN *St. George* 106 Here..he left off his roaguing, and began his Villanies. **1651** W. SHEPPARD *England's Balm* (1657) 28 The common offences of Swearing, Drunkenness,..Vagrancy or Roguing.

transf. **1681** OTWAY *Soldier's Fort.* II. i, Here's the ring you set a roguing.

2. Playing the rogue, knave, or rascal. †Also in phr. *to go a-roguing.*

1619 FLETCHER *Mons. Thomas* III. i, This was thy Roguing, For thou wert ever whispering; fye upon thee. **1697** VANBRUGH *Relapse* III. ii, You'll never leave roguing, I see that. **1706** ESTCOURT *Fair Example* II. ii, You are going a rogueing. **1719** DE FOE *Crusoe* II. (Globe) 546 Nothing else but the Hopes of going a Roguing brought him to do it.

3. *Hort.* The elimination of inferior plants.

1858 DARWIN in *Life & Lett.* (1887) II. 122 The 'roguing', as nursery-men call the destroying of varieties which depart from their type. **1859** —— *Orig. Species* i. (1860) 34 The destruction of horses under a certain size was ordered, and this may be compared to the 'roguing' of plants by nurserymen. **1968** *Punch* 18 Sept. 410/3 Any plants not true to type are removed by systematic 'roguing', which may account for a further ton per acre. **1978** HIDE & LAPWOOD in P. M. Harris *Potato Crop* xi. 432 Roguing (negative selection) and later multiplication from disease-free plants (positive selection) were used to improve the health of seed.

'roguing, *ppl. a.* [f. ROGUE *v.* + -ING².] Wandering, living, or acting like a rogue.

1581 HANMER *Jesuites Banner* cj b, I woulde..that you..sufred the roging Jesuites beyond the seas, to performe your vowes. *a* **1603** T. CARTWRIGHT *Confut. Rhem. N.T.* (1618) 75 You are found in that penury, that the rouing and roging stagers are. **1625** HART *Anat. Ur.* I. ii. 26 This base roguing and cozening Empiricke. **1672** MARVELL *Reh. Transp.* I. 53 Perhaps some roguing Boy that managed the Puppets, turned the City wrong.

fig. **1598** MARSTON *Sco. Villanie* II. v. 197 Faire age! When ..roguing vertue brings a man defame. *a* **1603** T. CARTWRIGHT *Confut. Rhem. N.T.* (1618) 610 This roguing sentence wee would haue suffered to wander still.

roguish ('rəʊgɪʃ), *a.* Also 6 **rogyshe,** 6–7 **rogish,** 6–8 **rogueish.** [f. ROGUE *sb.* + -ISH.]

1. Pertaining or appropriate to, characteristic of, rogues (†or vagrants); disreputable.

1572 *Act 14 Eliz.* c. 5 §4 Yf..they..do eftsones fall agaime to any kynde of Rogyshe or Vacabonde Trade of Lyef. **1592** GREENE *Black Bk.'s Messenger* Wks. (Grosart) XI. 17 So wee like two good Horse-corsers..swapt vp a Rogish bargaine. **1608** SHAKS. *Lear* III. vii. 104 (Q.²), Let's..get the bedlam To lead him where he would, his rogish madnesse Allowes it selfe to any thing. **1632** LITHGOW *Trav.* VIII. 360, I stayed in a Spaniards house..who kept a roguish Tauerne. **1667–8** PEPYS *Diary* 8 Feb., Bought an idle, rogueish French book, *L'escholle des filles.*

†**b.** Vile, wretched. *Obs.*⁻¹ (Cf. ROGUY *a.* 1.)

a **1625** BEAUM. & FL. *Love's Cure* II. ii, Lord how my head aches with this roguish hat.

2. Acting (†or wandering) like rogues; knavish or rascally in conduct.

1596 SPENSER *State Irel.* Wks. (Globe) 644/1 The persons, by whom it is used, be of better note then the former rogish sorte which ye reckned. **1641** HINDE *J. Bruen* lviii. 195 He abandoned and kept out of his house all roguish Players. **1687** A. LOVELL tr. *Thevenot's Trav.* I. 159 A great Noise of roguish Moors, both Men and little Boys. **1752** FIELDING *Amelia* XI. iii, A law very excellently calculated for the preservation of the lives of his Majesty's roguish subjects. **1798** *Anti-Jacobin* No. 2. 10 Or roguish lawyer, made you lose your little All in a lawsuit. **1828** P. CUNNINGHAM *N.S. Wales* (ed. 3) II. 207 As long..as England cannot keep her honest poor, so long will it be ner interest to turn all her roguish poor out from her bosom. **1863** *Confess. Ticket-of-Leave Man* 17 A roguish linen-draper..became bankrupt for £50,000.

3. Playfully mischievous; arch, waggish.

1681 DRYDEN *Span. Friar* I, The most bewitching leer with her Eyes, the most roguish Cast. **1712** ADDISON *Spect.* No. 269 ¶8 Will Wimble..shews a thousand roguish Tricks upon these Occasions. **1748** THOMSON *Cast. Indol.* I. xxv, The lad leap'd lightly at his master's call. He was, to weet, a little roguish page. **1781** BURNS *On Cessnock Banks* 4 Our lasses a' she far excels,—An' she has twa sparkling rogueish een. **1840** DICKENS *Old. C. Shop* xviii, Codlin..eyeing the landlord as with a roguish look he held the cover in his hand. **1886** SYMONDS *Renaiss. It.* (1898) VII. xiii. 223 He made himself a favourite by roguish ways and ready wit.

Comb. **1841** LEVER *C. O'Malley* x, With a sleek roguish-eyed priest.

4. Of plants: Inferior, degenerate.

1762 MILLS *Syst. Pract. Husb.* I. 472 There will always be, in every sort, some roguish plants, as the gardeners term them, which, if left to mix, will degenerate the kind.

roguishly ('rəʊgɪʃlɪ), *adv.* [f. prec. + -LY².] In a roguish manner; knavishly; mischievously.

1611 COTGR., *Meschamment,*..roguishly, knauishly, villanously. **1621** GRANGER *Expos. Eccles.* 303 His heir roguishly wasteth all, and is at last hanged. **1791** BOSWELL *Johnson* an. 1763 May 16, 'From Scotland,' cried Davies, roguishly. **1828** P. CUNNINGHAM *N.S. Wales* (ed. 3) II. 47 Nearly all the Currency criminals have, indeed, been furnished by three roguishly prolific families in the colony. **1863** GEO. ELIOT *Romola* i, A man of slim figure, whose eye twinkled rather roguishly.

roguishness ('rəʊgɪʃnɪs). [f. as prec. + -NESS.] The state or character of being roguish; knavery, roguery; also in later use, playfulness, archness.

1578 J. JONES *Preserv. Body & Soule* I. xxxvi. 73 What labours and trades be best for the communaltie to auoyde, as well roaguishnesse as idlenesse. [**1727** in BAILEY. **1755** in JOHNSON.] **1816** FORSYTH *Italy* (ed. 2) 393 These ladies.. seem to inherit from their lively grand-mothers a peculiar roguishness of look. **1859** GEO. ELIOT *A. Bede* vii, Her dark eyes hid a soft roguishness under their long lashes. **1875** M. G. PEARSE *Daniel Quorm* 146 A ripple of playful roguishness came over Dan'el's face.

†**'roguy,** *a. Obs.* Also 6–7 **roguie,** 7–8 **roguey.** [f. ROGUE *sb.* + -Y¹.]

1. = ROGUISH *a.* 1 and 1 b.

1598 MARSTON *Sco. Villanie* Prol. 167 Goe buy..some roguie thing, That thou maist chaunt unto the chamber-maid. **1614** B. JONSON *Barth. Fair* I. iv, The blacke boy in Bucklers-bury, that takes the scurvy, roguy tobacco, there. **1621** FLETCHER *Pilgrim* III. i, If I had open'd this when it was given me, This Roguy Box. **1680** R. L'ESTRANGE *Answ. to Litter of Libels* 6 Discoursing the Roguy Contrivances that were made use of for the gaining of Subscriptions to a Petition.

2. = ROGUISH *a.* 2.

c **1610** MIDDLETON, etc. *Widow* III. ii, To light upon a roguy flight of thieves. **1650** R. STAPYLTON *Strada's Low-C. Wars* v. 131 A few men of the poorest roguey sort of Hereticks. **1680** CROWNE *Misery Civ. War* I. i, A roguy Lawyer Will ruine all again with a meer quirk. **1707** E. FILMER *Defence Plays* 35 Keep those roguy Players at Arm's length. **1712–3** SWIFT *Jrnl. to Stella* 14 Mar., I doubt I shall not buy the library; for a roguey bookseller has offered sixty pounds more than I designed to give.

3. = ROGUISH *a.* 3.

1664 COTTON *Scarron.* I. Wks. (1715) 47 [This Cupid would] do a Thousand Roguy Tricks. **1692** R. L'ESTRANGE *Fables* I. lxxiv. (1714) 90 A Shepherd's Boy had gotten a Roguy Trick of crying a Wolfe. *a* **1704** T. BROWN *Lett. to Gent. & Ladies* Wks. 1709 III. II. 91 My dear Child, thou hast a smiling roguy Air.

rohȝe, the ray: see ROUGH *sb.*

Rohilla (rəʊ'hɪlə), *sb.* and *a.* Also †**Rohella, Rohila.** [Pashto 'inhabitant of Roh', f. placename *Rōh,* a district of Afghanistan: see also quot. 1885.] **A.** *sb.* A member of a people of Afghan origin inhabiting the Bareilly district of Northern India. **B.** *adj.* Of or pertaining to this people.

1773 W. HASTINGS *Diary* 21 Aug. (1948) 6 The Vizier added that the Abdallee maintained a Correspondence with the Rohellas. *Ibid.,* Money..due to the said Nabob by virtue of any engagement between him and the Rohilla chiefs. **1786** BURKE *Wks.* (1868) IV. 221 That the said Warren Hastings..did, in September, 1773, enter into a private engagement with the said Nabob of Oude..to furnish him..with a body of troops for the declared purpose of 'thoroughly extirpating the nation of the Rohillas'. **1829** J. TOD *Rajast'han* I. xxv. 672 The fragments were..placed in position to receive the flesh-pots of the sons of Ishmaël, the mercenary Rohilla Afghan. **1885** G. C. WHITWORTH *Anglo-Indian Dict.* 269/2 *Rohillá.* [Pashto, from *roh,* a mountain.] The name of a highland clan of Pathāns who early in the eighteenth century took possession of the district, now called after them, Rohilkhand. **1892** KIPLING *Barrack-Room Ballads* 104 We drove the black Rohillas back. **1921** G. A. GRIERSON *Linguistic Survey of India* X. 9 After the death of Aurangzēb, in 1707, the dissensions among the Hindūs of Bareilly enabled 'Ali Muhammed Khān, the leader of the Rōhilā Pathāns, to obtain possession of the country which is now called, after the name of the tribe, Rohilkhand... It is hardly necessary to point out the connexion between Rōh and Rōhilā. The latter word means literally an inhabitant of the Rōh. **1960** J. S. WATSON *Reign of George III* xii. 309 These Afghan soldiers of fortune, called the Rohillas, were suspected of co-operation with the Marathas. **1971** R. RUSSELL tr. *Ahmad's Shore & Wave* vi. 52 Some Rohillas had recently been arrested and charged with a series of burglaries and armed robberies.

rohly, obs. form of ROUGHLY *adv.*

‖**rohrflöte** ('ro:rfløːtə). *Mus.* Also **rohr flute;** *pl.* -n. [G., f. *rohr* tube + *flöte* flue-stop.] An organ stop having its pipes partly closed, the stopper at the top of each pipe being pierced by a thin tube.

1773 C. BURNEY *Present State of Mus. Germany* II. 305 Catalogue of stops in the Great Organ at Haarlem built by Müller 1738... 5. *Roer fluit,* 8 ft. with a funnel or small pipe upon the top. Eng. equivalent, Diap. half stopt. **1855** [see GEDACKT, GEDACT]. **1898** STAINER & BARRETT *Dict. Mus. Terms* 387/2 Rohrflöte, (Ger.) Reed-flute. An organ stop consisting of closed pipes, the tone of which is slightly reedy in quality, but very sweet. **1911** W. & T. LEWIS *Mod. Organ Building* v. 93 Many stops..occupy an intermediate position between two classes; as, for instance, a Rohr Flute. This stop is made to produce an upper harmonic which renders its timbre rather flutey in character, but at the same time, the fundamental tone is sufficiently obvious to link it with a Stopped Diapason. **1938** *Oxf. Compan. Mus.* 668/1 *Rohrflöte* or *Rohr Flute* (literally 'Reed Flute', but 'reed' here means a tube), of metal stopped pipes, with a slender tube through the stopper (hence the name). **1959** *Collins Mus. Encycl.* 554/1 *Rohrflöte,*..an organ stop of the flue type. The pipe is stopped at one end, but the stopper is pierced by a hole, in which is inserted a metal tube or chimney. **1966** P. WILLIAMS *European Organ 1450–1850* vii. 238 Organ-builders evidently brought with them new stops like *Rohrflöten.*

‖**rohun.** *Med.* [Hindī.] ***rohun bark*** (see quots.).

1858 SIMMONDS *Dict. Trade, Rohun bark,* the bark of the *Soymida febrifuga,* which is said to be a good substitute for cinchona. The nux vomica bark is often sold for it in the East. **1887** BENTLEY *Man. Bot.* (ed. 5) 509 The bark, which is official in the Pharmacopœia of India, is commonly known under the name of Rohun Bark... In the Bengal bazaars, the bark of *Strychnos Nux-vomica* is also known under the native name of *Rohun.*

‖**rohuna.** *Bot.* [Hindī *rohunna.*] (See quots. and prec.)

1846 LINDLEY *Veget. Kingd.* 462 The bark of Soymida febrifuga, the Rohuna of Hindostan, called on the Coromandel coast the Red-wood tree. **1887** BENTLEY *Man. Bot.* (ed. 5) 620 The febrifugal bark of *Soymida febrifuga,* the Rohuna tree.

roial, roially, etc., obs. ff. ROYAL(LY, etc.

roibek, var. ROOIBEKKIE.

roibok, var. ROOIBOK.

roid, *a. Obs.* exc. *dial.* Also 5 **roide, royd(e, rode** (rude). [a. OF. *roide, rode* (also northern *reide,* mod.F. *raide*):—L. *rigid-um* RIGID *a.,* but in some cases (esp. in Sc. texts) perh. a variant or scribal alteration of RUDE *a.*]

1. Stout, strong; violent, rough.

a **1400–50** *Alexander* (Dubl. MS.) 829* The kyng of þatt cuntree..Had rasyd vp a rode hoste. *c* **1400** *Destr. Troy* 1984 A rak and a royde wynde rose in hor saile. *Ibid.* 4428 A Roid beste vnreasonable, þat no Rule holdes. *c* **1425** WYNTOUN *Cron.* IX. i. 27 þus eftyr a royde harsk begynnynge Hapnyt a fast and gud endynge. *c* **1470** HENRY *Wallace* XI. 1362 For all thi roid rahress, Thow has na charge.

1883 *Huddersfield Gloss.* s.v., A *roid* night is a stormy one; *roid* work is a quarrel.

2. Rude, large, great, unwieldy.

a **1400** *Cursor M.* 23911 (Gött.), For-sake þu noght þis roide werk, For þou it roid [*Cott.* rude] and stubil be, It es in worschip wroght of þe. *c* **1400** *York Myst.* xxx. 175 Youre richesse schal be refte you þat is rude [*rime* noyed, stroyed]. *c* **1450** *St. Cuthbert* (Surtees) 6025 þe bell it was so grete and royde þat of þe caryage he was oft noyde. *c* **1470** HENRY *Wallace* v. 77 3hett schede he thaim, a full royd slope was maid.

3. Stiff. *rare*⁻¹.

c **1477** CAXTON *Jason* 25 The Geant roose also, but hit was not lightly for his legges were royde.

roid(e, obs. forms of ROOD, ROYD.

†**'roidly,** *adv. Obs.* Also 5 **royd(e)ly, rodely.** [f. ROID *a.* + -LY².] Rudely, roughly, severely.

1375 BARBOUR *Bruce* XIV. 305 That gret hoost roydly ruschit wes. *c* **1375** *Sc. Leg. Saints* xl. (*Ninian*) 1302 Quhen þu with me sa roydely chid. *a* **1400–50** *Alexander* (Dubl. MS.) 784* On þe rige with hys right hande hym rodely [he] strakez. *c* **1400** *Destr. Troy* 10298 þai..Rofe hit full roidly, rent hit in peses. **1480** CAXTON *Myrr.* II. xxiv, Yf ye meue it fast and roydly, it shal bowe anon.

roif, Sc. var. RO *sb.,* rest. *Obs.*

‖**roi fainéant** (rwa fɛneɑ̃). [Fr., lit. 'sluggard king': see FAINÉANT *sb.* and *a.*] One of the later Merovingian kings of France, whose power was merely nominal. Also *transf.* and *fig.*

1841 [see PESHWA]. **1879** *Encycl. Brit.* IX. 530/2 Children were kings in both Austrasia and Neustria; we reach the days of the 'do-naught' princes, the *rois fainéants,* and of the struggle between the mayors of Austrasia and Neustria. **1898** L. SERGEANT *Franks* xiv. 199 Dagobert's death.. marked the beginning of a series of Merovingian *rois fainéants.* **1929** W. R. INGE *Assessments & Anticipations* ii. 35, I have acquiesced in the undignified rôle of a *roi fainéant.* **1935** *Chambers's Encycl.* IV. 810/1 Charles Martel, *maire du palais* to the 'Rois Fainéants', defeated Arab invaders at Poitiers. **1966** *Economist* 1 Jan. 23/1 The launching of the Sputnik in 1957, in the reign of the *roi fainéant,* President Eisenhower, seemed to justify Krushchevian boasts that America's days of..supremacy were numbered. **1975** J. H. M. SALMON *Society in Crisis: France in 16th Cent.* viii. 193 The last years of Charles IX were those of a *roi fainéant.* The king ordered a new offensive against the Protestants of the south and La Noue in the west, but there were no resources to finance his armies.

roignous, var. ROINOUS *a.*

roik, obs. Sc. f. ROCK *sb.*¹, ROKE *sb.*¹

†**roil,** *sb.*¹ *Obs.* Forms: 6 roile, 6–8 royle, 7 royl, 8 roil. [Of obscure origin.]

1. An inferior or spiritless horse.

1523 SKELTON *Dk. Albany* 270 As it were a gote In a shepe cote,.. Therin, lyke a royle, Sir Dunkan, ye dared. **1576** GASCOIGNE *Philomene* (Arb.) 117 That horse which tyreth like a roile,.. Is better, much than is the harbrainde colte Which headlong runnes [etc.]. **1580** BLUNDEVIL *Horsemanship* I. xii. 16 b, If a faire Mare in old time had bene couered with a fowle roile, or had bene with fole out of season [etc.].

b. A draught-horse (of Flemish breed).

1587 HARRISON *Descr. Eng.* III. i, Such outlandish horsses as are dailie brought ouer vnto vs.., as the genet of Spaine, .. the Flemish roile, and Scotish nag.

2. A clumsy or stoutly-built female.

1533 UDALL *Floures* 61 b, There is not one crum or droppe of good fashion in all that great royles bodie... Catullus ther speaketh of a certaine mayden. **1577** B. GOOGE *Heresbach's Husb.* i. (1586) 46 And brought in therewithall his daughter, a iolly great royle. **1591** PERCIVALL *Sp. Dict.*, *Barragana*, a great ramping wench, a roile. **1746** *Exmoor Scolding* (E.D.S.) 16 Ya gurt Roile, tell ma,.. what Disyease dest mean? **1778** —— Gloss., *Roil*, or *Royle*, a big, ungainly Slam-makin; a great awkard Blowze or Hoyden.

roil, *sb.*[2] *rare.* Also 7 royl. [f. ROIL *v.*[2]] Agitation or stirring up (of water). Also *fig.*

1693 C. MATHER *Invisible World* (1862) 189 Some very great Saints of God, have sometimes had hideous Royls raised by the Devil in their minds. **1893** KIPLING *Many Invent.* 364 Port, port she casts, with the harbour-roil beneath her feet. **1895** *Outing* XXVI. 62/1 The roil disturbed the spot where the fish was endeavoring to escape.

†**roil**, *a.*[1] *Obs.*[−1] [Perh. related to ROIL *v.*[1] or *v.*[2]] ? Rich, luxuriant.

13.. *E.E. Allit. P.* B. 790 Bolde burnez wer þay boþe with berdles chynnez, Royl rollande fax to raw sylk lyke.

roil, *a.*[2] Now *dial.* (in form rile). [Related to ROIL *v.*[3]] = ROILED *ppl. a.*

1662 GURNALL *Chr. in Arm.* v. (1669) 83/1 How his spirit is royl and muddied. **1851** *N. & Q.* 1st Ser. IV. 317 The water is too rile to drink.

roil, *v.*[1] *Obs.* exc. *dial.* Forms: 4-6 (9 *dial.*) roil(e, 5 roille, roylle (roylyn), 5-7 (9 *dial.*) royl(e, 9 *dial.* rile, ryle. [Of doubtful origin: perh. the same word as next, but no similar sense appears in OF.]

It is not clear whether *royhland* (v.r. *rulȝeande*) in Wyntoun *Cron.* v. xii. 4644 belongs to this verb or the next.

†**1.** To roam or rove about; to gad about, wander; to stray. *Obs.*

c **1308** *Old Age* in *Rel. Ant.* II. 175 Hail be ȝe, freris,.. Evir ȝe beth roilend the londis al a-boute. **1387** TREVISA *Higden* (Rolls) I. 145 Armenius.. gadered knyȝtes þat roiled [*v.rr.* roillede, royled] aboute, and toke Armenia. **1483** CAXTON *Gold. Leg.* 115 b/1 Holde the in one place all stylle and walke not ne roylle aboute in the contree. **1532** MORE *Confut. Barnes* VIII. Wks. 747/2 Such apostatas woulde be bound to no cloyster, but haue all the worlde to royle in. **1555** W. WATREMAN *Fardle Facions* I. iii. 36 Thei ware sterne, and vnruly,.. roilyng and rowmyng vpon heade, heather and thether. **1565** GOLDING *Ovid's Met.* III. 55 When roiling safely in the vale before the herd alone He saw an heifar. **1619** BERT *Treat. Hawkes* 57 If thy hawke will not come, or not abide company.., or will royle or house.

†**2.** To move about vigorously. *Obs. rare.*

c **1400** *Laud Troy Bk.* 9192 Achilles loked to Troyle, And saw how he be-gan to royle.. a-monges Gregeis. *Ibid.* 13346 Then come theder douȝti Troyle And be-gan amonges hem royle.

3. *dial.* To play or frolic, *esp.* in a rough manner; to romp, rampage; to fidget.

1788- in various dial. glossaries.

†**roil**, *v.*[2] *Obs. rare.* In 4-5 royle, 5 roile. [ad. OF. *roillier*, *rooilier*, etc. (see Godefroy s.v. *roeillier*), related to *roelle* wheel.]

1. *intr.* Of a stream: To roll or flow.

c **1374** CHAUCER *Boeth.* I. pr. vi. (1868) 29 Þe fletyng streme þat roylep doun dyuersely fro heyȝe mountaignes.

2. *trans.* To roll (the eyes); to revolve (mentally).

c **1430** *Pilgr. Lyf Manhode* III. xliii. (1869) 158 Thanne j wole.. chide oon, blame an oother, and roile myne eyen as a bole. **1447** BOKENHAM *Seyntys* (Roxb.) 253 Inportunely he roylyd in hys mende How he myht best this matere ende.

roil, *v.*[3] Now *U.S.* and *dial.* Forms: 6-7 (8-9 *dial.*) royl(e, 7 (9 *dial.*) roile, 8- roil. See also RILE *v.* [Of obscure origin. An obs. F. *ruiler*, to mix up mortar, is cited by Godefroy.]

1. *trans.* To render (water or any liquid) turbid or muddy by stirring up the sediment; hence *fig.*, to perturb, disquiet, disorder. Cf. RILE *v.* 1.

1590 GREENWOOD *Answ. Gifford* 10 You.. haue nothing to say, if not to royle the doctrines.. with your feete, least others should drinke therof. **1616** T. SCOTT *Christ's Polit.* 8 Beasts of the fielde doe trouble the water, and roile it with their feete. **1662** GURNALL *Chr. in Arm.* VII. § 1 (1669) 49/1 Though the Devil throws the stone, yet 'tis the mud in us that royles our comforts. *a* **1734** R. NORTH *Lives* (1826) I. 195 The state was not very much roiled with faction. *Ibid.* III. 183 King William, having secured his own game, would not roil it to gratify them. **1771** J. ADAMS *Diary* 22 Aug., Wks. 1850 II. 290 His imagination is disturbed, his passions all roiled. **1854** THOREAU *Walden* xii. (1863) 245, I could dip up a pailful without roiling it. **1900** *Scribner's Mag.* Sept. 378/2 His nature was not always serene and pellucid; it was sometimes roiled by the currents that counter and cross in all of us.

2. To disturb in temper; to vex, irritate, make angry. Cf. RILE *v.* 2.

a **1734** NORTH *Lives* (1826) II. 168 That his friends.. should believe it, was what roiled him extremely. *Ibid.* III. 376 The doctor came out from the meeting (where probably he had been a little roiled). **1818** FEARON *Sk. Amer.* 97 Roads.. are unpopular in this state:.. we were mightily roiled (vexed) when they were first cut. **1866** BROGDEN *Prov. Linc.* **1907** *Springfield* (Mass.) *Weekly Republ.* 17 Jan. 6 The publication of such a work naturally roiled the publishers of Webster's international dictionary.

3. *intr.* To move in a confused or turbulent manner; to billow.

1939 W. FAULKNER *Wild Palms* 26 As something recognisable roils momentarily into view from beneath stagnant and opaque water, then sinks again. **1963** T. PYNCHON *V.* i. 22 Engine exhaust roiled in clouds around him. **1964** D. F. GALOUYE *Counterfeit World* xiii. 113 The waters roiled with the restless presence of thousands of—. **1977** *Time* 6 June 46/2 Strange currents flow for years in the deeps of the American society, then for reasons unclear suddenly roil to the surface.

Hence **'roiling** *ppl. a.*

1967 C. O. SKINNER *Madame Sarah* viii. 171 Sarah glanced down at the roiling flood water. **1976** U. CURTISS *Birthday Gift* xiv. 132 One thing stood clearly out of the whole roiling mess.

roil, *v.*[4] Also royl. [Of doubtful origin: connexion with prec. is not clear.] To salt (fish).

1870 M. GLOVER *Guide Isle of Man* 189 Such as are intended for red herrings are first 'royled', or rubbed with salt, in which they remain for two or three days.

roile, obs. variant of ROWEL.

roiled (rɔɪld), *ppl. a.* Also 7 royled. (See also RILED.) [f. ROIL *v.*[3]] Rendered turbid by stirring of sediment; also *fig.* esp. of the passions. Also with *up*.

1622 S. WARD *Life of Faith* (1627) 112 The speckled phantasies, darke obliuion, royled, soyled, affections. **1647** N. WARD *Simp. Cobler* 2 Sathan is now in his passions, hee feeles his passion approaching; he loves to fish in royled waters. **1648** J. BEAUMONT *Psyche* XX. cxcv, That which bubbles from a royled Mind. **1854** MISS BAKER *Northampt. Gloss.* s.v., How roiled the water looks. **1929** *Sun* (Baltimore) 12 June 1/1 It will be seen when the Senator gets roiled he can go the paces with the next one among the friends of the people. **1939** J. STEINBECK *Grapes of Wrath* x. 123 Your Pa's pa, he quoted Scripture all the time. He got it all roiled up, too. **1975** in W. Viereck *Lexikalische Ergebnisse des Lowman-Survey* I. iv. 279 If he lost his temper, you say he got.. roiled.

†**'roiler**[1]. *Obs.*[−0] In 6 roylar. [f. ROIL *v.*[1]] One who roams idly or dissolutely.

1565 COOPER *Thesaurus*, *Circumselliones*, tauerne haunters, roylars aboute.

'roiler[2]. *U.S.* [f. ROIL *v.*[4]] An apparatus, such as a revolving box, used in salting fish.

1890 in *Cent. Dict.*

'roiling, *vbl. sb.*[1] *rare.* [f. ROIL *v.*[1]] †The action or practice of roving or roaming about.

mare-roiling (see MARE[1] 6 b) may also belong here.

1398 TREVISA *Barth. De P.R.* IX. xxvi. (Bodl. MS.), Idel walking and roilingge aboute [was] forboode in þe saturdaie. **1567** HARMAN *Caveat* (1869) 31 These vnrewly rascales, in their roylynge, disperse them selues into seuerall companyes.

'roiling, *vbl. sb.*[2] *rare.* [f. ROIL *v.*[3]] The action of perturbing; agitation, turmoil; irritation.

1662 GURNALL *Chr. in Arm.* LV. § 1 (1669) 424/1 He is a rare Christian in whom the stream of his grace runs clear upon such royling. **1674** N. FAIRFAX *Bulk & Selv.* To Rdr., An ill will'd and frampled waspishness has broken forth, to the royling and firing of the age wherein we live.

roily ('rɔɪlɪ), *a.* Chiefly *U.S.* and *dial.* [f. ROIL *sb.*[2] or *v.*[3]] Muddy, turbid. *roily oil*, petroleum containing much emulsified water. Hence **'roiliness**.

1823 COOPER *Pioneers* xx, For fear you [the sap] should get roily. **1846** WORCESTER, *Roily*, *a.*, turbid;.. rily. **1866** BROGDEN *Prov. Linc.* **1880** *Scribner's Mag.* Aug. 484/1 If the water is very roily or brackish. **1895** *Outing* XXVI. 63/1 He abruptly departed, leaving behind him a trail of roily water. **1912** *Mem. Geol. Surv. India* XL. 121 [The well] being shut down at first on account of the 'roiliness' or emulsification of the oil. *Ibid.*, Two wells; one of these was a 'dry hole', but the other flowed during the first 24 hours 18,000 gallons of an emulsion of oil and water known in America as roily oil. **1915** REDWOOD & EASTLAKE *Petroleum Technol. Pocket-bk.* iv. 214 On recommencing pumping the well gave nothing but 'roily oil' for more than a month. **1920** E. H. C. CRAIG *Oil-Finding* (ed. 2) iii. 71 In a porous rock... oil and water may be inextricably intermingled... Such a rock struck in a well will probably yield 'roily oil', an emulsion very difficult to separate into its constituents, oil and water.

†**roin**, *sb.* *Obs.*[−1] In 5 royne. [a. OF. *roigne* (*roingne*, *roisne*), F. *rogne*, = Prov. *ronha*, *runha*, Cat. *ronya*, Sp. *roña*, Pg. *ronha*, It. *rogna*, of unknown origin.] A scab, scurf.

? *a* **1366** CHAUCER *Rom. Rose* 553 Hir nekke was of good fasoun.., Withoute bleyne, scabbe, or royne.

†**roin**, *v.*[1] *Obs.* In 4-6 royne. [ad. OF. *roignier* (mod.F. *rogner*), *rooignier*, for earlier **rodognier*:—pop. L. **rotundiāre*, f. L. *rotundus* ROUND *a.*] *trans.* To pare away; to clip; to cut short or curtail.

c **1315** SHOREHAM I. 973 Ase mot þe leche ine uoule sores, Wanne he roynep þe felþe. **1426** LYDG. *De Guil. Pilgr.* 17600 Thys hand kan Royne also florynes;.. Thys hand kan brake Cofer and cheste. **1573** TWYNE *Æneid* x. D d ij, Why now should any creature dare controul or hang down groyne To bend back your decrees, or destines now presume to royne.

†**roin**, *v.*[2] *Obs.* In 4, 6-7 royne. [Prob. ad. OF. **rognir* (cf. *rungier* in Godef. VII. 238/2), var. of *grognir* GROIN *v.*[1]] *intr.* To growl.

13.. *Coer de L.* 1083 The lyoun was hungry and megre,.. Abrod he spredde alle hys powes, And roynyd lowde, and gapyd wyde. **1596** SPENSER *F.Q.* v. ix. 33 Yet did he murmure with rebellious sound, And softly royne, when salvage choler gan redound. **1611** COTGR., *Ruir*, to rore, or to royne, like a Lyon.

Hence †**'roiner**; **'roining** *vbl. sb.* *Obs.*

1598 FLORIO, *Ruggiatore*, a roarer, a bellower, a royner. **1611** COTGR., *Ruissement*, a roaring, or Lion-like royning.

roineck, var. ROOINEK.

†**'roinish**, *a.* *Obs.* Forms: 4 roynyshe, -yssche, 6-7 roynish, 6 roinish. [f. ROIN *sb.* + -ISH. Cf. next.] Covered with scale or scurf; scabby, scurvy, coarse, mean, paltry, base.

13.. *St. Erkenwolde* 52 in Horstm. *Altengl. Leg.* (1881) 267 Þe bordure [was] enbelicit with bryȝt golde lettres, Bot roynyshe were þe resones þat þer one row stodene. **1393** LANGL. *P. Pl.* C. XXIII. 83 (M.), Re[u]mes and radegoundes and roynyssche [*al.* roynouse] scabbes, Byles and bocches and.. agues. **1573** TUSSER *Husb.* (1878) 191 The slouen and the careles man, the roinish nothing nice. **1592** NASHE *Four Lett. Confut.* Wks. (Grosart) II. 274 With none but clownish and roynish ieasts dost thou rush vppon vs. **1600** SHAKS. *A.Y.L.* II. ii. 8 The roynish Clown, at whom so oft, Your Grace was wont to laugh, is also missing. **1629** PARKINSON *Parad.* iii. 6 It must be taken vp and new set, or else it will grow too roynish and cumbersome. [**1814** SCOTT *Wav.* ix, Not much unlike one of Shakespeare's roynish clowns.]

†**'roinous**, *a.* *Obs.* In 4-5 royn(e)ous, roignous, ron-, runyous, ruynouse. [a. AF. *roinos*, *roynous*, *ruinus*, OF. *roigneux*, etc. (mod.F. *rogneux*), = Prov. *rognos*, *ronhos*, Cat. *ronyos*, Sp. *roñoso*, Pg. *ronhoso*, It. *rognoso*: see ROIN *sb.* and -OUS.] = ROINISH *a.*

? *a* **1366** CHAUCER *Rom. Rose* 987 The foule croked bowe hidous, That knotty was, and al roynous. **1377** LANGL. *P. Pl.* B. xx. 82 Rewmes & radegoundes and roynouse scalles, Byles, and bocches. *c* **1400** *Rom. Rose* 6190 This argument is al roignous; It is not worth a croked brere. **1474** CAXTON *Chess* 54, I sawe on a tyme a man that was royneous and ful of sores. **1491** —— *Vitas Patr.* (W. de W. 1495) I. xxxvii. 44/1 His body by straytnesse of lyffe became scabby and ronyous.

roiot, obs. f. ROYET.

rois(e, obs. Sc. ff. ROSE *sb.*[1]

†**roise**, *v.* *Obs.*[−1] In 5 royse. [Of obscure origin.] *intr.* ? To rave, talk nonsense.

c **1440** *York Myst.* xv. 69, I trowe you royse, For what it was fayne witte walde I, That tille vs made þis noble noyse.

‖**roi soleil** (rwa sɔlɛj). [Fr., lit. 'sun king'.] A title commonly used to designate Louis XIV of France, derived from a heraldic device used by him; applied *transf.* to any similarly pre-eminent individual, ruler, or divinity. Also *attrib.*

1890 G. BIRDWOOD *Rep. Misc. Old Rec. India Office* 222 The earliest coins minted by the English in India were of copper, stamped with a figure of an irradiated *lingam*, the phallic 'Roi Soleil'. **1943** E. M. W. TILLYARD *Elizabethan World Picture* vii. 83 The *roi soleil* is indeed one of the most persistent of all Elizabethan commonplaces. **1958** *Spectator* 6 June 721/2 Her rule is no longer the *roi-soleil* variety. **1961** *Listener* 31 Aug. 319/2 Popular books on Picasso in which the artistic *roi soleil* of the post-war years is still pictured as on some barricade or other. **1966** *Guardian* 31 Dec. 5/3 Cecil Harmsworth King, the *roi soleil* of Long Acre. **1978** *Times* 27 May 7/1 The palmy days of the Roi Soleil.

roist, dial. variant of RICE *sb.*[1]

1736 PEGGE *Kenticisms* (E.D.S.), *Roist*, a switch to beat a dog with; or long wood, for brushwood, before it is made up. Called also *Rice*.

roist, obs. form of ROAST *sb.* and *v.*

†**roist**, *v.* *Obs.*[−1] Also 6 (9 *arch.*) royst. [Back-formation from ROISTER *sb.*[1]] *intr.* To play the roister. Cf. ROISTER *v.*

1563 *Mirr. Mag.* II. 168 b, Traytours dyd triumphe,.. Reuing and robbing roysted euery where. *a* **1591** H. SMITH *Serm.* (1867) I. 361 They cannot be esteemed unless They royst. **1606** WARNER *Alb. Eng.* XVI. cii. 404 When their Retainors royst and wrong, yet out of Iustice leape. **1632** SHERWOOD, To roist,.. *comme* to swagger.

b. So *to roist it* (*out*).

1579 NORTHBROOKE *Dicing* (1843) 169 Nowe a dayes we see many seeke nothing but to royst it. **1583** STUBBES *Anat. Abus.* II. (1882) 75 Some of them haue.. foure or fiue benefices apeece, being resident.. at neuer a one, but roist it out elsewhere. **1601** DENT *Pathw. Heauen* 171 Borne onely to game, riot,.. ruffle it, and roist it out, and to spend their time in meere idlenesse.

roister ('rɔɪstə(r)), *sb.*[1] Now *arch.* Also 7-9 royster. [ad. F. *rustre* (†*ruistre*), 'a ruffin, royster, hackster, swaggerer' (Cotgr.), var., with excrescent *r*, of *ruste*:—L. *rustic-um* RUSTIC *a.*]

1. A swaggering or blustering bully; a riotous fellow; a rude or noisy reveller.

Very common *c* 1550-1700; now usually ROISTERER.

1551 T. WILSON *Logike* L vij b, Yf slaughter be not to be borne.. these roisters, and fighters, are not to be suffered to go vnpunished. **1579** TOMSON *Calvin's Serm. Tim.* 97/2 We must not play yᵉ iollie roysters, we must not spred abroad our wings. **1621** BP. MOUNTAGU *Diatribæ* 446 Such roysters and rake-shames as Mars is manned with. **1649** MILTON *Eikon.* IV, His adherents, consisting most of dissolute Swordmen and Suburb roysters, hardly amounted to one ragged regiment. **1687** T. BROWN *Saints in Uproar* Wks. 1730 I. 74 Why, how now, bully Royster, what's the meaning of this outrage in the face of Iustice? **1753–4** RICHARDSON *Grandison* (1781) VI. 269 Mr. Greville is a roister. **1797** BRYDGES *Hom. Trav.* II. 410 These roysters batter The walls and gates with dreadful clatter. **1820** W. IRVING *Sk. Bk.* I. 75 He now suspected that the grave roysters of the mountain had put a trick upon him. **1870** EMERSON *Soc. & Solit.* Wks. (Bohn) III. 26 If new topics are started, graver and higher, these roisters recede.

attrib. and *Comb.* **1573** TUSSER *Husb.* (1878) 188 Busie fault finder.. is roister like ruffen. **1611** COTGR., *Rustrement*, royster-like; sawcily. **1653** URQUHART *Rabelais* II. xiv. (1737) II. 113, I.. with my cords tied him royster-like both hand and foot. **1686** GOAD *Celest. Bodies* I. vii. 24 The Moon.. doth not so much as look as if she liked such Roister-company.

b. *dial.* A romp.

1790- in *Eng. Dial. Dict.*

2. 'A hound that opens on a false scent.'

1796 *Grose's Dict. Vulg. T.* (ed. 3).

'roister, *sb.*² *rare*⁻¹. [f. the vb.] The act of roistering.

1860 *Cornh. Mag.* Sept. 359 Some beau who had been on the roister all night.

'roister, *v.* Also royster. [f. ROISTER *sb.*¹] = ROIST *v.*

1582 [see ROISTERING *ppl. a.* 1]. **1663** J. H. *Hist. O. Cromwell* ii. 5 He was presently removed.. to Lincoln's Inne, where he might with less imputation.. royster it out. **1796** [see ROISTERING *ppl. a.* 1]. **1850** STRUTHERS *Poet. Wks.* II. 241 Who will may strut philosophizing, And, in his frenzied furor, royster. **1855** KINGSLEY *Westw. Ho!* xvi, He might have.. roystered it in taverns with Marlowe. **1893** BARING-GOULD *Cheap Jack Zita* I. 118 Acquaintances who had roistered or dealt with him.

transf. **1879** LOWELL *Poet. Wks.* 371 The wind is roistering out of doors.

†'roister-'doister. *Obs.* Also 6–7 royster doyster. [The name of the chief character in Udall's play, based upon ROISTER *sb.*¹] A roisterer or roistering fellow.

a **1553** UDALL (*title*), Ralph Royster Doyster. **1592** G. HARVEY *Four Lett.* iii. Wks. (Grosart) I. 214, [I] haue seene the madbraynest Roister-doister in a countrey dashte out of countenaunce. **1593** —— *Pierce's Super.* 71 Vnlesse he wrote onely to roister-doisters and hacksters. **1602** *2nd Pt. Return fr. Parnass.* I. ii. 276 Then royster doyster in his oylie tearmes, Cutts, thrusts, and foines at whomesoeuer he meets.

Hence **†'roister-'doisterdom; †'roister-'doistering** *a.*; **†'roister-'doisterly** *a. Obs.*

1592 NASHE *Four Lett. Confut.* Wks. (Grosart) II. 274 Thy roister-doisterdome hath not dasht vs out of countenance. **1593** G. HARVEY *Pierce's Super.* Wks. (Grosart) II. 131 If the world should applaude to such roisterdoisterly Vanity,.. what good could grow out of it? *Ibid.* 221 They that.. deuide their roister-doistering Iestes into Cuttes, slashes, and foines.

'roisterer. [f. ROISTER *sb.* or *v.*] A swaggering or noisy reveller. Cf. ROISTER *sb.*¹ 1.

1820 SCOTT *Abbot* xv, Carry thy roisterers elsewhere—to the alehouse if they list. **1827** LYTTON *Pelham* l, Like a lusty roisterer of the true kidney. **1849** MACAULAY *Hist. Eng.* iii. I. 360 If two roisterers met, they cocked their hats in each other's faces. **1877** BLACK *Green Past.* xlvi, There were no roysterers going home.

'roistering, *vbl. sb.* [f. ROISTER *v.*] The conduct of roisterers; a revel or racket.

1850 E. WARBURTON *R. Hastings* II. 49 The.. Lieutenant of the Tower will soon arrive, and if thou art not found in thine own cell, we shall have pretty roysterings. **1897** MARY KINGSLEY *Trav. W. Africa* 319 He keeps steadily at it in his way, reserving his roysterings until he is settled in life.

'roistering, *ppl. a.* [f. ROISTER *v.*]

1. Blustering, boisterous; associated with noisy revelling; uproarious, wild.

1582 STANYHURST *Æneis* II. (Arb.) 62, I thus muttred, with roystring phrensye betraynted. **1796** BURKE *Regic. Peace* iv. (1892) 337 The unfortunate antiquary.. may suffer in the roystering horse-play and practical jokes of the servants' hall. **1820** SCOTT *Abbot* xix, You sit singing your roistering songs about popes and pagans. **1879** MCCARTHY *Own Times* xxix. II. 403 The roystering adventures of Light Dragoons. **1898** BODLEY *France* II. IV. viii. 443 Those amazing trials.. which the whole community seems to enjoy as a roistering farce.

2. Of persons: Given to noisy revelling.

1824 W. IRVING *T. Trav.* I. 45 A roystering country squire of the neighbourhood. **1851** SIR F. PALGRAVE *Norm. & Eng.* I. 486 The roistering Danish men were living at free quarters in the monastery. **1883** LORD R. GOWER *Reminis.* II. 119, I found the only inn full of dirty militia-men and roystering farmers.

Hence **'roisteringly** *adv.*

1659 TORRIANO, *Alla-sbardelláta*, lavishly, swaggeringly, roistringly. **1868** *Morn. Star* Jan. 27 The students.. roysteringly kissed the fair revivalists. **1893** *Columbus Dispatch* 9 Mar., Sailors singing roysteringly or well.

†'roisterkin. *Obs.*⁻¹ [f. ROISTER *sb.*¹ + -KIN.] A petty roisterer.

a **1569** KINGESMYLL *Comf. Afflict.* (1585) C viij, The whole rablement of her bawdie bawdes, ruffling roysterkins with brawling bragges.

†'roisterly, *a. Obs. rare.* [f. ROISTER *sb.*¹ + -LY¹.] Roisterous, roistering.

1592 G. HARVEY *Four Lett.* Wks. (Grosart) I. 169 His plausible musteringe, and banquetinge of roysterly acquaintaunce at his first comminge. **1593** —— *Pierce's Super.* ibid. II. 116 Euery ruffianly Copesmate, that.. hanteth roisterly companie. *a* **1670** HACKET *Abp. Williams* I. (1692) 35 They delighted altogether in the garb and habit and roisterly fashions of men.

'roisterous, *a.* Also 6 roysterus, 7, 9 -ous. [f. ROISTER *sb.*¹ + -OUS.] = ROISTERING *ppl. a.*

1575 R. B. *Appius & Virg.* in Hazl. *Dodsley* IV. 135 Never was that mistress so furious nor curious, Nor yet her blows so boisterous, nor roisterous, nor dolorous. **1582** STANYHURST *Æneis* I. (Arb.) 21 One ship that.. was swasht wyth a roysterus heape-flud. **1681** OTWAY *Soldiers Fortune* I. i, Rampant, roysterous whores. **1843** CARLYLE *Past & Pres.* (1858) 156 Was the like ever heard of? The roysterous young dogs.. breaking the Lord Abbot's sleep. **1886** *L'pool Daily Post* 9 Feb. 4/6 Roysterous fellows who kick the shins or break in the helmets of constables.

†'roisting, *vbl. sb. Obs.* [f. ROIST *v.*] = ROISTERING *vbl. sb.*

c **1560** INGELEND *Disobedient Child* E ij, What cryinge was there for Cardes and Dyce! What roysting, what rufflyng made they within! **1584–7** GREENE *Carde of Fancie* Wks. (Grosart) IV. 14 What trouble can torment mee worse, then to see my sonne.. to consume his time in roysting and ryot. **1614** RICH *Honestie* (1844) 17 Wee must not condemne her.. by her perfuming, by her ryoting, by her roysting.

†'roisting, *ppl. a. Obs.* Also 6 ruysting, roystyng, 6–7 (9 *arch.*) roysting. [f. ROIST *v.*]

1. = ROISTERING *ppl. a.* 1.

1567 HARMAN *Caveat* (1869) 32 After their ruysting recreation. **1593** G. HARVEY *Pierce's Super.* 156 His Rauing Poetry, his Roisting Rhetorique. **1612** T. TAYLOR *Comm. Titus* i. 6 The ruffling, and roysting life of a number of our gallants, and lustie bloods. **1812** W. TENNANT *Anster Fair* IV. 2 With a roysting brazen clangour dire.

2. = ROISTERING *ppl. a.* 2.

a **1553** UDALL *Royster D.* Prol., Whose humour the roysting sort continually doth feede. **1594** LYLY *Mother Bombie* I. i, She is mewed vp.. least she should by some roisting courtier be stollen away. *a* **1661** FULLER *Worthies, London* (1662) 207 Not well pleased with some Roisting Company there, he embraced the next opportunity of departure after dinner.

Hence **†'roistingly** *adv. Obs.*

1571 GOLDING *Calvin on Ps.* lxxiv. 22 They.. spew out their blasphemies feerssely and roystingly. **1581** G. PETTIE tr. *Guazzo's Civ. Conv.* (1586) III. 126 Those women that love not to curle vp their haire roistinglie. **1614** LATHAM *Falconry* (1633) 71 It may be at the first seeing the Doue to stirre and flutter she may come roistingly to twitch or take it away.

roiston crow, variant of ROYSTON CROW.

†roit, *sb.*¹ *Obs.*⁻¹ In 5 royt. [Related to ROIT *v.*] (See quot.)

c **1440** *Promp. Parv.* 427/2 Reyke, or royt, ydylle walkynge abowt.., *discursus, vagacio, vagitas.*

roit, *sb.*² *Sc. rare.* Also royt. [? Related to ROIT *v.*] An abusive term applied to persons or cattle (see quot. 1825).

a **1585** POLWART *Flyting w. Montgomerie* 29 Thy ragged roundels, raueand royt, Some short, some lang, some out of lyne. **1728** W. STARRAT *Ep. to Ramsay* 63 But, lad, neist mirk we'll to the haining drive,.. The royts will rest. **1825** JAMIESON, *Roit, royt*, 1. a babbler. 2. A term of contempt for a woman. It is often conjoined with an adj. denoting a bad temper; as, *an ill-natured-roit*, Loth. It is also applied to a female brute, as to a cow. **1832–53** *Whistle-Binkie* Ser. I. 55 He has a wife,.. A randy royt ca'd Barmy Betty!

roit, *v.* Now *Sc.* and *dial.* In 5 roytyn, royt(e, 9 *Sc.* royt. [Of obscure origin.] *intr.* To roam or rove about. Hence **'roiting** *vbl. sb.*

c **1440** *Promp. Parv.* 436/1 Roytyn, or gon ydyl a-bowte, .. *vagor, discurro.* *a* **1450** MYRC (1868) 999 For goyng to þe ale on halyday, For syngynge, for roytynge, & syche fare. **1808** JAMIESON s.v., A beast, that runs through the fields, instead of keeping to its pasture, is said to *royt.*

roite, obs. form of ROOT *sb.*

roitelet ('rɔɪtəlɛt, ‖rwatlɛ). Now *arch.* Also 7–9 roytelet (8 -ett). [a. F. *roitelet*, †*roytelet*, f. OF. *roitel, roietel*, etc., dim. of *roi* ROY *sb.*] A petty or minor king.

1602 CAREW *Cornwall* 67 To their gentlemen they carrie a verie dutifull regard,.. holding them as Roytelets, because they know no greater. **1641** HEYLIN *Hist. Episc.* II. (1657) 58 It being probable that there were other petty Kings and Roytelets as well as he. **1722** D. COXE *Descr. Carolina* 96 Those who have.. obtain'd the favor of their petty royteletts. **1738–41** WARBURTON *Div. Legat.* (1788) II. 151 The difference between an Egyptian monarch, and a petty roitelet of the Philistines. **1815** J. C. HOBHOUSE *Substance Lett.* (1816) I. 154 Even the roitelets of Palermo, Brussels, Stockholm, and Stutgard, may have each an advocate at the Cabinet of St. James's. **1847–9** HELPS *Friends in C.* (1859) I. 82 The endless small bickerings.. of counts and dukes and roitelets.

†roiter. *Obs.* Also 6 royter. [ad. Du. *ruiter* (*ruyter*) in same sense.] A horseman, trooper.

1583 STOCKER *Civ. Warres Lowe C.* IV. 61 The Roiters of the Estates were at Gelumuide. *Ibid.* 64 The Royters of the Enemie were ouer hastie in the chargyng of them.

†'roitish, *a. Obs.*⁻¹ [? f. ROIT *v.* + -ISH.] ? Wandering, straggling.

1648 J. BEAUMONT *Psyche* VI. clx, No Weed presum'd to shew its roitish face On this fair stage.

‖Rōjū ('roːdʒuː). Also Rōchū, rōjiu, rōjū, etc. [Jap.] The senior councillors or ministers of state in Japan under the Tokugawa government (1603–1867).

1874 F. O. ADAMS *Hist. Japan* I. I. x. 71 The successors of Jyéyasû.. were mostly *fainéants*, as were their almost hereditary ministers, the rôjiu. **1893** F. BRINKLEY tr. *Hist. Empire Japan* viii. 329 In the event of the Shogun himself taking the field, he had to be accompanied by all the feudal barons, the Ministers of State (*Rochu*) becoming generals and the *Wakatoshiyori* holding chief command over the bannerets. **1912** E. LEE tr. *Saito's Hist. Japan* 147 The board of the 5 Rōchū, the treasurers.. controlled the imperial court officials and Daimiō. *a* **1922** J. MURDOCH *Hist. Japan* (1926) III. i. 4 These five constituted the Great Council, which was presently to become known as the Rōjū. **1970** J. W. HALL *Japan* x. 175 The *Rōjū* were given authority over matters of national scope. **1974** *Encycl. Brit. Macropædia* X. 71/2 By reorganizations in 1633–42 the executive.. was almost completed, as represented by the offices of senior councillors (rojū), [etc.].

†rok. *Obs.*⁻¹ (Of obscure meaning.)

Taken by Morris to mean 'crowd, throng': cf. RUCK *sb.*

13.. *E.E. Allit. P.* B. 1514 Þer was rynging on ryȝt of ryche metalles, Quen renkkes in þat ryche rok rennen hit to cache.

rok, obs. form of ROCK, ROOK.

rokat, obs. form of ROCKET.

roke (rəʊk), *sb.*¹ Now *dial.* Also 6 *Sc.* roik, royk, rok; *dial.* 8 rooac, 9 roac, ro(o)ak, rawk, rauk. See also ROOK, ROUK, ROWK. [Prob. of Scand. origin. The variants *roke, rawk, rowk* would normally arise from an OScand. **rauk(r)*, which has been superseded by a form with umlaut (ON. *reykr*, Sw. *rök*, Da. *røg*): see REEK *sb.*¹

It seems unlikely that MDu. *rooc* or MLG. *rôk* can have had any influence on the word. Icel. and Norw. *rok*, Icel. *roka*, 'driving spray or snow', which would account for the form *roke* only, are also unsatisfactory as regards the meaning.]

Smoke, steam; vapour, mist, fog; drizzling rain.

c **1250** *Gen. & Ex.* 1163 To-ward sodome he saȝ ðe roke, And ðe brinfires stinken smoke. **13..** *Sir Beues* 2647 Eueri seue ȝer ones.. comeþ a roke & a stink Out of þe water. *c* **1440** *Promp. Parv.* 436/1 Roke, myste, *nebula.* ? *a* **1500** *Battle Otterburn* in Child *Ballads* III. 298/1 Tyll the bloode from ther bassonnettes ranne, As the roke doth in the rayne. **1513** DOUGLAS *Æneis* III. iii. 95 The rane and roik reft fra ws sicht of hevin. *Ibid.* VII. Prol. 36 The firmament ourkest with rokis blak. **1535** STEWART *Cron. Scot.* I. 489 Winter come to hand,.. With mist and roik. **1570** LEVINS *Manip.* 160/2 Yᵉ Hore roke, *pruina.* **1781** HUTTON *Tour to Caves* Gloss. (ed. 2) 95 *Roke*, fog or mist. **1788** W. MARSHALL *Prov. Yorks., Rooac*, or *Roke*, a kind of smoke; a species of mist, fog, or small rain. **1828–** in dial. glossaries (Sc. Yorks., Linc., E. Angl., Suss., I. Wight, Wilts.). **1891** ATKINSON *Moorland Par.* 363 Spectacles.. are a bother in a thick mist or roke.

roke (rəʊk), *sb.*² Also roak. [Northern dial. *roke, rawk* scratch, flaw, etc.: see *Eng. Dial. Dict.* s.v. *Rauk.*] *Founding.* A fault in steel.

a **1890** MICHAELIS tr. Monthaye *Krupp & De Bange* 21 (Cent.), The [steel] bar.. would be so full of the imperfections technically called 'seams' or roaks as to be.. useless. **1914** [see LAP *sb.*³ 2 e]. **1923** GLAZEBROOK *Dict. Appl. Physics* V. 363/2 Rokes are formed from ingot cracks, blowholes at or near the surface, and certain kinds of surface defect of the ingot, and in the case of rolled bar they are usually radial when examined on a cross-section. **1945** GREAVES & WRIGHTON *Pract. Microsc. Metallogr.* x. 173 Rokes.. consist of fissures.. with their surfaces separated by a thin film of scale or other impurity. **1951** G. R. BASHFORTH *Manuf. Iron & Steel* II. x. 320 Subcutaneous blowholes, occurring very near the skin of the ingot, may become oxidized during reheating, resulting in the formation of 'roaks' and seams in the finished bars or blooms. **1967** A. K. OSBORNE *Encycl. Iron & Steel Industry* (ed. 2) 354/2 Rokes. (Roaks.) **1974** P. WRIGHT *Lang. Brit. Industry* xix. 184 Ingot defects have various names, for instance the *roke*, into which a surface blow-hole rolls out.

roke, obs. form of ROCK, ROOK, RUCK.

roke (rəʊk), *v.*¹ Now *dial.* Also 7 roak(e. [See ROKE *sb.*¹]

1. *intr.* To give off steam or vapour; to steam; to smoke; to be foggy or misty.

1613 WITHER *Abuses Stript* II. i, The using of Tobacco thus is vaine: I meane in those that daily sit and smoake Alehouse and Taverne till the windowes roake. **1614** W. BROWNE *Shepherd's Pipe* I. 132 A sticke, that taken is From the Hedge, in water thrust, Neuer rokes as would the first. *a* **1700** KEN *Edmund* Poet. Wks. 1721 II. 109 Her Tables with strong Broths and Sauces rok'd, Which gormandizing and foul Lust provok'd. **1790** GROSE *Prov. Gloss.* (ed. 2) s.v., He roked like a dunghill. **1876** *Mid-Yorks. Gloss.* s.v., He sweats and rokes like an old horse. **1883** in *Hants Gloss.*

2. *trans.* To expose to smoke. In quot. *fig.*

c **1620** Z. BOYD *Zion's Flowers* (1855) 6 That Gentiles roak't in sin might be respected.

†roke, *v.*², in obscure uses.

Perh. varr. of, or errors for, *rock, rouk* or *ruck*, and *rake.*

a **1400** *Sir Perc.* 1375 Were thay wighte, were thay woke, Alle that he tille stroke, He made thaire bodies to roke. *c* **1400** *Rom. Rose* 1906 The shaft I drow out of the arwe,

Roking for wo right wondir narwe. **1418–20** J. Page *Siege of Rouen* in *Hist. Coll. Citizen Lond.* (Camden) 33 There leve of Umfrevyle they toke, And in to the cytte the gon roke.

rokeage ('rəʊkɪdʒ). *U.S.* [Amer. Indian.] (See quot. and PINOLE.)

1848 Bartlett *Dict. Amer.* 278 *Rokeage*, or *Yokeage*, Indian corn parched, pulverized, and mixed with sugar.

'rokelay. *Sc.* Now *Hist.* Also rocklay. [ad. F. *roquelaire*, var. of ROQUELAURE.] A short cloak worn by women in the eighteenth century.

c **1805** Macneill *Poems* (1844) 97 He has coft me a rocklay o' blue. **1814** Scott *Wav.* xi, Having, moreover, put on her clean toy, rokelay, and scarlet plaid. **1821** —— *Pirate* vii, The best chance of getting a new rokelay and owerlay. **1881** *Blackw. Mag.* Apr. 526 Old women in white mutches and scarlet rokelays.

roker ('rəʊkə(r)). [? ad. Da. *rokke*, Sw. *rocka*, the ray: see ROUGH *sb.*] (See quots.)

1882 *Q. Rev.* Oct. 467 'Roker'—by which all fish of the Ray family, excepting skate, are meant, is a favourite food of the working classes. **1882** *Academy* 14 Oct. 280 Roker is used to denote the thornback-ray (*Raja clavata*, Lin.) exclusively... Rokers fetch a less price than skate in the markets, and are always quoted separately.

roket(e, obs. ff. ROCKET.

rokh, var. ROC.

†**'roking**, *vbl. sb.* *Obs.*[−1] In 5 rokynge, 6 rooking. [Prob. f. ME. **roke*, repr. OE. *hráca* spittle: see REACH *v.*[2]] Clearing of the throat.

1398 Trevisa *Barth. De P.R.* iv. ix. (Tollemache MS.), Full of spittynge, snyuel and rokynge [**1582** rooking].

rokk(e, obs. ff. ROCK *sb.* and *v.*

rokker, rokket, obs. ff. ROCKER, ROCKET.

rokki, rokky, obs. ff. ROCK *v.*[1], ROCKY *a.*

roky ('rəʊkɪ), *a.*[1] Chiefly *dial.* Also 8 *Sc.* **rocky**, 9 *dial.* **roaky, rokey.** [f. ROKE *sb.*[1] + -Y.] Misty; foggy; drizzly. Cf. RAWKY *a.*[2]

c **1440** *Promp. Parv.* 436/1 Roky, or mysty, *nebulosus.* **1722** Hamilton *Wallace* xii. iv. 229 (1786) 238 A rocky mist fell down at break of day. *a* **1825** Forby *Voc. E. Anglia, Roky*, foggy. **1828** Carr *Craven Gloss., Roaky*, drizzly. **1872** Tennyson *Last Tourn.* 502 [He] in a roky hollow, belling, heard The hounds of Mark. **1888** Rider Haggard *Col. Quaritch* xviii, He would take out a 'rokey' (foggy) looking bit of a picture.

roky ('rəʊkɪ), *a.*[2] *Founding.* [f. ROKE *sb.*[2] + -Y[1].] Possessing or characterized by rokes.

1932 E. Gregory *Metallurgy* ii. 58 Some of these cracks may escape detection in the forge, and unsound roky billets are thus produced. **1940** Simons & Gregory *Steel Manuf.* xix. 141 It is not uncommon for these cracks to be unnoticed in advance of forging or rolling, and they then elongate and 'open-out', producing 'roky' billets.

rol, obs. form of ROLL *sb.*[1] and *v.*[2]

rolag ('rəʊlæg). *Spinning.* [a. Gael. *rolag*, dim. of *rola* a roll.] A roll of carded wool ready for spinning.

1932 Simpson & Weir *Weaver's Craft* v. 30 The wool is now lifted lightly on the right-hand card, and placed on the back of the left, where it is rolled between the two card backs into a neat roll, or 'rolag'. **1964** H. Hodges *Artifacts* ix. 128 The roll of carded or combed fibres, the *rolag* or *sliver*, may be wound round a second rod. **1977** Y. Deutch *Weaving & Spinning* 129 The wool must first be teased and carded to separate the fibres and prepared for spinning by forming a roll of wool or rolag. *Ibid.*, Before spinning you will need to prepare by hand about 45 cm (18 in) of woollen thread from a rolag.

Roland ('rəʊlənd). Also 4 **Rouland (Rau-), Roulond,** 5 **Rowlonde,** 5–6 **Rowlande,** 6–9 **Rowland.** [OF. *Roland.*]

1. The legendary nephew of Charlemagne, celebrated in the *Chanson de Roland* and many other romances (frequently together with his comrade Oliver); hence, one comparable to Roland in respect of courage or warlike deeds; one who is a full match for another.

a **1300** *Cursor M.* 15 Hou king charlis and rouland faght. *a* **1330** *Otuel* 82 A kniȝt þat heet Roulond, & a noþer hatte oliuer, Kniȝtes holden wiþouten peer. **14..** *Sir Beues* (C.) 1910 Soche strokes were neuer seen yn londe Syth Olyuere dyed and Rowlonde. **1525** Ld. Berners *Froiss.* II. lxxx. [lxxvi.] 239 They were suche men that there were a iii. M. of them euery man worth a Rowlande or an Olyuere;.. nor we shall not fyght agaynst Rowlande nor Olyuer. *a* **1548** Hall *Chron., Hen. VI*, 146 b, To haue a Rowland to resist an Oliuer: he sent solempne Ambassadors to the kyng of Englande, offeryng hym his doughter in mariage. —— *Edw. IV*, 196 To haue a Rowlande for an Olyuer,.. he procured an amity with Henrie, king of Castell. **1591** Shaks. *1 Hen. VI*, i. ii. 30 England all Oliuers and Rowlands bred, During the time Edward the third did raigne. **1828** Scott *F.M. Perth* viii, There was some laughter.. when, as Henry Smith termed it, they saw their Oliver meet with a Rowland.

2. (*to give*) ***a Roland for an Oliver***, (to give) as good as one gets, a quid pro quo or tit for tat.

1612 in Birch *Crt. & Times Jas. I* (1848) I. 187 Howsoever it fall out, there is hope you shall have an Oliver for a Rowland. **1696** Southerne *Oronooko* ii. i, I have a Rowland for her Oliver, and so you may tell her. **1706** E. Ward *Wooden World Diss.* (1708) 97 For tho' she can write no more than a Mermaid, yet by the Help of some two-penny Scribbler, she will always return him a Rowland for his Oliver. **1773** *Life N. Frowde* 132 We resolved to give him a Rowland for his Oliver, if he attacked us. **1816** Scott *Antiq.* xxxv, He gave my termagant kinsman a *quid pro quo*—a Rowland for his Oliver, as the vulgar say. **1884** Rider Haggard *Dawn* xxxiii, Comforted.. by the thought that he had given Mrs. Carr a Roland for her Oliver.

Rolandic (rəʊ'lændɪk), *a.* *Anat.* Also **rolandic.** [f. next + -IC.] Used to designate various features of the central nervous system associated with Rolando (see next), as (*a*) the motor region or area of the cerebral cortex; (*b*) the fissure or sulcus of Rolando; (*c*) the angle at which the fissure of Rolando meets the median plane of the brain.

1881 C. G. Comegys tr. *J. M. Charcot's Lect. Dis. Spinal Cord* v. 49 We have enclosed within these pyramidal lines, what is known as the Rolandic region of the cerebral cortex, and which represents.. a region endowed with special physiological properties. **1883** W. B. Hadden tr. *J. M. Charcot's Lect. Localisation of Cerebral & Spinal Dis.* v. 193 The central, median, or, if you will so term them, the Rolandic convolutions. **1890** *Jrnl. Anat. & Physiol.* XXV. 3 In most hemispheres a small variable tertiary furrow may be detected below the lower end of the Rolandic fissure. *Ibid.* 19 By the 'Rolandic angle' I mean the angle which is formed by the meeting of the upper end of the sulcus with the mesial plane. **1908** H. E. Santee *Anat. Brain & Spinal Cord* (ed. 4) iii. 56 The average Rolandic angle is 71° 7'. **1910** G. G. Davis *Appl. Anat.* 36 The Rolandic area embraces the ascending frontal, or precentral, and posterior portion of the three frontal convolutions, the former being in front of the fissure of Rolando, or central fissure. **1921** Tilney & Riley *Form & Functions Central Nerv. Syst.* xxxvi. 643 The entire length of the Rolandic fissure is 8 cm. *Ibid.*, The *gyrus Rolandicus*... extended the entire length of the two Rolandic fissures. **1962** M. C. H. Dodgson *Growing Brain* vii. 55 The determination of Cunningham's Rolandic Index may be useful in doubtful instances. **1972** M. L. Barr *Human Nerv. Syst.* xiii. 207 The rolandic sulcus indents the superior border of the hemisphere about 1 cm behind the midpoint between the frontal and occipital poles. **1974** L. F. Sies *Aphasia Theory & Therapy* i. 54 The third area.. is located within the mid-saggital fissure, just anterior to the Rolandic motor foot area.

Rolando (rəʊ'lændəʊ). *Anat.* The name of Luigi *Rolando* (1773–1831), Italian anatomist, used with *of* and *attrib.* to designate: **a.** A fissure or sulcus of the brain separating the frontal lobe from the parietal lobe, described by him in 1825 (*Mem. d. R. Accad. d. Sci. di Torino* XXIX. 163). [tr. F. *sillon de Rolando* (F. Leuret 1839, in *Anat. Comparée du Syst. Nerv.* (1839–57) I. vi. 398).]

1839–47 R. B. Todd *Cycl. Anat. & Physiol.* III. 696/2 Two superior convolutions are met with above the fissure of Sylvius, between which is placed.. the fissure of Rolando. **1861** *Proc. Zool. Soc.* 248 Fig. 1 was drawn from an almost fresh brain, fig. 2 represents a brain which had been for several months in spirit. The roundness of outline of the latter as compared with the former, and the more transverse direction of the fissure of Rolando, are very remarkable. **1890** *Jrnl. Anat. & Physiol.* XXV. 139 It is a question if the fissure of Rolando is present in any other brains than those of Apes and Man. **1921** Tilney & Riley *Form & Functions Central Nerv. Syst.* xxxvi. 643 The fissure of Rolando has been found interrupted near its middle in the brains of several distinguished men. **1974** *Encycl. Brit. Macropædia* XII. 982/2 The two major grooves on the lateral surface of the brain are the lateral fissure (fissure of Sylvius), which starts at the base of the brain and extends upward and backward on the lateral surface, and the central sulcus (sulcus of Rolando), which runs from the middle of the dorsal border of the hemisphere downward almost to the lateral fissure.

b. The translucent gelatinous substance which fills the ends of the posterior grey horns of the spinal medulla.

1853 Busk & Huxley tr. *A. Kölliker's Man. Human Histol.* I. 408 The posterior, longer and thinner [horns].. at the free edge are invested with a more transparent layer, containing a preponderance of smaller nerve-cells—the substantia gelatinosa of Rolando. **1872** H. Power tr. J. Gerlach in S. Stricker *Man. Human & Compar. Histol.* II. xxx. 361 The posterior cornua are divisible into two portions,.. an anterior and a posterior, which last, owing to its peculiar translucency when examined with the naked eye, has long been known as the substantia gelatinosa of Rolando. **1929** Hewer & Sandes *Introd. Study Nerv. Syst.* vi. 20 Fibres.. giving off collaterals arborising round cells of the substantia gelatinosa of Rolando. **1976** *Expr. Brain Res.* XXVI. 77 Peripheral neurotomy.. induced a series of peculiar, *sui generis* alterations, both in the Rolando substance and in the dorsal column.

role (rəʊl). Also 7 rowle, roll, 8- rôle. [Fr. *rôle*, in the same sense, properly the 'roll' containing an actor's part.] **1. a.** The part or character which one has to play, undertakes, or assumes. Freq. *fig.*, with reference to the part played by a person in society or life. Also *spec.*, a part in a play, opera, film, or broadcast drama; = PART *sb.* 9. See also *title-role* s.v. TITLE *sb.* 11.

1606 S. Gardiner *Bk. Angling* 102 The Euangelist from God hath receiued such a rowle, it being inioyned him, to prepare the way of the Lord. **1692** L'Estrange *Fables* 281 The methods of Government and of humane Society must be preserved, where every man has his roll, and his station assigned him. **1790–1** Burns *Let. to C. Sharpe*, I value the several actors in the great drama of life, simply as they act their parts... As you, Sir, go through your *rôle* with such distinguished merit [etc.]. **1824** Byron *Juan* xvi. xcvi, Juan, when he cast a glance On Adeline while playing her grand rôle. **1858** Holland *Titcomb's Lett.* iii. 105 She was really very pretty, and took up her *rôle* with spirit and acted it admirably. **1888** Bryce *Amer. Commw.* I. 195 In order to support the *rôle* which they unconsciously fall into when talking to Europeans. **1886, 1900** [see *title-role* s.v. TITLE *sb.* 11]. **1912** M. B. Leavitt *50 Yrs. Theatr. Managem.* xiv. 184 Jennie Winston, an Australian, was likewise famous as a male impersonator and was also a favorite in leading operatic rôles. **1937** D. Frohman *Encore* xv. 199 In the course of his subsequent long career on the stage, he included in his repertoire more than a hundred and thirty difficult rôles. **1973** R. Roud in P. Noble *Favorite Movies* x. 103 In *Citizen Kane*.. Welles does indeed play a role in his film. **1980** D. Garfield *Player's Place* iv. 157 Studio actors have been found wanting in the performance of 'classical' roles.

b. The typical or characteristic function performed by someone or something; freq. in phr. ***to play a role.***

1875 H. C. Wood *Therap.* (1879) 535 As it is always employed in combination with other more active medicines.. the rôle it plays is somewhat uncertain. **1895** Parkes *Health* 35 The *rôle* of these microbes is to disintegrate.. organic bodies into simpler elements. **1944** J. S. Huxley *On Living in Revolution* 73 He [*sc.* Darwin] was aware that isolation might play a role in the production of new species. **1957** E. Lehrman tr. *N. A. Gorchakov's Theatre in Soviet Russia* v. 108 Did the Communist Party have any ideas of its own about the role of the theater before the Revolution of October, 1917? **1963** J. & E. Newson *Patterns of Infant Care* i. 21 One of the maternal grandmother's chief roles.. is being steadily taken over by the doctor, the midwife and the health visitor. **1973** A. R. Prest in Crick & Robson *Taxation Policy* ix. 129 A more recent study does seem to suggest a more positive role for these devices. **1981** *Newsweek* 4 May 74/3 The so-called hypothalamic-pituitary axis is the master-control center for hormones throughout the body and also plays an important role in emotions.

2. *Social Psychol.* The behaviour that an individual feels it appropriate to assume in adapting to any form of social interaction; the behaviour considered appropriate to the interaction demanded by a particular kind of work or social position.

1913 G. H. Mead in *Jrnl. Philos.* X. 377 This response to the social conduct of the self may be in the rôle of another—we present his arguments in imagination and do it with his intonations and gestures... In this way we play the rôles of all our group; indeed, it is only in so far as we do this that they become part of our social environment. **1936** R. Linton *Study of Man* viii. 114 Every individual has a series of rôles deriving from the various patterns in which he participates and at the same time *a rôle*, general, which represents the sum total of these rôles. **1949** R. K. Merton *Social Theory* iii. 110 A conception basic to sociology holds that individuals have multiple social roles and tend to organize their behavior in terms of the structurally defined expectations assigned to each role. **1950** T. M. Newcomb *Social Psychol.* viii. 280 A position has no meaning without its accompanying role. **1961** E. Goffman *Encounters* 85 In sociology there are few concepts more commonly used than 'role', few that are accorded more importance, and few that waver so much when looked at closely. **1967** M. Argyle *Psychol. Interpersonal Behaviour* iv. 73 By a 'role' is meant a pattern of behaviour which is shared by most occupants of a position, and which comes to be expected of them. The role usually includes a series of distinct relationships with people in other positions. **1977** R. Holland *Self & Social Context* v. 82 There is no attempt to explore the possibility that psychologists' and sociologists' own roles may influence their definitions and uses of the concept of role.

3. An expression, usu. in the form of a symbol or series of symbols, of the function or signification of a term appearing in an index or thesaurus, used esp. as a means of indicating its possible relevance to other terms with which it may be associated. Usu. *attrib.*, as ***role indicator, operator.***

1961 *Amer. Documentation* XII. 98 (*heading*) Notes on the use of roles and links in coordinate indexing. **1963** *Aslib Proc.* XV. 297 With 'roles' each keyword is classified by function. **1970** A. Chandor et al. *Dict. Computers* 332 *Role indicator*, a code associated with a keyword to identify it as a noun, verb, or adjective, etc. **1976** *Program* X. 18 *Prevulcanization* is stripped to *prevulcanis* (a) to *prevulcan* (a) to *vulcan* (da): the letters within parentheses indicate the role indicator. **1977** A. C. Foskett *Subject Approach to Information* (ed. 3) vi. 81 One of the rules used by Coates is that when we have a *thing* defined by the *material* of which it is made, the thing precedes the material, which is introduced by the role operator. **1979** J. E. Rowley *Mechanised In-House Information Syst.* i. 46 Roles or role indicators are appended to an index term at the indexing stage to indicate the use of the term in that context.

4. *attrib.* and *Comb.* (sense 2), as ***role absorption, -assumption, -creating, -differentiation, -expectation, -structure, -structuring, theory, theorist; role-assuming, -determined, -determining*** adjs.; **role conflict**, the difficulties encountered when one role makes conflicting demands on an individual or when an individual has several roles whose demands are conflicting; **role distance**, detachment from one's role; also (with hyphen) as *vb.*; **role model**, someone who, in the performance of a role, is taken as a model by others; **role-play**, the performance of a role, esp. the deliberate rehearsal or acting of a particular role, freq. used as a technique in training or psychotherapy; so **role-play** *v. intr.* and *trans.*, **role-player, role-playing** *vbl. sb.*; **role relation, relationship** (see quot. 1957); **role reversal**, the assumption of a role which is the reverse of that normally performed; **role-set** (see quot. 1957); **role-taking**, the imaginary assumption, leading to understanding, of another's role; hence (as back-formation) **role-take** *v. intr.*

1937 J. L. MORENO in *Sociometry* I. 51 The weaker the *role absorption by the ego, the more often can the ego soliloquize. **1932** *Amer. Jrnl. Sociol.* XXXVII. 378 Our habitual self, or character, is, however, a natural precipitate of this *rôle-assuming vocation. *Ibid.*, The technique here involved is that of '*rôle-assumption'. **1957** *Brit. Jrnl. Sociol.* VIII. 108 Theories of the middle range.., for example, of reference groups and social mobility, of communication, *role-conflict and the formation of social norms. **1964** M. ARGYLE *Psychol. & Social Probl.* xiv. 169 People are often exposed to role-conflicts, usually between the demands of different roles, such as how much time to devote to the job or family, sometimes to complexities in the position, as in the case of the military chaplain. **1977** M. EDELMAN *Polit. Lang.* iv. 75 The professional and the public official whose function it is to 'help' the inadequate, .. is .. eager to play his or her role, equipped with a built-in reason to discount or reinterpret qualms, role conflicts, and disturbing facts. **1943** *Role-creating [see *role-playing*]. **1956** C. W. MILLS *Power Elite* i. 25 Some elite men *are*.. typically *role-determined, but others are at times role-determining. **1968** B. MAYO *Moral Agent* in *R. Inst. Philos. Lect.* I. iii. 63 This cannot possibly be the sense of 'personal' which is contrasted with 'role determined', for his actions certainly are decided by .. his role. **1967** C. MARGERISON in Wills & Yearsley *Handbk. Managem. Technol.* 18 The owner-managers of the nineteenth century were largely *role-determining actors—they were able to control their factories and affairs very much in the manner that they wished. **1955** P. E. SLATER in A. P. Hare et al. *Small Groups* 499 What is the relationship of personality factors to *role differentiation? Are there factors which predispose an individual to assume a particular role? **1972** M. ARGYLE *Social Psychol. of Work* viii. 180 Role-differentiation appears in small social groups, as division of labour appeared in the earliest human communities. **1961** E. GOFFMAN *Encounters* 93 This 'effectively' expressed pointed separateness between the individual and his putative role I shall call **role distance*... The individual is actually denying not the role but the virtual self that is implied in the role. **1972** M. L. SAMUELS *Linguistic Evol.* (1975) vii. 146 R. B. Le Page suggests to me that in England there would be good reasons for the aristocracy of the late fourteenth and early fifteenth centuries to adopt affected forms of speech as a means of 'role-distancing' from the lower classes, from whom they had hitherto been differentiated by speaking French. **1978** A. RYAN in Hookway & Pettit *Action & Interpretation* 68 The question whether the crucial element in the dramaturgical picture is that cluster of insights which goes under the general heading of 'role distance'. **1979** *Internat. Jrnl. Sociol. of Law* VII. 289 Not that the average performer seems conscious of any evidence on his part of role-distance; on the contrary, such ritual commitment furnishes the core of his identity. **1951** PARSONS & SHILS *Toward Gen. Theory of Action* iv. 190 *Role-expectations are patterns of evaluation. **1969** in Halpert & Story *Christmas Mumming in Newfoundland* 142 Cat Harbour .. is normally characterized by rather rigid and formal role expectations. **1957** W. THIELENS in R. K. Merton *Student-Physician* II. 138 By the time students enter law or medical school, those whose decisions were made earliest are most likely to have a *role model. **1977** *N.Y. Times Mag.* 26 June 10/2 If the teacher was a 'role model', parents were obviously unaware of it. **1961** R. J. CORSINI et al. *Roleplaying in Business & Industry* i. 9 If they stopped now and then and discussed, evaluated, and practiced alternative ways of reacting, they *roleplayed. **1964** M. ARGYLE *Psychol. & Social Probl.* x. 133 Students role-play some of the situations they will meet on the job. **1970** *Peace News* 2 Oct. 3/4 During a strategy game, a situation may arise which is so interesting that the group may want to roleplay it. When the roleplay is over, people can return to the strategy game. **1979** *Lore & Lang.* Jan. 4 Dylan (5:3) is taking part in a 'spiderman' role-play, and another participant tries to drag him away. **1943** J. L. MORENO in *Sociometry* VI. 438 *Role-player is a literary translation of the German word 'Rollenspieler' which I have used. **1978** *Dædalus* Summer 137 He [*sc.* the bourgeois] is the man who, when dealing with others, thinks only of himself, and, in his understanding of himself, thinks only of others. He is a role-player. **1980** *Times Lit. Suppl.* 31 Oct. 1221/3 The hero of Anne Tyler's new novel, Morgan Gower, is an inveterate role-player. **1943** J. L. MORENO in *Sociometry* VI. 438 It may be useful to differentiate between *role-taking*.. —**role-playing*—which permits the individual some degree of freedom—and *role-creating*. **1951** *Amer. Sociol. Rev.* XVI. 181/2 In *role-playing* one does not pretend anything. A policeman arresting a person is .. performing or *playing* a role expected of one holding the position of public protector. **1960** W. H. WHYTE *Organization Man* v. 56 The role of slugger—not just a role-playing role, either—was assigned in advance. **1980** *Times Lit. Suppl.* 23 May 575/5 Role-playing is perhaps the true subject of the modern novel. **1940** *Sociometry* III. 20 The pattern of *rôle relations around an individual as their focus, is called his cultural atom. **1950** T. M. NEWCOMB *Social Psychol.* xiii. 453 These four kinds of *role relationships call for quite different sets of activities on his part. **1957** E. BOTT *Family & Social Network* i. 3 A *role-relationship* is defined as those aspects of a relationship that consist of reciprocal role expectations of each person concerning the other. **1977** R. HOLLAND *Self & Social Context* v. 97 The person with a strong ego can integrate experience of his past role-relationships and put it to the use of role-performance. **1951** *Occupational Psychol.* XXV. 65 The method of *role-reversal is designed to change the cognitive structure of disputants so that their social perception changes from divergence to convergence. **1967** M. ARGYLE *Psychol. Interpersonal Behaviour* x. 188 Role-reversal: here a trainee takes the reverse of the role he would take in real life, e.g. a foreman takes the role of a shop-steward. **1975** W. A. HAVILAND *Cultural Anthropol.* xiii. 319/2 During the installation rites of a chief among the Ndembu .., a different type of role reversal is manifest; the chief must sit in silent humility while he is reviled .. by anyone who feels so inclined. **1957** R. K. MERTON in *Brit. Jrnl. Sociol.* VIII. 110 Unlike Linton, I begin with the premise that each social status involves not a single associated role, but an array of roles. This basic feature of social structure can be registered by the .. term, role-set... By *role-set I mean that complement of role-relationships in which persons are involved by virtue of occupying a particular social status. **1968** P. K. BOCK in J. A. Fishman *Readings Sociol. of Lang.* 215 Radically different behavioral expectations *are* attached to the role of 'teacher' in connection with various members of the corresponding role-set. **1977** WARREN & PONSE in Douglas & Johnson *Existential Sociol.* x. 274 Instead, they have been concerned with social roles, role sets, and so on. **1940** *Sociometry* III. 21 This often produces a typical conflict in the *rôle-structures of two marriage partners. **1978** A. RYAN in Hookway & Pettit *Action & Interpretation* 67 The sociologist may, perhaps, rest content with giving a structural description of a society's role structure. **1967** D. COOPER *Psychiatry & Antipsychiatry* v. 84 There seemed an obvious need for a separate unit with less ritual and less rigid *role-structuring. **1972** *Jrnl. Social Psychol.* Dec. 247 The ability to *role-take accurately, or empathize, is the ability to see, feel, respond, and understand as if one were the other person. **1934** G. H. MEAD *Mind, Self & Society* IV. 254 The immediate effect of such *rôle-taking lies in the control which the individual is able to exercise over his own response. **1951** *Amer. Sociol. Rev.* XVI. 180/2 The term role-taking meant, for Mead, a strictly mental or cognitive or empathic activity, not overt behavior or conduct. **1964** M. ARGYLE *Psychol. & Social Probl.* x. 136 It [*sc.* indoctrination induced by Chinese 'thought reform'] can perhaps best be described as a piece of ego-involved role-taking, produced by extreme coercion, together with the temporary adoption of a new frame of reference. **1972** *Jrnl. Sociol Psychol.* Dec. 247 Role taking refers to the imaginative reconstruction by ego of alter's role. **1954** G. LINDZEY *Handbk. Social Psychol.* I. 238/1 More than any other single group, the *role theorists have developed and used the conception of the self as an intervening variable. **1977** R. HOLLAND *Self & Social Context* v. 91 Up to this point I have dealt with the *structural* role theorists represented in Coser and Rosenberg's book of readings. **1954** G. LINDZEY *Handbk. Social Psychol.* I. 238/1 The trend in role theory is in the study of the interactions of self and role as coordinates and not as parallels. **1972** W. C. COE *Challenges of Personal Adjustment* viii. 215 Role theory bridges the gap between the constructs of sociology and of psychology.

Hence **role** *v. trans.*, to provide (a term) with a role indicator; **'roling** *vbl. sb.*

1976 *Program* X. 14 (*heading*) A minicomputer retrieval system with automatic root finding and roling facilities. *Ibid.* 24 The presence of the connective merely ensures that the first word in the multi-word phrase is roled and stored.

role, obs. variant of ROLL *sb.*[1] and *v.*; obs. Sc. var. ROW *v.*

roleau, obs. var. ROULEAU.

roleo ('rəʊliːəʊ). *U.S.* Also **rolleo**. [f. ROLL *v.*[2] + ROD)EO.] (See quot. 1942.) Also *attrib.*

1933 *Nat. Geographic* Feb. 166 (*caption*) A floating log affords precarious footing; yet this expert woodsman .. rides it standing... Contests in this sport are a part of the 'Rolleo' celebration held annually. **1942** BERREY & VAN DEN BARK *Amer. Thes. Slang* §513 *Rolleo*, .. a log-rolling contest. **1948** *Chicago Tribune* 6 July I. 1/4 The others learned that the roleo is like a rodeo—except that instead of riding ornery bronchos, the contestants ride on floating logs that spin so fast the water churns up like a lawn sprinkler. **1949** *Boston Globe Mag.* 9 Oct. 8/1, I only wish your dad could see you roll at the Roleo. **1954** *Ocean Press* 24 Aug. 7/3 Running first won the world's championship at a 'roleo' in 1942 and has held the title ever since. **1956** *Sun* (Baltimore) 29 June 11/1 Lawrence Bergeron, .. president of the National Roleo Association, drowned today while competing in the 'old-timer' finals of the world championship log-rolling championships.

†**'roless**, *a. Obs. rare.* In 4 **roles, rooles.** [f. RO *sb.* + -LESS, or ad. ON. *rólauss*. Cf. also G. *ruhelos*.] Restless.

a **1300** *Cursor M.* 24447 Apon mi tas oft-sith i stod, Roles ramband to þe rode. *c* **1300** in Wright *Lyric P.* xii. 42 This world me wurcheth wo, Roo-les ase the roo, y sike for unsete.

Rolex ('rəʊlɛks). The proprietary name of a make of watch. Also *attrib.*

1912 *Trade Marks Jrnl.* 14 Aug. 1242 'Rolex'... Watches. Wilsdorf & Davis, .. London, .. ; watch manufacturers. **1957** J. BRAINE *Room at Top* iv. 40 A young man with sleek black hair, a shiny red face and a gold Rolex Oyster. **1970** W. WAGER *Sledgehammer* (1971) xvi. 99 He glanced down at the face of his gold Rolex. **1973** J. ROSSITER *Manipulators* xiv. 138 The watch on his wrist [was] an upper-bracket Rolex. **1977** B. FREEMANTLE *Charlie Muffin* xvii. 170 He looked at the heavy Rolex watch that had been part of the élite snobbism of the Green Berets in Vietnam.

roley-boley, -poley, obs. ff. ROLY-POLY *sb.*

Rolf (rɒlf). Also **rolf**. The name of Ida P. *Rolf* (1897–1979), U.S. physiotherapist, used *attrib.* to designate her technique of deep massage (also known as 'structural integration') aimed at reducing muscular, and consequently psychic, tension. Hence as *v. trans.* Also **Rolfed** (rɒlft) *ppl. a.*; **'Rolfer**, a practitioner of this technique; **'Rolfing** *vbl. sb.*, the Rolf technique.

1958 D. LAWSON-WOOD *Psycho-Logics & Posture* 11 The author is a fully qualified and registered masseur and physiotherapist, and is engaged .. in further intensive study and research in the Rolf Technique. **1970** *Psychol. Today* IV. 58/1 Rolf and the older rolf practitioners recognize the importance of this emotional component. *Ibid.* 88/3 In the case of the rolfed subjects there was no training. **1971** W. C. SCHUTZ *Here comes Everybody* 176 One man has been Rolfed many times and one area of difficulty is a rounded back. **1972** G. DOWNING *Massage Bk.* 155 The pain .. stops immediately when the Rolfer's hand is taken away. **1972** *New Yorker* 21 Oct. 34/2 Everyone under twenty-five discussed Rolfing... Rolfing is a system of deep massage that stretches and rearranges the tissue surrounding the muscles. **1977** *N.Y. Times* (City ed.) 15 July c. 22/2 We already spend far too much time practicing artificial modes of sociability, such as group encounters, sensitivity training, 'T' groups, Rolfing and the like. **1979** *Brit. Med. Jrnl.* 24 Mar. 796/2 There are also those .. who heal with rolfing, shiatsu, polarity treatment, aeriontherapy, or psionic medicine.

rolic, variant of ROLLICK *v.*

rolk, obs. Sc. variant of ROCK *sb.*[1]

roll (rəʊl), *sb.*[1] Forms: 3–7 **rolle**, 5–7 **rol, rowle**, 6–8 **rowl**, 6–7 **roule** (6 **roull**), 7–8 **roul**, 6–7 (9) **role**, 6–7 **roole** (7 **roale**), 6– *Sc.* **row**; 4– **roll**. [a. OF. *roolle, roulle, rolle, role* (mod.F. *rôle*: see RÔLE), = Prov. *rolle, rotlle*, Cat. *rotllo*, Sp. *rollo, rol*, Pg. *rolo*, It. *ruolo*:—acc. of L. *rotulus* (whence also It. *rotolo, ruotolo*, Sp. and Pg. *rotulo*). From OF. the word has also passed into the other Teut. languages, appearing as MDu. *rulle, rolle* (Du. *rol*), MLG. *rulle*, G. *rolle*, OIcel. *rolla*, Sw. *rulla, rulle*, Da. *rulle, rolle*.]

I. 1. A piece of parchment, paper, or the like, which is written upon or intended to contain writing, etc., and is rolled up for convenience of handling or carrying; a scroll.

a **1225** *Ancr. R.* 344 Nis non so lutel þing of þeos þet þe deouel naueð enbreued on his rolle. **1303** R. BRUNNE *Handl. Synne* 9287 Wyþ hys teþe he gan to drawe, .. þat hys rolle to-braste and rofe. *c* **1400** *Destr. Troy* 800 For to knele on his knes .. And the rolle for to rede. **1463** *Bury Wills* (Surtees) 20, iij merours of glas .., wiche be redy with my other glasys, and dyuerse rolles with scripture. **1526** *Pilgr. Perf.* (W. de W. 1531) 95 b, The thre verses wryten in the rowle that gothe aboute the tree. *a* **1586** SIDNEY *Ps.* XL. iv, Lord, .. in thy bookes rowle I am writ. **1605** CAMDEN *Rem.* (1623) 188 Atlas bearing Heauen with a roule inscribed in Italian. **1718** PRIOR *Solomon* II. 277 Busy Angels .. spread The lasting Roll, recording what We said. **1797–1805** S. & HT. LEE *Canterb. T.* I. 340 Several small rolls of vellum or parchment. **1844** DICKENS *Mart. Chuz.* v, 'You see' said Mr. Pecksniff, passing the candle rapidly from roll to roll of paper, 'some traces of our doings here'. **1867** LADY HERBERT *Cradle L.* 101 He showed them a roll containing a panoramic representation of his travels. **1888** W. P. FRITH *Autobiog.* III. vi. 144 A young lady—with .. a roll of music in her hand.

2. *spec.* **a.** Such a piece of parchment, paper, etc., inscribed with some formal or official record; a document or instrument in this form.

Freq. with defining term, as *rolls of Chancery, Court, Parliament*; also CHECKER, COURT-, RENT-ROLL, etc.

1377 LANGL. *P. Pl.* B. XIX. 460 With *spiritus intellectus* they seke þe reues rolles. **1433** *Rolls of Parlt.* IV. 479/1 That the rolles of accounte of the Baillifs, and the rentall rolle, .. and all Court rolles been putte and kepte in the cofre. **1444** *Ibid.* V. 74/1 To be enacted and enrolled of record, in the Rolle of the said Parlement. **1469** *Cal. Rec. Dublin* (1889) I. 333 Allso rollys to be made of the misis and costes. Allsoo rollis to be made of custumes. **1530** PALSGR. 537/1, I write a thyng in to a rolle of a courte, to remayne for recorde, *je enrolle*. **1591** LAMBARDE *Archeion* (1635) 55 The Chancellor had the keeping of the Rolls of Record, and the making out of Writs originall. **1611** BIBLE *Ezra* vi. 1 Search was made in the house of the rolles, where the treasures were laide vp. **1650** *Acts Sederunt* 2 Jan., The saids Lords .. ordaines the Lord, who is Ordinar in the Utter-house, to make ane roll, which he is to subscrive. **1712** ADDISON *Spect.* No. 447 ¶3 Being obliged to search into several Rolls and Records. **1765** BLACKSTONE *Comm.* I. 163 This law .. is much better to be learned out of the rolls of parliament, and other records. **1801** STRUTT *Sports & Past.* IV. ii. 296 In one of his wardrobe rolls we meet with the following entries. **1863** H. COX *Instit.* I. iv. 17 The practice commenced .. of entering the petitions .. on the Parliament Rolls.

fig. **1605** *Tryall Chevalry* I. i, He finds it written in the Rowles of time. *c* **1760** SMOLLETT *Ode Independence* 51 The rolls of right eternal to display.

b. ***Master*** (also †***Clerk*** or ***Keeper***) ***of the Rolls***, one of the four ex-officio judges of the Court of Appeal and a member of the Judicial Committee, who has charge of the rolls, patents, and grants that pass the great seal, and of all records of the Court of Chancery. Also *transf.* (quot. 1609).

A concise historical account of the office is given in the *Encycl. Brit.* (1886) XX. 628.

In quot. *c* 1687 the reference is to the Isle of Man.

1455 *Rolls of Parlt.* V. 301/2 The office of Keper of the Rolles of your Chauncerie. *c* **1460** J. RUSSELL *Bk. Nurture* 1017 Mastir of the rolles, riȝt þus ryken y, Vndir Iustice may sitte hym by. **1495** *Act 11 Hen. VII*, c 25 §3 The chief Justices of either Benche and the Clerke of the Rolles. **1509** in Leadam *Sel. Cases Crt. Requests* (Selden Soc.) 12 My lord Chaunceler comaundyd the Examynacyon vnto the master off the Rollys. **1581** LAMBARDE *Eiren.* I. v. (1588) 30 The Clearke of the Rolles (nowe called Maister of the Rolles). **1609** HOLLAND *Amm. Marcell.* XXIX. ii. 361 Having governed Syria, and gone through the Office of Master of the Rolles. *c* **1687** in Scott *Peveril* xi. *note*, One shill[ing] apiece to be giuen by them to the said cleark of the rolls, for .. engrossing these articles. *a* **1715** BURNET *Own Time* III. (1724) I. 381 He was soon after, without any application of his own, made Master of the Rolls. **1846** MCCULLOCH *Acc. Brit. Empire* (1854) II. 183 The Master of the Rolls ranks immediately after the Chief Justice of the King's Bench. **1889** GRETTON *Memory's Harkback* 141 Those who knew his value were fain to secure his services as Master of the Rolls.

fig. **1615** CROOKE *Body of Man* 502 Memory, which as a faithfull Recorder or Maister of the Rolles doth preserue, store vp [etc.].

c. *the Rolls*, the former buildings in Chancery Lane in which the records in the custody of the Master of the Rolls were preserved (now represented by the Public Record Office). Also = *Rolls Court* (see 5).

c **1430** LYDG. *Min. Poems* (Percy Soc.) 104 Unto the Rolls I gat me.., Before the clarkes of the chauncerye. **1598** STOW *Surv.* 319 Since the which time [1377] that house hath beene commonly called the Rolles in Chauncerie lane. **1610** HOLLAND *Camden's Brit.* (1637) 428 An house of Converts [[from Judaism]..which King Edward the Third appointed afterwards for rolls and records to be kept therein, and thereof at this day it is called The Rowls. **1668–9** PEPYS *Diary* 15 Mar., Thence to the Rolls, where I made inquiry for several rolls. *a* **1715** BURNET *Own Time* III. (1724) I. 596 When the fifth of November..came, in which we had always sermons at the Chapel of the Rolls. **1840** *Penny Cycl.* XVIII. 33/2 The order..(if presented at the Rolls) is at once drawn up by the secretary of the master of the Rolls. **1846** MCCULLOCH *Acc. Brit. Emp.* (1854) II. 182 The Master of the Rolls..administers justice in a separate court called the Rolls.

3. a. A register, list, or catalogue (of names, deeds, etc.); also phr. ***roll of fame***. Chiefly in fig. use.

In very frequent use from *c* 1800. The early examples are only contextual uses of sense 1.

c **1386** CHAUCER *Pard. T.* 911 Com vp, ye wyues, Youre names I entre heer in my rolle anon. **1393** LANGL. *P. Pl.* C. IV. 111 þei ouhten For to spure..What manere mester oþer merchaundise he vsede, Er he were vnder-fonge free and felawe in ȝoure rolles. **1433** *Rolls of Parlt.* IV. 479/1 That..all Burgeis rolles..been putte and kepte in the cofre. *a* **1529** SKELTON *Agst. Garnesche* 193, I rekyn yow in my rowllys, For ij dronken sowllys. **1598** BARRET *Theor. Warres* II. i. 18 To keepe a roll or list of all the souldiers of his company. **1610** HOLLAND *Camden's Brit.* (1637) 582 Registred in the roll of Saints. **1673** CAVE *Prim. Chr.* I. i. 10 Banished them out of the roll of their Deities. **1692** R. L'ESTRANGE *Josephus, Emb. to Caius* xii. (1733) 903 The Addition of one more to the Roll of our former Calamities. **1725** POPE *Odyssey* VIII. 418 Happy King, whose name The brightest shines in all the rolls of fame! **1768–74** TUCKER *Lt. Nat.* (1834) II. 415 Retained servants entered upon the steward's roll. **1828** SCOTT *F.M. Perth* vii, The merchants, shopkeepers, and citizens, who..filled up the roll of the ordinary magistracy. **1852** MISS YONGE *Cameos* (1877) II. iv. 46 The roll of the slain was brought to them as they sat down to supper. **1880** SWINBURNE *Stud. Shaks.* 118 The place occupied by *Bartholomew Fair* on the roll of Ben Jonson's [plays].

b. *Sc. Law.* A list of cases coming before a judge or court.

1826 SCOTT *Jrnl.* 31 Jan., There being nothing in the roll to-day, I stay at home from the Court. **1838** W. BELL *Dict. Law Scot.* 867 The roll itself is a list of the several causes, containing the surnames of the parties, and of the counsel, and in the weekly printed rolls, the name of the agent also.

c. The official list of those qualified to practise as solicitors (†or attorneys).

Commonly pl., and esp. in phr. ***to be struck off the rolls***, to be debarred from practising as a solicitor in consequence of some delinquency.

[**1835** *Penny Cycl.* III. 66/1 When the attorney is admitted, he subscribes a roll, which is the original roll of attorneys, of which the court takes notice as the recorded list of its officers.] **1840** DICKENS *Old C. Shop* xxxvi, His daughter could not take out an attorney's certificate and hold a place upon the roll. **1861** MRS. H. WOOD *East Lynne* v, He was on the rolls but had never set up for himself. **1862** A. TROLLOPE *Orley Farm* I. vii. 56 If I had..thrown over a client of mine by such carelessness as that, I'd—I'd strike my own name off the rolls.

4. A list of names used to ascertain whether each one of a set of persons is present; esp. *Mil.* (= MUSTER-ROLL) or in scholastic use.

1597 SHAKS. *2 Hen. IV*, III. ii. 106 Where's the Roll?..let them appeare as I call. **1598** BARRET *Theor. Warres* v. ii. 143 He taketh a roll of the bands committed to his charge. **1687** in *Magd. Coll. & Jas. II* (O.H.S.) 117 We called over the College Roll. **1799** WELLINGTON in Gurw. *Desp.* (1834) I. 37 It would surely be advisable to order the rolls to be constantly called, and to forbid any people to leave camp. **1828** SCOTT *F.M. Perth* xx, A royal pursuivant was dispatched..to call over the roll of Sir John Ramorny's attendants. **1859** THACKERAY *Virgin.* xii, The roll of each company is called at morning, noon, and night.

5. *attrib.*, as ***roll-bearer***; ***Rolls-Arbitrer***, ***-Buildings***, ***-Chapel***, ***-Court***, ***House***. Also, **Rolls Series**, a series of 'chronicles and memorials of Great Britain and Ireland published under the direction of the Master of the Rolls'; so ***Rolls edition***.

1598 SYLVESTER *Du Bartas* II. iii. *Captaines* 46 First a Student (under others' aw), Then Barister,..Then Queen's Solicitor, then Roules-Arbitrer. **1708** J. CHAMBERLAYNE *Pres. St. Gt. Brit.* II. III. (1710) 571 Six Clerks of the Rolls-Chappel. **1841** *Penny Cycl.* XX. 70/1 *Rolls-Court*, the Court of the Master of the Rolls, of which there are two, one at Westminster,..the other in the Rolls Buildings in Chancery Lane. **1849** ROCK *Ch. of Fathers* II. 381 A messenger, called from his office the Roll-bearer, carried it. **1884** MORRIS *Spec. Early Engl.* II. 340 The English text of Trevisa in the "Rolls" edition. **1887** FURNIVALL *Chron. R. Brunne* Introd. xix, So much worthless repetition in Latin as the Rolls Series must..contain.

II. 6. a. A quantity of material (*esp.* cloth), rolled or wound up in a cylindrical form, sometimes forming a definite measure. Also, a number of papers, etc., rolled together.

1378–9 *Durh. Acc. Rolls* (Surtees) 181 In tribus roll de worset..pro staminis faciend. **1391** *Earl Derby's Exped.* (Camden) 89 Pro vno rolle de satyn nigri. **1440–1** *Durh. Acc. Rolls* (Surtees) 627 Et pro 2 Rollez de Say pro camera Prioris. *c* **1489** CAXTON *Sonnes of Aymon* vii. 167 A hundred rolles of silke. **1540** *Act 32 Hen. VIII*, c. 14 For euery rolle, packe, or maunde of cony skynnes, xviii.s. sterlynge. **1612** A. HOPTON *Conservancy Yeares* 164 A Rowle of parchment is 5 dozen, or 60 skins, a dozen is 12 skins. **1660** *Act 12 Chas. II*, c. 4. Sched., Buckrams of the East country the roule or half-piece, v.s. **1719** DE FOE *Crusoe* I. (Globe) 85, I felt..the roll of English Lead,..but it was too heavy to remove. **1852** MRS. STOWE *Uncle Tom's C.* xiv. 127 The young man..had been making out a roll of bills while he was speaking. **1897** MISS KINGSLEY *Trav. Africa* 517 Quantities of gold dust, rolls of rich velvets, silks, satins, &c.

b. A quantity (usually small) of some soft substance formed into a cylindrical mass.

15.. HEN. VIII in *Vicary's Anat.* (1888) App. IX. 221 When it [*sc.* the plaster] is nere colde, make yt in rolles. *Ibid.*, Styrring it vntill it be plaster-wyse; and so make it vppe in rolles. **1641** MILTON *Animadv.* III. 63 It..was a pectoral roule we prepared for you to swallow down to your heart. **1717** ADDISON *Ovid's Europa's Rape* 27 Large rolls of fat about his shoulders clung. ? **1790** IMISON *Sch. Arts* II. 85 Pour it into water, and immediately make it up in rolls, and it is fit for use. **1809** POWELL tr. *Lond. Pharm.* (ed. 2) 324 [The soap plaster] must be formed into rolls when it begins to thicken. **1896** *Daily News* 30 July 5/2 Ireland sells its butter by the cask and firkin; England, by the pound, and 'roll' of 24 ounces, the stone, and the hundredweight.

c. A quantity of tobacco leaves rolled up into a cylindrical mass; tobacco in this form.

1633 *Virginia Stat.* (1823) I. 205 Noe tobacco..shall be made upp in rolle except betweene the first day of August and the last day of October. **1662** J. DAVIES tr. *Olearius' Voy. Ambass.* 203 That which the Ambassadors sent..consisted in..a Vessel of Aquavitæ, and a Roll of Tobacco. **1719** DE FOE *Crusoe* I. 42, I raised fifty great Rolls of Tobacco on my own Ground,..and these fifty Rolls being each of above a 100 Wt. were well cur'd and laid by. **1728** CHAMBERS *Cycl.* s.v., The generality of Tobacco in America is there sold in Rolls, of various Weights. **1809** R. LANGFORD *Introd. Trade* 127 Tobacco in the roll. **1843** *Penny Cycl.* XXV. 17/1 The finest tobacco however is made into rolls, which from their shape are called carrots. **1898** *Daily News* 23 Apr. 5/1 The rebate on tobacco..for the manufacture of cigars and roll.

d. *U.S.* The specific name of part of an ox.

1884 *Harper's Mag.* July 299/1 The division is made into ....loins, ribs, mess, plates, chucks, rolls, rumps.

e. A quantity of bills or notes rolled together; hence, the money a person possesses. *U.S.* and *Austral.* Also phr. ***a roll Jack Rice couldn't jump over***, a large quantity of money (*Austral. slang*).

1846 *Dollar Newspaper* (Philadelphia) 22 Apr. 4/6 He also had a roll which he said contained $600. **1904** *N.Y. Times* 16 May 5 It was as easy to be separated from one's 'roll' at a shell game there a quarter of a century ago as it was ten years ago. **1907** 'O. HENRY' *Trimmed Lamp* 171 He drew out his "roll" and slapped five tens upon the bar. **1912** J. SANDILANDS *Western Canad. Dict., Roll*, or *Wad*, a person's present supply of dollar bills or paper money. Roll him is to rob him of his money. **1919** H. L. WILSON *Ma Pettengill* ii. 62 [He] asked her how big her roll was, saying that he lived out there and it cost something to make a home. *a* **1925** [see CUT *v.* 56 q]. **1926** J. BLACK *You can't Win* iv. 35 No Missouri dip would take his roll, extract two fifty dollar bills, and put the rest back in his pocket. **1945** BAKER *Austral. Lang.* v. 107 A man..may even be fortunate enough to have a roll Jack Rice couldn't jump over. Jack Rice was a racehorse noted for his performances over hurdles. **1954** T. RONAN *Vision Splendid* II. 119 'I've got a roll Jack Rice couldn't jump over.' Marty produced one of those wads of currency Mr. Tappingham had seen only in the cruder American films and started peeling off ten-pound notes. **1960** 'N. CULOTTA' *Cop this Lot* v. 82 Man walks around with a roll in 'is kick Jack Rice couldn' jump over, an' 'e's not worth a zac.

f. A quantity of photographic or cinematographic film supplied rolled up; a spool of film.

1890 [see sense 14 c]. **1925** *Kodak Mag.* July 109 It is quite a good idea to develop just one or two rolls, to make sure that you are giving correct exposures. **1960** O. SKILBECK *ABC of Film & TV Working Terms* 110 Some Magazines hold..only two hundred feet of Stock and the Rolls are smaller than normal. **1973** C. MCCARRY *Miernik Dossier* (1974) 147 I'm sending you a roll of snaps to keep for me... You can have them developed. **1976** K. THACKERAY *Crownbird* v. 82 Priest was loading a roll of Tri-X into a black Nikon.

g. *spec.* = *music roll* (*b*) s.v. MUSIC *sb.* 13 d.

1902 *Encycl. Brit.* XXXI. 767/1 The use of the perforated roll acts by means of the ingenious and indeed faultless application of pneumatic leverage to the ordinary piano. **1906, 1913** [see *music roll*]. **1921** A. HUXLEY *Crome Yellow* x. 94 The music stopped... He..turned to the cabinet where the rolls were kept. He trod off the old roll and trod on the new. **1926**, etc. [see *piano roll*]. **1928** *Melody Maker* Feb. 161/3 Holding back the licenses of the 'Mechanical' reproductions on records and rolls. **1956** S. LONGSTREET *Real Jazz* 129 James P. Johnson was a great man on the rolls. Till 1920 he punched a lot of rolls. After that he recorded sides. **1972** *Jazz & Blues* Oct. 6/3 Changing the playing speed of the roll does not alter the pitch. **1977** *Times* 25 June 26/9 (Advt.), Pianola piano..100 rolls..£700.

h. A rolled-up quantity of a prohibited drug.

1962 'K. ORVIS' *Damned & Destroyed* v. 36 Loaded. Full of heroin. Carrying a roll, too. **1976** *Whig-Standard* (Kingston, Ontario) 21 Jan. 45/3 Bruce denied any knowledge of the roll, claiming his suitcase had been left unopened in the motel.

7. a. A small quantity of cloth, wool, straw, etc., rolled up into the form of a band or fillet. Now *spec.* a carding of this form.

a **1548** HALL *Chron., Hen. VIII*, 78 b, Gold and purple veluet, embrodered with little rolles of white sattin. **1553** BRENDE *Q. Curtius* D j, The diademe y[e] King ware upon his head..had a roule about it of white and grene. **1604** E. G[RIMSTONE] *D'Acosta's Hist. Indies* VI. xii. 456 A red rowle of wooll, more fine then silke, the which hung in the middest of his forehead. **1683** SALMON *Doron Med.* I. 318 Set it upon a Wreath, or rowl of Straw or Rushes. **1707** MORTIMER *Husb.* (1721) I. 328 To keep them [ants] from Trees, incompass the Stem four Fingers breadth with a Circle or Roll of Wooll newly pluck'd from a Sheep's Belly. *c* **1816** *Edin. Encycl.* VII. 286 Children are employed to lift the rolls or rowans from the carding engine, and unite them on the feeding-cloth. **1835** URE *Philos. Manuf.* 169 The fleece..is turned out in rolls called cardings, upon an endless cloth placed in front of and beneath the fluted cylinder. **1875** KNIGHT *Dict. Mech.* 1962/1.

†b. A form of bandage; = ROLLER *sb.* 10. *Obs.*

1541 R. COPLAND *Guydon's Quest. Chirurg.* L ij, Y[e] fore ende of the sayde rolle oughte to be sewed. And yf nede be there ought to take dyuers rolles. **1599** A. M. tr. *Gabelhouer's Bk. Physicke* 306/2 We must rowle the same.. with narrowe rowles, or with Fetles, according to the constitution of the disease.

8. †a. A round cushion or pad of hair or other material, forming part of a woman's head-dress.

1538 ELYOT, *Antiae*, the heare of a woman that is layde ouer hir foreheed, nowe gentylwomen do call them their rolles. **1579** LYLY *Euphues* (Arb.) 116 Take from them their ....Iewells, their rowles, their boulstrings, and thou shalt soone perceiue that a woman is the least parte of hir selfe. **1600** —— *Midas* I. ii, 'Now you can say no more of the head, begin with the purtenances...' 'The purtenances! it is impossible to reckon them vp... Hoods, frontlets,.. ribbons, roles' [etc.]. **1654** *MS. Diary*, For a silver Cawl and Rowl for my sister... For a black Cawl and Rowl. **1725** DE FOE *Voy. round World* (1840) 133 Large flat plates of gold upon the hinder part of her head, something in the place of a roll, such as our women wear. **1777** SHERIDAN *Sch. Scandal* II. i, Your hair combed smooth over a roll.

fig. **1597** MIDDLETON *Wisd. Solomon* xviii. 1 The pitchy night puts on a blacker rowl.

†b. A piece of cloth serving to form a turban.

1553 EDEN *Treat. Newe Ind.* (Arb.) 147 The gentlemen.. hauing theyr heades bounde aboute with listes and rowles of sundry coloures after the maner of the Turkes. **1572** in Feuillerat *Revels Q. Eliz.* (1908) 174 Bumbast to stuf Rowles for the Turkes heades. **1583** in Hakluyt *Voy.* (1904) V. 252 About his head a linen rowle.

c. An annular pad for placing on the head in order to facilitate or ease the carrying of heavy articles on it. Now *dial.*

1681 GREW *Musæum* II. i. i. 182 A..Ring of Wood, almost in the shape of a Womans Head-Roll, but not so big. **1681** W. ROBERTSON *Phraseol. Gen.* (1693) 1083 A roll for a woman's head, to carry things on, *arculus*. **1716** LADY M. W. MONTAGU *Let. to C'tess Mar* 14 Sept., Those rolls our prudent milk-maids make use of to fix their pails upon. **1855** [[ROBINSON] *Whitby Gloss.*, *Roll*, a circular pad, more or less annular in form, worn on the head by females who have to carry or support a heavy weight with that member.

†d. A support for a gown or petticoat, used instead of a farthingale. *Obs. rare*$^{-0}$.

1611 COTGR., *Hausse-cul*, a French Vardingale; or (more properly) the kind of roll vsed by such women, as weare.. no Vardingales. [**1632** SHERWOOD, *Roll* (which some women weare vnder their gownes), *hausse-cul*.]

†9. A billow, a roller. *Obs. rare*$^{-1}$.

1535 COVERDALE *Jonah* ii. 3 All thy wawes and rowles of water went ouer me.

10. a. A small loaf of bread, properly one which has been rolled or doubled over before baking.

1581 W. FULKE in *Conf.* III. (1584) Q ij, The sacramental bread..was..a rowle of bread. **1598** FLORIO, *Pane buffeto*, manchet bread or roule. *c* **1618** MORYSON *Itin.* IV. IV. i. 332 These wemen present them with Rowles baked like dry Fritters. **1674** JEAKE *Arith.* (1696) 74 Waster Bread seems to be Rowles or fine manchet Bread used principally in Victualling Houses to drink with. **1711** SWIFT *Jrnl. to Stella* 23 Dec., I have sat at home all day, and eaten only a mess of broth and a roll. **1741** *Compl. Fam.-Piece* I. ii. 98 Toast a whole French Roll, and put in the Middle of your Dish. **1790** *Trans. Soc. Arts* VIII. 155 It made very light breakfast rolls. **1832** *Blackw. Mag.* Jan. 11/2 New novels..are now looked for as regularly as rolls for the breakfast table. **1889** GUNTER *That Frenchman* iii, He sits down to his rolls, eggs, and coffee.

attrib. **1844** J. T. HEWLETT *Parsons & W.* xxxvii, The milkman, the rollman, the butterman.

b. With punning allusion to sense 2 b.

1649 J. TAYLOR (Water-P.) *Wand. West* 4, I left him in his shop, Lord Baron of the Browne Loaves, and Master of the Rolls (in that place). **1848** FORSTER *Goldsm.* III. vi. (1854) I. 310 He thought nature had meant him for a lord chancellor. "No,' whispered Derrick, who knew him to be a wealthy baker from the city, 'only for a master of the rolls.'

c. An item of food (other than bread) that is rolled up or doubled over before being cooked; chiefly with defining words, as ***fig-***, ***meat***, ***potato roll***. See also *jelly roll* s.v. JELLY *sb.*[1] 4, *pancake roll* s.v. PANCAKE *sb.* 3, *sausage roll* s.v. SAUSAGE 4 d, *Swiss roll* s.v. SWISS *a.* 2.

1845 E. ACTON *Mod. Cookery* xvi. 420 Excellent meat rolls. Pound..veal, chicken, or turkey... Form it into small rolls..fold them in good puff-paste, and bake them. **1922** JOYCE *Ulysses* 25 A bag of figrolls lay snugly in Armstrong's satchel. *a* **1944** K. DOUGLAS *Alamein to Zem Zem* (1946) 62 Meat roll and excellent ersatz coffee graced our menu. **1950** *Mrs. Beeton's Bk. Househ. Managem.* 1181 *Potato rolls*... Cut the potatoes into small pieces... Roll out the paste to the thickness of ⅛ of an inch, cut in rounds or squares 4 inches across, fill each with the vegetables, fold it over like a turnover, and bake.

11. a. *Arch.* A spiral scroll used in Corinthian and Ionic capitals; a cylindrical moulding; a curl, volute. ***roll and fillet***, 'a round moulding with a small square fillet on the face of it' (Francis).

1611 COTGR., *Volute*, the writhen circle, or curle tuft that hangs ouer, or stickes out of the chapter of a piller, &c.; and is tearmed by our workmen a Rowle, Cartridge, or

Carthouse. **1660** H. Bloome *Archit.* Ej, The lesser rowles. **1842** Gwilt *Encycl. Arch.* 1026 *Rolls*.. signifies in Gothic architecture mouldings representing bent cylinders. **1849** Ruskin *Seven Lamps* iv. §27. 116 It is a tracery of three orders;.. the second and third orders are plain rolls. **1879** *Cassell's Techn. Educ.* III. 40/2 A portion of the stone on either side was cut away, thus leaving the cylindrical roll clearly defined.

b. *Building.* A strip of wood, rounded on the top and fastened on the ridge or the lateral joints of a roof, to raise the edges of sheet-lead or zinc and so prevent the entrance of rain-water. ***hollow roll***, one formed by the edges of two sheets of lead or zinc being bent over together.

1833 Loudon *Encycl. Arch.* §1584 Lay on small joists.. and rolls (pieces of wood rounded, to dress the edges of the lead over). **1839** *Civil Eng. & Arch. Jrnl.* II. 78/2 The Water falling on such roof.. is carried off, and rolls and seams are rendered unnecessary. **1887** T. Hardy *Woodlanders* I. viii. 141 The grey lead roofs were quite visible.., with their gutters, caps, rolls, and skylights. **1904** Goodchild & Tweney *Technol. & Sci. Dict.* 288/2 *Hollow roll*, a lead roll made by bending over the edges of sheet lead, and so forming a tube. **1960** *B.S.I. News* May 23 Guidance on the use of lead sheet used as a covering for roofs... Design methods for both the woodroll and hollow-roll systems.

12. A part which is rolled or turned over.

1671 Grew *Anat. Pl.* I. iv. (1682) 31 The two Rowls beginning at each edge of the Leaf, and meeting in the middle. **1709** Steele *Tatler* No. 15 ¶4, I saw the Fellow.. hide Two Cards in the Roll of his Stocking. **1713** Swift *Frenzy of J. Denny* Wks. 1755 III. I. 139 The rolls of his stockings fell down to his ankles. **1821** tr. *Decandolle & Sprengel's Philos. Plants* 55 The roll (*ochrea*) is commonly a cylindrical membrane... It appears as a peculiar organ in the Polygoneæ and Cyperoideæ. **1841** S. Warren *Ten Thousand a Year* III. iii. 111 He had two waistcoats, the under one a sky-blue satin, (only the roll visible). **1898** *Hutchinson's Arch. Surgery* IX. 363 The first was in the roll of the reflected prepuce.

13. *Geol.* An ore body in sedimentary rock that has a C- or S-shaped vertical cross-section cutting across strata. Freq. *attrib.*

1942 *Bull. U.S. Geol. Survey* No. 936. 363 The vanadium-bearing hydrous mica is.. in part concentrated.. in thin zones that cut across bedding. As the zones.. are curved or wavy, they are called rolls by the miners. **1955** *Prof. Papers U.S. Geol. Survey* No. 300. 239/1 Similarities between roll ore bodies and the more prevalent tabular ore bodies in sedimentary rocks of the Colorado Plateau. *Ibid.* 239/2 In cross section, rolls commonly show C, S, and 'socket' shapes.., but in plan are linear. **1976** R. I. Rackley in K. H. Wolf *Hand-bk. Strata-Bound & Stratiform Ore Deposits* VII. iii. 116 The uranium 'roll' has long been known to uranium producers.

14. a. *attrib.*, in sense 'having the form of, made up in, a roll', as ***roll bread, brimstone, candle, film, -shutter, tobacco***, etc. Also †***roll-fashion***.

*c*1415 in *Rec. St. Mary at Hill* p. xcvi, Small wex Roll Candelles, to make .v. crosses vpon the awter. **1442** *Rolls of Parlt.* V. 61/1 Rolle Worsted xxx yardes long, and di. yard brode large. **1581** W. Fulke in *Conf.* III. (1584) Q ij, This thing is of long shape, or rowle fashion. **1665** Pepys *Diary* 7 June, I was forced to buy some roll-tobacco, to smell to and chaw. **1728** Chambers *Cycl.* s.v. *Roll*, Roll Tobacco is what is used both for chewing and rasping. **1764** *Museum Rust.* II. 174 Four ounces of roll brimstone. **1766** *Compl. Farmer* s.v. *Bread* T 2/1 We also meet with symnel bread, manchet or roll bread, and French bread:.. in roll bread there is an addition of milk. **1778** Aikin tr. *Beaume's Man. Chem.* (1786) 224 *Roll Sulphur.* During its fixing it takes the crystaline arrangement observed in the inside of rolls of brimstone. **1839** *Civil Eng. & Arch. Jrnl.* II. 358/1 Improvements in roll-lead and other soft metals. **1844** H. Stephens *Bk. Farm* III. 912 The other kind is called roll arnotto. **1880** *Nature* XXI. 210 The 'roll-cumulus' of the English Meteorological Office. **1895** *Montgomery Ward Catal.* Spring & Summer 217/1, 1 Roll Film, for 25 exposures—.20 1 Box of 5 Rolls of Film (for 25 exposures each) 1.00. **1902** *Encycl. Brit.* XXXI. 690/2 In many ways the most convenient and compact hand cameras are those made specially for use with the roll-film cartridges in many different sizes. **1911** *Chambers's Jrnl.* Feb. 141/2 At the kerb end the front is provided with a roll-shutter. **1913** I. Cowie *Company of Adventurers* 311 Accordingly Whitford placed on the dressed buffalo skin which they had placed on the ground before them, two pint measures of tea and a yard of thick Canadian roll tobacco. **1922** Rollshutter [see down-coming *ppl. a.*]. **1929** Moberly & Cameron *When Fur was King* 35 One and a half feet of Canadian roll tobacco sold for one.. made-beaver. **1933** *Discovery* Feb. 59/2 Roll films are used, each roll containing one hundred exposures. **1951** Yarsley & Kitchen in H. M. Langton *Synthetic Resins* (ed. 3) ii. 116 The bulk of the many millions of feet of cine film used throughout the world to-day is still celluloid, and $3\frac{1}{2}$ mil celluloid is the base for amateur roll film. **1977** J. Hedgecoe *Photographer's Handbk.* 10 By the 1890s George Eastman's rollfilm camera allowed many pictures to be taken at one loading.

b. *Arch.*, as ***roll-moulding, -tracery***. (Cf. 11 a.)

1830 Whewell *Arch. Notes German Churches* Pref. 11 The interior.. has.. abundance of small roll mouldings. **1835** R. Willis *Arch. Mid. Ages* 54 This enables us to divide it at once into two classes, Fillet-tracery and roll tracery. **1849** E. Sharpe *Dec. Window Tracery* 53 Roll-tracery is more common in Geometrical, than in Curvilinear Windows. *a*1878 Scott *Lect. Arch.* (1879) I. 248 The heaviness of large roll mouldings was often relieved by fillets.

c. *Comb.*, as ***roll-carding-engine, -end, -holder; roll-munching*** adj.; also **roll-boiling** (see quot. 1839 and roller *sb.* 24).

1835 Ure *Philos. Manuf.* 168 The finisher or roll-carding-engine differs from the scribbler in several particulars. **1839** —— *Dict. Arts* 1327 That part of the process where a permanent lustre is given usually by what is called roll-boiling; that is, stewing the cloth, when tightly wound upon a roller, in a vessel of hot water or steam. **1890** *Anthony's Phot. Bulletin* III. 322 There is no scope for so fixing the roll holder in its case. **1970** *Toronto Daily Star* 24 Sept. 27/1 (Advt.), Roll ends at cost. **1970** G. F. Newman *Sir, You Bastard* viii. 210 The bar was packed with fat roll-munching office workers. **1976** *Bridgwater Mercury* 21 Dec. 5/1 (Advt.), Room-size remnants. We must clear dozens of roll-ends to make room for new stocks.

III. 15. a. A cylindrical piece of wood or metal used to facilitate the moving of something; a roller; a windlass.

1426-7 *Rec. St. Mary at Hill* (1905) 64 Payd for a rolle & ij goiouns of Iron & a rope, xiiij d. *a*1547 Surrey *Æneid* II. 297 Underset the feet With sliding rolles. **1593** *Wills & Inv. N.C.* (Surtees, 1860) 229 A towele rowle of wood, 2ᵈ. **1603** Knolles *Hist. Turks* (1621) 539 [They] could not be out of their places removed, but.. with leavers and roules put under them. **1683** Pettus *Fleta Minor* I. 52 If you will have .. your Silver hollow and thin for separation.. granulate it over a Role. **1735** J. Price *Stone-Br. Thames* 8 The Ribs.. may be let down on Rolls. **1793** Smeaton *Edystone L.* §259 Fitted out with a roll proper for heaving up the anchor and chains. **1842** Gwilt *Encycl. Arch.* 1027 When blocks of marble.. are to be moved, they use what are called *endless rolls*. **1884** F. J. Britten *Watch & Clockm. Handbk.* 39 A roll or jumper.. keeps each wheel in its place.

b. *Weaving.* In the old hand-loom, a roller or beam round which the warp or the web was wound. Also *attrib.* and in combs. ***cane-, knee-, yarn-roll***.

1538 Elyot, *Panus*, also a weauers rolle, whereon the webbe of clothe is rolled or wounden. **1580** Hollyband *Treas. Fr. Tong, Loupe*, the roll of a weauers loome. **1728** Chambers *Cycl.* s.v., 'Tis on such Rolls that the Woollen, Silken, and other Threads are wound, whereof the Weaver's Works consist. **1797** *Encycl. Brit.* XVIII. 835/2 From this opening the web.. passes to the knee roll or web beam.., round which it is rolled by means of the spokes. *Ibid.*, Opposite to the breast-bar.. is the cane-roll or yarn-beam. **1823** *Mech. Mag.* 143 As he was turning on his cane at the cane spreaders, he missed his hold of the role stick. **1831** G. Porter *Silk Manuf.* 215 The beam, or yarn-roll, on which the threads are wound.

c. *Bookbinding.* A revolving patterned tool used in impressing and gilding; also, the pattern produced by a tool of this kind.

1656 Blount *Glossogr.* s.v., Books in Rolls are those which have a Roll of Gold on the edges of the Cover. **1687** Miége *Gt. Fr. Dict.* I, *Roulette, à faire le bord des Livres*, a Roll. **1818** *Art Bk.-binding* 25 Have a piece of rough calf leather to rub your tools, rolls, letters, etc. upon. **1879** *Cassell's Techn. Educ.* IV. 402 The fillets produce lines of various thicknesses.., whereas the rolls are covered.. with a complicated pattern. **1890** [see fillet *sb.* 11 c].

†**16.** *Naut.* (See quots.) *Obs.*

1611 Cotgr., *Molinet*,.. the roll wherein the whip of a Rudders tiller goes. **1627** Capt. Smith *Seaman's Gram.* II. 12 The Whip-staffe.. going thorow the Rowle, and then made fast to the Tiller with a Ring. **1644** Manwaring *Seaman's Dict.*, *Roll*, is that round piece of wood or iron, wherein the whip doth go. [Hence in later Dicts.]

17. a. A roller used for levelling soil or crushing clods.

1634 *Althorp MS.* in Simpkinson *Washingtons* (1860) App. p. lxvii, A stone roale for the walkes. **1651** Robert Child in Hartlib *Legacy* (1655) 107 This spreading of the Root is probable to be best effected by a Rowl, or some such thing. **1677** Plot *Oxfordsh.* 248 A weighty Roll, not cut round, but octangular, the edges whereof meeting with the clods, would break them effectually. **1707** Mortimer *Husb.* (1721) I. 28 In Oxfordshire they have Rolls made with Steel Edges, which as they go round cut the Turf. **1767** A. Young *Farmer's Lett. to People* 107 Oxen are precisely as convenient.. in the waggon, in carts, and tumbrills, in rolls, &c. **1805** R. W. Dickson *Pract. Agric.* I. 475 A one-horse roll then follows to level the flag, or furrow. **1854** *Jrnl. R. Agric. Soc.* XV. II. 483, I have found it advisable to use the roll occasionally to firm the soil. **1899** Rider Haggard *Farmer's Year* 148 First a roll drawn by one horse is passed over the land.

b. A roller used to crush, flatten, or draw out something, esp. in metal-working.

1656 Cromwell in *Grose's Antiq. Rep.* (1808) II. 411 Liberty to use all or any singular presses, rolls and cutters. **1676** J. Worlidge *Cyder* (1691) 103 Let the cylinders or rolls be about eight or ten inches in diameter. **1728** Chambers *Cycl.* s.v., Rolls, in Coining, are two Iron Instruments of a cylindrical Figure, which serve to draw or stretch out the Plates of Gold, Silver, and other Metal. **1753** in *6th Rep. Dep. Kpr. Rec.* App. II. 127 Cast metallic Rolls for the crushing.. or grinding of.. any kind of Grain. **1843** Holtzapffel *Turning* I. 184 The rollers or rolls of the ironworks are turned of a variety of forms. **1884** W. H. Greenwood *Steel & Iron* 319 The Rolls employed for the conversion of the shingled bloom of malleable iron into puddled bar, or into merchant bars, plates, sections, &c.

c. *Paper-making.* (See quot. 1875.)

1875 Knight *Dict. Mech.*, *Roll*, a cylinder mounted with blades for working paper-pulp in the tub. **1880** J. Dunbar *Pract. Papermaker* 29 The journals of the roll shaft should be frequently wiped, and no stuff.. allowed to escape at the ends of the roll or from below the edge of the roll cover.

18. *attrib.* and *Comb.*, as ***roll-carriage, -press, -printing, -train; roll-turner; roll-produced*** adj.; **roll feed**, a feed mechanism supplying paper, strip metal, etc., by means of rollers; so **roll-feeding** *vbl. sb.*; **roll-fed** *ppl. a.*; **roll-forming** *vbl. sb.*, cold forming of metal by repeated passing between rollers; so **roll-form** *v. trans.*; **roll-formed** *ppl. a.*; **roll mark**, a mark produced on sheet metal in flattening it with an imperfect set of rollers.

See also 17 c, and Knight *Dict. Mech.* (1875).

1793 Smeaton *Edystone L.* 196 The upright views of the *Roll carriage.. shew distinctly the manner of supporting the axis of the rolls on iron frames. **1967** Karch & Buber *Offset Processes* ii. 31 *Flexo-graphic.* This process involves the use of rotary (web or *roll fed) printing from rubber plates. **1968** *Gloss. Terms Mechanized & Hand Sheet Metal Work (B.S.I.)* 19 **Roll feed*, a feed mechanism that imparts continuous or intermittent motion to strip by means of rollers in contact with both surfaces. **1967** V. Strauss *Printing Industry* vi. 362/2 *Roll feeding was originally developed for the production of metropolitan newspapers by relief printing. *Ibid.* 363/1 Designers of roll-feeding machinery have devised a number of different roll-feeding methods. **1949** *Tool Engineers Handbk.* (Amer. Soc. Tool Engineers) 989 Most sheet and strip metals can be successfully *roll-formed. **1958** *Times Rev. Industry* June 20/1 The cylindrical body sections are made from two plates, roll-formed cold to shape and welded together. **1971** *Engineering* Apr. 59/1 Some permanent plastic coatings.. will endure the metal to which they are applied being drawn, roll-formed, bent, and pressed, without cracks developing or the coating peeling. **1949** *Tool Engineers Handbk.* (Amer. Soc. Tool Engineers) 989 Generally speaking, the sharpest corner practicable to maintain on a *roll-formed section would be one having an outside radius equal to the metal thickness. **1977** *Engin. Materials & Design* Aug. 50/3 Because the rivets are roll-formed, they are straighter than extruded rivets. **1932** E. V. Crane *Plastic Working of Metals* v. 91 Bending Operations.—Bar-folders, brakes, drawbenches, *roll-forming machines and bending dies in presses share the field. **1954** J. F. Young *Materials & Processes* (ed. 2) xix. 805 Roll forming consists of passing strip stock between sets of shaped driven rollers. **1967** S. Kalpakjian *Mech. Processing of Materials* vi. 202 A further development of roll forming is the production of welded tubing, starting with a flat strip. **1923** Glazebrook *Dict. Appl. Physics* V. 364/1 The effect of alternate heating and cooling is to cause small cracks in the surface of the rolls, which lead to slight ridges, or '*roll marks'. **1962** G. R. Bashforth *Manuf. Iron & Steel* (ed. 2) IV. iv. 138 Sections are liable to develop certain defects, such as.. 'roll marks' due to defective or badly worn rolls. **1866** *Tomlinson's Cycl. Usef. Arts* II. 461/2 Copper-plate and lithographic printing is performed at a *roll-press. **1890** W. J. Gordon *Foundry* 198 Printing from continuous paper is known as 'web-printing', '*roll-printing', or 'reel-printing'. **1952** J. B. Oldham *Eng. Blind-Stamped Bindings* i. 4 The use of a *roll-produced decoration. **1881** Raymond *Mining Gloss.*, **Roll-train*, the set of plain or grooved rolls through which iron or steel piles, ingots, blooms, or billets are passed, to be rolled into various shapes. **1884** *B'ham Daily Post* 24 Jan. 3/4 *Rollturners.—Journeymen Wanted.

roll, *sb.*² Also 7 rowle, 8 rowl. [f. roll *v.*¹]

1. a. The act of rolling; the fact of moving in this manner.

1743 Bulkeley & Cummins *Voy. S. Seas* 7 Upon the Rowl of a Sea, all the Chain-Plates to Wind-ward broke. **1847** C. Brontë *J. Eyre* xxv, I wish I could forget the roll of the red eyes. **1871** Tyndall *Fragm. Sci.* (1879) I. vi. 194 The roll of the Atlantic was full, but not violent. **1897** *Allbutt's Syst. Med.* II. 916 In tobacco intermittence the patient is, I believe, always conscious of the stop and roll-forward [of the heart].

fig. **1827** Scott *Jrnl.* 15 June, The conversation took its old roll. **1868** Tennyson *Spiteful Let.* 8, I hear the roll of the ages. **1884** G. Allen *Philistia* I. 5 Before he can set things fairly on the roll for better arrangement.

b. With *a* and pl. A single act, spell, or occasion of rolling. In ***go and have a roll***: go away, 'get lost' (*slang*).

1802-12 Bentham *Ration. Judic. Evid.* Wks. 1827 IV. 34 It has never yet been proposed that they should.. take a roll in the contents of a night-cart. **1820** T. Mitchell *Aristoph. Clouds* (1838) 8 These places of exercise for horses were strewed with dust,.. and a roll in them seems to have been allowed the Greek horses. **1877** Tennyson *Harold* v. i, If this war-storm in one of its rough rolls Wash up that old crown of Northumberland. **1941** Baker *Dict. Austral. Slang* 34 *Have a roll!, go and*, go to the devil! **1959** I. & P. Opie *Lore & Lang. Schoolch.* x. 192 Juvenile language is well stocked.. with expressions inviting a person's departure, for instance:.. go and have a roll.

c. A rolling gait or motion; a swagger. Esp. in phr. ***to have a roll on*** and varr.: to have a conceited bearing, to give oneself airs (*Eng. Public School slang*).

1836-7 Dickens *Sk. Boz, Characters* vii, That grave, but confident, kind of roll, peculiar to old boys in general. **1881** C. E. Pascoe *Everyday Life in our Public Schools* 160 Anything approaching 'swagger' is severely rebuked; there is no more objectionable quality than that understood by the expression, 'He's got such a horrid roll on'. **1908** D. Coke *House Prefect* i. 11 Brereton, they decided, had a bit of a roll on. **1913** A. Lunn *Harrovians* iii. 53 Ewen was an ugly lout, and was beginning to put on roll... after the game, his tendency to 'put on roll' was duly checked in the approved fashion.

d. (An act of) rotation of a vehicle or craft about an axis parallel to its direction of motion.

In the case of ships the movement consists of a partial rotation, immediately reversed, caused by wind or waves; with aircraft it is either a similar unintended movement or a deliberate manœuvre consisting of a complete turn through 360°; with motor vehicles and helicopters it is a tipping (outwards and inwards respectively) in cornering.

1862 W. Froude *Rolling of Ships* 75 All ships having the same 'periodic time', or period of natural roll, when artificially put in motion in still water, will go through the same series of movements. **1907** J. Masefield *Tarpaulin Muster* xvi. 161 At the last of her rolls there comes a clattering of tins, as the galley gear and whack pots slither across to leeward, followed by cursing seamen. **1912** *Techn. Rep. Advisory Comm. Aeronaut. 1911-12* 102 The pendulum movement from side to side.. misleads the pilot into operating his wing flaps to recover the vertical position of his body. By this he may aggravate the roll. **1918** W. G. McMinnies *Pract. Flying* x. 194 The roll, which consists of making the machine loop sideways and continue in the same direction as it was travelling before the manœuvre, is done with the engine on or off. **1920** *Nature* 11 Mar. 47/2 For use on board ship the compass must be mounted.. so that the rolls.. shall have but small effect on the compass. **1942** N. MACMILLAN *How to pilot Aeroplane* xv. 100 The full roll, the half roll, and the double half roll can all be made on the glide or during a zoom as well as on the level. **1945** J. M. LABBERTON *Marine Engineers' Handbk.* ix. 1389 The maximum velocity will occur at the vertical position and diminish to zero at the extremities of the roll... The maximum dynamic effect will occur at the maximum angle of roll. **1953** M. RAUSCHER *Introd. Aeronaut. Dynamics* 660/2 (Index), Roll or Bank, angle of. **1957** J. SHAPIRO *Helicopter* iii. 52 The sideways attitude of the helicopter against the horizon is known as its 'roll'. A more frequently used term for the same condition is 'bank'. **1961** *Times* 28 Mar. 4/6 There is a good deal of roll when cornering fast. **1967, 1974** [see PITCH *sb.*[2] 2 b]. **1974** *Physics Bull.* Jan. 11/1 The six component wind tunnel balance.. will be able to measure three forces (lift, drag and side force) and three moments (pitch, yaw and roll) on any aircraft model it supports. **1978** *Lancashire Life* Apr. 141/1 The Fiat 132-2000 rides very well indeed on all kinds of road surface and corners capably with a minimum of roll.

e. *Gymnastics.* An exercise in which the body is rolled into a tuck position and turned in a forward or backward circle.

1898 F. GRAF et al. *Hints to Gymnasts* III. 176 Before attempting any kind of.. rolls.. or handstands, the pupil should have mastered thoroughly all kinds of straight arm swinging exercises. **1920**, etc. [see *neck-roll* s.v. NECK *sb.*[1] 17]. **1935** *Encycl. Sports* 331/1 When half the roll has been accomplished the hands are changed from behind the head to a position in front, so that the body is then pivoted on the inside of the arms. **1955** *Simple Gymnastics* ('Know the Game' Series) (ed. 2) 25 *Forward Roll*—Bend forward and take the weight of the body on the hands. Tuck the head well under and roll with the knees on the chest. **1956** KUNZLE & THOMAS *Freestanding* ii. 32 From a forward roll to stand, to a cartwheel sideways down the same line as the roll.

f. A throw (at dice).

1926 G. ADE *Let.* 26 Oct. (1973) 114 This kind of party [*sc.* a 'Monte Carlo' party] is the wildest and most hilarious thing you ever heard. Before we got through Sunday evening the crap shooters were rolling for a hundred thousand a roll. **1966** O. NORTON *School of Liars* iv. 62 Ben rattled the dice-box. 'Now.. we'll have a quick roll before Hank the Bank comes, and I think Scott's in the chair.' **1969** R. C. BELL *Board & Table Games* II. v. 91 The first caster throws all five dice on his first roll. **1974** *Times* 20 Feb. 19/2 We are still schooling craps on this and we think we can make it on the next roll.

g. *colloq.* An act of sexual intercourse. ***a roll in the hay***: see HAY *sb.*[1] 3.

1942 BERREY & VAN DEN BARK *Amer. Thes. Slang* §362/1 *Copulation*,.. roll. **1962** P. GREEN tr. *S. de Beauvoir's Prime of Life* I. ii. 80, I had several unpleasant incidents with truck drivers, not to mention a commercial traveler who wanted me to have a roll with him in the ditch, and left me flat in the middle of the road when I refused. **1976** P. FERRIS *Detective* viii. 146 It involves State Security. Your Rosemary has been having a roll with a Cabinet Minister.

h. In colloq. phr. ***on a roll*** (orig. *N. Amer.*), enjoying a sequence of successes or a run of good fortune.

1976 [see *winning streak* s.v. WINNING *vbl. sb.*[1] 9]. **1979** *Tucson Mag.* Jan. 26/1 Now she is 26 and on a roll. **1983** *Christian Science Monitor* 5 Dec. 43/2 The paranoia of seeing the Soviets on a roll, the sense of the U.S. in decline, has about evaporated. **1984** *Times* 21 Mar. 19/2 The economy is on a powerful roll, but I am not worried about overheating. **1985** *New Yorker* 29 Apr. 55/2 Culpepper was on a roll... He could do no wrong.

2. *Mil.* Of a drum: A rapid, uniform beating, produced by alternate strokes of the sticks, and falling upon the ears as a continuous sound. ***long roll*** (see quot. 1802).

1688 HOLME *Armoury* III. xix. (Roxb.) 154/2 The maner of which beatings is performed by.. down right and rowling blows, for which they haue these termes: A Roofe. A Rowle [etc.]. **1802** JAMES *Milit. Dict.* s.v. *Role*, *Long roll*, a beat of drum by which troops are assembled at any particular spot or rendezvous or parade. **1842** LEVER *J. Hinton* v, Amid the thunder of cannon, the deafening roll of drums. **1861** in Post *Soldiers' Lett.* (1865) 56 We were so close to their batteries that we could hear.. the drums beating the 'long roll'.

transf. **1876** STAINER & BARRETT *Dict. Mus. Terms* s.v., In the case of a tambourine, the roll is produced by a rapid succession of blows from the knuckles.

3. a. Of thunder, etc.: A loud, reverberating peal; a continuous reverberation; a prolonged shout.

1818 KEATS *Endym.* I. 289 A shout from the whole multitude arose, That linger'd in the air like dying rolls Of abrupt thunder. **1839** DICKENS *Nich. Nick.* xxii, The roll of the lighter vehicles which carried buyers and sellers to the different markets. **1847** DE QUINCEY *Sp. Mil. Nun* v. Wks. 1853 III. 9 The crowd saluted her with a festal roll, long and loud, of vivas. **1889** CONAN DOYLE *M. Clarke* 3 The crash of guns, like the deep roll of a breaking wave.

b. *Phonetics.* = TRILL *sb.*[2] 3. Cf. ROLL *v.*[2] 4 c, ROLLED *ppl. a.* 4.

1950 D. JONES *Pronunc. of Eng.* (ed. 3) I. 95 Another variety of the 'burr' is a uvular fricative sound (without roll)... One may also hear a uvular roll with accompanying friction. **1973** J. D. O'CONNOR *Phonetics* ii. 47 Rolls consists of several rapidly repeated closures and openings of the air passage, as in the rolled *r*-sounds of Scottish or Italian... [The] uvular roll is common in Dutch for *r* and may be heard in French and German too—the sound is reminiscent of a gargling noise.

4. A rich sonorous or rhythmical flow of words in verse or prose.

1730–46 THOMSON *Autumn* 17 Thy tongue, Devolving thro' the maze of eloquence A roll of periods, sweeter than her song. **1858** FROUDE *Hist. Eng.* IV. 481 The beautiful roll of its language mingles with the memories of childhood. **1868** TENNYSON *Lucretius* 11 Fancy, borne perhaps upon the rise And long roll of the Hexameter. **1870** HUXLEY *Lay Serm.* iii. (1874) 49 The roll of Ciceronian prose.

5. a. *Mus.* The sounding of the notes of a chord in rapid succession; arpeggio.

1890 in *Cent. Dict.*

b. (See quot.)

1886 *Appleton's Ann. Cycl.* XI. 87 The roll is the most characteristic of all the canary-notes. This even and continuous roll is as perfect as the trill of any instrument.

6. An undulation or swell on the surface of land.

1874 KAY-SHUTTLEWORTH *Ribblesdale* III. 153 Drained into hollows between gentle rolls of land. **1902** 'LINESMAN' *Words Eyewitness* 285 As she looks for the form of her absent 'man' across the great yellow rolls of the veldt.

7. *Mining.* (See quots.)

1851 GREENWELL *Coal-trade Terms, Northumb. & Durh.*, *Roll*: see *Balk*. **1862** *Min. & Smelting Mag.* I. 313 'Swells', or 'rolls', and 'nips', are names given to a rising up in the floor of a coal bed, and where the roof and the floor both swell out, so as to reduce the thickness of the bed. **1883** GRESLEY *Gloss. Coal-mining*, *Roll*, see *Bump*. [A very sudden breaking, sometimes accompanied by a settling down, or upheaval of, the strata, during the working away of the mineral.]

8. *attrib.* and *Comb.*, as ***roll angle, plane***; **roll axis**, the axis about which a vehicle or craft rolls; **roll bar**, an overhead metal bar to protect the occupants of a motor vehicle in the event of its overturning; **roll cage**, in a motor vehicle, a centre box section designed to protect the occupants if the vehicle overturns; also *attrib.*; **roll cast** *Angling* (see quot. 1960[1]); hence as *vb. trans.* and *intr.*; ***roll-casting*** vbl. sb.; **roll rate**, the angular velocity of a vehicle or craft about its roll axis.

1961 *Which? Reports on Cars* 14 Published reports so far have been based on subjective assessment of *roll angle. **1970** *Motoring Which?* July 99/2 All three had low roll angles. **1950** NEWTON & STEEDS *Motor Vehicle* (ed. 4) xxxi. 566 The *roll axis for a car having axles at front and back will be some distance above ground level while that having independent suspensions at front and back will have a roll axis lying at ground level. **1962** Roll axis [see *pitch axis* s.v. PITCH *sb.*[2] 26]. **1954** *Amer. Speech* XXIX. 101 **Roll bar*, *n.*, a curved bar welded or bolted to the frame rails extending upward in back of the driver's seat to protect him in case he 'flips' over. **1957** *Life* 29 Apr. 133 In sanctioned meets cars must have roll bars over driver's seat. **1969** H. NIELSEN *Darkest Hour* xiii. 143 Goddard.. went over the embankment... The car has a roll bar, but you can see what happened. The door sprung open and he went out of it head first. **1979** *Tucson Mag.* Mar. 25/1 A removable forward hardtop and a convertible softtop rear window are separated by a Targa-style rollbar. **1972** *Sci. Amer.* Apr. 9/3 (Advt.), And '*roll cage' construction. The kind that soon, by law, may be required on all cars. **1973** *Times* 18 Oct. 35/3 The body comprises a one-piece glass-fibre outer shell on a steel monocoque centre section, with built-in rollcage. **1976** *Good Motoring* May 12/1 The roll-cage passenger compartment and anti-intrusion bars in the doors to help in side impacts. **1934** R. KELLY *Fishing* 9 (*heading*) The *Roll Cast. This cast is used where trees and brush overhang the banks of the stream. **1947** R. BERGMAN *With Fly, Plug & Bait* II. vi. 113 A skillful and long roll cast is essential. *Ibid.*, When roll casting I grease my line carefully. *Ibid.*, My torpedo head tapered line also has rather a stiff finish and roll-casts well. **1960** EDWARDS & TURNER *Angler's Cast* x. 101 The Spey cast .. is the simplest roll cast. *Ibid.* 105 If the angler is fishing the left bank of the river, with obstructions behind him, his only method of getting the line out is to roll cast. **1960** C. WILLOCK *Anglers' Encycl.* 158/2 *Roll-cast*, a fly cast in which the line is picked off the water without being thrown behind. **1972** *Trout & Salmon* June 58/3 Then make a roll-cast, but instead of roll-casting the line on to the water, roll it into the air. **1947** R. BERGMAN *With Fly, Plug & Bait* II. vi. 113, I have a special level line with a rather stiff finish which is especially fine for *roll casting. **1960** EDWARDS & TURNER *Angler's Cast* x. 101 The average angler.. thinks nothing of roll casting, with constant changes of direction, for half-a-day on his own trout stream. **1971** *Aeronaut. Jrnl.* LXXV. 295/2 Some selected type of manoeuvre, such as pitch attitude, or pitch rate, or normal acceleration, and corresponding quantities in the *roll plane. **1961** W. R. KOLK *Mod. Flight Dynamics* viii. 146 An airplane's ability to roll is properly a characteristic of its maneuverability, but is also a cornerstone of its flying qualities by reason of the unstable pitch-yaw resonance encountered at *roll rates exceeding the natural frequencies in either pitch or yaw. **1975** G. H. SAUNDERS *Dynamics of Helicopter Flight* v. 178 When the roll rate builds up to the point where the damping moment equals the control moment, no further increase in roll rate is achieved.

† **roll**, *sb.*[3] *Obs. rare.* In 5 rolle, 6 roule. [a. OF. *roele, roelle* (mod.F. *rouelle*), dim. of *roe, roue* wheel.] A flat, circular object; a disk.

c **1450** *M.E. Med. Bk.* (Heinrich) 214 Tak a gret rote of radysche, & pare hyt, & kytte hyt on fyfty Rounlettes,.. & on þe morowe ete ix rolles fastyngge. **1480** CAXTON *Myrr.* III. iv. 130 Thus.. she goth til she be al rounde, fayre, and clere in semblaunce of a rolle, and that we calle the ful mone. *c* **1550** H. LLOYD *Treas. Health.* N vj, To cause the stone to breke.., make ten or more roules of Radyshes rotes [etc.].

roll, obs. form of RÔLE.

† **roll**, *v.*[1] *Obs.* Also 4–5 rolle. [f. ROLL *sb.*[1]] To enrol; to write (a name, etc.) upon a roll, list, or register; to record (a statement or fact).

1377 LANGL. *P. Pl.* B. v. 278, I can þe nouȝte assoille, Til þow make restitucioun.., And sithen þat resoun rolle it in þe regystre of heuene. ? *a* **1400** *Morte Arth.* 2641 [I am] Kydd in his kalander a knyghte of his chambyre, And rollede the richeste of alle þe Rounde Table! *c* **1425** WYNTOUN *Cron.* VIII. xl. 6191 Of archeris thare assemblid were Twenty thowsand, that rollyd war. *c* **1450** *Cursor M.* 92 (Laud, 416), That is but fantasy of this world As yt is yn many boke roll. **1545** *Reg. Privy Council Scot.* I. 16 To pas to Lauder.., and ressave the saidis musteris.. and to roll thair names. **1597** SKENE *De Verb. Sign.* s.v. *Ballivus*, Quhen the Compter is charged.. conforme to ane former compt, rolled of before. **1651** JER. TAYLOR *Serm. for Year* I. (1678) 138 None of you all.. ever entered into this house of Pleasure, but he.. had his name roll'd in the chamber of Death.

absol. **1522** SKELTON *Why not to Court* 191 He rolleth in his recordes, He sayth, How saye ye, my lordes? Is nat my reason good?

roll (rəʊl), *v.*[2] Forms: α. 3–7 rolle, 4–7 role, 5 rollyn, 5–7 roll, 4 roll. β. 5–7 roule, 6–8 roul (7 rool), 6–7 rowle, 6–8 (9) rowl. γ. *Sc.* (and *north.*) 6 rou, 6– row, 8–9 rowe, 9 ro. [ad. OF. *roler, roller, rouler*, = Prov. *rolar* (*rotlar*), Sp. *rollar*, Pg. *rolar*, Catal. *rotolar*, It. *rotolare*:—pop. L. **rotulāre*, f. *rotula*, dim. of *rota* wheel. Hence also (M)Du. and G. *rollen*, Fris. *rolje, rôlje*, LG. *rullen*, Da. *rulle*, Sw. *rulla*.]

The following quotations illustrate the Scottish and northern forms:—**1513** DOUGLAS *Æneis* I. v. 72 Threty lang twelfmonthis rowing our. **1588** A. KING tr. *Canisius' Catech.* 97 To rou ȝour selfs in hair claith. **1677** *Lovers' Quarrel* 153 in Hazl. *E.P.P.* II. 259 In gold and silver thou shalt row. **1725** RAMSAY *Gentle Sheph.* III. ii, A fundling.. Right clean row'd up. **1787** BURNS *Brigs of Ayr* 120 In mony a torrent down the snaw-broo rowes. **1826** J. WILSON *Noct. Ambr.* Wks. 1855 I. 145 His collie, rowed up half asleep. **1885** STRATHESK *More Bits* ii, A clock is for keeping time if it's rowed up.

I. Transitive senses.

1. To move or impel forward (an object) on a surface by making it turn over and over; to shift about, to send down to a lower level, etc., in this manner. Also with *up* or *down, away*, etc. ***to roll the bones*** (*U.S. slang*), to play dice.

c **1375** *Sc. Leg. Saints* xlii. (*Agatha*) 255 þane bad he schellis & brynnand cole straw in þe floure,.. & nakyt þare-one hire rol. *Ibid.* xlv. (*Christina*) 218 He.. gert foure wicht men to ga þat suld rol hire to & fra. **1423** JAS. I *Kingis Q.* 163 So mony I sawe that than clymben wold, And failit foting, and to ground were rold. **1526** TINDALE *Mark* xvi. 3 Who shall rolle awaye the stone from the dore off the sepulcre? **1600** HOLLAND *Livy* XLII. II. 1124 They rolled downe two huge stones, whereof the one smote the King upon the head. **1665** SIR T. HERBERT *Trav.* (1677) 154 An Egg that fell from Heaven into Euphrates, and [was] by Fishes rolled on Land. **1726** SHELVOCKE *Voy. round World* (1757) 406 They rolled our casks down to the boat, but always expected a white face to assist them. **1743** BULKELEY & CUMMINS *Voy. S. Seas* 27 As Mr. Cozens was rowling up a steep Beech a Cask of Pease, he found it too heavy for him. **1832** MRS. MARCET *Seasons, Spring* (1847) 38 Off he would go, rolling along his hoop, and running after it. **1847** *Act 10 & 11 Vict.* c. 89 §28 Every Person who rolls or carries any Cask, Tub, Hoop, or Wheel.. upon any Footway. **1929** H. W. ODUM in *Amer. Mercury* Sept. 49/2 So we sets 'round in circle an' starts rollin' them bones. *Ibid.* 58/1 Gonna roll them bones. Gonna git some money an' play bad. **1945** L. SAXON et al. *Gumbo Ya-Ya* vii. 127 Today in the colored sections of the city there are always circles of men 'rollin' the bones' playing *Indian* Dice, which is any game of Craps unsupervised by a syndicate and without a player for the 'house'.

fig. **1581** R. GOADE in *Conf.* III. (1584) Q iiij, You heare his answere, this stone hath bene rowled enough. **1648** J. BEAUMONT *Psyche* I. cxxxii, Let their Wheels in any Circle run But that which might their homage roul to thee! **1651** HOBBES *Leviath.* III. xxxiii. 201 He had rolled off from the people the Reproach of Egypt. **1748** GRAY *Alliance* 49 Their Arms, their Kings, their Gods were roll'd away. **1857** HEAVYSEGE *Saul* (1869) 186 How light the heart whose weight is from it rolled!

b. To drive or draw (a vehicle); to wheel (a cycle); to move by means of rollers.

1513 DOUGLAS *Æneis* v. xii. 101 As the dirk nycht Rollit his cart ourthwort the polis brycht. *Ibid.* VI. ix. 115 By horssis four furth rollit wes his chair. **1535** COVERDALE *Jer.* xlvi. 9 Get you to horse backe, roll forth yᵉ Charettes. **1598** SYLVESTER *Du Bartas* II. i. III. *Furies* 268 Already all rowle-on their steely Cars On th' ever-shaking.. bars Of Stygian Bridge. **1648** HEXHAM II. s.v. *Rol*, Rolers wherewith a ship is Roled into the water, or into a haven. **1843** THACKERAY *Haggarty's Wife* Wks. 1898 IV. 499 Isn't he the most famous physician in Dublin, and doesn't he rowl his carriage there? **1894** *Outing* XXIV. 291/1 He carried a lantern and I rolled the wheel over a fair road and a large dike.

c. To convey in a wheeled vehicle.

1778 W. PRYCE *Min. Cornub.* 146 Room to roll back the broken deads in a wheel-barrow. **1842** LOVER *Handy Andy* xxi, The gig is round the corner, and the little black mare will roll us over in no time. **1889** BARRIE *Window in Thrums* ii, He'll be to row the minister's luggage to the post-cart.

d. To cover (a distance) by cycling.

1895 *Outing* XXVI. 361/1, I had rolled off seventy-seven miles from Allahabad.

e. *absol.* To bowl; to play at bowls. Also *trans.* To bowl (a game making a specified score, a number of strikes). *U.S.*

Cf. ROLLING *vbl. sb.*[2] 1, quot. 1583.

a **1864** HAWTHORNE *Amer. Note-bks.* 291 There is a bowling-alley on the island, at which some of the young fishermen were rolling. **1974** *Cleveland* (Ohio) *Plain Dealer* 13 Oct. c. 8/3 Marge Dimario, bowling in the Top Ten League at Ambassador Brookpark Lanes, rolled a 275 game. **1979** *Arizona Daily Star* 1 Apr. c2/6 Earl Anthony.. rolled nine strikes in the championship match yesterday.

f. Computers. ***to roll out***, (*a*) (see quots. 1954, 1962[1]); (*b*) to transfer (data held in a main memory) to an auxiliary store when a program of greater priority requires the former; similarly *to roll in* (in two senses).

1954 *Computers & Automation* Dec. 20/2 *Roll out*, to read out of a register or counter by the following process: add to the digits in each column simultaneously; do this 10 times (for decimal numbers); when the result in each column changes from 9 to 0, issue a signal. **1962** *Gloss. Terms Automatic Data Processing* (*B.S.I.*) 86 *Roll out* (*to*), for a counter which counts modulo *n*, to read its content by causing it to count a sequence of *n* pulses, determining at what stage in the sequence the content passes through zero. *Ibid.* 87 *Roll in* (*to*), to increase the content of a counter by causing it to count a sequence of pulses. **1969** P. B. Jordain *Condensed Computer Encycl.* 435 When main memory is released by any program, or a task terminates and its space becomes available, a task that had been rolled out can be rolled in and restarted. **1970** O. Dopping *Computers & Data Processing* ix. 123 The programs are..often stored in secondary memories, and the necessary program parts are rolled in to the primary storage when needed. When another program needs the memory space, some program parts may have to be rolled out to secondary storage again.

2. To form into a mass by turning over and over; to pile up in this manner. Also *fig.*

1547–64 Bauldwin *Mor. Philos.* (Palfr.) 97 Death.. rouleth both rich and poore folke together. **1553** Eden *Treat. Newe Ind.* (Arb.) 13 They rowled before them a bulwarke or countremure of earth. **1660** F. Brooke tr. *Le Blanc's Trav.* 106 The tide..flowes with such fury and impetuosity, as it were mountains rolled up in water. **1667** Milton *P.L.* vi. 594 Down they fell By thousands, Angel on Arch-Angel rowl'd, The sooner for thir Arms. **1757** W. Wilkie *Epigoniad* v. 122 Round the Theban walls, Heaps roll'd on heaps, the mingled forest falls. **1859** *La Crosse* (Wisconsin) *Union* 24 Oct. 2 He ought..to pitch in and help roll up a big majority for Randall. **1890** Hosmer *Anglo-Sax. Freedom* 360 The enormousness of the might which the autocrat of all the Russias is so rapidly rolling up. **1892** P. H. Emerson *Son of Fens* 13 The rollers are women who roll barley into ridges or tie the wheat. **1900** *Congress. Rec.* 23 Jan. 1103/2 They answered them by rolling up a plurality of 5,665 votes for the member from Utah out of a total of 67,805. **1951** *Sun* (Baltimore) 19 June 7/3 In the state elections of Lower Saxony..the SRP rolled up nearly 400,000 votes. **1976** *Billings* (Montana) *Gaz.* 4 July 11-A/1 The powerful PRI has always rolled up massive victories in every election during the past half century.

†**b.** To form (the brow) *into* wrinkles. *Obs.*⁻¹

1635–56 Cowley *Davideis* i. 130 Thrice did he knock his iron teeth, thrice howl, And into frowns his wrathful forehead rowl.

3. To drive or cause to flow onward with a rolling or sweeping motion. Also with *down*.

1667 Milton *P.L.* ii. 583 Farr off from these..Lethe the River of Oblivion roules her watrie Labyrinth. **1697** Dryden *Virg. Georg.* iii. 544 Where proud Ister rouls his yellow Sand. **1726–46** Thomson *Winter* 876 Where.., fring'd with roses, Tenglio rolls his stream, They draw the copious fry. **1792** Scott *Let.* in *Lockhart* (1837) I. vii. 190 The river rolls its waves below me of a turbid blood colour. **1802** *Edin. Rev.* I. 208 A river rolls down materials from every part of its channel. **1842** Tennyson *Locksley Hall* 186 Mother-Age..help me as when life begun: Rift the hills, and roll the waters. **1901** *Daily Express* 21 Mar. 5/6 Thames rolls the highest tide for two years.

refl. **1704** *The Sequel* xxxv, So Swelling Billows, when the Tempest cease, Foaming a while, they rowl themselves to peace. **1784** Cowper *Task* ii. 145 The waters of the deep shall rise, And..Shall roll themselves ashore.

fig. **1656** Cowley *Pindar. Odes, Praise of Pindar* ii, So Pindar does new Words and Figures roul Down his impetuous Dithyrambique Tide. **1833** Tennyson *Dream Fair Women* xlvii, Hearing the holy organ rolling waves Of sound on roof and floor Within.

b. To cause (smoke, etc.) to ascend in rolls.

1743 Francis *Horace's Odes* i. i. 5 In clouds th' Olympic dust to roll, To turn with kindling wheels the goal. **1840** Hawthorne *Biogr. Sk.* (1879) 173 The hearth..heaped with logs that roll their blaze and smoke up a chimney. **1887** Bowen *Æneid* ii. 758 Fierce fire by the wind to the rafters is rolled.

c. To bring *up* (wind) copiously.

1897 *Allbutt's Syst. Med.* III. 474 He..sits up in bed, and rolls up wind, belching it forth boisterously for many minutes.

4. *transf.* †**a.** *to roll up*, to recite rapidly. *Obs.*

1528 Tindale *Obed. Chr. Man.* 81 b, It is ynough yf thou canst rowle vpp a payre of matenses or an evensonge and mumell a few ceremonies. **1591** G. Fletcher *Russe Commw.* (Hakl.) 121 The boyes that are in the church answere all with one voyce, rowling it up so fast as their lippes can go.

b. To utter, give forth (words, etc.), with a full, rolling sound or tone. Chiefly with *out*.

1561 Hoby tr. *Castiglione's Courtyer* i. E iv, Yf in singing he roule out but a playne note. **1589** R. Harvey *Pl. Perc.* (1590) 16 A Preacher, if his conceipt be anything swift, that he can rolle it in the pulpit, must haue his reader at his elbow to fauor his voice. **1702** tr. *Le Clerc's Prim. Fathers* 289 To seek to be Admired by the ignorant Vulgar, by rowling, as it were, some words, and reciting with an extraordinary swiftness. **1814** Southey *Carmen Tri.* xvi, The happy bells, from every town and tower, Roll their glad peals upon the joyful wind. **1850** Thackeray *Pendennis* xvi[i], Pen,..who was a very excitable person, rolled out these verses in his rich sweet voice, which trembled with emotion.

c. To pronounce or sound with a trill.

1846 O. W. Holmes *Rhymed Lesson* Poet. Wks. (1895) 50 Don't, like a lecturer or dramatic star, Try over-hard to roll the British R. **1850** Thackeray *Pendennis* xxvii[i], Rolling out his *r* with Gascon force.

5. To turn round on (or as on) an axis; to cause to revolve or rotate; to turn over and over *in* something or between the hands; also, to carry *round* in revolving.

c **1400** *Brut* 253 Þai..toke a spete of Copur brennyng, & put hit þrouȝ þe horne into his body, and oftetymes rollede þerwiþ his bowailes. *c* **1430** *Two Cookery-bks.* 45 Þan rolle þin stuf in þin hond, & couche it in þe cakys. **1530** Palsgr. 693/1, I rolle a thyng bytwene my handes, *je roulle*. **1535** Coverdale *Lam.* iii. 16 He hath..rolled me in the dust. **1614** Markham *Cheap Husb.* i. iii, A branch or two of Saven anointed or rold in butter. **1667** Milton *P.L.* vii. 499 Now Heav'n in all her Glorie shon, and rowld Her motions. **1736** Gray *Statius* i. 41 And now in dust the polish'd ball he roll'd. **1799** Wordsw. *A slumber did my spirit seal* 7 No motion has she now,..She neither hears nor sees; Rolled round in earth's diurnal course.

fig. *c* **1400** in *Tundale's Vis.* (1843) 121 Thus gud feyth is rolled upso downe.

refl. **1596** Dalrymple tr. *Leslie's Hist. Scot.* I. 152 That he mycht..with the gretter confidence row him selfe in al filthines. **1611** Bible *Micah* i. 10 In the house of Aphrah rowle thy selfe in the dust. **1774** Goldsm. *Nat. Hist.* (1776) IV. 111 The porcupine..is said to roll itself upon the serpent, and thus destroy and devour it. **1796** H. Hunter *St.-Pierre's Stud. Nat.* (1799) III. 341 A mountain of water which approached us from the Sea, rolling itself over and over. **1864** Tennyson *En. Arden* 823 As the year Roll'd itself round again to meet the day When Enoch had return'd.

b. In literal renderings of Heb. *gālal*.

1560 Bible (Geneva) *Ps.* xxii. 8 He trusted [*marg.* roled] in the Lord. **1611** *Ibid.*, He trusted [*marg.* rolled himselfe] on the Lord. —— *Ps.* xxxvii. 5 *marg.*, Rolle thy way vpon the Lord. **1637** Sanderson *Serm.* (1681) II. 88 Roll thy self then upon His Providence, and repose thy self..upon His promises. **1659** Hammond *On Ps.* cxxxi. 3 To roll and repose themselves wholly upon God.

c. *Naut.* Of vessels: To cast (masts, etc.) overboard, to submerge (tackle, etc.), by rolling.

1633 T. James *Voy.* 107 Shee would haue rowled her Masts by the boord. **1799** *Naval Chron.* I. 11 One of the store ships rolled away her masts. **1805** in Nicolas *Disp. Nelson* (1846) VII. 168 *note*, The Santa Anna rolled over all her lower masts. **1868** *U.S. Rep. Munit. War* 266 Three times..did the ship roll her main chains right under, and threw the water on the upper deck. **1882** Nares *Seamanship* 198 Booms..have been..rolled overboard off the yards.

d. To cause to swing or sway from side to side.

1804 J. Grahame *Sabbath* 2 As his stiff unwieldy bulk he rolls, His iron-arm'd hoofs gleam in the morning ray. **1836** Sir G. Head *Home Tour* 208 Whenever..he gave the emphatic word of command 'Rowl her' the crowd..trotted across the deck. **1904** *Westm. Gaz.* 16 Aug. 8/1 The crew.. then tried the old whalers' dodge of rolling the ship with all hands.

refl. **1848** Dickens *Dombey* xxxiv, Then she..resumed her chair,..and rolling herself from side to side, continued moaning and wailing to herself.

e. To cause to fall and turn *over* by means of a blow, shot, etc.; to bowl *over*.

1850 R. G. Cumming *Hunter's Life S. Afr.* (ed. 2) I. 154, I got within range, and with a single ball I rolled him over in the dust. **1888** Henty *Cornet of Horse* xii, Falling back under a tremendous fire, which rolled over men and horses.

f. To rob (esp. someone drunk, drugged or sleeping). *slang*.

1873 A. S. Evans *À la California* xii. 298 When one of these fellows makes a raise by 'rolling a drunk' (i.e., taking the valuables from the pockets of a drunken man on the sidewalk), he will take a single bed at $37\frac{1}{2}$ cents. **1892** C. C. Jenkyns *Hard Life in Colonies* 165 To 'roll drunks' was to frequent drinking saloons, to follow any man who left drunk, roll him into the gutter and rob him. **1912** [see roll *sb.*[1] 6 e]. **1923** A. Price *Dreams* 3 My money, I kept in my cutter shoes, And I wasn't rolled the endurin' trip, So the whole ten days I hit the booze, With a downhill haul, and I let her rip. **1935** *Sun* (Baltimore) 2 July 1/1 We decided to get him drunk in his room the next night..and roll him. **1939** R. Chandler *Big Sleep* xx. 167 Here we are with a guy who..has fifteen grand in his pants... Somebody rolls him for it and rolls him too hard, so they have to take him out in the desert and plant him among the cactuses. **1949** *Life* 24 Oct. 23 She heard her new friends kidding about rolling guys. **1955** W. Gaddis *Recognitions* iii. v. 940 She paid all the bills at the George Sank and gave him a terrific time for a couple of days and then rolled him. **1958** G. Greene *Our Man in Havana* v. v. 245 In some of these places they try to roll you. **1960** *Times* 21 Sept. 3/7 We walked through a few back streets and Lutt suggested 'rolling' (robbing) someone. **1962** E. Lucia *Klondike Kate* iv. 107 The dames seldom rolled the miners or slipped them a Mickey. **1968** *Globe & Mail Mag.* (Toronto) 13 Jan. 7/4 If a hustler is not himself homosexual,..he is called 'trade'. Rough trade refers to hustlers who are liable to beat up or roll the homosexual, either after or instead of sexual relations. **1974** in W. R. Hunt *North of 53 Degrees* vii. 42 If you don't get drunk, you don't get rolled. **1978** *Courier-Mail* (Brisbane) 22 Apr. 10/4 He had given much thought before sentencing two aboriginal women..for 'rolling' a man in a hotel.

g. To start moving; *spec.* (esp. in command ***roll 'em***) to start (cameras) filming. *slang*.

1939 J. Dell *Nobody ordered Wolves* iv. 51 Someone shouted, 'Roll 'em,' and, someone else, 'Quiet there.' **1949** R. Chandler *Little Sister* xix. 131 He went back beside the camera. The assistant shouted 'roll 'em' and the scene went through. **1959** *Elizabethan* June 26/1 The director call out 'Action' to the actors, then 'Roll 'em' and the cameraman starts the camera. **1973** J. Drummond *Bang! Bang! You're Dead!* xxxi. 107 We may need the trucks at any time... I'll phone if I want you to roll 'em. **1977** *Rolling Stone* 21 Apr. 63/6 'Roll 'em'! crackled over the radio.

h. *fig.* To reduce, cut *back* (esp. prices). *U.S.*

1943 *Funk & Wagnalls New Stand. Encycl. Yearbk. 1942* 81/1 In many instances, wholesale or manufacturers' prices were 'rolled back' to an earlier date. **1943** *Sun* (Baltimore) 29 May 1/3 We are, therefore, confronted with the choice of rolling back the cost of living..or permitting an adjustment of wages and other income in line with the increase in the cost of living. **1944** *Ann. Reg. 1943* i. 287 Four 'pressure groups'..decisively vetoed the President's plan to 'roll back' farm prices to the level of the previous September. **1951** *Manch. Guardian Weekly* 15 Mar. 10/4 The Tampa *Tribune* in Florida..prominently reported,..the Government's promise to roll back meat prices. **1972** *Daily Tel.* 25 Apr. 4/7 From first reports, he thought perhaps 10 per cent. of America's large businesses would be required to 'roll back' prices because of excessive profits. **1975** *Washington Post* 26 Dec. A 22/1 The focus of this..bill is its attempt to roll back oil prices. **1977** *Time* 25 July 5/2 Fully 1.15 million workers were jobless in June... Unless the Giscard regime can roll back that figure, it could become a lethal weapon in the hands of the left.

i. *Econ.* With *over*. To finance the repayment of (maturing stock, or the debt it represents) by the issue of new stock.

1957 *Jrnl. Finance* Mar. 52 Since the success of a refunding offer is measured in terms of the percentage of the maturing obligation which is 'rolled over' into the new issue, it is required that the Treasury tailor its terms to the needs of the market. **1959** *Wall St. Jrnl.* 27 Jan. 17/3 Government bond dealers said that they expect the Treasury to announce late this week its plans for refunding nearly $15 billion of Federal debt maturing next month. How the Treasury will roll over these securities is anybody's guess. **1973** *Daily Tel.* 15 Sept. 23/3 Existing maturities are normally 'rolled over' (refinanced on their redemption date by the issue of further bonds at whatever the going rate of interest happens to be), thus giving the municipal treasurer a virtually perpetual access to the money market. **1976** *Economist* 16 Oct. 105/2 Even without any increase in interest rates since early April, 1976, the cost of servicing the national debt was bound to increase..from the need to roll over £2.8 billion of gilt-edged stock due to mature during the year.

6. *fig.* †**a.** To turn over in discourse. *Obs.*

c **1374** Chaucer *Troylus* v. 1061 O yrolled schal I be on many a tunge; Thurgh-oute þe worlde my belle schalbe runge.

b. To revolve, turn over (a matter) *in* the mind; †to consider, meditate upon (something).

c **1374** Chaucer *Boeth.* iii. met. xi. (1868) 100 Lat hym wel examine and rolle with inne hym self the nature and the propretes of the thing. *c* **1386** —— *Pard. T.* 839 Ful ofte in herte he rolleth vp and doun The beautee of thise floryns. *c* **1400** in *Babees Bk.* (1868) 333 Rolle faste this reasoun & thynke wele on þis clause. **1513** Douglas *Æneis* v. xi. 12 Juno,..Rolling in mynd full mony cankarit bloik, Has send adown.. Iris. *a* **1586** Sidney *Ps.* xxxv. ii, Those wrong doers..for my hurt each way their thoughtes did roule. **1687** B. Randolph *Archipelago* 36 We resolved on an excuse, after rowling a great many. **1710** Swift *Let.* 9 Sept. (Seager), I came home rolling resentments in my mind and framing schemes of revenge. **1855** Tennyson *Brook* 198 So Lawrence Aylmer,..rolling in his mind Old waifs of rhyme, ..Mused and was mute.

7. To turn (the eyes) in different directions with a kind of circular motion.

1513 Douglas *Æneis* x. viii. 23 On Turnus to behald, Our all his bustuus body, as he wald, Rollyng hys eyn. *c* **1550** Rhodes *Bk. Nurture* 174 in *Babees Bk.* (1868) 76 When thou shalt speake to any man, role not to faste thyne eye. **1593** Shaks. *Lucr.* 368 About he walks, Rolling his greedy eyeballs in his head. **1667** Milton *P.L.* xi. 616 Bred onely and completed to the taste Of lustful appetence, to..troule the Tongue, and roule the Eye. **1697** Dryden *Virg. Georg.* iii. 658 He..leaps upon the Ground; And hissing rowls his glaring Eyes around. **1781** Cowper *Expost.* 53 They..roll'd the wanton eye, And sigh'd for ev'ry fool that flutter'd by. **1852** Mrs. Stowe *Uncle Tom's C.* viii. 63 Sam, however, preserved an immovable gravity, only..rolling up his eyes, and giving..droll glances. **1899** *Allbutt's Syst. Med.* VII. 512 It was observed that 'he rolled his eyes'.

8. To coil round and round upon itself or about an axis; to form into a roll or a ball; to wind, fold, or curl up; also *fig.*, esp. in phr. ***to roll into one***, to combine; *spec.* To make (a cigarette) by rolling paper round loose tobacco; phr. ***to roll one's own*** (*sc.* cigarettes); also *fig.* Hence ***roll-your-own*** attrib. and ellipt.

1526 Tindale *Rev.* vi. 14 Heven vanysshed awaye, as a scroll when hitt is rolled togedder. **1593** Shaks. *2 Hen. VI*, iii. i. 228 As the Snake, roll'd in a flowring Banke, With shining checker'd slough. **1728** Chambers *Cycl.* s.v. Ribbonds, however, and Laces, Galloons, and Padua's of all Kinds, are thus roll'd. **1753** Chambers *Cycl. Suppl.* s.v. *Leaf, Revolute leaf*,..a leaf, the upper part of which rolls itself downward. **1791** 'G. Gambado' *Annals of Horsem.* v. (1809) 87 The genteelest method of rolling, strapping, and carrying their great coats. **1796** Withering *Brit. Pl.* (ed. 3) I. 386 Oval spots underneath the points of the leaf, which are rolled back. **1844** H. Stephens *Bk. Farm* III. 886 She then begins to roll the fleece from the tail towards the neck. **1859** Geo. Eliot *A. Bede* xxxii, 'I can't speak to that,' said Mrs. Poyser, in a hard voice, rolling and unrolling her knitting. **1860** Warter *Sea-board* II. 298 They shut themselves up like hedgehogs, or roll themselves into a ball.

fig. **1650** Hubbert *Pill Formality* 189 The very bowels of heaven been rowled together, and turned towards you. **1862** Mrs. Riddell *City & Suburb* 216 (Hoppe), You talk like a saint and a philosopher rolled into one. **1867** Freeman *Norm. Conq.* (1877) I. App. 768 Rolling together the Roman pilgrimage of Cnut, the marriage of Gunhild, and the Italian expedition of Conrad. **1879** T. Hardy *Let.* 26 Mar. (1978) I. 64 It is possible that he & the ancestor of your relative were two different persons who were in India at the same time, & so got rolled into one. **1887** *Spectator* 26 Feb. 287/2 Housemaid, butler, and footman rolled into one. **1907** G. B. Shaw *Major Barbara* 167 My methods..would be no use if I were Voltaire, Rousseau, Bentham, Mill, Dickens, Carlyle, Ruskin, George, Butler, and Morris all rolled into one. **1951** M. McLuhan *Mech. Bride* (1967) 135/2 He is the Supreme Court and human fate rolled into one. **1978** *N. & Q.* Feb. 94/1 Social and political historian, literary critic and man of the theatre rolled into one.

1885 Dickens *Dorrit* (1857) i. i. 6 He was now rolling his tobacco into cigarettes by the aid of little squares of paper. **1892** H. G. Parker *Pierre & his People* 128 He slowly rolled a cigarette. **1893** Leland *Mem.* I. 224 She rolled us each a cigarette. **1903** A. Bennett *Leonora* iii. 69 He had extraordinary aptitudes for drawing corks..and rolling cigarettes. **1930** *Amer. Speech* VI. 92 The following expressions belong to colloquialisms and slang, including movie and radio neologisms... *Rolls its own.* [Etc.]. **1932** J. D. Carr *Poison in Jest* xi. 157 He produced papers and tobacco... 'Good American,' he announced. 'I roll my own.' **1934** WEBSTER, *Roll one's own*,..to do things without outside aid. **1936** L. HELLMAN *Days to Come* I. 18 He has started to roll a cigarette. Quickly Julie offers him a box from the table. **1940** *Amer. Speech* XV. 335/2 Cigarettes.. may be *home-made, rolls*, or *roll-your-owns*. **1941** *N.Y. Times* 25 July 14/5 'Ghosting' is routine in public papers in the United States, and has been since our history began... Mr. Roosevelt proved again today that he can roll his own whenever he has the time and the inclination. **1952** *Arena* (N.Z.) XXXI. 2 But then Charlie would have rolled himself one, and looked up at the hills and pretended he didn't hear. **1960** J. MCNAMEE *Florencia Bay* 59 Looks sixty. Thin face. Dark. Looks a little Indian but not our kind of Indian. Rolls his own. **1975** R. L. SIMON *Wild Turkey* (1976) xx. 149, I.. took out some papers and started to roll a joint. **1977** *Daily Mirror* 30 Mar., Roll-your-own cigarette tobacco will also go up—but pipe tobacco and cigars escape. **1980** *Forest Products News* (Wellington, N.Z.) XVII. I. 6 He had come straight out of the bush with his roll-your-own.

b. With *up*. Also *Sc.* (in form *row*), to wind *up* (a clock).

1530 PALSGR. 537/1, I enrolle, I rolle up a writyng, or any other thyng rounde. **1608** TOPSELL *Serpents* (1658) 789 They take a Spiders web, rolling the same up on a round heap like a ball. **1671** GREW *Anat. Pl.* (16° 4) 32 The Labels [of fern are] all rowled up to the main Stem. **1725** *Fam. Dict.* s.v. *Paste*, Afterwards spread it [*sc.* paste] upon a Dish,.. and roll it up in large Rolls. **1728** CHAMBERS *Cycl.* s.v. *Leaf*, Instead of being plaited, they are rolled up. **1837** LOCKHART *Scott* I. ii. 74 The most venerable figure I had ever set my eyes on—tall and erect, with..stockings rolled up over his knees. **1848** DICKENS *Dombey* xviii, Rolling up his bed into a pillow.

fig. **1609** B. JONSON *Masque of Queenes* Wks. (1616) 947 To rowle up how many miles you haue rid. **1877** BRYANT *A Rain-dream* i, As the slow wind is rolling up the storm. **1895** *United Service Mag.* July 429 The overwhelming force.. could not fail to..roll up the Egyptian Army from that point. **1906** KIPLING *Puck of Pook's Hill* 221 Then the Winged Hats began to roll us up from each end of the wall. **1949** *Sun* (Baltimore) 25 Nov. 1/3 Capture of these critical defenses..placed the Americans in position to roll up the whole Yamashita defense front. **1963** 'J. LE CARRÉ' *Spy who came in from Cold* iii. 24 He had made a mistake in Berlin, and..his network had been rolled up.

refl. **1774** GOLDSM. *Nat. Hist.* (1776) VII. 303 They all, when touched, contract themselves, rolling themselves up like a ball. **1834** *Penny Cycl.* II. 353/2 Its..only defence when frightened or surprised, is to roll itself up.

c. Const. *about, on, upon, round.*

1530 PALSGR. 693/1 Rolle this towayle aboute your legge. **1683** MOXON *Mech. Exerc., Printing* xi. ¶9 A round Wooden-Rowler or Barrel.., to contain so much of the Girt as shall be rowled upon it. **1697** DAMPIER *Voy.* (1729) IV. x. 199 The Women..wear dried Thongs of the Sheeps Skins rouled round their Legs. **1753** J. BARTLET *Gentl. Farriery* (1754) 244 Rags..may be rowled on. **1868** TENNYSON *Lucretius* 82 Then would I cry to thee To..roll thy tender arms Round him.

9. To wrap, envelop, or enfold *in* something; to wrap *about* with something. Also *ellipt.*

c **1420** *Liber Cocorum* (1862) 38 Rere a cofyne of flowre so fre, Rolle in þo lampray. **1483** *Cath. Angl.* 311/1 To Rolle, *vbi* to falde or to lappe. **1530** PALSGR. 693/1 His arme was rolled aboute with grene sarcenet. **1588** HICKOCK in Hakluyt *Voy.* (1599) II. 220 Comming out of the water, she rowleth herselfe into a yellow cloth of foureteene braces long. **1613** PURCHAS *Pilgrimage* VIII. vi. 639 Their Kings, whose bodies are..lapped in white skinnes, and rowled in mats. **1721** RAMSAY *Morning Interview* 88 The nymph..rolls her gentle limbs in morning-gown. **1787** PEARSON in *Med. Comm.* II. 136 The belly was rolled as usual. **1833** TENNYSON *Two Voices* 156 What time the foeman's line is broke, And all the war is roll'd in smoke. **1861** C. READE *Cloister & H.* lxiv, Gerard rolled himself in the bed-clothes.

b. With *up*.

1602 MARSTON *Ant. & Mel.* I. Wks. 1856 I. 10 Could not the fretting sea Have rowl'd me up in wrinkles of his browe? **1607** CHAPMAN *Bussy d'Ambois* III. ii, Like a Rippiers legs rowl'd vp in bootes of haie ropes. *a* **1756** ELIZA HEYWOOD *New Present* (1771) 262 Rolling it up dry in another clean cloth. **1799** UNDERWOOD *Dis. Children* (ed. 4) II. 112 Keeping the fractured ends of the bones apposed to each other without rolling up the arm so tight as to occasion pain.

10. To spread out (paste) with a rolling-pin; to level or smooth (ground) with a roller; to render compact, smooth, or flat by means of pressure with a cylinder. Also with *out*.

c **1430** *Two Cookery-bks.* 46 Rolle it on a borde also þinne as parchement. **1523** FITZHERB. *Husb.* §15 They vse to role theyr barley-grounde after a shoure of rayne. **1573** TUSSER *Husb.* (1878) 99 Some rowleth their barlie straight after a raine. **1669** WORLIDGE *Syst. Agric.* (1681) 270 You may now rowl Wheat, if the weather prove dry. **1710** STEELE *Tatler* No. 203 ¶8 He may have Grass-plots in the greatest Perfection, if he will..water, mow, and roll them. **1786** ABERCROMBIE *Gard. Assist.* 92 Clean and roll gravel walks, and pole, roll, and mow the grass lawns. **1837** *Penny Cycl.* VII. 503/1 It [*sc.* the copper] is then cut..into pieces..of the required weight, which are heated in the muffle and rolled out. **1866** CRUMP *Banking* x. 227 The gold bars are rolled cold to the thickness of the coin. **1891** W. G. GRACE *Cricket* 270 The captain should see that the pitch is carefully and thoroughly rolled.

absol. **1801** *Farmer's Mag.* Apr. 128 Then harrow and roll repeatedly; hand-picking as before.

b. To reduce (stone or rock) to a smooth, rounded form by propulsion in flowing water and consequent attrition.

1811 PINKERTON *Petral.* II. 90 As those blocks..appeared to me rolled, I asked if they had been found in the beds of rivers. **1833** LYELL *Princ. Geol.* III. 265 Columns of basalt being undermined and carried down..the river, and in the course of a few miles rolled to sand and pebbles.

c. To make or form by passing a material between rollers.

1967 A. H. COTTRELL *Introd. Metall.* xxii. 442 This principle has been particularly developed in Rohn and Sendzimir mills for rolling thin foil. **1972** *Daily Tel.* 14 Apr. 21/2 This hid a 6 p.c. rise for the billets and nil rise for the reinforcing bars which are rolled from them.

11. ***to roll off***, to cause (the frequency response of audio apparatus) to decrease smoothly at the end of its range; also *to roll in* or *on*, to cause a similar increase. Cf. sense 25 below.

1970 J. EARL *Tuners & Amplifiers* v. 105 The receiver must incorporate a network which rolls the treble response off at the same rate as the transmitter rolls it on. **1975** *Hi-Fi Answers* Feb. 69/3 In a three-way speaker you've got to get the mid-range to cover the whole of the speech band all in one go,..and you've got to get it down to at least two octaves below the frequency at which you want to roll it in. **1975** G. J. KING *Audio Handbk.* ii. 38 Some designers prefer deliberately to roll-off the bass around 30 Hz. **1976** *Gramophone* Aug. 359/3 It also rolls off the curve sharply from 12·5 Hz to 6 Hz.

II. Intransitive senses.

12. To move by revolving or rotating on (or as on) an axis; to move forward on a surface by turning over and over. Also with advs., as *along, down, forth, round.*

13.. *Gaw. & Gr. Knt.* 428 þe fayre hede..felle to þe erþe, þat fele hit foyned wyth her fete, þere hit forth roled. **1390** GOWER *Conf.* III. 216 Me thoghte I sih a barli cake, Which fro the Hull..cam rollende doun at ones. **1485** CAXTON *St. Wenefryde* 3 The hede rolled doun to the chirche dore. **1533** UDALL *Floures* 111 b, [Sisyphus] coulde neuer cause it to lye, but that it rolled downe to the hylles foote agayne immediately. **1599** SHAKS. *Hen. V*, III. vi. 38 Her foot..is fixed upon a Sphericall Stone, which rowles, and rowles, and rowles. *a* **1616** BEAUM. & FL. *Wit without M.* v. iii, My head's a Hogshead still, it rowls and tumbles. **1681** CHETHAM *Angler's Vade-m.* xxvii. (1689) 157 The Lead dragging and rowling on the Ground. **1738** tr. *Guazzo's Art Convers.* 145 Round me circling Pleasures rowl. **1786** tr. *Beckford's Vathek* (1883) 36 Being both short and plump, he collected himself into a ball, and rolled round on all sides. **1812** CRABBE *Tales* xx. 99 Like Pluto's iron drop, hard sign of grace, It slowly roll'd upon the rueful face. **1836** DICKENS *Pickw.* vii, The ball..rolled between his legs. **1887** BOWEN *Æneid* VI. 181 Massive ash-trees roll from the mountains down the descent.

b. To advance with an easy, soft, or undulating motion. Also *fig.*

a **1400–50** *Alexander* (Dubl. MS.) 794* He als rekyndly ran, rolland hym vnder, As he þe sadyll hed sewyd seuenten wynter. **1586** B. YOUNG *Guazzo's Civ. Conv.* IV. 221 According to the Prouerbe, The tongue rolles there where the teeth aketh. **1607** TOPSELL *Four-f. Beasts* (1658) 452 The poor distressed panther rowled after him in humble manner. **1697** DRYDEN *Virg. Georg.* III. 649 In fair Calabria's Woods a Snake is bred..: Waving he rolls, and makes a winding Track. **1736** GRAY *Statius* vi. 26 A shining border round the margin roll'd. **1827** CARLYLE *Misc.* (1857) I. 10 Rolling after it in many a snaky twine.

c. Of vehicles: To move or run on wheels. Also (gen.), to start moving. Also *transf.* and *fig.*

a **1721** PRIOR *Down Hall* 58 Into an old Inn did this Equipage roll At a Town they call Hodsdon. **1803** LEMAISTRE *Sketch Mod. Paris* iii. 49 No carriage was allowed to roll that evening. **1843** LE FEVRE *Life Trav. Phys.* II. x. III. 4 Carriages..roll round and round, till they have been fully seen by the public. **1860** THACKERAY *Round. Papers, Thorns in Cushion*, The carriages of the nobility and guests roll back to the West. **1944** L. LARIAR *Man with Lumpy Nose* viii. 75 'Do me a favor and go home and write it!' McEmons stood over the reporter menacingly. 'Get rolling!' The reporter shuffled out of the room. **1952** S. KAUFFMANN *Philanderer* (1953) iv. 61 'Let's roll, dreamer', said Perry. **1956** A. H. COMPTON *Atomic Quest* i. 55 To help get the atomic program rolling. **1959** I. JEFFERIES *Thirteen Days* viii. 108, I..waved the drivers on. As they rolled I gave them one last treat..by taking my hat off. **1965** *New Statesman* 14 May 753/1 The private train is ready to roll. **1970** W. SMITH *Gold Mine* xii. 31 Wake up. Time to roll. **1977** *Observer* 3 Apr. 11/3 The PanAm captain then shouted: 'The bastard's not been given permission to roll. We're on the runway. We're on the runway.'

d. Of the foot: to slip on or upon an object.

1878 R. L. STEVENSON in *Temple Bar* LII. 55 His foot rolled upon a pebble. **1904** L. TRACY *King of Diamonds* ix. 123 Philip..almost fell too, for his left foot rolled on the constable's staff.

e. ***roll on*** ——: expressing a wish that time may pass quickly until a particular event; may (something) come soon.

1885 M. DAVITT *Leaves from Prison Diary* I. 150 'A burst in the City. Copped while boning the swag. 7 Stretch, 1869. Roll on 1876. Cheer up, pals.' Another—'Hook, 7 ys. Roll on time.' **1917** F. T. NETTLEINGHAME *Tommy's Tunes* 21 When this ruddy war is over, Oh! how happy we shall be!.. Roll on, when we go on furlough; Roll on, when we go on leave. **1936** J. CURTIS *Gilt Kid* ii. 19 'Well,' said the Gilt Kid, 'this is a whole lot better than making scrubbing brushes back in the old Monastery Garden.' 'Yes, and saying to yourself, "Roll on Cocoa".' **1958** M. K. JOSEPH *I'll soldier no More* xiii. 237 'What's your new gaffer like, Tom?' 'Like a barber's cat... I should worry—roll on my ticket.' **1962** *Sunday Express* 21 Jan. 15/5 Roll on the mid-twentieth century Venus. And the best of synthetic luck to her. **1970** M. TRIPP *Man without Friends* i. 15 He wakes at seven.. saying 'Roll on my retirement.' **1978** K. AMIS *Jake's Thing* x. 98 Roll on wrist-watch television.

f. To taxi in an aircraft. *Obs.* exc. *Hist.*

1910 *Flight* 24 Sept. 776/1 Messrs B. H. Barrington Kennett.., A. Aitken, and St. Croix Johnstone..are 'rolling' whenever the weather is suitable. **1915** KIPLING *Diversity of Creatures* (1917) 423 Wynn..had finished 'rolling'..and had gone on from a 'taxi' to a machine more or less his own. **1961** C. B. SMITH *Testing Time* iii. 48 It was still quite an event to leave the ground, and many would-be fliers spent their whole time 'rolling' (as taxying was then called).

g. ***heads will roll*** and varr.: there will be executions; also *fig.*, some will be ousted from power or position; also in extended and weakened uses.

1930 *Daily Herald* 26 Sept. 1/1 Giving evidence, Hitler declared..'If our movement is victorious there will be a revolutionary tribunal which will punish the crimes of November 1918. Then decapitated heads will roll in the sand.' **1940** *Time* 5 Aug. 22/1 Echoes of 'Heads will roll' Hitlerism were heard from Paris to Marseille. **1961** *Time* 1 Dec. 77/3 A.M.C. made it clear, too, that more heads would roll if the workers still failed to get the message. **1963** A. HOWARD in Sissons & French *Age of Austerity* 17 Mr Macmillan's head rolled at Stockton-on-Tees at 10.25 a.m. **1966** P. O'DONNELL *Sabre-Tooth* xvi. 225 'Suppose this improbable thing happens?'.. 'Then no doubt my head will roll.' **1972** *National Observer* (U.S.) 27 May 7/2 President Nixon decreed 'heads will roll' if 'petty bureaucrats' hinder Jaffe's war on narcotics. **1978** *Rugby World* Apr. 45/1 Wales lost, and heads rolled.

h. Of a movie camera or cameraman, etc.: to be in action; to start filming.

1938 'E. QUEEN' *Four of Hearts* iv. 53 'Then it's okay to shoot the works now, Butch?'.. 'We're rolling, Sam.' **1938** F. SCOTT FITZGERALD *Let.* 18 Apr. (1964) 28 It may come right at the crucial point of this picture (due to roll in June, but perhaps not starting till the fifteenth). **1958** *Punch* 17 Sept. 382/3, I can imagine the whole cast falling about with hysterical laughter the moment the cameras stop rolling. **1971** D. E. WESTLAKE *I gave at the Office* (1972) 178 'Okay, Jay,' Joe finally said, from behind the camera and lights and sound equipment. 'Let her roll.' **1978** G. VIDAL *Kalki* iii. 75 A man with a clapboard stood between the camera and the door. 'Start rolling,' said the director.

13. a. To wander, roam, travel or move about.

c **1386** CHAUCER *Wife's Prol.* 653 Man shal nat suffre his wyf go roule [*v.r.* roile] aboute. **1615** BRATHWAIT *Strappado* (1878) 37 So this surcharged soule rowl's here and there, And yet to comfort is no whit the neere. **1639** S. DU VERGER tr. *Camus' Admir. Events* 311 Hee begun to rowle up & down from house to house, & to visit the neighbourhood. **1726** LEONI *Alberti's Archit.* I. 100/1 A Trumpet if..too big, does not give a clear sound, because the air has room to rowl about in it. **1867** LATHAM *Black & White* 89 The 'Johnnies' who wounded or unwounded came rolling home. **1886** STEVENSON *Kidnapped* 284 You have rolled much..; what parish in Scotland..has not been filled with your wanderings?

b. ***to roll up***, to congregate, gather, assemble. Also, to arrive; to appear on the scene. *slang* (orig. *Austr.*).

1861 *Goulburn* (New South Wales) *Herald* 18 Sept. 2/2 It is not by accident that flags are unfurled with mottoes upon them, as 'roll up', 'no Chinese'. **1887** FARRELL *How He Died* 26 The miners all rolled up to see the fun. **1890** 'R. BOLDREWOOD' *Miner's Right* (1899) 47/1 They would 'roll up', so successfully that a crowd..would, on the appointed day, be seen marching..down the main street. **1920** G. BELL *Let.* 24 Oct. (1927) II. xix. 567 When the Mayor of Bagdad rolled up at 9 or the Naqib sent his son Saiyid Mahmud I was obliged to 'endosser' dressing-gown and go out to see them. **1929** 'SAPPER' in *Legion Bk.* 214 The man hasn't rolled up yet, but he won't be long. **1955** W. GADDIS *Recognitions* III. v. 863 The sight of a soiled limousine parked up the street..clouded his face with the memory of the girls from the American Embassy in Madrid who had rolled up the day before. **1968** M. WOODHOUSE *Rock Baby* xxiv. 232 They had to wait for me to roll up because I had the D.F. set, which meant I was the only one who could pin it down precisely. **1976** J. WAINWRIGHT *Who goes Next?* 161 A townie. A bit overdressed..he once rolled up in a velvet jacket. **1977** *Water Sport* (Austral.) Jan. 56/2 So please roll up and bring some of your friends.

c. ***to roll into***, to pitch into; *spec.* to thrash or drub (one). *Austr.* and *U.S.*

1890 'R. BOLDREWOOD' *Miner's Right* xxvi, If somebody had 'rolled into me' or *vice versâ*, it was doubtless my own affair. **1901** *Scribner's Mag.* XXIX. 500/1 Put her kites on and let her roll into it.

d. *U.S.* ***to roll out***: (see quot.).

1872 DE VERE *Americanisms* 223 *To roll out*..means..to begin a journey or commence an enterprise.

e. ***to roll along*** = sense 13 b.

1928 A. WAUGH *Last Chukka* 82 She entertains whoever there may be that chooses to roll along.

14. To ride or travel in a carriage.

1513 DOUGLAS *Æneis* X. v. 3 The mone intill hyr..cart of nycht Held rolland throw the hevynnis myddil ward. **1754** GRAY *Pleasure Vicissitude* 67 Mark where Indolence and Pride..Go, softly rolling side by side, Their dull but daily round. **1806** A. HUNTER *Culina* (ed. 3) 135 Providence has appointed few to roll in carriages. **1855** KINGSLEY *Glaucus* I You are going down by railway,..and as you roll along [etc.].

b. To be carried, or move, upon flowing water. Also *fig.*

1672 MARVELL *Reh. Transp.* I. 307 They rowl'd on a flood of wealth. **1697** DRYDEN *Virg. Georg.* I. 418 When..cakes of rustling Ice come rolling down the Flood. **1725** POPE *Odyssey* v. 469 Planks, Beams, dis-parted fly; the scatter'd wood Rolls diverse, and in fragments strows the flood. **1827** POLLOK *Course T.* x. 20 Rolling along the tide of fluent thought.

15. Of time or seasons: To elapse; to move *on* or *round*; to pass *over* or *away*. Also *fig.* and with compl. (quot. 1808).

1513 DOUGLAS *Æneis* I. v. 72 Than the ȝoung child.. Threty lang twelfmonthis rowing our sal be king. **1639** S. DU VERGER tr. *Camus' Admir. Events* 306 Thus rowles the event of humane things. **1697** DRYDEN *Virg. Past.* IV. 7 Saturnian times Rowl round again. **1738** GRAY *Propertius* iii. 38 Measured out the year, and bad the seasons roll. **1788** GIBBON *Decl. & F.* l. V. 174 Generations and ages might roll away in silent oblivion. **1808** SCOTT *Marmion* VI. Introd. 25 When the year its course had roll'd, And brought blithe Christmas back again. **1821** CLARE *Vill. Minstr.* I. 4 Thus labour's early days did rugged roll. **1883** S. C. HALL

Retrospect II. 461 Years rolled on and developed her intellectual power.

b. To succeed, follow *on*. *rare*$^{-1}$.

1838 LYTTON *Alice* IX. ii, Still day rolled on day and no tidings.

†**c.** (See quot. 1702.) *Obs.*

1702 *Milit. Dict.* s.v. *To Roul*, Officers of equal quality, who mount the same Guards, and do the same Duty, relieving one another, are said to Roul; as Captains with Captains, and Subalterns with Subalterns. **1737** *Common Sense* I. 161 No gentleman in the Army would have rowled upon Duty with such pitiful Officers. **1799** *Triumph of Benevolence* II. 412 They refused to roll with him, and he was obliged to sell out.

16. Of the heavenly bodies: To perform a periodical revolution. Also *fig.*

1604 T. WRIGHT *Passions* VI. 319 A stone by nature is inclined to descend, and the Sunne to rowle about the world. **1699** GARTH *Dispens.* III. 25 The Earth has rowl'd twelve annual turns, and more. **1713** BERKELEY *Guardian* No. 14, The earth..constantly rolls about the sun, and the moon about the earth. **1781** COWPER *Charity* 317 Philosophy.. Sees planetary wonders smoothly roll Round other systems under her control. **1842** BORROW *Bible in Spain* xxiv, The sun was rolling high in the firmament.

transf. **1601** DANIEL *To C'tess Cumbl.* 95 Wks. (Grosart) I. 206 The centre of this world, about the which These reuolutions of disturbances Still roule.

b. With compl. To traverse in revolving.

1667 MILTON *P.L.* VIII. 19 The Firmament..And all her numberd Starrs, that seem to rowle Spaces incomprehensible. *c* **1742** GRAY *Ignorance* 11 Thrice hath Hyperion roll'd his annual race.

17. Of seas, rivers, etc.: To flow with an undulating motion; to move in a full, swelling, or impetuous manner. †Also, to liquefy, melt.

1565 COOPER *Thesaurus* s.v. *Volutus*, A waue rollynge towarde the bankes. **1590** SPENSER *F.Q.* II. i. 24 Through midst thereof a little river rold. **1610** G. FLETCHER *Christ's Vict.* xii, If her clowdie browe but once growe foule, The flints doe melt, and rocks to water rowle. **1697** DRYDEN *Virg. Georg.* III. 367 Rolling from afar, The spumy Waves proclaim the watry War. **1706** PRIOR *Ode to Queen* xiii, So Volga's Stream..Rolls with new Fury down thro' Russia's Lands. *a* **1720** SEWEL *Hist. Quakers* (1795) I. III. 205 Presently a Wave came rolling. **1814** SCOTT *Diary* 5 Sept. in *Lockhart* (1837) III. viii. 271 The other, called Down Kerry, is a sea-cave,..a high arch, up which the sea rolls. **1848** DICKENS *Dombey* xvi, How steadily it rolled away to meet the sea. **1888** F. HUME *Mme. Midas* I. Prol., Half a mile of yellow sandy beach on which the waves rolled with dull roar.

fig. **1593** SHAKS. *Lucr.* 1118 Deep woes roll forward like a gentle flood. **1602** MARSTON *Antonio's Rev.* II. v, Thy tide of vengeance rowleth in. **1675** HOBBES *Odyssey* II. 155 Destruction is rowling toward ye. **1754** GRAY *Progr. Poesy* 10 The rich stream of musick..rolling down the steep amain. **1770** W. HODSON *Ded. Temple of Solomon* 4 The Battle roll'd against his Side. **1852** M. ARNOLD *Progress* viii. 30 Bright else, and fast, the stream of life may roll.

b. To move or sweep along or up with a wave-like motion; to advance with undulating movement; to ascend or descend in rolls or curls.

1626 BACON *Sylva* §31 As if Flame..would rowl and turn as well as move upwards. **1667** MILTON *P.L.* XII. 182 Fire must..wheel on th' Earth, devouring where it rouls. **1767** SIR W. JONES *Seven Fountains* Poems (1777) 34 His locks in ringlets o'er his shoulders roll'd. **1791** MRS. RADCLIFFE *Rom. Forest* ii, The dark mists were seen to roll off to the west. **1848** DICKENS *Dombey* xii, It..followed the example of the smoke in the Arabian story, as to roll out in a thick cloud. **1858** KINGSLEY *Lett.* (1878) I. 21 The fog rolled slowly upward.

c. *fig.* To pour *in*; to flow *in* in abundance.

1719 W. WOOD *Surv. Trade* 332 Commodities still rolling in in Trade. **1978** *Chicago* June 124/2 With money rolling in from the rest of the family empire..he began buying, parcel by parcel, the farmland around his family's estate. **1979** D. LOWDEN *Boudapesti 3* ii. 16 No, it's not money... We were quite well off... It was rolling in.

d. Of land: To undulate; to extend in gentle falls and rises. Cf. ROLLING *ppl. a.* 5.

1847 HERMANN MELVILLE *Omoo* vii, Across the water, the land rolled away in bright hillsides,..warm and undulating. **1856** STANLEY *Sinai & Pal.* (1858) 113 That 'great and terrible wilderness' which rolled like a sea between the valley of the Nile and..the Jordan. **1894** BLACKMORE *Perlycross* 128 Before them rolled the sweep of upland.

18. †**a.** To discourse freely or loudly *against* something. *Obs.*

c **1555** HARPSFIELD *Divorce Hen. VIII* (Camden) 82 To pour..out their..rhetoric, and..ryally to roule and revelle against God's owne..commandment. **1571** in Hakluyt *Voy.* (1904) V. 124 Persons, whose tongues too readily roule sometime against other men's painfull travels.

b. Of thunder, etc.: To reverberate, re-echo; to form a deep, continuous sound like the roll of a drum.

1598 SYLVESTER *Du Bartas* I. ii. 712 Loud it grones and grumbles, It rouls, and roars, and round..it rumbles. **1667** MILTON *P.L.* X. 666 They set..the Thunder when to rowle With terror through the dark Aereal Hall. **1757** W. WILKIE *Epigoniad* VII. 202 Then, bellowing deep, the thunder's awful sound..Far to the east it roll'd, a length of sky. **1797** SOUTHEY *Joan of Arc* VI, Deep through the sky the hollow thunders roll'd. **1817** BYRON *Manfred* I. i, O'er my calm Hall of Coral The deep echo roll'd. **1842** TENNYSON *Morte d'Arthur* 1 So all day long the noise of battle roll'd. **1848** DICKENS *Dombey* lvi, The organ rumbled and rolled as if the church had got the colic.

c. Of language, talk, etc.: To flow; to run *on*.

1743 FRANCIS tr. *Horace, Sat.* I. iv. 13 And as his verses like a torrent roll, The stream runs muddy. *a* **1764** LLOYD *Dial.* Poet. Wks. 1774 II. 15 A Poet only in his prose, Which rolls luxuriant, rich, and chaste. **1784** in *Johnsoniana* (1836) 325 His eloquence rolls on in its customary majestic torrent. **1850** THACKERAY *Pendennis* v, Mr. Pen again assented, and the conversation rolled on in this manner. **1861** J. PYCROFT *Ways & Words* 34 Fox..could..roll on for hours without fatiguing himself or his hearers.

d. Of sound: To flow in deep or mellow tones.

1819 SCOTT *Ivanhoe* xxxviii, The deep prolonged notes.. rolled on amongst its arches with the pleasing yet solemn sound of the rushing of mighty waters. **1850** THACKERAY *Pendennis* xx[i]v, She..sate there silent as the songs rolled by. **1862** MISS BRADDON *Lady Audley* xxix, The music still rolled on. The organist had wandered into a melody of Mendelssohn's.

e. Of birds: To trill or warble in song.

1886 *Appleton's Ann. Cycl.* XI. 87 The nightingale is one of the very few birds that share to some degree the faculty of rolling at any pitch of the voice uninterruptedly.

19. To turn over (and over). Esp. of persons or animals while lying on the ground. Also of motor vehicles. ***rolling in the aisles***: see AISLE 5 b.

c **1386** CHAUCER *Knight's T.* 2614 He rolleth vnder foot as dooth a bal. **1470–85** MALORY *Arthur* XIX. vii. 784 He trade on a trap and the bord rollyd, and there sir Launcelot felle doune. **1596** SPENSER *F.Q.* IV. vii. 32 Whom when on ground she groveling saw to rowle, She ran in hast his life to have bereft. **1810** CRABBE *Borough* iii. 4 In some fat pastures of the rich..May roll the single cow, or favourite steed. **1847** TENNYSON *Princ.* III. 165 Kittenlike he [*sc.* a leopard] roll'd And paw'd about her sandal. **1880** C. R. MARKHAM *Peruv. Bark* 207 The cargo-mules had played every kind of vicious trick..., running off..., and constantly trying to roll. **1954** *Amer. Speech* XXIX. 101 *Roll, v.i.*, to overturn. **1968** *Sun* 12 Nov. 8/4 While the world sleeps, they [*sc.* rally drivers] 'yump' and 'wrong slot' and sometimes have the misfortune to 'roll'. **1976** *Billings* (Montana) *Gaz.* 1 July 2-A/4 The patrol said American Horse's vehicle rolled three times after the collision.

b. Of the eyes: To move or turn round in the sockets; to revolve or rotate partially.

c **1386** CHAUCER *Prol.* 201 Hise eyen stepe, and rollynge in his heed, That stemed as a forneys of a leed. *a* **1529** SKELTON *Agst. Garnesche* 37 Your ien glyster as glasse, Rowlynge in yower..hede, vgly to see. **1590** SPENSER *F.Q.* III. i. 41 Her wanton eyes..Did roll too lightly. *a* **1631** DONNE *Poems* (1650) 46 Eyes which rowle towards all, weep not but sweat. **1676** D'URFEY *Mme. Fickle* III. iii, Look how his eyes rowle; how pale his lips are. **1811** SHELLEY *St. Irvyne* III. 26 His eyes wildly rolled, When the death-bell tolled. **1850** THACKERAY *Pendennis* xxvi[i], Her shoulders..were never easy..: nor were her eyes, which rolled about incessantly.

c. To turn or revolve upon an axis.

1646 SIR T. BROWNE *Pseud. Ep.* VI. v. 294 The Sun..hath also a dineticall motion and rowles upon its owne poles. **1692** BENTLEY *Boyle Lect.* viii. 273 The Earth rowls once about its Axis in a natural Day.

d. To hinge or depend *on* something (*obs.*); to turn or centre *on* a subject.

1707 *Curiosities in Husb. & Gard.* 140 The whole Secret of the Multiplication of Corn rouls on Nitre, which has the greatest Effect on all Corn-Lands. *Ibid.* 231 His whole Treatise of Nature rolls only on this Point. **1763** J. BROWN *Poetry & Music* §4. 37 Their Songs rowl principally on the great Actions and Events which concern their own Nation. **1842** BORROW *Bible in Spain* ii, Our conversation rolled chiefly on literary and political subjects.

e. *to roll out*: to get out of bed, to get up. *U.S. colloq.*

1884 W. SHEPHERD *Prairie Experiences* 237 The cook's voice shouts 'Roll out'... Before you have time to dress..it is 'Breakfast!' **1930** L. HUGHES *Not without Laughter* xv. 183 When his mother rolled out at six o'clock to go to work, he woke up again. **1942** Z. N. HURSTON in A. Dundes *Mother Wit* (1973) 223/1 All you did by rolling out early was to stir your stomach up. **1963** *Amer. Speech* XXXVIII. 271 The term *roll out* means 'to get out of bed in the morning'.

20. To turn oneself over and over *in* something; hence *fig.* to luxuriate or abound *in* riches, luxury, etc. Hence ***rolling-in-money*** absol. as *sb.*

1535 LYNDESAY *Satyre* 521 Ane Prince of..puissance Quhom ȝoung men hes in gouernance, Rolland into his rage. **1573** TUSSER *Husb.* (1878) 25 Away with such lubbers..that roules in expences. **1575** GASCOIGNE *Notes Instruction* Wks. (1575) T ij, It is not inough to roll in pleasant woordes. **1607** TOPSELL *Four-f. Beasts* (1658) 513 It rowleth and walloweth in the mire. **1671** MILTON *P.R.* III. 86 Rowling in brutish vices. **1696** TATE & BRADY *Ps.* cxxiii. 4 While they grow proud by our distress And roll in Ease. **1773** WESLEY *Wks.* (1830) XIII. 83 The English Methodists..do not roll in money, like the American Methodists. **1782** MISS BURNEY *Cecilia* v. x, Rolling in wealth which you do not want. **1809** MALKIN *Gil Blas* II. ix. ⁋4 The authors roll in luxury on the devastation of mankind. **1872** BLACK *Adv. Phaeton* xxiv. 332 We should all be rolling in wealth directly. **1960** AUDEN *Homage to Clio* 74 The rolling-in-money, The screamingly-funny.

†**b.** To dabble, speculate *in* (stocks). *Obs.*$^{-1}$

1711 STEELE *Spect.* No. 49 ⁋5 He lends, at legal Value, considerable Sums, which he might highly increase by rolling in the Publick Stocks.

21. Of thoughts, etc.: To revolve, come round again, in the mind.

1547 BOORDE *Introd. Knowl.* i. (1870) 117, I haue suche matters rolling in my pate, That I wyl speake and do. **1702** ADDISON *Dial. Medals* (1727) 42 She, pleas'd with secrets rowling in her breast. **1718** PRIOR *Solomon* II. 830 Here tell Me,..What diff'rent Sorrows did within Thee roll? **1818** G. JEBB *Corr.* (1834) II. 353 If I put forward anything which had not long rolled in my mind.

22. Of a ship: To sway to and fro; to swing from side to side. Also of masts: (cf. 5 c). Also with *down*.

Opposed to *pitch*, which signifies 'to rise and fall alternately at bow and stern'.

1600 HAKLUYT *Voy.* III. 552 The shippes doe roule very much in the harbour, by reason in foule weather the Sea will bee mightily growen. **1627** CAPT. SMITH *Seaman's Gram.* v. 21 To keepe the shrouds tight for the more safety of the mast from rowling. **1687** A. LOVELL tr. *Thevenot's Trav.* II. 3 We had a swelling Sea again which made us rowl all night long. **1711** W. SUTHERLAND *Shipbuild. Assist.* 34 Extream Breadths will be in the Nature of Ballances, and will cause a Ship to rowl. **1748** *Anson's Voy.* II. v. 245 The Sloop, having neither masts nor sails to steady her, rolled and pitched..violently. **1821** J. W. CROKER *Diary* 28 Aug., Went out..to see the steamboat arriving..; she rolled tremendously. **1867** LATHAM *Black & White* 2 We shipped great waves, and rolled to larboard, rolled to starboard, painfully. **1898** *Forest & Stream* 19 Feb. 156/2 Before the wind reached us the schooner rolled down at such an angle that her crew commenced to shorten sail. **1916** F. W. WALLACE *Shack Locker* (1922) 166 She rolled down an' came up with a dory a-hangin' on her fore-cross-trees.

b. To sail with a rolling motion. Also in phr. ***to roll down to St. Helena*** (see quot. 1796).

1796 T. TWINING *Trav. India*, etc. (1893) 355 The ship remained under nearly the same sail for many days,..rolling from one side to the other, the wind being directly astern. This is called 'rolling down to St. Helena' by the captains of Indiamen. **1834** MEDWIN *Angler in Wales* II. 19 You have heard of rolling down from the Cape to St. Helena; almost at all seasons of the year, it blows from the same quarter. **1890** CLARK RUSSELL *Marriage at Sea* vii, There are plenty of ships..rolling up Channel, and willing to land us.

c. To walk with a rolling gait; to swagger.

1843 CARLYLE *Past & Pres.* (1858) 139 Now rolling sumptuously to his place in the Collective Wisdom. **1887** RIDER HAGGARD *A. Quatermain* 250 Umslopogaas rolled along after us, eating as he went. **1890** CLARK RUSSELL *Marriage at Sea* iv, He rolled up to us and answered: 'No call, I think, sir, to haul in much closer'.

d. To sway heavily (with fat).

1890 'R. BOLDREWOOD' *Col. Reformer* (1891) 244 Grand-looking bullocks, all 'rolling fat'.

e. Of an aeroplane: to turn about its longitudinal axis.

1909 'AERO-AMATEUR' *Flying* ix. 55 If the wings of a soaring, or gliding machine are curved upwards in the form of a bow the machine certainly has a tendency to travel in a straight line, but will have also a tendency to roll badly. **1918** J. M. GRIDER *War Birds* (1927) 69 He was looping and rolling between the church spires. **1976** *Times* 17 July 12/3 The Pitts, a small and exceptionally manoeuvrable biplane ..can roll through more than 360° in a second.

f. ***to roll with the punches*** (and varr.), of a boxer: to move the body away from the opponent's blows in order to lessen their impact; *fig.*, to adapt oneself to difficult circumstances, take troubles in one's stride.

[**1941** F. GILMORE *Push Yourself* iv. 27 In boxing it is called 'rolling the punch' when a boxer, not having time to avoid being hit, deliberately moves with the punch when it hits him.] **1951** J. J. WALSH *Boxing Simplified* viii. 32 In an actual bout he will not have so much time to roll with the blow. **1956** H. KURNITZ *Invasion of Privacy* ii. 15 He had mastered the trick of rolling with the punches, rendering himself invisible when a crisis darkened the neighbouring skies. **1963** J. CROSBY *With Love & Loathing* 48 Madison Avenue rolls with the blow; it watches carefully which direction the cookie crumbles. **1979** *Now!* 21–27 Sept. 74/1 It would be possible to roll with such punches were it not for the fact that the 1980 election season has already begun and a seemingly invincible Democratic contender has suddenly launched himself into the fight.

23. To form into a roll; to shrink or fold *together*; to curl *up*.

1613 PURCHAS *Pilgrimage* v. (1614) xii. 507 The drying of the barke maketh it roll together. **1721** MORTIMER *Husb.* (ed. 2) II. 243 Which you may know by their Leaves lying down, rolling up, and wrinkling. **1901** *Blackw. Mag.* Sept. 337/2 There are stoppages..when the net has 'rolled'—but a net well shot..scarcely has a twist in it.

24. To turn out after being rolled. Usu. with *out*. Also *fig.*

1801 tr. *Gabrielli's Mysterious Husb.* II. 37, I should eat and drink more than I should earn..., supposing I ever did roll out to be good for anything. **1881** GEE *Goldsmith's Hdbk.* (ed. 2) 227 Imperfect bars of gold usually roll with a more extended jaggered edge as the process proceeds. **1896** *Daily News* 6 July 11/2 After a dry night, the wicket rolled out beautifully on Saturday morning.

25. ***to roll off***, (of audio apparatus) to exhibit a response decreasing smoothly to zero with increasing signal frequency; so to ***roll in***, to exhibit a response increasing similarly from zero. Cf. sense 11.

1959 *Consumer Reports* Sept. 452/2 The newer *Jansen* [tweeter] also rolled off slightly in the extreme high-frequencies. **1962** A. NISBETT *Technique Sound Studio* 253 The simplest form of filter (one resistor and one condenser) rolls off at 6 dB/octave above or below a certain frequency. **1970** J. EARL *Tuners & Amplifiers* i. 25 Many [loudspeaker] systems employ two units, one..going from about 30 or 40Hz and rolling-off due to the action of the crossover around 1 or 2 kHz and the other for treble rolling-in at about 1 or 2 kHz and responding up to 16 kHz or higher. *Ibid.* iii. 69 The majority of amplifiers have in-built high-pass filtering, rolling off around the 20 to 30Hz mark. **1976** *Gramophone* July 235/1 Further tonal correction is provided by push-buttons, to provide separate filters rolling off at 7 and 10kHz respectively.

†**roll**, *v.*³ *Obs.*$^{-1}$ [ad. OF. *roller, roler*, etc., f. *roil, rouil* rust.] *trans.* To polish, burnish.

c **1275** LAY. 22287 Hii wende to hire hinne;..hii rollede wepne and soide hire stedes.

roll, obs. Sc. variant of ROW *v.*

rollable ('rəʊləb(ə)l), *a.* [f. ROLL *v.*² + -ABLE.] Capable of being rolled.

1729 SHELVOCKE *Artillery* v. 390 These they rounded very exactly that they might be the more rollable. **1864** in WEBSTER. **1896** *Kodak News* II. 11/1 The use of rollable film in a roll holder.

'roll-about, *a.* and *sb. rare.* [f. ROLL *v.*²]

A. *adj.* Plump, podgy, roly-poly.

1815 SCOTT *Guy M.* xxvi, A little fat roll-about girl of six, holding her mouth up to be kissed.

B. *sb.* A wanderer; a rolling stone.

1893 BARING-GOULD *Cheap Jack Zita* I. 160 You are a rambler and a roll-about—never in one place.

rollar, obs. f. ROLLER *sb.*; obs. Sc. var. ROWER.

'roll-around, *a.* [f. *to roll around.*] That can be moved around on wheels or castors.

1973 *Sunday Bull.* (Philadelphia) 7 Oct. (Parade Suppl.) F12 (Advt.), The GE Countertop Oven is versatile in other ways, too. You can use it on a roll-around cart, or build it in. **1976** *Amer. Speech 1974* XLIX. 116 *Roll-around wet bar*, portable counter equipped with a sink.

'roll-away, *a.* Also rollaway. [f. *to roll away.*] That may be removed on wheels or castors. Also *absol.* as *sb.*, a roll-away bed.

1938 *Sun* (Baltimore) 13 Oct. 11/3 Mr. Latham invented the 'roll-away' stage over the footlights which is used in many motion-picture houses. **1941–2** *Sears, Roebuck Catal.* 689/4 Odora Roll-Away Chest... 4 easy-rolling ball bearing casters. *Ibid.* 1274/7 (Index), Roll-a-way Chests 689 Roll-a-way Cots 904C. **1958** *Daily Progress* (Charlottesville, Va.) 4 June 14/2 Cots and roll-aways donated by townspeople after a radio appeal. **1960** *Farmer & Stockbreeder* 29 Mar. 119/1 There are no litter problems, eggs are laid in rollaway nests, the floor area per bird is only 1 sq ft. **1960** *Washington Post* 27 Nov. E3 Three rollaway beds and a cot are stacked during the day on the back porch. **1966** A. CAVANAUGH *Children are Gone* II. iii. 30 A musty old building... Three rooms with a rollaway bed, which she and two other girls had taken turns occupying. **1969** *Islander* (Victoria, B.C.) 16 Nov. 2/2 The charming young hostess.. offered to get a roll-away cot for me. **1971** A. A. MICHELE *You don't have to Ache* ix. 188 Frequently the 'rollaways' that motels keep for the use of children are harder and better for your back than the regular bed mattress. **1974** *Country Life* 21 Nov. 1580/2 You get another big double bed down-stairs and a roll-away bunk.

roll back, roll-back, rollback. [f. *to roll back.*]

1. The action or fact of rolling backwards.

1937 *Times British Motor Number* 13 Apr. p. xxii/4 More than one method is available for automatically preventing roll back on an incline. **1949** SHURR & YOCOM *Mod. Dance* v. 181 The swift roll-back carries body weight onto the shoulders. **1978** *Daily Tel.* 4 Mar. 1/8 They died as nine Gnats swept across the airfield to practise a 'roll back'—a manoeuvre performed by the Red Arrows for several years without incident.

2. [ROLL *v.*² 5 h.] *U.S.* A reduction or decrease; *spec.*, a return (of commodity prices, etc.) to a lower level. Also *attrib.*

1942 *Time* 11 May 80 OPA have denied their [*sc.* retailers'] plea for a 'roll-back' of ceiling dates that would recognize the lag between rising wholesale and retail prices. **1943** *Funk & Wagnalls New Stand. Encycl. Year Bk. 1942* 373/1 For Price Roll Back and Price Squeezes, see *Business Review* under *Commodity Prices.* **1943** *Sun* (Baltimore) 19 May 7 Promised 'roll backs' on cabbage and lettuce will still leave prices of these foods, at the farm, three times as high as they were a year ago. *Ibid.* 1 July 14/3 Congress had been equally unkind to his eager plan to detour around the thornier difficulties of farm-price control by a rollback food-subsidy scheme. **1945** *Richmond* (Va.) *News Leader* 20 Aug. 10 The OPA is standing pat on its prediction of a clothing price rollback—eventually. **1959** *Time* 27 Apr. 15/2 The cold war's boundaries in 1959 were much as they had been in 1953—the rollback had been in men's minds, not real estate. **1972** *Fortune* Jan. 101/1 Even the 3.9 percent price increase the company posted for its 1972 models last July, before the price freeze forced a rollback, would have recovered only 65 percent of the unit cost increases anticipated for the current model year. **1973** *Black Panther* 21 Apr. 2/2 This decision provides a legal basis to begin a roll-back of that power. **1974** *Financial Times* 15 Aug. 17/6 We do need the 'roll back' which ex-President Nixon promised but (predictably) did not deliver. **1976** *Lebende Sprachen* XXI. 153/2 The pilot noticed an inflight engine roll back from 90 to 80% rpm.

roll-call ('rəʊlkɔːl), *sb.* [f. ROLL *sb.*¹ + CALL *sb.*]

1. a. The act of calling over a list of the names of persons forming a military or other body, in order to ascertain who are present; the marking of such a list at a particular time. Also (*U.S.*), a calling over of a list of members of a legislative or similar body in order to ascertain how each wishes to vote on a particular measure.

1775 *Essex Inst. Hist. Coll.* (1912) XLVIII. 61 This morning we went to rol col & then got our Brefust. **1777** *Ibid.* (1877) XIII. 118 Ordered that the Hour for Roll Call be altered to Nine o'clock in the morning. **1802** JAMES *Milit. Dict.* s.v., On critical occasions, and in services that require promptitude and exertion, frequent roll-calls should be made. **1834** HT. MARTINEAU *Demerara* ix. 124 There was no roll-call that night. **1883** V. STUART *Egypt* 3 Many of the poor fellows will never answer a roll call again. **1899** CROCKETT *Kit Kennedy* 304 The professor of that class.. was strict on roll-calls. **1902** *Ann. Rep. Amer. Hist. Assoc. 1901* I. 323 Except for the provision in the constitution there would have been no roll call on these votes. **1947** *Economist* 27 Dec. 1047/1 The sponsors of ERP avoided a roll-call on the first vote in order to take one on the agreed Bill. **1955** *Times* 4 Aug. 6/7 In foreign policy the President secured bipartisan support on nearly every occasion; in 32 Senate roll-calls the Democratic majority failed to agree with the Republican majority only once. **1972** *Computer & Humanities* VI. 184 The data are placed on cards with one record holding the yea.. or nay.. votes of one congressman on every roll-call.

transf. **1867** FREEMAN *Norm. Conq.* (1877) I. 2 Wiped out of the roll call of nations. *Ibid.* 406 In the roll-call of his titles England held the first place.

b. *attrib.*, as ***roll-call analysis, vote.***

1860 *Q. Rev.* Oct. 411 If the scapegrace of a public school is apt to lay the blame of his irreligion on his forced attendance on 'roll-call' chapels. **1899** *Westm. Gaz.* 1 July 5/3 The ruling of the President in respect to a roll-call vote. **1950** *N.Y. Times* 20 Apr. 1/6 The Senate adopted today, by a roll-call vote of 66 to 0, a resolution directing the Secretary of the Navy to confer appropriate posthumous decorations on the crew of the Privateer that presumably was shot down .. over the Baltic sea. **1963** *Midwest Jrnl. Polit. Sci.* VII. 156 (*heading*) A second look at the validity of roll-call analysis. **1970** *Computers & Humanities* V. 8 Several embarked on similar scalogram excursions into roll-call analysis of collegial bodies, both with and without computers. **1970** *Internat. & Compar. Law Q.* XIX. 1. 68 On a vote by show of hands, the required two-thirds majority was not obtained, but a second (roll-call) vote was taken, and the retention of the reference.. was confirmed. **1979** *Tucson* (Arizona) *Citizen* 20 Sept. 2A/4 Rep. Robert Bauman, R-Md., said the House voted against the bill because it came on a roll call vote, which puts each member on record as either supporting or opposing the measure to which the pay raise was attached.

2. *Mil.* The signal summoning men to be present at the calling of the roll.

1890 in *Cent. Dict.*

So **'roll-calling.**

1763 *Ann. Reg.* 159 The soldiers,.. immediately after roll calling,.. assembled to a man. **1891** *Daily News* 9 Nov. 3/1 The gathering of the five or six hundred children together in the morning for roll-calling and Bible-reading.

'roll-call, *v.* [f. the sb.] *trans.* To call the roll for (a group or body of persons). Also *fig.*

1928 *Daily Express* 19 Mar. 12/2 The German officers were counted or 'roll-called' in their rooms to save them the trouble of having to assemble or fall in with the other prisoners. **1962** V. NABOKOV *Pale Fire* 55 But who can teach the thoughts we should roll-call When morning finds us marching to the wall?

'roll-collar. [ROLL *sb.*¹] A turned-over collar on a garment. Also *attrib.*

1836 DICKENS *Sk. Boz, Scenes* vi, Embroidered waistcoats with large flaps, have yielded to double-breasted checks with roll-collars. **1841** S. WARREN *Ten Thousand a Year* I. i. 7 A queer kind of under-waistcoat, which in fact was only a roll-collar of rather faded pea-green silk. **1907** E. P. OPPENHEIM *Secret* ii. 15 He wore.. a made-up white tie, with the ends tucked in under a roll collar. **1922** JOYCE *Ulysses* 72 Stylish kind of coat with that roll collar. **1929** *Even. News* 18 Nov. 6/5 (Advt.), Below we show the D. B. Chester with long roll collar. **1963** *Times* 23 Jan. 12/4 The ubiquitous, exquisitely soft, reversible woollens were used for perfectly tailored, gently precise coats with tiny roll-collars. **1973** S. B. JACKMAN *Guns covered with Flowers* vi. 98 He dressed quickly—pants, T-shirt, roll-collar shirt, dark slacks.

Hence **'roll-,collared** *a.*, having a roll-collar.

1853 R. S. SURTEES *Sponge's Sp. Tour* (1893) 369 He sports.. a black satin roll-collared waistcoat. **1884** E. YATES *Recoll.* (ed. Tauchn.) I. 46 'Dandies' wore high-collared coats and roll-collared waistcoats, short in the waist.

'roll down, roll-down. [f. *to roll down.*] A game in which balls are rolled down a board into numbered holes, slots, or the like; a table or stall where this is played. Also *attrib.*

1926 *Variety* 29 Dec. 7/4 The outdoor show game with its 'rag front',.. 'roll downs', [etc.]. **1942** BERREY & VAN DEN BARK *Amer. Thes. Slang* §626/21 *Roll-down*, a gambling device using small balls rolling down between pins to holes in the bottom of the table. **1943** K. TENNANT *Ride on Stranger* vii. 61 But the Roll-Down Table was not doing too badly despite the rain... The players could shelter while they rolled the billiard balls down the green felt into shallow cups.

rolled (rəʊld), *ppl. a.* [f. ROLL *v.*²]

1. a. Turned over (and over) upon itself; formed into a roll; curled, coiled. Also with sbs. used *attrib.*

1467–8 *Rolls of Parlt.* V. 621/1 Rolled worsted, xxx yerds longe and di' yerde brode. *a* **1550** *Treat. Galaunt* 182 in Hazl. *E.P.P.* III. 159 Beholde the rolled hodes stuffed with flockes. **1728** CHAMBERS *Cycl.* s.v. *Bookbinding*, A double piece of roll'd Paper. **1819** M. EDGEWORTH *Let.* ? 10 Mar. (1971) 181 All the fashionable trimmings are of that rolled sort of flounces. **1844** H. STEPHENS *Bk. Farm* III. 887 The rolled fleece will.. be bulky in hand. **1861** BENTLEY *Man. Bot.* 144 Those in which the leaf is simply bent or folded; and.. Those where it is rolled. **1866** GEO. ELIOT *Felix Holt* III. xlvi. 221 The grandeur of barbaric forms—when rolled collars were not yet conceived. **1880** *Plain Hints Needlework* 125 Few.. teachers appear to know the difference between 'whipping' and 'rolled hem'. **1928** *Daily Mail* 3 Aug. 10/4 Members of the audience looked twice before they could.. appreciate the fact that she had rolled stockings. **1962** L. DEIGHTON *Ipcress File* xxv. 164 The British man.. put on his rolled brim hat. **1967** G. WATKINS in *Coast to Coast 1965–66* 208 The blue texture of his rolled-neck sweater was filled with sand. **1976** F. WARNER *Killing Time* I. vi. 18 Snowy my trainer turned up.. in his green rolled-neck sweater. **1977** S. BRETT *Star Trap* xi. 125 Dinner jacket, but not the old double-breasted or now-dated rolled-lapel style. **1978** D. DEVINE *Sunk without Trace* 6 The rolled umbrella was part of his stock-in-trade and was no index to the weather.

b. So ***rolled-up, rolled-in***; also ***rolled-down.***

1683 MOXON *Mech. Exerc., Printing* xxiv. ¶19 Small rowl'd-up bits may stick upon the Ball-leathers. **1728** CHAMBERS *Cycl.* s.v. *Leaf*, They are rolled up,.. as the Leaves of the Mountain Cowslip. **1815** KIRBY & SP. *Entomol.* xiii. (1818) I. 425 A little cell formed of the rolled-up leaf of a plant. **1844** H. STEPHENS *Bk. Farm* III. 886 The stance for the rolled up fleeces to lie upon. **1883** HUXLEY *Pract. Biol.* 95 The interval between the retracted disc and the rolled-in peristome. **1891** HARDY *Tess* II. xxiv. 35 Dairyman Crick kept his shirt-sleeves permanently rolled up past his elbows. **1916** JOYCE *Portrait of Artist* i. 47 He looked at Athy's rolled-up sleeves and knuckly inky hands. **1961** 'E. LATHEN' *Banking on Death* (1962) xviii. 145 Stan Michaels, clad in a blue work shirt with rolled-up sleeves. **1968** M. WOODHOUSE *Rock Baby* xvii. 160 She leaned against my rolled-up sleeping-bag. **1972** J. GORES *Dead Skip* (1973) vii. 43 The air coming in through the rolled-down window.. was wet and heavy. **1977** J. AIKEN *Last Movement* xi. 234 If he'd had a rolled-up Piero [*sc.* a painting] with him it would have been different.

†**c.** ***rolled hill***: (see quot. and cf. *rolling trench*).

1688 HOLME *Armoury* III. xvi. (Roxb.) 102/1 A Rouled Hill, is a great banke of earth made betwixt the face of a Bulwork and the besiegers; which being cast with shovels longer then ordinary, the lower part of this heap ouer the vpper, this hill is turned ouer and ouer, and is rouled on by degrees to fill the ditch.

2. a. Made to roll along.

1598 B. JONSON *Ev. Man in Hum.* Prol., Nor [is] roul'd bullet heard To say, it thunders.

b. Rounded by friction or attrition due to being moved by streams or tides.

1833–4 J. PHILLIPS *Geol.* in *Encycl. Metrop.* (1845) VI. 545/1 Sometimes it.. contains rolled and broken pieces of crystallized felspar. **1856** KANE *Arct. Expl.* I. xxxi. 427 Among the rolled-ice off Godsend Island. **1882** *Hardwicke's Sci. Gossip* 44 Rozel [bay] consists of a conglomerate of rolled pebbles.

3. a. That has been compressed by a roller, or between a pair of rollers; formed into sheets or bars by means of rollers.

1789 *Deb. Congress U.S.* 17 Apr. (1834) 167 It was agreed to lay an impost of seven and a half per cent.. on.. slit or rolled iron. **1806–7** J. BERESFORD *Miseries Hum. Life* (1826) II. xiv, Your newly-rolled gravel walk. **1836–41** BRANDE *Chem.* (ed. 5) 303 One of the plates is of cast and the other of rolled zinc. **1863** P. BARRY *Dockyard Econ.* 257 Rolled armour-plates are to be preferred. **1884** *Health Exhib. Catal.* 82/1 Rolled-iron Joists and Girders.

b. ***rolled gold***, a thin coating of gold applied to a baser metal by rolling.

1898 *Westm. Gaz.* 17 Nov. 2/1 Here's a lovely rolled gold watch. **1975** *Country Life* 20 Mar. 747/1 Rolled gold ballpoint pen. **1980** M. BOOTH *Bad Track* x. 182 He watched her.. light her cigarettes with a thin ladies' lighter of rolled gold.

c. ***rolled oats***: oats which have been husked and crushed.

1888 L. HARGIS *Graded Cook Bk.* 514 Tuesday. Breakfast. Rolled Oats. **1921** *Daily Colonist* (Victoria, B.C.) 29 Oct. 8/1 (Advt.), Robin Hood Rolled Oats, large drum 24¢. **1960** A. E. BENDER *Dict. Nutrition* 87/2 Rolled oats—crushed by rolling and partially pre-cooked. **1974** *Encycl. Brit. Micropædia* VII. 458/2 Rolled oats, flattened kernels with the hulls removed, are used mostly for oatmeal.

d. ***rolled asphalt*** (see quots.).

1938 B. H. KNIGHT *Mod. Road Construction* v. 56 Rolled asphalt is a mixture of sand and broken stone, slag or clinker bound together with asphaltic bitumen and laid hot. **1977** *Bitumen* (Shell Internat. Petroleum Co.) 4 Rolled asphalt contains a large proportion of sand, a relatively small amount of stones, and about equal proportions of medium-hard bitumen and filler. It provides a durable surface often lasting over 20 years, and is widely used in the United Kingdom for surfacing heavy-duty roads.

4. *Phonetics.* Articulated with a trill.

1909 D. JONES *Pronunc. Eng.* 25 There are no infallible rules for learning to pronounce the rolled *r*. **1935** [see APICAL *a.* 2]. **1962** A. C. GIMSON *Introd. Pronunc. Eng.* viii. 205 Any strongly rolled [r] sound, whether lingual or uvular, is not acceptable in RP. **1967** J. D. O'CONNOR *Better Eng. Pronunc.* iii. 78 Sometimes they [*sc.* foreign learners] use a *rolled* sound in which the tip of the tongue flaps very quickly several times against the alveolar ridge.. or the uvula taps against the back of the tongue in a similar way.

Rollei ('rɒlaɪ, -lɪ), proprietary abbrev. ROLLEIFLEX.

1950 *Trade Marks Jrnl.* 26 July 687/1 *Rollei*... Photographic, cinematographic and optical apparatus and instruments. Franke and Heidecke... Braunschweig, Germany. **1972** M. WOODHOUSE *Mama Doll* viii. 91 Sean-baby jumped down.. cranking the handle of a Rollei. **1976** T. ALLBEURY *Only Good German* ii. 10 'How did you sell it?' 'On the black market, got a Leica and a Rollei.'

Rolleiflex ('rɒlaɪflɛks, -lɪfl-). [Proprietary name.] A make of camera.

1930 *Trade Marks Jrnl.* 8 Jan. 44/2 *Rolleiflex*... Photographic cameras, optical instruments, optical lanterns and slides, kinematograph apparatus, stereoscopes and magnifying glasses, all being goods included in Class 8. Franke and Heidecke... Braunschweig, Germany. **1959** C. MACINNES *Absolute Beginners* 20 Around my neck hung my Rolleiflex.

rolleo, var. ROLEO.

roller ('rəʊlə(r)), *sb.*¹ Forms: 5–6 (9) rollar, 6–7 (9 *dial.*) rouler (6 rouller), 6–8 (9 *dial.*) rowler (6 rowlar), 9 *Sc.* rower, rouer; 5– roller (6 roler). [f. ROLL *v.*²]

I. 1. a. A rolling-pin. Now *dial.*

c **1420** *Liber Cocorum* (1862) 40 Make þy past With water, þer of þy fele [*read* fole] þou make With a roller, and drye hit. [**1648** HEXHAM II, *Een Rol-stock*, a Past-roler to make Pyes with.] **1882** *Jamieson's Dict.*, *Rower*, a roller for flattening dough;.. West of S.

b. A rubber-covered cylinder used for reducing one's weight.

1930 *London Mercury* Feb. 323 She makes the roller earn its keep, I can tell you! **1975** G. HOWELL *In Vogue* 55/2 The serpentine slimness was an essential... You bought rubber rollers with studs all over them.

2. a. A cylinder of wood or metal, revolving on pivots or a fixed axis, for lessening the friction of anything passed over it; also, a rounded piece of wood over which an endless towel is passed.

1434 *E.E. Wills* (1882) 102 Y bequethe my roller for a towell to Margery Bokeler. **1563-4** *Sarum Church-w. Accts.* (Swayne) 110 A roler to save yᵉ rope of yᵉ clock from fretyng, vj d. **1680** MOXON *Mech. Exerc.* x. 186 Guiding the String from the Pole to the Work by throwing it over a Rowler, moving on two Iron Center-pins. **1769** FALCONER *Dict. Marine* (1780), *Roller*, a cylindrical piece of timber, fixed.. so as to revolve about an axis. It is used to prevent the cables, hawsers, &c. from being chafed. **1780** J. HOWARD *Prisons* 331 They had every day a clean towel hung on a roller. **1867** SMYTH *Sailor's Word-bk.* 324 The pin is relieved of friction by three rollers in the coak, placed equilaterally. **1889** JESSOPP *Coming of Friars* vi. 298 The refinement of hanging a towel on a roller does not appear to have been thought of.

b. The revolvable drum, barrel, or axis of a winch or windlass.

1659 LEAK *Waterwks.* 25 Two Men with a Lever shall turn a Rowler to which a strong Cord is made fast. **1683** MOXON *Mech. Exerc., Printing* xi. 9 Upon that square is fitted a round Wooden-Rowler or Barrel. **1728** CHAMBERS *Cycl.* s.v. *Windlass*, The Axis or Roller goes thro' two of the Pieces, and turns in them. **1875** KNIGHT *Dict. Mech.* 2779/2 This is in cases where the windlass-roller is not solid, but consists of ratchet-heads [etc.].

3. a. One of a number of cylinders of wood or other material, either attached or free, for diminishing friction when rolling or moving a heavy body.

1565 COOPER *Thesaurus, Palangæ*,...rollers to conueigh thinges of great weight. **1606** SYLVESTER *Du Bartas* II. iv. *Magnificence* 1148 What mighty Rowlers, and what massie Cars Could bring so far so many monstrous Quars? **1687** A. LOVELL tr. *Thevenot's Trav.* II. 24 They have a kind of sled made of four pieces of Timber in square; two of which serve for an Axle-tree to two great rowlers. **1719** DE FOE *Crusoe* I. (Globe) 126, I went to the Woods, and cut Levers and Rollers. **1783** *Hull Gaol Act* 24 Any stall, shop, or shed.. that shall be moved upon wheels or rollers. **1837** W. B. ADAMS *Carriages* Introd. 6 This was doubtless the origin of rollers or round logs of wood, which are placed under heavy trees or beams in order to move them over the surface of the earth. **1884** W. H. GREENWOOD *Steel & Iron* 338 The rail ..is carried along upon a series of five rollers..to a circular saw.

b. (See quot.)

1837 W. B. ADAMS *Carriages* 95 Specimens of them may still be seen in the broad wheels of waggons, technically termed rollers.

c. A type of exercise wheel (see quot.).

1970 *Which?* Sept. 288/1 Once you got fit with skipping ropes and chest expanders... Now it is..rollers. Maybe you haven't seen one yet. It consists of a wheel about six inches in diameter, and a handle on each side. You kneel down, grasp the handles, roll forwards, and then roll back to the kneeling position.

4. a. A heavy cylinder of wood, stone, or (now usually) metal, fitted in a frame with shafts or a handle, for crushing clods, etc., and smoothing the ground by compression.

1530 PALSGR. 263/2 Rollar or rammer of husbandrie. **1563** T. HYLL *Art Garden.* (1593) 89 When the seedes be sowen and couered with earth, then to be pressed downe with a roller. **1623** J. TAYLOR (Water-P.) Wks. II. 241/1 Their exercise is priuately..to rowle the great rowler in the alleies of their garden. **1697** DRYDEN *Virg. Georg.* I. 260 Let the weighty Rowler run the round, To smooth the Surface of th' unequal Ground. **1707** MORTIMER *Husb.* (1721) I. 17 Where Meadows are flooded,..roll them with a large Barley Roller. **1787** W. MARSHALL *E. Norfolk* (1795) I. 145 The roller..is never used in Norfolk for the purpose of compression. **1855** DELAMER *Kitch. Gard.* (1861) 17 A roller, for gravel-walks and grass. **1899** RIDER HAGGARD *Farmer's Year* 145 One of the oldest and quietest horses..was dragging the wooden roller.

fig. **1864** LOWELL *Fireside Trav.* 212 There was no heavy roller of public opinion to flatten all character.

b. A rotating cylinder or roll for pressing, stamping, crushing, or rolling; one of a set of rolls for forming metal, etc., into bars or sheets; also, the revolving cylinder of a printing-machine for impressing the paper upon the printing-matter.

For various technical uses see Knight *Dict. Mech.*

1728 CHAMBERS *Cycl.* s.v. *Printing*, The Arms of the Cross are pull'd; and by that means, the Plate with its Furniture [is] pass'd thro' between the Rollers. **1738** *Patent* in *Encycl. Metrop.* (1845) VIII. 687/2 The wooll or cotton being thus prepared, one end..is put betwixt a pair of rowlers. **1825** J. NICHOLSON *Operat. Mech.* 335 Placed under a tilt-hammer, or passed through the rolls, or rollers, which consolidates it. **1838** *Penny Cycl.* XI. 256/1 The large mass of melted glass ..exhibiting changing colours in the sheet after the roller has been passed over it. **1882** *Encycl. Brit.* XIV. 385/2 Finally, the leather is rolled and compressed on a..wooden bed by a heavy hand roller.

c. *Printing.* A cylinder or roll of thick, elastic composition, mounted on a metal or wooden axis, for inking a form of letter, etc., before printing; also, a metal cylinder for distributing ink upon this.

1790 [see INKING *vbl. sb.* b]. **1824** J. JOHNSON *Typogr.* II. 532 From its being a cylindrical power, rollers were indispensably necessary. **1841** HANSARD *Printing* 118 If a printer employs six presses, and consequently six rollers. **1893** *Labour Comm. Gloss.* s.v., An iron roller covered with a composition of indigo. It works on a 'slab' ..and inks the type used in printing.

d. *Stationery.* A rolling blotter. Also *attrib.*

1875 KNIGHT *Dict. Mech.* 1963/1. **1899** *Westm. Gaz.* 28 Jan. 8/1 At present diplomatists invariably use the roller blotter for important documents. This, owing to its palimpsest character, is quite undecipherable.

5. a. A cylindrical piece of wood, etc.; esp. one on which cloth or other material is rolled up.

1567 MAPLET *Gr. Forest* 18 Ther is another..which hath yᵉ figure of a narrow Rowler. **1600** SURFLET *Countrie Farme* I. xxviii. 178 To fit the colt for the saddle, the good rider must first put vpon his head a halter, with a rouler of woode. **1691** RAY *Creation* (1692) II. 89 The long slender Worms,.. that breed between the Skin and Flesh.., are generally twisted out upon Sticks or Rowlers. **1802** JAMES *Milit. Dict.*, *Roller*,..a long piece of wood which is rounded and made taper to suit the regulated size of a military tail. **1889** T. HARDY *Mayor Casterbr.* xxxvii, A deal wand—probably the roller from a piece of calico. **1897** J. HOCKING *Mist on the Moors* iii, The calico blind, which was fastened to a roller, was pulled down.

b. A cylindrical device used for applying paint, wallpaper, etc., to a flat surface.

1955 *N.Y. Times* 12 June II. 16/6 Self-feeding rollers should be emptied, and the inside cleaned with whatever solvent is indicated for the kind of paint used. **1959** *Listener* 12 Feb. 311/1, I am often asked whether it is better to use a brush or a roller for painting. **1975** *Times* 28 Aug. 5/1 Embossed wallpapers..can be..applied in different manners (by roller, or by sponge..are just two of them).

6. a. *Organ-building.* A rounded slip of wood or piece of metal tube, turning, by the action of the key, on pins inserted into its ends, and having two or more arms at right angles to its length.

1632 [see ROLLER-BOARD]. **1797** *Encycl. Brit.* (ed. 3) XIII. 488/1 It pulls down the arm *b*, by the wire *d*, which turns about the roller *s* with the arm *a*. **1840-81** [see ROLLER-BOARD].

b. The toothed or studded revolvable barrel of a musical box.

1875 KNIGHT *Dict. Mech.* 1963/1.

7. a. A small wheel rotating on an axle or axis; a short cylinder serving as a wheel.

1802 JAMES *Milit. Dict.*, *Roller*, a small wheel placed at the foot of the hammer of a gun, or pistol lock, in order to lessen the friction of it against the hammer or feather spring. **1874** VANDERVELL & WITHAM *Syst. Figure-Skating* (ed. 2) iv. 63 There have been many attempts to imitate skating by means of small rollers or wheels attached to the feet.

b. *Bookbinding.* = ROLL *sb.*[1] 15 c.

1880 ZAEHNSDORF *Bookbinding* 122 A fine line worked on the centre of the edge of the board..requires more pains than simply running a roller over it.

8. a. (See quot.)

1856 'STONEHENGE' *Brit. Rural Sports* 544/1 The traces themselves either end with an eye, or, with a full fold upon themselves, with an iron eye, called a Roller, and intended to be used upon the Roller-bolt of the splinter-bar.

b. A roller-chain for a cycle (i.e. one in which flexibility is obtained by the use of small rollers in each link).

1897 A. C. PEMBERTON, etc. *Compl. Cyclist* 115 From a lengthy experience I can vouch for the old roller being by no means a bad chain.

II. 9. †**a.** ? A roll of paste. *Obs.*$^{-1}$

c **1420** *Liber Cocorum* (1862) 39 Lay hit in a roller as sparlyng fysshe, Frye hit in grece.

b. *dial.* A roll or cylinder of carded wool.

1844 W. BARNES *Poems Rural Life* 254 The whindlen chaps in town Wi' backs so weak as rollers.

c. *dial.* A line or row of hay, etc., raked ready for ricking.

1844 W. BARNES *Poems Rural Life* 107 A-riaken auver humps an' hollers To riake the grass up into rollers. **1901** *Longman's Mag.* July 209 The long rollers of newly-cut grass over which he stepped were touched..by arrows of light.

10. a. A long bandage, formed in a roll, for winding firmly round a limb, etc. Now more freq. ***roller-bandage***.

It is not certain that the first quot. belongs here.

1534 *Inv. Wardr. Katharine Aragon* in *Camden Misc.* (1855) 40 Item, two roullers, the one lynnene, the other wullen. **1575** TURBERV. *Faulconrie* 264 On everie side bynding them with the linnen rollers or fillets artificially. **1599** A. M. tr. *Gabelhouer's Bk. Physicke* 285/2 Applye it on the inflammation, and tye it with a Rowler, but not to stiffe. **1643** J. STEER tr. *Exp. Chyrurg.* vi. 21, I anointed the whole Arme.., and rowled about Rowlers dipped in Water and Vinegar. **1694** SALMON *Bate's Dispens.* (1713) 701/2 Holding it on with a Plaister..put over it, and binding it sufficiently fast with a Woollen Rouler. **1753** BARTLET *Gent. Farriery* (1754) 299 It would be very proper to keep the legs and pasterns rolled up with a firm bandage, or linnen rowler. **1783** H. WATSON in *Med. Comm.* I. 171 A flannel roller.. must..be applied after the operation. **1803** *Med. Jrnl.* X. 283 As this jacket produces but little sensible pressure, I should not altogether trust to it, without applying a roller over it. **1843** R. J. GRAVES *Syst. Clin. Med.* xxiv. 297 Using the moistened roller to keep the parts cool and retain the dressings.

†**b.** A swaddling-band. *Obs. rare.*

1656 W. DU GARD tr. *Comenius' Gate Lat. Unl.* 233 From sucking they proceed to weaning, and from the cradle to the rollers of the legs. **1706** PHILLIPS (ed. Kersey), *Roller*, a Swathing-band for young Children.

c. A broad, padded girth for a horse.

1688 HOLME *Armoury* III. 93/1 Rowler or Body Girth,.. which slippeth too and again on the body Girth, or Sursingle ..to keep the Girth from fretting of the hair. **1856** 'STONEHENGE' *Brit. Rural Sports* 347/1 When this has been done.., the side-reins are buckled on, and are attached also to the buckles in the roller, crossing them over the withers. *Ibid.*, The roller has been hitherto the only kind of pressure round the chest.

III. †**11.** A large cylindrical block of stone, capable of rolling easily down a slope. *Obs.*

1555 *Lydgate's Chron. Troy* II. xviii, Tyll the Troyans from the crestes caste The great stones..And Rollers [*MSS.* Callyon] eke grekes to oppresse. **1609** HOLLAND *Amm. Marcell.* 430 Overwhelmed with stones, fragments of pillars, and with Cylinders [*marg.* or Rollers], borne downe the steepe descent. **1654** HAMMOND *Fundam.* 187 When a man tumbles a cylindre or roller down a hill,..the man is the violent enforcer of the first motion of it.

†**12.** = GO-CART 1. *Obs.*$^{-1}$

1714 ALEX. SMITH *Lives Highwaymen* (ed. 2) II. 208 He was such a forward Child that he could run about without a Rowler, or Leading-Strings.

†**13.** A kind of stocking; = ROLL-UP *sb.* 1. *Obs.*$^{-1}$

1756 *Connoisseur* No. 115 ¶3, While I am employed in brushing the dust from my black rollers,..my wig is suddenly conveyed away.

14. a. *Zool.* Some infusorian.

1769 *Phil. Trans.* LIX. 149 Fig. 3 is the *volvox volutans*, or the roller.

b. *Conch.* The giant stromb, *Strombus gigas.*

1815 E. J. BURROW *Conch.* 202 [Strombus] Gigas. Large Conch; large Roller.

c. A variety of tumbler-pigeon.

1867 TEGETMEIER *Pigeons* xii. 127 The propensity to the performance of eccentric movements which distinguishes the breeds known as Tumblers and Rollers. **1879** L. WRIGHT *Pract. Pigeon Kpr.* 128 The true Birmingham Roller, which turns over backwards with inconceivable rapidity.

d. A cylinder-snake of the family *Tortricidæ*; a short-tail.

1890 in *Cent. Dict.*

15. a. A long, swelling wave, moving with a steady sweep or roll; a heavy billow.

1829 MARRYAT *F. Mildmay* xx, A..sloop of war was caught in the rollers. **1855** KINGSLEY *Westw. Ho!* vi, Not even a roller broke the perfect stillness of the cove. **1897** F. T. BULLEN *Cruise Cachalot* 90 The immense rollers setting in-shore..would soon carry a vessel up against the beetling crags.

fig. **1863** *Q. Rev.* CXIV. 567 The long rollers which followed the storm of the Reform Bill yet swelled heavily across the ecclesiastical waters.

b. A low rising or undulation on land. *U.S.*

1849 N. KINGSLEY *Diary* 29 Nov. (1914) 88 The land on the left rises in rollers from 10 to 50 feet and the soil appears rich.

†**16. a.** *Cant.* (See quot.) *Obs. rare*$^{-0}$.

1812 J. H. VAUX *Flash Dict.*, *Rollers*, horse and foot patrole, who parade the roads round about London during the night for the prevention of robberies.

b. *U.S. slang.* A policeman.

1964 *N.Y. Times Mag.* 23 Aug. 62/3 *Rollers*, police. **1967** 'I. SLIM' in T. Kochman *Rappin' & stylin' Out* (1972) 388 The rollers cruised by in a squad car. **1973** C. & R. MILNER *Black Players* v. 108 Look, for a roller (policeman) to come to this door—he's insane, he's gotta be a nut.

17. a. A ship that rolls or rocks.

1890 STEVENSON *Lett.* (1899) II. 185 The *Janet* is the worst roller I was ever aboard of. **1897** *Punch* 6 Nov. 207/2 Very few steamers in which I have..voyaged that have not been 'rollers'.

b. One who rolls, swings, or sways from side to side. ***Holy Rollers***: (see quot. 1893). Also *attrib.* and as *Roller*.

1842 *Southern Q. Rev.* (New Orleans) I. 400 It is a new species of religion, which sprang up..contemporaneously with the enthusiasm of the 'Holy Rollers'. **1891** *Pall Mall G.* 16 Nov. 1/3 All of them rolled from side to side like ducks on a common. In a great hall.. were fifty or sixty more of these rollers, smoking, laughing,..reading. **1893** LELAND *Mem.* I. 300 When the Holy Spirit seized them..the Holy Rollers.. rolled over and over on the floor. **1927** M. DE LA ROCHE *Jalna* v. 65 You'd make a good Methodist of the Holy Roller variety. **1928** *Amer. Mercury* Oct. 182/1 To the true Roller every word in his theological vocabulary..and every moral experience, no matter how trivial, is a symbol of forces whose presence inspires him to delirium. **1958** M. ARGYLE *Relig. Behaviour* iv. 34 The Baptists and other Evangelical groups were rather similar in 1850 to the Pentecostalists of today, and there are signs that the present Holy Rollers are becoming assimilated. **1961** C. MCCULLERS *Clock without Hands* x. 198 A part-time preacher who was able to make his Holy Roller congregation talk in strange tongues. **1969** *New Yorker* 14 June 78/2 They sound like fire-and-brimstone preachers in Holy Roller churches.

c. In baseball, a ball that rolls along the ground after being hit by the batter.

1880 *Chicago Inter-Ocean* 15 May 7/1 Flint sent a roller to Crane, and he touched the first batter on the way to second. **1949** *Fargo* (N. Dakota) *Forum* 23 July 8/8 Corcoran's roller, on which there was an error, enabled Erickson to count, making it 3 to 2. **1973** *Tucson* (Arizona) *Daily Citizen* 22 Aug. 57/6 Walslewski mishandled a slow roller by Burney. **1976** *Billings* (Montana) *Gaz.* 16 June 1-c/3 Martin beat out a slow roller over second base.

d. Formerly, a machine used in the early stages of a pilot's training (see quots.).

1917 J. R. MCCONNELL *Flying for France* iv. 143 First of all, the [flying] student is put on what is called a roller. It is a low-powered machine with very small wings. It is strongly built to stand the rough wear it gets, and no matter how much one might try it could not leave the ground. **1929** *Papers Mich. Acad. Sci., Arts & Lett.* X. 319/1 *Roller*.., an aviators' training machine which ran along the ground. Just about ready to fly, but which could not quite rise.

IV. 18. a. One who rolls up or forms into a roll or coil; one who compresses or shapes metal by passing it between cylinders or rolls.

1591 PERCIVALL *Sp. Dict.*, *Embolvedor*, a roller, a wrapper vp. **1793** *Regal Rambler* 76 The tall taylor, the six feet broad-shouldered roller of ribbands. **1832** HT. MARTINEAU *Hill & Valley* (1843) 83 They saw the roller and his catcher at work. **1871** *Daily News* 26 Sept., A meeting of all classes of ironworkers,.. shinglers, rollers, and puddlers, was held. **1890** *Melbourne Argus* 20 Sept. 13/7 The 'roller' now, after first gently shaking the fleece to rid it of any dirt or adhering locks, turns back the neck.

b. One who rolls a thing along. *rare*$^{-0}$.

1648 HEXHAM II, *Een Roller*, a Roler, or a Trundler.

c. *dial.* (See quot. and cf. ROLLER *v.* 2.)

1892 P. H. EMERSON *Son of Fens* 13 The rollers are women who roll barley into ridges or tie the wheat.

d. A thief; one who steals from drunken persons; a prostitute, esp. one who robs her customers. Cf. *jack-roller* s.v. JACK *sb.*[1] 34 a. Chiefly *N. Amer. slang.*

1915 *N.Y. World Mag.* 9 May 14/3 *Roller*, a pickpocket. **1935** *Amer. Speech* X. 14/1 *Creeper*, a prostitute who robs inebriated patrons. Modern *roller.* **1935** L. BOGAN in P. Oliver *Screening Blues* (1968) vi. 230 I'm just a stomp-down roller and I like to strut my stuff. **1948** [see LUSH *sb.*[2] 2]. **1973** *Daily Colonist* (Victoria, B.C.) 17 May 24/2 In addition to warning the public that rollers have been operating, the spokesman asked persons who are robbed to notify police.

19. *pl.* Curl-papers, hair-curlers. Also *sing.* Now usu. a metal or plastic cylinder round which the hair is rolled.

1795 tr. *C. P. Moritz's Trav.* 87 In the morning, it is usual to walk out in a sort of negligée [*sic*].. your hair not dressed, but merely rolled up in rollers, and in a frock and boots. **1799** MRS. J. WEST *Tale of Times* I. 143, I will put my hair in rollers this very evening. **1881** *Queen* 12 Mar. (Advt.), The Parisian leather roller, for curling the fringe, 1s. the dozen. **1940** C. MCCULLERS *Heart is Lonely Hunter* I. iii. 32 Her hair was done up in steel rollers. **1941–2** *Sears, Roebuck Catal.* 637/3 *Bob Roller*, a real aid in achieving the smooth, neat appearance of a well-groomed pompadour hair-do! Catches up all loose ends—..invisible when in hair. Makes neat, low rolls at the nape of your neck. *Ibid.* 637/4 *Hair Rollers.* Use these rayon and lastex tube rollettes to make those puffy, pompadour rolls at the front and the sides of your new hair-do. **1959** *Woman* 2 May 4/4 How do I keep my bouffant hair style looking just set? The secret lies in my home-made rollers—big, fat ones made from cotton wool wrapped round with paper hankies. **1960** *Sunday Express* 24 July 12/5 He was winding some of my hair on to a roller. Mr. Roger is my hair-dresser. **1971** *New Scientist* 19 Aug. 401/2 The inamorata..with hair in rollers, or hanging rat-tailed from the bath. **1977** P. CARTER *Under Goliath* iii. 17 The women in pink rollers nattered on the doorsteps.

20. A butterfly or moth which causes leaves to roll up (see quots.).

1832 J. RENNIE *Consp. Butterfl. & M.* 156 The Filbert Leaf Roller (*Lozotænia Anellana*, Stephens) appears [in].. July, but not common. *Ibid.*, The Gooseberry Leaf Roller.

21. A control in an aircraft for regulating roll.

1959 HOPKIN & THOMAS in *Jrnl. R. Aeronaut. Soc.* LXIII. 572/2 *Roller*, *pitcher*, *yawer* may well find general acceptance. **1961** *Shell Aviation News* Dec. 4/1 Instead of a stick,..we ought to have a motivator, or perhaps three motivators, namely a roller, a pitcher, and a yawer.

V. *attrib.* and *Comb.*

22. Attrib. with names of persons, as ***roller-boy***, ***-coverer***, ***-joiner***, ***-maker***, ***-man***, etc.

1896 HOWELLS *Impr. & Exp.* 27 He became a *roller boy, and served long behind the press before he was promoted to ..set type. **1851** *Census* (1854) 140 *Roller-coverer. **1894** *Labour Comm. Gloss.*, *Roller-Coverer*, a person who covers rollers for spinning purposes. **1858** SIMMONDS *Dict. Trade*, **Roller-joiners*, children employed in certain processes of the woollen manufacture. *Ibid.*, **Roller-maker*, a manufacturer of cylinders of different kinds. **1885** *Census Instruct.* Index 21 *Roller Man. **1893** *Westm. Gaz.* 24 July 2/7 A foreman roller-man in the employment of the South Wales Tin Plate Company.

23. Attrib. with names of things: **a.** In the senses 'of or pertaining to a roller or rollers', 'having the form or movement of a roller', 'operating as or by means of rollers', etc., as ***roller-belt***, ***-head***, ***machine***, ***shelf***.

See also Knight *Dict. Mech.* for other examples.

1877 RAYMOND *Statist. Mines & Mining* 430 To prevent the *roller-attachment of the lever from striking the body of the trip-wheel. **1967** E. CHAMBERS *Photolitho-Offset* ix. 127 A positive *roller-belt transport system is provided accepting any film base from 0·002 to 0·075 in. thick without the use of leaders, hangers, clips, etc. **1835** URE *Philos. Manuf.* 168 Being rubbed..by a fluted cylinder called the *roller-bowl. **1861** *Chambers's Encycl.* II. 512/2 The cloth.. is first brought in contact with *roller brushes. **1896** *Godey's Mag.* Apr. 375/2 A third has both *roller-chain and roller-sprocket. **1884** F. J. BRITTEN *Watch & Clockm.* 207 *Roller Edges for Lever and Chronometer Escapements. **1879** *Lumberman's Gaz.* Oct. 15 The abrogating of the old style of edging up on the log through the introduction of the *roller edger. **1967** M. CHANDLER *Ceramics in Mod. World* ii. 68 A rotating jigger-tool or *roller-head, which completes the shaping of the back. **1950** *Chambers's Encycl.* II. 788/1 In all printing processes, whether they use blocks, *roller machines or silk screens it is important to make use of special devices or expedients to ensure that the successive colour applications 'register' exactly. **1960** *Farmer & Stockbreeder* 22 Mar. (Suppl.) 8/2 The cost of running a mains-driven mower like the Ladybird roller-machine..works out at about 1d per hour. **1835** URE *Philos. Manuf.* 225 The *roller-pair..which receives the fine rovings from bobbins. **1866** *Tomlinson's Cycl. Usef. Arts* II. 399/1 The notes are printed..by means of *roller presses worked by steam. **1844** H. STEPHENS *Bk. Farm* II. 292 The corresponding end of the *roller-shaft. **1958** T. LANDAU *Encycl. Librarianship* 273/1 **Roller shelves*, large shelves for storing folios, etc., which rest on a series of small rollers. **1976** *Gloss. Documentation Terms* (*B.S.I.*) 57 *Roller shelves*, large shelves which rest on a series of rollers, designed for storing folios and other large volumes. Sometimes the volumes rest directly on the rollers. **1878** ABNEY *Photogr.* (1881) 217 Warnerke's *roller slide is of necessity only applicable to sensitive tissue.

b. In sense 'fitted with, coiling up on, a roller', as ***roller-blind***, ***caption***, ***-curtain***, ***door***, ***-map***, ***reefing***, ***shade***, ***shutter***, etc.

1833 LOUDON *Encycl. Archit.* §673 But the chief [kinds] are *roller blinds, Venetian blinds, and wire blinds. **1909** *Chambers's Jrnl.* Nov. 767/1 Also the hideous, cumbersome, expensive concomitant, the roller-blind? **1956** *Railway Mag.* Nov. 735/1 A large inward-opening aluminium door on which is mounted the roller-blind route indicator. **1973** *Times* 23 Mar. 13/5 In theory a roller-blind is a simple thing to make. **1960** D. WILSON in *Television Playwright* 259 We move in towards the painted Dove on the fuselage and hold for the *roller caption. **1904** *Westm. Gaz.* 4 Jan. 9/1 All theatres must be provided with steel *roller-curtains. **1976** *Star* (Sheffield) 26 Nov., The man walked up to the lorry.. pushed up the *roller door and walked off with two cartons of..cigarettes. **1897** KIPLING *Capt. Cour.* 199 He was looking earnestly at the vast *roller-map of America. **1924** *Trans. Newcomen Soc. 1922–3* III. 47 John Bywater (No. 2782 of 1804) patented a *roller reefing gear in which a hit-and-miss arrangement allowed the sweeps to be reefed or unreefed from inside the mill. **1945** *Archit. Rev.* XCVIII. 72/2 A further step forward was the invention, by Captain Stephen Hooper in 1789, of the 'roller reefing sail'. **1962** *Listener* 11 Jan. 85/3 Water-skiing with roaring speed-boats, and roller-reefing gear on yachts. **1976** *Yachts & Yachting* 20 Aug. 385/3 (Advt.), Proctor alloy spars, roller reefing, spinnaker and jib winches. **1961** WEBSTER, *Roller shade. **1962** *Amer. Speech* XXXVII. 173 The typically Southern coast expressions *lightwood*..for 'kindling wood', and *curtain* for 'roller shade'. **1937** *Times British Motor Number* 13 Apr. p. vi/3 There are more *roller shutters for vans instead of hinged doors, which are apt to swing out. **1938** *Archit. Rev.* LXXXIII. 81 Access to the window is by means of a roller shutter. **1978** *Cornish Guardian* 27 Apr. 5/3 (Advt.), Roller shutter garage doors.

c. In sense 4 c, as ***roller-box***, ***-composition***, ***-mould***, ***-stock***, etc.

1875 KNIGHT *Dict. Mech.* 1964/1. **1888** JACOBI *Printer's Vocab.* 114.

d. In sense 6, as ***roller-arm***, ***-frame***, ***-movement***, ***-peg***. Also ROLLER-BOARD.

1852 SEIDEL *Organ* 63 Instead of the roller-board, there is in some organs a roller-frame. **1881** C. A. EDWARDS *Organs* 73 The roller movement..requires a number of rollers in its construction. **1881** W. E. DICKSON *Organ-Build.* viii. 106 Iron roller-arms have some great advantages.

24. a. Objective, as ***roller-carrier***, ***-carrying*** adj., ***-making***.

1875 KNIGHT *Dict. Mech.* 1799/2 The arm *m s* is the roller-carrier, which swings on a pivot. **1887** *Daily News* 21 Oct. 3/5 My first phonograph consisted simply of a roller-carrying foil. **1888** *Encycl. Brit.* XXIII. 708/1 Since then glycerin has been introduced for roller making.

b. Instrumental, as ***roller-drying***, ***-grinding***, ***levelling***, ***-milling***, ***painting***, ***printing***, ***-spinning***; also ***roller-dried***, ***-driven***, ***-made***, ***-milled*** adjs.; ***roller-dry***, ***-paint***, ***-print*** vbs.

1939 *Jrnl. Dairy Res.* X. 202 *Roller-dried milk cannot be reconstituted so completely as spray-dried milk. **1932** *Bull. Hannah Dairy Res. Inst.* No. 3. 123 This milk was *roller-dried. **1950** J. G. DAVIS *Dict. Dairying* 486 Whey from cheese or acid casein manufacture can be successfully roller dried after neutralisation with calcium hydroxide. **1962** J. T. MARSH *Self-Smoothing Fabrics* xi. 174 In general, festoon chambers were very commonly employed until after World War II, when *roller-driven machines became more popular, particularly those with independent drive for each roller. **1932** *Bull. Hannah Dairy Res. Inst.* No. 3. 119 Broadly speaking, the successful commercial processes [for the manufacture of milk powder] may be reduced to three main types:—(1) *Roller-drying, (2) Spray-drying, (3) Dough-drying. **1939** *Jrnl. Dairy Res.* X. 202 The great heat to which milk is exposed in roller drying. **1879** *Encycl. Brit.* IX. 344/2 The various systems of *roller grinding. **1933** *Jrnl. Iron & Steel Inst.* CXXVII. 593 In order to eliminate these strains, the sheets are generally passed through *roller levelling machines just prior to the stamping operation. **1973** J. G. TWEEDDALE *Materials Technol.* II. iv. 97 Roller-levelling is a means for producing a reasonably-straight flat product from a long prismatic shape. The principle involves 'snaking' the section through a series of offset rolls which bend the section plastically, alternately in opposite directions. Starting first with a fairly severe bend and then with progressively less severe bends until the section is almost perfectly straight... The alternate bending irons out kinks and plastic flow difference left in the material from previous operations. **1892** *Daily News* 13 Sept. 5/4 Millers ..say that there is less nutriment in *roller-made flour. **1879** *Encycl. Brit.* IX. 344/2 *Roller milling or crushing. **1888** POWLES tr. *Kick's Flour Manuf.* 151 Not..that with roller milling larger bran is made than with stones. **1960** *Times* 12 Dec. 15/3 Having *roller-painted all her rooms herself. **1959** *House & Garden* July 94/3 *Roller painting, with all its attendant perils of upsetting the paint tray. **1959** *Manch. Guardian* 2 July 4/1 All London bus tickets were *roller-printed by the conductors. **1911** *Encycl. Brit.* XXVI. 696/2 In its simplest form the *roller-printing machine consists of a strong cast iron cylinder mounted in adjustable bearings capable of sliding up and down slots in the sides of the rigid iron framework. **1936** [see *hand block* s.v. HAND *sb.* 65]. **1963** A. J. HALL *Textile Sci.* iv. 203 Roller printing is the most convenient and satisfactory method of printing long 'runs' of a multi-coloured pattern on fabric. **1975** *Oxf. Compan. Decorative Arts* 281/1 Copper-plate printing replaced block printing in 1781 and roller printing followed shortly after. *a* **1854** RICKARDS in McCulloch *Acc. Brit. Empire* (ed. 4) I. 701 The wonderful discoveries.., such as *roller-spinning, the jenny, the carding-machine.

c. Parasynthetic, as ***roller-bearinged*** adj.

1922 *Encycl. Brit.* XXX. 36/2 Connecting-rods of rotary and radial engines consist usually of one master-rod, ball or roller-bearinged [etc.].

25. Special combs., as **roller arena**, a roller-skating rink; **roller bandage**, = sense 10; **roller-beam**, part of a drawing-frame for cotton; **roller bearing**, a bearing in which the journal is free to rotate round a ring of metal rollers; **roller bit** *Oil Industry*, a drilling bit in which the cutting teeth are on rotating conical or circular cutters; **roller-boiling**, = *roll-boiling* (see ROLL *sb.*[1] 14 c); **roller-bolt**, part of the splinter-bar of a carriage, serving also as a step; **roller box**, a box containing rollers; *spec.* (*a*) one containing drawing-rolls in a cotton-spinning machine; (*b*) (see quot. 1967); **roller-chair**, = *rolling-chair*; **roller-cloth** = *roller-towel*; **roller coaster**, a kind of switchback railway at an amusement park; also *transf.*, *fig.*, and *attrib.*; hence as *v. intr.*; so ***roller-coasting***; hence (as back-formation) ***roller-coast*** vb. trans. and intr.; **roller-coat** *v. trans.*, to apply with a roller (sense 5 b); **roller derby**, **Roller Derby**, a name for a type of speed-skating competition on roller-skates, now one with specified periods during which skaters can physically assist their own team members and impede opponents; such a competition; **roller disco**, a discothèque at which the dancers wear roller-skates; disco-dancing on roller-skates; **roller drier**, an apparatus in which milk is dried on the surface of one or more heated rollers, in the manufacture of milk powder; **roller hearth furnace** (see quot. 1970); **roller hockey**, a type of hockey played on roller-skates; = ROLLER-POLO; **roller-mill**, a mill in which the grinding is done by rollers; hence ***roller-miller***; **roller polo** = *rink polo* s.v. POLO 2; **roller print**, (*a*) a fabric with a design produced by roller-printing; (*b*) a roller for printing or impressing a design; **roller-shop**, the part of an iron-works where the metal is rolled; **roller steady** *Engin.* [STEADY *sb.* 2 b], a device which grips between rollers the article being turned on a lathe; **roller-top**, = ROLL-TOP *sb.* (also *attrib.*); **roller-towel**, a towel running on a roller; **roller-towelling**, a type of cloth used for roller-towels; **roller tube** *Biol.*, a tube which is continually rotated so as to moisten with nutrient solution the cells or tissue being grown in it; freq. *attrib.*; **roller-type** *a.*, of a kind that has the form or movement of a roller.

1971 *Islander* (Victoria, B.C.) 18 July 11/1 A large assemblage was at the *roller arena to see the sights. **1885** *Buck's Ref. Hand-bk. Med. Sci.* I. 470 The usual form of bandage is what is known as a '*roller-bandage'. **1835** URE *Philos. Manuf.* 118 The strong *roller-beam, on which are fixed several such drawing-heads. **1857** J. B. PASCAL *Brit. Pat.* 465 4 Figure 3 is an elevation of the *roller bearing of the axis. **1884** KNIGHT *Dict. Mech.* Suppl., Roller Bearing. **1886** *Bicycling News* 6 Aug. 664/1 Bicycle, Singer's roller bearings. **1915** V. W. PAGÉ *Model T Ford Car* iii. 117 The differential mechanism and the wheel end of the axle utilize roller bearings. **1958** *Times Rev. Industry* Aug. 32/1 The spindle..runs in pre-loaded taper roller bearings. **1970** B. PUGH *Pract. Lubrication* v. 45 An advantage of..roller bearings in preference to sleeve bearings is that they require the minimum of maintenance. **1918** *Oil Weekly* 27 July 25 (Advt.), Caddo bits will make more hole in hard rock for any given amount of money, than any other *roller bit on the market. **1924** L. C. UREN *Textbk. Petroleum Production Engin.* vi. 152 The Reed roller bit..is equipped with eight disc-shaped cutters having teeth milled around their circumference and mounted in a massive steel frame. **1966** *McGraw-Hill Encycl. Sci. & Technol.* II. 295/2 Penetration is by rotation of drill bits of two types: (1) roller bits, which have rolling cutters with projecting hard teeth; and (2) drag bits, with fixed chisel-type hard cutting edges. **1879** *Cassell's Techn. Educ.* IV. 376/1 This process, called '*roller boiling'.., effected a wonderful improvement on the finish. **1839** URE *Dict. Arts* 1294 Two splinter-bars, with their *roller-bolts, for connecting the traces of the harness. **1851** 'NIMROD' *The Road* 16 He placed his right foot on the roller-bolt,—i.e., the last step but one to the box. **1888** C. T. JACOBI *Printers' Vocab.* 113 **Roller box*, the receptacle in which rollers are kept to protect them from dust, etc. **1902** T. THORNLEY *Cotton Combing Machines* iii. 85 In times past a good deal of trouble has arisen in connection with the quadrant and roller box system. **1950** A. W. JUDGE *Centre, Capstan & Automatic Lathes* II. v. 204 Fig. 242 shows a roller box tool..in operation on a turret automatic. **1967** J. L. & G. H. F. NAYLER *Dict. Mech. Engin.* 299 *Roller box*, a cutting tool-holder used on capstan lathes and automatic lathes. The box holds a cutting tool and two rollers positioned so that part of the reaction force from the cutting tool is taken by the rollers, thus preventing distortion of the work. **1975** BRAM & DOWNS *Manuf. Technol.* v. 135 Various methods are used to set up the roller box, the one chosen depending on whether or not the work has been previously machined. **1897** *Westm. Gaz.* 21 June 7/1 She..was then placed in her *roller chair and wheeled out. **1862** 'G. HAMILTON' *Country Living* 11, I become acquainted..with the *modus operandi* of '*roller-cloths'. **1877** E. S. WARD *Story of Avis* 224 A roller-cloth would do, dear. **1973** *Nation Rev.* (Melbourne) 31 Aug. 1465/1 It is a ritual that defies time..and the giant forces that *roller-coast us at increasing velocity to some eerie destination. **1978** *Chatelaine* (Canada) Dec. 14/2 Canada's rates of inflation and cost of living are roller-coasting. **1888** *Pall Mall G.* 11 Sept. 4/2 The rage for rapid transit through the air,..by tobogganing, switchbacks, or *roller-coasters. **1903** *Boston Transcript* 7 Oct. 16 The cable cars run over routes that would shame a Coney Island roller coaster. **1931** [see JITTER *sb.* 1]. **1945** J. STEINBECK *Cannery Row* xvi. 100 Phyllis Mae had broken her leg getting out of the roller coaster. **1949** *Sun* (Baltimore) 1 July 28/5 Maryland found herself saddled with a system of 'roller coaster' roads. **1957** N. FRYE *Sound & Poetry* p. xx, Speeded-up metrical rhythms, such as Swinburne's roller-coaster anapests, are unmusical. **1961** *John o' London's* 6 July 21/1 The ever-accelerating roller-coaster of science. **1962** WODEHOUSE *Service with Smile* vii. 116 Her emotions were somewhat similar to those of a nervous passenger on a roller coaster at an amusement park who when it is too late to get off feels the contraption gathering speed beneath him. **1965** L. R. HUBBARD *Scientology Abridged Dict.* 26 A person 'roller coasters', i.e., gets better, then worse, etc., only when connected to a Suppressive Person or Group, and in order to cease roller coastering must receive processing intended to handle such. **1967** A. WEST in *Coast to Coast 1965–66* 214 They entered [the restaurant] through an underwater tunnel that began just next to the roller-coaster ticket office. **1968** *Surfer Mag.* Jan. 53/2 Martinson attempts a roller coaster down an Arpoador wave. **1969** *Observer* 3 Aug. 35/1 He may 'rollercoaster', bursting through a breaking wave, turning and bouncing down through the foam. **1970** *Studies in English* (Univ. Cape Town) I. 27 Yet another kind of wave is the rollercoaster... A rollercoaster wave is one that does not break continuously from one end to the other, but breaks in sections all along its length, thus offering the surfer a tricky, 'up and down' ride. **1971** G. G. LUCE *Body Time* v. 170 A physician who knew his patient's time print, the shape of his temperature and activity-rest cycle, and who knew where his patient was on this daily roller coaster, might have much less trouble interpreting the results of clinic tests. **1975** *New Yorker* 21 Apr. 36/1 She lost John—left him the way popcorn flies out of the bag on the roller coaster. **1977** *Time* 24 Jan. 14/2 Private sterling deposits have fluctuated little, while official deposits have roller-coastered. **1887** *Contemp. Rev.* May 733 Here are boating, fishing, .. *roller-coasting .. for boys. **1960** R. W. MARKS *Dymaxion World of B. Fuller* 27/2 Ducks, however, are anatomically unfitted for such aerial roller coasting. **1968** W. WARWICK *Surfriding in N.Z.* p. iv, *Roller coasting*, one way of dropping and climbing on a wave. **1961** WEBSTER, *Roller-coat *vt.* **1971** *Engineering* Apr. 61/2 Protectalac .. can be brushed, sprayed, roller or curtain coated. **1976** *Broadcast* 29 Mar. 8/3 An epoxy/polyurethane material .. was then roller-coated on to the .. floor space. [**1935** *Chicago Tribune* 13 Aug. 19/6 A 3000 mile roller skating derby will open at noon today when 50 skaters begin the long grind inside the main hall of the Coliseum.] **1936** *N.Y. Times* 11 Sept. 34/4 The *Roller Derby, first of the kind to be seen in New York, and in which fourteen teams of skaters composed of men and girls are entered, got well under way at the Hippodrome last night... The derby is a mythical race from Salt Lake City to New York. **1945** *Life* 21 May 81/1 The Chicago Coliseum fairly whistled with roller skates. The occasion was the tenth annual Roller Derby. **1972** *Guardian* 17 Feb. 10/1 A documentary study of a young man .. trying to become a Roller Derby star .. practising an amalgam of speed-skating and all-in wrestling. **1975** R. HOBAN *Turtle Diary* xxv. 115 She was American... She'd .. been a rodeo rider, done roller derbies, wrestled. **1979** *Tucson Mag.* Apr. 38/1 However, if you didn't know Tucson is the only city in America where roller derby is played on radials. **1978** S. BOORSTIN *Keep on Rollin'* 9/2 Skaters pursuing their passion .. under the strobe lights of a *roller disco. **1984** S. TOWNSEND *Growing Pains A. Mole* 54 Then the roller disco started and she sped off to do wild disco dancing on her skates. **1932** *Bull. Hannah Dairy Res. Inst.* No. 4. 61 The powder obtained from the standard *roller drier is not a high class product. **1963** A. W. FARRALL *Engin. for Dairy & Food Products* xiv. 410 The drum dryer, often called roller dryer. **1958** *Engineering* 11 Apr. 472/2 The mesh-belt type of furnace is satisfactory for strip of relatively low melting point material such as copper, but *roller-hearth or walking beam furnaces may be required for .. iron or nickel. **1970** *Gloss. Industr. Furnace Terms* (*B.S.I.*) 15 *Roller hearth furnace*, a furnace in which the charge is carried forward on driven alloy steel or refractory rollers. **1926** *Daily Colonist* (Victoria, B.C.) 9 Jan. 12/4 *Roller Hockey League entries close today. **1975** *Oxf. Compan. Sports & Games* 845/1 The roller hockey stick is similar in shape to a field hockey stick but flat on both sides of the blade. **1875** KNIGHT *Dict. Mech.* 1964/1 *Roller-mill. **1882** *Lancet* 10 June 967 To produce by means of roller mills the largest bulk of white flour from a given bulk of corn. **1892** *Daily News* 13 Sept. 5/4 Even *roller millers, however, have not got it all their own way. **1895** *Spalding's Official Roller Polo Guide for 1896* 5 New England is now the only section in which *roller polo rages. **1968** J. IRONSIDE *Fashion Alphabet* 246 **Roller print*: the colours for the design are applied directly to the cloth. **1969** E. H. PINTO *Treen* 100 Butter prints are of five distinct types and many patterns and sizes. The types are .. (5) roller prints. **1890** W. J. GORDON *Foundry* 111 In the same range as the *roller-shop is the laboratory. **1920** J. G. HORNER *Turret Lathe Practice* ii. 20 *Roller steadies were found essential at the time that attempts were being made to utilise the high-speed steel to the greatest advantage in turret practice. **1964** S. CRAWFORD *Basic Engin. Processes* v. 140 Many jobs require a special form on their end face... This can readily be produced with a roller steady ending tool which consists of two hardened-steel rollers which contact the finished diameter of the work and are closely followed by a form tool which produces the desired shape on the end of the component. **1975** BRAM & DOWNS *Manuf. Technol.* v. 135 The roller-steady turning tool-holder has two rollers incorporated into the design. **1897** KIPLING *Capt. Cour.* 198 The father .. laid his head down on the *roller-top of the shut desk. **1897** *Westm. Gaz.* 15 Jan. 9/2 Roller-top desks .. sell in Chemnitz for £14. **1845** *Knickerbocker* XXV. 444 Beside the window was the linen *roller-towel. **1862** MRS. H. WOOD *Mrs. Halliburton's Troubles* xix, Patience dried her hands upon the *roller-towel. **1980** D. WILLIAMS *Murder for Treasure* v. 46 A copious length of roller towel unhitched from its cabinet. **1881** C. C. HARRISON *Woman's Handiwork* i. 48 Among other washing fabrics used in art needlework are *crash*, **roller-towelling, bamboo-cloth*, [etc.]. **1932** D. C. MINTER *Mod. Needlecraft* 246/2 Roller towelling or Russian crash or zephyr. **1933** *Amer. Jrnl. Cancer* XVII. 753 With the *roller tube method these cells can be allowed to re-implant themselves in another portion of the tube. **1936** *Ibid.* XXVII. 49 Roller tubes of different types have been used with good results. **1947** *Anat. Rec.* XCIX. 157 We cultured the hearts of 10-day-old chick embryos and grew them in test tubes in a roller-tube apparatus. **1964** M. HYNES *Med. Bacteriol.* (ed. 8) xxiv. 353 An analogy to solid bacterial media was first provided by the roller-tube technique of tissue culture. Fragments of tissue are embedded in plasma clot in the tube, and continually moistened with culture medium by rotating the tube. Sheets of cells grow out from the tissue inoculum. **1960** *Farmer & Stockbreeder* 1 Mar. 72/1 For moving, the washer is mounted on *roller-type wheels. **1964** S. CRAWFORD *Basic Engin. Processes* xiv. 304 Similar in general principle to the above, but having roller-type anvils.

roller ('rəʊlə(r)), *sb.*[2] *Ornith.* [a. G. *roller*, f. *rollen* to roll. Hence also F. *rollier* in sense 1.]

1. An insessorial coracoid bird (usually the common roller, *Coracias garrulus*), having the form of a crow, and brilliant plumage.

The original source appears to be Gesner *Hist. Anim.* III. *Aves* (1604) 702, who says the bird was so called at Strasburg (*Argentoratum*) 'per onomatopœiam'. Later writers have variously explained the name as referring to a habit of rolling about in the air, or of rolling over sticks and stones in seeking food. A number of varieties, as *Angola*, *Indian*, *black*, *crimson*, etc., are enumerated in Shaw's *Gen. Zool.* (1809) VII. II. 387 ff.

[**1663** SKIPPON *Journ. Low C.* 21 Aug., We .. kill'd a curious bird call'd Rollar Argentoratensis, of the bigness of a dove, and of a blue colour.] **1678** RAY tr. *Willughby's Ornith.* 132, I am verily perswaded that this bird is no other than the Strasburgh Roller. **1752** HILL *Hist. Anim.* 388 The Corvus, with a blood-red back, a green tail, and black wings, the Roller... I think it the most beautiful of all European birds. **1774** GOLDSM. *Nat. Hist.* (1776) V. 242 The Roller .. may be distinguished from all others by a sort of naked tubercles or warts near the eyes, which still farther contribute to encrease its beauty. **1825** VIGORS & HORSFIELD in *Trans. Linn. Soc.* XV. 202 This bird [*Eurystomus orientalis*] .. was originally placed by Linnæus among the Rollers. **1873** TRISTRAM *Moab* xv. 294 In their flight these ravens often gambolled like the roller, dipping perpendicularly and performing somersaults in the air. **1893** SELOUS *Trav. S.E. Africa* 48 A pair of those rare and beautiful rollers (Coracias spatulatus) .. came and perched upon the tree.

attrib. **1855** KINGSLEY *Glaucus* (1878) 29 The blue and green Roller-birds, walking behind the plough.

b. Applied to other birds (see quots.).

1752 HILL *Hist. Anim.* 503 The grey Ampelis, with the head variegated with black, the Roller. This is of the size of the common black-bird. **1848** GOULD *Birds Austr.* II. pl. 17 *Eurystomus Australis*, .. Australian Roller. **1869** WALLACE *Malay Archip.* 42, I was rewarded by finding a splendid deep blue roller (Eurystomus azureus).

2. A variety of canary, remarkable for rolling or trilling in song.

1884 R. L. WALLACE *Canary Bk.*, The most valued of all [German canaries] are the variety known by the name of the Hartz Mountain Rollers.

'roller, *sb.*[3] *Oxford slang.* = ROLL-CALL *sb.*

1883 *Oxford Review* 26 April 345/1 Up to this time a nominal five, a practical four, and a possible three 'rollers' would suffice.

'roller, *v.* [f. ROLLER *sb.*[1]]

1. *trans.* To roll; to press or pass between rolls.

1827 *Patents* in *Ann. Reg.* 534/2 Machinery for rolling or rollering wool from the carding engine.

2. *dial.* To rake *up* (hay) into rows.

c **1830** MORTON *Glouc. Farm Rep.* 15 in *L.U.K.*, *Husb.* III, When the hay-making machine has done its work, the hay is hatched or rollered up, as it is called. *Ibid.*, When the field is all hatched or rollered, people with forks make up the hatches into cocks. **1893** DARTNELL & GODDARD *Wilts. Words* 77 Hay is 'put in rollers', or 'rollered up'.

'roller-board. 1. [ROLLER *sb.*[1] 6.] The board carrying the rollers in an organ. Also *attrib.*

1632 in J. Crosse *York Mus. Festiv.* (1825) App. 2 Item the rowler board carriages and keyes, xx *li.* **1840** *Penny Cycl.* XVI. 492/2 Figure 3 is a perspective view of a roller-board; AAA, the board on which the rollers are fixed. **1855** E. J. HOPKINS *Organ* x. 47 There are .. two distinct kinds of key-movement in common use in England; namely, the lever or fan-frame movement, and the roller-board movement. **1881** W. E. DICKSON *Pract. Organ-Building* viii. 96 Rollers are in sets, like backfalls and squares, and are arranged symmetrically on a board called a roller-board.

2. [ROLLER *sb.*[1] 7.] A board on rollers.

1958 J. KEROUAC *On Road* I. x. 58 Dean was frightfully waked up by the legless man on the rollerboard. **1963** *Lebende Sprachen* VIII. 106/3 *Roller-board* .., Rollbrett zur Reparatur unter dem Wagen.

roller-coaster: see ROLLER *sb.*[1] 25.

'roller-gin. [ROLLER *sb.*[1] 4 b.] A cotton-gin in which the cleaning was effected by rollers.

1825 J. NICHOLSON *Operat. Mechanic* 378 The roller-gin .. consists of two shallow fluted rollers .. placed so near to each other, that when the cotton is thrust against the line where they enter into contact, they immediately seize hold of it. **1851** *Art Jrnl. Illustr. Catal.* p. iii**/2 The machine now almost universally used .. is the saw-gin, the roller-gin having been supplanted even in India. **1888** *Encycl. Brit.* XXIII. 757/2 The 'roller gin' could clean only a half dozen pounds [of cotton] a day by slave labour.

'rollering, *vbl. sb.* Roller-skating.

1880 *World* 31 Mar. 12 The rinks at Brighton .. where 'rollering' has once more set in with unusual severity.

'roller-skate, *sb.* [ROLLER *sb.*[1] 7.] **1.** A skate mounted on small wheels or rollers, usually two pairs, instead of a metallic blade, for use in skating on smooth flooring, etc. Orig. *U.S.* Also *attrib.*

1863 *Rep. Comm. Patents 1861* (U.S.) I. 280 A roller skate provided with two rows of tubular adjustable rollers. **1874** VANDERVELL & WITHAM *Figure-Skating* (ed. 2) iv. 68 Good ice-skaters are usually under the impression that they can at once perform their .. evolutions on these roller-skates. **1887** *Encycl. Brit.* XXII. 105/2 The fatigue caused by these 'roller skates' is quadruple that of ordinary ice skating. **1893** KIPLING *Many Invent.* 5 The roller-skate rattle of the revolving lenses.

2. A vehicle considered to resemble a roller-skate, spec. (*a*) a tank; (*b*) a small car. *slang.*

1941 *Reader's Digest* Feb. 92 The boys of Britain's R.A.F. have developed a language all their own... 'roller skates' are tanks. **1961** PARTRIDGE *Dict. Slang* Suppl. 1127/2 *Roller skate*, a small, light waggon. **1976** LIEBERMAN & RHODES *Compl. CB Handbk.* vi. 135 *Rollerskate*, a small or foreign car.

Hence **'roller-skater, -skating** (also *attrib.*).

1874 VANDERVELL & WITHAM *Figure-Skating* (ed. 2) iv. 68 The operation of the ice skate seems variable and uncertain to the roller-skater. *Ibid.* 71 The exercise of roller-skating becomes .. as fascinating as ice-skating. **1884** *N.Y. Weekly Tribune* 13 Aug. 4/3 Down at the roller skating rink having an awfully good time. **1884** E. YATES *Recoll.* (ed. Tauchn.) I. 181 The London world went .. mad over the production of *Le Prophète* [1847–52], in which, by the way, roller-skating was first introduced. **1888** *Boston Jrnl.* 4 Oct. 2/4 The roller-skating craze .. has died out in this section. **1910** *Cycling* 2 Mar. 202 (*caption*) The roller-skating craze in Germany—a lady's race. **1949** *Time* 18 Apr. 25/1 The village board .. should wake up, give the kids a roller-skating rink. **1977** [see ROLLER-SKATE *v.*].

'roller-skate, *v.* [f. the sb.] *intr.* To use roller-skates; to travel on roller-skates. Also *fig.*

1928 *Daily Tel.* 7 Feb. 4/7 Splendid and Partner can roller-skate as agilely on one table as Barrie Oliver can dance on another. **1935** W. FORTESCUE *Perfume from Provence* 93 What more amusing than to watch the pompous Monsieur Jeannot slip on a piece of banana skin and skid into a heap of oranges, some of which scatter under the stalls and are swiftly prigged by alert urchins, while other marketers roller-skate on the remainder? **1942** BERREY & VAN DEN BARK *Amer. Thes. Slang* §728/4 *Drive fast*, .. roller-skate. **1967** in Cox & Grose *Organiz. Bibliogr. Rec. by Computer* VII. 185 The National Employee Index .. was referred to constantly—so much so that the messengers had to roller-skate through the file to gain access to it. **1973** *Times* 12 Nov. 18/6 Indeed children were roller-skating all over the place. **1977** J. CLEARY *High Road to China* vii. 226 The last event in the programme... A roller-skating race... Can you roller-skate?

'roller-ski, *sb.* [f. as ROLLER-SKATE *sb.*: see SKI *sb.*] A kind of ski, about three feet in length, fitted with small wheels like those on a roller-skate, and used for skiing on roads, etc. Hence as *v. intr.*; also **'roller-ˌskier, 'roller-ˌskiing** *vbl. sb.*

1978 *Skiing* Spring 58/1 Roller skiing has become *de rigueur* for dedicated cross-country skiers because .. 'it's the closest thing to skiing you can get without snow'. *Ibid.*, Tim roller-skis about 1,500 km .. between seasons. *Ibid.*, Roller skis don't have brakes. **1979** *Capital Times* (Madison, Wisconsin) 23 Nov. 45/1 That enthusiast was using rollerskis, a training tool champion skiers have employed for years to maintain form. *Ibid.*, Every championship cross-country skier relies on so many meters of rollerskiing during the off-season. *Ibid.* 45/2 One of the most avid rollerskiers around is Madison Police Chief David Couper. *Ibid.* 45/3 How did Koch keep his top form over the summer? He rollerskied.

rolley ('rɒlɪ). Also **rolly.** [Of obscure origin: perh. connected with ROLL *v.*[2], but cf. RULLEY.]

1. *Mining.* A kind of truck without sides, formerly much in use for carrying corves along underground horse-roads or upon rails to the shaft.

1825 [see b]. **1839** URE *Dict. Arts* 982 Each corve .. is lifted from the tram .., and placed on a carriage called a rolley, which generally holds two corves. **1851** GREENWELL *Coal-Trade terms, Northumb. & Durham* 43 The rolley was contrived as an improvement upon the tram, upon which a single corf was placed.

b. *attrib.* and *Comb.*, as ***rolley-driver, -horse, -way, -way-man, -wheel***, etc.

1825 J. NICHOLSON *Operat. Mechanic* 646 The plate railways employed in coal-mines, and there called tram and rolley-ways. *Ibid.* 649 A view of a rolley or tram-wheel. **1839** URE *Dict. Arts* 982 The rolley driver, with his horse, takes them to the bottom of the engine-shaft. *Ibid.*, The rolley horses have a peculiar kind of shafts. **1851** GREENWELL *Coal-trade terms, Northumb. & Durham, Rolleyway-man*, a man whose business is to attend to the rolleyway, and keep it in order.

2. A lorry; = RULLEY. Also *attrib.*

1886 *N. Eastern Daily Gaz.* 11 Aug. 1/6 Spring Rolleys for removing Furniture. *Ibid.* 1/4 Waterproof Cart and Rolley Covers. *Ibid.* 1/3 Wanted, .. steady Young Man as Rolleyman. **1894** HESLOP *Northumbld. Gloss.* s.v., 'A railway rolley,' a large, flat, four-wheeled waggon, used for the street delivery and carriage of merchandize.

rollick ('rɒlɪk), *sb.* [f. ROLLICK *v.*]

1. Exuberant gaiety or joviality; a very gay and jovial tone.

1856 *Titan Mag.* Nov. 403 The heat, the draughts, the bustle, rollick—all The genteel pleasures of a country ball. **1866** *Pall Mall G.* No. 446. 141/2 An unreal rollick in his voice and manner. **1886** *Macm. Mag.* Apr. 420 This snatch, .. in its mixture of sentiment, truth, and what may be excusably called 'rollick', is very characteristic of its author.

2. A sportive frolic or escapade.

1876 J. ELLIS *Cæsar in Egypt* 309 Off for a rollick—sweeter by stealth! **1883** J. PARKER *Tyne Chylde* 7 Once my life was a child's rollick, half trick, half dream. **1897** 'F. ANSTEY' *Trav. Comp.* ii, *Culd.* We might take a turn later on, and see the effect of St. Gudule in the moonlight. *Podb.* Something like a rollick that!

rollick ('rɒlɪk), *v.* Also *dial.* rollo(c)k. [Of obscure origin.] *intr.* To frolic, sport, or romp, in a joyous, careless fashion; to go off, move along, enter, etc., in this manner.

1826 SCOTT *Jrnl.* 2 Aug., Instead of writing me one other page.., you rollick into the woods till you have not a dry thread about you. **1854** MISS BAKER *Northampt. Gloss.*, *Rollock*, to romp about rudely. **1878** J. T. FIELDS in *Life & Lett. B. Taylor* I. iv. 76 We rollicked along into Washington Street. **1888** *Pall Mall G.* 28 Sept. 3/2 'Q.' appears as a rollicking humourist... He rollicks, perhaps, a little too laboriously.

b. *transf.* of things or animals.

a **1837** J. CLARE in *N. & Q.* 9th Ser. XI. 177/1 The wind is rollicking about to-day. Wild, but not stormy. **1846** T. B. THORPE *Myst. Backwoods* 13 Mounted by a rider..he [the mustang pony] goes rollicking ahead. **1853** KINGSLEY *Hypatia* xxix, The shrieks of his lute rose shrill..and rollicked on swifter and swifter as the old singer maddened.

c. To revel joyously *in* something.

1865 G. MEREDITH *R. Fleming* xxix, There was something desperately amusing to him in the thought that he had not even money enough to..provide for a repast. He rollicked in his present poverty.

Hence **'rollicker**.

1893 *Columbus* (Ohio) *Disp.* 19 Oct., It is the same..with the ragged, hungry little folk of the western isles as with the romping rollickers of Glasgow.

'rollicking, *ppl. a.* [f. ROLLICK *v.* + -ING[2].] Extremely jovial or gay; boisterously sportive:

a. Of persons.

1811 in E. Mathews *Mem. C. Mathews* (1838) II. viii. 148 Some of the 'rollicking fellows' (as they call themselves) who perform in that Court. **1832** LYTTON *E. Aram* II. v, Pray tell me all about him,—a wild, gay, rollicking fellow still, eh? **1858** DORAN *Court Fools* 117 The outlay of this rollicking Court even frightened the Commons. **1881** BESANT & RICE *Chapl. of Fleet* I. v, He was a rollicking, jovial, boon companion.

Comb. **1863** DICEY *Federal St.* I. 36 Suspicious glances directed towards a rollicking-looking clerk.

b. Of disposition, conduct, actions, etc.

1826 HONE *Every-day Bk.* II. 467 The 'tipsy toss' of that actor's head, his rollocking look. **1842** BARHAM *Ingol. Leg.* Ser. II. *Dead Drummer*, The pigeon-toed step, and the rollicking motion. **1874** BURNAND *My Time* vi. 50 He used to sing to us some rollicking songs with strangely worded choruses.

transf. and *fig.* **1857** B. TAYLOR *North. Trav.* xxv. 254 There was no lush, rollicking out-burst of foliage,..no easy unfolding of leaf on leaf. **1871** L. STEPHEN *Playgr. Eur.* (1894) viii. 186 It was a glacier of a rollicking spirit, given to plunge in broad curves over hidden ridges of rock.

Hence **'rollickingly** *adv.*; **'rollickingness**.

1842 *Fraser's Mag.* XXVI. 447 No man could sing a song more rollickingly. **1865** *Sat. Rev.* 25 Nov. 667 The jocose and rollicking chief is no more. His two successors hate jocosity and rollickingness.

rollicking, *vbl. sb.* [f. ROLLICK *v.*] **1.** The action of the vb.

1830–2 CARLETON *Traits* (1843) I. 113 There's no stop to their noise and rollokin. **1865** *Sat. Rev.* 25 Nov. 667/2 Lord Amberley..would never have to leave an administration headed by a Whig, for any amount of rollicking.

2. Also **rollocking**. A severe reprimand. *colloq.*

1938 F. D. SHARPE *Sharpe of Flying Squad* 332 *A rollicking*, a telling off. ('He gave the copper a real rollicking.') **1958** M. K. JOSEPH *I'll soldier no More* ii. 54 Someone's dropped a clanger. Someone's going to get a rollocking. **1970** G. F. NEWMAN *Sir, You Bastard* vi. 174 You were on the cards for one hell of a rollicking. **1973** *Observer* 18 Nov. 37/5 The unknown Fourth Division manager who gave his forward line a fearful rollicking.

'rollicksome, *a.* [f. ROLLICK *v.*] Rollicking. Hence **'rollicksomeness**.

1847 *Blackw. Mag.* July 67/2 The loud rolicsome sports in which he had hitherto been a leader. **1866** BLACKMORE *C. Nowell* xxxiii, Jack is obliged..to bottle up his money, his rollicksomeness and sentimentality.

'rollicky, *a. rare.* Given to rollicking. See also quot. 1942.

1881 W. S. GILBERT *Patience* (*c* 1891) I. 7 A smack of Lord Waterford, reckless and rollicky—Swagger of Roderick, heading his clan. **1889** J. K. JEROME *Idle Thoughts* 106 We men are supposed to be a bold and rollicky lot. **1942** BERREY & VAN DEN BARK *Amer. Thes. Slang* §278/20 *Hilarious*,.. rollicky.

†**'rolling**, *vbl. sb.*[1] *Obs. rare.* [f. ROLL *v.*[1]] An enrolling, enrolment; an entering upon a roll.

1303 R. BRUNNE *Handl. Synne* 9801 Syker ys, þat yn rolle ys leyde, For þan may hyt neuer be wypseyde; þe rollyng fordoþe croppe and rote. **1465** *Mann. & Househ. Exp.* (Roxb.) 298 My mastyr paid for the rollenge [of his patent], iij.s. iiij.d. *a* **1550** *Vox populi* 43 in Hazl. *E.P.P.* III. 269 By roulyng and by dating. **1552** *Reg. Privy Council Scot.* I. 32 That thair be Commissaris deput..to vesy the rolling of the futmen.

rolling ('rəʊlɪŋ), *vbl. sb.*[2] [f. ROLL *v.*[2]]

The sense is not clear in the following passage:

a **1440** *York Myst.* xxx. 234 Do rappe on the renkis, þat we may rayse with oure rolyng.

I. 1. a. The action of turning something over and over, or of causing it to roll; †bowling.

1451 CAPGRAVE *Life St. Gilbert* (E.E.T.S.) 93 þat þe onyment of vertue whech was with-inne him schuld be stered & rolled.. þat aftyr þat rollyng it schuld haue þe mor odour. **1483–4** *Durh. Acc. Rolls* (Surtees) 414 In 1 hoggeshede vini..cum cariag..et rollyng. **1583** *Burgh Rec. Edin.* (1882) 265 Proclamatioun to be maid discharging..all catchpulling, rolling, playing, drinking and taverning. **1615** CROOKE *Body of Man* 629 The Muscles of the Tongue are assistant vnto it in..his Functions of Speaking, Tasting and Rowling of the Meate. **1645** TOMBES *Anthropol.* 13 The rowling in sugar doth make the stomache swallow bitter pills. **1770** in J. Bulloch *Pynours* (1887) 76 To put a total stop to the rolling of all sorts of Casks. **1839** URE *Dict. Arts* 635 The body is..then dipped and rolled in the hot liquor. .. This is technically called rolling off, or roughing. **1862** ANSTED *Channel Isl.* II. xi. 286 The only reason why all are not rounded is that the work of rolling and wearing is still going on upon recently fallen material.

b. Short for LOG-ROLLING. *U.S.*

1819 [see *rolling bee*]. **1848** in H. Howe *Hist. Coll. Ohio* 358 Many times were we called from six to eight miles to assist at a rolling or raising, and cheerfully lent our assistance to the task. **1922** D. T. HERNDON *Centennial Hist. Arkansas* I. 209 The trees were felled, cut, or burned into lengths so that they could be handled, and then the neighbors were invited to the 'rolling'.

c. *slang.* Robbing. Cf. ROLL *v.*[2] 5 f.

1939 C. R. COOPER *Designs in Scarlet* i. 21 The 'rolling' or robbing of a man with whom they had been in company, on their alleged promise of sexual intercourse. **1948** *Sun* (Baltimore) 5 Jan. 9/5 Some of the more heavily doped victims of the fraulein 'rolling' racket have met the dawn clad in nothing more substantial than a pair of shorts. **1969** *Jeremy* I. III. 24/1 'Rolling' occurs most often in the lavatories of cinemas. **1973** *Times* 3 Apr. 14/7 Tony Bogle, a youth worker with Law's association, said: 'Mugging has been with us a long time. When the skinheads used to do it, they called it rolling.'

d. With *back*: see ROLL *v.*[2] 5 h.

1944 *Ann. Reg. 1943* 287 [An] organisation..strongly in favour of subsidies and the 'rolling back' of prices. **1979** *Daily Tel.* 2 Nov. 1 Stronger control of the economy and a rolling back of Socialist extravagance.

†**2. a.** A bandaging, enswathing, or binding up. **b.** A ligature or bandage. *Obs.*

c **1450** *M.E. Med. Bk.* (Heinrich) 233 3yf þe skyn be broke .., [use] oþer medycynes, and 3yf hyt nede, as on þe leg, rollyngges. **1541** R. COPLAND *Guydon's Quest. Chirurg.* Ljb, Howe many maners of lygatures or rollynges ben there? **1575** TURBERV. *Faulconrie* 264 This ligature and rolling of the member must be continued..xxx dayes. **1662** MERRETT tr. *Neri's Art of Glass* xxxviii, Rouling but once at a time, and letting it dry a little before the second rouling. **1676** WISEMAN *Surg. Treat.* (J.), By this rolling, parts are kept from joining together.

3. a. The operation of compressing, smoothing, or levelling a surface by means of a cylinder or roller; an instance of this.

1671 GREW *Anat. Pl.* (1684) 27 That which is sometimes also effected in Rowling of Corn. **1688** HOLME *Armoury* III. xv. (Roxb.) 24/2 Of the severall parts of a Book... Rowling, the printing the edges of the couer. **1765** A. DICKSON *Treat. Agric.* (ed. 2) 340 When land is laid down in grass for hay, rolling is of use in smoothing the surface. **1786** ABERCROMBIE *Gard. Assist.* 185 Give a good rolling after rain. **1801** *Farmer's Mag.* Apr. 129 After the..land has been effectually cleaned, by its harrowings, rollings, and pickings. **1837** *Penny Cycl.* VII. 503/1 Copper for the purpose of rolling leaves the smelting works in cakes. **1868** JOYNSON *Metals* 79 It is usually subjected to repeated hammerings and rollings at a low heat.

b. *rolling up* (Printing), preparing a lithographic plate for printing (see quots.).

1937 *Discovery* Oct. 300/1 Rolling up follows. The stone is kept damp, and the ink roller passed over it and the design charged with ink. **1967** E. CHAMBERS *Photolitho-Offset* xvii. 260 The transferred image requires strengthening before printing and the non-printing areas require fully desensitising to guarantee clean printing in the white areas. This operation in plate preparation is termed 'rolling up'. **1968** *Canad. Antiques Collector* June 6/2 The [lithographic] stone having been coated with 'etch' is left for 24 to 48 hours and then the original drawing is completely removed (washed out) and the crayons, inks, etc. replaced by the special printing inks required in the process. This stage is called 'rolling up' and is accomplished with a hand-made leather covered roller.

II. 4. The action (on the part of something) of turning over and over, revolving, etc., or of moving onwards in this way.

c **1440** *Promp. Parv.* 436/2 Rollynge, or turnynge a-bowte, *volucio*. **1548** ELYOT, *Petaurum*,..a kynde of game vsed in old tyme, wherin men by rollyng of wheles were cast vp alofte. **1613** PURCHAS *Pilgrimage* II. xiii. (1614) 182 Their rolling thorow the deepe and hidden vaults of the earth. **1662** HIBBERT *Body Divinity* I. 174 In an unconstant man there is..uncertain rollings of spirit. **1860** PUSEY *Min. Proph.* 386 The swift changes of man's condition in the rolling-on of time. **1879** THOMSON & TAIT *Nat. Phil.* I. I. §110 This motion is what we call rolling, or simple rolling, of the moveable body on the fixed.

b. Of the eyes: The action of moving or turning to and fro in the sockets.

? **1566** J. ALDAY tr. *Boaystuau's Theat. World* Q ivb, He had reproued..the mouing or rowling of their eyes. **1610** ATTERSOLL in *N. & Q.* 9th Ser. IV. 104 Many vse in their teaching,..hemming in the throat, rouling of the eyes [etc.]. **1647** N. BACON *Disc. Govt. Eng.* I. xli. (1739) 105 Not only the opening of the eye, but also the rowling of it about. **1728** YOUNG *Love of Fame* VI. 49 Mark well the rollings of her flaming eye. **1844** KINGLAKE *Eothen* xviii, The peculiar rolling of his eyes which I had remarked. **1848** DICKENS *Dombey* xxxi, The Native..who alarms the ladies..by the rolling of his eyes.

c. Wandering, roaming. *rare.*

1624 BP. MOUNTAGU *Gagg* To Rdr. 14 Let him come..to the poynts controverted, without rowling, rambling, raving.

d. *Surfing.* With *over*. (See quots.)

1962 T. MASTERS *Surfing Made Easy* 65 *Rolling over*, rolling beneath the board to get past larger broken waves. **1965** J. POLLARD *Surfrider* ii. 20 For the big ones start 'rolling over'. This is done by dropping underneath your board and hanging on by the 'rails', the sides, when a wave has broken and the white water is coming towards you.

5. a. A curve or spiral; a turning or folding.

1576 FLEMING *Panopl. Epist.* A iv, Flames in rowlings rounde, to sweepe the starres, the mouth dooth cast. **1611** COTGR., *Roulement*, a rowling, turning, foulding vp or inwards. **1660** H. BLOOME *Archit.* E j, *Voluta* hath a Circle, or rowling about of one part. **1883** HUXLEY *Pract. Biol.* 96 The movements which occur in contraction; the coiling up of the stalk; the rolling in of the disc.

b. = MAKING *vbl. sb.*[1] 8 b. Also, a hand-rolled cigarette. *N. Amer. colloq.*

1913 *Collier's* 1 Feb. 28 Forty 'rollings' in each 5 cent muslin sack [of tobacco]. **1940** *Amer. Speech* XV. 213/1 The day before payday, the camp's 'smoking' has become scarce and 'rollings' or 'makings' are at a premium. **1956** H. S. M. KEMP *Northern Trader* 89 The tobacco was medium cut, suitable for pipe or the 'rollings'. **1965** *Sun* (Vancouver) 31 Dec. 27/1 (*heading*) 'Rollings' are safer... Dr. E. R. Threthewie..said..that home-made cigarettes burn at a lower temperature..[which] reduces the amount of cancer-producing substances produced. **1973** B. BROADFOOT *Ten Lost Years* xix. 216 Enough money for rollings. You know, roll your own tobacco.

6. a. An oscillation or swinging from side to side in the nature of a partial revolution about the centre of gravity; *spec.* of ships (cf. ROLL *v.*[2] 22).

1635 A. STAFFORD *Fem. Glory* (1869) 18 The rowling of the Cradle, put her in mind that she was newly enter'd into the tempest of this life. *a* **1661** HOLYDAY *Juvenal* (1673) 232 This is called (as a long continuance at sea..taught me) the rowling of the ship. **1769** FALCONER *Dict. Marine* (1780), *Rolling*, the motion by which a ship rocks from side to side like a cradle. **1836** MISS MAITLAND *Lett. Madras* (1843) 24 Nothing but rolling by day and by night: but we are all looking forward to a week at the Cape to set us right again. **1847** W. C. L. MARTIN *Ox* 37/2 A grinding of the teeth, and a rolling about as if from extreme agony or colic. **1887** J. BALL *Nat. S. Amer.* 3 Forced to hold on with both hands during the rolling of the ship.

b. A turning movement of an aeroplane or motor vehicle about the direction of motion.

1911 G. H. BRYAN *Stability in Aviation* ix. 166 Devices such as fins or bent-up planes..may cause serious rolling when the aeroplane is suddenly struck by a side wind. **1922** *Encycl. Brit.* XXX. 18/1 French pilots again pointed the way in the art of 'rolling', a manoeuvre in which the aeroplane is rolled about its longitudinal axis. **1930** *Morning Post* 21 July 4/4 Sideway or rolling occurs at right angles to the propeller shaft. **1974** H. ASHLEY *Engin. Anal. Flight Vehicles* i. 4 Rolling is accomplished by ailerons and/or spoilers, placed near each wing tip and deflected in an antisymmetrical manner.

7. Of waves, etc.: The action of moving in a swelling or heaving manner.

1632 J. HAYWARD tr. *Biondi's Eromena* 158 The motion and rowling of the sea. **1651** JER. TAYLOR *Serm. for Year* (1678) 306 The wave of a Tide, which retired..and yet came farther upon the strand at the next rolling. **1832** MARRYAT *N. Forster* xxiv, The rolling of the surf. **1863** *Sat. Rev.* 6 June 729 When all this is brought into connexion with the rolling back of the stream, and the miraculous passage of the Israelites.

8. The sound produced by the motion of a wheeled vehicle, by the rapid, continuous beating of a drum, or by thunder.

1611 B. RICH *Honestie Age* (Percy Soc.) 18 Your eares againe shall be so incumbred with the rumbling and rowling of coaches. **1811** BUSBY *Dict. Mus.* (ed. 3) s.v., *Rolling*, that rapid pulsation of the drum by which the sounds..beat upon the ear with a rumbling continuity of effect. **1881** BESANT & RICE *Chapl. Fleet* I. vi, The noise..began in the early morning with the rolling of the carts.

b. Of canaries: (see ROLL *v.*[2] 18 e).

c **1890** tr. *Russ's Canary Birds* 99 They either depart from the 'rolling', or they do not achieve the desired duration and roundness of the melodies.

III. 9. *attrib.* and *Comb.*, as ***rolling action***, ***axis***, ***contact***, ***drag***, ***friction***, ***instability***, ***motion***, ***movement***, ***oscillation***, ***resistance***, ***stability***; (sense 1 b) ***rolling bee***; **rolling chamber**, a compartment for water-ballast extending across the beam of a ship; **rolling-house**, *U.S.* an inspection warehouse to which tobacco was conveyed by rolling; **rolling moment**, the moment acting on an aircraft about its longitudinal axis; **rolling paper** *U.S.* (usu. *pl.*), paper for making hand-rolled (esp. marijuana) cigarettes; †**rolling pear** (see quot. 1672); **rolling-road**, *U.S.* (see quot.); **rolling-room**, a room at the Mint in which the metal is rolled into strips; **rolling-table**, a table on which fleeces are rolled up.

1915 A. FAGE *Aeroplane* v. 68 We ignored the *rolling action due to the difference between the relative wind speeds of the wings. **1953** *New Biol.* XIV. 66 Stability can be related to any of the three axes—the *rolling axis (parallel to its direction of flight), the yawing axis.., and the pitching axis. **1819** W. KEYES *Jrnl.* 21 May in *Wisconsin Mag. Hist.* (1920) III. 463 Attended a *rolling bee this morning. **1900** *Geogr. Jrnl.* Jan. 34 The ship has a *rolling chamber to keep her steady. **1846** HOLTZAPFFEL *Turning* II. 581 Trusting to the surface or *rolling contact, to produce the rotation and traverse of the cylinder. **1976** *National Observer* (U.S.) 25 Sept. 17/1 'A lot of the problem is overcoming *rolling drag,' he says, a problem compounded because the aerobike's pedals are connected only to its propeller and not to its wheels. **1859** *Rolling friction [see *rolling resistance*].

1884 *Cent. Mag.* Jan. 446/2 The commonest mode of moving tobacco was yet more naked; the cask was strongly hooped, and then rolled..to the inspector's warehouse, known for this reason as a '*rolling-house'. **1921** *Rep. & Mem. Aeronaut. Res. Comm.* No. 745. 6 If, whenever one wing goes down due to a 'bump',..the wing tends to go down further, the motion shows '*rolling instability'. **1950** *Gloss. Aeronaut. Terms (B.S.I.)* I. 22 *Rolling instability*, the instability whereby the motion of the aircraft takes up an increasing oscillation after a rolling disturbance and does not settle down to a horizontal position. **1914** *Techn. Rep. Advisory Comm. Aeronaut. 1912–13* 117 Measurements of ..*rolling moment, for varying angles of yaw. **1939** L. BAIRSTOW *Appl. Aerodynamics* (ed. 2) iv. 188 Since L denotes rolling moment and *p* the angular velocity of roll. **1974** H. ASHLEY *Engin. Anal. Flight Vehicles* i. 4 At high speeds, rolling moment may be exerted simply by differential rotation of two all-movable horizontal stabilizers. **1923** *Rep. & Mem. Aeronaut. Res. Comm.* No. 846. 1 It was found necessary..to augment considerably the damping of the *rolling motion. **1912** *Techn. Rep. Advisory Comm. Aeronaut. 1911–12* 103 The one claim that is made for the 'lower centre of gravity aeroplane' is that, although it rolls, the *rolling movement is a steady one. **1958** D. PIGGOTT *Gliding* iii. 16 The ailerons control rolling or banking movements about the longitudinal axis. **1915** A. FAGE *Aeroplane* vi. 86 If the moments of inertia of the machine about the longitudinal and normal axes be small, the yawing and *rolling oscillations will be rapid. **1971** *Aeronaut. Jrnl.* LXXV. 297/2 The ability of an aircraft to maintain the desired direction of motion depends mostly on the roll response to aileron, the steadiness of the motion being influenced by the dutch-roll mode, which is a combined yawing and rolling oscillation. **1977** *Rolling Stone* 5 May 81/4 (Advt.), Includes *rolling papers and free legal-highs catalogue. **1979** *Christian Science Monitor* (Eastern ed.) 21 Nov. B2/2 The sale of rolling papers at supermarkets and the open sale of drug paraphernalia at head shops tend to signal children that the drug culture must be okay. **1664** EVELYN *Kal. Hort.* September 74 Emperours-pear, Cluster-pear,..*Rowling-pear. **1672** GREW *Anat. Plants* (1682) 15 Some Apples mend their Taste by Scoaping and Pears by Rowling, especially that called the Rowling Pear. **1859** RANKINE *Steam Eng.* 17 By the rolling of two surfaces over each other without sliding, a resistance is caused, which is called sometimes 'rolling friction', but more correctly *rolling resistance. **1696–1715** *Laws of Maryland* iv. (1723) 10 His Excellency..hath caused Four *Rolling Roads to be made and cleared for the Rolling or Transporting Tobacco or Goods by Land. **1884** *Cent. Mag.* Jan. 447/1 The road, which went round about to avoid hills, was called a 'rolling-road'. **1815** *Ann. Reg., Chron.* 84 The silver or *rolling room. **1921** *Rep. & Mem. Aeronaut. Res. Comm.* No. 745. 6 In still air, the test for rolling instability would be given by a jerk on the ailerons sufficient to depress one wing. If, after subsequent return of the control column the aeroplane tends to resume an even keel, there is '*rolling stability'. **1938** *Aircraft Engin.* Jan. 15/1 The effect on rolling stability of lowering the flaps..is quite small. **1900** H. LAWSON *Over Sliprails* 32, I was slipping past to the *rolling-tables, carrying three fleeces to save a journey.

†**b.** ***rolling hose*** or ***stockings***, stockings of which the tops could be rolled up or down on the leg. *Obs.* (Cf. ROLL-UP *sb.* 1.)

1683 *Lond. Gaz.* No. 1834/4 A pair of new rowling Worsted Stockings. **1686** *Ibid.* No. 2155/4 A Parcel of Rouling Silk Hose..supposed to be stolen. **1704** *Ibid.* No. 4067/7 A dark-coloured Coat, and rolling Stockings.

c. *Naut.* in **rolling-chock, -cleat, -rope, tackle**, applied to devices used to strengthen the yards against the strain produced by the rolling of the vessel.

1762 FALCONER *Shipwreck* II. 248 They furl the sail, and pointed to the wind The yard, by rolling tackles then confin'd. **1769** —— *Dict. Marine* (1780), *Rolling-tackle*, a pulley or purchase fastened to that part of a sail-yard which is to the windward of the mast, in order to confine the yard close down to..leeward when the sail is furled. **1840** R. H. DANA *Before Mast* xxv, We were hard at work..getting rolling-ropes on the yard,..and making other preparations for a storm. **1846** A. YOUNG *Naut. Dict.*, *Rolling-Chock*, or *Rolling-Cleat*, a piece of wood fastened to the middle of an upper yard, with a piece cut out of its centre so that it may half encircle the mast, to which it is secured by an iron parrel. *Ibid.*, *Rolling-Tackles*, tackles sometimes attached to a lower yard, to steady it in a heavy sea.

rolling ('rəʊlɪŋ), *ppl. a.* [f. ROLL *v.*[2]]

1. a. That turns over and over, esp. so as to move forward on a surface or down a slope.

c **1500** MORE *Fortune* in *Songs, Carols*, etc. (E.E.T.S.) 78 The rollyng dise in whom your lukk doth stonde. **1599** SHAKS. *Hen. V*, III. vi. 31 That Goddesse [*sc.* Fortune] blind, that stands vpon the rolling restlesse Stone. **1611** BIBLE *Ecclus.* xxxiii. 5 His thoughts are like a rolling axeltree. **1697** DRYDEN *Virg. Georg.* III. 66 Sisyphus that labours up the Hill The rowling Rock. **1742** GRAY *Eton* 29 What idle progeny succeed To chase the rolling circle's speed? **1847** EMERSON *Repr. Men, Goethe* Wks. (Bohn) I. 382 Nature will be reported... The rolling rock leaves its scratches on the mountain. **1882** MINCHIN *Unipl. Kinemat.* 71 The length of the arc..measured on the surface of the rolling body.

b. That moves or runs upon wheels.

1565 COOPER *Thesaurus* s.v. *Voluens*, *Plaustra voluentia*, rollynge wagons. **1648** HEXHAM II, *Een Rol-wagen*, a Roling wagon, to carry wares or commodities upon. **1853–** [see ROLLING STOCK]. **1891** *Daily News* 7 July 2/5, I have not thought it necessary to make rolling-load tests personally.

c. Of a person, his opinions: Changeable, shifting, variable, inconstant. Now *rare* or *Obs.*

1561 T. NORTON tr. *Calvin's Inst.* III. 179 Faith is not contented with a doutfull and rowling opinion. **1613** PURCHAS *Pilgrimage* II. xix. (1614) 219 Of which you have heard their rolling opinion before. **1652** N. CULVERWEL *Treat.* I. ix. (1661) 58 Had I met with this in a fluctuating Academick, in a rowling Sceptick. **1731** *Rape of Helen* Pref. p. vi, A man that has a rolling fancy, and can adapt his conceptions with pompous words and sounding epithets, is sure to carry the prize.

d. Of time or seasons: Steadily moving onwards, elapsing; also, moving round, recurring.

1695 PRIOR *Ode pres. to King* ii, Oft as the rolling Years return. **1700** ROWE *Amb. Step-Mother* I. i, Rolling Time, that gathers as it goes. *c* **1760** SMOLLETT *Ode to blue-ey'd Ann* 19 When rolling seasons cease to change. **1835** WORDSW. *On Death J. Hogg* 13 Nor has the rolling year twice measured..its steadfast course, Since [etc.]. **1850** TENNYSON *In Mem.* li, Ye watch..the rolling hours With larger other eyes than ours.

e. Progressive; increasing, accumulating. Also, renewable; subject to periodic review; responsive to changing conditions.

1719 W. WOOD *Surv. Trade* 41 The 17 or 18 millions lost ..by the French Trade..would by a continued rolling Encrease, have added more than sufficient to double the 56 Millions. **1887** *Times* 22 Apr. 7/6 He established rolling annuities which do credit to the ingenuity of the right honourable gentleman. **1959** *Daily Tel.* 8 July 10/3 Western policy, particularly as foreseen by Mr. Macmillan and Mr. Selwyn Lloyd, can be expressed as 'rolling negotiations'. **1960** *Guardian* 27 Oct. 1/5 His successful efforts to secure a three-year rolling programme for major [road] improvements. **1962** *Listener* 10 May 796/2 Nor is rolling planning, by which long-term targets are modified each year in the light of changing circumstances, any answer. **1971** *Guardian* 31 Mar. 13/6 The new rolling three year contract which gives the Authority an opportunity to warn a company to do better. **1972** *Times* 14 Sept. 18/5 The Post Office..has a five-year rolling programme (meaning that it is regularly reviewed) to spend £3,000 m on overall improvements and developments. **1978** *Broadcast* 9 Jan. 17/2 We disagree with their suggestion that the present system of rolling contracts be replaced by fixed term contracts. **1981** *Listener* 26 Feb. 290/3 Radio London.. cannot compete with LBC as a news station offering a 'rolling' format—regular bulletins linked by expanded news items..and local information.

f. Staggered, rotating; esp. of strikes, power-cuts, etc., that take place in different places in succession. orig. *U.S.*

1961 WEBSTER s.v. Rolling *adj.*, The economy was going through a rolling adjustment in which first one industry and then another was affected. **1969** *Age* (Melbourne) 24 May 3/8 The secretary of the Trades Hall Council..condemned threats of further rolling strikes. **1974** *Ebony* Feb. 36/1 If this phase fails, we will have no choice except to turn to mandatory cutbacks, and then perhaps rolling blackouts. **1979** 'A. HAILEY' *Overload* IV. xi. 351 'If we do have a serious oil shortage, almost certainly there will be rolling blackouts. You know what those are?'.. 'I think so. It means electric power will be off in different places for hours at a time.'

2. a. Revolving, rotating; turning on, or as on, an axis; moving round a centre.

1591 SYLVESTER *Du Bartas* I. i. 387 Let them deny..End and beginning to th' Heav'ns rowling roundnes. **1596** SPENSER *F.Q.* V. v. 2 Who so list..search the courses of the rowling spheares. **1670** MILTON *Brut* 2 Goddess of Shades .., who at will Walk'st on the rowling Sphear. **1678** R. CUDWORTH *Intell. Syst.* 882 Vulgar Opinion..supposes the Fixed Stars..to be the Utmost Wall, or Arched Roof, and Rowling Circumference thereof. **1707** PRIOR *Simile* 6 Didst Thou never see..A Squirrel spend his little Rage In jumping round a rowling Cage? **1784** COWPER *Task* v. 814 The God Who..wheels his throne upon the rolling worlds. **1848** DICKENS *Dombey* xxix, Aldermen and knights to boot: at whose sage nod..the rolling world stands still.

b. Of the eyes: Moving to and fro or up and down in the sockets.

1576 FLEMING *Panopl. Epist.* 245 When I..cast my rolling eyes from corner to corner,.. I see a liuely..image. **1598** DRAYTON *Heroical Ep.* iii. 29 Whilst I behold thy Globe-like rowling Eye. **1725** RAMSAY *Gentle Sheph.* II. iv, Thy..rowing eye that, smiling, tells the truth. **1875** BUCKLAND *Log-bk.* 195 Great rolling eyes. [**1899** *Allbutt's Syst. Med.* VII. 862 The ocular muscles have been implicated, causing rolling movements of the globes.]

Comb. **1848** BUCKLEY *Iliad* 305 The Trojans first drove back the rolling-eyed Greeks.

c. Turning round, turned over, in a coil or fold.

13.. *E.E. Allit. P.* B. 790 Bolde burnez wer þay boþe with berdles chynnez, Royl rollande fax to raw sylk lyke. **1611** COTGR., *Volute*, the rolling shell of a Snayle. **1842** *Fraser's Mag.* Dec. 657/1 To a white satin vest, fancy sprig, rolling collar, 1*l.* 15*s.* **1876** *Encycl. Brit.* IV. 496/2 To this old manner of forming shutters must be added the rolling shutters of Clark..and others. **1883** *Cent. Mag.* Sept. 725 The rolling scrolls, borrowed from the Romans.

d. Of thoughts: Revolving. *rare*⁻¹.

1677 SEDLEY *Ant. & Cl.* Wks. 1722 I. 165 Her rowling Thoughts on some dire Mischief bent.

e. Swinging, swaying.

1755 JOHNSON, *A Wallow*, a kind of rolling walk. **1899** *Allbutt's Syst. Med.* VI. 580 Extreme vertigo, a rolling gait, and lateral nystagmus.

3. a. Heaving, surging, swelling, flowing strongly and steadily onwards.

1633 T. JAMES *Voy.* 29 There came a great rowling Sea. **1642** H. MORE *Song of Soul* II. cxxix. Wks. (Grosart) 31 Woods rent from hence, its rowling rage bestows In other places that were bare before. **1721** RAMSAY *Prospect of Plenty* 28 Herrings..like best to play..In rowan ocean, or the open bay. **1773** WESLEY *Jrnl.* 23 Mar., We had..a strong gale, and a rolling sea. **1848** DICKENS *Dombey* iv, Think of the pitch-dark nights, the roaring winds, and rolling seas. **1850** TENNYSON *In Mem.* cxxix, Thy voice is on the rolling air.

fig. **1695** LD. PRESTON *Boeth.* I. 31 Toss'd on the rowling Waves Of giddy Chance. **1781** COWPER *Conversat.* 557 Its head is guarded as its base is sure; Fix'd in the rolling flood of endless years.

†**b.** Of sands: Moving, shifting. *Obs. rare.*

1632 LITHGOW *Trav.* VI. 293 A fiery faced plaine, scorch'd with burning heate, and deepe rolling Sand. **1665** SIR T. HERBERT *Trav.* (1677) 32 Afrique, where the greatest part is rowling sands, which permit no foundation of Towns nor long stations.

c. Ascending or moving in curls or rolls.

1664 POWER *Exp. Philos.* I. 21 A tremulous Motion and Agitation of rowling fumes. **1667** MILTON *P.L.* I. 671 A Hill ..whose griesly top Belch'd fire and rowling smoak. **1728** POPE *Dunc.* I. 248 He..lights the structure..: The rolling smoke involves the sacrifice. **1770** GOLDSM. *Des. Vill.* 191 Round its breast the rolling clouds are spread. **1906** *Temple Bar* Jan. 18 The old man looked..through the window at the rolling mist.

4. a. Producing a continuous swelling sound; reverberating, resounding. Also *fig.*

1652 J. WRIGHT tr. *Camus' Nat. Paradox* II. 37 Seeing.. the Rowling Thunder grumble, and the stormy clowds burst under his feet. **1688** HOLME *Armoury* III. xix. (Roxb.) 154/2 The manner of which beatings [of a drum] is performed by..down right and rowling blows. **1781** COWPER *Expost.* 499 Thy Druids.., while the victim..bled to death, Upon the rolling chords rung out his dying breath. **1842** TENNYSON *Sir Galahad* vii, A rolling organ-harmony Swells up, and shakes and falls. **1847** DE QUINCEY *Span. Mil. Nun* 11, Then came a rolling fire of thanks to St. Sebastian.

†**b.** Fluent, voluble. *Obs.*

1579 G. HARVEY *Letter-Bk.* (Camden) 71 The rowlinge tongue..of..ouer fine Cambridge barber. **1586** J. HOOKER *Hist. Irel.* in *Holinshed* II. 94/2 He was..in countenance amiable,.. a rolling tongue and a rich utterance.

c. Continuously sounded or trilled.

1863 A. M. BELL *Princ. Speech* 191 There is a difficulty.. to unaccustomed organs, in producing a rolling or vibrated R. **1872** COUES *N. Amer. Birds* 151 Its rolling notes recall those of the Carolina wren, but are stronger.

5. Of prairie-land, etc.: Having a succession of gentle undulations; wavy, undulating. Also *transf.* of mountainous scenery. Orig. *U.S.*

1819 SCHOOLCRAFT *Lead Mines* 26 The lands lie rolling, like a body of water in gentle agitation. **1835** W. IRVING *Tour Prairies* xvi, The land was high and undulating, or 'rolling', as it is termed in the West. **1890** 'R. BOLDREWOOD' *Col. Reformer* (1891) 154 A rolling, rugged down, flecked with patches of..heath. **1903** G. B. SHAW *Man & Superman* III. 71 Rolling slopes of brown with olive trees instead of apple trees in the cultivated patches. **1914** CHESTERTON *Flying Inn* xxi. 252 Before the Roman came to Rye or out to Severn strode, The rolling English drunkard made the rolling English road. **1949** *Boston Sunday Globe* 1 May (Fiction Mag.) 3/2 This was rolling prairie with mottes of timber and brush thickets. **1977** *Time* 14 Mar. 48/2 (Advt.), The majestic mountain views of Trinchera Peak and Mount Blanca..stand as silent sentinels protecting the rolling foothills.

6. In special collocations: **a.** Denoting that the thing in question rolls or is rolled in some way, as ***rolling barrel, book, bridge, chair, coulter, croquet, cultivator, ground, hitch, lamp, library, pendulum, plant, purchase, refinery*** (slang), ***road, table***, †***trench*** (cf. ROLLED *ppl. a.* 1 c), ***weed, wheel*** (see quots.). **rolling boil** *Cookery*, a continuous rapid boil. **rolling lift bridge**, a type of bascule bridge (see quot. 1930).

1875 KNIGHT *Dict. Mech.* 238/1 *Barrel*, a cylindrical vessel moving on an axis, for..making gunpowder. In the latter case it is partially filled with bell-metal balls, and is called a *rolling-barrel. **1969** *Daily Tel.* (Colour Suppl.) 5 Sept. 31 Heat fermented barley mash..to a '*rolling boil' in a portable boiler above the stove. **1972** K. LO *Chinese Food* I. 20 This soup is then brought to a rolling boil. **1646** SIR T. BROWNE *Pseud. Ep.* 244 An expression proper unto the paginall books of our times, but not so agreeable unto volumes or *rolling bookes in use among the Jews. **1666** *Lond. Gaz.* No. 36/1 The preparations of Waggons, *Rowling bridges and other Instruments of Warr. **1771** *Encycl. Brit.* II. 16/1 These rolling-bridges consist of a number of cylindrical rollers which turn easily on pivots. **1884** KNIGHT *Dict. Mech.* Suppl. 763/2 *Rolling Bridge*, one whose roadway traverses longitudinally on piers..or on rails. **1700** DRYDEN *Ovid's Met.* xv. 339 By slow degrees he [*sc.* a child] gathers from the ground His legs, and to the *rolling chair is bound. **1819** LADY MORGAN *Autobiog.* (1859) 275 This it was which sent me (dressed up in my rolling chair) to thank him on the eve of his departure. **1886** W. J. TUCKER *E. Europe* 114 His Excellency,..entering his rolling-chair, was wheeled off to bed. **1875** KNIGHT *Dict. Mech.*, **Rolling-colter*, a sharp-edged wheel which is attached to the beam of a plow, and cuts downwardly through the grass and soil. **1877** *Encycl. Brit.* VI. 609/2 **Rolling croquet*, in which the balls are sent together in nearly the same line, is made by trailing the mallet after the balls as soon as the stroke or tap is made. **1975** *N.Z. Jrnl. Agric.* Sept. 18/1 (Advt.), Yet the fact remains that the Lilliston-Lehman *rolling cultivator continues along in a class by itself. **1883** W. H. PARKER *Recoll. Naval Officer* iii. 22 On the third day toward sunset we succeeded in anchoring on the '*rolling ground' just outside the harbour [of Rio de Janeiro], and the most dangerous anchorage we could have selected. **1959** *Internat. Hydrogr. Bull.* VIII. 241 Subsequently when anchored in other offshore rolling grounds on the New Zealand coasts, *Lachlan*'s ship's company comforted themselves with the memory that this was not so bad as the Zephyr. **1769** W. FALCONER *Universal Dict. Marine* s.v. hitch, A *rolling-hitch. **1841** DANA *Seaman's Man.* 40 A bend, sometimes called a rolling hitch, is made by two round-turns round a spar and two half-hitches round the standing part. **1883** *Man. Seamanship for Boys' Training Ships R. Navy* (Admiralty) (1886) 87 Q. What is a rolling-hitch used for..? A. Bending a small rope to a large one, putting a tail jigger on a backstay. **1976** *Oxf. Compan. Ships & Sea* 719/2 A rolling hitch properly tied will never slip. **1797** *Encycl. Brit.* (ed. 3) IX. 517/1 *Rolling Lamp:..though the whole machine be rolled along the ground,..the flame will always be uppermost. **1920** R.

FROST *Let.* 19 Sept. (1972) 94, I ran into the *rolling library at Manchester Vt and had a good talk with Miss Frank who seemed to have been getting experience as well as selling books. **1930** F. J. TAYLOR *Mod. Bridge Constr.* viii. 124 Of the two types of bascule bridge, it may be well to deal with the Rolling Lift or Scherzer type first. The motion of this type of bridge is similar to that of a rocking chair as it rolls back at the same time as the end rises... The majority of *rolling lift bridges at the present day are of the single-leaf class. **1933** *Discovery* Apr. 129/2 The scheme must.. provide for rail and road cross-river traffic by means of viaducts and rolling lift bridges. **1849** CRAIG s.v., **Rolling-pendulum*, a cylinder caused to oscillate in small spaces on a horizontal plane; it has been applied to no important practical purpose. **1864** WEBSTER, **Rolling-plant*, the locomotives and vehicles of a railway. **1869** BOUTELL *Arms & Armour* viii. 141 Of these cross-bows..there were three varieties, severally named—the hind's foot, the lever, and the *rolling purchase [*arbalète à tour*]. **1975** L. DILLS *CB Slanguage Dict.* 51 **Rolling refinery*, truck hauling gas or oil (SW). **1976** PERKOWSKI & STRAL *Joy of CB* 174 *Rolling refinery*, a truck hauling gasoline or oil. **1969** 'D. RUTHERFORD' *Gilt-Edged Cockpit* vii. 117 Its tests on the '*rolling road' completed..the driver had taken it up to Silverstone. **1970** *Daily Tel.* 11 Feb. 14/5 A full diagnostic centre, including such refinements as a 'rolling road', to give engine and brake tests under simulated high speeds, involves considerable investment. **1971** *Timber Trades Jrnl.* 14 Aug. 71 (Advt.), Stenner VB 42in *rolling table log bandsaw machine, 20ft tables, VG type feed gear, with all electrics and control gear. **1603** KNOLLES *Hist. Turks* (1621) 797 The Turks..with a *rowling trench drew neerer and neerer unto the castle. **1641** MILTON *Animadv.* Pref., As if he had the surety of some rouling trench, [he] creeps up by this meanes to his relinquish'd fortresse of divine authority. **1888** *Cent. Mag.* Jan. 453/2 A 'tumble-weed' or '*rolling-weed'—one of those globular perennials of the plains that.. goes rolling around over the prairies at the mercy of the blast. **1863** S. R. GRAVES *Yachting Cruise Baltic* 48 These rocks..are ground together by a heavy *rolling-wheel worked by simple machinery.

b. Denoting that the thing causes rolling or flattening, as ***rolling girth, machine, muscle, stroke***.

This sense approximates to the attributive use of the vbl. sb., and is not always distinguishable from it.

1612 S. STURTEVANT *Met.* (1854) 76 The brasse plate and the *rowling girth are necessarie..additions in the Engine of the Printing Presse. **1832** HT. MARTINEAU *Hill & Valley* (1843) 83 The roller and his catcher stand on each side of the *rolling-machine. **1885** C. G. W. LOCK *Workshop Rec.* Ser. IV. 229 For modern work [in bookbinding], the rolling machine is..better than the hammer. **1615** CROOKE *Body of Man* 629 There are three kinde of Muscles..which wee may call *Locutorij*, *Gustatorij* and *Cibi reuolutores*, the Speaking, the Tasting and the *Rowling Muscles. **1874** J. D. HEATH *Croquet Player* 35 The *Rolling or Following Stroke. *Ibid.*, It is a mistake to suppose that a very great amount of force is required for rolling strokes.

Hence **'rollingly** *adv.*

1565 COOPER *Thesaurus*, *Volutatim*, with tumblynge and tossynge; rollingely. *Ibid.*, *Volubiliter*, rollingely; roundely. [Hence in later Latin and Italian Dicts.] *a* **1839** GALT *Demon of Destiny* VIII. (1840) 52 Waves on waves Rose rollingly. *a* **1842** MAGINN *Shaks. Papers* (1859) 152 Which may be rollingly Englished, Ladies [etc.].

rolling (rəʊlɪŋ), *pr. pple. colloq.* [f. ROLL *v.*[2] 20.] Short for *rolling in money, wealth*, etc.

1905 H. A. VACHELL *Hill* ix. 186 He's going to marry a girl who is simply rolling. **1921** G. O'DONOVAN *Vocations* xiii. 193, I wish the dear nuns would share some of their poverty with us. They must be rolling. **1922** C. SIDGWICK *Victorian* xxi. 163 He isn't a bad old thing at all and he's simply rolling. **1936** R. LEHMANN *Weather in Streets* III. 352, I ought to get quite a decent screw—these film people are rolling. **1967** E. LEMARCHAND *Death of Old Girl* iii. 31 She was rolling, and insisted on making him a decent allowance. **1976** *Listener* 6 May 574/4 Cyril at the forge, who started out shoeing plough-oxen for shillings, but who is now rolling due to horse-trials at Badminton and polo at Cirencester.

'rolling-mill. [ROLLING *vbl. sb.*[2] or *ppl. a.*] A mill or powerful machine in or by which metal, etc., is rolled out or flattened.

1787 M. CUTLER in *Life*, etc. (1888) I. 286 The force.. which is applied to the rolling and slitting mills by means of vastly large and double water-wheels. **1799** *Hull Advertiser* 27 July 4/3 The immense hammers, the wheels, the rolling-mills and the water-works. **1863** P. BARRY *Dockyard Econ.* 228 There are two rolling-mills at present working at Millwall, one for angles and bar iron, and the other for plates and heavy bars. **1884** KNIGHT *Dict. Mech.* Suppl. 763/2 The rolling mill for sole-leather has a small brass roller, driven by steam-power and passing over a concave bed covered with brass.

'rolling-pin. [f. as prec.]

†**1.** A cylindrical piece of wood round which a banner may be rolled to prevent creasing. *Obs.*[−1]

1497 in W. M. Williams *Ann. Founders' Co.* (1867) 47 Paid for iij Baners... Item, for a cofyn & a rollyng pin for the same Baners, xx d.

2. A roller or cylinder of wood, glass, or other material, for rolling out dough or paste to the required thickness for pie-crusts, etc.

1589 RIDER *Biblioth. Schol.*, A roling pinne, *magis, artopta*. **1594** PLAT *Jewell-ho.* III. 14 A rolling pinne of the same scantling. **1602** —— *Delightes for Ladies* xiii, Roule your paste vppon a sliked paper with a smooth and polished rowling-pin. *a* **1665** SIR T. MAYERNE *Archimag. Anglo-Gall.* No. 19 (1658) 14 As soon as the said Viands shall have bin beaten with the pestell or rowling pin. **1706-7** FARQUHAR *Beaux' Strat.* IV. i, You must take out the Bone, and beat the Flesh soundly with a rowling-pin. **1747-96** MRS. GLASSE *Art of Cookery* xxi. 337 With a little rolling pin roll them out as thin as tiffany. **1844** DICKENS *Mart. Chuz.* xxxix, She tripped downstairs..for the pie-board,..then for the rolling-pin. **1881** *Macm. Mag.* XLIV. 389 Flattening out a large flour cake..between her hands. There was a rolling-pin in the house, but she liked the old-fashioned way.

3. *Bookbinding.* An implement used for rolling leather.

1880 ZAEHNSDORF *Bookbinding* 89 Russia and calf require no setting up of the grain, but russia must be well rolled out with the rolling pin.

'rolling-press. [f. as prec.]

1. A copperplate-printers' press in which the plate passes in a bed under a revolving cylinder.

1625 NORDEN *Guide Eng. Trav.* To Rdr., The generall [tables] can hardly be enlarged, to be imprinted, but by cutting in copper, and to be printed in a Roling Presse. **1662** EVELYN *Chalcogr.* (1769) 48 One of his servants to attend only M. Antonio's rolling-press and to work off his plates. **1703** *Phil. Trans.* XXIII. 1516 The evident marks of pressure by the Plate,..and other Circumstances concurring, I thought this must needs be wrought off at the Rolling-press. **1778** COLMAN *Prose Sev. Occas.* (1787) II. 171 The Rolling-Press, at a very considerable expence, has added its assistance. **1837** *Penny Cycl.* IX. 438/2 A somewhat complicated machine, called a rolling-press. **1875** KNIGHT *Dict. Mech.* 619/1 The first copper-plate presses were simple pressure. The rolling-press was invented in 1545.

attrib. **1728** CHAMBERS *Cycl.* s.v. *Printing*, Rolling-Press-Printing, is employ'd in taking off Prints or Impressions from Copper-Plates engraven, or etch'd. **1771** LUCKOMBE *Hist. Print.* 87 This is the first English book embellished with rolling-press cuts. **1811** *Self Instructor* 552 Notice must be given to the rolling-press printer.

†**b.** A machine for printing designs on calico, etc. *Obs.*[−1]

1675 *Lond. Gaz.* No. 1728/4 A new Invention..for the Printing Broad Callicoes and Scotch Cloth, with a double-necked Rowling-Press.

c. A form of copying press. *rare*[−1].

1787 M. CUTLER in *Life*, etc. (1888) I. 269 Another great curiosity was a rolling press, for taking the copies of letters or any other writing.

2. A press which flattens, smooths, etc., by means of cylinders or rollers; a rolling-machine.

1833 HOLLAND *Manuf. in Metal* II. 236 The old wooden rolling press..is an exceedingly simple contrivance. **1839** URE *Dict. Arts* 858 After being thus annealed, the metal is passed through the rolling press. **1845** *Penny Cycl.* Suppl. I. 219/2 The 'rolling-press' has greatly improved the mode of proceeding [in bookbinding].

'rolling stock. [f. ROLLING *ppl. a.*] The locomotives, wagons, carriages, or other vehicles, used upon a railway. Also *attrib.*

1853 S. HUGHES *Gasworks* 335 Expenses necessary..for keeping in perfect order both the rolling stock and the permanent way. **1861** *Times* 22 Aug., The severity of the winter, which damaged their rolling stocks and seriously injured their roadways. **1878** F. S. WILLIAMS *Midl. Railw.* 127 In regard to the rolling stock..a deterioration of the value of the locomotives had taken place to the amount of ..£100,000. **1890** W. J. GORDON *Foundry* 152 The North-Western rolling-stock works.

fig. **1858** R. S. SURTEES *Ask Mamma* lxvi. 299 There is a regular rolling stock of bad farmers in every country.

'rolling stone. Also rolling-stone. [f. ROLLING *ppl. a.* or *vbl. sb.*[2]]

1. In the prov. ***a rolling stone gathers no moss***, or variants of this: see MOSS *sb.*[1] 3 b.

The proverb, with the same or similar wording, is found in various languages from at least the 15th century.

1546 HEYWOOD *Prov.* (1867) 26 The rollyng stone neuer gatherth mosse. **1581** MULCASTER *Positions* xxxvii. (1887) 156 [They] reape as much learning, as the rowling stone doth gather mosse. **1618** BRETON *Courtier & Countryman* Wks. (Grosart) II. 8/2, I haue heard that roling stones gather no mosse. **1720** T. BOSTON *Fourfold State* (1797) 305 A rolling stone gathers no fog. **1853** TRENCH *Prov.* 45 The old Greek proverb, 'A rolling stone gathers no moss'. **1886** 'SARAH TYTLER' *Buried Diamonds* xxii, The sudden turning up of Jack as a roving brother, who, like a rolling stone, gathered no moss.

2. A rambler, wanderer; a good-for-nothing.

1611 COTGR., *Rodeur*,..a rolling stone, one that does nought but runne here and there. **1621** SANDERSON *Serm.* I. 212 Some men are ever restless... But thes rowling stones carry their curse with them; they seldom gather moss. **1887** H. SMART *Cleverly Won* i. 1 It was odd that he should have been so much of a rolling-stone. **1892** *Boston* (Mass.) *Jrnl.* 6 Dec. 6/5 He was a shiftless fellow,—a rolling stone.

attrib. **1887** T. A. TROLLOPE *What I remember* I. ii. 41 One of the results of such a rolling-stone life as mine has been.

3. A cylindrical stone used for crushing, flattening, etc., esp. in the form of a heavy roller.

1611 COTGR., *Rollon*, a rowler, a rowling stone. **1664** EVELYN *Sylva* (1679) 26 Stubbed oak is the fittest timber for the case of a cider mill, and suchlike engines, as best enduring the unquietness of a ponderous rolling stone. **1709** J. WARD *Introd. Math.* v. (1734) 402 A Cylinder (or Solid, like a Rolling-stone in a Garden). **1768-74** TUCKER *Lt. Nat.* (1834) I. 474 A rolling stone, a wheel-barrow,..are fitted for peculiar uses of mankind. **1839** DE LA BECHE *Rep. Geol. Cornw.*, etc. xv. 494 The granite annually raised in the district and employed for bridges, pavements, rolling-stones [etc.]. **1846** KEIGHTLEY *Notes Virg.* 353 It [the threshing-floor] was then made solid and level with rammers or a rolling-stone.

rollio ('rɒlɪəʊ). Alteration of ROULEAU 3.

1816 *Ackermann's Repository* Oct. 241/1 The trimming is a rich rollio of intermingled gauze and satin at the bottom of the dress. **1960** C. W. CUNNINGTON et al. *Dict. Eng. Costume* 183/1 *Rollio*.., a trimming of material rolled into a very narrow tubular shape.

rollmops ('rəʊlmɒps). [Ger.] A rolled fillet of herring, flavoured with sliced onions, spices, etc., and pickled in brine.

Sometimes erroneously treated as a plural.

1912 G. FRANKAU *One of Us* 30 *Rollmops* is here, and *Hackfleisch*, *Speck* and *Huhn*. **1926** E. HEMINGWAY *Torrents of Spring* xii. 107 We lunched on rollmops. **1951** *Good Housek. Home Encycl.* 637/1 Rollmops are usually packed in brine. **1964** *Listener* 21 May 850/1 For the soused herring *à la crème* you will need: 8 roll-mop herrings [etc.]. **1973** L. HEREN *Growing up Poor in London* iii. 62 She would also buy roll-mops and soft cheese. **1975** *Courier-Mail* (Brisbane) 27 Sept. 15/7 He used to love her rollmops—fish things on skewers.

'roll-neck, *a.* [ROLL *sb.*[1] 14.] Having a roll-collar. Hence as *sb.*, a garment, usu. a sweater, with a roll-collar. So **'roll-necked** *a.*

1942 N. BALCHIN *Darkness falls from Air* vii. 127 The inspector was wearing a roll-necked Jaeger pull-over. **1948** *Melody Maker* 28 Feb. 4/3 The young chap..wore a blue roll-neck sweater. **1955** 'D. CORY' *Phoenix Sings* v. 89 A big fellow in a rollneck pullover. **1968** *Daily Mirror* 20 Aug. 9/1 And I got a couple of bright flowery roll-neck tops which will also go with the slacks. **1968** *Guardian* 19 Sept. 8/3 John Cranko came on stage after the première of his latest ballet in a white silk roll-neck. **1970** T. LEWIS *Jack's Return Home* 148 He had on a white silk rollneck and a bright red cardigan. **1977** *Time Out* 17–23 June 80/1 (Advt.), Former male model—but more the jeans and rollneck type.

rollock ('rɒlək). *slang.* [Alteration of BALLOCK, BOLLOCK.] **a.** *pl.* As *int.* = BOLLOCK 3. **b.** Comb., ***rollock naked*** adj. = ***ballock-naked*** adj.

1961 'B. WELLS' *Day Earth caught Fire* ii. 31 'Rollocks!' said Maguire and his voice was deliberately gruff to hide his embarrassment. **1962** A. WESKER *Chips with Everything* I. i. 11 Even if you're stark rollock naked, you'll all spring to attention.

rollock, var. ROLLICK *v.*; dial. f. ROWLOCK.

rollocking, var. ROLLICKING *vbl. sb.* 2.

rolloff, roll-off ('rəʊlɒf, -ɔː-). [f. *to roll off.*]

1. *Ten-Pin Bowling.* A game to resolve a tie or determine the qualifier for a later round of competition.

1947 *Richmond* (Va.) *News-Leader* 2 May 22 (*heading*) Scher wins Major Men's Pin Championship after rolloff. **1975** *Cleveland* (Ohio) *Plain Dealer* 6 Apr. 7-c/3 When they bowl in the rolloffs each contestant will be presented a Brunswick bowling bag as the prize for gaining the finals. **1976** *Eastern Even. News* (Norwich) 27 Aug., He won the roll-off competition with an eight game total of 1474 for a tournament average of 185. **1979** *Arizona Daily Star* 22 July c2/4 He won in the two-frame roll-off.

2. The smooth fall of response with frequency of a piece of audio equipment or the like at an end of its range. Cf. ROLL *v.*[2] 11 and 25.

1950 *Audio Engin.* Aug. 28/2 It is due to irregularities in the groove walls, and if heard through a flat system, sounds smooth or satiny, corresponding to initially white (flat spectrum) noise with perhaps some roll-off of the highs. **1956** *IRE Trans. Audio* IV. 35/2 To obtain the smooth transition between the woofer and tweeter, the two units should be designed to complement each other, both as to level balance and for obtaining the required rolloff in the low-frequency unit at the crossover frequency. **1959** KUH & PEDERSON *Princ. Circuit Synthesis* xiii. 212 In practice, the roll-off of the magnitude of the transfer function of an *m*-derived delay line is primarily due to the dissipation of the inductances. **1975** G. J. KING *Audio Handbk.* ii. 39 From the practical point of view, it is commonly necessary to introduce infrabass roll-off at least to attenuate rumble and other infrasonic noises which are often present on the programme signal.

3. First throw at dice.

1966 O. NORTON *School of Liars* vi. 94 [We] flipped for roll-off. Wally's ace took the box.

roll-on ('rəʊlɒn), *sb.* and *a.* [f. *to roll on.*]

A. *sb.* **a.** Also *pl.* A type of elasticated corset designed to be stepped into and rolled up on to the body. **b.** A deodorant, etc., applied by means of a rolling stopper at the mouth of the container.

a. 1941 *Amer. Speech* XVI. 96 Do you like these *Roll-ons*? **1945** *Richmond* (Va.) *Times-Dispatch* 29 Mar. 3/2 A start could be made by changing the corsets—reminiscent of cumbersome bone and lacing styles—and attracting young women with the idea of..roll-ons. **1960** M. CECIL *Something in Common* 40 Holding the base of her roll-ons firmly, she wriggled inside them optimistically. **1963** *Times* 7 June 8/1 He was searched and underneath a woman's roll-on was found to have 28 bars of gold weighing 61lb. in a belt. **1972** *Times* 26 June 13/5, I..found myself in a bedroom in which was a very surprised lady struggling into her roll-on.

b. 1960 *Which?* Feb. 35/2 Body mist, the only roll-on to contain hexachlorophane, weakened nylon and viscose rayon.

B. *adj.* That rolls on; involving rolling on.

1950 B. PYM *Some Tame Gazelle* i. 9 She liked her clothes to fit tightly and always wore an elastic roll-on corset. **1960** *Which?* Feb. 35/1 Most of those who commented preferred the roll-on method to either spray or stick. **1962** *Fuller Brush Products* Feb. 2/2 'Roll-On' anti-perspirant and deodorant. **1975** N. FREELING *What are Bugles blowing For?* xx. 118 Her mind was furnished with moisture cream and roll-on deodorants. **1981** *Radio Times* 16–22 May 26/2 (Advt.), Two-way stretch roll-on girdle.

'roll-on, 'roll-off. [f. *to roll on, to roll off.*] Used *attrib.* with reference to a method of transportation of vehicles by ship in which they are simply driven on to the vessel at the beginning of the voyage and off it at the end. Cf. *lift-on*, *lift-off* s.v. LIFT *v.* 14.

1955 *Sun* (Baltimore) 3 Nov. 10/2 At Palm Beach, he said, two major facilities of immediate value and interest are available to roll-on, roll-off shippers. **1958** *Engineering* 21 Mar. 354/3 Improvements are being made, including..the introduction of special containers, palletisation and of roll-on/roll-off methods. **1963** *Times Rev. Industry* Dec. 31 Collect a combined load from a number of British factories. Utilize the rollon-rolloff ferry services and deliver the goods direct to the continental buyer without using any expensive foreign warehouse space. **1967** *Sunday Times* 1 Jan. 24/6 Car-carrying liners with roll-on, roll-off facilities. **1969** *Guardian* 23 July 16/8 A ferry terminal for roll-on, roll-off passenger traffic. **1970** *Times* 2 June (Container Suppl.) p. ii/2 By the mid-1970s it is estimated that about 160 ocean-going purpose-built cellular container ships and roll-on roll-off ships with container capacity will be operating on the world's trade routes. **1972** *Guardian* 14 Aug. 20/2 Plans for a roll-on, roll-off ferry to Shetland from Aberdeen. **1976** *Southern Even. Echo* (Southampton) 16 Nov. 1/5 Dockers have threatened to close Portsmouth Docks in a move to stop Brittany Ferries from opening a freight service. They argue that yet another roll-on roll-off service would affect the jobs of dockers at ports like Poole.

'roll-out. Also rollout. [f. *to roll out.*]

1. An act of moving or wheeling out; *spec.* the official rolling out of a new aeroplane or spacecraft. Also *attrib.*

1957 *Britannica Bk. of Year* 512/1 *Rollout*, the rolling of an aeroplane from the production line. **1967** *Economist* 16 Dec. 1158/2 The roll-out ceremony and the preparations now being made for Concorde's first flight not only mark the half-way stage in the aircraft's development, but also the point at which costs begin to rise really sharply. **1973** *Nature* 9 Feb. 360/2 The landing of Luna-21 and roll-out of Lunokhod-2 into the Mare Serenitatis area..is already being hailed by the Soviet press as a precursor of cooperation in space between the United States and the USSR. **1976** *Daily Tel.* 18 Sept. 15 A milestone in the development of the next era of space travel was reached yesterday with the roll-out of America's first shuttle spacecraft.

2. The part of a landing during which an aircraft travels along the runway losing speed.

1959 *IRE Trans. Aeronaut. & Navig. Electronics* VI. 59/1 The objective..was to develop a full instrument-landing system which included touchdown and rollout. *Ibid.* 69/2 The roll out was accomplished by using the large hand-brake lever to keep the directional gyro centered until a full stop was completed. **1964** *Sci. Amer.* Mar. 33/1 If landings in Category III are adopted, however, the approach, flare decrab, touchdown and possibly rollout will be performed automatically. **1970** *Graphic* 12 Nov. 3 Two weeks following the first multiple flame-out, that same plane was loaded with 128 passengers headed for Mexico City. It landed safely. But no sooner was it on the ground—still on rollout—than all four engines quit again!

3. *Amer. Football.* A play in which a quarterback moves away from his protective blockers before attempting to pass. Also *attrib.*

1959 *Washington Post* 8 Nov. c6/4 A series of quarter-back roll-outs. **1969** D. Tallman *Directory of Football Defences* iii. 58 The roll-out pass is identical to the sprint-out, except that the quarterback, when clearing from the center will execute a roll-out or reverse-pivot technique. **1969** *Eugene* (Oregon) *Register-Guard* 3 Dec. 2D/1 The Spartans would run what looked like a rollout and then fire the ball from one side of the field to the other. **1970** *Globe & Mail* (Toronto) 28 Sept. 18/7 A rollout quarterback, with outstanding running ability, Gabler has had difficulty connecting with receivers. **1977** *Chicago Tribune* 2 Oct. III. 4/3 We switched from our regular 5-2 defense into a 4-3 in the second half to try to keep their quarterback from getting around the corner on rollouts.

'roll-over. orig. *U.S.* Also rollover, roll over. [f. *to roll over.*]

1. An overturning, a turning upside down; a complete revolution.

1945 *Richmond* (Va.) *Times-Dispatch* 19 Mar. 2/4 (*heading*) Yank describes B-29 roll over in Osaka raid. **1950** *Dance Mag.* Dec. 35/2 Her 'dance' included back-bends, cartwheels, splits and 'four successive rollovers'. **1955** *Sun* (Baltimore) 19 July 17/6 Crash rollovers, head on collisions and T-bone crashes. **1962** *Amer. Speech* XXXVII. 272 All sorts of strapping and cushioning devices to insure survival of the driver in case of a high-speed collision or roll-over. *c* **1973** J. Cholerton *Adv. Acrobatic Tricks & Dances* (Assoc. Amer. Tap Dancing) 11 Two backward rollovers, two nip-ups (to left), to centre. **1973** *Sci. Amer.* Feb. 80/1 Although frontal collisions are the most frequent accidents, side collisions and roll-overs are by far the most dangerous. **1977** *Time* 24 Jan. 2/3 (Advt.), The ESV's have proved their life-saving value in head-on and rear-end collisions, side-swipes and roll-overs.

2. *Econ.* Extension or transfer of a debt or other financial relationship; *spec.* reinvestment of money realized on the maturing of stocks, bonds, etc.; an issue of stocks or bonds replacing one which matures.

1958 *Fortnightly Rev.* (Anderson & Strudwick, Richmond, Va.) 27 June 4 *Roll-over*, a stock or bond issue which takes the place of one that is maturing (and into which the money realized on the maturing issue may be put). **1958** *Washington Post* 6 Nov. A18/1 We have..a roll-over, something in the order of $23 billion worth of short-term notes, I think four times, certainly three. **1972** *Times* 27 June (Tokyo Suppl.) p. v/4 The Japanese phrase 'circular-buying' covers the roll-over of speculative funds from one sector to another. **1976** *National Observer* (U.S.) 22 May 9/5 (Advt.), If you've been buying notes, bills or certificates of deposit for yourself or your organization, you'll find it's a lot easier to buy Dreyfus Liquid Assets. There's no paperwork, no worrying about maturity dates, roll-overs, safe-keeping or delivery—and there's no sales charge.

3. *attrib.* and *Comb.*, as (sense 1) ***roll-over accident, bar, protection***; (sense 2) ***roll-over contract, contribution, credit, facility, provision, relief.***

1970 *Motoring Which?* July 107/2 Door release buttons stuck out a little—might allow doors to open in a roll-over accident. **1970** *Daily Tel.* 15 June 6/5 Roll-over bars have long been standard fittings on open racing cars. **1973** P. Einzig *Roll-Over Credits* xv. 102 At the time of writing there is a complete lack of standardisation in the terms of roll-over contracts. **1976** *National Observer* (U.S.) 3 July 9/1 In such a situation the transfer of funds is treated as a 'roll-over contribution'. **1973** P. Einzig *Roll-Over Credits* i. 3 One of the most important changes has been the evolution.. of the system of roll-over credits—medium term credits with variable interest rates which are adjusted at fixed intervals to changes in the current market rates for short-term credits. **1975** *Daily Tel.* (Colour Suppl.) 25 July 30/3 If a creditor will only lend his money at short-term, but a debtor cannot hope to pay his debts for a long time, he is offered what is called a 'rollover facility'—a debt which is nominally short-term, but is automatically relent when it falls due for payment. **1972** *Times* 28 Dec. 21/1 Meeting all the foreseeable regulations on crash and roll-over protection. **1974** *Daily Tel.* 27 Apr. 21/2 Some developers had been hoping that the 'roll over' provisions would have been extended to the new tax. **1973** *Scotsman* 12 Jan. 6/2 Changes in capital gains tax should give either tapering relief on gifts or, if this is rejected, roll-over relief provisions on gifts. **1976** *Incorporated Linguist* XV. 72/2 The 'roll-over relief' where the gain on the disposal of an asset is transferred into the asset which replaces it, so that although the [capital gains] tax is payable, it is so only on the disposal of the final asset (eg on retirement). **1977** D. W. Healey in *Times* 30 Mar. 4/8, I propose an improved rollover relief for what is often called 'domestication', that is the transfer of an overseas branch to a separate non-resident company.

rolloway, var. ROLOWAY.

Rolls (rəʊlz), colloq. abbrev. ROLLS-ROYCE. Also *attrib.* and *fig.*

1928 E. Wallace *Double* i. 9 Dick knew the gentleman very well by name; indeed, he had recognised his big yellow Rolls standing outside the hotel. **1932** Auden *Orators* III. 101 In Rolls or on bicycle they bolt for mama. *a* **1963** 'Beachcomber' *Best of Beachcomber* (1963) ix. 102 She has a Rolls body and a Balham mind. **1965** *New Statesman* 14 May 753/3 He is essentially a working..journalist who sees the paper 'off the stone' in the composing room every night before driving by Rolls to his Greenwich home. **1977** C. McCullough *Thorn Birds* x. 224 Do you think Bob might let me borrow the old Rolls, if not the new one?

Rolls-Royce (rəʊlz 'rɔɪs). [Name of the manufacturing company.] **1.** A Rolls-Royce motor car.

1908 *Trade Marks Jrnl.* 26 Feb. 300 *Rolls Royce*... Motor cars and chassis included in this class. Rolls Royce, Limited, Cooke Street, Hulme, Manchester; Motor car manufacturers. **1915** 'I. Hay' *First Hundred Thousand* xiii. 173 Not long ago he was..driving a Rolls-Royce for a Duke. **1932** D. H. Lawrence *Last Poems* 256 Do you hear my Rolls Royce purr, as it glides away? **1936** J. B. Priestley *Walk in City* i. 5 So he popped into a long black Rolls-Royce. **1958** [see BISH]. **1975** *Sunday Times* 16 Nov. 44/3 The electric oven..has a dark glass front like a pop star's Rolls-Royce.

2. *fig.* **a.** Any product considered to be of the highest quality.

1916 W. A. Robson *Aircraft in War & Peace* xi. 161 None of the different machines made for these specialised purposes..will compare with the best pleasure aeroplane, the Rolls-Royce of the air. **1923** A. Bennett *Things that have interested Me* II. 107 The Row was flanked by processions of nun-like nursemaids pushing single prams and double prams—the Rolls-Royces of the pram-world. **1957** A. MacNab *Bulls of Iberia* ii. 28 The famous Murubes of old. Principal herd of main-line Vistahermosa. The 'Rolls-Royce' of taurine breeds. **1974** *Daily Mail* 24 Aug. 12/6 A lustrous Isphahan—the finest are the Rolls-Royces of rugs—size 6ft. by 4ft. might take two women two years to complete, and the value would be £1,800. **1977** *New Yorker* 19 Sept. 92/2 There was a nine-foot Bechstein—which many people feel is the Rolls-Royce of pianos—but when she opened the lid she found a mouse inside, eating the felt.

b. *attrib.* passing into *adj.*

1951 H. Hastings *Seagulls over Sorrento* in *Plays of Year 1950* IV. i. 45 Wot the 'ell's a bloke like 'im with a Rolls Royce accent..want to get mixed up in this mob for? **1960** *Sunday Express* 6 Nov. 16/6 Stanley Baker's rugged style has put him up in the Rolls-Royce class of actors. **1961** Partridge *Dict. Slang* Suppl. 1251/2 A bit Rolls Royce in his ideas. **1974** *Daily Tel.* 7 June 16 Vintage port— the Rolls-Royce end of the trade—accounts for only about one per cent. of port production. **1977** *Times* 23 Dec. 14/1 Norman Royce..disclaimed any pretensions to a 'Rolls-Royce performance', as a speaker.

Hence (*nonce-wds.*) **Rolls-'Royced** *a.* travelled in a Rolls-Royce; **Rolls-'Royceless** *a.*, without a Rolls-Royce, devoid of Rolls-Royces; **Rolls-'Roycey** *a.*, suggestive of a Rolls Royce; exceedingly wealthy.

1918 G. Frankau *One of Them* iii. 29 And the shrill cycle-bell's first tintillations Resounded from the dawning to the dark In a Rolls-Royceless, Peter Pan-less Park. *Ibid.* xxi. 162 For scarce a score of Rolls-Royced miles away..Miss Parker sat. **1926** D. H. Lawrence *Let.* 7 July (1932) 664 He was very nice; and apparently rich, too rich: Rolls-Roycey.

rollster, erron. form of ROSTER *sb.*

roll stone. *U.S.* A stone rounded by friction or attrition on a beach or in the bed of a river.

1845 J. C. Frémont *Rep. Exploring Expedition* 124 A swift current, over a bed composed entirely of boulders or roll stones. **1872** *Rep. Vermont Board Agric.* I. 688 A fine specimen of gold from a rollstone he found, while digging a well.

'roll-top, *a.* and *sb.* [f. ROLL *v.*^{2}]

A. *adj.* **1.** ***roll-top desk***, a writing-desk having a roll-over top or cover.

1887 *Trial H. K. Goodwin* (Massachusetts Supreme Judicial Court) 15 That shows the position of the roll-top desk which was in the front office. **1890** in *Cent. Dict.* **1901** *Westm. Gaz.* 7 Feb. 8/2 Ousting an old-fashioned table in favour of a roll-top desk. **1923** R. Herrick *Homely Lilla* xi. 173 A young woman looked up from the roll-top desk where she was running over a typed list of names. **1933** H. Nicolson *Jrnl.* 27 Jan. (1980) I. 47 Two brown-wood roll-top desks are pushed against the wall. **1977** C. McCullough *Thorn Birds* vii. 130 The roll-top desk stood alongside one of the big windows.

2. Applied to other items having a roll-over top or a top with a rolled shape.

1977 *Wandsworth Borough News* 7 Oct. 22/1 (Advt.), Kitchen/breakfast room..with Ascot sink water heater, solid fuel boiler, built-in larder, glazed china cupboard and small roll-top bath. **1977** *Time* 19 Dec. 43/1 A trendy new kitchen..may..include a Fasar range,..chopping-block islands with separate vegetable sinks, a rolltop condiment 'garage', [etc.].

B. *sb.* **1.** A roll-top desk.

1895 in *Funk's Stand. Dict.* **1912** W. Owen *Let.* 23 Mar. (1967) 125, I have suffered in being informed that the 'Roll Top' is sold. **1932** E. Bowen *To North* xii. 115 It was a relief not having her sprawling to telephone over Emmeline's roll top. **1980** *Family Handyman* Sept. 28/1 He'd priced rolltops in a downtown department store and knew he'd cut the cost in half.

2. The flexible top of a roll-top desk.

1913 in Webster. **1978** M. Kenyon *Deep Pocket* viii. 91 Peckover sat at the desk, slid the roll-top up.

'roll-up, *sb.* and *adj.* [f. ROLL *v.*^{2}]

A. *sb.* **1.** †**a.** = *rolling-hose* (see ROLLING *vbl. sb.*^{2} 9 b).

1755 Mason *Let. to Gray* 27 June, The altitude of his square-toed shoe heels, the breadth of his milk-and-watered rollups. **1824** Miss L. M. Hawkins *Mem.* I. 51 The exactitude with which his stockings preserved their place in the obsolete form of roll-ups.

b. = ROLY-POLY *sb.* 5. Also applied to salad, cooked food, etc., that is rolled up to form (part of) a dish. *U.S.*

1856 F. E. Paget *Owlet of Owlst.* 172, I whipped out, and got a puff, and a lump of raspberry roll-up. **1860** Geo. Eliot *Mill on Fl.* I. vi, I know what the pudden's to be—apricot roll-up. **1949** *New Yorker* 19 Nov. 94/3 Lunch box salad roll-ups. Roll up individual servings of finely shredded vegetable salad or coleslaw in a cabbage or lettuce leaf, fasten with a toothpick, [etc.]. **1952** *Sun* (Baltimore) 17 Jan. (B ed.) 12/1 (*heading*) Apple-ham rollups. **1977** *Chicago Tribune* 2 Oct. XI. 3/1 Place 2 tablespoons of mixture on each slice of roast beef; roll up. Place green beans on bottom of buttered shallow 10-by-6-by-2-inch casserole. Top with roll-ups.

c. An article of luggage coiled or rolled up and secured by means of a strap.

1831 M. Edgeworth *Let.* 6 May (1971) 536 A dressing-case—leather-roll-up which he preferred to a box. **1890** S. J. Duncan *Soc. Departure* 71 One portmanteau and a 'roll-up'.

d. A hand-rolled cigarette. *slang* (orig. *Prisoners'*).

1950 P. Tempest *Lag's Lexicon* 181 A 'good' roll-up is one that has a reasonable amount of tobacco in it. **1958** F. Norman *Bang to Rights* 55 A real snout, not even a roll up. **1963** T. Parker *Unknown Citizen* i. 23 The cigarette..was tasteless after the strong roll-ups in prison. **1967** *Daily Tel.* 21 Feb. 15/7 They smoked what one girl described as a 'roll-up', a loosely-rolled cigarette containing hemp. **1977** *New Society* 6 Oct. 24/2 An old man with one leg coughed in an agonising manner as he inhaled a very thin and slightly sad looking roll-up.

2. *Austr.* An assembly, a general gathering or meeting. (Cf. ROLL *v.*^{2} 13 b.)

1861 *Times* 9 Sept., No sooner was this fact known on the diggings than there was a 'roll-up' to demand their instant release. **1890** 'R. Boldrewood' *Miner's Right* xxxv, Making as much noise as if you'd hired the bellman for a roll-up.

B. *adj.* That can be rolled up; suitable for rolling up; made by rolling up.

1908 *Sears, Roebuck Catal.* 97/1 Two roll-up straps. **1923** *Daily Mail* 12 Feb. 2 (Advt.), Roll-up felts at half price. **1939–40** [see FOLD *v.*^{1} 1 e]. **1948** *Sunday Pictorial* 29 Aug. 6/4 A prisoner will do anything for tobacco. He will sell his dinner for two thin 'roll-up' cigarettes which have less tobacco in them than there is in a respectable cigarette-end. **1964** *McCall's Sewing* 168/1 The true roll-up sleeve..must be made of fabric with no right and wrong side. **1966** J. Gardner *Amber Nine* x. 148 Back down the cat-walk to the main roll-up garage-type door. **1974** *Camping & Caravanning* Sept. 12/3 The awning has a nylon zip arched 'stable door' type doorway and a complete roll-up front.

roll-uppable (rəʊl'ʌpəb(ə)l), *a. nonce-wd.* [f. *to roll up*, ROLL *v.*^{2} 8 b + -ABLE.] Able to be rolled up, suitable for rolling up.

1961 T. Hughes *Meet my Folks!* 33 Or the roll-uppable rubber ladder.

†**'roll-wagon, -wain.** *Obs.* [f. ROLL *v.*^{2}] A low-wheeled vehicle for conveying goods.

1502 *Arnolde's Chron.* (1811) 197 For a grete packe for the rolle wayne... Item for a lytill packe, the rolle wayne. **1647** Hexham I, A Role-waggon, *een rol-wagen.* **1675** Wycherley *Country Wife* IV. iii, I cannot make china for you all, but I will have a rol-waggon for you too.

'rollway. *U.S.* Also roll-way. [f. ROLL *v.*^{2}]

1. A natural slope on the bank of a river, or an inclined shoot, for expediting the descent of logs, etc., to the surface of the water or ice.

1878 *Lumberman's Gaz.* Mar. 16 There has been so little ice.. that the logs.. have floated off as fast as they have been banked. This will avoid the usual delay of breaking rollways. **1895** *Outing* XXVI. 392/1 The banks.. were.. lined with roll-ways, piled high with thousands of logs.

2. *transf.* The pile or stack of logs on a river-bank awaiting transportation.

1888 *Scribner's Mag.* Dec. 655 The logs.. are piled in great roll-ways, either on the ice or on a high bank. **1893** *Ibid.* June 714/2 This hook is driven firmly into a log at the foot of the rollway, and as it is pulled out the whole face of the rollway topples forward into the stream.

rolly ('rəʊlɪ), *a.* [f. ROLL *v.*^{2}] Somewhat rolling; inclined to roll or cause rolling. Also *Comb.*, as ***rolly-eyed*** adj.

1885 LADY BRASSEY *The Trades* 86 Tuesday and Wednesday were squally and 'rolly' days, and writing was a matter of extreme difficulty. **1887** —— *Last Voy.* 6 Jan., Left Bombay harbour at 2 A.M. and proceeded to sea under steam. Rather rolly. **1965** G. MCINNES *Road to Gundagai* xi. 197 Another.. known to us as 'The Rolly-Eyed Duke'.

Rolly ('rɒlɪ), *sb.* Representation of a popular pronunc. of ROLLEI.

1961 PARTRIDGE *Dict. Slang* Suppl. 1251/2 *Rolly*, a Rolliecord or Rollieflex [*sic*] camera. **1971** 'A. HALL' *Warsaw Document* xxi. 271 Let everyone know you're the press, take plenty of Rollies. **1973** K. BENTON *Craig & Jaguar* iii. 28 There was nothing of value.. only his Rolly, and that was broken.

†'**rolment.** *Obs.* Chiefly *Sc.* Also 5 **rollment**, 6 **rolmond**, 7 **rowmont**. [f. ROLL *v.*^{1} + -MENT.] = ENROLMENT 2.

1474 *Acta Audit.* (1839) 36 To bring the Rolment of þe court autentikly vnder a balȝeis sele. **1499** *Exch. Rolls Scot.* XI. 395 He sall put thaim in the rolment of his court. **1547–8** *Burgh Rec. Prestwick* (Maitland) 60 Produsyt ane rowmont of court of þe balȝe of Kyll. **1562–3** *Reg. Privy Council Scot.* I. 229 Ane pretendit decrete and rolment of Court. **1678** SIR G. MACKENZIE *Crim. Laws Scot.* II. viii. §vii, He was absolved by a Rolment of Court.

roloway. Also **rolloway.** [a. the specific name of *Simia roloway* (J. C. D. von Schreber *Säugthiere* (1774) I. 186), prob. f. the animal's native name in Ghana.] A large black and white guenon, *Cercopithecus diana roloway*, found in parts of tropical West Africa and distinguished from the Diana monkey by a longer, white beard. Also *attrib.*

1781 PENNANT *Hist. Quadrup.* I. 185 M[onkey] with a triangular black face, bordered all round with white hairs... Inhabits Guinea; is called there Roloway. **1792** KERR *Anim. Kingd.* 72 Palatine, or roloway... A gentle animal. **1894** R. LYDEKKER *Royal Nat. Hist.* I. iv. 102 The real name of the diana monkey in its native districts is said to be Roloway on the Gold Coast. **1910** W. P. WESTELL *Bk. Animal Kingdom: Mammals* ix. 163 The Roloway Monkey is often mistaken for the handsome Diana, to which it is very similar. **1966** W. C. O. HILL *Primates* VI. 531 This form has been much confused with the preceding; many authors.. having treated the Roloway as the Diana. **1966** R. & D. MORRIS *Men & Apes* viii. 234 Diana and rolloway monkeys have been considerably reduced in numbers.

rolp, obs. Sc. variant of ROUP.

rolster, erron. form of ROSTER *sb.*

rolwagen ('rəʊlwægən). Also **rollwagon, rollwaggon, row-waggon**, etc. [a. Du. *rolwagen*, lit. 'roll-wagon'.] A kind of Chinese cylindrical porcelain vase, or a Dutch imitation of this (see quot. 1960).

[**1675**: cf. ROLL-WAGON.] **1761** H. WALPOLE *Let.* 13 June (1928) II. 119 Don't trouble yourself about Delft—nay, I am now afraid you should get any, lest you should pack it up in an old china jar, and really find a meaning for that strange auctioneers word, a *rowwaggon*. **1786** *Catal. Portland Museum* 19 A 2-handled jar, and 2 row waggons. **1895** RIMBAULT & CLINCH *Soho & its Associations* ii. 35, 1 pair of blew china rowlwaggons. **1954** T. VOLKER *Porcelain & E. India Co.* v. 20 Two carrack flasks, one broken, 15, two small *rolwagens*. *Ibid.* [Note] *Rolwagen* is a name still in use in the porcelain trade in Holland, denoting a cylindrical vase, usually with a flat lip. **1957** *Apollo* June 251/1 'Rollwaggon' (or however you care to spell it) is still used of the cylindrical-bodied vases of the type frequently found in Transitional and K'ang Hsi blue-and-white. **1960** R. G. HAGGAR *Conc. Encycl. Continental Pott. & Porc.* 383/2 *Rolwagens*, corrupted in English to *row-waggons, roll-wagons*, the name given to cylindrical vases found in K'ang Hsi blue-and-white.

roly, abbrev. of ROLY-POLY *sb.* 5.

1892 MRS. H. WARD *David Grieve* II. 75 'He's like one of Aunt Hannah's suet rolies', she said.

roly-poly ('rəʊlɪ'pəʊlɪ), *sb.*, *a.*, and *adv.* Also **rolypoly.** Forms: 7 **rowle-powle**, 7–8 (9 *dial.*) **rowly-powly** (8 *Sc.* **-powl**), 8 (9 *dial.*) **rowley-powley**, 8 **rouly-pouly**, 9 *Sc.* **roulie-poulie**, 8–9 **rolly-pooly, -polly**, 9 **rol(l)ey-pol(l)ey (-boley), roly-poley**, 9 *dial.* **rolli-powley**, *Sc.* **rollie-poly**; 7– **roly-poly**, 9 **rolypoly.** [App. a fanciful formation on ROLL *v.*^{2} In sense 1 the second element may be based on POLL *sb.*^{1}]

†**1. a.** A worthless fellow; a rascal. *Obs.*

1601 B. JONSON *Poetaster* I. ii, How now, good man slaue? what, rowle powle [1692 rowly powly]? all riualls, rascall? **1602** DEKKER *Satirom.* Wks. 1873 I. 201 Ile have thee in league first with these two rowly powlies. **1609** ARMIN *Maids of More-Cl.* (1880) 107 Sause box, rowly powly, am I not your master?

†**b.** ? *adv.* Pell-mell, without distinction. *Obs.*$^{-1}$

1605 ROWLANDS *Hell's broke loose* (Hunterian Club) 17 Wee'le ayme our thoughts on high, at Honors marke: All rowly, powly; Tayler, Smyth, and Clarke.

†**c.** *adj.* ? Trifling, worthless. *Obs.*$^{-1}$

1679 *Sp. Miles Corbet* 5 That we have plotted and laboured long to turn this glorious Monarchy into a peddling roly poly, Independant Anarchy.

2. a. The name of various games, in most of which the rolling of a ball is the chief feature.

Johnson (1755), citing Arbuthnot, says 'A sort of game, in which, when a ball rolls into a certain place, it wins'. For later accounts of the various forms, see the *Eng. Dial. Dict.* s.v.

1713 ARBUTHNOT *John Bull* II. xv, If this be your Play.., let us begin some Diversion; what d'ye think of Rouly-pouly, or a Country Dance? **1730** in *Lett. C'tess Suffolk* (1824) I. 374 Lady Betty and herself play only at quadrille; but the Duchess of Marlborough takes to losing her money at roly-poly. **1745** *Act 18 Geo. II*, c. 34 §1 A certain pernicious Game called Roulet, or Roly-poly is daily practised. **1759** *Brit. Chron.* 17 Aug. 163 As some men were playing at Rolly poley at the Bird-cage alehouse. **1801** STRUTT *Sports & Past.* III. vii. (1810) 241 Half-bowl is practised to this day in Hertfordshire, where it is commonly called rolly-polly. **1807** E. S. BARRETT *Rising Sun* I. 76 To a luxurious supper succeeded wines,.. fire and flames, and rolly-polly on the floor. **1847** *Illustr. Lond. News* 6 Nov. 302/1 Restore *roulette* and rowley-powley to the Surrey hills, and the Knaves-mire flats. **1883** *Longman's Mag.* Apr. 655 [At Haddington Fair] there are.. travelling photographers, merry-go-rounds.., games of rolly-polly [etc.].

attrib. **1747** MRS. S. FIELDING *Lett. David Simple* I. 84, I did not go to the Roly-poly or Card-Tables.

b. *pl.* Billiard-balls. *nonce-use.*

1850 SMEDLEY *F. Fairleigh* vii, Going to have a touch at the rolley-polleys, I suppose.

3. A game in which children roll over and over down a bank or grassy slope.

1821 CLARE *Vill. Minstr.* I. 128, I.. often mark'd the place I play'd At 'roly poly' down the hill. **1894** HESLOP *Northumberld. Gloss.* 585.

4. A jocular name for a pea.

1784 *Cries of London* 32 Here's your large Rowley Powlies, no more than Six-pence a Peck. *Ibid.* 33 Rowley Powley, jolly Pease.

5. A kind of pudding, consisting of a sheet of pastry covered with jam or preserves, formed into a roll and boiled or steamed. *attrib.*

1848 THACKERAY *Bk. Snobs* xxxv, As for the roly-poly, it was too good. **1866** *Times* 2 Oct., He.. would have devoured a Charlotte Russe or a Nesselrode pudding as unthinkingly as a common rolly-pooly. **1894** ASTLEY *Fifty Yrs. Life* I. 247 Our *menu* not bad—carrot soup (potted), mutton pudding, .. and marmalade roly-poly.

attrib. **1841** THACKERAY *Gt. Hoggarty Diamond* (1849) xii. 168 You said I make the best rolly-polly puddings in the world. **1851** MAYHEW *Lond. Labour* I. 197 It is sometimes made in the rounded form of the plum-pudding; but more frequently in the 'roly-poly' style.

6. A roll or coil of hair (see quot.).

1866 *Daily Tel.* 16 Jan. 7/5 The German ladies are seen to be tremendous in back hair, front cascades, side bulbs, transverse roly-polies.

7. A kind of dance (see quots.).

1830–2 CARLETON *Traits* (1843) I. 341 The usual variety of Irish dances—the reel, jig, fling, three-part-reel, four-part-reel, rowly-powly. **1851** MAYHEW *Lond. Labour* (1861) III. 145 When I danced, it was merely a comic dance—what we call a 'roley poley'.

8. a. *Austr.* A salsolaceous plant having characteristics similar to those of the Rose of Jericho.

1859 D. BUNCE *Trav. w. Leichhardt in Austr.* 168 These weeds grow in the form of a large ball... No sooner were a few of these balls (or, as we were in the habit of calling them, 'rolly-poleys') taken up with the current of air [etc.]. **1865** TENISON-WOODS *Discov. & Expl. Austr.* II. 468 In the dry season it withers, and is easily broken off and rolled about by the winds, whence it is called roley-poley by the settlers. **1896** B. SPENCER *Thro' Larapinta Land* 13 On the loamy flats.. the most noticeable plant is *Salsola kali*, popularly known as the Rolly-polly.

b. ***roly-poly grass*** (see quots.).

1889 MAIDEN *Useful Native Pl.* 100 *Panicum macractinum*, .. 'Roly-poly Grass'. This species produces immense dry and spreading panicles. **1896** *Daily News* 11 June 3/1 The singular object labelled 'Roley-poley grass'.. is made up of tufts of a particular kind of grass, which, forming.. into a small ball, rolls away over the limitless prairie, gathering as it goes.

9. *adj.* Short and stout; podgy, dumpy, plump. Chiefly of children.

1820 MISS MITFORD in L'Estrange *Life* (1870) II. 85 The very reverse of the romping roly-poly thing, as round and blooming as a rose,.. which is my beau-ideal of a child of that age. **1853** MISS MULOCK *Agatha's Husb.* II. i. 13 Cottages, in the doors of which a few rolypoly, open-eyed children stood. **1865** —— *Christian's Mistake* 44 A little roly-poly woman, with a meek, round, fair-complexioned face. **1885** E. GARRETT *At Any Cost* vii, A beautiful beagle, watching.. over two roly-poly pups.

absol. **1836** *Backwoods of Canada* 216 One little girl, a fat brown roly-poly, of three years old, beat time on her father's knee.

Comb. **1874** COUES *Birds N.W.* 147 The plumage all.. puffy, making very pretty 'roly-poly' looking objects.

‖**Rom** (rɒm). Also *pl.* **Roma(s), Rom.** [Gipsy (Romany) *rom* man, husband; pl. *romá*.]

a. A (male) gipsy, a Romany.

1841 BORROW *Zincali* Introd. (1846) 20 He is to live in a tent, as is befitting a Rom and a wanderer. *Ibid.* III. 232 The .. speech of the Roma, or Zincali, as they style themselves. **1862** R. H. PATTERSON *Ess. Hist. & Art* 141 The Israelites have a peculiar religion, to which they are fanatically attached; the Romas (gypseys) have none. **1883** *Cent. Mag.* Apr. 909/1 She had known the chiefs of her people in the days.. when the Rom was a leader in the prize-ring, or noted as a highwayman. **1910** *Encycl. Brit.* XII 38/1 Only those who starting from the ancient Byzantine empire have travelled westwards.. call themselves by the name of Rom. **1973** *Guardian* 26 Mar. 7/1 The continued historical prejudice against the Rom—as the gipsies call themselves. **1976** *Sci. Amer.* Jan. 131/2 The Rom always try to cooperate.

b. *attrib.*

1973 *Guardian* 26 Mar. 7/2 The non-conforming way of life of the Rom people seems to attract increasing intolerance. **1976** *Sci. Amer.* Jan. 131/2 The Rom families that are studied here.. spent almost half of their time away from home, travelling.

rom., abbrev. of ROMAN *sb.*^{1} 4, used esp. as a proof-correctors' mark.

1824 J. JOHNSON *Typographia* II. 216 Rom. **1902** A. E. HOUSMAN *Let.* 30 Nov. (1971) 62 It ought to stand upright, not to slant (I have written 'rom.' in the margin). **1954** T. W. CHAUNDY et al. *Printing of Math.* ii. 53 Italic is restored to normal (i.e. roman) type by 'rom.' in the margin. **1973** S. BEALE *Collins's Authors' & Printers' Dict.* (ed. 11) 379/1 *Rom.*, roman type.

Rom., abbrev. of *Romans* ROMAN *sb.*^{1} 2 b.

romack, *v.*: see ROMMACK.

romage, obs. form of RUMMAGE *sb.* and *v.*

Romagnol, Romagnole (rəʊmə'njɒl, -'əʊl), *sb.* and *a.* Also in It. form **Romagnolo** (fem. **-ola**, pl. **-oli**). [ad. It. *Romagnolo*, f. *Romagna* (see below).] **A.** *sb.* A native or inhabitant of the Romagna, a district of northern Italy (now part of the region of Emilia-Romagna). **B.** *adj.* Of or pertaining to the Romagna or its inhabitants.

1821 BYRON *Don Juan* IV. 118 Juan's companion was a Romagnole. **1841** *Penny Cycl.* XX. 70/2 The Romagnoli are lively and quick, but they have the character of being hasty and violent. **1860** E. B. BROWNING *Napoleon III in Italy* in *Poems before Congress* 11 Piedmontese, Neapolitan, Lombard, Tuscan, Romagnole, Each man's body having a soul. **1901** M. CARMICHAEL *In Tuscany* iii. 115 A hot-headed Romagnol, Alfonso Cerquetti,.. had the hardihood to publish a pamphlet pointing out errors in the new Vocabolario of the Academy. **1926** *Contemp. Rev.* Mar. 297 General Pangalos might imitate the ancient Roman, rather than the modern Romagnole Dictator,.. and retire to his Eleusinian farm. **1934** E. POUND *Eleven New Cantos* xxxv. 25 The Romagnols wd. come here to Mantua. **1966** S. MANN *Collecting Playing Cards* i. 31 The Romagnole pack resembles the Piacentine in many ways. **1973** M. WEST *Salamander* i. 42 Ask that fellow over there, the street-cleaner, what he is. He will answer, 'I am a Sard, a Calabrese, a Neapolitan, a Romagnolo.' **1975** *Times Lit. Suppl.* 31 Oct. 1311/1 Even the title *Amarcord*, Romagnolo dialect for 'I remember', hints.. at the identity of the director and the subject of the memories.

So **Ro'magnan** [-AN] *a.*; **Roma'gnese** [-ESE] *sb.* and *a.*

1845 *Encycl. Metrop.* XII. 385/2 Demoralization has never, perhaps, sunk human nature lower than we find it among the Romagnese [*c* 1500]. **1931** M. YEO *St. Francis Xavier* vi. 62 Fogs from the Romagnan marshes enveloped the city. **1933** *Times Lit. Suppl.* 8 June 385/3 Already in Dante's 'Purgatorio' a Romagnese gentleman laments the days when 'ladies and knights,.. toils and ease, inspired love and courtesy'. **1972** *Sansoni-Harrap Stand. Italian & Eng. Dict.* I. II. 1120/2 Romagnese dialect.

Romaic (rəʊ'meɪɪk), *a.* and *sb.* [ad. Gr. Ῥωμαϊκός Roman (f. Ῥώμη *Rōma* ROME), used spec. of the Eastern empire.]

1. Forming, composed in, pertaining to, etc., the vernacular language of modern Greece.

1809 W. R. WRIGHT *Horæ Ionicæ* (1816) 61 The Romaic or modern Greek language. *Ibid.* 65 The Romaic dialect. **1811** BYRON (*title*), Translation of the Romaic Song. **1869** TOZER *Highl. Turkey* II. 184 Throughout these parts we found the Romaic language still spoken. **1872** C. W. KING *Gems & Rings* I. 311 The Greek legends.. perpetually exhibit the so-called Romaic pronunciation of the vowels.

b. *sb.* The vernacular language of modern Greece; a dialect of modern Greek.

1810 BYRON *Let. to H. Drury* 3 May, I speak the Romaic, or modern Greek. **1811** —— *Ch. Har.* II. lxxiii. *note*, The Albanians speak a Romaic as notoriously corrupt as the Scotch of Aberdeenshire. **1869** TOZER *Highl. Turkey* II. 43 The people of Nezero.. speak Romaic.

2. ***Romaic dance***, = ROMAIKA 2.

1830 H. G. KNIGHT *Eastern Sk.* (ed. 3) Pref. p. xxxi, The Romaic dance, said to have been the invention of Theseus.

Romaika (rəʊ'meɪkə). Also 7 **Romeica**, 9 **Romeka.** [ad. mod.Gr. ῥωμαϊκή: see prec.]

†**1.** = ROMAIC 1. *Obs.*$^{-1}$

1625 PURCHAS *Pilgrims* II. 1340 Many.. speake the vulgar Greeke, that is Romeica tongue.

2. A modern Greek dance.

1811 BYRON *Ch. Har.* II. xxxviii. *note*, The stupid Romaika, the dull round-about of the Greeks. **1841** HAMPSON *Med. Ævi Cal.* I. 259 The Romeka, a dance among the modern Greeks which imitates the tortuous passages of a labyrinth. **1869** TOZER *Highl. Turkey* II. 118, I never saw the Romaika worse danced.

romaine (rəʊˈmeɪn). [a. Fr. fem. of *romain* ROMAN.] **1.** *U.S.* = COS. Also *attrib.*

[**1885** W. MILLER tr. *Vilmorin-Andrieux's Veget. Garden* 309 The Paris market gardeners grow, under the name of *Romaine Plate*, a variety which appears to be intermediate between the Green and the Gray Paris Cos Lettuces.] **1907** H. W. WILEY *Foods & their Adulteration* VI. 284 Among the varieties which are most highly prized for this purpose [*sc.* salad] are the cabbage lettuce and the variety known as Romaine. *Ibid.*, The Romaine lettuce is more highly prized by most connoisseurs. **1942** E. PAUL *Narrow St.* vi. 50 Cabbages, cauliflowers,..potatoes, lettuce, romaine, *chicorée* and other salad leaves. **1966** T. PYNCHON *Crying of Lot 49* i. 11 The..garlicking of a bread, tearing up of romaine leaves. **1972** *New Yorker* 22 July 22/2 Fifteen romaine lettuces for four-fifty. **1978** *N.Y. Times* 30 Mar. C7/1 Cos or romaine..grows upright and forms tight sheaths of rich green leaves.

2. Any of various crêpe fabrics. ***romaine crêpe*** (see quot. 1968 and cf. quots. 1923 s.v. CRÊPE). Also *attrib.*

1922 *Glasgow Herald* 26 Apr. 10 The bride..wore a gown of white romaine. *Ibid.*, The two bridesmaids..wore white crepe romaine dresses. **1932** *Daily Tel.* 25 Apr. (Advt.), Coat of wool romaine. **1932** *Daily Express* 25 June 9/5 Lady Haslam..was in love-in-a-mist romaine armure. **1939** M. B. PICKEN *Lang. Fashion* 122/1 *Romaine*, sheer silk fabric in basket weave, made of fine yarns, having smooth surface and slightly more body than triple sheer. **1952** C. W. CUNNINGTON *Eng. Women's Clothing* 296 *Romaine*.., a lining fabric of French make, in warp satin weave. A sheer silk fabric in basket weave. Also 'a light woollen with dull surface and flat square weave'. **1957** M. B. PICKEN *Fashion Dict.* 277/1 *Romaine crepe*, heavy sheer crepe. **1968** J. IRONSIDE *Fashion Alphabet* 223 *Romaine crêpe*, a heavy, semi-sheer crêpe usually in a dull finish rayon, sometimes silk, made to resemble wool crêpe.

‖**romaji** (ˈroːmadʒi). Also **romazi**, and with capital initial. [Jap., f. *roma* Roman + *ji* letter(s).] A system of Romanized spelling for the Japanese language.

[**1888** B. H. CHAMBERLAIN *Handbk. Colloq. Japanese* i. 9 There is a party in favour of the adoption of the Roman alphabet. Its organ, the '*Rō maji Zasshi*', gives articles.. romanised according to a simple phonetic system.] **1903** R. LANGE *Text-bk. Colloq. Japanese* p. xviii, *Romaji* is designed to represent phonetically the standard pronunciation of the present day. **1935** *Amer. Speech* X. 274/2 Several movements for Romaji, Japanese written phonetically in Roman letters, are under way. [**1939** *Jrnl. Amer. Oriental Soc.* LIX. 99 The Japanese had long ago worked out a diaphonic spelling called *Nipponsiki* (Japanese-Style) *no Rômazi* and propagated it in competition with the reigning bastard English-Italian system named after Hepburn.] *Ibid.* 102 The present use of rômazi during an extended period is a hindrance rather than a help in the mastery of Japanese as it is normally written. **1950** D. JONES *Phoneme* 102 The name of the mountain which used to be written Fuji in the old Rōmaji system is now written Huzi. *Ibid.* 105 In the new Rōmazi orthography hi and si are distinguished. **1966** P. S. BUCK *People of Japan* (1968) x. 130 The Japanese have to master *romaji*, Japanese spelled in Roman letters.

‖**romal** (rəʊˈmɑːl). Also 7–9 **romall**, 8 **ro(e)maal**, 9 **roomal(l**, **-maul**, **romel**, **rumal**. [Urdū (Persian) *rūmāl*, f. *rū* face + *māl* wiping.]

1. A silk or cotton square or handkerchief, sometimes used as a head-dress; a thin silk or cotton fabric with a handkerchief pattern.

1683 *Lond. Gaz.* No. 1791/4, 12 Pieces of Romals or Sea Hankerchiefs. **1696** J. F. *Merch. Wareho. laid open* 35 Romals, of which there are usually three sorts,..there is Silk Romals, there is Romals Garrub and Cotton Romals. **1727** A. HAMILTON *New Acc. E. Ind.* II. xxxiii. 6 Radnugur, famous for manufacturing Cotton Cloth, and Silk Romaals, or Handkerchiefs. **1788** FALCONBRIDGE *Afr. Slave Trade* 54 Gold-dust, for which the Europeans give them goods, such as pieces of India chintz, basts, romals, guns. **1842** *Penny Cycl.* XXII. 12/2 The imports consisted in that year [1839] of 503,182 pieces of bandannoes, romals, and silk handkerchiefs.

2. The handkerchief or bandage used by Indian Thugs to strangle their victims.

1836 SLEEMAN *Ramaseeana* 145 It was Fatima who invented the use of the roomal to strangle the great demon Rukut-beej-dana. **1841** *P. Parley's Ann.* II. 374 He then seized the romel, and dexterously twisted it round the neck of his brother.

‖**Romalis** (rəʊˈmɑːlɪs). [Sp.] A Spanish gypsy dance (see quots.). Also, the music of this dance.

1841 BORROW *Zincali* I. vi. 317 Chicharona danced the Romalis (Gypsy dance) before her. **1846** [see OLE]. **1889** L. A. SMITH *Through Romany Songland* 54 The famous Romalis, the dance which Tiberius may have seen, and which no one but a gipsy dances in Spain. It is danced to the ancient Oriental music of hand-clapping, and to an old religious Eastern tune, low and melancholy, diatonic, not chromatic, and full of sudden pauses which are strange and startling. It is sung in unison, and has a chorus in which every one joins. **1967** 'LA MERI' *Spanish Dancing* (ed. 2) v. 74 This Romalis is part of a wedding ceremonial. The melody is Eastern; diatonic, low, melancholy and with sudden breathtaking pauses. Some..even identify it with the dance which Salome did before Herod.

Roman (ˈrəʊmən), *sb.*[1] Forms: α. 1 *pl.* **Romane**, **Romanan**. β. 3–4 **Romein**, 4–6 **Romayn(e**, 4–7 **Romain(e**. γ. 4–6 *pl.* **Romanys**, **-nis**, 6–7 **Romane**. δ. 5– **Roman**. [ad. L. *Rōmān-us*, f. *Rōma* ROME: cf. It., Sp., Pg. *Romano*. The β-forms, however, are a. OF. *Romain* (12–13th c.; so mod.F.), whence also MDu. *Romein*.]

I. 1. a. An inhabitant or native of ancient Rome; a Roman citizen or soldier; one belonging to the Roman state or empire.

α. *c* **893** K. ÆLFRED *Oros.* 2 Hu Romanum wearð an wundor oþiewed. *a* **900** *O.E. Martyrol.* 25 Dec., Romanan ʒesawon fyren cleowen ʒefeallan of heofonum. *Ibid.* 30 July, þa weop eall Romana duʒoð. *c* **1000** *Ags. Gosp.* John xi. 48 Romane cumað & nimað ure land.

β. **1297** R. GLOUC. *Chron.* (Rolls) 1201 Vor þe brutons woxe vaste, þe romeins bineþe were. *c* **1330** R. BRUNNE *Chron. Wace* (Rolls) 3295 Romayns dredden hem for to deye. *Ibid.* 3558 Neuere dirst Romayn stire in his stour. *c* **1380** WYCLIF *Sel. Wks.* I. 328 þis alien was kyng bi þe graunt of Romayns. *c* **1425** WYNTOUN *Cron.* IV. x. 1242 þe Romayn slew þe Frankis man. **1456** SIR G. HAYE *Law Arms* (S.T.S.) 46 A knycht askit justyng of a Romayn. **1526** TINDALE *Acts* xxv. 16 It is nott the maner off the Romayns [etc.]. **1581** SIDNEY *Apol. Poetrie* (Arb.) 22 Romaines, Saxons, Danes. **1611** SHAKS. *Cymb.* IV. iv. 47 The hazard.. fall on me by The hands of the Romaines.

γ. **13..** *Cursor M.* (Gött.) 21470 Fordon ʒe haue me wid ʒur dome, þat ʒe romanis broght fra rome. *c* **1425** WYNTOUN *Cron.* IV. ii. 150 He knyt hym to þe Tuskanys, And warrayide wiþe þaim þe Romanys. **1513** DOUGLAS *Æneis* VI. xv. 68 Bot thow, Romane, remember..To rewle the pepill. *a* **1591** H. SMITH *Arrow agst. Atheists* iv. I 2 b, Mahomet with his Arabians went, and first tooke part with the Romanes. **1611** BIBLE *Acts* xxii. 26 Take heede what thou doest, for this man is a Romane. **1658** SIR T. BROWNE *Hydriot.* ii. 15 Nor is it improbable that the Romanes early possessed this Countrey.

δ. *c* **1470** *Wyntoun's Cron.* IV. x. 1231 A Roman saw a Frankkis man. *Ibid.* xxiv. 2157 Silla þan a Roman wes. **1549** *Compl. Scot.* 98 Cheiffis and captans of the armye of the romans. **1565** COOPER *Thesaurus* s.v. *Gradus*, The Romans hadde waye..by Sicilie to atteine the empire of Afrike. **1601** SHAKS. *Jul. C.* III. ii. 78 Friends, Romans, Countrymen, lend me your ears. **1659** JER. TAYLOR *Ductor* Pref. (1676) p. xiii, Tribonianus the Lawyer, who out of the Laws of the old Romans collected some choice Rules. **1711** ADDISON *Spect.* No. 81 ¶7 When the Romans and Sabines were at War. **1788** GIBBON *Decl. & F.* liii. V. 511 In the lowest period of degeneracy and decay, the name of Romans adhered to the last fragments of the empire of Constantinople. **1811** BYRON *Ch. Har.* II. lxxiii. *note*, To give details of these nominal Romans and degenerate Greeks. **1871** RUSKIN *Fors* ii, The Romans did more, and said less, than any other nation that ever lived.

b. ***King***, or ***Emperor, of the Romans***, the sovereign head of the Holy Roman Empire.

c **1440** *Alph. Tales* 9 Philipp, þat was kyng of Romayns. **1492** *Acc. Ld. High Treas. Scot.* I. 200 To pass..to get the letteris subscriuit to the King of Rowmanis. *c* **1536** in *Songs & Carols*, etc. (E.E.T.S.) 152 This yer [sc. 1503] cam a gret embasset from þe Kyng of Romayns. *a* **1674** CLARENDON *Hist. Reb.* XIV. § 103 That meeting for the choosing a King of the Romans was of vast expense to every one of them. **1728** CHAMBERS *Cycl.* s.v., King of the Romans, in our Age, is a Prince elected, and design'd Successor to the German Empire. **1788** GIBBON *Decl. & F.* V. 151 They respectfully saluted the august Charlemagne with the acclamations of *basileus*, and emperor of the Romans. **1845** *Encycl. Metrop.* XII. 39/2 Again was a compromise effected, in which the King of the Romans appeared as a mediator. **1878** *Encycl. Brit.* VIII. 180/1 The German sovereign..called himself merely 'King of the Romans'..until he had received the sacred crown in the sacred city.

c. An inhabitant or native of later (mediæval or modern) Rome.

1547 BOORDE *Introd. Knowl.* xxii. (1870) 177 Naples is ioyned to Italy, wherfore they do vse the fashions..of Italyons and Romayns. **1788** GIBBON *Decl. & F.* lxix. VI. 552 The Romans were excluded from the election of their prince and bishop. **1808** STOWER *Printer's Gram.* 38 Aldus Manutius, by birth a Roman. **1835** LYTTON *Rienzi* V. vii, By birth a Frenchman, and full of the bitterest prejudices against the Romans. **1950** T. WILLIAMS *Roman Spring of Mrs. Stone* i. 34 Patience, said the Contessa. Rome was not built in a day! I am a Roman, said Paolo, but I am not Rome. **1967** C. SETON-WATSON *Italy from Liberalism to Fascism* ix. 334 He was an intelligent man, but vain and irresolute, with a Roman's liking for *combinazioni*.

†**d.** *Mil.* (See quots.) *Obs.*

1796 *Grose's Dict. Vulgar T.* (ed. 3), *Roman*, a soldier in the foot guards, who gives up his pay to his captain for leave to work; serving, like an ancient Roman, for glory, and the love of his country. **1802** JAMES *Milit. Dict.* s.v., A certain number of men were allowed to work in the metropolis, on condition they left their pay in their officer's hands. These men were called Romans.

2. a. *pl.* Those inhabitants of ancient Rome who had accepted the Christian faith.

a **1390** WYCLIF *Rom.* Prol., Here bygynneth the prologe of Jerome in to the epysteles of Poule to Romaynes. *a* **1420** *Ibid.*, Romayns ben thei, that of Jewis and of hethene men gaderid to gidere, bileueden in Crist. **1549** LATIMER *5th Serm. bef. Edw. VI* (Arb.) 139 The steppes thereof are set forthe in the tenth to the Romaynes. **1611** BIBLE *Rom.* i, Paul commendeth his calling to the Romanes. **1632** SANDERSON *Serm.* 21 The matter whereabout the eater and the not-eater differed in the case of the Romanes. *a* **1704** LOCKE *Par. & Notes Rom.* Synopsis, The Assurances he labours to give the Romans, that they are by Faith in Jesus Christ the People of God.

b. *ellipt.* St. Paul's Epistle to the Romans. Freq. abbreviated as *Rom.*

c **1420** *Wycliffite Bible* IV. 297 Here..bigyneth a prologe on the Romayns. **1660** JER. TAYLOR *Ductor* The Table s.v., Romans 14.14 that nothing is unclean of it self. *a* **1704** T. BROWN *Laconics* Wks. 1711 IV. 14 The Cavaliers..us'd to trump up the *12th* of the *Romans* upon the Parliament. **1824** CHALMERS in *Mem.* (1851) III. 38, I have now finished the eighth chapter of the Romans. **1902** DENNEY *Death of Christ* 180 Romans sixth has nothing to do with Romans third.

3. a. The language of the ancient Romans. *rare.*

1656 BULLOKAR *Eng. Expos.* s.v. *Romance*, That tongue, which was corrupted out of the Latine or Roman; which we now call French. **1862** LATHAM *Compar. Philol.* 650 The only Roman which is known to us, i.e. the Latin of the classics.

b. Romanic, Romance. *rare.*

1838 *Penny Cycl.* X. 432/2 The German monarch [in 847] took the oath in Roman, and the French in Teutonic.

c. The dialect of the modern Romans.

1598 [see NEAPOLITAN *sb.* d]. **1642** J. HOWELL *Instructions Forreine Trav.* xi. 138 There is in Italy the Toscan, the Roman, the Venetian, the Neapolitan,..and others..and all these have severall Dialects and Idiomes of Speech. **1973** *Daily Tel.* (Colour Suppl.) 22 Feb. 65/3 She..spoke such a flowery Roman that I wondered if this wasn't a sort of cultural or social dust thrown into one's eyes.

4. *Printing.* The style of letters distinguished by this name (see ROMAN *a.* 5); also *pl.* letters of a Roman fount.

1598 *Ord. Stationers' Co.* in *Hist. O.E. Lett. Foundries* (1887) 129 Those in pica Roman and Italic and in English. *a* **1625** FLETCHER *Nice Valour* IV. i, Did I not say this *wherrit*, and this *bob*, Should be both Pica Roman? **1676** MOXON *Print Lett.* 3, I..have elected them for a Patern in Romans and Italicks. **1683** —— *Mech. Exerc.*, *Printing* xiii. ¶1 Each of these several Sizes in the Roman,..for the Punches of Romans and Italicks..are not to be Forged to the same shape. **1706** PHILLIPS (ed. Kersey) s.v., *English Roman*, a sort of large Printing-letter. **1771** LUCKOMBE *Hist. Print.* 227 Roman is at present the most prevailing Letter used in printing. **1834–6** BARLOW in *Encycl. Metrop.* (1845) VIII. 771/2 No intermixture of Roman and Italic. **1848** HARE *Guesses* Ser. II. (1867) 393 The notion that one is to gain strength by substituting italics for romans.

attrib. **1888** JACOBI *Printers' Vocab.*, *Roman cases*, the cases for these founts as distinguished from italic cases.

5. a. A Roman nose. Cf. ROMAN *a.*[1] 4 c.

1838 DICKENS *Nich. Nick.* v, Snubs and romans are plentiful enough.

b. A Roman hyacinth.

1925 *Glasgow Herald* 26 Aug. 8/7 Early Romans are in, but at a very high price. **1934** 'E. M. DELAFIELD' *Provincial Lady in Amer.* 126 Early Romans should certainly be well above ground now.

II. 6. A member or adherent of the Roman Catholic Church; a Roman Catholic.

1547 BOORDE *Introd. Knowl.* xx. (1870) 172, I am a Greke. .. Yet the Romayns with me be mervellous wood. **1607** *Ld. Coke's Sp. & Charge* D 2 b, The true harted Protestants.. did quickly Cut the Throats of our English Romaines. **1689** *Prot. Garland* 3 As long as the Romans in Brittain bore sway, Good Men was Degraded, and in Prison lay. **1719** DE FOE *Crusoe* II. (Globe) 449 You will allow it to consist with me, as a Roman, to distinguish far between a Protestant and a Pagan. **1750** WESLEY *Wks.* (1872) II. 197 The congregation was four times larger than usual, in which were abundance of Romans. *c* **1816** MRS. SHERWOOD *Stories Ch. Catech.* 81, I..attended mass, which is the name the Romans give to the Lord's Supper. **1899** *Expositor* Oct. 285 A Puritan is satisfied with the *Pilgrim's Progress* and a Roman with the *Imitation of Christ.* **1936** S. DARK *Manning* iii. 101 Tory Romans were henceforth allowed to wear primroses in their button-holes on the anniversary of the death of Benjamin Disraeli. **1956** R. MACAULAY *Towers of Trebizond* xxii. 255, I decided that it should stick to Anglican churches, eschewing both Knox and the Romans. **1962** V. J. K. BROOK *Life Abp. Parker* xix. 343 He had constantly to entertain those given into his charge by the Council—Romans or others—that he might reason with them. **1965** M. SPARK *Mandelbaum Gate* ii. 45 Latest bulletin from the Holy Romans..they'll take at least another month to decide. **1975** BYFIELD & TEDESCHI *Solemn High Murder* (1976) i. 2 The Romans might have a nice large new..church right in town ..but the little Anglican wooden shack..had wine.

Comb. **1576** GASCOIGNE *Steele Gl.* (Arb.) 76 Some do (Romainelike) Esteme their pall and habyte ouermuche.

7. The Roman rite or liturgy.

1882 G. H. FORBES *Anc. Irish Missal* 28 *marg.*, The Postcommon in the Roman is different. *Ibid.* 35 *marg.*, This Service is not in the Sarum nor the Roman.

ˈRoman, *sb.*[2] = ROMANY[3].

1851 BORROW *Lavengro* lxxi, A daughter of mine, married out among certain Romans who walk about the eastern counties. **1871** M. COLLINS *Marq. & Merch.* I. ii. 94 We Romans have had Ashridge Common for our camps.

roman, *sb.*[3] *S. Afr.* Also **roo(i)man**. [Afrikaans, f. *rooi* red + *man* man.] **1.** A marine fish, *Chrysoblephus laticeps*, belonging to the family Sparidæ and having reddish skin. Also *attrib.*

1790 E. HELME tr. *Le Vaillant's Trav. Afr.* I. ii. 22 Among those [fish] in greatest estimation, they distinguish the *rooman*, a red fish [etc.]. **1801** [see STEENBRASS]. **1804** R. PERCIVAL *Acct. Cape of Good Hope* 43 The most common is the Roman fish... It is of a deep rose colour and of the perch kind. **1893** [see KINGKLIP]. **1957** S. SCHOEMAN *Strike!* iii. 32 It is universally known as 'roman', although some anglers and fishermen call it 'rooi roman' (red roman). **1971** *Cape Argus* 14 May 14 John Hughes shot a roman of 4,1 kg—which is equal to the South African spearfishing record.

2. A large nocturnal sun-spider belonging to the order Solifuga (or Solpuga) and having a sandy-coloured body.

1905 F. PURCELL in Flint & Gilchrist *Sci. in S. Afr.* III. iii. 178 The large nocturnal..species of *Solpuga*..are variously known by the name of Romans, Jagd-spinne-koppen (Hunting Spiders) or Haar-sheerders (Hair cutters). **1966** E. PALMER *Plains of Camdeboo* xiv. 233 On the farm we know ..the nocturnal species [of spiders] as Rooimans or Red Men, and of these latter I can neither think nor speak except in capitals.

‖**roman** (rɔmɑ̃), *sb.*[4] [Fr.: see ROMAUNT *sb.* and *a.*] A romance; a novel. Esp. in phrases: **roman à clef**, a novel in which actual persons are introduced under fictitious names; **roman à**

thèse, a novel that seeks to further a viewpoint or expound a theory; **roman d'aventure** = ROMANCE *sb.* 2; **roman de geste** = *chanson de geste*; **roman expérimental**, a realistic novel based upon deterministic theories of human nature of an alleged scientific character; also *fig.*; **roman fleuve**, a sequence of self-contained novels; **roman noir**, a Gothic novel, a shocker, a thriller; **roman policier**, a story of police detection.

1765 [see ROMAUNT *sb.* and *a.* 1]. **1868** Roman de geste [see CHANSON 2]. **1884** W. JAMES *Will to Believe* (1897) 173 Like the friends of M. Zola, we pique ourselves on our 'scientific' and 'analytic' character, and prefer to be cynical, and call the world a 'roman expérimental' on an infinite scale. **1889** E. DOWSON *Let.* 5 May (1967) 75 We..may..evolve a brilliant *roman.* **1893** H. JAMES *Let.* 23 Jan. in P. Gunn *Vernon Lee* (1964) x. 138 Her books of fiction are a tissue of personalities of this hideous roman-à-clef kind. **1905** Roman d'aventure [see LAI[1]]. **1913** G. TURQUET-MILNES *Influence of Baudelaire* v. v. 250 In his [*sc.* Arthur Machen's] works we again meet the distrust of nature from the documentary point of view —the distrust of 'Romans à Clef'. **1928** A. CHRISTIE *Mystery of Blue Train* x. 81, I see, Madame, that you have a *roman policier.* **1931** *Times Lit. Suppl.* 26 Feb. 151/4 The 'Radcliffian' novel, or *roman noir*, as the French call it. *Ibid.* 31 Dec. 1054/4 The study aims at giving a detailed analysis of the German criticism of Zola's Rougon-Macquart cycle and his theory of the *roman expérimental.* **1934** WEBSTER, Roman à thèse. **1936** *Times Lit. Suppl.* 15 Feb. 121/3 Those great *romans-fleuves* whose unnumbered volumes have no other purpose than to show us to ourselves as we appear. **1940** H. G. WELLS *Babes in Darkling Wood* 5 They pass at last..into more or less honest fact telling, into 'historical reconstruction', the *roman à clef*, biography, history and autobiography. **1954** K. TILLOTSON *Novels of Eighteen-Forties* I. 3 The *roman à thèse* is already establishing itself. **1955** *Times* 4 Aug. 10/3 *The Typewriter* is not great Cocteau, but it is fine melodramatic fare and strangely compelling emotionally. It has wit and good dialogue, but this is essentially a tragedy set in the frame of a *roman policier* and the answer to the mystery remains unanswered and unguessable until the very last scene. **1957** *Encycl. Brit.* I. 945/1 The inter-influence of French and English literature can be studied in the Breton romances and the *romans d'aventure* even better than in the epic poetry of the period. **1959** *Listener* 3 Dec. 1007/3 The re-creation of the medieval *roman*..in *The Story of Reynard.* **1965** *Ibid.* 27 May 799/1 *David in Silence*..is also in its way a *roman à thèse.* **1965** *Observer* 5 Sept. 21/5 The film is a *roman policier.* **1966** J. CARTER in Glover & Greene *Victorian Detective Fiction* p. xiv, The early *roman policier* writers. **1971** J. POPE-HENNESSY *A. Trollope* xvii. 364 We might claim..that *An Eye for an Eye* initiated the series of Trollope's *romans noirs.* **1972** V. GIELGUD *Black Sambo Affair* xxvii. 208 A fine collection of *romans policiers.* **1974** *Bookseller* 15 June 2696/3 He [*sc.* Anthony Powell] obviously feels reasonably protective towards the maestro of the *roman fleuve.* **1977** *New Yorker* 24 Oct. 184/2 A roman à clef whose skeleton key would seem to be the unsavory case of Alice Crimmins and her two murdered children. **1978** *Times Lit. Suppl.* 1 Dec. 1405/5 Success takes him to Hollywood, and there you feel a roman à clef, based on Puzo's profitable frustrations in movieland, is intended.

Roman ('rəʊmən), *a.*[1] Forms: 4 **Romein, -eyn**, 6 **-eyne**; 4–6 **Romayn**, 6 **-ayne**; 4–7 **Romain(e**, 5–7 **Romane**, 6– **Roman**. [In early use a. OF. *Romain*, *-ayn*, subsequently ad. L. *Rōmān-us*: see ROMAN *sb.*[1]]

I. 1. Of persons: Inhabiting, belonging to, or originating from the ancient city of Rome or its territory; holding the position of a citizen or member of the ancient republic or empire of Rome.

a **1300** *Cursor M.* 22343 Bot at þe last the romain king Sal of his ost mak gret gadering. *c* **1330** R. BRUNNE *Chron. Wace* (Rolls) 3366 Þey conseilled..þat Brenne scholde turne a-gayn To wyþstande þe host Romayn. **1390** GOWER *Conf.* I. 220 Paulus the worthi kniht Romein. **1533** BELLENDEN *Livy* Prol. (S.T.S.) I. 3 The empire..Fra romane kingis vnto consullis went. **1589** PUTTENHAM *Eng. Poesie* I. viii. (Arb.) 33 Horace the most delicate of all the Romain Lyrickes. **1600** SHAKS. *A.Y.L.* IV. ii. 4 Let's present him to the Duke like a Romane Conquerour. **1660** JER. TAYLOR *Ductor* III. iii. (1676) 574 The Roman Emperors residing in the East. **1712** STEELE *Spect.* No. 502 ¶1 Some perusing Roman Writers, would find [etc.]. **1756–7** tr. *Keysler's Trav.* (1760) II. 408 On the window-shutters are to be seen the heads of celebrated Roman ladies, as Martia, Julia, Aurelia. **1818** CRUISE *Digest* (ed. 2) I. 388 What the Roman lawyers called a *jus precarium.* **1841** *Penny Cycl.* XX. 80/2 Admixture of the northern people with the Roman population.

2. Of things: Of or pertaining to, connected with, ancient Rome, its inhabitants or dominion; practised or used by, current or usual among, the Romans, etc.

a **1300** *Cursor M.* 22255 Þat of þe romain sal Impire Hali lauerd be and sire. *c* **1386** CHAUCER *Wife's Prol.* 642 He often tymes wolde preche, And me of olde Romayn geestes teche. **1533** BELLENDEN *Livy* IV. xviii. (S.T.S.) II. 115 Skairslie mycht þe romane tentis be þat day defendit. **1565** COOPER *Thesaurus* App., *Romulus*, as the Romayne stories affyrme, the son of Mars. **1613** DEKKER *Strange Horse Race* Wks. (Grosart) III. 317 A Race,..with some triumphing in Chariots, after the Roman fashion. **1671** MILTON *P.R.* I. 217 To rescue Israel from the Roman yoke. **1738** *Gentl. Mag.* VIII. 233/2 A Robe somewhat resembling the Roman Habit. **1776** ADAM SMITH *W.N.* I. v. (1904) I. 43 The northern nations who established themselves upon the ruins of the Roman Empire. **1819** S. PARKES *Chem. Catech.* (ed. 9) 574/1 Tin, used in the Roman coinage. **1872** RUSKIN *Fors* xxi, Just where the Roman galleys used to be moored.

b. Of language, etc. = LATIN *a.*

c **1330** R. BRUNNE *Chron. Wace* (Rolls) 12538 He spak wel þe speche Romayn, For he had longe wiþ hem ben. **1390** GOWER *Conf.* I. 206 For Couste in Saxoun is to sein Constance upon the word Romein. *Ibid.* II. 90 The ferste lettres of Latin, Of which the tunge Romein cam. **1612** BREREWOOD *Lang. & Relig.* 50 The Spaniards call their language Romance till this day, which yet we know to differ much from the right Roman tongue. *c* **1620** A. HUME *Brit. Tongue* (1865) 8 Quhat was the right roman sound of them is hard to judge, seeing now we heer nae romanes. **1784** COWPER *Tiroc.* 605 'Tis not enough that Greek or Roman page, At stated hours, his freakish thoughts engage. **1841** LATHAM *Eng. Lang.* 45 At a given epoch between the first and fifth centuries the language of Gaul was more Roman and less Celtic than that of Britain. **1871** EARLE *Philol. Eng. Tongue* §590 The two great linguistic elements of Western civilization, the Roman and the Gothic.

c. ***Roman law***, the system or code of law developed by the ancient Romans, and still accepted in principle by many countries.

1660 JER. TAYLOR *Ductor* III. v. (1676) 715 The paternal power is defin'd by the measures of the Roman law. **1681** STAIR *Inst. Law Scot.* I. i. §10. 7 Oft-times by the Common Law, we understand the Roman Law, which in some sort is common to many Nations. *a* **1768** ERSKINE *Inst. Law Scot.* I. I. §i, The Roman law is always understood by way of excellency. **1804** RANKEN *Hist. France* III. III. iii. 292 By the consuetude of Roman and Gothic law in the south and west counties. **1842** T. ARNOLD *Lect. Mod. Hist.* (1860) 41 Many countries have adopted the Roman law.

3. Of antiquities, etc.: Belonging to, surviving from, the time of the Romans. Also *Comb.*, as ***Roman-looking*** adj.

a **1548** HALL *Chron., Hen. VIII*, 73 A pyller which was of auncient Romayne woorke. **1588** SHAKS. *L.L.L.* V. ii. 617 The face of an old Roman coine, scarce seene. **1663** BUTLER *Hud.* II. i. 310 Love in your heart as idly burns As Fire in antique Roman-Urns. **1699** *Phil. Trans.* XXI. 287 Some of the backermost part of which is an Ancient Roman building. **1705** ADDISON *Italy* Wks. 1721 II. 123 The workmanship of the old Roman pillars. **1774** PENNANT *Tour Scotl. in 1772* 82 Ride by the side of the Roman road. **1842** *Murray's Hand-bk. N. Italy* 251/2 A complete collection of all the Roman inscriptions found in the province of Brescia. **1864** *Chambers's Encycl.* VI. 23/1 As seen in ancient Egyptian, Greek, and Roman lamps. **1869** 'MARK TWAIN' *Innoc. Abr.* xlviii. 505 We came to a..Roman-looking ruin.

4. Of a type or kind characteristic of, or exemplified by, the Romans; Roman-like, esp. in respect of honesty, strictness, courage, or frugality. spec. ***Roman father***, a dominating head of a family.

1577 HELLOWES *Gueuara's Chron.* 43 Longinus vnderstanding thereof, dranke poison... This Romaine straunge act of Longinus gaue great admiration. **1596** SHAKS. *Merch. V.* III. ii. 297 One in whom The ancient Romane honour more appeares Then any that drawes breath in Italie. **1606** —— *Ant. & Cl.* I. ii. 87 He was dispos'd to mirth, but on the sodaine A Romane thought hath strooke him. **1750** W. WHITEHEAD *Roman Father* v. ii. 74 Has not a Roman father power to take The lives of all his children? **1762–71** H. WALPOLE *Vertue's Anecd. Paint.* Pref., It is not rigid nor Roman to say it, but a people had better be unhappy by their own fault, than by that of their government. **1784** COWPER *Task* IV. 168 A Roman meal;.. a radish and an egg. **1798** in *Poet. Anti-Jacobin* (1854) 217 Burke, in whose breast a Roman ardour glow'd. **1898** *Daily News* 6 Oct. 3/1 Europe may..resolve to place a sufficient force in the island to make a Roman peace. **1906** KIPLING *Puck of Pook's Hill* 148 There can't be much of the Roman Father about you! **1922** T. E. LAWRENCE *Let.* 26 Aug. (1938) 361 Perhaps I'm playing the Roman father trick, and it's not as bad as I think. **1940** H. G. WELLS *Babes in Darkling Wood* I. iv. 89 My Roman father! The Cadi of Clarges Street! **1962** *Listener* 25 Oct. 694/1 Dr Borosdin, the almost Roman father. **1977** P. G. WINSLOW *Ditch Hill Murder* II. 153 Richard had taken to playing the Roman father to Lerida.

†**b.** *transf.* Of language: Lofty, stately. *Obs.*

1619 J. DYKE *Caveat Archippus* 23 Others..affect.. such a Roman-English, as plaine Englishmen cannot understand. **1641** J. TRAPPE *Theol. Theol.* 227 Plainly to the capacity of the Hearers,..not in a stately stile, or Roman English.

c. Of a nose: Having a prominent upper part or bridge. Also *transf.* of a horse's nose.

1624 MASSINGER *Renegado* I. i, A third, An Austrian princess, by her Roman nose. **1650** BULWER *Anthropomet.* 84 We use to call such an high and eminent Nose, a Roman Nose. **1709** *Tatler* No. 75 ¶5 The Butler, who was noted for round Shoulders, and a Roman nose. **1780** COWPER *Progr. Err.* 396 Some Cæsar shows—Defective only in his Roman nose. **1831** YOUATT *Horse* viii. 117 In some horses, this arch is more than usually developed... These horses are said to have Roman noses. **1883** *Cassell's Nat. Hist.* I. 88 In man there is the Roman nose, the pug, the straight, the flat, the broken.

d. ***Roman holiday***, an occasion on which entertainment or profit is derived from injury or death; a scene of suffering considered as an object of amusement; a pitiable spectacle.

Orig. a holiday for a gladiatorial combat: see quot. 1818 s.v. HOLIDAY *sb.* 2.

1886 'S. COOLIDGE' *What Katy did Next* ix. 223 (*heading*) A Roman holiday. **1931** R. FERGUSON *Brontës went to Woolworth's* xxv. 220 There. I've made a Roman holiday of my dear little acquaintance, and I only hope I'm right. **1951** G. GREENE *Lost Childhood* 47 The critics..were perhaps influenced by horror at the Roman holiday. **1957** 'H. CARMICHAEL' *Put out that Star* x. 103 All you people ever think about is how you can turn any damn' thing at all into money: anything to make a Roman holiday. **1966** P. O'DONNELL *Sabre-Tooth* xv. 205 She had watched impassively, caring nothing for the man's death but loathing the Roman-holiday manner of it. **1967** A. WILSON *No Laughing Matter* III. 329 Was this what Picasso's wonderful Guernica stood for, this Roman holiday? **1972** A. HUNTER *Vivienne* x. 131 A Roman holiday was in the making, and the number of reporters had risen to five.

5. Of letters: Belonging to the modern type which most directly represents that used in ancient Roman inscriptions and manuscripts, esp. in contrast to *Gothic* (or *black letter*) and *Italic.*

1519 *Indent.* in *Philol. Soc. Trans.* (1867) 364 After thre dyverse letters, on for the englysh, an other for the laten, and the thyrde of great romayne letter. **1588** *Procl. for Waightes* 16 Dec., To be printed and marked with EL crowned, and a Romaine T with R. **1665** *Sarum Churchw. Acc.* (Swayne) 239 One large Bible in folio Buft and bost of a very faire Roman letter. **1683** MOXON *Mech. Exerc., Printing* ii. ¶2 Bodies are commonly Cast with a Romain, Italica, and sometimes an English Face. **1728** CHAMBERS *Cycl.* s.v. *Printing*, Hitherto there had been nothing printed but in Latin, and the vulgar Tongues; first in Roman Characters, then in Gothic, and at last in Italic. **1808** STOWER *Printer's Gram.* 35 Even in those nations works are printed..with Roman letters. **1857** *Lowndes' Bibliogr. Man.* I. 186/2 The first quarto edition of the authorised version, printed in the Roman letter.

b. Of handwriting: Round and bold.

1601 SHAKS. *Twel. N.* III. iv. 31, I thinke we doe know the sweet Romane hand. **1685** BOYLE *Enq. Notion Nat.* v. 155 If he should have made a Text-hand as fair as a Roman-hand. **1716** LADY M. W. MONTAGU *Lett.* I. xxvii. 89 Achmet Bey ..can already write a good Roman hand. **1893** *Daily News* 18 Jan. 5/2 People who have to write great quantities of 'copy' for the Press..find their hands, if Roman and fine at first, gradually disappearing in scrawl.

c. ***Roman uncial*** = SEMI-UNCIAL *a.* (*sb.*)

1897 [see *half-uncial* s.v. HALF- II. n]. **1906** E. JOHNSTON *Writing & Illuminating* i. 38 Roman uncials were fully developed by the fourth century.

6. a. Of the alphabet or its characters: Employed by the Romans, and (with various modifications) by all the modern nations of Western Europe and their (former) colonies.

1728 [see next]. **1744–5** *Phil. Trans.* XLIII. 285 The Letters in this Sculpture are mixed, being partly Roman, and partly Saxon. **1846** MONIER WILLIAMS *Skr. Grammar* 1 The following are the Devanāgarī letters, with their equivalents in the Roman character. **1879** *Encycl. Brit.* IX. 631/2 Many new sounds had to be represented which were not provided for in the Roman alphabet.

b. Of numeral letters: (see quot. 1728). Opposed to *Arabic.*

1728 CHAMBERS *Cycl.* s.v. *Character*, Roman Characters consist of the Uncial or Majuscule Letters of the Roman alphabet... The Numeral Letters that compose the Roman Character are in Number seven, *viz.*, I, V, X, L, C, D, M. **1735** *Phil. Trans.* XXXIX. 139 The Roman Numeral Ten, which was made in this Form, like an X. **1800** in *Archaeologia* XIII. 124 All the sums are specified in Roman characters. *Ibid.* 125 The churchwardens accounts of Shorne..are entered in Roman numerals as late as the year 1621. **1847** *Brit. Mag.* XXXII. 364 His singular intermixture of Arabic and Roman numerals.

7. *Arch.* = COMPOSITE *a.* 2.

1624 [see ITALIAN *a.* 1 c]. **1703** T. N. *City & C. Purchaser* 27 Composite, Compound, or Roman. *Ibid.* 28 Scamozzi makes the Roman Base 30 m. high. **1726** [see COMPOUND *a.* 2 c]. **1728** CHAMBERS *Cycl.* s.v. *Composite*, The Composite is also called the Roman and Italic Order. **1841** *Penny Cycl.* XX. 72/2 Roman architecture presents chiefly a corruption of the Doric and Ionic. **1842** *Murray's Hand-bk. N. Italy* 275/2 Neither the Roman Corinthian, nor the Roman Composite had any fixed type.

8. Used in combination with other adjs., as ***Roman-Alexandrian***, ***-British***, ***-Doric***, ***-Dutch***, etc.

Cf. the combs. in which *Roman* forms the second element, e.g. *Brito-*, *Gallo-*, *Græco-Roman.*

1802–12 BENTHAM *Ration. Judic. Evid.* (1827) 720 The maxim of the Roman-Gallic law. **1845** *Encycl. Metrop.* II. 855/1 The Roman Dutch law consists of the civil law and the ordinances and edicts issued by the supreme power in Holland. **1854** MILMAN *Lat. Chr.* IV. iii. (1864) II. 227 The gradual expulsion..of the British and Roman British inhabitants. **1901** E. NICHOLSON *Weights & Measures* 44 A weight two-thirds of the Roman-Alexandrian talent. **1928** R. NEVILL *Romantic London* ii. 39 The lower order is Roman-Doric. **1957** LD. HAILEY *Afr. Survey 1956* xxii. 1520 In South Africa ownership of the land is, in accordance with the principles of Roman-Dutch law, held to comprise all values in the land including mineral rights. **1964** J. SUMMERSON *Classical Lang. Archit.* 49/1 The Greek order has no base, nor is a base prescribed by Vitruvius, though in practice the Roman Doric always has a base, the Greek never. **1972** *Mod. Law Rev.* XXXV. I. 46 There is no warrant in Roman-Dutch law for a discretion as wide as that enunciated by the Appellate Division.

9. Engaged in the study of Roman law, antiquities, history, etc.

1845 *Encycl. Metrop.* II. 748/1 To the Roman lawyer the study of Roman antiquities is essential. **1879** *Encycl. Brit.* X. 65/1 Though public games..must be studied by the Roman historian.., yet [etc.].

II. 10. Pertaining to Rome in its ecclesiastical aspect; belonging to, connected with, etc., the Church of Rome. Cf. ROMAN CATHOLIC *a.*

Roman collar, a special form of collar worn by Roman Catholic, and some Anglican, clerics. ***Roman fever*** [transf. use of 13 c], a fondness for the Church of Rome, a desire to be converted to Rome.

1535 LYNDESDAY *Satyre* 237 First, at the Romane Kirk will ȝe begin. **1578** J. NELSON in Allen *Martyrdom Campion* (1908) 112 A voluntary departure from the unitie of the Catholike Roman faith. **1628** PRYNNE *Brief Suruay* Ep., The very pillars, and foundation stones of the Roman and Arminian Faction. **1659** JER. TAYLOR *Ductor* Pref., The Casuists of the Roman Church take these things for resolution. **1706** E. WELLS *Answ. Dowley* 48 Those called by you Roman Missionaries might with more accuracy have been called Romish Missionaries. **1788** GIBBON *Decl. & F.* xlix. V. 136 That name, with the addition of *saint*, is inserted in the Roman calendar. **1812** J. BRADY *Clavis Cal.* I. 250 The present method of chaunting..is frequently called the Gregorian chaunt, as well as the Roman chaunt. **1845** GLADSTONE *Glean.* (1879) VII. 192 Probabilism is by no means the universal or compulsory doctrine of the Roman theologians. **1877** O. WILDE *Lett.* (1962) 45 Poor Dunskie: I know he looks on me as a renegade; still I have suffered very much for my Roman fever in mind and *pocket* and happiness. *a* **1884** M. PATTISON *Mem.* (1885) vi. 226 The daughter had got the Roman fever in her veins. **1897** HALL CAINE *Christian* I. i, The younger clergyman wore a Roman collar. **1929** S. LESLIE *Anglo-Catholic* xii. 171 Edward.. assured him he had not left the Anglican Church, though the Anglican Church, he thought, had probably left him. The Canon only said, 'For Roman fever there is no cure and for Rome there is no leechdom.' **1952** R. MACAULAY *Let.* 12 Jan. (1961) 248, I am glad Dom Gregory Rees thinks 'Roman fever' abated; I don't notice it myself, anyhow among the laity.

fig. **1697** VANBRUGH *Relapse* v. iii, Come, no equivocation, no Roman turns upon us.

11. (*Holy*) ***Roman Empire***: the Romano-Germanic Empire which originated with Charlemagne in 800, and continued to exist down to 1806. So ***Roman Emperor***, = EMPEROR 2.

1610 *Elem. Armories* 146 These the present Armories of the Romaine Empire. *Ibid.* 147 The sacred Romane Empire. **1728** CHAMBERS *Cycl.* s.v. *Empire*, The Empire of Germany, call'd also, in Juridical Acts and Laws, the Holy Roman Empire. **1788** GIBBON *Decl. & F.* xlix. V. 167 In obedience to a secret treaty, the Roman emperor immediately withdrew. **1829** SCOTT *Anne of G.* vii, These dignitaries, because they held their fiefs of the Holy Roman Empire, claimed as complete sovereignty [etc.]. *Ibid.* xx, A system handed down to us from the most Christian and holy Roman Emperor, Charlemagne. **1864** BRYCE (*title*), The Holy Roman Empire.

†**b.** ***Roman months***, after G. *Römermonate*: (see quots.). *Obs.*

1670 *Lond. Gaz.* No. 525/2 The Contribution of the Empire, called the Roman Months, is not yet resolved. **1687** *Ibid.* No. 2284/1 This Grant of the Subsidy of 100 Roman Months hath met with another Perplexity. **1728** CHAMBERS *Cycl.* s.v. *Emperor*, He receives a Kind of Tribute from all the Princes and States of the Empire, call'd the Roman Month.

†**12.** = ROMANCE 1 b. *Obs.*

c **1425** *St. Mary of Oignies* II. xi. in *Anglia* VIII. 179 Alle þis she seyde in ryme and romayne tunge. *Ibid.*, þe louely songe of oure lady, þat is Magnificat, she rehercyd ful often .., expounynge hit in Romayne tunge. **1530** PALSGR. 44 Thoughe the olde Romayne tonge use many suche wordes, the trewe frenche tonge leaveth never the *e*..onwritten. **1612** [see ROMANCE *sb.* 1]. **1727** BAILEY (vol. II.), *Roman Language*, a mixture of Gaulish and Latin. **1804** [see ROMANESQUE *a.* 1].

III. 13. Of or pertaining to mediæval or modern Rome or its inhabitants; printed at Rome, etc.

1608 USSHER *Lett.* (1686) 22 We have long expected them from the Roman Press. **1647** YOUNG *Ibid.* 517 The Passage *Psal.* 142. 9. which I find in my Roman Edition. **1705** ADDISON *Italy* Wks. 1721 II. 127 In several of the Roman Churches and Chappels. *a* **1715** BURNET *Own Time* (1734) II. 546 He staid several Years at Rome, where he became acquainted with a Roman Lady. **1728** CHAMBERS *Cycl.* s.v. *Italian*, The Tuscan is usually preferred to the other Dialects, and the Roman Pronunciation to that of the other cities. **1841** *Penny Cycl.* XX. 134/1 A collection of popular Roman songs was published by the Cavaliere Visconti. **1853** HUMPHREYS *Coin-coll. Man.* II. 514 This modern Roman series has generally the name of the pope on one side.

b. ***Roman school***, the school of painting of which Raphael is the leading representative.

1797 *Encycl. Brit.* (ed. 3) XIII. 599/2 The artists in the Florentine and Roman schools painted most commonly in water colours or in fresco. **1841** *Penny Cycl.* XX. 76/2 The works of Raphael exhibit this style in its full development.. and he is accordingly the head or representative of the Roman school.

c. ***Roman fever***, a form of malarial fever prevalent at Rome.

c **1838** *Encycl. Metrop.* (1845) XXIV. 131/2 The Roman fever appears to differ in degree only from that of the West Indies. **1896** W. NORTH *Roman Fever* Pref. p. v, The nature and origin of the disease known as 'Roman Fever', a local form of a malady widely prevalent elsewhere.

d. Applied to a bidding system in Bridge orig. used by certain Italian players, or to various conventions and signals within this system.

1959 BELLADONNA & AVARELLI *Roman Club Syst. Distrib. Bidding* 2 In this fashion the person who is already playing bridge can learn one phase of the Roman Club expertly before going on to the next formula. **1959** REESE & DORMER *Bridge Player's Dict.* 190 *Roman system*... Opening bids of one diamond, one heart, and one spade, show a genuine suit and are forcing for one round. **1964** *Listener* 21 May 851/1 'Roman leads'..is a method whereby the lower of two touching honours, rather than the higher, is the normal lead. **1970** S. HUGHES *Art of Coarse Bridge* iv. 93 Patiently South explained that the Roman Club..meant that he had either a minimum balanced hand or a very strong one. **1975** *Times* 27 Sept. 10/7 Opening bids with double meanings which we now associate with the Roman and other artificial systems.

IV. In special applications.

14. †**a.** ***Roman herbs***: (see quot.). *Obs.*

1578 LYTE *Dodoens* 5 They do commonly call al such straunge herbes as be vnknowen of the common people, Romish or Romayne herbes, although the same be brought from Norweigh.

b. In names of species or varieties of plants, fruits, etc., as ***Roman apricot, bean, beet***, etc. (see quots. and these words).

1704 *Dict. Rust.* s.v. *Apricock*, The green *Roman-Apricock, the largest of all kinds and excellent for Compotes. **1766** *Compl. Farmer* s.v. *Apricok tree* E 3/2 The Roman is the next ripe apricot. **1578** LYTE *Dodoens* 474 In Englishe of Turner it is called kidney beane.., it may be also named Garden Smilax, or *Romaine Beanes. **1620** VENNER *Via Recta* vii. 143 The great red Beete, or *Romane Beete. **1815** F. P. CHAUMETON *Flore Médicale* II. 123 *Latin* Anthemis nobilis... *Anglais* Chamomile; *Roman Chamomile; Sweet-scented chamomile. **1856** WATTS tr. *Gmelin's Handbk. Chem.* X. 415 Fusing the oil of Roman camomile with hydrate of potash. **1861** BENTLEY *Man. Bot.* 580 The flowers [of the *Anthemis nobilis*] constitute the Roman or True Chamomiles of the Materia Medica. **1712** *Phil. Trans.* XXVII. 391 Tall *Roman Catch-Fly. **1648** HEXHAM II, *Romaine Coriander, or black Cummine-seed. **1731** MILLER *Gard. Dict.* s.v. *Geranium*, *Roman Crane's-bill, with strip'd Flowers. **1822** *Hortus Angl.* II. 189 *E[rodium] Romanum*. Roman Crane's Bill. **1860** WATTS tr. *Gmelin's Handbk. Chem.* XIV. 144 *Roman cumin oil is resinised by fuming nitric acid. *Ibid.*, Roman cumin seeds, distilled four times with water, yield 3·27 p.c. oil. **1665** REA *Flora* 123 The *Roman Cyclamen hath rounder leaves than the last. **1897** *Syd. Soc. Lex.*, *R[oman] fennel, a variety of *Fœniculum vulgare*, grown in Rome, characterised by its large fruit. **1877** D. T. FISH *Bulbs* 49 There are also *Roman hyacinths, of which very little indeed seems to be known, excepting that they are very early, sweet, and delicate. **1866** *Treas. Bot.* 663/2 *Roman laurel, *Laurus nobilis*. **1611** COTGR., *Lavande Romaine*, *Roman Lauender. *Ibid.* s.v. *Romain, Laictuë Romaine*, *Roman Lectuce, the greatest kind of Cabbadge Lectuce. **1706** LONDON & WISE *Retired Gard.* I. xv. 192 Now you may sow..the George Lettuce, the Roman, the Royal [etc.]. **1852** G. W. JOHNSON *Cottage Gard. Dict.* 531 *Lactuca*, Lettuce... Large Roman, Malta, for summer. **1796** C. MARSHALL *Gardening* xv. (1813) 243 The *Roman and Portugal [melons] are small but early. **1664** EVELYN *Kal. Hort.* (1729) 213 *Nectarines*,..Red *Roman, little Green Nectarine [etc.]. **1796** C. MARSHALL *Gardening* xvii. (1813) 284 The Newington, red Roman,.. and murry [nectarine], are good sorts. **1578** LYTE *Dodoens* 129 The first kind is now called..in English Greek or *Romayne Nettel. **1713** *Phil. Trans.* XXVIII. 35 Roman or Pill Nettle (*Urtica Romana*). **1834** *Penny Cycl.* II. 420/2 In the Roman nettle (*Urtica pilulifera*) they [the flowers] are collected into round heads. **1632** SHERWOOD s.v. *Nigella*, Ordinarie or *Romane Nigella. **1716** 'H. S. PHILOKEPOS' *Young Gard. Director* 89 *Roman Peach. **1726** *Dict. Rust.* (ed. 3) s.v. *Peach*, There are many other sorts of Peaches; as the Crown-Peach,.. Isabella, Roman. **1597** GERARDE *Herbal* 1047 The great Pease is called..in English *Romane Pease, or the greater Pease. *Ibid.* 247 *Romane Rocket is cherished in Gardens. **1796** C. MARSHALL *Gardening* xvi. (1813) 275 The round leaved sort [of sorrel], commonly called the *Roman, is reckoned the more grateful acid. *Ibid.*, Common sorrel likes a cool moist soil, but the Roman a dry one. **1578** LYTE *Dodoens* 5 Wormwood *Romayne groweth plentifully in Hungarie. **1866** *Treas. Bot.* 1237/1 Roman Wormwood, *Ambrosia artemisiæfolia*; also *Artemisia pontica*.

c. In some names of animals or birds, as ***Roman pigeon, runt, snail***; also ***Roman-lamp shell***.

1854 L. A. MEALL *Moubray's Poultry* 248 Roman Runt:.. mentioned by some writers as a separate subvariety. **1861** HULME tr. *Moquin-Tandon* III. ii. 84 The Helix Pomatia (Linn.) or Roman Snail. The shell of this species is $1\frac{1}{2}$ inch in height. **1870** GILLMORE tr. *Figuier's Reptiles & Birds* vii. (1892) 426 The Roman Pigeons, thus named because they are very common in Italy, are easily recognised from the circle of red which surrounds their eyes. **1898** MORRIS *Austral Eng.*, *Roman-Lamp Shell*, name given in Tasmania to a brachiopod mollusc, *Waldheimia flavescens*.

15. a. ***Roman balance, beam***, or ***steelyard***, the ordinary form of steelyard.

1611 COTGR., *Crochet*,..a Romane beame, or Stelleere. **1678** J. PHILLIPS tr. *Tavernier's Trav.* II. 9 They carry their weights always along with them, being like a Roman Beam, or a Stelleer. **1728** CHAMBERS *Cycl.* s.v. *Balance*, In the Roman Balance.., the Weight used for a Counterbalance is the same..; in the Common Balance, the Counterpoise is various. **1764** J. FERGUSON *Lect.* iii. 32 The..Roman steel-yard is a lever of this kind. **1858** HOMANS *Cycl. Commerce* 1758/2 The *Statera Romana*, or Roman steelyard, is mentioned in 315 B.C. **1875** KNIGHT *Dict. Mech.* 2370/1 A Roman balance found at Pompeii shows that they also had two centers of suspension for varying grades of weights.

b. With names of measures or weights, as ***Roman foot, mile, ounce***.

1607 TOPSELL *Foure-f. Beasts* 655 The hornes..are so lively expressed by Pliny... They are..long, about two Roman feet and three palmes... They are in breadth where they ioyne to the head, three Roman fingers and a half. **1705** ARBUTHNOT *Coins*, etc. (1727) Pl. 17 The Roman Ounce is the English Avoirdupoise Ounce. **1728** CHAMBERS *Cycl.* s.v. *Measure*, The Roman Foot, on the Monument of Cossutius. **1760** RAPER in *Phil. Trans.* LI. 774 An Enquiry into the Measure of the Roman Foot. **1776** GIBBON *Decl. & F.* ii. (1782) I. 62 *note*, The whole distance was 725 Roman, or 665 English miles. **1839** *Penny Cycl.* XV. 210/1 Taking the Roman foot at 11.62 English inches, the original Roman mile was therefore 1614 yards.

16. a. ***Roman alum***, a reddish native alum found in Italy, or a manufactured imitation of this.

1725 *Fam. Dict.* s.v. *Allom*, The Roman-Allom is dark red, transparent within, and of a sharp stiptick Taste. **1753** CHAMBERS *Cycl.* Suppl. s.v. *Alum*, Roman Alum properly denotes a rock Alum, of a red colour, prepared in the country near Rome. **1839** URE *Dict. Arts* 38 It is probable that Roman alum is a sulphate of alumina and potash, with a slight excess of the earthy ingredient. **1863** *Fownes' Chem.* (ed. 9) 317 Roman alum, made from alum-stone.

b. ***Roman vitriol***, blue vitriol, sulphate of copper.

1737 in Bracken *Farriery* (1749) 363 Vitriol, Roman, per Pound, [£]0 1 4. **1747** WESLEY *Prim. Physick* (1762) 42 A little Roman Vitriol dissolved in a Pint of Water. **1819** S. PARKES *Chem. Catech.* (ed. 9) 307 It [copper] is..combined with sulphuric acid to form Roman vitriol. **1839** URE *Dict. Arts* 337 The chemical preparations of copper which constitute distinct manufactures are, Blue or Roman vitriol .., Verditer and Verdigris.

c. ***Roman cement***, a cement or hydraulic mortar made by the addition of calcareous or argillaceous matter to lime, sand, and water = PARKER'S CEMENT. Also as *vb.*

The original *Roman cement* was that made by J. Parker from Sheppey stone and patented in 1796; the name, however, does not appear in the specification of the patent.

c **1800** PARKER & CO. (*heading of circular*), Roman Cement, artificial terras, and stucco. **1810** in Willis & Clark *Cambridge* (1886) II. 497 That the west Part [of Trinity Coll.]..be new fronted with Roman Cement. **1838** *Civil Eng. & Arch. Jrnl.* I. 245/1 When used as stucco, this lime is certainly superior to Roman cement. **1845** FORD *Handbk. Spain* I. 62 The cutaneous stucco by which his own illote carcass is Roman cemented. **1889, 1917** [see PARKER'S CEMENT]. **1919** A. T. BASSETT *S. Barnabas', Oxford* vi. 67 Some amusement was caused at the time by a box bearing the words 'Roman Cement', in large letters, being delivered at the Church for use in the connection with repairs to the campanile. **1970** H. BRAUN *Parish Churches* xix. 223 Roman cement is difficult to procure, but an admixture of lime with the Portland cement will help to improve the colour to some small extent. **1977** *Sci. Amer.* July 82/2 The high quality of Roman cements, which is evident in the number and solidity of the Roman structures still standing, was due in large measure to the added discovery that lime mixed with reactive siliceous material (in the form of crushed tiles or volcanic ash) gave a cement that developed superior strength and water resistance. 'Roman cement' made in this way enjoyed wide prestige and retained its popularity with little improvement or development until the end of the 18th century.

d. In names of colours, as ***Roman lake***, etc.

1835 FIELD *Chrom.* 99 An observation which applies to various lakes under the names of Roman Lake, Venetian Lake [etc.]. *Ibid.* 80 Roman Ochre is rather deeper and more powerful in colour [etc.]. *Ibid.* 69 Roman White is of the purest white colour.

e. ***Roman ring*** = *flying ring* s.v. FLYING *ppl. a.* 3.

1911 *Daily Colonist* (Victoria, B.C.) 26 Apr. 5/4 They [*sc.* vaudeville athletes] begin by drawing their body from the floor on Roman rings with snail-like slowness. **1965** F. SARGESON *Mem. Peon* vi. 165 The creak of parallel bars and Roman rings.

17. Misc. uses, as ***Roman mosaic, punch, sandal, satin, scarf, strings, water***. **Roman bath** = *Roman tub*; **Roman tub** *U.S.*, a large sunken bathtub.

1757 A. COOPER *Distiller* 213 Recipe for a Gallon of Roman water... Take the outer..peels of six Citrons; a gallon of Proof Spirit, and two quarts of water. **1828** *Lights & Shades* II. 79 Oh, William, can you tell us what Roman punch is? **1855** E. TWISLETON *Let.* 6 Apr. (1928) xiv. 266 Mrs. Carlyle was sumptuous, in a black velvet and Roman scarf. **1861** *Chambers's Encycl.* II. 677/2 The best [catgut] strings are used for musical instruments; and those which come from Italy, and are known as Roman strings, are the strongest. **1883** *Encycl. Brit.* XVI. 854/2 The modern so-called 'Roman mosaic' is formed of short and slender sticks of coloured glass. **1899** *Daily News* 21 Oct. 7/7 Roman satin is much used for ball and tea gowns, also dinner dresses. **1914** C. MACKENZIE *Sinister St.* II. III. iv. 559 Stella..was rushing from window to window, trying patterns of chintz and damask and Roman satin. **1934** WEBSTER, Roman sandal. **1939** M. B. PICKEN *Lang. Fashion* 130/2 *Roman sandal*, sandal with front composed entirely of straps, equally spaced. **1961** *Harper's Bazaar* Feb. 69 The splendid Roman striped satin of a Heppelwhite chair. **1971** *Sunday Nation* (Nairobi) 11 Apr. 20/1 (Advt.), Boots, Roman Sandals. **1972** *Fortune* Jan. 140c (Advt.), You'll have a cocktail lounge and restaurant on the premises. An outside elevator joining the opulent pool deck area and the beach. A Roman tub in your master bath. **1976** *Bathroom Ideas* 58/2 Blue, blue is this Roman bath set apart from the rest of the room. **1979** *Arizona Daily Star* 5 Aug. (Advt. Section) 16/9 Features formal dining, atrium, 2-way fireplace, roman tub in master bedroom.

'Roman, *a.*[2] = ROMANY *a.*[3] 3.

1851 BORROW *Lavengro* lxxi, You were always fond of what was Roman. **1857** —— *Romany Rye* vi, Mr. Petulengro was dressed in Roman fashion.

Romanaccio (roma'nattʃo). [It.] A modern dialect spoken in the city of Rome.

1963 *Guardian* 6 June 11/2 Cardinal Agagianian..speaks 11 languages including Romanaccio (Roman cockney). **1973** M. WEST *Salamander* ii. 163 A stable-boy laughed and I flew at him, clawing and punching and screaming in Romanaccio.

†**Roma'nality.** *Obs.*$^{-1}$ [f. ROMAN *a.*[1]] The Roman Catholic faith.

1637 BASTWICK *Litany* III. 19 Amongst the which are all those that are spaniolized and any wayes affect Romanality.

Roman candle. [ROMAN *a.*[1]]

1. A cylindrical fire-work, which throws out a succession of stars.

1834 MARRYAT *P. Simple* (1863) 51 There were silver stars and golden stars, blue lights and Catherine-wheels,.. Grecian-fires and Roman-candles. **1859** F. A. GRIFFITHS *Artil. Man.* (1861) 280 The signal rocket stars are also the best for Roman candles.

2. A parachute jump on which the parachute fails to open; a parachute which fails to open. Also (in full ***Roman candle landing***) an unsatisfactory landing by an aircraft. *slang.*

1943 HUNT & PRINGLE *Service Slang* 56 *Roman candles*. 'When a parachute simply fails to open. (Of course, on landing, you dash to the stores and get another.)' **1943** C. H. WARD-JACKSON *Piece of Cake* 52 *Roman candle landing*, a bad landing. **1952** *Chambers's Jrnl.* May 261/2 It is not so very long ago since parachute-jumping was a stunt indulged in by steel-nerved men of boundless courage performing in air circuses. In those days, the sight of some hapless individual streaming to earth with a 'Roman candle' (an undeveloped 'chute) was not exceptional. **1959** *Chambers's 20th Cent. Dict.* Add. 1389/1 *Roman candle*, a bad landing by aeroplane: a landing by parachute when the parachute fails to open. —v.i. to make such a landing. **1961** E. WAUGH *Unconditional Surrender* II. v. 141 The first thing the commandant asked when I reported Crouchback's accident. 'A Roman Candle?' he asked. **1976** A. WHITE *Long Silence* vii. 59, I experienced the sense of relief that says, 'This time, no roman candle!'

3. A Roman Catholic. *slang.*

1941 G. KERSH *They die with their Boots Clean* II. 57 There's services for C. of E-ers and Roman Candles. **1959** I. & P. OPIE *Lore & Lang. Schoolch.* xvi. 344 In Staines, Catholics are 'Roman Candles', and R.C. children call the Protestants 'Old Proddy Dogs'. **1974** P. HAINES *Tea at Gunter's* ii. 18 She said: 'I've noticed you lots—you're a Roman candle, aren't you?' 'What?'..'*R.C.*, silly.'

Hence **Roman-'candle** *v. intr.*, to make a parachute jump with a parachute that fails to open.

1959 [see sense 2 above]. **1975** tr. *Melchior's Sleeper Agent* (1976) III. 230 *He had roman-candled!* The chute had not opened! He was plunging toward oblivion.

'Roman 'Catholic, *sb.* and *a.* [ROMAN *a.* 10.

The use of this composite term in place of the simple *Roman, Romanist*, or *Romish*, which had acquired an invidious sense, appears to have arisen in the early years of the 17th century. For conciliatory reasons it was employed in the negotiations connected with the Spanish Match (1618–24), and appears in formal documents relating to this, printed by Rushworth (1659), I. 85–89. After that date it was generally adopted as a non-controversial term, and has long been the recognized legal and official designation, though in ordinary use *Catholic* alone is very frequently employed.]

A. *sb.* A member or adherent of the Roman Church; = CATHOLIC *sb.* 2.

1605 SANDYS *Europæ Speculum* K3b, Some Roman-Catholiques will not say grace..when a Protestant is present. **1615** DAY *Festivals* 159 Nor meant it Roman Catholiques, but good true Catholiques indeed. **1655** FULLER *Ch. Hist.* II. 146 There was a stiffe Roman Catholick (as they delight to term themselves) otherwise a man well accomplished. **1715** ADDISON *Freeholder* (1751) 12 Having been joined by a considerable Reinforcement of Roman-Catholicks. **1791** BOSWELL *Johnson* an. 1763, 5 Aug., In the afternoon the gentlewoman talked violently against the Roman Catholicks. **1849** MACAULAY *Hist. Eng.* ii. I. 231 His brother and heir presumptive was known to be a bigoted Roman Catholic. **1872** FREEMAN *Sk. European Hist.* xvii. §16 By the admission of the Roman Catholics to equal rights with Protestants.

transf. **1629** H. BURTON *Truth's Triumph* 51 To reconcile this Catholicke word Imputation, to the Church of Rome, and to make it a Roman-Catholicke.

B. *adj.* Of or belonging to the Church of Rome; = CATHOLIC *a.* 7.

1614 T. GENTLEMAN *England's Way to Wealth* 18 All those Romaine Catholicke and Papisticall countries. **1623** in Rushworth *Hist. Coll.* (1659) I. 86 That as well the most gratious Infanta as all her Servants and Family shall have free use and public Exercise of the Roman Catholick Religion. **1678** EVELYN *Diary* 15 Nov., Divers..were sent to the Towre, and all the Roman Catholic Lords were by a new act..excluded the Parliament. **1712** ADDISON *Spect.* No. 458 ¶5 English Gentlemen who travel into Roman-Catholick Countries. **1756–7** tr. *Keysler's Trav.* (1760) I. 14 The largeness and opulence of the lands in the Roman catholic districts. **1791** *Act 31 Geo. III*, c. 32 §11 Any Roman Catholick Ecclesiastick. *Ibid.* §16 As a Roman Catholick School-master or School-mistress. **1829** *Act 10 Geo. IV*, c. 7 (*R.C. Emancipation*), Certain Restraints and Disabilities..imposed on the Roman Catholic Subjects of His Majesty. **1872** FREEMAN *Sk. European Hist.* xiii. §10 This Council..fixed the Roman Catholic doctrines and practices in a much more rigid shape.

Hence **'Roman-Ca'tholically, -'Catholicly** *adv.*; **'Roman Ca'tholicism.**

1793 [see CATHOLICLY *adv.* 2b]. *a* **1823** D'ISRAELI *Cur. Lit.* (1866) 88 Sigismund lost both his crowns by his bigoted attachment to Roman Catholicism. **1842** MRS. TROLLOPE *Visit Italy* I. iii. 43 Many among them [*sc.* churches in Genoa] must be accounted, Roman-catholically speaking, as very rich. **1870–76** [see CATHOLICISM 1c].

'Roman Catho'licity. [f. ROMAN CATHOLIC *sb.* and *a.* + -ITY.] Roman Catholicism.

1806 M. B. PEMBRIDGE *R.C. Church Vindicated* i. 40 These edifices still bear the external signature of Roman Catholicity. **1965** E. O'BRIEN *August is Wicked Month* xvii. 218 'It's your Roman Catholicity,' he said.

romance (rəʊ'mæns, 'rəʊmæns), *sb.* and *a.* Forms: α. 4 **romanz, romaunz**, 4–6 (8–9) **romans(e**, 5–6 **romauns, romayns**; *Sc.* 5 **romanys**, 5–6 **romanis**. β. 4–5 **romaunce** (4 **ra-**), 5 **romawnce, -ounce**, 4– **romance**. [In ME., a. OF. *romanz, romans* (cf. ROMAUNT):—pop. L. **romanice* adv. f. L. *Rōmānicus*: see ROMANIC. Cf. Cat. *romans*, Sp. and Pg. *romance*, Prov. *roumanso*, It. *romanzo*, med.L. *romancia, -ium*. The spelling with *-aunce, -ance* was very early adopted in English, probably on the analogy of abstract sbs. In ME. verse the stress is commonly on the first syllable, except in rimes.

The same pattern of stress is reported in N. Amer. and non-standard British pronunciation; cf. the following: **1921** MENCKEN *Amer. Lang.* (rev. ed.) vii. 209 The chief movement in American..would seem to be toward throwing the accent upon the first syllable... I might add ..*defect, excess, address, magazine, decoy* and *romance.* **1939** N. MONSARRAT *This is Schoolroom* xvii. 385 The dance-band world..has given us a new pronunciation—'bokay' for bouquet, 'rómance' thus accented. **1966** C. MACKENZIE *My Life & Times* V. 193 The cinema audience wants rómance. We must give them rómance. **1971** J. FLEMING *Grim Death & Barrow Boys* vii. 87 It's the end of ro-mance, is marriage.]

I. 1. The vernacular language of France, as opposed to Latin. In later use also extended to related forms of speech, as Provençal and Spanish, and now commonly used as a generic or collective name for the whole group of languages descended from Latin.

c **1330** R. BRUNNE *Chron. Wace* (Rolls) 16701 Frankysche speche ys cald Romaunce, So sey þis clerkes & men of Fraunce. **1338** —— *Chron.* (1810) 205 Þis þat I haf said it is Pers sawe, Als he in romance laid, þer after gan I drawe. *c* **1400** *Rom. Rose* 2170 Til I..undo the signifiaunce Of this dreme into Romaunce. *c* **1407** LYDG. *Reson & Sens.* 4883 Swich a book in Romaunce Was neuer yet y-made in Fraunce. *c* **1450** LOVELICH *Grail* lii. 1064 It is ful Syker,.. that he which In Romawnce this drow Owte, he knew ful lytel Of Seynt Graal.

1612 BREREWOOD *Lang. & Relig.* 250 The Italian, French, and Spanish: all which in a barbarous word have been called Romanse, as you would say, Roman. **1614** SELDEN *Titles Hon.* 44 In the Prouinciall languages or Romances (as the French and Spanish are called). **1708** MADOX *Exchequer* Pref. Ep. p. xii, With them [Spaniards] Romance is used even at this day to signify the Castilian or genuine language of Spain. **1775** *Phil. Trans.* LXVI. 146 Authors, who deny that the Teutonic had any share in the composition of the Romance, since the Franks found it already established when they entered Gaul. **1823** ROSCOE tr. *Sismondi's Lit. Eur.* (1846) I. vii. 188 The two languages of the people, the rustic Romance, and the Theotisque, or German. **1838** GUEST *Hist. Eng. Rhythm* I. 316 The Romance of Oc. **1841** *Penny Cycl.* XX. 81/2 The process of corruption of the Latin into Romance [in Spain] was the same as in France and Italy. **1891** *Athenæum* 18 July 90/1 The tables of approximate synonyms from Saxon, Romance, and Latin.

Comb. **1882** E. A. FREEMAN *Lect. Amer. Audiences* I. v. 155 Did not the Norman Conquest..bring with it a settlement of strangers, of Romance-speaking strangers, enough to destroy all pretence on the part of the English nation to pure Teutonic descent? **1883** *Science* II. 115/1 The present Romance-speaking population of Roumania. **1964** Romance-based [see *Latin-based* s.v. LATIN *sb.* 5]. **1964** E. PALMER tr. *Martinet's Elem. Gen. Linguistics* v. 150 The Romance-speaking clerks of the eighteenth century..used ..variously a local Romance language and another language, Latin.

b. *attrib.* or as *adj.* Derived from, or representing, the old Roman tongue; descended from Latin. Also, composed in, using, etc., a vernacular tongue of Latin origin.

Cf. older F. *langue romance*, mod.F. *langues romanes.*

1420 *Durham Wills* (Surtees) I. 65 Item lego Matildi filiæ Roberti de Hilton..filiolæ meæ unum romance boke, is callyd ye gospelles.

1756–82 WARTON *Ess. Pope* I. v. 290 The Latin language ..was succeeded by what was called the Romance-tongue. **1776** BURNEY *Hist. Music* (1789) II. iv. 248 The Normans made it their boast..that they spoke the Romanse language with purity. **1841** *Penny Cycl.* XX. 81/1 That [12th] century was the brilliant age of Romance poetry. **1871** EARLE *Philol. Eng. Tongue* §351 Some substantives which have come to us through the French, from the southern Romance languages, Provençal or Spanish.

c. = ROMANSH.

1862 LATHAM *Compar. Philol.* 647 Of the Romance proper, the two main dialects are—1. That of the valley of the Rhine. 2. That of the valley of the Inn. *Ibid.*, At the present time the Romance phonesis is largely Slavonic.

II. 2. A tale in verse, embodying the adventures of some hero of chivalry, esp. of those of the great cycles of mediæval legend, and belonging both in matter and form to the ages of knighthood; also, in later use, a prose tale of a similar character.

Orig. denoting a composition in the vernacular (French, etc.), as contrasted with works in Latin.

α. **13..** *Coer. de L.* 7 Fele romanses men make newe Of good knyghtes, strong and trewe. **1375** BARBOUR *Bruce* I. 446 The romanys now begynnys her Off men that war in gret distress. *c* **1400** *Destr. Troy* 3896 Was neuer red in no Romanse of Renke vpon erthe So well louyt with all ledys. *c* **1475** *Partenay* 6417 Yf any man demaunde..What me shall call thys Romans souerain, hit name the Romans as of partenay. *c* **1500** *Lancelot* 209 One to my wit It war so gret o charg For to translait the romans of that knycht. **1530** PALSGR. 263/2 Romauns, *romant.*

β. *c* **1330** *Arth. & Merlin* 31 (Kölbing), Now ich ȝou telle þis romaunce: A king hiȝt while sir Costaunce. *c* **1374** CHAUCER *Troylus* III. 980 He..tok a lyght and fond his contenaunce, As for to loken vp on an old romaunce. *c* **1400** *Laud Troy Bk.* 18640 And thus was Troye dryuen doun.., As in this romaunce men may rede. *c* **1440** *Promp. Parv.* 436/2 Romawnce idem quod Ryme. **1589** PUTTENHAM *Eng. Poesie* II. [i]x. (Arb.) 97 Stories of old time, as the tale of Sir Topas, the reportes of Beuis of Southampton, Guy of Warwicke, Adam Bell, and Clymme of the Clough and such other old Romances or historicall rimes. **1662** J. DAVIES tr. *Olearius' Voy. Ambass.* 199 The Grand Rustam.. is also the only celebrated Heros of all their Romances. **1765** PERCY *Essay* in *Reliques* III. p. x, Proof that the old metrical Romances throw light on our old writers in prose. **1778** WARTON *Hist. Eng. Poetry* IV, The romance of the Squire of Low Degree. **1802** RITSON *Anc. Met. Rom.* I. p. xxxiv, The first metrical romance..is the famous *chanson de Roland.* **1844** HALLIWELL *Thornton Rom.* p. vi, The original of the English version of Perceval is an Anglo-Norman romance. **1881** HERRTAGE *Charles the Grete* (E.E.T.S.) Introd. v, A translation of the French prose romance of Fierabras.

b. Used without article.

In some cases perh. collectively or as a plural.

α. *a* **1300** *Cursor M.* 2 Man yhernes rimes for to here, And romans red on maneres sere, Of Alisaundur [etc.]. *a* **1310** in Wright *Lyric Poetry* ix. 34 Heo hath a mury mouht to mele, ..Romaunz forte rede. **1375** BARBOUR *Bruce* III. 437 The king..Red to thaim..Romanys off worthi Ferambrace. *a* **1400** *Emare* 215 To þe palys þey ȝede in fere, In romans as we rede. *c* **1470** *Golagros & Gaw.* 878 Oft in romanis I reid: Airly sporne, late speid. **1502** *Ord. Crysten Men* (W. de W. 1506) Prol., They y[t] loue bettir romayns of warres. **1513** DOUGLAS *Æneis* v. Prol. 14 Sum plesance takis in romanis that he redis.

β. **13..** *K. Alis.* 9 Off hey dedys men rede romance,.. Off Rowelond, and of Olyuer. **13..** *Gaw. & Gr. Knt.* 2521 As hit is breued in þe best boke of romaunce. *c* **1400** *Laud Troy Bk.* 13304 Iff he be ferd of any chaunce, Lete him sitte & rede romaunce!

3. A fictitious narrative in prose of which the scene and incidents are very remote from those of ordinary life; *esp.* one of the class prevalent in the 16th and 17th centuries, in which the story is often overlaid with long disquisitions and digressions. Also occas., a long poem of a similar type.

The immediate source of this use was app. F. *roman.*

1638 BAKER tr. *Balzac's Lett.* (vol. III.) 30, I make some choice, and runne not after all Spanish Romances with equal passion. **1666** BOYLE *Occas. Refl., Disc.* III. ii, Those voluminous Romances that are too often the only Books which make up the Libraries of Gallants, and fill the Closets of Ladies. **1727** GAY *Begg. Op.* I. xiii, I find in the Romance you lent me none of the great Heroes were ever false in love. **1759** JOHNSON *Idler* No. 84 ¶2 In romances, when the wide field of possibility lies open to invention, the incidents may easily be made more numerous. **1842** BRANDE *Dict. Sci.*, etc. s.v., In the seventeenth century Le Sage naturalised the Spanish romance in France. **1895** ARBER *Greene's Menaphon* Introd. xvi, In this Pastoral Romance..there is the least possible Plot.

b. A romantic novel or narrative.

1816 [see HISTORICAL *a.* 3]. **1831** SCOTT *Pirate* Introd., The very moderate degree of local knowledge..which he has endeavoured to embody in the romance of the Pirate. **1850** THACKERAY *Pendennis* li, He..made woful and savage onslaught on a poem and a romance which came before him for judgment. **1886** *Illustr. Lond. News* 10 July 26 My addictiveness to the perusal of modern romances.

c. *transf.* and *fig.* (perh. partly from 2).

1823 SCOTT *Let.* in *Westm. Gaz.* (1905) 22 Nov. 2/1 Abbotsford..is..a sort of romance in architecture. **1867** FREEMAN *Norm. Conq.* (1877) I. 267 In the hands of William of Malmesbury the story becomes a romance. **1883** *Cent. Mag.* Oct. 823/1 English associations are to us utterly delightful, and London especially a huge romance. **1894** H. DRUMMOND *Ascent Man* 1 The last romance of Science..is the Story of the Ascent of Man.

4. A Spanish historical ballad or short poem of a certain form.

From Sp. *romance*, whence also F. *romance*. Attributive uses, as ***romance-book, -verse***, etc., are common in works on Spanish literature.

1605 VERSTEGAN *Dec. Intell.* (1628) 200 The Spaniards calling to this day such Verses as they make in their language, by the name of Romances. **1706** STEVENS *Sp. Dict.*, *Romancero*, one that Composes that sort of Verses, call'd Romances. **1756–82** WARTON *Ess. Pope* I. v. 290 Every piece of poetry was at that time denominated a romance. **1832** IRVING *Alhambra* I. 297 For some time a vague intercourse was kept up by popular songs and romances. **1847** tr. *Bouterwek's Hist. Span. Lit.* 87 Another publication ..appeared in 1604, and contains upwards of a thousand romances and songs. **1893** H. B. CLARKE *Spanish Lit.* 45 The earliest printed romances appear in the *Cancionero General* of 1511.

b. *Mus.* A short vocal or instrumental piece of a simple or informal character.

[**1797** *Monthly Mag.* III. 306 The term Romance, as used by foreign musicians, is not so familiar with us as to be universally understood.]

1876 *Encycl. Brit.* V. 685/2 The concerto for pianoforte with accompaniment of the orchestra in E may be instanced. Here the adagio takes the form of a romance. **1881** *Grove's Dict. Music* III. 147 *Romance*, a term of very vague signification, answering in music to the same term in poetry, where the characteristics are rather those of personal sentiment and expression than of precise form.

5. That class of literature which consists of romances; romantic fiction. *spec.* a love story; that class of literature which consists of love stories.

1667 MILTON *P.L.* I. 580 And what resounds In Fable or Romance of Uthers Son. **1762** HURD *Lett. Chivalry & Romance* v. 39 The constant mixture..of pagan fable with the fairy tales of Romance. **1798** CHARLOTTE SMITH *Young Philos.* I. 110 A young lady..very deeply read in romance and novels. **1820** KEATS *Isabella* xlix, O for the gentleness of old Romance, The simple plaining of a minstrel's song! *a* **1854** H. REED *Lect. Eng. Lit.* ix. (1878) 273 Scott was to establish his fame as the great writer of historical romance. **1891** H. E. WATTS *Cervantes* 62 The chorus of detractors was swelled by all those..whose taste in romance had been ridiculed. **1936** 'G. ORWELL' *Keep Aspidistra Flying* x. 264 When a customer demanded a book of this category or that, ..'Sex' or 'Crime' or 'Wild West' or 'Romance' (always with the accent on the *o*), Gordon was ready with expert advice. **1954** [see FANTASY, PHANTASY *sb.* 4f].

personif. **1647** COWLEY *Mistr., Innocent Ill* iii, Though savage, and rock-hearted those Appear, that weep not ev'n Romances woes.

fig. **1800** WORDSW. *A narrow Girdle of rough Stones* 38 Lady of the Mere, Sole-sitting by the shores of old romance.

b. Romantic or imaginative character or quality; redolence or suggestion of, association with, the adventurous and chivalrous. *spec.* a love affair; idealistic character or quality in a love affair.

1801 MOORE *Morality*, In feeling's sweet romance. **1807–8** IRVING *Salmag.* (1824) 163 Oh! my romance of youth is past—Dear airy dreams, too bright to last. **1838** DICKENS *Nich. Nick.* xviii, Charity must have its romance. **1873** W.

BLACK *Pr. Thule* xxiv. 392 Romance goes out of a man's head when the hair gets grey. **1916** G. B. SHAW *Overruled* 81, I felt my youth slipping away without ever having had a romance in my life; for marriage is all very well; but it isnt romance. Theres nothing wrong in it, you see. **1922** JOYCE *Ulysses* 280 Chorusgirl's romance. Letters read out for breach of promise. **1942** T. RATTIGAN *Flare Path* I. 26 He was on a week's leave, and we were married before he went back to his Squadron. What the papers would call a whirlwind wartime romance. **1951** in M. McLuhan *Mech. Bride* (1967) 24/2 She loved him with another woman's body ..one of the tensest, most passionate romances you have ever experienced. **1960** *Times* 28 Sept. 15/4 Harry, undaunted by a succession of parties at which he has done nothing whatever, always attends in the hope of finding romance.

6. An extravagant fiction, invention, or story; a wild or wanton exaggeration; a picturesque falsehood. Also without article (cf. ROMAN CATHOLIC *sb.* and *a.*).

1497 in W. M. Williams *Ann. Founders' Co.* (1867) 46 Recvyed..of Maister Chamb[er]leyne of London for a fyne lost by Robt. Wells for romaunce, ij d. **1638** SIR T. HERBERT *Trav.* (ed. 2) 241 A drink..not so much regarded for those good properties, as from a Romance that it was invented and brew'd by Gabriel. **1667** DRYDEN & DK. NEWCASTLE *Sir M. Mar-all* II. ii, This is romance—I'll not believe a word on't. **1686** tr. *Chardin's Coronat. Solyman* 108 It was but a Romance, tho a pernicious Romance, which the General of the Slaves had compos'd to set those two Lords together by the Ears. **1717** J. KEILL *Anim. Œcon.* Pref. (1738) p. xli, The late Explications of Diseases are only Philosophical Romances. **1789** BELSHAM *Ess.* I. vii. 131 Such a view..of human life, appears to me no better than a romance. **1849** MACAULAY *Hist. Eng.* ix. II. 439 This romance rests on no evidence, and..seems hardly to deserve confutation.

7. *Comb.* **a.** Objective and obj. gen., as ***romance-maker***, ***-monger***, ***-writer***; ***romance-making***, ***-reading***, ***-weaving***, ***-writing***; ***romance-inspiring***, ***-making***, ***-wards*** adjs.

*c*1300 *Havelok* 2327 Romanz reding on þe bok. *c*1440 *Promp. Parv.* 436/2 Romawnce makare, *melopes.* **1713** ADDISON *Guardian* No. 139 ¶1 Your romance writers are likewise a set of men whose authority I shall build upon very little in this case. **1824** CAMPBELL *Theodoric* 53 Conscious of romance-inspiring charms. **1829** SCOTT *Wav.* Gen. Pref., A work which formed a sort of essay piece, and gave me hope that I might in time become free of the craft of Romance-writing. **1861** LD. BROUGHAM *Brit. Const.* xi. 153 The favourite theme of praise with all our romance-mongers. **1876** *Westm. Rev.* XLIX. 361 The novelist proper studies to represent his little world as the great world is; whereas the romance-writer..builds an ideal world. **1887** *Contemp. Rev.* LI. 172 Really good romance writing is the most difficult art practised by the sons of men. **1890** L. C. D'OYLE *Notches* 97 We were none of us..naturally of a romance-making bent of mind. **1904** 'MARK TWAIN' in *Harper's Weekly* 10 Dec. 11/1 There was no romance-reading that night. **1904** W. H. HUDSON *Green Mansions* 2 Let us hope that now, at last, the romance-weaving will come to an end. **1920** R. MACAULAY *Potterism* VI. iii. 228 He was also leaning romancewards and departing from the realm of pure truth. **1979** *N. & Q.* Feb. 90/2 Hanning tends to brush aside these technical difficulties of romance-writing.

b. Similative, as ***romance-like*** adv.; and instrumental, as ***romance-empurpled***, ***-like***, ***-hallowed*** adjs.

1620–55 I. JONES *Stone-Heng* (1725) 71 Romance-like hatched out of their own Brains. **1868** M. COLLINS *Sweet Anne Page* I. 232 Romance-empurpled Monte Cristo. **1888** SAXBY *Lads of Lunda* 127 The romance-hallowed regions of Robinson Crusoe and Mungo Park. **1971** K. MILLETT *Sexual Politics* (1972) I. i. 5 That Ida has dressed herself in a collapsible bathrobe and silk stockings is not only accommodating but almost romance-like.

8. *attrib.*, as ***romance-novel***, ***-literature***, ***thriller***; also passing into *adj.* with the sense: Having the character or attributes associated with romance; chivalrous; romantic.

1653 DOROTHY OSBORNE *Lett.* (1888) 116 He is resolved to be a most romance squire, and go in quest of some enchanted damsel. **1654** *Ibid.* 223 Can there be a romancer story than ours would make, if the conclusion prove happy? **1693** LOCKE in Fox Bourne *Locke* (1876) II. 243, I wonder, that..men should return again to the romance way of physic. **1820** T. MITCHELL *Aristoph.* I. p. lxxxv, The romance-novel..was a species of literary guilt, left for the invention of our own days. *a*1842 ARNOLD *Hist. Rome* (1846) II. xxvii. 89 The poetical or romance accounts of these last Gaulish invasions. **1890** 'R. BOLDREWOOD' *Col. Reformer* (1891) 113 An occasional romance gleam through the somewhat prosaic mist of his ordinary day-dreams. **1905** *N. Amer. Rev.* CLXXX. 5 You have made the American home..beautiful with your..noble romance-literature. **1961** *Times Lit. Suppl.* 8 Dec. 2/1 The growing success of the romance-thriller, where the basic plot of virgin-marries-older-man is sharpened..by often well-devised and dramatic villainy. **1975** *Listener* 20 Nov. 685/1 The many competent women writers of 'romance thrillers'.

Hence †**ro'mancealist**, a writer of romances. **ro'mancean** *a.*, pertaining to the period of old romances. **ro'manceful** *a.*, full of romance; romantic. **ro'manceishness**, tendency towards what is romantic. **ro'manceless** *a.*, unromantic. **ro'mancelet**, a short romance.

1652 URQUHART *Jewel* Wks. (1834) 256 Le Sieur de Balzak, who, by the quaintest *Romancealists of France,..was..esteemed in eloquence to have surpassed Ciceron. **1804** SOUTHEY *Lett.* (1856) i. 274 Is this only mere fiction; or had they in the *romancean days any 'second sight' of the diving bell. **1868** F. E. PAGET *Lucretia* 108 The *romanceful tragedy of the poor bride, Ginevra of Modena. **1835** BECKFORD *Recoll.* 53 At length he could bear with my *romanceishness no longer. **1856** *Leisure Hour* V. 67/2 He had just reached the quay, and—*romanceless as he undoubtedly was—was gazing with some interest on the placid water. **1876** F. HARRISON *Ess.* (1886) 219 Jane Austen would write little *romancelets to her girl correspondents.

romance (rəʊ'mæns), *v.* Also 4 **romauncen**. [f. the sb., or ad. F. *romancer* (OF. *romancier* to write, etc., in Romance), = Sp. and Pg. *romancear*, It. *romanzare*.]

†**1.** *intr.* To compose in verse. *Obs.*$^{-1}$

13.. *St. Gregory* (Vernon MS.) 19 Nou wol ich ariht biginne Romauncen of þis ilke song.

2. a. To exaggerate or invent after the fashion of romances; to talk hyperbolically.

1671 J. GLANVILL *Further Disc. Stubbe* 6 I'le be bound to believe you, yea even when you Romance about Jamaica. **1707** NORRIS *Treat. Humility* vii. 304 How strangely some vain people, when they are upon this bragging strain, will romance upon themselves and their families. **1764** SMOLLETT *Trav.* (1766) I. 264, I am apt to believe the fellow romanced a little, in order to render the adventure the more marvellous. **1807** G. CHALMERS *Caledonia* I. II. i. 232 It is quite allowable, for the chroniclers of the middle ages to romance in this manner. **1855** MACAULAY *Hist. Eng.* xviii. IV. 216 Now, when, for the first time, they told the truth, they were supposed to be romancing. **1877** 'RITA' *Vivienne* I. ii, 'Gaston is romancing as usual,' said a beautiful brunette.

b. To have romantic ideas; to use romantic language.

1849 C. BRONTE *Shirley* II. xii. 292 That I am a 'romancing chit of a girl' is a mere conjecture on your part: I never romanced to you. **1870** LOWELL *Stud. Wind., Condesc. Foreigners*, While I had been romancing with myself, the street lamps had been lighted.

3. a. *trans.* To say hyperbolically. *rare*$^{-1}$.

1729 FIELDING *Temple Beau.* III. x, You may justly say of them, what a certain philosopher romanced of learning—'That you know nothing at all'.

b. To persuade *into* something by romancing.

1825 *Examiner* 609/2 The merits and conduct of a family which we are to be romanced into a legitimate regard for.

4. To translate into a Romance tongue.

1878 tr. *Lacroix's Sci. & Lit. Middle Ages* 365 Various popular songs which had already been *romanced*—that is to say, written in the vulgar or Romance tongue.

5. *trans.* To have a romance or affair with, to court.

1942 BERREY & VAN DEN BARK *Amer. Thes. Slang.* §354/4 *Court*,..race, romance, run with, run *or* chase after, rush. **1956** B. HOLIDAY *Lady sings Blues* (1973) vi. 59, I was accused of romancing everyone in the band. **1970** M. BUTTERWORTH *Vanishing Act* xi. 125 A good-looking chap.. could do a bit of counter-jumping and romance the lady customers..if he had the cheek. **1976** T. GIFFORD *Cavanaugh Quest* v. 79 They were working on my kind of music... I'd romanced Anne to old stuff like that and we'd made love to Claude Thornhill recordings. **1980** N. DEMPSTER in *Daily Mail* 10 Apr. 19/3 He has been romancing Antonia for a year.

‖**romancé** (rɔmɑ̃se), *ppl. a.* Fem. **romancée**. [Fr., f. *romancer* (see ROMANCE *v.*).] Fictionalized, rendered in the form of a novel; *spec.* of a biography.

The fem. *romancée* is used in quot. 1962 because of Fr. *la biographie*.

1938 *Times Lit. Suppl.* 10 Sept. p. v/2 Signor Falta carefully avoids whatever may appear *romancé*. **1962** *Times* 5 July 17/4 The result is a solid, readable biography, slightly *romancée*.

romancer (rəʊ'mænsə(r)). Also 7 **romanzer**. [f. ROMANCE *v.* + -ER; in early use after OF. *romanceour*, later *romancier*, = Sp. *romancero*, It. *romanziere* (whence perh. the form in *-zer*).]

1. The author of a romance; a writer of romances or romantic fiction.

1338 R. BRUNNE *Chron.* (1810) 157 Þe Romancer it sais, R[ichard] did mak a pele, On kastelle wise alle wais, wrouht of tre fulle welle.

1654 VILVAIN *Th. Theol.* 191 Fancies as fabulous Poets or Romanzers devise. **1660** N. INGELO *Bentiv. & Ur.* I. Pref., He, as it may be said of other Romancers, hath made the fabulous rind so thick, that few can see through it into the useful sence. **1738** WARBURTON *Div. Leg.* I. 19 These political Romancers from Plato to this Author. **1756–82** WARTON *Ess. Pope* I. VII. 355, I can find none of this age, but barren chroniclers, and harsh romancers in rhime. **1830** SCOTT *Demonol.* x. 364 The tale might have made the fortune of a romancer. **1847** H. MILLER *Test. Rocks* ii. (1857) 80 Dragons as strange as were ever feigned by romancer of the middle ages. **1882** *Athenæum* No. 2828. 20 In him has passed away the last of the historical romancers who received their impulse from Scott.

transf. **1856** LEVER *Martins of Cro' M.* 14 Your fashionable architect is indeed a finished romancer.

2. One who deals in extravagant fictions; an inventor of false history; a fantastic liar.

1663 *Proposal to use no Conscience* 5 Those who are given to lying shall be called Romancers or Historians. **1671** J. GLANVILL *Further Disc. Stubbe* 7 So silly a Romancer are you. **1820** T. MITCHELL *Aristoph. Clouds* (1838) 65 See that romancer [*sc.* Philostratus] in his life of Apollonius. **1864** PUSEY *Lect. Daniel* viii. 552 Rationalists, like other romancers, 'ought to have good memories'.

3. A romantic person. *rare*$^{-1}$.

1748 RICHARDSON *Clarissa* (1768) V. 110, I..thought it to be a feigned or Love-name... Most of the fair Romancers have in their early womanhood chosen Love-names.

Hence **ro'manceress**. *rare*$^{-1}$.

1841 THACKERAY *Men & Pictures* Wks. 1900 XIII. 378 The mild compositions of the French romanceresses pall on the palate.

†**ro'mancial**, *a.* *Obs.*$^{-1}$ [f. ROMANCE *sb.* + -IAL.] Romance-like, romantic.

1653 R. SANDERS *Physiogn.* b 2 b, This subject is best seen in a homely and plain dress, and will not admit of a Romancial strain.

ro'mancical, *a. rare.* [f. ROMANCE + -ICAL.]

1. Of the nature of romances; romantic.

1656 DUCHESS OF NEWCASTLE *Natures Pictures* c 2 b, Those Tales I call my Romancicall Tales. **1667** —— *Life Dk. Newcastle* Pref. (1886) p. lvii, Telling romancical falsehoods for historical truths. **1825** LAMB *Lett.* (1888) II. 138 That all Spain overflowed with romancical books (as Madge Newcastle calls them).

2. Composing or inventing romances.

1822 LAMB *Elia* I. *Compl. Decay of Beggars*, The poets and romancical writers (as dear Margaret Newcastle would call them). **1886** *Academy* 31 July 69/1 The author of *Grandmother's Money* is an old romancical hand. **1889** *Sat. Rev.* 18 May 619/2 The representations of poets and romancical writers.

ro'mancing, *vbl. sb.* Also occas. with stress ('rəʊ-). [f. ROMANCE *v.* + -ING[1].] The action of the vb.; use of extravagant fiction or invention; fictitious narration.

1695 D. TURNER *Apol. Chyrurg.* 53 Launching out into a further liberty of romancing. **1719** WATERLAND *Vind. Chr. Div.* 102 Writing of History by Invention, is really Romancing. **1741** RICHARDSON *Pamela* (1824) I. 90 But this, to be sure, is horrid romancing! **1849** EASTWICK *Dry Leaves* 181 Commend me to a Persian for romancing. **1879** G. MEREDITH *Egoist* II. vii. 156 Oh! Mrs. Montague, that is what the country people call roemancing... **1884** *Publishers' Circular* 1 Nov. 1106/1 The mischief done by historical romancings has been very considerable.

ro'mancing, *ppl. a.* [-ING[2].] That romances; indulging in fanciful inventions; romantic.

1710 *Medley* No. 12. 2 This grave, yet sometimes pleasant and romancing Author, writ several Discourses. **1728** MORGAN *Hist. Algiers* II. iii. 246 The idle Story, picked up by Dr. Tassy out of that romancing Manuscript. **1766** GOLDSM. *Vic. W.* xxiii, A story, my child, told us by a grave, though sometimes a romancing historian. **1855** SMEDLEY *H. Coverdale* xxxi, If that had been my only reason for accepting my romancing husband. **1865** LIVINGSTONE *Zambesi* xix. 389 Marvels equal to the most romancing tales of ancient travellers.

ro'mancingly, *adv. rare.* [f. ROMANCING *ppl. a.* + -LY[2].] In a romancing manner.

1908 H. JAMES *Spoils of Poynton* p. xii, By just so much would the muse of 'dialogue', most usurping influence of all the romancingly invoked, be routed without ceremony.

ro'mancist. [ad. Sp. (and Pg.) *romancista*, or f. ROMANCE *sb.* + -IST.] A writer or composer of romances; a romantic novelist.

1656 BLOUNT *Glossogr.*, Romancist (from the Spa. *Romancista*), one that composes such Romances. **1866** READE *G. Gaunt* I. 101 He told his story like an attorney, and not like a Romancist. **1883** D. C. MURRAY *Hearts* I. 243 Much oftener than the romancist cares to fancy.

ro'mancity. *nonce-wd.* [f. ROMANCE *sb.* + -ITY.] A romantic quality or characteristic.

1828 *Sporting Mag.* XXII. 238, I scarcely know any groupe..in which there are more oddities, vanities, jealousies, romancities, fopperies and fancies.

ro'mancize, *v. nonce-wd.* [f. ROMANCE *a.* + -IZE.] *trans.* To invest with a Romance or Latin character.

1883 H. KENNEDY tr. *Ten Brink's E. Eng. Lit.* 127 When Lanfranc sat upon the archiepiscopal seat of Canterbury and began energetically to romancise the English church and clergy.

ro'mancy, *sb.* [Alteration of ROMANCE *sb.*; perh. after Sp. *romance* or It. *romanzo*.]

†**1.** A romance; = ROMANCE *sb.* 3. *Obs.*

1621 LADY M. WROTH *Urania* 504 Must..shee be named as if in a Romancy, that relates of Knights, and distressed Damosells, the sad Aduentures? **1652** URQUHART *Jewel* Wks. (1834) 293 A new coined romancy, or strange history of love adventures. **1716** M. DAVIES *Athen. Brit.* II. 394 Our Star-gazing Arian..has..a great many Papers and Manuscripts to prove the Arian Romancies.

2. Romance language. *rare*$^{-1}$.

1836 *Blackw. Mag.* XXXIX. 807 The 'clerk' who translated from the Latin into 'romancy' many a learned treatise.

†**ro'mancy**, *a. Obs.* [f. ROMANCE *sb.* + -Y.] Associated with, or redolent of, romance; romantic.

1654 *Gayton's Pleas. Notes* Pref. Verses, Where others Lamps have burnt long Attick nights, With ranck Romancie oyle to grease their Knights. **1659** WOOD *Life* (O.H.S.) I. 269 An old house situated in a romancey place. **1682** SHADWELL *Lanc. Witches* I, Canst thou think they are such romancy Knights, to take Ladies with nothing?

'**Romandom.** *rare*$^{-1}$. The Roman world.

1887 T. W. ALLIES *Throne Fisherman* 193 Nor did they reverence Rome..as the capital of Romandom.

Romane (rəʊ'meɪn), *a. rare.* [a. F. *romane*, fem. of *roman* ROMAN *a.*[1]] = ROMANCE 1 b.

1837 *Penny Cycl.* IX. 401/1 They speak the Ladin, a dialect of the Romane or Romance language.

Romanée (rɔmane). The name of a vineyard in the commune of Vosne-Romanée in the Côte d'Or department of France used *absol.* to designate the red wine produced there. Also, **Romanée-Conti, Romanée St. Vivant,** similar wines of this commune.

1833 [see MUSIGNY]. **1845** *Encycl. Metrop.* XXV. 1279/1 The Romanée St. Vivant comes from a vineyard called by that name, at a monastery so styled, where it was brought to perfection by the sons of the church. It is little, if any thing, inferior to Romanée-Cônti. **1858** THACKERAY *Virginians* I. xxix. 226 He..could distinguish between Clos Vougeot and Romanée with remarkable skill. **1904** A. BENNETT *Great Man* xvi. 174 He had gathered..that the greatest of all burgundies was Romanée-Conti. **1920** G. SAINTSBURY *Notes on Cellar-bk.* iv. 55 A Romanée of '87 which was good. **1936** BENTLEY & ALLEN *Trent's Own Case* xii. 143 The Romanée St. Vivant 1904 which was to follow the Meursault. **1976** G. MOFFAT *Over Sea to Death* xv. 175 Maynard..ordered a second bottle of Romanée-Conti.

Roma'nensian, *a.* and *sb.* [f. mod.L. *Romanens-is* (see quot.) + -IAN.

1571 *Thirty-nine Articles* xxii, Doctrina Romanensium de purgatorio, indulgentiis,..res est futilis.]

A. *adj.* Tending towards, taking the side of, the Church of Rome.

1885 DIXON *Hist. Ch. Eng.* III. 283 What is that but a Romanensian Antichristian adumbration of the Supper of the Lord? **1891** *Ibid.* IV. 233 The compliant princess.. relieved her devotions of all trace of English, calling to her side a Romanensian chaplain. **1894** FOOTMAN *Hist. Par. Ch. Chipping Lambourn* 92 The internecine struggle..between the Romanensian (to adopt Canon Dixon's phraseology) and the Reforming parties in the Church of England.

B. *sb.* A favourer or adherent of the Roman Church; a Roman Catholic.

1885 DIXON *Hist. Ch. Eng.* III. 385 They were found in the writings of Romanensians. **1891** *Ibid.* IV. 237 To Mary ..all were heretics who were not Romanensians.

†**'Romaner.** *Obs.*$^{-0}$ A Roman.

1570 LEVINS *Manip.* 84 Of Rome, Romaner, *Romanus.*

'Romanes. [Gipsy *Romanes* adv., f. *Romano*: see ROMANY[3].] The gipsy tongue.

1863 SMART in *Trans. Phil. Soc.* App. 5 All our Gypsies in speaking Romanes mix it to a greater or less extent with English. **1875** SMART & CROFTON *Dial. Eng. Gypsies* p. ix, The grammatical forms..of the 'deepest' extant English Romanes. **1898** WATTS-DUNTON *Aylwin* III. ix, She was one of the few Gypsies of either sex who could speak with equal fluency both the English and Welsh Romanes.

Romanesco (rəʊmə'nɛskəʊ), *a.* and *sb.* [It.] (Of or pertaining to) a modern dialect spoken in the city of Rome.

1967 P. E. H. DURSTON *Mortissimo* (1968) xvi. 135 The Romanesco accent had been perfect. **1973** M. WEST *Salamander* i. 56, I had friends there: Castiglione, who used to be a great locksmith.., Giuffredi, the poet, who wrote satires in Romanesco which nobody read any more.

Roma'nese[1]. *rare.* [f. ROMAN *sb.*[1] or *a.*[1] + -ESE, after the native designation.] = ROMANSH.

1841 LATHAM *Eng. Lang.* 392 The precise relation of the Romanese with the other Transalpine Languages has yet to be determined. **1863** *Chambers's Encycl.* V. 113/1 The Latin of the Engadine..and the Romanese differ greatly from Italian, but are far from being Latin.

Roma'nese[2]. *rare.* [f. ROMANY[3] + -ESE.] *pl.* Romany, gipsies.

1857 BORROW *Romany Rye* xii, That sign by which in their wanderings the Romanese gave..intimation as to the direction which they took.

Romanesh, obs. variant of ROMANSH.

Romanesque (rəʊmə'nɛsk), *a.* (and *sb.*) Also 9 -esk. [f. ROMAN *sb.*[1] or *a.*[1] + -ESQUE. Cf. F. *romanesque* romantic.]

1. = ROMANCE *sb.* 1 b.

1715 M. DAVIES *Athen. Brit.* I. 304 The old Norman Dialect was compos'd of those, Theudisque and the provincial and vulgar Romanesque Dialects. **1804** MITFORD *Inquiry* 237 Southern French, formerly distinguished from the northern by the name of the Roman, Romanesk, or Romance language. **1871** EARLE *Philol. Eng. Tongue* §647 The German language has taken more kindly to this Romanesque ornament than English has.

b. *absol.* as *sb.* = ROMANCE *sb.* 1.

1802 RANKEN *Hist. France* II. VII. i. 336 The two languages approached one another and by their union generated the Romanesque or Romans, a new tongue.

2. *Arch.* Prevalent in, or distinctive of, the buildings erected in Romanized Europe between the close of the classical period and the rise of Gothic architecture.

1819 W. GUNN *Inq. Gothic Archit.* 82 Capitals of different orders and magnitudes, surmounted with Romanesque arches. **1842** GWILT *Encycl. Archit.* §286 Strongly marked with the distinguishing features of the Byzantine and Romanesque styles. *a* **1878** SIR G. SCOTT *Lect. Archit.* (1879) I. 15 In England..the same Romanesque architecture had grown up with the new civilisation.

b. Built in the Romanesque style.

1830 WHEWELL *Arch. Notes German Ch.* 48 In the three great Romanesque cathedrals we have a horizontal moulding. **1842** *Murray's Handbk. N. Italy* 133 The early Lombard Romanesque churches exhibit a very peculiar character. **1883** 'OUIDA' *Wanda* I. 33 The prisons and clock tower are Romanesque.

c. Characterized by the use or prevalence of the Romanesque style.

1850 SIR G. SCOTT *Anc. Churches* 79 The architects of the later Romanesque period. **1882-3** SCHAFF *Encycl. Relig. Knowl.* 2139 The Romanesque period of Christian sculpture may be said to begin with the eleventh century.

d. *absol.* as *sb.* The Romanesque style of art or architecture.

1830 WHEWELL *Arch. Notes German Ch.* Pref. 13 Spires, Mentz and Worms, are spoken of..as three great examples of the Romanesque. **1850** SIR G. SCOTT *Anc. Churches* 79, I do not for a moment admit that Romanesque is other than a purely and truly Christian style. **1883** *Longman's Mag.* Nov. 45 Roman art had died and was not yet fully revived in the Romanesque.

3. *Painting.* (See quot.)

1842 BRANDE *Dict. Sci.*, etc., *Romanesque*, in historical painting it consists in the choice of a fanciful subject, rather than one founded on fact. The romanesque is different from romantic; because the latter may be founded on truth, which the former never is.

4. Romantic. ? *Obs.*

1799 MALTHUS *Diary* 24 June (1966) 87 He spoke of him [*sc.* Gustavus III] as..a little too romanesque and bizarre. **1850** C. M. YONGE *Kenneth* xx. 237, 'I know he thinks your point of honour rather romanesque,' said Effie, in her French-English. **1869** K. H. DIGBY *Little Low Bushes* 260 All fair things, lovely,..wild, or romanesque.

'Romanhood. [f. ROMAN *sb.*[1]] The quality of being a Roman.

1839 CARLYLE *Chartism* viii. 157 The red broad mark of Romanhood..has disappeared from the present.

Romani: see ROMANY[3] *sb.* and *a.*

Ro'manian, *a.*[1] [f. ROMANY[3].] Belonging to the Romany or gipsies.

1841 BORROW *Zincali* II. III. ii. 104 The curiosity of some learned individuals..induced them to collect many words of the Romanian language, as spoken in Germany, Hungary, and England. **1857** BORROW *Romany Rye* v, An iron bar, sharp at the bottom, with a kind of arm projecting from the top for..supporting a kettle or cauldron over the fire, and.. called in the Romanian language, 'Kekauviskoe saster'. *Ibid.* xii, The word for leaf in the Romanian language.

Ro'manian, *a.*[2] [f. the name *Roman-us* (*c* 790) + -IAN.] ***Romanian letters*** (see quot.).

1894 W. H. FRERE *Winchester Troper* p. xl, The so-called Romanian letters which were devised at St. Gall (perhaps by Romanus himself) to give directions as to singing.

Romanian (rəʊ'meɪnɪən), *sb.* and *a.*[3] Also **Roumanian, Rumanian.** Cf. ROUMAN *sb.* and *a.* [f. *România*, f. the native name *Român*:—L. *Roman-us*, and -AN, -IAN.

Until recently *Rumanian* was the dominant spelling in the twentieth century, but now *Romanian* is the officially preferred form.]

A. *sb.* **1.** A native or inhabitant of Romania (now the Socialist Republic of Romania).

1868 *Morn. Star* 28 Mar., The excellent Roumanians are doing their little best to make religion and constitutional government ridiculous. **1878** *Chambers's Encycl.* X. 709/1 The choice of the Rumanians fell upon Prince Charles of Hohenzollern-Sigmaringen, who was proclaimed Prince of R. on April 20, 1866. **1894** *Westm. Gaz.* 7 Sept. 2/3 Magyars and Roumanians alike have a right to call them by the names which they have borne..for generations. **1902** *Encycl. Brit.* XXXII. 312/1 As regards nationality [in Rumania], there are Rumanians, 5,469,036; foreigners, 171,063; and nondescript (principally Jews), 272,241. **1925** N. IORGA *Hist. Roumania* iii. 35 Anthropology and ethnography do not find the Slav type amongst the Roumanians. **1934** R. W. SETON-WATSON *Hist. Roumanians* i. 9 The Roumanians claim that they are the true descendants of Trajan's colonists. **1935** HUXLEY & HADDON *We Europeans* vii. 213 The largest nation in the Balkan peninsula is that of the Jugoslavs.., who are largely separated from their northern brethren by the Magyars and Rumanians. **1956** S. FISCHER-GALATI *Romania* I. i. 2 One [theory], proposed by the Romanians, is that most of the inhabitants 'took to the mountains' of Transylvania. **1964** *Whitaker's Almanack 1965* 913/1 By the *Treaty of Berlin*..the Principality was recognized as an independent State, and part of the *Dobrudja* (which had been occupied by the Roumanians) was incorporated. **1967** P. LATHAM *Romania* IV. 216 The Romanian from ancient times has embellished his surroundings with painting, carving, pottery and weaving. **1969** W. FORWOOD *Romanian Invitation* i. 18 Of their wines, Romanians are rightly boastful. **1971** O. MANNING *Romanian Short Stories* p. viii, The more the Romanians change, the more they are themselves. **1973** HOWAT & TAYLOR *Dict. World Hist.* 1313/2 Rumanians expected this to lead to union and autonomy. **1973** *Ann. Reg. 1972* 123 Possibly the replacement of Ulbricht by Honecker and the normalization of relations between the two Germanies made the move more acceptable to the Romanians. **1974** *Encycl. Brit. Macropædia* XV. 1053/2 The widespread rich folk costumes and the ancient folklore of Romanians..provide a reminder of the country's long traditions. **1974** M. B. BROWN *Econ. of Imperialism* xii. 296 What worries the Roumanians and other underdeveloped countries in the Soviet bloc is precisely the results of the artificial world division of labour in which they have for so long been held.

2. The language of Romania, a Romance language which has been exposed to many foreign, esp. Slavonic and Greek, influences.

1878 *Encycl. Brit.* VIII. 701/1 Roumanian is not only the national language of the country of that name, but is used by a considerable population in Servia. **1889** in Cent. Dict. **1902** *Encycl. Brit.* XXX. 396/2 The urban and most of the rural Vlachs are bilingual, speaking Greek as well as Rumanian. **1925** N. IORGA *Hist. Roumania* viii. 145 Coresi ..began to publish religious works in Roumanian, or in Roumanian and Slavonic. **1933** L. BLOOMFIELD *Language* xviii. 314 A feature common to both Roumanian and the western Romance languages is presumably guaranteed as Latin. **1948** A. L. KROEBER *Anthropol.* (rev. ed.) vi. 244 These Greek idioms and structure features recur in Latin-derived Rumanian. **1954** PEI & GAYNOR *Dict. Linguistics* 187 *Romanian*, a Romance language, the national tongue of Romania, and the native language of approximately 15,000,000 people. **1956** S. FISCHER-GALATI *Romania* I. i. 2 The Balkan Kutso-Vlach people speak a language akin to Romanian. **1964** *Whitaker's Almanack 1965* 913/2 Roumanian is a Romance language with many archaic forms and with admixtures of Slavonic, Turkish, Magyar and French words. **1968** J. LYONS *Introd. Theoret. Linguistics* v. 204 The so-called 'postpositive' articles of Swedish,.. Rumanian,..Macedonian, etc. **1969** W. FORWOOD *Romanian Invitation* ii. 25 The name Bucharest,..in Romanian Bucureşti, evokes the..days of leisurely railway journey across the Ruritanian map of Europe. **1972** M. L. SAMUELS *Linguistic Evol.* vi. 95 Romanian, Bulgarian and Albanian..share a number of features. **1974** K. KATZNER *Lang. of World* (1977) II. 95 Rumanian, more correctly spelled Romanian, is, as its name suggests, one of the Romance languages. **1975** *Language* LI. 411 In Rumanian, the polite pronoun..is 3rd person in form. **1976** 'D. FLETCHER' *Don't whistle 'Macbeth'* 48 None of us spoke Romanian.

B. *adj.* Of or pertaining to Romania, its inhabitants, or their language. ***Romanian stitch*** = *Oriental stitch* s.v. ORIENTAL *a.* 3 c.

1860 *Universe* 8 Dec. 1/2 His projects extend to the formation of a great Roumanian State. **1878** *Chambers's Encycl.* VI. 513/1 In 1877, the entire Rumanian military force numbered 144,668 men. **1881** MRS. E. B. MAWER (*title*), Roumanian Fairy Tales and Legends. **1883** *Science* II. 114/2 Roumanian ethnology. **1883** R. TORCEANU *Simplified Gram. Roumanian Lang.* p. vii, The Roumanian tongue can claim..attention on more grounds than one. **1885** MABEL COLLINS *Prettiest Woman* v, The Roumanian women are very beautiful. **1902** *Encycl. Brit.* XXXII. 313/2 The Rumanian Church is autocephalous, but holds the same dogmas as the Orthodox Greek Church. **1925** N. IORGA *Hist. Roumania* viii. 145 Religious manuscripts..in which the Roumanian text in red letters follows the Slavonic text in ink. **1927** PEAKE & FLEURE *Priests & Kings* xi. 177 The painted pottery people of the Rumanian plain spread along the foot-hills on the outside of the Carpathians. **1932** D. C. MINTER *Mod. Needlecraft* 10/1 Intergradating one stitch and colour with another, as is possible with Irish stitch ..and Roumanian..or satin stitch. **1934** M. THOMAS *Dict. Embroidery Stitches* 177 Roumanian Stitch consists of a long stitch across the shape tied down with a shorter slanting one in the centre. **1938** *Oxf. Compan. Mus.* 819/2 The Russian development of a national music..served to some extent as an incentive to Rumanian musicians. **1950** THEIMER & CAMPBELL *Encycl. World Politics* 372/1 On 7 October 1940 German troops occupied Rumania to secure Rumanian oil ..and agricultural surpluses for Germany. **1956** S. FISCHER-GALATI *Romania* I. i. 2 The Romanian nation was formed through the union of the Romans and the native population. **1957** M. B. PICKEN *Fashion Dict.* 279/1 *Rumanian-stitch*, series of parallel stitches intersected at center by shorter stitches. **1959** R. N. C. HUNT *Books on Communism* 37 An exhaustive study by a group of experts on aspects of Roumanian life under Communism. **1967** P. LATHAM *Romania* I. 18 The Romanian Black Sea coast faces east. **1968** J. LYONS *Introd. Theoret. Linguistics* v. 204 It is the criterion of 'interruptability' (or 'insertability') which distinguishes the English article as more 'word-like' than the Rumanian or Macedonian article. **1969** W. FORWOOD *Romanian Invitation* i. 17 The pleasures of the Romanian kitchen are very special. **1971** O. MANNING *Romanian Short Stories* p. ix, Romanian music is either gypsy music or peasant music. **1973** *Times* 2 Apr. 6/5 (Advt.), A fine quality Rumanian rug in superb Balkan colours. **1973** *Ann. Reg. 1972* 122 It was a relatively inward-looking year for the Romanian Communist Government and its leader. **1974** M. B. BROWN *Econ. of Imperialism* xii. 295 In the Roumanian dispute with Comecon, the basis of the Roumanian argument has been one that we have met before. **1976** P. CLABBURN *Needleworker's Dict.* 228/1 Romanian stitch has one cross at a slight angle, romanian couching has several crosses at the same angle. **1979** *Records & Recording* Aug. 61/2 The distinguished Romanian soprano sings the part quite beautifully.

Hence **Ro'manianism,** Romanian identity, Romanian nationalism.

1938 *Times* 1 Jan. 11/1 The new Government believed.. in the spiritual renaissance of Rumanianism through the Christian Church.

Romanianize (ruː'meɪnɪənaɪz), *v.* [f. ROMANIAN *a.* + -IZE.] *trans.* To make Romanian in character. Hence **Ro,maniani'zation.**

1922 O. JESPERSEN *Language* xi. 205 A Saxon village which had been almost completely Rumanianized. **1938** *Times* 1 Jan. 11/1 The laws for the protection of Rumanian labour, and of the Rumanianization of undertakings which.. employ foreigners instead of Rumanians.

Romanic (rəʊ'mænɪk), *a.* (*sb.*). [ad. L. *Rōmānic-us*, f. *Rōmānus* ROMAN *sb.*[1]]

1. Of languages: Descended from Latin; Romance. Also, composed, etc., in Romance; using a Romance language.

In quot. 1845 equivalent to ROMANSH.

1708 MADOX *Exchequer* Pref. Ep. p. xii, That signification in which they are used by the Romanick writers. **1845** *Proc. Philol. Soc.* II. 133 The Swiss in their northern districts.., before the Romanic tongue offends the ear with its indefinite misty compromises. **1859** HADLEY *Ess.* x. (1873) 194 The universality of this formation in the Romanic languages. **1888** P. SCHAFF *Hist. Ch.* VI. I. vi. 18 Several synods in Gaul, in the thirteenth century, prohibited the reading of the Romanic translation.

b. *absol.* as *sb.* = ROMANCE *sb.* 1.

1708 MADOX *Exchequer* Pref. Ep. p. xii, These kind of words..were originally Latin: Then were transmuted into Romanick. *Ibid.* p. xiii, The Latin word *Senior*, elder, hath a new import in the Romanick.

2. Derived or descended from the Romans; belonging to the Romance peoples.

1847 BUNSEN *Church of Future* 25 He of Romanic origin, the Reformer Calvin. **1867** PEARSON *Hist. Eng.* I. 269 The neighbourhood of a large Romanic population. **1876**

BANCROFT *Hist. U.S.* III. iii. 49 Shall the Romanic or the Teutonic race form the seed of its people?

†**Ro'manical**, *a.*[1] *Obs.*$^{-1}$ [f. ROMAN *a.*[1]] Belonging to the Roman Church.
1663 J. OWEN *Vind. Animadv.* Wks. 1852 XIV. 341 [If] great substantial parts of religion..be once rejected..as Romish or Romanical.

†**ro'manical**, *a.*[2] *Obs.*$^{-1}$ [f. F. *roman* romance.] Romancing, romantic.
1665 J. SERGEANT *Sure Footing* 218 Tradition, which gives that Book all its Authority, and secures its strange Contents from being held Romanical.

Romanichal: see ROMANY[3] 3 b.

Romanicist (rəʊ'mænɪsɪst). [f. ROMANIC *a.* (*sb.*) + -IST.] A student of Romance (sense 1); a scholar versed in Romance languages or literature.
1930 K. MALONE in *Studies in Honor of H. Collitz* 328 *Romanicist*..seems to be the only word that fits the case [of the Romance philologist]. **1937** J. ORR tr. *Iordan's Introd. Romance Linguistics* iv. 279 Ferdinand de Saussure..was an Indo-Europeanist, not a Romanicist. **1957** *Archivum Linguisticum* IX. 90 From the Romanicist's viewpoint.

Romanish ('rəʊmənɪʃ), *a.* and *sb.* [f. L. *Rōmānus*, or in later use ROMAN *sb.*[1] or *a.*[1] + -ISH. Cf. G. *romanisch*, MDu. *romeinsch.*]
†**1.** = ROMAN *a.*[1] 1. Also *absol.* as pl. *Obs.*
c **888** K. ÆLFRED *Boeth.* i, þa..yfel þe se cyning Ðeodric ..wið þam romaniscum witum dyde. *c* **1000** ÆLFRIC *Lives Saints* ix. 142 He wæs ær ʒewreʒed..to romaniscre leode. *c* **1200** ORMIN 6902 Biforr þe Romanisshe king. *Ibid.* 6911 Onnʒæn þe Romanisshe leode. *c* **1205** LAY. 5289 Al þat Romanisce folc ferde bi heore ræde. *c* **1275** *Ibid.* 7936 Loþliche hii fohte, and Romanisse fulden.
2. Belonging to, characteristic of, the Church of Rome; Romish; Roman Catholic.
seo romanisce cyrice occurs in the OE. translation of Baeda's *Hist. Eccl.*, but the later use is independent of this.
1591 TURNBULL *Expos. St. Jas.* 212 Who are now hote, now cold in religion: now professours, now Romanish Catholikes. **1636** MASSINGER *Bashful Lover* III. iii, I do not like The Romanish 'restitution'. **1688** (*title*), A brief but full Vindication of the Church of England, from the Romanish Charge of Schism. **1840** GLADSTONE *Ch. Princ. Consid.* 361 Affording a formidable display of Romanish versatility. **1882–3** SCHAFF *Encycl. Relig. Knowl.* 57 This city [Louvain] became the center whither all the Romanish emigrants from England gathered.
3. *absol.* as *sb.* = ROMANSH.
Perhaps to be stressed as *Ro'manish*.
1689 BURNET *Tracts* I. 89 In one half of the Country they Preach in High Dutch, and in other half in a corrupt Italian, which they call Romanish. **1825** *Encycl. Metrop.* (1845) XVII. 768/2 The Romansche (or Romanish) has a better claim to be considered as a Dialect of the French than of the Italian.

†**'romanisk.** *Obs.*$^{-1}$ (See quot.)
1542 BOORDE *Dyetary* x. (1870) 255 Also these hote wynes, as romanysk, romny, secke.

Romanism ('rəʊmənɪz(ə)m). [f. ROMAN *a.*[1]]
1. The Roman Catholic religion or doctrines, Roman Catholicism.
1674 BREVINT *Saul at Endor* i. 5 Thus Papists have the Common Faith,..and their own proper Romanism. **1837** WHATELY (*title*), Errors of Romanism. **1858** KINGSLEY *Lett.* (1878) II. 59 Romanism under the Jesuits became a different thing from what it had been before. **1871** —— *At Last* xiv, I am not likely..to be suspected of any leaning toward Romanism.
2. A feature of Roman architecture.
1827 *Gentl. Mag.* XCVII. II. 606/1 This we think a Romanism, injurious to the simple dignity of a pediment. **1851** RUSKIN *Stones Ven.* I. App. XVII. 392 Every stunted Grecism and stucco Romanism, into which they are now forced to shape their palsied thoughts.
3. a. Roman institutions; the prevailing spirit of the Roman world; Roman sway or influence.
1877 *Smith's Dict. Chr. Biogr.* I. 461/2 The coronation of Charles..symbolise[s] the recognition by Romanism of the victory of Teutonism. **1887** *Athenæum* 7 May 603 Hellenism and Romanism, how each began and ended, and the relation between the two.
b. Partiality for the Romans; tendency toward what is Roman; acceptance of Roman Law.
1880 L. WALLACE *Ben-Hur* 354 A woman, whose Romanism is betrayed by the colors flying in her hair. **1897** *Eng. Hist. Rev.* Jan. 152 A code of the common law, then, will buttress our ancient usages against the assaults of the modern Romanism.

Romanist ('rəʊmənɪst), *sb.* (and *a.*). [ad. mod.L. *Romanista* (Luther, 1520): see ROMAN *a.*[1] and -IST. So G. *Romanist* (Luther), F. *romaniste.*]
1. A member or adherent of the Church of Rome; a Roman Catholic.
1523 [COVERDALE] *Old God* (1534) F iv, The Romanistes do saye euen what soeuer they lyst of theyr own priuileges. **1547** *Life Abp. Canterb.* To Rdr. E j b, Idolatrous Archiflamines, the which were euery one..professed Baalites, and sworne Romanistes. **1620** USSHER *Serm.* 35 In vaine..doe the Romanists goe about to perswade vs, that their Images be no Idoles. **1676** GLANVILL *Ess. Philos. & Relig.* v. 27 We..grosly contradict our selves, in most of our Disputes against the Romanists. **1728** MORGAN *Hist. Algiers* I. iv. 77 The Christians in general, but more particularly the Romanists, they actually hate and abominate. **1761** HUME *Hist. Eng.* II. xxxv. 273 Southampton..stood at the head of the Romanists. **1832** PALMER *Orig. Liturg.* II. 254 Romanists may object that mission..is lost by schism. **1869** THIRLWALL *Lett.* (1881) I. 264 It is the Protestant cause that has most to hope from free discussion, in which I believe Romanists never engage willingly. **1879** HADDAN *Apost. Succession* Pref. p. viii, Romanists also, as a body, condemn our orders.
b. *attrib.* or as *adj.* Belonging or adhering to the Church of Rome.
1635 LAUD in *Ussher's Lett.* (1686) 477 By which means the Romanist, which is too strong a Party already, would both have strengthened, and made a scorn of you. **1687** LUTTRELL *Brief Rel.* (1857) I. 425 Mandamus's have been lately sent down to Magdalen colledge for 6 new Romanist fellowes. **1849** LYELL *2nd Visit U.S.* II. 291 Only half of these are Romanist churches. **1864** BURTON *Scot Abr.* I. iv. 191 A large portion of England was still Romanist. **1888** PATER *Ess. fr. Guardian* (1896) 85 On the whole actors fared better in England than in Romanist France.
2. One who is versed in or practises Roman Law; a lawyer of the Roman school. Also *attrib.*
1647 N. BACON *Disc. Govt. Eng.* I. xli. (1739) 68 The Saxons had not been long acquainted with the Romanists, but they had gotten that trick of theirs also of disheriting by last Will. **1802–12** BENTHAM *Ration. Judic. Evid.* (1827) I. 148 The Romanists, and after them the English lawyers [etc.]. *Ibid.* II. 381 The ecclesiastical and other Romanist lawyers..exhibit a perceptible distinction. **1893** MAITLAND *Township & Borough* 14 Foreign lawyers, Romanists and Germanists, are disputing strenuously.
3. A student of Roman antiquities.
1858 RAINE *Mem. J. Hodgson* II. 276 Horsley's *Britannia Romana* is the storehouse from which succeeding Romanists have drawn the most valuable information. **1889** *Archæol. Jrnl.* XLVI. 274 Archæology in England for a while went half mad upon the antiquity of man. The Romanists found themselves at a discount.
4. One who makes a special study of Romance languages or philology.
1886 *Encycl. Brit.* XX. 668/2 *Romania*..contains articles of the most eminent Romanists. **1888** *Jrnl. Educ.* Jan. 32 Those who claim to call themselves 'Romanists'..must make a much more complete and careful study of Latin than that commonly made by school-boys.

Roma'nistic, *a.* [f. prec. + -IC.]
1. Inclining to, tending towards, Romanism; of a Roman Catholic character.
1829 NEWMAN *Lett.* (1891) I. 206, I am used to think the country has not much to dread from Romanistic opinions. **1854** BP. WILBERFORCE in R. S. Wilberforce *Life* (1882) III. 329 Evasion seems to me the very clinging curse of everything Roman and Romanistic. **1884** URWICK *Nonconformity in Herts.* 173 Those conformists who are as Protestant as he, yet are content to use these Romanistic expressions.
2. Pertaining to Roman Law.
1802–12 BENTHAM *Ration. Judic. Evid.* (1827) II. 422 The German edition of Romanistic procedure is, on this head, more explicit than the Gallican.
3. = ROMANCE 1 b.
1882 MOZLEY *Remin.* II. lxxxiv. 103 In this he lets out rather than avows his preference for the Romanistic languages to the Greek.
So **Roma'nistical** *a. rare*$^{-1}$.
1684 H. MORE *Answ.* A iv, Whether this be to be deemed Romanistical or Anabaptistical.

‖**romanità** (romani'ta). Also with capital initial. [It., f. next.] **a.** = next. **b.** The spirit or influence of the central Roman authorities of the Roman Catholic Church; acceptance of papal policy.
1927 *Observer* 19 June 13/1 He [*sc.* Machiavelli] was too great a realist for his intellect to suffer imprisonment by humanist admiration for Rome, or, as we call it today, *romanità*. **1963** *Economist* 7 Dec. 1007/2 The assertion of collegial status for the bishops has been advanced jointly with a demand that the Curia should be internationalised... Yet internationalisation by itself is secondary. Indeed, it might sharpen the existing reasons for complaint: foreigners have been known to succumb to *Romanita*; they lack the engaging and emollient Italian supposition that laws are, on the whole, unlikely to be obeyed.

‖**romanitas** (rəʊ'mɑːnɪtɑːs, rəʊ'mænɪtɑːs). Also with capital initial. [late L.] The spirit or ideals of ancient Rome; Romanism.
1947 *Horizon* Feb. 84 The *romanitas* upon which Europe was founded. **1961** *Listener* 16 Nov. 814/1 The natural pride in *Romanitas* which has passed into his [*sc.* Pope Leo I's] thinking from secular tradition. **1975** *Times Lit. Suppl.* 25 Apr. 464/4 Amid the decline and fall of a civilization to which he owed both his religion and his *romanitas*, St Augustine inscribed..the charter of an enduring Christian culture. **1977** *History* LXII. 174 One would wish to know.. the extent to which there remained a concept of *romanitas* in Celtic Britain.

'Romanite. *rare*$^{-1}$. = ROMANIST 1.
1839 J. ROGERS *Antipopopriestian* II. §2. 119 Oh foolish Romanites, who hath bewitched you, that ye should not obey the truth?

Romanity (rəʊ'mænɪtɪ). [f. ROMAN *a.*[1]]
1. A Latin form of expression. *rare*$^{-1}$.
1740 GRAY *Let.* in Mason *Mem.* (1807) I. 240 Quitting my Romanities.., let me tell you, in plain English, that we come from Albano.
2. = ROMANISM 3 a.
1854 MILMAN *Lat. Chr.* I. 465 Not only was heathenism, but, excepting in the laws and municipal institutions, Romanity itself, absolutely extinct. **1877** MULLINGER *Schools Chas. Gt.* 52 Romanity, as a system, was at an end; and in its place monastic mediæval Christianity had arisen.

romanium (rəʊ'meɪnɪəm). [f. the name of the inventor, R. I. *Roman.*] An alloy of aluminium.
1897 *Cyclist* 8 Dec. 1412 The machines are built of tubes made of 'Romanium'. **1899** *Fortn. Rev.* LXV. 113 The Romanum cycle made of Romanium and Roman bronze.

romani'zation. [f. ROMANIZE *v.*]
1. Assimilation to Roman customs or models.
1876 WHITNEY *Study Lang.*, etc. 167 Italy after its first Romanization. **1885** *Archaeol.* XLIX. 127 We are struck by the evidence they supply of its thoroughgoing Romanization.
2. Alteration under Romance influence.
1899 F. H. SYKES *Fr. Elem. in M.E.* 7 Middle English underwent a romanization of its phrasal power more extensive than..the romanization of its vocabulary.
3. Alteration towards Romanism.
1893 *Advance* (Chicago) 7 Dec., With a view to a state-and-church Romanization of our public school system.
4. Transliteration into Roman characters; adoption of the Roman alphabet.
1894 *Athenæum* 10 Nov. 635/1 He [a Japanese] spends seven years in learning to read and write. Yet romanization, which would reduce the time to a year or so, is scouted by native and foreign scholars alike. **1925** C. H. BREWITT-TAYLOR *San Kuo* I. p. ii, The Wade system of romanisation, in which the vowels are Italian, has been used. **1934** *Bull. Int. Hist. & Philol. Acad. Sinica* IV. IV. 387 The French system of romanization of Chinese. **1961** *Amer. Speech* XXXVI. III. 177 Chang Ker Chiu gives both characters and the romanization ₒ*in*—'*yan* for 'craving for tobacco or opium'. **1963** [see PINYIN]. **1973** *Lancet* 14 July 78/1 Even this difficulty is compounded by the fact that there are about a dozen systems of romanisation (e.g., the same point may be described as Ho-ku, He-gu, or Ro-Kou). **1975** *Daily Colonist* (Victoria, B.C.) 22 Aug. 5/1 China is preparing to move into..romanization of the written Chinese language.

romanize ('rəʊmənaɪz), *v.* [f. ROMAN *a.*[1] + -IZE, or ad. F. *romaniser*, Sp. *romanizar*, med.L. *romanizare.*]
1. *trans.* To render Roman in character; to bring under the influence or authority of Rome.
1607 R. C[AREW] tr. *Estienne's World of Wonders* 58 The more a French-man is Romanized or Italianized. **1668** DRYDEN *Dram. Poesy* Ess. (Ker) I. 82 Perhaps too, he did a little too much Romanize our tongue, leaving the words which he translated almost as much Latin as he found them. **1762–86** H. WALPOLE *Vertue's Anecd. Paint.* (1786) II. 264 His ideas were all romanized; consequently his partiality to his favorite people..made him conclude it a Roman Temple. **1790** PENNANT *London* (1813) 9 Long before..it [London] was fully romanized. **1863** *Edin. Rev.* 66 The wide territory to the south of the wall of Severus..was thoroughly Romanized. **1874** STUBBS *Const. Hist.* I. i. 8 Both Franks and Visigoths had become Romanised.
b. To transliterate into Roman characters.
1836 [see ROMANIZED *ppl. a.* 1 b]. **1858** J. M. MITCHELL *Mem. R. Nesbit* vii. 179 *note*, Mr. Nesbit uses the Marathi character, which we have Romanized. **1884** *Athenæum* 2 Feb. 148/1 The Arabic article rendered 'al'..is written in a manner which should be romanized as 'lá'.
c. To render Roman Catholic in character or procedure.
1851 KINGSLEY *Lett.* (1878) I. 254 To Romanize the Church is not to reform it. **1862** *Q. Rev.* Apr. 325 The sympathizer with Rome has Romanized the services of his Church by his hymns.
2. *intr.* To follow Roman custom or practice; to accept the principles of Roman Law.
1629 LIGHTFOOT *Misc.* 137 Doth the Iew Romanize or the Roman Iudaize, in his deuotions? **1656** BLOUNT *Glossogr.* *Romanize*,..to imitate the speech or fashion of Rome, or the Romans. **1901** MAITLAND *Rede Lect.* 85 The medieval chancery has often been accused of romanizing.
b. To follow, tend towards, go over to, the Church of Rome; to become Roman Catholic.
1637 GILLESPIE *Eng. Pop. Cerem.* III. iii. 46 By the very same reasons prove we, that Formalists doe Romanize, by keeping the Popish Ceremonies. **1644** MILTON *Areop.* (Arb.) 40 So apishly Romanizing, that the word of command still was set downe in Latine. **1848** NEWMAN *Loss & Gain* 159 Any one who is inclined to Romanize should go abroad. **1855** BP. WILBERFORCE in R. G. Wilberforce *Life* (1881) II. 279 Miss —— very unsettled in mind. Fear that she will ultimately Romanize.

'romanized, *ppl. a.* [f. prec. + -ED.]
1. Drawn towards, affected by, Romanism.
1610 R. NICCOLS *England's Eliza* xxi, If your English Romanized hearts Gainst nature's custome swell with foule defame. **1628** PRYNNE *Brief Surv.* Ep., Some spurious and Romanized, if not Apostatized Sonnes, and Pastors of our Church. **1870** R. ANDERSON *Missions Amer. Bd.* IV. 78 The Syrian Catholic or Romanized Jacobite.
2. Assimilated to the Romans or to things Roman.
1695 EDWARDS *Perfect. Script.* 285 A battle against the Romans and Britains Romaniz'd. **1818** HALLAM *Mid. Ages* (1872) I. 285 The barbarians must have found nothing in Gaul but a Roman or Romanized aristocracy. **1844** *Proc. Philol. Soc.* I. 169 Welsh and Armorican are partially Romanized languages. **1893** W. M. RAMSAY *Ch. in Roman Emp.* 287 *note*, That a Jew..should write so Romanized a letter is even more improbable.
b. Expressed in Roman characters.
1836 (*title*), A Romanized-Singhalese and English Vocabulary. **1859** (*title*), The Lady's Tamil Book, containing..portions of the book of Common Prayer in Romanized Tamil. **1876** *Encycl. Brit.* V. 653/2 Text-books and dictionaries in Romanized Chinese.

'romanizer. [f. ROMANIZE *v.*]
1. One who favours the Church of Rome or the Roman usage.

1844 Hook *Take Heed* Pref. ii, Romanists and Romanizers.. are as much opposed to primitive doctrine as ultra-protestants can be. **1847** —— *Eccl. Biog.* III. 545 Wilfred, abbot of Ripon, was.. appointed to the bishopric; he was a Romanizer. **1852** Bp. Wilberforce in R. G. Wilberforce *Life* (1881) II. 149, I had opposed warmly the system of confession, and the whole system of the Romanizers.

2. One who advocates or accepts the principles of Roman Law.

1897 *Eng. Hist. Rev.* Jan. 152 A code which.. shall enlist the sympathies of at least one body of Romanisers, the students of the canon law.

'romanizing, *vbl. sb.* [f. as prec.] The action of the vb., in various sense. Also *attrib.*

1775 in Ash *Suppl.* **1836** (*title*), The Romanizing System. **1861** J. G. Sheppard *Fall Rome* 463 The Romanizing, so to speak, of Frank institutions. **1886** *Encycl. Brit.* XX. 696/2 A Romanizing of all their institutions was resorted to.

'romanizing, *ppl. a.* [f. as prec.] That Romanizes, in various senses.

1624 Gee *Foot out of Snare* vii. 54 To the great admiration of the stupid, gullifyed, Romanizing beholders. **1710** tr. *Werenfels's Disc. Logom.* 204 Our Romanizing Authors shall discover all the Roman Magistrates [etc.]. **1850** Bp. Wilberforce in R. G. Wilberforce *Life* (1881) II. ii. 68, I have been very generally blamed for encouraging Romanizing opinions. **1883** *Fortn. Rev.* Feb. 188 This lax rule especially favoured the views of the Romanizing party.

'Romanly, *adv.*[1] [f. Roman *a.*[1]] **a.** After the Roman fashion. **b.** Towards the Roman Church.

1606 *True & Perfect Relat.* P p ij, In as many kingdomes as are Romanly Catholique. **1652–62** Heylin *Cosmogr.* III. (1673) 157/2 Severus.. marched towards Persia with an army Romanly appointed. **1854** Lowell *Jrnl. Italy* Prose Wks. 1890 I. 144 The peasant, in his ragged brown cloak,.. still strides Romanly. **1899** Baring-Gould *Bk. West* I. 75 [Bishop] Grandisson was a man very Romanly inclined.

'Romanly, *adv.*[2] [f. Roman *a.*[2]] In the Romany or gipsy language.

1851 Borrow *Lavengro* lxxi, She has sung it Christianly, though perhaps you would like to hear it Romanly.

'Romanness. [-ness.] The quality of being influenced by Rome or by Roman Catholicism.

1959 *Catholic Times* 20 Mar. 5/4 His theory that the Welsh were profoundly conscious of their Roman-ness.

'Roman-nosed, *a.* [See Roman *a.*[1] 4 c.] Having a Roman nose. Hence **'Roman-nosedness** (*nonce*).

1832 Lytton *E. Aram* II. v, Fate had resolved to bait his Roman-nosed horse and refresh himself. **1848** Thackeray *Van. Fair* i, Biting her lips and throwing up her venerable and Roman-nosed head. **1912** J. S. Huxley *Individual in Animal Kingdom* iii. 80 In all Metazoa there is, before and during the sexual process, a shuffling and recombination of the chromosomes of the nucleus—those bodies which taken together appear to determine the characteristics of the offspring, or at least those which mark off from others of the same species,—whether it shall be tall or short, fair or dark, chubby or lanky, tip-tilted or Roman-nosed. **1912** D. H. Lawrence *Let.* 24 Dec. (1932) 87 If it's destined to have a snub nose, it's sheer waste of time to harass the poor brat into Roman-nosedness.

Romano (rəʊ'mɑːnəʊ). [It., = Roman.] In full *Romano cheese.* A strong-tasting hard cheese, orig. made in Italy.

1908 Doane & Lawson *Varieties of Cheese* 39 The Formaggio Pecorini are the sheep's-milk cheeses made in Italy... The most common cheese of this sort is the one designated Cacio Pecorino Romano, or merely Romano. *Ibid.*, In making Romano cheese the milk is heated to 100° F. and coagulated by rennet in fifteen minutes. **1918** J. L. Sammis *Decker's Cheese Making* (ed. 6) xxx. 218 *Romano.* This is usually made from skim milk [in America]. **1949** N. Standen *Art of Cheese Cooking* 30 Romano, in Italy, used to be made from sheep's milk which gave it a pungent flavor. In this country, though, it's made from cow's milk and is correspondingly milder. **1955** R. C. Brown *Compl. Bk. Cheeses* iii. 26 Romano is not as expensive as Parmesan. **1966** Marquis & Haskell *Cheese Bk.* II. 64 The black-rinded and.. grainy-looking Romano.. is much stronger than Parmesan. **1976** N. Thornburg *Cutter & Bone* viii. 199, I have.. some ridiculously expensive Romano cheese compliments of George.

Romano- (rəʊ'mɑːnəʊ, formerly rəʊ'meɪnəʊ), used as combining form of Roman *a.*[1], as in *Romano-British, -Briton, -canonical, -Celtic, -cosmopolitan, -Egyptian, -Germanic, -Hellenistic, -Saxon, Visigothic,* etc.

1847 J. Y. Akerman (*title*) An archaeological index to remains of antiquities of the Celtic, *Romano-British and Anglo-Saxon periods. **1871** Earle *Philol. Eng. Tongue* §39 By inheriting the relics of the Romano-British civilisation. **1963** *Times* 21 Feb. 5/7 Caerwent was the only fully developed Romano-British town in Wales. **1975** J. G. Evans *Environment Early Man Brit. Isles* vi. 157 There was some colonization by the Belgae and Romano-British people of areas not previously taken up. **1896** A. H. Keane *Ethnol.* II. xiv. 398 The Teutons merged everywhere in diverse proportions with the *Romano-Britons. **1956** Auden *Old Man's Road*, So thought (I think) the last Romano-Briton. **1909** Webster, *Romano-canonical. **1974** A. Watson *Legal Transplants* vii. 45 Some Roman law was creeping in primarily as a result of the acceptance of rules of romano-canonical procedure. **1861** J. G. Sheppard *Fall Rome* 422 In the dissolute atmosphere of *Romano-Celtic life. **1923** R. G. Collingwood *Roman Britain* iii. 68 Houses.. never losing their Celtic stamp or becoming *Romano-cosmopolitan instead of Romano-British. **1802–12** Bentham *Ration. Judic. Evid.* (1827) II. 202 In the English *Romano-ecclesiastical courts the evidence is on the same footing. **1934** Webster, *Romano-Egyptian. **1964** W. L. Goodman *Hist. Woodworking Tools* 33 Most of the adzes.. appear to be of a similar pattern to the Romano-Egyptian adze described earlier. **1802–12** Bentham *Ration. Judic. Evid.* (1827) I. 343 The technical system of *Romano-Gallic procedure. *Ibid.* II. 424 In *Romano-German, as in Romano-Gallic law. **1864** Bryce *Holy Roman Emp.* xx. (1866) 402 Though a simple revival of the old *Romano-Germanic Empire was out of the question. **1980** *Jrnl. R. Soc. Arts* July 534/2 In the Romano-Germanic tomb of a little girl, was found a decorated goose egg. **1859** Gullick & Timbs *Paint.* 63 The amalgamation of the Byzantine style with the old native Longobardian, produced a new school, which is known as the 'Romanesque' or *Romano-Greek. **1972** D. Dakin *Unification of Greece* i. 5 Many Byzantines began to see themselves not as heirs to the *Romano-Hellenistic traditions of the West but as the successors of ancient Hellas. **1796** *Archaeol.* (1800) XIII. 128 Ancient inscriptions.. in Roman, or *Romano-Lombardic characters. **1956** J. N. L. Myres in D. B. Harden *Dark-Age Brit.* 16 (*heading*) *Romano-Saxon pottery. **1970** J. L. Shneidman *Rise of Aragonese-Catalan Empire* I. v. 154 In the city of Urgel.. during the period of Arab domination the bishop had.. governed the city under the *Romano-Visigothic law called the *Fuero Juzgo.*

Romanowsky (rəʊmə'nɒfskɪ). *Histology.* Also **-ofsky, -ovski, -ovsky.** The name of Dmitriy Leonidovitch *Romanowsky* (1861–1921), Russian physician, used *attrib.*, in *Comb.*, and in the possessive to designate a stain and staining technique devised by him, and a class of derived stains and techniques, used for the detection of parasites in blood.

1903 *Brit. Med. Jrnl.* 30 May 1253/1, I was struck by the curious appearance.. of small round or oval bodies... On staining them by Romanowsky's method, they were found to possess a quantity of chromatin, of a very definite and regular shape, which clearly differentiated them from blood plates or possible nuclear detritus. *Ibid.* 28 Nov. 1401/1 The deep red of the Romanowsky-stained chromatin of the bodies is represented by black in the drawings. **1906** *Boston Med. & Surg. Jrnl.* CLIV. 643/1 A staining fluid, devised by me for use in the staining of blood films according to the method of Leishman, which gives the so-called Romanofsky polychrome staining. **1930** [see orthochromatic *a.* 2]. **1947** *Ann. Rev. Microbiol.* I. 48 They compared their findings made in this way with parallel studies employing the ordinary technics of smears stained with Romanowsky's stain. **1960** E. Gurr *Encycl. Microsc. Stains* i. 267 The azurs I, A, B and C, and methylene violet.. are present in varying degrees in the Romanowsky type of stains. The latter consists of methylene blue and its oxidation products in combination with eosin. **1970** J. C. Swartzwelder et al. in J. E. Blair et al. *Man. Clin. Microbiol.* xlix. 440/1 Stained with Giemsa or some other Romanowski dye. **1978** *Nature* 22 June 595/1 The cytoplasm stains a pale blue with Romanovsky stains, and the single nucleus.. a reddish-purple.

romans, obs. form of romance.

romansa, variant of romanza.

Ro'mansh, *sb.* and *a.* Forms: α. 8 **Romaun(t)sh,** 8– **Romansh, -sch(e,** 9 **Romanesh, Romonsch, Romuntch,** 9– **Romantsch.** β. 8 **Rumaunsch,** 9 **Roumansch, Rumansch, Rumansh, Rumonsh, -sch(e, -tsch.** [a. the native name *Rum-, Roman(t)sch, -on(t)sch,* etc.:—pop. L. *Romanice* adv.: see romance *sb.*] **a.** The language, of Latin origin, spoken in the Grisons or eastern district of Switzerland.

Sometimes restricted to the dialects of the north-western part, those of the Engadine being called Ladin. Cf. Rhæto-Romance. Also used of other Rhæto-Romance dialects and of this group of dialects as a whole.

α. **1663** Skippon *Journ. Low C.* in *Churchill's Voy.* (1732) VI. 696/1 The Engadine, where all the inhabitants.. speak an odd language, called Romauntsh. **1775** *Phil. Trans.* LXVI. 129 This language is called Romansh, and is now spoken in the most mountainous parts of the country of the Grisons. **1789** Coxe *Trav. Switzerland* III. 307 Titles of Earliest Books, and of the Bibles printed in the Romansh. **1802** Pinkerton *Mod. Geogr.* I. 573 Among the Grisons in Engadin, and in some other parts, is spoken what is called the Romansh. **1842** *Penny Cycl.* XXIII. 423/1 One-half of the population of the Grisons speak the Romuntch and Ladin. **1872** Dixon *Switzers* 58 In Graubunden.. nearly nine thousand families speak Romonsch. **1946** *Archit. Rev.* C. 58/1 It is for us a matter of course that the Alemanic part of the country would speak German, the French Swiss part French,.. and the Rhaetian districts Romansch, that, for instance, the Grisons, which comprise districts speaking German, Italian and Romansch, should publish their decrees in all three languages. **1969** *Language* XLV. 185 To counter Italian nationalist claims, Romansh was officially established as the fourth national language of Switzerland in 1939. **1971** *Language* XLVII. 797 (*heading*) Targets and paradigmatic borrowing in Romantsch.

Comb. **1887** *Encycl. Brit.* XXII. 781/1 The Romansch-speaking Leagues of Rhætia.

β. **1789** Coxe *Trav. Switz.* III. 282 *note*, It is called by the natives Arumansh, Rumaunsch, Romansch, Lingua Romanscha. **1825** *Encycl. Metrop.* (1845) XVII. 769/1 It.. is subdivided into two branches; the Rumonsche, spoken near the sources of the Rhine, and the Ladinsche near those of the Inn. **1841** *Penny Cycl.* XX. 83/1 The Rumonsch is a written language, and books have been published in it. **1875** Whitney *Life of Lang.* x. 184 Certain dialects of southern Switzerland are enough unlike Italian to be ordinarily ranked as an independent tongue, under the name of Rhæto-Romanic, or Rumansh. **1970** *Times Lit. Suppl.* 8 Jan. 40/2 He is fully conversant with the five national tongues—French, Spanish, Portuguese, Italian and Rumanian—and with their five regional varieties—Occitanian or Provencal.. Catalan.. Dalmatian.. Rumansch or Rhaetian (now strictly West Rhaetian, for that alone has evolved a recognized written language), and Sardinian.

b. *attrib.* or as *adj.*

In quot. 1920 referring to an ethnic group.

1663 Skippon *Journ. Low C.* in *Churchill's Voy.* (1732) VI. 696/1 The Lord's prayer in the Romauntsh language. **1775** *Phil. Trans.* LXVI. 129 An Account of the Romansh Language. **1828** *Encycl. Metrop.* (1845) XIX. 756/2 The most complete account of the Romansh language is that from the pen of Mr. Planta. **1880** [see Ladin]. **1920** *Q. Rev.* Apr. 443 Its population is not of German, but of Allemanic race, the only exception being that part which is of Romantsch origin. **1969** [see Rhæto-Romance].

romanso, romant: see romanzo, romaunt.

romantic (rəʊ'mæntɪk), *a.* and *sb.* Also 7 **romantique, 7–8 romantick.** [ad. F. *romantique*, f. *romant*, older form of *roman* romance, novel.]

A. *adj.* **1. a.** Of the nature of, having the qualities of, romance in respect of form or content.

1659 H. More *Immort. Soul* II. xi, I speak especially of that Imagination which is most free, such as we use in Romantick Inventions. **1665** Boyle *Occas. Refl.* (1848) 351 Your Friend Mr. Boyle.. was saying, that he had thoughts of making a short Romantic story. **1709** Hearne *Collect.* (O.H.S.) II. 199 In the Bodl. Library is a Collection of old Romantick Pieces. **1749** *Power & Harm. Prosaic Numbers* 45 Romances and Novels are often writ in this mixt Language, between Poetry and Prose: and hence it is sometimes called the Romantick Stile. **1777** Richardson *Arab. Dict.* Diss. p. xxix, Romantic Fiction has long been considered as of Eastern origin. **1829** Scott *Wav.* Gen. Pref., It was a step in my advance towards romantic composition. **1846** Wright *Ess. Mid. Ages* II. 38 Nothing can be more erroneous than the attempt to trace the origin of romantic literature to one particular source.

b. *Mus.* Characterized by the subordination of form to theme, and by imagination and passion.

1885 Fillmore *Pianof. Music* 80 In romantic music content is first and form subordinate. **1887** *Grove's Dict. Music* IV. 414 There were in romantic opera four principal elements—the imaginative, the national, the comic, and the realistic.

c. Of a work of modern literature, etc.: having romance as its subject; treating of a love affair.

1960 R. Rees *For Love or Money* ii. 30 The doctrine of D. H. Lawrence's *Fantasia of the Unconscious*: that sexual passion, unrelated to the religious impulse.. leads to sterility and death—as in *Anna Karenina*, in *Carmen*, and in the greater part of European 'romantic' literature. **1977** B. Pym *Quartet in Autumn* i. 3 Unable to find what she needed in 'romantic' novels, Letty had turned to biographies of which there was no dearth. **1981** S. Radley *Chief Inspector's Daughter* i. 15, I get depressed because I write romantic fiction instead of straight novels.

2. a. Of a fabulous or fictitious character; having no foundation in fact.

1667 Pepys *Diary* 10 Mar., These things are almost romantique, and yet true. **1673** *Vain Insolency Rome* 36, I marvel (though you read this, and much more as Romantick in the Popes Letters) that you can credit all this done by a person, about an hundred years since. **1728** Morgan *Algiers* I. 62 Nicephorus relates that.. S. Peter preached the Gospel in Mauritania: But this is looked upon to be intirely romantick. **1824** Dibdin *Libr. Comp.* 672 The notion of an early-printed edition of the Canterbury Tales, by Wynkyn de Worde, is purely romantic.

†**b.** Having no real existence; imaginary; purely ideal. *Obs.*

1660 Tatham *Charac. Rump* Dram. Wks. (1878) 290 Upon the onely security of Mr. Harrington's romantick Commonwealth. **1690** T. Burnet *Theory Earth* II. 171 We must not imagine that the prophets.. feigned an idea of a romantick state, that never was nor ever will be. **1711** G. Hickes *Two Treat. Chr. Priesth.* (1847) I. 214 He must give them priests without human infirmities; if I may say it, romantic priests.

3. Of projects, etc.: Fantastic, extravagant, quixotic; going beyond what is customary or practical.

1671 Sir W. Thompson in Feret *Fulham* (1900) I. 50 The romantic and visionary scheme of building a bridge over the river at Putney. **1719** W. Wood *Surv. Trade* 170 What is here represented, will be treated by some of our Planters, as Romantick. **1746** *Rep. Conduct Sir J. Cope* 50 Few crediting so 'romantick' an Enterprize. **1800** Mrs. Hervey *Mourtray Fam.* II. 67 It is his intention equally to share his future inheritance with his brother. A most romantic idea. **1854** Trench *Synon.* (ed. 2) 66 A romantic scheme is one which is wild, impracticable, and yet contains something which captivates the fancy.

4. a. Having a bent or tendency towards romance; readily influenced by the imagination.

1700 Rowe *Amb. Step-Moth.* II. i, How great a good by me sincerely offer'd Thy dull Romantick Honour has refus'd. **1778** Miss Burney *Evelina* lxii, I am not romantic;—I have not the least design of doing good to either of you. **1832** G. Downes *Lett. Cont. Countries.* I. 37 The Wood of Boulogne is the favourite resort of the Parisian when he wishes to be romantic. **1849** Macaulay *Hist. Eng.* ii. I. 199 To unhappy allies.. he extended his protection with a romantic disinterestedness.

b. Tending towards, characterized by, romance as a basis or principle of literature or art. (Opposed to *classical.*) Also of ballet (see quot. 1957). Hence used of persons connected with, or things relating to, literature, art, etc. of this kind.

1812 H. C. Robinson *Jrnl.* 19 May in E. J. Morley *Henry Crabb Robinson on Bks.* (1938) I. 84 We proceeded to Coleridge's first lecture... He spoke of religion, the spirit of chivalry,.. and a classification of poetry into ancient and romantic. **1813** *Edin. Rev.* Oct. 206 The poetry of the Spanish peninsula seems to have been more romantic and less subject to classical bondage than that of any other part of Europe. **1814** W. TAYLOR in *Monthly Rev.* Apr. 364 The eleventh [chapter] divides European poetry into two schools, the classical, and the romantic. **1819** [see CLASSICAL *a.* 6]. **1833** W. MAGINN in *Fraser's Mag.* VIII. 64 'The noticeable man [*sc.* Coleridge] with large grey eyes'—the worthy old Platonist—the founder of the romantic school of poetry. **1841** EMERSON *Ess., History* Wks. (Bohn) I. 11 The vaunted distinction between..Classic and Romantic schools, seems superficial and pedantic. **1851** GALLENGA *Italy* II. 65 That new school of literature to which the vague denomination of Romantic had been generally applied. **1878** DOWDEN *Stud. Lit.* 25 A leader of the Romantic movement. **1908** P. E. MORE *Shelburne Ess.* 5th Ser. 119 Like Friedrich Schlegel, he indulges in the romantic irony of smiling down upon himself and walking through life like a *Doppelgänger*. **1928** [see CLASSICAL *a.* 6d]. **1930** W. EMPSON *Seven Types of Ambiguity* i. 27 Before the Romantic Revival the possibilities of not growing up had never been exploited so far as to become a subject for popular anxiety. **1937** D. BUSH *Mythology & Romantic Trad. in Eng. Poetry* p. xiii, The effect of both the romantic and the industrial movements was to make the artist, if not an anti-social figure, at any rate an isolated one. **1938** *Oxf. Compan. Mus.* 810/1 By the 'Romantic School' in music is meant the group of active spirits in that movement which began in Germany with Weber (born 1786)... Or it can be carried back as far as Schubert (born 1797) and Beethoven (born 1770). **1951** F. KERMODE *Romantic Image* vii. 132 The next step forward in Romantic aesthetic depended upon a new theory of language. **1957** G. B. L. WILSON *Penguin Dict. Ballet* 230 *Romantic ballet*, used, somewhat narrowly, to describe the ballets produced during the period of the Romantic revival in literature in the early nineteenth century, or roughly from 1830–1850, taking as their theme the odyssey of mortal man in love with some female spirit of the air or water or with some maiden risen from her tomb... The dividing line is a slender one, i.e. in the romantic ballet the accent is on colour or mood rather than form and design which is predominant in the classical ballet. **1959** F. GADAN et al. *Dict. Mod. Ballet* 329/1 Several other great Romantic dancers appeared as La Sylphide. **1960** BECKSON & GANZ *Reader's Guide Lit. Terms* (1961) 108 Romantic irony occurs when a writer builds up a serious emotional tone and then deliberately breaks it and laughs at his own solemnity. **1977** J. A. CUDDON *Dict. Lit. Terms* 573 *Romantic revival*, a term loosely applied to a movement in European literature (and other arts) during the last quarter of the 18th c. and the first twenty or thirty years of the 19th c.

5. a. Characterized or marked by, invested or environed with, romance or imaginative appeal.

The examples given here illustrating the collocation of the adjective with *love, lover, friendship*, and the like, provide evidence of the emergence of its common present-day use to convey the idealistic character or quality of a love affair. Cf. ROMANCE *sb.* 5b.

1666 PEPYS *Diary* 13 June, There happened this extraordinary case—one of the most romantique that ever I heard of in my life, and could not have believed [etc.]. **1728** F. HUTCHESON *Ess. Passions* I. iv. 94 A Romantick Lover has ..no Notion of Life without his Mistress, all Virtue and Merit are summed up in his inviolable Fidelity. **1754** R. BERENGER in *World* 4 July 474, I know several unmarried ladies, who in all probability had been..good wives and.. mothers, if their imaginations had not been early perverted with the chimerical ideas of romantic love,..upon which principle, a footman may as well be the hero as his master. **1766** GOLDSM. *Vic. W.* i, The girl was..called Sophia; so that we had two romantic names in the family. **1769** J. USHER *Clio* (ed. 2) 82 Innocent and virtuous love..inspires us with heroic sentiments,..a contempt of life, a boldness for enterprize, chastity, and purity of sentiment... People whose breasts are dulled with vice, or stupified by nature, call this passion romantic love; but when it was the mode, it was the diagnostic of a virtuous age. **1778** S. TIGHE *Let.* 2 Apr. in G. H. Bell *Hamwood Papers* (1930) 27 There were no gentlemen concerned, nor does it appear to be anything more than a scheme of Romantic Friendship. **1806** BYRON *Fugitive Pieces* 23 And friendships were form'd, too romantic to last. **1813** SCOTT *Trierm.* I. xix, Yet e'en in that romantic age, Ne'er were such charms by mortal seen. **1854** RUSKIN *Lect. Archit. & Paint.* ii. 65 You feel that armour is romantic, because it is a beautiful dress, and you are not used to it. **1858** LYTTON *What will he do with It?* (1859) III. VII. xiv. 135 (*heading*) Romantic Love pathologically regarded by Frank Vance and Alban Morley. **1866** C. M. YONGE *Dove in Eagle's Nest* II. ii. 41 Good substantial wedded affection was not lacking, but romantic love was thought an unnecessary preliminary, and found a vent in extravagant adoration not always in reputable quarters. **1874** GREEN *Short Hist.* vii. §6. 407 The romantic daring of Drake's voyage..roused a general enthusiasm throughout England. **1942** T. BAILEY *Pink Camellia* vii. 50 The lovemaking was of the purely romantic kind, for Cecily would have no other. **1945** *New Statesman* 23 June 408/3 The book opens with a tale of romantic friendship at Oxford in the years following the first great war. **1966** *Listener* 7 Apr. 509/3 Nowadays, however, educated young West Africans have discovered the alleged virtues of romantic love. They stress the idea of marriage being a true union of husband and wife as well as an economic partnership. Love will be the most important thing when they marry. **1971** E. MAVOR *Ladies of Llangollen* v. 96 The strange ambivalence of the pre-Freudian romantic friendships. **1975** J. PLAMENATZ *Karl Marx's Philos. of Man* xiv. 400 The idea of romantic love has flourished in the same kind of society as the small family. Indeed, this family is quite often seen as the creature of romantic love: it is set up by a man and a woman who come to love one another and who choose each other as life partners. **1978** *Morecambe Guardian* 14 Mar. 17/2 Partnerships flourish. A romantic attachment is possible, but do not take it too seriously.

b. Of places: Redolent or suggestive of romance; appealing to the imagination and feelings.

1705 ADDISON *Italy* 2 It is so Romantic a Scene, that it has always probably given occasion to such Chimerical Relations. **1748** *Anson's Voy.* III. v. 337 An Island, which.. may in all these views be truly stiled romantic. **1816** PEACOCK *Headlong Hall* iii, To put his romantic pleasure-grounds under a process of improvement. **1864** SKEAT tr. *Uhland's Poems* 57 Still my heart no quiet knows; With him ..Tow'rds romantic isles it goes.

Comb. **1828** *Sporting Mag.* XXI. 224 The hunting events of the romantic-scened county. **1849** J. FORBES *Physician's Holiday* xiii. (1850) 123 It is a romantic-looking spot.

c. Similarly of persons, their character, etc.

1846 GROTE *Greece* I. xvii. (1862) I. 395 The exploits of many of these romantic heroes. **1856** STANLEY *Sinai & Pal.* (1858) 328 The grandest and most romantic character that Israel ever produced, Elijah the Tishbite.

Comb. **1847** H. MELVILLE *Omoo* lxxviii, He was a sunburnt, romantic-looking European.

B. *sb.* **1.** A feature, characteristic, idea, etc., belonging to, or suggestive of, romance.

1679 V. ALSOP *Melius Inquirendum* II. vi. 324 Some Legendary Fabler, that has stufft a Farce with Romanticks. *a***1846** A. RODGER *Poems, Lo'e me little* (1897) 12 Quat your romantics, your airs, and your antics, Tak' truth's honest track, and ye'll seldom gae wrang. **1887** BLACK *Sabina Zembra* 221 There you are with your romantics again.

2. A romantic person; *esp.* an adherent of romanticism in literature; a romanticist. Also, a composer of romantic music.

1827 CARLYLE in C. E. Norton *Two Notebks. of T. Carlyle* (1898) 111 Grossi..has written a new Epic... Grossi is a Romantic. **1865** *Reader* 3 June 619/1 This enthusiasm for enthusiasm..was natural to the whole race of romantics of that day. **1882** STEVENSON in *Longman's Mag.* I. 77 Walter Scott is out and away the king of the romantics. **1898** L. STEPHEN *Stud. Biogr.* II. iv. 142 The same view..made him dislike Carlyle and Froude as romantics, if not charlatans. **1927** R. H. WILENSKI *Mod. Movement in Art* 30 Nineteenth-century romantics deliberately left out all the features which the admirers of classical painting were accustomed to regard as indispensable to art. **1932** W. B. YEATS *Words for Music* 11 We were the last romantics, chose for theme Traditional sanctity and loveliness. **1933** A. DAVIDSON tr. *Praz's Romantic Agony* 4 The thirst for the infinite..animates the lines of the Romantics. **1938** *Oxf. Compan. Mus.* 113/1 Despite their sheer musical beauty, his [*sc.* Brahms's] compositions are strongly charged with what may be called an extra-musical emotion; hence the classification of their composer as a romantic. **1960** A. O. LOVEJOY in M. H. Abrams *Eng. Romantic Poets* 15 To be unsophisticated, to revert to the mental state of 'simple Indian swains', was the least of the ambitions of a German Romantic... The greatness of Shakespeare, in the eyes of *these* Romantics, lay in his Universalität. **1961** C. CLUTTON in A. Baines *Mus. Instruments* ii. 66 The [organ] works of Liszt and Franck,.. and of such late romantics as Reger, Jongen, and Elgar, rely upon a very large instrument. **1966** H. G. SCHENK *Mind of European Romantics* i. 6 Rationalism was attacked by the Romantics not on the grounds that the intellectual results yielded by it were false, but rather on the grounds that they were inadequate. **1977** *Times* 18 Oct. 24/9 White tuxedos are occasionally supplied to shipboard romantics.

ro'mantic, *v.* [f. the adj.] *trans.* = ROMANTICIZE *v.* 1. Also with *up*.

1969 G. LYALL *Venus with Pistol* xxii. 137 It was a fairly flat scene of somewhere in Venice, a bit romanticked up. **1972** *Guardian* 8 June 2/1 'Elizabeth R' starts a new run if you like your history romanticked.

ro'mantical, *a.* [f. ROMANTIC *a.* and *sb.* + -AL[1].] Having a romantic character or tendency.

1678 CUDWORTH *Intell. Syst.* I. ii. 60 This Theology of Epicurus was but Romantical. *a***1715** BURNET *Own Time* IV. (1724) I. 762 He represented the matter as so easy, that this appeared too romantical to the Prince to build upon it. **1759** STERNE *Tr. Shandy* I. xxi, Our knowledge physical, metaphysical,..romantical. **1829** MRS. S. C. HALL *Sk. Irish Char.* i. (1855) 29 It's mighty fine to be so romantical all for pure love. **1885** LADY BRASSEY *Trades* 206 The literature.. is written from a statistical, 'romantical', or 'missionarial' point of view. **1891** H. E. WATTS *Cervantes* 97 They brought the romantical way of writing into discredit.

ro'manticalism. *rare.* [f. ROMANTICAL *a.* + -ISM.] = ROMANTICALITY.

1922 W. J. LOCKE *Tale of Triona* xiii. 142 She..was driven by she knew not what idiot romanticalism into the grey worries of wifehood and motherhood.

romanti'cality. [f. ROMANTICAL *a.*] Romantic quality; a romantic thing or characteristic.

*c***1852** THACKERAY *Let.* in *Esmond* (Biogr. ed.) p. xxxiii, Take care not to be juggled by romanticalities and sentimentalities. **1881** *Scribner's Mag.* XXII. 391/2 She liked the excitement,—the romanticality of it.

ro'mantically, *adv.* [f. ROMANTICAL *a.*]

1. In a romantic manner; after a romantic fashion.

1687 BURNET *Cont. Reply Varillas* 98 After he had turned this as Romantically as he could, he makes her to dye. **1813** *Examiner* 11 Jan. 17/2 Romantically preferring his good conscience..to..a pension. **1856** DOVE *Logic Chr. Faith* VI. §4 Those who reject Revelation are the most romantically credulous on all other matters. **1865** E. C. CLAYTON *Cruel Fortune* I. 149, I should never have suspected you of being so romantically absurd.

2. In a romantic or picturesque way in respect of situation or scenery.

1772–84 *Cook's Voy.* (1790) I. 140 Two fortified villages. .. The smallest was romantically situated upon a rock. **1796** MORSE *Amer. Geogr.* I. 517 A small cascade, where the water falls 15 or 20 feet, very romantically between two rocks. **1817** J. SCOTT *Paris Revis.* (ed. 4) 270 The situation altogether is as romantically lovely as can be imagined. **1884** PENNINGTON *Wiclif* vi. 132 A place romantically situated on the bank of the Severn.

3. *Comb.*, as ***romantically-minded*** adj.

1952 'M. COST' *Hour Awaits* 227 It appears that this Professor..is romantically minded. **1965** HOUSE & STOREY *Lett. C. Dickens* I. p. xxi, The kind suggested here by the romantically-minded Kate.

ro'manticalness. [f. as prec. + -NESS.] Romantic quality or character.

1770 BARETTI *Jrnl. Lond. to Genoa* II. 134 This village.. has nothing remarkable but the romanticalness of its situation. **1902** *Westm. Gaz.* 28 June 3/1 A world of subdued romanticalness.

ro'manticism (-ɪsɪz(ə)m). [f. ROMANTIC *a.*]

1. A romantic fancy or idea.

1803 W. TAYLOR in *Ann. Rev.* I. 380 Public opinion heeds little the romanticisms of speculative philosophy.

2. Tendency towards romance or romantic views.

1840 THACKERAY *Paris Sk.-bk.* (1872) 43 The romanticism killed him. **1864** D. G. MITCHELL *Sev. Stor.* 7, I do not believe that such imaginative exaltation of feeling.. would beget..the very romanticism of charity. **1873** BLACK *Princ. of Thule* (1874) II. iv. 126 Although, doubtless, a girl's romanticism was a pretty thing, it would have to yield to the actual requirements of life.

3. The distinctive qualities or spirit of the romantic school in art, literature, and music.

1823 *New Monthly Mag.* IX. 175/2 The French Academy ..has determined never to receive within its bosom any one polluted by the dramatic heresy of romanticism. **1830** [see CLASSICISM 1]. **1844** H. F. CHORLEY *Music & Manners* III. 36 M. Liszt illustrates in himself the criticism, the pianism, the romanticism of the new schools. **1856** R. A. VAUGHAN *Mystics* (1860) II. 248 Side by side with the advocates of faith and feeling in the religious province, appeared German Romanticism in the field of art and literature. **1878** SEELEY *Stein* III. 437 Stein belonged to the class of society which naturally furnished recruits to Romanticism. **1934** C. LAMBERT *Music Ho!* II. 118 A title like the *Pathetic Symphony* is looked on as an example of decadent romanticism. **1937** D. BUSH *Mythol. & Romantic Trad. in Eng. Poetry* xii. 398 In various ways and for various reasons the broad deep stream of romanticism had run thin. **1941** P. H. LANG *Music in Western Civilization* xv. 746 In Beethoven classicism became romantic, and in Schubert romanticism became classic. **1957** F. KERMODE *Romantic Image* viii. 145 Romanticism is just the new disease at the stage of mania. **1960** A. O. LOVEJOY in M. H. Abrams *Eng. Romantic Poets* 5 The offspring with which Romanticism is credited are as strangely assorted as its attributes and its ancestors. **1978** *Times Lit. Suppl.* 25 Aug. 944/5 This..biography has its interest..as a portrait of a very unhappy man whom Romanticism destroyed.

ro'manticist. [f. as prec. + -IST.]

1. An adherent or romanticism in literature or art or music.

1827 CARLYLE in *Edin. Rev.* XLVI. 325 Their grand controversy, so hotly urged, between the Classicists and Romanticists..shows us sufficiently what spirit is at work in that long stagnant literature. **1830** *Blackw. Mag.* XXVII. 317 The much-disputed provinces of the Classicists and Romanticists. **1856** R. A. VAUGHAN *Mystics* (1860) II. 248 The Romanticists were the enthusiastic champions of the Ideal against Realism. **1883** GROVE *Dict. Mus.* III. 152/2 We cannot acquit the younger romanticists of the charge of an excessive realism. **1885** PATER *Marius the Epicurean* I. 100 A mere love of novelty.., as with the Euphuism of the Elizabethan age and of the modern French romanticists. **1938** *Oxf. Compan. Mus.* 810/1 It is..sometimes considered that the classical element..in the work of those two [*sc.* Schubert and Beethoven] was strong enough to rank them as the last of the Classicists rather than as the first of the Romanticists. **1941** P. H. LANG *Music in Western Civilization* xv. 746 If Weber, Chopin, and Schumann are accepted as full-blooded romanticists, we.. cannot enrol the composer of the *Unfinished Symphony*..in their company. **1970** W. APEL *Harvard Dict. Mus.* (ed. 2) 738/1 These traits need not imply that nonromantic music lacks emotional appeal. Nor does it mean that the romanticists were not form-conscious.

2. In appositive use, passing into *adj.*

1856 R. A. VAUGHAN *Mystics* (1860) II. 6 A few years ago some Romanticist littérateurs of Germany woke him up. **1875** DOWDEN *Shaks.* 227 The German Romanticist critic Franz Horn. **1888** PATER *Ess. Guardian* (1896) 104 Writers as unlike Wordsworth as the French romanticist poets.

Hence **romanti'cistic** *a.*

1889 *Harper's Mag.* Sept. 641/1 It was once for all accomplished by the romanticists of the romanticistic period. **1895** *Cent. Mag.* July 418, I had a visit from another romanticistic Englishman.

roman'ticity. Now *rare.* [f. ROMANTIC *a.*] Romantic quality or character; romanticism.

1782 ELIZ. BLOWER *Geo. Bateman* III. 139 Gave an air of romanticity to the scene, which greatly pleased them. **1811** MOORE *Mem.* (1853) I. 247 You must not be surprised if such a sweet and picturesque situation should inspire me with more than usual romanticity. **1832** J. P. KENNEDY *Swallow B.* xxx. (1860) 298 There was a moral romanticity in it.

ro'manticize, *v.* [f. as prec. + -IZE.]

1. *trans.* To render romantic in character.

1818 COLERIDGE *Lett.* (1895) 690 A wood..which the old workman..has romanticised with..fifty seats and honey-suckle bowers. **1836** *Fraser's Mag.* XIV. 720 The endless succession of Giaours, Childe Harolds, Laras, Corsairs,.. which have romanticised French taste. **1900** *British Weekly* 10 May 70/4 Modern feeling has greatly romanticised, we do not say raised, the idea of love.

2. *intr.* To indulge in romance.

1868 *Daily News* 21 Dec., A gentleman..may be led on, like Pendennis with Fanny Bolton, to flirt and romanticise beneath him.

Hence **ro,mantici'zation; ro'manticizing** *vbl. sb.*; **ro'manticized, ro'manticizing** *ppl. adjs.*

1855 MILMAN *Lat. Chr.* XIV. vii. (1864) VI. 246 The free prolix Epopee of the Trouvère, in its romanticised classic form. **1867** *Spectator* 6 Apr. 387 We cannot but marvel exceedingly that the romanticizing critics have not made the discovery for us. **1899** *Speaker* 14 Apr. 424/2 Enlivened by champagne and some grotesque romanticising on the part of the amorous Duchess. **1935** *Mind* XLIV. 95 His [*sc.* Nietzsche's] 'Dionysus philosophy' is a typically Germanic brutalisation, exaggeration, romanticisation of something borrowed. **1968** G. Ashe *Quest for Arthur's Britain* i. 28 Leland's romanticisation of Henry VIII was elaborately transferred to Elizabeth by Edmund Spenser.

ro'manticky, *a. rare.* [f. ROMANTIC *a.* + -Y^1.] Of a romantic character.
1912 D. H. Lawrence *Let.* ?5 Nov. (1962) I. 154, I want to read something romanticky—feel like it.

ro'manticly, *adv.* Now *rare* or *Obs.* [f. ROMANTIC *a.* + -LY^2.] In a romantic manner; romantically; †romancingly, falsely.
1681 H. More *Expos. Dan.* App. II. 289 The conceit looks almost as Romanticly or fabulously..as that of the Romanists. **1694** Strype *Cranmer* III. xxxviii. 465 He tells us Romanticly in the same Argument, That many Posts went [etc.]. **1749** Bp. Newton *Milton's P.L.* I. 57 *note*, King Arthur, son of Uther Pendragon, whose exploits are romanticly extoll'd by Geoffry of Monmouth. **1775** Burnaby *Trav.* 55 A small cascade, which falls about fifteen or twenty feet, very romanticly, from between two rocks. **1806** Surr *Winter in Lond.* III. 109 [She is] violently and romanticly in love with this young man.

ro'manticness. *rare.* [-NESS.] Romantic quality or character.
1748 Richardson *Clarissa* (1811) II. 40 Having heard me often praise the romanticness of the place. ?**1756** H. Walpole *Let. to Bentley* Aug., A whimsical mixture of devotion and romanticness. **1968** H. Koningsberger *Revolutionary* v. 13 The romanticness of..tears shed by women in Turgenev.

ro'mantico-, used as combining form of ROMANTIC *a.*, as in ***romantico-heroic*** adj., ***-history***.
1825 Carlyle *Schiller* II. (1845) 60 Hence..their subdivisions of 'romantic', and 'heroic', and 'romantico-heroic'. *a* **1849** Poe *Marginalia* Wks. 1864 III. 547 His romantico-histories have all the effervescence of his verse.

ro'mantism. [a. F. *romantisme*, f. *romantique.*] Romanticism; romance-writing.
1885 *Athenæum* 30 May 696 Victor Hugo [was] not so much the most glorious survival of romantism as romantism itself. **1890** F. M. Crawford *With the Immortals* 73, I do not like the frantic side of this modern romantism.

ro'mantist. *rare.* [f. after prec.; see -IST.] A romanticist; an idealist.
1887 *Macm. Mag.* June 143 Goethe was also a Romantist.

Romantsch, var. ROMANSH *sb.* and *a.*

†**'Romany^1.** *Obs.* Forms: 4 **Romani(e, -ye, Romaine**, 5 **Romaynge, Romayne.** [ad. OF. *Romanie*, ad. late L. *Rōmānia* (see Du Cange), f. *Rōmānus* ROMAN *a.*] The Roman Empire.
a **1300** *Cursor M.* 22319 He sal haue mikel lauerdhede Of romanie, and al þe impire. **13..** *Seuyn Sag.* 2093 (W.), In al Poile ne Romanye Ne is so mochel tresorie. **1377** Langl. *P. Pl.* B. xv. 559 Many man for crystes loue was martired in Romanye, Er any crystendome was knowe þere.

†**'Romany^2.** *Sc. Obs.* Also 5 **Romynis.** [a. OF. *romine, roumine, rommeine* (Godef.), of obscure origin: Palsgrave (200 and 559) gives it as *rommenis, -ys*, and equates it with *peaux de Lombardie.*] ***romany buge*** (also ***banes, skins***), some kind of small fur used for lining garments.
1495 *Acc. Ld. High Treas. Scotl.* I. 227 For Romany buge to lyne the sammyne gowne. **1498** Haliburton *Acc. Bk.* 74 Item a bred of Romany bowgh. *Ibid.* 171 Romynis bowgh. **1507–8** *Acc. Ld. High Treas. Scotl.* IV. 19 For I Romany skinnis to the samyn. **1513** *Ibid.* IV. 427 Half ane mantill of Romany banes. **1539** *Ibid.* VII. 27 Item,..to lyne ane goun .., vj dosane ane skyn les romany buge.

Romany^3 ('rɒmənɪ, 'rəʊmənɪ), *sb.* and *a.* Also **Rommany, -anee, Romeny, -ani.** [Gipsy *'Romani*, fem. and pl. of *'Romano* adj., f. *Rom* gipsy: see ROM.]
1. A gipsy; also *collect.*, the gipsies.
1812 J. H. Vaux *Flash Dict.*, *Romany*, a gypsy. **1841** Borrow *Zincali* Introd. (1846) 3 Some account of the Rommany, as I have seen them in other countries. *Ibid.* 12 The peculiar habits of the Rommanees. **1897** *Daily News* 27 Jan. 6/5 The Romanies, or gipsies, are working in the last stage of poverty, and are very poorly fed.
2. The language of the gipsies.
1812 J. H. Vaux *Flash Dict.* s.v., To patter romany, is to talk the gypsy flash. **1841** Borrow *Zincali* Introd. (1846) 5 Welcomes and blessings were poured forth in floods of musical Rommany. **1871** M. Collins *Marq. & Merch.* I. vii. 221, I understand Romany pretty well. **1972** *Guardian* 28 Nov. 14/3 The Gipsy Council is..printing readers..in Romani and English.
3. *attrib.* or as *adj.* = GIPSY 4 and 5.
1841 Borrow *Zincali* Introd. (1846) 5 One of the principal attractions of a Rommany choir at Moscow. *Ibid.* 21 Their tricks and Rommany arts. **1871** M. Collins *Marq. & Merch.* I. i. 47 The gipsy language—the Romany speech. **1877** M. M. Grant *Sun-Maid* i, The Spanish remnant of the old Romany tribes. **1899** F. H. Groome *Gypsy Folk-Tales* p. lxxx, *Bakht*, the Rómani word for 'luck' or 'fortune'. **1973** *New Society* 6 Dec. 595/1 Joint general secretary of the World Romani Congress. **1976** *Word 1971* XXVII. 357 Romani-English is distinctive because it has developed largely within a closed community.

b. Special Combs., as **Romany chal, Romanichal** [CHAL], a (male) gypsy; **Romany chi** (tʃaɪ) [Romany *chai* girl], a gypsy girl; **Romany rye** [RYE *sb.*^{3}], a man, not a gypsy, who associates with gypsies.
1843 Borrow *Zincali* (ed. 2) I. 32 Those were brave times for the Rommany chals. **1851** [see GORGIO]. **1953** J. de B. Levy *As Gypsies Wander* i. 38 His pleasure was extreme when he first heard that non-Gypsy people had written poems in praise of *Romanichals*. **1960** G. E. C. Webb *Gypsies* i. 19 Whoever heard of a *gorgio* coming up to a *Romanichal* and greeting him with words of the old language? **1857** Romany chi [see GORGIO]. **1876** [see CHAL]. **1933** K. Bercovici (*title*) The Romany chai. **1851** Borrow *Lavengro* II. xxvi. 236 Here the Gypsy gemman bee, With his Roman jib and his rome and dree—Rome and dree, rum and dry Rally round the Rommany Rye. **1857** —— *Romany Rye* II. ix. 113 'I'll bet a crown,' said the jockey, 'that you be the young chap what certain folks call "The Romany Rye".' **1915** F. Cuttriss *Romany Life* xi. 242 He introduced me as a Romany Rye. **1929** K. Bercovici *Story of Gypsies* x. 231 What is most astounding..is the mention made of the natives of England of good families who were found in the company of these Gypsies... Who could they be, these gentlemen, these first Romany ryes? **1973** *Cassell's Encycl. World Lit.* (rev. ed.) I. 489/1 The Gypsy Lore Society in Liverpool, which was founded by the American Romany Rye Charles Godfrey Leland.

romanye, variant of RUMNEY.

romanys, obs. form of ROMANCE.

ro'manza (ro'manza; in Sp. contexts also ro'manθa). Also **-ansa.**
†**1.** [ad. It. *romanzo*: see ROMANZO.] A romance; a romantic fancy. *Obs.*
1641 Earl Monm. tr. *Biondi's Civil Warres* IV. 54 The supposal..smels of a Romansa and inchantment. **1656** —— tr. *Boccalini's Advts. fr. Parnass.* I. lxxviii. (1674) 105 The Paladins of Spanish Romansa's. *a* **1661** Fuller *Worthies, Surrey* III. (1662) 87 Conceiving it rather a Romanza or Fiction than a thing really performed. *Ibid.*, *Yorks.*, It will sound Romanza-like to posterity.
‖**2.** *Mus.* [a. It., Sp. *romanza.*] A romantic song or melody; a lyrical piece of music; = ROMANCE *sb.* 4 b.
1834 *Chambers's Edin. Jrnl.* III. 110/2 Another youth.. begins singing a Spanish romanza. **1938** *Oxf. Compan. Mus.* 810/2 *Romanza..*, a song or song-like instrumental composition. **1970** J. Blades *Percussion Instruments* x. 196 Alexander Goehr scores for the lion's roar in his *Romanza for 'cello and orchestra* (1968). **1975** *New Yorker* 16 June 97/3 Then the romanza begins.

‖**romanze** (ro'mantsə). *Mus.* Pl. **romanzen.** [Ger., = romance.] A composition of a tender or lyrical character; *spec.* a slow, romantic instrumental piece or movement. Cf. prec. and ROMANCE *sb.* 4 b.
1883 Grove *Dict. Mus.* III. 147/2 The Romanze in Mozart's D minor PF. Concerto differs..from the slow movements of his other Concertos in the extremely tender and delicate character of its expression. **1947** A. Einstein *Mus. Romantic Era* xi. 130 It joins together five movements —Introduction, Allegro, Romanze, Scherzo, and Finale—into an uninterrupted whole. **1970** W. Apel *Harvard Dict. Mus.* (ed. 2) 736/2 The German *Romanze* is primarily an instrumental composition of a lyrical character. *Ibid.*, Vocal *Romanzen* occur mostly in operas.

†**ro'manzo.** *Obs. rare.* In 7 **romanso, romanço.** [a. It. *romanzo*: see ROMANCE *sb.*]
a. A romance. **b.** Romantic style.
1628–9 Digby *Voy. Medit.* Pref. (Camden) p. xxiii, Sweet boys and dear venturous knights, worthy to be put in a new romanso. **1647** Evelyn *Corr.* (1872) III. 5 (Stanf.), For I was expected all ribbon, feather, and romanço.

ro'manzovite. *Min.* Also **-owite, -ofite.** [Named by N. Nordenskiöld (1820) after Count *Romanzoff.*] A variety of grossularite.
1823 W. Phillips *Min.* (ed. 3) 33 Romanzovite. It is of a brown, brownish black, and black colour; and is described as occurring either compact or in crystalline plates. **1830** H. J. Brooke in *Encycl. Metrop.* (1845) VI. 491/1 Garnet... *Reddish-brown*, Essonite, Cinnamon-stone, Romanzovite. **1868** Watts *Dict. Chem.*

Romary ('rəʊmərɪ). [f. the name of the manufacturer.] The proprietary name of a brand of biscuits.
1926–7 *Army & Navy Stores Catal.* 8/2 Biscuits.. Romary Ginger Nuts. **1929** *Trade Marks Jrnl.* 4 Dec. 2029 Romary's... Biscuits. A. Romary & Company, Limited,.. Tunbridge Wells, Kent; manufacturers. **1934** E. Bowen *Cat Jumps* 192 The Romary biscuits. **1977** P. Harcourt *At High Risk* I. viii. 101 His secretary..placed beside me a plate of Romary biscuits.

romaunce, obs. form of ROMANCE.

romaunt (rəʊ'mɔːnt), *sb.* and *a. arch.* Forms: 6 **roma(u)nte**, 6–8 **romant**, 7 **romand**, 7, 9 **romaunt.** [a. OF. *romant* (later *roman*), an analogical variant of *romanz, romans* ROMANCE.]
1. A romance; a romantic tale or poem.
1530 Palsgr. 486/2 Though I fynde it moche used in the Romante of the Rose, it is..nowe lytle used. **1542** *Chaucer's Rom. Rose* 39 It is the Romaunte of the Rose, In whiche all the arte of loue I close. **1593** Drayton *Ecl.* vi. 37 Or else some Romant unto us areede. **1614** Selden *Titles Honor* 44 Take for it, this testimony out of an old Romaunt. **1682** Creech *Lucretius* (1683) 119 Ten thousand such Romants the Vulgar tell. **1765** Percy *Reliques* III. p. vi, As the Songs of Chivalry became the most popular compositions in that language, they were emphatically called Romans or Romants. **1812** Byron (*title*), Childe Harold's Pilgrimage, a Romaunt. **1828** Scott *F.M. Perth* vi, Then there are the minstrels, with their romaunts and ballads. **1884** Ruskin *Art of England* i. 5 The habit of regarding the external and real World as a Singer of Romaunts would have regarded it.
2. A Romance form of speech; also *attrib.*, Romance, Romanic, in respect of language.
In quots. applied to older French and to Romansh.
1530 Palsgr. *Introd.* 41 Mye is an olde Romant worde. *Ibid.* 446/1 *Je ruse*,..and in olde Romant *je lobe. Ibid.* 486/2 It [*adherdre*] is an olde Romant worde and nowe lytle used. **1855** Milman *Lat. Chr.* IX. viii. (1864) V. 396 *note*, But was the Romaunt version understood in Metz? *Ibid.* 405 The Romaunt among the peasants of the Alpine valleys.

romawnce, obs. form of ROMANCE.

Romayn(e, varr. ROMANY^1 *Obs.*

Romayne (rəʊ'meɪn), *a.* [See ROMAN *a.*]
1. Obs. form of ROMAN *a.*, q.v.
2. Applied to carving, etc. with a motif of heads in medallions.
1904 P. Macquoid *Hist. Eng. Furnit.* iii. 50 Chair.. decorated..with medallioned heads surmounted by conventional ornament in the Italian manner, and which in this century obtained the name 'Romayne Work'. **1955** R. Fastnedge *Eng. Furnit. Styles* 287 *Romayne carving*, decorative *motifs* taking the form of small profile heads in medallions, introduced in the early sixteenth century. **1961** *Times* 2 Dec. 11/7 Small objects, carved with Romayne heads. **1969** E. H. Pinto *Treen* 196/1 The first two snuff boxes of this type, carved with 'Romayne heads'..were very worn and I thought that they were genuinely mid or late 16th-century. **1975** *Oxf. Compan. Decorative Arts* 672/2 *Romayne work*, contemporary term for a decorative motif consisting of small profile-heads in medallions carved on furniture and panelling. This form of decoration was introduced into England from Italy in the time of Henry VIII and was often combined with Tudor roses and traditional Gothic tracery or linenfold.

romazi, var. ROMAJI.

†**romb**, *v.* (Origin and meaning obscure.)
c **1330** R. Brunne *Chron. Wace* (Rolls) 8198 (Petyt MS.), þe dragons..Wipped wyþ wenges, ouerwarpen & went, kracchid with clawes, rombed [*v.r.* rubbed] & rent.

romb(e, obs. ff. RHOMB.

rombel, -ble, obs. ff. RUMBLE *sb.* and *v.*

rombelow(e, obs. ff. RUMBELOW.

Romberg ('rɒmbɜːg). *Med.* The name of Moritz Heinrich *Romberg* (1795–1873), German physician, used in the possessive, *attrib.*, and *absol.* to designate (*a*) the test of requiring a patient to stand with feet together and eyes closed, and (*b*) the sign or symptom, diagnostic of ataxia, shown by a patient who then sways or falls (described by Romberg in *Lehrb. d. Nervenkrankheiten des Menschen* (1846) I. 795).
1885 *Jrnl. Nervous & Mental Dis.* XII. 354 'Romberg's symptom'—*i.e.* inability to stand with the eyes shut and the feet together—is not always present. *Ibid.* 355 'The Romberg symptom'. **1932** *Practitioners Libr. Med. & Surg.* II. xxiii. 809 The Romberg test for static ataxia is carried out by having the patient stand with heels and toes together with open eyes and then with closed eyes. The tendency to sway appreciably with the eyes shut constitutes a positive Romberg. **1961** *Lancet* 9 Sept. 569/1 Both legs were slightly weak, and Romberg's sign was positive. **1977** *Ibid.* 10 Dec. 1228/2 Neurological examination revealed a vertical gaze palsy,..and a tendency to fall backwards on Romberg's test.

rombowline. *Naut.* Also **r(h)um-.** [Of obscure origin.] (See quots.)
1841 R. H. Dana *Seaman's Man.* 120 *Rombowline*, condemned canvas, rope, &c. **1862** Nares *Seamanship* (ed. 2) 24 *Rhumbow-line*, soft rope for nippers, etc. **1864** Webster, *Rombowline*, old, condemned canvas, rope, &c., unfit for use except in chafing-gear. **1867** Smyth *Sailor's Word-bk.* 580 The refuse [is worked] into rumbowline for temporary purposes, not demanding strength.

†**romboyle**, *sb.* and *v. Cant. Obs.* (See quots.)
a **1700** B. E. *Dict. Cant. Crew*, *Romboyles*, Watch and Ward. *Ibid.*, *Romboyl'd*, sought after with a Warrant.

rombustical, rombustious, obs. forms of RUMBUSTICAL, -TIOUS.

†**'romby.** *Obs.*$^{-1}$ [ad. It. *rombi*, pl. of *rombo* RHOMB.] A lozenge or rhomb.
1592 R. D. *Hypnerotomachia* 67 b, The mouth of the arches were stopped with rombyes of cleare glasse.

Rome (rəʊm), *sb.* Also 4 **Rom**, 5–6 **Roome**, 6 **Room.** [a. OF. *Rome*:—L. *Rōma.*
The pron. (ruːm), indicated by the old spelling *Room(e* and by the rime with *doom*, etc., was retained by some educated speakers as late as the 19th cent.]
1. a. The city or state of Rome; the Roman empire. Freq. in personified use.
c **888** K. Ælfred *Boeth.* xxvii. § 1 Se Catulus wæs heretoȝa on Rome. **971** *Blickl. Hom.* 191 Ic wille gangan to Rome. *c* **1205** Lay. 5986 Brennes walde Rome fulle fiftene ȝere. *a* **1300** *Cursor M.* 22241 All kingrikes þat rome was vnder Fra lauerdhed o rome þam sundre. *c* **1330** R. Brunne *Chron. Wace* (Rolls) 3460 þyse wer gon to Lumbardye To procure Rome more partye. *c* **1425** Wyntoun *Cron.* v. xi. 3534 þe Saxonys..Agane Rome rasse wiþe mekyl mycht. **1490** Caxton *Eneydos* lxv. 166 The historyes of the romayns, and

of theym that founded roome. **1542** UDALL *Erasm. Apoph.* 248 b, One of the olde souldyours of Roome. **1588** SHAKS. *Tit. A.* I. i. 82 These that Suruiue, let Rome reward with Loue. **1624** QUARLES *Job Militant* x. xxix, Who, that did e're behold the ancient Rome, Would rashly give her Glorie such a doome? **1671** MILTON *P.R.* IV. 80 All Nations now to Rome obedience pay. **1741–2** GRAY *Agrippa* 17 The willing homage Of prostrate Rome. **1780** COWPER *Boadicea* 17 Rome.. Tramples on a thousand states. **1820** BYRON *Mar. Fal.* v. i, A wife's dishonour unking'd Rome for ever. **1841** ARNOLD *Lect. Mod. Hist.* (1860) 29 Rome.. has been the source of law and government.

b. In proverbs.

(*a*) **1545** R. TAVERNER tr. *Erasmus's Adages* sig. D iv Ye may use this prouerbe when ye wyll signyfye that one daye .. is not ynoughe for.. acheuynge.. a greate matter.. Rome was not buylt in one daye. **1562** HEYWOOD *Prov. & Epigr.* (1867) 168 Roome was not bylt on one day. **1705** HICKERINGILL *Priest-cr.* IV. (1721) 214. **1776** ABIGAIL ADAMS *Fam. Lett.* (1876) 202 But Rome was not built in a day. **1822** SCOTT *Fortunes of Nigel* II. x. 237 Rome was not built in a day—you cannot become used to your court-suit in a month's time. **1849** C. BRONTË *Shirley* I. v. 123 'As Rome,' it was suggested, 'had not been built in a day, so neither had mademoiselle Gérard Moore's education been completed in a week.' **1873** 'F. FERN' *Memorial Vol.* 347 Rome wasn't built in a day;—cooks can't be manufactured in a minute. **1901** S. LANE-POOLE *Sir H. Parkes* xvii. 316 The Japanese .. went too fast and fell into grave commercial, monetary, and administrative troubles. Neither Rome nor New Japan could be built in a day. **1941** P. CHEYNEY *Trap for Bellamy* iv. 58 Bellamy said: 'Life is what you make it. Rome wasn't built in a day.' **1950** T. WILLIAMS *Roman Spring of Mrs. Stone* I. 34 Patience, said the Contessa. Rome was not built in a day!

(*b*) **1599** PORTER *Angry Wom. Abingdon* (Percy Soc.) 50 Ile do as company dooth; for when a man doth to Rome come, he must do as there is done. **1670** G. H. tr. *Hist. Cardinals* I. I. 5 Whilst one is at Rome, one must live as they do there. **1817** BYRON *Beppo* ix, And you at Rome would do as Romans do, According to the proverb. **1863** W. C. BALDWIN *Afr. Hunting* vii. 267, I always do in Rome as Rome does, eat (if I can) whatever is set before me. **1976** N. THORNBURG *Cutter & Bone* i. 22 'When in Rome,' he said finally, shuddering. **1977** *Rolling Stone* 21 Apr. 73/3 He had a point —when in Rome and all that—but it was a point he was not exactly loath to make.

(*c*) **1721** KELLY *Sc. Prov.* 194 It is hard to sit in Rome, and strive against the Pope.

(*d*) *c* **1380** CHAUCER *Troilus & Criseyde* (1894) II. 36 For every wight which that to Rome went, Halt nat o path, or alwey o manere. *c* **1391** —— *Astrolabe* (1872) Prol. 29 Ryht as diuerse pathes leden diuerse folk the rihte wey to Rome. **1806** R. THOMSON tr. *La Fontaine's Fables* IV. XII. xxiv. 110 Three pious men, having one end in view, Their way to heaven with equal zeal pursue.—Three diff'rent roads the three concurrents chose, All roads alike conduct to Rome... —So those Thought they might part, and yet get on secure. **1861** C. READE *Cloister & Hearth* I. xxiv. 270 All roads take to Rome. **1872** W. BLACK *Strange Adv. Phaeton* vi. 111 'Surely the road to Oxford is easy to find.' 'It is,' I say to her. 'For you know all roads lead to Rome, and they say that Oxford is half-way to Rome—*argal*—.' But knowing what effect this reference to her theological sympathies was likely to have on Tita, I thought it prudent to send the horses on. **1911** J. A. THOMSON *Introd. Sci.* iii. 63 All roads lead to Rome, and he must be a bold man who will declare any of Nature's beckonings to be unworthy of attention. **1912** J. S. HUXLEY *Individual in Animal Kingdom* vi. 154 All roads lead to Rome: and even animal individuality throws a ray on human problems.

c. Applied to Constantinople, the capital of the eastern Roman empire.

1603 KNOLLES *Hist. Turks* (1638) 13 Yet haue the Sarasins attempted both Romes: they haue besieged Constantinople, and haue wasted.. the sea coasts of Italy.

2. The city of Rome as the original capital of Western Christendom, and the seat of the Pope; hence, the Roman Catholic Church, its influence or institutions, etc.

c **1380** WYCLIF *Sel. Wks.* III. 263 How falsely freris feyneþ ȝifte of þis tresore to ech pope of Rome. *Ibid.* 281 Dispensacion of þe Bischop of Rome. *c* **1400** *Apol. Loll.* (Camden) 12 In þe court of Rome mai no man geyt no grace, but if it be bowt. *Ibid.*, þe kirk of Rome. *c* **1425** WYNTOUN *Cron.* VI. xiii. 1096 þe auchtande Bennet tuk þe se Off Rome as pape. **1537** STARKEY *Let.* in *England* p. xlvii, The wych you perauenture wyl impute to thys defectyon from Rome. **1595** SHAKS. *John* v. ii. 70 King Iohn hath reconcil'd Himselfe to Rome. **1654** BRAMHALL in *Ussher's Lett.* (1686) 612 Your selves have preached so much against Rome, and his Holiness, that Rome and her Romanists will be little the better for that Change. **1749** GRAY *Installat. Ode* 47 The majestic lord, That broke the bonds of Rome. **1791** BOSWELL *Johnson* (Oxf. ed.) II. 548 He argued in defence of some of the peculiar tenets of the Church of Rome. **1840** NEWMAN in *Apol.* iii. (1904) 70/1 Rome, though not deferring to the Fathers, recognizes them. **1892** J. M. STONE *Faithful unto Death* vi. 119 It was also thought that many clergymen hesitated to marry,.. in case of a reconciliation with Rome.

transf. **1821–2** SHELLEY *Chas. I*, I. 58 That is the Archbishop... Rather say the Pope: London will be soon his Rome. **1899** *Daily News* 26 June 7/2 An imposing demonstration, in honour of Calvin, has just been held in the City of Geneva, which he raised to the proud position of 'the Rome of Protestantism'.

3. *Comb.* †**a.** Appositive, etc., as ***Rome-burgh***, ***city***, ***gate***, ***land***, ***-lede***, ***riche***, ***street***, ***-thede***, ***-ware***.

c **893** K. ÆLFRED *Oros.* II. iii. 68 Æfter þæm þe *Romeburȝ ȝetimbred wæs. *c* **1200** ORMIN 7010 þurrh þe king off Romeburrh. *c* **1330** R. BRUNNE *Chron. Wace* 12665 ȝow were wel bettere at Rome burgh, þan reyse baner a-geyn Arthurgh. **1606** HOLLAND *Sueton.* Annot. 31 Vpon which day, the foundation of *Rome Citie was laid. **1553** WILSON *Rhet.* 48 As farre as hence to *Rome gates. **1390** GOWER *Conf.* Prol. 715 Cesar Julius, which tho was king of *Rome lond. *c* **1205** LAY. 7187 Swa þat *Romleode comen to þissen þeoden. *c* **1200** ORMIN 8305 Fra þatt þatt he bigann to rixlenn I *Rome riche. **13..** *Seuyn Sag.* 1687 (W.), Thourgh *Rome stretes. *c* **1205** LAY. 9046 Kinbelin.. weorede *Rome-þeode wið vncuðe leode. *c* **888** K. ÆLFRED *Boeth.* xxvii. § 1 Hit wæs ða swiðe micel sido mid *Romwarum. *c* **1205** LAY. 7936 Laðliche heo foehten & Rom-ware feollen.

b. Objective, etc., as ***Rome-believer***, ***-bred***, etc.

1792 G. GALLOWAY *Poems* 40 Pit [= put] sandals on, Or bare-foot scud like Rome-believers. **1802–12** BENTHAM *Ration. Judic. Evid.* (1827) IV. 147 Such also has been the general practice under Rome-bred law on the continent of Europe. **1846** G. S. FABER *Lett. Tractar. Secess.* 68 He has told us, that.. a real Papist lay concealed beneath an outwardly professing and Rome-vituperating Anglican.

c. Special Comb.: **Rome-Berlin axis** [AXIS[1] 4 b], the association formed in 1936 between Fascist Italy and National Socialist Germany.

1936 [see AXIS[1] 4 b]. **1938** E. AMBLER *Cause for Alarm* viii. 128 The Rome-Berlin axis is one of the most effective principles of European power-politics that has ever been stated. **1939** 'G. ORWELL' *Coming up for Air* III. i. 182 Rubber truncheons, Rome-Berlin axis, Popular Front. **1976** S. HYNES *Auden Generation* vii. 193, 1936 is the peripeteia, the point where the action turned:.. the Rome-Berlin Axis was formed [etc.].

†**rome**, *v. Obs.*[−1] ? To stretch.

c **1340** *Nominale* (Skeat) 252 *Homme apres dormer se espreche*, Man aftur slepe romuth hym.

rome, obs. form of ROAM, ROOM, RUM *a.*; see also ROMY *v.*

romege(r, obs. ff. RUMMAGE(R.

romein(e, obs. ff. ROMAN *sb.* and *a.*[1]

ˈ**romeine.** *Min.* A former name for ROMÉITE.

1849 CRAIG, *Romeine*, a mineral occurring in small square octohedrons, in groups of minute crystals. **1852** BROOKE & MILLER *Phillips' Min.* 681 Romeine.. is found in the manganese mines of St. Marcel in Piedmont. **1868** WATTS *Dict. Chem.*, *Romeine*, or *Romeite*.

roméite (ˈrəʊmeɪaɪt). *Min.* Also **romeite.** [Named as *roméine* by A. Damour (1841) after the crystallographer *Romé de L'Isle*, later altered to form with -ITE[1].] An antimonate of calcium, $Ca_2Sb_2O_7$ (usu. also containing other elements esp. iron or titanium), which occurs as yellow or yellow-brown octahedral crystals. Formerly known as ROMEINE.

[**1850** J. D. DANA *Syst. Min.* (ed. 3) 416 (*heading*) Romeine, *Damour*,.. Romeit.] **1868** *Ibid.* (ed. 5) 547 Romeite was found by B. de Lom at St. Marcel in Piedmont. **1916** *Bull. U.S. Geol. Survey* No. 610. 96 The Brazilian so-called atopite is.. identical with the romeite from Italy. **1953** *Mineral Mag.* XXX. 101 The definition of stibiconite .. includes the mineral roméite, which has long been recognized as a calcium antimonate. **1968** I. KOSTOV *Mineral.* II. 265 Roméite and hydrocervantite.. have adsorbed water.

romekin, obs. form of RUMKIN.

ˈ**Romeless,** *a. rare*[−1]. [f. ROME *sb.* + -LESS.] Without Rome; destitute of Rome.

1885 FREEMAN *Chief Periods Europ. Hist.* 173 One of the most wonderful features of the age in which we live.. is that the world is Romeless.

romelynge, obs. form of RUMBLING.

romenay, -ey, variants of RUMNEY.

Romeo (ˈrəʊmiːəʊ). [Name of the hero of Shakespeare's tragedy *Romeo and Juliet*.]

1. A lover, a passionate admirer; a seducer, a habitual pursuer of women. Also *attrib.*

1766 C. ANSTEY *New Bath Guide* ix. 59 May I oft my Romeo meet, Oft enjoy his Converse sweet. **1867** TROLLOPE *Claverings* I. iii. 35 He has come out so strong in the Romeo line... We shall have him under your bed-room window with a guitar. **1917** E. O'NEILL *Long Voyage Home* in *Smart Set* Oct. 56/2 *Driscoll*.. Shut up, ye Rooshan baboon! A foine Romeo you'd make in your condishun. **1942** *Sun* (Baltimore) 26 Mar. 10/2, I think from the way I so often see his eyes cast far up and around through the open spaces that he is also playing a bit of Romeo. **1974** G. MITCHELL *Javelin for Jonah* iii. 48 Henry.. locked up the mansion to keep out any prospective Romeos who might fancy a visit to the women students' rooms. **1976** *Leicester Chron.* 26 Nov. 2/4 He's known as the studio's resident Romeo, with a social life and a string of girlfriends which must be exhausting rather than exhilarating.

2. (With small initial.) Also ***romeo slipper***. A type of high slipper, now only for men, usu. made of felt and with elasticated gores. *U.S.*

1895 *Montgomery Ward Catal.* Spring & Summer 514/2 Men's leather sole Romeo... This slipper is made of one piece of black felt. *Ibid.* 514/3 Ladies' Romeo... Made of toilet felt, fur trimmed. **1898** *Morse & Rogers Money Saver* Oct. 17 (Advt.), Men's romeo slippers. Don't be out of slippers. Romeos are becoming more and more popular. **1924** E. FERBER *Show Boat* i. 5 Peeping.. around this, the baffled eye could just glimpse oddments and elegancies such as.. a pair of scuffed tan kid bedroom slippers (men's) of the sort known as romeos. **1952** R. BISSELL *Monongahela* xix. 205 While sitting on the bunk pulling on your romeos you wonder what side of the family this madness comes from that makes you live like this.

3. ***Romeo and Juliet***: Anglicization of Sp. *Romeo y Julieta*, the proprietary name of a Havana cigar. (Also semi-Anglicized as ***Romeo and Julieta, Romeo y Juliet***.) Also *attrib.*

1904 *Trade Marks Jrnl.* 7 Sept. 1105 Romeo y Julieta... Tobacco, cigars, cigarettes and snuff. Rodriguez Argüelles & Co.,.. Havana, Cuba; cigar manufacturers. **1907** *Yesterday's Shopping* (1969) 64/2 *Havana cigars*... 'Romeo and Julieta'. **1945** A. HUXLEY *Time must have a Stop* v. 51 His Uncle Eustace lighted the massive Romeo and Juliet. **1957** J. OSBORNE *Entertainer* II. 43 Gave me a box of Romeo and Juliet cigars. **1966** *Guardian* 19 Mar. 6/6 The host had his mouth full of Romeo y Juliet cigar. *Ibid.* 12 Oct. 5/5 One could always finish with a cigar; say Romeo y Julieta, coronas, 660s the hundred, 5½ inches long.

Roˈmeoing. *nonce-wd.* [f. the Shakespearean *Romeo*.] Conduct resembling that of Romeo.

1827 HONE *Every-day Bk.* II. 133 This Romeoing is rendered more scenical by a tree.

ˈ**Rome-penny.** Now *Hist.* Forms: 1 **Rompæni(ȝ, -peniȝ, -peneȝ, 2 -peni; 4–5 Rome peny** (5 **Roome, Rume**), 9 **Rome-penny** (7 *dial.* **Ream-**). [f. ROME *sb.* 2 + PENNY.] = PETER('S)-PENNY.

a **1000** in Cockayne *The Shrine* 208 Siȝ ælc Rompeniȝ aȝifen be Petres mæsse dæȝe. *a* **1000** *Laws Northumbrian Priests* lvii. (Liebermann), We willaþ þæt ælc Rompæni beo ȝelæst be Petres mæssan to ðam bisceop stole. *a* **1023** WULFSTAN *Hom.* (1883) 113 Sulhælmessan and rompeneȝas and cyricsceattas. *a* **1193** BENEDICT OF PETERBOROUGH *Chron.* (Rolls) II. 226 Episcopus Dunelmensis jura ecclesiæ Eboraci, scilicet Le Rom-peni.. detinuit. **1377** *Rolls of Parlt.* III. 21/1 La charge de le Denier Seint Piere, appelle Rome-peny. *a* **1400** *Chron. J. Brompton* in Twysden *Decem Script.* (1652) 1235 Scilicet de Rume-peny, id est, de denario sancti Petri. *c* **1470** HARDYNG *Chron.* XCIX. viii, At his death he gaue to Roome eche yere The Roome pence, through Westsex all about. *Ibid.* CIII. vi, Offa [gave] through Mers the Rome peny Vnto the Church of Rome. **1674** RAY *N.C. Words*, *Ream-penny*; q. *Rome-penny*... 'He reckons up his ream-pennies', that is, tells all his faults. **1889** *Archaeol. Rev.* Aug. 43 It was called Rome-scot, Rome-penny, Hearth-penny.

romer (ˈrəʊmə(r)). Also **Romer.** [Named after Carrol *Romer* (1883–1951), British barrister, who invented it.] A small piece of plastic or card with scales along two edges meeting at a right angle, or (if transparent) bearing a grid, used for measuring the map reference of a point within the grid printed on a map.

1933 *Geogr. Jrnl.* LXXXII. 47 This Romer, as it was called after the gentleman who invented it. **1943** F. F. CROSSLEY *Map Reading* iii. 15 In order to facilitate the estimation of the last figure of the reference it is useful to construct a Romer... The sides of the Romer are subdivided into tenths. **1960** S. TURNER *Rallying* 38 The cross-roads might thus be given as 25401464. For plotting of this accuracy a romer is necessary. **1963** P. DRACKETT *Motor Rallying* iii. 41 Lining up the Romer so that one straight edge of the rectangle is in line with 386 and the straight edge meeting it is in line with 443, the point of bisection gives the place referred to. **1969** G. C. DICKINSON *Maps & Air Photographs* viii. 114 Of course a different romer is needed for each scale. **1975** J. B. HARLEY *O.S. Maps* ii. 24 A point.. can be indicated still more closely by estimating the tenths of the appropriate grid square either by eye or by means of a romer.

romer, obs. form of RUMMER.

†ˈ**Rome-raiker.** *Obs.* Chiefly *Sc.* Also 6 **Rome-raker (Roume-), -rakar, -raikar, Roome raiker.** [f. ROME *sb.* 2 + RAIKER.] = ROME-RUNNER.

1535 STEWART *Cron. Scot.* III. 276 Ane Rome-raiker that gane had mony gaittis. *c* **1550** LYNDESAY *Trag. Card.* 377 Off Rome rakaris, nor of rude Ruffianis, Off calsay Paikaris, nor of Publycanis. **1566** DRANT *Horace, Sat.* vi. D iv b, Not roumerakers, nor rente rackers nor staynde with vices mo. *a* **1585** POLWART *Flyting w. Montgomerie* 751 Gleyd glaiker roome raiker for releife.

römerite, var. ROEMERITE.

ˈ**Rome-runner.** *Obs.* exc. *Hist.* Also 4 **Rome-renner.** [f. ROME *sb.* 2 + RUNNER.] A person, esp. a cleric, who was constantly journeying to Rome to obtain benefices or other advantages.

1362 LANGL. *P. Pl.* A. IV. 111, I schal a-signe.. alle Rome Renners.. Bere no seluer ouer see. *c* **1380** WYCLIF *Wks.* (1880) 23 þus þes rome renneris beren þe kyngys gold out of oure lond. **1395** PURVEY *Remonstr.* (1851) 88 Though so great hil of gold were in Ingelond, and no man outake siche Rome-renneris toke of it. **1577** in J. Morris *Troubles Cath. Forefathers* (1872) I. ii. 79 Masters, you that are sworn, this fellow here, Cuthbert Maine, is, as you see, a Rome-runner.

1895 *Short Hist. Cath. Ch. Eng.* 258 Abuses chiefly caused by so called Rome-runners—priests thronging to Rome and importuning the Holy See for benefices.

ˈ**Rome-scot.** *Obs.* exc. *Hist.* Forms: 1 **Romȝescot**, 2, 6–7 **Romscot**, 7–8 **Roomscot**; 1 **Rome scott**, 1– **Rome scot**, 3– **Romescot**, 8– **Rome-scot** (also 5 **-scote**, 5–6 **-scotte**). [See ROME *sb.* 2 and SCOT *sb.* The OE. word was probably the source of MDa. *Romskud*, MSw. *Romskott*, *-skuth*, ON. *Rómaskattr*.] = ROME-PENNY.

c **1050** in Liebermann *Gesetze* 474 Romȝescot sy aȝifen on sanctus Petrus mæssedæȝ ær undern æfter middesumera. *c* **1050** *Laws Edw. Confessor* c. 10 (Liebermann), De denario Santi Petri (qui Anglice dicitur Romescot). **1127** *O.E. Chron.* (Laud MS.) an. 1127, þurh þæt he wæs legat of ðone Rome scott. *c* **1130** HENRY OF HUNTINGDON *Hist. Angl.* VI. (Rolls) 188 Rex vero Knut Romam splendide perrexit; et eleemosynam, quæ vocatur 'Romscot',.. perenniter assignavit. *c* **1237** ROGER OF WENDOVER *Flores Hist.* (1841) I. 258 Denarium beati Petri,.. quod Anglice 'Romescot' appellatur. **1387** TREVISA *Higden* (Rolls) VI. 213 He..

grauntede to seynt Peter of everiche hous of his kyngdom a peny, þat longe tyme of Englisshe men was i-cleped Rome scot. **1451** in T. Gardner *Hist. Dunwich* (1754) 148 Payd.. for Romescot in Fest. Paschae, 11 *ob.* **1512** *MS. Acc. St. John's Hospital, Canterbury*, Payd for romscot to Cosmas Bleune cherche, j d.

1631 Weever *Anc. Mon.* 157 Of Pardons, Pilgrimages, and Romescot. **1653** Milton *Hirelings* 57 They..might produce..that Romescot, or Peter's penny, was by as good statute law paid to the Pope. **1716** M. Davies *Athen. Brit.* I. 188 Such a Badge of the Romish Supremacy, that no other Nation ever wore.., viz. Peter-Pence or Rome-Scot. **1812** J. Brady *Clavis Cal.* II. 206 The confirmation he gave to the payment of the ancient Rome Scot, or Peter's Pence. **1875** Stubbs *Const. Hist.* II. xvi. 415 Even Peter's pence, the ancient Romescot,..was witheld for a time.

attrib. **1661** J. Stephens *Procurations* 103 The Cardinal is pleased..to collect, that a judgement fell upon this Land, when first it fell off from Rome-scot pay.

¶ (See quot.)

1596 Spenser *State Irel.* Wks. (Globe) 663 This was the course which the Romains used in the conquest of England, ..cutting upon everye portion of lande a reasonable rent, which they called Romescott.

So †**Rome-shot.** *Obs.*

c **1100** in Birch *Cartul. Sax.* III. 264 Relaxamus etiam eos qui intra villam ipsius procinctus commorantur a collecta denariorum quam *romeschot* appellant. *a* **1121** *O.E. Chron.* (Laud MS.) an. 1095, Man syððan þæt Romȝesceot be him sende. **1546** Bale *Eng. Votaries* I. 43 b, Thys Inas..clogged the west Saxons with payment of the Rome shott. **1550** *Ibid.* II. H iv, He also restrained the Rome shot. **1570** Foxe *A. & M.* (ed. 2) 177/1 Through which deuotion of the said kinges first came in the Peterpence or Romschots in this realme. *a* **1643** Sir J. Spelman *Life Alfred* (1709) 23 The same, it seems, was called Rome-shott or Peter Pence.

romesome, obs. form of ROOMSOME.

rometh(e, obs. forms of ROOMTH.

Romeward ('rəʊmwəd), *adv.* and *a.* [f. ROME *sb.* + -WARD.]

1. Towards, in the direction of, Rome.

c **1330** R. Brunne *Chron. Wace* (Rolls) 6810 How longe þe Romayns scholde soiourne, & whan þey scholde to Rome-ward tourne. **1390** Gower *Conf.* II. 200 Every lond, to Romeward which hadde be soubgit tofore. *c* **1412** Hoccleve *De Reg. Princ.* 1262 Seint Ambroses legende seith, how he Ones to Rome-ward took his viage.

1887 Bowen *Virg. Ecl.* I. 26 What was the mighty occasion that Romeward called thee to go?

2. Towards the Roman Catholic Church or Roman Catholicism.

1864 Newman *Apol.* iv. (1904) 135/1 As soon as I turned my face Romeward. **1871** E. Harrison in *Life & Lett. Jowett* (1897) II. 27 Newman stirred the soul of Oxford and drew all Romeward.

Comb. **1876** Fox Bourne *Locke* I. 459 Such a system of Church discipline as Stillingfleet and the Romeward-tending Church of England advocated and enforced.

3. a. As *adj.* Directed to, tending towards, the Roman Catholic Church.

1851 Bp. Wilberforce in R. G. Wilberforce *Life* (1881) II. 110 That Romeward tendency which, in many minds, is our present especial danger. **1887** *Spectator* 12 Mar. 360/2 His distinct repudiation of Romeward doctrine.

b. Directed towards or facing the city of Rome.

1850 J. Miley *Hist. Papal States* I. 6 Not less so on the Adriatic side of the Apennines than on the Romeward side. **1979** *London Rev. Bks.* 25 Oct. 5/3 Salim's flight to London can be compared..to the Romeward journey in Virgil.

So '**Romewards** *adv.*

1849 M. Arnold *Resignation* 9 So warriors said, Scarf'd with the cross..; so [said]..The Goth, bound Rome-wards. **1866** T. Harper *Peace thro' Truth* Ser. I. p. xcvii, Devout and earnest persons, casting a wistful glance Romewards.

'**Romewardness.** [-NESS.] Tendency towards Roman Catholicism.

1901 *Daily Chron.* 27 Aug. 5/1 The young Duchess was forgiven by her relatives for her Romewardness.

Romeyn(e, obs. forms of ROMAN *a.*[1]

Romic ('rəʊmɪk), *a.* and *sb.* [f. ROM-AN *a.* + -IC.] The distinctive epithet of a system of phonetic notation devised by Dr. H. Sweet.

1877 Sweet *Handbk. Phonetics* 102 This system, which I call 'Romic' (because based on the original Roman values of the letters). *Ibid.* 202 Detailed comparison of Glossic and Romic.

†'**Romified,** *ppl. a. Obs.* [See ROME *sb.* 2 and -IFY.] That has gone over to Rome.

1609 Sir E. Hoby *Let. to T. H[iggons]* 6 My readines is alwaies prest to answere you, or any Fugitiue Romified Renegado whomsoeuer. **1613** —— *Counter-Snarle* 66.

Ro'mipetal, *a.* [f. ROME *sb.*, after *centripetal.* Cf. med.L. *Romipeta.*] Tending towards Rome.

1897 *Eng. Hist. Rev.* Oct. 628 The kind of jurisprudence which is the outcome of this judicial system is likely to be a centripetal, Romipetal kind.

Romish ('rəʊmɪʃ), *a.* Also 6 **Romishe, Rhomish, Romysh(e.** [f. ROME *sb.* + -ISH. Cf. OFris. *Rumisk, -esk,* (M)Du. *Roomsch.* OHG. *Rômisc, Rûmisc* (MHG. *Rœmisch,* G. *Römisch*), MDa. *Romsk,* MSw. *Romsk, Römsk.*]

1. a. Belonging, pertaining, or adhering to Rome in respect of religion; Roman Catholic.

Chiefly in hostile or opprobrious use.

1531 Tindale *Exp. 1 John* iv, Examine the Romish bishop by this rule. **1560** Daus tr. *Sleidane's Comm.* 92 The Emperor chooseth out certen of the Romysh Relygion to make a decree. **1585** *Act 27 Eliz.* c. 2 §1 Priests..made.. according to the Order and Rites of the Romish Church. **1628** Prynne *Brief Surv.* Ep., Iesuiticall Treatises, or Romish prayer-bookes, Portuasses, and Mannuals. *a* **1674** Milton *Hist. Moscovia* iv. Wks. 1851 VIII. 491 Upon promise of the Duke to become Romish. **1725** Berkeley *Proposal* Wks. 1871 III. 225 Our neighbours of the Romish communion. **1791** Boswell *Johnson* (Oxf. ed.) II. 642 The charity in which he lived with good men of the Romish Church. **1814** Scott *Diary* 26 Aug. in *Lockhart,* Here, after 1745,..the priest of Egg used to perform the Romish service. **1850** Bp. Wilberforce in R. G. Wilberforce *Life* (1881) II. 91 An assurance sufficient to convince me that there is no danger of your acting in fact as a Romish confessor in the orders of the English Church. **1862** Furnivall *R. Brunne's Handl. Synne* (Roxb. Club) p. xlviii, The Romish second (Mosaic third) Commandment.

†**b.** *absol.* as *pl.* Roman Catholics. *Obs.*

1605 Sandys *Europæ Spec.* Y 3, In other points they seeme to stand..between the Romish and the Protestants. **1625** Pemble *Justification* (1629) 75 Against this the Romish contend, labouring to proue [etc.].

†**2. *Romish Catholic,*** = ROMAN CATHOLIC. *Obs.*

1606 *Proc. agst. Traitors* 28 In the names and for the behalfe of all the English Romish Catholiques. **1646** T. Temple *Irish Reb.* (1746) 24 The Romish Catholics now privately enjoyed the free exercise of their Religion. **1689** *Conn. Col. Rec.* (1859) III. 468 We doe aduise that..no romish catholick be suffered to keep armes within your government or citty. **1826** [see HOLY CROSS].

3. = ROMAN *a.* I. *arch.*

1567 Drant *Horace, Ep.* D v b, I, the romishe musicion. **1579** Spenser *Sheph. Cal.* Oct. 55 The Romish Tityrus, I heare, Through his Mecænas left his Oaten reede. **1600** Dekker *Gentle Craft* 18 Do this, and I will give thee..My cambricke apron, and my romish gloves. **1658** 'Optatus Ductor' *Quest. of Quest.* 23 S. Peter and S. Paul..caused no part of the bible to be translated into the Romish language. **1797** T. Holcroft tr. *Stolberg's Trav.* III. lxxi, A Romish squadron landed at Pompeii. **1816** T. J. Howell *Stranger in Shrewsbury* 182 During its subjection to the Romish yoke, this country formed part of the province of Flavia Cæsariensis. **1917** W. Owen *Let.* 14 Feb. (1967) 435 Do you need a Brooch? I saw an Egyptian one, rather huge,..and an Assyrian. No they wouldn't do since you no longer wear your Ancient British frocks. All the others in this town are either Romish, or nondescript.

†**4. *Romish alum*:** see ROMAN *a.*[1] 16 a. *Obs.*

1620 *Observ. on Silkwormes* D b, Roach-Allum, called Romish Allum.

†**5. *Romish herbs*:** see ROMAN *a.*[1] 14 a. ***Romish beans, peas*:** see ROMAN *a.*[1] 14 b. *Obs.*

1648 Hexham II. s.v. *Roomsch,* Romish Pease, or Pease growing about poles. *Ibid.,* Romish beanes.

Hence '**Romishly** *adv.*, '**Romishness.**

1658 Osborn *King Jas.* Wks. (1673) 484 Prayers and Fasts appointed to be used by those Romishly affected throughout this whole Realm. **1682** *Roxb. Ball.* (1884) V. 194 Lest they..be unto Newgate sent, There (Romishly) to keep a Lent. **1864** Mrs. Oliphant *Perpetual Curate* I. iii. 51, I think he has a bad attack of Romishness coming on. **1886** *Lett. from Donegal* 40 This contempt for what they call 'Romishness'.

'**Romist.** ? *Obs.* [f. ROME *sb.* 2 + -IST.] A Roman Catholic, a Romanist.

1592 Warner *Alb. Eng.* IX. xlviii. (1602) 222 One selfe-same Religion (such as Spanish Romistes haue). **1606** Dekker *Double P.P.* Wks. (Grosart) II. 159 Since so strange Commotion..Puffes the Romist vp in Armes. **1677** W. Hughes *Man of Sin* II. x. 177 This..consists in Words and Deeds. Now Romists have a Marvellous Stroak at both. **1716** M. Davies *Athen. Brit.* III. Diss. Drama 6 The Emblem of Geometry being apply'd to Presbytery, and the visionary Romists. **1784** J. Brown *Hist. Brit. Ch.* (1820) I. iv. 80 The Church of England's imitation of the Romists. **1821** *Fair Witch of Glasllyn* II. 349 The Dominicans were the ultra Romists.

†**b.** So *Romist Catholic. Obs.*[−1]

1661 Boyle *Style of Script.* 96 As much a nose of wax as the Romist Catholics say we make the other.

'**Romized,** *ppl. a. rare*[−1]. [See ROME *sb.* 2 and -IZE.] Siding with Rome.

1655 Fuller *Ch. Hist.* III. 52 The Romiz'd faction were zealous in his behalf.

'**rommack,** *v. dial.* In 8 romack, 9 rommak, -mock. [Of obscure origin: the variant *rammack* has a wide range, and *rummack* is current in north-western dialects.]

1. *trans.* To rummage or fish *up.*

1770 *Boston Rec.* (1887) XVIII. 30 Were it possible to romack up any absurd obsolete notion, which might have seemed calculated to propagate slavish doctrines.

2. *intr.* To romp or gambol boisterously or rudely. Hence '**rommacking** *ppl. a.*

a **1825** Forby *Voc. E. Anglia* s.v. *a* **1837** Clare in Miss Baker *Northampt. Gloss.* (1854) s.v., She's a rommaking, slommaking thing. **1854** Miss Baker *Northampt. Gloss.*

romme, obs. f. ROOM.

‖**rommelpot** ('rɒməlpɒt). Also **rommel pot, rommel-pot.** [Du., = rumble pot.] **a.** A type of drum used in southern Africa (see quot. 1840). **b.** A type of drum used in the Low Countries (see quots. 1964, 1976).

1840 B. Shaw *Memorials S. Afr.* iii. 44 The rommel pot is a bamboo over which a piece of skin is tightly stretched, and is used as a drum at their [*sc.* the Namaquas'] dances. **1881** *Encycl. Brit.* XII. 311/1 The 'rommel-pot' was a kind of drum. **1964** S. Marcuse *Mus. Instruments* 446/2 *Rommelpot*..., Dutch and Flemish friction drum with friction stick, made of an earthenware pot sometimes containing water, closed at the top by an animal bladder. The friction stick penetrates the center of the bladder and is rotated or pushed up and down. **1970** J. Blades *Percussion Instruments* x. 196 In Flanders the rommelpot is particularly associated with Christmas. **1976** D. Munrow *Instruments Middle Ages & Renaissance* v. 34/1 The rommelpot..is a type of friction drum... The action required is not scraping the stick to and fro but rubbing it gently with moistened fingers.

rommidge, obs. var. RUMMAGE *v.*

rommy, obs. var. ROOMY *adv.*

romnay, -ney, variants of RUMNEY.

Romney (Marsh) ('rʌmnɪ, 'rɒmnɪ mɑːʃ). The name of an area of rich grazing land on the coast of Kent, used *absol.* and *attrib.* to designate a stocky, long-woolled sheep of the breed so called.

1837 W. Youatt *Sheep* vii. 239 In some parts of the east of the county a polled breed of middle size, a cross between the Romney Marsh and the South Down, is found. **1861** I. Beeton *Bk. Househ. Managem.* 327 (*caption*) Romney-Marsh Ewe. *Ibid.,* The Romney Marsh..is a highly useful ..variety..of the English domestic sheep. **1891, 1894** [see KENT *sb.*[3]]. **1922** V. Sackville-West *Heir* iv. 42 It's like sheep..Oxfordshire don't do on Romney Marsh, and Romney Marsh don't do in Oxfordshire. **1923** [see LEICESTER]. **1926** *Daily Colonist* (Victoria, B.C.) 16 Jan. 15/5 Two handsome Romney rams, proud and bellicose,..were landed today. **1950** *N.Z. Jrnl. Agric.* Jan. 15/3 The Romney sheep was by then [*sc.* about 1890] the dominant breed. **1957** [see KENT *sb.*[3]]. **1974** T. Allbeury *Snowball* xiv. 72 It's been said that Romney Marsh sheep are bred only for survival. **1976** *Leicester Advertiser* 26 Nov. 11/5 The Animal Breeding Research Organisation is importing four hairy Romney rams from New Zealand. **1978** *Jrnl. R. Soc. Arts* CXXVI. 590/2 Factors limiting lamb production in New Zealand Romneys.

†**romongour.** *Obs.*[−1] [App. a comb. of *-monger,* but the first element is obscure. The French original has *maskignons.*] A (horse-) coper, corser, or dealer.

1340 *Ayenb.* 44þe zixte is: [to] hede þe zoþnesse of þe þinge þet me wyle zelle, ase doþ þe romongours of hors.

romour, obs. form of RUMOUR.

romp (rɒmp), *sb.* [Perh. a later form of RAMP *sb.*[1] with slight modification of sense.]

1. One who romps; *esp.* a play-loving, lively, merry girl (or woman).

1706 Vanbrugh *Prov. Wife* IV. iii, One that knows how to deal with such romps as you are. **1713** Arbuthnot *John Bull* II. i, Your Romps that have no regard to the common Rules of Civility. **1783** Johnson in Boswell *Life* (Oxf. ed.) II. 512 She was a better romp than any I ever saw in nature. **1806–7** J. Beresford *Miseries Hum. Life* (1826) XVIII. xv, The Matrons and Seniors of the Stage frisking and dashing through the parts of Romps and Rakes. **1846** De Quincey *Syst. Heavens* Wks. III. 171 Such a girl..you might call a romp; but not a hoyden, observe; no horse-play. **1862** Sala *Seven Sons* I. xi. 257 Another variety of the fat school-girl is there in the romp.

2. a. A piece of lively, boisterous play; a merry frolic. Freq. in *pl.*

1734 Fielding *Universal Gallant* III, What, are you at romps, good people? **1756–82** J. Warton *Ess. Pope* I. iv. 248 A game of romps was never so well dignified before. **1797** Mme. D'Arblay *Lett.* Dec., My little rogue soon engaged him in a romp. **1847** Ticknor *Life, Lett. & Jrnls.* II. xi. 229 The most thorough game of romps I have come across for many a day. **1882** Miss Braddon *Mt. Royal* II. x, I have been having a romp with my godson.

Comb. **1730–46** Thomson *Autumn* 528 Romp-loving Miss Is haul'd about, in gallantry robust.

b. Phr. ***in a romp,*** with the greatest ease.

1901 J. Ralph *War's Brighter Side* xv. 249 One said to me, as he pointed at Maghersfontain Kopje, 'Set a brewery upon top of that and my regiment will take the place in a romp.' **1904** 'O. Henry' in *Everybody's Mag.* Feb. 192/1 Rompiro will win in a romp... We'll carry the country by 10,000.

3. *attrib.*, as ***romp-suit*** = ROMPER 2.

1961 W. Sansom *Last Hours of Sandra Lee* iv. 70 A fresh-faced girl in a romp-suit.

romp (rɒmp), *v.* [Perh. a modification of RAMP *v.*[1] Cf. ROMP *sb.*]

1. *intr.* To play, sport, or frolic in a very lively, merry, or boisterous manner.

1709 Steele *Tatler* No. 15 ¶2 This careless Jade was eternally romping with the Footman. **1768–74** Tucker *Lt. Nat.* (1834) II. 143 How will you..prevent your sons from consorting with the blackguard, or your daughters from romping among the grooms? **1789** Mrs. Piozzi *Journ. France* I. 83 Gentlemen..romped with the girls of the house. **1842** J. Wilson *Chr. North* (1857) I. 143 The young people will have been romping about the parlours. **1881** H. Smart *Race for Wife* ii, They had romped together as children.

transf. **1891** 'J. S. Winter' *Lumley* ix, The big mare.., after romping about the road for a minute or two, tore away up a steep hill.

2. Chiefly *racing slang*: **a.** To move, cover the ground, easily and rapidly. Also *transf.*

1891 'J. S. Winter' *Mrs. Bob* 120 To use the language of the turf, she romped clean away from them. **1893** H. M. Doughty *Our Wherry* 70 In what was rough water to our little ship we romped along. **1928** *Sunday Express* 22 July 1/1 The child of 1928 simply romps through papers which were 'teasers' for the child of 1914. **1951** *People* 17 June 2 Petula Clark, who romps away with her first grown-up part with all-star honours. **1960** *Times* 16 May 19/1 He and Davies romped to a 5–1 lead. **1964** *Amer. Folk Music*

Occasional I. 40 Those..lists of Broadway..romp up past the million mark in a few months. **1968** J. SANGSTER *Touchfeather* ii. 8, I romped through the training, passing out eventually with the highest marks anyone could remember. **1976** *Southwest Times Record* (Fort Smith, Arkansas) 20 Sept. 1 B/1 The Dallas Cowboys overcame a rash of early errors and romped to a 24–6 National Football League victory over the New Orleans Saints.

b. To get *in* (or *home*), to win a race or prize with the greatest ease. Also *transf.*

1881 E. W. HAMILTON *Diary* 28 Oct. (1972) I. 178 The Liberal candidate, though a Roman Catholic and not supposed to be a good candidate, simply 'romped in'. **1888** 'THORMANBY' *Men of the Turf* 16 Eclipse..simply romped in, the easiest of winners. **1891** *Sporting Life* 20 Mar. (Farmer), I recall his recent half-mile at Oxford, when he romped home in the easiest possible manner. **1910** A. BENNETT *Clayhanger* III. xvii. 444 A demy poster..to inform the public that the true friend of the public was 'romping in'. **1927** *Observer* 18 Sept. 17/2 It is a bad blow to official Labour that Mr. Larkin should have romped home in north Dublin. **1950** *Sport* 22–28 Sept. 4/1 On Saturday the Forest 'stiffs' romped home to a 5–1 victory over Halifax. **1974** *Times* 2 Mar. 4/7 Mr Thorpe..romped home in his own constituency while Liberals elsewhere were generally less successful. **1977** *West Briton* 25 Aug. 18/1 Troon were handsome winners on Saturday when, facing a Hayle score of 200 for seven, they romped home by seven wickets.

3. *trans.* To drive or convey in a romping fashion.

1895 KIPLING *2nd Jungle Bk.* 78 Baloo..would shamble alongside a wavering line and half frighten, half romp it clumsily back to the proper road. **1897** *Daily News* 3 May 7/3 They were being romped back to Hanopoulo as fast as mules could take them.

rompe, obs. form of RUMP.

† **rompee.** *Her. Obs.* Also 7 rompe. [Alteration of F. *rompu* (pa. pple. of *rompre*), on the analogy of other heraldic terms in *-ee*.] Broken.

1610 GUILLIM *Heraldry* III. v. 133 He beareth, Sable, a cheueron Rompee, betweene three Mullets, Or, by the Name of Sault. *Ibid.*, This cheueron in Blazon is called Rompe or rather Rompu. **1728** CHAMBERS *Cycl.*, *Rompee*, or *Rompu*, in Heraldry, is applied to Arms, or other Ordinaries, that are represented broken; and to Chevrons whose upper Points are cut. [**1868** CUSSANS *Her.* (1893) 82 In this example..the Pales..are *rompu*, or broken by a Bend.]

romper ('rɒmpə(r)). [f. ROMP *v.* + -ER.]

1. One who romps.

1842 A. DE VERE *Song of Faith* 206 Boarding-school rompers, academic praters. **1876** T. HARDY *Ethelberta* (1890) 104 To look wistfully at the sitters when romping and at the rompers when sitting.

2. Usu. *pl.* Also ***romper suit.*** A one-piece garment for a child to wear at play; a casual one-piece garment worn esp. by young women. (See also quots. 1941, 1943.)

1909 *Dialect Notes* III. 364 *Rompers, n. pl.* A one-piece garment for children to play in. **1915** R. W. LARDNER *Bib Ballads* 3 Hark! A voice from the easy chair: 'He hasn't a romper that's fit to wear.' **1922** *Moving Picture Stories* 23 June 24/1 The dainty bit of femininity, by the way, wore a suit of gingham rompers. **1922** *Westm. Gaz.* 20 Oct. 9 (Advt.), An attractive romper suit for a small child is made of white washing material. **1928** L. NORTH *Parasites* 18 Many of them wore sweaters that would have put Joseph's coat to shame. And very long, very baggy knickers, Hollywood rompers. **1941** *Amer. Speech* XVI. 186/2 [British Army slang] *Rompers*, battle dress. **1943** 'T. DUDLEY-GORDON' *Coastal Command* 85 Sipping hot coffee as he took off his rompers (combined parachute harness and Mae West life-jacket) he told us of his first night raid. **1964** C. WILLOCK *Enormous Zoo* vii. 128 He wore his one-piece romper suit and his three-foot-wide straw hat. **1970** *Women's Wear Daily* 23 Nov. 31/2 We see little rompers..as a possible replacement. **1974** A. GODDARD *Vienna Pursuit* II. 77 A toddler in pale blue rompers.

† **'rompering.** *Obs.*$^{-1}$ (Meaning obscure.)

a **1616** BEAUM. & FL. *Wit without M.* v, I scorne sleepe... I scorne meate, I come for rompering, I come to waite upon my charge discreetely.

'romping, *vbl. sb.* [f. ROMP *v.* + -ING[1].] The action of the verb; boisterous play.

1711 STEELE *Spect.* No. 145 ¶6 His Pleasantry consists in Romping. **1731–8** SWIFT *Pol. Conv.* 56, I have torn my Petticoat with your odious Romping. **1825** J. NEAL *Bro. Jonathan* I. 27 She loved romping. **1825** HONE *Every-day Bk.* I. 135 The period that ushers in the carnival with rompings in the streets.

'romping, *ppl. a.* [f. ROMP *v.* + -ING[2].]

1. Of persons: That romps; engaged in, or given to, romping.

1711 STEELE *Spect.* No. 187 ¶3 The Air she gave herself was that of a Romping Girl. **1810** SIR A. BOSWELL *Edinb. Poet. Wks.* (1871) 53 There, romping miss the rounded slate may drop, And kick it out with persevering hop. **1869** TROLLOPE *He knew*, etc. xlvii. (1878) 260 Simply a romping girl, hardly more than a year or two beyond her teens.

fig. **1839–52** BAILEY *Festus* 253 Thine eyes are like two romping stars. **1887** HALL CAINE *Deemster* vi, And so five tearing, romping years went by.

2. Of actions, etc.: Having the character of a romp or romps.

1802 MAR. EDGEWORTH *Fr. Governess* Wks. 1832 III. 180 Miss Fanshawe, in a romping manner, pulled the paper out of her hands. **1835** *Politeness & Gd.-breeding* 48 Avoid all romping tricks. **1890** 'L. FALCONER' *Mademoiselle Ixe* iv, [She] listened respectfully to a denunciation of lawn tennis as a romping and unfeminine pastime.

Hence **'rompingly** *adv.* (Webster, 1864).

'rompish, *a.* [f. ROMP *sb.* + -ISH.] Inclined to romp; frolicsome.

1709 W. KING *Useful Trans. in Philos.* I. 37 The Dance was something Rompish. **1775** ASH, *Rompish*, inclined to rough play. **1824** MACTAGGART *Gallovid. Encycl.* s.v. *Ramp*, A creature is ramp that is rompish inclined. **1891** *Sat. Rev.* 14 Feb. 195/1 A rompish young personage. **1977** *Listener* 5 May 592/1 *Albert Herring* is altogether an awkward, disconcerting affair—so rompish on the surface.

Hence **'rompishly** *adv.*; **'rompishness**.

1711 STEELE *Spect.* No. 187 ¶3 She would..run into some other unaccountable Rompishness. **1847** WEBSTER, *Rompishly*. **1855** *Tait's Mag.* XXII. 220 Calculated to develope playful rompishness into boldness.

rompney, variant of RUMNEY.

'rompster. *rare*$^{-1}$. = ROMPER.

1893 *Pall Mall G.* 5 Jan. 3/1 Unfamiliar to the Yuletide rompsters of England.

rompt, obs. form of RUMP.

rompth, obs. var. ROOMTH.

rompu, *Her.*: see ROMPEE.

rompus, obs. f. RUMPUS.

rompy ('rɒmpɪ), *a.* [f. ROMP *sb.* + -Y.] Characterized by romps or romping; full of frolic.

1863 READE *Hard Cash* I. 134 Well, perhaps it is a little rompy. **1867** F. H. LUDLOW *Brace of Boys* 282 Everybody was permitted to be young again, and romp with the rompiest. **1877** DIXON *Diana, Lady Lyle* II. vi. i. 91 Bessie is..plump, rompy, bursting with health.

† **romsen,** obs. variant of RAMSON.

1647 HEXHAM *Eng.-Dutch Dict.* (Herbs), Romsens, *Knop loock, ofte wilde Loock.*

romth(y, variants of ROOMTH(Y.

romulea (rɒ'mju:lɪə). Also Romulea. [mod.L. (J. F. Maratti *Plantarum Romuleæ et Saturniæ in Agro Romano* (1772) 13), f. *Romul-us*, name of the mythical founder of Rome.] A small bulbous plant of the genus so called, belonging to the family Iridaceæ, native to coastal regions of southern Europe and South Africa, and bearing yellow, red, or purple flowers resembling a crocus.

1876 J. G. BAKER in *Jrnl. Bot.* XIV. 236 There are specimens in the herbaria either of Kew or the British Museum, with the exception of three of the *Romuleæ*. **1887** *Gardeners' Chron.* 5 Feb. 184/2 The hardier section of Romuleas belonging to the Mediterranean regions are also worthy our attention. **1909** R. FARRER *In Yorkshire Garden* viii. 148, I was quite terrified at the aspect of the Romulea clumps that my kind Cornish friend sent me the other day, so wild, so long and wiry-haired was their aspect. **1928** R. MACAULAY *Keeping up Appearances* ii. 14 Back from the beach stretched grassy slopes, purple and pink with romulea and silene. **1964** A. N. GRIFFITH *Collins Guide to Alpines* 243 Other romuleas, including the less hardy species from S. Africa, will be found described in detail.

Romu'leian, *a.* = next (sense 2).

1866 *Chambers's Encycl.* VIII. 309/1 In the Romuleian legend. *Ibid.*, The Romuleian myth.

Romulian (rəʊ'mju:lɪən), *a. rare.* Also 7 -ean. [ad. L. *Rōmuleus*, or f. *Rōmulus* the founder of Rome + -IAN.]

† **1.** Roman Catholic. *Obs.*$^{-1}$

1614 BP. HALL *No Peace with Rome* §3 What heresie is there in all times which that Romulean wolfe and her bawling clients are not wont to cast vpon vs?

2. Derived from, connected with, Romulus.

1842–3 *Smith's Dict. Grk. & Rom. Antiq.* 604 Six ancient Romulian years of 304 days each. **1886** *Encycl. Brit.* XX. 676/1 Exposure or killing of a child by its father contrary to the Romulian rules.

† **'Romulist.** *Obs. rare.* [f. *Rōmul-us* + -IST.]

1. A descendant of Romulus; a Roman.

1594 KYD *Cornelia* III. ii. 57 Why from Molossus and false Hanibal Haue yee reseru'd the noble Romulists?

2. A Roman Catholic.

1620 BP. HALL *Hon. Marr. Clergy* II. xvii, That sowre milke wherewith the shee-wolfe of the Seven Hills feeds the faction of her Romulists and Rhemists.

† **'romy,** *v. Obs.* Forms: 4 rumy-, rumi-, romi-, 4–5 romy, 5 romee, rome. [Of obscure origin. The synonymous Sc. form RUMMIS(H) may indicate an OF. **rumir*, **romir*, with lengthened stem **rumiss-*.] *intr.* To roar, to cry.

a **1300** *E.E. Ps.* ciii. 22 Lyoun whelpes romiand þat þai reue swa. *a* **1325** *Prose Psalter* xxi. 12 Hij maden her sautes vp me as a lyon rauissand and rumiand. **13..** *E.E. Allit. P.* B. 1543 He..romyes as a rad ryth[er] þat rorez for drede. ? *a* **1400** *Morte Arth.* 1124 Thane he romyed and rared, and ruydly he strykez. *c* **1440** *Alph. Tales* 300 Þis lyon wakend & myssyd his felow, & soght here & þer romyand & couthe not fynde hit. **1470–85** MALORY *Arthur* v. iv. 165 He rored and romed soo hydously that it were merueill to here. [Copying the allit. *Morte Arth.* 784.]

Hence † **'romying** *vbl. sb. Obs.*

c **1340** HAMPOLE *Pr. Consc.* 4774 Bot what þat romiyng sal signify, Na man may whit, bot God almyghty. *c* **1440** *Alph. Tales* 301 With a grete romying he ran opon þaim.

† **ron[1].** *Obs.* [Of obscure origin.

The word being app. southern, it is uncertain whether the original form is *ron* or *rǫn*:—**ran*: the latter would have a parallel in Ir. *rann* verse, poem, but any real connexion between the two is very doubtful. In *Cursor M.* 219 the form *ron* prob. stands for *roun*, *rūn*, but *riot ron* (riming with *don* done) in line 26938 may belong here.]

A short poem or song, *esp.* a love-song.

a **1225** *Leg. Kath.* 108 Nalde ha nane ronnes ne nane luue runes leornin ne lustnen. *c* **1275** *Luue Ron* 2 in *O.E. Misc.* 93 A mayde Cristes me bit yorne, þat ich hire wurche a luue ron [*rimes* -mon, con]. **1327** in *Rel. Antiquæ* I. 119 Herkne to my ron As ich ou telle con. *c* **1370** *Clene Maydenhod* (Vernon MS.) 2 Of a trewe loue clene and derne Ichaue I-write þe A Ron [*rimes* -mon, con, vppon].

† **ron[2].** *Obs.*$^{-1}$ [var. of RO *sb.* The *-n* is prob. not due merely to the rime-word *don*: cf. RONE *v.* and *mistrun* for MISTROW *sb.*] Rest.

a **1300** *Cursor M.* 24163 O[n] quam sal i nu cri and call, I redles vte o ron [*v.r.* ro]?

† **ron[3].** *Sc. Obs. rare.* Some kind of fish.

1525 in *Excerpta Lib. Dom. Jas. V* (Bann. Cl.) 7, ij ronis, lxxxiiij merlingis. *Ibid.* 8, j ron.

ron, obs. form of RONE *sb.*[1], ROUN, RUN.

ronagate, obs. form of RUNAGATE.

‖ **roncador** ('rɒŋkədɔə(r)). *U.S.* [Sp., agent-noun f. *roncar* to snore, snort.] One or other of several sciænoid fishes of the Pacific coast of North America (see quots.).

1882 JORDAN & GILBERT *Synop. Fishes N. Amer.* 572 *Sciæna stearnsi*,..Roncador. *Sciæna saturna*,..Red Roncador. **1884** RATHBUN *Nat. Hist. Aquat. Anim.* III. 379 *Corvina Saturna.* This fish is known where found as the 'Red Roncador'; less commonly as the 'Black Roncador' or 'Croaker'. **1888** GOODE *Amer. Fishes* 135 *Umbrina roncador*, generally known as the 'Yellow-tailed' or 'Yellow-finned Roncador'.

ronceval, variant of ROUNCIVAL.

ronchal, variant of RHONCHAL.

rond (rɒnd), *sb.*[1] Now *dial.* [var. of RAND *sb.*[1]]

† **1.** = RAND *sb.*[1] 2. *Obs.*

1393 LANGL. *P. Pl.* C. x. 148 When he ys rysen [he] romeþ out, and ryght wel aspieþ Whar he may raþest haue a repast oþer a ronde of bacon. **1466** *Mann. & Househ. Exp.* (Roxb.) 435 In ij. rondes of beffe, vj. d. **1572** J. JONES *Buckstones Bathes Benefyte* 9 b, Some in forme of Cakes, as at weddings: some Rondes of Hogs, as at vpsittings. **1623** *Althorp MS.* in Simpkinson *Washingtons* (1869) App. 46 For a sirloin, a rumpe, a buttocke, 2 necks, and a rond of beef.

2. In East Anglia, a marshy, reed-covered strip of land lying between the natural river-bank and the artificial embankment. Cf. RAND *sb.*[1] 1.

1865 [see REED *sb.*[1] 14]. **1878** MILLER & SKERTCHLY *Fenland* i. 8 In most parts of our country the rivers have their sloping shores and ronds. **1887** RYE *Norfolk Broads* 94 You will be run on to the rond so firmly.., that you will be unable to get off till the tide rises.

attrib. **1882** C. DAVIES *Norf. Broads & Rivers* xv. (1884) 110 The rond islands go floating up and down until they find a haven in some dyke or bay.

† **rond,** *sb.*[2] *Obs. rare.* [Of obscure origin.] A (dry) stick or rod.

a **1225** *Ancr. R.* 148 Þe grene bowes beoð al uordruwede, & forwurðen to druie hwite rondes. *Ibid.* 150 Hwonne þe rinde is aweie,..adruieð þe bowes, & iwurðet hwite rondes, to none þinge betere þen to fures fode.

† **rond,** *v. Obs. rare.* [? f. OE. *rǫnd* ROND *sb.*, RAND *sb.*[1]] *trans.* To cut or tear into strips. (Also with *to-*.)

a **1225** *St. Marher.* 6 Wið sweord scharpe ant wið eawles of irne hire leofliche lich rondin ant rendin. *a* **1225** *Leg. Kath.* 1974 Her..wes þis meiden iset, for to al torenden & reowðfulliche torondin.

rond, obs. form of ROUND.

‖ **rondache** (rɒn'dæʃ, ‖ rɔ̃daʃ). Also 7 ro(u)ndass. [F. *rondache*, †*rondace* (hence Du. *rondas*), f. *rond* ROUND *a.*]

1. A small circular shield or buckler.

1604 E. G[RIMSTONE] *D'Acosta's Hist. Indies* VI. xxvi. 487 For defensive armes they had little rondaches or targets. **1623** HEXHAM *Tongue-combat* 43 The Targets or Round-asses which some of these Gens-gallants did beare. **1672** DRYDEN *Assignation* II. i, Haunting her Street by Night, with Guittars, Dark-Lanthorns, and Rondaches.

1837 LOCKHART *Scott* (1839) VI. 351 This shield..being a round *rondache*, or highland target. **1897** *Daily News* 1 Feb. 6/2 A circular rondache of bright steel.

† **2.** *transf.* A foot-soldier. *Obs.*

1629 *S'hertogenbosh* 38 We..tooke in some Workes from the Enemies, and brought into the towne 2 Rondasses. **1646** HOWELL *Lewis XIII*, 122 He offer'd with his rondaches, and by an assault Seaward, to carry the Town.

‖ **rondavel** (rɒn'dɑ:vɛl). *S. Afr.* Also † rondabel, ronddawel. [a. Afrikaans *rondawel.*] A round tribal hut of primitive construction, usu. with a thatched, conical roof. Also *transf.*, a similar simple building used esp. as a holiday cottage; also as an outbuilding on a farm, etc.

1891 J. WIDDICOMBE *Fourteen Yrs. in Basutoland* 84 Mr. Charles Bell had very kindly engaged a Mosuto..to build us a round hut, or *rondavel*, as the whites usually call it. **1900** A. H. KEANE *Boer States* p. xviii, Rondabel, ronddawel, a round hut..; is now an outhouse detached from the dwelling, and used as a kitchen. **1904** A. WILMOT *Life & Times Sir R. Southey* iii. 69 At present the Land-drost lies in a 'Rondavel' of reeds and mud. **1910** J. BUCHAN *Prester John* iii. 53 There were some twenty native huts, higher up the slope, which the Dutch call *rondavels.* **1924** *Chambers's Jrnl.* Jan. 53/1 At the scene of operations rondavels have been constructed to accommodate the workers. **1936** 'THE IDLER' *Rolling Home* xxxi. 385 It consisted of a dozen rondavels grouped round a central thatched dining-room... A rondavel is a circular room built of brick or mud with a door and windows and is roofed with stout thatch. **1951** R. CAMPBELL *Light on Dark Horse* ii. 51 Even our Governor-Generals sleep, in the hot weather, in thatched rondavels walled with a mixture of cow-dung and mud. **1958** M. SPARK *Go-Away Bird* 102 She had used to squat with old Makata..outside his large rondavel. **1965** *Spectator* 8 Jan. 35/3, I slept in one of the rondavels..vacated for me for the occasion. There are twenty of these—tin huts twenty feet in diameter and partitioned to form two tiny semi-circular rooms. **1973** G. DURRELL *Beasts in my Belfry* vi. 121 The [bears'] dens, which were scattered among the bramble bushes that filled the enclosure, were beehive-like rondavels of stone covered with earth and turf. **1976** *Vogue* Jan. 114/3 Antigua..the Anchorage Hotel..accommodation units, ranging from rondavels to air-conditioned rooms with patios.

‖**rond de cuir** (rɔ̃ də kɥir). [Fr., lit. 'circle of leather'.] A round leather cushion, commonly used on office chairs in France; hence *transf.*, a bureaucrat.

[**1893** G. COURTELINE (*title*) Messieurs les Ronds-de-Cuir.] **1915** W. J. LOCKE *Jaffery* viii. 101 Do you think a leather seat for that hard wooden chair—what the French call a *rond-de-cuir*—would very greatly impair the poor fellow's imagination? **1938** *Times Lit. Suppl.* 28 May 368/3 Into the next twelve years he crowded all his life's work, his volumes of stories and novels..his good-bye to a *rond de cuir.* **1963** I. FLEMING *On H.M. Secret Service* xxiv. 259, I am just a pilot. I am not a 'rond de cuir', a chairborne flyer. **1969** *Punch* 5 Mar. 363/2 The island in this Octave is Barra, where he is in charge of the Home Guard and conducts a running fight on its behalf with the *ronds de cuir* of Whitehall. **1975** *Listener* 4 Sept. 314/4 How many *ronds-de-cuir* in peripheral *mairies*..must have lived through Robespierre!

‖**rond de jambe** (rɔ̃ də ʒɑ̃b). *Ballet.* Pl. **rond(s) de jambes, ronds de jambe.** [Fr., lit. 'circle of the leg'.] A circular movement of the leg in dancing. Freq. in *Comb.* (see quots.).

1830 R. BARTON tr. *Blasis's Code of Terpsichore* II. 101 Suppose it is the left leg that stands on the ground whilst the right, in the second position, is prepared for the movement, make it describe a semicircle backwards, which brings your legs to the first position, and then continue on the sweep till it completes the whole circle, ending at the place from whence it started. This is what we technically term *ronds-de-jambe. Ibid.* 102 The practice of *grands et petits battemens,* the *rond-de-jambes* on the ground and in the air,..&c. **1889** G. B. SHAW in *Star* 4 Oct. 2/4 The *entrechats, battements, ronds de jambes, arabesques, élévations,* and what's-his-names of the art of theatrical dancing. **1922** BEAUMONT & IDZIKOWSKI *Man. Classical Theatr. Dancing* II. i. 34 *Ronds de Jambe à Terre* serve to enable you to turn your leg well outwards. *Ibid.* 53 The celebrated dancers Gardel and Vestris are credited with the invention of the *rond de jambe en l'air.* **1930** CRASKE & BEAUMONT *Theory & Pract. Allegro in Classical Ballet* II. 70 Execute a *Double Rond de Jambe en dedans, sauté,* that is:- Spring upwards off the *right* foot. While the body is in the air—Execute with the *left* foot a *Double Rond de Jambe en l'air en dedans.* **1975** *New Yorker* 26 May 91/1 His passé leg in a multiple pirouette sweeps through rond de jambe en l'air into the opening battement of a series of grands jetés en tournant.

‖**ronde** (rɒnd). [a. F. *ronde,* fem. of *rond* ROUND *a.*]

1. *Typog.* A form of type imitating handwriting. Also *attrib.*

1838 TIMPERLEY *Printers' Man.* 63 Ronde Type, in imitation of secretary, has been very lately introduced to the notice of the profession. **1846** *Wood & Sharwoods' Spec. Bk. Type,* Great Primer Ronde. **1888** JACOBI *Printers' Vocab.* 115 *Ronde,* a fancy character of type somewhat similar to a script.

2. A round dance; a dance in which the participants move in a circle or ring.

[**1931** G. L. NUTE *Voyageur* 41 The call for *la ronde* was issued. This dance was another customary part of the journey, and it was entered into heartily despite the moralizing tone of the verses.] **1950** MARCEL-DUBOIS & ANDRAL *Dances of France* I. 21 In the Bourbonnais a peasant wedding is the great occasion for traditional Rondes, ring dances, by all the guests after the banquet. One such Ronde is..round a fire. **1974** *Islander* (Victoria, B.C.) 30 June 16/3 Wives and daughters of the traders joined in, and Warre partook of a Canadian ronde, a dance in which, he wrote, 'your admiration of your partner is expressed by kissing her openly as often as she will permit'. **1977** *Early Music* July 431/3 There are no descriptions of dances specifically called 'Ronde'. The name implies a round dance and rhythmically they fit either a Branle..or an Almaine.

3. A round or course of talk, activity, etc.; a treadmill. Cf. ROUND *sb.*[1] 13 c.

1957 *Economist* 19 Oct. 196/1 The subject has been completely submerged in the economic discussions which dominate the current *ronde.* **1977** *Times Lit. Suppl.* 1 Apr. 401/4 Heinz already represented the first step away from what was ultimately unbearable about the homosexual *ronde.*

ronde, obs. form of ROUND.

rondeal, obs. form of RONDEL.

‖**rondeau** ('rɒndəʊ, ‖rɔ̃do). Also 6 rund-, 8 roundeau. [F., later form of *rondel*: see next.]

1. A short poem, consisting of ten, or in stricter sense of thirteen, lines, having only two rimes throughout and with the opening words used twice as a refrain. (See also ROUNDO.)

1525 LD. BERNERS *Froiss.* II. xxvi. 71 A boke.. conteyninge all the songes, baladdes, rundeaux, and vyrelayes, which the gentyll duke had made in his tyme. **1691** DRYDEN *Amphitryon* IV. [*heading*], A rondeau. **1700** T. BROWN tr. *Fresny's Amusements* 132 Their most diversified Conversations are a sort of Rondeaus that end either in Artificial Slanders, or gross Flattery. **1710** POPE *Lett.* (1736) V. 87 This sort of writing call'd the *Rondeau* is what I never knew practis'd in our nation. **1837** HALLAM *Hist. Lit.* I. viii. §13 They dealt much in the rondeau, a very popular species of metre long afterwards. **1877** MISS YONGE *Cameos* III. vi. 46 She..used to sit up half the night writing ballads and rondeaux. **1889** A. LANG *Lett. on Lit.* ii. (ed. 2) 25 In his first volume Mr. Bridges offered a few rondeaux and triolets.

b. *transf.* A refrain.

1800 MAR. EDGEWORTH *Belinda* (1831) II. xxv. 178 This is the rondeau of your argument.

2. *Mus.* (See quot. 1841 and RONDO 1.)

1773 MME. D'ARBLAY *Early Diary* (1889) I. 186 Hetty.. began a rondeau in the overture to Sacchini's new opera. **1786** *Gentl. Mag.* LVI. I. 430 Rondeau. Sung by Mr. Weichsell and set by Mrs. Hook. **1841** *Penny Cycl.* XX. 142/1 *Rondeau* (Fr.) or *Rondo* (It.), a kind of air consisting of two or more strains, in which, after finishing the second strain, the first is repeated, and again after the third, etc., always returning to and concluding with the first.

rondel ('rɒndəl). Also 4 rondeal, 5 -delle, 6-7 rondell. [a. older F. *rondel* masc. (later *rondeau*: see prec.), or *rondelle* fem., f. *rond* ROUND *a.* Cf. ROUNDEL and RUNDLE.]

1. A circle; a circular object. Now *arch.* †Also *spec.* a round shield; the midriff.

The precise sense in quot. 1630 is not clear.

c **1290** *St. Michael* 452 in *S. Eng. Leg.* I. 312 A luyte rondel ase a sikel Men seoth þar-on liȝt. **1486** *Bk. St. Albans* e viij, In the mydref that callid is the rondell also. **1529** MORE *Dyaloge* II. Wks. 188/2 The ayre striken wt the breth of the spiker, & equally rolling forth in rondels to the eares of the hearers. **1549** *Compl. Scot.* vi. 42 Mak reddy ȝour.. halbardis, rondellis, tua handit sourdis and tairgis. **1593** Q. ELIZ. *Boeth.* 113 Hast thou not thus wrapt a rondell [L. *orbem*] of dyvine sinceritie? **1610** HOLLAND *Camden's Brit.* I. 654 They give a jirke, as if a twig bended into a rondle were sodainly let go. **1630** B. JONSON *New Inn* I. vi, Chalk, and renew the rondels, I am now Resolved to stay. **1871** R. ELLIS *Catullus* xvii. 26 As some mule [leaves] in a glutinous sludge her rondel of iron.

†**b.** *Fortif.* A round tower. *Obs.*

1686 *Lond. Gaz.* No. 2159/1 The Duke of Lorrain's Attack embraces three Rondels or Towers. **1687** B. RANDOLPH *Archipelago* 2 The maine castle is..fortified with six very large towers or rondells. **1704** J. HARRIS *Lex. Techn.* I, *Rondel,* in Fortification, is a round Tower sometimes erected at the Foot of the Bastions. [Hence in later Dicts.]

†**c.** A round or rung of a ladder. *Obs.*

1723 *Briton* No. 6 And make their Vices the only Rondels whereby they mount the Ladder of tow'ring Preferment.

2. A rondeau, or a special form of this.

1390 GOWER *Conf.* I. 133 He can carolles make, Rondeal, balade and virelai. *a* **1450** *Knt. de la Tour* (1868) 1, Y made for her loue songges, balades, rondelles, virallayes, and diuerse nwe thinges. **1604** E. G[RIMSTONE] *D'Acosta's Hist. Indies* VI. xxviii. 492 They haue likewise put our compositions of musicke into their language, as Octaves, Songs, and Rondells. **1811** BUSBY *Dict. Mus.* (ed. 3) s.v. *Roundelay,* Some writers speak of the Roundelay, or Rondel, as a kind of air appropriated to dancing. **1887** GLEESON WHITE *Ball. & Rondeau* Introd. p. lviii, In its origin the rondel was a lyric of two verses... With Charles d'Orléans the rondel took the distinct shape..of fourteen lines on two rhymes. *Ibid.,* Nor are these rondel-triolets exceptions; they are quite common till the beginning of the fifeenth century.

rondelai: see ROUNDELAY.

†'**rondelet.** *Obs. rare.* Also rondlette. [a. F. *rondelet,* dim. of *rondel* RONDEL 2.] A short rondeau. (Cf. ROUNDLET.)

1575 GASCOIGNE *Notes Instruction* Wks. U j b, Then haue you also a rondlette, the which doth alwayes end with one self same foote or repeticion, and was thereof (in my iudgement) called a rondelet.

rondelet, obs. variant of RUNLET[1].

‖**rondeletia** (rɒndə'liːʃ(ɪ)ə). Also -olecia. [mod.L., after the French naturalist *Rondelet* (1507-66).]

1. A tropical American genus of *Cinchonaceæ*; a plant or shrub of this genus.

1771 *Encycl. Brit.* III. s.v. **1819** *Pantologia* X. s.v., The species chiefly cultivated is..American rondeletia, with a woody stalk ten or twelve feet high;..flowers sessile, white. **1882** *Garden* 8 Apr. 242/2 Rondeletias..may now be struck from cuttings made of the young shoots.

2. A perfume resembling that which is characteristic of this genus of plants.

1840 HOOK *Fitzherbert* I. vii. 77 His yellow silk pocket-handkerchief scented..with a vile mixture of musk and bergamot, yclept rondolecia. **1866** *Treas. Bot.* 989/1 The perfume sold as Rondeletia takes its name from this plant, but is not prepared from any part of it.

rondelier (rɒndə'lɪə(r)). *nonce-wd.* [f. RONDEL + -IER.] A poet who composes rondels.

1878 G. M. HOPKINS *Lett. to R. Bridges* (1955) 49, I am very glad to hear the Rondeliers have come to see the beauty of your poetry.

rondell, obs. form of RONDEL, RUNDLE.

‖**rondelle** (rɒn'dɛl). [F., f. *rond* ROUND *a.* Cf. RONDEL.] A round; a circular piece.

In quot. 1839 the process described is a French one.

1839 URE *Dict. Arts* 328 The thick cake of congealed metal (*rondelle*) is lifted off with tongs. *Ibid.,* These *rondelles* are immediately immersed in cold water. **1879** G. PRESCOTT *Sp. Telephone* 288 A rondelle of firwood is fixed normally to the tube by its centre.

rondelle, obs. form of RONDEL.

'**rondelled,** *a. rare*⁻¹. [f. RONDEL 1 b.] Furnished with small towers.

1858 H. MAYHEW *Upper Rhine* (1860) 342 A belvidere built..at the cost of Herr Hofrath von Seyfried, whose rondelled residence is seen close by.

‖**rondeña** (ron'deɲa). [Sp.] A variety of song or dance native to Ronda in Andalusia.

1883 GROVE *Dict. Mus.* III. 599/2 Songs and dances often derive their names from the provinces or towns in which they are indigenous; thus *rondeña* from Ronda. **1954** *Ibid.* (ed. 5) III. 372 Most forms [of Andalusian song]..have four lines of eight syllables, and these include forms such as *granadinas, rondeñas,*..descended directly or indirectly from the *fandango.* **1967** 'LA MERI' *Spanish Dancing* (ed. 2) vi. 82 The Rondeñas originated as a lover's serenade under the window of his sweetheart, as did the Tarantos of the Levant.

‖**rondeur** (rɔ̃dœr). [Fr.] *pl.* Roundness, rounded forms or lines; *spec.* the curves of the female body.

1938 H. G. WELLS *Apropos of Dolores* iii. 113 A vast majolica plaque insisting upon the Rape of the Sabines, but always recalling to my mind, I don't know why—the rondeurs I suppose—that bustling cheese market at Alkmaar. **1966** *Guardian* 5 Aug. 8/4 These wide coats and dresses..will be able to take our rondeurs in their swing.

rondine ('rɒndiːn), *a. nonce-wd.* [f. F. *rond* ROUND + -INE[4], after *blondine.*] Made round, rounded.

1923 E. SITWELL *Bucolic Comedies* 70 Fat blondine pearls Rondine curls Seem.

rondle. Anglicized variant of RONDELLE.

1875 KNIGHT *Dict. Mech.* 1970/1 *Rondle* (Metal-working),..the crust or scale which forms upon the surface of molten metal in cooling, and which is removed..as it congeals.

rondlet, obs. f. RUNLET.

rondlette, var. RONDELET *Obs.*

rondnesse, obs. f. ROUNDNESS.

‖**rondo** ('rɒndəʊ). [It. *rondo,* a. F. *rondeau.*]

1. *Mus.* 'A piece of music having one principal subject, to which a return is always made after the introduction of other matter' (Grove).

1797 *Monthly Mag.* III. 227 A cantabile movement.., the subject of which is highly graceful; and is succeeded by a very pleasing rondo. **1811** BUSBY *Dict. Music* (ed. 3) s.v., The Rondo..takes its name from the circumstance of the melody going round, after both the second and third strain, to the first strain, with which it finally closes. In the vocal Rondo considerable discernment is requisite in the choice of proper words. **1861** *Sat. Rev.* 14 Dec. 610 The King..thus cuts the Gordian knot, and brings down the curtain upon a rapturous rondo from the *prima donna.* **1887** H. C. BANISTER *Mus. Anal.* ix. 218 When..there is more than one Episode, and therefore at least two returns to the Subject, the Episodical Movement is termed a Rondo.

attrib. **1874** OUSELEY *Mus. Form* 46 A tabular view of the Rondo Form..will sufficiently explain its structure. **1899** *Atlantic Monthly* LXXXIII. 753/2 The white distrusts the Indian,..the Greaser hates the white; there is a perfect rondo movement of dislike and antagonism.

2. A game of chance played with balls on a table. In quot. *attrib.*

1859 J. W. PALMER *New & Old* 229 (Cent.), With card and dice, roulette wheels and rondo balls, he fooled himself to the top of his bent.

‖**rond-point** (rɔ̃pwɛ̃). [Fr., f. *rond* ROUND + *point* centre.] **a.** In a garden: a circular space or centre whence paths radiate. **b.** In a town or city: a circus or roundabout where roads converge.

1884 H. JAMES in *Atlantic Monthly* May 631/2 A *jardin français*..with little blue-green perspectives and alleys and *rond-points.* **1903** A. H. BEAVAN *Tube, Train, Tram, & Car* x. 120 Sloane Street, where anyone approaching town by way of Kensington, meets the first of the numerous metropolitan 'rond-points'. *Ibid.* 121 A few doors from the 'rond-point' in Brompton Road. **1948** *Archit. Rev.* CIII. 158/2 Foremost in his mind he must have had such questions as where to place his rond-points and their radiating streets, and how to co-ordinate and integrate the various units of the plan. **1964** *Shell Gardens Bk.* 169 *Rond-Point,* a circular space or clearing from which avenues and alleys diverge or upon which they converge and from which one may get vistas of various parts of a garden or park. **1967** C. HUSSEY *Eng. Gardens & Landscapes 1700–1750* v. 41 The enclosing shrubberies were threaded by walks, straight for the most part but irregularly aligned, connecting sundry *rond-points* and mounds, to debouch at unexpected angles into the glade.

rondure ('rɒndjʊə(r)). [ad. F. *rondeur.*] A circle or round object; roundness. Cf. ROUNDURE.

c **1600** SHAKS. *Sonn.* xxi, All things rare, That heauens ayre in this huge rondure hems.
1868 BROWNING *Ring & Bk.* I. 27 The rondure brave, the lilied loveliness. **1874** SYMONDS *Sk. Italy & Greece* (1898) I. xi. 213 Cherubs clustered in the rondure of rose-windows.

rone (rəʊn), *sb.*[1] Now *dial.* Also 5-6 (9) ron, 6 *pl.* ronnis, -ys, 9 roan. [A northern word and prob. of Scand. origin, being phonetically equivalent to mod.Norw. dial. *rune*, var. of *runne*, *runn*, ON. *runnr* (mod.Icel. *runnur* and *runni*), in the same sense. The form *ranez* in the alliterative *Morte Arth.* 923 is no doubt an error.] A brake or thicket; thick bush or undergrowth. Also *attrib.*, as *rone-root.*

13.. *Gaw. & Gr. Knt.* 1466 He rechated, & rode þurȝ ronez ful þyk. *a* **1400** *Pistill of Susan* 72 Þe rose ragged on rys, richest on Rone. *c* **1470** HENRY *Wallace* v. 357 The rone wes thik that Wallace slepyt in. **1513** DOUGLAS *Æneis* VII. Prol. 69 Smal byrdis, flokand throw thik ronnis thrang. **1535** STEWART *Cron. Scot.* I. 359 With mos and mure and mony wodis wyld, And ron and roche. *a* **1585** MONTGOMERIE *Flyting* 288 The Weird Sisters.. Saw reavens rugand at that ratton be a ron ruit.
1820 *Blackw. Mag.* Nov. 145 The foot-path..conducting us through a roan of stunted oak and hazel. **1824** MACTAGGART *Gallovid. Encycl.* s.v. *Rossens*, The hounds could not uncover him, so the ron was set in flames about his lugs. **1846** BROCKETT *N.C. Gloss., Rone*, properly a thick plantation of bushes; but in the North usually applied to a thick cover of whins, which is called 'a rone of whins'. **1880** *Antrim & Down Gloss.* 83 'Hazely roans,' hazel brakes. 'Brackeny roans,' fern brakes.

†**rone,** *sb.*[2] Also 5 roone. Perh. early forms of *roan* ROWAN (the berry).

a **1440** *Sir Eglam.* 612, Y schalle geve the a nobylle stede, Also redd as ony roone [*rimes* stone, slon, upon]. **15..** in Pinkerton *Anc. Sc. Poems* (1786) 192 My rubie cheiks, wes reid as rone, Ar leyn. *a* **1586** MONTGOMERIE *Misc. Poems* xli. 12 Quhair lilies lyk lou is, Als rid as the rone [*rime* gone].

rone, *sb.*[3] *Sc. rare.* Also 7 ronn. [Of obscure origin.] A strip or patch of ice formed on the surface of the ground. Hence **'rony** *a.* (see quot. 1639).

1535 LYNDESAY *Satyre* 1050 Ʒe ar the lamps that sould schaw them the licht To leid them on this sliddrie rone of yce. **1639** SIR R. GORDON *Hist. Earls Sutherl.* (1813) 208 This wes called the Ronie rode, becaus it hapned in the wunter season, when as the ground wes full of ronns, or sheckles of yce. **1851** W. ANDERSON *Rhymes*, etc. (1867) 12 He slippit his foot on a rone i' the brae.

rone (rəʊn), *sb.*[4] *Sc.* Also ronn, rhone, roan. [Of obscure origin.] A pipe or gutter leading down from, or fixed under, the eaves of a roof to carry off the rain-water.

a. **1808** JAMIESON, *Rone*, the spout affixed to the side of a house, for carrying down the rain-water from the roof. **1822** GALT *Provost* xxvii, There being then no ronns to the houses,..the rain came gushing in a spout. **1859** M. FINDLATER *Betty Musgrave* 111 The drip from a broken rone falling into the hollowed doorstone. **1876** W. P. BUCHAN *Plumbing* i. 3 Simple half-circle iron rhones—*i.e.*, half-round eaves gutters made of cast iron.
β. **1821** GALT *Ann. Parish* xxxiii, Getting..the window cheeks painted, with roans put up. **1831** J. WILSON *Noctes Amb.* Wks. 1856 III. 152 You couldna hae been watter had you stood..under a roan. Say spout, James, roan is vulgar —it is Scotch. **1893** CROCKETT *Stickit Minister* 175 Climbing up a convenient roan or water pipe.

†**rone,** *v. Obs. rare.* [var. of RO *v.*, the *n* of the inf. being taken as part of the stem. Cf. *mistrun* for MISTROW *v.*, and see RON[2].] *trans.* To recreate; to comfort or console.

In the *E.E. Psalter* rendering L. *consolari.*
a **1300** *Cursor M.* 3351 Ysaac him yode to rone [*v.r.* ro], Thoght on thing he had to done. *a* **1300** *E.E. Psalter* lxxvi. 3, [I] Forsoke mi saule roned to be. *Ibid.* cxvii. 76 Be þi merci þat ite rone me.

Hence †**'roning** *vbl. sb. Obs.*

a **1300** *E.E. Psalter* xxii. 5 Mikel ronynge þai me do. *Ibid.* xciii. 19 Þine roninges fained mi saule in querte.

rone, obs. f. ROAN; obs. pa. t. RAIN *v.*

Roneo ('rəʊniːəʊ), *sb.* Also roneo. [f. the initial letters of ROTARY *a.* and *Neostyle* (see quot. 1901 below).] The proprietary name of various kinds of office equipment, esp. a duplicating machine. Freq. *attrib.* and *Comb.*

1901 *Trade Marks Jrnl.* 27 Nov. 1182 Roneo... Paper.., stationery and bookbinding. Neostyle Manufacturing Company, Limited. **1914** D. FRASER *Winning a Primitive People* III. xxvi. 272 A native clerk is there..turning on the Roneo hundreds of copies of some circular to the teachers. **1919** *Trade Marks Jrnl.* 13 Aug. 1138 Roneo... Type printing machines, type setting machines, and embossing machines. Roneo, Limited,..London. **1920** *Glasgow Herald* 3 Dec. 10 The staff of typists and Roneo operators required is very numerous and well paid. **1926** *Socialist Rev.* June 10 No printed newspapers (a few roneo bulletins), no trains. **1934** *Times Lit. Suppl.* 8 Mar. 162/3 *Roneo.*—As one must have it, why not have the derivation—Rotary Neostyle? **1941** E. R. EDDISON *Fish Dinner* xiii. 229 I'll go on for a bit: get my covering memorandum into shape... You've got the annexes all off the roneo now, have you? **1947** *Trade Marks Jrnl.* 5 Mar. 120/1 Roneo... Duplicating apparatus, duplicating machines..Roneo Limited,.. Romford, Essex, and..London,..; manufacturers and merchants. **1950** *Official Gaz.* (U.S. Patent Office) 12 Dec. 377/1 *Roneo.* Applicant claims ownership of British Registration No. 241,483 dated Oct. 23, 1901, and United States Registration No. 182,682. For duplicating machines and their parts, duplicating apparatus and their parts. **1958** S. HYLAND *Who goes Hang?* xxxi. 136 The complexities of the Roneo strip-index on which he was working. **1973** J. WAINWRIGHT *High-Class Kill* 119 An official statement; typed-out, Roneo-copied. **1977** *Gay News* 24 Mar. 22/4 One available in bookstores is Alain Huet's *Agence Tasse*, a roneotyped newssheet.

Hence as *v. trans.*, to copy or reproduce with a Roneo duplicating machine (usu. *pass.* with pa. pple. *roneo'd*); **'roneo'd** (also **roneo(-)ed**) *ppl. a.*, **'roneo-ing** *vbl. sb.*

1921 *Spectator* 7 May 584/1, I have had the memorandum 'Roneo'd' for circulation among near acquaintances. **1926** *Contemp. Rev.* June 682 Newspapers were reappearing in weird type-written or roneo-ed form. **1928** *Bull. Internat. Fed. League of Nations Societies* May–June 5 Among the documents which have been translated, roneoed and distributed by the Secretariat may be cited the following important Memoranda. **1934** *Planning* I. XXIII. 8 In addition to this broadsheet a roneoed bulletin goes round fortnightly to the hundred working members telling them what each group is doing. **1935** *Punch* 6 Mar. 262/2 He said he liked the little poem and was having some copies 'roneo'd'. **1940** W. S. CHURCHILL *Second World War* (1949) II. 631 The officials concerned in roneo-ing the various circulations. **1956** *Eng. Stud.* XXXVII. 146 The preface to the present (roneo'd, not printed) book. **1966** *Listener* 23 June 915/1 They studied the roneoed exam papers. **1974** D. SEAMAN *Bomb that could Lip-Read* xv. 144 Back would come a roneoed letter.

Rong (rɒŋ), *sb.* and *a.* [Native name.] = LEPCHA *sb.* and *a.*

1840 A. CAMPBELL in *Jrnl. Asiatic Soc. Bengal* IX. I. 379 The real Lepcha, or Rong proper, has no tradition whatever ..connected with the advent of his tribe into this part of the world. **1854** J. D. HOOKER *Himalayan Jrnls.* I. v. 127 They, or at least some of their tribes, call themselves Rong, and Arratt, and their country Dijong. **1876** G. B. MAINWARING *Gram. Róng (Lepcha) Lang.* p. vii, The proper name of the Lepchas, as they call themselves, is—Róng. *Ibid.* I. 1 The Róng (Lepcha) Alphabet may be divided into two parts. **1909** G. A. GRIERSON *Linguistic Survey of India* III. I. 233 The Lepchas are considered as the oldest inhabitants of Sikkim... They call themselves Róng... The number of speakers of Róng in Sikkim and Darjeeling were.. estimated. *Ibid.*, Róng literature comprises Buddhistic and other religious books. **1938** G. GORER *Himalayan Village* i. 35 The Lepchas do not call themselves Lepchas; they call themselves *Rong.*

rong, obs. f. RANK *a.*, RUNG *sb.*; obs. pa. t. REIGN *v.*, RING *v.*

ronge, variant of ROUNGE *v. Obs.*

rongeur (rɔ̃'ʒɜː(r)). *Surg.* [a. F. *rongeur* gnawing, a rodent, f. *ronger* to gnaw.] A strong surgical forceps with a biting action, used for removing small pieces from bone. Also *rongeur forceps.*

a **1884** KNIGHT *Dict. Mech.* Suppl. 764/1 Post's rongeur is specifically for the mastoid bone. **1888** *Buck's Handbk. Med. Sci.* VI. 176/2 The gnawing, or rongeur, forceps are necessary for the removal of the edges of bone and of diseased parts not otherwise accessible. **1908** J. W. SLUSS *Emergency Surg.* II. iv. 401 Provide, besides the ordinary instruments, Rongeur forceps, a mallet and chisel, or a trephine. *Ibid.* 405 The dura is now exposed, and if the opening..needs to be enlarged, the dura should be detached from the edge of bone and the chisel or rongeur employed. **1927** J. B. MACALPINE *Cystoscopy* xi. 160 The cystoscopic rongeur..may be used to break up stones which are very soft and friable. **1938** D. MUNRO *Cranio-Cerebral Injuries* vii. 90 At least 1 large and 1 small biting rongeur. **1966** G. L. HOWE *Minor Oral Surg.* xi. 221 The ease and speed..are due to the use of the side-cutting rongeurs (alveolotomy shears).

‖**ronggeng** ('rɒŋgɛŋ). [Malay.] **a.** A dancing-girl in Malaysia. **b.** A form of Malaysian popular dancing, often accompanied by singing.

1817 T. S. RAFFLES *Hist. Java* vii. 342 The common dancing girls of the country..are called *rông'geng*, and are generally of easy virtue... The *róng'gengs* accompany the dance with singing. **1849** ONG-TAE-HAE *Glance at Interior of China* 57 Native actresses are called ronggengs..they flourish a paper fan, sing native songs, and perform savage dances. **1910** R. J. WILKINSON *Papers on Malay Subjects: Life & Customs* III. 28 A *ronggeng* sings and acts. **1927** R. J. H. SIDNEY *In Brit. Malaya Today* xxiv. 281 We were treated to a pukkah Malay *ronggeng.* **1966** G. BLACK *You want to die, Johnny?* vi. 112 We got radio Binton, with *ronggeng* music. **1972** M. SHEPPARD *Taman Indera* 89 The most popular of these [dances] was called *Ronggeng*—a word which now means a professional dancing girl who dances and sings. **1976** LD. HOME *Way Wind Blows* vii. 116 Tunku Abdul Rahman..taught me—or rather tried to teach me— the ronggeng, the Malaysian dance in which the male, as far as I could see, plays a subordinate role to the female with hilarious results.

rongo-rongo ('rɒŋgəʊ'rɒŋgəʊ). *Archæol.* [Native name.] Hieroglyphic signs or script found on wooden tablets on Easter Island, a Chilean dependency in the eastern Pacific Ocean; the art of incising these. Also *attrib.* and *ellipt.*

1919 K. ROUTLEDGE *Mystery of Easter Island* xvi. 243 The tablets, known as 'kohâu-rongo-rongo', were an integral part of life on the island. *Ibid.* 244 Every clan had professors in the art who were known as rongo-rongo men ('tangata-rongo-rongo'). *Ibid.* 249 Kaara was servant to the Ariki, and had been taught rongo-rongo by him... The matters with which..the rongo-rongo would deal, such as genealogies, lists of ariki, or the wanderings of the people. **1947** D. DIRINGER *Alphabet* viii. 137 The script *rongo-rongo* was the monopoly of organized teachers; every clan had its own 'writing professors', that is, experts in the art who were known as *tangata-rongo-rongo*, 'rongo-rongo-men'. *Ibid.*, A less elaborate kind of rongo-rongo was called *tau.* **1957** M. BULLOCK tr. *Métraux's Easter Island* xii. 188 The spear carried by the leader..recalls the staff sometimes borne by the Easter Island *rongorongo. Ibid.*, The name given to these [hieroglyphic] tablets, *kohau rongorongo.* **1958** T. HEYERDAHL *Aku-Aku* vi. 164 The cave contained every possible thing except *rongo-rongo.*

rongue, obs. f. RUNG *sb.*

‖**ronin** ('rəʊnɪn). Also with capital initial. [Jap.] In feudal Japan, a lordless wandering samurai; an outlaw. Also *transf.* in recent use, a Japanese student who has failed and is permitted to retake a university (entrance) examination.

1871 A. B. MITFORD *Tales of Old Japan* I. 4 The word *Rônin*..is used to designate persons of gentle blood, entitled to bear arms, who have become separated from their feudal lords. *Ibid.* 18 Then the Rônins lost patience. **1876** W. E. GRIFFIS *Mikado's Empire* I. xxvii. 278 When too deeply in debt, or having committed a crime, they left their homes and the service of their masters, and roamed at large. Such men were called *rônins*, or 'wave-men'. **1899** KIPLING *From Sea to Sea* I. xxi. 415 And now let us go to the tomb of the Forty-Seven Ronins. **1947** R. BENEDICT *Chrysanthemum & Sword* vii. 138 The huge invincible *ronin* (a lordless samurai who lives by his own wits), the hero Benkei. **1967** D. & E. T. RIESMAN *Conversations in Japan* 17 Many had been *ronin* (the name given those who try again and again over a period of years to pass the exams), and finally when they made it were exhausted. **1970** *Observer* (Colour Suppl.) 8 Feb. 32/2 High school students who fail the university exam and are waiting to try again are called *ronin*, a reference to the landless samurai of old Japan which clearly describes their unhappy displaced position in a chronically status-sensitive society. **1974** *Encycl. Brit. Micropædia* VIII. 663/1 *Ronin*, in Japan, masterless samurai (warrior aristocrats) of the Kamakura (1192–1333) and Tokugawa (1603–1876) periods who were often vagrant and disruptive and sometimes actively rebellious.

ronk (rɒŋk), *a. dial.* [var. RANK *a.*] Unmanageable, refractory, unruly; depraved, libidinous; cunning. Hence **'ronkness.**

1877–1905 in *Eng. Dial. Dict.* **1908** E. M. SNEYD-KYNNERSLEY *H.M.I.* xvii. 191 'Well, sir, he is not a bad sort of boy, but he is—er—er—' I broke in to his relief: 'His mother says he is *ronk.*' The master jumped at it: 'That's exactly what he is, sir: he's ronk.' *Ibid.*, 192 Choir-boys have an established reputation for ronkness. **1972** *Times* 31 Oct. 14/7 'Ronk' means what the yokels of London would describe as 'randy'.

ronk(e, obs. ff. RANK *a.*

ronk-, var. RANK *v.*[1] *Obs.*

ronlet, obs. f. RUNLET.

ronne, obs. f. RUN *v.* (and *pa. pple.*).

ronneagate, obs. f. RUNAGATE.

†**ronnelles,** obs. var. RENDLES, rennet.

1530 PALSGR. 177 *Maisgue*, the ronnelles suche as chese is made with.

ronnen, obs. pa. pple. of RUN *v.*

ronner, obs. f. RUNNER.

ronnet, Sc. var. RUNNET *sb.*[1]

ronning, obs. f. RUNNING.

ronnogate, obs. f. RUNAGATE.

ronnon, -yn, obs. inf. RUN *v.*

ronnyng, obs. f. RUNNING.

ronnysh, var. of RUNISH *a.*[2]

ronquil ('rɒŋkɪl). *U.S.* [ad. Sp. *ronquillo* slightly hoarse, f. *ronco* hoarse.] One or other of a group of fishes found in the North Pacific.

1882 JORDAN & GILBERT *Synop. Fishes N. Amer.* 619 *Icosteidæ* (The Ronquils). *Ibid.* 623 *B[athymaster] signatus*, ..Ronquil.

ronsake, obs. form of RANSACK *v.*

Ron'sardian. *rare*$^{-1}$. [f. Pierre de *Ronsard* (1524–1585), the French poet.] = next.

1697 DRYDEN *Ded. Æneid* Ess. (ed. Ker) II. 206 To this the Ronsardians reply,..what remained for him, but, without delay, to pursue his first adventure?

'Ronsardist. [See prec. and -IST.] A follower of Ronsard; a poet who writes in the style of Ronsard.

1879 *Encycl. Brit.* IX. 651/1 He wrote sonnets and odes as became a Ronsardist. **1894** GOSSE *Jacobean Poets* 9 Barnaby Barnes, that isolated Ronsardist among our London poets, published no lyrics after 1595.

So **'Ronsardizing** *ppl. a.*

1879 *Encycl. Brit.* IX. 651/1 Desportes..and Bertaut.. continue the Ronsardizing tradition.

ronsee, -si, varr. ROUNCY *Obs.*

Ronson ('rɒnsən). The proprietary name of a brand of cigarette lighter. Also *attrib.*

1929 *Trade Marks Jrnl.* 11 Sept. 1516/1 Ronson... Pyrophoric lighters. The Ronson Art Metal Company, Limited. **1957** C. MACINNES *City of Spades* I. vii. 44, I.. held out my Ronson... when, hey presto! the lighter was flicked from my hand. **1961** C. WILLOCK *Death in Covert* xi. 199 Mr Goss took his Ronson lighter from his pocket and flicked it into flame. **1972** O. SELA *Bearer Plot* ii. 18, I leaned forward with my Ronson. The flame whooshed up.

ronsoune, obs. f. RANSOM.

ront(e, obs. ff. RUNT.

Röntgen: see ROENTGEN.

röntgenite, var. ROENTGENITE.

Ronuk ('rɒnʌk), *sb.* Also **ronuk**. The proprietary name of a make of polish; *spec.* a brand of floor polish. Hence as *v. trans.*, to polish with Ronuk. Also '**ronuked** *ppl. a.*; '**ronuker**, one who uses Ronuk.

1896 *Trade Marks Jrnl.* 8 Apr. 325 Ronuk... Polishing preparations. Thomas Mottley Fowler and Thomas Horace Fowler, trading as T. M. Fowler,.. Brighton; manufacturers. **1912** *Daily Chron.* 5 Mar. 4/5 'Ronuk' imparts a brilliant polish. *a* **1913** 'BARON CORVO' *Desire & Pursuit of Whole* (1934) i. 3 The profane vulgar who want.. brown boots properly ronuked, and linen stiffly starched. **1916** *Yorkshire Post* 29 June 10/3 In one hall three or four shovel-fuls of dirt are taken up by the ronukers as against one in any other hall, and twice as long is taken to ronuk this hall than any other hall, and three times the amount of ronuk is needed. **1918** KIPLING in *Story-Teller* Dec. 227/1 You'll often find half a dozen Brethren.. polishing and ronuking and sweeping everything they can get at. **1927** W. E. COLLINSON *Contemp. Eng.* 66 One curious development of some nouns is their power to form verbs: to zog a stain off (with a scouring powder), to ronuk [rɒnʌk] a floor (polish). **1929** *Trade Marks Jrnl.* 6 Mar. 404/2 Ronuk... Floor polish. Ronuk, Limited,.. Portslade,.. London,.. Manchester; and.. Cape Town, South Africa. **1955** N. BALCHIN *Fall of Sparrow* ii. 62 He was a big, bulky man, completely bald, and it was believed that the house matron polished his head every day with Ronuk.

rony *a.*: see RONE *sb.*[3]

ronyon: see RUNNION.

ronyous, variant of ROINOUS *a. Obs.*

†**roo**, *sb.*[1] *Obs.*[−1] [ad. OF. *roe* (mod.F. *roue*):—L. *rota*. Cf. ROW *sb.*[3]] A wheel.

?*a* **1400** *Morte Arth.* 3374, I salle redily rolle þe roo at þe gayneste. [Cf. 3388 Abowte scho whirles the whele.]

'roo, roo (ruː), *sb.*[2] *Austral. colloq.* [Shortened form of *kangaroo*.] **a.** = KANGAROO *sb.* 1.

1904 'S. RUDD' *Sandy's Selection* 11 Dead 'roos were common enough, but seldom was a live one thrown in Sandy's way. [**1926**: see KANGA[2].] **1933** *Bulletin* (Sydney) 30 Aug. 21/3 The whites have a kindly feeling for the 'roo. **1945** *Coast to Coast 1944* 80 First time he's seen a blasted roo. **1966** *Southerly* XXVI. 110 Possums and roos to trap. **1977** *Caravan World* (Austral.) Jan. 59/1 The river had brought emus and 'roos close to the road. **1979** *Daily Tel.* 23 Aug. 11/7 The baby roo tries to get herself adopted by other animals but they prove to be unsatisfactory means of transport.

b. *attrib.* and *Comb.*, as **roo bus, meat, shooter, steak**; **roo-bar** (see quot.); **'roo rat** = KANGAROO-RAT 1.

1976 *Car Facts & Feats* (ed. 2) III. 158 (*caption*) The cage in front of the head lamps is affectionately known as a 'roo-bar'. **1968** K. WEATHERLY *Roo Shooter* 12 The roo bus swept round a corner, into full view about twenty yards away; the shooter hit the brakes, depressed the clutch and grabbed the ·22 all in the same instant. **1977** *Weekly Times* (Melbourne) 19 Jan. 33/5 Not bad this 'tree veal. Not a touch on roo meat though. **1947** I. L. IDRIESS *Isles of Despair* xxxii. 212 Hungrily she.. satisfied her craving for land flesh. Kangaroo, wallaby.. flying fox, 'roo rat, porcupine. **1968** K. WEATHERLY (*title*) Roo shooter. **1980** *Age* (Melbourne) 1 Apr. 11/1 The national controversy between conservationists and those who want to increase the commercial exploitation of the kangaroo, notably the professional 'roo shooters and the farmers, [etc.]. **1926** K. S. PRICHARD *Working Bullocks* 21 When he had cooked and eaten the piece of 'roo steak he had been carrying.

Hence **roo** *v.*[2] *intr.*, to hunt kangaroos.

1932 K. S. PRICHARD *Kiss on Lips* 82 Rooin' this week, Colonel?... Cripes, that's something like!

roo (ruː), *v.*[1] *Orkn.* and *Shetl. dial.* Forms: 7–8 row, 8–9 rue, 9– roo. [Of Scand. origin, corresponding to Norw. dial. *rua*, Icel. *rýja* (pa. t. *rúði*, pa. pple. *rúinn*).] *trans.* To strip (sheep) of wool by hand; to pluck (wool) in this manner.

1612 [see *vbl. sb.* below]. **1615** *Acts Lawting Sheriff Orkney* (Maitland Cl.) 175 It is statut and ordanit that it sall nocht be lesum to no maner of persone nor persones to rowing [*sic*] ony scheip unto the tyme they be lawfullie warnit. **1629** *Ibid.* 205 That nane tak.. nor row sheip on Sonday. *a* **1733** *Shetland Acts 8* in *Proc. Soc. Ant. Scotl.* XXVI. (1892) 198 That none mark lambs or row sheep.. but at the sight of sufficient witnesses. **1809** A. EDMONSTON *Zetland* II. 211 About the middle of May, when the fleece begins to loosen spontaneously, it is pulled off with the hand; this operation is called *rooing* the sheep. **1856** ELIZA EDMONDSTONE *Sk. & Tales Shetland* xiv. 175 The wool is never shorn, but *rooed*, that is, pulled with the fingers from the creature's back, lock by lock.

Hence '**rooing** *vbl. sb.* Also *attrib.*

1612 *Acts Lawting Sheriff Orkney* (Maitland Cl.) 160 Act for Thift, Rowing and pulling of Scheip. **1807** J. HALL in *Bulwark* (1905) June 140/2 Nor does this operation, here called 'rooing', seem to give the animal the smallest pain, if performed at the proper season. **1822** HIBBERT *Descr. Shetl. Isl.* 439 At the same time the general *rueing* begins. **1883** R. M. FERGUSSON *Rambles* xvi. 104 It is the rooing day, when sheep are shorn.

roo, var. RO, rest; obs. f. ROE, ROW.

roob, obs. form of ROBE.

roocoocoo (ruːkuː'kuː), *v.* Also **roocooroo** (ruːkuː'ruː). [Imitative.] *intr.* Of a pigeon or a dove: to coo.

1922 JOYCE *Ulysses* 225 The.. porch.. where pigeons roocoocooed. **1960** C. DAY LEWIS *Buried Day* ii. 31 The roo-coo-rooing of doves.

rood (ruːd), *sb.* Forms: α. 1–6 rod, 3–6 rode (6 roide, rodde), 4–7 roode, 5 roed, rowd, 6 roud, 6– rood. β. *Sc.* 5 rwd, 5–6 rud, 5– rude, 6– ruid (9 reed). [OE. *ród* fem. (obl. cases *róde*, pl. *róda*), corresponding in sense 1 to OFris. *róde*, OS. *ruoda*, OIcel. *róða* (also *róði* masc.); the latter is prob. from OE. In the sense of twig or ROD (also measuring-rod, measure of land), the cognate forms appear as Fris. *roede* (*roe*), MDu. *ro(o)de*, *roede*, *ruede* (Du. *roede*), OS. *ruoda* (MLG. *rôde*, *rôdhe*, LG. *rôde*, *rôe*), OHG. *rouda*, *ruada*, *ruota* (MHG. *ruote*, *rûte*, G. *ruthe*, *rute*). In OE. the original application of this sense appears only in the compound *seȝlród* sail-yard, which corresponds to OHG. *segalrôda*.]

I. †**1.** A cross, as an instrument of execution; = CROSS *sb.* 1. *Obs.*

a **900** *O.E. Martyrol.* 30 Nov., On Patria þære ceastre he wæs ahangen on rode. **971** *Blickling Hom.* 191 Forþon þe he me of eorþan to heofenum laþaþ, þy sceal min rod onwended beon. *c* **1000** ÆLFRIC *Gen.* xl. 19 Æfter þam hæt Pharao þe ahon on rode [= 22 on gealȝan]. *a* **1154** *O.E. Chron.* (Laud MS.) an. 1137, þe Iudeus of Noruuic bohton an cristen cild .., & .. him on rode hengen. *a* **1225** *Ancr. R.* 122 Seint Andreu muhte iðolien þet te herde rode hef him touward heouene. *c* **1290** *Holy Rood* 75 in *S. Eng. Leg.* I. 3 Huy founden roden þreo: .. þe rode þat god was on ido, and þat þe tweie þeoues weren on an-honge. **13..** *E.E. Allit. P.* C. 96 Þaȝ I be nummen in Niniue & naked dispoyled, On rode rwly to-rent.

2. a. The cross upon which Christ suffered; the cross as the symbol of the Christian faith. Now only *arch.*

a **900** *O.E. Martyrol.* 25 Mar., Seo Cristes rod on þære he wæs ahongen. *c* **950** *Lindisf. Gosp.* John xix. 25 Ðestodun .. æt ðær rode hælendes moder.. & suoester. *c* **1000** ÆLFRIC *Saints' Lives* vi. 74 Mid haliȝ-dome of þæs hælendes rode. *c* **1205** LAY. 11165 þa rode, þe Crist ure lauerd alisden on þes middelærd. *c* **1290** *Holy Rood* 24 in *S. Eng. Leg.* I. 1 He seide me.. to burie þe rode op-on Caluarie hulle. *c* **1350** *Will. Palerne* 1669 Bi þat blisful barn þat bouȝt us on þe rode. **1387** TREVISA *Higden* (Rolls) VI. 427 þe foure irene nayles þat Crist was i-nayled with to þe rode. **1430–40** LYDG. *Bochas* I. i. (1544) 3 You for to saue He starf upon the roode. *c* **1530** *Hickscorner* 12 Whan she sawe her sone on the rode, The swerde of sorowe gave that lady a wounde. *a* **1600** MONTGOMERIE *Devot. Poems* iii. 41 When he wes rent vpon the rude, He boght belevers with his blude. **1609** J. DAVIES (Heref.) *Holy Roode* Wks. (Grosart) I. 22/2 We must endure the Racke, as he the Rood.

1801 WORDSW. *Cuckoo & Night.* xix, God,.. that died upon the rood, From thee and thy base throat, keep all that's good. **1868** MORRIS *Earthly Par.* (1870) I. i. 336 Good hope I have Of help from Him that died upon the rood.

fig. c **950** *Lindisf. Gosp.* Matt. xvi. 24 Ðif hua wil æfter meh ȝe-cyme.. ȝenimma roda *vel* unhælo his & ȝefylȝeð me. *c* **1175** *Lamb. Hom.* 147 He muneȝeð us an oðer rode to berene, þet is inemned.. fleises lensing. *c* **1200** ORMIN 5609 He take hiss rode, & bere itt rihht & follȝhe swa min bisne. *a* **1225** *Ancr. R.* 60 Þu schalt acorien þe rode, þet is, acorien his sunne.

†**b.** Used without article, esp. *on rood*. *Obs.*

c **825** *Vesp. Hymns* xiii. 16 Meȝen ðorh rode deaðes fordrestende. *a* **900** *O.E. Martyrol.* 25 Mar., Æfter þrym monðum wæs Crist ahangen on rode. *c* **950** *Lindisf. Gosp.* Matt. xxvii. 42 Ðif [he] cyniȝ israhela is, astiȝe nu of rode. *a* **1225** *St. Marher.* 1 Efter ure lauerd es pine, ant his passiun, ant his deð on rode. *c* **1250** *Gen. & Ex.* 386 Ne sulen it neuere ben un-don, Til ihesus bed on Rode don. *a* **1300** *Cursor M.* 10393 Iesu crist was tan And don on rode for our wite. **13..** *E.E. Allit. P.* A. 705 He on rode þat blody dyed. **1423** JAS. I *Kingis Q.* cxxxix, Be him that starf on rude. *c* **1470** HENRY *Wallace* IX. 151 'Mercy,' he said, 'for him that deit on rud'. **1500–20** DUNBAR *Poems* ix. 103 Thow, quhois blude on rude ran for my deid. **1567** *Gude & Godlie Ball.* (S.T.S.) 131 On Rude, thow sched thy blude.

1823 ROSCOE tr. *Sismondi's Lit. Europe* (1846) II. 139 The curse of God who died on rood, was on that sinner's head.

†**c.** In adjurations, *for the rood!* etc. *Obs.*

c **1320** *Sir Tristr.* 1766 For cristes rode! What haue y don wouȝ? **13..** *Sir Beues* 461 'Beues!' a seide, 'for þe rode, What dostow her?' *c* **1420** *Sir Amadace* (Camden) xiii, For the rode, On quat maner spendutte he his gud, That thusgate is a-way? *c* **1470** *Golagros & Gaw.* 124 Schir Gawyne, graith ye that gait, for the gude rude!

d. In asseverations, *by the rood!* etc. Now only *arch.*

13.. *Sir Beues* 968 'Bleþelich,' a seide, 'be þe rod!' **1377** LANGL. *P. Pl.* B. IV. 134 'And ȝet,' quod resoun, 'bi þe Rode I shal no reuthe haue'. *c* **1412** HOCCLEVE *De Reg. Princ.* 1459 Now, by the roode, fader, sothe sey ye. *c* **1450** HOLLAND *Howlat* 94 Be the rud, I am richt rad For to behald ȝour halyness. **1519** *Interl. Four Elem.* in Hazl. *Dodsley* I. 26 Yea, by the rood! even with the greatest. **1577–82** BRETON *Floorish upon Fancie* Wks. (Grosart) I. 17/1 And of such Beds, she hath such stoare of choise (by roode). **1602** SHAKS. *Ham.* III. iv. 14 *Qu.* Haue you forgot me? *Ham.* No by the Rood, not so.

1810 SCOTT *Lady of L.* I. xxii, Now, by the rood,.. Your courtesy has err'd. **1859** TENNYSON *Vivien* 374 Yea, by God's rood, I trusted you too much. **1896** A. AUSTIN *England's Darling* I. i, By the rood! they are wise enough.

3. a. A crucifix, *esp.* one stationed above the middle of a rood-screen; also *rarely*, a figure of the cross in wood or metal, as a religious object.

The roods at certain places are frequently mentioned as special objects of pilgrimage or worship. In some cases *rood* denotes especially the image of Christ as distinct from the cross itself.

c **1072** in Earle *Land Charters* 250 He hæfð þider ynn ȝedon.. ii mycele ȝebonede roda butan oðrum litlum silfrenum swur-rodum. *a* **1122** *O.E. Chron.* (Laud MS.) an. 1083, On þære rode þe stod bufon þam weofode. *Ibid.* an. 1102, þeofas.. breokan þa mynstre of Burh, & þær inne naman.. roden & calicen & candel-sticcan. *c* **1205** LAY. 22101 þe king nom ane rode [*c* 1275 an halidom]. **1297** R. GLOUC. *Chron.* (Rolls) 6594 He wende him uorþ to chirche & biuore þe rode com. **1362** LANGL. *P. Pl.* A. v. 145, I swere ..þat sunne wol I lete,.. And bidde þe Rode of Bromholm bringe me out of dette. *Ibid.* VII. 93, I bar hom þat I borwede,.. by þe Rode of Chestre! *c* **1449** PECOCK *Repr.* II. ix. 194 [To go] to the rode of the north dore at London rather than to ech other roode. **1496–7** *Rec. St. Mary at Hill* (1905) 224 Item, to the karvare.. for mendyng the Roode, the Crosse, þe Mary & Iohn. **1503** *Plumpton Corr.* (Camden) 179 That wold be the most joyfull tydings unto me.., as knoweth the blessed Rode of Rodeborne, who save you in His blessed keepinge. **1584** FENNER *Def. Ministers* (1587) 106 All Roodes, all Images of Saintes.., should.. be defaced. **1594** LYLY *Mother Bombie* v. iii, Get you gone, or I sweare by the roodes bodie Ile lay you by the heeles. **1625** PAGITT *Christianogr.* (1635) 22 Vouchsafe to blesse this Rood of the Crosse, that [etc.]. **1702** POPE *Wife of Bath* 245 He.. now lies buried underneath a Rood, Fair to be seen, and rear'd of honest wood. **1778** *Eng. Gazeteer* (ed. 2) s.v. *Wheathamstead*, Here are the remains of the popish image called the Rood, which is turned into the clerk's desk. **1812** BRADY *Clavis Cal.* II. 154 One of the most famous of these Crucifixes was found at Boxley Abbey in Kent, styled the Rood of Grace. **1853** RUSKIN *Stones Ven.* II. iv. 70 The great rood that crosses the church before the altar, raised in bright blazonry against the shadow of the apse. **1873** W. H. DIXON *Two Queens* III. XVI. xi. 243 Praying and going on a pilgrimage to shrine and rood.

b. A figure or representation of the cross.

1377 LANGL. *P. Pl.* B. xv. 506 Bothe riche and religious þat Rode þei honoure, þat in grotes is ygraue and in golde nobles.

4. *ellipt.* Holy Rood day. *Sc.*

1814 J. TRAIN *Mountain Muse* 30 [She told] How he, by lore obain'd at School, Each month could count from Rood to Yule.

5. Holy Rood: **a.** = sense 2. Now *arch.*

a **1100** *Leg. Rood* 3 þære halȝan rode ȝemetnes. *c* **1100** *O.E. Chron.* (MS. F) an. 200, On þysum ȝeare wæs ȝefunden seo haliȝe rod. *c* **1200** *Vices & Virtues* 33 Ac ðin lauerd hes ofearnede on ðare hali rode. *c* **1290** *Holy Rood* 1 in *S. Eng. Leg.* I. 1 þe holie rode i-founde was, ase ich eov nouþe may telle. *c* **1300** *Havelok* 431 Haue he þe malisun.. of þe leue holi rode. *a* **1515** *Interlud of Droichis* 173 in *Dunbar's Poems* (1897) 320 God bliss thame, and the Haly Rude. **1594** SHAKS. *Rich. III*, III. ii. 78 But by the holy Rood, I doe not like these seuerall Councels, I. **1648** HERRICK *Hesper.*, *Old Wives Prayer*, Holy-Rood come forth and shield Us i' th' citie, and the field.

1798 COLERIDGE *Anc. Mar.* VI. xx, And, by the holy rood! A man all light, a seraph-man, On every corse there stood. **1839** LONGF. *Celestial Pilot*, Then made he sign of holy rood upon them. **1842** TENNYSON *Day-dream, Revival* iii, By holy rood, a royal beard!

b. = sense 3. Now *arch.*

a **1122** *O.E. Chron.* (Laud MS.) an. 1070, Hi.. ȝeodon into þe mynstre, clumben upp to þe halȝe rode. **1583** FULKE *Def. Tr. Script.* iii. (1843) 187 Catholic Christians that reverently kneel in prayer before the cross, the holy rood, the images of our Saviour Christ and his saints.

1815 SCOTT *Ld. of Isles* II. xxiii, The Abbot on the threshold stood, And in his hand the holy rood. **1865** KINGSLEY *Herew.* ii[i], Under the altar behind the holy rood. **1899** E. J. CHAPMAN *Drama of Two Lives* 48 The Holy Rood With its crown'd Christ.

†**c.** = sense 4. *Obs. rare.*

c **1400** *Master of Game* (MS. Digby 182) ii, Aboute þe tyme of holy rode in Septembre. **1573** P. MORE *Alm. & Prognost.* A viij b, At holy Roode, and Gregorie, the nyght and day is equal.

d. *attrib.* (See also ROOD DAY.)

1023 in Kemble *Cod. Dipl.* IV. 25 Ic Ælfric.. ðas ilke kinges godne wille mid ðam haleȝan rode tacne ȝefæstni. *a* **1225** *Leg. Kath.* 193 [She] wrat on hire breoste.. þe hali rode taken. *c* **1400** *Brut* 292 In whiche ȝere, on Holy Roed ȝeue, deide Sere Iohn of Eltham.

6. *attrib.* and *Comb.*, as **rood-altar**, *Sc.* an altar of the Holy Rood; **rood-arch** (see quot. 1850); **rood-beam**, a transverse beam supporting the rood, usually forming the head of a rood-screen; †**rood-board**, *Sc.* an offertory-box in which collections for the rood were taken; **rood-cloth**, a cloth used to cover the crucifix over the rood-screen during Lent; †**Rood even**, the 13th of September (see ROOD DAY); **Rood-fair**, *Sc.* an annual fair held locally either in May or September; †**rood-light**, a light maintained before or beside the rood; †**Rood-mass**, a mass said in honour of the rood; also †**Rood(s)mas (day)**, = ROOD DAY; †**rood-pine**, the torment of the cross; **rood-priest**, a priest who officiated at a rood-altar; **rood-situation**, the position of a rood in a church; †**rood-soller**, a rood-loft; **rood-stair**, a staircase giving access to a rood-loft (1875 *Encycl. Brit.* II. 472); **rood-steeple** = *rood-tower*; **rood-stone** (see quot.); †**rood-token**, the sign of the cross; **rood-tower** (see quot.); †**rood-wold**, the rood or cross.

1472 *Extr. Aberd. Reg.* (1844) I. 31 Schir Androu,.. chaplan of ye *Rude altar in ye parisch kirk of ye said burgh. **1556** *Ibid.* 296 Maister Edward Menzies, cheplane of the ruid alter in the organ loft. **1650–1** *Extr. Rec. Stirling* (1887) 301 The annuell of the Rude altar. **1850** PARKER *Gloss. Arch.* (ed. 5) 393 The term *rood-arch is sometimes applied to the arch between the nave and chancel. *c* **1386** CHAUCER *Wife's Prol.* 496 He..lith y-graue vnder the *roode beem. **1850** PARKER *Gloss. Arch.* (ed. 5) 392 The rood..was supported either by a beam called the rood-beam, or by a gallery called the rood-loft. **1556** *Extr. Rec. Stirling* (1887) 68 Quhatsumevir persone being charget to gaddir with the *Rud brod. **1466** in *Archaeologia* L. I. (1887) 44 Item j *Rode clothe steyned w[t] the passioun of our lorde of the yifte of Iohne Crouton. **1566** in Peacock *Eng. Ch. Furniture* (1866) 159 One rood clothe, one banner clothe, one veale. **1375** BARBOUR *Bruce* XVII. 634 On the *Rude-evyn, in the dawing, The Ingliss host blew till assale. **1685** *Acts Parl. Scot.* (1820) VIII. 504 Ane free fair yearly to be holdin..at the paroch kirk of Killmanevock upon the Second Day of September called the *Ruidfair. **1790** MORISON *Poems* 11 When lads an' lassies..Came to the Rood Fair jauntin. **1832** CARLYLE in Froude *Life* (1882) II. 313 We despatched the animal to Alick, to make ready for the 'rood fair'. **1931** J. BUCHAN *Blanket of Dark* 86 Old John Naps was at the Rood Fair on Barton Heath. **1957** *Dumfries & Galloway Standard* 26 Jan. 3/2 The 'Reed' Fair, as we pronounced it in our Dumfries dialect—'Reed' was a corruption of Rude or Rood or Cross. **1442** in *Bucks., Berks., & Oxon. Archæol. Jrnl.* (1908) June 25 Ressevyd at Cristemas for ye *rode lyght of ye parishe, v[s]. vi[d]. **1529** *Test. Ebor.* (Surtees) VI. 21 The residue to the upholdynge of the rode light. **1545** *Ibid.* 235 For the *roode masse singinge everye Friday. *c* **1630** RISDON *Surv. Devon* §245 (1810) 258 Fairs they have on Roodmas day, and on St. James's day. **1825** JAMIESON *Suppl.*, *Rudesmess, Rudesmas*, a name given to a certain term in the year, Dumfr. *c* **1200** ORMIN 2018 Ne munnde he næfre letenn himm þurrh *rode-pine cwellenn. **1516** in Jeayes *Derbyshire Charters* (1906) No. 91 Indenture between Sir Thomas Russell, '*rood-prest,'..and John Knyvetone. **1618** in *Scottish Antiq.* XI. 21 Umquhill Sir Robert Meldrum, ruidpreist of Kinedvard. **1655** FULLER *Waltham Abbey* 16 Harpsfield..confesseth himself ignorant of the reason of the *Rood-scituation. *c* **1562** in *Shropsh. Parish Doc.* (1903) 61 To a peynetr for peynetyng the *rode soler, xii[d]. **1801** SCOTT *Eve of St. John* xx, By the black *rood-stone,..I conjure thee, my love, to be there! [*Note.* The black-rood of Melrose was a crucifix of black marble.] **971** *Blickling Hom.* 243 Hie ȝesawon Cristes *rodetacen on his onsiene. *c* **1000** ÆLFRIC *Hom.* II. 40 And wyrcan mid þæs lambes blode rodetacn on heora ȝedyrum. *a* **1225** *Ancr. R.* 20 Et te biginnunge of euerich tide..makieð rodentokne, also ich er tauhte. **1823** PUGIN *Gothic Arch.* Gloss., **Rood-tower, Rood-steeple*, the tower or steeple built over the intersection of the body and cross-ailes of a church. **1839** *Penny Cycl.* XIV. 8/2 Placed in the Rood (or central) tower. *c* **1250** *Gen. & Ex.* 255 Til ihesus was on werlde boren, And til he was on ðe *rode-wold.

II. 7. As a linear measure: A rod, pole, or perch. Now only in local use, and varying from 6 to 8 yards.

904 in Birch *Cart. Sax.* II. 266 Se [haȝa] is fram þære ea ..east wardes .xxviii. roda lang & þonon suþwardes .xxiiii. roda brad. **1466** *Mann. & Househ. Exp.* (Roxb.) 438, j. acre of lond conteynyth in lengthe .xl. rodes. **1543** in *Lett. & P. Hen. VIII*, XVIII. II. 118 For skoryn of a water souer.., cxx rud after id. ob. a rud. **1634–5** BRERETON *Trav.* (Chetham Soc.) 17 It is ten English rood long on the sides, eight rood broad. **1766** J. BARTRAM *Jrnl.* 7 Jan. 26 At about 200 yards from it runs out a large stream of water,..and may be smelt at some roods distant. **1790** W. MARSHALL *Rur. Econ. Midl. Co.* Gloss., *Rood*, a measure of eight yards in length. **1805** R. W. DICKSON *Pract. Agric.* I. 112 These [stones]..are commonly put about the middle of the work, in the proportion of nine or ten to every rood of seven yards. **1856** MORTON *Cycl. Agric.* II. 1126/1 *Rood*,..(Chesh.), of hedging, 8 yards;..(Derbys.), of bark, seems to be a pile 7 yards in length; of draining or fencing, 7 or 8 yards [etc.]. **1881** *Cheshire Gloss.* s.v., Such piece-work as hedging and ditching, draining, putting up posts and rails, &c., is done at so much per rood.

8. a. A superficial measure of land, properly containing 40 square poles or perches, but varying locally; a plot of land of this size.

A table of local variations from the statute rood is given in Morton *Cycl. Agric.* II. 939.

In OE. this use appears only in descriptions of boundaries, as the designation of particular strips of cultivated land. The ME. evidence is also very scanty, though the Latinized form *roda* occurs freely in charters.

889 in Birch *Cart. Sax.* II. 202 West be ðy wioda andlanges ðare rode oð ðane pyt. **961** *Ibid.* 292 Andlang þære rode innon syx æceras. **1058** in Earle *Land Charters* 248 Of ðære dune andlang þære rode oð hit cymð beneoðan stancnolle.

1139 in Dugdale *Monast. Angl.* (1655) I. 469/1 Una roda, ab aquilonari parte virgulti. ? **1231** *Ibid.* II. 40/2 Excepta una roda, quam retineo ad viam habendam juxta haiam meam. **1279** *Rot. Hundred.* (1818) II. 572/1 In mesuagio j rodam et xiiij acras terre. *a* **1377** in Dugdale *Monast. Angl.* (1655) II. 354/2 Unam virgatam lix. acras, tres rodas & xxxv. perticatas terræ. **1442** *Rolls of Parlt.* V. 59/1 The feerde parte of a Rode of Londe. *c* **1450** *Godstow Reg.* 287 The forsaid Rode of land, with all his pertynentis. **1538** tr. *Fitzherbert's Justyce Peace* 114 One rode, that is the 4 part of an acre of lande. **1571** DIGGES *Pantom.* II. xi. N ij, So manye perches you maye conclude the Area of that Figure, which ..bringeth 10 Acres 3½ Roodes. **1667** MILTON *P.L.* I. 196 His other Parts besides Prone on the Flood,..Lay floating many a rood. **1713** ARBUTHNOT *John Bull* II. vi, Nic... calculated the Acres and Roods to a great nicety. **1770** GOLDSM. *Des. Vill.* 58 A time there was..When every rood of ground maintained its man. **1805** *Trans. Soc. Arts* XXIII. 43, I had an acre and three rood of carrots. **1892** STEVENSON *Across the Plains* ii. 95 His old family estates, not one rood of which remained to him.

b. A measure (of land, paving, digging, building, etc.) corresponding to a square pole or perch, but with local and other variations. (See quots.)

1464 *Charters Peebles* (1872) 153 John Thomsoun..sal pay for his fredom x s. at Beltan, or a rud of causay. *c* **1470** HENRY *Wallace* VII. 826 Wallace..Romde him about a large rude and mar. **1532** *Extr. Rec. Edin.* (1871) 58 To the.. calsay makaris for ilk scottis rude, that is to say vj elnis of lenth and vj elnis of breid, xxx schillingis Scottis. **1597** SKENE *De Verb. Sign.* s.v. *Particata*, Sex elnes lang, and sex elnes broad, makis ane fall. To this fall the little ruid, or ruid of warke, or of buirdes, or of maisone, or sklait warke, is equal. **1609** —— *Reg. Maj., Burrow Lawes* cxix, Ane Ruid of land within ane Baronie, sould be measured be sax elnes... Ane Ruid of land within burgh, conteines twentie fute. **1829** *Glover's Hist. Derby* I. 91 Slate is sold by the rood, or in sufficient quantity to roof in 44 square yards. **1849** CRAIG, *Rood*... In Building, 36 square yards. In Flooring, 100 square feet. **1856** MORTON *Cycl. Agric.* II. 1126 *Rood*, ..(Chesh.),.. of land, 8 yards square = 64 square yards; of marl, 64 cubic yards... (Durham), of wall-building, 7 yards. .. (Berwicks.),..of masonry, 6 yards square, 2 feet thick [etc.].

†**c.** A measure of timber. *Obs.*

1391 *Mem. Ripon* (Surtees) III. 106 In j rod meremii sarrand. eodem tempore, 3*s.* 4*d.* **1534–5** *Durh. Acc. Rolls* (Surtees) 111 Pro sarracione j di. Rude meremii. **1597** [see b]. **1632** *Knaresb. Wills* (Surtees) II. 122, I discharge him of the payment of xxij*s.* enenst one rood of boardes he bought of me.

†**9.** A measure of wine. [MDu. *roede.*] *Obs.*

1502 ARNOLDE *Chron.* (1811) 190 The rood of reynysh wyne of Dordreight is x. awmes... Item the rood of Andwarp is xiiij awmes.

10. *Comb.*, as ***rood-breadth***; †**rood-fall** (cf. 8 b, quot. 1597). Also ROOD LAND.

1396 *Chron. de Melsa* (Rolls) II. 88, 3 perticatas terræ cum 7 rodefallis [*v.r.* rudefallis] in Suttona. **1806** J. GRAHAME *Birds of Scot.* I. 23 The oak majestical, whose aged boughs Darken a rood breadth.

rood, *v.* [var. of ROUD, *rudd*, etc.: see REDD *sb.*[2]] *intr.* To spawn.

1868 PEARD *Water-farm.* iv. 45 The heavier fish rood on the deeper runs.

rood, obs. pa. t. of RIDE *v.*

'Rood day. Now only *Hist.* [ROOD *sb.* 2.]

a. The Exaltation of the Cross (14 September). **b.** The Invention of the Cross (3 May). The earlier use is ***Holy Rood day*** in both senses.

a **1225** *Ancr. R.* 20 Þis winter schal biginnen ette holi rode dei ine heruest. **1297** R. GLOUC. (Rolls) 1932 Þe biginingge of may, As ȝe abbeþ ofte yhurd þe holi rode day. *c* **1380** WYCLIF *Sel. Wks.* I. 392 On Hooli roode Day. **1486** *Bk. St. Albans* E v, Tyme of grece begynnyth at mydsomer day And tyll holi Roode day lastyth. **1523** FITZHERB. *Husb.* §134 At any tyme between Martilmas and holyrode-day. **1596** SHAKS. *1 Hen. IV*, I. i. 52 On Holy-roode day. **1613** SELDEN *Illustr. Drayton's Poly-olb.* D.'s Wks. 1726 III. 1792 For the invention she is yet celebrated in holyrood day in May. **1641** *Art. Agreement* in *Harl. Misc.* (1811) VII. 216 That there shall be a league offensive and defensive, concluded and conformed by both parties, at or before Holyrood-day next. **1731** *Gentl. Mag.* (1732) 402 Sept. 14. Being Holy Rood Day, the King's Huntsmen hunted their Free Buck in Richmond new Park.

1520 *Extr. Rec. Stirling* (1887) 4 To be pait on the morne eftir the Rud day. **1597** *Return fr. Parnass.* II. i 739 And a drye cowe shall be 7 years oulde at the nexte roode daye. **1688** HOLME *Armoury* III. 187/2 The Dominican Monks.. Fast seven Months together from Rood Day in September to Easter. **1711** *Extr. Rec. Aberdeen* (1872) 344 The citizens to be advertised to enter ther children..at Roodday and Lambas. *a* **1779** D. GRAHAM *Hist. Buck-haven* in Writ. 1883 II. 235 Upon the Rood day..early in the morning. **1825** JAMIESON *Suppl.* s.v., The 14th of September is still called *Rude day* in Lanarkshire... In Roxb. *Rude-day* is the 25th September, which corresponds with the 14th old style. **1841** HAMPSON *Medii Ævi Cal.* I. 269 The day of the Invention of the Cross, and one of the Rode or Rood days.

roode, obs. pa. t. of RIDE *v.*

roode bec etc. (varr. of words of Afrikaans origin normally spelt *rooi-*): see ROOIBEKKIE etc.

roodge, *v.* Also 9 *dial.* **rooge, rouge, rudge.** [Of obscure origin.] *trans.* To push or lift; to move with effort.

1676 *Doctrine of Devils* 27 If as Demonologers say, a Devil ..can act mans body, so as to move, carry, roodge, hurry, transport it as he pleaseth. **1849–** in *Eng. Dial. Dict.* s.v. *Rooge* and *Rudge*.

rood goose. *Sc.* Also 8–9 **rude goose.** [Of obscure origin.] = ROAD-GOOSE.

The two earliest quots., which relate to Ross-shire, are the only real evidence for the name.

1791 *Statist. Acc. Scotl.* I. 265 A species of geese called rood geese, which are esteemed good eating. **1794** *Ibid.* XII. 274 Rude geese and swans sometimes come there in the winter and spring. **1817** FORSTER *Nat. Hist. Swallow Tribe* (ed. 6) 94 Rat or Road goose, Clatter goose, Brand goose, Rood goose. **1862** JOHNS *Brit. Birds* Index, Rood Goose, the Brent Goose.

†**rood land.** *Obs.* [f. ROOD *sb.* 8 + LAND *sb.*[1] 7.] A plot of land of one rood in extent.

14.. *Nom.* in Wr.-Wülcker 737 *Hec virgata*, a rodlande. *c* **1450** *Godstow Reg.* 556 The forsaid Rode lond. *c* **1510** *Reg. Burscough* lf. 4 (P.R.O.), On the Northe Syde of the sayd chapelle is viij acres and iij Rode londes and viij falle. **1594** in *Antiquary* XXXII. 118 Rent of a rode land, xv*s.* **1635** *MS. Indenture* (Lancs.), A parcel of land containing one roodland of land.

'rood-loft. Also **roodloft, rood loft.** [f. ROOD *sb.* 3 + LOFT *sb.* 4.] A loft or gallery forming the head of a rood-screen.

1399 *Mem. Ripon* (Surtees) III. 133 Pro j rodeloft de novo faciendo ex convencione, 3*l.* 6*s.* 8*d.*.. Et in j porcione meremii..pro prædicto rudeloft, 4*s.* **1431** *E.E. Wills* 90 For the reparacion of the chirch, and specially þe rodelofte of Stoke, C *s.* **1477–9** *Rec. St. Mary at Hill* (1905) 80 For scowryng of the Standardis candilstikkis, & the Rode loft,.. iij*s.* viij*d.* **1503** HAWES *Example Virtue* xiii. 242 The rood loft was yuery garnysshed with gold. **1579** NORTHBROOKE *Agst. Dicing* (1843) 148 Wheresoeuer they reade this worde crosse, they aduance out of hande their roode and roodeloft. *c* **1630** RISDON *Surv. Devon* §88 (1810) 86 It sheweth a fair church, with a rich..rood loft. **1719** ASHMOLE *Antiq. Berks.* I. 69 Under the King's Arms, placed over the Rood-Loft, is this Distich. **1797** NICHOLLS *Churchw. Acc.* 131 The rood-loft..was a gallery in popish times situate in every Church between the nave and the chancel. **1816** *Gentl. Mag.* LXXXVI. I. 500 Near the third window there are some steps remaining, which probably led to the rood-loft. **1840** PARKER *Gloss. Archit.* (ed. 3) 329 Roodlofts do not appear to have been common in this country before..the fourteenth century. **1872** ELLACOMBE *Bells of Ch.* in *Ch. Bells Devon* iv. 65 In some places there was a gable or turret over the Rood-loft to hold this sacring bell.

attrib. **1483–5** *Rec. St. Mary at Hill* (1905) 117 A newe holowe key to the Roode loffte dore. **1899** BARING-GOULD *Bk. of West* II. 224 A barrel of this explosive which had been placed in the rood-loft staircase.

'rood-screen. [f. ROOD *sb.* 3.] A screen, usually of richly carved wood or stone and properly surmounted by a rood, crossing the nave of a church beneath the chancel-arch and separating the nave from the choir.

1843 *Civil Eng. & Arch. Jrnl.* VI. 256/1 The inclosure of the altar by a screen or railing, answering to the rood-screen. **1861** *Archæol. Æliana* V. XVII. 157 The seats..are the residue of those which..occupied their appropriate place along the east front of the rood-screen. **1870** F. R. WILSON *Ch. Lindisf.* 61 A carved oak rood-screen has been recently placed at the chancel arch.

attrib. **1862** *Catal. Internat. Exhib., Brit.* II. No. 5983, A pair of rood-screen gates in hammered iron and brass.

rood-stake: see RUD-STAKE.

†**rood-tree.** *Obs.* [f. ROOD *sb.* 2.] The cross on which Christ died. Also *fig.*

c **1200** ORMIN 348 To wurrþenn offredd her O rodetreowwess allterr. *Ibid.* 5602 Þiss drædunng iss þatt rodetreo þatt Crist himm sellf spacc offe. *a* **1300** *Cursor M.* 16604 Apon þe mont of caluarie þai sett þis rode tre. *c* **1340** HAMPOLE *Pr. Consc.* 5260 Als he henged on þe rode tre,.. When he deyhed for mans trespas. **1390** GOWER *Conf.* II. 1161, I lieve and triste in Cristes feith, Which deide upon the Rode tree. *a* **1450** MYRC 248 Hyt ys goddes body þat soffered ded Vp on the holy rode tre. *c* **1485** *Digby Myst.* III. 1939 That for vs dyyd on þe rode tre.

roody, obs. form of RUDDY.

roof (ru:f), *sb.* Forms: α. 1 **hrof**, 3 **rhof**; 1–5 **rof**, 4–6 **roff, rofe**, 5 **roffe**; 4– **roof**, 4–7 **roofe**, 6 **rooff(e**; 5–6 **rouf**, 6 **rouffe, roughe, rowff(e**, 6–7 **rowfe, roufe.** β. 3–6 **roue**, 4–6 **rove**; *pl.* 4–5 **roaues** (5 **-ys**), 5, 20 **rooves, -is.** γ. *Sc.* 5–6 **ruf, rufe** (*north.* **ruffe**), 6 *pl.* **ruvis**, 6, 8–9 **ruif** (7 **ruiff**), 9 **reef.** [OE. *hróf*, = OFris. *rhoof* (Fris. *roef*), MDu. *roof, rouf, roef* (Du. *roef*, cabin, coffin-lid), MLG. and LG. *rôf*, OIcel. *hróf* boat-shed; the stem does not appear to be otherwise represented. English alone has retained the word in a general sense, for which the other languages use forms corresponding to OE. *þæc* thatch.]

1. a. The outside upper covering of a house or other building; also, the ceiling of a room or other covered part of a house, building, etc.

α. *Beowulf* 927 He to healle ȝeong..ȝeseah steapne hrof golde fahne. *a* **900** CYNEWULF *Crist* 14 Nu ȝebrosnad is hus under hrofe. *Ibid.* 495 Cyning ure ȝewat þurh þæs temples hrof. *c* **950** *Lindisf. Gosp.* Luke xii. 3 Þætte in eare sprecend ȝie woeron in cottum, aboden bið on hrofum. *c* **1000** ÆLFRIC *Hom.* I. 318 Entas woldon aræran..ænne stypel swa heahne þæt his hrof astiȝe oð heofon. *c* **1200** ORMIN 11351 Þe deofell ..sette himm heȝhe uppo þe rhof. *c* **1290** *S. Eng. Leg.* I. 187/99 Ȝwane is blod spreinde In þe rof an heiȝ. *c* **1300** *Havelok* 2082 A rof shal hile us boþe o-niht. **1390** GOWER *Conf.* I. 258 The Sparke fyred Up in the Rof;..whan the wyndes blowe, It blaseth out on every side. *c* **1440** *Promp. Parv.* 435/2 Roof, of an howse, *tectum, doma.* **1471** *Cal. Rec. Dublin* (1889) I. 347 And put a roffe of oke tymber therupon. *c* **1500** *Melusine* 297 She made it to touche..the rouf of the chambre that was ryght hye. **1535** COVERDALE *2 Kings* xxiii. 12 The altares vpon the rofe of Achabs perler, which the kynges of Iuda had made. **1600** J. PORY tr. *Leo's Africa* VII. 286 The walles of their houses are built of chalke, and the roofes are couered with strawe. **1610** HOLLAND *Camden's Brit.* (1637) 429 The Rowfe covered over with sheets of Lead. **1671** MILTON *P.R.* IV. 58 Thou may'st behold Outside and inside both, pillars and roofs Carv'd work. **1717** LADY M. W. MONTAGU *Lett.* I. xxxvii. 142 The roof was painted with all sorts of flowers. **1795** SOUTHEY *Joan of Arc* v, The shatter'd roofs Allow'd the dews of night free passage. **1815** J. SMITH *Panorama Sci. & Art* I. 254 Among the ancients, in those countries where it seldom rained, roofs were made quite flat. **1841** W. SPALDING *Italy & It. Isl.* I. 151 The introduction of columns..for the purpose of strengthening the roof. **1872** YEATS *Tech. Hist. Comm.* 132 Most houses in mediæval times were built high and narrow, with steep pointed roofs.

fig. *c* **1250** *Death* 155 in *O.E. Misc.* 178 Þi bur is sone ibuld þat þu schald wunien inne. Þe rof..schal ligge o þine chinne. *c* **1600** SHAKS. *Sonn.* x, Seeking that beautious roofe to ruinate, Which to repaire should be thy chiefe desire. **1781** COWPER *Table-T.* 625 The mind..Flew to its first position with a spring That made the vaulted roofs of pleasure ring.

β. *a* **1225** *Ancr. R.* 152 ȝet is ancre iefned her to sparuwe þet is one under roue. *c* **1384** CHAUCER *H. Fame* III. 1948 On the rove men may yet seen A thousand holes. **1387** TREVISA *Higden* (Rolls) VI. 55 Constantinus..unheled chirches roves [*v.r.* rooves] and coppes. *c* **1400** *Laud Troy Bk.* 17845 Aboute the roue That scholde be set the temple aboue. **1445** in *Anglia* XXVIII. 275 Vpon high bankys he makith new roovis. *a* **1500** *Nut Brown Maid* in *Arnolde's Chron.* (1811) 200 And vs abowe, noon other roue, but a brake bussh or twayne. *a* **1550** *Image Ipocr.* I. 87 in Skelton's Wks. (1843) II. 415 To runne in att the rove. **1903** *Dialect Notes* II. 352 *Roof, n. pl.* rooves. Common plural in Mass. **1938** C. HIMES *Black on Black* (1973) 165 W'en de panic cum an' de Lawd tek yo' food an' yo' clothes an' de rooves off'n yo' haids, den laff. **1939** [see *council (housing) estate* s.v. COUNCIL 17].

γ. *c* **1375** *Sc. Leg. Saints* xxvii. (*Machor*) 60 He saw angelis ..one þe ruf of þat house lycht. *c* **1440** *York Myst.* xiv. 18 Þe walles are doune,..Þe ruffe is rayned aboven oure hede. *c* **1475** *Rauf Coilȝear* 672 The rufe reulit about in reuall of Reid. **1513** DOUGLAS *Æneis* IV. viii. 112 The nycht oule, Heich on the ruif. *Ibid.* xii. 47 Of gretting..The rufis did resound. **1570** LEVINS *Manip.* 183 Yᵉ Ruffe of a house, *culmen.* **1633** *Extr. Rec. Stirling* (1887) 169 To repair thair grammer scoole..and putt on ane new ruiff thairon.

b. With *under*, *beneath*, †*within*, to denote entering, being or living in, a house.

Beowulf 403 þa secȝ wisode under Heorotes hrof. *c* **950** *Lindisf. Gosp.* Matt. viii. 8 Nam ic wyrðe þæt ðu inngae under rof min. **1382** WYCLIF *Ibid.*, That thou entre vndir my roof. **1596** DALRYMPLE tr. *Leslie's Hist. Scot.* I. 31 Thay nevir thair heid sett vndir the ruffe of ony hous. **1601** SHAKS. *Twel. N.* IV. iii. 25 Vnderneath that consecrated roofe, Plight me the full assurance of your faith. **1726–46** THOMSON *Winter* 483 Beneath his low illustrious roof, Sweet Peace and happy Wisdom smooth'd his brow. **1782** MISS BURNEY *Cecilia* VI. i, That since you were now under my roof, I could not refuse to receive their proposals. **1837** LOCKHART *Scott* I. ix. 317 They had both seen Scott frequently under their own roofs. **1888** BURGON *Lives 12 Gd. Men* I. iii. 302 For about two years they lived..under the roof of their father's youngest sister.

fig. **1642** FULLER *Holy & Prof. St.* IV. xxi. 353 Some maintain that Princes are too high to come under the roof of any Laws.

c. Used by extension to denote: (*a*) a house or chamber; chiefly *poet.*; (*b*) (rhetorically), a home, a household; a dwelling-place.

1591 SHAKS. *1 Hen. VI*, II. iii. 56, I tell you Madame, were the whole Frame here,..Your Roofe were not sufficient to contayn't. **1600** —— *A.Y.L.* II. iii. 17 Come not within these doores: within this roofe The enemie of all your graces liues. **1623** FLETCHER & ROWLEY *Maid in Mill* II. ii, My dwelling, sir? 'Tis a poor yeoman's roof scarce a league off. **1757** GRAY *Bard* 55 Shrieks of death thro' Berkley's roofs that ring. **1819** SHELLEY *Cyclops* 83 Whence come they,..approaching in ill hour The inhospitable roof of Polypheme? **1853** C. BRONTË *Villette* I. iii. 29 The evening, by restoring Graham to the maternal roof (his days were passed at school), brought us an accession of animation. **1922** D. L. SAYERS *Let.* 18 Dec. in J. Brabazon *Dorothy L. Sayers* (1981) ix. 96 He simply has not a red cent or a roof. **1979** J. RATHBONE *Euro-Killers* iii. 34 She had been happy to give them a free roof until they got work.

fig. **1617** HIERON *Wks.* II. 370 What is my heart, that Thou shouldest come within the roofe thereof?

†**d.** A story or floor in a house. *Obs.*

1617 MORYSON *Itin.* I. 18 The building..is all of free stone sixe or seven roofes high. *Ibid.* 112 The houses of the City are foure roofes high.

e. In phrases (chiefly *colloq.*). (*a*) ***to raise*** (or ***lift***) ***the roof***: to create an uproar, to make a resounding noise; (*b*) ***the roof falls in***: something disastrous occurs, everything goes wrong; (*c*) ***come off the roof***: don't put on airs; (*d*) ***to hit the roof*** = ***to hit the ceiling*** (CEILING *vbl. sb.* 5 b); (*e*) ***to go through the roof***: to become very angry (see also sense 2 a).

(*a*) **1860** M. J. HOLMES *Cousin Maude* 57 Ole master'll raise de ruff, case he put 'em away to sell. **1894** 'MARK TWAIN' in *Century Mag.* June 233/1 She was here to watch the trial now, and was going to lift up just one 'hooraw' over it... 'When dat verdic' comes, I's gwine to lif' dat *roof*, now, I tell you. **1905** *Eng. Dial. Dict.* V. 147/2 *Oxf.* Do be quiet, or you'll raise the roof (G.O.). **1922** WODEHOUSE *Girl on Boat* xvi. 253, I couldn't get within ten feet of that dog without its lifting the roof off. **1959** *Times* 19 Jan. 3/3 A good song to raise the roof. **1972** J. W. THOMPSON in W. King *Black Short Story Anthol.* 255 She flew from the kitchen like a startled sparrow, her hands perched nervously upon her hips—all set to raise the roof!

(*b*) **1866** D. BOUCICAULT *Flying Scud* in Nicoll & Cloak *Forbidden Fruit & Other Plays* (1940) 172 She undertook with all her veight to sit upon my knee... Fourteen stun six, I thought the roof had fell in. **1958** J. MORGAN *Expense Account* ii. 26 And it all worked out exactly right—up to the moment he walked into his office. Then the roof fell in. **1976** H. MACINNES *Agent in Place* xvii. 191 Georges said, 'I think the roof just fell in.' Tony had no reply. For once he was quite speechless.

(*c*) **1895** W. P. RIDGE *Minor Dialogues* ix. 86 She took up such a 'igh and mighty attitude..so I says to her, I says, 'Come off the roof.'

(*d*) **1925** FRASER & GIBBONS *Soldier & Sailor Words* 245 *Roof, to hit the*, to get into a temper. **1928** J. P. MCEVOY *Show Girl* ix. 133 Milton gave me a couple of drinks early in the evening out of his flask and Jimmy hit the roof. **1971** V. CANNING *Firecrest* x. 149 The P.M. and his cabinet..would hit the roof if they knew half of the things that went on.

(*e*) **1958** *Spectator* 25 July 133/1 Would it have hurt if someone had done it to you before? You'd have gone through the roof? **1975** J. SYMONS *Three Pipe Problem* xviii. 179 The company are simply wild. They have gone through the roof.

2. *fig.* **a.** The highest point or summit of something; that which completes or covers in; = CEILING *vbl. sb.* 6 d. ***to go through the roof*** (and varr.), of bids, prices, sales, etc.: to surpass the expected limit, to reach extreme heights.

c **888** K. ÆLFRED *Boeth.* xi. §2 Ic eow mæȝ..ȝereccan hwæt se hrof is ealra ȝesælð a. *a* **900** CYNEWULF *Crist* 749 þæt we to þam hyhstan hrofe ȝestiȝan, halȝum weorcum. *c* **950** *Lindisf. Gosp.* Mark xiii. 27 From hrof *vel* heum eardes wið to..heannise heofnes. *c* **1200** *Vices & Virtues* 95 Ðe faste hope hafð hire stede up an heih, for ði hie is rof and wrikð alle ðe hire bieð beneðen. **1377** LANGL. *P. Pl.* B. XIX. 324 Of al holywrit he made a rofe after, And called þat hous vnite. **1477** NORTON *Ord. Alch.* in Ashm. (1652) 22 Blessed is he that maketh due proofe, For that is roote of cunning and roofe. **1526** *Pilgr. Perf.* (W. de W. 1531) 142 The rofe yᵗ coureeth all, is the theologicall vertue hope. **1588** A. KING tr. *Canisius' Catech.* 80 Ye perfectione and ruif of yᵉ haill wark is Charitie. **1833** TENNYSON *Lotos Eaters* 69 Why should we only toil, the roof and crown of things? **1939** *Richmond* (Va.) *Times-Dispatch* 16 Aug. 17/8 Spokesmen for the shellers contended that since the price pegging program put a 'roof' on the price they must pay for peanuts they were entitled to a 'floor' against possible losses from 'innocent' over-buying. **1946** E. HODGINS *Mr. Blandings builds his Dream House* viii. 118 The Knapp sales curves were going through the roof. **1947** *Forum* (Johannesburg) 24 May 15/3 The Labour Party continues to snipe at the Government for refusing to take the roof off the maize price. **1962** *Listener* 28 June 1113/2 (Advt.), Starting salary from £11.10.0 per week to £12.16.0 per week according to qualifications, rising to roof of £14.2.0 per week. **1965** *New Statesman* 16 July 101/4 (Advt.), Starting salary £2,185–£2,445 according to relevant experience and qualifications rising to a roof of £2,835. **1972** *Times* 24 Oct. 10/3 Only a few special treasures were bid through the roof. **1973** *Times* 30 Oct. 19/6 On lots that were rare and undamaged they [*sc.* prices] went through the roof.

b. Applied to heaven, the upper air, etc., as covering the earth.

[*c* **700** CÆDMON *Hymn* 6 He aerist scop aelda barnum heben til hrofe.]

a **900** CYNEWULF *Crist* 60 þas sidan ȝesceaft, swylce rodores hrof. *a* **1300** *Cursor M.* 22170 Na land þat man kan neuen, Under þe rof o crists heuen. **13..** *K. Alis.* 513 (W.), He schal beo kyng al above Bytwene this and heven rove. **1399** LANGL. *Rich. Redeles* III. 248 Iche rewme vndir roff of þe reyne-bowe. **1602** SHAKS. *Ham.* II. ii. 313 This most excellent Canopy the Ayre,..this Maiesticall Roofe. **1815** SHELLEY *Alastor* 96 The varying roof of heaven And the green earth. **1821** —— *Epipsych.* 542 Under the roof of blue Ionian weather.

c. Something which in form or function is comparable to the covering of a house. Also, *spec.* in *Mountaineering* (see quot. 1963²).

Cf. OE. *pæs helmes hróf, beorȝes hróf* (Beowulf).

c **1611** CHAPMAN *Iliad* XVII. 326 The cruel steel afflicting all, the strongest did not dwell Unhurt within their iron roofs. **1633** MILTON *Arcades* 88 Under the shady roof Of branching Elm Star-proof. **1697** DRYDEN *Virg. Georg.* IV. 61 Nor Bees are lodg'd in Hives alone, but..Their vaulted Roofs are hung in Pumices. **1774** GOLDSM. *Nat. Hist.* (1776) VIII. 98 To prevent the earth from falling..they make a sort of roof with their gluey substance. **1817** SHELLEY *Rev. Islam* VII. xi, In that roof of crags a space was riven. **1834** WORDSW. *Noonday Hymn* 20 A church in every grove that spreads Its living roof above our heads. **1840** GEN. MERCER in R. J. Macdonald *Hist. Dress R.A.* (1899) 54 This elegant coiffure was ornamented with..a cockade in front of the roof. **1963** A. GREENBANK *Instructions in Rock Climbing* ix. 98 On the lip of an overhang which has no footholds immediately below... You jockey one boot up the rock, pressing on the flat face, then throw a knee over the edge of the 'roof'. *Ibid.* 151 *Roof*, the underside of an overhang. **1972** D. HASTON *In High Places* viii. 94 After an easy first pitch there was a series of overlapping roofs leading to a big ledge, followed by a line of cracks and chimneys to the top. **1976** *Newmarket Jrnl.* 16 Dec., Left-back Mickey Fordham latched on to a pass from Eley to fire home a third into the roof of the net.

d. *Mining.* The stratum lying immediately over a bed of coal; the stratum lying immediately over material that contains opal (*Austral.*); the top of a working or gallery.

1686 PLOT *Staffordsh.* 147 A roof of loose rotten stone without any certain beding or diping. **1708** J. C. *Compl. Collier* (1845) 30 Leave perhaps about a Foot thick of the Coal top for a Roof. **1778** W. PRYCE *Min. Cornub.* 79 When the Miners dig down or along in a large Lode, then the roof, i.e. the upper, the hanging wall, or incumbent wall of the Lode or Fissure, is..over their heads. **1789** J. WILLIAMS *Nat. Hist. Min. Kingd.* I. 72 Lime-stone may be reckoned among the very hard roofs of coal. **1833–4** J. PHILLIPS *Geol.* in *Encycl. Metrop.* (1845) VI. 590/2 This coal seam is covered by a 'roof' unlike that of any other coal bed above the mountain limestone in the British Islands. **1883** *Law. Rep.* 10 *Q.B. Div.* 553 Without leaving any pillars of coal or other support for the roof of the mine. **1931** M. S. BUCHANAN *Prospecting for Opal in Australia* 8 Almost all the sheet of potch containing opal lies within two ft. from the roof. **1960** *People* (Broadway, New South Wales) 27 Apr. 51 Pipe opal..is mostly found in soft, white clay between one and six inches below the overlying sandstone 'roof'.

e. A high mountain range or plateau; the highest part (*of* a region); ***the roof of the world*** [tr. Wakhani *bam-i-dunya*], orig. applied to the Pamirs, later also to Tibet or the Himalayas.

1842 *Chinese Repository* XI. 143 The Wakhanis name this plain Bam-i-Duniah, or 'Roof of the World', and it would indeed appear to be the highest table-land in Asia. **1876** T. E. GORDON (*title*) The roof of the world, being the narrative of a journey over the high plateau of Tibet to the Russian frontier and the Oxus sources on Pamir. *Ibid.* ix. 121 We were now about to cross the famous 'Bam-i-dunya', 'The Roof of the World', under which name the elevated region of the hitherto comparatively unknown Pamir tracts had long appeared in our maps. **1889** G. N. CURZON *Russia in Central Asia* v. 144 Descending from the hidden 'Roof of the world', its waters tell of forgotten peoples and whisper secrets of unknown lands. **1902** D. G. HOGARTH *Nearer East* 31 The course of this ridge in the Anatolian roof.. determines the parting of all the waters. **1953** J. MASTERS *Lotus & Wind* xix. 235 Few travellers used this route that arched over the roof of the world to link India with Chinese Sinkiang. **1956** G. N. PATTERSON *God's Fool* i. 13, I sat there in that remote valley in Tibet where no white man had ever been, fifteen thousand feet above sea-level on the roof of the world. **1959** *Listener* 15 Jan. 140/3 If you want to give yourself a test of stamina and skill in map reading you can walk the Roof of Wales. **1968** N. TRANTER *Cable from Kabul* ii. 29 Look—this area's called the Roof of the World. It's no place for aircraft. **1973** *Guardian* 20 Oct. 13/3 Identification of Church and State in Tibetan Buddhism dates from the 1640s. But the *feel* of an independent way of life on the battlemented roof of Asia is immensely older. **1979** *Yale Alumni Mag.* Apr. 2/3 (Advt.), Snow-capped peaks of the Himalayas along the roof of the world.

f. *Aeronaut.* = CEILING *vbl. sb.* 6 b. ? *Obs.*

1917 [see CEILING *vbl. sb.* 6 b]. **1940** *S.P.E. Tract* lv. 193 *Roof* is the zenith of a plane's ascent.

3. a. ***the roof of the mouth***, the palate. Also *ellipt.*

c **1000** ÆLFRIC *Gloss.* in Wr.-Wülcker I. 157 *Palatum, uel uranon*, goma, *uel* hrof ðæs muðes. *c* **1340** *Nominale* (Skeat) 30 *Iungyues et palet*, Gomes and the roof of the mouth. **1387** TREVISA *Higden* (Rolls) II. 257 Men of myddel londes [sownen her wordes] in þe roof of þe mouþ. *c* **1450** *Two Cookery-bks.* 78 Kutte a Swan in the rove of the mouthe. **1486** *Bk. St. Albans* c vj b, Put som in the Roofe of her mowth. **1535** COVERDALE *Job* xxix. 9 When their tonges cleued to the rofe of their mouthes. *a* **1586** SIDNEY *Ps.* XXII. ix, My cleaving tongue close to my roofe doth bide. **1611** COTGR., *Aluette*,..a little peece of flesh in the roofe of the mouth. **1644** Z. BOYD in *Zion's Flowers* (1855) App. 9 The tongues of all, did cleave unto their roof. **1741** A. MONRO *Anat. Nerves* (ed. 3) 132 The Base of the Nostrils and Roof of the Mouth. **1847** W. C. L. MARTIN *The Ox* 56/1 The roof of the mouth and the tongue are black. **1868** *Daily News* 26 Aug., A gold roof for false teeth. **1890** [see PALATE 1 b].

b. Similarly of other parts of the body, etc.

1863 HUXLEY *Man's Place in Nat.* §ii. 77 In the gorilla,.. the roofs of the orbits rise more obliquely into the cranial cavity. **1870** ROLLESTON *Anim. Life* 12 The removal of the roof of the cranium. **1872** COUES *N. Amer. Birds* 29 The scale forms the floor instead of the roof of the nostrils. **1888** FAGGE & PYE-SMITH *Princ. & Pract. Med.* (ed. 2) I. 56 The thinning of the roof of an abscess which is about to 'point'.

4. †**a.** *Sc.* A canopy or tester. *Obs.*

1505 *Exch. Rolls Scot.* XII. 673 Tua bosteris, vj werdoris, tua ruffis of carsay red and gren. **1533** *Acc. Ld. H. Treas. Scot.* VI. 182 To lyn the rufe of the said curtingis, iij elnis bukrame.

b. The top of a carriage, coach, or other covered vehicle.

1706 PHILLIPS (ed. Kersey), *Roof*, the top of a..Coach. **1806** J. BERESFORD *Miseries Hum. Life* VI. xiii, Seeing and hearing the roof of a crazy coach groan, crack, and bend, over your head. **1837** W. B. ADAMS *Carriages* 88 To form the roof, arching timbers are laid across from side to side. **1849** MACAULAY *Hist. Eng.* iii. I. 379 The passengers..were all seated in the carriage. For..it would have been most perilous to mount the roof.

5. The back or ridge (of a bull). *rare*⁻¹.

The Fris. *roef* is similarly used.

1808 *Compl. Grazier* (ed. 3) 9 The roof [of a bull ought to be] wide, particularly over the chine and hips, or hooks.

6. *slang.* **a.** A hat. **b.** The head.

1857 HUGHES *Tom Brown* I. v, Equipped in his go-to-meeting roof. **1897** MARSHALL *Pomes* 70 (Farmer), He..was bald upon the roof. **1926** MAINES & GRANT *Wise-Crack Dict.* 7/1 *Dropping one's roof*, losing one's hat. **1949** R. M. HOWE *H. Gross's Criminal Investigation* (ed. 4) viii. 162 *Titfa, roof, bonnet or tile*, hat.

c. An umbrella. ? *Obs.*

1844 E. HALL *Diary* in O. A. Sherrard *Two Victorian Girls* (1966) xi. 106 [A] family roof [umbrella] and a great blanket shawl.

7. *attrib.* **a.** In sense 1, with terms denoting some part, accessory, or feature of the roof, as ***roof-beam***, ***-board***, ***-capping***, ***comb***, ***-coping***, ***-cover***, ***-crest***, ***-deck***, ***-decking***, ***-glass***, ***-outlet***, ***-pane***, ***-ridge***, ***-roller***, ***-screen***, ***-shelter***, ***-slab***, ***-space***, ***-terrace***, ***-thatch***, ***-thatching***, ***-truss***.

1647 HEXHAM, The *roofe beame, *den dack balck*. **1873** MORLEY *Rousseau* I. vii. 258 My imagination..languishes and dies in a room and under roof beams. **1848** O. S. FOWLER *Home for All* (1851) 90 Since the *roof boards cross these rafters, so as to form an arch the other way, surely no greater solidity or strength can be required. **1940** *Chambers's Techn. Dict.* 730/1 *Roof boards*, boards laid on a roof to provide a foundation and an undercovering to the covering materials proper, such as slates, tiles, etc. **1968** O. S. NOCK *Railway Enthusiast's Encycl.* 246 (*caption*) G.W.R.: an early example of dining-car service, with rather flamboyant roof-boards, c. 1900. **1977** *36 Home Handyman Projects* (Austral. Home Jrnl.) 74/1 *Roof capping is usually put on with cement. After a few years of sun, wind and rain the cement cracks and falls out. **1908** *Encycl. Relig. & Ethics* I. 687/1 On the roof was a *roof comb—one of the most distinguishing features of Maya architecture. **1971** *Country Life* 4 Nov. 1219/2 A three-room temple surmounted by an enormous stone roof-comb originally carved with an impressive seated figure. **1890** A. J. C. HARE *S.-E. France* 577 Yellow and orange houses, each with..ornamented *roof-coping. **1875** KNIGHT *Dict. Mech.* 1973/2 Horizontal slats, slightly raised above the *roof-cover. *Ibid.*, Other kinds of *roof-coverings. **1862** *Catal. Internat. Exhib., Brit.* II. No. 2329, *Roof, cresting..glazed, and enamelled. Ventilating *roof crest tiles. **1947** *Archit. Rev.* CII. 117 The whole of the area on which this house is built is utilized for outdoor functions; above the living-room-kitchen part is an open *roof-deck, below the bedrooms a car-port. **1979** *Arizona Daily Star* 5 Aug. (Advt. Section) 20/1 The roof deck affords fantastic views. **1960** *Farmer & Stockbreeder* 16 Feb. (Suppl.) 40/1 When used as the *roof-decking to your new buildings or as a suspended ceiling to your existing ones, Stramit keeps temperatures constant. **1978** C. Tomlinson *Shaft* 39 Leaves might fall On to the *roof-glass. **1894** J. Watson *Jedburgh Abbey* (ed. 2) 119 The date of the earliest of the *roof-markings. **1967** *Gloss. Sanitation Terms* (*B.S.I.*) 41 **Roof outlet*, a rainwater fitting, normally provided with a grating, for building into a flat roof to receive rainwater for discharge into a rainwater pipe. **1922** Joyce *Ulysses* 265 Roll of Bensoul-benjamin rolled to the quivery loveshivery *roofpanes. *a* **1878** Sir G. Scott *Lect. Archit.* (1879) I. 53 They could not, under the same *roof-plane, introduce the intersecting vaults. **1833** Loudon *Encycl. Archit.* §153 One of them.. is called the *roof plate. *a* **1878** Sir G. Scott *Lect. Archit.* (1879) I. 251 Placed in a side wall and under a level roof-plate. **1844** Whittier *Bridal of Pennacook* 259 And, adown the *roof-pole hung,.. In the smoke his scalp-locks swung. **1855** Longf. *Hiaw.* xii. 179 The roof-poles of the wigwam Were as glittering rods of silver. **1849** *Ecclesiologist* IX. 15 The ends of the *roof-rafters. **1874** B. F. Taylor *World on Wheels* 218 There is singing everywhere:.. from the second rail of the fence, a gust of melody; from the *roof-ridge, a solo. **1881** Ruskin *Our Fathers have told us* I. (1884) 22 The Cathedral is seen beneath us,.. our gained hill-top being on a level with its roof-ridge. **1917** Conrad *Shadow-Line* II. 79 Here and there in the distance, above the crowded mob of low, brown roof ridges, towered great piles of masonry. **1936** *Discovery* Aug. 251/2 A *roof roller [excavated at Tell Duwein, near Jerusalem] was identical in form with that in use today in Palestine. **1688** Holme *Armoury* III. xii. 451/1 *Roofe Rooms. **1971** *Gloss. Terms Fire* (*B.S.I.*) II. 7 **Roof screen*, a vertical screen fitted internally to the roof of a building to divide the roof into bays, so that smoke and hot gases from a fire are contained within the bay of origin. **1848** Rickman *Styles Archit.* p. liii, The pendants, or vaulting shafts,.. would here be more correctly called *roof-shafts. **1928** D. H. Lawrence *Lady Chatterley* x. 145 Only one or two [chicks].. still dibbed about in the dryness under the straw *roof-shelter. **1963** *Gloss. Gen. Building Terms* (*B.S.I.*) 20 **Roof slab*, a slab forming the continuous loadbearing structure of a roof and spanning between supports. **1891** T. Hardy *Tess* xxiii. (1900) 55/2 Clinging to the roadside bank like pigeons on a *roof-slope. **1839** Ure *Dict. Arts* 624 Between the *roof-space over the pot.. a large passage is opened. **1960** *Farmer & Stockbreeder* 16 Feb. 49/2 (Advt.) Agrecon buildings give.. a maximum roof-space. **1970** J. Earl *Tuners & Amplifiers* i. 12 A simple indoor or roofspace aerial would be suitable for the reception of local stations. **1648** Hexham II, *Kap-raven*, *Roofe-sparrs. **1860** Dickens *Uncomm. Trav.* 78 The rain was jerking in gushes out of the old *roof-spouts. **1848** Thackeray *Van. Fair* lxv, The landlord.. led the way up the stairs to the *roof-storey. **1937** *Archit. Rev.* LXXXII. 119 (*caption*) The *roof-terrace is paved with 'Paropa' patent slabs. **1912** 'Q.' *Hocken & Hunken* xix. 239 With a rampant climber such as Rosa Devoniensis it is advisable to cut out each autumn, and clean remove some of the old wood; and this is no easy job when early neglect has allowed the plant to riot up and over the *roof-thatch. **1968** J. Arnold *Shell Bk. Country Crafts* 329 Hazel rods have many other uses, such as for salmon-traps on the Severn.. and pegs for *roof-thatching. **1828–43** Tytler *Hist. Scot.* (1864) I. 137 The third [stone].. shivered its strong *roof-timbers into a thousand pieces. **1839** *Civil Eng. & Arch. Jrnl.* II. 191/1 *Roof-trusses may be made entirely of cast-iron. **1875** Knight *Dict. Mech.* 1975/1 *Roof-truss*, the framework of a roof, consisting of thrust and tie pieces. **1964** W. L. Goodman *Hist. Woodworking Tools* 197 It may be, however, that the original French word *fermoir* has something to do with the *ferme* or roof-truss. **1805** R. W. Dickson *Pract. Agric.* I. 91 Two *roof-windows, at 6*s.* each.

b. In sense 2 d, as ***roof-coal***, ***-crag***, etc.

1821 Mander *Derbysh. Miner's Gloss.*, *Roof-work*, putting Slabs and other pieces of Timber to support the roof of Gabes and works in Mines. **1833–4** J. Phillips *Geol.* in *Encycl. Metrop.* (1845) VI. 704/1 An idea of the appearances of the Hutton roof crags. **1839** Ure *Dict. Arts* 978 The roof-stratum begins to break by the sides of the pillars. *Ibid.* 979 When a coal has a following or roof-stone,.. this facilitates the labour. **1883** *Science* I. 192/1 The exposure of the roof-shales is not sufficient to prove the absence of such detritus. **1887** P. McNeill *Blawearie* 134 The day on which I got my head crushed wi' the fa' o' roof-coal.

c. In sense 4 b, as ***roof-irons***, ***-seat***.

1894 *Daily News* 12 Dec. 8/4 Hansom cabs had got no roof irons to carry luggage. **1897** *Outing* XXX. 108/1 The scared old gent on the front roof-seat. **1900** F. Rogers *Man. Coaching* iv. 73 In the present coach, the roof-seats are fastened on the roof, with their edges fair with the front.

8. *Comb.* **a.** Objective, as ***roof-building***, ***-haunting***, ***-levelling***, ***-reaching*** adjs.; ***roof-draining***, ***-raising***; ***roof-tiler***, ***walker***.

1803 Han. More *Way to Plenty* (S.P.C.K.) 46 All the workmen were looking forward to the usual holiday of roof-raising. **1842** Tennyson *Day-Dream* 37 Roof-haunting martins warm their eggs. **1849** *Ecclesiologist* IX. 357 *note*, The metal-work required for roof-draining. **1860** Gen. P. Thompson *Audi Alt.* clxx. III. 197 A provision.. beneath the talents of the roof-building ape. **1863** G. M. Hopkins *Let.* 4 May (1956) 78 Leaving a candle burning, which I thought would keep the roof-walker in.. suspense. **1895** *Westm. Gaz.* 3 Sept. 8/1 Luxuriant shrubs, and roof-reaching roses. **1920** W. B. Yeats *Michael Robartes & Dancer* 20 And one bare hill Whereby the haystack and roof-levelling wind.. can be stayed. **1921** *Dict. Occup. Terms* (1927) §570 Roof tiler. **1973** *Times* 16 Oct. 4/8 Mr Walsh, aged 24, a roof tiler. **1976** *Star* (Sheffield) 29 Nov. 10/2 (Advt.), Roof tiler required in the very near future.

b. Similative, as ***roof-high***, ***-shaped*** adjs.; ***roof-like***, ***-wise*** advs.

1611 Cotgr. s.v. *Haultmuré*, A dish of brewes, whose soppes are heaped roofewise one vpon another. **1792** Wordsw. *Descrip. Sketches* 211 Mists.. Spread rooflike o'er the deep secluded vale. **1831** Carlyle *Sart. Res.* I. iii, Those thick locks.. overlapping roof-wise the gravest face we ever in this world saw. **1832** Ht. Martineau *Each & All* ii. 27 It will take a life time for our clumps to grow roof-high. **1860** Maury *Phys. Geogr.* (Low) ii. 39 The Gulf Stream is.. roof-shaped.

c. Locative, instrumental, etc., as ***roof-clustered***, ***-mired***, ***-rent***, ***-wrecked*** adjs.; ***roofward(s)*** adv.

a **1879** W. Howitt in M. Howitt *Autobiogr.* (1889) I. vii. 227 Clouds of smoke.. burst from the windows and streamed up roofwards. **1880** 'Mark Twain' *Tramp Abroad* xix. 171 A hill.. with.. its.. roof-clustered cap of architecture. **1922** Hardy *Late Lyrics & Earlier* 283 The bower we shrined to Tennyson, Gentlemen, Is roof-wrecked. **1932** Auden in *Rev. Eng. Stud.* (1978) Aug. 302 A sleepy liftboy swirled us roofward. **1933** C. Day Lewis *Magnetic Mountain* 50 Yet passing derelict mills and barns roof-rent. **1955** A. Clarke *Later Poems* (1961) 48 A cage-bird came among sparrows.. Plucked, roof-mired, all in mad bits.

9. Special combs., as **roof bolt** *Mining*, a tensioned rod anchoring the roof of a working to the strata above; so **roof bolting** *vbl. sb.*, the practice of using roof bolts; **roof-brain**, the cerebral cortex; **roof-cat**, an Indian species of wild cat; **roof-climb** *v. intr.*, to climb over the roofs of buildings; so *roof-climber*, *roof-climbing* vbl. sb.; **roof-drip**, a drip or dripping of water from a roof; **roof-garden**, (*a*) a garden, or collection of plants in large pots, etc., on the (flat) roof of a house or other building; freq. applied to a place for eating or entertainment situated on the roof of a building; also *attrib.*; (*b*) (see quot. 1932); **roof-jack**, (*a*) *Canad.*, a pole supporting the roof of a tent; (*b*) *Canad.*, a smoke vent of a chimney; (*c*) *U.S.*, a support for a house painter engaged in painting a roof; **roof-lorn** *a.*, roofless; **roof-man** = *gutter-man* (*c*) s.v. GUTTER *sb.*[1] 8; **roof-mask** (see quot.); †**roof-nail**, nails used to secure roofing material; **roof-nucleus**, *Anat.*, a part of the brain (see quots.); **roof organization** [tr. G. *dachsorganisation*], a parent organization; **roof pendant** *Geol.*, a mass of country rock projecting downwards into an intrusive body such as a batholith; †**roof-pincer**, a surgical instrument for raising the uvula; **roof-rack**, a framework upon the roof of a motor vehicle to which luggage is attached; **roof-rail** (see quots.); **roof rat** (Sc. *-rotten*), *Rattus rattus alexandrinus*, a climbing rat which has a brownish back and greyish underparts; **roof-scraper** (see quot.); **roof-snake**, an Indian snake infesting roofs; **roof-slate**, a roofing slate; **roof-spotter**, an observer posted at the top of a building to give warning of hostile aircraft; so **roof-spotting**; **roof-swell**, a variety of organ swell; **roof-top**; also used *attrib.* of something situated on top of a building; †**roof-trough** (with allusion of Chaucer *Miller's T.* 437); **roof-watcher** = *roof-spotter*; **roof-water**, rain-water collected from or falling from the roof of a building.

1955 *Trans. Inst. Mining Engineers* CXIV. 849 *Roof bolts cannot be used to replace normal supports at the face, but they have been used to advantage to bolt weak immediate beds together or to stronger beds above. **1973** L. J. Thomas *Introd. Mining* vii. 276 It is unwise to rely on roof bolts to hold up the roof bar and the lip of the entry. **1954** *Jrnl. Chem., Metall. & Mining Soc. S. Afr.* LIV 285/1 It was necessary to resort to *roof and side bolting and pig netting in order to protect the personnel. **1958** I. C. F. Statham *Coal Mining Pract.* II. ii. 144 An inversion of roof bolting, so-called floor bolting, in which bolts are inserted in holes drilled into the floor has proved successful in reducing floor lift. **1940** C. S. Sherrington *Man on his Nature* vii. 222 Observation indicates rather a *roof-brain which overseers subordinate mechanisms. **1960** *20th Cent.* Dec. 549 At the beck and call of those more primitive regions.. the roof-brain wakes or sleeps. **1895** Mrs. Croker *Village Tales* (1896) 52 He lay awake all night long, and listened to the wild *roof-cats stealing down the thatch. **1951** 'M. Innes' *Operation Pax* VI. vi. 286 If you *roof-climb,.. then you just can't.. sit in libraries too. **1932** *Daily Mirror* 28 May 6/4 An appeal to undergraduate *roof-climbers is made in the 'Cambridge Review'. **1932** G. Greene *Stamboul Train* III. i. 123 He intended to do no more roof-climbing that night. **1970** R. Lowell *Notebk.* 238 Thud of *roofdrip. **1893** M. Holley *Samantha at World's Fair* 286 Why, the very elevator you rode up to the *ruff garden on wuz made by a woman. **1894** R. H. Davis *Eng. Cousins* 112 On the top of the barge is a roof-garden of pretty girls. **1895** *N.Y. Dramatic News* 6 July 2/1 The growth of the roof garden idea has undoubtedly tended toward the obliteration of the regular forms of theatrical amusement during the heated term. **1898** *Daily News* 15 Aug. 3/1 The New York theatres are rejoicing in the possession of.. roof gardens. **1911** *Chambers's Jrnl.* Feb. 113/1 Thus the director.. has an opportunity to go to any part of the hotel, from the kitchen to the roof-garden, if he wants to look into matters. **1932** *Santa Fe Mag.* Jan. 34/1 A mallet type or a helper engine on a mountain job is a *sacred ox* or a *roof garden*. **1959** P. Oliver in M. T. Williams *Art of Jazz* (1960) xii. 110 The musicians and singers who had recently enjoyed a booming success at the.. dance-halls and roof-gardens, were now finding themselves 'laid off'. **1958** J. G. MacGregor *North-West of 16* iii. 42 Beside the *roof-jack it [*sc.* some animal] lay all night, and there.. was a bulge it made in the roof of the tent. **1970** R. & J. Paterson *Cranberry Portage* xiv. 88 Cranberry settlement squatted beneath a shifting smoke blanket, upheld by blue-grey columns spinning upwards from a hundred galvanized roof jacks. **1975** *Amer. Speech 1969* XLIV. 23 *Roofjack, n.* 1. A 12′ to 14′ plank with cleats affixed to shingles or embedded into roof material and which supports the painter; it serves as a platform from which steeply pitched roofs are painted. 2. A platform made for the pitch of a roof, flexible and made of wood; it is raised level against the pitch of the roof and thus allows the roof to be worked. **1804** Eugenia de Acton *Tale without Title* III. 127 To find himself conveyed to a *roof-lorn cottage. **1921** *Roof-man [see *gutter-man* s.v. GUTTER *sb.*[1] 8]. **1851** Ruskin *Stones Ven.* II. vi. 209 The *roof-mask, which protects this lower roof from the weather. **1350** in Riley *Mem. Lond.* (1868) 262, 2,600 de wyndounail,.. 23,000 de *rofnail. **1477–9** *Rec. St. Mary at Hill* (1905) 87 For sprigge, xij d, & for Rofe nayle, viij d. **1875** *Encycl. Brit.* I. 872/1 Two grey masses, named *roof nuclei. **1886** *Buck's Handbk. Med. Sci.* II. 329 The so-called roof-nucleus.. of the cerebellum. **1948** W. R. Benét *Reader's Encycl.* 541/2 s.v. *Institute of France*, It is a *roof organization and embraces these five academies. **1906** R. A. Daly in *Bull. Geol. Soc. Amer.* XVII. 336 The whole forms a huge irregular block of roof rock almost completely surrounded and probably underlain by.. granite. Such a block, once a downwardly projecting part of a roof in stock or batholith, may be named a '*roof pendant'; it is analogous to the pendant of Gothic architecture. **1934** C. R. Longwell et al. *Outl. Physical Geol.* ix. 173 Batholith: partly uncovered by erosion; P and P′ are masses of invaded country rock projecting deeply downward into the batholith. They are termed roof-pendants. **1961** *Amer. Mineralogist* XLVI. 249 Erosion has lowered the surface to the point where only patches of the metamorphics have been preserved, embedded in a matrix of the quartz diorite as roof pendants or 'curtains'. **1690** Blancard *Lex. Med.* 591 *Staphylepartes*,.. the *roof pincer. **1960** *News Chron.* 29 Apr. 10/5 Anyone.. can.. have his car fitted with.. a *roof-rack. **1976** P. Cave *High Flying Birds* i. 13 Just load the kites on to my roof-rack, drive down to the nearest Channel ferry service and go looking for the perfect hill. **1930** *Motor Body Building* LI. 105/1 'Coachwork Nomenclature' *Front *roof rail*, the cross bar joining the front ends of the cant rail. *Rear roof rail*, the cross bar at the back of the top of the body joining the rear ends of the cant rail. **1969** *Jane's Freight Containers 1968–69* 18/3 6. Freight container components. .. 6.8. *Roof rails*, longitudinal structural member situated at the top edge on either side of the freight container. **1882** D. C. Beard *Amer. Boys Handy Bk.* xxiii. 210 The *roof rat in the Southern States came originally from Egypt. **1926** *Genetics* XI. 456 The roof rat.. is common in the southern states, especially along the seaboard. **1957** O. Breland *Animal Friends & Foes* i. 17 The two most important kinds of house rats are the brown, or Norwegian, rat and the black, or roof, rat. **1971** *New Scientist* 15 Apr. 178/2 The term 'rat' could refer to.. the black rat.. and its colour varieties such as the roof rat. **1819** *Edin. Mag.* July 506 Black rotten, *Roof Rotten. **1909** J. R. Ware *Passing Eng.* 210/2 **Roof scrapers* (*Theatrical*), gallery boys—especially those standing behind the highest row of seats—and therefore nearer the roof. **1803** Plymley *Agric. Shropsh.* 43 The *roof-slate, or schistus tegularis, which contains more silex than argill. **1884** *Chambers' Jrnl.* Apr. 215/2 There are few bungalows the thatched roof of which is not the occasional abode of.. the *saukor*, or *roof-snake. **1940** *Manch. Guardian Weekly* 18 Oct. 288 If we are appointed *roof-spotters to our office, then we must have sharp eyes, good ears, shrewd judgment, and a knowledge of aeroplane types. *Ibid.* 1 Nov. 322 The reports to the Ministry show that the *roof-spotting system is welcomed by the workers. *Ibid.*, In the aggregate many thousands of man-hours have been saved by efficient roof-spotting. **1852** Seidel *Organ* 27 The *roof or door swell,.. when accurately constructed (of oak wood), is the best sort. **1611** Speed *Hist. Gt. Brit.* IX. xiv. §1. 746 Those fires.. taking hold of the *roof-tops of both the royall houses. **1887** Bowen *Virg. Æneid* IV. 185 When day comes, on the roof-top tall or the tower she alights. **1935** *Discovery* Apr. 94/2 He was cautious as to the advent of roof-top landings and city aerodromes. **1961** Conyn & Marten *Bali Ballet Murder* xxi. 220 One of those roof-top nightclubs [in New York]. **1963** *House & Garden* May 55/2 A rooftop garden in the Palazzo Wolkov. **1972** F. Forsyth *Odessa File* i. 9 The underground car park.. 200 yards from the house where he had his roof-top flat. **1979** *Tucson Mag.* Apr. 65 Distinguished by its.. rooftop solar collectors, the system has 621 square feet of flat plate collectors. **1665** Brathwait *Comment Two Tales* 23 Every one is to enter into their *Roof-trough or Kimelyn. **1941** *Roof-watcher [*see* Jim Crow[2]]. **1879** *Harper's Mag.* June 134/1 During storms the *roof water increases this action. **1910** W. De Morgan *Affair of Dishonour* iv. 55 To him who drinks no water, roof-water and well-water are welcome alike.

roof (ru:f), *v.* Forms: 5 rof(e, rove, 7 roofe, rooff(e, 6– roof. [f. the sb. Cf. older MG. *roeven*, *rueven* (Teutonista), Flem. *roeven*.]

1. a. *trans.* To provide or cover with a roof. Also with *in*, *over*.

c **1475** *Crabhouse Reg.* (1889) 61 She.. new rofyd it, and leyde therupon a fodyr of led. **1482** *Paston Lett.* III. 281, I wulle that the seid ele.. be newe rofed, leded, and glased. **1705** Addison *Italy* (Bohn) I. 444 Ancient Roman buildings .. roofed with either vaults or arches. **1726** Pope *Odyss.* XXIII. 196 Around the tree I rais'd a nuptial bower, And roof'd defensive of the storm and shower. **1775** *New Hampshire Prov. Papers* (1873) VII. 673, I think it would be much preferable to roofing them. **1819** Scott *Ivanhoe* xlii. *note*, The builders had attained the art of using cement, and of roofing a building. **1851** Carlyle *Sterling* I. xii, Next day, I had the passage at the entrance of the house repaired and roofed. **1886** H. F. Lester *Under two Fig Trees* 5 If you roof over the area, how on earth are they to get any light in the kitchen?

refl. and *fig.* **1634** Heywood *Maidenh. well lost* I. Wks. 1874 IV. 109 He has.. many a stormy night Beene forc'd to roofe himselfe i'th open field. **1872** Tyndall *Forms of Water* 133 The sea freezes, roofing itself with ice of enormous thickness.

b. To set as a roof *over* something.

1818 Shelley *Prometh. Unb.* IV. 113 The temples.. Of Man's ear and eye, Roofed over Sculpture and Poesy.

2. a. To be or form, to lie as, a roof over (something or (occas.) someone). Also *fig.* and with *in*, *over*.

1615 G. SANDYS *Trav.* 130 The stones so great, that eight floores it, eight rooffes it. **1662** ROWLEY *Birth of Merlin* IV. i, Know'st thou what pendulous mischief roofs thy head? **1819** BYRON *Juan* II. 115 As the new flames gave Light to the rocks that roof'd them. *a* **1820** BLAKE *Jerusalem* xix, in *Compl. Writings* (1972) 642 And Los was roof'd in from Eternity in Albion's Cliffs. **1833** TENNYSON *Eleanore* 99 As thunder-clouds that.. Roof'd the world with doubt and fear. **1865** KINGSLEY *Herew.* ii, Huge fir-trees roofed it in, and made a night of noon. **1891** E. ARNOLD *Light of World* 10 The impartial skies Roof one race in. **1935** A. J. CRONIN *Stars look Down* I. xxii. 211 The inrush had roofed in the Swelly: for fifty yards a barrier of water blocked the ropeway. **1972** R. ADAMS *Watership Down* ix. 36 Far around ..stood the orderly rows of beans,..roofing them over.

b. To shelter, house.

1820 SHELLEY *Sensit. Pl.* I. 57 Flow'rets which..Fell into pavilions,..To roof the glow-worm from the evening dew. **1883** JEFFERIES *Story of my Heart* 156 That his children may ..have sufficient to eat, drink, clothe, and roof them.

3. *intr.* To dwell under one roof. *rare*[−1].

1606 HEYWOOD *Challenge* V. i, Farewell world,..thou wilt not suffer Vertue And Beauty roofe together.

4. *trans.* To sit on the roof of (a coach).

1844 W. H. MAXWELL *Sports & Adv. Scot.* xxxi. (1855) 250 The accustomed process of *roofing* a stage-coach.

roof, obs. f. ROE *sb.*[2]; obs. pa. t. RIVE *v.*[1]

roofage (ˈruːfɪdʒ). [f. ROOF *sb.* + -AGE.] The material of a roof; roofing of any kind.

1865 E. BURRITT *Walk to Land's End* 205 The gracefulness of its roofage, the delicacy of its carved work. **1867** G. MUSGRAVE *Nooks & Corners Old France* II. 149 The dark slates that form the universal roofage. **1887** W. G. PALGRAVE *Ulysses* 237 A spacious raised wooden shed,.. roofed with thatch—your only *Shinto* wear for roofage.

transf. **1873** SYMONDS *Grk. Poets* x. 311 Branching limes, and elms with their..gnarled boles and sombre roofage. **1950** M. PEAKE *Gormenghast* xviii. 108 A posse of professors in a whirl of gowns and a shuffling roofage of mortar-boards.

roof-cast, obs. variant of ROUGH-CAST.

roofe, obs. variant of RUFF.

roofed (ruːft), *ppl. a.* [f. ROOF *v.* + -ED[1].]

1. Having a roof; covered with or as with a roof. Also with *in*, *over*.

? a **1500** *Chester Plays* III. 34 Three roofed chambers. **1555** EDEN *Decades* (Arb.) 116 Beinge roofed and paued with maruelous arte. **1605** SHAKS. *Macb.* III. iv. 40 Here had we now our Countries Honor, roof'd, Were the grac'd person of our Banquo present. **1673** RAY *Journ. Low C.* 39 The first publick Building that we saw so roofed since we left England. **1756–7** tr. *Keysler's Trav.* (1760) II. 466 Three detached parts of it, which are roofed, but very ruinous. **1792** WORDSW. *Descrip. Sketches* 184 She seeks a covert from the battering shower In the roofed bridge. **1832** G. DOWNES *Lett. Cont. Countries* I. 274 The Gallery of Kaltwasser, which is roofed like a house. **1863** GEO. ELIOT *Romola* xxxiii, A truncated tower roofed in with fluted tiles. **1896** W. BLACK *Briseis* xxiv, In the roofed-over portion of the Erectheum. **1909** C. F. G. MASTERMAN *Condition of England* viii. 254 The roofed-in labyrinthine airless ant-heaps of Mr. Wells's nightmare. **1923** D. H. LAWRENCE *Birds, Beasts & Flowers* 27 All your ponderous roofed-in erection of right and wrong. **1931** [see BREEZE-WAY, BREEZEWAY]. **1934** L. B. LYON *White Hare* 11 The roofed glade's a sieve That lets drip through sweet water. **1946** F. SARGESON *That Summer* 107 We all went under a little roofed-in part. **1976** 'G. BLACK' *Moon for Killers* vi. 83 A roofed-over area that looked almost big enough to be a bus depot.

2. As the second element in combs. denoting a particular form or kind of roof.

1600 HAKLUYT *Voy.* III. 391 Their houses are flat-rooffed. **1671** MILTON *P.R.* II. 293 He..entr'd soon the shade High rooft. **1703** NEVE *City & C. Purchaser* 271 All kind of flat Roof'd Buildings. **1804** *Europ. Mag.* XLV. 60/2 The thatch-roof'd village, and the busy town. **1857** DUFFERIN *Lett. High Lat.* (ed. 3) 139 To lie shivering inside a grass-roofed church. **1871** MORRIS in Mackail *Life* (1899) I. 245 Thorshaven, with its green-roofed little houses.

ˈroofer. [f. ROOF *sb.* or *v.*]

1. One who constructs or repairs roofs.

1855 OGILVIE *Suppl.* **1887** *Pall Mall G.* 15 Sept. 8/2 The metal workers show their processes, also roofers, plumbers, plasterers, leather-workers.

2. A hat. *slang.* Cf. ROOF *sb.* 6 a.

1859 G. W. MATSELL *Vocabulum* 74 Roofer, a hat. **1941** BAKER *Dict. Austral. Slang* 61 Roofer, a hat.

3. = COLLINS[1]. In full, ***hospitable roofer***. Also *attrib.*, as ***roofer letter***.

1914 *Sphere* 7 Mar. 312/3, I learn from *The Evening News* that that which some call..a 'roofer'—that is to say, a letter of thanks for hospitality—is also known as a Collins. **1935** F. M. FORD *Let.* 27 Sept. (1965) 243 They [*sc.* references] will at least serve as a hospitable-roofer. **1937** G. FRANKAU *More of Us* vii. 75 That bashful Hebe, too, received fair tip.. Sophie, red roses and a roofer letter, With 'kind regards to her young ladyship', And, 'hoping the old boy's catarrh is better'. **1971** C. WILLIAMS-ELLIS *Architect Errant* vii. 103, I felt that I really ought to write to the owner, Lord Townshend, at least some sort of a roofer or an apology. *Ibid.* xv. 217 In my roofer letter to Vita, I, of course, paid due homage to her so passionately loved Knole.

ˈroofing, (*vbl.*) *sb.* [f. ROOF *sb.* or *v.* + -ING[1].]

1. a. The act of covering with a roof; material used or suitable for roofs; that which forms a roof or roofs.

c **1440** *Pallad. on Husb.* I. 383 (Bodl. MS.), And lete hem drie er..rovyng [be] sette uppon, lest all be shent. **1598** STOW *Surv.* 180 Hee..gaue all the timber for the roofing of the two side Iles. **1611** CORYAT *Crudities* 163 Whiche forme of roofing is generally vsed in all those Italian cities that I saw. **1655** FULLER *Waltham Abbey* 19 Lead, Stone, and Timber, all devoured in the roofing, flooring, and finishing of their Steeple. **1725** *Fam. Dict.* s.v. *Thatching*, A thousand handfuls of Reed..will..cover about three square of Roofing. **1760–72** H. BROOKE *Fool of Qual.* (1809) III. 112 The hovel was of mud-walls, without any roofing. **1828–43** TYTLER *Hist. Scot.* (1864) I. 137 A huge machine was constructed, covered by a strong roofing of boards and hides. **1846** MCCULLOCH *Acc. Brit. Empire* (1854) I. 165 Thick and heavy slates..are used for building as well as for roofing. **1876** MISS BRADDON *J. Haggard's Dau.* III. 166 Arnold went up to an old farmhouse..to settle a question of roofing and thatching.

transf. **1883** GRESLEY *Gloss. Coal-mining* 206 *Roofing*, the upper 5 or 6 feet of the rock-salt beds.

b. *attrib.* ***roofing felt, material, slate, tile***, etc.

1815 J. SMITH *Panorama Sci. & Art* I. 191 In Holland, they frequently glaze their roofing tiles. **1833** *Penny Cycl.* I. 406/1 It is as hard as roofing slate. **1846** KEIGHTLEY *Notes Virg.* 375 It is of good size, for roofing-timber..is cut out of it. **1862** *Catal. Internat. Exhib., Brit.* II. No. 6029 Galvanized corrugated iron roofing sheets. **1886** C. SCOTT *Sheep-Farming* 98 There are now so many light roofing materials,—such as the Willesden roofing paper. **1894** *Country Gentlemen's Catal.* 269 *Roofing felt*.—The best known weather-resisting material yet introduced for roofing purposes. **1929** *Morning Post* 2 Oct. 6/5 These industries include electrical engineering, paint and varnish making, roofing-felts,..and the manufacture of linoleum. **1954** *Paper Terminol.* (Spalding & Hodge, Ltd.) 51 *Roofing felt*, a very porous, soft and thick paper made from low-grade materials and used as a base for impregnation with bitumen, tar, etc.

c. *attrib.* in other uses.

1867 *Chambers's Encycl.* IX. 439/1 The various kinds [of tiles] used for roofing purposes. **1875** KNIGHT *Dict. Mech.* 1973/2 *Roofing-machine*, one for preparing material for roofing purposes. **1896** *Daily News* 3 Aug. 3/5 Bridge and roofing firms have been busy.

2. *Mining.* (See quots.)

1747 HOOSON *Miner's Dict.* R iij, *Roofing* is rising upwards in the Work, be it either directly or by degrees. **1860** *Eng. & For. Mining Gloss.* (ed. 2) 78 *Roofing*, when the top of the loaded skip wedges against the top of the gate-road.

roofless (ˈruːflɪs), *a.* [f. ROOF *sb.* + -LESS.]

1. Of buildings: Having no roof.

1610 HOLLAND *Camden's Brit.* I. 402 At Luton I saw a faire church but the Quier then roofelesse. **1725** RAMSAY *Gentle Sheph.* II. iii, The wind made Glaud a roofless barn. **1793** COWPER *A Tale* 38 Within that cavity aloft Their roofless home they fixt. **1835** LYTTON *Rienzi* I. xii, He gazed around upon the roofless columns and shattered walls. **1877** WALLACE *Russia* xxviii. 436 But the great majority of the houses were still roofless.

2. Of persons: Not sheltered by a roof.

1829 LYTTON *Disowned* 13 The stolen feasts and the roofless nights of those careless vagabonds. **1839** F. A. KEMBLE *Resid. in Georgia* (1863) 7 Though the Irish peasant is starved, naked and roofless. **1863** W. B. JERROLD *Signals of Distress* 58 These roofless creatures.

3. Applied to poker played with no limit to the raise.

1912 R. W. SERVICE *Rhymes of Rolling Stone* (1913) 104 Your trouble was a roofless game of poker now and then.

ˈrooflet. [f. ROOF *sb.* + -LET.] 'A small roof or covering' (Ogilvie *Suppl.* 1855).

roof light. Also **roof-light, rooflight.** [ROOF *sb.*]

1. a. A flashing warning light that projects upwards from the roof of a motor vehicle. **b.** A small interior light attached to the underside of the roof of a motor vehicle.

1958 'CASTLE' & 'HAILEY' *Flight into Danger* viii. 107 At the turn-off..a police cruiser stood..its roof-light blinking a constant warning. **1961** *Times* 11 July 3/6 Coathooks, rooflights, clocks, and mirrors. **1970** A. ROSS *Manchester Thing* 58 The automatic roof light gave me a quick glimpse of two men, then the driver reached up to switch it off. **1977** *Daily Tel.* 13 Jan. 17/1 An RAF helicopter crew..were guided up a valley in thick fog and darkness by the roof-light of a Land-Rover.

2. A panel in or on the roof of a building or vehicle made of a material which admits light.

1961 *Engineering* 27 Oct. 552 A new series of rooflights have been designed. **1967** *Gloss. Caravan Terms* (*B.S.I.*) 2 *Rooflight*, for the purpose of expressing rooflight dimensions for catalogues, the roof aperture through which light and air pass. **1978** A. FENTON *Island Blackhouse* 18 All other windows..are fixed roof lights in the thickness of the thatch.

ˈroofline, roof-line. [ROOF *sb.* 7 a.] **1.** The outline or silhouette of a roof or a collection of roofs.

1857 C. VAUX *Villas & Cottages* 54 Some degree of picturesqueness can always be obtained by the treatment of the roof-lines. **1886** WILLIS & CLARK *Cambridge* III. 287 The tower is in four stages, the two highest of which rise above the roof-line of the adjoining chambers. **1936** W. FAULKNER *Absalom, Absalom!* ix. 366 It loomed, bulked, square and enormous, with jagged half-toppled chimneys, its roofline sagging a little. **1955** E. BOWEN *World of Love* i. 9 The long low roofline framed by too much sky. **1976** 'TREVANIAN' *Main* i. 14 Above the roofline, defused city-light glows in the damp, sooty air.

2. The outline of the roof of a car, usu. as seen in side elevation.

1967 [see *notch-back* s.v. NOTCH *sb.* 6]. **1971** *Daily Tel.* 20 Oct. 7/2 The styling competition winner is the Cirrus, a dart-shaped 2 + 2 GT car with a roofline only 49in high.

roofscape (ˈruːfskeɪp). [f. ROOF *sb.* + SCAPE *sb.*[3]] A scene or view of roofs.

1928 *Observer* 22 July 9/3 It appears I do not mention certain roofs and arcades that Mr. Gwynn has seen. Let me inform Mr. Gwynn that every week..I pass twenty wonderful roofscapes which are probably quite unknown to Mr. Gwynn. **1949** *Archit. Rev.* CV. 277/2 (*caption*) Roofscape: a view from the roof of almost any St. John's Wood house reveals at once the factor which contributes most to the character of the place—trees. **1954** L. P. HARTLEY *White Wand* 23 From my bedroom windows I enjoyed a roofscape. Domes and towers gave it grandeur and formal beauty, but what chiefly fascinated me was the roofs themselves. **1965** N. FREELING *Criminal Conversation* II. iv. 112 He was high..and possessed several roof- and streetscapes. **1975** C. N. MANLOVE *Mod. Fantasy* vi. 215 The actual shape and relief of Sark are throughout close to what we are told of those of Gormenghast, with its long wings, its broken tower and its huge flat roofscapes.

Also **ˈroofscaping** *vbl. sb.* [after LANDSCAPING *vbl. sb.*], (see quot. 1967).

1962 *Spectator* 30 Mar. 426 One characteristic of roof-scaping has all but vanished over the past decade or so—that of building rose-covered archways or pergolas. **1967** *Britannica Bk. of Year* (U.S.) 804/2 *Roofscaping*, the landscaping of rooftops (as of apartment houses and office buildings).

ˈroof-tile. Also 5 roff tyle, rofe-, rof tile; 6 roofe tyle. [f. ROOF *sb.*] A tile for covering the top ridge of a roof; a ridge-tile. In mod. use, a tile used as a roofing material; a roofing tile. Also *fig.*

1426–7 *Rec. St. Mary at Hill* (1905) 65 Also paid for a quartern roff tyle,..xv d. **1477** *Act 17 Edw. IV*, c. 3 Whityng & anelyng de tewle appellez pleintile autrement nosmez thaktile, roftile ou crestile, cornertile & guttertile. **1546** *Acc. St. Dunstan's, Cant.* (1885) 68 For playne tylle, iiij s. viij d.; for rwffe tylle, xj d. **1580** HOLLYBAND *Treas. French Tong*, *Enfestau*, or *festiére*, a roofe tile. **1611** COTGR., *Faistiere*, a ridge-tyle, Creast-tile, Roofe-tile. **1703** MOXON *Mech. Exerc.* 240 Roof Tiles..are laid upon the..ridge of the Roof. **1728** CHAMBERS *Cycl.* s.v. *Tyle*, Ridge, Roof, or Crease Tyles, are those used to cover the Ridges of Houses. **1793** J. WOODFORDE *Diary* 3 Mar. (1929) IV. 12 It blowed off many Tiles from the old part of the House, some Roof Tiles. **1936** *Discovery* May 142/2 The dangerous sprinkling of snow over the 'roof tile' slabs [of Mount Everest]. **1940** 'GUN BUSTER' *Return via Dunkirk* I. i. 11 The house was its old self even to the last brick, the last roof-tile. **1957** *Jrnl. Geol.* LXV. 239/1 The deeply trenched roof-tile shapes of figure 8 and the delicate fern-frond pattern..shown in figure 9 are two of several different shapes exposed in a single quarry of that area.

ˈroof-tree. Also 5 ruff tree, roffetre, 6 (8) *Sc.* rufe, ruif tre, 7 roufe, 20 rooftree. [f. ROOF *sb.*]

1. a. The main beam or ridge-pole of a roof. Also *fig.*

c **1440** *Promp. Parv.* 435/2 Roof tree (or ruff tree), *festum*. *c* **1475** *Pict. Voc.* in Wr.-Wülcker 777 *Hoc festum*, a roffetre. **1560** ROLLAND *Seven Sages* 14 The ruif tre of all this haill Maissoun. **1570** *Henry's Wallace* v. 209 A gret rufe tre [*v.r.* raftre] he had in till his hand. **1728** CHAMBERS *Cycl.* s.v. *Roof*, Roof-trees..is also used for the upper Timbers of any Building; whence in the Northern Counties, it is common to signify a whole Family, by saying, all under such a one's Roof-Tree. **1815** SCOTT *Guy M.* viii, Ye have riven the thack off seven cottar houses—look if your ain roof-tree stand the faster. **1857** DUFFERIN *Let. High Lat.* (ed. 3) 132 Instead of sleeping in the tent, he determined to seek shelter under a solid roof-tree. **1875–6** STEVENSON *Ess. Trav.* (1905) 146 Wood for the fire, or for a new roof-tree. **1923** T. S. ELIOT *Waste Land* v. 23 Only a cock stood on the roof-tree. **1950** D. GASCOYNE *Vagrant* 38 Entangled in the thicket of World Roof-Tree's dense leaves. **1955** E. POUND *Classic Anthol.* III. 184 High, pine-covered peak full of echos, Proud ridge-pole of Heaven, roof-tree Whence descended the whirl of spirits. **1969** *New Scientist* 13 Mar. 554/1 An enormous rooftree 558ft long has just been inched up from ground level to serve as the chief single member of the new hangar which is being built by BOAC.

b. *Sc.* in allusive use (see quots.).

c **1730** BURT *Lett. N. Scotl.* (1754) II. 41 As we say..—To your Fireside; he says much to the same Purpose—To your Roof Tree. **1837** LOCKHART *Scott* IV. vi. 191 Lord Melville proposed a bumper, with all the honours, to the Roof-tree. **1842** D. VEDDER *Poems* 141 We'll a' haud a ranting holiday, An' drink success to the laird's roof-tree.

2. *Naut.* (See quots. and cf. ROUGH-, RUFF-TREE.)

It is doubtful, in view of the variant forms, whether the first element here is really ROOF *sb.* The spelling does not appear to have been in actual use after the 17th century.

1626 CAPT. SMITH *Accid. Yng. Seamen* 13 They make a Iury-mast..with yards, rouftrees, or what they can. **1627** —— *Seaman's Gram.* vii. 32 The Roufe-trees..are..small Timbers to beare vp the Gratings from the halfe Decke to the fore-castle. **1688** HOLME *Armoury* III. xv. (Roxb.) 37/1 The Roofe trees are light wood that goes ouer the decks and fore-castle to beare vp the gratings and ledges wherein the netting ly. **1704** J. HARRIS *Lex. Techn.* I. s.v., That Peece of Timber which on Occasion is laid over the Half Deck to bear up Nettings, Sails, or Peeces of Canvas, is called a Roof-tree. [Also in Chambers (1728), Crabbe (1823), etc.]

ˈroofward, *adv.* [f. ROOF *sb.* + -WARD.] Toward, in the direction of, the roof.

1866 J. CONINGTON *Æneid* 55 Firebrands roofward dart. **1876** MORRIS *Sigurd* 2 A mighty tree, That reared its blessings roofward.

roofy (ˈruːfɪ), *a.* [f. ROOF *sb.* + -Y.]

1. Furnished with a roof.

1697 DRYDEN *Virg. Georg.* III. 634 Whether to roofy Houses they repair, Or sun themselves abroad in open air.

2. Abounding in roofs.

1884 *Harper's Mag.* 268/1 The roofy wilderness of the metropolis.

3. *transf.* High-pitched.

1897 HALL CAINE *Christian* I. ix, Capable of saying little humorous things in a thin 'roofy' voice.

roofye, variant of RUFFY.

roog, obs. form of ROGUE.

rooge, var. of ROODGE *v.*, ROUGE *sb.*[2]

rooi-aas ('rɔɪas). *S. Afr.* [Afrikaans, f. *rooi* red + *aas* bait.] = RED-BAIT.

1895, **1905** [see RED-BAIT]. **1913** W. THOMPSON *Sea Fisheries Cape Colony* ii. 48 Eastwards of Cape Point the place of this crustacean is filled by red-bait (*rooi-as*). **1930** [see RED-BAIT].

rooibaadjie ('rɔɪˌbaɪkɪ, -ˌbaɪcɪ). *S. Afr.* Also Roed Vatje, rooiba(a)tje, -baaitje. [Afrikaans, f. *rooi* red + *baadjie* jacket.] **1.** A British regular soldier, a redcoat. Now chiefly *Hist.*

1848 H. WARD *Five Yrs. in Kaffirland* I. v. 164 And how Umhala would laugh at the *Roed Vatjes*! **1858** [see sense 2]. **1885** J. NIXON *Compl. Story Transvaal* x. 183 First of all the officers, regular and irregular, should be fired at, and then the men with the puggarees round their hats (that is, the volunteers); and as for the rovi-baatjes [*sic*] (red-backs, i.e. regulars), it didn't matter about them—they would be sure to run when their officers were killed. *Ibid.* xi. 202 The moment the Boers rushed out to attack, after they saw their friends coming down the hill-side, the 'bastards' naturally took to flight, and sixty of his [*sc.* the Boer commandant's] men followed them, and thereupon the 'rooibatjes' fled also. **1897** E. GLANVILLE *Tales from Veld* xxvi. 200 Sonny, them *rooibaaitjes* can fight, but they're foolish. **1941** S. CLOETE *Hill of Doves* (1942) viii. 116 Why, our men were soldiers, veterans of wars, when these Rooibaadjies were but children. **1971** *Daily Dispatch* (East London, Cape Province) 18 Dec. 9 A young British rooibaadjie lurched towards him from the shadows!

2. A red larval form of the South African brown locust, *Locustana pardalina*.

1858 H. CALDERWOOD *Caffres & Caffre Missions* xii. 157 The youngest locusts..are then partly red and partly black. .. Sometimes they are called *roibatjes*—that is, red-coats, in allusion to the soldiers. **1875** C. B. BISSET *Sport & War in Afr.* 170 You see the very earth become alive with diminutive insects,..increasing in size and becoming the colour of the brightest red. At this stage they are called the Rooi baatyes or red soldiers. **1902** *Trans. S. Afr. Philos. Soc.* XI. p. xlv, The young of the migratory one [*sc.* a locust].. are so gaily coloured as to have earned for them the local name of '*rooi-batjes*', or redcoats. **1972** *Stand. Encycl. S. Afr.* VII. 21/1 Young crowded hoppers would develop into typical phase *gregaria* 'rooibaadjies'.

rooibekkie ('rɔɪbekɪ). *S. Afr.* Also roibek, rood(e)bec, -bekje, rooibe(c)k(ie), rooibekje. [Afrikaans, f. *rooi* red + *bek* beak + *-ie* dim. suff.] Either of two birds with red beaks, the waxbill, *Estrilda astrild*, or the pin-tailed whydah, *Vidua macroura*.

1793 tr. *C. P. Thunberg's Trav. Europe, Afr., & Asia* I. 312 The *Loxia Astrild*, on account of its red beak, was called Rood-beckje, or *Red-beak*, and was found in great numbers in the farmers gardens. **1822** W. J. BURCHELL *Trav. Interior S. Afr.* I. xii. 266 The *Roode-bekje* (Red beak), a small finch, ..is a very common bird. **1861** LADY DUFF GORDON *Let.* 10 Dec. in *Lett. from Cape* (1921) 60, I will try to bring home some cages of birds—Cape canaries and 'roode bekjes' (red bills), darling little things. **1868** J. CHAPMAN *Trav. Interior S. Afr.* II. i. 17 We shot and skinned some birds, among which was a long-tailed finch (king rooi bekkie). **1890** A. MARTIN *Home Life on Ostrich Farm.* i. 18 Another soft-voiced little singer is the *rooibeck*, or red-beak. **1899** R. B. & J. D. S. WOODWARD *Natal Birds* 66 This bird [*sc.* the pin-tailed widow bird] derives its name from its pretty wax-like red bill, which resembles that of the estrilda, and in common with them it is called *roibek*. **1900** A. C. STARK *Birds S. Afr.* I. 98 Common Waxbill..'Rodebec'..and 'Rooibeckie' of Dutch Colonists. **1913** [see KING *sb.* 7 a]. **1936** E. L. GILL *First Guide S. Afr. Birds* 32 Pin-tailed Widow-bird, King Rooibekkie,..is also parasitic; the eggs are laid in nests of the common Rooibekkie. **1952** *Cape Times* 15 Jan. 9/8 Farmers are demanding the extermination of the common rooibekkie, or waxbill. **1963** S. CLOETE *Rags of Glory* 548 The rooibekkies were still chattering in the trees.

rooibok ('rɔɪbɒk). *S. Afr.* Also roibok, roodebok, rooibuck, rooye bok. [Afrikaans, f. *rooi* red + *bok* buck.] = IMPALA.

1824 W. J. BURCHELL *Trav. Interior S. Afr.* II. xi. 215 One [antelope] is called *Paala* (Parla) by the Bichuanas, and is known by the name of *Roodebok* (Redbuck). **1835** A. SMITH *Diary* 27 Aug. (1940) II. 182 They had much difficulty in getting them to..carry the flesh of a rooye bok. **1866** T. LEASK *Diary* 12 May (1954) 44 Saw some rooibok, but felt too done up to go after them. **1875** [see IMPALA]. **1896** H. A. BRYDEN *Tales S. Afr.* 65 Smallfield..had shot a good rooibok. **1926** *Glasgow Herald* 31 Aug. 2/6 He had got a rooibuck (or impala) ram. **1932** FULLER & FOUCHE *Louis Trigardt's Trek* vi. 65 He told..about a *rooibok* and two geese they had shot. **1947** [see IMPALA]. **1968** L. G. GREEN *Full Many a Glorious Morning* 189 Palapye Road, named by an extinct tribe after the rooibok, was once the site of the 'post office tree'.

rooibos ('rɔɪbɔs). *S. Afr.* Also rooibosch, rooibostee. [Afrikaans, f. *rooi* red + *bos* bush.] **1.** An evergreen South African shrub of the genus *Aspalathus* (formerly *Borbonia*), belonging to the family Leguminosæ, and cultivated for its leaves which are used to make a kind of tea; also, the beverage made from the leaves. Also *attrib.*

1911 *S. Afr. Jrnl. Sci.* VII. 374 The author described..a *Borbonia*, the source of Cape 'rooibos' tea. **1932** WATT & BREYER-BRANDWIJK *Medicinal & Poisonous Plants S. Afr.* 70 *Borbonia pinifolia* Marl.,..Rooibostee..and *Borbonia cordata*..are also used as teas. **1946** [see *bush tea* s.v. BUSH *sb.*[1] 11]. **1948** *Cape Argus* 18 Dec. 7/9 Dr. Pieter le Fras Nortier..established a flourishing rooibos industry. **1949** L. G. GREEN *In Land of Afternoon* iii. 52 Bush tea is..an entirely different plant—a legume. You hear it called rooibos. *Ibid.* 53 The ants of the district collect rooibos seeds and store them underground. **1951** *Cape Times* 17 Oct. 2/6 Mr. Riordan was..a well-known rooibosch tea farmer. **1977** *Daily Tel.* 5 Mar. 18 Rooibosch is almost entirely free from tannin and contains no caffein.

2. A shrub or small tree, *Combretum apiculatum*, belonging to the family Combretaceæ, native to central and southern Africa, and bearing red or yellow foliage in winter, and spikes of scented yellow flowers.

1932 WATT & BREYER-BRANDWIJK *Medicinal & Poisonous Plants S. Afr.* 128 The Zulus regard *Combretum erythrophyllum* Sond., Bush willow,..Rooibos,..as poisonous. **1972** PALMER & PITMAN *Trees S. Afr.* III. 1633 The rooibos is a valuable fodder tree.

rooi-els ('rɔɪels). *S. Afr.* Also rood(e) els, elze. [Afrikaans, f. *rooi* red + *els* alder.] An evergreen tree, *Cunonia capensis*, belonging to the family Cunoniaceæ, native to southern Africa, and bearing compound leaves and racemes of fragrant cream flowers; also, the reddish wood of this tree. Cf. *red alder*, *red els* s.v. RED *a.* 17 d.

1801 J. BARROW *Acct. Trav. Interior S. Afr.* I. v. 339 Roode els..stands water well. **1822** W. J. BURCHELL *Trav. Interior S. Afr.* I. vii. 143 Its colonial name is *Rood Elze* (Red Alder), although the tree has not..the least resemblance to the Alder of Europe. **1948** *Cape Times* 5 Aug. 8/7 If trees must be planted, let them rather be the.. rooi els and other local forest trees. **1972** PALMER & PITMAN *Trees S. Afr.* I. 665 The rooi-els grows in moist mountain forests.

rooigras ('rɔɪxras). *S. Afr.* Also rooigrass. [Afrikaans, f. *rooi* red + *gras* grass.] A southern African grass, *Themeda triandra*, which goes a reddish colour in winter. Also *attrib.*

1889 H. A. BRYDEN *Kloof & Karroo* iv. 88 Much of the lower parts of these hills is clothed with rooi-grass. **1907** T. R. SIM *Forests & Forest Flora Cape of Good Hope* iv. 37 The rushes have given place to rooi-grass. **1929** J. W. BEWS *World's Grasses* vi. 253 'Rooi gras'..is a valuable forage grass. **1950** *Cape Times* 30 Oct. 9/6 A. C. Erasmus scattered the first *rooigras* seeds in the..bare land recently cleared. **1966** C. A. W. GUGGISBERG *S.O.S. Rhino* iv. 92 The dominant grass throughout the..range of the southern white rhino is *Themeda triandra*, which stands quite high and is popularly known as 'rooigrass'. **1972** *Stand. Encycl. S. Afr.* V. 320/2 A large number of species, e.g. Guinea grass .., rooigras.., the finger-grasses..are important pasture grasses.

rooihout ('rɔɪhəʊt). *S. Afr.* Also roodehout, roye-houtt. [Afrikaans, f. *rooi* red + *hout* wood.] One of several trees with reddish wood, esp. the Cape plane, *Ochna arborea*, or its wood. Also *attrib.*

1790 E. HELME tr. *Le Vaillant's Trav. Afr.* II. xiv. 288 Another tree, called *Roye-houtt*, (red wood) so named from its deep red colour, grows very thick. **1896** E. CLAIRMONTE *Africander* i. 2 A flock of long-tailed house birds..would dash past to settle in a *rooihout* tree. **1907** T. R. SIM *Forests & Forest Flora Cape of Good Hope* xiv. 163 Cape Plane.. Roodehout. **1973** *Eastern Province Herald* (Port Elizabeth) 28 May 13/2 No self-respecting woodcutter would have the handle of his axe made from any timber other than 'rooihout' (Cape plane) a reddish close grained wood.

rooikat ('rɔɪkat). *S. Afr.* Also roode-kat. [Afrikaans, f. *rooi* red + *kat* cat.] = CARACAL.

1785 G. FORSTER tr. *Sparrman's Voy. Cape of Good Hope* I. 150 Another kind of cat, as it is called, or the *roode-kat*, is ..supposed to possess a great medicinal power in its skin. **1880** J. NIXON *Life among Boers* vi. 142 There is another kind, known as the rooiket, whose skin is highly prized for making karrosses. **1939** S. CLOETE *Watch for Dawn* v. 70, I am as slim as a rooikat and this is my country. **1948** *Cape Times* 4 Dec. (Mag. Section) 3/4 A lithe red shape trotting through the bush ahead..was my first sight of the African lynx or rooikat. **1966** E. PALMER *Plains of Camdeboo* ix. facing p. 160 (*caption*) The brilliant coloured lynx or rooikat —rich red with jet-black ear tufts.

rooikrans ('rɔɪkrans). *S. Afr.* Also rooikran(t)z. [Afrikaans, f. *rooi* red + *krans* wreath, in allusion to the red aril of the seed.] A yellow-flowered shrub, *Acacia cyclops*, of the family Leguminosæ, native to Western Australia, and naturalized in southern Africa, where it is also called the golden willow. Also *attrib.*

1917 R. MARLOTH *Flora S. Afr. Suppl.: Common Names* 71 Rooikrans... From Australia..one of the Golden willows. **1920** *S. Afr. Smallholders' & Fruit Growers' Year Bk. 1920–1921* 175 Rooikrantz—A shrubby wattle useful for firewood. **1950** [see *Port Jackson willow* s.v. PORT JACKSON]. **1953** *Cape Times* 9 July 14/2 Silver trees are being choked by young self-seeded cluster pines and rooikrans. **1957** *Cape Times Mag.* 20 July 10/4 He wielded the chopper as easily as a man—severing the tough branches of the rooikrantz trees. *Ibid.* 10/6 On the outskirts of the rooikranz trees they began to dig.

rooiman, var. ROMAN *sb.*[3]

rooinek ('rɔɪnɛk). *S. Afr.* Also roineck and with capital initial. *Pl.* rooineks, rooinekke. [Afrikaans, f. *rooi* red + *nek* neck.] A term applied by Afrikaans-speaking South Africans to the British or to English-speaking South Africans.

1890 'S. ERASMUS' *Prinsloo of Prinsloosdorp* ii. 14 One morning he was on the market with his waggon when two men—English Rooineks— came and said: 'Piet, do you want to make £15?' **1896** H. A. BRYDEN *Tales S. Afr.* 210 Cornelis would open up, and yarn to me in a way that, until you know him well, the Boer seldom manifests to the *rooi-nek*. **1900** *Captain* III. 121/1 *Rooinek* scout. **1900** KIPLING in *Daily Express* 13 June 4/5 And you will see how we can shoot rooineks. **1921** *Chambers's Jrnl.* Jan. 32/1, I was thinking of the efforts that that infernal rooinek (red-neck) of a son of yours is making to deprive me of my only child. **1937** C. R. PRANCE *Tante Rebella's Saga* 47 A rascally Irish 'rooinek' whose real name had been Pat Murphy till he changed it to Piet van der Merwe when he turned Afrikander. **1947** H. C. BOSMAN *Mafeking Road* 117 But of course no rooinek can make a living out of farming, unless they send him money every month from England. **1962** [see LIMEY a]. **1963** S. CLOETE *Rags of Glory* xxxix. 316 The Englishmen were sunburned, red as lobsters. They did not go brown like the Boers. That's why we call them rooineks—rednecks—Renata thought. **1969** VISCT. BUCKMASTER *Roundabout* xviii. 279 An English taxi-driver told me that he had lived for twenty years in Cape Town, only still to be called 'A bloody roineck', the name given to our troops in the Boer war. **1972** *Daily Dispatch* (East London, S. Afr.) 2 Feb. 6 Nasty little racist jibes, which we South Africans have been listening to for the past 10 years, about Van der Merwe and the Rooinekke and 'a bantu'. **1975** 'D. JORDAN' *Black Account* v. 32 The Afrikaner industrialists..had emerged since 1948 to challenge the English *rooineks* and their dominance of South African finance.

rooing, *vbl. sb.*: see ROO *v.*

rooirhebok (rɔɪ'rɪəbɔk, -'riːbɒk). *S. Afr.* Also roode, rooye rheebok. [Afrikaans, f. *rooi* red + REEBOK.] The mountain reedbuck, *Redunca fulvorufula*. Also *attrib.*

1835 A. SMITH *Diary* 11 July (1940) II. 107 During this season the male and female of the rooye rheebok are generally apart. **1835** A. STEEDMAN *Wanderings S. Afr.* I. II. iv. 176 We observed, at some little distance, several antelopes of the description called *roode-rheebok*, which were running up the mountain. **1850** [see REEBOK]. **1904** [see NAGOR]. **1912** J. STEVENSON-HAMILTON *Animal Life Afr.* x. 157 Rooi rhebok favour the lower slopes of hills. **1957** *Cape Argus* 13 July 7/5, I have seen a rooi-rhebok ewe battling to save her kid from an eagle.

rook (rʊk), *sb.*[1] Forms: α. 1 hrooc, hroc, roc, 3 rok, 3–6 roke, 5–7 rooke, 5– rook. β. *Sc.* (and *north.*) 5–6 ruke, 6 reuk, rwik, 6–7 ruik(e. [OE. *hróc*, = MDu. *roec*, *roek-*, *rouc*, *rouk-* (Du. and Fris. *roek*), MLG. *rôk*, *rook* (LG. *rok*, *roke*, *rauk*, *rauke*), ON. *hrókr* (obs. Da. *rog*), OHG. *hruoh* (MHG. *ruoch*, G. *ruch*); cf. also MSw. *roka*, Sw. *råka*, Da. *raage*. The name may be of imitative origin.]

1. A black, raucous-voiced European and Asiatic bird (*Corvus frugilegus*), nesting in colonies; one of the commonest of the crow-tribe, and in the north of Britain usually called a *crow*.

The equation, in OE. and ME. glosses, with L. *graculus* (*grallus*), jackdaw, is probably inexact.

α. *c* **725** *Corpus Gloss.* G. 154 *Grallus*, hrooc. *c* **1000** ÆLFRIC *Saints' Lives* I. 492 Ðær fluȝ on sona to hrocas and hremmas. *a* **1250** *Owl & Night.* 1130 Golfinc, rok, ne crowe, ne dar þar neuer cumen i-hende. *c* **1290** *S. Eng. Leg.* I. 437/196 Blake foule huy seiȝe, Ase it crowene and rokes weren, fleon bi þe Eyr wel heiȝe. *c* **1340** *Nominale* (Skeat) 792 Roke, Rauen, and goldefynch. *c* **1384** CHAUCER *H. Fame* II. 1516 The halle was al ful y-wys Of hem..As ben on trees rokes nestes. *c* **1400** *Laud Troy Bk.* 17214 The Gregais wol not hir bodi grauen, But let hit ligge to roke & rauen. **1486** *Bk. St. Albans* d ij, That hawke that will slee a Roke or a Crow or a Reuyn. *a* **1529** SKELTON *P. Sparowe* 462 The roke, with the ospraye That putteth fysshes to a fraye. **1588** SHAKS. *L.L.L.* v. ii. 915 When Turtles tread, and Rookes and Dawes. **1601** HOLLAND *Pliny* x. xii. I. 276 The Crowes and Rookes have a cast by themselves. **1663** BUTLER *Hud.* I. i. 76 He'd prove..a Goose a Justice, And Rooks Committee-men, and Trustees. **1726–46** THOMSON *Winter* 141 A blackening train Of clamorous rooks thick urge their weary flight. **1768** PENNANT *Brit. Zool.* I. 168 Rooks are sociable birds, living in vast flocks: crows go only in pairs. **1802** MONTAGU *Ornith. Dict.* s.v., The Rook is partial to cultivated parts, as well as to the habitation of man. **1841** *Penny Cycl.* XX. 148/2 Grain, and insects especially, form the food of the Rook. **1870** MORRIS *Earthly Par.* I. II. 529 From hill to hill the wandering rook did sail, Lazily croaking.

β. *c* **1400** MAUNDEV. (Roxb.) viii. 31 Þer commes rukes and crakes and oþer fewles. **1424** *Sc. Acts Jas. I* (1814) II. 6 Rukes bigande in kirk ȝardis, orchardis or treis dois gret skaithe apone cornis. *c* **1450** HOLLAND *Howlat* 794 Sa come the Ruke with a rerd and a rane roch. **1500–20** DUNBAR *Poems* xxxiii. 117 Had he reveild bene to the rwikis, Thay had him revin all with thair clwikis. **1570** *Satir. Poems Reform.* xv. 53 Ȝe gleds and howlets, rauins and rukis.

2. a. Applied to persons as an abusive or disparaging term.

1508 DUNBAR *Flyting* 57 Revin, raggit ruke, and full of rebaldrie. **1593** *Tell-Troth's N.Y. Gift* (Shaks. Soc.) 13 Callinge his wittes together (of which he had no small neede, being mated with two such rookes). *Note.* They are rookes for their troubling tongs. **1603** DEKKER *Wonderfull Year* Wks. (Grosart) I. 89 So many Rookes, catchpolls of poesy, That feed vpon the fallings of hye wit. *a* **1661** FULLER *Worthies, Worcestershire* III. (1662) 168 In plain English, this Scotish Demster is an arrant rook, deplumimg England, Ireland and Wales, of famous Writers, meerly to feather his own Country therewith. **1721** RAMSAY *Ode to the Ph——* xii, Ye'll worry me, you greedy rook. **1784** BURNS *Rob Mossgiel* 4 Such witching books are baited hooks, For rakish rooks like Rob Mossgiel.

b. A cheat, swindler, or sharper, *spec.* in gaming.

1577 *Nottingham Rec.* IV. 173 For against thys Fayre evere noughte rooke wyll come. **1662** GURNALL *Chr. in Arm.* IV. §2 (1669) 77/1 They meet with many Rooks and Cheaters in their dealing. **1693** *Humours Town* 25 To shake away an Estate to known Rooks that live by the Dice, is an unaccountable piece of folly. **1705** WYCHERLEY *Let. to Pope* 7 April, So I am (like and old Rook, who is ruined by Gaming) forced to live on the good Fortune of the pushing young Men. **1767** COLMAN *Prose Sev. Occas.* (1787) II. 82 They need not be guilty of burglary, turn Rooks and Sharpers, commit fraudulent bankruptcies [etc.]. **1824** *Hist. Gaming* 50 We scarcely know whether yet to class him with the rooks or the pigeons. **1889** *Spectator* 18 May, To punish the rooks by positive fines and the pigeons by the public exposure of their folly.

appos. **1678** OLDHAM *Let. fr. Country* Wks. (1854) 74 Poets are cullies, whom rook fame draws in.

†**c.** A gull, a simpleton. *Obs.*

1598 B. JONSON *Every Man in Hum.* I. v, Hang him, rooke, he! why, he has no more iudgement then a malt-horse. **1601** —— *Poetaster* I. ii, What? shall I haue my sonne a stager now? an enghle for players? a gull? a rooke? **1611** CHAPMAN *May Day* III. ii, An arrant Rooke by this light; a capable cheating stocke; a man may carry him vp and downe by the eares like a pipkin. **1637** BASTWICK *Litany* I. 7 Such men as study by all means to serve God.. are by these varlets called rooks.

d. *slang.* A 'black-coat'. Cf. ROOKSHIP.

1859 *Slang Dict.* 82 *Rook*, a clergyman.

3. *Cant.* and *dial.* (See quots.)

1796 *Grose's Dict. Vulgar T.* (ed. 3), *Rook*,.. the cant name for a crow used in house-breaking. **1812** J. H. VAUX *Flash Dict.*, *Rook*, a small iron crow. **1879** MISS JACKSON *Shropsh. Word-bk.* 355 *Rook*, the iron key used for winding up a kitchen-grate when it is too wide.

4. a. *attrib.* and *Comb.*, as ***rook-babble***, ***-catcher***, ***-net***, ***-roost***, ***-scarer***; ***rook-crowded***, ***-delighting***, ***-haunted***, ***-like***, ***-racked***, ***-routed***, ***-tenanted*** adjs.; ***rook-scaring***, ***-shooting*** vbl. sbs.

1948 C. DAY LEWIS *Poems 1943–47* 21 The rook-babble of bathers. **1637** BASTWICK *Litany* I. 8 The Church-wardens through the Kingdome are the Prelats rook-catchers. **1964** *Listener* 24 Dec. 1009/2 Goal-posts, a public-house, a rook-crowded birch. **1914** W. B. YEATS *Responsibilities* 37 Suddenly I saw the cold and rook-delighting Heaven. **1872** MORRIS in Mackail *Life* (1899) I. 280, I am writing among the grey gables and rook-haunted trees. **1870** DICKENS *E. Drood* ii, Divers venerable persons of rook-like aspect. **1573–4** *Saffron-Walden Accs.* (MS.), For a rokenet, 8*s.* **1879** G. M. HOPKINS *Poems* (1967) 79 Lark-charmèd, rook-racked, river-rounded. **1937** J. W. DAY *Sporting Adventure* 88 The great rook-roosts of winter, the annual nightly gatherings of thousands of these birds, are breaking up. **1923** BLUNDEN *To Nature* 46 In the rook-routed vale. **1910** *N.E.D.*, *Rook-starver*, ... a rook-scarer. **1946** J. W. DAY *Harvest Adventure* xvi. 266 A rat-catcher is a Pest Control Officer and a rook-scarer a Corvine Operator! **1895** 'ROSEMARY' *Under Chilterns* i. 20 The poor child ain't fit for sech work as that there rewk-scarin' this weather. **1910** in *N.E.D.* s.v. *rook-starving*. **1969** G. E. EVANS *Farm & Village* v. 55 Some called it *bird-keeping* or *bird-tending*—keeping the birds off the newly sown land—while others referred to it simply as *rook-scaring*. **1837** DICKENS *Pickw.* vii, Your friend and I.. are going out rook-shooting before breakfast. **1874** LISLE CARR *J. Gwynne* I. i. 1 A cluster of old elms, rook-tenanted.

b. Special combs., as **rook-bolter** (see quot.); **rook-boy**, one employed in scaring rooks from corn; **rook-drive**, an expedition to shoot rooks; **rook-grove**, a clump of trees containing a rookery; **rook-hawk**, (*a*) a hawk trained to fly at rooks; (*b*) the hobby; **rook-hawking**, the sport of flying hawks at rooks; **rook-pie**, a pie made with (young) rooks; **rook-rattle**, a rattle used in scaring rooks; **rook rifle**, a rifle of small bore for shooting rooks; **rook-starver**, *dial.*, a rook-scarer; **rook-starving**, *dial.*, rook-scaring; **rook-worm**, a worm eaten by rooks; esp. the larva of the cockchafer, *Melolontha melolontha*.

1840 SPURDENS *E. Anglian Wds.*, *Quarrel*, a kind of bird-bolt,.. now only used by *rook-bolters for beating down rooks' nests. **1885** *Census Instruct.* Index, *Rook Boy. **1969** R. BLYTHE *Akenfield* 20 'Did you kill men, Davie?' 'I got several'—the same answer to a question on how he did on a *rook-drive. *a* **1682** SIR T. BROWNE *Norf. Birds* Wks. (Bohn) III. 321 By reason of the great quantity of corn-fields and *rook groves. **1855** SALVIN & BRODRICK *Falconry* 63 One of William Barr's best *rook Hawks in 1852 was an eyess Tiercel. **1887** A. C. SMITH *Birds of Wiltshire* 72 The Hobby... I am told that its provincial name in Wiltshire is the 'Rook Hawk'. **1855** SALVIN & BRODRICK *Falconry* 63 We now come to a somewhat similar sport, viz. *Rook hawking. **1769** MRS. RAFFALD *Eng. Housekpr.* (1778) 157 A *Rook Pye. Skin and draw six young rooks. **1837** DICKENS *Pickw.* vii, Indistinct visions of rook-pie floated through his imagination. **1892** 'Q.' *I saw three Ships* 163 Scattered among these were ox-bells, *rook-rattles, a fog-horn or two. **1859** STONEHENGE *Shot-Gun* 104 In *rook rifle-shooting at birds just fledged. **1900** E. GLYN *Visits of Elizabeth* 50 She amused herself.. by shooting at rabbits.. with a rook rifle. **1907** [see EJECTOR 2]. **1921** 'K. MANSFIELD' *Let.* 3 Feb. (1977) 215 My grandpa said a man could travel all over the world with a clean pair of socks and a rook rifle. **1972** *Shooting Times & Country Mag.* 4 Mar. 11/1 Somehow we got hold of a .300 rook rifle cartridge. **1976** *Ibid.* 16–22 Dec. 46/4 (Advt.), Holland and Holland .410 converted rook rifle, £70. **1895** BURROUGHS *White's Selborne* I. 143 A '*rook-starver'. **1766** *Compl. Farmer* s.v. *Red-worm* 6 K 3/1 It is called a grub, by others the large maggot, and the *rook worm, because the rooks eat it. **1841** *Penny Cycl.* XX. 148/2 The larvæ of the cock-chaffer (*Melolontha vulgaris*).. are called Rook-worms in many places. **1959** E. F. LINSSEN *Beetles Brit. Isles* II. 124 The larvae of the Cockchafer—sometimes called by farmers White Grubs or Rookworms—are exceedingly destructive. **1973** J. M. CHINERY *Field Guide Insects Brit. & N. Europe* 303 It is said that rooks are particularly fond of both adult and larval cockchafers and the larvae are often called rookworms.

rook (rʊk), *sb.*[2] *Chess.* Forms: 4–5 **rok**, 5–6 **roke** (5 roche), 6–7 **rock**; 5– **rook** (7 -ke). [a. OF. *roc(k, rok, ro(c)q*, = Sp. and Pg. *roque*, It. *rocco*, med.L. *rocus, rochus*, also MLG. *roch* (G. *roch, roche*), ON. *hrókr* (Icel. *hrókur*), MSw. *rokk*, obs. Da. *rok, rocke*. The ultimate source is Pers. *rukh*, the original sense of which is doubtful.] One of four pieces which at the beginning of the game are set in the corner squares, and have the power of moving in a right line forwards, backwards, or laterally over any number of unoccupied squares; a castle. Also in *fig.* contexts.

13.. *Guy Warw.* (1883) 426 Wiþ a roke he brac his heued þan. *c* **1330** R. BRUNNE *Chron. Wace* (Rolls) 11397 Somme ..Drowe forthe meyne for þe cheker Wyþ draughtes queinte of knight & rok. *c* **1407** LYDG. *Reson & Sens.* 6717 Hyr Rokys at eche corner oon Wer makyd of a ryche stoon. *c* **1450** *Treat. Chess* (MS. Ashm. 344), Draw thy knyght in a ande say chek, Sythen thy Roke in b and say chek. *c* **1489** CAXTON *Sonnes of Aymon* xxii. 478 Yonnet.. played wyth his roke that he sholde not be mated. **1562** ROWBOTHUM *Playe of Cheasts* A iv b, The Rooke is made lykest to the Kinge and the Queene, but that he is not so long. **1591** FLORIO *2nd Frutes* 75, I had beene taken napping, if I had plaid that rooke. **1622** FLETCHER *Span. Cur.* III. iv, Now play your best Sir, though I lose this Rook here, Yet I get libertie. **1656** BEALE *Chesse-play* 2 In the corner of the field the Rooke, Rock, or Duke, who is sometimes fashioned with a round head, sometimes like a Castle. **1735** BERTIN *Chess* 56 The bishop gives a check in his queen's rook's fourth square. **1812** CRABBE *Tales* xi. 363 Nor good nor evil can you beings name, Who are but rooks and castles in the game. **1870** HARDY & WARE *Mod. Hoyle, Chess* 39 The Rook.. may pass along the entire length of the board at one move.

rook, *sb.*[3] *Sc.* and *north. dial.* [Var. of ROKE or ROUK: the difference in the vowel is unusual.] Mist, fog.

c **1700** KENNETT in *MS. Lansd. 1033* fol. 327 b, A *Rook*, a steam or vapour. **1786** *Har'st Rig* (1794) 27 Mair scouthry like it still does look, At length comes on in mochy rook. **1825** in BROCKETT. **1894** HESLOP *Northumb. Gloss.* 584 Yonder's a rook on the law.

rook (rʊk), *sb.*[4] U.S. shortening of ROOKIE.

1905 *Bluejacket* Mar. 190/1 The sailors there said we were 'rooks'. **1927** *Amer. Speech* II. 278/1 *Rook*,.. novice. **1935** *Our Army* (U.S.) June 12 A life-long profession from club-footed 'Rook' to Top Soak. **1941** G. KERSH *They die with their Boots Clean* II. 85 This here Spencer drops weight... millions of stones that rook lost. **1942** *Yank* 23 Sept. 17 In the horse cavalry, recruits do not complain as loudly about kitchen police as do the rooks in other branches.

rook, *dial.*, a heap: see RUCK *sb.*

rook, obs. form of ROCK *sb.*[1]

rook (rʊk), *v.*[1] [f. ROOK *sb.*[1] 2 b.]

1. *trans.* To cheat; to defraud by cheating, *esp.* in gaming; to clean of money by fraud, extortion, or other means; to charge extortionately.

Chiefly in slang or colloquial use.

c **1590** [? LODGE] *Sir T. More* I. ii, Let them gull me, widgeon me, rook me, fopp me. **1598** B. JONSON *Ev. Man in Hum.* III. i, If he should prooue, *Rimarum plenus*, then s'blood I were Rookt. **1654** GAYTON *Pleas. Notes* IV. xviii. 261 How easily doth a brother rooke a brother, I mean the craftie brother the weaker? **1673** [R. LEIGH] *Transp. Reh.* 87 This may be a fair warning.. to take heed he be not rookt by such polititians. **1691** WOOD *Ath. Oxon.* II. 302 The unsanctified crew of Gamesters.. rook'd him sometimes of all he could wrap or get. **1710** PALMER *Prov.* 209 Drawn in by guinea-droppers, and rook'd of forty guineas and a watch. **1780** H. WALPOLE *Let. to Earl Harcourt* 10 June, Whether terrified.., or to rooke new legions.. of Infernals, the Gordon is fled. **1822** SCOTT *Nigel* xxi, It was this same Glenvarloch that rooked me, at the ordinary, of every penny I had. **1862** M. NAPIER *Life Visct. Dundee* II. 321 The Decreet of the Mint by which they had been so terribly rooked. **1897** ANSTEY *Trav. Comp.* ii, Not such a bad dinner! Expect they'll rook us a lot for it, though. **1938** *Sun* (Baltimore) 11 Oct. 24/2 There have been numerous complaints that the growers have been 'rooked'. **1969** *Listener* 10 Apr. 482/3 Because we had been rooked at the door, none of us ever thought of boycotting the desk where another seated veteran.. was selling post-cards. **1977** *Capital Times* (Madison, Wisconsin) 27 Jan. 10/3 The Federal Trade Commission thinks that a lot of people have been rooked by these buying clubs.

†**2.** To take by cheating, or by fraudulent means.

1648 SYMMONS *Vind. Chas. I*, 161 How they rooked to themselves all the Plate and Money. **1653** MILTON *Hirelings* Wks. 1851 V. 361 The Title of Gehazi.. to those things which by abusing his Master's name he rook'd from Naaman. **1695** COTTON *Martial* I. lxvi. 59 Dost hope.. For ten vile pence eternal glory rook?

†**3.** *intr.* To practise cheating. *Obs.*

1668 DRYDEN *Even. Love* III. i, In the gaming-house, where I found most of the town-wits; the prose-wits playing, and the verse-wits rooking. **1676** SHADWELL *Libertine* II, You women always rook in love, you'll never play upon the square with us. **1693** LOCKE *Educ.* §70 Learning to wrangle at Trap, or rook at Span-farthing.

†**4.** (Meaning uncertain.) *Obs.*

1632 SHIRLEY *Hyde Park* III. i, Ile rooke for once, my Lord, Ile hold you twenty more... Done with you too.

rook, *v.*[2] [f. ROOK *sb.*[2]] 'To castle at chess' (Ogilvie, 1850).

†**rook**, *v.*[3] *Obs.* (Exact meaning not clear.)

1616 in W. H. Wheeler *Hist. Fens* (1897) App. IV. 11 The Welland to be roaded, rooked, hooked, haffed, scowered, and cleansed.

rook, to crouch, cower: see RUCK *v.*

rooker[1]. *rare*[−1]. [f. ROOK *v.*[1] + -ER[1].] One who rooks or cheats.

1683 KENNETT tr. *Erasm. on Folly* 78 There is a pernicious destructive sort of flattery, wherewith rookers and sharks work their several ends upon such as they make a prey of.

ˈrooker[2]. (See quot.)

1851–3 *Tomlinson's Cycl. Arts* (1867) I. 179/2 The *rooker*, a tool resembling the letter L, fixed in a wooden handle, for the purpose of drawing out the ashes from the oven.

ˈrookeried, *a.* [f. next.] Having a rookery.

1836 R. FURNESS *Astrologer* II. Wks. (1858) 149 Descending by The rook'ried Holme, and to the town on Wye.

rookery (ˈrʊkərɪ). [f. ROOK *sb.*[1] + -ERY.]

1. a. A collection of rooks' nests in a clump of trees; a colony of rooks.

1725 *Fam. Dict.* s.v., They are commonly Groves and tall Trees near Gentlemens Houses in the Country that make your Rookeries. **1772** T. SIMPSON *Vermin-Killer* 21 Gentlemen keep rookeries for the sake of hearing a continual noise. **1822** SCOTT *Nigel* xvi, Like crows upon a falcon that strays into their rookery. **1842** TENNYSON *Locksley Hall* 68 The many-winter'd crow that leads the clanging rookery home. **1883** *Congregational Year Book* 58 To many, Church questions seem as trivial as the politics of a rookery.

b. The realm of rooks. *rare*[−1].

1738 *Gentl. Mag.* VIII. 301/2 This seemed to be no Breach of the Laws of Rookery, and was, I saw, practised by every one of the Rest.

2. A breeding-place, common resort, or large colony: **a.** Of sea-birds, *esp.* penguins.

1832 A. EARLE *Narr. of Residence on Tristan d'Acunha* 357 We visited what they call a 'penguin rookery'. **1838** POE *Narr. A. Gordon Pym* Wks. 1896 I. 441 Navigators have agreed in calling an assemblage of such encampments [of albatross] a rookery. **1840** *Penny Cycl.* XVII. 410/2 The towns, camps, and rookeries, as they have been called, of these birds [penguins]. **1897** *Westm. Gaz.* 20 Aug. 2/1 Further on.. we found a rookery of many thousands of the superb red-tailed tropic bird (*Phaeton phœnicurus*).

b. Of seals or other marine mammals.

1832 B. MORRELL *Four Voyages* p. xxiv, The word *rookery* ..has been applied by all our South Sea navigators to the breeding encampments of various oceanic animals, such as seal, penguins, &c. **1846** *McLean Papers* 22 Dec. 42 (typescript), A boat goes out in search of a 'rookery' as they term the collected seals on any spot. **1847** SIR J. ROSS *Voy. Antarctic Reg.* I. 47 Some of their [*sc.* seals'] haunts, or as the sealers term them 'rookeries'. **1860** *Merc. Mar. Mag.* VII. 208 The sea-elephants.. are gregarious, and.. will often congregate in 'rookeries' of hundreds. **1881** *Nature* XXV. 205 The 'rookery' of the sea-bears still found in abundance on St. Paul's Island. **1932** S. ZUCKERMAN *Social Life Monkeys & Apes* v. 69 Bull seals fight each other.. for territory in the rookery or mating ground. **1972** L. HANCOCK *There's a Seal in my Sleeping Bag* vii. 145 The rocky shores of Triangle Island itself are used by the Steller sea-lions as hauling-out grounds, while those of the large islets immediately off the main island are breeding grounds and rookeries.

3. a. A cluster of mean tenements densely populated by people of the lowest class. Also *attrib.*

1792 G. GALLOWAY *Poems on Various Subjects* 74 Then I begin my follies to repent, With naked elbows and a coat thread bare... So for to hide my gold I need no bags, While like to rookry dogs I'm cloth'd with rags. **1829** *Farmer's Jrnl.* 14 Sept. 294 This court is known by the name of the 'Rookery', (from there being a humble family in each room). **1851** H. MAYHEW *Lond. Labour* (1862) II. 331 We visited Market Street,.. a well known rookery of prostitutes. **1883** *Good Words* Aug. 542/1 A 'rookery' district in the great metropolis. **1887** JESSOPP *Arcady* Introd. p. xiii, A dozen families are.. in a rookery which grew up on the edge of a piece of waste. **1971** *Daily Tel.* 2 Dec. 6/4 The artisans, a potent radical force, were very different from the a-political desperate starvelings of the London rookeries. **1973** *N.Y. Law Jrnl.* 4 Sept. 5/3 Look at the city's unrepairable slums housing miserably over a million people... These rookeries are beyond repair. **1976** M. BUTTERWORTH *Festival!* vii. 106 Arnold.. lay in a crude shelter.. in the heart of a close-packed slum of some of the worst habitations at the festival; a rookery so vile that it had been totally rejected by all the rest.

b. (See quot.)

1860 *Slang Dict.* (ed. 2) 201 *Rookery*, in Military slang, that part of the barracks occupied by subalterns, often by no means a pattern of good order.

c. *transf.* in various applications.

1864 HERSCHEL *Fam. Lect. Sci.* 34 Java itself I should observe is one rookery of volcanoes. **1892** *Nation* LV. 480/1 The Inns of Court and of Chancery.. have been.. an immemorial rookery for authors. **1899** SOMERVILLE & ROSS *Irish R.M.* 252 Dr. Fahy's basement storey, with the rookery of paying guests asleep above.

4. *dial.* or *slang.* A row, disturbance.

c **1820** *Oh, What a Row!* (song) People toiling, roasting, boiling, bless us! such a rookery. **1824** *Spirit Publ. Jrnls.* (1825) 416 At this moment there was a terrible rookery and noise outside the court. **1838** HOLLOWAY *Prov. Dict.* s.v., 'To make a rookery' is to make a great stir about anything. **1925** *Dialect Notes* V. 340 *Rookery*, confusion, ruckus. **1942** BERREY & VAN DEN BARK *Amer. Thes. Slang* §5/1 *Disorder n.*, ..riz-raz, rookery, [etc.].

rookie (ˈrʊkɪ). *slang.* Also **rookey**, **rooky**. [Origin uncertain; perh. corruption of RECRUIT *sb.*] **1.** A raw recruit, *spec.* (*a*) an army or police recruit; (*b*) a novice at a sport, etc., esp. a first-year player in a particular team (chiefly *N. Amer.*).

1892 KIPLING *Barrack-Room Ballads* 68 So 'ark an' 'eed, you rookies, which is always grumblin' sore. **1893** —— *Many Invent.* 134 You can't drill, you can't walk, you can't shoot,.. you awful rookies. **1900** I. L. REEVES *Bamboo Tales* 100 One of his men, a green 'rookie'. **1909** R. A. WATSON *Happy Hawkins* 142 'Why, you blame rookie,' sez I, 'You don't really think I was mad do you?' **1913** *Chicago Record-Herald* 1 Mar. 12/2 Cal tried out Lefty Delano, a New Brunswick southpaw rookie. **1913** H. A. FRANCK *Zone Policeman 88* ix. 275 From the lieutenant to the newest uniformless 'rookie' every member of the police was swarming in and out of the building. **1918** I. CRUMP *Conscript 2989* 6 Oh, you rookey. **1929** *Daily Express* 15 Jan. 9/7 In 1915..he was a member of the Baltimore baseball team as a gawky 'rookie'. **1930** *Punch* 16 Apr. 443/1 The keen young rooky, just fresh from his public school. **1939** *Airman's Gaz.* Dec., Who was the Rookie here who thought ..Blanco was a Spanish General. **1956** 'E. MCBAIN' *Cop Hater* (1958) ix. 81 A squad car driven by a young rookie. **1961** F. H. BURGESS *Dict. Sailing* 173 *Rooky*, a brand new hand. **1966** *Time* 8 July 60/3 The new enlarged S. & S. will be in a more powerful position to bid for blockbusting authors, whose contracts have been escalating as rapidly as those of prize pro football rookies. **1975** *Listener* 16 Jan. 66/2 [He] flew with Hunt to Hong Kong, as a police rookie. **1976** *Billings* (Montana) *Gaz.* 16 June 5-c/1 Rookies Chris Evert ..and Rod Laver..headed the list of players named Tuesday to the World Team Tennis Western Division All-Star team. **1979** *Tucson* (Arizona) *Citizen* 20 Sept. 1 D/1 He was rookie of the year on the Professional Golfers Association tour in 1965.

2. *attrib.* passing into *adj.*

1930 E. H. LAVINE *Third Degree* (1931) 102 The shooting of 'rookie' Patrolman James A. Broderick. **1944** *Chicago Daily News* 21 Oct. 11/1 They expressed themselves..as willing to trade..for the rookie outfielder. **1954** L. ARMSTRONG *Satchmo* 37 They gave me the rooky greeting saying, 'Welcome, Newcomer'. **1963** *Listener* 4 Apr. 585/1 To the eye of the rookie policeman they were as unobtrusive as the pavement stones. **1968** [see CHARLEY-HORSE, CHARLEY HORSE]. **1972** M. WILLIAMS *Inside Number 10* xii. 322, I recall the times he was censorious with us about security and times when he treated us like the latest members of an awkward squad in a rookie army. **1974** *Spartanburg* (S. Carolina) *Herald* 18 Apr. C1/7 The Dallas Cowboys lost a fifth player to the World Football League Wednesday when rookie tight end John Kelsey of Missouri signed with the Honolulu Hawaiians. **1977** *Daily Mirror* 30 Mar., Rookie police constable Paul Weaver, 19, saved a 74-year-old widow from her blazing home. **1977** D. L. ALTHEIDE in Douglas & Johnson *Existential Sociol.* iv. 137 Rookie reporters..learn the ropes and eventually become bored with the questions of newcomers. **1980** *Washington Star* 18 July A6/3 Reagan's nomination is the penultimate step in a steady 12-year drive to the White House that began with a feeble tentative pass at the office in 1968 when he was derided as a Grade B Hollywood movie actor and a rookie right-wing fringe governor of California.

'rooking, *vbl. sb.*[1] [f. ROOK *v.*[1] + -ING[1].] The act or practice of cheating or defrauding.

1652 BROME *Damoiselle* IV. i, Though cheating there, and Rooking be as free As there is square play at the Ordinaries. **1707** *Reflex. upon Ridicule* 266 They consider themselves as in the Enemies Country, and think that Rooking is a kind of Lawful Profession. **1825** C. WESTMACOTT *Eng. Spy* II. 235 Most passive pigeon that ever submitted to rooking. **1936** *Sat. Even. Post* 19 Dec. 11/1 What else could we do but quit? Mel wasn't treatin' you square. Can you deny it? I won't speak for myself, though I was gettin' a fancy rookin', too, singin' and all. **1955** *Sun* (Baltimore) 10 Sept. 6/4 They submit to a rooking involving thousands of dollars.

attrib. **1659** *Invisible John made Visible* 4 The Tower, formerly a noble and unexpensive Prison, is..rendered a rooking Pinfold. *a* **1677** BARROW *Serm.* Wks. 1716 III. 287 This rooking Trick,..to dodge and shuffle with God.

'rooking, *vbl. sb.*[2] [f. ROOK *sb.*[1]] The driving away of rooks from fields.

1883 *Harper's Mag.* April 652 Other items are..weeding, and rooking, or employing a boy to drive away the rooks.

'rooking, *ppl. a.* [f. ROOK *v.*[1]] Cheating, swindling, dishonest.

16.. *Robin Conscience* 16, I walkt into St. Georges Field, Where rooking Rascals I beheld. **1641** MILTON *Reform.* I. Wks. (1851) III. 14 A band of rooking Officials, with cloke bagges full of Citations. **1680** COTTON *Compl. Gamester* (ed. 2) 9 A Crown the Rooking-winner lent him..to bear his charges homewards. **1934** DYLAN THOMAS *18 Poems* 20 A rooking girl who stole me for her side.

'rookish, *a.* [f. ROOK *sb.*[1] + -ISH.] Of or pertaining to rooks; resembling a rook.

1738 *Common Sense* II. 120 They seem now to be the Outcasts of the Rookish Race. **1869** *Daily News* 23 Jan., It gives a rookish look to a corpulent Frenchman, and makes a thin one spectral.

'rookle, *v.*, dial. var. of ROOTLE *v.* Hence **'rookler;** **'rookling** *ppl. a.*

1855 KINGSLEY *Westw. Ho!* viii, Such were then the pigs of Devon: not to be compared with the..game-flavoured little rooklers. **1857** —— *Two Y. Ago* II. 70 Rookling in their drains, like an old sow. **1865** —— *Poems, Martin Lightfoot's Song*, To the rookling sow took he.

'rooklet, -ling. [f. ROOK *sb.*[1]] A young rook.

1854 *Zoologist* XII. 4325 An attack is regularly made upon the rooklings by the..gamekeeper. **1897** *Badminton Mag.* IV. 427 Each time the old birds approach, the 'rooklets' positively quiver with excitement.

rookly, variant of ROKELAY.

'rookship. [Cf. ROOK *sb.*[1] 2 d.] A mock title applied to a clergyman.

1710 *Welchman's Tales* 7 He call'd him Knave in a Black Coat: which rais'd his Rookships Passion so.

†**'rookster.** *Obs.* [f. ROOK *v.*[1]] A cheat.

1697 POTTER *Antiq. Greece* I. xxv. (1715) 135 Beggars, Jack-puddings, Rooksters, and such like.

rookus ('rʊkəs). [Var. RUCKUS.] **a.** = RUCKUS.

1893 H. A. SHANDS *Some Peculiarities of Speech in Mississippi* 53 *Rookus*, a word signifying a quarrel or row. **1902** 'O. HENRY' in *Ainslee's Mag.* Mar. 130/1 He talks all spraddled out..'bout the rookuses he's been in. He claims to have saw the elephant and hearn the owl. **1924** W. M. RAINE *Troubled Waters* vi. 60 Course there'll be a rookus between him and Joe Tait.

b. rookus-juice *U.S. slang*, liquor.

1929 *Amer. Speech* IV. 385 Such terms as *rookus juice*, *third rail*,..and *bust-head* are evidently references to the potency or the effect of the liquor designated. **1942** BERREY & VAN DEN BARK *Amer. Thes. Slang* §99/1 *Liquor*..rinse, rookus-juice, [etc.]. **1951** *Western Folklore* X. 80 Give me a shot of:..rookus juice.

'rooky, *a.*[1] [f. ROOK *sb.*[1]] Full of, abounding in, consisting of, rooks; also *fig.*

1605 SHAKS. *Macb.* III. ii. 51 Light thickens, And the Crow makes Wing to th' Rookie Wood. **1800** HURDIS *Fav. Village* 157 The rooky tribe attend, and perched at hand, Watch the moist furrow. **1860** *Slang Dict.* (ed. 2) 201 *Rooky*, rascally, rakish, scampish. [**1890** *Temple Bar* Aug. 474 At this latening season most of the English are winging home to their rooky woods.]

'rooky, *a.*[2] *Sc.* and *north. dial.* [f. ROOK *sb.*[3]] Foggy, misty. Cf. ROKY *a.*[1]

1691 RAY *N.C. Words, Rooky*, misty. *c* **1700** KENNETT in *MS. Lansd. 1033* fol. 327 b, *Rooky*, misty or dark with steam and vapour. **1808** JAMIESON s.v. *Rak*, We say it is *a rooky day*, when the air is thick and the light of consequence feeble. **1825** BROCKETT *N.C. Gloss.*

rooky, var. ROOKIE.

rool, *v. rare.* (See quots.)

1828 CARR *Craven Gloss.*, *Rool*, to ruffle, to rumple clothes, by throwing them negligently about. **1886** *Jrnl. Microsc. Soc.* VI. 23 Whenever the balsam begins to 'rool' or cause hitching of the specimen. *Ibid.* 24 The balsam catches to the stone and 'rools', carrying the preparation with it.

rool(e, obs. forms of ROLL *sb.*[1] and *v.*[2]

room (ruːm, rʊm), *sb.*[1] Forms: (see below). [Common Teut.: OE. *rúm* neut., = MDu. *ruum, ruym, ruem* (Du. *ruim*), OS. *rûm* (LG. *rûm*), OHG. *rûm* (G. *raum*), ON. and Icel. *rúm* (Sw. and Da. *rum*, Norw. *rom*), Goth. *rūm*. The relationship to forms in *ru-* outside of Teutonic is uncertain.]

A. Illustration of forms.

α. 1–3 **rum,** 4 **rume.**

Beowulf 2690 Đa him rum aȝeald. *c* **1200** ORMIN 8489 Þe Laferrd haffde litell rum. *a* **1300** *Cursor M.* 20856 For þis bok has na noþer rume.

β. 4–6, 9 *dial.* **roum,** 4–7 **roume,** 5–6 **rovme.**

c **1330** *Arth. & Merl.* 6926 (Kölbing), On a swiþe grene roum. *c* **1340** HAMPOLE *Pr. Consc.* 9168 Þe roume and þe space..In þe cete of heven. *c* **1450** HOLLAND *Howlat* 475 With all the relykis raith, that in that rovme was. *c* **1495** *The Epitaffe*, etc. in Skelton's Wks. (1843) II. 389 Though the roume vnmete were for his pouer degre. **1526** TINDALE *Luke* ii. 7 Be cause there was no roume for them. **1577** B. GOOGE *Heresbach's Husb.* I. (1586) 13 These great rovmes that you see. **1639** SIR W. MURE *Ps.* civ. 9 The beames of all his high-raisd roumes. **1828** CARR *Craven Gloss.* s.v., Ith roum o comin to me, he went haam.

γ. 5–6 **rowm,** 5–7 **rowme,** 6 **rowlm(e.**

a **1400–50** *Alexander* 4920 He þat ristis in þat rowme. *c* **1440** *Promp. Parv.* 438/1 Rowm, space,..*spacium*. **1535** COVERDALE *2 Esdras* vii. 4 It was large of rowme. **1562** *Cal. Rec. Dublin* (1891) II. 21 The said rowlme of alderman of this cittie. **1608** *Church-w. Acc. Pittington*, etc. (Surtees) 150 For a rowme to build a stall on. **1654** in Campbell *Balmerino* (1899) 403 Finding that rowme and place not propriat.

δ. 5–7 **rome,** 5 **rom, rombe,** 5–6 **romme,** 7 **rum.**

c **1400** *Laud Troy Bk.* 3230 Ther myght thei alle stonde In romme. *c* **1440** *Generydes* 2044 In euery rome. *c* **1449** PECOCK *Repr.* III. xiii. 366 Dwelling ferther fro thens in rombe. **1530** PALSGR. 628/2 Make romme, maysters, here cometh a player. **1552** in *Vicary's Anat.* (1888) 119 As they in theire severall romes doo serve. **1603** OWEN *Pembrokeshire* (1892) 255 Their rarietie might have claimed rome in this place. **1684** *Pennsylv. Arch.* I. 86 One in the rum of Ralph withers Deceased.

ε. 5–7 **roome,** 5– **room.**

1494 in *Househ. Ord.* (1790) 109 To bee discharged of their roomes. **1497** BP. ALCOCK *Mons Perfect.* D iij b/2 His felowes in yᵗ room. **1549–62** STERNHOLD & H. *Ps.* lxxxiv. 3 The sparowes fynde a roome to rest. **1651** HOBBES *Leviath.* III. xxxiv. 211 Substances..take up roome. **1696** *Church-w. Acc. Pittington* 260 A new saxton to be chosen in his roome.

B. Signification.

I. 1. a. Space; dimensional extent.

a **1000** *Genesis* 1166 Þa his tiddæȝe under rodera rum rim wæs ȝefylled. *c* **1200** ORMIN 8489 Þe Laferrd haffde litell rum Inn all þatt miccle riche. *c* **1330** *Arth. & Merl.* 7896 (Kölbing), Her main þai kedde & large roume about hem redde. **1375** BARBOUR *Bruce* XI. 469 So fele battalis and so braid, That tuk so gret rowme as thai raid. *c* **1440** *Alph. Tales* 50 What was þe grettest mervayle & fayrest þing þat evur God made in leste rowme? **1523** FITZHERB. *Husb.* §26 Whan it is mowen, it..taketh more rowme in the barne than shorne corne dothe. *a* **1568** ASCHAM *Scholem.* II. (Arb.) 114 To draw other mens workes for his owne memorie sake, into shorter rowme. **1601** HOLLAND *Pliny* VII. xxxviii, A painted table,..which tooke up no greate roume. **1699** BENTLEY *Phal.* 414 Both Labour and Room was saved by their repeated Contractions. **1733** TULL *Horse-Hoeing Husb.* 91 It filling less room (by the breaking) is a proof of its specific gravity being increased. **1830** WORDSW. *Let. to Dyce*, In the edition of 1827 it was diligently revised, and the sense in several instances got into less room. **1847** C. BRONTË *J. Eyre* xxiv, Mr. Rochester won't, though there is so much room in the new carriage. **1855** DELAMER *Kitch. Gard.* (1861) 107 Cos lettuces will take up somewhat less room.

†**b.** *on* (or *by*) *room*, to or at a distance; apart. *Obs.* Cf. A-ROOM *adv.*

c **1250** *Gen. & Ex.* 4021 ȝede eft balaam up on-rum. **13..** *Prov. Hendyng* in *Pass. Christ* (E.E.T.S.) 54 Fle þou most and flitte on roume With eie and eke with herte. *c* **1400** *Destr. Troy* 2835 When the Grekes se the grete nauy, þai girdon o rowme. *a* **1440** *Sir Eglam.* 1087 By rome some stode and hur behelde. **1513** DOUGLAS *Æneis* v. x. 14 Eneas ..gaif command About the court the peple on rowm to stand.

2. a. Sufficient space; accommodation. (Also with addition of *ample, enough*, etc.)

c **1000** *Ags. Gosp.* Luke ii. 7 Hiȝ næfdon rum on cumena huse. **13..** *Seuyn Sag.* 599 (W.), The ympe had roum, and wexeth fast. *c* **1375** *Sc. Leg. Saints* ii. (*Paul*) 88 To here hym wes sik prese, þat fawt of rowme gret þar wes. *c* **1400** *Laud Troy Bk.* 3230 To the hauen of Athenes..For ther myght thei alle stonde In romme. **14..** *Sir Beues* (O) 3078 Than began Beuys..to get hym rowme wyth gode Marglay. **1535** COVERDALE *Isaiah* xlix. 20 This place is to narow, syt nye together, yᵗ I maye haue rowme. **1583** *Leg. Bp. St. Androis* 147 For laik of rowme, that rubiature Bespewit vp the moderator. **1665** BOYLE *Occas. Refl.* (1848) 50 How many thousand times more there might be without wanting room. **1671** in *12th Rep. Hist. MSS. Comm.* App. V. 22 It was so hard to get room that wee were forced to goe by four a clocke. **1791** COWPER *Retired Cat* 73 With hunger pinch'd, and pinch'd for room. **1858** LYTTON *What will He do* I. iv, All the men who rule England have room in that palace.

(*b*) Phr. *room at the top* (freq. *fig.*)

1900 W. JAMES *Let.* 2 Apr. (1920) II. 121 Verily there is room at the top. S—— seems to be the only Britisher worth thinking of. **1914** A. BENNETT *Price of Love* vii. 143 The Imperial had set out to be the most gorgeous cinema in the Five Towns; and it simply was. Its advertisements read: 'There is always room at the top.' **1929** *Times* 11 Jan. 13/4 When successful men give schoolboys their prizes they generally throw in a little advice. They recommend industry, neatness, punctuality, and other virtues, but they also dwell on the saying that there is always room at the top. **1933** W. S. MAUGHAM *Sheppey* III. 89 You have to be pretty smart with all the competition there is nowadays... There's always room at the top. **1947** 'G. ORWELL' *Eng. People* 22 The masses..know it is not true that 'there's plenty of room at the top'. **1957** J. BRAINE *Room at Top* xxviii. 230 You're the sort of young man we want. There's always room at the top. **1960** *20th Cent.* July 79 Academically speaking, the room at the top in sociology is lessening. **1980** *Times* 14 Jan. 5/5 In that last crisis, McEnroe suddenly looked young and vulnerable and Borg's tennis told him bluntly that, for the time being, there was no room at the top.

b. Const. *for*, or *to* with infin. ***no room to swing a cat in*** and varr.: see SWING *v.*[1] 7 a.

c **1385** CHAUCER *L.G.W.* 1999 *Ariadne*, He..hath roume & ek space To welde an axe. **1417** in *Surtees Misc.* (1890) 12 That Hesyll may have rowme thar to lay hys sole. **1478** EARL RIVERS in Gairdner *Rich. III* (1878) App. 396 If ye may get rome for iij or iiij men of thys contre..for to be in the parlement hows. **1535** COVERDALE *Ps.* xvii[i]. 36 Thou hast made rowme ynough vnder me for to go. **1587** in Feuillerat *Revels Q. Eliz.* (1908) 391 For Roome for the office and masters lodging at Grenewiche. **1611** BIBLE *Gen.* xxiv. 23 Is there roome in thy fathers house for vs to lodge in? **1662** STILLINGFL. *Orig. Sacræ* III. iv. §7 There would be room enough for them, and for provision for them. **1757** GRAY *Bard* 51 Give ample room, and verge enough The characters of hell to trace. **1795** *Gentl. Mag.* 542/2, I request you will spare room for one tribute more to his memory. **1833** HT. MARTINEAU *Loom & Lugger* II. i. 18 We must teach him.. that there is room in the wide world for all. **1840** *Penny Cycl.* XVII. 345/1 The plants..would then have room to grow out. **1868** HELPS *Realmah* xvii. (1876) 460 There was not sufficient room for the furniture.

3. ***to make room*****:** †**a.** To clear a space for oneself. *Obs.*

1375 BARBOUR *Bruce* VI. 234 He smertly raiss, And, strikand, rowm about him mais. *c* **1400** *Sowdone Bab.* 876 Tho Roulande Durnedale oute-drowe And made Romme abowte. **1470** HENRY *Wallace* III. 140 The Scottis on fute gret rowme about thaim maide With ponȝeand speris. **1535** COVERDALE *Josh.* xvii. 15 Make thy selfe rowme there in the londe of the Pheresites and Raphaim.

b. To make way, yield place, draw back or retire, so as to allow one to enter, pass, etc. Similarly *to give room*, and with imperative suppressed.

(*a*) *c* **1440** *York Myst.* xxii. 1 Make rome be-lyve, and late me gang. **1470–85** MALORY *Arthur* VII. i. 213 There was made pees & rome, & ryght so they yede with hym vnto the hyghe deyse. **1530** PALSGR. 628/2 Make romme, maysters, here cometh a player. **1596** SHAKS. *Merch. Ven.* IV. i. 16 Make roome, and let him stand before our face. **1613** PURCHAS *Pilgrimage* II. xx. (1614) 222 Make roome, I pray, for another Rabbi with his Bird. **1711** ADDISON *Spect.* No. 122 ¶6 Notwithstanding all the Justices had taken their Places upon the Bench, they made room for the old Knight. **1812** J. WILSON *Isle of Palms* IV. 251 In churchyard on the Sabbath-day They all make room for her.

(*b*) *a* **1400** *St. Alexius* (Laud 108) 481 ȝiueþ me roum, & lat me se þe body þat was boren of me. **1526** TINDALE *Luke* xiv. 9 Geve this man roume. **1592** SHAKS. *Rom. & Jul.* I. v. 28 A Hall, Hall, giue roome, and foote it Girles. **1601** —— *All's Well* I. ii. 67, I..wish..I quickly were dissolued from my hiue To giue some Labourers roome.

(*c*) **1588** SHAKS. *L.L.L.* V. ii. 703 Roome for the incensed Worthies. **1601** —— *Jul. C.* III. ii. 170 Roome for Antony, most Noble Antony. **1808** SCOTT *Marm.* I. xii, Room, lordings, room for Lord Marmion. **1827–35** N. P. WILLIS *The Leper* 1 Room for the leper! Room!.. The cry pass'd on.

c. To provide or obtain space or place for something by the removal of other things.

1666 Pepys *Diary* 10 Sept., Clearing out cellars, and breaking in pieces all my old lumber, to make room. **1778** C. Jones *Hoyle's Games* 27 Throwing out the best Cards in your Hand..in order to make Room for the whole suit. **1849** Macaulay *Hist. Eng.* vi. II. 142 He explicitly said..that room must be made for them by dismissing more Protestants. **1895** *Law Times' Rep.* LXXII. 861/2, 750 tons of the coal had been sold to make room for cargo at a South American port.

4. *transf.* or *fig.* Opportunity or scope *to* do something. Also in OE. without infinitive.

In 18th cent. examples the sense sometimes appears to be 'occasion', 'reason', 'cause'.

Beowulf 2690 Frecne fyrdraca fæhða ȝemyndiȝ ræsde on ðone rofan ða him rum aȝeald. *a* **1000** *Boethius Metr.* x. 30 Deað þæs ne scrifeð, þonne him rum forlæt rodora waldend. *c* **1205** Lay. 1003 þe riche haueð muchel rum, to ræsan biforen þan wrecchan.

1535 Coverdale *Wisdom* xii. 19 Euen when thou iudgest, thou geuest rowme to amende from synnes. **1637** Rutherford *Lett.* (1862) I. 364 Pray that the Lord w^d be pleased to giue me room to speak to His people in His name. **1703** Marlborough *Lett. & Disp.* (1845) I. 170 To give no room to the King of Portugal to fall off again, I should [etc.]. **1793** Smeaton *Edystone L.* § 183 As soon as the season would give us room to suppose we were likely to have success. **1827** Keble *Chr. Y.* 2 The trivial round, the common task Would furnish..Room to deny ourselves.

b. Opportunity, scope, or opening *for* something, by which it is rendered possible.

1692 R. L'Estrange *Fables* (1714) 29 There's room yet for a Distinction..betwixt what's done Openly..and a Thing that's done in Hugger-mugger. **1710** Steele *Tatler* No. 198 ¶ 6 Cælia had no more Room for Doubt. **1726** Swift *Gulliver* i. vii, Still there was Room for Mercy. **1828** Scott *F.M. Perth* xv, There is no room for pardon where offence must not be taken. **1855** Macaulay *Hist. Eng.* xi. III. 100 As to most of the provisions there was little room for dispute. **1875** Jowett *Plato* (ed. 2) V. 122 In such a commonwealth there would be less room for the development of individual character.

c. In uses similar to prec., but more directly *transf.* from the literal sense.

1577 *St. Augustine's Manuell* Q iiij, Hauyng thee in my hart..so as there may be no rowme in me for any counterfet or vncleane loue. **1596** Shaks. *1 Hen. IV*, iii. iii. 174 There's no roome for Faith, Truth, nor Honesty, in this bosome of thine. **1660** F. Brooke tr. *Le Blanc's Trav.* 285 Then there was amongst us such a tyde of tendernesses, there was not room for words. **1697** Dryden *Virg. Georg.* iv. 331 No room is left for Death, they mount the Sky. **1710** Steele *Tatler* No. 139 ¶ 1 Business and Ambition take up Men's Thoughts too much to leave Room for Philosophy. **1764** Goldsm. *Trav.* 268 But while this softer art their bliss supplies, It gives their follies also room to rise. **1868** Tennyson *Spiteful Letter* 14 What room is left for a hater?

†**d.** Leisure, time *to* do something. *Obs.*

1769 G. White *Selborne* xxvi, Where you spent..some considerable time, and gave yourself good room to examine the natural curiosities.

II. 5. a. A particular portion of space; a certain space or area.

c **1340** Hampole *Pr. Consc.* 9168 þe roume and þe space þat es contende In þe cete of heven has nane ende. *c* **1440** *Alph. Tales* 50, And all þe wittes of a man is sett in þat litle rowm. *a* **1483** Earl Rivers in Gairdner *Rich. III* (1878) App. 395 Ye will leve a rome..for a skochon of the armez of Wodevile and Scalis. **1509** Fisher *Funeral Serm. C'tess Richmond* Wks. (1876) 304 It is so grosse, that it occupyeth a rowme..and letteth other bodyes to be presente in the same place. **1587** Fleming *Cont. Holinshed* III. 1537/2 The roome within this close baie conteineth almost fortie acres. **1617** Moryson *Itin.* iii. 69 That the whole roome towards the streets may be reserved for shoppes. **1695** Woodward *Nat. Hist. Earth* iii. ii. (1723) 178 Which [Earth] he fancies ..to contract it self into a lesser Room. **1755** J. Shebbeare *Lydia* (1769) I. 55 When he was at leeward, he was equally cautious of allowing a proper room, through fear of receiving a shot betwixt wind and water. **1779** Johnson *Wks.* (1787) IV. 478 A journal of the weather..which exhibits in a little room, a great train of different observations. **1833** L. Ritchie *Wand. by Loire* 186 The squares, amounting to thirty-three, are not worth the room which their names would occupy. **1885–94** R. Bridges *Eros & Psyche* April 28 A Zephyr straying out of heaven's wide room Rush'd down.

†**b.** A (short) space of time. *Obs.*$^{-1}$

14.. *Sir Beues* (C) 1007 + 19 þe Sarsyns yn a rome At that tyme were ouercome.

†**c.** A space, compartment, or square on an abacus, chess-board, etc. *Obs.*

1542 Recorde *Gr. Artes* 120 When the summe to be abatyd, in any lyne appeareth greater then the other, then do they borowe one of the next hygher roume. **1562** Rowbothum *Playe of Cheasts* A vj b, The king..hath libertie to assault thre roumes or stepps as he listeth.

d. *Shipbuilding.* (See quots.)

1846 A. Young *Naut. Dict.*, *Timber-and-Room*, Room-and-Timber, Room-and-Space,..in shipbuilding, the distance from the moulding edge of one timber to the moulding edge of the timber next to it. *c* **1860** H. Stuart *Seaman's Catech.* 66 'Room and space'..is the distance occupied by each set of timbers, called a 'frame'; measured along the keel it varies from 2 ft. 6 in. to 3 ft. 9 in. in ships of war. **1874** Thearle *Naval Archit.* 86 These plates..are all in either three, four, or even six room and space lengths. *Ibid.* 92 Thus the intercostal portions are twice the room and space in length.

†**6. a.** A particular place or spot, without reference to its area. *Obs.*

c **1330** *Arth. & Merl.* 6926 (Kölbing), He fond cartes..& loges & pauilouns Telt on a swiþe grene roum. *c* **1440** *Generydes* 2044 The Sowdon..rideth streyte to his pavilion, With lordes abought hym in euery rome. **1470–85** Malory *Arthur* x. xxxviii. 474 Ye may kepe the rome of thys Castel this twelue moneth and a day. **1533** Bellenden *Livy* ii. v. (S.T.S.) I. 145 This cocles, set be aventure in ane rovme maid for defence of þe said brig. **1540** *Test. Ebor.* (Surtees) VI. 94 For my rowme where I shalbe buried. **1611** Bible *Wisdom* xiii. 15 And when he had made a conuenient roume for it, set it in a wall. **1674** N. Fairfax *Bulk & Selv.* 30 If the Soul..settles in some room whence it may best..sway the whole body.

†**b.** *Sc.* A place in a series, narration, or logical sequence. *Obs.*

1590 Bruce *Serm. Sacram.* C 3 b, In the third roume, it coms in to be considered, how [etc.]. **1616** in Sprott *Scott. Liturgies Jas. VI* (1901) 19 We seeking Thy Kingdom and the righteousness of it in the first room. **1721** Wodrow *Hist. Suff. Ch. Scot.* (1830) II. 139/2 Thus, in the first room, our religious and reformation-rights, and next our lives and civil liberties, are laid at the King's feet. **1724** —— *Life J. Wodrow* (1828) 4 In the last room I shall give account of his manuscripts.

c. *spec.* (See quots.) Cf. *fishing-room* s.v. fishing *vbl. sb.*[1] 5 b.

1620 R. Whitbourne *Discourse & Discovery of New-found-land* 30 [They] doe cut downe many of the best trees they can finde, to build their stages and roomes..; hewing.. and destroying many others that grow within a mile of the Sea, where they use to fish. **1858** Simmonds *Dict. Trade*, *Room*, a fishing station in the British North American Provinces. **1937** P. K. Devine *Folk-Lore Newfoundland* (Gloss.), *Room*, a fishing premises: stage, flakes and store. **1948** *Canad. Geogr. Jrnl.* Mar. 110/1 Fishing off Labrador is carried on by fishermen who leave Newfoundland in May or June and reside at 'rooms' (buildings used by the fishermen) on various parts of the Labrador coast until the close of the season. **1954** F. Briffett *Story of Newfoundland & Labrador* 32 A man's fishing property—flakes, stages and stores—was known as his room. **1963** J. T. Rowland *North to Adventure* iv. 54 Most of the schooner men had permanent stations, or 'rooms',..with storehouses and fish stages. **1975** *Canad. Antiques Collector* Mar.–Apr. 10/2 Of a crew of 40, there would be 24 to man eight small boats and 16 to work on the room.

7. *Sc.* †**a.** *pl.* Domains, dominions, territories, bounds. *Obs.*

c **1470** Henry *Wallace* vi. 270 Sa he begane with strenth and stalwart hand To chewyss agayne sum rowmys off Scotland. **1533** Bellenden *Livy* i. iii. (S.T.S.) I. 26 The romanis incresčit Ilk day in new mvnitioun, bringand new rowmes vnder þare dominioun. **1560** Rolland *Seven Sages* 1 Rome..Conquest grit realmes, lordschips and rowmes braid. **1570** *Satir. Poems Reform.* xviii. 39 Lat neuer þai Ruffians within ȝour rowmis reill.

b. An estate in land; a piece of ground held or occupied by one; a farm. Now *rare.*

1500–20 Dunbar *Poems* lxxix. 6 For rekkyning of my rentis and roumes, ȝe neid nocht for to tyre ȝour thowmes. **1546** *Reg. Privy Council Scot.* I. 22 In thair personis, landes, rowmes, possessionis, and gudis. **1570** *Satir. Poems Reform.* xxiii. 30 Thair was sum that tuik thy rowmis in few. *c* **1657** Sir W. Mure *Hist. Ho. of Rowallane* Wks. (S.T.S.) II. 242 Garnegep and Calder, rowmes now not knowne by these names. **1688** W. Scot of Satchell *Hist. Name Scot* (1776) 45 Ev'ry pensioner a room did gain, For service done and to be done. **1808** Jamieson s.v., Room is still commonly used for a farm. **1818** Scott *Hrt. Midl.* xlv, Zealous professors, ..to whom the preceding Duke of Argyle had given rooms in this corner of his estate. **1884** *Scotsman* 26 July 3/1 Three merks..of Land in the room of Gord, Keotha, and Bremer in the Parish of Cunningsburgh.

8. a. An interior portion of a building divided off by walls or partitions; *esp.* a chamber or apartment in a dwelling-house. †Formerly also, a compartment, bay, stall (of a barn, stable, etc.).

See also the combs. *bed-*, *dining-*, *drawing-room*, etc.

1457–8 *Durh. Acc. Rolls* (Surtees) 637, j grangie de 5 rowmez... Pro factura j rowme in tenemento. **1556–7** *Cal. Rec. Dublin* (1889) I. 460 None shall devyde the dwelling howses of this cittie into sondrie rowlms for their private gayn. **1598** Shaks. *Merry W.* v. v. 61 Search Windsor Castle... Strew good lucke (Ouphes) on euery sacred roome. **1617** Moryson *Itin.* i. 58 Under the fortification of the Castle round about, are stables for horses, and some roomes for like purposes. **1653** Dorothy Osborne *Lett.* (1888) 132 'Tis a very fine seat, but..Sir Thomas Cheeke.. told me there was never a good room in the house. **1703** Neve *City & C. Purchaser* 61 To distribute the whole Ground-plot..into Rooms of Office, or Entertainment. **1760** Wesley *Wks.* (1872) III. 12, I was obliged once more to coop myself up in the Room. **1791** Mrs. Radcliffe *Rom. Forest* ii, The room appeared to have been built in modern times upon a Gothic plan. **1841** Lane *Arab. Nts.* I. 122 Low seats which generally extend along three sides of the room. **1891** E. Peacock *N. Brendon* II. 67 The rooms of the cottage were low.

transf. and *fig.* **1579** Spenser *Sheph. Cal.* Dec. 68 The honey Bee, Working her formall rowmes in wexen frame. **1608** Topsell *Serpents* (1653) 643 The whole Combe containeth four orders of Cells; the first the Bees occupy... The last is appointed for the room of Honey-making. **1629** Sir W. Mure *True Crucifix* 30 Our harts for Him..A rowme should bee to rest in, and reside.

b. *spec.* (chiefly *pl.*) a room or rooms for public gatherings, an assembly room, auction room, gambling room, etc.; at Lloyd's of London, the area where insurance business is carried out.

1766 C. Anstey *New Bath Guide* vii. 45 The Captain is come, And so kind as to go with us all to the Room. *Ibid.* viii. 48 (*heading*) Mr. B-n-r-d goes to the Rooms. His opinion of Gaming. **1771** Smollett *Humph. Cl.* I. 115 In the forenoon, they crawl out to the Rooms or the coffee-house. **1779** F. Burney *Diary* Oct. (1842) I. 254 In the evening we all went to the rooms. The rooms, as they are called, consisted, for this evening, of only one apartment, as there was not company enough to make more necessary. **1822** W. Hazlitt in *New Monthly Mag.* IV. 112 An old gentleman.. who looked as if he had played many a rubber at the Bath rooms. **1876** Geo. Eliot *Dan. Der.* I. ii. xv. 291 They moved off together to saunter through the rooms, Sir Hugo saying as they entered the large *saal*—'Did you play much at Baden, Grandcourt?' **1904** A. E. W. Mason *Truants* xxiii. 217 She..bought a visitor's list at the kiosk in front of the rooms. **1928** A. Christie *Mystery of Blue Train* xxvii. 214 He found [him] in the Rooms, jauntily placing the minimum stake on the even numbers. **1931** *N. & Q.* 29 Aug. 155/2 Book auctions.—May I voice a long overdue protest against the pernicious and iniquitous custom prevailing in the 'Rooms' of doing up parcels of books with string. **1933** D. C. Peel *Life's Enchanted Cup* x. 121 The Rooms were so crowded that I could not get near enough to play at my chosen table. **1946** G. Stimpson *Bk. about Thousand Things* 51 This bell, which hangs in a clock-topped tower in 'Lloyd's Rooms' was salvaged from the frigate Lutine. **1962** H. O. Beecheno *Introd. Business Stud.* xvi. 153 He [*sc.* the broker] will then take this in to 'the Room' at Lloyd's and approach one or more leading underwriters. **1972** [see old boy].

c. *pl.* Chambers or apartments occupied by a person or persons; lodgings.

1837 Dickens *Pickw.* ii, I trust I shall have the pleasure of seeing you and your friend at my rooms. **1879** Miss Braddon *Cloven Foot* xxviii, Can I have his rooms for a few nights? I..don't want to go to a hotel. **1886** C. E. Pascoe *London of To-day* xxii. (ed. 3) 213 The rooms of the Society of Arts..are in John Street.

d. *Sc.* and *north. dial.* (See quots.)

1795 *Statist. Acc. Scot.* XV. 339 The rent of a room and kitchen, or what in the language of the place is stiled a but and a ben. **1829** Hogg *Sheph. Cal.* vi, The Room, which, in those days, meant the only sitting apartment of a house. **1877** *Holderness Gloss.*, *Room*,..the parlour or sitting-room.

e. The persons assembled in a room; the company.

1712 Addison *Spect.* No. 269 ¶ 12 His venerable Figure drew upon us the Eyes of the whole Room. **1898** Hewlett *Forest Lovers* vi, As for the..old soul by the fire, she kept her back resolutely on the room.

9. In various technical applications:

a. One of the passages or spaces for working left between the pillars of a coal-mine. Chiefly in phr. ***pillar and room***, Sc. ***stoop and room.*** Cf. pillar *sb.* 7, post *sb.*[1] 7 d.

1789 J. Williams *Min. Kingd.* I. 8 The boards or rooms in which the colliers are working. **1839** Ure *Dict. Arts* 960 Each miner continues to advance his room or working-place, till [etc.]. *Ibid.* 975 [The system of] working with pillars and rooms, styled post and stall. **1883** Gresley *Gloss. Coal-m.* 206 *Room and Rance* (S.), a system of working coal somewhat similar to double stall. **1893** *Labour Commission Gloss.* s.v. *Stoop*, In the stoop and room the seam is divided into pillars called *stoops* by passages at right angles to each other called *rooms.*

b. A measure of coals (see quot. 1883).

1800 Colquhoun *Comm. Thames* iii. 147 Coals are sometimes bought by what is called the Room. **1824** *Mech. Mag.* 90 Some merchants..will promise to give sixty-eight sacks to a room. **1883** Gresley *Gloss. Coal-m.* 206 *Room*,.. a weight of 7 tons of coal, or $5\frac{1}{4}$ chaldrons by measure.

c. *Naut.* (See quot.)

1805 Mast-room [see mast *sb.*[1] 4 b]. *c* **1850** *Rudim. Nav.* (Weale) 143 *Rooms*, the different vacancies between the timbers, and likewise those between the beams, as the mast-rooms, capstan-room, hatch-room, &c.

d. *local.* The space between the thwarts of a boat. (A Scandinavian sense.)

1855 *Norfolk Words* in *Trans. Phil. Soc.* 35 *Room*, the space between thwarts. **1896** *Good Wds.* Jan. 17/1 The sean is shot. It had lain a huge brown heap in its proper 'room' or compartment of the boat. **1899** Spence *Folk-Lore* 127 The boat was divided into six compartments, viz., fore-head, fore-room, mid-room [etc.]... The shott was double the size of a room.

10. *attrib.* and *Comb.* **a.** (in sense 8), as ***room air***, ***-bell***, ***-door***, ***-grate***, ***number***, ***paper***, ***rent***, ***ticket***; ***room-fellow***, ***maid***, ***-keeper***; ***room-breaking*** vbl. sb.; **room clerk**, in a hotel, guest-house, etc., a clerk who assigns rooms to patrons; **room divider**: see divider 9; **room service**, the provision of food or drink for a hotel guest in his room, or the department providing this; **room temperature**, the temperature of a, or the, room, esp. that which is comfortable for occupants, conventionally taken as about 20°C; also *attrib.* and *fig.*; **room-to-room** *attrib.*, (of a telephone) connecting rooms within the same building.

1957 *Encycl. Brit.* XI. 353/1 Louis Savot..developed for the Louvre a fireplace in which room air was drawn through passages under the hearth and behind the fire grate. **1975** *New Yorker* 22 Dec. 78/3 He decided to discontinue Berger's oxygen therapy. He wanted him breathing room air again. **1861** *Chambers's Encycl.* II. 12/2 The use of room-bells is universal. **1951** S. Spender *World within World* 36 After the room-breaking episode the attitude of my fellow freshmen towards me altered. **1916** W. A. Du Puy *Uncle Sam, Detective* 49 The room clerk had suggested that it was the custom of the hotel that guests without baggage should pay in advance. **1978** S. Sheldon *Bloodline* xxxiii. 315 Before Max left Chamonix, he stopped at the desk of the Kleine Scheidegg hotel and talked to the room clerk. **1866** J. Macgregor *Rob Roy on Baltic* 192 The rioter is my English room-companion of the Norway inn. **1824** Scott *St. Ronan's* xxxviii, I'll bring word to your room-door.. how she is. **1930** R. Macaulay *Staying with Relations* ix. 122 Snakes might be her companions, wild cats her room-fellows, but she..abandoned herself to these. **1828** Moir *Mansie Wauch* 53 The prices of the room-grate, the bachelor's oven, the cheese-toaster. **1722** De Foe *Col. Jack* ii, One of our room-keepers says, he saw a couple of young rogues..hanging about there. **1922** Joyce *Ulysses* 304 The meal should be divided..among the members of the sick and indigent roomkeepers' association. **1955** A. Ross *Australia 55* xv. 212 The room-maid says the world will end, not with an atom bomb, but with a flood. **1976** *Evening*

Standard 14 June 26/3 (Advt.), Room maids, m/f, required by London Penta Hotel. **1959** A. CHRISTIE *Cat among Pigeons* iv. 54 Must have given me the wrong room number. **1968** 'M. CARROLL' *Dead Trouble* ii. 22 The receptionist.. asked what room number. **1976** H. NIELSEN *Brink of Murder* xii. 94 Send up a fifth of Buchanan's... You know my room number. **1870** P. FITZGERALD in *All Year Round* V. 112/1 The decorations of the Jericho Theatre are rather of a homely cast, room paper garnished with bead mouldings. **1973** *Canad. Antiques Collector* Jan.–Feb. 20/1 A few scattered stories of the early elegance of room paper survive. **1818** *N. Amer. Rev.* Mar. 427 The room rent and wood are estimated upon the condition that two students live in a College room. **1851** C. CIST *Sk. Cincinnati in 1851* 65 The annual term bill for room-rent.. and incidental expenses is ten dollars. **1883** *Cent. Mag.* Sept. 739 It pays room rent and lights. **1942** *Amer. Mercury* July 90 That meant.. maybe room rent and a reefer or two. **1930** A. BENNETT *Imperial Palace* vii. 32 The head floors-waiter did not conceal his belief that the room-service was the basis of prosperity. **1935** WODEHOUSE *Luck of Bodkins* xxiv. 311 If you go to that phone and call Room Service, you can get all the champagne you want. **1949** O. NASH *Versus* 99 (*title*) Mrs. Purvis dreads room service. **1965** I. FLEMING *Man with Golden Gun* vii. 94 Order what you want from Room Service. **1971** R. THOMAS *Backup Men* xviii. 156 The room service waiter.. brought the hamburgers and coffee. **1974** P. GORE-BOOTH *With Great Truth & Respect* 155 The only way I found of getting any relaxation at all was to be extravagant and have 'room service' breakfast. **1978** *Time* 3 July 47/2 Half-eaten room-service sandwiches. **1924** J. G. A. SKERL tr. *Wegener's Orig. Continents & Oceans* 128 They can prove that the earth is about two or three times as rigid at room-temperature as steel. **1945** R. T. ROLFE *Dict. Metallogr.* 4 It may consist.. of a period of standing at room temperature. **1959** J. BRAINE *Vodi* xiv. 193 Of course the red wine should be at room temperature. **1962** SIMPSON & RICHARDS *Physical Princ. Junction Transistors* ix. 211 The effect of these two factors is to make it desirable to place the operating point at a lower point than would be decided by room-temperature conditions. **1974** *Times* 13 Nov. 12/5 Put the mixture.. overnight in the refrigerator. Allow to come up to room temperature again before baking. **1976** I. LEVIN *Boys from Brazil* v. 143 He wasn't accorded a warm or even room-temperature welcome. **1977** *Nature* 17 Feb. 660/2 The bK_{590} intermediate.. has a lifetime of 2 μs at room temperature. **1905** A. BENNETT *Tales of Five Towns* II. 264 She pushed his room-ticket across the page of the big book. **1938** Room-to-room [see BUZZ *sb.*[1] 1 d]. **1786** ABERCROMBIE *Gard. Assist.* 291 Placing the glasses.. in a room-window to the sun.

b. ***room-bound, -ridden*** ppl. adjs., confined to one's room. ***room-sealed*** ppl. adj. (see quot. 1967).

1855 DICKENS *Little Dorrit* I. xv, As the room-ridden invalid settled for the night. **1857** MRS. MATHEWS *Tea-Table T.* II. 62, I was generally room-bound, and therefore unable to attend public worship. **1963** *B.S.I. News* May 15/2 B.S. 3561 refers to fan-assisted air heaters,.. and room-sealed heaters, giving requirements for their construction and performance. **1967** *Gloss. Terms Gas Industry* (*B.S.I.*) 78 *Room-sealed appliance*, an appliance which, when in operation, has the combustion air inlet and the combustion products outlet isolated from the room in which the appliance is installed.

III. †**11. a.** A place in which one is stationed or seated; a particular place assigned or appropriated to a person or thing. *Obs.*

a **1400–50** *Alexander* 330 With þat rysis vp þe renke & his rowme lefys. *c* **1489** CAXTON *Blanchardyn* xxx. 113 Euery man cam forth for to doo his deuoyre, eche of hem in his rowme in defending the place. **1513** SIR T. MORE *Rich. III*, Wks. 42/1 To whome the Duke of Buckingham saide, goe afore Gentlemenne and yomen, kepe youre rowmes. **1565** JEWEL *Reply Harding* (1611) 213 Eustathius.. was the President, and the Bishop of Romes Legates.. sate in the fourth roome beneath. **1593** SHAKS. *Rich. II*, v. v. 108 Go thou and fill another roome in hell. **1610** FLETCHER *Faithf. Sheph.* IV. i, A blast.. by chance may come, And blow some one thing to his proper room. **1672** DAVIES *Rites Durham* 33 Were placed, in their several Rooms, one above another, the most excellent Pictures. **1698** [R. FERGUSON] *View Eccles.* 8 The Terms Mr. Lobb hath been contending for, are not hitherto allowed a room in the Confessions of Faith of the Reformed Churches. **1721** WODROW *Hist. Suff. Ch. Scotl.* (1830) II. 140/2 The 11th act of this session.. deserves a room in this collection.

transf. *c* **1611** CHAPMAN *Iliad* IX. 568 All the Greeks will honour thee, as of celestiall roome.

b. Contrasted with *company*, in phrases denoting that the absence of a person is preferred to his presence. Also *transf.*

1577 STANYHURST *Descr. Irel.* 7/2 For such a scoffing prelate, hys rowme had bene better then his company. **1603** HOLLAND *Plutarch's Mor.* 645 Better his roome, than company (quoth ech one). **1646** FULLER *Wounded Consc.* (1841) 283 Preferring his room, and declining his company, lest his sadness prove infectious to themselves. **1672** H. MORE *Brief Reply* 306, I must confess I had rather have their [*sc.* images] room than their Company. **1724** H. JONES *Virginia* 53 Felons.. whose Room they had much rather have than their Company. **1770** *Placid Man* II. 219 You would as lief have my room as my company. **1880** *Adam & Eve* 328 I'd rather have his room than his company.

†**c.** A place or seat in the theatre. *Obs.*

1599 B. JONSON *Ev. Man out of Hum.* II. i, Yet he pours them [names] out as familiarly, as if he had.. ta'en tobacco with them over the stage, in the lord's room. **1600** E. BLOUNT *Hosp. Incurable Fooles* Ep. Ded., I beg it with as forced a looke, as a Player that in speaking an Epilogue makes loue to the two pennie-roume for a plaudite. **1611** CORYAT *Crudities* 248 They sate on high alone by themselues in the best roome of all the Play-house. *a* **1619** [see *penny-room*, s.v. PENNY 12].

†**d.** *transf.* A settled place *in* a person's affection or regard. *Obs.*

1598–9 FORD *Parismus* I. (1636) 121 Let Pollipus.. be the man that shall possess the second room in your good liking. **1607** HIERON *Wks.* I. 211 Are these things strangers to thy thoughts, or doe they take vp a chiefe roome in thy affections? **1685** BAXTER *Par. N.T.* Phil. i. 7 You have a great room in my heart.

†**12. a.** An office, function, appointment; a post, situation, employment. *Obs.*

Exceedingly common in the 16th century.

c **1483** BARADOUN in *Pol., Rel., & L. Poems* (1903) 289 In the courte, is many noble Roome; But god knowith, I can noon soche cacche. **1485** *Rolls of Parlt.* VI. 357/2 Th' Office or Rowme of oon of the Yomen of oure Crowne. **1514** *Mem. Ripon* (Surtees) I. 303 We have yeven and graunted unto hym th' office and rowme of baner berer befor S. Wilfride. **1589** *Hay any Work* 19 To haue the romes of the true and natural members of the body. **1598** R. GRENEWEY *Tacitus, Ann.* VI. iii. (1622) 125 One is appointed over the rest to exercise the roome of a Consull. **1605** CAMDEN *Rem.* (1623) 249 He.. forsooke a right worshipfull roome when it was offered him. **1644** BULWER *Chirol.* 146 That none should be admitted into roomes of divine calling, but such who are called and are fit.

†**b.** Without article: Office, position, authority.

1480 *Robt. Devyll* in Hazl. *E.P.P.* I. 37 A Jue sate at the borde, that greate rowme longe In that house beare. **1509** BARCLAY *Shyp of Folys* (1874) II. 13 If that thou be hye of rowme and name If thou offende the more shall be thy shame. **1541** PAYNELL *Catiline* iv. 5 To some desirous therof he behight roume and auctoritie. **1582** N. T. (Rhem.) *John* x. 1 *note*, Calvin, Luther,.. and al that succede them in roome and doctrine.

†**c.** ***to bear* (*the*) *room***, to be in office or authority; to have all the power. *Obs.*

1526 SKELTON *Magnyf.* 786 Beryst thou any rome, or cannyst thou do ought? **1530** in Furniv. *Ballads fr. MSS.* I. 317 Marchaunte Straryngers beryth the Rowme. **1534** WHITINTON *Tullyes Offices* II. (1540) 99 In that yere that I bare roume.

†**13. a.** An office or post considered as pertaining to a particular person, *esp.* by right or by inheritance. *Obs.*

c **1450** HOLLAND *Howlat* 984 Bot thow reule the richtuiss, thi rovme sall orere. **1513** BRADSHAW *St. Werburge* I. 2517 This noble abbesse.. dylygently prepared to supple her rowme. **1586** J. HOOKER *Hist. Irel.* in *Holinshed* II. 151 He.. procured them to be remoued, and their roomes to be supplied with.. learned Englishmen. **1628** MILTON *Vac. Exerc.* 58 Then quick about thy purpos'd business come, That to the next I may resign my Roome. **1651** N. BACON *Disc. Govt. Eng.* II. i. (1739) 7 The Dukes.. forsake the Court, Favourites step into their rooms. **1699** T. C[OCKMAN] *Tully's Offices* (1706) 290 That Man.. that outs the rightful Heirs.. and procures himself to be put into their Rooms. **1751** LABELYE *Westm. Bridge* 83 The Rooms of those removed or dead, being filled up with Persons fully as honest.

b. ***in one's room***, in one's place, denoting substitution of one person or thing for another. (In early use with reference to offices or appointments.)

(*a*) **1489** CAXTON *Faytes of A.* III. viii. 183 Takynge his leue he sayth to the captayne that he shall putte another for hym in his rowme. **1560** DAUS tr. *Sleidane's Comm.* 279 In whose roume afterward succeded George Selde a Civilan. **1581** PETTIE tr. *Guazzo's Civ. Conv.* II. (1586) 53 b, That he may be put from his office, and some other placed in his roome. **1631** WEEVER *Anc. Funeral Mon.* 69 Detaining many of them in prison.. that others of his owne followers might bee placed in their roomes. **1667** MILTON *P.L.* III. 285 Be thou in Adams room The Head of all mankind. **1706** VANBRUGH *Mistake* 11, A proposal.. to take you (who then were just Camillo's age) and bring you up in his room. **1771** *Chron.* in *Ann. Reg.* 137 The names of the Earl of Granard.. and Lord Sudley.. to be added to the list in their room. **1800** SCOTT *Let.* in *Lockhart* (1837) I. x. 321, I refer you for particulars to Joseph, in whose room I am now assuming the pen. **1883** *Catholic Dict.* s.v. *Carthusians*, With grief he [St. Bruno] left his beloved companions, the most prudent.. of whom, Landwin, he appointed prior in his room.

(*b*) **1599** SHAKS. *Much Ado* I. i. 304 Warre-thoughts Haue left their places vacant: in their roomes Come thronging soft and delicate desires. **1673** AUSTEN *Fruit Trees* II. 148 As these are removed the husbandman plants others in their roomes. **1712** J. JAMES tr. *Le Blond's Gardening* 172 If several Elms should die successively in the same Place, you should put Lime-Trees.. in their Rooms. **1774** GOLDSM. *Nat. Hist.* (1776) III. 354 The old long hair falling off, and a shorter coat of hair appearing in its room.

c. ***in the room of***, in the place (†or office) *of*, in lieu *of*, instead *of*, a person or thing. (Cf. prec.)

(*a*) **1535** COVERDALE *Matt.* ii. 22 But when he herde that Archelaus did raynge in Iury, in ye rowme of his father Herode. **1599** HAKLUYT *Voy.* II. II. 60 So we placed other men in the roomes of those that we lost. **1667** PEPYS *Diary* 1 Sept., The Attorney General is made Chief Justice in the room of my Lord Bridgeman. **1709** STEELE *Tatler* No. 11 ¶9 Declared Alderman.. in the Room of his Brother,.. deceased. **1838** THIRLWALL *Greece* IV. 41 A Spartan named Leon.. had taken the command in the room of Pedaritus. **1854** MISS BAKER *Northampt. Gloss.* s.v., He went in the room of another.

(*b*) **1615** W. LAWSON *Country Housew. Garden* (1626) 30 An eye or bud, taken.. from one tree, and placed in the roome of another eye or bud. **1668** HALE *Pref. Rolle's Abridgment* 4 It is much out of use, and new Expedients substituted in roome thereof. **1736** BUTLER *Anal.* I. v, To substitute judgment in the room of sensation. **1749** FIELDING *Tom Jones* v. iv, You must let me have my old one again, and you may have this in the room on't. **1846** TRENCH *Huls. Lect.* Ser. II. i. 142 In the room of shifting cloud-palaces.. stands for us a City which hath come down from heaven.

d. Used with vbl. sbs. Now *dial.*

1802 MRS. E. PARSONS *Myst. Visit* III. 144 In the room of loitering about Paris.. I shall have the.. pleasure of being.. a little useful. **1828** CARR *Craven Gloss.* [see Forms β.]. **1861** *Macm. Mag.* Dec. 141/2 Missis would still keep going on with her parties and company, o' rum o' minding her farm and dairy.

room (ruːm), *sb.*[2] *Obs.* exc. *dial.* Also 6 rome, roome. [Of obscure origin.] Scurf on the head; dandruff.

1578 LYTE *Dodoens* 262 The same.. doth cure.. the scurffe or roome of the head. *Ibid.* 410 The lye.. is very good to washe the scurffe of the head,.. causing the rome and scales to fall off. **1847** HALLIW., *Room*, dandruff. *Somerset.* **1886** ELWORTHY *W. Somerset Wd.-Bk.* s.v.

room (ruːm), *a.* *Obs.* exc. *Sc.* Forms: 1, 3 rum, 3 rume; 4–5 roume (4 roumm), 4–6 rowm(e, 5 rowmme; 4–5 rome, 5 romme, rombe; 6–9 room (7 roome). [Common Teut.: OE. *rúm*, = OFris. *rūm* (mod.Fris. *rûm, rom*), MDu. *ruum, ruym* (Du. *ruim*), MLG. *rûm, ruem* (LG. *rûm*), OHG. *rûmi*, ON. *rúmr* (Sw. and Da. *rum*, Norw. *rom*): cf. ROOM *sb.*[1]]

†**1.** Spacious, large, ample in dimensions; wide, extensive. *Obs.*

Beowulf 2462 þuhte him eall to rum wongas & wic-stede. *c* **825** *Vesp. Psalter* xxx. 9 Ðu ȝesettes in stowe rumre foet mine. *Ibid.* ciii. 25 Ðis sæ, micel & rum. *c* **888** K. ÆLFRED *Boeth.* xix. §1 Behealde he.. hu neara þære eorðan stede is, þeah heo us rum þince. *c* **1000** *Ags. Gosp.* Matt. vii. 13 Se weȝ is swiðe rum, þe to forspillednesse ȝelæt. *c* **1200** ORMIN 3689 He wollde ȝifenn uss All heoffness rume riche. *c* **1250** *Owl & Night.* 643 Mi nest is holeuh & rum amidde. *a* **1300** *Cursor M.* 3318 Fodder and hai þou sal find bun; Na roummer sted in al þe tun. *a* **1340** HAMPOLE *Psalter* lxxvii. 15 In þe felde of thaneos, þat is, in þe rowme stede of meke comaundment. *c* **1386** CHAUCER *Reeve's T.* 225 Ther was no rommer herberwe in the place. ? *a* **1400** *Morte Arth.* 3470 A renke in a rownde cloke, with righte rowmme clothes. **1423** JAS. I *Kingis Q.* lxxvii, I was anon In broght Within a chamber, large, rowm, and faire. *c* **1470** HENRY *Wallace* VII. 986 A rowme passage to the wallis [thai] thaim dycht. **1535** STEWART *Cron. Scot.* I. 379 He set his feild furth on ane rowmar plane. **1560** ROLLAND *Seven Sages* 13 Lat vs þair mak ane hous baith rowme & squair. *c* **1635** CAPT. BOTELER *Dial. Sea Serv.* (1685) 133 It causeth a Ship to be much Roomer (that is larger) within Board.

†**b.** ***the room sea***, the open sea. *Obs.*[−1]

c **1400** *Sc. Trojan War* II. 1978 Tharfor in haist to þe rowme se Thai torned and held on þar way.

†**c.** Open to choice. *Obs.*[−1]

1481 CAXTON *Reynard* (Arb.) 108 Whan reynard herde that it stode so rowme that he shold chese to knowleche hym ouercomen and yelde hym Or ellis to take the deth.

†**2. a.** Distant, remote. *Obs. rare.*

c **1449** PECOCK *Repr.* I. xiv. 79 Doom of resoun.. as the next and best reule, and the power of resoun as for the rombe and ferther reule. *Ibid.* II. xx. 272 Into departing and disseuering and into rombe distaunt being.

†**b.** Of winds: = LARGE *a.* 14. *Obs.*

1632 LITHGOW *Trav.* II. 45 This hauen wherein we lay, expecting roome windes. *Ibid.* 59 Having roome windes, and a fresh gale, in 24. houres we discovered the Ile.

3. *Sc.* Clear, unobstructed, empty.

Some cognate uses are found in OE. texts.

1641 FERGUSON *Sc. Prov.* 4 b, A fair fire makes a roome flet. **1710** RUDDIMAN *Gloss. Douglas' Æneis* s.v. *Rowme*, We say, To make a room house, when one drives them out that are in it. **1810** J. COCK *Simple Strains* I. 142 (E.D.D.), When in their beds and snugly laid There's silence and a room fireside.

†**4.** *Comb.*: **room-handed, -hende** *adjs.*, liberal, generous; **room-house**, a privy (cf. *long-house* s.v. LONG *a.* 18). *Obs.*

c **1200** *Trin. Coll. Hom.* 29 ȝef þu.. best rum-handed to glewmen. *c* **1205** LAY. 6538 He wes.. radful and rihtwis and a mete rum-hende. *c* **1250** *Owl & Night.* 652 Men habbeþ among oþre iwende A rum-hus at heore bures ende.

room, obs. variant of RUM *a.*

room, *adv.* Forms: 1 rume, 4 romme, 4, 6–7 rome, 6–7 room(e. *Comp.* 6 rowmer, 6–7 romer, 7 roamer, rummore. [OE. *rúme*, f. *rúm* adj., = OS. and OHG. *rûmo*.]

†**1.** Widely; far and wide; to or at a distance. *Obs.*

a **1000** *Genesis* 1456 Heo wide hire willan sohte & rume fleah. *Ibid.* 1895 Sceoldan.. þa rincas þy rumor secan ellor eðelseld. **1340–70** *Alex. & Dind.* 80 Whi farest þou so fihtinge, folk to distroie, & for to winne þe word wendest so romme? *Ibid.* 581 Of richesse & of renoun romme be ȝe kidde. *c* **1449** PECOCK *Repr.* v. xiii. 553 Whilis thei stonden or sitten or knelen rombe fer ech from othir.

2. Amply; fully; to the full. Now *dial.*

a **1000** *Genesis* 1372 Drihten.. rume let willeburnan on woruld þringan. *c* **1000** *Saxon Leechd.* I. 282 Hyt rum þa wyrmas forð ȝelædeþ. **13..** *Sir Beues* 1860 þe geaunt was wonder-strong, Rome þretti fote long. **1969** G. M. BROWN *Orkney Tapestry* 134 Guidman, go to your bacon And cut us doon a daggon Cut it lucky, cut it room, Look 'at you dunno cut your toom.

3. *Naut.* **a.** = LARGE *adv.* 7 a.

Very common from *c* 1580 to 1630.

1564 SPARKE in *Hawkins' Voy.* (Hakl. Soc.) 10 He espied another Island,.. and being not able.. to fetch it by night, went roomer untill the morning. **1585** T. WASHINGTON tr. *Nicholay's Voy.* I. xi. 13 Leauing the coast.. we bare roome to seawards. **1597** J. PAYNE *Royal Exch.* 33 Hale bollinge to double the poynt, a luff from the rock, rowmer from the sand. **1622** *Relat. Eng. Plantation Plymouth* in Arber *Pilgr. Fathers* (1897) 435 We could not fetch the harbour, but were fain to put room again, towards Cape Cod. **1669** STURMY *Mariner's Mag.* I. ii. 19 The Chase pays away more room. *Ibid.*, The Chase goes away room, her Sheets are both aft. **1902** J. M. BARRIE *Little White Bird* xv. 163 He was drifted towards the far shore, where are black shadows he knew not the dangers of, but suspected them, and so.. went roomer of the shadows until he caught a favouring wind.

b. Const. *with* the land, etc.

1537 *Adm. Court Exemplifications* I. No. 174 Seeing a ship coming somewhat rome with theym. **1557** JENKINSON in Hakluyt *Voy.* (1599) I. 310 The wind vering more northerly, we were forced to put roomer with the coast of England againe. *Ibid.*, We were forced to beare roomer with Flamborow head.

room (ru:m), *v.*[1] Now *dial.* or *arch.* Forms: 1 rumian, 3–4 rumen, 3–5 rume (5 ruym); 4–5 roume (5 reume), 5–6 rowm(e, 6 rovm; 5 rom(e, 9 room. [OE. *rúmian*, f. *rúm* ROOM *a.*; perh. formed anew in ME. Parallel forms are Fris. *rûmje, romje*, Da. *rumme*, Fær. *rúma*, Norw. *roma*. The usual OE. verb was *rýman*: see RIME *v.*[4]]

†**1. a.** *intr.* To become clear of obstructions.

c **1000** *Saxon Leechd.* I. 76 Drince ðreo ful fulle on niht nistiȝ; þonne rumað him [*sc.* the man] sona se innað.

†**b.** *trans.* To clear (the throat). *Obs.*⁻¹

1483 CAXTON *Gold. Leg.* 372 b/1 Take a softe egge and bere hit to suster Andree of ferriere for to rume her throte.

2. *trans.* To clear (a space) from persons or things, esp. by superior force. Now *arch.*

a **1375** *Joseph Arim.* 597 Euer-more þe white kniht hem þe place roumede. *c* **1425** WYNTOUN *Cron.* IX. xxv. 3182 Quhen þe feld was rowmyt swa, The Duke of Burgone.. On a syd enterit in þe place. *c* **1489** CAXTON *Sonnes of Aymon* ix. 245 Guycharde and I shall rowme the waye afore you. *c* **1500** *Lancelot* 3385 Neuer mycht be sen His suerd to rest, that in the gret rout He rowmyth all the compas hyme about. **1513** DOUGLAS *Æneis* XII. xii. 38 Quhen voydit weill and rowmyt was the feild.

1816 W. TAYLOR in *Monthly Mag.* XLI. 527 For them the monks had room'd their eating hall.

†**b.** To remove, shift. *Obs.*⁻¹

13.. *Seuyn Sag.* 2468 (W.), Th' emperour had wonder of this, And let reume his bed.

†**3. a.** *intr.* To give way; to depart. *Obs.*

c **1330** R. BRUNNE *Chron. Wace* (Rolls) 13072 On alle sides he smot aboute, & made þeym roum [*text* rounn] þorow-out þe route. **1340–70** *Alex. & Dind.* 2 Whan þis weith at his wil weduring hadde, Ful raþe rommede he rydinge þedirre.

†**b.** *trans.* To vacate, leave, abandon. *Obs.*

1393 LANGL. *P. Pl.* C. I. 189 And yf he [a cat] wratthe, we mowe be war and hus way roume. **1481** CAXTON *Reynard* (Arb.) 31 Many of his lignage.. token leue soroufully, and romed the court. *Ibid.* 61 On the morow erly he ruymed his castel and wente with grymbart. **1513** DOUGLAS *Æneis* X. viii. 18 Seand Rutylianis Withdraw the feyld sa swyth, and rovm the planis. **1566** DRANT *Horace, Sat.* vi. D vj, I may rome my mastership, wheresoeuer lyketh me.

†**c.** *refl.* To betake (oneself) *off*; to give (oneself) free scope. *Obs.*

1598 W. PHILLIP tr. *Linschoten* I. xcii. 148 Comming with the ship,.. he had almost laid her on ye same place, where the other was cast away: but day comming on, they romde themselues off, and so escaped. **1621** R. BOLTON *Stat. Irel.* 313 He had a scope of a hundred and twentie miles long and a hundred and odd miles broade to runne and roome himself.

4. *trans.* To extend, enlarge. *Obs.* exc. *dial.*

a **1300** *Cursor M.* 14922 Es resun þat wee vr rime rume And set fra nu langer bastune. *c* **1325** *Chron. Eng.* 83 in Ritson *Metr. Rom.* II. 273 Fourti fet, roumede and grete, Into the see he made him lepe. *c* **1425** WYNTOUN *Cron.* VII. (Wemyss) 1936 Than Iohne bischop of Glasgw Rowmyt þe kirk of Sanct Mongw.

1894 HESLOP *Northumbld. Gloss.*, *Rooming-down*, extending the bottom of a bore hole. A term used by sinkers.

room (ru:m), *v.*[2] Also *Sc.* 6– roum, rowm. [f. ROOM *sb.*[1]]

†**1.** *Sc.* **a.** *trans.* To install. *Obs. rare.*

1567 *Reg. Privy Council Scot.* I. 533 To that effect that he may be inaugurat, placeit, and rowmit thairin. **1663** SIR G. MACKENZIE *Relig. Stoic* xii. (1685) 114 Nothing is roomed in our judgment and apprehension but what first entered.

†**b.** To assign (common pasturage) proportionally among the different 'rooms' or lands entitled to share in it.

Used only in connexion with SOUM *v.*; for illustrations see that word.

2. chiefly *U.S.* **a.** *intr.* To occupy rooms as a lodger; to share a room or rooms *with* another; to live *together* in the same room(s). Also *to room it.*

1828 MRS. STOWE *Let.* in *Life* (1889) ii. 41 She rooms with me, and is very interesting and agreeable. **1856** —— *Dred* ii, Clayton and Russel had.. roomed together their four years in college. **1860** *Ann. Amherst College* 47 Many of the students who roomed in the College lost their all. **1888** HOWELLS *A. Kilburn* iii, I didn't let him room in your part of the house; that is to say, not sleep there. **1912** F. M. HUEFFER *Panel* I. i. 19 She and me were on the old North Circuit. Roomed it and ate off the same old herring together. **1937** *Observer* 22 Aug. 7/2 He dressed like a hobo, hitch-hiked from San Francisco to Los Angeles, and roomed on the town's Main Street as a plain British seaman. **1969** L. MICHAELS *Going Places* 167 Slotsky helped him with chemistry and French—Finn's reason for rooming with him in the first place. **1973** *Time* 25 June 11/1 John.. roomed with Barry Goldwater Jr., who now is his neighbor. **1977** *Western Mail* (Cardiff) 5 Mar. (Rugby Suppl.) 4/2 It was on that tour that I developed a close friendship with many of the Welsh players... TGR and JPR I roomed with on many occasions, waiting on them hand and foot. **1979** *Yale Alumni Mag.* Apr. (Suppl.) cn12/1 Charlie, with whom I roomed, stayed through freshman year.

b. *trans.* To accommodate or lodge (guests).

1860 *Blackw. Mag.* Jan. 112/2 A miserable public house, where I was 'roomed', or in other words, put into the same room with, a rising medical practitioner. **1864** *Daily Tel.* 13 Oct., The door's open, and if they couldn't room any more guests they'd pretty soon close up, I guess. **1892** *Rep. Amer. Mission. Assoc.* 101 We have to room them with the normal and college students in the college buildings.

†**room**, *v.*[3] *Obs.*⁻¹ ? To stretch out, aim *at*.

a **1400–50** *Alexander* 2466 Roomes [*v.r.* rooues] noȝt at þe raynbowe þat reche ȝe ne may.

room, obs. form of ROAM *v.*, ROME.

'**roomage.** *U.S. rare.* [f. ROOM *sb.*[1] + -AGE.] Space; internal capacity; accommodation.

1843 WHITTIER *Cassandra Southwick* 110 Pack with coins of Spanish gold.. The roomage of her hold. **1865** BURRITT *Walk Land's End* vi. 209 Mat and seat the rotunda of St. Paul's, and the nave of Westminster, to every foot of their magnificent roomage. *Ibid.* xii. 399 It entertained Charles II in its best guest and banquet room, and William Prynne with coarser roomage and fare.

roomage, obs. variant of RUMMAGE.

roomal, variant of ROMAL.

rooman, var. ROMAN *sb.*[3]

†**roome**, obs. variant of RHOMB.

1627 CAPT. SMITH *Seaman's Gram.* xv. 73 For to learne to .. know the tides, your Roomes, pricke your Card, say your Compasse.

Roome, obs. form of ROME.

roomed (ru:md), *a.* [f. ROOM *sb.*[1] + -ED.] With defining word prefixed: Having rooms of a specified number or kind, as *one-*, *double-*, *many-roomed*; also *wide-roomed*, †spacious.

1548 UDALL, etc. *Luke* xiii. 115 b, Thei that are of suche sortes, dooe choose the brode and the wyde roumed waie. **1610** HEALEY *St. Aug. Citie of God* 566 The Arke had roomes below and roomes above, and therefore was called double roomed. **1840** LOUDON *Cottager's Man.* (L.U.K.) 30 Transforming every two-roomed hut into such cottages. **1890** [see FOUR C. 1 b]. **1895** SCULLY *Kafir Stories* 57 A little one-roomed building, set apart for guests.

roome(d)ge, obs. forms of RUMMAGE.

'**roomer**, *sb.* [f. ROOM *v.*[2] 2 a.]

1. A lodger who occupies a room or rooms without board. orig. *U.S.*

1871 L. H. BAGG *4 Years at Yale* 46 *Roomer*, a word used by landladies to designate a lodger or occupant of a room who takes his meals elsewhere. **1887** *Ohio State Jrnl.* 2 Sept., Complaint had been made by some of the roomers in the Mithoff block. **1889** *N.Y. Evening Post* 29 Dec., On the third floor were a number of roomers. **1905** 'O. HENRY' in *N.Y. World Mag.* 20 Aug. 4/2 There was rejoicing among the gentlemen roomers whenever Miss Leeson had time to sit on the steps. **1912** J. SANDILANDS *Western Canad. Dict.*, *Roomer*, a lodger who has living accommodation in a house and gets his food elsewhere. **1919** *Studies* VIII. 304 There is no 'board' provided, but simply a room... A 'roomer' has all the perfect liberty of a latchkey... She can entertain what visitors she likes in her own room. **1939** *Sun* (Baltimore) 6 Jan. 1/2 Held with Joseph Malone, 27, as a material witness was Elizabeth Gelula, 23,.. a third-floor roomer. **1959** M. CHAMBERLIN *Dear Friends & Darling Romans* v. 50 There were, besides me, two other roomers in the apartment. *a* **1968** M. RICHLER in R. Weaver *Canad. Short Stories* (1968) 2nd Ser. 151 'Meet your new roomer,' Mervyn said. **1973** *Kingston* (Ontario) *Whig-Standard* 5 Mar. 28 (Advt.), Roomers, $15 weekly with kitchen facilities. **1976** *National Observer* (U.S.) 25 Sept. 8/2 A roomer who had been helping to install some additional bathrooms was heating wax on a hot plate in his room.

2. With a numeral prefixed: a house with that number of rooms, as *six-roomer*.

1853 *Dickens Bleak Ho.* lxiv. 612 'It's a six roomer, exclusive of kitchens,' said Mr. Guppy, 'and in the opinion of my friends, a commodious tenement.' **1972** *Daily Tel.* 8 Mar. 22 Some high figures for Chelsea houses—£29,000 for a six-roomer in First Street.

†'**roomery.** *Obs.*⁻¹ [ad. Sp. *romeria*, f. *Roma* ROME.] A pilgrimage.

1665 SIR T. HERBERT *Trav.* (1677) 62 In his Roomery in the way to Medina.. he was wounded to death.

roo'mette. *N. Amer.* [f. ROOM *sb.*[1] + -ETTE.] A small sleeping-compartment on a train; also, a small bedroom for letting. Also *attrib.*

1938 *Sun* (Baltimore) 14 June 20/2 The roomettes are small, completely inclosed rooms with accommodations for one traveler. Washstands fold into the walls after use. **1945** *Sci. Amer.* Mar. 170 Two-Story Pullmans—.. the cost margin is reduced to a narrower point in the new duplex roomette car... Each roomette has individual control of heat, light, and air conditioning. **1957** *New Yorker* 26 Oct. 68/3 Seated in his roomette, he opened the paper nervously. **1960** *Times* 19 Jan. 16/5 Travellers seeking rest between planes will rent roomettes, containing bed and bath, by the hour. **1971** *Guardian* 15 Sept. 11/1 Wandering from my roomette to the observation car as Canadian National transported me through the Rockies. **1974** *News & Courier* (Charleston, S. Carolina) 17 Feb. 1-A/8 The 9:40 arrives at 9:55 and everyone piles on—except me. My reserved 'roomette' is gone because a car was taken off the train somewhere between Jacksonville and Savannah. **1976** *Billings* (Montana) *Gaz.* 30 June 5-D/6 (Advt.), Chalet Roomette, private bath, refrigerator, washing facilities, $75 + dep. **1980** *Times* 4 Feb. 12/5, I was in a single sleeper, which Amtrak [*sc.* an American railway corporation] call a 'roomette'—probably the ugliest composite word ever invented. **1980** *Daily Tel.* 7 Nov. 15/1 He settled into his cramped, double-glazed Australian train cabin ('Roomette' in Strine).

room-free, *a. Sc.* and *north.* Also 3–4 rum-, 4–5 roum-fre. [f. ROOM *sb.*[1] + FREE *a.*]

†**1.** Entitled to free accommodation in a mill for the purpose of having one's corn ground. *Obs.*

1279 *Percy Chartulary* (Surtees) 233 Erunt rumfre et multurfre ad molendinum de Wllouer de omnibus bladis suis. *a* **1300** in Hodgson *Hist. Northumb.* (1832) II. 118 Liberi sint a multura.. et sint Rumfre propinquius quod molant post me ipsum et post bladum inventum in trimodio. **1315–7** in *Laing Charters* (1899) 7 Quod ipsi sint rumfre in eodem molendino.. quandocunque voluerint molere blada. **1484–5** *Extr. Rec. Peebles* (1872) 31 We find at the cornes of Corscunnyngfeld aucht to be rowme free in the myln of Peblis to the fourti corne.

2. (See quot.)

1887 *Jamieson's Dict.* Suppl. s.v., To sit *room-free* in a dwelling-house means to sit *rent-free*; and to hold a property *room-free* is to hold it without paying the usual burghal duties.

'**roomful**, *sb.* [f. ROOM *sb.*[1] + -FUL 2.] As much or as many as a room will hold.

1710 SWIFT *Exam.* No. 25 ¶8 Where it is a Man's Business to entertain a whole Room-full, it is unmannerly to apply himself to a particular Person. **1772** FRANKLIN *Lett.* Wks. 1887 IV. 537 [Of books] I brought none with me, and have now a roomful. **1841** BROWNING *Pippa Passes* ii, This room-full of rough block-work. **1850** THACKERAY *Pendennis* xxv[i], One day he went to the Hall, and there was a roomful of visitors. **1884** 'EDNA LYALL' *We Two* xxvi, She.. had to serve her roomful of enemies.

'**roomful**, *a. rare.* [f. ROOM *sb.*[1] + -FUL 1.] Capacious, ample, roomy.

1601 DONNE *Progr. Soul* xxxiv. Wks. (Grosart) I. 82 Now in a roomefull house this soule doth floate. **1892** BROOKE *E.E. Lit.* II. xvi. 85 He reared aloft the Firmament and this roomful land stablished.

room-handed, -house: see ROOM *a.* 4.

'**roomie**, *sb. U.S. colloq.* Also roomy. [f. ROOM *sb.*[1] + -IE.] A room-mate.

1918 *Sat. Even. Post* 6 July 5/3, I wouldn't make no holler at that if they had of left us pick our own roomys. **1945** *Richmond* (Va.) *Times-Dispatch* 26 July 14/7 Short-stop Skeeter Newsome, 'Inky's' roomie on the road, went home because of illness in his family. **1967** 'E. QUEEN' *Face to Face* xvi. 76 The Temple girl is given an alibi by her roomie. **1973** J. WAMBAUGH *Blue Knight* viii. 122, I called Craz my old roomie because.. twenty years ago, I moved into this big house with him. **1976** 'B. SHELBY' *Great Pebble Affair* 77 One of the screws came and rattled the bars on my cage. 'Hey... We finally got you a roomie.'

'**roomily**, *adv.* [f. ROOMY *a.* + -LY[2].] With plenty of room; amply, spaciously.

1818 *Edin. Mag.* Oct. 329 We roomily dwell in the heather-bell. **1855** KINGSLEY *Westw. Ho!* xxi, Walls,.. some twelve feet high, between which the whole crew.. were housed roomily. **1884** RIDER HAGGARD *Dawn* 25 Her figure was so finely proportioned and so roomily made.

'**roominess.** [f. ROOMY *a.* + -NESS.] The quality of being roomy or spacious; capaciousness.

1840 MOORE *Mem.* (1856) VII. 275 Russell's berth was.. the chief object of our attention, and I was most agreeably surprised by its roominess. **1856** STONEHENGE *Brit. Rural Sports* II. III. i. 392/1 A bolder and fuller head, with great width and general roominess of skull. **1892** E. REEVES *Homeward Bound* 198 We prefer our old friend's saloon, passages, and general roominess.

fig. **1889** DIGGLE *Life Bp. Fraser* i. 13 This complete unselfishness gave Bishop Fraser great intellectual roominess.

'**rooming**, *vbl. sb.* [f. ROOM *v.*[2]] **1. a.** The letting of rooms to lodgers. **b.** The occupying or sharing of rooms. Chiefly *attrib.* See also ROOMING-HOUSE

1959 *Listener* 11 June 1012/1 Houses that are now usually converted into rooming apartments of inconvenient character. **1967** *Economist* 21 Oct. 264/2 The crowded rooming areas of central London. **1968** *Globe & Mail* (Toronto) 3 Feb. 41/1 (Advt.), Large family home 8 rooms huge kitchen 2 washrooms garage, walk-out basement to backyard. Perfect area for rooming. **1970** *Cape Times* 28 Oct. 20/2 (Advt.), Fine 7-roomed residence. Excellent rooming proposition. Fully furnished. **1977** *Rolling Stone* 5 May 50/1, I already have the rooming list.

2. rooming-in orig. *U.S.* (see quot. 1947); also *transf.* (see quot. 1978) and *attrib.*

1946 *Mod. Hospital* Dec. 44/2 Three Detroit hospitals.. have been.. experimenting in certain selected cases with a 'rooming-in' plan which permits the mother to have her baby at her bedside. **1947** JACKSON & THOMS in *Connecticut State Med. Jrnl.* XI. 175/1 Rooming-in is a term applied to that form of hospitalization where mother and newborn baby room together and in which the mother takes as much care of the baby as possible. **1950** *N.Y. Times* 30 Dec. 16/2 About 75 per cent of expectant mothers who plan to have their babies at Grace-New Haven Community Hospital.. now are requesting the rooming-in plan whereby they may keep their babies with them instead of having them cared for in the hospital nursery... Rooming-in is preferred by more women with higher education and by women with husbands in upper occupational classifications. **1960** F. W. GOODRICH *Maternity* vii. 103 Most ideal rooming-in set-ups make some provision for the baby to be returned to the nursery when the mother so desires. **1965** *Nursing Times* 5 Feb. 182/1 The siting of a nursery far distant from the wards added to the difficulties of the staff in spite of the fact that rooming-in was practised. **1974** G. B. LIPKIN *Psychosocial Aspects of Maternal-Child Nursing* x. 56/1 The nurses in the rooming-in unit stress their function as instructors in child care. **1978** *Who's Who* 1934/1 A 'Rooming-In' hospital for mother nursing of infants and small children with congenital defects requiring plastic surgery.

'rooming-house. orig. *U.S.* (See quot. 1893.)

1893 *Spectator* 16 Sept. 366/1 We go to no hotel, but look for what Americans call a 'rooming house', i.e., a house which lets furnished apartments. **1909** *Washington Times* 2 Mar. 1 Hundreds of persons who never slept in any but first-class hotels when away from home will tonight get their rest in rooming houses. **1911** *Daily Colonist* (Victoria, B.C.) 1 Apr. 13/1 (Advt.), 14 roomed house, just overhauled, repainted and in first class condition. One of the best rooming house propositions in the city. **1923** E. F. Wyatt *Invis. Gods* III. ii. 105 Fairfax Avenue was now a nondescript street of rooming houses, apartments and carpet-cleaning establishments. **1932** *New Yorker* 9 Apr. 36/2 Miss Cedarholm..succeeded..to the ownership of the brick dwelling at 338 Schermerhorn Street. This she continued to operate as a rooming-house. **1957** V. Nabokov *Pnin* iii. 64 There had been—in yet another rooming house—a still cozier bedroom-study. **1958** 'N. Shute' *Rainbow & Rose* iii. 76 Ma went there for the movies, and then when her contract ended she kept a rooming house. **1961** *Daily Tel.* 25 Mar. 16/5 The body of a woman.., was found by police officers last night in a rooming house in Lorenzo Street, King's Cross. **1973** *Sun-Herald* (Sydney) 26 Aug. 3/3 Police said another grandchild witnessed the stabbings in a rooming house. **1976** *Billings* (Montana) *Gaz.* 7 July 10-A/6 She moved to Washington D.C., where she was a proprietor of a rooming house for 20 years.

'roomless, *a. rare.* Also 6 roumles. [f. room *sb.*[1]] Lacking room or space; strait, confined; also, without rooms.

1548 Udall, etc. *Erasm. Par. Mark* iii. 28 The shyppe wherein Jesus preached is very narowe and roumles to vncleane and synfull persons. **1971** *Daily Tel.* 27 Sept. 6 (*heading*) Sleeping bags and camp beds for roomless students.

'roomlet. *rare*[−1]. [-let.] A small room.

1880 Miss Bird *Japan* II. 242 Steep, narrow staircases, nefarious-looking roomlets, irregular balconies.

†**'roomliness.** *Obs. rare.* [f. roomly *a.*] Roominess.

1744 *Lond. Mag.* 557 The primary Enquiry is to the Roomliness and Strength of the Ship. *Ibid.* 558 Roomliness and Strength of Decks.

†**'roomly,** *a. Obs.*[−1] [f. room *sb.*[1] + -ly[1]. Cf. OE. *rúmlic* abundant, plentiful, liberal.] Large.

1743 *Lond. & C. Brewer* III. (ed. 2) 191, I..boil it with two Pounds of Hops..in a roomly Canvas or such as they call Straining Cloth.

†**'roomly,** *adv.* [OE. *rúmlíce* (see room *a.* and -ly[2]), = MDu. *rumelike, -lijc* (Du. *ruimelijk*), MLG. *rumelik(en*, OHG. *rûmlihho*, MSw. *rumlika, -leka*.] Liberally, largely, abundantly.

*c***950** *Lindisf. Gosp.* Matt. *Introd.* 18/14 [He] rumlice foretacnas [L. *clementer informat*]. **971** *Blickling Hom.* 49 And ȝif we þonne lustlice & rumlice þa welan dælaþ earmum monnum. *c***1000** Ælfric *Saints' Lives* I. 514 Biȝe us.. rumlicor to dæȝ be hlafe. *c***1200** *Trin. Coll. Hom.* 213 Þe sullere doð narewere þane he sholde, and te biggere rumluker þan he sholde. *c***1205** Lay. 2452 Alle þa vncuðe to hire comen..for seoluere & for golde, & heo rumliche hit ȝef. *a***1300** *E.E. Psalter* xxx. 30 And roum-like sal he yhelde in land To þas þat ere pride doand. *c***1425** Wyntoun *Chron.* IX. ix. 1136 (Royal MS.), Til lordis rowmly he landis gave; His swnnys he mad rych and mychty.

'room-mate. orig. *U.S.* [f. room *sb.*[1]] One who lodges in or occupies the same room or rooms with another; a fellow-lodger.

1789 W. Dunlap *Father* IV. 42 We were room mates at Halifax. **1838** J. L. Stephens *Trav. Russ. & Turk. Emp.* I. 251 With a Frenchman and a Greek for my room-mates. **1849** W. S. Mayo *Kaloolah* (1850) 107 My interesting room-mates were so far recovered as to be able to take the air upon deck. **1873** C. M. Yonge *Pillars of House* III. xxx. 170 The room and the room-mate that had seemed so disgusting to home-bred Felix. **1899** Whiteing 5 *John St.* 210 Little Nance, the chum and room-mate of Tilda. **1912** A. Brazil *New Girl at St. Chad's* i. 19 One of my room-mates snored atrociously. **1923** *Jrnl. Exper. Psychol.* VI. 436 She admitted having sold..clothing taken from her roommate. **1949** A. Huxley *Let.* 11 May (1969) 598 It would be very unwise to try to pay back two thousand in the first year—particularly at the price of having a room mate. **1951** *Sport* 27 Apr.–3 May 8/3 Stan and Jack are fellow-Geordies who were England room-mates last summer. **1954** W. K. Hancock *Country & Calling* ii. 66 My room-mate, Percy Dicker, is now my brother-in-law and a man of renown in the Wangaratta district of Victoria. **1975** D. Lodge *Changing Places* ii. 101 His roommate freaked out on LSD. **1978** H. Wouk *War & Remembrance* xxviii. 287 The third roommate, the squadron exec, was writing in the ready room.

†**'roomsome,** *a. Obs.* In 6 romesome, 6–7 roomesome, 7 rowmsome, roomsom. [f. room *a.*] Ample, capacious, roomy.

1581 Pettie tr. *Guazzo's Civ. Conv.* I. (1586) 22 b, I know by this your exposition of this worde (*Ciuile*) the field wee haue to enter into is verie wide and roomesome. **1598** Florio *Dict.* To Rdr., A more..vnweildie and more roomesome vessell then the biggest hulke on Thames. **1602** J. Davies (Heref.) *Mirum in Modum* xxiii. Wks. (Grosart) I. 7 The Cells..Are made by right more rowmsome then the rest. *a***1642** Sir W. Monson *Naval Tracts* III. (1704) 357/1 She is Roomsom for her Men. **1671** Evelyn *Diary* 16 Oct., An old house..made..capable and roomesome.

'roomstead. Now *rare* or *Obs.* Also 7 roomesteade, 8 room stead. [f. room *sb.*[1]] A compartment or division; a certain space or length.

1641 Best *Farm. Bks.* (Surtees) 47 The greate roomesteade in the northende of the rye-barne helde all our winter corne this yeare. *Ibid.*, As much as could possibly be layed in that roomsteade. **1691** J. Gibson in *Archaeologia* XII. 188 Dr. Uvedale of Enfield... His greens take up six or seven houses or roomsteads. **1718** in *Trans. Cumb. & Westm. Archæol. Soc.* (N.S.) III. 200 Benjamin Farish hath one firehouse containing two room steads..to lett. **1764** *Skeffling Inclosure Act* 9 The pieces, parts, or room-steads of the earth-bank. **1800** Tuke *Agric.* 93 A roomstead (i.e. one post and two rails), being 1*s.* 7*d.* including carriage. **1820** W. Scoresby *Acc. Arctic Reg.* II. 461 The carpenters had completely cleared the roomstead. *Note*, Roomstead is the space between any two ribs or frames of timber in a ship.

†**'roomster.** *Obs.*[−1] An occupant of space.

1674 N. Fairfax *Bulk & Selv.* 181, I being at no agreement with this same hideous Roomster.., I may.. have my harmless mistake paid home by a vile mischance.

roomth (ru:mθ). Now *dial.* Also 6 rumeth, 6–7 rometh(e, roometh; 6 romth(e, rompth; 7 roumth, roomthe. [f. room *a.* + -th[1]: cf. Færöese *rúmd*. The earlier form is rimth.]

1. Space; *esp.* ample or unconfined space. †*to make roomth*, to make way.

1540 Bible (Cranmer) *2 Sam.* xxii. 20 For he brought me out into roumth, he delyuered me, because he had a loue vnto me. **1559** Aylmer *Harborowe* E iv b, All histories and monumentes canne not be conteined in so lyttle rometh. **1575** *Gammer Gurton* II. iv, Make here a little romth. **1612** Drayton *Poly-olb.* vi. 122 But Rydoll,.. Not finding fitting roomth upon the rising side, Alone unto the West directly takes her way. **1643** Trapp *Comm. Gen.* xliii. 25 A mans gift makes roomth for him. **1881–** in dial. glossaries (Leic., Warw., Sheff).

†**b.** Space occupied by an object; extent, bulk.

1603 Drayton *Bar. Wars* VI. xxviii, Whose romth but hinders others that would grow. **1622** Malynes *Anc. Law-Merch.* 40 Pease grinded weigh more than corne, the roundnesse giveth cause to have more roomth. **1674** N. Fairfax *Bulk & Selv.* 54 Having seen what the Worlds lastingness and roomth is.

†**c.** Extent; jurisdiction. *Obs.*[−1]

1601 Bp. W. Barlow *Defence* 188 Lastly, that the Church haue roometh vniuersally extended.

†**2.** Sufficient space or scope *for* or *to* do something. *Obs.*

*a***1540** Barnes *Wks.* (1573) 298 The false brethren..unto whom S. Paule gaue no romthe as concernyng to bee brought into subiection. **1596** Drayton *Legends* iv. 209 Where now my Spirit got roomth it selfe to show. **1615** W. Lawson *Country Housew. Garden* (1626) 10 So there be sufficient roomth left for walkes. **1639** H. Ainsworth *Pentateuch* Gen. ix. 27 'Inlarging' also, is not only of roomth to dwell in.., but oftentimes of the heart.

†**b.** A sufficient occupation. *Obs.*[−1]

1585 Dyer *Prayse of Nothing* C ij, It were a romth for some idle bodye, to looke into the accedents of euery state, which hath been diuersly afflicted for nothing.

†**3.** A defined or limited space. *Obs.*

1550 *Nottingham Rec.* IV. 98 In the est end of the Spyces Chamber a romthe for a p[r]esse. **1579** Twyne *Phis. agst. Fortune* I. 6 b, This narrowe roomth, and place of necessitie, is knowne without Astrologicall coniecture. **1596–7** S. Finche in *Hist. Croydon* (1783) 155 We..are now fillinge the voyde rometh therin with earth and rubbishe. **1639** H. Ainsworth *Pentateuch* Num. ii. 27 So many thousand tents as Israel had could not be pitched in a little roomth.

†**b.** A chamber, apartment. *Obs.*

1579 Fenton *Guicciard.* 415 A fire kindled..in their stoare house called the Arzenale, euen in the rometh where was their saltpeter. **1635** *Maldon Doc.* (Bundle 80, No. 2), vis. viiid. for dressing up the said moote-hall, counsell chamber, and other the Romethes there this yere.

†**4.** An office, function, or dignity. *Obs.*

1504 Lady Margaret tr. *De Imit.* IV. v. 267 By the puttynge to of the handes of the Bysshoppe thou arte admyttyd vnto that hye rometh. *a***1530** in Ellis *Orig. Lett.* Ser. III. II. 153 Very gladde I wolbe that he in that romethe myght doo your most excelent Grace service. **1586** in *10th Rep. Hist. MSS. Comm.* App. V. 439 The credytt, vocacion, rompth, promocion and callinge of Bayliefes. *a***1604** Hanmer *Chron. Irel.* (1633) 57 He preferred one Iohn his Deacon and disciple, to the roomth.

†**b.** A position or office pertaining to a person; one's place. *Obs.*

1544 A. Cope *Hannibal & Scipio* 40 They commanded to let the old Senatours go free, and use their romthes. **1573** Twyne *Virgil* Life ¶j b, When his voice failed him at eny time, Mecænas supplied his romth in readynge. **1600** S. Finche in *Hist. Croydon* (1783) 154 b, Margaret her daughter is in good hope to supplie her mothers romthe.

†**c.** *in the roomth of*, in the place *of*, instead *of*. Also with possessives. *Obs.*

1533 Wriothesley *Chron.* (Camden) I. 21 The Lorde William Howarde as deputie..in the romth of the Marshall of Englande. **1578** J. Stockwood *Serm.* 24 Aug. 78 It were farre better that they were vtterly remoued, and able Pastors put in theyr roomths. **1615** W. Lawson *Country Housew. Garden* (1626) 6 Our old fathers can tell vs, how woods are decaied, and people in the roomth of trees multiplied. **1624–5** *Nottingham Rec.* (1889) IV. 393 Annother Counceller to be ellected in his roomthe.

†**'roomthily,** *adv. Obs.*[−1] [f. roomthy *a.*] In respect of space; spatially.

1674 N. Fairfax *Bulk & Selv.* 103 God by making of a body and real space with it,..is thereby..no more roomthily there than he was before.

†**'roomthiness.** *Obs.* Also 7 roomethinesse, roomthyness(e. [f. roomthy *a.*] Roominess.

1553 Grimalde *Cicero's Offices* (1556) 55 Likewise in a noble mannes howse..ther must be made a provision for roomethinesse. **1570** T. Norton tr. *Nowel's Catech.* 60 Neither is there any thyng or place that is not enuironed and enclosed with the roomthinesse of heauen. **1627** Drayton *Agincourt* 8 Tents and Pauillions in the fields are pitcht, (E'r full wrought vp their Roomthynesse to try). **1674** N. Fairfax *Bulk & Selv.* 23 The everlasting time and boundless roomthiness. *Ibid.* 82 There is roomthiness between that and the other boundary or term.

†**'roomthsome,** *a. Obs.*[−1] In 6 romth-. [f. roomth.] Spacious, roomy.

1599 Nashe *Lenten Stuffe* 42 A cage or pigeon house, romthsome enough to comprehend her and..her nurse.

roomthy ('ru:mθɪ), *a.* Now *dial.* Also 6 romthie, romthy, room(e)thie, roomethy. [f. roomth + -y.]

1. Spacious, ample, roomy.

1578 Banister *Hist. Man* I. 30 With a slacke or romthy kynde of knitting. *Ibid.* 33 These bones in women [are].. much more ample, and romthy. **1612** Drayton *Poly-olb.* i. 210 After whom, cleere Enian in doth make, In Tamer's roomthier bankes their rest that scarcely take. **1655** Fuller *Ch. Hist.* II. 104 Because England was richer and roomthyer then their own Countrey. **1676** Hubbard *Happiness People* 55 God will rather have his people..pent up in a corner, then roomthy, and swoln with pride. **1726** S. Sewall *Lett.-bk.* (1886) II. 202 He has a situation roomthy and beautifull enough to build the New-Jerusalem in. **1854–** in dial. glossaries (Northamp., Warw., Oxf.).

†**2.** Pertaining to space; occupying space. *Obs.*

1674 N. Fairfax *Bulk & Selv.* 21 Time had not been if God had not made timesome beings, nor room if he had not made roomthy.

†**'roomward,** *adv. Naut. Obs.* Also 7 roome-. [f. room *adv.*] = room *adv.* 3.

1611 Cotgr., *Bouter au vent*, to beare roomeward; or, to fill the sayles with wind. **1647** W. Browne tr. *Polexander* II. III. 214 My Pilot was constrained to goe Roome-ward to Sea. *Ibid.* 226 This Fleet..put roome-ward to Sea, as soone as they had descried us. **1658** Earl Monm. tr. *Paruta's Wars Cyprus* 140 Having fallen much Roomeward at the beginning of the fight,..they kept aloof from the great gallie.

So †**'room-way** *adv. Obs.*[−1]

1627 Capt. Smith *Seaman's Gram.* ix. 44 When she would not come neere the land, but goeth more Roome-way than her course, wee say she beares off.

roomy ('ru:mɪ), *a.* and *adv.* Also 7 roumy, rommy. [f. room *sb.*[1] + -y. Cf. MLG. *rumich*, *ruymich*, G. *räumig*.]

A. *adj.* **1.** Of ample dimensions; capacious, large; wide.

1627 Capt. Smith *Seaman's Gram.* xi. 52 This makes a Ship more roomy. *a***1656** Bp. Hall *Rem. Wks.* (1660) 64 A place both more publick, roomy, and chargelesse. **1697** Dryden *Virg. Georg.* II. 388 Let thy Vines in Intervals be set, Indulge their Width, and add a roomy Space. **1743** Blair *Grave* 267 His roomy chest by far too scant To give the lungs full play. **1773** *Life N. Frowde* 199 He agreed..to accommodate us all on board his Ship, which was a very fine and roomy one. **1807** G. Chalmers *Caledonia* I. I. ii. 101 In this roomy currach, St. Cormac sailed into the north sea. **1855** Thackeray *Newcomes* viii. I. 77 A gentleman of bland aspect with a roomy forehead. **1883** J. Gilmour *Mongols* xxvii. 320 The outer garment of both sexes is a wide roomy coat which reaches down to the ground.

fig. **1693** Dryden *Juvenal* Ded. (1697) p. lxxxii, This sort of Number is more roomy: The Thought can turn it self with greater ease in a larger compass. **1827** Pollok *Course T.* (1854) 280 A roomy life, a glowing relish high.

2. Of female animals: Of large proportions internally.

1796 W. H. Marshall *W. Eng.* II. 202 Some roomy good cows. **1853** *Jrnl. R. Agric. Soc.* XIV. II. 430 A well-proportioned roomy cow. **1853** Stonehenge *Greyhound* 174 A large roomy bitch..will most probably 'throw' a lot of undersized greyhounds. **1894** *Field* 9 June 846/1 [A mare,] a fine, roomy daughter of Lincolnshire Lad II.

†**B.** *adv. Naut.* = room *adv.* 3. *Obs.*

1624 Capt. Smith *Virginia* 192 At last she bore up rommy for the Sea, and we heard of her no more. *Ibid.* 224 The next was a ship of Holland... She was put roumy. **1626** —— *Accid. Yng. Seamen* 18 Beare vp the helme, goe roumy.

roomy, var. roomie.

roon (røn). *Sc.* Also roen, roond, and rund. [Of obscure origin.] A piece of the list or selvage of cloth; a strip or shred. Also *roon-shoon* (see quot. 1824).

1785 Burns *To W. Simpson* Postscr. iii, They thought the Moon, Just like a sark, or pair o' shoon, Woor by degrees, till her last roon Gaed past their viewin. **1808** Jamieson, *Roon*, a shred, a remnant,..also *roond*. **1824** Mactaggart *Gallovid. Encycl.*, *Roon-shoon*, shoes made of the roons, or selvages of cloth. **1862** Hislop *Prov. Scot.* 179 The best o' wabs are rough at the roons.

roonde, obs. f. round.

roone, obs. f. roan.

roong, obs. pa. pple. of RING *v.*[1]

roop (ruːp), *sb.*[1] [var. of ROUP *sb.*[3]] Hoarseness; a hoarse sound.

1674 RAY *N.C. Words* 39 A *Roop*, a Hoarseness. **1788-** in northern dial. glossaries (Yks., Northumb.). **1898** *Daily News* 22 Feb. 3/3 That touch of noble hoarseness.. like the roop of the bow on the string of a violoncello.

roop, *sb.*[2], in northern and Sc. phrase ***stoop and roop***, completely: see STOOP *sb.*

roop, *v. rare.* [Cf. ROOP *sb.*[1]] *intr.* To utter a hoarse note or sound.

1894 CROCKETT *Love Idylls* (1901) 182 A sleepy hen rooped lazily in a hole under the hedge. **1894** —— *Raiders* (ed. 3) 234, I only rooped like a rough-legged fowl.

roop(e, obs. ff. ROPE; variants of ROUP.

rooped, *a. Sc.* and *north. dial.* Also 7 **roopt,** 9 **roopit, -et,** and ROUPED. [f. ROOP *sb.*[1]] Hoarse.

1677 NICOLSON in *Trans. R. Soc. Lit.* (1870) IX. 316 *Roopt*, hoarse with bawling. **1822** SCOTT *Nigel* xv, He had something of a catarrh, and spoke as hoarse as a roopit raven. **1881** J. L. ROBERTSON in Edwards *Mod. Sc. Poets* III. 35 The minister grew hearse and roopit.

roopee, obs. form of RUPEE.

roope-sicke: see ROPE-SICK *a.*

roopy (ˈruːpɪ), *a.* Chiefly *dial.* See also ROUPY *a.*[2] [f. ROOP *sb.*[1]] Hoarse.

1825- in dial. glossaries (Northumb., Durh., Yks., Berks, Hants). **1850** DICKENS *D. Copperfield* vii, He had observed I was sometimes hoarse—a little roopy was his exact expression. **1864** MISS BRADDON *J. Marchmont's Legacy* III. 179 The lonely hen set up a roopy cackle.

roopy, variant of ROUPY *a.*[1]

roor, obs. form of ROAR.

roorback (ˈrʊəbæk). *U.S.* Also **-bach, roarback.** [The name of the fictitious author Baron von *Roorback* (see quot. 1864).] A false report or slander invented for political purposes.

[**1844** *Republican Sentinel* (Richmond, Va.) 4 Oct. 3/3 The rapid succession of events in the 'Roorback' line, has satisfied us, that the whole matter is a *quiz* or a *forgery*.] **1855** I. C. PRAY *Mem. J. G. Bennett* 368 Among the efforts made to defeat the election of Mr. Polk was one to which allusion is frequently made in political discussion, politicians speaking of a political lie as a 'Roorback'. **1864** WEBSTER, *Roorbach*, a forgery or fictitious story published for purposes of political intrigue. [*Note.* The word originated in 1844, when such a forgery was published, purporting to be an extract from the 'Travels of Baron Roorbach'.] **1870** L. BAUGH *To Voters of Washington County* (broadside), Beware of 'Roarbacks' on the eve of the election. **1884** *Boston* (Mass.) *Jrnl.* 6 Sept., The Herald and Globe abound in roorbacks which are designed to influence the vote in Maine. **1913** A. B. REEVE *Poisoned Pen* xii. 367 Billy McLoughlin knows how to make the best use of such a roorback on the eve of an election. **1947** *Chicago Daily News* 27 Mar. 6/1 The roorback stage of the closing days of the campaign broke wide open today with appeals to racial and religious prejudice coming to the surface in many sections of the city. **1963** R. I. MCDAVID *Mencken's Amer. Lang.* 180 Since the exposure of the fraud actually helped Polk, it is sometimes spelled *roarback*.

roore, obs. form of ROAR.

Roorkee (ˈrʊəkiː). Also **Roorkhee, rhoorkee, Roorkie.** The name of a town, northeast of Delhi, in Uttar Pradesh, India, used *attrib.* in **roorkee chair**, a type of collapsible chair, with wooden frame and canvas back and seat, originally produced there; also *ellipt.*; **roorkee work**, a kind of canvas work associated with Roorkee.

1905 *Army & Navy Co-op. Soc. Rules & Price List* 15 Mar. 261/2 Roorkhee folding chair. Each 18/9 (Supply uncertain) Do. do., English make, of ash throughout, better finished. Each 21/6. **1907** *Yesterday's Shopping* (1969) 281/2 Roorkhee Folding Chair. English make, of ash throughout, well finished... Do., in green canvas with back... An improved form of Roorkee chair, it having a leg rest. **1936** J. CARY *Afr. Witch* viii. 158 Four chairs, including the Resident's well-known *rhoorkee*, taller than the rest, were empty. **1937** G. FRANKAU *More of Us* xiv. 147 Splendid sank Circe to a canvas throne Of rhoorkee work. **1953** J. MASTERS *Lotus & Wind* v. 69 There was no furniture left except a folding table and a Roorkie chair on which the colonel sat. **1973** 'B. MATHER' *Snowline* xvi. 189, I lay back in a long Roorkhee chair. **1975** C. ALLEN *Plain Tales from Raj* v. 65 Perhaps some Roorkee chairs, made of canvas stretched on wood.

roos, obs. form of ROUSE *sb.*

roosa, rusa (ˈruːsə). Also **roussa, rusha.** [Hindī *rúsá.*] ***roosa grass***, an Indian grass (*Andropogon Schœnanthus* or *Cymbopogon Martini*), from which ***roosa oil*** is distilled.

1853 T. C. ARCHER *Pop. Econ. Bot.* 279 Oil of Indian Grass, Roosa Oil, or *Roosa-ke-til*, is distilled from the leaves of *Andropogon Calamus aromaticus.* **1858** SIMMONDS *Dict. Trade*, Roosa-Grass Oil. **1885** WATT *Econ. Prod. India* 249 This is the roussa paper grass, abundant everywhere in the Deccan. *Ibid.* 250 Perhaps the name by which it is most generally known is rusa oil. *Ibid.*, Rusha oil.

roose, *sb.* ? *Obs.* Forms: α. 3–5 **ros,** 4 **rose,** 4–5 **roos,** 5 **roys(e.** β. 4–6 **rous,** 7 **rowze.** γ. *Sc.* 4–6, 9 **ruse,** 5 **rus(s,** 6 **ruys, ruiss(e.** δ. 8– **roose.** [a. ON. *hrós* (Icel. *hrós*, Fær. *rós*, Norw., Sw., and Da. *ros*): cf. ROOSE *v.*]

1. Boasting, vainglory; an instance of this, a boast, brag, vaunt.

α. *c* **1200** ORMIN 4910 All idell ȝellp & idell ros þu cwennkesst i þe sellfenn. *a* **1300** *Cursor M.* 11948 Nu þat i do þou it for-dos, And þar-of sal þou mak na ros. **13..** *Minor Poems fr. Vernon MS.* 505 Such þing as þou seyst and doos, þi Neiȝebor wol þerof make Roos. *c* **1400** *Song Roland* 650 Shall none of you mak your rose or ye go furþre. *c* **1450** *Cast. Perseverance* 1068 þerfore do as no man dos,.. & of þi-self make gret ros. **1486** *Bk. St. Albans* e vj b, The master to his man makyth his Roys That he knowith be kynde what the hert doys Att huntyng.

β. **1303** R. BRUNNE *Handl. Synne* 5158 Ne be nat proude þogh þou weyl dous, yn þyn herte to make a rous. **1463** G. ASHBY *Poems* 11 Goo forth, lytyll boke, mekely, without rous. **16..** *Sir Lambewell* 304 in *Percy's Folio MS., Ball. & Rom.* I. 154 Shee warned me be-forne, of all things that I did vse, of her I shold neuer make my rowze.

γ. *c* **1470** *Gol. & Gaw.* 98 Bot thow mend hym that mys.. Thow sall rew in thi ruse. **1513** DOUGLAS *Æneis* VIII. Prol. 50 Sum makis a tume ruse. *a* **1572** KNOX *Hist. Ref.* Wks. 1846 I. 242 What thei receaved we can nott tell; but few maid ruse at thare returnyng. **1596** DALRYMPLE tr. *Leslie's Hist. Scot.* II. 242 Johne Moydert.. maid meikle ruse that he him selfe was the cheif of Makdonelis kynd. **1808** JAMIESON, *To mak a tume ruse*, to boast where there is no ground for it, but the reverse.

δ. **1718** RAMSAY *Christ's Kirk Gr.* III. iv, Wha wins syn may make roose, Between you twa. **17..** *Maggie's Tocher* in Herd *Coll. Sc. Songs* (1776) II. 78 We'll mak nae mair toom roose.

†**2.** Commendation, praise. *Obs.*

a **1300** *Cursor M.* 13896 Quen he his aun roos has soght, In his muth sothfast es noght. *a* **1350** *St. Nicholas* 87 in Horstm. *Altengl. Legend.* (1881) 12 Noght for no ruse of erthli thing Bot allone vnto goddes louyng. *c* **1375** *Sc. Leg. Saints* xli. (*Agnes*) 114 þe prefet begane to spere.. quhat man it wes.. þat agnes þe ruse of mad. *c* **1470** *Gol. & Gaw.* 1241 All erdly riches and ruse is noght in thair garde.

roose, obs. form of ROSE *sb.*

roose (ruːz, *Sc.* røːz), *v.* Now *Sc.* and *north. dial.* Forms: α. 3 **rosenn,** 4 **ros,** 4–5 (9 *dial.*) **rose,** 5 **roys.** β. 4–9 **ruse,** 5–6 **rus(s,** 6 **rws, ruis,** 7–9 **ruze;** 6 **reuse,** 7 **reouse, reuze;** *Sc. dial.* 8 **reeze, rease,** 8–9 **reese.** γ. 6 **rowse,** 7–9 **rouse.** δ. 7– **roose** (*dial.* 8 **rooyse,** 9 **rooze, roois**). [a. ON. *hrósa* to boast of, praise (Icel. *hrósa*, Fær. *rósa*, Norw. and Sw. *rosa*, Da. *rose*): cf. ROOSE *sb.*]

†**1.** *intr.* To boast or be proud *of* something. *Obs.*

c **1200** ORMIN 4906 þatt iss hæfedd sinne.. To rosenn off þin haȝherrleȝȝc. *c* **1475** *Rauf Coilȝear* 481 Of that Ryall array that Rolland in raid, Rauf rusit in his hart of that Ryall thing.

†**2.** *refl.* **a.** To boast oneself; to vaunt. Const. *of, that* with clause, or infin. **b.** To praise or commend oneself. *Obs.*

α. *a* **1300** *Cursor M.* 28102 Ic ha me rosed in my mode bath o my werkes wyc and gode. *a* **1340** HAMPOLE *Psalter* xxxi. 3, I cried all þe day rosand me of rightwisnes.

β. **13..** *SS. Peter & Paul* 152 in Horstm. *Altengl. Leg.* (1881) 78 Simon.. rusid him þan þat he might raise Dede men to lyue. *c* **1340** HAMPOLE *Prose Tr.* 12 Noghte ruysand hyme of his reghtwesnes. *c* **1400** *Melayne* 956 So mot I spede, He sall noghte ruysse hym of this dede. *c* **1460** *Towneley Myst.* xxiii. 492 He has hym rused of great prophes. **1508** DUNBAR *Tua Mariit Wemen* 194 He.. makis repet with ryatus wordis, Ay rusing him of his radis. **1533** GAU *Richt Vay* 75 Mony spekis mekil and rwsis thayme of faith. *c* **1560** A. SCOTT *Poems* (S.T.S.) iii. 21 Reuse nocht ȝour self, latt vþiris preiss ȝour rentis.

γ. *c* **1440** *York Myst.* xxix. 271 Oure stiffe tempill,.. This rebalde he rowses hym it rathely to rayse.

δ. **1637-50** ROW *Hist. Kirk* (Wodrow Soc.) 476 Alledging that honest ministers that went to the Bishop roosed themselves little of it.

3. *trans.* To praise, extol, commend, flatter.

α. *a* **1300** *Cursor M.* 2417 Sua þai rosed hir to þe king þat he þam did befor him bring. **13..** *E.E. Allit. P.* B. 1371 To rose hym in his rialty rych men soȝtten. *c* **1460** *Towneley Myst.* ii. 95 What gifys god the to rose hym so? *Ibid.* xii. 234 Here is.. the leg of a goys, With chekyns endorde, pork, partryk, to roys. **1877** *N.W. Linc. Gloss.*, *Rose*, to praise, to flatter.

β. *c* **1460** *Towneley Myst.* xxi. 33 For if other men ruse hym, we shall accuse hym. *c* **1475** *Rauf Coilȝear* 80 Thank me not ouir airlie,.. For I haue seruit the ȝit of lytill thing to ruse. **1513** DOUGLAS *Æneis* I. ix. 84 This ilk Tewcer his enemyis of Troy Rusit and lovit. **1570** *Satir. Poems Reform.* xii. 132 Be my saule, my self culd neuer ruse ȝow. **1603** *Philotus* xxxiv, Bot be it gude ȝe do not spair, As royallie to ruse it. **1677** NICOLSON in *Trans. R. Soc. Lit.* (1870) IX. 316 *Ruze*, to flatter. **1691** RAY *N.C. Words* 59 To *Reuze*, to extol or commend highly. **1715** RAMSAY *Christ's Kirk Gr.* II. viii, They rus'd him that had skill. *a* **1800** in Skinner *Misc. Poet.* 110 There's nane that reads them.. But reezes Robie. *a* **1800** *Young Allan* ii. in Child *Ballads* IV. 378 Some there reasd their hawk, their hawk, And some there reasd their hound. **1879** JOHN WHITE *Jottings* 225 (E.D.D.), I've rus'd ye for yer head and heart.

γ. **1549** COVERDALE, etc. *Erasm. Par. 1 Cor.* 27 If such let passe nothing undone and unsuffered and all to be rowsed and commended of the lewde people. *a* **1553** UDALL *Royster D.* I. i, Prayse and rouse him well, and ye haue his heart wonne. **1766** A. NICOL *Poems* 104, I right fickle was and fain To be sae rous'd. **1842** CLARK *Rhymes* 23 Wi' flattery I'll no rouse thee.

δ. **1703** THORESBY *Yorkshire Wds.* (E.D.S.), *Rooyse*, to extol. **1723** RAMSAY *Fair Assembly* ix, These modest maids inspire the muse, In flowing strains to shaw Their beauties, which she likes to roose. **1785** BURNS *1st Ep. to J. Lapraik* 94 Friends an folk that wish me well, They sometimes roose me. **1786** —— *Ded. to G. Hamilton* 3 A fleechan, fleth'ran Dedication, To roose you up, an' ca' you guid. **1834** A. SMART *Rambl. Rhymes* 162 Let poets in their idle lays Roose up auld Scotland's early days. **1865** WAUGH *Lanc. Songs* 30 Aw roos't her, poor lass.

b. In various proverbs and sayings.

1710 RUDDIMAN *Gloss. Douglas Æneis* s.v., Every body ruses the ford as he finds it. **1721** KELLY *Scot. Prov.* 210 If it be ill, it is as ill rused. *Ibid.* 282 Ruse the fair Day at Night. **1818** SCOTT *Rob Roy* xxvii, Let ilka ane roose the ford as they find it.

ˈ**rooser.** *Sc. rare.* Also **rusar, ruser.** [f. ROOSE *v.* Cf. ON. *hrósari.*] A boaster, braggart.

1535 STEWART *Cron. Scot.* III. 440 [It] hapnis oft ane vanter to be liear,.. And ane gude rusar [is] seindill ane gude rydar. **1721** KELLY *Scot. Prov.* 36 A great ruser was never a good rider.

rooser, variant of ROUSER, a sprinkler.

Roosevelt (ˈrəʊz(ə)vɛlt, ˈruː-). The name of Theodore *Roosevelt* (1858–1919), President of the United States 1901–9, used *attrib.* or in the possessive in **Roosevelt('s) elk, wapiti** to designate a large, dark-coloured elk, *Cervus canadensis roosevelti*, found in coastal forests of north-western North America, and named in his honour by C. H. Merriam in 1897 (*Proc. Biol. Soc. Washington* XI. 271).

1897 *Proc. Biol. Soc. Washington* XI. 272 Roosevelt's Wapiti... Size large; head and legs black (probably only in winter pelage); skull and antlers massive. **1902** STONE & CRAM *Amer. Animals* 34 Roosevelt's Elk... Larger and darker coloured, with heavier horns. **1923** *Outing* Apr. 3/1 The Olympic peninsula.. contains vast, unmapped forests ..teeming with the lordly Roosevelt elk. **1975** *Islander* (Victoria, B.C.) 26 Jan. 16/4 The Olympic, or Roosevelt elk, are common in Olympic Park.

Rooseveltian (ˈrəʊz(ə)vɛltɪən, ˈruː-), *a.* [f. the family name *Roosevelt* + -IAN.] Of, pertaining to, or characteristic of Theodore Roosevelt (see prec.), or Franklin Delano Roosevelt (1882–1945), President of the U.S. 1933–45, or the Roosevelt family in general. Hence ˈ**Rooseveltism.**

1908 *Sci. Amer.* 25 Jan. 59/3 In this advanced twentieth century we had fondly hoped that the 'nature faker' at least was a product of the Rooseveltian age of literature. **1909** *Weekly Ardmoreite* (Ardmore, Okla.) 24 Feb. 8/1 Quarantine lifts Mar. 4... Get rid of Rooseveltism. **1915** *Fatherland* (N.Y.) 20 Dec. 346 We do not believe that the German Americans will have to chose between the devil of Rooseveltism and the deep sea of Wilson. **1923** A. HUXLEY *On Margin* 164 In true Rooseveltian style, he admired energy for its own sake. **1940** *Economist* 16 Nov. 601/2 He can make the official policy of the United States Government more completely Rooseveltian than it has been. **1948** *Chicago Tribune* 1 Feb. I. 37/3 It is a typical example of Rooseveltian democracy where charity is invited where it is not needed. **1953** *News* (Lynchburg, Va.) 6 May 6/1 That is not Rooseveltism. It is not New Dealism... It is good old-time Jeffersonian democracy. **1953** R. NIEBUHR *Christian Realism & Polit. Probl.* (1954) v. 59 The *status quo*, until the Rooseveltian era, permitted a degree of non-interference by the state.. which must make America a paradise for all true devotees of *laissez-faire.* **1965** *Economist* 16 Jan. 221/2 The profile.. bears a distinctly Rooseveltian chin. **1974** *Listener* 31 Jan. 148/1, I recall being the only child in my class who did not come from the Rooseveltian atmosphere of the homes of the Thirties. **1977** *National Observer* (U.S.) 22 Jan. 17/1 And Eleanor was an accomplished smiler in her own right, adding weight to the theory that smiling was a major Rooseveltian impulse. **1979** *N.Y. Rev. Bks.* 17 May 30/4 Schaller thus finds in early 1941, long before Pearl Harbor, the origin of the Rooseveltian program which wound up five years later in General Marshall's unavailing postwar mediation.

rooseveltite (ˈrəʊz(ə)vɛltaɪt, ˈruː-). *Min.* [ad. Sp. *rooseveltita* (R. Herzenberg 1946, in *Bol. Técnico* (Facultad Nacional Ingeniería, Univ. Técnica, Oruro, Bolivia) No. 1. 10), f. the name of Franklin D. *Roosevelt* (see prec.): see -ITE[1].] An arsenate of bismuth, $BiAsO_4$, which is found as a white or grey crust in veinlets of wood-tin in Bolivia and Argentina.

1947 *Amer. Mineralogist* XXXII. 372 (*heading*) Rooseveltite. **1949** *Mineral. Abstr.* X. 9 It is named rooseveltite, and is perhaps isomorphous with pucherite. **1972** *Tschermaks Mineral. und Petrogr. Mitt.* XVII. 65 Rooseveltite occurs in the weathering zone of the San Francisco de los Andes and Cerro Negro de la Aquadita mines, located in the San Juan Province, Argentina.

Rooshan, Rooshian, Roosian, varr. RHOOSIAN *sb.* and *a.*

ˈ**roosing,** *vbl. sb.* [f. ROOSE *v.*] **a.** Boasting, vaunting, vainglory. **b.** Commendation, praising.

c **1200** ORMIN 4564 Ʒæn rosinng, & ȝæn idell ȝellp. *Ibid.* 4902 Rosinng & all idell ȝellp.. iss hæfedd sinne. *a* **1300** *Cursor M.* 28524 þer-of haf i made rosyng. *c* **1340** HAMPOLE *Pr. Consc.* 7070 What avayld us pryde,.. rosyng of ryches or of ryche aray? *c* **1350** *St. John* 318 in Horstm. *Altengl. Leg.* (1881) 38 þe sext teches.. To refuys riches for ruseing. *a* **1800** *Redesdale & Wise William* in Child *Ballads* IV. 383 There fell a roosing them amang.

roosing, obs. form of ROUSING.

Roosky ('rʊskɪ), var. RUSSKI *a.* and *sb.*

roost (ruːst), *sb.*[1] Forms: 1 hrost, 4 rooste, 5 roist, 6 roust, rowst, ruste (7 roest), 6– roost. [OE. *hróst*, = MDu. and Flem. *roest*, and prob. OS. *hrôst* the spars of a roof (cf. sense 3). The further relationship is uncertain.]

1. a. A perch for domestic fowls; also *gen.* a perching- or resting-place of a bird.

a **1100** *Gerefa* in *Anglia* IX. 262 On odene cylne macian —ofn & aste & fela ðinga macian sceal to tune—ȝe eac henna hrost. **1398** TREVISA *Barth. De P.R.* XII. xvii. (Bodl. MS.), [The cock] setteþ nexte to hym one rooste þe henne þat is moste fatte and tendre. **1530** PALSGR. 264/1 Roost for capons or hennes, *jevssover*. **1565** HARDING *Confut. Apol.* 17 b, Gete ye now vp into your pulpettes, like bragging cockes on the rowst, flappe your winges, and crow out alowde. **1593** DRAYTON *Ecl.* iii. 46 Since good Robin to his Roost is gone. **1607** TOPSELL *Four-f. Beasts* 151 In a Dogge [the power of smell] is that sence which searcheth out and descryeth the roustes, fourmes, and lodgings of Wilde Beasts. **1700** DRYDEN *Cock & Fox* 46 Sooner than the matin-bell was rung, He clapp'd his wings upon his roost, and sung. **1751** JOHNSON *Rambler* No. 138 ¶ 12 When she is to see the hogs fed, or to count her poultry on the roost. **1820** W. IRVING *Sketch Bk.* II. 359 The sudden rustling in the thicket of birds frightened from their roost. **1884** ALLEN *Amer. Farm Book* 491 Swabbed along the roosts and laying boxes.. it has proved destructive to these vermin.

b. A hen-house, or that part of one in which the fowls perch at night.

1580 HOLLYBAND *Treas. Fr. Tong, Gelinier*, a hen house, a roust. **1589** *Hay any Work* 36 He sleepeth belike in the top of yᵉ roust. **1671** MILTON *Samson* 1693 As an ev'ning Dragon came, Assailant on the perched roosts, And nests in order rang'd Of tame villatic Fowl. **1784** COWPER *Task* v. 58 Now from the roost, or from the neighb'ring pale,.. Come trooping.. The feather'd tribes domestic. **1821** CLARE *Vill. Minstr.* I. 18 Sad deeds bewailing of the prowling fox; How in the roost the thief had knav'd his way. **1839** *Lincoln Gaz.* 12 Feb. 3/4 The rogues went to another roost adjoining the house. **1855** D. J. BROWNE *Amer. Poultry Yard* 83 The dormitory, or roost, should be well ventilated. *Ibid.*, To let air or light into the roost.

c. A collection or number *of* fowls, etc., such as may occupy a roost. Also without const.

1827 COL. HAWKER *Diary* (1893) I. 303, I killed a roost of small birds. **1966** D. LACK *Population Stud. Birds* ix. 156 At night they assemble in immense roosts, often in thorns.

d. *fig.* A resting-place; a lodging bed.

1818 *London Guide* p. xii, *Roost*, bed. *Ibid.* 225 Coming from roost one morning,.. I met old acquaintance, B——e, in Barbican. **1858** O. W. HOLMES *Aut. Breakf.-t.* (1883) 122 The world has a million roosts for a man, but only one nest. **1864** LOWELL *Fireside Trav.* 110 The only roost was in the garret, which.. contained eleven double beds, ranged along the walls. **1891** C. ROBERTS *Adrift Amer.* 23, I selected what appeared to me to be about the best spot for a roost, and.. made a fairly comfortable bed. **1930** R. CAMPBELL *Adamastor* 72, I.. Who now am but a roost for empty words. **1944** [see *robot roost* s.v. ROBOT 2]. **1946** MEZZROW & WOLFE *Really Blues* xii. 219, I know I'm gonna call some hogs soon as I hit my roost.

e. *to rule the roost*, now the more usual form of *to rule the roast* s.v. ROAST *sb.* 1 b.

1769 in *William & Mary Coll. Q. Mag.* (1908) Jan. 175 They say she rules the Roost, it is a pity, I like her Husband vastly. **1828** A. N. ROYALL *Black Bk.* II. 315 These priests will rule the roost. **1893** *Boston Jrnl.* 20 Apr. 5/3 England rules the roost. Her ships at Hampton Roads admittedly the finest. **1926** FOWLER *Mod. Eng. Usage* 509/1 *Rule the roast* (*roost*). The OED gives no countenance to *roost*, it does not even recognize that the phrase ever takes that form; but most unliterary persons say *roost* & not *roast*; I have just inquired of three such, & have been informed that they never heard of *rule the roast*, & that the reference is to a cock keeping his hens in order. **1931** R. CAMPBELL *Georgiad* ii. 29 The great Tu Quoque rules the golden roost. **1938** A. CHRISTIE *Appointment with Death* v. 37 Her husband thought a lot of her and adopted her judgment on almost every point. He was an invalid for some years before he died, and she practically ruled the roost. **1955** 'A. GILBERT' *Is she Dead Too?* vi. 114 'Miss Bannerman was very jealous, and she didn't care for children or animals.' 'Then she could have found herself some other lodgings. You'd scarcely let her rule your roost.' **1963** *New Yorker* 15 June 16/3 The London underworld, where Peter Sellers rules the roost. **1974** S. ELLIN *Stronghold* (1975) 36 My grandfather.. ruled the roost, and he was a firm ruler for all his mild manner.

2. Without article, in various phrases:

a. *to go*, etc., *to roost*. Also *fig.* of persons: To retire to rest. (Cf. Flem. *te roest gaan.*)

a **1529** SKELTON *E. Rummyng* 191 The hennes ron in the mashfat; For they go to roust Streyght ouer the ale ioust. *a* **1631** DRAYTON *Noah's Flood* 383 When the crowned cock ..Comes to roost by him. **1648** HEXHAM II, *Roesten*, to Jugge, or goe to Roest, as Hens, Patridges, &c. **1797–1808** VINCE *Astron.* xxi. 228 The birds went to roost. **1836** MACGILLIVRAY *Trav. Humboldt* viii. 109 These birds go to roost long before night. **1867** 'OUIDA' *Castlemaine's Gage* (1879) 20 The swallows were gone to roost amidst the ivy. *fig.* **1829** SCOTT *Jrnl.* II. 314 So to roost upon a crust of bread and a glass of small beer, my usual supper. **1852** THACKERAY *Esmond* I. xiii, 'Tis time for me to go to roost. I will have my gruel a-bed. **1879** STEVENSON *Travels in Cevennes* (1886) 212 Half an hour later, and I must have gone supperless to roost.

b. *at roost*, roosting, perched. Also *to take roost*, to perch.

1692 SIR R. L'ESTRANGE *Fables* ccclii, A Fox spy'd a Cock at Roost with his Hens about him. **1713** DERHAM *Phys.-Theol.* VII. ii, The Breast, and its Bone, made like a Keel.. to counterpoise the Body, and support and rest it upon at Roost. **1848** LYTTON *Harold* VII. ii, Where the falcon took roost. **1864** BROWNING *Mr. Sludge*, While you cling by half a claw To the perch whereon you puff yourselves at roost.

c. *to come home to roost*, to come back upon the originator.

1810 SOUTHEY *Kehama* Motto, Curses are like young chickens: they always come home to roost. **1838** LYTTON *Alice* 340 The curse has come home to roost. **1887** LOWELL *Democr.* 173 All our mistakes sooner or later surely come home to roost.

3. In various local applications (see quots.).

1790 MORISON *Poems* 105 (E.D.D.), Frae the roost a rung she drew. **1808** JAMIESON, *Roost*,.. the inner roof of a cottage, composed of spars of wood reaching from the one wall to the other... It is also vulgarly used to denote a garret. **1856** MORTON *Cycl. Agric.* II. 725/2 *Roost*, (Lancas.), the upper part of a cow-house; loft over stable.

4. *attrib.*, as ***roost-time***, ***-tree***; ***roost lay*** (see quot.).

1780 G. WHITE *Selborne* xciv, They happened to be suddenly roused from their roost-trees. **1823** EGAN *Grose's Dict. Vulg. T.*, *Roost Lay*, stealing poultry. **1884** JEFFERIES *Life of Fields* (1908) 97 A loud.. clamour of rooks and daws, who have restlessly moved in their roost-trees. **1889** —— *Open Air* 216 The partridges may run through to join their friends before roost-time on the ground.

roost (ruːst), *sb.*[2] Also 7–9 roust, 8–9 rost, 9 rust. [a. ON. *rǫst* (Norw. *røst*), in the same sense.] A tumultuous tidal race formed by the meeting of conflicting currents off various parts of the Orkney and Shetland Islands.

1654 BLAEU *Atlas, Scotia* 150 Exiguis scaphulis quas facile maris æstus ac fluctus, quem *Roosts* appellant, absorbet. **1693** J. WALLACE *Orkney* 93 *Roust*, a very tempestuous tide. **1774** LOW *Orkney* (1879) 14 Where the water breaks on Stroma, it goes off in vast whirls, and forms a roust by the dancing of the stream. **1821** SCOTT *Pirate* i, The current of a strong and furious tide, which.. is called the Roost of Sumburgh. **1841** *Penny Cycl.* XXI. 384/1 The majestic cliffs and towering headlands that frown over the dark and stormy seas and *rousts*. **1868** D. GORRIE *Summers & W. Orkneys* v. 161 The roosts are in their wildest state of agitation with ebb tides and westerly swells.

roost, obs. form of ROAST *sb.* and *v.*

roost (ruːst), *v.* Forms: 6 rust(e, roste, 6–7 roust(e, rowst, 7– roost. [f. ROOST *sb.*[1] Cf. Flem. *roesten* (Kilian).]

1. Of birds: To settle on a perch or the like for sleep or rest; to settle for sleep, go to rest.

1530 PALSGR. 696/1 These capons ruste whan it draweth towardes nyght, they be wyser than men be. **1577** B. GOOGE *Heresbach's Husb.* IV. (1586) 166 After the seuenth moneth, you may put them to roust in the house with the other Peacockes. **1600** SURFLET *Countrie Farme* I. xv. 96 By hauing rousted vpon the trees in the open aire. *a* **1682** SIR T. BROWNE *Tracts* (1683) 29 Sitting, roosting, covering and resting in the boughs. **1748** *Anson's Voy.* III. i. 400 The greatest part of the birds.. were such as are known to roost on shore. **1791** COWPER *Yardley Oak* 52 Time hath made thee what thou art—a cave For owls to roost in. **1852** M. ARNOLD *Empedocles* II. 432 On the cliff-side, the pigeons Roost deep in the rocks.

transf. **1567** TURBERV. *Epit.*, etc. 36 No sooner stirres Auroras Starre,.. But they that rousted were in rest.. Do pack apace to labours left. *a* **1661** FULLER *Worthies* (1840) I. 106 Verres.. never saw the sun either to rise or set, as roosted after or before.

b. Of persons: To seat oneself, to perch. *colloq.*

1816 SCOTT *Antiq.* viii, Down to the flat shelf on which the sufferers had roosted. **1852** MRS. STOWE *Uncle Tom's C.* vi, About a dozen young imps were roosting, like so many crows, on the verandah railings. **1897** FLANDRAU *Harvard Episodes* 60 She is the woman who, when you call, roosts discreetly at the extreme end of a long sofa.

2. To lodge, harbour, make one's abode or quarters. In mod. use: To pass the night.

1593 NASHE *Christ's T.* Wks. (Grosart) IV. 95 Banisht he was, and longer in Ierusalem might hee not roust. **1610** HOLLAND *Camden's Brit.* (1637) 366 A rabblement of Danes rousted heere one whole yeare. [**1664** J. WEBB *Stone-Heng* (1725) 206 Camden finds him and his Danes roosting afterwards for one whole Year at Cirencester.] **1716** B. CHURCH *Hist. Philip's War* (1865) I. 161 It was hard to tell where to find Annawon, for he never roosted twice in a place. **1813** SIR R. WILSON *Priv. Diary* (1862) II. 486, I am most anxious to be on the wing, and again roosted. **1855** THACKERAY *Newcomes* xxxix, Stopped to roost at Terracina. **1883** J. A. SYMONDS *Shaks. Predec.* v. (1900) 166 These vagrants wandered up and down the country, roosting in hedge-rows.

b. *fig.* or in fig. contexts.

c **1554** COVERDALE *Hope of Faithful* Pref. Aiij, It vnknowne, all vices swarm and roste in vs. **1598** MARSTON *Sco. Villanie* I. ii. 178 Modestie is rousted in the skyes. **1607** S. HIERON *Wks.* I. 262 Men haue euen determined with themselues, that, let the word of the kingdome roust where it will, sure with them it shall not harbour. **1660** BONDE *Scut. Reg.* 108 So great ignorance cannot roust in their pates, who are so worldly wise. **1730** YOUNG *1st Ep. to Pope* 10 Where speculation roosted near the sky. **1793** BURNS *Address spoken by Miss Fontenelle* 5 So [I] sought a Poet, roosted near the skies.

3. *trans.* To afford a resting-place to (one); to accommodate, harbour. Also *fig.*

1854 S. DOBELL *Balder* iii. Poet. Wks. 1875 II. 17 They defy the storms of heaven, and roost The weary-winged Ages. **1873** CARLETON *Farm Ball.* 43 You have often slept in pens; I've a mind to take you out there now, and roost you with the hens!

'roost-cock. Now *rare.* [f. ROOST *sb.*[1]] A domestic cock.

1606 H. PARROT *The Mous-Trap* (Halliw.), Gallus, that greatest roost-cock in the rout. **1627** E. F. *Hist. Edw. II* (1680) 88 The old Roost-cock in his Country-language. **1668** CHARLETON *Onomast.* 75 *Gallus Gallinaceus*,.. the House, or Roost-Cock. **1736** AINSWORTH II, *Gallinaceus*,.. a roost-cock, a cockerel. *c* **1750** [MRS. PALMER] *Devonsh. Dial.* (1837) 18 Their blowzy faces as rid as roost-cocks. **1789** G. WHITE *Selborne* cv, Roost-cocks, which had been silent, began to sound their clarions. **1858** POLSON *Law & Lawyers* 116 A beautiful roost-cock flew upon his head and crowed three times.

rooste, obs. form of ROAST *sb.* and *v.*

'roosted, *a. rare.* [f. ROOST *v.* or *sb.*[1]] Perched on a roost. Also *fig.*

1748 THOMSON *Castle Indol.* II. xl, Yet oft his anxious eye Mark'd them, like wily fox who roosted cock doth spy. **1779** SHERIDAN *Critic* II. ii, Is't thus your new-fledged zeal And plumed valour moulds in roosted sloth?

rooster ('ruːstə(r)). Chiefly *U.S.* and *dial.* [f. ROOST *sb.*[1] + -ER[1].]

1. a. A cock.

1772 A. G. WINSLOW *Diary* 14 Mar. (1894) 45 Their other dish.. contain'd a number of roast fowls—half a dozen, we suppose, & all roosters at this season no doubt. **1806** *Balance* (Hudson, N.Y.) 22 July 227 (Th.), The New York Rooster —may he continue to crow! **1822** J. FLINT *Lett. fr. Amer.* 264 Rooster, or he-bird.—Cock, the male of the hen. **1836** *Backwoods Canada* 308 The produce of two hens and a cock, or *rooster*, as the Yankees term that bird. **1847** H. MELVILLE *Omoo* lxvi, With a rooster's quill, therefore, a bit of soiled paper, and a stout heart, he set to work. **1870** J. H. B. NOWLAND *Early Reminisc. Indianapolis* 149 It was during this canvass [in 1840] that Tom gave to the Democratic party their emblem, which they have claimed ever since, the chicken cock, or rooster. **1882** *Garden* 20 May 348 At sunrise I was awakened by a sturdy old rooster. **1922** JOYCE *Ulysses* 646 Chalk a circle for a rooster. **1923** E. W. BENJAMIN *Marketing Poultry Products* iv. 120 Cock, or Rooster.—These are the mature males. **1951** M. A. JULL *Successful Poultry Managem.* (ed. 2) xi. 348 A cock or old rooster is a mature male chicken with coarse skin, toughened and darkened meat.

b. *transf.* of persons.

1785 GROSE *Dict. Vulgar T.*, *Queer rooster*, an informer that pretends to be sleeping, and thereby overhears the conversation of thieves in night cellars. **1821** P. EGAN *Life in London* II. v. 276 Roosters and the 'peep-o'-day boys' were out on a prowl for a spree. **1840** *Log Cabin* 5 Sept. 3/2 *Chapman*, the great Rooster of the Loco-Foco party,.. was formerly one of the editers [*sic*] of an Infidel paper, the Boston Investigator. **1855** *N. Amer. Rev.* CXLI. 434 The toughest set of roosters that ever shook the dust of any town. **1871** G. MEREDITH *H. Richmond* II. 214 Hang.. your talk of a fine girl, like my Janet, as a piece of poultry, you young rooster! **1881** *Philad. Rec.* No. 3428. 2 It is not.. in the nature of things that a rooster in the Legislature should quietly submit to be lectured by a rooster outside of the legislature. **1883** *Bird o' Freedom* 7 Mar. 3/1 Whether the returned member be a rooster or not time will tell. **1897** BARRÈRE & LELAND *Dict. Slang* II. 156 *Queer rooster* (American thieves), a man that lodges among thieves to pick up information for the police. **1923** R. D. PAINE *Comrades of Rolling Ocean* xiv. 252 What was that rooster's name?

c. *U.S.* A wild violet as used in a children's game.

1884 *Harper's Mag.* June 94/1 Purple violets.. were slaughtered by hundreds, for the projecting spur under the curved stem at the base of the flower enabled the boys to hook them together and 'fight roosters', as they termed it. **1946** C. RICHTER *Fields* 231 In April they played Hens and Roosters, yoking their wild white and blue violets to see which would get its head pulled off.

d. A bird that is roosting or about to roost.

1949 *Brit. Birds* XLII. 323 The more leisured flight of the roosters [*sc.* starlings] was in contrast to the steady procession of the migrants.

2. *U.S.* (See quot.)

1871 in De Vere *Americanisms* 262 Rooster.. indicates a bill, or proposed law, which will benefit the legislators—and no one else.

3. rooster comb *U.S.* = *rooster head*; **rooster('s) head** *U.S.*, the American cowslip, *Dodecatheon meadia*, or a wild violet of the genus *Viola*; also *attrib.*; **rooster tail** *N. Amer.*, the curved plume of water thrown up by a speedboat or surfboard.

1964 MRS L. B. JOHNSON *White House Diary* 21 May (1970) 142 One little girl.. offered me a bunch of red and yellow wildflowers—'snake tongue' and 'rooster comb'. **1894** *Jrnl. Amer. Folk-Lore* VII. 94 *Dodecatheon Meadia*, var., shooting stars, roosters' heads. **1934** H. VINES *This Green Thicket World* 171 One not thicketed might have felt sorry for the blue daisies, white daisies, roosterheads. **1947** *Atlantic Monthly* July 41/2 Spring not only brought tadpoles but.. big bunches of rooster-head violets that the children picked in the woods. **1953** *Marine Digest* 19 Sept. 29/1 She was boxed in on the first turn by Gale and the two Such Crusts and their combined rooster tails just about sank her. **1956** *Sun* (Baltimore) 26 Oct. 34/5 It ruled.. that it was 'highly probable' the wake or fall of water from the 'rooster tail' of the boat travelling at high speed had caused the damage. **1963** *Pix* 28 Sept. 62/4 *Rooster-tail*, wake of a board. **1976** *Telegraph-Jrnl.* (St. John, New Brunswick) 7 Aug. 3/3 The small craft skim the river at incredible speeds. Their giant rooster tails sometimes reach a height of 90 feet.

Hence **'roosterish** *a.*

1898 'MARK TWAIN' in *Harper's Mag.* Mar. 536/2 He stands vast and conspicuous.. self-satisfied and roosterish.

'roosting, *vbl. sb.*[1] [f. ROOST *v.*]

1. Perching for rest; places for perching.

1604 DRAYTON *Owle* Poems (1619) 423 By all signes.. The Birds therein their nightly roosting made. **1713** DERHAM *Phys.-Theol.* VII. i. §5 The Legs all curved for their easy Perching, Roosting, and Rest. **1820** SCOTT in *Lockhart* (1837) IV. 376 A great deal of valuable fir planting, which you may remember; fine roosting for the black game.

2. a. *attrib.*, as ***roosting area***, ***behaviour***, ***-cage***, ***habit***, ***-house***, ***site***, ***-stick***, ***-time***, ***-tree***.

1976 T. SOPER *Everyday Birds* v. 59 When birds reach the vicinity of the roosting area there will often be a spectacular flying display. **1953** *Brit. Jrnl. Animal Behaviour* I. 91 (*heading*) The winter roosting and awakening behaviour of captive Great Tits. **1964** A. L. THOMSON *New Dict. Birds* 709/1 Roosting behaviour varies from species to species, and to some extent within a species. **1976** H. M. DOBINSON *Bird Count* ix. 150 (*heading*) Roosting habits of our most common species. **1844** H. STEPHENS *Bk. Farm* I. 153 An opening.. in the outer wall of the roosting-house. **1840** *Penny Cycl.* XVIII. 477/1 The first roosting-perch..should be placed lengthways. **1874** J. W. LONG *Amer. Wild-fowl* ix. 161 In the evening the ducks will be seen coming from the roosting-ponds. **1953** *Brit. Jrnl. Animal Behaviour* I. 91/2 Aggressive behaviour over roosting sites was seen on a few evenings. **1927** W. DE LA MARE *Told Again* 287 The hens on their roosting-sticks. **1621–3** MIDDLETON & ROWLEY *Changeling* IV. i, At roosting time a little lodge can hold 'em. **1743** W. ELLIS *Mod. Husbandman* July xvi. 77, I..took the Hen and her Young at Roosting Time. **1825** C. WATERTON *Wanderings in S. Amer.* 119 All the Toucanets feed on the same trees... You will find it has only been a dinner party, which breaks up and disperses towards roosting time. **1953** *Brit. Jrnl. Animal Behaviour* I. 91/1 In England the changes in the roosting times [of Great Tits] are similar to those in the north but less marked. **1834** J. J. AUDUBON *Ornith. Biogr.* II. 41 These roosting-trees of the Buzzards are generally in deep swamps, and mostly in high dead cypress trees. **1879** JEFFERIES *Wild Life* 281 They [*sc.* rooks] stretch from here to the roosting-trees.

b. Esp. ***roosting-place***; also *fig.*

1725 *Fam. Dict.* s.v. *Poultry*, Being wont in a Morning early, to go out of the Hen-House or Roosting-Place. **1789** G. WHITE *Selborne* cvi, The poultry dared not to stir out of their roosting-places. **1809** MALKIN *Gil Blas* I. xiii. ¶6, I.. slunk to my roosting-place, where I fell asleep. **1844** ALB. SMITH *Adv. Mr. Ledbury* iii, Jack quitted his roosting-place amongst the baggage. **1874** J. W. LONG *Amer. Wild-fowl* xxiv. 245 When their feeding-grounds and roosting-places are near together.

† **'roosting,** *vbl. sb.*² *Obs.*⁻¹ In 6 roostynge. [Cf. ROOST *sb.*²] Turbulent flow or turmoil.

1555 EDEN *Decades* (Arb.) 382 We mette northerly wyndes and greate roostynge of tydes.

'roosting, *ppl. a.* [f. ROOST *v.*] That roosts or perches; going to roost.

1798 BLOOMFIELD *Farmer's Boy, Autumn* xlii, From each bough The roosting Pheasant's short but frequent crow Invites to rest. **1813** SCOTT *Rokeby* v. ii, Hoarse into middle air arose The vespers of the roosting crows. **1886** *Daily News* 24 Sept. 5/2 They..startle from its crumbling recesses the roosting doves.

root (ruːt), *sb.*¹ Forms: *α.* 1, 5 rot, 3–6 rote, 4 rotte, 5 roth, roytt, rowte, 6 rott, roite, rout(e, rowth, 9 *dial.* roit; 4–7 roote, 5– root. *β. Sc.* 5–6 rut, 6 ruite, rwit, 5– rute, 6– ruit, 9 reet, rit; *north.* 9 reut, rut, re(e)at. [Late OE. *rót*, a. ON. *rót* (Icel. and Fær. *rót*), Norw. and Sw. *rot* (MSw. *root*), Da. *rod* (†*rood*), NFris. *rôt*, *rut* (prob. from ODa.), LG. *rut*. The original stem **wrōt-* is connected on the one hand with L. *rādīx*, and on the other with OE. *wyrt*: see WORT. The usual OE. words for 'root' are *wyrttruma* and *wyrtwala*.]

I. 1. a. That part of a plant or tree which is normally below the earth's surface; in *Bot.*, the descending axis of a plant, tree, or shoot, developed from the radicle, and serving to attach the plant to and convey nourishment from the soil, with or without subsidiary rootlets or fibres; also applied to the corresponding organ of an epiphyte, and to the rootlets attaching an ivy to its support.

a **1150** in Napier *Contrib. O.E. Lex.* 54 Se Godes freond cwæð þæt he leofode be weode & be wyrtan roten & be wæteres drence. *Ibid.*, He leofede be wyrtan rotan. *a* **1175** in *Hist. Holy Rood-tree* 4 An fet..wæs ifylled of þæt ylce watere & þa ȝyrdæ þeron asette, forþan ðe he nolde þæt ða roten fordruȝode wæron. *c* **1200** ORMIN 10064 þatt axe shollde þa beon sett Rihht att te treowwess rote. *a* **1300** in *E.E.P.* (1862) 10 þer nis..no tre in erþ so fast, mid al har rotis so fast ipiȝt, þat [etc.]. *a* **1300** *Cursor M.* 1346 þis tre was of a mikel heght.., And to þe rotte [*Gött.* rote] he kest his he. **1362** LANGL. *P. Pl.* A. VII. 96 Mi plouh-pote schal be my pyk, and posshen atte Rootes. **1390** GOWER *Conf.* I. 7 Now stant the crop under the rote. *c* **1440** *Promp. Parv.* 437/2 Rote, of a thynge growynge, *radix*. **1483** *Cath. Angl.* 314/2 A Rute, *radix, radicula*. **1513** DOUGLAS *Æneis* IV. viii. 80 Als far his ruite doith spreid Deip ondir erth. **1573** TUSSER *Husb.* (1878) 98 Get..a parer..to pare away grasse and to raise vp the roote. **1613** SHAKS. *Hen. VIII*, I. ii. 97 Though we leaue it with a roote thus hackt, The Ayre will drinke the Sap. **1672–3** GREW *Anat. Pl.* (1682) 128 What the Mouth is to an Animal; that the Root is to a Plant. **1750** GRAY *Elegy* 102 Yonder nodding beech, That wreathes its old fantastic roots so high. **1792** J. BELKNAP *Hist. New Hampsh.* III. 108 When the roots have been loosened by the frost, they are..cut and dug out of the ground. **1815** SHELLEY *Alastor* 531 Ancient pines Branchless and blasted, clenched with grasping roots The unwilling soil. **1846** J. BAXTER *Libr. Pract. Agric.* II. 383 In transplanting walnuts, ..great care should be taken that their roots be as little injured as possible. **1884** BOWER & SCOTT *De Bary's Phaner.* 438 In the growing-point of the stem, branches, and roots, and in young rudimentary leaves.

b. In phr. ***by the root*(*s*)**, denoting the complete pulling up of a plant or tree. (Cf. 9 c.)

c **1385** CHAUCER *L.G.W.* 2613 *Hypermnestra*, The floure, the lefe, ys rent vp by the rote To maken garlandes. *c* **1400** MAUNDEV. (Roxb.) xvii. 79 So þat þai be taken vp by þe rutes. *c* **1440** *Promp. Parv.* 131 Drawe vp by þe rote, *eradico*. **1526** *Pilgr. Perf.* (W. de W. 1531) 23 He..plucketh vp the breers, wedes and grasse by the rotes. **1593** SHAKS. *3 Hen. VI*, v. iv. 69 Yonder stands the thornie Wood, Which.. Must by the Roots be hew'ne vp yet ere Night. **1648** MILTON *Ps.* lxxx. 54 The tusked Boar out of the wood Up turns it by the roots. **1667** —— *P.L.* II. 544 As when Alcides ..tore Through pain up by the roots Thessalian Pines. **1765** A. DICKSON *Treat. Agric.* (ed. 2) 112 The weeds themselves must be pulled up by the root. **1833** HT. MARTINEAU *Briery Creek* ii. 26 They could pull up a tall tree by the roots.

c. Used without article; also in phrases as ***to take root***, to settle properly in the ground, ***to make root, strike root.***

c **1386** CHAUCER *Squire's T.* 153 Euery gras that groweth vp on roote. **1432–50** tr. *Higden* (Rolls) I. 265 For a tree may not take þer [L. *ibi*] roote for saltenes of the erthe. *c* **1440** *Promp. Parv.* 437 Rotyn, or take rote, as treys, *radico*. *c* **1480** HENRYSON *Fables, Trial Fox* xxx, Ouer Ron and Rute thay ran togidder raith. *c* **1560** A. SCOTT *Poems* (S.T.S.) xxxv. 9 He sall haif brute, as tre on rute Endlang the rever plantit. **1573** TUSSER *Husb.* (1878) 83 Thy garden plot..Well clensed and purged of roote and of stone. **1611** BIBLE *Ps.* lxxx. 9 Thou..didst cause it to take deepe root, and it filled the land. **1707** MORTIMER *Husb.* 7 This will cause it to strike fresh Root. **1725** *Fam. Dict.* s.v. *Root-grafting*, Which Piece of Root will draw in Sap, and nourish the Graft. **1738** WESLEY *Ps.* LXXX. xi, Water'd with Blood, the Vine took Root. **1856** GLENNY *Everyday Bk.* 263 The object of this is to let them make root when inclined, but not to grow any until wanted. **1878** BROWNING *La Saisiaz* 29 Fruit Others reap and garner, heedless how produced by stalk and root.

d. In phr. ***on*** (***its***) ***own roots***, used to describe a plant whose tissues all developed from the same embryo; not grafted or budded.

[**1822** J. C. LOUDON *Encycl. Gardening* II. 436 The scion is a part of the living vegetable, which, united or inserted in a stock or other vegetable of the same nature, identifies with it, and grows there as on its natural stem and roots.] **1869** S. R. HOLE *Bk. about Roses* viii. 112 The two trees..are on their own roots, but the Rose thrives stoutly on the Brier and the Manetti, budded and grafted, wherever roses grow. **1914** H. H. THOMAS *Gardening for Amateurs* 696/1 Plants may grow rampantly on their own roots to the material disadvantage of any useful products. **1944** KAINS & MCQUESTEN *Propagation of Plants* (rev. ed.) xiv. 334 Why do not nurserymen sell us plants on their own roots? The answer is that in no other way [than grafting] can fruit trees true to name be propagated so rapidly. **1968** *Horticultural Abstr.* XXXVIII. 630/2 Gialla Precoce Morettini on its own roots flowered earlier on a sandy soil than on a clay soil.

2. The permanent underground stock of a plant from which the stems or leaves are periodically produced; also, by extension, a plant, herb.

c **1200** *Trin. Coll. Hom.* 161 [It] is cleped..wildernesse gef þare manie rotes onne wacseð. **1596** DALRYMPLE tr. *Leslie's Hist. Scot.* I. 36 The herb gude to give the cattel against the rute that thay cal trifoly. **1599** SHAKS. *Hen. V*, II. iv. 39 As Gardeners doe with Ordure hide those Roots That shall first spring, and be most delicate. **1664** EVELYN *Kal. Hort.* April (1671) 48 Transplant such Fibrous roots..as Violets, Hepatica, Primroses. **1786** ABERCROMBIE *Gard. Assist.*, *Arr.* 81 The propagation of bulbous and tuberous roots for general supply. **1847** MRS. LOUDON *Amateur Gard. Monthly Cal.* 22/1 Others succeed pretty well by buying imported roots from the nurseryman every year. **1858** KINGSLEY *Poems* 137 That roots, which parch in burning sand, May bud to flower and fruit again.

3. a. The underground part of a plant used for eating or in medicine; now *spec.* in *Agric.*, one of a fleshy nature, as the turnip or carrot, and by extension, any plant of this kind.

a **1150** [see sense 1]. *c* **1200** ORMIN 3213 Hiss drinnch wass waterr.., Hiss mete wilde rotess. *c* **1205** LAY. 31885 þat folc ..lufeden bi wurten, bi moren and bi rote. **13..** *Cursor M.* 4711 (Gött.), þe wrecched pore miht find na fode,..þat soght þaim rotis als þe suyn. **1393** LANGL. *P. Pl.* C. XVI. 244 Bestes [live] by gras & by greyn and by grene rotes. *c* **1400** MAUNDEV. (Roxb.) viii. 30 þai liffe with dates and rutes and herbes. *c* **1489** CAXTON *Blanchardyn* xxi. 70 He hath in his house a rote that ..shal gyf me help. *a* **1533** LD. BERNERS *Huon* xxi. 63, I haue eten none other thynge but rootes & frutes. **1551** TURNER *Herbal* (1568) 21 It is euidently knowen that water wyll wexe thycke, if this roite be brused and put in it. **1605** SHAKS. *Macb.* I. iii. 84 Or haue we eaten on the insane Root, That takes the Reason Prisoner? **1617** MORYSON *Itin.* I. 34 Corne fields set with cabbages and roots. **1671** MILTON *P.R.* I. 339 We here Live on tough roots and stubs, to thirst inur'd More then the Camel. **1704** F. FULLER *Med. Gymn.* (1711) 94 These Roots may be so manag'd by a good Hand as to eat as Food. **1763** *Museum Rust.* I. 332 This root would..fill them up with flashy fat. **1801** *Farmer's Mag.* Jan. 113 Very few turnips are with us this season; this root having generally failed. **1817** SHELLEY *Rev. Isl.* v. lvi. 5 Melons, and dates, and figs, and many a root Sweet and sustaining. **1879** *Cassell's Techn. Educ.* IV. 237/1 Cattle require their 'roots' to be carted from the field to the homestead.

b. With defining words: (see quots.).

1787 *Gentl. Mag.* Nov. 963/1 The Mangel Wurtz..or Root of Scarcity. **1789** *Trans. Soc. Arts* VII. 33 The cows fed on the Common Turnep gave most milk..and those on the Root of Scarcity the least. **1801** *Farmer's Mag.* Jan. 87 In the mean time, all, rich and poor, have the greatest abundance of the root of plenty, potatoes.

c. *U.S. dial.* A spell effected by the supposedly magical properties of certain roots. Cf. *root doctor, worker*, sense 23 below.

1935 Z. N. HURSTON *Mules & Men* 340 Nearly all of the conjure doctors practice 'roots'. **1962** *Jrnl. Amer. Folklore* LXXV. 313 Local synonyms for the spell are 'curse', 'trick', 'fix', 'conjure', 'root', and 'hoodoo'.

4. a. The imbedded or basal portion of the hair, tongue, teeth, fingers, nails, or other members or structures of the body.

a **1225** *Leg. Kath.* 2122 [To] þurhdriuen hire tittes wið irnene neiles, & renden ham up hetterliche wið þe breoste roten. *c* **1320** *Sir Tristr.* 1485 His tong haþ he ton And schorn of bi þe rote. **1398** TREVISA *Barth. De P.R.* v. xxviii. (Bodl. MS.), þese boones stonde of twey ordres in þe oone side with þe rootes of þe fingres. **1508** KENNEDIE *Flyting w. Dunbar* 374 The ravyns sall ryve na thing bot thy tong rutis. **1523** FITZHERB. *Husb.* §91 If they be not kilde, they wyl.. eate the rotes of the horse eares, and kil hym. **1580** BLUNDEVIL *Horsem.* IV. cxvii. 54 A malander..hath long haires with stubborne roots. **1607** SHAKS. *Timon* v. i. 136 Each false [word] Be as a Cantherizing to the root o' th' Tongue. **1681** GREW *Musæum* I. v. i. 85 Beneath, close by the Root of the Saw, are two oblique Nostrils. **1710** *Lond. Gaz.* No. 4672/4 A..Spanish Dog, with..one large Liver colour Spot at the Root of his Stern. **1798** COLERIDGE *Anc. Mar.* II. xiii, Every tongue, through utter drought, Was withered at the root. **1817** KIRBY & SP. *Entomol.* xix. (1818) II. 145 The rightful queen..seized her with her jaws near the root of the wings. **1856** STONEHENGE *Brit. Rural Sports* 479/2 The root of the thumb should be brought close up to the ribs. **1898** *Allbutt's Syst. Med.* V. 151 Most frequently it starts from the root of the lung. **1940** W. FAULKNER *Hamlet* III. ii. 198 The bleached hair darkening again at the roots since it had been a year now since there had been any money to buy more dye. **1970** G. F. NEWMAN *Sir, You Bastard* viii. 213 Brown roots growing through her split blonde hair.

b. The more or less 'muddy' base of a crystal or gem, esp. of an emerald.

1695 WOODWARD *Nat. Hist. Earth* IV. (1723) 192 Their Root, as the Jewellers call it; which is only the Abruptness at that End of the Body whereby it adhered to the Stone. **1867** BILLING *Sci. of Gems* 126 A large piece of veiny, cloudy root of amethyst, 2½ inches by 2 inches (not good enough to rank as a jewel).

c. That part of anything by or at which it is united to something else.

1632 LITHGOW *Trav.* I. 22 The breadth of Italy at the roote and beginning thereof,..from the Adriaticke coast, to the riviera di Genoa. **1840** *Civil Eng. & Arch. Jrnl.* III. 237/1 A wooden jetty has been run out from the root of the pier. **1869** SIR E. REED *Ship Build.* xx. 430 The angle iron ..is liable to open at the root under very heavy blows. **1884** F. J. BRITTEN *Watch & Clockm.* 289 In watches the roots of all the wheels and pinions are left square except the roots of the barrel or great wheel teeth and the roots of the centre pinion leaves. **1910** *Aëronaut. Jrnl.* XIV. 115 The angle of incidence of each wing gradually decreases from the root to the tip. **1948** H. CONSTANT *Gas Turbines* v. 77 The blades stall at the root and tip. **1978** D. KÜCHEMANN *Aerodynamic Design of Aircraft* vi. 429 The upwash generated by that part of the body ahead of the root of the gross wing should also be close to that generated by the portion of the gross wing ahead of the root and should again be small.

d. *slang* The penis.

1846 *Swell's Night Guide* 119/1 *Flash*, to sport, to expose, he flashed his root. **1902** FARMER & HENLEY *Dict. Slang* V. 289/2. **1970** K. MILLETT *Sexual Politics* III. vii. 329 It measures intelligence as 'masculinity of mind', condemns mediocre authors for 'dead-stick prose', praises good writers for setting 'virile example' and notes that since 'style is root' (penis), the best writing naturally requires 'huge loins'.

5. a. The bottom or base *of* something material; *esp.* the foot of a hill.

c **1386** CHAUCER *Clerk's T.* 58 At the West syde of Ytaille, Doun at the roote of Vesulus the colde. **1483** CAXTON *Gold. Leg.* 59 b/2 Whan moyses had brouht them forth unto the rote of the hylle they stode there. **1553** EDEN *Treat. New Ind.* (Arb.) 20 Mountaynes..at the rootes wherof are found Rubines, Hiacinthes. **1579** *Reg. Privy Council Scot.* III. 189 That na thing remane within the clois about the rute of the tour bot the dur thairof. **1635–56** COWLEY *Davideis* I. Poems (1905) 261 Numbers which still encrease more high and wide From One, the root of their turn'd Pyramide. **1687** LOVELL tr. *Thevenot's Trav.* II. 74 A rock.., at the root whereof there is a little spring of Water. **1726** LEONI *Alberti's Archit.* I. 11/1 That Stream..continually undermining and eating away the Root of the Mountain. **1817** SHELLEY *Rev. Isl.* VII. xi. 3 A burst of waters driven As from the roots of the sea. **1844** MRS. BROWNING *Drama of Exile* Poems 1850 I. 85 Split the charnel earth To the roots of the grave. **1897** GEIKIE *Anc. Volcanoes Grt. Brit.* I. 12 There will thus be a constant pressure of the molten magma into the roots of volcanoes.

b. The bottom of the groove of a screw thread.

1892 *Screws & Screw-Making* (Britannia Co., Colchester) iii. 39 The diameter at the root of the thread. **1920** F. J. CAMM *Screw Cutting* i. 6 In some instances American screws are measured at the bottom of the thread B; this portion is often called the root. **1964** S. CRAWFORD *Basic Engin. Processes* (1969) xiv. 299 The root is the bottom portion of the groove between the flanking surfaces of the thread.

II. 6. a. The source or origin *of* some quality, condition, tendency, etc. Also occas. without const.

Freq. with fig. context directly referring to sense 1.

c **1200** ORMIN 4976 Forr niss nan mahht tatt bettre maȝȝ þe winnen eche blisse þann allre mahhte rote maȝȝ. *a* **1225** *Ancr. R.* 54 Biginnunge & rote of þis ilke reouðe was a liht sihð e. *a* **1300** *Cursor M.* 28744 þou pain þe rotes as þou mai O þis man sin to do awai. **1390** GOWER *Conf.* III. 197 Pite, men sein, is thilke roote Wherof the vertus springen alle. **1423** JAS. I *Good Counsel* 2 Wertew floure and rut is of noblay. **1467–8** *Rolls of Parlt.* V. 622/2 It was shewed..that Justice was grounde well and rote of all prosperite. **1525** LD. BERNERS *Froiss.* II. clxxviii. [clxxiv.] 535 This rote and foundacion of hatred multyplyed greatly after. **1589** *Pasquil's Return* C iij b, This is the roote of all the mischife. **1611** SHAKS. *Wint. T.* II. iii. 89 The Root of his Opinion, which is rotten, As euer Oake or Stone was sound. **1639** S. DU VERGER tr. *Camus' Admir. Events* 34 To cut up the roote of all these fooleries in her sonne. **1711** STEELE *Spect.* No. 48 ¶4, I have several Follies which I do not know the Root of. **1720** RAMSAY *Prosp. Plenty* 145 Malicious envy! root of a' debates. **1821–2** SHELLEY *Chas. I*, I. i. 103 The root of all this ill is prelacy. **1884** tr. *Lotze's Metaph.* 513 The root of all these difficulties seems to be a confusion in our idea of.. an acting force.

b. Predicated of persons or material things.

1377 LANGL. *P. Pl.* B. xv. 98 Prestes, and prechoures.., That aren rote of þe riȝte faith. *c* 1386 CHAUCER *Can. Yeom. T.* 516, I wol it verifie In this Chanoun, roote of alle trecherie. *c* 1400 *Beryn* 4015 Saff the Burgeysis of the town, of falshede þat were rote. *c* 1485 *Digby Myst.* (1882) III. 1671 O blyssyd womman, rote of ower savacyon. 1549 LATIMER *2nd Serm. bef. Edw. VI* (Arb.) 64 These flattering clawbackes are originall rotes of all mischyue. 1590 SPENSER *F.Q.* II. vii. 12 All otherwise.. I riches read, And deeme them roote of all disquietnesse. 1667 MILTON *P.L.* IX. 645 To the Tree Of prohibition, root of all our woe.

7. a. A source of some quality, etc.; *esp.* a virtue or vice giving rise to some condition or action.

c 1200 ORMIN 11658 Alle fule lusstess Biginnenn þære & springenn ut Off gluterrnessess rote. *a* 1310 in Wright *Spec. P.* xviii. 57 Suete Jhesu,.. In myn huerte thou sete a rote Of thi love. *c* 1380 WYCLIF *Wks.* (1880) 173 This [covetousness] is a venymous rote þat makiþ here seruyce.. not acceptable to god. *c* 1400 *Apol. Loll.* (Camden) 91 Wene we not þe gospel to be.. in þe leuis of wordis, but in rot of resoun. 1564 *Reg. Privy Council Scot.* I. 291 Hir Majestie wald nocht that ony rute were left behind, quhilk mycht engender ony new displesour or grudge betuix thame. 1603 H. CROSSE *Vertues Commw.* (1878) 26 Considering those inconueniencies that rise out of the roote of aboundance. 1671 MILTON *Samson* 1032 Or was too much of self-love mixt, Of constancy no root infixt. 1781 COWPER *Expost.* 111 Faith, the root whence only can arise The graces of a life that wins the skies. 1823 MOORE *Loves Angels, 3rd Angel's Story* x, Humility, that low, sweet root From which all heavenly virtues shoot. 1876 MELLOR *Priesth.* ii. 77 The root of bitterness out of which all this strife has grown is simple.

†**b.** *to take root*, to spring *from* something.

a 1300 *Cursor M.* 43 Vr dedis fro vr hert tas rote, Quedur þai be worthi or bale or bote.

8. a. A person or family forming the source of a lineage, kindred, or line of descendants.

13.. *Seuyn Sages* 1072 (W.), I ne mai do thi sone no bot, But yif I wite the sothe rot, Of what man hit was biyete. *c* 1375 *Cursor M.* 10162 (Trin.), Ioachim bringere of bote, he was comen of dauid rote. 1388 WYCLIF *Isaiah* xi. 1 And a ȝerde schal go out of the roote of Jesse. 1555 HARPESFIELD in Bonner *Hom.* 6 For as much as they two were the very route, where of all men must ryse. 1582 STANYHURST *Æneis* I. (Arb.) 17 Thence flitted thee Latin ofspring, Thee roote of old Alban. 1605 SHAKS. *Macb.* III. i. 5 It was saide.. that my selfe should be the Roote, and Father Of many Kings. 1667 MILTON *P.L.* II. 383 To confound the race Of mankind in one root. 1766 BLACKSTONE *Comm.* II. 217 This taking by representation is called a succession *in stirpes*, according to the roots; since all the branches inherit the same share that their root, whom they represent, would have done. 1818 CRUISE *Digest* (ed. 2) III. 409 It was introduced with a view to discard the son; and that the father should become the *propositus* or *root*, to whom No 10 is exactly in the same relation as No 11 is to the son. 1873 DIXON *Two Queens* I. i. I. 4 Among the deputies were many who had sprung from Oriental roots.

transf. *a* 1653 GOUGE *Comm. Heb.* vii, Shem was the root of the Church.

b. A scion, offshoot. (Chiefly Biblical.)

13.. *Guy Warw.* (1883) 442 Þei he be þe deuels rote, Y schal nouȝt fle him a fot. 1382 WYCLIF *1 Macc.* i. 10 And there wente out of hem a roote of synne, Antiochus the noble. —— *Rev.* xxii. 16. 1526 TINDALE *Rev.* v. 5 A lion beinge off the tribe off Juda, the rott of David, hath obtayned to open the boke. 1611 BIBLE *Isaiah* xi. 10 In that day there shall bee a roote of Iesse, which shall stand for an ensigne of the people. 1632 LITHGOW *Trav.* x. 435 The plants of their Parishes, being the rootes of meere Irish. 1745 W. ROBERTSON in *Trans. & Paraph. Scot. Ch.* vi. 13 So in this cold and barren World That sacred Root arose.

9. a. That upon or by which a person or thing is established or supported; the basis upon which anything rests.

In 19th cent. use common in the phr. ***to have (its) root(s) in*** (something).

1340 *Ayenb.* 116 [To] strengþi his roten ine þe erþe of libbende. 1377 LANGL. *P. Pl.* B. xx. 53 Antecryst cam þanne and al þe croppe of treuthe Torned it vp so doune and ouertilte þe rote. 1523 COVERDALE *Old God & New* (1534) D iv, By so moche the more the christen fayth waxed stronge and gathered fast rotes. 1563 WINȜET *Wks.* (S.T.S.) I. 127 Sen it hes the grund and deip ruitis in the Scriptuir. 1612 SELDEN *Illustr. Drayton's Poly.olb.* xvii. (1876) II. 250 Some have referred the utmost root of the Lancastrian title to Edmund,.. eldest son to Henry III. 1679 NESS *Antichrist* 180 Two.. is the lowest number (for one is but the root of numbers). 1720 OZELL *Vertot's Rom. Rep.* II. XI. 179 Cato .. fell into Pompey's Hands, who to cut up the Root of the Civil War, put him to Death. 1784 COWPER *Task* v. 353 Our love is principle, and has its root In reason. 1787 —— *Stanzas Bills Mortality* 24 A worm is in the bud of youth, And at the root of age. 1820 SHELLEY *Prometh. Unb.* II. iii. 42 The nations echo round, Shaken to their roots, as do the mountains now. 1849–50 ALISON *Hist. Europe* II. vi. §63. 57 This prodigious change.. laid the axe to the root of the aristocracy. 1874 STEVENSON *Ess. Trav.* (1905) 245 A high wind under a cloudless sky.. seems to have no root in the constitution of things.

b. Of qualities, esp. with reference to their hold upon persons.

1340 *Ayenb.* 34 Of þe rote of auarice guoþ out manye smale roten. *c* 1400 *Sc. Trojan War* II. 396 In þe which dame Auaryce Festned hyr rotes at dewyce. 1556 J. HEYWOOD *Spider & Fly* xxxix. 17 Where honestnes or vertusnes bearth rout. 1570 DEE *Math. Pref.* *iiij b, What rotes.. vertue had fastened in his brest. 1605 SHAKS. *Macb.* IV. iii. 85 This Auarice.. growes with more pernicious roote Then Summer-seeming Lust. 1781 COWPER *Table Talk* 15 With a courage of unshaken root, In honour's field advancing his firm foot. 1841 TRENCH *Parables* xii. (1877) 241 Righteousness, both in its root of faith and its flower of charity.

c. In phrases denoting completeness or thoroughness, as ***to the root(s)***, ***by the root(s)***, etc. (Cf. 1 b.)

1388 WYCLIF *Ps.* li[i]. 7 Therfor God schal distrie thee in to the ende, he schal drawe thee out bi the roote. 1560 DAUS tr. *Sleidane's Comm.* 93 b, Wherby these newe spronge up sectes mayе be plucked up by the rotes. 1599 B. JONSON *Cynthia's Rev.* v. v, That so she might, more strictly, and to root, Effect the Reformation she intende. 1611 SHAKS. *Cymb.* I. i. 28 What's his name, and Birth? I cannot delue him to the roote. 1640–1 in Rushw. (1721) III. I. 187, I wonder not at all.. that they would have them [Bishops] up by the Roots. 1781 COWPER *Truth* 574 Since the dear hour that.. cut up all my follies by the root. 1818 CRUISE *Digest* (ed. 2) III. 12 This argument was quite cut up by the roots by the determination of the House of Lords in the case of Tong v. Robinson. 1860 RUSKIN *Unto this last* i. §22 He [the merchant] has to understand to their very root the qualities of the things he deals in. 1894 FENN *Real Gold* 89 As if he were enjoying himself right down to the roots.

10. a. The bottom or real basis, the inner or essential part, of anything.

the root of the matter, a literal rendering of Heb. *shōresh dābār* in Job xix. 28.

c 1386 CHAUCER *Can. Yeom. T.* 908 (Ellesm. MS.), Telle me the roote.. Of that water, if it be youre wille. 1393 LANGL. *P. Pl.* B. xv. 64 [He] þat þorw resoun wolde þe rote knowe Of god and of his grete myȝtes, his graces it letteth. 1426 LYDG. *De Guil. Pilgr.* 10033 Yiff the roote be wel out souht, Strengere than thow, that ys he nouht. 1565 COOPER *Thesaurus, Stirps quæstionis*, the roote, and foundation of a question. 1611 BIBLE *Job* xix. 28 Seeing the root of the matter is found in me. 1674 N. FAIRFAX *Bulk & Selv.* 168 That everlastingness which the soul has in the root.. is of the same kind. 1735 *Col. Rec. Pennsylv.* IV. 45 Until he advisedly looketh into the Roots of it and tries it by the Rule of Law. 1850 ROBERTSON *Serm.* Ser. III. v. (1872) 61 In every such case it may be taken for granted that the root of the matter has not been reached. 1875 SWINBURNE *Ess. & Stud.* 274 His resolute desire to get at the roots of things, and deeper yet if deeper might be.

†**b.** The bottom *of* the heart, in various figurative uses. *Obs.*

For earlier examples see HEART-ROOT 1. In latest examples perh. an alteration of *rote*.

1485 CAXTON *Paris & V.* (1868) 11 In hym I haue putte the rote of myn entyere herte. 1508 DUNBAR *Poems, Tua Mariit Wemen* 162, I sall a ragment reveil fra the rute of my hert. *c* 1560 A. SCOTT *Poems* (S.T.S.) xv. 1 Vp, helsum hairt! thy rutis rais, and lowp. 1607 SHAKS. *Cor.* II. i. 202 A Curse begin at very root on's heart. 1607 CHAPMAN *Bussy D'Ambois* Plays 1873 II. 82 As illiterate men say Latine praiers By roote of heart, and daily iteration. 1684 BUNYAN *Pilgr.* II. 11 That thou read therein to thy self, and to thy Children, until you have got it by root-of-Heart.

c. ***at (the) root***, at bottom, essentially.

1855 KINGSLEY *Westw. Ho!* ii, He was, at root, a godly and kind-hearted pedant enough. 1857 BORROW *Rom. Rye* xvi, At the root mad.

11. a. ***to take*** (or ***strike***) ***root***, to obtain a permanent footing or hold; to settle down *in* a place, etc.

1535 COVERDALE *2 Kings* xix. 30 And the doughter Iuda.. shall from hence forth take rote beneth, and beare frute aboue. 1560 DAUS tr. *Sleidane's Comm.* 92 b, No suche sectes can take roote or remayne emonges them. 1605 CAMDEN *Rem.* (1623) 10 This warlike.. Nation, after it had as it were taken roote here. 1784 COWPER *Task* II. 568 Prejudice in men of stronger minds Takes deeper root, confirm'd by what they see. 1809 MALKIN *Gil Blas* x. xi. ¶5 As soon as I had taken root in my new soil. 1840 DICKENS *Barn. Rudge* xlviii, The cause has taken a deep root, and has spread its branches far and wide. 1899 GARDINER *Cromwell* 36 The idea struck root.

†**b.** A hold upon a person's affections, confidence, or favour. *Obs.*

a 1715 BURNET *Own Time* (1724) I. 207 Such an attempt.. would give him a faster root with the King. 1756 HOME *Douglas* II, Let not thy jealousy attempt to shake And loosen the good root he has in Randolph.

c. A strong link or attachment.

1854 KINGSLEY *Lett.* (1878) I. 432 The awful feeling of having the roots which connect one with the last generation seemingly torn up.

d. *pl.* Established ties with a locality or region; one's social, cultural, or ethnic origins or 'background'. Also in colloq. phr. ***to put down roots***, to become established in a place, to settle down.

1921 R. MACAULAY *Dangerous Ages* iv. 82 The.. infinitely loved Barry, who was going to give her roots. 1949 G. B. SHAW *Buoyant Billions* II. 21 Plenty of money and no roots. No traditions. 1969 A. G. THOMAS in L. Durrell *Spirit of Place* 117 On three occasions, when he has bought a house and put down roots, the whole collection has been posted out to him. 1977 *Gay News* 7–20 Apr. 10/4 In Scots and Welsh schools children are taught about their national roots, culture and history. 1977 P. THEROUX *Consul's File* 184 Is it possible to put down roots here?.. The Chinese won't, the Tamils can't, the Malays pretend they have them.

12. ***root-and-branch***: see BRANCH *sb.* 6 b.

For *root and crop, root and rind*, in similar uses, see CROP *sb.* 5 and RIND *sb.*[1] 2.

1642 SIR E. DERING *Sp. on Relig.* 94, I never gave my name in to take away both root and branch.

b. In adverbial use: Completely, utterly.

1640 SLINGSBY *Diary* (1836) 66 Some do petition to reform them, others to abolish them root and branch. 1650 R. STAPYLTON *Strada's Low C. Wars* v. 141 Constantly to endeavour the extirpation of it, Root and Branch. 1777 J. ADAMS *Fam. Lett.* (1876) 299 If our people do not turn out now and destroy Burgoyne's gang, root and branch. 1829 SCOTT *Rob Roy* Introd., Cutting off the tribe of MacGregor root and branch. 1887 *Times* (weekly ed.) 23 Sept. 17/3 You may look forward.. to local government being dealt with by Parliament root and branch.

†**c.** *ellipt.* The policy of total abolition. *Obs.*

1679 EVELYN *Sylva* (ed. 3) 2 Professing themselves against Root and Branch.

d. In attributive use, of persons or things.

1737 *Gentl. Mag.* VII. 499 These are Root and Branch Men, and strike at the Foundation of all our National Happiness. 1788 *Ann. Reg., Misc.* 143, I have hit upon a plan which will make root and branch work of it, and do the business effectually. 1816 *Edin. Rev.* XXVII. 167 We have seen that our root-and-branch Reformer went a great deal farther. 1858 J. PAYN *Foster Brothers* xv, The boy had become at heart a root-and-branch democrat. 1887 *Dict. Nat. Biog.* IX. 249/2 The so-called root-and-branch bill for the total extinction of episcopacy.

III. †**13.** *Astrol.* = RADIX 2. *Obs.*

c 1386 CHAUCER *Man of Law's T.* 314 Of viage is ther noon eleccioun,.. Noght whan a roote is of a burthe yknowe? *c* 1391 —— *Astrol.* ii. §54 Consider thy rote furst, the wyche is made the begynning of the tabelis. 1575 F. WITHER tr. *Indagine's Chiromancy* III. N iv, They which haue Venus in the rote of their natiuity. 1603 [see RADIX 2]. 1647 LILLY *Chr. Astrol.* clvii. 654, I oft am enforced to name the Root of the Nativity, it were more proper to say the Radix, for our English doth not well expresse the sense of the words.

14. *Math.* **a.** A number, quantity, or dimension, which, when multiplied by itself a requisite number of times, produces a given expression. ***cube*** (or ***third***) ***root***: see CUBE *sb.*[1] 3. ***square*** (†***quadrate***) or ***second root***: see SQUARE *a.*

1557 RECORDE *Whetstone* C iv, Thei onely haue rootes, whiche bee made by many multiplications of some one number by it self. 1571 DIGGES *Pantom.* I. xxv. Hj b, The roote quadrat of the whole number, is the desired distance or line Hypothenusal. 1660 BARROW *Euclid* Expl. Signs, The Side or Root of a Square. 1679 MOXON *Math. Dict.* 38 *Cube Root*, the Root or Side of the third Power: So if 27 be the Cube, 3 is the Side or Root. 1706 W. JONES *Syn. Palmar. Matheseos* 47 The Root or First Power being taken as a Side, the Second Power will be a Square. 1753 *Chambers' Cycl.* Suppl. s.v., The extraction of the roots of algebraic quantities. *Ibid.*, Impossible Root is not only the square root of a negative quantity, but any other root denominated by any even number. 1798 HUTTON *Course Math.* (1799) I. 80 Roots are sometimes denoted by writing the character $\surd$ before the power, with the index of the root against it. 1859 B. SMITH *Arith. & Algebra* (ed. 6) 199 The Square Root of any proposed quantity. 1876 *Rep. Brit. Assoc. Adv. Sci. 1875* II. 13 (*heading*) Theorems on the *n*th roots of unity. 1898 G. CHRYSTAL *Introd. Algebra* (1902) 5 Special cases are the second root written $\sqrt{a}$; the third root or cube root [etc.]. 1941 COURANT & ROBBINS *What is Math.?* ii. 100 The complex cube roots of 1.. are the roots of the equation $x^2 + x + 1 = 0$. 1966 *Math. Rev.* XXXI. 29/1 If α is an algebraic integer, $\alpha \neq 0$, α not a root of unity, then at least one of the conjugates of α has absolute value greater than 1.

b. The value or values of an unknown quantity which will satisfy a given equation.

1728 CHAMBERS *Cycl.* s.v. If the Value of *x* be Negative, e.gr. $x = -5$, the Root is said to be false. 1798 HUTTON *Course Math.* (1799) I. 249 To find the root of the cubic equation $x^3 + x^2 + x = 100$, or the value of *x* in it. 1826 in *Encycl. Metrop.* (1845) I. 544/2 Both members of an equation may be raised to the same power, or the same root of them may be extracted. 1885 WATSON & BURBURY *Math. Th. Electr. & Magn.* 179 The three roots are always real. The equation is the same as that [etc.].

c. A unique node or vertex of a graph from which every other node can be reached. Also ***root node***.

1857 A. CAYLEY in *Phil. Mag.* XIII. 172 The inspection of these figures will show at once what is meant by the term in question, and by the terms *root, branches*,.. and *knots* (which may be either the root itself, or proper knots, or the extremities of the free branches). 1881 *Amer. Jrnl. Math.* IV 266 In a tree of N knots, selecting any knot at pleasure as a root, the tree may be regarded as springing from this root, and it is then called a root-tree. 1965 *Proc. Cambr. Philos. Soc.* LXI. 499 A tree is a connected topological graph without circuits. The vertices will also be called nodes or individuals. There is often one distinguished node called.. the root. 1973 C. W. GEAR *Introd. Computer Sci.* vii. 282 Formally, a tree is a set of nodes connected by branches such that there is one and only one way of going from one node to another via branch connections, and which has a distinguished node called the root node. 1973 S. EVEN *Algorithmic Combinatorics* vi. 109 A vertex *v* is called a root.. of the graph if every vertex of the graph is reachable from *v*. 1976 E. MINIEKA tr. *Berge's Graphs & Hypergraphs* (ed. 2) iii. 32 A graph does not always have a root. 1977 *Sci. Amer.* Apr. 70/1 The location of the first key to be examined in a binary tree is traditionally known as the root; in the 31-word example the root is 16.

d. ***digital root***: the digit obtained when all the digits of a number are added and the process is repeated on successive results until the outcome is a single digit.

1956 G. A. MONTGOMERIE *Digital Calculating Machines* vii. 140 One such check number is the 'digital root' obtained by adding all the digits of the number. 1973 *Sci. Amer.* Dec. 120/1 One way to do it makes use of the old accountant's trick for checking addition by digital roots.

15. *Philol.* **a.** One of those ultimate elements of a language, that cannot be further analysed, and form the base of its vocabulary; †a primary word or form from which others are derived.

1530 PALSGR. *Introd.* 31 His thre chefe rotes, that is to say, his theme, his preterit participle, and his present infynityve. 1599 *Broughton's Lett.* xii. 39 Recourse must be had to the Hebrew, euen to a false roote. 1615 BEDWELL *Index Ass.* O iij, The theame or roote, as they call it, from whence it is deriued, is.. *Kara'*, to reade. 1631 GOUGE *God's Arrows* I. §11. 15 The word.. is derived from the same roote. 1740 CHESTERF. *Lett.* lxiii. (1792) I. 177 The shortest and best way of learning a language is to know the roots of it; that is those original primitive words, of which many other words are made. 1760 STERNE *Tr. Shandy* IV. xxix, As it is a fault only in the declension, and the roots of the words continue untouch'd. 1837 G. PHILLIPS *Syriac Gram.* 20 The simplest forms of nouns are those which consist only of the letters composing the root. 1856 STANLEY *Sinai & Pal.* (1858) 260 Sharon, a name of the same root as that used to designate the table-lands beyond the Jordan. 1883 MORFILL *Slavonic Lit.* ii. 39 A Slavonic root, meaning dwelling.

b. With punning allusion to sense 1.

1663 BUTLER *Hud.* I. i. 59 Hebrew Roots, although th' are found To flourish most in barren ground, He had such plenty. 1812 COMBE *Syntax, Picturesque* XXIII. 20 What though by toil and pain, I know Where ev'ry Hebrew root doth grow. 1831 CARLYLE *Misc.* (1857) II. 328 No Greek Roots grew there.

16. *Mus.* (See quot. 1889.)

1811 BUSBY *Dict. Mus.* (ed. 3), *Root*, a term applied by theorists to the fundamental note of any chord. 1818 —— *Gram. Mus.* 314 The Triad may have its mediant either two whole tones, or a tone and a semitone, above its Root. 1867 MACFARREN *Harmony* (1892) 51 The inversion of a chord is the placing one of its other notes, instead of the root, in the bass. 1889 PROUT *Harmony* iii. §58 Much trouble is sometimes caused to students from the word *Root* being used in two senses by theorists—as the lowest note of any combination of thirds, and also as the fundamental tone in the key from which the combination is harmonically derived.

17. Miscellaneous senses of uncertain affinity. Cf. ROOT *v.*[1] 9.

a. *slang.* (orig. *Schoolboys'*). A forceful kick. Also **root about** (see quot. 1900).

1900 FARMER *Public School Word-Bk.* 169 *Root-about* ..(The Leys), promiscuous football practice. 1934 N. SCANLAN *Winds of Heaven* 46 Matt gave him 'a root in the gear' and told him not to talk like a stable boy. 1961 in WEBSTER, Caught him a great root with his boot on the backside.

b. *Austral. coarse slang.* An act of sexual intercourse. Also, a (female) sexual partner.

1959 in R. Chamberlain *Stuart Affair* (1973) xi. 111 Did you have a root? 1961 F. HARDY *Hard Way* iii. 77 The conversation led inevitably to women. Our shabby criminal struck a match revealing..a sign scrawled on the wall: 'Best American root—ring such and such a number.' 1969 *Private Eye* 4 July 14/3, I hear tell these *artists* in London don't exactly have to chase the odd *root.* 1973 A. BUZO *Rooted* I. 43 Hey, do you remember the time he got pissed out of his mind and fronted up to this old duck and asked her for a root? 1974 P. KENNA *Hard God* I. 33 Have you ever gone all the way with a girl?.. You know what I mean. Have you ever had a real root? 1976 D. IRELAND *Glass Canoe* 147 Johnny Bickel..thought she'd be an easy root and began to take notice of her.

IV. *attrib.* and *Comb.*

18. a. Attrib. in sense 1, with words denoting some part, appendage, or feature belonging to a root, as ***root-bark, -bud, -cap, -fibre, -system, -thread, -tip, -zone***, etc.

1832 *Planting* 7 in *Husb.* III. (L.U.K.), Should the soil be dry.., the bark in question is gradually converted into *root-bark. 1805 R. W. DICKSON *Pract. Agric.* II. 603 They are enabled to propagate their subterraneous wires or *root-buds. 1977 J. L. HARPER *Population Biol. of Plants* 290 Both sexes spread clonally by means of root buds. 1875 HUXLEY & MARTIN *Elem. Biol.* 71 Its lower end is covered by the *root-cap of the ultimate termination of the principal root. 1805 R. W. DICKSON *Pract. Agric.* II. 779 It is quite necessary that the sets have formed *root-fibres at the bottoms before they are removed. 1874 COOKE *Fungi* 9 A stray fragment of a *root-fibril. 1875 HUXLEY & MARTIN *Elem. Biol.* vi. 41 Appendages, consisting of leaves, branches, *root-filaments, and reproductive organs. 1882 *Garden* 25 Feb. 133/1 *Root fungus frequently attacks the Rose. 1868 *Rep. U.S. Commiss. Agric.* (1869) 249 The large amount of *root-growth in the deeper, central parts of the ridge. 1857 A. GRAY *First Less. Bot.* (1866) 31 The absorbing surface of roots is very much greater than it appears to be, on account of the *root-hairs. 1849 BALFOUR *Man. Bot.* §963 They [broomrapes] attach themselves to the roots of various plants, and are hence called *Root-parasites. 1805 R. W. DICKSON *Pract. Agric.* I. 550 Different new lateral stems or *root-scions are sent off. 1848 LINDLEY *Introd. Bot.* (ed. 4) II. 183 *Root secretions are now regarded as unimportant. 1805 R. W. DICKSON *Pract. Agric.* II. 620 The branching out of the stringy *root-shoots or wires. 1742 *Lond. & Country Brewer* IV. (ed. 2) 258 The *Root-spire.. will be so many Tails to increase the Measure. 1804 J. GRAHAME *Sabbath* (1827) 82 When the wren..from the *root-sprig trills her ditty clear. 1805 R. W. DICKSON *Pract. Agric.* II. 751 The earth being well laid upon the hills round the *root-stems of the plants. 1875 BENNETT & DYER tr. *Sachs' Bot.* 608 The cut surface of the *root-stump remains at first quite dry. 1786 ABERCROMBIE *Gard. Assist.* 17 To clear away all *root-suckers. 1902 *Encycl. Brit.* XXV. 439/1 The presence of a feeble absorptive *root-system and an extended surface of the shoot for transpiration and transudation are the outstanding points [of hydrophytes]. 1969 P. THROWER *Every Day Gardening* iv. 85/2 Budding is really a form of grafting and enables the grower to unite a garden rose with a root system or 'stock' obtained from a wild or vigorous rose. 1954 J. R. R. TOLKIEN *Fellowship of Ring* I. vii. 141 His grey thirsty spirit drew power out of the earth and spread like fine *root-threads in the ground. 1954 —— *Two Towers* 66 Something between *root-tip and leaf-tip. 1967 L. PICKEN *Organization of Cells* iv. 127 In the presence of low concentrations of phenolic compounds growing root tips also showed a temporarily increased frequency of fragmentation [of chromosomes]. 1953 J. RAMSBOTTOM *Mushrooms & Toadstools* xviii. 206 The microflora is greater in the region of actively growing roots than in the soil generally: this is perhaps particularly true of bacteria, but also holds for fungi. This *root-zone of increased population is known as a rhizosphere. 1805 R. W. DICKSON *Pract. Agric.* II. 625 The continued propagation of potatoes by subterraneous buds, or *root-wires.

b. In the sense 'made of roots'.

1853 LOWELL *Moosehead Jrnl.* Prose Wks. 1890 I. 9 Sometimes a root-fence stretched up its bleaching antlers. 1864 ATKINSON *Stanton Grange* 7 On the garden side, a root-bench was constructed against the bole of the tree. 1895 *Outing* XXVI. 389/2 The grass needs time to weave the deep, tough, root carpet so essential for sure footing. 1930 BLUNDEN *Poems* 318 Thus the sacred well Is passed, and now the far root-canopy Issues its people, swift and slippery.

c. Misc., as ***root-room, -sort; root-beset, -built, -inwoven; root-bitten, -eaten, -filled, -fringed, -pale, -stricken, -torn, -weary; root-devouring, -digging, -eating, -feeding, -forming; root-like.***

1897 MARY KINGSLEY *W. Africa* 554 A narrow, slippery, muddy, *root-beset bush-path. 1872 TENNYSON *Gareth & Lynette* 445 Wan-sallow as the plant that feels itself *Root-bitten by white lichen. *a* 1763 SHENSTONE *Economy* I. 167 Suffice the *root-built-cell, the simple fleece,..the crystal stream. 1817 KIRBY & SP. *Entomol.* xvi. II. 5 The males of another *root-devouring beetle. 1877 tr. *Tiele's Hist. Relig.* 17 Lowest in the scale stands the religion of the *root-digging Australians. 1915 *Proc. Soc. Antiquaries London* XXVII. 149, I have often picked up on the surface of the camp pieces of old *root-eaten human bones. 1882 *Garden* Mar. 147/2 The Cabbage fly is much of the same size as the *root-eating fly. 1892 LUBBOCK *Beaut. Nat.* 67 Others collect *root-feeding Aphides into their nests. 1918 *Atlantic Monthly* CXXII. 122 The Place d'Etoile was perhaps first adumbrated by wild boars concentrating on a *root-filled marsh. 1946 *Nature* 19 Oct. 555/1 The *root-forming capacity of penicillins G and X almost certainly resided in these substances themselves. 1944 BLUNDEN *Shells by Stream* 5 Upon the *root-fringed dais. 1792 S. ROGERS *Pleas. Mem.* I. 79 Yon *root-inwoven seat. 1832 LINDLEY *Introd. Bot.* III. v. 351 Generally the root or *root-like bodies are to be excluded from all characters higher than those of species. 1960 S. PLATH *Colossus* 63 *Root-pale her meagre frame. *c* 1887 G. M. HOPKINS *Poems* (1967) 103, I do advise You, jaded, let be; call off thoughts awhile Elsewhere; leave comfort *root-room. 1977 *Interim* IV. IV. 4 Strips of unripened green, retarded from maturity by the moisture and greater root-room in the ditch's silts below. 1960 T. HUGHES *Lupercal* 33 Worm-sort, *root-sort, going where it is profitable. 1860 CHRISTINA ROSSETTI *Poems* (1904) 191/1 Thou, *root-striken, shalt not rebuild thy decay On my bosom for aye. 1871 R. ELLIS *Catullus* lxiv. 288 Tall *root-torn beeches. 1931 A. HUXLEY *Cicadas* 51 Never a tortured flower Shudders, *root-weary, on the verge of flight.

19. In sense 3, as ***root-boat, -cellar, -crop, -culture, -cutting board, -field, vegetable***, etc.; also ***root-eater, -gatherer, -pedlar, -puller, -pulper, -woman; root-loving, -pulping*** adjs.

For names and descriptions of various implements or machines, as *root-bruiser, -cutter, -digger*, etc., see Knight *Dict. Mech.* (1875) and *Suppl.* (1884).

1636 *Maldon Borough Deeds* (Bundle 110, fol. 2), March 12. Re[ceived] for the groundage of a *Root boate at barrow hills, 4*d.* 1822 LOUDON *Encycl. Gard.* 378 The *root-cellar may have a few divisions on the ground to keep the different roots apart. 1872 Root-cellar [see *grain-box* s.v. GRAIN *sb.*[1] 18 a]. 1965 E. L. MYLES *Emperor of Peace River* II. ii. 184 After that we collected the potatoes and put them in the root cellar. 1834 *Husb.* I. 382 (L.U.K.), Regarding *root crops, Mr. Cuthbert Johnson also mentions [etc.]. 1847 W. C. L. MARTIN *Ox* 115/1 Of all these root-crops, it appears that the least exhausting to the land is that of the beet. 1901 L. H. BAILEY *Princ. Vegetable-Gardening* ix. 271 Root crops require a cool season and a deep soil. 1969 *Oxf. Bk. Food Plants* 172 (*heading*) Crucifer and composite root crops. 1840 BUEL *Farmer's Comp.* 163 The advantages of *root culture to the soil. 1969 E. H. PINTO *Treen* 95 The introduction and gradual increase throughout the 18th century, in the growing of root crops for animal winter feed, led to the importance of the well worn *root cutting board. *a* 1735 ARBUTHNOT *Misc. Wks.* (1751) I. 212 Any Daughter of a Waterdrinker and *Root-eater. 1932 BLUNDEN *Fall in, Ghosts* 9 The crucifix surmounting the steps of granite in the middle of the *rootfields. 1977 F. PARRISH *Fire in Barley* ii. 18 Dan heard the bloodhounds..race across the root field towards the farm. 1562 TURNER *Herbal* II. 56 b, Theyr *root gatherers digged not theyr rootes hole out of grounde. 1947 C. S. LEWIS in *Punch* 1 Oct. 324/1 Fruit-loving, *root-loving gods. 1562 TURNER *Herbal* II. 56 b, Ye Duche *root pedlers of Antwerp. 1699 EVELYN *Acetaria* App. P 5 b, So have you a Composition for any *Root-Pudding. 1856 *Trans. Mich. Agric. Soc.* VII. 54 D. O. & W. S. Penfield, Detroit, one iron *root puller. 1952 S. SELVON *Brighter Sun* ix. 161 With a root-puller attached the tractor would move up to a tree and the arms would reach down into the earth and wrest the tree out. 1940 *Chambers's Techn. Dict.* 730/1 **Root pulper*, a machine comprising a rotating steel disc furnished with cutters, to which roots that have been cleared of soil are fed. 1978 *Morecambe Guardian* 14 Mar. 22/3 (Advt.), Bale Sledge, Buck Rake, Root Pulper. 1910 *Chambers's Jrnl.* Mar. 207/2 The electricity furnished by this means serves to light the house.., and drives a chaff-cutter, a circular saw, and a *root-pulping machine. 1820 W. TOOKE *Lucian* I. 306 You are nothing but a *rootscraper and a mountebank. 1851 MAYHEW *London Lab.* I. 130/1 The '*root-sellers' (as the dealers in flowers in pots are mostly called). 1802 WILLICH *Dom. Encycl.* III. 503/2 *Root-Steamer, an useful machine ..for steaming potatoes, carrots, and other roots, with the view of feeding cattle. 1886 C. SCOTT *Sheep-Farming* 80 A *root store, a small hay shed,..and a comfortable hut for the shepherd, are all requisites of the lambing fold. *Ibid.* 66 Corn boxes do not need to be so large as the *root troughs. 1898 *Allbutt's Syst. Med.* V. 895 Raw fruits, *root vegetables, and bread must be avoided. 1957 P. WORSLEY *Trumpet shall Sound* 15 The people live by cultivating.. root-vegetables. 1976 *Southern Even. Echo* (Southampton) 1 Nov. 4/3 The sandy soil there, he reckons, suits root vegetables just fine. 1801 *Spirit Public Jrnls.* V. 304 Nor will he despise the filth and rubbish of a *root-woman's cellar.

20. In sense 4, as ***root-drawer, -forceps; root-affection, -centre, -sheath, -treatment; root-filling, -planing, -rising; root-filled*** adj.

1899 *Allbutt's Syst. Med.* VI. 894 As a rule the root-affection is most severe. 1899 *Allbutt's Syst. Med.* VI. 46 The painful impressions upon the root centres. 1597 A. M. tr. *Guillemeau's Fr. Chirurg.* b 4 b, The Roote-drawer, to drawe any roote of a toothe. 1963 C. R. COWELL et al. *Inlays, Crowns, & Bridges* viii. 84 A post-retained crown is commonly indicated for a root-filled anterior tooth the natural crown of which has become discoloured. 1977 *Proc. R. Soc. Med.* LXX. 439/1 Teeth root-filled or crowned before operation were excluded from these results. 1963 C. R. COWELL et al. *Inlays, Crowns, & Bridges* viii. 85 The root filling should be well condensed. 1969 *Gloss. Terms Dentistry (B.S.I.)* 23 *Root filling*, the permanent filling and sealing of the root canal of a tooth to avoid the accumulation within the root canal of fluids or micro-organisms. 1875 *Dental Cosmos* XVII. 509 The forcing of delicate beaks of a fine pair of root-forceps up between the root and the bone. 1962 BLAKE & TROTT *Periodontology* x. 105 For pockets under 3mm, only removal of calculus and root planing and polishing are necessary. 1922 D. H. LAWRENCE in *Poetry* XXI. 65 Until your veiled head almost touches backward To the root-rising of your erected tail. 1859 *Todd's Cycl. Anat.* V. 497 The..inner rootsheath lies in immediate contact with the outer rootsheath. 1872 HUXLEY *Physiol.* xii. 278 The superficial epidermic cells of the hair sac.. become converted into root sheaths. 1927 W. E. COLLINSON *Contemp. Eng.* 60 If a tooth is decaying or hollow we have it stopped or filled..or we have root-treatment (sterilization and withdrawal of nerve).

21. In sense 9 or 10, as ***root-cause, -conception, -confusion, -divergence, -evil, -fallacy, -idea***, etc. (Now passing into adj.)

1915 E. CARPENTER *Healing of Nations* i. 12 One might be on safer ground by trying to get at the *root-causes of this war. 1977 J. WAINWRIGHT *Day of Peppercorn Kill* 191 He didn't trust us, Dick—that's the root cause. 1862 R. VAUGHAN *Eng. Nonconf.* 194 These were the *root conceptions of their faith. 1934 *Downside Rev.* LII. 223 As to the second root-conception of Cistercianism, the mere enunciation of an opinion..cannot be allowed. 1940 W. EMPSON *Gathering Storm* 25 The mind..now less easily decides On a good *root-confusion to amass Much safety from irrelevant despair. 1927 AUDEN & DAY-LEWIS *Oxf. Poetry* p. vi, The logical conflict, between the denotatory and connotatory sense of words, which is the *root-divergence of classic and romantic. 1891 HIBBERT *Eng. Gilds* 143 That *root-evil of our present industrial system, irregularity of employment. 1872 MORLEY *Voltaire* 236 Without seeking to expose the *root fallacy of idea. 1847 *Proc. Philol. Soc.* III. 34 The writer is convinced that the *root-ideas..are few in number. 1866 DK. ARGYLL *Reign of Law* ii. 70 Force is the root-idea of Law in its scientific sense. 1933 E. PARTRIDGE *Words, Words, Words!* I. 88 The root-idea of blood as something vivid or distressing or both still colours the use of the adjective. 1923 D. H. LAWRENCE *Kangaroo* vii. 141 Hardly sympathy at all, but an ancient sort of *root-knowledge. 1960 *Spectator* 7 Oct. 518/2 Mr. Kimche is arguing against the consistent record, and against the very *root-logic of Zionism. 1681 FLAVEL *Method of Grace* xi. 233 Christ..the comprehensive *root-mercy, from whom are all other mercies. 1875 E. WHITE *Life in Christ* II. xiv. (1878) 155 S. Paul and the other apostles treat this as a *root-principle of the gospel theology. 1933 H. READ *Art Now* I. 47 This brings us down to the *root-problem of aesthetics. 1957 M. SWAN *Brit. Guiana* iv. 68 It is one of the root problems of the country. 1853 KINGSLEY *Hypatia* viii, He found himself face to face with the *root-questions of all thought. 1924 R. HICHENS *After Verdict* III. xiv. 491, I loved her Then because I loved you. That was the *root reason. *a* 1957 R. CAMPBELL tr. A. de Campos in *Coll. Poems* (1960) III. 138 Which, once constructed, announce themselves As Real-Things, Spirit-Things, or Entities of the Stone-Soul, Made ours at certain moments by *root-sensations. 1976 S. HYNES *Auden Generation* ii. 56 As the decade moved on, these images took on heavier symbolic meanings..but the *root-sense of the images remained the same. 1884 J. PARKER *Apost. Life* II. 213 You must find in yourselves the *root-thought of God. 1667 FLAVEL *Saint Indeed* Ep. Ded., There are multitudes of books indeed, and of them many concern not themselves about *Root-truths. 1898 G. MEREDITH *Odes Fr. Hist.* 61 Strength is of the plain *root-virtue born. 1855 KINGSLEY *Glaucus* 32 The great *root-wonder of a number of distinct individuals connected by a common life.

22. a. In sense 14, as ***root-factor, -limitation, -point.***

1857 *Trans. Cambr. Phil. Soc.* (1864) X. I. 263 We then, in the common way, establish the existence of the root-factor. *Ibid.* 266 The curves P = 0, Q = 0, the intersection of which determines the root-points. 1874 *Ibid.* (1879) XII. II. 395 On the geometrical representation of Cauchy's theorems of Root-limitation.

b. In sense 15, as ***root-accent, -character, -class, determinative, -element, -enlargement, -expansion, form, -language, -morpheme, -noun, -period, -play, -stem, stress, -syllable, -vowel, -word; root-accented, -final, -initial, -forming, stressed*** adjs.

1935 G. K. ZIPF *Psycho-Biol. of Lang.* 133 The explanation offered by Jespersen for extensive root-accent. 1975 *Language* LI. 140 The more commonly occurring root-accented forms *trāmane, dāmane, dhārmane, bhārmane.* 1871 *Public Sch. Lat. Gram.* §14. 21 The last letter of a Root, as g in flag-, is the Root-character. 1879 W. D. WHITNEY *Sanskrit Gram.* ix. 208 The root-class [of verbs]..its present-stem is coincident with the root itself. 1965 G. Y. SHEVELOV *Prehist. of Slavic* xxiv. 367 It is to be assumed that in these words the varying consonants had not been originally a part of the root but were the so-called root determinatives, a kind of suffixes whose function is no longer discoverable. 1935 G. K. ZIPF *Psycho-Biol. of Lang.* 145 When the accent..was not on the endings, it was always on the stem-formative (suffix or infix) and not on the root-element. 1976 *Archivum Linguisticum* VII. 63 The discrepancy between the consonants..is easily accounted for by the assumption of different root-enlargements. 1895 P. GILES *Short Man. Compar. Philol.* xxv. 370 The details of the theory of root-expansion are..as yet too little worked out. 1965 H. M. HOENIGSWALD in W. Winter *Evidence for Laryngeals* 93 Such extra-Indoiranian etymologies as have been advanced with any promise mostly involve root-final position for the voiceless aspirates. 1973 *Trans. Philol. Soc.* 1971 68 *sil-* is not a permissible Indo-European root form. 1933 L. BLOOMFIELD *Language* 275 Even our root-forming morphemes..have some flexibility. 1956 *Language* XXXII. 453 The root-initial verb aspect markers are most aptly described in terms of simulfixation. 1972 *Ibid.* XLVIII. 477 The alternations in the non-nasal prefixes are conditioned by the voicing of the root-initial consonant. **1885** *Encycl. Brit.* XVIII. 774/1 A Chinese monosyllable or an Egyptian or Polynesian dissyllable is radical, unless there can be demonstrated in some part of it a formative value; and a language wholly composed of such words is a root-language. **1935** G. K. ZIPF *Psycho-Biol. of Lang.* 177 The total magnitude of complexity of the root-morpheme *fac*, a typical example, was diminished. **1950** *Lingua* II. 241 He makes only a few isolated remarks about the morphemes that occur most frequently, i.e. the root-morphemes. **1972** *Language* XLVIII. 477 Such a proto-initial is very poorly attested by the comparative data in root-morphemes. **1879** W. D. WHITNEY *Sanskrit Gram.* xiii. 314 The root-noun used as infinitive has the same form, and the same accent,.. as in its other uses. **1962** C. WATKINS *Indo-European Origins of Celtic Verb* I. 185 The verbal root **med-* being identical with the athematic root noun **med-*. **1874** SAYCE *Compar. Philol.* vi. 227 The root-period is not inconsistent with a rudimentary inflection. **1970** M. DAHOOD *Psalms* III. 109 The rootplay evident in *yilbᵉšu* and *boštām*.. is of a piece with the wordplays that wryly characterize many biblical and Canaanite laments. **1879** W. D. WHITNEY *Sanskrit Gram.* v. 129 Root-stems, having in them no demonstrable element added to a root. **1979** T. BURROW *Problem of Schwa in Sanskrit* 66 The root stem *nās-* f. 'nostril, nose' inflects with long vowel in the only strong case which occurs in the Veda. **1965** G. Y. SHEVELOV *Prehist. of Slavic* iv. 68 In all these cases the Li[thuanian] F[alling] P[itch] type has root stress. *Ibid.* 69 Analogy with the root stressed instr[umental] and loc[ative] pl[ural]. **1845** *Proc. Philol. Soc.* II. 50 Those syllables which are dignified by the name of root syllables. **1900** H. SWEET *Hist. Lang.* vi. 103 The place of the accent [in Aryan] was not restricted by any considerations of quantity or distance from the end of the word,.. nor was it restricted to the root-syllable of a word, as was afterwards the tendency in the Germanic language. **1972** *Language* XLVIII. 477 Arranging the words in the alphabetical order of their root-syllables. **1852** *Proc. Philol. Soc.* V. 201 The root-vowel *a* of the Latin *fra-ter*. **1571** GOLDING *Calvin on Ps.* xxxiv. 6 All agree not in the woord ..which some supposing too bee derived of the roote-woord. **1587** —— *De Mornay* xxviii. 444 Now the word Silo (saith Kimhi in his booke of Rootewordes) signifieth the *Sonne of him*. **1865** TYLOR *Early Hist. Man.* iv. 61 Two divisions of the root-words of our Aryan language. **1918** R. BRIDGES in G. M. Hopkins *Poems* 100 Passages where, in a jungle of root-words, emphasis seems to oust euphony. **1954** H. READ *Anarchy & Order* 196 The root-word *vir* [in *virtue*] has the implication of masculinity.

c. In sense 16, as ***root-note***, ***-position***, ***-progression***.

1883 *Grove's Dict. Music* III. 158/1 The group of harmonics generated by their fundamental or root note. **1891** PROUT *Counterpoint* (ed. 2) 192 This will give us a most unpleasant mediant chord in root position in the fourth bar. **1901** —— *Harmony* v, We have several times made the bass fall a fifth, to impress upon the student the identity of the root-progression.

23. Special combs., as **root-alcohol** (see quot.); **root-aorist** *Philol.*, in certain Indo-European languages, an aorist formed by adding personal endings directly to the root-syllable of the verb; **root-ball**, (*a*) = NIGGER-HEAD 1 a; (*b*) the mass formed by the roots of a plant and the soil between and around them; hence **root-balled** *a.*; **root beer**, *U.S.*, a beverage prepared from roots; **root-beetle**, a beetle infesting the roots of trees; **root-bound** *a.*, †(*a*) bound or held by roots; (*b*) = POT-BOUND *a.*; also *fig.*; †**root bread** *U.S.*, the bulbs of *Camassia quamash* (cf. CAMAS, QUAMASH), formerly baked and eaten in western North America; **root canal**, the pulp-filled cavity within the root of a tooth; **root-climber**, a plant which climbs by the aid of rootlets developed on the stem; **root coal** (?); †**root colour**, a dye-colour produced by certain roots; hence †**root-coloured** adj.; **root cutter**, (*a*) an implement for cutting edible roots; (*b*) one for cutting tree roots underground; **root cutting**, a cutting taken from the root of a plant; **root-devourer**, a beetle living upon roots (see quot.); **root digger**, (*a*) a primitive implement for digging up edible roots; (*b*) a member of a North American indian people (cf. DIGGER 2 c); **root doctor** *U.S. dial.*, one who treats ailments by means of roots, a herb-doctor; also = *root worker* below; **root-footed** *a.*, rhizopodous; **root-form**, (*a*) a basal or primitive form (of something); (*b*) an insect form which infests the roots; **root gall** (see quot. 1902); **root-graft** *sb.*, (*a*) a graft of a scion on to a root; (*b*) a naturally occurring graft between the roots of neighbouring trees; hence **root-graft** *v. trans.*, to graft by means of a root-graft; **root-grafted** *ppl. a.*, **root-grafting** *vbl. sb.*; **root-hold**, attachment by means of roots (freq. *fig.*); **root-knot**, a disease of many crop and other plants, caused by infestation of the roots with the nematode *Heterodera marioni* producing characteristic swellings or nodules; freq. *attrib.*; **root-mean-square** *Physics*, a mean calculated as the square root of the arithmetic mean of the squares of a set of values; freq. *attrib.*; **root nodule**, a swelling on a root of a legume or other higher plant containing symbiotic micro-organisms which fix nitrogen; **root pressure** *Bot.* [tr. G. *wurzelkraft* (J. von Sachs *Handb. der Exper.-Physiol. der Pflanzen* (1865) IV. vii. 199)], the hydrostatic pressure generated in the roots of a plant, which helps the sap to rise in the xylem; **root-prune** *v.*, to prune (a tree) by cutting its roots; so **root-pruning**; **root rot**, a disease of plants, attacking the roots; **root-run**, the space over which the roots of a plant extend; **roots reggae**, a style of reggae music considered as an expression of the black Jamaicans' cultural identity; **root-stroke**, a decisive stroke, a fatal blow; **root swell(ing)**, an outgrowth of a tree above a root, forming a natural buttress; †**root tubercle** = *root nodule* above; **root worker** *U.S. dial.*, one who uses roots to work spells, a conjurer (cf. sense 3 c above); so **root work**; **root-worm**, a worm attacking the roots of plants.

1883 R. HALDANE *Workshop Rec.* Ser. II. 11/2 **Root-alcohol.*—A number of roots and tubers.. have been availed of for the manufacture of alcohol. **1879** W. D. WHITNEY *Sanskrit Gram.* xi. 276 Imperative forms of the *root-aorist are not rare in the early language. **1955** H. G. LUNT *Old Church Slavonic Gram.* iv. 89 The most wide-spread type of the older aorists was the so-called 'root-aorist', attested by over 650 examples with some 27 verbs. **1976** *Archivum Linguisticum* VII. 62 In Oscan-Umbrian *-e-* is the sign of a secondary thematization of the Indo-European root-aorist. **1930** *Sat. Even. Post* 13 Dec. 11/2 Bogs of black muck dotted with devilish, rotating *root-balls that throw a man waist-deep. **1956** X. FIELD *Housewife Bk. House Plants* I. 31 If the outside of the root ball is a network of roots re-potting is called for. **1973** J. L. FAUST *Bk. House Plants* 37 If the root ball of the plant is very tightly packed and hard, it can be squeezed a bit to break it apart. **1966** *Gloss. Landscape Work* (*B.S.I.*) IV. 19 **Root-balled*, with roots contained within a well-defined mass of soil (in practice usually wrapped with protective material). **1843** *Knickerbocker* XXII. 85 Let.. the temperance halls and the *root-beer perambulatories make answer. **1851** HAWTHORNE *Ho. Seven Gables* iii, No less than five persons.. enquired for ginger-beer or root-beer or any drink of a similar brewage. **1856** KANE *Arctic Expl.* I. xxix. 387, I will stay only long enough to complete my latest root-beer brewage. **1921** [see COCA-COLA]. **1974** E. BRAWLEY *Rap* II. xix. 250 Sucking on his root beer freeze through a red plastic straw. **1817** KIRBY & SP. *Entomol.* xxiii. II. 372 In the morning.. the *Hopliæ*, *root-beetles before mentioned, have their dances in the air. **1634** MILTON *Comus* 662 As Daphne was *Root-bound, that fled Apollo. **1885** R. T. COOKE *Root-Bound* 11 My plants do blossom well.. and I don't know why unless it is because they are root-bound. *Ibid.* 12 It's good for folks and flowers too to be root-bound.. sometimes; especially, if we want to bring forth good fruit. **1946** *Nature* 23 Nov. 762/2 Further experiments show the importance of.. the feeding of root-bound plants with a balanced fertilizer prior to transplanting. **1976** *S. Wales Echo* 27 Nov. 4/1 He informed the schoolmaster that finding a square root meant looking for limp leaves in seedlings or pot plants, this condition being caused by them being root-bound in box or pot. **1805** W. CLARK in *Orig. Jrnls. Lewis & Clark Expedition* (1905) III. 85 Traded for some *root Bread & skins to make shirts. **1806** J. ORDWAY in Lewis & Ordway *Jrnls. Western Explor.* (1916) 352 We bought a little dark couloured root bread which is not good but will Support nature. *c* **1840** D. THOMPSON *Narr. Explorations W. Amer. 1784–1812* (1916) II. iv. 413 An old Man made a short speech, and made a present of two cakes of root bread (not moss). **1893** *Dental Rec.* XIII. 523 (*heading*) Filling *root canals with coal wadding. **1923** *Ibid.* XLIII. 269 The root-canals afford excellent hold for posts. *Ibid.* 682 The first requisite for root-canal filling is the complete sterilisation of the root-canal and tubuli. **1978** S. SHELDON *Bloodline* xli. 356 A dental bill for root-canal work for Charles Martel. **1897** J. C. WILLIS *Flowering Pl. & Ferns* I. 177 **Root-climber.* **1813** VANCOUVER *Agric. Devon* 71 The *root coal has a broken and wavy texture. **1777** *Dict. Chem.* I. U 8 *note*, The stuffs intended to receive a *root color. *Ibid.*, The nuts and roots employed in the *root-colored dye. **1807** T. YOUNG *Lect. Nat. Phil.* II. 208/2 Scythes, chaff cutter, *root cutter. *a* **1877** KNIGHT *Dict. Mech.* II. 1975/2 To bring the roots to a convenient size for the stock and to remove the danger of choking, root-cutters were introduced. **1943** J. STUART *Taps for Private Tussie* xxii. 226 You could follow the mule behind a locust-beamed plow with a sharp root cutter in it and hear the roots pop. **1969** E. H. PINTO *Treen* 18 Root Cutters. The traditional type illustrated.. with pivoted knife at one end, was made in a considerable range of hardwoods.., and was used generally.. by apothecaries. **1954** A. G. L. HELLYER *Encycl. Garden Work* 68/2 As a rule *root cuttings are taken while the plant is dormant, which means generally, in winter. **1969** P. THROWER *Every Day Gardening* v. 108/1 Propagation by root cuttings is the best way of increasing many thick-rooted perennials like verbascums, Oriental poppies, phlox, anchusa and *Limonium latifolium*. **1817** KIRBY & SP. *Entomol.* xxiii. II. 349 The *root-devourers or tree-chafers (*Melolontha, Hoplia*, &c.) support themselves.. in the air and over the trees. **1831** W. GORDON *Let.* 3 Oct. in A. H. Abel *Chardon's Jrnl. at Fort Clark* (1932) 346 Many of these [Snake Indians] go by the name which signifies *Root digger, because they live by digging roots. **1837** W. IRVING *Capt. Bonneville* II. xii. 204 These are of that branch of the great Snake tribe called Shoshokoes, or Root Diggers, from their subsisting, in a great measure, on the roots of the earth. **1865** LUBBOCK *Preh. Times* 420 Root-diggers are either made of horns, or of crooked sticks pointed and hardened by fire. **1866** *Proc. Philad. Acad.* 225 The Shoshoni, or Root-Digger skulls, three in number, vary in form. **1947** B. A. DE VOTO *Across Wide Missouri* 432 'Root-digger'.. describes all the tribes, most of them superior tribes, that lived in localities where there were staple crops of edible roots and bulbs. **1821** J. HOWISON *Sk. Upper Canada* xii. 195 'Oh!' said the woman, 'if I had but the *root doctor that used to attend our family at Connecticut; he was a dreadful *skeelful* man.' **1890** *N.Y. Age* 19 Apr. 1/1 Carmier was what people call down here a root doctor... He only rode around the county.. and made his living curing the sick and selling his medicine. **1900** *Jrnl. Amer. Folklore* XIII. 228 People git conjur from the root-doctors and one root-doctor often works against another, the one that has the most power does the work. **1934** [see MOJO[1]]. **1962** *Jrnl. Amer. Folklore* LXXV. 315 She finally went to a root doctor and was informed that her husband and three women had placed a spell upon her. **1862** ANSTED *Channel Isl.* II. ix. 242 The rhizopoda or *root-footed animals. **1875** WHITNEY *Life Lang.* 13 The *root-form of the verb. **1884** W. K. PARKER *Mammalian Desc.* (1885) iv. 72 The primordial root-form of all the nobler creatures, now existing... A still lower root-form than the Tadpole. **1888** *Encycl. Brit.* XXIV. 239 A number of minute insects..; these are the root-forms (radicola) of *Phylloxera*. **1902** L. H. BAILEY *Cycl. Amer. Hort.* IV. 1545/2 The term *root-gall is usually applied to the abnormal enlargement of roots due to insects and other animal organisms. **1933** *Jrnl. R. Hort. Soc.* LVIII. 233 The absence of detailed information regarding the infective stage of the root-gall nematode and its life history has been remedied. **1977** J. L. HARPER *Population Biol. Plants* xvi. 484 (*caption*) *Biorrhiza pallida* forms root galls and meristem galls on the oak at different seasons. **1824** J. C. LOUDON *Encycl. Gardening* (ed. 2) II. 396 Such *root-grafts grow with uncommon vigour. **1900** L. H. BAILEY *Cycl. Amer. Hort.* II. 661/2 In the West apples at least are usually *root-grafted. **1951** F. J. CHITTENDEN *Dict. Gardening* II. 919/2 Rhododendrons.. are.. frequently root-grafted, using roots of common species of their genus as stocks. **1956** *New Biol.* XX. 101 There is evidence that the fungus can infect trees only through wounds that penetrate the bark. The disease spreads locally by means of natural root grafts. **1900** L. H. BAILEY *Cycl. Amer. Hort.* II. 663/2 In the East.. budded apple trees are preferable to *root-grafted trees. **1942** KAINS & MCQUESTEN *Propagation of Plants* (rev. ed.) xii. 294 Ten Walldow root-grafted trees were all dead but one limb on one tree. **1707** MORTIMER *Husb.* 513 *marg.*, *Root grafting. *c* **1820** *Edin. Encycl.* XI. 196/1 Recourse is sometimes had to root-grafting. **1886** G. NICHOLSON *Illustr. Dict. Gardening* II. 91/2 Plants largely propagated by Root-grafting are Bignonias, Clematis, Hollyhocks, and Wistarias. **1977** J. L. HARPER *Population Biol. of Plants* 235 It is doubtful whether any careful search has ever been made to detect the extent of root grafting in other communities of herbs. **1864** SPENCER *Illustr. Progr.* 372 It would become possible for plants of higher organization to find *roothold. **1880** MISS BIRD *Japan* I. 123 Even maples had found roothold in their gigantic stems. **1889** *Bull. U.S. Dept. Agric. Div. Entomol.* No. 20 (*title*) The *root-knot disease of the peach, orange, and other plants in Florida, due to the work of Anguillula. *Ibid.*, 9, I.. can find no mention of the root-knot.. prior to the year 1857. That year Hon. P. J. Berckmans.. found this disease prevalent. *Ibid.*, In 1876 I found the root-knot prevalent over Florida, and learned from old residents that as far back as 1805 it had been known. **1912** E. W. SWANTON *Brit. Plant-Galls* viii. 107 Miss Ormerod first reported the occurrence of this pest, known as the 'root-knot' eelworm, in Britain. **1954** *New Biol.* XVI. 113 The Root Knot Eelworm.. is a tropical or sub-tropical species which in Britain infests the soil of heated glasshouses... Its host-range includes almost all the decorative plants grown in conservatories. **1976** *Daily Times* (Lagos) 8 June 2/2 The workshop is discussing Integrated Crop Protection System with emphasis on root-knot diseases affecting economic crops. **1895** *Electrician* 27 Sept. 721/1 A short time ago Dr. Fleming published a new and ingenious method of plotting wave forms with polar co-ordinates, and of directly obtaining therefrom the *root mean-square value. **1927** S. H. LONG *Navigational Wireless* i. 7 Thus the effective value I equals the square root of the mean value of the squares of all the instantaneous values. This is often called the root-mean-square value, or R.M.S. value or virtual value. **1956** A. A. TOWNSEND *Struct. Turbulent Shear Flow* iii. 51 The rate of increase of the decay scale is proportional to the root-mean-square turbulent velocity. **1978** *Nature* 9 Mar. 143/2 We note here that sound pressures as well as displacement are expressed as root-mean-squares. [**1899** J. B. FARMER *Botany* ix. 44 Plants which have not these nodules on their roots are unable to utilize the free atmospheric nitrogen.] **1907** F. CAVERS *Plant Biol.* iii. 119 The *root-nodules of leguminous plants contain a micro-organism which fixes free atmospheric nitrogen. **1949** A. NELSON *Introd. Bot.* xxv. 391 The root nodule, so typical of this bacterial association with a legume, commences when the bacterium enters the root hair of the legume. **1976** BELL & COOMBE tr. *Strasburger's Textbk. Bot.* (rev. ed.) 293 In the root nodules of alder, *Hippophae*, *Eleagnus*, and also probably of *Myrica* and *Casuarina*, the organisms concerned are symbiotic actinomycetes, also capable of fixing atmospheric nitrogen. **1875** BENNETT & DYER tr. *Sach's Text-bk. Bot.* III. i. 600 (*caption*) Apparatus for observing the force with which water escapes under *root-pressure from the transverse section of a stem. **1896** *Phil. Trans. R. Soc.* B. CLXXXVI. 572 An important function of root-pressure, *i.e.*, to dissolve up and clear out the gaseous contents of such conduits as are occupied by bubbles. **1931** E. C. MILLER *Plant Physiol.* iv. 168 Under conditions of low transpiration or in the spring before the leaves are unfolded, water is forced into the conducting vessels of the root and up through the stem under pressures varying from a fraction of an atmosphere to several atmospheres. This pressure is evidenced by the bleeding of cut vines and branches of certain species of plants and is apparently connected with the exudation of water from the leaves of plants, which occurs under certain conditions. This pressure, which is set up in the fibrovascular bundles of the stem and root due to the water which is being forced in them is known as 'root pressure'. **1976** *Sci. Amer.* May 104/3 Although Hales had discovered the existence of root pressure, he concluded that the roots are not solely responsible for the pressure of the sap in the branches. **1851** *B'ham & Midl. Gardener's Mag.* Apr. 39 All plants that are breaking very strong should be *root-pruned. **1841** T. M. RIVERS (*title*), *Root Pruning of Pears and other Trees. **1883** *Science* I. 369/2 The cause of the *root-rot in grape-vines. **1933** *Jrnl. R. Hort. Soc.* LVIII. 280 The occurrence of root-rot of Sweet Peas.. is described as one of the causes possibly associated with the streak disease of Sweet Peas. **1978** EVANS & KUMM *Woman's Own Pot Plant Doctor* 21/1 The commonest reason for all house plants dying off is root rot. **1882** *Garden* Jan. 35/3 Roses.. cease to grow altogether if their *root-run remain saturated. **1977** MCKNIGHT & TOBLER *Bob Marley* x. 127 What reaches our ears is no longer *roots reggae. **1978** *Oxford Times* (City ed.) 24 Feb. 15 This is a good example of roots reggae complete with chunky rhythm and 'dub' echoes. *a* **1732** BOSTON *Crook in*

Lot (1805) 110 Even when the *root-stroke is given in believers, the rod of pride buds again. *a* **1732** —— *Mem.* xi. (1899) 361 The gospel-doctrine has got a root-stroke by the condemning of that book. **1932** *Sun* (Baltimore) 6 Sept. 6/11 The famous Wye oak..is reported to be 27 feet 8 inches in circumference four and a half feet above ground, but the measurement taken at this point is said to include large *root swells. **1902** *Forestry Q.* I. 56 The influence of the enlarged base of the bole (*root-swelling) is appreciable at the breast-high point, and gives the stem a neiloid form. **1954** W. E. Hiley *Woodland Managem.* ix. 134 By girthing at 6 feet instead of 5 feet it may be possible to get away from the root swelling which usually occurs at the base of a large tree and often gives rise to inaccurate estimating. **1887** H. Marshall-Ward in *Phil. Trans. R. Soc.* B. CLXXVIII. 539 The first close investigation of these *root-tubercles (as they may be shortly termed) is due to Woronin. **1894** *Knowledge* 1 Mar. 68/1 (*heading*) The root-tubercles of peas, beans, and vetches. **1897** W. G. Smith tr. *Tubeuf's Dis. Plants* ix. 101 First-year alders without tubercles do not thrive in soil free from nitrogen..; when, however, provided with root-tubercles they assimilate nitrogen. **1967** D. C. Tinling in *Psychosomatic Med.* XXIX. 483 (*heading*) Voodoo, *root work, and medicine. **1970** M. Walker *Prophets for New Day* 29, I run down to Sis Areny's And told her what I seen '*Root-worker's out to git me What you reckon that there mean?' **1883** *Science* II. 143/2 These observations refer chiefly to the crown-borer, the *root-worm, and the crown-miner.

root, *sb.*[2] *dial.* [f. root *v.*[2]] The action of the vb. root[2]; chiefly in phr. ***on the root.***

1846 in *N. & Q.* 4th Ser. V. 326, I can give these old bones a root. **1892** J. A. Owen *On Surrey Hills* 56 Fur, fish, and feather need all look alive when Toby was on the root. **1895** *Month* Oct. 248 One of our rustic friends had a sow, with a litter of pigs, out on the root, as he termed it.

root (ruːt), *v.*[1] Forms: 4–6 **rote** (5 **rotyn**), 4–7 **roote**, 7– **root** (6 **wroot**, **rowt**); 5–6, 9 *Sc.* **rute**, **ruit**, 9 *dial.* **reut**, **reeat**, **reet**, etc. [f. root *sb.*[1] Cf. MSw. *rota* to make rootfast, *rotas*, *rota sig*, obs. Da. *rode*, to take root.]

I. In pa. pple. *rooted*.

Perhaps to some extent directly f. root *sb.*[1]

1. a. Filled or covered with roots.

c **1200** *Trin. Coll. Hom.* 163 Þat lond..bicam waste, and was roted oueral, and swo bicam wildernesse.

b. Furnished or provided with roots; established or fixed by having taken root. Also *fig.*

c **1400** *Apol. Loll.* 92 As we watteren plantis til þey han ben rotid, and þan we cessen to watter. *c* **1425** *Eng. Conq. Irel.* 20 Ther-for we willen withstond..þe yuel whil hit is comyn, ar hit be Iroted. **1560** Daus tr. *Sleidane's Comm.* 321 b, Sence Luthers doctrine was depely roted & spred abrode. **1596** Dalrymple tr. *Leslie's Hist. Scot.* II. 290 Quhen heresie deiper was ruted. **1647** N. Bacon *Disc. Govt. Eng.* i. lxvi. (1739) 143 Edward the first pursued the same course, especially in his first times, when he was but tenderly rooted. **1670** R. Baxter *Cure Ch. Div.* iii. v. Pref., The sin may be multiplyed and rooted past all hope of remedy. **1782** Cowper *Poet, Oyster & Sensit. Pl.* 16, I envy that unfeeling shrub, Fast rooted against ev'ry rub. **1815** J. Smith *Panorama Sci. & Art* II. 584 The dissipation of prejudices, which are deeply rooted. **1868** J. H. Blunt *Ref. Ch. Eng.* I. 105 Her affection for him seems to have been very deeply rooted. **1888** Bryce *Amer. Commw.* III. 339 Present arrangements were far too deeply rooted for..alteration.

c. Fixed or firmly attached by the root or roots. Const. *in*, *between*, *to*, etc. Also *transf.* or *fig.* (cf. 2).

1398 Trevisa *Barth. De P.R.* v. xxxi. (Bodl. MS.), Suche postemes whanne þei beþ ibradde and iroted and ipiȝt in þe side. **1526** *Pilgr. Perf.* (W. de W. 1531) 133 b, The more it groweth and spredeth his braunches, the more surely it is roted and fastned in the grounde. **1597** A. M. tr. *Guillemeau's Fr. Chirurg.* 19/1 Some vlcerations are rotede betweene vaynes and tendones. **1681** Grew *Musæum* i. vii. ii. 165 His Horns rooted between the Eyes and the Snout. **1697** Dryden *Virg. Georg.* iii. 689 Hellebore, and Squills deep rooted in the Seas. **1717** Addison tr. *Ovid's Met.* ii. Wks. 1721 I. 165 She found Her self with-held, and rooted to the ground. **1748** *Anson's Voy.* ii. x. 244 The Jesuits being thus firmly rooted on California,..have already extended their jurisdiction quite across the country. **1801** Southey *Thalaba* xii. iii, The living flower that, rooted to the rock,..Shrunk down within its purple stem to sleep. **1837** Disraeli *Venetia* iii. vii, He remained rooted to the ground. **1861** Pattison *Ess.* (1889) I. 48 Another proof how entirely the German aliens were rooted in English soil.

2. *fig.* Firmly fixed or established, deeply implanted, *in* something: **a.** Of abstract things; esp. qualities, etc., in a person's nature.

a **1225** *Ancr. R.* 386 Alle Godes hesten..beoð ine luue iroted. **1340** *Ayenb.* 26 Þanne sseweþ hy þe kueades þet were y-hole and yroted ine þe herte. **1387** Trevisa *Higden* (Rolls) VII. 401 It is hard to worche uppon þoughtes þat is i-roted in of longe tyme. *c* **1430** *Pol., Rel., & L. Poems* (1866) 43 That pasaunt Goodnes..whiche Rotide is in youre femynete. **1530** Palsgr. 694/1 If a vyce be ones rooted in a man, it is harde to get it away. **1570** Golding *Justin* xxix. 129 b, The naturall hatred that was knowen to bee roted in him against the Romaynes euen from his very childhoode. **1651** Hobbes *Leviath.* ii. xxx. 179 By what means so many Opinions..have..been so deeply rooted in them. **1736** Berkeley *Discourse* Wks. 1871 III. 417 Obedience to all civil power is rooted in the religious fear of God. **1849** Macaulay *Hist. Eng.* iv. I. 456 The principle..was firmly rooted in the public mind. **1877** R. H. Hutton *Ess.* (ed. 2) I. 74 If the passion of avarice be not wholly rooted in him.

b. Of persons in practices, opinions, etc.

c **1325** *Minor P. fr. Vernon MS.* 663 Corteis knihthod and clergye, Þat wont were vices to forsake, Are nou..Rooted in Ribaudye. *c* **1380** Wyclif *Wks.* (1880) 131 Þus þes possessioners..ben out of feiþ, hope & charite, & harde rotid in heresie. **1447** Bokenham *Seyntys* v. 305 In Crystys feyth rotyd so wel was he. **1451** Capgrave *Life St. Aug.* (E.E.T.S.) 45 What þei had be with him ȝeres and were roted in religion. **1547** *Act 1 Edw. VI*, c. 3 §7 Children..brought vp in idlenesse..be so rooted in it. **1611** Bible *Eph.* iii. 17 That yee being rooted and grounded in loue, May be able to comprehend..the loue of Christ. **1661** A. Wright *Expos. Ps.* xcii. 13 We cannot root firmly there, unless we are rooted in Jesus Christ. **1724** A. Collins *Gr. Chr. Relig.* 35 The Jews were so rooted in their notion of a Temporal Deliverer. **1823** Gillies *Aristotle's Rhetoric* x. 210 The man rooted in villainy will be guilty of all sorts of enormity.

II. 3. a. *trans.* To furnish with roots; to fix or establish firmly; to implant deeply, attach strongly. Freq. *transf.* or *fig.*, and const. *in*, *into*, *to*, etc.

a **1340** Hampole *Psalter* xxii. 3 He gaf me lastynge in his biddyngis, and rotid me, and made me perfite in charite. *a* **1500** *Bernardus De Cura Rei Fam.* (E.E.T.S.) 226 For it fosteris and rutis þam in þar vice. **1591** Shaks. *Two Gent.* ii. iv. 162 Lest the base earth Should..Disdaine to roote the Sommer-swelling flowre. **1596** Dalrymple tr. *Leslie's Hist. Scot.* I. 210 To festne and to rute it into the hartes of wandireris by the way. *c* **1600** Shaks. *Sonn.* cxlii, Roote pittie in thy heart. **1647** Hammond *Power of Keys* vii. 137 This course being thus taken for the planting and rooting all good resolutions. **1691** Dryden *King Arthur* iv. i, Amazement roots me to the ground. **1725** Pope *Odyss.* xiii. 189 The God arrests her with a sudden stroke, And roots her down an everlasting rock. **1816** Scott *Old Mort.* xxxviii, All Jenny's efforts to remove him from the garden served only to root him in it. **1841** Lytton *Night & Morning* i. i, Our poor Caleb had for years rooted his thoughts to his village.

refl. **1393** Langl. *P. Pl.* C. iii. 55 Al þe riche retynaunce þat roteþ hem on fals lyuynge Were bede to þat brudale. *a* **1400** *Prymer* (1891) 27 And y haue rotid me in a worschipful puple. **1535** Coverdale *Ecclus.* xxiv. 8 Let thy dwellinge be in Iacob,..& rote thy self amonge my chosen. **1810** Scott *Lady of L.* ii. xix, Firmer he roots him the ruder it blow. **1856** Froude *Hist. Eng.* (1858) I. i. 10 One of many of the rising merchants who were now able to root themselves on the land. **1875** Jowett *Plato* (ed. 2) I. 188 Forms which have rooted themselves in language.

b. *Austral. slang.* (See quot. 1959.)

The placing of this sense is uncertain; it may be, or be apprehended as, a *fig.* use of sense 10 b below.

1945 Baker *Austral. Lang.* viii. 152 The authentic digger form is *Wouldn't it root you!* A regimental paper 'Wiry' (1941) took its name from the first letters of the words in this phrase. **1951** D. Stivens *Jimmy Brockett* 244 'It looks as though we're rooted, smacker,' I told Herb. **1959** Baker *Drum* ii. 140 *Root*,..to outwit, baffle, exhaust, utterly confound (someone). Whence, *to be rooted*, to be exhausted or confounded; *get rooted!* Go to blazes! **1961** M. Calthorpe *Dyehouse* (1962) xl. 186 'He can get rooted, for all I care,' Collins said bitterly. **1973** *Telegraph* (Brisbane) 15 Nov. 3/1 Mr. Whitlam later admitted having said in an aside: 'It is what he put in his guts that rooted him.' **1974** J. Powers *Last of Knucklemen* iii. ii. 93 'What the hell's goin' on here?' 'The Hun's rooted—that's what!' 'Done like a dinner!'

4. To cause (a cutting) to grow roots.

1824 J. C. Loudon *Encycl. Gardening* (ed. 2) ii. 400 All plants which are difficult to root..will be found in the first instance..to throw out roots only, from the ring of herbaceous matter. **1884** D. T. Fish *Pop. Gardening* I. 212/1 One strong argument in favour of rooting roses at that season [*sc.* spring] consists in the fact that they have all the summer before them to grow into plants. **1925** W. Watson *Gardener's Assistant* VI. 82/1 We root a Cactus by drying it in the sun. **1969** P. Thrower *Every Day Gardening* iii. 45/1 Cuttings which have been rooted under mist, or in a heated propagator, must be hardened off..before planting them in the open ground.

5. a. *intr.* Of plants: To take or strike root.

c **1440** *Promp. Parv.* 437/2 Rotyn, or take rote, as treys and herbys, *radico*. **1471** Ripley *Comp. Alch.* iii. xvii. in Ashm. (1652) 143 Then shall thy seeds both roote and spyre. **1577** B. Googe *Heresbach's Husb.* i. (1586) 30 The fyrst dooth roote all in length lyke the Radishe. **1599** Shaks. *Hen. V*, v. ii. 46 Her fallow Leas, The Darnell, Hemlock, and ranke Femetary, Doth root vpon. **1673** *Lady's Call.* i. v. §28 A tender plant, that will scarce root in stiff or rocky ground. **1707** Mortimer *Husb.* (1721) II. 125 They root very deep, therefore plant your sets pretty deep. **1763** Mills *Pract. Husb.* IV. 152 That no crop will thrive well.., unless the ground be trenched deeper than the thyme rooted. **1801** *Farmer's Mag.* Jan. 104 The potatoes continued to root well. **1846** J. Baxter *Libr. Pract. Agric.* (ed. 4) I. 315 There are several varieties of the Amaryllis that do not root so freely as others. **1860** Gen. P. Thompson *Audi Alt.* cx. III. 31 They may not come to fruit now, but they will begin to root.

b. *fig.* To take root; to settle, establish oneself. Freq. with *in*.

a **1340** Hampole *Psalter* xv. 2 Þai haf festid þaire hope in þe land of heuen, and rotid in luf. **1362** Langl. *P. Pl.* A. x. 78 Dowel..saueþ þe soule, þat sunne haþ no miht..ne to Reste, ne to Rooten in þe herte. **1382** Wyclif *Ecclus.* xxiv. 16 And I rootede in a pupl wrshipid. **1526** *Pilgr. Perf.* (W. de W. 1531) 132 So yᵗ the grace of god & his vertues may rote in our soules. **1571** Golding *Calvin on Ps.* lxxiv. 22 That comon errour of theirs, wherein they rooted, is quite dasshed. *a* **1625** Cope in Gutch *Coll. Cur.* I. 121 True honour will ever root, where false glories fade like flowers. **1688** Crowne *Darius* iv, Oh! thou art rooting deeper in my heart, Tear thyself from me. **1740** Somerville *Hobbinol* i. 77 What Love can decay That roots so deep! **1753** Foote *Englishm. in Paris* ii, Now I'll redeem my error, and root for ever here. **1869** McLaren *Serm.* Ser. ii. vii. 113 The small continuous vices, which root under ground and honeycomb the soul.

c. To have a basis *in* something.

1882 *New Eng. Hist. Reg.* XXXVI. 181 These local divisions..root in the military institutions of the ancient Teutons. **1941** *Sun* (Baltimore) 25 Nov. 14/3 The trouble into which he intervened roots in a controversy over whether welding is a separate 'art' or not. **1955** E. Pound *Section: Rock-Drill* lxxxix. 56 The Civil War rooted in tariff.

III. 6. *trans.* To pull, tear, drag, or dig *up* by the roots; to uproot. Also *fig.*

1398 Trevisa *Barth. De P.R.* xi. xiii. (Bodl. MS.), Þondre ..destroieþ hiȝe treen & roteþ hem vp wiþ here blostringe oute of grounde. *Ibid.* xvii. cl, Whan þei [thorns] beþ ifalle oþer roted [**1495** rotyd vp] þei beþ ibound..to fagettes & ibrende. **1565** Cooper *Thesaurus* s.v. *Extirpo*, *Extirpare & funditus tollere vitia*, to roote vp and take cleane away. **1611** Bible *1 Kings* xiv. 15 The Lord..shall root vp Israel out of this good land, which hee gaue to their fathers. **1697** Dryden *Virg. Georg.* ii. 414 Root up wild Olives from thy labour'd Lands. **1712** Addison *Spect.* No. 451 ¶3 It would ..root up the Corn and Tares together. **1737** *Gentl. Mag.* VII. 48/2 As if they intended.. to root up all Order and Harmony of Government. **1847** W. C. L. Martin *Ox* 37/2 The utility of rooting up as much as possible all noxious plants from pasture grounds, and the ditches around them, is palpable.

7. a. To pull, dig, or take *out* by the roots; hence *fig.*, to extirpate, exterminate, destroy.

Cf. outroot *v.*, and the variant rout *v.*

c **1450** tr. *De Imitatione* i. iii. 5 If men wolde yeue so gret diligence to rote oute vices. **1535** Coverdale *1 Kings* xviii. 4 Whan Iesabel roted out yᵉ prophetes of yᵉ Lorde. *a* **1586** Sidney *Ps.* v. ii, Thou..shall roote out the tongues to lyeing bent. **1610** Holland *Camden's Britain* (1637) 163 Under a faire pretence and shew of rooting out superstition. **1687** A. Lovell tr. *Thevenot's Trav.* ii. 23 So many Soldiers would be sent out against them, that they would be utterly rooted out. **1712** Addison *Spect.* No. 505 ¶5 It is the chief Business of this Paper to root out popular Errors. **1782** Miss Burney *Cecilia* ix. vi, Not all her unwillingness..could now root out her suspicions. **1853** Kingsley *Hypatia* xxix, You may root out your own human natures if you will. **1879** Froude *Cæsar* xvii. 288 The punishment fell on his tribe. The Eburones were completely rooted out.

b. Const. *of*, *from*.

1535 Coverdale *Job* xviii. 14 All his comforte and hope shal be roted out of his dwellynge. *Ibid.*, *Amos* ii. 3, I will rote out the iudge from amonge them. **1667** Milton *P.L.* vi. 855 He meant Not to destroy, but root them out of Heav'n. *c* **1715** Swift *Serm.* iii. Wks. 1751 XIII. 26 This would root out Envy and Malice from the Heart of Man. **1729** Law *Serious C.* xi. (1732) 164 He that is endeavouring to..root out of his mind all those passions of pride.

c. *intr.* To die *out* completely.

1828 P. Cunningham *N.S. Wales* (ed. 3) II. 2 By supposing..that their descendants gradually rooted out or became blended with the aborigines.

d. To raise completely *out* of something.

1844 Mrs. Browning *Drama of Exile* Poems 1850 I. 62 Root out thine eyes, Sweet, from the dreary ground.

8. a. To clear *away* (†*forth*) completely.

1398 Trevisa *Barth. De P.R.* xvii. clxxx. (Bodl. MS.), He schal be porled & perissched & rased and roted awey. **1567** *Gude & Godlie Ball.* (S.T.S.) 97 Quha..dois blaspheme the kynde and liberall, Sall rutit be furth of memoriall. **1570** *Satir. Poems Reform.* xiii. 21 Rutit furth clene out of memorie. **1871** Tyndall *Frag. Sci.* (1879) I. ix. 296 A glacier is undoubtedly competent to root such masses bodily away.

b. To drag, tear, remove by force, *from* a place.

1567 *Gude & Godlie Ball.* (S.T.S.) 104 Thay sall us rute from the ground. **1582** Stanyhurst *Æneis* iii. (Arb.) 71, I drew neere, mynding too roote fro cel earthye the thicket. **1624** Quarles *Sion's Elegies* iv. 21 To see thy brother's seede Ruin'd and rent, and rooted from the earth. **1746** P. Francis tr. *Horace, Sat.* i. iii. 106 Since we never from the breast of fools Can root their passions. **1805** Southey *Madoc* ii. xvi, Bear away These wretches!..And root them from the earth.

c. Without const. To uproot, outroot.

1582 Stanyhurst *Æneis* ii. (Arb.) 64 Yf you father also Youre self too murther, too roote your progenye purpose. **1629** Gaule *Holy Madn.* 203 We cannot root them, we must restraine them. **1773–83** Hoole *Orl. Furioso* xxiv. 346 The trees, and cave he view'd; Those lopt and rooted, this in fragments hew'd.

9. To lop the roots or rootlets from.

1844 H. Stephens *Bk. Farm* II. 19 A field of 25 acres of excellent Swedes was pulled, rooted, and topped.

10. Miscellaneous senses of uncertain affinity. (Perh. properly developments of root *v.*[2])

a. *trans.* and *intr.* To kick, esp. in the backside. *slang* (chiefly *Schoolboys'*).

1890 Barrère & Leland *Dict. Slang* II. 186/1 *Root*, *to* (schools and London), to give one a kick behind. **1914** 'I. Hay' *Lighter Side School Life* ii. 52 We rooted Sowerby afterwards for grinning. **1934** *Bulletin* (Sydney) 31 Jan. 32/2 Give the horse that can root a bit to the horse-breaker or the head stockman is the general rule, or, better still, to the blacks. **1946** B. Marshall *George Brown's Schooldays* xxxvii. 145 Rooting them [*sc.* new pupils] up the backside is the only way of dealing with them.

b. *Austral. coarse slang. trans.* (usu. with a male subject). To copulate with; *intr.*, to copulate, to engage in sexual intercourse. Also in phr. ***to root like a rattlesnake***, to copulate vigorously.

1958 R. M. Stuart in R. Chamberlain *Stuart Affair* (1973) ii. 12, I took her bathers off. Then I raped her. She was hard to root. **1966** P. White *Solid Mandala* 185 We'll root together so good you'll shoot out the other side of Christmas. **1969** *Private Eye* 1 Aug. 14 The Pope's a Jew if that jam tart doesn't root like a rattlesnake. **1974** K. Cook *Bloodhouse* 110 We found this bloody little poofter down on the beach fiddling with a bird... Couldn't even root her.

root (ruːt), *v.*[2] [Later form of wroot *v.*, probably through association with prec. See also rout *v.* in this sense.]

1. a. *intr.* Of swine: To turn up the soil by grubbing with the snout; to dig with the snout in search of food.

1538 Leland *Itin.* (1768) III. 19 If a Man do but cast corn wher Hogges have rotid, it wyl cum up. **1607** Topsell *Four-f. Beasts* 668 [Swine wiil] rise in flesh..the sooner if they be permitted to roote now and then in the mire. **1653** H. Cogan tr. *Pinto's Trav.* xlix. 190 Wild Boars, that were rooting in the earth near to a pond. **1727** Swift *To Delany*

Wks. 1751 VII. 235 A Sooterkin, Which..in the Soil began to root, And litter'd at Parnassus' Foot. **1850** *Jrnl. R. Agric. Soc.* XI. II. 599 Store-pigs..may be allowed to root in fallows or on the dung-heap. **1871** L. STEPHEN *Playgr. Eur.* (1894) ix. 212 The Alpine pig..roots contentedly round the châlets.

fig. **1809** *Ann. Reg.* 745 Whilst others were thus rooting for preferment, Mr. Paley was engaged in the composition of an important work.

b. *transf.* of certain fishes, worms, etc.

1653 WALTON *Angler* xi. 196 The Barbell..loves to live..where it is gravelly, and in the gravel will root and dig with his nose like a Hog. *c* **1730** SWIFT *Dick* Wks. 1751 XIII. 218 As when from rooting in a Bin,..A lively Maggot sallies out. **1883** *Science* II. 154/1 Many fishes..have the habit of rooting in the mud for their food. **1890** *Illustr. Lond. News* 13 Sept. 330/1 Disturbing the morning meal of the crows rooting in the litter-heaps.

c. *dial.* and *colloq.* To poke about, rummage; to pry or poke *into* a thing; to lounge or idle about, etc. Also const. *about*, *around*.

1831 LOVER *Leg. Irel.* Ser. I. 189 She run rootin' into every corner o' the room, lookin' for it. **1892** MRS. H. WARD *David Grieve* IV. xi, She took him about with her, 'rootin', as she expressed it, after the hens and pigs. **1896** CROCKETT *Grey Man* xxxvi, There I was rooting and exploring. **1904** in *Eng. Dial. Dict.* V. 151/2 They like to rute about the house. **1916** JOYCE *Portrait of Artist* v. 203 He allowed his mother to..root into the folds of his ears. **1920** R. MACAULAY *Potterism* I. ii. 20 Watching Tane's..hand with its short square fingers rooting in the sand for shells. **1943** V. PALMER in *Coast to Coast 1942* 29 Charlie rooted about in the nose of the dinghy drawn up above the tide. **1977** C. ROCKS *Winter's Tales 23* 132, I rooted around till I found the kettle.

d. *colloq.* (orig. *U.S. slang*) To cheer *for* a (baseball, etc.) team. Also *transf.*, to be active *for* a person or thing by giving support, encouragement, or applause. Also without const.

1889 *N.Y. Semi-Weekly Tribune* 5 Nov. 5/4 Murphy has done little but 'root' for the Giants this year. **1895** in *Funk's Standard Dict.* **1895** J. S. WOOD *Yale Yarns* 152 We rooted hard, too, and did a lot of shouting and yelling. **1897** FLANDRAU *Harvard Episodes* 164 The fellows who had promised to vote for Wolcott..were beginning now to 'root' for him vigorously. **1922** S. LEWIS *Babbitt* v. 66 Zilla keeps rooting for a nice expensive vacation. **1943** *Crisis* July 201/3 The papers of Los Angeles crowed... They rooted and cheered. **1951** *Sport* 30 Mar.–5 Apr. 3/1 If the rules of the tournament made it possible for Stan to be transferred to Newcastle tomorrow, then the whole country would be rooting for the 'Magpies' on April 28th. **1951** in M. McLuhan *Mech. Bride* (1967) 8/1 He rooted fiercely for the underdog, perhaps because he was so much the underdog himself. **1959** N. MAILER *Advts. for Myself* (1961) 400 If he dares not to castrate his hatred of society..then I would have to root for him because he may have been born to write a great novel. **1967** *Boston Sunday Herald Mag.* 9 Apr. 4/3 You'll find it becomes a whole different game from just sitting in your armchair, rooting blindly. **1971** A. BURGESS *M F* xii. 140 A popcorn-eating audience roots for two youths fighting a huge engulfing python. **1976** A. MILLER *Inside Outside* vii. 81, I..wound up in front of the Visiting Committee with the Governor rooting for me.

e. ***root hog or die***, used of or addressed to persons, implying the necessity of labour or exertion to maintain life or prosperity. Also as *attrib. phr. N. Amer.*

1834 D. CROCKETT *Narr. Life* viii. 60 We therefore determined to go on the old saying, root hog or die. **1843** *Amer. Pioneer* II. 419 This letter exhibits his as well as my own case in that day; for it was 'root hog or die', and hard times have come back again! **1879** A. W. TOURGÉE *Fool's Errand* xxv. 150 The 'root-hog-or-die' policy. **1904** *N.Y. Even. Post* 20 Aug. 4 'The school and college', explained plains President Eliot, 'cannot use the method of Nature—root, hog, or die.' **1931** J. T. ADAMS *Epic of Amer.* i. 37 At the beginning of most settlements it was 'root, hog, or die' for all. **1976** *Globe & Mail* (Toronto) 9 June 41/6 Many of that generation, however, no longer put up with that root-hog-or-die kind of motivation.

2. *trans.* **a.** To turn over, dig up, with the snout. Also *fig.*, to search *out*, hunt *up*.

1592 SHAKS. *Ven. & Ad.* 636 He..hauing thee at vantage ..Wold roote these beauties, as he root's the mead. **1607** —— *Timon* v. i. 168 Alcibiades.., Who like a Bore too sauage, doth root vp His Countries peace. **1691** RAY *Creation* I. (1701) 155 He is provided with a long and strong Snout.., conveniently formed for the rooting and turning up the Ground. **1717** POPE *Iliad* XII. 166 On every side..they..root the shrubs and lay the forest bare. **1802** *Sport. Mag.* XX. 64 Lonely watch'd he the grunters all day, As they rooted the stubbles for shack. **1866** *Daily Telegr.* 12 Jan. 5/5 There is a reason for everything,..if we will only strive to root and think it out. **1894** HALL CAINE *Manxman* v. v, From underneath the sofa in the parlour he rooted up a brown paper parcel.

b. To form (holes) by rooting. *rare*$^{-1}$.

1854 *Jrnl. R. Agric. Soc.* XV. I. 21 They enforced penalties for letting hogs root holes in embankments.

root, obs. form of ROT, ROTE; dial. f. RUT.

roota baga, obs. form of RUTABAGA.

'rootable, *a.* [f. ROOT *v.*[1]] (See quot.)

1611 COTGR., *Enracinable*, rootable, fit to take root.

rootage ('ru:tɪdʒ). [f. ROOT *sb.*[1] or *v.*[1]]

†**1.** The act of rooting *out*. *Obs.*$^{-1}$

1587 HARRISON *England* III. ii. (1878) 16 The like order is taken with us for our vermines, as with them also for the rootage out of their wild beastes.

2. Root-hold; firm rooting.

1874 MURDOCH *Sandy M'Tartan* 22 The thistle-flow'r o' Scotland!—It finds fit rootage there. **1878** B. TAYLOR *Deukalion* III. i. 101 Our seeds of total life Find rootage, and ..Redeem this desolation. **1885** *Homiletic Rev.* Sept. 232 Being destitute of rootage in the soil of faith.

3. A system of roots; a root-stock.

1895 in *Funk's Stand. Dict.* **1927** H. E. FOSDICK *Pilgrimage to Palestine* 60 The very rootage from which came Aaron's rod that budded..the solemn monks still show to the visitor.

roote, obs. form of ROT *v.*, ROTE, ROUT.

rooted ('ru:tɪd), *ppl. a.* [f. ROOT *v.*[1] and *sb.*[1]]

1. a. Having roots; furnished with roots. *spec.* Having been made to grow roots.

Chiefly of plants, but also in transf. uses.

1557 RECORDE *Whetst.* G iij b, Now will we..intreate more of rooted nombers. **1712** J. JAMES tr. *Le Blond's Gardening* 160 The best way of planting Woods, is to do it with rooted Plants. **1786** ABERCROMBIE *Gard. Assist.* 78 Plant either in full plants, or rooted slips. **1839** *Penny Cycl.* XV. 509/2 Grinders simple or compound, rooted. **1852** G. W. JOHNSON *Cottage Gardener's Dict.* 304/2 A rooted cutting is not a new plant, it is only an extension of the parent. **1870** ROLLESTON *Anim. Life* 4 The Squirrels..live on seeds and have, like most *Muridae*, rooted molars. **1882** VINES tr. *Sachs' Bot.* 848 We assume..that the..shoot is rooted. **1969** P. THROWER *Every Day Gardening* viii. 196/2 Give the rooted cuttings as much light as possible to prevent them from becoming drawn.

b. With qualifying adj. or adv. prefixed.

See also *bulbous-*, *fibrous-*, *tuberous-rooted*.

1611 COTGR. s.v. *Fendu*, *Radis fendu*, the..many-rooted Raddish. **1699** PETIVER in *Phil. Trans.* XXI. 293 The Radishes, both Garden and Spanish, (which is the large Black-rooted;)..and the round and long Rooted Turnep. **1707** MORTIMER *Husb.* (1721) II. 160 They shoot out during the Summer many well-rooted Suckers. **1731** MILLER *Gard. Dict.* s.v. *Adonis*, The Hellebore-rooted Pheasant's-eye. *a* **1822** SHELLEY *Ess. & Lett.* (1886) 58 The bare boughs of the marble-rooted fig-tree. **1883** *Grove's Dict. Music* III. 158/2 To decide whether G or F or D is the root, or whether indeed it is even a double-rooted chord.

2. a. Planted in the ground; attached or fixed by roots; firmly implanted; having taken root.

1390 GOWER *Conf.* I. 86 Ther was nevere rooted tre, That stod so faste in his degre. **1718** POPE *Iliad* XIV. 578 Full in his eye the weapon chanced to fall, And from the fibres scoop'd the rooted ball. **1784** COWPER *Task* II. 100 The fixt and rooted earth, Tormented into billows, heaves and swells. **1859** GEO. ELIOT *A. Bede* xlix, There's no more moving you than the rooted tree.

fig. **1878** CUYLER *Pointed Papers* 171 Nor will the drought affect a well-rooted Christian.

b. *transf.* Of habits, opinions, etc.

1526 *Pilgr. Perf.* (W. De W. 1531) 263 b, To be a conquerour of vyce, by holy roted loue & assured hope of yᵉ kyngdome of god. *a* **1548** HALL *Chron., Hen. IV*, 29 b, Nor rooted malice is not in hast plucked up. **1605** SHAKS. *Macb.* v. iii. 41 Can'st thou not..Plucke from the Memory a rooted Sorrow? **1693** *Apol. Clergy Scot.* 38 Single Acts may grow into rooted Habits. **1710** BERKELEY *Princ. Hum. Knowl.* §124 Ancient and rooted prejudices. **1777** BURKE *Addr. to the King* Wks. 1842 II. 396 This scheme being..set up in direct opposition to the rooted and confirmed sentiments and habits of thinking of an whole people. **1825** SCOTT *Jrnl.* 28 Nov., He..never moved from his rooted opinion, blow as it listed. **1883** F. M. CRAWFORD *Dr. Claudius* iii, Have you a very strong and rooted dislike to the society of women?

c. Of maladies: Deep-seated, chronic.

1744 BERKELEY *Siris* §119 Though not a perfect recovery from my old and rooted illness. **1807** *Med. Jrnl.* XVII. 270 Her complaint every day gained ground, and appeared of a very rooted nature.

3. Torn *up* by the roots.

1797 *Encycl. Brit.* (ed. 3) XVI. 252/2 These would have represented the river-gods as seated on ruins, brandishing rooted-up trees.

'rootedly, *adv.* [f. ROOTED *ppl. a.*] In a rooted or firmly grounded manner.

1610 SHAKS. *Temp.* III. ii. 103 They all do hate him As rootedly as I. **1653** HEMINGS *Fatal Contr.* I. ii, The Queen as rootedly does hate her sonnes As I her Ladyship. **1814** J. MURRAY in Smiles *Mem.* (1891) I. 230 Their praise is..rootedly confirmed on a second perusal. **1880** G. MEREDITH *Tragic Com.* xvi, At the age of forty, men that love love rootedly.

'rootedness. [f. ROOTED *ppl. a.*] Rooted or firmly grounded character or quality.

1642 W. PRICE *Serm.* 14 Rootednesse, groundednesse in knowledge. **1676** W. ALLEN *Addr. Non-Conform.* 153 This diffidence proceeds..from the rootedness and strength of your prejudice. **1860** W. G. WARD *Nat. & Grace* 142 The strength, earnestness, rootedness, of this recognition. *c* **1880** PUSEY in Liddon *Life* (1893) I. xii. 281 Evidence..of the sincerity and rootedness of his own conviction.

†**'rooten**, *v. Obs.*$^{-1}$ [f. ROOT *sb.*[1] + -EN.] *trans.* To furnish with a root.

1649 BLITHE *Eng. Improv. Impr.* (1653) 165 Untill they be so rootened and stifned so strong that they will endure a beast rubbing upon them.

root-end. [f. ROOT *sb.*] That end of a stem, hair, etc., which is next the root; the end of a seed from which the root is developed.

1636 SANDERSON *Serm.* II. 54 A heart hardned with long custom of sinning..is like the knotty root-end of an old oak. **1707** MORTIMER *Husb.* (1721) I. 343 When the Sprits come forth at the Root-end of the Corn. **1743** R. MAXWELL *Sel. Trans.* 331 When you take out the Lint..set it up on the Root-end in Rows. **1832** *Planting* 29 in *Husb.* III. (L.U.K.), The leaves should be cut off half way up from the root-end of the cutting. **1846** J. BAXTER *Libr. Pract. Agric.* (ed. 4) II. 403 Raising the first sheaf.., and passing it with the root-ends downwards to the ground. **1879** A. GRAY *Struct. Bot.* (ed. 6) 13 The root..originates in tissue just back of that which covers the root-end of the caulicle.

rooter[1] ('ru:tə(r)). [f. ROOT *v.*[1] or *sb.*[1]]

1. a. An extirpator, eradicater, uprooter (*of* something). Usually const. *out*, *up*.

1560 DAUS tr. *Sleidane's Comm.* 37 b, Whiche had alwayes ingendred the roters out of Heresyes. **1570** GOLDING *Justin* XVI. 85 b, Cassander the father of them, the rooter vp of the kynges house. **1622** MASSINGER & DEKKER *Virg. Martyr* I. i, The strongest champions of the Pagan gods, And rooter out of Christians. **1650** ARNWAY *Tablet* (1661) 154 The rooters up of religion and monarchy. *Ibid.* 184 Rooters of truth and order. **1862** RAWLINSON *Anc. Mon., Chaldæa* vii. 164 The destroyer of crops, the rooter-up of trees.

b. A machine for loosening the surface of the ground.

1950 *N.Z. Jrnl. Agric.* Oct. 333/2 At first a small rooter was used which was designed for scarifying pavements and roads and which could be drawn by a 40 h.p. tractor. **1965** G. J. WILLIAMS *Econ. Geol. N.Z.* Plate xxxix, This very pure calcareous material is soft enough to be excavated by rooters, and in consequence can be produced at low cost.

2. *spec.* A 'root-and-branch' man. Now *Hist.*

1642 SIR E. DERING *Sp. on Relig.* 161 The Rooters, the Antiprelaticke party declaim against me. **1660** SOUTH *Serm.* (1717) IV. 27 The Rooters and Through-Reformers made clean Work with the Church. **1824** SOUTHEY *Bk. of Church* xvii. I. 378 Vane and Cromwell, who now began to appear among the rooters as they were called. **1900** W. A. SHAW *Hist. Eng. Ch. 1640–60* I. 79 Its numbers included more than the mere Rooters.

3. *slang.* (See quots.)

It is not certain that these belong here.

1840 GEN. MERCER in R. J. Macdonald *Hist. Dress R.A.* (1899) 50 The remainder of the hair was gathered into a queue behind..and tied close to the head; this we called a rooter. **1860** *Slang Dict.* (ed. 2) 201 *Rooter*, anything good, or of a prime quality; 'that *is* a Rooter', i.e., a first-rate one of the sort.

'rooter[2]. *colloq.* (chiefly *U.S.*) [f. ROOT *v.*[2]]

1. A pig which roots. Also *transf.*

1648 HEXHAM II, *Een Wroeter*, a Rooter, or a Grubber. **1681** T. FLATMAN *Heraclitus Ridens* No. 29 (1713) I. 191 If he be not a Hog,..he is always a Rooter, whining, and grunting. **1864** *Daily Telegr.* 27 Sept., He is a very ugly pig —a cross between the Irish 'greyhound' and the Yankee 'rooter'. **1886** P. ROBINSON *Teetotum Trees* 25 The pig may ..grow gaunt and fierce, a rooter among strange wild foods.

2. *colloq.* (chiefly *U.S.*) One who cheers or 'roots' for a (baseball, etc.) team. Also *transf.*, one who supports or encourages another; a warm advocate, a partisan.

1890 *N.Y. Press* 8 July 6/1 At this juncture the New York rooters began to 'pull' for the home team, but the effort was useless, not a man..succeeded in reaching first base. **1895** in *Funk's Standard Dict.* **1901** *Speaker* 19 Jan. 439 At the first class cricket matches for years he has been what in the States they call a rooter. **1901** *Daily Colonist* (Victoria, B.C.) 31 Oct. 4/3 'What makes him look so very white?' inquired the fairy maid. 'He's had the starch knocked out of him,' the woolly rooter said. **1931** L. STEFFENS *Autobiogr.* II. III. xxxiii. 593 They..don't ask about, they don't hear of, the always existing few quiet students with concealed gifts in the rooters at a football game. **1939** G. ADE *Let.* 7 July (1973) 212, I attended the [1912 Republican] convention as a spectator and also as a rooter for Theodore Roosevelt. **1952** *Manch. Guardian Weekly* 12 June 3/3 General of the Army Eisenhower..came..to hold his first political press conference before the New York reporters... There was also present a motley and vociferous band of rooters. **1959** *Times Lit. Suppl.* 6 Nov. p. xix/1 The exclusive audience that goes to Twickenham or Lord's is replaced by millions of rooters. **1963** D. OGILVY *Confessions Advert. Man* i. 14 This will give us 49,700 rooters for Ogilvy, Benson and Mather. **1978** *N.Y. Times* 29 Mar. B 5/1 The Wildcats' coach..had walked back into the stands to embrace his family and shake hands with some rooters with blue and white buttons.

'rootery. [f. ROOT *sb.*[1]] A pile formed of tree-roots with interspersed soil for the ornamental growing of garden-plants. Cf. ROCKERY.

1882 in *Imperial Dict.* (Annandale). **1898** *Gardener's Mag.* 3 Sept. 572/2 Rosa Luciæ—R. Wichuraiana of American gardens—is already becoming popular in this country for covering ground, for rooteries, &c.

'root-fall, *sb. rare.* [ROOT *sb.*[1]]

1. A tree which has fallen owing to the roots giving way.

a **1634** COKE *On Litt.* IV. lxxiii. (1648) 300 That no trees other then..meerly windefals and rootfals may be thrown down or taken away.

2. The condition of being root-fallen.

1886 *Times* 18 Aug. 10/6 The Hessian Fly confines its injury to the joints of the straw, causing a disorder analogous to that of root-fall and 'gout' in the stems.

'root-fall, *v. rare*$^{-1}$. [Cf. next.] *intr.* To become root-fallen.

1813 in W. Marshall *Review* V. 35 In loose land subject in any degree to cause wheat to root-fall.

'root-fallen, *a.* [f. ROOT *sb.*[1]] Of grain-crops: (see quot. 1764).

1763 *Museum Rust.* I. 111 The wheat [is] on that account very much subject to be root-fallen. **1764** *Ibid.* III. 145 What I mean by root-fallen is, that when the plants become tall and weighty, the roots are apt to give way, and the plant come to the ground. **1807** A. YOUNG *Agric. Essex* (1813) I. 9 It is horrid land... It runs, by frosts, from the roots of wheat, which becomes root-fallen. **1854** *Jrnl. R. Agric. Soc.* XV. I. 124 The crop..was much root-fallen.

'rootfast, *a.* Forms: 2 rotfest, 4–6 rotefast, 5 rote faste, *Sc.* rutfast. [a. ON. *rótfastr* (Norw. and Sw. *rotfast*, Da. *rodfast*): see ROOT *sb.*[1] and FAST *a.*] Firmly settled or held by the roots; securely established.

1127 *O.E. Chron.* (Laud MS.) an. 1127, þa beþohte he him þæt ȝif he mihte ben rotfest on Engle land þæt he mihte habben eal his wile. *c* **1375** *Cursor M.* 11703 (Fairf.), Wiþ þis stert vp þis tree rotefast, and þer hit stode a welle oute-brast. *c* **1375** *Sc. Leg. Saints* xliv. (*Lucy*) 260 Scho mycht nocht steryt be mare þane ware a rutfast tre. *c* **1440** *Jacob's Well* 289 Stedfastnesse, þat makyth a mannys herte styff as..a rotefast tre þat no storme may ouyrthrowe. **1953** C. DAY LEWIS *Italian Visit* iii. 36 A character root-fast Like a man's in the deposit of all his acts.

Hence **'rootfastness**. *rare*⁻¹.

1526 *State P. Hen. VIII*, VI. 534 Whanne He shall perceeyue that the oolde tre for lakk of vegeetyue sprytis maye nott opteeyne perfect rotefastnesse.

roother, obs. form of RUDDER.

'root-house. [f. ROOT *sb.*[1]]

1. An ornamental building made principally of tree-roots, esp. in a garden.

1765 R. DODSLEY *Leasowes* in *Shenstone's Wks.* (1777) II. 289 Winding forward down the valley, you pass beside a small root-house, where on a tablet are these lines. *Ibid.* II. 294 Here, entering a gate, you are led through a thicket of many sorts of willows, into a large root-house, inscribed to ..the Earl of Stamford. **1802** MRS. E. PARSONS *Myst. Visit* II. 243 Behind it was a root house, where the fire-wood was kept. **1832** MISS MITFORD *Village* Ser. v. (1863) 440 They.. had adjourned to the root-house, a pretty rustic building at the end of the garden.

2. A house or barn for storing roots.

1790 *Pennsylvanian Packet* 30 Mar. 4/2 On the premises are..two arched stone root-houses. **1805** R. W. DICKSON *Pract. Agric.* I. 60 Root-Houses. Where a number of cows ..are fed on winter roots and vegetables,..it is highly necessary to have houses of this sort. **1847** W. C. L. MARTIN *Ox* 115/1 Where hay is scarce, carrots form a very economical substitute; they must be kept in dry root-houses or in trenches. **1961** W. O. MITCHELL *Jake & Kid* 28 'Bin a real fine summer fer vegetables,' he said then. 'Too bad yer ma don't have no root house.' **1970** *Islander* (Victoria, B.C.) 22 Nov. 13/2 Into the root house went the potatoes, carrots and other root vegetables.

'rootiness. [f. ROOTY *a.*] The quality of being rooty. Also *fig.* Cf. RACINESS.

1804 *Trans. Soc. Arts* XXII. 351 Its extreme rootiness may perhaps be occasioned by the hemp growing too thin on the land. **1937** G. M. YOUNG *Daylight & Champaign* 193 Here is exactly the harshness and rootiness, the integrity and objectivity that our poetry needed.

'rooting, *vbl. sb.*[1] [f. ROOT *v.*[1] or *sb.*[1]]

1. a. The action of taking or striking root; also *fig.*

c **1380** WYCLIF *Wks.* (1880) 201 And þat we falle not in-to dispeir of goddis mercy for olde rotynge & custome in synne. *c* **1440** *Promp. Parv.* 437/2 Rotynge, or takyinge rote yn waxynge, *radicacio*. **1611** COTGR., *Enracinement*, a rooting, or taking root. *a* **1620** DYKE *Right Receiving Christ* (1640) 170 Plants and trees first roote before they growe, & then growth followes after their rooting. **1725** *Fam. Dict.* s.v. *Carnation*, Let him..put the Earth down upon it to facilitate its Rooting. **1825** *Greenhouse Comp.* I. 223 Rooting generally takes place in six months, but with some species a year is required. **1849** *Beck's Florist* 297 That the plants which have been removed may get a chance of rooting before frosts set in.

b. *attrib.*, as *rooting-ground*, *medium*, *-place*.

1827 STEUART *Planter's G.* (1828) 451 In this way, in good rooting-ground, he would have roots sixteen or seventeen feet long. **1854** *Zoologist* XII. 4445 If all the seed that fell should find no rooting-place. **1935** A. F. HORT *Garden Variety* IV. 229 The rooting medium is about six inches of ordinary builders' sand.

2. a. A root; roots collectively; also, a firm hold or attachment by means of roots. Often *fig.*

a **1300** *Cursor M.* 9269 'Iesse,' he said, 'of his roting Sothfastle a wand suld spring'. **1526** TINDALE *Matt.* xiii. 6 Hitt cauth heet, and for lake off rotynge wyddred awaye. ? **1579** MONTGOMERIE *Misc. Poems* XLVIII. 7 Quhais ruiting sure and toppis reaching he Mot brek the storme. *a* **1619** FOTHERBY *Atheomastix* I. x. §5 A weake, and a flickring opinion,..hauing no rooting, nor footing. **1674** Z. CAWDREY *Catholicon* 17 This Parochial Combination would give the Royal interest the strongest rooting in the hearts of his subjects. **1707** MORTIMER *Husb.* (1721) II. 25 Ashes..are best transplanted young because of their deep Rooting. **1763** MILLS *Pract. Husb.* III. 349 That the grass may have time to get good rooting. **1858** *London Rev.* Oct. 28 The desire of gaining for oneself..a rooting, and a place of rest, on the soil of one's own land.

b. In phr. *to take rooting*.

1548 UDALL, etc. *Erasm. Par. Mark* iv. 32 Because it coulde not for stones take rootyng but lacked rootes. **1591** SPENSER *Ruins of Rome* 248 Thence th' Imperiall Eagle rooting tooke. **1613** PURCHAS *Pilgrimage* I. vi. (1614) 31 Religion..taketh naturally such rooting, that all politicall Lawes and tortures cannot pluck it vp. **1677** YARRANTON *Eng. Improv.* 62 The Linen Manufacture..will take deep rooting and get a good Foundation on a sudden. **1728** MORGAN *Algiers* II. ii. 234 He determined to nip in the Bud this dangerous Rival, before he took too firm Rooting.

3. The action of implanting.

1596 DALRYMPLE tr. *Leslie's Hist. Scot.* I. 225 He caused the croce of Christe to be placed in dorpes and in Tounis, to the ruiting of the Luife of Christe in the ground of the hartes of his awne.

4. The action of taking *out* or *up* by the roots.

1565 COOPER *Thesaurus*, *Extirpatio*, a pluckynge vp by the rootes; a rootynge out. **1617** FLETCHER *Valentinian* III. iii, Were it to save your worth, Or to redeem your name from rooting out,..I ought, and would dye for ye. **1632** SHERWOOD, A rooting vp, rooting out, or plucking vp by the roote, *desracinement*. **1846** GROTE *Greece* (1862) II. 334 The rooting up of an olive-tree in Attica was forbidden. **1876** FREEMAN *Norm. Conq.* V. 507 To attempt a deliberate rooting up of the speech of their island kingdom.

5. *coarse slang.* Of a male: the action or process of copulating. (Now chiefly *Austral.*: cf. ROOT *v.*[1] 10 b.)

1922 JOYCE *Ulysses* 754 All the poking and rooting and ploughing he had up in me. **1970** G. GREER *Female Eunuch* 41 All the vulgar linguistic emphasis is placed upon the *poking* element; *fucking*, *screwing*, *rooting*, *shagging* are all acts performed upon the passive female.

'rooting, *vbl. sb.*[2] [f. ROOT *v.*[2]]

1. The action of grubbing in the earth for food. Also *transf.*

1600 SURFLET *Countrie Farme* VII. xxvii. 853 The huntsman therefore shall know the fairenes of the bore..by his traces, rootings, soile, and dung. **1611** COTGR., *Fouge*, the rooting of wild Swyne among Fearne, &c. **1686** PLOT *Staffordsh.* 387 They have a pretty device here..to prevent their hogs from rooting. **1774** GOLDSM. *Nat. Hist.* (1776) VII. 108 The jaws..are extended, and evidently formed for rooting in the ground. **1893** KIPLING *Many Invent.* 319 After two hours of rooting through this desolation at an average rate of five miles an hour.

attrib. **1898** *Gardener's Mag.* 3 Sept. 572/1 A good pig has been known to indicate 40 lbs. weight of truffles in a rooting day.

2. *slang* (chiefly *U.S.*). Cheering, encouraging, or otherwise supporting. Also in *Comb.*, as *rooting interest*. Cf. ROOT *v.*[2] 1 d.

1937 D. RUNYON in *Collier's* 21 Aug. 32/4 No talking and no rooting from the spectators is permitted. **1971** L. KOPPETT *N.Y. Times Guide Spectator Sports* viii. 155 There is the team element as a rooting interest. **1977** *Time* 25 July 51/2 *One on One* is a picture that..transcends its humble conception and develops what movie people used to call a 'rooting interest' in its characters.

'rooting, *ppl. a.*[1] [ROOT *v.*[1]] That takes or strikes root. (See also quot. 1776.)

1766 *Compl. Farmer* s.v. *Orchard*, You should observe never to sow too near the trees, nor suffer any great rooting weeds to grow about them. **1776** J. LEE *Introd. Bot.* 378 *Radicans*, rooting, striking Root laterally and fixing to other Bodies. **1841** *Penny Cycl.* XX. 373/2 They possess rooting and floating stems. **1877** HULME *Wild Fl.* p. vi, Silverweed. —Flowers solitary on slender axillary peduncles, springing from the rooting nodes.

b. *spec.* in plant-names.

1841 *Penny Cycl.* XIX. 485/2 *Rhus radicans* (Rooting Poison-Oak). **1859** MISS PRATT *Brit. Grasses* 244 Rooting Bristle Fern. Fronds three or four times pinnatifid.

'rooting, *ppl. a.*[2] [f. ROOT *v.*[2]]

1. That roots or grubs.

1594 SHAKS. *Rich. III*, I. iii. 228 Thou eluish mark'd, abortiue, rooting Hogge. **1613–6** W. BROWNE *Brit. Past.* II. i, Nor boorish hog-heard fed his rooting swine. **1642** SIR E. DERING *Sp. on Relig.* 95 Many others of your rooting Tribe. **1870** MORRIS *Earthly Par.* III. IV. 296 The rooting swine Beneath the..oak-trees grunt and whine.

2. In redupl. Comb., as **rootin' tootin'**, (*a*) *dial. rare*, inquisitive, meddlesome; (*b*) *slang* (chiefly *N. Amer.*), noisy, rumbustious, boisterous; rip-roaring, lively. Cf. ROOTY-TOOT.

1875 NODAL & MILNER *Gloss. Lancs. Dial.* 228 He's a *rootin*' tootin' sort of a chap. **1924** L. B. KOZLOWSKI in *Catal. Copyright Entries* (U.S. Copyright Off.) III. 5698 (*song-title*) Roottin-toottin-Lou; from Kalamazoo. **1937** *Film Daily* 1 May 4/3 (*heading*) Gene Autry in Rootin' Tootin' Rhythm. **1948** *Sun* (Baltimore) 7 Jan. 13/1 Basketball games today have developed into rootin', tootin' contests, with more of the emphasis on the tootin'. **1949** *N.Y. Times Bk. Rev.* 27 Mar. 32 'Smoke up the Valley' is actually a rootin'-tootin' romance of blazing six-shooters and gore. **1963** *New Statesman* 24 May 786/3, I also.. expressed mild surprise about a rootin' tootin' night club that advertised 'Girls! Girls! Girls!'

rootle ('ruːt(ə)l), *v.* Also *dial.* routle. [f. ROOT *v.*[2] + -LE. See also ROOKLE *v.*]

1. *intr.* To root or grub; *transf.* to poke about. Also const. *about*, *round*.

1809 BATCHELOR *Anal. Eng. Lang.* 141 *Rootle*, to dig up roots like swine. **1854** MISS BAKER *Northampt. Gloss.* I. 181 How them children are rootling about! **1865** F. BOYLE *Dyaks of Borneo* 22 The backs of the pigs rootling among the débris almost brush the flooring. **1899** *Contemp. Rev.* Dec. 795 A pug, rootling about among the ivy, startled out a great fat rabbit. **1917** KIPLING *Diversity of Creatures* 261 There's a tin of cocoa in my study somewhere... Rootle round till you find it. **1929** V. WOOLF *Room of One's Own* i. 14 The chapel itself was marsh too, where the grasses waved and the swine rootled. **1936** A. CHRISTIE *Cards on Table* ix. 85 I'll leave you my keys and..you can rootle to your heart's content. **1943** *Theology* xlvi. 159 It is coming to be seen that he [*sc.* Nietzsche] rootled about in the subsoil of the modern mind to the profit of few things so much as the Christian Faith. **1959** *Elizabethan* Apr. 10/2 We rootled among the debris for something to eat. **1964** P. WHITE *Burnt Ones* 203 On the way, as she rootled after the lovely little lighter, I was relieved to see her bag was still stuffed with notes. **1977** *Zigzag* Apr. 43/3 He rootled about under the stairs and found an unopened Christmas present bottle of Glenfiddich.

2. *trans.* To root or grub *up*; to rout *out*. Also *transf.*

1863 MRS. GASKELL *Sylvia's Lovers* xxiii, A misdoubt me if there were a felly there as would ha' thought o' routling out yon wasps' nest. **1885** *Fishing* I. 415 Rootling up the sand and gravel for his livelihood. **1889** JESSOPP *Coming of Friars* 242 The litter of pigs that were rootling up the beechnuts in the woods. **1945** D. REES *Cambridge Murders* xiii. 135 He set one or two members of his staff to rootle out the past histories of all the people whose names had been mentioned. **1955** M. BANKS *Commando Climber* x. 189 Their [*sc.* the reindeers'] disappearance has been attributed to a late autumn thaw..which covered their winter pasture with a crust of ice that prevented them rootling out their fodder. **1978** *New Scientist* 20 July 171/2 Pigs which rootle out the eggs and eat the vulnerable young.

'root-leaf. [f. ROOT *sb.*[1]] A radical leaf.

1712 *Phil. Trans.* XXVII. 385 The Root-leaves [of sciatica cresses] stand on long foot-stalks. **1796** WITHERING *Brit. Pl.* (ed. 3) II. 198 The root-leaves..are never wing-cleft. **1847** W. E. STEELE *Field Bot.* 47 Root-leaves..long-stalked, divided into 3 deep. **1870** HOOKER *Stud. Flora* 359 *Spiranthes autumnalis*,..flowering-stem sheathed distinct from the root-leaves.

rootless ('ruːtlɪs), *a.* Also 5–6 rooteles, 7 rootlesse. [f. ROOT *sb.*[1] + -LESS: cf. ON. *rótlauss*, Norw. *rotlaus*, Da. *rodløs*.]

1. a. Without roots; destitute of roots.

c **1374** CHAUCER *Troylus* IV. 770 Ful oft a by worde here I seye, That rooteles mot grene soone deye. **1652** BENLOWES *Theoph.* VI. xxxi, As Aarons rootless Rod, so didst thou fructifie! **1781** BURNS *First Psalm* iv, Like the rootless stubble tost, Before the sweeping blast. **1839** *Penny Cycl.* XV. 509/2 Grinders compound or rootless. **1882** FARRAR *Early Chr.* I. 492 Like a rootless stalk on a thin soil.

b. *fig.* or in fig. contexts.

1656 JEANES *Fuln. Christ* 387 All terrestriall treasures, and riches, are rootlesse. **1754** YOUNG *Centaur* ii. Wks. 1757 IV. 139 We are for rootless joys, joys beyond appetite; which is the sole root of sensual delight. **1867** H. MACMILLAN *Bible Teach.* xi. (1870) 218 Separated from Him, man is an incomplete creature,..rootless, hungry, dry, and withered. **1890** *Spectator* 28 June, A rootless religion is no religion. **1934** A. WOOLLCOTT *While Rome Burns* 93 Those rootless widows who wear buttoned shoes. **1977** R. BARNARD *Blood Brotherhood* viii. 79 Rootless young men, without families.

2. *Mus.* (See ROOT *sb.*[1] 16.)

1867 MACFARREN *Harmony* (1892) 167 The seemingly rootless harmony of the 3rd and 6th of the supertonic..has been satisfactorily traced to the dominant as its generator.

Hence **'rootlessness**; **'rootlessly** *adv.*

1865 *Pall Mall G.* 29 Mar. 2 Mr. Disraeli's rootlessness of character as we have called it, probably contributes to his wit. **1927** E. BOWEN *Hotel* xiv. 167, I haven't had time for a feeling of rootlessness. **1929** A. HUXLEY *Do what you Will* 157 Nature-worship is..so refined, so rootlessly high-class. **1958** *Times Lit. Suppl.* 3 Jan. 4/4 Mr. Mellers characterizes the nineteenth century Russian Westernizers' music as 'rootlessly European' and believes that Stravinsky has merely made this rootlessness symbolic of the modern artist in general. **1978** P. MOORE *Man, Woman, & Priesthood* i. 4 In an age of rootlessness which is searching for significant tradition, we have much to offer if we have the courage to dig deep enough. **1980** *Church Times* 1 Aug. 2/4 Drinking problems are, more often than not, connected with other social problems such as homelessness and rootlessness.

rootlet ('ruːtlɪt). [f. ROOT *sb.*[1] + -LET.]

1. A branch of the root of a plant; a subsidiary root; also, one of the secondary roots thrown out laterally for support by ivy and a few other climbing plants.

1793 MARTYN *Lang. Bot.* s.v., Root-leaf and Rootlet are more proper in English than Radical leaf and Radicle. **1827** STEUART *Planter's G.* (1828) 237 Every effort must be made to preserve the minutest fibres and capillary rootlets entire. **1860** GOSSE *Rom. Nat. Hist.* 57 He tears up the reluctant tree, and..exposes the juicy and tender rootlets. **1888** J. INGLIS *Tent Life in Tigerland* 116 A fine old fig-tree, with numberless tendrils and rootlets hanging pendant.

fig. **1878** CUYLER *Pointed P.* 170 The soul thus reaches down through its every rootlet into Christ's deep, cool well.

b. Used *collect.* without article. *rare*⁻¹.

1894 BARING-GOULD *Deserts S. France* I. 23 To combine with their delicate lacings of rootlet to keep the soil in place.

2. *Malting.* The radicle of a steeped grain. Also *collect.*

1830 in M. DONOVAN *Dom. Econ.* I. 83 The moment the rootlet makes its appearance, the vegetation is stopped. **1860** E. S. WHITE *Maltster's Guide* 62 Floor charges occasionally arise from the rank growth of rootlet. *Ibid.* 92 It is necessary to separate the rootlets from the malt.

3. *Physiol.* A slender branch, fibre, etc., of some structure, such as a vein or nerve.

1875 *Encycl. Brit.* I. 903/1 The veins corresponding to them are rootlets of the inferior vena cava. **1876** BRISTOWE *Th. & Pract. Med.* (1878) 659 Membranous pellicles.. prolonged by rootlets into the Lieberkühnian follicles. **1899** *Allbutt's Syst. Med.* VI. 768 The rootlets of the third nerve pass archwise through the tegmentum cruris.

'rootling. [f. ROOT *sb.*[1]] = ROOTLET 1.

a **1706** EVELYN *Sylva* (1776) 106 Laying bare the whole root and then dividing it into four parts, in form of a cross, to cut away the interjacent rootlings. **1787** MARSHALL *E. Norfolk* I. 236 Its rootlings being unable to make the proper progress in a compact or a cold soil. **1861** *Macm. Mag.* June 126 A pea is planted, and there spring from it a rootling and a plantling.

'root-stock. [f. ROOT *sb.*[1]]

1. *Bot.* A rhizome; a stem that grows entirely underground; a creeping stem.

1832 *Planting* 132 in *Husb.* III. (L.U.K.), Fourteen large trees, growing from the same root-stock. **1861** MRS. LANKESTER *Wild Flowers* 43 The Large-flowered Hypericum, or St. John's Wort,..has a creeping, woody rootstock. **1877** F. G. HEATH *Fern World* 21 The lower leafy portion of the frond almost touches the crown of the root-stock.

2. A source from which offshoots have arisen; a primitive form.

1877 Dawson *Orig. World* xiii. 272 The Egyptians being .., if languages have one origin, likely to be near its root-stock. **1888** Clodd *Story of Creation* (1894) 128 Whether there was an ancestral form or rootstock from which both reptile and mammal branched off..is not clear.

3. A stock on to which another variety has been grafted or budded.

1933 H. H. Thomas *Pop. Encycl. Gardening* 392/1 The shoot of the required variety is united with a suitable rootstock or with a branch of an established tree of the same kind. **1954** A. G. L. Hellyer *Encycl. Garden Work* 208/2 An apple may be described as grafted upon paradise rootstock. **1969** P. Thrower *Every Day Gardening* iv. 84/2, I keep a close lookout throughout the season for suckers growing from the roots below the union of the rose and the rootstock.

rootte, obs. form of ROT *v.*

'root-walt, *v.* Now *dial.* Forms: 6 **rote walt**, 6, 9 **rootwalt**, 9 *dial.* **rootwelt, -wout, -waut, -wart.** [f. ROOT *sb.*[1] + WALT *v.*] *trans.* To overturn by the roots; to uproot.

1532 Whytford *Werke for Househ.* E, The curse of the parentes dothe eradicate, rotewalt and utterly destroy the possessyars and the kynred of the chylder. **1577-87** Holinshed *Chron.* II. 353 Much hurt was doone by..the rootwalting of trees, as well in woods as orchards. **1828** Carr *Craven Gloss., Root-welted*, torn up by the roots. **1862-** in dial. glossaries (Yks., Lanc., Chesh., Shropsh.).

'root-weed. [ROOT *sb.*] A weed which propagates itself chiefly by means of roots, as distinguished from weeds which originate from seed.

1765 A. Dickson *Agric.* (ed. 2) II. 270 To increase the food of plants, and destroy root-weeds. **1790** Marshall *E. Midl.* II. 43 Extirpating the roots of twitch and other root weeds. **1837** *Flemish Husb.* 71 in *Husb.* III. (L.U.K.), The root-weeds are necessarily cleaned out in the spreading.

'rooty, *sb. Mil. slang.* Also **rootey.** [ad. Urdū (Hindī) *rōṭī*. Cf. ROTI[2].] **a.** Bread.

1883 Sala in *Illustr. Lond. News* 7 July 3/3 At least eight years ago I heard of a private soldier complaining..that he had not had his 'proper section of rooty'. **1900** Kipling in J. Ralph *War's Brighter Side* (1901) xv. 253 And the 'umble loaf of 'rootey' Costs a tanner, or a bob. **1900** 'M. Thyme' in *Ibid.* xx. 316 Bully beef and rooty, and Something's give me a pain. **1957** [see JILDI]. **1959** *Listener* 5 Mar. 406/1 Eight ounces of 'rooty'—that is bread.

b. rooty gong (GONG[2] 2 a), a medal formerly awarded to members of the British Army in India (see quots.).

1925 Fraser & Gibbons *Soldier & Sailor Words* 245 *Rooty gong*, long service Medal. **1936** F. Richards *Old-Soldier Sahib* vi. 108 The Good Conduct medal or 'Rooty Gong'..was so called because it was a regular ration-issue, like bread or meat or boots. **1948** Partridge *Dict. Forces' Slang* 157 *Rooty gong*,..*Rooti* is the Indian Army word for bread, the implication being that the wearer has eaten a tremendous aggregate of Service loaves and therefore deserves it.

rooty ('ruːtɪ), *a.* Also 5 **ruty**, 6 **rutty**, 7 **rootie.** [f. ROOT *sb.*[1] + -Y.] Abounding in roots; full of roots; consisting of roots; also, belonging to or suggestive of roots.

1483 *Cath. Angl.* 314/2 Ruty, *radicosus.* **c 1611** Chapman *Iliad* XVII. 654 As a syluane hill Thrusts backe a torrent... Nor can [it] with all the confluence breake through his rootie sides. **1649** Blithe *Eng. Improver Impr.* (1653) 196 Lands above measure hard, rooty, rushy, twichy, or any way unfeacible. **1713** Derham *Physico-Theol.* x, Such Vegetables as are weak [support themselves] by striking in their rooty Feet. **1818** Keats *Endym.* IV. 793 There was.. not a tree, beneath whose rooty shade He had not with his tamed leopards played. **1853** G. J. Cayley *Las Alforjas* I. 176 Some embers which smouldered dimly round a huge rooty log. **1884** T. Hardy *Wessex Tales* (1889) 180 He retired down the rooty slope. **1905** E. F. Benson *Image in Sand* xviii. 292 The warm wind bore with it..the good, moist, rooty smell of the dusky heather.

rooty, var. ROWTY *a. dial.*

rooty-toot ('ruːtɪtuːt). *slang* (chiefly *U.S.*). Also **root-a-toot**, etc. [A redupl. form, ult. of echoic origin, usu. representing the sound of a trumpet; cf. *rootin' tootin'* s.v. ROOTING *ppl. a.*[2] and TOOT *v.*[2]] Something noisy, riotous, or lively; *spec.* an early style of jazz music. Also as *adj.* and (in various nonce-uses) *vb. intr.*

1887 T. Darlington *Folk-Speech of S. Cheshire* 319 There was a *rooty-tooty* at Cholmondeley last Setterday, an' everybody from raïnd about went bu' mey. **1907** G. B. Shaw in *Neolith* Nov. 9 The trumpet angel..root-a-tooted at the sky. **1931** O. Nash *Hard Lines* 24 Oh rooti-ti-toot for Smoot of Ut. **1936** *Amer. Mercury* XXXVIII. p. x/2 *Rooty-toot*,..razz-ma-tazz. **1937** G. Frankau *More of Us* iii. 38 So Izzy Cohen (y sus Boys) root-tooting Moved Innocent to choric rhapsody. **1938** *Brit. Empire Mod. Eng. Illustr. Dict.* 1257/2 *Rooty-toot* (Am.), old-fashioned jazz. **1951** W. Morum *Gabriel* I. iii. 39 He knew hambone and joanna meant trombone and piano, But what could be a rooty-toot, a gobstick, skins and skeletons? **1976** *Listener* 29 July 120/3 It's all done to the most cheerful, rooty-tooty music imaginable. **1977** *Time Out* 28 Jan.–3 Feb. 17/3 Ma, some of them songs are rooty-toot-toot but the whole damn show is as real as George Wallace fairy and as sassy as a pile of rocking horse sheet.

rooue, obs. f. ROOF.

roound, obs. f. ROUND.

roove (røv), *sb. Sc.* In 6 **rufe**, *pl.* **ruvis**, 9 *dial.* **ruove, röv.** [var. of ROVE *sb.*[2]] A burr for a rivet. Cf. REW *sb.*[3]

1513 Douglas *Æneis* I. iii. 49 [The ship] quhairin ancyant Alethes was, The storme ourset, raif ruvis and syde semis. **1535** Stewart *Cron. Scot.* I. 140 With..pleven plait with mony riall rufe, With courtlie cast of cot-armour abufe. *Ibid.* II. 167 Throw birneis bricht quhair all thair ruvis raue. **1892** George Stewart *Shetland Tales* (ed. 2) 70 Dey wir biggit wi' timmer pins, bit efter dey cam hame dey were clinkit wi' seam an' ruove.

roove, variant of ROVE *sb.*[3] and *sb.*[5]

roove (røv), *v.*[1] *Sc.* Also 6 **ruiff**, 9 *dial.* **riv.** [f. ROOVE *sb.*] *trans.* To rivet, secure with a rivet.

1587 *Sc. Acts Jas. VI*, c. 136 (1814) III. 522/1 Þat þer be a prik of Irne,..passing throw þe middis of þe said ovir corss bar, Ruiffit bayth onder and abone. **1646** Baillie *Lett. & Jrnls.* (1841) II. 403 If this naill be once rooved, we with our teeth will never gett it drawne. *a* **1678** A. Wedderburn *Serm.* xxx. 277 The Mediator..hath driven the nail, and rooved it so fast, that there were no possibility to draw it again. **1824** Mactaggart *Gallovid. Encycl.* s.v., My fellow went up and roov'd that nail on the other side. **1890** Service *Notandums* ix. 64 It was an airn ring rooved in a muckle stane.

fig. **1654** A. Gray *Serm.* (1755) viii. 141 The great Voice of our Consciences and of all the Convictions which God rooves upon them. **1725** Ramsay *Gentle Sheph.* v. iii, The Lord o' Heaven..Confirm your joys, and a' your blessings roove! **1791** Learmont *Poems* 58 Guid is roovit to nae state: It comes to us an' lea'es the great.

roove (ruːv), *v.*[2] *Mining.* (See quot.)

1883 Gresley *Gloss. Coal-mining* 206 *Roove*, to rub or knock against the roof.

rooved, *a. rare.* [f. ROOVE *sb.* or *v.*[1]] Riveted; in combs. ***silver-, brass-rooved.***

1661 *12th Rep. Hist. MSS. Com.* App. VII. 387 Seven silver-rooved daggers..; nine brass-rooved daggers.

roozer, dial. form of ROUSER.

ropalic, var. RHOPALIC.

roparie, obs. f. ROPERY.

rope (rəʊp), *sb.*[1] Forms: α. 1–4 **rap**, 2–5, *Sc.* 7–9 **rape**; 4 **rayp**, 6–9 **raip(e**, 6 **raipp**; 8–9 **raep**, 9 *dial.* **reap(e, reeap.** β. 3–4 **rop**, 4–7 **roop(e**, 5–6 **roppe**, 6–7 **roap(e**; 3– **rope.** [Common Teut.: OE. *ráp* masc., = OFris. *râp* (in *silrâp*; WFris. *reap*, EFris. *rôp*, but NFris. *riap*:—**rêp*), MDu. and Du. *reep*, MLG. *rêp*, *reep*, *reip* (LG. *rêp*), OHG. and G. *reif*, ON. *reip* neut. (Icel., Fær., Norw. *reip*, Sw. *rep*, †*reep*, Da. *reb*, †*reeb*, *reeff*, etc.), Goth. *raip* (in *skaudaraip* shoe-thong). In the Lex Salica (*c* 490) the Old Frankish form appears to be Latinized as *reipus* (only in a transferred sense), and from early Teutonic the word passed into Finnish as *raippa* rod, twig.]

I. 1. a. A length of strong and stout line or cordage, usually made of twisted strands of hemp, flax, or other fibrous material, but also of strips of hide, pliant twigs, metal wire, etc.

In technical use the name of *rope* is given to cordage above one inch in circumference, and the largest sizes are called *cables*. For the nautical names of special ropes, as *bolt-*, *breast-*, *bucket-*, *buoy-rope*, see the first element.

α. *c* **725**, *c* **825** [see sense 2]. *c* **888** K. Ælfred *Boeth.* xiii, Ne mæᵹ hit mon..mid rape ᵹebindan. *c* **950** *Lindisf. Gosp.* John ii. 15 [He] ᵹeworhte..suuopa of rapum. **971** *Blickl. Hom.* 241 Hraðe hie sendon rap on his sweoran, and hie hine tuᵹon ᵹeond þære ceastre lanan. **1154** *O.E. Chron.* (Laud MS.) an 1140, Me læt hire dun on niht of þe tur mid rapes. *c* **1175** *Lamb. Hom.* 47 Me nom rapes and caste in to him for to draᵹen hine ut of þisse putte. *c* **1205** Lay. 1099 Heo rihten heora rapes, heo rærden heora mastes. **1375** Barbour *Bruce* III. 691 Ankyrs, rapys, baith saile and ar, And all that nedyt to schipfar. *a* **1400-50** *Alexander* 1520 He..sammes þaim on aithire side with silken rapis. *c* **1470** Henry *Wallace* VII. 201 A bauk was knyt all full of rapys keyne. **1508** Dunbar *Tua Mariit Wemen* 331, I wald haif ridden him to Rome, with ane raip in his heid. *a* **1585** Montgomerie *Flyting* 403 Thir ladies lighted fra their horse, And band them with raipes. **1718** Ramsay *Christ's Kirk Gr.* III. xii, His young wife.. sneg'd the raips..We'er knife that day. **1783** Burns *Mailie's Elegy* vii, Wae worth that man wha first did shape That vile, wanchancie thing—a raep!

β. *c* **1275** Lay. 20333 Hii worpen vt one rop and Baldolf hine igrop. **1303** R. Brunne *Handl. Synne* 8055 Aboute þe body a rope þey wonde, And to þe bere fast þey bonde. **1387** Trevisa *Higden* (Rolls) III. 199 Meny yuy stalkes i-bounde in a schorp rope. *c* **1400** *Destr. Troy* 13020 Hir hondes bounden at hir backe bigly with ropes. **1489** Caxton *Faytes of A.* I. xvii. 49 Bounden togider and wel teyed with ropys. **1535** Coverdale *Judges* xvi. 8 The prynces of the Philistynes broughte vp vnto her seuen new roapes. **1581** J. Bell *Haddon's Answ. Osor.* 218 b, Chayned with an Iron Roape, and lying under hys table amongest dogges. **1607** Topsell *Four-f. Beasts* (1658) 249 Their daggers, and a rope of leather thongs, wherewithall they entred the battail. **1627** Capt. Smith *Seaman's Gram.* v. 20 The standing ropes are the shrouds and staies. **1673-4** Grew *Anat. Pl.* (1682) 139 The Barque of any Tree, as of Willow (whereof are usually made a sort of Ropes). **1720** Pope *Iliad* XXIII. 139 With proper Instruments they take the Road, Axes to cut, and Ropes to sling the Load. **1781** Gibbon *Decl. & F.* xix. (1787) II. 133 Tying their legs together with ropes, they dragged them through the streets. **1841** *Penny Cycl.* XX. 156/1 Ropes formed of iron wire have been..introduced to a considerable extent. **1872** Yeats *Tech. Hist. Comm.* 70 Ropes were used in the gymnasium by the ancient Greeks.

b. *fig.* or in fig. contexts.

c **1000** Ælfric *Hom.* I. 208 Anra ᵹehwilc manna is ᵹewriðen mid rapum his synna. *c* **1200** *Vices & Virtues* 45 For us te warnin þat ure ropes ne to-breken. *c* **1200** Ormin 15818 Þeᵹᵹ wrohhtenn rap þurrh sinnfull lif To draᵹhenn hem till helle. *a* **1300** *Cursor M.* 21920 Ded sal rug us til his rape. **13..** *K. Alis.* 6282 (Laud MS.), Now þe kyng haþ al þis in his rope, He shipped swiþe in to Ethiope. **1434** Misyn *Mending Life* 107 Abundance of Riches, flaterynge of wymmen, Fayrnes or bewte of ȝouthe: þis is þe threfold rope þat vnnethis may be brokyn. **1560** Rolland *Seven Sages* 88 Gif ȝe may not eschaip, Than ar ȝe baith but dout tane in the raip. **1624** Bedell *Lett.* xi. 156, I haue met with sundry that pull this roape as strongly the other way.

c. Used without article, as a material.

1769 Falconer *Dict. Marine* s.v. *Rope-bands*, Certain pieces of small rope or braided cordage. **1839** Ure *Dict. Arts* 1076 Two, three, or more strands of shroud or hawser-laid rope. **1876** Voyle & Stevenson *Milit. Dict.* 352/1 The strength of Manilla rope is less than that of hemp rope.

2. In various special uses:

a. A stout line used for measuring; a sounding line; hence in later use, a certain measure of length, esp. for walling or hedging. Now *local.* Also ***rope-length.***

c **725** *Corpus Gloss.* (Hessels) B 178 *Bolides*, sundᵹerd in scipe *vel* metrap. *c* **825** *Vesp. Ps.* civ. 11 Cweoðende ðe ic selle eorðan rap erfes eowres.

1562 *Act 5 Eliz.* c. 4 §15 What Wages every Workman.. shall take..for Ditching, Paving, Railing or Hedging, by the Rod, Pearch,..Rope or Foot. **1597** Skene *De Verb. Sign.* s.v. *Particata*, Ane rod, ane raip, ane lineal fall of measure, are all ane,..for ilk ane of them conteinis sex elnes in length. **1797** Billingsley *Agric. Somerset* 79 The expence of a list-wall may be thus calculated per rope of twenty feet running length. **1850** *Jrnl. R. Agric. Soc.* XI. II. 728 Dry walls, built 4 feet high at 1*d.* a foot (20*d.* per rope length). **1886** in *Eng. Dial. Dict.* s.v., To the Agricultural Labourer who shall best dig and lay a Rope and Half of Hedge.

b. A line stretched between two points at some height above the ground, upon which an acrobat performs various feats. (See also *tight-rope.*)

1620 Sir S. D'Ewes in *Coll. Life & T. Jas. I* (1851) 117 A pretty pastime called dancing upon the ropes. **1695** Dryden *Dufresnoy's Art Paint.* Pref. 49 Like a skilfull dancer on the Ropes (if you will pardon the meanness of the similitude). **1707** J. Stevens tr. *Quevedo's Com. Wks.* (1709) 434 She.. exercis'd her self upon the Streight Rope. **1740** Somerville *Hobbinol* I. 303 Thus on the slacken'd Rope The wingyfooted Artist..Stands tott'ring.

fig. **1612** Webster *White Devil* v. ii, See, see Flamineo.. Is dancing on the ropes there, and he carries A money-bag in each hand, to keep him even.

c. *pl.* The cords marking off a prize-ring or other enclosed space; the ropes marking the boundary of a cricket ground. Phr. ***on the ropes***: see quot. 1958; also *fig.*

1829 P. Egan *Boxiana* 2nd Ser. II. 158 Lenney found himself hanging on the ropes, where he was milled down. **1854** Dickens *Hard T.* ii, He would..bore his opponent.. to the ropes, and fall upon him neatly. **1859** Lever *D. Dunn* xxx, This unforeseen 'bolt over the ropes'. **1888** R. H. Lyttelton in Steel & Lyttleton *Cricket* xvi. 439 There is a strong cord running all round the ground, every decently hard hit is certain to reach the ropes if the ball once passes the fieldsman. **1892** *Sporting Life* 31 May 3/4 Among his hits were three drives over the ropes for 6. **1901** G. B. Shaw *Admirable Bashville* II. i. 302 The Australian Champion and his challenger..fought to a finish... The bold Ned Skene revisited the ropes to hold the battle for his quondam novice. **1904** A. A. Milne in *Punch* 18 May 358/1 Time was I cared for cricket,..Cutting a ball to the ropes for four. **1924** 'W. Fabian' *Sailors' Wives* xv. 175 You've got him on the ropes. They tell me he shows signs of matrimony. **1958** F. C. Avis *Boxing Reference Dict.* 78 *On the ropes*, said of a boxer who is forced back on to the ropes by his opponent, or is lying helpless on them. **1971** *Times* 27 Sept. 9/8 Griffith was defenceless against the ropes and his own corner as Monzon unleashed a string of straight rights and lefts. **1972** *Times* 16 May (Wall Street Suppl.) p. iv/2 A good section of the industry was on the ropes and there were times when I wondered if it would survive. **1976** J. Snow *Cricket Rebel* 168 (*caption*) Ray Illingworth hooks..in the England v West Indies Test at the Oval, 1973. The ball, arrowed, is on its way to the ropes. **1977** J. Laker *One-Day Cricket* 88 Three further perfectly timed shots had cleared the boundary ropes. **1977** *New Yorker* 25 July 70/3 Miss Wade was on the ropes several times in the first set, but she stayed in there and managed to win it, 7–5. **1980** *Tablet* 26 Jan. 81/3 There is talk that the Kennedy campaign is not just 'on the ropes', but that it is plain dead.

d. A clothes-line.

1833 Carlyle in Froude *Life* (1882) II. 365 To-day white sheets hang triumphantly on the rope.

e. *U.S.* A lasso.

1888 *Cent. Mag.* Feb. 506/1 The rope, whether leather lariat or made of grass, is the one essential feature of every cowboy's equipment.

f. *transf.* A type of lodging-house (see quot. 1836).

1836 Dickens *Pickw.* (1837) xvi. 160 The twopenny rope ..is just a cheap lodgin'house, vere the beds is twopence a night... They has two ropes, 'bout six foot apart, and three from the floor, which goes right down the room; and the beds are made of slips of coarse sacking, stretched across 'em... At six o'clock every mornin', they lets go the ropes at one end, and down falls all the lodgers. **1973** L. Heren *Growing up Poor in London* i. 10 One of the ropes, or lodging houses, was home for Indian pedlars... The rope was next to a pub.

g. A skipping-rope. Cf. *to jump rope* s.v. JUMP *v.* 1 f.

1874 R. L. Stevenson in *Portfolio* V. 116 A mistress of the art of skipping..the rope passed over her black head and under her scarlet-stockinged legs with a precision and regularity that was like machinery. **1927** C. V. Goddard in *Word Lore* II. 128 Never leave the rope empty Go to church on Ash Wednesday. **1959** I. & P. Opie *Lore & Lang.*

Schoolch. xii. 239 People from the surrounding villages bring great lengths of clothes-line with them, and skip ten and even fifteen abreast in each rope. 1978 J. IRVING *World According to Garp* vii. 133 Jumping rope for half an hour in a corner of the gymnasium.

h. *Mountaineering.* A climbing-rope. So *transf.*, a group of climbers, *esp.* one that is roped together. Also *attrib.* and *fig.*

1892 C. T. DENT *Mountaineering* ii. 71 There is no part of the Alpine equipment for those who intend to go above the snow line..more important than the rope. 1919 G. D. ABRAHAM *On Alpine Heights & Brit. Crags* i. 10 The legs of both were steadied by the second climber, who secured the rope around a projecting knob of rock. 1935 R. L. G. IRVING *Romance of Mountaineering* vii. 114 Tom de Lépiney runs out fifty metres of rope in crossing, held by the rope from as high as possible. 1935 D. PILLEY *Climbing Days* iv. 84 And for those who did not lead, but still desired to take the share of responsibility which falls to any genuine member of a *rope*, a climb would help. 1941 C. KIRKUS *Let's go Climbing* iii. 46 When a rope travelling south meets a rope travelling west the result is apt to be rather like a Maypole dance. 1955 M. BANKS *Commando Climber* v. 89 Lower down we passed under some tottering, unstable-looking séracs, in company with an Italian and a French rope. 1965 A. BLACKSHAW *Mountaineering* vii. 195 A wet rope should not be left coiled, as this will delay drying and encourage deterioration. 1968 P. CREW *Encycl. Dict. Mountaineering* 100/2 In artificial climbing rope management can become very complicated. 1972 D. HASTON *In High Places* iv. 52 We reckoned on teaming up two ropes of two, Eley with me and Geoff with Dennis English. 1979 D. CLARK *Dread & Water* ii. 33 It's up to you and your pals on the same rope to make your own decisions as the need crops up.

i. A rope suspended vertically in a gymnasium for climbing and other exercises.

1903 *Handbk. Physical Training* (Admiralty) I. 30 For rope climbing the class will be formed up about 4 paces from the ropes. 1940 MCCLOW & ANDERSON *Play Gymnastics* 87 Small boys who are free in the gymnasium show a great interest in equipment upon which they can climb or from which they can hang. They never seem to tire of swinging on the ropes. 1965 D. R. CASADY et al. *Handbk. Physical Fitness Activities* xii. 96/2 When climbing the rope, one must climb down as well as up.

3. a. A cord for hanging a person; a halter; the hangman's cord. So *transf.*, capital punishment. Also in phr. ***to take a rope***, to hang oneself.

c 1290 *St. James* 117 in *S. Eng. Leg.* I. 37 Ane Rop he dude a-boute is necke, and ladde him toward is dome. 1297 R. GLOUC. (Rolls) 9212 An rop me dude aboute is nekke, he suor honge he ssolde. *c* 1300 *Cursor M.* 16501 A rape he gatt al priueli,..þer-wit him-self he hang. *c* 1330 R. BRUNNE *Chron. Wace* (Rolls) 10010 þer ostages..he heng..wyþ rop & streng. *c* 1440 *Alph. Tales* 178 Sho hangid hur selfe. And as sho did it þe rape braste, & sho was still on life. *c* 1489 CAXTON *Sonnes of Aymon* xi. 281, I promyse..to lende you a rope, yf ye have nede of it. 1535 LYNDESAY *Satyre* 2450, I think to se thy craig gar ane raip crack. *a* 1585 MONTGOMERIE *Flyting* 96 Goe ride in a raipe for this noble new ȝeir. *a* 1649 DRUMM. OF HAWTH. *Hist. Jas. V*, Wks. (1711) 112 Because they could not agree among themselves about those who should stretch the Ropes,..they escaped all the Danger. 1670 COTTON *Espernon* I. III. 127 An old man..told me this story,..being one of those set apart for the Rope. 1713 ARBUTHNOT *John Bull* II. iii, When these Wretches had the Rope about their Necks. 1781 COWPER *Retirem.* 584 All had long suppos'd him dead, By cold submersion, razor, rope, or lead. 1857 BORROW *Romany Rye* xli, He used to say, that they were fools, who did not always manage to keep the rope below their shoulders. 1898 BESANT *Orange Girl* II. ix, I feel..as if the rope was already round my neck. 1934 H. N. ROSE *Thes. Slang* 18/1 Jim got a rope this morning. 1935 A. J. POLLOCK *Underworld Speaks* 98/2 *Rope*, hanging. 1935 J. HARGAN *Gloss. Prison Lang.* 7 *Rope, take a*, to hang oneself, to commit suicide. 1950 H. E. GOLDIN *Dict. Amer. Underworld Lingo* 180/2 *Rope*, capital punishment by hanging; (loosely) capital punishment by any means. 1976 *Leicester Mercury* 14 Oct. 4/4 The complete disregard for law and order which is so prevalent today is the direct result of the policies of himself and most members of the Labour Government which resulted in the cane being abolished for disobedient schoolboys, the birch for thugs and the rope for murderers.

†**b.** Used in angry exclamations. *Obs.*

1598 R. BERNARD *Terence, Andria* I. ii, What's the matter now with him? What a rope ailes hee? What a diuell would he haue? 1599 PORTER *Angry Wom. Abingdon* (Percy Soc.) 46 *Boy*. Hold fast by the bucket, Hodge. *Hod.* A rope on it! 1682 N. O. *Boileau's Lutrin* IV. 19 What the Rope ails you? (cry'd the testy Lacquey).

†**c.** As an allusive or derisive cry. *Obs.*

1591 SHAKS. *1 Hen. VI*, I. iii. 53 Winchester Goose, I cry, a Rope, a Rope. Now beat them hence. 1663 BUTLER *Hud.* I. i. 546 He understood..What Member 'tis of whom they talk when they cry Rope, and Walk Knave, walk.

4. In various figurative phrases:

a. ***to give one rope*** (***enough***, or ***plenty of rope***), to allow one free scope or action, esp. in order that he may embarrass or commit himself. So ***to have plenty of rope***, etc.

a 1659 BP. BROWNRIG *Serm.* (1674) I. iii. 42 Give them rope, and scope enough, let them do their utmost. 1672 R. WILD *Poet. Licent.* 28 The Papists swelling is the way to burst, Let them have Rope enough, and do their worst. 1687 SETTLE *Refl. Dryden* 67 Give our Commentator but Rope, and he hangs himself. 1855 [see HANG *v.* B. 3b]. 1887 J. HAWTHORNE *Tragic Mystery* xiv, Evidently, the best way..was to give him plenty of rope wherewith to hang himself. 1892 'ANSTEY' *Voces Populi, Free Speech*, I appeal to you, give this man rope—he's doing our work splendidly.

b. ***to come***, or ***run***, ***to the end of one's rope***, (*a*) to be finally checked in wrong-doing; (*b*) to come to the end of one's resources, to be at the end of one's tether. So ***at the end of one's rope***, ***one's rope is out***, etc.

1686 tr. *Chardin's Coronat. Solyman* 106 Being run to the end of his Rope, as one that had no more Excuses to make. 1898 BESANT *Orange Girl* Prol. 7 His rope is certainly long out, so that he is kept from Tyburn Tree by some special favour. *Ibid.* II. xii, They have come to the end of their rope: their time is up. 1931 F. L. ALLEN *Only Yesterday* ii. 32 Physically the President was almost at the end of his rope. 1943 M. CARPENTER *Experiment Perilous* 214 I've come, I think, to the end of my rope. 1954 N. COWARD *Future Indefinite* v. vi. 321 What I had been dreading for a long time happened. I collapsed finally and knew that I had come to the end of my rope. 1971 *Ink* 12 June 7/4 On Monday, 24 May, the Mans strikers—now at the end of their rope financially—voted to accept the compromise proposals. 1977 *Transatlantic Rev.* LX. 79 Judy was at the end of her rope.

c. ***to know the ropes***, to understand the way to do something; to be acquainted with all the dodges. So ***to learn, put one up to, the ropes***. Also ***to show one, understand, the ropes***.

1840 R. H. DANA *Bef. Mast* ix, The captain, who..'knew the ropes', took the steering oar. 1850 'J. TIMON' *Sketch* 18 Aug. in *Opera Goer* (1852) II. 186 The belle of two weeks standing, who has 'learned the ropes'. 1854 *Congress. Globe* 33rd Congress I Sess. App. 893/2 They are familiar with all the dodges of the season, understand the ropes about town [etc.]. 1860 T. C. HALIBURTON *Season-Ticket* viii. 226 Tell me..about Canada, and show me the ropes. 1874 *Slang Dict.* 271 'To know the ropes,' is to be conversant with the minutiæ of metropolitan dodges, as regards both the streets and the sporting world. 1876 BESANT & RICE *Gold. Butterfly* xliii, You've sought me out, and gone about this city with me; you've put me up to ropes. 1882 SALA *Amer. Revis.* (1885) 54 The foreigner who does not 'know the ropes'—that is to say, who is crassly ignorant. 1894 MASKELYNE *Sharps & Flats* 98 The circle was composed entirely of men who thought they 'knew the ropes' as well as he did. *a* 1911 D. G. PHILLIPS *Susan Lenox* (1917) II. ii. 20 I'll show you the ropes... You'll find the job dead easy. 1937 'G. ORWELL' *Road to Wigan Pier* ix. 182, I would find out about tramps and how you got in touch with them..and then, when I..knew the ropes well enough, I would go on the road myself. 1949 E. WAUGH *Loved One* 133 Mr. Schultz had found a young man to take Dennis's place and Dennis was spending his last week at the Happier Hunting Ground in showing him the ropes. 1973 G. GREENE *Honorary Consul* I. i. 26 Fortnum knew the local ropes. He saved the Ambassador a lot of trouble. 1976 J. I. M. STEWART *Young Pattullo* ii. 43, I was being made aware..that I didn't quite know the ropes.

d. ***on the high ropes***: see HIGH *a.* 17h.

e. ***to pull the ropes***, to direct or influence events. ? *Obs.*

1876 W. G. NASH *Century of Gossip* iv. 70, I cum purty near..tellin' 'em that Elton wouldn't pull a rope for him, if he got the nominashun. 1900 G. N. BOOTHBY *Maker of Nations* i. 19 You *do* require to know the ropes. And what is more, you require to be very careful how you pull those ropes when you are familiar with them.

f. ***money for old rope***: see MONEY *sb.* 6h.

II. 5. a. A quantity of some material twisted together in the form of a rope; a rope-like structure; a thing having the elongated form of a rope or cord.

1394 *Earl Derby's Exp.* (Camden) 158 Diuersis operariis facientibus ropez de dicto feno. 1523 FITZHERB. *Husb.* §25 For to knowe whanne it [hay] is wyddred ynoughe, make a lyttell rope of the same. 1610 MARKHAM *Masterp.* II. cx. 391 With a soft rope of hay. 1677 GREW *Anat. Fruits* (1682) 187 By the Length..do run a pair of little Vascular Ropes. 1686 GOAD *Celest. Bodies* I. ii. 2 A Fog which sometimes casts it self into Shreds or Ropes, and..furls up into Gossamere. 1731 MILLER *Gard. Dict.* s.v. *Asplenium*, Seed-pods..furnish'd with a little round Rope. 1759 MILLS tr. *Duhamel's Husb.* I. viii. (1762) 44 This would only raise a long unwieldy rope of turf. 1843 *Civil Eng. & Arch. Jrnl.* VI. 38/2 The effect of this..is to form a running rope of water in the pipe. 1891 T. HARDY *Tess* xxxix, An immense rope of hair like a ship's cable.

b. ***a rope of sand***, something having no coherence or binding power.

1624 GATAKER *Transubst.* 152 Like ropes of sand (as wee are wont to say) doe these things hang together. 1670 CLARENDON *Contempl. Ps.* Tracts (1727) 583 Which destroys all possible security and confidence in this rope of sand, which Tradition is. 1780 GOUV. MORRIS in Sparks *Life & Writ.* (1832) I. 222 Our union will become a mere rope of sand. 1800 J. ADAMS *Wks.* (1854) IX. 87 Sweden and Denmark, Russia and Prussia, might form a rope of sand, but no dependence can be placed on such a maritime coalition. 1894 MRS. F. ELLIOT *Roman Gossip* iv. 124 The alliance fell through of itself like a rope of sand.

c. (See quot. 1950.) Also *attrib.*, as ***rope silk***.

1880 L. HIGGIN *Handbk. Embroidery* i. 4 'Embroidery', or Bobbin Silk..is manufactured in what is technically called 'rope', that is, with about twelve strands in each thread. When not 'rope' silk, it is in single strands, and is then called 'fine' silk. 1910 *Art Needlework* 2/2 Arden's 'Hazel' Embroidery No. 3... As thick as (and closely resembling) those silks called 'Rope' and 'Cable', it can be used for merely outlining with long and short stitch. 1950 *Mercury Dict. Textile Terms* 430/1 *Rope silk*, an embroidery silk thread consisting of singles doubled into threads and these doubles again doubled to form a strong thread.

d. *U.S. slang.* A cigar.

1934 H. MCLELLAN in *Detective Fiction Weekly* 10 Nov. 29/2 He jerked a cigar out of her mouth... 'It burns my stomach to see a dame smoking a rope'. 1940 *Amer. Speech* XV. 335/2 A cigar is *rope*. 1960 WENTWORTH & FLEXNER *Dict. Amer. Slang* 433/2 *Rope*, a cigar... Occasional use in comic papers and by would-be wits. 1978 H. WOUK *War & Remembrance* vii. 66 Carter Aster was smoking a long brown Havana tonight. That meant his spirits were high; otherwise he consumed vile gray Philippine ropes.

e. *Anthrop.* A system of descent or inheritance in which the link is formed from father or mother to the children of the opposite sex (see quot. 1935).

1935 M. MEAD *Sex & Temperament* x. 176 Instead..of organizing people into patrilineal groups or matrilineal groups..the Mundugumor have a form of organization that they call a *rope*. A rope is composed of a man, his daughters, his daughters' sons, his daughters' sons' daughters; or if the count is begun from a woman..her sons, her sons' daughters..[etc.]. 1953 A. K. C. OTTAWAY *Educ. & Society* ii. 25 Inheritance [among Mundugumor] passes from father to daughter, and then to her son. This is known as a 'rope'. 1968 *Internat. Encycl. Social Sci.* VIII. 405/2 Men may be linked cross-sexually to their mothers, and women to their fathers, to produce the alternating or cross-sexual system of the 'rope'. 1976 H. READING *Dict. Social Sci.* 181 *Rope*, descent group resulting from alternating descent.

f. *slang.* Marijuana.

1944 D. BURLEY in A. Dundes *Mother Wit* (1973) 211 Marijuana-Weed—..*rope*. 1945 L. SHELLY *Jive Talk Dict.* 16/2 *Rope*... Marijuana cigarette. 1972 [see MUGGLE[3]].

g. *Astr.* A group of magnetic lines of force twisted together.

1961 H. W. BABCOCK in *Astrophysical Jrnl.* CXXXIII. 577 The fluid shear will be affected by the increased magnetic viscosity of local field concentrations, and these will be twisted into more or less discrete flux strands or 'ropes'... The flux ropes may be visualized as roller bearings. 1977 *Nature* 21 Apr. 686/1 More than 90% of the total magnetic flux, outside pores and sunspots, that emerges from the sun is confined to ropes that are only a few hundred kilometres across.

6. a. A number *of* onions, etc., strung or plaited together. Also *ellipt.*

1469–70 *Durh. Acc. Rolls* (Surtees) 93 Pro 14 Rapys del unyons. 1562 J. HEYWOOD *Prov. & Epigr.* (1867) 206 Wilt thou hand vp with ropes of ynions? 1622 MASSINGER & DEKKER *Virg. Mart.* II. iii, Let us both be turned into a rope of onions if we do not! 1674 JEAKE *Arith.* (1696) 66 Garlick. In 1 Hundred 15 Ropes. In 1 Rope 15 Heads. 1706 E. WARD *Hud. Rediv.* (1707) I. iv. 19 Be sure you never trust..The Value of a Rope of Onions With him that halts 'twixt two Opinions. 1794 STEDMAN *Surinam* (ed. 2) II. xix. 70 From the middle of the branches appears the seed, hanging down also in the form of a large rope of onions. 1890 *Pall Mall G.* 9 June 7/2 'Ropes' of ova being washed ashore from the weeds along the banks.

b. A thick string *of* pearls. Also *ellipt.*

1617 T. ROE *Jrnl.* 6 Oct. in Purchas *Pilgrimes* (1625) I. IV. xvi. 571, I told him I had a rich Pearle, and some other ropes faire. 1630 DAVENANT *Just Italian* III. i, This orient Roap is yours and you must wear't. 1632 MASSINGER *City Madam* III. iii, Rubies, sapphires, And ropes of orient pearl. 1665 SIR T. HERBERT *Trav.* (1677) 140 About his neck [was] a rope of carcanet of great Oriental Pearl. 1870 DISRAELI *Lothair* xxxiii, The Justinianis have ropes of pearls—Madame Justiniani..gives a rope to every one of her children when they marry. 1931 *Amer. Speech* VII. 113 Get this rope to the fence before we fall for receiving. 1966 A. LOOS *Girl like I* vii. 145 Gaby Deslys..wore 'ropes' of pearls, as they were then called.

†**c.** *fig.* A long series. *Obs.*

1621 BURTON *Anat. Mel.* III. iv. I. iii. (1651) 673 A rope of Popes, that by their greatness and authority bear down all before them. 1631 R. BOLTON *Comf. Affl. Consc.* (1635) 32 An aspersion..that not all the bloud of that rope of Popes, which constitute Antichrist, could ever be able to expiate.

7. a. A viscid or gelatinous stringy formation in beer or other liquid. Also *attrib.*

1747 MRS. GLASSE *Cookery* xvii. 150 The best Thing for Rope Beer. 1846 TIZARD *Brewing* (ed. 2) 532 The viscid and oily effect termed 'the rope'. 1857 G. BIRD *Urin. Deposits* (ed. 5) 278 They will..form dense masses in the urine, hanging in ropes like the thickest puriform mucus. 1869 BLACKMORE *Lorna D.* vii, I count him no more than the ropes in beer.

b. A bacterial condition of bread and the like in which it may be drawn into strands.

Cf. quot. 1850 s.v. ROPINESS.

1899 J. BLANDY *Baker's Guide* (ed. 4) iii. 169 (*heading*) Rope in cakes. 1921 W. & W. C. JAGO *Technol. Bread-Making* xvii. 345 During hot weather bread is liable to an outbreak of the disease called 'rope'. *Ibid.*, Modern writers agree in ascribing rope to bacterial activity. 1972 *Sci. Amer.* Mar. 18/1 Baked goods, for example, go stale rapidly. Once made, they are often exposed to mold spores that become active in warm weather or high humidity. In bread the spores produce a condition called 'rope'.

III. *attrib.* and *Comb.* (in senses 1–3).

8. a. Attrib. in sense 'made of rope', as ***rope-basket, bed, bedstead, -bit, -breeching, -bridge, -buffer, -cable, sling, sole, tow***, etc.

1848 tr. *Hoffmeister's Trav. Ceylon*, etc. ix. 330 We saw only a few solitary men, with rope-baskets on their arms. 1925 H. CRANE *Let.* 17 June (1965) 208 A lot of wonderful old rope beds and furniture came right along with it. 1972 E. WIGGINTON *Foxfire Bk.* 140 The rope bed was once the only bed to be found in this area. 1971 *Canad. Antiques Collector* Sept.–Oct. 15/1 Another early..bed is the low poster rope bedstead. 1940 C. DAY LEWIS tr. *Virgil's Georgics* III. 61 Try a rope-bit In his mouth now and then. 1816 SIR H. DOUGLAS *Milit. Bridges* 167 Rope-bridges were formerly much used in war. 1856 'STONEHENGE' *Brit. Rural Sports* 79/1 The former size [of gun] may be used with a rope-breeching, which is attached to the bows of the punt. 1923 Rope-bridge [see JHULA]. 1961 L. VAN DER POST *Heart of Hunter* 10, I was possibly the only person who could start this kind of interpretation; who could be this kind of improvised little ropebridge over the deep abyss between the modern man and the first person of Africa. 1965 A. NICOL *Truly Married Woman* 39 It used to take them about an hour to make a detour to cross..on the swinging rope bridge. 1876 PREECE & SIVEWRIGHT *Telegraphy* 171 The pad or rope-buffer *b* is next placed over this. 1836 *Penny Cycl.* VI. 260/1 If provided only with rope cables it is necessary to ride with a bower-anchor and a kedge. 1820 SCORESBY *Arc. Regions* II. 234 All the oars are fixed by rope-grommets to a single thole. 1882 'OUIDA' *Maremma* I. ii. 45 Its miserable horses straining at their rope harness. 1805 R. W. DICKSON

Pract. Agric. I. 415 The ploughman driving by means of rope reins. **1901** Merwin & Webster *Calumet 'K'* i. 5 'Slack away!' he called to the engineers, and he cast off the rope sling. **1957** Clark & Pyatt *Mountaineering in Brit.* xvi. 239 Rope-slings were used thus as early as 1931. **1971** C. Bonington *Annapurna South Face* xi. 127 Standing in a rope sling, suspended from a peg, he was able to reach up to another crack above the overhang and hammer in a further peg, clipped in another sling and pulled himself up. **1894** *T. Eaton & Co. Catal.* Spring & Summer 31/1 White canvas bathing shoes, rope soles. **1964** Rope sole [see *mess-boy* s.v. mess *sb.* 7]. **1965** *Economist* 25 Dec. 1416/3 In the [U.S.] National Forests there are 199 developed winter sports sites equipped with 164 chair lifts..312 rope tows and 48 ski jumps. **1968** *Globe & Mail* (Toronto) 13 Jan. 35/7 London's Ski Club with seven rope tows. **1978** W. F. Buckley *Stained Glass* xv. 147 He found it irresponsible that his thoughts should turn to skiing, which he longed to attempt in the lofty Alps after several winters of rope tows in Vermont during hectic weekends away from Yale.

b. Attrib. in misc. uses, as *rope-boy*, *-knout*, *-machinery*, *-manufacture*, *-pattern*, *skipping*, *socket*, *-traction*, *-trade*, etc.

1952 *Landfall* Sept. 206 Ropeboys just standing can feel cocky pride in shouting. **1970** *Guardian* 26 Nov. 13/2 A rope boy, in climbing diction, is a second man who spends patient hours securely belayed as he holds or pays out the rope for a leader. *a* **1918** W. Owen *Mental Cases* in *Poems* (1920) 8 Thus their hands are plucking at each other; Picking at the rope-knouts of their scourging. **1838** *Civ. Eng. & Arch. Jrnl.* I. 320/2 On Huddart's Rope Machinery. .. The above communication on the improvements in rope manufacture [etc.]. **1890** Sayce *Hittites* vii. 116 The so-called rope-pattern occurs once or twice on Babylonian gems. **1969** R. D. Abrahams *Jump-Rope Rhymes* p. xv, Rope skipping..with men..is now part of the training program for some athletic activity..rather than a game. **1889** *Cent. Dict.*, Rope-socket. **1935** *Discovery* Apr. 118/2 Actual drilling is done by a 'string' of tools... At the top of the string is the connecting rope socket, which permits the tools to turn freely, ensuring a round hole. **1841** *Penny Cycl.* XIX. 260/2 Rope-traction..is attended with great expense from the wear of the ropes. **1886** *Encycl. Brit.* XX. 845/1 A distinct branch of the rope trade.

c. Objective with agent-nouns, as *rope-bearer*, *-hauler*, *-layer*, *-spinner*, etc. Also rope-maker.

1599 Nashe *Lenten Stuffe* 27 Not a slop of a ropehaler they send forth to the Queenes ships, but hee is first broken to the Sea in the Herring mans Skiffe. **1640–1** *Canterb. Marriage Licences* (MS.), Robert Adman [of Wye] rope-layer. **1723** *Lond. Gaz.* No. 6186/10 William Buckland,..Ropespinner. *Ibid.* No. 6187/4 James Cleaver,..Rope-Weaver. **1801** Surr *Splendid Misery* I. 125 Her Ladyship is the best rope-skipper we have. **1841** *Penny Cycl.* XX. 154/2 Some of the principal rope-manufacturers of Great Britain. **1887** P. McNeill *Blawearie* 121 Straight to my companion went the rope-bearers.

d. Objective, with vbl. sbs. and pres. pples., as *rope-breaking*, *-climbing*, *-closing*, *-laying*, *-making*, *spinning*, etc.

1791 Bentham *Panopt.* i. Postscr. 162 Any rope-making legislator, or any legislator's rope-making friend. **1815** Kirby & Sp. *Entomol.* xiii. (1818) I. 406 A process more singular than that of rope-spinning. **1835** Ure *Philos. Manuf.* 62 Rope-making and wire-working belong also to this head. **1847** Halliw. s.v., The ancient custom of rope-pulling is always strictly observed in Ludlow on Shrove Tuesday. **1886** *Encycl. Brit.* XX. 846/1 An American rope-laying machine is in use. *Ibid.*, They receive no fore-twist in the rope-closing apparatus. **1903** [see sense 2 i above]. **1926** *Daily Colonist* (Victoria, B.C.) 17 July 10/2 Mr. Ash..had plenty of thrills among the Mexican bandits and cattle thieves, during which time he became expert with the revolver, the lasso, and rope spinning. **1965** D. R. Casady et al. *Handbk. Physical Fitness Activities* xii. 96/2 Rope climbing promotes the development of a strong grip. **1969** G. E. Evans *Farm & Village* xi. 126 This saddler's shop, with 'a rope-spinning ground' behind it was sold by auction in July 1875 at the Lion Inn, Debenham. **1975** F. Kennedy *Alberta was my Beat* viii. 92 Guy Weadick..when he found that he could not successfully ride outlaw horses, turned to rope spinning.

e. With pa. pples. or adjs., as *rope-fastened*, *-girt*, *-held*, *-muscled*, *-shaped*, *-soled*, *-swung*, etc.

1699 R. L'Estrange *Erasm. Colloq.* (1725) 269 He would take Care that this Tribe of Half-shod, and Rope-girt People should never fail. **1780** Fawkes tr. *Apollonius Rhodius, Argonautics* i. 1235 Here the rope-fasten'd stone they heave on shore, Which serv'd as anchor to the ship before. **1839** Lindley *Introd. Bot.* 450 *Rope-shaped*,..formed of coarse fibres resembling cords. *c* **1860** H. Stuart *Seaman's Catech.* 37 They have the advantage of rope-stropt leading blocks. **1876** M. Collins *Blacksm. & Scholar* II. 22 A huge brown rope-muscled hand. **1892** Sladen *Japs at Home* xxvi, Pilgrims of every degree, from the rope-shod pauper, to the swaggering plutocrat. **1920** *Blackw. Mag.* Apr. 507/2 He was dressed quaintly in well-washed dungarees,..a gaudy waist-cloth, rope-soled shoes [etc.]. **1955** M. Allingham *Beckoning Lady* iii. 39 She was wearing a bright blue dress .. and rope-soled shoes. **1973** G. Mitchell *Murder of Busy Lizzie* iv. 47 She pulled on a pair of rope-soled shoes. **1957** A. Clarke *Too Great a Vine* 23 Rope-swung victims ring that bell.

9. Special combs., as **rope-bark**, *U.S.*, the shrub *Dirca palustris*, also called leather-wood and moose-wood; **rope-barrel**, = *rope-roll*; **rope border** (esp. in *Basketry*), a border resembling the twisted strands of rope; **rope-boring**, the boring of wells with a drill suspended and worked by means of a rope; **rope brown**, a type of strong brown paper orig. made from old rope; **rope burn**, a burn caused by the friction of a rope; hence as *v. trans.*; **rope-chain**, an ornamental chain (for a watch, etc.) of a rope-pattern; † **rope-craft**, rope-making; **rope-dance**, a performance on the tight-rope; **rope-drill**, a form of military drill in which a stretched rope is used to represent part of a company; **rope embroidery silk** = sense 5 c above; **rope-end**, = rope's-end; **rope-ferry**, a ferry worked by a rope; **rope-grass** (see quot. 1848); **rope-ground**, a rope-walk; **rope horse**, a horse ridden by one roping an animal; † **rope-law**, hanging; † **rope-leap**, death by hanging; **rope-moulding**, a moulding of a rope-pattern; **rope-paper**, **-pump** (see quots.); **rope-quoit**, a quoit made of a ring of rope, used for playing on board ship; **rope race**, the compartment or passage through which a driving-rope passes; **rope-railway**, a railway on which rope-traction is employed; † **rope-rhetoric** (?); **rope rider** (see quot.); **rope-ring**, a ring for boxers marked off by a rope; **rope-roll**, a cylinder or drum on which drawing-ropes are wound; **rope-runner**, †one who has run from the rope; (see also quot. *a* 1886); **rope-sheaf** (see *rope-barrel*); **rope-sight**, in bell-ringing, facility in judging when to pull a rope, from the position and movement of others; **rope silk**: see sense 5 c above; **rope stitch** (see quot. 1882); **rope-trick**, † (*a*) ? a punning or illiterate distortion of 'rhetoric'; (*b*) a juggling trick or sleight-of-hand involving a rope or ropes; freq. in *Indian rope-trick*; also *fig.*; **rope-twine**, ?thick twine, or rope-yarn; **rope-twister**, an implement for making hay or straw ropes; **rope-walker**, a rope-dancer; hence *rope-walking* vbl. sb.; **rope-way**, (*a*) = *rope-railway*; (*b*) a rope used as a means of transport; **rope-weed**, **-wind** (see quots.); **rope wrapping** = *rope brown* above.

Various technical combs., such as *rope-clamp*, *-clutch*, *-elevator*, etc. are explained in Knight *Dict. Mech.*

1851 Dunglison *Med. Dict.*, *Rope Bark, *Dirca palustris*. **1811** Farey in W. H. Marshall *Review* (1817) IV. 110 A turn-tree, or *rope-barrel, for winding up the Ore in small tubs. **1839** Ure *Dict. Arts* 982 Inclined-plane machines, which are moved either by vertical rope-barrels, or horizontal rope-sheaves. **1897** *Private Life of Queen* xxiv. 201 A very simple cornice..composed of the conventional 'egg and dart' and '*rope' borders. **1912** T. Okey *Introd. Art of Basket-Making* ix. 100 *The Rope Border*—This, a modification of the plaited border, may be carried out by numbering six stakes in succession and doubling the first two. **1953** A. G. Knock *Willow Basket-Work* 26 The simplest and smallest rope border was used on the oval buff shopping basket. **1888** *Chambers's Encycl.* II. 331/2 The *rope-boring machinery of Mather and Platt of Salford..is in extensive use. **1902** *Encycl. Brit.* XXX. 763/2 In Europe rods, either of iron or wood, seem to be preferred, though rope boring is by no means unknown. **1908** R. W. Sindall *Manuf. of Paper* vi. 27 **Rope browns* are common papers made of fairly strong material of a miscellaneous character, this name having been derived from the fact that rope and similar fibre were at one time used exclusively. **1914** E. A. Dawe *Paper & its Uses* xvii. 115 Brown wrapping papers are made of various materials and in many qualities and substances. Rope browns, air-dried, cylinder-dried are three kinds. **1926** *Paper Terminol.* (Spalding & Hodge, Ltd.) 23 *Rope brown*, a quality of brown paper manufactured from old rope. **1955** S. C. Gilmour *Paper* xxii. 251 The thickness of a quality such as Rope Brown would appear to the touch to be much in excess of the same substance in an M. G. Pure Kraft. **1905** *Outing* July 415/1 Before we left that camp Rodney and Sue were sleek and fat, and my bruises and *rope-burns were healed. **1944** B. A. Botkin *Treas. Amer. Folklore* i. iv. 132 The red rope-burn that he wore about his permanently stiff neck, usually hidden by a bandana, was his only diploma. **1948** Faulkner *Intruder in Dust* vii. 159 A big saddleless black mule with a rope-burn on its neck. **1965** A. Blackshaw *Mountaineering* viii. 217 (*caption*) He is wearing gloves to protect his hands from rope burns should the leader fall. **1966** M. & O. Murie *Wapiti Wilderness* v. 54 There was such friction from the mule's wild lunges that my palms were rather badly *rope-burned. *a* **1490** Botoner *Itin.* (Nasmith, 1778) 167 Le domum de *rope-crafft. **1883** J. Parker *Tyne Chylde* 7 Life was a *rope-dance, a swing, a butterfly chase. **1844** *Regul. & Ord. Army* 295 Squad or Light Infantry Drill;..*Rope Drill, &c. **1895** *Montgomery Ward Catal.* Spring & Summer 90/3 *Rope Embroidery Silk..very coarse. **1897** *Sears, Roebuck Catal.* 321/2 Corticelli Rope Embroidery Silk..A course [*sic*] silk, for bold designs..when rapid work is required. **1859** Geo. Eliot *A. Bede* v, Hunting Will Maskery out of the village with *rope-ends and pitchforks. **1788** M. Cutler in *Life*, etc. (1888) I. 399 It is a *rope-ferry. **1897** *Outing* XXIX. 564/1 To cross the river by the old rope ferry. **1848** Craig, **Rope-grass*, the common name of the plants of the genus Restio, from the supple shoots of many of the species being used as withes at the Cape of Good Hope. **1799** *Hull Advertiser* 21 Dec. 1/1 To enter into partnership in a *Rope-Ground. **1841** *Penny Cycl.* XX. 154/1 Spinning rope-yarns ..in the rope-ground, or rope-walk. **1944** R. F. Adams *Western Words* (1945) 131/2 When running an animal to be roped, the educated *rope horse knows when the cowboy takes down his rope and what is expected of him. **1961** R. P. Hobson *Rancher takes Wife* i. 19 Rhino was a good rope horse. **1592** Warner *Alb. Eng.* vii. xxxvii, Both did fault in one same ill. Yeat *rope-law had the Youth, the Fryar liv'd Cleergie knaved still. **1611** Cotgr., *Demisaut*, a halfe-leape; also, the *roape-leape, or some mens last-leape. **1836** H. G. Knight *Archit. Tour Normandy* 199 The most common mouldings are the billet,..hatchet, nebule, star, *rope. **1875** W. McIlwraith *Guide Wigtownshire* 103 Quaint pepper-box turrets, rope mouldings, crow-stepped gables. **1888** Jacobi *Printers' Vocab.* 115 **Rope paper*, strong packing paper of various sizes made largely of old rope. **1815** J. Smith *Panorama Sci. & Art* II. 146 A *rope pump, which consists of a rope rapidly revolving over two pulleys, one of which is at the top and the other in the water of the well. **1893** F. F. Moore *I Forbid Banns* xii, He went amidships to where a game of *rope quoits was being played. **1892** J. Nasmith *Students' Cotton Spinning* xii. 400 In arranging the blowing rooms it is now customary to separate them from the main building by the *rope race. *a* **1890** *Engineer* LXVIII. 454 (Cent.), *Rope railways, as they were called, or rope-ways for transmitting..goods. **1596** Nashe *Saffron Walden* Ep. Ded., Vtterly thou bewrayest thy nonproficencie in the Doctors Paracelsian *rope-retorique. **1903** *Sci. Amer.* 23 May 392/2 In soft-coal mines the man in charge of the cable train is called a *rope rider. In bringing his cars out of the mine he sits upon the ring which connects the cable with the train. **1813** *Sporting Mag.* XLI. 40 A stand up fight in a twenty feet *rope-ring. **1851** Greenwell *Coal-trade Terms, Northumb. & Durh.* 45 The diameter of a *rope-roll should not be less than 8 feet. **1875** Martin *Winding Mach.* 64 We must give up using metallic ropes wound upon rope-rolls in working from great depths. **1612** Beaum. & Fl. *Coxcomb* ii. iii, Stand further friend: I doe not like your *rope-runners. *a* **1886** *All Year Round* (Cent.), A rope-runner is pretty much the same as a break-man on a goods-train. **1902** *Encycl. Brit.* XXVI. 521/1 He [*sc.* the bellringer] has to bear in mind,..what bell or bells are striking immediately before or after him—this being ascertained chiefly by '*ropesight' *i.e.*, the knack..of seeing which rope is being pulled immediately before and after his own. **1956** G. E. Evans *Ask Fellows who cut Hay* xviii. 143 The science of change-ringing is something of a mystery to the layman... 'It's all right once you get *rope-sight*,' one old ringer confided. **1975** *Islander* (Victoria, B.C.) 16 Mar. 12/3 He must start pulling his bell before the bell that he is following has sounded, so he must be able to recognize from the movement of the ropes (without hearing the sound) when he should start to pull his own rope, and this art of recognition is called 'ropesight'. **1977** *Church Times* 20 May 8/5 The ability to see one's path in this dancing maze is called ropesight, and is an essential attribute for a change ringer. **1880** L. Higgin *Handbk. Embroidery* iii. 28 *Rope stitch..should..have the appearance of a twisted rope. **1882** Caulfeild & Saward *Dict. Needlework* 192/2 Rope Stitch..is similar to Crewel and Stem Stitch in appearance, and only differs from those stitches in being worked from the top of the material downwards. **1899** Miss Masters *Bk. Stitches* 81 Knotted rope stitch is effective for coarse outlines. **1932** D. C. Minter *Mod. Needlecraft* 55/2 Chain, pekinese, appliqué, Portuguese border and rope stitch..are useful for working this type of letter. **1596** Shaks. *Tam. Shrew* i. ii. 112 That's nothing; and he begin once, hee'l raile in his *rope trickes. **1887** *Encycl. Dict.* VI. i. 182/1 *Rope-trick*.., a juggling feat, introduced into England from America by the Brothers Davenport, in 1864. The performer was bound with ropes in a cabinet, or to a chair; the lights were then lowered, and on their being raised he was discovered at liberty, having been released, it was said, by spiritual agency. **1894** A. Lang *Cock Lane* 106 Thus, when Ibn Batuta, the old Arabian traveller, tells us that he saw the famous rope-trick performed in India—men climbing a rope thrown into the air, and cutting each other up, while the bodies revive and reunite—he very candidly adds that his companion, standing by, saw nothing out of the way, and declared that nothing occurred. **1907** Maskelyne & 'Devant' in 'D. Devant' *My Magic Life* (1931) xii. 131 We are prepared to pay a salary at the rate of £5,000 a year to any man who can perform the Rope Trick as described in the papers... He is to stand out in the open air... He is to throw one end of a rope into the air, and the other end is to be on the ground. The rope is to become stiffened; a boy is to climb up it and disappear into space. **1922** L. H. Branson *Indian Conjuring* ix. 76 (*heading*) The Indian rope trick. **1953** —— *Lifetime of Deception* xxxviii. 206 The Indian '*Jadoo-wallah*' is a much over-rated performer, particularly as the world-famous Indian rope trick has never been performed. This is a statement of fact. **1958** *Times Lit. Suppl.* 17 Jan. 26/5 These are no ugly moral questions, no probings of primitivism: Sir Maurice blandly marshals the material..and the miracle (or rope trick, according to one's viewpoint) is duly performed. **1977** *Private Eye* 4 Mar. 17/3 For what such massive buying operations did was to ensure that the Slater share price resembled the Indian rope trick, defying gravity. **1719** De Foe *Crusoe* i. (Globe) 55 Small Ropes and *Rope-twine. *Ibid.* ii. (Globe) 395 One of the English Men with a Piece of Rope-Twine..ty'd his two Feet fast together. **1844** H. Stephens *Bk. Farm* III. 969 A hay-rope, twisted on the spot..with a *rope-twister or thraw-crook. **1615** Sandys *Trav.* 77 Grammarian, painter, *rope walker—All knowes The needy Greek—bid go to heaven, he goes. **1862** E. A. Hall *Diary* 2 Jan. in O. A. Sherrard *Two Victorian Girls* (1966) ii. 289 Spent an hour at the Crystal Palace and saw the rope-walker, Blondin. **1942** E. Sitwell *Street Songs* 11 We watched the sonambulists, rope-walkers, argonauts. **1881** *Gen. Statutes State of Michigan* (1882) I. 539 Any person..who shall apprentice, give away, let out or otherwise dispose of any such child to any person in or for the vocation, service or occupation of *rope or wire walking..shall be deemed guilty of a misdemeanor. **1890** [see act *sb.* 7 c]. **1957** *Encycl. Brit.* XIX. 547/1 *Rope-walking*, the art of walking, dancing and performing tricks on a rope or wire stretched between two supports. **1889** *Engineer* LXVIII. 454/1 Rope railways, as they were called, or *ropeways, for transmitting minerals and goods, seem to be rapidly growing in favour, especially for mining purposes. **1928** *Daily Mail* 7 Aug. 8/5 Next week's programme includes instruction in the use of heavy derricks and aerial ropeways. **1941** 'R. West' *Black Lamb & Grey Falcon* II. 925 If you have to have a rope-way, you have to have Germans... All the decent funiculars in the world are made by a German company. **1950** tr. *Mountaineering Handbk.* (Assoc. Brit. Members Swiss Alpine Club) x. 116 To transport loads, injured people or materials over precipices, ravines, large crevasses or torrents, where possible fix a rope over the obstacle..the anchorage at the ends of a ropeway should be firm enough to meet all eventualities. **1963** *Economist* 30 Nov. 911/1 Aerial ropeways and chairlifts can be pretty profitable. **1611** Cotgr., *Voluble*, Withiwind, Bindweed, *Roapweed. **1855** Miss Pratt *Flower. Pl.* IV. 17 Field Bindweed..has many country names, as *Ropewind, Withywind. **1937** *Rope wrapping [see *acid-proof* adj. s.v. acid *sb.* 4].

rope (rəʊp), *sb.*[2] Now *dial.* Forms: 1 rop (hrop), 4–5 *pl.* roppes (5 roppis), 7 rop, 7, 9 rap, 9 rapp; 5– *pl.* ropes (5 ropys), 7– rope. [OE. *rop* (*hrop*), = MDu. *rop*, of uncertain relationship; in later use becoming identical in form with prec.] A gut, entrail, intestine. Freq. in *pl.*

c **1000** *Sax. Leechd.* II. 230 On þære wambe & on þam roppe & smæl þearmum. *c* **1000** ÆLFRIC *Gloss.* in Wr.-Wülcker 113 *Colum*, hrop. **1340** *Ayenb.* 62 He is ase þe gamelos þet leueþ by þe eyr and naȝt ne heþ ine his roppes bote wynd. **13..** *E.E. Allit. P.* C. 270 He glydes in by þe giles,..Relande in by a rop, a rode þat hym þoȝt. **1398** TREVISA *Barth. De P.R.* XVII. lxiv. (Bodl. MS.), He þat eteþ benes alwey contynualli haþe ache & gnawinge in guttes & in roppes. *c* **1430** *Two Cooker-bks.* 39 Take þe Roppis with þe talour, & parboyle hem. *c* **1460** J. RUSSELL *Bk. Nurture* in *Babees Bk.* (1868) 149 Fried mete þat stoppes and distemperethe alle þe body, bothe bak, bely, & roppes. **1530** PALSGR. 263/2 Ropes in the small guttes. **1674** RAY *N.C. Words* 59 In the South the Guts prepared and cut out for Black Puddings or Links are called Ropes. *c* **1700** KENNETT in *MS. Lansd. 1033*, fol. 328 The guts of fowls are calld raps in Kent. **1772** GRAVES *Spir. Quix.* x. xi, A brace of ostriches roasted, at the upper end, with the ropes on a toast. *a* **1793** G. WHITE *Selborne* (1853) 275 The entrails..might have been dressed like the ropes of a woodcock. **1828–** in many dial. glossaries.

†**rope**, *sb.*[3] *Obs.* Forms: 1 hrop, 2 rop, 4 roupe. [OE. *hróp*, = Fris. *rop*, MDu. and Du. *roep*, OHG. *ruof* (G. *ruf*), ON. *hróp* (Norw. and Sw. *rop*, Da. *raab*), Goth. *hrôps*: cf. ROPE *v.*[2]] Outcry, clamour, cries of distress or lamentation.

The spelling *roupe* may be due to confusion with ROUP.

971 *Blickl. Hom.* 185 þær biþ a wop & hrop & toþa gristbitung. *c* **1205** LAY. 15066 þer wes wop, þer wes rop, & reuliche iberen. **13..** *Seuen Sag.* 1185 (W.), With lourand chere,..Hond wringging, and loud roupe, And here visage al biwope.

rope (rəʊp), *v.*[1] Also 4 *north.* raip(e. [f. ROPE *sb.*[1] Cf. ON. *reipa* to fasten with a rope (whence early northern ME. *raipe*), MLG. *repen*, *reepen*, MDa. *rebe*, to measure with a rope.]

1. a. *trans.* To tie, bind, fasten, or secure with a rope. Also with *up*.

a **1300** *Cursor M.* 24023 Vn-reufulli þai can him raipe, Ful snoberli him or to snaipe. *c* **1515** *Cocke Lorell's B.* 12 Some roped ye hoke, some ye pompe, and some ye launce. **1610** MARKHAM *Masterp.* II. cx. 391 Then rope his legs with a soft rope of hay. **1639** T. DE GREY *Compl. Horsem.* (1656) 373 Rope up all his legges to the body, not suffering him to lie down. **1787** MARSHALL *E. Norfolk* (1795) II. 387 *To Rope*, to tedder; as a horse. **1856** KANE *Arct. Expl.* II. xvi. 169 Every bag was, in sailor-phrase, roped and becketed; in ordinary parlance, well secured by cordage. **1873** BLACK *Pr. Thule* xxv. 417 The slain deer roped on to the pony. **1889** J. ABERCROMBIE *Eastern Caucasus* 3 In less than half an hour the baggage was in, every thing roped tight and we were jolting at a rapid pace.

transf. **1862** TYNDALL *Mountaineer.* xi. 90 We skirt a pile of moraine-like matter, which is roped compactly together by the roots of the pines.

b. In mountaineering, to attach (persons) to each other by means of a rope for greater safety. Also *absol.*, and with *up*.

1862 TYNDALL *Mountaineer.* ii. 14 We accordingly rope ourselves, and advance along the edge of the fissure. **1871** L. STEPHEN *Playgr. Eur.* II. iv. 312 Guides have sometimes objected to rope a party together. **1974** *Times* 18 Feb. 2/7 They had set out yesterday morning to climb Zero Gulley. About half way up Mr. Beattey slipped and fell 100ft, landing on a ledge. Mr. Thomas was roped to him. **1976** D. CLARK *Dread & Water* i. 8 Redruth was climbing solo on a pretty easy pitch... Silk was roped to a partner.

1865 *Sat. Rev.* 29 July 141/2 The question of roping or not roping is always a fertile source of discussion in the Alps. **1894** G. M. FENN *Alpine Valley* I. 133 Shall we rope together? **1922** E. R. EDDISON *Worm Ouroboros* xii. 177 They roped at the foot of the glacier that came down from the saddle, some five thousand feet above them. **1925** *Climbers' Club Jrnl.* XVII. 41 We roped up at the foot of the rocks at ten o'clock and serious climbing began at once. **1950** T. LONGSTAFF *This my Voyage* ii. 16 We struck the arête at seven fifteen and after a bite, roped up. **1952** MORIN & SMITH tr. *Herzog's Annapurna* ix. 138 We roped up in the same order in which we had camped. **1965** A. BLACKSHAW *Mountaineering* vii. 198 The party should rope at the bottom of the first pitch of the climb.

c. *to rope it*, to make use of the rope in order to proceed with greater safety.

1881 STEVENSON *Virg. Puerisque* (1895) 163 An Alpine climber roping it over a peril.

d. To assist with ropes.

1890 HALLETT *1000 Miles* 400 Just below the island..is a very long rapid, down which we were roped. **1925** E. F. NORTON *Fight for Everest: 1924* 115 It was one of our rules that any party of porters..must be met at the Col and escorted and roped over the intricate route into camp. **1976** A. WHITE *Long Silence* ii. 18 It had been a difficult climb... He..roped me most of the way.

e. *to rope down* (intr. and trans.), to descend by means of a double rope fixed above; to make an abseil.

1931 *Climbers' Club Jrnl.* XVII. 204 The next little excitement was when we came to the top of..the Grand Diable... One has to rope down it. **1935** D. PILLEY *Climbing Days* vi. 122 This roping down..is a trick one gets used to. **1943** E. SHIPTON *Upon that Mountain* iv. 78 We reached a gap about 30 feet deep, and roped down into it. **1945** G. W. YOUNG *Mountain Craft* (ed. 4) iv. 152 Climbers, shy still of claiming it as a national practice, still struggle alternatively with 'rappel' and 'Abseilung', so as to put a wrapper..of dark foreign distinction about new methods of roping down. **1955** P. BAUER *Kanchenjunga Challenge* I. i. 22 We roped down with flashes of lightning as our only illumination. **1965** A. BLACKSHAW *Mountaineering* viii. 239 (*heading*) Roping down (abseiling or rappelling).

2. To inclose or mark off (a certain space) with a rope. Usually const. *in*, *off*, *out*, *round*.

1738 in Waghorn *Cricket Scores* (1899) 20 The ground will be roped round as usual. **1809** *Sporting Mag.* XXXIII. 228 A thirty-feet ring, roped, was the field of blood. **1824** SCOTT *St. Ronan's* xvii, Traversing..as limited a space of ground as if it had been actually roped in for their pedestrian exercise. **1866** *Pall Mall G.* No. 450. 199/2 The ground is roped out. **1889** *Cent. Dict.* s.v. rope[1] v., A space in front of the pictures was roped off to prevent injury to them. **1921** A. HUXLEY *Crome Yellow* xxviii. 298 It was the hour for the dancing..a space had been roped off. **1976** *S. Wales Echo* 23 Nov., A section of the centre had to be roped off yesterday to enable schools to use the sports facilities.

3. *Naut.* (See quot. 1846.)

1846 A. YOUNG *Naut. Dict.* s.v., To rope a sail, is to sew the bolt-rope round its edges. **1882** NARES *Seamanship* (ed. 6) 12 A square sail is roped on the after side. *Ibid.* 130 All fore-and-aft sails are roped on the port side.

4. a. *U.S.* and *Austr.* To catch with a rope; to lasso. Also *fig.* (see ROPEABLE *a.*).

1848 RUXTON *Life Far West* (1849) 20 Maybe you'll get 'roped' by a Rapaho afore mornin'. **1884** 'R. BOLDREWOOD' *Melb. Mem.* xxi. 150 You could 'rope'..any Clifton colt or filly, back them in three days, and within a week ride a journey.

b. *to rope in*, to draw into some enterprise; to ensnare, to lure or decoy; to arrest (*rare*). Orig. *U.S.*

1848 BARTLETT *Dict. Amer.* 278 *To rope in*, to take or sweep in collectively; an expression much used in colloquial language at the West. **1859** —— (ed. 2) 370 *Rope in*, to decoy, viz., into a mock-auction establishment, a gambling-house, etc. **1899** SOMERVILLE & ROSS *Irish R.M.* 275, I won't be roped into this kind of business again. **1916** 'BOYD CABLE' *Action Front* 10 They..roped in my captain to identify me. **1925** D. G. MACKAIL in *Strand Mag.* Sept. 254/2 I'm sorry for you, my man, but..another twenty-four hours, and we might have been roping you in, too. **1929** —— *How Amusing!* 108 He remembered now; they'd roped him in as a godfather. **1970** *Nature* 2 May 395/1 Despite its ability to attract private funds, the zoo has been less successful at roping in the public. **1973** E. PAGE *Fortnight by Sea* xi. 120 I've roped in the Pagets for a game, it seems she plays golf too. **1978** *Lancashire Life* Mar. 96/2 Much of it can be a do-it-yourself operation, in which the whole family can be roped in to help. **1981** N. FREELING *One Damn Thing* iv. 30 The gendarmes..set the urban police to rope in the rest of the band.

5. *Racing.* **a.** To pull back or check (a horse) so as to prevent it from winning in a race.

1857 G. LAWRENCE *Guy Liv.* ix, Where the bold yeomen, in full confidence that their favourite will not be 'roped', back their opinions manfully for crowns. **1887** BLACK *Sabina Zembra* 311 They declare he roped Redhampton at Liverpool.

b. *absol.* To lose a race intentionally by holding back.

1882 *Sydney Slang Dict.* 7/2 *Rope*, to lose a race purposely: to swindle one's backers or the public by a 'cross' or prearranged race, in which the best man or best horse is made to 'rope' or run behind. **1887** *Cyclist* 14 Sept. 1203/1 In athletics the only men who can make it really worth while to 'rope' are the back-mark men. **1894** A. MORRISON *M. Hewitt, Investigator* ii, He wouldn't dare to rope under my very eyes. **1904** R. THOMAS *Swimming* ii. 44 A racer is said to rope when he does not exert himself to the utmost, in order to make out that he is not so good a swimmer as he really is, that he may thus get an advantage in the next handicap for which he enters.

6. a. *intr.* To be drawn out into a filament or thread; to become viscid or ropy.

1565 GOLDING *Ovid's Met.* I. (1593) 4 Then Isikles hung roping downe. **1584** R. SCOT *Discov. Witchcr.* XII. xxi. (1886) 229 It will rope like birdlime, that you maie wind it about a Sticke. **1601** HOLLAND *Pliny* XI. xv, If a man touch it, rope it wil and draw small slimie threds after it. **1644** PLATTES in *Hartlib's Legacy* (1655) 231 They put it into Coolers, and when it is well cooled it will rope like oyl. **1743** *Lond. & Country Brew.* III. (ed. 2) 167 It causes..their Bread to rope as well as their Beer. **1797** F. BAILY *Jrnl. Tour N. Amer.* (1856) 181 By trying whether it will rope betwixt the finger and thumb. **1854** *Pharmac. Jrnl.* XIII. 366 His syrups thicken (technically called *roping*).

b. *trans.* To pull, draw out, or twist into the shape of a rope.

1843 *P. Parley's Ann.* IV. 363 They dabbed the treacle into each other's eyes, and roped it over each other's shoulders. **1887** MEREDITH *Ball. & Poems* 9 Old Kraken roped his white moustache.

†**rope**, *v.*[2] *Obs.* [OE. *hrópan* (pa. t. *hréop*), = OFris. (*h*)*rôpa*, MDu. and Du. *roepen*, OS. *hrôpan* (LG. *rôpen*), OHG. *hruofan*, etc. (G. *rufen*), ON. *hrópa* (Norw. and Sw. *ropa*, Da. *raabe*): cf. Goth. *hrôpjan*. Prob. of imitative origin.] *intr.* To utter a cry or shout; to cry out. Hence '**roping** *vbl. sb.*

a **1000** *Guthlac* 878 þa wrohtsmiðas wop ahofun, hreopun hreðlease. *c* **1000** *Ags. Ps.* (Thorpe) cxlvi. 10 Se þe mete syleð..hrefnes briddum, þonne heo hropende him ciȝeað to. *a* **1225** *Ancr. R.* 330 Mid þus onwille halsunge [she] weopeð & gret [*T.* ropes; *C.* ropeð] efter sume helpe. *c* **1400** *Ywaine & Gaw.* 242 Lions, beres, bath bul and bare, That rewfully gan rope and rare. **1549** *Compl. Scot.* vi. 39 The ropeen of the rauynis gart the crans crope.

†**rope**, *v.*[3] *Obs. rare.* [? Related to REPE *v.*[1]] *trans.* To lay hold of. Hence '**roping** *vbl. sb.*, touching, probing (of a matter).

a **1225** *Ancr. R.* 128 þe uoxes..draweð al into hore holes, þet heo muwen arepen & arechen [*C.* ropin & rimen; *T.* repen & rinen]. *Ibid.* 314 Unneaðe, þauh a last, þuruh þen abbodes gropunge [*T.* ropinge; *C.* reping], he hit seide.

†**rope**, *v.*[4] *Obs. rare.* [Of obscure origin.] *intr.* ? To fall in torrents. Hence '**roping** *ppl. a.*

a **1400–50** *Alexander* 4176 þan fell þar fra þe firmament, as it ware fell sparkis, Ropand doun o rede fire, þan any rayn thikire. *c* **1400** *Destr. Troy* 3693 With a ropand rayne rugh was the se. *Ibid.* 4631, 9637.

rope, obs. f. RAPE *sb.*[4]; obs. pa. t. of REAP *v.*

ropeable ('rəʊpəb(ə)l), *a. Austr.* and *N.Z. slang.* Also **ropable.** [f. ROPE *v.*[1] + -ABLE.] Requiring to be roped; intractable, wild; violently angry.

1874 C. DE BOOS *Congewoi Corr.* 195, I don't know a nastier smell than the smeller new togs just fresh from the tailor's goose, and the thoughter that amost made me ropable. **1891** *Melbourne Argus* 10 Oct. 13/4 The service has shown itself so 'ropeable' heretofore that one experiences.. satisfaction in seeing it roped. **1898** 'R. BOLDREWOOD' *Romance of Canvass Town* 322 Your Aunt would be ropeable. **1919** H. LAWSON *Coll. Verse* (1969) III. 385 Don't get ropable, or moony—and, above all, don't get spoony. **1955** P. WHITE *Tree of Man* (1956) 278, I often remember how you broke that washstand at Yuruga. Mother was ropeable. **1957** D. NILAND *Call me when Cross turns Over* (1958) 216 God, she thought, as she sat down, he's ropable. **1958** *N.Z. Listener* 16 May 21/3 There was —— with a walking stick, his leg in plaster. And was he ropeable! He came down and ripped into them: 'Who do you think you're going to play—a kindergarten? You're playing New Zealand. Now get cracking.' **1963** J. CANTWELL *No Stranger to Flame* viii. 125 She was going to have my kid, but she dropped it when another bloke put the acid on. I got ropeable and did her.

'**rope-band**, etymologizing form of ROBAND.

1769 FALCONER *Dict. Marine* (1780), *Rope-bands*,.. pronounced roebins, certain pieces of small rope, or braided cordage, used to tie the upper edges of the great sails to their respective yards. **1792** *Falconer's Shipwr.* II. 324 *note*, They are passed..between the rope-band legs. **1846** A. YOUNG *Naut. Dict.*, *Rope-Bands*, or *Robands*, small pieces of two yarn foxes plaited, or of sennit or spun-yarn, sometimes used to confine the head of a sail to its yard or gaff. **1867** SMYTH *Sailor's Word-Bk.* 579.

roped (rəʊpt), *ppl. a.* [f. ROPE *sb.*[1] or *v.*[1]]

1. a. Formed into viscous threads. *rare*⁻¹.

1607 WALKINGTON *Optic Glass* 124 He..voided a great abundance of roped phlegme.

b. Twisted like a rope.

1880 *Archaeol. Cant.* XIII. 115 An oval-shaped Sign, containing, within a roped wreath, the figure of Sir John Schorne. **1901** *Illustr. London News* 22 June 912 The helmet, with slightly roped comb, opens down the centre of the chin-piece.

2. a. Girdled with a rope; tied or fastened with a rope; marked *off* by a rope, etc. Also *fig.*

1829 P. EGAN *Boxiana* 2nd Ser. II. 350 Harry Jones and Bob Simmonds entered a twenty-four-foot roped ring at one o'clock. **1834** MOTLEY *Corr.* I. 37 These are your true monks—none of your bare-footed, rosaried and roped friars. **1876** G. M. HOPKINS *Wreck of Deutschland* iv, in *Poems* (1967) 52, I steady as a water in a well, to a poise, to a pane, But roped with, always, all the way down from the tall Fells or flanks of the voel, a vein Of the gospel proffer. **1881** *Daily News* 13 April 2/8 The heats were decided in a roped ring of about 18 feet. **1894** *Persian Pict.* 17 Their donkeys laden with roped bundles of grass. **1921** A. HUXLEY *Crome Yellow* xxvii. 295 In a roped-off space beyond, Mary was directing the children's sports. **1927** WODEHOUSE *Meet Mr. Mulliner* iii. 70 He seemed to be always on the point of introducing into debates on parish matters the methods which had made him so successful in the roped ring. **1932** AUDEN *Orators* III. 109 To stand with the wine-dark conquerors in the roped-off pews. **1943** J. B. PRIESTLEY *Daylight on Saturday* iv. 23 They went..to the enormous canteen. There was a roped-off space in the middle. **1955** E. HILLARY *High Adventure* 10 George Band with Sherpas..on a roped cliff. **1965** F. SARGESON *Mem. Peon* vi. 163 His meagre, roped-off end of the..area. **1976** A. PRICE *War Game* II. 217 Posters directing motorists to roped-off fields. **1977** *Custom Car* Nov. 58/1, I can't help thinking a roped-off enclosure and a bit of creative parking for the various classes would have made for more interest.

b. Performed by means of roping.

1893 *Athenæum* 30 Sept. 460/1 Our roped ascent..was probably the first ever made. **1935** *Encycl. Sports* 431/2 No one should ever attempt a roped climb without at least one experienced mountaineer in the party.

'**rope-,dancer.** [ROPE *sb.*[1] 2b. Cf. Du. *reepdanser.*] One who 'dances' or balances on a rope suspended at some height above the ground; a funambulist. Also *fig.*

1648 WILKINS *Dædalus* II. vii, It [*petaminaria*] is probably derived from the Greek word πετασθαι, which signifies to Fly, and may refer to such kind of Rope-Dancers. **1670** EACHARD *Cont. Clergy* 33 Those usually that have been rope-dancers in the schools, oft-times prove Jack puddings in the pulpit. **1707** SIR W. HOPE *New Method Fencing* iii. 35 The surprising..Feats of Activity, performed by..Rope-Dancers, and Tumblers. **1760–72** H. BROOKE *Fool of Qual.* (1809) III. 143 Posture-master, rope-dancer, and equilibrist. **1822** HAZLITT *Table-t.* I. i. 18 To balance himself for any time in the same position the rope-dancer must strain every nerve. **1849** MACAULAY *Hist. Eng.* i. I. 102 All who live by amusing the leisure of others, from the painter and the comic poet, down to the rope-dancer.

'**rope-,dancing**, *vbl. sb.* [ROPE *sb.*[1] 2b.] The action of 'dancing' or balancing on a stretched rope; funambulism. Also *transf.*

a **1704** T. BROWN *Wks.* (1709) III. III. 142 As the Romans borrow'd their Comedy from the Græcians; so it is not improbable, that to them likewise they owe their Rope-Dancing. **1775** JOHNSON in *Boswell* 16 Oct., At the Boulevards saw nothing, yet was glad to be there.—Rope-dancing and farce. **1836–7** DICKENS *Sk. Boz, Scenes* xiv, There was a spectral attempt at rope-dancing in the little open theatre. **1871** KINGSLEY *At Last* v, The rope-dancing which goes on in the boughs of the Poui tree.

So **ˈrope-ˌdancing** *ppl. a.*

c **1825** *Encycl. Metrop.* (1845) XVII. 549 Rope Dancing Elephants were exhibited by Galba when Prætor. **1872** HOWELLS *Wedd. Journ.* (1892) 276 Every swaggering statue of a saint, every rope-dancing angel.

rope-end. Variant of ROPE'S-END *v.*

1872 BLACKMORE *Maid of Sker* vi, The corners such as, in the navy, we should have been rope-ended for. **1877** W. S. GILBERT *Foggerty's Fairy* (1892) 200 She was a precious bad lot as ought to be rope-ended.

†**ˈropefull.** *Sc. Obs.* In 6 rapfow, raipfull. [f. ROPE *sb.*[1]] A gallows-bird.

1567 *Satir. Poems Reform.* viii. 1 Renigat rapfow! thocht þow raif... Quhat sayis thow bot we knaw our sell? **1583** *Leg. Bp. St. Androis* 401 To help that raipfull, scho hes reft him Whairfore, ye say, my ladie left him.

ˈrope-house. [ROPE *sb.*[1]]

1. A building in which ropes are made and stored.

1571 A. JENKINSON *Voy. & Trav.* (Hakl. Soc.) II. 284 He hath giuen them ground..to place a rope house ioyning to their owne house. **1667** PEPYS *Diary* 30 June, They are fain to take the deals of the rope-house to supply other occasions. **1693** *Lond. Gaz.* No. 2846/3 For Building a New Rope-House, and some Store-Houses, at Their Majesties Yard at Portsmouth. **1777** (*title*), Trial of John the Painter for wilfully and maliciously setting Fire to the Rope House in the King's Yard at Portsmouth. **1812** *Chron.* in *Ann. Reg.* 82 The eastern rope-house of Plymouth dock-yard. **1877** RAYMOND *Statist. Mines & Mining* 132 A blacksmith-shop, a rope-house,..and one machine-shop.

2. A salt-house in which the brine is evaporated on suspended ropes.

a **1855** *Tomlinson's Cycl. Usef. Arts* II. 554/1 The *Maison de Cordes*, or *rope-house*, was invented by an ingenious Savoyard, named Buttel.

rope ˈladder. [ROPE *sb.*[1]] A ladder made of two long pieces of rope connected at intervals by pieces of rope, wood, or metal. Also *transf.*

1704 *Lond. Gaz.* No. 4008/2 Others climbed over the Walls by the help of some Rope-Ladders. **1788** GIBBON *Decl. & F.* lvi. V. 618 At the dead of night several rope-ladders were dropped from the walls. **1817** KIRBY & SP. *Entomol.* xxii. (1818) II. 291 It consists of little silken threads, which it has spun in a zigzag direction, forming a rope-ladder. **1875** KNIGHT *Dict. Mech.* 1980/1 Rope ladders are employed for enabling persons to ascend and descend from the deck of a ship or from her booms into boats alongside.

ˈrope-like, *adv.* and *a.* [ROPE *sb.*[1]] **a.** *adv.* After the manner of a rope. **b.** *adj.* Resembling a rope.

1840 EMERSON *Woodnotes* I, in *Dial* Oct. 244 The rope-like pine roots crosswise grown Composed the network of his throne. **1849** *Sk. Nat. Hist., Mammalia* III. 144 The left tusk..tapering gradually to a point, with a spiral twist (ropelike) throughout its whole extent. **1867** LATHAM *Black & White* 118 Parasitic plants and rope-like lianas begin to appear. **1883** W. S. KENT *Fisheries Bahamas* 37 The rope-like bundle of spicules, that in *Hyalonema* form a simple stalk.

ˈrope-ˌmaker. [ROPE *sb.*[1] Cf. Du. *reep-maker.*]

a. One who makes ropes; a roper.

1388 WYCLIF *Acts* xviii. 3 He dwellide with hem, and wrouȝte; and thei weren of roopmakeris craft. *a* **1490** BOTONER *Itin.* (Nasmith, 1778) 218 Circumferentia marisci XII brachia, ut relatum mihi per unum rope-maker. *c* **1515** *Cocke Lorell's B.* 5 Nycke crokence the rope maker, And steuen mesyll-mouthe muskyll taker. **1592** GREENE *Upst. Courtier* Wks. (Grosart) XI. 259 Now sir this Ropemaker hunteth mee heere with his halters. **1614** T. GENTLEMAN *Englands Way to win Wealth* 31 Houses and worke-yards erected for Coopers, and Rope-makers. **1622** PEACHAM *Compl. Gent.* i. (1634) 15 A Gardiner, Ropemaker, or Aquavitæ-seller. **1710** ADDISON *Tatler* No. 116 ¶3 They begged Leave to read a Petition of the Rope-Makers. **1769** [see ROPER 1]. **1842** DICKENS *Amer. Notes* (1850) 143/2 The men were employed as shoemakers, rope-makers,..and stonecutters. **1872** YEATS *Techn. Hist. Comm.* 46 A representation is extant of a rope-maker at work with his assistants.

b. *rope-maker's eye*: a special eye made on a rope.

1883 *Man. Seamanship for Boys' Training Ships R. Navy* (Admiralty) (1886) 127 A Rope-Maker's Eye is generally made in the end of a jibstay when fitted with a slip at the jib-boom end, and has a thimble in it to receive the slip. **1911** *Encycl. Brit.* XV. 874/1 *Ropemakers' Eye*..is formed by taking out of a rope one strand longer by 6 in. or a foot than the required eye, [etc.].

ˈropemanship. [ROPE *sb.*[1], after *horsemanship, seamanship.*] The art of walking along, or climbing up, a rope.

1869 *Daily News* 28 Sept., The cheering for both the performers in this daring act of ropemanship was tremendous. **1891** *Sat. Rev.* 23 May 612/2 Seamanship and 'ropemanship' were far more important than they are now.

†**Rope Monday.** *Obs.* [f. ROPE *sb.*[1]: see note to HOCKTIDE.] = HOCK MONDAY.

Occurs freq. in the Maldon records, and is clearly the Monday following the second Sunday after Easter.

1403 *Maldon Court-Rolls* Bundle 1 No. 5, Die lune proximo ante festum apostolorum Philippi et Jacobi videlicet Ropemoneday. **1463** —— *Liber B.* fol. viii b, At the Courte holde at Maldon, with the lete, on the Monday callyd Ropemonday. **1468** —— *Court-Rolls* Bundle 44 No. 4, Die lune vocata Ropemondaye secundo die Maii.

rope-over, *a. rare*[−1]. [ROPE *sb.*[1]] ? With muscles like twisted strands of rope.

1887 G. M. HOPKINS *Poems* (1967) 104 Lank Rope-over thigh; knee-nave; and barrelled shank.

roper (ˈrəʊpə(r)). [f. ROPE *sb.*[1] + -ER[1]. Cf. MDu. *reeper*, MLG. *reper.*]

1. a. One who makes ropes; a rope-maker.

1226 in J. T. Gilbert *Hist. & Munic. Doc. Irel.* (Rolls) 82 Philippus le ropere. **1321–2** *Rolls of Parlt.* I. 391/2 Pur les custages de VI Ropers alauntz de Brideport. **1362** LANGL. *P. Pl.* A. v. 166 A Ropere, a Redyng-kyng and Rose þe disschere. *a* **1450** *Knt. de la Tour* (1868) 79 An ensaumple of a ropers wiff that was not trew in kepinge of her mariage. **1497** *Naval Acc. Hen. VII* (1896) 185 Payed..Willyam Ellyott & Edmond White Ropers of Lynne for an hawser. **1540** *Act 32 Hen. VIII*, c. 14 Smithes, ropers, shypwrightes ..and other..handy craftes men. **1586** FERNE *Blaz. Gentrie* 21 Valentinian, the sonne of a roper, possessed the Romane Empire. **1622** *Relat. Plantation Plymouth. New Eng.* 8 Having a noose as artificially made, as any Roper in England can make. **1688** HOLME *Armoury* III. 113/1 Yarn spun by the Roper. **1769** FALCONER *Dict. Marine, Cordier*, a rope-maker, or roper. **1802** *Naval Chron.* VIII. 258 The..ropers, riggers, and riggers' labourers. **1860** *Macm. Mag.* I. 226 To begin a..discourse with him, and then walk backwards, like a roper.

†**b.** *John Roper's window*, a rope-noose. *Obs.*

1552 HULOET s.v., *Restio* is he that loketh in at John ropers window, by translation, he that hangeth him selfe.

†**c.** One who deserves the rope. *Obs.*

1615 THOMAS *Dict.*, A Roper or an vngracious fellow, *nequam.*

2. One who secures bales, etc., with a rope.

1850 OGILVIE *Imperial Dict.*

3. *Racing.* A jockey who prevents a horse from winning by holding it in; one who intentionally loses any race by similar methods.

1870 *Daily News* 31 Jan., Stick to his post he must,.. unless 'the ropers' are to have it all their own way in the Spring Handicaps. **1876** BESANT & RICE *Gold. Butterfly* xxxiii, He would go back to the old courses and become a Roper. **1887** *Cyclist* 14 Sept. 1203/2 The difficulty of establishing a case against a persistent 'roper' is very much greater in cycling.

4. chiefly *U.S.* One who uses a lasso.

1808 PIKE *Sources Mississ.* (1810) 160 Taking the wild horses, in that manner, is scarcely ever attempted, even with the fleetest horses, and most expert ropers. **1888** *Cent. Mag.* Feb. 506 A really first-class roper can command his own price. **1964** C. WILLOCK *Enormous Zoo* v. 92 At last her head was coming within range of the ropers. **1976** *Billings* (Montana) *Gaz.* 5 July 1-c/1 At Sunday's performance, cowboys in the calf roping event were the stars as each of the last five ropers managed to conquer Mike Cervi's rowdy black calfs to place in the money.

5. A gambling-house decoy. Also *roper-in.*

1840 *Picayune* (New Orleans) 31 Oct. 2/3 He had not well landed on the Levee, so famous for cotton bags, sugar, ..'ropers in', and other 'dry goods'. **1844** J. H. GREENE *Expos. Arts Gambling* (ed. 2) 158 Those secret partners, by gamblers, are termed *ropers*, or *stool-pigeons*: their business is to delude the inexperienced into their dens of iniquity. **1859** in Bartlett *Dict. Amer.* (ed. 2) 371 A young man at his hotel, who turned out to be a roper in of a gambling house. **1875** E. KING *Southern States* v. 61 The ropers for gambling-houses..haunt each conspicuous corner.

ˈrope-ripe, *a.* and *sb.* [ROPE *sb.*[1] 3.]

A. *adj.* Ripe for the gallows; fit for being hanged. *Obs.* exc. *arch.*

1552 HULOET, Roperype, or vngracious waghalter, *nequam.* **1562** J. HEYWOOD *Prov. & Epigr.* (1867) 206 Whether wilt thou hang vp with ropes of ynions? Or stifly stande vp, with roperipe minions? **1597** CHURCHYARD *Choice* Cciii, But gallows lucke, and rope ripe happe At length was guerdon for our paine. [**1892** H. V. MILLS *Lake Country Romances* 147 Thou art a rope-ripe rascal thyself.]

†**b.** Applied to language. *Obs.*

c **1530** *Prodigal Son* 61 Such ropperype terms. **1553** T. WILSON *Rhet.* 59 If we firste expresse our mynde in plaine wordes, and not seke these roperype termes. **1574** RICH *Mercury & Soldier* M ij b, When it pleaseth you to bestow so many nice names and other rope rype terms upon such as be my subjectes. **1611** CHAPMAN *May Day* Plays 1873 II. 368 Lord how you roule in your rope ripe termes.

†**B.** *sb.* One who is ripe for the gallows. *Obs.*

1573 TUSSER *Husb.* (1878) 183 Giue hardnes to youth and to roperipe a twig. **1600** ? LYLY *Maids Metam.* II. ii, How the diuel stumbled this case of rope-ripes in—into my way? **1632** SHERWOOD, A rope-ripe, ripe for the rope, or deseruing the rope, *grevolable, relasche de pendu, pendard.*

ropery (ˈrəʊpərɪ). Also 6 roppery, roparie, 6–7 -erie. [f. ROPE *sb.*[1] + -ERY.]

1. A place where ropes are made; a rope-walk.

In early quots. as a locality in London.

1363 *Lett. Bks. Lond.* G. fol. 133 De Grossers in Roperie, c *s.* [**1382** *Ibid.* H. fol. 138b, In parochia Omnium Sanctorum in Roperia.] **1598** STOW *Surv. London* vii. (1603) 42 Wolfes gate in the roparie in the Parrish of Alhallowes. **1744** J. WILSON *Synop. Brit. Plants* 55 Musk Thistle,..on the ropery, by the sides of the road to the glass-houses. **1775** SWINBURNE *Trav. Spain* (1779) xvii. 123 The new ropery, and the forges where they put fresh touch-holes into old cannon. **1839** URE *Dict. Arts* 1072 This rope is fixed at the head and foot of the ropery. **1885** *L'pool Daily Post* 30 June 4/5 He had a lease of a shipbuilding yard and ropery.

2. Trickery, knavery, roguery. Now only *arch.*

1592 SHAKS. *Rom. & Jul.* II. iv. 154 *Nur.* I pray you sir, what sawcie Merchant was this that was so full of his roperie? *Rom.* A Gentleman Nurse, that loues to heare himselfe talke, and will speake more in a minute, then he will stand to in a Moneth. **1618** FLETCHER *Chances* III. i, You'll leaue this roperie [*2nd fol.*, Roguery] when you come to my yeares. **1871** MEREDITH *Adv. Harry Richmond* liii. III. 187 Your wife, your son, your dupes, every soul that touches you, mildews from a blight! You were born of ropery.

rope's end, *sb.* [ROPE *sb.*[1]]

1. The end of a rope; *esp.* a piece from the end of a rope used as an instrument of punishment. Also in phr. *not to care a rope's end for.*

c **1460–70** *The Good Wyfe* 91 in *Bk. Precedence* 41 Take not euery roppys-end Witt euery man þat hallis. **1590** SHAKS. *Com. Err.* IV. iv. 16 To what end did I bid thee hie thee home? *E. Dro.* To a ropes end sir, and to that end am I return'd. **1663** PEPYS *Diary* 23 June, I beat him, and then went up in to fetch my rope's end. **1687** A. LOVELL tr. *Thevenot's Trav.* I. 196 With Ropes-ends laying one another over the Shoulders. **1769** FALCONER *Dict. Marine, Bouts de corde*, a cat of nine tails, colt or rope's end for punishment. **1828** P. CUNNINGHAM *N.S. Wales* (ed. 3) II. 287, I allow them to carry ropes-ends in their pockets to touch up the lazy fellows. **1847** H. MELVILLE *Omoo* xi, Fastening a rope's end to each sleeper, he rove the lines through a number of blocks. **1858** TROLLOPE *Three Clerks* II. viii. 178 Uncle Bat ..did not care a rope's end for Undy Scott. **1887** BESANT *The World Went* xiv, If you anger me more, you shall taste the rope's-end.

2. A halter; a hangman's noose.

1821 SCOTT *Pirate* v, I cannot see the pleasure men propose by dangling in a rope's-end betwixt earth and heaven. **1888** STEVENSON *Black Arrow* 200 If we fell to be recognised..I should be kicking in a rope's end.

Hence **rope's-end** *v.*, to flog with a rope's end; **rope's-ending** vbl. sb.

1825 *Gentl. Mag.* XCV. II. 397 'To leather,' 'to strap,' 'to ropes-end,' &c., speak for themselves. **1836** E. HOWARD *R. Reefer* xxxviii, I would..rope's-end those lubbers. **1840** H. COCKTON *Life Valentine Vox* xii. 88 You shall catch, my dear, the blessedest rope's-ending you ever had any notion on yet. **1885** RUNCIMAN *Skippers & Sh.* 75 He could not rope's-end the owner of the boat. **1887** BESANT *The World Went* iv, In such ships are floggings daily, and mutinous words, with rope's-ending and continual flogging.

†**rope-sick,** *a. Obs.* Also roope-sicke. [ad. Du. dial. *ropziek* (Boekenoogen *Zaansche Volkstaal* 857).] Of herring: Having the back infested with parasitic worms.

The pamphlet of 1614 is the source of later quots.

1614 T. GENTLEMAN *Eng. Way to win Wealth* 15 The roope-sicke Herrings that will not serue to make barreld Herrings. *Ibid.* 20 They [herrings]..do alwaies at that season become Roope-sicke and do spawne and become Shotten betwixt Wintertonness and Orfordness. *Ibid.* 29. **1622** MALYNES *Anc. Law-Merch.* 243 All those Herrings ..(which are rope-sicke) they may not bring home into Holland. *a* **1642** SIR W. MONSON *Naval Tracts* VI. (1704) 524/2 Betwixt Winterton and Orfordness they use to Spawn, and are called by the Hollanders the Rope-sick Herrings.

†**rope-tide.** *Obs.*[−1] [See ROPE MONDAY.] = HOCKTIDE.

1406 *Maldon Court-Rolls* Bundle 2, No. 2, Soluet ad Ropetyde prox. iiis. iiii*d.*

ˈrope-walk. [ROPE *sb.*[1]] A stretch of ground appropriated to the making of ropes. Also *attrib.*

1672 *Rec. Early Hist. Boston* (1881) VII. 72 John Harrisons rope walke. **1692** in Picton *L'pool Munic. Rec.* (1883) I. 312 The rope walke to be converted to no other use but a rope walke. **1716** *Lond. Gaz.* No. 5488/9 A Rope-Walk, and other Freehold Lands. **1761** *Brit. Mag.* II. 591 For the sake of peace, France will demolish the new works at Dunkirk,..and destroy the rope-walks. **1824** MISS MITFORD *Village* Ser. I. (1863) 8 A rope-walk shaded with limes and oaks. **1855** KINGSLEY *Westw. Ho!* xxviii, Bridgeland Street.., which then was but a row of rope-walks and sailmakers' shops. **1886** *Encycl. Brit.* XX. 844/1 *Ropewalk Spinning.*—The sequence of operations in this ancient but still greatly used method of working is—(1) heckling the fibre; [etc.]. **1963** G. BLAKE *Gourock* ii. 22 It is interesting to note that the site on which was built the original Gourock, Ropework Company's rope-walk in 1777 was already marked 'Ropework' in 1721. *Ibid.* 24 The original Gourock ropewalk, 200 fathoms long and slated for half its length ran down to a rocky spit. **1971** *Daily Progress* (Charlottesville, Va.) 21 July 23/4 Born in an era of sailing vessels with their need for miles and miles of rope for riggings, the Ropewalk flourished in both world wars and declined after each.

transf. **1851** H. MELVILLE *Whale* xxxi, He is never chased; he would run away with rope-walks of line.

ˈrope-work. [ROPE *sb.*[1]]

1. A place where ropes are made.

1797 *Encycl. Brit.* (ed. 3) XVI. 493/2 The methods practised in different rope-works are..exceedingly different. **1806** RENNIE in Smiles *Engineers* II. 239 Block-machinery and rope-works might likewise be worked by steam-engines. **1816** SCOTT *Antiq.* xix, The three strands of the conversation, to speak the language of a rope-work.

2. An arrangement of ropes.

1816 SIR H. DOUGLAS *Milit. Bridges* 176 The general rope-work to support the flooring of the bridge was made of hawsers.

3. Use of ropes in climbing.

1901 G. BELL *Let.* 8 Sept. (1927) I. vii. 127 After a great deal of complicated rope work we reached the Gemse Sattel. **1979** D. KYLE *Green River High* xvi. 211 All *I* had to do was shin a hundred feet up a rope! .. I've never been a one for rope-work, even in the gym.

4. Decoration with a rope motif.

1952 J. B. OLDHAM *Eng. Blind-Stamped Bindings* I. 11 Italian and Spanish blind bindings are so unlike English as to be easily distinguishable, with the former's characteristic leafy or rope-work frame, and the latter's rather unusual and fantastic stamps.

ropey, var. ROPY *a.*

'rope-yard. [ROPE *sb.*[1]]

†**1.** = ROBAND. *Obs.*$^{-0}$ (? Error for *rope-yarn.*)

1611 COTGR., *Rabans*, rope-yards; the ropes, or treble cordes whereby the sayles of a ship are tied vnto the yardes.

2. A yard where ropes are made.

1664 PEPYS *Diary* 19 July, Down by water to Woolwich, where coming to the rope-yarde..we are told that Mr. Falconer..is just dead. **1714** MANDEVILLE *Fab. Bees* (1733) I. 420 This article alone would yield many a tedious holiday to the anchor-smiths and the rope-yards. **1864** SPENCER *Illustr. Progress* 188 There are the vessels in which cotton is imported, with the building-slips, the rope-yards.

'rope-yarn. Chiefly *Naut.* [ROPE *sb.*[1]]

1. a. A single yarn forming part of a strand in a rope; a piece of yarn obtained by unpicking an old rope.

1623 J. TAYLOR (Water P.) *Hempseed* Wks. (1630) III. 66/2 Your mastlines, ropeyarnes, gaskets, and your stayes. **1627** CAPT. SMITH *Seaman's Gram.* v. 25 Rope yarnes..serue to sarue small ropes, or make Sinnet, Mats, Plats, or Caburnes. **1720** DE FOE *Capt. Singleton* (1906) 169 We..hauled home the topsail sheets, the rope-yarns that furled them giving way of themselves. **1769** FALCONER *Dict. Marine*, *Rope-yarn*,..the smallest and simplest part of any rope, being one of the threads of which a strand is composed. **1840** R. H. DANA *Bef. Mast* iii, These 'rope yarns' are constantly used for various purposes. **1885** RUNCIMAN *Skippers & Sh.* 259 He could clear a ropeyarn held four feet ten above the deck.

b. Used to denote a small or trifling thing.

1801 NELSON 23 May in Nicolas *Disp.* (1845) IV. 384 Not a Rope-yarn can be carried away or expended (except in Battle) between this period and September 1st. **1835** MARRYAT *J. Faithful* xiv, I can trust Tommy as far as keeping off the river sharks; he'll never let them take a rope-yarn off the deck. **1879** L. FARRAGUT *D. G. Farragut* v. 33 If you touch a rope-yarn of this ship, I shall board instantly.

2. Yarn obtained by untwisting an old rope, or such as is used for making ropes.

1626 CAPT. SMITH *Accid. Yng. Seamen* 16 Then, [cables serve] as the rest of the ouer-worne tackling, for rope yarne, caburne, sinnit, and okum. **1698** FRYER *Acc. E. India & P.* 37 The bended Planks are sowed together with Rope-Yarn of the Cocoe. **1719** DE FOE *Crusoe* I. (Globe) 85, I had made me a long Line of some Rope Yarn. **1766** *Compl. Farmer* s.v. *Trellis* 7 M 2/1 The shoots of the trees are fastened to this frame with ozier twigs, rope yarn, or any other soft bandage. **1805** *Sporting Mag.* XXV. 76 Bound with a thread of rope-yarn. **1859** CORNWALLIS *New World* I. 15 Attached to the rigging by pieces of rope-yarn.

3. Used *attrib.* to designate a day given as a holiday or, more usu., a half-holiday (see quots.). Chiefly *Naval slang*.

1886 H. BAUMANN *Londinismen* 159/1 *Rope-yarn..Sunday*, freie(r) Sonntag. **1914** *Dialect Notes* IV. 151 *Rope-yarn holiday, n. phr.*, a half holiday. **1929** F. C. BOWEN *Sea Slang* 113 *Rope Yarn Sunday*. In the British Navy, '*Make and Mend time*' q.v., on Thursday afternoon. The Americans use the term for Saturday afternoon when there are no drills or inspections, but ship's work is done. Their make and mend is on Wednesday, known as *Rope Yarn Holiday*. **1952** J. V. NOEL *Naval Terms* 184 *Rope Yarn Sunday*, any afternoon, except a week-end, that is free of work. Usually Wednesday afternoon is called *rope yarn Sunday* since liberty is often granted early on that day aboard ships in port. **1956** E. N. ROGERS *Queenie's Brood* 79 Rope-yarn Sunday is the seaman's Monday. Actually, it is a half day off and comes on a Wednesday afternoon. **1962** GRANVILLE *Dict. Sailors' Slang* 97/2 *Rope-yarn Thursday*,..the original Naval..half holiday.

ropia, obs. variant of RUPEE.

†**ropier**, obs. variant of ROPER.

1720 *Lond. Gaz.* No. 5908/9 Joseph Barnes, late of Killingworth, Ropier.

'ropily, *adv.* [f. ROPY *a.*] 'In a ropy manner; in a viscous or glutinous manner, so as to be drawn out like a rope' (Webster, 1864).

ropiness ('rəʊpɪnɪs). Also 7-8 roapiness. [f. ROPY *a.* + -NESS.] The condition or property of being ropy or viscous; stringiness.

1663 BOYLE *Usef. Exp. Nat. Philos.* II. xix. 285 Divers formidable diseases which seem to proceed from the coagulation, or ropinesse of the blood. **1682** *Art & Myst. Vintners* (1703) 15 The foulness and ropiness of Wines. **1733** *Phil. Trans.* XLI. 700 The Fetor and Roapiness in her Urine abated. **1742** *Lond. & Country Brew.* I. (ed. 4) 41 To prevent its running into Cohesions, Ropiness, and Sourness. **1839** URE *Dict. Arts* 1304 The tannin by this time will have separated the azotized matter from the liquor, and removed the ropiness. **1850** *Brit. Assoc. Rep.* Sections (1851) 60 Complaints respecting a disease in their bread termed ropiness. **1883** *Science* I. 367/2 The ropiness of milk ..is caused by the action of microscopic organism.

roping ('rəʊpɪŋ), *vbl. sb.* [f. ROPE *sb.*[1] or *v.*[1]]

1. Ropes collectively; cordage, rope-work.

1566 *Southampton Crt. Leet Rec.* (1905) I. 38 The pyleing and ropeing of the weste caye ys to be also amended. **1720** DE FOE *Capt. Singleton* v. (1840) 80 Roping made of mats and flags. **1844** H. STEPHENS *Bk. Farm* III. 975 The roping when completed has the appearance of a net with square meshes. **1883** WALSH *Irish Fisheries* 10 Oftentimes good nets are lost by reason of those nearer on the roping giving way. **1883** *Man. Seamanship for Boys' Training Ships R. Navy* (Admiralty) (1886) 50 Q. What is the roping? A. The bolt rope round the edges of the sail to prevent it from rending. **1977** D. JAMES *Spy at Evening* vi. 29, I jumped. Into the black spray, clawing wildly for the rope ladder..my outstretched fingers touched the stiff, wet roping.

2. A ropy or rope-like formation.

1658 tr. *Porta's Nat. Magic* VIII. iv. 221 Aloes..beat together [with waters] until it turn to water, and swim about in ropings. **1849** DANA *Geol.* iii. (1850) 190 With the usual ropings and twistings in the surface.

†**3.** The operation of rowelling. *Obs.*$^{-0}$

1611 COTGR., *Seton*, a rowell; or the rowelling, or roping of a bruised or strained horse.

4. Chiefly *U.S.* and *Austr.* The action of catching or securing with a rope. ***roping in, up***: (see ROPE *v.*[1] 4 b).

1848 BARTLETT *Dict. Amer.* 278 *Roping in*, cheating. A very common expression in the South-western States. **1849** in De Vere *Americanisms* (1872) 629 I'll lay bank, if you must have a game, but I'll make one condition: no roping in! **1890** 'R. BOLDREWOOD' *Col. Reformer* (1891) 119 The drafting, the roping, the branding,..were novelties and excitements of a very high order. **1907** S. E. WHITE *Arizona Nights* III. i. 241 The roping and throwing and branding.. filled our days with..the unusual. **1932** BLUNDEN *Face of England* 102 The last shocks are on the wagon, the roping-up is done. **1973** *Times* 2 Oct. 15/2 Giraffes are among the most difficult animals to capture. Straight-forward roping is unsuitable because a fall is more likely to break the neck of a giraffe than of a more compact animal. **1976** *Billings (Montana) Gaz.* 16 June 1-c/2 Cooper, who was being pressed in the second go-round of steer wrestling, held the lead in team roping with teammate Phil Longacre at 7.34 seconds. **1979** *Tucson Mag.* Apr. 68/3 The charreada is a fast-paced program of riding, roping, music, and dancing.

5. The action of fitting with haulage ropes.

1884 *Manch. Exam.* 16 Sept. 5/3 The permanent roping of the rapids is also talked of.

6. *Racing.* The action of holding back or checking a horse to prevent it from winning; also *transf.* (see quot. 1874).

1864 *Daily Telegr.* 6 May, The Chester Cup contest was perfectly fair; there was no suspicion of 'roping'. **1868** E. YATES *Rocks Ahead* I. vi, It was understood that..there was to be no more 'pulling', or 'roping', or any other chicanery. **1874** *Slang Dict.* 271 When a pedestrian or other athlete loses where he should have won, according to his backer's calculations, he is accused of roping.

7. *attrib.*, as ***roping arena, horse, -needle, -pole, stick, -twine.***

1979 *Farmington* (New Mexico) *Daily Times* 27 May 10 c/5 (Advt.), 40 acres with..iron fenced corral, roping arena, etc. **1949** *Los Angeles Times* 12 July II. 2/5 The final resting place of Soap Suds, once the greatest humorist's favorite roping horse. **1976** *Billings* (Montana) *Gaz.* 27 June 8-D/1 (Advt.), Saddle horses of all kinds & roping horses for sale. **1867** SMYTH *Sailor's Word-bk.* 580 *Roping-Needles*, those used for roping, being strong accordingly. **1890** 'R. BOLDREWOOD' *Col. Reformer* xii, A first-class stockman, and handy with the roping-pole. **1878** E. S. ELWELL *Boy Colonists* 190 Ernest..had to get behind the animal, and by dint of prodding with the roping stick..to force it to run up towards the corner. **1888** 'R. BOLDREWOOD' *Robbery under Arms* III. xiv. 201 He stuck to his roping-stick—good, heavy-ended gum sapling, six or seven feet long. *c* **1860** H. STUART *Seaman's Catech.* 53 The roping is sewn on to the sails with roping twine.

roping, variant of ROUPING *vbl. sb.*

'roping, *ppl. a.* [f. ROPE *v.*[1] + -ING[2].] Forming ropes or rope-like threads, *esp.* of a viscid or glutinous nature; turning ropy.

c **1440** *Promp. Parv.* 436/2 Ropynge, ale or oþer lycowre, *viscosus*. **1486** *Bk. St. Albans* A iij b, If it be glaymous and roping she engenderith an euel callid the Cray. **1577** B. GOOGE *Heresbach's Husb.* IV. (1586) 184 The best Hony..is ..fine, roping, if it be drawen in length. **1599** SHAKS. *Hen. V*, III. v. 23 Let vs not hang like roping Isyckles Vpon our Houses Thatch. **1614** LATHAM *Falconry* I. 49 No water, but a roaping froth in it. **1686** GOAD *Celest. Bodies* II. ii. 169 We shall number Fifty Fogs, and some Roping *Fila*, besides thinner mistiness. **1694** SALMON *Bate's Dispens.* (1713) 223/2 Adding of liquid or roping Pitch-like Soot ʒiij. **1820** CLARE *Rural Life* (ed. 3) 116 Let dust keep gathering on the ground, And roping cobwebs dangle round.

'ropish, *a.* [f. ROPE *sb.*[1] 7.] Somewhat ropy; tending to ropiness.

1855 OGILVIE *Suppl.*

'ropishness. *rare*$^{-1}$. [Cf. prec.] The quality or state of being ropish.

1664 EVELYN *Sylva* (1679) 27 The very saw dust is of use, as are the ashes and lie.., to cure the roapishness of wine.

roploch, obs. form of RAPLOCH.

roppe, obs. form of ROPE.

ropy ('rəʊpɪ), *a.* Also 6 ropye, 7 roapie, 7-8 roapy, 20- ropey. [f. ROPE *sb.*[1] + -Y.]

1. a. Forming or developing viscid, glutinous, or slimy threads; sticky and stringy.

1480 CAXTON *Trevisa's Higden* III. xx, Lentulus spat and þrewe ropy spotel in his face. *a* **1500** *Promp. Parv.* 436/2 Ropy as ale,..*viscosus*. *a* **1529** SKELTON *E. Rummyng* 24 Her lewde lyppes..slauer, men sayne, Lyke a ropy rayne. **1547** BORDE *Introd. Knowl.* i. (1870) 123 There ale is starke nought, lokinge whyte & thycke,..smoky and ropye. **1651** J. CLEVELAND *Poems* (1677) 87 Like Snakes engendring were platted her Tresses, Or like to slimy streaks of Ropy Ale. **1697** DRYDEN *Virg. Georg.* III. 759 Roapy Gore he from his Nostrils bleeds. **1721** BRADLEY *Philos. Acc. Wks. Nat.* 122 All that roapy, viscid gluten, separated there by the Glands. **1772** T. PERCIVAL *Ess.* (1777) I. 337 The mucilaginous or ropy substance which grows copiously on it. **1831** YOUATT *Horse* viii. 150 A considerable discharge of ropy fluid from the mouth. **1850** *Brit. Assoc. Rep.* Sections (1851) 60 Observations on Ropy Bread. **1877** BLACKMORE *Erema* III. xliii. 45 With a swirl and a curl of ropy mud. **1935** J. LAWRANCE *Painting from A to Z* xi. 103 Thick, ropey coats of paint look unsightly. **1940** H. L. HIND *Brewing* II. xxxvii. 917 The general consensus of practical brewing opinion in Great Britain seems to be that a species of coccus or 'sarcina' is nearly always to be found in samples of ropy beer. **1950** *N.Z. Jrnl. Agric.* Feb. 165/3 Stock should not be allowed to drink from stagnant pools, as these are a source of the organism responsible for ropey milk.

fig. **1768-74** TUCKER *Lt. Nat.* (1834) II. 534 If there be any thing of..selfishness, or other passion intermingled, it is ropy and imperfect. **1791** GIFFORD *Baviad & Mæviad* (1794) 44 The ropy drivil of rheumatic brains. **1815** J. C. HOBHOUSE *Substance Lett.* (1816) II. 187 The writers whose best pages seem but..ropy drivellings.

b. *transf.* of the air.

1726 LEONI *Alberti's Archit.* I. 64/1 You will find the Air ..thick and heavy, and perfectly ropy; so that..you shall sometimes see a sort of strings..like cobwebs. **1788** J. MAY *Jrnl. & Lett.* (1873) 106 My lungs..have been irritated for several days by the thick ropy air. **1789** *Ibid.* 125, I often find them [*sc.* beds] musty, and the air of the sleeping-rooms thick and ropy.

c. *fig.* Bad, unsatisfactory, unreliable, unwell. *slang* and *colloq.*

1942 *R.A.F. Jrnl.* 18 Apr. 10, I then commanded a scratch squadron of rather ropey machines. **1942** *Tee Emm* (Air Ministry) II. 131 It will probably show how ropy your judgement is on modern types. **1944** S. GIBBONS *Bachelor* xvi. 144, I think you must have a ropey time. Worrying about the poor, and giving all your money away and not eating much. **1945** *Gen* 30 June 51/1 He's feeling a bit ropey now, and he's going to have a bad night. **1953** E. HYAMS *Gentian Violet* iii. 42 Their aircraft are pretty ropey. **1957** *Daily Mail* 3 Dec. 14/1 It is, of course, very difficult to get waiters on New Year's Eve. If you hire them outside, you may get a few ropey types. **1959** W. D. PEREIRA *North Flight* ii. 33 You look a bit ropey, Dad, why don't you go home.. and relax? **1961** *Sunday Express* 15 Jan. 4/6, I feel a bit ropey... I think I've picked up some sort of virus. **1963** *Times* 20 May 6/5 Some of the acting is a bit ropy. **1971** J. AIKEN *Nightly Deadshade* iii. 22 Mother..was crippled and Father left her... Everything was one hundred per cent ropy except that she had a little money. **1978** F. MANN *Acupuncture* (ed. 3) ix. 138 Sometimes a ropy pulse occurs in elderly people who have had many illnesses affecting several bodily systems, all of which have been only partly cured.

d. Of a cow: producing ropy milk.

1960 *Farmer & Stockbreeder* 19 Jan. 60/3 But what did farmers do? They sent all their ropy cows to F[atstock] M[arketing] C[orporation] and flogged the best in the auction mart.

2. Having the form or tenacity of a rope; suggestive of a rope.

1765 *Museum Rust.* IV. 5 There still are grass and weeds remaining, that will the next ploughing cause the furrows to be ropy. **1823** ROSCOE tr. *Sismondi's Lit. Eur.* (1846) II. xxxii. 346 The massy heap of ropy ringlets his vast hands divide. **1851** RUSKIN *Stones Ven.* (1874) I. xxvi. 289 Spongy lavas, which the volcano blast drags hither and thither into ropy coils. **1881** JUDD *Volcanoes* iv. 98 Lavas which present this appearance are frequently called 'ropy lavas'. **1973** M. AMIS *Rachel Papers* 132 Otherwise it was mostly long whitened grass, frizzled bushes, and hundreds of ropey little trees, fifteen feet high. **1976** *Nature* 26 Feb. 650/1 Sample ARP 74-14-31, with a ropey surface showing flow direction, has a preserved glassy crust and a palagonite layer overlain by a thin manganese coating.

fig. **1878** MRS. STOWE *Poganuc P.* iii. 22 Zeph..is one o' them ropy, stringy fellers, jest like touch-wood.

roque (rəʊk). [An arbitrary alteration of CROQUET *sb.*; cf. ROQUET *sb.*] A form of croquet played in the U.S., differing from croquet chiefly in the use of a hard-surfaced, embanked court, ten hoops, and short-handled mallets. Also *attrib.*

1899 *Boston Even. Transcript* 15 Sept. 6/5 The players of the new croquet, having developed a new and scientific game, have adopted a new name, and call it roque. **1906** *Springfield* (Mass.) *Weekly Republ.* 30 Aug. 16 A 16-years-old lad who never before had played in a big-tournament won the national championship at roque. **1909** *Chicago Daily News* 12 Aug. 8/1 They are holding a roque tournament at Norwich, Conn. **1924** R. LARDNER in *Current Opinion* July 128/2 'Good gracious!' I said. 'Imagine being married to a woman that plays five hundred like she does and drops her teeth on the roque court!' **1954** J. STEINBECK *Sweet Thursday* viii. 55 Roque is a complicated kind of croquet. **1968** *Punch* 9 Oct. 495 Archery and golf and rackets and roque and lawn tennis have all been in and out again. **1976** *Webster's Sports Dict.* 356/2 *Roque*, a variation of croquet played with short-handled mallets on a hard-surfaced court.

roque, obs. variant of ROC.

Roquefort (rɒkfɔː(r)). [See def.] **a.** A kind of cheese made at Roquefort in the S.W. of France. (Now a proprietary name in the U.K.)

[**1766** W. C. CROKER *Compl. Dict. Arts & Sci.* I. s.v. *Cheese*, At Rochfort, in Languedoc, they make a cheese of ewe's milk.] **1837** *Penny Cycl.* VII. 15/2 In France the Roquefort cheese is compared to our Stilton, but is much inferior. **1882** *Bazaar* 15 Feb. 176 Roquefort is made with a mixture of goats' and ewes' milk, the manufacture being originally restricted to the plateau of Larsac. **1885** [see EDAM]. **1927** M. A. HULBERT *Treasures of Hundred Cooks* ix. 212 Use equal parts of Roquefort and Philadelphia cream cheese. **1933** *Gourmet's Bk. Food & Drink* ix. 136, I do not think a creamy or soft cheese is the best..nor, on the other hand, would I advise starting the meal with the brutal pungency of Roquefort. **1955** *Times* 10 May 12/4 Roquefort, a French blue veined cheese, is perhaps the best example of a cheese that is still to-day definitely 'regional'. **1963** *Trade Marks Jrnl.* 26 June 885 Roquefort... Roquefort cheese. Société Anonyme Des Caves & Des Producteurs Réunis de Roquefort (Aveyron). **1976** *National Observer* (U.S.) 23 Oct. 10/3 Other favorite menu frauds, Reeves reports, include substituting..blue cheese for Roquefort.

b. In full *Roquefort dressing*. A variety of salad dressing made with Roquefort cheese. Also used *attrib.* of a salad served with this. Chiefly *U.S.*

1943 D. POWELL *Time to be Born* ix. 210 Cheever must.. eat oysters Rockefeller and Roquefort salad dressing. **1961** J. HELLER *Catch-22* (1962) ix. 98 I've got some live Maine lobsters hidden away that I can serve you tonight with an excellent Roquefort salad and two frozen éclairs. **1962** *Listener* 11 Jan. 90/3 It is worth trying to order one of those marvellous green salads unaccompanied by the demand: 'Roquefort, thousand-isle or French?' **1968** C. DRUMMOND *Death & Leaping Ladies* i. 21 Plain salad, with a little touch of Roquefort dressing. **1973** M. & G. GORDON *Informant* xl. 152 A hamburger dinner with lettuce salad and Roquefort dressing. **1977** *Transatlantic Rev.* LX. 87 Andrea, in bad humor, portions out breakfast—leg of armadillo.., imitation roquefort dressing, a half-ration of water and sour mix.

roquelaure ('rɒkələə(r)). Now *Hist.* Also α. 8 rocquelaure. β. 8 roccelo (9 roccillo), rocolo, roquelo (9 roquello); 9 *dial.* rockalow, -elow, rockilo. γ. 9 ro(c)quelaire (cf. ROKELAY). [a. F. *roquelaure*, named after the Duke of Roquelaure (1656–1738). With the β-forms cf. Sp. *roclo*.] A cloak reaching to the knee worn by men during the eighteenth century and the early part of the nineteenth.

α. **1716** GAY *Trivia* I. 51 Within the Roquelaure's Clasp thy Hands are pent. **1760** STERNE *Tr. Shandy* VI. vi, I have a project.. of wrapping myself up warm in my roquelaure, and paying a visit to this poor gentleman. **1791** MRS. RADCLIFFE *Rom. Forest* (1820) II. 212 Presently he saw a gentleman, wrapped up in a roquelaure, alight and enter the inn. **1836** MARRYAT *Japhet* lxx, I went out and purchased a roquelaure, which enveloped my whole person. **1859** *All Year Round* No. 18. 432 Owens.. had constantly worn a large cloak, or roquelaure (as the article was called at that time), of a dark blue colour. **1901** GUY BOOTHBY *My Indian Queen* i, I donned my roquelaure, and descended to the street.

attrib. **1806** NOBLE *Contn. Granger* III. 490 The *roquelaure* cloak.. displaced the surtout.

β. **1754** *Connoisseur* No. 33. 136 Close by the parlour door there hung a pair of stag's horns, over which there was laid across a red Roccelo and an amber-headed cane. **1796** MME. D'ARBLAY *Camilla* IX. iii. She then saw.. a figure wrapt round in a dark blue roquelo. **1812** —— *Diary* (1846) VI. 353, I have often seen him.. muffled up in a plain brown rocolo. **1828** CARR *Craven Gloss.*, *Roccillo*, a cloak. **1860** *Slang Dict.* 201 *Rock a Low*, an overcoat. **1884** E. YATES *Recoll.* I. 47 Some old gentlemen wore cloaks, too, in my youth [1836–47],.. one kind.. [being] known to the London public as a 'rockelow'.

γ. **1825** HONE *Every-day Bk.* I. 1197 A sort of uniform coat and a plaid rocquelaire. *a* **1849** POE *Cask of Amontillado* 273 Drawing a *roquelaire* closely about my person.

roquesite ('rɒkeɪsaɪt). *Min.* [ad. F. *roquésite* (Picot & Pierrot 1963, in *Bull. de la Soc. franç. de Min. et de Crist.* LXXXVI. 7/2), f. the name of Maurice *Roques*, 20th-c. French geologist: see -ITE[1].] A sulphide of copper and indium, $CuInS_2$, occurring as small greyish blue crystals.

1963 *Mineral. Abstr.* XVI. 372/1 A new mineral determined by electron microprobe technique is named roquésite. It occurs as inclusions in bornite in the Charrier Cu, Sn, and Fe mine, Allier, central France. **1970** *Doklady Earth Sci.* CXCI. 138/1 During field investigation of ores from depth at a pyrite deposit in central Kazakhstan, we detected roquesite, a mineral reported in such ores for the first time. **1974** *Mineral. Abstr.* XXV. 329/1 Roquesite.. occurs in grains up to 1 mm in length in bornite associated with chalcopyrite, wittichenite,.. etc. in veins cutting a Devonian volcanic-sedimentary succession.

roquet: see ROCKET and ROCQUET.

roquet ('rəʊkeɪ), *sb.* [App. an arbitrary variation of CROQUET, perh. by a misunderstanding of the phr. *to take croquet*.] In croquet, the act of hitting another player's ball with one's own.

1866 LE FANU *All in Dark* I. xii. 101 Trevor and William Maubray played rather acrimoniously, making savage roquets upon one another. **1877** *Encycl. Brit.* VI. 609/1 When able to make a roquet at several yards with tolerable certainty, the learner should next practise rushing.

attrib. **1874** HEATH *Croquet-Player* 46 A ball can be sent off the ground in a roquet-stroke.. without incurring any penalty.

roquet ('rəʊkeɪ), *v.* [See prec.] *trans.* In croquet: †**a.** = CROQUET *v.*; also *absol.* **b.** Of a ball: To strike (another ball). **c.** To strike (another player's ball) with one's own; also *absol.*

1862 *Rules Croquet* 1 Miss Mallet shows the field how to Roquet. *Ibid.* §3 Should a player strike a ball, he is entitled to Roquet it in any direction he pleases. **1874** HEATH *Croquet-Player* 12 If his ball.. hits or 'roquets' another ball, he places it in contact with that ball. **1877** *Encycl. Brit.* VI. 609/1 Each ball can only be roqueted once during each turn. *Ibid.*, Roqueting with such force [etc.].

Hence **roqueted** ('rəʊkeɪd) *ppl. a.*, **roqueting** ('rəʊkeɪɪŋ) *vbl. sb.* and *ppl. a.*

1869 *Laws Croquet* 11 It is necessary that the roqueted ball should be perceptibly moved. **1869** BRADWOOD *The O.V.H.* (1870) 43 Far fetched differences between 'roqueting' and 'croqueting'. **1874** HEATH *Croquet-Player* 41 It is desirable that the touch of the roqueting ball should scarcely disturb it.

Ro-Railer (rəʊ'reɪlə(r)). Also **ro-railer**. [f. RO(AD *sb.* + RAIL *sb.*[2] + -ER[1].] The name of an experimental vehicle, introduced by the London, Midland, and Scottish Railway, which could be adapted to run on either road or railway. (No longer current.) Cf. *road-railer* s.v. ROAD *sb.* 12.

1931 *Times Educ. Suppl.* 31 Jan. p. iv/1 Trials of the 'ro-railer', a vehicle which.. can be driven either on the railway or on the road. **1934** *Discovery* Nov. 317/1 The L.M.S. have experimented with various types [of railcar], including a 'Ro-Railer' which can run equally well on road and on rail, and more conventional Diesel-engined car. **1959** H. ELLIS *Brit. Railway Hist.* II. III. i. 334 The L.M.S. tried out, on the Stratford upon Avon and Midland Junction line, a motor bus called a Ro-Railer, with two sets of wheels which could be very quickly substituted, one for another, according to whether it were to go on road or railway.

roral ('rɔərəl), *a. rare.* [f. L. *rōr-*, stem of *rōs* dew.] Dewy, roscid.

1656 BLOUNT *Glossogr.* **1737** M. GREEN *Spleen* 77 These see her.. With roral wash redeem her face, And prove herself of Titan's race. **1888** A. S. WILSON *Lyric of Hopeless Love* xcvi, The round dewdrop on the flower Absorbeth by its roral power The treasures of the air.

†**'rorant**, *a. Obs.* [ad. L. *rōrant-*, *rōrans*, pres. pple. of *rōrāre* to bedew.] Falling as dew.

1686 GOAD *Celest. Bodies* II. xiii. 337 Yet we must not necessarily infer, there is any Rorant Vapour descending.

ro'ration[1], perversion of ORATION *sb.*

1595 MUNDAY *John a Kent* II. i, The Lordes were so pontiffically pleased with your roration.

ro'ration[2]. [ad. L. *rōrātio*.] 'A Falling of Dew' (Bailey, vol. II, 1727).

rore, obs. form of ROAR.

†**rore**, *sb. Obs.* [ad. L. *rōr-*, *rōs*.] Dew.

c **1600** *Timon* III. v. (1842) 54 My words, neither aspersed nor inspersed with the flore or rore of eloquence.

rore (rɔə(r)), *v. rare.* Also 5 **roryn, rooryn**. [a. MDu. *roeren* or MLG. *rôren* to move, stir; but sense 2 may have some other origin.]

1. To turn over, to stir about or up, to trouble. Still E. Anglian in a special sense: see ROARER[2].

c **1440** *Promp. Parv.* 437/1 Rooryn, or ruffelyn, amonge dyuerse thyngys (*H.P.* rooryn or purlyn, amonge sundry thynges), *manumitto*. **1565** GOLDING *Ovid's Met.* III. 597 [He] rores the water with the teares and sloubring that he made.

†**2.** To exchange, barter. Hence **'roring** *vbl. sb.*

c **1440** *Promp. Parv.* 71/1 Chawngyn, or roryn. *supra in* Barteryn. *Ibid.* 437/1 Rooryn, or chaungyn on chaffare for a nother,.. *cambio*. Rorynge,.. *cambium*.

†**3.** To affect with some feeling. *Obs.*

1481 CAXTON *Reynard* (Arb.) 64, I am oftymes rored and prycked in my conscience as to loue god aboue all thynge.

†**'rorer**. *Obs. rare.* [a. MDu. *roerer* or LG. *rôrer*: see prec.] A disturber of the peace.

1311 *Lett. Bk. Lond.* D. fol. 133b, Simon Braban [indicted].. quia ipse est noctivagus et Rorere. *Ibid.*, Thomas de Bery.. quod ipse vivit de perquisitis de Rorers.

†**'rorid**, *a. Obs.* Also 7 **roride**. [ad. L. *rōridus*, f. *rōr-*, *rōs* dew.] Dewy; of the nature of dew. Very common in 17th cent., esp. in *rorid cloud*.

1602 DEKKER *Satirom.* Wks. 1873 I. 228 Rorid cloudes being suckt into the Ayre. **1646** SIR T. BROWNE *Pseud. Ep.* 345 The Rainebow.. caused by the rayes of the Sunne, falling upon a roride and opposite cloud. **1693** EVELYN *De la Quint. Compl. Gard.*, *Melons* 3 A little Rorid meazing out out of the Pulp, but by no means Watrish and Flashy. **1715** tr. *Pancirollus' Rerum Mem.* II. 306 It was known to the Greeks.., not under the Name of Manna, but of aerial or rorid Honey.

ro'riferous, *a. rare.* [f. L. *rōrifer* + -OUS.] Bringing or bearing dew. Also *transf.*

1656 BLOUNT *Glossogr.* **1672–3** GREW *Anat. Pl.* (1682) 67 The Succus or Sap they carry, seems to be a kind of Dewy Vapour, therefore, they may not improperly be called Roriferous or Vapour-Vessels. **1728** CHAMBERS *Cycl.* s.v., Roriferous-Duct, q.d. Dew-dropping Pipe; a Name given the Thoracick Duct, from its slow Manner of conveying.. the Chyle into the common Stream of Blood. **1851** DUNGLISON *Med. Dict.*, *Roriferous*, an epithet given to vessels which pour exhaled fluids on the surface of organs.

So **ro'rifluent** *a.*, 'flowing with dew' (Johnson, 1755); **ro'rifluous** [ad. L. *rōrifluus*], *a.*, 'flowing with dew' (Bailey, vol. II, 1727); **ro'rigenous** *a.*, 'produced of dew' (*ibid.*).

roring, obs. form of ROARING; see RORE *v.*

rori'torious, *a.* = RORY-TORY *a.* 2.

1821 EGAN *Real Life* I. 619 The Randallites were *roritorious*, and, flushed with good fortune, lined the public-houses on the road to *wet their whistles*.

‖**Roriz** (rɔ'riʃ). The name of a wine-growing estate in the Douro valley of Portugal, used *absol.* to designate a variety of port produced there.

1873 C. M. YONGE *Pillars of House* I. ii. 30 What right had you to know that I knew the taste of Cape from Roriz? **1907** *Yesterday's Shopping* (1969) 96/1 *Ports for laying down*.. Quinta Roriz. **1917** *Harrods Catal.* 1286/1 *Old bottled vintage ports*.. Kopke Roriz. **1920** G. SAINTSBURY *Notes on Cellar-Bk.* iii. 38 Kopke's famous 'Roriz' did not.. appeal to me.

ro-ro ('rəʊrəʊ), *a.* Abbrev. of ROLL-ON, ROLL-OFF.

1969 *Jane's Freight Containers 1968–69* p. iii/2 Ro-Ro berths were also included. **1969** *Australian* 30 Oct. 13/1 First the Scandias and now it's to be an even larger series of roll-on roll-off (Ro-Ro) ships for service in the Australia-Europe trade. **1974** *Times* 23 Jan. 16/7 Colonel Frank Bustard, one of the great shipping pioneers.. was the father of the 'ro-ro' revolution. **1975** *Globe & Mail* (Toronto) 2 Oct. B14/1 It is adapted for roll-on, roll-off operation and will be served by two.. ro-ro ships. **1978** *N.Y. Times* 30 Mar. D12 (Advt.), The new Farrell fleet incorporates the most sophisticated and efficient methods of cargo handling. We have breakbulk, container, LASH, RoRo and giant container vessels.

rorqual ('rɔːkwɒl). [a. F. *rorqual* (Cuvier), ad. Norw. *røyrkval*, repr. ON. **røyðar-*, OIcel. *reyðar-hvalr*, f. *reyðr* the specific name + *hvalr* whale.] A whale of the genus *Balænoptera*, having a dorsal fin; the finner.

1827 E. GRIFFITH *Cuvier's Anim. Kingd.* IV. 493 The Balænæ.. are divided into three sub-genera: The Whales Proper..; the Fin Fish..; and the Rorquals, the throat of which is channelled with folds in longitudinal furrows. **1840** *Cuvier's Anim. Kingd.* 149 The Rorquals (*Balænoptera*) have a dorsal fin, and are subdivided according as the belly is smooth or wrinkled. **1860** GOSSE *Rom. Nat. Hist.* 115 The species was no doubt the great rorqual. **1897** F. T. BULLEN *Cruise of 'Cachalot'* 61 Finbacks, a species of rorqual, were always pretty numerous.

†**rorra**. *Obs.*[−1] Some kind of dish or seasoning.

a **1450** *Tourn. Tottenham* The Feest iv, Ther was pestels in poyra And laduls in rorra For potage.

Rorschach ('rɔːʃɑːx). The name of Hermann *Rorschach* (1884–1922), Swiss psychiatrist, used *attrib.* and *absol.* to designate a type of projective personality test first devised by him, in which a standard set of ink blots of different shapes and colours is presented one at a time to a subject with the request that he should describe what they suggest or resemble. Also ***Rorschach* (*ink*) *blot, method***, etc. Also *fig.*

1927 MOIR & GUNDLACH in *Jrnl. Exper. Psychol.* Apr. 151 Each subject was given the Rorschach test. *Ibid.*, In a classification of the individual records according to the Rorschach diagnostic tables. **1935** *Amer. Jrnl. Psychiatry* July 109 The Rorschach test has recently received considerable attention in psychiatric and psychological circles. **1942** [see INSECURITY 1]. **1948** *Personnel Psychol.* I. 357 (*heading*) Can the Rorschach pick sales clerks? **1951** KOESTLER *Age of Longing* i. 40 The brandy.. expanded slowly into a Rorschach blotch on the marble surface. **1953** A. K. C. OTTAWAY *Educ. & Society* viii. 147 The Rorschach method of giving a verbal interpretation of ink-blots. **1956** *Publ. Amer. Dial. Soc.* XXVI. 121 The social or clinical psychologist will want to go still more deeply into the individual's imaginative response to the Rorschach ink blots. **1958** *Listener* 17 July 93/2 Rorschach blots and tapestries. **1960** *Commentary* June 486/2 Rorschach (inkblot) ratings. **1966** T. PYNCHON *Crying of Lot 49* i. 18 His [*sc.* a psycho-therapist's] theory being that a face is symmetrical like a Rorschach blot. **1971** *Jrnl. Gen. Psychol.* LXXXV. 295 Free associative responses and responses to ambiguous stimuli—a kind of auditory Rorschach. **1974** B. M. & D. D. BRAGINSKY *Mainstream Psychol.* vi. 118 The two most widely used psychological tests, the Rorschach inkblot test and the Draw-a-Person test (both projective tests), have also been widely researched. **1980** *Dædalus* Spring 136 The Rorschach test is effective.. because it forces people to be creative.

Rörstrand ('rørstrand). Also *erron.* **Rostrandt**. The name of a building in Stockholm in which a ceramics factory was opened in 1725, used *attrib.* and *absol.* to designate the varieties of pottery and porcelain manufactured there.

1881 C. SCHREIBER *Jrnl.* 7 Oct. (1911) II. 354 Stockholm, Rostrandt, and Marienberg pottery and porcelain. **1901** W. P. RIX tr. *E. Bourry's Treat. Ceramic Industries* I. i. 753 Rörstrand crockery ware. **1906** W. BURTON *Porcelain* xvi. 188 The body and the glaze of the Rörstrand porcelain are as beautiful as those of Copenhagen. **1925** B. RACKHAM tr. *E. Hannover's Pott. & Porc.* I. IV. iv. 482 Rörstrand faïence has not infrequently.. an even faint violet tone. **1961** *Guardian* 3 Mar. 10/5 Foreign buyers do not want Wedgwood or Doulton or Spode or Minton to look like Arabia, Rörstrand, or Rosenthal. **1974** *Encycl. Brit. Micropædia* VIII. 669/3 *Rörstrand faïence*, first faïence (tin-glazed earthenware) produced in Sweden.

rort (rɔːt), *sb. Austral. slang.* [Back-formation f. RORTY *a.*] **1.** A trick, a 'dodge'; a fraud or dishonest practice. Now freq. with qualifying word.

1936 J. DEVANNY *Sugar Heaven* 20 The cockies are supposed to pay this retention money into the bank.. but normally they don't pay it in... It's the greatest rort ever. **1958** *Sunday Mail Mag.* (Brisbane) 24 Aug. 4/4 'If they don't it will be a rort.' 'But why should it be a rort?' asks the man. **1973** *Nation Rev.* (Melbourne) 31 Aug. 1441/3 Items such as the health scheme have yet to be introduced and others—such as the removal of many of the more outrageous tax rorts—could still be frustrated were there to be an early election. **1979** *Sunday Sun* (Brisbane) 7 Jan. 20/3 Many professional people.. previously were denied access to the typical expense account rort.

2. A crowd; a wild party.

1941 BAKER *Dict. Austral. Slang* 61 *Rort*,.. a crowd. **1952** T. A. G. HUNGERFORD *Ridge & River* 81 Out we go on another bloody rort, so what's the use of saving a day? **1969**

G. Johnston *Clean Straw for Nothing* 78, I am not, strictly, a true devotee of the wild Australian 'rort' and always remorseful in my hangovers. **1972** *Sydney Morning Herald* 26 Aug. 20/3 One of her annual St Teresa's Day parties—a decorous..underworld rort in honour of St Teresa.

rort (rɔːt), *v. slang.* [Back-formation from RORTY *a.*] **1.** *intr.* To shout, complain loudly; to shout abuse. Also, to call the odds at a race-meeting. Also with *at.*

1931 T. H. Dey *Leaves from Bookmaker's Book* ii. 35 How he could 'rort', and keep his customers on the racecourse in a perpetual roar of laughter with his witty remarks. **1935** M. Harrison *Spring in Tartarus* III. 327 It isn't you..that I'm rorting at. **1962** Granville *Dict. Sailor's Slang* 97/2 *Rort*, to shout in argument or act truculently when charged with indiscipline... In Cockney Slang *to rort* is to 'shout the odds'.

2. (See quots.) *Austral. slang.*

1941 Baker *Dict. Austral. Slang* 61 *Rorting*, shrewd practices, confidence trickery. **1980** *Sunday Mail* (Brisbane) 15 June 6 (*heading*) Overseas tax havens and 'rorting' claimed. $3000m a year in tax dodges.

rorter (ˈrɔːtə(r)). *Austral. slang.* [f. RORT *sb.* or *v.* + -ER¹.] One who engages in dishonest practices; a professional sharper or trickster.

1941 Baker *Dict. Austral. Slang* 61 *Rorter*, a professional sharper: a hawker of worthless goods: one who practises sly dodges to obtain money. **1945**, **1961** [see *poofter rorter* s.v. POOFTER]. **1962** A. Marshall *This is Grass* 159 Rorters like Flogger prepared to fleece any man who stood staring around him.

rorty (ˈrɔːtɪ), *a. slang* (orig. *Londoners'*). Also **raughty.** [Of obscure origin.] Fine, splendid, jolly, etc.; (of persons and things) boisterous, rowdy, noisy; (of drinks) intoxicating; (of behaviour, speech, etc.) coarse, earthy, of dubious propriety; crudely comic. Also as quasi-*adv.*

c **1864** Vance *Chicaleary Cove* 1 (Farmer), I have a rorty gal. **1885** *Punch* 22 Aug. 86/2 It's nice, if it's naughty! I'm regular rorty. **1886** —— 28 Aug. 99/2 We'd a rorty old time. .... But Stonehenge, as I say, is a fizzle. **1888** ''Arry' in *Ibid.* 6 Oct. 156/1, I like to feel rorty and free. **1898** R. Hichens *Londoners* xvi. 280 'Tell us a good story, Rodney—one of your rorty ones.' Mr. Rodney shrivelled. 'I fear', he murmured—'I fear I am scarcely in the—the—er—rorty vein to-night.' **1899** R. Whiteing *No. 5 John St.* ix. 95 She is Boadicea..no 'British warrior queen' of nursery recitation, but a right-down 'raughty gal', leading her alley [[*sic*] to battle against the Roman 'slops'. **1904** G. B. Lancaster *Sons o' Men* 190 If Sandy or Towse get into a row we must back 'em up, of course. But it's been a rorty piece of work. **1914** 'Bartimeus' *Naval Occasions* xvii. 144 I've heard her talking like a Mother to a rorty Midshipman. **1923** —— *Seaways* vii. 96 Isn't he a little man?..Bettin' with bookies and actin' rorty. **1932** S. Gibbons *Cold Comfort Farm* xvi. 217 Compared with the heavy, muffling darkness of the night in which the countryside was sunk, the lights looked positively rorty. **1950** 'D. Divine' *King of Fassarai* xxix. 255 It [*sc.* coconut milk] comes rortier if you leave it.. to ferment, but it's got a kick now. **1969** W. Tute *Matter of Diplomacy* ii. 16 The rorty brigadier must have a taste for lean stringy meat, though of course she had been a baronet's daughter and that made up for a lot. **1971** *Sunday Nation* (Nairobi) 11 Apr. 29/3 The once-called 'power roar' from the engine compartment..never became obtrusive or 'rorty'. **1973** *Daily Tel.* 23 Aug. 6/8 He has a wide and rorty selection of illustrations. **1974** *Good Motoring* Mar. 22/1 It is..odd that such a comfortable car should have such brilliant performance..which is characterised by a 'rorty' exhaust note. **1978** C. Beaton *Parting Years* 160 Anne Tree is likewise an oversize personality and character—rorty, Hogarthian and with exquisite understanding of character.

Hence **ˈrortiness.**

1885 *Referee* 23 Aug. (Ware), She reminded me a little too much, in her rortyness, of the serio-comic lady [etc.].

ˈrorulent, *a. rare.* [ad. L. *rōrulent-us* dewy.]

1656 Blount *Glossogr.*, *Rorulent*, covered with, or full of dew. **1826** Kirby & Sp. *Entomol.* IV. xlvi. 275 *Rorulent*, covered like a plum with a bloom which may be rubbed off.

†**ˈrory,** *a.*¹ *Obs. rare.* Also 7 **roarie.** [f. L. *rōr-, rōs* dew.] Dewy.

1600 Fairfax *Tasso* I. xiv, On Libanon at first his foote he set, And shooke his wings with roarie May-dewes wet. **1621** Quarles *Argalus & P.* III. Wks. (Grosart) III. 273/1 A Crowne of burnisht Gold, beshaded o're With Foggs and rory mist.

rory (ˈrɔərɪ), *a.*² *Sc.* = RORY-TORY 1.

1866 Jas. Smith *Merry Bridal* 9 Wi' a' her falderals sae gay, An' rory ribbons fleein'. **1901** *Tailor & Cutter* 8 Aug., The time when large overcheck tweeds and designs distinctly 'rory' were the common style.

Rory O'More (ˈrɔərɪ əʊˈmɔə(r)). *Rhyming slang.* Also **Rory O'Moore** and *ellipt.* as **Rory, rory.** [The name of a legendary Irish rebel, the eponymous hero of a popular ballad (1826) and novel (1837) by S. Lover (1797–1868), Irish writer.] **a.** The floor; also *on the Rory*, poor, penniless. **b.** A door.

1857 'Ducange Anglicus' *Vulgar Tongue* 17 Rory-O'More, *n.* floor. **1859** Hotten *Dict. Slang* 145 *Rory O'Moore*, the floor. **1892** 'Doss Chiderdoss' in *Sporting Times* 29 Oct. 1/2, I fired him out of the Rory quick. **1935** A. J. Pollock *Underworld Speaks* 98/2 *Rory O'More*, the door. **1936** J. Curtis *Gilt Kid* xviii. 178 Some lousy berk must have been snooping around the place and found that rory open. **1938** F. D. Sharpe *Sharpe of Flying Squad* 332 *On the Rory*, penniless. **1953** Berrey & Van den Bark *Amer. Thes. Slang* (1954) §466/3 *Rory O'Moore*, a door. **1973** B. Aylwin *Load of Cockney Cobblers* x. 49 *Rory O'More*, floor or door, *Rory.*

ˈrory-ˈtory, *a. dial.* Also **rory-cum-tory.** [Cf. TORY-RORY.]

1. Loud or gaudy in colour.

1874 S. P. Fox *Kingsbridge* 266 *Rory tory*, tawdry. **1880** Mrs. Parr *Adam & Eve* vi. 89 Dressin' up in that rory-tory stuff.

2. Noisy, boisterous.

1893 'Q' *Delect. Duchy* 226 A great, red, rory-cum-tory chap. **1896** Baring-Gould *Dartmoor Idylls* 18 If he's fractious, you'll sing to him; but none of your Rory-Tory tunes.

ros, obs. pa. t. RISE *v.*; obs. f. ROOSE, ROSE.

†**rosabel.** *nonce-word.* [ad. L. *rosa bella.*] A beautiful rose.

1523 Skelton *Garl. Laurel* 977 My mayden Isabell, Reflaring rosabell, The flagrant camamell.

rosace (ˈrəʊzeɪs, ‖rozas). [a. F. *rosace* (1547 in Godef. *Compl.*), f. *rose* ROSE *sb.*]

1. A rose-window. Also *attrib.*

1849 Allies *Jrnl. France* 101 A vast decorated window terminating in a great rosace above. **1871** *Standard* 17 June 5/4 The Church is lightsome with its frequent rosace windows. **1889** A. M. F. Robinson *End Mid. Ages* 289 The Gothic front with its deep porch and rosace.

2. An ornament or design resembling a rose; a rosette.

1873 Ferguson in H. B. Tristram *Land of Moab* 384 The "rosaces" between the triangles at Mashita. **1883** *Grove's Dict. Music* III. 161/2 Under the head of Ruckers will be found illustrations of the rose or rosace as used by those great [violin-]makers.

‖**rosacea** (rəʊˈzeɪʃ(ɪ)ə). *Path.* [fem. of L. *rosāceus*, in the sense of 'rose-coloured'.] A hyperæmic form of acne; in full, ***acne rosacea.***

[**1833** *Cycl. Pract. Med.* I. 30/2 The treatment of acne *rosacea* demands great perseverance.] **1876** Duhring *Dis. Skin* 73 In rosacea of the nose, the skin has the appearance of being hot and inflamed. **1899** *Allbutt's Syst. Med.* VIII. 613 Rosacea is commoner in women than in men.

rosacean (rəʊˈzeɪʃən). *Bot.* [Cf. next and -AN.] A plant of the order *Rosaceæ*.

1854 S. Thomson *Wand. Wild Fl.* II. 105 In the strawberry,..a true rosacean, the carpels are borne on the receptacle. **1896** *Naturalist* 91 The main reason for investigating..the rosacean plants.

rosaceous (rəʊˈzeɪʃəs), *a.* [ad. L. *rosāceus*, f. *rosa* ROSE *sb.*]

1. *Bot.* Belonging to, characteristic of, the natural order *Rosaceæ*, of which the rose is the type.

1731 Miller *Gard. Dict.* s.v. *Chamænerion*, The Flowers are rosaceous, and consist of four Leaves. **1777** Lightfoot *Flora Scotica* II. 734 The leaves..form, at the summits of the branches, barren rosaceous stars. **1830** Lindley *Nat. Syst. Bot.* 82 No Rosaceous plants are unwholesome. **1861** Bentley *Man. Bot.* 232 Rosaceous [corolla]..is composed of five petals, without, or with very short claws, and spreading in a regular manner.

2. Resembling a rose in form; rose-like.

1783 Barbut *Vermes* 93 *Echinus Rosaceus* Linn., the Rosaceous Sea Urchin. **1896** Vizetelly tr. *Zola's Rome* 263 The spacious porch, whose lofty vaulted ceiling was adorned with panels displaying a rosaceous pattern.

3. *Path.* Of the nature of rosacea.

1900 *Archives of Surgery* XI. 209 The sting attaching to all acne of the rosaceous or tuberous types, is that a suspicion of intemperance is excited in all beholders.

†**roˈsacic,** *a. Chem. Obs.* [Cf. prec. and -IC.] ***rosacic acid***, the name given by Proust to a supposed acid forming a constituent of lateritious urinary sediment.

1807 T. Thomson *Chem.* (ed. 3) II. 317 The other three [[acids], namely, the uric, rosacic, and amniotic, are never employed as instruments of analysis. **1826** Henry *Elem. Chem.* II. 415 According to Proust,..this sediment contains, mixed with uric acid and phosphate of lime, a peculiar acid, which he terms the rosacic, from its resemblance in colour to the rose. **1841** *Penny Cycl.* XX. 161/2 If this opinion be correct, no such substance as the rosacic acid exists.

rosacrucian, obs. f. ROSICRUCIAN.

†**rosage,** *a. Obs.*⁻¹ [ad. L. *rosāce-us* or OF. *rosace.*] ***gum rosage***, = GOUT *sb.*¹ 2.

c **1450** in *Vicary's Anat.* 228 Vndir the nose lyes a wayne, There-wythe shall the frensi be sclayne, And the gome rosage [= gut roset, p. 229] alswa.

†**rosagine.** *Obs.*⁻⁰ [a. F. *rosagine.*] The oleander or rose-bay.

1545 Elyot, *Nerium*, a tree or shrub whyche hath leaues lyke an almonde, which some doo call Oleander, some Rosagine.

rosaie, var. REZAI.

†**rosair.** *Obs.*⁻¹ [ad. L. *rosār-ium* ROSARY.] A rose-bed, rose-garden.

c **1440** *Pallad. on Husb.* XII. 344 Rosair in Feueryeer al though me make, Now make hit ther is warme.

†**roˈsaker.** *Obs.* Also 6 **rosager,** 7 **rosacre.** [Alteration of ROSALGER.] Realgar.

1592 *Wills & Inv. Durh.* (Surtees) 212, iiij lbs. of arsnecke and rosager 8ᵈ. **1598** B. Jonson *Ev. Man in Hum.* III. v, A tabacco-pipe..will stifle them all in the end, as many as vse it; it's little better then rats bane, or rosaker. **1616** Bacon in A. Wilson *Jas. I* (1653) 86 Poyson after poyson: First Rosaker, then Arsnick, then Mercury sublimate. **1643** *Five Yrs. K. Jas.* in *Harl. Misc.* (Malh.) V. 378 He gets into his hands certain poisons, viz. rosacre, white arsnick [etc.].

ˈrosal, *a. rare.* [f. ROSE *sb.* + -AL¹. Cf. F. *rosal* rose (13th c. in Godef. *Compl.*), and ROSEAL.]

†**1.** Rosy, roseate, ruddy. *Obs.*

1566 Drant *Jeremiah* iv, Rosall ruddish reade within, clare rede as precioüse stones. **1620** Shelton *Quix.* IV. vii, And at the Time, we Phoebus may devise Shine thro' the Rosal Gates of th' Orient bright. **1641** Beedome *Poems* E 6 Thus from forth her rosall gate she sent, Breath form'd in words.

2. *Bot.* Rosaceous. *rare.*

1846 Lindley *Veget. Kingd.* 563 Rosal Exogens, with polypetalous flowers, and carpels both free from the calyx [etc.]. **1858** —— *Sch. Bot.* x. 160 The..Plane tree belongs to the Urtical, and the..Apple to the Rosal alliance.

†**rosalger.** *Obs.* Also **rosealgar, -alger.** [var. of RESALGAR (cf. Pg. *rosalgar*): see also ROSAKER.] Realgar, disulphide of arsenic.

14.. [see RESALGAR]. **1545** *Bk. of Rates* C iij b, Rosealgar the C. pound. **1580** Greene *Mamillia* I. Wks. (Grosart) II. 114 The mouse, if she feede vpon rose-alger for the glistering hue, deseruеth to be poysoned. **1662** *Stat. Irel.* (1765) II. 403 Rosalger, *vide* arsenick, the pound 4ᵈ.

†**rosalia**¹. *Path. Obs.* Also **rossalia.** [mod.L., prob. of Italian origin: cf. It. *rosellia, rosolia* measles, and see *rosillia* in Du Cange.]

1. (See quot.)

1676 Jas. Cooke *Marrow Chirurg.* IV. I. ix. (ed. 3) 740 Rossalia, red fiery spots, which break out at the beginning of Diseases all over the Body as if it were a small Erysipelas.

2. Scarlatina; scarlet fever.

Good wished to revive the name *rosalia* in place of the 'barbarous and unclassical term' *scarlatina.*

1822 Good *Study Med.* (1829) III. 13 The disorder.. evinced all the common symptoms of a mild rosalia; and, like rosalia, it proved itself contagious.

Rosalia² (rəʊˈzɑːlɪə). *Mus.* Also with small initial. Pl. **Rosalias, Rosalie.** [Prob. the personal name *Rosalia*, occurring in the title of an Italian popular song, *Rosalia, mia cara*, the melody of which employs this device.] The repetition of a phrase or passage one note higher, with the retention of the same intervals and a consequent change of key.

[**1773** C. Burney *Present State of Music in Germany* II. 327 The French have a term for this tediousness, which is wanting in other languages, they call it *Rosalie.*] **1801** Busby *Dict. Mus.* s.v., *Rosalia*, a term applied by the Italians to the repetition of a passage one note higher. **1883** Grove *Dict. Mus.* III. 160/1 *Rosalia*,..a form of Melody, Vocal or Instrumental, in which a Figure is repeated several times in succession, transposed a note higher at each reiteration. *Ibid.* 160/2 Schumann has been recently accused of writing Rosalie, *usque ad nauseam.* **1937** G. B. Shaw *London Music in 1888–89* 30 To give the orchestra symphonic work instead of rosalias and rum-tum. **1944** W. Apel Harvard Dict. Mus. 652/2 *Rosalia*, a disparaging term denoting the schematic and unimaginative application of sequential treatment... The word applies in particular to sequences which, owing to the exact repetition of the intervals, involve modulation of the key to the higher second. **1954** *Grove's Dict. Mus.* (ed. 5) VII. 230/2 *Rosalia*, the name given to the identical repetition of a melody a tone higher, keeping the exact intervals of the notes.

rosaline (ˈrəʊzəliːn). Also with capital initial. [App. of Fr. origin (see etym. note).] In full, ***rosaline point.*** A variety of fine needlepoint or pillow lace. Used esp. of Venetian or Belgian rose-point lace. Also *Comb.*

The word is not found in standard Fr. dicts., but occurs in specialist works (cf. C. Mague *Dentelles Anciennes* (1930)). Webster (1961) prefers to regard it as irreg. f. ROSE *sb.*, but its meaning and use in Eng. suggest a Fr. origin.

1900 E. Jackson *Hist. Hand-Made Lace* vii. 66 Richness of workmanship distinguished the early eighteenth century specimens, and the firm yet delicate laces such as Rosaline Point..were especially suitable for the purpose. **1921** Galsworthy *To Let* I. ii. 25 'There's a bit of rosaline point in here,' he said, stopping before a shop, 'that I thought you might like.' **1953** M. Powys *Lace & Lace-Making* vi. 47 In the Treasury of St. Marks in Venice there is Bas d'Aube of the finest quality with smaller flowers and detail, a type of Point de Venise which is called 'Rosaline', the whirls and picots sometimes rising up to the height of half an inch and giving a moss-like effect. *Ibid.* iv. 23 Rosaline is made with the same technique as the Point d'Angleterre and Duchesse, the only difference being that it has a winky pin at the border of the braid instead of the usual edge. **1966** 'E. Kyle' *Love is for Living* iii. 27 They hadn't any rosaline perlé... Their best lacemaker is ill. *Ibid.* vi. 51 This is rosaline perlé. Here is the real rose-point. You see that the first has these small knots like pearls to diversify the pattern? **1971** *Country Life* 4 Nov. 1197/3 This *rosaline* or *point de neige* is the summit of virtuosity.

rosaniline (rəʊˈzænɪlaɪn). *Chem.* Also **-in.** [f. ROSE + ANILINE. Named by Hofmann.] A powerful organic base, derived from aniline by treatment with a reagent, yielding crystalline salts much used in dyeing; a dye-colour obtained from this. Also *attrib.*

1862 Hofmann in *Proc. Roy. Soc.* XII. 5, I..propose the term Rosaniline for the designation of the new substance. *Ibid.* 7 Both classes of rosaniline-salts crystallize readily. **1872** J. P. Cooke *New Chem.* 321 Rosaniline is a base like ammonia. **1898** *Allbutt's Syst. Med.* V. 412 Here the rosaniline is the staining principle and not the hydrochloric acid.

†**rosare**, obs. var. of ROSARY 3 b or ROSIER.
c **1500** KENNEDIE *Poems* (Schipper) iv. 58 þocht we brek vowis.. To þe, Rosare, and rute of our remeid.

rosarian (rəʊˈzɛərɪən). [f. L. *rosāri-um* (see ROSARY) + -AN.]
1. One who is interested in the cultivation of roses; *esp.* an amateur rose-grower.
1864 HIBBERD *Rose Book* 12 To furnish the rosarian with an intelligible key to the catalogues [of roses]. **1882** *Garden* 25 Feb. 132/3, I have no doubt many rosarians.. have found swarms of the black ants on the top of Rose buds.
2. *R.C. Ch.* A member of a Confraternity of the Rosary.
1867 R. PALMER *Life P. Howard* 40 *note*, The Confraternity of the Holy Rosary, called 'Rosarians'. **1871–2** *Rosarian* I. 378 A Rosarian asks prayers for the conversion of her three brothers.

'**rosaried**, *ppl. a.* [f. ROSARY + -ED.] Provided with, or wearing, a rosary.
1834 MOTLEY *Corr.* I. 37 These are your true monks—none of your bare-footed, rosaried and roped friars, but jovial old gentlemen.

‖**ro'sario.** *Obs.* [It., Sp., or Pg. *rosario.*] = ROSARY.
1622 MABBE tr. *Aleman's Guzman d' Alf.* I. 118 It is a common practice amongst Theeves and Ruffians, to haue their *Rosario* still in their hand. **1652** HOWELL tr. *Giraffi's Rev. Naples* II. 70 The Nunnes.. made solemn processions, repeating the most holy *Rosario.* **1748** *Anson's Voy.* II. v. 186 She was deep laden with steel,.. *rosarios*, European bale goods.

†'**rosarist.** *Obs. rare.* [See ROSARY and -IST.] One who uses the rosary.
1657 A. C. & T. V. (*title*), Jesus, Mary, Joseph, or the Devout Pilgrim of the Ever Blessed Virgin Mary,.. published for the benefit of the Pious Rosarists.

‖**rosarium** (rəʊˈzɛərɪəm). [L. *rosārium*: see ROSARY.] A rose-garden.
1841 *Penny Cycl.* XX. 158/2 They form an elegant section of flowers for the rosarium. **1869** S. R. HOLE *Bk. about Roses* 48 The Rosarium must be both exposed and sheltered; a place both of sunshine and of shade.

rosarubie: see ROSE-A-RUBY.

rosary ('rəʊzərɪ). [ad. L. *rosārium* rose-garden, f. *rosa* ROSE *sb.* Hence also It., Sp., and Pg. *rosario*, F. *rosaire* (1611) in sense 5.]
†**1.** The title of a treatise on alchemy (*Rosarium philosophorum*) by Arnaldus de Villa Nova. *Obs.*$^{-1}$
c **1386** CHAUCER *Can. Yeom. T.* 876 Lo, thus seith Arnold of the new toun, As his Rosarie maketh mencioun.., Ther may no man Mercurie mortifie.
2. *Hist.* A base or counterfeit coin, of foreign origin, current in England during the thirteenth century at the value of a penny, and declared illegal by Edward I.
1387 TREVISA *Higden* (Rolls) VIII. 289 Kyng Edward dampned sodeynliche fals money þat was slyliche i-brouȝt up: men cleped þe money pollardes, crocardes and rosaries [*rosarios*]. *a* **1513** FABYAN *Chron.* VII. 401. **1568** GRAFTON *Chron.* II. 182. **1605** CAMDEN *Rem.* (1623) 176 Afterward Crocards and Pollards were decried downe to an halfe penny, Rosaries, Stepings and Staldings forbidden. **1749** J. SIMON *Ess. Irish Coins* 15 *note*, These.. foreign coins, called Mitres, Lionines, Rosaries,.. &c. from the stamp or figures impressed on them, were privately brought from.. beyond the seas, and uttered here for pennies.
3. a. A piece of ground set apart for the cultivation of roses; a rose-garden, rosarium. Also, a rose-bed, rose-plot.
c **1440** *Pallad. on Husb.* III. 526 This mone is eke rosaries to make With setes, or me may her sedes sowe. *Ibid.* IV. 126 Soone in this mone ek make vp thi rosary. **1570** LEVINS *Manip.* 105 A Rosarie, *rosarium.* **1608** MACHIN *Dumb Kt.* IV. i, What, is there a Hercules that dare to touch Or enter the Hesperian rosaries? **1657** G. THORNLEY *Daphnis & Chloe* 182 Alas, the Rosaries, how are they broken down! **1815** *Hist. J. Decastro* iv. 37 Coming to the rosary,.. I sat down upon the seat. **1822** LOUDON *Encycl. Gard.* §6555 In rosaries commonly but one plant of a sort is introduced, and the varieties which most resemble each other are placed together. **1869** S. R. HOLE *Bk. about Roses* 44 Men of moderate means may make or maintain a Rosary at a very moderate expense.
fig. c **1440** *Alph. Tales* 325/1 He was hedid & cristend in his awn blude, & broght vnto þe rosary of paradyce. **1671** J. WEBSTER *Metallogr.* 168 This is the key of all their secrets, and onely can open the door into the Philosophers Rosary. [Cf. sense 1.]
†**b.** A rose-bush or rose-tree. *Obs. rare.*
1523 SKELTON *Garl. Laur.* 979 The ruddy rosary, The souerayne rosemary, The praty strawbery. **1606** *Proceed. agst. Garnet* D d 3 The sweetest and the fairest blossome that euer budded, either out of the white, or the red Rosary.
†**4.** Used as the title of a book of devotion. *Obs.*
1526 *Pilgr. Perf.* (W. de W. 1531) 298 Here begynneth the Rosary of our Sauyour Jesu, gyuynge thankes and prayse to his holy name, by maner of meditacyon and prayer. **1533** (*title*), The Mystik sweet Rosary of the faythful soule: garnished rownde aboute.. with fressh fragraunt flowers. **1583** STUBBES (*title*), The Rosarie of Christian Praiers and Meditations for diuers Purposes.
5. *R.C. Ch.* **a.** A form of prayer or set of devotions consisting in the recitation or chanting of fifteen decades of Aves, each decade being preceded by a Paternoster and followed by a Gloria; Our Lady's Psalter; a book containing this.
There are also other rosaries, as that of St. Bridget, of the Seven Dolours, etc.: see the *Catholic Dict.* s.v.
1547 *Homilies* I. in *Good Works* III. (1859) 61 Let us rehearse some other kinds of papistical superstitions and abuses, as of Beads, of Lady Psalters and Rosaries. **1570** GOOGE *Pop. Kingd.* iii. (1880) 36 b, Used commonly as most of weight, the Rosaries do flourish wondrously. **1605–6** *Act 3 Jas. I* c. 5 §24 No person shall bring from beyond Seas.. any Popish Primers, Ladies Psalters, Manuels, Rosaries. **1679** J. SHARP *Serm. St. Margarets* 28 You may entertain yourselves with saying over your Rosary.. and other Private Prayers. **1715** BENTLEY *Serm.* x. 371 Nothing but Mass-books and Rosaries,.. dry Postills and fabulous Legends. **1792** J. TOWNSEND *Journ. thro' Spain* II. 17 We met twelve fine made fellows who came from Navarre singing the rosary. **1830–2** CARLETON *Traits* (1843) I. 240, I.. signalized myself frequently by taking the lead in a rosary. **1884** *Tablet* 11 Oct. 591/1 St. Dominic's Priory.. seems to be more and more recognised as the centre of the devotion of the Rosary.
transf. **1616** B. JONSON *Entertainment at Althorpe* Wks. 875 As the rosarie of Kisses, With the oath that neuer misses. **1649** MILTON *Eikon.* i. Wks. 1851 III. 347 To throw contempt.. upon this his Idoliz'd Book, and the whole rosarie of his Prayers.
b. In full *the Rosary of Our Lady*, etc.
1570 FOXE *A. & M.* (ed. 2) 860 Among the which Friers there was one named Alanus de rupe, a Blacke Frier, whiche made the Rosarye of our Ladyes Psalter (so they terme it). **1584** R. SCOT *Disc. Witchcr.* (1886) 445 An example taken out of the Rosarie of our Ladie, in which booke doo remaine ..ninetie and eight examples to this effect. **1635** A. STAFFORD *Fem. Glory* 235 The Sodalitie of the Rosary of this our blessed Lady. **1669** (*title*), The Method of Saying the Rosary of Our Blessed Lady.
6. a. *R.C. Ch.* A string of a hundred and sixty-five beads divided into fifteen sets (each having ten small and one large bead), carried on the person and used to assist the memory in the recital of the Rosary; also, a similar set of fifty-five beads (*the lesser rosary*). The small beads represent Aves and the large ones Paternosters and Glorias.
1597 BP. HALL *Sat.* VI. ii, When at the Corner-crosse thou did'st him meet, Tumbling his Rosaries hanging at his belt. **1744** OZELL tr. *Brantome's Sp. Rhodom.* (ed. 2) 175 A Death's Head at the End of a Gold or Diamond Rosary. **1794** MRS. RADCLIFFE *Myst. Udolpho* xxxi, I leave it to cowards like thee to carry rosaries. **1832** W. IRVING *Alhambra* II. 223 Information having been carried.. of the crosses and rosaries, and other reliques contained in the bag. **1858** tr. *Life of Xavier* 13 Each one wore his rosary hanging round his neck.
fig. **1820** KEATS *Isabella* xxiv, Come down,.. ere the hot sun count His dewy rosary on the eglantine. **1881** DUFFIELD *Don Quix.* II. 46, I came against a rosary or a string of people miserable and unhappy. **1951** N. MARSH *Opening Night* v. 106 Trying to cheer herself up by telling over her rosary of romantic memories. **1960** S. BECKER tr. *Schwarz-Bart's Last of Just* (1961) VI. 291 One day Fräulein Blumenthal arrived to visit, leading her rosary of tiny Levys.
b. A string of beads used by other religious sects in the recitation of their prayers.
1868 *Proc. Geogr. Soc.* 15 July 154–5 The Tibetans made use of the rosary and prayer-wheel... The rosary.. ought to have 108 beads. **1883** GILMOUR *Mongols* xvii. 204 Buddhism puts into his hand a rosary.
c. *Path.* (See quots.)
1897 *Allbutt's Syst. Med.* III. 115 The enlargement of the ends of the ribs at the junction with the costal cartilages—the 'beads' which collectively form what is called the 'rosary'—is the earliest of all the bone changes. **1901** *Dunglison's Med. Dict.* App., *Rosary, rachitic*, row of elevations like beads, on the cartilages of the ribs in rickets.
†**7.** A chaplet or coronet. (In quots. *fig.*) *Obs.*
1651 JER. TAYLOR *Holy Dying* iii. §1 Christ hath now knit them into Rosaries and Coronets. *a* **1667** —— *Diary* 1 Every day propound to your selfe a Rosary or a Chaplet of good Works, to present to God at night.
†**8.** (See quot.) *Obs.*$^{-0}$
1656 BLOUNT (copying Cotgrave), *Rosary*,.. an ordinary Limbeck for distilling Rose water.
9. *attrib.* and *Comb.*, as ***rosary bead, chain, confraternity, devotion.*** **Rosary-Sunday**, *R.C. Ch.*, the first Sunday in October, when the victory over the Turks at Lepanto (1571) is celebrated.
1748 *Earthquake at Lima* (ed. 2) 271 Rosary Devotion. **1834** *Penny Cycl.* IV. 78 Beads (Rosary Beads) are made of horn, ebony, ivory,.. and other materials. **1865** *Pall Mall G.* No. 206. 10/2 Sunset on Rosary-Sunday. **1871–2** (*title*), The Rosarian; a monthly organ of the Holy Rosary Confraternity. **1873** *Catal. Exhib. Jewellery* (S. Kensington Mus.) No. 770, Rosary-chain of pearls and diamonds with cross as pendant. **1884** *Tablet* 11 Oct. 591/1 Rosary Sunday has always been distinguished by a special observance.
b. ***rosary-palm, -pea, -shell***: (see quots.).
1684 tr. *Exquemeling's Bucaniers Amer.* I. 33 There be also in Hispaniola four other species of Palms, which are ..*Palma Espinosa* or Prickle-palm, *Palma a chapelet* or Rosary-palm [etc.]. **1866** *Treas. Bot.* 854/2 *Pea, Rosary*, the seed of *Abrus precatorius.* **1898** MORRIS *Austral Eng.* 394/2 *Rosary-shell.* In Europe, the name is applied to any marine gastropod shell of the genus *Monodonta.* In Australia, it is applied to the shell of *Nerita atrata.*

rosasite ('rəʊzəsaɪt). *Min.* [a. It. *rosasite* (D. Lovisato 1908, in *Atti d. R. Accad. d. Lincei* XVII. II. 726), f. *Rosas*, name of a mine at Sulcis, Sardinia: see -ITE¹.] A carbonate-hydroxide of copper and zinc, $(Cu,Zn)_2(OH)_2CO_3$, a secondary mineral found as a bluish-green deposit on copper and zinc ores.
1909 *Jrnl. Chem. Soc.* XCVI. II. 246 (*heading*) Rosasite, a new mineral from the mines of Rosas (Sulcis, Sardinia). **1958** *Mineral. Mag.* XXXI. 501 Rosasite has not so far been reported in Britain, but we are now able to record no less than seven occurrences. *Ibid.*, The rosasite generally forms small bluish-green wart-like aggregates.

‖**rosa solis.** *Obs.* Also rosa-solis. [mod.L., lit. 'rose of the sun' (f. *rosa* rose, and *sōlis*, gen. of *sōl* sun), but the original form is ROS SOLIS.
Rosasolis is also recorded as a Pg. form.]
1. The plant sundew, *Drosera rotundifolia.*
1568 TURNER *Herbal* III. 79 Rosa solis is a little small herbe that groweth in mossey groundes and in fennes. **1584** COGAN *Haven Health* 228 Take a pottel of good *Aqua vita*, ..and put into it two good handfuls.. of the herbe called *Rosa Solis.* **1597** GERARDE *Herbal* 1367 Let them lay the leaues of Rosa solis in the spirit of wine. **1626** BACON *Sylva* §495 The Herb called *Rosa-Solis* (wherof they make Strong Waters). **1796** WITHERING *Brit. Pl.* (ed. 3) II. 324 Round-leaved Sundew. *Rosa solis*, Redrot.
2. A cordial or liqueur originally made from or flavoured with the juice of the plant sundew, but subsequently composed of spirits (esp. brandy) with various essences or spices, sugar, etc.
In *Meeting of Gallants* (1604) 18 converted into *rose of solace.*
1563–4 *Will of Simon Smyth* (Somerset Ho.), A pottle of the best rosasolis. **1584** COGAN *Haven Health* 226 These sundrie others are.. rather vsed as medicines than with meates: such is *Aqua vitæ, Aqua composita, Rosa Solis.* **1597** GERARDE *Herbal* 1367 That liquor made thereof [*sc.* sundew] which the common people do call Rosa Solis. **1602** MIDDLETON *Blurt, Master Constable* III. iii, He so smells of ale and onions, and rosa-solis, fie. **1641** G. H. *Witts Recreations* Y 6 b, Wee abandon all Ale, and beare that is stale, Rosa-solis and damnable hum. **1702** FARQUHAR *Twin Rivals* II. ii, I an't for your hot spirits, your rosa solis, your ratafias, your orange-waters. **1760–72** H. BROOKE *Fool of Qual.* (1809) III. 145 [They] were regaling themselves with a glass of rosa solis. **1818** SCOTT *Hrt. Midl.* xxxviii, You winna be the waur o' a glass of the right Rosa Solis.
fig. **1601** BRETON *Longing of a Blessed Heart* Wks. (Grosart) I. 13/2 The Rosa solis the sicke soule reuiueth. **1643** *Merc. Brit.* No. 10. 76 (Stanf.), This Rosa Solis of Intelligence to comfort them in their agony of ill news.

†**rosat**, *a.* and *sb.* *Obs.* [a. F. *rosat* or ad. L. *rosātus.*] = ROSET *a.* Also as *sb.*, oil of roses.
1579 LANGHAM *Gard. Health* (1633) 539 Sugar rosat, dissolue sugar in Rose-water, and seeth it well, and cast it on a marble stone till it be cold. **1601** HOLLAND *Pliny* II. 83 As touching the oile Rosat, made by way of infusion, it was in request before the destruction of Troy. **1674** J. MOLINS *Anat. Obs.* 14 Sept., [He] applyed his Calchanthum to it.., continually renewing his Stupes diped in Rosat.

rosat, obs. form of RUSSET.

†**rosate**, *a. Obs.*$^{-1}$ [ad. L. *rosātus*: cf. prec.] = ROSEATE *a.* 1.
1601 HOLLAND *Pliny* XIV. i, In one place they [grapes] are of a fresh and bright purple, in another, of a glittering, incarnate, and rosate colour.

†**rosated**, *ppl. a. Obs.* [See prec. and -ED.]
1. Crowned with a chaplet of roses.
a **1661** FULLER *Worthies, Yorkshire* III. (1662) 207 He appeareth there neither laureated nor hederated Poet,.. but only rosated, having a Chaplet of four Roses about his head.
2. ? Treated with oil of roses.
a **1774** GOLDSM. *Surv. Exp. Philos.* (1776) II. 382 Rosated spirit of wine, quite limpid, and spirit of vitriol, almost so, produce a red.

‖**rosbif** (rɔzbif). [Fr., repr. ROAST BEEF.]
a. In *Gastronomy*, beef (and occas. other types of meat) roasted in the English manner. Also *Comb.* and *transf.*
1846 R. FORD *Gatherings from Spain* xi. 120 Our true love for the *ros-bif* of old England. **1877** E. S. DALLAS *Kettner's Bk. of Table* 7 In the most popular cookery books of France ..roast mutton and lamb are designated Rosbif de Mouton, and Rosbif d'agneau. **1897** A. BEARDSLEY *Let.* 15 Apr. (1970) 303 She.. has been lecturing me about diet. Hot water and rosbif make up her programme. **1923** JOYCE *Let.* 12 July (1966) III. 78 My complexion is now cinnabar and rosbif a l'anglaise. **1972** *Country Life* 20 Jan. 159/1 The Frenchman, if given the opportunity, prefers *le rosbif anglais.* **1972** J. AIKEN *Butterfly Picnic* i. 19 How about a nice grilled steak—chicken—rosbif?
b. A French pejorative term for an Englishman. *rare.*
1858 THACKERAY *Virginians* (1859) II. iii. 23 Only my white cockade and coat had saved me from the fate which the other *canaille* of Rosbifs had deservedly met with.

roscherite ('rɒʃəraɪt). *Min.* [ad. G. *roscherit* (F. Slavík 1914, in *Bull. internat. de l'Acad. tchèque des Sciences, Prague* XIX. 109), f. the name of Walter *Roscher* (fl. 1914), German apothecary and mineral collector: see -ITE¹.] A hydrated basic phosphate of beryllium, calcium, iron, and manganese, $(Ca,Mn,Fe)_3Be_3(PO_4)_3(OH)_3.2H_2O$, sometimes also containing magnesium, found as yellowish-green to brown crystals in granite and pegmatite.
The presence of beryllium in roscherite was not discovered until 1958, the mineral previously having been believed to contain aluminium.
1916 *Chem. Abstr.* X. 31 Roscherite is a new monoclinic mineral occurring as short thick plates and also as slender prismatic and thin tabular crystals. **1958** *Amer. Mineralogist*

XLIII. 824 Roscherite from the Sapucaia pegmatite mine occurs as single crystals, crystal aggregates, and granular crusts in vugs in muscovite. **1975** *Tschermaks Mineral. und Petrogr. Mitteilungen* XXII. 266 Roscherite from Lavra da Ilha, Taquaral, Minas Gerais is a magnesian roscherite.

Roscian (ˈrɒʃ(ɪ)ən), *a.* [f. the name of Quintus *Roscius* Gallus (†62 B.C.), a famous Roman actor.] Characteristic of Roscius as an actor; famous or eminent in respect of acting.

1636 HEYWOOD *Challenge for Beauty* Prol., Our (once applauded) Rosscian straine In acting such might be reviv'd againe. **1659** PECKE *Parnassi Puerp.* 180 That Ben, whose Head deserv'd the Roscian Bayes, Was the first gave the Name of Works, to Playes. **1861** DICKENS *Gt. Expect.* xxx, The celebrated provincial amateur of Roscian renown.

roscid (ˈrɒsɪd), *a.* Now *rare*. Also roscide. [ad. L. *rōscid-us* dewy, f. *rōs* dew: cf. RORID.] Dewy, moist, dank; resembling or falling like dew.

1626 BACON *Sylva* §55 The Spirits of the Wine, doe prey vpon the Roscide Iuyce of the Body. **1642** H. MORE *Immort. of Soul* I. iii. 18 In a roscid cloud I did espy A Lunar rainbow. **1684** tr. *Bonet's Merc. Compit.* XIX. 713 Roscid vapours..are restored..by such things as breed an halituous Blood. **1730–4** WATERLAND *Script. Vind.* Wks. 1843 IV. 183 The falling drops of small roscid rain. **1744** ARMSTRONG *Art Pres. Health* (1807) 49 The fine and subtle spirits cost too much To be profus'd, too much the roscid balm. **1819** H. BUSK *Vestriad* I. 312 No shout..Buoys him on tip-toe to their roscid heaven.

†**ˈroscidating**, *ppl. a.* *Obs.*⁻¹ [Cf. prec.] Having a dewy or cooling effect.

1638 RAWLEY tr. *Bacon's Life & Death* (1650) 64 Refrigeratours which passe not by the Stomach; Drinkes Roscidating, or engendring Oyly Juyces.

Roscius (ˈrɒsɪəs, ˈrɒsk-, ˈrɒʃ(ɪ)əs). Also **Roshus**, **Rossius**. The name of Quintus *Roscius* Gallus (see ROSCIAN *a.*), used to designate an actor, usu. one of outstanding ability, success, or fame (now chiefly *Hist.*, with reference to David Garrick). Also *fig.*

1647 HERRICK *Noble Numbers* 74 Thou art that Roscius, and that markt-out man, That must this day act the Tragedian. *a* **1661** FULLER *Worthies* (1662) London 224 Edward Allin..was the Roscius of our age. *a* **1706** EVELYN *Diary* an. 1662 (1955) III. 338 His best [painting] in my opinion is Lacy the famous Rossius or comedian, whom he has painted in three dresses. **1749** W. R. CHETWOOD *Gen. Hist. of Stage* 155 Mr. George Powel, a reputable Actor, with many Excellencies, gave out that he would perform the Part of Sir John Falstaff in the Manner of that very excellent English Roscius, Mr. Betterton. **1763** BOSWELL *Jrnl.* 21 Jan. (1950) 163, I was sitting with the great Roscius of the age [*sc.* Garrick]. **1793** W. B. STEVENS *Jrnl.* 13 May (1965) 82 The little Roscius of a Baronet tortures his *Crura Podilla* into Harlequin Agility. **1804** *Times* 27 Nov. 3/1 The Young Roscius was at Covent-Garden Theatre last night. **1826** HAZLITT in *New Monthly Mag.* Jan. 38 Of our party only two persons present had seen the British Roscius [*sc.* Garrick]. **1888** KIPLING *Soldiers Three* 58 Captain dear,.. the gallery have enjoyed the performinces av a Roshus. **1958** C. OMAN *David Garrick* xiv. 372 The Garricks set out for home next day... John O'Keefe, the Dublin playwright, saw Roscius for the last time 'walking very quick (his way)' up and down the Adelphi terrace. **1973** C. PRICE *Theatre in Age of Garrick* ii. 6 To the eighteenth century, Garrick was the outstanding actor of modern times, and to call him 'Roscius' as was so often done was merely to indicate that in one respect at least England could rival ancient Rome.

roscoe (ˈrɒskəʊ). *U.S. slang.* Also rosco and with capital initial. The surname *Roscoe* used as a term for a gun, usu. a pistol or revolver. See also *John Roscoe* s.v. JOHN 4.

1914 JACKSON & HELLYER *Vocab. Criminal Slang* 72 *Roscoe*,..a revolver... 'Stash your roscoe before you come back to the kip.' **1927** *Amer. Speech.* II. 387/2 During the harvest season, individuals and gangs harvested the harvesters at the point of the *rod* or *Roscoe* (gun). **1930** *Sat. Even. Post* 28 June 161 Slide back the shutters in the steel windows, jam your roscoes through and blast hell out of everything in sight. **1930** *Amer. Mercury* Dec. 457/2 They settle him on a rosco rap. **1941** *Sun* (Baltimore) 15 Oct. 10/16 Favorite roscoes and tommy guns of gangland's paladins. **1958** *Sat. Even. Post* 20 Sept. 86/1 Mickey and a sinister young hood..waved a couple of loaded roscoes at the cashier. **1965** E. LACY *Moment of Untruth* vii. 111 'I know you're a dick, but..'..'What makes you think that?' 'At the bull fight, when I stood up to let you pass—felt the roscoe on your hip.' **1979** E. NEWMAN *Sunday Punch* viii. 62 "You'll shoot me if I don't sell?'.. His hand went to the bulge again. 'Is that what they call a "roscoe"?'

roscoelite (ˈrɒskəʊlaɪt). *Min.* [f. the name of Sir Henry *Roscoe* (1833–1915), English chemist + -ITE¹.] A vanadium ore that is a basic silicate of potassium, vanadium, and aluminium belonging to the mica family and occurring as minute green or brown scales.

1876 J. BLAKE in *Amer. Jrnl. Sci.* CXII. 31 The mineral, to which I have given the name of Roscoelite,—in honor of Professor Roscoe, of Manchester, who has done so much for the chemical history of vanadium,—is a well marked species of mica, containing quite a large percentage of vanadium. **1943** R. D. GEORGE *Minerals & Rocks* iii. 92 As an ore of vanadium, roscoelite has been found chiefly in western Colorado. **1966** *Mineral. Abstr.* XVII. 670/1 Haradaite ($SrVOSi_2O_6$), goldmanite (calcium vanadic garnet $Ca_3V_2Si_3O_{12}$), and roscoelite ($KV_2AlSi_3O_{10}(OH)_2$) have been hydrothermally synthesized..at moderate *PT* conditions. **1974** *Encycl. Brit. Micropædia* X. 346/3 Vanadium is the 22nd most abundant element in the Earth's crust. Some commercial sources are the minerals carnotite, vanadinite, and roscoelite.

rose (rəʊz), *sb.*¹ and *a.*¹ Forms: 1– rose, 5 roos, 5–6 roose, ross, 5, 7 rosse, 6 ros, roase; *Sc.* 5 roise, 5–6 rois, roys(e; 9 *dial.* rooas(e, rwose. [OE. *rose* or *róse*, ad. L. *rosa* (It., Sp., Pg. *rosa*, F. *rose*); in ME. prob. reinforced from French. Cf. MDu. *rose* (Du. *roos*, Fris. *roas*), LG. *rose*, OHG. *rôsa* (G. *rose*), ON. *rósa* (MSw. *rosa*, Da. *rose*; Icel. *rós*, Sw. *ros*). L. *rosa* is prob. an adoption of Gr. ῥοδέα through intermediate Greek and Italian dialects (Brugmann, I. 684).]

A. *sb.* I. The flower or plant.

1. a. A well-known beautiful and fragrant flower which grows upon a shrub of the genus *Rosa*, usu. of a red, white, or yellow colour, and widely cultivated throughout the world.

The petals of the rose have been used for various economical purposes: cf. ATTAR, OTTO¹, ROSE-CAKE, ROSE-VINEGAR, ROSE-WATER, etc.

c **888** K. ÆLFRED *Boeth.* ix, Se stearca wind..toweorpð.. ..þære rosan wlite. *a* **1000** ÆLFRIC *Hom.* I. 444 Rosena blostman & lilian hi ymtrymedon. *c* **1055** *Byrhtferth's Handboc* in *Anglia* VIII. 299 þær we onfengon þære rosena swæc. *a* **1225** *Ancr. R.* 276 And breres bereð rosen, & berien, && blostmen? **13..** *Coer de L.* 3736 Ladyes strowe here boures With rede roses, and lylye flowres. **1390** GOWER *Conf.* I. 173 As the Netle..The freisshe rede Roses brenneth And makth hem fade. *c* **1450** *Godstow Reg.* 558 Yeldyng therof yerely to hym..j. Rose atte fest of seynt Iohn Baptist. **1526** *Pilgr. Perf.* (W. de W. 1531) 234 So longe it is called the budde of a rose, as it is not a perfyte rose. **1595** BARNFIELD *Cynthia* (1841) 10 Euer as she went she strew'd the place, Red-roses mixt with Daffodillies fine. **1620** VENNER *Via Recta* vii. 148 In the Red Roses, earthy parts are predominant. **1665** BOYLE *Occas. Refl.* (1848) 360 Roses.. do not onely keep their Colour longer than Tulips, but when that decays, retain a perfum'd Odour. **1742** GRAY *Propertius* ii. 10 There bloom the vernal rose's earliest pride. **1781** COWPER *Retirem.* 724 Flow'rs by that name promiscuously we call, But one, the rose, the regent of them all. **1809** BYRON *Bards & Rev.* 76 As soon Seek roses in December —ice in June. **1856** RUSKIN *Mod. Painters* IV. v. xiv. §25 A rose is rounded by its own soft ways of growth. **1882** *Garden* 11 Feb. 93/1 A bunch of green Roses gathered from a bush in the open air.

b. *oil of roses*, rose-oil (see sense 19 d).

c **1400** *Lanfranc's Cirurg.* 13 Aboute þe wounde leie a medicyn defensif,..oile of rosis, & a litil vynegre. **1541** COPLAND *Guydon's Quest. Chirurg.* O j b, Anoynte it with oyle of Roses or other oyntement to mytygate the smert. **1563** HYLL *Art Gardening* (1593) 88 The best making of the oile of Roses is on this wise, first clip off the rose leaues from the whites, and boiling the same in oyle Oliue, then sun the same in a glasse for fiftie daies. *c* **1623** LODGE *Poore Mans Talent* (Hunterian Cl.) 43 Mintts bruised and mixed wyth oyle of Roses, and applied to the stomacke, is good against ....vomytt. **1662** [see OIL *sb.*¹ B. 2]. **1725** *Fam. Dict.* s.v. *Wound*, Take..Pitch or Gum, Oil of Roses [etc.]. **1753** *Chambers' Cycl.* Suppl. s.v. *Rose*, How to gain a larger quantity of the essential oil of roses. **1868** WATTS *Dict. Chem.* V. 115 Oil of roses is often adulterated with oil of geranium.

c. *cakes, honey, sugar, syrup, water of roses* (cf. 19 d, and ROSE-CAKE, etc.).

c **1430** *Two Cookery-bks.* 27 Take Quynces,..caste hem on a potte, & caste þer-to water of Rosys. **1552** [see sense 19 d]. **1671** PHILLIPS, *Rhodomel*,..Honey of Roses. **1676** J. COOKE *Marrow Chirurg.* (ed. 3) 785 Manna dissolv'd in Syrup of Roses. **1680** OTWAY *Caius Marius* v. ii, Remnants of Pack-thread, and old Cakes of Roses. **1686** W. DENTON *Let.* in M. Verney *Mem.* (1899) IV. ix. 359, I could wish you would take sugar of roses with yr. asses' milke. **1725** *Fam. Dict.* s.v. *Appetite*, With a little Syrup of Roses make a small Lump of it. **1728** CHAMBERS *Cycl.* s.v. *Rose*, Sugar of Roses is made of Red-Rose Leaves, dried in an Oven. **1922** [see RINGOCANDY].

d. Used without article.

c **1440** tr. *Pallad. on Husb.* VI. 211 In euery pound of oil an vnce of rose Ypurged putte. *Ibid.* 216 In Iuce of rose. **1483** *Cath. Angl.* 312/1 Oyle of Rose, *rodolium*. **1839** URE *Dict. Arts* 1149 Three ounces of essence of rose. **1871** FARRAR *Witn. Hist.* ii. 63 The rocks should flow with honey, and the briars bloom with rose.

2. a. A rose-plant, rose-bush, or rose-tree.

In early quots. not clearly distinguishable from sense 1.

c **1380** WYCLIF *Sel. Wks.* I. 108 þis smelle is Crist, clepid plantinge of rose in Jerico. **1577** B. GOOGE *Heresbach's Husb.* (1586) 67 Roses..are diverslie planted. **1597** GERARDE *Herbal* 1080 We haue in our London gardens one of the red Roses, whose flowers are..of great estimation. **1664** EVELYN *Kalend. Hort.* 69 In mid June Inoculate Jasmine, Roses, and some other rare shrubs. **1725** *Fam. Dict.* s.v. *Rose-tree*, The Rose deserves as much care as any Shrub that grows in a Garden. **1731** MILLER *Gard. Dict.* s.v. *Rosa*, The next Sort of Rose which flowers in the open Air, is the Cinnamon. **1822** LOUDON *Encycl. Gard.* (1824) 892 Roses require some attention to pruning. **1845** *Beck's Florist* 137 The first prize for twenty Roses in pots. **1882** *Garden* 4 Mar. 142/2, I have a green Rose, evidently a climber.

b. *Austr.* A name given to the 'scrub-vine' (*Bauera rubioides*), and to a shrub (*Boronia serrulata*) of the order *Rutaceæ*.

1874 *Treas. Bot.* Suppl. s.v., Rose, Australian, *Boronia serrulata*. *Ibid.*, Rose, River (Tasm.), *Bauera rubioides*. **1891** W. TILLEY *Wild West Tasmania* 7 (Morris), The.. troublesome Bauera shrub; whose gnarled branches have earned for it the..expressive name of 'tangle-foot' or 'leg ropes'. [It] has been named by Spicer the 'Native Rose'.

3. a. With defining term prefixed (denoting either one of the numerous varieties of the common rose, or some other plant), as *Alpine*, *apple*, *Ayrshire*, *Banksian*, etc.

The more important of these, as *blush-*, *brier-*, *cabbage-*, *canker-*, *China-*, *Christmas-rose*, etc., are treated under the first element or as main words. Only a few of the many others in use are illustrated here.

1797 *Encycl. Brit.* (ed. 3) XVI. 495/2 The..*Alpine inermous rose, grows five or six feet high. **1725** *Fam. Dict.* s.v. *Rose-tree*, There are two other sorts of Striped Roses,.. one of which is call'd the York and Lancaster Rose, and the other, the *Apple Rose. **1837** RIVERS *Rose Amateur's G.* 42 The *Ayrshire Rose..is merely a seedling hybrid from our Rosa arvensis. *Ibid.* 52 The true *Banksian Roses are not adapted for pillar roses..: they require a wall. **1864** HIBBERD *Rose Bk.* 8 *R. Banksiæ* is the type of a restricted..section of climbing roses, natives of China; known in gardens as Banksian roses. **1837** RIVERS *Rose Amateur's G.* 20 Hybrid China roses..owe their origin to the China, Tea-scented Noisette and *Bourbon roses. *Ibid.* 50 The *Boursault Rose (Rosa Alpina)... This is a most distinct group of roses, with long, reddish flexible shoots. **1786** ABERCROMBIE *Gard. Assist., Arr.* 33/1 Indian or *Chinese rose. **1837** RIVERS *Rose Amateur's G.* 68 The common Chinese Rose, (Rosa indica), and the crimson Chinese Rose, or Rosa semperflorens. **1725** *Fam. Dict.* s.v. *Rose-tree*, The best Season in England to plant *Dutch Roses. **1786** ABERCROMBIE *Gard. Assist., Arr.* 33/2 *Eglantine rose, or sweet briar. **1647** HEXHAM I, An *Eglantire Rose. **1707** MORTIMER *Husb.* (1721) II. 165 The **Ever-green Rose, that grows like wild Eglantine. **1844** KITTO *Phys. Hist. Palestine* vii. 284 The principal species in that country are..the hundred-leaved (or damask) rose, the yellow rose, and the evergreen rose. **1725** *Fam. Dict.* s.v. *Rose-tree*, The *hundred-leav'd Rose, without smell. **1864** HIBBERD *Rose Bk.* 6 *R. Damascena*, *R. Gallica*, and *R. centifolia*, constitute together the section of *Centifolium*, or hundred-leaved roses. **1837** RIVERS *Rose Amateur's G.* 87 The single *Macartney Rose was brought from China, in 1795, by Lord Macartney. **1786** ABERCROMBIE *Gard. Assist., Arr.* 32/2 *Marbled rose. **1797** *Encycl. Brit.* (ed. 3) XVI. 495/1 Marbled rose.., having..large, double, finely-marbled, red flowers. **1797** *Encycl. Brit.* (ed. 3) VIII. 499/1 The seeds having been carried by the French to their West India settlements, it hath thence obtained the name of *Martinico-rose. **1807** *Miller's Gard. Dict.* s.v. *Rosa*, Double China Rose, commonly called in the West Indies, Martinico Rose. **1725** *Fam. Dict.* s.v. *Rose-tree*, The *Yellow Rose has broad Leaves of a yellow Lemon Colour, and has no smell.

b. With defining term (genitive phrase) added:

rose of the Alps, one of a small species of shrubs, *Rhododendron hirsutum* or *R. ferrugineum*, natives of the Alps; Alpine rose. **rose of Cayenne**: (see quot. 1874). **rose of heaven**, a beautiful garden-flower, *Lychnis* or *Viscaria Cœli-rosa*. **rose of Jerusalem**, a species of Amomum (see quot. 1598). **rose of May**, the common white narcissus; poets' narcissus (*N. poeticus*). **rose of the mount**, a variety of peony. **rose of the prime**, the primrose. **rose of Sienna**, Indian mallow. **rose of the sun** = ROSA SOLIS I. **rose of the Virgin**, the rose of Jericho. **rose of the world**, (*a*) a variety of the common rose; (*b*) a handsome rose-coloured flower, *Camellia japonica Rosa-mundi*. Also ROSE OF JERICHO, ROSE OF SHARON.

1598 FLORIO, *Amomo*, a sweete-smelling shrub in Armenia with leaues like the vine, called our Ladies Rose, or the Rose of Ierusalem, or Garden Pepper. **1611** COTGR., *Rose de nostre Dame*, Rose of the mount, Knights Bloome, Peonie, Pionie. **1628** WITHER *Brit. Rememb.* 137 Here plucks the Cowslips, Roses of the Prime, There Lavander, sweet Marjoram and Thyme. *a* **1653** GOUGE *Comm. Hebr.* ix. 121 There is a rose of Ierusalem, which is milk white, and called..Amomum. **1725** *Fam. Dict.* s.v. *Rose* (*Wild*), The Indian and Japan Mallows;..it's more known by the Name of the Rose of Sienna. **1731** MILLER *Gard. Dict.* s.v. *Rosa*, The Rose of the World, or *Rosa Mundi*. **1852** G. W. JOHNSON *Cottage Gard. Dict.* 790/1 Rose of Heaven, *Lychnis Coeli-Rosa*. *Ibid.*, Rose of the World. **1866** *Chambers's Encycl.* VIII. 337/1 Numerous superstitions are connected with this plant, which is called *Rosa Mariæ*, or *Rose of the Virgin*. **1866** *Treas. Bot.* 991/1 Rose of the Alps. *Ibid.*, Rose of May. **1874** —— Suppl. s.v., Rose of Cayenne, *Licaria guianensis*; or, according to some authorities, *Dicypellium caryophyllatum*. **1910** KIPLING *Rewards & Fairies* 275 Excellent herbs had our fathers of old—..Cowslip, Melilot, Rose of the Sun.

II. In allusive, emblematic, or figurative uses.

4. a. The flower as distinguished by its surpassing beauty, fragrance, or rich red colour.

971 *Blickl. Hom.* 7 Seo readnes þære rosan lixeþ on þe. *a* **1225** *Leg. Kath.* 1423 Se rudie & se reade ilitet euereuch leor as lilie ileid to rose. *a* **1300** *Cursor M.* 9927 It castes lem ouer al sa bright..Als ros þat es als in springing. *c* **1385** CHAUCER *L.G.W.* 613 *Cleopatra*, Sche was fayr as is the Rose in may. *c* **1420** *Anturs of Arth.* 161, I was reddere in rode þan rose in þe rayne. *c* **1470** *Golagros & Gaw.* 854 The blude.. As roise ragit on rise, Our ran thair riche vedis. **1597** SHAKS. *2 Hen. IV*, II. iv. 28 Your Colour (I warrant you) is as red as any Rose. *a* **1732** GAY *New Song on New Similies* 55 Sweet as a rose her breath and lips. **1798** COLERIDGE *Anc. Mar.* I. ix, Red as a rose is she. **1856** EMERSON *Eng. Traits, Race*, The old men are as red as roses, and still handsome.

b. With reference to the prickles (commonly called *thorns*) of the bush on which the flower grows. Also *fig.*

a **900** *O.E. Martyrol.* 2 Sept., He wæs cristen læce, and he eardode in hæðenra midlene swa swa rose sio wyrt bið on þorna midlynæ. *a* **1250** *Owl & Night.* 444 þe rose also myd hire rude þat cumeþ of þe þorne wode. *c* **1300** R. GLOUC. (Rolls) 6794 As þe rose springþ of þe brer þat ssarp & kene is. **1390** GOWER *Conf.* I. 62 That was a Rose is thanne a thorn. **1430–40** LYDG. *Bochas* Prol. ix, There is no rose..in garden, but there be sum thorne. **1535** COVERDALE *Song Sol.* ii. 1 As the rose amonge the thornes, so is my loue amonge the daughters. *a* **1586** MONTGOMERIE *Misc. Poems* xl. 46 Sen peircing pyks ar kyndlie with the rose. **1611** COTGR. s.v., No Rose without a prickle. **1667** MILTON *P.L.* IV. 256 Flours of all hue, and without Thorn the Rose. **1819** SCOTT *Ivanhoe* xviii, To gather life's roses, unscathed by the briar. **1882** CHRISTINA ROSSETTI *Poems* (1904) 174/1 Herself a rose,.. She bore the Rose and felt the thorn.

c. In miscellaneous uses.

1375 BARBOUR *Bruce* XI. 546 The king had said.. That ane rose of his chaplet Wes faldyn. **1423** JAS. I *Kingis Q.* 186, I pray for all the hertis dull, That.. has no curage at the rose to pull. **1546** HEYWOOD *Prov. & Epigr.* (1867) 21, I toke hir for a rose, but she breedth a burre. **1560** ROLLAND *Crt. Venus* I. 587 Of all vertewis, lufe is the crop and rois. **1600** S. NICHOLSON *Acolastus* (1876) 24 None must pluck the Redrose of her prime, But he that gaynes her with a golden voyce. **1842** TENNYSON *Vision of Sin* III. 5, I saw that every morning.. God made Himself an awful rose of dawn. **1877** —— *Harold* III. i, The Saints are virgins; They love the white rose of virginity.

d. ***bed of roses***: (cf. BED *sb.* 6 b).

[*a* **1593** MARLOWE *Pass. Shepherd* iii, There will I make thee a bed of Roses. **1648** HERRICK *Hesp.*, *Upon Eliz. Herrick*, In thy bed of Roses, then,.. Sleep, while we hide thee from the light. **1665** DRYDEN *Ind. Emp.* v. ii, Think'st thou I lie on beds of roses here.]

1806 *Cobbett's Parl. Deb.* VII. 1243 So that he.. does not imagine the directors lay on a 'bed of roses'. **1895** *Dict. Nat. Biogr.* XLIV. 396/2 These border commands were no beds of roses.

e. ***to pluck a rose***: see PLUCK *v.* 9.

f. ***not to be the rose but to be near it*** (and variants), phr. expressing a person's proximity to some admired person, ideal, or the like.

[**1808** F. GLADWIN tr. *Sâdy's Gûlistân* p. x, I was a worthless piece of clay, but having for a season associated with the rose, the virtue of my companion was communicated to me.] **1818** C. R. MATURIN *Women* I. x. 191 'I am not the rose,' said he, 'but I have been near the rose.' **1825** H. WILSON *Memoirs* (ed. 2) I. 234, I considered her with respect and admiration, unmixed with jealousy. This was not the rose; but she had dwelled with it. **1848** THACKERAY *Pendennis* (1849) I. ii. 11 If they were not the roses, they lived near the roses, as it were, and had a good deal of the odour of genteel life. **1866** MRS. GASKELL *Wives & Daughters* II. xviii. 181 The great reason why she did not hear of the gossip against Molly as early as anyone, was that, although she was not the rose, she lived near the rose. **1872** S. R. HOLE *Six of Spades* xii. 106 It seems to say, with the perfumed earth in the Persian fable, 'I am not the rose; but cherish me, for we have dwelt together.' **1899** H. JAMES *Awkward Age* II. viii. 84 Mrs. Grendon, though not perhaps herself quite the rose, is decidedly, in these days, too near it. **1907** E. GOSSE *Father & Son* iv. 91, I was not permitted to go forth and trade with this old person, but sometimes our servant-maid did, thereby making me feel that if I did not hold the rose of merchandise, I was very near it. **1917** 'O. DOUGLAS' *Setons* xiii. 151 It was not the rose but it was someone who at times was near the rose—and he went and sat down beside Jessie. **1979** *Country Life* 7 June 1863/4 Laura moves to Candleford Green, which, if not the rose of Candleford itself, is still nearer the rose than was Lark Rise.

g. *pl.*, expressing favourable circumstances, ease, success, etc., in various phrases, as ***roses, (roses,) all the way, not all roses, everything's roses, come up roses*** (U.S.).

[**1629** H. BURTON *Truth's Triumph* 285 The passage from earth to heauen is not strowed with roses.] **1855** BROWNING *Patriot* in *Men & Women* I. 191 It was roses, roses, all the way. **1899** W. E. NORRIS *G. Ingilby* vi, '[Entertaining] is not all roses, you see', the girl remarked. **1930** A. P. HERBERT *Water Gipsies* xiii. 173 The tunnel was too much for you, eh? Well, I told you it weren't all roses on the 'Cut'. **1938** G. GREENE *Brighton Rock* VII. i. 283 'Sometimes he's bad to me. Oh, I can tell you,' she urged, 'it's not all roses.' **1948** WODEHOUSE *Uncle Dynamite* vi. 84, I should have thought you would be so glad to get back from a ghastly country like Brazil that life would have been roses, roses all the way. **1969** *Times* 12 Dec. 24 If some disaster hit us.. we would have to soldier on, pretending that everything in the column was coming up roses. **1971** 'E. LATHEN' *Longer the Thread* (1972) vi. 60 'We don't have to worry about where the next thunderbolt will hit.' 'So everything's roses,' Eric Marten growled derisively. **1974** *New Yorker* 1 Apr. 95/2 (Advt.), There is a splendid hotel on a marvelous corner of Park Avenue where everything's coming up roses and crystal and gilt. **1976** C. WESTON *Rouse Demon* (1977) xviii. 89 This kid's from a good solid home. Parents are okay. Everything's roses. **1977** *Time* 7 Feb. 59/1 Aired over eight consecutive nights, *Roots* came up roses for ABC. **1977** *World of Cricket Monthly* June 42/2 Although Australia lost the Ashes, it was roses, roses, all the way for him.

h. ***the last rose*** (with allusion to quot. 1820), the last flowering *of* an era, an art form, or the like, before its end.

[**1820** T. MOORE *Irish Melodies* 119 'Tis the last rose of summer, Left blooming alone.] **1965** C. MACKENZIE *My Life & Times* IV. 147 The summer of 1912 blows in my memory like a flower of time that was; it is for me the last rose of a London that vanished during the First World War. **1978** *Times* 5 Aug. 14/6 The 'Pervigilium Veneris' is one of the most haunting incantations of love ever written. This last rose of pagan poetry is also appropriately mysterious. **1981** *Sunday Tel.* 14 June 12/8 This book is a literary curiosity. It is the last rose of a pre-Vatican II summer.

i. ***to come out smelling of roses*** (and variants): to emerge with an (apparently) unblemished record.

1968 'E. LATHEN' *Come to Dust* xvii. 167 No matter how you sliced it, the old grads.. were not going to come out of this smelling like roses. **1976** J. PORTER *Dover & Claret Tappers* xii. 146, I intend to emerge from this business smelling of roses. If, to achieve this, I have to wash my hands in your blood, that's perfectly OK by me.

j. ***roses round the door***, phr. used to denote marital (or rural) domestic happiness.

1934 L. GOLDING *Five Silver Daughters* xiii. 315 Talking about my mother and her pearls—it all sort of reminded me of the roses round the door. **1977** B. PYM *Quartet in Autumn* iv. 38 'Roses round the door and all that', as Norman used to say when Letty's retirement plans were mentioned.

5. *transf.* A peerless or matchless person; a paragon; *esp.* a woman of great beauty, excellence, or virtue. Also const. *of*.

Frequently used, *esp.* in early examples, to designate the Virgin Mary. ***English rose***: see ENGLISH *a.* 2 e.

a **1400** *Minor Poems from Vernon MS.* xxviii. 41 Heil Rose hiȝest of hyde and hewe. **1412** LYDG. *Chron. Troy* I. 2974, I ȝow beseche, O goodly fresche rose, Myn emprise to bringen to an ende. *c* **1450** *St. Cuthbert* (Surtees) 6440 Of Religioun he was þe rose. **1508** DUNBAR *Gold. Targe* 253 O reuerend Chaucere, rose of rethoris all. **1596** SHAKS. *1 Hen. IV*, I. iii. 175 To put downe Richard, that sweet louely Rose, And plant this Thorne. **1602** —— *Ham.* IV. v. 157 Oh Rose of May, Deere Maid, kinde Sister, sweet Ophelia. **1653** H. COGAN tr. *Pinto's Trav.* xxiii. 86 The same Priest.. began to sing aloud these words 'Virgin, you are a Rose'. **1683** *Whip for Devil* 118 By all the most blessed Names of the Virgin.., beautiful Soul, blessed Rose. **1720** T. M. tr. *Horstius' Parad. Soul* (1771) 453 Mystical Rose, Pray for us. **1731–8** SWIFT *Pol. Conv.* i, *Miss.* Well; here's a Rose between two Nettles. *Neverout.* No, Madam;.. here's a Nettle between two Roses. **1819** SCOTT *Ivanhoe* xiv, A Saxon heiress of large possessions.., a rose of loveliness, and a jewel of wealth. **1872** in Mrs. Somerville *Personal Recoll.* iv. (1874) 61 They called her the 'Rose of Jedwood'. **1882** [see 4 b].

6. *Eng. Hist.* The flower, white or red, which was respectively the badge, emblem, or symbol of the rival Houses of York and Lancaster. Also *transf.*, the parties thus symbolized.

Wars of the Roses, the civil wars in the fifteenth century between the Yorkists and Lancastrians.

For the reputed adoption of the emblem, see Shaks. *1 Hen. VI*, II. iv. 27 ff.

1509 HAWES *Past. Pleas.* (Percy Soc.) 1 Grace shal him [Prince Henry] well enclose, Whiche by true right sprange of the reed rose. *a* **1529** SKELTON *Sp. Parrot* 37 Cryst saue Kyng Henry the viii., our royall kyng, The red rose in honour to florysh and spryng! **1612** DRAYTON *Poly-olb.* v. 64 Whose marriages conioyn'd the White-rose and the Red. **1642** FULLER *Holy & Prof. St.* v. v. 378 The Red rose might become White, by losing so much bloud, and the White rose Red by shedding it. **1738** *De Foe's Tour Gt. Brit.* (ed. 2) III. 120 It proved a lucky Day to the White Rose of York and made the Red Rose of Lancaster look pale and wan. **1829** SCOTT *Anne of G.* vii, The civil discords so dreadfully prosecuted in the wars of the White and Red Roses. **1835** M. GRAHAM *Little Arthur's Hist. Eng.* II. xxxii. 3 For more than thirty years afterwards, the civil wars in England were called the wars of the Roses. **1841** S. BAMFORD *Passages Life Radical* (ed. 2) II. xxvi. 132, I passed the Obelisk at Barnet, where the famous battle was fought in the wars of the roses. **1878** STUBBS *Const. Hist.* III. xviii. 274 Henry VII, combining the interests of the rival roses. **1879** TROLLOPE *Eye for an Eye* I. ii. 30 They have held the same property since the wars of the roses. **1939** W. S. MAUGHAM in *Hearst's Internat.* Feb. 30/2 The barony held by the first earl dated from the Wars of the Roses. **1966** A. L. ROWSE (*title*) Bosworth Field and the Wars of the Roses.

b. As the emblem of England. Cf. 12 c.

1629 B. JONSON *Underwoods, To E. Filmer*, Who did this Knot compose Again hath brought the Lily to the Rose. **1825** A. CUNNINGHAM *German Lairdie* ii, He's pu'd the rose o' the English loons,.. But our thistle top will jag his thumbs.

7. a. ***under the rose***, privately, in secret, in strict confidence; SUB ROSA. Also *transf.* (quot. 1876).

So early mod.Du. *onder de roose* (Kilian), MLG. *under der rosen*, G. *unter der rose*: there is reason to believe that the phrase originated in Germany.

1546 *State Papers Hen. VIII*, XI. 200 The sayde questyons were asked with lysence, and that yt shulde remayn under the rosse, that is to say, to remayn under the bourde, and no more to be rehersyd. **1622** FLETCHER *Beggars' Bush* II. iii, If this make us speak Bold words, anon, 'tis all under the Rose Forgotten. **1644** HOWELL *Parables Times* 147 Being all under the Rose they had privilege to speak all things with freedom. **1687** T. BROWN in *Dk. Buckingham's Wks.* (1705) II. 131 Where under the Pulpit, as under the Rose, we may say what we please against either State or Church. **1708** *Brit. Apollo* No. 112. 3/1 But when we with caution a secret Disclose, We cry Be it spoken (Sir) under the Rose. **1775** J. ADAMS in *Fam. Lett.* (1876) 61 In Congress we are bound to secrecy. But, under the rose, I believe that ten thousand men will be maintained in the Massachusetts. **1818** SCOTT *Rob Roy* xxvi, Why, ye are to understand,.. I speak amang friends, and under the rose. **1876** GEO. ELIOT *Dan. Der.* xxviii, This fine fellow, whom he believed to be his cousin under the rose.

b. In allusions to the above phrase.

1730 FIELDING *Rape upon Rape* Wks. 1775 II. 51 The rose is ever understood over the drinking-room, and a glass is the surest turnkey to the lips. **1890** *Ch. Times* 21 Feb., If these persons are well informed (and some of them are very near the rose) the prospect of legislation is not too brilliant.

III. As a designation of colour.

8. A delicate red or light crimson colour.

1530 PALSGR. 264/1 Rose, colour. **1728** CHAMBERS *Cycl.* s.v. *Colour*, The same blue, with red half in grain, makes amaranth, tan-colour, and dry rose. **1761** *Poetry* in *Ann. Reg.* 234 Did they, no matter how, disturb their cloaths; Or, over lilied, add a little rose! **1834–6** in *Encycl. Metrop.* (1845) VIII. 463/1 Several different shades of enamel colours, rose, red, and brown. **1864** LOWELL *Fireside Trav.* 286 One great mountain that soaked up all the rose of sunset. **1882** *Garden* 23 Dec. 548/1 The flowers.. bright magenta shaded with warm rose.

9. Chiefly *pl.* The fresh pink or ruddy hue of the complexion, esp. in young women.

1590 SHAKS. *Mids. N.* I. i. 129 How now my loue? Why is your cheek so pale? How chance the Roses there do fade so fast? **1607** EARL STIRLING *J. Cæsar* III. ii, I see the Roses fading in thy face. **1622–1713** [see LILY 3]. **1775** SHERIDAN *Duenna* II. i, Then the roses on those cheeks are shaded with a sort of velvet down, that gives a delicacy to the glow of health. **1812** CRABBE *Tales* xvi. 266 In Anna's cheek revived the faded rose. **1877** MRS. OLIPHANT *Makers Flor.* vi. 172 The fresh country ladies had to be warned against spoiling their natural roses with paint.

10. ***the rose***, a popular term for a local inflammatory cutaneous disease, frequently accompanied by fever, in which the skin assumes a deep red colour; erysipelas; St. Anthony's fire.

Perhaps originally from Dutch or German.

1599 A. M. tr. *Gabelhouer's Bk. Physicke* 286/1 If then anye man get the Rose or anye other inflammation. **1658** A. FOX *Wurtz' Surg.* II. xxi. 134 There are other humours which fall into the Knee, even as the Rose or Anthonies Fire useth to fall. **1788** *Med. Comm.* II. 182 The Rose, or Erysipelas of the extremities, is commonly preceded by lowness. **1833** *Cycl. Pract. Med.* II. 105/2 Erysipelas.. is known in popular language by the name of *the Rose*, from the colour of the skin. **1900** *Hutchinson's Arch. Surg.* XI. 209 Local cyanosis, although less common than local roses, is often quite as definitely in association with the too liberal use of alcoholic beverages.

transf. **1799** W. BUTTER (*title*), On the Venereal Rose.

11. † **a.** A rose-coloured wine. *Obs.*$^{-1}$

c **1460** J. RUSSELL *Bk. Nurture* 115 þerfore a pipe of coloure de rose þou kepe..; the reboyle to Rakke to þe lies of þe rose, þat shalle be his amendynge.

b. A rose-coloured or reddish variety of apple, pear, potato, etc.

1676 WORLIDGE *Cyder* (1691) 179 Alexandrian Roses I have not heard of. **1822** LOUDON *Encycl. Gard.* §1434 Dessert Pears... Rose, Thorny Rose. **1860** R. HOGG *Fruit Manual* 214 (Pears) *Summer Rose* (Epine Rose; Ognonet; Rose; Thorny Rose).—Fruit medium sized, oblate. **1888** *Daily News* 10 Sept. 2/7 Potatoes... Early Roses are the freest from blight.

IV. A figure or representation of the flower.

12. a. *Her.* A conventional design or figure representing this flower, usu. consisting of five lobes or petals.

13.. *Sir Beues* 3786 Here armes were riale of siȝt..; þe chaumpe of gold ful faire tolede, Portraid al wiþ rosen rede. **1459** *Paston Lett.* I. 469 My maister helmet in the myddes, with rede roses of my maisters armes. *a* **1550** in Baring-Gould & Twigge *W. Armory* (1898) 6 Boscowne: Ermyn a rose gul[es]. **1562** LEGH *Armory* 170 b, The fielde Geules, a Rose. Or. **1610** GUILLIM *Her.* III. ix, A rose gules Barbed and Seeded. **1675** [see CHEVRON *sb.*[1] 2]. **1708** J. CHAMBERLAYNE *St. Gt. Brit.* (1710) 57 The White Rose was the ancient bearing of the House of York, and the Red Rose that of Lancaster. **1722** A. NISBET *Syst. Her.* I. 379 Crest, an Hand issuing from a Cloud, and reaching down a Garland of Roses proper. **1864** [see BARBED *ppl. a.*[1] 3]. **1868** CUSSANS *Her.* (1893) 105.

b. A representation of the flower in needlework or painting. Also printed on fabric, woven in a carpet, etc.

1434 *E.E. Wills* 102 A whit couerkell with roses & flourdeluces. **1466** *Records* in *Archaeologia* (1887) L. 1. 38 Item j vestment of blewe chamlet, enbraudet w[t] whyte Roses. **1542** *Ibid.* 46 Item a vestement blwe Chamlet w[t] rosis. *a* **1548** HALL *Chron., Hen. VIII*, 73 b, All the Copes and Vestementes wer.. poudered with redde Roses purled with fine golde. **1897** *Sears, Roebuck Catal.* 290/1 Imported Paris Organdies.. with colored roses, buds and leaves. **1955** R. P. JHABVALA *To whom she Will* xv. 102 She was very fine now in a pink silk kamiz with blue roses on it. **1964** C. MACKENZIE *My Life & Times* III. 13 The Surgeon's lessons [in putting] were given along the corridor.., the hole being one of the roses in the Brussels carpet. **1972** *Country Life* 6 Jan. 25/3 Many quilts [were] named after roses.. Cactus Rose, Desert Rose, Rose of Sharon, Rambling Rose (whose other name was Old Maid's Ramble).

c. As an emblem of the houses of York or Lancaster, or of England. Cf. 6. Also as an emblem of the rival sporting teams of Yorkshire and Lancashire.

[*a* **1475** G. CHASTELLAIN *Chron.* Œuvres 1864 IV. 155 Un chevalier.. portant le nouvel collier du roy, la rose blanche et le soleil.] **15..** *Sir Andrew Barton* in *Surtees Misc.* (1890) 67 When he saw the Lion of England out blaisse, The sterne [*read* streemers] and the roose about his eye. **1853** HUMPHREYS *Coin-coll. Man.* II. 463 The twopenny pieces [of Jas. I] have a rose on one side, and a thistle on the other, crowned. **1907** F. THOMPSON in *Athenæum* 23 Nov. 654/3 It is little I repair to the matches of the Southron folk, Though the red roses crest the caps, I know. **1954** A. W. LEDBROKE *Lancashire County Cricket* xxv. 244 The bank holiday Battle of the Roses provides.. the nearest approach to the atmosphere of Sydney or Melbourne—when the crowds are orderly. But there is more than tenseness to a match between Lancashire and Yorkshire.

† **13.** A kind of cup or bowl. *Obs. rare.*

1444 *Test. Ebor.* (Surtees) II. 112, I wil y[t] William my sone haue.. ij standing cuppis of a sute gilt, ij coveryd pecis callid rosis. **1459** *Paston Lett.* I. 469 Item, j. paire basyns, with gilt verges, and j. rose, with my maisters helmet enameled and gilt in the myddes.

14. a. A rose-shaped design of metal or other material; an imitation of a rose in metal-work, etc.

1459 *Paston Lett.* I. 469 Item, j. stondynge cuppe gilt, with j. kever, with j. rose in the toppe, weiyng xl unces. **1488** *Acc. Ld. High Treas. Scot.* I. 82 Item, ane vche of gold maid like ane ros of diamantis. *c* **1520** *Mem. Ripon* (Surtees) III. 206 Item pro ij rygges, roses, & key plattes, 16*d.* **1578** in Feuillerat *Revels Q. Eliz.* (1908) 293 For xxx[tie] dozen of Roases mowlded & guylded. **1611** COTGR., *Rosette*,.. the Rose at the end of the cheeke of a bitt, next to the reynes. **1655** MARQ. WORCESTER *Cent. Inv.* §70 A Key with a Rose-turning pipe and two Roses, pierced through endwise through the Bitt thereof. **1661** BOYLE *Style of Script.* (1675) 173 In roses of diamonds, the Jewels oftentimes keep us from minding the flower and the enamel. **1706** STEVENS *Sp. Dict.*, *Roséta*, a little Rose, such as is made upon curious Works in Silver, or the like to cover a rivet, or for such use. **1806** A. HUNTER *Culina* 54 Put on the upper crust with a hole in the middle, to be covered with a rose of the same paste. **1879** *Encycl. Brit.* IX. 254/2 The fish..are..packed with the heads outwards in hogs-heads, and a 'rose' of fish in the middle to keep the level.

b. ***golden rose***, an ornament of wrought gold, blessed by the pope on the fourth Sunday in Lent, and usually sent as a mark of favour to some notable Roman Catholic personage, city, or church. Also *ellipt.*

The ornament has been of various forms; the design finally adopted is a thorny branch with several leaves and flowers, surmounted by a principal rose—all of pure gold.

1560 DAUS tr. *Sleidane's Comm.* 50 The golden Rose, which the Pope had lately consecrated, he sendeth to Henry the eyghte. **1617** MORYSON *Itin.* I. 149 Vessels of gold and silver, Roses hallowed by the Pope (which these Princes hold for rich presents). **1696** PHILLIPS s.v. *Rose.* **1845** S. AUSTEN *Ranke's Hist. Ref.* I. 435 The legate..was at length prevailed upon to deliver to the elector the golden rose which had been entrusted to him. **1884** *Cath. Dict.* (1897) 413/1 Among the recipients of the rose have been.. Napoleon III, and Isabella II of Spain.

c. The card of a mariner's compass (now usu. ***compass rose***) or of a barometer; more generally, a circular pattern showing the points of the compass. Cf. WIND-ROSE 2.

1527 R. THORNE in Hakluyt *Voy.* (1589) 257 The roses of the windes or pointes of the compasse. **1594** R. ASHLEY tr. *Loys le Roy* 111 The inuention of the Sea-mans compas, consisting of a Rose, and a needle of steele. **1795** C. HUTTON *Math. Dict.* II. 373/1 The 32 lines in the rose or card of the compass. **1919** S. F. CARD *Air Navigation* ii. 11 When the chart or map contains the true and magnetic 'roses'..the conversion can be done by putting a straight edge from the centre to the true direction. **1937** M. COVARRUBIAS *Island of Bali* iv. 76 The Nawa Sangga, the magic rose of the winds, the Balinese cardinal directions. *Ibid.* ix. 280 A chicken with feathers of five colours was placed in the centre [of an offering], next to a small circular Rose of the Winds made of rice dyed in the eight different colours of the cardinal directions. **1943** [see PELORUS]. **1951** N. MONSARRAT *Cruel Sea* I. 13 The ship was his: he was to commission and to command H.M.S. *Compass Rose*... *Compass Rose* was nothing out of the ordinary; it had to be a flower name because she was one of the new Flower Class corvettes. **1960** E. L. DELMAR-MORGAN *Cruising Yacht Equipment & Navigation* ii. 30 The dial or, as we call it these days, Pelorus or dummy compass rose, was the navigator's instrument and was in use for many centuries long before it was given magnets and mounted on a pivot.

d. A knot or ornamental device inserted in the sound-hole or the table of certain stringed instruments of the guitar type.

1676 MACE *Mus. Monum.* 49 The Knot or Rose in the Lute Belly, would be little and smoothly cut. **1728** CHAMBERS *Cycl.* s.v. *Lute*, In the middle of the Table is a Rose or Passage for the Sound. **1883** *Grove's Dict. Music* III. 161/1 In the harpsichord and spinet there was usually but one soundhole with its rose.

e. *Arch.* = ROSETTE *sb.* 2.

1728 CHAMBERS *Cycl.* s.v. *Abacus*, Some Ornament, as a Rose, or other Flower,..in the middle of each Arch. *Ibid.* s.v. *Capital*, Twisting round towards the middle of the Face of the Capital, and terminating in the Rose. **1842** GWILT *Encycl. Arch.* s.v., The centre of the face of the abacus in the Corinthian capital is decorated with what is called a rose.

f. *Building.* A circular, sometimes ornamental mounting through which the shaft of a door-handle may pass.

1857 *Commissioners of Patents' Jrnl.* 16 Jan. 41 Patent 37, January 5, 1857, Andrew Brundish: for mounting knobs, and in constructing and mounting roses for locks, latches and other such like fastenings. **1902** J. T. REA *How to Estimate* xi. 217, 2-in cast brass knobs with solid necks, cast rose and escutcheon. **1945** N. W. KAY in R. Greenhalgh *Building Repairs* iv. 110/1 A knob may be held by its rose and be free to swivel in it. **1957** M. T. TELLING in *Pract. Building & Decorating* II. iii. 154 To cover holes for keys and spindles, escutcheon plates and roses are fixed with small brass nails or screws.

g. A circular mounting on a ceiling through which the wiring of an electric light passes; = *ceiling rose* s.v. CEILING *vbl. sb.* 7.

1889 *Illustr. Official Jrnl.* (Patent Office) 24 July 616/1 Improvements in roses for supporting electric lamps. **1944** A. C. GREENWOOD *Pract. Electr. Wiring & Contracting* v. 152/2 Covers of roses should screw down with an easy motion. **1967** *Times Rev. Industry* June 74/3 Electric fittings (e.g. switches, roses, lampholders, fuseboxes, junction boxes). **1977** L. R. WAKELIN *Home Electr. Repairs* 24/2 A neutral conductor must be taken to the light rose.

h. A figure in *Sword-dancing* (see quots.).

1913 C. J. SHARP *Sword Dances N. England* III. ii. 106 The leader should call 'Nut', a bar or two before the end of a strain, so that the Rose may be begun at the commencement of the next strain... The dancers leave the Nut in the hands of No. 1 and fall back into line facing the audience, returning to the original Rose position. **1933** E. K. CHAMBERS *Eng. Folk-Play* 129 There is a persistent figure..in which each dancer presses the hilt of his sword under the point of his neighbour's so as to mesh the swords together..in a form which may be anything from a pentagon to an octagon... This is called the Lock or Nut, which probably means Knot, and at Whitby the Rose. **1971** D. KENNEDY *North Skelton Sword-Dance* 9 *The Rose.* The leader raises the Lock in his right hand and all dance round clockwise.

i. An award (differentiated as the ***Golden***, ***Silver***, and ***Bronze Rose***) presented at the International Television Festival at Montreux for successful light entertainment programmes.

1961 *Times* 27 May 7/5 The B.B.C.'s 'Black and White Minstrel Show' won the main prize tonight in the Montreux international television festival's Golden Rose contest. The jury awarded the first prize of a 'golden rose' and 10,000 Swiss francs..to the B.B.C. show. **1964** *Ann. Reg. 1963* 457 The C.B.S. spectacular, *Julie and Carol at Carnegie Hall*, won the top prize for light entertainment—the Golden Rose—at the Montreux International Television Festival in May. **1972** *Times* 5 May 5/3 Britain carried off both the Golden Rose and the Silver Rose television awards here today for the best television light entertainment shows. **1975** *Times* 5 May 4 *The Goodies*, the BBC entry, has won the Silver Rose award at the television festival at Montreux... Italy won the contest and the Golden Rose... The Bronze Rose..went to Austrian television.

15. a. An ornamental knot of ribbon or other material in the shape of a rose, worn upon a shoe-front. Cf. ROSETTE *sb.* 1.

1602 SHAKS. *Ham.* III. ii. 288 Two Prouinciall Roses on my rac'd Shooes. **1650** T. B[AYLEY] *Worcester's Apoph.* 39 Silk stockings with roses and Garters suitable. **1774** *Westm. Mag.* II. 484 Undress...—Coloured Slippers, and small Roses. **1808** SCOTT *Marm.* VI. Introd. 42 The heir, with roses in his shoes, That night might village partner choose. *transf.* **1609** B. JONSON *Sil. Woman* II. i, All the yellow doublets, and great roses i' the towne will bee there.

b. A rosette worn on a cap or hat, *spec.* that of a clergyman. Also *Comb.*

1779 *Gentl. Mag.* XLIX. 190 How long has the Rose been part of the clerical habit? *Ibid.* 349 The rose, I apprehend, is peculiar to the English Clergy. **1796** PEGGE *Anonym.* (1809) 147 The Clergyman wears a rose in his hat. **1825–9** MRS. SHERWOOD *Lady of Manor* IV. xxviii. 402 A rose of lace lay on the table, it had been taken from the cap of Theophilus. **1837** SYD. SMITH *Let. Singleton* Wks. 1859 II. 277/1 The Bishop of Winchester was a Curate; almost every rose-and-shovelman has been a Curate in his time.

16. †a. A kind of star-fish. *Obs.*$^{-1}$

1668 CHARLETON *Onomast.* 59 *Stellæ marinæ*,..Star-fishes, Roses.

b. (See quot. 1881.)

c **1879** L. WRIGHT *Pigeon Keeper* 166 We see even now occasionally an all but circular 'rose' instead of a frill in some Owls. *Ibid.*, The round,..amply developed 'rose-frill'. **1881** J. C. LYELL *Fancy Pigeons* 184 The rose is formed by the feathers on the crown of the head growing out from the centre in regular form.

c. A formation suggestive of a rose; the circular protuberance round an animal's horn at its rise from the forehead; a growth around the eyes of certain birds.

1880 DAWKINS *Early Man* iv. 88 This most remarkable antler, characterised by the absence of a burr or rose. **1890** *Jrnl. Microsc. Sci.* XXX. 90 It [tetronerythrin] was first found in the so-called 'roses' around the eyes of certain birds by Dr. Wurm.

d. The rounded end of a potato, esp. one being used for sprouting.

1851 H. STEPHENS *Bk. of Farm* (ed. 2) I. 630/2 The sets should be cut with a sharp knife, be pretty large in size, and taken from the rose or crown end of the tubers. **1976** *Country Life* 5 Feb. 305/4 Seed tubers of earlies [*sc.* potatoes] will be stood 'rose' or blunt end uppermost..to sprout.

e. *Geol.* = ROCK-ROSE 5, ROSETTE 5 e.

1911 *Proc. U.S. Nat. Museum* XXXVIII. 19 In Rockenberg occur well-developed rosettes or 'roses', often uniting in extensive groups. **1954** R. L. PARKER tr. *Niggli's Rocks & Mineral Deposits* vii. 274 (*caption*) Rosette-like arrangement of tabular crystals of hematite, known as iron roses. **1955** F. H. POUGH *Field Guide Rocks & Minerals* (ed. 2) II. 182 [Barite] is found in perfect imitative 'roses' of a red-brown color and sandy texture near Norman, Oklahoma. **1973** A. F. L. DEESON et al. *Collector's Encycl. Rocks & Minerals* 122/3 Gypsum 'roses' occur in many areas where gypsum has been dissolved in percolating waters which are drawn to the surface by capillary action and evaporate.

17. A perforated metal cap or nozzle attached to the spout of a watering-pot, etc., to distribute water in fine sprays; also, a perforated plate fitted on the orifice of a water-pipe, etc., to serve as a sprinkler or strainer.

1706 LONDON & WISE *Retir'd Gard'ner* I. 251 This Vessel imitates exactly the Rain.., by shedding the Water it contains out of a Thousand little Holes that are in the Rose of it. **1756** C. LUCAS *Ess. Waters* I. 230 Pieces of tubes..with a rose, like that of a gardener's watering pot. **1846** A. YOUNG *Naut. Dict.*, *Rose*, or *Strainer*, a plate of copper or lead perforated with small holes, sometimes placed upon the heel of a pump to prevent any thing being sucked in which might choke the pump. **1892** *Phot. Ann.* II. 48 Use a rose on the tap for washing plates.

fig. **1861** A. WYNTER *Social Bees* 276 His whole body became in a few minutes one rose, from which the water previously imbibed transuded.

18. *ellipt.* **a.** = ROSE DIAMOND.

1678 *Lond. Gaz.* No. 1330/4 Four Roses, cut in India, weighing 3 carrets ¼, being good stones. **1703** *Ibid.* No. 3930/4 One [Ring] with 13 Diamonds set in a Lozenge, Roses. **1786** H. WALPOLE in Leslie & Taylor *Sir J. Reynolds* (1865) II. 480, 4600 diamonds, all roses. **1851–3** *Tomlinson's Cycl. Arts* (1867) I. 307/2 The brilliant and the rose lose in cutting and polishing somewhat less than half their weight. **1898** WIGLEY & STANSBIE *Art Goldsm.* 132 Roses are often cut with fewer facets than are shown in the illustration.

b. A rose-window.

1823 PUGIN *Gothic Archit.* Gloss. s.v. *Rose-window*, The gable-windows of many of the English churches may boldly claim a comparison with the finest roses. **1851** LONGF. *Gold. Leg.* iii. *Cathedral*, See, too, the Rose, above the western portal.., The perfect flower of Gothic loveliness! **1905** BOND *Gothic Archit.* 517 In France the rose was first put under a circular arch.

c. = ROSE-NAIL.

1851–3 *Tomlinson's Cycl. Arts* (1867) II. 206 A thinner sort, called *fine rose*, are used in pine and other soft woods. **1884** *Encycl. Brit.* XVII. 165/2 Thus we have the names tacks, sprigs, and brads for very small nails; rose, clasp, and clout, according to the form of head.

V. *attrib.* and *Comb.*

19. Attributive: **a.** In general uses, as ***rose-amateur***, ***-bloom***, ***-blossom***, ***-bough***, ***-breath***, ***-culture***, ***-dust***, ***-flake***, ***-flower***, ***-form***, ***-fruit***, ***-grower***, ***-petal***, ***-prickle***, ***-scent***, ***-stem***, ***-time***, ***-tribe***.

1837 RIVERS *Rose Amateur's G.* 19 Hybrid Provence roses are very robust and..useful to the *rose amateur. **1820** KEATS *Eve St. Agnes* xxv, *Rose-bloom fell on her hands, together prest. **1929** C. DAY LEWIS *Transitional Poem* II. 34 Heedless if truth maintain On the rose-bloom her station? **1878** SWINBURNE *Forsaken Garden* in *Poems & Ballads* (Ser. 2) 29 The foam-flowers endure when the *rose-blossoms wither. **1927** E. SITWELL *Rustic Elegies* 37 Beneath the twisted *rose-boughs of the heat. **1892** W. B. YEATS *Countess Kathleen* 93 Ah, leave me still A little space for the *rose-breath to fill. **1846** T. RIVERS *Rose Amateur's Guide* (ed. 4) II. 131 Modern gardening has made rapid strides in *rose culture. **1924** E. SITWELL *Sleeping Beauty* xiii. 44, I shall be but thin *rose-dust, He will be cold, unkind. **1951** L. MACNEICE tr. *Goethe's Faust* 294 That noble soul which gave me right of seizure They've filched by throwing rose-dust in my eyes. **1876** G. M. HOPKINS *Wreck of Deutschland* xxii, in *Poems* (1967) 58 Stigma, signal, cinquefoil token For lettering of the lamb's fleece, ruddying of the *rose-flake. *c* **1330** *Arth. & Merl.* 3061 (Kölbing), Violet & *rose flour Woneþ þan in maidens bour. *a* **1400** *Stockh. Med. MS.* i. 57 in *Anglia* XVIII. 296 Take an hand-full of rose-flowris. **1751** MEAD *Wks.* (1775) 372 To rub it often with vinegar, in which rose-flowers..have been infused. **1846** LINDLEY *Veget. Kingd.* 564 Perpendicular section of a Rose-flower. **1917** D. H. LAWRENCE *Look! We have come Through!* 60 To me it seems the seed is just left over From the red rose-flower's fiery transience. **1731** MILLER *Gard. Dict.* s.v. *Opulus*, The Flowers consist of one Leaf, which expands in a circular *Rose Form. **1917** D. H. LAWRENCE *Look! We have come Through!* 60 How will you have it?—the rose is all in all, Or the ripe *rose-fruits of the luscious fall? *a* **1963** S. PLATH *Uncoll. Poems* (1965) 9 First frost, and I walk among the rose-fruit. **1857** *Rose-grower [see *rose show*, sense 23 a below]. **1864** HIBBERD *Rose Bk.* 95 The rose grower must never confound together the idea of a climbing with that of a pillar rose. **1920** G. SAINTSBURY *Notes on Cellar-Bk.* iv. 57 A friend of mine..had some official business with one of the great rose-growers in the neighbourhood of London. **1960** R. CAMPBELL tr. J.-M. A. Gamo in *Coll. Poems* III. 85 Silken spectrum-blaze Which an eternity shot through with rays Showers with a thousand rose-petals of light. ? **1803** COLERIDGE *Recoll. Love* iv, As when a mother doth explore The *rose-mark on her long-lost child. **1850** OGILVIE, *Rose-bug*, a winged insect..which feeds on *rose-petals. **1611** BIBLE *Eccl.* xxiv. 14, I was exalted..as a *rose-plant in Iericho. **1822** LOUDON *Encycl. Gard.* (1824) 892 Rose-plants should be a year in pots..when it is intended to force them. **1944** E. SITWELL *Green Song* I Remember the *rose-prickles of bright paws Though we shall mate no more. **1601** HOLLAND *Pliny* II. 93 As for *Rose-rewes, the earth ought to be digged and opened about the roots. **1859** GEO. ELIOT *Adam Bede* I. xv. 279 The delicate *rose-scent of his hair. **1885** A. EDWARDES *Girton Girl* I. v. 111 Tintajeux Manoir with its..faded drawing-room, its half lights, its rose scents. **1960** S. PLATH *Colossus* 36 Thorns on the bloody *rose-stem. **1632** SHERWOOD, A *rose-still, *rosaire.* **1675** WOOLLEY *Gentlew. Comp.* 150 Then put it in a Rose-Still, with slices of Lemon-peel. *c* **1440** *Alph. Tales* 324 Þis man was passand ferd & compuncte, for als mekull as it was not *rose tyme. **1850** MRS. GASKELL *Let.* 26 Apr. (1966) 111 The Shaens begged me to come in rose-time to them. **1912** E. POUND *Ripostes* 33 Thou keep'st thy rose-leaf Till the rose-time will be over. **1924** E. SITWELL *Sleeping Beauty* v. 26 If none of the *rose-tribe can survive The snow, then how can our poppet live? **1837** RIVERS *Rose Amateur's G.* 82 It sold for a high price.., when first sent forth to the *rose world.

b. In the sense of 'used for cultivating roses', 'overgrown, overspread with roses', 'bordered with roses', as ***rose-alley***, ***-arbour***, ***-bank***, ***-bed***, ***-bower***, ***-farm***, ***-garden***, ***-hedge***, ***-land***, ***-walk***, ***†-yard***, etc.

1934 E. M. WRIGHT *Story of Joseph Wright* viii. 232 We formed a torchlight procession down the *rose-alley, and buried Mary's playfellow in her own plot of garden. **1580** HOLLYBAND *Treas. Fr. Tong*, *Vn Rosier*, a *Rose arbour. **1977** *Belfast Tel.* 22 Feb. 9/6 The rose arbor in Belfast's Botanical Gardens provides little shelter from the rain. **1591** PERCIVALL *Sp. Dict.*, *Rosal*, a *rosebanke. *a* **1849** BEDDOES *Wolfram's Dirge*, On a rose-bank to lie dreaming With folded eye. *a* **1100** in Napier *O.E. Glosses* xxiii. 8 *Rosetis*, *rosbeddum. **1610** GUILLIM *Her.* III. vii, Knights..whose worth must be tried in the field, not vnder a Rose-bed or in garden-plot. **1812** CRABBE *Tales* xiii. 418 Save where the pine..on the rose-beds threw a softening shade. **1883** R. W. DIXON *Mano* I. vi. 16 Winding walks along *rose-borders led. **1825** SCOTT *Talism.* xxiii, The song of the nightingale will sooner blight the *rose-bower she loves. **1876** O. WILDE *Kottabos* II. x. 269 Roses are white in the rose-bower. **1975** J. O'FAOLAIN *Women in Wall* iii. 46 'Please... Let me do it.' .. 'Tell,' he went to sit down in a rose bower, 'about the Call.' **1970** T. HUGHES *Crow* 31 The woodpecker drummed clear of the rotovator and the *rose-farm. **1535** COVERDALE *Ecclus.* xxxix. 13 Florish as the *rose garden, synge a songe of prayse. **1848** THACKERAY *Van. Fair* xxxix, Poor Lady Crawley's rose-garden became the dreariest wilderness. **1910** *Granta* 5 Feb. 201 It is said..that he keeps poultry and a cow, plays simple tunes on a pan pipe, bathes every evening at sunset, and takes all his meals in a rose garden. **1936** T. S. ELIOT *Burnt Norton* in *Coll. Poems 1909–35* 185 The door we never opened Into the rose-garden. **1867** A. J. EVANS *St. Elmo* xxi. 292 A Cherokee *rose-hedge is not more thickly set with thorns than a literary career with grievous, vexatious, tormenting disappointments. **1856** *N. & Q.* 2nd Ser. II. 72/2 [He] has a perfectly green rose in flower in his new *rose-house. **1929** R. BRIDGES *Testament of Beauty* III. 88 In the New World far Pasadena's *roseland. **1708** KERSEY, *Rosere*, a *Rose-plat. *c* **1765** T. FLLOYD *Tartarian T.* (1785) 55/2 Gulpenhe has placed a large dyke at the end of the *rose-walk. **1483** *Cath. Angl.* 311/2 A *Rose ȝerde, *rosetum.* **1530** PALSGR. 264/1 Roseyarde where roses growe, *rosier.*

c. In sense 'made of roses', as ***rose-crown***, ***-crants***, ***-garland***, ***-wreath***.

c **1375** *Sc. Leg. Saints* i. (*Peter*) 708 With lely and rose-cronis in hand. *c* **1384** CHAUCER *H. Fame* I. 135, I sawgh.. on hir hede..Hir Rose garlonde, white and rede. **1477–9** *Rec. St. Mary at Hill* (1905) 81 For Rose-garlondis and wodrove-garlondis on Saynt Barnebes day. **1513** DOUGLAS *Æneis* v. vii. 8 For the victor a bull, and all his heid Of..rois garlandis reid Buskit full weill. *a* **1634** CHAPMAN *Alphonsus* Plays 1873 III. 271 When thou hadst stoln her daintie rose Corance And pluck'd the flow'r of her virginitie. **1643** A. ROSS *Mel Helic.* 106 A Rose-crown was more fit For thee, and Thorns for this of mine.

d. In sense 'made from roses', 'flavoured or scented with essence of roses', as ***rose-camphor, -honey, -oil, -powder, -sugar***, etc.

1552 TURNER *Herbal* II. uiij, Rose oyle conforteth the same partes that the stilled water of roses doth. **1620** VENNER *Via Recta* vii. 129 The best way to eate them is with Rose-sugar. **1648** HEXHAM II, *Roosen-honigh*, rose-hony. **1657** T. REEVE *God's Plea for Nineveh* 123 Lawn, musks, civets, rosepowders, gessamy butter, complexion waters. **1725** *Fam. Dict.* s.v. *Ointment*, To have Rose Ointment, Take..fresh red Roses pounded [etc.]. **1839** URE *Dict. Arts* 1149 The most fashionable toilet soaps are, the rose, the *bouquet* [etc.]. **1841** *Penny Cycl.* XX. 160/1 A dirty oil results, which on standing for some time forms several distinct layers, the upper one of which is sold as rose-oil. **1855** OGILVIE *Suppl.*, *Rose-camphor*, one of the two volatile oils composing attar of roses. **1883** *Cassell's Dict. Cookery* 771/2 Rose Brandy, for flavouring Cakes and Puddings. *Ibid.* 772/1 Rose tea in some complaints is a useful tonic.

e. In sense 'designed or made in the form of a rose', as ***rose-band, -boss, -knot, -lashing***, etc.

1510 *York Fabric Rolls* (Surtees) 263 Also yt is ordeynd rose bandes and fillettes and other carrifying wark. **1611** FLORIO, *Rosette*, little Roses; also Rose purles or worke in bone-lace. **1769** FALCONER *Dict. Marine* (1780) s.v. *Knot*, The principal of these are the diamond-knot, the rose-knot, the wall-knot. **1841** R. H. DANA *Seaman's Man.* 13 The foot-ropes..should be..seized to the boom by a rose-seizing through an eye-splice. **1842** FRANCIS *Dict. Arts & Sci.*, *Rose Ornament*, a common ornament in cornices, around apertures, and in other parts of Gothic architecture. **1867** SMYTH *Sailor's Word-bk.*, *Rose-Lashing*, this lashing is middled, and passed opposite ways; when finished, the ends appear as if coiled round the crossings. **1873** TRISTRAM *Moab* xi. 199 On the flat wall itself runs a large pattern like a continued W, with a large rose boss between each angle. **1947** A. RANSOME *Great Northern?* i. 20 A hand..took hold of the rose knot worked in the end of the bit of rope that dangled from the clapper of a small ship's bell.

20. a. Attrib., in sense 'having the colour of a rose', passing into *adj.*, rosy, roseate, rose-coloured.

1816 BYRON *Ch. Har.* III. xcix, The snows above The very Glaciers have his colours caught, And sun-set into rose-hues sees them wrought. **1830** TENNYSON *Adeline* 7 Thy rose-lips and full blue eyes Take the heart from out my breast. **1850** THACKERAY *Pendennis* xxi[i], She was ordinarily pale, with a faint rose tinge in her cheeks. **1858** W. BAGEHOT in *National Rev.* Apr. 455 The harsh outlines of poverty will not bear the artificial rose-tint. **1870** F. KILVERT *Diary* 13 Mar. (1938) I. 56 The mountain clad in deep snow and tinged with rose colour... As the sun set a lovely rose tint stole over the snowy mountains. **1876** *Contemp. Rev.* June 48 The roselight of the morning sun. **1906** W. DE LA MARE *Poems* 124 From the day, The rose-light ebbed away. **1916** JOYCE *Portrait of Artist* (1969) v. 218 The dull white light spread itself east and west, covering the world, covering the roselight in his heart. **1922** C. MACKENZIE *Altar Steps* xxvii. 315 A set [of vestments] in old rose damask for mid-Lent. **1929** BLUNDEN *Near & Far* 47 And sounding works whose smoke lifts proud Through towers of force to yon rose-cloud. **1930** E. POUND *XXX Cantos* ii. 13 The coral face under wave-tinge, Rose-paleness under water-shift. **1932** BLUNDEN *Face of England* 85 And that far rose-reflection burns On the dusk water far too red. **1949** DYLAN THOMAS *Let.* 13 Oct. (1966) 328, I have the hot and cold rose-flush comings and goings after elderberry wine last night. **1965** F. SARGESON *Mem. Peon* iv. 82, I held her hand to examine its dusky rose-bloom.

b. Used predicatively.

1833 TENNYSON *Pal. of Art* 169 The lights, rose, amber, emerald, blue. **1871** J. HAY *Pike County Ball.* (1880) 54 A sky as glad as the smile of Heaven Blushed rose o'er the minster-glades.

c. With names of colours: cf. ROSE-PINK, -RED.

1812 SHAW *Gen. Zool.* VIII. II. 434 Green Parrakeet, with rose-blue head. **1845** *Beck's Florist* 232 Among the best were Ivery's Prince Albert [petunia], rose-crimson. **1882** *Garden* 15 July 58/2 Flowers large, semi-double, delicate rose-lilac. **1916** E. & O. SITWELL *20th-Cent. Harlequinade* 23 Rose-silver haze. **1928** *T. Eaton & Co. Catal.* Spring & Summer 1/1 Felt hat... Colors Sand; Rose-Beige; Gobelin Blue. **1930** E. POUND *XXX Cantos* xvii. 78 Stone trees, white and rose-white in the darkness. **1932** H. CRANE *Let.* 13 Feb. (1965) 399 Wine glasses of a smoky rose-purple transparency that set one dreaming. **1949** E. POUND *Pisan Cantos* lxxvi. 43 And within the crystal, went up swift as Thetis In colour rose-blue before sunset And carmine and amber. **1953** W. DE LA MARE *O Lovely England* 33 Rose-green the light where a hermit knelt, praying, His solitude verdurous, vision-like, still. **1966** C. MACKENZIE *My Life & Times* V. 21 Their rose-brown flesh burnt by the sun. **1977** *Horse & Hound* 10 June 41/3 (Advt.), 14 hands 1 in outstanding quality rose grey gelding, 4 yrs.

21. Parasynthetic: **a.** With reference to colour, as ***rose-bellied, -enamelled, -faced, -fingered, -finned, -flecked, -flushed, -footed, -impearled, -lit, -shadowed, -shot, -spotted, -stained, -veiled***, etc.

1809 SHAW *Gen. Zool.* VII. 377 **Rose-bellied crow.* *a* **1586** SIDNEY *Astr. & Stella* Sonn. XCIX, That sweete aire which is Morne's messenger, with *rose-enameld skies. **1826** DISRAELI *Viv. Grey* VI. ii, Rays of living fire flame over the rose-enamelled East. **1820** SHELLEY *Prometh. Unb.* I. 321 Golden-sandalled feet, that glow..Like *rose-ensanguined ivory. **1847** WEBSTER, **Rose-faced.* **1884** TENNYSON *Becket* Prol., The rosefaced minion of the King. **1920** BLUNDEN *Waggoner* 20 The *rose-finned roach and bluish bream. **1599** T. M[OUFET] *Silkwormes* 11 *Rose-fingred Dame no sooner had put out Nights twinckling fires. **1838** W. MAGINN *Homeric Ball.* (1850) 25 Until the rose-fingered queen of day Sprang from the dawn. **1965** E. BISHOP *Questions of Travel* 25 Hastily, all alone, a glistening armadillo left the scene, *rose-flecked, head down, tail down. **1913** C. MACKENZIE *Sinister St.* I. I. vi. 86 Over a red wall hung down the branch of a plum tree, loaded with creamy ovals of fruit, already *rose-flushed with summer. **1942** E. SITWELL *Street Songs* 31 Then, who knows *Rose-footed swan from snow, or girl from rose. **1812** SHAW *Gen. Zool.* VIII. II. 434 **Rose-headed parrakeet*... Green Parrakeet, with rose-blue head, black throat and collar. **1830** TENNYSON *Arab. Nts.* 140 Flowing beneath her *rose-hued zone. **1917** G. FRANKAU *City of Fear* 25 *Rose-impearled o'er a wonder-world Glowed the last of the sunset-gleams. **1910** A. BENNETT *Clayhanger* IV. iii. 479 He left the crowded and *rose-lit dining-room early. **1867** G. MEREDITH *Vittoria* I. i. 12 The gleam of the distant *rose-shadowed snows. **1957** R. CAMPBELL *Coll. Poems* II. 109 Freckled like rose-shot apricots. **1952** A. G. L. HELLYER *Sanders' Encycl. Gardening* (ed. 22) 73 Sepals with a white, *rose-spotted, ribbon-like appendage. *a* **1973** J. R. R. TOLKIEN *Silmarillion* (1977) xxiv. 250 Like a white bird, shining, *rose-stained in the sunset. **1875** M. COLLINS *Blacksmith & Sch.* I. 274 The eye is aroused by the beauty of her *rose-tinged cheek. **1952** R. CAMPBELL tr. *Baudelaire's Poems* 46 The balcony beneath a *rose-veiled sky.

b. With reference to form, as ***rose-flowered, -headed, -leaved, -shaped***, etc.

1703 in *Dampier's Voy.* (1729) III. 456 *Rose podded Rest-harrow*... Grows a Foot and half high. **1753** *Chambers' Cycl.* Suppl. s.v. *Pæonia*, The dwarf rose-flowered winter piony. **1805** R. W. DICKSON *Pract. Agric.* II. 597 Preventing the beans from becoming what is termed rose-headed. **1839–52** BAILEY *Festus* 189 By the bloom wherein thou dwellest, As in a rose-leaved nest. *c* **1850** *Rudim. Nav.* (Weale) 135 Boat-nails..are..generally rose-headed. **1887** BENTLEY *Man. Bot.* (ed. 5) 495 The true German Geranium Oil or Oil of Rose-leaved Geranium. **1933** E. SITWELL *Five Variations* 4 And many a rose-shaped heart must lie beneath The maps on strawberry leaves. **1945** C. L. B. HUBBARD *Observer's Bk. Dogs* 87 Ears rose-shaped.

22. a. Similative, as ***rose-ambrosial, -bright, -carved, -cut, -fragrant, frail, -fresh, -full, -heavy, -hot, -pale, -soft, -solemn, -towering***, etc.

1936 L. B. LYON *Bright Feather Fading* 54 Alas, no rose-ambrosial world men share Who fall from love and falling cease to be. **1839–48** BAILEY *Festus* XIV. 138, I could sit and set that rose-bright smile, Until it seem to grow immortal there. **1805** SCOTT *Last Minstrel* VI. xxiii, Blaz'd every rose-carved buttress fair. **1773** GOLDSM. *She Stoops to Conq.* III, A parcel of old-fashioned rose and table-cut things. **1927** JOYCE *Pomes Penyeach* 3 Frail the white rose and frail are Her hands that gave... Rosefrail and fair..My blueveined child. **1890** 'R. BOLDREWOOD' *Col. Reformer* (1891) 336 Antonia, cool, glistening, delicately robed, and rose-fresh. **1932** E. SITWELL *Bath* iv. 68 The rose-full, rose-soft, hooped dresses are wet with dew. **1895** W. B. YEATS in *Sat. Rev.* 2 Nov. 573/1 The rose-heavy twilight. **1922** D. H. LAWRENCE in *English Rev.* Feb. 101 The living steel In rose-hot tips, and flakes of rose-pale snow. **1951** W. DE LA MARE *Winged Chariot* 50 That rose-pale cheek, loose hair, and eager tongue. *c* **1860** J. R. LOWELL *Power of Sound* (1896) 9 So sang she, feeling in her bosom stir The rose-soft palms of that first murderer. **1916** JOYCE *Portrait of Artist* (1969) iv. 155 It was only..within rosesoft stuffs that he dared to conceive of the soul or body of a woman moving with tender life. **1932** [see *rose-full* above]. **1935** W. EMPSON *Poems* 22 Snow-puppy curves, rose-solemn dado band. **1609** J. DAVIES (Heref.) *Holy Roode* cxxv, Yet Rose-sweet is the ingresse to these Briers. **1949** S. SPENDER *Edge of Being* 16 To wake on peaks at dawn among the inhuman Rose-towering dreams. **1725** *Fam. Dict.* s.v. *Pears*, When they serve them up, they range them handsomely upon a Dish Roseways. *Ibid.* s.v. *Rasberry-Bush*, Five Leaves rose-wise. **1887** G. MEREDITH *Ball. & Poems* 155 This body stood rose-warm in the courts.

b. Instrumental, as ***rose-clad, rose-circled, -clustered, -covered, -crowned, -embowered, -entangled, -festooned, -garlanded, -lamped, -wreathed***, etc.

1975 G. EWART *Be my Guest!* I. 32 Or I see Gertrude waving from a cottage with a very attractive *rose-circled door. **1869** S. R. HOLE *Bk. about Roses* 142 Now we have passed through the *Rose-clad walls—through the Rose-wreathed colonnades and courts of the outer palace. **1971** B. MALAMUD *Tenants* 50 This flower-massed, *rose-clustered, floating island. **1849–50** ALISON *Hist. Europe* IV. xxvi. §71. 615 The *rose-covered fields of Fayoum..were..visited. **1598** SYLVESTER *Du Bartas* II. ii. II. 542 May still raigns, and *rose-crown'd Zephyrus..makes the green trees to buss. **1849** M. ARNOLD *Mycerinus* 93 Here came the king, holding high feast, at morn Rose-crown'd. **1910** R. BROOKE *Hill* in *Cambr. Rev.* XXXII. 181/1 We shall go down with unreluctant tread Rose-crowned into the darkness! **1918** G. FRANKAU *One of Them* 257 Screen me..From my sub-conscious Freudian profanity, That *rose-embowered private sitting-room. **1962** I. MURDOCH *Unofficial Rose* v. xxvi. 249 He wandered towards her through a *rose-entangled forest. **1929** M. LOWRY *Let.* 13 Mar. (1967) 5 Of course it was..merely a *rose-festooned illusion. **1917** A. WAUGH *Loom of Youth* IV. viii. 322 He had done what he set out to do, he would step *rose-garlanded out of the lighted room, in the flush of his success. **1868** MORRIS *Earthly Par.* (1870) I. I. 405 So far..That she a *rose-hedged garden could behold. **1925** C. DAY LEWIS *Beechen Vigil* 24 Like a queen of fable In *rose-lamped gardens. **1591** SYLVESTER *Du Bartas* I. v. 1029 An extream Fever..wanly did displace The *Rose-mixt-Lillies in her lovely face. **1818** SHELLEY *Rosal. & Helen* 820 His cheek became..fair, As *rose-o'er-shadowed lilies are. **1847** H. W. LONGFELLOW *Evangeline* II. iii. 108 *Rose-wreathed, vine-encircled, a broad and spacious veranda. **1869** [see *rose-clad*]. **1924** R. GRAVES *Mock Beggar Hall* 61 While incense burns beside the rose-wreathed couch.

c. With vbl. sbs. and ppl. adjs., as ***rose-bearing, -diffusing, gathering***, etc.

1756 DYER *Fleece* I. 470 A drear abode! from rose diffusing hours. **1863** S. R. HOLE in *Gardeners' Ann.* 109 One of the chief charms of rose-growing is the frequent..arrival of New Roses. **1869** —— *Bk. about Roses* 87 The teaching of those Rose-loving brothers over the Border. **1882** MISS BRADDON *Mt. Royal* ii, He had never paused in his rose-gathering.

23. a. Special combs.: **rose-berry**, a hip; **rose bit**, a countersink bit having a conical head with a number of radial cutting teeth that meet at the tip; †**rose blanket** *U.S.*, a blanket decorated with a rose motif; **rose box**, (*a*) a box for holding roses; (*b*) *Naut.* (see quot. 1976); **rose-burner**, = ROSETTE *sb.* 5 c; **rose-catarrh**, *U.S.*, rose-cold or rose-fever; **rose-cistern**, one receiving the rose of a pump; **rose-clinch**, a kind of nail (see quot. 1875); also *attrib.*; **rose-cold**, *U.S.*, a kind of fever resembling hay-fever; †**rose-cross** [F. *rose-croix*], = ROSICRUCIAN *a.*; †**rose-cup**, = sense 13; **rose diagram**, a diagram in which values of a quantity in various directions are shown graphically according to compass bearing, in the manner of a wind-rose; **rose-draught**, a drink made from or with the essence of roses; **rose-encrinite**, a rose-like fossil crinoid; **rose-eyed**, *a.* (see PIN-EYED *a.*); **rose-fever**, *U.S.*, the rose-cold; **rose-gall**, an excrescence produced on the dog-rose, etc., by certain insects; †**rose-garland**, a form of still; **rose gold**, an alloy of gold with a little copper, having a reddish tinge; **rose hatband**, a hatband decorated with a rosette; **rose head**, (*a*) a kind of nail (see quot. 1835); (*b*) an instrument used in dentistry; (*c*) = ROSE *sb.* 17; (*d*) a spreading top on an upright rain-pipe; **rose-hip**, = *rose-berry*; also = HIP *sb.*[2]; **rose hip syrup**, a syrup containing extract of rose hips, taken as a source of vitamin C; **rose-hip tea**, a beverage made from rose-hips and hot water; **rose-iron**, an iron-glance or hæmatite, occurring in rosette-like groups of tabular crystal found in Switzerland (*Cassell's Encycl. Dict.*); **rose-jar**, a jar for holding dried rose petals; †**rose-key**, a key in which the end of the hollow stem is of a rose-shaped pattern; †**rose-knight**, ? a Rosicrucian; **rose-lathe**, a rose-engine; **rose-nozzle**, = sense 17; †**rose-parley**, pleasant conversation or discourse; **rose-pear** (see quot. 1708); †**rose-pence**, coin of low value, bearing the figure of a rose, issued for currency in Ireland; **rose-petal**, used *attrib.* of various preserves, wine, etc., made from rose petals; †**rose-pipe**, the shaft or stem of a rose-key; **rose-point**, point-lace exhibiting the raised pattern of a conventional rose; **rose-pump**, one having a rose at the shaft-end; **rose-ring** (see quot. and sense 18 a); **rose show**, an exhibition mainly or entirely of roses; **rose-spot**, *Path.*, a red spot characteristic of certain fevers; **rose-sprinkler**, = sense 17; †**rose-stone** (see quot.); **Rose Sunday** *obs.* exc. *Hist.*, the fourth Sunday in Lent; **rose-temple**, a belvedere over which climbing roses may be trained; **rose-wine** = ROSOLIO; **rose-work**, work produced by or turned in a rose-engine; the process by which this work is produced; also *attrib.*

1856 CAPERN *Poems* 76, I track'd her where hawthorn and *roseberries burn To vie with the holly's rich glow. **1868** *Rep. U.S. Comm. Agric.* (1869) 178 Among them [*sc.* small fruits] may be noted red and black currants,..and rose-berries,..the fruit of the *Rosa cinnamomea*. *c* **1921** D. H. LAWRENCE *Mr. Noon* iv, in *Mod. Lover* (1934) 224 Gilbert helped her to pick scarlet rose-berries, and black privet berries. **1846** HOLTZAPFFEL *Turning* II. 565 The *rose-bit..is..very much used for light finishing cuts, in brass, iron, and steel; the extremity is cylindrical,..and the end is cut into teeth like a countersink. **1858** *Min. Proc. Inst. Civil Engineers* XVII. 178 A 'rose-bit'is..employed, to remove the intervening metal. **1875** SIR T. SEATON *Fret Cutting* 70 A rose-bit is a conical piece of steel, cut into a coarse file, and used for sloping off the edges of the screw-holes, so that the screw-head may not project above the metal. There is another kind of rose-bit for wood-work. **1966** A. W. LEWIS *Gloss. Wood-working Terms* 7 The chief type [of countersink bit] is the 'rose' bit which has radial flutes which shave away the edge of the hole. **1759** *Newport* (Rhode Island) *Mercury* 26 June 3/2 Just imported by Simon Pease, jun..best *Rose Blankets. **1820** *Columbian Centinel* 8 Jan. 3/4 A great variety of Dry Goods:..Rose Blankets. **1863** S. R. HOLE in *Gardeners' Ann.* 5 *Rose-boxes and tubes are ordered from London. **1923** *Man. Seamanship* (Admiralty) II. xviii. 305 *Gear Boxes*... Suction and delivery hoses with bends and rose boxes. **1972** L. M. HARRIS *Introd. Deepwater Floating Drilling Operations* App. B 238 Bilge drainage should be checked... The rose boxes and strainer plates are clear, clean and sound. **1976** *Oxf. Compan. Ships & Sea* 722/2 *Rose Box*, the name given to the strainer at the end of the suction pipe of a bilge pump... It is also widely known, particularly in yachts, as a strum box. **1879** WEBSTER *Suppl.* s.v. *Burner*, *Rose-burner. **1887** *Cassell's Encycl. Dict.*, *Rose-catarrh. **1778** PRYCE *Min. Cornub.* 170 A pump, that conveys the water from the *rose cistern to the tye pump. **1851–3** *Tomlinson's Cycl. Arts* (1867) II. 206 *Rose-clench is a sort much used in ship and boat-building. **1875** Knight *Dict. Mech.* 1506/1 Rose-clinch nail; rose head, square point, either clinched or riveted down on a washer or rove. **1879** Webster *Suppl.*, *Rose-cold. **1880** *Libr. Univ. Knowl.* (N.Y.) VII. 377 Two forms [of hay-fever], one called the rose cold or June cold, corresponding to the affection known in England. **1627** Drayton *Agincourt*, etc. 216 The *Rose-crosse knowledge which is much like that, A Tarrying-iron for fooles to labour at. **1438** *Will of Matilda Lane* (Somerset Ho.), My salt saler and my ij *Rose cowppes be delyvered to William Kirketon and to John Kirketon. **1938** *Bull. Geol. Soc. Amer.* XLIX. 1887 The orientation of the long axes are [*sic*] plotted as a conventional '*rose' diagram. **1956** *Q. Jrnl. Geol. Soc.* CXII. 71 A rose diagram is made showing the directions, in 10-degree classes, of the long axes of the stones. **1971** I. G. Gass et al. *Understanding Earth* xiii. 175 (*caption*) Rose diagram representing readings of dip directions of the cross laminae of either linguoid ripples or barchan dunes. **1849** *Blackw. Mag.* Jan. 40 One might as well take a *rose-draught for the plague. **1882** Ogilvie, *Rhodocrinus*,.. the *rose-encrinites. **1884** J. E. Taylor *Sagacity & Mor. Plants* 79 Common people have long distinguished such Primroses under the names of 'pin-eyed' and '*Rose-eyed'. **1851** E. S. Wortley *Trav.* III. 22 This complaint [*sc.* hay-asthma] is known in the United States, and is called there, *rose-fever. **1879** Webster *Suppl.*, *Hay-fever*.. is also called.. hay-cold, rose-cold, and rose-fever. **1884** M. Mackenzie *Dis. Throat & Nose* II. 306 In America the affection is sometimes called 'rose fever'. **1753** *Chambers' Cycl.* Suppl., **Rose galls*,.. certain unnatural productions of the *rosa sylvestris*, or dog rose. **1822** Loudon *Encycl. Gard.* (1824) 893 Some.. are attacked by the *Cynips rosæ*, which, by puncturing the bark, occasions the production of rose-galls. **1527** Andrew *Brunswyke's Distyll. Waters* b iv, Ye shall dystylle in common styllatoryes named *Rose-garlandys. **1708** *Lond. Gaz.* No. 4408/4 Lost.., a Gold Watch,.. with a *Rose-Gold Chain. **1901** Rose gold [see karat]. **1948** A. Selwyn *Retail Jeweller's Handbk.* (ed. 3) x. 137 Red gold had a revival when Paris jewellers re-introduced it in jewellery in 1937–38, and other countries followed. Pale shades are called pink or rose gold. **1708** *Lond. Gaz.* No. 5464/3 A *Rose Hat-band about his Hat. **1742** W. Ellis *Mod. Husbandman* July xxiv. 128 A Barrel.. that has an Arm of Tin fix'd in with a *Rose-head, that the Water may run on their Roots. **1835** *Partington's Brit. Cycl., Arts & Sci.* I. 862/2 To form the heads of horse-nails, called *rose heads. **1859** J. Tomes *Dental Surg.* 344 The rose-head is very serviceable in reducing to a cylindrical form the ragged opening of a small cavity. **1883** *Specif. Alnwick & Cornhill Railway* 51 Four-inch rain-pipes are to be provided, with proper roseheads. **1857** A. Gray *First Less. Bot.* (1866) 125 A *Rose-hip may be likened to a strawberry turned inside out. **1915** *Chambers's Jrnl.* 20 Mar. 271/2 These [*sc.* plants for feeding pigs and fowls] were supplemented in the autumn by non-fattening foods, such as acorns.. and rose-hips. **1976** *Norwich Mercury* 17 Dec. 3/7 They [*sc.* bird paintings] include a greenfinch with rosehips. **1942** *Q. Jrnl. Pharmacy* XV. 314 During the winter of 1941–42 the Ministry of Health experimented with two new large-scale sources of the vitamin, black-currant purée and *rose hip syrup. **1972** J. Mann *Mrs. Knox's Profession* x. 82 Gripe water, rose hip syrup and everything else a baby could conceivably need. **1964** G. Hauser *Treasury of Secrets* v. 52 The pink *rose hip tea.. is the great favorite at the famous Bircher-Brenner Sanatorium in Switzerland. **1973** C. Bonington *Next Horizon* xii. 175 John and Dougal settled down to their meal of dried meat and nuts, followed by rose-hip tea. **1894** *Harper's Mag.* Jan. 310/1 A *rose-jar stood on one [table] in the corner. **1655** Marq. Worcester *Cent. Invent.* (1663) E 3 b, A *Rose Key. **1631** R. Bolton *Comf. Affl. Consc.* (1640) 266 Let.. all the Physitians in the World, even the *Rose-Knights, as they call themselves, lay all their heads together for the cure. **1855** Ogilvie *Suppl.*, *Rose-lathe. **1879** Goode *Anim. Res. & Fisheries U.S.* 247 *Rose-nozzles (for washing eggs). **1582** Stanyhurst *Æneis* ii. (Arb.) 62 Shee claspt my righthand, her sweet *rose parlye thus adding. **1611** Cotgr., *Poire d'eau rose*, the *Rose-Peare. **1708** Kersey, *Rose-pear*, a kind of Pear whose Pulp eats short, and is ripe in August and September. **1556** *Proclam.* 19 Sept. in *Tudor Proclam.* (1897), Their sayde Maiesties.. do will and commaunde that all *rose pence shall.. be no more receyued nor taken for lawefull.. monye, within thys their realme of England, or any other their domynyons excepte.. Irelande. **1935** H. Edib *Clown & his Daughter* xxxvi. 201 I've brought stuffed vine-leaves and *rose-petal jam, Tewfik. **1963** M. McCarthy *Group* i. 18 An Armenian restaurant in the twenties, where you got rose-petal jelly for dessert. **1968** J. Rathbone *Hand Out* vi. 36 His breakfast.. consisted of sour grey bread, white cheese, rose-petal syrup and tea. **1970** *Rose Ann.* 93 Pot-pourri and rose petal jam from well-loved old recipes.. are often made at home... Home-made rose-petal wine has a delicious taste. **1975** P. Somerville-Large *Couch of Earth* vii. 115 The waiter.. came over.. the napkin over his arm stained with rosepetal jam. **1977** *Times* 25 Nov. (Christmas Bk. Suppl.) p. xxx/4 Experimenting with rose petal oils to soften the skin. **1655** Marq. Worcester *Cent. Invent.* §44 To make a Key of a Chamber door, which to your sight hath its Wards and *Rose-pipe but Paper-thick. **1865** *Athenæum* No. 1944. 132 *Rose-point and pillow lace. **1882** Caulfeild & Saward *Dict. Needlewk.* 454/2 Spanish point, or Spanish Guipure à Bride, or Rose Point, is a Needle Lace. **1778** Pryce *Min. Cornub.* 170 Old fire engine *rose pumps. **1838** *Civil Eng. & Arch. Jrnl.* I. 139/1 And the diameters of the tie and rose lift pumps were 11 inches. **1705** *Lond. Gaz.* No. 4121/4 Lost,.. a *Rose Ring, with a.. Brilliant in the middle, set round with.. small Diamonds. **1857** *Florist* Apr. 122 A suggestion to Rose growers—amateurs and professionals:—why should we not have, near some central station (such as Rugby) A Grand National *Rose Show? **1978** *Lancashire Life* Sept. 40 The Lakeland Rose Show this year cost £25,000 to stage. **1888** Fagge & Pye-Smyth *Princ. & Pract. Med.* (ed. 2) I. 172 It is often impossible to say.. whether they are really *rose-spots or.. ordinary pimples. **1890** *Anthony's Photogr. Bulletin* III. 22 The rubber tubing over the washing tank was removed, and a *rose sprinkler attached to the faucet. **1698** Fryer *Acc. E. India & P.* 213 The Names of Rough Stones [*i.e.* diamonds]. A *Rose Stone, if round; if long, a Fossel. **1880** McClintock & Strong *Cycl. Bibl. Lit.* IX. 130 It is not known when the ceremony of consecrating the rose was introduced... The day is always the fourth Sunday in Lent, which is consequently known as '*Rose-Sunday'. **1891** tr. *Pastor's Hist. Popes* I. 220 Golden roses were bestowed each year on Laetare Sunday, hence called Rose Sunday. **1864** S. Hibberd *Rose Bk.* vi. 125 To form a simple *rose temple is a matter of no great difficulty. **1894** *Country Gentlemen's Catal.* 295/2 Rose Temple.. Price— £5. With Openings filled in to form a Summer House. Price—£7 5/-. **1852** in *Venerabile* (1930) Apr. 357 A good dinner and caffe after with beautiful *rose-wine. **1680** Moxon *Mech. Exerc.* xiv. 241 Of *Rose-work, &c. Rose-Work Turning, or Works of any other Figure, are performed.. after the same manner as Oval Work is made. **1815** J. Smith *Panorama Sci. & Art* I. 81 Watch-cases, snuff-boxes, and various sorts of trinkets, are sometimes formed by what is called rose-work.

b. In names of plants, flowers, etc.: **rose acacia**, a tree (*Robinia hispida*) having rose-coloured flowers; the American moss-locust; **rose box**, a plant of the genus *Cotoneaster* (*Cent. Dict.*); **rose-briar**, a rose-bush or rose-tree; † **rose elder**, the Guelder rose; **rose geranium**, a rose-scented species of geranium, *Pelargonium capitatum*, or *P. graveolens*, or one of several varieties of them; also, a perfume resembling the scent of these flowers; **rose gum**, a large gumtree, *Eucalyptus grandis*, found in eastern Australia; **rose laurel**, the oleander; **rose lichen**, a kind of lichen, *Parmelia kamtschadalis*, used for giving a perfume and rosy hue to the fabric in calico-printing; **rose lily, lupine** (see quots.); **rose mahogany**, an eastern Australian timber tree, *Dysoxylum fraserianum*, of the family Meliaceæ, or its fragrant reddish wood; **rose mallow**, (*a*) the hollyhock, *Althæa* (or *Malva*) *rosea*; (*b*) the genus *Hibiscus* of the N.O. *Malvaceæ*; a plant of this genus; **rose oak**, ? some Indian species of rhododendron; † **rose parsley**, a species of anemone, *A. hortensis*; **rose pea**, a species of garden pea cultivated in the 17th and 18th centuries; **rose plantain**, the name of several species of plantain (see quots.); **rose poppy**, the corn rose; † **rose ribwort**, the rose plantain; **rose snowball tree, tangle, tulip** (see quots.); **rose vine**, *U.S.*, a climbing rose; **rose-willow**, one of several species of salicaceous trees or shrubs, as *Salix helix*, *S. rosea*, or *S. purpurea*; **rose-withy** (see quot.). Also rose-apple, -bay, etc.

1819 *Pantologia* s.v. *Robinia*, *Robinia hispida*, *rose acacia, or robinia. **1852** Motley *Corr.* (1889) I. v. 129 The acacias (rose acacias) under my window.. are not yet leafless. **1598** Florio, *Rosaio*, *Rosaro*, a *rose bryer. **1840** Hor. Smith *Cromwell* I. 109 A coppice,.. matted with wild rose-briars. **1932** D. H. Lawrence *Last Poems* 178 Rose-leaves to bewilder the clever fools And rose-briars to strangle the machine. **1597** Gerarde *Herbal* 1237 The *Rose Elder groweth in gardens, and.. is called in Latine, *Sambucus rosea*, and *Sambucus aquatica*, being doubtlesse a kind of the .. water Elder. **1832** *Chambers's Edin. Jrnl.* 7 Apr. 76/2 Thorburn bought a *rose geranium, intending to ornament his shop. **1867** Augusta Wilson *Vashti* xxxiii, A few violets, mignonette, and one very luxuriant rose-geranium. **1885** Lady Brassey *In the Trades* 426 The rose-geranium is here [in the Bermudas] called the 'grave-yard geranium', probably from the fact that it is grown in all the churchyards on the island. **1890–1** *T. Eaton & Co. Catal.* Fall & Winter 42/2 Perfumes.. Italian violet, rose geranium, white heliotrope. **1939** L. MacNeice *Autumn Jrnl.* 69 Clouding The cooling water with rose geranium soap. **1964** C. Loewenfeld *Herb Gardening* ii. 171 Rose geranium is a shrubby plant with deeply cut and divided leaves and clusters of pink and lavender flowers. **1971** *Vogue* 15 Sept. 85/1 Bubble Bath in four fragrances—Lemon Verbena, English Fern, Rose Geranium and Lavender Blue. **1947** R. H. Anderson *Trees New South Wales* (ed. 2) 158 Flooded Gum or *Rose Gum (*Eucalyptus grandis*). A tall, frequently majestic tree. **1967** A. Rule *Forests Austral.* iii. 36 Species such as tallowwood and rose gum, occurring in the humid coastal forests of eastern Australia. **1548** Turner *Names Herbes* (E.D.S.) 56 *Nerion*.. maye be called in englishe Rose bay tree or *rose Laurel. **1870** Morris *Earthly Par.* III. iv. 110 The bright rose-laurels trembled in the air. **1840** Browning *Sordello* ii. 30 If he stopped to pick *Rose-lichen, or molest the leeches quick. **1831** M. Russell *Egypt* (1832) 488 The *rose-lily of the Nile, or the Egyptian bean, .. is the *nymphæa nelumbo* of Linnæus. **1731** Miller *Gard. Dict.* s.v. *Lupinus*, The *Rose Lupine. **1822** *Hortus Anglicus* II. 229 *L*[*upinus*] *Pilosus*. Rose Lupine... Corolla pale flesh-colour, standard red. **1929** W. D. Francis *Austral. Rain-Forest Trees* 185 *Dysoxylum fraserianum* Benth. Rose-wood, *Rose Mahogany. **1958** *N.Z. Timber Jrnl.* June 59/1 Rose mahogany.. resembles Honduras mahogany. **1965** *Austral. Encycl.* III. 319/2 One of the best-known and most abundant of these [trees] is the rose mahogany. *Ibid.*, Its dust, like that of rose mahogany, has an irritating effect on tender parts of the skin. **1731** Miller *Gard. Dict.*, *Malva rosea*: *Rose Mallow, or Hollyhock. **1857** A. Gray *First Less. Bot.* (1866) 115 A pollen-grain.. of Hibiscus or Rose-Mallow, studded with prickly points. **1879** E. Arnold *Lt. Asia* 43 Lower grew *rose-oaks and the great fir groves. **1548** Turner *Names Herbes* (E.D.S.) 13 Anemone groweth muche about Bon in Germany;.. it is called of the common herbaries *Herba venti*, it may be called in english *rose perseley. **1601** Holland *Pliny* II. 227 This Argemony aforesaid hath leaues like to Anemony, *i.* Rose Persly or Windfloure: jagged they be in maner of garden Parsly. **1629** J. Parkinson *Parad.* lii. 522 The Scottish or tufted Pease, which some call the *Rose Pease, is a good white Pease fit to be eaten. **1690** L. Hammond *Jrnl.* 2 Apr. in *Proc. Mass. Hist. Soc.* (1892) 2nd Ser. VII. 154 Wedensday, I planted my Rose pease. **1725** *Family Dict.* s.v. *Pease*, Tufted or Rose Pease, of two Sorts. **1726** B. Townsend *Compl. Seedsman* 5 The Rose Pea, or Crown Pea, brings a Bunch of Peasecods on the Top of the Plant, and no where else. **1629** Parkinson *Paradisi* 352 *Plantago Rosea*, *Rose Plantane. **1741** [see plantain[1] 1 b]. **1876** *Encycl. Brit.* IV. 120/2 The variety of Plantago media, called the Rose-plantain in gardens. **1648** Hexham ii, *Koren-rose*, *Rose-poppie, that growes in Corne. **1597** Gerarde *Herbal* 342 *Rose Ribwoort hath many broade and long leaues. **1852** G. W. Johnson *Cottage Gard. Dict.* 790/2 *Rose Snowball Tree, *Viburnum Opulus roseum*. **1846** Lindley *Veg. Kingdom* 23 *Ceramiaceæ*.—*Rosetangles... Seaweeds of a rose or purplish colour, seldom olive or violet. **1850** Ogilvie, **Rose-tulip*, a species of tulip, the *Tulipa rosea*. **1879** Tourgee *Fool's Errand* (1883) 36 A little verandah, over which clambers a *rose-vine still wreathed with buds and blossoms. **1597** Gerarde *Herbal* 1204 The *Rose Willow groweth vp likewise to the heighth and bignesse of a shrubbie tree;.. the branches are many, whereupon do growe very many twigs of a reddish colour. **1789** E. Darwin *Bot. Gard.* ii. i. 75 *note*, The scales of the ament in the *salix rosea*, rose-willow, grow into leaves. **1855** Miss Pratt *Flower. Pl.* V. 72 Rose Willow.. owes its name.. to certain rose-like expansions at the end of the branches. **1671** Skinner *Etym. Bot.*, *Rosy-withy, *vel* Rose-bay; Willow-herb.

c. *Ent.* In the names of insects which frequent and feed upon the rose: **rose-aphis**, the plant-louse *Aphis* (or *Siphonophora*) *rosea*; **rose-beetle, bug**, the rose-chafer or rose-fly; **rose-cutter bee** (see quot.); **rose-fly**, the rose-chafer; **rose gall-fly**, an insect which produces galls on rose-leaves; **rose-grub, -maggot**, a grub or maggot of a rose-infesting insect; **rose-hopper, rose leaf-hopper**, a greenish-yellow sucking insect, *Typhlocyba* (or *Edwardsiana*) *rosæ*, of the family Cicadellidæ, which attacks the foliage of roses, making the leaves pale and mottled; **rose-megachile**, a species of leaf-cutting insect (cf. *rose-cutter bee*); **rose plume**, a species of moth (see quot.); **rose sawfly**, a hymenopterous insect which lays its eggs in rose-leaves. Also rose-chafer.

1806 Shaw *Gen. Zool.* VI. i. 171 *Aphis Rosæ* or *Rose Aphis is very frequent during the summer months on the young shoots and buds of roses. **1783** Latham *Gen. Syn. Birds* II. i. 3 Buffon asserts their fondness for the *Rose Beetle [*scarabeus auratus*]. **1884** *Leisure Hour* Jan. 48/1 The most expensive beetles are the Cetonias, or Rose-beetles, of the Eastern Archipelago and Africa. **1800** *Massachusetts Spy* 1 Oct. 3/4 He suggests that the *Rose-bug is the pre-existing state of those worms. *a* **1817** Dwight *Trav. New Eng.*, etc. (1821) II. 398 An insect.. not unlike a rosebug in form, but in every respect handsomer. **1868** *Rep. U.S. Comm. Agric.* (1869) 87 The much-dreaded rose-bug, *Macrodactylus subspinosus*. **1916** W. P. Eaton *Idyl of Twin Fires* 207, I frequently pick rose bugs.. before breakfast, very early, when they are still sleepy. **1864–5** J. G. Wood *Homes without H.* viii. (1868) 177 These cells are made of rose-leaves, and are the work of the *Rose-cutter Bee (*Megachile Willoughbiella*). **1753** *Chambers' Cycl.* Suppl., **Rose-fly*,.. a peculiar species of fly found very frequently on rose bushes. **1855** Ogilvie *Suppl.*, Rose-fly. **1882** *Garden* 25 Nov. 469/1 Very nearly allied to the gall-flies of the Oak is the *Rose gall-fly. **1863** S. R. Hole in *Gardeners' Ann.* 17 When all looks green and healthful, he will be searching for that worm i' th' bud, the *rose grub. **1920** Wodehouse *Damsel in Distress* i. 10 The small, yellowish-white insect.. sometimes called a *rose-hopper. [**1852** T. W. Harris *Treat. Insects New England Injurious to Vegetation* (ed. 2) 199 There is another little leaf-hopper that.. lives upon the leaves of rose-bushes. *Ibid.* 511/2 Rose-bush leaf-hopper.] **1890** *Insect Life* II. 340 Original figures are given of.. the *Rose Leaf-hopper. **1939** Metcalf & Flint *Destructive & Useful Insects* (ed. 2) xvii. 585 The rose leafhopper and another common apple leafhopper, pass the winter in the egg stage in the bark. **1970** L. Hollis *Roses* x. 106 Rose leaf-hopper .. sucks the sap and causes mottling to appear on the leaves. **1882** *Garden* 27 May 368 *Rose maggots are unusually plentiful. **1868** tr. *Figuier's Insect World* (1892) 366 *Rose Megachile (*Megachile centuncularis*). **1832** J. Rennie *Consp. Butterfl. & M.* 231 The *Rose Plume (*Pterophorus rhododactylus*, Fabricius) appears in gardens, about roses. **1840** Hereman *Gardener's Libr.* II. 169 *Zaraca Fasciata*, Red-bodied *Rose Saw-Fly.

24. a. Special collocations in sense 20: **rose-aniline**, = rosaniline; **rose breccia** (see quot. and breccia); **rose-comb**, a flesh-coloured caruncle lying flat upon the head of certain fowls, as in the Sebright cock; also, a bird bearing a comb of this kind; also *attrib.*; hence *rose-combed* adj.; **rose copper** (see quot. 1706); **rose-ear**, a dog's ear so hanging as to expose the flesh-coloured inner side; **rose fish**, a scorpænoid fish, *esp.* the Norway haddock, *Sebastes marinus*, or the red-fish; **rose-garnet**, *Min.*, a rose-red variety of garnet found in Mexico (*Encycl. Dict.*); **rose glass**, a rose-coloured kind of glass made in France (Knight); **rose-madder**, the rose colour produced by madder dye or pigment; † **rose madrepore** (see quot.); **rose manganese**, *Min.*, rhodonite; **rose-mole**, a mark or mole of a reddish colour; **rose opal**, *Min.*, a rose-hued opal occurring with quincite (*Encycl. Dict.*); **rose pearl** (see quot.); **rose quartz**, *Min.*, a translucent variety of quartz, of a rose-red colour; **rose sparus**, a Mediterranean fish (see quot.); **rose wing**, (*a*) a species of moth with rosy wings; (*b*) a variety of pigeon.

1879 Webster *Suppl.*, *Rose-aniline. **1839** *Civil Eng. & Arch. Jrnl.* II. 453/2 *Antique *Rose Breccia*. Clear red ground with little spots of rose and black, others white. **1850** D. J. Browne *Amer. Poultry Yard* 52 The fleshy *rose comb of the golden Hamburgh terminating in a sharp point behind..is seen in no other variety of fowl. **1889** *Cent. Dict.* s.v. *Comb*, A rose comb..is best illustrated in the Hamburg fowls. **1927** HALDANE & HUXLEY *Animal Biol.* ii. 68 The original pure-bred rose-comb stock gives nothing but rose-combs. *Ibid.* 69 The offspring will clearly be blue Andalusian.., with rose-combs. **1972** *Country Life* 16 Nov. 1265/1 Of the 11 [bantams] two were cockerels of rosecomb blood... One of the two rosecombs was supposed to be a hen. **1885** *Bazaar* 30 Mar. 1265 Black *rosecombed bantams, bred from noted prize winners. **1683** MOXON *Mech. Exerc., Printing* xvii. ¶1 *Rose Copper is commonly accounted the softest. **1706** PHILLIPS (ed. Kersey), *Rose-Copper*, a Copper melted several times, and separated from its gross and earthy Parts. **1839** URE *Dict. Arts* 823 The reverberatory furnace generally employed..for refining rose copper. **1883** G. STABLES *Our Friend the Dog* vii. 61 **Rose-ear.*—In this ear the tip turns downwards and backwards, and the inner side is exposed. **1731** R. HALE *Jrnl.* 18 June in *Essex Inst. Hist. Coll.* (1906) XLII. 223 Wee spy'd the Fin of a Whale..& Supposing it to be a *Rose fish, ran forward to see it. **1855** OGILVIE *Suppl.*, Rose-fish. **1888** GOODE *Amer. Fishes* 257 The Rose-fish, *Sebastes marinus*, is conspicuous among cold-water fishes by its brilliant scarlet color. **1947** *Richmond* (Va.) *Times-Dispatch* 4 May B15/2 Boston showed a two-month catch of rosefish. **1975** *Globe & Mail* (Toronto) 9 Aug. 8/3 The Russians.. pioneered in earlier years..such harvests as the rosefish catch off Labrador. **1886** H. C. STANDAGE *Artists' Man. Pigments* v. 52 *Madder Lakes* (Madder Carmine.., Lake or *Rose Madder). **1895** *Montgomery Ward Catal.* Spring & Summer 252/3 Winsor & Newton's Oil Colors..Pink Madder, Rose Madder. **1902** *Encycl. Brit.* XXXI. 773/1 Amongst the former [*sc.* natural colouring matters] may be named..rose-madder and the madder-lakes from the alizarin and allied bodies derived from the root of the ordinary madder plant *Rubia tinctorum*. **1933** H. NICOLSON *Diary* 16 Mar. (1966) 143 They [*sc.* the Rocky Mountains] are rose-madder and blue. **1799** SHAW *Naturalist's Misc.* X. pl. 383 *Rose Madrepore... This is one of the most elegant of the ramified Madrepores, being, when recent, of a beautiful rose-color. **1856** DANA *Rudim. Treat. Min.* 72 Rhodonite (Manganese spar; *Rose manganese) is of a beautiful rose colour, inclining sometimes to violet. **1877** G. M. HOPKINS *Poems* (1967) 69 Glory be to God for dappled things—..For *rose-moles all in stipple upon trout that swim. **1872** L. P. MEREDITH *Teeth* 233 '*Rose Pearl'. This romantic name is given to a base of comparatively recent introduction..intended as a substitute for continuous gum. **1819** BAKEWELL *Introd. Min.* II. 241 *Rose-quartz. **1844** *Civil Eng. & Arch. Jrnl.* VII. 77/2 Red granite, hornblende and rose quartz,..being exceedingly abundant. **1803** SHAW *Gen. Zool.* IV. II. 407 **Rose sparus*... Size and shape of a Perch: colour most beautiful rose-red. **1832** J. RENNIE *Consp. Butterfl. & M.* 46 The *Rose Wing (*Callimorpha rosea*, Latreille) appears [at] the end of June and beginning of July. c**1879** L. WRIGHT *Pigeon Keeper* x. 127 In the neighbourhood of Birmingham many fanciers prefer the Mottle..with no other marking than the mottled shoulder: these are often called Rosewings.

b. In names of birds: **rose cockatoo**, the rose-breasted cockatoo; **rose-finch**, a small European or Asian finch belonging to the genus *Carpodacus*, the males of which have red or pink plumage; **rose fly-catcher**, an American rose-coloured fly-catching warbler, as *Cardellina rubra* or *C. rubrifrons* (*Cent. Dict.*); so **rose fly-catching warbler**; **rose linnet, lintie**, (*a*) the red-breasted linnet; (*b*) the redpole; **rose ouzel**, the rose-coloured ouzel; **rose parrakeet**, = NONPAREIL 5 b (*Encycl. Dict.* 1886, s.v. *Parrakeet*); **rose pastor**, the rose ouzel; **rose pigeon** (see quot.); **rose starling**, the rose-coloured ouzel; **rose tanager, warbler** (see quots.).

1899 W. T. GREENE *Cage-birds* 78 The *Rose, or Rosy-breasted Cockatoo is a common Australian species, that is often palmed off on the unwary as a 'Grey Parrot'. **1863** T. C. JERDON *Birds India* II. 399 The *Rose-finch is found as a cold weather visitant throughout the greater part of India. **1890** E. W. OATES *Fauna Brit. India: Birds* II. 212 The genus *Propasser* belongs to the Rose-finches, the males of which are characterized..by rose-coloured plumage. **1953** D. A. BANNERMAN *Birds Brit. Isles* I. 175 The eastern races of the rosefinch also winter in India. **1884** COUES *N. Amer. Birds* 314 *Cardellina*,..*Rose Fly-Catching Warblers. **1825** JAMIESON, **Rose-lintie*, the red-breasted linnet. **1827** FLEMING *Brit. Anim.* 85 *Fringilla Linaria*, Rose Linnet. **1876** SMILES *Sc. Nat.* xiii. 260 The Reed Warbler, the Rose Linnet, the Twite..bred in suitable localities round the loch. **1831** RENNIE *Montagu's Ornith. Dict.* 436 *Rose ouzel (*Pastor roseus*). **1887** A. C. SMITH *Birds Wilts.* 214 In England it [the Rose-coloured Pastor] has been styled the 'Rose Ouzel'. **1841** SELBY in *Proc. Berw. Nat. Club* I. 253 *Rose-pastor, killed at Tweedmouth. **1819** *Shaw's Gen. Zool.* XI. I. 42 *Rose pigeon (*Columba miniata*)..; the under parts of the body of a hoary red. **1857** *Zoologist* XV. 5669 A young *rose-starling flew..into the room. **1884** COUES *N. Amer. Birds* 318 *P*[*yranga*] *æstiva*... *Rose Tanager. Summer Red-Bird. **1889** *Cent. Dict.* s.v. *Cardellina*, *C. rubra* is the *rose warbler, entirely red;..found in Texas and southward.

rosé (ˈrəʊzeɪ, ‖roze), *sb.*² (*a.*²) [*ellipt.* for F. *vin rosé* pink wine.] **1.** A wine that is light red or pink in colour.

1897 A. BEARDSLEY *Let.* 17 May (1970) 320, I have just vomited up the meals of the last two or three days. You see your Saint Marceau (royal rosé) has been avenged. **1932** E. HEMINGWAY *Death in Afternoon* 491 *Valdepenas* is.. excellent in both white and rosée [*sic.*]. **1951** E. DAVID *French Country Cooking* 26 Rosés of Anjou and Tavel. **1959** *News Chron.* 9 Dec. 6/6 It says of a Portuguese Rosé: '..Pale pink but sparkling'. **1960** *House & Garden* June 118/3 A Vin Rosé from the Côte du Rhône will cost you about 8s and a Rosé from Anjou a little more. **1974** *Guardian* 24 Jan. 13/5 True rosé is made from black grapes when the skins are left in the vat for the first one to three days of fermentation. *Ibid.* 13/6 The rosé makers can adjust acidity by early or late picking.

2. *attrib.* or as *adj.* Of a wine: that is a *vin rosé*; light red or pink in colour. Also *transf.*

1959 *Good Food Guide* 34 Rosé and white Bordeaux, 10/6. *Ibid.* 199 About three dozen wines, beginning with white and rosé ordinaires at 12/6 (oddly, no red). **1960** *Harper's Bazaar* Apr. 115/2 Add 1 bottle dry *rosé* wine. **1967** A. LICHINE *Encycl. Wines* 417/2 Not to be forgotten are the rosé wines of Portugal. **1974** *Harrods Christmas Catal.* 14 Ostrich feather boa..shades of mandarin/rosé £36. **1977** *Times* 12 Feb. 7/2 Pastry, rosé meat, rough-cut pâté and lambent juices.

rose (rəʊz), *v.*¹ [f. ROSE *sb.*; in sense 4 after F. *roser.*]

†**1.** *intr.* To blossom like a rose. *Obs.*⁻¹

The text has *ryseth*, but the rime requires *roseth*.

14.. LYDG. *Goodly Ballad* in Thynne *Chaucer* (1532) 234 b, Myn herte welkeneth thus sone, anon it roseth; Now hotte, nowe colde, and efte in feruence.

2. a. *trans.* To colour like a rose; to make rosy. Usually in *pa. pple.*

1610 G. FLETCHER *Christ's Vict.* I. xvli, Ros'd all in lively crimsin ar thy cheeks. **1614** SYLVESTER *Bethulia's Rescue* IV. 372 Her ruddy round Cheeks seem'd to be composed Of Roses Lillied, or of Lillies Rosed. **1773** *Gentl. Mag.* XLIII. 512 When once set free again,..We can be ros'd and lilly'd in a minute. **1847** TENNYSON *Princ.* vi. 324 She turn'd; the very nape of her white neck Was rosed with indignation. **1876** T. HARDY *Ethelberta* xxxi, Picotee's face was rosed over with the brilliance of some excitement.

b. *intr.* To become rosy; to blush. *rare*⁻¹.

1922 HARDY *Late Lyrics* 22 You grew elate, And rosed, as maidens can, For a brief span.

3. *trans.* To perfume with rose-scent.

1875 TENNYSON *Q. Mary* III. v, It shall be all my study for one hour To rose and lavender my horsiness.

4. To treat (wool, etc.) with a chemical mixture in order to impart a rosy tint.

1839 URE *Dict. Arts* 791 The wool is then removed and washed. It must be rosed the following day.

rose, *v.*² *dial.* (See quots. and RUSE *v.*)

1825 J. JENNINGS *Dial. W. Eng.*, *To Rose*, to drop out from the pod, or other seed vessel, when the seeds are over-ripe. **1847** HALLIW. s.v., When the upper part of a quarry or well falls in, it is said *to rose in*.

rose, pa. t. RISE *v.*; obs. f. ROOSE.

†ˈ**roseac**, *a. Obs.*⁻¹ In 7 roseack. [f. L. *rose-us* + -AC.] Rose-like, rosy.

1638 BRATHWAIT *Barnabees Jrnl.* IV. (1818) 173 Lips I relish richly roseack, Purely nectar and ambroseack.

†**roseager**. *Sc. Obs.* [? Misuse of *rosager*, var. of ROSAKER.] (See quot.)

1684 SYMSON *Galloway* in *Macfarlane's Geogr. Collect.* (S.H.S.) II. 103 Their Beir is commonly very oatie, and in some places mixt with darnel, which they call Roseager. *Ibid.*, This Roseager being narcotick occasions strangers to find fault with our ale.

roseaker: see ROSAKER.

roseal (ˈrəʊzɪəl), *a.* Now *arch.* Also 6–7 roseall, rosiall, 7 rosial. [f. L. *rose-us* + -AL¹, or from ROSE *sb.* + -IAL.]

1. = ROSEATE *a.* 1.

α. **1531** ELYOT *Gov.* II. xii, Beholding the rosiall colour, which was wont to be in his visage, tourned in to sallowe. **1595** *Blanchardine* (1890) 220 Seazing vpon the rosiall lips of his royall Queene. **1620** *Swetnam Arraigned* (1880) 25 Then I must blame you, Ladie, you doe ill, To blast those Rosiall blossomes. **1636** DAVENANT *Wits* Wks. (1673) 187 The Stones are Rosial and Of the white Rock.

β. **1587** M. GROVE *Pelops & Hipp.* (1878) 44 She whose roseall hue was staynde and hyd on euery cheeke. a**1592** GREENE *Jas. IV*, v. iii, The Roseall crosse is spred within thy field, A signe of peace. **1607** DEKKER *Whore of Babylon* Wks. 1873 II. 209 By that blest flower Vpon whose roseal stalke our peace does grow. **1622** PEACHAM *Compl. Gent.* (1661) 164 Sibilla Agrippa is to be drawn in a Roseall garment, a woman in years. **1747** *Gentl. Mag.* 242 Far in the roseal east, Aurora's seat. **1893** F. THOMPSON *Poems* 69 Child-angels, from your wings Fall the roseal hoverings..On the cheeks of Viola.

2. = ROSEATE *a.* 2.

1577–87 HOLINSHED *Chron.* I. 92/1 Cast vpon his sacred toome the roseall garlands gaie. **1893** F. THOMPSON *Poems* 59 They took the roseal chaplet up.

3. = ROSEATE *a.* 3.

a**1601** ? MARSTON *Pasquil & Kath.* II. 135, I did but softly sip The Roseall juice of your reuiuing breath. **1652** CRASHAW *Carmen Deo Nostro, Prayer*, The rich & roseall spring of those rare sweets.

rose-alger: see ROSALGER.

rose-apple. [f. ROSE *sb.* + APPLE *sb.*]

†**1.** A kind of apple having rose-coloured flesh.

1626 BACON *Sylva* §510 Few Fruits are coloured Red within: The Queen-apple is: and another apple, called the Rose-apple. **1693** EVELYN *De la Quint. Compl. Gard.* I. 126 The Rose-Apple extremely resembles the *Apis* in all its outside.

2. a. A small tree of the genus *Eugenia* (esp. *E. Jambos*, *E. malaccensis*, and *E. aquea*), extensively grown in the tropics for its beautiful foliage and fruit. **b.** The edible, sweet-scented fruit of this tree, used for making preserves, etc.

1790 W. BECKFORD *Descr. Acct. Jamaica* II. 190 The orange, the rose-apple, the papa..and other productions. **1812** [see JAMBO c]. **1830** LINDLEY *Nat. Syst. Bot.* 65 The balsamic odour of the eastern fruits called the Jamrosade and the Rose Apple. **1871** KINGSLEY *At Last* xvi, That with leaves like a great myrtle, and bright flesh-coloured fruit, [is] a Malacca-apple, or perhaps a Rose-apple. **1885** LADY BRASSEY *The Trades* 323 The islands also produce custard-apples, bread-fruit, rose-apples. **1975** I. & A. MANCINELLI tr. *Bianchini & Corbetta's Fruits of Earth* 168 The rose apple is about the size and color of an apricot, with one to three seeds inside.

3. *Austr.* The Queensland or sweet plum, *Owenia cerasifera*.

1889 MAIDEN *Useful Native Pl.* 49.

rose-a-ruby. Also 7 rosarubie. [App. f. ROSE *sb.* and RUBY *sb.*] The pheasant's-eye, *Adonis autumnalis*.

1597 GERARDE *Herbal* 310 Our London women do call it [Adonis flower] Rosearubie. **1629** PARKINSON *Parad.* 293 Some of our English Gentlewomen call it Rosarubie: we vsually call it Adonis flower. **1671** SKINNER *Etym. Bot.*, Rose a Ruby, *Flos Adonis Ruber*. **1753** *Chambers' Cycl.* Suppl. s.v. *Adonis*, There are three varieties of this plant [*sc.* Adonis], commonly called, 1. The common red bird's eye, or rose a ruby [etc.]. **1864** PRIOR *Plant-n.* 192.

roseate (ˈrəʊzɪət), *a.* Also 6–7 roseat, 7 rosiat. [f. L. *rose-us* + -ATE².]

1. a. Having the pink or light crimson hue of roses; rose-coloured, rose-red, rosy.

1589 LODGE *Scillaes Metam.* (Hunterian Cl.) 20 So maist thou..knit thy temples with a roseat twist. **1600** *Eng. Helicon* T j, The rich adorned rayes of roseate rising morne. **1725** POPE *Odyss.* IV. 784 The morn reveals the roseate East. **1794** MRS. RADCLIFFE *Myst. Udolpho* xxxv, The setting-rays tinged their snowy summits with a roseate hue. **1820** SHELLEY *Prometh. Unb.* II. i. 25 Through yon peaks of cloud-like snow The roseate sunlight quivers. **1874** SYMONDS *Sk. Italy & Greece* (1898) I. 133 The roseate whiteness of ridged snow on Alps.

Comb. **1830** *Encycl. Metrop.* (1845) XXI. 305/2 Chest and belly roseate red. **1839** DE LA BECHE *Rep. Geol. Cornw.* xv. 502 Among the innumerable varieties of elvans..we may notice that which is roseate-tinted.

b. In names of birds, as ***roseate spoonbill, tern, cockatoo***.

(*a*) **1785** LATHAM *Gen. Synop. Birds* III. I. 16 Roseate Spoonbill, *Platalea Ajaja*... The plumage is a fine rose-colour. **1838** AUDUBON *Ornith. Biog.* IV. 188 The Roseate Spoonbill is found for the most part along the marshy and muddy borders of estuaries. **1872** COUES *N. Amer. Birds* 264 Roseate Spoonbill. In full plumage rosy-red, whitening on neck.

(*b*) **1813** MONTAGU *Ornith. Dict.* Suppl. s.v. *Tern*, The length of the Roseate Tern is only fifteen inches and a half. **1835** AUDUBON *Ornith. Biog.* III. 296 Beautiful, indeed, are Terns of every kind, but the Roseate excels the rest. **1862** C. A. JOHNS *Brit. Birds* 565 Roseate Terns have been discovered..in the mouth of the Clyde, Lancashire, and the Farn Islands.

(*c*) **1877** *Nature* 16 Aug. 336 A Roseate Cockatoo (*Cacatua roseicapilla*) from Australia.

2. Formed of, consisting of, roses. ? *Obs.*

1607 HEYWOOD *Fayre Mayde Exch.* Wks. 1874 II. 66 Devise sweet roseat coronets. **1630** DRAYTON *Muses' Elys.* Nymphal iii. 12 The most renown'd With curious Roseat Anadems are crown'd. **1742** COLLINS *Ode Mercy* 25 To thee we build a roseate bow'r. **1783** O'KEEFE *Birth-Day* 22 With roseate chaplets crown'd.

†**3.** Rose-scented. *Obs. rare.*

1667 MILTON *P.L.* v. 643 Roseat Dews dispos'd All..to rest. **1720** POPE *Iliad* XXIII. 227 Celestial Venus hover'd o'er his Head, And roseate Unguents, heav'nly Fragrance! shed.

4. a. *fig.* Rosy; happy, smiling.

1873 W. BLACK *Pr. of Thule* v. 77 How bright, and roseate, and happy she looked. **1887** STEVENSON *Misadv. J. Nicholson* v, At which meal the re-assembled family were to sit roseate.

b. Rose-coloured, optimistic.

1868 G. DUFF *Pol. Surv.* 195 A very roseate account of the empire. **1881** GOLD. SMITH *Lect. & Ess.* 261 A persuasive person who could depict the merits of his scheme with roseate but delusive eloquence.

Hence ˈ**roseately** *adv.*

1834 W. TAYLOR in Robberds *Mem.* (1843) II. 556 Hope is like the first blush of dawn, roseately beautiful. **1859** *Chamb. Jrnl.* XI. 128 The golden bars..Soon leave the earth, but linger roseately.

ˈ**roseate**, *v. rare.* [f. prec.]

†**1.** *intr.* (See quot.) *Obs.*⁻⁰

1611 FLORIO, *Roseggiare*,..to roseate, to flower or bud as Roses.

2. *trans.* To render roseate or rosy.

1852 W. JERDAN *Autobiog.* II. ix. 100 He was a fine example of a rubicund Scotchman; fattened and roseated in London. **1898** TALMAGE in *Christian Her.* 20 Apr. 344/4 The millennial June which shall roseate all the earth.

rose-bay. [f. ROSE *sb.* + BAY *sb.*¹]

1. The oleander or rose-laurel, *Nerium Oleander*. Also ***rose-bay tree***.

1548 TURNER *Names Herbes* (E.D.S.) 56 Nerion, otherwyse called Rhododendron.., maye be called in englishe Rose bay tree or rose Laurel. **1597** GERARDE *Herbal* 1220 Rose-Baie is a small shrub of a gallant shewe like the Baie tree. *Ibid.*, This plant is named..Rose Tree, Rose Baie, Rose Baie tree. **1698** *Phil. Trans.* XX. 331 The Flowers seem to resemble the Oleander or Rose-Bay. **1725** *Fam. Dict.* s.v., Most hired Gardeners are apt to lay the Branches of Rose-Bays,..preferring their own Advantage to their Master's Pleasure, who would delight in seeing a Rose-Bay-Tree adorn'd with Branches at the Foot. **1846–50** A. WOOD *Class-bk. Bot.* 458 *Nerium Oleander*, Rose Bay-tree... This splendid shrub is common in Palestine.

2. a. The rhododendron (and azalea). **b.** A tree or plant of this genus.

1760 J. LEE *Introd. Bot.* App. 306 Bay, Mountain Rose, *Rhododendrum*. *Ibid.* 325 Rose Bay, Dwarf, *Rhododendron*.

1796 WITHERING *Brit. Pl.* II. 239 *Azalea procumbens*,.. Trailing Rosebay. Highland mountains. **1845–50** MRS. LINCOLN *Lect. Bot.* 164 Rhododendron,..sometimes called mountain laurel or rose-bay. **1846–50** A. WOOD *Class-bk. Bot.* 376 *Rhododendron maximum*, American Rose Bay. **1898** *Atlantic Monthly* LXXXII. 498 Purple rhododendron or mountain rose-bay (*R. Catawbiense*).

3. The willow-herb, *Epilobium angustifolium*. Also *attrib.*

1671 SKINNER *Etym. Bot.*, Rose-withy, *vel* Rose-bay; Willow-herb. **1760** J. LEE *Introd. Bot.* App. 325 Rose Bay Willowherb, *Epilobium*. **1777** JACOB *Catal. Pl. Faversham* 66. **1846–50** A. WOOD *Class-bk. Bot.* 262 *Epilobium angustifolium*... Willow Herb. Rose-bay. **1855** MISS PRATT *Flower. Pl.* II. 280 *Epilobium angustifolium* (Rose Bay, or Flowering Willow).

rose bowl. [f. ROSE *sb.* + BOWL *sb.*[1]]

1. A bowl designed to hold cut roses; *spec.* such a bowl offered as a prize in a competition.

1895 *Montgomery Ward Catal.* 545/2 Rose Bowl, 6½ inch, imitation of heavy cut glass. **1916** *Daily Colonist* (Victoria, B.C.) 25 July 7/1 (Advt.), Brilliant Beauty Glassware Assortment..Rose Bowls—Clear crystal, beautiful design. Special, each 50c. **1958** L. DURRELL *Mountolive* xii. 232 The room was full of the scent of the pastels burning in the great rose-bowl by the telephone. **1970** P. BAIR *Tribunal* III. ii. 161 For the winner a prize of two hundred pounds was waiting, together with a handsome rose bowl. **1972** *Daily Tel.* 10 Oct. 13 Today's young people hardly know what a rose-bowl is. **1976** *South Notts Echo* 16 Dec. 3/5 The winner will receive a silver rose-bowl which is competed for annually.

2. *U.S.* (With capital initials.) The name of a football stadium at Pasadena, California, used *attrib.* and *absol.* of a football match played between rival college teams annually on New Year's Day at the conclusion of the local Tournament of Roses.

1930 *Los Angeles Times* 2 Jan. (Sports section) 1/1 Southern California's smashing victory gives that institution two wins in as many Rose Bowl games... The other triumph was scored over Penn State in 1923. **1947** *Collier's* 29 Nov. 89/2 Getting to the Rose Bowl is even simpler this year because Illinois, as the winner last year, isn't eligible to go until three years are up. **1959** *Boston Herald* 1 Jan. 75/4 When you tune in the Rose Bowl, watch the quarterbacks. **1969** *Eugene* (Oregon) *Register-Guard* 3 Dec. 1D/3 Michigan's football team began working out without equipment Tuesday in preparation for the trip to Pasadena, Calif., for the Rose Bowl game against Southern California New Year's Day. **1971** J. HENDERSON *Copperhead* xx. 244 It was Lourdes, the Rose Bowl, and a Democratic Convention all in one gargantuan jumble. **1976** *Honolulu Star-Bull.* 21 Dec. H-5/1 Michigan football Coach Bo Schembechler agrees with Southern California's John Robinson that the Rose Bowl should decide the national championship.

rose-breasted, *a. Ornith.* [f. ROSE *sb.*] Having a breast of a rosy or carmine hue. In the names of various birds, as ***rose-breasted cockatoo, finch, fly-catcher, grosbeak***, etc.

1801 LATHAM *Gen. Synop. Birds* Suppl. II. 223 Rose-breasted Fly Catcher... N.S. Wales. **1810** A. WILSON *Amer. Ornith.* II. 135 The Rose-breasted Grosbeak is.. thirteen inches in extent. **1847** LEICHHARDT *Jrnl.* viii. 272 The rose-breasted cockatoo (*Cocatua eos*, Gould) visited the patches of fresh burnt grass. **1859–63** J. G. WOOD *Illustr. Nat. Hist.* II. 192 The Rose-breasted Nyctiornis, or Red-faced Night-feeder. **1884** COUES *N. Amer. Birds* 348 *Carpodacus frontalis rhodocolpus*,..Rose-Breasted Finch. *Ibid.* 389 *Zamelodia ludoviciana*,..Rose-Breasted Song Grosbeak.

'rosebud. Also rose-bud. [f. ROSE *sb.*]

1. The bud of a rose; the flower of a rose before it opens. Also *fig.*

1611 BIBLE *Wisd.* ii. 8 Let vs crowne our selues with Rose buds. **1647** CRASHAW *Steps to Temple, Tear* iv, Such a Pearle as this is..The Rose buds sweet lip kisses. **1727–46** THOMSON *Summer* 1587 The parted lip, Like the red-rose bud moist with morning-dew. **1773** *Phil. Trans.* LXIII. 129 The rose-tree..was covered with leaves and rose-buds. **1825** J. NEAL *Bro. Jonathan* I. 33 Her..mouth, like the wet rose-bud, was brimful of something like poetry. **1856** MRS. BROWNING *Aur. Leigh* II. 12 Rosebuds reddening where the calyx split.

attrib. **1798** WOLCOT (P. Pindar) *Tales Hoy* Wks. 1812 IV. 407 Her rosebud-lips expanded with a smile. **1890** 'L. FALCONER' *M'selle Ixe* v, Her rosebud-like beauty.

2. *transf.* **a.** A pretty maiden; a girl in the first bloom of womanhood; also as a term of endearment. Cf. BUD *sb.*[1] 3 b.

c **1790** BURNS *To Miss Cruikshank* 1 Beauteous rose-bud, young and gay, Blooming on thy early May. **1807–8** W. IRVING *Salmag.* (1824) 162 Two sister nymphs,..Twin rose-buds bursting into bloom. **1848** KINGSLEY *Saint's Trag.* II. vi, My fair rose-bud—A trifle over-blown, but not less sweet—I have been pining for you.

b. *U.S.* A débutante.

1885 *Harper's Mag.* Mar. 544/2 The girls have gone to a 'rose-bud' dinner. **1890** *Cent. Mag.* Aug. 582 They flutter their brief hour in society... Some of them hold on like grim death to rosebud privileges. **1973** *Times Lit. Suppl.* 1 June 608/1 He married..a college beauty queen (a 'Rosebud' of 1922).

†**c.** A member of the junior section of the Girl Guides Association, now called a 'Brownie' or 'Brownie Guide' (see BROWNIE[1] 2). *Obs.* exc. *Hist.*

1914 A. BADEN-POWELL in *Girl Guides' Gaz.* June 2/1 The age at which a Rose Bud may join the Baden-Powell Girl Guides is eight years. **1914** O. BADEN-POWELL in *Ibid.* July 3/1, I am so glad to hear that some of you are taking up the work of training Rosebuds, to follow in your footsteps. **1915** *Girl Guides' Gaz.* Jan. 15/2 Our 'Rosebuds' are growing rapidly in numbers..but we hear they are dissatisfied with their name. *Ibid.* June 3/2 (*heading*) Rosebuds or Brownies? **1973** *New Society* 27 Sept. 755/2 Brownies were started in 1910 by Baden-Powell's sister, under the name of Rosebuds.

3. ***rosebud-nail***: (see quot.).

1802 JAMES *Milit. Dict.*, *Rose-bud Nails*, are small round-headed nails, driven in the centre of the roses of the plates.

4. *Sc.* Some kind of small sea-shell.

1893 CROCKETT *Stickit Minister* (1895) 242 The lady teachers wandered about and..explored with their classes the great shell-heaps for 'rosebuds' and 'legs of mutton'.

'rose-bush. [f. ROSE *sb.* + BUSH *sb.*[1]]

1. A bush of the rose kind. Also *attrib.*

1587 GOLDING *De Mornay* xix. (1592) 296 There is not here so faire and sweet a Rosebush, which hath not very sharpe pricks. **1611** COTGR., *Rosier*, a Rose-tree, Rose-bush, Rose-brier. *a* **1691** BOYLE (J.), This way of procuring autumnal roses will, in most rose bushes, fail. **1707** *Curiosities in Husb. & Gard.* 259 The Buds of Rose-bushes. *c* **1765** FLLOYD *Tartarian T.* (1785) 65/2 A spring..takes it's source from the foot of a rose-bush. **1807** SOUTHEY *Lett.* (1850) III. 68 Here I am now planting garden-enclosures, rose-bushes,..and resolute to become a mountaineer. **1850** THACKERAY *Pendennis* xxviii, Her hands were guaranteed from the thorns of her favourite rose-bushes by a pair of gauntlets. **1897** *Outing* XXX. 244/2 A deep valley, where great trees were reduced to a rose-bush size.

2. *Austr.* A kind of timber-tree (see quot.).

1889 MAIDEN *Useful Native Pl.* 532 *Eupomatia laurina*, ..'Rose-bush', or 'Balwarra'. A small tree. The wood is soft, close, coarse-grained, and of a yellowish-brown colour.

rose-cake. [f. ROSE *sb.*]

†**1.** A preparation of rose-petals in the form of a cake, used as a perfume, etc. *Obs.*

1598 FLORIO, *Rosata*, a rose cake. **1607** TOPSELL *Four-footed Beasts* 91 Calves marrow with an equal quantity of whay, Oyl, Rose-cake and an Egge, do soften the hardness of the cheeks and eye-lids. **1615** J. STEPHENS *Satyr. Ess.*, *Country Bridegroom*, He must savour of gallantry a little; though he perfume the Table with Rose-cake. *a* **1676** HALE *Prim. Orig. Man.* III. iv. (1677) 271 The experience of the growing of Moths out of the Seeds of Lavender, and Worms in Rose-cakes. **1738** CHAMBERS *Cycl.* s.v. *Rose-water*, The rose-leaves, remaining at the bottom of the still, are kept under the name of rose-cakes for a perfume.

2. (See quot. and ROSETTE *sb.* 3.) ? *Obs.*

1670 PETTUS *Fodinæ Reg.* 4 When they are smelted and cast into a solid form, if Lead, they call them Pigs;..if Copper, Rose-cakes.

3. A kind of sweetmeat (see quot.).

1902 MRS. RATTRAY *Sweetmeat-Making* 114 Rose Cake... Flavour with oil of roses, and colour with cochineal.

rose-'campion. [f. ROSE *sb.* + CAMPION[2].] A pretty garden-plant of the genus *Lychnis* or *Agrostemma*, having rose-coloured flowers; esp. *L.* or *A. coronaria*; mullein-pink.

1530 PALSGR. 264/1 Rosecampyon a floure. **1548** TURNER *Names Herbes* (E.D.S.) 79 The third is called Thryallis, and Rosecampi[on] in englishe. **1626** BACON *Sylva* §560 Plants, that..have a Kinde of Downey or Velvet Rine, upon their Leaves; as Rose-Campion. **1688** [see CAMPION[2]]. **1728** GARDINER *Rapin on Gardens* (ed. 3) I. 35 Æthiopis, Woolfbane, red Rose-campions rise. **1786** ABERCROMBIE *Gard. Assist.*, *Arr.* 65 Rose campion (*agrostemma*). **1866** *Treas. Bot.* 700/2 *Coronaria*, in which the calyx is thickened in fruit; the Rose Campion (*Lychnis coronaria*) is a good example. **1872** TENNYSON *Last Tournament* 234 Glowing in all colours, the live grass, Rose-campion,..poppy, glanced About the revels.

'rose-,chafer. *Ent.* Also 8 chaffer. [f. ROSE *sb.* + CHAFER[1].] A beetle of the genus *Cetonia* (esp. *C. aurata*), of a burnished green or copper colour, frequenting roses and in the grub-state very destructive to vegetation; the rose-fly.

1704 PETIVER *Gazophyl.* iii. §23 *Scarabæus pectinarius viridis*,..the Rose Chaffer. **1817** KIRBY & SP. *Entomol.* xxiii. (1818) II. 321 Those enemies of vegetable beauty the rose-chafers (*Cetonia aurata*). **1844** H. STEPHENS *Bk. Farm* III. 779 The *Cetonia aurata*, Green rosechafer, is found on the flowers of the turnip plant. **1899** D. SHARP *Insects* 200 In Britain we have only four kinds of Cetoniides; they are called Rose-chafers.

rose-cheeked, *a.* [f. ROSE *sb.*]

1. Having ruddy or rose-coloured cheeks; rosy-cheeked.

1592 SHAKS. *Ven. & Ad.* i, Rose-cheek'd Adonis hied him to the chase. **1607** —— *Timon* IV. iii. 86 Bring downe Rose-cheekt youth to the Tubfast, and the Diet. **1642** H. MORE *Song Soul* II. App. xcix, Fair comely bodies, goodly beautifi'd, Snow-limb'd, rose-cheek'd. **1833** TENNYSON *Miller's Daughter* 133 Rosecheekt, roselipt, half-sly, half-shy, You would, and would not, little one.

2. *Ornith.* ***rose-cheeked kingfisher***, an Ethiopian species, *Ispidina picta*.

1868–71 R. B. SHARPE *Monograph Alcedinidae* 141.

'rose-,colour, *sb.* Also rose colour. [f. ROSE *sb.* or *a.*]

1. The colour of a rose; rosy or crimson tint or hue. Also *attrib.*

1382 WYCLIF *Esther* xv. 8 She forsothe thurȝshed the chere with rose colour [**1388** colour of roosis]. **1526** TINDALE *Revelation* xvii. 4 And the woman was arayed in purple and rose color. **1565** COOPER *Thesaurus* s.v. *Amethistus*, The more rose colour the better. **1611** FLORIO, *Rodite*, a precious stone of a Rose-colour. **1725** *Fam. Dict.* s.v. *Anemone*, The Turkish or Bizantine [anemone], of a Rose-colour. **1780** J. T. DILLON *Trav. Spain* (1781) 318 [It is] called Rosiclei by mineralogists, from its rose-colour appearance. **1793** T. BEDDOES *Calculus*, etc. 222 The blood contained in the left ventricle..was of a rose colour. **1828** STARK *Elem. Nat. Hist.* I. 452 Body shaded with rose-colour, and silvery. **1856** DANA *Rudim. Treat. Min.* 72 Rhodonite..is of a beautiful rose colour, inclining sometimes to violet.

transf. **1865** MRS. GASKELL *Wives & Daughters* (1866) I. xxv. 280 Such were the facts, but rose-colour was the medium through which they were seen. **1870** EMERSON *Soc. & Sol.*, *Farming*, The farmer's office is..important, but you must not try to paint him in rose-colour. **1883** *Harper's Mag.* Feb. 419/1 Lawson..was inclined to see things in rose-color.

2. *fig.* A pleasant or attractive experience or outlook. (So F. *couleur de rose*: see COULEUR.)

1857 TROLLOPE *Barchester T.* III. ix. 177 It was not all rose colour with Mr. Slope, although his hopes ran high. **1883** LORD R. GOWER *My Reminisc.* I. 313 Even a fashionable painter's life is not all rose colour. **1885** *New Bk. Sports* 222 A canoe trip cannot be warranted to be all rose-colour more than any other human undertaking.

So **'rose-,colour** *v.* (see quot.). *rare.*

1556 OLDE *Antichrist* 11 As for this beast, he hathe allready rose coloured him self a great while with payntes blood. **1974** M. C. GERALD *Pharmacol.* xv. 281 Stimulation of RAS results in an enhanced state of arousal to environmental stimuli,..'rose-coloring' the individual's subjective appraisal of the world around him.

'rose-,coloured, *a.* [f. ROSE *sb.*]

1. a. Having the pink or light crimson colour of a rose; roseate, rosy.

1526 TINDALE *Rev.* xvii. 3, I sawe a woman sytt apon a rose colored best. **1580** in *Liturg. Serv. Q. Eliz.* (1847) 578 Strengthen her hand..to double into the bosom of that rose-coloured whore that [etc.]. **1613** PURCHAS *Pilgrimage* VIII. ii. (1614) 733 First coloured blacke, then ash-coloured, then rose-coloured, then red. **1717** LADY M. W. MONTAGU *Let. to C'tess Mar* 1 Apr., The..drawers..are of a thin rose-coloured damask. **1789** PILKINGTON *View Derbysh.* I. 323 A dry, spongy, violet pulp, from which a rose-coloured pigment may be prepared. **1854** TOMLINSON *Arago's Astron.* 59 Several rose-coloured protuberances..beyond the dark limb of the moon. **1886** A. WINCHELL *Walks Geol. Field* 131 A second basin..has its bottom covered by.. rose-coloured salt-crystals.

b. In specific names, as ***rose-coloured algæ, cow-bird, flounder, ouzel, pastor, pelican, sea-anemone, spoonbill, starling, thrush, vervain***: see quots. and the sbs., and cf. ROSE *sb.* 23, 24, ROSEATE *a.* 1 b.

1861 BENTLEY *Man. Bot.* 717 *Rhodosporeæ*, *Florideæ*, or *Rose-coloured Algæ. **1837** MACGILLIVRAY *Hist. Brit. Birds* I. 613 The *Rose-coloured Cow-bird (*Turdus roseus* Linn.) is about the size of the Spotted Starling. **1795** SHAW *Naturalist's Miscellany* VII. pl. 238 The *Rose-coloured Flounder. **1766–1832** [see OUZEL 2 b and PASTOR *sb.* 4]. **1843** YARRELL *Brit. Birds* II. 52 The Rose-coloured Pastor is an accidental visiter to this country. **1785** LATHAM *Gen. Synopsis of Birds* III. II. 579 *Rose-coloured Pelican, the plumage wholly of a rose-colour. **1802** BINGLEY *Anim. Biogr.* (1813) III. 425 The *Rose-coloured Sea Anemone. On this species the Abbé Dicquemaire made several experiments, to ascertain its powers of production. **1870** GILLMORE tr. *Figuier's Reptiles & Birds* (1892) 325 The *Rose-coloured spoonbill, a native of South America, the plumage of which possesses the most beautiful tints. **1843** YARRELL *Brit. Birds* II. 51 *Turdus roseus*, *Rose-coloured Starling. **1792** PENNANT *Arct. Zool.* II. Index, *Rose-coloured Thrush. **1822** *Hortus Anglicus* II. 136 *V. Aubletia*. *Rose-coloured Vervain... Flowers pink or crimson, numerous, in stalked heads.

†**2.** Clad in red or scarlet robes. *Obs.*[−1]

1546 *Gasser's Prognost.* D 5 b, The roase coulered persons subject to Jupiter, as Patriarches, Cardinalles,..shable had in much estimation and honour.

3. *fig.* Characterized by cheerful optimism, or tendency to regard matters in a highly favourable or attractive light. ***rose-coloured spectacles***, used in *fig.* phrases to indicate that a person's view of something is unduly favourable, optimistic, or idealistic.

1854 C. M. YONGE *Castle Builders* iv. 56 The first rose-coloured light in which they had viewed everything, was wearing off. **1856** DICKENS *Dorrit* (1857) I. xxxiv. 299, I don't like to dispel your generous visions, and I would give any money..to live in such a rose-coloured mist. **1861** HUGHES *Tom Brown at Oxf.* II. 102 Oxford was a sort of Utopia to the Captain... He continued..to behold towers, and quadrangles, and chapels,.. through rose-coloured spectacles. **1863** *Sat. Rev.* 1 Aug. 165 All the facts of the case that might chance to interfere with the rose-coloured view of the 'Company of Jesus' that is habitual to him. **1867** A. J. EVANS *St. Elmo* xii. 157, I have a right to all my charming, rose-colored views of this world. **1875** MRS. TROLLOPE *Charming Fellow* I. vii. 84 This rose-coloured condition of things did not last. **1921** PRINCESS P. METTERNICH *Days that are no More* iii. 104, I was young and favoured by fortune, no troubles had yet befallen me, and I saw everything through rose-coloured spectacles. **1981** *Oxford Jrnl.* 15 May 8/2 Mrs M—— must be viewing Carterton crossroads through rose-coloured spectacles. Far from being vastly improved, it is becoming a ghastly eyesore.

Hence **rose-'colourist**, one who takes a rose-coloured view of things. *nonce-word.*

1852 C. READE *Peg Woffington* (1853) 135 'This day, in particular, is a happy one,' added the rose colourist.

Rosecrucian, obs. form of ROSICRUCIAN.

'rose-cut, *a.* and *sb.* Also rose cut. [ROSE *sb.* 18.] Of diamonds: (see quots.).

1842 FRANCIS *Dict. Arts.* **1850** HOLTZAPFFEL *Turning* III. 1322 The rose cut consists of triangular facets arranged upon and around a central hexagon. **1862** *Chambers's Encycl.* III. 536/1 Vertical and lateral appearance of rose-cut diamond. **1877** *Encycl. Brit.* VII. 165/2 The rose cut..is given to stones which have too little depth to be cut as brilliants; it has the whole upper curved surface covered with equilateral triangles.

rosed, (rəʊzd), *a.* [f. ROSE *sb.* or *v.*[1]]

†**1. a.** Flavoured or compounded with rose-petals. **b.** Rose-scented. *Obs.*

1562 TURNER *Herbal* (1568) II. 7 If ye take it inwarde, you must take it wyth rosed honye or wyth rose leaues. *a* **1586** SIDNEY *Arcadia* (1622) 234 A rosed breath, from lips more rosie proceeding. **1643** A. ROSS *Mel Helic.* 168 If Musk, Perfume, or rosed air, Or Balm could vaporate from thee. **1652** CADEMAN *Distiller of London* 147 The same quantity drunk with rosed Honey looseth the Belly.

2. Rendered red or rosy in colour; rose-coloured, rose-hued. (Cf. ROSE *v.*[1] 2.)

1588 SHAKS. *Tit. And.* II. iv. 24 Alas, a Crimson riuer of warme blood..Doth rise and fall betweene thy Rosed lips. **1880** G. MEREDITH *Tragic Com.* (1881) 134 He was a bridegroom, for whom the rosed Alps rolled out a panorama of illimitable felicity.

3. Adorned with representations of roses. Also *fig.*

1891 MISS DOWIE *Girl in Karp.* 143 A settee..covered in faded rosed-over tapestry. **1898** G. MEREDITH *Odes Fr. Hist.* 70 The rosed and starred Revolving Twelves [*sc.* hours].

4. Of a watering-pot: Having or provided with a (specified kind of) rose. In quots. ***fine-rosed.***

1850 *Beck's Florist* Mar. 67 They are watered with a little chilled water (using a fine-rosed pot). **1875** *Carpentry & Join.* 95 Made damp at pleasure by watering from a very fine rosed watering pot.

rose 'diamond. [f. ROSE *sb.*] A nearly hemispherical flat-bottomed diamond, having the upper surface cut into many triangular facets or planes; a rose-cut diamond.

1698 FRYER *Acc. E. India & P.* 214 A Rose Diamond that is very thick, it's good to set it close. **1705** *Lond. Gaz.* No. 4154/3 A large pair of Rose Earings, with a large Diamond in each, set round with 12 small Rose Diamonds. **1753** HANWAY *Trav.* (1762) I. VII. xcv. 437 Six dozen of buttons and six dozen of button-holes of rose diamonds. **1850** HOLTZAPFFEL *Turning* III. 1322 Diamonds that have defects are split by cleavage, and the pieces are cut into rose diamonds. **1898** WIGLEY & STANSBIE *Art Goldsm.* 132 Rose diamonds are frequently cut from rough chips.

attrib. **1707** *Lond. Gaz.* No. 4300/3 A Pair of Rose Diamond Ear-Rings. **1725** DE FOE *Voy. round World* (1840) 142 A ring of silver, with false stones in it, like a rose-diamond ring.

rose-drop. [f. ROSE *sb.* + DROP *sb.*]

†**1.** An ear-drop forming a rose-setting. *Obs.*$^{-1}$

1707 *Lond. Gaz.* No. 4300/3 A Pair of Rose Diamond Ear-Rings, with Rose Drops, containing 36 Rose Diamonds.

2. *Med.* (See quot., and cf. *rosy-drop.*)

1719 QUINCY *Phys. Dict.* (1722) 188 *Gutta Rosacea*, Rose-Drop, is an Eruption upon the Skin, chiefly in the Face, which marks it with red Blotches or Wheals of a red Colour. **1851** DUNGLISON *Dict. Med.*

3. A kind of lozenge or sweet (see quots.).

1858 SIMMONDS *Dict. Trade, Rose-drop,*..a lozenge flavoured with rose essence. **1889** R. WELLS *Bread & Biscuit Baker's Assist.* 71 Rose Drops..are made as in the preceding case. Flavour with essence of rose and colour with cochineal.

rose du Barry (rəʊz dju: 'bærɪ). Also rose du Barri. [f. the name of the Comtesse *du Barry* (1746–93), a patron of the Sèvres porcelain factory.] A soft shade of pink developed *c* 1757 for use as a ground colour on Sèvres porcelain. Also *attrib.* or as *adj.* Cf. ROSE POMPADOUR.

1856 [see CABARET[1] 3]. **1879** C. SCHREIBER *Jrnl.* 13 Oct. (1911) II. 227 Some very fine Rose du Barry Sèvres vases. **1902** *Encycl. Brit.* XXIX. 730/1 The experts of Tôkyô and Nagoya have produced many very beautiful specimens of monochrome enamels—yellow (canary or straw), *rose du Barry*, liquid-dawn red, [etc.]. **1912** C. MACKENZIE *Carnival* xxviii. 284 The two girls followed their host to his room which was hung with rose du Barri draperies prodigally braided with gold. **1931** J. CANNAN *High Table* iii. 36 His head making a grease mark on the *rose du Barri* brocade. **1934** *Historical Colours* (Thos. Parsons & Sons) 58 Du Barry Red is sometimes wrongly called Rose du Barry. **1960** H. HAYWARD *Antique Coll.* 243/2 *Rose du Barry*, a popular misnomer for the coloured ground used on Sèvres porcelain and properly known as rose Pompadour. **1974** *Country Life* 3 Oct. 939/3 Vases of delicate pink which we know now as rose Pompadour but which used to be called rose du Barry.

†**rosee.** Also rose, roseye. [ad. OF. *rosé*, f. *rose* ROSE *sb.*] A dish flavoured with rose-petals.

1381 in Pegge *Forme of Cury* (1780) 105 For to make Rosee. Tak the flowris of Rosys..and..bray hem wel in a morter [etc.]. *Ibid.* 43. *c* **1390** *Forme of Cury* No. 52 Rosee. Take thyk mylke,..Cast þerto suger.., Dates ymynced [etc.],..seeth it, and alye it with flours of white Rosis. *c* **1430** *Two Cookery-bks.* 24 Roseye.—Take..Red Rosys, an grynd fayre in a morter with Almaunde mylke.

'rose-,engine. [f. ROSE *sb.*] An appendage to a turning-lathe by means of which curvilinear or intricate patterns can be engraved.

1839 URE *Dict. Arts* 1161 Coloured transparent glass is applied as enamel in silver and gold bijouterie, previously bright-cut in the metal with the graver or the rose-engine. **1843** *Penny Cycl.* XXV. 424/2 Holding the headstock steady when the rose-engine is to be used as a common lathe. **1875** KNIGHT *Dict. Mech.* 549/1 A straight-line chuck is used in a rose-engine when the patterns are to be made to follow a straight instead of a circular direction.

attrib. **1841** *Penny Cycl.* XX. 168/1 Rose-engine turning. **1851–3** *Tomlinson's Cycl. Arts* (1867) II. 778/2 The rose-engine lathe differs from the common lathe in this [etc.].

roseer(e, obs. ff. ROSER.

rose-hill: see ROSELLA[1].

rosei, variant of REZAI.

'roseine. *Chem.* Also rosein. [f. L. *rose-us* + -INE[5], -IN[1].] One of the red salts derived from rosaniline; *spec.* acetate of rosaniline.

1862 HOFMANN in *Proc. Roy. Soc.* XII. 5 Mr. Nicholson designates the pure base of the red colouring matter by the name of Roseine. **1862** MILLER *Elem. Chem., Org.* (ed. 2) 449 When treated with peroxide of lead and sulphuric acid, aniline furnishes a delicate rose colour, which Dr. D. Price has called *roseine.* **1883** *Science* II. 143/2 Indigo, carmine, and roseine, mixed so as to produce the same tint.

†**rosel.** *Obs.*$^{-1}$ [a. OF. *rosel* (mod.F. *roseau*).] A reed.

c **1400** tr. *Secreta Secret., Gov. Lordsh.* 68 A..feble feer, þat vnnethes may to-brenne rosels and smal chippys.

'rose-leaf. [f. ROSE *sb.* + LEAF *sb.*[1]] The leaf of a rose; usually, a rose-petal.

? *a* **1366** CHAUCER *Rom. Rose* 905 And many a rose-leef ful long Was entermedled ther-among. *c* **1385** —— *L.G.W.* 228 A garlond on his hed of rose leuys Stekid al with lylye flourys newe. **1562** TURNER *Herbal* (1568) II. 7 You must take it wyth rosed honye or wyth rose leaues. **1598** BP. HALL *Sat.* IV. iv, Seest thou the Rose-leaues fall vngathered? **1721** YOUNG *Revenge* II. i, In ceaseless tears, and blushing with her love.., like a rose-leaf wet with morning dew. **1799** G. SMITH *Laboratory* I. 334 Take the distilled rose-leaves, from which all the spirit and oil is extracted. **1821** SHELLEY *Music, when soft voices die* 5 Rose leaves, when the rose is dead, Are heaped for the beloved's bed. **1895** *Atlantic Monthly* Mar. 294 That soft hand-pressure, like a pad of rose-leaves.

Comb. **1832** J. RENNIE *Consp. Butterfl. & M.* 156 The Rose Leaf Roller (*Lozotænia Rosana*, Stephens) appears the middle of June, in gardens about rose-trees. **1854** C. M. YONGE *Heartsease* II. xviii. 50 A little pair of socks, in delicate fancy-knitting for Johnnie. 'Dear, dear mamma! her own pretty rose-leaf pattern. Think of her knitting for my Johnnie!' **1908** [see HALVA]. **1913** C. MACKENZIE *Sinister St.* I. II. ii. 167 As for Dora's face, Michael found it beautiful with the long-lashed blue eyes and rose-leaf complexion. **1946** L. B. LYON *Rough Walk Home* 27 On rose-leaf heights we too were born, But spirit falters, or the proud foot slips.

fig. **1851** THACKERAY in *Scribner's Mag.* II. 132/2 A very little domestic roseleaf rumpled puts me off my work. **1870** MISS BROUGHTON *Red as Rose* I. 63 The velvet rose leaf of her cheek. **1897** MISS KINGSLEY *W. Africa* 489 It is sad to think of this thorn being added to the rose-leaves of a West Coast chief's life.

Hence **'rose-,leafy** *adj.*

1884 'MARK TWAIN' *Huck. Finn* xxii. 222 Every lady's rose-leafy dress flapping soft and silky.

'roseless, *a.* [f. ROSE *sb.*] Without or destitute of roses; pale, colourless.

1831 *Fraser's Mag.* III. 52 Her cheek was roseless and emaciated. **1882** *Garden* 14 Jan. 28/3 In this Roseless season it is pleasant to be able to pick bunches of white Roses, or what looks like them.

roselet[1] ('rəʊzlɪt). Forms: 5 roslett, 6 roselette, 9 roselet. [f. ROSE *sb.* + -LET.] A little rose; a figure or representation of this; †spec. in *Her.* (see quot. 1562).

1486 *Bk. St. Albans* b iij b, The threde baage is roslettys. **1562** LEGH *Armory* (1597) 37 The third badge are Roselettes, that is to say single Roses, that haue but v. leaues a peece. **1896** *Westm. Gaz.* 20 July 1/3 She rapidly gathers the simple open-hearted roselets wherever she can spy them.

So **'roselette.** *rare*$^{-1}$.

1870 ROCK *Text. Fabr.* I. 196 To take these roselettes for the Tudor flower would be a great mistake.

‖**roselet**[2]. [Norman dial.] The sand-smelt. (Cf. ROSERET.)

1862 ANSTED *Channel Isl.* II. ix. 212 The roselet (*atherina presbyter*), a kind of smelt, is abundant and delicious.

'rose-like, *a.* [f. ROSE *sb.* + -LIKE I.]

Resembling a rose in colour, appearance, or fragrance.

1530 PALSGR. 322/2 Roselyke, of the coloure of a rose, *rosaicque.* **1601** MARKHAM *Mary Magd. Lament.* Pref. 74 Marie shewes to maids.. How they should weepe, and decke their rose-like cheekes, With showers of greefe. **1661** LOVELL *Hist. Anim. & Min.* Isagoge, As the Thrush,.. black-bird, saxatile,..double-coloured, roselike, brassilian and indian stare. **1705** *Phil. Trans.* XXV. 1869 The Rose-like parts were not near so large upon the little Leaves. **1705** GARDINER *Rapin on Gardens* (1728) I. 28 Drest in white Robes she spreads a Rose-like Bloom. **1818** SHELLEY *Rosal. & Helen* 1010 The rose-like hues which flow From sunset o'er the Alpine snow. **1866** *Treas. Bot.* 978/1 It [the genus *Rhodorrhiza*] derives its name from the rose-like smell peculiar to the rootstocks.

rose-lipped, *a.* Also -lipt. [f. ROSE *sb.* + LIPPED *ppl. a.*] Having lips of a rosy hue.

1604 SHAKS. *Oth.* IV. ii. 63 Turne thy complexion there: Patience, thou young and Rose-lip'd Cherubin. **1750** WARTON *Ode to Fancy* 56 Where Laughter rose-lipp'd Hebe leads. **1796** *New Ann. Reg.* 165 See, as the rose-lipt Almé weave the dance, To melting airs they move, in amorous play. **1827** HOOD *Mids. Fairies* lxxxi, His pretty mouth.. Lay half way open like a rose-lipp'd shell. **1896** HOUSMAN *Shropshire Lad* liv, For many a rose-lipt maiden And many a lightfoot lad.

roselite ('rəʊzəlaɪt). *Min.* [f. Prof. G. *Rose*, a German mineralogist (1798–1873) + -LITE.] A rare hydrous arsenate of cobalt and calcium, of vitreous lustre, found in rose-red crystals at Schneeberg in Saxony.

1830 *Encycl. Metrop.* (1845) VI. 485/2 Roselite?.. Occurs in attached crystals on greyish quartz. Primary form a Right rhombic prism. **1857** DANA *Man. Min.* (1862) 268 *Roselite*, a rose-red mineral, related to, if not identical with, cobalt bloom. **1875** *Jrnl. Chem. Soc.* XXVIII. 240 On the crystalline form of roselite.

ro'sella[1]. [App. for *Rose-hiller*, f. *Rose-hill*, Paramatta near Sydney: see Morris *Austral Eng.*]

1. A brightly coloured seed-eating Australian parakeet belonging to the genus *Platycercus.*

1829 *Sydney Gaz.* 21 July 4/1 The doleful dying quails, And roselles [*sic*] golden. **1838** J. HAWDON *Jrnl.* 15 Mar. in *Journey New South Wales to Adelaide* (1952) 51 Parrots now appeared more numerous, Rosellas and others. **1847** LEICHHARDT *Jrnl.* III. 80 The common white cockatoo, and the Moreton Bay Rosella parrot, were very numerous. **1881** *Chequered Career* 167 The bright-plumaged paraquets and rosellas that are so familiar to the Australian eye. **1941** *Coast to Coast 1941* 86 Thither were transferred..the assortment of rosellas and grass parrots that had in one way or another fallen into captivity. **1966** EASTMAN & HUNT *Parrots Austral.* p. ix, I rather feel that the Blue-cheeked is a very beautiful connecting link between Pale-headed and Northern Rosellas.

2. *Austral.* and *N.Z.* A sheep whose wool is beginning to fall off naturally, and which is therefore easy to shear.

1849 D. MCLEOD in *Stephen's Adelaide Miscell.* III. 81 At shearing he..pick[s] all the 'Rosellas' (clean-bellied sheep). **1910** C. E. W. BEAN *On Wool Track* 193 If there is an old ewe in the pen, a 'rosella' as they call her, with most of the lower wool worn off, she goes the first. **1954** E. C. STUDHOLME *Te Waimate* (ed. 2) I. xv. 130 An old hand.. would..quickly catch and shear all the 'rosellas', or easily shorn sheep. **1972** J. S. GUNN in G. W. Turner *Good Austral. Eng.* iii. 60 Few shearers recognised *flyer, cop, gunbarrel*..as terms for what is usually called a *barebelly* or *rosella.*

ro'sella[2], **ro'selle.** Also rozelle. [Perh. a corruption of the French name *l'oseille* (sorrel) *de Guinée.*] The red or Indian sorrel, *Hibiscus sabdariffa.*

1857 *Tait's Mag.* XXIV. 164 (*India.*) Fields of the beautifully rosy-tinted roselle. **1858** SIMMONDS *Dict. Trade, Roselle...* Its calyxes..are much employed for making tarts, jellies, and refreshing drinks: a fibre, also known as gayal fibre, is obtained from the stem. **1887** MRS. DALY *Digging & Squatting* 122 Rosellas we grew most successfully... My mother managed to invent Rosella syrup, one of our most refreshing beverages. **1890** WATT *Dict. Econ. Prod. India* IV. 243 The seeds of the Rozelle are used medicinally.

‖**rosemaling** ('ro:sə,mɑ:lɪŋ, -,mɔ:lɪŋ). [Norw., f. *rose* rose + *maling* painting.] The art of painting (wooden implements, furniture, etc.) with decorative flower motifs. Hence **'rosemaled, -malt** (-mɑ:ld, -mɑ:lt) *ppl. a.* [Norw. *-malt* pa. ppl. of *male* to paint], decorated with rosemaling; **'rosemaler,** one who practises rosemaling.

1948 *School Arts* Mar. 223/1 The Rosemaling (flower painting) of Norway has been brought to this country [*sc.* the U.S.A.] and skillfully adapted to American living by Per Lysne of Stoughton, Wisconsin. **1950** H. MAJOR *Norwegian Holiday* 88 There will be a bowl or two decorated in the colorful rose-painting (*rosemaling*) design of the district. *Ibid.* 93 (*caption*) A student must first design his rosemaling. **1953** J. STEWART *Folk Arts of Norway* iv. 87 Rosemaling.. has a counterpart in the Swedish *blomstermålning* (flower painting), in the decorative painting of Russia, and in Pennsylvania Dutch art. **1956** T. BØHN in *Norwegian-Amer. Stud. & Rec.* XIX. 120 The multitude of Norwegian immigrant items grew, including such things as *rosemalt* chests, cupboards, boxes. **1972** DEAN & SMITH *Wisconsin* 145/1 Rosemaling, the colorful art of floral painting that grew up in Norway, is enjoying a booming revival in Wisconsin. **1975** LOVOLL & BJORK *Norwegian-Amer. Hist. Assoc., 1925–1975* v. 21 The museum has also conducted workshops in *rosemaling* (rose painting) and wood carving, with teachers from Norway. **1975** J. LANGLAND in *Massachusetts Rev.* (Univ. of Mass.) Summer 568 They stuffed their childhood into rosemaler trunks, clamped them with iron bands locked once and for all on the eastern hemispheres. **1976** P. VIRCH *Rosemaling in Round* i. 1/2 The largest public collection of rosemaled chests, bowls, furniture and boxes can be seen in Vesterheim, the Norwegian-American museum in Decorah, Iowa. *Ibid.*, (*caption*) This collection of bowls owned by the author was painted for her by..rosemalers of Norway.

rose-malloes. Anglicized form of RASAMALA.

1858 SIMMONDS *Dict. Trade, Rose-malloes,* a name in Bombay for the liquid storax obtained from *Liquidambar orientale* of Miller. **1881** *Encycl. Brit.* XII. 718/2 An American *Liquidambar* also produces a rose-malloes-like exudation.

rosemary ('rəʊzmərɪ). Forms: 5 rose mary, 6 rosmary, 6–7 rosemarie (6 -ye), 7 rosemery; 6– rosemary. [An alteration of ROSMARINE, ad. L. *rōs marinus* or late L. *rōsmarinum* (neut.), whence also It. *rosmarino*, F. *romarin* (OF. *romm-, roum-, rosmarin, rosamerine*), Prov. and Cat. *romani(n)*, Pg. *rosmaninho* (Sp. *romero*), and in the Teut. languages, MDu. *rosemarine, -ijn* (Du. *ros-, rozemarijn*), MHG. *rôsenmarîn,* *roszmarin* (G. *rosmarin*), MSw. *rosemarin* (Sw. and Da. *rosmarin*).

The L. name, which also appears as *marīnus rōs*, *rōs maris*, and simply *rōs*, means 'sea-dew', which has been supposed to have reference to the plant growing near the sea. In English, as in some of the older Teut. forms, the first element has been assimilated to ROSE *sb.*, and the second may have been taken as the name of the Virgin.]

1. An evergreen shrub (*Rosmarinus officinalis*), of the N.O. *Labiatæ*, native to the south of Europe, the leaves of which have an agreeable fragrance, and have been much used in perfumery, and to some extent in medicine.

c **1440** *Promp. Parv.* 437/1 Rose mary, herbe (*K.* rosemaryne), *rosemarinus, rosa marina.* **1523** SKELTON *Garl. Laurel* 980 The ruddy rosary, The souerayne rosemary, The praty strawbery. **1578** LYTE *Dodoens* 263 Rosemary floureth twise a yeare, once in the spring time of the yeare, and secondarily in August. **1603** DEKKER *Wonderfull Yeare* Wks. (Grosart) I. 114 Rosemary which had wont to be sold for 12. pence an armefull, went now for six shillings a handfull. **1671** GREW *Anat. Plants* (1682) 17 Some Vegetables lose their Smell, as Roses; others, keep it, as Rose-mary. **1712** tr. *Pomet's Hist. Drugs* I. 211 Aromatick Herbes, as Thyme, Rosemary, Lavender, and the like. **1785** MARTYN *Rousseau's Bot.* xii. (1794) 125 If you compare the flowers of sage and rosemary together, you will find them agree in most.. particulars. **1807** J. E. SMITH *Phys. Bot.* 190 It has been long ago asserted that wax may easily be gathered from the leaves of Rosemary. **1866** *Treas. Bot.* 992/1 Rosemary.. is employed in the form of lotion and wash for the hair. **1882** 'OUIDA' *Maremma* I. 115 Its sides were clothed with myrtle, aloe, and rosemary.

b. With pl. A plant or species of rosemary.

1866 *Cornhill Mag.* Nov. 537 A tangled growth of heaths and arbutus, and pines, and rosemaries.

2. In passages referring to the use of rosemary as an emblem, or on particular occasions (as funerals and weddings), or for decoration, etc.

(*a*) **1584** C. ROBINSON *Handefull Pleas. Delites* A ij b, Rosemarie is for remembrance, betweene vs daie and night. **1602** SHAKS. *Ham.* IV. v. 175 There's Rosemary, that's for Remembraunce. **1706** ESTCOURT *Fair Example* III. i, I dreamt last Night of Rosemary, that betokens Honour.

(*b*) **1592** SHAKS. *Rom. & Jul.* IV. iv. 79 Sticke your Rosemarie On this faire Coarse, and as the custome is, And in her best array beare her to Church. **1682** *Will of Tooker* (Somerset Ho.), My body to the earth without any ceremony then Rosemary and wine. **1700** T. BROWN tr. *Fresny's Amusem.* 22 There goes a Funeral with the Men of Rosemary after it. **1725** BOURNE in Brand *Pop. Antiq.* (1777) iii. 29 The carrying of Ivy, or Laurel, or Rosemary, or some of those Ever-Greens [at funerals], is an Emblem of the Soul's Immortality.

(*c*) **1601** SIR W. CORNWALLIS *Essays* II. I. [xlix.] Nn 6 As trim as a Brides rosemary. *a* **1652** BROME *City Wit* v. i, They passe as to the Wedding with Rosemary. **1663** KILLIGREW *Parson's Wedding* v. i, Go get you in then, and let your husband dip the Rosemary.

(*d*) **1611** BEAUM. & FL. *Kt. Burning Pestle* v. i, We will have.. a good piece of beef, stuck with Rose-mary. **17..** *Boy & the Mantle* xxxvi. in Percy *Reliques*, Where stood a boar's head garnished With bayes and rosemarye. **1808** SCOTT *Marm.* VI. Introd. 59 Then the grim boar's head frown'd on high, Crested with bays and rosemary. **1831** LYTTON *E. Aram* I. v, The ale, and the cider with rose-mary in the bowl, were incomparable potations.

3. Applied to various other plants, usually with qualifying word prefixed, as ***golden, poet's, Spanish, wild rosemary***: (see quots.).

1597 GERARDE *Herbal* III. vi. 1110 The Poets Rose-marie or Gardrobe, *Casia Poetica L'Obelij.* **1611** COTGR., *Rosmarin sauvage*, (the red-branched) wild Rosemarie. **1753** *Chambers' Cycl.* Suppl. *App.*, Spanish-Rosemary, a name sometimes given to the *Thymelæa* of botanists... Poet's-Rosemary, a name sometimes given to the *Cassia* of botanists. **1760** J. LEE *Introd. Bot.* App. 325 Rosemary, Wild, *Sedum. Ibid.*, Rosemary, Lesser Wild, *Andromeda.* **1860** PIESSE *Lab. Chem. Wonders* 172 In Sweden the marsh sedum or wild rosemary takes the place of the hop. **1862** C. A. JOHNS *Brit. Birds* 426 A shrub (popularly known on the coast of Norfolk by the name of 'Rosemary'), the *Suæda fruticosa*, Shrubby Sea Blite, of botanists. **1889** MAIDEN *Useful Native Pl.* 396 *Cassinia lævis*... Called 'Wild Rosemary' in parts of Queensland. A rather slender shrub. **1898** MORRIS *Austral Eng.* 395/2 Rosemary, Golden, name given in Tasmania to the plant *Oxylobium ellipticum.*

4. *attrib.* and *Comb.*, as ***rosemary branch, camphor, flower, oil***, etc.

1551 *Tottel's Misc.* (Arb.) 187 Of a Rosemary braunche sente. **1577** *F. de Lisle's Legendarie* B vj b, But as sone as she had gotten her desired pray, she gaue them a rosemarie wipe, dismissing them. **1611** FLORIO, *Rosmaro*,.. also a Rosemary-tree. **1674** PETTY *Disc. Dupl. Proportion* 75 A foot square of a Rosemary-Field may be smelt one Perch or Rod. **1706** [see HUNGARY]. **1728** CHAMBERS *Cycl.* s.v., Conserve of Rosemary Flowers, Essence of Rosemary, Rosemary-Water, &c. **1753** —— Suppl. s.v. *Thymelæa*, Short rosemary-like leaves. **1841** *Penny Cycl.* XX. 170/2 It deposits a stearopten, or rosemary-camphor. **1866** *Treas. Bot.* 807/2 *Oil, Rosemary*, the volatile oil distilled from the branches of *Rosmarinus officinalis.*

b. ***rosemary-stones***: (see quot.).

1686 PLOT *Staffordsh.* 155 A sort of friable stone of a deep yellow colour found *sparsim* in lumps amongst the stiffest and fattest Marles at Eardley.., used by the painters, and by the workmen all call'd by the general name of Rosemary-stones.

c. ***rosemary-leaved***, in plant-names.

1731 MILLER *Gard. Dict.* s.v. *Myrtus*, Rosemary-leav'd Myrtle. **1753** *Chambers' Cycl.* Suppl. s.v. *Thymelæa*, The rosemary-leaved African *Thymelæa*, with long flowers. **1786** ABERCROMBIE *Gard. Assist.*, *Arr.* 34 Santolina,.. Rosemary leaved. *Ibid.* 41 Lavender cotton,.. Rosemary leaved. **1855** MISS PRATT *Flower. Pl.* V. 88 Rosemary-leaved Willow.

† **'rosen**, *a. Obs.* Also 5 **rosene, rosyne.** [f. ROSE *sb.* + -EN[4].]

1. Formed or consisting of roses; pertaining to roses; distilled from roses.

c **1000** *Sax. Leechd.* I. 302 Ȝenim þysse ylcan wyrte seaw aglaofotis mid rosenan ele ȝemencȝed. ? *a* **1366** CHAUCER *Rom. Rose* 845 His leef a rosen chapelet Had maad. *c* **1374** —— *Boeth.* II. metr. iii. (1868) 39 Whan þe wode wexeþ redy of rosene floures. **1446** LYDG. *Nightingale Poems* (1900) 20 Gadre on an hepe these rosen-floures fyve.

2. Rose-coloured, rosy, roseate.

c **1000** ÆLFRIC *Hom.* II. 334 Þa betwux hancrede læȝ se halȝa wer ȝeedcucod, mid rose[n]um hiwe ofergoten. *a* **1100** *Anglo-Saxon Hymn.* (Surtees) 105 Mid ænlicum leohte & wlite rosenum. *a* **1100** *Gloss.* in Haupt *Zeitschrift* IX. 483 *In rosatum*, on rosenne [*altered to* ȝerosedne]. *c* **1374** CHAUCER *Boeth.* II. metr. iii. (1868) 39 Whan phebus.. bygynneþ to spreden his clerenesse with rosene chariettes. *Ibid.* III. metr. i. 64 þe day.. lediþ þe rosene horse of þe sonne. *c* **1402** LYDG. *Compl. Bl. Knt.* 656 Er the sonne to-morwe be risen newe, And er he have ayein his rosen hewe. **1412-20** —— *Troy-bk.* II. 3923 Allas! chaunged is hir rosen hewe!

rosen, obs. form of ROSIN.

rose-nail. [f. ROSE *sb.*] A wrought nail having a round head made with, or cut into, triangular facets.

1640 in Entick *London* (1766) II. 177 Chair nails, Copper nails, rose nails, and saddle nails. **1660** *Book of Rates* s.v. *Nailes*, Copper nailes, Rose nailes, and Sadlers nailes. **1703** R. NEVE *City & C. Purchaser* 212 Rose Nails.. are drawn four-square in the Shank. **1851-3** *Tomlinson's Cycl. Arts* (1867) II. 206/1 Rose nails are made from 1½ to 40 lbs. per thousand. **1879** *Cassell's Techn. Educ.* IV. 12/1 'A ten-pound rose' would signify a rose-nail, of which a thousand would weigh ten pounds.

Rosenante, var. of ROSINANTE.

rosenbuschite ('rəʊzənbʊʃaɪt, rəʊzən'bʊʃaɪt). *Min.* [ad. Norw. *rosenbuschit* (W. C. Brögger 1887, in *Geol. För. i Stockholm Förh.* IX. 254), f. the name of K. H. F. *Rosenbusch* (1836-1914), German mineralogist and geologist: see -ITE[1].] A fluorine-containing alumino-silicate of calcium, sodium, zirconium, and titanium occurring as radiating groups of slender triclinic crystals of an orange or grey colour.

1890 *Jrnl. Chem. Soc.* LVIII. 1079 Rosenbuschite.. presents sufficient analogies to pectolite for it to be described as a zircon-pectolite. **1966** W. A. DEER et al. *Introd. Rock-Forming Minerals* 60 Rosenbuschite occurs as an accessory mineral in nepheline-syenite, but is a more frequent constituent of nepheline-syenite pegmatites.

† **rosenet.** *Obs.*[−1] = CORNET *sb.*[1] 4.

1580 BLUNDEVIL *Horsemanship* IV. 55 b, Open the rift with a Rosenet or drawer.

rosenhahnite (rəʊzən'hɑːnaɪt). *Min.* [f. the name of Leo *Rosenhahn*, U.S. amateur mineralogist, who first found it in 1962 + -ITE[1].] A hydrous calcium silicate, $(CaSiO_3)_3.H_2O$, occurring as buff to white, tabular or lath-like, triclinic crystals.

1967 A. PABST et al. in *Amer. Mineralogist* LII. 336 (*heading*) Rosenhahnite, a new hydrous silicate from Mendocino County, California. **1973** *Nature* 5 Jan. 42/1 Thermal dehydration data showed that the molecule of water is given off very slowly at temperatures between 400 and 500°C and a single crystal of rosenhahnite transforms into an almost perfect single crystal of wollastonite, $CaSiO_3$.

Rosenkreuzian, var. ROSICRUCIAN *sb.* and *a.*

rosennie, obs. form of ROSINY.

rose noble. [f. ROSE *sb.* + NOBLE *sb.*[1] 2.]

1. A gold coin current in the fifteenth and sixteenth centuries, being a variety of the noble with the figure of a rose stamped upon it, and of varying value at different times and places. *Obs.* exc. *Hist.*

1473 *Acc. Ld. High Treas. Scot.* I. 64 A Franche croune and half a ross noble. **1488** *Ibid.* 90 Takin.. the saim tyme, viij royse nobillis. **1494** HALYBURTON *Ledger* 51 A fardyn of a ros nobyll, price 3*s.* 4½*g.* **1507** *Extr. Aberd. Reg.* (1844) I. 434 Thai prisit.. the weicht of the Rose noble till tua merkis. **1553** *Extr. Rec. Edinb.* (1871) 274 Gevin to the provest for the wyld aventurs,.. ane ross noble, iij[li] viij[s]. **1589** WOTTON *Lett.* (1907) I. 235 In receiving my money at Stoade I took rose nobles after 20*s.* 4*d.* **1630** *R. Johnson's Kingd. & Commw.* A 3, [The French] have thought to disgrace his whole storie, by calling him a Pensioner of England, and a man hired to write by the good Rose-nobles of England. **1688** HOLME *Armoury* III. 29/1 The Rose Noble.. is also termed the Rose Royal, or the Royal of England. **1710** *Lond. Gaz.* No. 4748/4 A Queen Elizabeth's Piece of 35*s.* 3 Rose Nobles. **1726-31** TINDAL *Rapin's Hist. Eng.* (1743) II. XVII. 157 The double Rose-Noble, or Rose-Rial, which is a noble Medal. **1820** SCOTT *Monast.* xxix, The knight cut short his argument, by throwing the landlord a rose-noble. **1853** HUMPHREYS *Coin Collector's Man.* II. 449 There was also the old noble, now called the 'rose noble', to distinguish it from the George noble which had been newly issued. **1888** RIDER HAGGARD *Col. Quaritch* xli, There were Rose Nobles of Edward IV.

transf. **1611** BEAUM. & FL. *Philaster* v. iv, *Capt.* Philaster. Cry my Rose nobles, cry. *All.* Philaster.

attrib. *a* **1668** DAVENANT *Man's the Master* Epil., You men with bright rose-noble hair. **1695** in J. W. *Drayton's Heroical Ep.* A iv, All is Standard, all Rose-noble Gold.

2. *dial.* or *local.* **a.** The hound's tongue (*Cynoglossum officinale*). **b.** The figwort, *esp.* the knotted figwort (*Scrophularia nodosa*).

1876- in BRITTEN & HOLLAND *Eng. Plant-names.* **1877** *Hardwicke's Science Gossip* 46/1 *Scrophularia nodosa* is known by the name of 'rose-noble'. **1900** MCILROY *Craiglinnie Burn* ix, Salutary herbs, such as rosenoble, dandelion,.. and hoarhound.

Rosenthal ('rəʊzəntɑːl). The name of Philip *Rosenthal*, founder of a porcelain factory at Selb in Bavaria *c* 1880, used *attrib.* of pottery made there.

1947 M. PENKALA *European Porcelain* 64 Rosenthal porcelain is carefully modelled and decorated. **1962** P. PURSER *Peregrination 22* XXX. 136 The tray was silver and the tea service Rosenthal china. **1970** E. PACE *Saberlegs* XVI. 152 Oranges heaped in an old Rosenthal bowl. **1977** C. MCFADDEN *Serial* (1978) i. 8/2 They spent it rapidly on.. Rosenthal china.

roseny, obs. form of ROSINY.

roseo-, combining form, repr. L. *rose-us* in the sense 'rose-coloured', in names of various salts, alkalis, etc., as ***roseochrome, -chromic, -chromium, -cobalt, -cobaltia, -rhodium.***

1853 *Chem. Gaz.* XI. 208 Fixed bases decompose the salts of roseocobaltia. **1857** *Ibid.* XV. 147 The salts of roseocobalt have a purely saline.. taste. **1859** *Ibid.* XVII. 84 A new ammoniaco-metallic base, which the author calls roseochrome. **1889** MORLEY & MUIR *Watt's Dict. Chem.* II. 160 Roseochromium chloride. **1894** *Ibid.* IV. 407 Roseorhodium compounds.

rose of Jericho. [Cf. *Ecclus.* xxiv. 14.]

1. A small annual cruciferous plant (*Anastatica hierochuntina*), native to the arid deserts of South-west Asia and North-east Africa, the dried fronds of which unfold under the influence of moisture; the resurrection plant, Mary's flower, or rose of the Virgin.

c **1400** *Three Kings Cologne* 90 In þis wey þat oure lady seynt Marie ȝede in to Egipt, and.. þat sche come aȝene, growe drye roses þe wich be cleped þe roses of Ierico. **1548** TURNER *Names Herbes* (E.D.S.) 12 For lacke of that, thys rose of hierico semeth to be amomis. **1597** [see HEATH *sb.* 5 b]. **1601** HOLLAND *Pliny* II. 258 Likewise the iuice of the herb Amomum [*marg.* Rose of Ierico]. **1687** LOVELL tr. *Thevenot's Trav.* I. 193 In the plain of Jericho, there are Roses of Jericho (as they call them).., they blow not unless they be put into water, and then they blow in all seasons. **1703** MAUNDRELL *Journ. Jerus.* (1721) 86 The Roses of Jericho were not to be found at this season. **1760** J. LEE *Introd. Bot.* App. 325 Rose of Jericho, *Anastatica.* **1849** BALFOUR *Man. Bot.* §762 Rose of Jericho,.. remarkable for the hygrometric property of the old withered annual stems. **1872** H. MACMILLAN *True Vine* vi. 257 Like the rose of Jericho, which.. is carried by the wind to some moist place where its seed may be sown.

†**b.** (See quot.) *Obs. rare*[−0].

1753 *Chambers' Cycl.* Suppl. *App.*, *Rose of Jericho*, a name by which some call the *Hesperis.*

†**2.** *transf.* The Virgin Mary. *Obs. rare.*

c **1430** LYDG. *Min. Poems* (Percy Soc.) 48 This rose of Jericho, ther grewh non suyche in May. *Ibid.* 96 This Rose of Jericho fresshest on lyve. *c* **1485** *Digby Myst.* I. 13 This glorious maiden.. of Ierico the sote rose Floure.

rose of Sharon ('ʃɛərən). [Heb. *Shārōn*, the name of a fertile level tract along the coast of Palestine between Joppa and Mount Carmel.]

1. a. An Eastern flower variously identified with the crocus, polyanthus narcissus, and cistus.

The identity of the flower is quite uncertain. The Hebrew word is *ḥabaççeleth*, which the translators of the Revised Version explain as 'the autumn crocus'.

1611 BIBLE *Song Sol.* ii. 1, I am the rose of Sharon, and the lillie of the valleys. **1764** CHURCHILL *Gotham* Poems 1767 II. 13 The Rose of Sharon which perfumes the Vale. *a* **1826** HEBER *'By cool Siloam's shady rill'* 4 How sweet the breath, beneath the hill, Of Sharon's dewy rose. **1835** V. MONRO *Ramble in Syria* I. 75 Unless the 'rose of Sharon' is the *Cistus roseus* of Linnæus, which grows abundantly, I know not what it may be. **1856** *N. & Q.* 2nd Ser. II. 437/2 Even less like a true-rose than *Helianthemum roseum*.., which Monro and Wilde think the 'Rose of Sharon'.

b. *U.S.* The Syrian hibiscus, *H. syriacus* or *Althæa frutex.*

1847 DARLINGTON *Amer. Weeds & Usef. Pl.* (1860) 67 Syrian Hibiscus. Rose of Sharon. Shrubby Althæa. **1876** E. G. WHITE *Testimonies for Church* (1948) I. 19 There was a beautiful pink flower in the garden called the rose of Sharon. **1974** *Daily Colonist* (Victoria, B.C.) 23 July 20/6 The other Rose of Sharon is a real beauty whose true name is *Hibiscus syriacus.*

c. A species of St. John's wort, esp. *Hypericum calycinum.*

1882 *Garden* 15 July 41/2 The Olympic St. John's Wort is .. nearly as large as the common Rose of Sharon. **1886** R. HOLLAND *Cheshire Gloss.* 291 Rose of Sharon, *Hypericum calycinum.* **1938** A. T. JOHNSON *Garden To-day* xl. 141 The old 'Rose of Sharon'.., a lowly carpeting shrub, is fairly well known. **1979** C. E. L. PHILLIPS *New Small Garden* xv. 243 There are 'carpeting' plants for covering rough places or growing under trees. The Rose-of-Sharon is one of the most useful of these.

2. Used figuratively. (See quots.)

1781 COWPER *Hope* 463 See Germany send forth Her sons to.. plant successfully sweet Sharon's rose On icy plains. **1819** SCOTT *Ivanhoe* xx[i]v, I am not an outlaw, then, fair Rose of Sharon.

3. Chiefly *U.S.* The name of a pattern used in quilting. Also *attrib.*

1894 *Scribner's Mag.* Sept. 363/1 Other floral designs, the sunflower, double peony, rose of Sharon hint at flower-borders lovingly tended by the over-taxed hands of a busy housewife. **1915** M. D. WEBSTER *Quilts* caption facing p. 75 Rose of Sharon. Made in Indiana about 65 years ago. It has a wool interlining instead of the usual cotton. **1929** R. E. FINLEY *Old Patchwork Quilts* xi. 126 The quilt shown.. presents the original somewhat crude but very old type of 'Rose of Sharon' block. **1964** D. BRIGHTBILL *Quilting as Hobby* 88/1 The most popular pattern [of Bride's Quilts].. was the Rose of Sharon... Its name was probably derived from the Song of Solomon: 'I am the Rose of Sharon And the Lily-of-the-Valley.' **1966** D. A. HINSON *Quilting Man.* iii. 45 The Rose of Sharon quilt patterns are legion. **1974** *Times* 11 Jan. 9/5 Quilting is a special craft of [the Mennonites]..and they love the traditional patterns like Rose of Sharon.

roseola (rəʊ'ziːələ). *Path.* [mod.L., f. *rose-us* rosy + dimin. suffix *-ola*; cf. F. *roséole.*] A rash of rosy spots or eruptions occurring in measles and similar diseases; also, false or German measles.

1818 E. THOMPSON tr. *Cullen's Nosologia* (ed. 3) 326 Roseola; Rose Rash. A rose coloured efflorescence, without papulæ or wheals. **1880** *Flint's Princ. Med.* 1071 The eruptive fever called roseola or rose rash, sometimes called false measles, is an affection of very little importance. **1889** E. SMITH *Treat. Dis. Childr.* (ed. 2) 31 Epidemic roseola, often called..German Measles, is a mild infectious complaint.

Hence **rose'oliform** *a.*

1899 *Allbutt's Syst. Med.* VIII. 485 The term includes.. erythematous urticaria in sheets (roseoliform, rubeoliform, scarlatiniform).

ro'seolar, *a. Path.* [f. prec. + -AR.] Of or pertaining to, of the nature of, roseola.

1877 F. T. ROBERTS *Handbk. Med.* (ed. 3) I. 110 Roseolar or erythematous eruptions have been observed in some instances, and in others certain bluish spots. **1896** *Allbutt's Syst. Med.* I. 820 The appearance of roseolar spots.

ro'seolous, *a. Path.* [-OUS.] = prec.

1861 BUMSTEAD *Ven. Dis.* (1879) 747 In some cases,.. punctae of a deeper color are seen on the surface of the roseolous patches. **1873** F. T. ROBERTS *Handbk. Med.* 1008 A roseolous rash. **1897** *Allbutt's Syst. Med.* II. 564 Roseolous and other eruptions.

'roseous, *a.* [f. L. *rose-us* + -OUS.] Rose-like.

1786 ABERCROMBIE *Gard. Assist., Arr.* 58 Hollyhock (*alcea*), Roseous or rose-flowered.

'rosepath. [f. ROSE *sb.* + PATH *sb.*] A pattern used in weaving.

1932 SIMPSON & WEIR *Weaver's Craft* x. 92 Other suitable 'threading drafts' will be given; but the 'Rose-path' entering offers plenty of scope for experiment and a great variety of patterns. **1960** A. GIBBS in G. Lewis *Handbk. Crafts* 103 Let us assume that we are going to use a simple pattern, Rosepath (this is a universal pattern, being found in peasant weaving throughout the world; it is capable of a very large number of variations).

rose-pink, *sb.* and *a.* [f. ROSE *sb.* + PINK *sb.*[5]]

A. *sb.* **1.** A pigment of a pinkish hue, produced by colouring whiting or chalk with a decoction of Brazil-wood, etc.

1735 J. PEELE *Perspective* 29 Rose-pink finely ground and powdered. **1795** *Gentl. Mag.* LXV. II. 741, I should suppose rose-pink no other than chalk or whiting tinged of a red colour. **1836–7** DICKENS *Sk. Boz, Scenes* xx, A dinner.. where clean faces appeared in lieu of black ones smeared with rose pink. **1847** SMEATON *Builder's Man.* 100 Take of linseed oil one quart, alkenett root one ounce, and rose pink half an ounce. **1877** E. S. DALLAS *Kettner's Bk. of Table* 338 The rose-pink, which is sometimes used for colouring..is obtained from the peach tree.

2. A pink tint or hue like that of roses. Also *fig.*, sentimentality, sentimental writing.

1864 in WEBSTER. **1872** G. MEREDITH *Let.* 3 Dec. (1970) I. 473 Read the first chapter for a specimen of modern rose-pink. **1882** *Garden* 1 April 223 Dense trusses of flowers of a lovely rose-pink. **1885** G. MEREDITH *Diana* i, Rose-pink and dirty drab will..have passed away.

B. *adj.* **1.** Of a pinkish colour resembling that of the rose; rosy pink, roseate.

1843 PORTLOCK *Geol.* 213 Arragonite is found..at Down Hill, of a rose pink shade. **1883** V. STUART *Egypt* 363 In the centre of the great hall is a beautiful rose-pink granite sarcophagus.

2. *fig.* = ROSE-COLOURED *a.* 3.

1837 CARLYLE *Fr. Rev.* I. II. iii, If we pierce through that rosepink vapour of Sentimentalism, Philanthropy, and Feasts of Morals. **1861** HUGHES *Tom Brown at Oxf.* xlii, Hardy..would test his new idea..and ruthlessly strip off any tinsel or rose-pink sentiment. **1891** FARRAR in *Harper's Mag.* May 903 The people of our slums will never be won by a rose-pink religionism.

Hence **'rose-pink** *v.*, to colour with rose-pink.

1836–7 DICKENS *Sk. Boz, Scenes* xiii. 117 'Where's the bleeding officer?'—'Here!' replies the officer, who has been rose-pinking for the character.

rose Pompadour ('rəʊz 'pɒmpədʊə(r)). [f. ROSE *sb.* + POMPADOUR.] = ROSE DU BARRY. Cf. POMPADOUR 2.

Considered by some authorities to be the more correct term.

1884 P. VILLARS tr. *Gasnault & Garnier's French Pottery* ix. 123 We must mention, among the most remarkable productions of the manufactory of Sèvres during the first period whose history we have briefly sketched, the beautiful ornamental vases with..the pink ground termed *rose carné* or *rose Pompadour* (sometimes erroneously called *rose Dubarry*). **1905** W. BURTON tr. *Auscher's Hist & Descr. French Porcelain* viii. 65 In 1757 the painter Xrowet invented that most famous ground-colour, rose-Pompadour. **1935** *Burlington Mag.* May 249/2 The 'claret-colour', which must have started as an attempt to ape the lovely rose Pompadour of Sèvres. **1936** *Ibid.* Dec. p. xix/2 The Sèvres porcelain especially the apple-green and *rose Pompadour* pieces. **1949** *Dict. Colours Interior Decoration* (Brit. Colour Council) III. 23/1 *Rose Pompadour.* This colour (matched to porcelain in the Wallace Collection, London) is named after Madame de Pompadour who took a great interest in the porcelain manufactury, first at Vincennes and later at Sèvres. **1960** R. G. HAGGAR *Conc. Encycl. Continental Pott. & Porc.* 386/2 *Rose Pompadour*.. was invented according to Garnier by Jean Hellot, or, according to Auscher by Xhrouet... It takes its name from the Marquise de Pompadour (died 1764). **1960** H. HAYWARD *Antique Coll.* 243/2 Coalport..produced a rose Pompadour in the 19th cent. **1975** *Oxf. Compan. Decorative Arts* 135/2 An outstanding result of this [development of Sèvres, fostered by royal privileges] was the development of a series of very splendid ground-colours: dark blue in 1749, ..pink ('rose Pompadour') in 1757 and so on.

†**'roser.** *Obs.* Also 5 roseer(e, 5–6 rosere. [a. AF. *roser, = OF. *rosier* ROSIER.] A rose-bush.

c **1300** *Havelok* 2919 þe heu is swilk in hire ler, So is þe rose in roser. ? *a* **1366** CHAUCER *Rom. Rose* 1651 In thilke mirour saw I tho..A roser charged ful of roses. *c* **1400** MAUNDEV. (Roxb.) ix. 35 þase braunchez þat ware brynnand become reed roseres, and þase braunchez þat ware noȝt kindled become whyte roseres. *c* **1450** LOVELICH *Grail* xliii. 239 Vndir a Roser thou wentest there To schonen the hete In alle Manere. **1523** SKELTON *Garl. Laurel* 656 The bankis enturfid with singular solas, Enrailid with rosers. *a* **1568** *Tayis Bank* 114 Roseris raiss on raw.

attrib. *c* **1485** *E.E. Misc.* (Warton Cl.) 67 The same maner throȝe anothere hole of a red rosere branche.

rose-rash. *Path.* [f. ROSE *sb.* + RASH *sb.*[3]] = ROSEOLA.

1818 [see ROSEOLA]. **1834** *Good's Study Med.* (ed. 4) IV. 420 *note*, For the annular rose-rash, the warm-bath, gentle laxatives, and the mineral acids are recommended. **1894** DUKES *Features Epid. Roseola* 15 To mistake roserash for measles causes infinite trouble.

'rose-red, *a.* and *sb.* [f. ROSE *sb.* + RED *a.* and *sb.*[1] Cf. MDu. *rose(n)root* (Du. *roze-*, *rozenrood*), MHG. *rose(n)rôt* (G. *rosenrot*), MSw. *roseneródh* (Sw. *rosenröd*, Da. *-rød*), Icel. *rósrauður*.]

A. *adj.* Red like a rose; rose-coloured.

a **1300** *K. Horn* 16 He was whit so þe flur, Rose red was his colur. *c* **1386** CHAUCER *Sec. Nun's T.* 254 Two corunes han we, Snow white and Rose reed, that shynen cleere. *a* **1400** *Lybeaus Disc.* 1538 Knyghtes..That beth armed sure In rose-reed armure. *c* **1425** *Orolog. Sapient.* vii. in *Anglia* X. 388 By þe vertue of þat rose-rede blode þat þou schaddest. **1796** KIRWAN *Elem. Min.* (ed. 2) I. 328 Redstone..—Its colour, by reflected light, is rose red. **1828** STARK *Elem. Nat. Hist.* I. 474 Body beautiful rose red, silvery on the sides and abdomen. **1871** R. ELLIS *Catullus* lxiv. 275 They..Swim in a rose-red glow.

B. *sb.* A red like that of a rose.

a **1400** *Pol., Rel., & L. Poems* (1903) 271 Wrout is on þe bok with-oute, V. paraffys grete & stoute Bolyd in rose red. **1839** URE *Dict. Arts* 53 The *l[ichen] physodes* gave a yellowish-gray; the *pustulatus*, a rose red. **1872** TENNYSON *Gareth & Lynette* 1061 Beyond a bridge of treble bow, All in a rose-red from the west. **1882** *Garden* 1 April 211 They are both of a uniform soft rose-red.

roseret. *rare.* (See quot. and ROSELET[2].)

1843 RICHARDSON in *Ann. Nat. Hist.* XI. 179 *Atherina presbyteroides* (Nob.), Tasmanian Roseret.

rose'rial. *Obs.* exc. *Hist.* [f. ROSE *sb.* + RIAL *sb.*[1] 3.] A gold coin of the value of thirty shillings, having the figure of a rose upon one side, coined by James I.

1617 MORYSON *Itin.* I. 283 Pieces of thirty shillings, called Rose Ryals... And the aforesaid Rose Ryall was nine penny-weight and five graines. **1695** LOWNDES *Ess. Amendmt. Silver Coins* 26 A Commission..To Coin Rose-Rialls..and Angels. **1710** J. HARRIS *Lex. Techn.* II. s.v., In 3 James I rose rials of gold were coined at 30s a-piece and spur-rials at 15s. **1853** HUMPHREYS *Coin-coll. Man.* II. 465 The rose rial of 30 shillings was similar to those of the preceding reigns. *Ibid.*, The motto on the reverse of the rose rial.

'rose-root. *Bot.* [f. ROSE *sb.* + ROOT *sb.*]

1. One of certain related herbaceous plants, esp. *Sedum rhodiola* or *Rhodiola rosea*, growing in rocky districts or on cliffs, the root of which emits a rose-like fragrance when bruised or dried; = ROSEWORT 1.

1597 GERARDE *Herball* 416 Doubtlesse it tooke his name *Rhodia radix*, of the roote, which smelleth like a Rose: in English Rose roote, and Rose woort. **1611** COTGR., *Racine sentant la rose*, Rosewort, Roseroot; an hearb. **1786** ABERCROMBIE *Gard. Assist., Arr.* 65 *Rhodiola rosea*, or rose root. **1806** [see ROSEWORT 1]. **1858** KINGSLEY *Misc.* I. 164 Sea-green rose-root, with its strange fleshy stems and leaves, which mark..the beginning of the Alpine world.

attrib. **1855** MISS PRATT *Flower. Pl.* II. 327 *Sedum Rhodiola*, Rose-root Stone Crop.

†**2.** = ORPINE 2. (Cf. ROSEWORT 2.) *Obs.*

1731 MILLER *Gard. Dict.* s.v. *Anacampseros*, *Telephium*, or *Rhodia Radix*; in English, Orpine, Live-ever, or Rose-root. **1753** *Chambers' Cycl.* Suppl. *App.*, *Rose-root*, a name by which some call the Anacampseros or Orpin.

'rosery. [f. ROSE *sb.* + -ERY.] A portion of a garden set apart for growing roses; a rosarium; a cluster or plantation of rose-bushes.

1864 HIBBERD *Rose Bk.* iv. 83 Those who form their roseries by planting small plants. **1883** J. PAYN *Thicker than Water* xiii, With walled gardens, a huge rosery and..a bowling-green. **1888** *Co-operative News* 4 Aug. 783 The hills are crowned..by art with..fairy-like roseries.

rose-scented, *a.* [f. ROSE *sb.*] Having the perfume of a rose.

1785 MARTYN *Rousseau's Bot.* xxiv. (1794) 335 The Rose-scented [geranium] has also lobed leaves. **1817** KIRBY & SP. *Entomol.* xxi. (1818) II. 249 The rose-scented capricorn (*Cerambyx moschatus*, L.) produced a similar effect. **1820** KEATS '*Bards of Passion and of Mirth*' 14 Where the daisies are rose-scented. **1852** G. W. JOHNSTON *Cottage Gard. Dict.* 819/1 *Sedum Rhodiola* (Rose-scented).

roset (rəʊ'zɛt), *sb.*[1] Also 5 rosytt, 6 rosett, 6–8 rosset. [Based upon ROSE *sb.* Cf. ROSET *a.* and ROSETTE *sb.*

F. *rosette* occurs in sense 1, but is app. not recorded till much later than the first English examples. A med.L. *rosetus* 'rose-coloured' is given by Du Cange (1279).]

†**1.** A rose-coloured pigment, or the colour produced by this. (Cf. ROSET *a.* 2.) *Obs.*

c **1485** *E.E. Misc.* (Warton Cl.) 72 To temper roset, grynd hit on a stone, with as myche gume and also myche water as of rosytt. **1558** WARDE tr. *Alexis' Secr.* I. v. 92 Than scrape the saied roset and kepe it, and whan you will write withall, stiepe it in gommed water. **1578** LYTE *Dodoens* 547 With the iuyce of this herbe (red Blite), one may write as faire a red, as with roset made of Brasill. **1612** PEACHAM *Gentl. Exerc.* I. xxiii. (1634) 80 Take Florey Blew, and grinde it with a little fine Roset, and it will make a deep Violet. **1674** LEYBOURN *Compl. Surv.* 309 Rosset, washed and tempered with Gum water, differs not much in Colour from Lake. **1688** HOLME *Armoury* III. 149/1 Rosset..is a soft and fadeing colour which will not continue long.

†**2.** ? The rose-pear (cf. ROSE *sb.* 23). *Obs.*

1600 SURFLET *Countrie Farme* III. xlix. 537 Garden, tender and delicate peares, such as are the Eusebian and the Marie peare, the roset, hasting,..butter peare.

3. = ROSETTE *sb.* Also *Comb.*

1807 in Georgiana Hill *Hist. Eng. Dress* (1893) II. 222 My shoes [are] of white satin with silver rosets. **1830** *Mech. Mag.* XIV. 31 By..again subjecting it to the hammer, a beautiful roset-shaped Damascus is obtained. **1831** DAVIES *Nat. Med.* 47 A number of small whitish crystals, disposed in rosets or in a radical form.

roset ('roːzɪt), *sb.*[2] *Sc.* Also 6 ros(a)it, rosett, 6, 9 rosit, 8–9 rozet, 9 rozit, rozzet. [Var. of ROSIN, perh. by a further alteration of ROSIL: cf. Sc. *groset*, *rangat*[2], with F. *groseille*, *ringaille*.] Rosin, resin. Also *attrib.*

1501 *Acc. Ld. High Treas. Scot.* II. 24 For vij pund of rosait to mak the clath thicht. **1513** DOUGLAS *Æneis* VI. iii. 45 Full of rosett doun bett is the fir tre. *Ibid.* 113 A huge heip ..Of dry aik schidis and fat rosit treis. **1536** BELLENDEN *Cron. Scot.* (1821) I. 136 With birnand flammis of pik, roset and brintstane. **1578** *Inventories R. wardrobe* (1815) 257 Ane barrell of auld rosett.

a **1774** FERGUSSON *Election* Poems (1845) 40 The canty cobbler quats his sta', His roset and his lingans. **1786** BURNS *To a Louse* v, O for some rank, mercurial rozet, Or fell, red smeddum. **1828** MOIR *Mansie Wauch* vii. 64, I was visibly convinced by the smell of burnt roset. **1884** D. GRANT *Lays & Leg. North* 16 The flame..as fiercely as a rozet log On winter hearth did flare. **1894** LATTO *Tam. Bodkin* iii, The rozet spread oot like a pancake i' his loof.

b. ***roset-end***, the rosined end of a shoemaker's thread.

1808 MAYNE *Siller Gun* I. xx, Sae, here and there, a rozit-end Held on their locks! **1868** G. MACDONALD *R. Falconer* xi, He had just cracked the roset-ends off his hands.

†**roset**, *a. Obs.* Also 5 rosett, roseet, rosete (russet), 5–6 rosette, 6 rosset. [In sense 1 ultimately repr. late L. *rosāt-us* (in *oleum rosātum*, whence also OF. *huile rosat*). Sense 2 may be an attrib. use of ROSET *sb.*[1]]

1. (Placed after the sb.) Compounded with the essence of roses; distilled from roses:

a. ***sugar roset.*** (Cf. OF. *sucre rosach.*)

1398 TREVISA *Barth. De P.R.* XVII. cxxxvii. (Bodl. MS.), Wiþ sugere is ymade succura rosacia suger rosette that haþ vertu to comforte and to binde. *c* **1450** BURGH *Secrees* 1712 Sugre Roseet with aloes mastyk Wel chawyd. **1450–80** tr. *Secreta Secret.* 31 Take sugir rosett with aloe, and mastyk and chewe alle harde. **1563** HYLL *Art of Garden.* (1593) 89 That which is called suger roset..helpeth the bloudy flixe. **1579** LANGHAM *Garden Health* (1633) 533 Sugar Roset is good for the bloudy flux, the chollerick vomitings. **1657** W. COLES *Adam in Eden* 82 Confections..which still retain with them the name of sugar, as Sugar Roset, Sugar Violet, &c.

b. ***oil, vinegar, honey roset.***

a **1400** *Stockh. Med. MS.* ii. 260 in *Anglia* XVIII. 314 3if it be lewkyd with oyle of [*sic*] roset. *c* **1450** *M.E. Med. Bk.* (Heinrich) 92 For to make oile roset [*v.rr.* rosete, rosette, russet; tr. L. *oleum rosaceum*]. **1541** ELYOT *Cast. Helthe* 93 b, Use to take whyte wine good, white vyneger rosette, water of roses, in equall portions. **1558** WARDE tr. *Alexis' Secr.* I. I. 8 b, You must adde unto it a lytle grene waxe and a very lytle Honye roset.

2. Rose-coloured, roseate.

1548 ELYOT, *Rubriceta*, rosette colour, suche as women vse to peincte theim with. **1558** PHAER *Æneid* I. B iv b, His mother..with a roset youth his eyes and countenance overcheard. *Ibid.* VII. 144 The golden morning bright with roset wheles dyd mounting rise.

ˈroset, *v. Sc.* Also 6 rosat. [f. ROSET *sb.*²] *trans.* To smear or rub (*esp.* a violin bow) with rosin. Hence **ˈroseting** *vbl. sb.*

1513 *Acc. Ld. H. Treas. Scot.* IV. 476 For a barrell of uley to the Margret for the rosatyn of hir, xlv s. *Ibid.* 477 For ane pot to the rosatyn of hir. *a* **1774** FERGUSSON *Poems* (1845) 5 Fiddlers! your pins in temper fix, And rozet weel your fiddlesticks. **1820** HOGG *Shepherd's Cal.* vi, Such a forenoon of cutting, and sewing, and puffing, and roseting. **1865** TESTER *Poems* 161 Roset weel yer fiddle bow.

roset, obs. form of RUSSET.

ˈrose-ˌtinted, *a.* [f. ROSE *sb.*] = ROSE-COLOURED *a.* spec. ***rose-tinted spectacles*** = *rose-coloured spectacles* s.v. ROSE-COLOURED *a.* 3.

1855 SINGLETON *Virgil* I. 247 She said, and, turning off, reflected sheen From her rose-tinted neck. **1885** 'MARK TWAIN' *Let.* 2 Mar. (1917) II. 452 He sold me $10,000 worth of another rose-tinted stock. **1956** C. WILSON *Outsider* viii. 245 The good-natured, eupeptic vulgarian who sees life through rose-tinted spectacles. **1966** *Listener* 20 Oct. 559/2 The official propaganda machine, whose task is to present every aspect of Soviet life through rose-tinted spectacles. **1977** *Church Times* 25 Feb. 7/2 There are no rose-tinted specs shading the very clear eyes of Elizabeth West as she describes life in her *Hovel in the Hills.*

ˈrose-tree. Also rose tree. [f. ROSE *sb.* + TREE *sb.*] A rose-bush.

c **1340** *Nominale* (Skeat) 667 *If, roser et cenelere,* Hw, rosetre and hawetre. **1398** TREVISA *Barth. De P.R.* XVII. cxxxvii. (Bodl. MS.), þe rose tree springeþ somtyme bi sowinge of sede. **1611** [see ROSE-BUSH]. **1664** EVELYN *Kal. Hort.* (1729) 195 It were profitable now also to top your Rose Trees. **1712** ADDISON *Spect.* No. 418 ⁋8 His Rose-trees, Wood-bines, and Jessamines, may flower together. **1774** GOLDSM. *Nat. Hist.* (1824) III. 305 They are to be met with ..upon the leaves of the ash, the poplar, and the rose trees. **1859** GEO. ELIOT *A. Bede* xx, The very rose trees, at which Adam stopped to pluck one, looked as if they grew wild. **1864** TENNYSON *Aylmer's F.* 157 One [hut] look'd all rosetree, and another wore A close-set robe of jasmine set with stars.

Rosetta stone (rəʊˈzɛtə stəʊn). [The name of a celebrated stone, bearing a trilingual inscription dating from the 2nd c. B.C., found in 1799 near Rosetta in Egypt.

The stone, now in the British Museum, bears an inscription in Greek, demotic, and hieroglyphics; the decipherment of the latter two parts of the inscription by Jean-François Champollion in 1822 led to the interpretation of all the other early records of the Egyptian civilization.]

Used *transf.* and *fig.* of something that resembles the Rosetta stone, usu. by acting as a key to some previously unattainable understanding (in quot. 1969, something indecipherable).

1902 *Encycl. Brit.* XXVI. 721/2 Although not the Rosetta stone which enabled him to decipher the minute structure of glucose and its congeners, this compound made possible for the first time the separation and identification of such compounds. **1933** H. G. WELLS *Shape of Things to Come* 24 About a third of the shorthand stuff was already represented by longhand or typescript copy in the folders. That was my Rosetta Stone. **1969** R. LOWELL *Notebk. 1967–68* 102 The typescript looked like a Rosetta Stone. **1975** *New Yorker* 29 Sept. 29/1 A knowledge of accounting is a kind of Rosetta stone. **1979** *Sci. Amer.* Mar. 72/1 The spectrum of the hydrogen atoms has proved to be the Rosetta stone of modern physics: once this pattern of lines had been deciphered much else could also be understood.

roˈsetta-wood. (See quot.)

1843 HOLTZAPFFEL *Turning* I. 103 Rosetta-Wood, is a good sized East Indian wood..; the general colour is a lively red-orange..; the wood is close, hard, and very beautiful when first cut.

rosette (rəʊˈzɛt), *sb.* [a. F. *rosette*, dim. of *rose* ROSE *sb.*: see -ETTE.]

1. a. A decoration consisting of a bunch or knot of ribbons, leather strips, worsted or the like, concentrically disposed so as to resemble a rose, and worn as an ornament or badge.

1790 *Pennsylvania Packet* 11 Dec. 3/2 Imported..Ladies ..elegant..beaded rosettes, for shoes. **1802** JAMES *Milit. Dict.*, *Rosette*, an ornamental bunch of ribands, or cut leather, which is worn both by officers and soldiers in the British service, on the upper part of their cues. **1838** DICKENS *Nickleby* xxiv, A pair of white soiled satin shoes with large blue rosettes. **1848** LAYARD *Nineveh* (1850) 325 The ornaments on his robes consisted of rosettes and fringes. **1871** G. MEREDITH *H. Richmond* xiii, The ladies were working rosettes for me. **1965** T. GUNN in *New Statesman* 14 May 768/1 To enter Jerusalem on an ass..or wear a rosette for Arsenal. **1967** *Listener* 26 Oct. 552/3, I walked up to one of the chaps and said.., pointing at the two Welsh rosettes upon his chest: 'Excuse me, what are these for?'

transf. **1863** TYNDALL *Heat* v. §195 We have our drop of water moulded to a most beautiful rosette.

b. *spec.* as a decoration of harness; *esp.* applied to such a decoration awarded to prize-winners at horse shows and similar events.

1858 SIMMONDS *Dict. Trade*, *Rosette*,..an ornament for a horse's head-stall. **1875** KNIGHT *Dict. Mech.* 1984/1 *Rosette*, ..a leather or metallic ornament placed on a bridle or halter at the point where the front joins the crown-piece. **1951** J. PULLEIN-THOMPSON *Radney Riding Club* ii. 31 When the ponies were fed and settled for the night Eric nailed the new rosettes beside the others in the saddle-room. **1957** R. FERGUSON *Rosettes for Jill* v. 52, I fastened my two red rosettes and the blue one on Black Boy's brow-band, and collected my prizes.

c. *Naut.* A form of knot.

1875 KNIGHT *Dict. Mech.* 1240/2.

d. *transf.* A rose- or star-shaped symbol used in guides to hotels and restaurants to indicate the standard of service or cuisine provided.

1966 P. V. PRICE *France* 318 The famous 'stars' of Michelin, which are indicated by rosettes in the guide book, refer *solely* to the standard of the food and drink. **1974** *Country Life* 24 Jan. 167/3 (Advt.), Our AA Rosette reflects ..the high standards of country house hotel-keeping of which we are justly proud. **1976** *Times* 2 Oct. 10/1 In Avignon..a truly Lucullan dinner at *Hiély-Lucullus*..the food worthy of its two rosettes in Michelin.

2. *Arch.* **a.** An ornament resembling a rose in form, painted, sculptured, or moulded upon, attached to, or incised in a wall or other surface.

1806 DALLAWAY *Obs. Eng. Archit.* 179 About the reign of Edward III..more ornament was introduced, and delicately carved orbs and rosettes were added. **1838** *Murray's Hdbk. N. Germ.* 493 The winding stair terminates, under a species of carved rosette. **1872** ELLABOMBE *Bells of Ch.* in *Ch. Bells Devon* 215 A girdle of twelve oval medallions containing, in relief, busts of the twelve Apostles, each divided by elegant rosettes.

b. A rounded ornamental perforation; a rosace or rose-window.

1836 LONGF. in *Life* (1891) I. 248 The two round windows or rosettes are exquisitely beautiful. **1851** RUSKIN *Stones Venice* (1874) I. xvii. 184 The arches in pairs, or in triple and quadruple groups,..with small rosettes pierced above them for light.

3. *Metallurgy.* One of the disk-like plates formed by successive sprinklings of water upon the molten copper in a crucible.

1797 *Encycl. Brit.* (ed. 3) XI. 467/1 By again sprinkling water on the mass of copper, it is all of it reduced into plates, which are called *rosettes*, and these plates are what is called *rosette-copper*. **1839** URE *Dict. Arts* 326 The *matt*..being sprinkled with water and taken off, leaves the black copper to be treated in a similar way, and converted into *rosettes*. **1875** KNIGHT *Dict. Mech.* 1970/1 Copper thus treated is known as *rose copper*, from its red color, and the disks are known as *rosettes*.

4. *Biol.* **a.** A cluster of organs or parts, a marking or group of markings, resembling a rose in form or arrangement.

1834 MᶜMURTRIE *Cuvier's Anim. Kingd.* 312 In the third section of the sedentary rectigrade spiders, the *Orbitelæ*, the external fusi are almost conical, slightly salient, convergent, and form a rosette. **1872** H. A. NICHOLSON *Palaeont.* 105 In another great group the ambulacral areas..simply form a kind of rosette upon the upper surface of the shell. **1888** ROLLESTON & JACKSON *Anim. Life* 723 'Ciliated rosettes,' or minute depressions into the mesoglaea.

b. A cluster of leaves naturally disposed like the petals of a rose. Also, a similar formation as a symptom of plant disease, the leaves on a stem being clustered owing to its greatly reduced internodal growth.

1847 W. E. STEELE *Field Bot.* 42 Scions short, terminating in a rosette of leaves. **1870** HOOKER *Stud. Flora* 359 Leaves ..in lateral rosettes. **1891** *Jrnl. Mycol.* VI. 143 The lower leaves on these tufts or rosettes roll and curl, turn yellow,.. and fall early. **1937** F. D. HEALD *Introd. Plant Path.* ii. 20 Rosettes, or closely grouped clusters of leaves caused by the failure of axes to make a normal elongation. This should not be confused with the normal rosette habit of certain plants. **1952** [see next sense]. **1980** *Amateur Gardening* 18 Oct. 21 The lovely wide-faced flowers..are held over the hairy rosettes of leaves in May and June.

c. Any of various plant diseases in which there are rosette-like malformations of leaves. Also ***rosette disease***.

1891 E. F. SMITH in *Jrnl. Mycol.* VI. 143 It seems best, therefore, to call it [*sc.* the disease] 'the peach rosette' until it can be determined whether it is identical with yellows. *Ibid.* 146 This rosette disease resembles yellows very closely. **1895** in *Funk's Stand. Dict.* **1923** *Phytopathology* XIII. 41 The symptoms of the rosette disease of wheat bear certain resemblances to the symptoms of corn mosaic as described by Kunkel. **1946** *Ann. Reg. 1945* 349 K. M. Smith..has shown that the two separable complexes of tobacco rosette disease may be transmitted..by Aphis. **1950** *Times* 2 Feb. 9/2 This new discovery brings within reach a means of prevention of virus diseases which are transmitted by aphids, such as yellow virus on sugar beet, strawberry virus and rosette disease in groundnuts. **1952** tr. *Gram & Weber's Plant Dis.* 489/2 Rosette is a disease of *Lilium longiflorum* and its varieties...Infected plants have yellow leaves which remain in a basal rosette. **1972** J. T. SLYKHUIS in Kado & Agrawal *Princ. & Techniques Plant Virol.* vii. 208 Evidence that pigeon pea sterility and rose rosette are caused by viruses rests on transmission of the disease by grafting.

d. *Med.* A group of red cells bearing one factor adhering to one red cell bearing another factor, produced in tests for antigens, antibodies, and related substances on the cell surfaces.

[**1958** *Jrnl. Clin. Invest.* XXXVII. 1216/2 The antibody-sensitized red cells were seen to cluster around individual leukocytes, often producing rosette-patterns.] **1964** *Immunol.* VII. 477 Many of the peritoneal cells were seen to be coated with sheep red cells, giving, in many instances, a characteristic 'rosette' appearance. **1966** *Jrnl. Exper. Med.* CXXIII. 144 (*caption*) Rosettes of sheep red cells adsorbed onto the surface of guinea pig lung macrophages. **1971** I. M. ROITT *Essent. Immunol.* iii. 50 When lymphocytes are incubated with, say, sheep red cells, those with surface receptors for the erythrocytes will bind them to form a rosette. **1976** *Nature* 15 July 216/1 This heat treatment does not destroy the ability of the macrophages to form rosettes with sheep red blood cells.

5. a. A circular rose-like pattern; also, one of the pattern-disks of a rose-engine.

1767 J. WEDGWOOD *Let.* 23 May (1965) 53 At Birmingham I saw a Lathe executed upon the plan of that which is full of Rosetts, and every Rosett had a projection from the edge. **1843** *Penny Cycl.* XXV. 424/2 Upon the mandril are mounted the pattern guides, or rosettes, circular plates of gun-metal or brass, each..having two patterns or waves upon its rim. **1867** *Chambers's Encycl.* IX. 594/2 A number of rosettes are generally strung at once on the mandrel. **1875** KNIGHT *Dict. Mech.* 963/2 The means by which the stars, rosettes, and ornamental tablets..are produced around the denominating figures, etc., of bank-notes. **1931** A. U. DILLEY *Oriental Rugs & Carpets* (caption to plate 33) India Rug of Persian star, palinette, rosette, and leaf design with border of realistic flowering plants.

b. = ROSE DIAMOND.

1865 BRANDE & COX *Dict. Sci.* etc., s.v. *Diamond*, They are cut chiefly into two forms, called brilliants, and rose-diamonds or rosettes.

c. Any object, or arrangement of parts, resembling a rose in form.

1856 *Orr's Circ. Sci., Pract. Chem.* 507 The gas must be burnt under a platinum rosette. **1875** KNIGHT *Dict. Mech.* 1984/1 *Rosette*,..a form of gas-burner in which the gas issues at a circular series of holes.

d. = ROSE *sb.* 14 g.

1896 R. ROBB *Electr. Wiring* v. 152 The holes in the socket bushing and in the rosette are little larger than enough to allow the cord to slide through them. **1904** *Electr. World & Engin.* 7 May 887/2 The finish and smoothness of the rosette are in every way admirable. **1961** C. C. CARR *Craft's Amer. Electricians' Handbk.* (ed. 8) iv. 126 The drop cord passes through the hole in the center and is attached to connections inside the body of the rosette.

e. *Geol.* = ROCK-ROSE 5, ROSE *sb.* 16 e.

[**1902** H. A. MIERS *Mineral.* IV. i. 249 Irregular conjunctions are distinguished as—... Rosette-shaped, when they overlap round a centre like the petals of a rose.] **1905** *Bull. U.S. Geol. Survey* No. 239. 59 The rosettes are sometimes a foot in diameter, while there is every gradation from this to submicroscopic size. **1923** *Proc. Oklahoma Acad. Sci.* III. 102 Barite and especially the form known as 'sand barite rosettes', has long attracted attention as one of the most widely disseminated of Oklahoma minerals. **1971** FEJER & WALKER tr. *H. Baegel's Collector's Guide Minerals & Gemstones* i. 31 Tabular minerals (gypsum, barite, hematite) may occasionally form rosettes ('desert roses').

f. *Engin.* An arrangement about a point of three or more coplanar lines that represent the axes of strain gauges used to determine the strain existing in a structure or material at that point.

1931 W. HOVGAARD in *Trans. Soc. Naval Architects & Marine Engineers* XXXIX. 26/1 We arrive thus at what may be called a 'rosette' of strain measurements consisting of one horizontal (longitudinal) strain, one vertical (transverse), and two at 45 degrees inclination. **1946** G. MURPHY *Advanced Mechanics of Materials* iii. 64 Valuable information concerning the stresses can be obtained by measuring the strains developed in a model or a trial design of the prototype and converting the strains into stresses. The usual procedure involves the measurement of the normal strains on a rosette of three or four intersecting gage lines at the point. **1950** M. I. HETENYI *Handbk. Exper. Stress Anal.* ix. 400 The four-gage 45° rosette combines all the advantages enumerated..for the equiangular and the rectangular rosettes. **1969** H. N. NORTON *Handbk. Transducers for Electronic Measuring Syst.* xiii. 559 Gages with multiple grids (rosettes) were developed for simultaneous measurement of strain in different directions.

6. *attrib.* and *Comb.*, as ***rosette bud, form, habit, plate, symptom, virus***; ***rosette-forming, -like*** adjs.; **rosette copper** (see sense 3); **rosette gauge** *Engin.*, an assembly of strain gauges whose axes correspond to the lines of a rosette (see sense 5 f); **rosette plant** (see quot. 1934).

1977 J. L. HARPER *Population Biol. of Plants* xviii. 543 Digitalis purpurea regenerate from rosette buds if the inflorescence is damaged before the seed is required. **1898** MANSON *Trop. Dis.* 25 In quartans and tertians.. sporulating rosette-forms are seen occasionally. **1977** J. L. HARPER *Population Biol. of Plants* xiv. 437 The flora of Port Meadow is composed of perennial grasses..plus laterally spreading clonal dicots..and some rosette-forming species. **1943** *Exper. Stress Anal.* I. I. 13/2 In connection with the use of wire resistance rosette gages..small corrections must sometimes be applied to the initial strain observations. **1969** H. N. NORTON *Handbk. Transducers for Electronic Measuring Syst.* xiii. 561 When using rosette gages, it is necessary to operate upon the output readings using Poisson's ratio to convert strain rates to stress. **1937** Rosette habit [see sense 4 b above]. **1857** HENFREY *Elem. Bot.* 23 The rosette-like off-shoots of House-leeks. **1903** W. R. FISHER tr. *Schimper's Plant-Geogr.* III. iv. 706 Perennial rosette-plants play a leading part, especially on alpine meadows. **1934** H. GILBERT-CARTER tr. *Raunkiaer's Life Forms of Plants* ii. 47 A transition is formed from the rosette plants in which..the foliage leaves are all gathered into a rosette at the base. **1965** *Austral. Encycl.* VII. 123/2 It [*sc.* the Western Australian pitcher-plant] is a small rosette plant. **1888** ROLLESTON & JACKSON *Anim. Life* 235 Two cords.. connect the rosette plates at one end with the corresponding plates at the other end. **1928** C. E. OWENS *Princ. Plant Path.* xix. 423 Potato plants which are attacked by the Rhizoctonia fungus on the underground parts sometimes show leaf-roll and rosette symptoms. **1937** K. M. SMITH *Textbk. Plant Virus Dis.* ii. 186 Numerous other [groundnut] plants in the Gambia have been observed showing typical rosette symptoms. **1960** J. E. VAN DER PLANK *Plant Path.* III. vii. 262 Rosette virus ordinarily spreads slowly from peach to peach. **1977** J. L. HARPER *Population Biol. of Plants* xvi. 488 The rosette virus of peach..kills the host rapidly.

rosette (rəʊˈzɛt), *v.* [f. ROSETTE *sb.*]

1. *intr. Med.* Of a cell: to form a rosette.

1969 [implied in ROSETTING *ppl. a.* below]. **1973** *Jrnl. Immunol.* CXI. 1834 Lymphocytes with binding sites for complement..do not rosette with R[abbit] R[ed] B[lood]

C[ells]. **1977** *Lancet* 5 Nov. 988/1, 2%..of the lymphocytes rosetted with sheep red blood-cells (T cells).

2. *trans.* To award a rosette-like symbol to, as a mark of excellence.

1974 *Guardian* 20 Mar. 1/3 Three restaurants much rosetted by English guides—the Ritz, the Savoy, and the Mirabelle.

So **ro'setting** *ppl. a.*

1969 *Internat. Arch. Allergy* XXXV. 220 Vicarious loss of potentially rosetting cells would distort the results.

rosette, obs. form of ROSET *a.*

ro'setted, *a.* [f. ROSETTE *sb.* + -ED².]

1. a. Having, furnished or ornamented with, rosettes; formed into rosettes.

1836 E. HOWARD *R. Reefer* xxviii, His laced cocked hat, with the rosetted corners. **1836-7** DICKENS *Sk. Boz, Scenes* xx, Knee cords and tops superseded nankeen drawers and rosetted shoes. **1871** *Figure-Training* 75 Balancing herself on the very tips of her rosetted and high-heeled slippers. **1901** *Bull. Geol. Soc. Amer.* XII. 166 Even the loose and less coherent matrix reveals, under the action of wind and rain, an ill-defined, though unmistakably radiate, or rosetted structure. **1955** *Mineral Abstr.* XII. 573 Rosetted crusts of silver-white semseyite on galena. **1966** D. VARADAY *Gara-Yaka's Domain* iv. 47 There they [*sc.* cheetahs]..glared up at their rosetted relative. The humourless leopard glared back at them. **1969** *Internat. Arch. Allergy* XXXV. 214 (*caption*) Typical appearance of rosetted cells obtained with the suspension-centrifugation technique. **1975** *Daily Tel.* 8 Sept. 13 Triumphantly rosetted and bristling with the familiar red-and-white battle insignia of Manchester United.

b. Of skin or pelt: marked with rosette-like blemishes.

1905 W. E. CASTLE *Heredity of Coat Characters in Guinea-Pigs & Rabbits* 75 A rosetted or rough coat is unknown in rabbits. **1960** O. MANNING *Great Fortune* I. 20 The skin was mottled purple and rosetted with yellow scabs.

c. Having been awarded a rosette.

1972 *Times* 6 May 9/3 As delicious as any rosetted *specialité.*

2. Affected with rosette disease.

1891 *Bull. U.S. Dept. Agric. Div. Veg. Physiol. & Path.* I. 48 Many of the roofs of rosetted trees were honey-combed by gum-pockets. **1937** K. M. SMITH *Textbk. Plant Virus Dis.* ii. 186 The rosetted plant may flower, but few of the pegs make any growth. **1949** BUTLER & JONES *Plant Path.* viii. 289 'Rosetted' peaches nearly always die the following autumn or winter.

rosetting (rəʊ'zɛtɪŋ), *vbl. sb.* [f. ROSETTE *sb.* and **v.* + -ING¹.] The occurrence or development of rosettes.

1948 MELHUS & KENT *Elem. Plant Path.* x. 246 These plants nearly always remain dwarfed and often show a 'rosetting' caused by the increase in the number of branches and the shortening of the internodes. **1970** *Internat. Arch. Allergy* XXXIX. 658 It is possible to obtain a rosetting reaction with antigen-coated erythrocytes around receptor-bearing dead lymphoid cells. **1978** T. T. KOZLOWSKI in Horsfall & Cowling *Plant Dis.* III. ii. 31 Symptons of mineral deficiencies include necrosis, dieback of shoots, rosetting, [etc.]. **1978** *Nature* 13 Apr. 619/2 (*caption*) Cells were tested for rosetting with IgG-OE immediately or after incubation overnight at 37°C, and with or without trypsin treatment.

'rosety, *a. Sc.* Also **-etty**. [f. ROSET *sb.*²] Rosined; resinous.

1882 *Jamieson's Sc. Dict.*, *Rosetty*, tipped or smeared with rosin; as, *rosetty sticks*, fire lighters. **1888** BARRIE *Auld Licht Idylls* iv. 94 'Rosetty (resiny) roots' for firewood. **1894** LATTO *Tam. Bodkin* xxvi, The tooth cud be easily pu'd oot by means o' a rosety string.

rose-'vinegar. [f. ROSE *sb.* + VINEGAR *sb.*] (See quot. 1866.)

1603 F. HERING *Cert. Rules* B 2 Let him wash his face.. with rose-water and rose-vinegar. **1610** B. JONSON *Alch.* v. ii, Purposing..T'haue burnt rose-vinegar, triackle, and tarre, And ha' made it sweet. **1713** *Phil. Trans.* XXVIII. 138 Moistned with Rose-Vinegar. **1725** *Fam. Dict.* s.v. *Roast-Meats*, Then they may be eaten with green Sauce,.. or with Rose-Vinegar. **1866** *Chambers's Encycl.* VIII. 335/2 Rose Vinegar, made by steeping rose petals in vinegar, is useful as an external application in headaches, for dissipating unpleasant smells in apartments.

rose-water ('rəʊz'wɔːtə(r)). [f. ROSE *sb.* + WATER *sb.* Cf. MDu. *rose(n)-*, *rooswater* (Du. *rozenwater*), MLG. *rosenwater*, MHG. *rôs(en)waȥȥer* (G. *rosenwasser*), MSw. *rosenvatn* (Sw. *-vatten*, Da. *-vana*).]

1. a. Water distilled from roses, or impregnated with essence of roses, and used as a perfume, etc.

1398 TREVISA *Barth. De P.R.* XVII. v. (Bodl. MS.), Men temper þe wyne wiþ rose water. **1456** *Cov. Leet-bk.* 292 He payde for a glasse of Rose water that my lord Ryvers had ij s. **1553** EDEN *Treat. Newe Ind.* (Arb.) 17 Their Priestes washe the Image of the deuyll with rose water. **1594** NASHE *Unfort. Trav.* Wks. (Grosart) V. 37 Their nere bitten beardes must.. be dewd euerie daie with rose water. **1620** VENNER *Via Recta* vi. 95 Orenges sliced and sopped in Rose-water and Sugar, are very good to coole..the stomacke. **1662** GURNALL *Chr. in Arm.* XI. 215/1 The Rose-water is not the less sweet, because one writes Wormwood-water on the glass. **1712** tr. *Pomet's Hist. Drugs* I. 111 It is of these Roses we make the best Rose-Water. **1782** MISS BURNEY *Cecilia* VI. xi, After dinner you shall bathe them in rose-water. **1850** THACKERAY *Pendennis* li, He..could scent his pocket-handkerchief with rose-water. **1856** DELAMER *Fl. Garden* (1861) 141 A well-known type is the medical rose, grown.. for the preparation of rose-water by distillers.

b. With *a* and pl. *rare.*

1582 LICHEFIELD tr. *Castanheda's Conq. E. Ind.* I. xiii. 33 So came they thether,..finding there..coralls, Rose waters, and all kinde of Conserues. *a* **1586** SIDNEY *Arcadia* (1622) 246 Haue you euer seene a pure Rosewater kept in a crystall glasse? how fine it looks? how sweet it smels? **1806** *Med. Jrnl.* XV. 70 A fragrant rose water is distilled from the root [of yellow rose-wort]. **1870** EMERSON *Soc. & Sol.* vii. 133 We may yet find a rose-water that will wash the negro white.

c. *attrib.*, as ***rose-water bottle, bowl, dish, ewer***, etc.; also **rose-water pear** (see quots. 1676, 1786); **rose-water pipe**, an oriental tobacco-pipe in which the smoke passes through rose water before reaching the mouth; **rose-water still**, a still for making rose-water.

1629 J. PARKINSON *Parad.* III. xxi. 592 The Rosewater peare is a goodly faire peare, and of a delicate taste. **1663** BOYLE *Usef. Exp. Nat. Philos.* II. ii. 79 Made by a bare distillation in a common rose-water still. **1676** WORLIDGE *Cyder* (1691) 214 The Rosewater-pear, the Shortneck,..are ..very good table fruit. **1698** FRYER *Acc. E. India & P.* 248 Also Rose-Water Bottles, the best Water whereof is Distilled here. **1786** ABERCROMBIE *Gard. Assist.*, *Arr.* p. xii, Pears,..Principal Varieties... Summer Pears Ripe in August and September... Rose-water [etc.]. **1835** N. P. WILLIS *Pencillings by Way* II. xxi. 234 A string of beads in one hand, and a splendid narghilé, or rose-water pipe, in the other. **1869** *Corporation & College Plate* 6 The fashion of ewers and rose-water dishes was introduced from the East to Europe. *Ibid.*, Rose-water Ewer. **1886** *Cakes & other Good Things* (ed. 2) 3 Rose-water Cake. **1898** JEANES *Mod. Confect.* 263 Rosewater Ice. **1956** G. TAYLOR *Silver* v. 97 A rose-water dish of 1672 belonging to St John's College, Oxford. **1960** H. HAYWARD *Antique Coll.* 243/2 *Rose-water ewer and dish or basin*, used for finger-washing at table. **1968** *Canad. Antiques Collector* June 9/3 The rose water bowl or basin was like an enormous soup plate, 12 to 20 inches in diameter. It had an extra wide rim, two inches or more, around the slightly depressed center and was usually ornately decorated.

2. *fig.* or in fig. context.

1590 GREENE *Never too late* (1600) 8 Wetting Cupids wings with rosewater, and tricking vp his quiver with sweete perfumes. **1598** E. GUILPIN *Skial.* (1878) 65 But I must.. haue A blessing of Rose-water, ere I goe. **1830** *Morn. Chron.* 4 Aug., But for the 1500 killed and wounded..this would almost have been what Mirabeau said was impossible: a revolution of rose-water. **1870** LOWELL *Study Wind.*, *Condesc. Foreigners* Wks. 1890 III. 241 We do not ask to be sprinkled with rosewater.

3. *attrib.* in fig. uses:

a. Of language: Fair, flattering. *rare*⁻¹.

1598 E. GUILPIN *Skial.* (1878) 37 Come to the Court, and Balthazer affords Fountaines of holy and rose-water words. .. Nothing but cossenage doth the world possesse.

b. Gentle, mild, sentimental.

1837 CARLYLE *Fr. Rev.* II. VI. i, It is not a Revolt, it is a Revolution; and truly no rose-water one! **1855** MRS. GASKELL *North & S.* xv, 'They are that,' replied Mr. Thornton. 'Rose-water surgery won't do for them'. **1872** BAGEHOT *Physics & Pol.* (1876) 213 This is no pleasant power, no 'rose-water' authority.

c. Elegant, superfine.

1840 THACKERAY *Catherine* iii, To paint such thieves as they are: not dandy, poetical, rose-water thieves; but real downright scoundrels. **1883** *Cent. Mag.* Sept. 738 Because you're not [rich], she will strike for one of them rose-water snobs on Algonquin Avenue.

d. Pleasant, comfortable. *rare.*

1889 GRETTON *Memory's Harkback* 21, I was to be cut adrift.., and sent to rough it among strangers in a new and anything but a rose-water life.

Hence **'rose-'water** *v.*, **'rose-'watered**, **'rose-ˌwatery**, *adjs.*

1600 ROWLANDS *Lett. Humours Blood* iv. 63 Mellfluuious, sweete Rose-watred elloquence. **1876** SIR R. F. BURTON in Lady Burton *Life* II. (1893) 72 My language is not rose-watered. **1893** *Edin. Rev.* July 59 Literary revolutionists have rosewatered Catiline. **1902** G. B. SHAW *Let.* 20 June (1972) II. 277 The comparatively rose-watery part of it [*sc.* a situation in *Mrs. Warren's Profession*].

'rose-ˌwindow. *Eccl. Arch.* [f. ROSE *sb.* + WINDOW *sb.*] A circular window, *esp.* one divided into compartments by mullions radiating from a centre, or filled with tracery suggestive of the form of a rose; a Catherine or marigold window.

1773 NOORTHOUCK *New Hist. London* 610 Those in the second stage are of the kind called rose windows. **1820** D. TURNER *Tour Normandy* I. 178 These large circular windows, sometimes known by the name of rose windows. **1849** FREEMAN *Archit.* 373 Some of the aisle windows at Oppenheim are little more than rose windows. *a* **1878** SIR G. SCOTT *Lect. Archit.* (1879) II. 218 The general idea..may be said to be parallel to that of a circular or rose window.

'rosewood. [f. ROSE *sb.* + WOOD *sb.*]

1. One of several kinds of valuable, fragrant, close-grained cabinet-wood, chiefly that yielded by tropical leguminous trees of the genera *Dalbergia* (esp. *D. nigra*) and *Machærium*; also, a tree yielding this wood.

The true rosewood of commerce is that imported from S. America, esp. from Brazil, where the name *Jacaranda* is applied to *Dalbergia* and to several species of *Machærium.*

1660 F. BROOKE tr. *Le Blanc's Trav.* 26 Here is likewise.. the most exquisite Rose wood. **1666** J. DAVIES tr. *Rochefort's Caribby Isles* 40 The wood called Rose-wood is fit not only for the Carpenter, but also for the Joyner. **1703** *Lond. Gaz.* No. 3917/4 The Loading of the Dorothy,..consisting of Canary Wines, Orchilla, Rosewood. **1745** P. THOMAS *Jrnl. Anson's Voy.* 252 There is also another particular Wood, which they call Rose-wood... Its colour is black, inclining to red. **1821** J. SMYTH *Pract. Customs* 294 Rose Wood is used principally by cabinet-makers for drawing-room furniture. The smell of real Rose Wood is very fragrant, resembling that of roses. **1843** HOLTZAPFFEL *Turning* I. 104 The colours of rose-wood are from light hazel to deep purple, or nearly black. **1870** YEATS *Nat. Hist. Comm.* 224 The best rosewood comes from Rio de Janeiro.

2. The fragrant wood of certain species of Convolvulus, as *C. floridus* and *C. scoparius*, and of the allied genus *Rhodorrhiza*, natives of the Canary Islands.

1671 SKINNER *Etym. Bot.*, Rose-wood, lignum Rhodium, Aspalathus, sic dictum quia odore omnino Rosam refert. **1718** QUINCY *Compl. Disp.* 85 Rosewood is accounted astringent and drying. **1797** *Encycl. Brit.* (ed. 3) II. 396/1 The rose-wood, whence the oleum rhodii is obtained. **1866** *Treas. Bot.* 978/1 *Rhodorrhiza*..derives its name from the rose-like smell peculiar to the rootstocks and lower part of the stems, which yield a kind of Rosewood (*lignum rhodii*). **1868** WATTS *Dict. Chem.* V. 116 Oil of Rosewood, a volatile oil obtained from rosewood (*Convolvulus scoparius*).

3. The West Indian candlewood, *Amyris balsamifera*; also *A. montana.*

1756 P. BROWNE *Jamaica* 208 White Candlewood, or Rosewood... The wood..bears a fine polish, and has a fine smell. **1797** *Encycl. Brit.* (ed. 3) I. 644/1 The [Amyris] balsamifera, or rose-wood, is found on gravelly hills in Jamaica and others of the West India islands. **1843** HOLTZAPFFEL *Turning* I. 104 *Amyris montana* is called Yellow candle-wood, or rose-wood. **1858** SIMMONDS *Dict. Trade.*

4. Applied to several Australasian trees, as the myall, pencil cedar, and sandalwood (see quots.).

1779 FORREST *Voy. N. Guinea* 256 Here grows a kind of rose wood, called narra, many dammer trees. **1838** MITCHELL *Three Exped.* I. 203 One or two trees of a warmer green, of what they call 'rosewood',..gave a fine effect. **1866** *Treas. Bot.* 992/1 Roswood, New South Wales. The wood of *Trichilia glandulosa.* **1889** MAIDEN *Useful Native Pl.* 126 *Eremophila Mitchelli*,..'Rosewood', or 'Sandalwood'. *Ibid.* 212 *Acacia glaucescens*,..a 'Rosewood'. *Ibid.* 419 *Dysoxylon Fraserianum*,..called variously 'Rosewood', 'Pencil Cedar', and 'Bog-onion'.

attrib. **1844** LEICHHARDT in J. D. Lang *Cooksland* (1847) 91 The Rosewood Acacia, the wood of which has a very agreeable violet scent like the Myal Acacia.

5. With defining terms:

African rosewood, the West African tree *Pterocarpus erinaceus*; also, the wood of this. **Burmese rosewood**, = LINGO. **Dominica rosewood**, a West Indian tree, *Cordia Gerascanthus*; also, the wood of this. **(East) Indian rosewood**, the blackwood of the East Indies, *Dalbergia latifolia.* **Jamaica rosewood**, the sweet-smelling wood of *Amyris balsamifera*, or of *Linociera ligustrina.* **Moulmein rosewood**, a species of *Millettia*, native to Burma.

1866 *Treas. Bot.* 380, 774, 991-2. **1886** *Encycl. Brit.* XX. 852/1. **1890** *Cent. Dict.* s.v.

6. A shade or tint of the colour of rosewood.

1853 *Heal & Son Catal.*: *Bedsteads* 33/1 Parisian Bedstead, with handsome cast iron side and ends, sheet iron head and foot board, japanned rosewood. **1897** *Sears, Roebuck Catal.* 22/3 Wood stains..Perfect imitations of natural woods, Cherry, Rosewood, Mahogany, Walnut [etc.]. **1907** *Yesterday's Shopping* (1969) 145/1 Stains..as used by the Working Ladies Guild, colours:—Rosewood, Satinwood, Oak, [etc.]. **1927** *Daily Tel.* 21 Feb. 14 (Advt.), Two-Piece Suits, Coats, &c. Available in shades of Light Grey, Rosewood, Fawn, Sand, &c. **1930** *Daily Express* 6 Oct. 13/1 (Advt.), Shades, beaver, brown, rosewood, and drab. **1971** [see MOSS *sb.*¹ 5 d].

7. *attrib.* and *Comb.*, as ***rosewood-coloured*** adj.; ***rosewood marble, oil, piano, shelf, tree.***

1842 TENNYSON *Talking Oak* 118 She left the novel half-uncut Upon the rosewood shelf. **1852-3** *Tomlinson's Cycl. Arts* (1867) II. 123/1 Rosewood marble, so called from its marking resembling that of rosewood, is extremely hard and of close texture. **1848** THACKERAY *Van. Fair* lv, She also left the fire-irons,..and the rosewood cottage-piano. **1868** WATTS *Dict. Chem.* V. 116 Rosewood-oil is sometimes used for adulterating oil of roses. **1874** STEWART & BRANDIS *Flora N.W. & Central India* 148 *Dalbergia latifolia*.., the Blackwood or Rosewood tree of Southern India.

Hence **'rosewoodize** *v.*, to suffuse or stain with a colour like that of rosewood.

1853 C. READE *Chr. Johnstone* v, A race of women that the northern sun peachifies instead of rosewoodizing.

'rosewort. *Bot.* [f. ROSE *sb.* + WORT *sb.* In sense 1 prob. ad. G. *rosenwurz*, Du. *roosen-wortel* (Kilian).]

1. = ROSEROOT 1. Now *rare.*

1578 LYTE *Dodoens* 341 Rosewurt or the roote savering like the Rose, groweth in Macedonia and Hungarie. **1597** GERARDE *Herbal* 416 Rosewoort hath manie small, thicke, and fat stems, growing from a thicke and knobby roote. **1611** [see ROSE-ROOT 1]. **1796** WITHERING *Brit. Pl.* (ed. 3) II. 389 Yellow Rose-wort, Rose-root. Mountains of Westmoreland [etc.]. **1806** *Med. Jrnl.* XV. 70 Yellow rose-wort. Rose-root. .. Leaves numerous,..fleshy, sea-green, sometimes tinged with purple. **1866** *Treas. Bot.* 992/1.

†**2.** = ORPINE 2. (Cf. ROSEROOT 2.) *Obs.*

1725 *Fam. Dict.* s.v., They dry the Leaves of Rose-Wort, and..hang 'em up in some high Place that is expos'd to the ..Sun. **1758** BORLASE *Nat. Hist. Cornwall* 233 Rose-wort, *Telephium roseum*, gathered..among the rocks at the Land's End.

3. *pl.* Lindley's name for the *Rosaceæ.*

1845 LINDLEY *Sch. Bot.* (1862) 58 Order XXIII. *Rosaceæ.* —Roseworts. **1846** —— *Veget. Kingd.* 564 That Roseworts have some intimate relationship with Myrtleblooms is proved by Appleworts.

Rosh Chodesh, Rosh Hodesh (‖rɔʃ 'xodeʃ, rəʊʃ 'xəʊdəʃ). [Heb., lit. 'head of the month'.] A Jewish half-holiday observed at the appearance of the New Moon, the beginning of the Jewish month.

1879 C. E. SACHAU tr. *Albîrûnî's Chronol. Anc. Nations* xiv. 274 (*heading*) Nîsan.. has only one Rosh-Ḥodesh and 30 days. **1934** WEBSTER, Rosh Ho'desh.. or Cho'desh. **1963** *Times* 24 Apr. 16/1 He initiated the delightful presidential custom of inviting to his residence a representative gathering of citizens from a different ethnic group each 'Rosh Chodesh', the start of a Hebrew calendar month. **1976** G. JESSUP *No Strange God* xi. 75 The first day of every month is a semi-festival, called *Rosh Ḥodesh*, when mourning and fasting are forbidden.

Rosh Hashana (‖rɒʃ haʃa'na, rəʊʃ hə'ʃəʊnəʊ). Also **Rosh Hashanah, Rosh Hashonoh,** etc. [Heb., lit. 'head of the year'.] The Jewish New Year, celebrated on the first and second day of the month Tishri.

1846 *Jewish Chron.* 21 Aug. 199/1 Rosh Hashana (New Year), and Yom Kippur (Day of Atonement), were kept by most of our co-religionists. **1862** *Chambers's Encycl.* IV. 304/1 The most exalted of new-moon festivals was that of the first day of the seventh month, 'the day of remembrance of the sounding' or 'of trumpets' (Lev. xxiii. 24), to which in later times.. the name of Rosh hashana (New Year) was given. **1907** I. ZANGWILL *Ghetto Comedies* 18 We lived somehow till *Rosh Hashanah* (New Year), hoping it would indeed be a New Year. **1957** L. STERN *Midas Touch* III. xx. 152 So this year you will come to *shul* maybe for *Rosh Hashona*? **1960** F. RAPHAEL *Limits of Love* II. i. 165 It's *Rosh Hashana*... I'm going to read some prayers. **1970** *Challenge* (Lubavitch Foundation) 281 *Rosh Hashonoh* is Coronation Day for G-d as our King and for Israel as His people. **1973** *Jewish Chron.* 19 Jan. 5/4 After the Munich massacre of Israeli Olympic sportsmen.. it was decided that memorial prayers would be recited at the Rosh Hashana service in Copenhagen's main synagogue. **1973** *Synagogue Light* Sept. 26 Jewish residents of New York State, will join on September 26, with others of their faith throughout the world, in the observance of Rosh Hashanah. **1978** *Detroit Free Press* 16 Apr. (Record) 9/5 On September 16, 1939, the eve of Rosh Hashana.. the *Luftwaffe*.. bombed the Jewish quarter of Warsaw.

Roshi ('rəʊʃɪ). [Jap.] The spiritual leader of a community of Zen Buddhist monks.

1934 D. T. SUZUKI *Training of Zen Buddhist Monk* iv. 31 Yinji-ryō which attends on the master known as Rōshi. **1949** C. HUMPHREYS *Zen Buddhism* vii. 142 Laymen, accepted for teaching by the Roshi, may come for a period... The whole of the monastery is locked in full meditation with a queue of .. monks waiting their turn for the Roshi to confirm, reject or make further suggestions for their inward labours. **1959** *Encounter* Jan. 21/1 The Zen Master, or *Roshi*, the spiritual head of the monastery. **1972** *Last Whole Earth Catalog* (Portola Inst.) 50/2 She's sort of like an elderly Zen priest, an old roshi who after years of work and study has distilled a large burden of 'knowledge' into a single gem of wisdom which he renders in a single haiku. **1974** R. C. ZAEHNER in *Times Lit. Suppl.* 6 Dec. 1389/4 Anglican priest turned Zen Rōshi, reconciled to his church shortly before his death, but belly-laughing, genial, infuriating Rōshi to the end. **1978** C. HUMPHREYS *Both Sides Circle* xv. 165 There is no likelihood of Zen roshis, in the full meaning of the term as used in the Rinzai School, arriving in Europe in sufficient numbers to give us expert training.

rosial(l, -iar, -iat, obs. ff. ROSEAL, ROSIER, ROSEATE.

†'**rosiar.** *Obs.*[−1] ? A rose-apple.

1620 VENNER *Via Recta* vii. 109 Such are our Queene-Apples, and Russetings,.. and next our Rosiars.

†**rosical,** *a.*, ? misprint for *rosial* ROSEAL *a.*

1635 R. JOHNSON *Tom a Lincoln* i, Thy.. Rosical cheeks surpassing Snow for whiteness.

rosi'cler. *rare.* Also 7 rosiclear, 8 rossicler. [a. Sp. and Pg. *rosicler* bright red, etc.]

†**1.** Used as a fanciful title. *Obs.*

1611 BEAUM. & FL. *Philaster* v. iv, My Royal Rosiclear, We are thy Mirmidons, thy Guard, thy Rorers.

2. *Min.* Any of the varieties of ruby silver ore, as proustite and pyrargyrite.

The Spanish name; not now in English use.

1728 CHAMBERS *Cycl.* s.v. *Silver*, The Rossicler is another black Mineral distinguished by whetting and rubbing it against Iron, which turns it red. **1780** J. T. DILLON *Trav. Spain* (1781) 318 One very curious specimen, like an incrustation of rubies, called Rosicler by mineralogists, from its rose-colour appearance.

‖**3.** (See quot.)

1883 BURTON & CAMERON *Gold Coast* I. 19 The Rosicler, or rosy dawn-light was that of a May morning.

Rosicrucian (ˌrəʊzɪ'kruːʃ(ɪ)ən), *sb.* and *a.* Also 7 Roso-, Rose-, Rosie-, 8 Rosy-, 7–8 Rosacrucian (7 -ant); 7 Rose-, 8 Rosy-, 7–9 Rosicrusian, 9- (after G. *Rosenkreuz*) Rosenkreuzian; 7 Rosicrutian. [f. mod.L. *rosa crucis* (Du Cange) or *crux*, as a rendering of G. *Rosenkreuz* (see def.): cf. F. *rose-croix*, Sp. *rosacruz*, and *rosy cross* s.v. ROSY *a.* 5.]

A. *sb.* A member of a supposed society or order, reputedly founded by one Christian Rosenkreuz in 1484, but first mentioned in 1614, whose members were said to claim various forms of secret and magic knowledge, as the transmutation of metals, the prolongation of life, and power over the elements and elemental spirits. Also, a member of a present-day Rosicrucian society (see sense B below).

1624 T. SCOTT *Vox Dei* 52 The bretheren of the invisible order of the Rosacru[ci]ants. **1653** WALTON *Angler* xii. 227 A mysterious knack, which.. lies locked up in the braine or brest of some chimical men, that like the Rosi-crutians, yet will not reveal it. **1663** SPENCER *Prodigies* (1665) 46 The Rosie-Crucians acted so hugely by imagination in Philosophy,.. are so invincibly resolved upon their hypotheses, that [etc.]. **1690** LOCKE *Hum. Und.* II. i. (1695) 48 This some may suspect to be a step beyond the Rose-crucians. **1714** ADDISON *Spect.* No. 574 ⁋1, I was once engaged in Discourse with a Rosicrusian about *the great Secret*. *c* **1740** BOLINGBROKE *Ess. Pope* Wks. 1754 IV. 85 All the folly and knavery.. of wizards, of witches, and of rosycrucians. **1820** SCOTT *Monast.* ix, 'I used to doubt the existence of Cabalists and Rosicrucians,' thought the Sub-Prior. **1856** R. A. VAUGHAN *Mystics* (1860) II. 98 The Rosicrucians pretended that they could prolong life indefinitely. **1891** *Myst. Rosie Cross* 5 It is commonly held .. that there is a close.. connection between the Alchymists and the Rosicrucians. **1957** *Encycl. Brit.* XIX. 560/1 That it is not always possible to prove the existence of the order in a given country at any particular moment does not disturb the Rosicrucians, for it seems to be recognized that there occur periods when the order is deliberately 'in sleep'.

B. *adj.* Belonging or pertaining to, connected with, characteristic of, this society. Now also applied to various societies that claim to continue the Rosicrucian tradition (see quot. 1959).

1662 SPARROW tr. *Behme's Rem. Wks., Apol. Perf.* 132 Not Tinctured, according to the Cabalisticall, Theophrasticall, Roso-Crucian kind. **1678** BUTLER *Hud.* III. iii. 15 Rosicrusian Virtuoso's Can see with Ears, and hear with Noses. **1710** ADDISON *Tatler* No. 243 ⁋2 To speak in Rosycrucian Lore, I have entered into the Clefts of the Earth. **1712–4** POPE *Rape Lock* To Mrs. A. Fermor, These Machines I determined to raise on a very new and odd foundation, the Rosicrucian doctrine of Spirits. **1815** MISS PORDEN *The Veils* Introd., On the Rosicrusian mythology, a system of poetical machinery might be constructed of the highest character. **1837** K. H. DIGBY *Mores Catholici* VIII. vi. 193 The cabalistic learning, expressed in the unintelligible language of Theosophy, which was in the seventeenth century to be the foundation of the Rosenkreuzian society. **1864** W. SMITH *Shaw's Hist. Eng. Lit.* xv. (1865) 294 The fantastic theories of Paracelsus and the Rosicrucian philosophers. **1959** *Chambers's Encycl.* XI. 840/2 In the mid-19th century there came into being a Rosicrucian Society in England, an offshoot of masonry, the leading figure being R. W. Little. The name has also been appropriated by American theosophy. None of these later developments can claim historical continuity with any original group. **1961** *Listener* 21 Sept. 443/2 Nothing of his marriage or his dealings with Rudolf Steiner, the Rosicrucian Order, or the Catholic Church. **1977** *Daily Times* (Lagos) 5 Jan. 2 (Advt.), Members of the Rosicrucian Order Amorc (Nigeria) have applied to be registered under the Land Perpetual (Succession) Act.

Hence **Rosi'crucianism, Rosicruci'anity, Rosi'crucianize** *v.*

c **1740** BOLINGBROKE *Ess. Pope* Wks. 1754 IV. 44 Had Arnobius.. lived in our days, you would have been.. made the father of *rosycrucianism. **1850** *Fraser's Mag.* XLII. 528 The Rosicrucianism of so vigorously-minded a man as Samuel Johnson. **1955** C. S. LEWIS *Surprised by Joy* iv. 62 She was.. floundering in the mazes of Theosophy, Rosicrucianism, Spiritualism; the whole Anglo-American Occultist tradition. **1961** *Listener* 21 Dec. 1089/1 For a time Satie dabbled in Rosicrucianism. **1838** *Blackw. Mag.* XLIV. 639 A circumstance occurred.. that by no means diminishes the *Rosicrucianity of my notions of the spiritual. **1833** *Edin. Rev.* LVII. 136 A constant endeavour to *rosicrusianize every subject.

'**rosied,** *a. rare.* [f. ROSY *a.* + -ED.] Made rosy or rose-red; decked with roses.

1855 OGILVIE *Suppl., Rosied*,.. adorned with roses or their colour. **1889** *Universal Rev.* Nov. 437 The northern streamers upon rosied wings Shimmer and wheel and fade. **1910** W. DE LA MARE *Three Mulla-Mulgars* xxii. 291 The faintly-rosied starlight.

Rosie Lee, var. ROSY LEE.

'**rosier.** *Obs.* exc. *poet.* Also 6 roysyer, rosyer, rosyar, rosiere, 6–7 rosiar. [a. F. *rosier*:—L. *rosārium*, f. *rosa* ROSE *sb.*: cf. ROSARY and ROSER.] A rose-tree, rose-bush.

1523 SKELTON *Garl. Laurel* 1178 Of Vertu also the soueráyne enterlude; The Boke of the Rosiar. *a* **1548** HALL *Chron., Hen. VIII*, 61 Yᵉ first an Oliue tree,.. yᵉ iii. a Roysyer with the armes of England [etc.]. **1590** SPENSER *F.Q.* II. ix. 19 Ne other tire she on her head did weare, But crowned with a garland of sweete Rosiere. **1620** T. GRANGER *Div. Logike* 120 How many flowers the rosiers bring.

1829 SOUTHEY *All for Love* III. xii, The nightingale.. Hath in the garden rosier trill'd A rich and rapturous song. *a* **1851** MOIR *Tower of Ercildoune* vii, The rosiers twain that shed their bloom In autumn o'er the lover's tomb. **1925** E. SITWELL *Troy Park* 88 Under a rosier Stood the Bishop Walked with a crozier.

'**rosiery,** irreg. variant of ROSERY.

1791 ANNA SEWARD *Lett.* (1811) III. 81 The rosiery will not, I trust, have exhausted all its bloom and fragrance.. before I reach you.

rosignell, obs. Sc. f. ROSSIGNOL.

rosil ('rɒzɪl, 'rɒz(ə)l), *sb.* Now *dial.* Forms: 5 rosell, 6 rossall, 6, 8 rossell (8 rossel); 5 rosyle, 7, 9 rosil, 8–9 rossil; 9 rozzel, rozzle. [Variant of ROSIN *sb.*]

1. Rosin, resin.

14.. *Nom.* in Wr.-Wülcker 683 *Hec rosina*, rosyle. **1485–6** *Durh. Acc. Rolls* (Surtees) 416 Pro 4ᵒʳ dd. de rosell, 3*s.* 4*d.* **1571** in *Eng. Hist. Rev.* XII. 447 For mixing white wax with rossall and turpentyne. **1579** *York Fabric Rolls* (Surtees) 117 For rossell to the plumber, 3s. **1691** RAY *S. & E.C. Words* s.v., I suppose from *rosin*, which here in Essex the Vulgar call *Rosill*. **1787–** in many dialect glossaries.

2. A kind of soil (see ROSILLY *a.*).

Hence '**rosil** *v. dial.*

1819 R. ANDERSON *Cumbld. Ball.* (*c* 1850) 95 He rozzelt the strings.

'**rosilly,** *a. dial.* Forms: 6 rosellie, 8 rosselly; 7- rosilly. [f. ROSIL *sb.* + -Y.] Of soil: (see quots. 1691 and *a* 1825). Cf. ROSINY *a.* 2.

1577 HARRISON *Descr. Brit.* I. xiii. in *Holinshed* I. 38 The red or white sandy [mould], the lomye, roselly, grauelly, chalky or blacke. **1691** RAY *S. & E.C. Words, Rosil* or *Rosilly* soil; Land between Sand and Clay, neither light nor heavy. **1721** MORTIMER *Husb.* (ed. 2) II. 42 That which I have observed to be the best is a rosselly top, and a brick earthy bottom. In general, a true Rossel or light Land, whether white or black, is what they are usually planted in. *a* **1825** FORBY *Voc. E. Anglia, Rosilly*, like rosin. It is applied to a soil both sandy and clayey.

'**rosily,** *adv.* [f. ROSY *a.* + -LY[2].] With a rosy hue; in a rosy manner.

1809 MALKIN *Gil Blas* x. x. ⁋22 They live like so many sons of the church, rosily, merrily, and fatly. **1852** M. ARNOLD *Empedocles* II. 81 The white Olympus-peaks Rosily brighten. **1893** E. H. BARKER *Wand. S. Waters* 7 The after-light of sunset was lingering rosily upon the naked crags.

'**rosin** ('rɒzɪn), *sb.* Forms: α. 4–6 rosyn, 5 roosyn, 6 rosing, 4, 6- rosin, 7–8 rozin. β. 4–6 rosyne (5 ross-), 4–7 rosine, 7 rozine. γ. 4 roseyne, 6 -eyn; 5 ros(s)ene. δ. 6 roasen, rossen, 6–8 rosen, rozen, 7 rozzen. ε. 6 rosome, 9 *dial.* rosum. [An alteration of RESIN *sb.* Further alterations are ROSIL and ROSET. For the change of vowel, which appears also in Anglo-L. *rosina*, cf. OF. *roisin* (G. *rosine*, Du. *rozijn*, Da. *rosin*) as a variant of *raisin*.]

1. a. = RESIN *sb.*; *spec.*, this substance in a solid state obtained as a residue after the distillation of oil of turpentine from crude turpentine.

The colour of the product (yellow, brown, or black) depends on the continuation of the heat employed.

α. *a* **1350** *St. Lucy* 183 in Horstm. *Altengl. Leg.* (1881) 19 Pik and rosyn he bad in cast, And oyle, to ger þe fire brin fast. **1382** WYCLIF *Ezek.* xxvii. 17 Bawm, and hony, and oyle, and rosyn. *c* **1400** *Lanfranc's Cirurg.* 132 An entreet maad of .ij. parties of whiȝt rosyn, & oon partie of wex. **1496** *Naval Accs. Hen. VII* (1896) 174 Laying on of piche, Rosyn & talow uppon the seid ship. *c* **1550** *Disc. Common Weal. Eng.* (1893) 246 Tarre, pitche, rosing whereof we haue none at all. **1570** LEVINS *Manip.* 134/15 Rosin, *resina.* **1611** BIBLE *Song Holy Children* 22 To make the ouen hote with rosin, pitch, towe, and small wood. **1660** BOYLE *New Exp. Phys. Mech.* Proem 11 A melted Cement, made of Pitch, Rosin, and Wood-ashes. **1712** E. COOKE *Voy. S. Sea* 204 A sort of Rozin, which is good for curing of Wounds. **1779** *Phil. Trans.* LXX. 17 The powder of rosin will be attracted by those parts only of the electro-phorus, which are electrified positively. **1821** CRAIG *Lect. Drawing*, etc. vii. 400 A solution of rosin or fine Burgundy pitch in pure spirit of wine. **1865** KINGSLEY *Herew.* x, They wore coats stiffened with tar and rosin. **1873** E. SPON *Workshop Rec.* Ser. I. 346/2 Black Rosin is a most important article in the composition of good [printing-] ink.

β. **1367–8** *Durh. Acc. Rolls* (Surtees) 386 In sex libris de rosine, 2*od.* **1390** GOWER *Conf.* II. 200 Thei go be nyhte unto the Myne With pich, with soulphre and with rosine. **1454** *Cal. Rec. Dublin* (1889) I. 283 No maner of man dwellynge in the said cite shulde.. by salte, ire, pych, rosyne, collys. **1551** TURNER *Herbal* (1568) 30 The small leues in the top broused or broken sauour lyke rosyne. **1604** E. G[RIMSTONE] *D'Acosta's Hist. Indies* IV. xxviii. 285 Liquors, oiles, gummes, and rozines. **1613** PURCHAS *Pilgrimage* VIII. xii. (1614) 803 All whiche they mingled together with.. the fume of Rosine. **1681** Rosine [see RESIN *sb.* 2].

γ. **1390** *Earl Derby's Exped.* (Camden) 64 Pro melle, lynesede,.. roseyne. **1465** *Waterf. Arch.* in *10th Rep. Hist. MSS. Comm.* App. V. 302 Yren, pitche, rosene, nor tarre. **1485** *Cely Papers* (Camden) 181 Paid be hym for a qwartt of rossene, xjd. **1533** ELYOT *Cast. Helthe* (1539) 58 They be somtyme made with roseyn. **1548** —— *Dict.* s.v. *Cedria*, The roseyn that renneth out of the great cedre tree.

δ. **1447** BOKENHAM *Seyntys* (Roxb.) 78 A vessel of bras.. Full of pyche, rosen oyle and smere. **1516** *Galway Arch.* in *10th Rep. Hist. MSS. Comm.* App. V. 397 Pich, canvas, rossen. **1582** STANYHURST *Æneis* IV. (Arb.) 109 Vessels, calcked with roasen smearye. **1602** MARSTON *Antonio's Rev.* III. iv, My fiddlestick wants rozzen. **1651** BIGGS *New Disp.* ⁋126 Aloes by ablution looseth the juice, and there remaineth a meer rozen. **1742** YARROW *Love at First Sight* 98 A piece of Rozen, and two Yards of Catgut. **1779** *Phil. Trans.* LXX. 16 Some powder of rosen.. is shaken upon the electrophorus.

ε. **1541–2** in Swayne *Sarum Churchw. Acc.* (1896) 269 A Torche of Rosome weynge ix li. ij *s.* iij *d.* **1872** DE VERE *Americanisms* 536 Rosum is a common corruption of rosin, which is almost universally pronounced ros'm by the mass of the people. **1880** *W. Cornw. Gloss.*, *Rosum*, rosin.

b. With *a* and pl. A particular kind of rosin.

1604 E. G[RIMSTONE] *D'Acosta's Hist. Indies* IV. xxviii. 285 Liquors, oiles, gummes, and rozines, which come from divers plants and hearbes. **1672–3** GREW *Anat. Pl.* II. iii. (1682) 67 In the dryed Root of Angelica, &c. being split, the Milk.. appeareth,.. condensed to a hard and shining Rosin. **1718** QUINCY *Compl. Disp.* 7 The former is the case of chrystallized Salts, Rosins, and the like.

c. *slang.* (*a*) Alcoholic drink. Cf. ROSIN *v.* 2. (*b*) A fiddler, a violinist; also, *rosin-the-bow*.

1734 *Select Trials* I. 227/1 Says I to the Gentleman, I hope, Sir, you won't forget your Coachman—a little Rozzam wou'd do very well. *Ibid.*, Rosin, strong Drink: A Metaphor first used among Fidlers. **1864** HOTTEN *Slang Dict.* 215 *Rosin*, beer or other drink given to musicians at a dancing party. *Ibid.*, *Rosin-the-bow*, a fiddler. **1901** F. E. Taylor *Folk-Speech S. Lancashire*, *Rozzin*, a jocular term for musician's drink. **1904** S. Watson *Wops the Waif* (1924) iii. 9/1 A short, lame man,..with a violin beneath his arm, suggesting the identity with the 'rosin' announced.

2. *attrib.* and *Comb.*, as ***rosin boiler, candle, -distiller, -flux, gas, size, soap***; ***rosin-weeping*** adj.; **rosin-back** *Circus slang*, (*a*) a horse used by a bareback rider or acrobat; (*b*) a bareback rider; **rosin-end** (see quot.); †**rosin flower**, a pine tree; **rosin oil, plant, rose, tin** (see quots.); **rosin-tree**, a South African shrub (*Cineraria resinifera*), which exudes resin; **rosin-weed**, *U.S.*, the compass plant (*Silphium laciniatum*).

1923 C. R. Cooper *Under Big Top* 170 She is trained to the '*rosinback', as the ring horse is called. **1931** *Amer. Mercury* Nov. 353/2 *Rosinbacks*, bareback riders. **1933** P. Godfrey *Back-Stage* xvii. 213 One of the least spectacular, yet most difficult, tasks is to train the trick-rider's horse, or 'rosin-back'. These horses are massive Flemish animals, capable of supporting on their broad backs several performers at a time. **1945** C. B. Cochran *Showman looks On* iii. 33 A 'rosin-back' is a ring-horse used by bareback riders.. Rosin is rubbed into the horse's back to help the rider to get a firm footing as he jumps from the ring on to the horse. **1974** V. Canning *Painted Tent* iii. 51 There were a few horses in the stable, a couple of rosin backs and a small black pony. **1880** J. Dunbar *Pract. Papermaker* 54 Cubic contents of small *rosin boiler. **1611** Cotgr. s.v. *Chandelle*, *Chandelles de Buchs*, *rosen candles, vsed by the poorer sort of people neere vnto Bourdeaux. **1885** *List of Subscribers, Classified* (United Telephone Co.) (ed. 6) 207 Tar, *rosin, benzole and naphtha distillers. **1828** Carr *Craven Gloss.*, *Rosin-end, a shoe-maker's waxed or rosinned thread. *c* **1611** Chapman *Iliad* xi. 434 As when a torrent..beares blasted Oakes, and witherd *rosine flowres,..into the Oceans force. **1960** Cooke & Marcus *Electronics & Nucleonics Dict.* 410/2 *Rosin-core solder*, solder made up in tubular or other hollow form, with the inner space filled with *rosin flux to serve as a noncorrosive flux for soldering joints. **1976** *S9* (N.Y.) May/June 101/3 For electronics work only rosin flux is used as it is non-corrosive. **1839** Ure *Dict. Arts* 562 *Rosin gas is cheaper than oil gas. **1866** *Treas. Bot.* 807/2 *Oil, *Rosin*, an oil obtained from the resin of the pine-tree, used by painters for lubricating machinery, and other purposes. **1856** A. Gray *Man. Bot.* (1860) 209 *Silphium*, *Rosin-Plant. Heads many-flowered, radiate. **1886** Britten & Holland, **Rosin Rose. Hypericum calycinum*, L., and *H. perforatum*, L., the smell of which is supposed to resemble that of rosin. *Yks.* **1880** J. Dunbar *Pract. Papermaker* 55 Take..10 gallons of the thick prepared *rosin size. **1839** Ure *Dict. Arts* 1144 Of Yellow or *Rosin Soap. **1867** Brande & Cox *Dict. Sci.*, etc. III. 310/2 **Rosin Tin*, a miner's name for pale-coloured translucent Tinstone with a resinous lustre. **1815** Anne Plumptre tr. *Lichtenstein's Trav. S. Africa* II. 176 A shrub, which grows from two feet to three feet and a half high, called by the colonists *harpuisbosjes*, the *rosin tree. **1834** Schoolcraft *Exped.* 297 Among the flowers, the plant called *rosin-weed attracts attention by its gigantic stature. **1608** Sylvester *Du Bartas* ii. iv. *Decay* 970 With a Pole of *rozen-weeping Fir.

rosin ('rɒzɪn), *v.* Forms: 5 rossyen, 6 roson, 7 rosen, rosin, rozen, 7–8 rozin, 9 *U.S.* rosum. [f. the sb.]

1. *trans.* To smear over, or seal up, with rosin; to rub (*esp.* a violin bow or string) with rosin.

1497 *Naval Accs. Hen. VII* (1896) 294, C weight Rosyn to Rossyen the seid Ship abouewater. **1588** Lambarde *Eiren.* iv. iv. 461 Well sewed with threed well twisted, waxed and rosoned. **1624** *Althorp MS.* in Simpkinson *Washingtons* (1860) App. p. liv, To the tinker for new rozening and mending 13 black jackes and 2 botles. **1642** Fuller *Holy & Prof. St.* iv. i. 240 Those, who make musick with so harsh an instrument, need to have their bow well rosend before. **1756** *Connoisseur* No. 128 ¶4 Not one of these people will open their mouths, or rosin a single string, without being very well paid for it. **1823** J. Badcock *Dom. Amusem.* 175 [Place layers,] till the jar is full, then bung and rosin it. **1896** Lumsden *Poems* 43 He screwed her up wi' conscious pride And rosin'd her.

absol. **1607** Dekker & Marston *Westw. Hoe* D.'s Wks. 1873 II. 341 They are but rozining, sir, and theile scrape themselues into your company presently.

fig. **1650** B. *Discollim.* 34 My..heart-strings are grown so feeble, that if I should not rozen them now and then (with a little mirth) they would soone crack quite asunder.

2. *fig.* To supply with liquor; to make drunk; also *intr.*, to indulge in drink. Now *dial.*

1729 Fielding *Pleasures Town* iii. i, A fiddlestick is a drunkard: Why? Because it loves ros'ning. **1828** Carr *Craven Gloss.*, *Rosinned*, drunk. 'He war purely rosinn'd.' **1869–** in dialect glossaries (Northumbld., Lanc., Linc.).

†**rosi'naceous**, *a.* *Obs.*$^{-1}$ [f. rosin *sb.* + -aceous.] Yielding resin; resinous.

1669 Worlidge *Syst. Agric.* (1681) 105 Roots of the Firs, Pines, or other Rosinaceous Trees.

Rosinante (rɒzɪ'næntɪ). Also 8–9 **rozinante**. [ad. Sp. *Rocinante* (f. *rocin* horse, jade: see rouncy), the name of the horse ridden by Don Quixote.] A poor, worn-out, or ill-conditioned horse; a hack, a jade.

Usually as a quasi-proper name.

1745 *Life & Adventures B.-M. Carew* 65 Who, enraged by their several Losses, began to curse the Doctor and his Rosinante. **1759** Sterne *Tr. Shandy* ii. xvii, Ill-fated sermon!..trod deep into the dirt by the left hind-foot of his Rosinante. **1788** J. May *Jrnl. & Lett.* (1873) 100, I felt queer enough mounted on my Rosinante, about thirteen hands high. **1816** *Sporting Mag.* XLVIII. 233 The more humble donkey and spare Rosinante trotting and snorting along the road. **1867** Lady Herbert *Cradle L.* 56 A wretched 'rosinante', such as would appear at a Spanish bull-fight.

Hence **Rosi'nantine** *a.*, lean, worn-out. *nonce-wd.*

1936 P. Fleming *News from Tartary* ix. 235 Plump and naked..they [*sc.* camels] were a great contrast to our shaggy, Rosinantine beasts.

†**ro'sine.** *Obs.*$^{-1}$ [f. L. *ros-a*, after *rēgīna*, etc. Cf. regine.] A rose; in quot. as a title of the Virgin Mary.

1500–20 Dunbar *Poems* lxxxv. 8 Our tern inferne for to dispern, Helpe rialest rosyne.

rosined ('rɒzɪnd), *ppl. a.* [f. rosin *v.* + -ed¹.] Smeared or rubbed with rosin; resinous. Also *fig.*

1598 Grenewey *Tacitus, Germania* (1622) 271 Amber.. will burn like unto wood pitched and rosened. **1613** Purchas *Pilgrimage* viii. xii. (1614) 804 Foure women attending with Torches of Pine tree Rosenned. **1714** Gay *Sheph. Week* vi. 24 That Bowzybeus who could..with the rozin'd Bow torment the String. **1774** Goldsmith in *London Chron.* 28–30 Apr. 416/3 And shall I mix in this unhallow'd crew? May rosin'd lightning blast me if I do. **1832** Brewster *Natural Magic* viii. 181 Its vibrations..may be kept up, by drawing a rosined fiddle-bow across it. **1887** Bowen *Æneid* v. 663 The God of the flames..Riots on bench, and on oar, and on rosined timbers of pine.

rosiner ('rɒzɪnə(r)). *Ir.* and *Austral. slang.* Also **rosner, rossiner, rozener.** [f. rosin *sb.* or *v.* + -er¹.] A drink of spirits; a stiff drink. Also *transf.*

1932 D. Johnston *Moon in Yellow River* i. 35 Well, you must step across to the store some time and we'll give you a rosner. **1933** *Bulletin* (Sydney) 10 May 20/1 Fill up the cup, a rozener, a hummer! **1934** S. Beckett *More Pricks than Kicks* 119 'And the rosiners' said Mrs. Tough, 'will you have that in the lav too?' Reader, a rosiner is a drop of the hard. **1947** H. D. Brockman *Fatal Days* 114 I've not had a solitary spot since four. I need a rosiner. **1954** T. Ronan *Vision Splendid* 345 Two nips that old Block had and the one I poured into Peter. They were rozeners I'll admit, but still the three I've had out of this second bottle haven't exactly been small ones. *a* **1966** 'M. na Gopaleen' *Best of Myles* (1977) 310 A rossiner wouldn't be bad, have a double one after this. **1973** D. Stuart *Morning Star, Evening Star* 53 There's no harm in a bit of rosiner after a hard day's travel, just once in a while.

'**rosiness.** Also 7 **rosyness.** [f. rosy *a.*] Rosy colour or complexion.

1651 Davenant *Gondibert* iii. i. 36 Orna now..breaks through her blushes so As the fair Morn breaks through her rosyness. **1824** Miss Mitford *Village* Ser. i. (1863) 133 Such a complexion,..so healthily fair with such a sweet rosiness. **1879** Christina Rossetti *Seek & Find* 65 Snow.. on mountain heights, flushed with pure rosiness at the fall of day.

'**rosing,** *vbl. sb.* [f. rose *v.*¹ 4.] The action of treating with chemicals in order to redden.

1839 Ure *Dict. Arts* 787 There next follows..the rosing by boiling in a bath of salt of tin. *Ibid.* 790 The rosing is given with solution of tin, mixed with soap water.

'**rosing,** *ppl. a.* *rare*$^{-1}$. [f. rose *sb.* or *v.*] Rose-like, rosy.

c **1480** Henryson *Test. Cres.* 464 Nocht is ȝour fairnes bot ane faiding Flour;..Ȝour roising reid to rotting sall retour.

†'**rosinish,** *a.* *Obs.*$^{-1}$ [rosin *sb.*] Resinous.

1600 Surflet *Countrie Farme* ii. xliv. 291 Take of the.. greenest, and most rosinish leaues of Nicotiana that can be chosen a pound.

'**rosinous,** *a.* Now *rare* or *Obs.* [f. rosin *sb.*] Resinous.

1651 R. Child in *Hartlib's Legacy* (1655) 50 The Countrey aboundeth much with Firs, and Pine-trees: which the Inhabitants usually cut, that the Gum, Rosinous, or Turpentine substance may sweat forth. **1707** *Curiosities in Husb. & Gard.* 93 There are Juices, 1. Aqueous,..5. Rosinous, 6. Bituminous. **1725** *Fam. Dict.* s.v. *Aloes*, Aloes Wood is Rosinous. **1794** *Phil. Trans.* LXXXIV. 388 The candles made of white lac also smoked and produced a rosinous smell.

rosiny ('rɒzɪnɪ), *a.* Also 6 **rosinie**, 7 **roziny**; 6–7 **roseny**, 7 **ros-, rozenny, -ie.** [f. rosin *sb.*]

1. Full of rosin; resinous.

1562 Turner *Herbal* ii. (1568) 89 A tede is a fat and roseny pece of a pyne or pich tre, which hewen of serueth for torches. **1576** G. Baker *Jewell of Health* 80 The lyke doe they describe of the fattes and rosinie substances. **1605** Timme *Quersit.* i. xiii. 62 Some whole trees are to be seene more sulphurus and roseny than other some. **1638** Rawley tr. *Bacon's Life & Death* (1650) 4 Trees Odorate,..and Trees Rozennie, last longer in their Woods, or Timber, than those abovesaid. **1669** [see resinaceous]. **1904** E. Nesbit *Phœnix & Carpet* i. 4 The rosiny fire-lighters that smell so nice.

†**2.** Of soil: Resembling, having the colour of, rosin. *Obs.* (Cf. rosilly *a.*)

1613 Purchas *Pilgrimage* i. xi. (1614) 59 The soile is of a rosennie clay. **1685** Temple *Ess. Gardening* Wks. 1720 I. 182 Of all sorts of Soil, the best is that upon a Sandy Gravel, or a Rosiny Sand.

'**rosion.** *rare*$^{-0}$. (See quot.)

1656 Blount, *Rosion*,..a gnawing, a griping, a biting.

'**rosist.** *rare.* [rose *sb.*] A grower or 'fancier' of roses.

1869 S. R. Hole *Bk. about Roses* 24 Passing from the bluecoat school of Rosists to the black.

'**rosland.** *dial.* [f. ross *sb.*³] (See first quot.)

1704 *Dict. Rust.* (1726), *Rosland*, heathy Land, or full of Ling;..Waterish, or Moorish Land. **1889** *Universal Rev.* Nov. 435 On river plain And smothered rosland stirs the snow and dies.

†**rosmarine**¹. *Obs.* Forms: (1 **rosmarim**,) 4–8 **rosmarine** (4 **-yne**), 5 **ros maryn, rosemaryn(e**, 4, 6, 8 **rosemarine.** [A more original form of rosemary.]

1. Rosemary.

[*c* **1000** *Sax. Leechd.* I. 184 Ðeos wyrt þe man rosmarim, & oðrum naman boþen nemneþ.]

13.. in *Reliq. Antiq.* I. 195 The rote of rosmaryne Man may set welle and fyne Betwene Aprile and the May. **1390** Gower *Conf.* III. 132 His herbe propre is Rosmarine, Which schapen is for his covine. **14..** *Med. MS.* in *Anglia* XIX. 79 Rosmarine. *c* **1450** *M.E. Med. Bk.* (Heinrich) 182 Tak þe rote of..rosmaryn, lauender, prymmerole. **1481** Botoner *Tulle on Old Age* (Caxton) f 5 Violettys, rosemarynes, maiorons, gylofres. **1591** Spenser *Muiopot.* 200 Colde Lettuce, and refreshing Rosmarine. **1598** Bp. Hall *Sat.* iv. iv. 118 Byting on Annis-seede, and Rosemarine. **1654** H. L'Estrange *Chas. I* (1655) 200 Mr. Prynne and Mr. Burton were brought into London in great pomp and state, being conducted with many thousands of horse and foot, having sprigs of Rosmarine in their hands. **1742** Shenstone *Schoolmistr.* 109 Trim rosemarine, that whilom crown'd The daintiest garden of the proudest peer.

2. Sea-dew. *rare*$^{-1}$.

1616 B. Jonson *Queenes Masques* Wks. 902 You shall.. steep Your bodies in that purer brine, And wholsome dew call'd Ros-marine.

†**rosmarine**². *Obs.*$^{-1}$ [f. mod.L. *rosmar-us* (16th cent., ad. Da. *rosmar*), or It. and Sp. *rosmaro*, Pg. *rosmar*; the ending may have been suggested by *morse marine*.] The walrus.

1590 Spenser *F.Q.* ii. xii. 24 The horrible Sea-satyre,.. And greedy Rosmarines with visages deforme.

Rosminian (rɒz'mɪnɪən). [See def.] **a.** *sb.* A member of the Institute of Charity, a religious congregation founded in 1828 by Antonio Rosmini-Serbati (1797–1855). **b.** *adj.* Of or pertaining to Rosmini, his Order, or his philosophy.

1837 L. D. Shrewsbury *Let.* 16 Apr. in D. Gwynn *Fr. Luigi Gentili* (1951) ix. 128, I thought the Rosminians would bring their means with them. **1843** M. Pattison *Diary* 1 Oct. in W. Meynell *John Henry Newman* (1890) iii. 32 Talk of some Rosminian Nuns coming to England. **1874** tr. *Überweg's Hist. Phil.* II. 496 Manzoni..applied the Rosminian principles to the art of composition. **1882** W. Lockhart in tr. *Rosmini's Sketch Mod. Phil.* Introd. p. ii, The preliminary difficulty in understanding the Rosminian philosophy. **1886** *W. Lockhart's Life Rosmini* xxxi. (ed. 2) I. 284 Here at present resides a small community of Rosminian Fathers. *Ibid.* II. 340 Notwithstanding all the accusations of *heterodoxy* against the Rosminians.

Hence **Ros'minianism**, the philosophical system or principles of Rosmini.

1874 tr. *Überweg's Hist. Phil.* II. 496 Pestalozza, whose *Elementi di Filosofia*, 1847, contain the best exposition of Rosminianism.

rosner, var. rosiner.

rosoch: see rosoth.

Roso-crusian, obs. form of Rosicrucian.

rosoglio, variant of rosolio.

'**rosolate.** *Chem.* [f. rosol-ic + -ate⁴.] A salt of rosolic acid.

1835 *R. D. & T. Thomson's Rec. Gen. Sci.* I. 50 The precipitation of the rosolate of lime.

rosolic (rəʊ'zɒlɪk), *a.* *Chem.* [f. L. *ros-a* + -ol + -ic.] ***rosolic acid*** = aurin.

1835 *R. D. & T. Thomson's Rec. Gen. Sci.* I. 50 Rosolic acid is a resinous mass which may be reduced to powder, and assumes an orange yellow colour. **1857** *Manch. Mem.* XV. 2 On the Composition and Derivation of Rosolic Acid. **1878** tr. *Ziemssen's Cycl. Med.* XVII. 520 The same holds good as regards corallin or pæonin, a red colour composed of rosolic acid.

rosolio (rəʊ'zəʊlɪəʊ). Also **ros(s)oglio, rossolio.** [a. It. *rosolio*, var. of *rosoli*: see ros solis. Cf. mod.L. *rossolium*.] A sweet cordial made in Italy and Southern Europe from spirits, raisins, sugar, etc.

1818 'A. Burton' *Adventures J. Newcome* iv. 238 At each Jew Agent's did he stop, Each Wine-house, and Rosolio-shop. **1819** T. Hope *Anast.* I. iv. (1820) 82 To support the ardour of my affections with rosoglio and spice. **1834** Marryat *P. Simple* xvii, I walked to a posada (that's an inn), and drank seven bottles of rosolio to keep myself quiet. **1850** [see *liqueur-glass* s.v. liqueur *sb.* 3]. **1864** Visc'tess Strangford *Adriatic* 269 The best liqueurs in the world, maraschino, rosoglio of several sorts [etc.]. **1901** Besant *Lady of Lynn* xi, The wine of Lisbon and Canary, the rosolio and the ratafia. **1973** *Times Lit. Suppl.* 14 Sept. 1064/2 He plied the abbot with sweet pink rosoglio and was then admitted to a closet in the cellar.

rosoth, a spurious word due to printers' errors for *rother-soil*: see rother 2.

1671 Phillips s.v. *Rother-beasts*, Whence *Ro-soil* [1678–1706 *Rosoth*] is used in Herefordshire, for the soil.. of those beasts. **1708** Kersey, *Rother-soil* or *Rosoth*. **1721** Bailey, *Rother-soil*, *Rosoch*.

†**rosp**, *v.*[1] *Obs.*[−1] [? var. of RASP *v.*[1] Cf. Norw. dial. *rosp* a rasp.] *trans.* To waste.

c **1250** *Gen. & Ex.* 2132 Al ðat ðise first .vii. maken, Sulen ðis oðere vii. rospen & raken.

†**rosp**, *v.*[2] *Obs.*[−0] [Cf. RASP *v.*[2], and Flem. *ruispen*, *ruspen* (Kilian), MLG. *ruspen*.] *intr.* To belch. Hence †'**rosping** *vbl. sb.*

c **1440** *Promp. Parv.* 437/1 Rospynge, or bolkynge (*S.* balkynge), *eructacio*.

†**rospeys, rospyse**, varr. RASPIS[1]. *Obs.*

c **1440** *Promp. Parv.* 437/1 Rospeys, wyne, *vinum rosatum*. **1465** *Mann. & Househ. Exp.* (Roxb.) 307 Item, for a botelle of rospyse, iiij.d.

Ross (rɒs), *sb.*[1] Also 6 Ros, 8 **Rosse**. The name of a county in the north of Scotland, used *attrib.* in ***Ross herald***, one of the six Scottish heralds.

1475–6 *Exch. Rolls Scot.* VIII. 372 Diligens signifero, nunc Ross heraldo nuncupato. **1526** *Acc. Ld. High Treas. Scot.* V. 266 Delivrit to Ros herrold, lettre requiring my lordis of Arrane and Murray to restor the Kingis gunis. **1566** *Cal. Scottish Papers* (1900) II. 250 Lettre..caried by Wm. Steward *alias* Ros harald of armes to the Q. of Scottes. **1641** *Reg. Privy Council Scot.* Ser. ii. I. 405 Befoir..Johne Malcome, Ross Herald. **1742** ALEX. NISBET *System of Heraldry* II. IV. xvi. 171 Rosse Herald, so named from the County of Ross, which was of old an Appendage of the Crown. **1863** G. SETON *Law & Pract. Heraldry in Scot.* 37 The Heralds attached to the Lyon Court are six in number, viz., Islay, Rothesay, Marchmont, Albany, Ross, and Snowdon.

ross (rɒs), *sb.*[2] Also 6 rose, 6–7 rosse, 9 *dial.* **rawse**. [App. of Scand. origin, corresponding to Norw. dial. *ros* (*rus*), small rubbish, scrapings.]

†**1.** Rubbish, refuse, dregs. *Obs.*

1577 HARRISON *England* III. viii. (1878) II. 53 The heads of saffron..being scowred from their rose [**1587** rosse or filth] ..are interred againe. **1587** *Ibid.* II. xx. (1877) I. 331 Either reserued in the house, or hauing the rosse pulled from their rootes, laid againe in the earth. **1630** LEVETT *Ordering of Bees* (1634) 51 Put the Combes and water together into a Canvas bagge,..and straine as much as you can.., casting away the rosse that remaineth in the bag.

2. The scaly outer portion of the bark of trees. Chiefly *U.S.*

The *Eng. Dial. Dict.* (1904) gives *rawse* or *ross* as a Sussex word, with the sense 'the scrapings of oak-bark, lichen, and moss'.

1778 J. CARVER *Trav. N. Amer.* 497 The ross or outside bark [of the ash] being near eight inches thick. **1828–32** WEBSTER, *Ross*, the rough scaly matter on the surface of the bark of certain trees. *New England*. *c* **1840** LANCE *Cottage Farmer* 23 Get then some oak bark, cut off the ross, and chop ..the inner rind. **1875** KNIGHT *Dict. Mech.* 1984/2 *Rossing-machine*, a machine for removing the ross, or rough scaly, exterior portion of bark, from the remainder.

ross, *sb.*[3] *dial.* [a. Welsh *rhos*.] A marsh, morass. Cf. ROSLAND.

1839 LEWES *Gloss. Hereford.*

Ross (rɒs), *sb.*[4] The name of Sir James Clark *Ross* (1800–62), Scottish explorer, used *attrib.* and in the possessive in **Ross('s) gull**, to designate a pinkish-white Arctic gull, *Rhodostethia rosea*, formerly named *Larus rossii* in his honour by J. Richardson in 1825 (*App. W. E. Parry's Jrnl. Second Voy. N.-W. Passage 1821–23* 359).

[**1872**: see ROSY *a.* 5.] **1902** *N. Amer. Fauna* XXII. 80 Ross Gull. The first known specimen of this beautiful species was killed at Alagnak, Melville Peninsula, by James Clark Ross, in June, 1823, during Parry's second voyage. **1926** A. THORBURN *Brit. Birds* IV. 70 The Wedge-tailed Gull... A specimen of this small and very beautiful species, known also as Ross's Gull, is said to have been obtained at Tadcaster, Yorkshire, in December, 1846. **1957** L. L. SNYDER *Arctic Birds Canada* 222 The rather fragmentary information pertaining to Ross's Gull has come largely from the Old World. **1971** *Country Life* 23 Sept. 751/1 The announcement of two rare arctic gulls sighted in the north east of England last December: a Ross's gull and an ivory gull. **1976** *New Yorker* 26 Jan. 25/3 Last year around this time, a Ross's gull—the only species of gull with a conspicuously pink breast—caused a considerable stir when it arrived at Salisbury, Massachusetts, thousands of miles from its normal home, in Siberia.

Ross (rɒs), *sb.*[5] The name of Bernard R. *Ross* (1827–74), factor of the Hudson's Bay Company, used in the possessive in **Ross'(s) goose** to designate a small Arctic goose, *Chen rossii*, formerly *Anser rossii*, named in his honour in 1861 by John Cassin (*Proc. Acad. Nat. Sci. Philadelphia* 72).

1874 E. COUES *Birds of Northwest* 553 Horned Wavy; Ross' Goose. **1908** C. MAIR *Through Mackenzie Basin* 320 At Fort Chipewyan..Ross's goose is the last to arrive in the spring. **1947** C. E. GILLHAM *Raw North* 175 He kindly interpreted for me while I interviewed his natives regarding the whereabouts of the Ross's goose. **1966** W. E. GODFREY *Birds of Canada* 52/2 White or greyish-white geese with black wing tips, they are likely to be confused with Ross's Goose.

Ross (rɒs), *sb.*[6] The name of Sir Charles A. F. L. *Ross*, Scottish-born engineer and soldier, used to designate a type of rifle used by the Canadian Army, esp. in the war of 1914–18.

1906 *Canadian Mag.* Dec. 66 (Advt.), Ross Rifles... The best in the World... 303 Calibre. **1917** *Grit* (Toronto) 7 Dec. 4/5 Think of the Ross Rifle, the lame horses, the sham shoes, the Allison rake-off. **1963** *Military Arms of Canada* 43 The Ross Rifle was a straight pull bolt action rifle that was made in calibre .303 British and .280 Ross for the Canadian Government. **1972** J. MINIFIE *Homesteader* xix. 169 We had been issued Ross rifles, a heavy weapon with a straight-draw action which jammed. **1973** J. QUICK *Dict. Weapons* 377/1 *Ross .303 rifle*... Under actual trench-warfare conditions it was found unsuitable. A serious problem with this weapon is the bolt. If reassembled wrong, it will permit firing in an unlocked position, resulting in serious injury or death to the shooter.

ross, *v.* *U.S.* [f. Ross *sb.*[1] 2.] (See quots.)

1853 S. STRICKLAND 27 *Yrs. Canada West* II. 230 As soon as the tree is felled, a person, called a liner, rosses and lines the tree on each side. **1864** WEBSTER, *Ross*, to divest of the ross, or rough, scaly surface; as, to ross bark. **1878** *Lumberman's Gaz.* Mar. 16 Removing the bark from the top of the log, or 'rossing' it, as it is termed by loggers.

Hence '**rossing** *vbl. sb.*

1875 KNIGHT *Dict. Mech.* 1984/1 Rossing-machine. *Ibid.* 1985/1 Rossing Attachment for Saw-Mill. **1958** *N.Z. Timber Jrnl.* June 59/2 *Rossing*, removing the bark from logs.

ross, obs. form of ROSE *sb.*

†'**rossals**. *Obs.*[−1] [ad. mod.L. *rossalia*: see ROSALIA.] = ROSALIA I.

1661 LOVELL *Hist. Anim. & Min.* 327 The measells..are cured as the small pocks; hereto belong the crystals, tubercles, rubeols, and rossals.

Rossby wave ('rɒsbɪ). *Physics* and *Meteorol.* [f. the name of Carl-Gustaf Arvid *Rossby* (1898–1957), Swedish meteorologist + WAVE *sb.*] A long wavelength fluctuation of a current in a fluid system having no divergence and subject to Coriolis force; *esp.* a lateral fluctuation of a jet stream, with wavelength comparable with the radius of the earth.

[**1951** *Jrnl. Meteorol.* VIII. 264/2 The velocity..of Rossby long waves relative to a basic current.] **1963** *Deep-Sea Res.* X. 735 Damped, stationary Rossby waves can occur in the ocean superimposed on a steady west to east flow. **1974** *Earth-Sci. Rev.* X. 203 Planetary or Rossby waves, though probably unimportant in the fluid interior of the Earth, are of interest to earth scientists in general, because of their pervasive role in the general circulation of oceans and atmospheres. **1974** *Nature* 5 Apr. 539/1 The intense Kuroshio current may generate a series of Rossby waves, which can propagate across the entire Pacific Basin. **1974** *Encycl. Brit. Macropædia* X. 163/1 If floor conditions are neither divergent nor convergent.., the absolute vorticity should not change with time... This explains the reason for the formation of long planetary waves, the so-called Rossby waves, in the upper-tropospheric flow patterns.

rosse, obs. form of ROSE *sb.*

rossel(l: see ROSIL and RUSSEL.

†'**rosseld**, *a.* *Obs.*[−1] (Meaning uncertain.)

? *a* **1400** *Morte Arth.* 2793 Thorowe a rownnde rede schelde he ruschede hym sone, That the rosselde spere to his herte rynnes!

'**rosselled**, *a.* *dial.* Also 8 rostled, 9 rossill'd. [Of obscure origin.] (See quots.)

1781 HUTTON *Tour to Caves* Gloss., *Rostled*, half rotten as apples sometimes are. **1828** CARR *Craven Gloss.*, *Rossell'd*, decayed,..a rossell'd apple. **1862** C. C. ROBINSON *Dial. Leeds* Gloss. 395 'A rossill'd apple.' Said only of this species of fruit.

rossellie, obs. form of ROSILLY.

rossen, obs. form of ROSIN.

'**rosser**. *U.S.* [f. ROSS *v.* + -ER.] A rossing-machine.

1875 KNIGHT *Dict. Mech.* 1984/2 A common use of the rosser is in saw-mills,..to remove the bark from the log in advance of the path of the saw.

rosset, obs. form of ROSET, RUSSET.

Rossettian (rə'zɛtɪən), *a.* [f. the name of D. G. *Rossetti* (see below) + -IAN.] Pertaining to or characteristic of Dante Gabriel Rossetti (1828–82), English poet and Pre-Raphaelite artist, or his work.

1881 'V. LEE' *Let.* in P. Gunn *Vernon Lee* (1964) vii. 79 All the Rossettian poeticules. **1905** G. B. SHAW *Let.* 11 Sept. (1972) II. 555 His [*sc.* W. Morris's] old Rossettian associates called him Topsy. **1908** D. H. LAWRENCE *Let.* 9 Oct. (1962) I. 30 What's the M.R.? Mary Rose? It sounds Rossettian. **1914** G. B. SHAW *Pygmalion* (1916) III. 144 One of the beautiful Rossettian costumes which..led to the absurdities of popular estheticism. **1927** E. SITWELL in *Daily Mail* 30 June 10/4 In provincial cities we may still find relics of Rossettian heads of fox-coloured hair. **1974** K. CLARK *Another Part of Wood* v. 179 An invitation to dine was in Rossettian language 'Come and grub with me', but dinner was more Beardsleyan.

So **Rossetti'ana** [ANA *suff.*], relics of, or information about, D. G. Rossetti.

1928 R. L. MEGROZ in *Daily Express* 28 Sept. 10/3 Sir Hall Caine has now made explicit what every careful student of Rossettiana has realised, that Lizzie Siddal committed suicide.

rossie ('rɒsɪ), *sb.* *Anglo-Ir.* [ad. Ir. *rásaidhe*, *rásaí*.] A wandering woman, a jilt; used as a disparaging term for a woman.

1922 JOYCE *Ulysses* 359 If they could run like rossies she could sit so she said she could see from where she was. **1927** P. S. DINNEEN *Irish-Eng. Dict.* (ed. 2) 879/1 *Rásach, -aighe, -acha, f.*, a rambling woman, a gipsy, a jilt; *cf.* rossie (*Dublin*); *rásaidhe, id.* **1939** JOYCE *Finnegans Wake* (1964) 327 All the prim rossies are out dress-parading. **1961** 'F. O'BRIEN' *Hard Life* v. 71 She told us all about her dear friend, Emmeline Pankhurst. Now there is a bold rossie for you if you like.

Rossi-Forel (ˌrɒsɪ fɒ'rɛl). Also **Rossi Forel**. [The names of Michele Stefano Conte de *Rossi* (1834–98), Italian geologist, and François-Alphonse *Forel* (1841–1912), Swiss physician and limnologist, who in 1883 collaborated in proposing the scale (a modification of Rossi's scale of 1873).] ***Rossi-Forel scale***: a ten-point scale used to measure the local intensity of an earthquake.

1885 *Science* 6 Mar. 197/1 The intensity of shocks is measured on the Rossi-Forel scale. **1900** *Jrnl. Geol.* VIII. 304 The continuous curves represent the isoseismal lines of intensities 4 and 3 of the Rossi-Forel scale. **1946** *Nature* 13 July 65/1 The shock on May 8 was apparently the most pronounced felt in Dunedin for many years. The intensity recorded there was IV–V on the Modified Mercalli Scale (equivalent to 5 on the Rossi-Forel Scale). **1976** *Daily Colonist* (Victoria, B.C.) 17 Aug. 1/1 The quake, measuring 7 on the Rossi Forel scale of 10, struck shortly after midnight.

‖**rossignol**. Also 6 rosignell. [F. *rossignol*:—pop.L. **lusciniolu*, a masc. form of L. *lusciniola*.]

†**1.** The nightingale. *Obs.*[−1]

1590 BUREL *Passage Pilgr.* in *Watson's Collect. Sc. Poems* (1706) II. 28 The Osill and the Rosignell, The Phœnix and the Nichtingell.

2. *Canada*. The song-sparrow (*Melospiza*).

1879 A. B. STREET in *Poems of Places, Brit. Amer.* 11 The brown rossignol's shrill carol.

†**rossin**, obs. Sc. pa. pple. of ROAST *v.*

1597 *Trials Witchcr.* in *Spald. Club Misc.* (1841) I. 85 The ane half of the day rossin in his bodye, as gif he hed bene rossin in ane vne.

rossiner, var. ROSINER.

rossing-machine: see ROSS *v.*

Rossinian (rə'siːnɪən), *a.* [f. the name of G. A. *Rossini* (see below) + -IAN.] Pertaining to or characteristic of Gioacchino Antonio Rossini (1792–1868), Italian operatic composer, or his music.

1869 H. S. EDWARDS *Life of Rossini* v. 55 The melody, as it now exists, is eminently Rossinian in form and style. **1897** G. B. SHAW in *Sat. Rev.* 20 Mar. 290/1 Passages which are Rossinian in their reliance on symmetry of melody and impressiveness of march to redeem poverty of meaning. **1927** *Daily Tel.* 14 June 12/6 The performance..was as full of spirit and élan as the delightful Rossinian 'snippets' that help to make this ballet [*sc.* La Boutique Fantasque] perhaps the most exhilarating thing in the whole of M. Diaghileff's repertory. **1955** E. DENT in H. Van Thal *Fanfare for E. Newman* 92 We sometimes find the most tragic situation set to the most cheerful music merely because the Rossinian style demands a big *finale* and the impression of a happy end. **1977** *New Yorker* 11 July 82/1 'Un Giorno di Regno', Verdi's first comic opera, which is a bit old-fashioned for its period and full of Rossinian idioms.

rossite ('rɒsaɪt). *Min.* [f. the name of Clarence Samuel *Ross* (1880–1953), U.S. geologist + -ITE[1].] A hydrated calcium vanadate, $CaV_2O_6.4H_2O$, found as yellow triclinic crystals occurring in glassy masses in sandstone.

1926 FOSHAG & HESS in *Amer. Mineralogist* XI. 66 (*heading*) Rossite, a new calcium vanadate from Utah. *Ibid.*, This mineral has been called rossite, in honor of Dr. C. S. Ross of the U.S. Geological Survey. **1963** *Canad. Mineralogist* VII. 713 The crystal structure of rossite, $Ca(VO_3)_2.4H_2O$, has been determined. **1968** I. KOSTOV *Mineral.* 470 Rossite group. The group comprises exclusively vanadates of aluminium, iron, sodium, and calcium, most of which are closely related to the montroseite group of oxides.

rösslerite, var. ROESSLERITE.

rosslynge, obs. form of RUSTLING.

‖**rosso antico** ('rosso 'antiko). [It., lit. 'ancient red'.]

1. The name given by Josiah Wedgwood (see WEDGWOOD) to the red stoneware produced at his Staffordshire factories.

1776 J. WEDGWOOD *Let.* 3 Mar. (1903) II. 163, I am afraid we shall never be able to make the *Rosso Antico* otherwise than to put you in mind of a red-Pot-Teapot. **1875** E. METEYARD *Wedgwood Handbk.* 28 Wedgwood made much red ware from the same Bradwell-wood clay as that used by Elers, only he glazed the insides of his vessels. Some of Wedgwood's earliest portrait medallions and bas-reliefs were in rosso antico, but the results were not satisfactory. **1976** *Times* 7 Dec. 16/3 The same American bidder paid £1,000..for a Wedgwood *rosso antico* pot-pourri vase of 1805.

2. A rich red marble found in Italy, and employed as a decoration. Also *attrib.* or as *adj.*

1816 J. DALLAWAY *Of Stat. & Sculpt.* 248 That [*sc.* the marble] of Lybia, is called, by the present antiquaries, 'rosso antico': of this marble there is no known quarry. **1848** MILL *Pol. Econ.* I. III. iv. 552 The materials of many of the ornamental articles manufactured in Italy are the substances called rosso, giallo, and verde antico. **1863** LYTTON

Caxtoniana II. 15 The columns of its lofty portico were of the *rosso antico* marble. **1882** *Athenæum* 30 Dec. 906/1 The material altogether Tuscan, the white marble having been brought from Serravezza, the red (like a fine *rosso antico*) from the neighbourhood of Siena. **1969** *Listener* 16 Jan. 79/1 Of marbles I have found *cipollino, pavonazzetto, giallo* and *rosso antico*, but no harder materials such as porphyry or serpentine.

rossolio, var. ROSOLIO.

‖**ros solis.** *Obs.* [L. *rōs* dew + *sōlis* gen. of *sōl* sun. The plant and liquor are also known in F. (and Pg.) as *rossoli(s*, whence Sp. and It. *rosoli* in sense 2 (cf. ROSOLIO).]

1. The plant sundew; = ROSA SOLIS 1.

1578 LYTE *Dodoens* 414 The Ros Solis and Woolfes clawe do growe in drie waterie Countries. **1621** BURTON *Anat. Mel.* II. iv. I. iii. 440 Rosemary, Ros Solis, Betony, Saffron. **1652** CADEMAN *Distiller of London* 34 ℞.. Ros solis, gathered in due season, and clean picked. **1728** CHAMBERS *Cycl.* s.v. *Rosolis*, It had its Name because antiently prepared wholly of the Juice of the Plant *Ros solis*. **1757** A. COOPER *Distiller* III. l. (1760) 215 The Ros-Solis or Sundew, from whence this Cordial Water has its name.

2. = ROSA SOLIS 2. *rare.*

1652 CADEMAN *Distiller of London* Table of Waters, *Aq. Roris Solis*, Ros solis proper. **1877** E. S. DALLAS *Kettner's Bk. of Table* 21 The Italians.. brought with them into France at least two liqueurs—this acqua d'oro with a predominant flavour of rosemary; and rossolis, with a predominant flavour of sundew.

†**rossome.** *Obs.*$^{-1}$ [G. †*roseme*.] Redness.

1527 ANDREW *Brunswyke's Distyll. Waters* L iv b, The same water is good agaynste the impetigines, and the rossome [G. *die röte*] in the face.

'rossy, *a. rare*$^{-1}$. [f. ROSS *sb.*[2]] Rubbishy; of the nature of ross.

1657 S. PURCHAS *Pol. Flying-Ins.* 68 The sap.. wherewith they temper the dry rossie dross, that they gnaw off from old decayed posts and pales.

rossy, obs. f. ROSY *a.*

rost(e, obs. ff. ROAST, ROOST, RUST.

rostel ('rɒstəl). *Bot.* [Anglicized f. ROSTELLUM.] The radicle of a seed.

1793 MARTYN *Lang. Bot.* s.v. *Rostellum*, The Rostel, or descending plane part of the Corcle or heart, in the first vegetation of the seed. **1832** *Planting* 13 in *Husb.* III. (L.U.K.), The *rostel*, or first radicle, which descends into the soil, and becomes the root of the tree. **1876** *Encycl. Brit.* IV. 266/2 The corcule (which includes the plumule or future stem and the rostel).

ro'stellar, *a. Bot.*, etc. [f. ROSTELL-UM + -AR.] Pertaining to, or constituting, a rostellum.

1877 HUXLEY *Anat. Inv. Anim.* iv. 212 The Diphyllidea have.. two armed rostellar prominences. **1885** H. O. FORBES *Wand. E. Archipelago* 93 An insect, to secure the pollinia, would require to alight on the margin of the rostellar platform.

ro'stellate, *a. Bot.*, etc. [f. ROSTELL-UM + -ATE.] Having a rostellum.

1826 KIRBY & SP. *Entomol.* IV. xlvii. 384 Mouth perfect, or rostellate. **1830** LINDLEY *Nat. Syst. Bot.* 257 Characterised by having.. a superior perianthium and rostellate seeds. **1866** *Treas. Bot.* 992/2 *Rostellate*,.. terminating gradually in a hard long straight point—as the pod of radish.

ro'stelliform, *a. Bot.*, etc. [f. ROSTELLUM.] Of the form or shape of a rostellum.

1819 SAMOUELLE *Entomol. Compend.* 292 Proboscis sheathed beneath a rostelliform process. **1830** LINDLEY *Nat. Syst. Bot.* 257 Seeds with a.. lateral rostelliform hilum.

‖**rostellum** (rɒ'stɛləm). [a. L. *rostellum* a small beak or snout (Pliny), dim. of *rostrum*.]

1. *Bot.* **a.** A radicle: cf. ROSTEL. ? *Obs.*

1760 J. LEE *Introd. Bot.* I. vii. (1765) 15 *Rostellum*, a plain Part of the Corculum; which descends. **1797** *Encycl. Brit.* (ed. 3) III. 435/2 The Corculum.. consists of two parts, viz. plumula and rostellum. **1832** LINDLEY *Introd. Bot.* (1839) 250 The radicle.. (*rhizoma* or *rostellum*); cotyledons..; and plumule.

b. (See quots.)

1841 *Penny Cycl.* XX. 175/2 *Rostellum*.. is applied to the short beak-shaped process found on the stigma of many violets, as *Viola hirta*, *V. odorata*, and *V. canina*, &c.; and Orchidaceæ, as *Orchis, Spiranthes, Listera*, &c. **1849** BALFOUR *Man. Bot.* §421 In Orchids, each of the pollen masses has a prolongation or stalk,.. which often adheres to a prolongation at the base of the anther, called *rostellum*. **1862** DARWIN *Orchids* Introd. 6 The rostellum either includes or is formed of viscid matter.

2. *Zool.* **a.** The tubule and enclosed siphuncle of the various species of louse, replacing the usual mouth apparatus of insects.

1826 KIRBY & SP. *Entomol.* III. 363.

b. The protruding fore-part of the head of tapeworms, armed with hooklets or spines.

1849 in CRAIG. **1856-8** W. CLARK *Van der Hoeven's Zool.* I. 180 *Tænia*... Head with four suctorial oscules, and mostly with a rostellum median, imperforate, retractile. **1888** ROLLESTON & JACKSON *Anim. Life* 225 *Taenia elliptica* .. also possesses a peculiar round rostellum beset with four irregular rows of sixty small hooks.

roster ('rɒstə(r), 'rəʊstə(r)), *sb.* Also 9 **rolster, rollster.** [ad. Du. *rooster* table, list, a transferred use of *rooster* gridiron (f. *roosten* to roast), in allusion to the parallel lines drawn on the paper.]

1. *Mil.* A list or plan exhibiting the order of rotation, or turns of duties and service, of officers, men, and bodies of troops.

Also, esp. *U.S.*, a simple list or register of officers, divisions of a regiment, etc., with various particulars relating to them.

1727 H. BLAND *Mil. Disc.* xix. 207 As each Nation had a different Number of Battalions in Flanders, their Duty was regulated by a Roster. *Ibid.* 283 At the Opening of the Campaign, he [the Adjutant-General] is to settle with the Majors of Brigade the Rosters for the several Duties. **1799** WELLINGTON in Gurw. *Desp.* (1834) I. 36 Major General Baird having desired to be relieved—Colonel Wellesley, being next on the roster, was ordered on the same night to command within the fort. **1824** —— *Suppl. Desp.* (1867) II. 332 The officers throughout the service.. perform the duty by what is called in the army a Roster, which is not kept by the commanding officer, but in the orderly room. **1857** SIR W. NAPIER *Life Sir C. Napier* I. 377 It was in strict accordance with the customs of the service, namely, to place some captains on to the field officers' rolster. **1884** LD. ROBERTS in *19th Cent.* June 1066 He becomes a duty man, and is on the roster for guards, &c.

2. *transf.* A list or table exhibiting the names of a set of persons, esp. as taking turns of duty with each other. Also in extended uses.

1858 SIMMONDS *Dict. Trade, Roster*, a list showing the turn or rotation of service or duty, as in the case of police-magistrates.. and others, who relieve or succeed each other. **1881** *Art Interchange* (N.Y.) 27 Oct. 89 On the feminine side of the [opera] company's roster there is more cause for apprehension. **1892** *Nation* 29 Dec. 493/1 The author's roster of the diplomatic body stationed at Berlin in 1837. **1930** *New Statesman* 3 May p. iii/1 One particular point is worth noting as to the names in this amazing roster of public enemies. **1942** E. PAUL *Narrow St.* xxxix. 337 Practically the entire roster of the Cagoulards was in the new Vichy Government. **1955** *Railway Mag.* May 365/2 This involves over 300 miles daily and is normally a 4-6-0 steam locomotive roster. **1967** W. W. NEWCOMB *Rock Art of Texas Indians* iv. 38/1 The roster of game animals which could figure prominently in human subsistence is not large. **1971** M. TAK *Truck Talk* 133 *Roster*. When the dispatch department has no immediate assignment for a driver, the driver's name is entered on the dispatch roster. **1978** *Detroit Free Press* 16 Apr. (Detroit Suppl.) 25/3 There he burned up American Association and made Tigers' roster in Spring Training, 1977.

3. *attrib.* and *Comb.*, as ***roster-board, game, sheet, system.***

1963 J. LUSBY in B. James *Austral. Short Stories* 233 Thwaites.. walked to the roster-board. **1977** *Weekly Times* (Melbourne) 19 Jan. 71/2 Feature of the roster games in the Kentish Cricket Association was the 6–15, including the hat-trick, by Railton's David Castles against Kimberley. **1977** R. LUDLUM *Chancellor MS.* xvii. 184 He kept mementoes... Photographs, roster sheets. **1976** B. JACKSON *Flameout* vii. 122 The roster system played unfair tricks on investigators: you could.. find yourself involved in two [air crash] investigations in three months.

roster ('rɒstə(r), 'rəʊstə(r)), *v.* [f. the sb.] *trans.* To place (someone or something) on a roster.

1922 *Glasgow Herald* 26 Jan. 8 The men can be rostered up to nine hours, with overtime paid after eight hours. **1962** *Mod. Railways* May 350/1 The day Birmingham–Glasgow trains in each direction are now rostered for Type 4 diesel haulage. **1967** *Times Rev. Industry* July 65/2 Even opening on Saturday morning is a vexed question among bank staffs. The board's suggestion that staffs might be rostered.. ignores the factors of personal convenience and prestige. **1970** *Railway Mag.* Oct. 561/2 The stud of 'Deltics' is regularly being rostered right up to the limit of locomotives in traffic. **1973** C. MASON *Hostage* ii. 34 Eighteen men.. had been rostered on for the two shifts of the guard. **1975** *New Yorker* 13 Oct. 152/3 One of McInally's replacements, Saxon, is rostered at five feet ten and a hundred and forty pounds. **1977** *Daily Tel.* 18 Feb. 2/5, I also found examples where more staff were rostered to work on Sundays than on week-days.

Hence **'rostered** *ppl. a.*, placed on a roster; assigned in accordance with a roster.

1973 *Daily Tel.* 13 Dec. 2/8 They [*sc.* train drivers] are continuing to do rostered overtime as agreed locally, and are only banning voluntary additional overtime and rest-day working. **1977** *N.Z. Herald* 8 Jan. 2-9/6 (Advt.), Fitter-turners will be required to work alternating shifts or a rostered day work scheme.

roster, obs. form of ROASTER.

rösti, var. ROESTI.

†**'rostle,** *sb. Obs.*$^{-0}$ [? ad. L. *rostellum*. Cf. ROSTEL.] (See quot.)

1585 HIGINS *Junius' Nomencl.* 300/2 *Vectis rostratus*,.. a barre or leauer with an iron point or end: a rostle.

†**'rostle,** *v. Obs.* Also 5 ro(o)styl, etc. [? f. OE. *rostian* to roast: see -LE.] *trans.* To burn slightly; to parch.

Perh. represented by mod. northern dial. *rossel, rozzel*, etc.; see *Eng. Dial. Dict.* s.v. *Rozzle*.

c **1440** *Promp. Parv.* 437/1 Rost[l]yd, sum what brennyd [*Winch.* rostylyd, sumwat brente], *ustillatus. Ibid.*, Roost[l]one [*Winch.* rostolone, *K.* rostelyn, *P.* rostlyn], *ustulo, ustillo. Ibid.*, Rostlynge [*Winch.* roostyllynge], *ustyllacio.*

rostral ('rɒstrəl), *a.* (*sb.*). Also 5 **rostrale,** 6 **rostralle.** [ad. late L. *rostrāl-is*, f. L. *rostr-um* beak: see -AL[1].]

†**1.** ***rostral bone***, the coracoid process. Also *absol.* as sb. *Obs.*

c **1400** *Lanfranc's Cirurg.* 156 For to fastne þe schuldre, þis boon rostral is putt in maner of a wegge. *Ibid.* (Addit. MS.), Two smale bonys whiche beþ y-clepyde rostralis. **1541** R. COPLAND *Guydon's Quest. Chirurg.* Gj, [One branch] byndeth & closeth these two addycyons called Rostralles.

2. Of columns, pillars, etc.: Adorned with the beaks of galleys or with representations of these. Also *transf.*

rostral crown, a golden crown, adorned with figures of ships' beaks, awarded to the person who first boarded an enemy's ship.

1709 ADDISON *Tatler* No. 161 ¶7 The Other wore a rostral Crown upon her Head. **1734** tr. *Rollin's Anc. Hist.* (1827) I. II. 377 A rostral pillar was erected in his honour. *c* **1800** MISS E. C. KNIGHT *Autobiogr.* I. 118 At the extremity of the saloon.. was a rostral column, on which were inscribed the names of the heroes of the Nile. **1860** MOTLEY *Netherl.* (1868) I. v. 258 The Genoese merchants had erected two rostral columns. **1883** *Cent. Mag.* Nov. 78/2 Its fountains, obelisk, allegorical statues of chief French cities, rostral and other lamp-posts.

3. *Zool.* Of or pertaining to, situated in or upon, the rostrum.

1826 KIRBY & SP. *Entomol.* IV. xlvi. 316 *Rostral*.., when seated on a rostrum. **1854** *Orr's Circ. Sci., Org. Nat.* I. 271 The compressed rostral teeth of the saw-fish are deeply implanted in sockets. **1880** GÜNTHER *Fishes* 335 The rostral cartilage is produced into an exceedingly long, flat lamina.

4. *Anat.* (See quot. 1975.)

1894 *Amer. Naturalist* XXVIII. 374 The two ends of the principal axis are respectively 'rostral' instead of 'cephalic' or 'oral' or 'proral'.. and.. 'caudal' [according to Schulze]. *Ibid.* 375 Among Ascidia.. there is perhaps a rostral extremity, but there is no caudal extremity in adults. **1953** *Brit. Jrnl. Psychol.* XLIV. 184 The procedures employed were.. transorbital leucotomy and thermocoagulation of the cerebral cortex in the rostral portion of the frontal lobes. **1954** T. L. PEELE *Neuroanat. Basis Clin. Neurol.* iv. 39/2 Running transversely across the rostral end of the cerebral peduncles are the optic tracts. **1975** E. GARDNER et al. *Anatomy* (ed. 4) i. 5/2 Rostral means nearer the 'front end', which is taken to be the hypophysical area in the early embryo and the region of the nose and mouth in post-embryonic life.

Hence **'rostrally** *adv.*, towards the rostral part.

1936 *Jrnl. Anat.* LXX. 208 Sagittal serial sections show that rostrally it runs into continuity with the medial preoptic nucleus. **1954** T. L. PEELE *Neuroanat. Basis Clin. Neurol.* iv. 38/1 Beginning at the caudal point of transection and proceeding rostrally, the following visible divisions can be made: medulla, pons,.. and cerebral hemispheres. **1970** *Brain* XCIII. 42 Most of the degeneration is a little more rostrally situated than in the preceding experiment. **1978** C. REID *Primer Human Neuroanat.* xvi. 149 A larger area of the reticular formation facilitates or augments reflexes at lower levels and this area extends rostrally through the pons and mid-brain and into the diencephalon.

rostrate ('rɒstrət), *a.* [ad. L. *rostrāt-us*, f. *rostrum* beak: see -ATE.]

†**1.** = ROSTRAL *a.* 2. *Obs.*

1601 HOLLAND *Pliny* VI. iv. I. 456 Forasmuch as we are light vpon the mention of Naual or Rostrate coronets, this would be noted [etc.]. **1674** EVELYN *Navig.* Misc. Writ. (1825) 645 Their rostrate crowns, and that pretty insolence by act of senate allow'd to C. Duillius.

2. Having, or furnished with, a rostrum; terminating in a rostrum: **a.** *Bot.*

1819 *Pantologia, Rostrate fruit*, in botany, a beaked fruit. Having a process resembling the beak of a bird: as in geranium, scandix, pecten. **1830** LINDLEY *Nat. Syst. Bot.* 61 The apex.. rostrate, and elongated in various ways beyond the insertion of the filament. **1870** J. D. HOOKER *Stud. Flora* 13 *Nuphar luteum*... Berry ovoid rostrate.

b. *Ent.*, *Zool.*, etc.

1826 KIRBY & SP. *Entomol.* IV. xlvi. 307 *Rostrate*.., when the anterior part of the head is elongated and attenuated into a cylindrical or many-sided rostrum or beak. **1848** *Proc. Berw. Nat. Club* II. 305 Body ovate-oblong, narrowed and rostrate in front. **1884** *Geol. Mag.* 560 In other forms, the anterior extremity becomes nasute or rostrate.

rostrated ('rɒstreɪtɪd), *a.* [See prec. and -ED.]

1. = ROSTRAL *a.* 2; also of a galley, having a beak.

1705 ARBUTHNOT *Coins*, etc. (1727) 249 He brought to Italy an hundred and ten rostrated Galleys of the Fleet of Mithridates. **1796** MORSE *Amer. Geogr.* II. 424 The rostrated column erected by Duillius. **1832** *Examiner* 324/2 With Roman temples and rostrated columns at the side scenes. **1839** *Civil Eng. & Arch. Jrnl.* II. 104 The rostrated decorations of the pedestal.. proclaim it at once to be a naval trophy.

2. = ROSTRATE *a.* 2.

1771 *Encycl. Brit.* II. 42/1 The antheræ are rostrated and barren. **1819** G. SAMOUELLE *Entom. Compendium* 230 Front as if truncated, vertical, not rostrated. **1849** *Proc. Berw. Nat. Club* II. 370 Head rostrated. **1866** R. TATE *Brit. Mollusks* iv. 71 The jaw of *Arion hortensis* contrasts strongly with the smooth rostrated jaw of *Limax*.

b. In specific names of fishes, etc.

1797 SHAW *Naturalist's Misc.* IX. pl. 304 The Rostrated whale.., Blackish sharp-snouted whale. *c* **1800** *Ibid.* XIV. pl. 586 The Rostrated Gymnotus:.. Long-snouted Gymnotus. **1803** —— *Gen. Zool.* IV. II. 337 Rostrated chætodon. *Ibid.* 401 Rostrated scarus.

rostrato-, combining form of ROSTRATE *a.*, occas. used to form adjs., as ***rostrato-nariform.***

1846 DANA *Zooph.* (1848) 432 In some instances the outer lip.. is elongate, producing a rostrato-nariform shape.

rostrifacture (ˈrɒstrɪˌfæktjʊə(r)). *rare*⁻¹. [f. L. ROSTRUM beak: after MANUFACTURE *sb.*] A structure made by a bird with its beak.

1884 E. COUES *Key to N. Amer. Birds* (ed. 2) 408 Distinguished as the orioles are for the dexterity and assiduity they display in their elaborate textile rostrifactures [etc.].

roˈstriferous, *a.* [f. *rostri-*, as combining form of L. *rostrum* + -FEROUS.] Having a rostrum (esp. as distinguished from a proboscis).

1852 DANA *Crust.* I. 440 Ophthalmic ring not rostriferous. **1888** ROLLESTON & JACKSON *Anim. Life* 482 With mouth.. at the end of a non-introversible snout, i.e. rostriferous.

ˈrostriform, *a.* [ad. mod.L. *rostriformis*: cf. prec. and -FORM.] Having the form or shape of a beak or a rostrum; beak-like.

1801 *Phil. Trans.* XCI. 260 Its beginning, with a rostriform point. **1826** KIRBY & SP. *Entomol.* III. xxviii. 17 With a maxilliferous mouth seldom rostriform. **1856–8** W. CLARK *Van der Hoeven's Zool.* I. 415 Head with anterior process mostly rostriform.

rostro-, used as combining form of ROSTRUM in some scientific terms, as ***rostro-antennary***, ***-branchial***, ***-lateral***; ***rostrocaudally*** adv.; **rostro-ˈcarinate** *a. Archæol.*, of or pertaining to stone implements of a keeled and beaked shape, esp. those characteristic of the Oldowan and Sangoan cultures of the African Pleistocene, and to flint objects from the Red Crag deposits of East Anglia, formerly thought to be hand tools of late Pliocene date, but now believed to be natural formations; also *ellipt.* as *sb.*

1888 *Huxley & Martin's Elem. Biol.* 225 A rostro-antennary branch;..distributed to the antennule and rostrum. **1912** R. LANKESTER in *Phil. Trans. R. Soc.* B. CCII. 295 We distinguish..an anterior surface, narrowed to the form of a keel and ending in a beak (hence we call the implement 'rostro-carinate') as a consequence of the oblique direction and convergence of the lateral surfaces, which approach one another so as to leave only a narrow keel-like ridge between them. **1934** *Jrnl. R. Anthrop. Inst.* LXIV. 337 Among these large tools (which were afterwards called Sangoan), a number of well-made rostro-carinate forms is to be distinguished. **1952** *Mem. Geol. Survey Uganda* VI. II. 64 The most finely finished product is somewhat canoe-like in shape—sharp prow, blunt stern..; the less finished or those not elaborately shaped, rather like a flat bottomed boat or rostro-carinate. **1957** J. K. CHARLESWORTH *Quaternary Era* II. xxxviii. 1016 The Cromerian implements..are ochreous or orange-brown artefacts, often striated as at East Runton. The tools are usually made from heavy flakes but include rostrocarinates and crude Abbevillean forms. **1964** K. P. OAKLEY *Frameworks for dating Fossil Man* iv. 176 Some [Oldowan flakes] were beak-shaped. [*Note*, p. 263] 'Rostro-carinate', a term which is better avoided since it suggests identification with the flaked flints well known under that name from the Crags of East Anglia which are now regarded to be of natural origin. **1960** *Jrnl. Compar. Neurol.* CXV. 166/2 In the medial nucleus a topographic organization is suggested in which the nucleus has effectively made a 180° rotation rostro-caudally. **1975** *Nature* 17 Apr. 617/2 There is also a gradient, though less steep, rostrocaudally along the eminentia. **1872** H. A. NICHOLSON *Palaeont.* 151 The one nearest the rostrum 'rostro-lateral'.

ˈrostroid, *a. rare*⁻¹. [f. ROSTR-UM + -OID.] Beak-like, rostriform.

1867 *Smithsonian Misc. Collect.* VII. 2 The head has the same long, rostroid appearance.

†**ˈrostrous,** *a. Obs.*⁻¹ [f. L. *rostr-um* beak + -OUS.] Having a beak or rostrum; beaked.

1651 BIGGS *New Disp.* ₱284 Therefore rostrous animals, as birds, because they want teeth, have need of a double stomack.

ˈrostrulate, *a. Ent.* [See next and -ATE.] Having a rostrulum.

1826 KIRBY & SP. *Entomol.* IV. xlvii. 383 Mouth rostrulate.

‖**ˈrostrulum.** *Ent.* [mod.L., dimin. of L. *rostrum* beak.] The mouth-organ of the *Pulicidæ* or fleas (see quot.).

1826 KIRBY & SP. *Entomol.* III. xxxiii. 362 *Rostrulum*,.. the oral instrument of *Aphaniptera*..in which the ordinary *Trophi* are replaced by a bivalve beak.

‖**rostrum** (ˈrɒstrəm). Pl. rostra, *rarely* rostrums. [a. L. *rostrum* beak.]

1. *Rom. Antiq.* The platform or stand for public speakers in the Forum of ancient Rome, adorned with the beaks of ships taken from the Antiates in 338 B.C.; also, that part of the Forum in which this was situated: **a.** In *pl.*

1542 N. UDALL tr. *Erasmus's Apophthegmes* II. f. 315ᵛ, The place called *Rostra* (where oracions wer made to the people). **1579** NORTH *Plutarch, Cicero* (1896) V. 366 Antonius.. commaunded his head and his hands should straight be set up over the pulpit for Orations, in the place called Rostra. **1600** HOLLAND *Livy* IV. xvii. 151 The Statues of these Embassadours which were at Fidene murdered, were set up openly at the charges of the citie in the Rostra. **1647** R. STAPYLTON *Juvenal* 61 The city of Rome had four great forums or piazzas, 1. *Forum Romanum* or *vetus*, wherein was the *comitium* or hall of justice, the rostra or pulpits for orations [etc.]. **1741** MIDDLETON *Cicero* I. v. 393 Before they met, he called the people likewise to the Rostra. **1765** SMOLLETT *Trav.* (1766) II. 128 Their rostra were generally adorned with the heads of some remarkable citizens. **1841** *Penny Cycl.* XX. 176/1 The rostra was between the Comitium, or place of assembly for the Curiæ, and the Forum, properly so called, or place of assembly for the Comitia Tributa. **1879** FROUDE *Cæsar* xv. 241 Pompey came forward on the Rostra to speak.

b. In *sing.*; also applied to the orators' stand in the Athenian assembly.

1713 ADDISON *Cato* II. ii, Myself will mount the Rostrum in his favour. **1751** EARL ORRERY *Rem. Swift* (1752) 185 What a glorious, what a consistent figure, must Swift have made in the rostrum at Rome. **1770** LANGHORNE *Plutarch* (1879) I. 191 When he came down from the rostrum, the women paid their respects to him. **1850** GROTE *Greece* II. lvi. (1862) V. 92 Hyperbolus is named by Aristophanes as having succeeded Kleon in the mastership of the rostrum in the Pnyx.

2. *transf.* A platform, stage, stand, etc., adapted for public speaking.

The singular form, though strictly incorrect, is the one commonly employed in this sense.

1766 CLAP *Hist. Yale C.* 77 It is built of Brick,..with a Steeple and Galleries, in which are three Rostra for Orations, Disputations, &c. **1776** H. WALPOLE *Let. to C'tess Ossory* 17 Dec., For want of Parliament General Burgoyne is..making an oration from the rostrum to the citizens of Westminster. **1813** *Examiner* 29 Mar. 198/2 From the old rostrum, he harangued the populace. **1840** DICKENS *Barn. Rudge* xxxix, Mr. Tappertit mounted on an empty cask which stood by way of rostrum in the room. **1877** BLACK *Green Past.* xxxix, The auctioneer had an improvised rostrum put up for himself at the end of the long table. **1974** R. ADAMS *Shardik* xxiv. 186 The rostra, barracoons and blocks of the slave market.

fig. **1886** LOWELL *Democracy* (1887) 11 This age of publicity, where the newspapers offer a rostrum to whoever has a grievance, or fancies that he has.

b. *spec.* A pulpit. Also *transf.* and *fig.*

1771 SMOLLETT *Humph. Cl.* (1815) 167 Humphry.. owned that he had been encouraged to mount the rostrum by the example and success of a weaver, who was much followed as a powerful minister. **1784** COWPER *Task* II. 409 The things that mount the rostrum with a skip, And then skip down again. **1816** SCOTT *Old Mort.* xxxi, As the worthy divine..was advancing towards the rostrum. **1873** M. DAVIES *Unorth. Lond.* (1876) 77 Mr. Banks glided into the Rostrum. *Ibid.* 100 Though mounted withal on the rostrum of Nonconformity. *a* **1964** G. UNDERWOOD *Pattern of Past* (1968) ix. 96 *Rostra* are sloping recumbent stones, sometimes projecting from a hillside, and sometimes half buried in a slanting position on level ground. At their upper points they mark small terminal blind springs, and their situation and appearance suggests that they may have been intended as pulpits. I have named them accordingly.

c. The platform as an institution.

1883 WHITTIER *Our Country* 43 Free press and rostrum, church and school.

d. A platform for a policeman when superintending the traffic at a crossing.

1930 *Morning Post* 16 July 12/5 First and foremost..there is the constable on the rostrum.

e. *Theatr.* (See quot. 1951.)

1930 W. G. FAY *Short Gloss. Theatr. Terms* 17 When it is necessary to use a rostrum to get elevation on the stage it is generally concealed behind a ground row. *Ibid.* 24 *Ramp*, a slope made of planks from a rostrum to the stage where steps are not used. **1951** *Oxf. Compan. Theatre* 678/1 *Rostrum*, any platform, from a small dais for a throne to a vast battlement, placed on the stage. It is usually made with a removable top and hinged sides, to fold flat for packing. It is reached by steps or a ramp, and quitted off-stage by 'lead-off' steps. A rostrum-front is a canvas-covered flat placed to conceal the front of the platform.

f. *Cinemat.* and *Television.* A platform used to support a camera employed in the filming of animated sequences and the like. Also *attrib.*

1951 HALAS & PRIVETT *How to Cartoon for Amateur Films* 105 Let's leave the camera on one side for the moment and consider the *rostrum*. That is the frame on which the camera and the board which holds the animation drawings are mounted. **1959** HALAS & MANVELL *Technique Film Animation* xix. 235 Such scenes as night bombing, wrecked aircraft, submarines under water and flying through cloud were done with one or two drawings, a little wood-carving, cotton-wool and the full use of single and multiplane shooting on the animation rostrum. *Ibid.*, *Rostrum camera*, apparatus for producing an image on cine-film. Its minimum requirements for animation work are that it must be capable of exposing one frame or film at a time when required. **1975** *Gloss. Terms Motion-Picture Industry* (*B.S.I.*) 9 *Rostrum*, adjustable but rigid support for the camera and the animation table, so constructed that they do not alter position relative to each other in an uncontrolled way. **1976** *Oxf. Compan. Film* 19/2 In the diagram, the camera (a) is shown mounted on the rostrum (US term 'animation stand'). **1977** *Broadcast* 18 Apr. 43/2 Vacancy for aerial image rostrum cameraman.

3. *Rom. Antiq.* A beak-like projection from the prow of a warship; = BEAK *sb.*¹ 7.

1674 EVELYN *Navigation & Commerce* Misc. Writ. (1825) 637 The Thasii added decks; Pisæus the rostrum, or beak-head. *a* **1700** —— *Diary* June 1645, The beakes of these vessells are like the ancient Roman rostrums. **1705** ADDISON *Italy* 14 An old Rostrum of a Roman Ship, that stands over the Door of their Arsenal. **1841** *Penny Cycl.* XX. 176/1 It pointed towards the Comitium, and the rostra were affixed to the front of it, just under the arches.

b. *transf.*

1782 H. WALPOLE *Let.* 18 May (1904) XII. 251 To-day we hear that Sir George Rodney has defeated—ay, and taken —Monsieur de Grasse in his own ship... These naval rostra arrived very opportunely to stay our impatience for a victory over the Dutch.

4. †**a.** The beak or nose of an alembic or still.

1660 BOYLE *New Exp. Phys. Mech.* viii. 64 The Rostrum or Nose of it..was Hermetically closed. **1684** tr. *Blancard's Phys. Dict.*, *Rostrum*, the Pipe to conveigh the Liquor distilling into the Receiver. [Also in various later Dicts.]

†**b.** The nozzle of a pair of bellows. *Obs.*

1706 BAYNARD *Cold Bathing* II. 236 Bellows to draw the Aereal Niter in at the Valve or Clack..which closing by the Pressure of the Hand, squeezeth it out of the Rostrum or Nose.

†**c.** (See quot.) *Obs.*

1722 QUINCY *Phys. Dict.* (ed. 2), *Rostrum*, is used..also for a crooked Scissars which the Surgeons in some Cases make use of for the Dilatation of Wounds. [Hence in Johnson, and various later Dicts.]

†**d.** (See quot.) *Obs.*

1740 J. GRASSINEAU *Mus. Dict.* 205 *Rostrum*, is the name of an instrument wherewith they rule paper for musical compositions. **1753** *Chambers' Cycl.* Suppl. s.v., Rostrum is also used to signify an instrument wherewith paper is ruled for musical compositions.

5. *Zool.*, etc. **a.** A beak or snout; an oral apparatus of an elongated form.

1753 *Chambers' Cycl.* Suppl. s.v., The *rostrum* or snout in fishes varies very much in figure. **1803** P. RUSSELL *Indian Fishes* II. 69 The length from the rostrum to the caudal fin. **1834** MᶜMURTRIE *Cuvier's Anim. Kingd.* 303 A sucker or siphon,..in the form of an acute inarticulated rostrum,.. fulfils the functions of a mouth. **1871** DARWIN *Desc. Man* I. viii. 255 In some weevil-beetles there is a great difference between the male and female in the length of the rostrum or snout.

Comb. **1826** KIRBY & SP. *Entomol.* III. xxxiv. 514 The Rhynchophorous or rostrum-bearing beetles.

b. A process or formation resembling a beak.

1815 BURROW *Conchol.* 33 *Cauda*, rostrum or beak; the elongated bases of the belly, lips and columella. **1831** KNOX *Cloquet's Anat.* 37 This aspect..presents on the median line a ridge, called the rostrum or azygous process. **1878** HOLDEN *Hum. Osteol.* (ed. 2) 79 The rostrum of the sphenoid would fit into the gap between them. **1884–5** *Riverside Nat. Hist.* (1888) I. 373 The apex of this phragmocone is enveloped in a second calcareous shell, the rostrum or guard.

6. *Bot.* (See quots.)

1832 LINDLEY *Introd. Bot.* (1839) 170 The whole mass of the corona is the *orbiculus*..; certain horn-like processes are *cornua*, or horns; the upper end of these is the beak, or *rostrum*. **1841** *Penny Cycl.* XX. 176/2 *Rostrum*, a botanical term applied to any rigid prolongation of remarkable length, or to any additional process at the end of any of the parts of a plant. **1866** *Treas. Bot.*, *Rostrum*, any beak-like extension; as in the stigma of some asclepiads.

rosulate (ˈrɒzjuːlət), *a. Bot.* [f. late L. *rosula*, dim. of *rosa* rose + -ATE².] (See quots.)

1832 LINDLEY *Introd. Bot.* 418 *Rosulate*, when parts..lie packed closely over each other, like the petals of a double rose. **1857** HENFREY *Elem. Bot.* 44 Where these so-called 'radical' leaves are arranged with some regularity, and spread out horizontally, as in the House-leeks, they are said to be *rosulate*. **1872** OLIVER *Elem. Bot.* II. 221 A low perennial, with tufted woody stock, rosulate linear leaves, and pedunculate capitate flowers.

rosum, U.S. and dial. variant of ROSIN *sb.*

rosy (ˈrəʊzɪ), *a.* Also 6 rossy, 6–8 rosie, 8 rosey. [f. ROSE *sb.* + -Y. Cf. MDu. *rosich* (Du. *rozig*), MHG. *rôsic* (G. *rosig*, *rösig*).

An OE. *rosiᵹ* has been inferred from the dat. sing. *roseum* in Thorpe's *Hom. Ælfric* II. 334. But this appears to be an error for *rosenum*, which is the reading in two Bodleian MSS.]

A. *adj.* **1. a.** Having the crimson or pink colour of a rose; rose-coloured, rose-red.

c **1374** CHAUCER *Troylus* III. 1755 Elementes..Holden a bond perpetuely duryngе, That Phebus mot his rosy day forth brynge. **1570** LEVINS *Manip.* 108/35 Rossy, *roseus*. **1615** CROOKE *Body of Man* 410 This spirit..blesseth all partes with ioy and iolitie and dies them with a Rosie colour. **1667** MILTON *P.L.* XI. 175 For see the Morn..begins Her rosie progress smiling. **1725** POPE *Odyss.* VII. 239 Alcinous gave the sign, And bade the herald pour the rosy wine. **1784** COWPER *Task* I. 495 The lark is gay, That dries his feathers ..Beneath the rosy cloud. **1823** CLISSOLD *Ascent Mt. Blanc* 23 The western arc of the misty circle kindled, from a rosy to a deep reddening glow. **1845** *Beck's Florist* 198 The dark crimson feathered upper petals..contrast prettily with the white centre and rosy under petals. **1871** R. ELLIS *Catullus* lxiv. 309 Wreaths sat on each hoar crown, Whose snows flush'd rosy beneath them.

b. Said of persons, their features, etc., especially as betokening good health.

1593 SHAKS. *Lucr.* 386 Her lily hand her rosy cheek lies under. **1611** —— *Cymb.* V. v. 121 That sweet Rosie Lad. **1697** DRYDEN *Æneid* II. 807 She held my hand,..Then from her rosy lips began to speak. **1736** *Gentl. Mag.* VI. 454/1 Dear Doctor, answered the Dean; you look well and rosy, your Colour is fresh. **1797–1805** S. & HT. LEE *Canterb. T.* II. 165 The carriage he was often pleased to fill with tired and rosy vintagers. **1807–8** W. IRVING *Salmag.* (1824) 276 Whenever he went a sparking among the rosy country girls of the neighbouring farms. **1848** THACKERAY *Van. Fair* xx, The honest Irish maid-servant..asked leave to kiss the face that had grown all of a sudden so rosy. **1875** H. G. WOOD *Therap.* (1879) 408 It is an every-day occurrence to see pale anaemic patients become, whilst taking it, rosy and plethoric.

c. Blushing; accompanied with blushes.

1611 SHAKS. *Cymb.* II. v. 11 She..pray'd me oft forbearance: did it with A pudencie so Rosie [etc.]. **1614** TOMKIS *Albumazar* I. i, Thou know'st my rosy modesty cannot do it. **1781** COWPER *Anti-Thelyph.* 87 She..turn'd her rosy cheek away. **1878** BROWNING *La Saisiaz* 10 Due return of blushing 'Good Night', rosy as a borne-off bride's.

d. *spec.* (See quot.)

1847 HALLIW. s.v., Hens, when they commence laying, and their combs look red and healthy, are said to be rosy.

e. *slang.* Drunk; tipsy.

1905 *Dialect Notes* III. 17 *Rosy*, *adj.* Slang. Drunk. **1931** *Princeton Alumni Weekly* 22 May 798/1 When 'the lid is off' one gets 'rosy',..and maybe 'passes out'. **1975** D. BAGLEY *Snow Tiger* xii. 104 Sure, there was drinking. Some of the boys..got pretty smashed... I was a bit rosy myself.

2. Resembling a rose; *esp.* sweet-smelling or fragrant as a rose, rose-scented.

a **1586** SIDNEY *Arcadia* III. (Sommer) 247b, Did not a rosed breath, from lips more rosie proceeding, say [etc.]. **1615** BRATHWAIT *Strappado* (1878) 83 If thy delicious breath I chaunce to sip, Being the rosie verdure of thy lip. **1616** B. JONSON *Epigr.* xcvii, His clok with orient veluet quite lin'd through, His rosie tyes and garters so ore-blowne. **1744** AKENSIDE *Pleas. Imag.* II. 168 That name indeed Becomes the rosy breath of love.

fig. **1820** KEATS *Lamia* I. 82 Whereat the star of Lethe not delay'd His rosy eloquence.

3. Abounding in, decorated with, roses; composed of roses.

1508 DUNBAR *Goldyn Targe* 40 The rosy garth depaynt and redolent.. Arayed was, by dame Flora the queene. **1590** SPENSER *F.Q.* I. ii. 37 A Rosy girlond was the victors meede. **1634** MILTON *Comus* 105 Braid your Locks with rosie Twine. **1697** DRYDEN *Virg. Past.* VI. 24 His rosie Wreath was dropt not long before. **1743** FRANCIS tr. *Hor., Odes* I. v. 2 What youth, the rosy bower beneath, Now courts thee to be kind?

fig. **1637** MONRO *Pract. Obs.* iv. in *Exped.* II. 194 As this life is Rosie, so it hath flowers mixed with thornes.

4. a. Of times, circumstances, etc.: Bringing happiness; bright, gladsome; promising, hopeful.

1775 SHERIDAN *Duenna* I. i, Her rosy slumbers shall not fly. **1820** KEATS *Lamia* I. 199 As though in Cupid's college she had spent Sweet days.., And kept his rosy terms. **1874** L. MORRIS *To a Child of Fancy* ii, My little dove,.. Who through the laughing summer day Spendest the rosy hours in play. **1887** H. SMART *Cleverly Won* ix, To be purposely knocked over when his chance of winning looked rosy, would be too provoking.

b. *transf.* Of temperament: Sanguine. *rare.*

1878 STEVENSON *Inland Voy.* (1902) 80 My companion, in a rosier temper, listened with great satisfaction to my Jeremiads.

5. a. In special collocations, as **rosy apple**, (*a*) used in skipping formulas; (*b*) (see quot. 1959[2]); **rosy-bill**, a South American pochard, *Netta peposaca*, which has a pink bill; **rosy cross**, the supposed emblem of the Rosicrucians (also *attrib.*); **rosy drop** (see quots. and ROSE-DROP 2); **rosy finch**, a bird of the genus *Leucosticte*, native to the northern parts of Asia and N.W. America; †**rosy gills** (see quot.); **rosy gull**, an American species of gull.

Also in various names of moths, as *rosy day, footman, minor, rustic*: see J. Rennie *Butterflies & Moths* (1832) 72, 86, etc.

1916 N. DOUGLAS *London Street Games* 64 *Rosy apples lemon and a pear A bunch of roses shall she wear. **1959** I. & P. OPIE *Lore & Lang. Schoolch.* xv. 339 The skipping formula usually begins.. Rosy apple, lemon tart, Tell me the name of your sweetheart. A, B, C, D, [etc.]. *Ibid.* xviii. 381 There are more than sixty established names for the pursuit of illegally knocking at doors... *Rosy Apple.* Derby. **1964** *Western Folklore* XXIII. 258 Rosy apples, Mama's little tart, Tell the initials Of your sweetheart! **1888** R. HUBBARD *Ornamental Waterfowl* II. v. 162 The *Rosy-bill is a native of South America. **1956** G. DURRELL *Drunken Forest* i. 16 Rosybills, immaculate in their gleaming black-and-grey plumage, their beaks looking as though they had been freshly dipped in blood. **1976** *Eastern Daily Press* (Norwich) 16 Dec. (Advt.), Sale, pairs black swans, Emperor, Barnacle, Egyptian, Tested, Gadwell, Shelduck, Rosybill, Carolinas, Pintails. **1631** BOLTON *Comf. Affl. Consc.* (1640) 90 In this conflict.. no new devise of the Knights of the *Rosie-crosse.. is able any whit, or at all, to revive, ease, or asswage. **1652** T. VAUGHAN (*title*), The Fame and Confession of the Fraternity of R.C. Commonly, of the Rosie Cross. **1664** BUTLER *Hud.* II. iii. 651 As for the Rosie-cross Philosophers, Whom you will have to be but Sorcerers. **1821** SCOTT *Kenilw.* xviii, Thou hast gulled the whole brotherhood of the Rosy Cross. **1891** [see ROSICRUCIAN A]. **1822** GOOD *Study Med.* (1829) II. 359 Carbuncled-face. *Rosy drop. **1871** NAPHEYS *Prevent. & Cure Dis.* III. xiii. 1081 Red swelling on the face of hard drinkers and high livers, known as 'rosy drop'. **1801** LATHAM *Synop. Birds* Suppl. II. 207 *Rosy finch. *Fringilla rosea*.. Inhabits among the willows.. in Sibiria. **1884** COUES *N. Amer. Birds* 350 *Leucosticte*,.. Rosy Finches. *a* **1700** B. E. *Dict. Cant. Crew*, **Rosy-gills*, sanguine or fresh-colour'd. **1831** *Wilson's Amer. Ornith.* IV. 353 *Larus Franklinii*, Franklin's *Rosey Gull. **1872** COUES *N. Amer. Birds* 316 Wedgetailed, or Ross' Rosy Gull,.. white, rosy-tinted.

b. In collocations used *attrib.* (see quots.).

1843 *Proc. Berw. Nat. Club* II. 49 *C. rosacea.*—Rosy Feather Star. **1865** GOSSE *Land & Sea* 257 The cones of pellucid rosy lilac, the Rosy Crumb Sponge. **1898** *Westm. Gaz.* 4 Nov. 9/2 Mandarin, Muscovy, and rosy-bill ducks.

6. With other adjs. (or sbs.) expressing colour, as ***rosy-blue, crimson, -gilt, -golden, -mauve, -red***; also ***rosy bright, -pale.***

1608 SYLVESTER *Du Bartas* II. iv. *Decay* 159 The Lillies of her breasts, the Rosie-red In either cheek. **1667** MILTON *P.L.* VIII. 619 With a smile that glow'd Celestial rosie red. **1725** POPE *Odyss.* III. 505 The racy wine,.. By ten long years refin'd, and rosy bright. **1832** TENNYSON *Œnone* 176 From the ground her foot Gleamed rosywhite. **1845** *Beck's Florist* 179 With large handsome foliage and.. flowers of a pleasing rosy-crimson colour. **1862** G. M. HOPKINS *Vision of Mermaids* (1929), Which, lightening o'er the body rosy-pale, Like shiver'd rubies dance. **1882** *Garden* 22 Apr. 271 The glowing rosy purple hue. **1925** V. WOOLF *Common Reader* 115 The apples rosy-gilt in the afternoon sun. **1926** D. H. LAWRENCE *Sun* iii. 11 The child and she were now both tanned with a rosy-golden tan, all over. **1952** A. G. L. HELLYER *Sanders' Encycl. Gardening* (ed. 22) 94 [*Cattleya*] *Harrisoniana*, light rosy-mauve, variable, summer, autumn. **1956** H. GOLD *Man who was not with It* (1965) xi. 89 His hungry mouth, rosy-red with fever. **1976** I. MURDOCH *Henry & Cato* I. 3 Leaving New York in daylight, his plane had soon risen into a sort of radiant rosy-blue stratospheric gloom. **1978** *New York* 3 Apr. 94/3 The terrine de poisson, a rosy-pale slice of fish pâté.

7. *Comb.*, chiefly parasynthetic, as ***rosy-billed, -bosomed, -cheeked, -coloured, -faced, -fleeced, -flowered, -footed, -lipped, -muzzled, -petalled, -rayed***, etc.; also ***rosy-blushing, -dancing, -glistening, -rising, -torturing, -warm.***

1876 *Proc. Zool. Soc.* 399 The *Rosy-billed Duck has been successfully introduced into Europe. **1598** SYLVESTER *Du Bartas* II. ii. IV. *Columns* 449 Heav'n's *Rosie-blushing cheeks. **1634** MILTON *Comus* 986 The Graces, and the *rosie-boosom'd Howres. **1728–46** THOMSON *Spring* 1007 The rosy-bosom'd Spring To weeping Fancy pines. **1603** BRETON *Packet Mad Lett.* I. iii, The beautifull lineaments of *rosie cheekt Ladies. **1824** MISS MITFORD *Village* Ser. I. (1863) 114 Rosy-cheeked apples, plums with the bloom on them. **1855** MACAULAY *Hist. Eng.* xxi. IV. 610 Foxhunting squires and their rosycheeked daughters. **1669** H. MORE *Exp. 7 Epist.* 78 The Cardinals should go in their *Rosie-coloured Hats and Robes. **1716** ROWE *Ode for New Year* viii, On the balmy air sits rosy-colour'd health. **1823** SCOTT *Quentin D.* xx, All the rosy-coloured ideas.. which flutter about the couch of a youth. **1754** GRAY *Poesy* 28 The *rosy-crowned Loves are seen On Cytherea's day. **1796** T. TOWNSEND *Poems* 31 O'er the *rosy-dancing tide. **1824** W. IRVING *T. Trav.* (1848) 5 In the opinion of the *rosy-faced butler. **1744** AKENSIDE *Pleas. Imag.* II. 634 O restore The *rosy-featur'd maid. **1936** R. CAMPBELL *Mithraic Emblems* 57 The *rosy-fleeced Arrival of the Moon. **1927** V. WOOLF *To Lighthouse* I. vii. 63 A *rosy-flowered fruit tree. **1728** THOMSON *Spring* 488 While the *rosy-footed May Steals blushing on. **1866** J. B. ROSE tr. *Ovid's Met.* 236 The rosy-footed maidens. **1928** O. GOGARTY *Wild Apples* 8 Fair skin and smooth as the rosy-footed dove's wing! **1809** MALKIN *Gil Blas* VIII. i. (Rtldg.) 276, I began to look like a *rosy-gilled son of the church. *a* **1918** W. OWEN *Poems* (1963) 127 The crunch of boots on blue snow *rosy-glistening. *c* **1374** CHAUCER *Troylus* II. 1198 Therwith al *rosy hewed tho wex she. **1773–83** HOOLE *Orl. Fur.* xxv. 347, I view'd Her sparkling eyes, her features rosy-hu'd. **1862** G. M. HOPKINS *Vision of Mermaids* (1929), The waves were *rosy-lipp'd. **1923** D. H. LAWRENCE *Birds, Beasts & Flowers* 63 Violets, Pagan, *rosy-muzzled violets. **1791** COWPER *Iliad* I. 588 The day-spring's daughter, *rosy palm'd. **1928** BLUNDEN *Retreat* 44 This retinue Of *rosy-petalled sauntering joys. **1925** —— *Eng. Poems* 90 Others like opals *rosy-rayed convene. **1916** —— *Pastorals* 19 Nothing Eastern come to us Save the *rosy-rising sun. **1595** WEEVER *Epigr.* IV. xxii. E vj, Their *rosie-tainted features cloth'd in tissue. **1598** DRAYTON *Heroical Ep.* (1695) 21 A *Rosie-tincted Feature is Heav'ns Gold. **1833** TENNYSON *Two Voices* 60 In tufts of rosy-tinted snow. **1929** BLUNDEN *Near & Far* 19 No *rosy-torturing desert. **1818** KEATS *Endym.* IV. 313 Let it mantle *rosy-warm With the tinge of love.

B. *ellipt.* or as *sb.* **1.** ***the rosy*** (*a*) wine; (*b*) blood; (*c*) a good time; phr. ***to do the rosy***, to have a good time. *slang.*

1840 DICKENS *Old C. Shop* vii, Richard Swiveller finished the rosy and applied himself to the composition of another glassful. **1891** *Sporting Life* 25 Mar. 7/3 Goddard was smothered in the rosy as he went to his chair, and Choynski bled at the mouth. **1892** E. J. MILLIKEN *'Arry Ballads* 69/2 A doin' the rorty and rosy as lively as 'Opkins's lot. *Ibid.* 77 Not *my* idea of the rosy.

2. *Naut. slang.* A ship's rubbish-bin.

1937 D. MARLOWE *Coming, Sir!* ii. 46, I struggled with the heavy garbage bins, called 'rosies'. **1962** GRANVILLE *Dict. Sailors' Slang* 97/2 *The rosy*, the Merchant Navy's *gash bucket*: a 'rose by any other name'. **1966** 'L. LANE' *ABZ of Scouse* 86 *Put a crust on ther Rosy fer 'im*, he has a good appetite. *Rosy*, a ship's swill bin.

rosy ('rəʊzɪ), *v. rare.* [f. the adj.]

1. *trans.* To render rosy; to tinge with rose-colour.

1652 COLLIER in Benlowe *Theoph.* B iv b, Fond Sense, cry up a rosie Skin, Sacrata rosy'd is within. **1864** A. DE VERE *Infant Bridal* 195 At first a gentle fear Rosied her countenance. **1883** JEFFERIES *Story of my Heart* iii, The purple of sunset rosied the sward.

2. *intr.* To become rosy or rose-red. Hence '**rosying** *vbl. sb.*

1862 THORNBURY *Life Turner* I. 28 The rosying in twilight of the reaches of the Thames. **1881** *Argosy* XXXII. 223 The sea-pinks rosying in ocean cave.

Rosycrusian, obs. form of ROSICRUCIAN.

rosy-fingered, *a.* Having rosy fingers. Chiefly *fig.*, after the Homeric ῥοδοδάκτυλος (ἠώς).

1590 SPENSER *F.Q.* I. ii. 7 The rosy fingred Morning faire. **1599** B. JONSON *Cynthia's Rev.* III. v, Take her by the Rosie-fingerd hand. **1657** J. SMITH *Myst. Rhet.* 9 Poets, that choose rather to say, rosie-fingered Aurora than red-fingered Aurora. **1685** DRYDEN *Albion & Alb.* II. i, The rosy-fingered morn appears. **1762** COWPER *To Miss Macartney* 97 So may the rosy-finger'd hours Lead on the various year. **1791** —— *Odyss.* IX. 194 The rosy-fingered daughter of the dawn. **1855** KINGSLEY *Heroes* IV. (1868) 45 Rosy-fingered Eos came blushing up the sky. **1871** PALGRAVE *Lyr. Poems* 83 Rosy-finger'd ye come, and golden-hair'd as the day.

Rosy Lee, Rosie Lee ('rəʊzɪ 'liː). Also with small initials. Rhyming slang for 'tea'. Also *ellipt.* as Rosie.

1925 FRASER & GIBBONS *Soldier & Sailor Words* 246 *Rosy Lee*, tea. (Rhyming slang.) **1929** J. B. PRIESTLEY *Good Companions* I. iv. 133 'Ow about a drop o' Rosie Lee? *Ibid.* 134 We'll 'ave the Rosie now, George. **1964** A. PRIOR *Z Cars Again* iv. 35 This is the best cup of rosy I get all day, Janey. **1968** J. BOLAND *Breakdown* I. 4 Want a drop of rosie, do yer, Dad? **1970** A. DRAPER *Swansong for Rare Bird* ix. 90 We were having a cup of rosy lee.

rosyn(e, obs. forms of ROSIN.

rot (rɒt), *sb.*[1] Forms: 4–6 rote, 4–5 rott, 5–7 rotte, 5 root; 4– rot. [App. of Scand. origin: cf. Icel., Fær., Norw. *rot*, Sw. dial. *råt*, obs. Da. *rodt, rod, raad* (16th c.), LG. *röt*, related to ROT *v.*, ROTTEN *a.*]

1. The process of rotting, or the state of being rotten; decay, putrefaction; also, rotten or decayed matter.

a **1300** *Cursor M.* 5921 For þe rotte þat þar-on fell.. Ne was in hus na vessel fre. *Ibid.* 19001 In hell Ne suld noght crist be left to duell, Ne neuer o rote his flexs ha sight. **13..** *E.E. Allit. P.* B. 1079 þer was rose reflayr where rote has ben euer. **1382** WYCLIF *Micah* ii. 10 For the vnclennesse therof it shal be corrupt with the warst rott. *c* **1440** *Promp. Parv.* 437/1 Rot, or rotynge, *corrupcio, putrefaccio.* **1483** *Cath. Angl.* 312/1 A Rote, *caria, caries, liuor.* **1750** *Phil. Trans.* XLVI. 444 It was a hollow Bag, as he thought, filled with Rot and corruption. **1854** S. DOBELL *Balder* i, Your rot Glimmers in corse-lights on the shuddering dark.

fig. **1538** STARKEY *England* II. ii. 194 Who ys so blynd that seth not.. the grete infamy and rote that remeynyth in vs? **1581** MULCASTER *Positions* 159 *marg.*, The main rot of the Romaine empire. **1601** WEEVER *Mirr. Mart.* A vij, Many headed Rumour, Vices preseruer, vertues festred rot. **1859** WHITTIER *Preacher* 65 From the death of the old the new proceeds, And the life of truth from the rot of creeds.

2. a. A virulent disease affecting the liver of sheep which are fed on moist pasture-lands; inflammation of the liver caused by the fluke-worm, liver-rot. Usually with *the.*

See also *foot-, hunger-, liver-, pelt-, water-, winter-rot.*

c **1400** *Rule St. Benet* 1331–2 For thurgh a schep þat rote hase hent May many schep with rote be schent. *c* **1460** *Towneley Myst.* xii. 26 All my shepe ar gone,.. The rott has theym slone. **1538** STARKEY *England* I. iii. 98 When they [i.e. sheep] are closyd in ranke pasturys & butful ground, they are sone touchyd wyth the skabe and the rotte. **1546** *Supplic. Poore Commons* (E.E.T.S.) 85 When it hath pleased God to punish vs with the rot of our shepe. **1647** TRAPP *Comm. Rom.* v. 12 As the rot over-runneth the whole flock. **1667** MILTON *P.L.* XII. 179 His cattel must of Rot and Murren die. **1712** E. COOKE *Voy. S. Sea* 69 Sometimes the Rot among Cattel is rather a Relief than a Damage. **1766** *Compl. Farmer* s.v. *Rabbit* 6 H 4/2 Rabbits are subject to.. the rot, which is caused by the giving them too large a quantity of greens. **1809** *Med. Jrnl.* XXI. 93 The rot in sheep often prevails to an alarming degree, in the up-lands that skirt these fens. **1846** J. BAXTER *Libr. Pract. Agric.* (ed. 4) II. 15 It is by summer flooding, where it is practised, that the fatal disease of rot is introduced. **1864** T. S. COBBOLD *Entozoa* 171 In the season of 1830–31, the estimated deaths of sheep from rot was between 1,000,000 and 2,000,000.

b. A particular form, instance, or epidemic, of this disease.

1538 STARKEY *England* I. iii. 98 Commynly they dye of skabe and rottys in grete nombur, wych cumyth.. bycause they are nuryschyd in so fat pasture. **1617** MORYSON *Itin.* II. 68 Many private men in England have in one yeere lost more cattel by a rot, then the Pale lost by this spoyling of the rebels. **1668** MORE *Div. Dial.* II. x. (1713) 116 Nor dare I adventure to propose to you the Murrain of Cattle or Rots of Sheep. **1763** MILLS *Pract. Husb.* III. 416 A farmer who kept four hundred sheep tried this receipt in the last general rot (about five years ago). **1768–74** TUCKER *Lt. Nat.* (1834) I. 535 The simple sheep licks up the autumnal dews hanging upon her pasture, which gives a rot to her flesh. **1864** J. FORSTER *Sir J. Eliot* I. 102 Was not the first rot or scab that came among English sheep brought by one out of Spain?

fig. **1667** DAVENANT & DRYDEN *Tempest* Epil. 4 Among the muses there's a general rot. **1765** H. WALPOLE *Lett.* (1892) IV. 432 There seems to be a rot among princes: the Emperor Don Philip and the Duke are dead.

c. ***red rot***: see RED *a.* and *sb.*[1] 19. ***white rot***, the plant *Hydrocotyle vulgaris*, belonging to the order *Umbelliferæ*; marsh pennywort, sheep-rot; also, rot-grass (*Pinguicula vulgaris*).

1597 GERARDE *Herbal* 424 Water Pennywoort is called.. in English Sheepes killing Pennygrasse, Pennyrot, and in the north countrie White rot. **1640** PARKINSON *Theat. Bot.* 534 They call it [butterwort] *White rot*,.. for the Country people doe thinke their sheepe will catch the rot, if for hunger they should eate thereof. **1806** GALPINE *Brit. Bot.* 21 *Hydrocotyle*, White-Rot. **1886** HOLLAND *Cheshire Gloss.* 389 White Rot, *Hydrocotyle vulgaris.*

3. a. A putrescent or wasting disease in persons. Also *fig.*

1388 WYCLIF *Prov.* xii. 4 Rot is in the boonys of that womman, that doith thingis worthi of confusioun. *a* **1585** MONTGOMERIE *Flyting* 323 The painfull poplesie,.. The rot, the roup, and the auld rest. *a* **1592** GREENE *Jas. IV*, IV. iii, Go, and the rot consume thee! **1607** SHAKS. *Timon* IV. iii. 64, I will not kisse thee, then the rot returnes To thine owne lippes againe. **1650** BULWER *Anthropomet.* 87 We most justly abhorre the Nose that is sunk into this figure by the Venerian rot. **1662** R. MATHEW *Unl. Alch.* 69 Abusing himself in all blasphemies, riot and excess, in due time the Rot, or the Pox overtook them. **1836** *Encycl. Brit.* (ed. 7) XIV. 510/2 The disease called grinder's rot, an incurable consumption. **1898** [see GRINDER 9].

†**b.** In the imprecation ***rot on*** or ***upon.*** *Obs.*

1624 HEYWOOD *Captives* II. ii. in Bullen *O. Pl.* IV, Rott on that villeyne! no. **1638** COWLEY *Love's Riddle* I, A rott upon you; you must still be humoured. *Ibid.* IV, Rot on your possibles.

4. Decay in timber or other vegetable products, stone, etc. See also DRY-ROT.

1830 LYELL *Princ. Geol.* I. 217 The rock may with propriety be said to have *the rot*, for it crumbles to pieces in the hand. **1841** EMERSON *Man the Reformer* Wks. (Bohn) II. 240 Every species of property is preyed on by its own enemies, as iron by rust, timber by rot. **1868** *Rep. U.S. Comm. Agric.* (1869) 214 Low, wet soils almost invariably produce rot in the berry. **1882** DE WINDT *Equator* 85 Enormous holes in the bamboo flooring occasioned by rot.

5. *slang.* Nonsensical rubbish; trash, bosh. Also used of activities, objects, etc. Also as *int.* Cf. *tommy-rot* s.v. TOMMY 6.

1848 SHILLETO in Whibley *In Cap & Gown* (1890) 228 Your Natural-rot, your Moral-bosh. **1857** HUGHES *Tom Brown* vi, Let's stick to him and talk no more rot. **1879** M. E. BRADDON *Cloven Foot* iv. 96, I thought he despised ballet-dancing. Yet this is the third time I have seen him looking on at this rot. **1880** HENLEY & STEVENSON *Deacon Brodie* IV. 79 Portrait of George as a gay hironmonger... O rot! Hand it over, and keep yourself out of that there thundering moonlight. **1882** MISS BRADDON *Mt. Royal* III. i. 13 You are just the sort of woman to believe in that kind of rot. **1894** G. MOORE *Esther Waters* xxxix. 302 All bloody rot; who says I'm drunk? **1905** H. JAMES *Golden Bowl* vi. 74 He had not many things, none of the redundancy of 'rot' they had elsewhere seen. **1914** G. B. SHAW *Fanny's First Play* 158, I quite agree that harlequinades are rot. *a* **1953** E. O'NEILL *Long Day's Journey* (1956) I. 35 It's damned rot! I'd like to see anyone influence Edmund more than he wants to be. **1977** C. MCCULLOUGH *Thorn Birds* ii. 36 'What if it isn't the Eyetie girl?'.. 'Rot!' said Paddy scornfully.

6. *Cricket.* A rapid break-down or fall of wickets during an innings. Also *transf.*: a decline (in resources, standards, behaviour, etc.). Usu. in phrases ***the rot set in, to stop the rot***.

1868 *J. Lillywhite's Cricketers' Compan.* 61 A terrible 'rot' set in at the commencement of their second 'venture'. **1882** *Australians in Eng.* 71 After the fall of Leslie's wicket, however, a complete 'rot' set in. **1884** *Lillywhite's Cricket Ann.* 64 After this came the rot, and the total only reached 118. **1901** *Westm. Gaz.* 24 Apr. 2/3 It is to be hoped that something can be done (as cricketers would say) to 'stop the rot'. **1912** P. F. WARNER *Eng. v. Austral.* ix. 100 Ransford.. had rendered great service to his side by helping to 'stop the rot'. **1926** G. M. TREVELYAN *Hist. Eng.* VI. ii. 642 By these all too drastic measures the rot of pauperism was stopped. **1930** J. B. PRIESTLEY *Angel Pavement* i. 38 He could not pretend to himself now that such pitiful economies as these could stop the rot. **1938** R. WARNER *Professor* v. 113, I really don't know how the rot set in, but the process may have been something like this. **1951** C. P. SNOW *Masters* xix. 157 We must take care that a rot doesn't set in. **1955** *Times* 6 June 3/1 The rot began when Appleyard came into the attack. **1958** *Spectator* 22 Aug. 251/1, I have a feeling that, recently, airlines have been allowing this precious asset to depreciate. The rot set in with the introduction of bus fares. **1969** *Listener* 17 July 68/1 The rot set in, I think, with the President's speech to the Air Force Academy at Colorado Springs in June. **1973** M. WOODHOUSE *Blue Bone* ii. 12, I went up to London.. and that, as the saying goes, is where the rot set in.

7. *Comb.*, as ***rot-disease, epidemic, -proof, -proofed, -stricken***; † **rot-bean** (see quot.); **rot-grass**, one or other of several plants supposed to cause rot in sheep (see quots.); **rot-heap**, a rubbish-heap; **rot-steep** (see quot. 1838); **rot-stone**, = *rotten-stone*.

1716 *Petiveriana* I. 180 Barbadoes *Rot-bean,.. *Jetaiba Barbad. lobis minoribus.* **1864** T. S. COBBOLD *Entozoa* 173 The main facts relating to the origin.. of the *rot-disease. *Ibid.* 172 The *rot epidemic of 1824. **1631** R. H. *Arraignm. Whole Creature* ix. 69 They are as *rot grasse to sheepe. **1794** HUTCHINSON *Hist. Cumb.* I. App. 39 *Pinguicula vulgaris*, Rot-grass, supposed highly injurious to sheep, on moist grounds. **1844** H. STEPHENS *Bk. Farm* I. 350 *Melica cœrulea*, .. fly-bent or rot-grass. **1863** PRIOR *Brit. Plants* 192 Rot-grass, from its being supposed to bane sheep, a grass in the sense of herbage, *Pinguicula vulgaris.* **1881** MISS ORMEROD *Man. Injurious Ins.* 43 Burning the infested old cabbage-stocks.., instead of throwing them into *rot-heaps. **1870** *Daily News* 19 Aug. 2 Blocks of wood on end, with gravel pounded between, the whole made permanently waterproof and *rotproof. **1884** *Health Exhib. Cat.* 90/1 Rotproof Non-poisonous Wall Linings. *Ibid.* 104/2 Hammock Awnings, comprising also *Rotproofed specimens. **1838** T. THOMSON *Chem. Org. Bodies* 396 The cloth is steeped in a weak alkaline ley to remove the weaver's dressing. This is technically called the **rot steep.* **1874** W. CROOKES *Dyeing & Cal.-printing* 45 The 'rot steep', so called because the flour or size with which the goods were impregnated was formerly allowed to ferment and putrefy. **1819** SCOTT *Leg. Montrose* vi, The soldier, who was.. burnishing his corslet with *rot-stone and shamois-leather. **1897** *Month* June 638 One who ..had allowed human beings to perish like *rot-stricken sheep.

† **rot**, *sb.*[2] *Obs.* [a. Du. *rot* neut., or G. *rotte* fem., a. OF. *rotte, rote, route*, ROUT *sb.*[1]] A file (of soldiers). Cf. RAT *sb.*[5] Also *attrib.*

1635 BARRIFFE *Mil. Discipl.* cxx. (1643) 417 The other thirty two rots of Muskettiers belonging to the middle squadron. **1637** MONRO *Expedit.*, etc. II. *Abridgm. Exerc.* 183 There must be nine Rots of Pikemen, which have the Right hand, and twelve Rots of Musketiers on the left hand. *Ibid.*, Two are esteemed as Leaders, being a Corporall a Rot-master or Leader, and an under Rot-master.

† **rot**, *a. Obs.* [f. ROT *v.* Cf. Du. *rot*, LG. *röt, rot.*] Rotten; decayed.

1598 BP. HALL *Sat.* IV. iv. 118 Byting on Annis-seede, and Rose-marine, Which might the Fume of his rot lungs refine. **1620** *Westward for Smelts* (Percy Soc.) 19 Her teeth were rot, Her tongue was not. **1631** R. H. *Arraignm. Whole Creature* xiv. 235 Those things.. are as rot as our Irish bogs, or English Quagmires. **1707** MORTIMER *Husb.* (1721) I. 189 A good quantity of.. well-rot Dung and Earth mixt together.

rot (rɒt), *v.* Forms: 1 rotian, 3 rotien, 3–4 rotie, 3–5 rotye, 5 rootye; 3–5 roten, 5 rotyn (rooton); 4 roote, 4–5 root, 5 royt; 4–6 rote, rotte, 4– rot. [Common Teut.: OE. *rotian*, = Fris. *rotsje*, MDu. *roten, rotten* (Du. *rotten*), OS. *rotôn* (MLG. *roten*, LG. *rötten*), OHG. *rozzên*; Icel. *rota* (trans.), obs. Da. *rodde, rǿde*: see ROTTEN *a.*, and cf. the etym. note to RET *v.*[2]]

1. a. *intr.* Of animal substances: To undergo natural decomposition; to decay, putrefy, through disease, mortification, or death.

c **897** K. ÆLFRED *Gregory's Past. C.* xxi. 153 Swa se læce, ðonne he on untiman lacnað wunde, hio wyrmseð & rotað. *c* **1000** *Sax. Leechd.* II. 264 Maneȝum men lungen rotað. *c* **1055** *Byrhtferth's Handboc* in *Anglia* VIII. 299 Mid þam man smyrað ricra manna lic þæt hiȝ rotian ne maȝon. *c* **1200** ORMIN 4773 He warrþ all.. secnedd, Swa swiþe þatt hiss bodiȝ toc To rotenn bufenn eorþe. *c* **1275** *Serving Christ* 72 in *O.E. Misc.* 92 Boþe him schal rotye þat body and þe bon. **13..** *Sir Beues* 2697 Her I legge al to-blowe, And roteþ me flesch fro þe bon. **1387** TREVISA *Higden* (Rolls) I. 363 Þere is an ilond, þere no dede body may roty. *c* **1440** *Jacob's Well* 125 þanne fell on his fote a maladye, þat it rotyd. *c* **1520** L. ANDREW *Noble Lyfe* L ij, Than the fedders of the goshawke rote of yᵉ dounge of ardea as far as it toucheth. **1548** UDALL, etc. *Erasm. Par. Acts* ii. 9 b, Although his bodye was laid in graue voyde of all lyfe, yet ther it did not rotte or putrify. **1602** SHAKS. *Ham.* v. i. 179 How long will a man lie i' th' earth ere he rot? **1737** *Gentl. Mag.* VII. 117/2 The rest are stark dead, and may rot when they list. **1791** COWPER *Iliad* IV. 212 Where he left his brother's bones to rot. **1887** MORRIS *Odyss.* XII. 46 Dead men rotting to nothing.

b. Similarly of other substances liable to natural decay, as timber, fruit, vegetable matter, etc.

c **897** K. ÆLFRED *Gregory's Past. C.* xxii. 171 Of ðæm treowe sethim, ðæt næfre ne rotað. *c* **1000** ÆLFRIC *Exod.* xvi. 24 Hit [*sc.* the manna] ne rotode. *c* **1200** *Vices & Virtues* 91 Hier is igadered swilch timber ðe næure rotien ne mai. *c* **1250** *Gen. & Ex.* 3342 It [the manna] wirmede, bredde, and rotede ðor. *a* **1300** *Cursor M.* 23893 þat þat besaunt rote noght in hord. **1382** WYCLIF *Isaiah* xl. 20 The stronge tree, and the vnable to roten, ches the wise craftes man. *c* **1400** MAUNDEV. (Roxb.) ii. 5 Cedre may noȝt rote in erthe ne in water. **1470–85** MALORY *Morte Arth.* XVII. vi. 698 She lete make a.. clothe of sylke that shold neuer rote for no maner of weder. **1530** PALSGR. 694/1 This peare wyll rotte if you eate it nat betyme. **1581** MULCASTER *Positions* vi. (1887) 40 Like corne not reaped, but suffered to rotte by negligence of the owner. **1630** *R. Johnson's Kingd. & Commw.* 540 Yet.. the Grasse groweth at least one yard high, and rotteth.. upon the ground. **1687** A. LOVELL tr. *Thevenot's Trav.* I. 136 Sycamore-Wood.. that does not rot so soon as other Wood. **1726** LEONI *Alberti's Archit.* I. 34/1 There will be some small unconcocted Stones in it, which afterwards coming to rot, throw out little Pustules. **1748** *Anson's Voy.* II. iv. 219 Several of her casks had rotted. **1822** SHELLEY *When the Lamp* iv, From thy nest every rafter Will rot. **1858** GLENNY *Everyday Bk.* 203/2 Piled in a stack, till the grass and fibre all rot together. **1876** J. SAUNDERS *Lion in Path* i, Still year after year the fruit has rotted and dropped.

c. In *pa. pple.* used predicatively.

c **1290** *St. James* 301 in *S. Eng. Leg.* I. 43 þis ȝoungue Man sixe and þritti dawes heng up-on þe galu-treo Are he fader a-ȝein to him come, þat i-roted he auȝte to beo. *c* **1350** *Will. Palerne* 4124 For many a day hade i be ded & to dust roted, nadde it be goddes grace. **1387** TREVISA *Higden* (Rolls) VI. 475 Whan here body was i-take up of þe erþ e it was i-founde al i-roted and i-torned into powder. **1419** in Ellis *Orig. Lett.* Ser. II. I. 69 The Kele.. is yrotyt and must be chaungyd. **1561** HOLLYBUSH *Hom. Apoth.* 27 If the iaundis were rotted in a man. **1593** SHAKS. *Lucr.* 823 The branches of another roote are rotted. **1668** [see next]. **1726** LEONI *Alberti's Archit.* I. 7/1 Stones.. in Buildings, if their Tops are.. rotted, shew the Intemperature of the Air. **1872** BUSHNELL *Serm. Living Subj.* 369 They are humbled to a point so low by their idols, rotted into falsehood, buried in lust and shame.

d. With *away, off, out.*

c **1440** *Alph. Tales* 64 þer happend a surans for to fall in hys lymbe, þat his fute rotid off. *a* **1548** HALL *Chron., Rich. III*, 28 Myles Forest, at sainct Martyns le graunde by pece meale miserably rotted awaye. **1607** SHAKS. *Timon* IV. iii. 63 Thy lips rot off. **1668** CULPEPER & COLE *Barthol. Anat.* III. ix. 149 Some Scythians, whose earlets ar mortified and rotted of with cold. **1678** ILLINGSWORTH (*title*), A Just Narrative, or Account of the Man whose Hands and Legs rotted off in the Parish of Kingswinford. **1802–12** BENTHAM *Ration. Judic. Evid.* (1827) I. 398 Say, you wish your tongue may rot off,.. if you ever saw any such thing. **1849** LYELL *2nd Visit U.S.* II. 137 Some of the trunks must have rotted away to the level of the ground.

e. *N. Amer.* Of sea or river ice: to melt or thaw. Cf. ROTTEN *a.* 4 c.

1892 [implied in ROTTING *vbl. sb.*[1]]. **1977** *New Yorker* 20 June 86/2 Ice was beginning to rot.

2. a. *fig.* in various contexts, chiefly denoting decay of a moral or abstract kind.

a **1225** *Ancr. R.* 84 þeo þet rotieð and stinkeð al ine fulðe of hore sunnen. **1382** WYCLIF *Jer.* xiii. 9 Thus to roten Y shal make the pride of Juda. **1393** LANGL. *P. Pl.* C. VI. 151 Ryght so religion roteþ and sterueth. **1460** *Rolls of Parlt.* V. 377/2 Though right for a tyme rest and bee put to silence, yet it roteth not ner shall not perissh. **1594** T. B. *La Primaud. Fr. Acad.* II. 271 If wee staye and as it were rotte in these base, brutish and supposed pleasures. **1707** M. HENRY *Serm.* Wks. 1853 II. 597/1 It is true of prayer, what we say of winter, that it never rots in the skies. **1838** LYTTON *Alice* VI. v, Take the history of any civilised state before she rotted back into second childhood. **1870** LOWELL *Study Windows* 25 If they are cheated, it is, at worst, only of a superfluous hour, which was rotting on their hands. **1891** *Spectator* 13 June, A kind of society.. which always ends, sooner or later, by rotting down.

b. *slang.* ***to rot about***, to fool about, waste time. Now *rare.*

1902 E. NESBIT *Five Children & It* viii. 198 When we're all rotting about in the usual way heaps of things keep cropping up. **1909** J. R. WARE *Passing Eng.* 211/1 *Rotting about*.., wasting time from place to place. **1927** W. E. COLLINSON *Contemp. Eng.* 116 'To play the fool' is to rag about, rot about, fool about, play the [giddy] goat, bucket around.

3. a. Of persons: To become affected with some putrescent or wasting disease, esp. as the result of confinement in jail. Also *fig.*, to languish (*in* a place).

1340 *Ayenb.* 32 þe ilke anlikneþ þane ssrewe þet heþ leuere rotye in a prison [etc.]. **1393** LANGL. *P. Pl.* C. XIV. 22 Lo, how pacience.. brouhte hem al aboue þat in bale rotede. **1542–3** *Act 34 & 35 Hen. VIII*, c. 8 §1 Many rotte, and perishe to death for lacke of helpe of surgery. **1587** GOLDING *De Mornay* xxvii. (1592) 437 If I in the meane whyle do rotte there [in prison]. **1692** *Covenant of Grace* 11, I might use extremity towards you, cast you into Prison, and there let you Rot. **1758** JOHNSON *Idler* No. 22 ¶5 Some will confess their resolution that their debtors shall rot in gaol. **1784** COWPER *Task* III. 805 He.. Can dig, beg, rot, and perish. **1889** JESSOPP *Coming of Friars* i. 6 The civil authorities took no account of them as long as they quietly rotted and died. **1927** *Scribner's Mag.* Feb. 168/1 A man must do something. It's better than rotting in the saloons in Casper. **1975** T. ALLBEURY *Special Collection* ii. 10 The Moscow Centre has just left them to rot. **1978** I. B. SINGER *Shosha* ii. 39, I asked for Dora and he replied 'Rotting in Siberia'.

b. Of sheep: To become affected with the rot.

1523 FITZHERB. *Husb.* §66 If thou waine thy calues with hey,.. the rather they wyll rotte whan they come to grasse. **1596** HARINGTON *Metam. Ajax* (1814) 3 The poor sheep would eat him without salt (as they say); but if they do, they will soon after rot with it. **1637** MILTON *Lycidas* 127 The hungry Sheep.. Rot inwardly, and foul contagion spread. **1683** TRYON *Way to Health* 88 Over-wet Weather will corrupt them, and cause them to Rot in moist low Grounds.

4. a. *trans.* To affect with decomposition, putrescence, or decay; to corrupt, make rotten.

c **1386** CHAUCER *Cook's T.* 43 Wel bet is roten Appul out of hoord, Than þat it rotie al the remenaunt. **1557** NORTH *Gueuara's Diall Pr.* 442 Let an apple have never so little a broose, that broose is ynough to rotte him quickely. **1572** BOSSEWELL *Armorie* II. 118 Her dung is poyson to the Hauke, and rotteth her fethers. **1604** HIERON *Wks.* I. 504 He shewed His iustice in rotting it at the other time. **1672** MARVELL *Reh. Transp.* I. 132 A Dart, that where it does but draw blood, rots the person immediately to pieces. **1726** LEONI *Alberti's Archit.* I. 58/1 To keep the mortar from rotting the Timber. **1733** TULL *Horse-hoeing Husb.* 68 It is long continual Rains that Rot or Chill the Blossoms. **1820** W. SCORESBY *Acc. Arctic Reg.* I. 271 The salt in the sea.. destroys the tenacity of the bay-ice.., and, in the language of the whale-fisher, completely rots it. **1889** *Anthony's Photogr. Bull.* II. 241 It is necessary to rot or sweat ink after it is ground from ten to twenty-four hours.

refl. **1606** SHAKS. *Ant. & Cl.* I. iv. 47 This common bodie .. Goes too, and backe,.. To rot itselfe with motion. **1649** BLITHE *Eng. Improv. Impr.* (1653) 113 Many of your Cold, Sowr, Rushy Pastures, Rot themselves though never plowed.

b. *fig.* Also const. with *off, down, out.*

1567 *Trial Treas.* in Hazl. *Dodsley* III. 284 The Ruler of all rulers will.. rot their remembrance off from the ground. **1579** TOMSON *Calvin's Serm. Tim.* 116/2 We shall see these vermine that seeke nothing else but to rotte or venime the Church of God. **1628** FORD *Lover's Mel.* I. ii, Why shouldn't I.. snarl at the vices Which rot the land. **1848** LYTTON *Harold* IX. ii, Better that we had rotted out our lives in exile. **1871** CARLYLE in *Daily News* 4 Jan., This I lay at the door of our spiritual teachers.., who thereby incalculably rot the world. **1912** GALSWORTHY *Inn of Tranquility* 79 'They don't do a stroke more than they're obliged,' he ended; ..'Yes,' he muttered, 'the nation is being rotted down.'

c. *spec.* To ret. Cf. ROTTING *vbl. sb.* 2.

1811 *Weekly Reg.* 5 Oct. 86/1 (*heading*) Process for rotting hemp. **1835–6** *Encycl. Metrop.* (1845) VIII. 702/1 The operation of rotting, or as it is most commonly called, water-retting, flax and hemp.

d. *slang.* To spoil, interfere with; to ruin. Also const. *up.*

1908 A. S. M. HUTCHINSON *Once aboard Lugger* VI. viii. 344 You rotted my show all right. **1908** D. COKE *House Prefect* viii. 104 You can see Bob's off you, and we don't want to rot the whole thing up, just when he's begun to be decent again. **1932** 'A. BRIDGE' *Peking Picnic* xxv. 323 I've got a complex about the whole business, and you know why. Well, that might rot it all up, at any moment. **1973** N. W. SCHUR *British Self-Taught* 335 To *rot* a plan is to *spoil* it. **1978** *Sunday Times* 15 Jan. 42/7 A turquoise velvet top (detested since I rotted up a quiz programme in it).

5. To affect (sheep) with the rot. Also *absol.*

c **1380** WYCLIF *Wks.* (1880) 408 þanne he ledip his sheep wel in hool pasture þat wole not rote. **1523** FITZHERB. *Husb.* §54 It is necessary that a shepeherde shoulde knowe what thynge rotteth shepe. **1588** SHAKS. *Tit. A.* IV. iv. 93 More dangerous Then baites to fish, or hony stalkes to sheepe, When as the one is wounded with the baite, The other rotted with delicious foode. *a* **1656** VINES *Lord's Supper* (1677) 221 No shepherd would call his sheep into such pastures as will certainly rot them. **1725** RAMSAY *Gentle Sheph.* I. ii, Blashy thows.. may rot your ews. **1794** *Trans. Soc. Arts* XII. 235 Produce of the land.. very rushy,.. and always rotted sheep. **1854** *Jrnl. R. Agric. Soc.* XV. I. 234 Apparently sound pastures.. have rotted sheep this Season.

6. Used in imprecations against a person or thing, sometimes merely an outburst of irritation or impatience.

1588 SHAKS. *Titus A.* v. i. 58 But vengeance rot you all. **1611** —— *Cymb.* II. iii. 136 The South-Fog rot him. **1664** COTTON *Scarronides* I. Wks. (1715) 37 Where once your what shall's call'ums—(rot em, It makes me mad I have forgot 'em), Liv'd a great while. **1682** DRYDEN *Prol. to Southerne's Loyal Brother* 5 Both pretend love, and both (plague rot 'em!) hate. **1709** STEELE *Tatler* No. 73 ¶2 Rot you, Sir, I have more Wit than you. **1756** FOOTE *Engl. fr. Paris* II, I'll be rot if we don't make them caper higher. **1767** S. PATERSON *Anoth. Trav.* II. 52 Rot the name of the first post! I have forgot it. **1817** KEATS *Lett.* Wks. 1889 III. 74 For, rot it! I forgot to bring my mathematical case with me. **1859** DICKENS *T. Two Cities* II. v, 'She was the admiration of the whole Court!' 'Rot the admiration of the whole Court!'

7. *slang.* To chaff severely; to abuse, denigrate. Also *absol.*, to talk nonsense; to joke. (Cf. ROT *sb.*[1] 5.)

1890 LEHMANN *H. Fludyer at Cambridge* 106 Everybody here would have rotted me to death. **1890** W. E. HENLEY *Let.* 6 June in J. Connell *W. E. Henley* (1949) vii. 182 He'd have given much to hear you rotting the Alien. **1899** PHILLPOTTS *Human Boy* 169 Freckles, who was an awfully sportsman-like chap really, said he was only rotting all the time. **1905** H. A. VACHELL *Hill* vii. 155 Has anybody been rotting you? **1914** 'I. HAY' *Lighter Side School Life* vii. 181 We don't do any *work*: we just rot Duck-face. We simply rag his soul out. **1914** G. B. SHAW *Fanny's First Play* III. 200 But I'm serious: I'm not rotting. Really and truly—. **1922** S. LESLIE *Oppidan* iii. 38 A sport taking the mysterious form of 'rotting the Flea'. **1934** R. MACAULAY *Going Abroad* xxx. 264 There are things one simply mustn't rot about, I feel.

rota ('rəʊtə). [a. L. *rota* wheel.]

1. A political club, founded in 1659 by J. Harrington, which advocated rotation in the offices of Government; also, a society of this type.

1660 HARRINGTON (*title*), The Censure of the Rota upon Mr. Milton's Book, entituled, The Ready and Easie way to Establish A Free Common-wealth. **1662** in J. Ogilby *King's Coronation* (1685) 3, I..With Common-wealths and *Rota's* fill their heads. *a* **1680** BUTLER *Characters, Politician*, A speculative Statesman,..that did all his Exercises in the late Times of cursed Memory at the *Rota*, but is not yet admitted to practise.

2. a. A rotation (of persons, etc.); a round or routine (of duties, etc.); †a rote.

1673 RAY *Journ. Low C.* 425 These [councillors] are taken out of the great Council, and go round in a *rota*. **1710** PALMER *Proverbs* 95 Such Formal Devotions that are nothing but a *Rota*. **1751** R. PALTOCK *P. Wilkins* (1884) I. 186 The..occurrences which happened during this period ..consisted chiefly of the old rota of fishing, watering [etc.]. **1800** COLQUHOUN *Comm. Thames* 631 Perambulating the River..agreeably to a rota which is laid down. **1844** in Ribton-Turner *Vagrants & Vagrancy* (1887) 254 The experience of those managers who have taken their rota of duty in the office. **1868** ROGERS *Pol. Econ.* xiii. (1876) 10 According to a rota to be agreed on between each other.

b. A list of persons acting in rotation; a roster.

1856 HUGHES *Tom Brown* I. vii, The senior fag who kept the rota. **1878** STUBBS *Const. Hist.* III. xx. 419 Pleas of debt, which required the attendance of the parties to suits and the rota of qualified jurors. **1882** KEARY *Outl. Prim. Belief* ix. 437 They heard names called over and voices answering as if by rota.

3. *R.C. Ch.* The supreme court for ecclesiastical and secular causes. (Cf. ROTE *sb.*[5] 2).

1679 BURNET *Hist. Ref.* I. 50 At that time Staphileus Dean of the Rota was there. **1685** *Lond. Gaz.* No. 2081/1 The Republick of Venice have named four Persons for the Pope to chuse one, to fill the Place of Auditor of the Rota. **1728** CHAMBERS *Cycl.* s.v., The *Rota* consists of twelve Doctors, chosen out of the four Nations of Italy, France, Spain, and Germany. **1765** BLACKSTONE *Comm.* I. Introd. 15 To tell the king's courts at Westminster, that their practice is.. conformable to the decrees of the Rota or Imperial Chamber. **1845** S. AUSTIN *Ranke's Hist. Ref.* III. 149 He also claimed the holidays of the Roman rota for himself. **1877** D. LEWIS tr. *Sander's De Schism. Anglica* Introd. p. lxxiv, The next day was the day of the Conference with the Dean of the Rota. **1908** *Westm. Gaz.* 6 July 5/1 A special law for regulating the working of the ancient tribunals, the Rota, and the Segnatura.

‖**4.** *Mus.* A musical composition which has the form of a round; this form itself. Used esp. of medieval English songs (as 'Sumer is icumen in', where this designation appears in the original manuscript). Cf. ROUND *sb.*[1] 19 b.

1876 STAINER & BARRETT *Dict. Mus. Terms* 381/1 *Rota*.., a Round, but the word is sometimes applied to anything with frequent repeats, as for instance a Hymn tune. **1883** GROVE *Dict. Mus.* III. 180/1 It..is written for six voices, four of which sing the round proper or 'rota' (as it is termed in the Latin directions for singing it). **1944** W. APEL *Harvard Dict. Mus.* 652/2 *Rota*,..medieval name for a round, particularly the Sumer-canon, probably with reference to the 'turnover' of the melody in the different parts. **1955** *New Oxf. Hist. Mus.* (rev. ed.) II. xi. 402 Its form, which is described in the manuscript itself as a *rota*, is that of an infinite canon. **1979** *Early Music* July 391/2 The piece in question is the famous *rota* 'Sumer is icumen in'.

5. *attrib.* and *Comb.*, as (sense 1) ***rota man, room;*** (sense 2) ***rota committee, system;*** **rota cut**, an interruption or reduction of power or water supplies which is imposed on different areas by rotation in time of shortage.

1935 *Planning* II. XLIV. 13 As much as possible of the actual assessment of need should be left to local rota committees, using the regional scale with fairly wide discretion. **1974** *Times* 15 Feb. 15/2 The third course..is to impose rota cuts designed..to avoid the working days of industry, and..essential services such as hospitals. **1977** *Times* 20 Apr. 5/2 Rota-cuts (when water supplies are cut off for a certain number of hours a day) might appear a less painful alternative than standpipes (involving total cut-off of domestic supplies). **1664** BUTLER *Hud.* II. iii. 1108 As full of tricks, As Rota-men of Politicks. **1691** WOOD *Ath. Oxon.* II. 439 Dr. Will. Petty was a Rota-man and would sometimes trouble Ja. Harrington in his Club. **1673** *Character Coffee-House* in *Harl. Misc.* (1745) VI. 429 A Coffee-House is..a Rota Room, that, like Noah's Ark, receives animals of every Sort. **1955** *Times* 25 Aug. 9/6 Only if a six-day shopping week is adopted, with a rota system to give staff a five-day week, will distribution costs be materially increased.

rota-, var. ROTO-.

rotacism, -ize, variants of RHOTACISM, -IZE.

rotal ('rəʊtəl), *a.* [ad. late L. *rotāl-is* wheeled, or f. *rota* (see prec.) + -AL[1].]

1. Pertaining to a wheel or wheels. Also *fig.*

1656 BLOUNT *Glossogr.*, *Rotal*, of or belonging to a wheel [ed. 1674 *adds*, also inconstant, now up, now down]. **1881** *Illustr. Lond. News* 5 Nov. 439/2 The Cannebière is in a chronic state of vocal and rotal tumult.

2. Pertaining to rotation or circular motion.

1855 OGILVIE *Suppl.*, *Rotal action of affinity*, a term applied to the inductive action of affinity, as exhibited in the voltaic circle, in which it assumes a circular direction or return upon itself.

3. *R.C. Ch.* Connected with the Rota.

1907 *Cath. Weekly* 8 Nov. 8/2 On November 12 the Sacred Congregation of Rites will hold a rotal meeting. **1960** *Tablet* 18 June 586/2 The Rotal sentence referred to by Dr. McReavy relies on the pronouncement of Benedict XIV.

rotalian (rəʊ'teɪlɪən), *sb.* and *a.* *Zool.* [f. mod.L. *Rotalia* (Lamarck, 1809), neut. pl. of late L. *rotālis*: see prec.]

A. *sb.* A foraminifer of the genus *Rotalia.*

1869 *Monthly Microsc. Jrnl.* 303 If one of the simple Rotalians were thickened and drawn out at the umbilici. **1879** CARPENTER in *Encycl. Brit.* IX. 380/2 The..spiral mode of growth differs entirely from that of ordinary Rotalians.

B. *adj.* Of or belonging to the genus *Rotalia.*

1862 CARPENTER *Micros.* (ed. 3) 517 The two great series which may be designated (after the leading forms of each) as the Textularian and the Rotalian. **1879** —— in *Encycl. Brit.* IX. 380/1 This intermediate skeleton..completely envelops the original rotalian shell.

rotalid ('rəʊtəlɪd), *sb.* and *a.* *Zool.* [See prec. and -ID.] **a.** *sb.* A foraminifer of the family *Rotalidea.* **b.** *adj.* Belonging to this family.

1888 ROLLESTON & JACKSON *Anim. Life* 886 Exceptions to this rule however occur among the Rotalid *Tinoporinae. Ibid.* 892 There appear within the adult minute young with calcareous tests,..three-chambered in the Rotalid.

ro'taliform, *a.* *Zool.* [See prec. and -FORM.] Having the typical form of the genus *Rotalia.*

1888 ROLLESTON & JACKSON *Anim. Life* 895 Typically spiral and 'Rotaliform', i.e. coiled so that the whole of the segments are visible on the superior surface.

rotaline ('rəʊtəlaɪn), *a.* and *sb.* [ad. mod.L. *Rotalina*: see ROTALIAN.]

A. *adj.* Of or belonging to the *Rotalina*, a subfamily of *Rotalidea.*

1862 CARPENTER, etc. *Introd. Foraminif.* 212 It is in the true *Rotaliæ*..that we meet with the highest development of the Rotaline type. **1888** ROLLESTON & JACKSON *Anim. Life* 889 Calcareous spicules..make up its Rotaline test.

B. *sb.* A member of the *Rotalina.*

1862 CARPENTER, etc. *Introd. Foraminif.* 200 Certain shells ranked by D'Orbigny under the genus *Valvulina* are true Rotalines. **1879** H. A. NICHOLSON *Palæont.* I. 116 One of the earliest representatives of the Rotalines.

rotamer ('rəʊtəmə(r)). *Chem.* [f. ROTA(TIONAL *a.* + -MER.] Any of a number of distinct conformations of a molecule which can be interconverted by rotation of part of the molecule about a particular bond; a rotational isomer.

1963 *Chem. & Industry* 29 June 1086/1 The single sharp N-methyl signal indicates magnetic averaging of signals and hence very rapid rotamer interconversion even at low temperatures. **1969** *Jrnl. Chem. Soc.* B. 1019/2 The near temperature-invariance of the n.m.r. spectrum over the range studied could be the consequence either of one minimum-energy rotomer being strongly preferred, or of insufficient difference in magnetic shielding at *N*-methyl for different rotamers. **1976** *Nature* 26 Aug. 780/1 The analysis of the side-chain rotamer population..shows that the Met, Phe, and Tyr side chains favour one of the two possible *trans-gauche* rotamers, but for each of these residues all three rotamers have significant populations.

Rotameter (rəʊ'tæmɪtə(r), 'rəʊtəmiːtə(r)). Also **rotameter**. [partial tr. G. *rotamesser* (*Chem. Rev. über die Fett- u. Harzind.* (1911) XVIII. 55), f. *rota*(*tion* ROTATION, etc.: see -METER.]

1. A proprietary name for a device with a transparent wall that is fitted into a pipe or tube and indicates the rate of flow of fluid through it.

1911 *Chem. Abstr.* V. 1695 (*heading*) The rotameter. **1914** G. LUNGE *Techn. Gas-Analysis* 50 The 'Rotameter' of the Deutsche Rotawerke, Aachen, allows of directly reading off the quality of gas (or liquid) passing through per hour. **1925** *Industr. Chem.* I. 474/2 In oxy-acetylene welding, if rotameters are inserted in the oxygen and acetylene tubes, it is possible to obtain perfect uniformity. **1949** E. CHAIN in H. W. Florey et al. *Antibiotics* II. xvii. 701 From the air-filter the air passed through a rotameter..and a check-valve.. into the fermenter through the sparger. **1952** *Trade Marks Jrnl.* 18 June 555/1 *Rotameter*... Apparatus for measuring, indicating, or recording the rate of flow of gases or liquids. Rotameter Manufacturing Co. Ltd., Derwent Works, Purley Way, Croydon, Surrey; Manufacturers—29th Nov. 1948. **1979** A. L. LYDERSEN *Fluid Flow & Heat Transfer* iii. 61 Standard rotameters are delivered for connection to pipes with diameters from 3 to 150 mm.

2. Var. ROTOMETER.

rotan (rəʊ'tæŋ), *sb.*[1] Also 7 rottang, 7–9 **rotang.** [ad. Malay *rōtan*: see RATTAN.] So F. and G. *rotang*, F. *rotin*, Du. *rotting*.] One of the rattan palms. Also *attrib.* with *cane, palm*, and of objects made of rotan.

[**1598** W. PHILLIP tr. *Linschoten* I. xvi. 28 There is another sorte of the same reeds which they call Rotà: these are thinne like twigges of Willow for baskets.]

1662 J. DAVIES tr. *Mandelslo's Trav.* 134 From their Neighbours they fetch Timber to build withall, Rottang, that is, cordage of Cocoe. **1697** *Phil. Trans.* XIX. 590 Anchors of Iron and Wood, Cables of Rotang Canes. **1771** *Encycl. Brit.* II. 8/1 There is but one species [of calamus], *viz.* the rotang, a native of India. **1821** J. LEYDEN tr. *Malay Annals* 124 The whole Siamese army retreated; and, as they took their departure, they threw down large quantities of their baggage rotans in the district of Moar, where they took root. **1846** LINDLEY *Veget. Kingd.* 135 The Calami, or Rotangs, and the siliceous secretions of their leaves, indicate an affinity with Grasses. **1884** *Longman's Mag.* June 191 Spindle-trees grew side by side with prickly Rotang palms. **1927** H. M. TOMLINSON *Gallions Reach* xxxi. 242 The climbing palms, the rotans, flourished about it. **1939** *Geogr. Jrnl.* XCIV. 419 It [*sc.* the nutmeg fruit] falls to the ground with a heavy 'plop', or is gathered in a rotan cage at the end of a long stick. **1954** R. H. HOLTTUM *Plant Life in Malaya* xiii. 186 The most important group of climbing monocotyledons are the Rotans or Rattan canes. **1959** *New Biol.* XXX. 51 The rotan lashings and ladders are renewed annually. **1963** J. KIRKUP *Tropic Temper* 23 The..hall of the hotel was full of bamboo and rotan furniture. **1972** *Straits Times* (Singapore) 28 Nov. 1/2 The Government is bringing in the rotan as a new weapon to fight the drug menace in Singapore.

†**rotan** *sb.*[2] *slang. Obs.*[−0] (See quot.)

1725 *New Cant. Dict.*, *Rotan*, a Coach, or Waggon, any thing that runs upon Wheels; but principally a Cart.

Rotarian (rəʊ'tɛərɪən), *a.* and *sb.* Also occas. with small initial. [f. ROTARY *a.* and *sb.* + -AN.]

A. *adj.* Of, pertaining to, or characteristic of the Rotary organization, a Rotary Club, or Rotarians. **B.** *sb.* A member of a Rotary Club. Cf. ROTARY *a.* 4.

1911 (*title of periodical*) The Rotarian. **1915** *Chicago Herald* 9 Nov. 10/5 The Rotarians will observe 'Moving Picture day' at a luncheon in the crystal room of the Hotel Sherman. **1921** *Glasgow Herald* 10 Feb. 9/4 The President ..said the Prince lived out consistently the motto of Rotarians, 'Service, not self'. *Ibid.* 15 June 11/1 An effective programme on education must produce a more intense study of Rotarian literature, a more liberal use of the Rotarian speakers available [etc.]. **1923** R. HERRICK *Homely Lilla* xi. 181 Lilla, on opening the newspapers, often found his name and a brief report of his remarks at a Rotarian lunch. **1928** L. NORTH *Parasites* 270 Rotarians and women's clubs wrote her letters applauding her patriotic stand for home-products. **1931** [see MAIN STREET, MAIN STREET b]. **1935** G. GREENE *Basement Room* 141 He wouldn't have recognized himself among the rotarians. **1939** W. FORTESCUE *There's Rosemary* lv. 313, I quietly repeated the *rondeau* he had written for the Rotarian garden-party we had so lately given at Admiral's House. **1947** *Britannica Bk. of Year* (U.S.) 704/1 Rotarians throughout the world devoted their programs during the month of November to the United Nations Educational, Scientific and Cultural Organization. **1955** *Times* 9 May 3/2 The father, a pillar of rotarian society, expects the worst and is won over. **1968** M. BRAGG *Without City Wall* xxiv. 225 There, too, was the herd, just as herd-like as the Institutes, Rotarians, Churches, and Social Activators. **1976** *Time* 27 Sept. 30/1 When a Southerner calls his territory 'God's country,' he is less Rotarian than religious. **1978** G. VIDAL *Kalki* iii. 53 Dr. Ashok detached himself from a group of American secret agents (or Rotarians or salesmen).

Hence **Ro'tarianism**, the Rotarian system; the way of life held to be characteristic of Rotarians.

1922 *Nation* (N.Y.) 19 Apr. p.v (Advt.), Do you know your state? How it stands in intelligence, rotarianism, bootlegging, evangelism, crime? **1928** *Daily Express* 20 June 2/5 A pantomime symbolising the story of the spread of Rotarianism throughout the world. **1942** BERREY & VAN DEN BARK *Amer. Thes. Slang* §231/1 *Rotarianism*, middle-class propriety.

rotary ('rəʊtərɪ), *a.* and *sb.* [ad. late L. *rotāri-us* (Quicherat), f. *rota* wheel: see -ARY.]

A. *adj.* **1.** Of motion: Circular; taking place round a centre or axis.

1731 BAILEY, vol. II, *Rotary*, of or pertaining to a wheel; whirling or turning round, as a rotary motion.

1815 J. SMITH *Panorama Sci. & Art* I. 330 A rotary motion is very frequently transmitted by means of an endless strap. **1853** KANE *Grinnell Exped.* xv. (1856) 113 During its rotary oscillations against the bottom of the sea. **1867** DENISON *Astron.* 10 But the rotary motion of the earth is of no use for measuring latitude.

Comb. **1883** *Wheel World* Mar. 185 The 'Orbi-cycle', a rotary-motioned front steerer.

2. a. Operating by means of rotation; rotative.

Used spec. to designate a large number of machines in which the action depends on the rotation of some part.

1844 GROVE *Contrib. Sci.* 351 Two sets of magnets are employed, the one set stationary, and the other rotary. **1884** J. BURROUGHS *Locusts & Wild H.* 118 All our general storms are cyclonic in their character, that is, rotary and progressive. **1906** *Daily Colonist* (Victoria, B.C.) 6 Jan. 7/3 Big rotary snowplows and gangs of men have been unable to cope with the conditions. **1939** *Archit. Rev.* LXXXV. 76/3 The laundry is all electric, and is equipped with a Rotary Washer and Spin Dryer, and Rotary Ironer. **1960** *Which?* Mar. 48/1 The rotary mower differs from the side-wheel and roller in the way it cuts, which is a chopping action, like a scythe, rather than a shearing action, like a pair of scissors. **1963** R. R. A. HIGHAM *Handbk. Papermaking* ii. 68 Rotary screens may be divided into inward and outward flow types which may be either oscillating or stationary. **1970** *Which?* Mar. 84/2 If you have got long, rough, grass, you will still need a rotary mower. **1977** *Evening Gaz.* (Middlesbrough) 11 Jan. 10/4 (Advt.), Kenwood rotary ironer, excellent condition, £20. **1979** *SLR Camera* June 39/3 Don't put the prints in a conventional flat-bed or rotary dryer designed for drying fibre-based papers.

b. *Printing.* Designating a press in which a cylindrical printing surface is rotated continuously in contact with moving paper, usu. from a web, and the resulting method of printing.

1880 F. J. WILSON *Typogr. Printing Machines* IV. 135 Owing to the speed at which rotary machines are driven, slight difficulties frequently arise. **1899** J. SOUTHWARD *Mod. Printing* III. xvi. 148 Rotary web printing was in England first rendered practicable by engineers employed in the office of *The Times*, who produced the 'Walter Press,' which was completed in 1866. **1926** R. W. POLK *Pract. Printing* xv. 114 There are rotary presses (called sheet-fed rotaries) which print sheets of paper previously cut to size, but most of them print from large rolls of paper which feed a continuous web through the machine at a high rate of speed. **1962** *Penrose Ann.* LVI. 103 It is still too early to predict what the future will hold for the letterpress rotary machine utilizing wrapround plates. **1968** J. R. BIGGS *Basic Typogr.* 80/2 With a rotary press, in which an impression is made at every revolution of the cylinder, very high speeds are possible. **1979** P. G. NEW *Bk. Production* vi. 81 Letterpress..is taking a leaf from litho's book by adopting some of the same techniques, such as rotary printing.

c. Designating or pertaining to a system of drilling, used esp. in drilling for oil, in which the drilling column with the bit attached to it is rotated; ***rotary table***, in rotary drilling, a power-driven steel turntable which is attached to the top of the drilling column and serves to rotate it.

1906 B. REDWOOD *Treat. Petroleum* (ed. 2) I. 287 The rotary system, which is in general use in the oil-fields of the coastal plain of Texas, is a modification of that invented by Fauvelle in 1845. *Ibid.* 288 There are three styles of rotary rigs in use. *Ibid.* 289 The lower end of the drilling-rod or casing with the bit attached is passed through the rotary table. **1912** E. H. C. CRAIG *Oil-Finding* viii. 150 Thus through a thick soft argillaceous group it may be found most profitable to use a rotary rig, while drop drills and under-reamers may suit a variable series containing hard calcareous bands. **1939** D. HAGER *Fund. Petroleum Industry* ix. 200 The drill is turned by means of the rotary table. **1944** B. A. BOTKIN *Treas. Amer. Folklore* IV. 493 Rivalries take such subtle forms as the feud between cable-tool drillers and rotary workers in the oil fields. **1974** *Petroleum Rev.* XXVIII. 724/3 Samples may be retrieved by conventional rotary coring. **1974** *BP Shield Internat.* Oct. 18/4 Once it's drilled all the way down to the 'rotary-table', we pull the kelly back, unscrew it, and then make it up to another 30 feet section of pipe.

3. Of persons: Acting in rotation.

1862 *Congregationalist* 30 May (Cent.), Several years since they..became an Independent Presbyterian church with a rotary board of elders.

4. (With capital initial.) Of or pertaining to a world-wide organization of clubs for business and professional men (of which the first, formed in Chicago in 1905, met at each member's premises in rotation) which have the aim of promoting unselfish service and international goodwill. ***Rotary Club***, a local branch of this organization.

1910 *Chicago Record-Herald* 10 June 2/4 'The National Association of Rotary Clubs will be one of the most powerful factors in the civic life of the nation,' declared Paul P. Harris... 'Its membership, limited to one man in each line of business,..fighting together in the seventeen largest cities of the country, will be able to win on about any proposition they undertake.' **1921** *Glasgow Herald* 10 Feb. 9/4 Sir Harry Lauder was the guest of honour at a Rotary Club luncheon at the Hotel Cecil, London, yesterday afternoon. *Ibid.* 15 June 11/1 The subjects under consideration included Rotary education, publicity, and business methods. **1930** G. O. THOMAS *Calm Weather* 61 The Rotary Club of which I am a member is very luckily composed of such persons as are engaged in different ways of life, and deputed as it were out of the most conspicuous classes of mankind. **1945** *Business Week* (U.S.) 30 June 44/3 But final decision is to be made..at the next fully attended Rotary convention. **1951** *Britannica Bk. of Year* 558/1 Eleven young men and one young woman nominated by Rotary Clubs in Great Britain and Ireland were awarded Rotary foundation fellowships. **1963** *Sat. Even. Post* (U.S.) 9 Feb. 60/2 A new club adopts the standard Rotary constitution in its native tongue. *Ibid.* 62/3 Rotary volunteers are setting up small-business clinics in backward areas. **1972** T. P. MCMAHON *Issue of Bishop's Blood* xii. 143 He was pudgy, five-seven—the type that would fit at any Rotary luncheon in the country. **1976** *S. Wales Echo* 25 Nov. 20/4 The Rotary Club of Cardiff run a Christmas bargain shop from Tuesday next to Saturday.

5. Special collocations: ***rotary camera***, a type of automatic camera, used to photograph documents, in which the subject material is moved automatically past the lens in synchronization with the film; ***rotary clothes-drier*** or ***-line***, an approximately circular clothes line supported by spokes from a central pole and capable of rotation; ***rotary converter***, an electric motor adapted for use with either alternating or direct current and capable of converting one to the other; ***rotary cutting*** or ***cut***, a method of making veneer by rotating a log longitudinally against a knife-edge so that a layer of wood is peeled off; hence ***rotary-cut*** adj.; ***rotary cutter***, the apparatus used in this method; ***rotary engine***, any engine which produces rotary motion or of which the action depends upon the rotation of some part or parts; *spec.* (*a*) an aircraft engine with a fixed crankshaft around which cylinders and propeller rotate; (*b*) a Wankel engine; hence ***rotary-engined*** adj.; ***rotary table***: see sense 2c above; ***rotary-wing***, used *attrib.* to denote any aircraft deriving its lift from aerofoils that rotate, usu. in an approximately horizontal plane.

1955 H. TEN EYCK *Gloss. Terms Microreproduction* 68 *Rotary camera*, any microfilm camera which photographs documents while they are being moved by some form of transport mechanism. **1962** A. GÜNTHER *Microphotogr. in Library* (Unesco) 18 For the production of roll microfilm.. there are rotary cameras in which separate original pages and the film move synchronously. **1974** G. G. BAKER et al. *Guide to Production of Microforms* iii. 15 Some rotary cameras have been specially designed to accept continuous line-printout stationery. **1971** *Guardian* 10 Apr. 4/1 (Advt.), Rotary clothes drier with 100 foot line. **1971** *Country Gentlemen's Mag.* May 222/2 Rotary Clothes Lines..offer more line space than the conventional fixed line. **1978** P. PORTER *Cost of Seriousness* 3 A camera, an eye Of memory is recounting inches along from the pea-trellis, The cement-block fence, the rotary clothes-line. **1899** FRANKLIN & WILLIAMSON *Alternating Currents* xiii. 166 An ordinary direct current dynamo may be made into an alternator by providing it with collecting rings..in addition to its commutator. Such a machine is called a rotary converter. *Ibid.* 167 The rotary converter may be used as an ordinary direct-current dynamo or motor. **1934** *Discovery* Nov. 324/2 Their products include D.C. to A.C. rotary converters,.. constant current changing dynamos and an entirely portable petrol-driven alternator. **1950** *Times Rev. Industry* Sept. 25/1 One of the first three locomotives is to have a rotary converter set and d.c. motors. **1927** KNIGHT & WULPI *Veneers & Plywood* xvii. 151 The modern methods of manufacturing veneer are practically three-fold, the oldest being sawn, the later, sliced, and the recent, rotary cut. **1974** *Encycl. Brit. Macropædia* XIX. 922/2 More than 90 percent of all veneer is rotary cut... Logs of hard woods, intended for rotary cut or sliced veneer, are softened by submersion in hot water or steam. **1799** *Repertory Arts* X. 303 Similar effects may be produced..by a rotary cutter. **1936** *Archit. Rev.* LXXX. 180/3 If you produce your veneers in any required size by the rotary cutter (invented about 1892).. you superimpose something on your materials which is not natural to them according to established standards. **1973** *Materials & Technol.* VI. i. 85 The handling of veneers as they are produced by the rotary cutters varies from factory to factory. **1927** KNIGHT & WULPI *Veneers & Plywood* xvii. 148 There are four ways of converting logs into veneer... If these are to be arranged according to volume of production, rotary cutting will easily stand at the head of the list. **1957** *Encycl. Brit.* XXIII. 42/2 Veneers are also produced by means of the rotary cutting process as a raw material for plywood. **1838** *Civil Eng. & Arch. Jrnl.* I. 139/1 The expansive principle would not answer for rotary or double engines. **1887** *Encycl. Brit.* XXII. 516/2 In all rotary engines, with the exception of steam turbines,—where work is done by the kinetic impulse of steam,—there are steam chambers which alternately expand and contract in volume. **1909** *Flying: the Why & Wherefore* x. 91 The recent successes of the seven-cylinder rotary Gnome engine. **1928** C. F. S. GAMBLE *Story of N. Sea Air Station* xiii. 216 Although rotary engines were falling gradually into disfavour owing to their heavy lubricating-oil consumption, lack of reliability, and large head resistance, one engine was designed during this year—the Bentley Rotary..which gave excellent service in single-seater machines in 1918. **1960** C. H. GIBBS-SMITH *Aeroplane* I. viii. 30 In 1887 he [*sc.* Lawrence Hargraves] invented the rotary engine (driven by compressed air) in which the cylinders and propeller revolved about a stationary crankshaft. **1968** S. E. ELLACOTT *Everyday Things in Eng. 1914–68* xii. 182 The Wankel rotary engine..was on show at Earl's Court in October 1967. **1969** J. D. STORER *Simple Hist. Steam Engine* i. 16 If the water or wind could be replaced by a man-made stream of steam, or hot gases, an ideal rotary engine would result. This type of heat engine is known as a turbine. **1973** H. JONES *Steam Engines* iv. 47 Between 1785 and 1800, Boulton and Watt supplied 110 rotary engines fitted with sun and planet gear to textile mills. **1909** *Westm. Gaz.* 23 Oct. 9/1 Delagrange brought out his rotary-engined Bleriot. **1973** *Times* 28 June 31/2 The Mazda RX3, now the cheapest rotary-engined car at £1,615 in Britain. **1908** Rotary-wing [see *gyropter* s.v. GYRO-]. **1935** *Jrnl. R. Aeronaut. Soc.* XXXIX. 53 The main objects of this invention is [*sic*] to increase the stability and manœuvrability of helicopter machines, to improve the controllability of rotary wing aircraft to reduce the drag of such aircraft. **1958** *Times* 1 Mar. 7/3 A company engaged in manufacturing rotary wing aircraft is seeking permission to operate a base which would consist of a small platform built over the Thames, connected to an aircraft parking area on the river bank.

B. *sb.* **1.** A rotary machine or apparatus. *spec.* A rotary printing machine or press.

1888 JACOBI *Printer's Vocab.* 115 *Rotary*, a short term for rotary printing machines. **1890** W. J. GORDON *Foundry* 203 This machine gives twice the speed of the early rotaries. **1926** *Penrose's Ann.* XXVIII. 135 A battery of reel-fed litho. offset rotaries are running most efficiently. **1978** R. CLAY in J. Moran *Clays of Bungay* xiii. 145 In 1938 the Company had purchased two old Cottrell sheet-fed rotaries.

2. (With capital initial.) The Rotary organization or its ideals; an individual Rotary Club. ***Rotary International***, the official title (since 1922) of the world-wide organization of Rotary Clubs.

1921 *Glasgow Herald* 10 Feb. 9/4 Sir Harry Lauder..said Rotary was like the lamplighter who came into a dark street. **1922** *Rotarian* May 234/1 No more important question can ever come before a Rotary convention than one which will be discussed at the convention in Los Angeles—a Constitution for International Rotary. **1935** D. FAHEY *Mystical Body of Christ in Mod. World* vi. 112 Let us see what attitude the Catholic Church has adopted towards Rotary. **1944** B. JOHNSON *As Much as I Dare* 275 When the members of the Denver Rotary attend Eastern conventions they wear ten-gallon hats. **1963** *Sat. Even. Post* 9 Feb. 58 Once a mutual-aid society for Midwestern businessmen, Rotary busily promotes peace and good brotherhood on a global scale. **1977** H. FAST *Immigrants* IV. 243 I'm due to speak to Rotary in thirty-five minutes.

3. *U.S.* = ROUNDABOUT *sb.* 4d.

1940 N. BEL GEDDES *Magic Motorways* v. 91 Progress around the rotary is slow, for all cars have to weave from lane to lane and are slowed down by the cars feeding in ahead. **1955** *New Yorker* 12 Mar. 38/2 At eight the next morning we came to the first traffic rotary outside New York, in New Jersey. **1966** *PMLA* LXXXI. II. 11/1 In my lifetime I have seen the *traffic circle* of the Middle Atlantic States become the *rotary* of New England. **1976** A. CROSS *Question of Max* i. 15 She executed..several rotaries which seemed specifically designed to enable cars going in opposite directions to meet head-on.

'rotascope. [f. L. *rota* wheel: see -SCOPE.] A kind of gyroscope.

1832 W. R. JOHNSON in *Silliman's Jrnl.* XXI. 265 Description of an Apparatus called the Rotascope, for exhibiting several phenomena and illustrating certain laws of rotary motion. **1873** *Spon's Dict. Engin.* VII. 2440 The gyroscope or rotascope, an instrument illustrating the tendency of rotating bodies to preserve their plane of rotation.

rotatable (rəʊ'teɪtəb(ə)l), *a.* [f. ROTATE *v.* + -ABLE.] Capable of being rotated; admitting of rotation or rotatory movement.

1875 KNIGHT *Dict. Mech.* 1926/1 Sims's uterine repositor consists of a short metallic sounder, rotatable on a long shaft. **1889** *Sci. Amer.* LX. 306/3 The rotatable blade is designed to do the general work of the pressman in making forms ready.

rotatably (rəʊ'teɪtəblɪ), *adv.* [f. ROTATABLE *a.* + -LY[2].] In a manner that allows rotation.

1918 H. SEYMOUR *Reproduction of Sound* 263 The stylus 9 is mounted in a lever 10 rotatably supported on a pivot 11.

rotate ('rəʊtət), *a.* *Bot.* [f. L. *rota* wheel + -ATE[2].] Wheel-shaped; *esp.* of a monopetalous corolla with a short tube and spreading limb.

1785 MARTYN *Rousseau's Bot.* xii. 129 This genus is easily known by the monopetalous, rotate or wheel-shaped corol. **1830** LINDLEY *Nat. Syst. Bot.* 206 Corolla superior, monopetalous or polypetalous, rotate or tubular. **1872** OLIVER *Elem. Bot.* II. 211 A perennial herb, with..scorpioid cymes of rotate bright-blue flowers.

†rotate, *pa. pple.* *Obs.* [ad. L. *rotāt-us*, pa. pple. of *rotāre*: see next.] Revolved.

1471 RIPLEY *Comp. Alch.* II. viii. in Ashm. (1652) 137 Thyngs into thyngs must therfore be rotate, Untyll dyversyte be brought to parfyt unyte.

rotate (rəʊ'teɪt), *v.* [f. L. *rotāt-*, ppl. stem of *rotāre* to turn or swing round, whirl about, roll round, revolve, f. *rota* wheel.]

1. *intr.* To move round a centre or axis; to perform one or more revolutions.

1808 *Med. Jrnl.* XIX. 899 Permitting the corresponding part of the bone to rotate upon it. **1853** KANE *Grinnell Exped.* xxxvii. (1856) 339 Our brig had..rotated considerably to the northward. **1868** LOCKYER *Elem. Astron.* §§104 The Sun, like the Earth or a top when spinning, turns round, or rotates, on an axis.

2. *trans.* To cause (a thing) to turn round or revolve on a centre or axis.

1831 KNOX *Cloquet's Anat.* 366 It brings the thigh toward that of the opposite side, bends it a little, and carries it outward by rotating it. **1844** G. DODD *Textile Manuf.* i. 38 The warper..rotates the vertical wheel or frame..by means of the wheel..and the rope. **1878** HUXLEY *Physiogr.* 193 Sometimes the masses of lava are rotated in their flight.

3. To change, or take, in rotation.

1861 *Trans Illinois Agric. Soc.* IV. 318 We must rotate crops. **1879** J. HAWTHORNE *S. Strome* I. iii. 36 She could mow a field, drain it, plough it, and rotate its crops. **1894** SPERRY *Talks w. Young Men* 159 It is wise to alternate, or rotate the various forms of life's duties so as to secure daily, restful change, both physical and mental. **1950** *N.Z. Jrnl. Agric.* Jan. 4/1 By rotating the calves through the paddocks ahead of the cows at intervals of 3 or 4 days. **1980** W. SAFIRE in *N.Y. Times Mag.* 20 Jan. 10/3 She explained, 'We're going to rotate the house and we even rotate the cars. We've been separated for four months, and it's a growing experience.'

4. To put *out* in turn.

1881 *Harper's Mag.* LXIII. 265 Both, after a brief service, were rotated out of office.

5. *U.S. Mil.* (See quot. 1973[2]: chiefly *pass.*) Also *intr.* for *pass.*

1944 *Yank* 4 Feb. 6 The policy on leaves and furloughs includes provision that individuals who have had two years Alaskan service and who do not desire to be rotated may volunteer for an additional Alaskan tour. **1951** *Sun* (Baltimore) 3 Nov. (B ed.) 6/2 The assurances to G.I.'s in Korea that they would be rotated home were regarded with unmodulated disbelief. **1954** *Britannica Bk. of Year 1953* 354/2 Each side might rotate up to 35,000 men a month on a man-for-man basis. **1973** *Washington Post* 13 Jan. A3/3 You look at an NLF..soldier, who can't..get R and R to Hong Kong, time off in Vungtau, and then rotate in a year back to the States. **1973** J. QUICK *Dict. Weapons* 377/2 *Rotate*, to remove a person, crew, unit, or the like from service in an overseas area, from combat service, or from service in a hardship environment and to return such person, crew, or unit to service in the zone of the interior or other less exacting environment. **1976** 'B. SHELBY' *Great Pebble Affair* 12 Donnely and I rotated back to the States together.

Hence **ro'tated** *ppl. a.*

1824 A. DODS (*title*), Pathological Observations on the rotated or contorted Spine,..called Lateral Curvature.

† **rotated**, *a. Bot. Obs.* = ROTATE *a.*

1753 *Chambers' Cycl.* Suppl. *App.* s.v. *Petal*, The second class is of the plants with..rotated, or wheel-like flowers. **1797** *Encycl. Brit.* (ed. 3) III. 442/2 The figure of Solids is either..Rotated, wheel-shaped, plain [etc.].

rotating (rəʊˈteɪtɪŋ), *ppl. a.* [f. ROTATE *v.*]

1. a. Turning round on a centre or axis.

1854 EMERSON *Lett. & Soc. Aims, Resources*, Our Copernican globe is a great factory or shop of power with its rotating constellations. **1863** TYNDALL *Heat* i. 10 The edge of a swiftly rotating wheel. **1875** BEDFORD *Sailor's Pocket Bk.* iv. (ed. 2) 82 If the veering of the former, and the marked fall of the latter prove the gale to be rotating, or cyclonic.

b. Causing rotation; rotatory.

1883 J. MILLINGTON *Are we to read backwards?* 67 The rotating muscles have a much more numerous amount of contractions to effect.

2. Acting in rotation; rotative.

1884 *Athenæum* 19 Jan. 82/3 Four rotating regents conducted the classes of philosophy or arts. **1975** *Saturday Night* (Toronto) July–Aug. 18/2 It has been the unions in the public service, not surprisingly, who have perfected the kind of random sniper-fire known as 'selective' strikes or 'rotating' strikes or 'twenty-four-hour' strikes. **1976** *National Observer* (U.S.) 21 Aug. 15/1 Asolo now offers nine plays in rotating repertory from mid-February to Labor Day.

rotation (rəʊˈteɪʃən). [ad. L. *rotātiōn-em*, n. of action f. *rotāre*: see ROTATE *v.* and -ATION. So F. *rotation*, Sp. *rotacion*, It. *rotazione.*]

1. a. The action of moving round a centre, or of turning round (and round) on an axis; also, the action of producing a motion of this kind.

1555 EDEN *Decades* (Arb.) 185 The rotation or impulsion of the heauens. **1594** PLAT *Jewell-ho.* II. 37 A trew & philosophicall rotation whereby the inwarde fire of nature may be stirred vppe in euery vegetable. **1605** TIMME *Quersit.* I. ii. 8 By the yearly and continual rotation and reuolution of the right heauen,..and thinges might be well gouerned. **1661** GLANVILL *Van. Dogm.* 158 [A] puzled Candidate,..being ask'd what a circle was, describ'd it by the rotation of his hand. *a* **1680** BUTLER *Rem.* (1759) I. 318 All Rotations and Wheelings cause a kind of Giddiness in the Brain. **1720** WELTON *Suffer. Son of God* I. viii. 200, I see ..all Things..as if they were whirl'd about by the Quick Rotation of a Wheel. **1784** COWPER *Task* III. 160 Some..tell us whence the stars;..what gave them first Rotation. **1815** J. SMITH *Panorama Sci. & Art* I. 559 His diurnal rotation is believed to be performed in 10 hours, 16 minutes, 2 seconds. **1851** WOODWARD *Mollusca* I. 64 Eyes fixed, incapable of rotation. **1876** TAIT *Rec. Adv. Phys. Sci.* xii. (ed. 2) 294 This property of rotation may be the basis of all that to our senses appeals as matter.

fig. **1647** MAY *Hist. Parl.* I. i. 4 The perpetuall Rotation of fortune. **1700** CONGREVE *Way of World* II. iv, She has that everlasting rotation of tongue. **1710** PALMER *Proverbs* 245 A jest keeps an ill story alive and in countenance, and gives it a rotation.

b. *Cryst., Math., Physics.* The conceptual operation of turning a system about an axis.

1899 W. J. LEWIS *Treat. Crystallogr.* iii. 19 When the least angle which gives interchangeability is 90°, the rotation can be effected four times before the crystal returns to its original position. **1965**, etc. [see REFLECTION 10].

c. *Math.* = CURL *sb.* 3 e.

1909 J. G. COFFIN *Vector Analysis* v. 117 The operator ▽ × applied to **F** or curl **F** (read del cross **F** or curl of **F**), also sometimes written in German books, rot **F** (read rotation of **F**), is a new vector derived from **F**. **1911** [see CURL *sb.* 3 e]. **1923** H. LEVY tr. *Runge's Vector Analysis* ii. 111 The vector field **f**, when its rotation is not zero, that is, when **f** is not the gradient of a scalar function, leads to a second vector field **g** = ▽ × **f**. **1972** A. G. HOWSON *Handbk. Terms Algebra & Anal.* xxxv. 175 In physical applications, curl represents some measure of rotation (older texts often describe curl **f** as the rotation of **f** and denote it by rot **f**).

d. *Statistics.* The mathematical rearrangement of a body of data, regarded as representing a set of points in a space, so that the axes of the space come to lie in directions of particular relevance.

1935 L. L. THURSTONE *Vectors of Mind* ix. 222 Each independent rotation may be regarded as a disturbance of a pair of columns in the factorial matrix. **1952** R. B. CATTELL *Factor Analysis* xxi. 411 A great advance in speed in rotation processes is available now through the I.B.M. multiplier (a rotation of a 15 × 18 factor matrix can be done in a day). **1972** *Jrnl. Social Psychol.* LXXXVII. 69 Rotation to simple structure was made for five factors in each case, though not all five could be interpreted.

2. a. The fact of coming round again in succession; return or recurrence; a recurring series or period.

1610 HEALEY *St. Aug. Citie of God* xxi. 17. 858 That rotation, and circumvolution of misery and blisse, which he [Origen] held, that all mankind should run in. *a* **1676** HALE *Prim. Orig. Man.* (1677) 150 That by a kind of circulation or rotation Arts have their successive invention and perfection. **1756** C. LUCAS *Ess. Waters* I. 172 Medicines..suffer a rotation of fashions like our cloaths. **1765** A. DICKSON *Treat. Agric.* (ed. 2) 47 It observes a constant rotation, and is conveyed regularly from the earth to the air, and from the air to the earth. **1779** J. MOORE *View Soc. Fr.* (1789) I. xxix. 244 There is a constant rotation of society at Ferney. **1847** W. C. L. MARTIN *The Ox* 33/1 It is not..until the close of the third [year] that the [teeth] next in rotation succeed.

b. Regular and recurring succession in office, duties, etc., of a number of persons. Freq. in phr. *by* or *in rotation.*

The recent adoption of this sense in general use is noticed in the *British Mag.* for April 1763 (IV. 542), and ascribed to 'advertisements from the Police relating to the justices sitting by rotation, the felony-rotation in Bow-street', etc.

1656 HARRINGTON *Oceana* (1700) 54 Equal Rotation is equal vicissitude in Government, or succession to Magistracy confer'd for such convenient terms..as take in the whole body by parts. **1660** MILTON *Free Commw.* Wks. 1851 V. 439 A numerous Assembly of them all form'd and conven'd on purpose with the wariest Rotation. *a* **1721** SHEFFIELD (Dk. Buckhm.) *Wks.* (1753) II. 180 This is no small advantage in Republicks, where a sort of rotation is necessary, by which men are seen under several capacities. **1762** FALCONER *Shipwr.* II. 483 So the brave mariners their pumps attend, And help incessant by rotation lend. **1800** COLQUHOUN *Comm. Thames* xiii. 366 Five of the twenty-one Directors shall go out of office by rotation every year. **1833** HT. MARTINEAU *Manch. Strike* 73 Three members..sit daily,..viz., the treasurer, secretary, and one of the other members in rotation. **1888** BRYCE *Amer. Commw.* (1890) II. 88 In America..the tendency is towards 'rotation' in office.

c. *Agric.* A change or succession of crops in a certain order on a given piece of ground, in order to avoid the exhaustion of the soil.

1778 [W. MARSHALL] *Minutes Agric.* Digest 76 A regular rotation of Crops and Fallow is, perhaps, more convenient than profitable. **1792** YOUNG *Trav. France* 346 The effects derived from the rotation of crops. *Ibid.*, The miserable rotations commonly practised in France. **1845** MᶜCULLOCH *Taxation* II. vi. (1852) 247 By narrowing the demand for barley, and obliging the farmers to adopt imperfect rotations. **1874** STUBBS *Const. Hist.* I. iii. 50 The proper rotation of crops and fallow might be observed.

d. *Forestry.* The cycle of planting, felling, and replanting; the period of this, the (actual or planned) time between the formation or regeneration of a crop and its felling.

1888 E. E. FERNANDEZ *Man. Indian Sylviculture* i. 6 The existence of a rotation implies the more or less simultaneous appearance of the old generation, and a similarly more or less simultaneous removal of that generation and the appearance of the new one. There can hence be no rotation in the case of selection-worked forests. **1889** W. SCHLICH *Man. Forestry* I. II. ii. 170 The selection of the rotation.. should be so fixed under the method of natural regeneration as to admit of a proper regeneration of the wood, whether by seed or coppice shoots. **1890** W. J. GORDON *Foundry* 127 The Earl of Seafield's forest.., which is regularly planted and felled so as to cut a thousand acres annually on a rotation of sixty years. **1927** *Forestry* I. 101 A more detailed investigation of the returns from quality class V forests showed that at 100 years (the financial rotation) the yield was 1.06 per cent., and at 120 years (the more usual rotation) it was 1.03 per cent. **1938** G. S. CANSDALE et al. *Black Poplars* 9 The poplar is essentially a tree to be grown on short rotation. **1977** M. CLAWSON *Decision Making in Timber Production* 26 For many sites, the earnings from the next rotation of timber growing are highly speculative or dubious, partly because it is so far in the future.

3. *attrib.* and *Comb.*, as ***rotation axis, group, -movement, -tide***; ***rotation-like*** adj.; † **rotation-office** (see sense 2 b, note); **rotation grasses**, grasses sown in a rotation of crops.

1768 *Ann. Reg., Chron.* 57/2 The sitting Magistrates..at the Rotation-office in Whitechapel. **1812** *Sporting Mag.* XL. 283 At the Leeds Rotation-office this month, John Waddington, of Farnley.., was convicted..for shooting a hare. **1865** *Proc. Amer. Phil. Soc.* X. 165 Evidences of rotation-tides. **1886** *Daily News* 11 Dec. 6/3 As temporary pastures, that is to say, rotation grasses (including clover), are included in the arable area, one would naturally look for a proportional diminution in rotation grasses. **1899** *Allbutt's Syst. Med.* VII. 883 The balancing, nodding, and rotation movements are more especially likely to preserve a definite rhythm. **1903** Rotation axis [see *holoaxial* s.v. HOLO-]. **1952** DYLAN THOMAS *Let.* 11 Dec. (1966) 388 It was, I think, originally a little 'organ'..full of rotation-like gossip. **1971** I. G. GASS et al. *Understanding Earth* i. 19/1 The stereogram of zircon..shows a four-fold rotation axis in the centre and also shows a number of reflection planes. **1974** G. REECE tr. *Hund's Hist. Quantum Theory* xiii. 177 These two-valued representations of the rotation group had been discovered by Hermann Weyl.

rotational (rəʊˈteɪʃənəl), *a.* [f. prec. + -AL[1].]

1. Acting in rotation; of or belonging to rotation.

1852 DE MORGAN in Graves *Life Hamilton* (1889) III. 394 Members to go out by rotation each year... The rotational electors to be distributed through the year. **1870** PROCTOR *Other Worlds* v. 111 The energies indicated by mere velocity of motion, whether orbital or rotational, must be equally disregarded. **1886** BALL *Story Heavens* 534 In a similar manner we find the rotational moment of momentum for each of the other planets.

2. *Physics.* Of, pertaining to, or designating the (quantized) energy possessed by molecules, etc., by virtue of their rotation.

1914 *Chem. Abstr.* VIII. 859 According to the quantum hypothesis the rotational energy of a mol[ecule] varies discontinuously, from which it follows that a band is made up of a series of lines whose vibration difference is a measure of the moment of inertia of a mol[ecule]. **1939** J. W. T. SPINKS tr. *G. Herzberg's Molecular Spectra* I. iii. 72 The rotational quantum number *J*..gives approximately the angular momentum in units $h/2\pi$. **1950** W. J. MOORE *Physical Chem.* xi. 327 A set of closely packed rotational levels is associated with each of these vibrational levels. **1973** C. SAGAN *Cosmic Connection* (1974) iv. 27 Molecules undergo rotational transitions, due to the free rotation of the molecule. **1978** P. W. ATKINS *Physical Chem.* xvii. 561 According to the gross selection rule, methane cannot give a rotational Raman spectrum, whereas the hydrogen molecule, and any other diatomic..can.

3. *Agric.* Applied to methods of land management in which animals are grazed on successive areas of land in turn, so that each area is empty for a time after having been grazed.

1931 H. E. WOODMAN et al. in *Jrnl. Agric. Sci.* XXI. 267 It may be inferred that a similar result would follow from a system of rotational grazing, where the pasture enclosures, after being closely grazed, are permitted a 3-weeks' interval of unchecked growth before being grazed again. **1950** *N.Z. Jrnl. Agric.* Apr. 307/1 Rotational cropping is now an excellent fertility builder. **1967** C. D. BLAKE et al. *Fundamentals Mod. Agric.* ix. 208/1 In the broad sense, rotational grazing is any system of handling animals which involves holding them for short periods on small sections of the total area of an available pasture and then regularly moving them, as a group, to other sections of the whole area. There is an infinite number of rotational grazing systems available.

ro'tationally, *adv.* [f. prec. + -LY[2].] In a rotational manner; by or with respect to rotation.

1894 *Phil. Trans. R. Soc.* A. CLXXXV. 817 A simple theory of free electrons in a rotationally fluid æther. **1946** *Nature* 3 Aug. 176/1 These velocities are so high that rotationally stable stars cannot be formed unless one of two conditions is fulfilled. **1950** *N.Z. Jrnl. Agric.* Jan. 4/2 Calves which are rotationally grazed. **1976** *Physics Bull.* July 292/2 Eddies of rotationally dominated turbulence. **1978** *Sci. Amer.* Jan. 122/3 The four letters p, b, d and q are rotationally similar.

rotative (ˈrəʊtətɪv), *a.* [f. L. *rotāt-*, ppl. stem of *rotāre*: see ROTATE *v.* So F. *rotatif, -ive.*]

1. Rotating, turning round like a wheel; acting or operating by circular motion.

1778 PRYCE *Min. Cornub.* 313 He completed both a reciprocating and a rotative or wheel engine. **1799** *Repertory Arts* X. 295 How, by means of a rotative saw, to shape a piece from the rough. **1822** *New Monthly Mag.* VI. 267 By means of rotative machinery, connected with..a steam-engine, or other rotative power. **1877** *Encycl. Brit.* VI. 499/2 No rotative engine had yet been erected at Manchester.

b. Produced by rotation; producing, connected with, rotation.

1823 P. NICHOLSON *Pract. Build.* 443 Mouldings, which may be generated by planes carried round their axis' in those planes, are called *rotative* mouldings. **1824** W. TAYLOR in *Monthly Rev.* CIII. 193 He first advanced..the rotative doctrine. **1879** NEWCOMB & HOLDEN *Astron.* 211 The rotative forces acting on A and B are as it were distributed.

c. Of the nature of rotation.

1846 HOLTZAPFFEL *Turning* II. 522 The general practice ..is to give the tool a constant rotative shuffling motion. **1868** LOCKYER *Elem. Astron.* §359 As the Earth's rotative movement is uniform.

2. Acting or coming in rotation; recurrent.

1813 T. BUSBY *Lucretius* II. v. Comm. p. xxv, By the rotative course of nature [the earth] is now enabled to bring forth some things which she did not yield at her beginning. **1864** R. A. ARNOLD *Cotton Famine* 372 Cotton was cultivated in India as a rotative and not as a special crop.

rotativism (ˈrəʊtətɪvɪz(ə)m, rəʊˈteɪt-). [f. ROTATIVE *a.* + -ISM.] A system whereby different political parties hold office in turn according to a pre-arranged plan.

1908 *Sun* (N.Y.) 3 Feb. 2/1 Each party held office by arrangement alternately. This arrangement was known as rotativism. **1921** *Edin. Rev.* Jan. 158 The country must in effect sink back into the slough of 'rotativism'. **1960** W. C. ATKINSON *Hist. Spain & Portugal* xiii. 313 The system in Portugal was known as rotativism. **1969** I. GILMOUR *Body Politic* I. i. 55 The party struggle was also a stage fight in Portugal, where the parties agreed under a system called rotativism to alternate in office.

rotativist (ˈrəʊtətɪvɪst, rəʊˈteɪt-), *a.* (and *sb.*) [f. as prec. + -IST.] **1.** Of, pertaining to, or characterized by rotativism in politics. Also *ellipt.* as *sb.* Also *transf.*

1909 *Spectator* 12 June 918/2 The late King [of Portugal] yielded to the intrigues of the 'rotativist' parties. **1917** G. YOUNG *Portugal* vi. 217 The collapse of the Portuguese colonial empire must come with the continuance of the struggle between rotativist Royalism and revolutionary Republicanism. **1926** *Glasgow Herald* 24 Dec. 4/7 They recalled the indifference of the electorate on the frequent occasions of general elections by order of the Rotativists. **1929** *Camb. Anc. Hist.* (ed. 2) III. 253 A regular 'rotativist' arrangement made by the son of Smendes with the Thebans by which he was to be succeeded by the Theban high-priest ..and he again by a Tanite.

2. That relates to rotative movement. *rare.*

1939 A. J. TOYNBEE *Study of Hist.* VI. 173 Stoic and Epicurean philosophers who apparently were not put out by the incongruity between their rotativist conception of the nature of Reality and their ethical aim of Detachment.

ro'tato-, used as combining form of mod.L. *rotātus* ROTATE *a.* in ***rotato-dentate, -plane.***

1760 J. LEE *Introd. Bot.* I. xiii. (1765) 34 *Rotato-dentate*, wheel-shaped and indented. *Ibid.* iii. 7 *Rotato-plane*, wheel-shaped and flat.

rotator (rəʊˈteɪtə(r)). [a. L. *rotātor*, agent-n. from *rotāre* to ROTATE. Cf. F. *rotateur.*]

1. *Anat.* A muscle by which a limb or part can be moved circularly.

1676 WISEMAN *Surg. Treat.* VII. viii. 494 The Triceps, together with the Levidus, and the four little Rotators. **1744** tr. *Boerhaave's Inst.* III. 254 There was no other Place where the Rotators of the Thigh could be fixed, which draw it partly outwards. **1808** BARCLAY *Muscular Mot.* 389 In rolling the arm, the rotators radiad co-operate with the muscles called supinators; the rotators ulnad, with the pronators. **1893** A. S. ECCLES *Sciatica* 74 The action will only be carried to the extent possible without using the external rotators of the thigh.

attrib. **1744** tr. *Boerhaave's Inst.* III. 254 The Rotator Muscles insert their Tendons into the Protuberant Process. **1899** *Albutt's Syst. Med.* VIII. 31 The spasmodic action shifted from one rotator muscle to another.

2. a. A thing, apparatus, part, etc., which has a rotatory motion or action.

1772 *Scots Mag.* XXXIV. 186/2 A..machine, which he [William Kenrick] says he has contrived and denominated a Rotator. **1803** *Naval Chron.* X. 191 The spring part..is fixed to a rotator, or revolving apparatus. **1875** BEDFORD *Sailor's Pocket Bk.* v. (ed. 2) 161 The rotator [of a log] is a continuation of the part that holds the wheelwork. **1884** W. H. GREENWOOD *Steel & Iron* xi. 214 In the front end of the rotator are the slag-holes. **1930** *Jrnl. Sci. Instruments* VII. 22 It is necessary, for the purposes of wool examination, to be able..to examine the filament completely at any point by rotating it through 360°, and for this purpose a fibre rotator has been designed. **1967** *Stain Technol.* XLII. 107 The rotator consists of a 12 inch disc to which 8 glass jars..are held firmly... It is rotated by means of a rubber belt driven by a small electric motor. **1971** *Sci. Amer.* July 85/2 Perhaps a much more massive rotating object in the core of a galaxy could account for the existence of quasars. In these models the rotator must have a mass of about a billion solar masses. **1977** *Lancet* 28 May 1150/2 This allows rapid separation of antibody-bound from free T_3/T_4 by simple inversion of the assay tubes in a rotator.

b. A device for rotating an aerial.

1959 *Sears, Roebuck Catal.* Spring/Summer 884/2 TV Antenna Rotators... Turns antenna 360° per min. **1970** *Globe & Mail* (Toronto) 28 Sept. 30/4 (Advt.), Al's TV, towers, color, rotator, U.H.F., Channel 17 installed. **1974** HARVEY & BOHLMAN *Stereo F.M. Radio Handbk.* vii. 163 For long-distance (DX) reception an aerial amplifier and/or aerial rotator are useful accessories to a high gain aerial in extracting the largest possible signal to drive the receiver into full amplitude limiting. **1977** *Gramophone* Nov. 965/1 Feeding the tuner/amplifier from a four-element J-Beam FM aerial mounted on a rotator, it was possible to receive several continental FM stations in mid-Surrey.

3. One of the *Rotatoria*; a rotifer.

1876 *Beneden's Anim. Parasites* 36 An animal..which is only an imperfectly described Rotator.

4. *Math.* (See quot.)

1879 THOMSON & TAIT *Nat. Phil.* I. I. §345 The reciprocal of this time we shall call..the rapidity of the system, for convenience of comparison with the frequency of a vibrator or of a rotator, which is the name commonly given to the reciprocal of its period.

rotatory ('rəʊtətərɪ), *a.* and *sb.* [See ROTATE *v.* and -ORY.]

A. *adj.* **1. a.** Of the nature of rotation; connected with rotation.

1755 JOHNSON, *To Wheel*,..to have a rotatory motion. **1777** *Phil. Trans.* LXVII. 266 A new Theory of the Rotatory Motion of Bodies affected by Forces disturbing such Motion. **1794** G. ADAMS *Nat. & Exper. Phil.* III. xxxii. 308 The obstacles in the rough road cause this rotatory motion in the wheel. **1833** HERSCHEL *Astron.* vii. 234 By a sufficient rotatory velocity. **1845** TODD & BOWMAN *Phys. Anat.* I. 145 A rotatory movement at the hip-joint. **1882** MINCHIN *Unipl. Kinematics* 22 The theory of the rotatory polarisation of quartz.

b. Rotating; working by means of rotation.

1812 H. & J. SMITH *Rej. Addr.* 89 Pure child of Chance, which still directs the ball, As rotatory atoms rise or fall. **1837** BREWSTER *Magnet.* 112 Trying if the magnetic needle would be dragged along by the rotatory plates. *c* **1850** *Rudim. Nav.* (Weale) 67 The track of five..rotatory storms. **1892** STEVENSON *Across the Plains* ii. 93 Urging their horses with cries..and cruel rotatory spurs.

c. Causing rotation.

1828 STARK *Elem. Nat. Hist.* II. 444 Rotatory organ quadrilobed. **1871** T. R. JONES *Anim. Kingd.* (ed. 4) 476 A small oval orifice situated near the sinuated disk formed by the rotatory organs. *Ibid.*, The rotatory apparatus.

2. Going round, or coming, in rotation.

1824 W. TAYLOR in *Monthly Rev.* CIII. 193 This principle of frequent rotatory election. **1831** W. GODWIN *Thoughts Man* 97, I become..wearied with the repetition of rotatory acts and every-day occurrences.

B. *sb.* A rotifer. (Cf. ROTATOR 3.)

1835 KIRBY *Hab. & Inst. Anim.* I. iv. 154 The Rotatories, to which the wheel-animalcules belong.

rotavate, rotovate ('rəʊtəveɪt, 'rəʊtəʊ-), *v.* [Back-formation from next.] *trans.* To prepare (a field, garden, etc.) with a Rotavator; to work (a substance) into the soil by means of a Rotavator. Hence **'rota-, 'rotovating** *vbl. sb.*; **'rota-, 'rotovation.**

1959 *Birmingham Post* 10 June 1/1 A new allotment..had been 'adequately fenced, roadways constructed and the site ploughed and rotavated'. **1960** *Farmer & Stock-breeder* 26 Jan. 78/3 It is not claimed that Rotavation is suitable for all cultivations, all the time, in all soils. **1962** *Times* 11 Apr. 24/3 Garden rotovated. **1962** *Times* 3 Dec. (Agric. Suppl.) p. vii/5 The usual procedure..is to rotavate the dead herbage. **1971** *Nature* 13 Aug. 446/2 The British Ministry of Agriculture suffered some criticism for suggesting that the best way of disposing of surplus and unwanted DDT..was to rotovate it into the soil. **1977** *Jersey Even. Post* 26 July 24/6 (Advt.), Subsoiling and rotovating undertaken at competitive rates. **1978** *Rescue News* Summer 4/2 Methods of working peat include rotovation.

Rotavator, Rotovator ('rəʊtəveɪtə(r), 'rəʊtəʊ-). Also with small initials. [f. ROT(ARY *a.* + CULTI)VATOR; see ROTO-.] Proprietary names of a machine with rotating blades designed to break up or till soil.

1936 *Trade Marks Jrnl.* 1 July 808 Rotavator... Ploughs, cultivators, diggers, harrows and hoes, all being agricultural machines. Rotary Cultivators Limited. **1951** *Official Gaz.* (U.S. Patent Office) 13 Mar. 362/2 Rotary Hoes Limited, East Horndon, England. Filed Dec. 27, 1949. *Rotavator*... For ploughs, cultivators, diggers, harrows, and hoes. **1954** *Encounter* Dec. 31/2 Nobody said..that it was a handicap to have a holding so large you could *choose between* a rotavator and a proper tractor. **1959** *Times* 13 Mar. 6/6 Mr. Merricks then bid £5 and the Rotovator was knocked down to him. **1963** *Times* 17 Jan. 3/7 The machine, a 'Rotavator', breaks up the packed snow and ice into powder, so that it can be swept away. The machine has been used on Watford's football ground and there are plans to use it at race-courses. **1970** T. HUGHES *Crow* 31 The woodpecker drummed clear of the rotovator. **1971** 'S. SMITH' *Grave Affair* vii. 102 They went back to the farm for the rotavator to break up the soil. **1977** *Trade Marks Jrnl.* 21 Sept. 1895/1 *Rotovator*... Agricultural machinery and power operated agricultural implements. **1978** *Morecambe Guardian* 14 Mar. 22/3 (Advt.), Agrotiller and Landmaster Rotovators.

rotavirus ('rəʊtəvaɪərəs). *Biol.* [mod.L., f. L. *rota* wheel + VIRUS.] Any one of a genus of wheel-shaped double-stranded RNA viruses.

1974 T. H. FLEWITT et al. in *Lancet* 13 July 61/1 Since these viruses differ morphologically both from reoviruses and orbiviruses, the name 'rotavirus' is suggested for them. **1977** *Lancet* 11 June 1263/2 Rotaviruses cause acute enteritis in man and animals. **1977** *Rec. Adv. Clin. Virol.* I. 158 Rotaviruses differ both in size and shape from the reoviruses... They resemble orbiviruses in the appearance of rings..seen on some particles..; but the [rotavirus] diarrhoea viruses also differ from the orbiviruses in their smooth outline. **1979** *Brit. Med. Jrnl.* 15 Dec. 1551/1 Rotavirus infection is the commonest cause of acute non-bacterial gastroenteritis in infancy and childhood.

R.O.T.C., ROTC ('rɒtsɪ; also ɑːrəʊtiː'siː). *U.S.* [Acronym f. the initials of *R*eserve *O*fficers' *T*raining *C*orps.] A military division with units established at civilian educational centres to qualify students for appointment as reserve officers.

1916 *N.Y. Times* 27 Dec. 6/1 The cap ornament for members of the Reserve Officers' Training Corps is to consist of a wreath inclosing the letters R.O.T.C. **1919** [see DRIP *sb.* 3 b]. **1925** *Scribner's Mag.* July 15/2 He goes to the R.O.T.C. and prepares himself for a berth in the adjutant-general's office. **1936** *N.Y. Herald Tribune* 1 June 17/3 (*heading*) Flint defends the R.O.T.C. in Syracuse talks. **1959** N. MAILER *Advts. for Myself* (1961) I. 35 He had been allowed to go to this university only on the agreement..that he..was to join the R.O.T.C. and to remain in it until after graduation. **1974** *Hartsville* (S. Carolina) *Messenger* 22 Apr. 2-A/8 Early in the school year he went to Myrtle Beach Air Force Base for a military physical that was sent to all the academics and to the ROTC headquarters. **1975** *Publishers Weekly* 26 May 57/1 Out of his campus experiences he examines ROTC from the academic viewpoint. He ponders the fairness of grading prospective draftees.

†rotch. *Sc. Obs.* In 6 roche, rotche. [Of obscure origin. For later examples see RATCH *sb.*[1] 1.] A gun or gun-barrel.

1571 BANNATYNE *Jrnl.* (1806) 147 There was in her..thre or four last of powder, some crosletis, and roches of small ordinance. **1598** *Reg. Privy Council Scot.* V. 438 Sic peceis as salbe of the lenth of ane elne in the rotche at the leist.

rotch(e, variants of ROCHE *sb.*[1]

rotche (rɒtʃ). *Ornith.* Also rotch, roach, and ROTCHIE. [A later form of ROTGE, but the precise source is not clear.] The little auk.

α. **1809** EDMONSTON *Zetland Isl.* II. 274 *Alca Alle*, Rotche, Greenland Rotche. **1843** YARRELL *Brit. Birds* III. 358 The Little Auk, or Common Rotche,..is only a winter visiter to the British Islands. **1894** NEWTON *Dict. Birds* 797 In Smith Sound the Rotche is said not to breed below lat. 68° or above 79°.

β. **1820** W. SCORESBY *Acc. Arctic Reg.* I. 536, I..have observed it in pursuit of the rotch. **1831** RENNIE *Montagu's Ornith. Dict.* 438 The Rotch has sometimes been found dead very remote from the sea. **1841** *Proc. Berw. Nat. Club* I. 255 The *Mergulus alce*, rotch, a species that breeds in very high latitudes.

γ. **1820** W. SCORESBY *Acc. Arctic Reg.* I. 528 *Alca Alle*, the Little Auk, or Roach. **1823** —— *Jrnl.* 142 An immense quantity of roaches..flew past the ship towards the west.

†rotchet, obs. form of RATCHET.

1764 *Ann. Reg.* I. 78/2 Barrel and main spring... Great wheel and rotchet.

rotchet(te, obs. forms of ROCHET.

'rotchie. *Ornith.* = ROTCHE.

1831 RENNIE *Montagu's Ornith. Dict.* 438. **1859** MACCLINTOCK *Voy. 'Fox'* 139 The rotchie or little auk lays its single egg upon the bare rock.

rote (rəʊt), *sb.*[1] Now only *Hist.* [a. OF. *rote* (*rothe, route*), = Prov. and med.L. *rota, rotta*; also MDu. *rote*, MLG. *rotte, rode*, MHG. *rote, rott(e*, OHG. *rota, rotta*. The original form was prob. **hrotta*, an early Teutonic adoption of the Celtic word recorded by Venantius Fortunatus (6th cent.) as *chrotta*, on which see CROWD *sb.*[1]] A mediæval musical instrument, probably of the violin class.

a **1300** *Cursor M.* 7408 Dauid cuth on sere-kin note, Bath he cuth on harpe and rote. **13..** *E.E. Allit. P.* B. 1082 Organes & pypes, & rial ryngande rotes & þe reken fyþel. **1390** GOWER *Conf.* III. 303 He tawhte hir til sche was certein Of Harpe, of Citole and of Rote. *c* **1407** LYDG. *Reson & Sens.* 2394 He kan..Touche be crafte, and nat be rote, Harpe and lute, fythel and Rote. *c* **1450** HOLLAND *Howlat* 759 The rote, and the recordour,..The trumpe, and the talburn. **1590** SPENSER *F.Q.* II. x. 3 Argument worthy of Mæonian quill; Or rather worthy of great Phoebus rote. **1596** *Ibid.* IV. ix. 6 There did he find..The faire Pœana playing on a Rote.

1814 SCOTT *Ld. of Isles* III. xxiii, The lad can deftly touch the lute, And on the rote and viol play. **1823** ROSCOE tr. *Sismondi's Lit. Eur.* (1846) I. v. 128 Psaltry, symphony, and rote, Help to charm the listening throng. **1859** JEPHSON *Brittany* vii. 93 To converse, or sing ancient Breton lays to the rote. **1884** HERON-ALLEN *Violin Making* 62 The only difference between the earliest crwths..and the latest rotes ..seems to be the addition of the bow and finger-board.

rote (rəʊt), *sb.*[2] Also 4–5 roote, 5–6 root, 5 rot, 5–7 roat(e. [Of obscure origin; there is no evidence to confirm the suggestions that it is a. OF. *rote, route* route, way, or ad. L. *rota* wheel.]

†1. a. Custom, habit, practice. *Obs.*

c **1315** SHOREHAM III. 210 Þy wykked rote, Wanne þou ne halst þy masseday, As god hyt haþ y-hote. **1390** GOWER *Conf.* III. 45 Thilke art which Spatula is hote, And used is of comun rote Among Paiens. *Ibid.* 50 He..broght hem into such a rote, That upon him thei bothe assote. *c* **1440** *Promp. Parv.* 437/2 Root, of vse and custome.

†b. Mechanical practice or performance; regular procedure; mere routine. *Obs.* (Cf. sense 2.)

1581 MULCASTER *Positions* xli. (1887) 242 By the meere shadow, and roat of these sciences. **1693** EVELYN *De La Quint. Compl. Gard.* I. 3 A presumptuous Pratling Ignorance, upheld by some wretched Rote. **1712** J. JAMES tr. *Le Blond's Gardening* 80 Experience, Tryal upon the Ground, and a certain Rote,..necessary to this End. **1768** *Woman of Honor* II. 81 His education had proceeded in the common rote through school and college. *Ibid.* II. 189 He took the rote of forms to be the very quintessence of affairs.

†c. A rigmarole. *Obs. rare.*

14.. *Sir Beues* (MS. S) 1191 Men seye..in olde roote þat wimmannes bolt is sone schote. **1681** *Peace & Truth* 14 The Church of Rome hath turned Prayer into a meer Rote or Charm of unintelligible Words.

2. ***by rote***, in a mechanical manner, by routine, *esp.* by the mere exercise of memory without proper understanding of, or reflection upon, the matter in question; also, †with precision, by heart.

a. With *say, sing, play*, etc.

The meaning of the first quot. is not clear.

13.. *Gaw. & Gr. Knt.* 2207 Þat gere as I trowe, Is ryched at þe reuerence, me renk to mete, bi rote. *c* **1394** *P. Pl. Crede* 377 A ribaut..þat can nouȝt wel reden His rewle ne his respondes, but be pure rote. **1444** *Pol. Poems* (Rolls) II. 217 Suych labourerys synge may be roote, 'Alle goo we stille, the cok hath lowe shoon'. **1526** *Pilgr. Perf.* (W. de W. 1531) 160 Yf it were, than I myght..saye my seruyce by rote and custome. **1577–82** BRETON *Toyes Idle Head* Wks. (Grosart) I. 27/1, I did not sing one noate, except it were by roate. **1628** EARLE *Microcosm., Shop-keeper* (Arb.) 54 Hee tels you lyes by rote. **1662** PLAYFORD *Skill Mus.* II. (1674) 110 To learn to play by rote or ear without Book. **1715** DE FOE *Fam. Instruct.* I. vi. (1841) I. 112 We can all repeat the Commandments by rote. **1773** HAN. MORE *Search after Happiness* ii. 141, I talk'd by rote the jargon of the schools. **1832** HT. MARTINEAU *Hill & Valley* vii. 111 The young ladies..played their duet more by rote than con amore this night. **1856** HAWTHORNE *Eng. Note-bks.* (1870) II. 160 This guide..did his business less by rote..than any guide I ever met. **1878** BOSW. SMITH *Carthage* 436 The college..where little boys learn to repeat by rote the Koran from end to end.

b. With *know, get, learn*, etc.

c **1386** CHAUCER *Prol.* 329 Ther-to he koude endite, and make a thyng,..And euery statut koude he pleyn by rote. —— *Prioress' T.* 1712 He..herkned ay the wordes and the noote, Til he the firste vers koude al by rote. *c* **1440** *Partonope* 3215 The maner of spyces I know by rote. **1531** TINDALE *Prol. Ep. Rom.* Wks. 39, I thinke it meete that euery christen man..know it, by roate and without the boke. **1596** SPENSER *F.Q.* IV. ix. 6 Singing all her sorrow to the note, As she had learned readily by rote. **1624** HEYWOOD *Gunaik.* VIII. 375 The Psalmes of David which shee had almost *ad unguem* and by roat. **1663** BUTLER *Hud.* I. i. 135 All which he understood by Rote, And as occasion serv'd, would quote. **1709** STEELE *Tatler* No. 38 ¶12 He has by Rote, and at Second-hand, all that can be said of any Man of Figure, Wit, and Virtue in Town. **1781** COWPER *Conversat.* 7 Words learn'd by rote a parrot may rehearse. **1840** CARLYLE *Heroes* (1858) 321 Their commonplace doctrines, which they have learned by logic, by rote, at secondhand. **1874** L. STEPHEN *Hours in Library* (1892) II. iii. 102 In time we learn by rote the lessons which we had to spell out in our youth.

3. *attrib.*, as ***rote knowledge, -learning, -lesson, -work; rote-learned, -like***, adjs.; †***by-rote babble, lesson***; **rote learning**, also *spec.* in *Psychol.*, the learning by rote of meaningless material designed to be free of associations, as a technique in the study of learning.

1598 E. GUILPIN *Skial.* (1878) 45 T' heare a Parrat cry Her by-roate lesson of like curtesie. **1641** MILTON *Animadv.* Wks. 1851 III. 201 To pray in his own words without being ..fescu'd to a formal injunction of his rote-lesson. **1669** PENN *No Cross* Wks. 1782 II. 197 A little by-rote-babble, with..an hour's talk in other men's words. **1848** ELIZA COOK *To Charlotte Cushman* iii, No rote-learned sighing. **1862** G. P. MARSH *Orig. & Hist. Eng. Lang.* 25 A rote-knowledge of paradigms and definitions. **1864** KNIGHT *Passages Work. Life* I. i. 23 The dreary life of a day-school ..., for the education was altogether rote-work. **1876** GRANT *Burgh Sch. Scot.* II. xiii. 401 The rote-learning of rules once so universal. **1914** *Brit. Jrnl. Psychol.* VII. 253 (*title*) The value of distributed repetitions in rote learning. **1940** G. KATONA *Organizing & Memorizing* 164 We shall study the classic material used in investigating the memory, that is, rote learning of nonsense syllables. **1954** W. FAULKNER *Fable* 35 He said, repeated, rote-like, cold, unemphasised, almost telegraphic: 'Comité des Forges'. **1970** *Jrnl. Gen. Psychol.* LXXXII. 54 The similarity of the present results to those in the rote literature argues against the sharp distinction drawn between meaningful and rote learning by Ausubel.

†**rote**, *sb.*[3] *Obs.*$^{-1}$ [a. OF. *rote*, var. of *route* ROUT *sb.*[1] Hence also MDu., MLG., MHG., MSw. *rote*, MDa. *rode*.] A company, squadron.
1387 TREVISA *Higden* (Rolls) I. 311 [Creta] was þe firste lond þat..tauȝte horse men to ryde in rotes [L. *turmas*].

†**rote**, *sb.*[4] *Obs. rare.* [ad. med.L. *rota* (Du Cange).] A certain measure or weight.
c **1400** tr. *Secreta Secret., Gov. Lordsh.* II. lxvii. 84 Take ..þe Ferthe party of a Rote, and put all in x Rotes of swete water. *Ibid.* 85.

rote (rəʊt), *sb.*[5] Now *rare*. Also 6 root. [ad. L. *rota* ROTA, or (in sense 2) a. F. *rote*.]
†**1.** A wheel used as an instrument of torture or punishment. *Obs.*
1526 R. WHYTFORD *Martiloge* (1893) 43 All theyr membres & hole body stretched vpon a rote or turnyng whele. *a* **1575** *Diurn. Occurr.* (Bann. Cl.) 250 James Cadder .., being..tane in Strlueling in maner foirsaid, wes brokin on the root.
†**2.** *R.C. Ch.* = ROTA 3. *Obs.*
1528 GARDINER in Burnet *Hist. Ref., Rec.* (Pocock) I. 106 One Jacobus Symonet, dean of the rote. **1529** MORE *Dyaloge* III. Wks. 216/1 Sauyng the premunyre, we myghte haue it tryed in the rote at Rome. **1787** CHARLOTTE SMITH *Romance Real Life* II. 130 At the court of Rome, the department called the Rote, allowed the validity of her marriage.
3. Rotation; turn. *rare*$^{-1}$.
1831 *Fraser's Mag.* III. 508 They at first resolved That each should govern in diurnal rote.

rote (rəʊt), *sb.*[6] Now *U.S.* [See RUT *sb.*[3]] The roaring of the sea or surf.
1610 R. NICCOLS *England's Eliza* cclxx. 837 While the seas rote doth ring their dolefull knell. **1682** FLAVEL *Fear* 24 Such a noise as the rote of the sea. **1855** HALIBURTON *Nature & Human N.* 210 When..the rote is on the beach, it tells me it is the voice of the south wind giving notice of rain. **1864** LOWELL *Fireside Trav.* 193 X. walked away, rumbling inwardly like the rote of the sea heard afar. **1869** T. W. HIGGINSON *Oldport Romance* xviii, She could only distinguish the rote on the distant beach. **1909** *Newfoundland Q.* Dec. 9/1 The fishermen are accustomed, in foggy weather, to find their bearings by carefully listening to the rout of the sea on the shore, which they (very correctly) call rote, or rut. **1941** T. S. ELIOT *Dry Salvages* i. 8 The menace and caress of wave that breaks on water, The distant rote in the granite teeth. **1965** S. E. MORISON in *Amer. Neptune* Oct. 236 Often have I heard a Maine man say, 'Sea's making up. Hear that rote!' *Ibid.*, T. S. Eliot doubtless listened to the rote from his parents' house, during the windless calm after a storm, or on a 'weather-breeder' day when swells from the eastward begin crashing on the 'granite teeth' of Cape Ann before a storm breaks.

†**rote**, *a.*, obs. variant of ROTTEN *a.*
c **1386** CHAUCER *Sec. Nun's T.* 17 (Cambr. MS.), ȝit seen men weel..That ydilnesse is rote slogardye. *Ibid.* 228 Neuere mo ne schal they rote be.

rote (rəʊt), *v.*[1] Also 7 roat. [f. ROTE *sb.*[2]]
1. *trans.* To repeat, to run *over*, to rattle *off*, from memory. Also *absol.*
1593 DRAYTON *Ecl.* i. 16 Ravish'd to heare the warbling Birds to roat. **1630** —— *Muses Eliz.* Nymphal ii. 121 If by chance a Tune you roate, 'Twill foote it finely to your note. **1681** BAXTER *Answ. Dodwell* iv. 57 Did you think that your roteing over the name to them that deny the thing, would make a wise man change his Religion? **1816** J. GILCHRIST *Philos. Etym.* 134 It is really to be wished that authors would think more and rote less. *Ibid.* 140 The usual violations of usage might be put into a sixpenny piece to be roted off by the grammatical disciple. **1838** TUPPER *Proverb. Philos., Of Memory* iii, Memory is not wisdom: idiots can rote volumes.
†**2.** To learn or fix by rote. *Obs. rare.*
1607 SHAKS. *Cor.* III. ii. 55 Now it lyes you on to speake to th' people..with such words That are but roated in your Tongue. **1775** T. SHERIDAN *Art Reading* 283 Not..able to repeat even what is perfectly roted on the memory.
Hence '**roting** *vbl. sb.* and *ppl. a.*
1816 J. GILCHRIST *Philos. Etym.* 186 Can our roting, repeating scholar make Latin as Cicero made it? **1817** —— *Intell. Patrimony* 15 You will witness much reading, roting and repeating among those who pretend to learning.

rote (rəʊt), *v.*[2] [ad. L. *rotāre*, f. *rota* wheel.]
†**1.** *trans.* To rotate. *Obs.*
1578 BANISTER *Hist. Man* I. 27 When the cubit is at furthest extended, the posteriour and great Processe thereof, is roted and wheeled.
2. *intr.* To go *out* or *in* by rotation or turn.
a **1697** AUBREY *Lives, J. Harrington* (1898) I. 291 Now this modell upon rotation was:—that the third part of the Senate should rote out by ballot every yeare. **1806** W. TAYLOR in *Ann. Rev.* IV. 240 Of three County Members one might rote out yearly. **1860** GEN. P. THOMPSON *Audi Alt.* clxxi. III. 199 Here the only way seems to be, that instead of roting out, as was the device of our ancestors, men should for once in a way rote in.

†**rote**, *v.*[3] *Obs.* [Cf. ROTTLE *v.*] ? To flutter.
c **1330** *Arth. & Merl.* 3867 (Kölbing), þer miȝt men se þe baners roten, þe stedes forþ wel ȝern schoten.

rote, obs. f. ROOT, ROT, ROUT, RUT.

†'**roted**, *a. Obs. rare*$^{-1}$. [app. f. ROTE *sb.*[2]] Skilled, practised, experienced.
1470–85 MALORY *Morte Arth.* x. xxxvi. 472 This malgryne was an olde roted knyghte, and he was called one of the daungerous knyghtes of the world to doo bataille on foot.

roted, obs. f. ROOTED, ROTTED.

rotel, obs. f. ROTTLE *v.*

†**rote-master.** *Obs.*$^{-1}$ [ad. Du. *rotmeester*, G. *rottmeister*: see ROT *sb.*[2]] One in command of a company of gunners.
1523 *Lett. & Pap. Hen. VIII*, III. II. 1526.

roten, obs. f. ROTTEN *a.*

rotenone ('rəʊtənəʊn). *Chem.* Orig. †-on. [ad. Jap. *rotenon* (K. Nagai 1902, in *Jrnl. Tokyo Chem. Soc.* XXIII. 753), f. *roten* derris: see -ONE.] A toxic crystalline polycyclic ketone, $C_{23}H_{22}O_6$, obtained from the roots of several species of plant (notably derris, cubé, and timbo), which is widely employed as an insecticide in the form of a powder or an emulsified spray. Also as *v. trans.*, to treat with rotenone.
1924 *Chem. Abstr.* XVIII. 408 From air-dried roots, 0·93% crude rotenon is obtained which is mixed with waxy impurities. **1925** *Ibid.* XIX. 1708 Further analysis of rotenone, an active insecticidal principle of the root of *Derris elliptica* Benth. **1962** GORDON & LAVOIPIERRE *Entomol.* ix. 57 Fine dusts containing pyrethrum or rotenone are highly successful when employed against various insects such as fleas and lice. **1975** *New Yorker* 19 May 45/3 We poison out a small reef by squirting in emulsified rotenone, a chemical poison derived from the root of a South American plant called cubé, originally used by Indians for fishing. *Ibid.* 46/1 You rotenone a reef, and for the next hour or two you pick the samplings up. **1977** LEWIS & ELVIN-LEWIS *Med. Bot.* ii. 45 *Tephrosia cinerea*, yielding rotenone and the toxic principle tephrosin, is used in Venezuela and Africa as a fish poison.

†'**roter**[1]. *Obs.*$^{-1}$ [a. OF. *rotier*, variant of *routier*, ROUTER *sb.*[1]] A robber, highwayman.
1297 R. GLOUC. (Rolls) 6032 Aboute heruest þis deneis as roters [*v.r.* rotours, rotors] arnde Bi chilterne & to oxenford.

roter[2] ('rəʊtə(r)). [f. ROTE *v.*[1]] One who repeats by rote.
1624 BP. MOUNTAGU *Gagg* 301 Such Roters as these, are the men that talk of Fathers amongst their Gossips and Proselytes. **1816** J. GILCHRIST *Philos. Etym.* 217 A canting, mystical, visionary race of roters, eternally saying after consecrated authorities. **1817** —— *Intell. Patrimony* 102 The sole reason must have been, that he was less of a reader and roter.

rotey-time: see RUTEY *sb.*

rotge(e. *Ornith.* [Given by Martens (1675) as the name current among Dutch or Frisian sailors, with the statement that it is derived from the bird's cry *rottet tet*; but perh. a misunderstanding of Fris. *rotgies*, pl. of *rotgoes*, brent-goose.] The little auk. See also ROTCHE.
1694 *Martens' Voy. Spitzbergen* in *Acc. Sev. Late Voy.* II. 76 The old Lumbs have a very tough and dry Flesh, not to disparage the Rotges, Kirmews and young Lumbs when boiled. *Ibid.* (1711) 91 The calling or crying of the Rotges amongst one another. **1859** *Cornhill Mag.* I. 109 Passing Cape Dudley Diggs, we landed at a breeding-place of rotges (little auks). **1882** *Nature* XXVI. 387 Many rotgees had their young among the basaltic columns.

'**rot-gut, 'rotgut.** [f. ROT *v.* + GUT *sb.*]
1. An adulterated or unwholesome liquor; *spec.* bad small beer, or (in *U.S.*) inferior whiskey.
1633 HEYWOOD *Eng. Trav.* IV. Wks. 1874 IV. 72 Let not a Teaster scape To be consum'd in rot-gut. **1666** G. HARVEY *Morb. Angl.* xxviii. (1672) 76 They overwhelming their panch daily with a kind of flat *Scarbier*, or Rot-gut; we with a bitter dreggish small liquor. **1715** ADDISON *Drummer* v. Wks. 1830 II. 208 *Sir George.* Drink nothing but smallbeer for a fortnight——. *But.* Smallbeer! Rot-gut! **1831** LOVER *Leg.* 222 To the divil I pitch sitch rot-gut. **1867** P. FITZGERALD 75 *Brooke St.* II. 67 What is it to me..if you fill your cellars with all the 'rotgut' in the kingdom? **1892** HENLEY & STEVENSON *Deacon Brodie* I. iv, What brings the man from stuff like this to rotgut and spittoons at Mother Clarke's. **1911** E. M. CLOWES *On Wallaby* vi. 164 The cattle-men, shearers, and shepherds get their internal machinery completely ruined in time by the quantity of inferior boiled sugar and fruit that they consume, and which they have inelegantly christened 'rot-gut'. **1923** C. E. MULFORD *Black Buttes* xiv. 220 Yes, even a drink of rot-gut would 'a' bought you! **1939** JOYCE *Finnegans Wake* (1964) 381 And suck up..whatever surplus rotgut, sorra much, was left by the lazy lousers of maltknights and beer-churls. **1946** *Time* 7 Oct. 10/2 For 50 years we have been hearing how the drought-smitten Jayhawkers were poisoning themselves on bootleg rotgut because we couldn't get decent liquor. **1952** E. O'NEILL *Moon for Misbegotten* IV. 173 That isn't Phil's rotgut. That's real, honest-to-God bonded Bourbon. **1969** *Private Eye* 4 July 14/3 But don't drink that rotgut. Here warm your gizzard with a tot of rum from my flask. **1976** *Times* 8 July 16/4 It was being killed mercilessly by the whisky posts with their rotgut.
2. *attrib.* or as *adj.* Of liquor: Unwholesome, deleterious, injurious to the system. Also *transf.* and *fig.*
1706 T. BAKER *Tunbridge Walks* III. i, Damn rotgut Rhenish: we'll have Mrs. Motion's health in a bumper of Barcelona. **1767** S. PATERSON *Anoth. Trav.* II. 42 Their only drink was a cursed rot-gut stuff, which they called wine. **1830** MARRYAT *King's Own* xxxiv, The rotgut French wines had given him a pain in the bowels. **1871** *Daily News* 19 Jan., To take glass after glass of rotgut rum, schnapps, or arrack. **1877** H. RUEDE *Let.* 24 Apr. in *Sod-House Days* (1937) 57 They have a brand called 'Old Style', some of Catlin's (St. Louis) cheap rotgut tobacco, and from that price up. **1927** L. BROMFIELD *Good Woman* xiii. 140 A glass filled many times with the rot-gut whisky that Hennessy sold. **1948** F. BLAKE *Johnny Christmas* I. 5 Not a man in that line but hated Santa Ana and his Mexicans, hated their talk, the way they killed, their rot-gut laughter. **1970** J. HOWARD *Please Touch* 6 Many kinds of wine: sweet, dry, nutty, fruity, insouciant, rotgut, presumptuous and noble. **1978** *Sunday Times* (Colour Suppl.) 18 June 42/3 Traders stack their boats with liquor, rotgut whisky and cachaca, cheap spirit.
b. *spec.* (See quot.) *U.S.*
1888 GOODE *Amer. Fishes* 432 Its flesh spoils very quickly after the fish is taken from the water, hence the name 'Rot-gut Minnow', applied to it in Alabama.

roth, obs. form of ROOT *sb.*[1]

†**rothe**, *v.*[1] *Obs.*$^{-1}$ [ad. ON. *ráða*, = OE. *rǣdan*: see REDE *v.*] *trans.* To counsel, advise.
c **1300** *Havelok* 2817 And siþen shal ich under-stonde Of you..Manrede, and holde oþes boþe, Yif ye it wilen, and ek rothe.

†**rothe**, *v.*[2] *Obs.*$^{-1}$ [Of obscure origin.] *intr.* ? To talk nonsense.
c **1440** *York Myst.* xvii. 122 Kyng! in þe deuyl way, dogges, Fy! Now I se wele ȝe roþe and raue.

†'**rothel**, *v. Obs. rare.* (Of obscure origin and doubtful meaning.)
13.. *E.E. Allit. P.* B. 59 Al is roþeled & rosted ryȝt to þe sete, Comeȝ cof to my corte, er hit colde worþe. *Ibid.* 890 þenne vch tolke tyȝt hem þat hade of tayt fayled, & vchon roþeled to þe rest þat he reche moȝt.

‖**rötheln** ('rø:təln). [G. *rötheln*, *röteln* pl., f. *rot(h)* red.] German measles.
1873 F. T. ROBERTS *Handbk. Med.* 179 Hybrid of Measles and Scarlatina—Röthelin. **1877** *Ibid.* (ed. 3) I. 147 Rötheln has been regarded either as a mild form of measles or scarlatina. **1889** E. SMITH *Pract. Treat. Dis. Children* (ed. 2) ii. 32 An attack of rötheln is then, as a rule, a very insignificant matter.

rother ('rɒðə(r)). *Obs.* exc. *dial.* Forms: α. 1 **hriðer, hryþer,** 1–2 **hryðer,** 4 **riþer.** β. 2–3 **reðer,** 4 **reþer,** 5–6 **rether.** γ. 2–3 **reoðer,** 3 **roþer,** 3– **rother,** 5 **rodder,** 6 **rowder.** δ. 1 **hruðer,** 3 **ruðer, ruþer,** 4, 6 **ruther,** 5 **rudder.** [OE. *hríðer*, *hrýðer*, = OFris. *(h)rither*, *reder* (NFris. *ridder*, *redder* young ox, WFris. *rier* heifer), a derivative from the stem *hríð-* (found in *hríðfald*, *-hiorde*), = OS. *hrîth*, for earlier **hrinþ-*, which is also represented by OHG. *hrind* (G. *rind*), MLG. and MDu. *rind-*, *rint* (Du. *rund*). The shortening of the vowel before the ending *-ther* (as in *mother*, *brother*) prob. took place in later OE., with subsequent variation due to the influence of *r*.
It is not clear whether OE. *hrýðer* is a mere variation of *hríðer*, or represents an original ablaut variant **hrunþ-*.]
1. An ox; an animal of the ox kind; *pl.* oxen, cattle, neat.
α. **805–31** *Charter* in *O.E. Texts* 444 An hriðer duȝunde. **971** *Blickl. Hom.* 199 He..ongan sceotan wiþ þæs þe he ȝeseah þæt hryþer stondan. *c* **1000** *Sax. Leechd.* II. 100 Ðenim cealfes scearn oþþe ealdes hryþeres wearm & leȝe on. *c* **1050** *Voc.* in Wr.-Wülcker 341 *Armenta*, hryðera heorde. *a* **1122** *O.E. Chron.* (Laud MS.) an. 1012, Hi..hine þa þær oftorfodon mid banum & mid hryðera heafdum. *c* **1400** *Trevisa's Higden* (Rolls) III. 205 Senewes of schepe and of reþeren [β. riþeren].
β. *c* **1200** *Trin. Coll. Hom.* 37 Ðet oref..beð shep and reðeren and get and swin. *a* **1290** *Leben Jesu* (Horstm.) 853 Fond he þer inne..Schep and reþren, and coluerene eke. *c* **1306** *Pol. Songs* (Camden) 220 Upon a retheres hude forth he wes y-tuht. **1387** TREVISA *Higden* (Rolls) II. 13 þis ilond ..bringeþ forþ..reþeren and oþer bestes. *a* **1400–50** *Alexander* 1239 Meliager with his men..Raschis with rethere & rydis bot a quyle [etc.]. **1509** *Will of Myll* (Somerset Ho.), Duos Retheres et viginti oues.
γ. *c* **1225** *Leg. Kath.* 60 þe riche reoðeren & schep.. brohten to lake. *c* **1290** *S. Eng. Leg.* I. 300/11 Garganes reoþeren and oþure bestes I-nowe..to heore lesewe heom drowe. **13..** *K. Alis.* 4719 Men to heom threowe drit and donge, With foule ayren, with rotheres lunge. **1398** TREVISA *Barth. De P.R.* XVIII. i. (Bodl. MS.), Bestes þat eteþ grete gras and herbes as roþeren. **1474** *Waterf. Arch.* in *10th Rep. Hist. MSS. Comm.* App. V. 311 Rodders or ony othre marchaundise. **1607** SHAKS. *Timon* IV. iii. 12 It is the Pastour Lards the rothers [*em. for* Brothers] sides. **1875** PARISH *Dict. Sussex Dial.*, *Rother*,..a horned beast.
δ. *c* **1050** in Kemble *Cod. Dipl.* IV. 275 þæron næs orfcynnes nan mare buton vii hruðeru. *c* **1205** LAY. 8106 Islaȝene weoren to þon mele twælf þusend ruðeren. **1297** R. GLOUC. (Rolls) 1209 King cassibel..sacrefize to hor godes ..Vourti þousend of ruþeren. **1485** *Waterf. Arch.* in *10th Rep. Hist. MSS. Comm.* App. V. 319 The said bouchers bye the same rudders in thar names. **1518** in *Trans. Kilkenny Arch. Soc.* Ser. II. IV. 112 An Indentur..vpon ij rudders to be payed..yerly to Gerald Erle of Kildare.
2. *attrib.* and *Comb.*, as *rother-cattle*, *-driver*, *-herd*, *-soil*.
c **1000** ÆLFRIC *Gen.* xlv. 10 Eowre sceap and eower hryðer-heorda. *c* **1000** —— *Hom.* I. 322 Amos hatte sum hryðer-hyrde. *c* **1175** *Lamb. Hom.* 97 Amos het a reoðer heorde. **1396** *Chancery Warrants* file 560 Quatre boefs, pris de quarante soulds, [stolen] de Johan ap Jakke, retherdryver. **1578** LYTE *Dodoens* 752 The leaves of Elme are good fodder for rother cattell. **1602** CAREW *Cornwall* 23 Beastes seruing for meate onely, are Pigs, Goates, Sheepe, and Rother cattell. **1670** BLOUNT *Glossogr.* (ed. 3) s.v., Hence Rother-soyle, also used in Hereford shire, for the soyle or dung of those beasts.

rother, obs. form of RUDDER.

† **rother-beast.** *Obs.* exc. *arch.* = ROTHER 1.

α. **1483** in *Somerset Wills* (1901) 254 Also two oxen..and all my rother bestes. **1533** in Weaver *Wells Wills* (1890) 61 Every child of my son Thos. a Rother beste. **1567** GOLDING *Ovid's Met.* VII. 89 b, The cruell Beare to fall Upon the herdes of Rother beastes had now no lust at all. **1630** *R. Johnson's Kingd. & Commw.* 78 You shall see Heards of Rother Beasts and Horses, and Flocks of Sheepe. *c* **1640** J. SMYTH *Hund. Berkeley* (1885) 19 Land's which suffice for the breedinge of an horse beast or Rother beast. **1670** BLOUNT *Glossogr.* (ed. 3), *Rother-beasts* (a word used both in our old Statutes, and still in the North of England). **1836** in A. R. Stedman *Marlborough & Upper Kennet Country* (1960) xxvii. 270 No burgess shall keep on the common more than two rother beasts...that is to say, kine or bullocks. **1933** *Catholic Bull.* Mar. 215 Let us read over again the overwhelmingly impressive reasonings of this great among the greatest pontiffs, then contrast the fruits of imperial connection, of Masonry, of that trade in pasturing and larding the sides of rother-beasts, to champion which the Knight of the Ranchers..has couched his lance.

β. **1561** HOLLYBUSH *Hom. Apoth.* 25 The mary of Hertes, Roes, or rudder beastes. **1596** HARINGTON *Metam. Ajax* Prol. A viij, The ruther beastes that eate too greedily hereof wil swell til they burst. **1610** GUILLIM *Heraldry* III. xiv. (1660) 163 The Bull is the ringleader amongst ruther beasts. **1698** FRYER *Acc. E. India & P.* 244 The Ruther Beasts with distended Bags grazing in the Meadows.

† **'rotheren,** *a. Obs.* Forms: 1 **hryþeren,** 4–5 **reþeren** (5 **-erne**), **rotheren** (**roþerne**), **rutheren.** [OE. *hrýðeren*, f. *hrýðer* ROTHER. Cf. OS. *hrîtherin*, MLG. *rindern*.] Of or belonging to oxen or cattle. ***retheren tongue***, bugloss.

c **1000** *Sax. Leechd.* II. 186 Ðenim hryþeren flæsc ȝesoden on ecede. **1387** TREVISA *Higden* (Rolls) II. 309 It was a grete abhomynacioun among þe Egipcians to sle reþeren or ete reþeren flesche. **1398** —— *Barth. De P.R.* XVIII. i. (Bodl. MS.), Roþeren flesche and gote flesche is better sode þanne rosted. *c* **1400** *Trevisa's Higden* (Rolls) VII. 504 The Danes ..slouȝ him with stones and with rutheren bones. **14..** *MS. Sloane* 5 lf. 5/2 Buglossa,..lingua bouis. *gallice*, Lange de boef. *Anglice*, reþerne tounge.

Rotherham ('rɒðərəm). Also **Rotheram.** The name of a parish and township in Yorkshire, formerly used *attrib.* to designate an improved form of plough introduced (app. from Holland) about the middle of the 18th century.

1762 MILLS *Syst. Husb.* I. 255 The Rotheran [*sic*], or patent plough,..deserves the husbandman's particular attention. **1763** *Museum Rust.* I. 24 To stir the intervals,.. the Rotheram plow may be used. **1805** R. W. DICKSON *Pract. Agric.* I. 7 An intelligent farmer..assures us, that the rotheram-plough..goes very light, and is very useful. **1844** H. STEPHENS *Bk. Farm* I. 406 About the middle of the past century, the Rotherham plough appears to have been partially introduced into Scotland.

† **'rotherish,** *a. Obs.*$^{-1}$ [f. ROTHER + -ISH.] Resembling oxen.

c **1200** *Trin. Coll. Hom.* 37 Sume men..winned wið þe eorðe, and tiliȝet michel to oðre mannæs bihofþe, and þese men beð icleped ruðerihsse men. Of þese shepishse and ruðerishse men specð þe prophete.

Rothesay ('rɒθseɪ). Also 5 **Roth(is)say,** 6 **Rothsey.** The name of an ancient castle in Scotland, used *attrib.* in ***Rothesay herald***, one of the six Scottish heralds. Also *ellipt.*

1401–2 *Exch. Rolls Scot.* (1880) III. 552 In partem pensionis.., videlicet Rothesay heraldo. **1488** *Sc. Acts Parl.* (1814) II. 214/1 The lettrez brocht fra him be Rothissay herrald. **1507** *Acc. Ld. High Treas. Scot.* III. 371 Item, to Blewmantill, now callit Rothsey, for to pas in France. **1581** *Sc. Acts Parl.* (1814) III. 286/1 His said office of Rothesay herauld. **1642** *Reg. Privy Council Scot.* VII. 331 The other two [were charged] by John Spence, Rothesay Herald,..to render their houses. **1742** A. NISBET *Syst. Heraldry* II. IV. xvi. 171 Rothsay has his Name and Title from the Castle of Rothsay,..an antient Residence of our Scots Kings in the Isle of Bute. **1863** [see ROSS *sb.*^{1}].

† **rothly,** *a. Obs.*$^{-1}$ (Meaning uncertain.)

a **1400** *Pistill Susan* 341 Þo þat roþly cherl ruydely rored, And seide bi-fore þe prophete: 'þei pleied bi a prine'.

Rothschild ('rɒθstʃaɪld). [Name of Mayer Amschel *Rothschild* (1744–1812) of Frankfurt, and his descendants, proprietors of an international banking firm.] **1.** One who resembles a member of the Rothschild family in being exceptionally rich; a millionaire. Also in colloq. phr. ***to come the Rothschild***: to pretend to be rich (see COME *v.* 29 c).

1833 CARLYLE *Sart. Res.* I. v, in *Fraser's Mag.* VIII. 670/2 All miracles have been out-miracled for there are Rothschilds and English National Debts. **1850** E. RUSKIN *Let.* 18 Apr. in M. Lutyens *Effie in Venice* (1965) I. 167 We ..called on Madame Chabrillan who is married to the Rothschild of the family. **1863** GEO. ELIOT *Romola* I. I. 74 The Bardi..[were] standing in the very front of European commerce—the Christian Rothschilds of that time. **1885** H. JAMES *Little Tour in France* xii. 92 Jacques Coeur..was a Vanderbilt or Rothschild of the fifteenth century. **1893** W. S. GILBERT *Utopia (Limited)* I. 32 Though a Rothschild you may be..As a company you've come to utter sorrow. **1905** FARMER & HENLEY *Dict. Slang* 111/2 *To come the Rothschild*, to pretend to be rich. **1910** W. J. LOCKE *Simon* xvi. 221, I had wealth—not a Rothschild or Vanderbilt fortune but enough to assure me ease and luxury. **1938** [see ROCKEFELLER]. **1974** J. GARDNER *Return of Moriarty* 57 A relatively young whore, Mary Jane Kelly, who sometimes came the Rothschild about her past, calling herself Marie Jeannette Kelly.

2. as *adj.* See MOUTON ROTHSCHILD.

† **rothun.** *Obs.*$^{-1}$ (Meaning uncertain.)

13.. *E.E. Allit. P.* B. 1009 Suche a roþun of a reche ros fro þe blake, Askez vpe in þe ayre & vsellez þer flowen.

‖ **rôti**^{1} (roti). [Fr.] In *Gastronomy*, a main course consisting of roasted meat; (a dish of) roasted meat. Also as *adj.* (with preceding sb.) and *Comb.*

1771 SMOLLETT *Humph. Cl.* III. 143 The rotis were scorched and stinking, for the honour of the fumet. **1806** J. PINKERTON *Recoll. Paris* II. vi. 102 Upon the appearance of the *roti*, the ordinary wine is changed for the richer kinds of Burgundy or Bordeaux. **1841** THACKERAY *Mem. Gourmandizing* in *Fraser's Mag.* XXIII. 714/1 Saddle of mutton rôti. **1864** MRS. GASKELL *French Life* in *Fraser's Mag.* LXIX. 440/2 The rôti and the salad follow. **1906** MRS. BEETON *Bk. Househ. Managem.* lxii. 1669 *Rôti* (Fr.), the roast..the course of a meal which is served before the entremets. **1951** *Good Housek. Home Encycl.* 639/1 *Rôti*, the meat, poultry or game course in a dinner. **1980** G. GREENE *Dr. Fischer* xvi. 114 With the Mouton Rothschild there was a *rôti de boeuf*.

‖ **roti**^{2} ('rəʊtiː). [a. Hindi, Urdu *roṭī* bread, ROOTY.] A cake of unleavened bread of a type originating in India. (Now also current in the W. Indies.)

1920 *Chambers's Jrnl.* 29 May 407/1 What are two hours to an Indian peasant? They had had their *roti* (bread), and, the stomach being full, having to wait was a small matter. **1952** [see JOHNNY-CAKE a]. **1958** J. CAREW *Black Midas* vi. 98 We bought fruit and roti from peddlers on the stelling. **1971** *Leader* (Durban) 7 May 9/1 (Advt.), Only the best is good enough... That's why I use only Bakers Homo Flour for my roti. **1971** *Advocate-News* (Barbados) 17 Sept. 6/4 Among the specialties to be presented to Barbadians by the Roti Shop are chicken, beef and shrimp roti, dholl puri and potato roti. **1974** *Socialist Worker* 9 Nov. 8/3 The starving stream in from all directions to receive a roti (a thin flat piece of bread) or perhaps two if they are lucky. **1976** *Sunday Standard* (Bombay) 11 July 4/3 Roti, the unleavened bread, is the stuff of our lives.

rotie, obs. form of ROT *v.*

rotifer ('rəʊtɪfə(r)). [mod.L. (Leeuwenhoek, 1702), f. L. *rota* wheel + *-fer* bearing.] An animalcule belonging to the class *Rotifera*.

1793 T. BEDDOES *On Calculus* 250 The phænomena displayed by the rotifer..appear inexplicable. **1835–6** *Todd's Cycl. Anat.* I. 608/2 Singular experiments on the apparent resuscitation of the Rotifer. **1846** DANA *Zooph.* ii. (1848) 11 Polyps are..even less complex in structure than the minuter Rotifers. **1872** NICHOLSON *Biol.* 15 The Rotifers are minute mostly microscopic creatures which inhabit almost all our ponds and streams.

‖ **rotifera** (rəʊ'tɪfərə). [mod.L., neut. pl. of *rotifer(us)*: see prec.] A class of minute (usually microscopic) animalcules, having rotatory organs which are used in swimming.

1830 R. KNOX *Béclard's Anat.* 18 Other animals somewhat more compound, as the rotifera..and the polypi. **1848** CARPENTER *Anim. Phys.* ii. (1872) 112 The group of Rotifera or Wheel-Animalcules, which is one of great interest to the Microscopist. **1896** tr. *Boas' Text-bk. Zool.* 157 The Rotifera lay two different kinds of eggs.

Hence **ro'tiferal** *a.*, **ro'tiferous** *a.*, of or belonging to the *Rotifera*.

1835–6 *Todd's Cycl. Anat.* I. 607 The..rotatory or wheel-like organs of the Rotiferous Infusoria. **1871** T. R. JONES *Anim. Kingd.* (ed. 4) 463 In the rotiferous animalcules. **1886** *Encycl. Brit.* XXI. 8/1 Possessing undoubtedly Rotiferal characters.

† **'rotified,** *ppl. a. Obs.*$^{-1}$ [f. ROTE *sb.*^{2}] Repeated by rote.

1719 D'URFEY *Pills* V. 242 Let 'em tire all that pass with their rotified Cant, 'Will you buy any Shoes, pray see what you want'.

'rotiform, *a. rare*$^{-0}$. [ad. mod.L. *rotiformis*, f. L. *rota* wheel.] (See quots.)

1855 OGILVIE *Suppl.*, *Rotiform*, shaped like a wheel. **1864** WEBSTER, *Rotiform*,..having a very short tube, and spreading limbs;—said of a monopetalous corolla.

rotine, obs. form of ROUTINE *sb.*

roting, obs. form of ROOTING, ROTTING.

rotisserie (rəʊ'tiːsərɪ). *orig. U.S.* Also **rôtisserie.** [a. F. *rôtisserie*, f. *rôtiss-*, stem of *rôtir* to roast + *-erie* -ERY.] **1.** A restaurant where meat is roasted or barbecued, freq. at a grill in the front window.

1868 *Overland Monthly* Nov. 470/1 At some of these French houses, especially designated as *rotisseriés* [*sic*], the kitchen is nominally open to inspection. **1914** S. LEWIS *Our Mr. Wrenn* i. 15 A rôtisserie, before whose upright fender of scarlet coals whole ducks were happily roasting to a shiny brown. **1925** *Restaurant News & Managem.* Dec. 10 (*caption*) An instance of successful catering to business and professional people The Rotisserie Inn, Salt Lake City. **1936** MENCKEN *Amer. Lang.* (ed. 4) 215 *Rôtisserie*, with the accent omitted, seems to be an Americanism. It signifies an eating-house wherein chickens and butcher's meat are roasted at a charcoal-grill, usually in the show-window of the establishment.

2. A cooking appliance which has a rotating spit for roasting and barbecuing meat. Also *attrib.* and *Comb.*

1953 *Home Beautiful* Apr. 133 Cooking on a rotating spit or rotisserie is high gourmet cooking. **1953** J. & M. ROBERTSON *Compl. Small Appliance Cookbk.* ii. 37 Rotisserie heat is *beside* or *above* the revolving food. *Ibid.* ii. 42 Serve with rotisserie-browned potatoes. **1960** *Guardian* 17 Mar. 9/4 All the glittering machines, the washers, the electric rotisseries. **1969** *Daily Colonist* (Victoria, B.C.) 6 Dec. 40/1 They borrowed a commercial rotisserie, got the charcoal white hot, and loaded the apparatus with 200 pounds of wild boar. **1973** *Times* 30 July 11/1 Rôtisserie spits, continuous cleaning ovens, the use of colour..these and other innovations..are maintaining..the popularity of the gas cooker. **1978** *Lancashire Life* Apr. 125/3 There are, in fact, three variations of this cooker, the most expensive one having a built-in rotisserie and kebab attachments.

Hence (as a back-formation) **ro'tiss(e)** *v. trans.* and *intr.*, to cook meat on a rotisserie; **ro'tissed** *ppl. a.*, **ro'tissing** *vbl. sb.*

1958 *Word Study* Dec. 5/1 The manufacturer has created the verb 'rotiss'. *Ibid.* 5/2 The housewife is advised to set her pointer according to what meat is being 'rotissed', and is informed that she needn't preheat when 'broiling or rotissing'. *a* **1963** P. BRACKEN *I hate to housekeep Bk.* (1969) viii. 72 She is a little scared of the rotisserie in her new double oven, so she continues to buy her chickens ready-rotissed. **1978** *Verbatim* Feb. 1/2 One San Francisco appliance dealer boasts of a stove which will not only roast and broil, it will also *rotisse*!

Rotissomat (rəʊ'tiːsəʊmæt). [f. ROTISS(ERIE + -O + -MAT.] The proprietary name of a commercial automatic cooking appliance with rotating spits for roasting meat.

1947 *Official Gaz.* (U.S. Patent Office) 8 July 187/1 Rotiss-o-mat Corporation, Astoria, Long Island, N.Y. *Rotiss-o-mat for electric rotisseries.* Claims use since January 1946. **1958** *Trade Marks Jrnl.* 9 Apr. 372/2 *Rotiss-o-mat*... Electric installations for cooking poultry and parts of such installations included in Class II. Harley Manufacturing Corporation..New York. **1960** *Observer* 13 Nov. 3/3 Chicken restaurants depend on a shiny piece of plant called a 'rotissomat', invented by the American, Sol Leder. **1961** *Times* 24 July 13/5 An Oxford supermarket has a rotissomat. **1963** M. BEADLE *These Ruins are Inhabited* xi. 160 The one near me on the London Road has installed a rotissomat.

‖ **rotl** ('rɒt(ə)l). Forms: 7 **rethel, rotte** (? **rotle**), **rotal,** 9 **rotol, rottle, rattle, rutl, rotl.** [a. Arab. *reṭl*, *raṭl*, which is supposed by some to be an alteration of Gr. λίτρα.] An eastern weight, varying in different places and for different commodities, but usually something between one and five pounds. Cf. ROTOLO.

1615 W. BEDWELL *Arab. Trudgman* s.v., An hundred Rethels do make a Cantar. **1685** POCOCKE *Comm. Hosea* iii. 2 It contained the weight of seventy-two thousand drachms, that is, five hundred common rotals. **1687** A. LOVELL tr. *Thevenot's Trav.* I. 262 The Quintal contains 150 Rottes, the Rotte 12 ounces. **1825** *Milburn's Oriental Commerce* I. 88 [At Judda] 15 Vakias make 1 Rattle; 2 Rattles 1 maund. **1826–7** *Encycl. Metrop.* (1845) XVIII. 438/2 The Greek *rotl* = 180 *dirhems* is used in weighing cotton thread; the common *rotl* = 144 *dirhems*. **1836** LANE *Mod. Egypt.* II. 8 The *rutl* is about $15\frac{3}{4}$ oz.

rotle, obs. form of ROTTLE *v.*

† **'rotness.** *Obs.*$^{-1}$ [Cf. ROT *a.*] Rottenness.

1387 TREVISA *Higden* (Rolls) VII. 149 Seint Laurence, whos chirche dissolved and lowsed þoruȝ longe rotnes [L. *carie*] he reparailde.

roto ('rəʊtəʊ). *N. Amer.* Abbrev. of ROTOGRAVURE 2, an illustrated or pictorial (section of a) newspaper or magazine.

1932 G. A. CHAPPELL *Evil through Ages* v. 70 To-day our Sunday illustrated sections are taken up by wives and mothers..who sign testimonials, exhibit dogs, dress up as colonial dames, anything to get into the rotos. **1942** BERREY & VAN DEN BARK *Amer. Thes. Slang* §522/17 *Rotogravure section*, roto, rotogravure, roto section. **1975** *Boston Globe* 22 Feb. 7/3 (Advt.), The Bride: a special roto magazine devoted to the newlyweds and soon-to-be-weds of '75 this Sunday in The Boston Globe. **1978** *Amer. Poetry Rev.* Nov./Dec. 30/1 He was writing for the roto section of a Sunday Newspaper. **1979** *Globe & Mail* (Toronto) 25 Jan. 7/3 A few publications such as Chatelaine and the rotos—Weekend and the Canadian—slept right through it, as far as ad revenues were concerned.

roto- ('rəʊtəʊ-), in some words also *rota-*, comb. form of L. *rōta* wheel, roller and Eng. ROTARY *a.*, ROTATION, etc., as in ROTOGRAPH, ROTOCHUTE, etc.

rotochute ('rəʊtəʊʃuːt). [f. ROTO- + PARA)CHUTE *sb.*] A mechanical device with rotating blades which can be attached to objects dropped from a great height so as to slow their fall.

1949 *Jrnl. Brit. Interplanetary Soc.* VIII. 139 A new type 'high-speed' parachute, intended for use in retrieving recording equipment from high-altitude rockets, was tested recently... Ordinary parachutes were ripped to shreds after falling free into the denser atmosphere... Expelled from A-4 rockets at altitudes up to 100 miles.., the rotochute attains supersonic velocity before atmospheric density builds up and the blades begin to revolve, gradually being forced out against air pressure to assume a horizontal position. **1955** *Sci. News Let.* 5 Mar. 160/3 Supplies can now be dropped to troops from low altitudes by a 'rotochute', a bomb-shaped device with rotor blades to slow the descent. **1962** *Aeroplane* CII. 45/2 In the recovery of space vehicles, the 'rotochute' is capable—according to this company—of satisfying three basic requirements not easily met in a single recovery system.

† **ro'tocracy.** *Obs.* [f. *rot(ten)*: see ROTTEN *a.* 7 c and -OCRACY.] The body of persons who had the control of rotten boroughs.

1831 *Examiner* 81/2 Why have a constituency, if the constituency is passively to subserve to the Rotocracy?—(we thank *The Times* for the word). **1831** FONBLANQUE *Eng. under 7 Administr.* (1837) II. 101 Lest the Rotocracy should imagine..that it has been the cause of the progress of society.

Rotodyne ('rəʊtəʊdaɪn). Also **Rotadyne** ('rəʊtə-). [f. ROTO- + -DYNE.] A proprietary name of an aircraft equipped with rotors, capable of vertical take-off and rapid flight.

1949 *Trade Marks Jrnl.* 17 Aug. 727/1 *Rotadyne* 676,644. Rotary wing aircraft. The Fairey Aviation Company Limited,..Hayes, Middlesex. *Ibid.*, *Rotodyne* 676,645... To be associated with No. 676,644. **1958** *Times* 9 Nov. 4/4 The..Rotodyne, the world's first vertical take-off and landing airliner. **1959** [see ASSAULT *sb.* 8]. **1959** [see CONVERTIPLANE].

rotograph ('rəʊtəgræf). [f. L. *rota* wheel + -GRAPH.] A photographic print (esp. of a page in a book or manuscript) made by exposing the object through a lens and prism, so that its reversed image is thrown upon part of a roll of sensitive paper. Also *attrib.*

1898 in *Trade Marks Jrnl.* No. 1098 (1899) 408. **1903** *H. S. Ward's Fig. Photogr.* (ed. 3) 95 'Rotograph' Papers. *Ibid.* 183 'Rotograph' formulæ. **1906** *Oxford Univ. Press Circular* (24 Nov.), Rotary Bromide Prints, or Rotographs.

rotogravure (ˌrəʊtəʊgrə'vjʊə(r)). *Printing.* Also ‖**rotogravur**, † **rotagravure**, and with capital initial. [orig. the name of the *Rotogravur* Deutsche Tiefdrück Gesellschaft (Berlin), said to be f. the names of two other companies, *Roto*phot (Berlin) and Deutsche Photo*gravur* AG (Siegburg), adopted in Eng. with assimilation of the ending to that of PHOTOGRAVURE. The form *rotagravure* (in sense 1) is an etymologizing re-formation f. L. *rota* wheel, roller + PHOTO)GRAVURE or F. *gravure* engraving.] **1.** A method of printing by means of a rotary press with intaglio cylinders, usu. used at high speed for long print runs.

1913 *Photography* 7 Jan. 2/1 The half-tone block..has advantages for certain purposes which it does not share.. with Rotogravure. **1913** *Illustr. London News* 8 Feb. (Suppl.) p. iii/1 The rotogravur method is that more generally called the carbon. **1914** *N.Y. Times* 29 Mar. 11/1 Advance copies of the rotogravure section of *The Times* of next Sunday..awakened enthusiasm. This is the first rotogravure section to be printed upon the new rotogravure presses of *The Times*, and it contains thirty-eight additional famous paintings from the Altman collection. **1919** S. H. MORGAN in *Inland Printer* July 407/1 The proper name for the process and its product is 'rotary photogravure', and it is quite natural that in these busy times there would be an effort to abbreviate these two words. So why not use ..'rota', meaning a wheel or roll, and 'gravure',..and by combining the two call it 'rotagravure' hereafter? **1940** *Chambers's Techn. Dict.* 731/1 Rotagravure. **1942** J. STEINBECK *Moon is Down* ii. 29 Lieutenant Prackle took from his pocket a folded rotogravure page and he unfolded it and held it up and looked at it. It was a picture of a girl. **1957** *Gravure* Mar. 38/3 The first use of rotogravure in a periodical occurred in 1897, when a gravure illustration was included with an article by W. Burger describing the Castle Kreuzenstein, and which appeared in the monthly bulletin of the Imperial Austrian Museum of Art and Industry. **1972** *Physics Bull.* Sept. 532/2 For high quality colour work with long runs (one million or more) rotogravure printing is universally used.

2. A sheet or other object, or a section of a newspaper or magazine, that has been printed by this process.

1914 *N.Y. Times* 29 Mar. 11/3 The rotogravures are superior to any group of reproductions I have ever seen issued in this way, except for the occasional photogravure that some publication has put forth. **1943** D. POWELL *Time to be Born* iv. 94, I suppose business experience never can quite make up for your picture in the Sunday rotogravure. **1968** L. J. BRAUN *Cat who turned on & Off* vii. 64 His pleasurable dreams were always in colour; others were in sepia, like old-time rotogravure. **1978** J. UPDIKE *Coup* (1979) v. 197 The American press loved this artful clown; in their rotogravures he looked like a negative print of Santa Claus.

‖**rotolo** ('rɒtələʊ). Forms: 7 **rottala, rotola, rotello,** 8 **rottel(l)o,** 8–9 **rotolo,** 9 **rottolo**; also *pl.* 7 **rottollies,** 8–9 **rotoli,** 9 **rottolis.** [a. It. *rotolo* (pl. *rotoli*), ad. Arab. *raṭl.*] = ROTL.

1625 PURCHAS *Pilgrims* I. IV. 347 The weight..is two Rottalas, a Rottala is a pound of their weight. *Ibid.* II. VII. 1188 Three hundred and sixtie Rottollies of Moha. *Ibid.* IX. 1644 Eight and twentie Rotellos of this place. **1698** FRYER *Acc. E. India & P.* 207, 1 Rotola is 16 Ounc. or 1 *l.* Averd. **1727** W. MATHER *Yng. Man's Comp.* 399 In Aleppo, some [commodities] are weighed by the Rotolo of 680 Drachms; some by that of 700, and others by that of 720 Drachms. **1765** *Ann. Reg.* I. 75 At Brundisi, a hundred rotoli (a weight of about 33 ounces English) of Roman silver denarii were lately discovered. **1853** W. B. BARKER *Lares & Penates* 75 From a rotolo of coffee, or a few rotolos of rice, the whole town became at length compelled to furnish a stated contribution. **1867** BAKER *Nile Trib.* vi. 116 [He] has always consumed daily throughout his life two rottolis (pounds) of melted butter.

rotombe, variant of ROTUMBE *Obs.*

rotometer (rəʊ'tɒmɪtə(r), 'rəʊtəʊmiːtə(r)). Also **rota-.** [f. ROTO- + -METER.] A hand-held measuring device incorporating a small wheel whose revolutions are registered in terms of distance travelled, e.g. on a map or plan.

1901 F. W. TAYLOR *Art of Cutting Metals* (ed. 3) 91 An instrument called a 'rotameter', which we have found the best appliance for practical use in measuring the cutting speed. *Ibid.*, The small wheel..which projects beyond the rim of the rotameter is firmly pressed directly against the surface of the rotating forging. **1913** T. W. CROFT *Amer. Electricians' Handbk.* 134 The rotometer (Fig. 141), is a convenient tool for scaling distances. The little wheel is run over the course of the circuit. The pointer indicates feet direct for drawings of certain scales. **1949** R. ASHLEY *Electr. Estimating* i. 14/1 The map measure, commonly known in the profession as the 'rotometer', is considered by most electrical estimators engaged in large construction work as the most valuable of tools. **1957** G. E. HUTCHINSON *Treat. Limnol.* I. ii. 166 The shore line may be measured on the map by means of a rotometer. **1971** W. N. ALERICH *Electr. Construction Wiring* xvii. 456/2 The measuring can be done with the aid of a rotameter or an architect's scale.

roton ('rəʊtɒn). *Physics.* [f. ROT(ATION + -ON[1].] A quantum or quasiparticle associated with vortical motion in a liquid, esp. in liquid helium.

1941 L. LANDAU in *Jrnl. Physics U.S.S.R.* V. 75/2 An 'elementary excitation' of the vortex spectrum might be called a 'roton'. [*Note*] This name was suggested by I. E. Tamm. **1947** *Physical Rev.* LXXII. 852/1 In Landau's theory, the excited atoms of the Bose-Einstein theory are replaced by 'rotons'. **1968** *New Scientist* 25 July 198/3 The evaporation of helium atoms due to the decay of 'rotons', the elementary rotational excitations of liquid helium. **1973** *Nature* 9 Nov. 66/1 A new type of elementary excitation, christened the ^{3}He roton, may exist in liquid ^{3}He–^{4}He mixtures. **1977** *New Scientist* 3 Mar. 507/1 The physical nature of the roton still remains a mystery some thirty years after their existence was first postulated by Landau, although they have been detected in numerous experiments.

‖**ro'tonda.** Now *rare.* [It., fem. of *rotondo* round. Hence also F. *rotonde.*]

1. *spec.* The Pantheon. Cf. ROTUNDA 1 b.

1670 LASSELS *Voy. Ital.* II. 235 From hence I went to the Rotonda otherwise called anciently, the Pantheon. *a* **1747** HOLDSWORTH *Remarks Virgil* (1748) 218 The doors to the Rotonda at Rome. **1756–7** tr. *Keysler's Trav.* (1760) II. 464 Behind the Pantheon or Rotonda are to be seen the ruins of those [baths] of Marcus Agrippa.

2. A round or circular object.

1711 ADDISON *Spect.* No. 127 ¶9 When I survey this new-fashioned *Rotonda* [the hoop-petticoat] in all its Parts.

3. = ROTUNDO 3.

1874 LADY HERBERT tr. *Hübner's Ramble* I. iv. (1878) 39 In the rotonda, a species of ante-room generally attached to the bed-carriages.

rotor ('rəʊtə(r)). [Irreg. for ROTATOR.]

1. *Math.* (See quot. 1873.)

1873 CLIFFORD in *Lond. Math. Soc. Proc.* IV. 381, I propose to use the name rotor (short for rotator) to mean a quantity having magnitude, direction, and position, of which the simplest type is a velocity of rotation about a certain axis. **1882** *Nature* XXVI. 218 Such a displacement is the same as a rotation about the polar of the given line, and is hence called by Clifford a Rotor.

2. The rotating part of a dynamo or motor.

1903 *St. James's Gaz.* 7 Feb. 17/2 Both the rotor, and what is usually known as the stator of the motor, are constructed so as to be capable of rotation about a common axis.

3. A rotor arm.

1920 V. W. PAGÉ *Useful Hints for Motorists* iii. 89 The distributor head and rotor are made of bakelite. **1959** *Motor Man.* (ed. 36) viii. 215 Before replacing the rotor, which should also be cleaned with a petrol-damped rag and dried with a soft cloth, apply a few drops of engine oil to lubricate the cam bearing. **1975** tr. *Melchior's Sleeper Agent* III. 212 Someone's been monkeying with the jeep... The rotor! Someone's pinched the distributor rotor.

4. A cylinder mounted vertically on a ship and designed to be rotated on its axis, so that the Magnus effect will provide a forward propulsive force in a cross-wind.

1924 *Public Opinion* 14 Nov. 483/3 Very little electric power is required to work the rotors. **1924** *Glasgow Herald* 17 Nov. 4 The navigational importance of Herr Anton Flettner's 'rotor' as an auxiliary. **1925** *Ibid.* 6 Feb. 9 These towers—technically called rotors—are supported on strong internal masts, about which they are revolved by small electric motors. **1943** [see MAGNUS EFFECT]. **1957** *Encycl. Brit.* XIX. 577/2 The inventor states that it is not intended to drive ships solely by wind rotors, but that they shall serve as an auxiliary power upon steam and motor vessels.

5. A hub with a number of radiating arms that is rotated in an approximately horizontal plane to provide the lift for a helicopter or other rotary-wing aircraft.

1930 *Jrnl. R. Aeronaut. Soc.* XXXIV. 915 The wings of the aeroplane and the rotor of the autogiro. **1945** *Tee Emm* (Air Ministry) V. 56 Note the main rotor, that is the big propeller affair on top... Get rid of any assumption that because the rotor is *above* the aircraft it is also above *you.* **1973** R. LEWIS *Blood Money* viii. 107 The helicopter.. dropped lower towards the surface of the tarn until finally the downthrust of air from the rotors churned the water into a maelstrom.

6. The rotating vessel in a centrifuge.

1939 *Industr. & Engin. Chem.* Sept. 1073 The rotor or bowl must be removed for cleaning when it becomes filled with bowl cake. **1958** M. G. LARIAN *Fund. Chem. Engin. Operations* (1959) xiv. 566 The centrifuge is shown in Fig. 24. It consists of a tubular bowl rotor enclosed in a stationary casing. **1978** *Nature* 14 Sept. 147/1 Brain homogenates..are centrifuged at 100,000*g* for 18h in a Beckman 42.1 rotor.

7. A part of an encoding or decoding machine, rotation of which changes numerous electrical circuits and thereby the code.

1946 *U.S. Patent 2,402,182* 3 The selected ratchet and pawl mechanism..then rotates the rotors one step while the contacts carried by the rotors are disengaged. **1973** H. GRUPPE *Truxton Cipher* xviii. 189 That moment in '42 when he had handed over the Truxton Cipher rotors to the Russians. **1979** *Books & Bookmen* Jan. 31/1 The object was to enable the recipient of the message to set the rotors of his own machine for deciphering that particular message.

8. A large eddy in which the air circulates about a horizontal axis. [a. G. *rotor*, introduced in this sense by J. Küttner 1938, in *Beiträge zur Physik der freien Atmosphäre* XXV. 108.]

1949 *Q. Jrnl. R. Meteorol. Soc.* LXXV. 54 The crests of waves may be capped by clouds under suitable conditions of humidity. Beautiful examples are the Helm Bars.., and the 'Rotors' associated with the Moazagotl. **1955** *Tellus* VII. 367 The stationary lee-waves produced by a big mountain often break up into turbulent whirls or 'rotors' in the lower layers of the air flow. **1960** *Aeroplane* XCVIII. 390/3 They moved downwind into the downdraught and at 2,500 ft. dropped into the rotor and its turbulence, which became especially violent from 1,500 ft. down to the ground. **1979** *Courier-Mail* (Brisbane) 15 June 6/10 It was believed that wind conditions against the cliff face caused what was known in the sport as a 'rotor'. 'The wind spins across from the hill face and grabs you,' he said.

9. *attrib.* and *Comb.*, as **rotor arm**, the part of the distributor of an internal-combustion engine which, by its rotation, successively makes and breaks electrical contacts so that each sparking plug fires in turn; **rotor blade**, each of the radiating arms of the rotor of a helicopter or other rotary-wing aircraft; **rotor cloud**, a turbulent cloud in a rotor (sense 8) in the lee of a mountain; **rotor disc**, (*a*) the space swept out by rotor blades as they rotate; (*b*) the rotor head; **rotor head, hub**, the structure at the upper end of a shaft of a rotorcraft, to which the rotor blades are attached; **rotor ship**, a ship whose motive power is derived from cylindrical rotors. See also ROTORCRAFT.

1919 FRASER & JONES *Motor Vehicles* xviii. 195 The rotor arms are placed at right angles to each other and project from both sides of the shaft. **1964** [see DISTRIBUTOR 2 a (ii)]. **1968** *Listener* 25 July 109/1, I stopped the jeep in the middle of the crowd while Kim automatically removed the rotor arm and padlocked the gears. **1931** DE LA CIERVA & ROSE *Wings of Tomorrow* viii. 118 This was the only Autogiro that ever broke a rotor blade in flight. **1947** *Times* 16 Apr. 2/1 An airscrew which can be extended to the dimensions of a rotor blade such as that used in helicopters has long been sought. **1973** R. LEWIS *Blood Money* viii. 106 Crow heard the chatter of rotor-blades and saw the helicopter coming in. **1959** *Gloss. Meteorol.* (Amer. Meteorol. Soc.) 487 *Rotor cloud*, a turbulent, altocumulus-type cloud formation found in the lee of some large mountain barriers. **1967** R. W. FAIRBRIDGE *Encycl. Atmospheric Sci.* 609/1 The moazagotl condition is set up by a standing wave established when the warm chinook or foehn-type air flows down the lee slope of the mountain range, initiating a series of undulations with eddies, the rising air of which develop cumuloform rotor clouds. **1974** T. BEER *Atmospheric Waves* iv. 182 The base of the rotor cloud is near the level of the crest while the top may be several thousand feet higher. **1944** H. F. GREGORY *Anything Horse can Do* xiv. 145 The direct-control Autogiro is controlled by tilting the rotor disk in the desired direction. Actually it is accomplished by rocking the hub. **1976** B. JACKSON *Flameout* (1977) iv. 54 Klein bent to stare at the forward stages of the compressor rotor. All the wing-like blades were rooted in the rotor disk. **1931** DE LA CIERVA & ROSE *Wings of Tomorrow* vi. 93, I propose to overcome the inequality of lift by building into the rotor head a device for changing the angle of incidence of the blades as they made their circle. **1958** LAMBERMONT & PIRIE *Helicopters & Autogyros of World* 32 The rotor head..was controlled by feathering and impressed flapping. **1931** DE LA CIERVA & ROSE *Wings of Tomorrow* viii. 118 The rotor hub is almost entirely a machine shop product. **1949** *Electronic Engin.* XXI. 292/2 The testing tower..was erected to provide a means of testing rotor hubs and blades independently of helicopter aircraft. **1924** *Glasgow Herald* 17 Nov. 4 (*heading*) The rotor ship. *Ibid.* 12 Dec. 8 The Rotor ship is apparently a thing devoid of beauty. It reminds one of a match-box with two cigarettes placed vertically on top. **1926** *Ibid.* 27 Apr. 11 The big new rotorship Barbara will be launched at Bremen tomorrow. Her tonnage is 3000, and she has three rotors, each measuring nearly 100ft. in height and 13ft. in circumference. **1949** O. G. SUTTON *Sci. of Flight* iv. 84 The idea of a rotor-ship does not seem to have appealed to ship-builders in general and it is now regarded as a scientific curiosity and no more. **1957** *Encycl. Brit.* XIX. 578/1 An ordinary sailing vessel requires to take down all her canvas in a hurricane, but the rotor ship could continue sailing, with more stability for manoeuvring.

rotorcraft ('rəʊtəkrɑːft). [f. ROTOR + CRAFT *sb.*] A rotary-wing aircraft.

1940 *Jrnl. Aeronaut. Sci.* VII. 444/1 Theoretical studies of rotorcraft vibration...were initiated about two years ago by the Kellett Autogiro Corporation. **1955** LIPTROT & WOODS *Rotorcraft* ii. 12 Rotorcraft, which is the generic name for rotary wing aircraft, may be classified under six categories. .. Helicopter... Gyroplane... Cyclogyro... Gyrodyne... Compound helicopter... Convertible aircraft. **1969** *New Scientist* 28 Aug. 421/1 At least 60 per cent of the loaded weight of a tactical monoplane is normally disposable... The corresponding figure for rotorcraft rarely exceeds 45. **1979** *Daily Tel.* 14 Sept. 10/5 Britain's only helicopter museum, the British Rotorcraft Museum at Weston-super-Mare, Avon, said yesterday that it had been forced to close because the local airfield lease has run out.

Rotoscythe ('rəʊtəʊsaɪð). Also **roto-scythe, rotoscythe.** [f. ROTO- + SCYTHE *sb.*] The proprietary name of a machine with rotating blades, designed to cut rough grass or vegetation.

1948 *Times* 20 Mar. 6/7 The roto-scythe..has come to take the place of the brushing-hook for the removal of grass and herbage too tall for the mowing machine. **1949** *Trade Marks Jrnl.* 19 Jan. 48 *Rotoscythe*... Lawn Mowers. Power Specialities Limited,..Slough, Buckinghamshire; manufacturers. **1955** *Radio Times* 22 Apr. 46/1 Rotoscythe cuts long or short, neater-quicker. **1966** 'J. BERRISFORD' *Wild Garden* i. 16 Rough grass..must be cut (by scythe or rotoscythe).

Rototiller ('rəʊtəʊtɪlə(r)). Chiefly *N. Amer.* Also **rototiller, roto-tiller.** [f. ROTO- + TILLER *sb.*[1]] A machine with rotating blades or prongs designed to break up or till soil (registered in the U.S. as a proprietary name). Hence **'rototilling**, the preparation of soil with a Rototiller.

1923 *Sci. Amer.* Dec. 411/1 From England comes the description of one which differs radically from the American variety in that the soil is worked by a revolving member called a miller... The rototiller is driven by a two-cycle, 8 to 10 horse-power engine. **1932** *Official Gaz.* (U.S. Patent Office) 25 Oct. 949/1 *Rototiller* for farm machine for soil cultivation. Claims use since Feb. 9, 1929. **1938** C. CULPIN *Farm Machinery* vii. 106 One of the most successful types of rotary cultivator is the small 'Rototiller' type, of which the best-known example is the Simar Rototiller... The loose tilth produced by the Rototiller is very suitable for much horticultural work. **1959** *Times* 13 Mar. 6/6 Another man bid £5 for a roto-tiller. **1969** *Daily Colonist* (Victoria, B.C.) 15 July 22/5 In cultivated ground, hoeing or rototilling doesn't help much—in fact, it can spread the pest. **1974** *Globe & Mail* (Toronto) 5 Mar. 29/5 A friend of mine who deals in roto-tillers tells me he has more orders and enquiries this year than he's ever had. **1976** *Casper* (Wyoming) *Star-Tribune* 29 June 17/7 (Advt.) Custom plowing and roto-tilling, dozer work. **1978** *Sunday Star* (Toronto) 21 May A3/6 Rental agencies reported that most..of their garden tools, and especially roto-tillers, were rented for the day.

†**ro'tound**, *a. Obs. rare.* [ad. It. *rotondo* or L. *rotund-us*: see ROTUND *a.*] Round.

1433 LYDG. *S. Edmund* III. 1447 Out off a chapel, that callyd was rotounde They took the martir. *c* **1440** *Stacyons of Rome* 745 At seynt mary Rotounde [*v.r.* þe Rounde] there is a chyrche fayre I-founde. **1619** H. HUTTON *Follie's Anat.* (Percy Soc.) 23 His circled panch, is barrell-like, rotound Like earths vast concaves hollow and profound.

†**rotour.** *Obs. rare.* [a. OF. *roteor, rote(e)ur*, f. *rote* ROTE *sb.*[1]] A player on the rote.

In last quot. perhaps an error for *riotour*.

1303 R. BRUNNE *Handl. Synne* 1042 Ʒyf þou euer with iogeloure, with hasadoure, or with rotoure, Hauntyst tauerne. **1394-5** *Durh. Acc. Rolls* (Surtees) 599 Uni Rotour de Scocia, 6*s.* 8*d.* *c* **1430** LYDG. *Min. Poems* (Percy Soc.) 35 He is a person, she thynkethe, of fair figure,—A yong rotour, redy to hir pleasier.

rotour: see ROUTER *sb.*[1]

Rotovator, var. ROTAVATOR.

†**rotship.** *Obs. rare.* [f. ROT *a.*] Rottenness.

c **1400** *Lanfranc's Cirurg.* 86 If..þei han greet putride & rotschipe, þanne þou nedist a ful drie medicyn. *Ibid.*, If þat he haue a litil putrede or rotschipe.

‖**rotta** ('rɒtə). *Hist.* Also **rota.** [med.Lat.: see ROTE *sb.*[1]] + ROTE *sb.*[1]

1883 GROVE *Dict. Mus.* III. 179/1 *Rota*, or *Rotta*.., not, as might be supposed from its name, a species of vielle or hurdy-gurdy, but a species of psaltery or dulcimer, or primitive zither, employed in the middle ages in church music. It was played with the hand, guitar-fashion, and had seven strings mounted in a solid wooden frame. **1942** E. BLOM *Music in England* i. 12 A miniature in an eighth-century codex in the British Museum..shows King David playing on a rotta (a generic link between the lyre and the harp). **1964** S. MARCUSE *Musical Instruments* (1966) 102/2 In the 8th c., Cuthbert had mentioned the cithara that 'we' call rotta. **1977** *Early Music* July 300/1 When the musicians and minstrels adopted it [*sc.* the ancient psaltery] for their own purposes,..they made its shape and form suitable to their convenience, applying additional strings and calling it by the vernacular name *rotta*.

rottack: see ROTTOCK.

rottan ('rɒt(ə)n). Now *Sc.* and *dial.* Also 6, 8-9 **rotten**, 6 **rotton.** [var. of RATTON. For the difference in vowel cf. Fris. *rôt, roat, rotte-*, MDu. and MLG. *rotte* (Du. *rot*), MSw., Norw., and Icel. *rotta* (Sw. *råtta*, Da. *rotte*).] A rat.

?*a* **1500** *Chester Pl.* III. 179 Here cattis maken it full crowse, here a rotten, here a mowse. **1575** *Gamm. Gurton* III. iii, Thou skald, thou bald, thou rotten, thou glutton! I will no longer chide thee. **1673** WEDDERBURN *Voc.* 15 (Jam.), *Glis*, a rotten. **1756** MRS. CALDERWOOD *Jrnl.* (1884) 53 Even the poor dancer creept out of bed like a poisoned rottan. **1815** SCOTT *Guy M.* xxii, I had them a' regularly entered, first wi' rottens—then wi' stots or weasels. **1886** BRIERLEY *Cast upon World* 162 They looken as hungry as two rottans. **1894** LATTO *Tam. Bodkin* vii, The squeekin' o' mice an' rottans.

b. *attrib.*, as *rottan-fall* (rat-trap), *-hole*.

1673 WEDDERBURN *Voc.* 13 (Jam.), *Decipula*, a rotten fall. **1839** MOIR *Mansie Wauch* (ed. 2) xxvii, Div ye keep rotten-fa's aboot your premises? **1865** G. MACDONALD *A. Forbes* ii, I hae been seekin' ye..i' the verra rottan-holes.

†**rotte**, obs. form of RAT. (Cf. prec.)

14.. *Voc.* in Wr.-Wülcker 624 *Rato*, rotte.

rotte, obs. form of ROT, RUT; see also ROTL.

rotted ('rɒtɪd), *ppl. a.* Also 3 **roted**, 4-5 **rotid, -yd(e**, 5 **rooted, -yd.** [f. ROT *v.* + -ED[1].]

1. That has undergone, or passed into a state of, decay or putrefaction.

a **1225** *Ancr. R.* 84 Yet wolde he teteren & pileken, mid his bile, roted stinkinde fleshs. **1340** *Ayenb.* 205 A roted eppel amang þe holen makeþ rotie þe yzounde. **1398** TREVISA *Barth. De P.R.* VII. xxxvi. (Bodl. MS.), Febris putrida, roted feuer, haþ þat name of roted humoures of the whiche it is ibredde. *c* **1400** *Lanfranc's Cirurg.* 86 Þouȝ þat þou clense þe rotid boon wiþ schauynge. **1681** CHETHAM *Angler's Vade-m.* iv. §14 (1689) 45 The body of a rotted alder. **1721** BRADLEY *Philos. Acc. Wks. Nat.* 130 These have always their Habitation in shady moist Places, chiefly in rotted Wood. **1812** SIR J. SINCLAIR *Syst. Husb. Scot.* I. 282 The manure.. was rotted dung, turned over and prepared for the purpose. **1855** CARLYLE in *E. FitzGerald's Lett.* (1889) I. 235 All the horrors of a half rotted ship. **1880** C. R. MARKHAM *Peruv. Bark* 78 The dead and rotted roots of the rasamala-trees were allowed to remain.

2. *spec.* Of sheep: Affected by the rot.

1837 YOUATT *Sheep* xi. 450 The liver of a rotted sheep. **1867** BRANDE & COX *Dict. Sci.*, etc. s.v. *Rot*, This difference ..occasions some rotted sheep to thrive well..to a certain stage, when they suddenly fall off.

Hence †**'rottedness**, rottenness. *Obs.*

1398 TREVISA *Barth. De P.R.* XIII. xxvi. (Bodl. MS.), þey haue reste in here rotednes and in filþe. *Ibid.*, Slyme..of rotednes þat is vpon þe water. **1688** HOLME *Armoury* III. 433/2 To scrape away the rottedness of the Cranium.

rottel, obs. form of ROTTLE.

rotten ('rɒt(ə)n), *a.* Forms: 3 **rotin**, 4-6 **roten**, 4-5 **rotun**, 5 **rotyn**, 5-6 **roton**, 6 **rotne**; 4, 6 **rottyn**, 6 **rottin(e, rotton**; 5- **rotten.** [a. ON. *rotinn* (Icel. *rotinn*, Fær. *rotin*, Norw. *roten*; MSw. *rotin, rutin*, Sw. *rutten*, Da. *raaden*, †*rodden*), which has the form of a strong pa. pple. belonging to the ablaut-series *reut-, raut-, rut-*: cf. ROT *v.* and the forms cited under RET *v.*[2]]

I. 1. Of animal matter: In a state of decomposition or putrefaction; decomposed, putrid.

a **1225** *Ancr. R.* 84 Roted [*T.* rotin] stinkinde fleshs. **13..** *Cursor M.* 22907 (Gött), Dede þar gun his carion li, And þat was rotin al to noght. *c* **1330** *Arth. & Merl.* 73 (Kölbing), When ich am dede & roten in clay. **1388** WYCLIF *Numb.* v. 21 The Lord make thin hipe to wexe rotun, and thi wombe swelle, and be brokun. *c* **1450** *Myrr. our Ladye* 320 The bodyes of al men and women.., thoughe they be roten or brente. *c* **1489** CAXTON *Sonnes of Aymon* xix. 439, I am sory that ye be not deed rotyn wythin the pryson. **1533** GAU *Richt Vay* 81 The same body quhilk vesz grawit & rottine. **1588** SHAKS. *L.L.L.* v. ii. 666 The sweet War-man is dead and rotten. **1651** HOBBES *Leviath.* IV. xliv. 348 To give life again to a dead man, and renew his inanimate and rotten Carkasse. **1692** *Christ Exalted* 79 Which I am sure have a worse Savour than the rottenest Egg in the Town. **1701** STANHOPE *St. Bernard's Medit. St. Augustine*, etc. VIII. iii. 365 Its boasted Charms shall sink into a rotten Carcass. **1893** W. R. GOWERS *Man. Dis. Nerv. Syst.* (ed. 2) II. 437 The sclerotic after death was rotten and discoloured.

2. a. Of vegetable or other substances: In a state of thorough decay.

a **1340** HAMPOLE *Psalter* i. 3 Auerous men..þat gifes froit, bot when it is rotyn & out of tyme. *c* **1374** CHAUCER *Anel. & Arc.* 314 Sheo that hem trustithe shall hem fynde als faste As in a tempeste is þe Roton maste. *c* **1400** MAUNDEV. (Roxb.) vii. 25 þai [*sc.* apples] will be roten within viii. dayes. **1495** *Naval Acc. Hen. VII* (1896) 259 Sayles olde & Rotyn, j;.. Cokke Botes to the seid ship olde & Rotyn, j. **1555** EDEN *Decades* (Arb.) 111 Those shyppes beinge nowe rotten for age. **1583** HOLLYBAND *Campo di Fior* 131, I have but a few nuttes, and those are broken and rotten. **1621** BURTON *Anat. Mel.* II. iii. v. (1651) 341 They start at the name of death, as a horse at a rotten post. **1697** DRYDEN *Virg. Georg.* IV. 62 In the rotten Trunks of hollow Trees. **1760** BROWN *Compl. Turner* II. 69 Rotten sawdust, or any other rotten wood. **1790** BURKE *Fr. Rev.* 323 The true pedigree of property, and not rotten parchments and silly substitutions. **1813** WELLINGTON in Gurw. *Desp.* (1838) X. 378 There is one pontoon quite rotten. **1870** F. R. WILSON *Ch. Lindisf.* 99 The interior was..full of rotten sittings of all sorts and sizes.

fig. *c* **1386** CHAUCER *Prol. Reeve's T.* 21 We olde men.. Til we be roten, kan we nat be rype. **1546-** [see RIPE *a.* 1 c]. **1579** SPENSER *Sheph. Cal.* Dec. 118, I..follies nowe have gathered as too ripe, And cast hem out as rotten and unsoote. **1600** SHAKS. *A.Y.L.* III. ii. 126 You'l be rotten ere you bee halfe ripe.

b. In fig. contexts.

1526 *Pilgr. Perf.* (W. de W. 1531) 54 We that be in religyon sholde..purge the rotten bowes by confessyon. **1567** *Gude & Godlie B.* (S.T.S.) 186 O cankerit carionnis, and o ȝe rottin stakis. **1602** MARSTON *Ant. & Mel.* IV. Wks. 1856 I. 46 O rotten props of the craz'd multitude. **1654** WHITLOCK *Zootomia* 36 What rotten Tenements are our Bodies? **1781** COWPER *Progr. Err.* 288 Sin's rotten trunk, concealing its defects.

c. *absol.* The decayed part.

1629 CHAPMAN *Juv.* Poems (Globe) 259 To pick out, like the rotten out of apples.., a poor instance or two. **1875** TENNYSON *Q. Mary* II. ii, My Lord, cut out the rotten from your apple.

3. Of air, water, etc.: Putrid, corrupted, tainted, foul. †***rotten fever***, putrid or septic fever.

c **1330** R. BRUNNE *Chron. Wace* (Rolls) 16435 A manqualm cam..þorow roten eyr, þorow wykkede wyndes. *c* **1440** *Gesta Rom.* lviii. 374 (Add. MS.), Be-fore hem all he caste oute the rotyn watyr. **1565** COOPER *Thesaurus, Putor*, a rotten sauour. **1567** *Gude & Godlie B.* (S.T.S.) 185 Stinkand pulis of euerie rottin synk. **1600** E. BLOUNT tr. *Conestaggio* 238 At which time Queen Anne his wife fell sicke of a rotten feuer. **1606** SHAKS. *Tr. & Cr.* v. i. 21 The rotten diseases of the South. **1671** SALMON *Syn. Med.* III. lxxxv. 737 The putrid or rotten Feaver. **1802** *Med. Jrnl.* VIII. 358 The room was on the ground floor, seemed very damp, and had a rotten smell.

4. a. Of ground, soil, etc.: Extremely soft, yielding, or friable by reason of decay.

c **1440** *Pallad. on Husb.* I. 64 A roten swerd and welnygh blak,..And tough to glewe ayeyn [etc.]. **1483** CAXTON *G. de la Tour* D viij b, So they tooke their waye thorough the medowe, where were old cloddes all roten. **1565** COOPER *Thesaurus, Cariosa terra*, rotten earth quickly fallen to duste. **1607** J. NORDEN *Surv. Dial.* III. 113 They are taken in bogges, and such rotten grounds as cattle cannot feed upon. **1697** DRYDEN *Virg. Georg.* I. 304 Sow Beans and Clover in a rotten Soil. **1806** PIKE *Sources Mississ.* (1810) 87 The ice [was] very dangerous, being rotten. **1860** TYNDALL *Glac.* I. viii. 60 Scattering with my axe..the rotten ice of the sharper crests. **1892** P. H. EMERSON *Son of Fens* 118 That's rotten (boggy) that side, aint it?

b. Of rocks: Partly decomposed.

1805 FORSYTH *Beauties Scot.* III. 112 Besides the hard sort, much is to be found of what is commonly called rotten whin. **1839** MURCHISON *Silur. Syst.* I. xxvii. 341 The subsoil ..consists of rotten shale with scarcely the vestige of a solid bed of stone. **1852** JOHNSTON *Elem. Chem. & Geol.* viii. 119 The decayed traps, under the local names of Rotten rock, Marl, etc. **1868** *Rep. U.S. Comm. Agric.* (1869) 69 The sand marls of the rotten limestone group of this State.

c. orig. *N. Amer.* Of ice: weak; melting, disintegrating. (Cf. ROT *v.* 1 e.)

c **1665** P. E. RADISSON *Voyages* (1885) 133 We cutt the ice wth hattchetts & we found places where [it] was rotten, so we hazarded ourselves often to sinke downe to our necks. **1746** T. WALKER *Diary* 20 Mar. (1889) 9 Went over ye River upon ye ice. It grew very rotten. **1795** E. P. SIMCOE *Diary* 7 Feb. (1911) 266 At Jacques Cartier the ice was so rotten I was obliged to go a league higher to cross the river with safety. **1849** J. E. ALEXANDER *L'Acadie* II. ii. 31 Thence we proceeded to Montreal, which we reached after four days and three nights of most unpleasant travel, and even dangerous, on account of exposure and the rotten ice. **1916** N. DUNCAN *Billy Topsail* xvi. 120 [The ice] had yielded somewhat—it must have gone rotten—in the weather of that day. **1935** *Monthly Weather Rev.* (Washington) LXII. 133/1 The boatman, fisherman, and lots of others..swear that at this season [*sc.* spring] surface ice becomes rotten, or honeycombed, and sinks. **1966** T. ARMSTRONG et al. *Illustr. Gloss. Snow & Ice* Fig. 7 (*caption*) Rotten ice. The puddles on the surface have mostly joined together and in places have melted right through the ice.

5. a. Of sheep: Affected with the rot.

c **1460** *Towneley Myst.* xii. 221 Both befe, and moton Of an ewe that was roton. **1523** FITZHERB. *Husb.* §55 To knowe a rotten shepe. *Ibid.*, Take the shepe,..and yf the skynne..be pale-coloured, and watrye, thanne is he rotten. **1555** EDEN *Decades* (Arb.) 80 They dyed yet dayly as it were rotton sheepe. **1697** DAMPIER *Voy.* (1729) I. 50 Many.., for want of being accustomed to such Hardships, died like rotten Sheep. **1704** *Dict. Rust.* s.v. *Sheep*, If they are rotten, the Eyes are pale and dark. **1810** PARKINSON *Live Stock* I. 422 The nineteen [sheep] all died rotten. **1844** C. W. JOHNSON in H. Stephens *Bk. Farm* II. 45 Mr. Rusher..purchased, for a mere trifle, 20 sheep, decidedly rotten.

transf. **1704** *Dict. Rust.* s.v. *Rot*, If he [the horse] be rotten, his Liver and Lights are so putrified, that they are not to be recovered.

b. Characterized by the occurrence or prevalence of sheep-rot.

1799 *Agric. Surv. Lincs.* 329 In rotten years, the sheep that feed on the salt marsh..sell very high. **1810** PARKINSON *Live Stock* I. 425 The farm..was deemed so rotten, that the oldest inhabitants advised my father..not to keep sheep.

6. Damp, wet, rainy.

1599 B. JONSON *Ev. Man out of Hum.* I. iii, Expectation Of rotten weather, and vnseason'd howers. **1828** COL. HAWKER *Diary* (1893) I. 347 A rotten pinching white frost. **1844** H. STEPHENS *Bk. Farm* I. 300 A raw rotten fog after frost. **1881** *Folk-Lore Rec.* IV. 131 A Saturday's rainbow is sure to be followed by a week of rotten (rainy) weather.

II. 7. a. Morally, socially, or politically corrupt.

c **1380** WYCLIF *Sel. Wks.* I. 7 For þei ben divydid fro þe comoun maner of lyvynge bi hir rotun rytys. *c* **1384** CHAUCER *H. Fame* III. 1778 Ye maisty Swyne, ye ydel wrechhes, Ful of roten slowe techches. *a* **1548** HALL *Chron., Hen. VII* (1809) 429 So perdurable..that they can never be clerely extirpate..out of their rotten hartes. **1555** in Strype *Eccl. Mem.* (1824) III. App. xl. 111 And root up the rotten race of the ungodly. **1602** SHAKS. *Ham.* I. iv. 90 Something is rotten in the State of Denmarke. **1661** J. DAVIES *Civil Wars* 372 Purging his army by casting off such officers as he conceived rotten. **1718** *Free-thinker* No. 14. 95 He is Rotten at the Core, and his Soul is dishonest. **1797** GODWIN *Enquirer* I. xii. 103 This rotten morality will not abide.. examination. **1851** GALLENGA *Italy* 61 A scheme of nationality having for its head a rotten papacy. **1890** 'R. BOLDREWOOD' *Col. Reformer* (1891) 148 The whole rotten sham which calls itself a prosperous colony.

†**b.** Of language: Morally offensive; obscene.

c **1620** MORYSON *Itin.* IV. (1903) 417 Blasphemous oathes and rotten talke are among their nationall vices. **1641** HINDE *J. Bruen* li. 165 To be pure in lips and tongue, never suffering any rotten speech to fall from him.

c. ***rotten borough***: see BOROUGH 3 c.

8. a. Weak, unsound.

1607 SHAKS. *Cor.* I. x. 23 Nor sleepe, nor sanctuary,.. shall lift vp Their rotten Priuiledge, and Custome 'gainst My hate to Martius. **1658** OSBORN *K. Jas.* Wks. (1673) 501 Upon a hope (though a rotten one) of a future preferment. **1737** WHISTON *Josephus, Hist.* I. xxvi. §2 This fellow perceived the rotten parts of the family, and what quarrels the brothers had.

b. *slang.* (*a*) In a very poor state, of a very bad quality, quite worthless; 'beastly'; also as a mere expletive (quot. 1892) and in weakened sense in

rotten luck, shame, etc. (*b*) quasi-*adv.* as intensifying word.

1880 'Mark Twain' *Tramp Abroad* xxiii. 226 I'm most rotten certain 'bout that. 1881 Stevenson *Let.* 5 Dec., You may imagine how rotten I have been feeling, and feel now. 1892 Henley & Stevenson *Deacon Brodie* iv. i, Just like you. Forgot the rotten centrebit. 1895 *Westm. Gaz.* 20 April 7/2 Outside the competition they were, comparatively speaking, a rotten team. 1911 G. B. Shaw *Blanco Posnet* 405 You that always talk as if He never did anything without asking your rotten leave first. 1914 —— *Fanny's First Play* i. 177, I was copped in the Dock Road myself: rotten luck, wasn't it? 1922 Joyce *Ulysses* 748 It was rotten cold too that winter. 1930 [see *electric blanket* s.v. electric *a.* 2b]. 1943 [see due *sb.* 4c]. 1952 E. O'Neill *Moon for Misbegotten* ii. 107 You rotten bastard! 1959 I. & P. Opie *Lore & Lang. Schoolch.* ix. 161 Juvenile repugnance continues to be expressed by the old standbys .. rotten, rotten shame, rotten swiz. 1964 *Daily Mail* 14 Dec. 1/3 The other girls sent me up rotten when they heard about my date. 1976 M. Machlin *Pipeline* xli. 446, I would not say that they are your friendliest people. And sometimes they are downright rotten. 1977 *Listener* 12 May 626/2 Mr Wood is not only brave enough to send himself up rotten, but also to make a hilarious series out of the whole literary game. 1980 *Jewish Chron.* 26 Dec. (Lit. Suppl.) p. vii/2, I was the only girl among 50 reporters and of course I was spoilt rotten.

c. *Printing.* (See quot.)

1888 Jacobi *Printers' Vocab.* 115 *Rotten*, term applied to unsound impression in printing.

d. ***to knock rotten***, to kill or stun. *Austral. slang.*

1919 W. H. Downing *Digger Dial.* 31 *Knocked rotten*, killed or stunned. 1941 *Coast to Coast* 179 'He pulled it down on top of him,' continued Jo... 'It knocked him rotten.' 1945 Baker *Austral. Lang.* vi. 120 The development of an extensive vocabulary of fighting terms ... *knock rotten*.

e. *Austral. slang.* Drunk. Also in phr. ***to get rotten***.

1941 Baker *Dict. Austral. Slang* 61 *Rotten, to get*, to become exceedingly drunk. 1953 T. A. G. Hungerford *Riverslake* 135 Monday to-morrow—blasted work again. God, could I get rotten! 1971 J. Famechon *Fammo* 145 A reporter from one of the Sydney papers—he was the last to leave, rotten.

†**9.** *fig.* More than ripe. *Obs. rare.*

1640 Shirley *Constant Maid* iii. ii, My part is rotten in my head, doubt not. —— *Humorous Courtier* iii. i, Pray let me have All these directions in manuscript. I'll not see her Till they be rotten in my head.

10. *attrib.* and *Comb.*

a. Parasynthetic, as ***rotten-boned, -chested, -fleshed, -fustianed, -livered, -planked, -throated, -timbered*** adjs. Also rotten-hearted.

1912 D. H. Lawrence *Let.* 3 July (1962) I. 134 My cursed, rotten-boned, pappy hearted countrymen, *why* was I sent to *them*. 1927 R. Graves *Poems (1914–26)* 210 As counterbalance in my mind To being rotten-boned and blind. 1969 L. Michaels *Going Places* 63, I ..coughed again, a rasping, rotten-chested hack. 1908 Hardy *Dynasts* III. iv. vi. 417 We kings? Kings of the under-ground country, then, by this time, if we hadn't been too rotten-fleshed to follow the drum. 1853 R. S. Surtees *Sponge's Sp. T.* (1893) 220 All the scowling, rotten-fustianed, baggy-pocketed scamps of the country. 1929 R. Graves *Poems* 20 Lame, rotten-livered, this and that canaille. 1855 Browning *Hugues of Saxe-Gotha* xxix, At the foot of your rotten-planked, rat-riddled stairs. 1598 E. Guilpin *Skial.* (1878) 55 You rotten-throated slaues, Engarlanded with coney-catching knaues. 1818 Keats *Endym.* ii. 18 Many old rotten-timber'd boats there be.

b. With adjs., as ***rotten-dry, -red, -rich, -ripe, -sweet***; also ***rotten-roasted, -woven***.

1596 Nashe *Saffron Walden* Wks. (Grosart) III. 93 By this time imagin him rotten ripe for the Vniuersitie. 1601 Holland *Pliny* I. 365 That they be not brittle, and rather ripe drie, than sere or rotten-dry. 1623 Middleton *More Dissemblers* iv. i, [Ducks] all rotten roasted and stuffed with onions. 1840 Browning *Sordello* ii. 731 Fruits like the fig-tree's, rathe-ripe, rotten-rich. 1861 L. L. Noble *Icebergs* 319 Stumps of all .. colors, from rotten-red and brown down to coal-black. 1868 G. M. Hopkins *Jrnls. & Papers* (1959) 184 In the train I was noticing that strange rotten-woven cloud. 1869 Lowell *Glance behind Curtain* vi, The time is ripe, and rotten-ripe, for change. 1947 M. Morris in B. James *Austral. Short Stories* (1963) 348 She stood over the bin inhaling the queer rotten-sweet smell of the blossoms.

c. ***rotten-egg*** vb., to pelt with rotten eggs.

1884 *B'ham Weekly Post* 25 Oct. 3/7 He was rotten-egged, stoned, and otherwise greaty abused. 1936 W. Greene *Death in Deep South* 69 You are rotten-egged out of a jerkwater town—rotten egged!—by a handful of hoodlums.

'rotten, *v. rare.* [f. prec. Cf. Icel. and Norw. *rotna*, Sw. *ruttna*, Da. *raadne*.] *trans.* To rot.

1611 Speed *Theat. Gt. Brit.* (1614) 2/2 How the Romans found it, held it, and left it, as times ripened and rottened their successe.

†**'rottenhead.** *Obs.*$^{-1}$ [-head.] Rottenness.

1603 Holland *Plutarch's Mor.* 697 It preserveth the flesh for a time from rottenhead and putrifaction.

rotten-hearted, *a.* [f. rotten *a.* + heart *sb.*] Of a thoroughly corrupt nature or character.

c 1386 Chaucer *Parson's T.* ¶689 Þis roten hertid synne of Accidie and of slouthe. 1620 Sanderson *Serm.* I. 136 A rotten-hearted hypocrite humbleth himself outwardly, but repenteth not truly. 1642–4 Vicars *God in Mount* (1844) 6 Perfidious and rotten-hearted Prelates. 1647 Clarendon *Hist. Reb.* iv. §111 The People .. affronted such Lords as came near them, .. calling them Rotten-hearted Lords. 1754 Hume *Hist. Gt. Brit., Jas. I & Chas. I*, I. 315 The cry continually resounded against bishops and rotten-hearted lords. 1788 Burns *Let. to W. Cruikshank* Dec., That puritanic, rotten-hearted, hell-commissioned scoundrel. 1840 Dickens *Barn. Rudge* lxvii, Abject things those rotten-hearted jails had made them.

'rottenish, *a. rare.* [f. rotten *a.* + -ish.] Somewhat rotten or decomposed.

a 1722 Lisle *Husb.* (1752) 24 A layer of wet and rottenish dung. 1831 *Blackw. Mag.* XXX. 507 Most of the said sticks are rather rottenish.

†**'rottenly,** *a. Obs. rare.* [-ly[1].] Rotten.

1435 Misyn *Fire of Love* 81 Als þis rotynly body suffyrs. 1573 Tusser *Husb.* (1878) 44 A rottenly mould is land woorth gould.

'rottenly, *adv.* [-ly[2].] In a rotten (sense 8b) manner; unsoundly, etc.

1847 in Webster. 1905 G. B. Shaw *Let.* 29 Nov (1972) II. 584, I see .. that the papers all say that .. Major Barbara [is] a rottenly undramatic play. 1927 H. Walpole *Jeremy at Crale* iii. 43 'They weren't half pleased at your playing so rottenly.' 'I didn't play rottenly.' 1934 D. L. Sayers *Nine Tailors* ii. 79 I'm afraid—if I go west this time—I'll be leaving you rottenly badly off, old girl.

rottenness ('rɒt(ə)nnɪs). Forms: 4–5 **roten(n)esse**; 5 **rotynes(se**; 6 **rottennes, rottinnes, rottynnesse**, 6–7 **rotten(n)esse**, 7, 9 **rotteness**; 7– **rottenness**. [f. rotten *a.* + -ness.]

1. The state of being rotten or decayed; unsoundness, corruptness; also *concr.*, decayed or putrid matter.

1382 Wyclif *Ecclus.* xix. 3 Rotennesse and wormes shuln eritagen hym. *c* 1400 *Lanfranc's Cirurg.* 82 Þat þe rotynes & þe quytture myȝte þe bettere goon out. 1483 Caxton *Gold. Leg.* 299 b/1 He clensyd hym from al rotynes. 1530 Palsgr. 264/1 Rottynnesse of any thynge, *pourriture*. 1579 W. Wilkinson *Confut. Fam. Love* Ep. Ded. *iij b, Their blossomes are as dust and their fruite as rottennesse. 1631 Widdowes *Nat. Philos.* 37 Distilled water of Oke leaves cureth Fluxes, and rottennesse of the Liver. 1662 Stillingfl. *Orig. Sacræ* i. i. §9 For the sake of the apparent rottenness of the Superstructures to question the soundness of the foundations. 1722 Wollaston *Relig. Nature* ix. 181 The vitious life .. usually ends ill; perhaps in rottenness and rags. 1781 Cowper *Expost.* 90 He found, conceal'd beneath a fair outside, The filth of rottenness. 1813 Shelley *Q. Mab* v. 8 Loading with loathsome rottenness the land. 1884 *Law Times* LXXVII. 384/2 The scaffolding .. gave way, owing to the rottenness of a putlog.

fig. 1548 Udall, etc. *Erasm. Par. Luke* xxiii. 174 b, He alone of all men was not corrupt with any rottennesse of vice or of inordinate desires. 1633 G. Herbert *Temple, Church Porch* iii, Continence hath his joy: weigh both; and so, If rottennesse have more, let Heaven go. 1859 Kingsley *Misc.* II. 45 Mr. Froude shows .. his deep sense of the rottenness of the Church. 1879 Farrar *St. Paul* I. 331 It was Rome at the epoch of her most gorgeous gluttonies and her most gilded rottenness.

†**2.** Ripeness (of an impostume). *Obs.*$^{-1}$

1607 Markham *Horsemanship* vii. 57 If by no meanes it will come to any head or rottennes, then you shall ouer night apply round about the wenne Bole-armonike and vineger mixt together.

3. The condition of sheep affected by rot.

1704 *Dict. Rust.* s.v. *Sheep*, It stirs up the natural Heat of the Sheep, that wasts the moisture, and prevents Rottenness. 1789 T. Wright *Meth. Watering Meadows* (1790) 41 In six weeks afterwards the lambs were killed, and discovered strong symptoms of rottenness. 1867 Brande & Cox *Dict. Sci.*, etc. s.v. *Rot*, The signs of rottenness are sufficiently familiar to persons about sheep.

'Rotten Row. [App. f. rotten *a.* + row *sb.*[1] The name was formerly applied to various streets in different towns, the reason for the application being usually obscure.

In Scotland and the north of England the older form is usually *ratton raw* (see ratton and rottan), and thus app. of different origin.]

1. A road in Hyde Park, extending from Apsley Gate to Kensington Gardens, much used as a fashionable resort for horse or carriage exercise. Now usually called *the Row*.

1799 Sheridan *Pizarro* Prol., Anxious—yet timorous too!—— his steed to show, The hack Bucephalus of Rotten-row. 1850 Thackeray *Pendennis* xxxix [xl], He had cantered out of Rotten Row into the Park. 1860 W. H. Russell *Diary India* I. 102 The ride in Rotten Row, the dreary promenade by the banks of the unsavoury Serpentine. 1882 *Encycl. Brit.* XIV. 824/1 Its Rotten Row alive with equestrians.

2. *Naut.* (See quots.)

1867 Smyth *Sailor's Word-bk.* 580 *Rotten Row*, a line of old ships-in-ordinary in routine order. 1891 H. Patterson *Illustr. Naut. Dict.* 378 *Rotten Row*, a certain place in a navy yard in which worn-out vessels are moored. 1975 *Listener* 30 Oct. 581/3 The majority of our line-of-battle ships had been rotting in reserve [by 1778]... Many of the battleships laid up in 'Rotten Row' were mere stacks of decayed timber.

'rotten-stone. Also **rottenstone.** [f. rotten *a.* + stone *sb.*] A decomposed siliceous limestone chiefly used as a powder for polishing metals.

1677 Plot *Oxfordsh.* 66 Nothing does brighten Copper so well, as a sort of stuff they call rotten stone. 1731 Fielding *Grub St. Op.* ii. iv, Your bills for tutty and rotten-stone, when you used nothing but poor whiting. 1777 G. Forster *Voy. round World* II. 355 A sort of tripoly, which is called rotten-stone by some miners. 1823 W. Phillips *Min.* (ed. 3) 50 Rottenstone .. is dirty grey, or reddish brown, passing into black: it is dull, earthy, soft, meagre to the touch, and fetid when rubbed or scraped. 1862 Ansted *Channel Isl.* i. vi. 127 The interstices of the rock are generally filled with a red friable stone, called rotten-stone. 1876 A. H. Green *Phys. Geol.* ii. §6. 73 When the calcareous part of such rocks has been dissolved out by the action of water a sort of siliceous skeleton is left called Rottenstone.

attrib. 1807 Vancouver *Agric. Devon* (1813) 57 A decomposition of the shaley rotten-stone rock. 1867 J. Hogg *Microsc.* i. iii. 159 The finest tripoli or rotten-stone powder.

Hence **'rotten-stone** *v.*, to polish with rottenstone (*Cent. Dict.*).

rotter ('rɒtə(r)). [f. rot *v.*]

1. A causer of rot. *rare.*

1611 Cotgr., *Pourrisseur*, a rotter; and, particularly, the spotted, .. short-tailed Serpent, *Seps*.

2. *slang.* In vaguely depreciative use: One who is objectionable on moral or other grounds.

1894 G. Moore *Esther Waters* xl, A regular rotter; that man is about as bad as they make 'em. 1899 Kipling *Stalky* 172 What d'you take any notice of these rotters for? 1900 'G. Swift' *Somerley* 155 He liked his mother and sisters .. : all other women he classed as 'rotters'.

3. Something which is rotten with age.

1901 Henley *Hawthorne & Lavender*, An old black rotter of a boat Lay stranded in mid-stream.

'rotting, *vbl. sb.* Also 1, 3 **rotung**, 4 **roting**, 4–5 **rotyng(e, rooting**, 5 *Sc.* **rutting**, etc. [f. rot *v.* + -ing[1].]

1. The process of decaying, decomposing, or putrefying; †also, decomposed or putrid matter. Also ***rotting-down*** (in quot. *fig.*).

c 1000 *Ags. Ps.* (Thorpe) xxix. 8 Hu nyt is þe .. min cwalu, oððe min rotung on byrȝenue? *c* 1230 *Hali Meid.* (Bodl.) 16 As þet swote smirles .. wit þet deade licome þet is þer-wið ismiret, from rotunge. *a* 1300 *Cursor M.* 11505 For roting es na better rede. *Ibid.* 11859 Þe roting Þat him rennes vte, .. Ne mai na liueand man it thole. 1398 Trevisa *Barth. De P.R.* v. xxxviii. (Bodl. MS.), Yuel humours schuld esilich þerein be gadered to corrupcion and rooting. *c* 1420 *Liber Cocorum* (1862) 33 Presse out þo blode for anythyng, Þat is cause for grete rotyng. *c* 1480 Henryson *Test. Cres.* 464 Ȝour roising reid to rutting sall retour. 1526 *Pilgr. Perf.* (W. de W. 1531) 240 b, That vile and stynkyng caryon .. lyeth in putrefaction or rottyng. 1597 A. M. tr. *Guillemeau's Fr. Chirurg.* 10 b/2 Least the ayre cause therine some corruptione and rottinge. 1611 Cotgr., *Pourris*, a suppuration, a rotting. 1726 Leoni *Alberti's Archit.* I. 75/2 The rotting of the weeds raises unwholesome vapours. 1837 W. B. Adams *Carriages* 306 The ordinary process of decomposition in wood by what is technically termed 'rotting'. 1892 W. Pike *Barren Ground N. Canada* 174 The ice now began to show signs of rotting. 1916 Galsworthy *Sheaf* 269 Economically .. such rotting-down of the boys is grievously short-sighted.

2. The process of retting (flax).

1862 *Chambers's Encycl.* IV. 367/1 The operation is called rotting or retting, and requires to be managed with great care. 1875 Knight *Dict. Mech.* 1993/2 *Rotting*, the steeping of flax-stalks to soften the gum and loosen the fiber from the woody portions.

'rotting, *ppl. a.* Also 4 **rotand**, 5 **roting**, 6 **roating.** [f. rot *v.* + -ing[2].]

1. Undergoing decomposition or decay; suffering from rot.

a 1300 *Cursor M.* 28823 Be þis lede þou ta bisning þis heui rotand werlds thing. 1435 Misyn *Fire of Love* 98 Þe rotyng flesch suffyrs not owr mynde in god bisily to be borne. 1638 Cowley *Love's Riddle* 111, Goe, get you gone, looke to your rotting cattell. 1746 Francis tr. *Hor., Sat.* ii. iii. 164 Of straw he made his bed, While moths upon his rotting carpet fed. 1798 Coleridge *Anc. Mar.* iv. v, I looked upon the rotting sea, .. I looked upon the rotting deck. 1817 Shelley *Rev. Islam* x. xxi, Each well Was choked with rotting corpses. 1859 Kingsley *Misc.* II. 40 He sketches for us the rotting and dying Church. 1883 R. W. Dixon *Mano* i. viii. 21 Life's rotting root in sadness lingers late.

2. Productive of rot or decay; causing rottenness.

1563 Pilkington *Burning S. Paul's* B ij, The good shepeherde will not lette hys shepe feede in hurtful and roating pastures. 1715 Leoni *Palladio's Archit.* (1742) I. 2 The rotting moisture we have spoken of. 1818 Shelley *Rosal. & Helen* 928 The prisoners .. in their rotting dungeons lay. 1846 J. Baxter *Libr. Pract. Agric.* (ed. 4) II. 275 An 'excess of fluid', which, in what are called 'rotting meadows', the sheep is obliged to take in with its necessary food. 1897 Mary Kingsley *W. Africa* 547 In a rotting climate like West Africa.

Hence **'rottingness**, rottenness. *rare*$^{-1}$.

1495 *Trevisa's Barth. De P.R.* xix. lxxviii. 908 Rotyngnesse is corrupcion of substauncyall moysture.

†**'rottle,** *sb. Obs.*$^{-1}$ [ad. OF. *ratelle*, dim. of *rate*: see rate *sb.*[4]] The spleen.

c 1450 Burgh *Secrees* 1744 Ache in the Rottle And ek in the haunches. [Cf. *Secreta Secret.* 31 Akyng of thyn haunchis and of thi mylte.]

rottle ('rɒt(ə)l), *v.* Now *dial.* Also 4–6 **rotle**, 4–5 **rotel**, 5 **rottill-**. [= MDu. and MLG. *rotelen*, G. *rosseln* (also Du. *reutelen*, LG. *röteln*, G. *rösseln*), prob. of imitative origin: cf. rattle *v.* and ruttle *v.*] *intr.* To rattle, in various senses.

13.. *K. Alis.* 930 Mony a baner, of gold and ynde, That day rotled with the wynde. *Ibid.* 1871 Mony scheld ther was y-founde, And mony baner was rotelande. 13.. *Pol., Rel., & L. Poems* (1903) 249 Whanne .. þe prote Roteletȝ, And þe hew Faleweȝ. *a* 1400 *Rel. Antiq.* I. 65 His teth shulle ratelen; And his throte shal rotelen. 1577 B. Googe *Heresbach's Husb.* iii. (1586) 132 b, It .. rotleth with much noise in the throte. 1608 Tourneur *Reveng. Trag.* iv. ii, He whurles and rotles in the throate. 1675 Cotton *Burlesque upon B.* Wks. (1725) 278 Hearing Blood in Throats to rottle, Like Liquor from a strait-mouth'd Bottle. 1688 Holme *Armoury* ii. 134/1 A Goat when he sendeth forth his Cry Rattleth or Rotteleth. 1719 Hamilton *Ep.* i. viii. in Ramsay *Poems*, Tho' I should baith reel and rottle, .. At Ed'nburgh we sall ha'e a bottle. 1841 Hartshorne *Salop. Ant.* Gloss.

551 Rottling in his throat. **1861** R. YOUNG *Rabin Hill's Visit Rlwy.* I. xvii, Dont'e hear The snarten creter rottlen on? **1898** RAYMOND *Men o' Mendip* vi, A..note, so crisp that he'll rottle 'twixt your vinger an' thumb.

Hence **'rottling** *vbl. sb.*

a **1400-50** *Alexander* 943 Alexander..Sees slike a rottillyng in þe rewme & ridis al þe faster. **14..** *Siege Jerusalem* 277 Þan was rotlyng in Rome,..Schewyng of scharpe stele and scheldes ydressed.

rotto ('rɒtəʊ), *a. nonce-wd.* [f. ROTT(EN *a.* + -O[2].] A jocular var. of ROTTEN *a.* 8

1922 JOYCE *Ulysses* 23 The father is rotto with money. *Ibid.* 630 There was the case of O'Callaghan..among whose other gay doings when rotto and making himself a nuisance to everybody all round he was in the habit of ostentatiously sporting in public a suit of brown paper.

'rottock. Now *Sc.* Forms: 4 **rottok**, 9 **-ack, -ick.** [? f. ROT *v.*] A decayed or musty thing.

13.. *St. Erkenwolde* 344 in Horstm. *Altengl. Leg.* (1881) 274 Alle þe blee of his body was blakke as þe moldes, As rotene as þe rottok þat rises in powdere.

1806 JAMIESON *Pop. Ball.* I. 293 Now a' their gear and ald rottacks Had faun to young Hab o' the Heuch. [*Gloss.* 'Old musty corn. Literally, the grubs in a bee-hive.'] **1844** T. ANDERSON in Edwards *Mod. Sc. Poets* 14th Ser. 164 He'd sic routh o' auld rotticks was left by his daddy. **1867** GREGOR *Banffshire Gloss.*, *Rottack*, anything stored up for a long time with the idea of mustiness.

rotton, obs. form of ROTTAN, -EN.

Rottweiler ('rɒtwaɪlə(r), -vaɪlə(r)). Also **Rottweiller.** [a. Ger., f. *Rottweil*, the name of a town in Württemberg, West Germany + *-er* -ER[1].] A large black-and-tan dog belonging to the breed so called, having a short, coarse coat, docked tail, and a broad head with pendent ears. Also *attrib.*

1907 R. LEIGHTON *New Bk. Dog* 521/2 The Rottweil Dog, usually called the *Rottweiler Metzgerhund*, or butcher's dog of the town of Rottweil in South Germany. **1917** *Policeman's Monthly* Jan. 5/3 Nowadays four breeds of dogs are being used for police purposes: the Continental Sheepdog,..the Airedale Terrier, the Doberman Pinscher and the Rottweillers. **1939** KINNEY & HONEYCUTT *How to raise Dog* ii. 73 Very large (Breeds such as Great Danes, Newfoundlands,..mastiffs, Rottweilers, Italian bulls, and Pyrenean mountain dogs). **1948** C. L. B. HUBBARD *Dogs in Brit.* xvi. 163 Although a comparatively new arrival to Britain the Rottweiler is a very well-known dog on the Continent. **1962** *Times* 24 Aug. 1/3 (Advt.), Very special homes required by 3 Rottweiler puppies. **1963** *Guardian* 5 Jan. 5/3 Among the dogs successfully trained for police work are the Rottweiler..and the Bouvier. **1971** 'L. EGAN' *Malicious Mischief* (1972) viii. 127 Katharine thought of Labrador retrievers,..Newfoundlands, and Rottweilers. **1978** *Daily Tel.* 11 Apr. 3/6 Dulwich College staff are alleged to have been attacked by Rottweilers—German hunting dogs—belonging to a neighbour.

‖**rotula** ('rɒtjʊlə). Pl. usu. **rotulæ** ('rɒtjʊliː). [L. *rotula*, dim. of *rota* wheel.]

1. *Anat.* **a.** The knee-cap, patella.

c **1400** *Lanfranc's Cirurg.* 177 A round boon..clepid rotula, & of summen it is clepid þe yȝe of þe knee. **1597** A. M. tr. *Guillemeau's Fr. Chirurg.* p. xij b/1 That which is rotundelye elevatede, is called Rotula, or the shive of the knee. **1715** S. SEWALL *Diary* 2 July, I..was grievously surpris'd to find Hannah fallen down the Stairs again, the Rotula of her Left Knee broken. **1741** MONRO *Anat. Nerves* (ed. 3) 291 The Substance of the *Rotula* is cellular. **1803** J. BARCLAY *New Anat. Nomencl.* 127 Those parts in the sacral extremities..are the *tibia*, *fibula*, *poples*, and *rotula*.

b. The point of the elbow.

1760-72 H. BROOKE *Fool of Qual.* (1809) I. 98 The ball.. lodged on the rotula of my left arm. **1900** *Daily News* 3 July 3/4 The rotula of the elbows form big balls like knots on a crabtree stick.

2. a. One of five radial pieces forming part of the oral skeleton of sea-urchins.

1877 HUXLEY *Anat. Inv. Anim.* ix. 576 Superiorly, the epiphyses of each pair of alveoli are connected by long radial pieces—the *rotulæ*, articulated with their edges. *Ibid.*, The radii and rotulæ are ambulacral. **1888** ROLLESTON & JACKSON *Anim. Life* 560 This apparatus consists of an interradial portion..and of a radial portion—viz. the *rotula* and the *radii.*

b. A calcareous formation in the integument of some holothurians.

1888 ROLLESTON & JACKSON *Anim. Life* 550 The calcareous deposits of the body are as a rule represented only by scattered spicules.., by wheels (= rotulae), e.g. in *Chirodota*,..or variously shaped plates.

3. A genus of sea-urchins.

1753 *Chambers' Cycl.* Suppl. s.v., The characters of the rotulæ are, that they are flat shells in form of a cake.

4. (See quot. 1760.)

1760 J. FERGUSON (*title*), The Description and Use of the Astronomical Rotula, shewing the Change and Age of the Moon, the Motions and Places of the Sun, Moon, and Nodes in the Ecliptic [etc.]. **1883** *Blackw. Mag.* Aug. 258 Rotulas, orreries, dials, everything he could think of, his patient hands elaborated.

Hence **'rotulad** *adv.* (See first quot.)

1803 J. BARCLAY *New Anat. Nomencl.* 166 In the sacral extremities,.. Rotulad will signify towards the rotular aspect. **1808** —— *Muscular Motions* 435 The vagina..is in passing the joint extended *rotulad* and *poplitead* of the centre of motion.

rotular ('rɒtjʊlə(r)), *a.* [See prec. and -AR.]

1. Of or pertaining to the rotula or knee-cap.

1803 J. BARCLAY *New Anat. Nomencl.* 166 Towards the rotular aspect. **1814** WISHART tr. *Scarpa's Treat. Hernia* Expl. Table p. xvi, The aspects and positions here are tibial, fibular, rotular, and popliteal.

2. Having the form of a roll.

1871 WRIGHT *Homes of Other Days* ix. 140 The number which remain lead us to believe that every gentleman's family possessed one of these rotular manuals of English history.

†**rotule.** *Obs.*[−1] [a. F. *rotule.*] = ROTULA 1.

1578 BANISTER *Hist. Man* I. 33 A common cauitie, wherein lyeth the hole, or rotule of the knee.

rotulet ('rɒtjʊlɪt). [f. L. *rotul-us* roll + -ET[1].] A small roll; one of the parts of a large roll.

1848 REEVES *Eccl. Antiq. Down* p. xii, The four rotulets which comprise the taxation of Armagh and Tuam are stitched together. **1887** WILLMORE *Hist. Walsall* 45 An error in the transcription from the original rotulet.

†**rotumbe.** *Obs. rare.* Also **rotombe.** [ad. med.L. *rotumba* (Du Cange).] Some vessel used in alchemy.

c **1460-70** *Bk. Quintessence* 10 þe which licour gadere togidere in a rotumbe. *Ibid.*, It nedit to be putrified in a rotombe.

rotun, obs. form of ROTTEN *a.*

rotund (rəʊ'tʌnd), *sb.* Now *rare.* [Subst. use of next: cf. F. *rotonde*, It. *rotonda.*]

†**1.** A globe or ball. *Obs.*[−1]

1550 J. COKE *Eng. & Fr. Heralds* §64 The..kyng of Englande..is fygured holdynge in his left hand a ronde rotunde, representyng his Impery.

†**2.** A circular company of persons. *Obs.*

1636 R. GRIFFIN in *Ann. Dubrensia* (1877) 53 Since that brave Heroe dy'd.., Arthur, with his rotund of Knights.

†**3.** A round building or space. *Obs.*

1740 DYER *Ruins Rome* 402 And Phœbus' temple nodding with its woods Threatens huge ruin o'er the small rotund. **1756** BURKE *Subl. & B.* II. ix, For in a rotund, whether it be a building or a plantation, you can nowhere fix a boundary. **1778** *England's Gazetteer* (ed. 2) s.v. *Wells*, The chapter-house is a rotund, supported by a pillar in the middle.

†**4.** A round *of* occupation. *Obs.*[−1]

1799 SICKELMORE *Agnes & Leonora* I. 2 She retired from the bustle and monotony which a diurnal rotund of company produces.

5. A round expanse or extent; one who, or that which, has a rounded form.

1802 MRS. J. WEST *Infidel Father* I. 16 The frown which gradually overcast the luminous rotund of Lady Fitz John's countenance. **1860** I. TAYLOR *Ult. Civiliz.* 183 The merry rotund of the front aspect. **1882** *Nature* XXV. 405 Not only do the worker-ants store the 'rotunds', but when they require food they go to the rotunds, which feed them.

rotund (rəʊ'tʌnd), *a.* [ad. L. *rotund-us*, related to *rota* wheel: cf. ROTOUND *a.* and ROUND *a.*]

1. Round, circular, orbicular. Now *rare* except in scientific use.

1705 ADDISON *Italy* 177, I..can't forbear thinking the Cross Figure more proper for such spacious Buildings than the Rotund. **1796** W. H. MARSHALL *W. England* II. 75 The Town.., surrounded with inferior streets, caps a rotund hillock. **1843** S. C. HALL *Ireland* III. 200 All the Mithraic.. temples were rotund. **1856-8** W. CLARK *Van der Hoeven's Zool.* I. 153 Test rotund or cordate. **1866** *Treas. Bot.* 993/1 *Rotund*, orbicular, a little inclining to be oblong. **1878** ANDERSON *Exp. Yun-nan* 210 The more rotund character of the parietals.

Comb. **1852** DANA *Crust.* II. 1270 Centre of posterior margin deeply rotund-excavate.

2. Of the mouth: Rounded in the act of utterance. Hence *transf.*, sonorous, full-toned.

After L. *ore rotundo* (Horace *Ars Poet.* 323).

1830 JAMES *Darnley* xl, A long detail of grievances poured forth from the rotund mouth of Jekin Groby. **1831** DE QUINCEY in *Blackw. Mag.* XXIX. 765 The style of Latin they affect is..too florid, too rotund. **1865** DICKENS *Mut. Fr.* IV. xiii, A most rotund and glowing negative. **1886** *Manch. Exam.* 14 Jan. 5/6 He read out, in a fine, rotund, elocutionary style, the message.

3. Rounded, plump, podgy.

1834 JAMES *J. Marston Hall* x, Various peculiar points in his rotund conformation. **1856** KANE *Arct. Expl.* II. xxiv. 243 If they would bring to me their rotund little companion within three days. **1866** GEO. ELIOT *F. Holt* xxx, This pink-faced rotund specimen of prosperity.

Hence **ro'tund** *v. trans.*, to make round, cause to become round.

1650 BULWER *Anthropomet.* 20 He would have them by some device to have their Heads rotunded or rounded. **1822** *Examiner* 187/1 A tall gaunt Scot, somewhat rotunded by good fortune and ministerial dinners.

rotunda (rəʊ'tʌndə). [var. of ROTONDA, after L. *rotunda*, fem. of *rotundus.* See also ROTUNDO.]

1. a. A building round in shape both inside and outside, *esp.* one with a dome.

a **1700** EVELYN *Diary* 7 Feb. 1645, Virgil's sepulchre erected on a steepe rock, in forme of a small rotunda or cupolated columne. **1753** HANWAY *Trav.* (1762) I. III. xliii. 199 These edifices are rotundas, of about thirty feet diameter. **1789** MRS. PIOZZI *Journ. France* I. 393 The Temple of Vesta..is a pretty rotunda. **1814** COL. HAWKER *Diary* (1893) I. 116 A grand and fine-built rotunda for wheat and flour. **1863** MARY HOWITT tr. *F. Bremer's Greece* II. xiv. 103 We were conducted through a garden into a large rotunda, with an arched roof. *a* **1878** SIR G. SCOTT *Lect. Archit.* (1879) II. 232 The Pantheon is..a simple rotunda.

transf. **1710** ADDISON *Tatler* No. 116 ¶1 It..covered the whole Court of Judicature with a kind of Silken Rotunda, in its Form not unlike the Cupola of St. Paul's.

b. As the name of particular buildings of this form, such as the Pantheon at Rome.

1687 A. LOVELL tr. *Thevenot's Trav.* I. 187 The Dome.., which is much like the Dome of the Rotunda at Rome. **1705** ADDISON *Italy* 176 After having survey'd this Dome, I went to see the *Rotunda*, which is generally said to have been the Model of it. **1775** *Ann. Reg.* I. 217/1 A temporary octagon kind of building, erected about 20 yards below the rotunda [at Ranelagh]. **1841** *Penny Cycl.* XX. 186/2 The Rotunda or Church of Santa Maria Maggiore at Nocera. **1872** R. B. SMYTH *Mining & Min. Statistics* 81 The gutter..had been traced under the rotunda in the Botanical Gardens.

2. a. A circular hall or room within a building.

1780 A. YOUNG *Tour in Ireland* I. 2 In the evening to the Rotunda, a circular room, 90 feet diameter, an imitation of Ranelagh, provided with a band of music. **1808** M. WILMOT *Russ. Jrnls.* (1934) III. 316 From the Gallery one enters a Green House..in the Center of which is a rotunda for Entertaining Company. **1828** J. F. COOPER *Notions of Amer.* II. 158 In the rotunda, or the great hall of the capitol. **1841** *Penny Cycl.* XX. 187/1 A better example of a rotunda may be seen in that of the Bank of England. **1901** *Daily Tel.* 18 Mar. 10/7 The Reading Room of the British Museum.., that immense rotunda.

b. *N. Amer.* The main hall of a public building; a lobby, a concourse.

1905 *Eye Opener* (Calgary) 28 Jan. 3/1 The hotels have no drinking-water tanks in their rotundas for the use of guests or local patrons—for obvious reasons. **1912** J. SANDLANDS *Western Canad. Dict.*, *Rotunda*, the hall or main entrance and waiting-room of a railway depot or an hotel. **1924** J. F. DORRANCE *Never Fire First* xiii. 134 The scene in the rotunda of Montreal's impressive Windsor Station was as lively as it was metropolitan. **1958** *Edmonton Jrnl.* 19 June 33/3 Place and Date of Sale [is] Rotunda, Fifth Floor, Natural Resources Building, Edmonton, Alberta. **1973** H. KEMELMAN *Tuesday Rabbi saw Red* vi. 41 Inside the enclosed area of the Marble, the marble-tiled rotunda, students were swarming about.

3. *Typogr.* A type-face of gothic inspiration used in some early printed books, based on a rounded script developed in the 13th century and popularized by the Bolognese law-school; also, the manuscript hand on which this type-face was based.

1929 A. F. JOHNSON in *Library* IX. 364 This is the rounded gothic of the Italians... In typography the Germans call it Rotunda. *Ibid.*, Jenson's Rotundas had a much wider vogue than his roman. **1954** R. STOKES *Esdaile's Student's Man. Bibliogr.* (ed. 3) iv. 141 The third class of *rotunda* types..is largely an Italian style of gothic and shows a much more open quality. **1969** H. CARTER *View of Early Typogr.* iii. 50 This Italian rotunda was a somewhat cramped letter with short ascending and descending strokes. .. It was ideally suited to printing and printing was ideally suited to it. **1976** *Times Lit. Suppl.* 22 Oct. 1328/3 Caxton's mainstay bâtardes 2, 4, and 6 are surely best understood as belonging to the great calligraphic types of the earliest period, in fourth place after the Gutenbergian or Mainz texturas and rotundas and the Venetian romans. **1978** *Jrnl. R. Soc. Arts* CXXVI. 378/1 The widely practised 'Rotunda' hand of the Marmion, Soane, Serristori and other manuscript Hours.

4. *attrib.* and *Comb.*, as ***rotunda form***, ***-house***, etc.

1813 *Sporting Mag.* XLII. 54 The rotunda form of stabling was originally recommended about seventeen years since. **1841** *Penny Cycl.* XX. 186/2 A rotunda-house, about 50 feet in diameter. *Ibid.* 187/1 The rotunda interior of St. Peter-le-Poor's, London. **1841** *Civil Eng. & Arch. Jrnl.* IV. 117/2 The tholus, or concave dome,..renders the rotunda-shape..the most complete for internal effect.

†**ro'tundal**, *a. Obs.*[−1] [f. ROTUND *a.* + -AL[1].] Round, circular.

1624 DARCIE *Birth of Heresies* xx. 81 Who did not institute for you these rotundall hosts, or that they should bee rather round then square.

†**ro'tundant.** *Obs.*[−1] [f. ROTUND *a.*, after *quadrant.*] A round thing.

1661 K. W. *Conf. Charac.*, *College Butler* §1 He measures not by the chaine nor the quadrant, no, by the retundant [*sic*] rather, i.e. the jugg.

rotundate (rəʊ'tʌndət), *a. Bot.* and *Zool.* [ad. L. *rotundāt-us*, pa. pple. of *rotundāre*, f. *rotundus* round.] Rounded off.

1776 J. LEE *Introd. Bot.* 383 *Rotundatum*, rotundate, rounded, or with Angles in a Circle. **1826** KIRBY & SP. *Entomol.* IV. xlvi. 261 *Rotundate*.., rounded at the angles or sides. **1847** *Proc. Berw. Nat. Club.* II. 239 Ligula membranaceous, rotundate. **1872** OLIVER *Elem. Bot.* II. 149 A biennial herb, with simple alternate stipulate rotundate leaves.

ro'tundi-, combining form of L. *rotundus* round, used in a few words, as **rotundi'foliate** *a.*, **-'folious** *a.*, having round leaves; **ro'tundiform** *a.*, rounded; **ro'tundify** *v.*, to make rotund.

1858 MAYNE *Expos. Lex.*, *Rotundifolius*, having round leaves; round-leaved: *rotundifoliate. **1727** BAILEY (vol. II), **Rotundifolious*, which has round leaves. **1846** MRS. GORE *Engl. Char.* (1852) 140 Not a note or letter passing through the hands of these worthies but assumes a *rotundiform shape. **1876** M. B. EDWARDS *John & I* 363 Sausages.. oleaginous and *rotundifying.

†**ro'tundious**, *a. Obs. rare.* [See ROTUND *a.* and -IOUS.] Rounded, spherical.

1630 J. TAYLOR (Water P.) *Wks.* II. 70 So your rare wit.. Lyes in the caue of your rotundious skull. *Ibid.* 169/2 Till Tytans glory the rotundious Globe with splendor filles.

rotundity (rəʊˈtʌndɪtɪ). [ad. L. *rotunditas*, f. *rotund-us* round: see -ITY. So F. *rotondité*, It. *rotondità*, Sp. *rotundidad*.]

1. The condition of being round or spherical; roundness, sphericity.

1597 A. M. tr. *Guillemeau's Fr. Chirurg.* 10 b/1 The heade.., the rotunditye and rowndnes therof. *Ibid.* 43/1 The hole as greate as the rotunditye of a bullet. **1610** HEALEY *St. Aug. Citie of God* 465 Which in the beginning gave rotundity both to the Heavens and Sunne. **1650** BULWER *Anthropomet.* 85 Some bring in another rotundity of face. **1660** F. BROOKE tr. *Le Blanc's Trav.* 348 They believe the rotundity of the earth. **1733** CHEYNE *Eng. Malady* II. ii. §7 (1734) 131 Gold.. having no innate Fluidity, nor natural Rotundity of Particles. **1837** W. IRVING *Capt. Bonneville* II. 52 Large tracts, which are probably concealed from view from the rotundity of the lake's surface. **1878** HUXLEY *Physiogr.* xix. 318 One of the most convincing proofs of this rotundity.

b. *concr.* A round or spherical mass; a round building, etc.

1744 J. ARMSTRONG *Preserv. Health* II. 544 This huge rotundity we tread grows old. **1799** CAMPBELL *Pleas. Hope* II. 211 The shrine where motion first began,.. From whence each bright rotundity was hurl'd. **1819** W. FAUX *Mem. Days Amer.* (1823) 95 Dr. Storton's chapel, an immense, elegant rotundity, like Rowland Hill's in the Surrey road. **1839** HAWTHORNE *Transformation* I, The.. black rotundity of the Pantheon. *a* **1864** —— *Amer. Note-Bks.* (1879) II. 81 The.. winter-squash.. turns up its big rotundity to ripen in the autumn sun.

2. Rounded fullness, *esp.* of language.

1589 PUTTENHAM *Eng. Poesie* II. xi[i]. (Arb.) 114 It must be slenderer in some part, and yet not without a rotunditie and smoothnesse to giue the rest an easie deliuerie. *a* **1661** FULLER (Annandale), For the mere rotundity of the number and grace of the matter it passeth for a full thousand. **1803** *Edin. Rev.* II. 245 In order to give their narrative smoothness and rotundity. **1819** G. S. FABER *Dispensations* (1823) I. 108 In order to give due rotundity to his grand system. **1879** FARRAR *St. Paul* (1883) 686 He began.. with true legal rotundity of verbiage.

3. Roundness or plumpness of the body or its parts; fullness of habit.

1786 tr. *Beckford's Vathek* (1883) 38 The cursed Indian, who still preserved his rotundity of figure. **1826** in *Sheridaniana* 88 The jolly rotundity of his Lordship. **1891** HARDY *Tess* xi, The faultless rotundities of a lusty country girl.

b. Used *concr.* (Cf. 1 b.)

1858 HAWTHORNE *Fr. & It. Note-bks.* II. 31 An ugly, old, fat, jolly Bacchus,.. a tipsy rotundity of flesh. **1900** G. H. KINGSLEY *Sport & Trav.* 425 That this cumbrous rotundity may attack a wounded whale is likely enough.

roˈtundly, *adv.* [f. ROTUND *a.* + -LY².]

†1. In a round form. *Obs.*

1597 A. M. tr. *Guillemeau's Fr. Chirurg.* p. xij b/1 That which is rotundelye elevatede, is called Rotula.

2. Roundedly, fully.

1863 *Sat. Rev.* 11 Apr., The French.. suppose that they are the most completely and rotundly civilized of all the nations of the world.

roˈtundness. *rare*⁻⁰. [-NESS.] Roundness.

1727 BAILEY (vol. II).

roˈtundo. Now *rare* or *Obs.* [Alteration of ROTUNDA.]

†1. A circular form or figure. *Obs. rare.*

1625 PURCHAS *Pilgrims* II. x. 1832 Builded in a *rotundo*, and open at the top with a large round. **1632** LITHGOW *Trav.* x. 428 The Iland lyeth almost in a Rotundo.

2. A circular building, chamber, or space.

1632 LITHGOW *Trav.* VIII. 368 The chiefest Mosque.. [has] many Iles, Quires, and circulary Rotundoes. **1686** PLOT *Staffordsh.* 338 A large Rotundo fenced about with a high wall of brick, opening.. against the Front of the house. **1804** EUGENIA DE ACTON *Tale without Title* III. 232 The open benches in this rural rotundo. **1845** PETRIE *Round Towers Irel.* I. iii. 33 The Persians.. may have worshipped fire in rotundos of above 30 feet diameter.

attrib. **1806** SURR *Winter in Lond.* II. 218 There was a pavilion erected in this garden,.. built in the rotundo form.

3. A rounded part of a coach. [F. *rotonde*.]

1867 DIXON *New Amer.* I. iii. 35 Cutting off the coupé of a French diligence, and bellying out the rotundo.

roˈtundo-, used as combining form of L. *rotundus*, in **rotundo-ovate** *a.*, **-tetragonal** *a.* (see quots.).

1775 J. JENKINSON tr. *Linnæus' Brit. Pl.* Gloss., *Rotundo-ovate*, oval, but rather roundish. *Rotundo-tetragonal*, having four angles rather roundish. **1847** W. E. STEELE *Field Bot.* 57 Leafl. rotundo-ovate, abruptly cuspidate.

‖**roture** (rɔtyr). [F., app.:—L. *ruptūra* breaking, rupture: see Littré.]

1. Plebeian tenure.

1682 WARBURTON *Hist. Guernsey* (1822) 89 This division is to be understood of estates that are in roture. **1818** HALLAM *Mid. Ages* (1868) 106 A nobleman might, and often did, hold estates in roture, as well as a roturier acquire a fief.

2. Plebeian rank.

1795 HELEN M. WILLIAMS *Lett. France* I. 194 The period was still remembered when a round cap was the badge of roture. **1882** *Encycl. Brit.* XIV. 177/1 He himself always signed the name Delabruyère in one word, thus avowing his *roture*.

‖**roturier** (rɔtyrje), *sb.* and *a.* Also 7 roturer, and 8–9 *fem.* -iere (-jɛr). [F., f. *roture*: see prec. and -IER.]

A. *sb.* A plebeian; a person of low rank.

1586 FERNE *Blaz. Gentrie* 12 Be he Marchaunt, Burgesse, Roturier, peysaunt or slaue. **1594** R. ASHLEY tr. *Loys le Roy* 56 Although.. it was not lawfull for any Roturier or common person, to possesse any fee simple. **1649** HOWELL *Pre-em. Parl.* 10 The poor Roturier and Vineyard man. **1660** —— *Parly of Beasts* 18 My profession was both a Vineyard-man, and a Roturer, a poor Peasan I was. **1756** NUGENT *Gr. Tour* IV. 13 The third are the *Roturiers*, and comprehends their tradesmen, yeomen, and husbandmen, or peasants. **1798** CHARLOTTE SMITH *Yng. Philos.* I. 104 Sinking into the rank of plebeians, roturiers, fellows who live by digging. **1807** *Edin. Rev.* II. 125 The roturier and the noble were pretty nearly equal. **1833** LYTTON *Godolphin* 38 She'll take in some rich roturier, I hope. **1868** MISS BRADDON *Dead Sea Fr.* I. iv. 61 Palaces are common enough.., and the roturier may find one ready for his occupation.

2. In Canada, one who holds real estate subject to an annual rent.

1861 MAY *Const. Hist.* (1863) II. xvii. 575 A representative assembly, to which freeholders or *roturiers* to the amount of £500 were eligible as members.

B. *adj.* Plebeian.

1614 SELDEN *Titles Hon.* 302 With the Roturier or base tenures, this place hath not to do. **1791** CHARLOTTE SMITH *Celestina* (ed. 2) IV. 227 Her mother was roturiere. **1792** —— *Desmond* I. 243 You, Sir, have owned that your family is *roturier*. **1817** LADY MORGAN *France* I. (1818) I. 73, I have heard Napoleon's *roturiere* origin quoted by the *royalistes purs*. **1835** H. GREVILLE *Diary* 2 May, His manners, though courteous.., are *roturier* and vulgar.

‖**Rotwelsch** (ˈroːtvɛlʃ). Also †**Rothwelsch**. [Ger., f. MHG. *rot* beggar or *rôt* red + *welsch* WELSH.] A form of slang or cant used by vagrants and criminals in Germany and Austria.

1841 BORROW *Zincali* II. III. ii. 130 The name of this [robber] jargon varies... In Germany [it is called] 'Rothwelsch' or red Italian. **1892** [see YIDDISH *a.*]. **1916** H. BRADLEY *Shakespeare's English* in *Shakespeare's England* II. xxx. 567 The Hebrew words that are so conspicuous in the contemporary *Rotwelsch* of Germany. **1934** PRIEBSCH & COLLINSON *German Lang.* 260 The lowest type of speech is the thieves' and beggars' cant known in German as *Rotwelsch* or *Gaunersprache*. **1961** *John o' London's* 30 Nov. 610 The *argot* of the French underworld, the *Rotwelsch* of Germany, is paralleled by the *Cant* of English rogues and vagabonds. **1973** *Reader's Digest* Feb. 122/2 'Please, put away that firecracker,' said the Major, lapsing into *Rotwelsch*—the slang of Vienna's underworld.

roty: see RUTTY.

rotyd(e, obs. ff. ROTTED.

rotye, obs. f. ROT *v.*

rotyn, obs. f. ROT *v.*, ROTTEN *a.*

rotyng(e, obs. ff. ROOTING, ROTTING.

rou, var. of RO, rest: obs. Sc. f. ROLL *v.*; var. of ROW *a.*²

roub, obs. form of RUB *v.*

rouble (ˈruːb(ə)l). Forms: α. 6 **rubbel**, 6–7 **rubbell, rubble, roble, robell.** β. 7–9 **ruble**, 8 **rubel.** γ. 7–9 **rouble** (8–9 **rooble**). [a. Russ. *rublĕ* (also *rublevik'* silver rouble), of doubtful origin. The current English spelling has been adopted from French.]

1. The Russian monetary unit, in early times a money of account equal in value to an English mark, or 13*s.* 4*d.*, subsequently a silver coin (worth, e.g. in 1897, 2*s.* 1½*d.*).

Florio (1611) defines *Robbone* as 'a coine of gold in Muscouy called a rubble or roble', but see quot. 1617 here. Roubles of gold and platina have been coined in the 19th cent.

α. **1554** HASSE in Hakluyt *Voy.* (1589) 293 There goeth.. 23 Altines, and two Dengaesto a Rubble. *Ibid.*, Three Rubbles of siluer. *a* **1584** S. BOROUGH *Ibid.* (1599) I. 1. 280 They held one tooth of a Morse.. at a roble. **1584** SIR J. BOWES in Tolstoy *Interc. Eng. & Russia* (1875) 227 None of theim had clothes on his back worth a robell. **1617** MORYSON *Itin.* I. 290 They make all contracts by a money called Rubble, which is altogether imaginarie, for they have no such coyne, and it is esteemed in England at thirteene shillings foure pence sterling. **1635** PAGITT *Christianogr.* (1639) 17 Some of their Bishops have 2000, some 3000 Rubbles per annum.

β. **1601** R. JOHNSON *Kingd. & Commw.* (1603) 154 They receive, some 1000, some 80 rubles a yeare. **1664** MARVELL *Corr.* Wks. (Grosart) II. 147 Is six thousand rubles yearly.. so necessary a summe to so great a Prince? **1710** LD. WHITWORTH *Acc. Russia* (1758) 75 In 1703, great quantities of specie, Rubles, half Rubles, &c., were made, though the mass of the money is still in Copecks. **1716** J. PERRY *State of Russia* 7 *note*, A Ruble is 100 Russ Copecks, which was then each Copeck full an English Penny Value; but since the Czar has recoined his money, it is little more than half the former Value. **1753** HANWAY *Trav.* (1762) I. VI. lxxxi. 371 They keep accounts in rubles and copeeks, one hundred copeeks to a ruble. **1811** P. KELLY *Univ. Cambist* 371 This gives the value of the old Ruble 3*s.* 2*d.* sterling, and of the new, 3*s.* 2½*d.* **1823** BYRON *Juan* IX. lxxix, Already they beheld the silver showers Of rubles rain, as fast as specie can, Upon his cabinet. **1855** *Englishwoman in Russia* 37 He came to borrow a few rubles, which she kindly gave him.

γ. **1662** J. DAVIES tr. *Olearius' Voy. Ambass.* 97 Though, in trading, the Muscovites use the words, Altin, Grif, and Rouble.., yet is there no Coins of that kind. **1728** CHAMBERS *Cycl.* s.v. *Money*, In Muscovy,.. the Rouble [is] equal to 100 Copecs, or 2 Rixdollars, or 9 Shillings Sterling. **1833** R. PINKERTON *Russia* 8 The support of this naval establishment costs the crown 30 millions of roubles annually. **1868** *Pall Mall G.* 23 July 8 Rye-flour now costs 1 rouble 20 kopecs (four shillings) the poud (thirty pounds). **1891** *Melbourne Argus* 7 Nov. 13/7 The yearly pay of a private [in the Russian army] is 2 roubles 70 copecks.

2. A paper money of less value than the silver rouble (see quots.).

The rouble is now available primarily in paper form.

1811 P. KELLY *Univ. Cambist* I. 375 In 1808,.. 1 Silver Ruble was worth 2 Rubles of Exchange, or 2 of Bank Paper. **1875** BEDFORD *Sailor's Pocket-bk.* ix. (ed. 2) 317, 100 Copecks = 1 Silver Rouble = 3*s.* 2*d.* Paper money is the chief medium of payment. The paper Rouble is worth about 2*s.* 6*d.* sterling.

roubt, obs. f. ROUT.

rouch(e, obs. ff. ROUGH *a.*

roucht, obs. pa. t. REACH *v.*

†**roucote.** *Obs.*⁻¹ Some kind of fish.

c **1640** J. SMYTH *Hund. Berkeley* (1885) 319 Sorts of sea fish [taken] in this river... An haddocke, a Roucote, the sea tad.

roucou (ruːˈkuː), *sb.* Also 7 rocour, 7–9 rocou, 8 rocow, rocko, 9 rocu; 8 rowcow, roucau. [a. F. *roucou, rocou*, ad. Brazilian (Tupi) *urucú*.]

1. A dye-yielding tree, *Bixa orellana*, of the West Indies and South America. Also *roucou-tree*.

α. **1666** J. DAVIES tr. *Rochefort's Caribby Isles* 43 The Roucou is the same tree which the Brasilians call Urucu. **1716** *Petiveriana* I. 176 Maucaw, or Roucou-tree. **1756** P. BROWNE *Jamaica* 254 The Roucou or Arnotto Tree... All the seeds of this plant are covered with wax. **1871** C. KINGSLEY *At Last* viii, This was a famous plant—*Bixa Orellana*, Roucou; and that pulp was the well-known Arnotta dye of commerce.

β. **1681** GREW *Musæum* II. i. i. 185 A Leaf of the Rocour-Tree. **1783** JUSTAMOND tr. *Raynal's Hist. Indies* V. 28 They painted all their bodies over with the juice of the rocou or arnotto, which gave them the appearance of a boiled lobster. **1848** tr. *Hoffmeister's Trav. Ceylon*, etc. iii. 128 Scattered groups of Magnolias, or *Rocu-trees*, in full flower.

2. The dye or dye-stuff obtained from this tree; also called *anatta* or *arnatto*.

α. **1666** J. DAVIES tr. *Rochefort's Caribby Isles* 255 A certain red composition they call *Roucou* from the name of the tree that produces it. **1712** tr. *Pomet's Hist. Drugs* I. 223 The savage Americans cultivate the Shrubs that bear the Roucou with great Industry. **1794** MORSE *Amer. Geogr.* 596 A red or yellow dye called Roucau, and some other trifles. **1825** WATERTON *Wand. South Amer.* iii. 190 They paint themselves with the Roucou, sweetly perfumed. **1890** *St. James's Gaz.* 21 Oct. 14/1 The peculiar tints.. are said to be due to the saffron, roucou, cayenne, and other savories used in food.

β. **1698** FROGER *Voy.* 126 The chief Commodity of the Country is Sugar and Rocou. **1706** *Lond. Gaz.* No. 4269/3, 65 Casks of Rocko, and 4 Barrels of Indigo. **1796** STEDMAN *Surinam* I. xv. 400 All the Guiana Indians disfigure themselves more or less by the use of arnotta or rocow. **1887** MOLONEY *Forestry W. Afr.* 277 The well-known orange dye known as 'Arnatto' or 'Rocou' is prepared from the red pulp covering the seeds of this plant.

Hence **rouˈcou** *v.*, to stain with roucou.

1871 KINGSLEY *At Last* viii, The Indian.., when he has 'roucoued' himself from head to foot, considers himself in full dress.

‖**roucoulement** (rukulmɑ̃). *rare.* [Fr.] The soft cooing sound made by doves. Also *transf.*

1863 J. A. SYMONDS *Let.* 12 Aug. (1967) I. 413 This *roucoulement* (cooing) in the throat is different from the yogel & seems to be peculiar to Swiss singing. **1926** E. SITWELL *Elegy on Dead Fashion* 2 Roucoulement of doves and veilèd belles.

roud, obs. or dial. var. of RUDD¹ (the fish).

roud, *sb. dial.* [Cf. next and RUD *sb.*] The act of spawning.

1893 COZENS-HARDY *Broad Nrf.* 82 (E.D.D.), The broad-land fishes are said to be on the roud.

roud (raʊd), *v. dial.* [Cf. RODDING *vbl. sb.*², ROOD *v.* and RUD *sb.*] *intr.* To spawn.

1882 *Blackw. Mag.* Jan. 101 The great time for bobbing is when the roach and bream are rouding or spawning. **1882** C. DAVIES *Norfolk Broads* xviii. (1884) 131 The 'rouding' or spawning time of the bream and the roach.

roudes, variant of RUDAS *Sc.*

†**roudge.** *Obs. rare.* [Of obscure origin.] Some kind of coarse cloth.

1547 BOORDE *Introd. Knowl.* v. (1870) 139 Symple rayment doth serue us full well; Wyth dagswaynes and roudges we be content. *Ibid.* vi. 142 They do were wylde beastes skinnes and roudges.

roue, obs. pa. t. RIVE *v.*¹; obs. f. ROOF, ROVE.

‖**roué** (ˈruːeɪ). [F. *roué*, pa. pple. of *rouer* to break on the wheel. The name was first given to the profligate companions of the Duke of Orleans (*c* 1720), to suggest that they deserved this punishment.] One who is given to, or leads, a life of pleasure and sensuality; a debauchee, a rake.

1800 MRS. HERVEY *Mourtray Fam.* III. 60 Madame Duplin thought.. it was much to be lamented, that so fine a young lady should fling herself away on a *roué*. **1831** *Society* I. 48 He associated with none but black-legs and roués of the worst description. **1847** C. BRONTË *J. Eyre* xv, I knew him for a young roué of a vicomte—a brainless and vicious youth. **1873** SYMONDS *Grk. Poets* v. 137 Anacreon died at the ripe age of eighty-five.., a hoary-headed *roué*.

attrib. **1837** J. F. COOPER *Europe* II. 79 There is a certain *roué* atmosphere about them.

Hence **rouéism**, rakish life.
1847 Mrs. Gore *Castles in Air* xxxi. (1857) 303 In spite of his vocation of rouéism.

Rouen ('ruːɒn, † ruɑ̃). **a.** The name of a city in Northern France, used to designate various things in some way connected or associated with it, as ***Rouen bushel, duck*** (a common domestic variety), ***lilac***. (See also roan *sb.*[3] and Rowan[3].) Also used to designate earthenware of a type made at Rouen (esp. in the sixteenth and seventeenth centuries), as ***Rouen faience, plate, ware***.
1728 Chambers *Cycl.* s.v. *Measure*, That of Archangel is equal to three Rouen Bushels. **1854** Meall *Moubray's Poultry* 355 The Rouen ducks are good sitters. **1863** W. Chaffers *Marks Pott. & Porc.* 94 From this period [*sc.* the early sixteenth century] until the middle of the XVIIth Century no notices of the Rouen Fayence have been discovered. **1869** C. Schreiber *Jrnl.* 11 Oct. (1911) I. 51 In all these shops there was a profusion of Rouen ware, or what pretended to be such, which proves how common it is. *c* **1877** L. Wright *Bk. Poultry* 539 The Rouen Duck.. almost exactly resembles the Wild Duck, or Mallard, in its plumage. **1882** *Garden* 13 May 322/1 The Rouen Lilac..is an extremely pretty shrub. **1971** J. R. Bernasconi *Collectors' Gloss.* 191 *Rouen ware*, an enamelled faience ware produced at Rouen in the 17th century. **1974** N. Freeling *Dressing of Diamond* 26 His valuable pieces of Nevers and Rouen faïence. **1977** *Western Mail* (Cardiff) 5 Mar. 14/1 Elwyn D. Thomas & Co., F.S.V.A. will Sell by Auction ..'Dresden', 'Mason', 'Delft', 'Rouen' plates and plaques.
b. *ellipt.* = Rouen duck.
1854 Meall *Moubray's Poultry* 309 The Rouen is of the largest size. *c* **1877** L. Wright *Bk. Poultry* 539 He beat all other ducks in weight with Rouens.

rouen, var. of rowen.

rouer, obs. Sc. var. roller; obs. f. rover.

rouf (rəʊf). Also roaf, rofe, roof. Backslang, esp. among costermongers and criminals, for 'four'; *spec.* four shillings, four pounds; a four-year prison sentence.
1851 H. Mayhew *London Labour* I. 23/1 *Rouf-yenep*, Fourpence. **1882** *Sydney Slang Dict.* 11/2 *Roaf Yanneps*, four pence. **1950** P. Tempest *Lag's Lexicon* 212 All [prison] sentences are referred to in slang... 4 years, a 'lagging' or a 'rofe' (pron. 'roaf'). **1957** *Evening News* 12 Nov. 6/6 Newcomers [to Cockney slang] are a 'rouf' (4s), 'a deuce' (£2), and 'anarf' (10s). **1958** F. Norman *Bang to Rights* III. 138, I tried to tell them that it had been a business deal, but you know what it's like talking to a moronic coszer, so that was it I got a rouf. **1972** K. Royce *Miniatures Frame* v. 64 From under a pottery sugar jar..protruded two jacks... I found a roof under them.

rouf, obs. f. roof *sb.*, rough *a.*

roufe, obs. var. rove *sb.*

rouffe, obs. f. roof.

rouffyn, obs. f. Ruffin.

rouful, obs. f. rueful.

rouge (ruːʒ), *a.* and *sb.*[1] Also 5 rowdge, *Sc.* rouch, roche, 6 ruge. [a. F. *rouge*:—L. *rubeum*, acc. of *rubeus*, related to *ruber* and *rūfus*, and ultimately to red. *a.* and *sb.*[1]]
A. *adj.* **1.** ***Rouge Croix*** (or †***Cross***), ***Rouge Dragon***, the titles of two of the Pursuivants of the English College of Arms, so called from their badges.
1485 *Rolls of Parlt.* VI. 384/2 Richard Greenwood, otherwise called Rowdgecrosse. **1491** *Acc. Ld. High Treas. Scot.* I. 179 To Roche Dragon purcyfant of Ingland. **1511** *Ibid.* IV. 318 Ane pursevant of England callit Rugecorce. **1512** *Ibid.* 348 To Rugecroce, Inglis pursevant. **1616** Bullokar *Eng. Expos.*, *Rougecrosse*, the name of an office of one of the Purseuants at armes. *Rouge dragon*. **1656** [see portcullis *sb.* 4]. **1691** Wood *Ath. Oxon.* I. 349 He had been Rouge Croix and Windsore Herald. **1722** *Lond. Gaz.* No. 6084/4 Rouge Croix, Pursuivant of Arms. Rouge Dragon, Pursuivant of Arms. **1766** Entick *London* IV. 27 The four pursuivants, who are, Rougecroix, Bluemantle, Rouge-dragon, and Portcullis, are also created by the earl-marshal. **1806** A. Duncan *Nelson's Funeral* 29 Rouge Croix Pursuivant of Arms in close mourning, with his Tabard over his Cloak. *Ibid.* 30 Rouge Dragon Pursuivant of Arms, habited as Blue Mantle. **1869** Furnivall *Q. Eliz. Acad.* p. xxiv, To Mr. G. E. Adams, Rouge Dragon,.. I tender hearty thanks.
2. ***rouge royal***, a Belgian marble of a reddish colour. (Cf. Littré, s.v. *Royal* 18.)
1858 Simmonds *Dict. Trade*, *Rouge Royal*, a kind of marble. **1896** *Westm. Gaz.* 30 Apr. 2/1 Columns of rouge-royal marble stand as sentinels at the foot.
B. *sb.*[1] **1. a.** A fine red powder prepared from safflower, and used as a cosmetic to give an artificial colour to the cheeks or lips.
1753 Ld. Chesterf. *World* No. 18 ¶ 12 To lay on a great deal of *rouge*, in English called paint. **1762** *Songs & Poems Costume* (Percy Soc.) 240 Let the world be the judge: Why you daub 'em all over with cold-cream and *rouge*. **1789** Mrs. Piozzi *Journ. France* I. 183 A custom..prevails here, of wearing..no rouge. **1807** Robinson *Archæol. Græca* v. xxv. 543 The Athenian women..applied to their faces a layer of ceruse or white lead, with deep tints of rouge. **1875** Mrs. Randolph *Wild Hyacinth* I. 19, I recollect I had rubbed rouge on my cheeks and white stuff on my nose.
fig. **1762–72** H. Brooke *Fool of Qual.* (1792) II. 188 The glow of modesty is the only rouge that will be allowed to any fair face. **1812** Miss L. M. Hawkins *C'tess & Gertr.* (ed. 2) I. 324 Illicit connections she seemed to consider as the *rouge* of modern character. **1882** 'F. Anstey' *Vice Versâ* xvii. 312, I saw through his rouge with half an eye.
b. *transf.* A rouged person.
1855 Thackeray *Newcomes* l, Miss Newcome rode away —back among the roses and the rouges.
c. *attrib.* and *Comb.*, as ***rouge compact, -pot; rouge-maker, -making; rouge-like*** adj.
1800 *Med. Jrnl.* III. 130 A small circular, rouge-like appearance on each cheek. **1813** Moore *Post-bag* viii. 12 Thy roseate days, When the rich rouge-pot pours its blaze Full o'er thy face. **1851–4** *Tomlinson's Cycl. Usef. Arts* II. 473/1 Dr. Ure's account of the process of rouge-making. **1858** Simmonds *Dict. Trade, Rouge and Carmine Maker*, a preparer of those colours. **1931** F. L. Allen *Only Yesterday* v. 107 For every adult woman in the country there were being sold annually over a pound of face powder and no less than eight rouge compacts.
2. a. A red preparation of oxide of iron, used as a plate powder. Also (usu. with qualifying adj.) applied to polishing powders other than ferric oxide (see quot. 1937).
1839 Ure *Dict. Arts* 309 The best sort of polishing powder called *jewellers' red rouge* or plate powder is..precipitated oxide of iron. **1850** Holtzapffel *Turning* III. 1082 The red and black oxides of iron..are prepared by manufacturing chemists..as polishing powders, commercially known as crocus, rouge, red stuff,..&c. **1884** W. H. Greenwood *Steel & Iron* 44 A bright red pulverulent powder, forming the 'rouge' or 'colcothar' of commerce. **1937** *Industr. Minerals & Rocks* (Amer. Inst. Mining & Metall. Engineers) i. 55 Briefly, they [*sc.* metallic oxide buffing materials] consist of various iron oxides such as crocus (red-brown), rouge (red), black rouge (magnetic iron oxide) mainly for glass, green rouge (chromium oxide) mainly for platinum and stainless steels; satin rouge (lampblack) for celluloid and bone; [etc.]. **1962** R. Webster *Gems* I. xx. 366 The polishing powder..may be either rouge (iron oxide), green rouge (chromium oxide), putty powder..or rotten-stone.
attrib. **1884** F. J. Britten *Watch & Clockm.* 50 Using a rouge leather to touch up highly polished surfaces.
b. ***rouge flambé*** (ruʒ flɑ̃be), a brilliant red glaze for porcelain, orig. Chinese, made from copper oxide.
1902 *Encycl. Brit.* XXXI. 875/2 Even the long-sought secret of the Chinese *sang de boeuf* and *rouge flambé* glazes has been worked out in Europe. **1912** A. Bennett *Matador of Five Towns* 4 A few specimens of modern *rouge flambé* ware made at Knype. **1960** R. G. Haggar *Conc. Encycl. Continental Pott. & Porc.* 124/1 He succeeded in producing a fine *rouge flambé* and an admirable turquoise blue glaze. **1967** M. Chandler *Ceramics in Mod. World* iii. 95 Copper oxide..can—under suitable conditions in a reducing atmosphere—produce the extremely brilliant red of rouge flambé. *a* **1977** *Harrison Mayer Ltd. Catal.* 14/2 *Rouge flambe, sang de boeuf*, a red glaze originating in China, its rich colour being due to a copper glaze fired under reducing conditions.
c. ***rouge de fer*** (ruʒ də fɛr), an orange-red enamel colour made from a base of ferric oxide and used on Chinese porcelain.
1922 *Daily Tel.* 12 June 20/5 (Advt.), A pair of famille verte baluster vases enamelled in birds and flowering prunus, in green, rouge de fer, yellow, and aubergine, 17½ in. high. **1939** *Burlington Mag.* Apr. p. xv/1 A pair of famille-verte jars and covers,..with *rouge-de-fer* borders. **1959** *Times* 3 Mar. 7/2 A pair of eighteenth century models of dogs enamelled in *rouge de fer* realized 170 guineas. **1980** *Catal. Fine Chinese Ceramics* (Sotheby, Hong Kong) 166 All in tomato-red 'rouge-de-fer' and gilding.
3. = red *sb.*[1] 6 b.
1821 *Sporting Mag.* VII. 285 So his men fac'd about and they fought, and gave all the rouges a good dusting. **1897** W. C. Hazlitt *Four Generations* II. 181 De Merger was in politics a Rouge, and belonged to a very advanced political club at Tours. **1900** *Q. Rev.* Apr. 339 Politically they [*sc.* Canadians] were divided into Conservatives, Liberals, Radicals, Clear-Grits and Rouges.
4. a. ***Rouge et Noir*** (ruʒ e nwar), a game at cards, so called because the table at which it is played has two red and two black diamond-shaped marks, upon which the players place their stakes according to the colour they favour. Also *fig.*
1791–8 [see c.]. **1808** *Sporting Mag.* XXX. 26 The foreign games of *Roulet* and *Rouge et Noir*. **1817** *Ibid.* L. 129 He.. allowed a game called *Rouge et Noir* to be played by various persons. **1823** Barnewall & Cresswell *Rep.* I. 272 A certain unlawful game of cards called 'Rouge et Noir'. **1850** Thackeray *Pendennis* xliv, If we'd gone to Rouge et Noir, I must have won. **1886** Hardy *Mayor Casterbr.* I. x. 123 The rich *rouge-et-noir* of his countenance underwent a slight change. **1920** H. Crane *Let.* 18 Aug. (1965) 41, I am sure there is more of a 'rouge et noir' cast to your surrender. **1958** L. Durrell *Balthazar* iii. 61 You are not the sort of man to stake everything on a single throw at *rouge et noir*.
b. *ellipt.* A ***rouge-et-noir*** table.
1850 Thackeray *Pendennis* xliv, You have been at the Rouge et Noir: you were there last night.
c. *attrib.* with *debt, game, table*.
1791 in A. C. Bower *Diaries & Corr.* (1903) 140 There is another new Table brought up, called the Rouge & Noir game. **1798** *Sporting Mag.* XII. 53 A *Rouge et Noir* table with its appendages. **1827** Lytton *Falkland* 23 The sons who had horses to sell and rouge-et-noir debts to pay. **1862** Burton *Bk. Hunter* i. 55 The billiard-room and the rouge-et-noir table.
5. a. The red colour in the game of *rouge et noir*.
1805 *New Pocket Hoyle* 117 Another parcel is then dealt for rouge in a similar manner. **1827** Lytton *Pelham* xix, He set them all at one hazard on the *rouge*. **1850** *Bohn's Hdbk. Games* (1867) 343 The first parcel of cards played is usually for noir, the second for rouge. **1867** [see couleur 2]. **1928**, **1964** [see noir 2 b].
b. The red numbers in the game of roulette.
[**1850** *Bohn's Hand-bk. Games* 348 The other chances are also designated on the green cloth,..on one side 'l'impair, la manque, et le rouge'.] **1923**, etc. [see manque]. **1928**, etc. [see noir 2 a].
6. French red wine; = red *sb.*[1] 3 b. Also in *Comb.*
1957 L. Durrell *Spirit of Place* (1969) 143 You should see..the care with which they select a good bottle of champagne..or even an ordinary rouge at a shilling. **1976** N. Roberts *Face of France* xv. 153 The accompanying glass of wine..is only *rouge supérieure*.

rouge (ruːdʒ), *sb.*[2] Also rooge, ruge. [Eton school-term, of obscure origin.]
1. *Eton Football*. A scrimmage. Also *transf.*
1863 Kinglake *Crimea* II. 412 He wedged his cob into the thick of the crowd—the 'rooge', he would call it in his old Eton idiom of speech. **1875** *Punch* 27 Feb. 88/2 Then followed a lively 'rouge', or 'scrimmage', in which most of the leading lawyers of the House took part. **1899** Sir H. West *Recoll.* II. xxi. 276 The Peers and under-the-Gallery people acting exactly as we used to in a 'rouge' at football at Eton.
2. a. *Eton Football*. (See quot. 1892.)
1864 [Hemyng] *Eton School Days* xxiii. 260 Next to a goal, a ruge is the best thing you can have. **1868** *Hurst Johnlan Mag.* X. 349 The School gained three rouges, but each time the place-kick at the goal was unsuccessful. **1892** F. Marshall *Football* 34 (Eton), Should..the ball go behind from the charge and be touched by one of the attacking side, a 'rouge' will be scored. Now three rouges make a goal.
b. *Canadian Football*. (See quots. 1895 and 1954.)
1895 *Outing* XXVII. 249/2 A 'rouge' occurs when a man, in order to save his team from a 'try' being tallied against them, himself touches the ball down behind his own goal, and thereby gives one point to the opposing side. **1954** *Sun* (Baltimore) 11 Dec. 11/7 The 'rouge' is a point scored when a kick into the end zone isn't run out or when the kick goes clear through the 25-yard-wide zone. **1959** *Times* 30 Nov. (Canada Suppl.) p. xx/1 In Canada we also have the rouge, which is a kicked single point. **1966** *Weekend Mag.* (Montreal) 27 Aug. 20/2 If only our rouge were added to the American game, football..wouldn't leave a thing to be desired as a game. **1976** *Webster's Sports Dict.* 357/1 *Rouge*, Canadian football, a score of one point awarded to the kicking team when a member of the receiving team fails to run a kickoff or a punt out of his own end zone.

rouge (ruːʒ), *v.*[1] [f. rouge *sb.*[1]]
1. a. *trans.* To colour with rouge.
1777 Mme. D'Arblay *Early Diary* (1889) II. 178 His face was very delicately rouged. **1812** H. & J. Smith *Rej. Addr.*, *G. Barnwell*, Her face was rouged up to the eyes. **1827** Lady Morgan *O'Briens & O'Flahertys* II. 28 Lady Knocklofty, dear, says I, I wish you would allow me to rouge you. **1902** Cornish *Naturalist Thames* 167 No sheep sent to shows are allowed to have their coats rouged.
b. *fig.* To cause to colour or blush.
1815 Mme. D'Arblay *Diary* (1876) IV. 284 Madame.., though *rouged* the whole time with confusion, never ventured to address a word to me. **1867** A. J. E. Wilson *Vashti* xxx, Her thin but still lovely features, rouged by a hectic glow.
2. a. *intr.* To employ rouge on the face.
1782 Miss Burney *Cecilia* i. iii, One of them asserting boldly that she *rouged* well, a debate ensued, which ended in a bet. **1822** Hazlitt *Table-t.* Ser. ii. v. (1869) 120 Rouge high enough, and never mind the natural complexion. **1848** Thackeray *Van. Fair* lxiv, She *rouged* regularly now. **1880** 'Ouida' *Moths* III. 17 Vera would be a sublime wax doll, if she rouged.
b. *fig.* To colour, to blush.
1780 Mme. D'Arblay *Diary* I. 321 They all stared, and to be sure I *rouged* pretty high. **1954** H. Gold in *New World Writing* VI. 13 You should have seen me rouge all over.

rouge, *v.*[2] *rare*[−1]. (Perh. the same as Cornish dial. *rooge*, to handle roughly.)
1612 W. Parkes *Curtaine-Dr.* 21, I am so valerous that I dare rate And rouge ten Sergeants at the Counter-gate.

rouged (ruːʒd), *ppl. a.* [f. rouge *v.*[1] 1 + -ed[1].] Coloured with rouge.
1813 *Sketches of Character* (ed. 2) I. 76 How lovely black hair looks on a rouged cheek! **1845** Mrs. S. C. Hall *Whiteboy* vi, The rouged, and ornamented, and perfumed remains dressed for the funeral as if for a feast! **1876** J. Saunders *Lion in Path* xvii, A bevy of rouged and powdered dowagers.
transf. **1820** *Edin. Rev.* XXXIV. 102 The prevailing tone of rouged and smiling folly.

'**rougedom.** *rare*[−1]. [f. rouge *sb.*[1]] The domain of the rouged; the demi-monde.
1861 A. Leighton *Storied Trad. Sc. Life* Ser. ii. 33 She flew to him and hugged him with the art of one of the denizens of Rougedom.

Rouge et Noir: see rouge *sb.*[1] 4.

rougeing, variant of rouging.

rougeless ('ruːʒlɪs), *a. rare.* [f. rouge *sb.*[1] + -less.] Lacking rouge (in quot. *fig.*).
1857 [see intime].

‖**rouget** (ruʒe). [Fr.] = *red mullet* s.v. red *a.* 17 c.
1885 A. Edwardes *Girton Girl* III. v. 83 He invited me to eat red mullet with him..Rougets en papillottes, accompanied by fine old graves. **1960** E. David *French Provincial Cooking* 286 *Rouget* proper..is red mullet. **1967** G. Greene *May we borrow your Husband?* 59, I ordered a small *rouget* and a half bottle of Pouilly. **1975** *Harpers & Queen* June 110/3 We ate *rougets* next; such *rougets*, simply

grilled. **1977** *Times* 28 Jan. 15/7 Loup, daurade and rouget are among the best local fish [in Nice].

Rouget cell (ruːʒeɪ). *Histology.* Also **Rouget's cell.** [tr. G. *Rougetsche zelle* (B. J. Vimtrup 1922, in *Zeitschr. f. Anat. u. Entwicklungsges.* LXV. 178), f. the name of C. M. B. *Rouget* (1824–1904), French physiologist, who described such cells in 1873 (*Arch. de Physiol.* V. 603).] = PERICYTE.

1922 A. KROGH *Anat. & Physiol. Capillaries* iii. 54 As there can be no doubt that the richly ramified muscle cells on the capillary wall are the same as those originally found by Rouget in the hyaloid membrane, Vimtrup has named them after the first discoverer, and we shall speak of them henceforth as Rouget cells. **1928** [see PERICYTE]. **1939** W. E. LE GROS CLARK *Tissues of Body* vii. 158 In appearance, Rouget cells (or pericytes, as they have been called), are quite similar to connective-tissue cells. *Ibid.* 159 Vimtrup ..reported that, in Amphibia, local contraction of capillaries always started at the site of one of the Rouget cells. **1961** G. BEVELANDER *Essent. Histol.* (ed. 4) x. 106 According to some authors the tubule is clasped at intervals by Rouget's cells. These are branching cells which are said to be contractile and to cause the constriction of the capillaries. **1970** T. S. & C. R. LEESON *Histol.* (ed. 2) xi. 217/1 Among the pericapillary elements, peculiar cells (Rouget cells) with long branching processes which surround the capillary wall have been described. Early studies indicated that these cells were contractile and were responsible for the contractility of capillaries. More recent work suggests that true capillaries in mammals do not possess Rouget cells and that capillary contractility is independent of them.

rough (rʌf), *sb.*[1] Forms: 3 **ruhe,** 4 **roȝ,** 5, 7 **roughe,** 6– **rough,** 9 **ruff;** *Sc.* 6, 9 **rouch,** 9 **roch.** [f. ROUGH *a.*]

I. 1. The roughness or rough surface *of* something. *rare*⁻¹.

12.. *Ancr. R.* 184 (Titus MS.), He is þi file, þet lorimers habben, & fileð awei al..ti ruhe of sunne.

2. a. Rough or broken ground.

c **1480** HENRYSON *Mor. Fab., Wolf & Wether* viii, He wald chace thame baith throw rouch & snod. **1667** MILTON *P.L.* II. 948 So eagerly the fiend..through strait, rough, dense, or rare,..pursues his way. **1799** WORDSW. *Lucy Gray* xvi, O'er rough and smooth she trips along. **1821** SHELLEY *Hellas* 646 To light us to the edge Through rough and smooth.

b. A stretch of rough ground; *esp.* a steep bank or slope covered with undergrowth or trees; a coppice. Now *local.*

1600 HOLLAND *Livy* XXVIII. ii. 668 A mountaine countrey it was, full of roughs and crags. **1621** G. SANDYS *Ovid's Met.* I. (1626) 13 These roughs are craggy: moderate thy haste. **1669** WORLIDGE *Syst. Agric.* (1681) 331 *Rough,* the rough Coppice. Wood, or Brushy-wood. **1736** PEGGE *Kenticisms* (E.D.S.), *Rough,* a wood. *c* **1811** JANE AUSTEN *Let.* in *Pearson's 81st Catal.* (1900) 6 We walked Frank last night to Crixhall ruff, and he appeared much edified. **1841** HARTSHORNE *Salop. Antiq.* Gloss. 551 *Rough,* a wood or copse. **1878** JEFFERIES *Gamekeeper at H.* ii. 31 This mere boy at snap-shooting in the 'rough' will beat crack sports-men hollow.

c. The rough ground at the edge of, or between the greens on, a golf-course.

1901 *Scotsman* 9 Sept. 4/7 Thanks to Vardon having pulled into the rough, the Scotsman secured the sixteenth [hole]. **1955** [see BUNKER *sb.*[1] 4]. **1971** 'D. HALLIDAY' *Dolly & Doctor Bird* iii. 29, I played well that morning, and the two balls I shot into the rough I recovered. **1977** *Cork Examiner* 6 June 7/2 At the 13th, Higgins was in the rough off the tee. **1980** *Guardian* 10 June 25/3 A spectator found another in the left rough and Cisco found the other in the right rough.

3. A spike inserted in each heel of a horseshoe in 'roughing' horses to prevent slipping.

1884 KNIGHT *Dict. Mech.* Suppl. 770/1 If this steel rough be made to fit the hole exactly, it remains firm in its place.

4. *Comm.* A particular make of linen.

1890 *Daily News* 20 Dec. 2/5 Flax and Linen... Roughs and drills are going off steadily.

II. †5. a. Roughness (of the sea). *Obs.*⁻¹

13.. *E.E. Allit. P.* C. 144 Fysches Durst nowhere for roȝ arest at þe bothem.

†b. A spell of stormy weather. *Obs.*

1633 P. FLETCHER *Pisc. Eclog.* I. xviii, In calms, to pull the leaping fish to land—In roughs, to sing and dance along the golden sand. *Ibid.* VII. xxxii, In calms you fish; in roughs use songs and dances.

6. a. The rough, disagreeable part, side, or aspect of anything; that which is harsh or unpleasant; rough treatment, hardship.

1642 HOWELL *For. Trav.* (Arb.) 86 In the rough of their fury the greatest execration they use to rap out, is [etc.]. **1725** VANBRUGH *Prov. Wife* IV. iii, *Justice*... Does he not use you well? *Sir John.* A little upon the rough sometimes. **1801** MAR. EDGEWORTH *Contrast* Wks. 1832 V. 134 His new foreman bore the rough well. **1861** GEN. P. THOMPSON *Audi Alt.* clvii. III. 164 When he is brought into court, and trailed through all the rough of calling a spade a spade. **1893** C. G. LELAND *Memoirs* I. 31 When doing rough and tough in West Virginia.

b. Used in contrast to *smooth.* Also *pl.*

1612 *Buccleuch MSS.* (Hist. MSS. Comm.) I. 126, I truly delivered as well the rough as the smooth of all my speech. **1822** IRVING *Bracebr. Hall* (1890) 147 Through the rough and the smooth, the pleasant and the adverse. **1829** SIR T. LAWRENCE in D. E. Williams *Life* (1831) II. 519 The boys.. must encounter the rough and the smooth of weather, as of life. **1900** J. K. JEROME *Three Men on Bummel* 190 One must take a little rough with one's smooth.

pl. **1804** *Europ. Mag.* XLV. 334/1 In this manner had Blair and his horse Pocket..travelled, and taken the roughs and the smooths of the world together. **1862** THACKERAY *Philip* ix, You and I will take..the roughs and the smooths of this daily existence.

c. The heavier, rougher part of housework; freq. in phr. ***to do the rough.***

1946 M. DICKENS *Happy Prisoner* vii. 114 Cosy discussions on clothes and curtains and women to do the rough. **1950** J. CANNAN *Murder Included* iii. 39 He.. suggested having a woman for the rough. **1959** *Times* 21 Nov. 1/3 No cooking or rough. **1974** 'A. GILBERT' *Nice Little Killing* v. 70 The woman who came to do the rough twice a week.

d. Sharp, acid, or harsh drink; *spec.* (*a*) *slang,* draught bitter beer; (*b*) rough cider.

1946 J. IRVING *Royal Navalese* 147 'Rough', draught bitter beer. **1960** 'R. EAST' *Kingston Black* xiii. 129 He was selling the rough at three shillings a gallon.

7. A man or lad inclined to commit acts of violence or disorder in public; a rowdy.

1837 BARHAM in *Life & Lett.* (1870) II. 39 There'll be lots of new policemen, To control the rogues and roughs. **1847** *Illustr. Lond. News* 27 Nov. 339/1 Will you let the jury know what 'Roughs' are? I believe it is an electioneering name for ruffians. **1853** *Croker Papers* (1884) III. 268 To be stoned by some of the thousand roughs with which the accesses to Parliament will be thronged. **1883** LD. R. GOWER *Reminisc.* II. 108 She is educating and civilising a little colony there of roughs and vagabonds.

8. *colloq.* Short for ROUGH-RIDER.

1899 *Daily News* 23 Feb. 6/2 The Roughs swore by Roosevelt. **1900** *Westm. Gaz.* 17 July 8/1 The 'Roughs' and the 'Sharps' of the 18th Battalion Imperial Yeomanry.

III. 9. a. Rough or refuse matter in the working of minerals. Cf. ROW *sb.*[5] 2.

1677 YARRANTON *Eng. Improv.* 59 In the Forest of Deane ..iron is made at this day of Cinders, being the rough and offal thrown by in the Romans time. **1778** PRYCE *Min. Cornub.* 223 The rough that is carried back with the stream, by drawing it over again, may be rendered merchantable at a lower rate than the crop; and the rough of this rough, is thrown aside to make leavings. **1839** URE *Dict. Arts* 1244 The ore, on issuing, deposits its rough in the first basin. **1875** J. H. COLLINS *Met. Mining* 111 Material of a mixed nature, called 'dredge', or 'roughs', or 'rows'. **1881** RAYMOND *Mining Gloss., Roughs,*..coarse, poor sands, resulting from tin-dressing. **1887** P. M'NEILL *Blawearie* 174 Then it was indeed difficult to detect the foul from the *roughs* of the main coal.

b. *Agric.* (See quot. 1853.)

1844 H. STEPHENS *Bk. Farm* II. 267 A second woman is required to riddle the roughs from the foul spout into a heap by itself. **1853** *Encycl. Brit.* II. 282/2 The unthrashed ears and broken straw called *roughs* or *shorts.*

c. Applied to alum used as an adulterant in bread.

1855 *2nd Rep. Comm. on Adulteration of Food* 47 in *Parl. Papers 1854–5* VIII. 373 There are several trade names for alum; one of them, being very characteristic of its effects on the mucous surface, is 'roughs', and another is 'seasoning'. **1909** *Practitioner* Feb. 263 All the samples of bread contained alum, and an instance was mentioned of flour, with which as much as ten per cent. had been mixed... In the trade, the adulterant received the name of 'roughs'.

10. a. A rough draft. Also, a rough sketch, layout, etc.

1699 S. SEWALL *Diary* 23 Sept., Agree for 15*l.* and draw a rough of it and take his hand to it. **1710** in *Publ. Colonial Soc. Mass.* (1925) XV. 395 A rough of sundry Articles wᶜʰ drawn up. **1796** J. STEELE *Papers* (1924) I. 144 A rough of a letter which may at some future period compose part of a circular. **1936** *Punch* 12 Aug. 170/2, I don't suggest for a moment that these are *finished* ideas. They are no more than artists' roughs. **1961** WEBSTER, ²*Rough,*..4d rough proof. **1970** R. K. KENT *Lang. Journalism* 114 *Rough,* a preliminary layout or drawing, without details. **1975** J. BUTCHER *Copy-Editing* iv. 48 Alterations to artwork are caused as often by authors' inadequate or incorrect roughs..as they are by draughtsmen's mistakes. **1976** *Vogue* 15 Mar. 24/1 The roughs of my column are completed.

b. The rough state or material of anything; the rough outline of a spoon, etc.; hence ***rough-maker.***

1799 *Repertory Arts* X. 295 How, by means of a rotative saw, to shape a piece from the rough. **1879** *Cassell's Techn. Educ.* IV. 413/2 The 'rough-maker'..smooths off the burr left by the stamp, strikes up finally the under side, and bends down the little curve at the end of the handle.

c. Unhusked rice; paddy. (Cf. ROUGH *a.* 21.)

1837 *Civil Eng. & Arch. Jrnl.* I. 54 An Improved Mortar for Dressing Rough or Paddy, or Redressing.

d. Uncut precious stone; an uncut gem, esp. a diamond.

1920 in WEBSTER. **1961** in WEBSTER s.v., A huge piece of rough was cut to a superb gem of 128 carats. **1974** L. ST. CLAIR *Emerald Trap* (1975) i. 6, I want lots of big roughs. Finsch, Top Wesselton, maybe some Jaeger. **1976** W. GREATOREX *Crossover* 162 No thefts of rough have been reported, so I suppose they're clean?

11. ***in the rough***: **a.** In a rough, imperfect, or unfinished state; in a preliminary sketch or design.

1823 P. NICHOLSON *Pract. Build.* 159 Every kind of surface is first formed in the rough, and then finished by means of tools. **1848** MILL *Pol. Econ.* II. xvi. §4 (1876) 259 We must never forget that the truths of political economy are truths only in the rough. **1879** B. TAYLOR *Germ. Lit.* 99 An unlettered minstrel, with great qualities in the rough.

b. In an untidy state; in disorder; in an everyday condition.

1825 MRS. CAMERON *Seeds of Greediness* 3 'We are all in the rough to-day, Sir,' answered the woman; 'for I am very busy with this job'. **1844** DICKENS *Mart. Chuz.* xxxiii, 'You'll have a party?' said Crimple. 'No, I won't,' I said; 'he shall take us in the rough'. **1865** —— *Mut. Fr.* II. i, I wish you'd come with me, and take her in the rough, and judge her for yourself.

c. Approximately, roughly.

1868 ROGERS *Pol. Econ.* iii. (1876) 29 In the rough, it may be said that the cost of producing a pound Troy of gold [etc.].

†rough, *sb.*[2] *Obs.* Forms: 2 **ruhha, roche** (?), 3 **rohȝe,** 5 **rowhe, rowe, rowghe,** 6 **roughe.** [? late OE. *ruhha,* ME. type *roȝe,* = MDu. *roch(e, rochghe, rogghe* (Du. *rog,* Fris. *roch*), MLG. *roche, ruche* (hence Da. *rokke,* Sw. *rocka*), G. *roche,* †*roch.* Obscurely related to OE. *reohhe* REIGH.] The fish called the RAY.

c **1110** in Napier *Contrib. O.E. Lex.* 60 *Fannus,* suhha [? *read* ruhha]. *a* **1200** *Voc.* in Wr.-Wülcker 543 *Fannus,* ro(che). *c* **1275** LAY. 29557 Hii..nemen rohȝe tayl..and honge[de on h]is cope. *c* **1440** *Promp. Parv.* 438/1 Rowhe, or reyhe, fysche (*K.* rowe-fysshe, *P.* rowghe), *ragadies.* **1530** PALSGR. 264/1 Roughe fysshe.

rough, obs. var. of RUFF (the fish); see also ROUGHY.

rough (rʌf), *a.* Forms: (see below). [OE. *rúh, rúȝ-,* = Fris. *rûch* (pl. *rûge*), †*ruwg,* MDu. *ruuch* (*rugh-*), *ruych* (Du. *ruig*), MLG. *rûch, rûge* (LG. *rûg;* hence Da. †*rug*), OHG. *ruuh, rûh, rûch, ruoch* (G. *rauh*). Varying notation of the vowel and final guttural gives rise to a large number of spellings in ME. In OE. the stem *rúȝ-* also appears (by a normal change) as *rúw-,* whence ME. and later ROW *a.*]

A. Forms.

α. 1–3 **ruh** (1 **hruh,** 3 **ruhh**), 3 **ruhe, ruchȝe,** 1, 4, 6, 8 *Sc.* **ruch,** 5 *Sc.* **reucht,** 6 *Sc.* **rwch;** 4 **roh, rohu, rohw,** 5–7 *Sc.* **roche,** 6 *Sc.* **rocht,** 5, 8–9 *Sc.* **roch;** 5 **rouh, rowh,** 5–9 *Sc.* **rouch,** 6 *Sc.* **rouche, rowch;** 6 **routh, rowth.**

c **1000** *Saxon Leechdoms* III. 170 þæt he habbe ruh lic. *a* **1100** in Napier *O.E. Glosses* 3250 *Nodosi cippi,* ruches.. stocces. *Ibid.* 5189 *Hirsutas lanas,* hruhȝe wulla. *c* **1200** ORMIN 9663 Ruhh & harrd & sharrp. **12..** *Ancr. R.* 184 (MS. C.), Of þi ruchȝe sunnen. **13..** *Cursor M.* 21962 (Edin.), þe toþir sal be ful ruch and reþe. *c* **1450** HOLLAND *Howlat* 616 The rouch Wodwyss wyld. **1477** *Paston Lett.* III. 186 Fixid so fast with hys prikks rowh. **1523** SKELTON *Garl. Laurel* 803 Florisshyng of flowris, With burris rowth. *c* **1560** A. SCOTT *Poems* (S.T.S.) v. 58 Quhair the gait is ruch. **1596** DALRYMPLE tr. *Leslie's Hist. Scot.* I. 28 A rouch rock or craig. **17..** RAMSAY *Vision* ii, The air grew ruch. **1808** JAMIESON s.v., A rouch hass, or throat. **1872** W. ALEXANDER *Johnny Gibb* viii, Your fader—the roch dyker.

β. 1 **ruȝ,** 3–5 **ruȝ(e,** 5 **ruȝhe;** 4 **roȝ(e;** 4–5 **rouȝ, rowȝ(e,** 5 **rouȝe.**

? *a* **1000** *Gloss.* in Wr.-Wülcker 273 ðeþuf ficbeam,..*uel* ruȝ. **13..** *E.E. Allit. P.* B. 1545 þe honde..rasped on þe roȝ woȝe. **1382** WYCLIF *Gen.* xxv. 25 And al in maner of a skyn rowȝ. **1398** TREVISA *Barth. De P.R.* v. xxiii. (Bodl. MS.), ȝif þey been rouȝe and..brode. *a* **1425** *Cursor M.* 21962 (Trin.), þe toþer shal be wondir rowȝe.

γ. 4 **rug(g,** 4–7 (9 *sc.*) **rugh** (5 **rughh, rught);** 4–6 **rughe** (4 **rughȝe,** 6 **ruyghe);** 4–6 **rogh(e,** 5 **roght;** 4–5 **rowgh,** 5–6 **rowghe;** 5– 7 **roughe** (5 **rought),** 4– **rough.**

a **1300** *Cursor M.* 3489 þe first..was rogh as hare,..He þat was rugh was rede wit-als. **13..** *Ibid.* 24838 (Edin.), þe wedir..bigan be rug and reþe. *a* **1340** HAMPOLE *Psalter* lxviii. 14 Wiþ þe haire þat is rughe & sharpe. *c* **1400** *Destr. Troy* 6632 With a rught batell. *c* **1400** MAUNDEV. xxviii. (1839) 285 Thei beren gret Wolle and roughe. *c* **1440** *Promp. Parv.* 437/2 Rowghe, scharp or knotty. **1495** *Trevisa's De P.R.* IV. iii. 82 The thynge is rough. **1559** W. CUNNINGHAM *Cosmogr. Glasse* 45 The bodye..beyng a rough stone.

δ. 6 **rouf, roffe,** 6–7 **ruffe,** 7–8 **ruff.**

1577 B. GOOGE *Heresbach's Husb.* I. (1586) 28b, The blades of both kindes are ruffe. **1665** SIR T. HERBERT *Trav.* (1677) 20 Winds and ruff Seas. **1683** PETTUS *Fleta Minor* I. (1686) 9 It was ruffe and sharp. *a* **1738** SWIFT *To Dr. Sheridan* 12 Compar'd with which..A Smoothing-Ir'n itself is ruff. **1787** *Minor* 53 Saw away the ruff corners of your mind.

B. Signification.

I. 1. a. Having a surface diversified with small projections, points, bristles, etc., so as to be harsh or disagreeable to the touch; not even or smooth.

a **1000** *Riddles* xxvi. 5 Staþol min is steap,..neoþan ruh nathwær. *c* **1000** *Sax. Leechd.* I. 254 Ðeos wyrt..hafað leaf neah swycle mistel; þa beoð ruȝe & brade. *a* **1225** *Ancr. R.* 284 Nis þet iren acursed þet iwurðeð þe swarture & þe ruhure so hit is ofture & more iviled? **13..** *E.E. Allit. P.* B. 1724 þe fyste..rasped renyschly þe woȝe with þe roȝ penne. **13..** *Gaw. & Gr. Kt.* 745 þe hasel & þe haȝþorne..With roȝe raged mosse rayled ay-where. *a* **1400–50** *Alexander* 3815 þai..findis all þe strandis Full of Reidis..rughere þan thornes. *c* **1460** *Wisdom* 1055 in *Macro Plays* 70 Tyll þi nakyde body were all rought, Ande evyn rent to þe bonys bare. **1526** SKELTON *Magnyf.* 453 Whan the noppe is rughe, it wolde be shorne. **1553** EDEN *Treat. New Ind.* (Arb.) 16 Theyr skinne is very rowghe and full of chappes, and riftes like the barke of a tree. **1667** MILTON *P.L.* v. 342 Fruit of all kindes, in coate, Rough, or smooth rin'd. **1670** in *12th Rep. Hist. MSS. Comm.* App. V. 15 The silke..will soone grow rough, gather dust and sullie. **1774** GOLDSM. *Nat. Hist.* (1776) III. 221 The tongue is rough, and beset with prickles. **1781** COWPER *Retirement* 230 Rough elm, or smooth-grain'd ash, or glossy beech. **1820** SHELLEY *Prometh. Unb.* III. iii. 21 The rough walls are clothed with long soft grass. **1873** J. RICHARDS *Operator's Hdbk.* 135 The lumber is guided by its rough surface before coming in contact with the cutters.

b. Of cloth: Coarse; having a long nap.

a **1000** *Ags. Hymn.* (Surtees) 103 Ruhne wæfels, *yrcum tegimen.* *c* **1000** ÆLFRIC *Gloss.* in Wr.-Wülcker 125

Amphibalum, ruhhrægel. **1426** LYDG. *De Guil. Pilgr.* 17168 Off rowh frese, she hadde..A garnement shape lyk a sak. **1530** PALSGR. 322/2 Roughe as course clothe is, *rude*. **1611** BIBLE *Zech.* xiii. 4 Neither shall they weare a rough garment to deceiue. **1648** HEXHAM II, *Rouw laken*, Rough, or Course cloth. **1848** J. RUSKIN *Let.* 29 June in M. Lutyens *Ruskins & Grays* (1972) xiii. 123, I beg very *particular* thanks for the *Rough* towels. **1886** C. D. WARNER *Their Pilgr.* 3 A gentleman clad in a perfectly-fitting rough travelling suit. **1939** *Army & Navy Stores Catal.* 623/1 'Christy' bath towels rough brown linen pile... 'Christy' bath towels in mixed linen and cotton..a semi-rough towel for hard wear.

c. ***a rough bone***, one with meat on it. *Sc.*

1826 SCOTT *Woodst.* xx, A hungry tyke ne'er minds a blaud with a rough bane.

d. Applied to the surface of a tennis- or squash-racket on which the loops formed by the string(s) looped around others project; freq. in context of spinning a racket to decide the choice of service or ends. Opp. SMOOTH *a.* 1 d.

1890 [see SMOOTH *a.* 1 d]. **1911** C. H. B. QUENNELL in L. Weaver *House & its Equipment* 204 It spoils the game if, as a result of guessing 'rough' or 'smooth' [etc.]. **1973** M. RUSSELL *Double Hit* xxv. 186 Nevil spun his racket. 'Smooth,' said Colleano. 'Rough. I'll serve.'

e. *Bacteriol.* Applied to a bacterial phenotype characterized by corrugated and irregular colonies, and by cells lacking polysaccharide capsules.

[**1920**: see R. II. 2 a.] **1921** J. A. ARKWRIGHT in *Jrnl. Path. & Bacteriol.* XXIV. 38 The irregularity of the surface has led to this variant being called the Rough ('R') form in distinction from the Smooth ('S') form. **1949** L. R. THOMPSON *Introd. Microorganisms* viii. 106 Rough (R-type) colonies are characterized by a dull appearance, and a folded or uneven surface. **1974** Q. N. MYRVIK et al. *Fund. Med. Bacteriol. & Mycol.* ii. 25 When freshly isolated gram-negative pathogens are cultivated in the laboratory, they often undergo a smooth to rough (S→R) colony mutation.

2. a. Having the skin covered with hair; hairy, shaggy, hirsute. In later use *spec.* unclipped, unshorn; having a rough coat of hair.

c **1000** ÆLFRIC *Gen.* xxvii. 11 Esau min broðor ys ruh and ic eom smeðe. *a* **1225** *St. Marher.* 12 [She] sette hire fot uppon his ruhe necke. *a* **1250** *Owl & Night.* 1013 Hi goþ bi-tiȝt mid ruȝe uelle. **13..** *K. Alis.* 5956 He was rughher than any ku. **1382** WYCLIF *2 Kings* i. 8 A rowȝ man, and with an hery gyrdyl gyrd to the reenys. *c* **1400** MAUNDEV. (Roxb.) xxxii. 147 Þe folk er all full of feþers and rugh. **1481** CAXTON *Myrr.* II. viii. 83 Men and wymmen alle naked and also rowhe as beeres. **1565** COOPER *Thesaurus* s.v. *Horridus*, *Sus horridus*, a rough hogge with bristles standynge vp. **1610** SHAKS. *Temp.* II. i. 250 Till new-borne chinnes Be rough, and Razor-able. **1637** MILTON *Lycidas* 34 Rough Satyrs danc'd, and Fauns with clov'n heel. **1708** *Lond. Gaz.* No. 4421/8 Both are Rough, having lain at Grass all the Winter. **1875** *Encycl. Brit.* I. 396/1 Few fat sheep are now sent to market *rough* after the 1st of April. **1897** *Daily News* 2 Feb. 9/4 Fat bulls and rough cows were a difficult sale.

†**b.** Of hides: Undressed, untanned. Also of shoes, etc.: Made of undressed hide. *Obs.*

c **1050** *Voc.* in Wr.-Wülcker 468 *Pero*, hemming *i.* ruh sco. *a* **1300** *Cursor M.* 3677 Wit a rugh skin sco hidd his hals. *c* **1375** *Sc. Leg. Saints* xxxvi. (*John Baptist*) 279 With a belte of reucht skine made. **1432–50** tr. *Higden* (Rolls) I. 265 Hauenge clothes of the ruȝhe skynnes of bestes. **1489** CAXTON *Faytes of A.* II. xxxv. Kj b, All rounde aboute are nayled rowhe hydes and all wete and fresshe. **1508**– [see RILLING *sb.*¹]. **1588–9** *Reg. Privy Council Scot.* IV. 365 Rouch hydis and barkit leddir. **1645** *Rec. Elgin* (1903) I. 179 Sex roche hyddes pertaining to the said Johne.

3. Of ground: Difficult to traverse; uneven, rugged, broken; uncultivated, wild.

c **1000** *Life St. Guthlac* (1848) 20 Ða ferdon beȝen þurh ða ruȝan fennas. *c* **1200** ORMIN 9211 Whærse iss all..sharrp, & ruhh, & gatelæs þurrh þorrness & þurrh breress. **13..** *Gaw. & Gr. Kt.* 1898 Renaud com richchande þurȝ a roȝe greue. **1387** TREVISA *Barth. De P.R.* XVII. cxxvii. (Bodl. MS.), Paliurus is a þistel..& growiþ in rowȝ londe and vntelied. **1526** TINDALE *Luke* iii. 5 And the rought wayes shalbe made smoth. **1553** EDEN *Treat. New Ind.* (Arb.) 14 This region is rough with mountaynes. **1593** SHAKS. *Rich. II*, II. iii. 4 These high wilde hilles, and rough vneeuen waies, Drawes out our miles. **1611** BIBLE *Deut.* xxi. 4 The Elders of that citie shall bring downe the heifer vnto a rough valley. **1686** tr. *Chardin's Trav. Persia* 386 The Road is somewhat crooked and rough. **1719** DE FOE *Crusoe* I. (Globe) 297 We had some rough Way to pass yet. **1791** COWPER *Odyss.* VII. 346 The shore presented only roughest rocks. **1820** SHELLEY *Sensit. Pl.* II. 44 Into the rough woods far aloof. **1865** RUSKIN *Sesame* i. §26 Most men's minds are indeed little better than rough heath wilderness. **1885** *Law Rep.* Weekly Notes 146/2 A small cottage and some 22 acres of rough land held therewith.

fig. **1671** MILTON *P.R.* I. 478 Hard are the ways of truth, and rough to walk. **1741–2** GRAY *Agrip.* 53 Gain the rough heights, and grasp the dangerous honour. **1821** SHELLEY *Epipsych.* 72 She met me, Stranger, upon life's rough way.

II. 4. a. Of the sea or water: Running high, agitated, turbulent.

13.. *E.E. Allit. P.* C. 147 Hit reled on round vpon þe roȝe yþes. *c* **1400** *Destr. Troy* 3693 With a ropand rayne rugh was the se. **1470–85** MALORY *Arthur* XIV. v. 648 He came to a rough water the whiche roryd. **1553** EDEN *Treat. New Ind.* (Arb.) 33 The sea was very rough. **1593** SHAKS. *Rich. II*, III. ii. 54 All the Water in the rough rude Sea. **1615** G. SANDYS *Trav.* 17 The winds grew contrary: and the seas..too rough to be brooked by so small a vessell. **1662** J. DAVIES tr. *Mandelslo's Trav.* 117 The sea is rough at all times, there is no Landing without danger. **1743** P. FRANCIS tr. *Hor.*, *Odes* III. xii. 9 When he rises with vigor from Tiber's rough waves. **1808** JAMIESON s.v. *Heis*, One is said to get a *heisie* in a rough sea. **1862** MISS BRADDON *Lady Audley* x, She had always been..afraid of a rough sea.

fig. *a* **1596** *Sir T. More* II. iii. 27 A quiet ebb will follow this rough tide. **1769** SIR W. JONES *Palace Fortune* Poems (1777) 23 And rough with tempests [is] his afflicted breast. **1887** *Times* (Weekly ed.) 16 Dec. 1/3 He will find rough waters very soon.

b. Of weather, wind, etc.: Stormy, tempestuous, violent; rigorous, severe.

13.. *Cursor M.* 24838 (Edin.), Þe wedir als in somer smeþe Son bigan be rug and reþe. **13..** *E.E. Allit. P.* C. 139 Roȝ rakkes þer ros with rudnyng an-vnder. **1470–85** MALORY *Arthur* XX. i. 797 Wynter with his rouȝ wyndes and blastes. **1530** PALSGR. 669/2, I pull in the sayle of a shyppe, as marryners do in a roughe wether. **1565** COOPER *Thesaurus*, *Dies turbidus*, a foule rough day. **1605** SHAKS. *Macb.* I. iii. 147 Time, and the Houre, runs through the roughest Day. **1663** COWLEY *Verses & Ess.* (1669) 108 The roughest season of the sky. **1764** GOLDSM. *Trav.* 166 Turn we to survey Where rougher climes a nobler race display. **1784** COWPER *Task* III. 441 That no rough blast may sweep His garlands from the boughs. **1818** SCOTT *Let.* in *Lockhart* (1837) IV. iv. 123 Should the weather be rough,..do not think of riding. **1852** M. ARNOLD *Empedocles* I. ii. 246 Nor is the wind less rough that blows a good man's barge.

c. Of a voyage or journey: Accompanied or attended with, performed in, rough weather.

1854 DOYLE *Brown, Jones & R.* 2 After a rough passage, ..landed at Ostend. **1877** [see PASSAGE *sb.* 4].

5. a. Of actions, etc.: Violent; marked by violence towards, or harsh treatment of, others.

a **1300** *Cursor M.* 21962 His first comme it was ful smeth, þe toþer sal be rugh and reth. *c* **1400** *Destr. Troy* 10161 With a rumour full roide & a roght hate. *Ibid.* 13902 The ruerde wax ranke of þat rught fare. **1591** SHAKS. *1 Hen. VI*, IV. vii. 8 Rough deeds of Rage, and sterne Impatience. **1611** —— *Cymb.* IV. i. 22 Her Father..may (happily) be a little angry for my so rough vsage. **1635–56** COWLEY *Davideis* IV. 83 Nor was their Lust less active or less bold, Amidst this rougher search of Blood and Gold. **1756** tr. *Keysler's Trav.* (1760) IV. 446 The elector..seemed highly provoked at this rough usage. **1861** HUGHES *Tom Brown at Oxf.* ix, There might be some reason for the rough handling he had got. **1881** STEVENSON *Virg. Puerisque* (1903) 65 Those who have..not learnt the rough lessons that youth hands on to age.

b. Of places or times: Riotous, disorderly; attended with, or marked by, rowdiness.

1863 MRS. GASKELL *Sylvia's Lovers* iv, The town was rough with a riot between the press-gang and the whaling-folk. **1884** *Western Daily Press* 2 June 3/1 In the language of the police the Derby Day was the 'roughest' which they had ever experienced.

c. Troublous, unpleasant, unfortunate, unreasonable, unfair.

c **1856** W. WHITMAN *Daybks. & Notebks.* (1978) III. 670 That's rough. **1867** 'MARK TWAIN' *Let.* 5 Dec. in C. Clemens *Mark Twain* (1932) 16 Another devilish thing is that the Alta [California] copyrighted the letters—that was rough. **1889** A. LANG *Letters on Lit.* 183 As we had also lots of..boomerangs..the poultry used to have rather a rough time of it. **1891** F. PAGET *Spirit of Discipline* 164 Things promised a rough time for the Church at Ephesus. **1941** BAKER *Dict. Austral. Slang* 61 *A bit rough*, unreasonable, unfair. **1942** *Yank* 23 Sept. 14 At best the going's very rough. **1944** *Yank* 4 Aug. 5 'We were 66 days on the beach at Anzio,' said Egan. 'It was rough.'

6. a. Of language or expression: Harsh, overbearing; uncivil, rude; angry, passionate.

c **1400** *Destr. Troy* 2031 Antenor..rekont by row all þere rogh speche. **1535** COVERDALE *1 Kings* xii. 13 The kynge gaue the people an harde rough answere. *a* **1548** HALL *Chron.*, *Rich. III*, 14 b, Letters of a more rougher and hawter sort, not without minatorie termes. **1599** SHAKS. *Hen. V*, V. ii. 313 Our Tongue is rough, Coze, and my Condition is not smooth. **1617** MORYSON *Itin.* I. 84 Austine Barbadici.., by faire and rough tearmes, kept the league unbroken. **1647** CLARENDON *Hist. Reb.* I. §27 The Duke, by his rougher Dialect, in the end prevailed. **1709** STEELE *Tatler* No. 31 ⁋2 [He] called him..Lyar, Dog, and other rough Appellatives. **1754** CHATHAM *Lett. Nephew* v. 39 Towards Servants, never accustom yourself to rough and passionate language. **1848** THACKERAY *Van. Fair* lix, The landlady reproached herself bitterly for ever having used a rough expression to her. **1891** BP. W. HOW *Lighter Moments* (1900) 22 He answered with a rough 'Yes'.

fig. **1611** SHAKS. *Wint. T.* III. iii. 55 Thou'rt like to haue A lullabie too rough.

b. So of features or looks.

1595 SHAKS. *John* III. i. 104 The grapling vigor, and rough frowne of Warre. **1849** JAMES *Woodman* v, My friend,.. whose looks are rougher than his intentions.

7. a. Of persons, their disposition, etc.: Inclined to be violent, harsh, rude, or ungentle.

to cut up rough: see CUT *v.* 60 l.

1530 PALSGR. 322/2 Roughe, boystous in dealyng, *royde*. **1535** COVERDALE *Wisdom* xviii. 15 As a rough man of warre. **1593** SHAKS. *2 Hen. VI*, IV. ix. 44 Be not to rough in termes, For he is fierce. **1600** E. BLOUNT tr. *Conestaggio* 23 Fearing more the Kings choler, by reason of his rough inclination. **1607** SHAKS. *Cor.* III. ii. 25 You haue bin too rough, somthing too rough: you must returne, and mend it. **1746** P. FRANCIS tr. *Horace*, *Ep.* II. i. 384 The bards..Who dare not trust the rough, contemptuous stage. **1802** MAR. EDGEWORTH *Moral T.* (1816) I. xvii. 142 So rough in my manner to him..that he thinks I have no feeling. **1867** PRINCESS ALICE *Mem.* (1884) 170, I am so afraid they will be too rough with her. **1875** JOWETT *Plato* (ed. 2) I. 231 Nay, ..do not be rough; good words, if you please.

transf. **1671** MILTON *Samson* 1066 A rougher tongue Draws hitherward, I know him by his stride. **1742** GRAY *Spring* 38 Brush'd by the hand of rough Mischance. **1821** SHELLEY *Dirge for the Year* 9 So White Winter, that rough nurse, Rocks the death-cold Year to-day.

b. ***the rougher sex***; the male sex.

1781 COWPER *Conversat.* 843 Divest the rougher sex of female airs. **1822** SCOTT *Nigel* Introd. Epist., I must abide by the general opinion, that he is of the rougher sex.

c. Of horses: Not properly broken in; not easy to ride on. *rare.*

1590 SHAKS. *Mids. N.* V. i. 119 He hath rid his Prologue, like a rough Colt. **1685** COTTON tr. *Montaigne* I. xlviii, The Prince of Sulmona, riding a rough horse at Naples. **1797** *Encycl. Brit.* (ed. 3) VIII. 666/1 The more he trots, and the more he rides rough horses, the better.

8. Of remedies, medicines, etc.: Violent in effect; strong, powerful.

a **1674** CLARENDON (J.), He..forced him to a quicker and rougher remedy. **1705** ARBUTHNOT *Coins*, etc. (1727) 284 His Purgative Medicines are generally very rough and strong.

9. *colloq.* **a.** Bearing or falling hardly *on* a person, etc.

1870 BRET HARTE *Luck Roaring Camp* 2 Sandy Tipton thought it was 'rough on Sal'. **1887** BESANT *Kath. Regina* iv, She is a governess somewhere, I believe. It's rough on her, isn't it?

b. Severe *on*, 'down' *on*, a person.

1870 BRET HARTE *Luck Roaring Camp* 15 They're mighty rough on strangers. **1895** HARDY in *Harper's Mag.* Mar. 579 The management had..been rough on cousins ever since.

10. *dial.* Unwell, sick, ill; miserable, dejected, in a bad way.

1883 'MARK TWAIN' *Life on Mississippi* lii. 513, I spent my last 10 cts for..cheese & i felt pretty rough. *a* **1893** *Story of Dick* viii. 85 (Wilts. Gloss.), She was took rough as it might be uv a Monday. **1961** M. DICKENS *Heart of London* II. 204 He looks rough. Someone ought to do something. Take im to ospital. **1971** C. BONINGTON *Annapurna South Face* xvi. 196 'I'll never make it to Camp VI,' said Nick. 'I feel dead rough.' **1972** *Times* 22 June 4/1, I felt really rough..before I was admitted to hospital.

III. 11. a. Of sounds: Discordant, harsh.

c **1400** *Lanfranc's Cirurg.* 197 Also her vois is rowȝ, ouþer sumtyme it is wondirly scharp. *c* **1450** HOLLAND *Howlat* 215 The Ravyne, rolpand rudly in a roche ran. **1580** SPENSER *Let. Harvey* in H.'s Wks. (Grosart) I. 35 Rough words must be subdued with Vse. **1608** SHAKS. *Per.* III. ii. 88 The rough and woeful music that we have. **1683** KENNETT tr. *Erasm. on Folly* (1709) 16 The delivery of Achilles was rough, harsh, and hesitant. **1751** JOHNSON *Rambler* No. 92 ⁋12 It requires very little skill to make our language rough. **1845** *Proc. Philol. Soc.* II. 139 In general it will be found to have affected broad, rough sounds. **1876** BRISTOWE *Th. & Pract. Med.* (1878) 505 The roughest and most grating murmurs.

b. *Gram.* Aspirated.

1736 AINSWORTH *Lat. Dict.* II. s.v. *H*, The original softer א and ה,..and the rougher ע and ח the parent of H. **1746** [see BREATHING *vbl. sb.* 9]. **1785** *Ess. Punctuation* 153 That letters over which it [ʽ] is placed, should be pronounced with a rough breathing. **1880** *Encycl. Brit.* XI. 355/1 H still remained as the rough breathing.

c. Of the sound of an internal-combustion engine: irregular, excessively noisy.

In quot. 1945 with a pun on sense 10.

1930 *Engineering* 24 Oct. 534/3 A state of affairs which would cause the engine to be 'rough' in its running. **1945** C. H. WARD-JACKSON *Piece of Cake* (ed. 2) 53 When an engine sounds rough it is not well.

12. Sharp, acid, or harsh to the taste, *esp.* of wine or cider.

1545 ELYOT, s.v. *Asper*, *Asperum uinum*, a rough wyne. **1583** STUBBES *Anat. Abus.* II. (1882) 25 Harshe, rough, stipticke, and hard wine. **1606** SHAKS. *Ant. & Cl.* I. iv. 64 Thy pallat the[n] did daine The roughest Berry on the rudest Hedge. **1743** P. FRANCIS tr. *Horace*, *Odes* I. xx. 6 'Twas rack'd into a Grecian cask, Its rougher juice to melt away. **1800** *Med. Jrnl.* IV. 252 Six pounds and a half of syrup, which had rather an unpleasant rough taste. **1834** *Good's Study Med.* (ed. 4) IV. 110 New and rough port-wine, diluted with an equal quantity of cold water. **1892** *Sat. Rev.* 15 Oct. 435/2 That..attraction that West-country folk find in rough cider.

13. a. Of diction, style, etc.: Wanting grace or refinement; rude, unpolished, rugged.

1535 STEWART *Cron. Scot.* I. 5 Thocht thi langage be bayth rouche and rude, ȝit neuirtheles the sentence is richt gude. **1599** SHAKS. *Hen. V*, Epil. 1 Thus farre with rough and all-vnable Pen, Our bending Author hath pursu'd the Story. **1638** JUNIUS *Paint. Ancients* 27 The Art of Painting hath been about the time of her infancy..rough and poore. **1709** POPE *Ess. Crit.* 338 Most by Numbers judge a Poet's song; And smooth or rough, with them is right or wrong. **1751** CHATHAM *Lett. Nephew* I. 1 Your translation..is very close to the sense of the original.., the numbers not lame, or rough. **1818** SCOTT *Hrt. Midl.* xxxii[i], Gifted with a sort of rough eloquence which raised him above his companions. **1881** JOWETT *Thucyd.* I. Introd. p. viii, The old version of Hobbes..is very rough and inaccurate.

b. Of language, expression, etc.: coarse, vulgar, indelicate.

1958 *Spectator* 1 Aug. 176/2 It badly needs its rough jokes. **1961** in WEBSTER s.v., A rough anecdote for such an audience. **1976** *Honolulu Star-Bull.* 21 Dec. E-1/4 You learn to live with the rough language so it doesn't bother you.

14. a. Of persons, their disposition, etc.: Lacking in culture or refinement; uncultivated; having rude manners or ways.

1588 SHAKS. *L.L.L.* v. ii. 306 Their shallow showes,.. And their rough carriage so ridiculous. **1688** PENTON *Guardian's Instruction* (1897) 20, I was pleased to see the ruff boyish humour filed a little. **1709** ADDISON *Tatler* No. 108 ⁋4 A plain, rough, honest Man, and wise, tho' not learned. **1781** GIBBON *Decl. & F.* xix. (1787) II. 134 Who, under the semblance of a rough soldier, disguised the most artful insinuation. **1821** SHELLEY *Epipsych.* 440 The mossy tracks ..(Which the rough shepherd treads but once a year). **1842** MIALL in *Nonconf.* II. 249 A rougher earnestness than is at present fashionable. **1888** F. HUME *Mme. Midas* I. Prol., The man at his feet was a rough, heavy-looking fellow.

absol. **1784** COWPER *Tiroc.* 341 Great schools suit best the sturdy and the rough.

b. ***rough and round*** or ***tough***: cf. ROUGH AND READY.

c **1813** I. POCOCK in M. R. Booth *Eng. Plays of 19th Cent.* (1969) I. 67, I suppose old rough-and-tough, master Grindoff, will be here presently. **1825** SCOTT *Jrnl.* 18 Dec., I love the virtues of rough and round men. **1848** DICKENS

Dombey ix, A blundering young rough-and-tough boy like me.

c. Unrefined (but kindly or friendly).

1848 Dickens *Dombey* xxxii, The generous..youth, whom he had loved, according to his rough manner. **1864** Tennyson *Aylmer's F.* 591 Being much befool'd..By the rough amity of the other. **1873** Black *Pr. Thule* (1874) 9 Mackenzie offered them a rough and hearty welcome.

d. In slang phrases ***rough as bags, guts***, etc., uncouth, coarse. Chiefly *Austral.* and *N.Z.*

1919 W. H. Downing *Digger Dial.* 42 Rough as bags. **1925** Fraser & Gibbons *Soldier & Sailor Words* 246 *Rough as a sandbag*,..a term for a person who behaves unpleasantly. Uncouth. Objectionable. **1929** K. S. Prichard *Coonardoo* ii. 22 Ted was as rough as bags..a good-looking, good-natured bloke who could neither read nor write. **1938** E. Lowe *Salute to Freedom* 318 Rough as bags. Cleared his throat..and spat, just missing a pile of ribbons. **1941** Baker *Dict. Austral. Slang* 61 *Rough as a sandbag*, as for next. *Rough as bags, rough as a bag*, unpolished, crude, coarse. Esp. applied to persons. 'Rough as a pig's breakfast' is an equivalent. **1941** —— *N.Z. Slang* 53 [20th cent. N.Z. slang includes] rough as a bag (the Australians also have rough as bags), and rough as a pig's breakfast. **1946** E. G. Webber *Johnny Enzed in Middle East* 23 Smarten 'em up... Rough as bags. **1948** P. White *Aunt's Story* 34 Tom Wilcocks was as rough as bags. His neck was red and strong. The pollard had caked hard on his hard hands. **1966** G. W. Turner *Eng. Lang. Austral. & N.Z.* vi. 115 There is simile:..'rough as bags' (which I know better in the variant 'rough as sacks'). **1966** B. Beaver *You can't come Back* 118 I'm shy all right, but I'm not smooth... I'm rough as guts. **1968** F. Hardy *Unlucky Australians* 11 The old Territorian is a good bloke, rough as guts but his heart's in the right place. **1970** *Guardian* 25 July 6/1 Behan was most obviously gross and cussed and tragic and rough as ould bags. **1977** C. McCullough *Thorn Birds* x. 235 Even Dot MacPherson, the Bingelly heiress,..was rough as bags, no posh Sydney boarding school and all that crap.

15. Of occupations or exercises: Requiring or associated with rude energy or strength.

1717 Lady M. W. Montagu *Let. to Pope* ¶5 The softness and warmth of the climate forbid..all rough exercises. **1797** *Encycl. Brit.* (ed. 3) VIII. 665/2 This rough work, all at once, is plainly..detrimental at first. **1865** Ruskin *Sesame* ii. §68 The man, in his rough work in open world, must encounter all peril and trial. **1906** *Temple Bar* Jan. 6 Living in a native hut and maintaining himself by the roughest labour.

IV. 16. a. Of materials: In a natural or crude state; undressed, unwrought; not brought by working into a finished condition or form.

1434 in Dugdale *Monast.* (1846) VI. 1414/1 All the inner side of rough stone, except the bench-table-stones. **1435** *Coventry Leet Bk.* 181 Here is a ston of rough-iron, the whiche must be tendurly cherysshet. **1485** *Nott. Rec.* III. 231, vj. lode of rugh plaster vnbrenned. **1545** *Bk. of Rates* d ij b, Blowynge hornes the dossen... Roughe hornes the M. **1582** in *Trans. Jewish Hist. Soc.* (1903) IV. 93 For everie quintall of rough Copper he made (being cxij *li.*) he must have vij. Kebulls of Copper ure. **1601** *Act. 43 Eliz.* c. 10 §2 Other Engine to stretche or straine any roughe and unwroughte Woollen Clothe. **1670** Pettus *Fodinæ Reg.* 5 In these Veins..are often found Loadstones,..Rough pearl and Soft diamond. **1766** *Compl. Farmer* s.v. *Queen-bee*, The intestines of these bees are found at times to be more or less distended with honey, and with rough wax. **1788** Gibbon *Decl. & F.* l. V. 227 A chair or pulpit of rough timber. **1839** Ure *Dict. Arts* 704 The bloom or rough ball, from the puddle furnace. **1897** Henty *On the Irrawaddy* 131 As they [*sc.* jewels] were in the rough state, he had no idea what size they would be when cut.

†**b.** *Sc.* Raw, uncooked. *Obs.*$^{-1}$

1793 T. Scott *Poems* 351 Nae mair a rive o' gait, or fowl, Ha'f rough, ha'f roastet on a coal, But guid sirloin.

17. a. Made in a general way without detailed minuteness; having an approximate accuracy or adequacy, rudely sufficient; also, in a preliminary form, to be further improved or elaborated.

1607 Shaks. *Timon* i. i. 43, I haue in this rough worke, shap'd out a man [etc.]. *a* **1766** G. Colman *Posth. Lett.* (1820) 336, I have drawn out the above rough sketch, merely to enable you to think in the same train with me. **1801** *Farmer's Mag.* Jan. 21 A subject susceptible only of a rough guess. **1819** Scott *Let.* in *Lockhart* (1837) IV. viii. 255, I add a rough drawing of the arms. **1866** Rogers *Agric. & Prices* I. xxiii. 601 The possible produce was in a rough way understood and attained. **1882** Floyer *Unexpl. Baluchistan* 70 The inhabitants seemed capable of a rough division into three classes.

b. ***rough draft, draught*** (cf. draught *sb.* 32).

1699 Temple *Ess. Pop. Discontent* Wks. 1720 I. 263, I shall ..trace upon this Paper the rough Draught of some such Notions as I have had long and often in my Head. **1706** E. Ward *Wooden World Diss.* (1708) To Rdr. A vj b, This rough Draught of my untutor'd Pencil. **1712** Steele *Spect.* No. 272 ¶1 The rough Draught of the Marriage Settlement. **1831** [see draught *sb.* 32]. **1879** Froude *Cæsar* xiii. 173 His Agrarian law, the rough draft of which had been already discussed.

c. ***rough copy*** (cf. copy *sb.* 6).

1781 Cowper *Table-T.* 614 A rough copy of the Christian face Without the smile, the sweetness, or the grace. **1811** Miss L. M. Hawkins *C'tess & Gertr.* (1812) I. 259 She could not always read his rough copy. **1888** M. Robertson *Lombard St. Myst.* xxii, The supposed deeds were only rough copies.

d. Of stationery, etc.: for use in writing rough notes or exercises; in which preliminary records are written.

1867, etc. [see *rough book*, sense 21]. **1884**, etc. [see *rough log(-book)*, sense 21]. **1928** E. Scott *War among Ladies* I. iv. 44 Blotting-paper, foolscap, 'rough' paper..were laid out. **1960** *Sc. Nat. Dict.* V. 343/2 *Jot-book*, a rough note-book. *Ibid.*, A pupil's rough exercise book. **1977** P. D. James *Death of Expert Witness* ii. 101 His rough notebook?.. Anything of importance was noted in that book, and subsequently transferred to the files.

e. Applied to a vacuum of the lowest degree of evacuation.

1927 G. W. C. Kaye *High Vacua* vi. 74 For industrial purposes, such as exhausting rough vacuum mains, furnaces, or ovens, the so-called 'dry air pump' of the engineer is normally employed. **1949** S. Dushman *Vacuum Technique* iii. 141 With a 'rough' vacuum of about 10 mm mercury, such a pump could reduce the pressure to about 1 micron. **1969** *Gloss. Terms Vacuum Technol.* (*B.S.I.*) I. 7 *Rough vacuum*, 10^5 N/m^2 to 10^2 N/m^2. 760 torr to 1 torr. [*Note*] Not intended to be precise definitions, but to provide convenient and practical subdivisions of the vacuum range. **1976** *Physics Bull.* Apr. 161/1 Medium vacuum is used extensively for freeze drying and rough vacuum is also used for specimen handling and sample transfer.

18. a. Not very good or perfect.

1812 *Examiner* 7 Sept. 563/2 Barley rather a rough sample. **1862** Miller *Elem. Chem., Org.* (ed. 2) 337 *Red liquor*, a rough acetate of alumina used by the calico-printer. **1868** Joynson *Metals* 22 The iron..run into rough moulds or channels made in sand.

b. *London slang.* Coarse or stale (food).

1851 Mayhew *Lond. Labour* I. 53/1 The 'dropped' and 'rough' fish is bought chiefly for the poor. **1859** *Slang Dict.* 82 'Rough fish', bad fish.

c. Lacking in comfort or refinement.

1859 Jephson *Brittany* i. 5 Who can put up with rough accommodation on an emergency. **1881** R. Buchanan *God & the Man* II. v, The rough fare of the ship's crew.

19. a. Comprising or requiring only the ruder degrees or processes of workmanship or skill.

1680 Moxon *Mech. Exerc.* xi. 211 We will not suppose that the Grooves are of equal depth with the Rough-working of the Gouge. **1704** Fuller *Med. Gymn.* Pref., We know.. their Pharmacy was Rough and Barbarous. **1746** P. Francis tr. *Horace, Sat.* II. iii. 34 Here the rude chisel's rougher strokes I trac'd. **1803** *Med. Jrnl.* X. 90 To avail themselves of those methods, however rough and unsightly they may appear, which experience shews to possess great power. **1845** *Penny Cycl.* Suppl. I. 674/1 After the first or rough boring the interior is fine-bored. **1860** Tomlinson *Arts & Manuf.* 2 Ser. *Cutlery* 61 The first, which is called rough buffing, is with Trent sand, and the second, gloss buffing.

b. Ignoring, or incapable of, fine distinctions; not entering into minutiæ or details.

1819 Scott *Ivanhoe* xlii, The natural and rough sense of Robin Hood. **1855** Pusey *Doctr. Real Presence* Note B 43 Such a rough, indefinite mind as Luther's. **1873** Hamerton *Intell. Life* xi. ii. 405 In this rough justice of the world there is a natural distribution of rewards.

20. *Sc.* Having abundance or plenty, *esp.* of a homely or plain sort. Also ***rough and round***, coarse but plentiful.

1721 Kelly *Sc. Prov.* 145 He has a Hole under his Nose that will never let him be rough. **1808** Jamieson s.v., *A gude rouch house*, a house where there is abundance of provisions. **1818** Scott *Hrt. Midl.* xlv[i], Plenty of all the requisites for 'a rough and round dinner'.

V. 21. a. In special collocations, as **rough arch**, a discharging arch; **rough band**, *dial.*, a band playing 'rough music'; †**rough bear**, a Scottish variety of barley; **rough bine**, a prickly hop-bine (see quot.); **rough book**, *Naut.* (*a*) (see quot. 1867); also = *rough log*(*-book*); (*b*) a book in which rough notes are written, a jotter; **rough bounds**, (*a*) the Scottish Highlands; (*b*) part of western Inverness-shire; **rough calf** (see quot. 1952); **rough coal** (see quots.); **rough coat**, the first coat of plaster on lath; **rough coating**, = rough-cast *sb.* 2; **rough cut** *Cinematogr.*, the first edited version of a film, the state of a film after preliminary editing; also *attrib.*; **rough Epsom** (see quot.); **rough file**, a file with a deep-cut face; **rough grazing**, uncultivated land used for grazing; an area of such land; **rough-knots**, 'unsophisticated seamen' (Smyth); **rough log(-book)** *Naut.*, a book in which the particulars of a ship's voyage are first entered, to be written up later in the main log-book; **rough-mast, mortar, plate, -rendering** (see quots.); **rough mix**, a preliminary blend of separately recorded parts of a piece of music; **rough pâté**, pâté made with coarsely-chopped or -minced meat; **rough rice**, unhusked rice, paddy; **rough scruff, rough-scuff**, *U.S.* (see quots.); †**rough setter**, a rough-stone mason; **rough-skins**, *U.S.* (see quot.); **rough-slant**, *U.S.*, a lean-to, a rude shelter; **rough spin** *Austral. slang*, a misfortune; **rough-stoning**, scouring with rubbing-stone; **rough strings** (see quots.); **rough stuff**, (*a*) the bottom stuff for boots and shoes; (*b*) coarse paint used before the final coat; (*c*) unruliness, violent behaviour; **rough timber** (see quot. 1711); **rough-tonguing**, rude speech; verbal abuse, disparaging; a scolding; **rough trade** *slang*, a tough or sadistic element among male homosexuals, esp. prostitutes; the activities of homosexual prostitutes; (see also quots. 1935, 1973); †**rough wall**, rubble work; **rough-waller**, a builder of rough-stone walls.

1833 Loudon *Encycl. Archit.* §1075 All the doors, windows, etc., to be saved with *rough arches (to have discharging arches) over the same. **1854** *Wilts. Arch. Mag.* I. 88 The procession was in each instance headed by what is called a '*rough band'. **1771** *Encycl. Brit.* I. 61/1 The common barley,..the Highland barley, more commonly called **rough bear* [etc.]. **1846** J. Baxter *Libr. Pract. Agric.* (ed. 4) I. 398 What is commonly called 'white bine', tolerably free from the rough barbs which are often found on the under part of the leaves, which constitute a '*rough bine'. **1867** Smyth *Sailor's Word-bk.* 580 **Rough Books*, those in which the warrant officers make their immediate entries of expenditure. **1902** Conrad *Typhoon* v. 47 He copied neatly out of the rough-book the number of miles, the course of the ship. **1969** A. Laski *Dominant Fifth* ii. 43 She had been drawing on her rough book. **1814** J. Grant *Orig. Gael* 288 The people or Gael of the mountains, expressed in English by *rough bounds. **1830** *Encycl. Metrop.* (1845) XXI. 54/1 The most rugged district is that.. between Argyleshire, Loch Lochy, and the sea, and generally called the *Rough-bounds*. **1862** Skene *Introd. Dean of Lismore's Bk.* p. xv, The Garbh chriochan or rough bounds, consisting of Arisaig, Moydart, Moror and Knoydart. **1912** Monk & Lawrence *Text Bk. Stationery Binding* 85 *Rough calf or its substitutes require the surface well cleaned before tooling. **1952** A. W. Lewis *Basic Bookbinding* ii. 17 *Rough calf*, calf skin finished on the flesh side and used on books with the flesh side outermost. **1963** B. C. Middleton *Hist. Eng. Craft Bookbinding Technique* 286 Rough calf was much used in the seventeenth and eighteenth centuries. **1975** *Sotheby & Co.* (*Hodgson's Rooms*) *Catal.* 31 July–1 Aug. 45 Abelard (Peter) and Heloise. Opera,..a few leaves slightly soiled, eighteenth century rough calf, slightly rubbed. **1789** J. Williams *Min. Kingd.* I. 244 *Rough, roch, or rock coal,..is a free coal of various degrees of strength and hardness, commonly of a good black colour. **1839** Ure *Dict. Arts* 962 The open-burning cubical coals are known by several local names; the rough coal or clod coal, from the large masses in which they may be had. **1855** J. Phillips *Man. Geol.* 204 The coal is partly 'splint', partly 'rough' or 'cheery'. **1875** Knight *Dict. Mech.* 1993/2, **Rough-coat*,..the first coat on lath. On brick it is termed *laying*..; on masonry, *rendering*. **1791** W. H. Marshall *W. Eng.* (1796) II. 297 Stucco is analogous to the materials of a dam,..*Rough Coating, to the puddle of Canal Makers. **1939** *N.Y. Times* 2 Apr. x. 4/4 The only demands we have made on the producers as a Guild were to have two weeks' preparation time for 'A' pictures, one week preparation time for 'B' pictures and to have supervision of just the first *rough cut of the picture. **1952** L. Ross *Picture* (1953) iii. 108 Actually, every director should make the rough cut—the film as assembled from start to finish for the first time—himself. **1957** Manvell & Huntley *Film Music* iii. 59 Functional music may be composed after the film has been shot and assembled in rough-cut. **1970** *Daily Tel.* 23 Sept. 12/3 There was no censorship apart from the cutting of a single frame at the request of an East German Government representative who saw the pictures at rough-cut stage. **1978** P. J. Kavanagh *People & Weather* vi. p. ciii, He returned to the studio with his film, triumphant... But when he put together the rough-cut he was appalled. **1853** Ure *Dict. Arts* I. 57 The alum mothers are boiled down to a crystallizing point, and afford a crop of '*Rough Epsom', which is a sulphate of magnesia and protoxide of iron. **1834–6** *Encycl. Metrop.* (1845) VIII. 275/2 Files of the very coarsest sort are called *rubbers*, and the next in order to these are called *rough files. **1932** *Jrnl. Min. Agric.* XXXIX. 37 White clover can be successfully established on certain types of *rough grazings without mechanical cultivation. **1953** E. Smith *Guide Eng. Traditions* 1 'Rough grazing', wild open land over which various owners of livestock have grazing rights. **1966** I. Moore *Grass & Grasslands* iv. 30 The transition from ley to permanent pasture or meadows, thence to rough grazing and scrub, and finally to forest, is an orderly, gradual process. **1970** *Sruth* (Inverness) 16 Apr. 3/1 The reconditioning of regenerated areas of heath land and rough grazings. **1884** *Naval Encycl.* 701/2 **Rough log*, the book in which the journal of the ship is originally written. A smooth copy, signed by the watch-officers, is inspected by the commanding officer, and forwarded to the Navy Department. **1917** D. Wilson-Barker *Man. Elementary Seamanship* (ed. 7) vii. 225 Every officer keeps an account of the work..during his watch. This record he enters on a log slate, scrap, deck, or rough log, as it may be called. **1922** F. Riesenberg *Stand. Seamanship for Merchant Service* xviii. 761 The *smooth log* is a copy of the *rough log*. The latter is the original and valuable record. **1961** F. H. Burgess *Dict. Sailing* 174 *Rough log*, the deck log. **1948** R. de Kerchove *Internat. Maritime Dict.* 667/2 *Ship's log book*, a nautical record compiled from entries taken from the *rough log book. **1961** F. H. Burgess *Dict. Sailing* 68 *Deck log*, a ship's rough log book, in which is recorded all information about working the ship, and other events as they occur. **1962** G. Danton *Theory & Pract. Seamanship* xiii. 288 The Chief Officer's logbook..is virtually a diary of the ship's activities. The information contained therein is derived from the rough logbook, which is kept by the individual Officers-of-the-watch. **1970** D. M. Henderson *Seamanship* xxvi. 464 The rough, original or chart room log-book is written up by the Officer of the Watch or Officer of the Deck. **1867** Smyth *Sailor's Word-bk.* s.v. *Mast*, **Rough-mast*, or *rough-tree*, a spar fit for making a mast. **1977** *Rolling Stone* 24 Mar., I'd sneak back in and listen to the *rough mix. **1977** *Zigzag* Apr. 6/2 The way Stevie likes to work is to record something, then take a rough mix down to the country where he's got a little demo studio, and work out what he's going to put down within what's already there. **1775** Ash s.v. *Roughcasting*, The *rough mortar on the surface of a building. **1823** Crabb *Technol. Dict.*, *Rough mortar*, a sort of sand which, when mixed with mortar, makes it look as red as blood. **1961** G. Smith *Business of Loving* xi. 222, I settled on a *rough paté, some pheasant with game chips. **1974** *Times* 4 Nov. 14/8 We chose rough country pâté and Vichyssoise to start with. **1977** P. Harcourt *At High Risk* i. 19 We had a rough *pâté de la campagne*. **1883** J. D. Weeks *Rep. Manuf. Glass* 20 *Rough plate is the crude plate-glass as it comes from the annealing oven. **1823** P. Nicholson *Pract. Build.* 393 *Rough-rendering..means one coat rough. **1763** *Ann. Reg.* I. 92, 776 bushels of *rough rice. **1831** *Boston Even. Transcript* 1 Oct. 1/2 The *roughscruf of St Louis called my deliverer a Watchenago. **1865** 'Mark Twain' in *Californian* 18 Mar. 8/2 The ruff-scruff and rag-tag-and-bob-tail of noble old Calaveras. **1859** Bartlett *Dict. Amer.* (ed. 2) 371 **Rough-Scuff*, the lowest people; the rabble. **1864** Webster, *Rough-scuff*, a rough, coarse fellow. **1435** in Dugdale *Monast.* (1846) VI. 1415/1 Will. Horwode shall nether set mo nor fewer free masons, *rogh setters ne leyes thereupon. **1859** Bartlett *Dict. Amer.* (ed. 2) 371 **Roughskins*, a gang of Baltimore bullies. **1924** *Truth* (Sydney) 27 Apr. 6 *Rough spin, bad luck. **1940** F. D. Davison *Woman at Mill* 150, I had a rough spin. **1855** Mrs. Gaskell *North & S.* xii, There had been *rough-stoning done in the middle of the floor. **1823** P. Nicholson *Pract. Build.* 189 The pieces of timber which are thus placed under the steps are called *rough strings. **1842** Gwilt *Encycl. Arch.* §2026 The framed timbers which support the steps of a staircase..generally consist of two pieces inclined to the pitch of the stairs, called the *rough strings*. **1889** *Charity Organis. Rev.* Jan. 7 Clickers cut out the leather for the uppers, *rough-stuff cutters that for the soles and heels. **1913** J. London *Valley of Moon* I. iv. 32 There's goin' to be rough stuff down there in a minute. **1915** H. L. Wilson *Ruggles of Red Gap* ii. 30 But you'll have to be firm, because he's full of tricks. And if he starts any rough stuff, just come to me. **1919** W. H. Downing *Digger Dial.* 42 *Rough stuff*, an undisciplined, reckless, indecent, disorderly or disrespectful person or thing. **1925** Chesterton *Everlasting Man* I. i. 24 His chief occupation..was..treating women in general with what is, I believe, known in the world of the film as 'rough stuff'. **1940** Wodehouse *Eggs, Beans & Crumpets* 238 Your aunt..has a right to early information about any rough stuff that is being pulled on the premises. **1959** 'M. M. Kaye' *House of Shade* xx. 275 I'd have got that pro-Red nancy-boy before he started any rough stuff. **1978** *Lancashire Life* Apr. 73/2 The presence of a girl in a group of tipsy young men keeps them in check, however: the laughs are there but the rough stuff isn't. **1607** *Nott. Rec.* IV. 284 The marketts of sawen and cloven tymber..excepting all *rough tymber. **1711** W. Sutherland *Shipbuild. Assist.* 163 Rough Timber; that which is only cut down, and the Boughs lop'd off. **1916** 'Boyd Cable' *Action Front* 98 An' I admit I felt easier after that *rough-tonguin'... That slobberin' an' kissin' business ..may be all right for a lot o' bloomin' Frenchies. **1919** J. Buchan *Mr. Standfast* xii. 217 He would relish the rough-tonguing of non-coms. **1956** N. Marsh *Off with his Head* (1957) ix. 191 Maids up to castle heard his great-auntie giving him a terrible rough-tonguing. **1935** A. J. Pollock *Underworld Speaks* 99/1 **Rough trade*, a person picked up on the street by a sexual pervert. **1965** *Playboy* Aug. 124/2 The gay boys call us 'rough trade'! We're the ones they date.... We're the ones they buy presents for. **1967** *Evening Standard* 11 July 10/3 The gradual destruction..of..Boyde Ashlar..as he gets involved with what I believe is called the Rough Trade. **1973** *Amer. Speech 1970* XLV. 58 *Rough trade* n, pick-up from one of the occupations typical of tough men, such as truck drivers or dock workers. **1976** M. Machlin *Pipeline* xxxviii. 412 There were no gay bars or hangouts, and very few gays dared walk the streets in the more extravagant, deviant-type-wardrobes. Any gay activity in Fairbanks was probably confined to rough trade. **1978** C. Beaton *Parting Years* vi. 159 He made friendships too easily with the 'rough trade'. **1980** *Times Lit. Suppl.* 7 Mar. 253/3 Auden was a homosexual who..seems to have had a greater craving for a settled relationship and being loved than for rough trade or other casual excitement. **1398** *Hist. Dun. Script. Tres* (Surtees) p. clxxx, Exterius de puro lapide vocato *achiler*.., interius vero de fracto lapide vocato **roghwall*. **1864** C. W. King *Gnostics* 174 The common workman who ran up the body of the wall..was called the '*Rough-waller'. **1885** Westall *Old Factory* i, He was a first-rate hedger and ditcher and rough waller.

b. In names or animals, esp. fishes and reptiles, as **rough aphrodite, bullhead, dab**, etc.; also **rough-tail, -wing**, etc. Also **rough collie**, a long-coated black and white, or black, tan, and white collie; **Rough Fell**, a large long-woolled sheep of the breed so called, found in parts of the Pennine area; **rough greyhound** = deerhound.

1783 Barbut *Vermes* 43 *Aphrodita Scabra*, the *Rough Aphrodite. **1803** Shaw *Gen. Zool.* IV. ii. 259 *Rough bullhead, *Cottus Scaber*... Native of the Indian seas. **1806** *Rough collie [see collie]. **1872** 'Stonehenge' *Dogs Brit. Islands* (ed. 2) ii. viii. 175 The rough or shaggy-coated colley ..has a fine foxlike muzzle. **1931** A. C. Smith *About our Dogs* xvii. 275 The Smooth Collie should be identical in all features with the Rough, except in coat. **1977** *Grimsby Even. Tel.* 5 May 3/5 (Advt.), Cairns, Westies, Rough Collies, Old English Sheepdogs. **1840** *Cuvier's Anim. Kingd.* 323 *P[leuronectes] leminoides*, the Long, or *Rough Dab. **1916** W. J. Malden *Brit. Sheep & Shepherding* vi. 58 The *Rough Fell sheep of the moors and hills of North-west Yorkshire..and adjoining districts are clearly allied to the Scotch Black-face. **1945** J. F. H. Thomas *Sheep* ii. 30 The Rough Fell. Again a breed not numerically strong. **1960** Rough Fell [see Exmoor]. **1843** R. T. Lowe *Fishes Madeira* I. 55 *Trachichthys pretiosus*, Black-mouthed affonsin or *Rough-fish. **1883** Day *Fishes Gt. Brit.* II. 342 Fuller's ray, ..*Rough flapper, Edinburgh. **1888** Rough greyhound [see *fleet-hound* s.v. fleet *a.*[1] 4]. **1948** C. L. B. Hubbard *Dogs in Brit.* xv. 122 The Deerhound, or Rough Greyhound as it was then called, was a prized possession of the Scottish chieftain. **1802** Shaw *Gen. Zool.* III. i. 229 *Rough lizard. *Lacerta Stellio*... This species is remarkable for the unusually rough..appearance of its whole upper surface. **1769** Pennant *Brit. Zool.* (1776) III. 75 *Rough Ray... The upper part of the body..entirely covered with small spines. **1883** Day *Fishes Gt. Brit.* II. 346 The Homelyn ray: rough ray: sandy ray. **1781** Pennant *Hist. Quadrup.* II. 524 **Rough Seal*... Perhaps what the Newfoundland Seal-hunters call Square Phipper. **1866** *Chambers's Encycl.* VIII. 585/1 The Rough..Seal (*P. hispida*) frequents quiet bays on the coasts of Greenland. **1802** Shaw *Gen. Zool.* III. ii. 494 *Rough snake, *Coluber Scaber*. **1803** *Ibid.* IV. ii. 408 *Rough sparus, *Sparus Dentex*. **1661** Lovell *Hist. Anim. & Min.* 234 *Rough-taile [= the horse mackarel]..is a dry fish and engendreth thick juyce. **1887** *Encycl. Brit.* XXII. 192/1 s.v. *Snakes*, Family 3. *Uropeltidæ* (Rough Tails). **1877** *Nature* 3 May 18/1 A *Rough Terrapin (*Clemmys punctularia*) from the Upper Amazons. **1802** Shaw *Gen. Zool.* III. i. 55 *Rough tortoise, *Testudo scabra*? **1819** G. Samouelle *Entomol. Compend.* 408 *Tortrix rugosana*, the *Rough-wing. **1832** J. Rennie *Consp. Butterfl. & M.* 184 The Rough-Wing..appears the beginning of June on hedges. *Ibid.* 180 The Grey Rough-Wing. **1648** Hexham ii, *Een Steen-worm*, a *Rough-worme in a mans foote, or a Lope.

c. In names of plants, as **rough bindweed, bristle-grass, cadlock**, etc.

1601 *Rough-bindweed [see bindweed 2]. **1611** Cotgr., *Liset picquant*, Rough Bindweed. **1823** Crabb *Techn. Dict.*, *Rough Bindweed*,..the *Smilax aspera* of Linnæus. **1859** Miss Pratt *Brit. Grasses* 82 *Rough Bristle-grass. **1611** Cotgr., *Langue de bœuf*,..Ox-tongue, *rough or small Buglosse. **1790** W. H. Marshall *Midl.* Gloss. (E.D.S.), *Cadlock*, **Rough*,..wild mustard. **1859** Miss Pratt *Brit. Grasses* 73 Tufted Hair-grass..is also termed **Rough-caps*, from its long, narrow, rough, twisting leaves. *Ibid.* 63 *Rough Cat's-tail. **1849** Craig, **Rough-chevril*, the plant *Anthriscus vulgaris*. **1562** Turner *Herbal* ii. 26 a, Lagopus maye be called in Englishe Haris foot or *rough clauer. **1611** Cotgr., *Treffle bas*, hares-foot, rough Clauer. **1771** *Encycl. Brit.* II. 304/1 *Dactylis..glomeratus*, or *rough cock's-foot grass. **1805** R. W. Dickson *Pract. Agric.* II. 832 Rough Cock's-foot Grass..is a coarse, rough grass, but very hardy and productive. **1859** Miss Pratt *Brit. Grasses* 97 Rough Cock's-foot. **1889** Maiden *Useful Native Pl.* 143 *Trema aspera*,..'*Rough Fig'... This shrub is firmly believed by some to be poisonous. **1886** Britten & Holland *Plant-n.*, *Rough Grass, *Dactylis glomerata*. **1833** Sturt *S. Australia* I. iii. 118 The *rough-gum abounded near the creek. **1898** Morris *Austral Eng.* 180/1 Rough-barked or Rough Gum, *Eucalyptus botryoides*. **1784** Cullum *Hist. Hawsted* 4 *Rough Horse-tail, or Shave-grass (*Equisetum hyemale*) in woods. **1861** Bentley *Man. Bot.* 705 *Equisetum hyemale*, Rough Horse-tail, which is largely imported from Holland under the name of Dutch Rushes. **1883** *Almondbury Gloss.* s.v. *Kex*, There are two sorts of kex—Shiny Kex, *Angelica sylvestris*; and *Rough Kex, *Heracleum spondylium*. **1877** E. Leigh *Cheshire Gloss.*, **Rough-nut*, the sweet or Spanish chestnut. **1548** Turner *Names Herbes* (E.D.S.) 76 It may be called in englishe Cow-persnepe or *rough Persnepe. **1797** Billingsley *Agric. Somerset* 116 The sorts [of potatoes] cultivated are the kidney,..*rough red, purple, and silver-skin. **1886** Britten & Holland *Plant-n.* 408 *Rough Robin, *Lychnis Flos-cuculi*. **1548** Turner *Names Herbes* (E.D.S.) 46 It maye be named in englishe *rough Trifoly or harefote. **1886** Britten & Holland *Plant-n.*, *Rough Weed, *Stachys palustris*.

22. With sbs. used attrib., as ***rough-board, -edge, -water, -weather, -wood***.

1833 *Chambers's Edin. Jrnl.* 1 June 141/1 Those who are tough, keep the deck in their rough-weather cloaks. **1862** Burton *Book-hunter* i. 18 He was not a black-letter man,.. or a rough-edge man. **1865** Dickens *Mut. Fr.* ii. xii, Rough-weather nautical clothes. **1893** *Outing* XXII. 122/1 Curiosities without number hide the rough-board walls. **1898** H. E. A. Coate *Realities of Sea Life* xiv. 124 All hands very busy in unbending rough-weather sails and bending fine-weather ones. **1921** W. de la Mare *Crossings* 67 A garden chair beside a roughwood table. **1967** *Gloss. Terms Air-Cushion Vehicles (B.S.I.)* 7 *Rough water drag*, the increment in the drag during operation in rough water over the drag, under otherwise identical conditions, in calm water. **1971** *Flying* Apr. 27/1 A deep V bottom provides lower impact loads on rough-water landings. **1978** J. A. Michener *Chesapeake* iv. 184 The entire group of Quakers went..to the rough-wood house of James Lamb.

23. *Comb.*, forming parasynthetic adjs., as ***rough-backed, -barked, -bearded, -edged, -faced, -grained, -mouthed, -surfaced***, and sbs. derived from these, as ***rough-handedness, -heartedness***; also ***rough-looking***.

1836 J. G. Whittier *Mogg Megone* 11 The gnarlèd trunk of the *rough-barked oak. **1837** *Penny Cycl.* IX. 396 Any other rough-barked plant. **1612** Webster *White Devil* v. i, No *rough-bearded comet Stares on thy mild departure. **1828** J. E. Smith *Engl. Flora* II. 49 Leaflets ovate, pinnatifid, *rough-edged. **1932** D. Gascoyne *Roman Balcony* 36 Glittering, rough-edged shadows on the dull lawn. **1970** *Daily Tel.* 23 Jan. 6 Rough-edged men who cannot complete a sentence without a four-letter word. **1978** J. Carroll *Mortal Friends* ii. vii. 216 He threw himself into the fray with a fierceness that was rough-edged and merciless even for him. **1812** E. Weeton *Let.* 25 May (1969) II. 15 A *rough-faced fellow, a journeyman saddler. **1895** F. M. Crawford *Casa Braccio* xvii, The lower story was built of rough-faced blocks of travertine stone. **1849** D. J. Browne *Amer. Poultry Yd.* (1855) 243 One short, squat, *rough-feathered, ill-marked goose. **1611** Cotgr., *Perche de mer*, the sea Perch; a wholesome, *rough-find, and tongue-lesse, rocke-fish. **1703** J. Philips *Splendid Shilling* 128 Walnut in *rough-furrow'd Coat secure. **1704** *Dict. Rust.* (1726) s.v. *Oak*, The *rough-grain'd Body of a stubbed Oak. **1840** Dickens *Old C. Shop* xv, A gentle hand—rough-grained and hard though it was. **1962** in E. E. Evans-Pritchard *Ess. Social Anthropol.* v. 115 He represented a sultan who excels the ordinary people in body and spirit, and one gained the impression that one was dealing with a rough-grained, able and cunning man. **1548** Elyot, *Hispidus*, bristled, or *rough heared. **1648** Hexham ii, *Ruydigheydt*, Scabbinesse, Scurvinesse, or Rough-haired. **1793** Martyn *Lang. Bot.*, *Hirtus*, rough-haired. **1863** *Life Normandy* II. 224 A couple of big rough-haired deer-hounds. *a* **1680** Butler *Charact., A Bumpkin* (1908) 41 He is never without some *rough-handed Flatterer, that rubs him, like a Horse, with a Curry-Comb. **1870** J. B. Brown *Eccles. Truth* 269 The age of conquest and rough-handed violence. **1889** Gretton *Memory's Harkback* 22 One instance as well as a hundred will tell my babyism and their *rough-handedness. **1856** Lever *Martins of Cro' M.* 244 To rub shoulders with the coarse-minded, the *rough-hearted, and the vulgar. **1615** Byfield *Coloss.* iii. 12 The first is fear .., as it is opposed unto boldness, conceitedness, *rough-heartedness. **1860** Ruskin *Unto this Last* iv. §79 These *rough-jacketed, rough-worded persons. **1806** Surr *Winter in London* III. 226 A *rough-looking sea-faring man, about four-and-thirty years old. **1630** *R. Johnson's Kingd. & Commw.* 279 More *rough mannerd than the Silesians and Bohemians. **1899** A. Bennett *Jrnl.* 29 Oct. (1932) I. 96 The actual coarse, ignorant, crude-thinking, *rough-mouthed maiden of past times. **1594** Nashe *Unfort. Trav.* Wks. (Grosart) V. 104 Boulstered out with *rough plumed siluer plush. **1690** Norris *Beatitudes* (1692) 83 The World is made for the bold and violent, the *rough-spirited and turbulent. **1926** *Rough-surfaced [see offset *sb.* 10 b]. **1962** *Science Survey* XI. 166 There are smooth-surfaced vesicles, vacuoles and tubules; flattened sacs whose limiting membranes are encrusted with particles and therefore 'rough'-surfaced. **1593** Nashe *Christ's T.* Wks. (Grosart) IV. 248 Hee wil sende a *rougher stringed scourge amongst vs. **1533** *Rough-tasted [see apple *sb.* 1]. **1731** Miller *Gard. Dict.* s.v. *Wines*, Of the same Sort are certain austere or rough-tasted Substances. **1872** Tennyson *Gareth & Lynette* 885 *Rough-thicketed were the banks and steep. **1598** Marston *Sco. Villanie* iii. ix. 217 Higher straines Then well beseemes a *rough-tongu'd Satyres part. **1855** Kingsley *Heroes, Argonauts* v. 165 They were rough-tongued. **1728** Chambers *Cycl.* s.v. *File*, Some cutting faster, as the *rough-tooth'd file. **1818** Keats *Endym.* ii. 864 No longer did he wage A *rough-voic'd war against the dooming stars. **1865** Morris *Jason* xvii. 79 The shout Of rough-voiced sea-folk endeth every song.

b. In specific names of animals, birds, etc.

1890 *Cent. Dict.* s.v., The *rough-backed cayman, *Alligator* or *Caiman trigonatus*, of South America. **1785** Latham *Gen. Synop. Birds* VI. 586 *Rough-billed Pelican. **1803** Shaw *Gen. Zool.* IV. ii. 191 *Rough-finned band-fish, *Cepola Trachyptera*. **1901** *Nature* 19 Sept. 523/2 Seven *rough-keeled snakes (*Dasypeltis scabra*). **1843** R. T. Lowe *Fishes Madeira* I. 155 *Mugil corrugatus*, Common or *Rough-lipped Grey Mullet of Madeira. **1887** *Cassell's Encycl. Dict.*, *Rough-necked jacare..from Demarara. **1758** Borlase *Nat. Hist. Cornw.* 276 *Rough-ridged limpet. *c* **1711** Petiver *Gazophyl.* vi. 58 *Rough-scaled Cape Lizard. **1801** Shaw *Gen. Zool.* I. i. 134 *Rough-Tailed Bat. **1871** Darwin *Desc. Man* ii. xii. (1890) 332 The rough-tailed stickleback (*G. trachurus*). **1838** Audubon *Ornith. Biog.* IV. 593 *Rough-winged Swallow, *Hirundo Serripennis*. *Ibid.* 595 In its general appearance..the Rough-winged Swallow is extremely similar to the Bank Swallow. **1872** Coues *N. Amer. Birds* 114 *Stelgidopteryx*, Rough-winged Swallow.

c. In specific names of plants. ***rough-stalked meadow-grass***.

1882 *Proc. Berwick Nat. Club* IX. 430 There is a fine cluster of *rough-barked Spanish chestnuts among the oaks. **1889** Maiden *Useful Native Pl.* 441 The former [was called] by the colonists 'Rough-barked Bloodwood'. *Ibid.* 85 *Echinopogon ovatus*,..*Rough-bearded Grass. **1833** *Proc. Berwick Nat. Club* I. 29 *Hieracium prenanthoides*—*Rough-bordered Hawkweed. **1753** *Chambers' Cycl.* Suppl. s.v. *Tithymalus*, The wart-Spurge, or *rough-fruited Spurge. **1822** *Hortus Anglicus* II. 7 *P. Argemone*, Long *Rough-headed Poppy. **1789** J. Pilkington *View Derbysh.* I. 443 *Lathyrus hirsutus*, *Rough podded Vetchling, or Pease-everlasting. **1796** Withering *Brit. Plants* (ed. 3) III. 640 *Ervum hirsutum*, Rough podded Tare. **1822** *Hortus Anglicus* II. 246 *L. Hirsutus*, Rough-podded Lathyrus. *Ibid.* 463 *T. Dactyloides*, *Rough-seeded Tripsacum. **1805** R. W. Dickson *Pract. Agric.* II. 826 The Common or *Rough-stalked Meadow Grass. **1901** H. M. Ward *Grasses* iii. 42 *Poa trivialis*. (Rough-stalked Meadow-grass.) Conspicuous in deep rich pastures. **1960** *Farmer & Stockbreeder* 8 Mar. 117/1 Rough-stalked meadow grass, bent, and wild white clover together with a few so-called 'weeds'. **1854** H. Miller *Sch. & Schm.* (1858) 398 The characteristic vegetable is the *rough-stemmed tangle—*Laminaria digitata*.

rough (rʌf), *adv.* Also 7–8 ruff; *Sc.* 6 (8) ruch, 9 rouch, roch. [f. the adj. Cf. the earlier form row *adv.*]

1. a. In a rough manner; roughly, rudely; without special care or accuracy, etc.

1560 Rolland *Seven Sages* Prol. iii, Scho..Meruellit at me how I durst..Aganis wemen to speik sa ruch and rude. **1610** Holland *Camden's Brit.* (1637) 759 The river Cam, which running rough upon stones, cutteth through it. **1680** Otway *Orphan* ii. iv, Should you charge me rough I should but weep. **1687** *Lond. Gaz.* No. 2289/7 A plain brown cropt Nag,..Walks and trots well, gallops rough. **1762** Mills *Syst. Husb.* I. 92 Before the land is plowed rough for a spring crop. **1780** *Mirror* No. 97 They should be taught..to speak their own language rough and round. **1858** Kingsley *Poems* 62 As we pledge the health of our general, Who fares as rough as we. **1897** *Outing* XXX. 481/2 In polo, a man rides rough all the time. **1954** L. Klemantaski tr. *Fraichard's Le Mans Story* v. 52 'The engine is running rough!' he cried. **1978** J. Gardner *Dancing Dodo* xxxviii. 308 The port engine faltered... She had started to run rough.

b. *to lie (live, sleep) rough* (see quots.).

1697 Dryden *Virg. Georg.* iii. 357 Rough upon the flinty Rock he lyes. *a* **1700** B. E. *Dict. Cant. Crew*, *To lie Rough*, in one's Clothes all Night. **1796** *Grose's Dict. Vulg. T.* (ed. 3), *To lie rough*,..to sleep on the bare deck of a ship. **1824** Scott *Redgauntlet* ch. xii, Job will take you to a place where you may sleep rough till he calls you. **1893** *Wiltshire Gloss.*, 'To sleep rough', or 'lay rough', to sleep about out of doors like a vagabond. **1960** *Guardian* 7 Dec. 1/4 He had been sleeping rough with the others on a haystack. **1974** *Whig-Standard* (Kingston, Ontario) 11 Jan. 7/1 A 'dosser'.. Sleeps on a bench, wrapped in a newspaper, living 'rough'. **1974** J. I. M. Stewart *Gaudy* ix. 172 We neither of us had a bean, you see, and I was just going to sleep rough. **1977** *Jrnl. R. Soc. Arts* CXXV. 148/2 There are going to be 2000 single people in London without homes sleeping rough this Christmas.

2. *Comb.* **a.** With verbs, as ***rough-bore***, to bore roughly, ***rough-dig, -edit, -enter, -hull, -lay, -land, -school, -sketch, -sort***, etc.

1565 Cooper *Thesaurus*, *Crustare parietes*,..to rough lay; to pariette walles. **1593** Nashe *Christ's T.* Wks. (Grosart) IV. 69 Now the raine wil rough-enter through the crannies of theyr wauering. **1679** Moxon *Mech. Exerc.* ix. 155 They generally Rough-plain their Boards for Flooring. **1776** G. Semple *Building in Water* 3 They..could not conveniently get the Ruins at that Time removed, therefore, they only just rough-levelled them. **1793** Smeaton *Edystone L.* §81, I immediately rough-turned a piece of wood. **1812** Sir J. Sinclair *Syst. Husb. Scot.* ii. App. 50 After kiln-drying the barley, it is put into the mill, and rough hulled. **1829** A. Cunningham *Lives Brit. Painters* I. 111 Having received an agreeable letter from Dr. Franklin he rough-wrote an answer. **1881** Miss Braddon *Asphodel* II. 66 [He] had rough-ploughed a thousand acres or so of his best land. **1890** W. J. Gordon *Foundry* 18 At first it is rough bored, should it not have been cast hollow. **1909** *Country Life* 23 Oct. 577/1 One could see him rough-schooling younger brothers and companions. **1910** W. J. Locke *Simon* xxiv. 315 The story of his marriage is a little lunatic drama all to itself and I will tell it some day. But now I can only rough-sketch the facts. **1950** Partridge *Here, There & Everywhere* 166, I should like to rough-sketch the position occupied by him and Lewis Carroll in the chronology of the subject. **1960** *Aeroplane* XCIX. 541/2 Turning to lunar and interplanetary research, Mr. Stoller said that in 1962 three Ranger vehicles were planned to rough-land payloads on the surface of the Moon. These will be followed by the soft-landing mission. **1962** A. Nisbett *Technique Sound Studio* vii. 124 It will often be possible to rough edit without bothering to mark the tape. **1969** W. Rutherford *Gallows Set* iv. 55 This film has already been rough-edited... That means that the editor will have done all the obvious things, taken out false starts, put in the cutaway questions. **1972** H. Evans *Newsman's Eng.* i. 1 The international news..has been checked, rough-edited. **1976** *Norwich Mercury* 19 Nov. 11/3 It is advisable to rough-dig all uncropped land. **1978** *Cahiers de Lexicologie* XXXII. 31 Assembling and rough-sorting a citation collection.

b. With pa. pples. used attributively or predicatively, as ***rough-bedded, -bound, -built, -clad, -cut, -dug, -hurled, -plucked, -scored, -split, -trimmed***, etc.

1593 Shaks. *Lucrece* 1249 As in a rough-grown grove. **1612** Drayton *Poly-olb.* i. 52 Thou Jersey, bravely crown'd With rough-imbattl'd rocks. **1683** Moxon *Mech. Exerc., Printing* xiii. ¶3, I have Fil'd the Face..with a Rough-Cut-File. **1727–46** Thomson *Summer* 1761 A savage ..with the unfashioned fur Rough-clad. **1793** Smeaton *Edystone L.* §148 The second step rough bedded. **1818** Scott *Rob Roy* xix, The crowd..forced its way up a steep and rough-paved street. **1864** Tennyson *Enoch Arden* 95 His face, Rough-redden'd with a thousand winter gales. **1865** G. M. Hopkins *Poems* (1967) 20 Those crookèd rough-scored chequers may be pieced To crosses meant for Jesu's. **1870** D. G. Rossetti *Let.* 21 Apr. (1965) II. 851, I suppose the inscription at the back of the rough-bound copy sent is from the real block. **1877** R. J. More *Under the Balkans* 215 A small bit of woollen carpet laid on the red rough-plastered floor. **1882** W. D. Hay *Brighter Britain!* I. v. 120 Rough-split sections of the great logs. **1887** Ruskin *Præterita* II. 400 Floors and partitions all of rough-sawn larch. *a* **1892** J. G. Whittier in S. T. Pickard *Life & Lett. Whittier* (1894) I. i. 13 And lo! in the midst of a clearing stood The rough-built farmhouse, low and lone. **1909** *Daily Chron.* 18 Oct. 4/5 Fowls are sold both dead and rough-plucked, and alive for fattening. **1925** Blunden *Eng. Poems* 31 As wave-wise Rough-hurled they rose, With a sweet sureness. **1965** G. J. Williams *Econ. Geol. N.Z.* xiv. 221/1 During the second world war about $1\frac{1}{2}$ tons of rough-trimmed mica were won from this area. **1967** E. Short *Embroidery & Fabric Collage* ii. 38 Woven silks were embellished with rich all-over embroidery which incorporated pearls and rough-cut gem stones. **1973** R. Adams *Watership Down* xx. 125 The Honeycomb was still rough-dug and half-finished. **1976** *Cumberland News* 3 Dec. 35/3 (Advt.), Oven ready and rough plucked birds.

c. With pres. pples., as ***rough-blustering, -clanking, -living, -rising***.

1605 Sylvester *Du Bartas* ii. iii. *Lawe* 1003 Rough-blust'ring Boreas nurst with Riphean snow. **1729** Savage *Wanderer* ii. 15 Rough-rising from yon sculptur'd wall, Bold prophets nations to repentance call! *Ibid.* v. 460 His chains rough-clanking to discordant groans. **1743** Francis tr. *Hor., Odes* iii. vii. 28 The rough-swelling tides. **1808** Jamieson s.v. *Rouch*, A profane swearer, a drunkard, &c. is called a rouch, or a rouch-living man.

d. With vbl. sbs., as ***rough-boring, -editing, -landing, -rolling, -schooling***.

1853 Ure *Dict. Arts* (ed. 4) II. 509 Shingling..costs, in wages, 1*s.* 9*d.* per ton; and rough-rolling, 1*s.* 2*d.* **1890** *Rep. Brit. Assoc.* 939 The mild steel..is after forging and rough-boring subjected to the process of oil-hardening. **1909** *Spectator* 30 Oct. 678/2 Sir Percy Fitzpatrick is certainly right in picking out..the 'rough-schooling of younger boys and companions'. **1959** *Fortune* July 157/1 A somewhat more difficult trip..will be the rough landing of a fifty-pound payload on the moon. **1962** A. Nisbett *Technique Sound Studio* vii. 117 *Rough editing* is assembling the main body of the programme in the right order and taking out the longer stretches of unwanted material.

rough (rʌf), *v.*[1] Also 8 ruff. [f. the adj.]

I. 1. *trans.* †**a.** To raise a nap on (cloth); = row *v.*[7] *Obs.*

1483–4 *Act 1 Rich. III*, c. 8 §13 Tayntours..for evenynge of cloth onely after it commeth from the Mille and before it be roughed [*AF. text* roughez].

b. To turn, pull, scrape or rub *up*, so as to make rough. Also *fig.*

1763 Mills *Pract. Husb.* III. 125 The wheat..felt a little rough in the hand, because, not having been stirred for six years, the little hairs that are at the extremity of the grain, and the particles of the bran, were roughed up. **1850** Holtzapffel *Turning* III. 1121 The face of the polisher is roughed up, or thoroughly scraped with an old razor blade or knife. **1879** Jefferies *Wild Life* 124 If the hurricane roughs up the straw on all the ricks in the parish. **1884** —— *Life of Fields* (1891) 171 It roughs them up the wrong way.

c. To make rough; to ruffle.

1844 Mrs. Browning *Dead Pan* x, Thine eagle, blind and old, Roughs his feathers in the cold. **1875** R. Browning *Aristoph. Apol.* 114 Go ask my rivals..how they roughed my fleece. **1887** *Daily News* 29 Sept. 3/1 The salt water caused it to blister and roughed her bottom.

d. *spec.* (See quots.)

1825 Jennings *Dial. W. Eng.* p. xviii, *To Rough*, to roughen; particularly a horse's shoes. **1838** Holloway *Prov. Dict.*, *To rough*, to put long headed nails into a horse's shoes to make them rough, and so prevent the horse from slipping in frosty weather. **1889** Gretton *Memory's Harkback* 152 The ordinary remedy was to 'rough' your horse; that is, to turn up the heels of the shoes, and fasten them with great-headed nails.

2. a. To offend, grate upon (the ear).

1623 H. Sydenham *Serm.* (1637) 133 Those eares which have been stockt hitherto with the supple dialect of the Court..will not be rough't now with the course phrase of a reproofe.

b. To use rough language to (a person); to ruffle (one).

1861 Hughes *Tom Brown at Oxf.* iii, [He] lost no chance of roughing him in his replies. **1883** *Cent. Mag.* Sept. 737, I didn't mean to rough you when I said that. I don't want to hurt your feelings.

c. To deal roughly with, ill-use. See also sense 6g.

1845 W. G. Simms *Wigwam & Cabin* 1st Ser. 58 She [*sc.* a bear] roughed me once or twice more with her paws. **1868** *Pall Mall G.* 5 Oct. 4 This year a band of these Hungarians ..were considerably roughed and mishandled. **1869** T. B. Aldrich *Story Bad Boy* 191 How tenderly the years touched him..!—all the more tenderly..for having roughed him so cruelly in other days. **1904** *Baltimore American* 1 Aug. 2 (*heading*) Badman roughs a train, but is shot in the hand by a plucky trainman. **1928** *Daily Mail* 25 July 12/4 Tunney knows he will be roughed and bustled around for the first few rounds. **1957** D. Niland *Call me when Cross turns Over* vi. 153 They grabbed Shelton and roughed him outside into the rising wind. **1971** *Frendz* 21 May 2/4 Cant put the rest down because the tin hats will rough my kin. **1978** *N.Y. Times* 29 Mar. b 6/5 The Mets..roughed Pete Falcone with a pair of runs apiece in the fourth, fifth and sixth innings.

3. *intr.* **a.** To become rough or stormy. *rare*[−1].

1876 Capt. R. F. Burton *Gorilla L.* I. 21 The cruel crawling sea began to rough, purr, and tumble.

b. To bristle or ruffle *up*.

1904 Sladen *Lovers Japan* xii, When a snake is drawn backwards, its scales rough up like cogs and hold it.

II. 4. a. ***to rough it***, to face or submit to hardships, rough or casual accommodation, etc.; to do without ordinary conveniences or luxuries; to live in a rough way.

1768 J. Byron *Narr. Patagonia* 205 We were obliged to ruff it the whole passage. *c* **1771** M. Suckling *Let.* in Southey *Life of Nelson* (1813) I. i. 5 What..has poor Horatio done,..that he..should be sent to rough it out at sea? **1796** Washington *Writ.* (1892) XIII. 341 Never having been accustomed to shift or rough it. **1826** Scott *Jrnl.* 20 Nov., The expense of travelling has mounted high. I am too old to rough it. **1879** Geo. Eliot *Theo. Such* ii. 37 Roughing it with them under difficulties.

b. *to rough* (*it*) *out*: (see out *adv.* 7b).

1821 Scott *Pirate* xxix, We have no other course for it but to..rough it out as well as we can. **1833** Marryat *P. Simple* (1863) 404, I determined, to use a nautical expression, to rough it out. **1836** *Backwoods of Canada* 41, I might..have roughed out a year or so.

5. *trans.* **a.** To break in (a horse).

1802 James *Mil. Dict.*, *To Rough Horses*, a word in familiar use among the dragoons to signify the act of breaking in horses, so as to adapt them to military purposes.

b. To expose (an animal) to rough weather and hard or scanty fare.

1858 *Jrnl. R. Agric. Soc.* XIX. i. 147 The idea..that 'roughing' calves (which means exposing them to cold and hunger) makes them hardy.

c. *Austral.* and *N.Z.* To shear (a sheep) badly.

1878 'Ironbark' *Southerly Busters* 180, I allus roughs 'em when the boss Ain't on the shearin' floor. **1897** D. McK. Wright *Station Ballads* 37 But he wouldn't shear at Maimai, started in to rough them through. **1956** G. Bowen *Wool Away!* (ed. 2) 156 *Rough 'em*, the opposite to 'pink 'em', and meaning rough shearing and a bad job of the sheep.

III. 6. With various advs. **a.** To trim or work *off* in a rough fashion.

1789 G. Keate *Pelew Isl.* 96 Timber..which being cut down at the back of the island and roughed off, they could easily manage to bring round.

b. To shape or cut *out* roughly; to plan or sketch *out* roughly.

1770 C. Carroll *Let.* 25 Apr. in *Maryland Hist. Mag.* (1917) XII. 352, I think you are wrong to Have the Capitalls &c. finished there, they may be defaced in the Carriage, w[h] Danger would be avoided if they only roughed out there. **1793** Smeaton *Edystone L.* §144 The two new steps..and all the dovetails were roughed out. **1820** W. Scoresby *Acc. Arc. Reg.* I. 232 In the formation of these lenses, I roughed them out with a small axe. **1843** Holtzapffel *Turning* I. 168 The stone is first roughed out with a point and mallet. **1875** *Carpentry & Join.* 113 He will rough out these at his own saw pit with the usual felloe saw. **1955** *Times* 4 Aug. 7/6 The first act has been already roughed out. *a* **1974** R. Crossman *Diaries* (1975) I. 370 By the early hours I had roughed out a reasonably intelligent script.

c. To fill or work *in*, to sketch *in*, roughly.

1864 Blackmore *Clara Vaughan* xxi, I had just roughed in my outline. **1891** Kipling *Light that Failed* (1900) 129, I must rough 'em in with the pencil.

d. To work *down* (iron) into rods.

1839 Ure *Dict. Arts* 707 A steam engine of thirty-horse power can rough down in a week 200 tons of coarse iron.

e. *Mus.* To tune *up* roughly.

1889 *Grove's Dict. Music* IV. 554 As much proficiency in tuning as enabled him to 'rough up', the technical term for the first tuning of a pianoforte.

f. To dig *out* in a rough manner.

1887 *Daily News* 8 Feb. 6/3 Miners rough out the clay in the first place with pick and shovel, and..machinery finishes the circular cutting with mathematical accuracy.

g. Const. *up.* To deal roughly with, assault, damage, upset, intimidate; = sense 2c.

1942 Berrey & Van den Bark *Amer. Thes. Slang* §341/2 *Treat roughly*; *'manhandle'*...rough (up), rough-house, strong-arm, treat 'em rough. **1943** R. Chandler *Lady in Lake* (1944) xxxvi. 192 You know how to rough up a bum that hasn't any money. **1959** 'M. M. Kaye' *House of Shade* iii. 29 When am I supposed to have roughed up your room? **1963** *Times* 14 Jan. 3/1 They had roughed-up France's pack a year ago. **1970** M. Braithwaite *Never sleep Three in Bed* xi. 135 They began to rough us up and we kicked and pulled and yelled about what our dads would do if they didn't leave us alone. **1973** *Time Out* 2–8 Mar. 15/1 A lot of teachers got roughed up, but that's not to say beaten up. **1977** M. Goulder in J. Hick *Myth of God Incarnate* iii. 58 Not only must he be prepared to be roughed up by southern policemen; he must also risk assassination. **1978** *N.Y. Times* 30 Mar. d 19/4 But at that point, the Phillies dealt Bruhert a cruel blow. They roughed him up with six rapid-fire singles. **1978** J. A. Michener *Chesapeake* xiv. 864 Amos Turlock..led an expedition to Caveny's home, which had been roughed up but not destroyed.

h. ***to rough down***, to give (wood) a rough, preliminary planing. Cf. roughing *vbl. sb.* 2b.

1960 *McGraw-Hill Encycl. Sci. & Technol.* XIV. 543/1 Flat or uniformly contoured surfaces of wood are roughed down, smoothed, or made level by the shaving and cutting action of a wide-edged blade or blades.

7. a. To work or shape in a rough preliminary fashion.

1770 C. Carroll *Let.* 20 Apr. in *Maryland Hist. Mag.* (1917) XII. 351 The stone cutters wish to have a draft of the Bases & Capitalls, they could rough the stones to that draft, & save a great deal of carriage. **1815** Scoresby in *Mem. Wernerian Soc.* II. 270, I roughed them with a small axe. **1839** Ure *Dict. Arts* 596 The piece of glass is now roughed into a circular form. **1850** Holtzapffel *Turning* III. 1034 The alabaster is roughed, or roughly ground on what the lapidary terms a roughing or lead mill. *a* **1890** E. L. Wilson *Quarter Cent. Photogr.* 35 (Cent.), In the grinding of a lens the first operation consists in roughing it, or bringing it approximately to the curvature it is ultimately to assume. **1937** *Times* 13 Apr. (British Motor No.) p. xii/2 Machines of particular interest are the Gleason completing machine for producing differential pinions, roughed and finished at a speed of 65 seconds each, and the lapping machines.

b. To clean (grain) roughly.

1851 *Jrnl. R. Agric. Soc.* XII. ii. 412 He..'chaffs' or 'roughs' the corn once over with a roughing-machine.

c. To heckle (flax) roughly. See also ruff *v.*

1882 *Encycl. Brit.* XIV. 665/1 In the case of heckling by machinery, the flax is first roughed and arranged in stricks, as above described under hand heckling. **1902** *Brit. Med. Jrnl.* 31 May 1341 The process of roughing, sorting, and hackling the flax.

d. To subject to a partial or preliminary evacuation. Also with *down, out.*

1948 [implied in *roughing down* s.v. roughing *vbl. sb.* 2b]. **1971** *Physics Bull.* July 423/2 This consists of a large ion pump and liquid N_2 cooled titanium sublimation pump combination, 'roughed' by two high capacity sorption pumps and an oil free mechanical roughing pump. **1976** A. Roth *Vacuum Technol.* v. 200 The removal of the atmospheric air from the system to some acceptable operating pressure is referred to as roughing out the system. .. Mechanical rotary pumps, and ejectors are the typical roughing and backing pumps.

†**rough**, *v.*[2] *Obs.* Forms: 4 rouwen, 5 row(w)hyn, rewyn, 5–6 rough. [ME. type **roȝen* (*rowen*), corresponding in form to OHG. and MHG. *rohen* (*ruhen*) to roar, and in meaning to (M)Du. *rochelen*, G. *röcheln*.] *intr.* To cough, to hawk, to clear the throat.

13.. *Old Age* in *Reliq. Antiq.* II. 211, I rivele, I roxle, I rake, I rouwe. *c* **1440** *Promp. Parv.* 249/1 Hostyn, or rowhyn, or cowghyn (*H.*, rowwhyn..), *tussio.* *a* **1470** H. Parker *Dives & Pauper* (W. de W. 1496) iv. iv. 164/1 He cought & roughed so, that his sone..myght haue no reste by hym in the chambre. *a* **1529** Skelton *Col. Cloute* 1223 Let hym cough, rough, or sneuyll.

rough, obs. var. of roe, roof; var. of ruff *v.*

'roughage. [f. rough *a.* + -age.] **1.** The less useful or refuse part (of crops); rough grass or weeds. *dial.*, *U.S.* and *N.Z.*

1883 *Encycl. Amer.* I. 98 The 'roughage' of crops has been neglected, the entire straw and stalks being burned. **1890** *Glouc. Gloss.*, *Roughage*, rubbish; the clearings off the land or out of ditches would be so called. **1940** E. C. Studholme *Te Waimate* x. 80 The first work of the settlers was to burn off the roughage on large areas of country. **1950** *N.Z. Jrnl. Agric.* Feb. 122/3 On much of the country a fairly high proportion of cattle to sheep is carried, the cattle being used largely to clean up roughage left by the sheep.

2. a. The indigestible fibrous matter or cellulose in vegetable foodstuffs. Also *attrib.*

1927 *Lancet* 16 July 106/1, I suspect that the advocacy of this bread was begun on the ground that the extra cellulose which it contains, forming what has been termed 'roughage', is of advantage as a mechanical irritant to the mucous membrane of the colon. **1932** *Times Lit. Suppl.* 7 Jan. 1/3 French art has had in the past its extra-artistic responsibilities, its burdens and entanglements, leading to the presence in the work of art of what corresponds to 'roughage' in food. **1948** *Good Housek. Cookery Bk.* 13 Much constipation is due to insufficient quantities of roughage in the diet. **1963** *Times* 4 Feb. 4/7 Roughage diets. **1976** *Which?* Nov. 244/3 Wholemeal bread is a simple and effective source of roughage.

b. *fig.*

1931 *Musical Times* Jan. 74/1 This was another of the oddities that we have to accept as roughage to the Hallé [orchestra] fare. **1948** C. S. Lewis *Lit. & Life* 58 There is no roughage in a Kipling story—it is all unrelieved vitamins from the first word to the last. **1962** [see funk *sb.*[2] 2]. **1963** *Punch* 23 Jan. 141/3 Twelve months in jail provided the roughage for his first book. **1974** *Times* 28 Feb. 15/3 The electorate..finally gagged on their traditional roughage of internecine strife.

rough-and-ready, *a.* Also unhyphened.

1. Of things: Not elaborately or carefully ordered, contrived, or finished; just good enough to serve the purpose.

1810 F. J. Jackson in Sir G. Jackson *Diaries & Lett.* (1873) I. 120 A more rough and ready state of things.. than we had before been accustomed to. **1858** R. S. Surtees *Ask Mamma* xlv, The hunting establishment was of the rough and ready order. **1893** Sir R. Ball *Story of Sun* 222 The rough-and-ready compass so invaluable to the navigator. *Comb.* **1856** Stonehenge *Brit. Rur. Sports* 414/1 Sharp spurs are on the heels—rough and ready-looking prads these.

2. Of persons: Ready to take things as they come; not finical or particular; working in a rough but prompt and effective manner.

1843 in *Amer. Speech* (1965) XL. 132 But Rough and Ready made dem smell Gunpowder a la Poker. **1846** *Congress. Globe* 24 May 865 Col. [Zachary] Taylor.. had won for himself by his gallant conduct in the field the soubriquet of 'Old Rough and Ready'. **1849** E. E. Napier *Exp. S. Afr.* I. 163 If you can catch a sober, rough-and-ready 'Totty', who is able to.. put his hand to any thing. **1870** W. Thornbury *Tour round Eng.* I. ii. 44 In a few days his rough and ready hand was on their collars. **1894** Mrs. F. Elliot *Roman Gossip* iv. 94 A sort of leer, as of a rough-and-ready cynic.

3. Of manner, etc.: Roughly efficient or effective, without entering into minutiæ or observing a regular procedure.

1860 Emerson *Cond. Life* ii. (1861) 39 The rough and ready style which belongs to a people of sailors, foresters, farmers, and mechanics. **1868** Freeman *Norm. Conq.* (1877) II. 495 A rough and ready way of repaying themselves. **1897** *Allbutt's Syst. Med.* II. 880 Instead of all this rough-and-ready turbulence, relays of attendants should be.. organized.

Hence **rough-and-readiness**.

1956 *Essays in Crit.* VI. 185 Beliefs that allow Pound to be satisfied.. with a surprising emotional rough-and-readiness. **1960** *Guardian* 30 Nov. 7/1 The rough-and-readiness of such Italian neo-realists as Rossellini.

rough-and-tumble, *a.*, *sb.*, and *adv.* Also unhyphened. [Orig. boxing slang.]

A. *adj.* **1.** Characterized by rough informality or disregard of usual rules; having the character of a scuffle or scramble; rude and disorderly.

1832 J. P. Kennedy *Swallow B.* xv. (1860) 138 Rough-and-tumble fights in which they were often engaged. **1859** Bartlett *Dict. Amer.* (ed. 2) 371 A rough and tumble fight is said to be one in which all the laws of the ring are discarded. **1872** O. W. Holmes *Poet. Breakf.-T.* x, That circle of rough-and-tumble political life where the fine-fibred men are at a discount. **1887** Stevenson *Underwoods* I. iv. 7 Their rough-and-tumble play they shared. *transf.* **1899** Callow *Old Lond. Tav.* I. 3 There was always a more or less rough-and-tumble air about the place.

2. Of persons: Practising irregular or informal methods of boxing, etc.; inclined to be rough or violent.

1848 B. D. Walsh *Aristoph.* 157 *note*, The victories of.. wrestlers, boxers, and rough-and-tumble gentlemen. **1860** O. W. Holmes *Elsie Venner* (1887) 39 The rough-and-tumble fighters all *clinch*. **1890** F. W. Robinson *Very Strange Family* 18 Rough-and-tumble lads, with no fine feelings.

3. *transf.* Riotous, disorderly, forming a confused mass or group.

1858 O. W. Holmes *Aut. Breakf.-t.* (1883) 237 Dare-devil impudence of rough-and-tumble vegetation. **1879** Stevenson *Trav. Cevennes* (1886) 49, I.. found.. another marish bottom among rough-and-tumble hills.

4. Roughly constructed or improvised; makeshift. *rare.*

1912 Kipling *Land & Sea Tales* (1923) 70 They heaved up their rough-and-tumble anchor, and made after a.. sailing-ship.

B. *sb.* **1.** Haphazard or random fighting, struggling, or adventure; scuffle, scramble.

1810 *Edin. Rev.* XV. 447 When two persons fight, it is generally 'according to the rule of rough and tumble'. **1840** R. H. Dana *Bef. Mast* xxviii. 92 The old brig.. in which I had spent nearly a year, and got the first rough and tumble of a sea-life. **1875** Whyte-Melville *Katerfelto* i, The Cornish hug, the Devonshire shoulder-grip, and the West Somerset rough-and-tumble.

2. With *a.* A random or free fight or set-to.

1821 Southey in *Q. Rev.* XXIV. 494 The Coalheaver.. closed with him at once for a rough-and-tumble. **1887** Rider Haggard *A. Quatermain* viii, He had been successful in his rough and tumble with the Elmoran.

C. *adv.* In a rough, informal manner.

1818 J. Palmer *Jrnl. Trav.* 131, I understand the question is generally asked, will you fight fair, or take it rough and tumble? **1825** J. Neal *Bro. Jonathan* III. 270 A bit of clear tussle with a redhot Mohawk or so—rough an' tumble—would be a relief to me. **1935** Z. N. Hurston *Mules & Men* (1970) I. viii. 178 Mr. Allen might have eaten by the rules but Cliffert and I went at it rough-and-tumble with no holds barred.

Hence **rough-and-tumbling**. *rare.*

1808 Ashe *Trav.* I. 296 No fighting, no racing, no rough and tumbling, or anything to be observed but industry. **1832** *Chambers's Edin. Jrnl.* I. 130/2 The scene can only be compared to a rough-and-tumbling in the back woods of America.

roughback ('rʌfbæk). [f. rough *a.* + back *sb.*[1]] One of several flatfishes with rough skins, esp. the long rough dab, *Hippoglossoides platessoides.* Also *attrib.*

1795 J. Sinclair *Stat. Acct. Scotland* XVI. 548 Flounders of all kinds, roughback, plaise. **1815** J. Arbuthnot *Hist. Acct. Peterhead* 15 Dab, vulgarly called Rough Back Fluke, Rochie. **1903** G. Sim *Vertebr. Fauna of Dee* 244 Long Rough Dab. 'Rochie'.. 'Rough-back Fluke'.. is not looked upon with much favour as an article of food. **1935** *Fisheries Notice* (Min. Agric.) No. 23.4 Suggested Trade Name. Rough-back... General English Equivalent. Long Rough Dab. **1973** J. Grigson *Fish Cookery* 281 Roughback (i American plaice) (ii rock sole; flat-fish).

rough-board, *v.* [rough *a.* 21.] *trans.* To cover with rough boards.

1849 D. J. Browne *Amer. Poultry Yd.* (1855) 87 Rough-board it from the apex downward by the sills to the ground.

rough-cast, roughcast ('rʌfkɑːst, -æ-), *ppl. a.* and *sb.* Also 7 **ruff-cast**. [f. rough *adv.* and *a.* See cast *v.* 57, 45, and *sb.* 25.]

I. 1. a. *ppl. a.* Of walls, etc.: Roughly coated with a mixture of lime and gravel.

1519 Horman *Vulg.* 241 Some men wyll haue theyr wallys plastered, some pergetted.., some roughe caste. **1617** Moryson *Itin.* I. 188 The building of the City is.. of unpolished stone with the outside plastered, and rough cast. **1655** Fuller *Ch. Hist.* I. 7 As white-limed houses exceed those which are only rough cast. **1704** Swift *T. Tub* xi, He rubbed.. against a rough-cast Wall. **1830** Miss Mitford *Village* Ser. IV. (1863) 259 A low, white, irregular, rough-cast building. **1861** Neale *Notes Dalmatia* 97 Arbors running along the top of rough-cast walls.

b. *transf.* or *fig.* Also const. *with.*

1606 Sylvester *Du Bartas* II. iv. *Magnificence* 1266 Where Wals are rough-cast wth the richest Stones. **1655** Vaughan *Silex Scint.* I. *Regeneration*, My walke a monstrous, mountain'd thing, Rough-cast with rocks and snow. **1681** Grew *Musæum* I. iv. iv. 76 The Shell underneath or within is white: without, it is all over rough-cast.

c. Of glass: cast in a particular manner (see 2 d).

1939 *Archit. Rev.* LXXXV. 99 (*caption*) Bent dome of 'rough-cast' glass used, at the Saint-Gobain pavilion, Paris 1937, as a simple and elegant alternative to the ordinary opaque basin. **1973** *Technical Translation Bull.* XIX. 103 *Plate glass*.. is expensive to produce owing to the need for grinding and polishing of the 'rough cast plate' produced as a first stage... Indeterminate patterns such as 'rough cast' or 'cathedral' are normally called 'cast.'

2. a. *sb.* A composition of lime and gravel, used as a plastering for the outside of walls.

1590 Shaks. *Mids. N.* III. i. 71 Let him haue some Plaster, or some Lome, or some rough cast about him, to signifie wall. **1622** Mabbe tr. *Aleman's Guzman d'Alf.* I. 39 The face of her.. looked like an old wall all to bedawbed with rough-cast. **1663** Gerbier *Counsel* 79 Rough-cast upon Lath being very well done, is worth eighteen pence the yard. **1789** M. Madan tr. *Persius* (1795) 120 *note*, The plaster, parget or rough cast of a wall. **1810** Wordsw. *Prose Wks.* (1876) II. 277 The house must be covered with rough-cast, otherwise it cannot be kept dry. **1850** *Ecclesiol.* XI. 74 Both tower and spire are covered with rough-cast. **1883** Mrs. Banks *Forbidden to Marry* I. v. 85 Black beams intersecting.. the weather-stained roughcast.

b. *transf.* or *fig.* Also with *a.*

1609 J. Davies (Heref.) *Holy Roode* D 2 b, A Rough-cast of thicke Gore his Body shrouds. **1648** J. Beaumont *Psyche* XXII. ccxcix, Her scurfy Roughcast scaled off, and all Her Skin to fresh and tender smoothness left. **1658** Rowland tr. *Moufet's Theat. Ins.* 922 [The wasp's nest is] well fenced above with a certain rough-cast to keep off all wind and weather.

c. *attrib.* Consisting of rough-cast. Also *fig.*

1599 Nashe *Lenten Stuffe* Wks. (Grosart) V. 201 With light cost of rough cast rethoricke it may be tollerablely playstered ouer. *c* **1670** Wood *Life* (O.H.S.) I. 280 Two or three stones, and some rough-cast stuff were blown from off the tower. **1828** *Lights & Shades* II. 122 A decent-looking inn with a rough-cast coating.

d. A type of glass (see quot. 1962).

1962 *Gloss. Terms Glass Industry* (*B.S.I.*) 31 *Rough cast*, rolled translucent glass, one surface of which has a definite texture, made by rolling molten glass either on a table or between rollers. **1973** [see sense 1 c].

II. †**3.** *sb.* A rough sketch or outline. *Obs.*

Properly in two words, as in the earlier quots.

1579 Gosson *Sch. Abuse* (Arb.) 24 To show you that in a rough cast, which I see in a cloude. **1641** Milton *Ch. Govt.* I. vii, If we look at his native towardlinesse in the rough cast without breeding. **1644** Digby *Nat. Bodies* a iv b, A loose modell and roughcast of what I designe to do.

4. *ppl. a.* Roughly or rudely contrived, designed, or made; of a rough, imperfect type.

1591 Nashe *Prognostication* Wks. (Grosart) II. 151 Vttering in their furye such rough cast eloquence. **1635–56** Cowley *Davideis* I. 811 He smooth'd the rough-cast Moons imperfect mold. **1693** Dryden *Disc. Satire* Ess. (Ker) II. 55 This rough-cast unhewn poetry was instead of stage-plays for the space of an hundred and twenty years together. **1714** R. Fiddes *Pract. Disc.* II. 367 This brightest jewel and ornament of human nature is so rough cast. **1880** Stallybrass tr. *Grimm's Teut. Myth.* I. 103, I can only look upon Cæsar's statements as a half-true and roughcast opinion. **1892** J. Tait *Mind in Matter* (ed. 2) 159 The rough-cast 'goodness' of the *bonus homo* of Christianised heathenism.

rough-cast ('rʌfkɑːst, -æ-), *v.* Also 7 **rogh-**, **roof-**. [f. rough *adv.* + cast *v.* Cf. prec.]

1. *trans.* To coat, cover, or fill in, with rough-cast.

1565 Cooper *Thesaurus*, *Incrusto*, to parget, or to roughe cast. **1584** in Willis & Clark *Cambridge* (1886) I. 294 To Parkes seruant for roughcasting and filling the place behind the armes and Creast. **1639** [see parget *sb.* I.]. **1757** *Phil. Trans.* I. 199 The steeple is.. roughcasted on the outside. **1797** Mme. D'Arblay *Let.* July 27 Our cottage is now in the act of being rough cast. **1833** Loudon *Encycl. Archit.* §478 It is brought to an even surface by rough-casting it with a mixture of lime and fine gravel. **1875** W. McIlwraith *Guide Wigtownshire* 31 Some of the houses have been carefully rough-cast and white-washed.

transf. and *fig.* **1593** Nashe *Christ's T.* Wks. (Grosart) IV. 210 With blacke boyling Pitch, rough cast ouer her counter-feite red and white. **1609** J. Davies (Heref.) *Hum. Heauen on Earth* Wks. (Grosart) I. 43/2 Rogh-cast the skin of smooth-fac'd glozing Guile With burning blisters to consume the same. **1640** Bastwick *Lord Bishops* ii. C, Thus did they *incrustare vitia*, parget, or roughcast their vices.

2. To mould, fashion, or shape roughly; to prepare in a rough form.

The first quot. may belong to sense 1.

1586 T. B. *La Primaud. Fr. Acad.* I. Ep. Ded., This Platonical Academie & schoole of moral philosophy, which .. was raised up & set togither in France, & is newly rough-cast (as you see) by an English workman. *a* **1613** Overbury *Characters, Taylor*, Wks. (1856) 78 A Taylor is a creature made up out of threds, that were pared off from Adam, when he was rough-cast. *a* **1658** Cleveland *Poems* (1677) 58 Nor bodily, nor ghostly Negro could Roughcast thy Figure in a sadder mold. **1751** Warburton & Hurd *Lett.* (1809) 85, I have so imperfect an idea of my subject, and rough-cast my composition so loosely, that my works, if they escape damning, are yet in a state of purgatory. **1835** W. Irving in *Life & Lett.* (1866) III. 72, I have commenced, and have rough-cast several of the chapters.

Hence **'rough-caster**, a workman who puts on rough-cast.

1594 in *Antiquary* XVII. 211 Itm. to the roughcaster, xxvjs., viijd. **1855** in Ogilvie *Suppl.*

'rough-casting, *vbl. sb.* [f. rough-cast *v.*]

1. The action of coating with rough-cast.

1565 Cooper *Thesaurus*, *Tectorium*, the plaisteryng, pargettynge, or rough castyng of walles. **1611** Cotgr., *Crespissement*, a pargetting, rough-casting. **1703** R. Neve *City & C. Purchaser* 236 River-sand is very good for Rough-casting of Walls. **1795** W. H. Marshall *W. Eng.* II. 296 An admirable theory of the operation of roughcasting. **1833** Loudon *Encycl. Archit.* §529 *Roughcasting*, or *Harling* as it is called in Scotland, is a mode of outside finishing well calculated to protect walls from the weather. **1977** *S. Wales Echo* 18 Jan. (Advt.), Pebble Dashing, Spar Dashing, Rough-casting, all types of Plastering carried out.

2. *concr.* = rough-cast *sb.* 2.

1703 *Art's Improvement* I. 8 Of a Serviceable and useful Plaster.., the which they call Rough-casting. **1823** P. Nicholson *Pract. Build.* 380 Rough-casting is an outside finishing cheaper than stucco. **1875** W. McIlwraith *Guide Wigtownshire* 80 On the inside of the walls the plaster still clings here and there,—coarse, however, as modern rough-casting.

'rough-coated, *a.* [rough *a.*] Having a rough coat. Chiefly of animals.

1687 *Lond. Gaz.* No. 2303/4 A large grey Gelding,.. rough Coated. **1742** *De Foe's Tour Gt. Brit.* III. 257 Rough-coated Fish, such as Rousses, Haus, &c. the coarsest of all. **1843** Holtzapffel *Turning* I. 89 Lance-wood.. is called one of the rough-coated woods. **1852** C. W. H[oskins] *Talpa* 133 His hot and rough-coated nag jumped with some alacrity.

'rough-draft, *v.* [Cf. rough *a.* 17 b.] *trans.* To draft in a rough form.

1879 Miss Braddon *Cloven Foot* x. 101, I am ready to rough-draft any form of settlement you dictate. **1975** I. K. Martin *Regan & Manhattan File* 110 Regan wrote his own report and rough-drafted Cassidy's report as a favour.

'rough-draw, *v.* ? *Obs.* [rough *adv.*] *trans.* To draw, draft, or design roughly. Hence **'rough-drawn** *ppl. a.*

1672 Dryden *Conq. Granada* I. II. i, His Victories we scarce could keep in view, Or polish 'em so fast as he rough-drew. **1679** —— *Troil. & Cress.* Prol., In this my rough-drawn Play, you shall behold Some Master-strokes. **1716** M. Davies *Athen. Brit.* II. 21 The Author of such Legal Formularies, tho' they had been rough-drawn by his Clerk or some Body else. **1779** Johnson *L.P.*, *Cowley*, 'The Guardian,' a comedy which Cowley says was neither written nor acted, but rough-drawn by him.

'rough-dry, *v.* [rough *adv.*] *trans.* To dry (clothes) without smoothing or ironing. Now more generally, to dry roughly or imperfectly.

1837 Dickens *Pickw.* xvii, The process of being washed in the night-air, and rough-dried in a close closet. **1978** P. Harcourt *Agents of Influence* xii. 146 She.. continued to rough-dry her hair on the towel.

Hence **'rough-dried** *ppl. a.*, **'rough-dry** *a.*

1856 Mrs. Stowe *Dred* I. 181 Clothes look rough-dry, as if they had been pulled out of a bag. **1865** M. Eyre *Lady's Walks S. of France* i. 8 The articles.. are neither starched nor ironed, but simply sent home rough dry. **1890** *Cent. Dict.*, *Rough-dry*, dry but not smoothed or ironed: as, rough-dry clothes. **1900** Kipling in *Daily Express* 12 June 4/5 Sweating men, rough-dried sweating horses with wisps of precious forage. **1942** Z. N. Hurston in A. Dundes *Mother Wit* (1973) 222/1 He was born with this rough-dried hair. **1952** 'J. Tey' *Singing Sands* i. 8 Service.. had lost its starch and its high glaze. It had become what housewives call rough-dried.

roughed (rʌft), *ppl. a.* [f. rough *v.*[1]]

1. *Plastering.* (See quot. 1823.)

1823 P. Nicholson *Pract. Build.* 393 Rendered, Floated, and Set, for paper, should be termed roughed-in. **1829** Elmes *Dilapid.* App. p. lxvi, Repair the defective and damaged brick-work, roughed and guaged arches.

2. Rendered rough, in various senses.

1866 J. B. Rose *Virg. Ecl. & Georg.* 30 Their foreheads fair were roughed with horn. **1888** *Cent. Mag.* Nov. 83/1 A roughed woman who will eat our provender and bring us no profit.

roughen ('rʌf(ə)n), *v.* [f. ROUGH *a.* + -EN⁵.]

1. *trans.* To render or make rough; to bring into a rough state. Also with *up*.

1582 STANYHURST *Æneis* III. (Arb.) 79 Whilst..seas, with north blast and wynter frostye, be roughned. **1720** A. HILL *Wks.* (1753) I. 16 That no harsh technical terms should be introduc'd to roughen poetry with the dryness of philosophy. **1755** *Connoisseur* No. 83 ¶8 To roughen the verse and make it roar again with reiteration of the letter R. **1820** SHELLEY *Prometh. Unb.* II. i. 128 Its rude hair Roughens the wind that lifts it. **1844** G. DODD *Textile Manuf.* iii. 105 The nap of the cloth is roughened up by a brush. **1873** SPON *Workshop Rec.* Ser. I. 2/2 The surface of the paper is roughened by using the erasing knife.

refl. **1855** DICKENS *Dorrit* I. xvi, There are times when that girl's whole nature seemed to roughen itself against seeing us so bound up in Pet.

b. To 'rough' (a horse).

1864 MRS. CARLYLE *Lett.* III. 238, I had him roughened the first day of the frost.

c. *fig.* To irritate, ruffle.

1859 DICKENS *T. Two Cities* II. v, What has roughened your temper? **1896** MRS. H. WARD *Sir G. Tressady* 190 The creditor's temper had been roughened.

2. To grind *down* roughly.

1839 URE *Dict. Arts* 955 *Pointing*, is executed on two iron or steel grindstones, by two workmen, one of whom roughens down, and the other finishes.

3. *intr.* To become rough, in various senses.

1730–46 THOMSON *Autumn* 577 The cap, the whip, the masculine attire, In which they roughen to the sense. **1794** MRS. PIOZZI *Synon.* II. 327 The wild scenery roughens at every step. **1813** EUSTACE *Class. Tour* (1821) I. viii. 309 The river roughening into a torrent. **1865** THIRLWALL *Lett.* (1881) II. 37 The wind was rising and the sea roughening.

fig. **1821** SHELLEY *Hellas* 282 Latmos, and Mycale, roughen With horrent arms.

b. To have a rough feel. *rare*⁻¹.

1829 LANDOR *Imag. Conv., Penn & Ld. Peterborough*, Something that roughens in the hand, like gold.

Hence **'roughener**, one who or that which roughens; **'roughening** *vbl. sb.* and *ppl. a.*

1582 STANYHURST *Æneis* III. (Arb.) 87 Graunt to vs milde passadge, and tempest mollifye roughning. **1728–46** THOMSON *Spring* 640 Far in the grassy dale, Or roughening waste. **1744** J. ARMSTRONG *Art Pres. Health* iii, The roughening deep expects the storm. **1825** L. HUNT *Bacchus in Tuscany* 82 This letter [*r*]..he had learnt..most probably in Tuscany, where it is in great request, as the roughener of a soft language. **1898** *Allbutt's Syst. Med.* V. 706 There is often some evidence of recent endocarditis about the stricture in the form of roughening or small vegetations.

'roughened ('rʌf(ə)nd), *ppl. a.* [f. ROUGHEN *v.*] That has been made rough, in various senses.

1810 SCOTT *Lady of L.* IV. xxi, The voice..though strain'd and roughen'd, still Rung wildly sweet to dale and hill. **1830** HERSCHEL *Study Nat. Phil.* 161 Thus, roughened iron, especially if painted over or blackened, becomes dewed sooner than varnished paper. **1876** PREECE & SIVEWRIGHT *Telegraphy* 14 The hydrogen, being readily discharged from its roughened surface, rose in bubbles.

Comb. **1888** RUTLEY *Rock-forming Min.* 36 The wrinkled or roughened-looking surfaces of sections of olivine crystals.

'rougher ('rʌfə(r)). [f. ROUGH *v.* or *a.* + -ER.]

1. A workman who makes something in the rough; one who carries out the less finished operations of a work.

1885 *Census Instruct.* Index. *a* **1890** E. L. WILSON *Quarter Century in Photogr.* 35 (Cent.), When the glass [for a lens] is handed to the rougher, it is round in shape. **1893** *Labour Comm. Gloss.*, *Roughers*, the workers in the iron industry employed at the 'rolls'.

2. *Weaving.* A piece of cloth taken from the loom and ready for perching.

1888 *Encycl. Brit.* XXIV. 661/2 Woollen cloth from the loom, called 'roughers', has an irregular, slack aspect.

3. A board studded with steel spikes or teeth for heckling flax. Cf. RUFFER².

1882 *Encycl. Brit.* XIV. 665/1 The heckler..dashes the fibre into the teeth or needles of the rougher or 'ruffer' heckle. The rougher is a board plated with tin [etc.].

4. *colloq.* A rough-rider.

1901 *Daily Express* 28 Aug. 6/6 Lord Maitland..served at the Cape as adjutant of the prototype 'Roughers'.

roughet ('rʌfɪt). *dial.* Also 9 roughit, 6, 9 ruffet. [f. ROUGH *a.*] **a.** A field overgrown with bracken or bushes; a stretch of waste land; a copse. **b.** Coarse dried grass left on pasturelands as winter fodder for cattle (cf. ROWET).

1616 LANE *Cont. Sqr.'s T.* IV. 414 Right perfect in the skilles Of ridinge goiles, plaines, ruffetes, dales, and hills. **1788** W. H. MARSHALL *Yorks.* I. 236 The old well-timbered woods..have..got up fortuitously from seedling-plants, rising in neglected roughets. **1796** —— *W. Eng.* II. 68 The produce—arable crops, grass, wood, and roughets of furze, and rubbish. **1847–** in dial. glossaries (Heref., Glouc., Kent).

'rough-foot, *a. rare.* [Cf. next.] **a.** = ROUGH-FOOTED 2. **b.** Having hairy feet.

a **1352** MINOT *Poems* ii. 19 Rughfute riueling, now kindels þi care. **1617** DRUMM. OF HAWTH. *Forth Feasting*, The rough-foot Hair safe in our Bushes shrouds.

'rough-footed, *a.* Also 5 rouh-, roghe-, 6–7 ruffe-, and see ROW *a.*¹ 3. [ROUGH *a.*]

1. Having feathered feet. Chiefly in spec. names of birds, as ***rough-footed dove, eagle***, etc.

1495 *Trevisa's De P.R.* XII. vii. 417 Therfore rouh foted [1398 rowe-fotid, 1535 roughfoted] douues brede well nyghe in euery month. **1530** PALSGR. 264/1 Roughe foted dove, *coulomb*. **1594** BARNFIELD *Affect. Sheph.* II. vii, Ile giue thee fine ruffe-footed Doues to keepe. **1611** COTGR., *Cheveche*,..th'ordinarie rough-footed, and short-taild Owle. **1668** CHARLETON *Onomast.* 63 *Morphno congener*,.. the Rough-footed Eagle. *Ibid.* 75 *Alba, Lagopus*,..the white and rough-footed Partridge. **1678** RAY *Willughby's Ornith.* 156 A rough footed Cock and Hen. **1725** *Fam. Dict.* s.v. *Pigeon*, The tame Rough-footed ones differ not much from the wild [pigeons]. **1783** LATHAM *Gen. Synop. Birds* IV. 709 Rough-footed Cock. **1834** MUDIE *Brit. Birds* I. 74 The principal [fancy pigeons] are the Barbary, the Laced, the Norway, the Rough-footed [etc.].

2. Wearing shoes of undressed hide with the hair on. Now *Hist.*

a **1529** SKELTON *Agst. Scottes* 170 Of the out yles the roughe foted Scottes. **1542** ELDER *Let. to Hen. VIII* in *Bannatyne Misc.* (1827) I. 13 They call ws in Scotland Reddshankes, and in your Graces dominion of England roghe footide Scottis. **1818** [see RED-SHANK 1]. **1825** SCOTT *Talisman* xv, Though the rough-footed knaves be our enemies in Cumberland.

'rough-grind, *v.* [ROUGH *adv.*] *trans.* To grind roughly or so as to leave an unsmoothed or uneven surface.

1660 INGELO *Bentiv. & Ur.* II. (1682) 120 Two rows of teeth to rough-grind the Meat. **1850** HOLTZAPFFEL *Turning* III. 1317 The stone is rough-ground to the rounded form. **1863** W. PHILLIPS *Sp.* v. 83 Ordered to rough-grind their swords.

Hence **'rough-grinder**; **'rough-grinding** *vbl. sb.*, **'rough-ground** *ppl. a.*

c **1790** IMISON *Sch. Arts* II. 155 This tool, or rough-grinder, should be of an elliptical form. **1850** HOLTZAPFFEL *Turning* III. 1298 The first process in glass-cutting, or the rough grinding, is performed with cast-iron wheels, called mills. **1901** KIPLING *Kim* xi. 289 A clothful of *atta*—grayish, rough-ground native flour,—twists of down-country tobacco.

'rough-head. *Sc.* and *U.S.* [ROUGH *a.*]

1. *Sc.* A grass-turf. ? *Obs.*

1765 in W. Hunter *Biggar & Ho. of Fleming* (1862) ii. 14 [A complaint..was lodged against certain feuars for cutting Roughheads]. **1862** *Ibid.* xv. 183 Large supplies of peats and divots, or, as they are generally called, roughheads.

2. The red dace or red-fin.

1886 in *Cassell's Encycl. Dict.*

3. 'The iguanoid lizard of the Galapagos, *Trachycephalus subcristatus*' (Cent. Dict.).

rough-hew ('rʌfhjuː), *v.* [ROUGH *adv.* Cf. Fris. *rûchhouwen* rough-hewing.] **a.** *trans.* To hew (timber, etc.) roughly; to shape out roughly, give crude form to; to work or execute in the rough.

1530 PALSGR. 694/2, I rougheheawe a pece of tymber to make an ymage of, or to put to some byldyng, *je charpis*. **1598** FLORIO, *Scappezzare*, to rough hewe a peece of timber or stone. **1640** BP. HALL *Episc.* III. vii. 254 It appeares then, that Farell and Viret rough-hew'd this statue, which Calvin after polished. **1711** ADDISON *Spect.* No. 215 ¶8 To return to our Statue in the Block of Marble, we see it sometimes only begun to be chipped, sometimes rough-hewn.

b. *transf.* or *fig.*

1565 COOPER *Thes.* s.v. *Exascio*, It is rough hewed, or squared out, or it is begunne. **1592** NASHE *Four Lett. Confut.* Wks. (Grosart) II. 197 He..speakes not that sentence in the Pulpit, which before he rough-hewes not ouer with his penne. **1602** SHAKS. *Ham.* v. ii. 10 There's a Diuinity that shapes our ends, Rough-hew them how we will. **1651** *Fuller's Abel Rediv.* (1867) II. 284 And first he rough-hewed, and after polished and published, his exquisite tract. **1829** SCOTT *Abbot* xxxviii. Note T, The supernatural machinery with which his plan, when it was first rough-hewn, was connected. **1860** SMILES *Self-Help* xiii. 340 Daily life being the quarry from which we..rough-hew the habits which form it.

absol. *a* **1680** BUTLER *Rem.* (1759) I. 174 This proves that Wit does but rough-hew, Leaves Art to polish, and review.

Hence **'rough-hewer** [cf. Fris. *rûchhouwer*]; **'rough-hewing** *vbl. sb.*

1573 BARET *Alv.* s.v. *Hew*, A rough hewer, *lapicida*. **1587** FLEMING *Contn. Holinshed* III. 1272/1 If things be not in perfection vpon this first rough hewing. **1855** OGILVIE *Suppl.*, *Rough-hewer*, one who rough-hews. **1868** *Westm. Rev.* Jan. 188 Both were engaged in rough-hewing an empire... And though Miss Martineau regards some parts of the rough-hewing process as 'a national calamity' [etc.].

'rough-hew, *sb. rare.* [f. the vb.] Something lacking the finishing process; a preliminary version.

1889 G. M. HOPKINS *Lett. to R. Bridges* (1935) 301 It was only a sketch, a rough-hew of a song.

'rough-hewed, *ppl. a.* ? *Obs.* = next.

1591 LYLY *Wks.* (1902) I. 424, I mette I know not with what rough-hewed Ruffian. **1598** MARSTON *Pygmal. Sat.* iii, Now grim Reprofe, swell in my rough-heu'd rime. **1611** COTGR. s.v. *Graces*, Hee is a harsh, vnpleasant, rough-hewed, currish, or churlish, fellow. **1652** ASHMOLE *Theatr. Chem. Brit.* Prol. 13 Ancient Rough-hew'd Expressions.

rough-hewn ('rʌfhjuːn), *ppl. a.* [ROUGH *adv.* Cf. ROUGH-HEW *v.*]

1. Roughly hewn or shaped out, roughly wrought; lacking the finishing process.

1530 PALSGR. 694/2 It is rough hewen all redy, I wyll nowe fall a karvynge of it. **1592** NASHE *P. Penilesse* Wks. (Grosart) II. 35 Their heads, like rough hewen Gloabes, are fit for nothing but to be the blockhouses for sleepe. *a* **1631** DONNE *Elegy* viii, Thy head is like a rough-hewen statue of jeat. **1800** WORDSW. *Hart-Leap Well* I. xvii, Three several pillars, each a rough-hewn stone. **1833** HT. MARTINEAU *Charmed Sea* ii. 16 The holes between the rough-hewn logs were stuffed with moss. **1852** MRS. CARLYLE *Lett.* II. 179 A statue that had been perfectly polished in front, and left rough-hewn behind.

b. *transf.* and *fig.*

1593 G. HARVEY *Pierce's Super.* Wks. (Grosart) II. 300 Smooth voyces do well in most societies.., when rough-hewne words do but lay blockes in their own way. **1608** D. T. *Ess. Pol. & Mor.* 66 b, To polish and fashion out his then rough-hewen fortune, with the edge of his subduing sword. **1672** DRYDEN *Assignation* III. i, Lord, what a Monster of a Man is there! With such a Workiday, rough-hewn Face too! **1718** POPE *Arachne* 172 In a strong satyr's rough-hewn form he came. **1856** R. A. VAUGHAN *Mystics* (1860) I. 41, I give these remarks just as I find them, brief and rough-hewn. **1865** KINGSLEY *Herew.* ii, Envy and hatred, like all other vices in those rough-hewn times, were apt to take very startling..shapes.

2. Of persons: Lacking in refinement; uncultivated, plain, blunt; †rough-natured, cruel.

1600 HOLLAND *Livy* II. lvi. 82 Being a rough hewen souldiour, and not used to make Orations. **1609** —— *Amm. Marcell.* xxx. i. 380 A barbarous and rough hewen fellow,.. shaking a drawne sword in his hand. **1660** WILLSFORD *Scales Commerce* 149 But leaving the rough-hewn and cross-grain'd people to their own imaginations. **1719** DE FOE *Crusoe* II. (Globe) 356 The English Man reply'd like a true rough-hewn Tarpaulin. **1744** OZELL tr. *Brantome's Sp. Rhodom.* 95 A brave, bold, rough-hewn Gentleman of Britany. **1831** SCOTT *Ct. Rob.* iii, The rough-hewn native of the north. **1892** *Month* Nov. 310 Rough-hewn rustics without manners.

transf. **1604** F. HERING *Mod. Defence* 16 Medecines... The third and last are termed Violent, churlish or rough-hewen.

rough-hound. [ROUGH *a.*] A dog-fish, *esp.* of the large and small spotted species. Cf. *row-hound*, s.v. ROW *a.*¹

1602 R. CAREW *Surv. Cornw.* I. 32 Of flat [fish there are] Brets, Turbets, Dories,..Guilthead, Rough-hound, &c. **1674** RAY *Coll. Words*, Fishes 98 Rough Hounds, *Mustelus*. **1710** SIBBALD *Fife & Kinross* 117 *Catulus major vulgaris*, the Rough Hound. **1740** R. BROOKES *Art of Angling* 191 Of the Bounce, Rough-Hound or Morgay. **1848** *Zoologist* VI. 1973 Small Spotted Dog, *Scyllium canicula*. Frequently called 'rough' or 'row-hound'. **1854** BADHAM *Halieut.* 430 The dog-fish tribe.., whether the white, blue, or basking shark, the..rough-hound or Bounce, &c.

rough house, rough-house, *sb. slang* (orig. *U.S.*). [ROUGH *a.* 21.] An uproar, a disturbance, a row; horseplay, boisterous behaviour; a fight, a struggle.

1887 M. ROBERTS *Western Avernus* 54 He called the bridgeman a very opprobrious name, and for a moment there was great danger of a 'rough house' out of hand. **1895** *Harper's Mag.* Mar. 540/2 They might be goin' to hev considerable rough house—a fuss, I mean, sir. **1900** *Dialect Notes* II. 55 *Rough-house, n.* 1. A disorderly class. 2. Rough play. **1902** G. H. LORIMER *Lett. Merchant* xvi. 238 [He] said he liked things lively, but there was altogether too much rough house on Beacon Hill for him. **1906** *Dialect Notes* III. 154 *Rough-house, n.* Scuffle (in a room). 'The room looked like they had a roughhouse.' Common slang. **1908** A. J. DAWSON *Finn* xix. 292 Seems to me you've been havin' a pretty rough house with somebody. **1911** R. D. SAUNDERS *Col. Todhunter* iii. 49 But an ominous cry rose from his front. 'Rush 'em, boys! Make a rough-house.' **1913** R. H. BARBOUR *Around the End* xxi. 258 The audience..indulged in wild 'rough-house'. **1919** 'ETIENNE' *Strange Tales from Fleet* 136, I need not enlarge on the subsequent entertainments, which consisted of a sing-song followed by a 'rough house', in which a certain amount of furniture was broken. **1923** H. L. FOSTER *Beachcomber in Orient* xi. 240, I ..watched Singapore fade into the distance with its memories of vice, iniquity, and general rough-house. **1933** E. O'NEILL *Ah, Wilderness!* I. 25 That's enough, now. No more roughhouse. You sit down here, Richard. **1941** *Penguin New Writing* II. 87 Someone being funny and turnin' off your juice and you keep striking at your electrode and wondering why the hell it doesn't strike and flash, and losing your temper, and then seeing the rest laughing and having a rough house for a while. **1952** [see BOCHE]. **1973** 'B. GRAEME' *Two & Two make Five* xiii. 123 He's smaller and lighter than me; not nearly so useful in a rough house.

b. *attrib.* or as *adj.* (Also *roughhouse*.)

1898 F. P. DUNNE *Mr. Dooley in Peace & War* 25 Other gin'rals iv th' r-rough-house kind, like Napoleon Bonypart, th' impror iv th' Frinch, Gin'ral Ulis S. Grant, an' Cousin George Dooley, hired coarse, rude men. **1901** *Official Basket Ball Rules* (Spalding's Athletic Library) 49 Mr. Naismith never invented the game for 'rough house' work. **1906** *N.Y. Globe* 22 Aug. 6 On that rough-house occasion more force than was necessary was used to eject the Bryanite faction. **1919** H. L. WILSON *Ma Pettengill* ii. 74 Two or three other directors..had put him into rough-house funny plays where he got thrown downstairs or had bricks fall on him. **1932** *Amer. Speech* VII. 241 Jazz is free, Jazz is roughouse. **1938** E. BOWEN *Death of Heart* II. iv. 240 Mr. Bursely was shoved against the bookcase by Wallace Parker shoving, that rude way... I didn't like him to see us so rough house. **1938** R. GRAVES *Coll. Poems* 121 Time and Space Do but amuse us with their rough-house turn. **1946** *Casper* (Wyoming) *Tribune-Herald* 29 Mar. 9/3 Rocky, with his striking black hair and roughhouse tactics in the ring, has become a gallery idol.

'rough-house, *v. slang* (orig. *U.S.*). Also rough house, roughhouse. [f. the sb.] **1.** *intr.* To make a disturbance or row; to behave or act boisterously or violently; to fight or engage in horse-play *with*. Also quasi-*trans.* with *it*.

1900 *Dialect Notes* II. 55 *Rough-house, v.i.* To put a room in disorder. **1904** R. L. MCCARDELL *Show Girl & her Friends* 107 When they teased him about having to keep him out of the place if he did not stop rough-housing it, poor Dopey smiled..and asked if he had hurt anybody very bad. **1908** U. B. SINCLAIR *Metropolis* 57 She's always wanting to rough-house it. **1920** 'SAPPER' *Bull-Dog Drummond* ix. 239 Somebody has been rough-housing by the look of things. **1928** *Chambers's Jrnl.* Apr. 211/2 He had a veteran in combat to deal with, a man who had 'rough-housed' it all over the world. **1929** E. L. RICE *Street Scene* II. 167 Rough-housing with your kid brother. **1971** *Daily Colonist* (Victoria, B.C.) 5 May 43/2 Police spokesmen said the boys were 'rough-housing' on the grass. **1977** *Time* 10 Jan. 13/1 Twice, a broken leg set him back—once when he was caught in an avalanche while skiing, later while roughhousing with friends.

2. *trans.* To handle (a person) violently; to assail roughly; to maltreat by rough usage.

1902 H. L. WILSON *Spenders* xxxvi. 436 You rough-housed the boy considerable yesterday. **1903** *N.Y. Times* 6 Oct. 1 After the rush the classes adjourned to Massachusetts Avenue and began to 'rough house' the passing street cars. **1925** H. L. FOSTER *Trop. Tramp with Tourists* 188 The S[ocial] M[anager] must not risk the loss of their future patronage by mauling or roughhousing such as might not enjoy it, or at least tolerate it. **1928** *Daily Express* 4 Sept. 9/5 Harvey as a boxer of exceptional skill should not have allowed West to rush into close quarters and 'rough-house' him. **1938** X. HERBERT *Capricornia* (1939) xxvi. 389 He explained that when he had tried to keep order at the station he had been rough-housed. **1952** in Wentworth & Flexner *Dict. Amer. Slang* (1960) 434/1 The question of whether.. gun-toting bodyguards rough-housed Swedish citizens.

Hence **'rough-houser** (also *attrib.* and *fig.*); **'rough-housing** *vbl. sb.*

1904 *N.Y. Even. Post* 2 Jan., In fiction, whether it is historic, society, or the work of literary rough-housers. **1927** *Blackw. Mag.* June 843/2 It is more than mere rough-housing. **1933** D. L. SAYERS *Murder must Advertise* v. 90 Stand by..in case there's any rough-housing. **1949** KOESTLER *Promise & Fulfilment* I. xii. 131 Apart from some rough-housing..the troops found no occasion for any martial activity. **1951** *Sun* (Baltimore) 2 Mar. 19/2 In some sections, wrestling is outdrawing boxing... Lord Carlton, who poses as a titled Englishman; the Golden Terror, a roughhouser type..have contributed to the success. **1974** H. L. FOSTER *Ribbin'* vi. 244 Many male teachers relate physically to male students through playful roughhousing where some form of physical body contact is made.

roughie ('rʌfɪ). *dial.* and *slang.* Also **roughy**. [f. ROUGH *sb.*[1] + -IE, -Y[6].] **1.** A rough or rowdy; a brawler; a hooligan.

1905 *Eng. Dial. Dict.* V. 158/1 Roughy, *sb.* Sc. Irel. 1 A coarsely made, bullying fellow. Ant. GROSE (1790) *MS. add.* (C.) **1933** *Bulletin* (Sydney) 15 Nov. 33/1 With such a lot of roughies in the hall. **1953** *Amer. Speech* XXVIII. 118 *Rough, roughy, n.* A carnival roustabout, a manual labourer. **1966** W. S. RAMSON *Austral. Eng.* iv. 62 Roughie, meaning 'a coarsely made, bullying fellow' was used in both Scotland and Ireland. **1971** P. DRISCOLL *White Lie Assignment* vii. 60, I know a roughie when I see one... He's just one of those blokes who can't stay away from trouble.

2. *Austral.* In dog- and horse-racing: an outsider.

1934 'S. RUDD' *Green Grey Homestead* 155 Those who had lost a wager or two will turn to Bell and say: 'You knew something about the roughie!' **1951** CUSACK & JAMES *Come in Spinner* 40 He's a roughie so 'e'll go out at long odds. **1958** F. HARDY *Four-Legged Lottery* 14, I might just have a shilling on a roughie. **1973** *Sun-Herald* (Sydney) 26 Aug. 58/2 Punters were reluctant to support him... Consequently Pepper Moss went out as a 12-1 'roughie'.

3. *Austral.* A trick, an unfair practice; esp. in phr. ***to put a roughie over.***

1939 K. TENNANT *Foveaux* II. i. 122 Kelly put a roughie over Charlie to-day. *Ibid.* III. ii. 151 'They're putting over a roughie at Central,' the secretary..mentioned casually. **1945** BAKER *Austral. Lang.* xv. 265 A *roughie, toughie, hottie, crookie, swiftie, smartie* will all be heard in male conversation to describe a joke or trick that is either agreeable or disagreeable. **1970** R. BEILBY *No Medals for Aphrodite* 269, I bluffed him, put a roughie over him.

roughing ('rʌfɪŋ), *vbl. sb.* [f. ROUGH *v.*]

1. a. The action of making rough. Also *fig.*

1755 *Mem. Capt. P. Drake* II. i. 6 She would not even receive some Presents I offered her, but stood Proof against my Ruffing and Smoothing. **1876** VOYLE & STEVENSON *Milit. Dict.* 353/1 The term *roughing* is applied to the action of a rasp on a fuze, to make it bite in the fuze-hole.

b. The process of treating horse-shoes in such a manner as to prevent slipping.

1865 *City Press* 25 Mar., In consequence of the late severe weather, and the evil results of roughing. **1889** GRETTON *Memory's Harkback* 153 His horse..being badly pricked in the roughing.

2. a. The action or operation of preparing roughly or treating in a preliminary manner. In various technical uses (see quots.).

1839 URE *Dict. Arts* 635 The body is now put into a coarse hair cloth, then dipped and rolled in the hot liquor, until the root ends of the beaver are thoroughly worked in. This is technically called rolling off, or *roughing*. **1850** HOLTZAPFFEL *Turning* III. 1314 For large stones, the roughing is generally commenced with grinding emery. **1854** *Jrnl. R. Agric. Soc.* XV. II. 378 The first separation of the chaff and pulse (usually called roughing). **1882** *Encycl. Brit.* XIV. 665/1 The flax is, after roughing, broken or cut into three lengths.

b. With advs., as *down, in, off, out, up.* (cf. ROUGH *v.*[1] 6 b; also *attrib.*).

1825 J. NICHOLSON *Operat. Mechanic* 617 The stucco..is rubbed over the wall with a flat brush of hogs' bristles. When this process, called *roughing in*, has been performed [etc.]. **1839** URE *Dict. Arts* 591 The apartment in which the roughing-down..is performed, is furnished with a considerable number of stone tables. **1846** HOLTZAPFFEL *Turning* II. 519 The gouge or roughing out tool for brass-work. **1873** SPON *Workshop Rec.* Ser. I. 122/2 Bastard stucco is of three coats, the first is roughing in or rendering. **1881** *Mechanic* §567. 263 It is used for 'roughing down' or taking off the bulk of the superfluous wood. **1883** *Proc. Inst. Mech. Engineers* 226 They are used in different machine tools principally for 'roughing out', or..rapidly reducing castings, forgings, &c., from their rough state to nearly their finished forms. **1884** *Pall Mall G.* 4 Mar. 9/1 The 'roughing-up' of the dog was finished, and he then went back to the studio. **1901** *Jrnl. Inst. Electr. Engineers* XXXI. 312 Two drills should in all cases be provided, one a roughing-out drill, and the other a finishing drill. **1947** J. C. RICH *Materials & Methods of Sculpture* ix. 252 The bushhammer is a very useful and fairly rapid tool, which may be employed from the coarse, initial roughing-out stages almost to the very delicate or final stages of the carving. **1947** DYLAN THOMAS *Let.* Jan. (1966) 292 And I also worked upon the preliminary roughing-out of the script with Taylor. **1948** *Rev. Sci. Instruments* XIX. 15/1 The holding pump serves as a fore-pump for the diffusion pump during the roughing-down portion of the cycle. **1969** E. H. PINTO *Treen* 388/1 A mid-19th-century roughing off plane. **1970** R. J. SMALL *Study of Landforms* iv. 128 Many of these joints are evidently post-denudational, having appeared since the 'roughing-out' of the main elements in the landscape by Tertiary erosion.

c. *concr.* (See quots.)

1834-6 BARLOW in *Encycl. Metrop.* (1845) VIII. 760/2 The nap, or, to use the technical word, the *roughing*, consists chiefly of beaver down [etc.]. *Ibid* 762/1. **1875** KNIGHT *Dict. Mech.* 1993/2 The first coat..on masonry [is termed] *rendering* or *roughing*.

3. The fact of undergoing hardships, or living under hard conditions.

c **1823** BYRON *Don Juan* XII. lxiii. variant line 6 in Hagelman & Barnes *Concordance to Byron's Don Juan* (1967) 682 But those who have been a little used to roughing. **1836** T. POWER *Impressions Amer.* II. 211 This little city [*sc.* Mobile] was to me one of the most attractive spots I visited south of the Potomac. I came upon it..after a severe roughing, and found a fine climate and old friends. **1841** B. HALL *Patchwork* I. 45 Abundant opportunities..to gratify the taste of the greatest lover of roughing. **1854** J. L. STEPHENS *Centr. Amer.* 376 Pawling with the experience of seven years 'roughing' had expedients. **1893** A. H. S. LANDOR *Hairy Ainu* 2 A man who could stand any amount of hardships and roughing.

4. *Boxing.* ? Rough or foul handling; also *N. Amer.*, in *Football, Ice Hockey,* and *Lacrosse*: foul tackling, punching, or pushing. Also, ***roughing-the-kicker attrib.***

1866 in *Encycl. Brit.* (1888) XXIV. 691/1 *Boxing*... That no wrestling, roughing, or hugging on the ropes be allowed. **1938** *Sun* (Baltimore) 27 Oct. 12/6 Brooks, of Yale, broke through and rushed the kicker... Being unable to stop himself in midair, he naturally crashed into the kicker, and Michigan was given the ball for roughing the punter. **1958** F. C. AVIS *Boxing Reference Dict.* 96 *Roughing*, questionable tactics in a boxing contest, and likely to involve disqualification of the offender. **1958** *Herald-Tribune* (Grande Prairie, Alberta) 28 Feb. 5/6 Bryan McCurdy.. and Bill Oakford..went off together for roughing and slashing at the 18:55 mark. **1961** J. S. SALAK *Dict. Amer. Sports* 371 *Roughing the kicker* (football), making unnecessary bodily contact with the punter, which is illegal. *Roughing the passer* (football), unnecessary roughness to a player who has thrown a forward pass. A penalty is involved for this infraction. **1968** *Globe & Mail* (Toronto) 15 Jan. 20/2 The skirmish provoked a pushing duel that netted every player on the ice, with the exception of the goalkeepers, minors for roughing. **1973** *Houston* (Texas) *Chron.* (Suppl.) 14 Oct. 5/1, I was unaware of just how specialized pro football had become until..discovering that one team's kicker had not punted the entire evening. He had, however, drawn eight roughing-the-kicker penalties... It's 15 yards and an automatic first (five yards and an automatic first for the less flagrant 'running into the kicker'). **1976** *Webster's Sports Dict.* 357/1 *Roughing the kicker* (*football*), a personal foul that results when a defensive player runs into or knocks down the kicker on a scrimmage kick without first touching or deflecting the ball... When it is called, the penalty is 15 yards from the previous spot. *Roughing the passer* (*football*), a personal foul in professional play that results when a defensive player runs into or tackles a passer after a forward pass has been thrown... When it is called, the penalty is 15 yards from the previous spot.

b. With *up*: see ROUGH *v.*[1] 6 g.

1960 *Sunday Express* 23 Oct. 17/4 His roughing-up of George Bernard Shaw can't compare for butchery with what Mr. Mankowitz did last week to Robert Louis Stevenson. **1973** J. PATTINSON *Search Warrant* iv. 67 He could already feel the stiffness in his limbs that was the result of the roughing-up. **1977** R. BARNARD *Blood Brotherhood* xvi. 181 Their gang knifings and roughings-up.

5. *attrib.* (in sense 2), as ***roughing-cylinder, filter, -gouge, -lathe, -machine, -mill, plane, -roll, -roller, shop, -tool.*** **roughing pump**, a pump for evacuating a system from atmospheric pressure to a lower pressure at which a second pump can operate.

1839 URE *Dict. Arts* 705 These roughing cylinders are generally 7 feet long. *Ibid.* 706 The shingling mill..consists of two sets of grooved cylinders, the first being called *puddling rolls* or *roughing rolls*. **1850** HOLTZAPFFEL *Turning* III. 1034 The alabaster is roughed, or roughly ground on what the lapidary terms a roughing or lead mill. **1851** *Jrnl. R. Agric. Soc.* XII. II. 412 He..'chaffs' or 'roughs' the corn once over with a roughing-machine. **1873** J. RICHARDS *Operator's Hdbk.* 163 A roughing gouge, to reduce the piece so that it will fit the rest. **1889** G. FINDLAY *Eng. Railway* 112 An interesting feature of this shop is the 'roughing lathe'. **1904** *Rep. Brit. Assoc. Adv. Sci.* 1903 761 The other two original tanks were converted into six roughing filters containing 3 feet in depth of fine gravel, to intercept particles which have escaped the precipitation process. **1910** *Daily Chron.* 15 Jan. 7/2 The cause of the fire was the fusing of an electric motor in the 'roughing' shop [of an opticians' factory]. **1960** *McGraw-Hill Encycl. Sci. & Technol.* XIV. 543/1 The scrub or roughing plane..has heavy, rounded blades making it suitable for cleaning up rough boards. **1958** *Rev. Sci. Instruments* XXIX. 368/1 With the roughing pump pinched off..and the system then thoroughly baked out while pumping with the electronic pump, very low pressures can be achieved. **1971**, **1976** Roughing pump [see ROUGH *v.*[1] 7 d].

roughings ('rʌfɪŋz). *dial.* Also 8 roughin. [App. a var. of ROWEN, influenced by ROUGH *a.* through the variant ROW *a.*[1]] (See quots.)

1674 RAY *N.C. Words, Eddish,* Roughings. **1691** —— *S. & E.C. Words, Roughings*, latter grass, after-mathes. **1694** KENNETT *Par. Antiq.* Gloss. s.v. *Ernes*, Roughings and Aftermaths. **1736** J. LEWIS *Isle of Thanet Gloss.* (E.D.S.), *Roughin*, the grass after mowing. **1736** PEGGE *Kenticisms* (E.D.S.), *Ersh*,..the stubble after corn is cut. In Derbyshire they call it *edidge*, and restrain it to roughings or aftermaths. **1843** WAY in *Promp. Parv.* 424 *note*, In Hampshire and Sussex it is called rowings or roughings. **1875** PARISH *Sussex Gloss., Rowens*, or *Roughings*. **1883** *Hampshire Gloss., Roughings*, winter dried grass.

roughish ('rʌfɪʃ), *a.* [f. ROUGH *a.* + -ISH.] Somewhat rough.

1764 GRAINGER *Sugar Cane* III. 227 *note*, The nut [of the hiccory] whose shell is thick, hard, and roughish. **1796** WITHERING *Brit. Pl.* (ed. 3) II. 93 Straw 3-cornered, angles acute, roughish. **1813** JANE AUSTEN *Lett.* (1884) II. 202 It is but roughish weather for any one in a tender state. **1850** L. HUNT *Autobiog.* xv. 226 Mr. Wordsworth had a deep, roughish, but not unpleasing voice. **1888** 'R. BOLDREWOOD' *Robbery under Arms* i, He could..ride a roughish horse too.

Comb. **1847** WM. DARLINGTON *Amer. Weeds*, etc. (1860) 297 Leaves..roughish-puberulent beneath. **1852** GRAY in *Smithsonian Contrib. Knowl.* V. VI. 77 Stems..2–3 feet high, roughish-hirsute. **1855** LEIFCHILD *Cornwall* 268 In steps a shrewd, roughish-looking man.

rough leaf. [ROUGH *a.*]

1. The first true leaf of a (garden or field) plant, as distinguished from the cotyledons; a foliage leaf.

1754 JUSTICE *Scots Gard. Direct.* 95 In about three Weeks Time these Plants will begin to put out their rough Leaves. **1763** MILLS *Syst. Husb.* IV. 174 Soon after it has put out it's third, or what the gardeners call it's rough, leaf. **1801** *Farmer's Mag.* Nov. 413 As soon as they have put out the rough leaf, they should be transplanted. **1844** H. STEPHENS *Bk. Farm* III. 749 Its cotyledons then expand upwards into two rudimentary smooth leaves, and immediately thereafter two true or rough leaves appear.

2. The stage of growth when the true leaves have appeared.

1733 TULL *Horse-Hoeing Husb.* x. 95 They are so long in such dry poor Land before they get into Rough Leaf. **1787** WINTER *Syst. Husb.* 239 The fly too frequently destroys the young [turnip] plants before they grow into rough leaf. **1805** R. W. DICKSON *Pract. Agric.* II. 660 After..the plants have formed considerable tops, and are in what is usually termed *rough leaf*. **1848** *Proc. Berw. Nat. Club* II. 323 A healthy braird being produced, nearly in a state approaching to the 'rough leaf'.

rough-leaved, *a.* [ROUGH *a.*] Having rough leaves. Often in plant-names, as ***rough-leaved fig.***

1668 WILKINS *Real Char.* 80 Herbs considered according to the Superficies of their Leaves,..may be distinguished into such as are Rough leaved. **1731** MILLER *Gard. Dict.* s.v. *Ulmus*, The common rough-leav'd Elm. **1797** *Encycl. Brit.* (ed. 3) III. 421/2 Rough-leafed plants. **1834** AUDUBON *Ornith. Biogr.* II. 448 The Rough-leaved Cordia.., one of the most beautiful of the West Indian trees. **1868** WHITTIER *Among the Hills* Prel. 54 Nightshade and rough-leaved burdock. **1889** MAIDEN *Useful Native Pl.* 30 *Ficus aspera*, ..'Rough-leaved Fig'.

rough-legged, *a.* [ROUGH *a.*] Having hairy or feathered legs; *esp.* of birds: having the tarsi feathered.

1611 COTGR., *Coq de bois*, a blacke, and rough-legd Moore-cocke. **1691** *Lond. Gaz.* No. 2647/4 A chesnut Gelding.., rough Legg'd, having all his Paces. **1776** PENNANT *Brit. Zool.* II. App. 529 Roughleg'd Falcon. This species is a native of Denmark. **1811** A. WILSON *Amer. Ornith.* IV. 60 The Rough-legged Hawk measures twenty-two inches in length. **1830** *Cumb. Farm Rep.* 57 *Husb.* III. (L.U.K.), The farm horses in greatest repute in this district are the rough-legged Clydesdale or Lanarkshire breed. **1840** *Cuvier's Anim. Kingd.* 171 The Rough-legged Buzzard... One of the most widely diffused of Birds. **1896** LYDDEKER *Brit. Mammals* 42 The rough-legged bat, *vespertilio dasycneme.*

roughling, obs. form of RUFFLING *a.*

rough lock, rough-lock. *N. Amer.* [LOCK *sb.*[2] 4.] A device, as a chain, for slowing the passage down a slope of a vehicle or of logs. So **'rough-lock, 'roughlock** *v. trans.*, to slow a vehicle by means of a rough lock, to attach chains to a vehicle so as to slow it; **'rough-locking** *vbl. sb.*

1859 MARCY *Prairie Trav.* iii. 93 Rough-locking is a very safe method of passing heavy artillery down abrupt declivities. **1884** W. SHEPHERD *Prairie Experiences* 197 The hind wheels were rough-locked, that is, a large linked chain was tied round the rim of the wheel in such a way that the wheel rides upon the chain, which drags along and cuts into the ground. **1913** E. MACLENNAN in MacLennan & Snow *Songs of Neukluk* 15 She had a skookum load of logs, but I couldn't understand With the rough-lock and the gee-pole how it scaped from her command. **1962** J. ONSLOW *Bowler-Hatted Cowboy* v. 46 The rough-lock bit deep into the softening ice and mud. **1973** R. D. SYMONS *Where Wagon Led* I. viii. 128 The stout sleigh groaning in protest against the logging chain rough-locked around a hind runner.

†**'roughly**, *a.* *Obs.*$^{-1}$ In 5 roghlych. [f. ROUGH *a.* + -LY[1].] Harsh-sounding.

13.. *E.E. Allit. P.* C. 64 Goddes glam to hym glod,.. With a roghlych rurd rowned in his ere.

roughly ('rʌflɪ), *adv.* Forms: 4 ruchli, rohly, 6 *Sc.* rouchly; 4 rughli, 4, 6 rughly, 6 rughtly, 6– roughly, 7 ruffly. [f. ROUGH *a.*]

1. In a rough, ungentle, or violent manner; with roughness or violence.

a **1300** *Cursor M.* 22151 þe wind to do rughli to rise. *c* **1325** *Metr. Hom.* (1862) 23 Kinric sal rohly rise Igain kinric. **1526** SKELTON *Magnyf.* 1910, I rushe at them rughly, and make them ly full lowe. **1560** DAUS tr. *Sleidane's Comm.* 365 He dealeth so sharply and roughly with him. **1601** SHAKS. *Twel. N.* III. iv. 124 The Fiend is rough, and will not be roughly vs'd. **1638** SANDERSON *Serm.* (1681) II. 113 God in His dispensations commonly.. dealeth roughliest with us at the first. **1680** *Hatton Corr.* (1878) I. 219 The K. received them but ruffly. **1712** STEELE *Spect.* No. 427 ¶ 1 One whose own Character has been very roughly treated. **1778** MISS BURNEY *Evelina* lxxxii, Shaking him roughly by the hand. **1844** THIRLWALL *Greece* lxiv. VIII. 305 When it appeared that the ambassadors had received no instructions on this head, they were roughly dismissed. **1884** W. C. SMITH *Kildrostan* 87 Give me the calm of Tempe where no wind Blows on the vine-stocks roughly.

Comb. **1856** KANE *Arct. Expl.* II. ix. 95 There are emotions among rude, roughly-nurtured men which vent themselves in true poetry.

2. Without much care, skill, or finish; in a rude or imperfect manner.

1607 NORDEN *Surv. Dial.* III. 120 The Surueyor and his Clarke may enter them roughly in a booke, and afterward inroll them faire in a booke of Parchment for Continuance. **1662** J. DAVIES tr. *Olearius' Voy. Ambass.* 10 The Miracles of S. Nicholas, painted according to the mode of the Country, very roughly; and without proportion. **1797** MRS. RADCLIFFE *Italian* vi, The walls were roughly painted with subjects.. tending to inspire melancholy awe. **1810** SOUTHEY *Kehama* II. viii, It was an Idol roughly hewn of wood. **1851–3** *Tomlinson's Cycl. Arts* II. 169/1 The man then gets out a mass of rock and dresses it roughly into a cylinder. **1889** JESSOPP *Coming of Friars* ii. 54 The smaller strips of parchment.. have been roughly bound together in volumes.

Comb. **1826** KIRBY & SP. *Entomol.* IV. l. 546, I placed under a wine-glass several of each along with roughly-powdered camphor. **1875** SIR T. SEATON *Fret-Cutting* 67 The iron [is] run along the roughly-cut moulding.

3. Without strict accuracy or precision; only in an approximate or general way.

1841 *Penny Cycl.* XXI. 287/2 The population of Servia is roughly reckoned at about half a million of inhabitants. **1849** MACAULAY *Hist. Eng.* iii. I. 420 *note*, King.. roughly estimated the common people of England at 880,000 families. **1865** RUSKIN *Sesame* i. §33 Now, £700 is to £50,000,000 roughly, as sevenpence to two thousand pounds. **1893** EARL DUNMORE *Pamirs* I. 36 The Vedas.., which date back, roughly speaking, some 3000 years.

†**rough mason.** *Obs.* [ROUGH *a.*] A mason building only with unhewn stone.

Common in 16th c., with various spellings.

1444 *Act 23 Hen. VI*, c. 12 Les gagez ascun frank mason ou maister Carpenter nexcede pas par le jour iiij *d*... un rough mason & mesne Carpenter.. iii *d.* par le jour. **1504** *Bury Wills* (Camden) 99 Herry Brown, rough mason. **1538** ELYOT, *Cementarii*, daubers, pargetters, rowghe masons, whiche do make onely walles. **1554–5** in Willis & Clark *Cambridge* (1886) II. 470 Covenauntted with Scott the ruyghe mayson to make vpp the new wall and chimnays. **1602** *Burford Reg., Hist. Mss. Comm., Varr. Collect.* I. 165 For a maister free Mason, *vd.* For a maister rough Mason, *vd.*

rough music. [ROUGH *a.*] Noisy uproar; usually, a din produced by knocking together pots, pans, and other domestic utensils for the purpose of annoying a neighbour. Hence **rough-music** *v.*, to subject (a person) to this form of annoyance.

1708 *Brit. Apollo* No. 56. 3/2 Excuse the Rough Musick of Tongs and of Hammer. **1770** *Ann. Reg., Chron.* 74 A number of boys attended with shovels, playing the rough music. **1796** GROSE *Dict. Vulg. T.* (ed. 3), *Rough Music.* Saucepans, frying-pans, poker and tongs, marrow-bones and cleavers, bulls horns, etc. beaten upon and sounded in ludicrous processions. *a* **1845** HOOD *Public Dinner* ii, 'Mr. Tempest-one guinea, Mr. Merrington-twenty,' Rough music in plenty. **1847** MRS. GORE *Castles in the Air* I. xiii. 284 Poor Nixon.. had been more than once rough-musicked by his neighbours. **1854** KNIGHT *Once upon a Time* II. 250 The offender was rough-musicked. **1862** *Standard* 1 Dec., Those boisterous exhibitions of popular indignation known as rough music. **1867** SMYTH *Sailor's Word-Bk.* 580 *Rough Music*, rolling shot about on the lower deck, and other discordant noises, when seamen are discontented, but without being mutinous.

rough neck, rough-neck, roughneck. *colloq.* (orig. *U.S.*). [ROUGH *a.*] **1. a.** A rough or rowdy; a person of rough habits or quarrelsome disposition; an uncultivated or ignorant person.

1836 *Col. Crockett's Exploits & Adventures Texas* iv. 58 You may be called a drunken dog by some of the clean shirt and silk stocking gentry; but the real rough necks will style you a jovial fellow. **1903** *Sun* (N.Y.) 25 Nov. 2 The police were kept on the jump chasing away gangs of 'rough necks' (the pet name for the rowdies in Sam Park's late union) who went from building to building trying to intimidate members of the new union. **1903** *N.Y. Evening Post* 17 Aug. 7/7 His [*sc.* Sam Park's] stated income amounts to union wages from his union of 'rough-necks', as the iron-workers call themselves, as walking delegate. **1917** J. M. GRIDER *War Birds* (1927) 30 But there are a few rough-necks in every outfit that will cause trouble and get the whole bunch in wrong. **1918** [see *non-academic* s.v. NON- 3]. **1929** J. BUCHAN *Courts of Morning* I. iii. 51 The water-front was a perfect rat-hole for every criminal in the Pacific—every brand of rough-neck and dope-smuggler and crook. **1940** E. N. TEALL *Putting Words to Work* I. xxi. 147 The business man will say that if a university can afford to write such letters there is no need for a roughneck like him to bother. **1959** 'J. CHRISTOPHER' *Scent of White Poppies* vi. 91 She has me tabbed for a roughneck... She has enough on with civilizing you, without having me to cope with as well. **1972** D. HASTON *In High Places* i. 14 Jimmy was twenty-eight, and already a qualified architect; we were seventeen-year-old roughnecks. Basically I think.. he was at heart a roughneck himself. **1979** *Time* 13 Aug. 28/3 Like Lewis, countless other managers and entrepreneurs are coming to Denver to live amid its comfort and culture while their hired roughnecks and miners squeeze the energy from the rural out-posts.

b. *transf.* and *fig.*

Some examples are hardly distinguishable from sense 1 a.

1916 *Rio Grande Rattler* 13 Sept. 1 Ten buck [private] packers, known in the army as 'rough necks'— a title that usually fits the situation nicely. **1916** H. L. WILSON *Somewhere in Red Gap* v. 208 And so the party moved on for an hour or two, with the roguish young rough-necks cutting up merrily at all times, pretending to be cowboys coming to town on pay day. **1918** *Dialect Notes* V. 27 *Rough-neck*, n. 1. A rowdy. 2. A woman or girl of easy morals but not a prostitute. 3. A dance, open to anyone who 'has the price', at which 'anything goes'. General. **1926** MAINES & GRANT *Wise-Crack Dict.* 13/1 *Razor back*, roughneck or stake driver in a circus. **1926** F. SCOTT FITZGERALD *Great Gatsby* iii. 59 I'm Gatsby, he said... I was looking at an elegant young roughneck. **1941** E. P. O'DONNELL *Great Big Doorstep* iv. 59 'Are you a rough-neck?' 'Yes. I'm in the bull-gang so far. I'm trying to get in the office.' **1960** [see MAUVAIS COUCHEUR]. **1978** *Amer. Poetry Rev.* July/Aug. 36/2 He was also an intellectual roughneck.

c. A worker on an oil-rig, esp. a labourer on the floor of a rig.

1917 *Dialect Notes* IV. 421 *Roughneck, n.* A man who works about an oil derrick. **1932** *Amer. Speech* VII. 270 *Roughneck*, n., the regular term for a member of a driller's crew on a rotary rig; not applied to the driller. **1948** *Chicago Tribune* 5 Dec. I. 14/3 Among today's roughnecks you'll find college men—petroleum engineers and geologists. **1958** *Times* 15 May 14/6 Any such rig [for oil drilling] is known throughout the industry as a wildcat, and unskilled members of drilling crews are technically classified as 'roughnecks'. **1972** *Guardian* 11 Feb. 12/1 A Dutch oilman endorsed this. 'When the exploration is over, the 'roughnecks' (local labour) will go.' **1976** M. MACHLIN *Pipeline* xi. 135 He.. had worked as a Roughneck in the Louisiana area and in East Texas on the oil rigs. **1977** *Time* 14 Mar. 37/1 The centre of the rig's activities is the mud-slicked drill floor, where half a dozen roughnecks struggle day and night with heavy chains and power-driven winches to shove 90-ft.-long pieces of drill pipe into the narrow hole.

2. *attrib.* Rough; rowdy; uncultivated; characteristic of a rough-neck.

1916 H. L. WILSON *Somewhere in Red Gap* vii. 288 He really wanted.. to study insect life and botany and geography and arithmetic,.. instead of being killed off in a sudden manner by his rough-neck parent. **1920** C. SANDBURG *Smoke & Steel* 7 The others were rough-neck singers a long ways from home. **1931** 'R. WEST' in *Time & Tide* 19 Sept. 1091, I commend to every reader the essay on 'Foreheads Villainous Low', with its entertaining satire on the new 'roughneck' movement among the intellectuals. **1973** A. HUNTER *Gently French* xiv. 128 Those risks.. would be part of the fun for a roughneck Romeo. **1976** R. SANDERS in D. Villiers *Next Year in Jerusalem* 209 The roughneck genius of a Walt Whitman.

So **'rough-neck** *v. intr.*, to work as a rough-neck on an oil-rig; **'rough-necking** *vbl. sb.*

1932 *Amer. Speech* VII. 270 *Roughneck*, intr. v., to work as a member of a rotary driller's crew. **1976** *Globe & Mail* (Toronto) 16 Feb. 3/1 About 200 a year are beginners ready to try roughnecking, the industry's term for the beginners' job. **1977** *New Yorker* 6 June 47/2 One.. roughnecked in the oil fields near Houston.

roughness ('rʌfnɪs). Forms: 4 rowȝnes, 6 rowghnes, 5–7 roughnesse, 6–7 -nes, 6– roughness; 6 rouf-, roff-, ruffenesse; *Sc.* 6 rowchnes, 9 ro(u)chness. [f. ROUGH *a.* + -NESS.]

1. a. The quality of being rough to the touch.

1398 TREVISA *Barth. De P.R.* v. xxvii. (Bodl. MS.), þey be nought itaried and ilette, by meting and feling of rowȝnes. **1495** *Ibid.* IV. iii. 82 Roughnesse is not elles but an vneuynnesse in an harde thynge. **1572** BOSSEWELL *Armorie* II. 61 A beaste so called for the roughnesse and sharpenesse of his prickes. **1577** B. GOOGE *Heresbach's Husb.* I. (1586) 29 b, Cattell can not away with it, for the sharpenesse and ruffenesse of the eares. **1601** HOLLAND *Pliny* XIII. xii, The roughnesse of Paper is pollished and smoothed either with some tooth, or els with a Porcellane shell. **1648** MILTON *Observ. Peace Ormond* Wks. 1851 IV. 571 For that hairy roughness assum'd won Jacob the Birthright both Temporal and Eternal. **1700** DRYDEN *Ovid's Met.* I. 545 While yet the roughness of the stone remains. **1796** WITHERING *Brit. Pl.* (ed. 3) III. 649 Teeth.. long, expanding, sharp, and giving the plant its roughness to the touch. **1846** GREENER *Sci. Gunnery* 275 This roughness.. answers the same as friction by relief. **1875** JOWETT *Plato* (ed. 2) III. 647 Roughness is hardness mingled with inequality.

b. Ruggedness, brokenness (of ground).

1565 COOPER, *Loci iniqua asperitas*, vneuen roughnesse. **1585** T. WASHINGTON tr. *Nicholay's Voy.* I. xv. 16 By reason .. of the roughnesse of the place being ful of rocks. **1686** tr. *Chardin's Trav. Persia* 341 By reason of the Roughness and Height of the Mountaines. **1781** COWPER *Conversat.* 699 They.. From such communion.. Feel less the journey's roughness and its length. **1811** PINKERTON *Mod. Geogr.* (ed. 3) 82 The rich roughness of an English prospect, diversified with an abundance of wood. **1878** BROWNING *La Saisiaz* 45 If Roughness of the long rock-clamber lead not to the last of cliff.

c. A rough part or place.

1674 N. FAIRFAX *Bulk & Selv.* 151 Those thick roughnesses that sence beholds them with. **1747** *Gentl. Mag.* 209 To call these scabbed roughnesses scales.. is a great inaccuracy. *a* **1774** GOLDSM. *Surv. Exp. Philos.* (1776) II. 192 The resined bow.. being drawn along the string, its roughnesses catch the string at very small intervals. **1834–6** BARLOW in *Encycl. Metrop.* (1845) VIII. 664/2 The threads .. remove every roughness and inequality from the inside of the barrel. **1858** HAWTHORNE *Fr. & It. Note-bks.* I. 242 Trees and shrubbery.. mantle a host of rocky roughnesses, and make all look smooth.

fig. **1885** SPURGEON *Treas. David* Ps. cxxxi. 2 The Psalmist .. had smoothed down the roughnesses of his self-will.

d. *local* (chiefly *U.S.*) Fodder, hay, corn-husks, etc., as used to feed cattle or horses, as opp. grain. Also *transf.*

1813 J. HARTSELL *Jrnl.* 29 Oct. in *East Tennessee Hist. Soc. Publ.* (1939) XI. 99 Did not draw aney rufness for our teeme. **1846** *Knickerbocker* XXVIII. 313 The truck's all soaked, and there can't nobody stay here to save souls without some kind of *roughness* to keep up natur'. **1859** W. DICKINSON *Gloss. Dial. Cumberland* 93 *Roughness*,.. grass left for winterage. **1872** DE VERE *Americanisms* 536 Roughness in South Carolina denotes shucks or cornhusks, on account, probably, of the roughness of the serrated blades. **1888** C. D. WARNER *On Horseback* iv. 142 'Roughness', we found out at the other house, meant hay in this region. **1938** J. STUART *Beyond Dark Hills* iv. 88 We don't feed the cattle anything but roughness. **1949** *Publ. Amer. Dial. Soc.* XI. 10 *Roughness*,.. fodder; roughage. **1966** *Ibid.* *1964* XLII. 22 *Roughness*, rough fodder, corntops, coarse hay.

e. *Bacteriol.* The quality of being rough in sense 1 e of the adj.

1929 TOPLEY & WILSON *Princ. Bacteriol. & Immunity* vii. 191 The property of colonial roughness is associated.. with a characteristic change in the method of cell division. **1934** *Jrnl. Bacteriol.* XXVII. 559 Roughness is a relative term when applied to colonial form for many rough colonies may have a smooth appearance on ordinary media. **1960** L. PICKEN *Organization of Cells* iii. 63 The roughness expresses itself in the formation of dry, membranous, or brittle colonies, with irregular margins and corrugated surface, and a granular appearance under the microscope; in contrast to the colonies of the Smooth type which are creamy or butter-like in consistency, with even margins and homogeneous in texture.

2. Harshness, unpleasantness, crudeness (of sound, taste, colour); inelegance (of diction, etc.).

1495 *Trevisa's Barth. De P.R.* v. xxiv. 134 Roughnesse of voyce comyth of dryenes of ayre. **1579** E. K. *Ded. Spenser's Sheph. Cal.*, Now,.. for al the compasse of the speach, it is round without roughnesse, and learned without hardnes. **1646** SIR T. BROWNE *Pseud. Ep.* 338 Divers plants containe a gratefull sharpenesse.., or an austere and inconcocted roughnesse. **1675** A. BROWNE *App. Art of Limning* 10 Let not the Roughness of the Colour discourage you from proceeding. **1697** DRYDEN *Ded. Æneid* Ess. (Ker) II. 215 Wherever that [the cæsura] is used, it gives a roughness to the verse; of which we can have little need in a language which is overstocked with consonants. **1730** MILLER *Gard. Dict.* s.v. *Wine*, The coarse Wines.. by reason of their great Austerity and Roughness. **1818** KEATS *Endym.* II. 818 O dearth Of human words! roughness of mortal speech! **1884** R. W. CHURCH *Bacon* ix. 216 Their roughness gives a flavour which no elaboration could give. **1897** *Allbutt's Syst. Med.* II. 843 Roughness [of wines] is due to tannic acid.

pl. **1804** W. TAYLOR in Robberds *Mem.* (1843) I. 513 Ease usually results from polishing away roughnesses. **1874** H. R. REYNOLDS *John Bapt.* ii. 111 The grammatical roughnesses .. favour the idea. **1883** A. ROBERTS *O.T. Revision* xi. 232 Its provincial roughnesses were smoothed and softened.

3. Storminess, inclemency (of weather, etc.).

1545 ASCHAM *Toxoph.* I. (Arb.) 48 The.. winter, for the roughnesse of it, is cleane taken away from shoting. **1553** EDEN *Treat. New Ind.* (Arb.) 28 Partly enforced by roughnes of the sea. **1600** E. BLOUNT tr. *Conestaggio* 274 They made great reckoning of the roughnes of the sea. **1634** W. TIRWHYT tr. *Balzac's Lett.* I. 351 The roughnesse of the season.. makes mee over apprehensive to stirre out of my Chamber. **1687** A. LOVELL tr. *Thevenot's Trav.* II. 3 The roughness of the Sea.. was occasioned by the violence of the Wind.

4. Harshness of tone or manner; severity.

1530 PALSGR. 264/1 Roughnesse, *impetuosité*, *rudevr*, *rudesse*. **1548** UDALL, etc. *Erasm. Par. Matt.* xi. 50 b, They that be not moued with austeritie and roughnes, be wonte to bee wonne by fayre speakyng and gentilnes. *a* **1572** KNOX *Hist. Ref.* Wks. 1846 I. 195 The hardis in Baptisme signifie the rowchnes of the law, and the oyle the softnes of Goddis mercy. **1649** *Nicholas Papers* (Camden) 156 Sec. Nicholas.. should come againe unto the King as before, but with much more roughnes and sharpnes. **1683** BURNET tr. *More's Utopia* (1685) 92 Religion, notwithstanding its Severity and Roughness. **1741** RICHARDSON *Pamela* I. 55 Having been crying, at his Roughness in the Entry, I turn'd away my Face.

5. Rudeness or ruggedness of character or manners; lack of politeness or refinement.

1605 SHAKS. *Lear* II. ii. 103 This is some Fellow, Who hauing beene prais'd for bluntnesse, doth affect A saucy roughnes. **1683** D. A. *Art Converse* Pref., The Citizens of Edenborough have laid down the greatest part of their former Roughness. **1747** CARTE *Hist. Eng.* I. 14 He was.. well qualified by these talents to polish the roughness of the people he was to govern. **1784** COWPER *Task* v. 480 What were left of roughness in the grain Of British natures, wanting its excuse That it belongs to freemen, would disgust And shock me. **1818** HALLAM *Mid. Ages* (1872) II. 253 With all the national roughness and honesty. **1865** TROLLOPE *Belton Est.* iii, With something of the promised roughness of the farmer. **1886** *Tip Cat* xv. 200 None of them noticed the roughness of the serving up.

6. *Sc.* and *north. dial.* Abundance or plenty in a rough kind of way.

1803 *Anderson's Cumb. Ball.* 55 We've roughness amang hands, we've kye i' the byre. **1832–53** *Whistle-Binkie* Ser. II.

58 He said he was a lairdie, O' riggs and roughness plenty. **1880** *Antrim & Down Gloss.* s.v., 'There's a great roughness about his farm,' i.e. great plenty.

roughometer (rʌˈfɒmɪtə(r)). *U.S.* [f. ROUGH *a.* + -O + -METER.] = PROFILOMETER 2 (*b*).

1926 *Public Roads* VII. 144/2 The roughometer consists of a rack which is attached in a vertical position to the front axle of the vehicle. **1947** *Daily Progress* (Charlottesville, Va.) 20 Mar. 8 (*caption*) State Highway Department engineers have developed the 'rough-o-meter' pictured above to detect some of the tiniest irregularities in the surface of highways.

rough-out, roughout (ˈrʌfaʊt). [ROUGH *v.*[1]]

1. *Archæol.* A prototype of an artefact. Cf. ROUGH *v.*[1] 6 b.

1936 *Proc. Prehist. Soc.* II. 214 Some sixty odd specimens were found most of which were implements gone wrong in the manufacture or rough-outs never proceeded with. **1959** J. D. CLARK *Prehist. S. Afr.* v. 120 Unfinished roughouts are found associated with factory debris and many finely-made developed Acheulian and even later transitional forms. **1980** *Rescue News* Sept. 4/3 Many large fragments of stone roof slates in various stages of rough-out were found in the fill.

2. Used *attrib.* to designate informal outdoor clothing. *U.S.*

1963 *New Yorker* 29 June 75 Chinos, shirts, roughout jackets. **1976** *National Observer* (U.S.) 10 Apr. 21/5 One scuffed cowboy boot sits poised atop the other; the baggy, rough-out trousers are now slung low beneath the prodigious belly.

ˈrough-ride, *v.* [Back-formation from ROUGH-RIDER.] *intr.* To ride an unbroken horse; also *fig.*, to domineer *over.*

1890 'R. BOLDREWOOD' *Col. Reformer* (1891) 92, I can rough-ride a bit. **1896** MRS. CAFFYN *Quaker Grandmother* 32 She rough-rides over every one and everything.

rough-rider (ˈrʌfˌraɪdə(r)). Also *Sc.* rouch-rider. [ROUGH *a.*]

1. a. A horse-breaker.

1733 J. BRAMSTON *Man of Taste* 17, I would with Jockies from Newmarket dine, And to Rough-riders give my choicest wine. **1791** WOLCOT (P. Pindar) *Rights of Kings* Wks. 1812 II. 392 That every Subject ought to wear a Saddle O'er which those great Rough-Riders, Kings may straddle. **1804** *Sporting Mag.* XXIII. 288 Advised him to send the horse to be broke in by a rough-rider. **1857** BAGEHOT *Biogr. Studies* 63 You might as fitly employ some delicate lady as a rough-rider. **1887** SIR R. H. ROBERTS *In the Shires* i. 11 There, too, is..the rough-rider, in a pair of old brown leather breeches.

b. *Mil.* (See quot. 1853.)

1802 JAMES *Milit. Dict.*, Rough Riders are the assistants of the riding master, and one should always be appointed to each troop. **1847** ALB. SMITH *Chr. Tadpole* xxxvii, I've ridden colts that have thrown all the best rough-riders in the Blues. **1853** STOCQUELER *Mil. Encycl.* 236/2 *Rough Rider*, a non-commissioned officer in the cavalry regiments, whose business it is to break in refractory horses, and assist the riding-master when required. **1876** VOYLE & STEVENSON *Milit. Dict.* 353/1.

2. a. A horseman of a rough type; one engaged in rough work or who can ride an unbroken horse; also *Sc.*, a circus-rider. Also *fig.*

1828 SCOTT *F.M. Perth* xvi, Thou shalt answer the challenge, as good right thou hast, having had injury from this rough-rider. **1860** EMERSON *Cond. Life* ii. (1861) 40 These rough riders,—legislators in shirt-sleeves. **1888** ROOSEVELT in *Cent. Mag.* Feb. 505/2 The rough-rider of the plains, the hero of rope and revolver. **1890** 'R. BOLDREWOOD' *Col. Reformer* (1891) 94 A matchless rough-rider, and wellnigh impossible to be thrown. **1977** T. ALLBEURY *Man with President's Mind* vi. 62 At the Pentagon end Langham's going to need a man who grinds away diplomatically. Not a rough-rider.

b. *Mil.* An irregular cavalryman.

1884 *Manch. Exam.* 30 Oct. 5/5 The Cape roughriders will be more suitable for this employment than the regular troopers. **1891** MOULLIN *Surg.* I. v. 126 Cavalry soldiers and rough-riders. **1899** ROOSEVELT in *Scribner's Mag.* XXX. 7/1 When finally the Generals of Division and Brigade began to write in formal communications about our regiment as the 'Rough Riders', we adopted the term ourselves.

ˈrough-riding, *vbl. sb.* [f. after ROUGH-RIDER.] The action of a rough-rider. Also *fig.*

1776 G. COLMAN *Let.* 21 July in *Private Corr. D. Garrick* (1831) I. 231 After a great deal of rough riding, I have got him to accept bills of exchange payable in two and four months. **1844** DISRAELI *Coningsby* v. iii, The Prince Colonna, who, since the steeple-chase, had imbibed a morbid predilection for such amusements, and indeed for every species of rough-riding. **1864** KNIGHT *Passages Work. Life* II. vi. 121 He did me..good in his rough-riding when I was learning my paces in this intellectual manège. **1969** *Telegraph* (Brisbane) 17 May 3/2 Thrill-seeking boys..have discovered a dangerous new pastime—riding in tall buildings on the top of a lift cage... The boys call it 'rough-riding'.

So **ˈrough-riding** *ppl. a.*

1881 J. RUSSELL *Haigs* xiv. 426 With the rough-riding men on both sides of the frontier, to meet was to fight. **1898** *Daily News* 31 May 2/3 Qualifying themselves to become rough-riding sergeants and instructors of young recruits.

roughshod (ˈrʌfʃɒd), *a.* and *pa. pple.*

1. Of horses: Having shoes with the nail-heads projecting; chiefly *fig.* in phr. ***to ride roughshod over***, to domineer or tyrannize over, to treat without any consideration.

1688 HOLME *Armoury* III. 90/1 Rough shod,—when the nails are not yet worn that holds on the shoes. **1790** BURNS *Ball. Dumfries Election* xxiii, Lord, send a rough-shod troop o' Hell O'er a' wad Scotland buy or sell, To grind them in the mire! **1813** MOORE *Post-bag* i. 20 'Tis a scheme of the Romanists, so help me God! To ride over your most Royal Highness roughshod. **1861** *Sat. Rev.* Nov. 547 We remember that we have ridden roughshod over neutrals in our time. **1896** A. DOBSON *18th C. Vignettes* Ser. III. v. 149 The Doctor rode rough-shod over him with an inaccurate illustration.

transf. **1891** SMILES *Mem. J. Murray* I. v. 92 The rough-shod way in which it [the Edinburgh Review] endeavoured to crush down rising authors.

2. As *pa. pple.* Provided with shoes which are roughed to prevent slipping.

1826 SCOTT *Jrnl.* 26 Nov., Horses..gone to the smithy to be roughshod in this snowy weather.

rough shoot. [SHOOT *sb.*[1]] An act of shootng game without beaters; an area in which one has a right to shoot in this manner. So **ˈrough-shoot** *v. intr.*; **rough-shooter; rough-shooting.**

1900 *Field* 29 Sept. Advt. p. vi/2 Wanted, a good rough shoot, commencing season 1901–1902, on Lease; plenty of rabbits essential; 2000 to 5000 acres. **1934** F. ELLIS *Summers of Yesterday* II. 78 It was a wild bit we had taken, sea-trout fishing, brown trout, and rough shooting, that was all. **1937** L. DURRELL *Panic Spring* vii. 113 They used to..rough-shoot across the parklands. **1943** G. GREENE *Ministry of Fear* II. i. 122 The Home..had its own hens and pigs and a good many acres of rough shooting. **1972** 'M. INNES' *Open House* v. 42 Manage you a bit of rough shooting, too. Brought your gun? **1976** *Shooting Times & Country Mag.* 18–24 Nov. 28/2 (Advt.), A perfect fowler's or roughshooter's gun. *Ibid.* 16–22 Dec. 48/2 (Advt.), Yellow dog, 2 years, trained for rough shoot. **1976** *Evening Post* (Nottingham) 16 Dec. 21/8 (Advt.), Rough shoot wanted, 30 miles radius of Nottingham.

rough-skinned, *a.* [ROUGH *a.*] Having a rough skin or bark. ***rough-skinned plum***, the grey plum (PLUM *sb.* 3 b).

1598 SYLVESTER *Du Bartas* II. ii. I. *Ark* 412 The proud Horse, the rough-skinn'd Elephant. **1752** J. HILL *Hist. Anim.* 292 The compressed, roundish, rough-skinned Ostracion.., the Sunfish. **1846** LINDLEY *Veget. Kingd.* 543 The Rough-skinned, or Gray plum of the same colony [Sierra Leone] is the produce of Parinarium excelsum. **1902** CORNISH *Naturalist Thames* 49 In the crevices of pines, oaks, elms, and other rough-skinned timber.

ˈroughsome, *a. Sc.* [f. ROUGH *a.* + -SOME.] Somewhat rough; rough-mannered, unpolished.

c **1660** LIVINGSTONE in *Sel. Biogr. Wodrow Soc.* I. 265 The rubbish of a roughsome nature. **1713** WODROW *Corr.* (1843) I. 502 Satirical jesting, taunting or roughsome ways in conversation. **1836** *Fraser's Mag.* XIV. 433 That's a roughsome way o' ganging to work. **1884–** in *Eng. Dial. Dict.*

rough-spoken, *a.* [ROUGH *adv.*] Blunt or rough in speech.

1633 FORD *Broken H.* IV. i, A gallant man at arms is here; ..blunt and rough-spoken, Vouchsafing not the fustian of civility. **1815** SCOTT *Guy M.* xlv, He was..the queerest rough-spoken deevil too that ever ye heard! **1856** R. A. VAUGHAN *Mystics* (1860) I. VI. iv. 180 At last a voice cried out..(I think it was that roughspoken Carvel, the butcher).

rough-spun, *a. Sc.* and *north. dial.* [ROUGH *adv.*] Of persons: Rough-mannered, unpolished.

1822 HOGG *Perils of Man* II. 228 A gay rough spun cout he was. **1828** *Craven Gloss., Rough-spun*, blunt, unpolished, clownish. [Also in later glossaries.]

rought, obs. pa. t. of REACH, RECK, WORK; obs. f. ROUGH, ROUT, RUTH.

†**ˈroughtless,** *a. Obs.*$^{-1}$ In 5 roghtlesse. [App. f. **rought**, obs. pa. t. of RECK *v.*] Heedless.

c **1500** in Halliw. *Nug. Poet.* 69 Dreding ye were of my woos roghtlesse, That was to me a grevous hevinesse.

ˈrough-towel, *v. rare.* [ROUGH *a.*] *trans.* To rub or dry with a towel of long-napped material.

1889 E. SAMPSON *Tales of Fancy* 23 He sponged his men ..and rough-towelled them.

rough-tree. *Naut.* [In earlier use a var. of RUFF-TREE and ROOF-TREE 2; later also f. ROUGH *a.*] (See quot. 1769.)

1629 *Admiralty Court Exam.* 48 Took the rough trees of the shipp and nayled deales upon them and launched them overboard. **1671** PHILLIPS, *Rough-trees*, in Navigation, are small timbers to bear up the gratings from the half-Deck to the forecastle. **1769** FALCONER *Dict. Marine* (1780), *Rough-tree*, a name given in merchant-ships to any mast, yard, or boom, placed as a rail or fence above the ship's side, from the quarter-deck to the fore-castle. It is, however, with more propriety, applied to any mast, &c. which remains rough and unfinished. **1846** A. YOUNG *Naut. Dict., Rough-Tree*, an unfinished spar. **1867** SMYTH *Sailor's Word-bk.* 581 [copying Falconer and Young; hence also in later Dicts.].

b. *Comb.* **rough-tree rail, timber** (see quots.).

1794 *Rigging & Seamanship* 141 They are extended from the rough-tree-rail of the quarter-deck. *c* **1860** H. STUART *Seaman's Catech.* 70 What is meant by the rough-tree rail? It covers the heads of the timbers, and forms the bottom of the hammock netting. **1867** SMYTH *Sailor's Word-bk.* 581 *Rough Tree Timber*, upright pieces of timber placed at intervals along the side of a vessel, to support the rough-tree.

rough-up. *slang.* [f. ROUGH *v.*] **a.** An informal encounter or contest. **b.** A trial race.

1889 *Referee* 26 Jan. (Farmer), In a similar rough up with the gloves to that under notice. **1902** *Times* 26 Nov. 4/5 In his opinion there was no difference between a rough-up and a trial. **1933** *Bulletin* (Sydney) 6 Dec. 24/4 [Bridge] The council, while signifying approval, wants to make it clear that in future all inter-State rough-ups will be *its* pigeon. **1951** E. RICKMAN *Come racing with Me* x. 85 This one may be fit enough in a week or two to be given a 'rough-up' (a good gallop with companions but not a formal trial).

c. A fight; a brawl.

1896 *Sessions Papers Cent. Criminal Court* 22 June, There was a little rough up, and I found myself stabbed in my arm. **1950** K. S. PRICHARD *Winged Seeds* 26 There'd 've been a rough-up in no time, and only half a dozen of us with Paddy against forty or fifty men.

d. (See quot.)

1919 V. MARSHALL *World of Living Dead* 69 The 'donkey-dipper' is another kind of pick-pocket. He works alone, and his methods are to grip, to rip, and to run. 'A dead rough-up'—thus the more scientific of the fraternity designate him in their scorn.

rough-wrought, *pa. pple.* [ROUGH *adv.*] Roughly worked, shaped, or prepared.

1680 MOXON *Mech. Exerc.* xii. 211 Till you have rough-wrought all your Work from end to end. **1764** *Museum Rust.* II. 136 When the scantlings are large, I lay them, after they are rough-wrought, to soak in a pond of water. **1821** SHELLEY *Ess. & Lett.* (1852) II. 249 It is a sort of flattish dome, rough-wrought within by the chisel.

roughy[1] (ˈrʌfɪ). *Sc.* [Cf. RUFFY.] A withered bough; a dry stick or splinter, *esp.* one used as a light or torch.

1815 SCOTT *Guy M.* liv, Laying the roughies to keep the cauld wind frae you. **1829** *Ibid.* xxvi. *foot-note*, When dry splinters, or branches, are used as fuel to supply the light for burning the water, as it is called, they are termed, as in the text, Roughies.

ˈroughy[2]. Also **ruffie, ruffy.** [? f. ROUGH *a.*] An Australian fish (*Arripis georgianus*) of the perch family.

1875 *Spectator* (Melbourne) 19 June 81/1 Common fish, such as trout, ruffies, mullet,..and others.

roughy, var. ROUGHIE.

rouging (ˈruːʒɪŋ), *vbl. sb.* Also **rougeing.** [f. ROUGE *v.*] The action or practice of applying rouge to the face. Also *transf.*

1816 J. SCOTT *Vis. Paris* (ed. 5) 80 Gilding, like rougeing, suggests the very reverse. **1830** N. S. WHEATON *Jrnl.* 368 The practice of rouging..is confined to actresses and women of pleasure. **1892** *Daily News* 1 Mar. 5/4 Unless indeed this natural rougeing is as attractive to the opposite sex as the artificial kind is supposed to be in our species.

rougy (ˈruːʒɪ), *a.* [f. ROUGE *sb.* + -Y.] Full of, sprinkled with, rouge; resembling rouge.

1884 BRITTEN *Watch & Clockm.* 50 Particles of dust, and even hard rouge,..may be removed by a clean rougy brush. **1886** LINSKILL *Haven under Hill* I. viii. 105 It was all dusty with red rougy dust.

rouh, obs. form of ROUGH *a.*

‖**rouille** (ruj). [Fr., lit. 'rust'.] Mayonnaise flavoured with pimento or the like.

1951 R. CAMPBELL *Light on Dark Horse* xix. 275 No decent fisherman will eat bouillabaisse without the *rouille*. **1976** N. ROBERTS *Face of France* ix. 101 A fish soup..a *bourride*, with a spoonful of *rouille* stirred into it.

rouk (raʊk, ruk), *sb. Sc.* and *north.* [Var. of ROKE *sb.*[1], and of ROOK *sb.*[3]] Mist, fog.

c **1500** *Rowlis Cursing* 168 in Laing *Anc. Poet. Scotl.* 215 Quhair thair is hunger, cald and thrist, Dirknes, mirknes, rouk and mist. *a* **1510** DOUGLAS *K. Hart* I. 10 For wes he never ȝit with schouris schot, Nor ȝit ourrun with rouk, or ony rayne. **1659** HAY *Diary* (S.H.S.) 170 Thick rouk in the morning. **1808** in JAMIESON. **1825** in BROCKETT. **1861** J. BROWN *Horæ Subs.* Pref. p. vii, Now, the rouk (mist born of early frosts) is lying white and chill. *a* **1870** H. S. RIDDELL *Poet. Wks.* (1871) I. 199 Yon rouke that's floating by sae grey.

†**rouk,** *v. Obs. north.* and *Sc.* Also 5–6 rowk. [Perh. a special sense of *rouk* RUCK *v.*[1], but see also RUNK *v.*] *intr.* Only in phrase ***rouk and roun(d)***, to talk privately.

c **1440** *York Myst.* vii. 48 Me liste noȝt nowe to rouk nor rowne. *a* **1500** in *Ratis Raving*, etc. 103 A woman suld..with no ȝonge men rouk [*v.r.* rowk] na roune. **1529** LYNDESAY *Compl.* 185 Roundand and rowkand, ane tyll vther. *a* **1575** *Diurn. Occurr.* (Bann. Cl.) 45 The Inglismen begouth to gif bakkis, and to rouk and round, sayand it was ane greit matter to brek the Scottis.

Hence †**ˈrouker**, a whisperer, tale-bearer.

1551 ABP. HAMILTON *Catech.* 71 A rowkar and rownar sall fyle his awin saule. *Ibid.*, Ane rowkar and doubil toungit.

rouk(e, obs. or dial. ff. RUCK *sb.* and *v.*

roukere: see RUCKER.

ˈrouky, *a. Sc.* and *north.* [f. ROUK *sb.* + -Y. Cf. ROKY and ROOKY.] Misty, foggy.

1808 JAMIESON, *Rouky*, misty. **1813** PICKEN *Poems* II. 130 Blae was the mornin', an' rouky an' raw. **1829** BROCKETT *N.C. Gloss.* (ed. 2) 249 *Rouky*, misty, damp, foggy.

roul(e, obs. ff. ROLL *sb.* and *v.*, RULE.

‖**roulade** (ruːˈlɑːd). [F., f. *rouler* to roll.]

1. *Mus.* A quick succession of notes, properly as sung to one syllable.

1706 PHILLIPS (ed. Kersey), *Roulade*, (Fr.) a Trill, Trilling, or Quavering. **1728** in CHAMBERS *Cycl.* **1818** BUSBY *Gram. Mus.* 150 A *Roulade* is a smooth but rapid course of notes, interspersed in the course of an air without breaking the measure. **1839** COL. HAWKER *Diary* (1893) II. 166

Vercellini was..singing his roulades in the garden. **1894** *Times* 11 June 8/1 The roulades in which the soprano part of Donizetti's once popular opera abounds.

transf. **1859** *All Year Round* No. 36. 219 There are no rattling roulades of cabs, no rolling thunder waggons of omnibuses. **1872** GEO. ELIOT *Middlem.* xliii, A few notes from a man's voice and then a piano bursting into *roulades.* **1895** MISS MULHOLLAND *Striking Contrast* 313 The birds sang joyous roulades through the shady woods.

2. *Cookery.* A dish prepared by rolling up a slice of meat or a sponge or similar base, esp. with a filling (see quots. 1969, 1975[1]). Also *attrib.*

1885 *Tasty Dishes* (James Clarke & Co.) 151 Roulades of Beef. **1958** *Catal. County Stores, Taunton* June 3 *Pâté de foie gras*..Roulade for slicing—a tin 14/9, 22/3. **1965** A. R. DANIEL *Up-to-Date Confectionery* (ed. 4) xxviii. 407/2 Roulade Slices. *Ibid.* 408/1 Spread the sheet or roulade with pink-coloured kirsch-flavoured butter icing. *Ibid.* 409/1 The Swiss..make a special type of butter-sponge sheet from which to make roulade and dresden slices. **1969** R. & D. DE SOLA *Dict. Cooking* 194/2 *Roulade,*..slice of meat, covered with forcemeat or other savoury filling, rolled up, and cooked. **1975** J. CHILD *From Julia Child's Kitchen* III. 109 A *roulade* is a flat soufflé baked in a rectangular shape, then rolled up with a filling. **1975** *Times* 18 Dec. 7/5 The roulade of avocado is..delicious. **1980** *Times* 24 May 24/3 Puddings include chocolate roulade.

Hence **rou'laded, rou'lading** *ppl. adjs.*

1860 *All Year Round* No. 41. 342 A rouladed piano scale, fired off by the swiftest and most dexterous of Thalberg's hundred fingers. **1867** MISS BROUGHTON *Cometh up as a Flower* vii, The trilling, roulading carpenter.

‖**rouleau** (ruːˈləʊ). Also 8–9 roleau. Pl. rouleaus, -eaux. [F., repr. OF. *rolel* (pl. *roleaux*), f. *rôle* roll.]

1. a. A number of gold coins made up into a cylindrical packet.

In 1694 (*Ladies' Dict.*) defined as 'a paper of Guineas, to the number of 39'; in 1796 (*Grose's Dict.*) the number is given as 'from twenty to fifty or more'.

1693 SOUTHERNE *Maid's Last Prayer* I. i, I must.. send some *rouleaus* to the bank, to pay my damn'd debts. *a* **1694** ETHEREDGE *Song of Basset* Wks. (1735), 'Tis only Cony can redress Her Grief with a *Rouleau.* **1716** POPE *Basset-Table* 81 In bright Confusion open Rouleaux lie, They strike the Soul, and glitter in the Eye. **1772** FOOTE *Nabob* II, Teach him the best method of making a rouleau. **1823** BYRON *Juan* XII. xii, How beauteous are rouleaus! how charming chests Containing ingots, bags of dollars, coins. **1884** MRS. C. PRAED *Zéro* ii, She held towards him a rouleau of gold.

fig. **1775** SHERIDAN *Duenna* III. vii, A walking rouleau—a body that seems to owe all its consequence to the dropsy!

b. *transf.*, esp. of blood-corpuscles. Also *attrib.*

1858 BIRCH *Anc. Pottery* II. 269 The moulds were then piled in rouleaux or stacks. **1877** F. T. ROBERTS *Handbk. Med.* (ed. 3) I. 54 The red corpuscles show a marked tendency to run together, and under the microscope are seen to form 'rouleaux'. **1897** *Allbutt's Syst. Med.* II. 750 Rouleaux formation may be absent altogether.

2. A roll; a coil.

1795 in W. Roberts *Mem. Han. More* (1835) I. 467 (Stanf.), The charming rouleau of Cheap Repository poetry which you bestowed upon me. **1825** J. NICHOLSON *Operat. Mechanic* 351 Into the third, or upper place, they slide a rouleau of wire, weighing 150 kilogrammes. **1861** *Times* 25 Sept., The great-coat is worn in a rouleau round the body. **1876** GEO. ELIOT *Dan. Der.* xxxiv, Her yellow face with its darkly-marked eyebrows and framing rouleau of grey hair.

3. A trimming of a rolled form (see quot. 1882). Also in extended use (see quot. 1976). Also *attrib.* and *Comb.*

1820 M. EDGEWORTH *Let.* 8 June (1979) 160 Muslin gowns each trimmed with rouleaux of sattin. **1827** *Souvenir* I. 13 (Stanford), Skirt trimmed with two flounces each,.. with one satin rouleaux on the lower edge. **1835** *Court Mag.* VI. p. vi, Dark brown velvet mantle lined with swansdown, a rouleau of which edges the collar, sleeves, and round of the cloak. **1882** CAULFEILD & SAWARD *Dict. Needlewk.* 427/1 *Rouleau,* a French term denoting a large Piping, or rolled trimming, sometimes used as a decorative covering for the heading round a Flounce, or any such kind of Hem. **1968** J. IRONSIDE *Fashion Alphabet* 105 *Rouleau,* a rounded padded belt which may be finished with a knot or bow. **1970** *Kay & Co.* (Worcester) *Catal. 1970–71* Autumn/Winter 173/1 Deep back opening with rouleau tie fastening. **1972** *Country Life* 23 Mar. 737/3 A tweed suit..has a rouleau belt. **1974** *Janet Frazer Catal.* Spring & Summer 184/3 Nylon slip with lace trimmed rouleau straps. **1975** *Times* 14 Oct. 9/5 The hand made rouleau belts and the gold and ivory buttons. **1976** P. CLABBURN *Needleworker's Dict.* 228/3 *Rouleau,* any trimming or part of an article which is rounded or rolled. It may be in the form of piping or may mean a turned hollow tube as in the 'shoelace' shoulder straps of the 1930s and 1940s. **1977** *Daily Tel.* 4 Apr. 15/1 She wears a charming little rouleau-edged cap tilted over her brow. *Ibid.* 15/3 There were..dresses of black cotton.., and the academic robe, with high, padded rouleau neck, shone out.. in most unacademic tangerines.

4. Used *attrib.* to designate a type of vase with a cylindrical body and narrow neck, made in China from the late seventeenth century, or an imitation of such a vase.

1915 R. L. HOBSON *Chinese Pott. & Porc.* II. x. 165 (*caption*) Club-shaped (*rouleau*) Vase finely painted in famille verte enamels. **1936** *Burlington Mag.* Nov. p. xix/1 *Famille-verte* vases..a large *rouleau* specimen. **1937** *Ibid.* June p. xxv/2 Other specimens of K'ang-hsi in brilliance and quality are a pair of large rouleau vases. **1964** M. MEDLEY *Handbk. Chinese Art* 81/2 *Rouleau vase* is a vase with cylindrical body, short rather flat shoulders, a short thick neck, also cylindrical, and a slightly spreading mouth, which sometimes turns up a little at the rim. The term applies to a type of vase produced from the late 17th century onward. **1977** *Times* 17 May 16/4 Two large ($17\frac{1}{2}$ inches) *famille verte* rouleau vases.

†**roulekere.** *Obs.*[−1] A name for the hare.

Perhaps for *rou-lokere*, but *lekere* occurs below.

13.. *MS. Digby 86* fol. 168b, þe westlokere, þe waldeneie, þe sid-lokere, And eke þe roulekere.

‖**roulement** (rulmɑ̃). [Fr., lit. 'roll, roster'.] A movement of members or equipment of the armed services; rotation of units, relief of troops. Also *attrib.*

1918 W. S. CHURCHILL in M. Gilbert *Winston S. Churchill* (1977) IV. Compan. I. 290 Although *roulement* can proceed on both sides, this is a formidable preponderance and it tells more and more as reserves are used up. **1930** *Times Lit. Suppl.* 10 July 567/1 After the Lys offensive he was in what was known as the *roulement,* the transfer of troops to the Rheims area. **1941** W. S. CHURCHILL *Second World War* (1950) III. 735 Reserves of pilots and machines should be disposed in squadrons, and thus allow *roulement* to be extended in the event of protracted fighting. **1971** H. WILSON *Labour Govt.* (1974) xix. 467 Moreover, there was a problem of rotating troops, what is known in the West as *roulement.* **1977** *Guardian Weekly* 14 Aug. 4/2 Their individual battle tours on Irish soil..Roger spent four months here once with his *roulement* unit.

rouler, obs. or dial. var. ROLLER *sb.*

†**roulet.** *Obs.*[−1] [a. OF. *roulet, rolet,* dim. of *rôle* roll.] A small roll.

c **1540** *Practyse Cyrurg. Mountpyller* Aj, Then he putteth and layeth betwene those partyes and the Skul roulettes [*printed* Ronlettes], stupes, or plagettes made of lynte.

‖**roulette** (ruːˈlɛt). Also 8 rowlet, 8–9 roulet. [F., dim. of *rouelle* wheel.]

†**1.** A small wheel. *Obs. rare.*

a **1734** NORTH *Life Lord Keeper North* (1742) 137 The Manner of the Carriage [of coal] is by laying Rails of Timber from the Colliery, down to the River,..and bulky Carts are made with four Rowlets fitting these Rails. *Ibid.* 294 Wherever there was like to be a Friction, a Roulet was placed to receive it.

2. a. A game of chance played on a table with a revolving centre, on which a ball is set in motion, and finally drops into one of a set of numbered compartments.

1745 *Act 18 Geo. II,* c. 34 §1 A certain pernicious game called roulet or roly-poly is daily practised. **1808** *Sporting Mag.* XXX. 26 The foreign games of *Roulet* and *Rouge et Noir.* **1860** LD. LYTTON *Lucile* II. i, The duke..turn'd to roulette, And sat down, and play'd fast, and lost largely. **1882** SERGT. BALLANTINE *Exper.* iv, Roulette..was to be found at all the lower description of [gambling] houses.

b. *attrib.*, as ***roulette ball, box, system, table, -wheel.***

1827 DISRAELI *Viv. Grey* v. vi, The Roulette table opens immediately. **1844** *Rep. Sel. Comm. Gaming* 210 in *Parl. Papers* VI. 1 Seized..2 roulette balls, 2 dice-boxes, 2 bags containing 366 counters, [etc.]. *Ibid.* 211, I seized a roulette-wheel and a quantity of gambling apparatus. **1851** MAYHEW *Lond. Labour* I. 371 The raffler of the China ornaments produces a portable roulette box or table. **1863** TREVELYAN *Compet. Wallah* (1866) 59 Foreign noblemen..turning the crank instead of the roulette-wheel. **1926** A. CHRISTIE *Murder of R. Ackroyd* iii. 26 Caroline visibly wavered.. much as a roulette ball might coyly hover between two numbers. **1976** 'J. FRASER' *Who steals my Name?* xi. 134 A roulette ball has no memory... In the South of France a ball went into the same slot seven times running. **1976** P. CAVE *High Flying Birds* iv. 47, I once sold a foolproof roulette system to a professional gambler for 500 francs.

c. The centre part of a roulette table; a box used for a simple form of roulette. Also *Comb.*

1850 *Bohn's Hdbk. Games* (1867) 348 He throws an ivory ball into the concavity of the Roulette, in a direction opposite to the movement which he has given to the movable bottom. **1851** MAYHEW *Lond. Labour* I. 371 What may be called 'the board' of some of these 'roulettes' is numbered to thirty-two. *Ibid.* 189, I'm a roulette-maker now.

d. ***Russian roulette:*** see RUSSIAN *a.* 2e.

3. *Math.* A certain curve (see quots.).

1867 BRANDE *Dict. Sci.,* etc. III. 314/2 *Roulette,* the curve traced by any point in the plane of a given curve when the latter rolls, without sliding, over another fixed curve. **1879** SALMON *Higher Plane Curves* vii. 284 Roulettes or curves generated by a point on a rolling curve.

4. A device to keep the hair in curl.

1860 FAIRHOLT *Costume* (ed. 2) 571 To 'put a wig in pipes' was a phrase descriptive in the last century of a wig whose curls were kept in order by *roulettes.* **1874** *Temple Bar* XLI. 54 Their hair..is piled up in a wonderful pyramid of..rolls all so stiff that they stand alone without the aid of pads, roulets, puffs, or hair-pins.

5. *Engraving.* (See quots.)

1835 *Brit. Cycl. Arts & Sci.* I. 508/1 A more expeditious way of multiplying the dots has been contrived in the instrument called a *roulette,* a toothed wheel, fixed to a handle which, by being rolled forcibly along the copper, produces a row of indentations. **1854** FAIRHOLT *Dict. Terms Art* 376 *Roulette,* a small instrument..used by engravers to produce a series of dotted lines on a plate. It takes two forms, one like a spur-rowel.., and another which rolls at right angles with the shaft of the tool. **1875** KNIGHT *Dict. Mech.* 1994/1 Engravers' roulettes, principally used in mezzotinting to raise the burr when the original ground produced by the cradle has been too much scraped or burnished away.

6. A revolving toothed wheel used for perforating adhesive postage stamps.

1867 *Philatelist* I. 102 The next sort [of perforation]..is that not made by a fixed machine, but by what is called the *roulette,* or revolving wheel. *Ibid.* 103 A line..which acts as guidant to the roulette.

7. A light roller used in massage.

1895 *Syd. Soc. Lex., Pressions,* in massage, methods of pressing or compressing the muscles, by means of the whole hand, the tips of the fingers, or the roulet.

Hence **rou'letter**, a player at roulette.

1891 *Pall Mall G.* 3 June 6/1 We should have whole courts full of titled rouletters.

rou'letted, *pa. pple.* [f. prec.] **a.** Of postage stamps: Perforated by means of a roulette.

1867 *Philatelist* I. 166 Some of the rouletted specimens are but an apology for it. **1870** *Routledge's Ev. Boy's Ann.* Feb. Suppl. 3 Not being rouletted, they may be considered proofs. **1891** WESTOBY *Post. Stamps Gt. Brit.* 3 Unused rouletted specimens exist.

b. Of archaeological objects: impressed with lines or dots by means of a cogged wheel or a comb.

1938 *Oxoniensia* III. 28 Sherd with shell-grit; fine stabs and rouletted horizontal lines. **1939** V. G. CHILDE *Dawn European Civilization* (ed. 3) xii. 214 The 'rouletted' decoration is executed with a comb with very short teeth, separated by extremely narrow interstices, and probably with a curved edge. It yields a practically continuous line of round or, more often, rectangular dots, separated by low septa. **1969** G. BIBBY *Looking for Dilmun* xv. 323 They were Attic ware, imports from Greece itself. Some of them were even rouletted, decorated with a close pattern of semi-circles made with a toothed wheel, a characteristic which proved their Greek origin beyond a doubt. **1977** *Antiquaries Jrnl.* LVII. 381 Fine wares include bowls..with a foot-stamp within rouletted circles (second century A.D.), and lead-glazed wares.

c. *gen.*

1975 J. B. HARLEY *O.S. Maps* v. 72 It..was characterized by National Grid lines rouletted in black. [*Note*] That is, the line consists of small, closely spaced dots.

rou'letting, *vbl. sb.* [f. as prec.] **a.** Perforating by means of a roulette. **b.** Decorating pottery, etc., with dotted lines by means of a cogged wheel or comb; ornamentation produced in this way.

1895 *Pop. Sci. Monthly* Mar. 604 Rouletting is done with a tool very much like those sold on the streets..to cut glass. **1937** *Oxoniensia* II. 19 It contained a great quantity of Roman pottery, mostly early grey ware jars but including part of a butt-beaker in fine buff ware with two zones of rouletting, and a bit of a buff amphora handle. **1973** A. H. WHITEFORD *N. Amer. Indian Arts* 148 Coins and ingots were hammered into sheets and decorated by stamping and rouletting. **1979** *Archaeology* July–Aug. 31/1 The carinated bowls were stamped with palmettes inside concentric spirals of rouletting, a technique of producing hatch lines around the central design.

rouliche, obs. form of RULY.

roulie-poulie, Sc. variant of ROLY-POLY *sb.*

†**roulk,** ? error for RAUK *a.*, hoarse.

c **1450** HOLLAND *Howlat* 45 (Bann. MS.), [It] rowpit rewth-fully roch in a roulk rud rane.

roull, obs. f. ROLL *sb.*[1]

rouller, obs. var. ROLLER *sb.*

rouly-pouly, obs. f. ROLY-POLY *sb.*

roum, obs. or dial. f. ROOM *sb.* and *v.*

Rouman (ˈruːmən), *sb.* and *a.* Also Ruman. [ad. F. *Roumain,* ad. the native name *Român:* cf. ROMANIAN *sb.* and *a.*]

A. *sb.* **1.** = ROMANIAN *sb.* 1.

1856 H. STANLEY *Rouman Anthol.* Pref. p. ix, The descent of the Roumans from the legionaries of Trajan and Aurelian. **1878** *Chambers's Encycl.* VI. 512/2 Every Ruman who possesses a small yearly income is eligible for a seat in parliament. **1888** *Encycl. Brit.* XXIV. 269/2 These peculiarities are common to the Roumans north of the Danube. **1957** *Encycl. Brit.* XIX. 637/1 Tradition, embodied in a local chronicle of the 16th century entitled 'History of the Ruman land since the arrival of the Rumans'..gives 1290 as the date of the founding of the Walachian state.

2. = ROMANIAN *sb.* 2.

1856 H. STANLEY *Rouman Anthol.* Pref. p. xi, The Latinity of Rouman is..sadly disguised under the Cyrillic alphabet.

B. *adj.* = ROMANIAN *a.*

1856 H. STANLEY (*title*), Rouman Anthology; or, Selections of Rouman Poetry. *Ibid.* Pref. p. xi, The leading peculiarity of the Rouman language. **1883** *Science* II. 114/2 The Rouman language and Rouman institutions were examined in detail. **1957** [see sense A. 1 above].

Hence **Rou'manicize, 'Roumanize** *v.*, to make Romanian in character or form; **'Roumanish,** = ROMANIAN *sb.* 2.

1876 WHITNEY *Lang. & Its Study* 296 Romance Languages:..(7) Roumanish, (8) Wallachian. **1894** *Westm. Gaz.* 7 Sept. 2/3 Towns of purely German foundation and name,..which it is impossible either to 'Magyarise' or to 'Roumanize'. **1903** *Contemp. Rev.* Feb. 242 The principle of Roumanicising the Jews in the schools succeeded.

Roumanian: see ROMANIAN *sb.* and *a.*[3]

roumanite, var. RUMÄNITE.

Roumansh, var. of ROMANSH.

roumbill, obs. f. RUMBLE.

roume, obs. f. ROOM.

Roumelian (ruːˈmɛlɪən, -ˈmiːlɪən), *a.* (*sb.*) Also **Rumelian.** [f. as ROUMELIOTE: cf. Turk. *rum* Byzantine Greek (of Turkish nationality), *il* province.] Of or pertaining to Roumelia (see ROUMELIOTE), with particular reference to Ottoman territories of the southern Balkans inhabited by Greeks and now forming parts of northern Greece and Bulgaria; of or pertaining to the form of Greek spoken there. Also as *sb.*, a Greek inhabitant of Roumelia.

1859 J. F. MAGUIRE *Rome* (ed. 2) xxviii. 323 The different languages in which poetical compositions were recited at the Polyglot Academy, for Epiphany, 1858 [were]..Danish, Roumelian, Albanian, Polish, [etc.]. **1880** E. W. HAMILTON *Diary* 29 Aug. (1972) I. 41 Colonel Wilson who is reporting on the state of the Bulgarian and Eastern Roumelian provinces finds..a better state of affairs than he expected. **1888** *Encycl. Brit.* XXIII. 655/2 This is due partly to the Christian communities, notably the Maronites and others in Syria, the Anatolian and Roumelian Greeks, and the Armenians. **1902** D. G. HOGARTH *Nearer East* 155 Most thinly peopled are the mountainous districts between the Vardar and the Rumelian plains. **1935** H. EDIB *Clown & his Daughter* xxi. 114 Why should they insult him and spit at him because he was a Rumelian?

Roumeliote (ruːˈmiːlɪəʊt). Also **Rum-, -iot.** [ad. mod.Gr. Ῥουμελιότης: see def. and -OTE.] A native of Roumelia, or that part of the Balkan peninsula lying immediately to the north of the Morea and Ægean. Also *attrib.* or as *adj.*

Normally used of the area corresponding to Aetolia and Acarnania. Cf. ROUMELIAN *a.* (*sb.*).

1835 N. P. WILLIS *Pencillings* II. xxii. 248 At the Adrianople gate, we found a large troop of horsemen..who had accompanied a Roumeliote chief from the mountains. **1838** *Penny Cycl.* XI. 432/2 The Moreotes have not in general the frank boldness of the Roumeliotes. *Ibid.* 434/2 Dissensions between the Roumeliote chiefs. **1845** S. AUSTIN *Ranke's Hist. Ref.* 217 The Rumeliotes and Bosniaks. **1886** *Times* 5 Apr. 5/1 Instinctively the Roumeliots prefer to blame Turkey rather than Russia. **1939** A. TOYNBEE *Study of Hist.* VI. 331 The Rumeliot Greek Armatole and Klephtic ballads. **1964** A. A. PALLIS *Greek Miscellany* 144 He took the side of the Roumeliots against the party of the primates of the Morea. *Ibid.*, His hero was that greatest of Roumeliot captains, George Karaiskakis. **1969** C. M. WOODHOUSE *Philhellenes* iv. 118 The same feelings were expressed by an old Rumeliot whom James Emerson met. **1973** —— *Capodistria* xv. 347 Two Roumeliote *kapetánioi*, Grivas and Stratos, were bombarding each other..to settle a private feud. *Ibid.* xvi. 382 The Roumeliotes..were eager for action.

‖**Roumi** (ˈruːmiː). Also 6 **Rumi**, 9 **Roumy**. Fem. **roumia**. [ad. Arab. *rūmī* Byzantine, Pers. *rūmi* Turk, Greek.] Among Arabs, a term for a European.

1576 R. EDEN tr. *Vertomannus's Navigation & Vyages* VI. xiv. 401 They affyrmed also, that there are certayne Christian kynges (whiche they call Rumi) of great power, confynyng or borderyng on the dominions of the great Turke. **1819** J. L. BURCKHARDT *Trav. Nubia* 542 Such a misfortune had never been heard of in the time of the Islam, and before them no Roumy had ever come into these parts. **1867** 'OUIDA' *Under Two Flags* II. iii. 74 Not but what our *Roumis* are brave fellows enough; better comrades no man could want. **1924** *Public Opinion* 27 June 619/3 The Roumis had got round the flanks and were attacking the Arab Camp. **1927** *Daily Express* 17 June 9 An intelligent and up-to-date caid..in the Sahara..answered..'most of my people are unaccustomed to the ways of the roumia (foreign woman).' **1958** *Times Lit. Suppl.* 11 July 393/4, I did happen to be the first *roumia* allowed to a remote branch of the sect who live off the beaten track.

roumm(e, obs. forms of ROOM.

†**roun.** *Obs.* Forms: 1, 3-4 **run**, 2-4 **rune**, 3-5 **roune**, 4-5 **roun**, 5-6 **rowne**. [Common Teut.: OE. *rún* str. fem., = MDu. *rune, ruun* (*ruen*), whisper, secret counsel, etc., OS. *rûna* (MLG. *rûne, rûn*), OHG. *rûna* (MHG. *rûne*, G. *raun*, dial. *rûn*), ON. *rún*, Goth. *rûna* (rendering Gr. μυστήριον, συμβούλιον, and βουλή). See also RUNE *sb.*[2]

The normal modern spelling both of the sb. and the related verb would have been *rown*; but the sb. barely survived beyond ME., and the verb by developing a final *d* assumed the form *round* (ROUND *v.*[2]).

The use of the word is largely poetic, and the precise sense intended is often very uncertain.]

1. A dark or mysterious saying; a secret or mystery.

c **950** *Lindisf. Gosp.* John *Intr.* 4/4 Æt uaelle Iacobes mið meniȝum deȝlum runum [he] spræc. *a* **1000** *Elene* 333 (Gr.), ðehyrað, hiȝegleawe, haliȝe rune, word & wisdom. *c* **1200** ORMIN 18786 Godess dærne rune Nass nohht tohh-wheþþre whilwendlic, Acc aȝȝ onn ane wise. *a* **1225** *Leg. Kath.* 1333 Crist..schawde..suteliche þe deopschipe & te derne run of his deað on rode. *c* **1400** *Beryn* 1529 Engrosid was the covenaunte be-twen hem bothe to, In presence of þe Emperour,—in opyn, & no roun.

2. A runic letter, a rune.

c **900** tr. *Baeda's Hist.* IV. xxii. (1890) 328 Se ȝesiþ..hine ascode hwæðer he ða alysendlecan rune [L. *litteras solutorias*] cuðe. *a* **1000** *Proverbs* in Grein I. 349 Ræd sceal mon secȝan, rune writan, leoþ ȝesingan. *c* **1205** LAY. 3196 Þis writ com to Fraunce, to þan freo kinge. he hit lette raden, leof him weren þa runen [*v.r.* roune]. *Ibid.* 25340 Þan kaisere heo radden þat he write runen [*c* 1275 writes makede].

3. That which is written; writing; a writing, a book, an epistle.

a **1000** *Daniel* 542 (Gr.), Hæðen heriȝes wisa..bæd him areccan, hwæt seo run bude. *a* **1000** *Andreas* 134 Hæfdon hie on rune & on rimcræfte awriten..wera endestæf. *a* **1300** *Cursor M.* 15230 Þan he tok þe bred and brack, Als it es redd in run. *c* **1320** *Sir Tristr.* 2040 Bi water he sent adoun Liȝt linden spon. He wrot hem al wiþ roun.

4. Counsel, consultation, *esp.* of a private or secret nature.

Beowulf 172 Moniȝ oft ȝesæt rice to rune, ræd eahtedon. *a* **1000** *Wanderer* 111 (Gr.), Swa cwæð snottor on mode, ȝesæt him sundor æt rune. **1006** in Kemble *Cod. Dipl.* III. 351 Ic Siward cinges þeȝen æt ræde and æt runan. *c* **1200** ORMIN 6397 Þeȝȝ þa comenn to þe king, & he þeȝȝm droh to rune. *a* **1300** *Cursor M.* 3987 Thoru mi moder red and run, I stal him fra his benisun. *c* **1330** *Arth. & Merl.* 1218 (Kölbing), Yuel þe bifalle,..þou hast yseyd to loude þi roun!

5. A speech or discourse.

In early use with implication of secrecy (cf. sense 1). In the two latest quots. the meaning appears to be 'popular talk or rumour, report'.

c **1200** *Moral Ode* 89 (Trin. Coll. MS.), Elche rune he hereð and he wot alle dade. *a* **1250** *Owl & Night.* 1170 Dahet euer suich budel in tune, þat euer bodeþ un-wreste rune, An euer bringeþ vuele tiþinge. **13..** *K. Alis.* 806 (W.), For he wolde, in schort roune, Alisaundre his sone croune. *c* **1320** *Sir Tristr.* 945 Þe ferþ ȝere, (a ferly roun!) Þre hundred barnes fre. *a* **1400-50** *Alexander* 244 A riall roune þou me redis, a reson of blis. *c* **1470** HARDING *Chron.* CXVIII. (MS. Douce 354 fol. 80 b), For whom þer was amonge the comonte A grete byworde, as fele on þe wondre and Roun As did vpon the Erle Edryke of Stractoun. **1567** TURBERV. *Epit.* etc. 76 By reauing breath and rowne in worldly stage..Of him that well deserude..For worship and renowne to haue his share.

b. A song; a cry or call.

a **1310** in Wright *Lyric P.* vi. 29 Geynest under gore, herkne to my roune. *Ibid.* xiii. 43 Lenten ys come with love to toune, With blosmen ant with briddes roune. *c* **1320** *Sir Tristr.* 510 Þai blewen þe riȝt kinde And radde þe riȝt roun. *a* **1400** *Lybeaus Disc.* 1029 Sir Giffroun..Was bore hom on his scheld Wiþ care and rufull roun.

6. A form of speech; a language.

c **1205** LAY. 32000 Þa nomen of þan tunen on Sexisce runen. *c* **1330** R. BRUNNE *Chron. Wace* (Rolls) 13757 Egle ys ern on Englische roun.

roun, obs. f. ROUND *v.*[2]; obs. pa. pple. of RUN *v.*

rounce (raʊns), *sb.*[1] *Typog.* [ad. Du. *ronds(e, ronse* in the same sense: it is not quite certain whether this is a derivative of *rond* round.]

1. The handle of the winch by which the spit and wheel are turned so as to run the carriage of a hand-press in and out.

1683 MOXON *Mech. Exerc.*, *Printing* vi. 68 On the straight Shank of this Winch is fitted the Rounce. *Ibid.* xxi. 323 Having Pull'd the first Pull, and having the Rounce still in his Left Hand, He turns the Rounce about again. **1728** CHAMBERS *Cycl.* s.v. *Printing*, To the outside of the Spit is fix'd a Handle, or Rounce, by which the Press-man turns the Plank in or out at pleasure. **1795** *Trans. Soc. Arts* XIII. 248 By a gentle motion of the rounce.., fixed on the end of the spit. **1808** STOWER *Printer's Gram.* 323 On the square pin is fitted a winch, on which is placed the rounce, five inches long. **1825** J. NICHOLSON *Operat. Mechanic* 294 The carriage is moved by the rounce or handle K, with a spit and leather girts very similar to the wooden press. **1888** JACOBI *Printers' Vocab.* 115 *Rounce*, the handle by means of which the press carriage is run in and out.

2. The spit and wheel (or girth-barrel) of a printing-press.

1683 MOXON *Mech. Exerc.*, *Printing* xxiv. ⁋3 In winding the Girts off or on the Barrel of the Rounce. **1808** STOWER *Printer's Gram.* 343 The girths should be nailed on the barrel of the rounce. **1858** SIMMONDS *Dict. Trade, Rounce*, a wooden cylinder, to which is attached a belt and handle, for rolling in and out the bed or coffin of a printing-press. **1892** OLDFIELD *Man. Typog.* xxi, The rounce should now be fixed and followed by the table, to which the girths of the rounce must be attached.

b. *attrib.*, as ***rounce-barrel, -handle, -spindle.***

1683 MOXON *Mech. Exerc.*, *Printing* xxiv. ⁋3 The Carriage-board, Frame of the Coffin, and the Rounce-barrel. *Ibid.* ⁋6 Both ends of the Rounce-Spindle. **1896** T. L. DE VINNE *Moxon* 411 With a rounce handle on the end of this spindle.

rounce, *sb.*[2] *U.S.* [Perh. ad. G. *ramsch* a variety of Skat.] A card-game in which the winning is determined by subtracting from an initial score. Also, a similar domino game. Hence **rounce** *v.*[2] (see quots. 1864, 1868).

1855 in *Calif. Hist. Soc. Q.* (1929) VIII. 352 Had a great rounce game, a little noise but no fun. **1857** *Hoyle's Games* 99 The Game of Rounce is played by each player taking five pieces, (after having turned for the trump, the highest piece turned deciding that point); the trump is then turned up for the trump-holder by his right hand adversary, the highest end being trump. **1864** W. B. DICK *Amer. Hoyle* 397 Rounce. This is a pleasant game [of dominoes], and from two to four may participate in it. *Ibid.*, The player who fails to take a trick with his hand is 'Rounced', i.e., sent up five points. **1868** —— *Mod. Pocket Hoyle* 196 The game of Rounce, as played in the United States, is derived from the German game of *Ramsch*, and in its principal features resembles Division Loo. *Ibid.* 197 Each trick taken in play counts one point, and if a player fail to take a trick after entering to play his hand, he is *Rounced*, that is, sent up five points, which adds a X to his score. **1890** in *Cent. Dict.* **1897** R. F. FOSTER *Compl. Hoyle* 281. **1975** *Way to Play* 66/1 Forty-two, or domino rounce, is an adaptation of a card game for play with dominoes. The object is to score points by winning tricks.

rounce, *v.*[1]: see ROUNCING *ppl. a.*

rounce, *v.*[2]: see ROUNCE *sb.*[2]

rounce, obs. form of ROUNCY.

†**rounce robble hobble.** *Obs.* [Imitative.] Stanyhurst's attempt to represent the sound of thunder, copied allusively or derisively by some later writers.

1582 STANYHURST *Æneis* VIII. (Arb.) 137 A clapping fyerbolt (such as oft, with rownce robel hobble, Ioue toe the ground clattreth). **1589** NASH in Greene *Menaphon* (Arb.) 13 Then did he make heauens vault to rebounde, with rounce robble hobble Of ruffe raffe roaring, with thwick thwack thurlery bouncing. **1602** MARSTON *Ant. & Mel.* II, Was't not rare sport at the sea-battle, whilst rounce robble hobble roared from the ship sides. **1622** MASSINGER & DEKKER *Virg. Martyr* IV. ii, I'll come upon her with rounce, robble-hobble, and thwick-thwack-thirlery bouncing. **1656** *Choyce Drollery* 7 Rounce, Robble, Hobble, he that writ so big.

rouncing (ˈraʊnsɪŋ), *ppl. a.* Now *dial.* [? Imitative.] Roaring, noisy.

A verb *rounce* occurs in some dialects with the sense of 'to bounce', 'to flounce about'.

1596 HARINGTON *Metam. Ajax* (1814) 69 Sir Andrew Flamocke.., at the very time the king drew his horn from his mouth, lets me fly a rouncing F. from his T——. **1851** STERNBERG *Folk-Lore & Dial. Northants* 87 'A rouncing fire'. 'A rouncing wind'. **1879** MISS JACKSON *Shropsh. Word-Bk.* s.v.

rouncival (ˈraʊnsɪvəl). Forms: α. 6 **rownseual, rounceuall, -vall**, 7 **rounse-**, 7-9 **rounceval**; 6 **rounsefal**, 7 **rouncefall**. β. 6-7 **rounsiual** (7 **-val**), 7-8 **rouncival** (7 **-ual(l, -vall**); 7 **rownsifall, rouncifold**. γ. 6 **runciual(l**, 7 **-vale, runsivill**. δ. 8 **ronce-, roncival**. [Perhaps from the place-name *Roncesvalles* (*Roncevaux*), as stated by Blount (see quot. 1674 in sense 1), but there appears to be no outside confirmation of this, and the development of the later senses is obscure. In sense 4 there is prob. association with *rounce* (see prec.) and *fall* sb.]

1. Used *attrib.* as the specific designation of a large variety of garden or field pea.

1573 TUSSER *Husb.* (1878) 78 Set (as a daintie) thy runciuall pease. *Ibid.* 95 Runciuall pease set in winter. **1654** in F. L. Hawks *Hist. N. Carolina* (1858) II. 19 There was one Indian had two beads of gold in his ears, big as rounceval peas. **1674** BLOUNT *Glossogr.* (ed. 4), *Rounceval Peas*, a sort of great Peas, well known, and took name from Ronceval, a place at the foot of the Pyrenean Mountains, from whence they first came to us. **1725** *Fam. Dict.* s.v. *July* ⁋43 Ronceval Pease, Garden Beans, and French Beans. **1742** JARVIS *Don Quix.* II. III. vi, Each grain would have been the size of a good Ronceval-pea. **1856** MORTON *Cycl. Agric.* II. 575/2 Gray Rouncival, Giant, or Dutch Pea.—This is the latest of the field varieties.

b. *ellipt.* Also *pl.*, peas of this variety.

1573 TUSSER *Husb.* (1878) 51 But rather sowe otes, or else bullimong there, gray peason, or runciuals, fitches, or tere. *Ibid.* 87 Sowe runciuals timelie, and all that be gray. **1622** DRAYTON *Poly-olb.* xx. 46 The Rouncefall, great Beans, and early-ripening Peason. **1660** SHARROCK *Vegetables* 14 Rounsevals, if sowed never so early, will scarce come before the latter part of the month of June. **1707** MORTIMER *Husb.* (1721) I. 138 In Staffordshire they sow Garden-Rouncivals in the Fields. **1786** ABERCROMBIE *Gard. Assist.* Feb. 32 Also marrowfats to succeed the above, and rouncivals, or other larger kinds. **1824** LOUDON *Encycl. Gard.* 618 The egg, the moratto, the Prussian blue, and the rouncivals..are all very fine eating peas. **1856** MORTON *Cycl. Agric.* II. 577 White Rouncival..[with seeds] large, irregularly shaped, and white.

†**c.** *transf.* A wart. *Obs.*[−1]

1656 MENNIS & SMITH *Musarum Deliciæ* (ed. 2) 12 Cicero, (that wrote in Prose) So call'd, from Rouncival on's Nose.

†**2. a.** *attrib.* Gigantic, huge; robustious. *Obs.*

1582 STANYHURST *Æneis* III. (Arb.) 92 Then runs from mountayns and woods thee rownseual helswarme Of Cyclopan lurdens. **1602** DEKKER *Satirom.* Wks. 1873 I. 243 Dost roare? th' ast a good rouncivall voice to cry Lanthorne and Candle-light. **1668** WILKINS *Real Char.* II. i. 33 Crassitude, gross, deep, incrassate, rouncival.

†**b.** A monster. *Obs.*[−1]

1641 A. SCOTT *Journ.* in *Misc. Sc. Hist. Soc.* (1904) 278 So for a curious glover straite he calls To flea the rownsifall, and stuffs his hyde.

†**3.** A woman of large build and boisterous or loose manners. *Obs.*

1596 NASHE *Saffron Walden* Wks. (Grosart) III. 52 It was so fulsome a fat Bonarobe and terrible Rounceuall. **1611** HEYWOOD *Golden Age* II. i, I am not yet of that giant size but I may pass for a bona roba, a rounceval, a virago, or a good manly lass. **1654** GAYTON *Pleas. Notes* III. ii. 72 The reaking, sweaty Rouncifolds of Py-Corner.

†**4. a.** A heavy fall, a crash. *Obs.*[−1]

1582 STANYHURST *Æneis* II. (Arb.) 63 Then the tre deepe minced... At leingth with rounsefal, from stock vntruncked, yt harssheth.

†**b.** A form of alliterative verse. *Obs.*[−1]

1585 JAS. I *Ess. Poesie* (Arb.) 68 For flyting, or Inuectiues, vse this kynde of verse following, callit Rouncefallis, or Tumbling verse.

rouncy[1] (ˈraʊnsɪ). *Obs.* exc. *arch.* Forms: α. 4 **runci, runce, runcy**, 5-6 **runsy**. β. 4 **ronsi**, 5 **ronsy, ronsee**. γ. 4 **rouncyn, rounce, rounci**, 4-5 **rounsy**, 5 **rownsy, -se, -cy, rounsey**, 5, 6 **rounse**, 5 (9 *arch.*) **rouncy** (9 *arch.* **rouncey**). [a. OF. *ronci, roncin, runcin* (mod.F. *roussin*), = Prov. *roci, rossi, roncin*, Sp. *rocin*, Pg. *rocim, rossim*, It. *ronzino*, med.L. *roncinus, runcinus*, etc. (see Du Cange): the origin of these forms is unknown. The word also appears in MDu. *runsine, ronside, rosside*, etc., and in Welsh *rhwnsi* (from English).] A horse, esp. a riding-horse.

a **c 1300** *Havelok* 2569 For he him dredde swiþe sore, So runci spore. **1338** R. BRUNNE *Chron.* (1810) 177, I salle do him hang hie, or drawe with runcys. *c* **1475** *Rauf Coilȝear* 791 Vpon ane rude Runsy he ruschit out of toun. *Ibid.* 870 The gentill Knicht..ruschit fra his Runsy. **1508** DUNBAR *Flyting* 228 Quhill runsyis rynnis away with cairt and quheilis.

β. **13..** *Sir Beues* 757 Beues let sadlen is ronsi. *a* **1400–50** *Alexander* 2887 þis renke with his Ronsees he ridis ouire & leuys. *c* **1475** *Rauf Coilȝear* 479 He was the Ryallest of array, On Ronsy micht ryde.

γ. *c* **1305** *Pol. Songs* (Camden) 188 Hue nomen huere rouncyns out of the stalle. *Ibid.* 190 Ther hue loren huere stedes, ant mony rouncyn. **1338** R. BRUNNE *Chron. Wace* (Rolls) 11422 Bowes, arewes, he gaf to archers, Rounsyes gode vnto squiers. **13..** *Gaw. & Gr. Knt.* 303 þe renk on his rounce hym ruched in his sadel. *a* **1400–50** *Alexander* 817 þis renke & his rounsy þai reche vp a croune. *c* **1450** LOVELICH *Graal* lii. 585 Down he alyhte of his rownsy. *a* **1529** SKELTON *P. Sparowe* 1314 Of Dyomedes stable He brought out a rable Of coursers and rounses.

1875 BROWNING *Aristoph. Apol.* 145 Race-horse sired, not rouncy born. **1881** DUFFIELD *Don Quixote* I. xxxviii, It is the rouncy of Master Miguel de Cervantes.

†**rouncy**[2]: see ROUNCE-ROBBLE-HOBBLE.

1616 B. JONSON *Masque of Queenes* Wks. 954 Rouncy is ouer, Robble is vnder, A flash of light and a clap of thunder.

†**rouncy**[3]. *Obs.*$^{-0}$ = ROUNCIVAL 3.

1647 HEXHAM *Eng.-Du. Dict.*, Rouncie, or rouncevall, *een mannelick wijf.*

round (raʊnd), *sb.*[1] Forms: α. 4 **roonde**, 6 *Sc.* **ronde, runde**, 9 *Sc.* **roond**; 5 **rownde**, 5–7 **rownd**; 5–6 **rounde** (6 **rovnde**), 6– **round** (7 **rovnd**). β. 5–7 **rowne**, 5 **rown**, 8–9 *dial.* **roun', roon'**. [Partly a. F. *rond* masc. or *ronde* fem., and partly absolute uses of ROUND *a.* Cf. Du. *rond*, Da. and Sw. *rund*, G. *runde*.]

I. 1. a. A spherical or globular body; a sphere, globe, planet. Somewhat *rare*.

c **1330** *King of Tars* 544 Lymes hedde hit non; But as a roonde of flesche icore In chaumbre lay hire bifore. **1604** EARL STIRLING *Crœsus* v. i, She 'twixt her bosomes Rounds entomb'd his head. **1614** —— *Doomsday* III. i, Immortall Monarch, ruler of the rounds. **1642** H. MORE *Song of Soul* I. xxx. Wks. (Grosart) 16 As those farre shining Rounds in open skies. **1807** J. BARLOW *Columb.* I. 253 To yon dim rounds first elevate thy view.

b. *this* (*earthly*, etc.) *round*, the earth.

c **1586** C'TESS PEMBROKE *Ps.* LXXII. ix, Lett all this round Thy honor sound. **1594** KYD *Cornelia* II. 347 The Monarchies, that couer all This earthly round with Maiestie. **1607** J. DAVIES (Heref.) *Summa Totalis* Wks. (Grosart) I. 21/2 The Delvge (that did rince this Rovnd). **1667** MILTON *P.L.* VII. 267 Elemental Air, diffus'd In circuit to the utter-most convex Of this great Round. **1831** CARLYLE *Sart. Res.* I. iv, Some incarnate Mephistopheles, to whom this great terrestrial and celestial Round, after all, were but some huge foolish Whirligig.

c. The vault of heaven.

c **1590** MONTGOMERIE *Sonn.* xxxi. 7 Behind the..tuinkling round of burning rubies rare, Quhair all the gods thy duelling do desyre. **1629** MILTON *Hymn Nativ.* x. 102 Nature that heard such sound Beneath the hollow round Of Cynthia's seat. **1697** DRYDEN *Virg. Past.* III. 160 The round of Heav'n, which all contains. **1808** SCOTT *Marm.* I. Introd. 50 The wild birds carol to the round. **1879** BURROUGHS *Locusts & Wild Honey* 99 Not a speck or film in all the round of the sky.

2. a. An object of a circular form. In early use in spec. senses, as a heraldic roundle, a round piece of metal, a round mark in archery, etc.

c **1500** *Sc. Poem on Her.* 107 in *Bk. Precedence* 97 In armis ar sertene rondis, as ball. **1508** *Acc. Ld. High Treas. Scot.* IV. 121 To Will Raa, cultellar, for viij roundis to the Kingis suordis and grinding of thaim. **1531** in Butt *Ford's Archery* (1887) 141 Paied to Byrde Yoeman of the Kinges bowes for making the Roundes. *c* **1555** EDW. VI *Jrnl.* (Roxb.) 312, I lost the chaling of shoting at roundes, and wane at rovers. **1615** G. SANDYS *Trav.* 109 Ouer their shashes the men weare rounds of stiffned russet to defend their brains from the piercing feruour. **1688** HOLME *Armoury* I. vi. 60/2, I shall in the first place speak of the Rounds, Roundles, or Roundlets. **1757** W. WILKIE *Epigoniad* II. 46 The Theban spear;..Full to the center of the shield, it came; And, rising swiftly from the polish'd round, His throat transfix'd. **1810** SIR A. BOSWELL *Poet. Wks.* (1871) 54 Those polish'd rounds which decorate the coat, And brilliant shine upon some youth of note.

†**b.** Some species of flat sea-fish. *Obs.*$^{-1}$

1602 CAREW *Cornwall* 32 Of flat [fish there are] Brets, Turbets, Dories, Round, [etc.].

c. A large round piece *of* beef, usually one cut from the haunch.

In Langl. *P. Pl.* C. x. 148, where one MS. gives *rounde of bacon*, the correct reading is clearly *ronde*: see ROND *sb.*[1] I.

1660 W. DENTON *Let.* 29 Feb. in M. M. Verney *Mem.* (1894) III. xiii. 469 The Beef the best that ever was eat, I eat a whole Round last night my self. **1771** J. WOODFORDE *Diary* 5 Jan. in *Parson Woodforde Soc. Q. Jrnl.* (1970) III. I. 24, I gave them for Dinner..a Round of Beef boiled. **1821** SCOTT *Pirate* xvii, The board groaned with rounds of hung beef. **1853** R. S. SURTEES *Sponge's Sp. Tour* liv. 309 A magnificent cold round of home-fed beef, red with saltpetre. **1870** E. PEACOCK *Ralf Skirl.* I. 16 A round of cold spiced beef.

attrib. **1934** WEBSTER *Round steak.* **1972** 'L. EGAN' *Paper Chase* (1973) x. 161 Athelstane was..condescending to eat the best round steak cut into bite-size pieces. **1975** *Evening Herald* (Dublin) 8 May 6/7 Round steak..dropped by 10p per pound.

transf. **1861** G. F. BERKELEY *Eng. Sportsman* xv. 246 The quarters of the animal are indeed 'rounds of beef'.

d. *Brewing.* A large vessel or cask employed in the final process of fermenting beer.

1806 *Hull Advertiser* 11 Jan. 2/2. **1830** M. DONOVAN *Dom. Econ.* I. 173 Cleansing is generally performed in a number of vessels like hogsheads, called the *rounds*, from which the drink, if porter, is, when sufficiently purged, pumped up into immense store vats. **1880** *Spons' Encycl. Manuf.* II. 406 It was at one time the practice amongst the Scotch brewers to employ fermenting rounds only, and to cleanse from these directly into the casks.

e. pl. *Comm.* Articles that are naturally or artificially produced in round shapes.

1911 *Chambers's Jrnl.* 8 Apr. 297/1 Formerly 'flats' and 'rounds' used to be spoken of to distinguish the imports of this drug [*sc.* rhubarb]. **1928** *Daily Mail* 25 July 19/3 Potatoes.—Spitalfields: English Kidneys 6s to 7s, rounds 5s to 5s 6d per cwt.

3. a. A rung or rundle of a ladder.

1548 ELYOT, *Climacter*, the rounde or step of a ladder. **1579–80** in W. H. Turner *Select. Rec. Oxford* (1880) 410 Item, for the ladder rownes, vj*d.* **1615** W. LAWSON *Country Housew. Gard.* (1626) 40 A Ladder of eight or moe rounds. **1667** L. STUCLEY *Gospel Glass* xxvi. (1670) 253 They should be but as the rounds of a Ladder. **1709** *Tatler* No. 42 ¶13 A Ladder of Ten Rounds. **1854** MISS BAKER *Northampt. Gloss.* s.v., The common mode of describing the length of a ladder is to call it 'a ladder of so many rounds'. **1875** KNIGHT *Dict. Mech.* 1245/1 The collapsing-ladder..has rounds pivoted to the side-rails.

b. *fig.* or in fig. context.

1577–82 BRETON *Floorish upon Fancie* Pref., To make my Ladder of such stuffe As I may trust... But then the Rovndes must not be made of Rimes. *a* **1601** ? MARSTON *Pasquil & Kath.* (1878) I. 127 Let who will climbe ambitions glibbery rounds. **1661** J. DAVIES *Civil Warres* 152 They.. pursue their..intentions to the very uttermost round of the ladder. **1742** RICHARDSON *Pamela* III. 173, I should scorn to make myself a Round to any Man's Ladder of Preferment. **1786–7** *Microcosm* (ed. 2) 437 Having arrived at the 'topmost round' of that learning which this seminary was capable of bestowing. **1858** LONGF. *Ladder St. Augustine* ii, Our pleasures and our discontents Are rounds by which we may ascend. **1875** MRS. TROLLOPE *Charming Fellow* I. xiii. 170, I may consider myself on the first round of the ladder.

†**c.** The rounce of a printing-press. *Obs.*$^{-0}$

1648 HEXHAM II, *Rondtse*, the Wheele or Round of a presse.

d. A tooth or stave of a trundle.

1731 *Phil. Trans.* XXXVII. 6 To this is applied a Trundle, or Pinion,..of six Rounds, or Teeth. **1764** J. FERGUSON *Lect.* iii. 35 A winch six inches long, fixt on the axis of a trundle of 8 staves or rounds. **1805** BREWSTER *Ferguson's Lect.* I. 82 *note*, The cylindrical bars of trundles ..are called staves, or rounds. **1875** KNIGHT *Dict. Mech.* 2634/1 *Trundle-wheel*, a wheel acting as a pinion, in which the cogs consist of rounds or trundles fastened in disks which are secured to an axle.

e. A round cross-bar connecting the stilts of a plough, or legs of a chair; a stretcher.

1875 KNIGHT *Dict. Mech.* 1746/2, 1994/1, 2426/2. **1905** MARY E. WILKINS *Debtor* 266 Eddy sat down and swung his feet, kicking the round of the chair.

f. An iron bar of circular section.

1891 *Times* 5 Oct. 4/4 Engineers are sending in good orders for turning rounds, &c., and the demand for the general run of sizes in rounds, flats, squares, &c., is steadily increasing.

4. †**a.** A piece of sculpture or statuary executed in the round (see 5 a). *Obs.*

1622 PEACHAM *Compl. Gent.* xii. (1634) 110 Besides, Rounds (so Painters call Statues and their fragments) may be had when the life cannot. *Ibid.*, A Round is better to draw by..than any flat or painting whatsoever. **1662** EVELYN *Chalcogr.* 116 Rounds, Busts, Relievos and entire Figures. *a* **1700** —— *Diary* 22 Oct. 1644, Over the door is a round of M. Angelo.

b. *Arch.* A rounded moulding. (Cf. *quarter-round*, s.v. QUARTER *sb.* 31.)

1673 MOXON tr. *Barozzi's Arch.* 44 The Astragaloes, or Rounds. **1728** CHAMBERS *Cycl.* s.v. *Volute*, In others, the Round is parallel to the Abacus, and springs out from behind the Flower thereof. *a* **1878** SIR G. SCOTT *Lect. Archit.* (1879) I. 249 Its practical use being to strengthen the hollows rather than to enrich the rounds.

†**c.** A quantity of material made up in a roll.

1696 J. F. *Merch. Wareho. laid open* 5 The Cambricks are sold..in a Parcel, the Kentings are sold by Rounds, as four or five in a Round.

d. A plane with a convex bottom and iron, for working hollows or grooves.

1846 HOLTZAPFFEL *Turning* II. 483 Concave and convex planes, called hollows and rounds, include the fifth or sixth ..of the circle. **1875** KNIGHT *Dict. Mech.* 1113/1 The illustration shows the use of hollows and rounds, in the molding of a panel door.

5. ***the round***: **a.** That form of sculpture in which the figure stands clear of any ground, as distinguished from *relief*. Also *fig.*, a condition which displays a given subject from all aspects; three-dimensionality. Usu. in phr. ***in the round.***

1811 *Self Instructor* 512 The art of drawing, both from the round and from life. **1873** FORTNUM *Maiolica* xv. 171 Many early pieces, modelled in high relief and in the round, are probably of this origin. **1900** A. S. MURRAY *Catal. Sculpt. Parthen.* 113 In slab xxxviii. the cow's right horn must have been carved in the round, only the tip being attached to the background of the relief. **1931** *Times Lit. Suppl.* 31 Dec. 1052/3 One cannot tamper with a screen character who speaks like a human being..and has his being 'in the round'. **1933** *Punch* 12 July 51/2 It is not an easy part, seeing that it is the only character in the whole cast to be drawn in the round. **1948** 'M. WESTMACOTT' *Rose & Yew Tree* ix. 72 Up to now Lord St. Loo had been a name, an abstraction... Now he came into the round— a living entity. **1959** *Spectator* 7 Aug. 164/3 The camera also gives an impression in the round of the man who seems one-dimensional in print.

b. A rounded or convex form.

1797 *Encycl. Brit.* (ed. 3) XVII. 407/1 Lay the bend mould upon it, so as may best answer the round according to the grain of the wood. **1876** *Encycl. Brit.* IV. 43/1 The back springs back into its rounded form, and thus the face presents the appearance of having been cut in the round.

c. The natural form of timber, without being squared in any way.

1813 VANCOUVER *Agric. Devon* 251 Beech about the same, and sycamore 1*s.* 3*d.* all in the round, and where the trees were fallen.

d. *Theatr.* In phr. ***in the round***, alluding to performance on a stage or arena surrounded by the auditorium, as distinguished from a proscenium; esp. in ***theatre-in-the-round***. Cf. ARENA 5.

1944 *Bull. National Theatre Conf.* (U.S.) Apr. 19 In this country, Glen Hughes out in Seattle has operated his Studio and Penthouse theatres, playing sophisticated comedies to small audiences 'in the round'. **1948** *Sat. Rev.* 3 Apr. 24/1 'Theatre-in-the-round' is the way it is described by John Rosenfeld, who is not *a* czar but *the* czar in matters dramatic and musical in the Southwest. **1950** *Sun* (Baltimore) 8 June 16/1 The New York debut of theatre-in-the-round was off to a rousing start last week. **1958** *New Statesman* 22 Feb. 228/3 At the Mahatma Gandhi Hall, Fitzroy Square, Miss Margaret Rawlings is giving *Phèdre* in English In-the-Round. **1963** *Listener* 28 Mar. 559/2, I do object to playing to them in the round, because it gives them a chance to get at the actor physically. **1963** 'E. MCBAIN' *Ten Plus One* (1964) vii. 73 We did the play in the round...we banked rows of rented bleachers on the stage, and the performers worked in the centre. **1967** *Oxf. Compan. Theatre* (ed. 3) 941/2 Modern theatre-in-the-round first came into prominence in Russia, where in the 1930s Okhlopkov in his Realistic Theatre produced a number of Soviet plays on stages set up in the central area with the audience pressing close on all sides. **1980** *Times Lit. Suppl.* 5 Sept. 973/1 Audience involvement was not new to Tudor Drama: medieval theatre-in-the-round had already thrived on it.

e. ***out-of-round*** sb., the extent to which an object departs from being circular in section; also as *adj.* Hence ***out-of-roundness.***

1951 C. W. KENNEDY *Inspection & Gaging* iv. 67 Standards for allowable taper, out-of-round or eccentricity should be established in every shop. **1955** W. H. CROUSE *Automotive Engines* xiv. 403 Some bearing failures may result..from a tapered or out-of-round crankpin. *Ibid.* 412 Bearings working against out-of-roundness or taper of more than 0·0015 inch will not last long. **1962** *Mod. Petroleum Technol.* (Inst. Petroleum) (ed. 3) xxvi. 848 'Out-of-roundness'..must always be expected [in a pipe] as a result either of poor manufacture or of damage in transit. **1970** K. BALL *Fiat 600, 600D Autobk.* xi. 130/2 The out-of-round must not exceed ·0004 inch. **1975** BRAM & DOWNS *Manuf. Technol.* iv. 110 Disadvantages of self-centring chucks are that they cannot clamp blank or out-or-round items to maintain accuracy. **1979** *B.S.I. News* Jan. 4/1 Yielding in stiffeners due to out-of-roundness and buckling.

II. 6. The circumference or outer bounds *of* some circular object; the complete circle *of* something (with or without implication of the included area).

14.. *Voc.* in Wr.-Wülcker 600 *Paritonius*, the rownde of the erth. **1593** SHAKS. *Lucr.* 952 To..turn the giddy round of Fortune's wheel. **1615** G. SANDYS *Trav.* 32 On the left side stands the round of an ancient Chappell. **1707** MORTIMER *Husb.* (1721) I. 357 The ring or round of the Wheel is more flat. **1730** A. GORDON *Maffei's Amphith.* 211 That of Rome was built of Travertine Stone..in the Circuit or exterior Round. **1784** COWPER *Task* IV. 258 The moon.. Resplendent less, but of an ampler round. **1821** SCOTT *Pirate* xxv, The wide round of earth..holds nothing that I would call a recompense. **1833** TENNYSON *Miller's Daughter* 102 The dark round of the dripping wheel. **1856** STANLEY *Sinai & Pal.* (1858) 476 The 'circles' or the 'round' of the oases of the Jordan.

fig. **1865** NEALE *Hymns Paradise* 66 There the soul, in fullest tenour, Graspeth Wisdom's total round. **1870** LOWELL *My Books* Ser. I. (1873) 170 Shakespeare, the vast round of whose balanced nature seems to have been equatorial.

7. a. A circle, ring, or coil; an annular enclosing line or device. †***in round***, in a circle.

1382 WYCLIF *Lev.* xix. 27 Ne ȝe shulen in rownde [L. *in rotundum*] dodde heer, ne shaue beerde.

1589 FLEMING *Virg. Georg.* I. 9 The serpent huge with winding bowts and rounds Slides downe..in maner of a riuer. **1605** SHAKS. *Macb.* IV. i. 88 What is this, that..weares vpon his Baby-brow, the round And top of Soueraignty? **1667** MILTON *P.L.* IX. 183 The Serpent..fast sleeping soon he found In Labyrinth of many a round self-rowld. **1742** tr. *Heister's Surg.* III. (1768) II. 386 Then the Roller ascends gradually by spiral Rounds towards the Inguen. **1817** J. EVANS *Excurs. Windsor*, etc. 169 At each end, in a round, is a knight on horseback, in the manner of ancient seals. **1884** *Times* (weekly ed.) 28 Dec. 7/1 Upon which was engraved in a round, an inscription of a star with six rays.

fig. **1868** NETTLESHIP *Ess. Browning's Poetry* viii. 291 We cannot each finish our lives to a perfect round.

†**b.** ? A single turn of a chain. *Obs.*

1693 *Lond. Gaz.* No. 2838/4 Lost.., a Gold Chain with 7 Rounds. **1708** *Brit. Apollo* No. 8. 4/2 A Gold Chain containing six Rounds with a Gold Locket.

c. A single turn of yarn, etc., when wound as on a reel.

1753 HANWAY *Trav.* II. I. v. 18 A moss, which is about 60 inches in the round, can be most conveniently reeled off. **1880** *Plain Hints* 58 All materials in skeins are divided above into 'rounds' as they are comparatively easily counted.

8. a. A structure, or part of one, a building, enclosing wall, etc., having a circular form.

a **1578** LINDESAY (Pitscottie) *Chron. Scot.* (S.T.S.) I. 336 Ane greit round as it had bene ane blokhouse. *Ibid.*, Farder thair was tua great roundis in ilk syde of the ȝeit. 1602 MARSTON *Antonio's Rev.* Prol., If any spirit breathes within this round [*sc.* the theatre], Uncapable of weightie passion. 1632 LITHGOW *Trav.* I. 16 A rotundo.. open at the top with a large round. 1706 tr. *C'tess D'Anois Trav.* 127 The old Walls.. are yet standing: There are of them four Rounds, built at divers times. 1725 J. HENLEY tr. *Montfaucon's Antiq. Italy* (ed. 2) 21 A Round of Walls fortified with Towers. 1820 SCOTT *Monast.* v, The small *round*, or turret closet,.. was accessible by another door. 1865 HUNT *Pop. Rom. West Eng.* (1896) 275 Then it was that they constructed the rounds.. to protect their tin ground. 1881 FREEMAN *Venice* 133 The arches of the round rest on heavy rectangular piers of truly Roman strength.

b. A circular part, form, or arrangement of natural origin.

1602 CAREW *Cornwall* 107 The Iland is square with foure rounds at the corners like Mount Edgecumb. 1632 LITHGOW *Trav.* IX. 397 High are thy rounds, steepe, circled, as I see. 1741 LADY POMFRET *Lett.* (1805) III. 269 A vast round of mountains, joined, and covered with fir-trees. 1784 BECKFORD *Vathek* (1868) 68 She passed the large round of honeysuckles, her favourite resort.

c. A curve or bend, as of a river, bay, etc.

1616 B. JONSON *Queenes Masques* Wks. II. 908 Those curious Squares and Rounds Wherewith thou flow'st betwixt the grounds Of fruitfull Kent. 1728 POPE *Dunc.* II. 165 So Jove's bright bow displays its watry round. 1799 NELSON 30 Apr. in Nicolas *Disp.* (1845) III. 343 Castel-a-Mare, which is opposite Naples, and, by the Round of the Bay, twelve miles distant. 1807 J. BARLOW *Columb.* I. 262 The yielding concave bends sublimer rounds. 1890 *Murray's Lincolnshire* 177 The Trent makes some eccentric windings, called 'rounds', in this parish.

†**d.** *in round*, round about. *Obs.*[−1]

1618 BOLTON *Florus* III. x. (1636) 205 That most spacious city.. was girt in round by Cæsar with workes, stakes, and a ditch.

9. a. A circular group, knot, or assemblage of persons. Freq. in phr. ***in a round***, in a ring.

With quots. 1590, 1887 cf. sense 11.

1590 SPENSER *F.Q.* I. vi. 7 A troupe of Faunes and Satyres far away Within the wood were dauncing in a rownd. 1623 BINGHAM *Xenophon* 96 The Souldiers.. gathered together, and stood in rounds. 1655 STANLEY *Hist. Philos.* (1687) 52 From midst of that learn'd Round come I. 1711 ADDISON *Spectator* No. 1 ¶5 Sometimes I am seen thrusting my Head into a Round of Politicians at Will's. 1725 POPE *Odyss.* VIII. 518 The peers encircling form an awful round. 1887 RUSKIN *Præterita* II. 215 The dance of four sweet Pisan maids, in a round.

fig. 1784 COWPER *Task* II. 385 Constant at routs, familiar with a round Of ladyships. 1826 LAMB *Pop. Fallacies* xiii, Cannot we.. know Sulpicia without knowing all the round of her card-playing relations?

b. A circular group of things; a number of things set or arranged in a ring.

1598 SHAKS. *Merry W.* IV. iv. 50 (My daughter) and my little sonne, And three or foure more of their growth,.. With rounds of waxen Tapers on their heads. 1620 J. PYPER tr. *Hist. Astrea* I. II. 7 He made a Round of dead bodies about Clidaman. 1663 CHARLETON *Chor. Gigant.* 33 Encompassed only with a round of Columns. 1700 T. BROWN tr. *Fresny's Amusem.* 131 A Grave Assembly, but ill seated upon Low Stools set in a Round.

fig. 1767 YOUNG *Farmer's Lett. to People* 2 In a round of different professions, all must either immediately or relatively depend on each other. 1865 GEO. ELIOT *A. Bede* xxxvi, Repeating again and again the same small round of memories.

III. †**10.** A swinging stroke or cut. *Obs.*

c 1450 *Fencing w. two handed Sword* in *Rel. Antiq.* I. 309 A gode rounde with an hauke and smyte ryȝt doune. *Ibid.*, Gedyr up a doblet and spare not hys croune, With a rownde and a rake abyde at a bay. *a* 1627 SIR J. BEAUMONT *Bosworth F.* 547 Erects his weapon with a nimble round, And sends the Peasant's arm to kiss the ground.

11. a. A dance in which the performers move in a circle or ring, or around a room, etc.

1513 DOUGLAS *Æneis* XII. Prol. 193 Sum sing sangis, dansis ledys, and rovndis. *a* 1548 HALL *Chron., Hen. VI*, 108 To tel you.. what roundes were daunced in large and brode places.. it were a long woorke. 1605 SHAKS. *Macb.* IV. i. 130 Ile Charme the Ayre to giue a sound, While you performe your Antique round. 1636 J. STRATFORD in *Ann. Dubrensia* (1877) 49 Keeping their Revells now on Cotswold downes, In thy great honour, dancing Masques, and Rownes. 1695 BLACKMORE *Pr. Arth.* I. 702 The Jocond Fairies dance their silent round. 1798 WORDSW. *Peter Bell* I. 223 Peter, by the mountain rills, Had danced his round with Highland lasses. 1819 SCOTT *Ivanhoe* xliv, A good fellow and a merry, who will.. draw a bow, and dance a Cheshire round, with e'er a man in Yorkshire. 1892 SYMONDS *M. Angelo* (1893) I. vii. 34 Ballats for women to chant as they danced their rounds on the piazza.

fig. 1579 GOSSON *Sch. Abuse* (Arb.) 45 There are other which haue a share with them in their Schooles, therefore ought they to daunce the same Rounde. *a* 1593 MARLOWE *Edw. II*, IV. iii, With him is Edmund gone associate? And will Sir John of Hainault lead the round? 1799 WORDSW. *Three years she grew* 28 Where rivulets dance their wayward round.

b. The music for such a dance. *rare*[−1].

1626 BRETON *Pasquil's Madcappe* Wks. (Grosart) I. 7/2 A Fidler.. Who.. can but play a Round or Hey-de-gey, And that perhaps he onely hath by roate.

†**c.** ***Sallinger's*** (prob. = *St. Leger's*) ***round***. *Obs.*

1607 HEYWOOD *Wom. killed w. Kindn.* Wks. 1874 II. 98 Wee'l have Sellengers round. *c* 1645 CLEVELAND *Let.* Wks. (1677) 126, I look upon your Letter as a Spittle-Sermon; Salinger's Round, the same again. 1698 E. WARD *Lond. Spy* II. (1709) 30 'Twill make a Parson Dance Sallingers-round, a Puritan Lust after the Flesh.

12. a. Movement in a circle, or about an axis; motion round a certain course or track.

1604 E. G[RIMSTONE] *D'Acosta's Hist. Indies* V. xxviii. 415 The children with the old men made a certaine shew, with rounds and turnings. 1647 COWLEY *Mistr., Love & Life* iv, [The sun] does three hundred Rounds enclose Within one yearly Circles space. 1725 POPE *Odyss.* XIV. 339 In giddy rounds the whirling ship is tost. 1738 WESLEY *Hymns, Eternal Power* i, Where Stars revolve their little Rounds. 1820 SHELLEY *Witch of Atl.* 490 Those streams of upper air Which whirl the earth in its diurnal round. 1821 SCOTT *Pirate* i, His kill-joy visage will never again stop the bottle in its round. 1877 R. J. MORE *Under the Balkans* xv. 216 At the end of the third round they all marched out of the house.

fig. 1846 KEBLE *Lyra Innoc.* (1873) 108 The rounds of restless Love When high and low she searches. 1850 ROBERTSON *Serm.* Ser. III. ix. (1853) 115 In a constant round from the capital to the watering place, and from the watering place to the capital.

†**b.** ***in (a) round***, in a circle. *Obs.*

1626 BACON *Sylva* §9 This Motion worketh in round at first.. and then worketh in Progress. 1632 J. HAYWARD *Biondi's Eromena* 37 He ranne always in a round, going.. very little wide from the same place.

c. A roundabout way or course; one which turns round in a circle.

1590 SHAKS. *Mids. N.* III. i. 109 Ile leade you about a Round.. through bush, through brake, through bryer. 1719 DE FOE *Crusoe* I. (Globe) 269, I bad them.. then, keeping out of Sight, take a round, always answering when the other hollow'd. 1722 —— *Journ. Plague* (Rtldg.) 25, [He] fetch'd a Round farther into Buckinghamshire.. to a Retreat he had found out there. 1773 GOLDSM. *Stoops to Conq.* v, You took them in a round, while they supposed themselves going forward. 1841 JAMES *Brigand* xxxviii, You have given yourself a long round, and forced me to take a long round in order to meet you.

13. a. A recurring or revolving course *of* time.

1710 STEELE *Tatler* No. 181 ¶1 We make it [the clock] strike the Round of all its Hours. 1710 CONGREVE *To Cynthia* 27 Thro' each returning Year, may that Hour be Distinguish'd in the Rounds of all Eternity. 1798 ROGERS *Epistle to Friend* 12 The gay months of Carnival resume Their annual round of glitter and perfume. 1818 KEATS *Endym.* I. 983 What a calm round of hours shall make my days. 1842 TENNYSON *Love & Duty* 4 Shall Error in the round of time Still father Truth?

b. A recurring or continuous succession or series *of* events, occupations, duties, etc.

1655 VAUGHAN *Silex Scint., Repentance* E 4, In all this Round of life and death. 1667 MILTON *P.L.* VI. 6 A Cave.., Where light and darkness in perpetual round Lodge and dislodge by turns. 1729 BUTLER *Serm.* Wks. 1874 II. 195 Care and sorrow and the repetition of vain delights which fill up the round of life. 1752 JOHNSON *Rambler* No. 191 ¶11 This is the round of my day; and when shall I.. so change it as to want a book? 1813 F. J. JACKSON in *Sir G. Jackson's Diaries & Lett.* (1873) II. 191 The noisy round of the so-called pleasures of a London season. 1841 B. HALL *Patchwork* II. 209 The same causes bring a perpetual round of company to Malta. 1883 E. PENNELL-ELMHIRST *Cream of Leicestersh.* 337 The Quorn had a round of sport from noon till dark.

c. *spec.* A recurring succession or series *of* meetings for discussion or negotiation; one stage in such a process. Also without *const.*

1964 *Ann. Reg. 1963* 252 They disagreed on what should be the approach of the Six in preparation for the forthcoming 'Kennedy round' of negotiations. 1977 *Economist* 22 Oct. 89/1 There is still no sign (two months into the current wage round) that wages are about to go through the roof. 1978 *Internat. Relations Dict.* (U.S. Dept. State Library) 42/2 The talks, which opened in Geneva in October 1973, were called the 'Tokyo Round' because they were initiated by a declaration signed in Tokyo.

14. *Mil.* **a.** The walk or circuit performed by the watch among the sentinels of a garrison, camp, etc., esp. during the night. Chiefly in phr. ***to go*** (†***make, take, tread***), ***pace***, or ***walk the round***.

After F. *ronde*, whence also Sp., Pg., and It. *ronda*.

1598 BARRET *Theor. Warres* VI. iv. 244 The first [soldier] in the time of winter maketh his Rounds & counter Roundes for sixe houres. 1616 J. LANE *Contn. Sqr.'s T.* VIII. 434 So gettinge vp, he quicklie trode the rowne,..and crie[d] revenge, which pleasd the soldiers tooth. 1646 H. P. *Medit. Seige* 92 He that hath the charge of the Guard in the night time is to walke the round at times. 1728 CHAMBERS *Cycl.* s.v., In strict Garrison, the Rounds go every Quarter of an Hour. *a* 1791 LANGTON in *Boswell* (Oxf. ed.) II. 272 He accompanied the Major of the regiment in going what are styled the *Rounds*, where he might observe the forms of visiting the guards. 1813 SCOTT *Trierm.* III. x, As when a guard Of some proud castle, holding ward, Pace forth their nightly round. 1868 *Regul. & Orders Army* §859 Commanders of Guards are to go their rounds twice by day and twice by night.

fig. 1855 BROWNING *Master Hugues* iv, You may challenge them, not a response Get the church-saints on their rounds!

b. A watch under the command of an officer, which goes round a camp, the ramparts of a fortress, etc., to see that the sentinels are vigilant, or which parades the streets of a town to preserve good order; a military patrol.

1581 BLANDY *Castle of Policy* 18 b, Corporall, gentleman in a company or of the Rounde, Launce passado. 1598 BARRET *Theor. Warres* IV. ii. 107 The Round finding the Sentinell vigilant, neede not alwayes approch neare him. 1627 R. BERNARD *Isle of Man* (1635) 152 Divers times meeting the Gentlemen of the round.., he would stop their passages and turne them backe againe. 1652 WADSWORTH tr. *Sandoval's Civ. Wars Spain* 151 After which they kept their Rounds and Guards in the Citie, and sent Hors to the relief of Segovia. 1711 E. WARD *Quix.* 193 Don Vincent fearing to be taken up by the Rounds,.. left that Street with all possible speed. 1802 JAMES *Mil. Dict.* s.v., As soon as the sentry.. perceives the round coming, he shall give notice to the guard. 1878 STEVENSON *Inland Voy.* 84 It was just the place to hear the round going by at night in the darkness, with the solid tramp of men marching.

c. *pl. Naut.* Inspection.

1902 L. DELBOS *Naut. Terms* (ed. 4) 140/1 *Rounds*, inspection. 1914 'BARTIMEUS' *Naval Occasions* xviii. 158 The Sub-Lieutenant, 'standing the rounds' in the doorway. 1916 'TAFFRAIL' *Stand By!* 13 Except on Sundays, when the latter is specially tidied up for the 'rounds', it will not bear close investigation. 1961 F. H. BURGESS *Dict. Sailing* 174 *Rounds*, inspection.

15. A customary circuit, walk, or course; the beat or course traversed by a watchman, constable, vendor, etc.; also *transf.* Freq. in phr. ***to walk, take, go***, etc., ***one's round***(***s***). Also *spec.*, a visit to each of the in-patients in a ward or under the care of a particular doctor or nurse.

1607 J. DAVIES (Heref.) *Summa Totalis* Wks. (Grosart) I. 10/2 Ere once the Sunne his Round perambulate. 1688 PENTON *Guard. Instr.* (1897) 43, I could willingly have heard him [a Proctor in Oxford] longer but that he was to go his Rounds. 1709 STEELE *Tatler* No. 2 ¶2 The watchful Bellman march'd his Round. 1742 RICHARDSON *Pamela* IV. 74 In the Account she gave us of her benevolent Round, as Lady Davers calls it. 1815 SCOTT *Guy M.* xvii, The regularity with which the keeper makes his rounds with a loaded fowling-piece. 1861 DICKENS *Gt. Expect.* xxxii, A pot-man was going his rounds with beer. 1878 J. MILLER *Songs of Italy* 36 If a dead man should be found By these same fishers in their round. 1904 *Sci. & Art of Nursing* I. iv. 99 There is always the danger that in the haste and pressure to have all in order for the rounds of the medical staff, the minor requests of patients may be postponed. 1928 A. T. SCHOFIELD *Behind Brass Plate* xiii. 94 Samuel Fenwick, in his rounds, was very droll... After the usual examination of a new patient he performed his well-known trick. 1954 A. HUXLEY *Let.* 9 May (1969) 706 He [*sc.* a physician] takes foreign pupils—mostly doctors..—young men who live near by and go the rounds with him and learn by listening, answering questions and doing. 1965 SPENCER & TAIT *Introd. Nursing* vii. 31 It is generally considered that visitors can be in a main ward outside main meal times, sanitary rounds, rest times and doctors' rounds. 1974 G. B. MAIR *Confessions of Surgeon* v. 58 When added to routine clerking, ward rounds, night rounds, dealing with emergencies,.. no day had enough hours.

attrib. 1897 CROCKETT *Lad's Love* xxv, These irregular and uncovenanted halts, not entered in the round book.

16. a. A turn, a walk or drive, round a place or to a series of places, for the purpose of recreation, sight-seeing, purchasing, etc.; esp. in phr. ***to make, go, take a round***. Also *fig.*

1611 BEAUM. & FL. *Philaster* II. iv, Come, Ladies, shall we talk a round? As men Do walk a mile, women should talk an hour After supper. 1698 FRYER *Acc. E. India & P.* 100 Thence we took a Round.. to the English Tombs. *Ibid.* 137 Liberty to take a Round about the Castle. 1709 STEELE *Tatler* No. 13 ¶1, I went into Lincoln-Inn-Walks; and having taken a Round or Two, I sate down. 1765 FOOTE *Commissary* I, Mercy upon me, what a round I have taken! .. don't you see I am tired to death? *a* 1822 SHELLEY *Faust* II. 364 Yet I will take a round with you, and hope.. To beat the poet and the devil together.

slang. *c* 1848 'JUDSON' *Myst. N.Y.* I. 113 Taking a cruise about town, or going on a spree, is called taking a round.

b. A series *of* visits or calls.

1772 MME. D'ARBLAY *Early Diary* 30 Apr., We went yesterday to make a round of visits. 1843 DICKENS *Mart. Chuzz.* xxvii, I had a round of visits to make. 1866 G. MACDONALD *Ann. Q. Neighb.* xi, I.. made another round of visits.

c. *Golf.* A spell of play in which the player goes right round the course, or plays all the holes.

1775 C. B. CLAPCOTT *Rules of Golf* (1935) 24 No member of this Society pay the Cadies more than one penny per round. 1834 P. BUCHAN *Peterhead Smugglers* 63 To gang wi' you to the links ilka morning at five o'clock to a round o' the golf. 1866 *Golfer's Year Bk.* 65 The order of play was the reverse of the wonted 'round' over Bruntsfield, in order that strangers might cope on equal footing with players who were up to the green. Each round consisted of 7 holes, and four rounds were fixed on for the decision of the Tournament. 1879 *Encycl. Brit.* X. 766/2 A 'round', as it is termed, of the links [at St. Andrews] is very nearly four miles. 1897 *Encycl. Sport* I. 473 *Medal play*, the method of playing a game of golf by counting the number of strokes taken to the round by each side.

17. a. The circuit *of* a place, etc. †Also in early use without const.

1609 B. JONSON *Sil. Wom.* IV. ii, He walks the round up and down, through every room o' the house. 1655 tr. *Sorel's Com. Hist. Francion* IV. 11 The principal was by that time in the court and walked the round with a great lanthorn before him. 1712 ARBUTHNOT *John Bull* I. x, You have danc'd the Round of all the Courts. 1779 JOHNSON in *Boswell* 27 Oct., I am glad that you made the round of Lichfield with so much success. 1843 LE FEVRE *Life Trav. Phys.* II. II. ii. 189 In a short time we made the round of the Society. 1861 PEACOCK *Gryll G.* xxxi, Lord Curryfin..—in his official capacity—taking the round of the rooms. 1883 J. GILMOUR *Mongols* xviii. 211 You will find him.. going the rounds of the sacred place, prostrating himself at every shrine.

fig. 1867 SMYTH *Sailor's Word-bk.* 582 *Rounds of the Galley*,.. is figurative of a man incurring the expressed scorn of his shipmates.

b. ***to go the round***, of communications, news, etc., to be passed or handed on round a whole set of persons, etc.; also const. *of*. Now usu. *pl.*; also ***to make the rounds***.

1669 W. SIMPSON *Hydrol. Chym.* 124 The rest.. communicate it one to another, till it hath gone the round. 1833 HT. MARTINEAU *Tale of Tyne* v. 79 No light sayings of his upon the matter were going the round of his neighbourhood. 1837 *Jamestown* (N.Y.) *Jrnl.* 22 Mar. 3/2 There is a story going the rounds in relation to the president-elect. 1840 THACKERAY *Paris Sk.-bk.* I. 66 The following anecdote, that is now going the round of the papers. 1861 HUGHES *Tom Brown at Oxf.* ii. (1889) 9 This celebrated epistle.. created quite a sensation.. as it went the round after tea. 1862 O. W. NORTON *Army Lett.* (1903) 55 Everything of the kind has to go the rounds, you know. 1934

H. L. ICKES *Secret Diary* (1953) I. 254 He expressed the fear that in some way I connected him with all of these stories that are going the rounds about me. **1977** *Rolling Stone* 13 Jan. 39/2 The rumor that the FBI started about her being a Soviet spy is still making the rounds at parties she no longer attends.

c. *pl.* (See quots.; and cf. ROUNDSMAN 1.)

1795 SIR F. M. EDEN *State Poor* II. 29 Most labourers are, (as it is termed,) on the Rounds; that is, they go to work from one house to another round the parish. **1813** BATCHELOR *Agric.* 608 (E.D.D.), The increase of population has caused a deficiency of employment, which is so remarkable in some seasons, that a great proportion of the labourers 'go the rounds'. **1854** MISS BAKER *Northampt. Gloss., Rounds-Men*, labouring poor, who are taken into employment by the farmers in rotation; when they are said to be 'on the rounds'.

IV. †**18.** ***in round***, in turn or rotation. *rare.*

1527 *Churchw. Acc. St. Giles, Reading* 32 At this accompte hath bene dismissed John Beke and chosen in round Richard Body.

19. *Mus.* †**a.** A kind of song sung by two or more persons, each taking up the strain in turn.

1530 PALSGR. 264/1 Rounde a songe, *rondeau, uirelay*. **1586** W. WEBBE *Eng. Poetrie* (Arb.) 61 The sixt kinde, is called a round, beeing mutuallie sung betweene two: one singeth one verse, the other the next, eche rymeth with himselfe. **1603** HARSNET *Pop. Impost.* x, He had beene..the master setter of catches or roundes vsed to be sung by Tinkers, as they sit by the fire with a pot of good ale betweene theyr legges. **1641** BROME *Joviall Crew* IV. i, A Round, a Round, a Round, Boyes, a Round, Let Mirth fly aloft, and Sorrow be drown'd. **1683** SOAME & DRYDEN *Boileau's Art Poet.* II. 366 Each poem his perfection has apart; The British round in plainness shows his art.

b. (See quot. 1872.)

1776 BURNEY *Hist. Mus.* (1789) III. 348 A round is no more than a song of as many strains or sections as parts. **1811** BUSBY *Dict. Mus.* (ed. 3), *Round*, a species of fugue in the unison, composed in imitation of a catch, and so called because the performers follow each other through the several parts in a circulatory motion. **1872** BANISTER *Music* (1885) xxxv. 188 A Round is a species of Canon, for three or more equal voices, in which one voice sings a short complete melody, which is then sung by a second voice, the first voice proceeding to another accompanying melody.

20. a. A quantity of liquor served round a company, or drunk off at one time by each person present. †*to* ***keep the round***, to drink equally with the others.

1633 G. HERBERT *Temple, Ch. Porch* v, Drink not the third glasse... It is most just to throw that on the ground, Which would throw me there, if I keep the round. **1667** DAVENANT & DRYDEN *Tempest* II. i, This is prize brandy... Let's have two rounds more. **1716** ADDISON *Freeholder* No. 8 ¶2 The Tories..can scarce find beauties enough of their own side, to supply a single round of October. **1760** C. JOHNSTON *Chrysal* (1822) I. 71 A round or two of loyal toasts. **1799** GEO. IV in *Paget Papers* (1896) I. 150 Every Round was a Bumper to you in the very best Claret I had. **1821** SCOTT *Pirate* iv, A round of cinnamon-water serving only like oil to the flame. **1883** STEVENSON *Treas. Isl.* xxi, Serve out a round of brandy to all hands. **1928** C. MACKENZIE *Extraordinary Women* x. 176 Two rounds of stingers brought the evening to a close. **1960** M. SPARK *Ballad of Peckham Rye* (1964) vii. 107 Dixie, at first under the impression that Humphrey was buying the round, asked for a ginger ale. **1970** G. F. NEWMAN *Sir, You Bastard* viii. 255 Just a slag avoiding his round. **1978** J. PORTER *Dead Easy for Dover* xii. 125 The local chap had proved himself more than willing to stand his round, and Dover didn't ask more than that of anyone.

b. A piece cut right across the loaf. Also, a sandwich or sandwiches made of two slices cut from a loaf of bread.

1840 DICKENS *Barn. Rudge* iv, A couple of rounds of buttered toast. *a* **1845** BARHAM *Ingold. Leg., Knt. & Lady*, A round and a half of hot buttered toast. *a* **1902** S. BUTLER *Way of All Flesh* (1903) lxxii. 330 She..had made him a round of toast. **1947** A. RANSOME *Great Northern?* xix. 232 Peggy was cutting rounds of bread to make potted meat sandwiches. **1974** L. DEIGHTON *Spy Story* xvi. 162 'Have you come for your sandwiches?'.. 'Last night's pork, and one round of cheese.'

21. A quantity representing a single turn of work by a set of men; each man's contribution to this.

1708 J. C. *Compleat Collier* (1845) 37 Those Sticks immediately show him how many Rounds the Barrow-Men have put.

22. a. A single discharge of each piece of artillery or firearm; each of the shots fired by a single piece.

1725 *Lond. Gaz.* No. 6378/4 The great Guns..fired several Rounds. **1794** NELSON 30 July in Nicolas *Disp.* (1845) I. 462 The Garrison fired one general round, when they nearly all left their guns. **1821** SCOTT *Kenilw.* xxx, A round of artillery..was discharged from the battlements. **1846** GREENER *Sci. Gunnery* 58 The number of rounds that each gun fired averaged 1,249. **1878** *19th Cent.* Mar. 446 Of the men sent to Malta..a considerable proportion..had never even fired a round of ball cartridge.

b. A single charge of ammunition for a firearm.

1747 *Gentl. Mag.* 345 Wolfe's regiment carried into the field 24 rounds a man... Afterwards they had a supply of 8 rounds a man more. **1815** WELLINGTON 6 May in Gurw. *Desp.* (1838) XII. 355, I have thought it expedient to lodge in the fortress..1,000,000 rounds of musket ammunition. **1868** *Regul. & Orders Army* §630 For every trained soldier in the infantry 90 rounds of ball Cartridges, and 300 rounds per Battery for Artillery. **1879** *Cassell's Techn. Educ.* I. 66/1 The reduction in the weight of the arm with sixty rounds of ammunition was three pounds.

23. a. *Card-playing.* A single turn of play by all the players.

a **1735** GRANVILLE *Epigr. & Char., Women*, Women to cards may be compar'd; we play A round or two, when us'd we throw away. **1742** HOYLE *Whist* 22 You must play three Rounds of Trumps, otherwise you may have your strong Suit trumped. **1850** *Bohn's Hand-bk. Games* (1867) 137 At the fourth round of trumps, he revokes, and afterwards trumps your suit. **1885** R. A. PROCTOR *Whist* i. 27 The first round may show it to be unadvisable to continue the suit.

b. *Pugilism.* A single bout in a fight or a boxing-match. Also *transf.*, *fig.*, and in attrib. phr. ***round-by-round***.

1812 *Sporting Mag.* XXXIX. 187 The round lasted three minutes. **1846** C. ST. JOHN *Wild Sports Highl.* 248 We heard the clash of horns as two rival stags met and fought a few rounds together. **1886** CAROLINE HAZARD *Mem. J. L. Diman* i. 16 This friendship, which dated from a round of fisticuffs and bloody noses on both sides. **1937** 'M. INNES' *Hamlet, Revenge!* II. iii. 137 Gott sighed. 'You certainly know the habits of your friends. Round Two to you.' **1955** T. H. PEAR *Eng. Social Differences* 246 Championship fight..with a leading article and a back-page 'round-by-round' report. **1959** *Listener* 22 Oct. 681/2 He began round two by making a fresh application for *habeas corpus*. **1961** *Times* 25 May 15/4 It is a remarkable round-by-round study in the art of politics. **1967** *Listener* 3 Aug. 147/3 By quoting, selectively, two rounds of a three-round controversy..[you] gave an inaccurate picture of the course of the argument.

c. *Archery.* The discharge of a certain number of arrows by each archer.

1875 *Encycl. Brit.* II. 373/2 The origin of 'The York round', on which all public competitions by archers are now conducted. *Ibid.*, Two days' shooting, or the result of a 'double round'. **1879** M. & W. H. THOMPSON *Archery* 12 The 'National Round'..consists of 48 arrows at 60 yards, and 24 arrows at 50 yards.

d. *Sport.* A spell of play forming a definite stage in a competition or match.

1902 *Encycl. Brit.* XXVIII. 425/2 All the clubs entered are drawn by lot, in pairs, to play together in the first round; the winners of these ties are then similarly drawn in pairs for the next round. **1921** [see END *sb.* 20b]. **1951** *Sport* 30 Mar.–5 Apr. 2/4 In the Amateur Cup they reached the second round, losing to Pegasus.

24. a. A separate or distinct outburst *of* applause, cheers, etc.

1794 C. MATHEWS *Let.* 28 Dec. in A. Mathews *Mem. Charles Mathews* (1838) I. vi. 129 He came forward at the end of the play.., and he had six successive rounds of applause. **1808** *Monthly Mirror* Mar. 268 The audience.. with not three, but six rounds of applause, greeted his return. **1815** SCOTT *Guy M.* xxxvi, The gravity with which he accommodated himself to the humour of the moment.. procured him three rounds of applause. **1867** DICKENS *Let. to Miss Hogarth* 29 March, The roars of welcome and the rounds of cheers. **1884** *Western Daily Press* 21 Oct. 8/1 Mr. Chamberlain, on rising to reply, was received with several rounds of hearty cheers.

b. A single stroke in succession from each bell of a set or peal. Also *transf.*

1826 LAMB *Pop. Fallacies* ix, Ringing a round of the most ingenious conceits. **1872** ELLACOMBE *Bells of Ch.* in *Ch. Bells Devon* iii. 35 The ringing 'rounds', and 'call changes' was a good deal cultivated. **1897** JANE *Lordship* xiii, A man well practised in all that pertained to bells, whether rounds, changes, eights, twelves.

25. *ellipt.* = *round-the-houses* s.v. ROUND *prep.* 1 a. *slang.*

1893 P. H. EMERSON *Signor Lippo* xiv. 55 One day he walked straight into this kitchen clobbered in a black pair of rounds, tight to his legs.

round (raʊnd), *sb.*[2] [f. ROUND *v.*[1]] The act of rounding. Chiefly *Naut.* with *aft, down.*

1769 FALCONER *Dict. Marine* (1780) s.v. *Architecture*, The horizontal curve, or round-aft, of the first transom. **1846** A. YOUNG *Naut. Dict., Round-Aft*, in shipbuilding, the outward curve or convex form of the stern from the wing transom upwards. **1869** SIR E. REED *Shipbuild.* xii. 241 A stringer angle-iron is worked at the beginning of the round-down in order to form a finish to the deck planking. **1876** *Encycl. Brit.* IV. 44/1 The pressure of the roller against the back gives the required 'round', which can be varied by raising or lowering the pitch of the roller. **1943** T. HARSLEY *Find, fire, & Strike* 38 The 'round down' at the stern where the aircraft ready to take off are ranged.

round (raʊnd), *a.* Forms: α. 4 rund(e, 4–5 rond(e; 3– round, 4–6 rounde (5 rouned, rovnd), rownd(e, 5 rowndde, rowunde; 5 roende, 6 roound(e, 8–9 *Sc.* and *north.* roond. β. 4–5 roon, 5 roune, rowne, 8–9 *Sc.* and *north.* roon', roun'. [a. OF. *rund-*, *rond-*, *round-*, etc. (mod.F. *rond* masc., *ronde* fem.), representing earlier **redond*, **rodond*, = Prov. *redon*, *redun*, Sp. and Pg. *redondo*, It. *ritondo*, *rotondo* (and *tondo*):—L. *rotundus*: see ROTUND *a.* The French word is also the source of MDu. *ront*, *rond-* (Du. *rond*), MHG. *runt*, *rund-* (G. *runa*), (M)Sw., Da., Norw. *rund*, Fris. *roun*, †*ruwn*.]

I. 1. a. Having all parts of the surface equidistant from the centre; spherical, globular; resembling a ball.

c **1290** *S. Eng. Leg.* I. 311/407 Ase an Appel þe eorþe is round. *Ibid.* 318/654 þe eorþe a-midde þe grete se ase a luyte bal is round. *a* **1300** *Cursor M.* 293 In þe sune..Es a thing and thre thingys sere; A bodi rond, and hete, and light. *c* **1386** CHAUCER *Frankl. T.* 500 This wyde world which that men seye is round. *c* **1400** MAUNDEV. (Roxb.) i. 4 þis ymage was wont to hald in his hand a rounde appel of gold. *c* **1470** *Gol. & Gaw.* 886 Armyt in rede gold, and rubeis sa round. **1565** COOPER *Thesaurus* s.v. *Globus*, The rounde earth appearyng aboue the sea. **1590** SPENSER *F.Q.* I. v. 35 An huge round stone did reele Against an hill. **1631** WIDDOWES *Nat. Philos.* 18 Hayle is rayne, made hard in the fall, the higher the fall, the rounder and lesser. **1688** HOLME *Armoury* II. 114/2 Bolle of a Poppy is the round seed Pod. **1753** *Chambers' Cycl.* Suppl. s.v. *Leaf*, A sage leaf appears like a rug, or shag,..embellished with fine round crystal beads. **1760–72** H. BROOKE *Fool of Qual.* (1809) IV. 110 The motions whereby the round universe continues its course. **1800** tr. *Lagrange's Chem.* II. 238 By dissolving in this manner it becomes round, and acquires transparency. **1864** TENNYSON *Voyage* 7 We knew the merry world was round, And we might sail for evermore.

fig. **1583** STUBBES *Anat. Abus.* II. (1882) 10 To lawe go they, as round as a ball, till..both, or at least the one, become a beggar all daies of his life.

b. ***round shot***, spherical balls of cast-iron or steel for firing from smooth-bore cannon.

1616 J. LANE *Contn. Sqr.'s T.* v. 245 Powder, crosse barrs, round shott, pikes. **1627** CAPT. SMITH *Seaman's Gram.* xiv. 67 Round Shot is a round Bullet for any Peece. **1728** CHAMBERS *Cycl., Shot*..are of several Sorts; as Round-shot, or Bullets fitted to the Bore of the Piece. **1748** *Anson's Voy.* II. ix. 227 The great guns loaded with two round-shot for the first broadside, and after that with one round-shot and one grape. **1847** MARRYAT *Childr. N. Forest* xxiii, Duke Hamilton having his leg taken off by a round shot. **1883** STEVENSON *Treas. Isl.* xvii, The round shot and the powder for the gun had been left behind.

Comb. **1832** GEN. P. THOMPSON *Exerc.* (1842) II. 175 But a mathematical formula, when right, is a terrible modification of truth, a round-shot-like method of conveyance, which..tells dangerously on arriving at its destination.

ellipt. **1707** *Lond. Gaz.* No. 4380/2 We gave him..our Broadside with Double and Round. **1736** [CHETWOOD] *Voy. Vaughan* (1760) II. 214 We fir'd upon 'em with our Double and Round. **1804** MONSON in Owen *Wellesley's Desp.* (1877) 544 We..charged the enemy's advanced party under a most tremendous discharge of round, grape, and chain. *c* **1860** H. STUART *Seaman's Catech.* 13 When loading with round and grape.

2. a. Cylindrical; circular in respect of section.

1297 R. GLOUC. (Rolls) 1172 Stakes of ire monion,.. Aboue ssarpe & kene inou, bineþe grete & rounde. *c* **1375** *Sc. Leg. Saints* ii. (*Paul*) 850 þai..þe padok fand In a rownd tour still ȝelland. **1389** in *Eng. Gilds* (1870) 8 þer shul be founde v. tapres rounde,..for to ben liȝt on heye feste dayes. *c* **1440** *Promp. Parv.* 438/1 Rownde, as a spere or a staffe,..*teres*. **1486** *Bk. St. Albans* a vij, This hawke has..a flat leg, or a rownde legge. **1530** PALSGR. 264/1 Rounde tothe. **1577** B. GOOGE *Heresbach's Husb.* II. (1586) 106 Such as are flawed, seruing for Pillers of Churches, or other round woorkes. **1667** MILTON *P.L.* VI. 484 Hollow Engins long and round Thick-rammd. **1680** MOXON *Mech. Exerc.* xiii. 223 Turners work with a round String made of Gut. **1728** CHAMBERS *Cycl.* s.v. *File*, Those in common use are the Square,..Half-round, Round, Thin File, &c. all which are made of different Sizes. **1796** H. HUNTER tr. *St.-Pierre's Stud. Nat.* (1799) III. 16 That tower in the horizon..is blue, small and round. **1843** CARLYLE *Past & Pres.* (1858) 94 Rounder than one of your own sausages. **1884** F. J. BRITTEN *Watch & Clockm.* 36 A Round Broach is used for burnishing brass holes.

†**b.** *Sc.* Of cloth: Made of thick thread. *Obs.*

1488 *Acc. Ld. High Treas. Scot.* I. 139 For thre elne of rownde braide clayth. **1503** *Ibid.* II. 212 For x elne roundair claith, to be tua sarkis. **1566** in Hay Fleming *Mary Q. of Scots* (1897) 500 Tuelf elne of rownd cleith to be schetis to the servandis. **1589** *Exch. Rolls Scot.* XXII. 72 Small lyning .., round lining..at 6*s.* 6*d.* the eln.

c. Having a convex surface. *rare*$^{-1}$.

1523 FITZHERB. *Husb.* §33 This shall cause the lande to lye rounde,..and than shall it not drowne the corne.

d. Of the shoulders: Having a forward bend from the line of the back.

1709 *Tatler* No. 75 ¶5 The Butler..was noted for round Shoulders, and a Roman Nose. **1784** COWPER *Task* IV. 634 His awkward gait,..round shoulders, and dejected looks. *a* **1890** T. C. CRAWFORD *Eng. Life* 87 (Cent.), He is of medium height, with sloping, round shoulders.

3. a. Of persons (or animals): Plump, free from angularity; also, stout, corpulent.

c **1290** *S. Eng. Leg.* I. 351/227 ȝwane heo cam hom at eue, fair and round heo was. **1297** R. GLOUC. (Rolls) 8570 þikke mon he was ynou, round & noȝt wel long. **1390** GOWER *Conf.* II. 40 Hou sche is round, hou sche is smal. *c* **1440** *Promp. Parv.* 438/1 Rownde, for fetnesse, *obesus*. **1576** FLEMING tr. *Caius' Dogs* (1880) 8 Such a one..as is.. smoothe, full, fatte, and round. **1596** SHAKS. *1 Hen. IV*, II. iv. 155 Why you horson round man? what's the matter? **1748** THOMSON *Cast. Indol.* I. lxix, A little, round, fat, oily man of God. **1828** TICKNOR in *Life*, etc. I. xix. 381 She is a nice round lively little girl. **1856** EMERSON *Eng. Traits, Race*, They are round, ruddy, and handsome,..and there is a tendency to stout and powerful frames.

b. Of limbs, or parts of the body: Plump, full filled-out; well-shaped. Also *fig.* of character.

c **1386** CHAUCER *Knight's Tale* 1278 Hise lymes grete,.. Hise shuldres brode, hise armes rounde and longe. **1390** GOWER *Conf.* III. 27 He seth hire necke round and clene, Therinne mai no bon be sene. **1600** SHAKS. *A.Y.L.* II. i. 25 And yet it irkes me the poore dapled fooles [*sc.* deer].. Should..Haue their round hanches goard. **1614** SYLVESTER *Bethulia's Rescue* IV. 372 Her ruddy round Cheeks seem'd to be composed Of Roses Lillied, or of Lillies Rosed. **1832** IRVING *Alhambra* I. 29 The play of a graceful form and round pliant limbs. **1859** TENNYSON *Elaine* 1177 Take.. These jewels, and make me happy, making them An armlet for the roundest arm on earth. **1927** E. M. FORSTER *Aspects of Novel* iv. 106 The test of a round character is whether it is capable of surprising in a convincing way. If it never surprises, it is flat.

c. Of garments: Made so as to envelope the body or limbs in a circular manner; cut circularly at the bottom, so as to have no train or skirts. See also quot. 1960.

? *a* **1400** *Morte Arth.* 3470 A renke in a rownde cloke, with righte rowmme clothes. *a* **1548** HALL *Chron., Hen. VIII*, 239 A ryche goune of cloth of golde reised, made rounde without any trayne after the Dutche fassyon. **1592** GREENE *Conny Catch.* Wks. (Grosart) XI. 95 The round hose bumbasted close to the breech..is now common to euery cullion in the country. **1596** NASHE *Saffron Walden* Wks.

(Grosart) III. 55 If you aske why I haue put him in round hose, that vsually weares Venetians? **1687** A. Lovell tr. *Thevenot's Trav.* II. 91 [The vest] is cut very round before, so that the right side of it reaches over the Stomack. **1788** E. Sheridan *Jrnl.* 22 Dec. (1960) vi. 138 As to gowns all kinds—Chemises—Round gowns with flounce or not. **1796** in A. C. Bower *Diaries & Corr.* (1903) 163, I have bought a spotted muslin round gown. **1815** *La Belle Assemblée* June 274/1 *Morning-Dress.* Round dress of jacconet muslin. **1836** Dickens *Sk. Boz* (1837) 2nd Ser. 100 They were decent people, but not over-burdened with riches, or he would not have so outgrown the suit when he passed into those corduroys with the round jacket. **1872** Geo. Eliot *Middlem.*, Finale, When he wore a round jacket, and showed a marvellous nicety of aim in playing at marbles. **1882** L. Campbell *Life Clerk Maxwell* iii. 48 A round cloth jacket for winter wear. **1960** C. W. Cunnington et al. *Dict. Eng. Costume* 184/2 *Round dress* or *gown*, . . a term indicating a dress with joined bodice and skirt, the latter closed all round. . . 18th c. Occasionally made with a slight train. 19th c. No train, the term now meaning a dress without a train.

d. Of sails: Distended, bellied.

1881 *Daily Tel.* 28 Jan., Our old patched sails overhead were as round as the brig's bows.

e. Designating any of several styles of circular, conical, or pill-box hat.

1795 tr. *C. P. Moritz's Trav.* 141 A fellow in a brown frock and round hat. **1804** *Med. Jrnl.* XII. 76 Forming somewhat the shape of a round hat. *c* **1806** D. Wordsworth *Jrnl.* (1941) I. 303 A fine fellow . . in tight clean clothes and a nice round hat. **1825** H. Wilson *Mem.* II. 175 Down came Colonel Palmer . . his laced jacket covered with an old, short, brown great coat, and a shabby round hat. **1828** D. Wordsworth *Jrnl.* (1941) II. 403 Women often with round hats, like the Welsh. **1890** C. M. Yonge *More Bywords* 137 Those foolish girls thought me too fine a lady to like to be seen with her in her round hat on a Sunday. **1968** [see pill-box b].

4. a. Having all parts of the circumference equidistant from the centre; circular, formed like a circle; also, annular, spiral.

a **1300** *St. Edmund* 232 in *E.E.P.* 77 Þreo rounde cerclen heo wrot in þe paume amidde. **1338** R. Brunne *Chron.* (1810) 146 Of penyes rounde to Richard gan he bede Sexti þousand pounde. *c* **1380** Wyclif *Wks.* (1880) 357 Þe sacrid oost whijt & round þat men seen in þe preestis hondes. *c* **1430** *Two Cookery-bks.* 42 Þan take fayre brede, & kytte it as troundez rounde. **1466** in *Archaeol.* L. I. (1887) 35 Item j Rowne hope for the curtyne of oure lady in the chapell. **1530** Palsgr. 264/1 Rounde buckeler, *rodelle.* **1597** Shaks. *2 Hen. IV*, II. i. 95 Sitting in my Dolphin-chamber at the round table, by a sea-cole fire. **1634** Sir T. Herbert *Trav.* 97 The low-roome was round and spacious. **1660** F. Brooke tr. *Le Blanc's Trav.* 98 The Wizard makes a round hole in the ground. **1683** Temple *Mem.* Wks. 1720 I. 387 He wou'd be glad to see . . the Spanish Territories lie closer and rounder than they were then left. **1747** Gray *Death favourite Cat* 8 The fair round face, the snowy beard, The velvet of her paws. **1774** Goldsm. *Nat. Hist.* (1776) IV. 55 The ears are like those of a rat, being short and round. **1841** Lane *Arab. Nts.* I. 122 A round cloth, spread in the middle of the floor. *a* **1878** Sir G. Scott *Lect. Archit.* (1879) I. 155 In both countries the round abacus was . . used from an early period.

fig. **1576** Fleming *Panopl. Epist.* 402 Thus haue I runne about a round row of writers, and haue shewed wherein they are to be marked.

†b. Of vessels: Broad in the beam and with blunt stem and stern. *Obs.*

1600 E. Blount tr. *Conestaggio* 183 With threescore galleis, and some round vessels. **1632** J. Hayward tr. *Biondi's Eromena* 11 He might then either leave the Galley . . or send her backe againe, and there hire or buy a round vessell.

c. Exhibiting a curvilinear form or outline; curved; forming a segment of a circle.

1662 Evelyn *Chalcogr.* 5 Some round cheezil or lathe perhaps it was. **1669** Sturmy *Mariner's Mag.* I. ii. 24 Figure A is contained under one Limit or Term, which is the round Line. **1678** Moxon *Mech. Exerc.* iv. 70 There are several other Plains in use among Joyners, called Molding-plains; as, the Round, the Hollow [etc.]. **1842** Gwilt *Encycl. Arch.* §397 Sometimes we find one [pointed arch] . . inserted between several round ones. **1875** Knight *Dict. Mech.*, *Round chisel*, an engraver's tool having a rounded belly. *Ibid.*, *Round-plane*, a plane with a round sole for making rounded work.

d. Of measure: Circumferential.

1707 Mortimer *Husb.* (1721) II. 98 This Table of Round Measure shews how much in length makes a solid Foot of Timber in any round piece.

e. Of vowels: Produced by contracting the lips towards a circular form.

1867 A. J. Ellis *E.E. Pronunc.* I. iii. §3. 160 Round or Labialised Vowels. **1888** Sweet *Hist. Eng. Sounds* 20 The unrounding of back round vowels is rare.

5. a. Going round in, tracing out, a circle. ***round dance***, (*a*) = ring-dance (see also quot. 1868); also ***round dancer, dancing***; (*b*) [tr. G. *rundtanz* (K. von Frisch 1923, in *Zool. Jahrb., Abt. f. Allgemeine Zool. u. Physiol. der Tiere* XL. 31], a circular movement performed by bees at their hive or nest, believed to indicate a source of food to other bees.

1530 Palsgr. 264/1 Rounde daunce. **1565** Cooper *Thesaurus*, *Vertigo cæli*, the rounde course of celestiall bodies. **1648** Winyard *Midsummer-Morn* 2 His blood rides the round post, or dances the Morrice through him. **1683** Penn in R. Burton *Eng. Emp. Amer.* (1685) 117 The other part is their Cantico, performed by round-Dances. **1868** Whyte Melville *White Rose* I. i. 3 The lightest mover that ever turned a partner's head in a waltz (we did not call them round dances then). **1891** *Scribner's Mag.* Sept. 287/1 Each vessel making a complete circuit of the world on the round voyage. **1919** *Ladies' Home Jrnl.* May 31/1 My dear lady, are you going to give up round dancing? **1947** A. Einstein *Mus. Romantic Era* x. 110 The sharp rhythm of round dances and torch dances. **1950** K. von Frisch *Bees* iii. 71 The round dance and the wagging dance are two different terms in the language of bees, the former meaning a source of food near the hive and the latter a source at 100 metres or more. **1952** C. R. Ribbands *Behaviour & Social Life of Bees* xix. 153 The characteristic of the 'round dance' is that the bee performs a complete circle, whereas the 'waggle dance' is a figure-of-eight. **1973** R. A. Morse *Compl. Guide Beekeeping* xiii. 203 Certain races of bees use a dance intermediate between the round dance and the wag-tail dance incorporating parts of both. **1976** *Columbus* (Montana) *News* 3 June 1/2 Mr. and Mrs. Robert Shanks, Columbus, are ardent and avid square and round dancers.

†b. Round-about; to the opposite quarter. *Obs.*

1611 Cotgr., *Revirade*, a wheeling, or round turne; a backe iert. *Ibid.*, *Virevoulte*, a veere, whirle, round gambol.

c. Of time: Recurrent. *rare*$^{-1}$.

1860 Emerson *Cond. Life* vii, The round year Will bring all fruits and virtues here.

6. *Boxing.* Of blows: Delivered with a swing of the arm. Also *transf.* of persons.

1808 *Sport. Mag.* XXX. 247 Giving a round blow. **1810** *Ibid.* XXXVI. 195 He is a slow round hitter. **1861** Dickens *Gt. Expect.* iii, [He] made a hit at me—it was a round weak blow that missed me and almost knocked himself down. **1901** Edgeworth-Johnstone *Boxing* 42 The left elbow must be raised outwards until in a line with the shoulder. . . The blow is a round one.

II. 7. a. Of numbers: Full, complete, entire; esp. ***round dozen.*** Also *transf.* expressed roundly.

1340 *Ayenbite* 1 Blind, and dyaf, and alsuo domb. Of zeuenty yer al uol rond. *a* **1572** Knox *Hist. Ref.* Wks. 1846 I. 40 Yitt have I haid the round desone; and sevin of thame ar menis wyffis. **1638** Baillie *Lett. & Jrnls.* (1841) I. 125 On Thursday . . we had no scant of protestations; more than a round dozen were inacted. **1677** W. Hughes *Man of Sin* II. ii. 25, I will stint at Twelve. . . When the round Dozen is pay'd off, . . I mean no more than bare Interest thereby. **1711** *Country-Man's Let. to Curate* 4 This he pretends to make good by an enumeration of a round Dozen of our Reformers. **1748** *Anson's Voy.* II. ix. 227 This Manila ship, whose wealth . . we now estimated by round millions. *c* **1829** D. Jerrold in M. R. Booth *Eng. Plays of 19th Cent.* (1969) I. 175, I deserve a round dozen [*sc.* thirteen lashes] for the question. **1837** Hawthorne *Twice-told T.* (1851) I. xvi. 249 A round half dozen of pretty girls. **1867** Smyth *Sailor's Word-bk.* 581 *Round Dozen*, a punishment term for thirteen lashes. **1883** Stevenson *Treas. Isl.* xxi, There was a round score of muskets for the seven of us.

b. ***round number***, a number which is only approximately correct, usually one expressed in tens, hundreds, etc., without precise enumeration of units.

1646 Sir T. Browne *Pseud. Ep.* VI. i, Nor is it unreasonable to make some doubt whether . . Moses doth not sometime account by full and round numbers. **1649** Roberts *Clavis Bibl.* 57 It's usuall in Scripture to put the round number, for the punctual number. **1727** Newton *Chronol. Amended* (1728) i. 64 Appion . . tells in round numbers that Carthage stood seven hundred years. **1770** Langhorne *Plutarch* (1879) I. 491/2 It is common for historians to make use of a round number, except in cases where great precision is required. **1824** Jefferson *Writ.* (1830) IV. 389, I shall speak in round numbers, not absolutely accurate. **1858** Doran *Walpole's Last Jrnls.* I. 485 It is now, in round numbers, fifty-five millions. **1871** Earle *Philol. Eng. Tongue* (1880) §456 An abstract substantive which . . has a peculiar utility in expressing the more conventional quantities or Round numbers.

Comb. **1851** Mayhew *Lond. Labour* (1861) II. 526 This, still pursuing the round-number system, would supply nearly five articles of refuse apparel to every man.

fig. **1850** Thackeray *Pendennis* xlv, Such may be stated, in round numbers, to be the result of the information which Major Pendennis got. **1874** T. Hardy *Far fr. Mad. Crowd* x, Well, ma'am, in round numbers, she's run away with the soldiers.

c. Of computation, etc.: Approximately exact; roughly correct. *rare.*

In quot. 1746 perhaps = 'high', 'liberal'.

1631 Gouge *God's Arrows* II. §1. 131 He would in a round reckoning have beene said to have raigned one and forty yeares. **1746** *Acc. French Settlements N. Amer.* 18 In the year 1700, it was computed, that there were about five thousand able, effective men in Canada; . . some judicious people think it is a pretty round computation. **1831** Scott *Cast. Dang.* vii, 'I may form a round guess,' answered the stranger, 'what I might have to fear'.

8. a. Of a sum of money: Large, considerable in amount.

1579 *Nottingham Rec.* IV. 192 The londe lorde shall be bownde to . . the towne in a good round somme of money. **1599** Sandys *Europæ Spec.* (1632) 138 Their Annates and tenths doe still runne current . . : and amount no doubt unto a good round summe. **1613** Shaks. *Hen. VIII*, v. iv. 84 Ile lay ye all By th' heeles, . . and on your heads Clap round Fines for neglect. **1673** T. L. *Remarques Humours Town* 35 A round summ of ready money. **1711** Steele *Spect.* No. 41 ¶5 At length he was forced to the last Refuge, a round Sum of Money to her Maid. **1769** Blackstone *Comm.* IV. 218 It being usual in those courts to exchange their spiritual censures for a round compensation in money. **1817** Scott *Let.* in *Lockhart* (1837) IV. ii. 67 My sum is L.1700, payable in May—a round advance, by'r Lady. **1822** —— *Pirate* xxxiv, The burgh will be laid under a round fine. **1887** T. A. Trollope *What I remember* II. 21, I came home from my ramble with a good round sum in my pocket.

†b. So of quantities. *Obs. rare.*

1622 Malynes *Anc. Law-Merch.* 129 A Merchant in Spaine dealing for . . America, will buy a round quantitie of Germanie commodities or manufactures made there. **1659** Rushw. *Hist. Collect.* I. 464 To get in a good and round supply of Provision into the Citadel.

†c. Ample, generous. *Obs.*$^{-1}$

1592 Nashe *P. Penilesse* Wks. (Grosart) II. 64 If any Mecænas . . extend some round liberalitie to mee worth the speaking of.

9. a. Brought to a perfect finish or completeness; neatly turned or finished off.

a **1568** Ascham *Scholem.* II. (Arb.) 112 All his sentences be rownd and trimlie framed. **1616** B. Jonson *Epigr.* xcviii, He that is round within himselfe. **1660** Bp. Fell *Life Hammond* H.'s Wks. 1674 I. 23 His stile, though round and comprehensive, was incumbred sometimes by Parentheses. **1781** Cowper *Table-t.* 517 If sentiment were sacrific'd to sound, And truth cut short to make a period round. **1839–52** Bailey *Festus* 332 Ere yet he could . . foresee Life's round career accomplished in the skies. **1840** Carlyle *Heroes* iii. (1858) 263 It is truly a lordly spectacle how this great soul [*sc.* Shakspere] takes-in all kinds of men and objects, . . sets them forth to us in their round completeness.

†b. Thoroughly accomplished; carried out to a proper finish. *Obs. rare.*

1596 Nashe *Saffron Walden* 37 Wee might haue made round worke, and gone thorough stitch. **1625** Bacon *Ess.*, *Simulation & Diss.* (Arb.) 510 Simulation and Dissimulation commonly carry with them a Shew of Fearfulnesse, which in any Businesse doth spoile the Feathers of round flying vp to the Mark. **1665** in Strype *Eccl. Mem.* IV. 352 These instructions to make round work were backed with a commission to the justices to hear and punish.

c. Of the voice, sounds, etc.: Full and mellow; sonorous, full-sounding.

1832 L. Hunt *Poems* 201 The rounder murmur, fast and flush, Of the escaping gush. **1837** Dickens *Pickw.* xxviii, The merry old gentleman, in a good, round, sturdy voice, commenced [a song]. **1884** F. M. Crawford *Mr. Isaacs* ix, His voice . . was wonderfully smooth and round.

III. †10. a. Of blows, etc.: Heavy, hard, severe, swingeing. *Obs.*

Perh. originally = 'swinging': cf. sense 6.

c **1380** *Sir Ferumb.* 632 Helmes & hauberkes þay kutte a two, wiþ hure strokes rounde. *c* **1425** *Cast. Persev.* 2069 in *Macro Plays* 139 To rounde rappys ȝe rape, I rede! **1426** Lydg. *De Guil. Pilgr.* 16228 Hys Strokys wern so Fel and Rounde. **1586** J. Hooker *Hist. Irel.* in *Holinshed* II. 87/2 What a round fall he caught in his owne turne. *c* **1595** Capt. Wyatt *R. Dudley's Voy. W. Ind.* (Hakl. Soc.) 58 Wee had franklie bestowed upon her verie rownde and sownde vollies of shott. **1760–72** H. Brooke *Fool of Qual.* (1809) III. 20 She gave me a round cuff on the side of my head.

†b. Of fighting: Vigorous; general. *Obs.*

1601 Ld. Mountjoy in Moryson *Itin.* (1617) II. 156 The enemy one day . . began a round fight with us, close to our trenches. **1633** T. Stafford *Pac. Hib.* III. xiii. (1821) 368 Seeing them likely to draw on a round Skirmish. **1654** *Nicholas Papers* (Camden) II. 65 Lambert . . is for having a perfect league with Spaine and a round war with these Countries.

c. Of measures, etc.: Summary, vigorous; severe, harsh.

1617 *Fortescue Papers* (Camden) 21 If it will not be fitt that order be given for a speedye and rownde proceeding. **1670** Baxter *Cure Ch. Div.* Pref. 3 It is sharper and rounder dealing than all this, that must cure the Schismes in the Church. **1713** Arbuthnot *John Bull* II. xiii, A good round Whipping. *a* **1715** Burnet *Own Time* (1735) V. 147 The round proceeding of the Lord Godolphin reconciled many to him.

11. a. Of movement: Quick, brisk, smart. Chiefly in phr. ***a (good) round pace.***

1548 Patten *Exped. Scotl.* F vj, We cam on spedily a both sydes . . , but ye Scots indede wt a rounder pace. **1565** Cooper *Thesaurus*, *Citum agmen*, . . an armie marchyng a rownde pase. **1631** Massinger *Emperor East* III. ii, But, when we are entered, We shall on, a good round pace. **1710** *Lond. Gaz.* No. 4779/4 Trots all, and at a round Rate. **1771** Mackenzie *Man of Feeling* xiv, He walked a good round pace. **1806** A. Hunter *Culina* (ed. 3) 135 The same effect will scarcely be produced by four hours round trotting. **1859** Tennyson *Enid* 33 Round was their pace at first, but slacken'd soon. **1870** Peacock *Ralf Skirl.* II. 214 He . . proceeded on his way at a round trot.

†b. Of delivery: Fluent, easy. *Obs.*

1565 Cooper *Thesaurus*, *Volubilitas linguæ*, rounde or quicke speakyng, without impediment or staggerynge. **1573** Baret *Alv.* s.v., A man that hath a rounde and flowing vtterance. **1736** Ainsworth *Eng.-Lat. Dict.* s.v., To have a round delivery, *expedite loqui.*

†c. Of the tongue: Ready, prompt. *Obs.*

a **1568** Ascham *Scholem.* II. (Arb.) 115 Those that haue ye inuentiuest heades, for all purposes, and roundest tonges in all matters and places.

12. Plain, honest, straightforward.

1516 Bp. Fox *Rule of St. Benet* A ij b, We haue translated the sayde rule into oure moders tonge, commune, playne, rounde englisshe. **1579** E. K. *Ded. Spenser's Sheph. Cal.* §2 The speach . . is round without roughnesse. **1604** Shaks. *Oth.* I. iii. 90, I will a round vn-varnish'd Tale deliuer. **1625** Bacon *Ess.*, *Truth* (Arb.) 501 It will be acknowledged, . . that cleare and Round dealing, is the Honour of Mans Nature. **1628** Feltham *Resolves* (1647) 235 It is good to be just and plausible. A round heart will fasten friends, and linke men to thee in the chaines of love. *a* **1700** B. E. *Dict. Cant. Crew*, *Round-dealing*, Plain, Honest Dealing. [Hence in later Dicts.] **1814** Chalmers *Evid.* iii. 96 They deliver what they have to say in a round and unvarnished manner.

13. a. Of persons: Plain-spoken, not mincing matters, uncompromising, severe in speech (†or dealings) *with* another.

1524 *State Papers, Hen. VIII*, IV. 225 Onles ye see some likelihode that she woll falle to folowe the Kingis mynd, the sonner ye be round with her the better. **1539** Cromwell in Merriman *Life & Lett.* (1902) II. 177 The said bishop hath bene very playn and Rownde with Messieurs of the counseill there. **1579–80** North *Plutarch* (1612) 747 Upon land they [*sc.* pirates] found he [Cæsar] was very round with them, as also their iudge at Sea. **1607** Shaks. *Timon* II. ii. 8 He will not heare, till feele: I must be round with him. *a* **1639** W. Whateley *Prototypes* II. xxvi. (1640) 33 He is plaine and duly round with him; a plaine laying open of the fault of the offendor, is necessary to bring him to the sight of his fault. **1867** TROLLOPE *Chron. Barset* II. lvii. 135 Must he not be round with her, and give her to understand in plain words? **1869** —— *He knew*, etc. ii, We all know what a husband means when he resolves to be round with his wife.

b. Similarly without const. Somewhat *rare*.

1565 T. STAPLETON *Fortr. Faith* 112* S. Augustin vehement and rounde as you see, after his maner. **1633** EARL MANCH. *Al Mondo* (1636) 50 A man may be mannerly in the form, but must be round in the matter. *a* **1649** WINTHROP *New Eng.* (1853) I. 99 The deputy began to be in passion, and told the governour that, if he were so round, he would be round too.

c. Of speech, esp. reproof or chiding.

c **1425** WYNTOUN *Cron.* IX. xviii. 1763 The Erle maid ansuere rownd, He walde nocht for a thowsand pownd. **1570** *Henry's Wallace* XI. 1362 For all thi round reheirs Thow has na charge. **1599** SHAKS. *Hen. V*, IV. i. 216 Your reproofe is something too round. **1641** MILTON *Animadv.* Wks. 1851 III. 230 To deale by sweet.. instructions, gentle admonitions, and sometimes rounder reproofs. **1655** *Nicholas Papers* (Camden) II. 234 Card[inal] Mazarine writ a round and peremptory lettre to Monsr de Bourdeaux to conclude ye peace or come away. **1749** FIELDING *Tom Jones* VIII. iv, Gave her servants a round scold. **1809** W. IRVING *Knickerb.* VII. ix. (1849) 428 A memorial addressed to the governor, remonstrating in good round terms on his conduct. **1864** M. EYRE *Lady's Walks S. France* v. (1865) 55 She tells you home truths in the roundest manner.

14. a. Of lies or oaths: Bold, arrant, downright; not toned down in any way.

1645 *Liberty of Conscience* 28 Yet Hushai made a round lie. *a* **1714** SHARP *Serm.* Wks. 1754 IV. 309 Either a round oath, or a curse, or the corruption of one. **1843** DICKENS *Mart. Chuz.* xlii, To swear a few round oaths. **1874** *Slang Dict.* 272 *Round un*, an unblushingly given and well-proportioned lie.

†**b.** Gross, heinous. *Obs. rare*.

1638 MEDE *Wks.* (1672) 311 If thou makest not thy mouth a glorious organ,.. thou art a deep and a round offender.

c. Of assertions, etc.: Positive, unqualified.

1737 *Gentl. Mag.* VII. 494/2 This B. J. is a round Asserter when he said [etc.]. *a* **1814** BURNEY in *Boswell's Johnson* (Globe) an. 1780 *note*, This assertion concerning Johnson's insensibility to the pathetic powers of Otway is too round. **1822** SCOTT *Peveril* xxi, Julian made no answer whatever to this round intimation.

IV. 15. a. In special collocations: **round-back**, a person having a rounded back; **round ball**, (*a*) a kind of musical instrument for beating; (*b*) a particular form of ball-game; also *spec.* an early alternative name for BASE-BALL; **round barrow** *Archæol.*, a Bronze Age burial mound of circular form; **round bilge**, a curved, as distinct from an angular or stepped, hull; also *attrib.*; hence **round-bilged** *a.*; **round bolt**, a forelock bolt; **round bone** (see quots.); **round cap**, one who wears a round cap; †an undergraduate of Cambridge; **round cell** *Path.*, used *attrib.* = next; **round-celled** *a. Path.*, (of a neoplasm) characterized by round, undifferentiated cells; **round coal**, coal from which the small has been separated; large or 'lumpy' coal; **round corn** (see quot.); **round dropstone**, = DROPSTONE; **roundeye** *slang*, a European, as distinguished from a *slant-eye* (SLANT *a.* 3); **round frock** (see quot. 1875); hence ***round-frocked*** adj.; **round game**, any game, esp. at cards, in which each of a number of persons plays on his own account; **round haddock** (see quot.); †**round hale** (see quot. and HALE *sb.*^{5} 1); **round heels** chiefly *U.S.*, rounded heels that allow the wearer to rock backwards easily; usu. *transf.* and *fig.* (*slang*) implying the inability to remain upright, as in an incompetent boxer or sexually compliant woman; hence **round-heeled** *a.*; **round-heeler**; **round iron**, a bulbous soldering iron; **round log** *U.S.*, a log that has been felled but not hewn; also *attrib.*; †**round-long** *a.*, oblong; **round lot** *U.S.*, a unit of trade (see quot. 1962); **round meal**, coarse oatmeal; **round O**, (*a*) a 'round' lie; (*b*) a circle or number *of* persons; (*c*) *Cricket* (see quot.); †**round peal** (see quot.); **round-ridging**, ploughing in rounded ridges; †**round ringing** (see quot.); †**round salad** (?); **round seam, seizing, sewing, splice, stern** (see quots.); **round text**, large round-hand; **round tilth** (see quots.); **round timber** *U.S.*, timber that has been felled but not hewn; also *transf.*; †**round tire**, some part or form of woman's head-dress; **round tool** (see quot.); **round towel**, one which has the two ends sewed together; **round tower**, *Archæol.*, one of a number of high circular towers, somewhat tapering from the base to a conical roof-crowned top, which are found in certain countries, esp. Ireland; **round trade** (see quot.); **round turn, work** (see quots.); also in colloq. (orig. *Naut.*) phr. ***to bring* (*fetch*) *up with a round turn***, to check or stop suddenly; **round wood**, (*a*) = *round timber*; (*b*) short logs of small diameter from the tops of pine and spruce trees, used for box-making.

1605 BEN JONSON *Volpone* v. i, But your clarissimo, old *round-back, he will crump you like a hog-louse, with the touch. **1688** HOLME *Armoury* III. xvi. (Roxb.) 55/2 The third sort consists in striking, as Tabor, Timbrell,.. Bell, Cymball, *Round Ball, Jews Harp. **1834** R. CARVER *Bk. of Sports*, This game is known under a variety of names. It is sometimes called 'round ball', but I believe that 'base', or 'goal ball' are the names generally adopted in our country. **1856** *Porter's Spirit of Times* 27 Dec. 276/3, I have thought .. a statement of my experience as to the Yankee method of playing 'Base', or 'Round' ball, as we used to call it, may not prove uninteresting. **1871** CUTTING *Student Life Amherst* 112 'Wicket' and 'Round Ball' were quite common once, though of late years, 'Base Ball' has entirely superseded them. **1869** J. THURNAM in *Archaeologia* XLII. 168, I propose to classify the barrows of this part of England according to the following scheme:.. I. Long Barrows. (*Stone period*)... II. *Round Barrows. (*Bronze period*). *Ibid.*, In none of the.. long barrows.. have objects of metal .. been found... In the.. round barrows, not only are there objects of stone, but.. chiefly, those of bronze, and.. iron... They may be regarded.. as belonging to the Bronze period. **1926** M. C. BURKITT *Our Early Ancestors* vi. 151 In England we have.. passage graves (generally called 'Long Barrows' ..) in many places.., and stone kists (generally called Round Barrows from the circular shape of the tumuli). **1975** J. G. EVANS *Environment Early Man Brit. Isles* vi. 130 Two Bronze Age round barrows known as the Burton Howes. **1980** *Encounter* May 59/1 Long barrows and causewayed camps signal the territories of the early and middle Neolithic groupings, with the henges and round barrow cemeteries appearing in the late Neolithic/early Bronze Age. **1951**, **1961** *Round bilge [see *hard chine* s.v. HARD *a.* (*sb.*) 22]. **1977** *Austral. Sailing* Jan. 38/2 The round-bilged 'mouldie' hull has virtually disappeared. **1703** R. NEVE *City & C. Purchaser* 33 *Round-bolts (or long Iron-pins) with a Head at one end, and a Key-hole at the other. **1831** YOUATT *Horse* 262 The joint of the upper bone of the thigh with the haunch is commonly called the whirl or *round bone. **1856** STONEHENGE *Brit. Rur. Sports* 673/2 Round-Bone Disease is not uncommon... When the horse is lame behind,.. the farrier [often] fixes upon the round-bone as the seat of the mischief. **1719** *Freethinker* No. 153 Many a Damsel, who has marry'd a *Round-Cap, has dearly repented of her Bargain... An Undergraduate should no more be allowed to venture upon Wedlock, than an Apprentice. **1889** *Round cell [see sense 17]. **1961** R. D. BAKER *Essent. Path.* xix. 533 Malignant tumors of the thymus may arise from epithelial structures (carcinoma) or from a fibrous component (fibrosarcoma) but are perhaps most often round-cell tumors and presumably lymphomas. **1873** T. H. GREEN *Introd. Pathol.* (ed. 2) 120 A small *round-celled sarcoma of the liver. **1907** J. H. PARSONS *Dis. Eye* xxix. 605 Sarcoma is rare; it may be round or spindle-celled, pigmented or non-pigmented. **1961** R. D. BAKER *Essent. Path.* xiii. 302 The undifferentiated sarcomas must be classified according to how they look microscopically, and may be described as spindle-celled or round-celled. **1706** J. C. *Compl. Collier* (1845) 38 If the Coals be Hewed or Wrought pretty *Round and Large Coals. **1764** *Museum Rust.* III. xx. 84 The common custom, of calling large coals *round coals*. **1883** GRESLEY *Gloss. Coal-m.* 207 *Round Coal*, coal in large lumps, either hand-picked or after passing over screens to take out the small. **1889** *Cent. Dict.* s.v. *Corn*, **Round corn*, a trade-name for the grain of a class of yellow maize with small, round, very hard kernels. **1668** CHARLETON *Onomast.* 252 *Stalagmites*,.. *Round Dropstone. **1967** *Guardian* 16 Aug. 6/5 Many Europeans have been assaulted simply because they were '*roundeyes'. **1977** 'J. LE CARRÉ' *Hon. Schoolboy* vi. 125 In the East a roundeye could live all his life in the same block and never have the smallest notion of the secret tic-tac on his doorstep. **1797** *Sporting Mag.* X. 98 Members of the Agriculturean Club, or *Round-Frock Society. **1875** PARISH *Sussex Dial.*, *Round-frock*, a loose frock or upper garment of coarse material, generally worn by country-people over their other clothes. **1809** W. STEVENSON *Agric. Survey* 88 The '*round-frocked farmers' (for they pride themselves on frequenting the markets in the dress of their forefathers). **1790** SCOTT in *Lockhart* (1837) I. vi. 169 At night [we] laugh, chat, and play *round games at cards. **1838** DICKENS *Nickleby* i, Speculation is a round game; the players see little or nothing of their cards at first starting. **1883** LD. R. GOWER *Reminisc.* I. 122 What splendid round games we used to play in the evenings! **1883** *19th Cent.* July 162 The fish intended for the table are not eviscerated, hence they are called '*round' haddocks to distinguish them from the others which are called 'kit' haddocks. **1607** J. CARPENTER *Pl. Mans Plough* 209 The *Round-Hale is the plaining and polishing of the carnall mans actions. **1957** J. KERR *Please don't eat Daisies* 118, I know I'm just a broad, Mike. I'm a *round-heeled babe. **1975** 'R. ROSTAND' *D'Artagnan Signature* (1976) xiv. 83 You said that as if I'm some round-heeled little chippie who dragged you to the floor. **1927** *Vanity Fair* (N.Y.) Nov. 67/2 Others contend that 'a *round-heeler' was applied to street-walkers many years ago. **1926** ABBOTT & WEAVER *Love 'em & leave 'Em* III. 109 You want people to say you got *round heels. Why don't you go on the streets and be done with it? **1926** *Variety* 29 Dec. 7/4 A push-over, which means a fighter with round heels along cauliflower alley, was, by the same token, a dame on rockers. **1929** E. WILSON *I thought of Daisy* i. 16 Myra Busch is a push-over!.. She's got round heels! **1944** R. CHANDLER *Lady in Lake* v. 35 You'd think.. I'd.. pick me a change in types at least. But little roundheels over there ain't even that. **1963** 'G. BAGBY' *Murder's Little Helper* (1964) viii. 84 Little Miss Roundheels.. specialized in gentlemen who were otherwise committed. **1975** P. DE VRIES *Glory of Humming Bird* xiii. 192 Her famous round heels did not seem to rule out a stern morality on other counts. **1875** KNIGHT *Dict. Mech.* 2242/1 Plumbing and Soldering Tools. ..*d*, *round iron. **1869** S. HAYCRAFT *Hist. Elizabethtown, Kentucky* (1921) ii. 15 In the winter time they met in the *round log cabins with dirt floors. **1871** E. EGGLESTON *Hoosier Schoolmaster* 95 He came upon a queer little cabin built of round logs. **1884** 'MARK TWAIN' *Huck. Finn* xxxii. 329 Phelps's was one of these little one-horse cotton plantations.. round-log kitchen. **1668** CULPEPPER & COLE *Barthol. Anat.* I. xviii. 49 Their shape is *round-long and somwhat square. **1942** *Sun* (Baltimore) 27 Feb. 17/5 The rates charged by brokers for '*round lots' (units of 100 shares) range from 3 cents a share.. to 13 cents. **1962** S. STRAND *Marketing Dict.* 638 *Round lot*, a trading unit. 1) On the New York Stock Exchange, 100 shares. 2) On the Chicago Board of Trade, 5000 bushels. *a* **1843** SOUTHEY *Doctor* Interch. xxiv. (1847) VII. 79 It was *round Meal. **1844** H. STEPHENS *Bk. Farm* II. 365 There is no doubt that the round meal makes the best porridge when properly made. **1605** *London Prodigal* III. ii, My maisters mind is bloody, thats a *round O (*aside*), And therefore, syr, intreatie is but vaine. **1845** *Athenæum* Feb. 110 The playhouse additions and omissions were all very well for the round O of admirers who went to see and hear. **1863** C. READE *Hard Cash* vii, Alfred told her 'the round O', which had yielded to 'the duck's-egg', and was becoming obsolete, meant the cipher set by the scorer against a player's name, who is out without making a run. **1688** R. HOLME *Armoury* III. 462/2 A *Round Peale, is to ring the Bells what space of [time] the Ringers please. **1786** *Young's Ann. Agriculture* V. 107 We reject up-setting, which is here called *round-ridging..; and we plough the land flat. **1688** R. HOLME *Armoury* III. 462/2 *Round Ringing, when the Bells are up at set, that is with their mouths upright, both in the Fore stroak and Back stroak. **1578** LYTE *Dodoens* 422 They do mingle it amongst other herbes, in *rounde salades, and Iunkettes with egges. **1626** CAPT. SMITH *Accid. Yng. Seamen* 17 Twyne, a munke seame, a *round seame, a suit of sayles. **1839** URE *Dict. Arts* 598 What is called round-seam sewing.., which permits the leather to expand but in one direction, when the needle is passed through it, namely, upwards. **1867** SMYTH *Sailor's Word-bk.* 581 *Round-Seam*, the edges or selvedges sowed together, without lapping. **1841** R. H. DANA *Seaman's Man.* 8 Seizing the parts together with a *round seizing. **1867** SMYTH *Sailor's Word-bk.* 581 *Round Seizing*, this is made by a series of turns, with the end passed through the riders, and made fast snugly. **1879** *Encycl. Brit.* X. 692 *Round sewing or ordinary glove stitch, piqué stitch, and prick seam. **1753** *Chambers' Cycl.* Suppl. s.v. *Splice*, **Round-Splice*, is when a rope's end is so let into another, that they shall be as firm as if they were but one rope. **1867** SMYTH *Sailor's Word-bk.* 582 *Round Splice*, one which hardly shows itself, from the neatness of the rope and the skill of the splicer. *c* **1850** *Rudim. Nav.* (Weale) 143 **Round stern*, the stern of a vessel whose bottom, wales, &c. are wrought quite aft, and unite in the stern-post. **1766** SERLE *Art Writing* 6 The large *Round Text.. cannot be considered as a distinct Hand. **1849** LYTTON *Caxtons* 22 Designed for the less ambitious purposes of round text and multiplication. **1763** *Museum Rust.* I. 112 They keep their lands constantly cropped without fallow, which they call sowing a *round-tilth. **1796** BOYS *Agric. Kent* (1813) 73 The .. rich sandy loam.. cultivated under the round tilth system of East Kent, viz. Beans, Wheat, Barley. **1874** J. F. RUSLING *Across Amer.* xxvii. 429 Snow galleries consumed in all nearly forty-five million feet, board measure, of sawed timber, and over a million and a quarter feet of *round timber. **1905** *Bull. Bureau of Forestry* (U.S.) No. 61. 45 *Round timber*, pine trees which have not been turpentined. **1964** *Times Rev. Industry* Mar. 56/1 The firm has arranged with Boys and Boden to reopen the sawmill section of British Sawmills at Welshpool from March 1 for the conversion of round timber. **1972** *Gloss. Terms Timber* (*B.S.I.*) 8 *Round timber*, felled trees, logs or poles. **1657** REEVE *God's Plea* 123 How much girdles, gorgets,.. slippers, *roundtires, sweetballs, rings,.. do cost in our daies, many a sighing husband doth know by the years account. **1875** KNIGHT *Dict. Mech.*, **Round-tool*, a round-nose chisel.. for making concave moldings. **1845** *Ainsworth's Mag.* VIII. 71, I at last became quite tired of him and his string of repetitions, or *round towel speaking. **1896** *Allbutt's Syst. Med.* I. 452 A pulley is firmly fastened to the foot of the bed (an ordinary round towel is a useful one). **1908** G. JEKYLL *Children & Gardens* ii. 12 If it can have a small pantry containing a water supply and a sink,.. and a round towel handy, it will be better than if these necessaries were in the kitchen itself. **1827** G. HIGGINS *Celtic Druids* Pref. p. xlvi, Throughout Scotland and Ireland there are scattered great numbers of *Round Towers. *a* **1878** SIR G. SCOTT *Lect. Archit.* (1879) II. 14 The Early Irish remains are mainly of three classes: the.. domestic buildings of the monks; the oratories and churches; and the round towers. **1858** SIMMONDS *Dict. Trade*, **Round-trade*, a term on the river Gaboon and neighbourhood for a description of barter, comprising a large assortment of miscellaneous articles. **1841** R. H. DANA *Seaman's Man.* 53 Haul well out, and take a *round-turn with the earing round the cringle. **1846** A. YOUNG *Naut. Dict.* s.v., To take a round turn of a rope, means to pass it completely round any thing in order to hold on. **1867** SMYTH *Sailor's Word-bk.* 582 *Round-Turn in the Hawse*, a term implying the situation of the two cables of a ship, which, when moored, has swung the wrong way three times successively; if after this she come round till her head is directed the same way as at first, this makes a round turn and elbow. *a* **1910** in *Amer. Speech* (1979) LIV. 99 *Round turn*, ..'fetched up with a round turn'. Suddenly. **1920** GALSWORTHY *In Chancery* II. vi. 175 The end came swiftly on the 20th of January with a telegram... It brought him up with a round turn. **1961** F. H. BURGESS *Dict. Sailing* 174 *Round turn, Bring up with a*, stop someone or something abruptly. **1910** *Timber Trades Jrnl.* 8 Jan. 37/1 The wood shipped from Archangel is the now well-known *roundwood. **1930** *Aberdeen Press & Jrnl.* 3 Apr. 8 So far as the 'round wood' or 'pulp wood' is concerned, most of the Aberdeen contracts for the season are now fixed-up. **1971** *Country Life* 25 Nov. 1450/1 The cash value.. from the sales of roundwood and timber.. in East Anglia. **1750** W. ELLIS *Mod. Husbandm.* I. 16 This we call *round work, because the ploughman begins in the middle of so much ground as he intends for one broad-land.

b. In names of plants, etc.: **round Adam's apple** (see ADAM'S APPLE 1); **round aristolochia, birthwort**, = *round heartwort*; **round dock**, †(*a*) monk's rhubarb; (*b*) *dial.*, the common mallow (by error for *round hock*); **round edder** (see EDDER *sb.*); **round heartwort**, a variety of birthwort (*Aristolochia rotunda*), having round roots; **round radish**, the common radish; **round rape, round turnip**, the common turnip.

1729 *Dampier's Voy.* III. 444 *Round Adam's Apple. Its Flowers five leaved with Purple Veins; the Fruit round. **1548** TURNER *Names Herbes* (E.D.S.) 15 Aristolochia is of three sortes. The fyrst.. may be named in englishe *round .. astrolochia or round hertworte. **1728** CHAMBERS *Cycl.* s.v. *Aristolochia*, The round [aristolochia] is of a sub-acrid.. Taste. **1551** TURNER *Herbal* (1568) 43 *Aristolochia rotunda* ..may be called in Englyshe..*round byrthwurte. **1725**

Fam. Dict. s.v. *Wounds*, Aloes, Round Birthwort. **1712** tr. *Pomet's Hist. Drugs* I. 27 The great, common *round Dock, which many People cultivate. **1825** JENNINGS *Dial. W. Eng.* 64 The round-dock leaves are used at this day as a remedy ..for the sting of a nettle. **1729** DAMPIER *Voy.* III. 449 *Round Edder. Has a round cordated milky Leaf. **1548** *round hertworte [see *round aristolochia*]. **1580** BLUNDEVIL *Horsem.* v. 5 b, Take of.. round Hartwood, one ounce. **1611** COTGR., *Rave ronde*,.. the *round Raddish. **1562** TURNER *Herbal* II. 113 The great *round rape called commonly a turnepe. **1578** LYTE *Dodoens* 593 The round Rape or turnep at the beginning hath great rough brode leaues. **1731** MILLER *Gard. Dict.* s.v. *Rapa*, *Round Garden Turnip, with a white Root.

c. In names of fishes, etc., as **round fish**, fish of a rounded (as opposed to flat) form; **round-fish**: (*a*) the pilot-fish, *Coregonus quadrilateralis*; (*b*) the common carp; **round herring, landcrab, -mouth, -oyster, tail** (see quots. and sbs.).

1630 R. JOHNSON *Kingd. & Commonw.* 124 Upon the coast of Bretaigne, where it is muddy, store of *round fish, as Lamprey, Conger, Haddocke. **1895** *Daily News* 25 Nov. 5/3 The immature fishes caught by line are almost entirely round fishes, such as haddock and cod. **1836** SIR J. RICHARDSON *Fauna Bor. Amer.* III. 204 Our voyagers named it the *round-fish, and I have given it the specific appellation of *quadrilateralis*. **1882** JORDAN & GILBERT *Synop. Fishes North America* 298 C[*oregonus*] *quadrilateralis*, ..Pilot-fish;..Shad Waiter, Round-fish. *Ibid.* 263 *Etrumeus*... *Round Herrings. **1729** DAMPIER *Voy.* III. 419 The *Round Land-Crab. Runs Side-ways and Swiftly. **1886** *Athenæum* May 618/3 The *round-mouths, such as the lamprey, which differ from all other vertebrates in the constitution of their mouth. **1681** GREW *Musæum* I. vi. ii. 144 The *Round-Oyster with similar sides produced from an oblique Navle. **1836** YARRELL *Brit. Fishes* II. 32 The posterior edge [of the tail] becomes convex;..which has caused this fish [bull-trout] to be designated in the Annan by the name of *Roundtail when old, and Sea-Trout when young. **1832** J. RENNIE *Consp. Butterfl. & M.* 159 The *Round tip (*Ditula rotundana*..). Wings six lines, very bluntly rounded, smoke-coloured. *Ibid.* 114 The *Round Wing (*Cabera rotundaria*..); wings one inch one-twelfth to one-fourth, snow-white, rounded.

16. a. Parasynthetic combs., as ***round-backed, -barred, -barrelled, -bellied, -bodied, -bottomed, -browed, -budded, -celled, -cheeked, -cornered, -edged, -ended, -eyed, -footed, -hatted, -hoofed, -lipped, -necked, -paned, -pollened, -soled, -spectacled, -sterned, -walled***, etc.; also ***round-looking, -made, -shapen***; ROUND-ARCHED, -EARED, etc.

1844 H. STEPHENS *Bk. Farm* II. 403 If the field has a *round-backed form, the dunghill should be placed on the top of the height. **1923** D. H. LAWRENCE *Birds, Beasts & Flowers* 143 The upstart of your *round-barred, sun-round tail! **1682** *Lond. Gaz.* No. 1768/4 A white grey Roan Gelding,..*round barrel'd, full gascoign'd. **1828** SCOTT *F.M. Perth* viii, A strong black horse,..strong limbed, well-coupled, and round-barrelled. **1611** COTGR., *Matrac*, a.. wide, *round-bellied bottle. **1738** CHAMBERS *Cycl.*, *Retort*, ..a round-bellied vessel, either of earth or glass. **1756** NUGENT *Gr. Tour, Germany* II. 323 Large, round-bellied vessels of great burthen. **1919** J. MASEFIELD *Reynard the Fox* 9 Round-bellied like a drinking-cup. **1963** R. P. DALES *Annelids* ii. 42 *Sternapsis* is a small, *round-bodied burrower in which the septa have mostly broken down. **1826** KIRBY & SP. *Entomol.* III. xxix. 93 The *round-bottomed phial sometimes used by chemists. **1909** B. LUBBOCK *Deep Sea Warriors* 37 Three men came...each shouldering a 'round-bottomed chest', as the sailor's bag is called. **1964** V. J. CHAPMAN *Coastal Veg.* iii. 73 Round-bottomed flasks are completely filled with sea water. **1921** *Round-browed [see *firm-lipped* s.v. FIRM *a.* C. 1 b]. **1925** W. DE LA MARE *Two Tales* 95 Minute plants, their round-budded clusters showing. **1605** MARSTON *Dutch Courtezan* I. i. sig. B 1, A softe plumpe *round cheekt froe. **1871** GEO. ELIOT *Let.* 17 June (1956) V. 153, I hope she will be round-cheeked and strong. **1704** *Dict. Rust.* (1726) s.v. *Mallows*, Great white Roots, from whence arise *round-corner'd Leaves. **1967** KARCH & BUBER *Offset Processes* xii. 503 Round-cornered cards are usually purchased already round-cornered, die cut and absolutely rectangular. **1843** HOLTZAPFFEL *Turning* I. 228 A piece of flat iron..is thinned..by..a *round-edged fuller. **1951** WHITBY & HYNES *Med. Bacteriol.* (ed. 5) xx. 314 The *Clostridia* in their most typical form are straight or slightly curved *round-ended bacilli 0·4μ–1·2μ × 3μ–8μ. **1960** *Farmer & Stockbreeder* 2 Feb. (Suppl.) 8/3 Square or round-ended sticks are also useful..in building up a design. **1848** DICKENS *Dombey* xxiii, Rob the *round-eyed..looked on and listened. **1923** D. H. LAWRENCE *Birds, Beasts & Flowers* 160 Yellow eyes incomprehensible with thin slits To round-eyed us. **14..** in *Harrow. Hell* Introd. 25 After the asse, well-mouthid, well-wyndyd,..and *rownd-foted. **1962** *Times* 21 Dec. 10/7 A *round-hatted drummer. **1593** SHAKS. *Ven. & Ad.* l, *Round-hoofed, short-jointed, fetlocks shag and long,..Look, what a horse should have, he did not lack. **1672** JOSSELYN *New. Eng. Rarities* 20 The *Maccarib*,..a kind of Deer, as big as a Stag, round hooved. **1898** R. BRIDGES *Prometh.* Wks. I. 50 Round-hoofed or such as tread with cloven foot? **1866** GEO. ELIOT *F. Holt* (1868) 19 The little *round-limbed creature that had been leaning against her knees. **1906** HARDY *Dynasts* II. IV. i. 230 The Archduchess, a fair, blue-eyed, full-figured, *round-lipped maiden. **1958** S. SPENDER *Fool & Princess* 161 *Round-looking lips. **1820** SCOTT *Abbot* xx, The falconer..mounted his stout, *round-made, trotting nag. **1776** DA COSTA *Elem. Conchol.* 222 Both the *round-mouthed [shells] and these. **1962** L. DEIGHTON *Ipcress File* xxxi. 198 Jean wore a new *round-necked, sleeveless..dress in tangerine linen. **1974** *Country Life* 17 Jan. 107/1 A round-necked, sleeveless top. **1661** R. W. *Conf. Charac.* (1860) 37 The byasse of all his wooden headed *roundnodled associates. **1937** DE LA MARE & JONES *This Year, Next Year* 39/1 Through its *round-paned window. **1704** *Dict. Rust.* (1726) s.v. *Ranunculus*, *Round-pointed Leaves, of a pale, yellow blush on the inside. **1825** J. NICHOLSON *Operat. Mechanic* 330 Driving a round-pointed bar into a sort of loam. **1909** W. BATESON *Mendel's Princ. Heredity* I. v. 93 It was..more usual to find whites exclusively produced by the cross of two extracted F_2 whites, long-pollened and *round-pollened respectively. **1852** MUNDY *Antipodes* (1857) 195 Many of these..were mounted on rough, *round-ribbed cart mares. **1874** J. W. LONG *Amer. Wild-fowl* v. 94 By well-bred I..mean..a long, ..round-ribbed, and broad loined dog. *c* **1400** MAUNDEV. (Roxb.) xxii. 100 þaire mouthes er *round schapen, lyke a hors scho. **1523** FITZHERB. *Husb.* §77 The .ix. propertyes of a foxe. The..thyrde, to be *rounde-syded. **1862** 'VANDERDECKEN' *Yacht Sailor* 143 A beamy, round-sided vessel. **1690** *Lond. Gaz.* No. 2579/4 A *round-skirted Saddle stitch'd with Silver. **1964** W. L. GOODMAN *Hist. Woodworking Tools* 73 It is a *round-soled plane, 14in. long, with a type (b) mouth carving enclosing the date 1706. **1945** W. DE LA MARE *Burning-Glass* 53 *Round-spectacled Chardin's Passion for life. **1897** J. L. ALLEN *Choir Invisible* xiii. 195 Where some *round-sterned packet from New England or New Amsterdam was unloading its cargo. **1861** WHYTE MELVILLE *Mkt. Harb.* 81 The person's boots..were neat, *round-toed Wellingtons. **1866** STEPHENS *Runic Mon.* I. 305 Bone Combs,..more or less *roundtopt. **1892** E. REEVES *Homeward Bound* 12 The hills around Auckland.. are nearly all round-topped. **1683** *Lond. Gaz.* No. 1837/4 He is a *round trussed Man. **1677** *Ibid.* No. 1208/4 Of a low stature, *round visaged. **1931** G. O. RUSSELL *Speech & Voice* 67 A..*round-walled organ pipe. **1605** SHAKS. *Lear* I. i. 14 She grew *round womb'd, and had..a Sonne for her Cradle.

b. In generic or specific names of animals, birds, etc., as ***round-billed, -bodied, -crested, -furrowed, -horned, -lipped, -mouthed, -tailed, -toed, -winged***.

1688 *Phil. Trans.* XVII. 990 These Birds more than any other *Round-bill'd Birds seem to grope for their Meat in Cow-dung. **1774** GOLDSM. *Nat. Hist.* (1824) II. 408 One species of round-billed water fowl. **1752** J. HILL *Hist. Anim.* 16 *Tænia teres*, the *round-bodied Tænia: it is common in the mud of ponds and ditches. **1748** CATESBY *Nat. Hist.* (1754) 94 The *round-crested Duck... The head is crowned with a very large circular crest. **1783** LATHAM *Gen. Synop. Birds* II. I. 362 Round-crested Flycatcher: the crown of the head is furnished with a remarkable rounded crest. **1681** GREW *Musæum* 142 The *Round Furrow'd Escallop, with smooth Shells or Valves. **1782** JEFFERSON *Notes Virginia* (1787) 88 The flat-horned elk, or original. The *round-horned elk. **1776** PENNANT *Brit. Zool.* III. 52 **Roundlipped* [*whale*]. The character of this species is to have the lower lip broader than the upper, and of a semi-circular form. **1801** SHAW *Gen. Zool.* II. II. 495 Under-jawed Mysticete... Round-lipped Whale. **1945** STEP & WELLS *Shell Life* 228 Such a form as *Littorina rudis* ..was probably the ancestor of the *Round-mouthed Snail (*Cyclostoma elegans*), which is clearly a marine snail that has been so modified that it lives far inland on the dry chalk-downs. **1766** *Complete Farmer* s.v. *Insect* X. 3/2 Those *round-tailed worms, which are found in the intestines of men, horses, &c. **1781** PENNANT *Hist. Quadrup.* II. 540 Manati, Round-tailed. **1804** SHAW *Gen. Zool.* V. I. 228 Round-tailed Chub. **1752** HILL *Hist. Anim.* 112 The *round-toed Rana, with the body narrow behind. **1907** R. SOUTH *Moths Brit. Isles* 1st Ser. 175 (*heading*) The *round-winged muslin. **1908** *Ibid.* 2nd Ser. 257 In most of such aberrations the tips of the fore wings are rather more rounded than in typical specimens, and these are referable to ab. *rotundaria*, Haworth (Round-winged Wave).

c. In names of plants, etc., as ***round-fruited, -podded, -rooted, -seeded***. Also ROUND-LEAVED.

1855 MISS PRATT *Flower. Pl.* V. 296 **Round-fruited Rush*. Stem erect,..capsule roundish. **1725** *Fam. Dict.* s.v. *Blowing*, The *Round-Podded of Carnations..will begin to crack their Husks on one side. **1611** COTGR., *Pied-poul*, the *round-rooted, or Onion-rooted Crowfoot. **1731** MILLER *Gard. Dict.* s.v. *Raphanus*, The small round-rooted Radish is not very common in England. *Ibid.* s.v. *Aristolochia*, The round-rooted Birthwort. **1729** *Dampier's Voy.* III. 442 The *Round seeded Sensible. **1970** *Daily Tel.* 10 Jan. 7/3 Round-seeded peas lack the flavour of the wrinkled varieties.

17. In comb. with nouns used *attrib.*

1591 SYLVESTER *Du Bartas* I. v. 666 Where She..may rear Her round-Front Palace in a place secure. **1688** HOLME *Armoury* III. 358/2 The fourth [sort of turner's tool] is termed a round edge Grooving Hook. **1728** CHAMBERS *Cycl.* s.v. *Nails, Round-head Nails*, proper to fasten in Hinges. **1815** J. SMITH *Panorama Sci. & Art* I. 111 One which is convex, is sometimes called a roundsole [plane]. **1851–3** *Tomlinson's Cycl. Arts & Manuf.* (1866) I. 642/1 Round edge equalling file, and round-edge joint file. **1856** Round-bend [see LIMERICK 2 b]. **1875** KNIGHT *Dict. Mech.* 1995/1 *Round-joint File*, a kind of clockmaker's file. *Ibid.*, Round-nose chisel, Round-nose plane. **1889** D. J. HAMILTON *Text-bk. Path.* I. 363 The large round-cell sarcoma. **1895** *Model Steam Eng.* 90 It is..'roughed down' with a round-end tool to the required form. **1936** J. STEINBECK *In Dubious Battle* iv. 64 A roundwick Rochester lamp. **1940** E. MOLLOY *Electric Wiring* vi. 156 The British Standard Specification for domestic plugs and sockets is confined to the round-pin type. **1941** H. I. CHAPELLE *Boatbuilding* 44 The round-bottom model is considered by most amateur builders too difficult to construct. **1946** *Fortune* Apr. 142/1 [He] obviously doesn't want the job or he wouldn't have put in any round-figure bid that size. **1956** 'J. WYNDHAM' *Seeds of Time* 231 The doctor's round-figure price made him frown. **1967** KARCH & BUBER *Offset Processes* xii. 504 Perforating machines allow round-hole perforating, like that found on postage stamps and grocery store stamps. **1968** J. ARNOLD *Shell Bk. Country Crafts* 160 Later wagons, built after 1850 or so, had round-section ironwork. **1970** *Which?* Sept. 280/2 We have criticised this plug before since it will fit into a 5-amp round-pin socket which leaves the appliance unearthed. **1976** *Woman's Day* (U.S.) Nov. 158 Following construction detail, assemble legs and stretcher with 3" roundhead stove bolts and nuts. **1979** *Nature* 7 June 537/1 (*caption*) The 5-doxylstearic acid..was dried down from chloroform/methanol (2:1 v/v) solution in a round-bottom flask. **1979** *Jrnl. R. Soc. Arts* Nov. 746/1 The round-hole capsules resemble round-hole tea ceremony rooms.

round (raʊnd), *adv.* and *prep.* [f. ROUND *a.* or *sb.*[1] In early use perh. for *around*, after F. *en rond, au rond*.]

In both adv. and prep. the strengthened forms *all round, right round, round and round*, are common.

A. *adv.* (For idiomatic uses with *bring, come, get, go*, see these verbs.)

I. 1. a. Of motion: With a circular course, so as to return again to the point of departure. Also *transf.* of time, and in phr. ***round and round***.

a **1290** *Beket* 2125 in *S. Eng. Leg.* I. 167 Al round it orn aboute is heued, ase it were a dyademe, And al-round þare-abouten it lay. **1565** COOPER *Thesaurus* s.v. *Orbis*, To go rounde or in a rynge. **1591** SYLVESTER *Du Bartas* I. ii. 712 Loud it grones and grumbles, It rouls, and roars, and round-round-round it rumbles. **1611** COTGR. s.v. *Circulation*, The vapour..seemes to goe round, or circle-wise. **1743** P. FRANCIS tr. *Horace, Odes* IV. XI. 21 Mecænas counts a length of years To roll in bright succession round. **1746** —— *Epist.* II. i. 289 As the year brought round the jovial day. **1798** COLERIDGE *Anc. Mar.* I. xvii, It ate the food..And round and round it flew. **1863** WHITTIER *Mithridates at Chios* 32 Once more the slow dumb years Bring their avenging cycle round. **1875** JOWETT *Plato* (ed. 2) IV. 253 Thus we go round and round in a circle and make no progress. **1898** A. B. GOMME *Tradit. Games* II. 143 Round and round went the gallant, gallant ship. **1936** *Billboard* 11 Jan. 12/4 That latest contagion, *Music Goes Round and Round*,..is selling at the rate of 16,000 copies daily. **1977** *Washington Post* 26 Dec. c8/2 The music sells the movie. The movie sells the albums. The TV and radio and newspapers sell both. Round and round we go.

fig. **1704** SWIFT *Tale Tub* Pref., He may ring the Changes as far as it will go, and vary his Phrase 'till he has talk'd round.

b. To each in turn of an assembled company (orig. as seated at a table); hence, with (successive) inclusion of all those belonging to a company, body of persons, etc.

1613 SHAKS. *Hen. VIII*, I. iv. 97 A health Gentlemen, Let it goe round. **1713** SWIFT *Cadenus & Vanessa* 350 She nam'd the ancient Heroes round, Explain'd for what they were renown'd. **1786** BURNS *Halloween* vii, The auld Guidwife's weel-hoordet nits Are round an' round divided. **1826** LAMB *Pop. Fallacies* ix, When a money subscription is going round. **1863** SPEKE *Disc. Nile* 36 One pig, enough to feed the whole camp round. **1883** STEVENSON *Treas. Isl.* (1886) 5 Sometimes he would call for glasses round.

†**c.** From all sides; all over. *Obs. rare.*

1634 SHIRLEY *Opportunity* v. ii, *Pis.* Looke better on me. *Lau.* We have seene you round, Sir. **1726** SWIFT *Gulliver* I. ii, When he alighted, he surveyed me round with great Admiration. **1766** GOLDSM. *Vic. W.* xiv, After he had for a good while examined the horse round, finding him blind of one eye, he would have nothing to say to him.

†**d.** On all four feet. *Obs.*

1687 *Lond. Gaz.* No. 2290/4 A black..Colt..shoed round. **1711** *Ibid.* No. 4875/4 Shod all round. **1768** WESLEY *Jrnl.* 31 Oct., I procured one to shoe my horse all round. *fig.* **1731–8** SWIFT *Polite Conv.* 95 This is his Fourth Wife; then he has been shod round.

e. Through, throughout; from beginning to end.

Chiefly in phr. ***all the year round*** (also used *attrib.* or as sb. phr.). The use approaches that of the prep. following the sb.

1753 *Chambers' Cycl.* Suppl. s.v. *Yellow*, The flowers of the acacia..may be kept all the year round. **1851** MAYHEW *London Lab.* II. 112 Some [buyers] collect the skins all the year round. **1872** *Dublin Univ. Mag.* Feb. 224 The San Franciscans now eat the best of grapes, cherries, and pears, almost the year round. **1883** HARDY in *Graphic* Summer 4/2 One of those curious summer shelters sometimes erected on exposed points of view, called an all-the-year-round. **1893** K. SANBORN *S. California* 188 Pasadena is the greatest all-the-year-round health-resort in the world. **1910** *Busy Man's Mag.* Feb. 58/2 Vancouver is becoming an all-the-year-round resort. **1939** G. GREENE *Confidential Agent* IV. i. 269 We want to make it an all-the-year-round resort. **1963** *Times* 5 Feb. 7/5 Equipped for all-the-year-round motoring.

f. So as to include or visit in succession a number of places or persons.

1821 CLARE *Vill. Minstr.* II. 117 Seeking, hirpling round from time to time, Her harmless sticks from hedges hung with rime. **1861** [see GO *v.* 90 c]. **1884** DOWELL *Taxation & Taxes* (1888) III. 33 Employing a number of young men to go round with samples. **1897** ANSTEY *Trav. Comp.* ii, Mr. Podbury, who's kindly volunteered to conduct us round.

g. = ABOUT *adv.* 9. (Chiefly *U.S.*)

1857–8 in W. WHITMAN *Daybks. & Notebks.* (1978) III. 676 The Doctor has evidently been 'round some'. **1860** O. W. HOLMES *Elsie V.* xvi, Those unwholesome..creatures, that look not fit to be round among live folks. **1890** 'R. BOLDREWOOD' *Col. Reformer* (1891) 111 There were no wild beasts, or robbers, likely to be 'round'. **1894** MRS. DYAN *Man's Keeping* (1899) 25 That sickening old brute..has been fooling round making up to the General and Mrs. Yorke lately.

2. a. In a ring or circle; so as to encompass, encircle, or enclose something; on each wall or side (of a room, etc.).

a **1290** [see sense 1]. *a* **1539** *Cart. Rievalle* (Surtees) 341 The iii romys north therof seelyd round with waynscot. **1565** COOPER *Thesaurus*, *Orbem facere*,..to stande rounde, that they may be ready for their enemies euery way. **1593** SHAKS. *3 Hen. VI*, III. ii. 171 Vntill my mis-shap'd Trunke, that beares this Head, Be round impaled with a glorious Crowne. **1615** G. SANDYS *Trav.* 234 The..principall houses were stucke round on the outside with lampes. **1667** MILTON *P.L.* VII. 90 How first began..the ambient Aire wide interfus'd Imbracing round this florid Earth. **1732** BERKELEY *Alciphr.* i. §1 Fields planted round with plane-trees. **1797** COLERIDGE *Kubla Khan* 7 So twice five miles of fertile ground With walls and towers were girdled round. **1817** KEATS '*I stood tip-toe*' 166 He had found A little space, with boughs all woven round. **1859** TENNYSON *Geraint &*

Enid 335 My followers ring him round. **1893** C. G. Leland *Mem.* I. 36 A hall, hung round with many old family portraits.

b. So as to form a ring or circle; so as to have a circular form or section.

c **1386** Chaucer *Prol.* 589 His heer was by his erys ful round yshorn. **1542–3** *Act 34 & 35 Hen. VIII*, c. 6 Pinnes ..shal..haue..the point well and rounde filled canted and sharped. **1580** Blundevil *Horsem.* v. 40 b, When the horse lieth down, he spreadeth himselfe abrode, not being able to lie round togither on his bellie.

3. a. In every direction from a centre; on all sides; all about.

c **1440** *York Myst.* xxx. 165 He will..refe vs þe remys þat are rounde. *c* **1500** *World & Child* 5 For I am kynge and well knowen in these realmes rounde. **1513** Douglas *Æneis* v. vi. 79 As this ȝonkeir heirin tred and fut sett,..wenyng hym victour round. **1626** Bacon *Sylva* §201 All Sounds move Round; That is to say; on all Sides. **1719** Young *Busiris* I. i, Which will rise in flames At the least breath, and spread destruction round. **1781** Morison in *Sc. Paraphr.* xxxv. 5 As dew upon the tender herb diffusing fragrance round. **1808** Scott *Marm.* I. x, As Lord Marmion cross'd the court, He scatter'd angels round. **1852** M. Arnold *Tristram & Iseult* 247 All round the forest sweeps off, black in shade. **1884** *Graphic* 18 Oct. 398/1 We have managed to annoy foreigners all round.

b. By measurement in all directions from a given centre.

1656 H. Phillips *Purch. Patt.* (1676) 112 Within 20 miles round off London. **1766** Goldsm. *Vic. W.* iii, Scarce a farmer's daughter within ten miles round but what had found him successful and faithless. **1833** Ht. Martineau *Loom & Lugger* I. vi. 93 They will wake up all the sheep in the pens for a mile round. **1842** Louisa S. Costello *Pilgr. Auvergne* II. 158 Hundreds of peasants..hurrying to mass from every village for leagues round.

c. In the neighbourhood or vicinity; round about.

1785 Burns *Cotter's Sat. Nt.* iv, Belyve the elder bairns come drappin in, At Service out, amang the Farmers roun'. **1865** Kingsley *Herew.* xli, Hardly a French knight or baron round but had a blood-feud against him.

4. a. By a circuitous, roundabout, or indirect way or course.

1668 Pepys *Diary* 7 July, We are fain to go round by Newgate because of Fleet-bridge being under rebuilding. **1718** S. Sewall *Diary* 2 July, Lt. Govr. came home round in Mr. Gore's Calash. **1766** Goldsm. *Vic. W.* x, The horse-way..was five miles round, though the foot-way was but two. **1801** *Farmer's Mag.* Nov. 396 For exporting cattle, too large for sending round by the heads of the Friths. **1850** Mrs. Browning *Romance Swan's Nest* xv, Ellie..rose up gaily,..And went homeward, round a mile.

b. Denoting arrival or presence at some point or place reached by an indirect route.

1698 Fryer *Acc. E. India & P.* 175 The rest [of the seaports] are Possessed by the Malabar Raja's round to Porto Novo. **1755** Washington *Writ.* (1889) I. 208 Doctor Craik is expected round to Alexandria in a vessel. **1822** Shelley *Prose Wks.* (1880) IV. 270, I suppose..that you will not be round here until the middle of summer. **1841** J. T. Hewlett *Parish Clerk* I. 97 The carriage was ordered round. **1897** Flandrau *Harvard Episodes* 179 If I'd only known.., I could have asked some of the fellows round to meet you.

5. *Cricket.* **a.** In the direction lying behind the batsman; 'to leg'.

1857 Hughes *Tom Brown* II. viii, A beautifully pitched ball for the outer stump, which the..unfeeling Jack..hits right round to leg for five. **1882** *Daily Telegr.* 20 May, Murdoch hit him round and drove him for a brace of 4's.

b. = round-arm 1.

1859 *All Year Round* No. 13. 305 Southey bowled slow twisters at one end, and I bowled 'round' at the other.

II. 6. With a rotatory or whirling movement.

c **1500** *World & Child* 79 Lo, my toppe I dryve in same, —Se, it torneth rounde! **1565** Cooper *Thesaurus, Roto*, to tourne a thing rounde like a wheele. **1596** Shaks. *Tam. Shr.* v. ii. 20 He that is giddie thinks the world turns round. **1638** Brathwait *Barnabees Jrnl.* II. (1818) 65 Who will drink till th' world run round-a. **1679** Prance *Add. Narrative* 26 The Compendiarist's head turns round. **1719** De Foe *Crusoe* II. (Globe) 509 The whole World is in Motion, rouling round and round. **1782** Cowper *J. Gilpin* 41 Smack went the whip, round went the wheels. **1860** Tyndall *Glac.* I. iii. 30, I struck my staff into the snow, and turned it round and round. **1869** Ruskin *Q. of Air* i. §39 Their [dolphins'] black backs roll round with exactly the slow motion of a water-wheel.

7. In a curve, spirally.

1611 Cotgr., *Chantourné*, turned round, as the shell of a snayle.

8. a. In the opposite direction; to or towards the opposite quarter.

a **1765** *Sir Andrew Barton* I. iii. in Percy *Reliques* II. 177 King Henrye frownd, and turned him rounde. **1787** 'G. Gambado' *Acad. Horsem.* (1809) 38 If his horse has stopt and turned round five thousand times with him. **1842** Macaulay *Horatius* lviii, Round turned he, as not deigning Those craven ranks to see. **1875** Jowett *Plato* (ed. 2) I. 464 Socrates looked round at us as his manner was.

b. To the opposite view; to a different opinion, frame of mind, etc.

1825– [see come *v.* 71 c]. **1855** Kingsley *Westw. Ho!* xv, He submitted for the nonce, and Cary thought..that he had talked him pretty well round. **1859** Geo. Eliot *A. Bede* xxi, The only way to bring him round would be to show him what was for his own interest. **1874** Green *Short Hist.* viii. §2. 461 England veered round again to Protestantism under Elizabeth. *a* **1887** Jefferies *Field & Hedgerow* (1892) 318 It was no little matter to coax him round to unchain his vessel.

III. †9. a. Roundly; with a round or full utterance; in round terms. *Obs.*

c **1386** Chaucer *Pard. T.* Prol. 3 In chirche whan I preche, I peyne me to haue an hauten speche; I rynge it oute as rounde as eny belle. **1565** Cooper *Thesaurus, Clausulæ rotundæ*, full and perfitte clauses of sentenses fallyng rounde. **1575** *Gamm. Gurton* IV. ii[i], Yet take hede, I say, I must tel you my tale round. **1682** N. O. *Boileau's Lutrin* II. 73 Thus spoke our Lover whining, plain and round. **1780** *Mirror* No. 97 They should be taught..to speak their own language rough and round.

b. *spec.* (See quot.)

1774 *Ann. Reg., Nat. Hist.* 65/2 When a bird is thus become perfect in his lesson, he is said to sing his song round, or in all its varieties of passages, which he connects together, and executes without a pause.

†10. a. With a free or easy motion; with celerity or freedom. *Obs.*

c **1386** Chaucer *Sir Thopas* 175 His steede..gooth an Ambil in the way Ful softely and rounde. **1586** B. Young *Guazzo's Civ. Conv.* IV. 189 We are after meate merier, giue more pleasant aunsweres, and goe rounder away with anie matter, then when we are fasting. **1597** T. Morley *Introd. Mus.* 27 You must begin againe and sing..in halfe tyme (that is, as rounde againe, as you did before).

†b. Copiously; without restraint. *Obs. rare.*

1582 Stanyhurst *Æneis* II. (Arb.) 64 Round fel I too weeping,..with al eke thee sorroful houshold.

†c. Openly; in a straightforward manner. *rare.*

1602 Shaks. *Ham.* II. ii. 139, I went round to worke, And (my yong Mistris) thus I did bespeake. **1650** Milton *Tenure Kings* 32, I question not the lawfullness of raising War.., for no Protestant Church but have don it round and maintain'd it lawful.

†d. *round or rattle*, in any case. *Obs.*$^{-1}$

a **1670** Hacket *Abp. Williams* II. (1692) 206 In conjunction with them, or out of conjunction; round or rattle, if he were rich he must be a booty, or a compounder.

11. *Comb.* (in various senses), as ***round-blazing***, ***-burning***, ***-rolling***, ***-turning*** adjs.; ***round-stirring*** sb.; ***round-beset***, ***-fenced***, ***-girdled***, adjs.; **round-spun** *a.*, of strong stuff; sturdy.

1581 Mulcaster *Positions* xxvi, This exercise do I like best of any rounde stirring without the dores. **1591** Sylvester *Du Bartas* I. iv. 130, I see not how, in those round-blazing beams [etc.]. **1598** *Ibid.* II. ii. i. 38 Though round-fenc't with guard of armed Knights. **1611** *Sec. Maidens Trag.* III. i, The house is round-beset with armed men. **1642** H. More *Song Soul* I. i. 60 Round-turning whirlwinds on Olympus steep. **1729** Savage *Wanderer* III. 19 Yet reddening, yet round-burning up the air, From the white cliff, her feet slow-rising glare! **1783** Cowper *Epitaph on Hare* 29 Eight years and five round-rolling moons He thus saw steal away. **1818** Scott *Hrt. Midl.* xii, He's weel kend for a round-spun Presbyterian, and a ruling elder to boot. **1878** O. Wilde *Ravenna* 5 A moon of fire Round-girdled with a purple marriage-ring. **1923** D. H. Lawrence *Birds, Beasts, & Flowers* 25 Am I not blind, at the round-turning mill?

B. *prep.*

1. a. Of motion: So as to encircle, or make the complete circuit of; so as to go around. Also in phrr. ***round and round***, ***round-the-world***; **round-the-** (also †**me**) **houses**, (*a*) *Rhyming slang*, trousers (see also round *sb.*[1] 25); (*b*) *attrib. phr.* applied to a motor race or circuit following the streets of a city.

1602 Shaks. *Ham.* III. ii. 165 Full thirtie times hath Phœbus Cart gon round Neptunes salt Wash. **1667** Milton *P.L.* IV. 661 Those have thir course to finish, round the Earth. **1727–46** Thomson *Summer* 1495 A Drake, who.. bore thy name in thunder round the world. **1763** J. Brown *Poetry & Music* vi. 125 Holding a Branch of Myrtle in their Hand, which was sent round the Table. **1820** Keats *Lamia* I. 43 The God, dove-footed, glided silently Round bush and tree. **1865** Kingsley *Herew.* vi, Then he rode back to the ship, and round and round her. **1880** Haughton *Phys. Geogr.* ii. 17 Her day is now equal to her periodic revolution round the earth. **1898** A. B. Gomme *Tradit. Games* II. 122 Round and round the village, As we have done before. **1951** in *Oxf. Dict. Nursery Rhymes* 184 Round and round the garden like a teddy bear; One step, two step, Tickle you under there! **1977** *Washington Post* 26 Dec. c8/2 Travolta himself..is going round and round the country with a cordon of publicists.

Comb. **1857** 'Ducange Anglicus' *Vulgar Tongue* 17 *Round me houses*,..trousers, pronounced trouses [ed. 2, 1859, trousies]. **1858** A. Mayhew *Paved with Gold* II. x. 169 Philip intimating that, as soon as he had put on his *trousers*, he would blacken Bill's *eyes*, roared out, 'Wait till I've togged my 'round-the-houses', and then I'll cook your 'mince-pies' for you'. **1872** C. King *Sierra Nevada* vii. 134 A weather-beaten round-the-worlder. **1889** *Advance* (Chicago) Jan. 24 As travelers come home from a round-the-world tour. **1898** J. D. Brayshaw *Slum Silhouettes* 220 An' as fer 'is rahnd-the-'ouses, they 'ad a crease right dahn 'em. **1906** E. Dyson *Fact'ry 'Ands* xiii. 164 No man that wore 'ome-made round-th'-'ouses ever done wonders in this world. **1932** A. Christie *Peril at End House* xi. 131 It was he who financed..the expenses of the round-the-world flight. **1935** Eyston & Lyndon *Motor Racing* iv. 38 The introduction of events run over short circuits planned within the confines of a town. These have become known as 'round-the-houses' races, the first of which was the Grand Prix of Monaco, inaugurated in 1929. **1957** S. Moss *In Track of Speed* i. 14 The Manx Cup race in the Isle of Man, which was a sort of 'round-the-houses' contest in the environs of Douglas. **1970** *N.Z. News* 21 Jan. 16/1 Champion of the American circuit, British-born Ron Grant revelled in conditions he had not experienced before in the Wanganui annual round the houses motorcycle race. **1974** *Times* 10 Jan. 12 The West German round-the-world racing yacht, Peter von Danzig, is putting into Bluff, on New Zealand's South Island. **1974** P. Wright *Lang. British Industry* x. 87 Some of it [*sc.* rhyming slang] apparently doesn't even rhyme properly; e.g. *round the houses* (trousers).

b. So as to include, traverse, visit, etc., in turn or successively; also, all about (a certain area).

1605 Shaks. *Macb.* III. iv. 12 Anon wee'l drinke a Measure The Table round. **1689** Burnet *Tracts* I. 77 All those offices go round the several Communities, who have the right of nomination in their turn. **1697** Dryden *Virg. Georg.* II. 526 Round the Streets the reeling Actors ran. **1713** Swift *Cadenus & Vanessa* 366 A Party next of glitt'ring Dames, From round the Purlieus of St. James. **1849** Macaulay *Hist. Eng.* iii. I. 338 Three coaches..were sent every afternoon round the city to bring ladies to the festivities. **1867** Smyth *Sailor's Word-bk., Round the Fleet*, a diabolical punishment, by which a man, lashed to a frame on a long-boat, was towed alongside of every ship in a fleet, to receive a certain number of lashes. **1895** *Bookman* Oct. 16/2 Several gentlemen..who make a very good living by hawking these nightingales round the cafés.

c. Throughout, all through; from beginning to end of (a period of time). ***round the clock***, ***the clock round***: see clock *sb.*[1] 4. Also *Comb.*, as ***round-the-year***.

a **1715** Burnet *Own Time* (1734) I. 472 The King..was often weary of time and did not know how to get round the day. **1725** Pope *Odyss.* VII. 151 Verdant olives flourish round the year. **1839–52** Bailey *Festus* 317 Oh, thou wouldst promise me the clock round. **1959** *News Chron.* 28 Nov. 3/1 Round-the-year sea bathing.

2. a. Around; about; on the circuit or outer bounds of; so as to surround or envelop.

1662 Evelyn *Chalcography* 32 Put it round the brims of your plate. **1687** A. Lovell tr. *Thevenot's Trav.* I. ii. 3 On the Shoar, round this Port, there are several fair Palaces. **1725** Pope *Odyss.* v. 475 The chief..binds the sacred cincture round his breast. **1766** Goldsm. *Vic. W.* viii, Our family dined in the field, and we sate..round a temperate repast. **1831** Carlyle *Sart. Res.* III. x, Round one of those Book-packages..come..various waste printed-sheets. **1861** Pattison *Ess.* (1889) I. 45 Round the apartment,..on every projecting ledge.., was displayed..the silver and pewter plate. **1887** Bowen *Æneid* I. 649 The veil Woven with a border round it of yellow acanthus.

b. Having (some person or thing) as the central figure or subject.

1898 *Echo* 1 July 1/6 An American author..has written a novel round the author of the famous Persian 'Rubáiyát'.

c. *colloq.* Of time: About; approximately. Cf. around *prep.* 4 b.

1928 F. N. Hart *Bellamy Trial* iii. 92 It must have been round quarter to nine. **1942** Partridge *Usage & Abusage* 277/1 *Round* for *on* or *about* is a characteristic of Cockney speech: e.g. 'Meet me round seven o'clock'.

3. In all (or various) directions from; on all sides of.

1729 J. Rogers *12 Serm.* (1730) 347 When we come to look round us from the Ascent we have made. **1775** R. King *Life & Corr.* (1894) I. 18 The Sheep & Cattle belonged to Men in Chelsea and round the same. **1816** J. Wilson *City of Plague* I. i. 53 When round me silent Nature speaks of death. **1849** Macaulay *Hist. Eng.* iii. I. 339 In the language of the gentry many miles round the Wrekin, to go to Shrewsbury was to go to town. **1885** *Harper's Mag.* Feb. 445/2 She looked round her, and backed against some one coming up the street.

4. So as to revolve about (a centre or axis).

1728 Chambers *Cycl.* s.v. *Venus*, Her Motion round her own Axis [is performed] in 23 Hours. **1771** *Encycl. Brit.* I. 442 Jupiter turns round his axis in 9 hours 56 minutes. **1866** *Chambers's Encycl.* VIII. 361/2 The pressure..will..cause the ship to revolve round the centre of gravity.

5. a. So as to make a turn or partial circuit about, or reach the other side of. Also in *comb.* ***round-the-corner***.

1743 Bulkeley & Cummins *Voy. S. Seas* 1 This Squadron was design'd round Cape Horn into the South Seas. **1787** 'G. Gambado' *Acad. Horsem.* (1809) 34 In turning sharp round a post. **1833** Herschel *Astron.* i. 20 The effect of refraction, by which we are enabled to see.. round the interposed segment. **1852** Dickens *Bleak Ho.* iii, We went round the corner. **1894** Hall Caine *Manxman* 408 They brought up a carriage and drove him round the bay.

Comb. **1820** *Edin. Rev.* XXXIV. 305 Round-the-corner sort of personal satire. **1881** [see lazy-tongs]. **1915** A. Conan Doyle *Valley of Fear* I. vii. 121 You get to your point, I admit, but you have such a deuced round-the-corner way of doing it.

b. *to come* or *get round* (a person): see come *v.* 47, get *v.* 47 a.

c. ***round the wicket***: see bowl *v.*[1] 4 b.

1867 G. H. Selkirk *Guide to Cricket Ground* iv. 61 The discretion allowed to the bowler to deliver the ball either over or round the wicket. **1894** N. Gale *Cricket Songs* 26 If round the wicket, medium pace, Won't make the batsman budge,..Sling him a grub. **1956** N. Cardus *Close of Play* 14 Macaulay bowled off-spin from round the wicket. **1966** B. Johnston *Armchair Cricket* 109 *Round the wicket*, a method of delivery where the bowler has his back to the stumps at the bowling end as he delivers the ball, i.e. a right-arm bowler bowls on the right-hand side of the stumps, a left-arm bowler on the left-side. **1974** *Sunday Tel.* 9 June 34/6 Titmus, fancying his chances, went round the wicket and induced the predictable catch to short leg.

d. Phr. ***round the bend***: see bend *sb.*[4] 10 c.

round (raʊnd), *v.*[1] Forms: 4 rown-, 5 rownd(e, 6 rounde, rond(e; 4– round. [f. round *a.*, in early use perh. after OF. *rondir*. Cf. MDu. and Du. *ronden*, G. (late MHG.) *runden*, *ründen*, Da. *runde*, Sw. *runda*.]

I. *trans.* **1. a.** To make round; to invest with a circular or spherical form. Also *refl.*, to contract into a circle or ball.

c **1375** *Cursor M.* 7531 (Fairf.), He toke v. stanes rowned wiþ gynne. *c* **1430** *Pilgr. Lyf Manhode* II. cxlvii. (1869) 133, I am þe..irchownes douhter, rownded to gideres wiche roundeth him for vertu with hise broches. **1608** Topsell *Serpents* (1653) 697 This Serpent..climbeth up into trees where it roundeth it self round into a circle. **1670** Pettus *Fodinæ Reg.* 41 The Moniers, who are some to sheer the Monie,..some to round it, and some to stamp or coin it. **1806** J. Grahame *Birds of Scot.* I. 5 Even now he sits,..Half-hid, and warps the skep with willow rind, Or rounds the lid, still adding coil to coil. **1847** Tennyson *Princess* II. 350 On the lecture slate The circle rounded under female hands With flawless demonstration. **1871** Tyndall *Fragm. Sci.* (1879) II. x. 211 What rounded the sun and planets?

b. To draw together, or expand, into a rounded form. Also *refl.*

1867 A. J. Ellis *E.E. Pronunc.* I. iii. §3. 161 By more or less rounding the lips while the lingual position is held. **1890** Clark Russell *Ocean Trag.* II. xx. 156 Amazement.. rounded her eyes. **1894** Mrs. F. Elliot *Roman Gossip* viii. 225 Her eyes rounded themselves in her head.

c. To labialize (a vowel).

1867 A. J. Ellis *E.E. Pronunc.* I. iii. §3. 162 Hence we have this relation..that (u) is almost (ə) labialized or rounded. **1890** Sweet *Primer Phonetics* (1902) 17 Back and mixed vowels..are rounded by lateral compression of the corners of the mouth and, apparently, of the cheeks.

2. †**a.** To deface (coin) by cutting or paring. *Obs.*

c **1400** *Brut* clxiii, Kyng Edward..chaungede his mony, þat þo was foule cotte & rounded. **1602** Fulbecke *1st Pt. Parallel* 89 Such as clip, wash, round, or file mony, are only to forfeit their lands during their life. *a* **1625** Sir H. Finch *Law* (1636) 222 To clip, wash, round, or file, any mony of this Realme.

†**b.** To cut (the hair) short round the head; to trim, crop (the head, a person) in this way. *Obs.*

Common in 16th cent.; in later use only as an echo of Lev. xix. 27.

1432-50 tr. *Higden* (Rolls) VII. 183 Barbosus..was put from Yrlonde in that he did rownde the maydes after the consuetude of men. **1508** Kennedie *Flyting w. Dunbar* 399, I sall degraid the,..Ger round the hede, transforme the till a fule. **1577-87** Holinshed *Chron.* II. 8 To shave their beards, to round their heare, and to frame themselves..after the Norman manner. **1611** Bible *Lev.* xix. 27 Ye shall not round the corners of your heads. **1637** Gillespie *Eng. Pop. Cerem.* III. iii. 38 The law..simply forbiddeth to round the head. **1781** S. Peters *Hist. Connecticut* 69 The Levitical law forbids cutting the hair, or rounding the head.

fig. *a* **1548** Hall *Chron., Rich. III*, 36 He was rounded shorter by the whole head without attaynder or judgement.

absol. **1546** Langley tr. *Pol. Verg. de Invent.* III. xii. 80 b, Barbours to shaue and rounde were instituted by the Abantes.

†**c.** To cut or pare (the nails). *Obs.*$^{-0}$

1570 Levins *Manip.* 220/46 To Rond the nayls, *putare*.

d. To crop (the ears of dogs).

1781 P. Beckford *Th. Hunting* (1802) 70 *note*, It may be better..to round them [*sc.* a dog's ears] at their quarters, when about six months old... Dogs must not be rounded at the time they have the distemper upon them. **1845** Youatt *Dog* ix. (1858) 258 Some sportsmen are accustomed to *round* the ears, that is to cut off the diseased part. **1856** Stonehenge *Brit. Rur. Sports* 120/2 The Young Hounds will require to be Rounded,..an operation for the removal of a portion of their ears, so as to prevent their being torn by the briars and thorns.

3. a. To make convex or curving in outline; to raise to a relief; to form into a cylinder.

1677 Moxon *Mech. Exerc.* ii. 29 Hammer down the corners of..this shank,..and round it as near as you can with the hammer. **1702** Addison *Dial. Medals* Wks. 1766 III. 165 The figures on several of our modern Medals are raised and rounded to a very great perfection. **1719** De Foe *Crusoe* I. 144 Getting one [block of wood] as big as I had Strength to stir, I rounded it. **1876** *Encycl. Brit.* IV. 43/1 When the glue is quite dry the back is rounded by beating with a hammer.

refl. **1872** O. W. Holmes *Poet Breakf.-t.* ii, The sail.. swelled and rounded itself like a white bosom that had burst its bodice.

b. To develop or fill out to a rounded form.

a **1839** Praed *Poems* (1864) II. 23 Slender arms before my face Are rounded with a statue's grace. **1847** W. C. L. Martin *The Ox* 65/2 These cows..become full-fleshed and rounded. **1884** Augusta J. E. Wilson *Vashti* i, Sixteen years had ripened and rounded the girlish form.

4. a. To finish off, bring to completeness or to a perfect form.

1610 Shaks. *Temp.* IV. i. 158 We are such stuffe As dreames are made on; and our little life Is rounded with a sleepe. **1674** N. Fairfax *Bulk & Selv.* 73 These hidden working laws that round the world. **1778** *Ann. Reg.* 35 They ..took such measures..as strongly indicated a design of.. entirely rounding his possession of Silesia. **1848** L. Hunt *Jar of Honey* x. 127 We shall round our subject by finishing the circle where we began it. **1895** Mrs. Oliphant *Makers of Mod. Rome* I. vi. 97 The history of the first dedicated household..is thus rounded into a perfect record.

b. To frame or turn (a sentence, etc.) neatly or gracefully.

a **1732** Swift *Misc.* (J.), A quaint, terse, florid style, rounded into periods and cadencies, without propriety or meaning. **1791** Boswell *Johnson* (Oxf. ed.) I. 151 His periods, though not diligently rounded, are voluble and easy. **1842** J. H. Newman *Par. Serm.* V. ii. 23 The introduction..of serious and solemn words..to round, or to give dignity to, a sentence. **1875** Jowett *Plato* (ed. 2) I. p. xii, In framing an English sentence or in rounding a paragraph.

c. To finish or end (a sentence, etc.) *with* something.

1780 *Mirror* No. 97 He rounded this pathetic period with one of his best oaths. **1838** Dickens *Nickleby* xiv, Kenwigs was going to say 'house', but he rounded the sentence with 'apartments'. **1866** *N. & Q.* 3rd Ser. IX. 486/1 Rounding his challenge with a sweeping attack upon Archbishop Laud. **1883** F. M. Crawford *Dr. Claudius* xiii, Having rounded it [the conversation] neatly with a couple of anecdotes,..he rose to go.

d. To approximate (a number) by expressing it in fewer significant figures (the rightmost digit(s) being replaced by 0 and the last unaltered digit being increased by 1 when the digit that followed is 5 (or 6) or more); to express (a number) in a less exact but more convenient form. Also with *down*, *off*, *up* (see senses 5 h, 6 e, 8 d below).

1934 in Webster. **1935** Shuster & Bedford *Field Work in Math.* iv. 14 Round the following numbers to three significant figures. *Ibid.* 15 Multiply 2·87 ft. (*a*) by 3·14, (*b*) by 3·142... Round in each case to three figures. **1956** G. A. Montgomerie *Digital Calculating Machines* vii. 129 The usual rule is to ignore a digit less than five and to add one in the next place for five or more. 3·54 would be rounded to 3·5, 3·55 to 3·6, 3·56 to 3·6. **1962** *B.S.I. News* Jan. 25/1 The results are either exact or have been rounded by the accepted convention to the number of significant figures given. **1966** *Rep. Comm. Inquiry Univ. Oxf.* II. p. xxxii, In the tables each figure is rounded separately. **1971** *Jrnl. Gen. Psychol.* LXXXV. 72 The loadings have been rounded to two figures.

5. *round up*: a. To collect or gather up in a round mass or ball. Also *refl.*

1615 T. Adams *Black Devil* 71 Innumerable plagues of Hell are rounded up together in one. **1642** Fuller *Holy & Prof. St.* v. xviii. 429 He rounded himself up in his own prickles. **1650** W. D. tr. *Comenius' Gate Lat. Unl.* §43 The milkie-circle throngeth together a world of little small stars crouded, (rounded) up close into one heap.

†**b.** To rebuke or reprove (a person). *Obs.*$^{-1}$

1678 Bunyan *Pilgr.* I. (1900) 99 Then Christian roundly answered, saying, Demas [etc.]. *marg.* Christian roundeth up Demas.

c. To make up, complete (a number).

1806 Cumberland *Mem.* I. 262 [Johnson added] 'I want one of the dozen, and I must request Mrs. Cumberland to round up my number'.

d. *Naut.* (See quot. 1886.)

1846 [see sense 7 a]. **1886** *Encycl. Brit.* XXI. 604 *Round up*, to shorten up a tackle; to pull up a slack rope through a block. **1947** A. Ransome *Great Northern?* viii. 111 The *Sea Bear* slipped on in silence towards the big white motor yacht... She rounded up perhaps forty yards away.

e. To collect (cattle, etc.) by riding round the scattered herd and driving it together. Orig. *U.S.* and *Austr.* Cf. 7 c. Also *absol.*

1847 Capt. C. Sturt *Narr. Exped. C. Australia* (1849) I. 228 We rounded up the cattle till the moon should rise. **1869** *Overland Monthly* III. 126 At night they 'round up' or 'corral'. **1881** Grant *Bush-Life Queensland* II. xxxiv. 198 As the eager stock-horse rounded up the panting mob. **1891** C. Roberts *Adrift Amer.* 175 Before we turned in the horses were all rounded up. **1907** C. E. Mulford *Bar-20* 15 They shore outer be here now. They rounded up last week. **1925** E. F. Norton *Fight for Everest 1924* 26 Kingston and I amused ourselves by trying to round up some kiang [*sc.* wild donkeys]. **1949** *Sky Line Trail* Oct. 18/1, I met some cowboys rounding up strayed horses.

transf. **1885** *Weekly New Mexican Rev.* 15 Jan. 2/5 Mr. Twitchell went down to 'round up' the gang and was so far successful as to spot the leader. **1889** *Boston* (Mass.) *Jrnl.* 27 May 4/5 All the suspects will be rounded up for the coroner's inquest. **1903** *Times* 21 Sept. 4/5 The endless stretches of country..to be 'rounded up' by the cowboy at the end of the season. **1910** *Chambers's Jrnl.* June 384/1, I have seen groups of these unfortunates 'rounded up' and marched off to the nearest police-station. **1931** *Daily Express* 15 Oct. 6/3 The star-traders of the talkies have been out rounding up fresh material from which to carve the box-office idols of the future. **1944** M. Laski *Love on Supertax* xii. 118 They delay.. arrests in the futile hope of 'rounding up the whole gang'. **1975** P. G. Winslow *Death of Angel* vi. 136, I heard about your difficulty and immediately rounded up Cecil.

f. Similarly without *up*.

1865 Tucker *Austral. Story* 108 In the act of rounding some cattle for the purpose of yarding them. **1885** Mrs. C. Praed *Head Station* 54 A stockman and a brace of black boys rounded the mob.

g. To increase (a number) when rounding it (cf. sense 4 d above) by adding 1 to its rightmost remaining digit, or by expressing it as the next higher round number.

1956 G. A. Montgomerie *Digital Calculating Machines* vii. 129 In a long calculation, all these increases may accumulate, and it is better to round some of them up and some of them down. **1963** *Rep. Comm. Inquiry Decimal Currency* iv. 30, in *Parl. Papers 1962–3* (Cmnd. 2145) XI. 195 The custom with some of these goods is to round up, sometimes down, to the nearest halfpenny. **1969** *Guardian* 30 July 16/1 The Shell-Mex and BP group..will not be advising the 17,000 stations it supplies whether to 'round-up' or 'round-down' petrol prices when the halfpenny ceases to be legal tender. **1975** *Language for Life* (Dept. Educ. & Sci.) xxi. 310 Some Authorities with schools of under 100 pupils round up the number on roll to the nearest 50 and calculate their *per capita* allowance on that basis. **1976** [see rounding *vbl. sb.* 1 c].

6. *round off*: a. To make round, convex, or curved by trimming off edges or angles; to cut off (points, etc.) so as to make round.

1680 Moxon *Mech. Exerc.* xii. 207 With the Draw-knife round off the Edges, to make it fit for the Lathe. **1683** —— *Printing* xi. ¶22 The two upper corners of these Rails are rounded off that they may not mark the Paper. **1723** Chambers tr. *Le Clerc's Archit.* I. 8 Vitruvius orders the Plinth of the Tuscan Column to be rounded off. **1725** *Lond. Gaz.* No. 6356/3 A Slit in her Right Ear, if not rounded off since lost. **1814** Scott *Diary* 16th Aug. in *Lockhart*, The lower [stone]..is shorter, and rounded off, instead of being square at the corners. **1846** Brittan tr. *Malgaigne's Oper. Surg.* 217 An oval wound with the anterior angle rounded off. **1875** *Carpentry & Join.* 62 Do not round off the upper edge of these.

transf. **1807** J. Opie *Lect. Art* iii. (1848) 304 Classing his colours,..gently rounding off his light.

b. To finish off, complete (an estate, etc.) by addition of adjacent lands.

1820 Scott in *Lockhart* (1837) IV. xi. 376 It is £200 too dear, but..it rounds the property off very handsomely. **1876** Freeman *Norm. Conq.* V. 28 An unscrupulous grantee would sometimes round off his estates by seizing small parcels of land. **1890** *Spectator* 8 Mar., Those efforts at 'rounding off' dominion which so constantly result in disaster.

c. To finish or complete appropriately; to end neatly or elegantly.

1748 Richardson *Clarissa* V. 135, I gave him..a frown.. as much as to say, Swear to it, Captain. But the varlet did not round it off as I would have had him. **1818** Scott *Rob Roy* i, He had picked up..a convenient expression, with which he rounded off every letter to his correspondent. **1874** Deutsch *Rem.* 62 Prefacing, and rounding it off by an epilogue. **1887** Creighton *Hist. Ess.* xii. (1902) 334 Mr. Symonds has wished to round off his book too completely.

d. To cause to pass pleasantly.

1824 Byron *Juan* xv. xx, A conversational facility, Which may round off an hour upon a time.

e. = sense 4 d above. Also *absol.*

1935 Shuster & Bedford *Field Work in Math.* iv. 14 The product given above, 20·671728 ft., should be 'rounded off' to 20.7 ft. **1945** J. P. Eckert et al. *Description of ENIAC* (PB 86242) (Moore School of Electr. Engin., Univ. Pennsylvania) B-5 The products c_i are rounded-off to the same number of places. **1977** K. M. E. Murray *Caught in Web of Words* xi. 211 James had rounded off sums downwards rather than upwards—writing £900 for an actual £975 for example. **1978** Green & Lewis *Sci. with Pocket Calculators* ii. 21 Many calculators..round off automatically when displaying results.

7. *round in*: a. *Naut.* To haul in. (See quots. 1627 and 1846.)

1627 Capt. Smith *Seaman's Gram.* ix. 42 Let rise the maine tacke and fore tacke, and hale aft the fore sheat to the cats head, and the maine sheat to the cubbridge head, this is Rounding in, or rounding aft the saile. **1769** Falconer *Dict. Marine* (1780) s.v., Round-in the weather-braces! **1825** H. B. Gascoigne *Path to Naval Fame* 53 While some to ease the Tacks and Sheets are found, The Weather Braces in again they Round. **1841** R. H. Dana *Seaman's Man.* 49 Sometimes, if the weather brace cannot be well rounded in, ..the sail may be clewed up to leeward a little, first. *Ibid.*, Ease off the lee brace and round the yard in. **1846** A. Young *Naut. Dict.*, *Round in*, to haul in on a rope; especially on a weather brace. To round in a Tackle, means to haul in the slack of it in a horizontal direction; the term round up is applied in a similar manner when the tackle is in a vertical or sloping direction.

b. To round off (= 6 c).

1889 Stevenson *Edinburgh* 142 A martial swan-song,.. fitly rounding in the labours of the day.

c. To round up (= 5 e).

1900 *Daily News* 15 May 3/3 Perhaps it would be difficult to find men better fitted to 'round in' Republican stragglers. **1907** *Month* July 65 The cattle must be rounded in before breakfast.

8. a. *round out*, to finish or complete; to fill out, make plump. Also *fig.* and *refl.*

1856 Hawthorne *Eng. Note-bks.* (1870) II. 18 Her dream is half accomplished now, and..the remainder may soon be rounded out. **1867** Oliphant *Madonna Mary* II. 223 Your native air will soon round out your dear cheeks. **1926** *Publishers' Weekly* 29 May 1789/2 Presently we came away. The inquiry was rounding itself out. **1937** A. L. Rowse *Sir Richard Grenville* 10 New discoveries..helping to round out and present at length a fairly full portrait of the man. **1947** J. C. Rich *Materials & Methods of Sculpture* Pl. 35/4 (*caption*) Rounding out the forms from the front of the sheet. **1966** *Listener* 24 Nov. 763/1 Now, with three full-length plays behind him..it is possible to round out a little that first impression. **1972** *Daily Tel.* 30 Nov. 21 Lloyds Bank's new merchant bank, set up yesterday to round out the bank's services, has no name. **1979** *Arizona Daily Star* 5 Aug. I. 1/4 The third act very satisfactorily rounds out what has long been a frustrating, partially finished production.

b. *round down*, = overhaul *v.* 1. *Naut.*

1886 *Encycl. Brit.* XXI. 604/2 *Round down*, to overhaul, to slack by hand.

c. *round over*, to turn over so as to close at the end.

1895 *Westm. Gaz.* 22 Jan. 8/2 A new automatic machine, for rounding over, turning in, or closing cartridges.

d. *round down*, to decrease (a number) when rounding it (cf. sense 4 d above) by making no alteration to its remaining digits, or by expressing it as the next lower round number.

1956, etc. [see sense 5 h above]. **1970** *Guardian* 19 Feb. 13/6 The new conversion table would enable prices sometimes to be rounded down, although some may be rounded up. **1971** *Daily Tel.* 9 Nov. 14 It is Post Office practice for telephone bill totals ending in ½p to be rounded down to the nearest whole penny. **1976** [see rounding *vbl. sb.* 1 c].

II. 9. a. To make the complete circuit of, to pass or travel round (the world, a place, etc.).

1592 Greene *Conny Catch.* Pref. p. i, I haue seene the world, and rounded it, though not with trauell, yet with experience. **1615** G. Sandys *Trav.* 84 A hundred Knights Circling the sad pile... Thrice it they round, Their weapons clash. **1667** Milton *P.L.* x. 684 While the low Sun To recompence his distance, in thir sight Had rounded still th' Horizon. **1707** J. Stevens tr. *Quevedo's Com. Wks.* (1709) 232, I saw the Man round and round him, as a Dog does before he lies down. **1799** Southey *Eng. Ecl.* Poet. Wks. III. 169 With Cook he rounded the great globe. **1850** Tennyson *In Mem.* lxiii, The circuits of thine orbit round A higher height, a deeper deep.

fig. **1726-46** Thomson *Winter* 19 To thee..The Muse.. renews her song. Since has she rounded the revolving year.

b. To walk round, take a turn round, make the rounds of (a place, etc.). ? *Obs.*

1622 MABBE tr. *Aleman's Guzman d'Alf.* I. 70 Taking the care vpon him to round the house three or foure times aday. **1648** GAGE *West Ind.* 58 With two servants he would round the City. **1668** DRYDEN *Even. Love* I. ii, Prythee, let's round the street a little; till Maskall watches for their women. *a* **1734** NORTH *Examen* III. vii. §93 (1740) 577 Before I settled in my Quarters, I rounded the Crowd, to observe, as well as I could, what was doing. **1736** CARTE *Ormonde* I. 273 The vigilant governor..had caused all the watches to be twice or thrice rounded that night.

10. a. To pass round so as to get to the opposite side of (a place).

1743 BULKELEY & CUMMINS *Voy. S. Seas* 60 Keeping along Shore, and rounding every Bay. **1803** NELSON 23 May in Nicolas *Disp.* (1845) V. 73 She rounded Ushant yesterday afternoon. **1869** TOZER *Highl. Turkey* I. 201 The road.. penetrating from time to time into the mountain side to round a gorge. **1874** GREEN *Short Hist.* vii. §6. 407 The daring adventurer..rounded the Cape of Good Hope.

b. *slang* or *dial.* To 'get round' a person; to obtain information about or from (one) by artifice, etc.

1854 MISS BAKER *Northampt. Gloss.* s.v., I'll round her, and get the secret out before I've done with her.

11. a. To surround or encircle; to encompass *with* something.

1593 SHAKS. *Rich. II*, III. ii. 161 The hollow Crowne That rounds the mortall Temples of a King. **1599** T. M. *Silkwormes* 60 Rounding themselues ten thousand times and more Yet spinning stil behind and eke before. **1629** MAXWELL tr. *Herodian* (1635) 253 Protracting the time, till his whole army had rounded them. **1698** FRYER *Acc. E. India & P.* 296 They rounding their Cook Rooms with small Furnaces. **1765** J. BYRON *Voy.* in *Hawkesworth* (1773) I. 77 We cut it [*sc.* a cable] into junk and bent a new one, which we rounded with old rigging. **1844** MRS. BROWNING *Drama of Exile* 977 This is the zodiac of the earth, Which rounds us with a visionary dread. **1854** —— *Virgin Mary to the Child Jesus* iv, How motionless Ye round me with your living statuary.

b. In pa. pple. ***rounded.***

1500–20 DUNBAR *Poems* lix. 26 Cuddy Rig the Drumfress fuill May him resave agane this ȝuill, All roundit in-to ȝallow and reid. **1594** GREENE & LODGE *Looking Gl.* G.'s Wks. (Rtldg.) 117/1 Great Nineveh, Rounded with Lycus' silver-flowing streams. **1648** GAGE *West Ind.* 57 A white mantle of lawn or cambrick rounded with a broad lace. **1660** F. BROOKE tr. *Le Blanc's Trav.* 32 The town is large,..well rounded both with walls, and gardens and Arable land. **1871** G. MACDONALD *Wks. Fancy & Imag.* I. 285 Soon was she.. rounded with dead glitter.

c. To hem or shut *in.*

1606 SHAKS. *Tr. & Cr.* I. iii. 196 To weaken and discredit our exposure, How ranke soeuer rounded in with danger. **1911** W. JAMES *Some Probl. Philos.* vi. 99 Rationalistic philosophy has always aspired to a rounded-in view of the whole of things, a closed system of kinds.

12. To cause to turn round, or move in a circle; to bring round. Also with *off.*

1728 CHAMBERS *Cycl.* s.v., Hence, to round a Horse upon a Trot, Gallop, &c. is to make him carry his Shoulders and Haunches roundly or compactly upon a larger or smaller Circle, without traversing or bearing to a Side. **1833** TENNYSON *Mariana in the South* 79 The day..slowly rounded to the east The one black shadow from the wall. **1852** LEVER *M. Tiernay* xxxi, 'She's a stout boat to stand this,' said Tom, as he rounded her off, at a coming wave. **1890** CLARK RUSSELL *Ocean Trag.* III. xxxiv. 241 Rapidly averting his glance when she chanced to round her face towards him on a sudden.

III. *intr.* **13. a.** To walk or go about; *spec.* of a guard, to go the rounds. Now *rare.*

c **1532** DU WES *Introd. Fr.* in *Palsgr.* 938 To ronde or go about, *arondir.* **1598** BARRET *Theor. Wars* IV. iv. 115 The Gouernour..rounding extraordinarily is to giue the Word first vnto the Round. **1605** BACON *Adv. Learn.* I. i. §3 The wise mans eyes keepe watch in his head whereas the foole roundeth about in darknesse. **1667** MILTON *P.L.* IV. 685 Oft in bands While they keep watch, or nightly rounding walk .., thir songs Divide the night. **1941** *Penguin New Writing* II. 14 Early as it is women and old men are hunting for scraps of coal on the side of the incline. They have to be away before the police start to round.

b. To take a circular or winding course; to make a turn, curve, or sweep; to turn round, in various senses. Also const. *in.*

1674 *Boston Rec.* (1881) VII. 89 A high way..to runn.. betweene his other lands and soe roundinge about the side of the hill. **1679** MOXON *Mech. Exerc.* ix. 153 These four Winding steps aforesaid, rounding one quarter about the Newel, turns your Face in your Ascent. **1726** LEONI *Alberti's Archit.* II. 36/1 Those flutings..must round clear round the Column. **1757** W. WILKIE *Epigoniad* I. 2 Time's oblivious gulf,..In whose wide vortex worlds themselves are tost, And rounding swift successively are lost. **1834** MARRYAT *P. Simple* (1863) 392 We tore clear from her, and rounding to the wind shot a-head. **1859** TENNYSON *Pelleas & Ettarre* 138 The men who met him rounded on their heels And wonder'd after him. **1872** JENKINSON *Guide Lakes* (1879) 333 Rounding to the left, and attaining the top of Whiteside, the tourist [etc.]. **1924** GALSWORTHY *White Monkey* I. xiii. 109 He rounded-in from the Embankment towards home.

fig. **1750** FIELDING *Amelia* VIII. ii, Booth had a little mercy on the poor bailiff when he found him rounding in this manner, and told him he had made the matter very clear.

c. To curve *off.*

1677 MOXON *Mech. Exerc.* i. 5 The Heads of Pins that round off towards the edges. **1825** J. NICHOLSON *Operat. Mechanic* 509 The back of it [*sc.* the discharging pallet] a little rounding off from the centre.

d. *Naut.* ***round to,*** to come to the wind and heave to.

1830 MARRYAT *King's Own* xiii, The frigate..now prepared to round-to. **1840** R. H. DANA *Bef. Mast* xviii, She rounded-to and let go her anchor. **1890** CLARK RUSSELL *Marriage at Sea* vi, As she rounded-to, a whole green sea struck her full abeam.

e. *slang.* To become an informer; to peach. Usu. const. *on* (a person).

1859 *Slang Dict.* 82 *Round*, to tell tales, to 'split'..; 'to Round on a man', to swear to him as being the person, etc. **1869** *Times* 19 Jan. 11/6 He said 'I suppose Calvin has "rounded" on me, and I will "round" on him'. **1877** BESANT & RICE *Harp & Cr.* xxiv, You know I would not be such a bad lot as to round on your cousin, whatever he's done.

f. To turn round *on*; to assail, assault, esp. with words; to abuse, berate.

1882 *Sydney Slang Dict.* 7/2 *Round* (*on a man*),..to abuse. **1909** *Blackw. Mag.* Sept. 413/1 On one occasion..she had rounded on him and scolded him for a full half-hour. **1932** E. BOWEN *To North* xx. 211 Cecilia did not round on Julian. **1966** *Listener* 24 Nov. 764/2 It may be possible to find a parallel in the work of other writers whose first impulse, as young men, was to round on society. **1973** *Times* 16 Nov. 4 Professor Peters also rounds on the Inner London Education Authority for exceeding its brief.

14. a. To become round, circular, or spherical; to grow or develop to a full round form. Also with *out.*

1611 SHAKS. *Wint. T.* II. i. 16 The Queene..rounds apace: we shall Present our seruices to a fine new Prince One of these dayes. **1807** CRABBE *Par. Reg.* III. 554 Here clothed and fed, no sooner he began To round and redden, than away he ran. **1877** TENNYSON *Harold* I. i, Albeit no rolling stone,..Thou hast rounded since we met. **1893** *Chamb. Jrnl.* 19 Aug. 514/1 The little green apples grew and rounded and yellowed. **1912** *Red Mag.* Apr. 510/2, I guess she didn't know how she had rounded out in the mountain air.

fig. **1850** TENNYSON *In Mem.* xlv, So rounds he to a separate mind From whence clear memory may begin.

b. To have or assume a curved or rounded form; to curve or inflect. Also with *away* or *up.*

1670 NARBOROUGH *Jrnl.* in *Acc. Sev. Late Voy.* I. (1694) 42 Over the Cliff the Hill rounds up to the top. *Ibid.* 62 The South part rounds away in a Foreland: The South-shore rounds away South-east from this Foreland. **1711** W. SUTHERLAND *Shipbuild. Assist.* 45 If the Beams are required to round equal and alike. **1797** *Encycl. Brit.* (ed. 3) XVII. 411/1 In such a manner that the sheer rounds up, and the highest part is in the midships. **1832** L. HUNT *Poems* 196 That recess, Rounding from the main stream. *c* **1850** *Rudim. Navig.* (Weale) 129 The ledges..arch or round-up.

fig. **1859** WHITTIER *My Psalm* 64 All the angles of its strife Slow rounding into calm.

c. Of a whale: To prepare or make ready to dive by arching the back.

1889 in *Cent. Dict.* s.v.

d. ***to round up,*** to collect in a body.

1879 *Missouri Republican* 22 Oct. 3/7 Are you going to 'round up' at Maj. B.'s tonight? **1890** 'R. BOLDREWOOD' *Col. Reformer* (1891) 239 They are off at full speed..until..they can halt and 'round' up in the beloved camp. *Ibid.* 241 The ..cattle..being permitted to round up on the camp. **1896** BADEN-POWELL *Matabele Campaign* vii, I sounded my whistle and started along on the spoor, the scouts rounding up to me and taking up the trail.

round (raʊnd), *v.*[2] Now *arch.* Forms: α. 1 runian, 2 runien, 3 runen, 3–4 rune, 4 run; 3 rouny, 3–7 roune (4 -en, rone, 5–6 rovne), 4–6, 8 *Sc.* roun. β. 5 rownen, -yn, 4–7 rown(e. γ. 5 ronde, 5–7, 9 round, 6–7 rounde; 6 rownd, *Sc.* rund. [OE. *rúnian* (f. *rún* ROUN), = MDu. *rūnen, ruynen*, OS. *rûnôn* (MLG., LG. *rûnen*), OHG. *rûnên*, MSw. *runa*, to whisper. The normal modern form would have been *rown*; for the excrescent *d* cf. SOUND *sb.* and BOUND *ppl. a.*[1]]

In senses 1–3 very common down to the 17th cent., freq. with the addition of *in the* (or *one's*) *ear.*

1. *intr.* To whisper, to speak in a whisper; to converse or talk privately; †also occas., to mutter or murmur.

α. *c* **1000** ÆLFRIC *Gram.* xxxvi. (Z.) 217 *Susurro*, ic runiȝe. *c* **1000** *Ags. Ps.* (Spelman) xl. 8 Toȝeanes me ðohtan [*Cambr. MS.* runedon] ealle fynd mine. *c* **1250** *Lutel suth Serm.* 59 in *O.E. Misc.* 188 þeos prude maidenes þat..runeþ togaderes and spekeþ of derne luue. *c* **1290** *Beket* 1188 in *S. Eng. Leg.* I. 140 He rounede in is wiues ere, and tolde hire al is þouȝt. *c* **1320** *Sir Tristr.* 169 Mekeliche he gan mele, Among his men to roun. **1390** GOWER *Conf.* I. 161 Whan thei rounen in hire Ere. *c* **1407** LYDG. *Reson & Sens.* 4583, I say yt out, me lyst nat rovne, Thus ye shuld hir name expovne. *a* **1450** *Knt. de la Tour* (1868) 40 He turned towarde the peple, & sawe hem roune, iape, counsaile, and iangle, eche with other. *a* **1548** HALL *Chron., Edw. V*, 22 b, The duke rouned with the Maire and sayed, this is a marueileous obstinate silence. **1570** LEVINS *Manip.* 220 To Roune, *in aurem loqui.*

β. **13..** *Coer de Lion* 2142 The steward on knees him set adown, With the emperour for to rown. **13..** *E.E. Allit. P.* C. 64 Goddes glam to hym glod,..With a roghlych rurd rowned in his ere. **1415** HOCCLEVE *Sir J. Oldcastle* 93 Rowne in the preestes ere & the grace Of thy soule meekly to him confesse. *c* **1440** CAPGRAVE *Life St. Kath.* IV. 2096 Eche to other ful preuely thus dede rowne. **1526** SKELTON *Magnyf.* 1664 Yf it lyke you that I myght rowne in your eyre.

γ. *a* **1450** *Mankind* 292 (Brandl), He wyll ronde in yowur ere. **1526** *Pilgr. Perf.* (W. de W. 1531) 93 Preuy backbytynge ..is whan one whyspereth or roundeth with an other & secretely spekeᵺ..euyll of theyr neyghbour. **1592** GREENE *Conny Catch.* III. Wks. (Grosart) X. 170 Then hearken in thy eare, saide the Nip, and so rounding with him, cut the poore mans purse. **1620–6** QUARLES *Feast for Wormes* 517 My sacred Muse hath rounded in mine eare, And read the myst'ry of a twofold feare. **1822** SCOTT *Nigel* iii, So they let me go, and rode out, a' sniggering, laughing, and rounding in ilk ither's lugs.

†**b.** *transf.* Of the wind: To whistle. *Obs.*—[1]

c **1440** *Pallad. on Husb.* VI. 156 But ther the place is cloos is hem tenclude, And holde out wynde, although he rowne, or crie.

2. *trans.* To whisper (something); to utter or communicate in a whisper.

α. *c* **1000** in *Salomon & Saturn* (Kemble) 258 þeah þe mon hwylces hlihȝe..ne rehst þu hwæt hy rædon, oððe runion. **1303** R. BRUNNE *Handl. Synne* 6930 A man..Rouned yn seynt Ihons ere, þat he hadde broght..þyrty pounde. **1390** GOWER *Conf.* II. 209 The mannes herte anon is there, And rouneth tales in hire Ere. **1721** RAMSAY *Lucky Spence* xiii, I ..Roun'd in his lug, that there was a Poor country Kate [etc.].

β. *c* **1386** CHAUCER *Wife's T.* Prol. 241 (Ellesm.), What rowne ye with oure mayde? *c* **1412** HOCCLEVE *De Reg. Princ.* 1273 Seint Ambrose..Anon right rowned to his compaignye, 'Sires, it is tyme þat we hennes hye'. *c* **1450** *Myrr. Our Lady* 47, I rowned to the in the quyer halfe wordes, & therfore I am byden to satysfaccion. **1683** E. HOOKER in Pordage *Mystic Div.* Pref. Ep. 81 When thei rown in their maids ears so frequently and fiercely, What slow haste make yee?

γ. *a* **1529** SKELTON *Bouge of Court* 513, I haue an errande to rounde in your ere. **1552** in *Vicary's Anat.* (1888) App. XVI. 292 Certeyne busie bodies..rounded into the eares of the preachers..their tender consideracion. **1611** SHAKS. *Wint. T.* I. ii. 217 They're here with me already; whisp'ring, rounding: Sicilia is a so-forth. *c* **1680** Row *Suppl. Blair's Autobiog.* (Wodrow Soc.) 547 The Prelates did round and whisper among themselves what was spoken or done. **1823** SCOTT *Quentin D.* xxxvi, Bringing out honest De la Marck's plan.., instead of rounding it in my ear. **1858** CARLYLE *Fredk. Gt.* IX. x. (1865) III. 173 Ill Margraf rounded things into the Crown-Prince's ear, in an unmannerly way.

3. To address (a person) in a whisper; in later use *esp.* to take (one) privately to task.

α. β. *c* **1400** LOVE *Bonavent. Mirr.* (1908) 106 Sche wente ..to hir sone Jesu..and rowned hym in the ere and seyde. **1535** COVERDALE *Job* xxxiii. 15 In dreames and visions of the night season..he rowneth them in the eares. **1597** J. KING *On Jonas* (1618) 145 They shall euen feel themselues to be touched, and so closely rouned in the eare, as they cannot deny their offence. **1649** R. HODGE *Plain Direct.* 18 She went round about, and rowned him in his ear.

γ. **1530** PALSGR. 694/2 Go rounde hym in the eare and bydde him come and suppe with me. **1577–87** HOLINSHED *Chron.* III. 1149/1 George Gilpin..came to him and rounded him in his eare. **1606** S. GARDINER *Bk. Angling* 85 Elias thought himself the only remainder of the Church of Israel..: But God otherwise rounded him in the eare. *a* **1689** MRS. BEHN *Novels* II. 260 At first he thought to round him severely in the ear about it. **1731** MEDLEY *Kolben's Cape G. Hope* I. 82 The king of the country sent for him and rounded him in the ear on his purpos'd treachery. **1815** *Hist. John Decastro* I. 49 Old Crab did not let slip so favourable an opportunity to round his brother a little in the ear upon this subject. **1855** KINGSLEY *Westw. Ho!* xviii, He rounded his friend Mr. Brimblecombe in the ear, and told him he had better play the man a little more.

b. With double object: To whisper (something) to (a person).

1579 GOSSON *Sch. Abuse* (Arb.) 74 His Pypers were ready too rounde him in the eare, what he should speake. **1604** MIDDLETON *Black Bk.* Wks. 1885 VIII. 29 This rammish penny-father I rounded in the left ear..the place and hour. **1688** *Vox Cleri Pro Rege* 53 We have oft of late been rounded in the Ears, That the Priests Lips do keep Knowledge. **1823** LAMB *Elia* II. *New Year's Coming of Age*, He slily rounded the first lady in the ear, that an action might lie against the Crown. **1868** BROWNING *Ring & Bk.* IV. 600 Then round us in the ears from morn to night,..That you are robbed, starved, beaten and what not.

†**c.** To whisper into (the ear). *Obs. rare.*

1624 QUARLES *Job Militant* VII. 13 Did Record ever round thine eare, That God forsooke the heart, that was sincere? **1646** —— *Judgement & Mercy* Wks. (Grosart) I. 93 But, hark, my soule, there's something rounds mine eare.

†**4.** *intr.* To speak, talk, discourse (*of* something). *Obs.*

c **1200** *Trin. Coll. Hom.* 107 His eȝen to sen, his earen to listen,..his muð to runien. **13..** *Sir Beues* 4 Lordinges, herkneþ to me tale!.. Of a kniȝt ich wile ȝow roune. *c* **1375** *Cursor M.* 14922 (Fairf.), For-þi in rime wille we roun.

†**b.** *trans.* To say, speak, tell (something). *Obs.*

a **1300** *Cursor M.* 28110 Oft ic ha roned soth or lese þat i wyst noiþer queþer it wese. *c* **1386** CHAUCER *Sir Thopas* 124, I wol yow rowne How sir Thopas..Is comen agayn to towne.

†**5.** *intr.* To take counsel, deliberate, meditate.

c **1205** LAY. 5817 þer innen heo speken, þer inne heo runden ane lutle while. *Ibid.* 19340 Cnihtes gunnen runen, cnihtes gunnen ræden. **1430–40** LYDG. *Bochas* V. vii. (1554) 127 Perseueraunce, who list muse and roun, Graunteth to them..The triumph.

†**b.** *trans.* To talk about (or *over*); to discuss.

c **1205** LAY. 9860 Al niht heo runden, Whæt heom weoren to ræde. *Ibid.* 24887 þer men gunnen rune..wulc andswere he ȝiuen wolde. *c* **13..** *Cursor M.* 19713 (Gött.), þair redis þarfor gun þai rune wid all þe kepers of þat tune. *c* **1450** *Cov. Myst.* (Shaks. Soc.) 401 Rapely ye renne your resonys to rowne. **1535** STEWART *Cron. Scot.* II. 629 Syne quietlie togidder tha did roun The fassoun how he wald gif ouir the toun. **1637** RUTHERFORD *Lett.* (1862) I. 294 Oh how many black accounts have Christ and I rounded over together in the house of my pilgrimage!

†**c.** To take or give as counsel. *Obs.*

c **1205** LAY. 13189 Heo redden, heo runden [*c* **1275** rouneden],..þat Ambrosie heo wolden habben. *Ibid.* 16997 He þe wolde runen selest ræden.

round about, *adv.* and *prep.* [See ROUND *adv.* and ABOUT.]

In Gower *Confessio Amantis* and Spenser *F.Q.* the inverted form *about round* is also used.

A. *adv.* **1.** In a ring or circle; all round; on all sides or in all directions.

1338 R. Brunne *Chron. Wace* (Rolls) 8783 Rounde aboute, þer ar þey [stones] set. 1390 Gower *Conf.* I. 54 A litel plein, All round aboute wel besein With buisshes. c1420 Lydg. *Assembly of Gods* 386 Thus was the table set rownde aboute With goddys & goddesses. 1490 Caxton *Eneydos* xxxi. 117 Euery chambre was walled and closed rounde aboute. 1526 Tindale *Rom.* xv. 19 From Jerusalem and the costes rounde aboute, vnto Illiricum. 1581 Blandy *Castle of Policy* 16b, The souldiar standes readely furnisht to fight in the fielde, where he may looke round aboute. 1617 Moryson *Itin.* I. 58 Under the fortification of the Castle round about, are stables for horses. 1655 Stanley *Hist. Philos.* (1701) 86/2 Frequently looking back and round about, as greedy to be Revenged of the Enemy. 1703 Maundrell *Journ. Jerus.* (1707) 17 On the other side.. stood a great square Tower, and round about, the rubbish of many other Buildings. 1725 *Fam. Dict.* s.v. *Marchpane* ¶2 The Paste must be carefully stirr'd to the Bottom, and also round about. 1768 Ross *Helenore* 66 When day was up, an' a' clear round about. 1859 Geo. Eliot *A. Bede* x, They work at different things—some in the mill, and many in the mines, in the villages round about. 1878 Browning *Poets Croisic* i, Yon hollow, crusted roundabout With copper where the clamp was.

2. With a circular or encircling movement; so as to pass or turn right round.

1500–20 Dunbar *Poems* lvi. 14 Let anis the cop ga round about. 1535 Lyndesay *Satyre* 824 Me think the warld rinnis round about. 1586 B. Young *Guazzo's Civ. Conv.* iv. 188 Euerie one beganne to drink round about. 1611 Cotgr., *Vireuoulter*, to..turne or wheele round about. 1648 Hexham ii, *Rondt-om gaen*, to goe Round about.

3. To the opposite direction.

1582 Allen *Martyrdom Campion* (1908) 115 Which [psalms] finished turning himself round about to all the people, [he] said unto them in this sort. a1800 *Lady Maisry* xii, She's turnd her right an roun about. 1901 M. Carmichael *Life Walshe* vi. 82 And do but turn round about and behold the gentle city of Lucca.

4. By a circuitous path or route.

1870 Spurgeon *Treas. David* Ps. xxx. 2 He went at once to head-quarters, and not roundabout to fallible means. 1886 Holland *Chesh. Gloss.* s.v. *Raind-abait*, To go reawnd-abeawt for th' next road.

B. *prep.* **1.** So as to move or pass round; so as to encircle by moving round.

1484 Caxton *Fables of Æsop* v. ix, I haue gone round aboute the countre and prouynce. a1548 Hall *Chron., Edw. IV*, 8b, The lord Scales roade round aboute hym. 1598 Shaks. *Merry W.* iv. iv. 31 An old tale goes, that Herne the Hunter..Doth..Walke round about an Oake. 1605 —— *Macb.* iv. i. 4 Round about the Caldron go: In the poysond Entrailes throw. a1639 Carew *Beautiful Mistress* 12 The darkness flies, and light is hurl'd Round about the silent world. 1735 Pope *Prol. Sat.* 186 He who now to sense, now nonsense leaning, Means not, but blunders round about a meaning. a1833 *Battle of Otterburn* iv, He marchd up to Newcastle, And rode it round about. 1882 Blackmore *Christowell* ii, Tim went round about it,..and avoided the village.

2. In a ring or circle about; on all sides of; in all directions from.

1535 Coverdale *Exod.* vii. 24 The Egipcians dygged rounde aboute yᵉ ryuer, for water to drinke. 1590 Spenser *F.Q.* ii. ii. 25 Attonce he wards and strikes; he takes and paies;..Before, behind, and round about him laies. 1632 Milton *Penseroso* 48 And hears the Muses in a ring, Ay round about Joves Altar sing. 1676 Grew *Anat. Pl.* (1682) 175 Sometimes they [*sc.* flowers] are placed round about the Branch, that is, Coronated. 1728 Chambers *Cycl.* s.v. *Horse-Shoe*, Shoes with swelling Welts or Borders round about them. 1833 Tennyson *Lady of Shalott* iv. i, Round about the prow she wrote 'The Lady of Shalott'. 1871 Earle *Philol. Eng. Tongue* (1873) 8 Round about these, in a broken curve, are found the representatives of the Low Dutch family.

3. Of time, amount, etc.: about; approximately; = around *prep.* 4b.

1913 P. Reeves (*title*) Round about a pound a week. 1926 W. R. Inge *Lay Thoughts* 182 In the Middle Ages the births and deaths in the undrained towns were both round about 50 per thousand in each year. 1961 N. Cardus *Sir T. Beecham* 64 It was round about 1931 that he told me he was about to form a new orchestra in London.

roundabout ('raʊndəbaʊt), *sb.* and *a.* Also round-about. [f. prec.]

A. *sb.* **1. a.** A circle; a circular course or object; a circular encampment, a surrounding hedge, etc.

c1535 in *Dugdale's Monast.* (1825) V. 184/2 There is in the seid close a motte called the round abowte. 1591 Sylvester *Du Bartas* i. vi. 911 An Iron Fly flew out; Which having showne a perfect Round-about,..return'd unto her Master. 1674 Fairfax *Bulk & Selv.* 199 All the round-about of earthly beings. 1795 *Statist. Acc. Scot.* XV. 84 There are a great many round-abouts in the parish, commonly called Picts Works. 1816 Scott *Antiq.* i, A Pict's camp, or Round-about. 1854 Miss Baker *Northampt. Gloss.*, *Round-About*, the boundary-hedge of a coppice. 1894 *Murray's Handbk. Oxf.* 136 The Camp, locally the 'Round-about', is 140 yds. in diameter.

b. A plump, rounded figure. *rare*⁻¹.

1812 Combe *Syntax, Picturesque* i, Her face was red, her form was fat, A round-about, and rather squat.

c. *Sc.* 'An oatcake of a circular form, pinched all round with the finger and thumb' (Jam.).

1824 *Tournay* 31 (Jam.), Nackets and round-abouts to your coffee. 1828 Moir *Mansie Wauch* iii. (1849) 18 Round-abouts and snaps brown and white quality.

2. †**a.** A farthingale. *Obs.*⁻¹

1552 Latimer *Serm.* xxxv. (1584) 281 In the old tyme women were content with honest and single garments. Now they haue found out these round-aboutes.

b. *U.S.* A short jacket.

1823 J. F. Cooper *Pilot* i. vi. 66 The young sailor.. slipped his arms into the sleeves of a morning round-about, covered with the trappings of his profession. 1825 in *Trans Illinois State Hist. Soc. 1910* (1912) 177, I have twelve shirts six pair Pantaloons 6 vests..two round-abouts. 1843 Marryat *M. Violet* xliv, To wear their light nankeen trousers and gingham round-abouts. 1876 'Mark Twain' *Tom Sawyer* i, She turned just in time to seize a small boy by the slack of his roundabout. 1904 *N.Y. Even. Post* 7 Jan. 7 Only yesterday this young man was playing about the streets of Washington, a schoolboy in roundabouts.

c. *U.S.* An armchair with a rounded back.

1844 *Lowell Offering* IV. 175 [He sat] in a large flat-bottomed 'roundabout' on the opposite side of the fire-place. 1864 in Webster.

†**d.** *U.S.* A loose dressing-gown worn by women. †**e.** *N.Z.* (See quot. 1861.) *Obs.*

1841 *Southern Lit. Messenger* VII. 525/1 The garment is a long, loose roundabout, connecting in front with strings, and is much worn, even at the present time. 1856 V. Lush *Jrnl.* 17 Jan. (1971) 176 The whole lot stood quietly looking at us, clothed from top to toe in their long full roundabouts. 1861 R. B. Paul *N.Z.* 17 [The Maori women's] usual dress is..a shapeless sack of printed calico, called a 'roundabout', tied round the neck but loose at the waist. 1874 W. M. Baines *Narr. E. Crewe* 118, I also gave [the Maori girl] 8 yards of Navy blue print (which everyone knows is enough for a 'roundabout'). 1890 P. A. Philips *Reminisc. Early Days* 7 The hostess did not dress for dinner..her usual attire being a Maori roundabout. 1895 K. D. Wiggin *Village Watch-Tower* 103 Mother had let her slip on her new green roundabout over her nightgown.

3. †**a.** A shifty person. *Obs.*⁻¹ Cf. B. 1a.

1605 Breton *I pray you be not Angrie* Wks. (Grosart) II. 8/1 This rascal round-about, without good complexion or good condition.

b. A circuitous or indirect way; a detour.

1755 Washington *Writ.* (1889) I. 152 A very fatiguing ride and long round about, brought me to the General..at Frederick-Town. 1786 Cowper *Let. Lady Hesketh* 17 Apr. (1904) III. 18 A door opening out of our garden..will save the roundabout by the town. 1827 Scott *Jrnl.* 10 July, I went to Cadell's by the Mound, a long roundabout. 1858 Mrs. Carlyle *Lett.* II. 384 A bridge burnt down over the Trent, which occasioned a great roundabout. 1879 Browning *Martin Relph* 126 The floods were out, he was forced to take such a roundabout of ways!

fig. 1734 North *Examen* iii. vi. §10 (1740) 430 We must be excused for walking the Author's Pace, in all his Round-abouts, though it be out of all known Track of Truth.

c. An indirect utterance; a circumlocution.

1616–61 Holyday *Persius* (1673) 340/2 Wherefore, not to trouble our selves with these round-abouts, the old and ordinary exposition..seems to me most easie. 1753–4 Richardson *Grandison* (1781) II. 77, I began with my roundabouts and my suppose's. 1775 S. J. Pratt *Liberal Opin.* cxxv. (1783) IV. 143 Unsettle by systems and long-laboured literary roundabouts, the very marrow in the hollow of your bones. 1802 Mrs. E. Parsons *Myst. Visit* III. 243 After several roundabouts leading to the subject. 1875 Browning *Aristoph. Apol.* 148 All my roundabout Ends at beginning, with my own defence.

4. †**a.** A kind of round dance. *Obs.*

1766 Goldsm. *Vic. W.* ix, Though the Miss Flamboroughs..understood the jig and round-about to perfection, yet they were totally unacquainted with country dances. 1815 P. Roberts *Cambrian Antiq.* 46 The Roundabout, or more precisely the Cheshire-round.., is danced by two only.

b. A merry-go-round. ***to gain on the swings and lose on the roundabouts***: see swing *sb.*²

1763 *Brit. Mag.* IV. 50 There was a round-about for children to ride in, and all sorts of toys sold as at other fairs. 1813 *Sporting Mag.* XLII. 20 There were the usual swings, ups-and-downs and roundabouts. 1879 Sala *Paris Herself Again* (1880) II. 320 The great roundabouts, worked by steam, made a fearful clatter.

transf. 1780–2 Cowper *Jackdaw* 25 He sees, that this great roundabout—The world, with all its motley rout,..Is no concern at all of his.

c. A circular tour or excursion.

1894 *Westm. Gaz.* 20 Oct. 7/2 The general manager.. personally conducted the party on a 'roundabout', which took in fifty..miles of the Cambrian Railway.

d. A junction at which traffic moves one way round a central island. Cf. rondpoint b, rotary *sb.* 3.

1927 *Glasgow Herald* 3 Jan. 7/2 There is only one draw-back to the roundabout, and that is the inconvenience caused to pedestrians. 1937 *Times* 13 Apr. (British Motor No.) p. viii/1 Roundabouts..have the advantage of keeping vehicles on the move. 1947 *Daily Mail* 22 May 3/4 Removal of the Mansion House to make room for a big round-about. 1955 *Times* 2 Aug. 9/7 Makeshift tactics are particularly evident in the proposed treatment at Hyde Park Corner which includes an extremely complicated roundabout. 1967 *Listener* 28 Sept. 398/1 People make only occasional use of their speedometer..on such critical occasions as the approach to roundabouts. 1977 *Belfast Tel.* 14 Feb. 5/9, 12 shots were fired at an armoured police vehicle near the roundabout at Narrow-water Castle.

5. a. A burglar's tool: (see quot.).

1796 *Grose's Dict. Vulg. T.* (ed. 3), *Round About*, an instrument used in house-breaking... It will cut a round piece, about five inches in diameter, out of a shutter or door.

b. A rotatory vessel used in tanning.

1852 Morfit *Tanning & Currying* (1853) 411 In some places the tanning process is slightly modified..by the use of a large barrel-churn, or *roundabout*, which receives both the skins and alum-bath.

6. *Sc.* (See quot. and B. 5.)

1825 Jamieson, *Round-About*,..a fire-place,..in which the grate is detached from the walls, and so placed that persons may sit around it on all sides.

B. *adj.* **1.** Not following a straight course; not straightforward; circuitous, indirect.

a. Of persons. *rare.* Cf. A. 3a.

1608 Middleton *Mad World* ii. i, You progressive round-about rascal. 1823 Coleridge *Table-t.* 4 Jan., A rogue is a roundabout fool.

b. Of a way or journey.

1701 J. Norris in *Pennsylv. Hist. Soc. Mem.* IX. 43 We had a roundabout journey. 1710 Steele *Tatler* No. 234 ¶7 To carry them a dark Round-about Way to let them in at a Back-Door. 1834 James *J. Marston Hall* xi, I informed him that I enjoyed a roundabout more than a straightforward track. 1893 Selous *Trav. S.E. Africa* 56 After a hard day's walk over a very roundabout road.

c. Of methods or procedure.

1704 Norris *Ideal World* ii. i. 7, I need not argue this roundabout way. 1778 Miss Burney *Evelina* xxvi, She declared that she would have nothing to do with any round-about ways, but go openly and instantly to law. 1833 L. Ritchie *Wand. by Loire* 241 Why move towards your object in this round-about manner? 1864 Bowen *Logic* vii. 204 The Logicians invented the awkward, roundabout, and operose process which they called Reduction per impossibile.

d. Of statements or utterances.

1737 *S. Carolina Gaz.* 30 Apr.–7 May 1/1 [Drunkenness] bears no kind of Similitude with any sort of Virtue, from which it might..borrow a Name; and is therefore reduc'd to the wretched Necessity of being express'd by distant round-about Phrases. 1755 Smollett *Quix.* (1803) II. 193, I would not willingly disclose myself of a sudden, but prepare him by some round-about insinuation. 1818 Hazlitt *Eng. Poets* v. (1870) 114 A flimsy, round-about, unmeaning commencement. 1861 T. A. Trollope *La Beata* I. ix. 254 Before the old wax-chandler had got a quarter through his hints and round-about explanations. 1885 Clodd *Myths & Dr.* i. vi. 105 The savage..will use all sorts of roundabout phrases to avoid saying it.

e. Of a blow. *rare.*

1830 Lytton *Paul Clifford* vi, That round-about sort of blow with the left fist is very unfavourable towards the preservation of a firm balance.

f. Of or pertaining to a junction at which traffic moves one way around a central island. Cf. sense A. 4d above.

1927 *Rep. Commissioner Police Metropolis, 1926* 18 During the past year round-about systems of traffic have been put into operation at Parliament Square [etc.]. 1939 *War Illustr.* 7 Oct. 127 This car was found abandoned the morning after colliding with the posts of a 'roundabout' island. 1976 *Alyn & Deeside Observer* 10 Dec. 1/6 From there it runs to Broughton in the Welsh county of Clwyd and ends at a roundabout junction.

2. Taking a complete survey. *rare.*

a1704 Locke *Wks.* (1724) III. 391 Those who readily and sincerely follow Reason, but for want of having that which one may call large, sound, round about Sense, have not a full view of all that relates to the Question. [1876 Bancroft *Hist. U.S.* VI. li. 467 Hamilton was excelled by Madison in wisdom, large, sound, roundabout sense and perception of what the country would grant.]

3. a. Of garments: Cut circularly round the bottom; without a train or tails; going right round.

1710 Steele *Tatler* No. 245 ¶2 Six round-about Aprons with Pockets. 1837 Hook in *New Monthly Mag.* XLIX. 468, I hear the rustling of Mrs. Brandyball's roundabout silk gown. 1854 J. L. Stephens *Centr. Amer.* 6, I took my seat in a roundabout jacket upon a chair exceedingly comfortable.

b. Designating a type of chair with a rounded seat or back (see quots.). Cf. sense A. 2c.

1741 in J. S. Moore *Goods & Chattels of our Forefathers* (1976) 286 Six India Back Chairs and a Round about Ditto with Leather seats £2 os od. 1840 *Knickerbocker* XVI. 115, I sat in my roundabout chair the other evening. 1936 F. C. Morse *Furniture* 170 'Roundabout' chairs are met with in inventories from 1738 under various names,—'three-cornered chair', 'half round chair', 'round about chair'. 1952 J. Gloag *Short Dict. Furnit.* 398 The round-about chair has a circular seat, either upholstered or caned, a semi-circular back, and six legs. 1960 H. Hayward *Antique Coll.* 84/1 Corner chairs were known in the 17th cent. and were sometimes called elbow chairs or roundabout chairs. 1966 M. M. Pegler *Dict. Interior Design* (1967) 380 *Roundabout chair.* This chair is usually designed to fit into a corner, the square seat diagonally set and the back extending across two adjoining sides.

4. Of persons: Plump or stout in figure.

1806 Scott *Fam. Lett.* (1894) I. ii. 35 We have..a little roundabout girl with large dark eyes. 1840 Bremner *Excurs. Denmark*, etc. II. 406 The easy round-about men seen in Copenhagen, would excite a smile if seen side by side with these handsome fellows. 1892 Tennyson *Foresters* i. i, Each of 'em..as sleek and as round-about as a mellow codlin.

5. Allowing persons to sit all round. (Cf. A. 6.)

1802 C. Findlater *Gen. View Agric. Peebles* 40 The round-about fire side..was universally in use in the kitchen. 1815 Pennecuik *Descr. Tweeddale* 82 The round-about fireside..was universally in use in the kitchen. 1978 T. Henderson *Shetland* 142 (*caption*) A round-about fire in Walls about 1910.

6. That surrounds or encircles.

c1860 H. Stuart *Seaman's Catech.* 49 The head of the sail is brought to the gaff by an earring and roundabout lacing.

'roundabout, *v. rare.* [f. the adv.] *intr.* (with *it*). To wander about. Similarly (or from the adj.), **roundabou'tation,** circumlocution; **rounda'boutedly** *adv.*, = *roundaboutly*; **rounda'boutedness, roundabou'tility,** = *roundaboutness*; **'rounda,bouting** *vbl. sb.*, the action of going round about; **'rounda,boutly** *adv.*, in a roundabout manner; **'rounda,boutness,** the quality of being roundabout.

1812 Byron *Waltz* To Publ., Away they went, and *roundabouted it till supper-time. 1812 H. & J. Smith *Rej. Addr.* xix, To finish my tale without *roundaboutation. 1833 M. Scott *T. Cringle* xv, You had better say boldly that you do not without any roundaboutation. **1870** DICKENS *E. Drood* ix, What..was euphuistically, not to say *roundaboutedly, denominated 'the apartment allotted to study'. **1840** *Fraser's Mag.* XXII. 346 The lengthiness and '*roundaboutedness' which distinguish the effusions of diplomatists. **1863** *Examiner* 5 Sept., A precious example of *roundaboutility worthy of note. *a* **1860** J. YOUNGER *Autobiog.* (1881) xviii. 212 Its friskings, wanderings and *round-aboutings. **1876** MISS BROUGHTON *Joan* i, He said it ..more lengthily and *roundaboutly. **1810** SOUTHEY in C. C. Southey *Life* (1850) III. 274 The vice of the *Friend* is its *roundaboutness. **1826** MISS MITFORD *Village* Ser. III. (1863) 479 Woody lanes, which wind along from farm to farm,..meandering with such a surprising round-aboutness. **1891** *Athenæum* 18 Apr. 505/2 Coleridge replies in a letter intensely characteristic in its roundaboutness.

roundal, obs. form of ROUNDEL.

round-all. (See quot.)
1851 MAYHEW *Lond. Labour* III. 112 Doing..round-alls (that's throwing yourself backwards on to your hands and back again to your feet).

roundar, variant of ROUNER *Obs.*

round-arch. *Arch.* [ROUND *a.* 17.] *attrib.* Characterized by arches of a semicircular or rounded form, as in the Romanesque style.
1840 *Penny Cycl.* XVI. 275/1 There is quite as much dissimilarity as resemblance between the Lombardic or round-arch style of Italy and that of this country. **1853** RUSKIN *Stones Venice* II. vi. 215 Romanesque: Round-arch Architecture. Never thoroughly developed until Christian times. *a* **1878** SCOTT *Lect. Archit.* (1879) I. 18 The round-arch variety [was perfected] in the twelfth century.

round-arched, *a.* [ROUND *a.* 16.] Having rounded arches; *spec.* = ROUND-ARCH.
1606 SYLVESTER *Du Bartas* II. iv. *Magnificence* 887 Then ..they come Into a stately, rich, round-arched Room. **1849** FREEMAN *Archit.* 137 Consistent round-arched architecture took a leap from Etruria to Germany and England. **1887** RUSKIN *Præterita* II. 199 Two of the churches representing the perfectest phase of round-arched building in Europe.

round-arm, *a.* and *adv.* [ROUND *a.* 17.]
1. *Cricket.* Of bowling: Performed with an outward swing of the arm; also *ellipt.* (Cf. BOWL *v.*[1] 4.); or of a bowler who delivers the ball thus.
[**1833** J. MITFORD in *Gentl. Mag.* Sept. 238/2 Ashby.. introduced the round bowling, by throwing the arm in a sweeping circular position.] **1836** *New Sporting Mag.* Oct. 358 Mr. Lowth is a round-arm, left handed bowler. **1850** 'BAT' *Cricket. Man.* 33 Upon the introduction of what was defined 'round arm' [bowling], the path of the ball assumed a curvilineal form. *Ibid.* 34 Mr. J. Wills..devoted much time in maturing the round-arm system. **1889** in Lucas *Hambledon Men* (1907) 184 My opinion is..that with the present grounds round-arm must be depended upon.
2. Of blows: Dealt with a circular sweep of the arm. Also as *adv.*
1886 *Daily News* 4 Sept. 6/6 The blow was a round-arm one, and was done purposely. **1898** DOYLE *Trag. Korosko* v, He hit like a girl, round arm, with an open palm.
Hence **round-armed** *a.*; **round-armer**, a round-armed delivery.
1854 Round-armed [see BOWL *v.*[1] 4b]. **1863** *Lillywhite's Cricket Scores* III. 43 A medium-paced round-armed bowler. **1884** *Sat. Rev.* 26 Jan. 108/1 The clumsy round-armed hit..is not esteemed so highly as a straight hit made correctly from the shoulder. **1951** R. ROBINSON *From Boundary* ii. 39 He rings in a leg-break or a round-armer now and again. **1954** J. FINGLETON *Ashes crown Year* 255 Then came Miller's..appeal..as he rapped May's pads with a round-armer.

†**round-bow**, *v. Obs.* [ROUND *adv.* 2b.] *intr.* To curve convexly.
1591 SYLVESTER *Du Bartas* I. iii. 436 If in every coast Seas' liquid Glass round-bow'd not every where, With sister Earth, to make a perfect Sphear.

†**round-dealing**, *a. Obs.* [ROUND *adv.* 10c.] Dealing plainly or honestly.
1642 CHAS. I *Answ. to Printed Bk.* 1 Who..like Round-dealing men tell Us in plain English, That they have done Us no wrong. **1653** R. SANDERS *Physiogn.* 162 A round-dealing friendship, without deceit or circumvention. **1667** O. HEYWOOD *Heart-Treas.* viii. Wks. 1827 II. 88 Such are the chastising words of a round-dealing ministry, bitter at present, but profitable afterwards.
Comb. **1674** FAIRFAX *Bulk & Selv.* 37 To this we answer round-dealing-wise.

round-eared, *a.* [ROUND *a.*] Having round ears, or ear-like appendages.
a. In names of plants (see quots.).
1704 *Dict. Rust.* (1726) s.v. *Withy*, The round-ear'd shining Willow. **1841** *Penny Cycl.* XX. 359/2 *Salix aurita*, round-eared sallow:..stipules roundish, convex, toothed. **1855** MISS PRATT *Flower. Pl.* V. 98 Round-eared Sallow, or Trailing Sallow;..sometimes becomes a bushy tree, but is more commonly a shrub.
b. Of a cap.
1740 RICHARDSON *Pamela* I. 50, I bought of a Pedlar, two pretty enough round-ear'd Caps, a little Straw Hat. **1742** FIELDING *J. Andrews* IV. xvi, She wore one of her own short round-eared caps. **1815** SCOTT *Guy M.* xxxvi, The mistress of the place, with her..hair straggling like that of Megæra from under a round-eared cap. **1847** MRS. SHERWOOD *Life* xiii. 232 A gentle, quiet, old-fashioned looking girl, in a white apron and round-eared cap.

'rounded, *ppl. a.* [f. ROUND *v.*[1]]
I. † **1. a.** Of persons or their heads: Tonsured; shorn, cropped. **b.** Of the hair: Closely cut or trimmed. *Obs.*
1430–40 LYDG. *Bochas* IX. xiv, Like a byshop rounded and yshorne. **1432–50** tr. *Higden* (Rolls) I. 263 The men of that londe be rowndede in the maner of a cercle, as moche as men be of moore nobilite, in so moche thei be rowndede more hye. **1500–20** DUNBAR *Poems* lix. 19 He wantis nocht bot a rowndit heid. **1577–87** HOLINSHED *Chron.* I. 120/1 For he was rounded or shauen after the maner of the East church. **1605** CAMDEN *Rem., Epigr.* 10 Among whom long bushie haire was the signale mark of Maiestie,..when as all subiects were rounded, and the Kings only long haired.
2. a. Of a convex form; rising with an outward curve or swell on all sides.
1712 PARNELL *Spect.* No. 460 ¶6 The Top of the Building being rounded, bore so far the Resemblance of a Bubble. **1795** SOUTHEY *Joan of Arc* VII. 349 Where the buckler was beneath Rounded, the falchion struck. **1869** TOZER *Highl. Turkey* I. 19 These tents were circular in form, and rounded towards the top. **1878** HUXLEY *Physiogr.* xix. 337 The rounded surface of the earth.
b. Esp. of hills or rising ground.
1841 SPALDING *Italy & It. Isl.* I. 30 The mountains..are rounded in shape. **1853** KANE *Grinnell Exped.* xxviii. (1856) 229 At another time, you travel over rounded dunes of old seasoned hummock. **1871** KINGSLEY *At Last* i, A rounded hill some fifteen hundred feet high.
3. Of limbs, etc.: Having a full, swelling form; symmetrical, finely shaped.
1830 TENNYSON *Sea-Fairies* 4 The weary mariners..saw ..Sweet faces, rounded arms, and bosoms prest To little harps of gold. **1855** KINGSLEY *Westw. Ho!* xxiii, Her stature was taller, her limbs were fuller and more rounded. **1863** MISS BRADDON *Eleanor's Victory* i, The ankle so revealed was rounded and slender.
4. a. Having a roundish or circular, globular or spherical, form.
1834 MCMURTRIE *Cuvier's Anim. Kingd.* 351 The body is rounded and convex in some, oval or oblong..in others. **1851** CARPENTER *Man. Phys.* (ed. 2) 184 All stages of gradation may be traced, between simple rounded cavities.. and the lenticular lacuna. **1899** *Allbutt's Syst. Med.* VIII. 926 The individual lesions..may form large rounded patches.
b. *Geol.* Made round and smooth by attrition.
1802 PLAYFAIR *Huttonian Th.* 51 The fragments of the primary rock..are many of them rounded and worn. **1839** URE *Dict. Arts* 830 Portions of rounded gravel and organic remains. **1893** SIR H. H. HOWORTH *Glacial Nightmare* I. 36 While rounded boulders occur on the mountains, unrounded ones occur in the river beds.
c. Formed into a coil or round. *rare.*
1845 S. JUDD *Margaret* I. xvii, Bull, the dog, lies rounded on the hearth, his nose between his paws, fast asleep.
d. Trimmed to a cylindrical form.
1890 'R. BOLDREWOOD' *Col. Reformer* (1891) 225 The 'cap'..always of rounded and not of split timber like the lower bars.
5. a. Made round or curved, *esp.* at an extremity or end.
1796 WITHERING *Brit. Pl.* (ed. 3) IV. 106 Clefts differing in depth, generally three at the end, which is rounded. **1831** KNOX *Cloquet's Anat.* 137 At its fore part it is surmounted by a blunt and rounded edge. **1846** HOLTZAPFFEL *Turning* II. 629 Those angular threads which are rounded at the top and bottom, and which are thence called rounded or round threads. **1884** F. J. BRITTEN *Watch & Clockm.* 133 The teeth on the under side of the wheel..should be rounded.
b. Curved *off*.
1856 STONEHENGE *Brit. Rural Sports* 476/2 The inside hand lays hold of the loom just where the rounded-off part joins the square. **1897** *Allbutt's Syst. Med.* II. 1087 The members of which..are characterised by..a rounded-off head carrying a terminal mouth.
c. Of arches; also of architecture, = ROUND-ARCH(ED).
1859 RUSKIN *Two Paths* i. §33 The whole great French school of rounded architecture. **1874** SYMONDS *Sk. Italy & Greece* (1879) 92 Remains of Roman architecture..induced them [*sc.* artists] to adopt the rounded rather than the pointed arch. **1885** E. SANDERSON *Outl. World's Hist.* 365 The rounded arch of the Norman style..began to give place ..to the pointed arch of..the Gothic architecture.
II. 6. a. Brought to a full, complete, finished, or perfect state; showing no lack or defect.
1746 FRANCIS tr. *Horace, Epist.* I. vi. 60 A thousand talents be the rounded sum You first design'd. **1808** SCOTT *Let.* 2 Nov. in *Lockhart*, They have begun in a truly manly and rounded manner. **1845** E. HOLMES *Life Mozart* 258 Hummel was seated at Mozart's piano, and..made such progress as to delight every one with his smooth, brilliant, and rounded execution. **1888** BURGON *Lives 12 Good Men* II. xii. 421 His seemed a perfectly rounded life.
b. Of periods: Neatly finished; well turned.
1772 *Town & C. Mag.* 99 To introduce a rounded period or a smart antithesis. **1793** BURNS *Address spoken by Miss Fontenelle* 13 Can you..With..solemn-rounded sentence, Rouse from his sluggish slumbers fell Repentance? **1898** G. W. E. RUSSELL *Coll. & Recoll.* xii. 161 An inexhaustible supply of sonorous phrases and rounded periods.
c. Of a number: having been approximated by rounding; expressed in fewer significant figures. Also with advb.
1947 *Math. Tables & Other Aids Computation* II. 286 He had taken 10-figure logarithms of rounded-off quantities containing only five or six significant figures. **1953** *Proc. IRE* XLI. 1271/1 *Long Right* places the bits to be dropped into the *MQ* register; *Round* then leaves a rounded number in the accumulator. **1956** G. A. MONTGOMERIE *Digital Calculating Machines* vii. 129 A convenient rule to ensure this is to make the rounded digit even rather than odd in case of doubt. **1973** PHILLIPS & TAYLOR *Theory & Applic. Numerical Anal.* 359 If the amount neglected is exactly $\frac{1}{2}10^{-t}$ we can avoid statistical bias by forcing the last digit in the rounded number to be even.
7. Of sounds or the voice: Sonorous, mellow, harmonious.
1860 TYNDALL *Glac.* I. ii. 11 The sound was..sometimes broken into rounded explosions. **1891** KIPLING *Light that Failed* (1900) 222 The voice was fuller and more rounded, because the man knew he was speaking of his best work.
8. Of vowels: Affected by labialization.
1867 A. J. ELLIS *E.E. Pronunc.* I. iii. §3. 162 Applied to the rounded or labialised forms of these vowels. **1890** SWEET *Primer Phonetics* (1902) 17 Such a vowel..will still retain much of its distinctive rounded character. *Ibid.* 26 Pairs of rounded and unrounded vowels.
Hence **'roundedly** *adv.*; **'roundedness**.
1867 *Contemp. Rev.* VI. 266 The very roundedness of intellectual surface he presents..at first sight. **1868** TENNYSON *Lucretius* 190 Rosy knees and supple roundedness. **1878** T. SINCLAIR *Mount* 81 [It] made Milton's work indefinite and grandiose instead of simply freely roundedly grand.

roundel ('raʊndəl). Also 5 roundele, 5–6 -elle, 5–7 -ell, 7 -ill; 5 roundul, *Sc.* -all, 6–8 -al, 7 -ill; 5 rowndel, 6 -ale, 6–7 -ell. [ad. OF. *rondel* masc. or *rondelle* fem., f. *rond* ROUND *a.* Hence also med.L. *rondellus*, *-um* and *rondella*, It. *rondello*, *rondella*, MDu. and Du. *rondeel*, MLG. *rondel*, *rundel*, G. *rundel* (*rondel*), Sw. *rundel*, Da. *runddel*, †*rundel*. For varying adoptions of the word in English see RONDEL, ROUNDLE, and RUNDLE.]
I. 1. a. A circle drawn, marked out, or formed in any way. Now *dial.*
a **1290** *Beket* 2128 in *S. Eng. Leg.* I. 167 ȝwane men peyntiez an Anletnesse,..þere is depeint a Roundel al a-boute þe heued. *c* **1384** CHAUCER *H. Fame* II. 791 Yf that thow Thorwe on water now a stoon,..hyt wol make anoon A litel roundell as a sercle. *c* **1425** WYNTOUN *Cron.* I. ix. 533 As men may be a roundall se Merkit to be delt in thre. *c* **1440** *Promp. Parv.* 438/1 Rowndel, *rotundale.* **1529** MORE *Dyaloge* I. Wks. 121/1 Those nygromancers..that put theyr confydence in the roundell and cercle on the grounde. **1561** EDEN tr. *Cortes' Art Navig.* I. xx. 22 The Epicicle, is a circle or little roundel. **1634** WITHER *Embl.* 157 These roundells helpe to shew the mystery Of that immense and blest Eternitie. **1875** PARISH *Dict. Sussex Dial., Roundel*, a circle; anything round. **1876** F. K. ROBINSON *Whitby Gloss.* s.v., 'A witches roundel,' that within which she performs her rites.
b. Something forming a circle or ring; a number of things or persons disposed or grouped in a circle. Now *rare.*
1486 *Bk. St. Albans* E vij b, All theys oder, crokes and Roundulis bene. *Ibid.*, The crokes and the Roundellis of the Nombles of þe dere. **1532** MORE *Confut. Tindale* Wks. 707/2 A mainy of leud mocking knaues, which..woulde gette them into a roundell turnynge theym backe to backe. **1598** HAKLUYT *Voy.* I. 95 The roofe whereof consisteth..of wickers meeting aboue in one little roundell, out of which roundell ascendeth vpward a necke like vnto a chimney. **1613** W. BROWNE *Brit. Past.* I. iii. 55 It was a Roundell seated on a plaine,—Enuiron'd round with Trees. **1657** W. COLES *Adam in Eden* l, The white Flowers grow in spoaky roundels. **1713** J. WARDER *True Amazons* 49 Cut a notch in your Straw-hive, not through the Roundal as before, but somewhat less. **1893** KIPLING *Many Invent.* 133 B Company..gathered itself into a thing like a decayed aloe-clump..; and in that clump, roundel, or mob, it stayed.
†**c.** The outer circuit or rim *of* anything. *Obs.*
1534 MORE *Treat. Passion* Wks. 1347/2 Into all the worlde is gone out the sowne of them, and into the endes of the roundel of the earth the wordes of them. **1633** BP. HALL *Hard Texts* 430 As for the outmost roundells of those wheels they were of a vast and dreadful height.
†**d.** A round hole or hollow. *Obs.*
1578 BANISTER *Hist. Man* I. 8 [The] Suture..creeping.. through the middest of yᵉ eyes roundell. *Ibid.* 12. **1614** B. JONSON *Barth. Fair* IV. vi, Come put in his legge in the middle roundell, and let him hole there.
2. †**a.** *Sc.* A small round table. *Obs.*
c **1500** *Priests of Peblis* 23 Befoir them was sone set a roundel bricht, And with ane clene claith finelie dicht, It was ouir-set. *Ibid.* 579 Ane Roundel with ane cleine claith. **1548** *Extr. Rec. Edinb.* (1871) 136 Ane buyrd and form, stule and rowndale, xlviii s.
†**b.** A round mat for vessels to stand on. *Obs.*
1548 ELYOT, *Orbis*, a roundell to sette dysshes one for soylynge of the table clothe. **1725** *Fam. Dict.* s.v. *Distillation*, D.I. is a Glass or earthern Vessel nam'd the *Recipient*; they place it upon a Roundel of Straw, that it may have the firmer Footing.
c. A circular wooden trencher. Now only *Hist.*
1797 *Gentl. Mag.* LXVII. I. 281/1 The circular beechen plates, called roundels. **1827** *Ibid.* XCVII. II. 592 They are called roundels, are always twelve in a full set, and are made of beech-wood. **1851** *Archaeologia* XXXIV. 225 Account of some 'Roundells' or Fruit Trenchers of the Time of James I. **1971** R. HOWE *Mrs. Groundes-Peace's Old Cookery Notebk.* 56 Wooden trenchers were also known as treen roundels.
3. a. A small round shield. Now *Hist.*
1538 *Acc. Ld. High Treas. Scot.* VII. 13 Gevin for four roundellis to speris, vj cronis. **1562** J. SHUTE tr. *Cambini's Turk. Wars* 17 The Turkes covered their heades with roundels and targes. **1585** T. WASHINGTON tr. *Nicholay's Voy.* IV. v. 116 [They] are armed with..bucklers, roundels and targets of steele. **1846** FAIRHOLT *Costume in Eng.* 592 *Roundel*, the small circular shield of the fourteenth century.
b. (See quots.)
1846 FAIRHOLT *Costume in Eng.* 163 He has *roundels* at the bend of the arm, and upon the shoulders, which are sometimes chased and ornamented. **1879** PLANCHÉ *Cycl. Costume* 128 The plate-gorget, and circular gussets of plate to which English antiquarians have given the names of palettes and roundels, protect the arm-pits.

†**c.** *Anglo-Indian.* An umbrella; a sunshade. Recorded earlier as *rondell* (1676), *rundell* (1680): see Yule & Burnell (1886) 850/2.

1716 in J. T. Wheeler *Madras in Old. Time* (1861) II. 230 Cooks, water bearers, coolies, Palankeen boys, roundel men. **1773** IVES *Voy.* 21 To hire a Roundel-boy, whose business is to walk by his master, and defend him with his Roundel or Umbrella from the heat of the sun.

4. a. A small circular object; a little disk or rounded piece.

1542 UDALL *Erasm. Apoph.* 29 A maiden..did with woondreous sleight..cast vp and receiue again one after another, twelf trendles or rowndelles. **1545** RAYNOLD *Byrth Mankynde* II. x. (1634) 150 Temper the whole masse into little roundels or trochisks, each waying a dram. **1649** BP. HALL *Cases Consc.* 176 The first verses of that divine Gospell are singled out, printed, in a small roundell, and sold to the credulous ignorants. **1725** *Fam. Dict.* s.v. *Scorzonera*, The Flower..when it fades, leaves a Cottonny Roundel behind where the Seed is. **1812** SIR J. SINCLAIR *Syst. Husb. Scot.* II. App. 46 The right hand or lesser handle, attached to the larger one by the iron rod F, and the wooden roundels G, H. **1863** WYNTER *Subtle Brains* 15 Again rummaging, I come upon roundels formed from the bottoms of earthen-ware vessels. **1883** *Athenæum* 5 May 572/3 The prehistoric practice of trepanning the skull might have been performed..by removing a roundel.

b. *spec.* A perforated iron disk placed between the stock and cheeks of a gun.

1875 KNIGHT *Dict. Mech.* 1994/1.

5. †**a.** An ornamental circle sewn or embroidered on a garment. *Obs.*

1546 *Inv. Ch. Goods* (Surtees) 139 Three albes with parrettes of blak satten with roundelles. **1577** HARRISON *England* II. v. (1877) 124 Those [mantles] of the chanons are of Murreie with a roundell of the arms of S. George. **1609** DEKKER *Rauens Alm.* Wks. (Grosart) IV. 180 Do not those Roundels hang about him, shew like so many pardons, tyed to the partes of his body with Labels?

b. *Her.* = ROUNDLE 1 b.

1562 LEGH *Armory* 149 Whether are Roundells of all suche colours, as ye haue spoken of here before? or shall they be named Roundelles of those colours? **1655** M. CARTER *Honor Rediv.* (1660) 165 If these roundals are charged in counter-changes as before, then they are only called Roundals. **1880** *Encycl. Brit.* XI. 697/2 The Roundel, if of metal, is a simple disk.

c. A decorative panel, plate, medallion, etc., of a round form.

1859 GULLICK & TIMBS *Paint.* 307 [The altar piece] has also gables and medallions or roundels. **1875** FORTNUM *Maiolica* iii. 26 Each roundel is a massive disc of terra-cotta, of a single piece. **1891** *Proc. Soc. Antiq.* Jan. 223 A copper roundel, once gilt, with a shield of the arms of England.

d. A circle of painted glass; a small round pane or window.

1865 *Athenæum* No. 1974. 285/1 The allegorical figures in the roundels. **1885** [see BULLION[3] 2]. **1886** *Pall Mall G.* 31 Aug. 4/2 Occasionally white roundels, or bottle ends on a ground of blue or green. **1898** W. GANDY *Romance of Glass-Making* ix. 145 Now and then one comes across an old window—generally a cellar window—where the panes have been filled with bull's-eyes, 'roundels', or the waste centres left from the discs of crown glass after cutting. **1908** A. L. DUTHIE *Decorative Glass Processes* i. 28 Circular in form.. are *roundels*, which have always been largely used in leaded lights and are characteristic of German and Italian windows. They are made in an infinite variety of colour and size. **1933** R. MOLLET *Leaded Glass Work* ii. 13 Bullions are very popular... The smaller sizes (2 or 3 in. in diameter) are sometimes called 'roundels'.

e. An identification disc painted on an aeroplane; *spec.* that of the Royal Air Force and Royal Naval Air Command, comprising a design of concentric red, white, and blue circles.

1948 *Daily Tel.* 5 July 1/1 The R.A.F. plane—I could see the roundel—was spiralling down without a tail. **1963** J. LUSBY in B. James *Austral. Short Stories* 225 Wingtip clear of the next man's, able to move forward or back and level with his roundel. **1975** T. ALLBEURY *Palomino Blonde* xxiii. 142 A helicopter came..across the bay. The RAF roundels looked fresh and clean.

6. †**a.** A sphere or globe. *Obs.* (Cf. ROUNDLE 2.)

c **1590** in Nichols *Progr. Q. Eliz.* (1823) III. 53 A general resemblance of the Roundel to God, the World and the Queene. *Ibid.*, The Roundell hath no bonch or angle Which may his course stay or entangle. **1591** SYLVESTER *Du Bartas* I. iv. 328 More or less their roundels wider are, As from the Center they be neer or far. **1601** HOLLAND *Pliny* I. 188 Anacharsis the Scythian..inuented the cast of turning the roundell or globe.

b. A ball or bead-moulding.

1535 COVERDALE *2 Chron.* iv. 12 The two pilers with the roundels and knoppes aboue vpon both the pilers. **1609** BIBLE (Douay) *1 Kings* vi. 18 Al the house was covered within with ceder, having roundels. **1850** PARKER *Gloss. Arch.* (ed. 5), *Roundel*, the bead or astragal moulding.

†**c.** The ball of the elbow- or the knee-joint.

1541 COPLAND *Guydon's Quest. Chirurg.* G ij b, In suche maner that the sayde roundelles entre in to the holownesse of the sockettes. **1643** J. STEER tr. *Exp. Chyrurg.* xv. 60 It is necessary that part which belongeth to the rowndell of the knee be made hollow.

†**7.** A cylinder (of wood); a rung of a ladder. *Obs.* (Cf. ROUNDLE 3.)

1585 T. WASHINGTON tr. *Nicholay's Voy.* IV. xxxiii. 156 Solon..made them to be written in boords or roundelles of wood (which roundels, according to Aristotle, were called Cyrbes). **1589** NASHE *Martin Marprelate* Wks. (Grosart) I. 156 These men must needs (and so doo) dislike of all degrees; worthie themselues to proceede by no degrees, but roundels.

8. a. *Sc.* A round turret.

1738 *De Foe's Tour Grt. Brit.* III. 248 [The castle of Drumlanrig] is Four-square, with Roundels in the inner Angles of the Court. **1821** SCOTT *Pirate* xxx, The window of the west roundel of the auld house.

b. *Fortification.* A circular bastion.

1853 STOCQUELER *Mil. Encycl.* 237/1.

II. 9. A rondeau or rondel.

c **1385** CHAUCER *L.G.W.* Prol. 423 Manye an ympne.. That hightyn baladis, roundelys, & vyrelayes. *c* **1386** —— *Knt.'s T.* 1529 Whan that Arcite had..songen al the roundel lustily. *c* **1407** HOCCLEVE *Min. Poems* 60 This rowndel shul we synge. **1483** CAXTON *G. de la Tour* aj, I made songes, layes, Roundels, balades..in the mooste best wyse I cowde. **1513** DOUGLAS *Æneis* VIII. Prol. 67 The railȝear..ratlis furth ranis,..baith roundalis and ryme. **1530** PALSGR. 264/1 Roundell, *rondeau.* **1644** MILTON *Areopagitica* (Arb.) 37 A higher straine then their owne souldierly ballats and roundels could reach to. **17..** RAMSAY *Richy & Sandy* 26 A summer day I never thought it lang, To hear him make a roundel or a sang. **1835** LYTTON *Rienzi* II. i, I think one troubadour roundel worth all that Petrarch ever wrote. **1868** MORRIS *Earthly Par.* (1870) I. I. 209 He rode, scarce touched by care.., Humming a roundel with a smile. **1883** SWINBURNE (*title*), A Century of Roundels.

transf. **1582** STANYHURST *Æneis* IV. (Arb.) 111 The skrich howle..Her burial roundel..cruncketh in howling.

10. A round dance. Cf. ROUNDELAY 3.

1590 SHAKS. *Mids. N.* II. ii. 1 Come, now a Roundell, and a Fairy song. **1825** *Encycl. Metrop.* (1845) XVII. 548/2 The Roundel or Country Dance seems to be purely English. **1863** COWDEN CLARKE *Shaks. Char.* iv. 103 Rousing the mole-cricket with their midnight roundels upon the pearly grass.

roundelay ('raʊndəleɪ). Also 6-7 **-laye**, 7 **-laie**; 6 **rundelaye, -ley, roundley**, 7 **roundellay**. [ad. F. *rondelet* ROUNDLET, f. *rondel* ROUNDEL, with the ending assimilated to LAY *sb.*[4]]

1. A short simple song with a refrain.

1573 G. HARVEY *Letter-bk.* (Camden) 105, I beseeche you marke my roundelaye. **1589** GREENE *Menaphon* (Arb.) 37 Menaphon..began, after some melodie, to carroll out this roundelay. **1612** DRAYTON *Poly-olb.* To Rdr., Shepheards.. singing roundelaies, to their gazing flockes. *a* **1664** KATH. PHILIPS *Poems* (1667) 189 At our Feast he gets the Praise, For his enchanting Roundelayes. **1700** DRYDEN *Pal. & Arc.* 688 Who, listning, heard him while he search'd the Grove And loudly sung his roundelay of love. **1765** STERNE *Tr. Shandy* VII. xliii, The sister of the youth..sung alternately with her brother—'twas a Gascoigne roundelay. **1808** SCOTT *Marm.* III. viii, Now must I venture, as I may, To sing his favourite roundelay. *c* **1860** LONGF. *Whither?* v, The water-nymphs that are singing Their roundelays under me. **1877** A. B. EDWARDS *Up Nile* 449 The two crews met every evening to smoke, and dance, and sing their quaint roundelays together.

b. *transf.* A bird's song or carol.

1641 BEEDOME *Poems, Constant Maid* lix, The winged birds..Each one by turne did sing his rounde-lay. **1653** WALTON *Angler* iii. 78 The Cuckoe and the Nightingale.. with their pleasant roundelayes bid welcome in the Spring. **1813** SCOTT *Rokeby* II. xvi, While linnet, lark, and black-bird gay, Sing forth her nuptial roundelay. **1863** LONGF. *Wayside Inn* I. *Poet's T.* xviii, The whirr Of meadow-lark, and her sweet roundelay.

†**c.** The competitive singing of such songs. *Obs.*

1655 VAUGHAN *Silex Scint.* (1858) 242 Here many garlands won at roundel-lays Old shepherds hung up in those happy days, From Daphnis.

2. The music of a song of this type.

1593-1600 BRETON *Daff. & Prim.* Wks. (Grosart) I. 16/1 The muses all haue chose a settinge-place To singe and play the sheppherdes rundeley. **1604** —— *Passionate Shepherd* ibid. 5 While yee tune your pipes to play But an idle Roundelay. **1820** KEATS *Isabella* xxxii, The breath of Winter ..plays a roundelay Of death among the bushes and the leaves.

3. A kind of round dance.

1589 WARNER *Alb. Eng.* VI. xxxi. 135 When as they fel to Rowndelaies,..Not Satires, or the Naiades, were halfe so nimble. *a* **1633** T. TAYLOR *God's Judgem.* I. II. xxxvi. (1642) 288 They fell a dancing, men and women mixtly together,.. a ridiculous roundelay. *c* **1800** H. K. WHITE *Poems* (1837) 126 Dance, dance away, the jocund roundelay! **1867** LONGF. tr. *Dante, Inf.* vii. 24 So here the folk must dance their roundelay.

†**b.** A fairy circle or ring. *Obs.*[−1]

a **1635** CORBET *Poems* (1648) 8 Those Rings and Roundelays Of theirs, which yet remain, Were footed..on many a grassy plain.

rounde'leer. *nonce-wd.* [f. ROUNDEL 9.] A writer or composer of roundels.

1888 STEVENSON *Epil. to Inland Voy.*, Mr. Lang, Mr. Dobson, Mr. Henley, and all contemporary roundeleers.

roundeles, rennet: see RUNDLES.

roundelet(e, etc., obs. forms of ROUNDLET.

rounder ('raʊndə(r)). [f. ROUND *sb.*[1] and *v.*[1]]

I. 1. One who goes round, in special senses:

†**a.** One who goes the round of a watch or sentinels; esp. *Mil.*, an officer or soldier of the round. *Obs.*

1624 T. LUSHINGTON *Serm.* I. 41 In our modern Wars.. sometime the Rounder will clap a musket-shot through a sleepy head. **1650** R. ELTON *Art Mil.* (1659) 188 Severall Rounders..are..to admonish the Sentinels (in case of neglect). **1672** VENN *Mil. & Mar. Discipl.* 5 And upon his return there are four other Rounders to be sent twice in a night, to discover round the quarters. **1770** *Gentl. Mag.* XL. 369 The boundary of the dockyard..visited once if not oftener in the night by the Rounders (those who have the immediate superintending of the watchmen).

b. A Methodist local preacher.

1820 POLWHELE *Introd. to Lavington's Enthus. Meth. & Papists* p. lxxxviii, Many..prefer..even the Rounder, whether male or female,..to the accredited and licensed Minister. **1893** 'Q.' *Delect. Duchy* 116 On Sundays he.. became a Rounder, or Methodist local preacher.

c. = ROUNDSMAN 1.

1896 in *Eng. Dial. Dict.*

d. *N. Amer.* One who makes the round of prisons, workhouses, drinking saloons, etc.; a habitual criminal, loafer, or drunkard. Also *transf.*

1854 *Congress Globe* 33rd Congress 1st Sess. App. 1220/3 I have always found him a very kind and agreeable man—what the 'rounders' in New York would term a 'glover'. **1879** A. DALY *Let.* 20 Oct. in J. F. Daly *Life A. Daly* (1917) xxi. 330 [We] are old 'rounders' and familiar with the voice, gait and peculiarities of most of the actors and actresses on the American stage. **1884** [see REPEATER 5 b]. **1891** *Boston* (Mass.) *Jrnl.* 7 July 2/4 The regular rounders who are beginning to receive long sentences under the new drunkenness law. **1894** *Outing* XXIV. 440/2 A gay young bravo, one of New York's many 'rounders', or all-nighters. **1920** C. SANDBURG *Smoke & Steel* 51 A rounder leered confidential. **1935** Z. N. HURSTON *Mules & Men* (1970) I. iv. 93 'What make de rooster crow every morning at sun-up?' 'Dat's to let de pimps and rounders know de workin' man is on his way.' **1943** W. H. CHASE *Sourdough Pot* v. 24 [She] possessed all the earmarks of a 'rounder'—the evidence of much dissipation was remarkably developed. **1962** 'K. ORVIS' *Damned & Destroyed* iv. 29 An all-night dive patronized by cheap women and rounders and drunks. **1975** *Globe & Mail* (Toronto) 7 Oct. 4/5 He agreed that rounders—a term used to describe criminals whose haunts include hotels in the Jarvis Street–Dundas Street area of Toronto—have a great fear they will be seen talking to the police.

e. *U.S. slang.* (See quot. 1903.)

1881 *Bradstreet's* 29 Jan. 51/4 The 'rounder' in alms-taking is headed off. **1903** *Charities* 3 Oct. 283 The class of persons known as 'rounders', people who go from one hospital to another seeking advice and treatment, a species of medical mendicants.

f. *U.S. slang.* A transient railway worker.

1908 *Casey Jones* (song) in *Railroad Man's Mag.* May 764/1 Come all you rounders, for I want you to hear The story told of an engineer, Casey Jones was the rounder's name, A heavy right-wheeler of a mighty fame. **1939** F. J. LEE *Casey Jones* 287 The word 'rounder' as applied to Casey must be taken as a light, affectionate appellation. **1961** *Listener* 24 Aug. 270/2 His was a six-pipe job whose moans sent every coloured 'rounder' from Chicago to New Orleans into ecstasies.

2. a. *pl.* A game, played with bat and ball between two sides, in which each player endeavours to hit and send the ball as far away as he can, and to run to a base or right round the course without being struck by the fielded ball.

For a full description of the game see Gomme *Trad. Games* (1898) II. 145-6.

1828 W. CLARKE *Boy's Own Book* (ed. 2, London) 20 *Rounders.* In the west of England this is one of the most favourite sports with bat and ball... In Rounders, the players divide into two equal parties, and chance decides which shall have the first innings. **1854** DICKENS *Let.* 12 July (1938) II. 566 The keeping up of a 'home' at rounders. **1856** STONEHENGE *Brit. Rural Sports* 500/1 Rounders, besides an ordinary field, requires only a ball and a stick resembling a common rolling-pin. **1862** *Dublin Univ. Mag.* I. 642 What schoolboy has not played rounders in his youth? **1894** ASTLEY *50 Years Life* I. 7 Rounders and marbles were our principal amusements. **1939** *Bull. N.Y. Public Libr.* Apr. 303 Is baseball an offshoot of rounders? **1969** I. & P. OPIE *Children's Games* 5 At Sedgley Park School in Staffordshire, about 1805, the boys were content with Kites, Marloes (marbles),..Rounders,..and even with 'playing horses'. **1977** *Cleethorpes News* 27 May 18/1 In addition to exploring the mines, they played rounders among the sheep on the hillside.

b. A complete run at the game of rounders.

1856 STONEHENGE *Brit. Rural Sports* 501/1 When only one of the side is left in, the others being all put out, he may call for 'three fair hits for the rounder'. **1898** ALICE B. GOMME *Trad. Games* II. 146 When a complete rounder is obtained, the player has the privilege of..counting the rounder to the credit of his side.

3. A round of thanks, applause, etc.

1882 BLACKMORE *Christowell* II. xv. 299 Mrs. Cork..was off, amid a rounder of 'Thank'e, ma'am; thank'e'.

4. A round blow.

1883 READE in *Harper's Mag.* Dec. 132/1 The carter,.. while endeavoring a tremendous rounder,..received a dazzler with the left.

II. 5. A round tower. Cf. ROUNDEL 8 a.

1774 T. PENNANT *Tour in Scotl. & Voy. Hebrides 1772* I. 99 On each side the gateway..are two rounders. **1782** PENNANT *Journ. Chester to London* 11 A strong wall fortified with round towers... Some of the walls, and about six or seven rounders, still exist.

6. A round oath.

1885 MRS. C. PRAED *Head Station* I. vii. 120 Though we can all swear a rounder in the stockyard or on the drafting camp.

III. 7. *slang.* One who rounds on others.

1884 *Good Words* June 399/2 'Rounders'—that is, informers—..will quietly give 'the tip' to a detective.

8. One who rounds any kind of work; *esp.* in shoemaking (see quot. 1893).

1881 *Instructions Census Clerks* (1885) 40 Bookbinding:.. Rounder. *Ibid.* 45 Needle Maker:..Rounder. *Ibid.* 76 Boot and Shoe Making:..Rounder and all Rounder. **1889** *Daily News* 23 Dec. 2/6 The manufacturers determined..to suspend clickers, machinists, and rough stuff cutters, and the rounders and finishers. **1893** *Labour Comm. Gloss.*, *Rounders*, a country expression for the youths in the boot and shoe industry who cannot be trusted to cut the best materials, and who therefore cut such materials as common outsides, fittings, and linings. In London they are termed improvers.

9. a. A kind of boring-tool.

1839 URE *Dict. Arts* 966 The boring tools are represented in the following figures:—..10. The rounder. **1869** GREENWELL *Mine Engin.* 139 The rounder resembles a bêche externally, but it is solid and well steeled at the bottom. **1894** HESLOP *Northumbld. Gloss., Rounder*, a boring tool used for breaking or cutting off any projection which may have occurred in the hole.

b. A tool by which a rounded form is given to something.

1846 HOLTZAPFFEL *Turning* II. 642 A rod of wood.. reduced to a cylinder by a rounder or witchet. **1875** KNIGHT *Dict. Mech.* 1994/2 *Rounder*,.. a plane used by wheelwrights for rounding off tenons.

10. *Phonetics.* A sign used to indicate the rounding of a vowel.

1888 SWEET *Hist. Eng. Sounds* 2 When a mid vowel is formed with the rounding of a high vowel, it is said to be over-rounded, which is denoted by adding the 'rounder'.

11. *Newfoundland.* Small unsplit cod, freq. eaten as a delicacy.

1908 C. W. TOWNSEND *Along Labrador Coast* v. 132 The very small cod are not boned, but are salted whole. These are called 'leggies' or 'rounders'. **1966** A. R. SCAMMELL *My Newfoundland* 32 School fees could not be put on the account and the schoolmaster wouldn't accept fish, tomcods or rounders. *Ibid.* 91 When the last rounder was aboard he gave a quizzical glance at the sun. **1974** *National Geogr. Mag.* Jan. 129/2 We dined sumptuously on native dishes ..'rounders' (baby cod, salted and dried whole like kippers, and boiled for breakfast).

rounder: see ROUNDURE.

round-faced, *a.* [ROUND *a.* 16.]

1. Having a round face.

1676 WYCHERLEY *Pl. Dealer* v. ii, He was pretty tall, round-faced, and one..I ne'er had seen before. **1678** BUTLER *Hud.* II. iii. 713 The Roman Senate..Did cause their Clergy..The round-fac'd Prodigy [*sc.* an owl] t'avert. **1832** DOWNES *Lett. Cont. Countries* I. 530 A round-faced man, of rather low stature. **1843** HOLTZAPFFEL *Turning* I. 228 The edges are..trimmed with a round-faced hammer. **1888** *Riverside Nat. Hist.* V. 517 On the island of Formosa also occurs an allied round-faced species.

2. ***round-faced macaque, monkey***, the Formosan rock-macaque (*Macaca cyclopis*), having a flat, round face, and resembling the Bengal macaque.

1872 *Proc. Zool. Soc.* 777 It would seem that our Round-faced Monkey, in the proportionate dimensions of fore limb to spine's length, presents closest agreement with man. **1887** in *Cassell's Encycl. Dict.* s.v.

roundgar, obs. form of ROUNGER.

'round hand. [f. ROUND *a.* + HAND *sb.*]

1. A style of handwriting in which the letters are round, bold, and full.

1682 *Lond. Gaz.* No. 1732/4 The Bastard Italians (commonly) called the new A-la-mode Round-hands, with Round-mixt Running-hands, and mixt Secretaries. **1686** W. ELDER (*title*) in Arber *Term Catal.* II. 158/1 A Book of Copies for Learners of Round-hand. **1748** HARTLEY *Observ. Man* I. iii. 302 The common Round-hand, various Law-hands, and various Short-hands. **1766** SERLE *Art Writing* 3 Round Hand... In writing this Hand, let the Slope be inclining to your Right Hand. **1848** THACKERAY *Van. Fair* i, The orphan, little Laura Martin (who was just in round-hand). **1899** *Allbutt's Syst. Med.* VII. 436 A word written in the 'round hand' of the copy books.

attrib. and *transf.* **1766** SERLE *Art Writing* 61 The capital Round Hand Letters. **1844** ALB. SMITH *Adv. Mr. Ledbury* xxiv, 'Time flies quickly,' as we learn from the roundhand copies. **1888** PATER *Apprec.* (1890) 2 Something very tamely ..confined to mainly practical ends—a kind of 'good round hand'.

2. *attrib.* Of bowling: Performed with a horizontal swing of the hand or arm; round-arm.

1851 LILLYWHITE *Guide Crick.* 14 Mr. Willes..first introduced round-hand bowling, and Lambart first practised it.. forty years ago. **1884** *Harper's Mag.* Jan. 299/2 Oh, for..the round-hand bowling of our fathers' day!

So **'round-hander**, a 'round-arm' blow.

1892 W. S. GILBERT *Foggerty's Fairy* 169 He planted a round-hander on the Sergeant's left ear.

roundhead, round-head ('raʊndhɛd). Also 7-8 **Round-head, -Head, Round head.** [ROUND *a.*]

1. *Eng. Hist.* A member or adherent of the Parliamentary party in the Civil War of the 17th century, so called from their custom of wearing the hair close cut.

In this sense now usu. with capital and as one word.

The name appears to have arisen towards the end of the year 1641: see Clarendon *Hist. Reb.* IV. §121. Rushworth *Hist. Coll.* (1692) III. I. 463 attributes its origin to an officer named David Hide, who (app. on 27 Dec. of that year) threatened to 'cut the Throat of those Round-headed Dogs that bawled against Bishops'. Brathwait's use, if earlier than this, may be only an accidental anticipation of it.

1641 BRATHWAIT *Merc. Brit.* IV, See..how these notted and round heads with their prick eares doe listen and stare on their predicating Pinner. **1642** *Heads of all Fashions* 4 A Round-head is a man whose braine's compact, Whose Verilies and Trulies are an Act Infallible. **1651** [see CAVALIER *sb.* 3]. *a* **1671** LD. FAIRFAX *Mem.* (1699) 95 Those of the array exceeded their commission in oppressing many honest people, whom, by way of reproach, they called Roundheads. **1735** BOLINGBROKE *On Parties* 53 The Whigs were not Roundheads, tho' the Measures They pursued.. gave Occasion to the Suspicions I have mentioned. **1816** SCOTT *Old Mort.* viii, My cockade and my broadsword are my commission, and a better one than ever Old Nol gave to his roundheads. **1842** TENNYSON *Talking Oak* 299 Far below the Roundhead rode, And humm'd a surly hymn.

transf. **1643** in Swainson *Prov. Names Brit. Birds* (E.D.S.) 110 Her colour is most comely, And a Round-head is she [*sc.* a cuckoo], And yet no sect She doth respect. **1973** D. AARON *Unwritten War* 345 Southern magazines featured articles contrasting invidiously planter 'Cavaliers' and Yankee 'Roundheads'. **1976** *Listener* 5 Feb. 140/3 Under the Cromwellian leadership of Peter Hall, the roundheads of the new professionalism drove the cavalier dilettanti largely from the scene.

attrib. **1845** JAMES *Arrah Neil* i, The roundhead rascals, I wish I had my sword in their stomach. **1855** MACAULAY *Hist. Eng.* xv. III. 520 They would have been pointed at in the street as Roundhead knaves. **1963** *Times* 11 Feb. 6/7 Now that industry is 'dishoarding' labour and achieving results more effectively than Roundhead policy at the Treasury.

b. *N. Amer. slang.* An immigrant from northern Europe, *spec.* a Swede.

1895 *Dialect Notes* I. 393 *Roundhead*, a Swede. **1902** S. CLAPIN *New Dict. Americanisms* 341 *Roundhead*, in the North-West, frequently said of a Swede. **1931** 'D. STIFF' *Milk & Honey Route* iii. 38 Swedes are 'roundheads' or 'salve eaters'. **1976** 'TREVANIAN' *Main* (1977) iii. 57 'He's not a bad type, for a Roundhead,' Gaspard says.

c. *Ethnol.* One of a race or type of man characterized by roundness of the head. Cf. ROUND-HEADED *a.* 1 b. *rare.*

1896 A. H. KEANE *Ethnol.* I. v. 106 Mounds differing in type from those of the round-heads.

†**2.** A kind of weapon: (see quot. 1643). *Obs.*

1643 *Mercurius Civicus* No. 11. 84 A thousand of those weapons which the Papists call Round-heads, for that with them they intended to bring the Round-heads into subjection. **1643** [ANGIER] *Lanc. Vall. Achor* 22 A new-invented mischievous Instrument... An head about a quarter of a yard long, a staffe of two yards long put into their head, twelve iron pikes round about, and one in the end to stop with; This fierce Weapon they called, *A Round-head.* **1644-5** *Rec. Nottingham* (1900) V. 232 Paid to Richard Smith for roundheads for the towne, Vˡⁱ. *Ibid.* 233.

3. a. A siluroid fish of S. America. **b.** The weakfish of N. America.

1842 *Penny Cycl.* XXII. 17/1 It is said that the other species, the round-head (*Callichthys littoralis*, Hancock), has not been known to attempt such excursions. *Ibid.*, The round-head forms its nest of grass.

4. *attrib.* or as *adj.* Round-headed; puritanical.

1840 *Penny Cycl.* XVI. 276/1 Columns..are employed as piers to support the arches (not round-head, but pointed). **1907** *Mem. Old Derbyshire* 55 The intrusion of a round-head people upon the Neolithic long-heads. **1908** A. W. TILBY *Eng. People Overseas* I. ii. 72 The former was strongly cavalier and episcopal; the latter was as strongly roundhead and puritan.

Hence **'roundheader** = sense 1 b above.

1934 J. O'HARA *Appointment in Samarra* iii. 80 The schwackies, the roundheaders..—regional names for non-Latin foreigners—probably were inside getting drunk.

round-headed, *a.* [ROUND *a.* 16.] Having a round head, in various senses.

In the following quot. the precise meaning is not quite clear:—**1633** ROWLEY *Match at Midn.* III. i, Marry who thou woot to make a shew to shrowd thee from the storme round headed opinion, that swayes all the world, may let fall on thee.

1. a. Of persons: Wearing the hair closely cut; *spec.* belonging to the Roundhead party.

1642 in *N. & Q.* 10th Ser. X. 357/2 That Mr. Seldon.. had more learning than a thousand round-headed Pims. **1643** PRYNNE *Gag for Long-haired Rattle-Heads* L j b, The honour of our ancient Kings, who were Roundheaded, like to the Cœlestiall spheare. **1650** COWLEY *Guardian* v. iv, You have invited..the widdows round-headed kindred? **1816** SCOTT *Old Mort.* xxxv, I thought I had to do with the son of an old round-headed rebel. **1826** —— *Woodst.* i, Those round-headed commonwealth knaves.

b. *Ethnol.* Designating a race or type of man characterized by possessing a skull of rounded shape, usu. distinguished from a LONG-HEAD (sense 2). *rare.*

1896 A. H. KEANE *Ethnol.* I. v. 106 Mr. W. K. Moorehead ..recognises two distinct mound-building races, the old long-headed, and the later round-headed intruders.

2. a. In specific names of animals.

1729 *Dampier's Voy.* III. 399 Roundheaded Armadillo. **1768** PENNANT *Brit. Zool.* (1776) III. 56 Roundheaded cachalot: this species was taken on one of the Orkney Isles. **1855** *Orr's Circ. Sci., Org. Nat.* III. 410 The Round-headed Porpoise (*Phocœna melas*)..is distinguished by its very convex rounded head. **1897** H. O. FORBES *Hand-bk. Primates* I. 89 The round-headed sportive-lemur.

b. In specific names of plants.

1753 *Chambers' Cycl.* Suppl. s.v. *Mushroom*, The round-headed spring Mushroom. **1789** J. PILKINGTON *View Derbysh.* I. 380 *Juncus conglomeratus*, Round headed Rush. **1796** WITHERING *Brit. Pl.* (ed. 3) II. 333 Round-headed Garlic. *Ibid.* III. 522 Round-headed Mint. *c* **1833** *Swanland Farm Rep.* 127 in *Husb.* III, *Dactylis glomerata*, Round-headed cock's-foot. **1855** MISS PRATT *Flower. Pl.* III. 345 Round-headed Rampion. **1859** —— *Brit. Grasses* VI. 22 Round-headed Cotton-grass. *Ibid.* 40 Round Headed Sedge.

3. Of arches, windows, etc., or building characterized by these.

1758 BP. LOWTH *Life William of Wykeham* vi. 209 With round pillars.., round-headed arches and windows. **1827** *Gentl. Mag.* XCVII. II. 497 This recess was originally illuminated by five narrow round-headed windows. **1881** FREEMAN *Subj. Venice* 104 Above was a simple round-headed clerestory.

4. Of things which assume a rounded form towards the top or end.

1818 SCOTT *Rob Roy* v, The Cheviots rose before me;.. huge, round-headed, and clothed with a dark robe of russet. **1818** —— *Let.* in *Lockhart* (1837) IV. iv. 135 To plant birches, oaks, elms, and suchlike round-headed trees along the verges of the Kaeside plantations. **1866** G. STEPHENS *Runic Mon.* I. 227 These round-headed grave-stones can be traced back in England to the 11th or 12th century.

5. Of nails, etc., ending in a round disk or knob.

1802 JAMES *Mil. Dict.* s.v. *Nail, Rose-bud Nails* are small round-headed nails, driven in the centre of the roses of the plates. **1841** *Penny Cycl.* XIX. 256/1 The screws..are round-headed and countersunk. **1875** DARWIN *Insectiv. Pl.* vii. 139 A considerable number of the round-headed tentacles were inflected.

Hence **round-'headedness**, the state of being round-headed; the condition of having a round head.

1935 [see HIGH FREQUENCY 1 b].

Roundheadism. *rare*⁻¹. [f. ROUNDHEAD.] A Roundhead fashion.

1650 BULWER *Anthropomet.* 258 The City-Flat-Cap imitates the Brasilean Flat-Head, and is no other then a Grecian or Gallo-Grecian Round-headnisme [*sic*].

'round-house, *sb.* [In sense 1 app. f. ROUND *sb.*¹ 14 b (cf. Du. *rondhuis* guard-house); in other senses f. ROUND *a.*]

1. A lock-up; a place of detention for arrested persons. Now only *Hist.*

1589 in *Antiquary* XXXII. 373 [Rent of] the rounde house, iiijd. **1684** *She-Wedding* (title-p.), For which Fact the said Parties were both Committed, and one of them remains now in the Round House at Greenwich. **1697** VANBRUGH *Prov. Wife* IV. i, Out of respect to your calling, I shan't put you into the round-house. **1707** CIBBER *Double Gallant* I. I sit up every night at the Tavern: and in the Morning lie rough in the Round-house. **1791** WOLCOT (P. Pindar) *Remonstrance* Wks. 1812 II. 455 Thence at the Round-house, in about an hour Renews his poor debilitated power Of comprehending. **1817** MISS EDGEWORTH *Harrington* (1832) 17 The beggars..were led in captivity to round-houses. **1840** DICKENS *Barn. Rudge* lxxiv, Mr. Dennis, having been made prisoner late in the evening, was removed to a neighbouring round-house for that night. **1863** KINGSLEY *Water-Babies* v, Put him in the round house till he gets sober.

attrib. **1747** HOADLY *Suspicious Husb.* II. iv, If this should prove a Round-House Affair.

2. *Naut.* **a.** A cabin or set of cabins on the afterpart of the quarter-deck (cf. quot. 1769).

More recently, in use only on old sailing vessels (where it forms the quarters of the sailmakers, carpenters, and apprentices), and in connexion with Board of Trade tonnage measurements, when it generally includes all cabins built on deck.

1626 CAPT. SMITH *Accid. Yng. Seamen* 10 The Captaines Cabben or great Cabben, the steerage, the halfe Decke, the round house, the Forecastle. **1627** —— *Seaman's Gram.* II. 6 The Masters Cabin called the round house..is the vtmost of all. **1691** T. H[ALE] *Acc. New Invent.* 126 The Guns in the Fore-castle and steerage clear the Deck, as those of the Round-house do the Quarter deck. **1725** DE FOE *Voy. round World* (1840) 28 We..secured the Steerage, as also the roundhouse, so that we could not possibly be surprised. **1769** FALCONER *Dict. Marine* (1780), *Round-house*, a name given, in East-Indiamen, and other large merchant-ships, to a cabin..built in the after part of the quarter-deck, and having the poop for it's roof. The apartment is usually called the coach in our ships of war. **1834** MEDWIN *Angler in Wales* I. 229 One of my cabin-windows (for I had half the round-house) was open. **1852** MRS. STOWE *Uncle Tom's C.* xiv, The steersman at the wheel paused and smiled, as the picture-like head gleamed through the window of the round-house. **1906** *Temple Bar* Jan. 76 The reefers in the half-deck also start their sing-song, and the supernumeraries, in 'the round-house', make what melody they can.

attrib. **1846** YOUNG *Naut. Dict.* s.v., The beams on which the poop rests are called the round-house beams.

b. (See quot. *c* 1850.)

1808 J. DAVIS *Post Captain* (ed. 3) i. 5, I..was obliged to get up in the night to go to the roundhouse. *c* **1850** *Rudim. Navig.* (Weale) 143 *Round-house at the Head*, conveniences or seats of ease for the officers.

3. a. A round shed or building in which machinery is worked by circular movement.

1656 W. DU GARD tr. *Comenius' Gate Lat. Unl.* 133 Hee that..turneth about a draw-beam with levers; or walking in the round-hous whirleth the crane. **1886** ELWORTHY *W. Somerset Word-Bk.* s.v., Few farms are without a round-house in which the horses go round and round. **1971** *Country Life* 11 Nov. 1325/1 An example..is a farm building specifically termed the wheelhouse, but more popularly known as roundhouse or gin gan.

b. Part of a windmill (see quot.).

1876 MRS. EWING *Jan of the Windmill* iii, The projection is..an additional passage, encircling the bottom story of the windmill. It is the round-house. The round-house is commonly used as a kind of store-room.

4. orig. *U.S.* A circular shed for locomotives, with a turn-table in the centre. Also *fig.* and *attrib.*

1856 W. FERGUSON *Amer. by River & Rail* 249 The engine-house..is open in the centre; and this arrangement ..is much less expensive, than the 'round house', where all is covered in. **1875** KNIGHT *Dict. Mech.* 1994/2. **1881** *Scribner's Mag.* XXII. 833 The narrow-gauge of the N.P.C.R.R. crawls like a snake from the ferry on the bay to the roundhouse over and beyond the hills. **1891** C. ROBERTS *Adrift Amer.* 225, I found a quiet corner to sleep in, in the round-house, as they call the engine-sheds. **1895** *Rep. Chicago Strike 1894* (U.S. Strike Comm.) 214 A number of switch tenders, yard clerks, flagmen, tower men, and roundhouse men left their work. **1945** F. H. HUBBARD *Railroad Avenue* ii. 10 Many runners considered it smart to keep roundhouse work on an engine down to a minimum —the fewer the defects they reported, the better standing they had at the roundhouse. **1953** *Manch. Guardian Weekly*

5 Nov. 15/1 This restoration of power [over the money supply] was hailed by a writer in 'Harper's Magazine' as a.. guarantee that 'the engine of inflation has been stowed firmly in the roundhouse'. **1966** M. R. D. FOOT *SOE in France* ix. 269 Six large engines in the Troyes locomotive roundhouse. **1980** *Dædalus* Spring 121 Myths provide a conceptual system through which we may understand.. a roundhouse where we can move from the track of one person's reality to another's.

5. a. *U.S. Baseball.* A pitch made with a sweeping side-arm motion. Also *attrib.*

1910 *Amer. Mag.* June 224/2 The first curves discovered were of the variety now known as the 'barrel hoop' or 'round house'. **1912** C. MATHEWSON *Pitching* 19 When I first joined the Giants, I had what is known as the 'old round-house curve', which is no more than a big, slow outdrop. **1926** *Amer. Speech* I. 369/2 Pitched balls are designated by obvious terms. A 'spitter', a 'hook',.. a 'round-house'.

b. *slang* (orig. *U.S.*). A blow delivered with a wide sweep of the arm. Also *fig.* Freq. *attrib.*, esp. as ***roundhouse left, right.***

1920 *Collier's Mag.* 3 July 34/4 He swung a roundhouse left, square to the Kid's unprotected face. **1927** *Daily Express* 16 Dec. 3 It is necessary to take the [golf] ball cleanly, and with something akin to a 'round-house' swing from this position. **1932** J. T. FARRELL *Young Lonigan* iii. 133 They fought, slugging, socking away, rushing, swinging with haymakers and wild swishing roundhouses. **1945** *Tee Emm* (Air Ministry) V. 51 Discourage him by jabbing his snout or gills with an oar,.. and don't take round-house swings that may upset you. **1946** *Sun* (Baltimore) 14 Dec. 2/6 Mr. Collins leaped to his feet and swung a round-house right at the witness. **1948** *Ibid.* 12 May 17/6 Trainer Jimmy Jones obviously was disappointed at failure to have Coaltown [*sc.* a horse] on hand to deliver Columet's [*sic*] winning jab and round-house... Jimmy will saddle the Calumet starter. **1958** J. KEROUAC *On Road* iv. 126 Damion's girl suddenly socked Damion on the jaw with a roundhouse right. **1967** *Boston Herald* 1 Apr. 17/7 Harris built up an early lead over the baffled 29-year-old veteran with his roundhouse blows. **1976** M. MACHLIN *Pipeline* lvii. 573 Doheny's arm drew back, as though to launch a roundhouse upper-cut.

Hence **'round-house** *v.*, (*a*) to confine in a round-house; (*b*) *slang*, to hit (a person) with a round-house blow.

1889 CONAN DOYLE *Micah Clarke* xiii. 117, I have been round-housed many a time by the watch. **1974** W. GARNER *Big Enough Wreath* xi. 137 She roundhoused Smith with a white plastic handbag that must have had a brick in it.

'rounding, *vbl. sb.*^{1} [f. ROUND *v.*^{1} + -ING^1.]

I. 1. a. The action of the vb. in trans. senses. Also with *off*, *out*, *up*.

1562-3 *Act 5 Eliz.* c. xi. §1 Clipping, washing, rounding, or filing.. of any the proper Moneys or Coines of this Realme. **1611** COTGR. s.v. *Arrondissement*, The pieces, or shreds that are cut off in the rounding of a garment. **1794** *Rigging & Seamanship* 56 *Rounding* is giving the rope an additional turn after being closed. **1867** A. J. ELLIS *E.E. Pronunc.* I. iii. §3. 161 When the labial passage is large and unconstrained by rounding or narrowing of the labial orifice. **1876** M. WHILLDIN *Descr. Western Texas* 16 It soon became evident that a place near us had been selected for 'rounding up'. **1885** C. G. W. LOCK *Workshop Rec.* Ser. IV. 236/1 'Rounding' applies to the back of the book, and is preliminary to backing. **1886** T. FROST *Reminisc. Country Journalist* xi. (1888) 121 Canning.. was so extremely fastidious about the rounding of his periods. **1916** *Daily News* 6 Sept. 4 There can rarely.. have been a better example of the insolence of Zabernism than the 'rounding up' of crowds of unoffending people at the stations. **1932** W. C. HOLDEN *Rollie Burns* xiii. 172 Our rounding-up outfit was camped about eight miles from the Yellow House Canyon. **1936** *Trans. Philol. Soc.* 78 The rounding of *ā* to [ɔ] is in Middle English generally held to be a West Midland feature. **1947** A. EINSTEIN *Mus. Romantic Era* xi. 127 The perfect rounding-out of the form, which from the musical standpoint is entirely self-contained. **1949** *Jrnl. R. Aeronaut. Soc.* LIII. 957/1 The cabin floor angle in the steeper types, such as Dakotas and Lancastrians, is changed as slowly as possible by slow rounding out and by landing with the tail just off the ground. **1961** E. A. POWDRILL *Vocab. Land Planning* iii. 38 The private developer refers to most forms of peripheral development as 'rounding-off', whilst the planning authority merely contends that it is not, usually without saying what rounding-off really means. **1971** P. GRESSWELL *Environment* 132 Development will be severely restricted except for a reasonable amount of infilling and/or rounding off. **1977** *Canad. Jrnl. Linguistics 1976* XXI. 176 At this level we want to state, for example, that a language has vowels which are opposed in rounding.

b. *Naut.* with *in*, *up* (see quots.).

1769 FALCONER *Dict. Marine* (1780), *Rounding-in*, generally implies the act of pulling upon any rope which passes through one or more blocks, in a direction nearly horizontal. *Ibid.*, *Rounding-up*.. is expressed of a tackle which hangs in a perpendicular position, without sustaining or hoisting any weighty body: it is then the operation of pulling the blocks closer to each other, by means of the rope which passes through them. **1890** CLARK RUSSELL *Marriage at Sea* xiii, The sailors fell to *rounding-in*, as it is called, upon the main and main-topsail braces.

c. The action of ROUND *v.*^{1} 4 d. Also with *down*, *off*, *up* (cf. ROUND *v.*^{1} 5 g, 6 e, 8 d).

1935 SHUSTER & BEDFORD *Field Work in Math.* iv. 14 In computation with approximate numbers, rounding off should be done by these rules. **1953** *Proc. IRE* XLI. 1270/1 Different calculations may require different methods of rounding in order to reduce the residual rounding error to an acceptably low level. **1963** *Rep. Comm. Inquiry Decimal Currency* iii. 18 in *Parl. Papers 1962-3* (Cmnd. 2145) XI. 195 Outstanding balances would convert exactly on the changeover date, with no discrepancies which might or might not be explained by decimalisation roundings. **1973** C. W. GEAR *Introd. Computer Sci.* vi. 249 The errors introduced by rounding and truncation are initially small, but sometimes their effect is amplified by subsequent operations. **1976** C. BIRTWISTLE *Electronic Calculator* iii. 35, 23 is rounded down to 20 and 28 is rounded up to 30. Where is the critical point at which rounding down changes to rounding up? Obviously it is the half-way mark, 25.

2. The action of the vb. in intrans. senses. Also with *up*.

1674 FAIRFAX *Bulk & Selv.* 90 Suppose.. the Planets still holding their rooms, and holding on their roundings as they did before. **1732** WHALEY *Poems* 48 With happy Roundings swell'd the Breast. **1862** *Cornh. Mag.* Nov. 646 'Rounding' or treachery is always spoken of very indignantly, and often severely.. punished. **1868** VERNEY *Stone Edge* x, Come, Roland, I'll none waste my time with such roundings. **1906** *Brit. Med. Jrnl.* 13 Jan. 70 A little rounding up of the abdomen.

3. *attrib.*, as ***rounding-brass, -iron, -knife, plane***, etc.; **rounding error** = *round-off error* s.v. ROUND-OFF *sb.* 1.

1688 HOLME *Armoury* III. 383/1 *Rounding Knife*, a short broad Blade like a Turkish scimitar, a thick back and short handle. **1843** HOLTZAPFFEL *Turning* I. 232 The top and bottom rounding tools.. are made of all diameters for plain cylindrical works. **1845** YOUATT *Dog* iii. 83 When the time comes, the ears of the dog should be rounded; the size of the ear and of the head guiding the rounding-iron. **1851-4** *Tomlinson's Cycl. Useful Arts* (1866) I. 838/2 When quite dry, the proper width is given to the brim by means of a rounding-brass, or gauge. **1876** *Encycl. Brit.* IV. 44/1 The backing-machine is worked by the hand, and its action is somewhat similar to that of the rounding-machine. **1940** *Chambers's Techn. Dict.* 732/2 Rounding plane. **1948** *Math. Tables & Other Aids to Computation* III. 79 The operator is concerned with numerous questions of digital accuracy and the accumulation of rounding errors. **1962** A. BATTERSBY *Guide to Stock Control* 115 Allowing for rounding errors, the stockholding cost at ½ per cent would be £15. **1969** E. H. PINTO *Treen* 389 Different versions of the same tool, known as a stail-engine, witchet, or rounding and tapering plane. **1973** C. W. GEAR *Introd. Computer Sci.* vi. 249 The first source is called rounding error, and is due to the fact that only a finite set of all of the real numbers can be represented in the computer as floating-point numbers.

b. So ***rounding-up machine, tool***; **rounding-off error** = *round-off error*.

1884 KNIGHT *Dict. Mech.* Suppl. 831/2 A rounding up machine can shape 100 pairs of soles per hour. **1884** BRITTEN *Watch & Clockm.* 125 The fraises do not supersede the Rounding Up Tool. **1945** J. VON NEUMANN in B. Randell *Origins Digital Computers* (1973) 362 A reasonable precision for many differential equation problems is given.. by keeping the relative rounding-off errors below 10^{-8}. **1974** W. T. WELFORD *Aberrations Symmetrical Optical Syst.* vi. 84 The difference between them is to be calculated to a fraction of a wavelength; this may make a heavy demand on the computer when rounding-off errors are allowed for, since the computer word length may correspond to only about eight decimal digits.

II. 4. A rounded edge or surface; a curvature; a curved part or outline; †a tonsure.

1551 ROBINSON tr. *More's Utop.* I. (1895) 70 He shoulde be dyscryued by hys rounding and his eare marke. *a* **1583** in Halliwell *Rara Mathem.* (1841) 38 That Glasse woulde make the face.. narrowe accordinge vnto the roundinge of the glasse. **1680** MOXON *Mech. Exerc.* xiii. 226 A Tooth of Steel with such Roundings and Hollows in the bottom of it as I intended to have Hollows and Roundings upon my Work. **1760-72** H. BROOKE *Fool of Qual.* (1809) III. 149 Never did I behold such.. symmetry, such roundings of angles. **1771** LUCKOMBE *Hist. Print.* 309 A mortise.. from within an inch of the rounding to an inch and an half of the bottom. **1833** LOUDON *Encycl. Archit.* §602 The rounding of the chimney breast. *a* **1842** SIR C. BELL *Anat. & Phil. Express.* (1872) 223 He makes roundings merely; he is incapable of representing the elegant curved outline of beauty. **1897** *Westm. Gaz.* 8 Jan. 8/3 The cork disc is driven.. down into the rounding outside the bottle top.

5. *Naut.* A service of small rope or cordage, wound round a cable, spar, etc., to prevent chafing.

1748 *Anson's Voy.* II. i. 115 An iron chain, or good rounding,.. to secure them [*sc.* cables] from being rubbed by the foulness of the ground. **1769** FALCONER *Dict. Marine* (1780) *Fourrer*, to serve the cables as with plat, rounding, keckling, &c. **1840** R. H. DANA *Bef. Mast* iii, This chafing gear consists of.. roundings, battens, and service of all kinds. **1867** SMYTH *Sailor's Word-bk.* s.v. *Mat*, Rounding is now used instead of mats, it being neater and holding less water. **1882** NARES *Seamanship* (ed. 6) 229 Take a piece of.. stout rounding to the topmast.

†6. *pl.* Some part of a woman's head-dress. *Obs.*

1732 *Lond. Mag.* Oct. 351/1 The Head-Dresses, with the Peeks, Lappets, and Roundings.

7. *pl.* Clippings; parings.

1883 HALDANE *Workshop Receipts* Ser. II. 300/2 'Wet' materials:.. roundings of hides previously limed. **1889** *Charity Organis. Rev.* Jan. 9 [They] are forced.. to sell the 'roundings' (inferior portions).. at a considerable loss.

'rounding, *vbl. sb.*^{2} [Later form of ROUNING *vbl. sb.*: cf. ROUND *v.*^{2}] Whispering, private talk.

1509 BARCLAY *Shyp of Folys* (1570) 85 Within the Churche the seruice to encomber With their lewde barking, rounding, din and cry. *Ibid.* (1570) 208 They flatter their lorde with wordes fayre and gay And vayne roundinges. **1609** LD. BALMERINOCH *Narr.* in Pitcairn *Crim. Trials* II. 586 Then, be his Ma. countenance, and some rounding that past betuixt his Ma. and Sir A. Hay, I beganne to be in some suspicione.

'rounding, *ppl. a.* [f. ROUND *v.*^{1} + -ING^2.]

1. Surrounding, encircling.

1600 TOURNEUR *Transf. Metam.* lxvi, All with their poyson like a rounding ring; The good encombred Knight encompassing. **1830** TENNYSON *Mariana* 44 For leagues no other tree did mark The level waste, the rounding gray.

2. Assuming or having a circular or convex form; tending towards roundness.

1670 NARBOROUGH *Jrnl.* in *Acc. Sev. Late Voy.* I. (1694) 24 Upon which rounding Point stand black Rocks. **1709** *Lond. Gaz.* No. 4510/7 The Hoy Burthen 9 or 10 Tun,.. with a clean Tail, a rounding Wale. **1786** ABERCROMBIE *Gard. Assist.* 94 Turning.. the clean fresh gravel to the top, levelling it even in a rounding manner. **1869** WHITTIER *Norembega* 14 Unbroken over swamp and hill The rounding shadow lay.

b. In predicative and quasi-adv. use.

1683 MOXON *Mech. Exerc., Printing* xv. ¶2 It hath two of its Fore-Angles.. cut off either straight or rounding, according to the pleasure of the Work-man. **1712** J. JAMES tr. *Le Blond's Gardening* 155 You.. fill them with Mold.., which you lay rounding in the Middle like an Ass's Back. **1793** SMEATON *Edystone L.* §80 In some degree rounding, like the Rockers of a cradle. **1846** HOLTZAPFFEL *Turning* II. 499 If it [*sc.* a board] should be obviously higher.. at the edges from being 'cast and rounding'. **1858** *Skyring's Builder's Prices* 4 Care should be taken to allow for the remedy of that defect, by laying the joist rounding.

3. Circular, circuitous; moving round.

1711 *Milit. & Sea Dict.* (ed. 4), *Caracol*, as Wheel by Caracol; used only among the Horse, and is a Serpentine or Rounding Motion of Wheeling. **1728** MALLET *Excursion* Wks. 1759 I. 101 Where these huge globes Sail undisturb'd, a rounding voyage each. **1883** WHITTIER *Our Country* 35 Alone, the rounding century finds Thy liberal soil by free hands tilled.

'roundish, *a.* [f. ROUND *a.* + -ISH.]

1. Somewhat round.

1545 RAYNOLD *Byrth Mankynde* 25 The backe or outer syde therof roundysshe and smothe. *a* **1608** DEE *Relat. Spir.* I. (1659) 357 They.. break up the rock.. in roundish lumps as big as a twopeny loaf. **1683** MOXON *Mech. Exerc., Printing* xi. ¶15 The edges a little Bevil'd roundish away. **1733** TULL *Horse-Hoeing Husb.* xxiii. (Dubl.) 355 The Corner of the Plate.. we make a little roundish. **1755** MASON *Let. to Gray* 27 June, Mynn Herr—is of a roundish, squab figure. **1826** KIRBY & SP. *Entomol.* III. xxxv. 600 An oblong and sometimes roundish spot. **1875** BUCKLAND *Log-Book* 34 The mark of the foot is of a roundish form. **1897** *Allbutt's Syst. Med.* III. 80 Some osteophytes are flat and roundish.

2. *Comb.* **a.** Parasynthetic, as ***roundish-faced, -featured, -leaved, -shaped.***

1670 NARBOROUGH *Jrnl.* in *Acc. Sev. Late Voy.* I. (1694) 64 These People are.. roundish Faced, and well shaped. **1753** *Chambers' Cycl.* Suppl. s.v. *Ranunculus*, The roundish leaved ranunculuses. **1836-9** *Todd's Cycl. Anat.* II. 485/2 When they are viewed in an aggregate form, the semblance of roundish-shaped granules is seen. **1881** CARLYLE *Reminisc.* II. 35 She was roundish-featured.

b. With adjs., as ***roundish-deltoid, -obovate, -oval, -ovate.***

1828 J. E. SMITH *Eng. Flora* II. 263 Leaves roundish-oval, always longer than they are broad. *Ibid.* 265 Leaves roundish-obovate, serrated. **1847** STEELE *Field Bot.* 134 Leaves roundish-ovate, toothed, wrinkled. *Ibid.* 214 Rachis green, fronds linear; pinnæ roundish-deltoid.

Hence **'roundishness**, 'the state of being roundish' (Webster, 1828-32).

roundle ('raʊnd(ə)l). [var. of ROUNDEL.]

1. A ring or circle; an object of circular form; a disk, round plate, etc. (Cf. ROUNDEL.) Now *rare*.

1559 MORWYNG *Evonym.* 206 Take the rout of Dragons made cleen and cut in to thin roundles. **1601** HOLLAND *Pliny* II. 128 Good it is also to cut them into roundles. **1632** SIR S. D'EWES *Autobiog.* (1845) II. 72, I caused them all [*sc.* coins] to be put into roundles of ivory, and placed them in drawers in a box. **1688** HOLME *Armoury* II. 88/1 The flowers grow in roundles, towards the top of the stalk. **1855** tr. *Labarte's Arts Mid. Ages* p. xxix, Painted roundles or fruit trenchers. **1887** PARISH & SHAW *Kent Gloss.*, *Roundle*,.. the part of a hop-oast where the fires are made, which is generally circular.

b. *Her.* One of various circular changes distinguished by their tincture. (Cf. ROUNDEL 5 b.)

1610 GUILLIM *Her.* IV. xix, Of the first sort are Roundles, of which Leigh giueth examples of nine sundry. **1688** HOLME *Armoury* I. 60/2, I shall in the first place speak of the Rounds, Roundles, or Roundlets. **1728** CHAMBERS *Cycl.*, *Pellets*, in Heraldry, a Name given those Roundles which are Black; call'd also *Ogresses* and *Gun-stones*. **1864** BOUTELL *Her. Hist. & Pop.* xvii. (ed. 3) 260 He charged this group upon a roundle. **1868** CUSSANS *Her.* (1893) 73 *Roundles* are small circular figures—of frequent occurrence in Heraldry —forming a distinct group of Charges.

c. = ROUNDEL 3 b.

1869 BOUTELL *Arms & Armour* x. 193 The roundles at the elbows and shoulders sometimes assumed the form of lions' faces. *Ibid.* 196.

†2. A sphere or globe. *Obs.* (Cf. ROUNDEL 6 a.)

1601 HOLLAND *Pliny* I. 30 We speake.. [of] the round ball of the earth; and confesse that it is a globe... But yet the forme is not of a perfect and absolute roundle. **1609** —— *Amm. Marcell.* XX. iii. 145 The Sunne.. and the roundle of the Moone. **1674** FAIRFAX *Bulk & Selv.* 182 To find out a scantling beyond which the roundle or globe of the earth is not.

†3. A round of a ladder. *Obs.* (Cf. ROUNDEL 7.)

1643 SIR T. BROWNE *Relig. Med.* 25 Things.. which.. serve.. to judicious beliefs as scales and rondles to mount the pinnacles.. of Divinity. *a* **1663** SANDERSON *Serm.* (1681) II. 310 When they are in the top of their Jollity and gotten to the uppermost Roundle of the ladder.

†4. = ROUNDEL 9. *Obs.*

1544 *Lydgate's Bochas* Prol. li, Complaintes, ballades, roundles [*Bodl. MS.* roundelis], virelaies. **1579** SPENSER *Sheph. Cal.* Aug. 125 Sike a roundle never heard I none.

round-leaved, *a. Bot.* Also 8 round-leafed. [ROUND *a.* 16c.] Having round leaves. Chiefly in specific names of plants.

The number of varieties distinguished by this name is very large; only a few are given here.

1634 T. JOHNSON *Merc. Bot.* 19 Round leaved water Pimpernell. **1725** *Fam. Dict.* s.v. *Sallow*, The vulgar round Leav'd Sallow proves best in drier Banks. **1731** MILLER *Gard. Dict.* s.v. *Mentha*, The Great Round-leaf'd Water-Mint, with a variegated Leaf. **1786** ABERCROMBIE *Arr.* in *Gard. Assist.* 64 Round leaved winter green. **1809** KENDALL *Trav.* III. 146 The lumberers..meaning by *soft wood* all the evergreens; and by *hard wood* all deciduous or as they call them *round-leaved* trees. **1847** W. C. L. MARTIN *The Ox* 37/2 The great round-leaved willow (*salix caprea*). **1882** *Garden* 28 Oct. 375/2 Round-leaved Catchfly, with deep scarlet flowers.

'roundlet. Forms: 4 rownde-, 4–8 roundelet (5 -lett, 5–6 -lete); 4 rondlet, 5 rowndlet, rounlet, 5, 7– roundlet (7 -lett). [ad. OF. *rondelet*, dim. of *rondel* ROUNDEL. Cf. ROUNDELAY.]

†**1.** A short roundel. *Obs.*

*c***1386** CHAUCER *Frankl. T.* 220 (Corpus MS.), Of such matiere made he many layes, Songes, compleigntes, roundeletis, virrelayes. **1589** GREENE *Tullies Loue* Wks. (Grosart) VII. 136 So Terentia taking the Lute in hir hand beganne to warble out this roundelet.

2. A small circle or circular object; a little disk or round ornament; a circular clump, etc.

1380–1 *Durh. Acc. Rolls* (Surtees) 389 In vj Roundeletys empt. pro magno altare, ix d. **1385** *Ibid.* 265 In tribus rondlettys emptis pro rasturis. iv d. *c***1450** in Aungier *Syon* (1840) 367 Torches, mattes, uattes [? *read* nattes], and roundlettes for the chirche. *c***1450** *M.E. Med. Bk.* (Heinrich) 196 Drawe hyt two & fro, as þou woldest tempre wax, & mak hyt in roundeletes. *Ibid.* 214 Tak a gret rote of radysche..& kytte hyt on fyfty Rounlettes. **1603** DRAYTON *Bar. Wars* v. lx, The troubled Teares..Made them to seeme like Roundlets, that arise By a Stone cast into a standing Brooke. *a***1646** J. GREGORY *Posthuma* (1650) 310 The little Circles or Roundlets dispersed here and there about the Hemispheres. **1892** BRIGHTON *Sir P. Wallis* 103 The figure-head of the *Shannon*, a colossal female bust, ornamented with a necklace of gilded roundlets. **1906** *Dollar Mag.* June 91 The roundlet of trees presents the appearance of a fortification.

†**b.** A part of a hood (see quots.). *Obs.*

1603 STOW *Surv.* 545 These hoodes were worn, the Roundelets vpon their heades, the skirtes to hang behind in their neckes. **1834** PLANCHÉ *Hist. Brit. Cost.* 191 The alteration of the chaperon..into a regularly-formed crown within a thick roll called the roundlet.

c. *Her.* = ROUNDLE 1 b.

1688 HOLME *Armoury* I. vi. 61/1 He beareth Party per Pale Vert and Argent, three Roundletts counterchanged. **1738** CHAMBERS *Cycl.*, *Pellets*, in heraldry, a name given those roundlets which are black. **1766** [see OGRESS[2]]. **1838** *Penny Cycl.* XII. 140/2 There are nine roundlets, or balls, also used in heraldry.

†**3.** A small cask; a runlet. *Obs.*

1388 *Durh. Acc. Rolls* (Surtees) 48 In duo Rowndelet' de Sturgeown, 7s. **1435–6** in Heath *Grocers' Comp.* (1869) 418 The costis of x butts & vi roundeletts of resins of Corent. **1466** *Paston Lett.* II. 267 A roundlet of red wine of xv. gallonys. **1538** FITZHERB. *Justyce Peas* 109 The price of the But, Tone, Hoggeshede, Punchion, Tierce, Barel or Roundelet to be sold in grosse. **1594** PLAT *Jewell-ho.* 70 Set your roundelet in the sunne. **1656** BLOUNT, *Roundlet*, a certain measure of Wine, Oyle, &c. containing eighteen Gallons and an half. *c***1730** BURT *Lett. N. Scotl.* (1760) II. xviii. 83 Horses loaded with Roundlets of Usky.

roundley, obs. form of ROUNDELAY.

'roundliness. *rare*$^{-1}$. [Cf. ROUNDLY *a.*] Rounded outline or contour.

1870 G. H. KINGSLEY *Sp. & Trav.* (1900) iv. 75 The 'roundliness' and development of the upper part of the back and arms are superb.

†**'roundling.** *Obs.*$^{-1}$ [f. ROUND *a.* + -LING.] A variety of apple.

1655 MOUFET & BENNET *Health's Improv.* 196 Roundlings are called *mala Sceptiana*.

'roundly, *a. rare*$^{-1}$. [f. ROUND *a.* + -LY[1].] Somewhat round.

1613 W. BROWNE *Brit. Past.* I. iv, A Scyte, About the edges of whose roundly forme In order grew such trees as doe adorne The sable hearse.

roundly ('raʊndlɪ), *adv.* Also 5 roundliche, *Sc.* rondely, 6 roundely, roundlye, 6–7 roundlie. [f. ROUND *a.* + -LY[2]. Cf. MDu. *rondelic* (Du. *-lijk*), G. *rundlich*, MSw. *rundeliga* (Sw. *rundligen*), Da. *rundelig(en.*]

†**1.** At a quiet but steady pace. *Obs.*

*c***1430** *Pilgr. Lyf Manhode* I. cxxxv. (1869) 71 Soonere is the mule ofte at seynt james that goth roundliche [F. *qui va rondement son train*] than is thilke smiteth and sporeth his hors, and maketh him go sharpliche.

2. To the full; completely, thoroughly; in a thoroughgoing manner.

*c***1450** in *Househ. Ord.* (1790) 75 And to awnswere roundly there to every gallon, pottell, and pynte, by measure. **1579–80** NORTH *Plutarch, Lycurgus* (1612) 52 He that was taken with the maner, had his payment roundly, and was punished with fasting besides. **1597** SHAKS. *2 Hen. IV*, III. ii. 21, I was call'd any thing: and I would haue done any thing indeede too, and roundly too. **1640** BROME *Sparagus Garden* III. vii, And a man had come to London for nothing else but to be Cheated, hee could not bee more roundlier rid of his money. **1692** SOUTH *Serm.* (1744) II. 287 Every hypocrite..who never comes up roundly to the whole compass of his duty. **1784** COWPER *Task* VI. 606 God..Will reckon with us roundly for th' abuse Of what he deems no mean or trivial trust. **1825** SCOTT *Talism.* ix, The blame rests..with those with whom..I hope to reckon roundly. **1872** RUSKIN *Eagle's N.* §88 The result of our instruction is only that we are able to produce the most perfectly and roundly ill-done things that ever came from human hands.

3. Plainly, outspokenly, without mincing the matter, bluntly.

1528 GARDINER in Burnet *Hist. Ref.* (Pocock) *Rec.* I. li. 127 On the morrow we returned unto the pope's holiness and spake roundly unto him. **1589** GREENE *Menaphon* (Arb.) 58 Pleusidippus..gaue him the lie roundly in this replie. **1614** RALEIGH *Hist. World* II. (1634) 456 They told the Prophet roundly, that they would worship the Queene of Heaven. **1682** DRYDEN & LEE *Dk. Guise* II. i, And, pr'ythee, tell him roundly of his faults. **1745** P. THOMAS *Jrnl. Anson's Voy.* 276 Our Commodore..roundly answer'd..that he would go when he saw it convenient. **1775** SHERIDAN *Rivals* I. ii, Let me beg you..to enforce this matter roundly to the girl. **1821** J. W. CROKER *Diary* 17 Aug. in *C. Papers* (1884), He renewed all his complaints..and said roundly that he would not go on any longer. **1874** SYMONDS *Sk. Italy & Greece* (1898) I. 275 He told his father roundly that he would not go.

b. Frankly, openly, without concealment.

1593 R. HARVEY *Philadelphus* 19 Morgan began roundly to make open warre agaynst him. *a***1616** BEAUM. & FL. *Little French Lawyer* III. ii, [He] has challeng'd me down-right, defied me mortally... What a bold Man of War! he invites me roundly. **1642** *Compl. to Ho. Commons* 17 Wee must now deale roundly for the truth. **1851** HUSSEY *Papal Power* i. 39 The claim which he advanced somewhat roundly, and beyond his predecessors apparently.

4. Without circumlocution; straight.

1534 MORE *Treat. Passion* Wks. 1303/2 He went roundly to the matter, and sayd vnto them: what wyl ye gyue me and I shal delyuer hym to you. **1597** MORLEY *Introd. Mus.* 143 Then (to go to the matter roundly without circumstances) here be two parts. **1622** BP. ANDREWES *Serm.* (1841) IV. 160 They go roundlier to the point than doth Suarez, or any of them have been blundering about this gear of late. **1625** PEEKE *Three to One* A 4, Not to weary you with long Præambles,..I will come roundly to the matter.

b. Without qualification; absolutely.

1596 BELL *Surv. Popery* III. vi. 310 When cardinall Allen, in his notes vpon this place, auoucheth roundly that this text conuinceth praier for the dead. **1633** G. HERBERT *Temple, Affliction* v, I scarce beleeved, Till grief did tell me roundly, that I lived. **1671** J. WEBSTER *Metallogr.* vii. 116 But we may as roundly say, that the *Lapis Lazuli* is the Marchasue of Gold. **1709** SWIFT *Vind. Bickerstaff* Wks. 1751 IV. 219 He very roundly asserts, That he is not only now alive, but was likewise alive upon that very 29th of March. **1773** WESLEY *Wks.* (1872) X. 418, I do not roundly affirm this of every sentence..in the fifty volumes. *a***1817** DWIGHT *Trav. New Eng.*, etc. (1821) II. 155 When I ventured to question the soundness of these assertions, he roundly replied that they were certain truths. **1888** BURGON *Lives 12 Gd. Men* II. 424 [He] prints..certain discreditable words which he roundly asserts that I wrote.

5. Sharply, severely; unsparingly.

1570 GRINDAL *Let.* Wks. (Parker Soc.) 324 The Vice-chancellor and heads of houses proceed not so roundly in this case as were requisite, in my judgment. **1588** J. UDALL *Diotrephes* (Arb.) 27 The Queene shall..take them vp roundly, that they shall not dare to speake any more. **1607** HIERON *Wks.* I. 233 He takes them vp very roughly and very roundly, calleth them a generation of vipers. **1687** A. LOVELL tr. *Thevenot's Trav.* III. 2 They must also expect to be roundly fined, and some have been fined in above Ten thousand Livres. **1752** FIELDING *Amelia* VII. ii, I took the young lady herself very roundly to task. **1810** SCOTT in *Lockhart* (1839) II. 302 This said Kehama..will get it roundly in the Edinburgh Review. **1892** W. PIKE *Barren Gr. N. Canada* 96, I..abused him roundly when I found he had come without it.

†**6.** Fluently, glibly; readily. *Obs.*

1561 T. NORTON *Calvin's Inst.* III. 222 They falsly, yea & wrongfully pretende the knowlege of Christ, although they can eloquently & roundely talke of the Gospell. **1593** SHAKS. *Rich. II*, II. i. 122 This tongue that runs so roundly in thy head. *c***1620** MORYSON *Itin.* IV. (1903) 393 All the Polonians ..can speake the lattin tounge, and that roundly, but most falsly. **1696** S. PATRICK *Comm. Exod.* iv. 11 Cannot I..take away this Impediment.., and make thee to speak as roundly and gracefully as any Man living?

7. Rapidly, smartly, briskly, promptly.

1548 ELYOT, *Cursim legere*, to reade a pase, to reade roundely. **1573** G. HARVEY *Letter-bk.* (Camden) 46 He never made ani bones at it, but trudgd up roundely to work the feat. **1607** T. WALKINGTON *Opt. Glass* xiii. (1664) 138 He fell roundly to his victuals, having not eat any in a seven night before. **1639** LD. DUNGARVAN in *Lismore Papers* Ser. II. (1888) IV. 45 Wee had neither foote nor artillery yet was it resolued wee shold charge them roundly. *a***1715** BURNET *Own Time* III. (1724) I. 362 Lord Shaftesbury reckoned himself gone at Court, and acted more roundly. **1794** *Rigging & Seamanship* II. 322 The main sheet [is] eased off roundly. **1821** SCOTT *Pirate* xxxi, I..enforced my commands with a blow, which he returned as roundly. **1882** NARES *Seamanship* (ed. 6) 209 Slack off the studding-sail sheets roundly.

8. In a circular manner; in a circle; rotundly.

1565 JEWEL *Reply Harding* (1611) 204 And thus M. Hardings reasons run roundly against himselfe. **1590** SPENSER *F.Q.* II. ii. 15 Her golden lockes she roundly did uptye In breaded tramels. **1591** SYLVESTER *Du Bartas* I. ii. 1024 But the Heav'ns course, not wandring up nor down Continually turns only roundly round. **1648** HEXHAM II, *Rondelik*, roundly, or in the forme of a round. **1806** FORSYTH *Beauties Scotl.* III. 349 One third of the county [Dumbarton]..is yet open, or but roundly inclosed; that is, the farms are inclosed but not subdivided. **1851** HAWTHORNE *Twice-told T.* II. xi. 161 Sometimes a lady passed, swelling roundly forth in an embroidered petticoat. **1865** *Reader* No. 139. 242/3 Round and roundly oval cells. **1873** RUSKIN *Love's Meinie* iii. §82 Its beak..is bent down so roundly that the angriest parrot cannot peck, but only bite.

b. In a finished or polished style.

1709 POPE *Ess. Crit.* 359 Leave such to tune their own dull rhymes, and know What's roundly smooth or languishingly slow.

9. Generally; on a general estimate.

1699 BENTLEY *Phal.* 74 That seems to be spoken roundly and in the gross, without taking notice of odd years.

round-mouthed, *a.* [ROUND *a.* 16.] Having a round mouth.

1681 GREW *Musæum* I. vi. i. 134 The Lesser Round-Mouth'd Snail, with a shorter knobed Turban. **1752** J. HILL *Hist. Anim.* 137 The deeply-sulcated, round mouthed Turbo. **1776** DA COSTA *Elem. Conchol.* 222 Gualtieri has arranged all the taper shells together, both the round-mouthed and these. **1830** *Cumb. Farm Rep.* 65 in *Husb.* III. (L.U.K.), The round-mouthed spades used in forming canals, etc., called here navigation spades. **1851** WOODWARD *Mollusca* I. 12 The round-mouthed sea-snails are nearly all vegetarians. **1906** RAVEN *Bells* 36 The bells seem round-mouthed.

roundness ('raʊndnɪs). Also 4 rond(e)-, 5 rownde-, 4–6 rounde-, 5–6 rownd-. [f. ROUND *a.*]

1. a. The quality of being round; rotundity.

*c***1374** CHAUCER *Boeth.* V. pr. iv. (1868) 164 þe same roundenes of a body O, oþer weyes þe syȝt of þe eye knoweþ it, and oþer weyes þe touching. *c***1400** MAUNDEV. (1839) xiv. 159 And righte as the Perl of his owne kynde takethe Roundnesse, righte so the Dyamand..takethe squarenesse. *c***1400** *Pilgr. Sowle* (Caxton, 1483) V. xiv. 107 In a round spere ne ben mo partes of shap but only the roundenes. **1545** ASCHAM *Toxoph.* (Arb.) 127 Roundnesse..is fittest shappe and forme..for fast mouing. **1590** STOCKWOOD *Rules Construction* 48 The depth, height, squarenes, roundnes, of a thing. **1642** FULLER *Holy & Prof. St.* III. xxii. 213 The diamond hinders the roundnesse of the ring. **1701** NORRIS *Ideal World* I. ii. 99 Roundness being comprehended in the idea of a circle. **1774** GOLDSM. *Nat. Hist.* (1776) VIII. 149 A figure which bears some resemblance to..the roundness of a kernel. **1832** BREWSTER *Nat. Magic* vi. 148 Distant objects concealed by the roundness of the earth.

fig. **1845** MAURICE *Mor. Philos.* in *Encycl. Metrop.* II. 604/1 It is a set-off against this consideration, that roundness and completeness are the great characteristics of Aristotle. **1927** E. M. FORSTER *Aspects of Novel* iv. 98 Dickens's people are nearly all flat (Pip and David Copperfield attempt roundness, but so diffidently that they seem more like bubbles than solids).

b. Fullness, plumpness (of figure, etc.).

1829 LYTTON *Devereux* I. ii, His figure..destitute of the roundness and elasticity of youth. **1838** —— *Leila* I. iv, Leila was of the lightest shape consistent with the roundness of womanly beauty. **1886** G. R. SIMS *Ring o' Bells* II. iv. 64 Of late the little face had lost its roundness.

c. Of numbers: (see ROUND *a.* 7 a).

1841 MYERS *Cath. Th.* IV. §34. 352 A certain roundness of numbers..we may readily anticipate, when whole centuries are in question.

d. *out-of-roundness*: see ROUND *sb.*[1] 5 e.

2. Compass; circumference. Now *rare* or *Obs.*

1382 WYCLIF *Wisd.* i. 7 The Spirit of the Lord fulfilde the rondnesse of londis. *Ibid.*, *Dan.* iii. 45 Thou art the Lord God alone, and glorious vpon the roundenesse of erthes. *c***1400** MAUNDEV. (Roxb.) xx. 90 We schuld hafe sene all þe roundenesse of þe firmament, þat es to say bathe þe emisperies. *Ibid.* 93 So mykill hase þe erthe in roundenes all aboute. **1527** R. THORNE in Hakl. *Voy.* (1589) 253 Under the which is comprehended all the roundnesse of the earth. *a***1596** SPENSER *Ruines of Rome* viii, One would weene that one sole Cities strength Both land and sea in roundnes had survew'd. **1604** E. G[RIMSTONE] tr. *D'Acosta's Hist. Indies* I. ii. 6 These two elements, having their bounds and limits within their own roundnes and greatnes. **1664** EVELYN *Pomona* vii. (1729) 72 Let the reserved Branches be divided at a convenient roundness.

3. †**a.** A circular course; an orbit; a spiral or ring. *Obs.*

*c***1374** CHAUCER *Boeth.* IV. metr. vi. (1868) 144 ȝif þat he ne clepiþ nat aȝein þe ryȝt goynge of þinges, and ȝif þat he ne constreynede hem nat eftesones in to roundenesse enclined. **1572** J. JONES *Bathes Ayde* II. 14 They framed brasen pypes, which they rouled into many roundnesses, so ye pypes did resemble the Spyres of a Dragon.

b. A round object or formation; a rounded projection.

1382 WYCLIF *1 Kings* vii. 35 In the cop forsothe of the foot was a maner roundnes, of a cubite and a half, so forgid, that the watir vessel myȝte be sette there aboue. **1541** COPLAND *Guydon's Quest. Chirurg.* G ij b, Towarde the elbowe ben receyued ye roundnesses. **1549** *Compl. Scot.* vi. 55 Ane grit roundnes of lycht sal gyf lycht to mair nor the half of ane les roundnes. **1580** HOLLYBAND *Treas. Fr. Tong*, *Condyle*, the roundenesse or knots in the knee, ankle, elbow, and knuckles. **1631** WIDDOWES *Nat. Philos.* 45 Lettise hath his leaves gathered into a curled roundnesse. **1708** *Phil. Trans.* XXVI. 112 'Twas all over cover'd with a great number of exceeding small rising roundnesses.

4. Fullness or careful finish of language or style.

1557 SIR J. CHEKE in Hoby tr. *Castiglione's Courtier* ad fin., The roundnes of your saienges and welspeakinges of the saam. **1579** E. K. *Ded. Spenser's Sheph. Cal.* §1 The whole Period and compasse of speache so delightsome for the roundnesse. **1622** *Fotherby's Atheom.* Pref. p. xx, I haue.. hindered not the context, and roundnesse of the speech. **1727** BAILEY (vol. II) s.v. *Stile*, The roundness of periods charms the ear, and affects the mind. **1741** MIDDLETON *Cicero* (1742) III. xii. 321 That roundness of speaking, as the ancients called it, where there was nothing either redundant or deficient. **1856** EMERSON *Eng. Traits, Literature*, A good writer, if he has indulged in a Roman roundness, makes haste to chasten and nerve his period by English monosyllables. **1875** JOWETT *Plato* (ed. 2) II. 110 Are you and I expected to praise..only the clearness and roundness of the language?

†**5.** Uprightness, straightforwardness, openness.

1557 N.T. (Genev.) *Rom.* Argt., Euery man to walke in roundnes of conscience in his vocation. **1586** T. B. *La Primaud. Fr. Acad.* I. 400 Let all faining and dissimulation be banished from us, and all roundnes and integritie of hart and maners appeere in all our actions. **1628** Le Grys *Barclay's Argenis* 126 Gelanorus knowing him to be of a most clear roundness, turned out of his way to him. *a* **1649** Drumm. of Hawth. *Hist. Scot.* (1655) 38 The roundness of his intentions and his honesty.

6. Plainness or severity (of speech).

1619 Visc. Doncaster in *Eng. & Germany* (Camden) 103 I returned this rough answere.. For which roundnes, though I have sufficient warrant.., yet it may be I should have spared some part of the harshnes.

†7. Energy, activity; thoroughness. *Obs.*

1629 *Decl. Apprehension Bp. Chalcedon* 36 [That] they and every of them proceed with all diligence and roundness.. against the said Smith. **1709** Strype *Ann. Ref.* I. iv. 83 Had it not been for Cecyl's Widsom, Diligence, and Interest with the Queen, in all likelihood it had not proceeded with that Roundness it did.

round-nosed, *a.* [ROUND *a.* 16.] Having a round nose. Chiefly of tools (cf. *round-nose*, s.v. ROUND *a.* 17).

1611 Cotgr. s.v. *Teste*, A kind of blunt, and round-nosed Porpose. **1677** Moxon *Mech. Exerc.* i. 5 Plyers are of two Sorts, Flat Nos'd, and Round Nos'd. **1766** *Compl. Farmer* s.v. *Surveying* 7 G 1/2 Good iron-wire and curtain-rings to make it of, and a sharp-edged file, and round-nosed plyers to make it with. **1875** Knight *Dict. Mech.* 1742/2 Pliers with peculiarly shaped or proportioned jaws are called long-nosed pliers, round-nosed pliers, ..etc. **1898** *Archaeol. Jrnl.* V. 270 Among the relics were a few stone hammers or polishers, a number of 'round-nosed' chisels of bone.

†'**roundo.** *Obs.* Also 8 **Round O.** [Anglicized form of F. *rondeau.*] = RONDEAU.

1710 Pope *Lett.* (1735) I. 94 The vulgar spelling and pronouncing it Round O, is a manifest Corruption. **1751** Earl Orrery *Remarks Swift* (1752) 55 On Roundos hereafter your fiddle-strings spend, Write verses in circles, they never shall end. **1765** Percy *Reliq.* II. 11 The versification is of that species, which the French call Rondeau, very naturally englished by our honest countrymen Round O.

round O: see ROUND *a.* 15.

round-off, *a.* and *sb.* [f. ROUND *v.*[1] + OFF *adv.*]

A. *adj.* ***round-off file***: (see quot.).

1846 Holtzapffel *Turning* II. 826 Nicking and piercing files.. are called round-off files, and are used for rounding or pointing the teeth of wheels. **1875** Knight *Dict. Mech.*

B. *sb.* **1.** = ROUNDING *vbl. sb.*[1] 1 c. Freq. *attrib.* as ***round-off error***, the error introduced thereby.

1946 Goldstine & von Neumann in J. von Neumann *Coll. Wks.* (1963) V. 17 A very complicated calculation in which the accumulation and amplification of the round-off errors threatens to prevent the obtaining of results of the desired precision. **1947** *Bull. Amer. Math. Soc.* LIII. 1026 The transition from the true operations to their pseudo-operations is effected by any one of the familiar methods of round off. **1962** *Times Lit. Suppl.* 20 Apr. 268/1 Whenever approximations due to round-offs or other reasons are indicated, the degree of approximation is perfectly well determined. **1973** C. W. Gear *Introd. Computer Sci.* vi. 258 Sometimes a bad choice of method will make the solution very sensitive to round-off or truncation errors.

2. The act of rounding off or completing an operation appropriately.

1964 *Trampolining* ('Know the Game' Ser.) 40/1 It is similar in action to the round-off in ground work tumbling.

round 'robin. Also **Round Robin.**

†**1.** (See quots.) *Obs.*

1546 Coverdale tr. *Calvin's Treat. Sacr.* Pref. A ij, Certayne fonde talkers.. applye to this mooste holye sacramente, names of despitte and reproche, as to call it Jake in the boxe, and round roben, and suche other not onely fond but also blasphemouse names. **1555** Ridley in Foxe *A. & M.* (1570) 1924/2 There were at Paules.. fixed railing bils against the Sacrament, terming it Jacke of ye boxe, the sacrament of the halter, round Robin, with lyke unseemely termes.

†**2.** Applied to persons. *Obs.*

1592 Greene *Conny Catch.* Wks. (Grosart) X. 36 There in faith round Robin his deputie, would make them, like wretches, feel the waight of his heauiest fetters. **1636** R. N. in *Ann. Dubrensia* (1877) 66 Thou art he in whom All the brave Robins meet to make vp one, Round-Robin. *a* **1671** Hacket *Abp. Williams* II. (1692) 177 These Wat Tylers and Round-Robins being driven or persuaded out of Whitehall.

3. a. A document (esp. one embodying a complaint, remonstrance, or request) having the names of the subscribers arranged in a circle so as to disguise the order in which they have signed. Now used loosely of any such document signed by many persons, freq. in alphabetical order to indicate that responsibility is shared.

Originally used by sailors, and frequently referred to as a nautical term.

(*a*) **1730** *Weekly Jrnl.* 3 Jan. 3/4 A Round Robin is a Name given by Seamen, to an Instrument on which they sign their Names round a Circle, to prevent the Ring-leader being discover'd by it, if found. **1731** *Gentl. Mag.* I. 238 The Method used by Sailors when they mutiny, by signing their names in an orbicular manner, which they call a round Robin. **1742** J. Campbell *Lives Admirals* (1750) II. 98 The sailors on board the fleet, signed, what is called by them, a round Robin, that is, a paper containing.. their names subscribed in a circle, that it might not be discerned who signed first. **1828** *Lancet* 21 June 382/2 If thirteen physicians.. had written what seamen call a round robin to an authority. **1847** H. Melville *Omoo* xx, I proposed that a 'Round Robin' should be prepared and sent ashore to the consul. **1870** Thornbury *Tour rd. Eng.* I. 192 [He] so tormented his crew that they signed a round robin, and sent it to the Admiralty.

(*b*) **1755** Chesterf. in *World* No. 146 ¶8 If I thought it could be of any use, I could easily present them with a round robin to that effect of above a thousand.. names. **1791** Sir W. Forbes in *Boswell* (Oxf. ed.) II. 60, I enclose the Round Robin. This *jeu d'esprit* took its rise one day at dinner at our friend Sir Joshua Reynolds's. **1829** *Farmer's Jrnl.* Oct. 330 Last week the whole of the tenants.. sent a round-robin to his lordship's steward. *a* **1859** Macaulay *Biog.* (1867) 217 He tried to induce a large number of the supporters of the government to sign a round robin desiring a change. **1896** J. D. Coleridge *Eton in the Forties* 133 The headmaster suggested our signing and sending a round robin of congratulation. **1978** B. Levin in K. Gregory *First Cuckoo* 13 Writers of round robins ('We, the undersigned, each in his or her personal capacity..') also choose *The Times* for preference, the second elevens being accommodated elsewhere.

transf. **1816** Coleridge *Lay Serm.* (Bohn) 349 Such a round robin of mere lies, that you knew not which to begin with. **1977** *N.Y. Rev. Bks.* 4 Aug. 7/1 As if to point up the homosexual theme, rather than to offer a round robin of sexuality.

b. orig. *U.S.* A tournament in which every player or team competes once with each of the others. Freq. *attrib.*

1895 *Official Lawn Tennis Bull.* 3 Jan. 1/2 The so-called round-robin tournament, where each man plays every other, furnishes the best possible test of tennis skill. *Ibid.* 3/1 No one would.. argue that a man of that rating could win in a round-robin. **1904** J. P. Paret *Lawn Tennis* iii. 24 Invitation tournaments are of American origin, and the matches are generally played on what is called the 'round robin' system, each of the players meeting all of the others in turn. *Ibid.* iv. 65 The British visitors next played a round-robin at Chicago. **1943** M. Kraitchik *Math. Recreations* ix. 231 In a round-robin tournament among teams of four or two we must arrange a schedule by which every team meets every other just once. **1952** E. Lasker *Chess Secrets* 379 Arrange the players in groups, and have the winners, or the first two or three of each group, play a final round robin. **1974** *Times* 20 Apr. 11/1 The 'Aces' of America [*sc.* a bridge team] held their own against the Italians in the preliminary round-robin to decide who should compete in the final. **1978** *Time* 3 July 50/1 In June, the 14 survivors and the West German team.. moved to Argentina to join the host country's team in an exhausting series of round-robin matches.

c. (See quot. 1976.)

1972 J. Wambaugh *Blue Knight* (1973) x. 171 Would you care for a round robin or a three-horse parley to-day? **1976** *Daily Tel.* (Colour Suppl.) 26 Mar. 31/4 *Round robin*, three horses linked in Up and Down bets on each pair, plus three doubles and a treble (10 bets).

†**4.** (See quot.) *Obs.*[—0]

1688 Holme *Armoury* III. 97/2 *Round Robins*, narrow Ruffs only about the Doublet Collar.

5. *Mech.* (See quots.)

1794 W. Felton *Carriages* (1801) II. 195 The round Robin is a broad rim fixed to the end of the axletree bed, to prevent dirt falling in to injure the Arms of the Axletree. **1875** Knight *Dict. Mech.* 669/1 *Cuttoo-plate*,.. otherwise called a dirt-board, or round robin.

6. a. *U.S.* The fish *Decapterus punctatus.*

1876 Goode *Fishes Bermudas* 46 The Round Robin is seined in great numbers in Hamilton Harbor.

b. The angler-fish, *Lophius piscatorius.*

1880 *E. Cornwall Gloss.* (E.D.S.).

7. *Devon dial.* **a.** A small pancake.

1847 Halliwell.

b. Herb Robert; Ragged Robin.

1882 *Devonsh. Plant Names.*

Hence **round-robi'neer**, a subscriber to a round robin (sense 3 a), an importuner; **round-'robining**, the act of subscribing to a round robin (sense 3 a).

1933 H. P. Long *Every Man a King* xii. 179 If ever again you fifteen round-robineers find me drowning, for Heaven's sake, let me drown! **1968** *Guardian* 13 July 8/6 On Tuesday —after much round-robining—hundreds of BBC secretaries and studio staff intend boycotting the corporation's canteen.

round-shouldered, *a.* [ROUND *a.* 16.] Of persons: Having round shoulders; round-backed.

1586 Wynkfeilde in *Trial*, etc. *Mary Q. of Scots* (1889) 2 Y[e] Q. of S. being of stature tall and bodie corpulent, round shouldered. **1682** *Lond. Gaz.* No. 1737/4 A middle sized man, a little round shouldered. **1753** Hanway *Trav.* (1762) II. xvi. i. 437 *note*, The oriental people generally are round-shouldered, arising from their manner of sitting. **1825** J. Neal *Bro. Jonathan* I. 191 He stood.. regarding his vulgar .. round-shouldered brother opposite. **1865** Dickens *Mut. Fr.* I. v, A broad, round-shouldered, one-sided old fellow in mourning.

transf. **1895** Rider Haggard *Heart of the World* xiv, To the right and left of us the huge, round-shouldered mountains stretched in a majestic sweep. **1950** H. L. Lorimer *Homer & Monuments* v. 262 Here the round-shouldered short-tanged blade [of a sword] which alone was found at Arkalochon is in the majority, but side by side with it a more serviceable type is developed.

Hence **round-'shoulderedness**, the state or quality of having round shoulders.

1940 S. Spender *Backward Son* 14 References to.. his round-shoulderedness.

'**roundsman.** [f. ROUND *sb.*[1]]

1. A labourer in need of parochial relief, who was sent round from one farmer to another for employment, partly at the expense of the farmer and partly at the cost of the parish.

1795 Eden *State of the Poor* (1797) II. 384 Persons working in this manner are called rounds-men, from their going round to village or township for employ. **1820** Syd. Smith *Wks.* (1859) I. 302/2 The system of roundsmen is much complained of. **1830** Cobbett *Rur. Rides* (1885) II. 350 The labourers here who are in need of parochial relief, are formed into what are called roundsmen. **1854** *Jrnl. R. Agric. Soc.* XV. II. 262 The surplus labourers are employed in turns by the farmers..: these odd men were called 'rounds-men'.

attrib. **1834** *Tait's Mag.* I. 37/2 At present the roundsman system is a wasteful and unequal tax.

2. One who makes rounds of inspection; esp. *U.S.* a police-officer in charge of a patrol.

1868 *N.Y. Herald* 31 July 6/5 Patrolman Jas. Mee.. is hereby appointed roundsman on the force. **1870** 'Mark Twain' in *Galaxy* Sept. 430/1 The rank of constable or even roundsman. **1883** *Daily News* 18 Oct. 3/2 A roundsman and five patrolmen were present to preserve order. **1888** *Pall Mall G.* 9 Mar. 2/3 Shortly before the Emperor left the palace two roundsmen and two detectives patrolled the road. **1902** *Chambers's Jrnl.* Oct. 674/1 The first grade of promotion is to roundsman... The roundsman is an important man, for on him the discipline of the patrolmen largely depends. **1937** *Sun* (Baltimore) 1 Dec. 3/1 John McAdams, a former customs roundsman, who was dismissed recently, also was accused of being a member of the smuggling ring.

3. A person employed by a tradesman to go the round of his customers for orders and the delivery of goods.

1884 *Weekly Notes* 29 Nov. 216/2 The defendant agreed to serve the plaintiff as 'roundsman' and assistant. **1935** *E. Anglia Daily Times* 18 Dec. 4/2 A Lowestoft milk roundsman, who persuaded his customers to buy more than 12 per cent. more milk in three months, has won the £25 and cup awarded for salesmanship. **1977** 'M. Underwood' *Fatal Trip* xix. 106 It did not take long to discover the name of the dairy [and].. that Frey Chaytor was the roundsman.

Round Table, *sb.* Also round table, Table Round.

1. a. The table, celebrated in mediæval legend, round which Arthur and his chosen knights were supposed to have sat, and which was made round so that there might be no pre-eminence or rivalry.

The earliest mention of the table is that in Wace's *Roman de Brut* (1155). From at least the 15th century (see quot. 1485) the name has been given to a large circular table preserved at Winchester, bearing the names of Arthur and his most famous knights.

a **1300** *Cursor M.* 14 O kyng arthour þat was so rike,.. O ferlys þat hys knythes fell, þat aunters sere I here of tell,.. For to were þe ronde tabell. *c* **1330** R. Brunne *Chron. Wace* (Rolls) 10525 For his barons þat were so bolde.. Dide Arthur ordeyne þe rounde table [F. *la roonde table*] þat ȝit men telle of many a fable. **1470–85** Malory *Arthur* III. i. 101 For I shalle gyue hym the table round, the whiche Vtherpendragon gaue me. **1485** Caxton *Malory's Arthur* Pref., In dyuers places of Englond many remembraunces ben yet of hym... At wynchester the rounde table. **1589** Nashe *Anat. Absurd.* Wks. (Grosart) I. 14 The feyned no where acts of Arthur of the rounde table. **1612** Drayton *Poly-olb.* iv. 299 Then sing they how he first ordain'd the Circled-board, The Knights whose martial deeds far fam'd that Table-round. **1728** Chambers *Cycl.* s.v. *Table*, The Round Table.. was an Invention of that Prince, to avoid Disputes about the upper and lower End. **1802** Ritson *Metr. Rom.* I. p. xlvi, Neither.. does this impostour [Geoffrey of Monmouth] ever mention the round table.

b. In *Knight* (etc.) ***of the Round Table.***

c **1330** *Arth. & Merl.* 6518 (Kölbing), Next hem, wiþ outen fable, Sat þe kniȝtes of þe rounde table. ? *a* **1400** *Morte Arth.* 17, I salle telle 3ow a tale.. Off the ryealle renkys of the Rowunde Table. **1430–40** Lydg. *Bochas* VIII. xxv. (1494) E ij, Arthure.. Amonge his knightes of the round table. *Ibid.* E ij b, By othe and promyse bounde To brotherhede of the table rounde. **1470–85** Malory *Arthur* IV. iv. 124 By my hede said Arthur he is best worthy to be a knyght of the rounde table of ony that ye haue reherced. **1589** Puttenham *Eng. Poesie* I. xix. (Arb.) 57 Old adeuntures and valiaunces ..of king Arthur and his knights of the round table. **1671** Phillips, Knights of the Round-Table, or King Arthur's Knights. **1728** Chambers *Cycl.* s.v. *Table*, Paulus Jovius says, 'twas under the Empire of Frederic Barberosa, that the Knights of the Round Table first began to be talk'd of. **1781** Gibbon *Decl. & F.* xxxviii. (1787) III. 619 The gallantry and superstition of the British hero,.. and the memorable institution of his Knights of the Round Table. **1802** Ritson *Metr. Rom.* III. 240 Queen Guinever,.. with certain knights of the round-table, clothe'd all in green. **1859** Tennyson *Geraint* 3 The brave Geraint,.. one Of that great Order of the Table Round.

c. The body of knights of this order.

c **1330** *Arth. & Merl.* 2196 (Kölbing), Afterward.. Our king bigan þe rounde table.. Of kniȝtes, þat men wist best In þis warld. ? *a* **1400** *Morte Arth.* 93 That thow bee redy at Rome with alle thi Rounde Table. **1470–85** Malory *Arthur* IX. i. 339 All your courte and alle your Round table is by sire launcelot worshipped.. more than by ony knyghte now lyuynge.

1842 Tennyson *Morte d'Arth.* 234 But now the whole Round Table is dissolved.., And I, the last, go forth companionless.

†**d.** A meeting or assembly of Arthur's knights and nobles. *Obs.*

1297 R. Glouc. *Chron.* (Rolls) 3916 Þer nas bituene þis & spayne no prince wiþoute al þis, þat nas at þis rounde table, & at is feste ywis. ? *a* **1400** *Morte Arth.* 53 Whene he thys rewmes hade redyne.., Then rystede that ryalle and helde the Rounde Tabylle. *Ibid.* 74 Thus one ryalle araye he helde his Rounde Table. *c* **1470** Harding *Chron.* lxiii. 25 He [*sc.* Arthur] held his houshold, and the rounde table, Some time at Edenburgh, some tyme at Striueline.

e. *attrib.*, as ***Round Table cycle, hero, knight, legend***, etc.

1700 Dryden *Wife of Bath's T.* 352 Is this the custom of King Arthur's court? Are all Round-Table Knights of such a sort? **1798** C'tess Purgstall *Let.* in Lockhart *Scott* (1837) I. ix. 288 Don't.. give him a name out of your list of round-table knights. **1883** *Encycl. Brit.* XV. 523/1 He [Walter Map] was..one of the principal creators of the Round Table legends. **1886** *Ibid.* XX. 646 Pedigree of the Round-Table Heroes. **1897** AMOURS *Scot. Allit. Poems* (S.T.S.) p. lxxii, One of the stock stories so common in the Round Table cycle.

2. An imitation of Arthur's Round Table as an institution; an assembly of knights for the purpose of holding a tournament and festival, esp. that instituted by King Edward III in 1345.

The statements in Dugdale, Warton, etc., in regard to the tournament held by Mortimer at Kenilworth in 1279 are based on misunderstandings of the older authorities (see Wykes in *Ann. Monast.* (Rolls) IV. 281–2 and Rishanger *Chron.* 94).

[**1232** *Patent Rolls* (1903) 492 De rotunda tabula prohibenda.—Rex omnibus fidelibus suis qui conventuri sunt ad rotundam tabulam, salutem. *c* **1330** *Ann. Lond.* in *Chron. Edw. I & II* (Rolls) I. 46 Tabula rotunda apud Waldene, ubi Ernulphus de Mounteneye a Rogero de Leyborne lancea interfectus est.] *c* **1400** *Brut* (1908) 296 When þe Iustes were don, King Edward made a grete soper, in þe wiche he ordeyned feest, and bygan þe Rounde Table, & ordeyned & stefastyd þe day of þe forsaide Rounde Table to be holde þer at Wyndissore in Whitesen-wike euermore after erly. **1483** CAXTON *G. de la Tour* C ij, A good lady that gat a grete blame at a grete feste of a round table atte Joustes. **1523** LD. BERNERS *Froiss.* I. c. 120 The king of Englond toke pleasure to newe reedefy the Castell of Wyndsore,..and ther firste begonne the table rounde. **1552** in *Archaeologia* (1863) XXXIX. 34 To the knights of the Round Table (if I do it not in my lifetyme) xxs. to be spent at Myle end. **1765** PERCY *Reliq.* I. 35 Any king was said to 'hold a round table' when he proclaimed a tournament attended with some peculiar solemnities. **1803** GODWIN *Life Chaucer* I. 133 Edward III..purposing from the knights whose prowess on this occasion should be the most approved, to select the members of his new order, to be styled knights of the Round Table. **1846** *Archaeologia* XXXI. 106 The feast of the Round Table..in March, 1345.

†**b.** (See quot.) *Obs.*

The quotation is a direct translation from Walsingham *Historia Brevis* (1574) 154.

1592 STOW *Ann.* (1595) 367 King Edward [III in 1345] caused to be called together a great many Artificers, to the Castell of Windsore, and beganne to builde an house, which was called the round Table.

3. A name applied locally to various natural or artificial antiquities, freq. reputed to have associations with King Arthur.

1375 BARBOUR *Bruce* XIII. 379 Beneth the castell [of Stirling] went thai soyne, Richt by the Rownde Tabill thair way. **1530** LINDESAY *Test. Papyngo* 634 Adew, fair Snawdoun, with thy touris hie, Thy Chapell royall, Park, and tabyll rounde! **1612** SELDEN *Illustr. Drayton's Polyolb.* iv. 302 In Denbighshire..is a circular plain, cut out of a main rock, with some twenty-four seats unequal, which they call Arthur's Round Table. **1813** SCOTT *Trierm.* I. vii, He pass'd red Penrith's Table Round, For feats of chivalry renown'd. **1836** *Penny Cycl.* VI. 106/2 A space of ground [at Caerleon], which it is believed was a Roman amphitheatre, is commonly called Arthur's Round Table. **1872** HARDWICKE *Trad.*, etc. *Lancs.* 216 Several circular mounds in various parts of England..are..honoured with the name of 'King Arthur's Round Table'.

4. (Freq. with lower-case initials.) Used generally (alone or as *attrib.* phrase) to denote a number of persons seated round a circular table, or imagined as forming a gathering of this kind; *spec.* an assembly of people for a conference or discussions at which all participants are accorded equal status (in this sense freq. *attrib.*). Also *transf.*, a collection of opinions or remarks on a particular subject.

1826 MISS MITFORD *Village* Ser. II. (1863) 342 For cards she had no genius. Even the noise and nonsense of a round-table could not reconcile her to those bits of painted pasteboard. **1852** *Life in Bombay* 33 The snug round-table dinner-party. **1885** *Encycl. Brit.* XVIII. 656/2 Those four hundred poets who formed the famous 'Round Table' in the sultan's..palace. **1889** *Pall Mall G.* 6 Nov. 4/1 The 'New Round Table' is a symposium on Home Rule—a collection of remarks..from persons of various standpoints. **1892** *Review of Reviews* Feb. 148/1 The subject of the 'Round Table Conference'..is what part churches should take in labour problems. **1901** H. W. PAUL *Life Gladstone* xxi. 245 The year 1887 opened with an attempt to reconcile the conflicting elements of the Liberal Party, which came to be known as the Round Table Conference. **1910** (*title of periodical*) The Round Table: a quarterly review of the politics of the British Empire. **1928** *Daily Express* 3 July 2/4 The Archbishop of Canterbury made a striking proposal yesterday for a 'round table' to discuss the future relations of Church and State. **1929** *Times* 31 Oct. 14/3 Mr. Benn himself proposed to visit India forthwith for..a round-table conference. **1943** M. MCCARTHY in *Partisan Rev.* May–June 280 The problems..are..opened for discussion in an atmosphere reminiscent of the Chicago Round Table. **1943** *Times* 8 July 5/5 In certain instances we stayed overnight to enjoy the free and easy of a 'round table conference'. **1947** *Radio Times* 14 Mar. 1/2 Round-table controversial political discussions, which the BBC will continue to originate. **1952** D. RIESMAN in *Antioch Rev.* Dec. 418 A roundtable..of which he was chairman at the Corning Conference. **1955** *Times* 30 July 5/1 Round-table talks may be held in London about a year hence to consider a new constitution for a self-governing Singapore. **1973** *Word 1970* XXVI. 120 He took an active part in the linguistic and anthropological life of Mexico, attending conferences, round tables, and the like. **1976** *National Observer* (U.S.) 10 Apr. 1/3 The Observer convened an informal round-table talk involving six young people with differing perspectives. **1978** *Jrnl. R. Soc. Arts* CXXVI. 768/1 In 1930–31 he was Adviser to the Indian States Delegation to the Round Table Conference in London.

5. A formal association whose members meet regularly for discussion, *spec.* an organization (or a branch of it) founded in 1927, in which professional people between the ages of 18 and 40 hold discussions, debates, and similar activities, and undertake community service and the promotion of international understanding. Also allusively as *adj.*, designating the qualities or characteristics associated with the Round Table or its members.

1917 L. CURTIS *Let. to People of India* 13 The Round Table organisation..is merely a system for enabling people to unite for the study of their duties as citizens of this Commonwealth, as a guide to their own individual action. **1928** *Review of Reviews* Mar.–Apr. 253/2 At Norwich..an Association of Young Men has established a Club for young business men, meeting once a week in the evening for the reading of papers, discussions, and debates, under the title of 'The Round Table'. **1955** A. HUXLEY *Let.* 25 Mar. (1969) 739 Possibly also to go up..and stay a few days near Puharich's Round Table Foundation outfit. **1968** *Guardian* 10 Sept. 2/7 Mr Powell was speaking to the Rowley Regis Round Table at Cradley Heath, Staffordshire. **1972** J. BURMEISTER *Running Scared* xvii. 213 The woman was..wearing carefully bleached out jeans... Round Table, thought Ginny, with a touch of country. 'I'm terribly sorry.' The voice was Round Table too. **1973** *Stand. Encycl. S. Afr.* IX. 412/2 The Round Table movement in South Africa was founded in East London in 1948. **1977** *Times of Zambia* 7 Sept. 2/4 The committee is made up of the Rotary, Round Table and Lions clubs members.

Hence **round-table** *v.*, to take part in a round-table conference; **round-tabler**.

The use in quot. 1923 is with allusion to the periodical *The Round Table* (see quot. 1910 under sense 4 above).

1887 *Pall Mall G.* 3 Feb. 1 When Mr. Goschen goes over to the Tories on one side, Mr. Chamberlain round-tables on the other. **1889** *Ibid.* 6 Nov. 4/1 Other round tablers are Mr. Andrew Reid.., Lord Monkswell.., and others. **1923** T. E. LAWRENCE *Let.* 27 Mar. (1938) 413 You [*sc.* Lionel Curtis] have tried (Round Tabling and by mouth) to tell all whom you can reach. **1976** *National Observer* (U.S.) 1 May 19/3 They might squabble bitterly from time to time, but in the main the Round Tablers quoted each other, promoted each other, wrote books and plays and articles about each other with an incestuous zeal. **1976** *Norwich Mercury* 10 Dec., Children of Round Tablers sing for the 250 old folk from Wymondham and Attleborough who attended a Christmas party in Wymondham Central Hall on Sunday.

round-top. Also roundtop. [f. ROUND *a.*]

1. *Naut.* A platform (formerly circular) about a mast-head.

1706 PHILLIPS (ed. Kersey), *Top-Armours*, are a kind of Clothes, &c., set about the Round-tops of the Masts. **1722** DE FOE *Col. Jack* xi, A man on the roundtop cried out, Au voile, a sail. **1769** R. WOOD *Ess. Genius Homer* p. xxxi, As I looked from the round-top of the main mast, the fresh water appeared like an immense muddy pond. **1855** KINGSLEY *Westw. Ho!* xxi, The fog was up to our round-tops at sunrise this morning. **1876** BANCROFT *Hist. U.S.* VI. xl. 242 Jones could use only their nine-pounders and muskets from the round-tops.

2. *attrib.* Having a rounded top.

1825 J. NICHOLSON *Operat. Mech.* 644 [A railway] known ..by the denomination of the edge rail, round-top rail, fish-backed rail, &c. **1897** *Sears, Roebuck Catal.* 251/2 Black enameled iron, round top trunk. **1962** L. S. SASIENI *Princ. & Pract. Optical Dispensing* xii. 312 Round Top Fused [Trifocals]. **1966** J. S. COX *Illustr. Dict. Hairdressing* 129/1 *Round-top butch*, a hair style for men in which the hair is cut very short to a round contour.

round-towner. [f. ROUND *prep.*] One who loafs about a town.

1778 [W. MARSHALL] *Minutes Agric.* 10 Oct. 1775, I hope I shall never pay-off another 'Round Towner. *Ibid.*, Digest 36 The Roundtowners are wholly ineligible as indoor Servants.

round trip. orig. *U.S.* Also round-trip. [f. ROUND *a.* 15.] **a.** A circular tour or trip; an outward and return journey.

1860 *Railroad Guide* (Dinsmore & Co.) Sept. 142 Round trip tickets. **1868** *Putnam's Mag.* Mar. 351/1 Time for the round trip..44 hours. **1892** *Pall Mall G.* 4 July 7/2 A stated fare will be charged for the round trip. **1923** R. D. PAINE *Comrades of Rolling Ocean* xiii. 223 We signed for the round trip in the *Liberty Chimes*, but we don't feel like taking her all the way home. **1956** *People* 13 May 9/4 The 30-mile round trip to the lonely isle took seven hours. **1976** SCOTT & KOSKI *Walk-In* (1977) iii. 21 'Round trip?' the ticket seller asked... 'You want to go and come back?'

b. *transf.* and *fig.*

1932 *Amer. Speech* VII. 270 *Round-trip*.., one *pull-out* and the subsequent *run-in* of the drill pipe in rotary drilling. **1935** *Econ. Geol.* XXX. 739 Very deep wells may require as much as eight hours to make the 'round trip'. **1938** *Amer. Speech* XIII. 220/2 Round-trip words, i.e. from O[ld] F[rench] to Eng[lish], thence to French. **1945** L. SHELLY *Jive Talk Dict.* 33/1 *Round trip*, anything unusually good or outstanding. **1963** *Gloss. Mining Terms* (*B.S.I.*) III. 12 *Round trip*, the operation of with-drawing the drill rods and bit, etc., from the hole, of extracting core, replacing rods and bit and resuming drilling. **1973** *N.Y. Law Jrnl.* 20 July 5/1 The..Stock Exchange said yesterday it would like to attract small investors back to the stock market with a 'round trip' rate.

c. *attrib.*

1860 [see sense a above]. **1890** *Brighton* (Colorado) *Reg.* 25 Jan. 1/4 The railway company has rehashed its round-trip rate, from suburban towns to Denver. **1939** G. GREENE *Another Mexico* ii. 31 He had got a round-trip ticket to Mexico City. **1976** 'M. BARAK' *Secret List H. Roehm* v. 58 Enclosed was an Air France round-trip ticket to Montevideo. **1978** *Detroit Free Press* 5 Mar. D21/3 (Advt.), Commodore's unique Fly Free/Cruise Easy program..pays half of the lowest applicable round-trip air fare..to Miami.

Hence **round-'tripper**, (*a*) a traveller who makes a round trip; (*b*) in *Baseball*, a home run; a batter who hits a home run; **round-'tripping** *Econ.*, the practice of earning profit by borrowing on overdraft and relending in money markets.

1944 D. BURLEY in A. Dundes *Mother Wit* (1973) 219 That's why I'm out here..instead of being a round-tripper. **1962** P. PURSER *Peregrination 22* xii. 60 He was a tourist..the only genuine round-tripper in the first-class. **1974** *Saturday* (Charleston, S. Carolina) 20 Apr. 5-B/4 Jeff Grantz.. powered four round-trippers in one inning. **1974** *Daily Tel.* 25 May 20/3 Interest arbitrage operations, otherwise known as round tripping. **1977** *Times* 23 Nov. 29/8 It is believed there has been a good deal of 'round tripping'—borrowing in the money markets to finance purchases of CTDs at a profit. **1978** J. A. MICHENER *Chesapeake* 649 Home Run Baker.. would hit in one year the unheard-of total of twelve round-trippers. **1980** *Boston Globe* 30 Mar. 76 Home runs were circuit clouts. Then they became round trippers, until George Scott renamed them taters. **1980** *Times* 5 Sept. 15/2 It becomes attractive for blue-chip corporate borrowers to take loan from their banks and re-lend the funds to the short-term money markets. This is known as 'round-tripping'.

round-up. [See ROUND *sb.*[2] and *v.*[1]]

1. a. *Ship-building.* (See quot. 1846.)

1769 FALCONER *Dict. Marine* (1780) s.v. *Transom*, The former of these is called..the round-up, and the latter the round-aft. *Ibid.*, *Tonture des baux*, the round-up, or convexity of a ship's beams. **1833** RICHARDSON *Merc. Mar. Arch.* 8 Short curved line for the round-up and round-aft of the wing transom. **1846** A. YOUNG *Naut. Dict.*, *Round-up* of the Transoms; the segment of a circle to which they are sided; of beams, that to which they are moulded. **1869** SIR E. REED *Shipbuilding* xx. 431 While the frames and keel of the ship are in progress, beam moulds, with the round-up and lengths marked on them, are given out to the workmen to guide them in making beams.

b. *transf.* (in quot. *attrib.*)

1926 J. MASEFIELD *Odtaa* 214 He took one of the big round-up stew cauldrons which lay against a wall.

2. a. orig. *U.S.* The driving of cattle, etc., together or into an enclosure, usually for the purpose of registering ownership, counting, etc. Also *fig.*

1873 in *Ann. Wyoming* (1927) V. 74 The herders of this Co. start a Round-up tomorrow... Each man picks out his stock and drives them in. **1878** J. H. BEADLE *Western Wilds* xxviii. 437 These cattle, having run wild upon the plains of western Texas, are collected by a grand 'round-up'. **1879** *Tinsley's Mag.* XXIV. 353 One's companions, when camping out on the 'round up' are often anything but desirable. **1882** BAILLIE-GROHMAN *Camps Rockies* xii. 339 To collect these stragglers and to take a census,..the annual 'round-up' is held. **1887** T. R. *Ranche Life Montana* 160 When they have gone some miles, the captain of the round-up tells them to spread out into a wide half-circle, driving-in all the horses. **1907** S. E. WHITE *Arizona Nights* iii. 60 We had our first round-up, found the natural increase much in excess of the loss by Indians. **1909** [see PAY *v.*[1] 10]. **1951** E. PAUL *Springtime in Paris* xv. 287 Busse, rattled as a rabbit in a roundup, bounced back to the pavement just in time to bump into the burly Chestnut Man. **1976** *Billings* (Montana) *Gaz.* 10 June 1-c/1 At the Spanagel ranch west of Forsyth all hands are in the middle of roundup and putting up hay.

b. A meeting or social gathering of acquaintances or friends; a reunion.

1880 *Harper's Mag.* Feb. 380/2 We old fellows have a round up 'most every year in Denver. **1887** A. A. HAYES *Jesuit's Ring* 270 We'll have a round-up of your old friends. **1895** *Daily News* 16 Sept. 6/4 The good bishop had a family reunion or 'round up' on the lawn of one of his estates. **1936** L. C. DOUGLAS *White Banners* iv. 70 An unexpected invitation to read a paper at the first monthly round-up of the University Club.

c. The group of men and horses engaged in a round-up.

1878 in *Colorado Mag.* (1939) XVI. 152 Most of the round-up gone; a few still lingered at the bar. **1903** 'O. HENRY' in *Everybody's Mag.* June 519/1 The round-up had ridden on but a few moments before. *a* **1918** G. STUART *40 Yrs. on Frontier* (1925) II. 178 It was a novel sight to witness the big spring roundup pull out.

d. A survey of opinion; a résumé of facts or events; *spec.* in *Broadcasting*, a summary of newsworthy items.

1886 *Philadelphia Times* 3 May 1/1 That exception..will probably be included in the general round-up by tomorrow. **1892** *Boston Jrnl.* 29 Nov. 3/1 Round-Up of the Boston Aldermanic Districts. **1904** F. CRISSEY *Tattlings of Retired Policeman* ii. 42 A hatchet-faced lawyer..made a quick round-up of the representatives of the corporate interests and vested rights of the state. **1932** *Sun* (Baltimore) 21 Dec. 8/2 The 'round-ups' of Congressional opinion on the war debts issue. **1949** *Lincoln County News* (Oceanlake, Oregon) 4 Aug. 3/4 Another periodic survey of censorship conditions ..shows no major barriers have come down since the last roundup of the situation. **1958** *Spectator* 1 Aug. 159/1 The BBC's Middle East round-up on Saturday night was a notable project. **1962** *Listener* 22 Mar. 528/1 He presented a brilliant newsreel round-up 'Cease-fire in Algeria'. **1967** *Economist* 2 Dec. 915/1 A round-up of how America has reacted to the first rush into gold. **1974** *Radio Times* 21 Feb. 46/2 Commentary from Trinidad on the final day's play in the Second Test, together with a round-up of the day's sport.

e. The systematic rounding-up of people or of objects; *spec.* the arrest of people suspected of crime.

1899 *Chicago Rec.* 17 Jan. 12/1 A 'round-up' of all suspicious characters was begun. **1927** A. CHRISTIE *Big Four* v. 54 A short time ago a round-up was made of certain crooks and gunmen. **1943** *Sun* (Baltimore) 17 Nov. 6/1 The collection today will be of all tins accumulated since June 9, when the last such roundup took place. **1966** M. R. D. Foot *SOE in France* ix. 264 Contacts in the Rouen police.. provided reliable warnings of impending round-ups. **1978** *Detroit Free Press* 16 Apr. (Record) 9/3 The round-up began Aug. 26 at the command of the Germans, who at the same time began arresting 20,000 foreign Jews in the occupied zone.

f. = RODEO 3 b.

1914 *World's Work* Feb. 444/2 During the three days of The Round-Up, a constant stream of humanity pours into Pendleton. **1948** *Great Falls* (Montana) *Tribune* 18 Sept. 5/4 Malta is preparing to welcome at least 5,000 people this weekend when the two-day fall roundups will be staged.

g. In *fig.* phr. ***the last round-up***, death, resurrection, or the Last Judgement.

1932 G. Brown (*song-title*) The last round up. **1940** *Hoofs & Horns* Dec. 11/1 Tom Mix.. has laid down his honors.. and taken the sunset trail that leads to the Last Roundup.

3. *U.S.* A settlement, clearance.

1886 *Philadelphia Times* 3 May (Cent.), That exception.. will probably be included in the general round-up tomorrow.

4. *attrib.*, as (sense 2 a) ***round-up boss, camp, captain, outfit, party, wagon***; (sense 2 d) ***round-up article, programme, review***; (sense 2 f) ***round-up pennant, week***.

1960 V. Jenkins *Lions down Under* 14 'Potentially the greatest team ever to tour New Zealand,' was how Graeme Jenkins.. described them in a *round-up article. **1977** *Irish Times* 8 June 4/7 A round-up article on the celebrations written by the agency's court correspondent was delivered by hand to some London offices last night. **1920** J. M. Hunter *Trail Drivers of Texas* 313 The *round-up boss would let no one drive through the herd. **1923** R. Pocock in *Outward Bound* Mar. 410/2 Seventeen miles across the Mesa la Sal, in Utah, brought me to a *round-up camp. **1907** *Round-up captain [see CUT *sb.*[2] 24 c]. **1890** *Stock Grower & Farmer* 14 June 5/3 The herder was found by the Long S *roundup outfit, about six miles west of Sulphur draw. **1885** *Weekly New Mexican Rev.* 26 Mar. 1/6 *Round-up parties have already been started for that section. **1891** *Fur, Fin & Feather* Mar. 188 Wolves naturally follow in the wake of round-up parties. **1931** Y. Winters *Coll. Wks.* (1952) 66, I remembered.. The sprawling streets,.. The *Round-up pennants. **1979** *Jrnl. R. Soc. Arts* CXXVII. 358/1 What is reported on the news, and current affairs, something very different indeed from.. election *round-up programmes. **1978** *Amer. Poetry Rev.* Nov./Dec. 32/3 A *round-up review by George Dillon in *Poetry*. **1893** T. Roosevelt *Wilderness Hunter* ii. 23 Close beyond the trees on the farther bank stood the two *round-up wagons. **1973** R. D. Symons *Where Wagon Led* I. i. 10 Two of the three men.. were out in the south country with the roundup wagon. **1924** W. M. Raine *Troubled Waters* iv. 40 A poster .. announced *Round-up Week,.. roping, and other Western sports.

roundure (ˈraʊndjʊə(r)). Also 7 rowndure. [f. ROUND *a.* Cf. RONDURE.] Roundness; rounded form or space.

In Shaks. *K. John* II. i. 259 the reading of the first folio is *rounder*.

1600 Dekker *Fortunatus* Dram. Wks. 1873 I. 90 Your cries to me are Musicke, And fill the sacred roundure of mine eares With tunes more sweete then moving of the Spheres. **1620** —— *Dream* Wks. (Grosart) III. 40 Were all the Rowndure betwixt Hell and Heauen One Clowd condens'd, and into blackness driuen. **1623** Favine *Theatr. Honour* I. ii. 12 The frightfull eye of the Gyant Polyphemus, great and wide as the roundure of the Sunne. **1818** Keats *Wks.* (1889) III. p. cxxxix, You might suppose that the fair roundure of her fingers reached back to heaven.

ˈroundward, *a.* and *adv.* [f. ROUND *adv.*] **A.** *adj.* Circular. **B.** *adv.* In a circular direction.

1893 *Scribner's Mag.* XIII. 376/1 There was a bolt.. rearward, roundward, upward, downward. *Ibid.* 376/2 There was the same rearward, roundward bolt. **1927** D. H. Lawrence *Mornings in Mexico* 80 The reeling, roundward motion of tree-tips in a wind.

ˈroundway, *a. rare.* [f. ROUND *a.* 17.]

1. ? Having a round passage-way.

1862 *Catal. Internat. Exhib. Brit.* II. No. 2409 Improved extra strong round-way screw-down bib and stop cocks.

2. Moving round in the arena.

1875 Morris *Æneid* VIII. 636 From concourse of the hollow seats where roundway games were wrought.

ˈroundways, *adv. rare.* = ROUNDWISE.

1644 Digby *Nat. Bodies* xxvi. §5. 236 The second, go crosse or roundwayes about the ventricles within the hart. **1769** Mrs. Raffald *Eng. Housekpr.* 9 Skin and cut roundways in slices six large Spanish onions.

round-winged, *a.* [f. ROUND *a.* 16.]

†**1.** *Arch.* = PERIPTERAL *a. Obs. rare*$^{-1}$.

1715 Leoni *Palladio's Archit.* (1742) II. 8 This prospect is call'd *Peripteros*, that is, wing'd round.., the same round-wing'd prospect remaining.. to every one that saw the Temple in flank.

2. *Ent.* In the names of moths, as **round-winged muslin, (white-)wave** (see quots.).

1832 J. Rennie *Consp. Butterfl. & M.* 275/1 Round-Winged Wave [114, The Round Wing, *Cabera rotundaria*]. **1869** E. Newman *Brit. Moths* 27 The Round-winged Muslin (*Nudaria Senex*). **1887** *Cassell's Encycl. Dict.* s.v., Round-winged white-wave, a British geometer moth, *Cabera exanthemaria*. **1907** R. South *Moths Brit. Isles* Ser. I. 175 The Round-winged Muslin (*Comacla senex*)..; the wings of this moth are rounder in outline than those of the Muslin.

3. Applied to certain hawks, as those of the genera *Accipiter* and *Astur*.

1890 in *Cent. Dict.*

ˈroundwise, *adv.* and *a.* Now *rare.* [f. ROUND *a.* + -WISE.]

1. *adv.* In a circular form, disposition, or arrangement; circularly.

1577 Harrison *Eng.* II. xxv. (1877) 364 King Edward the first.. did first coine the penie and smallest peeces of siluer roundwise. **1609** Bible (Douay) *Lev.* xix. 27 Neither shal you cut your heare roundwise; nor shave your beard. **1675** Han. Woolley *Gentlewoman's Comp.* 146 Take Apples sliced thin round-wise. **1725** *Fam. Dict.* s.v. *Larch-Tree*, It produces its Branches roundwise, at some equal Distance from each other.

2. *adj.* **a.** Circular, round. *rare*$^{-1}$.

1633 P. Fletcher *Purple Isl.* II. xxviii, The form (as when with breath our bagpipes rise, And swell) round-wise, and long, yet long-wise more.

b. = ROUNDWARD *a. rare*$^{-1}$.

a **1930** D. H. Lawrence *Apocalypse* (1932) 42 The roundwise moving of the cosmos.

round-wood: see ROWAN[1].

1857 Thoreau *Maine W.* (1894) 79 Mountain-ash, or round-wood, as the Maine people call it.

round-worm. *Zool.* Also **round worm.** [f. ROUND *a.* + WORM *sb.* In early examples only descriptive, later a specific name.] A parasitic worm of a rounded form infesting the human intestines: **a.** A worm of the genus *Lumbricus* or *Ascaris*, esp. *A. lumbricoides*.

1565 Cooper, *Lumbricus*, a longe rounde woorme.. in mans body. **1611** Cotgr., *Ascaride*, a kind of small round worme, which breeds in the bowels. **1658** *Moufet's Theat. Insects* II. xxxii, Round worms [breed] only in the small guts, Ascarides in the Longanum, the Gourd-worms.. in all. **1683** *Phil. Trans.* XIII. 154 The *Lumbricus teres*, that common Round Worm which Children usually are troubled with. **1797** *Encycl. Brit.* (ed. 3) XI. 343/1 The long round worms seem to be the most dangerous which infest the human body, as they often pierce through the stomach and intestines. **1822** Good *Study Med.* (1829) I. 345 The head of the long round worm is slightly incurved. **1829** Cooper *Ibid.* 344 It is calculated one-half of the total number of children have either the round, or thread-worm. **1896** tr. *Boas' Text Bk. Zool.* 160 The Common Round-worm (*Ascaris*), often of considerable size.

b. A nemathelminth, or a nematode worm.

1836-9 *Todd's Cycl. Anat.* II. 116/2 *Nematoidea*,.. Round-worms... Body elongated, rounded, elastic. **1864** *Chambers's Encycl.* VI. 704/1 The N[ematelmia] are sometimes termed *Round-worms*, just as the Platyelmia.. are called *Flat-worms*. **1896** tr. *Boas' Text Bk. Zool.* 158 *Nemathelminthes* (Round-worms).

ˈroundy, *a.* Now *dial.* [f. ROUND *a.*]

1. Rounded; of a round shape.

a **1586** Sidney *Arcadia* (1891) 310 Her roundy sweetly swelling lippes a little trembling. **1821** Clare *Vill. Minstrel* II. 55 Welcome, red and roundy sun, Dropping lowly in the west. **1882** G. M. Hopkins *Poems* (1918) 54 As tumbled over rim in roundy wells Stones ring.

2. *dial.* Of coals: (see ROUND *a.* 15).

1868- in northern dial. glossaries.

roune, var. of ROUN *sb.*, ROUND *v.*[2]; obs. f. RUNE *sb.*[2]

†**ˈrouner.** *Obs.* Forms: 1 runere, 4-6 rowner (5 -ere, 6 *Sc.* -ar), 5 rouner (6 *Sc.* -ar, roundar). [OE. *rúnere*, f. *rúnian* to whisper, ROUND *v.*[2] Cf. MDu. *runer* (*ruyner, runaer*, etc.), MLG. *runer*, OHG. *rûnari* (G. *rauner*).] A whisperer; a tatler, tale-bearer.

c **1000** Ælfric *Gram.* xxxvi. (Z.) 217 *Hic susurro*, ðes runere oþþe wroht. **1388** *Pol. Poems* (Rolls) I. 271 Rowners and flatreres. *c* **1425** Lydg. *Assembly of Gods* 687 Rowners, uagaboundes, forgers of lesynges. *a* **1470** H. Parker *Dives & Pauper* (W. de W. 1496) IV. v. 199/2 A preuy rowner, that pryuely telleth false tales amonges the people. **1500-20** Dunbar *Poems* xx. 33 Be thow not ane roundar in the nwke. *Ibid.* xxvi. 52 With.. rownaris of fals lesingis. **1551** Abp. Hamilton *Catech.* 71 Of thame that ar quysperaris, rowkaris and rounaris.

roung, obs. Sc. pa. pple. of REIGN *v.*; obs. f. RUNG *sb.*

†**rounge**, *v. Obs.* Also 6 *Sc.* runge, ronge, rownge. [ad. OF. *roungier*, *rungier*, *rongier* (mod.F. *ronger*): of obscure formation.]

1. *intr.* To roar, cry out.

a **1375** *Joseph Arim.* 361 He roungede an heiȝ, and rorede so harde, his eiȝen flowen out of his hed.

2. *intr.* and *trans.* To gnaw; to champ.

1390 Gower *Conf.* I. 177 For evere on hem I rounge and gknawe And hindre hem al that evere I mai. *c* **1400** *Pilgr. Sowle* (Caxton) I. xx. (1859) 20 Lyke a worm I am woned to bvte and to rounge them that wrongly thew selue. *c* **1430** *Pilgr. Lyf Manhode* I. lv. (1869) 33 It wolde neuer stinte to rounge [*printed* raunge] so michel til it hadde slayn his mayster. *Ibid.* II. cxxxvi. 129 As the wolf that hath strangled the shepe.. and hath rounged his chekes. **1513** Douglas *Æneis* III. iv. 93 With ȝour chaftis to gnaw ȝe sall be fane, And runge ȝour tabillis all and burdis. *Ibid.* IV. iv. 11 Hir fers steid stude stamping,.. Rungeand the fomy goldin bitt.

b. *intr.* To chew the cud.

c **1410** *Master of Game* (MS. Digby 182) xxxiv, For euermore she [the hare] fumeth and croteth and roungeth and bereth talowe and grece. **1486** *Bk. St. Albans* e iij b, All [beasts] that bere skyne and talow and Rounge.. shall be flayne safe the hare.

3. *trans.* To clip (coin). *Sc.*

1540 *Sc. Acts Jas. V* (1814) II. 373 Þat na maner of man tak vpoun hand for to Ronge the croun of wecht. **1619** in C. Innes *Sk. E. Scot. Hist.* App. (1861) 522 Thair wes tuo of the xx mark peceis rounged and far les then the thrid wes.

Hence †**rounged** *ppl. a. Obs.*

a **1572** Knox *Hist. Ref.* Wks. 1846 I. 404 Thair clyppit and rowngeit Soussis.. ar commandit to have course in this realme. **1622** W. Scot *Course Conformitie* x. 43 To attaine thirteen rounged and dilapidate Bishoprickes.

†**ˈrounger.** *Obs.* Also 5 roungere, roundgar. [f. ROUNGE *v.* 3, or ad. AF. **roungere*, OF. *rongeur*.] A clipper of coins.

1338 R. Brunne *Chron.* (1810) 238 Edward.. wille wite certeyn, who schent has his mone. Of clippers, of roungers [F. *roygnurs*], of suilk takes he questis. *c* **1430** *Pilgr. Lyf Manhode* III. xvii. (1869) 144 This hand is an.. vnhelere and brekere of cofres, and a roungere of floreyns. *a* **1600** in Drake *Eboracum* I. vi. (1736) 189 Roundgars of gold, washers of gold.

†**ˈrouning**, *vbl. sb. Obs.* Also 1 runung, 3 runing, roning; 4-6 rounyng(e, 5 rounn-, rovn-); 4-6 rownyng(e, 5 rowyn-), 5-6 rowning(e, 6 rowening). See also ROUNDING *vbl. sb.*[2] [f. OE. *rúnian*, ME. *rounen*: see ROUND *v.*[2]] Whispering; private conversation or consultation, etc.

c **1000** Ælfric *Hom.* (ed. Assmann) vi. 161 Hi.. on synderlicum runungum þæt riht eall rædd on. *c* **1205** Lay. 14070 He wolde wið þan kinge holden runinge. *c* **1275** —— 3249 Þe Scottene king and þe duk.. mid hire stille rouning nemen heom to reade. **13..** *K. Alis.* 7604 (Laud MS.), After þis queynt rounyng Alisaunder spedde in þis doyng. *c* **1384** Chaucer *H. Fame* III. 1960 And ouer alle the houses Angles Ys ful of rovnynges. *c* **1450** tr. *De Imitatione* III. i. 64 Blessid be þo eres þat receyueþ of goddys rounynge, & takiþ non hede of þe rounyng of þis worlde. *c* **1475** in *Babees Bk.* (1868) 4 Withe-oute lowde lauhtere or Iangelynge, Rovnynge, Iapynge, or other Insolence. **1533** More *Apol.* 240 Castyng abrode a suspicyouse bablynge, of gatheryng, and assemblynge, and rownynge, and talkynge.

†**ˈrouning**, *ppl. a. Obs.* Also 1 runiende, 4 rownande, rownende. [Cf. prec.] Whispering, murmuring.

c **1050** *Voc.* in Wr.-Wülcker 441 *Musitantes*, þa runiendan. **13..** *E.E. Allit. P.* A. 112 Swangeande swete þe water con swepe, Wyth a rownande rourde raykande aryȝt. **1382** Wyclif *Ecclus.* xxi. 31 The rownende grucchere shal defoule his soule.

Hence †**ˈrouningly** *adv.*, in a whisper. *Obs.*

c **1380** Wyclif *Wks.* (1880) 328 Sum confessioun is made to man, and þat may be on many maneres; outher opynly & generaly.. or priuely & rownyngly. **1406** Hoccleve *La Male Regle* 172 Cloos kepte I me; no man durste I depraue But rownyngly; I spak no thyng on highte.

rounsefal, obs. form of ROUNCIVAL.

†**ˈrounsepike.** *Obs. rare.* In 5 rounse-, rownsepyk. [Of obscure origin: cf. RAMPIKE and RAMPICK.] A leafless branch.

1470-85 Malory *Arthur* VI. xvi. 209 Ouer his hede he sawe a rownsepyk, a bygge bough leueles. *Ibid.*, Syr Launcelot putte aweye the stroke with the rounsepyk.

rounseval, obs. form of ROUNCIVAL.

rounsy, obs. form of ROUNCY.

†**rount**, *a. Obs.*$^{-0}$ Roan.

1688 Holme *Armoury* II. 155/1 Colours of Horses... Rount, is a kind of flesh colour, or a Bay intermixt with white and gray; a Roan-colour. *Ibid.*, Grissel, is a light Rount.

rountree, obs. variant of ROWAN-TREE.

roup (raʊp), *sb.*[1] *Sc.* and *north.* Also 7 roop, 8 roupe, 9 *north.* raup. [f. ROUP *v.* 2.] An auction; the act of selling or letting by auction.

1693 Stair *Instit.* I. xvi. (ed. 2) 135 A Roup at the half or major part of the Owners against the rest. **1698** A. Fletcher *Two Disc. Aff. Scot.* 36 The letting of Farms.. by Roop or Auction. **1700** Law *Council of Trade* (1751) 9 All other effects that shall be sold by public roupe in this kingdom. **1785** Mrs. Grant *Lett. fr. Mountains* (1813) II. 114 Every article of cattle and furniture was sold. The roup lasted a week. **1833** *Act 3 & 4 Will. IV*, c. 46 §70 The said collector is.. to sell by public roup.. such part of the said goods and effects. **1878** C. Gibbon *For the King* i, Bauldy's chief business had been to announce roups.

attrib. and *Comb.* **1785** Mrs. Grant *Lett. fr. Mountains* (1813) II. 110 Roups, then, are a source of great amusement here and a very expensive one to the roup-makers. **1829** Hogg *Sheph. Cal.* ii, This cow.. is valued in my roup-roll at fifteen pounds. **1890** Service *Notandums* 5 Shall I reprint the roup bills o' my ryegrass parks?

roup (ruːp), *sb.*[2] Forms: 6 roupe, 6-7 roope, 7 rup, roupp, 6- roup, 7- roop. [Of obscure origin.] A disease in poultry characterized by morbid swellings on the rump.

1551 Turner *Herbal* I. B v, Garlyke.. is also good for the pype or roupe of hennes and cockes, as Pliny wryteth. **1578** Lyte *Dodoens* 638 They cure the pipe or roupe of Pultrie and Chickens with Garlyke. **1614** Markham *Cheap Husb.* (1623) 141 The roupp is a filthy bile or swelling on the rumpe of Poultrie, and will corrupt the whole body. **1765** *Treat. Dom. Pigeons* 34 The wet roop next falls under our consideration. **1805** R. W. Dickson *Pract. Agric.* II. 1210 The Roup is known by the rump becoming swelled and enlarged. *c* **1858** Eliz. Watts *Poultry Yard* 167 Inflammation and Intumescence of the Rump Gland.. To this affection the term 'roup'.. is often applied.

attrib. and *Comb.* **1748** Richardson *Clarissa* (1768) VI. lxxvi. 324 Thou droopest like a pip or roup-cloaking chicken. *c* **1858** Eliz. Watts *Poultry Yard* 168 Baily's roup pills are almost universally known and appreciated.

roup (ruːp), *sb.*[3] Also 8 roupe, and ROOP *sb.*[1] [Prob. of imitative origin.]

1. *Sc.* and *north.* Hoarseness, huskiness; †some disease affecting the throat.

a **1585** MONTGOMERIE *Flyting* 323 The rot, the roup, and the auld rest. **1674-** [see ROOP *sb.*[1]]. *c* **1770** BEATTIE *To Alex. Ross* iii, O may the roupe ne'er roust thy weason. **1773** FERGUSON *Poems* (1789) II. 77 To fleg frae a' your craigs the roup, Wi' reeking het an' creeshy soup. **1811-** in northern dial. glossaries.

2. A form of purulent catarrh affecting domestic poultry.

1808 JAMIESON, *Roup*..also denotes a disease which affects hens in the mouth or throat. **1849** D. J. BROWNE *Amer. Poultry Yd.* (1855) 267 The symptom most prominent in the roup, is difficult and noisy breathing, beginning with what is termed the gapes, as in the pip. *c* **1877** L. WRIGHT *Bk. Poultry* 200 In very aggravated cases of roup the entire throat is sometimes filled with the diseased secretion.

roup (raʊp), *v. Sc.* and *north.* Also 4 roupe, 5-6 rolp, 6 rowp, 9 *north.* raup, rawp, etc. [Of Scandinavian origin: cf. Icel. *raupa* (Fær. *reypa*) to boast, brag, MSw. *röpa* to shout, Da. *røbe* to disclose, reveal.]

1. *intr.* To cry, shout, roar; to croak. Now *arch.*

13.. *St. Alexius* 566 in Horstm. *Altengl. Leg.* (1881) 187 Scho beganne to roupe & rare. *c* **1450** HOLLAND *Howlat* 215 The Ravyne, rolpand rudly in a roche ran. **1513** DOUGLAS *Æneis* IX. viii. 44 Taikand..na maner schame, Sua amangis men to ryn, and roup or rame. **1535** LYNDESAY *Satyre* 3075 Thir ruiks thay roupit wonder fast. **1571** *Satir. Poems Reform.* xxviii. 89 Rowpand for riches..Sum benefice I bocht or euer it vaikit.

1841 LYTTON *Nt. & Morn.* (1851) 111 There they were, romping and rouping in the garden, like a couple of gaol birds. **1892** MRS. STUART MENTEATH *Lays Kirk & Covenant* 24 Let heretics both rave and roup.

†**b.** *trans.* To proclaim or utter with a loud voice. *Obs.*

1513 DOUGLAS *Æneis* III. i. 129 The lattir halsing syne lowde [we] schowtit thrise, Rowpand at anis, adew! *Ibid.* IV. viii. 129 Or lyk Orestes,..Rowpit and sung quhow he his modir fled. *a* **1572** KNOX *Hist. Ref.* Wks. 1846 I. 96 These slaves of Sathan..rowped as thei had bein ravinis, yea, rather thei yelled and rored as devillis in hell, 'Heresy! heresy!'

†**c.** To invoke loudly. *Obs. rare.*

1513 DOUGLAS *Æneis* IV. ix. 75 Thre hundreth goddis with hir mouth rowpit sche. *Ibid.* xi. 51 Thow Proserpyne, quhilk, by our gentile lawis, Art rowpit hie, and ȝellit lowd by nycht.

2. To sell or let by auction.

1568 LAUDER *Minor P.* II. 37 Iustice is rowpit, as vtheris waris; This is most plane, and nocht obscure. **1574** *Reg. Privy Council Scot.* II. 391 To caus rowp the said croft and myre. **1590** *Ibid.* IV. 534 That the small custumes..micht be yeirlie roupit and sett to the best availl. **1637** RUTHERFORD *Lett.* (1862) I. lxxxviii. 225 If men and angels were rouped and sold at the dearest price. **1693** STAIR *Instit.* I. xvi. (ed. 2) 135 Either to take his part at such a rate,..or Roup his own part when he pleases. **1733** P. LINDSAY *Interest Scot.* 213 Those poor Fishermen..must pay it,..or have their Houshold furniture distrained and roupt for the Payment of it. **1827** SCOTT *Jrnl.* 11 Apr., The parks were rouped for £100 a year more than they brought last year. **1879** *Scotsman* 22 Mar., The Linlithgow town and bridge customs were rouped yesterday. **1889** BARRIE *Window in Thrums* 90 His effects were rouped before I knew him.

b. To sell up (a person).

c **1817** HOGG *Tales & Sk.* VI. 61 He has since heard..that they had been rouped out at the door. **1824** MACTAGGART *Gallovid. Encycl.* 342 Squire Kirtle..May roup his farmers. **1871** C. GIBBON *Lack of Gold* viii, It was not Angus's fault that he was rouped.

Hence ˈ**rouping** *ppl. a.*

1530 LYNDESAY *Test. Papyngo* 1083 The rowpand Reuin said: sweit syster, lat se ȝour holy intent.

rouped, *a. Sc.* and *north.* Also 8-9 roupet, -it, and ROOPED. [f. ROUP *sb.*[3] + -ED.] Affected with hoarseness; hoarse.

1677- [see ROOPED *a.*]. **1786** BURNS *Earnest Cry & Prayer* ii, Alas! my roupet Muse is haerse! **1806** A. DOUGLAS *Poems* 29 Is your throat no dry an' roupit Whistlin a' day loud an' sweet? **1897** BEATTY *Secretar* xli, He had a voice like a roupet craw.

roupee, obs. form of RUPEE.

rouper (ˈraʊpə(r)). *Sc.* Also 6 rowper. [f. ROUP *v.* + -ER[1]. Cf. Icel. *raupari* braggart.]

1. One who cries or shouts.

a **1585** POLWART *Flyting w. Montgomerie* 757 Ragged rowper like a raven.

2. One who sells goods by auction.

1799 W. THOM *Wks.* 447 A rouper is pursuing his interest when he pays the bell-man to intimate his roup.

roupie, obs. form of RUPEE.

rouping (ˈraʊpɪŋ), *vbl. sb. Sc.* and *north.* Also 6 rowp-, 7 roupeing, roping. [f. ROUP *v.*]

1. The action of selling or letting by auction; also, an auction, a roup.

1593 *Sc. Acts Jas. VI* (1816) IV. 30 The commoun guid and patrimonie of all Burrowis within this Realme,..efter the ȝeirlie rowping and setting thairof, as vse is. **1646** R. BAILLIE *Anabaptism* (1647) 17 One..in a public roping did seem to use some couzenage in buying of a house. **1685** *Min. Bk. New Mills Cloth Manuf.* (1905) 85 Appoynts [that] a roupeing be called upon Monday. **1786** FRASER TYTLER *The Lounger* No. 79 ¶4 Was you ever at a sale,—a rouping you call it in this country? **1818** SCOTT *Hrt. Midl.* xlii, After the rouping is ower, and the bills paid. **1888** BARRIE *Auld Licht Idylls* ii, Then took place the rouping of seats in the parish church.

b. *Comb.*, as **rouping-clerk**, an auctioneer's clerk; †**rouping-wife, -woman**, a woman who holds auctions, or who buys at auctions for the purpose of selling again.

1782 SIR J. SINCLAIR *Observ. Scot. Dial.* 127 *Rouping-wife*, a female auctioneer. **1785** *Gentl. Mag.* LV. I. 201 The furniture of the house being previously sold to a rouping-woman, as she called it. **1818** SCOTT *Hrt. Midl.* iv, His neighbour the rouping-wife, or saleswoman. **1882** J. WALKER *Jaunt to Auld Reekie* 180 Would'st [thou] be degraded to a rouping clerk.

2. Crying, yelling.

c **1865** S. S. JONES *Northumb.* 115 Ilka bairnie spite o' its roupin' an' skirlin' had getten washed an' busked up.

roupy (ˈruːpɪ), *a.*[1] Also 9 roopy. [f. ROUP *sb.*[2]] Of poultry: Affected with the roup (inflammation of the rump-gland).

1722 DE FOE *Plague* (Bohn) 165 The breath of such a person would poison..even a cock or hen:..it would cause them to be roupy, as they call it. **1823** *New Monthly Mag.* VIII. 501 Fast he sat as roopy turkey-poult. **1830** 'B. MOUBRAY' *Poultry* (ed. 6) [73 Imposthume upon the rump is called roup. *Ibid.*] 74 Roupy hens seldom lay.

roupy (ˈruːpɪ), *a.*[2] [f. ROUP *sb.*[3]]

1. Hoarse, husky.

1808 JAMIESON s.v. *Roup*, A peculiar sense,..denoting..hoarseness of voice, as the adj. *roupy* is now used. **1872** F. W. ROBINSON *Bridge of Glass* II. i, The sheep grew wheezy and roupy and unnaturally dispirited. **1898** MUNRO *J. Splendid* iv. 48 The crows..complained in a rasping roupy chorus.

2. Of poultry: Affected with the roup (purulent catarrh). Also, pertaining to the roup.

1830 'B. MOUBRAY' *Poultry* (ed. 6) 32 Cocks..are liable to become aguish,..perhaps, in the end, turning roopy or glandered. *Ibid.* 74 When the malady becomes confirmed, with running at the nostrils, swollen eyes, and other well-known symptoms, they are termed Roupy. *c* **1877** L. WRIGHT *Bk. Poultry* 199 The characteristic roupy discharge.

fig. **1863** QUINN *Heather Lintie* 64 Wi' dark, bedimmed, dull roupy e'en..We slowly staumer on.

roupy, obs. form of RUPEE.

rourde, variant of RERD(E *sb. Obs.*

†**rous**, *sb.*[1] *Sc. Obs.*[−1] [Of obscure origin: cf. next.] A heavy fall or crash.

1535 STEWART *Cron. Scot.* III. 135 His hors hapnit to snapper and to fall, With sic ane rous quhill that him self flew wnder.

Rous (raʊs), *sb.*[2] *Biol.* The name of Francis Peyton *Rous* (1879–1970), U.S. physician, used *attrib.* to designate (*a*) a type of virus-induced sarcoma which afflicts birds, described by him in 1910 (*Jrnl. Exper. Med.* XII. 696); (*b*) an RNA virus which causes such sarcomata (its existence was suggested by Rous et al. in 1912 (*Jrnl. Amer. Med. Assoc.* 20 Nov. 1794/1)). So ˈ**rousvirus**.

1911 *Jrnl. Exper. Med.* XIII. 389 We succeeded..in cultivating malignant tissues such as the Rous chicken sarcoma. **1925** W. E. GYE in *Lancet* 18 July 109/2 It has now been shown that Rous tumour No. 1 is caused by a virus which has been cultivated. **1931** *Brit. Jrnl. Exper. Path.* XII. 127 To decide whether the fragility of the Rous virus were due to its inability to resist oxidation, or whether a proteolysis were the inactivating cause. **1945** DURAN-REYNALS & SHRIGLEY in *Res. Conf. on Cancer* (Amer. Assoc. Adv. Sci.) 13/1 When the Rous tumor virus is inoculated into ducks two sets of lesions occur. **1945** H. S. N. GREENE in *Ibid.* 19/1 Dr Shrigley has succeeded in transplanting the Rous sarcoma in the anterior chambers of guinea pigs' eyes, and this is the first instance in which a virus-induced tumor has been proved to be a cancer. **1961** R. D. BAKER *Essent. Path.* xiii. 311 Carcinogenic viruses are known to produce the Rous sarcoma in chickens and the Shope papilloma of rabbits. **1961** *Lancet* 5 Aug. 301/1 The ability of cells infected with Rous-sarcoma virus to multiply has been demonstrated, but such chronically infected tumour cells cannot be considered to have recovered. **1972** *Sci. Amer.* Jan. 26/1 The rousviruses do not transfer information from RNA to RNA, as other RNA viruses do. **1977** *Nature* 15 Dec. 631 The genome of Rous sarcoma virus (RSV) is a 30–40S RNA of 10,000 nucleotides.

rous (raʊs), *adv. rare.* Also 9 rouse. [Echoic.] With a bounce or bang.

1672 VILLIERS (Dk. Buckhm.) *Rehearsal* III. ii, 'Slife, Sir! you should have come out in choler, rous upon the Stage, just as the other went off. **1888** ELWORTHY *W. Somerset Word-bk.* s.v., Down come the roof, rouse.

rous, variant of ROUSE *a.*, red. *Obs.*

rousable (ˈraʊzəb(ə)l), *a.* [f. ROUSE *v.*[1] + -ABLE. Cf. AROUSABLE *a.*] Capable or admitting of being roused.

1910 *Daily Chron.* 7 Mar. 8/1, I thought her endowed with a temper that might be very violent when roused, though not easily rousable. **1961** *Lancet* 5 Aug. 323/1 She was semicomatose but rousable.

rousant (ˈraʊzənt), *a. Her.* [f. ROUSE *v.*[1] + -ANT[1].] (See quot. 1780.)

1688 HOLME *Armoury* II. xix. 479/1 A Falcon rowsant to the Sinister, is the Crest of Falckenstein of Bavaria. **1780** EDMONDSON *Compl. Body Her.* II, *Rousant*, a term given by some Heralds to a bird rising, as if preparing to take wing. **1868** CUSSANS *Heraldry* (1893) 95 *Rising*, or *Rousant*... This term is usually employed in blazoning Swans.

rousch, obs. form of RUSH *v.*

†**rouse**, *sb.*[1] *Obs.* [Of obscure origin.] Mirth.

c **1400** *Beryn* 1669 The todir burgeyse rose hym vp, for to make Rouse, And axid of his felawe [etc.]. *Ibid.* 3610 Beryn & his feleshipp wer within the house, And speken of hir answer, & made but litill rouse.

rouse (raʊz), *sb.*[2] Also 6-7 rowse. [f. ROUSE *v.*[1]]

†**1.** A shake (of the feathers, etc.). *Obs.*

1589 PUTTENHAM *Eng. Poesie* III. xxiii. (Arb.) 272 These fowles in their moulting time, when their feathers be sick, and be so loase in the flesh that at any little rowse they can easilie shake them off. **1600** BRETON *Melanch. Humours* Wks. (Grosart) I. 14/1 But all in feare to make so farre a flight, Vntill his pennes were somewhat harder growne; He gaue a rowse. **1614** LATHAM *Falconry* (1633) 53 If her stomacke..be cold and dull, she will flie wilde and carelesly, and on plains and rowses. **1672** JOSSELYN *New Englands Rarities* 17 The Porcupine.., a very angry Creature and dangerous, shooting a whole shower of Quills with a rowse at their enemies.

2. *Mil.* The signal for arousing; the réveille.

1802 JAMES *Milit. Dict.*, *Rouse*, one of the bugle-horn soundings for duty. **1821** JOANNA BAILLIE *Metr. Leg.*, *Wallace* xxxvii, No more again the rouse of war to hear. **1863** *Cornh. Mag.* VII. 446 The first notes of the rouse are dismal, ..but they are succeeded by a few others of an encouraging and lively character. **1894** WOLSELEY *Marlborough* II. 198 When the 'rouse' had sounded that morning.

3. A violent stir. Also ***rouse-out***.

1824 W. IRVING *T. Trav.* I. 61 He revolutionized the whole establishment, and gave it such a rouse that the very house reeled with it. **1881** C. A. STEPHENS *Knockabout Club in Woods* (1882) xi. 122 The result was a most unwelcome rouse-out shortly after ten o'clock. **1916** C. SANDBURG *Chicago Poems* 125 The silk and flare of it [*sc.* a red scarf] is a great soprano leading a chorus Carried along in a rouse of voices reaching for the heart of the world.

4. *attrib.*, as (sense 2) ***rouse-parade***.

1937 D. JONES *In Parenthesis* I. 4 We've got too many buns —and all those wads—you knew they were going—why did you order them—they won't be in after rouse-parade even —they've gone.

rouse (raʊz), *sb.*[3] Now *arch.* Also 7 rouce, rouze, 7, 9 rowse. [Prob. an aphetic form of *carouse*, due to the phrase *to drink carouse* having been apprehended as *to drink a rouse*.

It has been suggested that the word is ad. Da. (also Sw. and Norw.) *rus*, = Du. *roes*, LG. *rûse*, G. *rausch* intoxication, drunken fit; but both form and meaning are more easily accounted for by the above explanation. 'The Danish rowsa' in Dekker *Gull's Hornbook* may be simply due to the passages in Shaks. *Hamlet*.]

1. A full draught of liquor; a bumper.

1602 SHAKS. *Ham.* I. ii. 126 And the Kings Rouce, the Heauens shall bruite againe. **1626** J. TAYLOR (Water P.) *Trav.* Wks. (1630) III. 80/2 Because death should not terrifie him, they had giuen him many rowses and carowses of wine and beere. **1640** GLAPTHORNE *Wallenstein* V. ii, My Lord,.. take me off This lusty rowse to your owne health.

1820 SHELLEY *Let. to Maria Gisborne* 65 Then all quaff Another rouse, and hold their sides and laugh.

2. A carousal or bout of drinking.

1602 SHAKS. *Ham.* II. i. 58 There was he gaming, there o'retooke in's Rouse. **1619** FLETCHER *Mons. Thomas* I. ii, She has heard..The gambols that you plaid.., your several mischiefs, Your rowses and your wenches. **1654** GAYTON *Pleas. Notes* IV. viii. 217 After a good rouze, or good dose of *Nepenthe*, they are in a trance.

1855 KINGSLEY *Westw. Ho!* viii, Amyas..invited..his old schoolfellows..to a merry supper and a 'rowse' thereon consequent. **1863** COWDEN CLARKE *Shaks. Char.* v. 131 It was natural that a free, open-hearted soldier should welcome the arrival of his brother-officers with a rouse.

3. In the phrases ***to take one's rouse, have a rouse, give a rouse***.

(*a*) **1602** SHAKS. *Ham.* I. iv. 8 The King doth wake to night, and takes his rouse. **1616** *Marlowe's Faustus* (Rtldg.) 122/2 He took his rouse with stoops of Rhenish wine. **1623** MASSINGER *Dk. Milan* I. i, Your lord, by his patent, Stands bound to take his rouse.

(*b*) **1609** B. JONSON *Sil. Wom.* III. vi, We will haue a rouse in each of 'hem, anon, for bold Britons, yfaith. **1667** DAVENANT & DRYDEN *Tempest* IV. iii, I long to have a rouse to her grace's health. **1815** SCOTT *Guy M.* xxxiv, Rambling up and down this d——d vault, and thinking about the merry rouses we have had in it. **1842** TENNYSON *Vision of Sin* IV. ix, Fill the cup, and fill the can: Have a rouse before the morn. **1864** BURTON *Scot Abr.* II. 181 Patrick's neighbour,..with whom..he has a merry rouse.

(*c*) **1604** SHAKS. *Oth.* II. iii. 66 'Fore heauen, they haue giuen me a rowse already. **1609** HEALEY *Discov. New World* 84 Giue me one rouse, my freind, and get thee gone. **1842** BROWNING *Cavalier Tunes* II. i, Give a rouse: here's, in Hell's despite now, King Charles!

†**rouse**, *a. Obs.* Also 5 rous, rowse. [a. OF. *rous* (mod.F. *roux*):—L. *russum*, acc. of *russus* red.] Red-haired. (Only in personal names.)

c **1400** *Ywaine & Gaw.* 1146 Pray to hir..That sho forgif the, in this stede, Of Salados the rouse ded. *c* **1400** *Brut* cxxxiv. 138 After þis William Bastard regnede his sone William [þe] Rous. *c* **1425** in Maskell *Mon. Rit.* (1847) III. 345 For the soules of the kyngis William Rowse, Herry the firste [etc.]. **1531** ELYOT *Gov.* I. xii, William called Rouse.

rouse (raʊz), *v.*[1] Also 5-8 rowse, 6-8 rowze, 6-9 rouze (7 rouz), 7, 9 *Sc.* roose. [Orig. a technical term in hawking and hunting, and so presumably of AF. or OF. origin, but the precise source is obscure. In general use common after *c* 1585, and freq. strengthened by *up*. Cf. also AROUSE *v.*[1]

I. † 1. *refl.* **a.** Of a hawk: To shake the feathers. *Obs. rare.* Cf. sense 9.

1486 *Bk. St. Albans* A vi, And whanne she hathe doone she will rowse hire myghtyly. [**1825** SCOTT *Betrothed* xxiii, The..vigour with which they pruned their plumes, and shook, or, as it was technically termed, roused themselves.]

†b. (See quot.) *Obs. rare.*

1530 PALSGR. 694/2, I rowse, I stretche my selfe, as a man dothe whan he gothe to prove a maystrye, *je me coppie*. It was a sporte to se him rowse him selfe and stretche out his armes, or ever he began to wrestyll.

2. *trans.* To cause (game) to rise or issue from cover or lair. Cf. RAISE *v.*[1] 4 b.

1531 ELYOT *Gov.* I. xviii, If they wold use but a fewe nombre of houndes, onely to harborowe, or rouse, the game. **1575** TURBERV. *Venerie* 106 The huntesman..shall then go before them and rowze the Deare. **1596** SHAKS. *1 Hen. IV*, I. iii. 198 The blood more stirres To rowze a Lyon, then to start a Hare. **1627** TAYLOR (Water P.) *Armado* Wks. (1630) I. 93 So hath this Woodmanship diuers and sundry tearmes of Art..as you must say, Rowse a Bucke, Start a Hare, and vnkennel a Foxe. **1697** DRYDEN *Virg. Georg.* III. 624 Thou mayst..Rouze from their Desart Dens, the bristled Rage Of Boars. **1709** PRIOR *Henry & Emma* 397 To beat the woods, and rouse the bounding prey. **1774** GOLDSM. *Nat. Hist.* (1776) III. 121 The chief huntsman, entering with his hounds within the lines, rouzed the game with a full cry. **1831** SCOTT *Cast. Dang.* vi, He proposes to go to rouse the wild cattle. **1858** KINGSLEY *Poems* 160 They roused a hart, ..A hart of ten.

fig. **1589** GREENE *Menaphon* (Arb.) 15 When they want certaine liquid sacrifice, to rouze her [the muse] foorth her denne. **1593** SHAKS. *Rich. II*, II. iii. 128 To rowze his Wrongs, and chase them to the bay.

†3. a. To raise or set up, to ruffle. *Obs.*

1590 SPENSER *F.Q.* I. xi. 9 An Eagle, seeing pray appeare, His aery plumes doth rouze. *Ibid.* II. iii. 35 He.., standing stoutly up, his lofty crest Did fiercely shake, and rowze as comming late from rest. **1604** DRAYTON *Owle* 732 As he stands proudly rowzing up his Plumes.

†b. To raise or lift up. Also *fig. Obs.*

1507 SHAKS. *2 Hen. IV*, IV. i. 118 Henry Bullingbrooke and hee Being mounted, and both rowsed in their Seates. **1633** P. FLETCHER *Purple Isl.* XI. xxix, She strives..to.. rouze her fainting head, which down as oft would fall. **1650** EARL MONM. tr. *Senault's Man bec. Guilty* 310 When he heard the comfort of birds or the noyse of the waters he rowsed up his soul to his Creator.

refl. **1599** SHAKS. *Hen. V*, I. ii. 275, I will..shew my sayle of Greatnesse, When I do rowse me in my Throne of France.

4. To cause to start up from slumber or repose; to awaken from sleep, meditation, etc. Also with *up*, *out*.

1593 SHAKS. *Rich. II*, I. iii. 134 Rouz'd vp with boystrous vntun'd drummes. **1601** —— *Twel. N.* II. iii. 60 Shall wee rowze the night-Owle in a Catch? **1632** MILTON *L'Allegro* 54 The Hounds and horn Chearly rouse the slumbring morn. **1711** ADDISON *Spect.* No. 55 ¶1 A young Fellow who was rouzed out of his Bed, in order to be sent upon a long Voyage. **1757** W. WILKIE *Epigoniad* VII. 231 The stars descend; and soon the morning ray Shall rouse us to the labors of the day. **1819** SHELLEY *Cenci* IV. iv. 18, I must rouse him from his sleep, Since none else dare. **1853** KINGSLEY *Hypatia* xxviii, At last a low whistle roused her from her dream. **1896** BADEN-POWELL *Matabele Campaign* iii, Here I roused out Pyke, the officer in command. *Ibid.* xvi, At 2.30 we were roused up.

absol. **1846** TRENCH *Mirac.* xiv. (1862) 244 Christ rouses from the bier as easily as another would rouse from the bed.

b. To disturb, chase away (sleep). *rare.*

1667 MILTON *P.L.* III. 329 The cited dead Of all past Ages to the general Doom shall hast'n, such a peal shall rouse thir sleep.

5. *fig.* **a.** To awaken or startle (one) from a state of ease or security.

1594 T. B. *La Primaud. Fr. Acad.* II. 577 Although some men..fall sometimes into this senslesnesse, yet..God afterwards rowseth them vp well enough. **1627** DRAYTON *Agincourt* 100 And in vpon Northumberland doth breake, Rowzing the Sluggish villages from sleepe. **1650** HUBBERT *Pill Formality* 90 It rowsed him out of his Bed, in order.. *a* **1740** WATERLAND *Serm.* xxxiii. Wks. 1823 IX. 412 His present fears, rather than any thing of true penitence, roused him up, and made him have recourse to God. **1770** PITT in Almon *Anecd.* (1810) II. xxxix. 194, I mean to rouse, to alarm the whole nation—to rouse the Ministry, if possible, who seem awake to nothing but the preservation of their places.

b. To stir up, excite to vigorous action or thought, to provoke to activity.

c **1586** C'TESS PEMBROKE *Ps.* LV. iv, Purple morn,..and midday cleare, Shall see my praying voice to God enclin'd, Rowzing him up. **1612** T. TAYLOR *Comm. Titus* i. 16 When the holy Ghost would rowse vp the slothfull seruant, he threateneth him his portion with hypocrites. **1678** R. L'ESTRANGE *Seneca's Mor.* (1702) 120 Philosophy..rouzes, us where we are faint and drouzy. **1710** STEELE *Tatler* No. 2 ¶2 The Emperor is rouzed by this Alarm. **1777** WATSON *Philip II* (1793) II. XIII. 173 The Spaniards, rouzed by the danger which threatened them,..made a bold and vigorous resistance. **1808** *Med. Jrnl.* XIX. 161 Emetics..I thought might rouse the liver from its state of torpor. **1860** TYNDALL *Glac.* I. xxvii. 197 Vainly the postilion endeavoured to rouse them [*sc.* horses] by word and whip. **1888** BRYCE *Amer. Commw.* II. 413 To excite the voters by..the sense of a common purpose, rousing them by speeches or literature.

c. Const. *to* or *into*.

1701 DE FOE *Trueborn Eng.* 45 Till Pity rowz'd him from his soft Repose, His Life to unseen Hazards to expose. **1715** POPE *Iliad* II. 94 Unite, and rouze the sons of Greece to arms. **1743** R. BLAIR *Grave* 319 Enough to rouse a dead man into rage. **1831** SIR J. SINCLAIR *Corr.* II. 181 They roused the population to action, and armed them. **1847** MARTIN *Ox* 130/2 The animal is roused to fury. **1863** GEO. ELIOT *Romola* vi, His pride was roused to double activity.

d. To provoke to anger.

1843 *P. Parley's Ann.* IV. 355 He felt a delight..in plaguing the nursemaid, and in rousing the cook.

6. *refl.* in senses 4 and 5.

1590 LODGE *Rosalynde* (Hunterian Cl.) 85 With that his Brother began to stirre, and the Lion to rowse himselfe. **1606** SHAKS. *Tr. & Cr.* III. iii. 222 Sweete, rouse your selfe; and the weake wanton Cupid Shall from your necke vnloose his amorous fould. **1656** SANDERSON *Serm.* (1689) 141 Rowzing up himself and his spirits with zeal as hot as fire. **1726** SWIFT *Gulliver* IV. ii, I roused myself, and looked about me in the Room where I was left alone. **1794** MRS. RADCLIFFE *Myst. Udolpho* iv, He seemed by an effort to rouse himself. **1842** TENNYSON *Ld. of Burleigh* 21 From deep thought himself he rouses.

b. Const. *to*.

1587 GOLDING *De Mornay* Pref. (1592) p. vi, That reason rowseth up her selfe to rest vpon trueth. **1606** SHAKS. *Ant. & Cl.* V. ii. 287, I see him rowse himselfe To praise my Noble Act. **1693** OWEN *Holy Spirit* 114 Let such Souls rouze up themselves to lay hold on him. **1746** P. FRANCIS tr. *Horace, Epist.* I. ii. 48 Will you not rouse you to preserve yourself? **1848** DICKENS *Dombey* xxxii, The Captain.. roused himself to a sustained consciousness of that gentleman's presence. **1880** MRS. FORRESTER *Roy & V.* I. 2 He too rouses himself to acknowledge the general homage.

7. To stir up, agitate, put into motion, bring into an active state.

1582 STANYHURST *Æneis* II. (Arb.) 50 Thee water is rowsed, they doe frisk with flownse to the shoare ward. **1667** MILTON *P.L.* II. 287 The sound of blustring winds, which all night long Had rous'd the Sea. **1728** T. SHERIDAN tr. *Persius* vi. (1739) 84 In rouzing the Strings of the Lyre. **1785** BURNS *Ep. to Rev. J. M'Math* 11 Lest they shou'd blame her, An' rouse their holy thunder on it. **1810** *Sporting Mag.* XXXVI. 277 All the charges which they and the prosecutor had roused up against him. **1836** *Backwoods of Canada* 79 The landlady..led me to a blazing fire, which her damsels quickly roused up.

b. To stir up, excite, inflame (a feeling).

1589 GREENE *Menaphon* (Arb.) 68 He began thus to rowze vp his furie. **1637** HEYLIN *Answ. Burton* 184 You call upon the nobles to rowze up their noble Christian zeale. **1666** DRYDEN *Ann. Mirab.* cxc, But sharp remembrance..And shame..Rouse conscious virtue up in every heart. **1752** HUME *Ess. & Treat.* (1777) I. 12 The spirit of the people must frequently be rouzed. **1777** ROBERTSON *Hist. Amer.* II. (1778) I. 116 Those unprovoked injuries rouzed their courage. **1841** ELPHINSTONE *Hist. Ind.* II. 605 This crime only roused the indignation of the Marattas, without weakening their power. **1875** JOWETT *Plato* (ed. 2) IV. 156 The passions of religious parties have been roused to the utmost.

c. To stir (a liquid, *esp.* beer while brewing).

1823 J. BADCOCK *Dom. Amusem.* 101 Having poured boiling water on the suspected sample, rouse it well. **1839** URE *Dict. Arts* 118 Rouse the beer as the hops are gradually introduced. **1876** *Encycl. Brit.* IV. 275/2 This is done by 'rousing' the gyle every two hours with a utensil made for the purpose.

8. *Naut.* To haul *in*, *out*, or *up* with force.

c **1625** *Nomenclator Navalis* (MS.), *Rowse in* is a worde theie use particularlie when as a Cabell or Hawser doth lie slack in the water and they would have him made tawght. *Ibid.*, To keepe it [the cable] stiff and tawght, they will hale in soe much as lies slack, and this they call Rowsing-in the Cabell or Rowse-in the Hawser. [Hence in various 17th cent. nautical works.] **1769** FALCONER *Dict. Marine* (1780), *Recouvrer*, to rowse-in, or haul any rope into the ship. **1832** MARRYAT *N. Forster* v, You and the boy, rouse the cable up .., and bend it. **1841** R. H. DANA *Seaman's Man.* xv. 85 Rouse the cable out through the hawse-hole. **1886** J. M. CAULFIELD *Seamanship Notes* 3 Rouse out reef pendant.

transf. **1890** 'R. BOLDREWOOD' *Col. Reformer* (1891) 193 You cut a straight sapling while we rouse out the saddle-straps for a splice.

II. *intr.* **†9.** Of hawks or other birds and animals: To shake the feathers or body. *Obs.*

1486 *Bk. St. Albans* C viij, She Rousith when she shakith all hir federis. **1575** TURBERV. *Faulconrie* 149 Then suffer hir until she rowse or mewte, and when she hath done either of them unhoode hir. **1639** T. DE GRAY *Compl. Horsem.* 216 You shall perceive him either to shake his head, or to winch with his tayle, to rouze, or shake. **1657** R. LIGON *Barbadoes* (1673) 4 The Turtles..there, mute, prune, and oyl their feathers; rouse, and doe all their offices of nature. **1678** PHILLIPS, *Rowze*, in Faulconry is when a Hawk lifteth up, and shaketh her self.

10. Of game: To rise from cover. *rare.*

1575 TURBERV. *Venerie* 106 All the horsemen must quickly cast abrode about the couert, to discouer yᵉ Harte when he rowzeth and goeth out of his hold. **1590** SIR T. COCKAINE *Treat. Hunting* C iv b, This done, you may begin to tuft for a Bucke, and finding him single, especially if he rouse foorth of a great brake, put your hounds softly upon. **1826** HONE *Every-day Bk.* II. 1031 A red buck roused, then crossed in view.

11. To move with violence; to rush. *rare.*

1582 STANYHURST *Æneis* I. (Arb.) 19 A king he placed, throgh whose Maiestical Empyre Theese blasts rouze forward, or back by his regal apointment. **1818** *Sporting Mag.* II. 279 The Paddington boy..tried again to rouse in upon Doly's victualling-office.

†12. To rise up, stand on end. *Obs.*⁻¹

1605 SHAKS. *Macb.* V. v. 12 My Fell of haire Would at a dismall Treatise rowze, and stirre As life were in't.

13. To get up from sleep or repose; to waken up.

1605 SHAKS. *Macb.* III. ii. 52 Good things of Day begin to droope, and drowse, Whiles Nights black Agents to their Prey's doe rowse. **1642** MILTON *Apol. Smect.* Wks. 1851 III. 266 Up, and stirring..with the Bird that first rouses. **1682** CREECH *Lucretius* (1683) 131 And softer Curs, that lie and sleep at home, Do often rouse, and walk about the Room. **1707** J. STEVENS tr. *Quevedo's Com. Wks.* (1709) 229 Day came, and we all rouz'd. **1719** DE FOE *Crusoe* II. (Globe) 488 Rouzing..from Sleep with the Noise, I caus'd the Boat to be thrust in. **1882** FLOYER *Unexpl. Baluchistan* 99, I gradually roused up on hearing this, and..put my head out of the tent door. **1890** *Illustr. Lond. News* 13 Dec. 746/1 When I roused, the yellow sun was pouring in at my lattice.

b. *fig.* To become active; to bestir oneself, take heart or courage, etc.

1589 L. WRIGHT *Hunting of Antichrist* 13 Shortly after began to rowse our noble and valiant Lion of England, Henrie the eight of famous memorie. **1611** SPEED *Hist. Gt. Brit.* VII. xxxvi. (1623) 386 Hubba that had harried the English, and now rouzed upon the newes of King Elfred's victory and life. **1624** QUARLES *Job Militant* xix. 6 Rouze up, fond man, and answere my replies. **1740** *Johnson's Debates* (1787) I. 91 It is surely time for this nation to rouse from indolence, and to resolve to put an end to frauds that have been so long known. **1791** COWPER *Iliad* IV. 498 Be it ours to rouse at once To action. **1831** SCOTT *Cast. Dang.* xiii, In God's name, rouse up, sir; let it not be said that [etc.].

c. Of qualities or feelings.

1671 MILTON *Samson* 1690 His fierie vertue rouz'd From under ashes into sudden flame. **1759** ADAM SMITH *Moral Sent.* (1804) I. 181 Our indignation rouses and we are eager to refute..such detestable principles. **1850** THACKERAY *Pendennis* lxxi, Arthur..felt his anger rousing up within him.

rouse (raʊz), *v.*[2] Also *Sc.* and *north.* roose, rooze. [Aphetic form of ARROUSE *v.*]

1. *trans.* To sprinkle (herring, etc.) with salt in the process of curing.

17.. in *Lauder's Suppl. Decis. Lds. Council* IV. 845 His charter not mentioning that it was for export, he was not bound to rouse them with salt upon salt. **1800** *Chron., Ann. Reg.* 110/2 Herrings sprinkled (or as it is termed 'roused or corned') with a moderate quantity of salt will continue perfectly good at least two months. **1854** H. MILLER *Sch. & Schm.* (1858) 43 We could see..the curers going about rousing their fish with salt, to counteract the effects of the dog-day sun. **1894** R. LEIGHTON *Wreck Golden Fleece* 57 While I go below and roose the fish.

2. To cause (water) to overflow (see quot.).

1794 DAVIS *Agric. Wilts* 38 In the catch-meadows..the great object is to keep the 'works of them' as dry as possible between the intervals of watering;..care is necessary to make the most of the water by catching and rousing it as often as possible.

†rouse, *v.*[3] *Obs. rare.* [Of obscure origin.] ? To rest, settle.

1563 FOXE *A. & M.* 1393/2, I was caryed to my Lordes Colehouse agayne, where I with my syxe fellowes do rouse together in the straw, as cherefullye..as other doo in theyr beds of downe. **1616** *Rich Cabinet* 153 The maister of the house began to rouse his shoulders in a rich chaire.

rouse (raʊs), *v.*[4] *Austral.* and *N.Z. colloq.* Also rous. [Cf. ROUST *v.*[1]] *intr.* To scold. Freq. const. *at*, *on*, *onto*: to upbraid (someone). Hence **'rousing** *vbl. sb.*[3]

c **1910** in G. A. WILKES *Dict. Austral. Colloquialisms* (1978) 279/2 *Rouse*, abuse or vilify. **1911** L. STONE *Jonah* v. 47 It's gittin' late; 'ow'll yer ole woman rous w'en yer git 'ome? *Ibid.* xi. 126 'E niver rouses on me. W'en 'e gits shirty, I just laugh, an' 'e can't keep it up. **1915** C. J. DENNIS *Songs of Sentimental Bloke* 88 If she 'ad only roused I might 'a' smiled. She jist seems 'urt an' crushed; not even riled. **1934** V. PALMER *Sea & Spinifex* 182 Combo's one of those sulky devils that forget nothing... Can't take a bit of rousing as part of the day's work. **1940** F. SARGESON *Man & his Wife* 27 Then Mrs Bowman roused on to me for putting too much sugar in her tea. **1951** D. CUSACK *Say No to Death* 30 Auntie used to rouse on me frightfully because I spent so much time on the beach. **1961** R. LAWLER *Piccadilly Bushman* 31 Don't rouse at me, Alec.

rouseabout ('raʊzəbaʊt), *sb.* [f. ROUSE *v.*[1]]

1. *dial.* (See quots. 1778 and 1886.)

1746 *Exmoor Scolding* (E.D.S.) 30 A rubbacrock, rouze-about..swashbucket. **1778** —— *Gloss.*, A Rouzabout, a restless Creature never easy at Home, but roaming from Place to Place. Also, a Sort of large Pease [etc.]. **1886** ELWORTHY *W. Somerset Word-bk.* 633 *Rouse-about*.. implies coarseness, roughness, awkwardness, yet withal bustling activity.

2. *Austral.* and *N.Z.* **a.** A man or boy employed on a sheep station; an odd man on a farm. Cf. ROUSTABOUT *sb.*

1861 [see *fleece-picker* s.v. FLEECE *sb.* 6]. **1881** *Chamb. Jrnl.* Mar. 157 Rouseabouts are men and boys who pen the sheep, pick up the fleeces as they are shorn, sort and pack the wool [etc.]. **1890** *Melbourne Argus* 20 Sept. 13/6 The shearers hold themselves as the aristocrats of the shed, and never associate with the 'rouse-abouts'. **1893** J. A. BARRY *S. Brown's Bunyip* 280 The everlasting drudgery of the rouseabout. **1901** M. FRANKLIN *My Brilliant Career* xvii. 150 Joe Slocombe, the man who acted as groom and rouseabout, was waiting for me. **1909** 'S. RUDD' *From Selection to City* ix. 76 Numbers of shearers and rouseabouts had arrived on the scene before us, and the station was all astir. **1917** A. B. PATERSON *Saltbush Bill* 8 Come all you little rouseabouts and climb upon my knee. **1936** A. RUSSELL *Gone Nomad* iii. 19, I..was able to throw, skirt, and roll a fleece with the crack rouseabout of the shed. **1947** D. M. DAVIN *Gorse blooms Pale* 81 I'm not letting Joe get buggered about by any bloody fly-by-night rouseabout. **1961** *N.Z. Listener* 26 May 8/1 The rouseabout and presser had just finished clearing up. **1966** 'J. HACKSTON' *Father clears Out* 181 As a boy milker, manager, rouseabout, stud-master, and jackeroo on our place I became aware of the prevailing bad manners among some cows.

b. *transf.* An odd-job man or general worker; a casual labourer. *Austral.* and *N.Z.*

1906 E. DYSON *Fact'ry 'Ands* ii. 15 Billy the Boy, the juvenile rouseabout from the printer's flat. **1911** E. M. CLOWES *On Wallaby* iii. 64 It is to land so won and so held that every casual 'rouseabout' or street loafer feels that he has a perfect right. **1933** *Bulletin* (Sydney) 7 June 20/1 The rouseabout at Casey's pub was sacked. **1951** Cusack & James *Come in Spinner* 39 They'll probably stick you in as rouseabouts in a lunatic asylum, seeing the experience you've 'ad 'ere.

c. *attrib.*, as ***rouseabout swiper, work.***
1887 J. Farrell *How he Died* 19 It may be that the rouseabout swiper who rode for the doctor that night Is in Heaven with the Hosts of the Blest, robed and sceptred, and splendid with light. **1906** E. Dyson *Fact'ry 'Ands* xii. 148 A man was engaged to assist at the guillotines and do the rouseabout work of the factory. **1934** J. Lilico *Sheep Dog Mem.* 27 [The dogs] would head, lead, huntaway, force and back, though.. they were best at rouseabout work.

3. ***rouse-about block***, a large snatch-block.
1875 Knight *Dict. Mech.* 2230/1.

rouseabout ('raʊzəbaʊt), *v. Austral.* [f. rouseabout *sb.* 2.] *intr.* To work as a rouseabout. Hence **'rouseabouting** *vbl. sb.*
1914 *Bulletin* (Sydney) 17 Dec. 44/2, I never done no shearin'; but I rouseabouted one year in a shed near Muttaburra. **1945** Baker *Austral. Lang.* ii. iii. 61 We.. now speak of *jackerooing* (just as we speak of *rouseabouting*), for work as a station-hand. **1967** *Southerly* XXVII. 205 Writing, he said, came easier than.. shearing, station rouseabouting.

roused (raʊzd), *ppl. a.*^{1} [f. rouse *v.*^{1} + -ed^1.] Disturbed; aroused, awakened.
1590 Spenser *F.Q.* iii. i. 62 The whole family.. Rashly out of their rouzed couches sprong. **1602** Shaks. *Ham.* ii. ii. 510 So after Pyrrhus pause, A rowsed Vengeance sets him new a-worke. **1716** *Loyal Mourner* 10 And rouz'd Sea-Monsters in the Tempest play. **1820** Shelley *Witch Atl.* l, The flagging wing Of the roused cormorant. **1856** Stonehenge *Brit. Rural Sports* 129/1 The fine fresh scent of a newly-roused fox. **1894** Mrs. H. Ward *Marcella* II. 245 He leant over her in his roused strength.

roused, *ppl. a.*^{2} (See rouse *v.*^{2} 1.)
1899 *Shetland News* 22 July (E.D.D.), Two small cargoes of 'roused' herrings were sent south from Lerwick.

rousedness ('raʊzɪdnɪs, -zd-). *rare.* [f. roused *ppl. a.*^{1} + -ness.] The state of being aroused; a roused condition, alertness.
1915 D. H. Lawrence *Rainbow* iv. 94 And there was a kind of bristling rousedness in the room. *Ibid.* x. 261 Everywhere was a sense of mystery and rousedness.

†**rousee.** *Obs.* [a. OF. *rousee, rosee* (mod.F. *rosée*), ultimately f. L. *rōs*.] Dew.
1481 Caxton *Godfrey* cxl. 208 How oure men reioysed them of a dew or rousee descendyng thenne fro heuen. *Ibid.*, Thenne began to falle a rayne or a dewe, so swete a rousee was neuer seen.

rousement ('raʊzmənt). *U.S.* [f. rouse *v.*^{1} + -ment.] A rousing up of religious excitement.
1883 *Congregationalist* 27 Sept. (Cent.), Deep strong feeling, but no excitement. They are not apt to indulge in any more rousements. **1885** *Home Missionary* Apr. 473 The 'rousement' as the religious excitement was called, was not long in coming.

rouser ('raʊzə(r)). [f. rouse *v.*^{1} + -er^1.]
1. a. One who, or that which, rouses or stirs up.
1611 Cotgr., *Esveilleur*,.. a rowser, a raiser from sleepe. **1612** Shelton *Quix.* i. iii. vi, All this which I have depainted to thee, are inciters and rowsers of my mind. **1783** J. Young *Crit. Gray's Elegy* (1810) 44 The rousers to morning labour are also enumerated as four. **1801** Scott *Glenfinlas* xxxv, Within an hour return'd each hound; In rush'd the rousers of the deer. **1898** Monson *Trop. Dis.* xii. 212 A fine stream of iced water poured on the forehead from an elevation will act as a stimulant and rouser.
b. An implement or apparatus used for stirring (*esp.* beer in brewing).
1765 H. Jackson *Ess. on Brit. Isinglass* 56 Previous to cleansing, conquassate the whole Aggregate with a Rouser. **1830** M. Donovan *Dom. Econ.* I. 165 A vertical rod plunges down the copper... This rod terminates in a horizontal bar, carrying an extended chain, called, on account of its duty, a *rouser*. The rod and rouser are both kept in continual motion. **1839** Ure *Dict. Arts* 585 The inter-mixture may be effected either by lading the glass out of one pot into another ..or by stirring it up with a rouser. **1854** Ronalds & Richardson *Chem. Technol.* (ed. 2) I. 287 The contents can be constantly agitated by the rouser.
attrib. **1839** Ure *Dict. Arts* 116 The rouser shaft may be lifted by means of the chain.
2. a. One who, or that which, is remarkable in some respect.
1839 C. F. Briggs *Adventures H. Franco* I. xiv. 127 We never exchanged another word until we reached the fire, and then, says he to me, I tell you what, Smith, it is going to be a rouser. **1859** Bartlett *Dict. Amer.* (ed. 2) 372 *Rouser*, something very exciting or very great. Thus an eloquent speech or sermon, a large mass-meeting, or a big prize-ox, is a rouser. **1868** *Putnam's Mag.* Jan. 70 He's a rouser to make punch, I assure you. **1895** Crockett in *Cornh. Mag.* Dec. 578 For a' the leers in the pairish—and there are some rousers—ye beat them clean. **1977** *Time* 24 Oct. 8/3 It cleared the way for a rouser of a speech by Thatcher.
b. An outrageous falsehood.
1825–9 Brockett *N.C. Gloss.* s.v. *Ruze*. **1838** Holloway *Prov. Dict.*, *Rouser*, or a Rousing Lie, is such a monstrous lie as rouses the wonder and astonishment of every one who hears it. **1873** Leland *Egypt. Sketch-Bk.* 176, I like a man to tell a rouser while he is about it.
3. A loud noise; a noisy person, song, etc.
1731 Swift *Strephon & Chloe*, He.. Let fly a Rouzer in her Face. **1872** De Vere *Americanisms* 225 The rouser is.. a man who talks very loud and occasionally yells. **1893** Milliken *'Arry Ballads* 64 (Farmer), We made the whole place ring a rouser, till Jolter implored us to stop.
4. *Austral.* = rouseabout *sb.* 2.
1897 H. Lawson *While Billy Boils* 85 They are all shearers, or at least they say they are. Some might be only 'rousers'. **1900** —— *Verses, Popular & Humorous* 168 The 'rouser' has no soul to save. Condemn the rouseabout! **1902** —— *Children of Bush* 241, I must get some more money for the rouser from some of those chaps. *a* **1964** E. Harrington in *Penguin Bk. Austral. Ballads* (1964) 262 The rousers gave a billycan and brand new tucker bag.

rousette, variant of roussette.

rousie ('raʊzɪ). *Austral.* and *N.Z. colloq.* Also **roussie, rousy.** [Abbrev. of rouseabout.] = rouseabout *sb.* 2.
1933 *Bulletin* (Sydney) 29 Nov. 20/1 The rousie entered the office to be paid off. **1952** [see dagger *sb.*^{2} b]. **1956** F. B. Vickers *First Place to Stranger* ix. 135 He tried to run all the rousies till Ivor stopped him. *a* **1964** H. P. Tritton in *Penguin Bk. Austral. Ballads* (1964) 228 Then try to catch the rousy's eye, and softly whisper, 'Tar'. **1966** G. W. Turner *Eng. Lang. Austral. & N.Z.* vii. 147 There are names for woolshed workers,.. the *rousie* or rouseabout and the *sheepo* who fills the catching pens.

rousing ('raʊzɪŋ), *vbl. sb.*^{1} [f. rouse *v.*^{1} + -ing^1.] The action of the verb in various senses.
c **1580** Jeffere *Bugbears* Epil., With sowcynges, with rowsynges, with bownsynges. **1587** Golding *De Mornay* xvii. (1617) 290 A rouzing of her feathers & a vaine flapping of her wings. **1627** Capt. Smith *Seaman's Gram.* vii. 31 Rousing is.. pulling the slacknesse of any Cables with mens hands into the Ship. **1634** W. Burton (*title*), The Rowsing of the Sluggard. Deliuered in seuen Sermons. **1719** Baynard *Health* (1740) 19 Ferments in the body pent, which early rowzing may prevent. **1756** Burke *Subl. & B.* Wks. I. 265 That without this rousing they would become languid and diseased. **1823** J. Badcock *Dom. Amusem.* 22 The addition of lime to the pyrolignous acid.. is done in a large vessel by frequent rousings up. *c* **1870** Stubbs *Lect. Europ. Hist.* ii. x. (1904) 258 A sort of rousing appears to take place.

'rousing, *vbl. sb.*^{2} [f. rouse *v.*^{2}] The action of sprinkling, etc.
1706 A. Boyer *Ann. Q. Anne* IV. 51 The clause relating to the rousing of herrings with foreign salt. **1842** J. Wilson *Voy. Scotl.* II. 158 The necessities of gutting and rousing. **1887** Moloney *Forestry W. Afr.* 127 It is recommended that new resins should be subject to a rough sifting and rousing in common soda-and-water.

rousing ('raʊzɪŋ), *ppl. a.* [f. rouse *v.*^{1}]
In the following quotation the precise sense is not clear.
1606 *Wily Beguiled* E ij, Ile.. wrap me in a rousing Calue-skin suite, and come like some Hob-goblin, or some Diuell Ascended from the grisly pit of Hell.
1. That rouses, awakens, or stirs up.
1641 Milton *Animadv.* Wks. 1851 III. 230 Against negligence or obstinacy will be requir'd a rousing volie of Pastorly threatning. **1665** Boyle *Occas. Refl.* iv. ix. (1848) 222 The careless Sensualists, that fly a rowzing Sermon. **1755** *Connoisseur* No. 92 ¶8 Justice Silence.. has no sooner swallowed the rousing cup, than he roars out a catch. **1791** Mrs. Radcliffe *Rom. Forest* ii, He gave the fire a rousing stir. **1889** *Spectator* 14 Dec. 830 He was the most rousing of our poets.
transf. **1799** Robertson *Agric. Perth* 181 A rousing furrow should be given to it, and the rough stubble turned down.
2. a. Of a lie: Outrageous, gross.
1664 H. More *Myst. Iniq.* viii. 133 It were likewise a good roosing miracle, and bigger then belief, that a certain Holy House.. should be carried out of Palestine into Italy. **1677** Coles *Eng.-Lat. Dict.*, A rousing lye, *mendacium magnificum.* **1706** Phillips (ed. Kersey), *Rousing Lie*, a whisking great one. **1791** Burns *Death & Dr. Hornbook* i, Ev'n Ministers, they hae been kenn'd.. A rousing whid, at times, to vend. **1828** Carr *Craven Gloss.*
b. Of a fire: Roaring, blazing strongly.
1682 Tate *Abs. & Achit.* ii. 547 For our wise rabble ne'er took pains to inquire, What 'twas he burnt, so it made a rousing fire. **1760–72** H. Brooke *Fool of Qual.* (1809) II. 151 The weather was very cold.., and I had a rousing fire. **1838** Dickens *Lett.* (1880) I. 9 A rousing fire halfway up the chimney. **1887** R. N. Carey *Uncle Max* vi, Come into the parlor: there is a fine rousing fire that will soon warm you.
c. Of trade, etc.: Brisk, lively.
1767 Sterne *Tr. Shandy* ix. v, A Jew.. had the ill luck to die of a strangury, and leave his widow in possession of a rousing trade. **1895–** in *Eng. Dial. Dict.* in various contexts.
3. Of the nature of, connected with, awakening or rising.
1671 Milton *Samson* 1382, I begin to feel Some rouzing motions in me. **1712–14** Pope *Rape Lock* i. 15 Now lapdogs give themselves the rowsing shake.
4. That is awakening or rising.
1821 Clare *Vill. Minstr.* I. 13 Meeting objects from the rousing farm.
Hence **'rousingly** *adv.*
1664 H. More *Myst. Iniq.* 376 To act more rousingly. **1847** Webster, *Rousingly*, violently, excitingly.

Rousseauan (ruː'səʊən), *a.* (*sb.*) [f. the name of the French author Jean Jacques *Rousseau* (1712–78).] Pertaining to Rousseau or his views on religion, politics, education, etc. Also as *sb.* So **Rousseau'esque** *a.*^{1}, **Rou'sseauian, Rou'sseauish** *adjs.*; similarly **Rousseau'istic, Rou'sseauvian** *adjs.*; **Rou'sseauism,** the principles or doctrines of Rousseau; **Rousseau'arian, Rou'sseauist** (also as *adj.*), **Rou'sseauite,** one who follows Rousseau.
1775 H. Walpole *Let.* 3 Apr. (1904) IX. 174 The Rousseaurians [*sic*] will imagine that I interpolated the condemnation of his *Eloïse.* **1806** J. Mackintosh *Let.* 24 Dec. in R. J. Mackintosh *Mem. Life Sir J. Mackintosh* (1835) I. vi. 306 It is certainly a most ingenious, and the only reasonable, modification of the Lockian and Rousseauvian principle. **1865** *Pall Mall G.* 12 Dec. 10 It is mere Rousseauism which induces men.. to overlook the former while they reprobate the latter. **1873** Morley *Rousseau* II. 132 Writing Rousseau-ite essays. **1879** Dowden *Southey* 53 A creature overflowing with Rousseauish sensibility. **1881** *World* 28 Dec., His confessions.. are not at all Rousseauian, save, perhaps, in style. **1889** *Q. Rev.* Apr. 545 This Rousseauan fiction of man's essential goodness. **1889** *Cent. Dict.*, *Rousseauist*.., a follower or an admirer of J. J. Rousseau. **1905** H. G. Wells *Mod. Utopia* v. 171 The sweetish, faintly nasty slops of Rousseauism. **1914** *Blast* 20 June 18 Blast.. Rousseauisms (wild Nature cranks). **1928** C. Hollis *Dr. Johnson* iii. 67 The Rousseauan argument was that man was good. *Ibid.* 68 Rousseauans had been responsible for the generalisation that man was good. **1930** H. Read *Wordsworth* iii. 131 They had taken a ward to educate.. but they did not take their duties any more seriously than a pair of Rousseauites should. **1935** D. Fahey *Mystical Body of Christ in Mod. World* iv. 30 The Rousseauist dogma of the natural goodness of man. *a* **1937** J. L. Stocks *Reason & Intuition* (1939) vi. 84 In modern times the Rousseauistic strain still survives. **1937** 'C. Caudwell' *Illusion & Reality* v. 98 Wordsworth, like Shelley profoundly influenced by French Rousseauism. **1938** R. Graves *Coll. Poems* 96 And being no Rousseauist, Nor artists-of-the-world-unite. **1947** A. Einstein *Mus. Romantic Era* xviii. 339 This Rousseauesque theory of the linguistic origin of music, basically wrong as it is, still reappears even in professional psychological literature of the 19th century. **1962** Gregor & Nicholas *Moral & Story* v. 144 This somewhat Rousseauistic view of nature contrasts strangely with the determinist one, which Hardy runs alongside it. **1962** C. Walsh *From Utopia to Nightmare* ix. 126 Americans are Rousseauans by temperament. **1965** M. Hodgart *Faber Bk. Ballads* 12 We are all Rousseauists or Wordsworthians to the degree that we are discontented with the artificiality of our culture. **1967** B. W. Alderson tr. *Hürlimann's Three Cent. Children's Bks. in Europe* ix. 120 The Romanticism and Rousseau-ish idealism in books about America and the Indians. **1969** J. Mander *Static Society* 170 The 'good' Indian myth of Rousseauvian Europe. **1971** Rousseauian [see *neo-primitivism* s.v. neo- 1 a]. **1971** G. Steiner *Bluebeard's Castle* i. 24 What needs close attention is the extent to which critiques of urban society tend to become indictments of all formal, complex civilization as such ('civilization', of course, has in it the word for city). Rousseauist naturalism has an obvious destructive edge. **1974** *Listener* 21 Mar. 372/3 The editor of his [*sc.* Aaron Burr's] journal calls it 'Rousseauistic'... Couldn't one just call it unselfconscious? **1977** *Times Lit. Suppl.* 11 Feb. 148/2 The Machiavellian and Rousseauesque hints of subordination of church to state. **1977** in *Private Eye* 10 June 5/2 In the name of directness, of authenticity, of courage, of any number of Rousseauian virtues that belong exclusively to the noble savage. **1977** *Listener* 16 June 790/3 Throngs of Indonesians who.. appear to conform to the most elevated models of Rousseauvian *noblesse.* **1978** *Dædalus* Summer 2 The Rousseauan longing for a pastoral idyll is not yet dead.

Rousseauesque (ruːsəʊ'ɛsk), *a.*^{2} [f. the name of Henri 'le Douanier' *Rousseau* (1844–1910), French primitive painter + -esque.] Characteristic of the style of Rousseau.
1962 *Guardian* 9 July 5/3 She is also extremely successful in depicting Rousseau-esque foliage. **1978** A. Huxley *Illustr. Hist. Gardening* iii. 76 (*caption*) This Rousseauesque painting from the Jodphur [*sic*] school depicts a lush private garden.

rousset, obs. form of russet.

‖**roussette** (ruː'sɛt). [F., a derivative of OF. *rous* (F. *roux*) red.]
1. The frugivorus bat, *Pteropus vulgaris.*
1774 Goldsm. *Nat. Hist.* (1862) I. 473 Of foreign bats, the largest we have any certain accounts of, is the Roussette, or the Great Bat of Madagascar. **1781** Pennant *Hist. Quadrup.* II. 550 Many of the Roussettes are of an enormous size. **1833** *Penny Cycl.* I. 184/1 The common roussette.., which inhabits Madagascar and the Isle of France. **1839** *Cuvier's Anim. Kingd.* I. 70/2 Some of the Cheiroptera, such as the Roussette Bats. **1845** *Encycl. Metrop.* XXIII. 670/2 [The] Edible Roussette is the largest of the genus.
2. A shark of the family *Scylliidæ.*
1882 Jordan & Gilbert *Synop. Fishes N. Amer.* 58 *Scylliidæ* (The Roussettes).
3. A white wine produced primarily in the French departments of Savoy and Jura.
1926 P. M. Shand *Bk. of Wine* v. 171 Frangy and Digny-Musièges belong to the more or less immediate neighbourhood of Seyssel, as does also a good, rusty-coloured wine called Roussette, named after the informing grape of the Savoy vineyards. **1946** G. Millar *Horned Pigeon* xx. 309 With the *fondue* we drank *Roussette*, an excellent local white wine which was then new to me. **1967** A. Lichine *Encycl. Wines* 459/1 *Roussette*, the principal wine of Seyssel, in Haute-Savoie, France. It is white, flinty-dry, and made from Roussette grapes. **1968** *Vogue* 15 Apr. 121/1 To the South of the Jura lie the vineyards of the Savoy. Both red and white wines are grown, but it is the latter that are worth looking for, especially seyssel and.. crépy and roussette.

roussie, var. rousie.

‖**Roussillon** (rusijɔ̃). [See def.] A red wine made in the old province of Roussillon (now the department of Pyrénées-Orientales) in the south of France.
1768 *Phil. Trans.* LXI. 287 The Malaga, Migraine, Roussillon, began to freeze. **1865** 'Ouida' *Strathmore* II. xxii. 281 Draughts of fierce Roussillon, or above-proof cognac.

‖**roussin.** *rare*⁻¹. [F.] = ROUNCY¹.

1653 URQUHART *Rabelais* I. xxiii, He rode a Naples courser, a Dutch roussin, a Spanish gennet.

roust (raʊst), *sb.*¹ Now *Sc.* Forms: 3 rowwst, 5 rowste, 6, 9 roust. [a. ON. *raust* (Norw. *raust*, Fær. *reyst*, Sw. *röst*, Da. *røst*) voice.] Voice, cry; shout, roar.

c **1200** ORMIN 9197 þe rowwst iss herrd off ænne mann þatt epeþþ þuss i wesste. *a* **1400-50** *Alexander* 488 Anectanabus..drafe thurȝe þe sale With slike a rowste & rerid. **1513** DOUGLAS *Æneis* IV. Prol. 67 The feildis all doith of thar roustis resound. **1808** JAMIESON, *Roust*, the act of roaring or bellowing. *c* **1820** G. BEATTIE *John of Arnha* (1882) 34 (E.D.D.), To ilk bellow, roust and roar.

roust (raʊst), *sb.*² *N. Amer.* (orig. *Criminals'*) *slang.* [f. ROUST *v.*²] The act of jostling (see quot. 1942); harassment, roughing up, esp. by the police; a police raid.

1942 BERREY & VAN DEN BARK *Amer. Thes. Slang* §490/5 *Roust, rousting, rowdy-dowdy*, the act of causing a crush in a crowd or jostling the victim in order to pick his pockets. **1961** RIGNEY & SMITH *Real Bohemia* p. xvi, *Roust, a*, a bust, an arrest, a raid. **1978** R. THOMAS *Chinaman's Chance* xxiii. 234 'I'm.. your friendly, conscientious chief of police.' Wu nodded slowly. 'And this is a roust, huh?'

roust (raʊst), *v.*¹ *Sc.* [f. ROUST *sb.* Cf. Norw. *rausta, rousta*, in the same sense.] *intr.* To shout, bellow, roar, make a loud noise.

1513 DOUGLAS *Æneis* X. vi. 79 As Pharon cryis and dois rowst Wyth haltand wordis. *Ibid.* XII. xii. 69 Of thar rowsting all the large plane And woddis rank rowtis and lowis agane. **1813** W. BEATTIE *Poems* (1871) 34, I hear the stirkies roustin'. **1819** TENNANT *Papistry Storm'd* (1827) 119 He had a trumpet braw, Whairwi' he 'gan to roust and blaw. *Mod.* Dinna roust an' roar like that.

roust (raʊst), *v.*² orig. *dial.* and *U.S.* [? Alteration of ROUSE *v.*¹] **1. a.** *trans.* To rout *out*; to rouse or stir *up*, to raise or arouse (*from* one's bed, etc.).

1658 D. LUPTON *Flanders* 9 Who will..ere long roust them out of this Hole, and make them look out another kennel. **1850** W. COLTON *Deck & Port* 299 We rousted our anchors this afternoon from the bed in which they have slumbered for the last six weeks. **1858** BEECHER *Life Thoughts* (1859) 115 To roust out all the vermin and the nibbling mice and turn up the yellow dirt to the sun. **1871** J. HAY *Little Breeches* 12 But we rousted up some torches, And sarched for 'em far and near. **1883** *Peterson Mag.* June 469/2 Awhile ago you was all rousted-up about goin' to New York village to see Mrs. Larne. **1890** H. M. STANLEY *In Darkest Africa* I. xiii. 333 They were thoroughly rousted out, and their camps were destroyed. **1905** J. C. LINCOLN *Partners of Tide* xi. 221 'Now, then,' he added, 'while we're waitin' for the tide to turn we might's well roust out a little more of the cargo.' **1939** J. STEINBECK *Grapes of Wrath* 123 Don't roust your faith bird-high an' you won't do no crawlin' with the worms. **1972** E. WIGGINTON *Foxfire Bk.* 169 You get up and roust up your fire. **1978** R. LUDLUM *Holcroft Covenant* xliii. 496 I've been rousted from my bed to take additional scrapings from the dead man's room.

b. *intr.* To get *up*, turn *out*; to rummage *around*.

1884 J. C. HARRIS *Mingo & Other Sk.* 162 It twon't never do in the roun' worl' for to be a-makin' faces at 'im frum the groun'. Roust up, roust up. **1900** C. C. MUNN *Uncle Terry* 172, I ginerally roust out by daylight. **1912** R. A. WASON *Friar Tuck* 67, I knew it was my duty to roust out an' keep Horace from gettin' more sleep'n my treatment for his nerves called for. **1941** J. STREET *In my Father's House* i. 19 Suppose you were a dominecker rooster—I mean hen... And you were in a coop and just outside the coop was a heap of grass that you wanted to roust around in. **1977** 'O. JACKS' *Autumn Heroes* v. 67 He made them go over the check lists with him... He rousted around.

2. To jostle (see quot. 1942); (esp. of police) to harass, rough up. *N. Amer.* (orig. *Criminals'*) *slang.*

1904 'No. 1500' *Life in Sing Sing* 252/1 *Roust*, to jostle. **1942** BERREY & VAN DEN BARK *Amer. Thes. Slang* §490/12 *Roust*,..to cause a crush in a crowd or jostle the victim in order to pick his pockets. **1972** J. WAMBAUGH *Blue Knight* (1973) v. 68, I can't take this kind of heat. I can't take being rousted and hurt. **1976** N. THORNBURG *Cutter & Bone* viii. 193 He ran into Sergeant Verdugo, one of the detectives who had rousted him the night of the murder. **1978** *Globe & Mail* (Toronto) 11 Jan. 8/1 Like one afternoon last spring,.. when plain-clothes cops are rousting us when we're trying to do business. At the same time the bank at Church and Carleton gets robbed and the robber got away on foot.

roust (raʊst), *v.*³ *Austral. colloq.* [var. of ROUSE *v.*⁴; cf. ROUST *v.*¹] *intr.* = ROUSE *v.*⁴ Also with quasi-obj. in phr. *to roust hell out of.* Hence **'rousting** *vbl. sb.*¹

1916 C. J. DENNIS *Songs of Sentimental Bloke* 124 *Roust* or *rouse*, to upbraid with many words. **1918** —— *Digger Smith* 82 All me roustin' leaves 'em both serene. **1938** X. HERBERT *Capricornia* xviii. 250 'All dem sister proper humbug.' 'How's that?' 'All time roustin'. All time tink we go out wid boys. We no can talk boys. But dem sister proper mad long boys demself.' **1941** S. CAMPION *Mo Burdekin* 139 And 'avin 'im roust hell outa me for it. **1970** P. WHITE *Vivisector* i. 11 He hung around Mumma, waiting for her to settle, and she didn't roust on him.

roust, obs. form of ROOST, RUST.

roustabout ('raʊstəbaʊt), *sb.* [f. ROUST *v.*²] **1.** *U.S.* A wharf labourer or deck hand.

1868 *Putnam's Mag.* Sept. 342 As the steamer was leaving the levée, about forty black deck-hands or 'roustabouts' gathered at the bows. **1872** DE VERE *Americanisms* 225 The Western rough is frequently a roustabout. **1891** C. ROBERTS *Adrift Amer.* 216 On all these river boats most of the men employed are what is termed roustabouts, and are just ordinary labourers who are picked up anywhere.

2. a. orig. *U.S.* A handy man. Cf. ROUSEABOUT *sb.* 2. Also, a casual or unskilled labourer; a vagrant or layabout.

1877 *Harper's Weekly* 17 Mar. 3/3 The vagabonds, the roustabouts, the criminals, and all the dregs of society seem to be Democrats. **1880** A. A. HAYES *New Colorado* v. 77 He was a kind of rostabout [*sic*], or dish-washer, to a camping outfit. **1883** *Longm. Mag.* June 178 This poor young man had been a 'roustabout' hand on a station. **1883** 'MARK TWAIN' *Life on Mississippi* li. 454 Do you mean the Roman army?—those six sandalled roustabouts in nightshirts? **1896** *Daily Chron.* 15 Aug. 11/1, I was working on a Queensland gold-field once, first as 'feeder' and general 'roustabout', then as engine-driver. **1896** J. MCDOUGALL *Saddle, Sled & Snowshoe* xv. 187, I have been Mr. Woolsey's interpreter, guide, and general 'roust-about', his confidante and friend, for the past two years. **1911** H. S. HARRISON *Queed* 35 It takes a Whitney to invent the cotton gin, but the dullest negro roustabout can operate it. *a* **1918** G. STUART *40 Yrs. on Frontier* (1925) II. 179 Every man, whether owner of the largest herd or a humble roustabout, takes his orders from the captain. **1942** E. H. PAUL *Narrow St.* xix. 152 Butchers, roustabouts and helpers..toiled steadily in the lamplight. **1960** H. MILLER *Nexus* (1964) xiv. 237 I've got a good wife, only we're temperamentally unsuited to one another. I'm too common for her. Too much of a roustabout.

b. *spec.* A workman in a circus. *N. Amer.*

1931 *Amer. Mercury* Nov. 353/2 *Razorbacks*,..Workmen who load and unload the circus train; never called *roustabouts* or *flunkeys*. **1949** *Los Angeles Times* 9 Apr. 2/3 Roustabouts from the Clyde Beatty circus appeared to offer any manual labor needed. **1957** *Harper's Bazaar* Feb. 175 He may earn his living as a petty criminal, a hobo, a carnival roustabout or a free-lance moving man in Greenwich Village. **1976** *Telegraph-Jrnl.* (St. John, New Brunswick) 4 Sept. 32/1 From a carnival *roustabout* to owner of the show in 25 years.

3. A general or manual labourer on an oil installation.

1948 H. L. MENCKEN *Amer. Lang.* Suppl. II. 763 *Roustabout*, a laborer on an oil lease, not a member of the rig crew. **1959** LARSON & PORTER *Hist. Humble Oil & Refining Co.* xii. 291 The next annual crop of new engineers was.. put to work for a year as roughnecks or roustabouts. **1971** C. SIMPSON *New Australia* 518 The average young oilfield worker, called a 'roustabout', needed to have more than muscles. Technical competence was also called for. **1972** L. M. HARRIS *Introd. Deepwater Floating Drilling Operations* iv. 35 Drilling and roustabout crew requirements differ little from rig to rig. **1975** *Offshore Engineer* Dec. 54/1 (Advt.), The clothing was tested on the rig Sedco 700, operating close to the 62nd parallel, by supervisors and roustabouts on the nightshift.

roustabout ('raʊstəbaʊt), *v.* [f. prec.] *intr.* To be, or work as, a roustabout.

1907 'O. HENRY' in *Everybody's Mag.* Nov. 593/1, I hurried the rest of the way up the river, roustabouting on a lower coast packet that made a landing for every fisherman that wanted a plug of tobacco. **1934** in *Amer. Ballads & Folk Songs* 494 When Jack is old and weather-beat, Too old to roustabout.

'rouster. [f. ROUST *v.*²] **1.** *U.S.* = ROUSTABOUT *sb.* 1.

1883 *American* VI. 40 Men..who used to be rousters, and are now broken down and played out. **1929** B. L. BURMAN *Mississippi* iii. 47 A rouster, with two coffee sacks tied around his body..lay on the boiler deck strumming a guitar. **1938** —— *Blow for Landing* xiv. 236 Barrels began to roll swiftly down the gang-plank, like a bass-drum accompaniment for the feet of the negro rousters. **1941** [see COONJINE *sb.* and *v.*].

2. *U.S.* and *Austral.* = ROUSTABOUT *sb.* 2.

1890 in BARRÈRE & LELAND *Dict. Slang.* **1911** C. E. W. BEAN *'Dreadnought' of Darling* xxxviii. 338 There tumbled out of it all the sweepings of Sydney, all the old cripples, and beggars, and rousters in Christendom.

rousti, obs. form of RUSTY.

rousting *vbl. sb.*¹: see ROUST *v.*³

rousting ('raʊstɪŋ), *vbl. sb.*² *U.S. colloq.* [f. ROUST *v.*² + -ING¹.] (An act of) police harassment, a police raid (see also quot. 1942).

1942 BERREY & VAN DEN BARK *Amer. Thes. Slang* §490/5 *Rousting*,..the act of causing a crush in a crowd or jostling the victim in order to pick his pockets. **1960** *Washington Post* 25 Jan. 1 There's more vice on Pacific Heights and Nob Hill and there's no rousting (police raiding) up there. **1968** S. ELLIN *Valentine Estate* II. vi. 51 Rousting was the word for it. Keep pushing a man until he either left the territory or did something he could be nailed for. **1972** B. GARFIELD *Line of Succession* I. 75 The prisoners each morning complained to their lawyers of the nightly roustings. **1975** *High Times* Dec. 31/1 So far, however, the little hungo town has been spared the midnight roustings.

roustlynge, obs. form of RUSTLING.

rousty, obs. form of RUSTY.

rousy, var. ROUSIE.

rout (raʊt), *sb.*¹ Forms: α. 3-4 rute, 4 rut(te; 3- route, 4-7 rowte, 5 rouwte, 5-6 routte; 4- rout (6 routt), 4-7 rowt. β. 3 rouȝte, 5 roughte; 4 rouht, 5-6 rought; 5 rowght, 5-6 rowth. [a. AF. *rute*, OF. *route* (also *rote, rotte*, whence ROT *sb.*²):—L. *rupta*, fem. of *ruptus* broken, the original sense being 'division, detachment'.]

I. 1. A company, assemblage, band, or troop of persons. Now chiefly *poet.*

In later use usually with some tinge of sense 5.

12.. *Ancr. R.* 92 Ure Lefdi mid hire meidenes, & al þe englene uerd [*C.* rute]. *a* **1300** *Cursor M.* 13503 þis bred and fische was delt a-bute, Had nan defaut in al þat rute. *c* **1386** CHAUCER *Knt.'s T.* 1636 To the paleys rood ther many a route Of lordes, vp on steedes and palfreys. *c* **1430** LYDG. *Min. Poems* (Percy Soc.) 104 Beneth them sat clarkes a great rout, Which fast dyd wryte. *c* **1450** *Mirour Saluacioun* (Roxb.) 149 Telle nowe of alle this rovte be prophie who stroke the. **1523** SKELTON *Garl. Laurel* 240 To se if Skelton wyll put hymselfe in prease Amonge the thickeste of all the hole rowte. **1553** BRENDE *Q. Curtius* Ff vij, The souldiours were not sturred to eny sedicion, but repayred by rowtes unto theyr capitaynes. **1600** FAIRFAX *Tasso* XI. ii, The helpe obtaine Of all the blessed of the heau'nly rout. **1616** B. JONSON *Forrest* iii, The rout of rurall folke come thronging in. **1710** J. PHILIPS *Pastorals* i. 25 'Mong rustick Routs the chief for wanton Game. **1810** SCOTT *Lady of L.* III. xx, A blithesome rout, that morning tide, Had sought the chapel of St. Bride. *a* **1839** PRAED *Poems* (1864) II. 39 And now, amid that female rout, What scandal doth he buzz about? **1866-7** J. THOMSON *Naked Goddess* 25 All the people swarming out, Young and old a joyous rout.

b. A number of animals going together; a pack, flock, herd, etc. Now *rare.*

c **1275** LAY. 2598 þar he balu funde vppen one route of wolues awedde. ? *a* **1366** CHAUCER *Rom. Rose* 909 Nyghtyngales a full grete Route, That flyen ouer his heed aboute. **1377** LANGL. *P. Pl.* B. Prol. 146 Wiþ þat ran þere a route of ratones at ones. *c* **1440** *Pallad. on Husb.* I. 851 Al the route [of snails, etc.] A trayne of chalk or askis holdith oute. **1486** *Bk. St. Albans* e ij, My chylde, callith..a Rowte of Wolues where thay passin inne. **1576** TURBERV. *Venerie* 100 Of fallow beasts the company is called an heard, and of blacke beasts it is called a rout, or a Sounder. **1598** MANWOOD *Lawes Forest* iv. (1615) 45 Foresters and good woodmen do use to say..A rout of Wolfes. **1674** JOSSELYN *Two Voy.* 67 They commonly go in routs, a rout of wolves is 12 or more. *a* **1732** GAY *Fables* II. ii, Around him throng the feather'd rout. **1774** J. BRYANT *Mythol.* II. 365 Nothing can represent more happily..the rout of animals first bursting from their place of confinement. **1821** CLARE *Vill. Minstr.* I. 89 Noisy bark of shepherds' dogs, The restless routs of sheep to stop.

c. A large number or collection of things.

? *a* **1366** CHAUCER *Rom. Rose* 1667 To pulle a Rose of all that Route To bere in myn honde aboute. **1390** GOWER *Conf.* II. 296 His Ape..hadde gadred al aboute Of stickes hiere and there a route. **1513** DOUGLAS *Æneis* VIII. v. 53 The serpent of Lern..of heidis wyth hyr mekle rout. **1561** T. NORTON *Calvin's Inst.* IV. 151 That which is of God scarcely glimmereth through at holes, among the rout of the inuentions of men. **1624** CAPT. SMITH *Virginia* II. 39 With an infernall rout of words and actions.

†**2.** Without article: Assemblage, gathering, array, etc. Chiefly in prepositional phrases. *Obs.*

c **1275** LAY. 25416 Sone a-ȝein come cnihtes to route, mid wepne wel idiht. *c* **1290** *S. Eng. Leg.* I. 101/14 Folk wende þudere..bi manie scor to-gadere... þo seinte lucie þis i-saiȝ al dai so gret route [etc.]. *a* **1300** *Cursor M.* 7537 Quen dauid went him forth in route, He sagh þe folk, þai war in dute. *c* **1375** *Sc. Leg. Saints* xxiv. (*Alexis*) 516 In ilke syd þai gadryt owt, to thet sancte, In-to gret rowt. *c* **1430** *Hymns Virgin* (1867) 84 At mydday y was dubbid knyȝt, In route y lerned for to ryde. *c* **1440** *York Myst.* xix. 149 Gars gadir in grete rowte Youre knyghtis kene be-lyue. **1609** SKENE *Reg. Maj.* 136 Na man within burgh dwelland, salbe bound in man-rent, nor ryde in rout, in feir of weir, with any man.

†**b.** *in rout*, in succession, in order. *Obs.*

c **1375** *Cursor M.* 7047 (Fairf.), Esebon..toke israel to lede and loke; he led ham vij ȝere in rowte. *c* **1450** *Bk. Curtasye* 670 in *Babees Bk.*, þenne comes þe pantere with loues thre, ..And saller y-coueryd and sett in route; With þo ouemast lofe hit shalle be sett.

3. *in* (or *on*) *a rout*, in a troop, body, etc.

a **1300** *Cursor M.* 5155 þai come all wit in a rutte [*Gött.* apon a route]. **1387** TREVISA *Higden* (Rolls) I. 409 They leueþ so esiliche in a rowte, þat seelde þey bereþ purse aboute. *c* **1400** *26 Pol. Poems* 143, I fonde there byrdys with feders shene, Many oon sittyng apon a rowte. **1423** JAS. I *Kingis Q.* cliii, Lytill fischis..In a rout can swym So prattily. *c* **1500** *Lancelot* 2956 Furth by o syd assemblyng on a rout Whar that one hundereth knychtis was, & mo. **1513** DOUGLAS *Æneis* I. iv. 51 The mekle hirdis followit in a rowt. *a* **1529** SKELTON *E. Rummyng* 362 There came an hepe Of mylstones in a route.

4. An attendant company; a suite, retinue, train.

a **1300** *Cursor M.* 5311 Iacob went þan wit his rute, His tuelue him al abute. **13..** *K. Alis.* 181 (Laud MS.), Forþ she ferde, myd her route. *c* **1430** *Syr Gener.* (Roxb.) 116 In his route He broght .iii. M¹ knightes stoute. *c* **1477** CAXTON *Jason* 118 As Peleus and the gentill men of his route sawe the noble flees..they were all ameruailed. **1538** LELAND *Itin.* (1769) VI. 35 Willyam Tresham..was cruelly slayne by one Salisbyri and Glin of Wales with their Route. **1577-87** HOLINSHED *Chron.* I. 9/1 An Ile..Most meet where thou maist plant thy selfe with all thy rout. **1763** J. BROWN *Poetry & Mus.* vi. 108 The accidental Adventure of Thespis and his Rout.

II. 5. A disorderly, tumultuous, or disreputable crowd of persons.

c **1290** *S. Eng. Leg.* I. 211/392 þare comen blaste op of þe putte, deuelene a gret rouȝte. **13..** *E.E. Allit. P.* B. 1782 þenne ran þay in on a res, on rowtes ful grete. **1399** LANGL. *Rich. Redeles* I. 16 By rewthles routus þat ryffled euere. *c* **1450** *St. Cuthbert* (Surtees) 5265 Of men and women so grete a route, And childer, lay þe kirke aboute, And made slyke noys and cry. **1538** STARKEY *England* I. iii. 77 Loke what an idul route our nobul men kepe and nurysch in theyr housys. **1568** GRAFTON *Chron.* II. 119 Foulkes.. assemblyng together a great rowte of Ruffians and Robbers issued out of the Castell of Bedford. **1621** BURTON *Anat. Mel.* I. ii. III. xv. (1651) 135 An honest man knows not in what sort..to carry himself with credit in so vile a rout. **1655** MILTON *Soc. Defence* 291 A hireling rout scraped together from the dregs of the people. **1737** WHISTON *Josephus, Antiq.* XIV. xi. §5 Hyrcanus..alledged that a rout of strangers ought not to be admitted. **1750** JOHNSON *Rambler*

No. 48 ⁋9 To the noisy route of bacchanalian rioters. **1816** SCOTT *Old Mort.* xxxiv, 'Ay—the trumpeter to the long-ear'd route, I suppose,' replied Claverhouse. **1854** MILMAN *Lat. Chr.* VI. iii. (1864) III. 478 A great rout, at least 5000, ..marched forth to Settimo. **1876** BANCROFT *Hist. U.S.* I. xiv. 450 Revelling with a luxurious and abandoned rout.

b. *Law.* An assemblage of three or more persons proceeding to commit an unlawful act.

[**1379–80** *Rolls of Parlt.* III. 81 Les routes & assembles venantz issint hors de Gales. *Ibid.*, Que en cest present Parlement les ditz Mesfesours, & les Route-leders, soient restreintz de lour grante malice.]

1429 *Rolls of Parlt.* IV. 345/2 The saide trespassours come ..with grettur rowtes and riotes thenne ever thay dede byfore. **1464** *Cov. Leet Bk.* 331 If any personnes..vexe thair neyghbours, oure subgittes, with-in oure seid Cite,..or make any Routes or conuenticles within the same. **1530–1** *Act 22 Hen. VIII*, c. 15 All ryottes, rowtes, and vnlawfull assemblies committed and done aboue the nomber of twenty persones. **1581** LAMBARDE *Eiren.* II. v. (1588) 185 A Route is a disordered assembly of three or moe persons, mooving forward to commit by force an unlawfull acte. **1641** in Rushw. *Hist. Coll.* III. (1692) I. 465 All good and lawful ways and means for preventing of Tumults and Routs. **1682** *Sec. Plea Nonconformists* Ded. A 3 b, Punish not Religious Assemblies of peaceable Men, under the odious names of Routs and Riots. **1743** in Wesley *Jrnl.* (1749) 120 Several disorderly persons, stiling themselves Methodist-preachers, go about, raising routs and riots. **1774** JEFFERSON *Autobiog.* Wks. 1859 I. 140 Our laws, for the suppression and punishment of riots, routs, and unlawful assemblies. **1841** *Penny Cycl.* XX. 17/1 Two minor offences of rout and unlawful assembly, which are similar to riot, are generally treated on under that head. **1886** *Encycl. Brit.* XX. 564/2 A rout is an unlawful assembly which has made a motion towards the execution of its common purpose.

6. The whole number of persons constituting a certain (disreputable) class.

a **1400** *Minor Poems fr. Vernon MS.* 598/532 Doute wel more wikked men, And come not in heore route. *c* **1410** *Sir Cleges* 261 (W.), Thou chorle, withdrawe the smertly,..Go stond in beggers rowght! *c* **1480** *Cokwolds Daunce* 227 in Hazl. *E.P.P.* I. 47 Many schall dance in the cokwolds rowte, Both by nyght and day. **1561** T. NORTON *Calvin's Inst.* I. 65 The deuell and all the route of the wicked. **1579** E. K. *Ded. Spenser's Sheph. Cal.*, I scorne and spue out the rake-hellye route of our ragged rymers. **1616** R. C. *Times Whistle* (1871) 18 You shalbe cast Into that pitt, with the ungodlie rout. **1651** *Fuller's Abel Rediv., Luther* (1867) I. 62 Whom the pope of Rome and the rout of the wicked persecute and dishonour. **1896** HOUSMAN *Shropshire Lad* xix, Now you will not swell the rout Of lads that wore their honours out.

†**7.** *the rout*, the common herd, the rabble. *Obs.*

1375 BARBOUR *Bruce* IX. 504 Renownit of so hye prowes, That he of vorschip passit the rout. *c* **1400** *Apol. Loll.* (Camden) 61 Þu schal not folow þe rowt to do iuel. **1550** CROWLEY *Last Trumpet* 402 It is God that appointeth Kings and rulers ouer the route. **1593** BILSON *Govt. Christ's Ch.* 349 Did ever God or Mans Lawe preferre the feete before the head, the rowt before the ruler. **1633** G. HERBERT *Temple, Sacrifice* 185 Thus trimmed forth they bring me to the rout, Who 'Crucifie him', crie. **1673** *Remarques Humours Town* 50 Such easie representations were then..for the Rout and Plebeans. **1708** MRS. CENTLIVRE *Busie Body* I. i, 'Tis a vast Addition to a Man's Fortune, according to the Rout of the World, to be seen in the Company of leading Men. **1730** SWIFT *Traulus* Wks. 1751 X. 148 Tho' perhaps among the Rout, He wildly flings his Filth about.

†**b.** With adjs., esp. *common* or *vulgar*. *Obs.*

1590 SHAKS. *Com. Err.* III. i. 101 That [will be] supposed by the common rowt. **1621** T. WILLIAMSON tr. *Goulart's Wise Vieillard* 103 The base rabble, and rascally route of the world. **1637** R. ASHLEY tr. *Malvezzi's David Persecuted* 187 The vulgar rout breede such kinde of people by applauding them. **1693** SOUTH *Serm.* 454 The multitude or common rout, like a drove of sheep. **1700** ASTRY tr. *Saavedra's Royal Politician* I. 112 To be Born, only to make One in the World, is for the Vulgar Rout.

†**c.** *to rule the rout*, to have full sway. *Obs.*

1570 *Satir. Poems Reform.* xii. 76 Sen double murther markis to reule the rout.

8. Riot, disturbance, stir, uproar.

1439 *Rolls of Parlt.* V. 16/2 In manere of Werre, Riote, Route and Insurrection arraied. **1557** *Tottell's Misc.* (Arb.) 239 He in the midst of all this sturre and rout, Gan bend his browes, and moue him self about. **1591** SPENSER *M. Hubberd* 558 Then made they revell route and goodly glee. **1604** SHAKS. *Oth.* II. iii. 210 Giue me to know How this foule Rout began: Who set it on. *c* **1690** *Ld. Delamere* iii. in Child *Ballads* IV. 113/1 Such a rout has been in the parliament, as I hear, Betwixt a Dutch lord and my lord Delamere. **1728** SWIFT *Jrnl. Mod. Lady* Wks. 1751 VII. 195 Not School-boys at a Barring-out Rais'd ever such incessant Rout. **1766** [ANSTEY] *Bath Guide* v. 53 Are the Fiddlers come hither to make all this Rout? **1804** FESSENDEN *Democracy Unveiled* (1806) II. 84 Who and what are ye, Patriots stout, For Freedom, who make such a rout? **1872** BLACKIE *Lays Highl.* 80 The winds without kept whistling rout.

b. Fuss, clamour, noise. Formerly common in phrase *to make a rout about* (something).

1684 LUTTRELL *Brief Rel.* (1857) I. 300 'Twas strange any man should..make all this rout that was about it. *a* **1714** M. HENRY *Acts* xii. 6 Tradition makes a mighty rout about these chains. **1771** T. HULL *Sir W. Harrington* (1797) II. 206 There used to be a great rout made about some very high piece of service the Captain was to do for him. **1824** LADY GRANVILLE *Lett.* (1894) I. 326, I cannot..help feeling nervous about my presentation, because they all make such a rout about it. **1854** MISS BAKER *Northampt. Gloss.* s.v., 'What a rout she's making over it!' 'She needn't make such a rout about such a trifle.'

†**c.** Sway, influence. In phr. *to bear a* (or *the*) *rout*. *Obs.*

1550 in Tytler *Hist. Scot.* (1864) III. 383 The Scots bear a fell rout in this court, and be much made of. **1616** J. LANE *Contn. Sqr.'s T.* v. 40 The man at Fregiley bears all the rowt.

9. A fashionable gathering or assembly, a large evening party or reception, much in vogue in the eighteenth and early nineteenth centuries. (Cf. DRUM *sb.*[1] 10.)

1742 FIELDING *Amelia* IV. vi, She went directly to a rout where she spent two hours. **1751** JOHNSON *Rambler* No. 84 ⁋11 Ladies of my age go to assemblies and routes without their mothers. **1771** SMOLLETT *Humph. Cl.* 31 May, She keeps a small rout at her own house, never exceeding ten or a dozen card-tables. **1810** SIR G. JACKSON *Diaries & Lett.* (1873) I. 128 Last night I was at a really grand rout at Lady Rowley's. **1858** KINGSLEY *Poems* (1878) 236 As if the sum of joy to you Were hunt and pic-nic, rout and ball. **1887** RUSKIN *Præterita* II. 390 One rarely heard..of her going to a theatre, or a rout, or a cricket-match.

b. *attrib.* and *Comb.*, as ***rout biscuit, -chair, -china, day***, etc.

1775 MME. D'ARBLAY *Early Diary, Lett.* Nov., He was obliged to go in..to Lady Harrington's before he came, it being her Rout Day. **1785** TRUSLER *Mod. Times* III. 202 All the rout-going men and women of rank. **1812** MISS L. M. HAWKINS *C'tess & Gertrude* I. 265 She had not hired rout-chairs, rout-glasses, rout-china, to accommodate her guests. **1813** *Examiner* 15 Mar. 171/1 The usual lumber of a rout-party. **1858** DICKENS *Lett.* (1880) II. 52 He is transformed into a rout-furniture dealer of Rathbone Place. **1875** *Encycl. Brit.* III. 252/2 The dough for rout biscuits is placed in a strong metal box or chamber in which a piston is tightly fitted.

c. ***rout-cake***, a rich cake originally made for use at receptions.

1807 J. BERESFORD *Miseries Hum. Life* xv. §6. 60 Such feminine bon-bons as sweet-meats, rout-cakes, and the choicer kinds of fruit. **1848** THACKERAY *Van. Fair* iii, He managed a couple of plates full of strawberries and cream, and twenty-four little rout cakes. **1873** MISS BRADDON *Lucius Davoren* I. Prol. ii, Think of the macaroons and rout-cakes we have trampled under our heels.

d. ***rout-seat*** (see quot. 1858).

1836–7 DICKENS *Sk. Boz, Tales* iii, The furniture was taken out, and rout-seats were taken in. **1858** SIMMONDS *Dict. Trade, Rout-seats*, slight cane-top benches let out to hire for dances and evening parties. **1898** BESANT *Orange Girl* II. iii, Some of them rolled upon the rout seats, and so fell fast asleep.

Hence **ˈrouting** *vbl. sb.*, the frequenting of routs; also ***routing-day***, a day for holding a rout.

1750–1 MRS. DELANY *Autobiog.* (1861) III. 2 The day is tomorrow; but that not being a proper routing day, I choose to have them on the eve. **1754** SHEBBEARE *Matrimony* (1766) II. 84 Lady Sapplin returned to the London Life of Visiting, Routing, Carding. **1767** LADY S. LENNOX *Life & Lett.* (1901) I. 211, I own I am wore to death with routing.

rout (raʊt), *sb.*[2] Also 7 **rowt(e**, 7–8 **route**. [ad. obs. F. *route* (cf. F. *déroute* DEROUT *sb.*):—L. *rupta*: see prec.]

1. Disorderly or precipitate retreat on the part of a defeated army, body of troops, etc.

1598 BARRET *Theor. Warres* I. i. 4 Men once disordered.. commonly fall to rout. **1600** E. BLOUNT tr. *Conestaggio* 50 Manie of the Nobilitie,..seeing the armie in route, sought the King. **1667** MILTON *P.L.* II. 770 Wherein remaind..to our Almighty Foe Cleer Victory, to our part loss and rout. **1764** GRAY *Triumph of Owen* 34 Where he points his purple spear, Hasty, hasty Rout is there. **1814** SCOTT *Ld. of Isles* III. xxvii, Of rout and rally, war and truce,— As heroes think, so thought the Bruce. **1873** LONGF. *Wayside Inn* III. *Sp. Jew's Second T.* 5 In rout before his path From the field of battle red Flee all. **1878** J. MILLER *Songs of Italy* 64 There was rout Of ships like the breaking of regiments.

transf. **1743** P. FRANCIS tr. *Horace, Epist.* II. i. 351 Chairs, coaches, carts, in rattling rout are roll'd. **1807** J. BARLOW *Columb.* III. 261 Our scanty feast; Which, driven in hasty rout, our train supplied.

b. Esp. in phr. *to put to (the) rout*.

1612 *North's Plutarch* 1124 Men..who so plied the Athenians, that they brake them, and put them all to rout. **1667** MILTON *P.L.* IV. 3 The Dragon, put to second rout, Came furious down. **1770** LANGHORNE *Plutarch* (1879) II. 683/2 Against him, Pompey sent Afranius, who put him to the route. **1844** H. H. WILSON *Brit. India* III. 36 The entrenchment was carried, and the Burmas were put to the rout. *c* **1850** LANE *Arab. Nts.* (Rtldg.) 477 They instantly put them in disorder, and very soon to rout.

fig. **1596** SIR J. DAVIES *Orchestra* xxxii, How doth Confusions Mother, headlong Chance, Put reasons noble squadron to the rout? **1843** LE FEVRE *Life Trav. Phys.* III. III. viii. 183 Napoleon put to rout all these things when he inhabited the palace. **1873** M. ARNOLD *Lit. & Dogma* (1876) 237 To baffle and put to rout their false dogmatic theology.

2. An instance of this; a complete overthrow and flight.

1611 SHAKS. *Cymb.* v. iii. 41 Then beganne..A Rowt, confusion thicke: forthwith they flye. **1647** CLARENDON *Hist. Reb.* I. §86 The Retreat had been a Rout without an Enemy. **1704** ADDISON *Campaign* Misc. Wks. 1726 I. 79 The rout begins, the Gallic squadrons run. **1748** *Anson's Voy.* II. xii. (1776) 361 The other two Squadrons..were calm spectators of the rout of their comrades. **1836** THIRLWALL *Greece* III. 281 A body of Locrian cavalry, which came up as the rout began, aided the Bœotians in the slaughter of the flying enemy. **1849** MACAULAY *Hist. Eng.* v. I. 580 The retreat soon became a rout. **1874** GREEN *Short Hist.* iv. §i. 162 The rout of an English detachment.. prolonged the contest into the winter.

fig. **1651** CULPEPPER *Astrol. Judgem. Dis.* (1658) 114 Nature gets strength over the disease, and will at last put him to a total rout. **1667** PEPYS *Diary* 1 Sept., Sir H. Cholmly tells me there are hopes that the women also will have a rout.

3. A defeated and fleeing band or army.

1621 LADY M. WROTH *Urania* 301 He disordered the ranck, and brake Antissius order, whereupon their men were in routs. **1647** SPRIGGE *Anglia Rediv.* I. ii. (1854) 12 The lieutenant-general..pursued the enemy, lodged most of the remains of the rout in Blechingdon house. **1828** SCOTT *F.M. Perth* ix, Therefore was he given to be a rout and a spoil to his enemies.

rout, *sb.*[3] *Sc.* and *north.* ? *Obs.* [Related to ROUT *v.*[6]]

†**1.** A violent movement. *Obs.*[−1]

13.. *Gaw. & Gr. Knt.* 457 With a runisch rout þe raynez he tornez, Halled out at þe hal-dor, his hed in his hande.

2. A (heavy) blow or stroke.

1375 BARBOUR *Bruce* II. 356 [They] plungyt in the stalwart stour, And rowtis ruyd about thaim dang. **14..** *Sir Beues* (MS. O) 3957 Sir Beues..gaue kynge Iour suche a rout, That he neuer rose. *c* **1480** HENRYSON *Fables, Wolf & Fox* xx, The cadgear wald haif raucht the foxe ane rout. **1513** DOUGLAS *Æneis* XIII. Prol. 148 Syne to me wyth his club he maid a braid, And twenty rowtis apoun my rigging laid. **1583** *Leg. Bp. St. Androis* 703 Ane porter..to the bischop his blissing gave, Betuixt the schoulders a royall route, Turning him wodderschins about. **1728** RAMSAY *Fables, Monk & Miller's Wife* 246 With a great rung..to lend him a sound rout. *a* **1779** GRAHAM *Writ.* (1883) II. 98, I gave her such a rout over her long snout. **1824** MACTAGGART *Gallovid. Encycl.* 414 *Rout*, a heavy blow with a stick.

†**rout**, *sb.*[4] *Sc. Obs. rare.* [Origin and real meaning obscure.] In phrases ***bone and rout, stout and rout***, completely.

Cf. the later form *stoop and roop*, s.v. STOOP *sb.*

c **1375** *Sc. Leg. Saints* xxxvii. (*Vincent*) 353 Þane gert he his body bere..to bestis & foulis..til ete hyme bath stout & rout [*rime* doute]. *Ibid.* xlvii. (*Effame*) 92 For þane þe gret fir suld brek oute, & bryne þe madyne bane & route.

rout (raʊt, *Sc.* rut), *sb.*[5] Chiefly *Sc.* Also 9 **rowt**. [f. ROUT *v.*[2] Cf. Norw. *rut* in the same sense.] A loud noise or shout.

In some cases not clearly separable from next, owing to the similarity of the senses and the ambiguity of the spelling.

1513 DOUGLAS *Æneis* I. iii. 52 In the mene quhile, with mony rout and roir The see thus trublit. **1515** *Scottish Field* 633 in *Chetham Misc.* (1856), For there was shott at a shotte, a thousand at once, That all rang with that rowte, roches and other. *a* **1774** FERGUSSON *King's Birthday* Poems (1845) 2 The hills in terror would cry out And echo to thy dinsome rout. **1813** PICKEN *Poems* I. 45 They mak' sic rout an' rair Soun' thro' ilk region o' the air. *a* **1878** AINSLIE *Land of Burns* (1892) 218 Wi' eerie rair an' rowt Cried the wakrife spirit out. **1882** J. WALKER *Jaunt to Auld Reekie* 170 The limmer's [= cannon's] rout wad ding them maistly deaf.

rout (raʊt), *sb.*[6] *Sc.* [f. ROUT *v.*[3] Cf. Norw. *raut*.] A bellow or low (of an ox, etc.).

1513 DOUGLAS *Æneis* XII. ii. 136 Lyke as the bull..Gevis terribill rowtis and lowis monyfald. **1817** *Lintoun Green* 49 A crummie's rowt! The english call a low! **1866** J. SMITH *Merry Bridal* 17 The Bull rins wild amang the nowte, An' funkin daft wi' merry rowt. **1880** J. E. WATT *Poet. Sk.* 64 (E.D.D.), Her voice it resembles the rowte o' a coo.

†**rout**, *sb.*[7] *Sc. Obs. rare.* Also 6 **rute**. [Of obscure origin: cf. ROOD-GOOSE, and Icel. *hrota, hrotgás*, Norw. *rotgaas*, Fris. *rotgoes*, Du. *rotgans*, the brent-goose.] A species of wild goose.

The misprint *routhurrok* in quot. 1578 is evidently the ultimate source of *routheroock-goose* in P. Neill *Tour Orkney & Shetland* (1806) 196.

1551 *Sc. Acts Mary* (1814) II. 484 The wylde guse of the greit bind, ijs. The claik, quink, and rute, the price of the peece, xviij *d.* **1578** LESLIE *De Orig. Scot.* 37 Alia sex Anserum genera apud nos inueniuntur. *marg.* Vulgus his uocibus distinguit Quinck, Skilling, Claik, Routhurrok [*read* Rout, Hurrok], Ridlaik. **1639** SIR R. GORDON *Hist. Earls of Sutherland* 3 In all this province ther is great store of..wildgouse, ringouse, routs, whaips,..and all other kinds of wildfowl.

†**rout**, *sb.*[8] *Obs. rare.* Also **rowt**. [Of obscure origin.] A close or field.

1615 SIR R. BOYLE in *Lismore Papers* (1886) I. 82, I bought the lease..of Drombegg rout, half a ploughland. **1635** *Ibid.* IV. 127 An enclosed rowt abowt 4 irishe acres of meddow.

†**rout**, *sb.*[9] *Obs. rare*[−1]. [Of obscure origin.] Some kind of horse.

1697 VANBRUGH *Æsop* I. IV. ii, Your Worship has six Coach-Horses,..besides Pads, Routs, and Dog-Horses.

rout (raʊt), *sb.*[10] [f. ROUT *v.*[8]] The act of searching, or of turning *out* something.

1821 CLARE *Vill. Minstr.* II. 32 There came the snail from his shell peeping out, As fearful and cautious as thieves on the rout. **1880** MRS. PARR *Adam & Eve* II. 138, I didn't count 'pon this rout-out comin' yet whiles, for..Eve. **1912** C. MACKENZIE *Carnival* xxxiv. 358 'I'm going to have a rare old rout-out this morning,' Jenny announced.

rout, obs. variant of ROUTE.

rout (raʊt), *v.*[1] *Obs.* exc. *dial.* Forms: 1 **hrutan**, 4–7 **rowte** (5 **rowtyn**), 4–6 **route**, 6– **rout** (9 *dial.* **routy**). Also *pa. t.* 4 **rout**, *pl.* **rout(t)en**. [OE. *hrútan*, = OFris. *hrūta, rhūta, rūta*, OS. *hrūtan*, MDu. *rūten*, OHG. *rûȝan, rûȝen* (G. *ruszen, rauszen*), prob. of imitative origin. An ablaut-variant appears in ON. and Icel. *hrjóta*, Norw. *rjota, ryta*.] *intr.* To snore.

In common literary use from *c* 1300 to 1600.

c **725** *Corpus Gloss.* 1923 *Stertens*, hrutende. *c* **1000** ÆLFRIC *Gram.* xxviii. (Z.) 168 *Sterto*, ic hrute. **13..** *Coer de L.* 4229 They slepte faste and gun to route. **13..** *E.E. Allit. P.* C. 186 He..Slypped vpon a sloumbe sclepe, & sloberande he routes. **1390** GOWER *Conf.* II. 111 He wot noght..hou the day is come aboute, Bot onli forto slepe &

route Til hyh midday. *a* **1450** *Knt. de la Tour* (1868) 81 The good man.. made semblaunt that he had slepte, and routed. **1483** CAXTON *Gold. Leg.* 97/2 Thenne he fylle a slepe and rowted so fast, that noman myght awake hym. **1532** MORE *Confut. Tindale* Wks. 595/1 Tyndal of likelyhode lay nere him and heard hym all the while snorte & rowte. **1581** J. BELL *Haddon's Answ. Osor.* 50b, Ye route so soundly in these drousie dreames, that you cannot bee awakened out of them: and therefore I will leave you snortyng in them. **1601** HOLLAND *Pliny* I. 309 The Dolphins and Whales be heard to rout and snort again, they sleepe so soundly. **1644** BULWER *Chirol.* 73 A soulder, that.. routeth and snorteth.. in his sleep. **1815** SCOTT *Guy M.* i, Are ye lying routing there, and a young gentleman seeking the way to the Place? **1851** T. STERNBERG *Dial. & Folk-Lore Northants* 88. **1888** ELWORTHY *W. Somerset Word-bk.* s.v. *Routy.*

Hence ˈ**routing** *vbl. sb.*

c **1386** CHAUCER *Reeve's T.* 246 His wyf bar him a burdon a ful strong, Men myghte hir rowtyng heere two furlong. *c* **1440** *Promp. Parv.* 438/2 Rowtynge, yn slepe, *stertura.* **1519** HORMAN *Vulg.* 46b, Thy routtynge awaked me. *Ibid.*, Thy routtynge is harde hither. **1601** HOLLAND *Pliny* IX. x, They.. keepe such a snorting and routing in their sleepe, that they bewray where they be. **1650** VENNER *Via Recta* 304 Offensive rowtings and oftentimes untimely awakings do ensue.

rout (raʊt, *Sc.* rut), *v.*[2] Now *rare.* Chiefly *north.* and *Sc.* Forms: 4 **rute,** 5 **rut;** 4 **route, rowte,** 6 **rowt,** 8 **rout.** [Prob. of Scand. origin: cf. Norw. *ruta* in the same sense, an ablaut-variant of ON. *rjóta*, MSw. *riuta*, Sw. *ryta.*

MDu. *rûten*, MHG. *rûzen, russen* (G. *rauszen*) in related senses may be of distinct origin from the forms cited under ROUT *v.*[1], which originally had initial *hr-*.]

intr. Of the sea, winds, thunder, etc.: To roar, make a loud noise.

a **1300** *Cursor M.* 21869 Þe see sal rise and rute; Mani man sal dei for dute. **13..** *Coer de L.* 4304 That stone whanne it out fleygh,.. 'Allas!' they cryede.., 'It routes as it wer a thondyr'. **13..** *St. Cristofer* 370 in Horstm. *Altengl. Leg.* (1881) 459 Þe water bygane to bolne & rowte. And ofte-tyms hym turnede abowte. *c* **1374** CHAUCER *Troylus* III. 743 The sterne wind so loude gan to route That no wight other noyse mighte here. **1513** DOUGLAS *Æneis* I. ii. 64 Dyrknes as nycht besett the seis abowt; The firmament gane rummeling rair and rowt. *a* **1776** *Lowlands of Holland* ii. in Child *Ballads* II. 318 The weary wind began to rise, and the sea began to rout [*rime* about].

Hence ˈ**routing** *vbl. sb.* and *ppl. a.*

c **1384** CHAUCER *Ho. Fame* III. 1933 Ryght so hyt ferde, As dooth the rowtynge of the ston, That from thengyne ys leten gon. **1513** DOUGLAS *Æneis* I. iv. 75 Passit eke haue ȝe The evir rowtand Caribdis rolkis fell. *Ibid.* VII. ii. 132 Ane cheif gret forest.. namyt from a haly routand well. **1795** *Statist. Acc. Scot.* XVI. 9 A Routing Well at Monktoun, that is said always to predict a storm. **1901** SAVAGE-ARMSTRONG *Ballads of Down* 371 Dangerous eddies.. named, from their loud and ominous roaring sound, 'the Routing Rocks.'

rout (raʊt), *v.*[3] *north.* and *Sc.* Also 4–6, 8–9 **rowt(e,** 5, 9 **rote,** 7, 9 **rawt,** 9 **raut.** [a. ON. *rauta*, Norw. *rauta*, MSw. and Sw. dial. *röta*, in the same sense.]

1. *intr.* Of cattle: To bellow, roar, low.

c **1300–** [implied in sense 2]. **1483** *Cath. Angl.* 313/1 To Rote (to Rowt, *sicut bos* A.); *boare, mvgire.* **1533** BELLENDEN *Livy* I. iii. (S.T.S.) I. 23 The ky.. lowit [*v.r.* rowtit] agane on þe samyn maner. *a* **1585** MONTGOMERIE *Flyting* 501 All the ky in the countrey.. routed in a reane. **1620** T. GRANGER *Div. Logike* 66 The Swine grunteth, The Cow rowteth. **1674** RAY *N.C. Words* 39 To *Rowt* or *Rawt*, to lowe like an Ox or Cow. **1721** RAMSAY *Richy & Sandy* 72 Nuckle kye stand rowting in the loans. **1786** BURNS *Ordination* vi, Nae mair thou'lt rowte out-owre the dale, Because thy pasture's scanty. **1820** SCOTT *Monast.* iii, To see poor Grizzie and Crumbie.. turning back their necks to the byre, and routing. **1851** MAYNE REID *Scalp Hunt.* iv, The animal 'routed' with extreme terror; and, plunging forward, soon headed the band. **1893** CROCKETT *Stickit Minister* 229 After him thundered the bull, routing in blood-curdling wrath.

b. Of other animals. *rare.*

1560 ROLLAND *Crt. Venus* IV. 406 Scho.. findis it deid: that scho dois rout and rair.

2. *transf.* Of persons: To roar or cry loudly.

c **1300** *Havelok* 1911 He maden here backes al so bloute Als here wombes, and made hem rowte Als he weren kradelbarnes. *a* **1340** HAMPOLE *Psalter* lxxvi. 1 He is all in silence bifor god, þof he rowt and rare all day. *c* **1425** WYNTOUN *Cron.* III. vii. 953 To rare Swa þat he lik was.. For to til his ded thraw til a nowte. **1787** BURNS *The Calf* v, To hear you roar and rowte, Few men o' sense will doubt your claims To rank amang the Nowte. **1816** SCOTT *Old Mort.* xiv, The carle gae them a screed o' doctrine!.. he routed like a cow in a fremd loaning. **1868–** in *Eng. Dial. Dict.* **1893** STEVENSON *Catriona* 323 It is quite needless to rowt at a gentleman in the same chamber with yourself.

b. To make a roaring noise.

1834 M. SCOTT *Cruise Midge* (1863) 53 One or two of the demon-like Savages were routing on bullock's horns.

3. *trans.* To utter in roars; to shout *out.*

1807–10 TANNAHILL *Poems* (1846) 83 Hearing a lively outfiel' sermon, Even though rowted by a stirk. **1886** STEVENSON *Kidnapped* xxix, 'I have no manner of inclination to rowt out my name to the countryside,' said Alan.

Hence ˈ**routing** *vbl. sb.* and *ppl. a.*

1483 *Cath. Angl.* 313/1 A Rowtynge, *boatus, boema, mugitus.* **1570** GOOGE *Pop. Kingd.* I. (1880) 8 They laugh and with a rowting noyse, their greefe they plaine discrye. *a* **1609** ALEX. HUME *Day Estivall* 228 Of bleiting sheepe.., Of calues and rowting ky. **1641** BEST *Farm. Bks.* (Surtees) 117 That they may not hear the rowtinge and blaringe one of another, for feare that the kyne breake over to them. **1644** in Ritchie *Churches of St. Baldred* (1880) 263 The sikness among beastis, callit the routing evil. **1778** *Gentl. Mag.* XLVIII. 408 In Rutting time, bucks keep a continual routing, or bellowing. **1818** SCOTT *Rob Roy* xiv, They cou'dna get a word o' sense out o' him, for downright fright at their growling and routing. **1867** CARLYLE *E. Irving* 303 Especially one [bridge] called 'rowting', i.e. bellowing or roaring 'Brig', spanning a grand loud cataract.

†**rout,** *v.*[4] *Obs.* Forms: 4 *pa. t.* **rutte, routte;** 6 **rought, rowte, rout(e.** [a. OF. *router* (*roucter, roupter*), *ruter, roter* (mod.F. *roter*):—L. *ructāre*: cf. ERUCTATE *v.*] *intr.* To belch, to bring up wind.

1377 LANGL. *P. Pl.* B. v. 398 He.. roxed and rored, and rutte [*v.r.* routte] atte laste. *c* **1500** *World & Child* 800, I cough and rought, my body wyll brest, Age dothe folowe me so. **1530** PALSGR. 695/1, I rowte, I belche, as one dothe that voydeth wynde out of his stomacke, *je roucte.* **1535** LYNDESAY *Satyre* 4353 Scho riftit, routit, and maid sic stends. *c* **1550** H. LLOYD *Treas. Health* Y vij, Whatsoeuer helthful man.. losyth his voyce & routeth withall, he dyeth wythin seuen dayes.

†**rout,** *v.*[5] *Obs. rare.* Also 5 **rouȝte.** [f. OF. (*a*) *route* (see ROUTE *sb.*), used as a cry to direct hunting-dogs: see Godefroy VII. 251/3.] Of a huntsman: **a.** *intr.* To shout to the dogs. **b.** *trans.* To direct (a dog) by shouting.

c **1410** *Master of Game* (MS. Digby 182) Prol., He shall se the hert passe byfore hym and shall halowe and route myghtlich. *Ibid.*, He shall route and blowe as lowde as he may. *Ibid.* xxxiv, As ofte as any hounde caccheth it, he shulde hue to hym by his name and route hym to his felawes.

†**rout,** *v.*[6] *Obs.* Forms: 1 **hrutan,** 3 **ruten,** 4 **rute,** *pa. t.* **rut;** 4–5 **route,** 5 **rowte.** [OE. *hrūtan*, of obscure relationship. Cf. ATROUT *v.* and REAT *v.*]

1. *intr.* To rush, dash; to move with great force or violence.

a **1000** *Riddle* xxxvi. 7 Ne æt me hrutende hrisil scriþeð. *a* **1225** *Leg. Kath.* 2005 Hit bigon to claterin,.. ba þe treo & te irn; & ruten forð wið swuch rune þe stucchen of baðe [etc.]. *c* **1380** *Sir Ferumb.* 1343 To a wyndowe wente þes barouns fre & ther þay loked oute, þay seȝe þe waȝes of þe se harde to-gadre route. *c* **1400** *Laud Troy Bk.* 6806 Cariolus.. And Theseus kyng to-geder routed With speres scharpe, that men myȝt here. *c* **1400** *Destr. Troy* 912 The dragon.. rut out roidly with a rede hete. *Ibid.* 5699, 12691. *c* **1450** *Fencing w. two handed Sword* in *Rel. Ant.* I. 309 Thy rakys, thy rowndis, thy quarters abowte, Thy stoppis, thy foynys, lete hem fast rowte.

2. *trans.* To throw, cast, hurl.

c **1400** *Laud Troy Bk.* 3662 Thei sette engynes al aboute, And grete stones thei did in route. *c* **1460** *Promp. Parv.* (Winchester) 388/2 Rowtyn or throwyn, *proicio.* *c* **1460** *Play Sacram.* 701, I shalle.. shake thys cake owt of thys clothe & to the ovyn I shall yt rowte.

b. To stir vigorously.

c **1440** *Pallad. on Husb.* XI. 299 Aftir dayes iij they goth therto, And myghtyly they route [L. *commovent*] hit to and fro.

3. To beat severely. (Cf. ROUT *sb.*[3] 2.)

1398 TREVISA *Barth. De P.R.* VI. xv. (Tollem. MS.), He routeþ and beteþ him ofte.. leste he drawe to euyl maneris and tacchis. *c* **1440** *York Myst.* xxxiii. 155 Þou bes lassched lusschyd, and lapped. Ʒa, rowted, russhed, and rapped. **1768** ROSS *Helenore* I. 44 Their task was mair nor they cud well mak out, An' as they promis'd, they their backs did rout.

Hence ˈ**routing** *vbl. sb.* and *ppl. a.*

13.. *E.E. Allit. P.* B. 354 I sende out.. Such a rowtande ryge þat rayne schal swyþe. *c* **1400** *Destr. Troy* 1986 With a routond rayn ruthe to beholde. *c* **1450** *Cast. Persev.* 1829 (Macro Plays), I schape þese schrewys to mekyl schame: iche rappyth on oþer with rowtynge rele.

†**rout,** *v.*[7] *Obs.* Forms: 4 **rute,** 4–6 **route,** 5–6 **rowt(e,** 5 **rought,** 6–7 **rout.** [In part at least a. OF. *router* (also *arrouter*), f. *route* ROUT *sb.*[1] and ROUTE *sb.*; but sense 2 may have some other origin.]

1. *intr.* To assemble, to gather or herd *together*; also, to take part in a gathering.

Quot. *c* 1350 may belong to, or indicate the development of, sense 2.

a **1300** *Cursor M.* 11633 Quen maria sagh þaa bestes rute, First sco was gretli in dute. *Ibid.* 14618 Son wit þam he was vmsett; þar bigan þai for to rute And for to gadir him a-bute. *c* **1350** *Will. Palerne* 5478 Robboures ne reuowres miȝt route none, þat þei nere hastili hange. *c* **1418** *Pol. Poems* (Rolls) II. 246 Where shuld he other route or ride Agayns the chief of chivalrie. **1457** *Sc. Acts Jas. II* (1814) II. 50 At na man.. ride nor rowt in feir of weir w[t] na man bot w[t] þe king or his officiaris. **1530** PALSGR. 695/1, I rowte, I assemble togyther in routes, or I styrre aboute, *je me arroute.* I lyke nat this geare that the commens begynneth to route on this facyon. **1562** LEGH *Armory* 77 Where other beastes do herde and rowte together,.. the Lyon wyll not so do. **1622** BACON *Hen. VII* (1876) 66 The meaner sort routed together, and suddenly assailing the earl in his house, slew him, and divers of his servants.

2. To stir, move; to make a movement.

c **1380** WYCLIF *Sel. Wks.* I. 209 He pursueþ a preest.. and somoniþ him and traveiliþ him, þat it is hard to him to rowte. *c* **1386** CHAUCER *Man of Law's T.* 540 In al that lond no cristen dorste route; Alle cristen folk been fled fro that contree. **14..** *Sir Beues* (MS. C) 2626 No man durste yn þat cuntre rowte, Be hoole xx myle abowte. **1436** *Pol. Poems* (Rolls) II. 167 Gode see-menne.. bete theme home, and made they myght not route. *c* **1500** *World & Child* 396 He is in euery dede doughty, For hym dare no man rowte. *a* **1553** UDALL *Roister D.* IV. vii, Nowe sirs, keepe your ray, and see your heartes be stoute, But where be these caitifes, me think they dare not route.

3. To be riotous, behave riotously.

c **1400** *Beryn* 2766 This gardeyn is.. ful of may flouris,.. The wich been so redolent, & sentyn so a-boute, That he must be ryȝte lewd, þat þerin shuld route. *c* **1460** *Wisdom* 505 (Macro Plays), Yeue to yowur body þat ys nede, Ande euer be mery; let reuell rowte! **1570** LEVINS *Manip.* 228/38 To Route, or royst, *grassari.* **1591** SPENSER *Vis. Bellay* xii. 166 When from nigh hills, with hideous outcrie, A troupe of Satyres in the place did rout.

4. *trans.* To scour, ride over, in a troop.

1500–20 DUNBAR *Poems* xlii. 92 Sklandir.. him aganis Assemblit ane semely sort full sone, And raiss and rowttit all the planis.

Hence ˈ**routing** *vbl. sb.* and *ppl. a.*

1513 in Pitcairn *Crim. Trials* (Bann. Cl.) I. 95 For riding furth of burgh in warlike manner in 'routing', and for thereby breaking the Acts of Parliament. **1583** GOLDING *Calvin on Deut.* iii. 16 When folke.. keep rowtings in Tauerns or Alehouses. **1634** C. DOWNING *State Eccles.* 97 In that routing-rush of reformation, who could expect but the part corrected must needs be for the time neare to utter ruine. **1650** (*title*), The Routing of the Ranters, a true Relation, with some of their abominable.. behaviour.

rout (raʊt), *v.*[8] Also 6–7 **rowte,** 9 *dial.* **routy.** [Irregular var. of ROOT *v.*[2]]

1. a. *intr.* Of swine: To turn up the soil with the snout in search of food. Now chiefly *dial.*

1547–64 BAULDWIN *Mor. Philos.* (Palfr.) 22 Swine had rather lie routing in durt & in mire, then in cleare & faire water. **1576** GASCOIGNE *Steele Gl.* (Arb.) 70 They did not rowte (like rude vnringed swine) To roote nobilitie from heritage. **1656** BAXTER *Reformed Pastor* 21 To take us up into heaven,.. while we think of no such matter, but are routing in the earth. **1688** HOLME *Armoury* II. 135/2 Boar and Swine are said to Rout, or be Routing, or Worming, if they break into Gardens. **1864** KINGSLEY *Rom. & Teut.* 287 If.. you find pigs routing in your enclosure, you may kill one. **1886** ELWORTHY *W. Somerset Word-bk.* 633.

b. To poke about, rummage. (Cf. ROOT *v.*[2] 1 c.)

1711 SWIFT *Jrnl. to Stella* 22 Oct., I must rout among your letters, a needle in a bottle of hay. **1760–72** H. BROOKE *Fool of Qual.* (1809) III. 67 The company staid routing and searching the house below. **1836** MOORE *Mem.* (1856) VII. 170 Performed some of my home commissions, besides routing away for a couple of hours at the British Museum. **1897** BEATTY *Secretar* 37 We heard them routing about, and swearing, amongst the butts of ale.

2. a. *trans.* To turn over, or dig *up*, with the snout.

1571 TUSSER *100 Points Husb.* 9 For rowting thy pasture, ring Hogs thou hast nede. **1621** *Nottingham Rec.* IV. 378 For soffering the medow to be routted vp. **1726** LEONI *Alberti's Archit.* II. 54/2 They used to raise something of a fence about it [*sc.* a dead body] to keep off the beasts from routing it up. **1787** BECKFORD *Italy* II. 269 Routing up the moss at their roots in search of acorns. **1818** KEATS *Endymion* I. 282 When snouted wild-boars routing tender corn Anger our huntsmen.

fig. **1836** SIR H. TAYLOR *Statesman* xxxii. 251 A lawyer.. busy.. in routing and tearing up the soil to get at a grain of the subject.

b. *transf.* To tear *up*, scoop *out.* Also with *away* and without const. *spec.* to cut a groove in (a wooden or metal surface), to machine or work with a router.

1726 LEONI *Alberti's Archit.* I. 72/2 The water that rushes down precipitately, routs up the bottom, and.. carries away every thing that it can loosen. **1818** *Trans. R. Soc. Arts* XXXV. 123 In the old way of routing the wood the grooves are torn and uneven at the bottom. **1843** HOLTZAPFFEL *Turning* I. 135 The elastic tool.. is put in motion, and.. routs or cuts out the shallow recess. **1884** JEFFERIES *Life of Fields* (1908) 117 Like the claws of some prehistoric monster, the shares [of the steam-plough] rout up the ground. **1934** *Woodworker* XXXVIII. 158/3 He first routs out his templet as suggested to the.. shape he desires. **1946** C. H. HAYWARD *Light Machines for Woodwork* xii. 155 It is of special value for routing the ends of pieces.. of odd shape. **1948** H. MISSINGHAM *Student's Guide Commerc. Art* II. 100 The line block is finished by first routing away all unwanted metal from the work. **1958** *New Scientist* 17 July 441/2 (*caption*) Routing an aircraft bulkhead from a solid billet of high-tensile aluminium alloy. **1960** 'N. SHUTE' *Trustee from Toolroom* vi. 131 You routed each plank all along its length to fit the next one?

3. a. To fetch or turn (a person) out of bed; to cause to get up. Also with *out.* Also to fetch (a person) out of a house, etc.

c **1776** H. NEWDIGATE *Let.* in A. E. Newdigate-Newdegate *Cheverels* (1898) i. 9 My Lord routed us out y[e] moment we had breakfasted to pass sentence upon some trees that are to be fell'd. **1787** M. CUTLER *Life*, etc. (1888) I. 287 The people at the White House were gone to bed, but I soon routed them. **1856** MRS. STOWE *Dred* xxx. 303, I took a notable turn this morning, and routed them up to an early breakfast. **1892** *New York Sun* 8 May 2/7 He ran to a neighbouring farmhouse, routed out the people.

b. To search out, bring to light Also, to turn *out* (a room, etc.).

1805 G. M'INDOE *Million of Potatoes* 149 Syne routed up a glass for John. **1814** JANE AUSTEN *Let.* Aug. (1952) 397 as soon as my Trunk & Basket could be routed out from all the other Trunks & Baskets in the World, we were on our way. **1836** MARRYAT *Midsh. Easy* xviii, The soldiers will soon have our description and rout us out. We shall be pinned in a couple of days. **1859** MEREDITH *R. Feverel* xvi, Have you more of them, sir; of a similar description? Rout them out! **1929** J. MASEFIELD *Hawbucks* 101 He went home to his cellar and routed out a bottle of port. **1938** M. K. RAWLINGS *Yearling* iv. 31 He dashed in to his room and routed out his heavy cowhide brogans. **1950** R. MOORE *Candlemas Bay* III. 142 Ordinarily, he would have enjoyed routing out the fishhouse. **1973** A. CHRISTIE *Postern of Fate* I. v. 39, I shall go up and rout him out.

c. To drive out *from* a place.

1812 H. & J. SMITH *Rej. Addr.* v. (1873) 38 Who routed you from a rat-hole. **1820** W. IRVING *Sketch Bk., Rip van Winkle* §12 From this strong hold the unlucky Rip was routed by his termagant wife.

4. To turn over; to toss or drive about.

1845 HOOD *Tale of a Trumpet* 121 After poking in pot and pan, And routing garments in want of stitches. **1856**

STONEHENGE *Brit. Rural Sports* 59/2 Let him be put on the scent of pheasants.., and let him rout them about well for a few minutes.

Hence **'routing** *vbl. sb.* and *ppl. a.*; also with *out*.

1572 *Schole-ho. Women* 344 in Hazl. *E.P.P.* IV. 118 Plant them round with many a pin, Ringed for routing of pure golde. **1579** FULKE *Heskins' Parl.* 124 Leauing.. M. Heskins with his groyne serching in that swill, I will chase him from routing in the holy auntient garden of Irenæus. **1758** EDWARDS *Sonn.* xliv. (Todd), Do thou the monumental hillock guard From trampling cattle, and the routing swine. **1820** CLARE *Rural Life, Poet's Wish* 43 Curse upon that routing jade, My territories to invade. *a* **1852** MOORE *Moral Positions* iii, To guard the frail package from tousing and routing, There stood my Lord Eld-n, endorsing it 'Glass'. **1875** BLACKMORE *Alice Lorraine* III. vi. 89, I would give a month's tithes for a good day's routing among that boy's accumulations. **1946** C. H. HAYWARD *Light Machines for Woodwork* xii. 147 For such work as the free-hand routing out of.. the ground-work of a piece of carving it is essential that the wood is laid flat.. and the machine passed over it. **1953** E. G. HAMILTON *Power Tools for Home Craftsman* vii. 231 Routing with a pattern is a fast and simple method of doing production work. **1958** *New Scientist* 17 July 441/1 The chief applications of the intricately shaped parts produced from solid metal by routing are in the aircraft industry. **1976** C. H. GRONEMAN *Gen. Woodworking* (ed. 5) xlvi. 224 (*caption*) Freehand routing of a penciled design.

attrib. **1846** HOLTZAPFFEL *Turning* II. 737 The stringings ..are inlaid with the routing gage. **1875** KNIGHT *Dict. Mech.* 1995/2 Routing-machine. *Ibid.* 1996/1 Routing-tool. **1935** *Times* 9 Nov. 4/4 Blind men.. use, unaided, the circular saw and the routing machine (a speed of 15,000 revolutions a minute) to carve the animals.

rout (raʊt), *v.*⁹ [App. an alteration of ROOT *v.*¹, but cf. MDu. *rūten* (later *ruyten, ruiten*) in the same sense. In later use perh. associated with *v.*¹⁰] *trans.* To root *out*, to extirpate.

1591 NASHE *Prognostication* 12 If God or the king rout them not out with a sharpe ouerthrow. *c* **1605** ? ROWLEY *Birth of Merlin* IV. i, With an utter extirpation To rout the Brittains out and plant the English. **1670** G. H. *Hist. Cardinals* I. II. 52 The Jews were.. routed out of Jerusalem. **1700** ASTRY tr. *Saavedra's Royal Politician* I. 199 The ill Seed be routed out before it take Root. **1754** A. MURPHY *Gray's Inn Jrnl.* No. 89 Whole Families are entirely routed out of House and Home. **1800** J. MILNER *Lett. to Prebendary* (1815) 98 It was to repress and rout out these.. that the crusade.. and the Inquisition were set on foot. **1865** KINGSLEY *Hereward* xxi, Make the most of her before I rout thee out. **1907** *Blackw. Mag.* Dec. 758/2 One may see the agents of Shems-ed-Dulal.. passing along to rout out Christianity from Nubia.

†**b.** With *out* omitted. *Obs. rare*⁻¹.

1682 LUTTRELL *Brief Rel.* (1857) I. 162 The magistrates there have quite routed the meeting houses in that citty, and severall of the hearers sent to prison.

rout (raʊt), *v.*¹⁰ Also 7 root, route, rowt(e. [f. ROUT *sb.*²]

1. *trans.* To put (an army, body of troops, etc.) to rout; to compel to flee in disorder.

c **1600** [see the *vbl. sb.*]. **1611** SHAKS. *Cymb.* v. ii. 12 Stand, .. The lane is guarded: Nothing rowts vs, but The villany of our feares. **1617** MORYSON *Itin.* II. 178 The Irish.. were suddenly routed, and our men followed the execution. **1644** *10th Rep. Hist. MSS. Comm.* App. IV. 69 Col. Ludlowe with a regiment.. of about 300 [horse] did charge and route 1400 of the King's forces. **1680** HICKERINGILL *Curse Ye Meroz* 14 The French-men who rooted his Army. *a* **1727** NEWTON *Chronol. Amended* iv. (1728) 299 They routed the army of Pharaoh. **1781** GIBBON *Decl. & F.* xli. IV. 167 They were routed at the first onset. **1839** THIRLWALL *Greece* xlviii. VI. 127 The Egyptians.. were routed and fled toward the fortress. **1874** GREEN *Short Hist.* iv. §6. 205 A small English force.. sufficed to rout the disorderly levies.

b. *fig.* To discomfit, defeat utterly.

1676 D. GRANVILLE *Lett.* (Surtees) 159 A sound Arch-deacon sure.. will rowte him. *a* **1704** T. BROWN *Satire upon French King* Wks. 1730 I. 60 But now I'm clearly routed by the treaty. **1850** THACKERAY *Pendennis* xxvii. 179 This gravity and decorum routed and surprised the Colonel more than any other kind of behaviour probably would.

c. To disperse, dispel, scatter, drive away.

1648–9 *Eikon Bas.* 109 They think no Victories so effectuall to their designs as those that most rout and waste my Credit with my People. **1683** TRYON *Way to Health* 536 'Tis certain that such diseases.. are not to be routed by all their Regiments [etc.]. **1840** DICKENS *Old C. Shop* v, A few whispered words.. routed these symptoms effectually. **1850** THACKERAY *Pendennis* vii, He.. routed his mother's objections with infinite satisfaction to himself.

†**2. a.** *intr.* To break into rout; to flee in disorder. *Obs.*

1631 CHAPMAN *Cæsar & Pompey* Plays 1873 III. 163 The souldiers.. Euery way routing: as th' alarme were then Giuen to their army. *a* **1680** BUTLER *Rem.* (1759) I. 6 The gallant Subvolvani.. make a Sally Upon the stubborn Enemy, Who now begin to rout and fly.

†**b.** *refl.* in the same sense. *Obs.*

1636 E. DACRES tr. *Machiavel's Disc. Livy* II. 333 If the first front be broken,.. they fall together into a confusion, and rout themselves. **1647** CLARENDON *Hist. Reb.* VII. §195 The whole Body Routed themselves, and fled.

Hence **'routing** *vbl. sb.*

c **1600** EDMONDS *Observ. Cæsar's Comm.* 80 The disorder or rowting of an enemie which is caused by the bow-men. **1650** FULLER *Pisgah* IV. v. 85 So vain is it, for men to outvie Gods routings, with their recruitings.

routable ('raʊtəb(ə)l), *a.* [f. ROUT *v.*¹⁰ + -ABLE.] Capable of being routed.

1853 G. J. CAYLEY *Las Alforjas* I. 5 The most formidable of French impossibilities are always routable by a charge of cavalry.

rou'tation. *nonce-word.* = ROUT *sb.*¹ 9.

1809 *Spirit Public Jrnls.* XIII. 178 Lady A.. chooses a distant night which does not interfere with any then declared routations.

route (ruːt), *sb.* Forms: 3 rute, 4–6, 8– route (6 roote, 7 rote, routte); 6–9 rout (6 *Sc.* rowt). [a. F. *route* (OF. also *rute*):—L. *rupta* (sc. *via*), fem. of *ruptus* broken: cf. ROUT *sb.*¹ and *sb.*² for other developments of meaning.

Found in ME., and in the end of the 16th cent., but not finally adopted until the beginning of the 18th; from that time down to *c* 1800 the usual spelling was *rout*. The pronunciation (raʊt), which appears in early 19th cent. rimes, is still retained in military use, and by many speakers in the U.S. and Canada.]

1. a. A way, road, or course; a certain direction taken in travelling from one place to another; a regular line of travel or passage. Also, used in various countries, esp. the U.S. and France, with a following numeral to designate a particular highway (also *fig.*).

a **1225** *Ancr. R.* 350 Þe gode pilegrim.. ne etstont nout ase foles doð, auh halt forð his rute. *c* **1315** SHOREHAM I. 1358 Wo-so lokeþ, ne geþ he nauȝt derk, Ac lyȝt ine lyues route. *c* **1410** *Master of Game* (MS. Digby 182) xxii, Hunters also beyonde þe see callen of an herte or of a boore þe routes and þe paas;.. paas þei clepe þe goynges where a beeste gooth, and þe routes where as he is ypassed.

? **1568** *Satir. Poems Reform.* xlvi. 52 Steir be the compas, and keip hir rowt. **1582** N. LICHEFIELD tr. *Castanheda's Conq. E. Ind.* I. ii. 5 b, The Captaine generall commaunded, that.. they shuld euery one make, and keepe, their roote or course to Cabo Verde. **1594** BLUNDEVIL *Exerc.* (1597) 204 The Mariners.., to bee the better assured of their routes and courses on the sea, do deuide euery quarter of the Horizon into 8 seuerall windes. *Ibid.* 330.

α. **1677** *Phil. Trans.* XII. 880 The Routs, Courses and Distances of the principal Ports. **1710** *Lond. Gaz.* No. 4732/1 We were to take the Rout through the Sarfana. **1774** J. BRYANT *Mythol.* II. 58 He is said to have persevered in his rout westward. **1808** PARSONS *Trav. Asia*, etc. iv. 77 We still remained in camp, the ground being too swampy to continue our rout. **1835** WILLIS *Pencillings* I. iii. 28 It is impossible to conceive a rout of more grandeur than this famous road along the Mediterranean from Nice to Genoa.

β. **1748** *Anson's Voy.* Introd., The chart of that northern Ocean, and the particulars of their route through it. **1749** CHESTERF. *Lett.* clxiv. (1774) II. 469, I leave the choice of the route to you. **1794** PALEY *Evid.* (1800) 80 They parted from one another, and set forwards upon separate routes. **1840** THIRLWALL *Greece* lix. VII. 359 Antigonus.. attempted to overtake him, by a different route, which traversed the plains north of the Sangarius. **1877** FROUDE *Short Stud.* (1883) IV. I. x. 113 They had gone by separate routes to separate ports. **1924** *N.Y. Times* 21 Dec. VIII. 9/7 Route 2 is the high-way from Scranton Pa... to Montreal. **1933** KIPLING *Souvenirs of France* i. 18 That was the Rhone Road, Route 7. **1938** *Travel* June 37/1 From New York there are three delightful motor routes.. all picking up Route 6. **1962** 'K. ORVIS' *Damned & Destroyed* v. 41 You haven't fooled me. You're on Route Zero. **1970** *Washington Post* 30 Sept. B4/1 Fredericksburg location is just off route 95.

b. In *transf.* or *fig.* uses.

1630 LORD *Banians* 88 As some report, the River Ganges was carried from her wonted Rote, to runne in a new chanell. **1673** O. WALKER *Educ.* 6 The narrow, rough, and unbeaten routtes of Industry and labour. **1738** WARBURTON *Div. Legat.* I. 377 This Emulation disposed him to take a different Rout to Fame. **1781** COWPER *Conversat.* 213 At ev'ry interview their route the same, The repetition makes attention lame. **1824** BYRON *Juan* xv. li, It wearies out. So the end's gain'd, what signifies the route? **1884** tr. *Lotze's Metaph.* 374 Nature seems.. to reach many of her ends by long circuitous routes. **1899** *Allbutt's Syst. Med.* VII. 547 Micro-organisms may sometimes enter by this route and thus invade the meninges.

c. *U.S.* An established stage by which post is conveyed prior to delivery.

1792 *Deb. Congress U.S.* 10 Jan. (1849) 58 The route by which the mails are at present conveyed shall in no case be altered. **1821** *Ibid.* 31 Dec. (1855) 47 Praying that the route of the mail from Savannah to Augusta.. may not be altered. **1874** *Ann. Rep. Postmaster-General* (U.S. Post-Office Dept.) 209 Each railway post-office clerk.. is required to attach to each package of letters he makes up a facing or label-slip bearing the address of the package, the office or route upon which it was made up.

d. *N.Amer.* A round travelled regularly by someone collecting, delivering, or selling goods, such as newspapers or milk.

1841 *Jamestown* (N.Y.) *Jrnl.* 5 May 2/4 He succeeded in obtaining possession of a route for a morning penny paper. **1849** C. MATHEWS *Moneypenny* xiii. 119 Go up-stairs, and tell Wages to give you the St. John's Park route. He'll fix your pay. **1868**, etc. [see *paper route* s.v. PAPER *sb.* 12]. **1874**, etc. [see *milk-route* s.v. MILK *sb.* 10]. **1939** J. P. MARQUAND *Wickford Point* x. 108 Her father ran a milk route and drank hard cider. **1976** *Washington Post* 19 Apr. C14/4 (Advt.), Routes are available in the metropolitan Washington area to aggressive persons who are experienced Route Sales people.

e. Phr. *to go the route*, in *Baseball*, to pitch for an entire game; also *transf.* in *Boxing*; *fig.*, to go the full distance, to go all the way. *U.S.*

1913 *Chicago Record-Herald* 16 Mar. VIII. 1/5 This was the first complete battle Cicotte has pitched, and he was watched closely to see if he could go the route. **1926** J. BLACK *You can't Win* xvi. 230 If a Chinese doesn't like you he will keep away from you; if he does like you he will go the route. **1933** *Amer. Speech* Oct. 36/1 He went the route without being kayoed. **1948** *Chicago Tribune* 8 May II. 3/3 Bill Voiselle went the route for the Braves. **1963** I. FLEMING *On H.M. Secret Service* iv. 45 She made love with the fervour and expertness of a girl who, in the American phrase, had 'gone the route'. **1974** *Index-Jrnl.* (Greenwood, S. Carolina) 18 Apr. 11/3 Steve Rogers went the route, giving up six hits.

2. Routine, regular course. *rare.*

1725 *Fam. Dict.* s.v. *Blood*, Those who use sick Persons only by a certain Rout, order them to be bled. **1803** *Med. Jrnl.* X. 293 It seems to me there was pretty much regularity in the rout of the disease. **1854** THOREAU *Walden* Concl., It is remarkable how.. insensibly we fall into a particular route, and make a beaten track for ourselves.

3. *Mil.* **a.** The order to march.

1751 FIELDING *Amelia* I. I. ix. 68 This Letter was from his Captain, to acquaint him, that the Rout, as they call it, was arrived, and that they were to march within two Days. **1784** R. BAGE *Barham Downs* II. 118, I was under the care of a surgeon, and our route came for a march. **1796** *Grose's Dict. Vulgar T.* (ed. 3), *Rout*, an order from the Secretary at War, directing the march and quartering of soldiers. **1826** G. R. GLEIG *Subaltern* iii, Nor was it till the evening of the 27th that the long-expected route arrived. **1878** MAJOR GRIFFITHS *Eng. Army* iii. 67 'Routes', or marching orders, are issued by the Quarter-master-General's people.

fig. **1844** W. H. MAXWELL *Sports & Adv. Scot.* xxxix. (1855) 306 Old Daly found his route had come.

b. In phr. *to get*, or *give, the route*, to receive, or issue, marching orders.

1848 THACKERAY *Van. Fair* xxiv, As transports were in plenty, they would get their route before the week was over. *Ibid.* xxxii, 'I don't move till O'Dowd gives me the route,' said she. **1886** MRS. RIDDELL *For Dick's Sake* ii, We are expecting to be sent on active service immediately, and.. I don't care how soon we get the route. **1890** 'R. BOLDREWOOD' *Col. Reformer* (1891) 120 A feeling of.. satisfaction possessed him when he got the route for Warbrok.

c. *column of route*, the formation assumed by troops when on the march.

1802 C. JAMES *New Mil. Dict.*, s.v. *March*, His next care must be the arrangement of all its different component parts, with which he will form his column of route. **1844** *Queen's Regul. & Ord. Army* 179 A Column of Route is to proceed with as extensive a front as the road will permit. **1976** *Broadcast* Dec. 17/2 There can be few occupations so completely degrading as marching in column-of-route.

4. *attrib.*, as (sense 1) ***route book, card, check, -form, -map, marker, -mile, -mileage, number, planning, proficiency***; ***route-proving*** adj.; (sense 3) ***route column, march*** (hence as *vb. intr.*), ***-marching***; **route-goer** *Baseball*, one who goes the route (see sense 1 e above); hence **route-going** *a.*; **routeman, route man** *N.Amer.* = ROUNDSMAN 3; also, a salesman who works a particular route (see sense 1 d above); hence **routemanship; route salesman** *N.Amer.*, a salesman who works a particular route (cf. *routeman*); so **route sales, route salespeople; route sheet** *N.Amer.*, an engagement itinerary for a touring company or artist.

1910 (*title*) *Route book for the British Isles. **1975** *Oxf. Compan. Sports & Games* 702/2 The correct route, which the organizers convey to the crew in route-books. **1931** *Amer. Speech* VI. 335 *Route-card,.. a table or schedule issued to show people giving the 'stands' for about ten days in advance. **1963** P. DRACKETT *Motor Rallying* iii. 39 British rallies require only the accurate plotting of six-figure map references plus the ability to.. read from a simple route-card. *Ibid.* 37 *Route checks, or passage controls, are also a feature of the majority of rallies. **1954** W. FAULKNER *Fable* 6 It was a whole battalion.. emerging from the *Place de Ville* in close *route column. **1888** PENNELL *Sent. Journ.* 99 The *route-form was passed from one to the other. **1967** *Boston Sunday Herald* 26 Mar. II. 3/1 The Philadelphia 76ers had five *route-goers.. while Hal Greer missed only one game. **1976** *Billings* (Montana) *Gaz.* 17 June 2-H/4 Doug DeCinces and Lee May each hit three-run homers to support 39-year old Mike Cuellar's first *route-going performance of the season. **1918** *Nat. Laundry Jrnl.* 1 May 56/1 It really matters little whether he be known as a *route man, salesman, or representative... Good route men are scarce. **1943** *Daily Progress* (Charlottesville, Va.) 29 May 8 (Advt.), In the face of a 40% reduction in gasoline mileage your routeman will call on you three times each week as in the past. **1976** *Billings* (Montana) *Gaz.* 2 July 9-C/1 (Advt.), Excellent opportunity for a Route Man to take over present route & expand. **1945** *U.S. Armed Forces Educ. Man.* EM 991. xiii. 136 This chapter explains the elements of *routemanship. **1883** *Science* II. 86/1 A *route-map of Russia in Europe. **1895** W. S. CHURCHILL *Let.* 27 Feb. in R. S. Churchill *Winston S. Churchill* (1967) I. Compan. I. viii. 559, I went out with the regiment on Friday to a *route march—which was very fine. **1909** *Blackw. Mag.* Sept. 396/1 They have all been called out to some absurd inspection, or route march, or manœuvres, or something. **1934** WEBSTER, Route-march, v.i. **1939** *Airman's Gaz.* Dec., You route march into the local swedeville. **1977** D. BAGLEY *Enemy* xxix. 231 Benson had a cushy billet for a soldier in wartime. Not for him route marches in the pouring rain. **1789** *Rules & Regulations Field Exercises & Movements Army in Ireland* I. 54 In Common *Route marching the same regularity of step cannot be required, as is necessary in the operation of manœuvre. **1868** *Queen's Regul. & Ord. Army* §1118 The Troops on home Service are to be practised in route marching once a week. **1925** *N.Y. Times* 5 Aug. 8/3 The shield of the United States was adopted today as a model for the outline of *route markers for the system of national highways. **1968** M. WOODHOUSE *Rock Baby* xv. 148 Plenty of people cross various borders.. when they can't see the route-markers. **1911** *Encycl. Brit.* XXII. 824/2 In Europe the average *route-mile capital is £27,036. **1962** *Observer* 25 Mar. 1/5 Route-mileage is the length of routes, as distinct from the length of individual sets of tracks. British Railways cover about 18,500 route-miles. **1967** *Listener* 26 Jan. 123/1 A maximum of 100 m.p.h. is now possible over about 360 route-miles of British Rail. **1924** *N.Y. Times* 21 Dec. VIII. 9/7 The *route number is painted in figures five inches high. **1973** D. WESTHEIMER *Going Public* iv. 64 He memorized the route numbers of the buses. **1967** *Jane's Surface Skimmer Syst.* 1967–68 51/1 The Central Electricity Generating Board.. is constantly faced with *route-planning problems. **1959** WALLIS & BLAIR

Thunder Above iii. 15 His first trip as captain would be a *route-proficiency check. **1957** *Times* 21 Dec. 5/3 The flight ..completed their *route-proving programme before the beginning of commercial operations. **1937** DEARMOND & GRAF *Route Sales Managem.* 4 Another factor in *route sales distribution, the accurate anticipation of customer demand. **1937** *Job Descriptions of Laundry Industry* 253 Route-Man, Route Driver, *Route-Salesman... Drives a Delivery Truck over an established route to collect washing from and deliver it to customers' houses. **1968** *Globe & Mail* (Toronto) 13 Feb. 33/7 (Advt.), Route Salesman..required by supplier of industrial garments. **1976** *Washington Post* 19 Apr. C14/4 (Advt.), *Route Sales.* Routes are available..to aggressive persons who are experienced *Route Sales people. **1916** *Variety* 27 Oct. 12/2 Sam Sidman's Own Show is on the Columbia *route sheet to play there. **1941** W. C. HANDY *Father of Blues* xiv. 195 Each one..had been copying other pluggers' borrowed route-sheets and submitting them to me as evidence of work done by themselves.

‖**5.** ***en route*** (ãrut) (also ***en-route***, N. Amer. ***enroute***), on the way.

1779 in Jesse *Geo. Selwyn*, etc. (1844) IV. 112 On which day he would certainly be *en route* with Mie Mie. **1857** *Tait's Mag.* XXIV. 165 Bread, biscuits, jams, and other things not procurable *en route.* **1867** LATHAM *Black & White* 34 Informing a friend..that certain goods were *en route* to him from England in a certain ship. **1872** SHAND *Shooting Rapids* I. vii. 119 They changed horses twice en route. **1955** *Times* 10 May 10/3 In the course of his journey to Leeds the Prime Minister made several speeches *en route.* **1956** R. BRADDON *Nancy Wake* ix. 93 He would attempt to escape somewhere en route to Gerona. **1967** *Boston Sunday Herald* 26 Mar. VI. 4/1 (Advt.), Enroute to Miami with overnight stays in Wash., D.C., [etc.]. **1976** *National Observer* (U.S.) 7 Feb. 11/3 You can take advantage of Sitmar's 'Cruise Plus' feature which allows stopovers enroute home. **1978** *Nature* 5 Oct. 363/2 US spacecraft are now en-route to Venus, Jupiter, Saturn and Uranus.

route (ruːt), *v.* [f. the sb.] **a.** *trans.* To mark as available, to send or forward, to direct to be sent, be a certain route.

For the pronunc., see the sb.

The pres. pple. is spelt *routeing* (the better form: cf. note s.v. ROUTEING *vbl. sb.*) or *routing.*

1890 *Whitby Gaz.* 21 Nov. 3/5 Passenger tickets used on the Scarborough and Whitby Railway.., whether such tickets be routed or not. **1893** *Pall Mall G.* 25 Jan. 2/1 Goods routed this way are taken by rail to Duluth. **1893** M. H. CUSHING *Story of our Post Office* 235 Here are the carriers themselves, engaged in 'routing' the mail. **1926** J. BLACK *You can't Win* ix. 113 The papers were carefully read at night, and the next morning 'routed' through the prison. **1926** *N.Y. Times Mag.* 15 Aug. 6 Complaints were routed past the complaint department to the President's office. **1952** *Oxf. Mag.* 24 Jan. 142 An attempt is made to govern, by routing it through the Proctors, the growing spate of information. **1959** *Daily Tel.* 17 Mar. 13/2 A minute later he routed the Liverpool Street–Norwich train through. **1960** *Washington Post* 16 Nov. A16 West Germany's share of a greater European effort in NATO would have to be routed through NATO organs. **1961** L. MUMFORD *City in Hist.* (1966) xvi. 567 Major through-traffic streams must be routed around residential areas. **1971** P. GRESSWELL *Environment* 105 Others [*sc.* footpaths] might be better routed round field edges than through the middle of fields. **1971** D. POTTER *Brit. Eliz. Stamps* xiii. 142 Very large postings in bulk attract substantial discounts. They are routed by second-class mail. **1977** *Daily Tel.* 20 Jan. 17/4 The organising committee intends to prevent a repetition by routeing the procession through wide streets.

b. To schedule or bill.

1916 *Variety* 22 Oct. 12/2 Rud Hynicka's show..will not play the Star and Garter next week as routed. **1932** L. C. DOUGLAS *Forgive us our Trespasses* (1937) xiii. 253 Deducing from time-tables, Dinney hypothetically routed Joan to arrive at six-thirty on Thursday evening.

c. To direct (an electrical signal or transmission of any kind, as a telephone call) over a particular circuit or path, or *to* a particular location.

1948 J. ATKINSON *Telephony* I. xii. 234/2 The group centre extends the call to the zone centre where it is routed to the distant zone centre exchange. **1956** *B.B.C. Handbk.* *1957* 50 The sound components of the various contributions are routed and switched simultaneously with the vision. **1962** *Listener* 3 May 770/2 If one operator on the lunar surface wished to communicate with another operator a dozen miles away, his only method would be to route his signal by way of the Earth. **1964** F. L. WESTWATER *Electronic Computers* i. 6 By means of electronic switching devices a word is routed to the correct address in the store. **1973** *Daily Tel.* 22 Jan. 2/1 The dialling code for Rome is 010 39 6. The digits 010 route the call to the international automatic exchange in London, 39 routes to Italy, and the final 6 is the code number for Rome. **1973** *Physics Bull.* Feb. 109/1 The reference channel plug-in..accepts a reference signal derived from a chopper, which enables the plug-in to control and route the signal pulses to two counting channels.

route, obs. form of ROOT.

† **route**, perh. an error for ROOK *sb.*[1]

a **1529** SKELTON *P. Sparowe* 449 The churlysshe chowgh; The route and the kowgh.

routed (ˈraʊtɪd), *ppl. a.* [f. ROUT *v.*[10] + -ED[1].] Put to rout; compelled to flee in disorder.

1606 SHAKS. *Ant. & Cl.* III. i. 9 Spurre through Media.. and the shelters, whether The routed flie. **1678** SIR R. L'ESTRANGE *Seneca's Mor.* (1696) 124 It fares with us in Humane Life, as in a Routed Army. **1724** DE FOE *Mem. Cavalier* (1840) 200 The..remains of his routed regiments. **1770** LANGHORNE *Plutarch* (1851) I. 293/1 The poor remains of his father's routed forces. **1849** MACAULAY *Hist. Eng.* v. I. 614 The routed army came pouring into the streets of Bridgewater. **1874** GREEN *Short Hist.* v. §1. 224 The routed soldiery turned into free companies of bandits.

routeing (ˈruːtɪŋ), *vbl. sb.* [f. the vb.] Also **routing**. Delineation of routes, etc. Also, the action of the vb.: direction along, or allocation to, particular routes.

Routeing is the better form to distinguish it from ROUTING *vbl. sb.* and *ppl. a.* (pronounced (ˈraʊtɪŋ)).

1881 *National Baptist* XVII. 374 The coloring and routeing of the map..add greatly to its value. **1903** *Electr. World & Engineer* 23 May 856/1 The facility which such combination lends to through routing of cars. **1930** M. CLARK *Home Trade* xxiv. 198 All waste of time in the passage of any piece of work through the factory, scientific management methods endeavour to eliminate by 'routeing'. **1947** A. HARRIS *Bomber Offensive* 188 Against this we devised a new kind of routeing. **1964** F. L. WESTWATER *Electronic Computers* iii. 28 The routing and control of a sequence of pulses throughout a computer depends on an appropriate assembly of switching circuits. **1975** *Daily Tel.* 12 Feb. 14 Postal addresses are in effect routing directions. **1976** P. R. WHITE *Planning for Public Transport* vii. 139 The weakness is that journey times between major towns are often far too long, especially in relation to potential direct routeings.

‖**route nationale** (rut nasjɔnal). Pl. **routes nationales**. [Fr., = national highway.] In France, a main or trunk road constructed and maintained by the central government.

1896 A. P. ROCKWELL *Roads & Pavements in France* 26 The 22,000 miles of *Routes Nationales* are periodically examined with great care in order to ascertain the actual thickness of the stone layer. **1906** C. NEVILLE *Round France in Motor* vi. 39 The next morning we ought to have continued along the Route Nationale, which goes to Macon *via* Châlon. **1924** KIPLING in *N.Y. World* 23 Apr. 15/2 Route Nationale No. 20 conducts from Paris to the Spanish frontier at Bourg-Madame. **1949** M. LASKI *Little Boy Lost* iii. 49 This isn't Paris—it's some shabby village away from all the *routes nationales.* **1973** G. SIMS *Hunters Point* xix. 177 The frontier town of Menton..where the French Route Nationale meets the Italian Via Aurelia.

† **router**, *sb.*[1] *Obs.* Forms: 4 roto(u)r, 5 *Sc.* rw-, rutowr, 6 rutour; 5 rowter, 6 rout(t)er. [a. AF. *routour*, OF. *routeur*, f. *route*, in the sense either of 'band, troop' (ROUT *sb.*[1]) or 'road' (ROUTE *sb.*): cf. RUTTER[1].]

1. A lawless person; a robber, ruffian.

[**1379** *Rolls of Parlt.* III. 62/2 En grant confort & abaundissement des tielx malfeisours & routours.]

a **1400** [see ROTER[1]]. *c* **1425** WYNTOUN *Cron.* v. xiii. 4648 Qwhar Bellyal barnys ar bulȝeande And rutowris raggit þar rulȝeande. **1481** CAXTON *Godfrey* xx. 51 To venge vpon thyse false rowters, and theuys the oultrage that they had don. *Ibid.* xxxi. 67 They toke alle the maydens of the town lyke rowters & theues. **1536** BELLENDEN *Cron. Scot.* (1821) I. 32 Than sal thay corruppit rutouris his minions, be salut as kingis.

2. A swaggering soldier or bully.

1557 *Welth & Helth* 388 (1907), Who cummeth there? Hance bere pot, Ascon router. **1576** BP. WOOLTON *Chr. Man.* I v b, They set them out wyth sumpteous and gorgeous apparell of dyuers colors, some tyme lyke Routters, some tyme lyke Rouffyns.

ˈrouter, *sb.*[2] [f. ROUT *v.*[1]] (See quot.)

1611 COTGR. *Ronfleur*, a snorer, a snorter, a rowter.

router (ˈraʊtə(r)), *sb.*[3] [f. ROUT *sb.*[1] 5 or *v.*[7]] One who takes part in a rout; a riotous person.

1670 *Tryal of Rudyard, Moor*, etc. in *Phœnix* (1721) I. 369 They never had been guilty of being Rioters and Routers. **1788** W. MARSHALL *Prov. Yorksh.*, *Rooter*,..a person rushing into company abruptly, or rudely.

ˈrouter, *sb.*[4] *nonce-word.* [f. ROUT *sb.*[1] 9.] One who gives a rout or reception.

1809 *Spirit Public Jrnls.* XIII. 179 Very considerable losses exalt the character of a rout prodigiously; and if a young heir is done over, it is a stamp of honour to the router.

router (ˈraʊtə(r)), *sb.*[5] [f. ROUT *v.*[8] 2 b.]

1. a. A cutter that removes wood from a groove or recess, as in a router plane.

1818 *Trans. R. Soc. Arts* XXXV. 123 With my plane, as fast as the cutters pierce the wood, the router follows after, and clears the wood out of the groove. **1846** HOLTZAPFFEL *Turning* II. 488 The central plate of the plough is retained as a guide for the central positions of the router and cutter.

b. A router plane.

1846 C. HOLTZAPFFEL *Turning & Mech. Manipulation* II. 979 Mr. Wm. Lund has constructed the router..with a screw adjustment to the cutter. **1875** SIR T. SEATON *Fret-Cutting* 111 To assist in smoothing the ground and getting it level in all parts, carvers frequently make use of a 'router', a species of plane. **1923** R. GREENHALGH *Pract. Joinery & Carpentry* xix. 245 A number of grooves are first run round the wreath [of a handrail] in suitable places, a useful tool for this purpose being the router. **1954** W. E. KELSEY *Carpentry, Joinery & Woodcutting Machinery* i. 14 Router or old woman's tooth... This is a tool for cleaning out and levelling the bottoms of trenches. **1974** G. BLACKBURN *Illustr. Encycl. Woodworking Handtools* 169 The Pattern Maker's Router is similar to the Router Plane, but with a machined, larger sole.

c. (See quot. *a* 1877.)

a **1877** KNIGHT *Dict. Mech.* I. 288/2 The center-bit consists of three parts: a center point or pin..; a thin cutting point or nicker that..circumscribes the hole; and a broad chisel-edge or router, placed obliquely, and tearing up the wood within the circle marked out by the point. **1947** H. E. KING *School Cert. Woodwork* vi. 63 Boring Bits... The router and nicker are sharpened on the inside only. **1955** M. M. WATERS *Woodwork* 107 The nicker extends lower than the router and so engages the wood slightly ahead of it.

d. A woodworking machine similar to a spindle moulder but using a much higher speed of rotation and able to produce finished work; also, a portable hand-held version of this.

1946 W. B. MCKAY *Joinery* i. 24 Another form of vertical boring machine is known as a router or recessing machine or overhead spindle moulder. **1954** W. E. KELSEY *Carpentry, Joinery & Woodcutting Machinery* xvii. 517 The router has taken over a great deal of the lighter work up to 1 in. or 1¼ in. thick which was formerly done on the spindle-moulder. *Ibid.* 546 Portable electric router... This machine works on the same principle as the overhead-router. **1958** *Wall St. Jrnl.* 30 Sept. 7/4 An official..enthuses over a new power wood-working tool called a 'router'. **1976** *Arizona Republic* (Phoenix) 9 May K2/6 Harman uses a router (similar to an electric drill..) to make a hole in the center of the slice for the hand shaft to go through. **1976** *S. Wales Echo* 23 Nov. 11/5 (Advt.), One overhead router £200. Various other items for woodworking shop.

2. One who routs *out* or draws forth.

a **1890** in *Cent. Dict.*, He is a fair scholar, well up in Herodotus, and a grand router-out of antiquities.

3. *attrib.*, as **router bit, cutter** = sense 1 c above; **router plane**, a plane with a cutter projecting below the sole so that the bottom of a groove or recess can be planed.

1953 E. G. HAMILTON *Power Tools for Home Craftsman* vii. 230 Small router bits are usually of the single-flute type. **1976** C. H. GRONEMAN *Gen. Woodworking* (ed. 5) xlvi. 220 Most routers use ¼- or ⅜-in.-shank (6·35- or 9·52-mm-shank) router bits. *a* **1877** KNIGHT *Dict. Mech.* III. 1995/2 *Routing-machine*, a shaping-machine which works by means of a router-cutter..revolving above a bed with universal horizontal adjustment. **1846** HOLTZAPFFEL *Turning* II. 488 The router-gage..has a tooth like a narrow chisel. *Ibid.* 487 A router plane..has a broad surface carrying in its center one of the cutters belonging to the plough. **1934** *Planecraft* (C. & J. Hampton Ltd.) xiv. 105 The Record Router Plane ..is made both with an open and with a closed mouth. **1966** A. T. COLLINS *Newnes Compl. Pract. Woodworking* 30 Router planes are used for levelling and smoothing the surface on the bottom of a groove, slot or cavity which is inaccessible to an ordinary grooving plane. **1974** [see sense 1 b above].

Hence **ˈrouter** *v.*, to cut away, hollow out, with a router.

1890 in *Cent. Dict.*

routh (raʊθ), *sb. Sc.* and *north.* Also **rowth.** [Of obscure origin.] Abundance, plenty.

1720 RAMSAY *Edinb.'s Salut. to Ld. Carnarvon* iv, But routh for pleasure and for use..You's hae at will. **1725** —— *Gentle Sheph.* III. iv, Nor does he want o' them a rowth at will. **1785** BURNS *Scotch Drink* 123 Fortune! if thou'll but gie me..rowth o' rhyme to rave at will, Tak a' the rest. **1816** SCOTT *Antiq.* xl, I trow there was routh o' company. **1842** J. AITON *Domest. Economy* (1857) 144 An unfavourable impression..which requires more hospitality and routh to remove than should be gone into at a manse. **1894** CROCKETT *Raiders* (ed. 3) 215 He has a barren heritage and routh of heather.

Prov. **1737** RAMSAY *Scot. Prov.* (1797) 14 A houndless hunter, and a gunless gunner, see aye rowth of game.

routh (raʊθ), *a. Sc.* Also **rowth, ruth.** [Cf. prec.] Abundant, plentiful; well supplied.

1791 LEARMONT *Poems* 28 [They] rue the day wi' wailin's rowth. **1822** GALT *Provost* xxxv, She..had aye a ruth and ready hand for the needful. **1863** QUINN *Heather Lintie* 225 Tae keep us rowth I've meal eneuch.

routh, obs. f. ROUGH *a.*, var. of ROWTH (rowing), obs. f. RUTH *sb.*

routher, obs. f. RUDDER.

routhero(o)ck: see ROUT *sb.*[7]

routhless, obs. f. RUTHLESS.

ˈrouthy, *a. Sc.* [f. ROUTH *sb.*] Plentiful, abundant, possessed of plenty.

1792 BURNS *Country Lassie* 12 Then wait a wee, and cannie wale, A routhie butt, a routhie ben. *a* **1880** in Edwards *Modern Sc. Poets* I. 291 O'Siller I've never been routhy.

Hence **ˈrouthiness**.

1872 J. PATERSON *Autobiogr. Remin.* iv. 87 This was not enough to account for her evident rowthiness.

‖**routier**[1], obs. or *Hist.* variant of RUTTIER.

1677 *Phil. Trans.* XII. 880 The Author hath, for the Sake of Merchants, annexed the Routier of the East and West-Indies. **1962** J. NEEDHAM *Sci. & Civilisation in China* IV. I. 285 Huang Shêng-Tsêng named as one of his sources a *Chen Wei Pien* (Collection of Needle Positions), which may or may not have been a specific printed book. If it was, it must have been a 'routier' or 'rutter' like the *Yüeh Yang Chen Lu Chi* (Record of Courses Set by the Needle in the Cantonese Seas), which is known to have still existed in the 18th century. **1971** S. E. MORISON *European Discovery Amer.: Northern Voy.* xiv. 465 Alfonce attributes the discovery of this river to the Portuguese, and the rhymed *routier* of 1547 by Jean Mallart agrees.

‖**routier**[2] (rutje). [Fr., f. *route* ROUTE *sb.*]

1. *Hist.* A member of any of numerous companies of mercenary soldiers that were active in France during the later Middle Ages.

1845 *Encycl. Metrop.* XI. 620 They [*sc.* the mercenary adventurers] were named also..*Routiers*, for numerous reasons too unsatisfactory to deserve quotation. **1910** *Encycl. Brit.* II. 683/1 Arthur now resumed the war against the English, and at the same time took vigorous measures against the plundering bands of soldiers and peasants known as *routiers* or *écorcheurs.* **1924** K. NORGATE *Richard the Lion Heart* ii. 53 If these Routiers could have been controlled by their employers, Henry and Richard might probably have been easily surrounded and captured. **1951** W. B. WELLS tr. *Perroy's Hundred Years War* IV. i. 149 When he entered the king's service,.. Duguesclin was no more than a captain of *routiers*, fond of pillage and raids. **1961** P. GREEN tr. *Oldenbourg's Massacre at Montsegur* iv. 105 The *routiers*, or mercenary companies, who formed a large part of the infantry. **1965** AUDEN *About House* (1966) 17 Conventional Blunderbuss war and its routiers. **1970** M. JONES *Ducal Brittany* vi. 167 The payments made by John IV to the *routier* companies in 1368–9 were..rather of protection money.

2. In France, a long-distance lorry driver. Also *attrib.*

In the *attrib.* examples the reference is usually to the *Guide des Relais Routiers*, a guide-book originally designed for lorry-drivers in France.

1961 L. DURRELL in *Holiday* Feb. 114 We planned to stop somewhere on the road to Béziers and have a bite of supper —Raoul knew a little place patronized by the *routiers*. **1971** *Guardian* 18 Aug. 10/5 One hotel (Routiers) stop in each direction including dinner and breakfast..[£]9.00. **1975** *Ibid.* 27 Jan. 7/5 Setting out with your Green Card and your Routier Guide to storm the Alpine passes. **1976** *Times* 14 Feb. 13/4 A cheap and cheerful *routier* halt where..the *café au lait* came in something more like a *pot de chambre* than a cup.

routi'narity. *nonce-word.* [Cf. next and -ITY.] Tendency to routine.

1868 VISC. STRANGFORD *Select.* (1869) I. 215 By their apathy, or their stupidity, or selfishness, or routinarity,..if I may use the terms.

rou'tinary, *a.* [f. ROUTINE *sb.* + -ARY.] According to routine or custom. Also, in wider senses: that acts according to routine; occurring, performed, etc., routinely.

1870 EMERSON *Soc. & Solit.* vii, He retreats into his routinary existence, which is quite separate from his scientific. **1963** V. NABOKOV *Gift* ii. 105 Some sort of routinary hallucination, like a harmless domestic ghost that sits down..every evening by the fireside. **1967** D. FLAKOLL tr. *Asturias's Cyclone* iii. 33 'The second ball is routine... Perhaps you can tell us where..routine commences.' 'It ends the instant the ball leaves your hand. You are no longer a rutinary [*sic*] bowler. The adventure begins.' **1976** *Word 1971* XXVII. 61 The exceptionality, for today, of prenatal assessment of foetal neurophysiology will be the routinary procedure of the future.

routine (ruː'tiːn), *sb.* (*a.*) Also 7 rotine, routin. [a. F. *routine* (†*rotine*), f. *route* ROUTE *sb.*]

1. a. A regular course of procedure; a more or less mechanical or unvarying performance of certain acts or duties.

a **1680** BUTLER *Rem.* (1759) II. 29 The general Business of the World lies, for the most Part, in Rotines and Forms. **1751** CHESTERF. *Lett.* cclx. (1792) III. 195 Haunt the Courts particularly in order to get that routine. **1777** J. ADAMS *Fam. Lett.* (1876) 247, I have got into the old routine of war office and Congress. **1808** SCOTT in *Lockhart* (1837) I. i. 31 Our class was, in the usual routine of the school, turned over to ..the Rector. **1846** GREENER *Sci. Gunnery* 126 More intimately acquainted with the routine of iron manufacturing than any other person. **1871** R. H. HUTTON *Ess.* II. 393 His external career was..identified with all the dullest routine of commercial duties.

b. A set form (of speech); a regular set or series (of phrases, etc.). *rare.*

1676 SHADWELL *Virtuoso* I. i, To have a form, a fashion of wit, a rotine of speaking, which they get by imitation. **1681** R. L'ESTRANGE *Casuist Uncas'd* Pref. p. vi, They have a certain Routin of Words, and Sayings, that have the tone of Magique in the very Sound of them. **1822** HAZLITT *Table-t.* Ser. II. v. (1869) 123 A routine of high flown phrases.

c. *Theatr.* A carefully rehearsed act or sequence of actions (in dancing, singing, dialogue, etc.); a sketch, turn, or 'number'; the manner in which an act is performed. Similarly in *Gymnastics*, a performance comprising a sequence of exercises carried out either on the floor or on apparatus, usu. in competition. Also *transf.* and *fig.*

1926 *Dance Mag.* June 25/3 No one ever taught him a routine. When he hummed a tune, dance steps just came to him. **1930** *Dancing Times* July 354/2 If a student goes through the same routine of steps (I am not talking of exercises, but of combined steps constituting a dance) [etc.]. **1932** N. COWARD *Words & Music* I. 9 Don't do a pratfall in your first routine. **1949** N. MARSH *Swing, Brother, Swing* xii. 280 He wasn't meant to fall. They'd altered the routine. **1956** H. KURNITZ *Invasion of Privacy* xiv. 92 Do you know the blackmail routine that Jarrold gave me tonight? **1959** LOKEN & WILLOUGHBY *Compl. Bk. Gymnastics* xvii. 196/1 For example, a fast, snappy mass tumbling act would be good following a slow, precise doubles balancing routine. **1963** 'E. MCBAIN' *Ten plus One* vi. 78 What the hell is this? .. A vaudeville routine at the Palace? **1975** *Oxf. Compan. Sports & Games* 452/1 In C-difficulty routines he may perform movements such as going from a handstand between the bars and then resting again in another handstand. **1977** *Time* 22 Aug. 43/1 A teacher in Peoria had encouraged him to become a performer, and when he returned from Germany he started a routine there at a little club.

d. *Computers.* A set of instructions which performs a specific task and is stored so that it may be executed many times; now esp. one which may be part of a longer, self-contained program.

1945 J. P. ECKERT et al. *Description of ENIAC* (PB 86242) (Moore School of Electr. Engin., Univ. Pennsylvania) B-3 Suppose it is desired to..carry out a computational routine of m line steps, print the final results, and then perform the same routine n times. **1948** GOLDSTINE & VON NEUMANN in J. von Neumann *Coll. Wks.* (1963) V. 217 We call the coded sequence of a problem a routine, and one which is formed for the purpose of possible substitution into other routines a subroutine. **1948** *Proc. IRE* XXXVI. 1453/1 The iterative methods of numerical analysis involve the repeated performance of computing routines. **1951** M. V. WILKES et al. *Preparation of Programs for Electronic Digital Computer* iii. 22 A 'closed' subroutine is one which is called into use by a special group of orders incorporated in the master routine or main program. **1967** *Technology Week* 23 Jan. 11/2 (Advt.), Software for Sigma 5 includes..a library of mathematical, business and utility routines. **1971** DUDRAP & EMERY in R. A. Wisbey *Computer in Lit. & Linguistic Res.* III. 90 It is often better to provide a few assembly-code routines than to try doing character editing in 'raw' FORTRAN. **1980** K. D. WISE *Microcomputers* v. 102 Transfers of data or control between routines should occur only when the programmer specifically requests them and only as called for in the specification of the routines.

2. Without article: Regular, unvarying, or mechanical procedure, discharge of duties, etc.

1789 MRS. PIOZZI *Journ. France* II. 25 The laws of insipid and dull routine. **1830** D'ISRAELI *Chas. I*, III. iv. 39 He was an honest man, but the harness of routine had rusted on his back. **1848** MILL *Pol. Econ.* I. vii. §5 (1876) 67 Any process which cannot be reduced almost to an affair of memory and routine. **1877** FROUDE *Short Stud.* (1883) IV. I. viii. 87 The succession to the English crown had not yet settled into fixed routine.

3. a. *attrib.* (now passing into *adj.*). Of a mechanical or unvaried character; performed by rule. Also, in wider senses: of a customary or standard kind; usual, typical, standard.

1817 J. SCOTT *Paris Revisit.* (ed. 4) 8 To quit for a time their natural track, and respite their routine tasks. **1845** LD. CAMPBELL *Chancellors* xxxvii. (1857) II. 137 Somerset resolved..to place the Great Seal in the hands of some one who might do its routine duties. **1890** 'R. BOLDREWOOD' *Col. Reformer* (1891) 177 The routine life..would be unendurably dull. **1940** H. SPENCER *Art & Life W. Shakespeare* v. 197 No routine braggart-soldier he. **1960** 'E. MCBAIN' *Give Boys Great Big Hand* vi. 59 'Maybe you can find some of Karl's skull on it. Isn't that what you'd like to find?' 'This is just a routine investigation, Mrs. Androvich.' **1961** W. SARGEANT in WEBSTER s.v. *routine* adj., The level of artistry..was altogether routine and uninspired. **1964** L. DEIGHTON *Funeral in Berlin* xxvii. 146, I shouldn't worry about it. It's just a routine check. **1979** *Sci. Amer.* Dec. 112 Recently it has become routine in many laboratories and hospitals to record evoked potentials from the brain stem.

b. *Comb.*, as ***routine-chained***, ***-ridden***, ***-sodden*** adjs.

1920 *Chambers's Jrnl.* 19 June 453/2 Routine-chained staffs worked on into the night. **1929** A. HUXLEY *Holy Face* 64 Our routine-ridden, mechanized world of flabbily sub-human sentimentalists. **1964** M. MCLUHAN *Understanding Media* x. 103 The need for advanced knowledge presses on the spirits of the most routine-ridden minds. **1920** *Contemp. Rev.* June 866 The Soviet authority had to destroy everything in this department—the laws themselves, the routine-sodden institutions.

routine (ruː'tiːn), *v.* [f. prec.] *trans.* To apply a routine to; to organize according to a routine. Hence **rou'tining** *vbl. sb.*

1897 G. B. SHAW in *Sat. Rev.* 18 Dec. 712/1 No actor can possibly play leading parts of the first order six nights a week all the year round unless he underplays them, or routines them mechanically in the old stock manner. **1941** W. C. HANDY *Father of Blues* iv. 39, I was consulted by Whalen and Martelle relative to routining their shows. **1948** 'LA MERI' *Spanish Dancing* iv. 43 There are a variety of typical steps which can be routined at the will of the dancer. **1959** R. CONDON *Manchurian Candidate* ii. 31 Yen Lo got three implantation teams started on them, staying with each team through the originating processes until he had assured himself that all had been routined with smoothness. **1976** W. GOLDMAN *Magic* II. 65 He spent the intervening days working out his routining. Start with the flashy stuff or save those for the end?

routined (ruː'tiːnd), *ppl. a.* [f. ROUTINE *v.* + -ED[1].] Subjected to or regulated by (a) routine.

1913 E. F. BENSON *Thorley Weir* i. 22 The gleaming romance and glory that lie so close below the surface of the most routined and rutted life. **1928** *Manch. Guardian Weekly* 23 Nov. 407/2 Criticism will do well not to base on this routined output a judgment which leaves out of account the Schubert of the year of his death. **1948** 'J. TEY' *Franchise Affair* xiii. 138 One result of stepping out of a routined life was..that you couldn't..stroll home at four o'clock of an afternoon. **1964** F. BOWERS *Bibliogr. & Textual Crit.* VI. iii. 180 An inexperienced..compositor might be supposed to feel the influence of copy more strongly than a thoroughly routined workman.

routineer (ruːtiː'nɪə(r)). [f. ROUTINE *sb.* + -EER[1], perh. after F. *routinier*.] One who acts by, or adheres to, routine.

1875 JOWETT *Plato* (ed. 2) I. 422 He has been a true mystic and not a mere routineer or wand-bearer. **1878** R. WILLIS *Life of Harvey* 166 The routineer, with an appropriate salve for every sore. **1928** G. B. SHAW *Intelligent Woman's Guide Socialism* lxx. 340 The civil servant, the judge, the navy captain, the field marshal, the archbishop, however extraordinary able, gets no more than any routineer of his rank and seniority. **1956** 'H. MACDIARMID' *Stony Limits & Scots Unbound* 129 The routineer Haig, Whose lack of imagination carried him through. **1977** *National Observer* (U.S.) 22 Jan. 6/1 The innovator, in both business and the arts, is always to be contrasted..with the routineer.

routinely (ruː'tiːnlɪ), *adv.* orig. *U.S.* [f. ROUTINE *sb.* (*a.*) 3 a + -LY[2].] As a matter of course or of routine; according to (a) routine; by rote, mechanically.

1924 *Scribner's Mag.* Aug. 216/1 Even now I think we take policemen, professors, conductors, etc., much too routinely. **1948** A. COOKE in *Manch. Guardian Weekly* 29 Apr. 13/2 It has been routinely filed away and incorporated in the body of American dogma. **1956** *Nature* 25 Feb. 383/1 The inhibition of the enzyme by the osmium tetroxide fixative routinely used for electron microscopical preparations. **1965** *Economist* 10 July 137/3 Such infractions are routinely settled with a small bribe for the policeman. **1968** J. D. WATSON *Double Helix* xviii. 129 He was only routinely enthusiastic as he went over Griffith's quantum-mechanical arguments. **1971** D. LAMBERT in C. Bonington *Annapurna South Face* 289 Appendicectomy is done routinely on members of expeditions to the Antarctic. **1974** J. HELLER *Something Happened* 101 'What did you do today?' I ask routinely (before she can ask me).

routiner (ruː'tiːnə(r)). [f. ROUTIN(E + -ER[1].]

†**1.** = ROUTINEER. *Obs. rare*[—1].

1875 W. CORY *Lett. & Jrnls.* 400 Those good things of the mind which the old routiners reserved for Masters of Arts.

2. *Teleph.* A set of equipment for testing circuits and switching apparatus in an exchange.

1929 *P.O. Electr. Engineers Jrnl.* XXII. 24 Routiners are composed of two main parts: the test and control apparatus, and the access equipment. **1948** J. ATKINSON *Telephony* I. xxi. 453/1 Specially designed test boxes or routiners..are arranged to apply test conditions somewhat more onerous than the conditions normally encountered in practice. **1973** *P.O. Electr. Engineers Jrnl.* LXVI. 44/2 Trunk circuit routiners..are used to verify that a call can be established to a distant answering relay-set over each outgoing trunk circuit in turn and that the transmission loss..is within maintenance tolerance.

routing, *vbl. sbs.* and *ppl. adjs.*, see ROUT *sb.*[1], ROUT *v.*[1], etc., and ROUTEING *vbl. sb.*

‖**routinier** (rutinje), *a.* and *sb.* *Mus.* [Fr.: cf. ROUTINEER.] **A.** *adj.* Of a piece of music: composed in a routine or orthodox manner. *rare.* **B.** *sb.* A conductor who performs in a mechanically correct, but uninspiring, way.

1934 C. LAMBERT *Music Ho!* v. 279 Walton's..mature but regrettably consonant *Belshazzar's Feast* was dismissed, particularly by the older critics, as 'routinier', conventional, and unworthy of its place in so selectly revolutionary a festival. **1970** *Guardian* 1 Jan. 8/2 Everything was first-rate with the exception of Boris himself..and the conductor Boris Khaikin, a tired routinier. **1970** *New Yorker* 26 Sept. 114/3 A new conductor..didn't seem to arouse much tension. He proved to be what is usually described as a useful *routinier*.

routinish (ruː'tiːnɪʃ), *a.* [f. ROUTINE *sb.* + -ISH.] Of the nature of routine. So **rou'tinism**, prevalence or domination of routine; **rou'tinist**, one who acts by routine.

1830 *Blackw. Mag.* XXVII. 425 There was nothing routinish in his Pilgrimage. He did not stroll about with cicerones and guide-books. **1852** C. MORFIT *Tanning & Currying* (1853) 163 The old routinists..give the hides a soaking of ten, twelve and even fifteen months. **1860** SMILES *Self-Help* viii. 218 The late Duke of Wellington was a great routinist. **1883** *Jrnl. Educ.* XVII. 151 Where 'stony routinism' prevails. **1889** *Lancet* 5 Oct. 703/1 He deprecated routinism, automatism, mechanical prescription in medicine.

routinization (ruːˌtiːnaɪ'zeɪʃən). [f. ROUTINIZE *v.* + -ATION.] The being or becoming routine in character or operation; the action of superimposing a routine upon that which was previously less systematized or controlled.

1934 in WEBSTER. **1946** GERTH & MILLS *From Max Weber* (1947) iii. 54 By tracing out the routinization of charisma, Weber is able to assign a heavy causal weight to institutional routines. **1954** *Encounter* June 12/1 Coal mining..now—with the mechanisation of cutting and conveying—takes on much of the routinisation of factory work. **1960** *Guardian* 29 Apr. 11/1 Beatnik Tanya..excoriates the routinisation of sex in marriage. **1965** H. KAHN *On Escalation* xiii. 258 It is a major purpose of current command-and-control efforts to facilitate the 'routinization'..of the various aspects of crisis management. **1972** A. GIDDENS *Politics & Sociol. in Thought of Max Weber* iii. 39 The 'routinisation' of politics —that is to say, the transformation of political decisions into decisions of administrative routine..—is specifically foreign to the demands which are most basic to political action. **1976** *National Observer* (U.S.) 26 June 17/3 We are all equally liable to the lumpish routinization of compassion both maddening and necessary.

routinize (ruː'tiːnaɪz), *v.* [f. ROUTINE + -IZE.] *trans.* To subject to (a) routine; to make into a (matter of) routine.

1928 *Amer. Speech* III. 434 An investigator of nurses' training asks whether nurses are to become 'machinized and routinized'. **1937** J. DOLLARD *Caste & Class in Southern Town* xv. 344 All such behavior patterns have emotional value, even when they seem most routinized. **1960** W. H. WHYTE *Organization Man* xxvi. 364 They know how to routinize crisis. **1965** *Listener* 24 June 925/2 Ours is a time in which man..has been mechanized and routinized. **1973** J. S. BRUNER *Beyond Information Given* (1974) xvii. 300 When..the child has routinized the task of holding two objects, one in each hand, there then occurs a first storage activity. **1978** *Dædalus* Summer 70 Duty emerges..as an attempt to codify, systematize, and routinize behavior which springs from desire.

rou'tinized, *ppl. a.* [f. prec.] Subject to (a) routine; made into a (matter of) routine.

1938 *Sun* (Baltimore) 21 July 18/1 There was nothing to indicate an approaching disaster in the routinized handling of the dynamite before the blast. **1945** G. WILLIAMS *Women & Work* ii. 41 Women.. were mostly confined to the lower-grade, more routinised categories. **1949** M. MEAD *Male & Female* xiii. 269 The baby would not eat, having very doubtfully enjoyed the routinized, cloth-enveloped experience. **1952** B. ULANOV *Hist. Jazz in Amer.* xiii. 151 The fairly tight, routinized Nichols sessions set the style. **1978** *Jrnl. R. Soc. Arts* CXXVI. 412/2 Administration is the conduct of affairs in a routinized fashion. **1981** *Times Lit. Suppl.* 27 Feb. 216/1 The twentieth century may be the century of.. routinized labour.

†**'routious**, *a. Obs.*⁻¹ [f. ROUT *sb.*¹] Disorderly, riotous.

1602 WARNER *Alb. Eng.* XIII. lxxvii. 320 Their most incestious, lecherous, and routious Drinke-mad Feasts.

†**'routish**, *a. Obs.*⁻¹ [f. ROUT *sb.*¹ 5 b.] Resembling a rout.

a **1734** NORTH *Examen* I. ii. §115 The Common Hall.. became a routish Assembly of sorry citizens.

routous ('raʊtəs), *a. Law.* Now *arch.* [f. ROUT *sb.*¹ 5 b.] Of the nature of, concerned in, constituting, a rout.

1632 *Star Chamber Cases* (Camden) 139 Thomas Broughton, joyning.. with divers others.., came in a riotous and routous manner armed to the said chappell. **1672** *Life & Death of J. Alleine* vi. (1838) 64 As for riotous, routous and seditious assemblies he did abhor them. **1846** DE QUINCEY *Wellesley* Wks. 1858 VIII. 29 To be routous is nothing like so criminal in law as to be riotous. I never go beyond the routous point.

routously ('raʊtəslɪ), *adv. Law.* Now *arch.* [f. prec. + -LY².] In a routous or disorderly manner.

1663 in *Life & Death J. Alleine* vi. (1838) 64 That he.. did riotously, routously and seditiously assemble. **1680** *New Jersey Archives* (1880) I. 304 Capt. Phillip Carteret.. hath persisted and riotously and routously with Force and Arms, endeavoured to assert and maintain the same. **1776** GOUVR. MORRIS in Sparks *Life & Writ.* (1832) I. 99 Many hard names.. of which I believe the very gentlest and smoothest kind are riotously and routously. **1800** ADDISON *Rep.* 274 These men were indicted for having unlawfully, riotously and routously assembled together. **1880** *Times* 28 Oct. 11/3 'Unlawfully, riotously, and routously' assembling together.

routy, form of ROWTY *a. dial.*

rouwe, obs. form of ROUGH *a.* and *v.*², ROW *v.*

rouwte, obs. form of ROUT *sb.*¹

‖**roux** (ruː). [F. *roux* red, browned.] A mixture of melted butter and flour used for thickening soups and gravies.

1813 L. E. UDE *French Cook* vi. 140 Cut your chops.., then fry them in a little butter, of a nice brown colour, drain this butter, and make a *roux* very *blond*. *Ibid.* xiii. 297 Put a lump of butter into a stew-pan... Then make a *roux* by mixing a little flour. When your *roux* begins to get brown, put in two large onions cut [etc.]. *Ibid.* xiv. 361 After having stewed your oysters.., you make a *roux blanc* into which you put a few small onions, [etc.]. **1845** E. ACTON *Mod. Cookery* (ed. 2) iv. 97 Sauce tourneé is.. rich pale gravy.. thickened with delicate white roux. **1861** MRS. BEETON *Bk. Househ. Managem.* 251 *White roux*, for thickening White Sauces... Allow the same proportions of butter and flour.. and proceed in the same manner as for brown roux. **1882** MRS. H. REEVE *Cookery & Housek.* xxiii. 271 Sauces require to be bound together, and for this purpose either roux, arrowroot, potato flour, or eggs are used. **1945** *ABC of Cookery* (Ministry of Food) xiii. 51 This mixture of fat and flour is called a roux. **1965** *House & Garden* Dec. 84/4 Cook for a further few minutes to dispel the raw flour taste, then stop, if you want the *roux* white, carry on a little longer for the blonde, and longer still for a brown. **1976** *National Observer* (U.S.) 6 Nov., The roux should be brown but not burned. Do not burn or you will ruin the gravy.

rouz(e, obs. forms of ROUSE *v.*¹

†**rouze**, *v.* ? *nonce-word.* (See quot.)

1681 OTWAY *Soldier's Fort.* I. i, To see a pretty Wench and a young Fellow touze and rouze and frouze and mouze.

†**rouzie-bouzie**, *a. Obs.* ? Uproariously drunk.

1693 SOUTHERNE *Maid's last Prayer* III. i, I may return most rouzie-bouzie, and if I find you have injur'd me, I'll swinge you all, by Hercules.

†**rouzle**, *v.* ? *nonce-word.* To rumple.

a **1722** MRS. CENTLIVRE *Platonick Lady* IV, Well, I protest you are a waggish Man; Lord how you have rouzl'd and touzl'd one!

rov, var. RAV.

rovcaste, obs. variant of ROW-CAST *v.*

rove (rʌv), *sb.*¹ Now *dial.* Also 6 rofe, 7 roufe. [a. ON. *hrufa* (Norw. *ruva*, Sw. *rufva*, Da. *roe*) or MDu. *rove* (Du. *roof*), MLG. *rove*, *roffe* (LG. *rove*, *rave*, etc.), MHG. (and G.) *rufe*, related to OHG. *riob*, ON. *hrjúfr*, OE. *hréof* scabby, leprous.]

1. †**a.** A scabby, scaly, or scurfy condition of the skin. *Obs.*

a **1400** *Stockholm Med. MS.* in *Anglia* XVIII. 117 For hym þat hath skabbe or roue. **1425** *26 Pol. Poems* 111 From worldis worschipe y am shoue, And brouȝt abas from al astat; My skyn is cloþed al on roue.

b. A scab; the scaly crust of a healed or healing wound.

1590 BARROUGH *Meth. Physick* II. iv. (1639) 76 The unskilfull.. pull away the scab or rove, which they ought not to do before they see the rove lifted up. **1601** HOLLAND *Pliny* II. 448 The gall likewise of the Sea-scorpion, taketh off the roufe of sores. **1823** E. MOOR *Suffolk Wds.* 320. **1897** *N. & Q.* 7th Ser. XI. 67.

†**2.** A rind, hard skin, or crust. *Obs. rare.*

1530 PALSGR. 263/2 Rofe of baken or befe. **1601** HOLLAND *Pliny* I. 377 The very pure and perfect Baulme.., when it hath gum mingled among,.. will gather soon a brittle roufe or crust vpon it, which quickly cracks and breaks.

rove (rəʊv), *sb.*² Forms: α. 5 rewe, rowe. β. 5 rofe, roff(e, 6 rugh, 7 roue, rooue, 5- rove. See also ROOVE *sb.* [a. ON. *ró* (Norw. *ro*, Fær. *rógv*), in the same sense. On the excrescent *v* of the usual forms cf. the etym. note to RO *sb.*]

1. A small metal plate or ring on which the point of a nail or rivet is clinched or beaten down in the building of boats or small ships; a burr.

α. *c* **1440** *York Myst.* viii. 109 Take here a revette, and þere a rewe [*rime* newe]. ? *a* **1500** *Newcastle Play* 26 All things I him fulfill, Pitch, tar, seam, and rowe [*rime* therto].

β. **1406** *Durh. Acc. Rolls* (Surtees) 606 Item in exp. Ricardi Couhird.. pro seme et Rufe. **1474-5** *Ibid.* 645 Cum seme, rove, clavis ferr. et lign. pice, et bitumine emp. pro eadem. **1486-95** [see 2]. *a* **1625** *Nomenclator Navalis* (Harl. MS. 2301), The Rove is that little iron plate into which the clinch nails are clinched. **1750** BLANCKLEY *Nav. Expos.* 137 *Roves*, are small square Pieces of Iron, with a Hole punched in the Middle of them, through which the Nail goes, where it is clenched, and fastens the Boards of Pinnaces, Yawles, or Wherries to one another. **1794** *Rigging & Seamanship* 8 *Rove*, a small square piece of iron, with a hole in the middle, whereon is clenched the point of a nail, to prevent its drawing. **1860** TOMLINSON *Arts & Manuf.* Ser. II. *Steel* 43 They are clenched either by hammering down the extremity, or by placing over it a little diamond-shaped plate of metal called a rove, and rivetting the end of the clench nail down upon it. **1889** [see CLINCH *sb.*¹ 1]. **1894** HESLOP *Northumb. Gloss.*, *Seam-nail*, a nail without a point,.. on to which a rove is rivetted.

†**2.** ***rove and clinch (nails)***, nails provided with roves for clinching. *Obs.*

1486 *Naval Acc. Hen. VII* (1896) 15, lxj lb di. of long Rofe & clenche. **1495** *Ibid.* 152 Roff & clynche nayles xliiij lb... In clynche worke Roff & nayle xijˡ. **1598** STOW *Surv.* (1603) 139 Nayled with rugh and clench. **1626** CAPT. SMITH *Accid. Yng. Seamen* 3 The Carpenter and his Mate is to haue the Nayles, Clinches, roue and clinch-nailes.

ellipt. **1644** MANWARING *Seaman's Dict.* 86 The Planckes of Clincher-boates, are thus fastned together, which kind of work is called Rove and Clinch.

†**rove**, *sb.*³ *Obs.* Also 7-8 roove. [ad. F. *arrove*, obs. var. *arrobe*, ad. Sp. and Pg. *arroba*.] = ARROBA.

α. **1588** PARKE tr. *Mendoza's Hist. China* 350 You shall haue foure roues of wine.. for foure rials of plate,.. foure roues of suger for five rials. **1596** MELLIS *Recorde's Gr. Artes* 543 Forraine wools, to wit, French, Spanish, and Estrich, is also sold by the pound or C. weight, but most commonly by the Roue, 25 pounds to a Rove. **1632** LITHGOW *Trav.* x. 482 Two Roves of Figges and Rasins. **1699** J. DICKENSON *Jrnl. Trav.* 69 We had five Roves of Ammunition-Bread..; twenty Roves of strung Beef; sixty Roves of Indian-Corn. **1720** *Lond. Gaz.* No. 5911/1 A Rove.. is 32 Pounds.

β. **1656** PHILLIPS *Purch. Patt.* (1676) 213 There are some other denominations of these weights in several places, as.. Rooves. **1712** W. ROGERS *Voy.* (1718) 39 Our boat returned and brought a present, being a Roove of fine sugar. **1714** *Lond. Gaz.* No. 5190/2 Fifty Rooves of Gold.

rove (rəʊv), *sb.*⁴ [f. ROVE *v.*¹]

1. A ramble or wandering.

1742 YOUNG *Nt. Th.* IX. 673 In thy nocturnal rove, one moment halt. **1840** BROWNING *Sordello* II. 269 Sordello's paradise, his roves Among the hills and valleys, plains and groves. **1870** *Pall Mall G.* 24 Aug. 10, I have not set off on my day's rove without taking precautions.

fig. **1786** BURNS *Ep. to Young Friend* vi, Never tempt th' illicit rove, Tho' naething should divulge it.

b. In phr. ***on*** or ***upon the rove***; dial. ***a rove***.

1828 CARR *Craven Gloss.* s.v., Cattle are.. said to be all a rove when they are running about in hot weather. **1830** GALT *Lawrie T.* VIII. xii, He went upon the rove. **1876** BESANT & RICE *Gold. Butterfly* xx, Isaac went around on the rove.

2. *Sc.* A mental wandering or raving. *rare*⁻¹.

1789 J. BROWN *Rem.* (1807) 274 In his roves he was often about that place.

3. *dial.* A method of light ploughing.

1702 *Farm Lease* (Essex), The Landlord is to allow the tennant 4/- an acre for every acre plowed to clean, and 2/- an acre for every Rove for what land is fallowed, the tennant not exceeding three earths and 1 Rove. **1740** in Cullum *Hist. Hawsted* (1784) 217 Three clean earths and a rove. **1784** *Ibid.*, A rove is half a ploughing: two furrows are made instead of four. **1808** *Young's Ann. Agric.* XLV. 342 Instead of an entire clean earth of four furrows, the plough goes over it, making only two, this slight kind of ploughing is sometimes.. called a rove. **1823-** in E. Anglian and Essex glossaries.

rove (rəʊv), *sb.*⁵ Also 9 roove. [Related to ROVE *v.*³]

1. A sliver of any fibrous material (esp. cotton or wool) drawn out and very slightly twisted.

1789 E. DARWIN *Bot. Gard.* (1791) II. 58 With quicken'd pace successive rollers move, And these retain, and those extend the rove. **1801** *Encycl. Brit.* Suppl. II. 518/1 Such is the state of the slab or roove of the first formation. **1839** URE *Dict. Arts* 357, 30 coils of the sliver or roove are laid in one length of the bobbin barrel. **1884** W. S. B. MCLAREN *Spinning* (ed. 2) 54 The carriage.. drawing out the rove which has been thus delivered.

2. *collect.* Textile material in this form.

1901 *Scotsman* 9 Oct. 11/3 Rove is quiet at £9. 10*s.* for 200 lb.

rove (rəʊv), *v.*¹ Forms: 5-7 roue, 6 roaue, 6-8 roave, 5- rove. [Of doubtful origin: possibly a Midland form of RAVE *v.*² to stray (cf. note to ROVER¹). In senses 5 and 6 perhaps partly influenced by ROVE *v.*²]

I. †**1.** *intr.* To shoot with arrows *at* a mark selected at pleasure or at random, and not of any fixed distance. Also without const. *Obs.*

The object of roving was evidently to give practice in finding the range of the mark, while shooting at the butts and pricks taught accuracy of aim.

1474 *Coventry Leet Bk.* 389 þat no maner persone of þis Citie frohensfurth rove, but shote at stondyng prikkes & buttes. **1586** WARNER *Alb. Eng.* II. ix. 39, I see him roue at others marke, and I vnmarkt to be. **1622** DRAYTON *Poly-olb.* xxvi. 122 At Markes full fortie score, they used to Prick and Rove. **1633** BP. HALL *Hard Texts, N.T.* 123 A certain man drew a bow without any aim or intention of any speciall marke but only roving in common at the army.

†**b.** *fig.* or in fig. context. *Obs.*

1565 JEWEL *Reply Harding* (1611) 412 Which purpose if he neuer vouchsafe once to touch, but range abroad, as his manner is, & roaue idlely at matters impertinent, then must wee needes say he bewraieth his want. **1579** SPENSER *Sheph. Cal.* Aug. 79 She rovde at me with glauncing eye. **1602** FULBECKE *2nd Pt. Parallel* 55, I would first that Anglo-nomoph. should shew.. in what sort partition is made: otherwise I should but roue at an vncertaine marke. **1615** T. ADAMS *White Devil* 3 His hypocrisie that roaved at the poore, but levelled at his profit.

†**c.** *esp.* To form a conjecture, to guess (*at* a thing). *Obs.*

1558 in Feuillerat *Revels Q. Eliz.* (1908) 17 The chardge may be roved at. **1600** HAKLUYT *Voy.* (1810) III. 46 Yet did he but rove at the Matter, or (at the least) gathered the knowledge of it by Conjectures only. **1627** BP. HALL *Epist.* III. v. 324 Then I could tell how to take a direct aime, whereas now I must roue and coniecture. **1674** N. FAIRFAX *Bulk & Selv.* 168 That Centaur and Meremaid, that never were but in the wildest thoughts of him that sometimes roved at them.

†**d.** With complement expressing distance. *Obs.*

1590 SIR J. SMYTH *Disc. Weapons* 46 b, Two or three scores off; and rouing sixe, seauen, or eight scores. *c* **1590** GREENE *Fr. Bacon* (1630) 7 But Bacon roues a bow beyond his reach, And tels of more then Magicke can performe.

†**2.** To shoot away *from* a mark; hence, to wander *from* the point; to diverge, or digress. *Obs.*

c **1555** HARPSFIELD *Divorce Hen. VIII* (Camden) 52 Thus you see how far and wide the adversaries rove from the mark and matter they should shoot at. **1581** W. CHARKE in *Conf.* IV. (1584) D d iiij, Roue not in generall discourses, that come not neere the marke. **1633** BP. HALL *Hard Texts, N.T.* 304 From which graces some having roved, and taken a wrong aime.., have turned aside into vain jangling. **1648** MILTON *Sonn.* xii. 13 But from that mark how far they roave we see.

†**3.** *trans.* **a.** To aim at (a mark). *Obs.*⁻¹

1546 J. HEYWOOD *Prov.* (1867) 30 Yet haue ye other markis to roue at hand.

†**b.** To shoot (an arrow, etc.) without fixed aim. Hence *fig.*, to utter at random. *Obs.*

1581 J. BELL *Haddon's Answ. Osorius* 161 If Osorius require this at our handes, that whatsoever his lavishe tounge shall rashly roave at large, be coyned for an unreproveable oracle. **1596** HARINGTON *Apol. Ajax* (1814) 39 After they had roved three or four idle words to praise a man, straight they marr all at the buts. **1607** —— in *Nugæ Ant.* (1804) II. 47 Manie bowlts were roved after him, and some spitefullie feather'd.

†**c.** To pierce *with* arrows, etc. *Obs.*

Perhaps by confusion with *rove*, pa. t. of RIVE *v.*¹ 3.

a **1575** tr. *Pol. Verg. Eng. Hist.* (Camden) I. 44 He roved the olde man throughe with his swerde. *Ibid.* 143 They roved him throughe with arrowse.

4. *intr. Angling.* To troll with live bait.

1661 WALTON *Angler* (ed. 3) xii. 184 If you rove for a Pearch with a Minnow, then it is best to be alive. **1787** T. BEST *Angling* (ed. 2) 49 If you rove for him, with a minnow or frog (which is a very pleasant way) then your line should be strong. **1867** F. FRANCIS *Angling* ii. (1880) 71 Roving for barbel is not often resorted to.

II. 5. *intr.* To wander about with no fixed destination; to move hither and thither at random or in a leisurely fashion; to stray, roam, ramble.

1536 *Act 27 Hen. VIII*, c. 28 §1 A greate multytude of the Relygyous persons in suche smale Houses doo rather chose to rove abrode in apostasy than to conforme them to the observacion of good Relygyon. **1568** GRAFTON *Chron.* II. 156 The Souldiours that lay in Southwarke.. roued ouer vnto Westminster, and spoyled there the kinges Palace. **1627** HAKEWILL *Apol.* (1630) 282 On Sea we rou'd three dayes as darke as night. **1650** FULLER *Pisgah* I. v. 12 Such the store of ravenous beasts freely roaving up and down the countrey. **1711** STEELE *Spect.* No. 254 ¶3 One would think you.. roved among the Walks of Paradise. **1798** WORDSW. *Peter Bell* I. 241 He roved among the vales and streams, In the green wood and hollow dell. *c* **1835** WILLIS *Florence Gray* 48, I have roved From wild America to Bosphor's waters. **1879** FROUDE *Cæsar* ix. 98 They roved over the waters at their pleasure, attacking islands or commercial ports.

transf. *a* **1691** BOYLE *Hist. of Air* (1692) 249 The numerous sorts of saline corpuscles that rove up and down in the air. **1850** W. COLLINS *Antonina* iv, The rich light roved over the waters.

b. *fig.* or in fig. context.

1579 GOSSON *Sch. Abuse* (Arb.) 16 When Ouid had roaued long on the Seas of wantonnesse, hee became a good Pilot to all that followed. **1598** BARRET *Theor. Warres* III. i. 32, I haue in generall roued ouer some part thereof alreadie. **1658-9** in *Burton's Diary* (1828) IV. 37, I had rather that this House were laid aside by a question, than rove up and down thus, and do nought. **1667** DUCHESS OF NEWCASTLE *Life Dk. N.* (1886) IV. 253 For though my judgment roves at random, yet it can never miss of errors. **1738** WESLEY *Hymns*, '*Infinite Power, Eternal Lord*' ix, Then shall my Feet no more depart, Nor my Affections rove. **1784** COWPER *Task* IV. 232 Roving as I rove, Where shall I find an end, or how proceed? **1812** CRABBE *Tales* ii. 399 Then roved his spirit to the inland wood.

c. Of the eyes: To look in various directions; to wander. Also *transf.*

a **1656** BP. HALL *Rem. Wks.* (1660) 951 Durst we give our eyes leave to rove abroad in wanton glances? **1737** *Gentl. Mag.* VII. 697/1 Her eyes rove fast his wish'd approach to hail. **1838** JAMES *Robber* i, The stranger's eye roved on to the landscape. **1902** 'LINESMAN' *Words Eyewitness* 126 A Boer searchlight..which roved like an angry eye from end to end of our line of march.

d. To extend, stretch out. *rare*⁻¹.

1639 FULLER *Holy War* v. xviii. (1840) 273 North Eastward, it [the kingdom] roued ouer the principalities of Antioch and Edessa.

6. *trans.* To wander over, traverse.

1634 MILTON *Comus* 60 Comus..Roaving the Celtick and Iberian fields, At last betakes him to this ominous Wood. **1667** —— *P.L.* IX. 575 On a day roaving the field, I chanc'd A goodly Tree farr distant to behold. **1725** POPE *Odyss.* x. 335 O blind to fate! what led thy steps to rove The horrid mazes of this magic grove? **1783** W. THOMSON *Watson's Philip III*, VI. (1793) II. 248 He had also ships of war under his command which roved the sea. **1807** WORDSW. *Misc. Sonn.* II. xviii, A labyrinth, Lady! which your feet shall rove. **1859** TENNYSON *Elaine* 35 Roving the trackless realms of Lyonnesse.

†**7.** *refl.* To betake oneself to wandering. *Obs.*⁻¹

1653 CHISENHALE *Cath. Hist.* 376 They quit the harbor adjoyning to that Rock, and rove themselves upon the billows of strange contests.

8. *dial.* To wander in mind or in speech, to rave; to be light-headed or delirious. Chiefly *Sc.*

1720 PENNECUIK *Helicon* 15, I roave, all sense is gone, I'll fly away. **1766** SHIRRA *Deathbed Dial.* in *Rem.* (1850) 26 He roved much through this day. **1824** MACTAGGART *Gallovid. Encycl.* 414 When one talks while sleeping, we are said to be roving in our sleep. **1897** J. HAMMOND *Cornish Parish* 339 If we are distracted with pain, we are 'roving'.

†**rove**, *v.*² *Obs.* Also 6–7 roue. [ad. MDu. or MLG. *roven* to rob (see REAVE *v.*¹), but perh. not clearly distinguished from prec.] *intr.* To practise piracy; to sail as pirates.

a **1548** HALL *Chron., Edw. IV* 222 The bastard..made sayle with all haste & Roued on the sea. **1553** BRENDE *Q. Curtius* B iiij, He became a Pirate, and roved on the sea, where he toke .170. shippes. **1613** PURCHAS *Pilgrimage* VI. viii. (1614) 601 Tripolis,..a receptacle of the Pyrats, which roue and rob in those seas. **1698** FRYER *Acc. E. India & P.* 42 With fourteen Sails of Ships they roved on the Coasts of Malabar.

rove (rəʊv), *v.*³ [Of obscure origin: cf. ROVE *sb.*⁵] *trans.* To form (slivers of wool or cotton) into roves or rovings.

1789 *Trans. Soc. Arts* I. 34 The Cotton is carded, roved and spun into threads. **1796** MORSE *Amer. Geogr.* I. 543 Machinery to sliver, rove, and spin flax and hemp. **1835** URE *Philos. Manuf.* 215 Although both [flax and wool] must be roved and spun upon similar principles, each requires peculiar modifications in its machinery. **1879** *Cassell's Techn. Educ.* I. 214/1 The cotton is..cleaned... After that it is roved, a process by which each ribbon is greatly attenuated.

†**rove**, *v.*⁴ *Obs.*⁻¹ (Meaning not clear.)

c **1330** *Arth. & Merl.* 1935 (Kölbing), A beggar þer com in... Wiþ his scholder he gan roue & bad gode, for godes loue.

rove, *v.*⁵ *dial.* Also 9 roove. [Of obscure origin.] (See quots.)

1711 *Brit. Apollo* No. 143. 2/1 It is Bacon before it is roved or dry'd. **1847** HALLIW., *Roove*, to dry meat in a chimney, or over a kiln. *Glouc.* **1890** *Glouc. Gloss.*, *Rove*, to smoke-dry meat.

rove (rəʊv), *v.*⁶ [Of obscure origin.] *trans.* To reduce (a grindstone) in diameter by means of a special tool.

1850– [see ROVING *vbl. sb.*⁴]

rove (rəʊv), *ppl. a. rare*⁻¹. [irreg. pa. pple. of RIVE *v.*¹] *rove-ash*, made of riven ash-wood.

1802 *Naval Chron.* IX. 293 A rove-ash oar that will dress clean and light, is too pliant.

rove, pa. t. and pa. pple. of REEVE *v.*¹; pa. t. of RIVE *v.*¹ and *v.*²; Sc. var. of RO, rest; obs. f. ROOF *sb.*

'rove-beetle. [? f. ROVE *v.*¹] A beetle of the family *Staphylinidæ*.

1781 BARBUT *Insects* 95 They are by some called Rove-Beetles. **1784** PENNANT *Arct. Zool.* Suppl. 155. **1817** KIRBY & SP. *Entomol.* xxiii. (1818) II. 322 The anterior tarsi of many of the larger rove-beetles. **1868** *Rep. U.S. Comm. Agric.* (1869) 307 Many of the rove beetles, *Staphylinidæ*, are found in decaying animal and vegetable substances. **1883** *Good Words* Dec. 762/2 Many of the Rove or Cock-tail Beetles found it out nearly as soon.

†**roveison.** *Obs. rare.* In 4 roueiso(u)n, rouyson. [a. OF. *roveison*, etc.:—L. *rogātiōn-em*: see ROGATION.] *pl.* Rogations.

c **1300** *S. Eng. Leg., Litany* (MS. Harl.), þe feste of þe Roueisons þe lasse Letanie is. *Ibid.* (MS. Ashm.), Wen me aboute feldes goþ wiþ baners as ȝe iseþ þre dawes & uasteþ ek, þat me clupeþ þe rouysons. *Ibid., St. Edmund* in *E.E.P.* (1862) 80 In o tyme of þe roueisouns þis holi man also Prechede a dai at Oxenford.

rovelling. *rare.* = ROVE *sb.*⁵

1805 LUCCOCK *Nature of Wool* 146 The object here is to break the wool completely,..and to form it into a thin roll, or 'rovelling', of the slightest texture imaginable. *Ibid.* 147 The particles..produce no rovelling, and cannot be spun in the same manner as a woollen thread.

roven, var. pa. pple. REEVE *v.*¹

rover¹ ('rəʊvə(r)). Also 6–7 rouer, 6 roauer; *Sc.* rever. [f. ROVE *v.*¹ The Sc. form *rever* may stand for **raver*, or be due to confusion with ROVER² and REAVER.]

1. a. *Archery.* A mark selected at will or at random, and not of any fixed distance from the archer. Also in later use, a mark for long-distance shooting (contrasted with *butt*). Most frequently in phr. *(to shoot) at rovers.*

α. **1468** *Coventry Leet Bk.* 338 Hit is ordeyned..þat noman within þis Citie frohensfurth shote at Rovers, but at buttis & standyng prikkis. **1531** ELYOT *Gov.* (1580) 82 At rovers or pryckes, it is at his plesure that shoteth, howe faste or softly he listeth to goe. **1541–2** *Act 33 Hen. VIII*, c. 9. §2 Noe Man under thage of xxiiij yeres shall shoote at any standinge prick excepte it be at a Rover whereat he shall chaunge at every shoote his marke. **1615** MARKHAM *Country Contentm.* 108 The Roauer is a marke incertaine,..and..must haue arrowes lighter or heauier, according to the distance. **1638** J. UNDERHILL *News fr. Amer.* in *Mass. Hist. Colls.* (1837) VI. 26 They..shot remote, and not point-blank, as we often do with our bullets, but at rovers. **1700** DRYDEN *Iliad* I. 77 The god nine days the Greeks at rovers kill'd. **1728** RAMSAY *Archers diverting themselves* 1 The Rovers and the Butts you saw. **1797** *Encycl. Brit.* (ed. 3) II. 214/1 All these prizes are shot for at what is termed rovers, the marks being placed at the distance of 185 yards. **1819** SCOTT *Ivanhoe* xiv, The distance between that station and the mark allowing full distance for what was called a shot at rovers. **1856** FORD *Archery* 104 Concerning roving, or shooting at rovers, very few words will suffice.

β. *c* **1560** A. SCOTT *Poems* (S.T.S.) v. 44 To schute at buttis, at bankis and brais; Sum at the reveris, sum at the prikkis. *a* **1578** LINDESAY (Pitscottie) *Chron. Scot.* (S.T.S.) I. 340 The said Inglischemen sould schute aganis thame ether at prickis, reveris or at buttis.

b. *fig.*, chiefly in phr. *to shoot at rovers.*

1551 CRANMER *Answ. Gardiner* 63 Where you pretende to shoote at the butte, you shoote quite at the rouers, and cleane frome the marke. **1572** CHURCHYARD in J. Jones *Bathes of Bathes Ayde* To Rdr., At rovers they but shot their shafts. **1600** WATSON *Decacordon* (1602) 67 Note this, that popularitie is the rover they ayme at, in all their proceedings. **1661** GLANVILL *Van. Dogm.* 107 But Nature shoots not at Rovers. **1702** *Exam. Burnet's Expos. 39 Art.* 34 He will be found to shoot all the while at Rovers, and wide of the Mark.

†**c.** A kind of arrow used in roving. *Obs.*

1599 JONSON *Cynthia's Rev.* v. x, Here be [arrows] of all sorts, flights, rouers, and butt-shafts. **1624** QUARLES *Sion's Elegies* III. iv, His Bowe is bent, his forked Rouers flye.

d. *attrib.*, as *rover mark, -shooting, shot.*

1566 WITHALS *Dict.* 64 The rouer markes, *incerta.* **1598** SYLVESTER *Du Bartas* II. ii. III. *Colonies* 118 Here, if I list, or lov'd I rover-shooting,..I could derive the lineall Descents Of all our Sires. **1643** HERLE *Answ. Ferne* 11 Such another rover shot as wide in the..extent of both the termes, as time it selfe Hath and Will. **1685** TEMPLE *Ess., Gardens* II. 11 Perhaps..these fine Schemes would prove like Rover Shots, some nearer and some further off.

†**2.** *at rovers* (rarely *at rover*), without definite aim or object; at random, haphazard. Chiefly in phr. with *run, talk, live*, etc. *Obs.*

(*a*) **1532** MORE *Confut. Barnes* VIII. Wks. 786/2 Either their dede and declaracion must nedes stande and be firme, or els all runne at rouers and nothing be certain or sure. **1562** J. HEYWOOD *Prov. & Epigr.* (1867) 56 Leat not your toung roon at rouer. **1625** BP. MOUNTAGU *App. Cæsar* 288 Walk at random and at rovers in your by-paths, if you please. **1697** J. SERGEANT *Solid Philos.* 362 Which, let loose to fly at rovers, are too hard for their Reason Unestablish'd by Principles.

(*b*) **1542** UDALL *Erasm. Apoph.* 288 b, Thy dooynges o Cato dooen more nere approche vnto the spirite of prophecie... Menyng that Cato talked at rouers. **1587** GOLDING *De Mornay* xxvi. (1592) 405 These particularities ..do euidently shew that Moyses spake not at rouers. **1606** *Sir Gyles Goosecappe* I. i. in Bullen *Old Pl.* III. 11 A good bustling Gallant, talkes well at Rovers. **1686** tr. *Chardin's Trav. Persia* 337 After several Discourses at Rovers, he told me, He was very much troubl'd for me. **1725** WODROW *Corr.* (1843) III. 178 Unless I had then a fuller view of circumstances than I have, I can only talk at rovers in it.

(*c*) **1555** WATREMAN *Fardle of Facions* I. v. 55 The Kinges of Egipte..liued not at rouers as other kinges doe. *a* **1658** CLEVELAND *Rebel Scot* iii, Hence 'tis they live at Rovers and defie This, or that place, Rags of Geography. **1691** J. NORRIS *Pract. Disc.* 3 A Man were better have no Mark before him, but live at Rovers.

(*d*) **1611** COTGR., *À veuë de païs*, at random, roaming, at rovers, at large. **1654** VILVAIN *Theorem. Theol.* vii. 205 A giddy Ostrich..having laid hir first Eg at rovers on the sands. **1681–6** J. SCOTT *Chr. Life* II. 489 We must necessarily think of God at Rovers without any certain aim or rule to..direct our apprehensions.

3. a. One who roves or wanders, *esp.* to a great distance; a roving person or animal. Also *spec.* (see quot. 1944).

1611 SHAKS. *Wint. T.* I. ii. 176 Next to thy selfe, and my young Rouer, he's Apparant to my heart. **1700** BLACKMORE *xxxiv Ch. Isaiah* 259 Vultures and all the rovers of the air To the red fields of slaughter shall repair. **1742** YOUNG *Nt. Th.* IX. 1612 Yet why drown Fancy in such depths as these? Return, presumptuous rover! **1835** W. IRVING *Tour Prairies* 172 The Indian of the west is a rover of the plain. **1849** *Sk. Nat. Hist., Mammalia* III. 70 These young rovers the French hunters call bêtes de compagnie. **1872** TENNYSON *Last Tourn.* 542 Harper, and thou hast been a rover too. **1933** H. G. WELLS *Bulpington of Blup* v. 177 They were to go as 'Rovers' to the Russian Ballet. **1944** G. B. SHAW *Everybody's Political What's What?* xxxi. 279 Complaisant critics were welcomed in the theatre even when all the stalls were sold out and they had to be content as 'rovers' without allotted seats, sitting or standing about wherever they could.

transf. **1895** WORKMANS *Algerian Mem.* 29 We wheeled the rovers out, and mounted for our journey of over 1500 miles.

†**b.** An inconstant lover; a male flirt. *Obs.*

c **1690** STEPNEY *Spell* 4 Whene'er I wive,..Wit, beauty, wealth, and humour give, Or let me still a rover live. **1710** ADDISON *Tatler* No. 157 ¶4 An old Friend of mine, who was formerly a Man of Gallantry and a Rover. *a* **1721** PRIOR *Song* xix, Phillis, give this Humour over,..I shall turn an errant Rover, If the favour's still refus'd.

c. *Australian Rules Football* (see quot. 1969¹). *Rugby Football*, formerly, an extra forward performing some of the functions of the scrum half and fly half. *Amer. Football*, a defensive linebacker who is assigned to move about to anticipate opponents' plays.

1894 A. SUTHERLAND in M. Shearman *Athletics & Football* (ed. 4) II. vii. 422 The rover is an individual chosen for his quickness and readiness to go wherever he is wanted. He observes the turn of the game, and follows when he sees his own followers being over-weighted by their adversaries [in Australian Rules Football]. **1909** E. G. NICHOLLS *Mod. Rugby Game* iv. 54 A fifth three-quarter..as the 'rover' or flying half is frequently styled. **1916** *Colliers* 30 Dec. 30/3 He is all over the field as a rover, diagnosing the play quickly and with unfailing accuracy. *a* **1917** J. E. RAPHAEL *Mod. Rugby Football* (1918) xvii. 225, I played 'rover' for England on a memorable day at the Crystal Palace. **1927** WAKEFIELD & MARSHALL *Rugger* II. vi. 268 The formation used in New Zealand... In this formation..the outsides consist of the extra forward, who may be described either as a rover or a half-back, a scrum-half, two five-eighths, a centre, [etc.]... The rover puts the ball into the scrum, while the scrum-half stands at the base of the scrum to take it out. **1954** J. B. G. THOMAS *On Tour* 26 They [*sc.* the All Blacks] packed 2-3-2, with Gallaher acting as a 'rover', whose duty it was to put the ball into the scrum while the scrummage half back waited behind the scrum. **1969** EAGLESON & MCKIE *Terminol. Austral. Nat. Football* III. 10 *Rover*, a member of the ruck, usually smaller than the other two members (*followers*), and selected for agility in capturing the ball. **1969** *Australian* 24 May 39/4 Essendon has Barry Davis back as a ruck-rover, to help captain Don McKenzie, and this should strengthen the side's following division and provide more opportunities for rovers Bob Greenwood and Don Gross. **1970** *Univ. of Alabama Football Press Guide* 17 The rover slot was very similar to linebacking. **1975** *Oxf. Compan. Sports & Games* 385/1 A team [in Australian Rules Football] is made up of three full-forwards [etc., and]..the 'ruck'. The ruck consists of two followers and a rover, who moves with the flow of play.

d. Formerly, a member of a senior branch of the Scout Association (see SCOUT *sb.*⁴ 2 c). Also *rover scout.*

In 1967 this branch of the Scout Association was replaced by the venture scout branch (see quot. 1966).

1922 R. BADEN-POWELL *Rovering* 210 Rovers are a Brotherhood of the *Open Air* and *Service.* **1933** A. G. MACDONELL *England, their England* xiii. 235 Lots of the young chaps are Rovers and don't drink so as to be an example to the Scouts and Cubs. **1959** *Chambers's Encycl.* II. 481/2 The movement in Great Britain is divided into four groups: rover scouts, i.e. young men of 18 and over; [etc.]. **1966** *Times* 10 June 11/1 The Scout Association will have three main sections—cub scouts.., aged 8 to 11; scouts, aged 11 to 16; and venture scouts (replacing senior scouts and rovers), aged 16 to 20. **1972** K. BONFIGLIOLI *Don't point that Thing at Me* i. 7 His bedroom is..full of fresh air; just what you would wish your Rover Scout son's room to be.

e. The name given to an R.A.F. reconnaissance patrol flown in 1940 and 1941. Also *attrib.*

1942 *R.A.F. Jrnl.* 3 Oct. 18 'Strike' and 'rover' patrols were on the board every day. **1957** R. BARKER *Ship-Busters* ii. 35 The Rover was a roving commission, an armed reconnaissance against enemy shipping..carried out by a small number of aircraft working independently.

f. Also **Rover, 'Rover.** *ellipt.* A Land-Rover (see LAND *sb.*¹ 12).

1961 A. WILSON *Old Men at Zoo* iv. 207 You hop into the rover, Carter. You're frozen. **1973** G. MOFFAT *Lady with Cool Eye* vi. 66 Slade was taking the spare wheel off the 'Rover's bonnet. **1975** *Country Life* 13 Feb. 373/1 Some elderly sportsmen have high seats constructed on their 'rovers'..for shooting.

4. *Croquet.* **a.** (See quot. 1869.)

1869 *Laws Croquet* 9 *Rover*, a ball that has gone through all its hoops and is ready to peg out. **1874** HEATH *Croquet Player* 81, I have seen many a game won, even when the adversary had both balls rovers, and the other side had scarcely started.

b. A player whose ball is a rover.

1874 HEATH *Croquet Player* 71 The adversary is supposed ..to be a good player, and likely, if he gets in, to make a long break, become a rover.

5. A remote-controlled surface vehicle for extraterrestrial exploration.

[**1967** *Jrnl. Spacecraft & Rockets* IV. 209/1 A dynamic analysis in preliminary design of a lunar roving vehicle should have at least two basic aspects.] **1970** *Science Jrnl.* Jan. 16 The first rover is scheduled to take four trips of up to 32 km each with travel limited to 4·8 km radius from the landing site. **1971** [see *moon buggy* s.v. MOON *sb.*¹ 16]. **1971** *Nature* 19 Nov. 125/3 The rover had a responsive steering, and..climbed slopes where the dust layer was deep enough to make walking difficult. **1972** [see LUNAR *a.* and *sb.* A. 1 c]. **1978** *Sci. Amer.* Mar. 89/3 Another possibility is an unmanned surface rover capable of traversing hundreds of kilometers over a period of several years, which would be able to analyze the regolith in more detail than any satellite in orbit could.

rover[2] ('rəʊvə(r)). Also 4 rovere, 5 rovare, rowar, 5–7 rouer. [a. MDu. or MLG. *rover*, f. *roven* to rob: see REAVER.]

1. A sea-robber, pirate.

In later use tending to coalesce with ROVER *sb.*[1] 3.

1390 GOWER *Conf.* I. 359 It fell per chance upon a day A Rovere of the See was nome. **1436** *Libel Eng. Policy* in *Pol. Poems* (Rolls) II. 164 Of this Bretayn.. Are the grettest rovers and the grettest thevys that have bene in the see many oone yere. *c* **1460** FORTESCUE *Abs. & Lim. Mon.* vi. (1885) 123 It shalbe nescessarie þat the kynge haue alway some ffloute apon the see, ffor the repressynge off rovers. *a* **1548** HALL *Chron., Hen. VIII* 91 The kynges subiectes.. were greuously spoyled and robbed on the sea, by Frenchemen, Scottes and other rouers. **1576** FLEMING *Panopl. Ep.* 385 You are in peril of Pyrates and Rouers to spoyle you. **1613** PURCHAS *Pilgrimage* v. ix. (1614) 609 Algier hauing beene of olde, and still continuing a receptacle of Turkish Rouers. **1653** H. COGAN tr. *Pinto's Trav.* xxiii. 81 This Rover, believing that we were Chineses, came and assailed us with two great Juncks. **1700** S. L. tr. *Fryke's Voy. E. Ind.* 193 These Rovers had several Oars with them. **1752** HUME *Ess. & Treat.* (1777) I. 552 The early Romans really exercised piracy,.. and.., like the Sallee and Algerine rovers, were actually at war with most nations. **1807** G. CHALMERS *Caledonia* I. III. vii. 378 The Danish rovers had also considerable establishments at Waterford. **1855** MACAULAY *Hist. Eng.* xv. III. 547 To ransom a Christian captive from a Sallee rover was.. a highly meritorious act. **1867** FREEMAN *Norm. Conq.* I. 295 There appears by his side another rover of the North.., the famous Olaf Tryggwesson.

†**b.** A pirate ship; a privateer. *Obs.*

1590 E. WEBBE *Trav.* (Arb.) 19, I went againe into Russia ..: in which our voyage we met with v. Rovers or men of war, whom we set vppon, and burnt their Admirall. **1692** LUTTRELL *Brief Rel.* (1857) II. 423 Algier, 12 March. All our rovers except 2 are laid up, and the men employed in the army. **1720** DE FOE *Capt. Singleton* i. (1906) 3 Coming home again from the banks of Newfoundland, we were taken by an Algerine rover, or man-of-war. **1726** *Adv. Capt. R. Boyle* (1768) 21 We found ourselves within half a Mile of a Rover of Barbary.

†**2.** A marauder, robber. *Obs.*

1550 BALE *Eng. Votaries* II. Hiiij, Anselmus.. obstinately withstode him to the very face like a ruffelinge rouer. **1570** FOXE *A. & M.* (ed. 2) 2286/1 Thomas Horton iourneying.. between Mastrick and Cullen, chanced to be taken there by certayne Rouers. **1609** BIBLE (Douay) *2 Kings* xiii. 20 The rovers of Moab came into the land the same yeare. **1638** BRATHWAIT *Barnabees Jrnl.* III. (1818) 99 As these privately conferred, A rover took them unprepared. *a* **1707** S. PATRICK *Autobiogr.* (1839) 7 They declared neither for King or parliament; intending only to stand upon their guard against rovers.

rover[3] ('rəʊvə(r)). [f. ROVE *v.*[3]]

1. One who makes cotton, etc., into roves; an attendant at a roving-frame.

1742 RICHARDSON *De Foe's Tour Gt. Brit.* (ed. 3) III. 165 On the first Stage were the Teazer, Carder, Rover, Spinner, Reeler of the Cotton Wool. **1881** *Daily News* 17 Nov. 2/5 The rovers and slubbers got 8s. a week, and they are getting 14s. a week now. **1885** *Manch. Exam.* 7 Apr. 4/4 A carder and.. a rover were remanded on a charge of setting fire to.. the mill.

2. A roving-frame.

1897 *Traill's Social England* VI. 73 In the preparing frames, known as slubbers or rovers, the bobbins were necessarily large and weighty.

†'**rovery**[1]. *Obs. rare.* [a. MDu. or MLG. *roverie*: cf. REAVERY.] Piracy.

1600 HOLLAND *Livy* XL. xlii. 1086 He laid the whole fault of all the roverie and piracie at sea upon Gentius the king of the Illyrians. **1610** —— *Camden's Brit.* II. 205 These Norwegians who with their manifold roberies and roveries did most hurt.

'**rovery**[2]. *rare*[-1]. [f. ROVE *v.*[1]] Roving.

a **1653** BINNING *Sinner's Sanct.* Wks. 1839 I. 304 How many impertinences and roveries and wanderings.

roving ('rəʊvɪŋ), *vbl. sb.*[1] [f. ROVE *v.*[1]]

1. a. *Archery.* The action or practice of shooting at a random mark.

1480 *Coventry Leet Bk.* 457 þe people of þis Citie yerely breken the hegges & dykes of þe seid Priour in diuerse places in þeir shotyng cald Rovyng. *Ibid.* 458 Although such rovyng about the Citie of London & all oþer grete Cities is suffred. **1562** J. HEYWOOD *Prov. & Epigr.* (1867) 184 Of an archers rouyng. **1626** SHIRLEY *Maid's Revenge* I. ii, *Montenegro.* How now, are thy arrows feathered? *Velasco.* Well enough for roving. **1665** J. FRASER *Polichron.* (S.H.S.) 150 Few or none could compeat or cop with him in arching, either at butts, bowmarks or roaving. **1856** [see ROVER[1] 1]. **1887** BUTT *Ford's Archery* 137 When there is sufficient space for golf links, roving might still be practised.

fig. **1674** N. FAIRFAX *Bulk & Selv.* 76 Some low and underly rovings at.. that height and depth of workmanship.

b. *attrib.*, as ***roving arrow, course, shaft.***

1479 in Longman & Walrond *Archery* (1894) 119 Shoyting shaftes, rowying shaftes, childre shaftes, clense arrows un-nykt. **1562** J. HEYWOOD *Prov. & Epigr.* (1867) 184 What a shafte shootes he with a rouyng arrowe? **1622** DRAYTON *Poly-olb.* xxvi. 330 With Broad-arrow, or But, or Prick, or Rouing shaft. **1939** P. H. GORDON *New Archery* iii. 21 Royal edict set aside places for shooting in the towns and provided long roving courses over the distances between towns.

2. a. The action of wandering or roaming.

1611 COTGR., *Escumement*,.. also, a raunging, rouing. **1637** RUTHERFORD *Lett.* I. xc. (1664) 184 Galloping after our own night-dreams, (such are the roving of our miscarrying hearts). **1691** HARTCLIFFE *Virtues* 185 It doth answer to all the numberless Rovings of men's Fancies. **1741** WATTS *Improv. Mind* xv. Wks. (1813) 103 If we indulge the frequent rise and roving of passions. **1789** BELSHAM *Ess.* I. x. 191 The study of Mathematics contributes to.. check the rovings of fancy. **1837** W. IRVING *Capt. Bonneville* I. 296 Every year this animal's rovings are restricted.

b. *attrib.* (passing into the *ppl. a.*). **roving commission** (see quot. 1846); also *transf.* and *gen.*, (a body given) authority to pursue any inquiry or investigation in whatever quarters it may be considered necessary.

1820 W. IRVING *Sketch Bk.* (1859) 2 It has been either my good or evil lot to have my roving passion gratified. **1846** A. YOUNG *Naut. Dict.*, *Roving-Commission*, an authority granted by the Admiralty to the officer in command of a vessel to cruise wherever he may see fit. **1867** *Congress. Globe* 22 Mar. 273/2, I think it would be safer to leave this matter [of certain state claims] to the direct inspection of the War Department, than to send out a roving commission. We have had enough of these roving commissions. **1892** *Daily News* 19 Feb. 7/4 A new sort of roving power had been obtained by the War Office under the Ranges Act. **1894** *Congress. Rec.* 25 Apr. 4098/1 Is it a legitimate expenditure of the public money to send up consuls with roving commissions to hunt out commerce for a certain class of our people? **1930** W. S. CHURCHILL (*title*) My early life: a roving commission. **1936** A. CHRISTIE *ABC Murders* xviii. 130, I had a kind of roving commission to purchase things for my brother. **1954** 'N. BLAKE' *Whisper in Gloom* I. ii. 31 Who'd you put him on to? Or was it a roving commission? **1959** *Ann. Reg. 1958* 179 The Russians opposed the Western proposal that they should be mobile and on a permanent footing on the ground that such 'roving commissions' would engage in espionage. **1981** *Listener* 1 Jan. 12/1 For several years as West Africa correspondent he had what was in effect a roving commission.

†'**roving**, *vbl. sb.*[2] *Obs.* [f. ROVE *v.*[2]] The pursuit of, an act of, piracy or robbery.

a **1513** FABYAN *Chron.* VII. (1811) 361 Natwithstandynge the great harmys they had done by rouing vpon the see. **1585** T. WASHINGTON tr. *Nicholay's Voy.* I. viii. 8 Most of them .. lyuing onely of rouings, spoyles, and pilling at the Seas. **1611** COTGR., *Piraterie*, piracie, roving. **1660** F. BROOKE tr. *Le Blanc's Trav.* 17 They are there much vext with the continuall rovings and robberies of the Arabians.

roving ('rəʊvɪŋ), *vbl. sb.*[3] [f. ROVE *v.*[3]]

1. The process of converting cotton, wool, etc., into roves.

1825 J. NICHOLSON *Operat. Mech.* 390 Three such skeins being passed through another drawing-frame, and stretched in their progress, become fitted for roving, the last step in the preparatory processes. **1853** URE *Dict. Arts* (ed. 4) I. 758 The first operation is called 'spreading',.. the second and third 'drawings',.. and lastly the 'roving'. **1861** FAIRBAIRN in *Rep. Brit. Assoc.* p. lxi, Improvements in carding, roving, combing, spinning, and weaving.

2. *concr.* **a.** A rove.

1802 PALEY *Nat. Theol.* vii. (ed. 2) 96 He sees.. the wool in rovings ready for spinning into threads. **1835** URE *Philos. Manuf.* 20 Drawing these out into slender spongy cords, called rovings, with the least possible twist. **1884** W. S. B. McLAREN *Spinning* (ed. 2) 231 The spindles also begin to turn comparatively slowly, putting a little twist for the first time into the roving. **1960** *New Scientist* 10 Mar. 597/1 The quantity of glass fibre applied.. is governed by the rate of operation of the rollers that feed the multi-ply coil of glass fibre rovings to the cutter block. **1964** H. HODGES *Artifacts* ix. 128 Sometimes the rolag may be drawn out to a thickness approaching that of the required thread, and even given a slight twist before winding on to the distaff. Prepared fibres in this state are usually called rovings. **1972** *Physics Bull.* Nov. 663/3 The glasses are produced in continuous strands, consisting of 204, or multiples of 204, filaments which are subsequently processed into rovings or into yarns for weaving purposes. **1977** *Austral. Sailing* Jan. 51/2 The construction.. sounds strong, including a hand-laid layer of woven rovings and additional strengthening in stress areas.

b. Roves collectively.

1844 G. DODD *Textile Manuf.* i. 31 The 'tube-roving frame'.. produces a much larger quantity of roving..; but the roving produced is inferior. **1946** A. J. HALL *Stand. Handbk. Textiles* iii. 105 The roving at this stage is about as thick as coarse string. **1972** *Physics Bull.* Nov. 663/3 S-Glass is most commonly employed in 'roving' or other unwoven forms. **1972** *Sci. Amer.* Dec. 47/2 Roving, on bobbins, is put into spinning frames, where it receives a final drawing out and the twisting necessary to make it into yarn.

3. *attrib.* **a.** In names of machines (or parts of these), as ***roving-billy, -bobbin, -box, -frame***, etc.

1795 *Edin. Advert.* 6 Jan. 15/1 Five.. carding engines.., four roving billies. **1825** J. NICHOLSON *Operat. Mechanic* 390 The loosely twisted thread from the roving bobbin. *Ibid.* 387 The spinning-frame.. is more closely allied to the bobbin and flier roving-frame. **1835** URE *Philos. Manuf.* 111 The bobbin and fly frames, or roving-machines. **1884** W. S. B. McLaren *Spinning* (ed. 2) 120 The dandy roving boxes arranged in any number of spindles and boxes that are convenient.

b. Misc., as ***roving-department, -room, -waste.***

1835 URE *Philos. Manuf.* 414 There was no appearance of dirt or of impure air in the preparing or roving-rooms. **1862** *Athenæum* 30 Aug. 264 In the so-called 'roving'.. department of flax-factories. **1894** *Times* 17 Aug. 9/3 Slubbing waste, roving waste, ring waste, yarn waste.

'**roving**, *vbl. sb.*[4] [f. ROVE *v.*[6]] The action of reducing the diameter of a grindstone. Also *attrib.* as ***roving-plate.***

1850 HOLTZAPFFEL *Turning* III. 1109 The roving plate.. jumps, and appears to fill the stone with minute furrows. **1875** KNIGHT *Dict. Mech.* 1023/2 Turning or roving is effected by reversing the motion of the stone and holding a hooked flat tool against its edge.

roving, corruption of ROBAND.

c **1860** H. STUART *Seaman's Catech.* 47 Take one of the robands next to the midship one.., and take the midship roving for a stop. **1867** SMYTH *Sailor's Word-bk.* s.v. *Rovens.*

roving ('rəʊvɪŋ), *ppl. a.* [f. ROVE *v.*[1]]

†**1.** Random; conjectural. *Obs.*

1635 *Court Min. E. India Co.* (1907) 64 A roving estimate. **1649** HEYLIN *Relat. & Observ.* I. 57 By a roaving Accusation shot at randome at me. **1687** RYCAUT *Hist. Turks* II. 258 The occasion of this unexpected.. resolution caused many roving guesses and opinations of the reasons of it.

2. a. That roves; wandering, roaming; nomadic.

1634 MILTON *Comus* 485 Som roaving Robber calling to his fellows. **1667** —— *P.L.* III. 432 Imaus.., Whose snowie ridge the roving Tartar bounds. **1749** JOHNSON *Irene* I. ii, A roving soldier seiz'd.. A virgin shining with distinguish'd charms. **1788** GIBBON *Decl. & F.* l. V. 174 The same life is uniformly pursued by the roving tribes of the desert. **1837** W. IRVING *Capt. Bonneville* I. 29 Roving bands of independent trappers. **1856** STANLEY *Sinai & Pal.* xi. (1858) 395 Up this rich plain came the roving Danites from the south.

Comb. **1838** DICKENS *Nickleby* xxiii, There was a roving-looking person in a rough great-coat.

b. ***roving blade***: see BLADE *sb.* 11 b.

1828 SCOTT *F.M. Perth* xvi, I shall have the renown of some private quest, which may do me honour as a roving blade. **1886** 'SARAH TYTLER' *Buried Diamonds* xxviii, Whatever you like to call my fine, roving blade of a brother-in-law.

c. ***roving sailor***, a local name of various plants, as the ivy-leaved toadflax, and the creeping saxifrage or loosestrife.

1882 *Devon. Plant-names* (E.D.S.). **1891** 'MAXWELL GRAY' *Heart of Storm* I. 173 A low stone wall, over which the dainty little 'roving sailor' spread its shining trails.

d. Of an ambassador, journalist, etc., required to travel to various locations to deal with events as they occur.

1938 E. WAUGH *Scoop* III. i. 258 Will you accept five year contract five thousand year roving correspondent. **1946** *R.A.F. Jrnl.* May 147 This month our roving reporter.. went back to Germany. **1958** *Listener* 26 June 1043/2 He was in the recent past Mr. Kishi's roving trade ambassador in south-east Asia. **1965** B. SWEET-ESCOTT *Baker St. Irreg.* iii. 98 Staying in the Middle East as 'a kind of roving ambassador'. **1967** *Boston Sunday Globe* 23 Apr. 29/2 Boston's roving inspectors—who check on city services for the mayor. **1968** J. DRUMMOND *Gantry Episode* ix. 72 It can't be done. Not by ordinary methods. That's why Purnell wants you as his roving reporter. **1970** A. SINCLAIR *Guevara* vi. 71 From 1960 onwards, Che had often served as a roving ambassador for Fidel Castro. **1972** D. BLOODWORTH *Any Number can Play* xii. 111 She would return.. as a roving correspondent for the Worldover Syndication Service.

3. *transf.* **a.** Of the eyes or sight.

1596 SPENSER *F.Q.* IV. iv. 7 His roving eie did on the Lady glaunce. **1728–46** THOMSON *Spring* 504 Nature,.. undisguis'd by mimic Art,.. spreads Unbounded beauty to the roving eye. **1769** SIR W. JONES *Palace of Fortune* Poems (1777) 24 Maia.. Cast on an emerald ring her roving sight. **1841** BARHAM *Ingol. Leg.* Ser. II. *Smuggler's Leap*, He has curling locks, and a roving eye. **1951** N. MITFORD *Blessing* I. ii. 17, I'm afraid she's deeply romantic, and Valhubert has a roving eye. **1968** D. GRAY *Died in Red* xiv. 73 The man with the roving eye comes along, and he tells you you're wonderful. **1970** V. GIELGUD *Candle-Holders* xi. 98 Angela Baynes had caught Tarzan's permanently roving eye.

b. Of the thoughts, affections, discourse, etc.

c **1630** MILTON *Passion* 22 These latter scenes confine my roving vers. **1660** GOUGE *Chr. Direct.* ii. (1831) 21 Though roving thoughts, as birds, will hover about thee.., yet suffer them not to lodge and nestle in thee. **1693** STEPNEY in Dryden *Juvenal* viii. (1697) 211 Such Frollicks with his Roving Genius suit. **1784** COWPER *Task* II. 525 Their rules of life.. prov'd too weak To bind the roving appetite. **1812** CRABBE *Tales* xi. 401 Yet pride still lived, and struggled to sustain The drooping spirit and the roving brain. **1885** *Law Times Rep.* LII. 586/2 Such a general and roving interrogatory as this should not be allowed.

4. Characterized by, inclined to, wandering or roaming. (Cf. *vbl. sb.*[1] 2 b.)

1725 BERKELEY *Proposal* Wks. 1871 III. 227 The Americans, so long as they continue their wild and roving life. **1821** SCOTT *Pirate* xxxi, I hope a gentleman of the roving trade has as good a right to have an alias as a stroller. **1851** MAYHEW *Lond. Labour* I. 321 This passion for 'a roving life' (to use the common expression by which many of the street-people themselves designate it). **1863** W. C. BALDWIN *Afr. Hunting* i. 2 Being of a roving turn of mind, I was placed in the large merchant's office of an ex-M.P., with a view of being fitted for going abroad.

'**rovingly**, *adv.* [f. ROVING *ppl. a.*]

†**1.** Without fixed mark or definite aim. *Obs.*

1601 DEACON & WALKER *Answ. Darel* 189 Are you not ashamed thus rouingly to raunge with your penne? *a* **1691** BOYLE *Wks.* (1772) V. 522 What, by reason,.. he can either not at all, or but rovingly, guess at.

2. In a wandering fashion; towards roaming.

1701 WOLLEY *Jrnl. N. York* (1860) 45 As to their way of living, it's very rudely and rovingly, shifting from place to place, according to their exigencies. **1849** *Blackw. Mag.* LXVI. 706 We can assure all who are rovingly inclined.

row (rəʊ), *sb.*[1] Forms: α. 1, 4–5 (6–9 *north.* and *Sc.*) raw (4 rau), 3–5 (6 *Sc.*) rawe. β. 4–7 rowe, 5– row, 5–6 roo, 7 roe. [? OE. *ráw* (see sense 9 b), var. of *rǣw* REW *sb.*[1], which may be related to MDu. *rīe* (Du. *rij*), MHG. *rîhe* (G. *reihe*).]

I. 1. a. A number of persons or things set or arranged in a (straight) line. Freq. const. *of*. *spec.* A line in a chorus.

When used without *of*, the context generally makes clear the composition of the 'row'; examples like quot. 13.. are rare.

α. *a* **1225** *Leg. Kath.* 1930 þæt al þe hweoles beon þurh-spitet mid kenre pikes..rawe bi rawe. *a* **1300** *Cursor M.* 23043 þe formast rau sal stan him nere, Als þaa þat er his dughti dere. **13..** *E.E. Allit. P.* A. 105 þe playn, þe plonttez, þe spyse, þe perez, & rawez & randez & rych reuerez. **1423** JAS. I *Kingis Q.* cliv, On euery syde, a longe rawe Off treis saw I. **1483** *Cath. Angl.* 301/1 Rawe, *series*. *c* **1730** RAMSAY *Fables, Ram & Buck* 4 Leading his family in a raw. **1786** BURNS *Toothache* v, [Where] ranked plagues their numbers tell, In dreadfu' raw. **1800-** in common Sc. and northern use.

β. *c* **1440** *Promp. Parv.* 438/1 Rowe, or reenge, *series, linea.* **1526** TINDALE *Mark* vi. 40 They sate doune here a rowe and there a rowe, by houndredes and by fyfties. **1582** N. LICHEFIELD tr. *Castanheda's Conq. E. Ind.* I. lxxi. 146 The Captaine.., returning to shoot the Saker againe, did carrie away another row of beams. **1610** HOLLAND *Camden's Brit.* (1637) 429 A new Church..supported with sundry rowes of marble pillars. **1697** DRYDEN *Virg. Georg.* IV. 213 He knew to rank his Elms in even Rows. **1707** MORTIMER *Husb.* (1721) I. 347 One which hath four Rows of Grain on the Ear, ..and the other two Rows. **1779** COWPER *Pine-apple & Bee*, The pine-apples, in triple row, Were basking hot. **1810** CRABBE *Borough* i. 292 The lads who tow Some enter'd hoy, to fix her in her row. **1848** LYTTON *Harold* XI. ii, Row by row, line by line, all the multitude shouted forth [etc.]. **1849** THACKERAY *Pendennis* I. xiv. 125 Who's that gal in the second row, with blue ribbons, third from the stage. **1887** MORRIS *Odyssey* XII. 91 Threefold rows of teeth. **1932** D. L. SAYERS *Have his Carcase* xxiii. 303 O.K. darling. 'Aeroplane Girl', first row, song and dance. **1967** A. WILSON *No Laughing Matter* II. 85 The thousands of silly boys who join the back row of the chorus every year.

b. A number of persons or things arranged in a circle. *rare.*

1576 FLEMING *Panopl. Epist.* 402 Thus haue I runne about a round row of writers, and haue shewed wherein they are to be marked. **1617** MORYSON *Itin.* III. 137 Some sixe miles from Salisbury is a place in the fields where huge stones are erected..standing in three rowes after the forme of a crowne. **1719** DE FOE *Crusoe* I. 129, I..surrounded myself with a Row of Stakes set upright in the Ground.

c. *transf.* A string or series *of* something.

c **1510** MORE *Picus* Wks. 13/1 Thy prayer..rather interrupted and broken,..then drawen on length with a continuall rowe and noumber of woordes. **1559** in Strype *Ann. Ref.* (1824) I. App. XI. 36 Let them shew me their busshoppes; they are so far off, as to bringe a rowe in order unto St. Paul. **1674** N. FAIRFAX *Bulk & Selv.* 106 By which kind of Mathematical parts..he does all his great feats in his whole row of Answers. *a* **1691** BOYLE *Wks.* (1774) IV. 75 There can be no ingredient assigned..that may not be derived either immediately, or by a row of decompositions, from the universal matter.

2. a. An array or set of persons (or things) of a certain kind; a class or category. † ***the lower row***, the populace. Now *rare.*

a **1300** *K. Horn* 1086 (R.), Horn..sette him doun wel lowe In the beggeres rowe. **1390** GOWER *Conf.* I. 225 That I mai stonde in thilke rowe Amonges hem that Saundres use. *Ibid.* II. 76 The lord nomore hath..Than hath the povereste of the rowe. **1483** CAXTON *G. de la Tour* k v b, To putte her self in the Rowe or companye of them that were re-nommed. **1581** PETTIE *Guazzo's Civ. Conv.* I. (1586) 24 The error of the world, which esteemeth them in the row of the tollerable. **1601** R. JOHNSON *Kingd. & Commw.* (1603) 200 In the rowe of these potent princes inhabiting betweene Indus and Ganges dwelleth the King of Narsinga. **1654** H. L'ESTRANGE *Chas. I* (1655) 128 To allow the use of lawful pastimes in the lower row upon that day. **1678** CUDWORTH *Intell. Syst.* 13 Democritus..was of the Italick Row, or Pythagorick Succession. **1738** tr. *Guazzo's Art Conversation* 71 Those whom you have now described, I think should stand in the Row of the Desirable and Commendable. **1787** M. CUTLER in *Life*, etc. (1888) I. 225 She has an only daughter,..who is, at least, approaching the old-maid's row. **1821** W. LIDDLE *Poems* 31 If ye'd been o' the batch'lor row, It ne'er wad bred up sic a strow.

†b. Place, position, or rank. *Obs.*$^{-1}$

a **1310** in Wright *Lyric P.* iv. 25 He byt us buen of hyse; Ant on ys ryht hond hente rowe.

†c. A company. *Obs. rare.*

c **1450** LOVELICH *Arth. & Merl.* 1416 Mochel wers schal I sein aforn al this rowe! *c* **1460** *Towneley Myst.* xiii. 109 God looke ouer the raw, Full defly ye stand.

d. *Mus.* = *tone-row* s.v. TONE *sb.* 11. Also Comb., as ***row-note***.

1936 *Musical Q.* XXII. 14 The chief contribution towards the organization of the twelve-tone system is that peculiarly Schoenbergian concept—part abstract theory and part pure inspiration—the 'row': a semi-arbitrary arrangement of the twelve chromatic tones into a horizontal motival structure. *Ibid.* 31 Examples could be multiplied indefinitely, but,..most of them would boil down to some similar types of random distribution of the row-notes. **1958** A. JACOBS *New Dict. Mus.* 390 This method works through the 'note-row' (or 'series'), in which all the twelve notes are placed in a particular order as the basis of a work. No note is repeated within a row, which accordingly consists of twelve different notes and no others. **1965** *Listener* 20 May 757/3 An important aspect of the work is the extraction from the note-series of innumerable motivic elements and of the great variety of ways in which the row is itself presented. **1971** *Times Lit. Suppl.* 1 Oct. 1180/2 He [*sc.* Webern] was particularly partial to rows whose second half is a mirror inversion of the first.

†3. a. A ray or beam. *Obs.* (Cf. DAY-RAWE.)

a **1225** *Juliana* 21 þe rawen rahten of luue þurh euch lið of his limes, & inwið bearnde of brune. **1412-20** LYDG. *Chron. Troy* I. 1199 Whan þat þe larke..Gan to salue the lusty rowes rede Of Phebus char. **15..** *Tayis Bank* 26 The reid sone rais with rawis.

†b. A (written or printed) line. *Obs.*

c **1384** CHAUCER *H. Fame* I. 448 He most rede many a Rowe On Virgile or on Claudian. *a* **1400-50** *Alexander* 2843 Quen he þis rawis had rede he rewfully wepid. **1598** BP. HALL *Sat.* IV. i. 6 Which who reads thrise,..And deep intendeth every doubtfull row, Scoring the margent.

†c. *Chess.* A file or rank. *Obs.*

a **1500** *MS. Ashmole 344* fol. 10 b, Then fayne a drawght in the same rowe w[t] þi Roke.

†d. The letters of the alphabet. Cf. (CHRIST-) CROSS-ROW. *Obs.*

1570 FOXE *A. & M.* (ed. 2) 175/1 This Charles builded so manie monasteries as there be letters in ye row of A.B.C. **1611** J. DAVIES (Heref.) *Sco. Folly, To C'tess Pembroke* Wks. (Grosart) II. 63/1 But I Am little i, the least of all the row.

4. a. A number of houses standing in a line; a street (esp. a narrow one) formed by two continuous lines of houses. (Cf. REW *sb.*[2])

Chiefly *Sc.* and *north.*, being common in local names of particular streets in various towns (cf. next). Also *Comb.*, as **row house** *N. Amer.*, a terraced house; also (with hyphen) *attrib.*; hence **row housing**.

c **1450** *St. Cuthbert* (Surtees) 1881 Of þat towne on þe este rawe A house bren. *c* **1470** HENRY *Wallace* VII. 558 Haist þow fast... Behynd thaim cum, and in the Northast raw. **1531** *Test. Ebor.* (Surtees) VI. 19 The third part of one Raw called Scherome Raw. **1564** *Extr. Burgh Rec. Edin.* (1875) 185 The hie passege quhilk ledys fra the West Port to the Commoun Mwre throuch the raw and streit callit [*blank*]. **1663** *Providence Rec.* (1894) V. 205 Being in the Towne of Providence afores[ai]d, and in the Rowe of the Towne. **1753** W. MAITLAND *Hist. Edin.* I. vi. 97 The Brewery in the Candlemaker Row. **1807** CRABBE *Par. Reg.* I. 169 This infected row we term our street. **1832** W. STEPHENSON *Gateshead Poems* 50 When he got up to the raw, An open door and light he saw. **1900** GUTHRIE *Kitty Fagan* 43 Passing down the row, her passage was like a procession. **1936** H. HAGEDORN *Brookings* i. 10 So the Brookings children moved to Baltimore..and went to live in a pleasant brick row-house with the canonical white stoop which Baltimoreans cherished. **1940** *Sun* (Baltimore) 16 Feb. 24/1 Mr. Pagon, in proposing that the entire area be rezoned from a row-house status, pointed out that [etc.]. **1949** *Ibid.* 29 Nov. 12/1 The Housing Authority's plans call for row housing. **1952** *Ibid.* 11 Jan. 12/3 The narrowest row house will be 16 feet across the front..and there will be only seven to a group. **1957** W. H. WHYTE *Organization Man* xxiii. 305 A study of several new Philadelphia row-house neighborhoods. **1968** *Globe & Mail* (Toronto) 13 Feb. B2/4 There is no doubt that municipalities..would be agreeable to more realistic zoning in respect to smaller lots, row housing, etc. **1979** *Kingston* (Ontario) *Whig-Standard* 29 Mar. 21/4 The township has called for ten feet of yard between the end of a line of row houses and the next building.

b. ***the Row***, used *ellipt.* for Goldsmith's Row(?), Paternoster Row, and Rotten Row, in London. Also *attrib.*

1607 MIDDLETON *Michaelmas Term* III. iv, Where grows this pleasant fruit? Says one citizen's wife in the Row. **1812** COMBE *Picturesque* XXIII, 'Tis not confined..To vulgar tradesmen in the Row. **1822** BYRON *Let. to Moore* 27 Aug., The shipwreck..'took', as they say in the Row. **1871** J. M. LANGFORD *Let.* 2 Dec. in *Geo. Eliot Lett.* (1956) V. 223 Some of the Row Houses whose subscription was partially delivered have been in for more. **1884** *Eng. Illustr. Mag.* Oct. 25/2 There are bad riders in the Row.

c. In Yarmouth, one of a number of narrow lanes connecting the main streets.

1599 NASHE *Lenten Stuffe* 19 Yarmouth. Her sumptuous porches and garnisht buildings.., the spanbroad rowse running betwixt. **1742** RICHARDSON *De Foe's Tour Gt. Brit.* (ed. 3) I. 61 The Streets [of Yarmouth] are all exactly strait .., with Lanes or Alleys, which they call Rows, crossing them in strait Lines also. **1865** *Daily Telegr.* 25 Aug., These 'rows' are simply alleys running from one main thoroughfare to another. They are almost inconceivably narrow.

d. In Chester, one of several raised and covered galleries running along the sides of the four main streets.

1610 HOLLAND *Camden's Brit.* (1637) 605 Galleries or walking places, they call them Rowes having shops on both sides. **1777** *Phil. Trans.* LXVIII. 132 There is a form of building peculiar to Chester, called the Rows, which are covered galleries that make a complete communication between most of the principal streets. **1847** ALB. SMITH *Chr. Tadpole* Introd. (1879) 3 The wind came..brawling along the covered rows.

e. Chiefly *U.S.* A line of cells in a prison; esp. in phr. ***death row***, the part of a prison where condemned prisoners are kept.

1950 in M. McLuhan *Mech. Bride* (1967) 4/2 The doomed men..were filmed in death row yesterday afternoon. **1968** *Listener* 15 Feb. 210/2 Until he arrived, the ten prisoners in death row never left their cells, not even for exercise. **1971** *Black Scholar* Apr.-May 19/1 He is now waiting on Death Row in the Ohio Penitentiary. **1973** *Philadelphia Inquirer* 7 Oct. (Today Suppl.) 26/3 After all that time, you'd think we would all be exhilarated to be off the row. But everyone of us wanted, on some level, to go back. We didn't want to face the responsibilities of being out and having to fend for ourselves. **1973** *Publishers Weekly* 27 Aug. 231/2 Sentenced to death, he cut off his penis and has spent 23 years in a cage on a row reserved for lunatics. **1980** *Sci. Amer.* Apr. 63/3 Texas, which already has such a capital-punishment law on the books, currently ranks second in the nation, with 119 on death row.

5. a. A line of seats in a theatre, etc.

1710 STEELE *Tatler* No. 130 ¶12 They shall have a Place kept for them in the first Row of the Middle Gallery. **1758** JOHNSON *Idler* No. 18 ¶6 She [was]..among those that sat in the first row. **1792** BOSWELL *Johnson* (Oxf. ed.) II. 573 An appearance so improper in the front row of a front box. **1888** *Encycl. Brit.* XXIII. 223/1 The chief priestesses..occupied marble thrones in the προεδρία or front row.

b. *U.S.* A story or flat in a building.

1873 'SUSAN COOLIDGE' *What Katy Did* iii, 'Which row are you going to have a room in?' she went on.

6. a. A line of plants in a field or garden. Also *Comb.*, as **row boss** *U.S.* (see quot. 1937); **row crop** (see quot. 1930).

1733 TULL *Horse-hoeing Husb.* (Dubl.) 127 Servants are apt to Hoe too far from the Rows. **1786** ABERCROMBIE *Gard. Assist.* 328 Dig the ground between the plants, raising the earth ridge-ways along the rows on both sides. **1855** E. S. DELAMER *Kitchen Garden* (1861) 41 Set another row parallel to, and a foot apart from, the former; and then a couple more rows, which will complete the bed.

attrib. **1778** [W. MARSHALL] *Minutes Agric., Digest* 63 A comparative view of the Row and Random Cultures. **1805** R. W. DICKSON *Pract. Agric.* I. 466 Others accustomed to the row system. **1832** *Planting* 23 in *Husb.* III. (L.U.K.), For these crops..the row and ridge system of culture should be adopted. **1884** KNIGHT *Dict. Mech.* Suppl., *Row Marker*, an implement for marking out ground for planting in rows. **1930** *Amer. Speech* VI. 11 Irrigation farmers call beets, potatoes, and beans *rowcrops* in distinction from alfalfa and the grains, the *flood* crops, for in the former case the water is directed down rows instead of being allowed to flow over the whole field. **1937** *Sun Mag.* (Baltimore) 11 July 9/3 'The young ones aren't as good as their parents,' said the row boss. *Ibid.*, The term 'row boss' comes..from his being in charge of the pickers when they are working along the rows of vegetables. **1943** J. S. HUXLEY *TVA* 45 Indian corn and other row crops. *Ibid.* 58 Row crops are confined to the more level spots. **1950** *Engineering* 5 May 505/3 Light, medium and heavy tractors were all represented, and each group was subdivided into rowcrop and general-purpose tractors. **1960** *Farmer & Stockbreeder* 1 Mar. 125/1 We pioneered pneumatic tyred row-crop wheels. **1971** *Arable Farmer* Feb. 29/1 Wheel tractors on the farm being used solely for haulage and row-crop work. **1977** *New Yorker* 29 Aug. 48/1 So much for row-boss supervision, so much for harvest labor, so much for trucking, so much for tractor overhead, so much for fertilizer and pesticides.

b. orig. *U.S.* ***to have a hard*** (***long***, etc.) ***row to hoe***, to have a difficult task to perform.

1835 D. CROCKETT *Tour Down East* 69, I never opposed Andrew Jackson for the sake of popularity. I knew it was a hard row to hoe. **1848** LOWELL *Biglow P.* Ser. I. Wks. (1884) 213 You've a darned long row to hoe. **1892** GUNTER *Miss Dividends* ix, I am afraid Harry Lawrence has a hard row to hoe. **1912** J. MASEFIELD *Widow in Bye St.* IV. 56 Bessie, the gipsy, got with child by Ern... 'I hear the gipsy has a row to hoe.' **1955** *Times* 2 Aug. 4/6 The lecturer then set himself a hard row to hoe; the scholarly correction of everything his audience may have been taught at school about King John, Runnymede, and Magna Carta. **1961** B. FERGUSON *Watery Maze* v. 119 Mountbatten had therefore no easy row to hoe; but he had a definite course to steer: the invasion of France. **1969** *Listener* 26 June 894/2, I recognise full well that there are many people who always find life a pretty difficult row to hoe and our society must be a compassionate society. **1976** *New Yorker* 26 Apr. 62/3 Women have a God-damned hard row to hoe.

c. *U.S.* ***to hoe one's own row***, to do one's own work; to mind one's own business.

1871 in De Vere *Americanisms* 608 Now that I have hoed my own row.., they deluge me with congratulations.

7. a. (See quot.)

1807 SEWELL in Young *Agric. Essex* II. 60, 24 of the bunches [of teazle] are fixed on a small stick, and called a row, 240 of which make a load in bulk.

b. A hedgerow. Also *U.S.* a wall.

a **1825** FORBY *Voc. E. Anglia*, *Row*, a hedge. **1883** *Cent. Mag.* Sept. 686 A pair of brown-thrashers..were flitting from bush to bush along an old stone row in a remote field.

8. In knitting, one line of stitches.

1800 M. EDGEWORTH *Parent's Assistant* (ed. 3) II. 79 Her mother's unfinished knitting lay upon a table near the bed, and Susan sat down in her wicker arm chair and went on with the row, in the middle of which her hand stopped the preceding evening. **1872** GEO. ELIOT *Middlem.* II. III. xxvi. 69 Mrs Taft who was always counting stitches and gathered her information in misleading fragments caught between the rows of her knitting. **1909** W. J. LOCKE *Septimus* i. 4 She counted the rows of her knitting. **1932** [see KNIT *sb.* 1 a]. **1970** M. HAMILTON-HUNT *Knitting Dict.* 19 Cast on in usual way, work a few rows of st st, the depth of the hem required.

II. In prepositional phrases. (See also AROW.)

†9. ***on row***: **a.** In a line. *Obs.*

α. *c* **1330** *Arth. & Merl.* 5408 Her names to tellen ȝou in sawe Hou þai wenten al on rawe. First wenten þre wiþ gret honour [etc.]. **1375** BARBOUR *Bruce* XI. 431 Thai stude than rangit all on raw, Reddy for till byde battale. *c* **1400** MAUNDEV. (Roxb.) xxii. 102 He mase þam to sitt on rawe and delez þam þis relefe. *c* **1470** HENRY *Wallace* IV. 430 In a dern woode he stellit thame on raw. **1513** DOUGLAS *Æneis* VII. xi. 91 He drivis furth the stampand hors on raw Vnto the ȝok. **1530** LYNDESAY *Test. Papyngo* 643 Sum tyme in the I led ane lustye lyfe, The fallow deir, to see thame raik on rawe.

β. *c* **1320** *Sir Tristr.* 779 Lat mo men wiþ þe ride On rowe. *c* **1330** *Amis & Amil.* 1900 When thai were semly set on rowe.

†b. In order, in succession. *Obs.*

[A doubtful example occurs in *Saxon Leechd.* II. 238 Sele þonne drincan on sume rawe (? *read* sume on rawe) niȝon daȝon.]

α. *a* **1300** *Cursor M.* 221 þis are the maters redde on raw, þat I thynk in þis bok to draw. *Ibid.* 5460 Quen he endid had his sau His suns blessed he on rau. *a* **1400** *Sir Perc.* 1193 Thus he dalt thame on rawe Tille the daye gunne dawe. **1483** *Cath. Angl.* 301/1 On Rawe, *gradatim, ordinatim, seriatim.* **1513** DOUGLAS *Æneis* V. iii. 56 By cuttis than per ordour, all on raw, Thair place thai chesit.

β. *c* **1320** *Sir Tristr.* 504 þe rauen he ȝaue his ȝiftes..On rowe. *a* **1450** MYRC 123 And say the wordes alle on rowe, As a-non I wole ȝow schowe. *c* **1470** HARDYNG *Chron.* CCXXXII. ii. 3 The Frenche assembled..And gate the lande ay by and by on rowe. **1509** HAWES *Past. Pleas.* XXVII. (Percy Soc.) 132

Full wofull was my herte, Whan all on rowe they toke me by the hande.

†**10.** ***by row***, in order, one after another. *Obs.*

c **1330** *Arth. & Merl.* 8632 (Kölbing), Þer he was of Arthour biknawe & of his feren al bi rawe. *c* **1374** CHAUCER *Troylus* II. 970 Right as floures..spreden in hire kynde cours by rowe. **1442** *Cursor M.* 9712 (Bedford), To haue Recorde no dome owe, Or we assent all be Rowe. *c* **1460** *How the Goode Wif* 158 in Hazl. *E.P.P.* I. 191 Take a smerte rodde, and bete hem alle by rowe. **1533** MORE *Debell. Salem* Wks. 1031/1 Thus haue I..now replied to euery chapyter of hys booke by row. *c* **1555** HARPSFIELD *Divorce Hen. VIII* (Camden) 78 Consider all these parts of the decalogue by rowe as diligently..as you may.

†**11.** ***in row***, in line, in order. *Obs.*

c **1460** *Vrbanitatis* 37 in *Babees Bk.* (1868) 14 Do hem no Reuerens, but sette alle in Rowe. **1542** UDALL *Erasm. Apoph.* Pref. **ij, The ordre of regions and kyngdomes as thei stand in rowe. *c* **1650** in *Percy's Folio MS., Ball. & Rom.* I. 277 To whom there did succeed in row 8 heyres of his successiuelye.

†**12.** ***on a row***: **a.** = 9 a. *Obs.*

α. **13..** *E.E. Allit. P.* A. 545 Set hem alle vpon a rawe, & gyf vchon in-lyche a peny. *c* **1400** *Laud Troy Bk.* 2925 Thei sayled alle on a rawe, Til thei were come ther thei were knawe. *c* **1440** *Alph. Tales* 292 Hym þoght þat he saw in a vision a grete multitude of virgyns goyng on a raw by hym. *a* **1500** *Gest of Robin Hood* 1222, I wolde not that..For all the golde in mery Englonde, Though it now lay on a rawe.

β. *a* **1310** in Wright *Lyric P.* ix. 35 Hire gurdel of bete gold is al..; Al whith rubies on a rowe. *c* **1330** R. BRUNNE *Chron. Wace* (Rolls) 1683 Coryneus..busched þem on a rowe. **1430–40** LYDG. *Bochas* IX. xxxi. (MS. Bodl. 263) fol. 433 That thei sholde be pleyn confessioun Requere mercy knelyng on a rowe. *a* **1500** *Gest of Robin Hood* 237 And nowe they renne away fro me, As bestis on a rowe. *a* **1548** HALL *Chron., Hen. VIII* 22 b, Thei frapped together .xxiiij. greate Hulkes..and set them on a rowe. **1621** T. WILLIAMSON tr. *Goulart's Wise Vieillard* 90 Their vertuous children..About their table all on a rowe. **1682** DRYDEN *Dk. Guise* V. ii, Five Hundred Popular Figures on a Row.

†**b.** In order or succession; one after another; all together. *Obs.*

c **1400** *Sowdone Bab.* 390 That he myght the Romaynes kille, Playnly on a rowe. *c* **1450** LOVELICH *Merlin* v. 1474 (Kölbing), For thinges, that ben past, I knowe, And thinges, that ben comeng vppon a rowe. *c* **1552** in Strype *Cranmer* (1694) II. 137 The child that is yet unborn Shal them curse al on a rowe. **1597** BEARD *Theatre God's Judgem.* (1612) 202 They slew their lawfull King, and set vp three other on a row. **1610** WILLET *Daniel* 446 All the Popes vassals..so haue beene of late the kings of France on a rowe.

13. ***in a row***, so as to form, or be in, a line. Also *transf.* of occurrences: in succession, consecutively. *colloq.*

c **1369** CHAUCER *Dethe Blaunche* 975 She wolde have be.. A cheef mirour of al the feste Thogh they had stonden in a rowe. **1557** RECORDE *Whetst.* H ij, Men call a line of Brickes ..when many bee laied in a rowe. **1697** DRYDEN *Virg. Georg.* IV. 252 They..chime their sounding Hammers in a Row. **1719** DE FOE *Crusoe* II. (Globe) 385 When the poor Women saw themselves set in a Row thus. **1843** *Penny Cycl.* XXVII. 237/2 [The shores] north of the island are beset with almost innumerable islets, which lie along it in a row. **1855** MRS. CARLYLE *Lett.* II. 251 Near the sea..are three houses in a row. *a* **1961** in WEBSTER s.v.⁴ *row*, Won the state tourney for four years in a row. **1969** 'E. LATHEN' *When in Greece* xiii. 139 Acute gastric distress..kept him awake..for a second night in a row. **1979** M. BABSON *So soon done For* i. 10, I burnt the clothes he'd been wearing yesterday, and I shampooed his hair three times in a row.

14. †**a.** ***by*** or ***on rows***, = 9 b, 10. *Obs.*

c **1440** *York Myst.* xx. 50 Maistirs, takes to me intente, And rede youre resouns right on rawes. *c* **1460** *Towneley Myst.* xviii. 60 In som mynde it may the bryng To here oure sawes red by rawes.

b. ***in*** (or †***on***) ***rows***, in lines.

c **1450** HOLLAND *Howlat* 244 Quhen thai war rangit on rawis. **1508** DUNBAR *Tua Mariit Wemen* 35 Ane marbre tabile..With ryale cowpis apon rawys. **1694** *Acc. Sev. Late Voy.* II. (1711) 126 Round about this Star are small black Spots, in rows. **1706** LONDON & WISE *Retir'd Gard.* I. 332 Planted in Rows at Five Inches Distance from each other. *a* **1822** SHELLEY *Faust* II. 254 An hundred bonfires burn in rows.

15. Special Combs.: **row matrix** *Math.*, a matrix consisting of a single row of elements; **row vector** *Math.*, a vector represented by a row matrix.

1941 BIRKHOFF & MACLANE *Survey Mod. Algebra* viii. 203 The coordinates of a vector ξ relative to a given basis in an *n*-space *V* form a one-rowed array $X = (x_1, \ldots, x_n)$, *X* a 'row matrix'. This may be considered as a vector in $V_n(F)$ or as a $1 \times n$ 'row matrix'. **1954** BEAUMONT & BALL *Introd. Mod. Algebra & Matrix Theory* i. 23 Any *m* by *n* matrix.. may be thought of as an *m* by 1 column matrix with elements which are 1 by *n* row matrices. **1928** H. W. TURNBULL *Theory of Determinants* iii. 36 There are two distinct types of vector, the row vector, and the column vector. **1978** *Nature* 13 Apr. 605/2 A row vector..may be derived which has elements representing the magnitude of growth response to each climatic variable.

row (raʊ), *sb.*² [A slang or colloquial word, of obscure origin, in common use from *c* 1800. Noted by Todd (1818) as 'a very low expression'.]

1. a. A violent disturbance or commotion; a noisy dispute or quarrel. Freq. in phr. ***to make***, or ***kick up, a row***.

1746 S. BARRY *Let.* 6 June in D. Garrick *Private Corr.* (1831) I. 41 This occasioned a pleasant scene, for immediately, a terrible 'Row' ensued, between the few who paid ready money, and those who brought in his benefit-tickets. **1753** J. POULTER *Discoveries* (ed. 2) 13 He would prick again for thirty [Guineas]; we were afraid he would make too big a Row when he lost that, that is, a great Noise. **1787** in A. C. Bower *Diaries & Corr.* (1903) 76 The man makes a row and sayes he cannot get others without money. **1789** *Loiterer* No. 12. 12, I shall..now and then kick up a row in the street. **1806** SURR *Winter in Lond.* III. 203 It was reserved for the present winter..to introduce in the pit of the opera a *row*, in the lowest sense of that vulgar word. **1820** BYRON *Juan* IV. xcix, As boys love rows, my boyhood liked a squabble. **1857** HOLLAND *Bay Path* xii, She was not prepared for so terrific a row as he said had taken place. **1885** ANSTEY *Tinted Venus* 25 You can do no good to yourself or any one else by making a row. **1955** *Times* 11 May 14/3 The Barons Court contest gains piquancy from a big local row which both sides expect to favour the Conservatives.

Comb. c **1840** MITFORD *Lett. & Rem.* (1891) 130 It was a case like that of the row-loving Irishman.

b. In phr. ***what's the row?*** What is all the noise about? What is the matter? What is doing?

1837 DICKENS *Pickw.* ii, What's the row, Sam? **1838** —— *O. Twist* viii, Hullo, my covey! What's the row? **1849** THOREAU *Week Concord Riv.* Friday 357 Come to see the sport and have a hand in what is going,—to know 'what's the row', if there is any.

2. Noise, din, clamour.

1845 FORD *Handbk. Spain* I. 23 The varied and never-ceasing din.., the dust, the row, which Spaniards, men as well as beasts, kick up. **1863** KINGSLEY *Water Bab.* (1874) 34 Never was there heard..such a noise, row, hubbub, babel, shindy, hullabaloo. **1864** HEMYNG *Eton School Days* ii, Chudleigh was going to speak.., when Chorley cried, 'Hold your row, will you?'

row (rəʊ), *sb.*³ [f. ROW *v.*¹] A spell of rowing; a journey on the water in a rowing-boat.

[Hexham (1647) gives *rowe* in the sense of 'oar': there appears to be no other evidence for this.]

1832 F. TROLLOPE *Dom. Manners Amer.* (ed. 2) I. xvi. 249 A row upon the Ohio was another of our favourite amusements. **1847** in WEBSTER. **1864** LOUISA S. COSTELLO *Tour Venice* 310 Re-entering the gondola [we] resumed our row. **1873** HELPS *Anim. & Mast.* i. (1875) 3 He asked me to go out for a row with him.

†**row**, *sb.*⁴ *Obs. rare.* [OE. *rów*, = ON. *ró*: see RO *sb.*] Rest.

a **1000** *Guthlac* 184 Ðonne hy of waþum werʒe cwoman,.. rowe ʒefeʒon. *a* **1450** MYRC 447 In goddes body I be-leue nowe A-monge hys seyntes to ʒeue me rowe.

row (raʊ), *sb.*⁵ [See ROW *a.*¹]

†**1.** Roughness. *Obs. rare.*

a **1225** *Ancr. R.* 184 He is þi uile, & uileð awei al þi rust & al þi ruwe of þine sunnen. **1330** R. BRUNNE *Chron.* (1810) 215 Þou has frendis inowe.., If þou turne to þe rowe, þei salle drede þe chance.

2. *Cornish mining.* 'Coarse, undressed tin ore; refuse from the stamping mills.'

1860 *Eng. & For. Mining Gloss.* (ed. 2) 21 *Row*, large stones, rough. *a* **1863** TREGELLAS *Cornish Tales* (1868) 94 Go athurt the floors ovver to a laarge pile of Row. **1875** J. H. COLLINS *Met. Mining* 111 Material of a mixed nature, called 'dredge', or 'roughs', or 'rows'.

†**row**, *sb.*⁶ *Sc. Obs. rare.* In 6 roow. [a. F. *roue*:—L. *rota*.] A wheel.

1582–8 *Hist. & Life Jas. VI* (1804) 154 To be publickly punisht, brokin upoun the roow, and thus pynit to the death.

row, *sb.*⁷ Also 6 rowe. [Cf. ROW *v.*³] A rove of wool or cotton.

1673 WEDDERBURN *Voc.* (Jam.), *Filum*, a thread. *Naeta*, a rowe. **1825** J. NICHOLSON *Operat. Mechanic* 385 The portions thus rolled are called rows, rolls, or rowans. *Ibid.* 391 The rows or rowans are taken to a roving-billy.

row, obs. form of ROE *sb.*

row (raʊ), *a.*¹ *Obs.* exc. *dial.* or *arch.* Forms: α. 1–3 ruw- (1 ru-), 3 ru. β. 1 row-, 3–5 rowe (4 rouwe), 4– row. [An inflectional variant of ROUGH *a.*: cf. MDu. and MLG. *ruw-*, *ru* (Du. *ruw*). See also ROW *sb.*⁵]

1. Rough, in various senses. (Common from *c* 1300 to 1450.)

α. **931** in Birch *Cartul. Sax.* II. 364 To ðære ruwan hecgan. **944** *Ibid.* 557 On ðone ruwan hlync. *c* **1000** in Cockayne *Narrat.* (1861) 22 Wæron hie swa ruwe and swa ʒehære swa wildeor. *c* **1000** ÆLFRIC *Genesis* xxvii. 23 Þa ruwan handa wæron swilce þæs yldran broður. *c* **1225** *Ancr. R.* 120 Þet ruwe vel abute þe heorte. *c* **1250** *Gen. & Ex.* 1544 Ysaac wende it were esau, for he grapte him and fond him ru.

β. **944** in Birch *Cartul. Sax.* II. 557 Andlang þæs rowan linces. *a* **1300** *Owl & Night.* 1013 Hi goþ bytuht myd rowe felle. *c* **1350** *Ipomadon* 6147 Hys hed ys row wyth feltred here. **1362** LANGL. *P. Pl.* A. x. 120 Þe rose..Out of a ragged roote, and of rouwe breres springeþ. *c* **1400** *Beryn* 520 He axid his staff spitouslich with wordis sharp & rowe. *c* **1440** CAPGR. *Life St. Kath.* I. 942 Cande þe rych, whech hath a see ful rowe. *a* **1529** SKELTON *Agst. Garnesche* iii. 124 Thow a Sarsens hed ye bere, Row and full of lowsy here. **1746–** in south-western dial. use (see *E.D.D.*).

2. In special collocations, as ***row cheer*** (†), ***dashle, dog, hound, smith*** (†): (see quots.).

1403–4 in Bickley *Little Red Bk. Bristol* II. 183 No Smyth yclepid a Rowsmyth of the towne of Bristow. *c* **1440** *Promp. Parv.* 437/2 Rowchere, *acrimonia*. **1848** *Zoologist* VI. 1973 Small Spotted Dog, *Scyllium canicula*. Frequently called 'rough' or 'row-hound'. **1891** CHOPE *Hartland Gloss.* s.v. *Dashle*, The milk-thistle is called Milky-dashle, and the Scotch thistle Row-dashle. *Ibid.*, *Row-dogs*.., Rough men (Clovelly).

3. *Comb.*, as **row-foot(ed)**, = ROUGH-FOOT(ED). Now *arch.*

1398 TREVISA *Barth. De P.R.* XII. vi. (Tollem. MS.), Rowe-fotid dowues bredeþ euery monþe. **1564–78** BULLEIN *Dial. agst. Pest* (1888) 6, I had better bee hangad in a withie or in a cowtaile, than be a rowfooted Scot. *a* **1802** *Kinmont Willie* xxv. in Scott *Border Min.* (1869) 269 'Why trespass ye on the English side? Row-footed outlaws, stand!' quo' he. **1896** KIPLING *Seven Seas* 118 What care I for your row-foot earls?

row (raʊ), *a.*² Now *north. dial.* Forms: 1 hreow, 5–6 rowe, 5–7, 9 *dial.* row, 9 *dial.* rou. [OE. *hréow*, app. an ablaut-variant of *hréaw* RAW *a.*] Raw, uncooked, untanned, etc. Also ***row-eyed, -nosed*** adjs.

c **1000** ÆLFRIC *Exod.* xii. 9 Ne eton ʒe of þam nan þing hreowes. **1483** *Cath. Angl.* 312/1 Rowe, *crudus, incoctus. Ibid.*, To be Rowe, *crudere.* **1489** CAXTON *Faytes of A.* II. xxxv. 152 Ayenst brenninge yron may haue no defence row leder nor also lamynes of yron. **1551** TURNER *Herbal* I. (1568) B v, Garlyke..swageth the olde coughe, taken row or soden. **1562** *Ibid.* II. 72 The rowe iuice..dronken softeneth the belly. **1686** *Lond. Gaz.* No. 2156/4 A white cropt Gelding with a whisk Tail, Row-nosed and Row-eyed. **1829** BROCKETT *N.C. Gloss.* (ed. 2), *Rou*, cold, bleak and damp; especially as applied to a place, or to the weather. **1894** HESLOP *Northumb. Gloss.*, *Ro, roa, row*, raw, as meat that is under-cooked.

†**row**, *adv. Obs.* Also 4–5 rowe. [f. ROW *a.*¹] Roughly; angrily, fiercely. Chiefly in phr. ***to look row.***

1297 R. GLOUC. (Rolls) 590 King lotrin..dude al is wille, vor he lokede so rowe. **13..** *Coer de L.* 4661 Kyng Richard ..on hym gan to look rowe. *c* **1386** CHAUCER *Can. Yeom. T.* 861, I haue yow toold ynowe To reyse a feend al looke he neuer so rowe. *c* **1440** *Eng. Conq. Irel.* 89 The kynge henry ..was a man..row [*v.r.* roghly] lokynge, and rede in wreth. *c* **1450** *Merlin* xi. 168 He was grete and longe, and blakke and rowe rympled. *a* **1500** *Chaucer's Dream* in C.'s Wks. (1598) 358/1 His heavy brow He shewed the Queene, & looked row.

row (rəʊ), *v.*¹ Forms: 1 rowan, 3 rowen, rouwen, roʒen, reowe, 3–6 rowe (4 rowwe), 4– row, 6 roa; *Sc.* 5 rou-, roy, 6 roll. Also *pa. t.* 1 reow, 3 rue, 3–4 rewe; *pl.* 1 reowon, -un, hrowun, hræuun, reon, 2 reowan; *pa. pple.* 6 rowen. [OE. *rówan*, = OFris. **rôia* (WFris. *roeije*, EFris. *rôi, roie*, NFris. *rui, rö*), MDu. *royen, roeyen* (Du. *roeijen*), MLG. and LG. *rôjen, rojen*, MHG. *rüejen*, ON. and Icel. *róa* (Norw. *roa, ro*, Sw. and Da. *ro*). The root *rō-* is also the base of OE. *rōðor* RUDDER, and various forms of it appear in the related languages, as OIr. *ráme* (Ir. *rámh*), L. *rēmus*, Gr. ἐρετμόν oar, ἐρέτης rower.]

I. 1. a. *intr.* Of persons: To use oars, sweeps, or similar means, for the purpose of propelling a boat or other vessel.

c **950** *Lindisf. Gosp.* Luke viii. 23 Hrowundum..ðæm (*vel* miððy ʒehrowun) [he] slepde [*c* **1000** þa hiʒ reowun, þa slep he]. *c* **1000** ÆLFRIC *Colloq.* in Wr.-Wülcker 96 Ic astiʒe min scyp..and rowe ofer sælice dælas. *a* **1122** *O.E. Chron.* (Laud MS.) an. 1046, His sciperes..wurpon hine on þone bat..& reowan to scipe. *c* **1205** LAY. 7813 Nu þohte Julius Cezar.. rouwen swa longe, þat he come to Londen. *c* **1290** *S. Eng. Leg.* I. 139 Heo roweden forth al þane dai. *c* **1320** *Sir Tristr.* 1656 So he was þe kniʒtes trewe; Tristrem, so rewe he. **13..** *E.E. Allit P.* C. 216 Þay ruyt hym to rowwe & letten þe rynk one. *c* **1400** *Destr. Troy* 4521 Þus went þay to water,..Sesit vp þere sailes, & in sound Rowet. *c* **1477** CAXTON *Jason* 38 They made redy their oores and rowed by the force of their armes. **1553** EDEN *Treat. New Ind.* (Arb.) 39 They were enforsed to gather vppe theyr sayles, and to rowe only with the maste. **1578** T. N. tr. *Conq. W. India* 38 Having rowen little more then halfe a league, they espied a greate Towne. **1582** STANYHURST *Æneis* III. (Arb.) 76 Oure sayls are strucken, we roa furth with speedines hastye. **1617** MORYSON *Itin.* I. 3 All Passengers without difference of condition must help to rowe. **1700** DRYDEN *Ceyx & Alc.* 92 The sailors ship their oars, and cease to row. **1706** E. WARD *Wooden World Diss.* (1708) 57 They pray as they row, backwards. **1810** CRABBE *Borough* xxii. 325 To row away with all my strength I try'd. **1865** J. THOMSON *Sunday up River* v. i, Boating on our river. I to row and you to steer.

transf. **1655** MARQ. WORC. *Cent. Inv.* §15 The course.. according to which the Oars shall row.

b. *fig.* or in fig. context. (See also 2.)

c **1380** WYCLIF *Wks.* (1880) 411 We shulden be pilgryms heere & rowe wisely in þis boot to heuene. **1393** LANGL. *P. Pl.* C. xi. 52 To repenten and ryse, and rowen out of synne, To contricion. *c* **1586** C'TESS PEMBROKE *Ps.* CVII. xi, To wisshed port with joy they row. **1630** J. TAYLOR (Water-P.) *Cast over Water* Wks. II. 161 To their iournies end all Creatures rowes. **1663** BUTLER *Hud.* I. i. 874 Whatsoe're we perpetrate We do but row, we are steer'd by Fate. **1728** EARL OF AILESBURY *Mem.* (1890) 650 Certain it was that in her Court there were persons that looked one way and rowed another. **1736** AINSWORTH *Eng.-Lat. Dict.*, To row one's own course, or do as one pleaseth.

c. ***to row dry***, to perform merely the action of rowing either in pretence or as an exercise; also, to row without splashing, or (jocularly) without getting wet. Also *fig.*

1833 MARRYAT *P. Simple* xxviii, 'He's rowing *dry*, your honour—only making bilave.' 'Do you call this rowing dry?' cried another, as a sea swept over the boat. **1867** SMYTH *Sailor's Word-bk.* 583 *Row Dry*, the order to those who row, not to splash water into the boat.

d. ***rowed of all!*** (See quot. 1867.)

1836 MARRYAT *Midsh. Easy* ii, 'In bow—rowed of all.' The boat was laid alongside. **1867** SMYTH *Sailor's Word-bk.* 583 *Rowed of all*, the orders for the rowers to cease, and toss their oars into the boat simultaneously, in naval style.

e. With complement denoting the place of the rower in the boat.

1856 STONEHENGE *Brit. Rural Sports* 476/2 A companion who will not mind a few splashes..should be put in to 'row stroke'. **1883** C. READE in *Harper's Mag.* Dec. 131/2 [He] rowed six in the college boat. **1889** J. K. Jerome *Three Men in Boat* vii, I gave it up at last; I said I'd row bow.

f. *to row over*, to go over the course without a competitor, thus winning a race or heat.

1888 Woodgate *Boating* (Badm.) 243 Winners of the Wing-field Sculls: 1834. A. A. Julius rowed over.

2. a. *to row against the flood, stream, wind and tide*, etc. Freq. in fig. use, to undertake a difficult or arduous task; to work in adverse circumstances or in the face of opposition.

a **1250** *Prov. Alfred* 145 in *O.E. Misc.* 110 Strong hit is to reowe ayeyn þe see þat floweþ. **1311** *Pol. Songs* (Camden) 254 Whoso roweth aȝein the flod, Off sorwe he shal drinke. **1390** Gower *Conf.* II. 61 Betre is to wayte upon the tyde Than rowe ayein the stremes stronge. **1470–85** Malory *Arthur* x. xxviii. 458 They must be foughten with alle, or els we rowe ageynst the streme. *c* **1485** *Digby Myst.* iv. 491 Ya, I wyll no more row ageyn the Flode, I wyll sett my soule on a mery pynne. **1677** Horneck *Gt. Law Consideration* v. (1704) 373 He that can row against the stream, may with great facility row with it. **1679** Petty in Ld. E. Fitzmaurice *Life* (1895) 244, I have been travailing in dark dirty crooked ways, and have been rowing against wind and tide. **1822** Scott *Nigel* Introd. Ep., No one shall find me rowing against the stream... I write for general amusement. **1855** Kingsley *Westw. Ho!* iv, I am not going to be fool enough to row against wind and tide too.

†**b.** *to row past one's reach*, to attempt more than one can do. *Obs.*

1557 *Tottel's Misc.* (Arb.) 129, I rowe not so farre past my reache. **1575** Gascoigne *Hearbes, Weedes, etc.* Wks. (1587) 131 Hold wyth the head, and row not past thy reach. *Ibid.* 150 Thus can I.. adventure for to teach The falcon fly, and yet forwarne she row not past her reach.

c. *to row in the same* or *in one boat* (see quots.). Also *to row in*, to conspire. *slang.*

1796 *Grose's Dict. Vulg. T.* (ed. 3), *To row in the same boat*, to be embarked in the same scheme. **1801** Col. Hanger *Life* II. 347 This society (pardon the vulgarity of the expression!) all rowed in one boat, passing bills from one to the other. **1812** J. H. Vaux *Flash Dict.*, *Row in the boat*, to go snacks or have a share in the benefit arising from any transaction to which you are privy. **1867** Smyth *Sailor's Word-bk.* 583 *To Row in the same Boat*, to be of similar principles. **1897** *Daily Tel.* 12 Feb. 5/7 It's very likely the sellers and the general public concerned in auction sales are anything but satisfied with the results of sales by auction where a 'knock-out' is arranged, and especially where the auctioneer 'rows in' with the crew. **1909** J. R. Ware *Passing Eng.* 211/2 *Row in*,.. unfair conspiracy. From Thames life through centuries. A man 'rowed in' in a river robbery, or even a murder. **1934** P. Allingham *Cheapjack* xvi. 202, I think these boys had better row in with us... We may as well stick together. **1970** G. F. Newman *Sir, You Bastard* vii. 194 What if they try to row in? **1977** P. Moyes *To kill Coconut* vii. 99 'Rowing in' is slang for implicating somebody in a crime.

3. a. Of a boat or other vessel: To move along the surface of water by means of oars.

c **1375** *Sc. Leg. Saints* xvii. (*Martha*) 33 As fysche wald he dwel in þe flud, & our-tyrwit batis, þat rowyt þare. **1398** Trevisa *Barth. De P.R.* xiii. xii. (Bodl. MS.), [In the Dead Sea] maye no schip rowe noþer sayle. **1500–20** Dunbar *Poems* lxxxviii. 29 Where many a barge doth saile, and row with are. **1590** Sir J. Smyth *Disc. Weapons* 12 All the long boates.. do rowe with all furie towards the land. **1750** Blanckley *Nav. Expos.* 14 Barge—Rows with twelve Oars. **1793** Smeaton *Edystone L.* §226 We therefore agreed that the light yawl should row the headmost... Each boat rowed with four oars. **1794** Mrs. Radcliffe *Myst. Udolpho* xvi, Montoni's gondola rowed out upon the sea.

b. *to row guard, the rounds*, of a guard-boat: to go the rounds amongst warships in harbour.

1758 *Ann. Reg.* i. 81/1 The boats from every ship in commission.. attended, and rowed guard round the Royal Anne. **1769** Falconer *Dict. Marine, Guard-boat*, a boat appointed to row the rounds amongst the ships of war which are laid up in any harbour. **1799** *Naval Chron.* I. 258 The Terrible's cutter in Rowing Guard got among the breakers.

c. *trans.* To be fitted or rowed with, to carry (so many oars).

1769 Falconer *Dict. Marine* s.v. *Boat*, Pinnaces.. are somewhat smaller, and never row more than eight oars. **1799** Nelson in Nicolas *Disp.* (1845) I. 11 The Spanish barge rowed twenty-six oars, besides Officers, thirty in the whole. **1806** A. Duncan *Life Nelson* 178 In a small boat rowing six oars. **1854** H. Miller *Sch. & Schm.* (1855) 508, I purchased.. a light little yawl.. that rowed four oars.

4. Of waterfowl, fish, etc.: To swim, paddle.

Similarly used of persons in *Beowulf* 512, 539.

1631 Widdowes *Nat. Philos.* 65 Geese, Duckes, Swannes, have whole feete to rowe in the water. **1694** *Acc. Sev. Late Voy.* ii. (1694) 119 When they [i.e. starfish] swim in the Water they hold their Legs together, and so they row along. **1728–46** Thomson *Spring* 777 In the pond The finely-checker'd duck before her train Rows garrulous. **1827** Hood *Mids. Fairies* iv, Others [*sc.* fish] with fresh hues row'd forth to win My changeable regard. **1885–94** R. Bridges *Eros & Psyche* Sept. 6 Down he dived, And rowing with his glistening wings arrived At Aphrodite's bower.

II. 5. a. *trans.* To propel (a boat or other vessel) by means of oars. (See also quot. 1788.)

c **1340** *Nominale* (Skeat) 316 *Homme neef de veroun nage*, [Man] Schippe with ore rowith. **1390** Gower *Conf.* I. 223 The barge Envie stiereth.. Wher Falssemblant with Ore on honde It roweth. **1466** *Mann. & Househ. Exp.* (Roxb.) 211 To the men of the Kervelle for rowenge the bote to Manytre. *a* **1513** Fabyan *Chron.* (1516) ii. 205 Rowe the bote Norman, rowe to thy lemman. **1590** Spenser *F.Q.* ii. vi. 10 In this wide Inland sea,.. my wandring ship I row. **1728** Chambers *Cycl.*, *Oar*,.. an Instrument whereby a Boat, Barge, Galley, &c. is row'd, or advanc'd along the Water. **1788** Franklin *Wks.* (1888) X. 17 A large boat rowed by the force of steam is now exercised upon our river. **1810** Crabbe *Borough* xxii. 167 Alone he row'd his boat; alone he cast His nets beside. **1884** Pae *Eustace* 77 The arrangement was that Willy should row one boat and Eustace the other.

b. To make (a stroke), to use (an oar), in the course or exercise of rowing.

1866 Woodgate *Rowing & Training* 55 He must impress upon all his crew the necessity of not rowing a single stroke carelessly. *Ibid.* 58 In these.. two men row a pair of oars.

c. With *race, heat*, etc., as complement.

1888 Woodgate *Boating* (Badm.) 252 This [1846] was the first race rowed in keelless boats. *Ibid.*, This [1877] is the only dead heat ever rowed in this race.

6. To convey (persons) on the water in a boat propelled by oars. Also *refl.*

1375 Barbour *Bruce* iii. 425 Þe thrid wes ane þat rowyt þaim our deliuerly, and set þaim on þe land. **1470–85** Malory *Arthur* i. xxv. 73 Go ye into yonder barge, and rowe your self to the swerd. *a* **1513** Fabyan *Chron.* (1516) ii. 205 This Mayer.. was rowed thyther by water. **1812** Byron *Ch. Har.* i. lxx, Some o'er thy Thamis row the ribbon'd fair. **1832** G. Downes *Lett. Cont. Countries* I. 392, I had to be rowed out a little from the shore. **1839** Fr. A. Kemble *Resid. in Georgia* (1863) 62 We rowed the doctor over to see some of his patients.

7. *transf.* To convey, transport, propel, move, in a manner or with a movement similar to rowing. Also, to take as payment for rowing (see quot. 1607).

1607 Dekker *Knights Conjuring* Fj, At Westminster-bridge.. ready to be torne in peeces to haue two pence rowed out of your purse. **1667** Milton *P.L.* vii. 439 The Swan.. Rowes Her state with Oarie feet. **1707** Mortimer *Husb.* (1721) I. 24 'Tis a vast quantity of Water that their turning will row along upon a flat. **1713** Derham *Phys. Theol.* vii. i. §5 [The legs] somewhat out of the Center of Gravity.. for the better rowing their Bodies through waters. **1787** T. Best *Art of Angling* 1 The tail an instrument of progressive motion which serves to row them forward. **1884** *Mil. Engin.* I. ii. 78 With the lever it is *rowed* to the right or left as may be required.

8. *U.S. slang.* **a.** *to row* (one) *up Salt River*, see salt river 2 b.

b. *to row* (one) *up*, to treat (one) to a severe verbal castigation.

1845 in Bartlett *Dict. Amer.* (1848) 279 We should really like, of all things, to row up the majority of Congress as it deserves in regard to the practice. **1850** Lowell in Scudder *Life* I. 303, I am tired of controversy, and, though I have cut out the oars with which to row up my friend Bowen, yet I have enough to do.

9. a. To make (one's way) by, or as by, rowing.

1821 Scott *Kenilw.* xxv, Joan.., with robust pace, and red sturdy arms, rowed her way onward, amongst those prim and pretty moppets.

b. To have, make use of, in a rowing-match.

1888 Woodgate *Boating* (Badm.) 245 The winners only rowed seven oars in the final heat. **1900** Sherwood *Oxford Rowing* 160 Corpus.. rowed an untrained man.

c. To row against (another person or crew).

1888 Woodgate *Boating* 237 Beach.. rowed Wallace Ross for the championship.

d. *to row down*, to overtake by rowing.

1869 in Sherwood *Oxford Rowing* 156 What is allowed to be the strongest crew upon the river.. has been rowed down every day.

e. *to row out*, to exhaust by rowing.

1928 *Daily Express* 7 Aug. 12/6 Both pairs finished in a distressed condition, Boardman being completely rowed-out.

row (rəʊ), *v.*[2] *Obs.* exc. *dial.* Also 4–5 rowe. [Related to, or formed on, row *sb.*[1]]

†**1.** *intr.* ? To run in a straight line. *Obs.*

c **1300** *Maximon* in *Rel. Ant.* I. 120 Hunten herd y blowe, Hertes gonne rowe, Stunte me no ston.

†**2.** To send out rays; to shine; to dawn. *Obs.*

c **1320** *Pol. Songs* (Camden) 239 The rybaudz a-ryseth Er þe day rewe. **1377** Langl. *P. Pl.* B. xviii. 123 Eyther axed other.. Of the dyne and of the derknesse, and how þe daye rowed. **1390** Gower *Conf.* I. 315 Whan the dai began to rowe, Tho mihten thei the sothe knowe.

fig. *c* **1374** Chaucer *Compl. Mars* 2 Loo Venus rysen amonge yow rowes rede And floures fressh honouren thee this day.

3. *trans.* To arrange, put or place in a line or row. Now *dial.* Also in pa. pple., set *with* something in a row or rows.

For other purely dialect senses, see the *Eng. Dial. Dict.*

1657 Thornley *Daphnis & Chloe* 197 His mouth rowed with Elephant-pearl. **1703** R. Neve *City & Country Purch.* 42 They Row them up, like a Wall.., with some small Intervals betwixt them. *a* **1717** Parnell *Poet. Wks.* (1833) 59 Bid her wear thy necklace rowed with pearl. **1824–** in *Eng. Dial. Dict.*

b. *intr.* To come up in rows; to form in a row or rows.

c **1830–** in *Eng. Dial. Dict.*

row (raʊ), *v.*[3] *slang* or *colloq.* [f. row *sb.*[2]]

1. a. *trans.* To attack or assail (a person) in a rough manner; to rag (a man or his rooms). ?*Obs.*

1789 *Loiterer* 14 Nov. 10 We.. looked into every coach, *rowed* the waggons, examined both the boxes, the roofs, and the baskets. **1790** *Loiterer* No. 55. 11 'Let's row him, Racket,' exclaimed a third; upon which they unanimously turned their horses against me. **1803** *Gradus ad Cantab.* s.v., To row a room; to break the furniture. **1825** Westmacott *Eng. Spy* I. 158 Rowing a fellow—going with a party in the dead of night to a man's room, nailing or screwing his oak up [etc.]. **1863** E. Hitchcock *Rem. Amherst Coll.* 335 The smart stories told by collegians about 'rowing Freshmen'.

b. To rouse *up* by making a noise.

1789 *Loiterer* 21 Feb. 11 Racket *rowed* me up at seven o'clock—sleepy and queer but forced to get up to make breakfast for him.

2. a. To rate or scold (a person) angrily or severely; to take sharply to task. Also const. *out, out of.*

a **1809** J. Palmer *Like Master* (1811) I. xv. 212 Helen will row you well.. if you are not as good as your word. **1856** Miss Yonge *Daisy Chain* i. xix, I suppose you think I have no right to row you, but I do it to save you from worse. **1863** Gladstone in Morley *Life* (1905) I. 738 She rowed me for writing to Lord Palmerston about her accident. **1908** *Smart Set* June 143/1 Most fathers would have rowed me out of the house. **1976** *New Mus. Express* 31 July 6/4 But you get these weird, insecure feelings that they might be trying to row you out, which wasn't the case. No one was talking about sacking me.

absol. **1843** Sir J. Paget *Mem. & Lett.* vi. 150, I have succeeded I trust in reproof—rowing in good earnest, till a culprit even wept.

b. To criticize sharply or severely.

1826 Froude *Rem.* (1838) I. 197, I.. will try my best to set to rights the places you row.

3. *intr.* To make a row or disturbance; †to engage in a rag. Now usu. in the more limited sense 'to have a row, to quarrel noisily or heatedly'.

1797 Louisa Gurney in A. J. C. Hare *Gurneys of Earlham* (1895) I. 66 After scolding, rowing, bickering,.. we all agreed to go. **1851** B. H. Hall *College Words* s.v., Flushed with the juice of the grape, all prime and ready for rowing. **1868** *Daily Telegr.* 31 July 5/6 The noisy, ill-bred herd of greedy Germans that stormed, rowed,.. and upset benches. **1882** Bret Harte *Flip* iv, You forget how you used to row .. because tramps.. came to the ranch. **1890** T. A. Janvier *Aztec Treasure-House* xvi. 195 Some of these Indians are friendly, and we don't want to start a row with them if they are willing not to row with us. **1914** S. Lewis *Our Mr. Wrenn* xvii. 227 Why, Mouse! I thought you'd be glad to see me. I've never rowed with you, have I? **1970** G. F. Newman *Sir, You Bastard* viii. 209 He couldn't remember rowing. Rows were usually loud demonstrative things. **1978** R. Rendell *Sleeping Life* viii. 73 We row, of course we do, that's healthy in a marriage, but we love each other.

†**row**, *v.*[4] *Obs.*[−1] (Meaning doubtful.)

Phonetically it might belong to row *v.*[1], but the context rather suggests connexion with row *a.*[1]

c **1330** R. Brunne *Chron. Wace* (Rolls) 10338 Þenne bygynnes þe lough to flowe, & ouer þe bankes to renne & rowe.

†**row**, *v.*[5] *Obs.*[−1] [Related to row *sb.*[4] Cf. ro *v.*] *intr.* To rest.

c **1400** *Beryn* 284 Madam! wol ye stalk Pryuely in-to þe garden, to se the herbis growe? And aftir, with our hostis wyff, in hir parlour rowe.

row, *v.*[6] Now *dial.* [Of obscure etym.]

†**1.** *trans.* To thrust the fingers, to poke (*in* something). *Obs.*

? **14–** *Stasyons of Jerus.* 561 in Horstm. *Altengl. Leg.* (1881) 363 [Jesus] bad hym pute his hond in his ryȝht syde; When Thomas had rowyd in his wonde, He wepe full sore. **1600** Cawdray *Treas. Similies* 517 Hee that roweth in an eye for the getting out of a moate, when a beame is sticking, there is small hope that he shall cleare that eye.

b. *dial.* 'To make a vigorous investigation' *into* something.

1877 in *Holderness Gloss.*

2. To stir, to mix by stirring; to poke or rake about. Freq. with *up*.

1641 S. Smith *Herring Buss Trade* 10 One Boy doth row and stirre them up and downe in the salt. **1704** *Dict. Rust.* (1726) s.v. *Brewing*, Afterwards it [liquor] is to be put into the Mashing-Tub to wet the Malt, as stiff as you can well row it up. *Ibid.*, The same rowed as before. **1765** *Compl. Maltster & Brewer* 7 When the first mash is quite done rowing up. **1788** W. H. Marshall *Prov. Yorksh.*, *To row*, to rake or stir about, as ashes in an oven. **1877** *Holderness Gloss.*, *Row-up*, to stir up a sediment until it becomes equally diffused.

row (rəʊ), *v.*[7] Now *dial.* Also 6–7 rowe; *pa. pple.* 5 rowen. [f. row *a.*[1]] *trans.* To raise a nap on (cloth). Cf. nap *v.*[2] 2.

In quot. 1604 confused with the shearing process.

1487 *Rolls of Parlt.* VI. 403/1 An Act that no Stranger or Denizen shall carry any Woollen Clothes out of this Realme, before they be Barbed, Rowed and Shorne. **1511–2** *Act 3 Hen. VIII*, c. 6 §1 The Walker.. shall not rowe nor werke any Clothe or Webbe with any Cardes. **1543** *Act 1 Rich. III*, c. 8 §13 (Publ. Gen. Acts), Teyntours whiche hereafter shalbe vsed.. for due stretchyng of cloth onely, after that it commeth fro the myll, and before it be rowen. **1557** in Hakluyt *Voy.* (1599) I. 298 Whether our set clothes.. be rowed and shorne; because ofttimes they goe vndrest. **1604** *Maldon Borough Deeds* (Bundle 126, No. 1), Ad eskurand. et tondend. (*Anglicè*, to thick and to rowe) apud molendinum suum. **1624** in Strype *Stow's Surv.* (1720) I. 130 My twelve Cloth-workers, that usually row and sheere my Clothes. **1886** Elworthy *W. Somerset Wd.-bk.*, *Row*, to roughen cloth, *i.e.* to comb or teaze out a nap on it, as on a blanket.

row, *v.*[8] *Sc. rare.* [App. a var. of rove *v.*[3] Cf. row *sb.*[7]] *trans.* To make (wool) into roves.

17.. *Tarry Woo* in Herd *Scots Songs* (1776) II. 100 When 'tis carded, row'd, and spun Then the work is haflens done.

row, Sc. var. roll *sb.*[1] and *v.*; obs. f. roll *v.*, rue *v.*

rowable ('rəʊəb(ə)l), *a. rare.* [f. row *v.*[1]] Capable of being rowed, or rowed upon.

1570 Levins *Manip.* 3 Rowable, *remigabilis.* *a* **1637** B. Jonson *Horace, Art Poet.* 94 That long narrow fen Once rowable, but now doth nourish men. **1886** *Camb. Univ. Mag.* Nov. 108 The only piece of rowable water on the Cam.

rowage (ˈrəʊɪdʒ). [f. ROW *v.*[1] + -AGE.]

†**1.** Rowing dues or charges. *Obs.*$^{-1}$

c **1680** DALLAS *Stiles* (1697) 414 Merchant of the said Towage, Rowage, Anchorage,..and other dues.

2. Provision or equipment for rowing. *rare*$^{-1}$.

1859 LEWIN *Invas. Brit. by Cæsar* 76 The vessels could lie in shallow water.., and the rowage would make them independent of wind and tide.

rowal, obs. form of ROWEL *sb.*

rowan[1] (ˈrəʊən, *Sc.* ˈraʊən). *north.* and *Sc.* Also roan, rown, etc. (see ROWAN-TREE). [Of Scand. origin, corresponding either to Norw. *rogn* (cf. ROWN), or more probably to *raun* (*roun, raon*, Sw. *rön*, Da. *røn*), of which Icel. *reynir*, MSw. *röne*, MDa. *røne*, are derivative forms.]

1. The mountain ash; = ROWAN-TREE I.

1804 J. GRAHAME *Sabbath* 443 The sloe, or rowan's bitter bunch. **1810** SCOTT *Lady of L.* III. iv, A heap of wither'd boughs was piled, Of juniper and rowan wild. **1861** D. H. HAIGH *Conq. Brit. by Saxons* 78 *note*, The tree of which he speaks is probably the mountain-ash, rown or witch. **1887** R. BUCHANAN *Heir of Linne* iii, The rowan or mountain-ash shook its scarlet berries and dipped its tasselled hair.

2. The berry of the mountain ash. Also *attrib.*

1880 H. TODD *Poet. Wks.* (1907) 213 Still shine the rowans red. **1897** SARAH GRAND *Beth Bk.* xxix, Hips and haws and rowans also rioted in red. **1899** *Daily News* 4 Nov. 7/6 Rowan jelly with game.

3. *rowan-berry*, = prec.

1814 SCOTT *Diary* 23 Aug. in Lockhart (1836) III. vii. 227 A pennon of silk, with something like round red rowan-berries wrought upon it. **1845** *New Stat. Acc. Scot.* XIV. 191 The native fruits found in the parish are brambles,.. roanberries and hazelnuts. **1891** BARRIE *Little Minister* (1890) 6 Rowan berries in your black hair.

rowan[2] (ˈraʊən). *Sc.* [For *rowin'*, ROWING *vbl. sb.*[6]] A roving (of wool or cotton).

c **1816** *Edin. Encycl.* VII. 286 Children are employed to lift the rolls or rowans from the carding engine. **1825** J. NICHOLSON *Operat. Mechanic* 391 The rows or rowans are taken to a roving-billy. **1890** *Scott. N. & Q.* Aug. 53 The 'piecers' attended to the Billy and 'pieced' or mended the 'rowans' or rovings as they were drawn in by the slubber.

†**Rowan**[3]. *Sc. Obs.* In 5–6 Rowane (-nis). App. the place-name *Rouen* (cf. ROAN *sb.*[3]), used *attrib.* to designate various kinds of cloth.

1488 *Acc. Ld. High Treas. Scot.* I. 153 For ij elne j quartar of Rowane gray for a gowne to the Duke. **1494** *Ibid.* 231 To Robert Lundye and the ȝong Lard of Ardross, vij ellis of Rowane tanne. **1500** HALYBURTON *Ledger* (1867) 260, 5 ell of Rowanis clath to be hym a gon. **1502** in Pitcairn *Crim. Trials* I. *29 Unius toge de Rowane-tanne.

rowan, variant of ROWEN.

rowan-tree. *north.* and *Sc.* Forms: α. 6–9 **roun-**; 6, 8 **rown-**; 8 **rowen-**; 8– **rowan-**. β. 7– **roan-**, 8 **roane-**, 9 **royn(e-**. γ. 7, 9 **rauntree**; 9 **rauntry**; 8–9 **rantree**, **rantry**; 9 **ranter**, **rantle**. [See ROWAN[1].]

1. The mountain ash, *Pyrus Aucuparia*.

α. **1548** TURNER *Names Herbes* (E.D.S.) 75 The seconde kynde [of sorbus] is called..in Englishe a rountree or a Quicken tree. **1597** JAS. I *Dæmonol.* I. iv. 12 Such kinde of Charmes as commonlie daft wiues vses, for healing of forspoken goodes,..by knitting roun-trees..to the haire or tailes of the goodes. **1615** W. LAWSON *Orch. & Gard.* (1623) 13 Ashes, Rountrees, Burt-trees, and such like. **1788** PICKEN *Poems* 59 *note*, Alluding to the vulgar opinion of rountree being efficacious against all sorts of charms. **1828** SCOTT *F.M. Perth* xxvii, Amid extensive forests of oak-wood, hazel, rowan-tree, and larches. **1842** *Proc. Berw. Nat. Club* II. x. 7 The rowan-tree assumed a taller habit. **1895** CROCKETT *Love Idylls* (1901) 172 The rowan tree which used to grow from a cleft to the right.

β. **1671** SKINNER *Etymol. Bot.*, Roan-tree, *Sorbus sylvestris Alpina*. **1762** BP. FORBES *Jrnl.* (1886) 164 You can see Ash, Oak, Birch, Roan-tree. **1791** W. GILPIN *Forest Scenery* I. 37 The mountain-ash, often called the roan tree, should be mentioned. **1814** HUDDLESTON *Toland's Hist. Druids* 283 Roan tree and red thread, Put the witches to their speed. **1828** CARR *Craven Gloss.* s.v., Pointing, it may be supposed, at the royn-tree in her hand. **1859** W. S. COLEMAN *Woodlands* (1866) 57 From very early times, the Roan Tree enjoyed a wide reputation..for the inherent magical powers attributed to it.

γ. *a* **1694** SIR A. BALFOUR *Lett.* (1700) 31 A kind of Fruit tree called Cormes, not much unlike our Raun-tree. **1801** HOGG *Scot. Pastorals* 26 Mark yon rauntree spreading wide. **1811** WILLAN *Yorks. W. Riding*, Rantry. **1822** W. IRVING *Braceb. Hall* II. 165 A branch of rauntry or mountain-ash. **1853** JAMIE *Emigrants Family* 40 (E.D.D.), Though they had used the rantree's branch.

2. *attrib.* with *berry*, *branch*, *cross*, etc.

α. **1722** NISBET *Heraldry* 372 Three Rowentree Branches sliped proper. *c* **1770** *Laidley Worm* in Evans *Old Ball.* (1784) III. 175 Crying, that witches have no power Where there is rown-tree wood. **1820** SCOTT *Abbot* xxvii, A rowan-tree switch for a whip. **1821** —— *Kenilw.* i, The Eldorado, where..country-wenches thread rubies for necklaces, instead of rowan-tree berries. **1832** CARLYLE in *Froude* (1882) II. 278 The 'rowan-tree gate' and all gates but the outer one are removed.

β. **1825** MISS KENT *Sylvan Sk.* 251 A roan-tree cross, which he bears in the left hand.

γ. **1768** ROSS *Helenore* I. 6 The jizzen-bed wi' rantree leaves was sain'd. **1768** —— *Rock & Wee Pickle Tow*, I'll gar my ain Tammie..cut me a rock..Of good rantry-tree for to carry my tow. **1884** D. GRANT *Lays & Leg. North* 103 A rantree stick Was quickly cut fae coppice thick.

rowar, variant of ROLLER, ROWER.

rowball. ? *Obs.* [ad. Pg. (also Sp.) *robalo*, the name of a fish resembling a bream, also applied to several American fishes.] (See quots.)

1803 P. RUSSELL *Indian Fishes* II. 68 Both fishes, especially the first, are esteemed for the table, and are known to the English under the name of Rowball. **1804** SHAW *Gen. Zool.* V. I. 155 Indian Polyneme, *Polynemus Indicus*... Rowball. *Ibid.* 156 Four-Fingered Polyneme, *Polynemus Tetradactylus*;..like the former, called Rowball by the English.

row-barge. Now only *Hist.* [f. ROW *v.*[1]] A barge propelled by oars or sweeps.

c **1513** in Ellis *Orig. Lett.* Ser. III. I. 155 The one was Coke the Qwenys servant in a row barge. *a* **1548** HALL *Chron.*, *Hen. VIII*, 23 The said Admirall put hymself in a small rowe barge, with three other small rowyng shippes and his awne ship boate. **1653** H. COGAN tr. *Pinto's Trav.* xxiii. 83 After these vessels followed a number of row-barges. *a* **1656** USSHER *Ann.* (1658) 288 The rest were of the nature of Row-barges. **1716** *Lond. Gaz.* No. 5464 Going in the Chertsey Row-barge from London. **1737** *Gentl. Mag.* VII. 370/1 No Tilt-Boat or Row-Barge to take at one Time more than 37 Passengers. **1761** HUME *Hist. Eng.* xxvii. II. 128 He was followed by some row-barges and some crayers. **1860** MOTLEY *Netherl.* I. v. 165 Teligny ventured forth in a row-barge.

row-boat (ˈrəʊbəʊt). [f. ROW *v.*[1] Cf. Du. *roeiboot* (Fris. *-boat*).] A boat propelled by oars; a rowing-boat.

1538 *Acc. Ld. High Treas. Scot.* VI. 421 Item, to Johne Bertane for grathing of the Kingis row boit in tymmer werkmanschip. **1648** HEXHAM II, *Een Roey-schip, ofte schuyte*, a Rowe-boate. **1697** *Lond. Gaz.* No. 3315/1, I lay there 3 days after, but could see nothing, except a Row-boat. **1728** MORGAN *Algiers* II. i. 218 Well-known and often frequented creeks serve now to conceal their Brigantines and Row Boats. **1753** HANWAY *Trav.* (1762) I. II. xvi. 70 These robbers..go..in row-boats which carry from twenty to thirty hands. **1801** COL. HANGER *Life* II. 394, I pressed a strong row-boat, with two men. **1867** CARLYLE *E. Irving* 107 Our vessel was a rowboat belonging to some neighbours. **1893** 'Q.' *Delect. Duchy* 13 A fishing-boat with a small row-boat in tow.

rowbour, variant of RUBBOUR *Obs.*

†**row-bowls.** *Sc. Obs.* [f. *row* ROLL *v.*[2]] The game of bowls.

1501 *Acc. Ld. High Treas. Scot.* II. 112 Giffin to the King himself that he playit at the row bowlis,..lvjs. **1505** *Ibid.* III. 134. **1507** *Ibid.* 392.

row-cast, dial. variant of ROUGH-CAST.

a **1517** *Merton Coll. Doc.* (MS.), Shall Rovcaste and pargett all the Stone walls. **1746** *Exmoor Scolding* (E.D.S.) 46 More an zo, thee wut rowcast, nif et be thy own Vauther. **1778** —— *Gloss.*, *To Row-cast* (i.e. to rough-cast), to throw Dirt that will stick. **1881**- in dial. glossaries (Glouc., Som., Devon, Isle of Wight).

rowch, obs. f. ROUGH *a.*

rowche, var. of ROCHE *sb.*[1] 3.

rowchnes, obs. Sc. form of ROUGHNESS.

rowde, obs. f. RUDD[1].

row-de-dow (raʊdɪˈdaʊ). [Echoic: cf. ROW *sb.*[2] and ROW-DOW-DOW.] Noise or din, uproar, disturbance. Also *attrib.*

1790 R. TYLER *Contrast* III. i. 42 There was a soldier fellow, who talked about his row de dow, dow, and courted a young woman. **1832** *Deb. Congress U.S.* 13 Mar. (1833) 2128 The rub-a-dub and row-de-dow excitement. **1848** LOWELL *Biglow P.* Ser. I. Poems 1890 II. 102 Let 'lone the rowdedow it saves To hev a wal-broke precedunt. **1885** *Referee* 8 Mar. 5/1 With regard to the Prince and Princess's visit to Ireland, the 'row-de-dow'—that is, we believe, the Hibernian term for it—which took place [etc.]. **1887** *Scottish Leader* 19 Oct. 4 He seems to have braced himself for a superior effort in his favourite row-de-dow line.

So **row-de-'dowing** *vbl. sb.*

1832 LADY GRANVILLE *Lett.* (1894) II. 130, I think there will be a great row-de-dowing amongst them all.

rowdge, obs. form of ROUGE *a.*

rowdiness (ˈraʊdɪnɪs). [f. ROWDY *a.* + -NESS.] The quality of being rowdy; disorderliness.

1862 TROLLOPE *N. Amer.* I. 309 They have learned to dislike the rowdiness of their country's politics. **1895** BESANT *Westminster* ix. 229 For downright bludgeon rowdiness and riot, the rabble at Westminster..was equalled by few towns.

row-dow-dow (ˈraʊdaʊdaʊ). [Echoic.] An imitation of the sound produced by beating a drum.

1814 SCOTT *Wav.* xxxiv, As this was beyond the capacity of the drubber of sheep-skin, he was fain to have recourse to the inoffensive row-dow-dow. **1863** *Life in Normandy* I. 25 The band ceased to play, and the drums struck up a rōw-dōw, rōw-dōw-dōw, all striking at the same moment.

rowdy (ˈraʊdɪ), *sb.*[1] and *a.* Also 9 **rowdey**. [Of American, but otherwise quite obscure, origin.]

A. *sb.*[1] Originally, a backwoodsman of a rough and lawless type; hence, a rough, disorderly person; one addicted to quarrelling, fighting, or disturbing the peace:

a. In American use, or with ref. to America.

1808 W. LITTELL *Festoons of Fancy* (1814) 62 But it seems to this court that the loss to him would be the same, as if he had lost it among those, whom his gentlemanship is pleased to call *rowdies*. **1819** W. FAUX *Mem. Days Amer.* (1823) 179 No legal inquiry took place, nor, indeed, ever takes place amongst the Rowdies, as the Back-woodsmen are called. *Ibid.* 277 The hunters, or Illinois Rowdies, as they are called, are rather troublesome. They come rudely with their hats on into the parlour, and, when drunk, threaten Mr. Flower's life. **1824** H. C. KNIGHT *Lett. fr. South* 93 The riotous roisters, or, as they are here [Kentucky] called, rowdies, will fight..from mere love of fighting. **1864** NICHOLS *40 Years Amer. Life* II. 89 A mob of Boston rowdies went over to Charlestown and plundered and burnt the Ursuline Convent of Mount Benedict. **1871** in De Vere *Americanisms* s.v., Roughs and rowdies are multiplying fearfully in our borders.

b. In general use.

1865 *Sat. Rev.* 15 July 74/2 The organization of the rowdies was perfect, all Conservative rowdies being massed on one side of the hustings, and all Liberal rowdies on the other. **1887** *Westm. Rev.* June 280 When he assures us that these Belfast rowdies are the most intelligent of the Irish people, we take leave to exercise our own judgment a little. **1905** J. B. FIRTH *Highw. & B. Derbyshire* 390 A horde of callous rowdies.

B. *adj.* **1. a.** Belonging to the class, having the manners or conduct, of rowdies; of a rough and disorderly type.

1819 W. FAUX *Mem. Days Amer.* (1823) 316 When the English first came to Evansville settlement, these Rowdey labourers had nearly scared them out. *Ibid.* 332 He could not find a man to serve the warrant,..and means to impanel a Rowdey jury, and try the matter before himself. **1844** MRS. HOUSTON *Voy. Texas* II. 106 The rowdy fellow (*anglice* scamp) is held in check by the consciousness, that should he offend.., tarring and feathering would be his portion. **1863** HAWTHORNE *Our Old Home* I. 38 Transforming him..from the most decorous of metropolitan clergymen into the rowdiest and dirtiest of disbanded officers. **1883** LORD R. GOWER *Reminis.* II. 53 A town of steep streets crowded with a rowdy mob.

b. *transf.* Of animals: Refractory; inclined to give trouble.

1872 C. H. EDEN *My Wife & I in Queensland* iii. 69 Branding or securing a troublesome or, colonially, a 'rowdy' bullock. **1895** A. B. PATERSON *Man fr. Snowy River* (1896) 125, I can ride a rowdy colt.

2. Characteristic of rowdies; *esp.* marked by disorderly roughness or noise.

1852 BRISTED *Upper Ten Thousand* 33 My red wheels are rather rowdy, I must own; not exactly the thing for a gentleman. *Ibid.* 239 Low, shabby, dirty men...alike in their slang and rowdy aspect. **1863** E. DICEY *Federal St.* 251 A regular noisy, rowdy, glorious, Fourth of July. **1882** MISS BRADDON *Mt. Royal* vi, I think I should go to-night to the most rowdy theatre in London.

'rowdy, *sb.*[2] *slang.* ? *Obs.* [Of obscure origin.] Cash, coin.

1841 LEMAN REDE *Sixteen String Jack* I. iv, *Kit.* He's got the rowdy, hey? *Theo.* Rowdy! What's rowdy, I wonder? **1850** THACKERAY *Pendennis* lxxvi, But he has got *the rowdy*, which is the thing. **1856** *Punch* 23 Aug. 79 The Queen of Oude May spend her Rowd-y, careless and *sans souci*.

rowdy (ˈraʊdɪ), *v.* [f. ROWDY *sb.*[1]] **a.** *intr.* To play the rowdy; to act in a noisy, disorderly manner.

1896 A. MORRISON *Child Jago* 282 You came in drunk, and rowdied about the church with your hat on.

b. *trans.* To treat in a rowdy manner.

1825 J. K. PAULDING *John Bull in Amer.* xii. 209 Notwithstanding..their being regulated and rowdied, and obliged to cut down trees as big round as a hogshead.

rowdy-'dow, *sb.* [Cf. ROW-DE-DOW.] Boisterous noise; uproar. Also *attrib.* passing into *adj.* and quasi-*adv.* So **rowdy-dowy** *a.*

1852 J. LABERN *Popular Comic Song Bk.* 75 While Spifflicating Charlie Coker and Jane of the Hatchet-face divine, Just did the Rowdydowy Poker. **1935** W. STEVENS in *Poetry* XLV. 245 The heavy bells are tolling rowdy-dow. **1946** *Time* 22 July 40 This rowdy-dow roundup is the wild-cow milking contest. **1950** *N.Y. Times* 9 July II. 1/1 To restore the old rowdy-dow of burlesque, Mr. Mike Todd and Mr. Clark have gathered a handful of authentic drolls.

rowdy-dow, *v.* [f. prec.] *intr.* To be noisy or boisterous.

1966 T. PYNCHON *Crying of Lot 49* v. 110 She collided with a gang of guided tourists come rowdy-dowing out of a Volkswagen bus.

'rowdy-'dowdy, *a.* *slang.* [Cf. ROW-DE-DOW.] Characterized by noisy roughness.

1854 M. S. CUMMINS *Lamplighter* 260 To offer herself as a champion for that rowdy-dowdy child. **1882** in OGILVIE. **1898** J. K. JEROME *Sec. Thoughts* 293 In Rook-land the rowdy-dowdy, randy-dandy, rollicky-ranky boys get up very early. **1901** *Daily News* 10 Jan. 9/3 They commenced a music hall song—'A Little Bit Off the Top', and other rowdy dowdy songs. **1928** [see NIGHTMAN 2].

rowdying (ˈraʊdɪɪŋ), *vbl. sb.* [f. ROWDY *v.* + -ING[1].] Causing a disturbance.

1839 *Picayune* (New Orleans) 26 Feb. 2/4 There *is* more quiet and less rowdying..here than in Boston, with all its anti-drinking, anti-bellringing and other anti-noise making laws. **1887** *Courier-Jrnl.* (Louisville, Kentucky) 18 Feb. 1/3 There was a good deal of noise and 'rowdying'. **1913** D. H. LAWRENCE *Sons & Lovers* xiii. 430 'We've heard that song before,' snapped the old man. 'Now you get off, and don't be long about it. Comin' *here* with your rowdying.'

rowdyish (ˈraʊdɪɪʃ), *a.* [f. ROWDY *a.* + -ISH.] Somewhat rowdy.

1850 HAWTHORNE *Amer. Note-Bks.* (1883) 389 A brandy-burnt and rowdyish sort of personage. **1874** W. R. GREG *Rocks Ahead* 201 The administration has fallen into the hands of men too rowdyish, too infamous, or too incapable to be endured.

rowdyism (ˈraʊdɪɪz(ə)m). [f. ROWDY *sb.*¹ + -ISM.] Conduct characteristic of rowdies.
1842 S. LONGFELLOW *Let.* 8 Feb. in *Lett. Charles Dickens* (1974) III. 40/1 [Charles Dickens was] very animated and talkative,.. with.. the slightest tincture of rowdyism in his appearance. **1857** B. TAYLOR *N. Trav.* xx. 205 The purposed rowdyism of the man's style shows a little too plainly. **1874** BURNAND *My Time* xxxi. 310 Door-knocker wrenching, street-fighting, and suchlike rowdyism. **1893** LELAND *Mem.* I. 302 The degrading influences of this rowdyism. **1936** I. L. IDRIESS *Cattle King* xx. 189 Perhaps the hostility and rowdyism that the Salvation Army had to suffer.. aroused his sympathy. **1955** *Times* 20 Aug. 6/1 The seriousness with which the commission regards the situation.. from the relatively minor demonstration in Saarbrücken last Saturday night to the rowdyism in Neunkirchen on Wednesday night. **1976** *Southern Even. Echo* (Southampton) 15 Nov. 2/8 The problems presented by late night rowdyism.

rowdyon (*Promp. Parv.* 437): see RODION.

rowe, variant of RO (*obs.*); dial. and Sc. var. ROLL *v.*; obs. f. ROW *sb.*, *a.*, and *v.*; obs. f. RUFF (the fish); var. WRO (*obs.*).

rowed (rəʊd), *a.* [f. ROW *sb.*¹]
1. Having stripes of a specified colour.
15.. in *Percy's Folio MS., Ball. & Rom.* I. 391 The red blood in her face did rise; it was red rowed for to see. **1552** *Invent. Ch. Goods* (Surtees) 41 One suyt of vestmentes of whyt rowyd sarsnet.
2. Having (a specified number of) rows.
1762 MILLS *Syst. Pract. Husb.* I. 419 Both the four rowed and the six rowed barley are generally sown in the autumn. **1844** H. STEPHENS *Bk. Farm* II. 360 The natural classification of barley by the ear is obviously..4-rowed, 6-rowed, and 2-rowed. **1866** *Chambers's Encycl.* VIII. 393/2 *Rye-grass*.., a two-rowed, flatly-compressed spike.

rowed, *ppl. a. rare*⁻¹. [f. ROW *v.*⁶] Of herrings: Stirred up and down (in salt).
1641 S. SMITH *Herring Buss Trade* 10 One boy takes the rowed Herring, and carries them in Baskets to the Packers.

rowed, variant of ROWET *dial.*

roweite (ˈrəʊaɪt). *Min.* [f. the name of George *Rowe*, 20th-cent. U.S. mine official and mineralogist + -ITE¹.] A basic borate of calcium and manganese, usu. also containing magnesium and zinc, first found as light brown elongated orthorhombic crystals in zinc ore at Franklin, New Jersey; $(Mn,Mg,Zn)_2Ca_2B_4O_7(OH)_6$.
1937 BERMAN & GONYER in *Amer. Mineralogist* XXII. 301 The crystals of roweite are light brown in color, lath shaped and without measurable terminations. **1975** *Soviet Physics: Doklady* XX. 244/1 The isostructural nature of the (Mn,Mg) and Mn roweites and the $[B_4O_5(OH)_4]$ tetraradical.. met in sodium borate.

rowel (ˈraʊəl), *sb.* Forms: 5 roile; 5 rewel-, 6 ruel; 5 rowelle, 5–8 rowell, 6 rowyll, 6–7 rowal, 5– rowel; 6 rowle, 7 roule. [ad. OF. *roel*, *rouel* masc., or *roele*, *rouele*, *ruele* (etc.) fem., dim. of *roe*, *roue* (see ROW *sb.*⁶):—L. *rota* wheel. Cf. med.L. *rotella*.]
I. 1. a. A small stellar wheel or disk with sharp radial points and capable of rotation, forming the extremity of a spur.
c **1400** *Destr. Troy* 1258 He Richet his Reynes and his roile stroke. *c* **1430** *Pilgr. Lyf Manhode* II. xcviii. (1869) 111 A peyre spores she hadde on, with longe rewelles wel arayed. **1483** *Cath. Angl.* 312/2 A Rowelle of a spore, *perpetra, stimulus*. **1512** *Act 4 Hen. VIII*, c. 19 §14 Lyke dyverse Rowles of Spurres betwyxte the barres of the Crosse. **1562** TURNER *Herbal* II. (1568) 43 Lupine hath.. a lefe with v. or seuen iaggers, which.. haue the lykenes of a ruel of a spor. **1616** BRETON *Good & Bad* xv, When to maintaine valor his spurres haue no rowels nor his sword a point. **1688** HOLME *Armoury* III. 304/1 A Scotch Spur.. is an old way of making Spurs, Rowels not then being in fashion. **1784** COWPER *Task* VI. 527 With sounding whip, and rowels dyed in blood. **1808** SCOTT *Marm.* VI. xiv, Lord Marmion turn'd,.. And dash'd the rowels in his steed. **1833** J. HOLLAND *Manuf. Metal* II. 310 The rowel occurs for the first time in a sketch belonging to the latter end of the thirteenth century. **1877** BLACK *Green Past.* xiii, The rowels of his spurs were an inch and a half in diameter.
fig. **1602** MARSTON *Ant. & Mel.* v. Wks. 1856 I. 62 Your wits spurs have but walking rowels; dull, blunt, they will not drawe blood.
b. *Her.* (See quot. 1562.)
1562 LEGH *Armory* 185 He beareth Argent a Mollet of v. pointes, Azure. If the pointes be euen they be called Rowelles. **1603** STOW *Surv.* (1908) I. 52 A Crosse double to the ring, betwene fower rowals of sixe poyntes. [**1610** GUILLIM *Her.* III. v.]
c. The rowel-head (see next).
1844 DISRAELI *Coningsby* IV. xiv, The yeoman struck his spurs to the rowels. **1863** THORNBURY *True as Steel* I. 155 Up to the rowel went every spur.
d. *attrib.* and *Comb.*, as ***rowel-deep*** adv., ***-head***, ***-maker***, ***-spur***.
1597 SHAKS. *2 Hen. IV*, I. i. 46 He.. strooke his able heeles Against the panting sides of his poore Iade Vp to the Rowell head. **1686** PLOT *Staffordsh.* 377 The Rowell maker.. makes the 5, 6, 7, 8, or 10 pointed rowells, of iron or steel. **1820** SCOTT *Abbot* xviii, I will remain here, with bridle in hand, ready to strike the spurs up to the rowel-heads. **1832** W. C. BRYANT *Poems* 45 His spurs are buried rowel-deep, he rides with loosened rein. **1870** LOWELL *Study Windows* 2 All the couriers in Europe spurring rowel-deep make no stir. **1880** in Mrs. O'Donoghue *Ladies on Horseback* (1881) 232 A correspondent.. advises ladies to use a rowel spur, with five prongs.
†**2. a.** The rim of a wheel. *Obs.*
? *a* **1400** *Morte Arth.* 3262 Abowte cho whirllide a whele..; The rowelle whas rede golde with ryalle stonys;.. The spekes was splentide alle with speltis of siluer.
†**b.** A small wheel or pinion. *Obs.*
1599 T. M[OUFET] *Silkwormes* 35 Ingenious Germane, how didst thou convey Thy Springs, thy Scrues, thy rowells, and thy flie?
†**3.** *Eccl.* ? A wheel-shaped chandelier. *Obs.*
Occurs as *ruele* in Latin context in 1249–52 (*Camden Misc.* IX. 10); also in Latin form *rotella* (ibid. 23).
1451 in Gardner *Hist. Dunwich* (1754) 149 For Wax ȝens Estern, and filling the Rowel. **1505** *Will of Joan Longe* (Somerset Ho.), I bequeth to the makyng of a Rowell in the same church. **1565** in Peacock *Eng. Ch. Furniture* (1866) 159 Item one Pax, candellsticks, Rowelles, Mass bookes.
attrib. **1542** *Masham Parish Acc.* (MS.), Resauyd and gathryde in the Church for the rowell Candell afore the rood, xx^d.
II. †**4. a.** The end of a pig's snout. **b.** The knee-pan. **c.** A vertebra. *Obs.*
c **1410** *Master of Game* (MS. Digby 182) v, And whan alle þat faileth hem, þei wrote in þe grounde with þe rowell of hir snowte, þe whiche is reght herde. **1543** TRAHERON *Vigo's Chirurg.* 183 b, Of the dislocacion of the panne or rowell of the knee. **1586** BRIGHT *Melanch.* xxvi. 149 The rowels of the neckbone with their snagges hinder that inclination.
†**5. a.** A small knob on a scourge. *Obs.*⁻¹
1540–1 ELYOT *Image Gov.* xxxix. 98 Whipped throughoute the citie of Rome with whyppes full of ruelles called Scorpions. [Cf. Elyot (1538), *Scorpio*,.. a whyppe hauing plummetts of leade at the endes of the cordes.]
†**b.** A knob on a horse's bit. *Obs.*
1590 SPENSER *F.Q.* I. vii. 37 The yron rowels into frothy fome he bitt. **1598** FLORIO, *Mellone*,.. rowels in the mouth of a horses bit like melons. **1607** MARKHAM *Caval.* II. (1617) 106 By the cruelty of their bytts, as by hie ports with Trenches, and rough roules or buttons.
6. *Farriery.* A circular piece of leather or other suitable material, with a hole in the centre, inserted between the flesh and skin of a horse or other animal to cause discharge or humours; also, any kind of insertion used for this purpose.
Properly distinct from a *seton*, but the two are sometimes confused.
1580 BLUNDEVIL *Horsemanship* v. 51 Two round rowels made of the vpper leather of an old shoo,.. and let such rowels be three inches broad. *Ibid.* 51 b, When he goeth vpright, pull out the rowell. **1607** MARKHAM *Caval.* VII. (1617) 42 After the sore hath runne eight or tenne dayes, you shall heale it by taking away the rowell. **1610** —— *Masterp.* II. clviii. 464 Tye the two ends of the tampins or rowels together. **1714** *Phil. Trans.* XXIX. 48 Putting.. a Rowel or Seton under the Chin, in the Dewlaps. **1761** EARL OF PEMBROKE *Mil. Equitation* (1778) 127 When horses are out of case,.. a rowel, and two ounces of the following powder,.. are of great service. **1802** WILLICH *Domest. Encycl.* III. s.v., Rowels are eminently useful in carrying off rheums or defluxions from the eyes. **1846** J. BAXTER *Libr. Pract. Agric.* (ed. 4) II. 141 A seton or a rowel should be retained for three or four weeks. **1885** G. FLEMING *Vet. Surg.* I. 195 The rowel itself is simply a small piece of thin leather, felt, indiarubber, gutta-percha, or even lead.
attrib. **1678** *Lond. Gaz.* No. 1295/4 A black Gelding,.. with a Rowel Mark on the farther Buttock. **1704** *Ibid.* No. 4068/4 A grey Mare.., Ewe-Neck'd,.. and hath six Rowel-Marks.
†**7.** ? A circular drain-cover. *Obs.*⁻¹
1601 *Nottingham Rec.* IV. 262 To carry away our meanor, to th'end rowells be nott stopped when the[y] sweepe downe ther channels.
†**8.** A round or rung of a ladder. *Obs.*
1652 STERRY *Eng. Deliv. North. Presb.* 46 A ladder joyning heaven and earth, in which ladder every Rowel is a spiritual, a living glory. **1836** *Col. Crockett's Exploits & Adventures Texas* i. 1 Though they start at the lowest rowel of the ladder.
9. ? A radiating group of twigs.
1869 BLACKMORE *Lorna D.* xvii, To fill the tips of the spray-wood and the rowels all up the branches with a crowd of eager blossom. **1894** HALL CAINE *Manxman* II. vii, The rowels of the thin boughs overhead.

rowel (ˈraʊəl), *v.*¹ [f. ROWEL *sb.* 1.]
1. *intr.* and with *it*. To use the spur-rowels.
1599 NASHE *Lenten Stuffe* Wks. (Grosart) V. 249 The dust that they raise in hot spurd rowelling it on to performe complementes vnto him. **1890** KIPLING in *Fortn. Rev.* XLVII. 681 He'll answer to the whip, and you can rowel enough for both.
2. a. *trans.* To spur (a horse) with the rowel.
1833 *Fraser's Mag.* VII. 270 Carl.. rowelled his horse sharply. **1863** W. C. BALDWIN *Afr. Hunting* vi. 200, I nursed my nag to the best of my judgment, rowelling him well, but holding him fast by the head. **1893** *Scribner's Mag.* XIII. 378/1 He rowelled the horse with his burnished spurs.
b. To prick with rowels.
1891 KIPLING *Light that Failed* (1900) 271 He was rummaging among his new campaign-kit, and rowelling his hands with the spurs.
c. *fig.*
1918 F. HACKETT *Ireland* xii. 331 The indecency and indignity of personal subjection rowelled Parnell like a spur with teeth in it. **1931** E. LINKLATER *Juan in Amer.* II. xii. 137 Now the staccato ear-splitting *rafale* of cheering rowels them afresh. **1967** S. BECKETT *Stories & Texts for Nothing* 42 Between the caressing voice and the fingers rowelling my neck the contrast was striking. **1975** E. BERCKMAN *Indecent Exposure* viii. 94 Her visit.. was strong enough to rowel and disturb her.

rowel (ˈraʊəl), *v.*² Also 6–7 rowell. [f. ROWEL *sb.* 6.] *trans.* To insert a rowel in (a horse or other animal).
1580 BLUNDEVIL *Horsemanship* v. 51 Rowell the two slittes or cuttes with two round rowels. *Ibid.* 51 b, It shall be needefull to rowell him with a leather rowell vpon the shoulder point, and to keepe him rowelled the space of fifteene daies. **1657** W. COLES *Adam in Eden* ccii, The root serveth to rowell Cattle and to cure them of the Cough. **1675** *Lond. Gaz.* No. 1049/4 Lost.., a small white hound Bitch,.. having been roweled in the Breast three dayes since. **1711** *Ibid.* No. 4917/4, 2 spots on her farther Hip as if she had been Rowell'd. **1771** SMOLLETT *Humph. Cl.* 24 May, I can dress a horse.., and bleed and rowel him. **1818** SCOTT *Rob Roy* vii, I could attain no information beyond what regarded worming dogs, rowelling horses, and following foxes. **1841** HARTSHORNE *Shropsh. Gloss.* 552.

rowel-bone: see RUEL-BONE.

ˈrowelled, *a. rare*⁻¹. [f. ROWEL *sb.* 1.] Of a spur: Furnished with a rowel.
1834 PLANCHÉ *Brit. Costume* 99 The rowelled spur is first seen on the great seal of Henry III, but it is not common before the reign of Edward I.

ˈrowelled, *ppl. a. rare.* [f. ROWEL *v.*²]
a. Having a rowel inserted.
1580 BLUNDEVIL *Horsemanship* v. 56 b, So as the rowelled place may be in the verie middest thereof.
b. Pricked by rowels (in quot. *fig.*).
1924 R. CAMPBELL *Flaming Terrapin* ii. 29 Rowelled by that sharp prow to hissing hate, The waves washed round her.

ˈrowelling, *vbl. sb.* [f. ROWEL *v.*²] The operation of inserting a rowel in a horse, etc.
1601 HOLLAND *Pliny* II. 218 Take a sliuing or slip of the root and draw it through the eare of sheep or horse in manner of rowelling. **1688** HOLME *Armoury* III. 90/2 Rowelling of Horses is putting of Hair Rings through the Horse skin to draw out Corruption. *c* **1720** GIBSON *Farrier's Guide* II. lvii. (1738) 216 Rowelling is an artificial vent made to discharge noxious humours. **1747** *Gentl. Mag.* 488 If this method is observed, with rowelling,.. it probably will prevent the mortality. **1831** YOUATT *Horse* 399 The manner of rowelling has been described at page 186.
attrib. **1725** *Fam. Dict.* s.v. *Rowelling*, Take some Horse-hair,.. put it into the Rowelling-Needle. **1834** PERCIVALL *Hippopath.* I. 136 With a pair of rowelling scissors, we first slit the skin sufficiently to admit of the finger. **1885** G. FLEMING *Vet. Surg.* I. 74 A special form of scissors named rowelling scissors, or rowelling bistoury.

rowen (ˈraʊən). Now chiefly *dial.* and *U.S.* Forms: α. 4 **rewayn**, 5 **ryweyn**, 6 **rewen**. β. 5 **raweyne**, **rawen**, 8–9 **rawing** (9 **rawn**). γ. 5 **rowayne**, **roweyn**, 6– **rowen**, 9 **rouen**, **rowan**; 7 **rowin**, 7–9 **rowing**. [a. ONF. **rewain* (cf. mod.Picard *rouain*, Norman *revouin*), = OF. (and mod.F.) *regain*: for the etymology of the second element see GAIN *sb.*² and *v.*² An Anglo-Latin *rewaynum* occurs in the 14th cent.]
1. The second growth or crop of grass or hay in a season; aftermath, eddish. Cf. ROUGHINGS.
The precise application of the term (esp. with regard to cutting the aftergrowth or leaving it for pasture) varies to some extent in different localities.
α. *a* **1345** in *Bp. Hatfield's Survey* (Surtees) 201 Et de 10s. rec. de rewayno omnium pratorum in parco post falcacionem. **1382** *Ibid.* 170 Pastura prati, post asportationem feni de Rewayn. *c* **1470** *Hors, Shepe, & G.* (Roxb.) 7 The second croppe they carye home of ryweyn. **1577** [see γ].
β. *c* **1440** *Promp. Parv.* 424/2 Raweyne, hey (*P.* rawen), *fenum serotinum*. **1710** HILMAN *Tusser Rediv.* xvi. 25 Ther is a Water-retting and a Dew retting, which last is done on a good Rawing, or aftermath of a Meadow Water. **1866** *Athenæum* 23 June 827/2 The 'rawing' of our East Anglian farmers. **1895** RYE *E. Angl. Gloss.*, *Rawn*, a second growth of meadow grass.
γ. *c* **1440** *Hors, Shepe, & G.* 140 The secunde crop, thei carie home Roweyn [*v.r.* Rowayne]. **1514** BARCLAY *Cyt. & Uplondyshm.* (Percy Soc.) 9 Gyve to the bestes good rowen in pleynte. **1580** TUSSER *Husb.* (1878) 126 Which euer ye sowe, that first eat lowe. The other forbare for rowen [**1577** rewen] to spare. **1656** BLOUNT *Glossogr.*, *Edish*,.. the rowen or aftermath. **1669** WORLIDGE *Syst. Agric.*, *Rowen*, rough Pasture full of Stubble or Weeds. **1710** HILMAN *Tusser Rediv.* (J), *Rowen* is a field kept up till after Michaelmas, that the corn left on the ground may sprout into green. **1796** J. ADAMS *Diary* Wks. 1851 III. 417 A soft fine rain.. will.. lay the foundation of fine rowen and after feed. **1805** R. W. DICKSON *Pract. Agric.* II. 972 Cow-keepers find great advantage in keeping the animals constantly fed with.. fresh cut grass, and soft green rouen. **1846** *Jrnl. R. Agric. Soc.* VII. I. 61 Sainfoin.. will yield a good crop of hay..; and the rowen is most valuable for lambs. **1880** HOWELLS *Undiscov. Country* xx. 309 The sunny glisten of meadows where the Shakers' hired men were cutting the rowan.
fig. **1875** *Galaxy* XIX. 560 The rowen of Democratic victory has been as plenteous as the harvest.
b. In *pl.* form.
1638 QUARLES *Hieroglyph.* XIV. iii. Wks. (Grosart) III. 196 By the low-shorn Rowins doth appear The fast-declining year. **1639** HORN & ROB. *Gate Lat. Unl.* xxxv. §419 The lateward crop (eddish, rowings) shoots out afresh of grass springing up the second time. **1721** MORTIMER *Husb.* (ed. 3) I. 233 For the Wintering of Cattle, about September you must turn them out.. into your Rowens. **1805** R. W. DICKSON *Pract. Agric.* II. 1030 In order to their being fattened out on the rouens. *a* **1825** FORBY *Voc. E. Anglia*, *Rawings*, after grass. **1850** MRS. BROWNING *Lady Geraldine's Courtship* xxxix, And across it from the rowans A brown partridge whirring near us, till we felt the air it bore. **1876** *Surrey Gloss.* s.v., To put the cattle into the *rowens* is to turn them out into the fields lately mown.

fig. *a* **1644** QUARLES *Virgin Widow* Wks. (Grosart) III. 292/2 When we had taken the first crop of his exuberous baggs, you might have then made bold to eate the Rowens.

†**2. a.** = *rowen partridge*. Also *transf.* of a woman. *Obs.*

1603 HOLLAND *Plutarch's Mor.* 219 As for the partridges, ..the old rowens full subtilly seeme to wait the comming of the said hunters [etc.]. **1603** *Philotus* xxxiii, The deuill cum lick that beird auld rowan; Now sie the trottibus and trowane, Sa busilie as sho is wowane.

†**b.** Rowen butter or cheese. *Obs.*

1675 HAN. WOOLLEY *Gentlew. Comp.* 215 When your Rowens come in,..do not lavish away your Milk-butter or Cheese.

3. *attrib.* and *Comb.*, as ***rowen crop***, ***grass***, ***hay***; also †**rowen butter** (see quot. 1745); †**rowen (-tailed) partridge**, a partridge frequenting a field of rowen grass or hay: cf. RUIN-TAIL(ED).

With quot. 1882 cf. ROWET, quot. 1893.

1523 *Acc. St. John's Hosp.*, *Cant.* (MS.), For the rowen grass of the appull garden. **1600** HOLLAND *Pliny* XVIII. xxviii, The rowen grasse afterwards commeth up..thicke and high for pasture and forrage. *Ibid.*, To the end there may be a second math of rowen hay in Autumne. **1603** —— *Plutarch's Mor.* 570 The old rowen partridges teach their yoong ones how to runne awaie from before the fowler. **1626** BRETON *Fantastickes* Wks. (Grosart) II. 7/1 Bucks now are in season, and Partridges are Rowen-taild. **1745** *De Foe's Eng. Tradesm.* iii. (1841) I. 23 You bargain for the right rowing butter, which is the butter that is made when the cows are turned into the grounds which have been mowed. **1765** *Museum Rust.* IV. 275, I shut that up for a rowen (aftermass) crop of hay. **1801** HUNTINGTON *Bank of Faith* 91 This I feared would fall heavy upon me, as my rowen hay keeps my cows. **1866** BROGDEN *Prov. Linc.* s.v. *Rowen*, The rowen hay season affords..an extra employment. **1882** JEFFERIES *Bevis* III. xvii. 268 Grey rowen grass at the verge of the ditch showed that frost had wandered thither.

rowen (-cheese): see RUEN.

rower[1] ('rəʊə(r)). Also 5 roware, -ere, 6 *Sc.* rollar. [f. ROW *v.*[1] Cf. MDu. *royer*, *roeyer* (Du. *roeijer*), MLG. *royer*, *roier*, Norw. *roar*.]

1. One who rows; an oarsman.

c **1374** CHAUCER *Boeth.* IV. met. iii. (1868) 122 þe rowers and þe maryners hadden by þis..dronken þe wickede drynkes. **1382** WYCLIF *Ezek.* xxvii. 6 Thei maden to thee thi seetis of rowers of yuer of Ynde. *c* **1440** *Promp. Parv.* 437/2 Roware, yn a water, *remex*. **1513** DOUGLAS *Æneis* x. iv. 118 Furth held..Aulestes..with gret strenth of rowaris in that pres. **1565** COOPER *Thesaurus* s.v. *Remex*, To ease or healpe the rowers with settinge vp a sayle. **1600** HOLLAND *Livy* XXXVII. x. 950 Polyxenidas..would neither have rowers nor other mariners in any number about his fleete. **1689** BURNET *Trav.* II. (1750) 102 Which runs with such a Force, that we went thirty Miles in three Hours, having but one Rower. **1732** LEDIARD *Sethos* II. VIII. 140 Other accommodations.. for the slaves, sailors, and rowers. **1775** JOHNSON *West. Isl.* Wks. X. 497 Sir Allan victualled it for the day and provided able rowers. **1832** DOWNES *Lett. Cont. Countries* I. 113 We ..embarked in a covered boat, after a battle with the rowers, who wanted to force us into a wet one. **1877** A. B. EDWARDS *Up Nile* xvii. 470 A crew of steady rowers can do thirty miles a day.

2. *pl.* = REMEX 2.

1884 COUES *N. Amer. Birds* 115 Rudders, or true tail-feathers, like the remiges or rowers, are usually stiff, well-pronounced feathers.

†**rower**[2]. *Obs.* [Origin obscure.] A dead or fallen tree.

1404 in *Wilts. Archæol. Mag.* (1879) XVIII. 164 Sept. Kiesnes [= chênes] appellez 'rowers' pour foaile. **1413** *Patent Roll 1 Hen. V*, Arbores mortuas vocatas Rowers. **1455** *Rolls of Parlt.* V. 306/1 Nor of the undrewode and Rowers in a woode..for theire perpetuell fuell.

†'**rower**[3]. *Obs.* [f. ROW *v.*[7] + -ER[1].] One who puts a nap on cloth.

1598 DELONEY *Jacke Newb.* ii. 38 There were shearemen everie one,..And hard by them there did remaine Full foure score rowers taking paine.

rower, Sc. variant of ROLLER *sb.*[1]

†**rower-back.** *Obs.*[−1] [a. Du. *roerbak*: see RORE *v.*] A trough in which herrings are stirred among salt.

1641 S. SMITH *Herring Buss Trade* 9 One man takes the full Baskets, when they [*sc.* herrings] are gipt, and carries them to the rower backe, wherein is salt. [Hence in later Dicts. and Encycls.]

rowet ('raʊɪt). *dial.* Also 7 roet, ruet, 9 rou(e)t, rowett, rowed. [App. f. ROW *a.*[1]; cf. ROUGHET.] Aftermath, winter-grass; also, coarse grass growing on waste land or in ditches, etc.

c **1700** KENNETT in *MS. Lansd. 1033* fol. 326 *Roet* or *Ruet*, pasture ground fed with cattle as distinguisht from hay-ground. *a* **1722** LISLE *Husb.* (1752) 251, I was afraid they would have been much pinched, their rowet being gone. **1823** E. MOOR *Suffolk Words*, *Rout*, coarse grass, which looks brown and sare in the meadows in spring. **1850** OGILVIE, *Aftermath*..is also called latter math, rowen, or rowett. **1893** MRS. KENNARD *Diogenes Sandals* ix, Gale walked..mile after mile, over 'rowett' and 'burnett'.

attrib. **1766** *Compl. Farmer* s.v. *Dairy*, The foddering season in the former holds so much longer, occasioned by the rowet-grass falling of a month sooner. **1893** *Wiltshire Gloss.*, *Rowet-grass*, the long rough grass in hedges, etc., which cattle refuse; rowan or coarse aftergrass.

'**rowety**, *a. rare.* Also **rowetty**. [f. prec.]

†**1.** ***rowety grass***, rowen or rowet-grass. *Obs.*

a **1722** LISLE *Husb.* (1752) 19 They will not..encourage a rowety grass to arise.

2. = ROWTY *a. rare.*

1878 JEFFERIES *Gamekeeper at H.* 31 The body hidden by the tangled dead ferns and 'rowetty' stuff. **1879** —— *Wild Life* ii. 26 A little of that rowetty grass seen in the damp furrows of the meadows.

rowfe, rowff(e, obs. forms of ROOF *sb.*

row-footed: see ROW *a.*[1]

'**row-galley.** Now *Hist.* [f. ROW *v.*[1] + GALLEY *sb.*] A galley moved or propelled by oars.

a **1548** HALL *Chron.*, *Hen. VIII*, 22 Three Galies of force, with diuerse Foystes & Rowgalies. **1577–87** HOLINSHED *Chron.* I. 28/1 Cesar..got together 80 saile of great ships and row gallies. **1596** DALRYMPLE tr. *Leslie's Hist. Scot.* II. 326 A rowgaylay weil furnist. **1748** *Anson's Voy.* II. vi. 202 Two Row-gallies of thirty-six oars a-piece. **1795** NELSON 7 Feb. in Nicolas *Disp.* (1845) II. 5 The Enemy would have had the Ports of this Island full of Row-galleys. **1836** MARRYAT *Midsh. Easy* (1863) 215 It is a galley, sir—one of the row galleys—I can make out her bank of oars. **1876** BANCROFT *Hist. U.S.* V. x. 439 Two British ships..captured or destroyed the four American row-galleys in the river.

rowgh(e, rowȝ(e, obs. ff. ROUGH *a.*; var. ROUGH *sb.*[2] *Obs.*

rowght, obs. var. ROUT *sb.*

rowh(e, obs. ff. ROUGH *a.*, var. ROUGH *sb.*[2] *Obs.*

rowhyn, var. ROUGH *v.*[2] *Obs.*

rowiness ('rəʊɪnɪs). [f. ROWY *a.* + -NESS. Cf. ROE[3] and ROEY.] The state of being rowy or streaked; streakiness.

1875 LASLETT *Timber* 178 That [mahogany] cut in the province of Tabasco has generally some rowiness or figure to recommend it. **1885** W. L. CARPENTER *Soap & Candles* 174 Lest any portions of lye should be accidentally entangled in the soap, producing want of homogeneity, called 'rowiness', seen when the soap is cut up.

rowing ('rəʊɪŋ), *vbl. sb.*[1] [f. ROW *v.*[1] + -ING[1].]

1. a. The action (or †occupation) of propelling a boat, etc., by means of oars.

c **950** *Lindisf. Gosp.* Mark vi. 48 He..ȝesæh hia wynnennde in rowincg. *Ibid.* John xxi. 8 Oðri..ðeȝnas on scip *vel* on rouing cuomon. **1382** WYCLIF *Mark* vi. 48 He syȝ hem trauelinge in rowynge. *c* **1400** MAUNDEV. (Roxb.) xxxiii. 151 Sum..died for weryness of rowyng and ower trauaillyng. **1436** *Pol. Poems* (Rolls) II. 197 Suche another rowynge..Was not sene of princes many a day. **1555** *Act 2 & 3 Phil. & Mary* c. 16 § 1 Watermen exercising, using and occupying Rowing upon the River of Thames. **1585** T. WASHINGTON tr. *Nicholay's Voy.* II. xi. 46 With strength of rowing we coasted along. **1642** FULLER *Holy & Prof. St.* V. xviii, Here what tugging, what towing, what rowing! **1653** H. COGAN tr. *Pinto's Trav.* x. 30 They gave over rowing, and ..asked us what we desired of them. **1769** FALCONER *Dict. Marine* (1780), *Vogue*, the rowing of a galley. **1825** J. NICHOLSON *Operat. Mechanic* 55 The very best and most effectual posture in a man is that of rowing. **1863** *Sat. Rev.* 4 Apr. 438 Such rowing as that of Oxford is always worth going to see. **1887** STEVENSON *Merry Men* i. 13 Sea-cloth polished on the bench of rowing.

fig. **1638** RAWLEY tr. *Bacon's Life & Death* (1650) 63 The continued Course of Nature, like a running River, requires a continuall rowing and sailing against the stream.

b. *fig.* (See ROW *v.*[1] 8 b.)

1856 in De Vere *Americanisms* (1871) s.v., We hope the President gave his Secretary a good rowing up; he certainly deserved it for his imbecility.

2. *attrib.* and *Comb.* **a.** Denoting 'propelled by oars', as ***rowing-barge***, ***-boat***, ***-ship***.

a **1548** HALL *Chron.*, *Hen. VIII*, 23 A small rowe barge, with three other small rowing shippes. **1647** HEXHAM I, A rowing berge, *een roey-jacht*. **1820** CROKER *Diary* 11 Mar., Went out in a rowing-boat to the breakwater. **1863** *Sat. Rev.* 4 Apr. 437 A severely-contested match between two well-manned rowing-boats. **1901** *Westm. Gaz.* 11 Feb. 10/1 Two 40ft. steam pinnaces and one 30ft. rowing barge.

b. Denoting 'connected with, used in, rowing', as ***rowing-gear***, ***-seat***, ***-wheel***; **rowing machine**, an appliance in which exercises may be done that simulate rowing; **rowing stick** *poet.*, an oar; **rowing tank** (see quot. 1976).

1613 in *Scot. Hist. Rev.* (1905) July 360 Ane gailley..with her sailling and *rowing geir. **1884** KNIGHT *Dict. Mech.* Suppl. 770/2 *Rowing Gear*, outriggers and various devices to assist the oarsman. **1848** J. DE C. LOCKE tr. *Montolieu's Swiss Family Robinson* 2nd Ser. I. x. 95 (*heading*) The *rowing-machine. **1894** *Outing* Mar. 458/1 The exercises consist of hard work on rowing-machines or in the tank, vigorous dumb-bell exercise, and a run of two miles per day. **1935** C. ISHERWOOD *Mr. Norris changes Trains* iv. 68 The Baron made a hobby of his figure. He tortured himself daily on an electric horse, a rowing-machine and a rotating massage belt. **1944** T. RATTIGAN *While Sun Shines* II. 58 If you want exercise I've got a rowing machine in the bathroom. **1977** 'E. CRISPIN' *Glimpses of Moon* i. 20 Exercising on a rowing-machine. *c* **1440** *Promp. Parv.* 438/1 *Rowynge sete yn a schyppe, *transtrum*. **1648** HEXHAM II, *Een Riem-banck*,..the Seats, or Rowing-seats in a Galley or Boate. **1923** E. POUND *XXX Cantos* xx. 93 Their names are not written in bronze Nor their *rowing sticks set with Elpenor's. **1892** *Outing* Jan. 277/2 In 1887 the *rowing tank was first put into practical use in the Yale gymnasium. **1939** NICKALLS & MALLAM *Rowing* iv. 87 The object of the rowing tank is to allow oarsmen to indulge in..rowing without going out on the river.... Tank rowing originated in America, where ice prevents any outdoor rowing for a considerable part of the year. **1976** *Webster's Sports Dict.* 360/1 *Rowing tank*, a large tank of water containing a mock-up of a shell in which an oarsman or sculler can practice his stroke and work on technique. The effectiveness of a stroke is indicated by a meter which measures the turbulence of the water. **1808** TREVITHICK & DICKINSON *Patent Spec.* No. 3148 In a ship ..we place a *rowing wheel shaped like an undershot water-wheel furnished with floats or pallets.

c. Misc., as ***rowing-club***, ***-match***, ***-room***, ***-shirt***, ***-song***, ***-supper***.

1801 STRUTT *Sports & Past.* II. ii. 70 Rowing matches were substituted..upon the Thames during the summer season. **1850** THACKERAY *Pendennis* xxx, Those ferocious dandies, in rowing shirts and astonishing pins and waistcoats. **1856** KANE *Arct. Expl.* II. xxvi. 264 A stretch of the land-water wide enough to give us rowing-room. **1866** WOODGATE *Rowing & Training* 86 The private races of the numerous rowing clubs in the kingdom. **1888** L. A. SMITH *Music of Waters* p. xxvii, Rowing-songs should..also be included in this class. **1889** GRETTON *Memory's Harkback* 67 As to these rowing suppers, he would set them down at once. **1956** M. W. STEARNS *Story of Jazz* ix. 96 Whereas early travelers heard rowing songs and sea shanties, later specialists found work songs.

†'**rowing**, *vbl. sb.*[2] *Obs.*[−1] [f. ROW *sb.*[1] or *v.*[2]] Becoming rowy or streaky.

1750 W. ELLIS *Mod. Husbandm.* III. I. 136 (E.D.S.), [Others make a strong brine,] and therein put pounds of fresh butter, and it will preserve them from rowing.

rowing ('raʊɪŋ), *vbl. sb.*[3] [f. ROW *v.*[3] + -ING[1].] A rating, scolding, or severe talking to.

1832 E. GROSVENOR *Let.* 15 Dec. in G. Huxley *Lady Elizabeth & Grosvenors* (1965) iv. 103 To some magistrates who behaved shabbily B. gave what was called 'a proper rowing'. **1836** MRS. SHERWOOD *Henry Milner* III. v, That quizzing and rowing which he had experienced. **1841** LEVER *C. O'Malley* lxxxiv, He gave him a devil of a rowing a few days ago. **1896** GUY BOOTHBY *In Strange Company* II. vi, When I saw that my rowings proved useless, I ironed him for a couple of days.

†'**rowing**, *vbl. sb.*[4] *Obs.*[−1] [Cf. ROW *v.*[4]] ? Violent blowing.

13.. *Propr. Sanct.* (Vernon MS.) in *Herrig's Archiv* LXXXI. 112/93 þe Rouwyng in Contrariusnesse Of þeose wyndes more and lesse Bitokneþ diuers trauayle Of holi churche.

'**rowing**, *vbl. sb.*[5] [f. ROW *v.*[7] + -ING[1].] The process of putting a nap on cloth.

c **1475** *Pol. Poems* (Rolls) II. 284 As myche for gardyng, spynnyng, and wevyng, Fullyng, rowyng, dyyng, and scheryng. **1582** HAKLUYT *Voy.* (1599) II. 162 The faults in Walking, Rowing and Burling, and in Racking the Clothes aboue measure vpon the Teintors. **1592** GREENE *Upst. Courtier* Wks. (Grosart) XI. 278 The Cloth worker what with rowing and setting in a fine nap, with powdering it and pressing it, with shering the wooll to the proofe of the threed, deale so cunningly [etc.]. **1964** H. HODGES *Artifacts* x. 145 Finally, the clean felted cloth was often brushed with teazles (*teazling*, *rowing*) to raise a nap of fine hairs on the surface.

[The entry in Phillips (ed. Kersey, 1706) '*Rowing of Clothes*, is the smoothing of them with a Roller, &c.', is prob. an erroneous explanation of this.]

'**rowing**, *vbl. sb.*[6] [f. ROW *v.*[8]] Roving (of wool or cotton); also *concr.* a roving or rowan.

1748 RICHARDSON *De Foe's Tour Brit.* (ed. 4) II. 335 The Number of Hands which it employs..in Spinning, Carding, Rowing,..is almost incredible. **1824** MACTAGGART *Gallovid. Encycl.*, *Rowings*, wool made up in long rolls, with cards, before it is spun.

rowing, dial. variant of ROWEN.

rowing ('rəʊɪŋ), *ppl. a.*[1] [f. ROW *v.*[1]] Using, or accustomed to use, oars.

1716 GAY *Trivia* I. 163 The rowing crew, To tempt a fare, clothe all their tilts in blue. **1850** THACKERAY *Pendennis* xxx, There were rowing-men, whose discourse was of sculling matches. **1884** *Harper's Mag.* Feb. 338/2 The undisturbed slumber of rowing-men.

rowing ('raʊɪŋ), *ppl. a.*[2] *rare.* [f. ROW *v.*[3]]

a. Rowdy; disposed to make a row.

1812 *Examiner* 9 Nov. 719/2 The defendant..made a promise to send some *rowing* lads on the next Sunday.

b. Quarrelling; disposed to quarrel.

1961 *Guardian* 20 Oct. 7/6 The grey Depression background, the rowing parents.

Rowism ('raʊɪz(ə)m). [See next and -ISM.] The principles of the Rowites.

1846 McCULLOCH *Acc. Brit. Empire* (1854) II. 297 Rowism in Scotland is somewhat akin to what is known as Irvingism in England.

Rowite ('raʊaɪt). [See def.] A member of a religious sect which accepted the teachings of the Rev. J. M. Campbell, minister of Row in Dumbartonshire, Scotland, from 1825 to 1830.

1834 J. M. CAMPBELL *Mem.* (1877) I. 113 They would say Rowites like Quakers dispensed with the ordinances altogether. **1846** McCULLOCH *Acc. Brit. Empire* (1854) II. 297 The Rowites impute extraordinary influence to the Holy Spirit.

rowith, obs. f. RUTH.

rowk, rowkar (obs. Sc.): see ROUK *v.*

rowke, obs. var. RUCK *sb.* and *v.*

rowl, obs. f. ROLL *sb.*[1] and *v.*

Rowland ('rəʊlənd). *Physics.* The name of H. A. *Rowland* (1848–1901), U.S. physicist, used *attrib.* and in the possessive to designate certain devices and concepts associated with his work, as **Rowland('s) circle**, a circle on which must lie the entrance slit, (curved) grating, and photographic plate of a spectrograph if all the spectral lines are to be brought to a focus on the plate; **Rowland ghost**, a spurious spectral line produced by a periodic error in the spacing of the lines of a diffraction grating; **Rowland grating**, a diffraction grating ruled on a machine built by Rowland; **Rowland('s) mounting** (see quot. 1966); **Rowland ring**, a torus made of a magnetic material whose properties it is wished to investigate and linked with a coil of current-carrying wire.

1932 *Jrnl. Optical Soc. Amer.* XXII. 245 Symmetric adjustment of the grating about the point of tangency to the *Rowland circle. **1952** R. W. DITCHBURN *Light* vi. 196 If then a point source of light is placed at a point Q on the circle whose diameter is equal to the radius of the grating, and which touches the grating at its centre, the spectra will be focused along the circle. This circle is known as the 'Rowland circle'. **1967** G. W. STROKE in S. Flugge *Handbuch der Physik* XXIX. 477 Eq. (25.27) is clearly satisfied on Rowland's circle. *Ibid.*, The best foci are obtained on the Rowland circle when the source is also placed on that circle. **1922** *Jrnl. Optical Soc. Amer.* VI. 419 The separations of the *Rowland ghosts from the parent lines are readily deduced from the characteristics of the ruling engine. **1969** D. RICHARDSON in R. Kingslake *Appl. Optics & Optical Engin.* V. ii. 27 In contradistinction to Rowland ghosts, which usually arise from errors extending over large areas of the grating, each satellite usually originates from a small number of misplaced grooves in a localized part of the grating. **1910** *Phil. Mag.* XX. 773, I had a polished flat plate of speculum metal, such as is used for making *Rowland gratings, silver-plated and polished. **1926** R. W. LAWSON tr. *Hevesy & Paneth's Man. Radioactivity* IV. i. 44 The grating space of a Rowland grating is about 10^{-4} cm. **1974** *Encycl. Brit. Macropædia* II. 235/1 Some Rowland gratings are still in use. **1901** *Physical Rev.* XII. 10 The second grating..was of 21 ft. radius, 14,438 lines to the inch. It was arranged on *Rowland's mounting. **1914** *Astrophysical Jrnl.* XL. 205 It provides for a grating of 15 ft. (4·57 m) radius, and, optically considered, is the Rowland mounting with the plane of the focal circle vertical. **1966** *McGraw-Hill Encycl. Sci. & Technol.* IV. 141/1 In the Rowland mounting, camera and grating are connected by a bar forming a diameter of the Rowland circle. **1953** J. D. KRAUS *Electromagnetics* v. 232 (*caption*) *Rowland-ring method of obtaining magnetization curve. **1966** *McGraw-Hill Encycl. Sci. & Technol.* VIII. 51/1 When the core of the Rowland ring is initially demagnetized, B = 0 and H = 0.

† **rowland-hoe.** *Obs.*$^{-1}$ Some kind of game.

1622 WITHER *Christmas Carol* xii, Some Yovths will now a Mvmming goe, Some others play at Rowland-hoe.

rowlar, obs. var. ROLLER *sb.*[1]

rowle, obs. var. RÔLE, ROLL, and ROWEL.

rowle-powle, obs. var. ROLY-POLY *sb.*

rowler, obs. or dial. var. ROLLER *sb.*[1]

rowlet, obs. form of ROULETTE.

rowley-powley, obs. or dial. var. ROLY-POLY.

rowley rag: see RAG *sb.*[2] 2.

rowling, obs. f. ROLLING.

rowlm(e, obs. ff. ROOM *sb.*[1]

rowlock ('rʌlək, 'rɒlək). Forms: α. 8 rowluck, 8– rowlock. β. 9 **rollock**, **rullock**. [Prob. an alteration (after ROW *v.*[1]) of the earlier OARLOCK.

The etymological pron. ('rəʊlɒk) is recognized by many Dictionaries, in some cases without mention of the usual forms.]

a. A contrivance or device, usually consisting of a notch, two thole-pins, or a rounded fork, on the gunwale of a boat, forming a fulcrum for the oar in rowing.

α. **1750** BLANCKLEY *Nav. Expos.* 138 *Rowlucks*, are spaces left on the Gunwale, where two Thoals are let in at such a Distance from each other, as to admit the Oar, at the End of the Loom to lie on, for rowing the Boat. **1769** FALCONER *Dict. Marine* (1780) s.v. *Oar*, In large vessels, this station is usually called the *row-port*; but in lighters and boats it is always termed the *row-lock*. **1857** P. COLQUHOUN *Oarsman's Guide* 29 The *rowlock* is composed of 3 parts; the *thouel*, against which you row; the *stopper* which is opposite to it; and the *filling* on which the oar rests. **1878** JEFFERIES *Gamekeeper at H.* 107 The regular sound of oars against the tholepins or rowlocks of a boat.

β. **1821** SHELLEY *Let.* Prose Wks. 1888 II. 326 The rullock, or place for the oar, ..ought to be nearer to the mast. **1834** M. SCOTT *Cruise Midge* (1859) 355 We distinctly heard ..the rumble of the rollocks. **1864** RAWLINSON *Anc. Mon. Assyria* vii. 177 Assyrian vessels had no rullocks.

b. *attrib.*, as *rowlock-filling*, *-leather*, *-pin*, *-plate*.

1840 *Penny Cycl.* XVIII. 395 In those ribands are fixed row-lock pins. **1853** HICKIE *Aristoph.* (Bohn) I. 6 A rowlock-leather you have..about your eye. **1857** P. COLQUHOUN *Oarsman's Guide* 12 Box-wood and brass have been tried for the rowlock filling. *c* **1860** H. STUART *Seaman's Catech.* 7 Ship the rowlock plates.

† **'rowly**, *adv.* *Obs.*$^{-1}$ [f. ROW *a.*[2] + -LY[2].] = RAWLY *adv.* 2 or 3.

1562 TURNER *Herbal* II. (1568) 70 He setteth out an other herbe, but by hys leue a lytle to rowly described, for Hormino.

rowly-powly, dial. f. ROLY-POLY *sb.*

rowm, obs. f. ROOM *sb.*[1], *a.*, and *adv.*

row-man, erron. var. of ROUNDSMAN 1.

1833 *Farm Rep.* 152 in *Husb.* III. (L.U.K.), In the winter season some labourers are unable to meet with employment, and are sent about as 'row-men'.

rowme, obs. f. ROAM *v.*, ROOM *sb.*[1], *a.*, and *adv.*

rowmer, obs. f. ROAMER.

rowmont, var. ROLMENT *Obs.*

rown (raʊn). Now *dial.* Forms: α. 5 rowne, 6 *pl.* rounis, 8 roon, 9 rowan; 8– rown. β. 5, 9 rownd (9 round). [a. ON. *hrogn* (Icel. *hrogn*, Fær., Norw., and Da. *rogn*; MSw. *rughn*, *rompn*, Sw. *rom*), = OHG. *rogan* (G. *rogen*): cf. ROE[2], ROAN *sb.*[4], and RAWN.]

1. The roe of a fish.

α. *c* **1440** *Promp. Parv.* 438/2 Rowne, of a fysche, *liquamen*. **1483** *Cath. Angl.* 311/1 A Rowne of Fysche, *lactis*. **1536** BELLENDEN *Cron. Scot.* (1821) I. xliii, The hie fische spawnis his meltis, and the scho fische hir rounis, and incontinent coveris thaim ouir with sand. **1596** DALRYMPLE tr. *Leslie's Hist. Scot.* I. 50 The hie Salmonte haueng castne the meltis, and the sche salmonte the Rounis. **1796** LAUDERDALE *Poems* 64 As lang's ye pay our annual fees in milts an' rowns. **1824** MACTAGGART *Gallovid. Encycl.* s.v. *Milts*, Herrings..with milts, are said to be the male herring, the other with rowns, the female. **1894** HESLOP *Northumbld. Gloss.*, *Rowan*, *Rown*, the roe of a fish.

β. *c* **1475** *Pict. Voc.* in Wr.-Wülcker 765 *Hoc laquamen*, rownd. **1868–** in dial. glossaries (Cleveland, Whitby, E. Anglia).

2. The turbot; = RODDEN-FLUKE. ? *Obs.*

1793 *Statist. Acc. Scot.* IX. 337 Formerly there was a very plentiful fishing upon the coast here, consisting of cod, ling, haddock, rowan or turbot, skait, &c... But..none are now caught but a few cod, rowan, and skait.

Hence **'rowning-time**, the spawning season.

1893 COZENS-HARDY *Broad Norf.* 77.

rown, obs. f. ROUND.

rownce, var. ROUNCE.

rownd(e, obs. ff. ROUND.

rowne, var. or obs. f. ROUN, ROUND; see also RUN *v.*

† **'rowness**[1]. *Obs.* [f. ROW *a.*[1]] Roughness; also, hoarseness (*of* the voice).

1398 TREVISA *Barth. De P.R.* v. xxxv. (Bodl. MS.), Diuers passiouns ibrad by diuers fleting of humours to þe principal of þe lunges as..cowȝe, hoosenes, rownes of þe voice. *c* **1450** *M.E. Med. Bk.* (Heinrich) 222 For scabnesse & rownesse of body & of skyn.

† **'rowness**[2]. *Obs.* [f. ROW *a.*[2]] Rawness.

1483 *Cath. Angl.* 312/2 A Rownes, *cruditas*.

† **rownfol(d.** *Obs.* (Meaning obscure.)

1481–90 *Howard Househ. Bks.* (Roxb.) 463 My Lord.. paide hym for iij. rownfollis ij.s. iiij.d. the rownfolde.

rownsepyked ('raʊnspaɪkɪd), *ppl. a.* *rare*$^{-1}$. [f. ROUNSEPIKE.] Of a tree, having branches stripped of leaves.

1937 D. JONES *In Parenthesis* III. 39 More leper-trees pitted, rownsepykèd out of nature, cut off in their sap-rising.

† **rown-wheel.** *Obs.* *rare*$^{-0}$. (See quot.)

1688 HOLME *Armoury* III. 340/2 The Rowne Wheel..of a Wind-Mill..turns the upper Mill-stone.

'row-off. [f. ROW *v.*[1] + OFF *adv.*] In rowing, a race giving the losers in previous heats a second chance to qualify for the final.

1928 *Daily Tel.* 7 Aug. 12/1 Under the repechage system of rows-off between previous losers, J. Wright..and T. D. A. Collet..had another chance in the sculling event.

'row-over. [f. ROW *v.*[1] + OVER *adv.*] An instance of rowing over. Cf. ROW *v.*[1] 1 f.

1868 W. BROUGH *Field of Cloth of Gold* v. 41 Here I am you see, Coming to trial, should the plaintiff halt, Defendant claims a judgement by default. So you are mine; and I my rival crow over. It's what they call in boat-racing a row over.

rowp, obs. form of ROUP.

rowpee, obs. form of RUPEE.

row-port. *Naut.* [f. ROW *v.*[1] + PORT *sb.*[3] 2. Cf. *rowlock* and *oar-port*.] (See quots.)

1769 FALCONER *Dict. Marine* (1780) s.v. *Row-lock*, In the sides of the smallest vessels of war, a number of little square holes, called row-ports, are cut for this purpose, parallel to the surface of the water. **1846** A. YOUNG *Naut. Dict.*, *Row-port*, ports cut through the sides of any small vessel that may have occasion to use sweeps during calm weather. *c* **1850** *Rudim. Navig.* (Weale) 144 *Row-ports*, square scuttles cut through the sides of frigates, sloops, and small vessels, one between each port in midships.

rowsant, obs. form of ROUSANT.

rowse, obs. form of ROOSE, ROUSE.

rowser, variant of ROUSER.

† **'rowsey**, *a.* *Obs. rare.* [Of obscure origin.] ? Disorderly, uncouth, frowsy.

1567 HARMAN *Caveat* (1869) 19 The abhominable..and ..detestable behauior of all these rowsey, ragged rabblement of rakehelles. **1661** K. W. *Conf. Charac.* (1860) 74 That Fryday face of his, whose rowsey whiskers and brischy turnpikes make him resemble..some borish Turk.

† **rowsgray.** *Obs.* (Uncertain.)

Perhaps two words, the second being GREY *sb.* 6.

1619 MIDDLETON *Love & Antiq.* Wks. (Bullen) VII. 331 The names of those beasts bearing fur, and now in use with the..Skinners. The ounce, rowsgray, ginnet.

row-slave. *rare*$^{-1}$. [f. ROW *v.*[1]] A slave engaged in rowing.

a **1618** SYLVESTER *Mem. Mortality* xvi. Wks. (Grosart) II. 217 The World's a Sea, the Galley is the life,..And man the Row-Slave, to the Port of Death.

rowst(e, obs. ff. ROOST, ROUST, RUST.

† **rowsting.** *Obs.*$^{-1}$ (Obscure.)

1581 *Act 23 Eliz.* c. 10 §1 [No person shall take] Fesauntes or Partridges with..Snares, Ginnes, Enginnes, Rowsting, Lowffing or other deuices whatsoeuer.

rowsty, obs. form of RUSTY *a.*

rowt(e, obs. ff. ROOT, ROUT, ROUTE.

† **rowte-weir.** *Obs.*$^{-1}$ (Obscure.)

1584 in Binnell *Descr. Thames* (1758) 63 Wears, Engines, Rowte Wears, Pight Wears, Foot Wears.

† **rowth.** *Sc. Obs.* Also routh. [f. ROW *v.*[1] + -TH[1]. Cf. OE. *rówet*, *réwet*.]

1. Rowing.

c **1425** WYNTOUN *Cron.* VI. 2114 (Wemyss), Toward þe north þe traid haldand, Ouþer with saill or routh passand. **1467** *Reg. Dunfermline* (Bann. Cl.) 359 þe man..passis vp and set owre þare nettis with routh with a tow of xxiiij fadome. **1513** DOUGLAS *Æneis* V. iii. 24 The swifte Pristis with spedy routh..Furth steris the stern Mynestheus.

2. A stroke of the oar(s).

1513 DOUGLAS *Æneis* III. v. 15 Swepand the fluide with lang rowthis belife. *Ibid.* v. iv. 76 Thai pinglit ayris wp to bend, and haill With sa strang rowthis.., The mychty kervell schudderit at euery straik.

rowth, obs. f. ROOT *sb.*[1], ROUGH *a.*; var. ROUTH; obs. var. WROTH.

rowthe, obs. f. RUTH.

Rowton ('raʊtən). The name of Montague William Lowry-Corry, 1st Lord *Rowton* (1838–1903), used *attrib.* in **Rowton (lodging-) house**, a type of cheap lodging-house intended to provide better conditions than a common lodging-house.

1892 *Times* 16 Dec. 8/1 Yesterday a large model lodging-house which has been erected by Lord Rowton at Bond-street, Vauxhall, for the accommodation of working men, was opened for the inspection of visitors. The building, which has been named 'Rowton-house', stands upon a site within a few yards of Vauxhall-cross. **1911** *Encycl. Brit.* XXIII. 789/1 In 1894 a company, Rowton Houses (Limited), was incorporated to extend the scheme, a main characteristic of which was that the houses should not be charitable institutions but should be on a paying commercial basis. **1932** KIPLING *Limits & Renewals* 388 In what they call a Rowton lodging-house. **1937** H. G. WELLS *Brynhild* vi. 74 One man wrote from a Rowton lodging-house on ruled paper torn from an exercise book. **1956** A. WILSON *Anglo-Saxon Att.* II. ii. 355 He had drifted from lodgings to Salvation Army hostels and Rowton Houses. **1960** C. WILSON *Ritual in Dark* I. ii. 41 It would have destroyed his appetite, like a meal in a Rowton House. **1968** *Listener* 28 Nov. 735/2 Eventually we drove him round Camden Town looking for a night's lodging. We went first to the local Rowton House. **1972** *Guardian* 19 Feb. 9/3 He ended up in a hostel, like Rowton House, for the down and out. **1977** *Vole* No. 3. 23/2 Gone is the once normal category of 'the lodger' and gone are such institutions as Rowton House, providing decent short-term accommodation for single people.

rowty ('raʊtɪ), *a.* Now *north. dial.* Forms: 6 rowtie, 7– rowty, 9 routy. [App. related to ROWET, but found earlier: cf. ROWETY *a.*] Of grass, etc.: Coarse, rough, rank.

1587 HARRISON *Descr. Brit.* I. xviii, The haie of our low medowes is not onelie full of sandie cinder,..but also more rowtie, foggie, and full of flags. *Ibid.* III. i, The hinderance by rot is rather to be ascribed to..their licking in of mildewes, gossamire, rowtie fogs, and ranke grasse. **1691** RAY *N.C. Words*, *Rowty*, over-rank and strong: spoken of Corn or Grass. **1788** W. H. MARSHALL *Prov. Yorksh.*, *Rowty*, rank, overgrown, as beans or other corn. **1855** ROBINSON *Whitby Gloss.* s.v., Thick rowty grass.

row-waggon, var. ROLWAGEN.

rowwe, obs. form of ROW.

rowwhyn, variant of ROUGH *v.*[2] *Obs.*

rowy ('rəʊɪ), *a.*[1] [f. ROW *sb.*[1] + -Y. Cf. ROEY.]

1. Of cloth: (see later quots.).

1552 *Act 5 & 6 Edw. VI*, c. 6 §40 If any Searcher..find any of the Clothes..cockely, pursy, bandy, squally or rowy. *a* **1825** FORBY *Voc. E. Anglia*, *Rowy*, of uneven texture, having some threads stouter than others. **1854** MISS BAKER *Northampt. Gloss.*, *Rowy*, of uneven texture; like linen cloth which has some threads coarser and thicker than others. **1883** in *Cent. Dict.* s.v., For which reason it is styled *rowey*, as the thin places extend across the piece [of cloth] similar to the lines on writing-paper.

2. Striped, streaky, streaked (*esp.* of bacon).

1750 ELLIS *Mod. Husbandm.* IV. iii. 78 (E.D.S.), If butter is made of clover.. it is apt to be rowy. **1895** T. PINNOCK *Black Co. Ann.* (E.D.D.), Hauf a pound o' bacon in rashers, an'.. it must be rowy.

rowy ('raʊɪ), *a.*[2] [f. ROW *sb.*[2] + -Y[1].] Noisy; characterized by quarrelling.

1922 JOYCE *Ulysses* 763 Hes running wild now out at night away from his books and studies and not living at home on account of the usual rowy house.

rowze, obs. form of ROUSE.

†**rox**, *v.*[1] *Obs.*[−1] Also 4 rosk. (Origin and precise sense not clear: cf. ROXLE *v.*)

1377 LANGL. *P. Pl.* B. v. 398 He bygan *benedicite* with a bolke,.. And roxed [*v.r.* roskid, raxed] and rored and rutte atte laste.

rox, *v.*[2] *dial.* [Of obscure origin.] **a.** *intr.* To decay, soften, slacken. **b.** *trans.* To make soft or slack. Hence **roxed** *ppl. a.*, decayed, etc.

1847- in dial. glossaries (Northamp., Leic., Glouc.).

Roxburghe ('rɒksbərə). [Named after the 3rd Duke of Roxburghe (1740–1804).] A style of bookbinding consisting of plain leather backs with gilt lettering, cloth or paper sides, and leaves with untrimmed edges and bottoms.

1877 *Quaritch's Gen. Catal.* 569 Burton's (J.H.) Book-Hunter... 12mo. hf. Roxburghe, uncut. **1890** *Academy* 24 May p. ii, In limp covers, 10s. 6d. net; in roxburghe, 13s. 6d. net.

Roxbury ('rɒksbərɪ). The name of a town in Massachusetts, used *attrib.* in **Roxbury russet** to designate a variety of green-skinned apple with russet markings, originally grown in New England.

1822 J. THACHER *Amer. Orchardist* 136 Roxbury russeting .. is one of the best known, and most valuable fruits in Massachusetts. **1834** *N.Y. Sun* 23 Sept. 4/1 The sweet side of the apple is of a bright yellow colour, and the sour side of the same colour as the Roxbury Russet. **1861** [see BALDWIN]. **1880** *Harper's Mag.* Mar. 573/2 She set right to a-parin' them Roxbury russets. **1949** *Amer. Forests* Sept. 20/1 Some of the apples sound familiar: Smoke House, Roxbury Russet, Jonathan, Baldwin. **1975** *New Yorker* 11 Aug. 35/1 The first American apple of which there is any record is the now all but forgotten Roxbury Russet.

†**roxle**, *v. Obs.*[−1] (See ROX *v.*[1])

13.. *Old Age* in *Reliq. Antiq.* II. 211, I rivele, I roxle, I rake, I rouwe.

roxy ('rɒksɪ), *a. dial.* [f. ROX *v.*[2]] (See quots.)

1833 LOUDON *Encycl. Archit.* 620 The fruit being what is called mosy, roxy, or sleepy, nearly synonymous terms, and all signifying fruit beginning to decay. **1854** MISS BAKER *Northampt. Gloss.*, *Roxy*, decaying, as fruit or rotten cheese. **1881–96** in Leic. and Warw. glossaries.

Roxy ('rɒksɪ), *sb.* The nickname of Samuel Lionel Rothafel (1882–1936), U.S. radio and film entrepreneur, used *attrib.* of persons and things connected with the chain of cinemas built by him.

1940 F. SCOTT FITZGERALD *Let.* 12 July (1964) 84 It's very modern to be taking dramatic criticism although it reminds me vaguely of the school for Roxy ushers. **1957** *Encycl. Brit.* XV. 868/1 The Roxy theatre,.. which opened in 1927 in New York city, with a 6,250 seating capacity, cost $8,000,000 and grossed in one week $144,267. **1961** A. BERKMAN *Singers' Gloss. Show Business* 76 *Roxy ending*.., the fanfare ending of a song, first used at the Roxy Theatre in New York. The Roxy Ending is sometimes played at the end of a production number, or where majestic fullness is required. (Also *Paramount ending*, *Publix ending*).

†**roy**, *sb.*[1] *Obs.* Also 5–6 roye. [a. OF. *roy*, F. *roi*, = ONF. *rei* (see RAY *sb.*[8]):—L. *rēg-em*, *rex* king.]

1. A prince; a sovereign, a royal person.

Common in Sc. poetry of the 16th century.

?*a* **1400** *Morte Arth.* 2372 The roy ryalle renownde, with his Rownde Table. *c* **1440** *York Myst.* xxvi. 1 Vndir þe ryallest roye of rente and renowne. *c* **1470** *Gol. & Gaw.* 301 The roy rial raid withoutin resting. **1500–20** DUNBAR *Poems* lxxvii. 34 Syne the Bruce,.. Thow gart as roy cum rydand vnder croun. *c* **1557** ABP. PARKER *Ps.* cxlix. 421 Let Syons youth and childer ioy In their most princely roy. **1584** HUDSON *Judith* vi. 65 Abash not reader, though this reckless Roy.. Was thus beguilde. **1611** H. BROUGHTON *Require of Agreement* 52 The Apostles.. wrote in most roiall Greeke, to tell that the Roy of all wisedome ruled their penne.

2. *ellipt.* = COLOUR-DE-ROY.

1549 *Act 3 & 4 Edw. VI*, c. 2 §1 Clothe called Russettes, Musters, Marbles, Grayes, Royes and suchelyke colors.

†**roy**, *sb.*[2] *Obs.*[−1] (Meaning doubtful.)

Perh. a misuse of prec. (cf. RAY *sb.*[8] b); but the passage appears to be an echo of *York Myst.* xv. 69–71, in which *royse* belongs to ROY *v.*

14.. *Shrewsb. Fragm.* in *Non-Cycle Myst. Plays* (1909) 1 ȝe lye, bothe, by þis liȝt, And raues as recheles royes!

Roy (rɔɪ), *sb.*[3] *Austral.* [f. the personal name *Roy*.] A smart, fashionable, or 'smooth' person. Also *attrib.*

1960 *Encounter* May 28 The Australian business-man or big land-owner, the button-down shirt, lightweight suit type of smoothie from the North Shore line in Sydney or the Toorak Road in Melbourne, with his spurious 'taste' and 'culture'... In current Australian terminology, this is the 'Roy' type. **1965** *Nation* (Austral.) 27 Nov. 21 Middle-class 'Roys' in sports cars and yachting jackets. **1971** F. HARDY *Outcasts of Foolgarah* xi. 143 The young executives, the in-people, call them what you like, the Roys, the jet set, the status symbol seekers from Perisher Valley to Palm Beach, and none of them worth a pinch of shit if it comes to doing an honest day's work.

roy, *v. north.* and †*Sc.* [Of obscure origin.]

†**1.** *intr.* To talk nonsense. *Obs.*

a **1440** *York Myst.* xv. 69, I trowe þou royse, For what it was fayne witte walde I, That tille vs made þis noble noyse. **1508** DUNBAR *Flyting* 54 Renunce, rebald, thy ryming, thow bot royis.

2. (See quots.)

1828 CARR *Craven Gloss.*, *Roy*, to bluster, to domineer. **1847** HALLIW., *Roy*,.. to swagger; to boast; to indulge in convivial mirth. *North.* **1876-** in northern glossaries.

royal ('rɔɪəl), *a.* and *sb.* Forms: 4–7 **roial** (5 **-ale**), 5–7 **roiall** (5 **-alle**); 5–6 **royalle**, 5–7 **royall**, **-ale**, 5– **royal**. [a. OF. *roial* (mod.F. *royal*):—L. *rēgāl-em* REGAL *a.* In ME. the variants REAL (*a.*[1]) and RIAL were also in common use.

The French origin of many ME. and early modern uses is shown by the adj. being placed after the noun.]

A. *adj.*

In a number of Shaksperian passages (see Schmidt) the adj. has a purely contextual meaning, the precise force of which is not always clear.

I. 1. a. Of blood, etc.: Originating from, connected with, a king or line of kings.

c **1374** CHAUCER *Troylus* I. 435 In hym ne deynede sparen blood royal The fyr of loue. *c* **1386** —— *Knt.'s T.* 1018 As they that weren of the blood roial Of Thebes. **1413** [see BLOOD *sb.* 10]. **1500–20** DUNBAR *Poems* xlviii. 167 Haill, blosome breking out of the blud royall. **1590** SPENSER *F.Q.* I. i. 5 She.. by descent from Royall lynage came Of ancient Kinges and Queenes. **1665** MANLEY *Grotius' Low C. Wars* 321 One was sent to govern them that was of Royal Blood, and by Kinred allyed to the King. **1667** MILTON *P.L.* XII. 325 Of the Royal Stock Of David.. shall rise A Son. **1737** *Gentl. Mag.* VII. 499/2 Endeavouring to alienate the Affections of the People from the Royal Family. **1749** GRAY *Installat. Ode* 37 High potentates, and dames of royal birth. **1841** ELPHINSTONE *Hist. Ind.* II. 271 His house, alone, of the Rájpút royal families, has rejected all matrimonial connections with the kings of Delhi. **1871** *Burke's Peerage* 836 This ducal house [of Norfolk] stands, next to the blood-royal, at the head of the peerage of England.

Comb. **1607** TOURNEUR *Rev. Trag.* I. i, Royal-blood monster!

b. Of persons: Having the rank of king or queen; belonging to the royal family.

Royal Highness: see HIGHNESS *sb.* 2 b. ***Royal Majesty***: see MAJESTY 2. ***Princess Royal***: see PRINCESS *sb.* 3.

1513 MORE in Grafton *Chron.* (1568) II. 767 Which Lordes were.. appointed as the kinges nere friends to the tuition of his royall person. **1535** LYNDESAY *Satyre* 177, I am ane sportour and playfeir To that Royall ȝoung King. **1591** SHAKS. *1 Hen. VI*, v. ii. 4 Then march to Paris, Royall Charles of France. **1606** —— *Ant. & Cl.* v. ii. 321 It is well done, and fitting for a Princesse Descended of so many Royall Kings. **1655** *Nicholas Papers* (Camden) II. 182 The first word that her highnesse Royale euer heard of it. **1765** BLACKSTONE *Comm.* I. 225 The prince of Wales,.. and also his royal consort, and the princess royal. **1788** GIBBON *Decl. & F.* xlix. V. 146 The royal youth was commanded to take the crown from the altar. **1809** WORDSW. *Sonnet*, Call not the royal Swede unfortunate, Who never did to Fortune bend the knee. **1838** LYTTON *Leila* II. i, The small grey eyes of the friar wandered over each of his royal companions with a.. penetrating glance.

transf. **1526** TINDALE *1 Peter* ii. 9 But ye are a chosen generacion, a royall presthod, an holy nacion, and a peculiar peple. **1837** NEWMAN *Par. Serm.* III. xvii. 272 The royal dynasty of the Apostles is far older than all the kingly families which are now on the earth.

c. Of parts of the body.

1598 SHAKS. *L.L.L.* IV. ii. 146 (Q.[1]), Deliuer this Paper Into the royall hand of the King. **1611** BIBLE *Transl. Pref.* ¶3 His Royall heart was not daunted. **1625** in Rushw. *Hist. Coll.* (1659) I. 206 God in his mercy soon repair this breach by your Royal head. **1865** RUSKIN *Sesame* ii. §87 The power of the royal hand that heals in touching.

transf. **1698** FRYER *Acc. E. India & P.* 176 [A tiger] Disrobed of its Royal Hide.

2. a. Of rank, etc.: Of or pertaining to a sovereign, or the dignity or office of a sovereign.

In quots. under (*a*) the adj. follows the sb.

(*a*) *c* **1374** CHAUCER *Troylus* I. 435 Myn estat royal here I resigne In-to hire hond. *c* **1430** LYDG. *Minor Poems* (Percy Soc.) 25 Where is Pirrus, that was lord and sire Of Ynd, in his estate royall? **1514** BARCLAY *Cytizen & Uplondyshm.* (Percy Soc.) 17 From cotes, & houses pastorall, They have ascended to dygnyte royall. **1579** LYLY *Euphues* (Arb.) 193 The Empresse keepeth hir estate royall. **1600** E. BLOUNT tr. *Conestaggio* 250 In a manner exempte from the iurisdiction royall. **1683** CHAS. II in *Var. Collect., Hist. MSS. Comm.* IV. 194 By the authority of our Power Royall to be executed in such order.. as We think most convenient.

(*b*) *c* **1460** FORTESCUE *Abs. & Lim. Mon.* vii. (1885) 125 Other suche nobell and grete costes, as bisitith is roiall mageste. **1475** *Bk. Noblesse* (Roxb.) 7 Conquest or victorie by violence or by roialle power. **1523** [COVERDALE] *Old God* (1534) G ij, Sechinge and goynge about to get royall & proude tytles. **1593** SHAKS. *Rich. II*, II. i. 120 By my Seates right Royall Maiestie. **1667** MILTON *P.L.* II. 1 On a Throne of Royal State, which far Outshon the wealth of Ormus and of Ind. **1681–6** J. SCOTT *Chr. Life* (1747) III. 202 By all which it is abundantly evident that Christ hath a royal Power delegated to him from the Father. **1784** COWPER *Task* v. 551 His [God's] other gifts All bear the royal stamp that speaks them his. **1815** ELPHINSTONE *Acc. Caubul* (1842) II. 257 These divisions.. have fallen off from the royal authority, in a greater proportion than those under the Haukims.

b. So of insignia or emblems of royalty.

1422 tr. *Secreta Secret., Priv. Priv.* 200 Of this Came tythynges to the kynge of the Cite, and he anoone arose fro his roial Siege. *c* **1450** *Merlin* iii. 42 When thei of the portes saugh the baners roiall of kynge Constance, thei hadden grete merveile. *a* **1533** LD. BERNERS *Huon* xlii. 141 Thou art not worthy to sytt in a sete royall. **1593** SHAKS. *Rich. II*, II. i. 40 This royall Throne of Kings, this sceptred Isle,.. this England. **1611** SPEED *Hist. Gt. Brit.* IX. xv. §52. 632/1 Before him in gold and glorious colours the Royall Standard was borne. **1674** BREVINT *Saul at Endor* 63 The Gift of Miracles being to Teachers, what both Credential Letters and Roial Colors are to public Officers. **1708** J. CHAMBERLAYNE *St. Gt. Brit.* (1710) 56 The Royal Arms of Scotland. *Ibid.*, Her Majesty's Royal Motto. **1715** *Lond. Gaz.* No. 5310/1 The Royal Standard was display'd. **1832** MACAULAY *Armada* 20 As slow upon the labouring wind the royal blazon swells. **1844** *Regul. & Ord. Army* 36 Every ship and vessel of war meeting her shall fire a Royal Salute. **1899** *Daily News* 2 Dec. 6/6 Ermine is especially useful. The two sketches given here show modes of introducing the royal fur.

c. Of persons: In the service of the king or sovereign. Also *transf.* of pawns in chess.

1648 MILTON *Ps.* lxxxv. 13 Before him Righteousness shall go His Royal Harbinger. **1763** SIR W. JONES *Caissa* Wks. 1799 VI. 502 The chief art in the Tacticks of Chess consists in the nice conduct of the royal pawns. **1849** MACAULAY *Hist. Eng.* vii. II. 224 Two royal messengers were in attendance during the discussion.

3. a. Belonging to, occupied or used by, a king or kings; forming part of the possessions or property of a sovereign.

1412–20 LYDG. *Chron. Troy* II. 5636 He was lord of eyr, of lond, & see, Hys royal kyngdam deuidyng into þre. *a* **1548** HALL *Chron., Hen. VIII*, 25 [He] departed from his manour royall of grenewich the xv. daye of June. **1593** SHAKS. *Rich. II*, II. iv. 45 We are inforc'd to farme our royall Realme. *a* **1618** RALEIGH *Apology* 27 If you find it [*sc.* the mine] Royall,.. then let the Serjeant Major repell them. *a* **1676** HALE *De Jure Maris* I. vi. in *Hargrave's Law Tracts* (1787) I. 36 This great and solemn tryall for the right of a royall river. **1746** FRANCIS tr. *Horace, Ep.* I. xii. 8 Are you with food, and warmth, and raiment blest? Not royal treasures are of more possesst. **1784** COWPER *Task* v. 157 Nor wanted aught within, That royal residence might well befit, For grandeur or for use. **1815** J. MAYNE *Jrnl.* 3 Feb. (1909) xi. 270 The Princess of Wales was present, and towards the end of the opera she went round into the royal box. **1820** SHELLEY *Œd. Tyr.* II. ii. 111, I am a famous hunter, And can leap.. Even the palings of the royal park. **1835** THIRLWALL *Greece* vi. I. 169 Most of the great families seem to have resided in the same town which contained the royal mansion. **1867** SMYTH *Sailor's Word-bk.* 583 *Royal Yacht*, a vessel built and equipped expressly for the use of the sovereign. **1874** W. P. LENNOX *My Recoll.* I. iii. 77, I.. upon reaching the theatre dismounted, and followed the royal party into the anteroom of the royal box. **1930** E. WALLACE *Lady of Ascot* x. 105 Julian had a Royal Enclosure badge, and was the only member of the party possessed of this privilege. **1958** *Spectator* 8 Aug. 201/1 The physicists, who sometimes exercise their sovereignty by barring psychology from the Royal Enclosure of the physical sciences. **1963**, **1968** [see ENCLOSURE 4 a]. **1971** H. TREVELYAN *Worlds Apart* xxiv. 282 My wife did her part, showing great endurance and invariable good humour, finding herself, while I was in England, on Khruschev's right at a lively dinner in the 'Royal Box' in the Bolshoi Theatre during the celebration of Shakespeare's four hundredth anniversary. **1974** 'G. BLACK' *Golden Cockatrice* vii. 113 The kind of people who might one day get him into the Royal Enclosure at Ascot.

transf. **1768** WILDMAN in *Encycl. Brit.* (1771) I. 335/1 If this is done.. the operator should examine the royal cells. **1835** *Penny Cycl.* IV. 152/1 The royal cells are very different from those of the male or worker. **1899** D. SHARP *Insects* 66 When the denizens of a hive are about to produce another queen, one or more royal cells are formed.

b. ***royal fish***: (see quots. and FISH *sb.*[1] 2).

Cf. Bracton II. v. 7 ('balena, sturgio, et alii pisces regales'), Fleta I. xlv, and Britton I. xviii.

1570–6 LAMBARDE *Peramb. Kent* (1826) 257 Any fish (called a Craspeis, that is,.. a great or roiall fishe, as whales, or suche other, which by the Lawe of Prerogative perteined to the King himselfe). **1623** WHITBOURNE *Newfoundland* 9 The Sea likewise all along that Coast, doe plentifully abound in other sorts of fish, as Whales,.. Hogs, Porposes, Seales, and such like royall fish. *a* **1676** HALE *De Jure Maris* I. vii. in *Hargrave's Law Tracts* (1787) I. 43 These royal fish extended to other than whale and sturgeon, viz. to porpoise, and *grampise*, or great fish. **1756**, **1776** [see FISH *sb.*[1] 2]. **1818** CRUISE *Digest* III. 270 Royal fish consist of whale and sturgeon, to which the King, or those entitled by grant from him, or by prescription, have a right, when either thrown on shore, or caught near the coast. **1843** *Penny Cycl.* XXVII. 290/2 The Dugong is considered by the Malays as a royal fish, and the king has a right to all that are taken. **1883** *St. James's Gaz.* 9 Nov., The term 'royal fish' includes the three varieties of sturgeon, whale, and porpoise.

4. Pertaining to the king (or queen) as civil or military head or representative of the state.

Common in special designations, as ***Royal Artillery***, ***Engineers***, ***Marines***, ***Naval Reserve***, ***Navy***, etc.

1593 SHAKS. *3 Hen. VI*, III. iii. 253 And thou Lord Bourbon, our High Admirall, Shall waft them ouer with our Royall Fleete. **1604** E. G[RIMSTONE] *D'Acosta's Hist. Indies* IV. vii. 226 Not reckoning the Silver.. that hath been entred in other roiall custome houses. *c* **1648** MILTON *Sonnet* xviii, Cyriack, whose Grandsire on the Royal Bench Of Brittish Themis, with no mean applause Pronounc't. **1667** —— *P.L.* I. 677 As when bands Of Pioners with.. Pickaxe arm'd Forerun the Royal Camp, to trench a Field. **1748** *Earthquake Peru* i. 58 The Government of the Kingdom depends on that of the Royal Court. **1765** BLACKSTONE *Comm.* I. 408 The method of ordering seamen in the royal fleet. **1592**, **1769** [see NAVY[1] 3]. **1786** [see ARTILLERY *sb.* 5]. **1852** DICKENS *Bleak Ho.* xxxiv, I don't care a pinch of snuff for the whole Royal Artillery establishment. **1862** ANSTED *Channel Isl.* IV. xxiii. 525 The Royal Court in each of the two principal islands consists of the Bailiff, who presides, and the twelve Jurats. *a* **1865** SMYTH *Sailor's Word-bk.* (1867) 583 Royal naval reserve. **1876** VOYLE & STEVENSON *Milit. Dict.* 471/2 Woolwich.. is also the head-quarters of the royal regiment of artillery. **1889** [see ENGINEER *sb.* 2 c]. **1911** *Shipping World* 15 Mar. 276/1 The Royal Fleet Auxiliary

Burma..is a vessel with considerable claims to notice. **1913** [see *flying officer* s.v. FLYING *vbl. sb.* 3]. **1918** *Times* 16 Mar. 10/2 It is Our Will and Pleasure that the Air Force to be established pursuant to the said Act shall be styled the 'Royal Air Force'. *Ibid.* 28 Nov. 9/3 The three Corps will henceforth be known as the 'Royal Army Service Corps', the 'Royal Army Veterinary Corps', and the 'Royal Army Ordnance Corps'. **1922** JOYCE *Ulysses* 48 Her fancyman is treating two Royal Dublins in O'Loughlin's of Blackpitts. **1935** *Ann. Reg. 1934* 23 The Minister announced that a new branch of the Territorial Army, under the name of the Royal Defence Corps, was to be formed. **1937** *Ann. Reg. 1936* 65 The King had approved the creation of a new Reserve called the Royal Air Force Reserve, which would be open only to men in civil life. **1943** [see R.E.M.E., REME]. **1946** *Times* 10 Dec. 4/4 The King has approved that the following regiments and corps shall in future enjoy the distinction of 'royal', their new titles being..Royal Army Educational Corps. Royal Army Dental Corps. Corps of Royal Military Police. Royal Pioneer Corps. **1950** *Jrnl. R. United Service Inst.* XCV. 289 In the same Army Order it was also stated that on transfer to the R.A.C. the R.T.C. would be re-designated Royal Tank Regiment. **1955** *Times* 20 July 8/7 The Queen has approved the promotion of Prince Bernhard of the Netherlands to the honorary rank of Air Vice-Marshal Royal Air Force Volunteer Reserve, with effect from July 8. **1965** *Oxford Mail* 29 June 1/4 A new Army corps will come into being next month. It is the Royal Corps of Transport made up of the Royal Army Service Corps..the Royal Engineers' transport units and the Movement Control Service.

5. a. ***Royal Burgh***, a Scottish burgh which derives its charter directly from the Crown.

1648 *Sc. Acts* (1872) VI. II. 83 For erecting of þe samyne [burgh] in ane frie burgh royall. **1672** *Ibid.* (1820) VIII. 77/2 þat they..be freed in all tyme comeing from beiring burden with the royall burroues. **1693** STAIR *Instit.* IV. xlvii. §19 (ed. 2) 726 Bailies of Regality, Bailies of Burghs-Royal, or of Burghs of Regality. **1708** J. CHAMBERLAYNE *St. Gt. Brit.* II. II. ii. 505 These Royal Boroughs are not only several distinct Corporations, but they are also one entire Body, governed by.. one general Court. **1734** *Treat. Orig. & Progr. Fees* 34 That Duty which Burghs-Royal, by their Charters of Erection, owe to the King. **1806** *Gaz. Scot.* Introd. p. xxxiii, The royal boroughs of Scotland also form, as it were, a commercial parliament, which meets once a year at Edinburgh. **1866** (*title*), Records of the Convention of the Royal Burghs of Scotland.

b. ***Royal Borough***, part of the title of three English boroughs (Kensington (and Chelsea), Kingston-upon-Thames, and Windsor) that have a royal connection.

1897 *Private Life of Queen* xxvii. 226 Our Queen..gave the plot of land..to the people of the 'Royal Borough' [of Windsor] for a recreation ground. **1901** *London Gaz.* 19 Nov. 7472/2 The King has been pleased to direct Letters Patent to be passed..granting the title 'Royal' to the Metropolitan Borough of Kensington, and ordaining and declaring that the said Borough shall henceforth be called and styled the 'Royal Borough of Kensington'. **1923** *Victoria Hist. Co. Berkshire* III. 56/2 The borough of Windsor..was from the first, as it has since remained, a royal borough, owning no overlord but the King. **1930** G. B. SHAW *Apple Cart* II. 75 It is my intention to offer myself to the Royal Borough of Windsor as a candidate at the forthcoming General Election. **1975** G. EVANS *Kensington* p. xvi, Although the granting of the title 'Royal' does not carry with it any special precedence or privilege, there are only three English Boroughs—Kensington, Kingston-upon-Thames..and Windsor—on which the Sovereign has conferred the title. **1976** *Equals* Dec. 8/1 She is one of four Conservative councillors for the St. Mary's ward of the Royal Borough of Windsor and Maidenhead.

6. Founded or established by, under the patronage of, a sovereign or royal person.

Royal Society, a Society incorporated by Charles II in 1662 for the pursuit and advancement of the physical sciences. ***Royal Academy*** (see ACADEMY 6).

1509 BP. FISHER *Funeral Serm. C'tess Richmond* Wks. (1876) 308 She that buylded a college royall to the honour of the name of crist Ihesu. **1671** GLANVILL *Further Disc. M. Stubbe* 11 A malevolent, envious humour against the Royal Society, and its Friends. **1759** in Hodges & Hughes *Sel. Naval Documents* (1927) 135 Whereas Mr. Nathaniel Peacock has been educated in the Royal Academy at Portsmouth, and is well qualified to serve His Majesty at sea. **1769** *Ann. Reg., Chron.* 106/2 The Royal Academicks gave an entertainment at their house in Pall-Mall. **1784** COWPER *Tiroc.* 503 Shall royal institutions miss the bays, And small academies win all the praise? **1802** JAMES *Milit. Dict.* s.v. *Academy*, We have in England two royal military academies, one at Woolwich, and one at Portsmouth. **1834** *Times* 25 Jan. 5/3 The mayor and other members were willing to show proper deference to the Royal commission. **1865** RUSKIN *Sesame* i. §49, I hope it will not be long before royal or national libraries will be founded in every considerable city. **1871** [see COMMISSION *sb.*[1] 6]. **1873** *London Gaz.* 21 Jan. 265/1 We do therefore beg leave to recommend that your Majesty will be graciously pleased, by your Order in Council, to approve of the closing of the Royal Naval College at Portsmouth, and the founding of a College at Greenwich, to be styled 'The Royal Naval College'. **1886** PASCOE *London of To-day* xxv. (ed. 3) 233 One of the so-called royal hospitals of London. **1894** *Times* 19 May 7/3 A report by Mr. R. Hunter Pringle, Assistant-Commissioner to the Royal Commission on Agriculture, has been laid before Parliament. **1907** *Times* 9 Mar. 12/2 The ninth annual dinner of the Automobile Club was held..last evening... The chairman announced that a letter had been received from the Home Office stating that his Majesty had been pleased to command that the club should be henceforth known as the Royal Automobile Club. **1926** *Daily Chron.* 13 May 1/7 The proposals in this direction tentatively made in the report of the Royal Commission should be pressed and the powers of the proposed board enlarged. **1926** *Encycl. Brit.* II. 1020/1 The constant vigilance and activity of the Royal Society for the Protection of Birds and the Selborne Society have secured legislative and administrative protection for birds. **1927** T. M. LONGSTRETH *Silent Force* 344 We are members of the Royal Canadian Mounted Police..and I'm going to seize your ship and cargo. **1928** *Times* 24 May 11/4 The Royal Colonial Institute, which celebrates its diamond jubilee this year, has decided to change its name to 'The Royal Empire Society'. **1930** [see *National Trust* s.v. NATIONAL *a.* 5]. **1955** *Times* 15 June 8/7 The executive committee of the Royal Automobile Club, which is responsible for the conduct of motor races in the United Kingdom, is to meet to-day. **1958** *Times* 9 May 7/7 The Queen has approved, by Order in Council, that henceforth the Royal Empire Society shall be known as the Royal Commonwealth Society. **1965** *Listener* 17 June 892/6 Three royal commissions are at this moment examining the general parts of the local government body. **1971** *Whitaker's Almanack 1972* 1098/2 Royal British Legion, Headquarters, Pall Mall, S.W.1. **1976** *Fundy Tourist* (St. Stephen, New Brunswick) 1 July 1/1 The Royal Canadian Mounted Police —the words conjure up visions of red knights on slick black steeds. **1977** *R.A.F. News* 11-24 May 5/6 The collection.. in aid of the Warboys Branch of the Royal British Legion Honorary Association. **1977** *Western Morning News* 1 Sept. 6/1 The following..adhere to a code of conduct laid down by the Royal Institute of Chartered Surveyors. **1980** *Brit. Med. Jrnl.* 29 Mar. 925/1 The obvious and only course of action was a Royal Commission.

7. a. Proceeding from, performed by, a (or the) sovereign.

1611 BIBLE *1 Kings* x. 13 Besides that which Solomon gaue her of his royall bountie. **1613** SHAKS. *Hen. VIII*, I. iv. 86 By all your good leaues Gentlemen; heere Ile make My royall choyce. **1704** J. HARRIS *Lex. Techn.* I, *Royal Assent*, is that Assent which the King gives to a thing formerly done by others, to the Election of a Bishop by Dean and Chapter. **1708** J. CHAMBERLAYNE *St. Gt. Brit.* (1710) 54 When he shall please in his Royal Progresses to visit these parts. **1780** T. DAVIES *Life David Garrick* I. xvi. 180 The king was prevailed upon to give a kind of sanction to this entertainment, by a royal command, on the first night of representation. **1784** COWPER *Tiroc.* 416 The royal letters are a thing of course—A king, that would, might recommend his horse. **1849** MACAULAY *Hist. Eng.* v. I. 592 A building which had been honoured by several royal visits. **1861** *Chambers's Encycl.* II. 229/1 In 1556..the Stationers' Company of London was constituted by royal charter. **1863** [see ASSENT *sb.* 2]. **1869** *Bradshaw's Railway Manual* XXI. 298 The Fusion Bill..was..carried through both Houses of Parliament and received the Royal assent on the 31st of July. **1876** VOYLE & STEVENSON *Milit. Dict.* 354/1 Royal warrants, where the army is concerned, relate to all matters touching the soldier. **1976** *Times* 1 Sept. (Fashion Suppl.) p. ii/5 Norman Hartnell and Hardy Amies, both royal warrant holders.

b. Of the king or sovereign.

1821-2 SHELLEY *Chas. I*, I. i. 117 You torch-bearers.. attend the Marshal of the Masque Into the Royal presence. **1845** PATTISON *Ess.* (1889) I. 25 His innocence, however manifest, could not save him from the royal vengeance. **1849** MACAULAY *Hist. Eng.* vii. II. 219 A proof that the dominion of the Jesuits over the royal mind was absolute.

II. 8. a. Befitting, appropriate to, a sovereign; *esp.* stately, magnificent, splendid. Also applied to the use of the plural pronoun 'we' by a single person to denote himself. Cf. WE *pron.* 2 a.

c **1386** CHAUCER *Squire's T.* 59 This Cambynskan..In roial vestiment sit on his deys. *a* **1400** *Sqr. lowe Degre* 94 In her oryall there she was, Closed well with royall glas. *c* **1430** *Syr Gener.* 2534 He wedded hir with grete solemnitie; A royaler fest did neuer man see. **1470-85** MALORY *Morte Arth.* VII. ii. 215 The kynge helde hit [the feast] att Carlyon in the moost royallest wyse. **1534** MORE *Treat. Passion* Wks. 1286/2 Thus say they,..God tooke from the posteritye of Adam, the roiall duchye, that is to wytte the ioyes of heauen. **1542** UDALL *Erasm. Apoph.* 345 Some folkes..esteme feastes whiche are drawen of a greate length..to bee royall deintie geare. **1601** SHAKS. *Twel. N.* II. iii. 187 Sport royall I warrant you. **1607** —— *Timon* III. vi. 56 Royall Cheare, I warrant you. **1652** CRASHAW *Carmen Deo Nostro* Wks. (1904) 247 Rich, Royall food! Bountyfull Bread! **1702** N. ROWE *Tamerlane* IV. i. 1614 Is this the Royal Usage, thou didst boast? **1835** [see WE *pron.* 2 a]. **1931** *N. & Q.* 6 June 414/1 The writer uses 'we' throughout—rather unfortunately, as one is sometimes in doubt whether it is a sort of 'royal' plural, indicating only himself, or denotes himself and companions. **1960** J. RAE *Custard Boys* II. xv. 175 'In the absence of the accused we will continue with the trial.'.. He used the royal 'we', but he spoke for us all. **1964** R. H. ROBINS *Gen. Linguistics* vii. 287 Somewhat similar is the use of the 'royal *we*'; in strictly ceremonial circumstances reigning sovereigns in some countries (of which Great Britain is one) use what are otherwise first person plural pronouns in reference to themselves in their official or constitutional capacity. **1966** J. CLEARY *High Commissioner* ii. 26 'May we ask whom you wish to see?' Monarchs and butlers, Malone thought: who else has the right to speak in the royal plural? **1975** M. BABSON *There must be Some Mistake* i. 1 '*We* simply can't take it in,' Lydia drawled, her '*we*' not only royal, but universal.

b. Finely arrayed; resplendent; grand or imposing.

c **1420** *Anturs of Arth.* 332 All þat royalle rowte to þe qwene ryds. *c* **1440** *York Myst.* xvii. 43 A sodayne sight was till vs sente, A royall sterne þat rose or day Before vs on the firmament. **1500-20** DUNBAR *Poems* lxxvii. 53 Thair lady.. was convoyed with ane royall routt Off gryt barrounes. **1613** SHAKS. *Hen. VIII*, IV. i. 37 A Royall Traine beleeue me. **1871** R. BROWNING *Pr. Hohenstiel* 1143 Those happy heights where many a cloud Combined to give you birth and bid you be The royalest of rivers. **1892** SLADEN *Japs at Home* xxvi, Nikko with its..awestruck pilgrims, and its shrines, royal of the royal.

c. Having rank comparable to that of a king. Also *fig.* (in quot. 1526 tr. Gr. βασιλικός).

c **1386** CHAUCER *Sir Thopas* 136 And gestours for to telle tales..Of Romances that been Roiales [*v.r.* reales]. **1526** TINDALE *Jas.* ii. 8 Yf ye fulfill the royall lawe acordynge to the scripture which sayth: Thou shalt love thyne neghbour as thy silfe, ye do wele. **1593** G. HARVEY *New Lett.* Wks. (Grosart) I. 265 An immortall Memoriall as some noble and royall witts haue bestowed vpon the euer-renowned Lepanto. **1596** SHAKS. *Merch. V.* III. ii. 242 How doth that royal Merchant good Antonio? **1624** MASSINGER *Renegado* II. iv, Like a Royall Marchant to returne Your great magnificence. **1725** *Family Dict.* s.v. *Sweet-Basil*, It worthily deserving to be term'd a Royal Plant, from its fragrant Smell and great Vertues.

d. *colloq.* Noble, splendid, first-rate. Also (chiefly *U.S. colloq.*) used as an intensifier, freq. with ironic force.

1583 *Leg. Bp. St. Androis* 703 Ane porter..to the bischop his blissing gave, Betuixt the schoulders a royall route. **1853** KANE *Grinnell Exped.* xxx. (1856) 261 The wind blowing a royal breeze, but gently. **1883** F. M. CRAWFORD *Dr. Claudius* xix, And they cantered away in royal spirits. **1890** *Cent. Mag.* Nov. 105 The soldiers..have given to woman's loyalty and ministrations a 'royal three times three'. **1938** G. GREENE *Brighton Rock* III. i. 99 She remembered: a face in a bar. She had a royal memory. **1951** J. D. SALINGER *Catcher in Rye* iv. 27 He gave out a big yawn while he said that. Which is something that gives me a royal pain in the ass. I mean if someone *yawns* right while they're asking you to do them a goddam favor. **1960** WENTWORTH & FLEXNER *Dict. Amer. Slang* 435/1 *Royal*... Used as a term of emphasis, esp. before taboo words and expressions, most freq. in 'a royal screwing'. **1972** *Dict. Contemp. & Colloq. Usage* 24/2 *Royal screw* (*fuck*),..an ultimate or complete put-down; total failure where success was expected; an unmitigated defeat or deception. **1976** *Times Lit. Suppl.* 9 July 841/2 Life principle Elspeth may be, but she is also a royal pain in the neck. **1977** C. MCFADDEN *Serial* x. 26/2 Kate had been Harvey's idea of a royal Bengal pain in the ass for the last year.

9. a. Of persons: Having the character proper to a king; noble, majestic; generous, munificent.

14.. LYDG. in *Pol., Rel., & Love P.* (1901) 52, I founde a liknesse depict vpon a wall, Armyd in vertues,..The hede of thre, full solempne and roiall, Intellectus, memorye, and resoune. **1594** SHAKS. *Rich. III*, I. ii. 245 That braue Prince, ..Yong, Valiant, Wise, and (no doubt) right Royal. **1601** —— *Jul. C.* III. i. 127 Cæsar was Mighty, Bold, Royall, and Louing. **1616** *Rich Cabinet* 54 Hee..can readily recount, what a royall house-keeper his great grandfather was in euery particular. **1861** MAY *Const. Hist.* I. i. (1863) 50 Louis the Great himself could not have been more royal:—he..felt himself every inch a king.

b. Said of animals or birds. (Cf. 13.)

c **1430** LYDG. *Minor Poems* (Percy Soc.) 23 The royall lyon lete call a parlement. *Ibid.* 151 The royalle egle with his fetherys dunne. **1562** LEGH *Armory* (1597) 60 Plinie writeth that the Cocke is the royallest birde that is, and of him selfe a king. **1873** BROWNING *Red Cott. Nt.-cap* 1404 A stag-hunt gives the royal creature law.

c. Of character, feelings, etc.

1565 COOPER *Thesaurus*, *Animus regalis*, a royal harte. **1600** SHAKS. *A.Y.L.* IV. iii. 118 'Tis The royall disposition of that beast To prey on nothing, that doth seeme as dead. **1625** K. LONG tr. *Barclay's Argenis* V. i. 325 It was the royallest bounty, to give presently. **1704** TRAPP *Abra-Mulé* III. i. 1060 Now you're indeed a Prince: 'Tis Royal Anger, But Threats do nothing. **1781** COWPER *Retirement* 774 No womanish or wailing grief has part, No, not a moment, in his royal heart. **1843** LONGF. *Spanish Student* I. i, Her step was royal,—queen-like. **1865** CARLYLE *Fredk. Gt.* V. XVIII. iii. 71 Pitt's bearing, in this grand juncture and crisis, is royal.

10. In various military and related uses, denoting something on a grand scale, or of great size or strength:

a. ***battle royal*** (see BATTLE *sb.* 3); also †***joust, siege, voyage royal***; ***royal war***.

c **1489** CAXTON *Sonnes of Aymon* xvii. 396 To see where he myghte best pitche his tentes and his pavylions, for to kepe sege royall afore the castell of Mountalban. **1494** *Lett. Rich. III & Hen. VII* (Rolls) I. 394 The justys roiaulx in the kyngis palaice of Westmester. **1594** SHAKS. *Rich. III*, IV. iv. 538 Away towards Salsbury, while we reason here, A Royall batteil might be wonne and lost. **1601** R. JOHNSON *Kingd. & Commonw.* 141 They are able to raise or vnder-take any voyage royall. **1602** LD. MOUNTJOY *Let.* in Moryson *Itin.* (1617) II. 214 Such necessaries as your Lordships were perswaded were onely fit for a more royall warre. **1672-1860** [see BATTLE *sb.* 3].

†**b.** ***army royal*** or ***royal army*** (see quot. 1731). ***camp royal*** (see CAMP *sb.*[2] 2 c). Also ***battalion royal***. *Obs.*

a **1548** HALL *Chron., Hen. IV*, 15 An armye royall appoyncted with all spede to inuade England. **1590** SIR J. SMYTH *Disc. Weapons* 10 b, They do discouer that they haue very seldome or neuer seene an Armie royall march in the field. **1602** MARSTON *Ant. & Mel.* III. Wks. 1856 I. 33 He who hath that hath a battalion Royal, armour of proofe. **1617** MORYSON *Itin.* II. 69 The weakning of the royallest Army that ever went out of England. **1728** CHAMBERS *Cycl.* s.v., A Governor who has the assurance to hold out a petty Place against a Royal Army. **1731** BAILEY (vol. II), *Royal Army*, is an army marching with heavy cannon, capable of besieging a strong, well-fortified city.

†**c.** ***royal bastion, fort*** (see FORT-ROYAL), ***parapet***. Also ***lists royal***. *Obs.*

a **1548** HALL *Chron., Edw. IV*, 8 The kyng..caused lystes royall for the champions..to be newly erected. **1642** HEXHAM *Art Mil.* (ed. 2) II. 54 A small Fort Royall, where the proportion of the Polygones are of 55, 50, or 45 rodd. **1665** SIR T. HERBERT *Trav.* (1677) 89, It is as Royal a Fort as any in India. **1704** J. HARRIS *Lex. Techn.* I, *Royal Parapet*, or, *Parapet of the Rampire*, in Fortification, is a Bank about three Fathoms broad, and six Foot high, placed upon the Brink of the Rampire. **1721** DE FOE *Mem. Cavalier* (1840) 183 Seven royal bastions, with ravelins and outworks.

d. †***cannon royal*** (see CANNON *sb.*[1] 2). ***royal mortar*** (see quot. 1867).

[*a* **1575** *Diurn. Occurr.* (Bann.) 330 Ane cannone ryell.] **1687** A. LOVELL tr. *Thevenot's Trav.* I. 8 Upon this Bastion there is a fair Basilick, or Canon-Royal. **1728** CHAMBERS *Cycl.* s.v. *Cannon*, Cannon royal;..Weight..8000*lib.* Length..12 Feet. **1867** SMYTH *Sailor's Word-bk.* 583 *Royal Mortar*, a brass one of $5\frac{1}{2}$ inches diameter of bore, and 150 lbs. weight, throwing a 24-pounder shell up to 600 yards.

11. a. ***royal paper***, † ***paper royal***, paper of a size measuring 24 by 19 inches as used for writing and 25 by 20 for printing. (Cf. RIAL *a.* 4.)

(*a*) **1497** *Naval Acc. Hen. VII* (1896) 128 A reame of paper roiall. **1529** in *Trevelyan Papers* (Camden) 139 To a Stacyoner, for vj bokes of paper royall. **1583** *Rates of Customs* D vj, Paper royall the reme. **1630** J. TAYLOR (Water-P.) Wks. (N.), His shirt may be transform'd to paper-royall. **1669** STURMY *Mariner's Mag.* v. xii. 63 Cartredges are usually made of Canvas and Paper-Royal. (*b*) **1578** in Feuillerat *Revels Q. Eliz.* (1908) 296, iiii quire of Royall paper. **1601** HOLLAND *Pliny* XIII. xii, That kind which was called Macrocola, or large Roiall Paper. **1659** GAUDEN *Tears Ch.* 45 As a church in folio; as a fair book of royall paper. **1710** ADDISON *Tatler* No. 216 ¶ 12, I bequeath my English Weeds pasted on Royal Paper. **1786** COWPER *Wks.* (1837) XV. 187 You will observe that they have all made the full payment, and all subscribe for royal paper. *ellipt.* **1712** *Lond. Gaz.* No. 5018/3 For all Paper called.. Royal fine.., fine Holland Royal.., Blue Royal.., Genoa Royal. **1855** R. HERRING *Paper & P. Making* 103 Middle Hand, 22 by 16;.. Royal Hand, 20 by 25.

b. Hence ***royal folio, quarto, octavo***, † ***sheet***.

1673 *Term Catal.* 7 Feb. (1902) I. 132 A new Map of England in a Royal Sheet. **1797** *Monthly Mag.* III. 59 It will be comprized in three or more volumes. royal quarto. **1873** MORLEY *First Sk. Eng. Lit.* (1892) 508 In 1611 he published, in royal folio, his Chronicle. **1877** *Quaritch's Gen. Catal.* 907 Cureton (W.) Spicilegium Syriacum.., roy. 8vo. cloth.

12. *Naut.* **a.** ***royal sail***, a small sail hoisted above the topgallant sail.

1769 FALCONER *Dict. Marine* App. (1780), *Boulingue*, the royal-sail. **1794** *Rigging & Seamanship* 135 *Royal Staysails* .. are the same as a top-gallant-staysail, only with one or two cloths less, and are hoisted next above them. **1858** *Merc. Mar. Mag.* V. 354 Royal and top-gallant sails in.

b. ***royal mast***: (see quot. 1867). Also ***royal pole*** (quot. 1899).

1794 *Rigging & Seamanship* 16 *Royal Masts* line similar to the stump-head of topgallant masts... They are seldom used. **1820** W. SCORESBY *Acc. Arct. Reg.* II. 197 It is usual to take down royal masts. **1867** SMYTH *Sailor's Word-bk.* 471 *Royal-mast*, a yet smaller mast, elevated through irons at the head of the topgallant-mast; but more generally the two are formed of one spar. **1899** F. T. BULLEN *Log of Sea-waif* 192 Like all American-built ships, we carried very long 'royal poles', or bare tapering extensions of the masts above the highest part of the rigging.

attrib. **1840** R. H. DANA *Bef. Mast* ii, I took my bucket of grease and climbed up to the royal-mast-head.

13. a. In names of birds, as ***royal cuckoo, duck, eagle***, † ***milan, tern, tody***.

1575 TURBERV. *Falconrie* 41 The Eagle royall, which is the yellow and tawnie Eagle,.. doth as muche differ from the yellowe Eagle, as the blacke Mylion doth from the Mylion Royall. **1728** CHAMBERS *Cycl.* s.v. *Eagle*, Eagle-Royal. **1787** LATHAM *Gen. Synop. Birds* Suppl. II. 349 Royal Duck. **1792** SHAW *Mus. Leverianum* 167 The Royal Cuckow (*Cuculus regius*). **1809** —— *Gen. Zool.* VII. I. 56 Royal Eagle, *Falco regalis*. **1811** PINKERTON *Mod. Geogr.* (ed. 3) 701 The brilliant plumes of the royal goose do not save it from destruction, the flesh being exquisite. **1812** SHAW *Gen. Zool.* VIII. I. 124 Royal Tody, *Todus regius*. **1872** COUES *N. Amer. Birds* 319 Royal Tern. Bill Orange. Mantle pearly grayish-blue.

b. In specific names of insects, reptiles, etc., as ***royal leopard, mantle; royal boa, python; royal monkey, tiger*** (see quots.); **royal antelope**, a tiny antelope, *Neotragus pygmæus*, found in forested areas of West Africa; **royal Bengal (tiger)**, an Indian variety of the tiger, *Panthera tigris*, distinguished by unbroken stripes.

For *cygnet* and *hart royal* see the sbs. *royal stag*: see ROYAL *sb.* 3 c.

1711 *Phil. Trans.* XXVII. 344 Two varieties of very curious English Moths, which for their Beauty and Spots are call'd Royal Leopards. **1771** T. PENNANT *Synopsis Quadrupeds* 28 Antelope.. Royal.. with very short strait horns. **1781** PENNANT *Hist. Quadr.* 200 Royal [Monkey]. A variety of a ferruginous or reddish bay color, which the Indians call the king of the monkies. **1800** SHAW *Gen. Zool.* I. II. 344 The largest are those of India, and are termed Royal Tigers. **1802** *Ibid.* III. II. 347 Royal Boa, *Boa Regia*. **1815** BURROW *Conchol.* 196 *Ostrea, Pallium*, Royal Mantle. **1832** RENNIE *Consp. Butterfl. & M.* 122 The Royal Mantle .. appears in July. **1871** E. G. E. WARD *Jrnl.* 3 June in D. P. Carew *Many Years, Many Girls* (1967) i. 52 One lady.. had arrayed herself in a complete suit of tiger-stripes.. so that she looked like a Royal Bengal. **1872** *Proc. Zool. Soc.* 639 The type of the former I believe to have been a genuine specimen of the Royal Antelope. **1876** *Nature* 14 Dec. 150/2 A Royal Python (*Python regius*).. from West Africa. **1964** L. S. CRANDALL *Managem. Wild Mammals in Captivity* 675 The royal antelope.. was represented in the Zoological Gardens of London in 1914. **1964** R. PERRY *World of Tiger* xv. 233 The.. very rare Royal Bengal tiger is distinguished by unbroken black stripes.

14. a. In plant-names, as ***royal bay, bracken, catch-fly, comfrey, fern, moonwort, palm***, † ***satyrion***, † ***standergrass, water-lily***. (See also OSMUND², PALMETTO b, PEACOCK *sb.* 6 b.)

1849 CRAIG, **Royal bay*, the plant Laurus Indicus, a native of Madeira. **1777** LIGHTFOOT *Flora Scotica* (1792) 653 Flowering Fern, or Osmund Royal. *Anglis.* *Royal Brachens. *Scotis.* **1882** *Garden* 28 Oct. 375/2 The *Royal Catchfly,.. also with scarlet flowers. **1725** *Fam. Dict.* s.v. *Plant*, In this Month [July] appear..*Royal Comfrey, Poppies. **1860** LOWE *Ferns* VIII. 7 The *Royal Fern, Osmund Royal, or Flowering Fern, is one of our handsomest British species. **1796** WITHERING *Brit. Pl.* (ed. 3) III. 763 Osmund Royal. Flowering Fern. *Royal Moonwort. **1890** *Cent. Dict.* s.v. *Palm*, *Royal palm, *Oreodoxa regia* of the West Indies and Florida. **1894** MAX O'RELL *J. Bull & Co.* 30 The well-named royal palm that raises its tall, straight trunk high into the air. **1578** LYTE *Dodoens* 226 The *royall Satyrions are found in certayne medowes and moyst woodes of England. *Ibid.* 225 *Royall Stander-grasse or Palma Christi. **1867** H. MACMILLAN *Bible Teach.* vii. (1870) 148 The gigantic leaf of the *royal water-lily of South America.

b. Applied to special varieties of fruit or vegetables. ***Royal Ann(e)*** (U.S.) a variety of bigarreau cherry, having red skin and white flesh, or a tree bearing fruit of this kind; ***Royal Sovereign***, a variety of strawberry or its large, early-ripening fruits.

1620 VENNER *Via Recta* vii. 128 The great Royall Walnut doth for wholesomnesse in all respects far exceed the rest. **1706** LONDON & WISE *Retir'd Gard.* 35 The Winter Royal Pear is of a new Date. *Ibid.* 38 The Royal Peach is of a middle Size. **1707** MORTIMER *Husb.* (1721) II. 148 In June and July come on the Royal Bellgards, or Fair Looks..: Others are called Imperial Lettices from their size. **1731** MILLER *Gard. Dict.* s.v. *Apple Tree*, Royal Russetting. *Ibid.*, Devonshire Royal Wilding. *c* **1814** *Edin. Encycl.* XI. 202/2 The Royal George is an excellent peach. *Ibid.* 209/2 The Royal russet, or leathercoat russet. **1892** *Proc. R. Hort. Soc.* XV. p. lxvii, First Class Certificate. To Strawberry Royal Sovereign (votes, unanimous), from Mr. T. Laxton, Bedford. **1897** S. T. WRIGHT *Fruit-Culture* xviii. 116 For early forcing, Royal Sovereign is a grand acquisition, as it is remarkably early and prolific, with large fruit of excellent quality. **1900** L. H. BAILEY *Cycl. Amer. Hort.* I. 293/2 The Napoleon Bigarreau (locally known as Royal Ann) is the ideal for a white cherry. **1930** V. R. GARDNER *Cherry* xiii. 111 The outstanding light-fleshed sweet cherry is the Napoleon,—also known as Napoleon Bigarreau and Royal Ann. Indeed it is the *one* white-fleshed sweet cherry of real commercial importance in the United States. **1941** M. L. SMITH *Going to God's Country* iv. 175 It was very beautifull with all the groves of tall fir trees and the Royal Ann cherys. **1946** *Nature* 6 July 24/2 The virus.. produces faint chlorotic spots on the leaves of Royal Sovereign strawberry. **1957** M. McCARTHY *Memories Catholic Girlhood* viii. 202 Two kinds of cherry trees, black and Royal Anne. **1960** B. K. WILSON *Lovely Summer* i. 11 Slade is going to pick the Royal Sovereigns this afternoon.

15. a. In various special collocations, as **royal antler** (see B. 3 b); **royal arch**, one of the degrees of freemasonry; **royal bark**, a variety of cinchona bark; **royal binding** (see quot. 1952); † **royal bob**, gin; **royal cocoon** (see quot.); **royal evil** = KING'S EVIL; **royal flush** (see quots.); formerly also = *straight flush* s.v. STRAIGHT *a.* 9 b; **royal icing**, a hard, shiny icing, the ingredients of which include egg whites; **royal jelly**: see JELLY *sb.*¹ 2; **royal pendulum, poverty, preventive, scamp** (see quots.); **Royal Scot**, a familiar name for the London to Glasgow express; also, the name of the class of locomotive designed to haul this train; **Royal Stewart (tartan)**: (see quot. 1975); also known as *dress Stewart* or *Royal tartan*; **royal stitch** (see quots.); **royal straight (flush)** in Poker, = *royal flush*; also *fig.*; **royal suture** (see quots.); **royal tennis** = *real tennis* s.v. REAL *a.*² 4 e.; **royal tine** (see quots.).

For *royal road* see ROAD *sb.* 6 c.

1849 CRAIG s.v., **Royal antler*, the third branch of the horn of a hart or buck, which shoots out from the rear. **1778** DERMOTT *Ahiman Rezon* 52 Having.. mentioned that Part of Masonry commonly called the *Royal Arch, (which I firmly believe to be the Root, Heart, and Marrow of Free-Masonry). **1823** (*title*), Laws and Regulations, for the Order of Royal Arch Masons. **1869** *Findel's Hist. Freemasonry* (ed. 2) 182 The Royal Arch Degree, now the fourth degree in England, is in its essential elements decidedly French in its origin. **1876** *Encycl. Brit.* V. 782/1 The yellow, *royal, or Calisaya bark.., the produce of *Cinchona Calisaya*. **1929** G. D. HOBSON *Bindings in Cambr. Libraries* 141 More *royal bindings were turned out at this bindery [*sc.* Samuel Mearne's] than at any other. **1939** *Guide Exhib. in King's Library* (Brit. Mus.) 119 The later royal bindings do not, perhaps, maintain the same high level of excellence. **1952** J. CARTER *ABC for Book-Collectors* 157 A book described as being in a 'royal binding' may be expected to have a sovereign's arms on one or both covers; but it must not necessarily be supposed that it therefore has a royal provenance. **1729** A. BLUNT in Tovey *Brit. & For. Spirits* (1864) 68 Well from thee may it assume The glorious modern name of *Royal Bob. **1770** in Masson *Chatterton* II. iii. (1874) 163 A person.. who had drunk so much royal-bob .. that she was now singing herself asleep. **1797** *Encycl. Brit.* (ed. 3) XVII. 485/2 The cocoons which are kept for breeding are called *royal cocoons. **1836** R. FURNESS *Astrologer* II. Wks. (1858) 150 With the Confessor, touch'd the *royal evil. **1868** W. B. DICK *Amer. Hoyle* (ed. 5) 177 **Royal Flush*, a Straight or Sequence, all of the same suit. *Ibid.* 178 *Straight Flush*, the same as Royal Flush. **1888** B. MATTHEWS *Pen & Ink* 197 The Straight Flush (called a Royal Flush when it begins with the ace and ends with the ten). *Ibid.* 198 The Royal Flush is not often seen; like other exalted monarchs it does not make itself common in men's eyes. *c* **1895** THOMPSON *Poker Club* 6 A Royal Flush—Ace, King, Queen, Jack (or Knave) and Ten Spot of the same suit. **1922** [see FULL HOUSE 2]. **1845** E. ACTON *Mod. Cookery* xvi. 423 (*heading*) Tourte meringuée, or, tart with *royal icing. **1974** *Times* 13 Nov. 12/5 Royal icing or glacé icing must be made with proper icing sugar. **1851-3** *Tomlinson's Cycl. Manuf. & Arts* s.v. *Horology*, The most important invention of this period was the anchor escapement... The seconds pendulum with this escapement was called the **royal pendulum*. **1726** BAILEY, **Royal Poverty*, a modern Nick-name for the Liquor call'd Geneva or Genevre, because when Beggars are drunk they are as great as Kings. **1858** MAYNE *Expos. Lex.*, **Royal Preventive*,.. Name of a quack lotion, being a solution of the acetate of lead. **1796** *Grose's Dict. Vulg. T.*, **Royal Scamps*, highwaymen who never rob any but rich persons, and that without ill-treating them. **1927** *Times* 27 Sept. 16/2 With the beginning of the winter train service yesterday the London, Midland and Scottish Railway introduced a non-stop run of 299½ miles... This run will be made daily by the 10 a.m. *Royal Scot from London to Carlisle, which proceeds to Edinburgh and Glasgow. **1933** *Triumph of Royal Scot* 16 The locomotive which hauled the train throughout the tour was LMS Number 6100 Royal Scot, the first of 50 locomotives of the Royal Scot class to be constructed in 1927. **1942** *Model Railway News* Jan. 9/1 The exhaust steam injector on the 'Royal Scot' was omitted on the model. **1953** *Manch. Guardian* 15 Aug. 3/3 Good fortune and the fact that all the coaches were of the new all-steel type reduced casualties when the Royal Scot was derailed near Abington last Saturday. **1977** *Times* 30 Apr. 12/3 On Monday.. the Royal Scot is making a celebration run from Euston to Glasgow —50 years.. after the first train of that name chugged its way out of London. **1783** P. POTT *Chirurg. Wks.* II. 184 The *royal stitch was performed in this manner: the intestines being emptied,.. an incision was made [etc.]. **1849** CRAIG s.v., *Royal stitch*, an old operation for the cure of inguinal hernia. **1842** J. S. STUART in *Vestiarum Scoticum* Pl. III (*caption*) The *Royal Stuart. **1855, 1969** [see HUNTING *vbl. sb.* 3 b]. **1975** J. SCARLETT *Scotland's Clans & Tartans* 94 The origin of the Royal Stewart tartan is unknown... There is no record of the Royal Stewart sett having borne that name before the nineteenth century—little that it even existed... General Stewart of Garth.. stage-managed George IV's visit in 1822 and costumed him in 'Royal Stewart'. **1895** W. STEVENS *Let.* 4 Aug. (1967) 7 Girls charming lots of money but am always open to engagements in finance where I hold a *royal straight. **1907** J. C. HARRIS in *Uncle Remus's Mag.* Oct. 28/3 The hand I've dealt to you is known as a royal straight flush, an' it sweeps ever' thing before it. **1962** R. COOK *Crust on its Uppers* iii. 40 They're all *diamonds*, ace, king, queen... Suppose he makes royal straight flush? *Ibid.* 41 He hasn't made royal straight. **1846** BRITTAN tr. *Malgaigne's Oper. Surg.* 416 The **royal suture*. For this the sac was exposed entirely; it was then raised and sewn up by a suture. **1902** E. MILES *Racquets, Tennis, & Squash* v. xi. 270 *Note on the name 'Tennis'*.—In Tasmania the game is called *Royal Tennis; in England it is occasionally called Real Tennis; and in America it is always called Court Tennis. **1912** G. INGLIS *Sport & Pastime in Australia* xii. 175 Tennis—or Royal Tennis as it is often called in Australia—was first introduced into the Commonwealth by Mr. S. S. Travers about 1875... The Hobart court was originally built by Mr Travers as a private court. In 1882 it was taken over by the 'Royal Tennis' Club. **1965** *New Statesman* 6 Aug. 185/1 The royal tennis court, which is enclosed. **1977** *Times* 19 Aug. 12/8 Playing royal tennis at Hampton Court. **1882** *Jrnl. R. Soc. Bengal* LI. II. 44 Further up the beam is a third snag..; this snag.. I take to be analogous to the *royal tine. **1893** LYDEKKER *Horns & Hoofs* 270 The royal tine is properly the same as the trez-tine.

b. Following the sb., as ***cement, cider, purl royal***; † ***metre royal*** = ***rhyme royal*** (RHYME *sb.* 2 c).

1548 W. FORREST in *Starkey's England* p. lxxxiii, A notable warke.. composed of late in meatre royall by.. sir William forrest preeiste. **1684** HAINES (*title*), Aphorisms upon The New Way of Improving Cyder, or making Cyder-Royal. **1707** MORTIMER *Husb.* (1721) II. 341 By adding Wormwood to Cyder-Royal.. you may make it as good.. as the best Purl-Royal. **1825** J. NICHOLSON *Operat. Mechanic* 767 A cement.., composed of 4 parts of bricks powdered..; of one part of green vitriol..; and of one part of common salt... It is called the Cement Royal.

c. With names of colours, as ***royal blue, green, purple, red***.

1661 COWLEY *Cromwell* Ess., Plays, etc. (1906) 374 And seventy times in nearest blood he dy'd.. his Royal Purple Pride. **1789** J. WOODFORDE *Diary* 9 Sept. (1927) III. 139, I took 2 Inside Places in the Royal Blue Coach.. to London. **1820** J. H. REYNOLDS *Fancy* (1906) 74 I'm an Officer,.. a sailor with old Jervis—A man of royal blue. **1835** FIELD *Chromatogr.* 111 Royal Blue is a deeper coloured and very beautiful smalt, and is also a vitreous pigment, principally used in painting on glass and enamel. **1881** C. C. HARRISON *Woman's Handiwork* I. 61 The cushion-cover.. has a ground of royal purple velvet. **1890** *Pall Mall G.* 2 Feb. 4/1 Purple, blood-orange, royal red, and sun colour. **1902** *Recipes for Colour, Paint, Varnish, Oil, Soap & Drysaltery Trades* i. 36 Royal Green. Prussiate of potash.. Sulphate of iron, [etc.]. **1913** C. L. UEBELE *Paintmaking & Color Grinding* x. 171 Foremost in the line of greens is what we [*sc.* Americans] call chrome green, which, however, is known on the other side as Brunswick or royal green, an intimate mixture of chrome yellow and Prussian blue. **1951** R. MAYER *Artist's Hand-bk. Materials & Techniques* ii. 60 *Royal green*, chrome green. **1956** G. DURRELL *My Family & Other Animals* 18 The endless, meticulous curves of the sea flamed for an instant and then changed to a deep royal purple flecked with green.

16. *Comb.*, as ***royal-chartered, -hearted, -sized, -souled, -spirited, -towered; royal-rich***.

1600 BRETON *Strange Fortunes of Two Princes* Wks. (Grosart) II. 27/1 This roiall-spirited youth.. fell thus to talke to himselfe. **1628** MILTON *Vac. Exerc.* 100 Whether thou be the Son Of.. Medway smooth, or Royal Towred Thame. **1785** *Hist. York* II. 110 The Company of Linen-Weavers, which is a Royal-chartered Company. **1833** TENNYSON *Palace of Art* 191 In this great house so royal-rich, and wide. **1836** J. H. NEWMAN in *Lyra Apost.* (1849) 118 Royal-hearted Athanase, With Paul's own mantle blest. **1883** J. PARKER *Apost. Life* II. 69 A great-hearted, royal-souled man. **1974** *Publishers Weekly* 26 Aug. 302/1 A royal-sized volume containing a spectacular gallery of 306 illustrations in full colour.

17. ***royal-cousin, -highness***, used as vbs., to address (one) by these titles.

1831 TRELAWNY *Adv. Younger Son* cxiii, De Ruyter bantered me about this Princess of Yug, and Royal Highnessed me unceasingly. **1875** TENNYSON *Q. Mary* III. iv, Their two Graces Do so dear-cousin and royal-cousin him.

B. *sb.*

1. † **a.** A king or prince. *Obs.*

c **1420** *Anturs of Arth.* 345 Scho rydes vp to þe heghe desse, by-fore þe royalle. *c* **1450** LOVELICH *Grail* lv. 260 Alle the Royalles Comen hem vnto, and there to Ioswe diden they homage. *c* **1470** HARDING *Chron.* VII. viii, Hercules slough kynge Lamadone, And led awaye the royalles of the towne.

b. *colloq.* A member of the royal family; a royal personage.

1774 [see *sub-governess* s.v. SUB- 6]. **1788** MME. D'ARBLAY *Diary* IV. IV. 169 We were too soon for company, except the Royals. **1807** T. CHALMERS in Hanna *Mem.* I. 80, I was conducted..to a room through which the royals pass in their way to the drawing-room. **1894** *Westm. Gaz.* 30 May 6/1 Any allusion to the indisposition of a 'Royal' appears to be considered at Court a species of treason.

†**2.** The name of various coins. *Obs.*

a. An English gold coin: = RIAL *sb.*^{1} 3 a. *rose royal*, = ROSE-NOBLE.

a **1513** FABYAN *Chron.* VII. (1811) 655 This yere, was a newe coyne ordeyned by the Kynge, the whiche was namyd the royall, & was & yet is in value of .x. shillynges, the halfe royall .v. s. **1542** RECORDE *Gr. Artes* (1575) 197 A Royall containeth an Angell and a halfe, that is to say: 11*s.* 3*d.* **1608** MIDDLETON *Trick to Catch Old One* III. i, There's a brace of royals; prithee, help me to th' speech of her. **1642** ROGERS *Naaman* 392 As much as Crownes or Royalls out-bid brasse farthings. **1688** [see ROSE-NOBLE 1].

b. = RIAL *sb.*^{1} 3 b.

a **1513** FABYAN *Chron.* VII. (1811) 471 To pay for euerych of y^e^ sayd thre monethes...x. M. royalles of Fraunce, which at that tyme were in value after the rate of sterlynge money, euery royall .xxi. d. or .xiiii. sous Parys.

c. = REAL *sb.*^{1} 1, RIAL *sb.*^{1} 4.

1577–87 HOLINSHED *Chron.* III. 1211/1 Good store of Spanish roials of plate. **1608** WILLET *Hexapla Exod.* 693 Arias Montanus valueth the shekel at foure Spanish royals. **1653** MILTON *Lett. State* Wks. 1851 VIII. 306 The Damages..amounting to 298555 Royals ½ which is of our Money—74638*l.* 15*s.* 00*d.* **1719** DE FOE *Crusoe* I. 229, I found in this Seaman's Chest about fifty Pieces of Eight in Royals, but no Gold. **1755** MAGENS *Insurances* II. 43 We insure to you N upon Gold and Silver, Royals, and Pearls.

d. = REAL *sb.*^{1} 2, RIAL *sb.*^{1} 4 c.

1615 G. SANDYS *Trav.* 86 The Sultanies, and especially the Royals of eight,..is what they most seeke for. **1626** SIR R. COTTON *Sp. Alteration Coyn* in *Posthuma* (1651) 297 The said Royall of Eight runnes in account of Trade at 5.s. of his Majestie's now English money. **1634** SIR T. HERBERT *Trav.* 182 A Royall of eight, or foure shillings and foure pence.

e. A name projected, but not adopted, in Great Britain and Australia, for a decimal unit of currency.

1920 *Rep. R. Comm. Decimal Coinage* 11 in *Parl. Papers* (Cmd. 628) XIII. 467 The second scheme (Lord Leverhulme's) proposes the creation of a new unit of 100 halfpennies to be called a Royal. *Ibid.* 12 We must regard the halfpenny and Royal scheme as impracticable. **1962** A. C. AITKEN in *Listener* 26 Jan. 159/1, I would rectify this..by simply having a pound of a dozen shillings. I will call it a 'royal'—for that has the proper sound and connotation, and, besides, a stag of twelve points is a 'royal'. **1963** *Guardian* 6 June 11/2 The Cabinet decided today that Australia's main currency units will be the Royal and the Crown... The royal, equal to 10 of the present Australian shillings, will be subdivided into 100 cents.

3. †**a.** The second branch or tine of a stag's horn, lying above the brow-antler. *Obs.*

[*c* **1410** *Master of Game* (MS. Digby 182) xxiv, þe reals, þe whiche be þe secunde tyndes, be nere þe aunteleres. **1486** (see RIAL *sb.*^{1} 2).] **1576** TURBERV. *Venerie* (1908) 238 The lowest Antliere is called The Brow Antliere,..the next Royall. **1611** COTGR., *Surendouiller*, the royall of a Stag, the Beancler of a Bucke; the second branch on either of their heads. **1623** COCKERAM I. s.v. *Pollard*, Royall is the next [start] growing aboue the Broach.

†**b.** (See quot. 1576.) *Obs.*

App. a mistake on the part of Turberville.

1576 TURBERV. *Venerie* (1908) 54 This fyrst is called Antlier. The second Surantlier. All the rest which growe afterwardes, vntill you come to the crowne, palme, or croche, are called Royals and Surroyals. **1610** GUILLIM *Her.* III. xiv. 179 Skilfull Wood-men describing the head of a Hart, doe call the..*c*. Lowest antlier the Browanteliers, *d.* Next aboue therevnto the Bezanteliers, *e.* Next aboue that the Royall. **1627** J. TAYLOR (Water-P.) *Navy of Landships*, Wks. I. 93 As a Hart hath..the Antliers, the Surantlers, the Royals, the Surroyals, and the Croches.

1883 *Science* I. 181/2 The fourth and fifth [tines] correspond somewhat closely to the 'royal' and 'sur-royal' of the Wapiti.

c. A stag having a head of twelve points or more.

1848 QUEEN VICTORIA *Jrnl.* 18 Sept. (1980) 64 A magnificent stag, 'a royal', which had dropped, soon after Albert had hit him. **1857** Q. VICTORIA *Jrnl. Highlands* 6 Oct., He had very fine horns, a royal on one side. **1883** *Longman's Mag.* Nov. 74 A grand eleven-pointer, if not a 'Royal', standing out alone.

†**4.** *ellipt.* A royal boat or vessel. *Obs.*$^{-1}$

1632 J. HAYWARD tr. *Biondi's Eromena* 40 The Prince taking her for some Pirats ship..commanded the Galley-slaves of his Royall, to row amaine.

5. *Naut.* **a.** A royal sail. Also, a royal mast.

1769 FALCONER *Dict. Mar.* (1780), *Royal*, a name given to the highest sail..in any ship. It is spread..above the top-gallant-sail. **1798** CAPT. BERRY in Nicolas *Disp. Nelson* (1845) III. 50 It was necessary to take in the royals when we hauled upon a wind. **1834** CAPT. MARRYAT *P. Simple* (1863) 340 We clapped on the royals to follow her. **1840** R. H. DANA *Bef. Mast* iv, We spread more canvas than she did, having royals and sky-sails fore and aft. **1937** C. S. FORESTER *Happy Return* I. i. 10 He had..noted that the wind was from the west, and just strong enough to give the ship steerage way, with all sail set to the royals. **1970** *Parade* (Austral.) June 26/2 The ship must have sunk almost instantly because when she was found two days later, only the top of one of her royals was just visible out of the water.

b. *attrib.* (also for *royal mast*).

1839 *Knickerbocker* XIII. 42 Send him some ratlinstuff, so that he can set up brace-backstays abaft, and cross his royal yards, and call all hands up anchor. **1840** R. H. DANA *Bef. Mast* xiv, We were called up at night to send down the royal yards. **1841** —— *Seaman's Man.* 11 The royal shrouds..are fitted like those of the top-gallant masts. *Ibid.* 18 The royal clewlines are single. **1927** G. BRADFORD *Gloss. Sea Terms* 146/1 *Royal yard*, the next above the topgallant yard.

6. A kind of small mortar (see quot. 1802).

1790 BEATSON *Naval & Mil. Mem.* II. 78 The enemy, on their taking possession of Fort St. Phillip's, found..seventy mortars including royals and cohorns. **1802** JAMES *Milit. Dict.*, *Royals*, in artillery, are a kind of small mortars, which carry a shell whose diameter is 5.5 inches.

7. *pl.* **a.** (See quot. 1802.)

1762 *Cal. Home Office Papers* (1878) 168 The King approves of the succession in the Royals on Col. Masterton's retiring. **1802** JAMES *Milit. Dict.* s.v., The First Regiment of Foot..is likewise sometimes called *Royal Scotch* and *Royals*. **1840** GEN. MERCER in R. J. Macdonald *Hist. Dress R.A.* (1899) 53 The 1st Royals long retained their queues after every other regiment had discarded them.

b. (See quot. 1867.)

1867 SMYTH *Sailor's Word-bk.* 583 *Royals*, a familiar appellation for the marines since the mutiny of 1797, when they were so distinguished for the loyalty and steadiness they displayed. **1977** *Navy News* June 4/1 Next opportunity for the Hermes and 845 Squadron to work with the Royals was during Exercise Dawn patrol in the first weeks of May.

c. (See quot. 1893.)

1883 SIMS *How the Poor Live* xii, His big book with the list of the names of regular men, or 'Royals', open before him. **1893** *Labour Comm. Gloss.*, *Royals*, men who get the first chance of dock work, and, like a casual labourer, can be paid or taken on at any time, but receive no week's notice as permanent men do.

8. Short for *royal blue*.

1885 *Queen* 24 Oct. (Advt.), *Ladies' gloves*... Shades, Tan, Golden, and Royal. *c* **1900** in *American Mail Order Fashions* (1961) 30 *Sweater*, made with alternate stripes..of ..red and royal, or royal with red stripes. **1922** *Daily Mail* 11 Dec. 1 (Advt.), Beautifully made in Duvetyn or Monchon,..Black, Grey, or Royal. **1939** J. B. PRIESTLEY *Let People Sing* iv. 82 It [*sc.* a van] had been generously rather than neatly painted, in a manly scheme of crimson and royal. **1974** *Harper's & Queen* Sept. 35/1 Crêpe dress. Black, sand, mink, red, emerald or royal.

9. *ellipt.* for: **a.** The Royal Society. Also *attrib.* **b.** The Royal Show (of the Royal Agricultural Society).

1951 C. P. SNOW *Masters* v. 45 There's not been a day pass in the last three years when he hasn't reminded me that he is a Fellow of the Royal, and that I am not. *Ibid.* 49 He would not get into the Royal Society now. But as March came round each year, he waited for the announcement of the Royal elections. **1958** *Spectator* 27 June 829/2 The Royal is the shop-window of British farming. **1966** 'W. COOPER' *Mem. New Man* II. vi. 172, I was not agreeing off the cuff that Bill's getting into the Royal would necessarily enhance his prospects. **1975** *Country Life* 26 June 1676/1 Beneath the surface of a highly professional modern 'Royal', one may sense the old-time garden-party atmosphere... Verona and the Royal Show are each unique in their own way because they have evolved.

‖**royale** (rwajal). [Fr., lit. 'royal', in same sense.] = IMPERIAL *sb.* 8.

1842 W. C. MACREADY *Diary* 26 May (1912) II. 171 A middle-aged man..with moustache and royale oiled to points which curled up at considerable distance from his face. **1877** E. CREER *Lessons in Hairdressing* 95/2 *Royale* (or *Imperiale*), tuft of beard just below the under lip.

royalet ('rɔɪəlɛt). Now *rare*. Forms: 7 royalett(e, royallet, royolet, 7, 9 royalet. [f. ROYAL *sb.* 1 + -ET^1, perh. after F. *roitelet*.] A petty king or chieftain; a kinglet, princelet.

Used by several writers in the 17th cent., and revived by Southey and Landor in the 19th.

1650 FULLER *Pisgah* I. viii. 22 These royolets contented themselves, that their crowns..were as bright..as those of the mightiest monarchs. **1660** —— *Mixt Contempl.* II. xli. 60 King Hen. the Seventh was much troubled..with Idols, Scenecal Royaletts, poor, petty, pittifull Persons, who pretended themselves Princes. **1690** LEYBOURN *Curs. Math.* 460 b, Causing the Royalets to become Homagers to the Crown of England.

1808 SOUTHEY *Chron. Cid* 432 Royalets swarm in the barbarous ages of society. **1829** LANDOR *Imag. Conv.* Wks. 1853 I. 501/2 Defend me from being carried down the stream of time among a shoal of royalets. **1872** R. F. BURTON *Zanzibar* II. 63 At Kikuzu the caravan found a royalet,.. whose magical powers were greatly feared.

royalism ('rɔɪəlɪz(ə)m). [f. as next + -ISM, or ad. F. *royalisme*.] Attachment or adherence to the monarchy or to the principle of monarchical government.

1793 BURKE *Policy of Allies* Wks. VII. 133 Suspected of royalism, or federalism, moderantism [etc.]. **1795** *Ann. Reg.*, *Hist.* 99 Accusing them of inclining to royalism. **1814** W. TAYLOR in *Monthly Rev.* LXXIII. 51 Like Hume, he inspires pity for royalty, rather than royalism. **1865** MAFFEI *Brigand Life* I. 260 Royalism in this district is sometimes real fanaticism. **1891** *Spectator* 11 July, That is the very essence, not of royalism,..new or old, but of modern democracy.

royalist ('rɔɪəlɪst). Also 7 royallist. [f. ROYAL *a.* + -IST, or ad. F. *royaliste* (1611 Cotgr.).]

1. A supporter or adherent of the sovereign or the sovereign's rights, esp. in times of civil war, rebellion, or secession; a king's man; a monarchist; *spec.* in Canada, a United Empire Loyalist (see LOYALIST).

1643 PRYNNE *Sov. Power Parl.* II. 12 His Majesty and all Royalists must necessarily yeeld, that the Ports, Forts, Navy,..are not his, but the Kingdomes in point of right. **1651** *Nicholas Papers* (Camden) I. 278 There are abundance of Royalists gone for England from these parts and many more are going. **1737** *Gentl. Mag.* VII. 166/1 Notwithstanding what may be urg'd in his Favour as a Royalist. **1785** R. HUNTER *Quebec to Carolina* (1943) 65 The Royalists have settlements along Lake St. Francis and up to Cataraqui. **1812** *Ann. Reg.*, *Hist.* 209 He appears to have made no effectual resistance to the progress of the royalists. **1860** MOTLEY *Netherl.* v. I. 154 Of the royalists a single man was killed. **1972** J. MOSHER *Some would call it Adultery* IV. xxi. 176 'Oh, a Royalist, eh?' said the admiral, using the Yankee term for United Empire Loyalist, as they were known in Canada.

transf. **1675** BAXTER *Cath. Th.* II. I. 295 He [i.e. the devil] will be..a zealous Royalist for Cæsar.

b. *attrib.* or as *adj.*

1817 LADY MORGAN *France* II. (1818) I. 237 In the course of the same evening; *assisting* at a *royalist* dinner, drinking *ultra* tea, and supping *en républicaine*. **1838** MILL *Diss. & Disc.* (1859) I. 289 This conflict between a Royalist education, and the spirit of the modern world. **1848** W. H. KELLY tr. *L. Blanc's Hist. Ten Y.* I. 293 Observing a royalist post, he advanced towards it alone. **1867** FREEMAN *Norm. Conq.* (1877) I. 228 Rheims was restored to the royalist Archbishop.

2. *nonce-use.* A Royal Academician.

1841 *Civil Eng. & Arch. Jrnl.* IV. 20/1 Such a squeeze of frames, as we invariably find in the Architectural Room of the Royalists.

Hence **roya'listic, roya'listical** *adjs.*

1802 W. TAYLOR in Robberds *Mem.* (1843) I. 411 Effacements both of royalistical and pietistical inscriptions. **1867** *Contemp. Rev.* VI. 43 We wonder at his royalistic zeal. **1891** J. K. CHEYNE *Orig. Psalter* VII. ii. 339 The royalistic form of the Messianic Conception.

†**ro'yality.** *Obs. rare.* Also 7 royallity. [f. ROYAL *a.* + -ITY, perh. after *regality*.] = ROYALTY.

1607 J. REYNOLDS *Haggai* viii. (1649) 94 Amidst his royallity, his goodly apparell, his golden chaines. **1652** H. L'ESTRANGE *Amer. no Jewes* 51 The Royality in Lacedemonia hath predominated both in War and Sacrifices. **1678** SIR G. MACKENZIE *Crim. Laws Scot.* II. xi. §3 It was found, that His Majesties Palaces..were in Law no part of the Regality, but off the Royality.

royali'zation. *rare*$^{-1}$. [f. next + -ATION.] Conversion to royalism.

1881 SAINTSBURY *Dryden* 13 The complete royalization of nearly the whole people.

royalize ('rɔɪəlaɪz), *v.* Also 6–7 roialize, royallize, 7, 9 royalise (9 *Sc.* -eese). [f. ROYAL *a.* + -IZE.]

1. *trans.* To render royal; to invest with a royal character or standing.

c **1590** GREENE *Fr. Bacon* ix, Rich Alexandria drugges.. Shall royallize the table of my king. **1629** N. CARPENTER *Achitophel* II. (1640) 122 Our Saviour.., whose least alliance could have royalized the basest family. **1647** N. BACON *Disc. Govt. Eng.* I. lxiv. (1739) 136 All the King's labour was to royalize Gaveston into as high a pitch as he could. **17..** *Winning of Isle of Man* in Evans *O.B.* (1784) I. 279 The princely garter.., An order..Which brave king Edward did devise, And with his person royalize. **1809** COBBETT *Pol. Reg.* XV. 102 We royalized the cause of Spain; we made it a contest between king Ferdinand and king Joseph. **1859** W. ANDERSON *Disc.* (1860) 34 When they shall be royalized and glorified in the Kingdom of their Father.

transf. **1861** *Medical Times* 20 Apr. 421/2 An antelope comes from the Queen, and Royalises the collection.

b. To render famous, celebrate.

1586 MARLOWE *1st Pt. Tamburl.* II. iii, For fates and oracles [of] Heaven have sworn To royalize the deeds of Tamburlaine. **1605** BRETON *Soule's Immort. Crowne* Ded., The Patrone of all vertue will so Royallize your praise in the Heauens. **1636** BALLARD in *Ann. Dubrensia* (1877) 35 To Royalize thy glory: The world turnes Chronicle, and speakes a story.

2. *intr.* To bear rule as a monarch; to play the king. Also with *it*.

1606 SYLVESTER *Du Bartas* II. iv. *Magnificence* 79 Even hee..must be both Just and Wise, If long hee look to Rule and Royalize. **1652** E. BENLOWES *Theoph.* VI. xxxv. 85 The glorious list Of heirs of God,..Who royalize it there by Grace's high acquist. **1819** W. TENNANT *Papistry Storm'd* (1827) 24 In elbuck-chair He sat and royalees'd it there.

Hence **'royalized** *ppl. a.*, **'royalizing** *vbl. sb.*

1651 N. BACON *Disc. Govt. Eng.* II. xxvi. 213 The Crown of England, for ever now made triple by the Royallizing of that of Ireland amongst the rest. **1660** MILTON *Free Commw.* Wks. 1851 V. 445 The new royaliz'd Presbyterians.

royally ('rɔɪəlɪ), *adv.* Also 4 roialliche, 4–7 -ally, 5 -aly; 6 royallie, -aly. [f. ROYAL *a.*]

1. With the pomp or splendour appropriate to a king or sovereign; magnificently, splendidly.

c **1386** CHAUCER *Prol.* 378 It is ful fair to..haue a Mantel roialliche ybore. *c* **1386** —— *Knt.'s T.* 1687 On huntyng be they riden roially. *c* **1420** LYDG. *Assembly of Gods* 1487 In a chayar, apparaylyd royally, There sate Dame Doctryne. *c* **1489** CAXTON *Blanchardyn* liv. 211 The beautifull Queene was royally led to and from the Church..by two Kings. **1508** DUNBAR *Tua Mariit Wemen* 72, I suld at fairis be found ..To schaw my renoun, royaly. *a* **1548** HALL *Chron.*, *Hen. VIII*, 73 All the..quadrantes, bayes and edificies, were royally entrayled. **1611** SHAKS. *Wint. T.* IV. iv. 603 It shall be so my care, To haue you royally appointed, as if The Scene you play, were mine. **1638** KNOLLES *Hist. Turks* (ed. 5) 52 Isaac.., royally mounted vpon one of the Emperors horses,..was by them brought from the temple to the court. **1812** *Examiner* 14 Sept. 578/1 His children were not royally brought up. **1864** SKEAT tr. *Uhland's Poems* 412 Around him he gazes, and ne'er can tire Of the pomp so royally bright. **1871** R. ELLIS tr. *Catullus* vii. 6 Where royally Battus old reposeth.

2. With the power or authority of a king; in a manner befitting a king.

c **1485** *Digby Myst.* (1882) I. 58 A-boue all kynges.. Royally I reigne in welthe with-out woo. *a* **1513** FABYAN *Chron.* VII. (1811) 258 Kyng Henry ouercame the Frenshe Kynge royally in bataylI. **1535** LYNDESAY *Satyre* 1712 Greit King Humanitie, That in my Regioun Royally dois ring. **1593** SHAKS. *Rich. II*, III. iii. 21 The Castle royally is mann'd, my Lord, Against thy entrance. **1795** SOUTHEY *Joan of Arc* I. 367 When Desolation royally careers Over thy wretched country. **1848** THACKERAY *Van. Fair* xxvi, George pooh-poohed the wine and bullied the waiters royally. **1885** *Mag. of Art* Sept. 452/1 His grandparents had a good right to leave their mark on the town. They conquered it right royally.

b. *colloq.* Gloriously (*drunk*).

1836 E. HOWARD *R. Reefer* v, Getting royally drunk.

3. With royal munificence or liberality.

1601 LD. MOUNTJOY in Moryson *Itin.* (1617) II. 134 If in those two kinds we be not royally supplied, men and money will serve us to little purpose. **1653** H. COGAN tr. *Pinto's Trav.* ii. 3 The soldiers considering how this captain entreated them very royally [etc.]. **1781** COWPER *Hope* 118 Bestow'd on man.. Royally, freely, for his bounty sake. **1865** KINGSLEY *Herew.* xxvi, Hereward is a man of his word, and pays his soldiers' wages royally.

†**4.** In a monarchical manner; monarchically.

c **1460** FORTESCUE *Abs. & Lim. Mon.* i. (1885) 110 Wereby it may appere.. that it was bettir to the peple to be ruled politekely and roialy, than to be ruled only roialy. **1600** E. BLOUNT tr. *Conestaggio* 250 They shoulde returne into Portugall more roially affected.

†**royalme.** *Obs.* Forms: α. 4–7 roialme (5 -elme); 4–6 royalme (5–6 -aulme). β. 4 roiame, 5 -aume; 4–5 royam(m)e, 5 -aume. γ. 5 royme. [a. OF. *roialme, roiaume* (mod.F. *royaume*), var. of *reialme*, etc. REALM. Cf. also RIALM.] A kingdom, realm.

α. *c* **1350** *R. Brunne's Chron. Wace* (Rolls) 14321 Al þe roialme was in speyr. *Ibid.* 14763 Þe seueþe roialme. **1389** in *Eng. Gilds* (1870) 23 Þe Roialme and holy chirche and here owen soules.. to reulen and kepen. **1422** tr. *Secreta Secret., Priv. Priv.* 135 That he be.. obeyaunte to the laue of god, and al his roielme. **1489** CAXTON *Faytes of A.* III. xix. 211 Noon ought to come within the roialme without a gode saufconduyte. **1512** *Act 4 Hen. VIII*, c. 9 Preamble, Henry the vij[th] late King of this Roialme of Englond. **1556** ROBINSON tr. *More's Utopia* (Arb.) 39 The whole royalme is fylled.. with hiered souldiours. **1606** HOLLAND *Sueton.* 5 The Alexandrianes had driven their King out of his Roialme.

β. *c* **1350** *R. Brunne's Chron. Wace* (Rolls) 1954 Als þe þre royames lys. *Ibid.* 14325 Constantyn.. tok hym þe roiame in kepyng. **1475** *Bk. Noblesse* (Roxb.) 7 To destroie Roiaumes and countreis by roialle gret power. **1493** HEN. VII in *Four C. Eng. Lett.* (1880) 9 To the subversion of this our royaume.

γ. **1474** in *Coventry Leet Bk.* 413 Concernyng the well of vs, oure Royme, and subgettes of the same. **1482** in Rymer *Fœdera* (1711) XII. 166/1 Gevyng to theym.. Auctorite to go and adresse theymself unto the Royme of Scotlond.

b. The kingdom *of* heaven or paradise.

1483 CAXTON *Gold. Leg.* 192/2 The royame of heuen is nyghe to them that doo penaunce. **1502** *Ord. Crysten Men* (1506) I. iii, The chirche of the royalme of paradyse.

royal oak.

1. A sprig of oak worn to commemorate the restoration of Charles II in 1660. Hence ***Royal Oak Day***, the 29th of May, Oak Apple Day. (Now only in local use.)

The name of 'the Royal Oak' was given to the tree at Boscobel in Shropshire, in which Charles II hid himself during his flight after the battle of Worcester in 1651.

17.. in Brand *Pop. Antiq.* (1777) 354 Royal Oak The Whigs to provoke. **1777** BRAND ibid. App. 353 Of Royal-Oak Day. **1853** *N. & Q.* 1st Ser. VIII. 490 Each young loyalist is armed with a nettle.. with which.. are coerced those unfortunates who are unprovided with 'royal oak'. **1884** *Folk-Lore Jrnl.* II. 382 Those who did not conform to the usages of the 'Royal Oak day' were pelted with rotten eggs.

b. (With capital initial.) The constellation *Robur Carolinum*.

1771 *Encycl. Brit.* I. 487/1 The new Southern Constellations... *Robur Carolinum*, The Royal Oak.

2. The species *Quercus regia*.

1841 *Penny Cycl.* XIX. 215/1 *Q. regia*, the Royal Oak. Leaves stalked,.. heart-shaped, wavy... From Koordistan.

royalty (ˈrɔɪəltɪ). Forms: 4–6 royalte, 5–6 -tee, 6 -tye (5 royalltye), 6–7 -tie, 6– royalty; 5 ro(i)alte, 5–6 roialtie. [a. OF. *roialté*: see ROYAL *a.* Cf. also REALTY[1] and RIALTY.]

1. a. The office or position of a sovereign; royal dignity; royal power, sovereignty.

c **1398** CHAUCER *Fortune* 60 Whi sholdist thou my Roialte oppresse? **1422** tr. *Secreta Secret., Priv. Priv.* 151 Of the roialte and riches of goode men comyth goodnys. **1526** *Pilgr. Perf.* (W. de W. 1531) 156 b, Though the kynge were before hym in his robes of golde, he wolde lytell regarde his royalte. **1595** SHAKS. *John* v. ii. 130 Heare our English King, For thus his Royaltie doth speake in me. **1605** CAMDEN *Rem.* (1623) 47 Vpon which name of Basilides, deriued from Basilius, signifying a King, he assured himselfe of royalty. **1704** TRAPP *Abra-Mulé* II. i, Exert your Royalty, and be your self. **1769** GOLDSM. *Hist. Rome* (1786) I. 39 Tarquin.. added also the ensigns of royalty, in imitation of the Lydian kings. **1813** *Ann. Reg., Hist.* 16 He might live many years, though incapable of the functions of royalty. **1860** RUSKIN *Unto this Last* (1862) 79 All true royalty is ruling power.

transf. and *fig.* **1844** KINGLAKE *Eothen* xvii, The Arab superbly stalking under his striped blanket that hung like royalty upon his stately form. **1873** HAMERTON *Intell. Life* x. ix. 382 The splendour of a recognized intellectual royalty.

†**b.** The personality of a sovereign; (his or her) majesty. *Obs.*

1581 DERRICKE *Image Irel.* D iij, Her Maiestie.., whose royaltie not only wisheth them good, but also doth them good. *c* **1590** GREENE *Fr. Bacon* ix, I came to have your royalties to dine With Friar Bacon here in Brazen-nose. **1611** SHAKS. *Wint. T.* I. ii. 15, I haue stay'd To tyre your Royaltie.

†**c.** The sovereignty or sovereign rule *of* (a state).

1592 *Nobody & Somebody* C iv b, Which of you will perswade my Elidure To take vpon him Englands royaltie? **1594** SHAKS. *Rich. III*, III. iv. 42 His Masters Child, as worshipfully he tearmes it, Shall lose the Royaltie of Englands Throne.

†**d.** Authority or warrant *to* do something. *Obs.*

1633 FORD *Broken Ht.* III. ii, Your fiery metal, or your sprignal blaze Of huge renown, is no sufficient royalty To print upon my forehead the scorn, cuckold.

2. a. Magnificence, pomp, splendour. ? *Obs.*

c **1400** *Sowdone Bab.* 54 He roode tho vppon a Foreste stronde With grete rowte and roialte. **1470–85** MALORY *Arthur* III. i. 101 And so they rode freshly with grete royalte.. tyl that they came nyghe vnto london. **1508** FISHER 7 *Penit. Ps.* cxlii. Wks. (1876) 249 Salomon in all his royalte was neuer cladde with so fayre a colour and beaute. **1594** PLAT *Jewell-ho.* I. 9 Nature, which dooth heere present hir selfe in all hir royaltie. **1642** J. EATON *Honey-c. Free Justif.* 465 Who is able to value the royalty of this marriage accordingly?

†**b.** *pl.* Royal qualities. *Obs.*[−1]

1586 T. B. *La Primaud. Fr. Acad.* I. 171 As manie as have written of the praises and roialties of that vertue.

3. Kinglike or majestic character or quality; greatness, lordliness; munificence, generosity.

a **1548** HALL *Chron., Hen. VIII*, 74 b, The Frenchemen made bokes, shewyng the triumphant doynges of the Cardinalles royaltie. **1605** SHAKS. *Macb.* III. i. 50 In his Royaltie of Nature reignes that Which would be fear'd. **1611** —— *Cymb.* IV. ii. 178 'Tis wonder That an inuisible instinct should frame them To Royalty vnlearn'd. **1629** GAULE *Holy Madn.* 102 In a certaine royalty of Speech. **1769** GRAY *Ode Installat.* 81 Profane thy inborn royalty of mind. **1836** LYTTON *Athens* (1837) II. 522 He ascribes her fears to the royalty of her spirit. **1878** SIMPSON *Sch. Shaks.* I. 51 A notorious spendthrift, without money of his own, but famous for his royalty to men at arms.

4. a. Royal persons collectively or individually.

1480 *Robt. Devyll* 496 in Hazl. *E.P.P.* I. 238 There lyeth the Duches of Normandye, With many a lorde of her counsell, Of all thys greate lande the royalltye. **1599** SHAKS. *Hen. V*, v. ii. 5 As a branch and member of this Royalty, By whom this great assembly is contriu'd. **1605** —— *Macb.* IV. iii. 155 To the succeeding Royalty he leaues The healing Benediction.

1743 R. BLAIR *Grave* 133 Proud Royalty! how altered in thy looks! **1752** MASON *Elfrida* let. i, Affections rais'd rather from the impulse of common humanity, than the distresses of royalty and the fate of kingdoms. **1809** MALKIN *Gil Blas* VIII. xi. ¶4, I had to beat the hoof so long, that I began to suspect.. royalty had gone another way. **1865** KINGSLEY *Herew.* iv, Treating him very much, in fact, as English royalty during the last generation treated another Irish bard.

b. *pl.* Royal persons; members of the royal family. Also *transf.*

1813 LADY BURGHERSH *Lett.* (1893) 51 They are just like the Windsor Royalties, for they literally know every thing. **1865** RUSKIN *Sesame* i. §42 If less than this, they are.. dramatic royalties. **1885** RIDER HAGGARD *K. Solomon's Mines* xvi. 269 This long line of departed royalties (there were twenty-seven of them).

c. *pl.* Anecdotes about royal persons. *nonce-use.*

1748 H. WALPOLE *Lett.* (1846) II. 221, I have told you royalties enough!

5. a. *pl.* Prerogatives, rights, or privileges pertaining to, or enjoyed by, the sovereign. Also rarely in *sing.*

? *a* **1400** *Morte Arth.* 4005, I salle neuer.. regnne in my royaltez, ne halde my Rownde Table. **1480** CAXTON *Chron.* VII. (1520) 85 b, Other royaltees that perteyne unto the crowne. **1585** ABP. SANDYS *Serm.* xv. 260 Forgetting quite the losse of all other royalties whatsoeuer, he maketh mone for nothing, but onely this. **1595** SHAKS. *John* II. i. 176 Thou and thine vsurpe The Dominations, Royalties, and rights Of this oppressed boy. **1623** BURROUGHS *Sov. Brit. Seas* (1651) 6 It were strange to thinke that Princes.. will relinquish the possession of those Royalties which they and their Ancestors have held beyond all memory. **1667** MILTON *P.L.* II. 451 Wherefore do I assume These Royalties, and not refuse to Reign? *c* **1670** HOBBES *Dial. Com. Laws* (1681) 75 The Wages heretofore shall stand, so as the Kings Royalty be saved. **1855** W. H. MILL *Applic. Panth. Princ.* (1861) 185 The heir to the deserted throne and lost royalties of David.

†**b.** *pl.* Emblems or insignia of sovereignty. *Obs.*

1607 R. C[AREW] tr. *Estienne's World of Wonders* 122 This iolly Iupiter clothed in his royalties. **1716** B. CHURCH *Hist. Philip's War* (1865) I. 173 He told Capt. Church, these were Philips Royalties which he was wont to adorn himself with when he sat in State. **1769** GOLDSM. *Hist. Rome* (1786) I. 39 He assumed a crown of gold.. and robes of purple. It was, perhaps, the splendour of these royalties that first raised the envy of the late king's sons.

6. a. A royal prerogative or right, esp. in respect of jurisdiction, granted by the sovereign to an individual or corporation.

1483 *Rolls of Parlt.* VI. 255/2 Seased of the Lordships and Mannours of Coverton, and the Roialtie of the Hundred of Penwith. **1576** in W. H. Turner *Select. Rec. Oxford* (1880) 383 The Maior and Burgesses of Oxon do stande so muche.. uppon theire right and royaltie of the Thames. **1634–5** BRERETON *Trav.* (Chetham Soc.) I. 151 Sir Henry Wallope.. hath a very brave command and royalty and revenue hereabout. **1708** CHAMBERLAYNE *St. Gt. Brit.* (1710) 333 Its Royalty was transmitted to Jedburgh, the Chief Royal Burgh of the Shire. **1767** *Ann. Reg.* I. 92 The bill for extending the royalty of the city of Edinburgh over certain adjoining lands. **1849** GREENWELL *Coal-trade Terms* 45 *Royalty*, the minerals, with the right of working them... Beneath copyhold land, the royalty is vested in the lord of the manor. **1878** STUBBS *Const. Hist.* III. xx. 433 The lordship of Man was accounted as a royalty and conveyed within the island itself certain sovereign rights.

b. *pl.* (In later use chiefly denoting rights over minerals.) Also *fig.*

1580 DEE *Diary* (Camden) 8, Sept. 10th Sir Humfry Gilbert graunted me my request to him made by letter, for the royalties of discovery all to the North above the parallell of the 50 degree of latitude. **1598** BP. HALL *Sat.* v. iii. 81 Buy out the remnant of his royalties. **1610** HOLLAND *Camden's Brit.* (1637) 589 The Kings authority hath.. abrogated all those royalties, prerogatives, and priviledges, which the Lords Marchers enjoyed. **1647** N. BACON *Disc. Govt. Eng.* I. xvi. (1739) 32 Mines of Gold and Silver, Treasure trove, Mulcts for offences, and other privileges, which being originally in the Kings, were by them granted, and made Royalties in the hands of Subjects. **1676** MARVELL *Gen. Councils* Wks. (Grosart) IV. 145 The sufferings of the Laity were become the royalties of the Clergy.

1855 MACAULAY *Hist. Eng.* xxi. IV. 647 With the property were inseparably connected extensive royalties. **1878** F. S. WILLIAMS *Midl. Railw.* 580 Landed proprietors here as elsewhere became anxious to lease their royalties.

c. A payment made to the landowner by the lessee of a mine in return for the privilege of working it. Also, a payment made, or a portion of the production given, by a producer of minerals, oil, or natural gas to the owner of the site or of the mineral rights over it. Also *attrib.*

1839 *Penny Cycl.* XV. 231/1 This payment, which is denominated 'dues' or 'royalty',.. is.. a matter of right, and claimed.. whether the mine is profitable to the parties working it or not. **1883** GRESLEY *Gloss. Coal-mining* 1 Royalty or rent paid by the lessee for working and disposing of minerals. **1896** B. REDWOOD *Petroleum* I. v. 250 Such leases are often transferred at a larger royalty, especially after the territory has been proved productive. **1949** *Our Industry* (Anglo-Iranian Oil Co.) (ed. 2) i. 8 Oil companies wishing to prospect in a foreign country have first to make an agreement with the Government of that country... This agreement determines the royalties payable. **1971** WILLIAMS & MEYERS *Oil & Gas Terms* (ed. 3) 390 The landowner's royalty is typically 1/8th of production.

attrib. **1892** *Daily News* 15 Mar. 6/1 The enormous royalty rents paid.. for the right to get coal. **1977** *Time* 5 Dec. 59/1 What had really blown was a giant natural-gas well that probably will make Lucy and her husband, Walter Parlange, royalty rich.

d. A sum paid to the proprietor of a patented invention for the use of it.

1864 in WEBSTER. **1879** *Cassell's Techn. Educ.* IV. 103 For share of royalties given by a foreign patentee to his agent in England.

e. A payment made to an author, editor, or composer for each copy of a book, piece of music, etc., sold by the publisher, or for the representation of a play. Also *attrib.*

1857 MRS. GASKELL *Let.* 26 Nov. (1966) 484 He was to have the sale of them for three years.. paying me a royalty of 3d on each copy sold. **1867** J. SPEDDING *Publishers & Authors* 25 In order to translate the substance of the bargain into a percentage upon the sale, (or a 'royalty', as we call it,) it is only necessary to divide the total estimated profit by the number of copies through the sale of which it is to be made. **1875** HARDY *Let.* 4 Nov. (1978) I. 40 Name of book. Copies sold in the half year. Retail price of same. 10 per cent royalty. **1880** *Scribner's Mag.* May 138 Houses which.. paid no royalty to authors. **1883** *Manch. Exam.* 22 Nov. 5/3 If people could not sing these songs in private houses,.. the publisher would lose his trade and the author his royalty. **1885** *Times* 3 April 4/4 Abt's compositions.. seldom rise above the level of what in England is called the 'royalty song'. **1894** *Daily News* 6 June 2/4 The royalties, that is to say the payments made during the year 1893 for permission to represent the play. **1974** R. RENDELL *Face of Trespass* iv. 43 He began worrying about his royalty statement. *a* **1976** A. CHRISTIE *Autobiogr.* (1977) VI. iv. 318, I had not kept any of the royalty statements sent me.

f. A periodic payment for the right or privilege of using another person's know-how under a know-how or trade secrets agreement.

1962 *Conveyancer* XXVI. 368 Some sort of lump-sum payment on the signing of the agreement will usually be appropriate, since it must be recognised that the seller runs a risk when he hands over the initial batch of information and documents. Beyond that, it is common to provide for some sort of royalty on turnover. *Ibid.* 369 The seller.. will be willing to accept a reasonably widely drawn royalty clause on the basis that if the seller's methods turn out to be usable.. they are certain to incorporate a good deal of indispensable information. **1973** J. P. CUNNINGHAM *Competition Law of E.E.C.* viii. 172 The know-how agreements between Happich and Gallino and between Happich and Maglum contained provisions requiring the licensees to pay royalties to Happich.

7. a. *Sc.* = RIALTY 2 c.

1597 SKENE *De Verb. Sign.* s.v. *Schireff*, The indwellers within the schireff-dom and royaltie thereof. **1765–8** ERSKINE *Inst. Law Scot.* I. iv. §7 Royal palaces, though locally situated in boroughs of regality, were adjudged to be no part of the regality, but of the royalty. **1839** *Blackw. Mag.* XLVI. 299 There are within the city of Glasgow, properly so called, technically named 'the royalty', one hundred and two thousand inhabitants. **1860** CAIRNS *Mem. J. Brown* vi. 179 All beyond the bounds of what is called the royalty were exempted.

b. A domain, manor, etc., in possession of royal rights or privileges. ? *Obs.*

1652 NEEDHAM *Selden's Mare Cl.* 94 For a man to bee forbidden to Fish before my Hous or Royaltie is the common custom, although grounded upon no Law. **1677**

PLOT *Oxfordsh.* 202 An ancient Custom of the Royalty of Ensham. **1710** STEELE *Tatler* No. 169 ¶ 5, I have bought that little Hovel which borders upon his Royalty.

c. *Mining.* (See quots.)

1867 W. W. SMYTH *Coal & Coal-mining* 120 The roads which should remain open as thoroughfares for the working of the distant parts of the 'royalty' or field of operations. **1883** GRESLEY *Gloss. Coal-mining* 207 *Royalty*, the mineral estate or area of a colliery, or a portion of such property. A field of mining operations.

d. *Ir.* (See quot.)

App. a nonce-use based on Ir. *Ráth na Ríoghradh* the rath of the royalty, a name for the rath at Tara (A. J. Bliss).

1893 W. B. YEATS *Celtic Twilight* 104 They came to a royalty (a name for the little circular ditches, commonly called raths or forts, with which Ireland is covered since Pagan times).

8. a. A royal domain; a kingdom, realm; a monarchical state.

1638 SIR T. HERBERT *Trav.* (ed. 2) 88 In quondam times her royalties were more spacious, as soveranizing over many Townes of quality a great way removed. **1727** DE FOE *Syst. Magic* I. ii. (1840) 38 This petty royalty,.. raised upon the foot of chance, rather than blood. *a* **1754** CARTE *Hist. Eng.* (1755) IV. 3 All republicks were formed upon the ruin of such little royalties. **1758** *Ann. Reg.* 6 She raised herself.. to an electorate, and at last to a royalty, not only in name but in power. **1878** STUBBS *Lect. Mod. Hist.* (1886) 204 The titles of the several royalties which thus came to an end were claimed.. by other competitors.

transf. **1812** SOUTHEY in *Q. Rev.* VII. 72 Each [raven] taking a particular district as their peculiar royalty.

b. Monarchical government.

1878 STUBBS *Const. Hist.* III. xviii. §365 The politic royalty of England, distinguished from the government of absolute kingdoms by the fact that it is rooted in the desire and institution of the nation. **1898** BODLEY *France* II. III. i. 1 While the Chief of the Executive has.. been called King or Emperor, there has been no royalty in France.

royd, *Sc.*: see ROYET *a.*

royd(e, obs. forms of ROID *a.*, RUDE *a.*

royed, *a. Sc.* [f. Gael. *ruaidhe* 'a defect in fir timber'.] (See quot.)

1870 SMITH *New Hist. Aberdeenshire* I. 348 The old larch trees.. are often found 'royed' or affected with heart rot.

† **'royet**, *sb. Obs.* Also 6 **royat**, 7 **roiot**. [App. an irreg. var. of RIOT, but cf. also OF. *ruit* noise.] Riot, extravagance, dissipation.

1567 J. MAPLET *Gr. Forest* 85 b, To the intent that their youth should keepe good rule and not go at royat. **1587** GOLDING *De Mornay* xv. (1592) 238 Now and then they passe their boundes, suffering their wits to runne royet. **1600** HOLLAND *Livy* XXXVI. xi. 925 The like roiot and loosenesse of life tooke hold of the rest of the Kings captaines.

royet ('rɔɪət), *a. Sc.* Also 8–9 **royit**, 9 **royat**, **roy't**, **royt**. [Cf. prec. and RIOT *a.*]

† **1.** Extravagant, nonsensical. *Obs.*$^{-1}$

1553 *Douglas' Æneis* VIII. Prol. 147 To rede I begane The royetest ane ragment with mony ratt rime.

2. Riotous, wild; *esp.* of children.

The synonymous *roid*, *royd*, may be a variant of this, but cf. also ROID *a.*

1737 RAMSAY *Prov.* (1750) 83 Royet lads may make sober men. *a* **1773** FERGUSSON *Elegy J. Hogg* xvi. Poems (1789) II. 84 Ye royit louns! just do as he'd do. **1819** W. TENNANT *Papistry Storm'd* (1827) 55 Wi' spraichs o' bairns, a royat pack, Loupin' and shoutin' at his back. **1865** G. MACDONALD *A. Forbes* 12 Believing that at last the awful something or other had happened to the royt lassie.

'royet, *v. Obs.* exc. *Sc.* Also 6 **royot**, 9 **royat**, etc. [Cf. prec. and RIOT *v.*] *intr.* To riot, be riotous, live riotously.

1591 LODGE *Catharos* (Hunterian Cl.) 20 Alcibiades may royot, Timon may curse, Diogenes may bite. **1824** MACTAGGART *Gallovid. Encycl.* 414. **1866** GREGOR *Dial. Banff.*

'royetness. *Sc.* Also 6 **royitnes**. [f. ROYET *a.*] Wildness; romping.

1513 DOUGLAS *Æneis* VIII. Prol. 177 Neuer word in veritie, but all in waist went, Throu royitnes and raving that mayd myne ene reyll. **1825** JAMIESON *Suppl.*, *Royetness*, romping.

† **'royetous**, *a. Obs.* [f. ROYET *sb.*] Riotous. Hence † **'royetously** *adv. Obs.*

1526 TINDALE *Luke* xv. 13 There he wasted his goodes with royetous livinge. **1536** LYNDESAY *Answ. King's Flyting* 48 Lyke ane boisteous Bull, ȝe rin.. Royatouslie lyke ane rude Rubeatour.

† **'royishly**, *adv. Obs.*$^{-0}$ (See quot.)

1598 FLORIO, *Alasgangherata*, lauishly, at randon, royishly, out of frame.

royl(e, obs. forms of ROIL *sb.* and *v.*

† **'roylet.** *Obs. rare.* [f. ROY *sb.*^{1} + -LET.] = ROYALET.

1658 OSBORN *Adv. Son* Wks. (1673) 215 Whether Inferiour Commonalties and small Roylets be not as great a Bar to an Universal Tranquility. **1685** COTTON tr. *Montaigne* I. 519 Cæsar calls all the Lords of France, having free-franchise within their own demesnes, Roylets.

royme, variant of ROYALME *Obs.*

royn, *a. Sc. Obs.*$^{-1}$ (Meaning uncertain.)

1513 DOUGLAS *Æneis* XII. Prol. 121 Gymp gerraflouris thar royn [*v.r.* thareon] levys vnschet.

royne. *Sc.* [Cf. ROON.] A strip of cloth.

1821 GALT *Legatees* vii. 199 An orthodox corn, or bunyan, that could as little bear a touch from the royne-slippers. **1823** —— *Entail* xxvii, A mahogany cradle shod wi' roynes.

royne, obs. f. RHINE^{1}, var. ROIN *sb.* and *v.*

roynish, -ous, varr. ROINISH, -OUS.

roynows, obs. f. RUINOUS.

royolet, obs. f. ROYALET.

roys, obs. f. ROOSE, ROSE.

roysche, obs. f. RUSH.

royson, obs. f. RAISIN.

royst, etc., obs. f. ROIST.

royster, var. ROISTER.

Royston crow ('rɔɪstən). Also 7 **Roiston**. [f. the place-name *Royston* on the borders of Hertfordshire and Cambridgeshire.] The hooded or grey crow (*Corvus cornix*).

1611 COTGR. s.v. *Corneille*, *Corneille emmantelée*, the Roiston Crow, or winter Crow, whose backe, and bellie are of an ashie colour. **1617** MORYSON *Itin.* III. 160 Crowes of mingled colour, such as wee call Royston Crowes. **1734** ALBIN *Nat. Hist. Birds* II. 22 The Royston Crow..; on the Heathes about Newmarket, Royston, and elsewhere in Cambridgeshire it is frequently seen in Winter Time. **1771** G. WHITE *Selborne* xlii, Royston, or grey crows, are winter birds that come much about the same time with the wood-cock. **1841** *Proc. Berw. Nat. Club* I. 253 The royston or grey-backed crow (*Corvus cornix*). **1880** BARING-GOULD *Mehalah* i, At all times they are haunted with sea mews and roysten [*sic*] crows.

royt, obs. var. ROIT *sb.* and *v.*

roytelet, obs. f. ROITELET.

royter, var. ROITER.

royther, obs. f. RUDDER.

roz (rɒz). Abbrev. ROZZER.

1971 J. WAINWRIGHT *Dig Grave* 79 Not that he gave a fart about the roz crowd. **1977** —— *Do Nothin'* v. 83 The roz has removed his helmet.

rozelle, var. of ROSELLE.

rozen, rozin, obs. ff. ROSIN.

rozener, var. ROSINER.

rozet, var. ROSET *sb.*^{2}

Rozinante, var. ROSINANTE.

rozye, var. of REZAI.

rozzer ('rɒzə(r)). *slang.* [Origin unknown.] A policeman, a detective.

1893 P. H. EMERSON *Signor Lippo* xviii. 87 If the rozzers was to see him in bona clobber they'd take him for a gun. **1903** A. M. BINSTEAD *Pitcher in Paradise* iii. 75 He.. nearly knocked down the rozzer in the mackintosh suit who was regulating the traffic from the middle of the road. **1936** M. ALLINGHAM *Flowers for Judge* xiii. 193 Aven't seen 'er since she went off with a rozzer. **1942** WODEHOUSE *Money in Bank* (1946) xiv. 126 You mean a rozzer? A detective? **1958** E. HYAMS *Taking it Easy* III. iii. 298 Then some nosy rozzer come up on a motorbike. **1962** R. GORDON *Doctor in Swim* v. 36 You can always try a bit of give and take with an English rozzer, and no hard feelings. **1977** 'E. CRISPIN' *Glimpses of Moon* xii. 236 The rozzers were after him, not a doubt about that.

r-process: see R III. 7.

-rrhaphy, formative element [ad. Gr. -ρραφία, f. ῥάπτειν to sew: see -Y^{3}], used to form words denoting surgical suturing of a wound or part, as *gastrorrhaphy*, *hysterorrhaphy*.

-rrhoea, -rrhea, formative element [ad. Gr. -ρροια (as in διάρροια DIARRHŒA, γονόρροια GONORRHŒA), f. ῥοία flux, flow], used in various medical terms, as LOGORRHŒA, MUCORRHŒA.

ru, obs. form of ROW *a.*, RUE.

Rualla (ruː'alə), *sb.* and *a.* Also **Ruála**, **Ruwalla**, etc. **A.** *sb.* A Bedouin people; a member of this people. **B.** *adj.* Of or pertaining to this people.

1831 J. L. BURCKHARDT *Notes on Bedouins & Wahábys* I. 6 *El Raualla*.. generally occupy the desert from Djebel Shammar towards the Djof, and thence towards the southern vicinity of the Hauran; but they frequently encamp between the Tigris and Euphrates. **1875** *Encycl. Brit.* II. 247/2 First, the Anezah clan, whose pasture-grounds extend from Syria southward to the limits of Jebel Shomer... Their principal subdivisions are the Sebaá on the north, the Woold-Alee on the west, and the Ruála on the south. **1888** C. M. DOUGHTY *Trav. Arabia Deserta* I. vii. 194 The poor man had been maimed thus by a Ruwàlla lance-thrust in the mouth, when riding in the North. **1917** [see HOWEITAT]. **1918** T. E. LAWRENCE *Lett.* (1938) 248 We decided to carry out a flying attack.. with our regular troops, the Rualla horse.., and such Hauran peasants as should be brave enough to declare for us. **1926** —— *Seven Pillars* (1935) III. xxx. 174 His was the chief family of the Rualla, but Nuri had no precedence among them at birth, nor was he loved. *Ibid.*, One of the chief men of the Ruwalla. **1959** W. THESIGER *Arabian Sands* iii. 54 In Syria I.. had visited the summer camp of the Rualla, a city of black tents.

ruana (ruː'ɑːnə). [Amer. Sp.] A type of Colombian and Peruvian cape or poncho.

1942 F. CARPENTER *Our S. Amer. Neighbors* iii. 63 Men and women dressed in elegant clothes.. meet Indians wearing native straw hats, and bright home-woven ponchos which are here called 'ruanas'. **1971** *Sat. Rev.* (U.S.) 31 July 55/2 'Knee-rugs' (about 38" × 54") which double for long skirts, ruanas, jumpers. **1974** *Times* 22 Aug. 9/3 Macindo .. [is] an ethnic shop specializing in the handwork of the Northern Andes... For the winter there will be heavier wool ponchos, ruanas and serapes. **1977** *Western Living* (Vancouver) Apr. 28/3 The women folk [in Peru], dressed in broad full length skirts, rainbow coloured *ruanas* (cape-like shawls) and a variety of masculine hats.

Ruanda, var. RWANDA.

rub (rʌb), *sb.*^{1} Also 6–7 **rubbe**, 7–8 **rubb**. [f. RUB *v.*^{1}]

1. a. An act or spell of rubbing.

1615 W. LAWSON *Country Housew. Gard.* (1626) 23 That no tree.. touch his fellowes... If they touch, the winde will cause a forcible rub. **1706** E. WARD *Wooden World Diss.* (1708) 96 It costs him many a Rub with his Paws, before he can make his Top-Lights to shine clearly. **1812** SIR J. SINCLAIR *Syst. Husb. Scot.* II. App. 13 It got a good rub of harrowing, so as to fill up the seams betwixt the furrows. **1839** URE *Dict. Arts* 597 For every six turns of circular motion, it must receive two or three rubs across the diameter. **1891** C. ROBERTS *Adrift Amer.* 138 By doing this the feathers all came off with a rub.

b. *spec.* The act of rubbing down a horse.

1662 *Dk. Newcastle's Racing Rules* (MS. Wood 276 a, fol. 149), The reliefe is to be onely water, the Rub but halfe an houre, and then the Judge is to bid them mount.

c. *Naval slang.* A loan *of.* Also const. *at.*

1914 'BARTIMEUS' *Naval Occasions* xxi. 193 'Don't you take on, Taff,' said another, pushing over his pannikin of rum. ''Ave a rub at this lot.' **1919** W. LANG *Sea Lawyer's Log* xiii. 162 'Innyone as hasn't had a letter can have a rub of mines,' says Moriarty, the big Irishman, generously. **1946** J. IRVING *Royal Navalese* 147 'The rub of a dollar' means the loan of a dollar. **1948** PARTRIDGE *Dict. Forces' Slang* 158 Give us a rub of five bob till pay day!

2. a. *Bowls.* An obstacle or impediment by which a bowl is hindered in, or diverted from, its proper course; also, the fact of a bowl meeting with such impediment.

In 16–17th cent. freq. in figurative contexts.

1586 HOOKER *Hist. Irel.* in *Holinshed* II. 97/1 Whereby appeareth how dangerous it is to be a rub, when a king is disposed to sweepe an alleie. **1593** SHAKS. *Rich. II*, III. iv. 4 *La.* Madame, wee'le play at Bowles. *Qu.* 'Twill make me thinke the World is full of Rubs, And that my fortune runnes against the Byas. *c* **1613** MIDDLETON *No Wit like Woman's* II. iii, There's three rubs gone, I've a clear way to the mistress. **1642** FULLER *Holy & Prof. St.* V. xix. 440 He would not.. lay the unexpected rubs in the allie to the bowlers fault, who took good aim though missing the mark. **1681** FLAVEL *Right. Man's Ref.* 196 It spoils their game by an unforeseen rub in the green. **1757** J. ABERCROMBIE in R. Rogers *Jrnl.* (1883) 73 It is impossible to play at bowls without meeting with rubs. **1876** *Encycl. Brit.* IV. 180/2 A 'rub'.. is when a jack or bowl, *in transitu*, comes in contact with any object on the green.

† **b.** In general use: Any physical obstacle or impediment to movement. Also *fig. Obs.*

1679 PRANCE *Add. Narrative* 16 A Bowl thrown from the Top of an Hill, leaps over all Rubs, Lets, and Impediments, till it comes to the bottom. **1715** DESAGULIERS *Fires Impr.* 59 Water.. passes along.. whilst it has no resistance before it; but if it meets with any rub, it spreads all round about. **1734** —— *Exp. Phil.* I. 220 The Pole [of a carriage] that bends sends back the Wheel a little when there is a Rub to be overcome. **1753** HOGARTH *Anal. Beauty* x. 61 The point of the pencil.. would perpetually meet with stops and rubs. **1760–72** H. BROOKE *Fool of Qual.* (1809) III. 131 Men.. who would be perpetually putting rubs before the wheels of good government. **1821** SCOTT *Kenilw.* xvi. There will be rubs in the smoothest road, specially when it leads up hill.

c. *rub of* (or *on*) *the green*, in golf, an accidental interference with the course or position of a ball. Also *fig.*

1842 in R. Clark *Golf* (1875) 140 The green has its bunkers, its hazards, and *rubs*. *a* **1875** *Ibid.* 276 Whatever happens to a ball by accident.. must be reckoned a rub of the green. **1881** FORGAN *Golfer's Handbk.* 35 Rub on the Green. **1931** *Times Lit. Suppl.* 31 Dec. 1048/4 If he is unfortunate in having finished his task before his problem was knocked completely out of shape by England's suspension of the gold standard, that is just the 'rub of the green'. **1962** *Guardian* 5 Nov. 2/2 If applications.. reached fantastic proportions, the Government would have to consider the matter. 'At present we treat it as a rub of the green.'

3. An obstacle, impediment, hindrance, or difficulty, of a non-material nature: † **a.** With addition of *in* (or *on*) *one's way*, *course*, etc. *Obs.*

Very common from *c* 1590 to *c* 1775.

1590 NASHE *Pasquil's Apol.* I. Wks. (Grosart) I. 214 Some small rubs, as I heare, haue been cast in my way to hinder my comming forth, but they shall not profit. **1599** SHAKS. *Hen. V*, II. ii. 188 We doubt not now, But euery Rubbe is smoothed on our way. **1621** BURTON *Anat. Mel.* III. ii. VI. v. (1651) 580 They are well inclined to marry, but one rub or other is ever in the way. **1641** SIR R. BAKER *Apol.* 115 The Clergie man hath.. many Imployments which are as rubs in his course of Learning. **1697** J. SERGEANT *Solid Philos.* 62 Some Rubs I have put in the way of this Pretence. **1728** VANBR. & CIB. *Prov. Husb.* II. i. 49 If it is not too far gone; at least it may be worth one's while to throw a Rub in his way. **1790** *Bystander* 25 If the sister throws any rub in my way, so much the worse for her.

b. In general use. Now *rare* or *Obs.*

Very common during the 17th and 18th centuries.

1607 Middleton *Michaelmas Term* iv. iii, I have no sense to sorrow for his death, whose life was the only rub to my affection. **1640** Sir K. Digby in *Lismore Papers* Ser. ii. (1888) IV. 135 Your father..is at euery rubb called vpon by the King, as yf nothing could be well done, that he did not dictate. **1686** Goad *Celest. Bodies* i. xviii. 116 We must look for some Rubs in pursuit of Natural Knowledge. **1724** Swift *Drapier's Lett.* iv. Wks. 1751 VIII. 354 Which is a great Smoother of Rubs in publick Proceedings. **1793** Smeaton *Edystone L.* §176 These unexpected rubs were not however insuperable. **1806** Scott 11 Feb. in *Lockhart* II. iii. 93 Notwithstanding some little rubs, I have been able to carry through the transaction. **1814** Lady Burghersh *Lett.* (1893) 179 We had then just heard of the rub which Sacken's corps, under Blücher, had received.

c. In phr. ***there's*** (or ***here lies***) ***the rub***.

1602 Shaks. *Ham.* iii. i. 65 To sleepe, perchance to Dreame; I, there's the rub. **1712** Steele *Spect.* No. 533 ⁋1 But her Relations are not Intimates with mine. Ah! there's the Rub. *c* **1769** Goldsm. *Epil. to 'The Sisters'* 11, I will. But how? ay, there's the rub! **1821** Scott *Pirate* xxxiv, Here lies the rub... When she hears of you she will be at you. **1887** Jessopp *Arcady* i. 28 Oh, the labour market! there's the rub!

†**4.** A roughness; an unevenness or inequality.

1605 Shaks. *Macb.* iii. i. 134 To leaue no Rubs nor Botches in the Worke. **1647** H. More *Cupid's Confl.* xxxii, Nor rub nor wrinkle would thy verses spoil, Thy rhymes should run as glib and smooth as oyl. **1682** Sir T. Browne *Chr. Mor.* ii. ix, Able to discover the inequalities, rubbs, and hairiness of the Skin. **1747** *Gentl. Mag.* 78 It may be drawn over a floor with such notches, or rubs.

5. a. An intentional wound or chafe given to the feelings of another; in later use *esp.* a slight reproof or teasing.

1642 Rogers *Naaman* 89 Both the former rubs, and this affront..wrought a marvellous abasement in his soule. **1677** *Govt. Venice* 277 They many times give them such rubs and mortifications, that they are quickly taken down. **1720** De Foe *Capt. Singleton* x. (1840) 182 You have always one dry rub or another to give us. **1780** Mme. D'Arblay *Diary* May, He failed not to give me a rub for my old offence. **1841** Barham *Ingol. Leg.* Ser. ii. *Auto-da-Fé*, Each felt the rub, And in Spain not a Sub Much less an Hidalgo, can stomach a snub. **1851** Mayhew *Lond. Labour* III. 135 Then I'd give 'em a rub up on the smoking mania. **1887** Service *Life Dr. Duguid* xvi. 102 She seldom saw me but she gied me a bit rub aboot Leezie.

b. An encounter with something annoying or disagreeable; an unpleasant experience in one's relations with others.

1645 Quarles *Sol. Recant.* ix. 48 Then chear, my soul; Let not the rubs of earth Disturb thy peace, or interrupt thy mirth. **1733** Miss Kelly in Swift *Lett.* (1768) IV. 41 Your friendship..makes me bear the common rubs of life with patience. **1766** Goldsm. *Vic. W.* i, We sometimes had those little rubs which Providence sends to enhance the value of its favours. **1822** Earl Dudley *Lett.* 23 Aug. (1840) 352 A man of business should be quick, decisive, and callous against small rubs. **1862** Thornbury *Turner* I. 336 The Téméraire had doubtless had its rubs as a French battle-ship. **1899** *Speaker* 29 July 106/2 His deanery palled on him..; its quasi-episcopal rubs and worries..were to him intolerable.

6. *pl.* = rubbers. *rare*⁻¹.

1799 *Young's Annals Agric.* XXXIII. 418 (E.D.S.), A complaint [in sheep]..called by the shepherds [in Suffolk] the rubs or rubbers, because of their seeming to rub themselves to death.

7. a. *dial.* A mower's whetstone.

1823 E. Moor *Suffolk Words* 321 *Rub*, the gritty, silicious aggregate with which the lusty mower whets his sythe. **1892** P. H. Emerson *Son of Fens* xiv. 110 Ha' you got a good old rough rub? My cutter is rather thick.

b. A plater's tool used for smoothing the silver.

1870 *Eng. Mechanic* 25 Feb. 573/1 We now come to the 'rubbing', which is a sort of burnishing with a rough burnisher called a rub.

8. A sound as of rubbing.

1907 R. H. Babcock *Dis. Lungs* xxvi. 511 If the chest be examined a friction-rub is likely to be detected on the side corresponding to the pain... The symptoms are the result of a dry, circumscribed pleurisy. *Ibid.* xxxv. 726 The so-called pleuritic friction sound or pleuritic rub..is a succession of fine crackling sounds..produced by the separation of the two pleural surfaces or by their rubbing together when rendered sticky. **1950** *Audio Engin.* Aug. 15/3 When the cause of the noise is mechanical, as in defective or ill-designed speakers, pickups and microphones, we may hear rattles,..rub, and wheeze. **1976** *Lancet* 13 Nov. 1083/1 Bronchial breath sounds and a pleural rub were present over the right middle lobe.

9. Special Combs.: **rub resistance**, the degree to which print will withstand rubbing without becoming smudged or detached; so **rub-resistant** *a.*

1958 E. A. Apps *Printing Ink Technol.* xxvii. 431 A high standard of rub-resistance is necessary in inks used for food cartons which are jostled in transport, and for display cards which are frequently handled. *Ibid.* 432 Inks which tend to give gloss and very level films are also usually fairly rub-resistant. **1967** E. Chambers *Photolitho-Offset* xvi. 240 Anti-driers retard drying on the machine and modifiers such as waxes and oils control setting, flow,..and rub-resistance.

†**rub**, *sb.*² *Obs. rare.* (See rub *v.*²)

1613 *Uncas. Machiav.* 9 At Ruffe and Trumpe note thou the dealers rubs. [**1613** *Answ. Uncas. Machiav.* F 2 For deale or rub, whose hap so ere it be to haue, The knaue of Clubs will euer be a knaue.]

rub (rʌb), *sb.*³ Abbrev. of rubber *sb.*² 2.

1830 H. Lee *Mem. Manager* II. vii. 28 Play an occasional rub or two at whist. **1859** Lang *Wand. India* 9 The good players are playing high..—five gold mohurs on the rub. **1887** Ashby Sterry *Lazy Minstrel* (1892) 139 We've heaps of friends, a quiet 'rub', A pleasant dinner at the Club.

rub (rʌb), *v.*¹ Also 4–7 rubbe (4 robbe), 5–6 rube, 6 roub. [ME. *rubben*, = LG. *rubben* (whence prob. Da. *rubbe*, Sw., Norw., and Icel. *rubba*): the further etym. is obscure.]

I. *trans.* **1. a.** To subject (a surface or substance) to the action of something (as the hand, a cloth, etc.) moving over it, or backwards and forwards upon it, with a certain amount of pressure and friction. Also with compl. (quots. 1377, 1697).

1377 Langl. *P. Pl.* B. xiii. 99 Þus sone þis doctour, As rody as a rose rubbed [*v.r.* robbed] his chekes. *c* **1440** *Promp. Parv.* 438/2 Rubbyn, or chafyn, *frico.* **1483** *Cath. Angl.* 313/1 To Rub, *fricare.* **1530** Palsgr. 695/1 Rubbe the chyldes heed, nouryce, to bring hym aslepe. **1553** Bale *Vocation* 35 b, A gentilman of the contraie..rubbed me on the elbowe and bad me..lete him alone. **1611** Bible *Tobit* xi. 12 And when his eyes beganne to smart, he rubbed them. **1678** Lady Chaworth in *Hist. MSS. Comm.* 12th Rep. App. V. 48 A wolfe's tooth..to rub his teeth with for easier breeding them. **1697** Dryden *Virg. Georg.* iv. 542 Th' officious Nymphs..rub his Temples, with fine Towels, dry. **1719** De Foe *Crusoe* i. (Globe) 244, I..caused Friday to rub his Ankles. **1826** F. Reynolds *Life & Times* I. 145 Sending our horses to the stables, and seeing them well rubbed, and fed. **1842** Tennyson *Day-Dream, Revival* 19 The king awoke,..And yawn'd, and rubb'd his face. **1875** Jowett *Plato* (ed. 2) I. 432 Socrates, sitting up on the couch, began to bend and rub his leg.

Prov. **1596** Spenser *F.Q.* iv. i. 40 My selfe will for you fight, As ye have done for me; the left hand rubs the right. **1652** J. Wright tr. *Camus' Nat. Paradox* ix. 196 In the Country, one hand rubb's the other as in Citties.

absol. **1662** *Dk. Newcastle's Racing Rules* (MS. Wood 276 a, fol. 149), There must be three heats, the first to Sparton-hill, there to rub halfe an hour.

b. To press (ears of corn) with friction between the hands, in order to extract the grain. (Cf. 11 b.)

1508 Dunbar *Flyting* 117 Fane at evin for to bring hame a single, Syne rubb it at ane vthir auld wyfis ingle. **1526** Tindale *Luke* vi. 1 His disciples plucked the eares of corne, and ate them, and rubbed them in their hondes.

c. To make (one's hands) move over and press upon each other, as a sign of satisfaction. Also *fig.*

1778 Miss Burney *Evelina* lxxxii, [He] rubbed his hands, and was scarce able to contain the fullness of his glee. **1831** Scott *Ct. Rob.* vi, He sighed and rubbed his hands with pleasure, like a man newly restored to liberty. **1893** Forbes-Mitchell *Remin. Gt. Mutiny* 220 Sir Colin..jumped to his feet, rubbing his hands. **1922** Joyce *Ulysses* 324 The *Times* rubbed its hands and told the whitelivered Saxons there would soon be as few Irish in Ireland as redskins in America. **1966** *Listener* 30 June 936/1 The British Government has invested half a million pounds on this display of international sport and the London hotel-keepers are rubbing their hands. **1973** *Times* 30 Apr. 5/4 Cloth manufacturers of all sorts must be rubbing their hands just now, because fashion definitely calls now for a greater volume of material per garment.

d. To press with friction against (a thing).

1821 Clare *Vill. Minstr.* I. 154 Idle cows rubbing the post.

e. *spec.* (See quot. 1861.)

1861 *Sat. Rev.* 22 June 647/1 These brasses are capable of being 'rubbed', that is, of having an impression taken of them..by covering them with paper, and rubbing with some fitting substance upon the paper. A likeness of the brass is thus produced, the plain portions being dark, and the incisions remaining..white. **1879** Westwood *Lapid. Walliæ* 157 She placed the stone in the south porch of the church, where I carefully examined, drew, and rubbed it.

2. a. To subject to pressure and friction in order to clean, polish, make smooth, or sharpen. Also const. *with*.

1382 Wyclif *Lev.* vi. 28 If it were a brasun vessel, it shal be rubbid, and washe with water. *c* **1386** Chaucer *Miller's T.* 561 Who rubbeth now, who froteth now his lippes With dust, with sond, with straw, with clooth, with chippes? **1526** *Pilgr. Perf.* (W. de W. 1531) 138 The more it is polysshed or rubbed, the more perfytly it receyueth the lyght. **1530** Palsgr. 695/1, I rubbe thynges with a cloute to make them cleane, *je torche.* **1601** Shaks. *Twel. N.* ii. iii. 128 Goe sir, rub your Chaine with crums. **1667** Primatt *City & C. Build.* 75 That this sort of work to be Rubbed..is worth thirty four or thirty five shillings a Rod. **1678** Moxon *Mech. Exerc., Handyworks* I. iv. 64 When you have occasion to take your Iron out of the Stock to rub it, that is to whet it. *a* **1756** Eliza Heywood *New Present* (1771) 252 To rub the stove and fire-irons. **1796** Morse *Amer. Geogr.* I. 491 They are kept very neat, being rubbed with a mop almost every day. **1843** *Penny Cycl.* XXV. 426/1 The two faces of the tool must be rubbed to such an obtuse angle as to appear almost straight. **1853** Kane *Grinnell Exp.* xxii. (1856) 172 The masses..have been rubbed as round as pebbles. **1861** Flor. Nightingale *Nursing* (ed. 2) 61 The old-fashioned polished oak floor, which is wet-rubbed and dry-rubbed every morning to remove the dust.

fig. **1749** Chesterf. *Lett.* cxlv. (1774) I. 398 You will now, in the course of a few months, have been rubbed at three of the considerable Courts of Europe.

b. *fig.* To revive, stir up, in respect of memory or recollection. More freq. with *up*: see 13 a, b, c.

1580 Lyly *Euphues* (Arb.) 248 If at our arriuall thou wilt renew thy tale, I will rub my memorie. **1622** Fletcher *Span. Cur.* ii. i, The Mony rubbs 'em into strange remembrances. **1634** Sir T. Herbert *Travels* 110 This would rub afresh his former iniustice..that all men might see apparantly his auarice. **1813** Scott 25 July in *Lockhart*, You should rub him often on this point, for his recollection becomes rusty.

†**c.** To examine closely. *Obs. rare.*

a **1614** D. Dyke *Myst. Self-deceiving* (1614) 340 To haue the conscience rubbed and ransacked. So that with Dauid it cryeth: Try mee, O Lord. **1653** Z. Bogan *Mirth Chr. Life* 21, I will not rub the questions whether these angells can contract themselves.

3. a. To affect painfully or disagreeably; to annoy, irritate. Chiefly in various phrases.

1523 [see gall *sb.*² 1 c]. **1581** Sidney *Apol. Poetrie* (Arb.) 44 Is it the bitter, but wholsome Iambick, which rubs the galled minde? **1604** Shaks. *Oth.* v. i. 11, I haue rub'd this yong Quat almost to the sense, And he growes angry. **1610** —— *Temp.* ii. i. 138 You rub the sore, When you should bring the plaister. **1660** R. Coke *Power & Subj.* 270, I have rubbed some sores which are not convenient to bee touched at this time.

1868 Whyte Melville *White Rose* II. v. 66 It is no unusual drawback to married life, this same knack of 'rubbing the hair' the wrong way. **1883** J. Hawthorne *Dust* xxviii, Philip..was always rubbed the wrong way by Lady Flanders.

†**b.** To impede, hinder. *Obs.*⁻¹ (Cf. rub *sb.*¹ 3.)

1605 Shaks. *Lear* ii. ii. 161 'Tis the Duke['s] pleasure, Whose disposition all the world well knowes Will not be rub'd nor stopt.

c. To chafe, abrade, make rough or ragged.

1805 *Naval Chron.* XIV. 331 She got a little rubbed. **1808** *Med. Jrnl.* XIX. 454 Where the vesicle from neglect has been much rubbed, or otherwise injured. **1880** J. Dunbar *Pract. Papermaker* 29 The continual vibration of the cover rubs the stuff.

4. To treat (a surface) *with* some substance (esp. in a soft or liquid form) applied by means of friction and pressure.

1535 Coverdale *Ezek.* xvi. 4 Thou wast nether rubbed with salt, ner swedled in cloutes. **1566** Drant *Wail. of Jeremiah* K iiij, Fayre Tsyons elders..sytte downe in silence deepe, Theyr heade yrubde with ashes pale. **1599** Shaks. *Much Ado* iii. ii. 50 A rubs himselfe with Ciuit. **1667** Milton *P.L.* i. 774 The suburb of thir Straw-built Cittadel, New rub'd with Baume. **1726** Leoni *Alberti's Archit.* I. 25/1 Beams made of..Thorn rub'd over with Oyl. **1799** *Med. Jrnl.* II. 42 The practitioner..directed him to rub every evening, a certain part of his body with the oxygenated ointment. **1847** W. C. L. Martin *Ox* 172/1 The affected quarter..should be well rubbed with a weak camphorated mercurial ointment. **1860** Tyndall *Glac.* i. xxv. 191 He continued to rub his hands with snow and brandy.

fig. **1663** S. Patrick *Parab. Pilgr.* xx, There is none but either commends a vice, or impresses it on us, or secretly rubs us with it.

5. a. To bring into contact with another body or surface by means of friction accompanied with pressure. Const. *against*, *on*, *over*, and *together*. Joc. phr. ***not to have two pennies to rub together***, and varr., expressing lack of money or poverty.

c **1400** Maundev. (Roxb.) xvii. 80 Rubbe it on þe saphir or on cristall. **1523** Fitzherb. *Husb.* §18 The sheepe wylle rubbe them on the stakes. **1530** Palsgr. 695/1, I rubbe..one thynge agaynst an other, *je frotte.* **1565** Cooper *Thesaurus* s.v. *Frico*, To rubbe their sides agaynst the tree. **1697** Dryden *Virg. Georg.* iii. 401 He rubs his Sides against a Tree. **1774** Goldsm. *Nat. Hist.* (1776) VII. 334 Others are of opinion the sound is produced by rubbing its hinder legs against each other. **1811** Thomson *Lond. Disp.* (1818) 547 Rub them together until the globules disappear. **1847** W. C. L. Martin *Ox* 161/1 The tormented animal rubs itself against posts, palings, gates, or the boles of trees. **1863** Geo. Eliot *Romola* xxvii, [He] closed his eyes and rubbed his hands over his face and hair. **1929** M. de la Roche *Whiteoaks* vii. 98 George, like Finch, was always hard up. Sometimes they had not between them two coins to rub together. **1977** K. O'Hara *Ghost of T. Penry* xvii. 172 I've known Mrs Bathhurst without two pennies to rub together, and always..concerned about others.

b. To bring (a part of the body) into reciprocal contact; hence ***to rub shoulders*** (etc.) ***with***, to come into contact, to associate, *with* others. Also ***to rub elbows*** (***with***) (chiefly *U.S.*).

1645 Rutherford *Tryal & Tri. Faith* (1845) 4 We cannot but rub skins with corruption. **1834** *Tait's Mag.* I. 39/2 Against how many hundreds a-day does not such a thing rub shoulders. **1848** Thackeray *Bk. Snobs* xxv, She had rubbed shoulders with the great. **1851** Carlyle *Life J. Sterling* i. viii. 74 One right peal of concrete laughter at some convicted flesh-and-blood absurdity, one burst of noble indignation at some injustice or depravity, rubbing elbows with us on this solid Earth. **1863** *Sat. Rev.* 4 April 437 The river is wide enough..to allow..steamboats to keep within view of the race without absolutely rubbing sides. **1906** U. Sinclair *Jungle* xxvi. 327 Young white girls from the country rubbing elbows with big buck Negroes with daggers in their boots. **1916** L. N. Parker *Disraeli* ii. 56 You would pass him in the street without the faintest idea you had rubbed elbows with one of the world's greatest powers! **1922** Joyce *Ulysses* 497 Have we cold feet about the cosmos? No... You have that something within, the higher self. You can rub shoulders with a Jesus, a Gautama, an Ingersoll. **1946** Mezzrow & Wolfe *Really Blues* ii. 21, I got my kicks out of rubbing elbows with all those bigtime gamblers. **1956** B. Holiday *Lady sings Blues* (1973) i. 8 A whorehouse was about the only place where black and white folks could meet in any natural way. They damn well couldn't rub elbows in the churches. **1961** in Webster s.v. *rub* vb., Reports on social products rub shoulders with book reviews and notes. **1976** E. Maclaren *Nature of Belief* iii. 20 I'm rubbing shoulders with questions of religious philosophy all the time. **1979** *Yale Alumni Mag.* Apr. (Suppl.) cn20/3 As a piano played show tunes of the 1930's, Teng rubbed elbows with George Weyerhauser of the Weyerhauser Co.

†**c.** *fig.* To fix (a charge, etc.) *on* one. *Obs.*

1618 Abp. Spottiswoode in *Spottiswoode Misc.* (1844) I. 86, I feare it be the purpose of many to rubbe this waye vpon his Majesty the imputation of tyrannie. *c* **1690** J. Fraser *Mem.* in *Sel. Biog. Wodrow Soc.* (1847) II. 184 It offends God by rubbing a lie on him, and calling the work of his spirit a natural work.

d. ***to rub noses (with)***, to touch noses in greeting, in token of friendship. Also *fig.*

This custom was practised among Eskimos, Maoris (see HONGI), and elsewhere in the Pacific Islands. Among Eskimos it has practically died out.

1822 G. F. LYON *Jrnl.* 28 July (1824) vi. 247 When the principal [Eskimo dancer] had pretty well exhausted himself, he walked gravely up to him, and taking his head between his hands, rubbed noses with him amidst the plaudits of all present. **1832** A. EARLE *Narr. Residence N.Z.* 159 He..rubbed noses so forcibly with me that I felt his friendship for some time. **1858** R. M. BALLANTYNE *Coral Island* xx. 242 Tararo went up to Jack and rubbed noses with him... Seeing that this was their mode of salutation..we rubbed noses heartily with the whole party. **1891** *Guardian* 25 Feb. 312/2 Bringing the most different people to 'rub noses' with one another. **1945** D. LEECHMAN *Eskimo Summer* 240 Before they had much contact with white men, the Eskimos used to rub noses on meeting old friends after a protracted absence. **1964** MRS. L. B. JOHNSON *White House Diary* 15 June (1970) 169 Lynda Bird..had enjoyed Hawaii hugely, rubbing noses with Maori children. **1973** 'D. JORDAN' *Nile Green* xx. 82 He's got three daughters and an Eskimo au pair girl... It's all this rubbing noses... It gets him down.

e. ***to rub one's nose in it***: see NOSE *sb.* 9 e.

6. Const. with various prepositions.

a. To remove, take or clear away, *from*, *off*, or *out of*, by rubbing.

1508 DUNBAR *Flyting* 64 Wit and wisdome ane wisp fra the may rub. **1545** ASCHAM *Toxoph.* (Arb.) 109 Some wyth holdynge in the nocke of theyr shafte too harde, rub the skyn of there fingers. *a* **1676** HALE *Prim. Orig. Man.* IV. vii. (1677) 348 Mankind..never rubs the Corn out of the Ear. **1798** JOANNA BAILLIE *Tryal* IV. iii, Hav'nt you rubbed the skin off your shins, Sir Loftus? **1816** SCOTT *Old Mort.* xliii, Were he once rubbed out of the way, all, he thinks, will be his own. **1886** MRS. RIDDELL *For Dick's Sake* i, Before London..has begun to rub the sleepy dust out of her great eyes.

b. To reduce *to* powder by rubbing.

1726 SWIFT *Gulliver* I. viii, Some of his best Bisket, which rubbed to Powder,..was their constant Food. **1753** *Chambers' Cycl.* Suppl. s.v. *Copper*, This may be rubbed to powder. **1811** THOMSON *Lond. Disp.* (1818) 698 Rub them together to a powder.

c. To force *into* or *through*, spread *over*, a surface by rubbing. Also *fig.* (cf. 9 c).

1778 *Encycl. Brit.* (ed. 2) III. 2293/2 Covering it as thin as possible, and rubbing it into the paper with a leather-stump. **1843** R. J. GRAVES *Syst. Clin. Med.* xx. 231, I ordered the nitro-muriatic acid liniment to be rubbed over his chest. **1857** T. MOORE *Handbk. Brit. Ferns* (ed. 3) 26 Rub the soil through a sieve with half-inch square meshes. **1869** CLARIDGE *Cold Water Cure* 86 What pain will he not endure; what poisons swallow or rub into his flesh? **1879** H. JAMES *Bundle Lett.* No. iv, The other one rubs it into me too; but in a different way. **1894** *Athenæum* 10 March 316/2 The following lesson..cannot be too thoroughly rubbed into the present as well as the rising generation.

II. With adverbs.

7. ***rub away***, to remove by rubbing.

c **1400** *Rule St. Benet* 2275 þat whils scho rubes a-way þe rust, þe vessel fal not al to dust. **1481** CAXTON *Reynard* (Arb.) 106 It smerted so sore that he muste rubbe and washe it a way. **1893** J. ASHBY STERRY *Naughty Girl* vi, [She] tried to rub her tears away with the back of her hand.

8. ***rub down***: **a.** To clean (a horse) from dust and sweat by rubbing.

1673 [R. LEIGH] *Transp. Reh.* 101 Not that I would have him to do..so much as to rub down a bishops horses heels. **1693** STEPNEY tr. *Juvenal* VIII. 271 When his Fellow-Beasts are weary grown, He'll play the Groom, give Oats, and rub 'em down. **1779** *Mirror* No. 62, I just ordered my horse to be rubbed down. **1844** H. STEPHENS *Bk. Farm* II. 180 After the horses are rubbed down, the men proceed to the straw-barn.

b. To make smooth, to reduce, grind down, etc., by rubbing.

1794 *Rigging & Seamanship* 88 Rubber, a small iron instrument..to rub down or flatten the seams. **1850** TENNYSON *In Mem.* lxxxix, Ground in yonder social mill We rub each other's angles down. **1852** MRS. CARLYLE *Lett.* II. 175 He has rubbed it all down with pumice-stone. **1887** D. A. LOW *Machine Draw.* (1892) 3 The colour should be rubbed down in a dish.

c. *colloq.* To search (a person) by passing the hand all over the body and limbs.

1887 *19th Cent.* XXII. 487 The custom of 'rubbing down' each labourer as he passes the dock gates. **1903** W. B. NEVILL *Penal Serv.* v. 42 A man who had been in prison over a year, and who must therefore have been 'rubbed down' at least a thousand times.

9. ***rub in***: **a.** To apply (dry colours) by rubbing; to draw or sketch in this way.

1811 *Self Instructor* 556 Rub in your crayons according to their proper colours. **1857** J. H. STEGGALL *Hist. Suffolk Man* x. (1859) 166 To rub in the dead colour, and your own figure more particularly. *Ibid.*, And rapidly indeed did the facetious fellow rub me in, and make a good likeness of me. **1882** *Gd. Words* 604 Here again, while I am out-tackling, Crayon rubs in a few outlines.

b. To apply (an ointment, etc.) by means of continued rubbing.

1837 *Penny Cycl.* IX. 439/1 Having rubbed in the charcoal and oil. **1865** MRS CARLYLE *Lett.* III. 259 Geraldine rubbed it [the liniment] in for an hour. **1899** *Allbutt's Syst. Med.* VIII. 859 Chrysarobin is rubbed in for ten minutes.

c. *slang.* To emphasize or reiterate (*esp.* something disagreeable). (Cf. 6 c.)

1870 *Daily News* 26 May (Farmer), Rubbing it in well is a well-known phrase amongst the doubtful portion of the constabulary. **1897** KIPLING *Capt. Cour.* ix, Ye needn't rub it in any more.

10. ***rub off***, to remove by rubbing.

1591 SYLVESTER *Du Bartas* I. vi. 71 His Enemy..Hastes to some Tree..whereon To..rub-off his detested Zone. **1615** W. LAWSON *Country Housew. Gard.* (1626) 37 When he puts a bud in any place where you would not haue him, rub it off with your finger. **1655** FULLER *Ch. Hist.* III. 4 His Rythmes, which we here set down, with all the rust thereof, without rubbing it off. **1779** *Mirror* No. 3 Without any danger of this colouring being rubbed off. **1810** CRABBE *Borough* x. 82 We to our neighbours and our equals come, And rub off pride that man contracts at home. **1875** JOWETT *Plato* (ed. 2) I. p. xiii, Modern languages have rubbed off this inferential and adversative form.

11. ***rub out***: **a.** To efface, erase, obliterate by rubbing. Also *fig.* (chiefly *U.S.*), to wipe out, kill.

1567 MAPLET *Gr. Forest* 93 He rubbeth out the print of his bodie and steps. **1570–6** LAMBARDE *Peramb. Kent* (1826) 323 May we utterly rubbe out the old blemish. **1638** JUNIUS *Paint. Ancients* 208 The pencil doth sometimes help the art, as well by rubbing out what was painted, as by painting. **1679** V. ALSOP *Anti-sozzo* III. iv. 321 It's as possible..for the Leopard to rub out his Dapples, as for such an one to doe good. **1706** E. WARD *Wooden World Diss.* (1708) 41 Why should a Man rub out good Things, without a solid Consideration for it. **1819** SHELLEY *Peter Bell 3rd* VII. iii, Like one who rubs out an account. **1894** A. ROBERTSON *Nuggets* 179 There wasn't a figure in the landscape. She was rubbed out of the drawing.

fig. **1848** RUXTON *Life in Far West* i. 13 Five of our boys got rubbed out that time. **1890** 'R. BOLDREWOOD' *Col. Reformer* (1891) 303 You seem to have seen these poor fellows..just before they were rubbed out. **1936** E. AMBLER *Dark Frontier* vii. 111 Rovzidski rubbed out by Red Gauntlet mob... Government fail to take action against slayers. **1946** L. B. LYON *Rough Walk Home* 24 Again the random child by robot thumb Of war rubbed out. **1950** A. LOMAX *Mr. Jelly Roll* 220 The gangsters..had promised to rub him out if he didn't stop trying to hire away their star New Orleans side-men. **1957** WODEHOUSE *Over Seventy* xii. 125 The heavy goes to his asylum, and two months later is released as cured. Upon which, he dresses up as a Siberian wolf-hound and hurries off to rub out another citizen. **1961** B. FERGUSSON *Watery Maze* xiv. 333 The first task was to destroy the enemy's radar organisation, and the R.A.F. addressed themselves to the job of rubbing out as many stations as they could. **1979** E. NEWMAN *Sunday Punch* xxiv. 214, I learned what the man muttered when the fight ended and Aubrey was declared the winner. It was: 'That Philpott-Grimes. I maybe rub him out.'

b. To extract (corn) from the ear by rubbing.

1719 DE FOE *Crusoe* I. (Globe) 146 My Corn, which I always rubb'd out as soon as it was dry.

c. *Printing.* (See quot. 1888.)

1683 [see RUBBED]. **1787** *Printer's Gram.* 350 Before the Pressman goes to work, he rubs out his Ink. **1888** JACOBI *Printers' Vocab.* 115 *Rub out ink*, to rub by means of the brayer the ink on the ink table previous to distribution.

†**d.** (See quot.) *Obs.*

a **1793** J. PEARSON *Polit. Dict.* 50 *Rubbing-out*, a cursed hawking, and spitting, and shuffling of the feet, at any Member the House does not like to hear speak. Sir Joseph Mawbey was rubbed out the last Parliament.

12. ***rub over***, to go over (with the hand, a tool, etc.) in the process of rubbing.

1647 N. WARD *Simp. Cobler* 84, I come to rubbe over my work. **1778** *Encycl. Brit.* (ed. 2) III. 2292/2 With some fine-pounded charcoal..rub over the pierced lines. **1876** PREECE & SIVEWRIGHT *Telegraphy* 18 Zinc may be amalgamated by being first cleaned..and then rubbed over with mercury.

13. ***rub up***: **a.** To revive, recall to mind (some recollection, incident, etc.).

1572 BUCHANAN *Detection Mary Q. Scots* I j b, I had rathest rubbe vp the remembrance of that day quhen the Quene..came to the nobilitie. **1586** T. B. *La Primaud. Fr. Acad.* I. 673 We spake of it before, but we must of necessitie often rub up the remembrance thereof. **1603** KNOLLES *Hist. Turks* (1621) 596 Rubbing up the slaughters at Caire, Eubœa, Methoni, and Constantinople. **1647** N. BACON *Disc. Govt. Eng.* I. lxvi. (1739) 147 Then the Clergy rub up old sores, and exhibit their complaints to their holy Father. **1680** SIR C. LYTTELTON in *Hatton Corr.* (Camden) I. 232 If you have a mind to rubb up yͤ memory of yʳ old loves, I can help you a little in it. **1715** *Disc. on Death* 7 They..began to rub up their Memories of their past. **1827** SCOTT *Diary* in *Lockhart* (1839) IX. 126 We rubbed up some recollections of twenty years ago. **1840** HOOD *Up Rhine* 7 We rubbed up our old stories and old songs.

b. To refresh (one's memory, etc.); to make clearer or stronger.

1643 LIGHTFOOT *Glean. Ex.* (1648) 11 Moses..rubbeth up his faith againe. **1663** S. PATRICK *Parab. Pilgr.* 314 To rub up my memory and to fasten those things in my mind which hung loose before. **1778** MME. D'ARBLAY *Diary* 26 Aug., There can be no better house for rubbing up the memory. **1815** SCOTT *Guy M.* xxxix, An East Indian must rub up his faculties a little..before he enters this sort of society. **1818** LADY MORGAN *Autobiog.* (1859) 126, I..have begun a course of history, ancient and modern, to rub up my memory before I touch on classic ground.

c. To brush up, revive or renew one's knowledge of (a subject).

1775 SHERIDAN *Rivals* III. iv, I must rub up my balancing, and chasing, and boring. **1799** HAN. MORE *Fem. Educ.* (ed. 4) I. 232 Some profession, which should oblige him, as we say, to rub up his Greek and Latin. **1813** MACAULAY in Trevelyan *Life* (1880) I. 45, I shall have..to rub up my Mathematics. **1861** HUGHES *Tom Brown at Oxf.* xiii, On the whole, I must rub up my history somehow. **1884** RIDER HAGGARD *Dawn* xx, I shall be glad of the opportunity of rubbing up my classics a little.

absol. **1863** J. COLDSTREAM in Balfour *Biogr.* (1865) v. 190, I was far behind and very much needed to 'rub up'.

d. To mix or prepare by rubbing.

1697 DAMPIER *Voy.* (1699) 2 We..rubb'd up 20 or 30 pound of Chocolate, with Sugar to sweeten it. **1843** R. J. GRAVES *Syst. Med.* xi. 127 The camphor should be previously triturated..and the whole must be rubbed up into the form of an emulsion. **1873** E. SPON *Workshop Rec.* Ser. I. 3/1 No ink should be used except indian ink, rubbed up fresh every day upon a clean palette.

e. With *the wrong way*: (cf. 3 a). Also *ellipt.* without phr.

1862 H. AÏDÉ *Carr of Carrlyon* III. 55 Don't rub her prejudices up the wrong way,..if you can help it. **1882** E. W. HAMILTON *Diary* 31 Aug. (1972) I. 328 Lord Dufferin is half inclined to advise that we should concede this to them in order not to rub up the Sultan more than we can help. **1897** *Catholic Mag.* Sept. 169, I did not answer, for I felt completely rubbed up the wrong way. **1971** *Weekend World* (Johannesburg) 9 May 6/7 Judges, magistrates, prosecutors, defence lawyers treat everybody alike, but the minor officials sure know how to rub up a non-White.

f. To caress (a person) in order to excite him or her sexually. *slang.*

1656 R. FLETCHER tr. *Martial's Epigrams* II. 102 Me thinks I scarcely am wound up by thee..to the height of Venerie. ..Thus Phillis rub me up, thus tickle mee. **1937** PARTRIDGE *Dict. Slang* 710/2 *Rub up*,..so to caress a person that he or she becomes actively amorous. **1939** JOYCE *Finnegans Wake* (1964) I. 203 Rubbing her up and smoothing her down, he baised his lippes in smiling mood.

g. To make clean, clear, or bright (again) by rubbing.

1847 C. BRONTË *Jane Eyre* III. viii. 183 My first aim will be..to *clean down* Moor House..; my next to rub it up with bees-wax, oil, and..cloths, till it glitters again. **1859** MRS. STOWE *Minister's Wooing* xviii. 179 He rubbed up his optical instruments to see whether they were rising in right order. **1886** F. R. STOCKTON *Casting away of Mrs. Lecks & Mrs. Aleshine* III. 111 In the mornin' I'll rub up that floor till it's as bright as new. **1974** A. ROSS *Bradford Business* 76 Even the short heavy bolts had been rubbed up with a wire brush.

III. *intr.* **14. a.** To exert or employ friction accompanied by pressure; to move and at the same time press *upon* or *against* something.

c **1330** R. BRUNNE *Chron. Wace* (Rolls) 8198 When þey hadde longe to-gyder smyten, Spatled, spouted,..rubbed, & brent. **1393** LANGL. *P. Pl.* C. x. 81 To karde and to kembe ..To rubbe and to rely. *c* **1460** *Stans Puer ad Mensam* 14 Byfore thy soueraуne cracche ne rubbe nought. **1580** BLUNDEVIL *Horsemanship* Xvij, If you see that..he [*sc.* a horse] leaue not rubbing, then marke in what place he rubbeth. **1615** W. LAWSON *Country Housew. Gard.* (1626) 23 If boughs or armes touch and rub,..they make great galls. **1660** F. BROOKE tr. *Le Blanc's Trav.* 320 Where the fish lye so thick, the ship brushes, and rubbes upon them as 'twere sayling through a shelf of sand. **1687** DRYDEN *Hind & P.* III. 132 This last allusion galled the Panther more, Because indeed it rubbed upon the sore. **1765** A. DICKSON *Treat. Agric.* (ed. 2) 189 The left side of the sock rubs upon the firm land. **1830** R. KNOX *Béclard's Anat.* 239 The fibro-cartilages which are met with wherever a tendon rubs against a bone. **1840** LARDNER *Geom.* 189 As the surface of the cylinder is prevented from rubbing or slipping on the surface on which it rests.

fig. **1887** O. W. HOLMES *Hundred Days Eur.* v. 191 It always rubbed very hard on my feelings.

b. Of a bowl: To encounter some impediment which retards or diverts its course.

1588 *Marprel. Epist.* (Arb.) 39 When Iohn of London throwes his bowle, he will runne after it, and crie rub, rub, rub. **1606** SHAKS. *Tr. & Cr.* III. ii. 52 So, so, rub on, and kisse the mistresse. **1611** COTGR., *Saulter*,..to rub (at Bowles). *a* **1700** B. E. *Dict. Cant. Crew*, *Rub-rub*, us'd on Greens when the Bowl Flees too fast, to have it forbear, if Words wou'd do it. **1770** J. LOVE *Cricket* 5 Where, much divided between Fear and Glee, The Youth cries Rub; O Flee, you Ling'rer, Flee! **1875** 'STONEHENGE' *Brit. Rural Sports* (ed. 12) 684 Every bowl which shall rub or set after it has run two yards past the parallel [etc.].

fig. **1609** *Ev. Woman in Hum.* II. ii. in Bullen *O. Pl.* IV, They rub at everie mole-hil.

†**c.** *fig.* To touch *upon* a thing or person closely or disadvantageously. *Obs.*

1628 LAYTON *Sion's Plea agst. Prelacy* (ed. 2) 27 This learning is not to be rub'd upon to boldly. **1637–50** ROW *Hist. Kirk* (Wodrow Soc.) 165 No more nor the miscariages of a man byassed can rub justlie upon an honest man walking straightlie.

d. ***to rub up***: to masturbate. *slang.*

1937 PARTRIDGE *Dict. Slang* 710/2 *Rub up*, the v. corresponding to *rub off*, 2 [*sc.* a masturbation]. **1963** C. MACKENZIE *My Life & Times* II. 115 Just as I was going down the steps into our area B—— asked me if I ever rubbed up... In bed that night I tried the experiment recommended by B——.

e. ***to rub off***, of qualities, etc.: to have influence *on* through close or continued contact; to be transmitted to others.

1959 N. MAILER *Advts. for Myself* v. 463 He spent years hobnobbing with gentlemanly shits and half-ass operators and some of it had to rub off on him. **1965** *Listener* 11 Nov. 761/1 There is no evidence that anything of Sickert's powerful teaching rubbed off on him. **1969** 'G. NORTH' *Procrastination of Sgt. Cluff* v. 44 How long was it since he'd begun to work with the Sergeant? How much of the Sergeant had rubbed off on him? Could he think any more except as the Sergeant thought? **1971** *Times* 9 Sept. 3/2 One hopes that something of their Christian charity and principles would rub off. **1976** E. MACLAREN *Nature of Belief* ii. 16 Jews come in contact with Zoroastrians and certain ideas rub off. **1978** *Jrnl. R. Soc. Arts* CXXVI. 185/1 Morale was lower, there was apathy and this was rubbing off on new entries.

15. *fig.* To continue in a certain course with more or less difficulty or restraint; to contrive, or make shift, to get *on*, *through*, *along*, live or last *out*, pass or go *off*, etc.

(*a*) **1469** *Paston Lett.* II. 392, I wyle rubbe on as long as I maye..tyll better pese be. **1611** COTGR. s.v. *Passer*, He hath goods enow to rub on, or to serue his turne, with. **1679** V. ALSOP *Melius Inq.* II. ix. 381 Whosoever shall teach us the Art to rub on with a doubting Conscience has paved a broad Causey for..his Holiness. **1704** F. FULLER *Med. Gymn.* (1711) 241 Most People are supinely content..to rub on in a Sickly Condition. **1776** FOOTE *Capuchin* I. Wks. 1799 II.

389 We be contented, Sir Harry, to rub on in our rust. **1846** J. G. LOCKHART 16 Dec. in *Croker Papers* (1884), [They] thought Government would rub on with this Parliament till August. **1880** MISS BRADDON *Just as I am* xvii, I hope we shall always manage to rub on somehow.

(*b*) **1570** FOXE *A. & M.* (ed. 2) 1892/1 He thus in great care and vexation endured.., rubbyng out as well as hee could. **1587** ROBT. MORTON *Let.* 17 June in *Cath. Rec. Soc. Publ.* V. 139 He is nott able to live havynge made harde shifte heare to rubbe owt this deare tyme. **1602** *2nd Pt. Return fr. Parnass.* I. iv. 429 Let vs proue Cony-catchers, Baudes, or any thing, so we may rub out. **1616** HIERON *Wks.* I. 586 A man makes a shift to rub out an houre, and to haue somewhat stil to say. **1670–98** LASSELS *Voy. Italy* II. 7 A poor widow of Rome..rub'd out poorly, but yet honestly.

(*c*) **1680** V. ALSOP *Mischief Imposit.* 103 Thus have I at length rub'd through the Reverend Authors Discourse. **1683** KENNETT tr. *Erasm. on Folly* 16 There is not any one Country whose inhabitants..rub through the world with more ease and quiet. **1706** E. WARD *Wooden World Diss.* (1708) 55 Having liv'd in various Regions, and rubb'd through many Callings. **1780** HAMILTON *Wks.* (1886) VIII. 6 We are entered deeply in a contest on which our all depends. We must endeavor to rub through it. **1815** EARL DUDLEY *Let.* 17 Jan. (1840) 85 Winter..he rubs through as well as he can by the help of patience and a cloak. **1849** M. ARNOLD *Resignation* 138 They rubb'd through yesterday In their hereditary way; And they will rub through, if they can, To-morrow on the self-same plan.

(*d*) **1818** W. IRVING *Life & Lett.* (1864) I. 396, I feel confident that I shall be able to rub along with my present means of support. **1851** MAYHEW *Lond. Labour* (1865) II. 555 It's got very bad now. I used to manage to rub along at first. **1888** BRYCE *Amer. Commw.* II. xliv. 156 The reason.. why the system..rubs along in the several States is, that the executive has little to do.

(*e*) **1784** MME. D'ARBLAY *Diary* 17 Jan., The evening rubbed on and rubbed off till it began to break up. **1818** SCOTT 14 Jan. in *Fam. Lett.* (1894) II. xiv. 4 The book is very well liked here, and has rub'd off in great stile.

b. Without const. *rare*$^{-1}$.

1706 ESTCOURT *Fair Example* v. i, Merrily is the word, and let the World rub.

16. To go, run, make *off*. Now *rare* or *Obs.*

c **1540** BANSLEY *Pryde of Women* in Hazl. *E.P.P.* IV. 238 Rubbe forthe, olde trottes, to the devyl worde. **1676** SHADWELL *Virtuoso* v, Who held my sword while I danc'd? .. A curse on him! he's rubb'd off with it. **1700** T. BROWN tr. *Fresny's Amusem.* viii. Wks. 1709 III. 82 He made a Dive into my Pocket, but encountering a Disappointment, Rub'd off, cursing the Vaccuum. **1710** *Brit. Apollo* No. 91. 2/2 Your..Club With ready Cash to Tavern rub. **1844** W. H. MAXWELL *Sports & Adv. Scot.* xxiii. (1855) 192 The curate ..left Æneas, and rubbed off in haste.

17. To bear rubbing; to admit of being rubbed (*off*, *out*, etc.).

1683 MOXON *Mech. Exerc.*, *Printing* xxiv. 389 When the Shank of a Letter has a proper Thickness, Founders say, It Rubs well. **1726** LEONI *Alberti's Archit.* I. 33/2 It is very soft, and will easily rub to pieces. **1765** *Compl. Maltster & Brewer* 51 Every maltster knows, that when the chive will rub off in his hand, it has been dried enough. **1859** *Handbk. Turning* 120 They [marks] will easily rub out. **1870** LOWELL *Study Wind.*, *Condesc. Foreigners*, When the plating of Anglicism rubs off..we are liable to very unpleasing conjectures about the quality of the metal underneath. **1877** SPURGEON *Serm.* XXIII. 492 Dirt will rub off when it is dry.

18. In comb. with sbs., as **rub-board**, (*a*) a board fitted with teeth, between which linen is drawn; also *attrib.*; (*b*) *N. Amer.*, a wash-board; **rub-iron** (see quot. 1875); **rub-rail**, a rail to protect (a vehicle, etc.) against rubbing.

1780 A. YOUNG *Tour Irel.* I. 180 Thence into the *rub boards; if coarse cloth one rub sufficient. **1885** *Census Instruct.* Index, Rubboard Man (Bleach Works). **1964** *Amer. Folk Music Occasional* I. 28 Clifton Chenies is no doubt the best known of the so-called 'Zydeco' musicians. This music..usually features the accordion with drum or rub-board accompaniment. **1972** *Daily Colonist* (Victoria, B.C.) 13 Feb. 22/2 Building furniture and washing clothes on a rub board in a small tub. **1875** KNIGHT *Dict. Mech.* 1998/2 **Rub-iron*, a plate on a carriage or wagon-bed against which the fore-wheel rubs when turning short. **1961** WEBSTER, *Rub rail. **1969** *Jane's Freight Containers 1968–69* 550/2 Products: G-85 fifth wheel container and general purpose trailer with cushioned rub rails. **1980** *Reader's Digest* Feb. 226/2 The car skidded..25 feet up the bridge, jumped a 5½-inch-high rub rail and hurtled..into the water.

† **rub**, *v.*[2] *Obs.* Also 6 roub. [var. of ROB *v.* 6.] *intr.* In certain card-games: To take all the cards of one suit.

a **1597** *Groome-Porters Lawes at Mawe* in *Anc. Broadsides & Ball.* (1867) 124 If you roub (not hauing the ace) you lose fower and al the vied cardes. **1607** HEYWOOD *Wom. killed w. Kindn.* Wks. 1874 II. 123 *Anne.* What's trumpes? *Wend.* Harts: Partner, I rub. **1611** COTGR., *Piller*,..to rub, or rob, at cards. **1642** FULLER *Holy & Prof. St.* v. vii. 386 Thus three aces chance often not to rub.

† **rub**, *v.*[3] *Cant. Obs.* [Of obscure origin.] *trans.* To carry off (to prison).

1676 *Warn. Housekeepers* 5 They rub us to the whitt. *a* **1700** B. E. *Dict. Cant. Crew*, *Rubs us to the Whit*, sends us to Newgate. **1737** *Old Ballad* (Farmer), Toure you well; hark you well, see Where they are rubb'd.

rub, obs. or Sc. form of ROB *v.*

rubabah, var. REBAB.

rubaboo, var. RUBBABOO.

rubace, rubacel(le: see RUBICELLE.

rub-a-dub (ˈrʌbəˌdʌb), *sb.* [Imitative.]

1. The sound of a drum being beaten; a drumming sound.

1787 COLMAN *Inkle & Yarico* II. i, Little Cupid's his drummer: he has been beating a round rub-a-dub on our hearts. **1833** HT. MARTINEAU *Manch. Strike* i. 16 A rub-a-dub on the drum woke him up. **1891** BARRIE *Little Minister* (1892) 53 The quick rub-a-dub of a drum was heard.

attrib. **1863** W. PHILLIPS *Speeches* iii. 36 A 'rub-a-dub agitation', as ours is contemptuously styled.

2. A pub, a hotel.

c **1926** 'MIXER' *Transport Workers' Song Bk.* 81, I gazed upon the motley crowd Within this 'rub-a-dub'. **1963** H. SLESAR *Bridge of Lions* iii. 52 He could fathom why rub-a-dub meant a pub.

Hence **rub-a-dub** *v.*; **rub-a-dub-dub**, (*a*) the sound of a drum; also *attrib.*; (*b*) *Austral.* and *N.Z. rhyming slang.*, a pub.

1814 SCOTT *Wav.* xxxiv, The drum advanced, beating no measured martial tune, but a kind of rub-a-dub-dub. **1831** *Lincoln Herald* 16 Dec. 3/6 The rub-a-dub-dub sound of these grand instruments. **1837** CARLYLE *Fr. Rev.* II. v. v, Sergeants rub-a-dubbing openly through all manner of German market-towns. **1887** W. S. PRATT in Gladden *Parish Prob.* 426 A player whose taste is limited to the rub-a-dub-dub class of music. **1941** [see RUBBEDY]. **1945** BAKER *Austral. Lang.* xv. 270 A hotel becomes known in rhyming slang as a *rub-a-dub-dub*—by rhyme on 'pub'. **1971** *National Times* (Austral.) 13 Dec. 20 'Let's grab some Kate and Sydney and a pint of apple fritter at the rub-a-dub-dub.'.. Translated: 'Let's grab some steak and kidney and a pint of bitter at the pub.'

rubage, obs. form of RUBBISH.

‖ **ruba'i** (ruˈbɑːiː). Also ruba'iy. Pl. rubaiyat (ˈruːbaɪ(j)æt, ˈruːbeɪ(j)æt). [Arabic *rubāʿīyah*, f. *rubāʿīy* composed of four elements.] In Persian poetry, a quatrain.

The pl. is chiefly familiar in the title of the work by Omar Khayyam (cf. OMARIAN *a.* and *sb.*), known to English speakers esp. in FitzGerald's version.

1859 E. FITZGERALD *Rubáiyát of Omar Khayyám* p. xii, The original Rubáiyát (as, missing an Arabic Guttural, these *Tetrastichs* are more musically called), are independent Stanzas, consisting each of four Lines of equal, though varied, Prosody; sometimes *all* rhyming, but oftener (as here attempted) the third line suspending the Cadence by which the last atones with the former Two. **1885** *Encycl. Brit.* XVIII. 656/1 Those principal forms of poetry now used in common by all Mohammedan nations—the forms of ..the *rubáʿí* or quatrain (our epigram, for which the Persians invented a new metre in addition to those adopted from the Arabs), [etc.]. **1934** [see QASIDA]. **1959** *Chambers's Encycl.* X. 202/1 *Omar Khayyam*.., Persian poet and master of the *ruba'i* (quatrain)... The *Rubaiyat* have now been translated into almost all the literary languages of the world.

† **ruban.** *Obs.* Also 6 rubande, rub(b)en, 7 rubin, 8 rubban. [a. F. *ruban*: see RIBAND and RIBBON.] A ribbon.

1474 *Acc. Ld. High Treas. Scot.* I. 21 Item..v elne of rubanis. **1516** *Invent. R. Wardrobe* (1815) 26 Item, ane certane of rubenis & sewing silk. **1530** PALSGR. 264/1 Rubande of sylke, *rubant*. **1533** *Acc. Ld. High Treas. Scot.* VI. 182 For rubanis to be latchatis to the samyn courtennis. **1651** [see BLUE RIBBON 1]. **1661** COWLEY *Verses & Ess.* (1669) 78 Across his Breast an azure Ruban went. **1695** BLACKMORE *Pr. Arth.* IX. 298 A flaming Ruban of Sydonian Dy. **1713** C'TESS WINCHILSEA *Misc. Poems* 350 To rise with new appearing Day, And..With various Rubans Nosegays tye. **1774** PENNANT *Tour Scotl.* 272 The rubbans, and other trifles I had brought, would have been insults to people in distress.

rub-and-go. *rare*$^{-1}$. = TOUCH-AND-GO.

1825 W. COBBETT *Rur. Rides* (1885) II. 12 With present prices..it is rub-and-go with nineteen twentieths of the farmers.

rubarb, obs. form of RHUBARB *sb.*

† **ru'barbative**, *a. Obs.* Also 6 -if, 7 rew-. [a. F. *reubarbatif* (Rabelais), obs. var. of *rébarbatif*, REBARBATIVE.] Crabbed, cross-grained.

The form may be due to association with *rhubarb*, to which quot. 1600 punningly alludes.

1600 O. E. (M. SUTCLIFFE) *Repl. Libel* III. i. 5 As appeereth by their Rubarbatif or as they call them expurgatorie indexes. **1603** FLORIO *Montaigne* II. xxxvii. 441 The same rewbarbative and severely-grave looke of theires. **1631** DEKKER *Match me in London* III. 32 A man were better to lye vnder the hands of a Hangman, than one of your rubarbatiue faces.

Rubarth's disease (ˈruːbɑːt). *Vet. Sci.* [Named after C. S. *Rubarth* (b. 1905), Swedish veterinary scientist, who described it in 1947 (*Acta Path. & Microbiol. Scand.* Suppl. No. 69).] An infectious disease of dogs, caused by an adenovirus, that affects chiefly the liver and is sometimes fatal; infectious canine hepatitis.

1951 *Vet. Record* 15 Dec. 833/2 We wish..to place before you certain data which we have been able to collect.. regarding virus hepatitis in dogs, or Rubarth's disease, within our own kennels. **1961** C. H. D. TODD *Popular Whippet* x. 147 There are four common canine diseases, viz. two virus diseases—distemper (including hard pad variety) and Rubarths disease (a liver affection), and two bacterial diseases which affect the kidneys. **1970** A. R. JENNINGS *Animal Path.* vi. 118 Intranuclear inclusion bodies are a feature of Rubarth's disease and the inclusions have diagnostic significance.

‖ **rubashka** (ruˈbaʃka). Pl. rubashkas, rubashki. [Russ.] A type of blouse or tunic worn in Russia.

The pl. *rubashka* in quot. 1956 is *erron.*

1921 *Glasgow Herald* 29 Nov. 6 In North Russia during the summer the men, young and old, clean-shaven or whiskered and bearded, wear rubashkas, or blouses, of various colours, some of them even set off with touches of bright embroidery. **1924** *Blackw. Mag.* Feb. 149/1 She had opened her khaki rubashka and shown the subaltern the scar. **1956** WALLIS & BLAIR *Thunder Above* (1959) ii. 11 An orchestra, colourful in their rich silk *rubashka*, providing music that seemed to flow from the Volga. **1972** *Nat. Geographic* Sept. 401 The bearded men wore *rubashki*, the hand-embroidered blouses of old Russia.

‖ **rubato** (ruˈbato). Ellipt. for *tempo rubato* (lit. 'robbed time'): see TEMPO. Also *transf.*

1883 GROVE *Dict. Mus.* III. 188/1 *Rubato*,..referring to the values of the notes, which are diminished in one place and increased in another. **1887** BROWNING *Parl. w. Cert. People*, *Charles Avison* ix, Love once more Yearns through the Largo, Hatred as before Rages in the Rubato. **1921** G. SAMPSON *English* III. 94 The natural *rubato* of civilised speech. **1925** J. A. JOHNSTONE (*title*) Rubato, or the secret of expression in pianoforte playing. **1946** J. CARY *Moonlight* ii. 9 Her old-fashioned style, indeed, with its exaggerated rubato, her swayings, murmurings, tosses of the head, might have amused or disgusted a modern audience. **1955** *Times* 9 May 3/7 His use of rubato sounded nonchalant instead of expressive in Mozart. **1977** *N.Y. Rev. Bks.* 13 Oct. 6/2 He remarks that Victorians had moved away from the hard clear notes of Wordsworth's *Lyrical Ballads*: the ballad had moved into the rubato and vibrato of the drawing room. **1979** *Early Music* July 341/1 In the Vivaldi example the *fermate* over the semiquaver rests can only be indications of *rubato*.

‖ **rubb**[1]. *Obs.* Also rubbe. [LG. *rubbe*, = Du. *rob* (hence G. *robbe*).] A seal.

1694 *Marten's Voy.* in *Acc. Sev. Late Voy.* II. 103 The Sea-Dogs, called Rubbs and Seales. **1725** *Brice's Weekly Jrnl.* 27 Aug. 2 The Sea-Dog, or Dog-fish, commonly called a Seal, or Rubbe, which was lately brought from Greenland.

‖ **rubb**[2]. *Obs.* [a. Piedmontese *rub*, *rubbo*, ad. Arab. *rubʿ*: see ARROBA.] (See quot.)

1756 tr. *Keysler's Trav.* I. 288 Many peasants in Piedmont sell annually four or five Rubbs of raw silk (each Rubb weighing twenty-five pounds).

rubbaboo (rʌbəˈbuː). *N. Amer.* (*Obs.* exc. *Hist.*) Also rababoo, robiboo, rubaboo, rubeiboo, etc. [ult. ad. Algonquian.] A kind of soup or porridge made from pemmican.

1821 N. GARRY *Diary* 22 Aug. in *Trans. R. Soc. Canada* (1900) VI. 151 Our men are now eating Rababoo made of Pemican and Flour. **1857** P. JACOBS *Jrnl.* 72 The food that is generally prepared and eaten in these regions by voyagers is what is called 'ahrubuhboo'. I do not know what the word itself means. I spell it as I hear it pronounced. **1862** R. KENNICOTT *Jrnl.* Jan. in J. A. James *First Sci. Exploration Russ. Amer.* (1942) ii. 85 Rubbaboo is a favorite dish with the northern voyageurs, when they can get it. It consists simply of pemmican made into a kind of soup by boiling in water. Flour is added when it can be obtained, and it is generally considered more palatable with a little sugar. **1865** MILTON & CHEADLE *N.-W. Passage by Land* xv. 289 Our fare was what the half-breeds call 'rubaboo', which we made by boiling a piece of pemmican the size of one's fist in a large quantity of water thickened with a single handful of flour. **1881** E. S. FARROW *Mountain Scouting* xiii. 200 When required for use, it [*sc.* pemmican] is cut from the hard mass and either eaten cold, or is mixed with flour forming a porridge called '*robiboo*'. **1935** *Beaver* Sept. 135 One of the tastiest forms, and one more often mixed than any other for table use, was 'rubeiboo', consisting of pemmican boiled down with a mixture of potatoes, onions and other vegetables. This, when properly seasoned, was very palatable. **1969** E. W. MORSE *Fur Trade Canoe Routes* I. ii. 23 The pemmican was either sliced off and munched raw, or made with flour and water into a *potage* called 'rubbaboo'.

ˈ**rubbacrock.** *dial.* [app. f. RUB *v.*[1] + CROCK *sb.*[1] 2.] (See quot. 1778.)

1746 *Exmoor Scolding* (E.D.S.) 30 A rubbacrock, rouze-about, platvooted, zidlemouth'd Swashbucket. **1778** *Ibid.* Gloss., *Rubbacrock*, a filthy Slattern that is as black as if she were continually rubbing herself against a Boiler or Kettle. **1888** ELWORTHY *W. Somerset Word-bk.* 634.

rubbage, obs. or dial. form of RUBBISH.

rubbed (rʌbd), *ppl. a.* [f. RUB *v.*[1]] Subjected to rubbing; smoothed or polished by rubbing, etc. Also with *out*.

1508 DUNBAR *Flyting* 205 Now vpaland thow leivis on rubbit quheit. **1663** GERBIER *Counsel & Adv. Builders* 56 Good London Bricklayers will work the Rod for forty shillings, rubbed Bricks. **1683** MOXON *Mech. Exerc.*, *Printing* xxiv. ¶ 19 He keeps the Rubb'd out Inck on the Inck-block of an equal Fatness. **1704** *Dict. Rusticum* s.v. *Hop*, The Root being dress'd, then the rub'd Mould is to be applied. **1774** M. MACKENZIE *Maritime Surv.* 101 Rub the Back of the Draught..with Charcoal; lay the rubbed Side on clean Paper. **1825** J. NICHOLSON *Operat. Mechanic* 555 Rubbed and gauged work is set in putty or mortar. **1842** GWILT *Encycl. Arch.* 519 When the surface of stone is required to be perfectly smooth, it is accomplished by rubbing with sand or gritstone, and it is called rubbed work. **1892** C. R. B. BARRETT *Essex Highways*, etc. 64 The rubbed-brick mouldings would seem to be of the same date as the brick tower.

rubbedy, rubberdy, rubbidy (ˈrʌbədɪ) *Austral.* Altered f. RUB-A-DUB *sb.* 2. Cf. RUBBITY.

1941 BAKER *Dict. Austral. Slang* 62 *Rubberdy*.., a public house. Rhyming slang on 'rub-a-dub-dub' for 'pub'. **1957** D. NILAND *Call me when Cross turns Over* iv. 101 How about a gargle? Down to the rubberdy, come on. **1962** 'D. FORREST' *Hollow Woodheap* i. 11 'Where..is "The Eagle on the Hill"?' 'A rubbedy in South Australia.' **1969** *Melbourne Herald* 8 May 15, I was having a gargle with a cobber in a Fleet St. rubbedy. **1970** K. GILES *Murder Pluperfect* ii. 46, I met another of the Fennels down at the rubbidy. **1971**

Australian Post 8 Apr. 40/5 There's the story of the barman in the rubbedy.

rubbee[1] (rʌˈbiː). *rare*⁻¹. [f. RUB *v.*[1]] One who is rubbed. In quot. *fig.*

1757 BYROM *Rem.* (1857) 592 The Enthusiasm epistle..I guess is the rubbing one that you mean; for the bishop, perhaps, if anybody, was the rubbee..in the other.

‖**rubbee**[2] (ˈrʌbiː), **rubbie**, varr. of RABI.

These spellings represent more correctly the real Urdū pronunciation.

1850 *Directions Rev. Off. N.W. Prov.* 211 When the attachment takes place before the rubbee crops are cut,..the collections must be credited to the coming rubbee kists. **1885** *Times* (weekly ed.) 2 Oct. 5/3 The 'rubbee' consists chiefly of pulse, and grains other than rice, and is harvested about March.

rubbel(l, obs. forms of ROUBLE, RUBBLE.

rubber (ˈrʌbə(r)), *sb.*[1] [f. RUB *v.*[1] + -ER[1].]

I. 1. a. A hard brush, a cloth, or the like, used for rubbing in order to make clean. Now *rare.*

1536 *Wardr. Acc. Hen. VIII* in *Archaeol.* IX. 245 One dussen brushes, and one dussen and a halfe of rubbers delyvered to like use into oure saide warderobe of our roobis. **1558** WARDE tr. *Alexis' Secr.* I. v. 90 To die hogges brystels and other thinges, for to make rubbers and brusshes. **1598** FLORIO, *Scuraccio*, a skouring cloth, a dish-clout, a skourer, a rubber. **1634** *Althorp MS.* in Simpkinson *Washingtons* (1860) App. p. lxviii, For small cordes to bynde the rubbers for the parlour. **1730** BAILEY (fol.). **1793** WOLCOT (P. Pindar) *Ep. to the Pope* Wks. 1812 III. 206 Make a good Rubber of the Virgin's Wig. **1880–** in *Eng. Dial. Dict.*

†**b.** A strigil. *Obs.*

1581 MULCASTER *Positions* xxxiv. (1887) 123 They disrobed themselues, and were chafed with a gentle kinde of rubber. **1603** HOLLAND *Plutarch's Mor.* 170 Like as Theocritus served twaine who would seeme to borrow of him his rubber or currying combe in the very baine. **1623** BINGHAM *Xenophon* 4 Xenias the Arcadian solemnized the Playes, called *Lycæa*, and proposed games. The games were Golden rubbers.

c. A towel used for rubbing the body after a bath. (See also quot. 1875.)

1577 tr. *Bullinger's Decades* (1592) 103 Let vs forbid to bring napkins and rubbars to Jupiter. **1598** FLORIO, *Pannetto*, a little cloth,..a towell, a rubber, a kercher. **1637** MASSINGER *Guardian* II. v, I must not forget..The silver bathing-tub, the cambric rubbers, The embroider'd quilt. **1693** DRYDEN *Juvenal* iii. (1697) 66 The..servants lay The Rubbers, and the Bathing-sheets display.

1875 KNIGHT *Dict. Mech.* 1997/1 *Rubber*,..a coarse, unbleached flax toweling for rubbing the body after bathing. *b.* A coarse towel used for drying horses.

†**2.** A tooth-powder or dentifrice. *Obs. rare.*

1558 WARDE tr. *Alexis' Secr.* Table, Dentifrices or rubbers for the teeth, of great perfection for to make them cleane. **1594** PLAT *Jewell-ho.* III. 74 Sweet and delicate dentifrices or rubbers for the teeth.

3. A whetstone, RUBSTONE. Now *dial.* †Also ***rubber-stone.***

1566 WITHALS *Dict.* 19/2 A rubber stone to sharpe the sieth, hooke, or other instrumentes with, *cos acuaria.* **1609** C. BUTLER *Fem. Mon.* (1634) 36 Rub it [the hive] well with a Rubber; which is a piece of rough grind-stone or sand-stone, as great as your hand can hold. *a* **1728** WOODWARD *Nat. Hist. Fossils* (1729) 18 This..is used for whetting of Scithes, and..is call'd Sand-Stone, Coarse-Scithe-Stone, or Rubber. **1854** MISS BAKER *Northampt. Gloss.*, *Rubber*, a coarse sandstone whetstone, for a scythe... The name is also given to a shoemaker's whetstone. **1880** JEFFERIES *Hodge & M.* II. 122 [He] searches for the rubber or whetstone, stuck somewhere in the side of the rick.

4. a. An implement of metal or stone used for rubbing, esp. in order to smooth or flatten a surface.

1664 EVELYN *Sylva* xxx. 102 Two or three days it will only require for cooling, which..they resist, by taking now off the outward covering with a Rabil or Rubber. **1794** *Rigging & Seamanship* 88 *Rubber*, a small iron instrument, in a wooden handle, to rub down or flatten the seams. **1850** HOLTZAPFFEL *Turning* III. 1089 The Rubber used by Masons and Statuaries is frequently a slab of grit stone, to which a handle is attached by means of an iron strap. **1852** MORFIT *Tanning*, etc. (1853) 166 It is a bad practice to use the slate, or rubber.., which being rough, may scratch and damage the hide upon its grain side. **1875** KNIGHT *Dict. Mech.* 1997/1 In the moldings of stone, an iron rubber mounted on a wooden stock is employed for fillets, beads, and astragals.

b. A piece or quantity of some soft material made into a pad or roll and used for rubbing and polishing.

1816 W. Y. OTTLEY *Inquiry Origin & Early Hist. Engraving* I. 81 The friction of a rubber, made of hair, or of pieces of cloth, was then applied to the paper, which was thus rubbed backwards and forwards till the impression of the engraving was transferred to the paper. **1837** *Penny Cycl.* s.v. *Engraving*, A *rubber* is a roll of cloth tied up tight, one end being kept in olive oil. **1839** URE *Dict. Arts* s.v. *Marble*, The polishing rubbers are coarse-linen cloths, or bagging, wedged tight into an iron planing tool. **1865** BRANDE & COX *Dict. Sci.*, etc. s.v. *Engraving*, Engravers use a roll of woollen or felt called a *rubber*, which is put in action with a little olive oil. **1875** *Ure's Dict. Arts* s.v. *Pottery*, It is ..rubbed..afterwards with a rubber formed of rolled flannel.

c. An article usu. consisting of a soft pad attached to a wooden handle, used for erasing chalk from a blackboard.

1880 [see BLACKBOARD]. **1978** P. MARSH et al. *Rules of Disorder* ii. 38 They just started..chucking wooden dice at her..and blackboard rubbers.

5. A large, coarse file. Also ***rubber-file.***

1677 MOXON *Mech. Exerc., Handyworks* i. 14 The Rough or Course Tooth'd File (which if it be large is called a Rubber). **1837** WHITTOCK *Bk. Trades* (1842) 225 The very heavy files, such as smiths' 'rubbers', are made of the inferior marks of blistered steel. **1846** HOLTZAPFFEL *Turning* II. 825 Rubbers..measure from 12 to 18 inches long,..and are made very convex. **1875** KNIGHT *Dict. Mech.* 1997/2 *Rubber-file*, a heavy, fish-bellied file, designated by weight, which varies from four to fifteen pounds.

6. A part of some apparatus which operates by rubbing; a machine which acts by rubbing. Also, †a brake acting by friction on the wheels of a vehicle.

1771 *Encycl. Brit.* II. 475/1 The best rubbers for globes are made of red basil skins. **1787** *Phil. Trans.* LXXVIII. 22 A part of the rubber..must serve to furnish the electric fluid to the glass. **1819** *Gentl. Mag.* LXXXIX. I. 351 Instead of a straight edge and levers for the adjustment of the ink, a leather rubber and screws have been adopted [in printing]. **1825** J. NICHOLSON *Operat. Mechanic* 160 Every article required to be broke or ground is exposed to the application of rubbers or crushers, resting on their fulcrums. **1844** H. STEPHENS *Bk. Farm* II. 328 The drum, or, as I would call it, the *rubber*,..does not..thrash by beating, but by rubbing the grain against a wire grating. **1850** R. GLISAN *Jrnl. Army Life* (1874) iv. 32 The third one [*sc.* vehicle], having no rubbers or brakes to the wheels, went so fast, down a steep hill, that the driver was thrown from his seat. **1881** RAYMOND *Mining Gloss.*, *Rubber*, a gold-quartz amalgamator, in which the slime is rubbed against amalgamated copper surfaces. **1894** T. B. SEARIGHT *Old Pike* 145 The 'rubber', called brake at this day, was not in use when the National Road was first thrown open for trade and travel. Instead,..saplings, cut at the summit of the hills, were shaped and fashioned to answer the ends of the 'rubber', and at the foot of the hills taken off and left on the roadside.

attrib. **1834–6** in *Encycl. Metrop.* (1845) VIII. 704/1 The most essential part of this machine consists of the rubber-boards. **1843** *Penny Cycl.* XXV. 425/1 The rubber-carriage T being moved along the bar B [etc.].

7. A brick which is rubbed smooth.

1825 J. NICHOLSON *Operat. Mechanic* 535 The best kind are used as cutting bricks, and are called red rubbers. In old buildings they are very frequently to be seen ground to a fine smooth surface. **1898** *19th Ann. Rep. U.S. Geol. Survey* VI. B. 407 A second kind, and one much used in London for fronts, is a large, light-red brick, so soft as to be readily scratched by the knife. These are called 'rubbers'. **1977** *Listener* 20 Oct. 519/4 There is quality, too, in the kind of bricks still known as 'rubbers'—ones that have been hand-rubbed on all surfaces to achieve an immaculate join.

II. 8. a. One who applies friction or massage as a curative process; a masseur or masseuse; *spec.* one who massages sportsmen or athletes (chiefly *N. Amer.*).

1610 BEAUM. & FL. *Scornf. Lady* I. i, Yonder's Mistres Younglove, Brother, the grave rubber of your Mistresses toes. **1680–4** DINGLEY *Hist. from Marble* xliii, A masculine sort of Bona roba Women which attend you at your lodgings and are called Rubbers. **1822–34** *Good's Study Med.* III. 336 Long continued and daily friction by a skilful rubber. **1857** MRS. CARLYLE *New Lett. & Mem.* (1903) II. 139 Mr. Erskine wrote me strong regrets about your going so far away from his rubber, who he thinks was certainly doing George good. **1887** C. BENNETT *Massage Case* II. 8 Many cases..had a nurse to wait on them, and a rubber and electrician besides. **1895** J. L. WILLIAMS *Princeton Stories* 185 Another sub and William, the negro rubber, picked Wormsey up. **1911** *Daily Colonist* (Victoria, B.C.) 6 Apr. 9/5 A 'rubber' has been engaged by Manager Wattalet. Perhaps the use of such a term would shock the sensibilities of our ball players. The correction, therefore, is made with all haste. It is a 'masseur', who has become attached to the Victoria baseball club. **1949** *Sun* (Baltimore) 14 Oct. 27/6 The schools have hired some of the best men in the training profession. Today, they are not just rubbers; they know anatomy, physiology and chemistry. **1950** J. DEMPSEY *Championship Fighting* xxiv. 192 The 'rubber' (rub-down man) applies soothing lotions to the muscles as he kneads them with his fingers.

b. An attendant who rubs the bathers at a Turkish bath.

1680 *Lond. Gaz.* No. 1556/4 Whereas the Proprietors of the Royal Bagno, are sensible that their Servants who attend Gentlemen, both Rubbers and Barbers, have been very troublesome. **1712** STEELE *Spect.* No. 332 ⁋3 Some of those Fellows, who are employ'd as Rubbers to this new-fashioned Bagnio. **1881** *Daily News* 13 April 2/2 When he married the prisoner she was a rubber at some Turkish baths.

9. a. One who rubs in any way; a workman specially engaged in rubbing in order to smooth or polish something. Also ***rubber-off.***

1611 COTGR., *Frotte-botte*,..boot-rubber, maker of boots cleane. **1654** WHITLOCK *Zootomia* 144 Some rubber of Horses heels. **1709** ADDISON *Tatler* No. 121 ⁋4 Grooms, Farriers, Rubbers, &c. **1775** J. ADAMS *Diary* 25 Oct. in Wks. 1850 II. 430 Duane says, that Jefferson is the greatest rubber off of dust that he has met with. **1820** J. H. REYNOLDS *Fancy* (1906) 74 He'll be no more a rubber Of wet sockets. **1839** URE *Dict. Arts* 1261 The types are taken to the rubber, a man who sits in the centre of the workshop with a grit-stone slab on a table before him. **1860** TOMLINSON *Arts & Manuf.* II. 55 The welder and rubber; the rib forger. **1893** *Times* 14 Dec. 8/2 The adoption of the respirators..for mixers; the provision of gloves and aprons for rubbers.

b. One who takes rubbings of brasses, etc.

1861 *Sat. Rev.* 22 July 647 A zealous 'rubber'..asking whether there were any 'brasses' in a church. **1897** WATTS-DUNTON *Aylwin* II. ii, My sudden enthusiasm for the rubber's art astonished even my father.

10. *fig.* A rebuke or irritating remark; a source of annoyance.

1706 E. WARD *Wooden World Diss.* (1708) 90 One or two Rubbers for such a horrid Negligence, makes him ever after look..sharp out to all Boats. **1786** WOLCOT (P. Pindar) *Bozzy & Piozzi* Wks. 1812 I. 348 This for the Rambler's temper was a rubber. **1884** in *Eng. Dial. Dict.*

III. Ellipt. for INDIA-RUBBER.

11. a. Caoutchouc. Now also applied to any of a large range of synthetic organic polymers having properties of elasticity, etc., resembling those of natural rubber.

Rubber is the base of various recent trade-names denoting preparations of caoutchouc, or substitutes for it, as *rubberide, rubberine, rubberite, rubberoid.*

1855 J. SCOFFERN in *Orr's Circ. Sci.*, *Chem.* 356 The mouth-pieces..are elongated tubes of vulcanized rubber. **1879** G. PRESCOTT *Sp. Telephone* 22 The diaphragms are placed on opposite sides of a short cylindrical piece of hard rubber. **1897** MARY KINGSLEY *W. Africa* 295 The pure rubber, when it is made, looks like putty. **1912** *Jrnl. Soc. Chem. Industry* 15 July 617/1 There can now be no doubt that rubber may actually be obtained synthetically by the polymerisation of isoprene and its homologues and that the synthetic product is really rubber and strictly comparable with natural rubbers. **1941** *Jrnl. R. Aeronaut. Soc.* XLV. 145 Mechanically, natural rubber is not surpassed by any synthetic rubber. However, in resistance to swelling by organic liquids..and deterioration by sunlight or oxidising agents, synthetic rubbers have been found superior. **1961** L. MUMFORD *City in Hist.* (1966) xv. 545 The new régime was based on..new synthetic materials, like rubber, bakelite, and the plastics. **1973** *Nature* 6 Apr. 420/1 Natural rubber is still the preferred polymer for many high performance applications.

b. *pl.* (*a*) Overshoes or galoshes made of india-rubber (orig. *U.S.*); (*b*) plimsolls, esp. plimsolls worn for climbing.

(*a*) **1842** *Southern Lit. Messenger* VIII. 516/2 The *younkers* who would go 'a Maying', very prudently provided themselves with rubbers and tippets before encountering the rough southeaster. **1856** S. ROBINSON *Kansas* xii. 160 The snows..are fast melting, and mingling with the clayey soil. So, besides the burden of rubbers, one has to carry no little portion of the native earth. **1859** BARTLETT *Dict. Amer.* (ed. 2) 373. **1872** DE VERE *Americanisms* 536. **1901** *Daily Colonist* (Victoria, B.C.) 22 Oct. 4/6 (Advt.), Special sale of rubbers today at 2.30 p.m. **1904** *Daily Chron.* 4 Jan. 5/2 In America 'rubbers' are worn almost universally in wet.. weather. *c* **1921** D. H. LAWRENCE *Mr Noon* iv, in *Mod. Lover* (1934) 221 He went out to his motor-cycle and got it ready. He went indoors and put on his rubbers. **1951** E. PAUL *Springtime in Paris* iii. 53 An umbrella rack with a porcelain tray for rubbers. **1972** J. MINIFIE *Homesteader* xvii. 145 It [*sc.* gumbo] was notorious for its adhesive quality; it stuck to everything, pulled off rubbers—galoshes as people were beginning to call them [in 1914]. **1974** M. Z. LEWIN *Enemies Within* iv. 17 Snow made it look beautiful. I put on my rubbers and walked around.

(*b*) **1925** *Jrnl. Fell & Rock Climbing Club* VII. 12 Arrowhead Ridge..Leader needs about 60 feet of rope. Rubbers. **1933** G. D. ABRAHAM *Mod. Mountaineering* v. 107 Rubbers are usually used, but I have also made the ascent in nailed boots, and in either footgear dry rocks are advisable. **1941** C. KIRKUS *Let's go Climbing* vi. 95 A climb of such difficulty is not done in boots, but in rubbers. These are ordinary plimsolls or gym shoes. **1950** T. LONGSTAFF *This my Voyage* xiv. 282 To the right of Kern Knotts Crack is a narrow vertical cracklet... It..is now a recognised climb. It is led, generally in rubbers, without any moral support of a rope from above. **1957** CLARK & PYATT *Mountaineering in Brit.* vii. 134 For the climb,..for which rubbers are recommended, all the party wore boots. **1968** P. CREW *Encycl. Dict. Mountaineering* 103/2 With the advent of P.A.'s and similar footwear, and their widespread use in Britain, the use of rubbers has diminished considerably.

c. A rubber tyre for a wheel. Also *collect.*, the tyres of a vehicle; occas. used in colloq. phrases expressing speed or acceleration. Chiefly *U.S.*

1882 *Bazaar, Exch. & M.* 15 Feb. 174 The wheels are of ordinary construction, red rubbers, crescent rims,..&c. *a* **1961** G. FELSEN in WEBSTER s.v., I'll road test her for you after we get new rubber on. **1976** N. THORNBURG *Cutter & Bone* iv. 91 The huddled figure..going round the car and out of sight for a few moments and then back into it almost immediately and laying down rubber again. **1977** *Hot Car* Oct. 61/1 There really is an incredibly large number of cars and vans cruisin' round on completely the wrong sort of rubber for the type of vehicle. **1980** J. BALL *Then came Violence* (1981) i. 7 Every patrol and supervisory car.. would be burning rubber within seconds.

d. A piece of rubber for erasing pencil or ink marks. Also used of erasers made of other substances

1788–9 HOWARD *New Royal Encycl.*, s.v. *Caoutchouc*, Very useful for erasing the strokes of black lead pencils, and is popularly called rubber, and lead-eater. **1891** *Catal. & Price List* (Waterlow & Sons Ltd.) 169 (*caption*) Artists' Rubber. Stationer's Rubber... Grey Vulcanised Rubber. **1907** A. E. ZAPF *Cycl. Drawing* I. 14 In making drawings, but little erasing should be necessary. However, in case this is necessary, a soft rubber should be used. **1928** [see BUNGIE, BUNGY]. **1952** PRICE & BISHOP *Art School Self-Taught* II. iii. 275 For erasing errors, a harder rubber is needed. **1968** F. G. HOLLIDAY *Man. Stationery* v. 113 Erasers are often called 'rubbers', but today a surprisingly small proportion of them actually consists of rubber. **1973** M. AMIS *Rachel Papers* 139 Between my finger and thumb I take a rubber and bounce it up and down on the desk.

e. *U.S. Baseball.* (*a*) The home plate; (*b*) the pitcher's plate (now the usual sense).

1891 *Chicago Herald* 5 May 6/1 Those same errors.. hustled two runs over the rubber. **1895** *Evening Star* (Washington, D.C.) 2 Oct. 9/3 Twirler Magee once more tried to 'make good', in a pitching sense, but..he was put out of the running, and Billy Dineen sent to the rubber. **1910** O. JOHNSON *Humming Bird* v. 54 In the breakaway Tyrell, the first to dust the rubber for the Chaperons, selected a hole in the circumambient and poked a buzzer over short. **1919** *Chicago Daily Tribune* 12 Apr. 19/2 An unfairly delivered ball is a ball delivered by the pitcher to the batsman with the bases unoccupied, while no foot is in contact with the rubber. **1950** A. DALEY *Times at Bat* 106

He hit the first pitch a mile... Still seething inwardly he crossed the rubber and returned to the dugout. **1975** *New Yorker* 14 Apr. 92/2 Seaver, too, restored memory—the cold, intelligent gaze; the unwasteful windup; the sudden forward, down-dropping stride off the rubber.

f. *slang.* A contraceptive sheath made of rubber; a condom. Cf. *rubber goods*, *shop* below.

1947 C. Willingham *End as Man* xiv. 173 Maybe next time you'll use a rubber. **1955** W. Gaddis *Recognitions* I. v. 184 What are you reading?.. Malthus, for Christ sake... The next thing, you'll be peddling rubbers in the street. **1968** B. Turner *Sex Trap* viii. 53, I need more rubbers. There's only enough for about a couple of good days left. **1978** J. Irving *World According to Garp* iv. 71 'Oh, Garp,' Cushie said. 'Don't you have any *rubbers*?'

12. *attrib.* **a.** In sense 'made of rubber', whether natural or synthetic, as ***rubber apron***, ***bag***, ***band*** (hence as *v. trans.*), ***bed***, ***boat***, ***bone***, ***boot***, ***bullet***, ***clothing***, ***coat***, ***dinghy***, ***garment***, ***glove***, ***hose***, ***nozzle***, ***pants***, ***ring***, ***sheet***, ***sheeting***, ***shoddy***, ***shoe***, ***sole***, ***suit***, ***tyre***, ***truncheon***, etc.

In very common use from about 1875.

1926 *Daily Colonist* (Victoria, B.C.) 10 Jan. 7/1 (Advt.), Women's *rubber aprons. Save your frocks and save your laundry bills, too. **1977** 'M. Underwood' *Fatal Trip* xviii. 102 'Caught me just in time,' the pathologist said, peeling off his rubber apron. **1866** *Robert Ware* (Harvard Mem. Biogr.) I. 240 With me and the horse came a *rubber bag containing much Sanitary knowledge. **1895** *Montgomery Ward Catal.* Spring & Summer 117/1 Cabinet of assorted pure *rubber bands for home and office use. Assortment of sizes up to one-half inch wide and 2½ inches in length. **1919** F. Hurst *Humoresque* 128 'I asked you why you was like a rubber band.' 'Aw, I give up, Miss Sadie.' ''Cause you're so stretchy, see?' **1947** J. C. Rich *Materials & Methods Sculpture* v. 121 Tape or rubber bands can be used to hold sections of a mold together for casting positives. **1962** D. Lessing *Golden Notebk.* IV. 488, I found a stack of letters rubber-banded together in one corner. **1973** 'E. McBain' *Let's hear It* xv. 216 He removed the rubber band from the roll, and spread the plans on the floor. **1849** N. Kingsley *Diary* 26 Oct. (1914) 78 Some of the fellows went in swimming this afternoon by takeing rubber beds. **1943** J. B. Priestley *Daylight on Saturday* xxix. 219 Sometimes they got into little *rubber boats and so weren't found for a day or two. **1976** J. Lee *Ninth Man* 5 The billowy outlines of the rubber boat, rapidly filling with air. **1949** N. Streatfeild *Painted Garden* v. 48 His spare collar and lead, his water bowl, his *rubber bone. **1973** E. Lemarchand *Let or Hindrance* viii. 91 A dog basket with a rubber bone in it. **1852** S. C. Davis *Jrnl.* 16 Dec. in B. A. Richards *Calif. Gold Rush Merchant* (1956) 85 Arrived at San Francisco and purchased 200 books, pamphlets, magazines, &c., also some *Rubber Boots, &c. **1975** *Ecology* LVI. 538/1 In very dry years the whole bog surface.. may be dry enough to walk on without rubber boots. **1971** *Guardian* 14 June 1/8 The soldiers, wearing gas masks and riot helmets, fired nine rounds of *rubber bullets. **1976** P. Ferris *Detective* viii. 150 You're half hoping I've got.. a patrol group coming in with gas and rubber bullets. **1980** *Jrnl. R. Soc. Arts* July 486/1 Fire hoses as favoured on the Continent or rubber bullets favoured by the Army in Ireland. **1895** *Montgomery Ward Catal.* Spring & Summer 296/3 Medium and heavy weight *rubber clothing. **1967** G. Freeman *Undergrowth of Lit.* x. 151 Talcum powder is also useful to apply to the body before squeezing into rubber clothing. **1850** N. Kingsley *Diary* 21 Nov. (1914) 157, I put on my *Rubber Coat and built a chimney outside the tent. *a***1918** G. Stuart *40 Yrs. on Frontier* (1925) I. 69 Rubber coats and shoes were unknown at that time. **1939** *Rubber dinghy [see dinghy 2 c]. **1953** *News Chron.* 2 June 2/6 Nothing had been forgotten by the crowds... Even rubber dinghies had been brought to keep off the rain. **1973** E. Lemarchand *Let or Hindrance* v. 54 Can't we get hold of an RAF rubber dinghy, or inflatable raft? **1921** *Dict. Occup. Terms* (1927) §608 Garment maker, rubber. **1967** G. Freeman *Undergrowth of Lit.* x. 152 There is a wide belief among women that sweating in *rubber garments makes them slim. **1895** *Montgomery Ward Catal.* Spring & Summer 297/1 Ladies' *Rubber Gloves... Men's Rubber Gloves. **1914** 'E. Bramah' *Max Carrados* 96 Here is a rubber glove. I have cut the wire but you had better put it on. **1932** E. Hemingway *Death in Afternoon* xii. 138 The doctor.. picked up the pistol in his rubber gloves. **1975** *Listener* 24 July 125/3, I have peeled off my rubber gloves and put the Fairy Liquid back on the shelf. **1892** *Photogr. Ann.* II. 48 A length of *rubber hose, about twelve inches, is a capital substitute. **1939** *N.Y. Sunday News* 4 June 68/3 What do you think, they're using a rubber hose on her? Piffle! **1976** H. Tracy *Death in Reserve* xii. 100 Why don't you get your bloody rubber hoses out and your hallucinogens.. and your flashing lights. **1898** *Allbutt's Syst. Med.* V. 433 The mixing pipette is provided with a *rubber nozzle. **1897** *Sears, Roebuck Catal.* 783/3 *Rubber pants. **1936** F. M. Ford *Let.* 6 Sept. (1965) 261 She [*sc.* Pennsylvania] led the Universe in the production of rubber pants. **1872** L. P. Meredith *Teeth* (1878) 63 *Rubber rings are much used around the teeth. **1895** *Montgomery Ward Catal.* Spring & Summer 537/3 Rubber rings, for Mason fruit jars. **1970** W. H. Parker *Health & Dis. in Farm Animals* v. 50 A more recent method of 'bloodless castration' is the use of the rubber ring. **1976** H. Tracy *Death in Reserve* xix. 146 Free bucket-and-spade, beachballs, rubber rings. **1922** *Encycl. Brit.* XXXII. 300/1 In very exacting work, such as the vulcanizing of *hard-rubber sheets, curing is effected by immersion of the material in hot water. **1957** *Ibid.* XIX. 610/1 The rubber sheet is firmly pressed against the prepared fabric. **1966** May & Moss *New Math for Adults Only* xii. 71/2 Such geometry.. is known as topology. Youngsters call it rubber-sheet geometry because the figures can be twisted and stretched and still remain the same. **1975** I. Stewart *Concepts Mod. Math.* x. 144 Topology is sometimes described as 'rubber-sheet geometry', a whimsical and somewhat misleading description. **1976** M. Millar *Ask for me Tomorrow* (1977) xiii. 107 She gave him a sponge bath.. on a rubber sheet on the bed. **1895** *Montgomery Ward Catal.* Spring & Summer 108/2 Nursery *rubber sheeting. **1965** M. Thomas *Grannies' Remedies* 16 Another.. poultice is a piece of soft thick sheet-lint.. squeezed out in hot water, and laid over the part, covered with a larger piece of thin rubber-sheeting. **1907** *Sci. Amer.* 5 Oct. 240/2 Scrap rubber, or *rubber 'shoddy' as it is called, is made up principally of worn-out boots and shoes. **1844** *Knickerbocker* XXIV. 287 Old *rubber-shoes! old rubber-shoes! Humble theme for heavenly muse! **1931** M. Allingham *Look to Lady* xvii. 178 They heard the soft scrape of his rubber shoes on the bole of the tree. **1897** *Sears, Roebuck Catal.* 208/1 Royal *rubber soles. **1901** E. W. Hornung *Black Mask* vi. 112 There had been no warning step.. and my suspicious eye had searched his feet for rubber soles. **1975** G. Seymour *Harry's Game* iv. 66 A night patrol, their faces blackened, rubber soles on their shoes. **1948** H. Innes *Blue Ice* viii. 205 Sweating underwater in a *rubber suit. **1872** *Carriage Builder's Gaz.* 1 Mar. 40/1 A wheel with a *rubber tire upon it. **1931** M. Allingham *Look to Lady* v. 66 A small but wicked looking *rubber truncheon and.. [a] Colt revolver. **1959** J. Braine *Vodi* iv. 69 They beat him up with rubber truncheons. The marks don't show. **1973** W. Fairchild *Swiss Arrangement* viii. 94 Give this one a pair of jackboots.. and he'd be just like the rest... Drench you with charm first and, if that failed, slug you with a rubber truncheon. **1883** *Cent. Mag.* Sept. 733/1 The *rubber tubing.. is a great convenience.

b. In sense 'producing rubber', as ***rubber plant***, ***tree***, ***vine***.

1872 De Vere *Americanisms* 420 Gum-trees are not unfrequently called Rubber-trees. **1880** C. R. Markham *Peruv. Bark* 461 The Ceará rubber-tree would thrive perfectly over a very wide area of the drier regions of British India. **1884** Knight *Dict. Mech.* Suppl. 771/1 Unlike the juice of the American rubber tree this milky sap will not run into a vessel placed to receive it. **1887** Moloney *Forestry W. Afr.* 233, I may single out as an example the rubber vine. **1888** H. Drummond *Trop. Africa* iii. (1889) 62 The well-known rubber plant abounds on Lake Nyassa.

c. In miscellaneous uses.

1875 Knight *Dict. Mech.* 1998/1 Rubber gage, knife, mould, saw. **1887** Moloney *Forestry W. Afr.* 78, I.. furnish separately the Gambia rubber export. *Ibid.* 92 The rubber industry is in its infancy as regards Her Majesty's Possessions on the Gambia. **1891** *Pall Mall G.* 21 Jan. 7/1 An American syndicate has been formed to control the rubber trade. **1907** *Chem. Abstr.* I. 1326 (*heading*) On the action of iodine and bromine on the resins in rubber latex. **1911** *Encycl. Brit.* XXIII. 798/2 The experience of planters in general is in favour of the complete removal of weeds from a rubber plantation. **1911** Rubber substitute [see *artificial rubber* s.v. artificial *a.* 5]. **1923** in M. Box *Trial of Marie Stopes* (1967) 166 A. As a matter of fact.. these things have been used by the hundreds... *Q.* Bought at rubber shops, rubber goods' shops? *Ibid.* 254 Contraceptives are for sale at what have been called, I think, rubber shops? **1935** *Chambers's Encycl.* VI. 123/2 Paints, varnishes, rubber-substitutes, oil-cloth, soft soap, &c. **1936** 'G. Orwell' *Keep Aspidistra Flying* i. 13 He'd slink into one of the rubber-shops and buy *High Jinks in a Parisian Convent*. **1940** Graves & Hodge *Long Week-End* vii. 105 Contraception['s] ..association with the pornographic literature of rubber-shops. **1948** M. Laski *Tory Heaven* i. 6 James had.. been sent to try his luck on an uncle's rubber-plantation in Malaya. **1967** G. Freeman *Undergrowth of Lit.* x. 152 To the rubber addict 'slimwear' is a key word. **1972** *Materials & Technol.* V. iv. 80 Rubber latex is not naturally very stable: the rubber particles coagulate spontaneously in course of time.

13. *Comb.* **a.** Objective, with agent-nouns, as ***rubber-collector***, ***-gatherer***, ***-hunter***, ***-planter***.

1880 C. R. Markham *Peruv. Bark* 459 The tracks of the rubber collectors through the dense forests. **1882** Moloney *Forestry W. Afr.* (1887) 86 The wasteful custom.. rubber-hunters have of cutting down.. every tree from which they extract the rubber. **1894** *Outing* XXIII. 356/1, I proposed to accompany the rubber-gatherer on his rounds. **1937** *Discovery* May 143/2 The rubber planter uses coconut shells for collecting the raw latex from his trees.

b. Objective, with ppl. adjs., as ***rubber-cutting***, ***-growing***, ***-producing***, ***-yielding***; also with vbl. sbs., as ***rubber-collecting***.

1875 Knight *Dict. Mech.*, *Rubber-cutting Machine*, a machine for making threads of caoutchouc for shirrs. **1884** *Harper's Mag.* Nov. 836 The rubber-yielding plants of South America. **1887** Moloney *Forestry W. Afr.* 89 The juice of rubber-producing trees. **1897** *Westm. Gaz.* 25 May 8/1 The rubber-growing territory of Appaboomah. **1910** *Blackw. Mag.* May 729/1 Rubber-collecting is less laborious, but takes you into dangerous parts.

c. Instrumental, as ***rubber-boned***, ***-booted***, ***-caped***, ***-coated***, ***-cored***, ***-covered***, ***-cushioned***, ***-faced***, ***-gloved***, ***-insulated***, ***-jointed***, ***-legged***, ***-lipped***, ***-mounted***, ***-mouthed***, ***-necked***, ***-soled***, ***-stoppered***, ***-tipped***, ***-tyred*** (also *fig.*), ***-treaded***.

1958 *New Statesman* 22 Feb. 227/2 Especially fantastic is the dance of a *rubber-boned neighbour (Stephen Preston). **1943** J. W. Day *Farming Adventure* xx. 228, I dined and went down to the quay, oil-skinned and *rubber-booted. **1935** W. Cather *Lucy Gayheart* I. ix. 75 When the *rubber-caped boy was gone, Lucy stood looking at the yellow envelope. **1934** Webster, *Rubber-coated. **1959** *Chambers's Encycl.* XII. 30/2 Some of the earliest known products of rubber, observed in Brazil, shoes and rubber-coated garments for example, possessed these faults. **1972** *Classification of Occupations* (Dept. Employment) III. 244/1 Operates machine to wind.. rubber coated wire round core. **1902** *Amer. Golfer* Apr. 102/1 The advent of the *rubber-cored ball has made this [*sc.* an official golf ball] a question of practical interest to all golfers. **1929** W. Deeping *Roper's Row* xxxv. 398 Sillocks was a golf maniac, and went from Rye to Hoylake.. smiting a rubber-cored ball. **1935** *Chambers's Encycl.* VI. 122/1 Innumerable other new applications, as in rubber-cored golf-balls and vulcanite fountain-pens, have caused an enormous increase in the importation of rubber. **1897** *Outing* XXX. 370/1 Strapping my *rubber-covered roll on the handle-bars, I was ready to start. **1971** *Flying* Apr. 40/1 The free-floating *rubber-cushioned engine cowling. **1911** *Encycl. Brit.* XXIII. 803/2 The required thickness of the spread sheet is very often secured by the *rubber-faced surfaces of two cloths being united before curing. **1965** F. Sargeson *Mem. Peon* vii. 241 It was more as though he aimed at captivating me with his abilities as a rubber-faced comedian. **1970** *Motoring Which?* July 107/4 Bumpers lightly mounted; rubberfaced overriders front and back. **1956** P. Scott *Male Child* II. vii. 174 Handled by sterilized, *rubber-gloved hands. **1977** B. Pym *Quartet in Autumn* x. 91 Her pink rubber-gloved hands plunged in the washing-up water. **1965** *Motor* 17 July 6/1 The wiring was *rubber insulated and in poor condition. **1934** J. A. Lee *Children of Poor* (1949) 200 People go to the circus to see the *rubber-jointed wonder. **1942** Berry & Van den Bark *Amer. Thes. Slang* §702/32 '*Punch-drunk*'; *dazed*,.. *rubber-legged. **1950** J. Dempsey *Championship Fighting* xxv. 200 He becomes '*rubber-legged' as he lurches about the ring. **1960** *Times* 24 Feb. 16/5 A right to the head had Luukkonen rubber legged as he stood against the ropes. **1898** *Cycling* 71 The flap and the *rubber-lined inside of the jacket.. are anointed with soft soap. **1973** M. Amis *Rachel Papers* 180 Once, I affectionately imitated her pout; she veered away in pained bewilderment, so I changed it to an imitation of *rubber-lipped Norman, claiming I had heard him on the stairs. **1947** Crowther & Whiddington *Science at War* iv. 166 A *rubber-mounted dome was found. **1969** *Jane's Freight Containers 1968–69* 245/1 Two rubber-mounted gantry cranes are used to transfer containers. **1968** *Times* 15 Nov. 16/1 The American designers swing-a-ding-ding with such vivacity and with such *rubber-mouthed, beady-eyed professionalism as to render our homemade brand soft-in-the-head amateurs by comparison. **1928** D. H. Lawrence *Lady Chatterley* x. 168 There was a toughness, a curious *rubber-necked toughness and unlivingness about the middle and upper classes. **1932** Blunden *Face of England* 114, I came to an old tree over the stream, and crossing with some disadvantage to its rubber-necked lichens, I was in an open meadow. **1957** R. Campbell *Coll. Poems* II. 126 The rubbernecked, Hell-touring Thracian. **1884** *Harper's Mag.* Jan. 304/2 A pair of *rubber-soled shoes. **1913** E. C. Bentley *Trent's Last Case* v. 123 He wore rubber-soled tennis shoes. **1973** J. Leasor *Host of Extras* iii. 49, I had not heard his rubber-soled shoes. **1927** C. B. Neblette *Photography* xx. 465 The potassium pentasulphide solution thus formed is then allowed to cool, filtered and kept in a *rubber-stoppered bottle tightly closed. **1913** *T. Eaton & Co. Semi-Ann. Sale Catal.* No. 36. 17/2 *Rubber tipped pencils. **1926** 'C. Barry' *Detective's Holiday* xi. 97 A sallow, unhealthy-looking man of about thirty years, who walked with the help of a stout stick and a rubber-tipped wooden stump. **1976** M. Gilbert *Night of Twelfth* i. 8 He.. walked.. with the aid of a rubber-tipped stick. **1886** *Bicycling News* 17 Sept. 748/2 The popularity of our *rubber-tyred steel wheels. **1901** Kipling *Let.* May in Ld. Birkenhead *R. Kipling* (1978) xiv. 235 We were bung full of beastly spiritual pride... We went about despising things and people, unconsciously turning our ideals to mean an easy life... soft rubber-tyred. **1980** A. Cromie *Lucky to be Alive* i. 9, I would be leaving the rubber-tired life behind. **1936** J. Steinbeck *In Dubious Battle* i. 11 He went in a dark entrance and climbed the narrow stairs *rubber-treaded, the edges guarded with strips of brass.

14. Special Combs.: **rubber boa**, a short, stout, brown snake, *Charina bottæ*, belonging to the family Boidæ and found in western North America; **rubber cement**, a cement or adhesive containing rubber in a solvent; hence **rubber-cemented** *a.* (also *fig.*); **rubber cheque** *slang* (orig. *U.S.*), a cheque that 'bounces'; **rubber-chicken circuit** *N. Amer. slang*, an after-dinner-speaking circuit; **rubber dam**, **rubberdam**: see dam *sb.*[1] 4 e; **rubber fetishism**, sexual fetishism which is centred on objects made of rubber; hence **rubber fetish**; **rubber goods** *pl.*, articles made of rubber; freq. *spec.* contraceptive devices; also *attrib.* and *fig.*; **rubber gum**, the sap or latex of rubber trees; **rubber ice** *N. Amer.*, thin, flexible ice; **rubber johnny** *slang*, a condom (cf. sense 11 f above); **rubber kite** *slang* = *rubber cheque*; **rubber-leather** *a.*, consisting of rubber and leather; **rubber-like** *a.*, resembling or suggestive of rubber; **rubber plant**, a tree, *Ficus elastica*, belonging to the family Moraceæ, and native to south-east Asia, the juvenile form of which is widely cultivated as a house plant for the sake of its large leathery leaves which are dark green above and pale yellowish-green beneath; **rubber-proofed** *a.*, coated or treated with rubber for water-proofing; **rubber snake** = *rubber boa*; **rubber solution**, a solution of rubber, *spec.* one used as an adhesive in the repair of tyres; **rubberware**, rubber goods; **rubberwear**, rubber clothing.

1907 R. L. Ditmars *Reptile Bk.* xxv. 211 The *Rubber Boa... Size moderate. Form very stout. **1977** *Westworld* (Vancouver, B.C.) May–June 46/2 Another snake common around the lake is the rubber boa. **1895** *Montgomery Ward Catal.* Spring & Summer 525/2, 1 can *rubber cement. **1939** R. Stout *Some Buried Caesar* xii. 175 I'll close it forever and seal the crack with rubber cement. **1965** Zigrosser & Gaehde *Guide Coll. Orig. Prints* vii. 107 Synthetic adhesives, such as rubber cement. **1961** W. Sansom *Last Hours S. Lee* 246 Bossom was already home, *rubber-cemented to his favourite comedian on the telly. **1962** 'E. McBain' *Like Love* (1964) vi. 82 Grossman turned over the lucite-encased sketch and studied the typewritten key rubber-cemented to its back. **1927** *Rubber cheque [see bounce *v.* 6 c]. **1936** Wallace & Curtis *Mouthpiece* i. 9 By now the woman has exhausted her credit in Vienna, issued a few rubber checks and passed on to Budapest or somewhere. **1955** J. Potts *Death of Stray Cat* xv. 157 Jimmy was going to have a lot more to explain than just a handful of rubber cheques. **1973** R. Busby *Pattern of Violence* vi. 94 Have you got that blighter who's been trying to put me out of business with rubber cheques? **1959** *Maclean's Mag.* 23 May 1/1 Next year's *rubber-chicken circuit is being sewed up by three Toronto women with a public-speaking agency called Canadian Celebrity Bureau.

1977 *Rolling Stone* 5 May 47/3 He spent the winter making speeches on the rubber-chicken circuit. **1954** B. KARPMAN *Sexual Offender* xix. 352 Another *rubber fetish in a case reported by Payne was a mackintosh, and in this case also the patient preferred one that had been stolen. **1930** S. PARKER tr. *Stekel's Sexual Aberrations* I. v. 105 During the two years that he was engaged, he continued his *rubber and glove fetishism unabated. **1951** HARTWICH & BURBURY tr. *Krafft-Ebing's Aberrations of Sexual Life* x. 173 Despite this strong rubber-fetishism he had a normal sexual relationship. **1971** E. CHESSER *Human Aspects Sexual Deviation* iii. 51 Although rubber fetishism features largely in pornographic literature, if it makes for married happiness it is impossible to see how any moral issue can arise. **1853** *Pathfinder Railway Guide* Sept. (Advt.), Goodyear's patent vulcanized *rubber goods. **1897** *National Police Gaz.* (U.S.) 26 May 15/4 (Advt.), T. W. Harrison's rubber, cigar, and book stores. List of all kinds of rubber goods, French & American specialities, pessaries of every description. **1922** JOYCE *Ulysses* 533 Rubber goods. Neverrip. **1928** D. H. LAWRENCE *Lady Chatterley* x. 141 She wasn't all tough rubber-goods and platinum, like the modern girl. **1951** G. GREENE *End of Affair* III. vii. 143 They ought to have opaque glass in their doors like rubber-goods shops. **1973** A. BROINOWSKI *Take one Ambassador* xii. 187 The rubber goods factory next door. **1910** *Chambers's Jrnl.* Mar. 153/2 In these forests grow the trees which yield the finest quality of *rubber-gum. **1896** *Dialect Notes* I. 423 **Rubber ice*, thin ice that bends when skated upon. **1916** *Ladies' Home Jrnl.* Apr. 101/2 'Soft as Cheese!' Doctor Rolfe concluded. 'Rubber ice and air holes.' **1962** W. O. MITCHELL *Kite* xiv. 171 Jimmy Sangster had gone through rubber ice, to be found far downstream in a back-water. **1980** *Private Eye* 29 Feb. 13/1 Even the *rubber johnny merchants gave him the thumbs down. **1961** *John o' London's* 30 Nov. 610/3 A worthless cheque is a **rubber kite*. **1923** *Daily Mail* 28 May 3 A new process for the manufacture of *rubber-leather compounds. **1922** *Encycl. Brit.* XXXII. 299/1 Isoprene undergoes polymerization on exposure to light with the production of a *rubber-like mass. *a* **1930** D. H. LAWRENCE *Last Poems* (1932) 156 The vibration of the motor-car has bruised their insensitive bottoms Into rubber-like deadness. **1959** *Times* 27 Apr. (Rubber Industry Suppl.) p. ii/4 Some of the earliest research work on a synthetic product with rubberlike properties was carried out in this country. **1888** *Rubber plant [see RUBBER *sb.*[1] 12 b]. **1908** 'O. HENRY' *Gentle Grafter* 138 The little wine-stained table..between the rakish rubber plant and the framed palazzio della something. **1959** C. MACINNES *Absolute Beginners* 81 The rubber-plants in the espressos had been dusted. **1971** *New Scientist* 9 Sept. 554/1 The prime atmospheric essential that they should be places fit for rubber plants to live in. **1934** J. A. SINCLAIR *Airships* iii. 65 The envelopes were composed of *rubber-proofed fabric, two fabrics being used with rubber interposed between them, and also on the inner or gas surface. **1960** *Textile Terms & Definitions* (Textile Inst.) (ed. 4) 123 Rubber-proofed sheeting. **1897** J. VAN DENBURGH *Reptiles Pacific Coast & Gt. Basin* 156 The *Rubber Snake..is not rare in the moister portions of California. **1954** R. C. STEBBINS *Amphibians & Reptiles Western N. Amer.* 352/2 Rubber Snake... Usually found in moist locations, often near, or within, coniferous woods. **1894** ALBERMARLE & HILLIER *Cycling* (rev. ed.) 471 The hole [is] discovered..and a small patch of rubber stuck over it with *rubber solution. **1911** *Encycl. Brit.* XXIII. 802/1 The best solvents for rubber are carbon bisulphide, benzol and mineral naphtha, carbon tetrachloride and chloroform. These liquids, either alone or mixed, are employed in making the rubber solutions used for technical purposes. **1967** E. SHORT *Embroidery & Fabric Collage* ii. 45 It is also a useful precaution to put a spot of rubber solution onto the endings of threads on the back of the work. **1972** *Materials & Technol.* V. xiv. 516 Sometimes rubber cements are made for impregnating or proofing of fabrics, or rubber solutions are prepared for dipping or adhesive purposes. **1950** *N.Z. Jrnl. Agric.* Oct. 300/1 During the war..*rubberware of any kind was very scarce. **1977** *Hot Car* Oct. 71/2 A full range of butch and beefy rubberware is also stocked both State-side and UK. **1967** G. FREEMAN *Undergrowth of Lit.* x. 150 There is also a comprehensive catalogue of the latest range of *rubberwear called 'Black Panther'. **1972** *Guardian* 2 Dec. 10/1 Allen Jones's search for potent imagery has led him into a vicarious world..[of] rubber-wear and lingerie catalogues.

rubber ('rʌbə(r)), *sb.*[2] Also 6-7 rubbers. [Of obscure origin: there is no evident connexion with prec. Hence Du. and G. *robber*, F. *robre*.

It is not quite clear whether the original form is that with or without *-s*, and except where *a* or *one* precedes, it is uncertain whether *rubbers* in the earlier quots. is to be taken as sing. or pl.]

In various games of skill or chance, a set of (usually) three games, the last of which is played to decide between the parties when each has gained one; hence, two games out of three won by the same side. Sometimes, a set of five games, or the winning of three of these by one side.

1. a. In bowls. †Also, in early use, the additional decisive game.

α. **1599** PORTER *Angry Wom. Abingdon* (Percy Soc.) 8 Weele to the greene to bowles... Phillip, come, a rubbers, and so leaue. **1602** DEKKER *Satirom.* Wks. 1873 I. 263 *Min.* I, a match, since he hath hit the Mistris so often i'th foregame, we'll eene play out a rubbers. *Sir Van.* Play out your rubbers in God's name.

β. **1606** *Choice, Chance*, etc. (1881) 33 Will you make one at bowles for a rubber or two? **1611** MIDDLETON & DEKKER *Roaring Girl* III. ii, When your husband comes from his rubbers in a false alley.., his bowls run with a wrong bias. **1650** T. B[AYLEY] *Worcester's Apoph.* 14 Presuming more upon his good bowling, then good manners, [he] continued the familiarity that should have ended with the rubbers. **1688** HOLME *Armoury* III. xvi. (Roxb.) 70/2 Bowl out the Rubber is to bowl a third game for the betts, when the players haue gotten one apeece. **1855** KINGSLEY *Westw. Ho!* xxx, There, Vice-Admiral, you're beaten, and that's the rubber.

fig. **1635** QUARLES *Embl.* I. x. Wks. (Grosart) III. 53/1 Who breathes that boules not;..every sinner Has plaid his rubbers: Every soule's a winner. **1659** *Burton's Diary* (1828) III. 475 Here is a rubber playing in Christendom. Can you, by law or conscience, undertake to assist either party? **1666** D. LLOYD *State Worthies* (1670) 199 This Lord was the only Person I have read of, who thus in a manner played Rubbers, when his Head lay at stake; and having lost the fore, recovered the after-game.

b. *Prov.* (See quots.)

Rubbers here is app. a late alteration of *rubs*.

1797 NELSON Feb. in Nicolas *Disp.* (1845) II. 350 They who play at balls must expect rubbers. *a* **1842** DE QUINCEY *Whiggism in Relat. Lit.* Wks. 1857 VI. 163 They who play at bowls must look for rubbers. **1874** L. STEPHEN *Hours in Libr.* (1892) I. 384 Those who play at bowls must look out for rubbers. **1888** 'R. BOLDREWOOD' *Robbery under Arms* (1890) 348 If you play at bowls, you must take rubbers.

2. At whist (also cribbage, backgammon, bridge).

1744 S. FIELDING *Adventures D. Simple* I. II. i. 140 The best Expedient to be found out is, to play a Rubbers at one place, and then drive their Horses to death, to get to the other time enough not to disappoint their Friends. **1749** FIELDING *Tom Jones* XV. iii, They were engaged in a rubber at whist. **1764** in *Priv. Lett. Ld. Malmesbury* (1870) I. 105, I played one rubber of crown cribbage. **1798** CHARLOTTE SMITH *Yng. Philos.* I. 108 A lonely residence..where a rubber was with difficulty made up. **1850** THACKERAY *Pendennis* xv, There was a party in Clavering..who held him up to odium because he played a rubber at whist. *Ibid.*, A dreary rubber at backgammon with the widow. **1886** *Biritch* 3 After each rubber there is a fresh cut for partners. **1892** 'F. ANSTEY' *Voces Pop.* Ser. II. 116 Well, I won't say 'no' to a quiet rubber. **1908** *Laws of Auction Bridge* § 11 At the end of the rubber the total scores..are added up. **1930** [see AUCTION *sb.* 2 b]. **1960** J. BETJEMAN *Summoned by Bells* vi. 56 Depositing their wraps and settling down To a nice rubber. **1965** *Listener* 20 May 758/3 Even a 33 per cent. chance of game is worth taking if the reward is a 700 rubber.

fig. **1798** *Anti-Jacobin* 2 Apr. (1852) 93 Play the Long Rubber of connubial life. **1847** S. R. HOLE *Hints to Freshmen*, etc. (ed. 2) 38 In the rubber of University life.. Clubs are no longer trumps.

3. In cricket, lacrosse and miscellaneous uses.

1792 in H. T. Waghorn *Dawn of Cricket* (1906) 118 The first game of the rubber. **1807** PIKE *Sources Mississ.* (1810) 100 When either party gains the first rubber, which is driving it quick round the post, the ball is again taken to the centre. **1833** T. HOOK *Parson's Dau.* I. vi, Harbottle and Harvey..retired to the adjoining room, and began a rubber at billiards. **1874** HEATH *Croquet Player* 91 Each pair plays a rubber of three games, the side which wins two out of the three winning the rubber. **1882** *Standard* 11 Sept. 3/3 The Stow-in-the-Wold Club has beaten the Royal Forest of Dean Lawn-tennis Club by sixteen rubbers to five. **1895** J. N. PENTELOW *Eng. v. Austral.* 76 Shaw's team thus winning the rubber in fine style. **1897** *Westm. Gaz.* 9 June 9/3 As in the case of America Cup, a rubber of races has to be sailed. **1912** J. B. HOBBS *Recovering 'Ashes'* 120 England thus decisively winning the match and the rubber by an innings and 225 runs. **1955** *Times* 10 June 4/1 It was not a sparkling partnership, but it was a sober and extremely serviceable start to the new rubber. **1975** *Cricketer* May 8/1 His side won four to one in the recent rubber in Australia.

†**4.** *fig.* or *transf.* **a.** ***to hold out rubbers***, to hold one's own, keep one's ground. *Obs.*

1593 G. HARVEY *Pierce's Super.* Wks. (Grosart) II. 76 Calumny and her coosen-german Impudency, wil not alwaies hould-out rubbers. **1597** *Return fr. Parnass.* I. i. 396 How hast thou held out rubbers ere since thou wentest from Parnassus? *Ibid.* 400 As for my holdinge out rubbers [etc.].

†**b.** An additional turn or spell at something; also simply, a spell, round, turn. *Obs.*

a **1643** W. CARTWRIGHT *Chambermaid's Posset* xv. in Wks. (1651) 231 The Glass was Compell'd still Rubbers to run, And he counted the fift Evangelist. **1661** A. BROME *Songs & Poems* 189 So here's t' you (Charles) a Rubbers too't. Here's a Cast more; if that wont do't, Here's half a dozen more. **1691** MOUNTFORT *Greenwich Park* II. iii, Agreed, then we'll first to Supper, and for a Rubbers at scampring.

†**c.** ***a rubber at cuffs***, a scuffle or fight in which only the hands are employed. *Obs.*

1668 R. L'ESTRANGE *Vis. Quev.* (1708) 129 The Thief, after a great struggle, and a good lusty Rubber at Cuffs, has made a shift to save himself. **1691** SOUTHERNE *Sir Ant. Love* I. i, Never offer'd at..a quarrel above a rubber at Cuffs. **1692** R. L'ESTRANGE *Fables* ccclxxvi. (1694) 396 These Two Boobies try their Title to him by a Rubber at Cuffs. **1694** JER. COLLIER *Misc., Duelling* 37.

†**d.** A quarrel; a turn or bout of quarrelling or recrimination. *Obs.*

1688 SHADWELL *Sqr. Alsatia* II. i, This is the old fellow I had like to have had a rubbers with in the morning. *a* **1700** B. E. *Dict. Cant. Crew, Rubbers*,..a Rencounter with drawn Sword, and Reflections made upon any one. **1705** VANBRUGH *Confederacy* II, If you please to drop yourself in his way, six to four but he scolds one rubbers with you.

5. *attrib.* and *Comb.*, as (sense 2) ***rubber player, saver, -value***; **rubber bridge**, a type of bridge in which the hands are not replayed and in which settlement is made after each rubber; **rubber game**, a game played to determine the winner of a series; **rubber match**, a match to determine the winner of a series; also *fig.*

1936 R. LEDERER *Mod. Contract & Duplicate* 10 At *Rubber Bridge you are faced by a variety of partners. **1951** E. CULBERTSON *Bidding & Play in Duplicate Contract Bridge* xv. 194 The strategy of bidding and play in total-point duplicate is almost exactly the same as the strategy of bidding and play in rubber bridge. **1977** *Times* 29 Aug. 6/4 The real experts preferred rubber bridge at which they could win hard cash. **1908** R. FOSTER *Auction Bridge* 32 It is very important not to let players make a declaration that will put them out, especially on the *rubber game. **1946** J. CARY *Moonlight* ix. 68 'Of course it was always a *rubber match,' Robin was saying to Amanda. 'From the first night. It didn't seem to matter at first. The really *interesting* thing was how it went bad on us.' **1976** *National Observer* (U.S.) 20 Nov. 5/1 In the rubber match this year, he seems to have sneaked by the same Sam Young with those 201 votes. **1977** *New Yorker* 25 July 58/1 In their rubber match the following year it was Miss Sutton, 6-1, 6-4. **1974** *Times* 16 Feb. 15/2 Without..a code, even the strongest *rubber player..will fail to find the perfect answers. **1928** A. E. M. FOSTER *Auction Bridge for All* 201 Z's bid was a good and cheap *rubber saver. **1912** F. IRWIN *Fine Pts. Auction Bridge* 166 The *rubber-value is 250 points above the line.

rubber, obs. Sc. f. ROBBER; var. RUBBOUR *Obs.*

rubber ('rʌbə(r)), *v.* [f. RUBBER *sb.*[1] 11. In sense 1 abbrev. for RUBBERNECK.]

1. a. *intr.* To turn the head round in order to look at something. Also const. *around, for. U.S. slang.*

1896 ADE *Artie* xi. 100 About a dozen ringers followed us in and stood around rubberin. **1899** [see RUBBERNECK]. **1899** W. J. KOUNTZ *Billy Baxter's Lett.* 4 Up there you are likely any minute to come face to face with an Apache or some leftover Aztec rubbering around among the trees. **1901** H. MCHUGH *John Henry* 10 Glancing out in the dining-room to see if mother was rubbering. *Ibid.* 92 She almost cracked her throat trying to rubber at him and play cards at the same time. **1910** 'O. HENRY' *Whirligigs* viii. 108 Every few minutes he would pick up his stick rifle and tiptoe to the mouth of the cave to rubber for the scouts of the hated paleface. **1916** H. L. WILSON *Somewhere in Red Gap* ii. 58 So I rubbered awhile,..and then I forgot 'em, looking at some other persons that come in. **1929** WODEHOUSE *Gentleman of Leisure* xiii. 107 Shall I rubber around and find out where is dey kept, boss? **1930** *Living Age* 1 Apr. 183 Bill Coyote.. was loping around the trail and rubbering for eats. **1950** *Chicago Tribune* 24 Jan. III. 1, I just saw Moon Mullins out in the alley rubbering up here. **1974** P. DE VRIES *Glory of Hummingbird* (1975) ii. 13 The oncoming cleric who could be seen from the curtained window at which we all rubbered to be even now approaching.

b. To listen or listen *in* (on a party telephone line). *N. Amer. colloq.*

1920 S. LEWIS *Main St.* 189 Say, did you hear me putting one over on these goats that are always rubbering in on party-wires? I hope they heard me! **1948** *Southern Folklore Q.* Sept. 191 She's always rubberin' on a party line. **1963** G. H. THOMSON *Crocus Country* xxxviii. 237 No one thought it much of a crime to 'rubber', as it helped to pass the time for isolated people.

2. *trans.* To coat or cover with rubber.

1903 *Motor. Annual* 301 These tyres consist of a..canvas layer, very thickly rubbered on the edge. **1907** *Westm. Gaz.* 20 Nov. 4/2 A series of layers, composed of rubbered cords.

rubberdy, var. RUBBEDY.

rubber heel, *sb.* (*phr.*) [RUBBER *sb.*[1] III + HEEL *sb.*[1]]

1. A shoe heel made of rubber.

1916 *Daily Colonist* (Victoria, B.C.) 23 July 10/6 The best rubber heel costs only 10¢ more. **1921** *Dict. Occup. Terms* (1927) § 602 *Rubber heel maker*,..a moulder..engaged in moulding rubber soles and heels. **1922** *Encycl. Brit.* XXXII. 301/2 To a large degree the rubber heel has also displaced leather in medium-grade footwear.

2. One who investigates the conduct of members of his own organization; *spec.* an internal police investigator. *slang.*

1942 BERREY & VAN DEN BARK *Amer. Thes. Slang* § 458/16 'Spotter.' (One who spys upon employees.)..rubber-heel. **1970** G. F. NEWMAN *Sir, You Bastard* 12 It was the detail that led the Rubber Heels to Shepherds Market. **1975** *Listener* 6 Feb. 163/3 'Have those five-day wonders and rubber heels never copped a drop or fitted someone up?' (Have those graduates from the Police College investigating a complaint against an officer never accepted a bribe or planted evidence?)

3. *attrib.* and *Comb.*, as (sense 2) ***rubber-heel boy, inquiry, mob***.

1962 PARKER & ALLINSON *Courage of his Convictions* iv. 152 Stamper thought he'd be clever and he phoned the rubber-heel mob at Scotland Yard. **1971** *Daily Tel.* 18 Sept. 1/7 They led to investigations into the conduct of police officers by senior detectives. To all British police forces this type of investigation is known as a 'rubber heel' inquiry. **1976** P. FERRIS *Detective* vii. 110 They were the rubber-heel boys, the policemen who investigated policemen.

Hence **'rubber-heel** *v. intr.* and *trans.*, to investigate (a colleague), to keep (an associate) under surveillance, to spy *on*; **'rubber-heeler** = sense 2 above; **rubber-heeling** *vbl. sb.*

1959 M. PUGH *Chancer* 91 'So,' he said, 'you fancy yourself as a rubber-heeler?' The phrase usually applied to a policeman, sent to check on another policeman, and to get his facts from the underworld. The 'rubber-heeler' was disliked by criminals as much as he was disliked by the police. **1968** 'B. MATHER' *Springers* xiv. 157 But Sonia? Was she here only for her own safety—or was she rubber-heeling on me to make certain there were no slip-ups? *Ibid.* xv. 168, I was under the closest rubber-heeling and I certainly couldn't afford to interest myself in something that was no longer in my parish. **1973** —— *Snowline* iv. 49 To a brothel? Not with me rubber-heeling on him, he wouldn't... Anyhow, as a copper he'd want it for free. **1976** R. BUSBY *New Face in Hell* viii. 114 He..had..been rubber-heeled for flagrantly fabricating evidence, demoted to sergeant and sent back into uniform. **1977** F. WEBB *Go for Out* v. 71 The Metropolitan Police owned four such vehicles for use by their crime squads, rubber-heelers, or the Special Branch.

rubberie, obs. variant of ROBBERY.

'rubberiness. [f. RUBBERY *a.* + -NESS.]

Rubber-like quality.

1952 E. HEMINGWAY *Old Man & Sea* 125 The old man swung the club down on him..and hit only the heavy solid rubberiness. **1959** *Times* 27 Apr. (Rubber Industry Suppl.) p. vi/6 Embrittlement caused by high temperature oxidation or by loss of rubberiness in the cold must therefore be avoided. **1972** P. W. ALLEN *Natural Rubber & Synthetics* i. 1 All [rubbers] are high polymers, but of a special type possessing distinctive chemical structural characteristics which enable them to be transformed by one means or another into materials having the property of 'rubberiness'.

rubberize ('rʌbəraɪz), *v.* [f. RUBBER *sb.*[1] + -IZE.] *trans.* To treat, coat, or impregnate with rubber. Hence **'rubberized** *ppl. a.*; **'rubberizing** *vbl. sb.*

1912 *Chem. Abstr.* VI. 1554 Hides and skins..are rubberized by treatment with hot rubber soln. consisting of Para rubber, [etc.]. **1918** *Sphere* 2 Feb. 109/2 The rubberised cotton envelope has a capacity of 77,000 cubic ft. **1925** *Sunday at Home* Mar. 346/1 The balloon..is of rubberised fabric. **1936** *Lancet* 10 Oct. 865/2 The airman wore a two-piece suit of rubberised fabric. **1951** *Oxf. Jun. Encycl.* VII. 466/1 Putting on the rubber, or 'rubberizing', takes place in several stages. **1953** J. Y. COUSTEAU *Silent World* 8 To protect myself from cold I spent days tailoring and vulcanizing rubberized garments. **1963** A. J. HALL *Textile Sci.* v. 235 Water repellency obtained by means of silicones retains its permeability to air..—this advantage is not possessed by textile materials which have been rubberised. **1967** *Jane's Surface Skimmer Syst. 1967–68* 2/2 The skirts can be manufactured simply by cutting up and bonding strips of standard rubberised cloth. **1972** *Materials & Technol.* V. xiv. 454 (*caption*) Fabric being rubberised on calender for use as conveyer belt carcase. **1977** *Field* 13 Jan. 66/4 What is the best way to clean a white rubberised riding mackintosh?

'rubberless, *a.*[1] [f. RUBBER *sb.*[1] II.] Lacking rubber, or rubber tyres.

1884 *Longman's Mag.* Mar. 486 The terrible jar which its rubberless wheels..communicated to the system of the rider. **1894** *Ibid.* Sept. 495 A rubberless world, a hideous reality.

'rubberless, *a.*[2] [f. RUBBER *sb.*[2]] Without playing a rubber (at whist).

1891 MISS C. MITFORD *Lett. & Rem. J. Mitford* 99 Mr. Mills..had not undertaken a journey of some half-dozen miles..in order to be sent rubberless away.

'rubberneck, *v.* and *sb. colloq.* (orig. *U.S.*). [f. RUBBER *sb.*[1] II.]

A. *vb.* **a.** *intr.* To crane the neck in curiosity, to gape; also, to look around, to sight-see. **b.** *trans.* To stare at. Hence **'rubbernecking** *ppl. a.* and *vbl. sb.*

1896 ADE *Artie* iii. 23, I stood around there on one foot kind o' rubber-neckin to find an openin. **1899** *Pall Mall Mag.* Sept. 195 'To rubberneck' or, more concisely, 'to rubber'..is to crane the neck in curiosity, to pry round the corner. **1902** GREENOUGH & KITTREDGE *Words* 255 Recent slang has coined the word 'rubber-neck' for a gaping fellow in the street, who turns his head this way and that. **1927** H. V. MORTON *In Search of England* ix. 173 Here's a great sight going on that hundreds of rubber-necking tourists would pay anything to see. **1932** D. L. SAYERS *Have his Carcase* iv. 59 She..could not waste time rubber-necking round Wilvercombe with Lord Peter. **1939** *Daily Mail* 12 Apr. 8/4 Thousands of people..have 'rubber-necked' this monstrosity [*sc.* Ming, the giant panda] until their eyes ached. **1939** *Times Lit. Suppl.* 20 May 293/3 Mr. Graves resembles some of the professional guides who showed him round when he went 'rubber-necking'. **1946** *Sun* (Baltimore) 5 Nov. 10/7 The long, vaulted central hall..was crowded with chairs for invited guests with probably five times as many more people standing behind them. Londoners love to rubberneck on tiptoe. **1958** *Observer* 27 Apr. 6/7 Mr. Gunther has the born tourist's eye, and he can put down what he sees. He carries his rubber-necking from the pavements and the cafés to every corner into which he is allowed to penetrate. **1969** *Daily Tel.* (Colour Suppl.) 21 Nov. 73/2 Hortensio was rubber-necking like an American tourist, admiring the scenery, sniffing the breeze. **1973** J. MANN *Only Security* vi. 61 'You're not itching to get your hands on the site?'..'Not a bit, lovely just to rubberneck for a change.' **1977** *Time* 16 May 54/1 Wisconsin motorists may never see a purple cow, but they are rubbernecking at an enormous piebald blue one emblazoned on Farmer Hilbert Schneider's 75-year-old barn at Johnson Creek.

B. *sb.* **a.** Someone who stares; an inquisitive person; a sight-seer, a tourist.

1899 *Amer. Jrnl. Sociol.* May 726 Oh, no! in the language of the shop, she was only a 'rubber-neck'. **1909** G. B. MCCUTCHEON *Truxton King* iii. 41 They are the nobility—the swells. They don't hang around the streets like tourists and rubbernecks. **1918** 'I. HAY' *Last Million* xii. 188 Attended by a respectfully interested cohort of disciples, or rubbernecks. **1937** *Daily Herald* 6 Feb. 6 One of its valuable features will be to deprive the rubber-necks, who gloat over the domestic troubles of their neighbours in the local police court, of their entertainment. **1941** J. SMILEY *Hash House Lingo* 46 *Rubber neck*, tourist. **1974** P. MCCUTCHAN *Call for Simon Shard* xiii. 119 Can you clear the place up, Inspector? Move the rubbernecks on, back to bed? **1975** C. WESTON *Susannah Screaming* (1976) xxiv. 123 Without apology, Krug shoved through the rubbernecks.

b. *attrib.* and *Comb.*, as ***rubberneck party, ride, tour, tourist***; **rubberneck auto, bus, car, wagon,** a vehicle for taking people on a sight-seeing tour.

1906 'O. HENRY' *Four Million* (1916) xix. 192 The *Rubberneck Auto was about ready to start. The merry top-riders had been assigned to their seats by the gentlemanly conductor. **1949** *Chicago Daily News* 13 Aug. 5/6 That's the relatively harmless impression of Skid Row seen from the *rubber-neck busses. **1951** E. PAUL *Springtime in Paris* x. 175 Large rubberneck buses from travel agencies drive through, packed with sightseers from various States of the Union. **1915** *Dialect Notes* IV. 245 **Rubber-neck car, n. phr.*, sight-seeing vehicle. 'We saw several *rubber-neck cars* in Yellowstone Park.' **1916** GALSWORTHY *Sheaf* 276 There exists in America a vehicle called the 'rubber-neck' car. **1925** H. L. FOSTER *Trop. Tramp with Tourists* 326 The tourists go riding through town in *rubberneck parties. **1927** *New Republic* 12 Oct. 210/2 'The Manhatters' is founded upon the idea of a *rubberneck ride through this island. **1915** *Chicago Herald* 8 Nov. 4/2 The black and tans from the southern states..have been taken on a *rubberneck tour. **1949** *Nat. Geogr. Mag.* Dec. 783/2 Twice daily a horse-drawn stage leaves the Plaza on a 'rubberneck' tour. **1926** *Glasgow Herald* 27 July 10 As somebody has to get it in the neck, it may as well be..the *rubberneck tourist. **1942** BERREY & VAN DEN BARK *Amer. Thes. Slang* §424/2 *Rubberneck tourist*, a sight-seeing tourist. **1908** G. H. LORIMER *Jack Spurlock* xi. 321 The Major inquired loudly of Horton, the Governor's secretary, whether he was 'runnin' a blank *rubber-neck waggon'. **1932** *New Yorker* 11 June 38/2 The one who stepped from the rubberneck wagon happened to be the first [Japanese lady] they had ever seen. **1943** M. FLAVIN *Journey in Dark* 174 On the rubberneck wagons the fellow with the megaphone would point it out and say: 'Residence of Stanley Adams, financier and banker.'

Hence **'rubbernecker** = RUBBERNECK *sb.*

1934 in WEBSTER. **1942** BERREY & VAN DEN BARK *Amer. Thes. Slang* §765/8 *Rubbernecker*, a sight-seer. **1958** *N.Y. Times* 19 Apr. 16/5 He..completed a swing that lofted the ball over the barrier. He grinned apologetically at the rubber-neckers. **1969** S. HYLAND *Top Bloody Secret* i. 61 The usual crowd of rubberneckers on the far pavement. **1974** *Spartanburg* (S. Carolina) *Herald* 22 Apr. A4/2 American rubber-neckers in Moscow or Leningrad or elsewhere, with their free and easy manners, will leave as much an impression on the Russians they meet as they will take away with them.

rubberoid ('rʌbərɔɪd). Also **Rubberoid.** [f. RUBBER *sb.*[1] III + -OID.] A substitute for rubber. Also *attrib.*

Formerly a proprietary name in the U.S. Quot. 1968 seems to denote a different substance (cf. RUBEROID, with which there may have been confusion).

1884 *Official Gaz.* (U.S. Patent Office) 8 Jan. 112/1 Composition as a substitute for hard rubber—The James D. Frary & Son Co., Bridgeport, Conn. Application filed November 26, 1883. 'The word Rubberoid.' **1910** [mentioned s.v. RUBBER *sb.*[1] II]. **1951** R. BRADBURY *Illustrated Man* (1952) 160 The city awaited the soft tread of their rubberoid boots. **1968** S. E. ROBERTS *Of Us & Oxen* x. 137 We also lost a piece of rubberoid. I don't know how such a heavy thing could have gotten away.

'rubbers. *dial.* [f. RUB *v.*[1]] (See quots.)

1779 A. YOUNG *Agric. Lincs.* 329 The rubbers, a sort of itch; they [*sc.* sheep] rub themselves to death; no cure. **1799** [see RUB *sb.*[1] 6].

rubber stamp, *sb.* (*phr.*) and *v.* [RUBBER *sb.*[1] III.] **A.** *sb.* (*phr.*) **1.** (See quot. 1888.) Also, the imprint of such a stamp.

1881 *Instructions Clerks Census Eng. & Wales* (1885) 158/2 Rubber Stamp Maker. **1888** JACOBI *Printers' Vocab.* 115 *Rubber stamps*, hand stamps cast in vulcanized india-rubber. **1954** KOESTLER *Invisible Writing* IV. xxxix. 420 Queuing up each time..to obtain the rubber-stamp which granted a further stay of a day or a week. **1957** E. H. GOMBRICH *Story of Art* xiv. 203 The result looked like any rubber stamp we use today, and the principle of printing it on paper was practically the same. **1975** J. VAN DE WETERING *Outsider in Amsterdam* (1976) ii. 24 They looked at the imprint of the rubber stamp and the signature.

2. *fig.* Used of a person or institution whose power is formal but not real; a person who or body which endorses uncritically.

1919 W. R. THAYER *Theodore Roosevelt* xxi. 334 He may have heard the exhortation 'Be your own President; don't be anybody's man or rubber stamp.' **1943** *Ann. Reg. 1942* 235 This new body..was not to have any of the traditional attributes of a Spanish Cortes. It was to be..an assemblage of Government nominees and notables, a rubber stamp. **1956** A. WILSON *Anglo-Saxon Att.* II. i. 196 The danger of the oldest of all representative bodies becoming a mere rubber stamp. **1965** *Listener* 3 June 823/2 The regional councils were attacked as being mere rubber stamps for the regional boards. **1976** *Survey* Winter 66 The governmental assemblies..are most certainly not rubber stamps for the decisions of their respective executives.

b. *attrib.* or as *adj.*

1931 *Government of Oxford* 5 Others believe that..interest would be stimulated if Congregation could be relieved of its 'rubber stamp' duties. **1940** *Manch. Guardian Weekly* 29 Mar. 252 Lord Samuel transfixed the 1931–5 Parliament in a phrase: he called it 'The rubber-stamp Parliament'. **1946** W. S. CHURCHILL *Victory* 197 Equal opportunity for all, under free institutions and equal laws—there is the banner for which we will do battle against all rubber-stamp bureaucracies or dictatorships. **1953** *Manch. Guardian Weekly* 8 Oct. 7 The President does not want a 'rubber-stamp' Congress. **1977** *Time* 14 Mar. 23/1 This month's session of the People's Assembly, Burma's rubber-stamp parliament.

B. *vb.* (With hyphen.) *trans.* **a.** To mark with the imprint of a rubber stamp; to print with a rubber stamp.

1922 *Hotel World* 13 May 2 No hotel would rubber-stamp its stationery. **1965** M. SPARK *Mandelbaum Gate* iv. 113 Abdul went to start rubber-stamping the soles of smuggled sandals. **1973** *Radio Times 50th Anniv. Souvenir* 66/1 I'd written a fan letter to Bing Crosby... I received a photo of him back—with his autograph rubber-stamped across it.

b. *fig.* To endorse or approve uncritically; to pass routinely or automatically.

1934 WEBSTER, *Rubber-stamp, v.t.* a. To sign with a rubber stamp. b. Hence figuratively, to approve, endorse, or dispose of (as a document or policy) as a matter of routine, usually without the exercise of one's judgment. **1935** *Ann. Reg. 1934* 304 Moreover the Democrats in Congress were completely at one with the Republicans..in their dislike at appearing merely to 'rubber-stamp' measures drafted by the President. **1959** *News Chron.* 8 July 1/1 We do not believe that the purpose of a conference of our type is to rubber-stamp every declaration. **1978** S. BRILL *Teamsters* i. 15 The current trustees..had rubber-stamped loans to mob fronts.

Hence **rubber-'stamping** *ppl. a.* and *vbl. sb.*; **rubber-'stampish** *a.* [-ISH[1]], quasi-automatic, almost purely formal.

1932 L. C. DOUGLAS *Forgive us Our Trespasses* (1937) ix. 183 An hour and a half was spent..in a rubber-stampish approval of the 'tentative suggestions' sent from the faculty 'as a basis of discussion'. **1952** 'M. COST' *Hour Awaits* 24 The first letter of 1919—its address almost obliterated by rubber-stampings. **1958** *Sunday Times* 20 Apr. 16/4 He is, in a sense, a dictator, for..the Constituent Assembly is virtually a rubber-stamping body. **1969** *Daily Tel.* 26 Aug. 14 A fresh round of repressive legislation, including instant loss of employment for all who question the official line in deed or word, was all ready for rubber-stamping. **1979** *China Now* Mar./Apr. 3/3 A central working conference..took decisions of far-reaching importance. These decisions were..not just a rubber-stamping of proposals.

rubbery ('rʌbərɪ), *a.* [f. RUBBER *sb.*[1] III + -Y[1].] Resembling or suggestive of rubber. Also *fig.* and *Comb.*

1907 GALSWORTHY *Country House* II. v. 147 He left his hand against the animal's warm, soft, rubbery mouth. **1928** *Collier's* 10 Nov. 20/2 He..wrapped a thick hairy arm about Dan's neck in a chancery hold and squeezed his Face into the thick rubbery flesh of his side. **1935** W. CATHER *Lucy Gayheart* I. viii. 67 Even his white skin looked harder, somewhat rubbery. **1950** J. D. MACDONALD *Brass Cupcake* (1974) x. 95 He paid off with a very rubbery check. **1959** *Washington Post* 19 Jan. A12/2 Mr. Mikoyan's responses to questions on the television program, 'Meet the Press', last evening were..as evasive and rubbery a performance as one could imagine. **1962** *Times* 9 Apr. 4/1 His legs went rubbery as Pender smashed him with lefts and rights to the head. **1973** *Country Life* 1 Nov. 1322/1 Palms and rubbery-leaved banana plants. **1977** *People Weekly* 10 Oct. 44/2 There..are the two rubbery faces mugging through those unforgettable sketches that kept America home Saturday nights from 1950 until 1954.

rubbidge, dial. variant of RUBBISH.

rubbidy, var. RUBBEDY.

rubbie, variant of RUBBEE[2].

'rubbing, *vbl. sb.* [f. RUB *v.*[1] + -ING[1].]

1. a. The action of the vb. in various senses.

1398 TREVISA *Barth. De P.R.* XVII. clxi. (Bodl. MS.), Wiþ many brakingges, hechelinge, & rubbingge, hurden beþ deperted fro hempe. *Ibid.* XVIII. xliii, þat oþer [tooth] is ispared leste he schulde waxe dulle wiþ contynual smytinge and rubbinge. *c* **1440** *Promp. Parv.* 438/2 Rubbynge, *confricacio*. **1528** PAYNELL *Salerne's Regim.* A iij, Rubbyng of the body, exercise, & digestion. **1580** BLUNDEVIL *Horsemanship* X viij, The signes be apparant by the itching & rubbing of the Horse. **1617** MORYSON *Itin.* I. 114 It was presently made yellow, and with no rubbing could be made white againe. **1683** MOXON *Mech. Exerc., Printing* xix. ¶4 Rubbing of Letters is also most commonly Boys-work. *Ibid.* xxiv. ¶11 This Rubbing is only to spread the Inck pretty equally. **1742** MIDDLETON *Cicero* (ed. 3) III. xii. 286 The care that he employed upon his body, consisted chiefly in bathing and rubbing. **1784** TWAMLEY *Dairying Exempl.* 20 Turning, rubbing, washing, and cleaning, is more than one Man can easily perform. **1850** THACKERAY *Pendennis* xxxvii, That sort of bloom wears off with the rubbing of the world. **1899** *Allbutt's Syst. Med.* VII. 740 Rubbing of the limbs and passive exercises are of much importance.

b. With advs., as *down, off, out, over, up.*

1648 HEXHAM II, *Bestrijckinge*, a Stricking or a Rubbing over, or an Annointment. **1687** T. BROWN *Saints in Uproar* Wks. 1730 I. 77 Vermin, bred up to..rubbing out of milk-scores, and bilking of their landladies. *a* **1704** —— *Laconics* Wks. 1711 IV. 20 He ought to have preach'd against Swearing, Pilfering, rubbing out of Ale-house Scores. **1771** LUCKOMBE *Hist. Printing* 233 Whether it be well scraped, so as not to want rubbing down. **1837** LOCKHART *Scott* (1839) IX. 369 He perhaps had been a good housemaid to Scotland and given the country a rubbing up. **1875** *Encycl. Brit.* II. 635/1 The rubbing off of arsenical particles in cleaning wall-papers.

2. *Bowls.* (See RUB *v.*[1] 14 b and *sb.*[1] 2.)

1588 SHAKS. *L.L.L.* IV. i. 141 Sir challenge her to boule. *Boy.* I feare too much rubbing. **1609** *Ev. Wom. in Hum.* II. i, Lets leave rubbing a while, since the byas runs so much the wrong way.

3. *techn.* The process of straightening the wires in needle-making.

1833 J. HOLLAND *Manuf. Metal* II. 356 This operation, which is called rubbing, straightens the lengths perfectly. **1860** TOMLINSON *Arts & Manuf.* 2 Ser. *Needles* 6 The noise given out by this process of rubbing, as it is called, is very similar to that of filing.

4. An impression or copy made by rubbing. (See RUB *v.*[1] 1 e.)

1845 MISS MITFORD in L'Estrange *Life* (1870) III. xi. 199 Taking rubbings of the different brasses in the churches round. **1854** *N. & Q.* 1st Ser. IX. 369/1, I send you this copy from a rubbing of a quaint epitaph. **1872** ELLACOMBE *Bells of Ch.* in *Ch. Bells Devon* ix. 320, I have a rubbing of a legend with the cross and stop.

5. *attrib.* **a.** In sense 'used for, or in connexion with, rubbing', as ***rubbing alcohol, -bed, -block, -board, -cloth,*** etc. Also ***rubbing-place, -stroke, -surface, table.***

1955 T. STERLING *Evil of Day* iii. 37 Celia checked her vanity case to see that she had enough *rubbing alcohol. **1971** *Sci. Amer.* Aug. 114/3 Spray the wax joints one at a time with rubbing alcohol. **1850** HOLTZAPFFEL *Turning* III. 1196 Slabs of marble..that are required to have flat surfaces..are laid upon the *rubbing-bed. **1875** KNIGHT *Dict. Mech.* 1392/2 A *rubbing-block is used for carrying the grit or powder for grinding..the faces of marble slabs. **1788** *Abridgm. Patents, Bleaching* (1859) 46 *Rubbing boards used in bleaching. **1835–6** *Encycl. Metrop.* (1845) VIII.

704/2 For the purpose of setting this machine to work..the tops of all the rubbing boards are movable. **1596** Nashe *Saffron Walden* Wks. (Grosart) III. 135 Head-brushes and beard-brushes.., *rubbing cloathes of all kindes. **1611** Cotgr., *Frottoir*,..a rubber, a rubbing cloth. **1861** Reade *Cloister & H.* lv, A cupboard to keep his comb and rubbing clothes. **1701** *Lond. Gaz.* No. 3723/4 The Horses to be shewn and entred at the *Rubbing-house 9 days before. **1828** Darvill *Treat. Race horse* 240 So necessary part of a racing establishment as a rubbing-house. **1565** Cooper *Thes.*, *Strigilecula*, a..*rubbynge instrument. **1884** McLaren *Spinning* (ed. 2) 227 From the doffers, the ends are taken in the regular way to the *rubbing leathers, and on to the bobbins. **1834–6** in *Encycl. Metrop.* (1845) VIII. 704 *Rubbing machine.—This is used immediately after the preceding breaking process. **1600** [Dekker] *Shoemakers Holiday* iv. (1862) 15 A good *rubbing pin, a good stopper, a good dresser, your four sorts of awls. **1683** Moxon *Mech. Exerc., Printing* xix. ¶4 They pick up the Letter to be Rub'd, and lay it down in the *Rubbing place. **1854** Miss Baker *Northampt. Gloss.*, **Rubbing-pole*, the pole with which the ashes are stirred and dispersed over an oven. **1782** W. H. Marshall *Minutes* in *Rur. Econ. Norf.* (1795) II. 115 It is an excellent custom of the Norfolk farmer to erect *rubbing posts in the different parts of the inclosure. **1833** Loudon *Encycl. Archit.* §16 Pigsty, with a rubbing-post in the open area or feeding-place. **1881** Hardy *Laodicean* I. v, At the rubbing-post was another groom. **1817** W. H. Marshall *Review* IV. 441, I have been..erecting *rubbing rails in various parts of the island. **1849** Claridge *Cold Water Cure* 50 The *rubbing-sheet... The term 'rubbing' is used, because when the sheet is thrown on the body, great rubbing is used outside of it. **1622** Malynes *Anc. Law-Merch.* 289 The triall is made by the touch-stone onely, with an obseruation of the *rubbing-strokes vpon it to bee alike and of the same strength. **1862** *Catal. Internat. Exhib., Brit.* II. No. 2285 The taps are lined with the anti-corrosive alloy; and the density of their *rubbing-surfaces is so varied, that the friction is reduced to a minimum. **1883** Gresley *Gloss. Coal-mining* 207 Rubbing Surface,..the total area of a given length of airway, i.e. areas of sides, top, and bottom, all added together. **1939** 'E. Queen' in *Blue Bk.* Oct. 21/2 Koyle slipped from the *rubbing-table, and Barney Hawks began shooing men out of the shower-room. **1976** *N.Y. Rev.* 24 June 8/3 Lyndon Johnson liked to talk to people while.. lying in bed, on his rubbing table, skinny-dipping.

b. In sense 'exposed to rubbing', as ***rubbing-paunch***, ***-piece***, ***plate***, ***-strake***.

c **1860** H. Stuart *Seaman's Catech.* 13 The mast is ready for the piece of timber called a *rubbing paunch made of fir, to receive the chafe of the lower yard. **1839** *Civil Eng. & Arch. Jrnl.* II. 122/1 A *rubbing piece of wrought iron or other metal may be introduced into the under side of the shoe. **1869** Sir E. Reed *Shipbuild.* xv. 282 The outer edges of the wings are fitted with rubbing-pieces, or fenders. **1879** *Encycl. Brit.* IX. 247/2 The purse..has some protection provided by layers of old netting called 'rubbing pieces' laced to its under surface. **1969** *Jane's Freight Containers 1968–69* 550/3 The front end incorporates a *rubbing plate and retractable king pin. **1875** Bedford *Sailor's Pocket Bk.* vi. (ed. 2) 227 A jackstay should be fitted round the boat, underneath the *rubbing strake for the rain awning to be laced down to. **1928** G. Campbell *My Mystery Ships* iii. 36 The hinges were outboard, and had to be covered with rubber and made to look like a *rubbing strake for going alongside a jetty. **1975** *Daily Colonist* (Victoria, B.C.) 24 May 7/3 Her hull mostly white down to the rubbing strake then black to the waterline.

'rubbing, *ppl. a.* [f. Rub *v.*[1] + -ing[2].]

1. That rubs; that exerts friction.

1739 C. Labelye *Piers Westm. Bridge* 22 To have the Gudgeons or Pivots, and all the rubbing Parts made smooth. **1825** J. Nicholson *Operat. Mechanic* 79 The rubbing parts thus bear long on each other, with enormous pressures. **1900** Hasluck *Mod. Eng. Handybk.* 74 The rubbing faces of guide-bars are..filed up as true as possible before the block is ground in.

b. Such as results from rubbing.

1853 Kane *Grinnell Exp.* xxxii. (1856) 279 Every now and then a harsh rubbing creak along her sides.

†**2.** ***rubbing shift***: (cf. Rub *v.*[1] 15). *Obs.*

1675 V. Alsop *Anti-Sozzo* ii. 53 Though he can make a shift with him, he could have made a Rubbing shift without Him. **1679** —— *Melius Inq.* ii. viii. 371 Many sincere Christians make a rubbing shift to get them [i.e. the ceremonies] down, accounting them tolerable though not illigible.

Hence **'rubbingly** *adv.*

1891 Duncan *Amer. Girl in London* 277 [A cat] besought small favours rubbingly with purrs.

'rubbing-brush. [Rubbing *vbl. sb.* 5 a.] A hard brush, such as is used for rubbing with.

1559 in Feuillerat *Revels Q. Eliz.* (1908) 103 Toe rubbing brusshes. **1577** Harrison *England* ii. vii. (1877) i. 169 Some beards are made round like a rubbing brush. **1606** *Choice, Chance*, etc. (1881) 38 His haire of the color of a roane horse, and as hard as the stumpe of a Rubbing brush. **1645** in Carte *Ormonde* (1735) III. 423 If he doe, he will spoil the proverb, in making a rubbing-brush of a goat's taile. **1730** Bailey (fol.), *A Rubber*, one that rubs, or a Rubbing-Brush.

'rubbing-stone. [Rubbing *vbl. sb.* 5 a.] A stone used for rubbing, in order to sharpen or smooth something. Cf. Rubstone.

1648 Hexham ii, *Een Wrijf-steen*, a Rubbing-stone. **1657** S. Purchas *Pol. Flying-Ins.* 59 A peece of a rubbing stone, such as Mowers use to whet their sithes withall. **1703** Moxon *Mech. Exerc.* 240 Rubbing them on a rubbing Stone with sharp Sand. **1823** P. Nicholson *Pract. Build.* 389 The headers and stretchers in returns, which are not axed, are likewise dressed upon the rubbing-stone. **1842** Gwilt *Encycl. Arch.* §1890 After the bricks for the guaged work have been rough-shaped by the axe, they are rubbed smooth on the rubbing stone.

rubbish ('rʌbɪʃ) *sb.* (and *a.*) Forms: α. 4 rubbous, 5 rubus(s, robous(e, -ows, -eux. β. 5 robys, -iis, rubbes, 6 ruby(e)s, rubbis. γ. 5 robishe, -issh, robyshe; 5–6 rubbusshe, rubushe; 6 rubys(c)he, roobysche; 5–6 rubbysh, 6 rubbi(s)she, -eshe, 6– rubbish. δ. 5 rubrysche, 6 robrisshe, rubbrysshe. ε. 6 rubbyge, 6–7 rubbidge (9 *dial.* -idge, -ige, -itch). ζ. 6–8 (9 *dial.*) rubbage, 8 rubage. [Of obscure origin: app. related in some way to Rubble, but it is difficult to regard the early forms as AF. plurals of *robel*, *rubel*, esp. in the absence of any evidence that these are themselves of F. origin.]

1. a. Waste or refuse material, in early use esp. such as results from the decay or repair of buildings; debris, litter, refuse; rejected and useless matter of any kind. †Also, a heap of rubbish.

α. [**1392–3** *Rolls of Parlt.* III. 306/2 Qe nulle..gette ne mette..ascuns fymes, ordures, mukes, rubbouses, ou lastage, en la dite ewe..entre les lieux sus ditz.] *c* **1400** *Brut* ccviii. 238 þai toke stone, and made þerwiþ þe tour; and miche sande and morter, and olde robous þer was lefte. **1429–30** *Rec. St. Mary at Hill* (1905) 72 For cariage of ij lodys robous, viij d. *c* **1440** *Promp. Parv.* 435/2 Robows, or coldyr, *petrosa, petro.* **1480** *Wardrobe Acc. Edw. IV* (1830) 121 A grete loode of robeux that was left in the strete after the reparacion.

β. **1429–30** *Rec. St. Mary at Hill* (1905) 74 Also for ledyng awey of Robys in a lyghtere, xvj d. **1495** *Naval Acc. Hen. VII* (1896) 154 For euery ton Tyght of Rubbes & Stones iiij[d]. **1531** *Lett. & Pap. Hen. VIII*, V. 184 Cartes..caryng of rubys out of the towne to the towne wharffis. **1577** Harrison *England* ii. xiii. (1877) i. 252 He had no sooner begun to dig among the rubbis, but he found an exceeding number of pillers.

γ. **1477–9** *Rec. St. Mary at Hill* (1905) 85 For Cariage of v lood of Robishe from Forster lane and Estchepe, x d. **1497** *Naval Acc. Hen. VII* (1896) 171 Dyggyng of the clay and other Rubbysh bytwene the gates. **1528–30** in R. G. Marsden *Sel. Pl. Crt. Adm.* (1894) 35 All chawkerys castyng thar rubysche in the kyngs strem we do present. **1562** Turner *Herbal* ii. (1568) 22 Iris groweth..amongest olde rubbishe and remnantes of olde walles. **1593** Shaks. *Rich. II*, v. ii. 6 Rude mis-gouern'd hands, from Windowes tops, Threw dust and rubbish on King Richards head. **1611** Bible *Neh.* iv. 10 There is much rubbish, so that we are not able to build the wall. **1687** B. Randolph *Archipelago* 2 A dry ditch which is almost filled up with rubbish. **1712** Addison *Spect.* No. 512 ¶6 A Tree that grew near an old Wall out of an Heap of Rubbish. **1767** A. Young *Farmer's Lett. to People* 58 It is surprising what great benefit coal-ashes and mortar rubbish are of to stiff lands. **1838** Dickens *Nickleby* ii, A few hampers, half a dozen broken bottles, and such-like rubbish, may be thrown there when the tenant first moves in, but nothing more. **1870** F. R. Wilson *Ch. Lindisfarne* 61 The floor was covered with light rubbish.

δ. **1487–8** *Rec. St. Mary at Hill* (1905) 137 Makyng clene of the houssis, beryng owte & castyng oute the Rubrysche. **1519** W. Horman *Vulgaria* xxix. 240 b, Battz and great rubbrysshe serueth to fyl vp in the myddell of the wall. **1530** Palsgr. 263/2 Robrisshe of stones, *plastras, fourniture.*

ε. **1551–52** in Willis & Clark *Cambridge* (1886) II. 469 For carrying rubbyge owt of ij chambers. **1595** J. Chardon *Fulfordo et Fulfordæ* 34 [She] hath caused the..rubbidge and whatsoeuer was noysome to be remooued. **1603** Knolles *Hist. Turks* (1621) 1136 Not much better than rude heapes of rubbidge and stones. **1646** J. Hall *Poems* i. 9 Ere since poore Cheapside Crosse in rubbidge lay. **1684** J. Peter *Siege Vienna* 49 We perceiving from the Walls several Arms and Legs in the Air, mingled with the Smoke and Rubbidge. **1828** Carr *Craven Gloss.*, *Rubbidge*, rubbish, any worthless articles. **1854** [see ζ].

ζ. **1583** Stubbes *Anat. Abus.* ii. (1882) 25 Gold..mixt with other drossie rubbage, and refuse mettal. **1608** *Church-w. Acc. Pittington* (Surtees) 287 For careying the rubbage out of the double porche. **1657** Tomlinson *Renou's Disp.* 309 On stone walls, old edifices, and rubbages. **1670–98** Lassels *Voy. Italy* II. 122 The old round rubbage of brick which is here..was anciently a fine Fountain. **1730** A. Gordon *Maffei's Amphith.* 220 The Ground being raised round about it..by reason of Rubbage fallen down. **1791** T. Newte *Tour Eng. & Scot.* 321 That the earth and rubbage should be disposed of in this manner. *a* **1825** Forby *Voc. East Anglia*, *Rubbage*, rubbish. **1854** Miss Baker *Northampt. Gloss.*, *Rubbage* or *Rubbidge*, rubbish.

b. Const. *of* (a thing or place).

a **1513** Fabyan *Chron.* vii. 429 There in the rubbusshe & sande of the same [tower] they buryed..these .iii. bodyes. **1558** Warde tr. *Alexis' Secr.* i. vi. 118 b, Let this fylinge or rubbysh of yron become almoste redde. **1590** Greene *Orl. Fur.* (Rtldg.) 111 So rich shall be the rubbish of our barks, Ta'en here for ballass to the ports of France. **1791** Newte *Tour Eng. & Scot.* 321 This terrace is formed by the rubbage of old houses. **1813** Sir H. Davy *Agric. Chem.* (1814) 328 The rubbish of mortar from houses.

2. *fig.* **a.** Worthless stuff; trash. Also, a worthless person.

γ. **1601** Shaks. *Jul. C.* i. iii. 109 What trash is Rome? What Rubbish, and what Offall? **1649** G. Daniel *Trinarch., Rich. II*, cccxxxiv, What the Landlord then shall Rubbish call, Will be throwne out; and you are Rubbish All. *a* **1656** Bp. Hall *Rem. Wks.* (1660) 17 The body is but meer rubbish to the soul. **1790** Burke *Fr. Rev.* 254 The French builders, clearing away as mere rubbish whatever they found. **1792** A. Young *Trav. France* 266 Here is a character uncontaminated with that rubbish which we see in so many other men. **1846** Greener *Sci. Gunnery* 214 The consequence is that iron of the most inferior nature, the veriest rubbish is used. **1881** 'Rita' *My Lady Coquette* i, I wonder how people can trouble to send such rubbish. **1976** W. Trevor *Children of Dynmouth* v. 114 Stringer, the headmaster, was rubbish; the P.E. man went after the girls.

ε, ζ. *a* **1631** Donne *Progr. Soul*, 2nd Anniv. 82 What fragmentary rubbidge this world is Thou know'st. **1645** Howell *Twelve Treat.* (1661) 328 They wold make Gods House cleane.., but 'tis visibly found that they haue brought much more rubbage into it. **1716** M. Davies *Athen. Brit.* II. 242 Unless..a few such like rubbage can be made answerable for Primitive Christianity. **1885** R. Holland *Gloss. County of Chester* (1886) 293 They're nowt bu' *rubbitch*.

b. Worthless, ridiculous, nonsensical ideas, discourse, or writing.

γ. **1612** T. Taylor *Comm. Titus* i. 6 The Romanists were ready inough to take it vp, and stil reserue it among the rest of their rubbish. **1692** Washington tr. *Milton's Def. People* M.'s Wks. 1851 VIII. 249 From hence to the end of your Book, I find nothing but Rubbish and Trifles. **1734** Waterland *Wks.* (1823) V. 102 Others might be named who have gradually..come to reject Christianity itself, as needless and useless, and all revealed religion as mere rubbish. **1799** Southey *St. Gualberto* xxiv. Poet. Works VI. 201 Dost thou deem the legendary deeds Of saints like this but rubbish, a mere store Of trash, that he flings time away who reads? **1858** Lytton *What will He do* i. xvii, Vance talked such republican rubbish. **1899** *The Month* May 539 What is all this rubbish about a spirit-woman staying with the Duchess?

ε, ζ. **1624** Wotton *Elem. Archit.* i. 13 Such conceits as these seeme somewhat too fine among this Rubbage. **1711** *Medley* No. 32. 2 Every body must be persuaded, that all the Atheistical Rubbige..proceeded originally from the Revolution.

c. Const. *of*.

1602 Marston *Ant. & Mel.* v. Wks. 1856 I. 64 Staind and trampled on, As worthlesse rubbish of nobilitie. **1655** Fuller *Ch. Hist.* iii. 75 Otherwise..certainly this Colledg had been swept away, as Rubbish of superstition. **1704** F. Fuller *Med. Gymn.* (1711) Preface, The removing of the Rubbish of a Vulgar Error. **1742** Young *Nt. Th.* ii. 349 Embruted every faculty divine; Heart-buried in the rubbish of the world. **1859** Tennyson *Merlin & V.* 345 Ev'n in the jumbled rubbish of a dream. **1871** Burr *Ad Fidem* ix, The rubbish of exploded scientific theories.

d. *spec.* (See quot.)

1773 *Phil. Trans.* LXIII. 258 This robin afterwards sung three parts in four *nightingale*; and the rest of his song was what the bird-catchers call *rubbish*, or no particular note whatsoever.

e. In interjectional use.

1863 Thackeray *Round. Papers, Strange to Say*, One old boy..with..a murmur of 'Rubbish' slinks away. **1888** Rider Haggard *Col. Quaritch* xli, 'Oh, rubbish,' said the Colonel. 'How can a skeleton sit and air himself?'

3. *attrib.* and *Comb.* **a.** Appositive, passing into *adj.*: Of a refuse or worthless kind (*obs.* by late 18th c.) In mod. colloq. use = Rubbishy *a.* 2.

1594 Nashe *Terrors of Night* Wks. (Grosart) III. 261 To stand all his whole life sifting and winnowing dry rubbish chaffe. **1596** —— *Saffron Walden* Wks. (Grosart) III. 161 The verie excrements of the rubbishest wits that are. **1675** Cocker *Morals* 37 They refine His Rubbish Nature to a Golden Mine. **1722** Hearne *Collections* (O.H.S.) VII. 338 Those [coins], too, poor, brass, rubbish Stuff. **1979** M. Boyce *I was There!* 83/2 A side that can be easily beaten.. a rubbish side, Bedworth or Nuneaton.

b. Attrib., in sense 'composed of, given up to, rubbish', as ***rubbish-ballast***, ***dump***, ***-heap***, ***-mound***, ***-pile***, ***-tip***, etc.

1851 Mayhew *Lond. Labour* II. 287/1 The *rubbish-ballast..was only 3*d.* to 6*d.* a ton. **1888** *Pall Mall G.* 9 May 4/2 Not allowing this country to become the *rubbish-bin of European labourers. **1976** W. Trevor *Children of Dynmouth* iii. 72 It's hardly irrelevant that the country for which men were prepared to give their lives has become a *rubbish dump. **1878** *Jrnl. Speculative Philos.* XII. 12 In the *failures* to 'adjust'—in the *rubbish-heap, according to Spenser—lies, for them, the real key to the truth. *c* **1887** Miss W. Jones *Games Patience* iii. 11 Lay out nine cards in three rows; then proceed to form a rubbish-heap. **1932** Kipling *Limits & Renewals* 299 He very rarely went down into what had now become a rubbish-heap. **1959** C. Fremlin *Uncle Paul* iv. 33 The five of spades would have to go on the rubbish heap after all. **1864** Skeat tr. *Uhland's Poems* 82 So many a right may prove our own, Long hid beneath some *rubbish-mound. **1884** 'Mark Twain' *Huck. Finn* xxxvii. 375 The *rubbage-pile in the backyard. **1889** —— *Connecticut Yankee* xix. 235 Just a rubbish-pile of battered corpses. **1851** Mayhew *Lond. Labour* II. 286/2 *Rubbish shoots. **1839** Ure *Dict. Arts* 852 Schist proper for the construction of the *rubbish-terraces. **1922** Joyce *Ulysses* 422 On a step a gnome totting among a *rubbishtip crouches to shoulder a sack of rags and bones. **1971** *Country Life* 24 June 1597/3 Wayside flowers..are still plentiful enough..especially in waste places like rubbish tips.

c. Objective, as ***rubbish-cartage***, ***-carter***, ***-collector***, etc.; also ***rubbish-dumping*** ppl. adj. Instrumental, as ***rubbish-filled*** adj.

1851 Mayhew *Lond. Lab.* II. 288/1 The summer..is the 'brisk season' of *rubbish-cartage. **1851** Mayhew *Lond. Lab.* II. 293/1 A brief description of the *rubbish-carter, and the scene of his labours. **1885** *Census Instruct.* Index, *Rubbish Clearer, Weigher, Unloader. **1965** F. Sargeson *Mem. Peon* iii. 47 It was said that one [absent-minded scholar] had arrived at the college with his household rubbish after leaving his umbrella outside his gate to be collected by the *rubbish-collector. **1937** Blunden *Elegy* 84 By mysterious law each place Where Nature looks most gentle and glad Attracts the *rubbish-dumping race. **1954** W. Faulkner *Fable* 385 The corporal's body..went over backward..onto the edge of the *rubbish-filled trench behind it. **1851** Mayhew *Lond. Lab.* II. 289/1 The *Rubbish-Shovellers, or 'gangers'.

d. Special combs., as **rubbish-price**, a paltry price, such as might properly be paid for rubbish; **rubbish pulley** (see quot.); **rubbish shop, store**, a junk shop; **rubbish walling** (see quots.).

1805 W. Taylor in Robberds *Mem.* (1843) II. 107 Style which resembles what the masons call rubbish-walling, where fragments of anciently hewn and sculptured stone are built in with modern brick-bats and the pebbles of the soil. **1869** C. Schreiber *Jrnl.* 17 June (1911) I. 17 We found a small teapot, Venetian,..in a rubbish shop in the Spaderia. **1872** *Ibid.* 14 Apr. 156 He took us to a rubbish store.., from which we got nothing but a 'Davenport' plate. **1884** KNIGHT *Dict. Mech.* Suppl. 771/2 *Rubbish Pulley*, a simple form of tackle-block used with a rope in hoisting materials from a foundation or excavation. **1894** *Times* 19 Dec. 11/4 At the present time they thought sales undesirable, as it rarely paid to throw away stock at rubbish prices.

Hence **'rubbisher**. (See quot.)

1892 *Min. Evid. Labour Comm.* Group A. II. 2/2 A rubbisher, or labourer,..is the man who carries away all the material from the rock-men to the place where the slates are made.

'rubbish, *v.* orig. and chiefly *Austral.* and *N.Z.* [f. the sb.] **1.** *trans.* To disparage, criticize severely. Hence **'rubbished** *ppl. a.*; **'rubbishing** *vbl. sb.*

1953 T. A. G. HUNGERFORD *Riverslake* ii. 20 It Verity was going to tramp you for burning the tucker..he would have rubbished you long before this. **1965** *Telegraph* (Brisbane) 26 Feb. 13, I knocked him down and I hope he dies. He rubbished me to a mate of mine. **1968** *Comment* (N.Z.) June 33/2 The paper..was recently rubbished in the Catholic *Tablet*. **1972** *Guardian* 16 Oct. 8/1 This live show had a live and participating audience; so Hockney got briefly rubbished the moment his film ended. **1975** *Observer* 12 Jan. 17/1 His plight, and that of the cricketers, have both been latched on to as a chance, not to be missed, of rubbishing the Poms. **1977** *Bulletin* (Sydney) 22 Jan. 14/3 To that extent the much rubbished figures of the CES are consistent with the quite independently determined estimates of the Bureau of Statistics. **1979** *Spectator* 14 July 28/2 A conventional rubbishing of the Left and applause of the Right.

2. *Surfing.* (Chiefly in *pass.*) To tip (a surfer) off a wave.

1962 *Austral. Women's Weekly* 24 Oct. (Suppl.) 3/3 *Rubbished*, to be thrown off wave and dumped on shore. **1963** *Sun-Herald* (Sydney) 22 Sept. 84/5 The fate the board rider dreads is the 'wipe out'. This is when he is 'rubbished' or tipped violently off a wave.

'rubbishing, *a.* [f. RUBBISH *sb.* + -ING².] Paltry, worthless, rubbishy.

1808 ELEANOR SLEATH *Bristol Heiress* I. 157 Young ladies of fortune used to keep themselves to themselves..and not flaunt about with such rubbishing sort of gentry as those. **1849** ALB. SMITH *Pottleton Legacy* (1854) 174 He..had some rubbishing woods, where people went to make a noise with guns. **1863** THACKERAY *Round. Papers, Strange to Say* (1899) 437 I've seen literary fellows at Clubs writing their rubbishing articles. **1884** MISS BRADDON *Ishmael* xxix, What rubbishing music it is!

Hence **'rubbishingly** *adv.*

1837 *Athenæum* 236 They are childishly, rubbishingly, ridiculously otherwise.

'rubbishly, *a. rare.* Also *dial.* **rubbidgly**. [f. as prec. + -LY¹.] Rubbishy, worthless.

1796 W. H. MARSHALL *W. England* II. 47 Some rubbishly ill bred Cattle, on these Commons. **1819** LAMB *Letters* (1888) II. 29 Shakspeare has thrust such rubbishly feelings into a corner—the dark dusky heart of Don John. **1828** CARR *Craven Gloss.* s.v. *Rubbidgly*, A parcel o' rubbidgly stuff. **1889** *N.W. Linc. Gloss.* (ed. 2) 449.

rubbishry ('rʌbɪʃrɪ). *rare.* [f. RUBBISH *sb.* + -RY.] Rubbish; a collection of rubbish.

1894 KIPLING in *Scribner's Mag.* Dec. 670 Fillin' my bunk wi' rubbishry the Chief put overside.

rubbishy ('rʌbɪʃɪ), *a.* Also 9 **rubbishey**. [f. RUBBISH *sb.* + -Y¹.]

1. Abounding in, covered with, rubbish or litter.

1795 ANNA SEWARD *Lett.* (1811) IV. 143 The fruit-trees, to whose luxuriance the rocky, and..rubbishy soil, below the surface, has proved very inauspicious. **1842** SIR H. TAYLOR *Edwin the Fair* IV. i, To be reviled By shallow coxcombs whom I daily..snatch from a rubbishy tomb Amongst the ruins of their wits. **1853** G. JOHNSTON *Nat. Hist. Eastern Borders* I. 87 The true plant is common in hedges and rubbishy places. **1860** SIR H. ACLAND in J. B. Atlay *Mem.* (1903) x. 290 Washington..has a few palaces shied down upon a rubbishy heath.

2. a. Of the nature of rubbish; paltry, contemptible, worthless.

1824 SCOTT *St. Ronan's* xii, Like your rubbishy Birmingham pieces, that will..go off at half-cock. **1841** MARRYAT *Poacher* xxiii, Only look what a rubbishy affair this is. **1862** 'SHIRLEY' (J. Skelton) *Nugæ Crit.* xi. 487 A rubbishy conceit is more invaluable to them than a finished design. **1893** LELAND *Mem.* I. 27 She spoke of the building as a rubbishy piece of architecture. **1946** [see LEAVABLE *a.*].

b. *Comb.*, as ***rubbishy-looking*** adj.

1874 'MARK TWAIN' *Lett. to Publishers* (1967) 81 You notice that the Gilded Age is a rather rubbishy looking book.

rubbity ('rʌbɪtɪ), shortened f. next. Cf. RUBBEDY, etc. *Austral.*

1941 BAKER *Dict. Austral. Slang* 62 *Rubbity*.., a public house. **1957** 'N. CULOTTA' *They're a Weird Mob* (1958) vii. 104 'Where's Jimmy an' Pat?' 'Down the rubbity.' **1963** *Australasian Post* 8 Aug. 47/3 The proprietor of the local rubbity was a woman. **1968** D. O'GRADY *Bottle of Sandwiches* 54 Roebourne boasted one pub..—the rubbity—we soon became aware of what was doing around the little joint. **1973** A. BUZO *Rooted* 63 'Been down to the rubbity lately?' 'No, I haven't hit the hops for a couple of weeks.'

rubbity-dub (ˌrʌbɪtɪ'dʌb), altered f. RUB-A-DUB-DUB (b). *Austral.*

1957 'N. CULOTTA' *They're a Weird Mob* (1958) vii. 104 'What is a rubbity?' Joe said scornfully, 'Rubbity-dub.' **1971** *National Times* (Austral.) 13 Dec. 20/2 'Let's grab a do-or-die, have a couple of inky stinks at the rubbity dub...' Translated: 'Let's grab a pie, have a couple of drinks at the pub.'

rubble ('rʌb(ə)l), *sb.* Forms: 4 **robyl**, 5 **-oyll, robill, -el(l, -elle**; 5 **rubel**, 6 **rubell**, 7 **ruble, rubbil**, 6–7 **rubbel(l**, 6– **rubble**. [Of obscure origin; app. related in some way to RUBBISH.]

1. Waste fragments of stone, esp. as constituting the rubbish of decayed or demolished buildings; †also, rubbish, or refuse in general.

a **1400** *Little Red Bk. Bristol* (1900) II. 31 Cum fimo et robyl quod admouere faciant infra tres dies. **1436–7** *Abingdon Rolls* (Camden) 113 Pro roboyll extra domum cariando. *c* **1440** *Pallad. on Husb.* I. 340 On part of lyme and tweyne of rubel haue. *c* **1495** *The Epitaffe*, etc. in *Skelton's Wks.* (1843) II. 390 In a graue in the grounde Deth depe hath [him] drounde Among robel and stonys. **1531–2** *Act 23 Hen. VIII*, c. 8 §1 Whiche persons..conueied..grauell, stone, robell, earth, slime, and filthe in the said portes. **1593** NORDEN *Spec. Brit., M'sex* II. 25 A hautie citie..smothered in the ashes of her owne rubble and ruynes. **1614** RALEIGH *Hist. World* II. 311 There are found..goodly Marble pillars, with other hewne and carved stone in great aboundance among the Rubble. **1666** in *Misc. Curiosa* (1708) III. 182 One can see nothing..but old ruined Walls with Rubbel, Bricks and Stones.

1855 KINGSLEY *Westw. Ho!* xxx, A pop-gun fort, which a third class steamer would shell into rubble for an afternoon's amusement. **1863** TREVELYAN *Compet. Wallah* (1866) 260 Those are..the sand and rubble that overspread the land. **1879** *Cassell's Techn. Educ.* IV. 363/1 Other kinds of ballast, such as rubble, are sometimes difficult to obtain.

fig. **1567** JEWEL *Def. Apol.* To the Queen Aiiij, To refourme his Churche from that..lothesome heape of filthe, and rubble. **1589** COOPER *Admon.* 249 Casting out the rubble of the Synagogue of Antichriste. *a* **1618** SYLVESTER *Panaretus* 621 Even while I raze, I raise; and, of the Rubble Of petty States, I build one hundred double.

†**b.** *Med.* Fragments of a calculus. *Obs.*

1545 RAYNOLD *Byrth Mankynde* 29 When it is broken,.. the grauel, rubbell, or peecis therof, descend from the raynes or kydnees in to the bladder. **1561** HOLLYBUSH *Hom. Apoth.* 39 If the rubbel or shardes of the stone do put the to payn, then vse that bath.

2. Pieces of undressed stone used in the construction of walls, esp. as a filling-in.

1565 COOPER *Thesaurus, Caementitius*,..made of rubbell or ragge stones. **1608** J. KING *Serm.* Ps. xi. 2–4. 20 Peeces of timber, barres of iron, massy stones, together with all..the rubble and stones in the wals of that great and glorious pile. **1764** SMOLLETT *Trav.* (1766) I. xxiii. 353 The houses are built of a ragged stone dug from the mountains, and the interstices are filled with rubble. **1793** SMEATON *Edystone L.* §114 The interior filling of the walls was with rough Rubble, and fragments of the quarries. **1839** STONEHOUSE *Isle of Axholme* 265 In the walls, which are scarcely ten feet high and built chiefly of rubble, are great ashlar stones. *a* **1878** SIR G. SCOTT *Lect. Archit.* (1879) I. 20 They were equally at home in the use of brick, or flint, or rubble.

b. *ellipt.* Rubble-work.

1815 J. SMITH *Panorama Sci. & Art* I. 223 The best kind, or coursed rubble, admits of bond timbers without difficulty. **1879** *Cassell's Techn. Educ.* I. 97/1 In uncoursed rubble.., stones of any size..are used without any reference to their heights.

3. *Geol.* Loose angular stones or fragments of broken material forming the upper covering of some rocks, and found beneath alluvium or overlying soil; also, water-worn stones.

[*a* **1728** WOODWARD *Fossils* I. 12 Those call'd Rubble-Stones. *Note.* They owe their Name, Rubble, to their being thus rubb'd and worn.] **1796** W. H. MARSHALL *W. Engl.* II. 5 The subsoil is also similar:—namely, a slatey rock, and a kind of rusty rotten slate, or rubble. **1852** LYELL *Elem. Geol.* (ed. 4) vii. 81 To this mass the provincial name of 'rubble' or 'brash' is given. **1860** MAURY *Phys. Geog.* i. 15 Treating the rocks less gently, it..rolls, and rubs them until they are fashioned into pebbles, rubble, or boulders. **1879** D. M. WALLACE *Australasia* iv. 74 The few inches of surface soil and rubble overlying the Silurian rock on the slopes and spurs of the hills.

b. *local.* A hard chalk often used in making field-roads.

1879 JEFFERIES *Wild Life* ii. 20 The byroads and paths made with the chalk or 'rubble' glare in the sunlight.

c. *pl.* Small coal; slack.

1883 GRESLEY *Gloss. Coal-mining* 207.

d. (See quots.)

1876 *Nature* 9 Nov. 31/1 The head of the bay..was filled with pack ice consisting of numerous small floe pieces.. intermixed with 'rubble', or 'boulder' ice. **1886** A. W. GREELY *3 Years Arctic Service* II. xxxiii. 45 Broken irregular piles of ice are known as rubble, which is the worst of all ice for travel.

4. (See quot. 1858.)

1858 SIMMONDS *Dict. Trade, Rubbles*, a miller's name in some counties for the whole of the bran or outside skin of the wheat, before being sorted into pollard, bran, sharps, etc. **1876** A. H. HASSALL *Food* 361 The principal adulterations of oatmeal..are those with the refuse matter of oats, of barley, and even wheat, termed 'rubble' and 'sharps'.

5. *attrib.* **a.** 'Of the nature of, consisting of, rubble', as ***rubble ballast, coal, granite***, etc.; also ***rubble ice*** (see 3 d).

1712 *Phil. Trans.* XXVII. 542 A dark, gray, hard Iron Oar, called the Rubble Iron-Stone. **1844** A. W. PUGIN in Purcell *Life & Lett. A. P. de Lisle* (1900) I. iv. 82 From the nature of the material used—a sort of rubble granite. **1855** J. PHILLIPS *Man. Geol.* 193 Heathen and rubble coals and partings. **1889** WELCH *Text Bk. Naval Archit.* ii. 27 A ship having this characteristic may be rendered stable in the upright position by the introduction of rubble or water ballast low down in the ship.

b. 'Constructed of, making use of, rubble', as ***rubble building, masonry, wall***, etc.

1825 J. NICHOLSON *Operat. Mechanic* 537 A wall built of unhewn stone, whether it be built with mortar or otherwise, is called a rubble wall. **1835** RICKMAN *Styles Archit. Engl.* (ed. 4) 308 Rubble walling is generally of pieces more nearly approaching a cube. **1844** H. STEPHENS *Bk. Farm* I. 170 To test if rubble masonry is well built. **1856** MORTON *Cycl. Agric.* II. 386/1 Breaking joint over every small stone in the wall in rubble building. **1881** S. WALPOLE *Rep. Salmon Fish.* App. 77 A rubble weir..has recently been built across the Severn at Llanidloes.

'rubble, *v.* [f. prec.]

†**1. a.** *trans.* ? To bring to ruin. *Obs.*⁻¹

c **1425** *Cast. Persev.* 1944 in *Macro Plays* 135 ȝone rappokis I ruble, & al to-rase; boþe with schot & with slynge I caste with a sleyt, with care to ȝone castel to crachen & to crase.

b. *trans.* To reduce to rubble. Also *fig.* Chiefly in *pass.* and as **'rubbled** *ppl. a.*

1926 F. M. FORD *Man could stand Up* I. ii. 37 Things had become more rubbled—mixed up with alarums. **1945** *Daily Progress* (Charlottesville, Va.) 2 Mar. 1/8 Cologne, rubbled anew after dawn by a thousand British heavy bombers. **1953** *Encounter* Nov. 52/1 Places like Priam's, scarcely now to be identified among the rubbled trenches that were Ilium. **1978** *Islands* (N.Z.) Aug. 67 O Brave New World..without cities and the bombs to rubble them.

2. *intr.* To poke or crawl about among rubbish or refuse. Also *fig.* Now *dial.*

1637 BASTWICK *Litany* III. 22 By rubbling and grubbing in those old errors and heresies, you may perhaps get some infection. **1896** *Warwickshire Gloss.* 196 Don't let the child rubble among them 'ere dusty things.

3. (See quot.) Now *dial.*

1863 J. R. WISE *New Forest* Gloss., *To Rubble*, to remove the gravel, which is deposited throughout the Forest in a thick layer over the beds of clay or marl.

rubble, obs. form of ROUBLE.

'rubbler. [f. RUBBLE *sb.*] (See quots.)

1865 BOWER *Slate Quarries* 19 Writing Slates are generally put into the hands of young boys, for the purpose of teaching them the art of slate-making. These youngsters are called rubblers. **1893** *Labour Commission Gloss.*, *Rubbler*, an irregular workman in a slate quarry. *Ibid.*, All boys and beginners are rubblers at first.

'rubble-stone. Also **ruble, rubble stone, rubblestone**. [f. RUBBLE *sb.*]

1. = RUBBLE *sb.* 2 and 3.

1707 MORTIMER *Husb.* (1721) I. 71 In Oxfordshire, where they have a lean Earth and a small rubble Stone, or a sowre sort of Land mixed with it. **1787** G. WHITE *Selborne* i, What is called a white malm, a sort of rotten or rubble stone, which, when turned up to the frost and rain, moulders to pieces. **1817** KEATINGE *Trav.* I. 208 The whole country is covered..with rubble-stone—strongly hinting at a Neptunian process. **1833** LOUDON *Encycl. Archit.* 545 The walls may be of rubblestone, bricks, or clay lumps. **1888** RIDER HAGGARD *Col. Quaritch* xli, A..vault..built of rubble stone.

attrib. **1853** R. S. SURTEES *Sponge's Sp. Tour* xxix. 178 An armless sign-post on one side, and a rubble-stone bridge.. on the other.

2. *pl.* Stones of the nature of rubble.

a **1728** WOODWARD *Fossils* I. 13 Neither the Bowlders, nor Rubble-Stones, are ever invested with an exterior stony Crust or Skin. **1789** J. WILLIAMS *Min. Kingd.* II. 7 Whinstone..is frequently too hard and strong to be commonly quarried for ruble-stones. **1822** SCOTT *Let.* in *Lockhart* (1839) VII. 38 The ruble stones would do much more than pay the labourers. **1849** JAMES *Woodman* xxxv, [He] had to traverse a considerable number of round rubble stones.

'rubble-work. Also **rubblework, rubble work**. [f. RUBBLE *sb.*] Masonry composed of rubble or unwrought stones; also, fragments of stone mixed with mortar and used as a filling-in.

1823 P. NICHOLSON *Pract. Build.* 309 The core of the rubble-work of the Grecian walls is impenetrable to a tool. **1849** CURZON *Vis. Monasteries Levant* 133 The roof..is supported by four square modern piers of plastered brick or rubble work. **1888** RIDER HAGGARD *Col. Quaritch* xl, It appeared to be rubble work built in the form of an arch.

attrib. **1862** BURTON *Bk. Hunter* I. 41 A sort of rubble-work inner wall of volumes, with their edges outwards.

rubbly ('rʌblɪ), *a.* [f. RUBBLE *sb.*] Abounding in, consisting of, rubble or loose broken material; having the nature or form of rubble.

1733 TULL *Horse-Hoeing Husb.* xxi. 304 The Concavity of the Fin..must be greatest in a stony rubbly Soil. **1758** BORLASE *Nat. Hist. Cornw.* 152 Where nature has been more sparing of her cement, the ore is found in a lax, arenaceous, and rubbly state. **1829** *Geol. Trans.* 2nd Ser. II. 41 The next bed, called the Rubbly Bed, is remarkable for the quantity of casts of shells which it contains. **1839** *Civil Eng. & Arch. Jrnl.* II. 209/1 The chalk in this district is of a rubbly description. **1894** *Ramsay's Phys. Geol.* 148 Near the surface, it assumes a rubbly character, and forms a fertile soil.

†**rubbon**, variant of RUBAN, ribbon.

1781 PENNANT *Hist. Quad.* II. 523 Rubbon Seal..Marked ..with a stripe of a pale yellow color, exactly resembling a rubbon laid on it by art.

†**'rubbour**. *north.* and *Sc. Obs.* Also 4 **robbour** (?), 6 **rowbour**, 6–7 **rubber**. [Of obscure origin.] A cask or keg.

1362–3 *Durh. Acct. Rolls* 178 In uno pari de Rebbours [? *read* Robbours] de novo fact. cum ligatur. earundem. **1404** *Ibid.* 397 In..ij par' de rubbours, j par de costrell, j par de magnis flaketis.

1492 *Acta Dom. Conc.* (1839) 280, x merkis for certane panȝell crelis & Rubbouris. **1494** *Acc. Ld. High Treas. Scot.* I. 252 Item, for ane rubbour to the ter, xiiij *d.* **1501** *Ibid.* II. 44 For vj gallonis thre pointis Ryns wyne send to Ternway and for rubbouris to the samyn and carying of it, . . iij *li.* vij *s.* **1504** *Ibid.* 430 Item, for iiij rubbouris to put powder in . . viij *s.* **1552** LYNDESAY *Monarche* 2224 Sax gret Rowbouris [*v.r.* rubbouris] of wycht wyne. **1597** D. WEDDERBURN *Compt Buik* (S.H.S.) 87 The fynest wynes in rubberis or fyn Muskedallis. **1608** *Ibid.* 117 James Myln in Elgyn hes my flacon or rubber to fill with aquavitie.

rubby ('rʌbɪ). *Canad.* [f. *rubbing* (*alcohol*) s.v. RUBBING *vbl. sb.* 5a: see -Y[6].] **1.** A habitual drinker of rubbing alcohol (see sense 2 below).
1950 A. PALMER *Montreal Confidential* 102 The police department has probably given up keeping score of rubbies they have fished out of the river. **1965** *Vancouver Sun* 18 Oct. 35/6 Most of the dinner guests were men off the street, rubbies, derelicts, the jobless, alcoholics, the lost ones, residents of Vancouver's Skid road. **1978** W. S. AVIS in *Occasional Papers Dept. English R. Military Coll. Canada* No. 2. 45 Both skid roads remained to become run-down, unsavoury slums . . , the hangouts of drifters, rubbies, and other unfortunates.

2. Rubbing alcohol, sometimes mixed with wine, etc., used as an intoxicant.
1961 *Maclean's Mag.* 29 July 36/1 A gallon of wine and two bottles of rubby and you can throw a party in the jungles that'll last all night. **1974** D. RICHARDS *Coming of Winter* i. 29 And there in the shacks the old men hard on rubby, telling stories of the war.

Also ˌ**rubby-'dub** [cf. also DUB *sb.*[6]] = sense 1 above.
1950 A. PALMER *Montreal Confidential* 101 If the bum looks a bit plastered don't stop. . . Chances are he's a 'rubby-dub' and his mind is no doubt clouded with smoke. **1957** *Maclean's Mag.* 25 May 68/2 'We've got everything here from ex-cons to rubby-dubs,' says . . one of Elliot's six provincial policemen. **1972** *Daily Colonist* (Victoria, B.C.) 7 Mar. 31/8 Mr. Minister, don't talk nonsense—don't suggest the rubby-dub has to gather up enough money for his own treatment.

rubby-dubby ('rʌbɪˌdʌbɪ). *Angling.* [? f. RUB *v.*[1], DUB *v.*[1] 5: see -Y[6].] Minced fish such as pilchards, mackerel, etc., placed in a net-bag and used as a lure for shark and other large fish. Also *attrib.*
1957 R. ARNOLD *Compl. Sea Angler* xi. 176 As the rubby-dubby moves through the water, the oil from the broken-up bait spreads out from behind the boat, leaving an ever-widening channel down which the hungry sharks . . will cruise searching their prey. **1959** *Angling Times* 27 Feb. 6/3, I, drifting with a rubby-dubby trail, soon had a shark. **1960** *Sunday Express* 24 July 13/1 Two net bags stuffed with old pilchards and mackerel (the skipper calls it 'rubby-dubby'). **1970** *Daily Tel.* 2 May 9/3 Large fish can be attracted, like shark, with the 'rubby dubby' method. **1971** *Angling Times* 10 June 24 Ivan got over the rubby-dubby bags, and started a drift.

'rub-down. [f. vbl. phr. *to rub down*: RUB *v.*[1] 8.] An act of rubbing down in any sense.
1885 *Boy's Own Paper* 21 Mar. 305/1 When the stick has dried in shape, trim it to taste with a sharp knife, and give it a good rub down with sand-paper. **1896** S. HALE *Let.* 4 June (1919) 299 We reached here reeking, just in time for a rubdown. **1903** NEVILL *Penal Serv.* v. 43 The search parade and the 'rub down' four times a day constitute a sort of drill. **1917** M. T. HAINSSELIN *Grand Fleet Days* xv. 104 To think that I should get a rub-down like this from the Admiral. **1936** J. CURTIS *Gilt Kid* xiii. 133 Just imagine getting a rubdown at the copper-house and the bogies dragging a lump of coal out of his sky. **1936** 'P. QUENTIN' *Puzzle for Fools* viii. 63 We took rubdowns and other uncomfortably beneficial treatments. **1963** X. FIELD *Under Lock & Key* xi. 143 They and their cells are searched every fortnight or so, at irregular intervals and at an unexpected moment. The 'rub downs' usually lead to their precious belongings being removed. **1965** MRS. L. B. JOHNSON *White House Diary* 5 Oct. (1970) 325 Lyndon on the table getting a rubdown and holding them in conversation. **1977** 'E. MCBAIN' *Long Time no See* viii. 123 A hawker for one of the rubdown emporiums handed her a leaflet.

Rube, var. REUB.

rubeanic acid ('ruːbɪænɪk 'æsɪd). *Chem.* [tr. G. *rubeanwasserstoffsäure*, f. L. *rube-us* red + G. *-an* (as in *cyanwasserstoffsäure* hydrocyanic acid) + *wasserstoff* hydrogen + *säure* acid.] Dithio-oxamide, $[CS(NH_2)]_2$, an orange-red crystalline solid formed by reaction of cyanogen and hydrogen sulphide, and employed in analysis as a reagent to detect copper.
[**1884** *Jrnl. Chem. Soc.* XLVI. 1109 (*heading*) The so-called rubeanhydric acid (cyanogen bisulphydrate).] **1891** *Ibid.* LX. II. 1008 The following experiments show that the red compound ('rubeanic acid, rubeanwasserstoff') obtained by the combination of cyanogen and hydrogen sulphide behaves in many reactions as if it were dithi-oxamide, $NH_2{\cdot}CS{\cdot}CS{\cdot}NH_2$. **1928** *Q. Jrnl. Indian Chem. Soc.* III. 118 Rubeanic acid may be regarded as a tantomeric compound consisting of an equilibrium mixture of sym.-dithio-oxamide and sym.-di-imido-dithio-oxalic acid. **1967** *New Scientist* 2 Feb. 272/3 A test plate subjected to 500 hours accelerated weathering while protected with a polyurethane resin containing rubeanic acid shows no sign of tarnishing. **1981** *Sci. Amer.* Feb. 127/1 For a more sensitive test [for copper in silver coins] Epstein suggests using a saturated solution of rubeanic acid (dithiooxamide) in alcohol and a 20 percent solution of malonic acid.

ru'bedinous, *a. rare*[−1]. [f. late L. *rubēdo, -dinis.*] Reddish.
1864 WEBSTER (citing M. STUART).
So **ru'bedinousness,** redness. *rare*[−1].
1599 A. M. tr. *Gabelhouer's Bk. Physicke* 48/1 A tryede water for inflammatione, and rubedinousnes of the Eyes.

†**rubee.** *Obs.*[−1] [med.L. gen. of *rubea*, var. of L. *rubia.*] Madder.
c **1540** in *Vicary's Anat.* (1888) App. ix. 225 Take the Iuce of nightshade, the Iuce of plantaigne, the Iuce of Rubee.

rube'facience. *Med. rare*[−1]. [See next and -ENCE.] The fact of making red.
1843 GRAVES *Syst. Clin. Med.* xx. 240 Its effects are not limited to temporary rubefacience.

rubefacient (ruːbɪ'feɪʃənt), *a.* and *sb. Med.* [ad. pres. pple. of L. *rubefacĕre*: see RUBIFY *v.*]
A. *adj.* Producing redness or slight inflammation; *spec.* of counter-irritants.
1804 ABERNETHY *Surg. Obs.* 16 By means which also excite some counter-irritation, as rubefacient plasters. **1830** R. KNOX *Béclard's Anat.* 147 To protect the skin from the rubefacient effect of the sun's rays, which is commonly called sun-burning. **1896** *Allbutt's Syst. Med.* I. 421 In whooping-cough the use of rubefacient embrocations is held in high esteem as a domestic remedy.
B. *sb.* An application producing redness of the skin; *esp.* a counter-irritant having this effect.
1805 *Edin. Rev.* VII. 45 The more durable stimulus of heated salt with millet seed and other rubefacients. **1843** GRAVES *Syst. Clin. Med.* xx. 231 This liniment we are much in the habit of prescribing where a rubefacient is required. **1899** *Allbutt's Syst. Med.* VIII. 777 This may best be effected by rubefacients.

rubefaction (ruːbɪ'fækʃən). [See RUBIFY and -FACTION. So F. *rubéfaction.*]
1. *Med.* The action of making (the skin) red; redness of the skin, esp. as produced by some application.
1658 PHILLIPS, *Rubefaction*, a making red.
1831 J. DAVIES *Mat. Med.* 171 Applied to the skin it produces rubefaction, pain, and all the symptoms of inflammation. **1875** H. C. WOOD *Therap.* (1879) 568 Capsicum and the stronger spices afford excellent materials for rubefaction.
2. The production of a red colour in water.
1860 GRIFFITH & HENFREY *Microgr. Dict.* (ed. 2).

Rube Goldberg (ruːb 'gəʊldbɜːg). *U.S.* The name of the American humorous artist Reuben ('*Rube*') Lucius *Goldberg* (1883–1970), used *attrib.* of any unnecessarily complicated, impracticable or ingenious device of the kind illustrated by this artist. Hence **Rube Gold'bergian** *a.*
1956 RICE & STEINMETZ *Amish Year* 69 The whole Rube Goldberg device is hitched to a wire which runs through ringbolts attached to short poles stuck in the ground, all the way to the house. **1961** WEBSTER, Rube Goldbergian. **1962** *Time* 22 June 38 It [*sc.* Bertrand Russell's *History of the World in Epitome*] consists of a page with seven words, a drawing of the Garden of Eden, . . a drawing of a Rube Goldbergian battle scene, and a few final words. **1963** *Johns Hopkins Mag.* Jan. 20 Insofar as Congress' Rube Goldberg machinery is contrived to help it wait for the propitious moment, it is much to be valued. **1977** *Time* 26 Sept. 33/1 It contains a Rube Goldbergian arrangement of pulleys, ropes and rollers. **1978** *Nature* 9 Nov. 122/3 Orchids are Rube Goldberg machines; a perfect engineer would certainly have come up with something better.

rubeiboo, var. RUBBABOO.

rubel, obs. form of ROUBLE, RUBBLE *sb.*

†'**rubelet.** *Obs.*[−1] [irreg. f. RUBY *sb.* + -LET.] A little ruby.
1648 HERRICK *Hesper., To Closet-Gods*, In the midst, to grace it more, was set A blushing-pretty-peeping Rubelet.

†**rubell.** *Obs.*[−1] (Origin and meaning obscure.)
1621 BURTON *Anat. Mel.* II. iv. II. i, Scilla or Sea onion . . is an ordinary vomit, . . mixt with rubell in a little white-wine.

‖**rubella** (ruː'bɛlə). *Path.* [mod.L., neut. pl. of *rubellus* reddish.] German measles. Cf. RUBEOLA 3. Also *attrib.*
1883 QUAIN *Dict. Med.* 927 The rash of . . *rubella* closely resembles the eruption of measles. **1897** *Allbutt's Syst. Med.* II. 118 As a rule rubella runs its course without complications. **1962** A. SORSBY in A. Pirie *Lens Metabolism Rel. Cataract* 298 Congenital cataract . . can be caused by such frankly environmental disturbances as maternal rubella. **1970** *Nature* 11 Apr. 172/1 Growth retardation occurs in rabbits congenitally infected with rubella virus. **1971** *Where* Sept. 271/1 Blindness . . in an increasing proportion of cases . . is linked with additional handicaps such as deafness, cerebral palsy or mental retardation (for example, 'rubella' babies often have more than one handicap).

rubellan ('ruːbələn). *Min.* Also **rubellane.** [f. L. *rubell-us* reddish.] (See quot. 1868.)
c **1830** *Encycl. Metrop.* (1845) VI. 508/2 *Rubellan*, Red Mica? **1868** WATTS *Dict. Chem.*, *Rubellan*, an altered biotite . . occurring in small hexagonal forms, or a red colour, in a kind of wacke. **1888** RUTLEY *Rock-forming Min.* 197 Some varieties, as rubellane, show dark reddish-yellow or orange tints.

rubelliform (ruː'bɛlɪfɔːm), *a. Med.* [f. RUBELL(A + -I- + -FORM.] Resembling the characteristic rash of rubella.
1959 *Amer. Jrnl. Trop. Med. & Hygiene* VIII. 104/1 The rash occurs . . as blotchy, maculopapular, rubelliform or occasionally petechial lesions. **1969** *Amer. Jrnl. Epidemiol.* LXXXIX. 665/2 A rubelliform rash . . mild upper respiratory symptoms and absence of Köplik's spots were the clinical diagnosis criteria. **1976** *Lancet* 6 Nov. 990/1 Three children had a rash, rubelliform in 2 cases and localised and purpuric in 1.

rubellite ('ruːbəlaɪt). *Min.* [f. L. *rubell-us* reddish + -ITE[1] 2b.] A variety of tourmaline.
1796 KIRWAN *Elem. Min.* (ed. 2) I. 288 *Rubellite*, red shorl of Siberia. Its colour, crimson, blood, or peach red. **1823** W. PHILLIPS *Min.* (ed. 3) 126 The Rubellite . . is of various shades of red, from a slight tinge to a fine pink; it is sometimes of a violet colour. **1837** DANA *Min.* 323 Rubellite occurs in a species of lithomarge. **1897** *Edin. Rev.* Oct. 345 The rubellite is . . much worn in Russia.

Rubenesque: see RUBENSESQUE *a.*

Rubens ('ruːbɪnz). The name of the Flemish painter Sir Peter Paul *Rubens* (1577–1640), used *attrib.* in **Rubens brown,** a brown earth-colour; **Rubens hat** (see quot. 1960); **Rubens madder,** madder brown.
1860 Rubens brown [see CASSEL]. **1885** A. EDWARDES *Girton Girl* I. xiii. 250 A distant lovely head . . its waves of amber hair set off against the soft velvet of a Rubens hat. **1886** H. C. STANDAGE *Artists' Man. Pigments* vi. 67 Rubens brown is a native earth of an ochreous character. *Ibid.* 69 Rubens madder, otherwise known as Orange Russet, [etc.]. **1934** H. HILER *Notes on Technique of Painting* ii. 125 *Madder*, . . *Rubens madder*, . . etc. These names are now applied both to products from the genuine madder root, and also to those made from its synthetic colouring principles alizarin and purpurin. **1960** C. W. CUNNINGTON et al. *Dict. Eng. Costume* 185/1 *Rubens hat* . . , a hat with a high crown and brim turned up on one side. **1969** R. MAYER *Dict. Art Terms & Techniques* 341/1 Rubens madder is now made from synthetic alizarin. *Ibid.* 414/1 Rubens brown is a variety of Van Dyke brown.

Rubensesque (ruːbən'zɛsk), *a.* [f. prec. + -ESQUE.] Characteristic or suggestive of the paintings of Rubens; esp. of a woman's figure: full and rounded. Also **Rube'nesque** *a.*
1913 *Maclean's Mag.* July 106/2 There are, no doubt, eccentric artists who prefer a Rubensesque figure, but these are the exceptions, and for most private work and school work a spare figure is far more valuable. **1925** W. DEEPING *Sorrell & Son* xx. 185 He had a view of her broad back, and her robust curves. . . A Rubenesque figure, sumptuous and solid. **1927** *Observer* 17 July 15/4 The models of his choice are of rather Rubenesque fullness. **1952** G. RAVERAT *Period Piece* v. 87 She had auburn hair . . a charming Rubenesque complexion, and a deep rich voice. **1957** W. CAMP *Prospects of Love* II. xiv. 89 'Was she about as big as me?' . . 'Yes, I think she was. Slightly more Rubensesque hips, if anything. But I should think her waist was the same.' **1971** R. HILL *Advancement of Learning* i. 13 The nude was Rubensesque. **1976** L. DEIGHTON *Twinkle, Twinkle Little Spy* viii. 78 The artless gesture of the *ingénue*, inappropriate for this Rubenesque wife and mother.

Rubensian (ruː'bɛnzɪən), *a.* [f. RUBENS + -IAN.] Of, pertaining to, or characteristic of Rubens or his work.
1890 *Athenæum* 18 Jan. 90 The composition is distinguished by the true Rubensian 'swing' and emphatic movement. **1940** *Burlington Mag.* June 193/2 This family, with all its Rubensian attributes, as plainly inherits something from each of Rubens's three masters. **1964** *Punch* 1 Apr. 490/2 A voluptuous Rubensian still-life. **1976** *Jrnl. R. Soc. Arts* CXXIV. 624/2 The *composition* of Constable's picture is perhaps the least Rubensian thing about it. **1979** *Amer. N. & Q.* Oct. 29/1 Rubensian themes that appear in the earlier part of Van Dyck's career.

†'**rubent,** *a. Obs.*[−1] [ad. pres. pple. of L. *rubēre* to be red.] Reddening, red.
1562 A. SCOTT *Poems* (S.T.S.) i. 4 Welcum, oure rubent roiss vpoun þe ryce!

‖**rubeola** (ruː'biːələ). *Path.* [mod.L., neut. pl. of **rubeolus*, dim. form of L. *rubeus* reddish. Cf. F. *rubéole.*]
†**1.** (See quots. and RUBEOLS.) *Obs.*
1676 JAS. COOKE *Marrow Chirurg.* IV. I. ix. 739 *Rubeola*, small red pimples among the Small-Pox and Measles, which sometimes happens to persons in health. **1693** tr. *Blancard's Phys. Dict.* (ed. 2), *Rubeola*, a sort of Small Pox, or Measles.
2. Measles.
1803 *Med. Jrnl.* IX. 38 Neither were the symptoms of rubeola in the least lessened or retarded. **1834** *Cycl. Pract. Med.* III. 625/1 By the term rubeola, or measles, in modern times, is understood a contagious inflammatory disease [etc.]. **1843** SIR T. WATSON *Princ. & Pract. Physic* II. 748 Another of these blood diseases is the measles; called also by nosologists, *rubeola*, and *morbilli*. **1883** J. N. HYDE *Pract. Treatm. Dis. Skin* IX. i. 389 The distinction between rubeola and rötheln will be given later. **1909** C. B. KER *Infectious Dis.* ii. 21 It would be simpler if every one referred to measles as 'morbilli' and to German measles as 'rubella', and if the term rubeola were allowed to drop. *Ibid.*, Unfortunately the term 'rubeola' is . . freely used to designate measles. **1947** K. WIENER *Skin Manifestations of Internal Disorders* iv. 90 The latin term rubeola is used for this disease [*sc.* German measles] in the German literature, while in the English-American terminology, rubeola designates true measles. **1969** A. B. CHRISTIE *Infectious Dis.* xii. 346 The term rubeola still lingers on as a synonym of measles, though this usage was condemned as long ago as 1909 by Ker. **1973** *Sci. Amer.* Sept. 105/1 The same principle now allows very effective immunization against poliomyelitis, tetanus, diphtheria and both kinds of measles (rubella and rubeola).
3. German measles; rubella; rötheln.
1858 J. COPLAND *Dict. Pract. Med.* III. I. 655 *Rubeola* holds a place between measles and scarlet fever, the name being derived from its deep red colour. **1863** AITKEN *Pract. Med.* (ed. 2) I. 340 The following table . . shows that rubeola, rötheln, or the mixed disease has every right to be

considered as a distinct affection. **1901** FAGGE & PYE-SMITH *Text Bk. Med.* (ed. 4) I. 185 It is often difficult to distinguish rubeola from 'ordinary rose-rash'.

Hence **ru'beolar** *a.*, of the nature of, characteristic of, pertaining to, rubeola. **rube'oliform** *a.*, having the form or appearance of rubeola. **ru'beoloid** *a.*, resembling, similar to, rubeola; *sb.*, a disease resembling rubeola. **ru'beolous** *a.*, rubeolar.

1898 P. MANSON *Trop. Dis.* xv. 249 An exanthem, erythematous on the face, *rubeolar on the trunk and limbs. **1899** *Allbutt's Syst. Med.* VIII. 485 Erythematous urticaria in sheets (roseoliform, *rubeoliform, scarlatiniform). **1857** DUNGLISON *Med. Lex.* (rev. ed.) 806 s.v. *Roseolæ*, *Rubeoloid, a term which is applicable to any eruption resembling rubeola. **1898** P. MANSON *Trop. Dis.* ix. 168 Being attended with a well-marked rubeoloid eruption. **1899** *Allbutt's Syst. Med.* VIII. 464 The first group which they call Rubeoloids and Scarlatinoids. **1822–34** *Good's Study Med.* (ed. 4) II. 334 If..*rubeolous contagion should have been previously received into the system. **1880** A. FLINT *Princ. Med.* 1066 Occasionally vesicles are intermingled with the rubeolous papules.

† **'rubeols.** *Obs.*$^{-1}$ [ad. mod.L. *rubeola*: see prec.] The red spots of measles.

1661 LOVELL *Hist. Anim. & Min.* 327 The measells, which are little swellings,..hereto belong the crystals, tubercles, rubeols, and rossals.

Ruberoid ('rʌ-, 'ru:bərɔɪd). Also **ruberoid.** A proprietary name applied esp. to a roofing material composed of felt impregnated with bitumen. See also RUBBEROID.

1901 *Official Gaz.* (U.S. Patent Office) 28 May 1848/1 Certain named substances of the nature of rubber. The Standard Paint Co., New York, New York. Filed Nov. 22, 1900. Ruberoid. **1902** *Trade Marks Jrnl.* 14 May 599 *Ruberoid*..Roofing pasteboard or paper and roofing felt. The Standard Paint Company Zweigfabrik Hamburg. **1910** *Ibid.* 8 June 894 *Ruberoid*... Paint and varnish included in Class 1.., and sheathing material included in Class 1 for heat insulating purposes. The Ruberoid Company Limited London. **1911** R. F. SCOTT *Jrnl.* 10 Jan. in *Last Exped.* (1913) I. iv. 111 On the outside [of the roof] is a matchboarding, then a layer of 2-ply 'ruberoid'. **1916** *Cornh. Mag.* Apr. 504 Myself and a chum had just returned ..laden with 3″ by 4″ timbers and ruberoid which we found. **1921** H. G. PONTING *Gt. White South* 123 The roof..was covered with a thicker layer of ruberoid, and was lined with a single thickness of boards. **1925** *Glasgow Herald* 3 Aug. 5 The hut..was timber-built and roofed with rubberoid [*sic*]. **1934** *Trade Marks Jrnl.* 21 Nov. 1504/2 *Ruberoid*... Nails; and sectional sheets of ordinary metal for use in building. The Ruberoid Company Ltd. **1958** *House & Garden* Mar. 66/2 Roofs can be of shingles, clay tiles or, as shown here, Ruberoid felt. **1975** *Cricketer* May 47/1 (Advt.), Ruberoid Cricket Pitch is the year round match or practice wicket which can be used out of doors then lifted and re-laid for internal use.

ruberythric (ru:bə'rɪθrɪk), *a. Chem.* [f. L. *rubia* madder + ERYTHRIC *a.*] ***ruberythric acid***, a yellow, crystalline compound contained in madder-root.

1857 MILLER *Elem. Chem., Org.* viii. 521 Rochleder's Ruberythric Acid was obtained in crystals from an infusion of madder. **1879** ROSCOE *Elem. Chem.* xxxviii. 354 Alizarin, the colouring principle of madder, is contained in the root as a glucoside (called ruberythric acid).

ru'bescence. *rare*$^{-1}$. [Cf. next and -ENCE.] The fact of becoming red.

1798 W. YONGE in Beddoes *Contrib. Phys. & Med. Knowl.* (1799) 299 Pain, heat and rubescence determine the degree of this excess.

rubescent (ru:'bɛsənt), *a.* [ad. pres. pple. of L. *rubescĕre*, f. *ruber* red. So F. *rubescent.*] Tending to redness; reddening, blushing.

1731 in BAILEY, vol. II. (ed. 2). **1803** SHAW *Gen. Zool.* IV. II. 190 Rubescent Band-Fish, *Cepola Rubescens*,..is said to have a pointed rather than a rounded head. **1876** MISS HAY *Nora's Love Test* I. 177 His idea was at once confirmed by Will's rubescent face.

† **'rubetude.** *Obs.*$^{-1}$ [irreg. f. L. *ruber* or *rubēdo*: cf. *nigritude*.] Redness.

1657 TOMLINSON *Renou's Disp.* 302 This plant from its rubetude is..called Rubia.

rubiaceous (ru:bɪ'eɪʃəs), *a. Bot.* [f. mod.L. *Rubiaceæ* (Jussieu, 1789), f. *Rubia* (L. *rubia*) the genus madder.] Pertaining to, or characteristic of, an order of plants of which madder (*Rubia*) is the typical genus.

c **1832** *Encycl. Metrop.* (1845) VI. 177 *Rubiaceous shrubs. **1852** TH. ROSS tr. *Humboldt's Trav.* I. vi. 212 The trees of the rubiaceous family. **1863** BATES *Nat. Amazon* vii. (1864) 203 Members of the Laurel, Myrtle, Bignoniaceous, and Rubiaceous orders.

rubiacic (ru:bɪ'æsɪk), *a. Chem.* [f. next: see -IC. So F. *rubiacique.*] ***rubiacic acid***, an acid obtained from rubiacin.

1857 MILLER *Elem. Chem., Org.* 522 A brownish red liquid, which on the addition of an acid deposits flocculi of *rubiacic acid.* **1868** WATTS *Dict. Chem.* s.v., *Rubiacic acid*, an acid produced..by boiling rubiacin..with ferric nitrate or chloride.

rubiacin ('ru:bɪəsɪn). *Chem.* Also **-ine.** [f. L. *rubia* + -(*c*)*in*: named by E. Schunck (*Ann. Chemie* LXVI. 176).] A yellow colouring matter obtained from madder-root.

1848 J. HIGGIN in *Phil. Mag.* XXXIII. 284 When heated, rubiacine fuses, blackens, and gives off orange vapours. **1868** WATTS *Dict. Chem.* s.v., Rubiacin is found partly in the precipitate produced by acids in the decoction of madder, partly in the residue left after exhausting the root with water.

rubian ('ru:bɪən). *Chem.* [f. L. *rubia* + -AN: named by E. Schunck (cf. prec.).] The bitter principle of madder-root.

1851 SCHUNCK in *Phil. Trans.* CXLI. 436 The intensely bitter taste of madder and its extracts is due to a peculiar substance, to which I have given the name of *Rubian.* **1868** WATTS *Dict. Chem.*, Rubian is a hard, dry, brittle, perfectly amorphous mass, resembling dried varnish or gum-arabic.

Hence **rubi'anic** *a.*; **'rubianin(e.** (See quots.)

1851 SCHUNCK in *Phil. Trans.* CXLI. 445 The orange-coloured flocks..now consist of four different substances..; the fourth substance I shall denominate *Rubianine.* **1868** WATTS *Dict. Chem., Rubianin*, a body obtained..by boiling aqueous rubian..with dilute sulphuric acid. *Ibid., Rubianic acid*,..an acid, produced..by the oxidation of rubian in contact with alkalis.

'rubiate. *rare.* [f. L. *rubia* madder + -ATE^{1}.] (See quots.)

1835 FIELD *Chromatogr.* 97 Rubric, or Madder Lakes.., have obtained..the various names of rose rubiates, rose madder, pink madder, and Field's lakes. *Ibid.* 98 Liquid rubiate..is a concentrated tincture of madder.

† **rubiator.** *Sc. Obs.* In 6 rube-, rubi-, rubyatour; rubiature. [Of obscure origin.] An unprincipled person; a scoundrel or villain.

1500–20 DUNBAR *Poems* xiv. 44 Sa mony tratouris, sa mony rubeatouris, Within this land was nevir hard nor sene. **1535** LYNDESAY *Satyre* 4254 Tak me an rackles rubyatour, Ane theif, ane tyrane, or ane tratour, Of everie vyce the plant. **1583** *Leg. Bp. St. Androis* 147 For laik of rowme, that rubiature Bespewit vp the moderator.

rubible, variant of RIBIBLE *Obs.*

† **'rubican**, *a. Obs.* [a. F. *rubican*, earlier *rabican.*] (See quot.)

1704 *Dict. Rust.* s.v. *Colours of a Horse, Rubican*, is when a Black or Sorrel-Horse has white Hairs here and there scatter'd over his Body, more especially upon his Flanks. [Also in various other dicts. of the 18th cent., but app. never in actual English use.]

rubicelle ('ru:bɪsɛl). Also 7 rubacel, 8 -celle; 8–9 rubicel(l. [a. F. *rubicelle, rubacelle*, app. a dim. of *rubis* ruby, or of *rubace* in the same sense.] A variety of spinel, of a yellow or orange-red colour.

1671 PHILLIPS, *Rubace*, and *Rubacel*, the name of a pretious stone that hath usually a kind of yellowish colour about the extremities of it. **1748** J. HILL *Hist. Fossils* 590 They also know two other Stones under the same general name of Rubies, calling them the Rock Ruby and the Rubacelle; but these are not of the Ruby kind. **1802** WILLICH *Dom. Encycl.* III. 512/1 The rubicell is of a reddish-yellow, and is..obtained from the Brazils. **1856** DANA *Min.* (ed. 3) 130 Jewellers..call the paler ones, balas ruby; and those which incline to an orange tint, they denominate rubicelle. **1897** *Edin. Rev.* Oct. 342 Several other colours are distinguished, as for instance the rubicelle.

Rubicon ('ru:bɪkən), *sb.* [The ancient name of a small stream on the east coast of northern Italy, forming part of the southern boundary of Cisalpine Gaul; the crossing of it by Cæsar marked the beginning of the war with Pompey.]

1. a. ***to cross*** or ***pass the Rubicon***, to take a decisive or final step, *esp.* at the outset of some undertaking or enterprise.

1626 J. MEAD in Birch *Crt. & Times Chas. I* (1848) I. 180 Queen Dido did never more importune Æneas's stay at Carthage, than his mother and sister do his continuance here at London... But now he is past the Rubicon. **1643** J. OWEN *Death of Death* Wks. 1852 X. 150 The die being cast and Rubicon crossed. **1672** DRYDEN *Conq. Granada* I. III, This noyse may chill your Blood, but mine it warms: We have already past the Rubicon. **1722** DE FOE *Col. Jack* (1840) 214 Giving her to understand..that she had passed the Rubicon; that she had taken such a step of her own accord. **1771** *Junius Lett.* liv. (1788) 301 *note*, The very soliloquy of Lord Suffolk before he passed the Rubicon. **1827** SCOTT *Napoleon* IV. 21 [Bonaparte] would,..like Cæsar, have crossed the Rubicon at the head of the popular party. **1847** C. BRONTE *J. Eyre* vii, A pause—in which I began to steady the palsy of my nerves, and to feel that the rubicon was passed.

b. *attrib.* in † ***Rubicon die*** (alluding to Cæsar's words ***alea jacta est***).

a **1628** F. GREVIL *Life Sidney* (1907) 113 [He] rather thought good to venture upon the cast of a Rubicon Dy.

2. A boundary, bounding line, or limit, in *lit.* or *fig.* senses.

1690 CROWNE *Eng. Friar* v. Dram. Wks. 1874 IV. 101 I'll be hang'd if this fellow got me. Some Cæsar pass'd my mother's Rubicon; wou'd I had his commentaries. **1711** in *10th Rep. Hist. MSS. Comm.* App. V. 132 The bancks of the Boyn.., the ould Rubicon of the Pale. **1738** DE FOE *Tour Gt. Brit.* (ed. 2) III. 19 Having thus passed the Rubicon (Trent) and set my Face Northward. **1829** SYD. SMITH *Wks.* (1859) II. 29/2 The moment the punishment passes this Rubicon, it becomes less and less, instead of greater and greater. **1862** MISS BRADDON *Lady Audley* xxvi, He was behindhand in his education, and had not yet passed the intellectual Rubicon of words of two syllables. **1895** BOSCAWEN *Bible & Monuments* (1896) 112 The Deluge formed the rubicon between the mythic period and the heroic and polyarchal age.

3. *attrib.* Applied to varieties of bezique and piquet. Also *absol.* (see quots.).

1882 'CAVENDISH' (*title*) The laws of Rubicon piquet, adopted by the Portland Club. **1887** 'CAVENDISH' (*title*), The Laws of Rubicon Bezique. **1890** BERKELEY *Bezique & Cribbage* 4 The game came much into vogue in France, under the name of Japanese or Rubicon Bezique. **1897** R. F. FOSTER *Compl. Hoyle* 438 Rubicon piquet, for two players. The chief difference between this game and the usual form, Piquet au cent, is in the manner of declaring... Rubicons. If either or both players fail to reach 100 points in the six deals, the one having the most is the winner, and adds to his own score all the points made by the loser, with 100 in addition for game. **1950** *Hoyle's Games Modernized* (ed. 20) 76 It is only necessary to discuss the Rubicon Game, the game of 100 or 101 points being in disuse. *Ibid.*, There is another condition, namely, the establishment of 100 as a 'Rubicon'. **1973** J. SCARNE *Encycl. Games* 604 Rubicon (*piquet*), failure of the loser of a game to reach 100 points. **1975** *Way to Play* 105/1 The procedure then depends on whether these totals exceed the 'rubicon' of 100 points.

Hence **'rubicon** *v.* (see quot. 1890).

1890 BERKELEY *Bezique & Cribbage* 10 If the loser's score, with his brisques, is less than 1,000, he is said to be rubiconed. **1897** R. F. FOSTER *Complete Hoyle* 623 Rubiconed, lurched, defeated before getting half way.

rubicund ('ru:bɪkʌnd), *a.* Also 6 rubicond, -cound, rubycund. [a. F. *rubicond* (= It. *rubicondo*, Sp. and Pg. *rubicundo*), or ad. L. *rubicund-us*, f. *rubēre* to be red.]

† **1.** Of things: Inclined to redness; tending towards a red colour; red. *Obs.*

1503 HAWES *Examp. Virt.* III. xxxvii, Rubyes moost pure and rubicound. **1509** —— *Past. Pleas.* XXVII. (Percy Soc.) 127 Broudred with perles and rubies rubicond. **1590** BARROUGH *Meth. Physick* III. xxxvii. (1596) 162 The inflammation waxeth worse, it [the urine] is more rubicund. **1669** W. SIMPSON *Hydrol. Chym.* 65 The chyle..meeting with the blood is dasht with a rubicund colour. **1671** J. WEBSTER *Metallogr.* xxv. 309 Of pure Minium, or native Cinnober he had two sorts; one rubicund, like the crude Ore of red silver.

2. Of the face, etc.: Reddish, flushed, highly coloured, esp. as the result of good living.

1696 PHILLIPS, *Rubicund*, Blood-red. Said of a jolly red countenance coloured with Wine. **1766** SMOLLETT *Trav.* ii. 12 A sleepy eye, a rubicund face, and carbuncled nose. **1798** HELEN M. WILLIAMS *Tour Switzerland* I. 195 It was evident from their rubicund faces and sparkling looks. **1807** DOUCE *Illustr. Shaks.* I. 58 Falstaff alludes to Pistol's rubicund nose, which..carried fire in it. **1835** WILLIS *Pencillings* II. li. 100, I found that my rubicund complexion was something uncommon among these dark-skinned Orientals. **1867** MRS. CHILD *Miria* xxvi. 317 His face, usually rubicund.., became redder.

b. Of persons: Having a complexion of this kind; red-faced (with good living).

1827 LYTTON *Pelham* vii, The attics..were thronged with rubicund damsels. **1886** RUSKIN *Præterita* (1887) II. 60 One was a rather short, rubicund, serenely beaming person.

transf. **1880** MISS BRADDON *Just as I am* xv, A room as portly, rubicund, and pompous as its owner.

Hence **'rubicundly** *adv.*

1599 A. M. tr. *Gabelhouer's Bk. Physicke* 187/1 Decocte it agayne till such time as it wexeth rubicundlye colourede. **1980** *Daily Tel.* 6 Oct. 3/1 'We can't go on living in the 19th century,' says the rubicundly amiable secretary of St Stephen's [Club].

rubicundity (ru:bɪ'kʌndɪtɪ). [f. prec. + -ITY, or ad. med.L. *rubicunditas.*] The state of being rubicund; redness (of face) from good living.

1599 A. M. tr. *Gabelhouer's Bk. Physicke* 48/1 It expelleth all rubicundity, and dolour of the Eyes. **1727** BAILEY vol. II. **1765** H. WALPOLE *Let. to G. Montagu* 19 Feb. (1846) V. 1, I do not wish you to parade your rubicundity and grey hairs through the mobs and assemblies of London. **1786** *Francis the Philanthropist* I. 61 Her rotundity of figure and rubicundity of countenance. **1831** MACAULAY 7 June in Trevelyan *Life*, His rector-like amplitude and rubicundity. **1882** J. HAWTHORNE *Fort. Fool.* I. v, An extra-ordinary change had come over his countenance. Its rubicundity was gone.

transf. **1844** *Blackw. Mag.* LV. 500 The stair carpet also added its contribution to the rubicundity of the scene.

† **rubi'cundous**, *a. Obs.* [ad. L. *rubicundus.*] 'Very red or ruddy, blood red' (Blount, 1656).

'rubid, *a.* [ad. L. *rubid-us.*] (See quots.)

1656 BLOUNT *Glossogr., Rubid*, reddish, somewhat red or ruddy. **1858** MAYNE *Expos. Lex., Rubidus*, that which is reddish, or approaching a red colour: rubid.

rubidine ('ru:bɪdaɪn). *Chem.* [f. L. *rubid-us* red + -INE.]

1. A compound belonging to the pyridine series.

1868 WATTS *Dict. Chem.* s.v., Rubidine..is a colourless liquid, having a faint odour and oily consistence. **1875** *Ibid.* Suppl. 2 Rubidine..has been detected in tobacco-smoke.

2. 'A red crystalline compound forming the colouring-matter of melons, etc.'

1895 *Funk's Stand. Dict.* s.v.

‖ **rubidium** (ru:'bɪdɪəm). [f. L. *rubid-us* red, in allusion to the two red lines in its spectrum: coined in Ger. by Bunsen in *Ann. d. Chem.* (1861) CXIX. 107.] **1.** A soft silvery-coloured metal belonging to the group which includes cæsium, lithium, potassium, and sodium. Atomic number 37; symbol Rb.

1861 H. E. ROSCOE in *Proc. R. Inst.* III. 326 A few days ago the speaker received a letter from Bunsen, which contains the following most interesting information:—'The substance which I sent you as impure tartrate of Cæsium contains a *second* new alkaline metal... I propose to call the new metal "Rubidium".' **1861** *Chem. News* 27 July 44/2 Both rubidium and cæsium, the two alkali metals recently discovered by means of spectrum analysis, have a great chemical similarity to potassium. **1862** TIMBS *Year-bk. of Facts* 188 Cæsium and Rubidium. **1868** WATTS *Dict. Chem.* s.v., Rubidium is a white metal, with a tinge of yellow, and a silvery lustre. **1885** GOODALE *Physiol. Bot.* 256 Cæsium and Rubidium have been detected by the spectroscope in minute amounts in many plants. **1912** J. W. MELLOR *Mod. Inorg. Chem.* xix. 359 Metallic rubidium is prepared by heating an intimate mixture of the carbonate with finely divided carbon. **1946** *Nature* 2 Mar. 269/1 Minerals richest in rubidium are the lithia micas (lepidolites) which quite frequently contain as much as 2–3 per cent Rb_2O. **1950** N. V. SIDGWICK *Chem. Elements* I. 65 Rubidium and caesium catch fire at once on exposure to air. **1974** *Encycl. Brit. Micropædia* VIII. 705/3 Rubidium, because of its electropositiveness, is second only to cesium as a proposed working fluid in plasma propulsion for deep-space probes.

2. *attrib.* and *Comb.*

1862 *Phil. Mag.* XXIV. 46 (*heading*) On the preparation of the rubidium compounds. **1911** *Encycl. Brit.* XXIII. 809/1 The rubidium salts are generally colourless, mostly soluble in water and isomorphous with the corresponding potassium salts. **1950** F. E. ZEUNER *Dating Past* (ed. 2) x. 334 Other minerals like hydrothermal microclines, pollucite, and rubidium-rich varieties of muscovite, may in due course become important. **1950** *Thorpe's Dict. Appl. Chem.* (ed. 4) X. 637/2 Rubidium Sulphate, Rb_2SO_4, forms rhombic crystals. **1962** F. I. ORDWAY et al. *Basic Astronautics* iv. 127 A rubidium-vapor magnetometer to measure magnetic fields in space. **1971** I. G. GASS et al. *Understanding Earth* ii. 44/2 A small amount [of strontium] is usually also incorporated into calcium-poor, rubidium-bearing potassium minerals. **1977** *Broadcast* 13 June 6/3 The MSF time signals are derived from what is loosely described as an atomic pendulum but is more correctly known as a rubidium vapour oscillation.

b. Special Comb.: **rubidium-strontium**, used *attrib.* to denote a method of isotopic dating, or results obtained from it, based upon measurement of the relative amounts in rock of rubidium 87 and its beta decay product, strontium 87.

[**1946** *Nature* 2 Mar. 269/1 By means of this standard, Rb/Sr ratios of five samples of lepidolite and one of pollucite were determined spectrochemically.., the resultant ages being as follows.] **1950** F. E. ZEUNER *Dating Past* (ed. 2) x. 334 Minerals suitable for the rubidium/strontium method must be rich in Rb and free from non-radiogenic Sr. **1961** *Times* 25 Apr. 2/6 The Department..is at present using both the potassium-argon and rubidium-strontium methods. **1977** A. HALLAM *Planet Earth* 184/2 Rubidium-strontium and uranium-lead measurements conclusively show that all these rocks were formed between about 3700 and 3800 million years ago.

rubied (ˈruːbɪd), *a.* [f. RUBY *sb.* + -ED[2].] Coloured like a ruby; ruby-tinged.

1608 SHAKS. *Per.* v. Prol. 8 Euen her art sisters the naturall Roses; Her Inckle, Silke, Twine with the rubied Cherrie. **1634** MILTON *Comus* 915 Thrice upon thy fingers tip, Thrice upon thy rubied lip. **1667** —— *P.L.* v. 633 Tables are set,..and rubied Nectar flows. **1775** S. J. PRATT *Liberal Opin.* cix. (1783) IV. 38 Complexions clear, eyes brilliant, lips rubied. *c* **1817** HOGG *Tales & Sk.* II. 231 The rubied west lost its dyes. **1856** RUSKIN *Mod. Paint.* IV. v. App. iii, Take your vase of Venice glass.., and recover that to its clearness and rubied glory.

ruˈbiferous, *a.* *rare*[−1]. [irreg. f. L. *rubi-* (cf. next) + -FEROUS.] Rubicund.

1841 J. T. HEWLETT *Parish Clerk* II. 168 Mrs. Bibulus, the respectable and rubiferous landlady.

†**ruˈbific**, *a.* *Obs.*[−1] [ad. L. type *rubific-us: cf. next.] Causing redness.

1701 GREW *Cosmol. Sacra* II. ii. §14 The several Species of Rays, as the Rubifick, Cerulifick, and others.

†**ruˈbificate**, *a.* *Obs.* [ad. pa. pple. of med.L. **rubificāre*: see RUBIFY *v.*] Heated to redness.

1471 RIPLEY *Comp. Alch.* v. iv. in Ashm. (1652) 149 To powder dry unprofytably Rubyfycate.

†**rubifiˈcation.** *Obs.* [See prec. and -ATION.]

1. The process of heating to redness.

1592 LYLY *Gallathea* II. iii, It is a very secrete Science, for none almost can vnderstand the language of it. Sublimation, Almigation,..Rubification [etc.]. **1645** HOWELL *Lett.* II. 55 To pass all the degrees and effects of fire—as distillation,.. dealbation, rubification, and fixation.

2. = RUBEFACTION 1.

1661 LOVELL *Hist. Anim. & Min.* 273 Soranus used them with alcyonium,..after shaving and rubification.

†**rubificative**, *a.* and *sb.* *Obs. rare.* [See prec. and -ATIVE.] **a.** *adj.* Reddening, rubifying, rubefacient. **b.** *sb.* A rubefacient application.

1601 HOLLAND *Pliny* XXIX. vi. II. 364 A sinapisme or rubificative made of mustard seed, untill the place look red. *Ibid.* II, *Rubified*,..when by application of mustard plastres, ..it recouereth a fresh colour againe, whereupon such plastres be called Rubificatiue.

rubiform (Johnson, etc.), error for RUBRIFORM.

rubify (ˈruːbɪfaɪ), *v.* Also α. 5–6 rubyfy(e, 6 -fie. β. 5 rubefy, 5–6 -fie. [a. OF. *rubifier*, *rubefier* (mod.F. *rubéfier*), = Sp. and Pg. *rubificar*, It. and med.L. *rubificare*, a Romanic form replacing L. *rubefacĕre*, f. *rube-us* red: see -FY.] *trans.* To make red; to redden. Now *rare.*

α. *c* **1386** [see below]. *c* **1430** LYDG. *St. Thomas* 1 Blissed Thomas rubyfyed with blood. **1471** RIPLEY *Comp. Alch.* in Ashm. (1652) 188 After thou rubify and into Glassys let hym be don. **1530** PALSGR. 695/1, I rubyfye, I make reed, *jeschaufe*, and *je rubifie*. This terme is nat yet admytted in comen spetche. **1576** BAKER *Jewell of Health* 215 Let all be calcined until the whole be come unto a rednesse, and being thus rubified, let all be brought into a fine powder. **1620** VENNER *Via Recta* Introd. 2 It maketh the colour yellow, because it corrupteth the bloud which rubifieth the colour. **1683** MOXON *Mech. Exerc., Printing* xi. ¶23 The Varnish.. so Burns and Rubifies the Blacking, that it loses much of its brisk and vivid black complexion. **1728** CHAMBERS *Cycl.* s.v. *Rubifying*, Red Arsenic is supposed to be no more than the common yellow Arsenick rubified by Fire. **1831** J. DAVIES *Mat. Med.* 159 This oil may be used likewise to rubify the skin.

β. *c* **1480** *St. Ursula* A viij, The bankes with blode were rubefyed all a longe. **1620** VENNER *Via Recta* vi. 94 It is.. much the better for the stomacke.., if it be rubefied, by macerating the leaues of red Roses in it. **1658** A. FOX *Würtz' Surg.* IV. ii. 312 Calcine it to a red colour: being thus rubefied, then pulverise it.

Hence ˈ**rubified** *ppl. a.*; ˈ**rubifying** *vbl. sb.* and *ppl. a.*

c **1386** CHAUCER *Can. Yeom. Prol. & T.* Preamble 797 Watres rubifying, and Boles galle, Arsenyk, sal Armonyak, and Brymstoon. **1622** MASSINGER & DEKKER *Virg. Martyr* II. i, The armado of pimpled, deep-scarleted, rubified, and carbuncled faces. **1646** SIR T. BROWNE *Pseud. Ep.* III. iii, Their dung and intestinall excretions..Topically applyed become a Phænigmus or Rubifying medicine. **1658** FRANCK *Northern Memoirs* (1821) 242 Over whose rubified sands we must plough the ocean to those delectable flourishing ports. **1728** CHAMBERS *Cycl.*, *Rubifying*, in Chymistry, etc. the act of turning a thing Red by Force of Fire.

rubiginose (ruːˈbɪdʒɪnəʊs), *a.* [See next and -OSE.] Rubiginous; *spec.* in *Bot.* (see quot. 1866).

1727 BAILEY vol. II, *Rubiginose*, rusty. **1866** *Treas. Bot.* 995 *Rubiginose*, brown-red; a term usually employed to denote a surface whose peculiar colour is owing to glandular hairs.

rubiginous (ruːˈbɪdʒɪnəs), *a.* [f. L. *rūbīgin-*, *rūbīgo* rust, blight + -OUS. The variant *robiginous* is given by Blount (1656).]

1. Rusty, rust-coloured, ferruginous.

1671 J. WEBSTER *Metallogr.* xvii. 246 Here and there portions of rubiginous iron. **1785** MARTYN *Rousseau's Bot.* xxi. (1794) 293 Sweet-Briar has..the leaves rubiginous or rusty underneath. **1800** HURDIS *Fav. Village* 64 The hue rubiginous of fast decline. **1871** COOKE *Hdbk. Fungi* I. 318 Pileus effuso-reflexed,..velvety, rubiginous.

b. In specific names of birds, etc.

1809 SHAW *Gen. Zool.* VII. I. 170 Rubiginous Falcon, *Falco rubiginosus*. *Ibid.* II. 313 Rubiginous Shrike, *Lanius rubiginosus*. **1881** *Proc. Zool. Soc.* 818 A specimen of the Rubiginous Cat (*Felis rubiginosa*) from Ceylon.

†**2.** Of plants: Affected by rust or blight. *Obs.*

1656 BLOUNT *Glossogr.*, *Rubiginous*, foule, musty, blasted.

†**ruˈbiginy.** *Obs.*[−1] [ad. L. *rūbīgin-*, *rūbīgo*: see prec.] Rustiness.

1657 TOMLINSON *Renou's Disp.* 224 It effects nigritude, mobility and rubiginy of them [*sc.* the teeth].

†ˈ**rubigo.** *Obs.*[−1] [? Misuse of L. *rūbīgo*.] The virile member.

1583 *Leg. Bp. St. Androis* 404 Fra scho had sayned it tuyss or thrise, His rubigo began to ryiss.

Rubik (ˈruːbɪk). [The name of E. *Rubik*, Hungarian teacher, who patented the puzzle in Hungary in 1975.] ***Rubik('s) cube***: a puzzle consisting of a cube seemingly formed by 27 smaller cubes, uniform in size but of various colours, each layer of nine or eight smaller cubes being capable of rotation in its own plane; the task is to restore each face of the cube to a single colour after the uniformity has been destroyed by rotation of the various layers.

1980 D. E. TAYLOR (*title*) Rubik's cube. **1980** D. SINGMASTER *Notes Rubik's 'Magic Cube'* (ed. 5) p. i, This edition has been retitled since the Magic Cube is now being sold as Rubik's Cube. *Ibid.* 37 Ideal [*sc.* the Ideal Toy Corp.] has renamed the cube as 'Rubik's Cube' on the grounds that 'magic' tends to be associated with magic. **1981** *Sci. Amer.* Mar. 14/1 Bűvös Kocka—the Magic Cube, also known as Rubik's Cube—has simultaneously taken the puzzle world, the mathematics world and the computing world by storm. **1981** *Bookseller* 4 July 45/1 Rubik's cube is the latest game/puzzle aimed at driving both parents and children to madness. **1981** *Daily Tel.* 9 July 14/1 Those who in recent months have been driven potty by the clicking of the intellectual's worry beads, the multi-coloured and multi-faceted Rubik Cube, will be glad to know that help has arrived.

ˈ**rubinate.** *Chem.* [f. RUBIN-IC + -ATE.] A salt formed by the action of rubinic acid.

1838 T. THOMSON *Chem. Org. Bodies* 118 Rubinate of potash thus obtained, throws down the earthy and metallic salts of a red colour. **1868** WATTS *Dict. Chem.* s.v. *Rubinic acid*, The rubinates are red and slightly soluble: their solutions blacken during evaporation.

†ˈ**rubine.** *Obs.* Also 6 rubin. [var. of RUBY, corresponding to OF. and Sp. *rubin* (Pg. *rubim*), It. *rubino*, med.L. *rubinus*; also MHG. *rubîn* (G. *rubin*), MSw. *robin* (Sw. and Da. *rubin*), MDu. *rubijn*, *robijn* (Du. *robijn*).] A ruby.

c **1511** *1st Eng. Bk. Amer.* (Arb.) Introd. 34/1 Precyous stones. As..Dyamant, Topasius, Carbonkel, Rubin. **1553** EDEN *Treat. New Ind.* (Arb.) 20 At the rootes wherof are found Rubines, Hiacinthes,..and suche other precious stones. **1590** SPENSER *F.Q.* II. iii. 24 Twixt the perles and rubins softly brake A silver sound. **1651** FRENCH *Distill.* vi. 186 It will be like to an orientall Rubine. **1691** RAY *Creation* I. (1692) 81 The Carbuncle or Rubine shining with red, the Sapphire with blue.

attrib. **1576** BAKER *Jewell of Health* 142 The oyle will become of a Rubine colour. **1617** T. CAMPION *Wks.* (Bullen) 83 Her rubine lips, when they their pearl unlock [etc.]. **1651** FRENCH *Distill.* v. 169 Five or six graines thereof give..a most incomparable rubine colour.

b. A ruby colour.

c **1700** in Dampier *Voy.* (1729) III. 405 The Head and Throat being of an admirable Rubine surpassing Description.

Hence **ruˈbineous** *a.* *rare*[−0].

1826 KIRBY & SP. *Entomol.* IV. xlvi. 283 *Rubineous*, the red splendour of the ruby.

‖**rubinetto** (rubiˈnetto). *rare.* [It.] A tap, a faucet (in quot. *fig.*).

a **1930** D. H. LAWRENCE *Last Poems* (1932) 157 The half-hidden private parts just a little brass tap, rubinetto, turned on for different purposes.

rubinglimmer (ˈruːbɪŋglɪmə(r)). *Min.* [a. G. *rubinglimmer*, f. *rubin* ruby + *glimmer* mica, GLIMMER *sb.*[2]] = *lepidocrocite* s.v. LEPIDO-.

1836 T. THOMSON *Outl. Min., Geol.* I. 439 Rubinglimmer. **1837** J. D. DANA *Syst. Min.* VI. 380 Brown iron ore... The crystallized variety has been called Onegite, rubinglimmer, pyrosiderite, and Göthite. **1879** *Encycl. Brit.* X. 229/1 Hæmatite (peroxide of iron) occurs crystallized in veins through crystalline rocks,..and sometimes in minute scales (rubin-glimmer) disseminated through the minerals of many crystalline rocks. **1919** [see *lepidocrocite* s.v. LEPIDO-]. **1944** C. PALACHE et al. *Dana's Syst. Min.* (ed. 7) 683 Goethite... Found at numerous localities in Nassau, Westphalia, and the Rhine Provinces, Germany, especially at Siegen (does not include the rubinglimmer = lepidocrocite, found at Siegen), [etc.].

rubinic (ruːˈbɪnɪk), *a.* *Chem.* [ad. F. *rubinique*, f. *rubine*, a red metallic preparation.] ***rubinic acid***, an acid formed by the action of alkalies upon catechin.

1838 T. THOMSON *Chem. Org. Bodies* 118 The evaporation, when we wish to obtain rubinic acid, must be spontaneous. **1850** *Fownes' Chem.* (ed. 3) 468 Rubinic acid ..is said to form red insoluble compounds with the earths and certain oxides of the metals. **1871** GARROD *Mat. Med.* (ed. 3) 257 Catechin..is converted by the action of alkalies and their carbonates into Japonic and Rubinic acids.

rubio (ˈruːbɪəʊ). [Sp., lit. 'fair, blond(e), golden'.] Limonite mined in northern Spain.

1892 *Trans. Fed. Inst. Mining Engin.* III. 611 A feature of the rubio deposits is the occurrence of numerous clay 'backs' in the ore. **1901** E. H. DAVIES *Davies's Treat. Metalliferous Minerals & Mining* (ed. 6) xxviii. 280B 'Rubio' ore continues to be the principal class of ore produced [in Bilbao]. **1923** R. H. RASTALL *Geol. of Metalliferous Deposits* xv. 340 One of the most important groups of mines is that of Somorrostro in Viscaya, west of Triano. In this region four types of ore are recognized: (1) Vena... (2) Campanil... (3) Rubio, limonite, often siliceous and aluminous. (4) Carbonato. **1935** *Economist* 2 Feb. 292/2 Business in foreign ore is quiet. Whilst best rubio is nominally 17s. per ton c.i.f. Middlesborough, the tendency is upward.

rubious (ˈruːbɪəs), *a.* [f. RUBY *sb.* + -OUS.] Ruby-coloured.

1601 SHAKS. *Twel. N.* I. iv. 32 Dianas lip Is not more smooth, and rubious. **1819** KEATS *Otho the Great* IV. ii, Pout her faint lips anew with rubious health. **1837** *Blackw. Mag.* XLII. 550 When the two Roses, in one blossom met, Twined with the Thistle's rubious coronet. **1885** MEREDITH *Diana* xiv, Romantic accessories of rubious vapour.

Comb. **1820** KEATS *Lamia* I. 163 She was undrest Of all her sapphires, greens, and amethyst, And rubious-argent.

ruble, variant of ROUBLE; obs. f. RUBBLE.

ˈ**rub-off.** *slang.* [f. vbl. phr. *to rub off*: RUB *v.*[1]] An act of masturbation or manual stimulation to orgasm.

1937 PARTRIDGE *Dict. Slang* 710/2 *Rub-off*.., a masturbation. **1969** T. PARKER *Twisting Lane* 202 She charges three quid for sex, two quid for a rub-off.

‖**rubor** (ˈruːbə(r)). Also 6 rubour. [L. *rubor*, related to *ruber* red.] Redness, ruddiness.

1656 BLOUNT *Glossogr.*, *Rubor*, shamefac'dness, redness, blushing. **1657** TOMLINSON *Renou's Disp.* 202 The Sinapism ..should be often looked at, to see if it have contracted rubour enough by its admotion. *a* **1734** NORTH *Examen* III. vii. §78 (1740) 563 Mr. Justice Jones,..when much offended, often shewed his Heats in a Rubor of his Countenance. **1794** COLERIDGE *Lett.* (1895) I. 87 He is obliged to drink three bottles of claret a day in order to acquire a stationary rubor. **1866** *Treas. Bot.* 995/1 *Rubor*, redness of any sort. **1886** FAGGE *Princ. & Pract. Med.* I. 57 Hæmorrhages also play an important part in the production of rubor.

ˈ**rub-out.** *U.S. slang.* Also rubout. [f. vbl. phr. *to rub out* s.v. RUB *v.*[1] 11 a.] A murder, an assassination, esp. of one gangster by another. Also *attrib.*

1927 D. HAMMETT in *Black Mask* May 11/2 The hombre she blamed for Paddy's rub-out. **1934** *Sun* (Baltimore) 21 Aug. 7/1 Another..witness is Mrs...Fontaine, alleged 'gang-girl' associate of 'Big George' Phillips wounded in one 'rub out' attempt. **1953** *Ibid.* 12 June 34/3 Police marked down the Messina murder as one of Baltimore's extremely rare gangland rubouts. **1959** *Washington Post* 15 Aug. A3/1 Two hoodlums were gunned to death on Chicago's West Side today and police said at least one of the executions was probably a crime syndicate 'rubout'. **1977** *Time* 10 Jan. 22/1 In what was clearly a political rub-out, the couple—who were discovered by Mrs. Tayyeb's sister, sometime Skyjacker Leila Khaled—had been killed by at least a dozen shots.

rubral ('ruːbrəl), *a. Anat.* [f. L. *ruber*, *rubr-* red + -AL.] Of or pertaining to the red nucleus of the brain.

1954 [see RUBRO-]. **1972** M. L. BARR *Human Nervous System* vii. 110/2 A few rubral efferents enter the cerebellum through the superior peduncle to end in cerebellar nuclei.

rubredoxin (ruːbrɪ'dɒksɪn). *Biochem.* [f. L. *rub-er* red + REDOX + -IN[1]: cf. FERREDOXIN.] Any of a class of natural proteins having an iron atom co-ordinated to the sulphur atoms of four cysteine residues, and concerned in intracellular electron-transfer processes.

1965 LOVENBERG & SOBEL in *Federation Proc.* XXIV. 233/2 This protein, which we tentatively named rubredoxin has been isolated in pure form. **1970** *Nature* 4 July 16/1 An interesting set of metalloproteins, which occur in plants and bacteria, are the non-haem iron proteins, such as the ferredoxins and rubredoxins. **1977** *Jrnl. Amer. Chem. Soc.* XCIX. 3505/1 (*heading*) Theoretical studies of the oxidized and reduced states of a model for the active site of rubredoxin.

rubric ('ruːbrɪk), *sb.* and *a.* Forms: 4 robryk, 4-5 rubryke, 5, 7 rubrike, 7 rubrique; 6-7 rubricke, 7-9 rubrick, 7- rubric. See also RUBRISH *sb.* [ad. F. *rubrique* or L. *rubrīca*, f. *ruber* red. Cf. It., Sp., Pg. *rubrica*; G., Da., Sw. *rubrik*, Du. *rubriek*. In senses 2 and 3 the usual form before the 16-17th cent. was RUBRISH.]

I. 1. a. Red earth, red ochre, ruddle. Now *arch.*

c **1440** *Pallad. on Husb.* IV. 512 Aysel and askis tempred with rubrike Ykest on hem sleeth doun this auntis alle. **1558** WARDE *Alexis' Secr.* I. 118 Mingle it with..xiiii or xvi carattes at the most of Rubricke, or sparkes of copper. **1607** TOPSELL *Four-f. Beasts* (1658) 104 This marrow [of a hart], ..in sheeps milk, with rubrick and soft pitch, drunk every day,..helpeth the ptisick and obstructions. **1652** J. FRENCH *Yorkshire Spa* v. 53 Rubrick, or a certain red earth (for so sometimes it signifies). **1677** PLOT *Oxfordsh.* 56 As if it were now in the transmutation..first into Rubrick, or Ruddle, and thence at last into..black chalk. **1868** BROWNING *Ring & Bk.* II. 767 Once a dwelling's doorpost marked and crossed In rubric by the enemy on his rounds As eligible, as fit place of prey.

†**b.** A red preparation for heightening the complexion. *Obs.*[−1]

1650 BULWER *Anthropomet.* 156 Now they have too little colour, then Spanish-paper, Red-Leather and other Cosmetical Rubriques must be had.

2. a. A heading of a chapter, section, or other division of a book, written or printed in red, or otherwise distinguished in lettering; a particular passage or sentence so marked.

c **1450** *St. Cuthbert* (Surtees) 1317 Of þis chapiter þe sext, In þe rubryke is þe text, How bosilus bare witnes [etc.]. **1658** PHILLIPS, *Rubrick*,..a noted sentence of any book marked with red Letters. **1778** T. WARTON *Hist. Eng. Poetry* xix. II. 9 Then follows a rubric 'How Aristotile declareth to kynge Alysandre of the stonys'. *Ibid.* 22 He mentions Dante only, who in the rubric is called 'a certain poet of Italy named Dante'. **1815** SCOTT *Guy M.* vii, The rubrick, with an emphatic *nota bene.* **1885** *Manch. Exam.* 13 Jan. 5/1 The event is so unusual that it deserves to be printed as a rubric in the official report.

transf. **1655** tr. *Sorel's Com. Hist. Francion* x. 30, I have indeavoured to make him abandon..those scattered Latin Rubricks, with which he always intermingles his discourse.

fig. **1838** LONGF. in *Life* (1891) I. 308 Autumn has written his rubric on the illuminated leaves.

b. *transf.* A descriptive heading or title; a designation, category. Also, an injunction, a general rule.

1831 CARLYLE *Sart. Res.* iv, Many sections are of a debatable rubric, or even quite nondescript and unnameable. **1887** STEVENSON *Misadv. J. Nicholson* i, Colette's was not a hell; it could not come..under the rubric of a gilded saloon. **1891** *N.Y. Times* 28 Sept. 4/5 It is the duty of independents—the duty of all voters—..to..'weigh the merits and demerits of each candidate and each party.'.. No better rubric of conduct could be laid down. **1934** J. W. POWELL in *Webster* s.v. rubric, The groups of opinion inculcated by instruction are again found to fall into five 'rubrics'—animism, cosmogony, mythology, metaphysic, and science. **1962** W. NOWOTTNY *Lang. Poets Use* viii. 202 There are no critical rubrics or Queensberry rules about this game. **1965** G. MCINNES *Road to Gundagai* i. 13 'Don't go out too far!' A censorious well-worn rubric and I barely heard it. **1970** I. L. HOROWITZ *Masses in Lat. Amer.* i. 3 To understand the processes that go under the rubric of social development it is necessary to study masses as well as elites.

3. a. A direction for the conduct of divine service inserted in liturgical books, and properly written or printed in red.

c **1375** *Lay Folks Mass Bk.* 624 þo robryk [*v.r.* rubryke] is gode vm while to loke, þo praiers to con with-outen boke. **1583** FOXE *A. & M.* 1398 The whole Canon of the Masse, with the Rubricke thereof, as it standeth in the Masse-booke. **1641** MILTON *Ch. Govt.* I. v, Anselme also of Canturbury..acknowledges from the cleerenesse of the text, that Ierome and the Church Rubrick hath before acknowledg'd. *a* **1699** STILLINGFL. (J.), They had their particular prayers according to the several days and months; and their tables or rubricks to instruct them. **1704** NELSON *Fest. & Fasts* ix. (1739) 585 Our holy Mother..by her Rubricks and Canons..trains us up. **1746** WESLEY *Princ. Methodist* 37 As a Minister, I teach her Doctrines. I use her Offices. I conform to her Rubricks. **1795** MASON *Ch. Music* II. 157 These Chaunts, succeeding one another in the allotted portions of the Rubric for the day. **1837** SYD. SMITH *Wks.* (1859) II. 289/1 His own most respectable Chaplain.. will tell him that the prayers are strictly adhered to, according to the rubric. **1879** T. F. SIMMONS *Lay Folks Mass Bk.* p. lxvii, The rubrics are in a smaller character.., but are not written in red, being only underlined in red throughout.

attrib. **1685** D. GRANVILLE *Rem.* in *Surtees Misc.* (1861) 209 Meaning by that expression, that his lordship would in short while become a good rubrick man.

Comb. **1699** T. BAKER *Refl. upon Learning* 207 That it has been taken from such a Copy, appears from the..Lessons markt in the Margin Rubrick-wise.

fig. **1605** SYLVESTER *Du Bartas* II. iii. *Lawe* 1118 While.. th' Eternall..him (faithfull) did inform In a new Rubrick of the Rites Divine. **1649** MILTON *Eikon.* xiii. Wks. 1851 III. 441 Was it not he, who..with his Sword went about to engraue a bloody Rubric on thir backs? **1699** FARQUHAR *Constant Couple* I. i, Who thought to find you out of the rubric so long? I thought thy hypocrisy had been wedded to a pulpit-cushion long ago. **1780** COWPER *Progr. Error* 185 Let Comus rise archbishop of the land; Let him your rubric and your feasts prescribe.

b. The rule of a religious order. *rare*[−1].

1809 MALKIN *Gil Blas* I. viii. ¶2 A Dominican friar, mounted, contrary to the rubric of those pious fathers, on a shabby mule.

4. A red-letter entry (of a saint's name) in the Church calendar; hence, a calendar of saints. Also *fig.* (quot. 1669) and *attrib.* ? *Obs.*

a **1618** J. DAVIES (Heref.) *Commend. Poems* Wks. (Grosart) II. 5/1 A Chappell and a Curate for the same..shall make thy Name In Rubricke of the Saints enrold to be. **1646-8** G. DANIEL *Poems* Wks. (Grosart) I. 196 Wee may..place His, as the cheif State-Martir's Day, Of all our Rubricke. **1669** HOPKINS *Serm.*, *1 Pet. ii. 13* (1685) 11 St. Jerome assigns no less than the blood of five thousand martyrs to every day in the year: only excepting the first of January from so deep a rubrick. **1754** H. WALPOLE *Lett.* (1846) III. 85, I don't know whether my father won't become a rubric martyr, for having been persecuted by him.

transf. **1611** J. DAVIES (Heref.) *Sco. Folly* Wks. (Grosart) II. 53/1 Mars or Minerua..so do shine That they in thee are glorious for thy grace, Which in Fames rubrick thus I enterline. **1671** MILTON *P.R.* IV. 393 For no date prefixt Directs me in the Starry Rubric set. **1700** ASTRY tr. *Saavedra-Faxardo* I. 239 How oft has Bloodshed been a kind of Rubrick inscribed with Injuries? **1813** J. FORSYTH *Rem. Exc. Italy* 282 *note*, The obscure, queer, filthy, and obscene gods in the ancient rubric.

5. The title or heading of a statute or section of a legal code (originally written in red).

1604 R. CAWDREY *Table Alph.* (1613), *Rubrike*,..a lawe, or title. **1634** in Row *Hist. Kirk* (Wodrow Soc.) 378 When this Act came to be heard in open Parliament, his Majestie gave ordour to read onlie the rubricks of it. *a* **1661** HOLYDAY *Juvenal* (1673) 263 The law (whose titles were written in red letters, and thence called rubriques, as Persius speaks). **1726** AYLIFFE *Parergon* 304 Then we should have no Occasion for particular Rubricks and Titles in Law to distinguish Proof made by Witnesses from such as is made by Instruments. **1790** BURKE *Fr. Rev.* (1898) 22 Repeating as from a rubric the language of the preceding acts of Elizabeth and James. **1829** SCOTT *Rob Roy* Introd. ¶24 It is neither mentioned in the title nor the rubric of the Act of Parliament. **1845** J. T. GRAVES in *Encycl. Metrop.* II. 780/1 The section beginning with the words *fratris vero*, of that title in the *Institutes* which has the rubric *de Nuptiis.*

6. [After Sp. *rúbrica.*] (See quot.)

1881 B. HARTE *Story of Mine* vi, The Spanish 'rubric' is the complicated flourish attached to a signature, and is as individual and characteristic as the handwriting.

II. *attrib.* passing into *adj.*

7. a. Written or printed in red.

c **1475** *Cath. Angl.* (Add. MS.) 313/1 To make Rubrike, *rubricare.*

1636 W. DURHAM in *Ann. Dubrensia* (1877) 9 That day which to posterity shall shine In Almanackes, writ, with a Rubricke-line. **1648** J. BEAUMONT *Psyche* XIII. ccxxxvi, At least that Lesson of Compassion they..might have plainly read, Which in large Rubrick Letters open lay. **1682** MRS. BEHN *City Heiress* 54 This happy day, to be inroll'd In Rubrick-letters and in Gold. **1735** POPE *Prol. Satires* 215 What tho' my Name stood rubric on the walls. **1781** CRABBE *Library* 188 Many an emendation show'd the age Look'd far beyond the rubric title-page. **1820** LAMB *Elia* I. *South-sea House*, Thy great dead tomes..with their..decorative rubric interlacings.

fig. **1829** *Sporting Mag.* XXIV. 49 The Belvoir kennel.. now stands rubrick in the Sporting World.

†**b.** Inscribed with the titles of books. *Obs.*

1728 POPE *Dunc.* I. 38 Here springs each weekly Muse, the living boast Of Curl's chaste press, and Lintot's rubric post. **1746** FRANCIS tr. *Hor., Sat.* I. iv. 92 No rubric pillar sets my works to sale. **1755** *Connoisseur* No. 86 ¶2, I was enabled to make out..the titles on rubric-posts.

8. a. Red, ruddy, rubicund. Now *arch.*

1659 W. CHAMBERLAYNE *Pharronida* III. iv. (1820) II. 71 And now I see her blood's low water doth allow Me only time to launch my soul's black bark Into death's rubric sea. **1694** CROWNE *Regulus* I. ii, He has the marks of a jolly rich priest, a rubrick nose, and a canonical belly. **1866** J. B. ROSE tr. *Ovid's Met.* 35 Father Titan marked the rubric sky. **1867** —— tr. *Virgil's Æneid* 348 Him they invest With sword, and shield, and helm of rubric crest.

b. As an epithet of certain lake-colours.

App. by error for *rubic, from *Rubia* madder.

1835 FIELD *Chromatography* 97 Rubric, or Madder Lakes. These pigments are of various colours. **1859** GULLICK & TIMBS *Painting* 292 The colours extracted, called rubric or madder lakes,..vary in tint from the most delicate rose to the deepest purple.

'**rubric**, *v.* Now *rare.* Also 6-8 rubrick. [f. the sb.] *trans.* To rubricate. Chiefly *fig.*

1599 NASHE *Lenten Stuffe* Wks. (Grosart) V. 221 William the Conquerour..firmed and rubrickt the Kentishmens gauill kinde of the sonne to inherite at fifteene. **1629** T. ADAMS *Wks.* 941 He [the pope] is too sawcie.., Stretching his arme to heauen, in rubricking what Saints hee list. **1681** RYCAUT tr. *Gracian's Critick* 236 That Cavalier who Rubricks his Executions with the Bloud he hath drawn by the instrument of Extortion from the Poor.

1883 *Ch. Times* 20 April 283 Mediæval Mass Books, rubricked chiefly with respect to plain, unsung services.

rubrical ('ruːbrɪkəl), *a.* Also 7 rubricall. [f. RUBRIC *sb.* + -AL[1].]

1. Pertaining to the colour red. *rare*[−1].

1641 MILTON *Animadv.* Wks. 1851 III. 240 You thus persecute ingenuous men over all your booke, with this one over-tir'd rubricall conceit still of blushing.

2. Marked by red letters. *rare*[−1].

1666 *Let.* in Harwood *Lichfield* 1806 442 The 17th Day of ..January, (a day ever to be rubrical amongst our City Remembrances).

3. Of or pertaining to liturgical rubrics; conforming to, enjoined by, the rubrics.

a **1754** WARBURTON *Nature & End Lord's Supper* Wks. 1788 V. 552 A lifeless rubrical piety. **1781** WARTON *Hist. Eng. Poetry* xxviii. III. 184 As the singing-psalms were never a part of our liturgy, no rubrical directions are any where given for the manner of performing them. **1851** RUSKIN *Stones Ven.* I. App. xiii. 377 The want of evangelical, and the excess of rubrical, religion among the tutors. **1870** ROCK *Text. Fabr.* I. 85 The rubrical colour for episcopal mitres is white. **1881** R. G. WILBERFORCE *Life Bp. Wilberforce* II. xiii. 437 How far clergymen were bound to canonical as apart from rubrical obedience.

Hence **rubri'cality**, observance of rubrics.

1848 KINGSLEY *Yeast* vi. Among high art and painted glass,..rubricalities, and sanitary reforms.

'**rubrically**, *adv.* [f. prec. + -LY[2].] In accordance with (liturgical) rubrics.

1696 COLLIER *Def. Absolution* 10, I hope a Form is better than no Form, Especially when it was a Form Rubrically appointed. **1844** *Ecclesiologist* III. 163 Morning and Evening Prayer ought rubrically to be said in the Chancel. **1883** *Times* 3 Jan. 6 In my judgment, it is rubrically illegal for a clergyman to make any addition of his own to the notice of Holy Communion required by the rubric.

rubricate ('ruːbrɪkeɪt), *v.* [f. L. *rubrīcāt-*, ppl. stem of *rubricāre*, f. *rubrica* RUBRIC *sb.*]

1. *trans.* To mark or colour with red; to write, print, or mark in red letters.

1570 FOXE *A. & M.* (ed. 2) 693 The one he doth rubricate, onely with his read letters, the other hee doth rubricate with their owne bloud. **1638** SIR T. HERBERT *Trav.* (ed 2.) 90 Curroone rubricates this in the Kalendar of his greatest dangers and deliverances. **1656** BLOUNT *Glossogr.*, *Rubricate*,..to make, or colour red with Oaker. **1849** ROCK *Ch. of Fathers* I. 96 Nine crosses are rubricated..in the prayer '*Per Quem haec omnia*'. **1872** O. SHIPLEY *Gloss. Eccl. Terms* 69 Those days which are not rubricated in our Calendar. **1892** *Athenæum* 12 May 624/2 A singularly handsome volume, with all the stage directions and names of characters rubricated.

b. To place in the calendar as a red-letter saint.

1570 FOXE *A. & M.* (ed. 2) 693 Dunstanus, who was rubricated with a *duplex festum.* **1638** SIR T. HERBERT *Trav.* (ed. 2) 33 St. Francis Shyvier the Navarrean Jesuit, who died *anno* 1552.., and rubricated by Pope Gregory 15.

c. To furnish with rubrics or red-letter headings; to regulate by rubrics. Also *transf.*

1846 J. C. HARE *Mission of Comforter* (1850) 212 A formal ..religion, according to which the thoughts of men were to be clast and rubricated for ever after. **1892** STOPFORD BROOKE *Early Eng. Lit.* II. xiii. 3 The MS. of the Gospels in the Bodleian..is rubricated.

2. *intr.* To sign by mark instead of name.

After Sp. *rubricare*: cf. RUBRIC *sb.* 6.

1846 R. FORD *Gatherings from Spain* (1907) 222 Although he could barely write his name, he could rubricate as well as any other Spaniard in Command.

Hence '**rubricating** *vbl. sb.* and *ppl. a.*

1842 *Wds. Churchwardens* (Cambr. Camd. Soc.) I. 9 They should be painted in large black letters, with all those letters in red which are printed in capitals in the Prayer Book: this is called rubricating. **1884** *Athenæum* 26 April 542/1 Probably the real artist..of the Bayeux tapestry was one of the rubricating draughtsmen whose works on vellum greatly resemble it. **1897** *Atlantic Monthly* LXXIX. 131 The fancy is restricted to the form, the cover, the borders, and the rubricating.

†'**rubricate**, *ppl. a. Obs. rare.* [ad. L. *rubrīcāt-us*, pa. pple. of *rubrīcāre*: see prec.] = next.

1604 R. PARSONS *3rd Pt. Three Convers. Eng.* 180 The principall [martyrs] are there rubricate, sett forth in redd letters. *a* **1641** SPELMAN *Originat. Terms.* v. ii. (1684) 63 Other Festivals I enquire not after, as of St. Dunstan and the rest that stand rubricate in old Kalendars.

'**rubricated**, *ppl. a.* [f. RUBRICATE *v.* + -ED[1].] Marked or signalized by red letters; written or printed in red; provided with rubrics.

1604 R. PARSONS *3rd Pt. Three Convers. Eng.* 408 This moneth also hath no rubricated Saint at all among Fox his Martyrs. *a* **1641** BP. MOUNTAGU *Acts & Mon.* (1642) 55 Many rubricated and double feasted Saints, in the Romane Calendar. *a* **1661** FULLER *Worthies, Oxford* II. (1662) 332, I ..may term them a week of brethren, whereof this Rubricated Cardinal was the Dominical letter. **1861** *Sat. Rev.* 7 Dec. 591/1 Adorned with elaborate borders and a rubricated initial letter to each psalm. **1864** RAINE *Priory of Hexham* (Surtees) I. Pref. I. p. lviii. *note*, In the rubricated title of a copy of this deed I have seen Hexham mentioned.

rubri'cation. [f. RUBRICATE *v.*: see -ATION.] The action or result of rubricating.

[**1658** PHILLIPS, *Rubrication*, a making red]. **1880** *Academy* 14 Aug. 110 An édition de luxe with all the charms of black-letter and rubrication. *c* **1900** J. E. HODGKIN *Rariora* II. 65 The rubricator has added in the space at the end of the second column of Fol. 6a his initials and the date of rubrication 1466.

rubricative (Phillips, 1658): an error for RUBRIFICATIVE.

'rubricator. [Agent-noun, on L. types, f. RUBRICATE *v.* So F. *rubricateur*.] One charged with the execution of the rubrics in manuscripts or early printed books.

1847 MADDEN *Layamon* I. 386 *note*, The rubricator here and below has omitted to insert the capital letters, for which a space has been left. **1884** SKEAT *Gamelyn* Introd. p. xvi, The rubricator and the scribe were usually different people, and we constantly find . . that the rubricator inserts a wrong capital letter.

rubrice, -ich(e: see RUBBISH.

rubrician (ruːˈbrɪʃən). [f. RUBRIC *sb.* + -IAN.] One who studies, or adheres to, liturgical rubrics.

1843 H. MOZLEY *Let.* 23 Aug. in D. Mozley *Newman Family Lett.* (1962) 135 The notion of Puseyites or Rubricians . . slipping unawares into popery is too absurd. **1849** ROCK *Ch. of Fathers* I. 97 The doubts as to their exact number and right places felt by such scrupulous rubricians as St. Boniface. **1861** —— in Manning *Ess. Relig. & Lit.* Ser. I. (1865) 89 The rubrician, too, will not overlook the fact [etc.]. **1866** *Clerical Jrnl.* 24 May 448/2 If Rubricians are allowed to do what is right in their own eyes, why should not all other parties do the same?

rubricism (ˈruːbrɪsɪz(ə)m). [f. as prec. + -ISM.] Tendency to adhere too closely to liturgical rubrics.

1862 *Macm. Mag.* V. 203 Its congregational worship affected no revolutionary Rubricism. **1978** C. HOWELL in C. Jones et al. *Study of Liturgy* II. III. x. 241 Trent ushered in four centuries of rigidity and fixation; it was an era of rubricism.

rubricist (ˈruːbrɪsɪst). [f. as prec. + -IST.]

1. One (excessively) devoted to the observance of liturgical rubrics; one who adheres strictly to the letter of the rubric.

1857 J. HAMILTON *Less. from Gt. Biogr.* 195 The stinted and external compliance of the rubricist and rule-monger. **1902** *Pilot* 7 June 600/2 He was the despair of finicking rubricists.

2. *nonce-use.* (See quot.)

1862 BURTON *Book Hunter* I. 59 Some collectors may be styled Rubricists, being influenced by a sacred rage for books having the contents and marginal references printed in red ink.

3. A rubricator.

1868 HINDE in *Symeon of Durham* (Surtees) I. Pref. p. xiv, It induced the rubricist to ascribe to Symeon the matter which follows.

rubricity (ruːˈbrɪsɪtɪ). [f. as prec. + -ITY.]

1. Assumption of a red colour.

1800 GEDDES *Critical Remarks* I. 183 The periodical feculency and rubricity of the Nile happen in July and October.

2. Adherence to liturgical rubrics.

1876 W. A. BUTLER *Mrs. Limber's Raffle* iv. (Cent.), Rubricity . . is the sheet-anchor of the Church. . . The rubric is explicit here, and settles the case. **1885** *Ch. Times* 20 March 220/1 Nobody . . ever questioned their regularity and (pardon the word) 'rubricity'.

rubricize (ˈruːbrɪsaɪz), *v. rare.* [f. RUBRIC *sb.* + -IZE.] **a.** *trans.* To provide with a rubric or rubrics. **b.** *intr.* To make general categorizations. Hence **'rubricizing** *ppl. a.*

1920 R. HARRIS *Testimonies* II. vii. 65 There is no reason to alter the opinion that the *Testimony* material should be rubricized. **1951** [see CONSTELLATE *v.* 2 b].

'rubricked, *ppl. a. rare*⁻¹. [f. RUBRIC *v.* + -ED¹.] Rubricated.

1834 SOUTHEY *Lett.* (1856) IV. 370 What talk there has been about the book, as yet has been chiefly owing to the rubricked copies.

rubrie, obs. Sc. form of ROBBERY.

†**ru'brific,** *a. Obs.* [See RUBRIFY and -FIC.] Conferring a red colour.

1704 NEWTON *Optics* I. (1721) 108 The homogeneneal Light and Rays which appear red, or rather make Objects appear so, I call Rubrific or Red-making.

†**rubrifi'cation.** *Obs.*⁻¹ In 6 rubryfycacyon. [ad. med.L. **rubrificātio*: see RUBRIFY *v.*] The action of making red; rubefaction.

1541 COPLAND *Galyen's Terap.* 2 Djb, Thou vsest rubryfycacyon in all sores.

†**rubrificative.** *Obs.*⁻⁰ (See quot.)

1611 COTGR., *Rubrificatif*, a rubrificatiue; a plaister of so strong, or strongly-drawing simples, that it . . makes red the place it is applied vnto.

†**'rubriform,** *a. Obs.* [Cf. next and -FORM.] Of a red nature.

1704 NEWTON *Optics* (1721) 156 Of those Rays which pass close by the Snow, the Rubriform will be least refracted, and so come to the Eye in the directest Lines.

†**'rubrify,** *v. Obs.* [f. *rubri-*, comb. stem of L. *ruber* red + -FY, prob. after a med.L. **rubrificāre*.] *trans.* To make red; to redden.

1634 T. JOHNSON *Parey's Chirurg.* XXVI. xxxiii. (1678) 653 Vesicatories . . which onely rubrifie, so that the part may onely become red, and not be burnt. **1657** TOMLINSON *Renou's Disp.* 203 The Sinapism . . either ulcerates or at least rubrifies it. **1689** T. PLUNKET *Char. Good Commander* 55 Have they not resolv'd our blood to spill, . . And Rubrifie the Streets in every Town?

rubrique, obs. form of RUBRIC.

†**'rubrish,** *sb. Obs.* forms: α. 4–5 rubrich(e, roberych (5 ribrusch); 5 rub-, 6 robrisshe; 5–6 rubryssh(e. β. 5 rubryce, 5–6 rubrice; 5 *pl.* rubryis. [a. OF. *rubriche*, *rubrice*, ad. L. *rubrica* RUBRIC *sb.*] A rubric.

α. *c* **1386** CHAUCER *Wife's Prol.* 346 After thy text, ne after thy Rubriche I wol nat wirche as muchel as a gnat. *c* **1440** LYDG. *Secrees* (1894) 7 This Rubryssh rehersith name of the philisoffre Callid philip, born in parys, which was translator of this book. **1451** CAPGRAVE *Life St. Aug.* (E.E.T.S.) 5 The rubrich be-for þe bok is writyn þus: The book Seynt Augustin, þe bischop, on-to his sistir, a widow. **1483** CAXTON *Cato* V j b, Thus endeth the table and Rubrisshes of this present boke. **1509** FISHER *Sermon C'tess Richmond* Wks. (1876) 292 Of latyn . . she had a lytell perceyuynge, specyally of the rubrysshe of the ordynall. **1530** PALSGR. 263/2 Robrisshe of a boke, *rubriche*.

β. **1456** SIR G. HAYE *Law Arms* (S.T.S.) 1 Into the quhilk buke thare salbe foure partis efter as the rubryis schawis. *Ibid.* 100 The chapitris of the ferde buke efter the quotacio̜uns of the rubricis. **1483** *Cath. Angl.* 313/1 A Rubryce, *rubrica*, *rubricus*. **1489** CAXTON *Faytes of A.* II. 88 Here begynneth the table of the Rubrycys of the seconde partye of thys boke. **1547** *Articles of Enquiry* (Grafton) A iv, Whether they haue put out of their churche bokes . . prayers hauynge rubricies conteyning Pardons or indulgences.

Hence **'rubrish** *v.*, to rubricate. *Obs.* Also **'rubrisher**, a rubricator. *arch.*

? **1469** *Paston Lett.* II. 335 Item, for Rubrissheyng of all the booke, iii *s.* iiij *d.* **1483** *Cath. Angl.* 313/1 To Rubryce, *rubricare*. **1863** BLADES *Caxton* II. p. liii, The illuminator, the rubrisher, and the wood-engraver.

rubro- (ˈruːbrəʊ), comb. form of L. *ruber* red, forming adjs. in *Anat.* with the sense 'relating to the red nucleus of the brain and (another part)', 'passing from the red nucleus to (another part)', as ***rubrobulbar, -frontal, -oculomotor, -parietal, -reticular, -spinal.***

1902 H. MORRIS *Treat. Human Anat.* (ed. 3) v. 769 The rubro-spinal tract is formed by a number of fibres which are scattered in the anterior part of the lateral pyramid, in the posterior part of the lateral ground bundle, and in the posterior part of Lowenthal's tract. **1937** J. H. GLOBUS *Pract. Neuroanat.* 150 Others . . descend to the brain stem and spinal cord as the rubroreticular and rubrospinal tracts. **1954** T. L. PEEL *Neuroanat. Basis Clin. Neurol.* xvii. 386/2 The rubro-oculomotor fibers to the third, fourth, and sixth cranial-nerve nuclei . . form the most mediodorsal part of the capsule of the red nucleus. *Ibid.* 387/1 Fibers to other cranial-nerve motor nuclei, a rubrobulbar tract, are probably included in the rubral outflow. *Ibid.*, Rubrofrontal and rubroparietal fibers are described as leaving the dorsolateral surface of the nucleus and passing . . to frontal and parietal lobes. **1972** M. L. BARR *Human Nervous System* vii. 110/2 Neuronal activity in the red nucleus . . influences lower motor neurons through the rubrospinal tract and through rubroreticular and reticulospinal connections. **1974** D. & M. WEBSTER *Compar. Vertebr. Morphol.* xii. 290 The rubrospinal tract leaves the red nucleus, and the reticulospinal tract leaves the reticular formation.

rubrysche, obs. variant of RUBBISH.

†**'rubster.** *Obs.*⁻¹ [f. RUB *v.*¹ + -STER.] A means of rubbing.

1697 *View Penal Laws* 69 No Clothworker shall use . . any Rubster or Rubsters, Pumicestone, or any other device whatsoever.

rubstone (ˈrʌbstəʊn). Also 6 *north.* rebstone. [f. RUB *v.*¹ + STONE *sb.*] A stone used for rubbing with, in order to sharpen or make smooth; *esp.* a kind of whetstone.

14.. *Domesday Bk. Ipswich* in Gross *Gild Merch.* (1890) II. 122 Quernstonys, gryndstonys, rubstonys. **1571** *Wills & Inv. N.C.* (Surtees, 1835) 352 Item I gyue to John Stephen in money fyue markes . . ij dosen knyff stones & iiij dosen rebstones. **1573** TUSSER *Husb.* (1878) 37 A brush sithe and grasse sithe, with rifle to stand, a cradle for barlie, with rubstone and sand. **1600** in Welford *Hist. Newcastle* (1887) III. 141 The loading and better disposing of sea-coals and pit-coals, grindstones, rubstones, and whetstones. **1697** in Brand *Newcastle* (1789) II. 300 [The mayor of Newcastle granted a warrant to four persons to seize on coals, grindstones, and rub-stones, sold by foreigners]. **1703** MOXON *Mech. Exerc.* 245 A Rub-stone, which is round, and is about fourteen Inches Diameter, . . on which they rub the Bricks which they cut into several shapes. **1850** HOLTZAPFFEL *Turning* III. 1098 The rubstones employed [in rubbing slate], depend principally on their relative abundance in the respective districts. **1866** BROGDEN *Prov. Lincs.*, *Rub-stone*, a white stone for sharpening scythes. **1875** KNIGHT *Dict. Mech.* 1998/2 *Rub-stone*, the flat stone on which the currier's knife is ground to an edge.

'rub-up. [f. vbl. phr. *to rub up*: RUB *v.*¹ 13.] The act of rubbing up in any sense.

1928 G. CAMPBELL *My Mystery Ships* xiii. 245 We . . went out to the Sound for a good 'rub up' in our drill and to get everything tested. **1943** 'TAFFRAIL' *White Ensigns* 26 He would take voluntary classes of men who wanted a rub-up in gunnery or seamanship before passing for higher rating. **1953** *Chambers's Jrnl.* June 355/1 Back then to the purgatory of waiting—with no text-books for a final rub-up permitted. **1967** KARCH & BUBER *Offset Processes* vi. 227 Plates are repaired: . . 4. By 'rub up'—to bring back or strengthen spots or areas that may become weak from an unknown cause.

rubus, -ushe, obs. forms of RUBBISH.

ruby (ˈruːbɪ), *sb.* and *a.* Forms: α. 4– ruby, 4–6 rubye, 5–7 rubie, rubey; 5 ro(o)by, rube(e, rubu. β. 4 rybe, 5 rybee, 6 rybwe; 4 ribe, 6 ribie; 5 rebe, reby. [a. OF. *rubi* (= Sp. and Pg. *rubi*, Prov. *robi*), more commonly *rubis*, repr. the Romanic stem *rubin-* (see RUBINE), obscurely related to L. *rubeus*, *ruber* red.]

I. 1. a. A very rare and valuable precious stone (the *true* or *Oriental* ruby), of a colour varying from deep crimson or purple to pale rose-red; now classed as a variety of corundum. Also, a less valuable stone (an aluminate of magnesium), distinguished as the *spinel* ruby, or a rose-pink variety of this, the *balas* ruby.

α. *a* **1310** in Wright *Lyric P.* v. 25 Ase gernet in golde, ant ruby wel ryht. *c* **1380** CHAUCER *To Rosemounde* 4 And lyke ruby ben your chekys rounde. **1530** PALSGR. 264/1 Ruby a precious stone, *ruby*. **1535** COVERDALE *Ezek.* xxviii. 13 Thou art decte . . with Ruby, Topas, Christall, Iacyncte. **1579** LODGE *Def. Poetry* ⁋1 The Rubie is discerned by his pale rednes. **1667** MILTON *P.L.* III. 597 If stone, Carbuncle most or Chrysolite, Rubie or Topaz. **1727–46** THOMSON *Summer* 147 At thee the Ruby lights its deep'ning glow. **1801** *Encycl. Brit.* (ed. 3) Suppl. II. 781/1 Pallets of ruby, driven by a hard steel swing wheel, need no oil. **1849** CAMPBELL *Inorganic Chem.* 150 The sapphire and ruby are alumina with a little colouring oxide. **1886** *Encycl. Brit.* XXI. 48/1 By this test the true ruby may be distinguished from spinel and garnet.

β. **13..** *E.E. Allit. P.* A. 1007 Þe sexte þe rybe he con. hit wale. *c* **1420** *Anturs of Arth.* xxxi. (Douce MS.), His gloues, his gamesons glowed as a glede, With graynes of rebe þat grai[th]ed bene gay.

b. With *a* and pl.

α. *a* **1310** in Wright *Lyric P.* ix. 35 Whith rubies on a rowe. *c* **1340** HAMPOLE *Pr. Consc.* 8904 Alle þe walles war made . . of cristalle schene, . . And þe garettes aboven of rubys and curalle. **1362** LANGL. *P. Pl.* A. III. 24 Rynges with Rubyes, and Richesses I-nouwe. *c* **1400** MAUNDEV. (Roxb.) xxi. 97 He beres . . a ruby, fyne and gude and orient. **1463** *Bury Wills* (Camden) 36 A doubyl ryng departyd of gold, with a ruby and a turkeys. **1500–20** DUNBAR *Poems* xlviii. 132 A radius croun of rubeis scho him gaif. **1545** *Test. Ebor.* (Surtees) VI. 228 A flower of golde . . with a rubie. **1603** SHAKS. *Meas. for M.* II. iv. 101 Th' impression of keene whips, I'ld weare as Rubies. **1700** DRYDEN *Pal. & Arc.* III. 54 His ample forehead bore a coronet, With sparkling diamonds and with rubies set. **1756–7** tr. *Keysler's Trav.* (1760) III. 185 A large golden heart hanging at a gold chain set with rubies and diamonds. **1813** SCOTT *Trierm.* III. xxvi, Here are rubies blazing bright. **1875** *Ure's Dict. Arts* II. 633 An imitation of the finest oriental rubies.

fig. a **1649** DRUMMOND OF HAWTH. *Wks.* (1711) 6 The Sun is fair, when he, with crimson Crown And flaming Rubies, leaves his Eastern Bed.

β. **13..** *Owain Miles* (1837) 37 Ribes and salidoines, Onicles and causteloines. *c* **1420** *Anturs of Arth.* ii. (Douce MS.), With riche ribaynes reuersset, . . Rayled withe rybees of rialle aray. *a* **1500** in Ashm. *Theatr. Chem. Brit.* (1652) 211 Thys ryche Reby, that ston of pryce. **1558** *Lanc. Wills* (Chetham Soc.) I. 88 A ring of gold wᵗ a broken ribie.

c. An artificial gem imitating the ruby.

1875 *Ure's Dict. Arts* II. 633 Frequently this mixture only yields an opaque mass . . : in that case rubies may be made of it.

d. The jewel of a watch (in the finest work usually a variety of ruby).

1875 KNIGHT *Dict. Mech.* 1998/2.

†**2.** *fig.* Applied, chiefly to women, as a term of high commendation. *Obs.*

a **1310** in Wright *Lyric P.* xvi. 53 Heo is rubie of ryhtfulnesse. *c* **1386** [see GEM *sb.* 2]. *c* **1485** *Digby Myst.* (1882) III. 959 Now godamercy, berel brytest of bewte! godamercy, rubu rody as þe rose! **1500–20** DUNBAR *Poems* lxxxvi. 42 Haile, redolent ruby, riche and radyuss! . . Haile, moder of God!

3. A red pimple on the face.

1558 WARDE tr. *Alexis' Secr.* II. 45 b, To take awaye red rubies that growe in the face by reason of the heate of the Liuer. **1590** SHAKS. *Com. Err.* III. ii. 138 Vpon her nose, all ore embellished with Rubies, Carbuncles, Saphires. **1611** COTGR., *Couperose*, . . extreame rednesse of the face, accompanied with many pimples, and rubies, especially about the nose. **1625** HART *Anat. Ur.* I. v. 46 May it not . . make their faces flourish with some orientall carbuncles and rubies? **1673** R. HEAD *Canting Acad.* 165 The rich Rubies on his Nose. **1770** FOOTE *Lame Lover* III. Wks. 1799 II. 82 The rubies with which his cheeks are enrich'd! **1841** BARHAM *Ingol. Leg.* Ser. II. *Old Wom. in Grey*, Certain rubies That garnished the nose of the good Father Hilary.

4. The colour of the ruby; a glowing purple-tinged red. †Also *Her.* = GULES.

1572 BOSSEWELL *Armorie* II. 67 b, The fielde is the Rubie, a Cheuron topaze, betwene iij Eaglettes displaide, with two heades, of the Pearle. **1592** WYRLEY *Armorie* 148 Sir William Luzie did here a partie hold In rubie armd, three Lucie fishes. **1605** SHAKS. *Macb.* III. iv. 115 When now I thinke you can behold such sights, And keepe the naturall Rubie of your Cheekes. **1634** RAINBOW *Labour* (1635) 27 If this be to labour, . . to flush their complexions to the drunkards ruby. **1847** EMERSON *Ode to Beauty* 28 The swinging spider's silver line, The ruby of the drop of wine.

5. *transf.* Applied to various things of a colour similar to the ruby: **a.** *pl.* The lips.

1592 DANIEL *Compl. Rosamund* 124 Wks. (Grosart) I. 85 As the saddest tale.. Makes silent listning vnto him that told it, So did my speech when Rubies did vnfold it. **1611** SHAKS. *Cymb.* II. ii. 17 That I might..kisse, one kisse. Rubies vnparagon'd, How deerely they doo't: 'Tis her breathing that Perfumes the Chamber thus.

b. Red wine.

1671 MILTON *Samson* 543 Nor did the dancing Rubie.. Allure thee from the cool Crystalline stream. **1859** FITZ GERALD tr. *Omar* v, Still the Vine her ancient Ruby yields.

c. *Pugilistic slang.* The blood.

1860 *Chamb. Jrnl.* XIII. 348 The fluid of which Harvey demonstrated the circulation in the human body, he [the pugilist] speaks of as 'claret', or 'carmine', or 'ruby'. **1888** *Sporting Life* 11 Dec. (Farmer), Saunders stopped a flush right-hander with his organ of smell, the ruby duly making its appearance.

d. *ellipt.* Ruby port (see sense 11).

1938 G. GREENE *Brighton Rock* I. iii. 37 'Give me a glass of Ruby,' the sombre man said. **1959** W. JAMES *Word-bk. Wine* 148 Ruby is a young, deep-red wine, or a tawny which has been refreshed with a younger wine.

6. †**a.** *Alchemy.* (See quot.) *Obs.*$^{-1}$

1610 B. JONSON *Alch.* II. i. 48 He that has once the flower of the sunne, The perfect ruby, which we call elixir.

b. (See quots.)

1696 PHILLIPS s.v. *Arsenic, Ruby of Arsenic*, is a Preparation of it with sulphur by means of several repeated sublimations. **1728** CHAMBERS *Cycl., Ruby*, in Chymistry, is a Name given to several Preparations of natural Bodies, because of their red Colour; as, Ruby of Arsenick, &c. **1753** *Chambers' Cycl.* Suppl. s.v., *Arsenical Ruby*,.. a name given to a sublimation of a mixture of arsenic and common sulphur. **1797** *Encycl. Brit.* (ed. 3) XVI. 544/1 What is called ruby of arsenic or of sulphur is the realgar; the ruby of zinc is the red blend; and the ruby of silver is the red silver ore.

c. *ellipt.* Ruby glass (see 11).

1839 STONEHOUSE *Isle of Axholme* 227 Even the ancient ruby is not lost to those artists who can and will patiently seek after it. **1862** *Catal. Internat. Exhib., Brit.* II. No. 6781 The group on the right is half-cased with ruby.

7. *Printing.* A size of type, intermediate between nonpareil and pearl. (Cf. AGATE *sb.* 4.)

There is no evidence to support the two earliest quots., which place ruby between pearl and diamond.

1778 MORES *Dissert. Eng. Typog. Founders* 26 So we exclude Minion, Nonpareil, Pearl, Ruby and Diamond, so named from their smallness and fancied prettiness. **1824** J. JOHNSON *Typographia* II. 76 Independent of the above sizes, we have just been informed, that Mr. Miller, of Edinburgh, has introduced another, which he designates by the name of Ruby; it is a size between Pearl and Diamond. **1839** HANSARD *Print. & Type-founding* (1841) 228 Ruby.., used for pocket dictionaries, prayer-books, &c.; but it is too small for any but the strongest sight. **1888** JACOBI *Printers' Vocab.* 116 *Ruby*, a size of type..equal to half a Small Pica in body.

II. *attrib.* and *Comb.*

8. a. Attributive, as ***ruby chain, cylinder, hole, laser, mine, ring, rock, roller, spark, stone.***

1508 DUNBAR *Golden Targe* 24 With hevinly beriall droppis, Throu bemes rede, birnyng as ruby sperkis. **1508** —— *Tua Mariit Wemen* 367 In ringis ryally set with riche ruby stonis. *a* **1700** KEN *Edmund* Poet. Wks. 1721 II. 150 Seven polish'd Ruby Rocks the columns were, Into bright Seraphs carv'd. **1710** *Lond. Gaz.* No. 2691/4 A Ruby Ring with three Brilliant Diamonds on each side. **1829** CRAWFURD *Jrnl. Emb. to Crt. of Ava* (1834) II. 203 The sapphire and ruby mines are considered the property of the King. **1843** HOLTZAPFFEL *Turning* I. 173 Ruby holes are also employed for rounding the leads of even-pointed pencils. **1872** TENNYSON *Last Tourn.* 409 He..show'd them both the ruby-chain. **1884** F. J. BRITTEN *Watch & Clockm.* 97 The.. teeth..lock the wheel by pressing on a hollow ruby cylinder or roller... There is a notch in the ruby roller. **1961** *Ann. Reg. 1960* 396 One drawback of the ruby laser was that it produced light only in bursts. **1974** *Encycl. Brit. Micropædia* VIII. 707/1 The chromium atoms responsible for the ruby's colour are also responsible for the emission of red light when ruby is excited by radiation, as in the red light produced by a ruby laser. **1977** *Jrnl. R. Soc. Arts* CXXV. 765/1 The first ruby laser of Maiman in 1960.

b. Similative, as ***ruby-like, -wise.*** Also ***ruby-ripe, -sweet.***

1694 SALMON *Bate's Disp.* (1715) 560/1 So will you have a Ruby-like Tincture. **1832** TENNYSON *Dream of Fair Women* ii, All faces turn'd to where Glows rubylike the far-up crimson globe. **1871** RUSKIN *Fors Clav.* vii. 11 Not merely..a colour on the outside, but going through and through, ruby-wise. **1918** W. DE LA MARE *Sam's Three Wishes* in *Twelve Poets* 27 Ruby-ripe to see, The pixy-pears burn on yon hawthorn tree. **1920** E. SITWELL *Wooden Pegasus* 21 As isles of the cherry Or ruby-sweet berry.

c. Instrumental, as ***ruby-circled, -headed, -studded.***

1872 TENNYSON *Last Tourn.* 364 Before him fled the face of Queen Isolt With ruby-circled neck. **1875** BEDFORD *Sailor's Pkt. Bk.* i. (ed. 2) 38 The two ruby-headed pivots are made exclusively for the heavier card J. **1895** SWETTENHAM *Malay Sketches* 180 Her hair fastened in a knot with four ruby-studded hairpins.

9. As *adj.* Having the colour of the ruby; of a dark glowing red, usually tinged with purple.

1508 DUNBAR *Gold. Targe* 38 The ruby skyes of the orient. **1515** *Acc. Ld. High Treas. Scot.* V. 9 Ane vnce of ruby silk to thair quaiffs. **1592** GREENE *Quip for Upstart Courtier* Wks. (Grosart) XI. 242 His face somthing Ruby blush, Cherry cheeked, like a shreed of scarlet. **1601** SHAKS. *Jul. C.* III. i. 260 Thy wounds... Which like dumbe mouthes do ope their Ruby lips. **1644** PRYNNE & WALKER *Fiennes's Trial* 115 Though he might haply view his ruby Nose without a Mirrour. **1648** J. BEAUMONT *Psyche* VIII. cclv, Their whiter Names Being dyed deep in ruby Martyrdom. **1712** tr. *Pomet's Hist. Drugs* I. 108 It will give the transparent Red, a Ruby Colour. **1764** GRAY *Triumph Owen* 22 High he rears his ruby crest. **1801** SOUTHEY *Thalaba* VI. xxiv, Vessels of wine, alternate placed, Ruby and amber. **1864** TENNYSON *Islet* 13 With a satin sail of a ruby glow. **1887** *The Lady* 20 Jan. 37/2 One lady had a ruby velvet, trimmed with costly lace.

10. a. In parasynthetic adjs., as ***ruby-berried, -budded, -coloured, -eyed, -faced, -hued, -lipped, -tasselled***, etc.

1866 GEO. ELIOT *F. Holt* (1868) 2 The purple-blossomed *ruby-berried nightshade. **1855** TENNYSON *Maud* I. iv. 1 A million emeralds break from the *ruby-budded lime. **1592** SHAKS. *Ven. & Ad.* 451 Once more the *rubi-colour'd portall opend. **1817** KIRBY & SP. *Entomol.* xxi. (1818) II. 223 The inequalities of its ruby-coloured surface. **1919** R. C. PUNNETT *Mendelism* (ed. 5) ix. 95 In canaries, again, there are *ruby-eyed cinnamon forms corresponding to the various green and yellow varieties. **1950** D. GASCOYNE *Vagrant* 38 Fatalist, Ruby-eyed. **1711** *Lond. Gaz.* No. 4813/4 He is..*Ruby Faced. **1741** *Chinese Lett.* i. 7 A jolly ruby-fac'd Prelate, lolling at Ease in his Coach, hinders his Progress. **1896** MARY BEAUMONT *Joan Seaton* 50 A great water-butt, its sides deep in *ruby-hued nasturtiums. **1642** H. MORE *Song Soul, Infin. Worlds* xcix, Fair comely bodies, ..rose-cheek'd, *ruby-lip'd. **1648** HERRICK *Hesper., Short Hymn to Venus*, I do love a Girle Rubie-lipt, and tooth'd with Pearl. **1878** LONGF. *Kéramos* 143 Little towns..*ruby-lustered with the light Of blazing furnaces by night. **1920** BLUNDEN *Waggoner* 55 And *ruby-tasselled shepherd's rose. **1708** J. PHILIPS *Cyder* II. 88 The elder Year, Pomona, pleas'd, shall deck With *ruby-tinctur'd Births. **1740** SOMERVILLE *Hobbinol* III. 45 The ruby-tinctur'd Corinth clust'ring hangs, And emulates the Grape. **1876** ROCK *Text. Fabr.* 63 Raised or cut *ruby-toned velvet of a rich soft pile. **1827** T. HAMILTON *Youth & Manhood C. Thornton* (1845) 76, I..gladly consigned the remains of the dish to the care of my *ruby-visaged neighbour.

b. In specific names of birds, as ***ruby-crested, -crowned, -headed, -necked.*** Also RUBY-THROATED.

1782 LATHAM *Gen. Synop. Birds* I. II. 780 *Ruby-crested Humming Bird. **1758** G. EDWARDS *Glean. Nat. Hist.* I. 95 The *Ruby-crowned Wren. **1785** PENNANT *Arct. Zool.* II. 413 Ruby-crowned Warbler. **1834** AUDUBON *Ornith. Biog.* II. 547 The Ruby-crowned Wren is found in Louisiana and other Southern States, from November until March. **1872** COUES *N. Amer. Birds* 78 Ruby-crowned Kinglet. Crown with a rich scarlet patch. **1811** SHAW *Gen. Zool.* VIII. I. 329 *Ruby-headed Humming-bird... This is one of the most beautiful of the straight-billed Humming-Birds. **1782** LATHAM *Gen. Synop. Birds* I. II. 779 *Ruby-necked Humming Bird.

11. a. In special collocations, as **ruby anniversary**, a fortieth anniversary; **ruby-back**, used *attrib.* to designate fine Chinese porcelain enamelled on the reverse in pink or crimson; so **ruby-backed** adj.; **ruby blende, copper** (see quots.); **ruby coral**, ? red coral; **ruby-dazzler** *Austral.* and *N.Z. slang*, something exceptionally fine (cf. BOBBY-DAZZLER); **ruby glass**, glass coloured by the oxides of copper, iron, lead, tin, etc.; **ruby port**, port of a deep red colour, *spec.* that matured in wood for only a few years and fined before bottling; **Ruby Queen** *Forces' slang* (see quot. 1925); **ruby silver**, proustite; **ruby spar** (see quot.); **ruby spinel**, = *spinel ruby*; **ruby sulphur, topaz**; (see quots.); **ruby wedding**, a fortieth (occas. forty-fifth) wedding anniversary; **ruby wood, zinc** (see quots.).

1962 *Guardian* 17 Nov. 5/2 The celebration of the BBC's *ruby anniversary. **1915** R. L. HOBSON *Chinese Pott. & Porc.* II. xii. 213 A *ruby-back saucer dish delicately painted. **1935** *Burlington Mag.* Jan. 25/2 At that period the Chinese kilns produced the ruby-back egg-shell porcelain. **1960** H. HAYWARD *Antique Coll.* 115/1 A new delicate painting style began to oust that of the *famille verte*..about 1720, and was applied especially to plates, bowls and cups and saucers of 'egg-shell' thin procelain. The 'ruby-back' variety is coloured deep rose-pink on the reverse. **1980** *Catal. Fine Chinese Ceramics* (Sotheby, Hong Kong) 180 Compare the ruby-back cups painted with fruit in the interior sold in these rooms 29th November, 1977. **1900** F. LITCHFIELD *Pott. & Porc.* vii. 113 The most highly-prized egg-shell, which is termed '*ruby backed' china. **1970** G. C. WILLIAMSON *Bk. of Famille Rose* vii. 104 Ruby-backed pieces can be marked off as belonging to a particular group, but the division must be confined exclusively to the ruby back. **1855** *Orr's Cir. Sci., Geol.*, etc. 501 *Proustite* —— Red Silver, *Ruby-blende. **1815** A. AIKIN *Mineralogy* (ed. 2) 88 Red Copper. *Ruby Copper. **1837** *Penny Cycl.* VII. 503/1 This oxide..occurs in Cornwall in the form of beautiful transparent crystals of a fine red colour, and is hence frequently called *ruby copper.* **1632** LITHGOW *Trav.* IX. 393 The Marine here [Trapani, Sicily] excelleth in *Ruby Corall. **1941** BAKER *N.Z. Slang* vi. 51 Expressions..in constant use by our youngsters:..bobbydazzler, *rubydazzler, dag, swinjer, [etc.]. **1941** —— *Dict. Austral. Slang* 62 *Rube*,..something esp. fine. *Rubydazzler pivots* as for 'rube'. **1977** W. S. RAMSON in *Quadrant* (Sydney) May 67/1 The *Australian Pocket Oxford*..is a real *beaut*, a *ryebuck* dictionary, a *ringer*, a *ripper*, a gem amongst dictionaries if not a *rubydazzler*. **1797** W. JOHNSTON tr. *Beckmann's Invent.* I. 205 In 1684 Orschall..wrote..of the manner of making *ruby-glass. **1860** LONGF. *Tales Wayside Inn, Falcon of Ser Federigo* 186 The ruby glass, the silver, and the gold. **1885** A. J. BUTLER tr. *Dante's Paradise* 268 *note*, Until the fifteenth century only 'ruby' glass was 'coated'. **1921** A. L. SIMON *Wine & Wine Trade* v. 59 It also happens sometimes that a vintage Port..will be kept in wood for a more or less extended number of years before it is bottled. The result will be a wine with less colour and strength than the early bottled vintage Port, but with more body and colour than tawny Port. This wine is often described as '*Ruby' Port. **1938** G. GREENE *Brighton Rock* I. iii. 47 Life was sunlight on brass bedposts, ruby port. **1967** A. LICHINE *Encycl. Wines* 411/2 A bottle of Vintage Port..will suffer if it is open to the air very long, though a Ruby Port or Tawny will survive better. **1925** FRASER & GIBBONS *Soldier & Sailor Words* 246 **Ruby Queen*,..an occasional nickname for any young nurse or Sister of fresh complexion. **1934** BLUNDEN *Choice or Chance* 31 With Ruby Queens We once crowned feeds of pork and beans. **1815** A. AIKIN *Mineralogy* (ed. 2) 79 Red or *Ruby Silver..occurs crystallized, dendritic, membranous, massive, and disseminated. **1882** *U.S. Rep. Prec. Met.* 177 The vein..contains black sulphurets and ruby silver. **1796** KIRWAN *Elem. Min.* (ed. 2) I. 254 The stone imported from Ceylon, called **ruby spar*,..is an iridescent sort of spinell ruby. **1839** URE *Dict. Arts* 570 The purchaser must ascertain if it be not a Siberian tourmaline, or *ruby spinel. **1868** WATTS *Dict. Chem.* V. 400 Precious spinel is distinguished by several names, according to its colour, the deep red variety being called ruby spinel. **1837** DANA *Syst. Min.* VI. 434 Realgar,..Red Orpiment or *Ruby Sulphur... Red Sulphuret of Arsenic. **1885** HORNADAY *2 Yrs. in Jungle* xxiv. 287 The island produces..garnets, 'Ceylon ruby' (*ruby topaz), star stones. **1911** WEBSTER s.v. ruby *a.*, **Ruby wedding*, the forty-fifth wedding anniversary. **1963** B. SMITH *Etiquette* vii. 117 According to a former convention..the interim anniversaries are..fortieth year, Ruby Wedding. **1977** *Times* 15 Apr. 12/5 This year marks his ruby wedding as well as his retirement. **1843** HOLTZAPFFEL *Turning* I. 103 Red Sanders, or *Ruby Wood, an East Indian wood, the produce of *Pterocarpus santalinus*. **1896** CHESTER *Dict. Min.* 237 **Ruby-zinc*, a popular name for..sphalerite of a deep-red color, and also for zincite with the same characteristics.

b. (See quots.)

1832 J. RENNIE *Consp. Butterfl. & Moths* 28 The Ruby Fly Hawk... Very rare. *Ibid.* 43 The Ruby Tiger..appears the beginning of July. **1868** J. G. WOOD *Homes Without Hands* xiii. 238 A specimen of the Ruby and Topaz Humming Bird (*Chrysolampis moschitis*).

ruby ('ru:bɪ), *v.* [f. the sb.] *trans.* To dye or tinge with the colour of the ruby.

1725 POPE *Odyss.* XX. 426 With sanguine drops the walls are rubied round. **1832** J. BREE *St. Herbert's Isle* 10 Her cheeks were rubied with the rose's hue. **1844** CORNISH *Select fr. Serm.*, etc. (1850) 374 So intense a gleam Rubied the oaken copse.

ruby-red, *a.* [RUBY *sb.*] **a.** As red as a ruby; having the red colour of ruby.

1591 GREENE *Farewell to Follie* Wks. (Grosart) IX. 266 A lip sweete rubie red, gracd with delight. **1611** FLORIO, *Rosseggiante*, ruby-red. **1796** WITHERING *Brit. Plants* (ed. 3) IV. 229 Gills ruby red, 4 in a set. **1847** C. BRONTË *J. Eyre* xi, The ornaments..were of sparkling Bohemian glass, ruby red. **1899** tr. *Jaksch's Clin. Diagnosis* (ed. 4) v. 186 An oily substance forms, from which ruby-red needles..slowly separate.

b. quasi-*sb.* A ruby-red colour or tint.

1885 [see ISOCHROMATIC *a.* 2]. **1899** tr. *Jaksch's Clin. Diagnosis* (ed. 4) viii. 410 The fungus threads are stained a ruby-red.

ruby-tail. [RUBY *a.*] **a.** *attrib.* = next. **b.** (See quots. and next.)

1837 *Penny Cycl.* VII. 136/2 The Chrysididæ are most of them, if not all, of parasitic habits... Some of these species are called ruby-tail flies. **1863** J. G. WOOD *Illustr. Nat. Hist.* III. 497 The beautiful Ruby-tail Flies, or Cuckoo Flies, so plentiful in summer about old walls and similar localities. **1881** *Cassell's Nat. Hist.* V. 384 This insect, the Common Gold Wasp, or Ruby-tail,..is of a deep metallic bluish green colour, except the upper surface of the abdomen, which is bright red.

ruby-tailed, *a.* [RUBY *a.*] Having a ruby-red hinder part; applied to hymenopterous insects of the genus *Chrysis*, esp. the golden wasp.

1862 *Chambers's Encycl.* III. 23/1 They sometimes receive the English names of Golden-tailed and Ruby-tailed Flies. **1868** J. G. WOOD *Homes without Hands* xxv. 481 Those splendid insects which are popularly called Ruby-tailed Flies, or Firetails, and scientifically termed Chrysididæ.

ruby-throat. [RUBY *a.*] A ruby-throated humming-bird or warbler. Also *attrib.* = next.

1783 LATHAM *Gen. Synop. Birds* II. I. 463 Ruby-Throat, *Motacilla calliope*. **1817** *Shaw's Gen. Zool.* X. II. 644 Ruby-throat warbler (*Sylvia Calliope*). **1872** *Routledge's Ev. Boy's Ann.* 201/1 What was our surprise to see the ruby-throat.. remain with the young ones.

ruby-throated, *a.* [RUBY *a.*] Having a ruby-red gorget. In names of birds (see quots.). Also occas. used of people.

1782 LATHAM *Gen. Synop. Birds* I. II. 769 Ruby-throated Humming-bird, *Trochilus rubineus*. Inhabits Brasil and Guiana. **1872** COUES *N. Amer. Birds* 184 Ruby-throated Hummingbird,..metallic gorget reflecting ruby-red. **1900** *Westm. Gaz.* 3 Dec. 10/2 Two specimens of the *Calliope Camtschatkensis*, or ruby-throated warbler. **1957** O. NASH *You can't get there from Here* 68 Our ruby-throated playgirls and madcap millionaires.

ruc, obs. form of ROC.

rucas, ruccus, *varr.* RUCKUS.

rucervine (ru:'sɜ:vaɪn), *a. Zool.* [f. mod.L. *Rucerv-us*: see RUSA and CERVINE *a.*] Of or belonging to a genus (*Rucervus*) of East Indian deer.

1881 *Cassell's Nat. Hist.* III. 60 Its antlers are large, and of the intermediate rucervine type. **1891** FLOWER & LYDEKKER *Mamm.* 321 The Rucervine group..is represented by the Swamp Deer.

ruch, obs. f. ROUGH *a.* and *adv.*

ruche (ruːʃ, F. ryʃ), *sb.* Also **rouche.** [a. F. *ruche* (†*rouche, rusche*), bee-hive, and (in allusion to the plaits of a straw hive) frill, etc.] A frill or quilling of some light material, as ribbon, gauze, or lace, used to ornament some part of a garment or head-dress. Also *attrib.*

a **1827** *Souvenir* I. 127/3 (Stanf.). A bonnet..with a blue and white ruche of gauze at the edge. **1862** *Engl. Wom. Dom. Mag.* IV. 236/1 The front of the body..was trimmed with white satin ruches laid over white blonde. **1881** *Truth* 31 March 446/1 The inevitable ruche of Mechlin lace makes the dress becoming to the neck. **1882** CAULFEILD & SAWARD *Dict. Needlewk.* 427/2 For silk the Ruche flutings should measure from half inch, to 1 inch.

transf. **1865** MRS. BEETON *Dict. Cookery* 210 Place a paper ruche on the bone.

β. **1858** SIMMONDS *Dict. Trade, Rouche,*..a goffered quilling of net, ribbon, blonde, or any other material. **1864** *Daily Tel.* 11 March, Her Royal Highness..wore a white satin dress with rouches of tulle.

Hence **ruche** *v.*[1], to trim with a ruche.

1892 *Daily News* 8 March 2/1 A black moiré silk was ruched with pink round the border of the skirt.

†**ruche (ruchche),** *v.*[2] *Obs.* Var. of RICH *v.*[2]

13.. *E.E. Allit. P.* C. 101 Þay her tramme ruchen, Cachen vp þe crossayl, cables þay fasten. **13..** *Gaw. & Gr. Knt.* 303 Þe renk on his rounce hym ruched in his sadel. *Ibid.* 367 He ful radly vp ros, & ruchched hym fayre.

ruched (ruːʃt), *ppl. a.* [f. RUCHE *v.*[1]] Trimmed with a ruche. Also *fig.*

1847 E. GRAY *Let.* 5 May in W. James *Order of Release* (1947) iii. 31 Cloaks of pale glacé silk with ruished frills round them. **1848** —— *Let.* 10 May in *Ibid.* v. 107 A stone silk dress with two broad flounces Ruched and a Brussells lace cape. **1896** *Boston* (Mass.) *Jrnl.* 3 Dec. 5/2 It had ruched sleeves. **1900** *Ann. Rep. Board of Regents Smithsonian Inst. 1898* II. 703 In a broad way we may distinguish as leading types [of hemipenis] the following: The smooth; the plicate, or flounced; the calyculate, or ruched; and the disk-bearing. **1923** E. SITWELL *Bucolic Comedies* 61 Ruched as their country waterfalls, The cherried maids walk beneath the dark walls. **1932** *Woman's Weekly* 19 Mar. 467/1 The..skirt is cut in wide scallops and trimmed with ruching. Little ruched pieces..give the frock quaintness and charm. **1978** *Detroit Free Press* 5 Mar D7/5 (Advt.), This terrific coat with its softly ruched back.

ruchet, obs. variant of ROCHET[2].

ruching (ˈruːʃɪŋ). [f. RUCHE *sb.* + -ING[1].] A trimming consisting of ruches. Also *fig.*

1862 *Engl. Wom. Dom. Mag.* IV. 236/1 A blue tulle skirt, trimmed with blue silk ruchings. **1888** MRS. H. WARD *R. Elsmere* 50 Her marvellous drab poplin, adorned with fresh pink ruchings. **1894** H. GAMLIN *G. Romney* 200 The cuffs edged with narrow white ruching. **1914** C. MACKENZIE *Sinister St.* II. IV. iv. 914 The beginning of the street ran between two high brown walls crowned with a ruching of broken glass. **1932** [see prec.]. **1971** *Homes & Gardens* Sept. 61/2 And not only have they pounced on all the lace, all those bibs and tuckers and ruchings and veils and shawls and scarves and yard after yard of flouncing.

ruchli, obs. form of ROUGHLY *adv.*

ruchy (ˈruːʃɪ), *a. rare.* [f. RUCHE *sb.*] Of the nature of a ruche.

1884 *Bazaar, Exch. & M.* 19 Dec. 658/1 Sleeves are sometimes..one puff, with a soft ruchy trimming at the end.

ruck (rʌk), *sb.*[1] Forms: α. 3 **ruke,** 5 **roke,** 6 *Sc.* **rouk,** 6–7 **rooke,** 7 **rowke,** 9 *dial.* **rook, rouk.** β. 6 **ruk,** 6–7 **rucke,** 7 **rukk(e,** 6– **ruck.** [App. of Scand. origin, corresponding to Norw. *ruka* (Aasen) with the same meanings, perh. repr. ON. **hruka* and so related to *hraukr* RICK *sb.*[1]]

1. a. A heap or stack of fuel or combustible material of any kind.

a **1225** *Ancr. R.* 214 Þe ȝiscare..fareð abuten asken & bisiliche stureð him uorte rukelen muchele & monie ruken togedere, & bloweð þerinne. *c* **1440** *Destr. Troy* 7149 All the Remnond and Roke radly þai broght, And brent vp the bodies vnto bare askis. **1549** COVERDALE, etc. *Erasm. Par. St. James* II. 34 Like as a litel fyre is mingled with a greate rooke of fewell, so that by lytel and litell it setteth al the whole rooke on fyre. **1556** OLDE *Antichrist* 177 The hole beast..is cast in to the burnyng streame or burnyng rooke of fyre. **1621** *Sc. Acts Jas. VI* (1814) IV. 628 That they nor nane of thame..keip any stakis, or Rukkes of haither, broome, Quhynnes, or vther fewall, within anye of the Closses. **1879** E. WAUGH *Chimney Corner* 251 I've made fourpence, to-day, wi' gettin' a rook (a lot) o' coals in. **1883** GRESLEY *Gloss. Coal-mining* 207 Ruck, the stock of coals on the bank.

†**b.** A particular measure or quantity of coals (see quot. 1611). *Obs.*

1483 *Nottingham Rec.* II. 421, 10 wain-loads of coals called 'pytte coles', every wain-load containing a whole 'roke' of coals. **1486** *Ibid.* III. 257 For half a roke of colys to brenne þe seid plaster with. **1611** *Rutland MSS.* IV. 484 in *Rep. Hist. MSS. Comm.* (1905), A rooke of colles ought to bee ij yeardes high and a yeard and quarter square by measure. **1651** *Publ. Gen. Acts* 1326 Such..of the said Coals as have been, or usually are sold by the Stack, Ruck, Fathom, or other uncertain Denomination.

2. A rick or stack of hay, corn, etc.; †a shock or stook. *Sc.* and *north. dial.*

1546 in *Cal. Laing Charters* (1899) 135 Onto the tyme the said medow be mawyn and put into rouk. **1570** *Wills & Inv. N.C.* (Surtees, 1835) 341 In wheat in the staggarth ij ruckes by estymac'on Fiftye thraves. **1611** COTGR., *Treseau,* a shocke, stowke, halfe-thraue, rowke, or heape of sheaues in a corne-field. **1725** RAMSAY *Gentle Shepherd* I. ii. 125 The spate may bear away Frae aff the howms your dainty rucks of hay. **1773** FERGUSSON *Poems* (1807) 229 Our rucks, fu' thick, are stackit i' the yard. **1804** R. COUPER *Poetry* I. 152 Strong on the ruck-head [I've] heard your voice Whan mid-night's tempests blew. **1871** ALEXANDER *Johnny Gibb* vi, Twa' or three aul' rucks to thrash oot.

3. a. A heap or pile of any material. Freq. in phr. ***in a ruck.*** Now *dial.*

a **1601** ? MARSTON *Pasquil & Kath.* IV. 117 So huge a Ruck Of heap'd vp fortunes. **1627** DRAYTON *Agincourt* 9 There in another Rucke Princes and Peasants lay together mixt. **1688** HOLME *Armoury* III. 312/1 They can neither Stand, Sit, Kneel, nor lie down, but be all in a ruck, or knit together. **1790** W. H. MARSHALL *Rur. Econ. Midl.* Gloss., *Ruck,* a rough bundle or heap of any thing. **1828** CARR *Craven Gloss., Ruck,* a great quantity; a heap of stones. **1851–** in many dial. glossaries (see *Eng. Dial. Dict.*). **1870** E. PEACOCK *Ralf Skirl.* I. 130 He doesn't care two pence about the bit of a rouk o' cobble stones and sand.

b. *transf.* A large number or quantity; a multitude, crowd, throng. ***in a ruck,*** in *Racing*: in one group.

1581 MULCASTER *Positions* vi. (1887) 47, I shall not neede to name the partes, all in one ruk, as of set purpose. *a* **1601** ? MARSTON *Pasquil & Kath.* III. 327 Rucks of rich Pearle, and sparkling Diamonds Shall fringe thy garments with Imbroadrie. **1657** G. THORNLEY *Daphnis & Chloe* 26 Sheep and Goats,..some ran on rucks, and hurried down to the Sea-shore. **1829** J. HUNTER *Hallamsh. Gloss., Ruck,* a multitude, as applied to people; a great assemblage, as applied to anything else. **1840** *Spirit of Times* 10 Oct. 380 When Randal blew his bugle, away they all flew in a ruck. **1847** ALB. SMITH *Chr. Tadpole* ii. (1879) 29 Finishing with a ruck of figures all at once. **1856** 'STONEHENGE' *Brit. Rural Sports* 377/1 When judgment is wanted in getting through a ruck of horses. **1884** *Pall Mall G.* 11 Aug. 4/2 There is a ruck of ambitious Gambettists in the prime of life.

c. (*a*) *Rugby Union.* (Also ***loose ruck.***) = ***loose scrummage*** s.v. LOOSE *a.* 9. (*b*) ***Australian Rules football.*** (See quot. 1969.)

1906 GALLAHER & STEAD *Compl. Rugby Footballer* ix. 134 What we call a loose ruck..represents the disordered state of things occurring, for example, when..a back has slipped and stopped the play when trying to block a forward rush. One man is down, and all his other colleagues in the back division are induced to come up to his assistance. **1955** *Times* 8 Aug. 2/2 With the South African pack controlling the line outs..and driving hard from the rucks the home side looked to have a firm grip on the game. **1956** V. JENKINS *Lions Rampant* xii. 180 On the muddy ground they made rush after rush, and piled into the loose rucks as if their lives depended on it. **1967** *Australian* 17 Apr. 12 Terry Waters ..was moved into the ruck in the third quarter. **1969** EAGLESON & MCKIE *Terminol. Austral. Nat. Football* III. 10 *Ruck.* 1. The three members of a team who do not occupy fixed positions but are free to follow the play wherever it goes around the field; the ruck consists of a rover and two followers. *Ibid.* 11 *Ruck.* 2. A member of a team selected to play in the ruck, other than the rover. **1973** [see MAUL *sb.*[1] 4]. **1979** *Times* 12 Dec. 9/1 Oxford..won most of the rucks or mauls that mattered.

4. ***the ruck:* a.** *Racing.* Those horses which are left behind in a body by the fastest goers. Also *fig.*

1846 *Punch* XI. 15 Who headed the Ruck? 'I,' said Lord George. **1852** BRISTED 5 *Years Eng. Univ.* (ed. 2) 85 The ruck falls off rapidly, and the good men settle down to their pace. **1862** WHYTE MELVILLE *Inside the Bar* I. 224 'What one horse can do another can.' Self-esteem implores us not to fall back into the 'ruck' behind. **1884** 'H. COLLINGWOOD' *Under Meteor Flag* 180 Summers came panting in with the ruck, after all was over. **1922** E. WALLACE *Flying Fifty-Five* xii. 70 Its jockey had given up all attempt at winning and was content to finish with the ruck.

b. The undistinguished crowd or general run (of persons or things).

1849 ALB. SMITH *Pottleton Legacy* (1854) 324 The uneducated and socially-unplaced ruck. **1859** M. NAPIER *Life Visc. Dundee* I. p. x, Far more honest, and..more right-minded than the ruck of their sect. **1879** *Contemp. Rev.* XXXVI. 291, I write simply as one of that common ruck of ordinary practical working men. **1894** MRS. F. ELLIOT *Roman Gossip* xii. 290 A great name, rising out of the feeble ruck of modern Italian sculpture.

5. *U.S. colloq.* Nonsense, rubbish.

1885 'MARK TWAIN' *Let.* 11 Sept. (1917) II. xxv. 460 Flowers and general ruck sent to him by Tom, Dick, and Harry from everywhere. **1890** *Scribner's Mag.* Aug. 159 He ..wears gloves, and take his meals private in his room and all that sort of ruck.

6. *attrib.*, as (sense 3 c (a)) ***ruck ball;*** (sense 3 c (b)) ***ruck man, -rover.***

1976 *Scotsman* 24 Dec. 16/4 The ruck ball was promptly knocked on by a centre. **1963** *Sunday Mail* (Brisbane) 24 Feb. 24/5 Dr. Eric Laithwaite,..senior lecturer in electrical engineering at Manchester University,..looks more like an uncomplicated ruckman than an ingenious scientist. **1969** EAGLESON & MCKIE *Terminol. Austral. Nat. Football* III. 11 *Ruckman,* a member of the ruck whose function it is to take marks, and to knock the ball to the rover when the ball is thrown up or bounced by the umpire. **1977** *Age* (Melbourne) 18 Jan. 26/4 (*caption*) Fumbling is embarrassing anytime for a famous VFL ruckman and Jones covers his face in despair. **1967** *Australian* 24 Apr. 12 The brilliant Polly Farmer is now being used as a ruck-rover. **1969** EAGLESON & MCKIE *Terminol. Austral. Nat. Football* III. 12 *Ruck-rover,* a mobile member of the ruck who is usually intermediate in size between a follower and rover.

ruck (rʌk), *sb.*[2] [a. ON. *hrukka* (Norw. *rukka*), for earlier **hrunka*: see RUNKLE *sb.*] A crease, fold, or wrinkle; a ridge.

1787 GROSE *Prov. Gloss., Ruck,* a wrinkle or plait. *Ibid.,* Your gown fits all in a ruck. **1811** WILLAN *West Riding Yorksh., Ruck,* a fold, or plait, made in cloth by crushing it. **1839** *Civil Eng. & Arch. Jrnl.* II. 76/1 The vessel..was found to be..without even a single strain or so much as a ruck in her copper. **1863** *Q. Rev.* July 97 He observed there also a number of large transverse ridges or rucks or the glacier. **1878** T. BRYANT *Pract. Surg.* I. 35 Careful attention should be paid to keep the bed smooth, and the sheets free from rucks.

ruck (rʌk), *sb.*[3] *dial.* A rut.

1823 [see *cart-ruck,* s.v. CART *sb.* 6]. **1839** LEWIS *Hereford Gloss., Ruck,* a rut of a road. **1858** *Zoologist* XVI. 5941 Deep, dirty ditches or rucks. **1869** *Lonsdale Gloss.* s.v.

†**ruck,** *sb.*[4] *Obs.*$^{-0}$ (See quot.)

1838 W. BELL *Dict. Law Scot.* 325 In addition to his subscription, the notary was formerly in use to add his *signum,* which was a flourish of penmanship, called a *paraph* or a *ruck.*

ruck (rʌk), *sb.*[5] *colloq.* [Perh. f. RUCK *v.*[6] or shortening of RUCTION or RUCKUS.] A quarrel, a row.

1958 F. NORMAN *Bang to Rights* I. 15, I didn't feel like having a ruck about this. **1960** *Times* 15 Mar. 7/7 All that gun business is—silly isn't it. I mean they were only having a ruck to start with. **1963** T. & P. MORRIS *Pentonville* vi. 144 The prisoner said that he had 'had a bit of a ruck with the instructor over this'. **1964** *Listener* 31 Dec. 1055/2 Squaddies and Teds, personal rucks forgotten, are fleeing from a common enemy—the law. **1976** 'P. B. YUILL' *Hazell & Menacing Jester* vi. 66 'I heard him and her having a ruck about Nicholas, that's all.' 'What kind of a row?'

ruck (rʌk), *v.*[1] Now *dial.* Forms: α. 3 **ruken,** 4–6 **rouke,** 5–6 **rowke,** 7–9 **rook.** β. 4 **rucken,** 5 **ruckyn (rukkun),** 6–7 **rucke,** 6– **ruck.** γ. *dial.* 8 **ruckee,** 9 **ruckey, rucky.** [Perh. of Scand. origin: cf. Norw. dial. *ruka* to crouch (Ross).] *intr.* To squat, crouch, cower, huddle together. Also *refl.* and in *pa. pple.*

α. *a* **1225** *Ancr. R.* 266 Vor þeo hwule þet heo stont upriht ne mei he [the fiend] nouðer on hire ne ruken ne riden. *c* **1340** HAMPOLE *Pr. Consc.* 6897 Þ e horribel vermyn venemus. Þe whilk sal on þe synful rouke, And ever-mare þam gnaw and souke. *c* **1386** CHAUCER *Knt.'s T.* 450 What is mankynde moore vn to you holde Than is the sheepe, þat rouketh in the folde? *c* **1430** *Pilgr. Lyf Manhode* III. xl. (1869) 156 In the kichene thei wolden rouken, an hol day gladliche, for to roste a smal hastelet. *c* **1440** LYDG. *Hors, Shepe & G.* 439 This sheepe rowkyng in his fold, Set litill stoor of swerd or Arwis keene. **1555** W. WATREMAN *Fardle Facions* I. v. 51 In the easemente of vrine, the men rowked doune, the women stoode vprighte. **1593** SHAKS. *3 Hen. VI,* v. vi. 47 The Rauen rook'd her on the Chimnies top, And chatt'ring Pies in dismall Discords sung. **1743** R. BLAIR *Grave* 35 Night's foul bird, Rook'd in the spire, screams loud.

fig. **1582** STANYHURST *Æneis* Ded. (Arb.) 7 As I can not deuine vpon such bookes, that happlye rouke in studentes mewes.

β. **1390** GOWER *Conf.* II. 57 Bot now thei rucken in here nest And resten as hem liketh best. *c* **1430** LYDG. *Min. Poems* (Percy Soc.) 118 The wolfe in fieldis the shepe dothe grete duresse, Rukking in foldis for fere dar nat arise. *c* **1440** *Promp. Parv.* 439/1 Rukkun, or cowre down, *incurvo.* **1567** GOLDING *Ovid's Met.* VI. (1593) 141 On the house did rucke A cursed owle the messenger of ill successe and lucke. **1573** G. HARVEY *Letter-bk.* (Camden) 118 Here ruckes my mistrisse makinge cleene the pan. **1583** GOLDING *Calvin on Deut.* xxiii. 136 Now their wit styeth not high but rather rucketh beneath vpon the ground. **1619** BERT *Hawkes* 56 Sometimes he..will..stop of his forefeet, without either rucking behinde, or aduancing before. **1691** RAY *N.C. Words* (ed. 2) 59 To *Ruck,* to squat or shrink down. **1820** WILBRAHAM *Gloss. Wds. Chesh., Ruck,* to get close or huddle together as fowls do. **1823–** in dial. glossaries (E. Anglia, Northampton, Cheshire).

γ. **1746** *Exmoor Scolding* (E.D.S.) 40 But thee, thee wut ruckee..in the Chimley Coander. **1842** PULMAN *Rustic Sketches* 41 Ee'd grasp th' rod..An' ruckey down quite low. **1886** ELWORTHY *W. Somerset Word-bk.* 635 *Rucky-down,* to stoop low by bending the knees;..to crouch low in any posture.

Hence **ˈrucker; ˈrucking** *vbl. sb.*

13.. *Names of Hare in MS. Digby* 86 fol. 168 b, Þe wint swifft, þe sculkere, þe hare serd, þe heg roukere [= hedge-rucker]. *c* **1440** *Promp. Parv.* 439/2 Rukkynge (*Harl. MS.* rukklyng), *incurvacio.*

ruck (rʌk), *v.*[2] [f. RUCK *sb.*[2] Cf. Norw. *rukka* in the same sense.]

1. *intr.* To slip *up* or work into creases or ridges; to become creased or wrinkled.

1812 *Monthly Mag.* XXXIV. 234 The motion of walking soon occasioned it to slip from its place, to ruck. *a* **1825** FORBY *Voc. E. Anglia, Ruck,* to have a folded, creased, ridgy, or uneven surface. **1842** *Fraser's Mag.* XXVI. 544 The sleeves ruck up and present his white, soft, and dimpled arms. **1888** JACOBI *Printers' Vocab.* 116 A sheet is said to 'ruck' when it gets creased or doubled in laying on.

2. *trans.* To crease; to wrinkle or cause to work *up* into ridges.

1828–32 WEBSTER, *Ruck,*..to wrinkle; as, to ruck up cloth or a garment. **1860** WHYTE MELVILLE *Mkt. Harb.* iii, Mr. Sawyer..lost his flat shooting-hat, and rucked his plaid trousers up to his knees. **1876** MISS BROUGHTON *Joan* I. i, An arm-chair..not at all rucked up or disarranged.

b. To draw or gather into small folds.

1896 *Westm. Gaz.* 16 June 9/1 The sleeves rucked and puffed in yet another new way. **1901** *Illustr. Lond. News* CXVIII. 910 The sleeves are of chiffon rucked with a band of the gold worked down the centre.

ruck (rʌk), *v.*[3] *dial.* [f. RUCK *sb.*[1] Cf. Norw. *ruka* in the same sense.] *trans.* To stack, to heap or pile up.

1720 RAMSAY *Wealth* 95 When autumn's stores are ruck'd up in the yard. **1841–** in dial. glossaries (Leic., Shropsh., Warw., Banff).

† **ruck**, *v.*[4] *Obs. rare.* [ad. L. *ruct-āre*: cf. ERUCT *v.*] To belch.
15.. LYNDESAY *Play* 1435 (Bann. MS.), Sche riftit, ruckit, and maid sic stendis. **1624** QUARLES *Job Militant* xix. 47 Wks. (Grosart) II. 96/1 His Belching rucks forth flames, his mouing Eye Shines like the glory of the morning Skie.

ruck (rʌk), *v.*[5] *slang.* [Of unknown origin.] *intr.* **a.** To inform *on* a criminal. **b.** To give information about a crime or a criminal. **c.** *gen.* To abandon, to repudiate a person. With *on.*
1884 *Daily News* 20 Sept. 2/2, I told the prisoner that I was not going to ruck on an old pal. **1889** *Session Paper Cent. Criminal Court, 1729–1913* CX. 871 He said 'Has Cleasby *rucked*? If he has, I will b–y well kill him when I come out'—ruck means telling. **1898** J. D. BRAYSHAW *Slum Silhouettes* 207 Yer won't tell Mo that I told yer—will yer? If he knew as I'd rucked on him, he'd kill me. **1903** A. M. BINSTEAD *Pitcher in Paradise* iv. 96 Your worthy parent..isn't going to ruck on you in the golden autumn of his life, just bcause you were denied the keen commercial instincts that led him to make a pile! **1906** E. PUGH *Spoilers* viii. 92 'I don't care,' said Deuce, defiantly... 'I ain't goin' to ruck on Dad.'

ruck, *v.*[6] *slang.* Also rux. [Of obscure origin.]
1. *trans.* To take severely to task; to row.
1899 T. M. ELLIS *Cats'-eye Rings* 93 Your dress is so slovenly that you would be ruxed by the examining officer. **1936** G. INGRAM *Muffled Man* i. 13 'Oh, all right,' sulked Sonny. 'You ain't going to "ruck" me, are you?' **1959** C. MACINNES *Absolute Beginners* I. 109, I saw I mustn't keep on rucking him, because, after all, this was a party. **1966** P. WILLMOTT *Adolescent Boys* vi. 112 The governor of my place is horrible... He rucks you if you take more than ten minutes for a quarter of an hour's job.
2. To vex, worry. *rare.*
1887 KIPLING *Plain Tales* (1888) 60 'E [was] too busy to rux 'isself about p'raids.

ruck, obs. form of ROC.

rucked (rʌkt), *ppl. a.*[1] [f. RUCK *sb.*[2] or *v.*[2]] Having rucks or small folds. Also with *up*: rumpled; caught up.
1600 *Newe Metamorphosis* (MS.) in Nares (1859) s.v., A rucked barke ore grewe their bodye and face. **1895** *Athenæum* 26 Jan. 124/2 The freedom with which he swings his leg, the 'rucked' trousers and easy shoes. **1898** *Westm. Gaz.* 30 June 3/2 Rucked satin, quite objectionable for millinery, makes a charming evening cloak. **1944** J. D. CARR *Till Death do us Part* vi. 64 A light-haired young man..lying on a rucked-up sofa. **1964** D. FRANCIS *Nerve* i. 7 Mr Brewer pulled down his unconscious wife's rucked-up skirt. **1980** C. FREMLIN *With no Crying* iv. 20 She'd..straightened her rucked-up skirt.

rucked, *ppl. a.*[2] [cf. RUCK *sb.*[1] 3 c (a).] Passed from a loose scrummage.
1976 *Wymondham & Attleborough Express* 3 Dec. 26/3 The youthful, fit students started in an attractive manner while Diss resisted with strong tackling and counter attacking from rucked possession.

rucker, rucking: see RUCK *v.*[1]

rucking, *vbl. sb.*[2] The action of RUCK *v.*[2]
a **1915** in W. H. Chantrey *Theatre Accounts* (1915) 67 Druggets or crumb cloths where used must be secured so as to be in no way liable to rucking.

rucking, *vbl. sb.*[3] [cf. RUCK *sb.*[1] 3 c (a).] Loose scrummaging.
1958 [see *loose scrummaging* s.v. LOOSE *a.* 9]. **1963** *Times* 31 May 3/4 He told New Zealanders: 'I think we can learn much from your game—particularly your forwards' rucking and driving over the ball, which we are trying to practise.' **1966** *Sunday Times* 2 Oct. 20/6 Their captain, Matthews, set an example with his rucking and gained them some valuable balls.

rucking, *vbl. sb.*[4] *slang.* [f. RUCK *v.*[6] + -ING[1].] A reprimand; a scolding, telling-off.
1958 F. NORMAN *Bang to Rights* I. 41 I'll have to give her a right rucking about that. **1974** T. BARLING *Shooter Man* iii. 23 Ask him. It'll only cost you a few coppers and a rucking for calling him back. **1976** E. DUNPHY *Only a Game?* v. 146 Perhaps all the rucking he was taking was getting through to him, and he started doing a little bit more.

ruckle (ˈrʌk(ə)l), *sb.*[1] *Sc.* and *north. dial.* [dim. of RUCK *sb.*[1] Cf. Norw. dial. *rukle* a small heap of twigs on a hearth.] A pile or heap; a bundle of sheaves; a stack of peats or the like.
1828 CARR *Craven Gloss.*, *Ruckle*, a great quantity; a heap of stones. **1848** *Jrnl. R. Agric. Soc.* IX. II. 507 A piece of rye-grass is pulled out of the top and tied round the head of the 'ruckle', as it is called. *Ibid.* 508 In a dry time it is carted directly from the 'ruckles' to the stack. **1867** LIVINGSTONE in *Proc. R. Geogr. Soc.* (1868) 180, I am a mere ruckle of bones. *c* **1882** J. LUCAS *Studies in Nidderdale* 119 After a time..they pile them [*sc.* peats] into stacks, which are called 'ruckles'.

ruckle (ˈrʌk(ə)l), *sb.*[2] [dim. of RUCK *sb.*[2] Cf. Norw. dial. *rukla* wrinkle, ridge.] A small ruck or ridge.
1853 G. J. CAYLEY *Las Alforjas* I. 37 There is a ruckle in the bed-clothes over his breast as if his arms were crossed.

ruckle (ˈrʌk(ə)l), *sb.*[3] [Cf. RUCKLE *v.*[3], and Norw. dial. *rukl* in the same sense (Aasen).] A rattling or gurgling noise, *esp.* in the throat of a dying person; the death-rattle.
1815 [see DEATH *sb.* 19]. **1825** JAMIESON *Suppl.*, *Ruckle*, a noise in the throat seeming to indicate suffocation. **1905** F. W. BAIN *Draught of the Blue* Introd. p. xiii, In the silence, broken only by the ruckle of the rushing water.

ruckle (ˈrʌk(ə)l), *v.*[1] Now *dial.* Also 3 rukelen. [freq. of RUCK *v.*[3]] *trans.* To pile up, heap together; *spec.* to form (clover) into a sheaf.
a **1225** *Ancr. R.* 214 Al þet he rukeleð & gedereð togedere.., al schal ine helle iwurðen to him tadden & neddren. *Ibid.* 406 Weop for his sunnen. Þu þu schalt..rukelen on his heaued bearninde gleden.
1800 TUKE *Agric. North Riding* 156 When the crop is large.., a small armful is taken up by the top, which is united by a twist; three of these are placed together... This operation is termed 'ruckling'. **1833** *Ridgemont Farm Rep.* 143 in *Husb.* III. (L.U.K.), When the season is precarious for drying the clover hay, the excellent..plan..of 'ruckling' is adopted. **1892–** in *E.D.D.* (Yks., Som.).

ruckle (ˈrʌk(ə)l), *v.*[2] [f. RUCK *v.*[2] + -LE 3.]
1. *intr.* To work (*up*) into folds or wrinkles.
1839 LEWIS *Hereford Gloss.*, *To Ruckle*, to rumple, to crease. **1853** CAYLEY *Las Alforjas* I. 4, I..buttoned the straps of my trousers to prevent them ruckling up. **1854** MISS BAKER *Northampt. Gloss.* s.v., The bandage ruckles up so, it must come off.
2. *trans.* To form, draw together, into folds.
1889 *Blackw. Mag.* Sept. 295 His face is shiny and is ruckled with high ridges and low furrows. **1903** *Daily Chron.* 23 May 8/4 The lace is arranged up on a frame of chiffon ruckled by hand.

ruckle (ˈrʌk(ə)l), *v.*[3] Also 6 rucle. [Of Scand. origin: cf. Norw. dial. *rukla* in the same sense.] *intr.* To make a rattling or gurgling sound; to rattle in the throat. Hence **ˈruckling** *ppl. a.*
1530 LYNDESAY *Test. Papyngo* 668, I am ane blak Monk, said the ruclande reuin; So said the gled, I am ane holy freir. **1731** MILLER *Gard. Dict.* s.v. *Wind*, If Water ruckles much, and frequent Bubbles arise, the Storm is but of a short Continuance. **1824** SCOTT *St. Roman's* xxxviii, The deep ruckling groans of the patient satisfied every one that she was breathing her last. **1859** *Out of the Depths* 162 Her glassy eyes, her ruckling breath,..told me plainly that she was dying fast. **1877** *N.W. Linc. Gloss.*, *Ruckle*, to breathe with difficulty, like one dying.

† **ˈruckle**, *v.*[4] [f. RUCK *v.*[1]] To crouch.
a **1500** [see *rucking* vbl. sb., under RUCK *v.*[1]]

ruckling, dial. variant of RECKLING.

ˈrucksack (ˈrʌksæk, ˈrʊksæk). Also rucsac, rucsack, 9 rücksack. [ad. G. *rucksack*, f. *rucken*, dial. var. of *rücken* back + *sack* SACK *sb.*[1]] A bag or knapsack carried on the back by walkers, climbers, etc.; = BACKPACK.
1866 *Nature & Art* I. 192/2 We therefore confidently recommend a perusal of it to all those about to grasp the 'Alpen-stock', and shoulder the 'Rücksack'. **1882** W. A. BAILLIE-GROHMAN *Camps in Rockies* 411 '*Rücksack*', or *Stalker's Bag* is..for all sporting purposes a most useful article. **1895** *Contemp. Rev.* Aug. 199 We divided our loads into two rucksacks. **1904** *Athenæum* 6 Aug. 175/1 One does not usually carry a bulky volume in one's rucksack. **1932** *Pontings Catal.* Whitsun, Rucksacks made of a..rubber proofed twill material. **1955** *Times* 31 Aug. 6/5 She wore shorts and rode a man's bicycle, on the back of which was strapped a heavy rucksack and a spare wheel. **1969** W. H. LITTLE in C. Cullingford *Man. Caving Techniques* iii. 33 A rucsac of a suitable kind and size will often be necessary to carry the caver's needs to the cave entrance. **1976** *Liverpool Echo* 7 Dec. 5/1 An electric drill, a sanding machine and two rucksacks worth a total of £110. **1978** *Vole* No. 7 29/1, I did manage to corner a walker in Dorset, whose rucsac nearly broke my arm when I tried to lift it.

ˈrucksacked, *a.* [f. prec. + -ED[1].] Provided with or carrying a rucksack.
1909 H. G. WELLS *Ann Veronica* xvi. 322 To walk beside him, dressed akin to him, rucksacked and companionable, was bliss in itself. **1973** A. PRICE *October Men* i. 8 Holidaying couples and rucksacked students.

ˈrucksackful. [f. RUCKSACK + -FUL.] As much as a rucksack will contain.
1971 C. BONINGTON *Annapurna South Face* xi. 126 Ian was therefore carrying up the entire load of fixed rope left by Nick and Martin, a rucksackful weighing around forty pounds.

ruckus (ˈrʌkəs). orig. and chiefly *U.S.* Also rucas, ruccus, rucus, rukus. [cf. RUCTION and RUMPUS *sb.*] An uproar, a disturbance; a row, a quarrel; fuss, commotion. Also *attrib.*
The earliest examples, spelt with a single *c* or *k*, may possibly represent the variant usually spelt ROOKUS.
1890 *Dialect Notes* I. 66 *Rucus* (rūkɐs): for *rumpus*. [Kentucky.] **1902** *Ibid.* II. 244 Rukus. **1909** 'O. HENRY' *Roads of Destiny* xiii. 210 There shall be rucuses in Salvador ..and the monkeys had better climb the tallest cocoanut trees. **1923** C. E. MULFORD *Black Buttes* ii. 20 Them two bummers [*sc.* restless cattle] was raisin' more of a ruckus than usual to-night. **1934** *Sun* (Baltimore) 17 May 10/1 The ruccus in the City Hall over discharge of a municipal employé by the Mayor. **1948** F. BLAKE *Johnny Christmas* II. 69 With this Kiowa-'Rapaho ruckus and these picture-book soldiers that just showed up, we don't want anything more on our hands. **1963** *Economist* 12 Oct. 147/2 The ruckus kicked up by the outraged wives and mothers of America. **1972** *Time* 10 July 38/1 But then ruckus raising is Fischer's speciality. **1977** *Times Lit. Suppl.* 1 July 792/1 World Team Tennis..now actively encourages..'audience participation', a polite phrase that covers barracking, beer-cans, and the kind of ruckus that England normally only sees after a Cup Final. **1979** *Dædalus* Spring 162 Like the *graeculi* of the Roman Empire, we Europeans are still capable of raising a little cultural ruckus.

rucky (ˈrʌkɪ), *a. rare.* [f. RUCK *sb.*[2]] Full of rucks or creases.
a **1825** FORBY *Voc. E. Anglia*, *Rucky*, full of rucks. **1883** MRS. F. MANN *Parish of Hilby* vii. 85 A big young man in a dress-coat and large rucky white gloves.

† **ruct**, *v. Obs. rare.* [ad. Sp. *ructar*, L. *rectāre*: cf. next.] *intr.* To belch, bring up wind. Hence † **ˈructer**, and † **ˈructing** *vbl. sb. Obs.*
1620 SHELTON *Quix.* II. xliii. 279.

† **rucˈtation.** *Obs.* [ad. late L. *ructātio*, f. *ructāre.*] = ERUCTATION.
1623 COCKERAM, *Ructation*, belching. **1651** BIGGS *New Dispens.* 206 Salutes the nose with an acid ructation. **1726** SWIFT *Gulliver* III. vi, Senates and great Councils are often troubled with..peccant Humours,..with sour frothy Ructations. **1771–2** *Ess. fr. Batchelor* I. 112 Troubled with sower, frothy, ructations, which proceed from a foul stomach.

ruction (ˈrʌkʃən). *dial.* or *colloq.* Also 9 'ruction. [Of obscure origin: in quot. 1831 associated with *insurrection.*] A disturbance, riot, or tumult; a disorderly dispute or quarrel; a row.
1825 JAMIESON *Suppl.*, *Ruction*, a quarrel; *to raise a ruction*, to be the cause of a quarrel. **1831** LOVER *Leg. Irel.* 148 It was in the time of the 'ruction [1798]. **1852** *Election Song* in *N.W. Linc. Gloss.* s.v., Four hundred dirty vagabonds All ready for a ruction. **1878** A. HUME *Remarks Irish Dial.* 111 When a..ruction has been 'riz'. **1886** *Sat. Rev.* 22 May 695/1 The ruction has been hardly in the fearless old Hibernian manner. **1890** *Spectator* 27 Dec. 933/1 Whisky which produces motiveless ructions at fairs and social gatherings. **1900** F. P. DUNNE *Mr. Dooley's Philos.* 24 That's life in America. 'Tis a gloryous big fight, a rough an' tumble fight, a Donnybrook fair three thousan' miles wide an' a ruction in ivry block. **1905** [see PAVVY]. **1913** [see RIPPIT]. **1921** E. O'NEILL *Diff'rent 1*, in *Emperor Jones* 218 That brown gal took an awful shine to Caleb and when she saw the ship was gittin' ready to sail she raised ructions, ..howlin' and screamin' and beatin' her chest with her fists. **1943** *Sun* (Baltimore) 17 Nov. 14/1 As a result of this little ruction, Baltimore is freed..from the grip of a political coalition which boded no good for the city. **1964** D. VARADAY *Gara-Yaka* xii. 103 The ructions of a clash between rival tribes.

† **ructuˈation.** *Obs. rare.* [f. late L. *ructuāre* for *ructāre.*] = RUCTATION.
1539 ELYOT *Cast. Helthe* (1541) 94 b, Let them..abstein from meates that ingender..fumous ructuacions or vapours.

† **ructuˈosity.** *Obs.*—[0] [f. L. *ructuōsus.*] 'A belching much' (Bailey, 1721).

† **ˈructure.** *Obs. rare.* [f. L. *ruct-āre* + -URE.] = RUCTATION.
1657 TOMLINSON *Renou's Disp.* 620 It solves all inflations of the stomack and belly into ructures. **1669** W. SIMPSON *Hydrol. Chym.* 97 With a sudden noise of a ructure or belch.

rucul (Palladius): see RUKEL.

rud (rʌd), *sb.*[1] Now *dial.* and *arch.* Forms: α. 1 rudu (*obl.* rude), 3, 6, 8–9 *Sc.* rude. β. 4–5 (9 *dial.*) rode, 4 rod. γ. 5–6 rudde, 5–7, 9 rud, 6–7, 9 rudd. [OE. *rudu* fem., related by ablaut to OE. *rēod* REOD *a.* and *rēad* RED *a.* and *sb.* The same grade of the stem is represented by ON. *roði* masc. (Norw. *rode*), redness.]
1. Red or ruddy colour; redness, ruddiness.
α. *c* **1000** *Apollonius of Tyre* (1834) 22 Ða ʒeseah se cyngc ðæt apollonius mid rosan rude wæs eal oferbræded. *a* **1225** *Ancr. R.* 330 Þe rude of monnes nebbe þet seið ariht his sunnen. *a* **1250** *Owl & Night.* 443 Þe rose also mid hire rude þat cumeþ ut of þe þorne wode. **1513** DOUGLAS *Æneis* XII. ii. 29 Lavinia..Hir moderis wordis felt deip in hir hert, So that the rude dyd hyr vissage glow.
β. *c* **1375** *Cursor M.* 18841 (Fairf.), His visage sumdel wiþ rode was blende. **1390** GOWER *Conf.* III. 27 He seth hire rode upon the cheke. *c* **1420** *St. Etheldred* 843 in Horstm. *Altengl. Leg.* (1881) 301 Hurre lures weron white as ony lely floure Ymeynde with rod.
γ. *c* **1400** *Destr. Troy* VII. 3048 Hir chekes [were] full choise;..As the rose, was the rud þat raiked hom in. **1430** LYDG. *Min. Poems* (Percy Soc.) 32 Farwele the rudde that was upon thi lippes. **1541** HYRDE tr. *Vives' Instr. Chr. Wom.* I. ix. 23 b, The one counterfaiteth the rudde of precious stones in the lyppes, the other whitenesse of face and necke. **1565** STAPLETON tr. *Bede's Hist. Ch. Eng.* 13 The dye of crymson, whose rudd will be appalled nether with heate of sonne nether with wette of wether. **1898** MEREDITH *Poems* I. 94 When mantles a tender rud In maids that of youths have sight.
2. Complexion (of those parts of the face which are naturally reddish or ruddy).
α. *c* **1000** ÆLFRIC *Gloss.* in Wr.-Wülcker 156 *Uultus*, and wlita, *uel* rudu. **12..** *Prayer to Our Lady* 20 in *O.E. Misc.* 193 Mi brune her is hwit bicume..and mi tohte rude iturnd al in-to oðre dehe. **15..** *Christ's Kirk* 21 in *Bann. MS.* 283 As ony ross hir rude wes reid. **1836** WILSON *Tales of Borders* IV. 34 Yon bloomin hizzy wi' the rose rude.
β. *a* **1310** in Wright *Lyric P.* v. 26 Hire rode is ase rose that red is on rys. **1340–70** *Alisaunder* 178 Rose red was hur rode, full riall of schape. *c* **1386** CHAUCER *Miller's T.* 131 His rode was reed, hise eyen greye as goos. *c* **1420** *Anturs of Arth.* xiii, Reddere in rode þan rose in þe rayne.
γ. **14..** *26 Pol. Poems* 145 My rudde was rede, my colour clere. *c* **1460** *Towneley Myst.* xxxi. 145 Youre rud that was so red, youre lyre the lylly lyke. **1519** HORMAN *Vulg.* 169 They whyte theyr face..with cerusse: and theyr lyppis and ruddis with purpurisse. *a* **1529** SKELTON *Ballad* Wks. 1843 I. 25 Your ruddys wyth ruddy rubys may compare. **1867** L. JEWITT *Derb. Ballads* 23 That lady so fair and free With rudd as red as rose in May.

3. Chiefly *dial.* Ruddle; †a red cosmetic.

c **1000** ÆLFRIC *Saints' Lives* I. 404 Gezabel..ȝehiwode hire eaȝan and hire neb mid rude. **1651** R. CHILD in Hartlib *Legacy* (1655) 73 Here is found ..white and yellow Marle, Plaister, Oker, Rudd [etc.]. **1691** RAY *Coll. N.C. Words* (ed. 2) 136 *Rud*, a sort of Blood-stone used in marking Sheep; from the red colour. **1788** W. H. MARSHALL *Prov. Yorksh.*, *Rud*, red ochre; used in giving a temporary mark to sheep. **1797** BRYDGES *Hom. Trav.* II. 290 Jove..mix'd a shower of rain with rud, To make 'em think it rain'd sheer blood. **1854** MISS BAKER *Northampt. Gloss.*, *Reddle*,..called also rud and ruddle. **1895** T. ELLWOOD *Lakel. & Iceland* 79 The smit marked upon the sheep with this Rud or Ruddle is generally the initial letter or letters of the owner's name.

Comb. *a* **1794** *Marriage of Sir Gawaine* lxv. in Percy *Reliques*, Sweet blushes stayn'd her rud-red cheeke. **1876** G. M. HOPKINS *Poems* (1967) 177 The blood-gush blade-gash Flame-rash rudred..and dingle-a-dangléd Dandy-hung dainty head.

rud, *sb.*² *Obs.* exc. *dial.* Forms: 5 **rode(s**, 6 **ruddis**, 6–7 **ruddes**, 7, 9 *arch.* **ruds**. [Of obscure origin.] The marigold (*Calendula officinalis*). Chiefly in *pl.* form. (Cf. RODE-WORT.)

14.. *Ms. Sloane* 5, lf. 9b/1 *Oculus Christi, calendula, solsequium*,..Seynte Marie rode. *c* **1450** *Alphita* (Anecd. Oxon.) 88 *Kalendula, sponsa solis*,..golduurt *vel* rodes. *c* **1475** *Pict. Voc.* in Wr.-Wülcker 786 *Hoc solsequium*, a rode. **1526** *Grete Herball* cxxxii. (1529) H v, Calendula is an herbe called ruddes. **1578** LYTE *Dodoens* 163 They be now called ..in English Marygoldes, and Ruddes. **1601** HOLLAND *Pliny* I. 20 Some take it [*Heliotropium*] for Ruds or Wert-wort: others for Turnsol, or the Marygold. **1647** HEXHAM I. (Herbs), Ruddes, or Marigolds, *Goudt-bloemen*. **1863** in *Isle of Wight Gloss.* (1881) 52 Among greens, small fruits, and ruds.

rud, *sb.*³ *dial.* Also 6 **rod, roid, rude**, 8–9 **rudd**. [Obscurely related to REDD *sb.*², RID *sb.*², ROUD *sb.*]

1. The spawn of frogs or toads. Usu. in combs. ***paddock-, toad-rud.***

1508 KENNEDIE *Flyting w. Dunbar* 342 Thou come..till a pule, and drank the paddock rod [*v.r.* rude, roid]. **1803** R. ANDERSON *Cumbld. Ball.* (1805) 82 Auld Grizzy the witch.. Meks paddoc-rud ointment for sair een. **1850** BAMFORD *Dial. S. Lancs.* 215 *Twod-rudd*, the spawn of toads. **1887** *Cheshire Gloss.*, *Rud*,..spawn of toads or frogs.

2. The act of spawning.

Cf. RODDING *vbl. sb.*, ROOD *v.*, ROUD *v.*

1794 W. HUTCHINSON *Hist. Cumb.* I. 459 They [*sc.* salmon] will take a bait of roe, or small fish, while upon the rudd, or laying their spawn.

rud, *sb.*⁴ *rare.* [var. of READ *sb.*¹: cf. RODDIKIN.] (See quot.)

1847 W. C. L. MARTIN *Ox* 2/1 The rud, or abomasum, which is the true digestive stomach... The huge paunch, for instance, is, at this early period, far less capacious than the fourth stomach, or rud.

rud, *v.*¹ *Obs.* exc. *dial.* Also 8 **rudd**; *pa. pple.* 3 **irud(d)ed**, 4 **roded**. [Related to RUD *sb.*¹ and RUDDY *a.* In sense 2 from RUD *sb.*¹ 3.]

†**1.** *trans.* To make red or ruddy. *Obs.*

a **1225** *Ancr. R.* 50 þeo þet beoð, uor Godes luue, mid hore blodshedunge irudded & ireaded, ase þe martirs weren. *Ibid.* 332 þe soule þet was bloc, & nefde bute dead heou, haueð ikeiht cwic heou, & is iruded feire. *a* **1400** *Langland's P. Pl.* C. xvi. 108 (Laud MS.), As rody as a rose roded were hus chekes.

1595 SPENSER *Epithal.* 173 Her cheekes lyke apples which the sun hath rudded. **1609** HEYWOOD *Brit. Troy* III. lvi, Many an anticke flake With rich Inamell azure green and Rudded. ? *a* **1700** in Child *Ballads* IV. 28/1 It's little matter what they do now, My life-blood rudds the heather brown.

2. *dial.* To colour or mark with ruddle.

1680 in Best *Farm. Bks.* (Surtees) 156 *note*, Put to the fell and rudded 55 weathers. **1876–** in dial. glossaries.

†**rud**, *v.*² *Obs.* Forms: 3–5 **rodden**, 4–5 **rudden** (5 **ruddon**). [Of obscure origin.] *trans.* To rub.

Halliwell gives '*Rud*, to rub, to polish. *Devon*', but there appears to be no confirmation of this.

c **1290** *St. Goerge* 41 in *S. Eng. Leg.* I. 295 Sethþe with a clout of here [they] roddeden þe woundes faste... þo men selten so is quike flesch and roddeden so with here! *c* **1305** *St. Edmund* 172 in *E.E.P.* 75 Fet & honde..He ruddede [*Laud MS.* roddede] a niȝt wiþ his here. **1393** LANGL. *P. Pl.* C. XVI. 108 Thus sone þis doctour, As rody as a rose roddede [*v.r.* ruddede] hus chekes, Kowede and carpede. *c* **1440** *Promp. Parv.* 438/2 Ruddon, *idem quod* rubbyn. **1495** *Trevisa's De P.R.* XVII. xcvii, Flexe is..rodded [*Bodl. MS.* irudded] and gnodded, ribbyd and herkelyd, and at the laste sponne.

rud, obs. form of RUDD¹, RUDE.

rudaceous (ruːˈdeɪʃəs), *a. Geol.* [f. L. *rūd-us* rubble + -ACEOUS.] Of a rock: composed of larger grains than is an arenaceous rock.

1904 A. W. GRABAU in *Amer. Geologist* XXXIII. 242 In the further subdivision of the clastic rocks, texture or size of grain takes precedence over chemical composition... We commonly recognize these sizes of grain, 1st that larger than what is commonly considered the normal sandgrain, 2d, the sand-grain, and 3d, the rock flour or impalpable powder. The first texture is most appropriately called rudaceous. **1920** —— *Gen. Geol.* xviii. 570 Rocks of all textures may be argillaceous, those of rubbly (rudaceous) texture and those of arenaceous texture generally carrying the clay as an admixture or as part of the cement. **1949** F. J. PETTIJOHN *Sedimentary Rocks* vii. 196 The rudaceous subtypes..are marked by characteristic compositional and textural features. **1977** A. HALLAM *Planet Earth* 168 Most sedimentary rocks, classified as either detrital or chemical-organic, are also classified according to their grain-size as rudaceous rocks, arenaceous rocks or argillaceous rocks.

rudas (ˈruːdəs), *sb.* (and *a.*). *Sc.* Forms: 8 **roudes**, 9 **rudous, roudas, rudas**. [Of obscure origin.] A coarse, unmannerly (old) woman; a termagant, virago, hag.

1725 RAMSAY *Gentle Sheph.* IV. i, Ye leed, auld roudes! **1824** SCOTT *Redgauntlet* ch. xx, I followed the auld rudas through twa Courts. **1844** W. CROSS *Disruption* xxiii. (E.D.D.), What can the auld roudas want wi' me?

b. As *adj.* Hag-like; coarse, unmannerly.

a **1802** *Prince Robert* iv, in Scott *Minstrelsy*, She has put it to her roudes lip, And to her roudes chin. **1816** SCOTT *Antiq.* xxvi, The auld carlin (a rudas wife she was). **1818** —— *Rob Roy* xxix, That auld rudas jaud of a gudewife. **1856** G. HENDERSON *Pop. Rhymes Berwick* 57 Rudous wives, grim, gaunt, and stark.

rudbeckia (rʌd-, ruːdˈbɛkɪə). [mod.L. (Linnæus *Systema Naturæ* (1735)), f. the name of Olaf *Rudbeck* (1660–1740), Swedish botanist + -IA¹.] A perennial herb of the genus so called, belonging to the family Compositæ, native to North America, and bearing yellow or orange flowers with a prominent conical disc of dark florets in the centre of each one.

1759 P. MILLER *Gardeners Dict.* (ed. 7) s.v. Rudbeckia with oval, Spear-shaped, undivided Leaves, placed alternate. **1789** W. AITON *Hortus Kewensis* III. 250 Broad jagged-leav'd Rudbeckia. Nat[ive] of Virginia and Canada. **1821** *Bot. Reg.* VIII. tab. 525 (*heading*) Eight-rayed Rudbeckia. **1870** W. ROBINSON *Wild Garden* II. 86 Newman's Rudbeckia... A very showy vigorous plant. **1908** G. JEKYLL *Colour in Flower Garden* ix. 79 The fine double Rudbeckia called Golden Glow is treated in the same way. **1931** *Daily Mirror* 27 Aug. 7/3 Among the best of autumn-flowering perennials for the mixed border, or the wild garden, are the rudbeckias. **1962** *Amateur Gardening* 17 Feb. 5 A flower which makes for a bold display in the garden and as a cut flower is the rudbeckia. **1974** C. MILNE *Enchanted Places* vi. 49 The penstemons, the bergamots,.. the rudbeckias, the dahlias..were still looking as lovely as ever.

rudd¹ (rʌd). Forms: α. 7 **rowde**, 7, 9 *dial.* **roud**. β. 7–9 **rud**. γ. 7 **rudde**, 7– **rudd**. [app. related to RUD *sb.*¹] A freshwater cyprinoid fish (*Scardinius erythrophthalmus*) somewhat resembling the roach; the red-eye.

α. **1606** S. GARDINER *Bk. Angling* 131 The Roche, Dace, Breame, Rowde doe but pingle, to the Pearche, and Pike. *a* **1672** WILLUGHBY *Hist. Pisc.* IV. vii. 252 Rutilus latior vel Rubellio fluviatilis,..Nostratibus a Rudd vel Roud; quibusdam locis Angliæ a Finscale. **1836** YARRELL *Brit. Fishes* I. 362 It is abundant in the broads of Norfolk, where it is called Roud. **1882** C. DAVIES *Norfolk Broads* iii, The rudd, or roud as it is generally called in Norfolk, is very abundant.

β. **1526** in 'Antiquary' *Forme of Cury* (1780) 177 Fresh Sammon... Great Ruds... Baken Turbuts. **1661** WALTON *Angler* (ed. 3) xvi. 218 There is a kind of bastard small Roch ..with a very forked tail..; knowing-men know their difference, call them Ruds. **1740** R. BROOKES *Art of Angling* I. xix. 54 The Rud or Finscale..is broader than a Carp, and thicker than a Bream. **1769** PENNANT *Brit. Zool.* III. 310 The Rud... This fish is found in the Charwell, near Oxford, and in the Witham in Lincolnshire. **1804** SHAW *Gen. Zool.* V. I. 198 [The roach is] Much allied to the Rud, but of a shape somewhat less deep. **1856** 'STONEHENGE' *Brit. Rural Sports* 251 Rud require rather a larger hook.

γ. **1672** [see α above]. **1685** RAY *Corresp.* 29 April (1718) 180 The Rudde is the Rotele of Baltner. **1753** *Chambers' Cycl.* Suppl., *Rubellus*,..a name given by some authors to the common roach, and by others to the rudd or finscale. **1836** YARRELL *Brit. Fishes* I. 361 The Rudd, or Red-eye, is a very common fish in Europe. **1883** *Fisheries Exhib. Catal.* (ed. 4) 104 Glass Case containing Stuffed Specimen of a Rudd. **1925** J. T. JENKINS *Fishes Brit. Isles* 297 The Rudd is usually deeper in the body than the Roach. **1966** *Studia Neophilologica* XXXVIII. 130 The English name of the rudd obviously refers to the red colour of the lower fins of the fish.

Rudd² (rʌd). [Perh. f. the name of Margaret Caroline *Rudd* (d. 1779), a notorious courtesan, for whom the table may have been invented.] Used *attrib.* and in the possessive in ***Rudd('s) table***, an elaborately appointed lady's toilet table of the late eighteenth century.

1788 in R. Fastnedge *Shearer Furnit. Designs from Cabinet-Makers' London Bk. of Prices* (1962) 14 A three foot 4 inch, rudd table, all solid, with astragal, or 2 beads, and hollow round the edge of the top, the 2 outside drawers with no quadrant boxes, a glass hung to each drawer, supported by quadrants.., plain Marlbro' feet, and an astragal round the bottom of the frame. **1793** *Cabinet-Makers' London Bk. of Prices* (ed. 2) 161 *A Rudd, or Lady's Dressing Table*.. Three feet four inches long, two feet wide, three drawers in front, a glass frame hing'd to each end drawer, and supported by quadrants, a moulding on the edge of the top, plain Marlbro' legs, and an astragal round the bottom of the frame. **1892** F. LITCHFIELD *Illustr. Hist. Furnit.* vii. 186 The names given to some of these designs [in Hepplewhite's *Guide*] appear curious; for instance: 'Rudd's table or reflecting dressing table,' so called from the first one having been invented for a popular character of that time. **1902** W. H. HACKETT *Decorative Furnit. 16th, 17th & 18th Cent.* x. 124 About the year 1788, Shearer also published ..'Household Furniture'... The nineteen plates consist of designs for secretaires, bookcases, bureaux..and what was known as a Rudd or lady's dressing table. **1970** [see *lobby chest* s.v. LOBBY *sb.* 4].

†**'rudden**, *v. Obs. rare.* In 3–5 **rudnen**. [f. the stem of RUD *sb.*¹ and *v.*¹ Cf. OIcel. *roðna*, MSw. *rudhna*, Sw. *rodna*.] *intr.* To become red. Hence †**'ruddening**, redness (in the sky).

a **1225** *Juliana* 26 þe reue rudnede [*Bodl. MS.* feng to rudnin], ant ogrome grede [etc.]. **13..** *E.E. Allit. P.* C. 139 Roȝ rakkes þer ros with rudnyng an-vnder, þe see souȝed ful sore.

rudder (ˈrʌdə(r)), *sb.* Forms: α. 1 **rothor, roðor, roðr**, 2 **roðer, roþur**, 3–5 **roþer**, 4–7 **rother**; 5 **rothere, rothir, -yr, royther**. β. 4 **roothur**, 6–7 **roother**, 7 **routher**. γ. 5 *Sc.* **ruthire, ruthyr**, 6 *Sc.* **ruthir**, 6–7 (9 *Sc.* and *north.*) **ruther**; 6 **rither**. δ. 5 **rodyr, rod(d)er**; 5 **rudyr**, 6 **-ir**, 5–7 **ruder**, 6– **rudder**. [OE. *róðor*, = OFris. *roder* (WFris. *roer*), MDu. *roder*, *roeder* (Du. *roer*), MLG. *roder*, *rôr* (LG. *rôr*), OHG. *ruadar*, *ruodar* (MHG. *ruoder*, G. *ruder*):—Teut. **rōþra-*, from the stem of ROW *v.* MSw. *rodher*, Fær. *róður*, Da. and Norw. *ror* in this sense are from LG.; the ON. *róðr* (Icel. *róður*, Norw. *ror*) denotes the act of rowing.]

†**1.** A paddle or oar used for steering or propelling a vessel. *Obs.*

c **725** *Corpus Gloss.* P. 178 *Palmula*, steorroðor. *Ibid.* T. 206 *Tonsa*, roðr. *c* **897** K. ÆLFRED *Gregory's Past. C.* lviii. 445 Ne mæȝ hit [*sc.* a ship] no stille ȝestondan, buton hit ankor ȝehæbbe, oððe mon mid roðrum onȝean tio. *c* **1000** ÆLFRIC *Gloss.* in Wr.-Wülcker 167 *Palmula*, roðres blæd. *a* **1100** *Voc.* ibid. 311 *Remus*, roðer. *a* **1300** *K. Horn* 202 Dai hit is igon and oþer, Wiþute sail and roþer. **1483** *Cath. Angl.* 313/1 A Ruder (Rudyr, *A.*), *vbi* a are. **1602** DRAYTON *Heroical Ep.* 82 b, The Swans with musick that the Roothers make..come gliding on the lake.

2. a. A broad, flat piece or framework of wood or metal, attached vertically to the sternpost of a boat or ship in such a way that it can be employed in steering it. Also in fig. contexts.

α. **1303** R. BRUNNE *Handl. Synne* 4624 A shyppe þat ys turned with þe roþer. **13..** *E.E. Allit. P.* B. 419 Hurrok, oþer hande-helme hasped on roþer. **1398** TREVISA *Barth. De P.R.* XII. xii. (Bodl. MS.), In swymmynge he sveþ þat one foote in stede of an ore and þe oþer in stede of a roþer. **1447** *Rolls of Parlt.* V. 135/1 They toke..the Rother of the Ship, the Saile, and all the Bonnettis. **1486** *Naval Acc. Hen. VII* (1896) 14 Tymbre..in makyng of a newe Rother. *Ibid.* 15 A pyntell & a gogeon for the Rother. **1549** COVERDALE, etc. *Erasm. Par. James* 33 Whither so ever the shippe maisters mynde that governeth the rother will set it. **1622** R. HAWKINS *Voy. S. Sea* (1847) 188 His boate fitted with sayle, oares,..windles and rother. **1632** J. HAYWARD tr. *Biondi's Eromena* 37 The Barke abandoned of her Rother, ranne whither the wind carried her. **1682** *Lond. Gaz.* No. 1720/7 While our Rother held, we bore away W. and upon every lift of the Sea, went off.

fig. **1340** *Ayenb.* 160 þe roþer of þe ssipe of þe zaule. **1390** GOWER *Conf.* I. 243 The Schip of love hath lost his Rother.

β. **13..** *Minor Poems fr. Vernon MS.* 716 Into þat schip þer longed a Rooþur. **1647** LILLY *Chr. Astrol.* xxvi. 158 The Roother of Sterne of the Ship.

transf. **1551** RECORDE *Cast. Knowl.* (1556) 269 The bright starre in the foote of the roother of Argus.

γ. *c* **1470** HENRY *Wallace* VII. 1067 A hundreth schippys, that ruthyr bur and ayr. **1513** DOUGLAS *Æneis* X. v. 8 Eneas ..sat in propyr persoun..To steir hys carvell and to rewill the ruther. **1570** *Satir. Poems Reform.* xvii. 122 Vagabounds we wander in miserie & wo, As ship but Ruther. **1582** STANYHURST *Æneis* I. (Arb.) 21 The oars are cleene splintred, the helme is from ruther vnhafted. **1613** M. RIDLEY *Magn. Bodies* 16 As a ship upon the water is directed even forward by the sterne and ruther. *a* **1656** USSHER *Ann.* (1658) 860 They burned the owners themselves in a fire made of the ruthers, oares, and plankes, of the ships. **1819** W. TENNANT *Papistry Storm'd* (1827) 38 And sieg'd his boat frae stem to ruther.

δ. *c* **1440** *Promp. Parv.* 438/2 Rodyr, of a schyppe, ..*amplustre*. *c* **1450** *Castle Persev.* 1741 (Macro Plays), I go ..swyfter þanne schyp with rodyr! **1457** *Nottingham Rec.* II. 366 To mak a rodder of. **1548** UDALL, etc. *Erasm. Par. Acts* xxvii, They toke vp the ankers..and leused withall the joyntes of the sterne and the rudder. **1555** EDEN *Decades* (Arb.) 108 She broke the rudder of the shyppe in peeces. **1582** N. LICHEFIELD tr. *Castanheda's Conq. E. Ind.* 52 To bring his Sailes and the Rudder of the Shippes a lande. **1634–5** BRERETON *Trav.* (Chetham Soc.) 169 The helm consists of rudder, tiller, and whipstaff, and except the ship move and make way the rudder is of no use. **1668** HOPKINS *Serm., Vanity* (1685) 118 Overflowing estates are but like huge enormous rudders, that rather serve to sink the ship, than steer it. **1722** WOLLASTON *Relig. Nat.* iii. 51 The pilot should direct the vessel by the use of the rudder he has fitted to it. **1774** GOLDSMITH *Nat. Hist.* (1776) V. 12 The tail, which is composed of quill feathers,..guides the animal's flight like a rudder. **1815** J. SMITH *Panorama Sci. & Art* I. 297 The oars and rudders of vessels are levers of the second kind. **1877** BRYANT *Odyss.* v. 307 He shaped a rudder next, To guide the raft along her course.

transf. **1872** COUES *N. Amer. Birds* 277 The natatorial limb becomes a rudder as well as an oar.

b. *fig.* One who or that which guides, directs, or controls.

α. *c* **1400** *Beryn* 212, I shuld be a rothir To set ȝewe in governaunce. **1509** HAWES *Pastime of Pleasure* xxix. (1555) R iij, Let not thy lady of thy harte be rother. **1509** —— *Joyful Med.* 29 God onmypotent Whiche is aboue, of all the worlde the rother. **1616** J. LANE *Contn. Sqr.'s T.* VI. 159 Yet so as wisdome holdinge our loves rother, Wee lovinglie and iustelie yeeld t' each other. **1637** H. SYDENHAM *Serm.* 20 Speech is the..sterne and rother of the soule.

β. **1613** J. DAVIES (Heref.) *Muses Teares* Wks. (Grosart) I. 8/2 Eloquence (the Routher of our Minde, Swaying th' Affects thereof, which way it lists). **1658** LENNARD tr. *Charron's Wisd.* III. cliii. (1670) 523 It [*sc.* eloquence] is.. the stern or roother of our souls, which disposeth the heart and affections.

δ. *a* **1578** LINDESAY (Pitscottie) *Chron. Scot.* (S.T.S.) I. 8 Ane new courteour that rullit so the ruddar and causit the king to discord with his broder. **1606** S. Gardiner *Bk. Angling* 3 The Rudder wherwith the Arke of Gods Church is guided, is the word of God. **1663** Butler *Hud.* i. i. 457 Rhime the Rudder is of Verses, With which like Ships they stear their courses. **1685** Barrow *Wks.* 1830 I. 363 Speech is indeed the rudder that steereth human affairs. **1727** *Philip Quarll* 79 The elevated Sailors..had lost the Rudder of their Reason. **1797** *Encycl. Brit.* (ed. 3) XIII. 506/1 The Tail is the director, or rudder, of birds in their flight. **1868** H. Law *Beacons of Bible* (1869) 119 It [*sc.* vain-glory] is the common rudder of man's life.

c. The representation of a rudder.

1538 Leland *Itin.* (1769) VII. 87 The Windowes be full of Rudders. Peradventure it was his Badge or Token of the Amiraltye.

d. An analogous flat movable structure used for controlling the motion of an aircraft; now usu. a vertical flap, hinged at its leading edge, forming part of the tailplane of an aeroplane.

The 'boat' in quot. 1804 is the gondola of a balloon.

1804 G. Cayley in J. L. Pritchard *Sir G. Cayley* (1961) 220 Fixed upon a universal joint a Rudder of considerable length opposing both an horizontal and vertical surface.. intersecting each other in right angles to the air. A handle to direct this Rudder must communicate with the Boat. **1843** *Mechanics' Mag.* XXXVIII. 278 The broad horizontal rudder, or tail, H, capable of being turned on its hinge to any angle, at pleasure, gives the power of ascent and descent when the propellers are used, and forms also the chief means of stability in the path of the flight. The small vertical rudder I, is for the purpose of lateral steerage. **1879** *Encycl. Brit.* IX. 321/1 M. Pénaud succeeded in overcoming the difficulty in question by the invention of what he designates his automatic rudder. This consists of a small elastic aero-plane placed aft or behind the principal aero-plane which is also elastic. **1910** R. Ferris *How it Flies* vi. 116 The rudder for steering to left or right is mounted at the extreme rear end of the body. **1966** D. Stinton *Anat. Aeroplane* viii. 163 Aerobatic aeroplanes usually have a large portion of the fin surface lying ahead of the tailplane, or a large portion of the fin and rudder lying behind its trailing edge. **1969** K. Munson *Pioneer Aircraft 1903–14* 9 The operator lies prone on the lower surface, his hips resting in the cradle, and his hands grasping the roller, D_1, which actuates the front rudder, D.

e. Use or turning of the rudder, the extent to which the rudder is turned.

1918 W. G. McMinnies *Pract. Flying* 218 If you are turning to the right and notice wind striking your left cheek, you are side-slipping outwards, so give a little more bank or take off some rudder. **1936** W. H. McCormick *Mod. Bk. Aeroplanes* x. 86 In order to turn an aeroplane to the right, right rudder is put on by moving the right-hand end of the rudder bar gently forward by means of the right foot. **1958** 'N. Shute' *Rainbow & Rose* ii. 49 She needed quite a bit of rudder. **1978** J. S. Evans *Pilot's Manual* iv. 151 Let it be assumed that our aeroplane is in cruising flight, with sufficient rudder applied to prevent propwash-induced yaw.

3. *Brewing.* A kind of paddle used in stirring malt in the mash-tub. Also *transf.* (quot. 1847).

c **1440** *Promp. Parv.* 328/1 Maschel, or rothyr, or masch-scherel, *remulus, palmula, mixtorium.* **1566** Withals *Dict.* 43 A rudder or instrument to stire the mashe fat with, *rutabulum.* **1615** G. Markham *Eng. Housew.* ii. ix. (1668) 187 Let..another with a mash rudder stirre some of the flower with it. **1648** *Inventory* in *Spottiswoode Misc.* (1844) I. 372 Ane maskeine fatt, ane taptrie and ane maskine rudder. **1707** Mortimer *Husb.* (1721) II. 322 You must press it down with your Hands or Rudder, with which you use to stir your Malt or Moaks. **1763** *Museum Rust.* I. 202 This is to be well mashed, and stirred about with the rudder for near half an hour. **1847** *Jrnl. R. Agric. Soc.* VIII. ii. 329 The stirrer, or 'rudder', is similar to those used by brewers.

4. A mining implement: (see quot.).

1747 Hooson *Miner's Dict.*, *Rudder*, an Instrument of Iron, or at least the end of it; 'tis much like the Head of a Lance,..but made somewhat broader..; the handle about two Foot long; this we use to let in the ends of Sliders or Head-trees.

5. a. *Ornith.* = rectrix 2. (Cf. 6 b.)

1884 Coues *N. Amer. Birds* 115 *Rectrices*, Rudders, or true tail-feathers,..are usually stiff, well-pronounced feathers, pennaceous to the very base of the vexilla.

b. The tail of an otter.

[**1903** H. Johnston *Brit. Mammals* vii. 138 The otter.. swims and dives with great facility, and propels itself with all four limbs, using the tail as a great rudder.] **1907** *Yesterday's Shopping* (1969) 694 Horses' hoofs, deer slots, fox, hare, or otter pads cured and mounted in various styles; also fox brushes and otter rudders. **1941** H. Cory *Mammals Brit. Isles* 34 When swimming submerged the animal uses the forefeet for paddling and the hind feet, assisted by the rudder, for steering. **1965** P. Wayre *Wind in Reeds* xi. 151 Canadian otters are larger and bulkier [than British ones] with broader and deeper heads and thicker rudders. **1976** *Scotsman* 24 Dec. (Weekend Suppl.) 2/2 He [*sc.* an otter] was coiled..with his jaws clenched, and his rudder curled round the webs of his hindfeet.

6. *attrib.* and *Comb.* **a.** Attrib. with words denoting some part of the rudder or apparatus connected with it, as ***rudder-band, -case, -chain, pedal, post***; **rudder-bar**, a bar operated by the pilot's feet which controls the position of an aircraft's rudder.

For enumerations and descriptions of many such terms see A. Young *Naut. Dict.* (1846 and 1863), Smyth *Sailor's Word-book* (1867), Knight *Dict. Mech.* (1875 and 1884).

1526 Tindale *Acts* xxvii. 40 They..lowsed the rudder bondes and hoysed vppe the mayne sayle to the wynde. **1598** W. Philip tr. *Linschoten* 167 So that our Ruther-staffe brake and two more..broke likewise..on being put into it. *a* **1620** Z. Boyd *Zion's Flowers* (1855) 10 The force of seas hath broke the Rudder-band. **1627** Capt. Smith *Seaman's Gram.* ii. 12 The Rudder..is..hung at the sterne vpon hookes and hinges, they call Pintels and Gudgions, or Rudder-irons. *Ibid.* vi. 28 The Rudder rope is reeued thorow the stern post, and goeth thorow the head of the Rudder. **1691** T. H[ale] *Acc. New Invent.* 82 To sheath the Rudder-Post. **1703** R. Neve *City & C. Purch.* [212] 235 *Rother-nails*..are principally to fasten Rother Irons to Ships, and require a full Head. **1769** Falconer *Dict. Marine* (1780), *Boite du gouvernail*, the rudder-case, or the box placed above the rudder-head,..through which the tiller passes. **1796** Nelson in Nicolas *Disp.* (1846) VII. p. xxxix, The ship..shipped a deal of water, which blew up the rudder coat. **1805** Capt. Crumby *Let.* in *19th Cent.* No. 273. 722 Captain Cooke joined us in partaking of some cold meat, &c. on the rudder head. **1837** Marryat *Dog Fiend* x, He makes his appearance at the rudder-chains. **1865** Dickens *Mut. Fr.* i. i, The man, with the rudder-lines slack in his hands,..kept an eager look out. **1874** Thearle *Naval Archit.* 67 Rudder-pendants, which secure the rudder to the vessel. **1889** Welch *Text Bk. Naval Archit.* xiii. 137 The rudder framing tapers in thickness from the front edge. **1912** *Q. Rev.* July 240 Machines like Dunne's, which have no separate rudder-bar allowing of foot-correction. **1918** W. G. McMinnies *Pract. Flying* 234 *Rudder post*, the upright member to which the rudder is hinged. **1919** Pippard & Pritchard *Aeroplane Struct.* v. 36 In some aeroplanes..the rudder bar is replaced by pedals and directional control is obtained by pressing the appropriate pedal. **1935** C. G. Burge *Compl. Bk. Aviation* 537 *Rudder post*, the main vertical member of a rudder to which the rudder hinges are attached. **1959** Rudder-bar [see 'n[3], 'n']. **1966** D. Stinton *Anat. Aeroplane* viii. 139 If hinge-moments are too high to be handled efficiently, artificial forces may be transmitted through the stick and rudder-pedals by an artificial feel-system. **1976** B. Jackson *Flameout* iv. 63 The flight data recorder..tape-recorded..the pilot's movements of the control yokes and rudder pedals, [etc.].

b. Attrib., etc., in other uses, as ***rudder-fan, flutter, -man, -part, power, -quill, -tail; rudder-making; rudder-like*** adj.

1549 *Compl. Scotl.* vi. 41 Than the master cryit on the rudir man. **1611** Cotgr., *Heaulmiere*, the Rudder-part of a ship. **1681** Grew *Musæum* i. iv. i. 61 His [*sc.* a humming-bird's] Tail an inch and ½. In which there are ten black Rudder-Quills ½ of an inch broad. **1804** J. Larwood *No Gun Boats* 14 Mast and rudder making at the root of the trees. **1835** Kirby *Hab. & Inst. Anim.* II. xvii. 163 The rudder-tail here described is that of the male bull-finch. **1851** Mantell *Petrifactions* v. §2. 421 The rudder-like, or heterocercal tail, is shown in many of the Ichthyolites. **1915** S. H. Carden in M. Gilbert *Winston S. Churchill* (1972) III. Compan. i. 625 Large rudder power makes her sufficiently handy although starboard engines out of action. **1928** *Daily Tel.* 13 Mar. 11/3 The machine dived into the sea from a height of about 100 ft. after developing what appeared to be rudder flutter. **1930** J. S. Huxley *Bird-Watching* vi. 102 They became birds through the evolution of feathers out of scales... The other peculiarities of modern birds, such as..the transformation of their originally long and awkward tail, like a kite's, into an efficient rudder-fan..came later.

c. In specific names of birds or fishes: **rudder-bird, -duck, -perch** (see quots.).

1828–32 Webster (citing Latham), *Rudder-perch*, a small fish..[which] is said to follow the rudders of ships in the warm parts of the Atlantic. **1884** Coues *N. Amer. Birds* 715 *Erismatura*,..Rudder Ducks. Remarkably distinguished from other *Fuligulinæ*..by the stiffened, linear-lanceolate tail-feathers. **1894** Newton *Dict. Birds* 797 *Rudder-bird* or *-duck*, a name for *Erismatura rubida*, one of the Spiny-tailed Ducks.

rudder ('rʌdə(r)), *v.* [f. the sb.] *trans.* and *intr.* To steer; to use the rudder. Also *fig.*

1856 Emerson *Eng. Traits, Wealth*, Steam..already..is ruddering the balloon, and the next war will be fought in the air. **1875** 'Stonehenge' *Brit. Rural Sports* ii. viii. i. (ed. 12) 613 In sailing to windward, a vessel not only requires her sails to be very carefully trimmed, but she must be 'ruddered' with equal care. **1940** 'N. Shute' *Landfall* 210 He glanced quickly at the cruiser to check the direction, ruddering slightly to maintain his course. **1942** *Tee Emm* (Air Ministry) II. 65 Do a quick barrel half roll..pulling the stick back..when you are on your side, and then rudder into a steep dive. **1952** M. Tripp *Faith is Windsock* ii. 35 Hamish pulled back on the throttles, strangling life from the engines; Bergen ruddered and braked hard. **1954** W. Faulkner *Fable* 107 He..ruddered the tracer right onto it. **1960** S. Plath *Colossus* 66 A pigeon rudders down. **1973** M. Amis *Rachel Papers* 71 That afternoon,..ruddered by perceptive questions, encouraging smiles and apt generalizations from myself, Rachel Noyes told the story of her life.

rudder, variant of ridder *sb.*[1] and *v.*[1]; obs. form of rother.

ruddered ('rʌdəd), *a.* [f. rudder *sb.*] Provided with a rudder.

1860 Emerson *Cond. Life, Fate*, The secrets of water and steam,..the chariot of the air, the ruddered balloon are awaiting you. **1865** E. Burritt *Walk to Land's End* 254 That little ruddered ark.

'rudder-fish. [rudder *sb.*] The name of several species of fish which follow or accompany vessels; *esp.* (*a*) the rudder-perch, a West Indian sea-fish; (*b*) the pilot-fish, *Naucrates ductor*; (*c*) the log- or barrel-fish (*Lirus* or *Palinurus perciformis*) of America; (*d*) a bluish fish (*Seriola zonata*), native to the Western Atlantic.

1734 in *Phil. Trans.* XXXVIII. 316 *Perca marina, Sectatrix*, the Rudder-Fish, so called because they are always seen following Ships, or sticking to the Rudders. **1792** Mar. Riddell *Voy. Madeira* 69 The hog-fish, the pilot or rudder-fish, whiting, bream. **1859** P. H. Gosse *Lett. fr. Alabama* 11 The spotted rudder-fish and the purple-banded pilot were often seen beneath the stern. **1888** Goode *Amer. Fishes* 221 The Rudder-Fish family, *Stromateidæ*, is represented on the coast by three species. *Ibid.* 234 The Banded Rudder-fish, *Seriola zonata*, has been observed as far north as Salem and Beverly.

ruddering ('rʌdərɪŋ), *a.* [f. rudder *sb.* + -ing[2].] That acts as a rudder; that guides or steers. Cf. rudder *sb.* 5 b.

1960 T. Hughes *Lupercal* 46 With webbed feet and long ruddering tail. **1960** R. W. Marks *Dymaxion World of B. Fuller* 29/2 As with the pulled (rather than pushed) wheelbarrow, the ruddering tail wheel was lifted over, rather than shoved into the traveled terrain.

'rudderless, *a.* [f. rudder *sb.* + -less. Cf. MDu. *roeder-*, Du. *roerloos*, MLG. *ro(d)erlos*, G. *ruderlos.*] **a.** Having no rudder; without a rudder.

1605 Sylvester *Du Bartas* ii. ii. iii. *Lawe* 168 Though Rudder-lesse, not Pilot-lesse this Boat Among the Reeds by the Floud's side did float. **1845** Hirst *Poems* 68 Vessels rudderless and courseless range. **1880** J. R. Macduff *In Christo* i Vessels tossed, unpiloted and rudderless, in the thick darkness.

b. *fig.* Without guidance or control.

1827 Lytton *Pelham* xl, The countess, whose thoughts wandered..in the most rudderless manner. **1850** Kingsley *Alt. Locke* xi, I felt myself in a most distracted rudderless state. **1864** Bowen *Logic* xii. 384 That same rudderless and purposeless crowd of primeval atoms. **1887** W. B. Yeats *Let.* 11 Mar. (1954) 32 Please excuse this somewhat rudderless scrawl. **1977** *Oxf. Mission Q. Paper* Jan.–Mar. 15 Young folk, often rudderless in their religious thinking and experience of life.

rudders: see ruders.

ruddervator ('rʌdəveɪtə(r)). *Aeronaut.* [f. rudder *sb.* + ele)vator.] A control surface designed to act as both rudder and elevator.

1962 *Flight Internat.* LXXXI. 172/1 The ruddervators are controlled from a control column horizontally mounted under the right side of the couch. **1966** D. Stinton *Anat. Aeroplane* 244 Flaps, ailerons, and 'ruddervators' were designed to incorporate the minimum number of ribs.

ruddick, dial. form of ruddock.

'ruddied, *ppl. a.* [f. ruddy *v.*] Rendered ruddy; reddened.

1847 Webster, *Ruddied*, made ruddy or red. **1850** Allingham *Poems, Morning* i, The wind shakes up the sleepy clouds, To kiss the ruddied morn.

'ruddily, *adv.* [f. ruddy *a.* + -ly[2].] In a ruddy manner; with a ruddy hue.

1816 Byron *Siege of Corinth* xxvi, Many a hand's on a richer hilt, But none on a steel more ruddily gilt. **1860** Tyndall *Glac.* i. xvi. 106 The fire was gleaming ruddily. **1884** *Contemp. Rev.* Aug. 336 Deep, narrow water-courses, ruddily stained by the ironstone beds whence they spring.

'ruddiness. [f. ruddy *a.* + -ness.] The quality of being ruddy; ruddy hue; ruddy or healthy complexion.

1541 Hyrde tr. *Vives' Instr. Chr. Wom.* i. ix. 23 b, They taught to peynt the blacke of eies, and ruddynes of chekes. **1565** Cooper *Thesaurus* s.v. *Purpureus*, Purple colour; blacke mixed with a certaine ruddinesse. *c* **1610** *Women Saints* 160 That ruddines onelie liked her, which shame-fastnes and bashfullnes produced. **1663** Boyle *Usef. Exp. Nat. Philos.* ii. App. 317 A face whose ruddiness argued a perfect recovery. **1775** Harris *Philos. Arrangem.* Wks. (1841) 363 He that increases in bulk, commonly increases with ruddiness. **1836** J. Grant *Random Recoll. Ho. Lords* ix. 197 His complexion is fair, mingled with a good deal of ruddiness. **1860** Tyndall *Glac.* i. xxi. 146 As the sun sank lower the ruddiness of his light augmented.

†'ruddish, *a. Obs.* [f. ruddy *a.*] Somewhat red or ruddy; reddish.

1563 Foxe *A. & M.* 1060/2 Hee was neuer knowen..to loke with so chereful & ruddish a countenaunce as he did at that present. **1573** P. More *Almanack & Prognostication* D vj b, The Sunne during that day his ruddishe rayes in the morning. **1588** Parke tr. *Mendoza's Hist. China* 207 The one of them was a white man, the other was ruddish. **1689** *Lond. Gaz.* No. 2415/4 John Dobbins a Shoemaker,..full fac'd, with ruddish Complexion.

ruddle ('rʌd(ə)l), *sb.*[1] Also 6 ruddell, 6–7, 9 *dial.* rudle. [Related to rud *sb.*[1] and *v.*[1] See also raddle and reddle.] A red variety of ochre used for marking sheep and for colouring; red ochre, reddle.

1538 Elyot, *Rubrica*,..ruddle wherwith shepe are marked. **1565** Cooper *Thesaurus*, *Sinopis*, a redde stone commonly called Sinoper, or Ruddle. **1576** Baker *Jewell of Health* 42 The redde chalke (that we name Ruddell). **1601** Holland *Pliny* I. 147 They colour and paint their bodies with a kind of red chalk or rudle called Rubrica. **1684** tr. *Bonet's Merc. Compit.* ix. 329 The mixture of the white of an Egg and Carpenters ruddle. *a* **1722** Lisle *Husb.* (1757) 499 Tho' the ruddle, if the sheep be much ruddled, weighs to our loss, yet that washes out. **1777** Forster *Voy. round World* I. 138 Their hair was black, and curling, and smeared with oil and ruddle. **1848** B. D. Walsh *Aristoph.* 11 *note*, To sweep the market-place with a rope covered with vermilion or ruddle. **1873** Browning *Red Cott. Nt.-Cap Country* ii. 477 The florist bedded thick His primrose-root in ruddle.

fig. **1697** D. Baker *Poems* 11 His Skin..All over Ruddle is, and from His flaming Eyes quick glances come.

attrib. and *Comb.* **1647** Hexham i. (Precious stones), A Ruddle stone, *een Vermillioen steen.* **1837** Wheelwright tr. *Aristophanes* II. 106 Fly to avoid the ruddle-colour'd rope.

'ruddle, *sb.*[2], var. of riddle *sb.*[2] i. Now *dial.*

1582 in Best *Farm. Bks.* (Surtees) 172 In þe ketchenge 2 wynder cloes, 9 seckes, 3 ruddles, and a seife. **1603** Holland *Plutarch's Mor.* 86 They will not passe thorough the holes of the sieve, ruddle or trie, if they be narrow. **1703**

THORESBY *Let. to Ray*, *Rudle*, a ridle. **1877** *Holderness Gloss.*, *Ruddle*, a sieve; a riddle.

ˈruddle, *sb.*³ [Of obscure origin.] (See quots.)

1823 E. MOOR *Suffolk Wds.* 323 *Rudle*, a beverage composed of warm beer and gin with sugar, and a slice of lemon peel. **1889** *Sat. Rev.* 9 Nov. 519/1 Dog's-nose, egg-hot, ruddle, and the like are agreeable stimulants on a frosty night.

ruddle (ˈrʌd(ə)l), *v.* [f. RUDDLE *sb.*¹] *trans.* To mark, smear, or paint with ruddle. Also *absol.*

1718 LADY M. W. MONTAGU *Lett.* II. 81, I am apt to believe, that they took the first hint of their dress from a fair sheep newly ruddled. **1755** SMOLLETT *Quix.* (1803) IV. 43, I learned to make such letters as are ruddled into packs. **1804** W. TAYLOR in *Ann. Rev.* II. 280 A severer criticism construes the epithet to mean ruddled, or painted red. **1859** W. WHITE *Northumbld. & Border* xxviii. 440 A woman.. was ruddling her doorstep. **1876** R. F. BURTON *Gorilla L.* I. 206 A fan of palm frond redolent of grease and ruddled with ochre.

fig. **1860** H. MAYHEW *Upp. Rhine* iv. 178 [A] red ribbon on his coat to ruddle him with the mark of a superior breed. **1960** S. PLATH *Colossus* 52 Imagine their deep hunger, deep as the dark For the blood-heat that would ruddle or reclaim.

Hence **ˈruddled** *ppl. a.*

1861 THACKERAY *Four Georges* i. (1862) 53 Kielmansegge and Schulenberg with their ruddled cheeks. **1882** MISS BRADDON *Mt. Royal* I. i. 28 One of the deeply ruddled sheep that spent their lives on those precipitous slopes.

ruddle, var. RADDLE *sb.*¹

ˈruddleman. [f. RUDDLE *sb.*¹] A digger of, or dealer in, ruddle; a raddleman.

1623 BURTON *Anat. Mel.* III. ii. II. ii. (ed. 4) 471 Besmeared like a ruddleman, a gypsy, or a chimny-sweeper. **1832** MISS MITFORD *Village* Ser. v. (1863) 411 He joined a troop of ruddle-men.

ruddock (ˈrʌdək). Forms: α. 1 rudduc, 5 (9 *dial.*) -uck; 4 ruddoc, 4–5 -ok (5 rod(d)ok), 5–6 -oke, 5–7 -ocke, 6– ruddock (7 rudock); 8–9 *dial.* ruddick. β. 6 ridduck, -ocke, 8 *dial.* ryddick, 9 *dial.* hirdick; 7 reddocke (9 *dial.* -ock, -ick), raddocke. [OE. *rudduc*, related to RUD *sb.*¹, RUDDY *a.*: see -OCK.]

1. The redbreast or robin, *Erithacus rubecula.* Now chiefly *dial.*

α. *c* **1000** ÆLFRIC *Gloss.* in Wr.-Wülcker 131 *Rubisca*, rudduc. *a* **1100** *Voc.* ibid. 286 *Rubisca*, salthaȝa, *uel* rudduc. *c* **1340** *Nominale* (Skeat) 784 *Musscherom*, *verder et lalowe*, Sparwe, ruddoc and larke. *c* **1381** CHAUCER *Parl. Foules* 349 The tame rodok & the coward kyte. *c* **1400** *Beryn* 685 Herke eek the fowles syngyng,.. The ruddok & the Gold-fynch. *c* **1440** *Promp. Parv.* 438/2 Ruddok, reed brest, *viridarius*, *rubellus*, *frigella*. **1528** PAYNELL *Salerne's Regim.* N ij, The .xj. is a ruddocke, called robyn red brest. **1595** SPENSER *Epithal.* 82 The Ouzell shrills; the Ruddock warbles soft. **1654** VILVAIN *Theorem. Theol.* Suppl. 230 Men may catch Ruddicks or Thrushes in Pitfals. **1688** HOLME *Armoury* II. 245/2 The Robin Red Breast, or Ruddock, is a small Bird generally pricking up his Tail. **1750** HEATH *Isles of Scilly & Cornwall* 299 (E.D.D.), They have linnets, gold-finches, ruddocks,.. and many other common birds. **1806** E. RUSHTON *Poems* 106 From his grounds may the lark never soar, On his boughs may the Ruddock be mute. **1827** HOOD *Plea Mids. Fairies* lv, The sweet And shrilly ruddock, with its bleeding breast. **1882** *Garden* 11 Nov. 424/1 The wood robin.. takes the place with us of the red-breasted ruddock.

β. **1611** SHAKS. *Cymb.* IV. ii. 224 The Raddocke would With Charitable bill.. bring thee all this. **1639**, **1825** [see ROBIN RUDDOCK]. **1877** *N. & Q.* 5th Ser. VIII. 45 *Reddick*, the robin-redbreast. **1886** ELWORTHY *W. Somerset Word-Bk.* 341 *Hirdick*, ruddock, the robin; generally called Rabin hirdick.

†**2.** *Cant.* A gold coin; hence *pl.*, gold, money.

1567 TURBERV. *Of two Desperate Men* Poems 134 b, The greedie Carle.. saw the Pot.. Where Ruddocks lay, and in the Ruddocks place A knottie Cord, but Ruddocks could not find. **1580** *Bugbears* I. i. 17 in *Archiv Neu. Spr.* XCVIII. 304 You have store of pence & riddockes in great plentie. **1592** LYLY *Midas* II. i, If.. he haue golden ruddocks in his bagges, he must be wise and honourable. **1622** MABBE tr. *Aleman's Guzman d'Alf.* II. 147 Three thousand crownes, in good, dainty braue ruddocks, all good double pistolets. **1628** R. HOBART *Life & Death Edw. II*, lv, The solace of the wayning yeares To view their ruddocks and their heapes of treasure.

†**3.** A variety of cider apple. *Obs.*

1600 SURFLET *Countrie Farme* III. xlix. 535 These kindes of cyders are made principally of the apples called small ruddocke. **1611** COTGR. s.v. *Rouveau*, *Pomme de rou[veau]*, the Ruddocke, Redding, Summer Goulding.

†**4.** A species of toad. *Obs.*

Cf. Cotgrave, '*Rubette*, a greene earth-Frog, or red Toad; very full of poyson, and of great vse among witches'.

1668 CHARLETON *Onomast.* 24 *Ranunculus viridis*, *Calamites*,.. the Green Frog, or Ruddock. **1726** LEONI *Alberti's Archit.* I. 51/1 We are told, that the Land-toad, or Ruddock, if.. burned in a Field, will drive away the Birds from devouring the Seeds. **1749** G. WEST *Odes Pindar* (1753) I. 253 The pois'nous Ruddock some, and Shrew-Mouse boil.

†**ˈruddon.** *Obs.*⁻¹ [App. related to next; cf. also RUDDEN *v.*] Redness.

13.. *E.E. Allit. P.* B. 893 Ruddon of þe day-rawe ros vpon vȝten, When merk of þe mydnyȝt moȝt no more last.

ruddy (ˈrʌdɪ), *a.* (*sb.*) and *adv.* Forms: α. 1, 3 rudi, 3 rudie, 5 rudy; 4–5 rodi, rody, 5 rodye, roddy, roody, 6 roudy, β. 6 ruddye, 6–7 ruddie, 5– ruddy. [OE. *rudiȝ*, f. the same stem as RUD *sb.*¹ and *v.*¹]

A. *adj.* **1. a.** Of the face, complexion, etc.: Naturally suffused with a fresh or healthy redness.

a **1100** in Napier *O.E. Glosses* i. 2932 *Uultus purpureus*, *i. rubicundus*, nebb rudi. *a* **1225** *Juliana* 20 As he biheold.. hire leofliche leor lilies iliche & rudi as þe rose. *c* **1230** *Hali Meid.* 35 þi rudie neb schal leanen, & as gres grenen. **13..** *K. Alis.* 7821 (Laud MS.), þe leuedyes shene als þe glas And þise maidens wiþ rody faas. **1390** GOWER *Conf.* III. 339 The descoloured pale hewe Is now become a rody cheke. *c* **1425** LYDG. *Assembly of Gods* 806 Roody as a roose ay he kept hys chere. **1490** CAXTON *Eneydos* xxix. 112 [Dido had] a lytell mouthe with roddy lyppes. **1535** COVERDALE *Gen.* xlix. 12 His eyes are roudier then wyne, and his teth whyter then mylck. **1594** T. B. *La Primaud. Fr. Acad.* II. 251 The cheekes become ruddy, and the lippes gather in themselues. **1700** DRYDEN *Pal. & Arc.* III. 75 Ruddy his lips, and fresh and fair his hue. **1712** BUDGELL *Spect.* No. 425 ⁋3 His Complexion was sanguine and ruddy. **1774** GOLDSM. *Nat. Hist.* (1776) II. 241, I found.. the visage white and ruddy and the lips of a proper redness. **1848** LYTTON *Harold* I. i, His complexion was extremely fair and his cheeks ruddy. **1876** BESANT & RICE *Gold. Butterfly* Prol. i, He was a youth of a ruddy and a cheerful countenance.

b. Of persons: Having a fresh red complexion.

c **1250** *Hymn* in *Trin. Coll. Hom.* 255 Nis non maide of þine heowe, swo fair, so sschene, so rudi, swo bricht. *c* **1369** CHAUCER *Dethe Blaunche* 905 Thus moche I dare sayn, that she Was.. rody, fresshe, and lyefely hewed. **1390** GOWER *Conf.* II. 14 Sche was rody on the cheke And red on bothe hire lippes eke. *c* **1450** *St. Cuthbert* (Surtees) 7360 þe tothir stode on his ryght syde, Rudy bathe of hewe and hyde. **1483** CAXTON *G. de la Tour* C ij b, I was wonte to be whyte, Rody, fatte, and the world preysed my beaute. **1577–87** HOLINSHED *Chron.* I. 195/2 He was of person comelie,.. of face ruddie. **1613** PURCHAS *Pilgrimage* V. xvii. (1614) 539 The Inhabitants comely and tall, rather ruddie then blacke. **1711** ADDISON *Spect.* No. 123 ⁋1 We were met by a fresh-coloured ruddy young Man. **1764** GOLDSM. *Trav.* 18 Where all the ruddy family around Laugh at the jests. **1859** GEO. ELIOT *A. Bede* xxxvi, The driver.. now came forward—a large ruddy man, with a sack over his shoulders.

c. Red with blushing. *rare*⁻¹.

a **1225** *Ancr. R.* 330 þet we moten þuruh rudi scheome passen to þe heouene.

d. Characterized by, or associated with, healthy redness of feature.

1820 KEATS *Lamia* I. 40 Love, and pleasure, and the ruddy strife Of hearts and lips! **1833** HT. MARTINEAU *Briery Creek* v. 98 The ruddy health attendant on a country life. **1860** MOTLEY *Netherl.* ii. I. 45 A figure.. instinct with ruddy vigorous life.

2. a. In general use: Red or reddish.

c **1386** CHAUCER *Doctor's T.* 33 Right as sche can peynte a lili white And rody a rose. *c* **1400** *Rom. Rose* 3629, I saw the rose,.. Fresh, rody, and fair of hewe. *c* **1440** *Pallad. on Husb.* VII. 25 Yf hit be ripe, is forto se If al the lond attonys rody grete, Enclyne, and thonke. **1477** NORTON *Ord. Alch.* iii. in Ashm. (1652) 41 A subtill Earth, browne, roddy, and not bright. *a* **1529** SKELTON *Knoledge, Aquayntance*, etc. 16 Your ruddys wyth ruddy rubys may compare. **1577** B. GOOGE *Heresbach's Husb.* I. (1586) 32 b, The leaues thereof ruddy, the seede white. **1601** SHAKS. *Jul. C.* II. i. 289 You are .. As deere to me, as are the ruddy droppes That visit my sad heart. **1697** DRYDEN *Virg. Past.* III. 107 Ten ruddy Wildings in the Wood I found. **1725** POPE *Odyss.* II. 382 Here ruddy brass and gold refulgent blaz'd. **1784** COWPER *Task* III. 573 The ruddier orange, and the paler lime. **1841** *Penny Cycl.* XXI. 85/2 All the feathers surrounded by a ruddy border. **1873** BLACK *Pr. Thule* 37 The snow peaks that rose above certain ruddy châlets. **1889** BUCHANAN *Heir of Linne* xii, Large earrings of ruddy gold hung in his ears.

transf. **1871** PALGRAVE *Lyr. Poems* 75 Now in the ruddy autumn Together already we stand.

b. As an epithet of light or fire, of the heavenly bodies, the sky or clouds, etc.

c **1386** CHAUCER *Squire's T.* 394 The vapour.. Maketh the sonne seme rody and brood. **1388** WYCLIF *Matt.* xvi. 2 ȝe seien, It schal be clere, for heuene is rodi. **1412–20** LYDG. *Chron. Troy* I. 3081 Atwen þe tweyliȝt and þe rody morwe þei toke her leue. **1423** JAS. I. *Kingis Q.* 1 The rody sterres twynklyng as the fyre. *c* **1449** PECOCK *Repr.* I. v. 24 Whanne heuen is rody in the euentid, a cleer dai schal be the morewe. **1554** F. VAN BRUNSWIKE tr. *Montulmo's Facies Cæli* B j, Faire and whitish ruddie cloudes sparkeling aboute the skie. **1589** GREENE *Menaphon* (Arb.) 51 As bright as siluer Phœbe mounted on the high top of the ruddie element. **1613** CHAPMAN *Maske Inns Court*, Ouer this.. the ruddy Sunne was seen ready to be set. **1667** MILTON *P.L.* II. 889 So wide they stood, and like a Furnace mouth Cast forth redounding smoak and ruddy flame. **1761** GRAY *Fatal Sisters* 21 Ere the ruddy sun be set. **1791** MRS. RADCLIFFE *Rom. Forest* ii, Till a ruddy glow, which fired all that part of the heavens, announced the rising sun. **1840** DICKENS *Barn. Rudge* i, Shading his eyes that his sight might not be affected by the ruddy glow of the fire. **1858** G. MACDONALD *Phantastes* vi. (1878) 88 The rays of the setting sun overflowed with a ruddy splendour the open place.

transf. **1646** BUCK *Rich. III*, I. 11 By this provident truce, that ruddy storme.. was diverted.

c. Qualifying other names of colours.

1565 COOPER *Thesaurus* s.v. *Candico*, Beyng a ruddy white. **1611** COTGR., *Roux*,.. a ruddie or sad yellow.

†**d.** Causing redness in vegetation. *Obs.*

1693 EVELYN *De La Quint. Compl. Gard.* II. 157 If the Ruddy or Dry Winds Reign, as they generally do this Month, we must.. water every thing in our Kitchen-Garden. **1719** LONDON & WISE *Compl. Gard.* 270 'Tis the Moon of this Month that is vulgarly call'd, the Ruddy-Moon, it being very subject to be windy, cold and dry.

3. *spec.* In names of birds and animals, as ***ruddy bunting***, ***duck***, ***goose***, ***plover***, ***sheldrake***, ***shelduck***, ***shoveler***, ***squirrel***, ***turnstone*** (see quots. and the sbs.).

1816 STEPHENS in *Shaw's Gen. Zool.* IX. II. 381 The *Ruddy Bunting is found among willows on the borders of the Onon in Siberia. **1814** A. WILSON *Amer. Ornith.* VIII. 128 The *Ruddy Duck is fifteen inches and a half in length, and twenty two inches in extent. **1872** COUES *N. Amer. Birds* 295 Ruddy Duck.. with the neck all round and the upper parts brownish-red. **1785** LATHAM *Gen. Synop. Birds* III. II. 456 *Ruddy Goose... This is larger than a Mallard. **1843** YARRELL *Brit. Birds* III. 140 It [ruddy sheldrake] has also been called the Ruddy Goose. **1785** PENNANT *Arct. Zool.* II. 486 *Ruddy Plover. **1813** A. WILSON *Amer. Ornith.* VII. 129 The Ruddy Plover is eight inches long, and fifteen in extent. **1872** COUES *N. Amer. Birds* 257 Ruddy Plover..; head, neck and upper parts varied with black, ashy and bright reddish. **1824** STEPHENS in *Shaw's Gen. Zool.* XII. II. 71 *Ruddy shieldrake (*Tadorna rutila*). **1862** C. A. JOHNS *Brit. Birds* 490 The Ruddy Sheldrake... Only a few specimens of this bird have been obtained in Great Britain. **1852** *Ruddy shelduck [see SHELDUCK]. **1954** J. DELACOUR *Waterfowl of World* I. 250 The Ruddy Shelduck is a strong and successful species which.. occupies a very large range. **1824** STEPHENS in *Shaw's Gen. Zool.* XII. II. 120 *Ruddy Shoveler (*Rhynchaspis rubida*). **1781** PENNANT *Hist. Quadrup.* II. 409 *Ruddy Squirrel. **1801** SHAW *Gen. Zool.* II. I. 132 Ruddy squirrel, *Sciurus Erythræus*... It is said to be a native of India. **1909** J. & M. MACOUN *Catal. Canad. Birds* (ed. 2) 212 *Ruddy Turnstone... This species is a common migrant in Newfoundland. **1938** P. A. TAVERNER *Birds of Canada* 185 The turnstone is represented in America by the Ruddy Turnstone.., rather smaller than the European form. **1972** S. BURNFORD *One Woman's Arctic* iv. 92 Only about fifty yards away, were the.. nests of two pairs of ruddy turnstones.

4. Orig. a euphemistic substitution for BLOODY *a.* 10; now freq. used as an intensive in its own right: damnable, blasted, confounded. *colloq.*

1916 'TAFFRAIL' *Pincher Martin* ii. 28 Go on, Ginger!.. Slosh 'im one on the ruddy boko! **1924** GALSWORTHY *White Monkey* II. i. 121 Only why didn't Mr. Elderson say: 'You ruddy liar!'? **1945** [see EUSTON ROAD]. **1968** [see GIVE *v.* 16 c]. **1969** I. KEMP *Brit. G.I. in Vietnam* ii. 31 'Oh no!' I thought. 'The ruddy thing won't have time to open before I hit.' **1977** *Radio Times* 12–18 Nov. 69/4, I carted my ruddy topee all over India and finally abandoned it under a bed in Fort William in Calcutta.

5. *absol.* or as *sb.* Ruddy colour.

1387 TREVISA *Higden* (Rolls) II. 15 Margery perles of alle manere colour and hewe, of rody and rede, of purpur and of blew. **1633** G. HERBERT *Temple, Church-rents & Schismes* i, Calamities Turned your ruddie into pale and bleak. **1758** BORLASE *Nat. Hist. Cornw.* 67 Steatites.. veined with green, ruddy, and purple. **1823** GALT *R. Gilhaize* xii, The ruddy of youth had fled his cheek.

6. *Comb.* **a.** Parasynthetic, as ***ruddy-bodied***, ***-cheeked***, ***-clustered***, ***-coloured***, ***-complexioned***, ***-faced***, ***-finned***, ***-haired***, ***-muzzled***, etc.

1542 UDALL *Erasm. Apoph.* 270, I feare not these ruddie coloured & fatte bealyed feloes. **1576** FLEMING *Panopl. Epist.* 376 He was ruddie coloured, much like the damaske rose. **1622** MABBE tr. *Aleman's Guzman d'Alf.* I. 31, I was a yong Lad, ruddy-cheek't, full-fac't, and plumpe withall. **1758** BORLASE *Nat. Hist. Cornw.* 276 The white ruddy-spotted snail with a circular mouth. **1816** in *Cent. Mag.* (1900) LIX. 629/1, I said she looked like a German, being fair and ruddy complexioned. **1848** THACKERAY *Van. Fair* liii, The ruddy headed youth brought him.. a fine silver dressing-case. **1888** H. MORTEN *Sk. Hospital Life* 17 An elderly woman, grey-haired, stout, and ruddy-cheeked. **1916** D. H. LAWRENCE *Twilight in Italy* 89 The many ruddy-clustered oranges beside the path remind me of the lights of a village. **1916** BLUNDEN *Harbingers* 34 Ruddy-finned roach and bronze carp swam. **1922** JOYCE *Ulysses* 291 The figure seated on a large boulder at the foot of a round tower was that of a broadshouldered.. ruddyfaced sinewyarmed hero. **1923** D. H. LAWRENCE *Birds, Beasts & Flowers* 62 Cyclamens, ruddy-muzzled cyclamens. **1960** S. PLATH *Colossus* 79 Bronze dead dominate the floor, Resistive, ruddy-bodied.

b. With adjs., as ***ruddy-bright***, ***-brown***, ***-dark***, ***-golden***, ***-orange***, etc.

1746 FRANCIS tr. *Horace, Sat.* II. viii. 39 Apples are more ruddy bright If gather'd by fair Luna's waning light. **1758** BORLASE *Nat. Hist. Cornw.* 109 A stone.. of a ruddy-purple ground. **1841** *Penny Cycl.* XX. 191/2 Wings ruddy-brown; bill lead-colour. **1897** SARAH GRAND *Beth Bk.* xxi, The wonderful ruddy-gold tones that shone on its trunk as the day declined. **1927** D. H. LAWRENCE *Mornings in Mexico* 35 Calico pantaloons round his ruddy-dark waist. *Ibid.* 126 The men are naked to the waist, and ruddy-golden. *a* **1930** —— *Last Poems* (1932) 266 Green moonlight And ruddy-orange limbs stirring the limbo Of the unknown air.

B. *adv.* Used, usu. preceding an adj., as an intensifier (orig. a euphemistic substitute for BLOODY *adv.* 2: cf. sense A. 4 above): confoundedly, damnably, damned.

1914 C. BERESFORD *Mem.* I. xiii. 119 All I've got to say, is to say you've got a ruddy good billet. **1922** JOYCE *Ulysses* 420 Lay you two to one Jenatzy licks him ruddy well hollow. **1933** M. LINCOLN *Oh! Definitely* iii. 23 I'd have ruddy well ..locked the door. **1959** M. GILBERT *Blood & Judgement* xiii. 139 Culver Street's been pulled down and a ruddy great block of flats put up. **1979** *Oxford Times* 28 Dec. 9/2 Most of the groups I heard there and elsewhere played too ruddy loud.

ruddy (ˈrʌdɪ), *v.* [f. RUDDY *a.*]

1. *trans.* To render ruddy in hue; to redden.

1689 HICKERINGILL *Ceremony-Monger* Wks. 1716 II. 468 Others.. whose Vertues and true Learning, must necessarily (if set near him) ruddy his Cheeks, and make him blush for shame. **1805** SCOTT *Last Minstr.* VI. xxiii, A wondrous blaze was seen to gleam;.. It ruddied all the copse-wood glen. **1837** CARLYLE *Fr. Rev.* III. IV. iv, As the coming Sun ruddies the East. **1889** *Universal Rev.* Nov. 432 A breath Of sundown ruddying the maple seeds.

2. *intr.* To turn red; to blush. *rare.*

1845 JANE ROBINSON *Whitehall* xix, Mrs. Chaloner, smiling and ruddying all over. **1938** W. DE LA MARE *Memory*

49 See, how the sun Ruddies through his filmy grey, Turns to light the dreaming one.

ˈruddyish, *a. rare.* [f. RUDDY *a.* + -ISH.] Somewhat ruddy.

1880 *Jrnl. Linn. Soc., Zool.* XV. 90 Colour,—a ruddyish white, with dark purple spirals above.

†**ˈruddyless.** *a. Obs.*⁻¹ In 5 **rodylese.** [f. RUDDY *sb.* + -LESS.] Pale.

c **1400** *Beryn* 951 When Fawnus was I-come, and sawe so rodylese His wyff þat was so dere.

rude (ruːd), *a.* and *adv.* Forms: 4 **ruide**, 4-5 **ruyde** (5 *Sc.* **royde**), 5 **ruyd**, 6 *Sc.* **ruid**; 5 **reude**, 5-6 **rewde**; 4- **rude**. [a. OF. *ruide, rude* (F. *rude*), or ad. L. *rudis* unwrought, unformed, inexperienced, etc. Cf. MDu. *ruud-, ruut.*

In some ME. and early Sc. texts there appears to be a certain amount of confusion between *rude* and ROID *a.*]

A. *adj.* **I. 1. a.** Uneducated, unlearned; ignorant; lacking in knowledge or book-learning.

?*a* **1366** CHAUCER *Rom. Rose* 752 She was nought rude ne vnmete, But couthe ynow of sich doyng As longeth vnto karolyng. **1390** GOWER *Conf.* II. 33, I am so rude in my degree And ek mi wittes ben so dulle. *c* **1430** LYDG. *Minor Poems* (Percy Soc.) 81 To voyde al errour fro folkis that ben rude. **1508** DUNBAR *Tua Mariit Wemen* 368 Hely raise my renovne amang the rude peple. **1536** CROMWELL in Merriman *Life & Lett.* (1902) II. 27 They shall leave their cure not to a rude and unlerned person but to a good, lerned & experte curate. **1609** BIBLE (Douay) *Gen.* xvi. *Comm.*, Some obey whilest they are rude or in a low state, but having got a little knowledge or advancement disdaine their advancers. **1651** HOBBES *Leviath.* II. xxvi. 141 The rude people taking pleasure in singing, or reciting them. *c* **1710** CELIA FIENNES *Diary* (1888) 11 The Country people being a Clownish rude people. **1849** MACAULAY *Hist. Eng.* vi. II. 107 The London clergy..set an example which was bravely followed by their ruder brethren all over the country. **1865** MOZLEY *Miracles* 209 The new religion was first promulgated by rude men unacquainted with learning and rhetoric.

b. *absol.* as *pl.* The unlearned or ignorant.

c **1400** *Rom. Rose* 2268 Loke..that they sitte so fetisly, That these ruyde may vttirly Merveyle. *c* **1460** G. ASHBY *Dicta Philos.* 534 He muste abstene from Rude & Unkunnyng, And al suche vnthrifty folkys despise. **1515** BARCLAY *Egloges* iv. (1570) C vj b, His sight infourmeth the rude & ignorant. **1568** T. HOWELL *Arb. Amitie* (1879) 53 Unto the weake shee was a strength,..Unto the rude, a lamp of light. **1655-60** STANLEY *Hist. Philos.* (1701) 121/2 Whatsoever they have, to the good seems sufficient, to the rude too little. [**1892** PATER *Wks.* (1901) VIII. 228 Fritillaries.., Snake's heads, the rude call them, for their shape.]

c. Of the mind, understanding, times, etc.

c **1386** CHAUCER *Miller's T.* 41 He knew nat Catoun, for his wit was rude. *c* **1425** WYNTOUN *Cron.* I. Prol. 39 Ruyde is my witt, And semple to put all in wryte. *c* **1500** *Melusine* 371 The vnderstanding of humayne Creature is to rude to vnderstande the spyce espirytuel. *a* **1547** SURREY in *Tottel's Misc.* (Arb.) 218 In the rude age when knowledge was not rife. **1638** JUNIUS *Paint. Ancients* 8 Young children..follow the tender imaginations of their rude and unexercised conceits in making of..images out of clay. **1648** WILKINS *Math. Magic* II. iii. 168 So much were all these kind of inventions admired in those ruder and darker times. **1788** PRIESTLEY *Lect. Hist.* IV. xxvi. 204 The fifteenth century was one of the most rude and illiterate ages. **1858** HAWTHORNE *Fr. & It. Note-bks.* (1872) I. 22 His first rude and ignorant prejudice. **1867** DK. ARGYLL *Reign of Law* vii. (1871) 376 The stage of rude ignorance which led to the breaking of machinery.

†**d.** *transf.* Of animals: Irrational. *Obs.*

1377 LANGL. *P. Pl.* B. xv. 453 As in wilde wildernesse wexeth wilde bestes, Rude and vnresonable rennenge without croperes. **14..** in *Tundale's Vis.* (1843) 124 To se the bestes that so humble bee.., The rude asse and the ox also. **1426** LYDG. *De Guil. Pilgr.* 16779 As wel thes Rude beestes, as Men that were Resounable.

2. a. Unexperienced, inexpert, unskilled. Now *arch.* and *rare.*

1382 WYCLIF *2 Chron.* xiii. 7 Bot Roboam was rude, and with ferde herte, and myȝt not aȝeinstonden to hem. **1489** SKELTON *Death Earl Northumbld.* 142 What nedeth me for to extoll his fame With my rude pen? **1529** WOLSEY in *Cecil P.* (Hist. MSS. Comm.) I. 7 At the Loge with the rude hand and hevy hert of hym that ys assurydly yours with herte and prayer. **1533** in Ellis *Orig. Lett.* Ser. III. II. 276 Scribled yn hast..with the rewde honde of your owne.., John Tregonwell. **1700** DRYDEN *Ovid's Met.* I. 544 Imperfect shapes, in marble such are seen, When the rude chisel does the man begin. **1746** FRANCIS tr. *Horace, Sat.* II. iii, Here the rude chisel's rougher strokes I traced. **1831** DIGBY *Mores Cath.* (1845) I. II. i. 107/1 The blessed Pasuntius..fled to..far-distant monasteries, dissembling his name, that there, as if a rude and new monk, he might discharge the lowest offices.

b. Lacking experience or skill *in*, without proper knowledge †*of*, unaccustomed *to*, something. Now *arch.* and *rare.*

a **1400** in Horstmann *Hampole* (1895) I. 165 A fleshle saule þe wilk is ȝitte rude in gastele studys. **1526** TINDALE *2 Cor.* xi. 6 Though I be rude in speakynge, yet I am not so in knowledge. **1534** WHITINTON *Tullyes Offices* I. (1540) 1 Suche as be rude of the greke tongue. **1561** WINȜET *Wks.* (S.T.S.) I. 9 Albeit we be ruid of letteris and iugement. *a* **1639** WOTTON *Dk. Buckingham* 20 We must consider him ..yet but rude in the profession of Arms. **1841** MACAULAY *Ess., Leigh Hunt* (1897) 592 He was altogether rude in the art of controversy. **1844** —— *Misc. Wks.* (1889) 295 It [the National Assembly] was no longer, as on the day when it met, altogether rude to political functions.

c. Inexact, superficial.

1691 RAY *Creation* (1714) 94 He confesses he has been but a rude observer of them.

3. a. Devoid of, or deficient in, culture or refinement; uncultured, unrefined.

In some cases not clearly distinguishable from (and partly implying) sense 4 or 5.

c **1386** CHAUCER *Wife's T.* 316 Al were it that myn auncetres wer rude, Yit may the highe God..Graunte me grace to lyve vertuously. **1426** LYDG. *De Guil. Pilgr.* 8691, I am be-kome an Erde man,..A rud shepperde, thorgh my folye, And ha for-sake chyualrye. *c* **1475** *Rauf Coilȝear* 935, I rek nocht of thy riches,..Said the rude Saraȝine. **1526** *Pilgr. Perf.* (W. de W. 1531) 2 My wytte is grosse, my selfe rude, and my tonge very barbarouse. **1596** SPENSER *F.Q.* VI. iii. 38 The rude Porter that no manners had Did shut the gate against him in his face. **1604** SHAKS. *Oth.* I. iii. 81 Rude am I, in my speech, And little bless'd with the soft phrase of Peace. **1624** BURTON *Anat. Mel.* To Rdr. (ed. 2) 9, I am..a loose, plaine, rude writer.., I call a spade a spade. **1750** GRAY *Elegy* 16 Beneath those rugged elms..The rude forefathers of the hamlet sleep. **1810** SCOTT *Lady of L.* I. xxx, 'Twere strange in ruder rank to find Such looks, such manners, and such mind. **1849** MACAULAY *Hist. Eng.* iii. I. 424 When he is a rude and thoughtless schoolboy and when he is a refined and accomplished man. **1864** TENNYSON *The Islet* 10 A crew that is neither rude nor rash, But a bevy of Eroses apple-cheeked.

b. Uncivilized, barbarous.

1483 CAXTON *Gold. Leg.* 146/1 He coude not conuerte the euyll, rude and wylde peple. **1568** GRAFTON *Chron.* II. 355 They..spake shamefully..of them, like to rude people without all humanitie. **1586** HOOKER *Hist. Irel.* in *Holinshed* II. 141/2 The rude people he framed to a civilitie, & their maners he reformed and brought to the English order. **1697** DRYDEN *Virg. Georg.* III. 588 Skins of Beasts, the rude Barbarians wear. **1732** BERKELEY *Alciphr.* VIII. §15 If we suppose rude mankind without the use of language. **1788** GIBBON *Decl. & F.* xlix. V. 158 It was the design of Otho the third to abandon the ruder countries of the north. **1815** ELPHINSTONE *Acc. Caubul* (1842) II. 135 Their dress, food, and manners are like those of the rudest Dooraunees. **1865** LUBBOCK *Preh. Times* iii. 60 We must now revert to still earlier times and ruder races of men.

c. Of things, feelings, actions, practices, etc.

?*a* **1400** *Morte Arth.* 1049 Thare ware rostez fulle ruyde, and rewfulle bredez. *c* **1532** DU WES *Introd. Fr.* in *Palsgr.* 1017 Grose folke of rude affection, dronkerdes, banysshed of trewe felyng [etc.]. *a* **1548** HALL *Chron., Edw. IV*, 37 Not content with hys grosse rudenesse, and rude dissimulacion. **1600** J. PORY tr. *Leo's Africa* v. 240 The citizens are valiant, though they bee of rude behauior. **1687** A. LOVELL tr. *Thevenot's Trav.* I. 15 The Women are Apparelled in a fashion that seems to be rude and clownish. **1746** FRANCIS tr. *Horace, Art Poet.* 319 The tragic bard,..Though rude his mirth, yet labour'd to maintain The solemn grandeur of the tragic scene. *Ibid.* 552 A rude genius of uncultur'd strain. **1819** SCOTT *Ivanhoe* iii, The other appointments of the mansion partook of the rude simplicity of the Saxon period. **1861** READE *Cloister & H.* xxxviii, With kind force and words of rude consolation, they almost lifted Denys on to the mule.

d. Of life, conditions, or times.

1538 STARKEY *England* I. i. 9 [City vice] wych al in the cuntrey and rude lyfe of them ys avoyded, by the reson that they lyfe not togydur aftur your cyuylyte. **1565** COOPER *Thesaurus* s.v. *Rusticus*, Rude and vplandish life in the countrey.

1769 ROBERTSON *Chas. V*, Wks. 1813 V. 462 Most of the American Tribes..are in a ruder and more simple state than the ancient Germans. **1777** —— *Hist. Amer.* IV. (1778) I. 257 In the New World, the state of mankind was ruder, and the aspect of Nature extremely different. **1827** HALLAM *Const. Hist.* iv. (1876) I. 191 A disorderly state of the church, arising from..the rude state of manners and general ignorance of the clergy. **1844** DISRAELI *Coningsby* VII. ii, Parliamentary representation was the happy device of a ruder age. **1883** *Fortn. Rev.* May 695 Englishmen have ceased to watch over their local interests with the jealous vigilance of ruder times.

4. Unmannerly, uncivil, impolite; offensively or deliberately discourteous: **a.** Of speech or actions.

c **1386** CHAUCER *Prol. Nun Priest's T.* 42 Then spak our Ost, with rude speche and bold,..'Com neer, thou preest'. ?*a* **1400** *Morte Arth.* 1332 Thou sulde repent fulle rathe of thi ruyde wordez. *a* **1533** LD. BERNERS *Huon* lxvi. 225 Gerarde began to fall at rude wordes with Huon. **1588** SHAKS. *L.L.L.* v. ii. 431 Teach vs sweete Madame, for our rude transgression, some faire excuse. **1617** MORYSON *Itin.* I. 36 Neither their murmuring nor rude speeches could make me yield the place to them. **1652** MILTON *Sonn.* xvi. 2 Through a cloud Not of warr onely, but detractions rude. **1711** STEELE *Spect.* No. 109 ⁋5 He..never said a rude thing in his Life. **1781** GIBBON *Decl. & F.* xix. (1787) II. 135 The profound respect..was insensibly changed into rude familiarity. **1847** MRS. KERR tr. *Ranke's Hist. Servia* 330 The haughty insolence of the Ottomans displayed itself in the rudest and most offensive conduct.

transf. **1784** COWPER *Task* II. 258 That no rude savour maritime invade The nose of nice nobility.

b. Of persons.

1590 SHAKS. *Mids. N.* III. ii. 262 Why are you growne so rude? **1617** MORYSON *Itin.* I. 197 He..did..call me backe, and surely would have been rude with me, had I not gone up faster than he could follow me. **1687** A. LOVELL tr. *Thevenot's Trav.* I. 277 These Slaves have power to beat the Turks if they are rude and insolent in their Taverns. **1718** *Free-thinker* No. 57. 12, I hope you will not think me rude in what follows. **1778** JOHNSON in *Boswell* (Oxf. ed.) II. 206 We have done with civility. We are to be as rude as we please. **1855** MACAULAY *Hist. Eng.* xviii. IV. 228 The crowd of rustics who had been rude to James when he was stopped at Sheerness. **1891** 'J. S. WINTER' *Lumley* xii, 'We haven't found Blackwood rude at all,' said Vere.

5. Ungentle, violent, harsh, rugged; marked by unkind or severe treatment of persons, etc.

a. Of personal qualities, the hands, etc.

1390 GOWER *Conf.* I. 165 This Geant with his ruide myht Part of the banke he schof doun riht. ?*a* **1400** *Morte Arth.* 1057 He..Raykez to-warde the renke reghte with a ruyde wille. *c* **1470** HENRY *Wallace* VIII. 1054 The rude low rais full heych abown that hauld. **1591** SHAKS. *Two Gent.* v. iv. 60 Ruffian: let goe that rude vnciuill touch. **1596** —— *1 Hen. IV*, I. i. 41 The Noble Mortimer..Was by the rude hands of that Welshman taken. **1632** MILTON *Penseroso* 136 Where the rude Ax with heaved stroke Was never heard. **1637** —— *Lycidas* 4, I com to pluck your Berries.., And with forc'd fingers rude, Shatter your leaves before the mellowing year. **1746** HERVEY *Medit.* (1818) 8 A sort of religious dread,..such as hushed every ruder passion. **1813** BYRON *Br. Abydos* II. xxviii, Hands more rude than wintry sky. **1850** S. DOBELL *Roman* i. Poet. Wks. (1875) 12 Like the shy Scared bird, to which the serpent's jaws are better Than his rude eyes. **1861** TULLOCH *Eng. Purit.* i. 94 The rude determination of this man made him master of every successive exigency.

b. Of acts, esp. blows, assaults, etc.

c **1375** BARBOUR *Bruce* II. 356 [They] plungyt in the stalwart stour, And rowtis ruyd about thaim dang. *c* **1470** *Gol. & Gaw.* 850 Rude reknyng raise thair renkis betuene. *a* **1533** LD. BERNERS *Huon* lviii. 198 The strokes was so rude that both knyghtes & horses fel to yᵉ erth. **1593** SHAKS. *Rich. II*, v. v. 106 How now? what meanes Death in this rude assalt? **1660** F. BROOKE tr. *Le Blanc's Trav.* 326 The chief Bachir unbinds him, gives him three rude lashes with a whip. **1671** MILTON *Samson* 1567 Lest evil tidings with too rude irruption Hitting thy aged ear should pierce too deep. **1743** FRANCIS tr. *Horace, Odes* I. xvii. 24 Nor here shall Mars intemperate wage Rude war with him who rules the jovial vine. **1799** CAMPBELL *Pleas. Hope* I. 105 'Twas his to mourn misfortune's rudest shock. **1849** MACAULAY *Hist. Eng.* vi. II. 46 If he attempted to subdue the Protestant feeling of England by rude means. **1868** M. PATTISON *Academ. Org.* vii. 329 We have lately had some rude reminders..that something is wrong, somewhere.

c. Involving hardships or discomfort.

a **1734** tr. *Rollin's Anc. Hist.* V. 107 The rude fatigues they had suffered during the storm. **1814** SCOTT *Ld. of Isles* I. xxv, For, to ourselves, the deck's rude plank Is easy as the mossy bank. **1820** SHELLEY *Death* iv. 3 Such is our rude mortal lot. **1861** READE *Cloister & H.* xxxix, Rude travel is enticing to us English.

d. Of persons: Acting in a rough or harsh manner; violent in action.

a **1800** *Lads of Wamphray* 65 in Child *Ballads* III. 460/2 O but these lads were wondrous rude, When the Biddess-burn ran three days blood! **1837** CARLYLE *Fr. Rev.* III. III. vii, With fire-words the exasperated rude Titan rives and smites these Girondins. **1863** MARY HOWITT tr. *F. Bremer's Greece* I. vi. 162 The old classical soil was trampled underfoot of the rude conqueror.

e. Fig. phr. ***rude awakening***, a severe disillusionment or arousal from complacency.

1895 G. ALLEN *Woman who Did* vi. 71 Alan was often quite alarmed in his soul when he thought of the rude awakening that no doubt awaited her. **1912** T. DREISER *Financier* v. 47 Life had given him no severe shocks nor rude awakenings. **1971** *Daily Tel.* 12 June 18/1 Anyone visiting this year's Grosvenor House Antique Fair..with the object of buying antiques on the cheap is in for a rude awakening. **1975** SHEA & WILSON *Golden Apple* IV. 248 Then comes the rude awakening: food riots, industrial stagnation, a reign of lawless looting and plunder.

6. a. Turbulent, violent, boisterous, rough. Chiefly of the sea, winds, etc.

a **1400-50** *Alexander* 5595 Þan ridis he to a Reuere, a ruyde & a hoge. **1523** LD. BERNERS *Froiss.* I. ccxxxv. 135 b, These men of armes..came to the ryuer of Marke, the whiche is rude and depe. **1597** SHAKS. *2 Hen. IV*, III. i. 20 In Cradle of the rude imperious Surge. **1605** —— *Lear* IV. ii. 30 You are not worth the dust which the rude winde Blowes in your face. **1667** MILTON *P.L.* x. 1074 The Clouds..pusht with Winds rude in their shock. **1742** GRAY *Propertius* ii. 37 How the rude surge its sandy Bounds control. **1775** SHERIDAN *Rivals* II. i, If the wind be keen, some rude blast may have affected her! **1807** J. BARLOW *Columb.* I. 275 Rude thunders rake the crags. **1851** CARLYLE *J. Sterling* III. ii. (1872) 182 Again, before long, the rude weather has driven him Southward. **1871** R. ELLIS *Catullus* lxiv. 179 A rough rude space of flowing water.

†**b.** ***rude air***, the open air. *Obs.*

1784 *Unfortunate Sensibility* II. 57, [I] had rarely been out but in a coach or a chair, so that I was almost a stranger to rude air.

c. Of health: Robust, vigorous.

1792 in *Ld. Auckland's Corr.* (1861) II. 461, I flatter myself you are restored to rude health. **1848** KINGSLEY *Yeast* xiii, The majority seemed under-sized, under-fed, utterly wanting in..what the penny-a-liners call 'rude health'. **1871** —— *At Last* ii, Health, 'rude' in every sense of the word, is the mark of the Negro woman.

7. Of sounds: Discordant, harsh, unmusical.

c **1350** *Will. Palerne* 1851 þe werwolf ful wiȝtli went to him euene, wiþ a rude roring as he him rende wold. *c* **1450** HOLLAND *Howlat* 45 Rolpit reuthfully roth in a rude rane. *c* **1470** HENRY *Wallace* v. 180 So hard thai blaw rude hornys wpon hycht. **1535** STEWART *Cron. Scot.* II. 56 So rude ane reird Wes neuir hard with no man in this erd. **1606** SHAKS. *Tr. & Cr.* I. i. 92 Peace you vngracious Clamors, peace rude sounds. **1697** CONGREVE *Mourn. Bride* I. i, There's not a Slave..But should have..shook his Chains in Transport and rude Harmony. **1746** FRANCIS tr. *Horace, Art Poet.* 484 We laugh at him who constant brings The same rude discord from the jarring strings. **1757** WILKIE *Epigoniad* IV. 91 His rude voice like thunder shakes the shore. **1822** SCOTT *Peveril* v, This man's rude and clamorous grief. **1843** WHITTIER *To J. P.* 15 Even thy song Hath a rude martial tone, a blow in every thought.

II. 8. a. Of language, composition, etc.: Lacking in elegance or polish; deficient in literary merit.

c **1340** HAMPOLE *Pr. Consc.* 9585, I rek noght, þogh þe ryme be rude, If þe maters þar-of be gude. **1390** GOWER *Conf.* III. 383 Y have do my trewe peyne With rude wordis and with pleyne..This bok to write. **1412-20** LYDG. *Chron. Troy* I. 3090 After þe maner of my rude stile. **1481** CAXTON *Reynard* (Arb.) 120 My copye whiche was in dutche, and by me william Caxton translated in to this rude and symple englyssh. **1551** ROBINSON *More's Utopia* Ep. Transl., Rude and vnlearned speche defaceth and disgraceth a very good matter. **1572** MASCALL *Plant. & Graff.* Ep., To commende this my simple and rude woorke vnto your Lordship. **1703** MAUNDRELL *Journ. Jerus.* (1732) 15 Only from this rude tradition. **1763** J. BROWN *Poetry & Music* §5. 50 The oldest Compositions among the Arabs are in Rythm or rude Verse. **1849** MACAULAY *Hist. Eng.* vii. II. 225 His rude oratory roused and melted hearers who listened without interest to the laboured discourses of great logicians and Hebraists. **1861** STANLEY *East. Ch.* viii. (1869) 271 The Apostles used freely a rude version of the Old Testament.

b. Of drawings, etc.: Rough, imperfect; not very accurate or finished.

1679 BURNET *Hist. Ref.* I. 282 A long letter, which the reader will find in the Collection, copied from the rude draught of it. **1681** GLANVIL *Sadducismus* 35 Those seemingly rude Lines and Scrawls which he intends for the Rudiments of a Picture. **1746** FRANCIS tr. *Horace, Sat.* II. vii. 110 Some rude design In crayons or in charcoal. **1748** *Anson's Voy.* II. iii. 140 The memorandums and rude sketches of the Master and Surgeon, who were not..the ablest draughts-men. **1888** *Poor Nellie* 176 People would often recognize the whereabouts of her rough rude sketches. **1890** DOYLE *White Company* xxv, He held a pen..with which he had been scribbling in a rude school-boy hand.

c. Roughly accurate or correct.

1854 H. ROGERS *Ess.* (1874) II. i. 53 A rude metaphorical or analogical approximation to exact expression. **1882** *Encycl. Brit.* XIV. 601/1 Fig. 27 shows in a rude way the absorption by cobalt glass cut in wedge form, and corrected by an equal prism of clear glass.

9. Coarse, inelegant, rough. *rare.*

*c*1386 CHAUCER *Clerk's T.* 956 Right nought was sche abaissht of hir clothing, Though it were ruyde and som del eek to-rent. *Ibid.* 1060 These ladys..strippen hir out of hir rude arraye. *a*1500 *Bernardus De Cura rei fam.* (E.E.T.S.) 83 Geffe þame enwcht of drynk and metis rude Quhilk may suffice to seruandis and þer fude. **1700** DRYDEN *Cymon & Iph.* 74 Rude work well suited with a rustic mind. **1831** SCOTT *Cast. Dang.* i, Their wants, with a very few exceptions, were completely supplied..by the rude and scanty produce of their..mountains and holms. **1849** MACAULAY *Hist. Eng.* iii. I. 332 The other section was destined to ruder and humbler service.

10. Of natural scenery or objects: Rugged, rough; uncultivated, wild.

*c*1386 CHAUCER *Manciple's T.* 66 (Ellesm.), Yet hath this brid..Leuere in a Forest, that is rude and coold, Goon ete wormes and swich wrecchednesse. *c*1475 *Rauf Coilȝear* 14 That Ryall raid ouir the rude mure. **1578** LYTE *Dodoens* 127 The first kinde of Veruayne groweth in rude places, about hedges, walles, wayes, streates and diches. **1606** SHAKS. *Ant. & Cl.* I. iv. 64 Thy pallat the[n] did daine The roughest Berry, on the rudest Hedge. **1634** MILTON *Comus* 352 Where may she wander now, whether betake her From the chill dew, amongst rude burrs and thistles? **1756** C. LUCAS *Ess. Waters* II. 95 In the middle of an open, rude common ..stands a spring. **1794** GODWIN *Caleb Williams* 234, I arrived at the termination of this ruder scene, and reached that part of the county which is inclosed and cultivated. **1816** SHELLEY *Mt. Blanc* 70 How hideously Its shapes are heaped around! rude, bare, and high, Ghastly, and scarred, and riven. **1867** LADY HERBERT *Cradle L.* iii. 79 The rude rock remains uncovered.

11. a. Imperfect, unfinished; not reduced to shape, order, or regularity. Now *rare* or *Obs.*

1382 WYCLIF *Mark* ii. 21 No man seweth a pacche of rude, or newe, clothe to an old clothe. **1387** TREVISA *Higden* (Rolls) V. 411 For þe staat of holy chirche in Engelond, þat was ȝit ruyde and boistous, shulde nouȝt flecche. **1595** SHAKS. *John* v. vii. 27 You are borne To set a forme vpon that indigest Which he hath left so shapelesse, and so rude. **1631** WIDDOWES *Nat. Philos.* 57 Spirits having roote in the heart, be either absolute or rude, and to be finished in other parts. **1692** RAY *Disc.* i. (1732) 3 A rude and inordinate Heap. **1704** ROWE *Ulysses* III. i, So Jove look'd down upon the War of Atoms And rude tumultuous Chaos.

b. Of natural products: Unwrought; unmanufactured, raw.

1555 EDEN *Decades* (Arb.) 72, I my selfe sawe a masse of rude goulde (that is to say, such as was neuer molten). **1609** BIBLE (Douay) *Ecclus.* xl. 4 Even to him, that is covered with rude linen [L. *lino crudo*]. **1621** BURTON *Anat. Mel.* To Rdr. 50 Let him..suffer no rude matter vnwrought as Tinne, Iron,..To bee transported out of his country. **1776** ADAM SMITH *W.N.* II. v. (1904) I. 401 Either the rude or manufactured produce. **1812** SIR H. DAVY *Chem. Philos.* 58 The production of metals from rude ores. **1844** DISRAELI *Coningsby* IV. ii, The cotton..in its rude state. **1865** LUBBOCK *Preh. Times* (1878) iii. 66 Iron in a 'rude' state.

c. Left in a natural rough state; undressed.

1800 WORDSW. *Hart-Leap Well* I. 83 Three pillars of rude stone Sir Walter reared. **1862** STANLEY *Jew. Ch.* (1877) I. iii. 50 There were rude stones at Delphi..anterior to any temple. **1878** C. STANFORD *Symb. Christ* i. 3 Conscious of such a spell upon our spirits at the sight of the rudest stone, the simplest mound.

12. a. Of a rough, inelegant, or rugged form; in early use, big and coarse; strong but ill-shaped.

?*a*1400 *Morte Arth.* 1096 Brade in the scholders,..Ruyd armes as an ake with ruslcede sydes. *c*1475 *Rauf Coilȝear* 794 Vpon ane rude Runsy he ruschit out of toun. *a*1533 LD. BERNERS *Huon* xciii. 300 Huons spere was bygge & rude. **1595** SHAKS. *John* II. i. 262 Tis not..your old-fac'd walles Can hide you.., Though all these English..Were harbour'd in their rude circumference. **1629** MILTON *Hymn Nativ.* i, The Heav'n-born-childe, All meanly wrapt in the rude manger lies. **1748** GRAY *Alliance* 26 How rude so e'er th' exterior Form we find. **1768** SIR W. JONES *Laura* Poems (1777) 79 Steep arching rocks..Form her rude diadem, and native throne. **1796** WITHERING *Brit. Pl.* (ed. 3) I. 233 Petals 4, rude, upright, blunt. **1805** WORDSW. *Prelude* XIII. 228 How oft high service is performed within, When all the external man is rude in show. **1846** KEBLE *Lyra Innoc.* (1873) 141 Who is this that comes with mantle rude? **1899** O. SEAMAN *In Cap & Bells* (1900) 87 Not that I wear, like Bergerac, A nose of rather rude dimensions.

b. Roughly made or formed; imperfect in design or execution.

1612 STURTEVANT *Metallica* (1854) 40 Rude-ware are such sort of Press-ware which after they are pressed and moulded require no further ornament: as Prest-pipes, Prest-tiles, Prest-brickes, Prest-stones. **1711** POPE *Temple Fame* 125 There on rude iron columns..The horrid forms of Scythian heroes stood. **1748** *Anson's Voy.* III. x. 415 The masts, sails, and rigging of these vessels are ruder than their built. **1814** SCOTT *Diary* 10 Aug. in *Lockhart*, It is easy to descend into it by a rude path. **1842** BORROW *Bible in Spain* xxiv, We saw others in the fields handling their rude ploughs. **1879** LUBBOCK *Sci. Lect.* v. 155 It is an error to suppose that the rudest flint implements are necessarily the oldest.

13. Of an imperfect, undeveloped, or primitive character.

1600 J. PORY tr. *Leo's Africa* III. 146 Other games there are also, but very rude. **1667** MILTON *P.L.* IX. 391 With such Gardning Tools as Art yet rude, Guiltless of fire had formd. **1728** R. MORRIS *Ess. Anc. Archit.* p. ix, Ghiberto..brought Architecture from that rude Gothick manner. **1788** GIBBON *Decl. & F.* l. V. 203 In the rude idolatry of the Arabs. **1839** URE *Dict. Arts* 983 This very rude and dangerous mode of exploding the inflammable gas, is still practised in a few mines. **1849** MACAULAY *Hist. Eng.* iii. I. 386 A rude and imperfect establishment of posts for the conveyance of letters had been set up by Charles the First. **1875** JOWETT *Plato* (ed. 2) V. 29 He has traced the growth of states from their rude beginning in a philosophical spirit.

†**14.** Large in amount. *Obs.*$^{-1}$

*c*1470 HENRY *Wallace* IX. 1506 Thai lugyt thar At rud costis, to spend thai wald nocht spar.

15. *Comb.*, as ***rude-featured***, ***-tongued***; ***rude-like***, ***-looking***, ***-spoken*** adjs. **rude boy**, one of a class of unemployed black youths inhabiting the poorer areas of Jamaica and typically seen as indolent and apt to commit petty crimes.

1632 LITHGOW *Trav.* v. 226 The Carauan presented his rude like maiesty with water, bread, [and] hearbes. **1795** *Fate of Sedley* II. 61 He arose with an heart of gladness; and ..pursued the rude fanged boar. **1797** SOUTHEY *Joan of Arc* VII, On his head A black plume shadow'd the rude-featured helm. **1803** J. RENNY *Society* 22 Stern as he was, rude-thoughted and untamed. **1876** *Nature* XIV. 176/1 It is a rude-looking machine. **1877** BLACK *Green Past.* xxvii, The rude-spoken German ex-lieutenant. **1967** *Caribbean Q.* Sept. 39 Rude bwoy is that person, native, who is totally disenchanted with the ruling system; who generally is descended from the 'African' elements in the lower class... Rude bwoys are largely centred in those urban areas that suffer from chronic depression. **1975** *Globe & Mail* (Toronto) 11 June 3/1 The rude boys, rudies or just plain rudes are the street corner toughs, hustlers, petty thieves and dealers in ganja (marijuana). **1976** D. HEBDIGE in Hall & Jefferson *Resistance through Rituals* 152 The exotica of Rastafarianism provided distractive screens behind which the rude boy culture could pursue its own devious devices unhindered and unseen. **1977** LOGAN & WOFFINDEN *New Musical Express Bk. of Rock* 414 The rude boys (outlaws) of Jamaica's shanty towns began to move into the studios, celebrating their own chosen lifestyle, which resulted in a spate of rudeboy records.

B. *adv.* **a.** In a rude manner; rudely. *rare.*

*c*1475 *Partenay* 3257 Then to the abbot, which that balled was, hath Gaffray spokyn rude and bustesly. **1607** TOPSELL *Four-f. Beasts* (1658) 483 The hair of Men grew rude, and in length like Womens. **1616** SURFL. & MARKH. *Country Farme* III. ii. 336 In this case you shall by no meanes bestow them into the earth thus rude and carelesly. *c*1788 BURNS *When Guilford good our Pilot stood* ix, Caledon..swoor fu' rude..To mak it guid in law, man. **1795** J. WOODFORDE *Diary* 8 Sept. (1929) IV. 226 Jane behaved quite rude this Evening. **1885** G. M. HOPKINS *Poems* (1967) 99 But ah, but O thou terrible, why wouldst thou rude on me Thy wring-world right foot rock?

b. *Comb.*, as ***rude-carved***, ***-fashioned***, ***-growing***, ***-made***, ***-masoned***, ***-ripened***, ***-rounded***, ***-spun*** adjs.

1588 SHAKS. *Tit. A.* II. iii. 199 What subtile Hole is this, Whose mouth is couered with Rude growing Briers. **1610** B. JONSON *Alchemist* II. i. 16 The couetous hunger..for a rude-spun cloke. **1796** TOWNSHEND *Poems* 23 Down the foaming rude-wash'd hills. **1797** SOUTHEY *Joan of Arc* IV, A massy stone And rude-ensculptured effigy. **1812** BYRON *Ch. Har.* I. xxi, Mark many rude-carved crosses near the path. **1840** MRS. NORTON *The Dream* 196 Lift some poor wounded wretch..Forth in some rude-made litter. **1867** SMYTH *Sailor's Word-bk., Skew*,..a rude-fashioned boat. *a*1889 G. M. HOPKINS *Poems* (1967) 185 Who built these walls made known The music of his mind, Yet here he had but shewn His ruder-rounded rind. **1928** BLUNDEN *Japanese Garland* 20 Over the rude-ripened vale. **1930** —— *Poems* 128 There is a sluice through whose rude-masoned stones And fissured planks our timid river falls.

rude (ruːd), *sb. colloq.* [f. RUDE *a.* and *adv.*]

a. An impolite or unsophisticated person. **b.** = *rude boy* s.v. RUDE *a.* 15.

1961 J. DAWSON *Ha-Ha* iv. 74 No Brains' Trust will work so long as you've always got to have a gaggle of rudes and silly old sages to balance the bright young men. **1975** [see *rude boy* s.v. RUDE *a.* 15].

rude, obs. form of ROOD, RUD *sb.*[1]

†**ˈrudeful**, *a. Obs.*$^{-1}$ [f. RUDE *a.*] Full of rudeness.

1587 R. ROBINSON *Golden Mirrour* (Chetham Soc.) 33 Of all my wandring wilfull dayes, And rechlesse rudefull toyes.

rudel, obs. form of RIDEL.

rudely (ˈruːdlɪ), *adv.* Forms: 5 ruydlyche, -(e)ly; 4 rudli, 5–6 *Sc.* -ly, 6 -lie, 7 -lye; 5 rewdly; 5 rudeli(che, 6 -lie, 7– rudely. [f. RUDE *a.* + -LY[2]. Cf. MDu. *rudelike*, *-lijc*, *-lic*.]

1. With great force or violence; violently, roughly.

13.. *Cursor M.* 22151 (Gött.), þe wind to do rudli to rise, And stormes do men sare to grise. **1375** BARBOUR *Bruce* II. 349 That..swa ruydly gan samyn ryd, That speris all tofruschyt war. ?*a*1400 *Morte Arth.* 794 He rawmpyde so ruydly that alle the erthe ryfez. *c*1470 HENRY *Wallace* IV. 247 Rudely fra him he reft it. *a*1533 LD. BERNERS *Huon* lxxxi. 242 He rose vp then sodeynly so rudely that he ouerthrewe cuppes and dysshes. **1590** SPENSER *F.Q.* I. i. 25 Soone as their Parent deare They saw so rudely falling to the ground. **1607** SHAKS. *Cor.* IV. v. 148 Whether to knocke against the Gates of Rome, Or rudely visit them in parts remote. **1660** F. BROOKE tr. *Le Blanc's Trav.* 325 They use them but rudely, and beat them till they cry like children. **1723** DART *Westmonasterium* I. 86 Chaucer..would never have fallen so rudely foul on the whole Order. **1792** S. ROGERS *Pleas. Mem.* II. 92 Oft in the saddle rudely rocked to sleep. **1813** SHELLEY *Q. Mab* IX. 185 And wilt thou rudely tear them from thy breast? **1864** NEWMAN *Apol.* i. (1904) 9/1, I was rudely awakened from my dream..by two great blows—illness and bereavement.

2. With harsh or discordant sound. ? *Obs.*

*c*1350 *Will. Palerne* 3270 þe cry rudli a-ros þat reuþe it was to hure. *a*1400 *Pistill of Susan* 341 þo þat roþly cherl ruydely rored. *c*1450 HOLLAND *Howlat* 215 The Ravyne rolpand rudly in a roche ran. **1535** LYNDESAY *Satyre* 4128 My sone..for me will rudelie rair, Fra tyme he se me hangit. *c*1586 C'TESS PEMBROKE *Ps.* LXVI. v, Swelling streames did rudely roare.

3. In an uncultured, uncivil, discourteous, or unmannerly fashion.

*c*1386 CHAUCER *Prol.* 734 He moost reherce..Every word, ..Al speke he never so rudely ne large. *c*1430 *Pilgr. Lyf Manhode* I. xxxix. (1869) 24 For toward grace dieu she wente, and rudeliche spak to hire. **1489** *Barbour's Bruce* IX. 750 Sen þow spekys sa rudly, It is gret skill men chasty Thy proud words. **1500–20** DUNBAR *Tua Mariit Wemen* 481 Sum raiffis furght rudly with riatus speche. **1568** GRAFTON *Chron.* II. 332 These people came to her Chayre, and dealt rudely with her, whereof the good Lady was in great doubt. **1601** SHAKS. *Twel. N.* I. v. 228 *Vio.* My words are as full of peace as matter. *Ol.* Yet you began rudely. **1669** R. MONTAGU in *Buccleuch MSS.* (Hist. MSS. Comm.) I. 451, I never saw anything in my life done so rudely and so uncivilly. *a*1704 T. BROWN *Decl. Advs.* Wks. 1730 I. 42 It seems you had never very good breeding thus to laugh at my ingenuity, and sport so rudely with my wit. **1781** COWPER *Table-T.* 158 To win no praise when well-wrought plans prevail, But to be rudely censur'd when they fail. **1806** SURR *Winter in Lond.* II. 240, I imagined he stared very rudely at lady Beauchamp. **1875** JOWETT *Plato* (ed. 2) V. 198 There is no reason why we should rudely quarrel with one another.

4. In an unskilful or imperfect manner; roughly, clumsily.

*c*1375 *Sc. Leg. Saints* Prol. 80 Of his modire syne sad I sume thing, þo It be rudly. *c*1430 LYDG. *Min. Poems* (Percy Soc.) 48 This litel schort dyte, Rudely compyled, lat it be noon offence. **1447** BOKENHAM *Lyvys of Seyntys* (Roxb.) 3 The matere wych I wyl of wryte, Althow but rudely I kun endyte. **1668** CULPEPPER & COLE *Barthol. Anat.* I. x. 23 The Stomach Nerves embracing this Orifice, rudely expressed. **1695** DRYDEN *Du Fresnoy's Art Paint.* Ess. (Ker) II. 122 In this manner, as I have rudely and briefly shewn you, painters and sculptors..perfectionate the idea. *a*1711 KEN *Divine Love* Wks. (1838) 215 The love of God is a grace rather to be felt than defined, so that I can do no more than rudely describe it. **1797–1805** S. & HT. LEE *Canterb. T.* I. 336 You will see [them] rudely delineated in the *relievo* that time has yet spared. **1822** W. IRVING *Braceb. Hall* xvii. 144 We heard the sound of a fiddle rudely played. **1847** W. C. L. MARTIN *The Ox* 57/1 In former times, when agriculture was practised rudely. **1865** TYLOR *Early Hist. Man.* v. 83 The place which they can only fill very partially and rudely.

b. With rough or unskilful workmanship.

14.. *Leg. Holy Rood* 86 Thre nayles war made ful tite..; þai war full grete and rudely wroght. **1594** SHAKS. *Rich. III*, I. i. 16, I, that am Rudely stampt, and want loues Maiesty. **1610** HOLLAND *Camden's Brit.* (1637) 312 A fort compassed about with a banke rudely cast up. **1613** PURCHAS *Pilgrimage* IV. xvii. (1614) 434 They haue..many idols rudely carved. **1810** SCOTT *Lady of Lake* I. xxvi, Their hoar trunks bared, And by the hatchet rudely squared. **1835** MARRYAT *J. Faithful* xxxiii, There was a bridge, rudely constructed of old ship plank. **1868** HELPS *Realmah* v. (1876) 80 The insignia consisted of a coronet rudely formed of dark polished stones, and feathers.

c. With rough or approximate accuracy.

1748 *Anson's Voy.* II. vi. 202 The total amount..can only be rudely guessed at. **1853** KANE *Grinnell Exped.* xliii. (1856) 401 A hummock hill..gave me the opportunity of measuring rudely the height of the swell. **1868** GLADSTONE *Juv. Mundi* i. (1870) 3 Means of estimating, however rudely, the lapse of years.

†**5.** Without refinement or elegance; coarsely, rustically. *Obs.*

1484 CAXTON *Fables of Æsop* II. vi, Better is to lyue surely and rudely in sewrte than swetely in peryll & daunger. **1538** STARKEY *England* I. i. 10 We may not therfor..dryue man to the woodys agayne and wyld forestys, wherin he lyuyd at the fyrst begynnyng rudely. *a*1568 ASCHAM *Scholem.* (Arb.) 117 If yow be borne or brought vp in a rude contrie, ye shall not chose but speake rudelie. **1617** MORYSON *Itin.* I. 178 These Citizens [of Bergamo] speake the Italian tongue, but more rudely then any other of Italy. **1701** WOLLEY *Jrnl. N. York* (1860) 45 As to their way of living, it's very rudely and rovingly.

6. In a rugged or irregular manner or form.

1602 MARSTON *Ant. & Mel.* v. Wks. 1856 I. 60 When men ..forsake taking of tobacco, and cease to weare their beardes so rudely long. **1694** *Marten's Voy. Spitzbergen* in *Acc. Sev. Late Voy.* II. 23 The other Rocks look rudely. **1732** POPE *Ess. Man* II. 4 The proper study of Mankind is Man... A Being darkly wise, and rudely great. **1793** HODGES *Trav. in India* 85 This is the last of a long range of mountains, which, at this place, rudely decline to the plain. **1843** PORTLOCK *Geol.* 511 The beds still retain, though rudely, their lamination.

b. Without definite order; irregularly.

1655–60 STANLEY *Hist. Phil.* (1701) 186/2 When matter was put into those Figures by God, first it was moved rudely without order. **1668** CULPEPPER & COLE tr. *Barthol. Anat.* I. 68, I cannot as yet perswade my self, that all things are done rudely and mechanically in the Body.

7. *Comb.*, as ***rudely-blustering***, ***-carved***, ***-chiselled***, ***-molten*** adjs.

1648 J. BEAUMONT *Psyche* XX. cccvi, She saw her rudely-blustering servants, who Disturb'd her Region, in one Calm united. **1835** *Penny Cycl.* IV. 339/1 The rudely-chiselled forms of several colossal figures. **1838** DICKENS *Nickleby* vi, With overhanging gables and balconies of rudely-carved oak. **1848** BUCKLEY *Iliad* 441 Then the son of Peleus deposited a rudely-molten mass of iron.

'ruden, *v.* *rare*⁻¹. [f. RUDE *a.* + -EN⁵.] *trans.* To render rude.

1897 NUTT in *Voy. of Bran* II. 120 The design was gradually rudened and simplified.

rudeness ('ruːdnɪs). Forms: 4–7 **rudenesse**, 5–7 **-nes**, 6– **rudeness;** 5 **rudines**, **rewd-**, **rudnesse**, 6 **rud-**, *Sc.* **ruidnes.** [f. RUDE *a.* + -NESS.]

†**1.** Lack of knowledge or education; want of learning; ignorance. *Obs.*

c **1380** WYCLIF *Wks.* (1880) 291 Vnderstond, ȝe kyngis; and schaak of ȝou rudenesse, ȝe þat jugen londis. **14..** in *Tundale's Vis.* (1843) 90 My wyttis be so dull with rudenesse, And in the cheynes of ignoraunce gyved. **1447** BOKENHAM *Lyvys of Seyntys* (Roxb.) 43 Nor of ye sugird welle In elicona my rudeness to leche I nevere dede taste. **1535** COVERDALE *Bible* Prol., Though it [Scripture] be not worthely ministred vnto the in this translacyon (by reason of my rudnes). **1551** ROBINSON tr. *More's Utopia* Ep. Transl., Through my rudenes and ignoraunce in our english tonge. *a* **1626** BP. ANDREWES *96 Serm.* (1661) 414 Whom they should have received, Him they had not heard of. This was a great rudeness. **1662** H. MORE *Philos. Writ.* Pref. Gen. (1712) 11 It is a piece of Rudeness and Unskilfulness in the nature of things to conceit that [etc.].

2. Want of culture or refinement; roughness of life or habits; uncouthness.

c **1386** CHAUCER *Clerk's T.* 397 It ne semyde not by liklynesse That sche was born and fed in rudenesse, As in a cote or in an oxe-stalle. *c* **1430** LYDG. *Min. Poems* (Percy Soc.) 218 A cherl of nature wil brayde on rewdnesse. **1500–20** DUNBAR *Poems* lxx. 18 We ar so beistlie, dull, and ignorant, Our rudnes may nocht lichtlie be correctit. **1579** E. K. *Ded. Spenser's Sheph. Cal.* ¶ 1, Thinking them fittest for such rusticall rudenesse of shepheards. **1630** *R. Johnson's Kingd. & Commw.* 534 So unspeakable is the rudenesse of either, that through all their Cities you shall not finde a Schoole to instruct their youth. **1673** RAY *Journ. Low C.* 119 The Negligence and Rudeness of the People who mind nothing that is Curious. **1741** MIDDLETON *Cicero* II. viii. 236 That state of rudeness and barbarism. **1774** WARTON *Hist. Eng. Poetry* I. Pref. p. i, We are pleased to mark the steps by which we have been raised from rudeness to elegance. **1807** G. CHALMERS *Caledonia* I. III. x. 458 Those similarities, which the same state of rudeness, or civility, will ever produce. **1888** BRYCE *Amer. Commw.* (1890) III. 290 The rudeness of the times, in which physical force counted for so much.

†**b.** Absence of virtue or goodness. *Obs.*

1451 CAPGRAVE *Life St. Gilbert* (E.E.T.S.) 74 þorw his wordis and his dedes þe rudenesse of many a soule was reformed. *a* **1513** FABYAN *Chron.* I. xxii. (1811) 17 This also is vnmynded of wryters outher for restfulnesse of tyme, or ellys for rudenesse of his dedes. **1538** BALE *God's Promises* II, I knowe thy mercye is farre above hys rudenesse.

3. Roughness, harshness, or violence in action or in the treatment of others.

a **1450** *Knt. de la Tour* (1868) 24 A woman may..make hym do welle, withe fairnesse rather thanne with rudenesse. **1606** SHAKS. *Tr. & Cr.* I. iii. 207 The Ramme that batters downe the wall, For the great swing and rudenesse of his poize, They place before his hand that made the Engine. **1638** R. BAKER tr. *Balzac's Lett.* (vol. II) 40 There are even beastes of so generous a disposition, that it would be rudenesse to carry a hard hand over them. **1682** NORRIS *Hierocles* 70 Not to doe it with violence and rudeness, but to follow the truth with mildness. **1704** *Pennsylv. Hist. Soc. Mem.* IX. 318 A difference arose, that ended with some rudeness.

†**b.** Austerity, severity, rigour, violence. *Obs.*

1649 JER. TAYLOR *Gt. Exemp.* I. Disc. iv. 120 John the Baptist..did violence to himself,..the rudenesses of Camels hair and the lowest nutriment of Flyes, were instances of that violence. **1664** EVELYN *Kal. Hort.* (1729) 224 The not observing of this, destroys more Plants than all the rudenesses of the season. **1665** BOYLE *Occas. Refl.* (1848) 59 The Gardener do's..secure the Tree from being blown down, or torn, by the rudeness of boisterous Winds.

c. A rough or violent act. *rare.*

1691–2 WOOD *Life* 14 Jan., Many rudenesses and rogueries committed by them. **1790** G. WALKER *Serm.* II. 99 Many an impotent encounter with the rudenesses and selfishness and cruelty of undisciplined passion.

4. Lack of civility or courtesy; bad manners.

c **1532** DU WES *Introd. Fr.* in *Palsgr.* 1035 The rudenesse that I yvel manerd have used toward your hyghnesse. **1566** PAINTER *Pal. Pleas.* (1569) I. 445 He prayed him not to take it in ill parte the rudinesse of his servauntes. **1601** SHAKS. *Twel. N.* I. v. 230 The rudenesse that hath appear'd in mee, haue I learn'd from my entertainment. **1634** MILTON *Comus* 178, I should be loath To meet the rudenesse, and swill'd insolence Of such late Wassailers. *a* **1691** BOYLE *Christian Virtuoso* Wks. 1774 V. 509 The seeming rudeness of the angel to St. Peter, when he struck him on the side, and hastily rouzed him. **1741** WATTS *Improv. Mind* (1801) 101 It is a piece of rudeness to interrupt another in his speech. **1778** MISS BURNEY *Evelina* lxxxi, The rudeness of his manner..springs from the same cause. **1822** LAMB *Elia* I. *Modern Gallantry*, A pattern of true politeness to a wife—of cold contempt, or rudeness, to a sister. **1875** JOWETT *Plato* (ed. 2) IV. 290, I hope..that I am not betrayed into rudeness by my love of conversation.

b. An instance of this.

1699 BENTLEY *Phal.* Pref. p. lxxviii, There's one Rudeness, that I ought not to omit; because it falls upon others, as much as my self. **1718** *Free-thinker* No. 61. 39 Contradiction of every Kind is a Rudeness. **1754** *World* No. 95 III. 223 This particular way of thinking very frequently subjects me to little rudenesses and affronts.

5. Roughness of style or workmanship.

c **1555** *Sloane MS. 261* fol. 3, I doubtede whether the rudenes of the worke weare not a..sclaunder to the authour. **1612** MONNIEPENNIE *Abr. Chron.* in *Misc. Scot.* I. 3 The plainnesse and rudenesse of my stile. **1636** *Recorde's Gr. Arts* Pref. A 3, I had rather..vtter the rudenesse of my translation, then to defraud them the benefit of so good a lesson. **1756** BURKE *Subl. & B.* Wks. 1842 I. 44 The rudeness of the work increases this cause of grandeur, as it excludes the idea of art and contrivance. **1783** BLAIR *Lect.* xliii. (1812) III. 225 It has certainly softened some of his rudenesses. **1838** THACKERAY *Strictures on Pictures* Wks. 1900 XIII. 264 This picture is executed with the utmost simplicity, and almost rudeness. **1872** R. F. BURTON *Zanzibar* I. 97 The windows are loop-holes, and the doors are miracles of rudeness.

6. Unfinished, imperfect, or primitive state; roughness, ruggedness.

1645 USSHER *Body Div.* (1647) 99 It seemeth that the rudenesse was in the earth onely; containing the water and the dry land. **1710** STEELE *Tatler* No. 179 ¶10 Two Grotto's, set off with all the pleasing Rudeness of Shells and Moss. **1769** E. BANCROFT *Guiana* 24 Nature sports in primæval rudeness. **1793** *Trans. Soc. Arts* V. 12 So much land may be truly said to have been made for ever, out of a mass of rudeness, which yielded no profit to its owner.

rudent, *a.* *Arch.* = next.

1697 EVELYN *Acc. Archit.* Misc. Writ. (1825) 408 This column is fluted..to about a third part downward, where they are convexly staved, and thence nam'd *radiant*, by some *rudent*, tho' of old we find them fluted the whole length.

rudented, *pa. pple.* *Arch.* [ad. F. *rudenté*, f. L. *rudent-*, *rudens* rope.] (See quots.)

1723 CHAMBERS tr. *Le Clerc's Treat. Arch.* I. 73 Their Flutings must be rudented, or cabled..as far as one third of their height; that is they must be filled up in part to that height, with..Rudentures. **1728** —— *Cycl.* s.v. *Column*, Cabled, or Rudented Column, is a Column having Projectures in form of Cables, or Canes, in the Naked of the Shaft [etc.].

rudenture. *Arch.* [a. F. *rudenture* (16th c.): cf. prec.] (See quots.)

There is no evidence that this or the two prec. words have ever been in actual English use.

1723 CHAMBERS tr. *Le Clerc's Treat. Arch.* I. 73 By a Rudenture we mean the Figure of a Rope or Staff cut, on some occasions, in the Flutings, to strengthen their sides. **1728** —— *Cycl., Rudenture*,..the Figure of a Rope or Staff, sometimes plain sometimes carv'd, wherewith a third Part of the Flutings of Columns are frequently filled up. [Hence in various later Dicts.]

‖**'rudera.** *Obs.* [a. L. *rūdera*, pl. of *rūdus* broken stone.] Fragments or ruins of a building.

1662 RAY *Three Itin.* (1738) III. 181 By the testimony of an ancient people thereabouts who have seen the vestigia and rudera of the walls. **1737** G. SMITH *Curious Relat.* I. iii. 402 None can equal the Rudera's of that once most magnificent Bridge which the Emperor Trajan caused to be built over the Danube. **1798** *Brit. Critic* XI. 226 The author's reasons for asserting.., though it does not appear in the rudera, that chimneys were common in the Roman houses.

Hence **'ruderal** *a.* [mod.L. *rūderālis*], *Bot.*, growing on or among stone-rubbish; peculiar to rubbish-heaps; also as *sb.*, a ruderal plant. **'ruderary** *a.* [late L. *rūderārius*], pertaining to rubbish. **'ruderate** *v.* [L. *rūderāre*], **rude'ration** [L. *rūderātio*], (see quots.). †**'ruderous** *a.*, abounding in rubbish.

1858 MAYNE *Expos. Lex.* s.v., *Ruderalis*,..which grows in rubbish and by walls..: *ruderal. **1878** HOOKER & BALL *Morocco* 144 What may be termed the ruderal vegetation throughout the Mediterranean region. **1905** F. E. CLEMENTS *Research Methods Ecol.* iv. 263 The pioneers in impoverished or exhausted fields are uniformly ruderal plants. **1929** J. W. BEWS *World's Grasses* vi. 226 Most of the species of *Digitaria* tend to become ruderals. **1963** *New Scientist* 20 June 677/2 The more permanent colonisers [on Lake Kariba, East Africa] appear to fall into two groups, those of semi-aquatic habitats,..and ruderals of open ground. **1970** *Watsonia* VIII. 175 Weeds or ruderal plants. **1979** *Nature* 20–27 Dec. 780/2 An ecological classification of plants into competitors, stress-tolerators and ruderals. **1727** BAILEY (vol. II), **Ruderary*, belonging to Rubbish. [Hence in later Dicts.] **1623** COCKERAM, **Ruderate*, to cast on rubble. **1823** P. NICHOLSON *Pract. Build.* 592 Ruderated; in paving, &c. laid with pebbles or little stones. **1730** BAILEY (folio), **Ruderation*, the laying of a Pavement with Pebbles or little Stones. **1813** FORSYTH *Rem. Italy* 142 Their successors..in some parts omitted the ruderation, in others the statumen, in others both. **1842** GWILT *Encycl. Arch.* Gloss., *Ruderation*,..a method of laying pavements, mentioned by Vitruvius, and according to some, of building walls with rough pebbles and mortar. **1657** TOMLINSON *Renou's Disp.* 318 All Horehound delights in *ruderous places.

†**'ruders** (also **rudders**), Anglicized form of RUDERA.

1608 TOPSELL *Serpents* (1658) 638 These..keep their trade of Honey-making in old trees, caves, holes, and in the ruders, and rubbish of old walls and houses. **1695** KENNETT *Par. Antiq.* iii. 8 A..watch-tower, the ruines or rudders whereof still appear in a plat of Meadow ground.

rudery ('ruːdərɪ). [f. RUDE *a.* and *adv.* + -ERY.] Rudeness; rude or impolite speech or behaviour; a rude remark, comment, practical joke, etc.

1932 R. ACKLAND *Strange Orchestra* II. 71 Just been having a bit of rudery, dear. **1933** DYLAN THOMAS *Let.* 25 Dec. (1966) 77, I have..been averse to including such obvious rudery in my letters to you. **1940** 'N. BLAKE' *Malice in Wonderland* II. xvi. 235 What's this? Some new rudery taken place? **1960** S. W. C. PACK *Admiral Lord Anson* i. 3 Although a superficial courtesy existed, coarseness and rudery were common. **1968** *Blackw. Mag.* CCCIII. 454/1 The lane twisted and turned, and small Sikh boys kept pace with us, their long hair tied in top-knots, chanting songs in Punjabi which I trust were not ruderies. **1979** J. SMYTH *Milestones* xviii. 230 Then suddenly he would uncoil, spring to the despatch box and reply pungently to some rudery which had appeared to float over his head.

rudesby ('ruːdzbɪ). Now *arch.* Also 7 **-bey.** [f. RUDE *a.*: see -BY 2.] An insolent, unmannerly, or disorderly fellow.

1566 DRANT *Horace, Sat.* II. i. F ij, A rudesbie, and vnruly ..man. **1567** —— *Ep.* II. i. G vj, To bearebaytinges or pricke playings our Rudesbies must awaye. **1581** G. PETTIE tr. *Guazzo's Civ. Conv.* II. (1586) 77b, As he which is ceremonious may be thought to be a dissembler, so he which is not so, may be taken to be a clowne, a rudesby, or a contemner of others. **1601** BP. W. BARLOW *Defence* 89 Those jangling rudesbies, titular Doctors in S. Paules time. **1820** SCOTT *Monast.* xv, Commoved by the speech of this rudesby. **1882** G. MACDONALD *Castle Warlock* I. xviii. 289 The rudesby was too old to be served as he had served the schoolmaster!

Rudesheimer ('ruːdəsˌhaɪmə(r)). Also *erron.* **Ruders-**, **Rhudes-.** [ad. G. *Rüdesheimer* (sc. *wein*), f. *Rüdesheim*: see def.] A fine white wine produced at Rüdesheim on the Rhine.

1797 *Encycl. Brit.* (ed. 3) XVI. 548/1, I should prefer the worst Burgundy..to any Rudesheimer I met with. **1829** SCOTT *Anne of G.* xxiii, I drink..in a cup of Rudersheimer, to the continuance of her sagacity. **1843** *Penny Cycl.* XXVII. 456/2 The differences between the Johannisberger and Rudesheimer wines. **1862** MISS BRADDON *Lady Audley* xxxix, Pleasant little dinners, that were washed down with sparkling Moselle and Rhudesheimer.

†**'rudeship.** *Obs. rare.* [f. RUDE *a.* + -SHIP.] Roughness, ungentleness.

c **1430** *Pilgr. Lyf Manhode* I. xv. (1869) 10 Of to gret rudeship mys befalleth,..rudeshipe mihte hurte more than the oynement shulde helpe.

rudesmas, -mess: see ROOD *sb.* 6.

†**rudesse.** *Obs.* [a. OF. *rudesse*, f. *rude* RUDE *a.*] = RUDENESS, in various senses.

1471 CAXTON *Recuyell* (Sommer) I. 188 En entencion to auenge hym..of that rudesse. **1490** —— *Eneydos* xlvii. 139 They that were without, assailled strongly, & by grete rudesse. *c* **1500** *Melusine* 28 Hit commeth to you of grette pryde or of grette rudesse for to passe byfore ony ladyes without spekyng or somme salutacion.

rudge, dial. var. RIDGE *sb.*, ROODGE *v.*

rudget, dial. var. *ridge-with*, RIDGE *sb.*¹ 8.

†**rudge-wash(ed):** see quots. and RIDGE *sb.*¹

1593 *Act 35 Eliz.* c. 10 A Rudge Wash Kersie, that is to say, being made of Fleece Wooll washed only on the Sheeps back. [**1607** COWELL *Interpreter, Rudge-washed Kersey* i. made of fleece-wool washed onely on the sheepes backe. Hence in later Dicts.]

rudi, obs. form of RUDDY.

†**'rudicle.** *Obs.*⁻¹ [ad. L. *rudicula.*] A wooden spoon, a spatula.

1657 TOMLINSON *Renou's Disp.* 531 They expose the pot to the Sun.., agitating the mixture with a rudicle.

Rudie ('ruːdɪ). *Jamaica.* Also **rudie.** [f. RUDE *a.* and *adv.* + -IE.] = *rude boy* s.v. RUDE *a.* 15.

1967 *Caribbean Q.* Sept. 41 The number of rudie tunes on the air-waves reflects the increased status accorded Rudies by this other Afro-Jamaican society. **1974** *Howard Jrnl.* XIV. 48 This theme is a strong one in West Indian culture and is reinforced by the image of the rudie in Reggae—the super cool hooligan who always come[s] out on top. **1976** *Daily Mirror* 2 Apr. 21/2 Unemployment was, and is, constantly high, with the Rudies being the main sufferers. Their problems became a theme of ska. **1977** *Westindian World* 3–9 June 13/4 'Steppin Razor'..is a little reminiscent of the rudie tunes of the sixties.

rudiment ('ruːdɪmənt), *sb.* [ad. L. *rudīmentum* beginning, first principle, etc., f. *rudis* imperfect, RUDE *a.* So F. *rudiment* (16th c.).]

1. a. *pl.* The first principles or elements of a subject; those points which are first taught to, or acquired by, one commencing the study or practice of a branch of knowledge, art, etc.

1548 UDALL, etc. *Erasm. Par. Matt.* vii. 50 They shoulde by suche maner (as a manne would say) of shadowes and rudimentes, be by litle and litle enstructed to those thinges that belonge vnto true godlynes. *c* **1590** MARLOWE *Faustus* i, First I'll instruct thee in the rudiments, And then wilt thou be perfecter than I. **1612** WOODALL *Surg. Mate* Wks. (1653) 2 When they had received their first rudiments from you as Apprentices. *a* **1680** BUTLER *Rem.* (1759) I. 150 From these first Rudiments he grew To nobler Feats. **1727** SWIFT *Hist. Vanbrugh's House*, From such deep Rudiments as these, V-- is become by due degrees For Building fam'd. **1824–8** LANDOR *Imag. Conv.* Wks. 1846 I. 469 We should at least be taught our rudiments before a hard lesson is put into our hands.

b. Const. *of* (the thing to be learned).

a 1548 HALL *Chron., Edw. IV*, 34 b, Chyldren whyche bee there.. taught the rudimentes and rules of Grammer. 1548 UDALL, etc. *Erasm. Par. Acts* ii. 13 Teache them that muste be christened the rudimentes and first beginninges of the gospell. 1600 SHAKS. *A.Y.L.* v. iv. 31 This Boy.. hath bin tutor'd in the rudiments Of many desperate studies. 1638 SIR T. HERBERT *Trav.* (ed. 2) 22 Necessity has taught them some parts of the rudiments of Arithmetick. 1726 SWIFT *Gulliver* I. vi, At which Time they are supposed to have some Rudiments of Docility. 1772 PRIESTLEY *Inst. Relig.* (1782) I. 143 Here we acquire.. rudiments of knowledge. 1841 YOUNG *Math. Diss.* Pref. p. xii, This class of equations will hereafter be admitted even among the rudiments of algebraic science. 1880 L. STEPHEN *Pope* i. 4 He picked up some rudiments of learning from the family priest.

transf. 1751 JOHNSON *Rambler* No. 114 ¶14 If those.. had been detected in their rudiments of robbery.

c. *sing.* A first principle; an initial step or stage, etc. Somewhat *rare*.

1548 UDALL, etc. *Erasm. Par. Luke* ix. 95 This was the first rudimente and entreaunce of the Apostles preachyng. 1579 W. FULKE *Heskins' Parl.* 9 The law.. of leauing the old bird ..was a good rudiment to teach them to abhor.. couetousnes. 1615 CROOKE *Body of Man* 31 The Veynes of the Mesentary giue the blood a kinde of rudiment or initiation. 1811 JEFFERSON *Writ.* (1830) IV. 160 The political rudiment of the young, and manual of our older citizens.

d. Pl. (With capital initial.) The name of the lowest class in certain Roman Catholic schools and colleges, freq. divided into the 'third', 'second', and 'first' class (of) Rudiments. Cf. FIGURE *sb.* 22 b.

1716 [see FIGURE *sb.* 22 b]. a 1799 in C. Butler *Acct. Life Alban Butler* (1799) 6 The year after Mr. Alban Butler's arrival at Douay, I was placed in the same school, under the same master, he being in the first class of rudiments, as it is there called, and I in the lowest. 1846 in *Stonyhurst Mag.* (1933) Dec. 415/2 July 25th Sun. Themes judged Rhet... 29th. Themes judged Rudiments. 1885 J. GILLOW *Lit. & Biogr. Hist. Eng. Catholics* II. 553 At the period of his liberation Robert Gradwell was in second-class Rudiments. 1893 B. WARD *Hist. St. Edmund's Coll.* iv. 58 The two classes of 'Figures' were changed very shortly after this into three classes of 'Rudiments', and this term has survived at St. Edmund's to the present day. 1912 B. WARD *Eve Catholic Emanc.* III. xxxiv. 2 He was a boy in the 'Second of Rudiments' [*Note*] Equivalent to the Second or Third form at an English school. 1936 M. TRAPPES-LOMAX *Bishop Challoner* i. 5 The 'classes', or forms, were named Figures or Rudiments, Grammar, Syntax, Poetry, and Rhetoric, names which originally were related to the work of the class... This nomenclature is still retained in some of the English Catholic schools. 1972 *Publ. Catholic Rec. Soc.* LXIII. 142 The vast majority of students began their course.. in one or other of the Rudiments classes.

2. a. *pl.* The imperfect beginnings of some (material or immaterial) thing; those parts which are the foundation of later growth or development.

1566 PAINTER *Pal. Pleas.* I. 78 The same bloude.. is readie to nourish the rudimentes of lyfe and lighte. 1603 HOLLAND *Plutarch's Mor.* 219 Certeine raw and unperfect rudiments ..of good and kinde fruits. 1664 EVELYN *Sylva* (1679) 4 To raise Trees for Timber.. from their Seeds and first Rudiments. 1710 STEELE *Tatler* No. 189 ¶1 The first Rudiments of Thought which they shew in their Letters. 1766 BLACKSTONE *Comm.* II. 9 It was calculated merely for the rudiments of civil society. 1777 PRIESTLEY *Matt. & Spir.* (1782) I. xxii. 282 Brutes have the rudiments of all our faculties. 1839 MURCHISON *Silur. Syst.* I. xxvii. 349 This fault has produced only the rudiments, if I may so speak, of a transverse valley. 1871 DARWIN *Desc. Man* I. i. 18 Rudiments, however, may occur in one sex, of parts normally present in the other sex.

b. *sing.* A beginning; an initial or imperfect form or stage.

1626 BACON *Sylva* §316 This [maturation of fruits] is effected.. by a Rudiment of putrefaction. 1625 K. LONG tr. *Barclay's Argenis* II. xx. 135 Care must be had, that these warres against Lycogenes, be.. a rudiment against Radirobanes. 1778 [W. H. MARSHALL] *Minutes Agric., Observ.* 120, I found a Copper Tunnel,.. which I was told was the Rudiment of a Rain-Gage. 1796 WITHERING *Brit. Pl.* (ed. 3) I. 146 The rudiment of a third floret standing upon a little fruit-stalk betwixt the other two florets. 1859 DARWIN *Orig. Spec.* v. (1860) 148 The whole anterior part of the head is reduced to the merest rudiment. 1880 HAUGHTON *Phys. Geogr.* vi. 282 Several species have been found.. with a rudiment of a thumb.

3. ***rudiments of the world***, in renderings or echoes of Biblical passages.

The Gr. original has τὰ στοιχεῖα τοῦ κόσμου, the Vulgate *elementa mundi*.

1557 N.T. (Genev.) *Gal.* iv. 3 We, as longe as we were children, were in bondage vnder the rudiments of the worlde. 1577 VAUTROULLIER *Luther on Ep. Gal.* 180 Paule .. speaketh here euen of the law of God, which he calleth the elements or rudiments of the world. [1628 PRYNNE *Love-lockes* 35 God commands us.. not to subiect our selues to the Rudiments, Lusts, and Ordinances of Carnall, or Worldly men.] 1665 BUNYAN *Holy Citie* 176 Not every babbling fellow, nor those that look for their abilities from the rudiments of the world. 1881 BIBLE *Gal.* iv. 3.

Hence **'rudiment** *v.*, to initiate. *rare*⁻¹.

1654 GAYTON *Pleas. Notes* II. ii. 37 It is the right discipline of Knight-Errantry, to be rudimented in losses at first.

rudimental (ru:dɪ'mɛntəl), *a.* [f. RUDIMENT *sb.* + -AL¹.] = next.

1597 MORLEY *Introd. Music* Annot. ¶1 b, Musicke is diuided into two parts, the first may be called Elementarie or rudimental, teaching to know the quality and quantity of notes. 1647 COTTON *Singing of Psalms* v. 23 It appeareth.. that there was something typicall or rudimentall in the manner of singing some of the Psalmes. 1664 POWER *Exp. Philos.* I. 60 If you take Nature at the rise and critically observe her in her rudimental and obscure beginning. 1688 HOLME *Armoury* III. 296/1 He that would discern the Rudimental stroak of a Plant.. may behold it [etc.]. 1711–4 *Spectator* (J.), Your first rudimental essays in spectatorship were made in my shop, where you often practised for hours. 1833 CHALMERS *Const. of Man* (1835) I. ii. 140 In this rudimental and incipient stage of human existence. 1847 J. WILSON *Lands of Bible* I. i. 24 In some of the animals.. we noticed a rudimental tendency to a dewlap. 1871 DARWIN *Desc. Man* II. xii. (1890) 354 The throat pouch.. is present in the female, though in a rudimental condition.

rudimentary (ru:dɪ'mɛntərɪ), *a.* [f. RUDIMENT *sb.* + -ARY¹. Cf. F. *rudimentaire*.]

1. Pertaining to, connected with, the rudiments of knowledge.

1839 HALLAM *Hist. Lit.* II. i. 35 They.. put the rudimentary study of the languages on a better footing. 1865 MAFFEI *Brigand Life* II. 47 To declare publicly that it was not necessary to provide rudimentary instruction.

2. Of the nature of a rudiment; undeveloped, immature, imperfect; esp. **a.** Of organic structures.

1840 E. WILSON *Anat. Vade M.* 9 At its middle is a rudimentary spinous process. 1851 RICHARDSON *Geol.* viii. 217 The digestive organs have an intestine and rudimentary gland. 1873 MIVART *Elem. Anat.* vi. 216 The 'perforated' transverse processes of man's cervical vertebræ consist, in part, of rudimentary ribs.

b. Of immaterial things.

1846 GROTE *Greece* I. xx. II. 107 A scene in harmony with the rudimentary political fabric just described. 1865 TYLOR *Early Hist. Man.* iv. 75 A rudimentary form of word language. 1884 F. TEMPLE *Relat. Relig. & Sci.* ii. (1885) 59 To live by duty is in itself rudimentary religion.

c. Of states or conditions.

1851 WOODWARD *Mollusca* I. 25 In the attached bivalves it .. exists only in a rudimentary state. 1861 BENTLEY *Man. Bot.* 417 The embryo.. contains within itself in a rudimentary condition all the essential organs of a plant. 1880 *19th Cent.* Apr. 617 Reducing to a rudimentary condition the eyes of.. fish and crustacea.

Hence **rudi'mentariness**.

1899 W. JAMES *Talks to Teachers* (1904) 233 No modern person ought to be willing to live a day in such a state of rudimentariness and denudation.

rudish ('ru:dɪʃ), *a.* [f. RUDE *a.* + -ISH.] Somewhat rude.

1774 FOOTE *Cozeners* III. ii, For man and wife to quarrel before folks is rather rudish, I own. 1822 *Blackw. Mag.* XI. 163 For most are but rudish. 1881 CARLYLE *Remin.* II. 158 Nothing but rudish hands, rude though kind enough, being about.

rudist ('ru:dɪst). Also **Rudista**. [a. mod.L. family name *Rudista* (J. E. Gray in *Synopsis Contents Brit. Mus.* (ed. 21, 1823) 62), f. L. *rudis* unformed + *-t-* + -A 4.] A fossil pelecypod bivalve mollusc belonging to the superfamily Rudistacea, which included cone-shaped reef-forming animals. Also *attrib.* Also **Ru-, ru'distid** [-ID³], in the same sense.

1889 NICHOLSON & LYDEKKER *Man. Palæont.* (ed. 3) I. xxxvi. 734 The *Rudistæ* are.. entirely extinct. 1890 *Mem. Boston Soc. Nat. Hist.* IV. 322/1 The Rudistæ are conical or cup-shaped Pelecypods with a superficially marked radial symmetry. 1935 TWENHOFEL & SHROCK *Invertebr. Paleontol.* ix. 403 The various Rudistids are especially noteworthy. 1959 *New Scientist* 1 Jan. 16/1 A good collection of fossil reef-forming corals, rudistids, and related atoll fauna. 1969 BENNISON & WRIGHT *Geol. Hist. Brit. Isles* xiv. 332 The coral-like Rudists are important, forming reef environments in Tethys. 1978 *Nature* 26 Oct. 779/2 Future editions could be improved by the inclusion of a few famous foreign examples such as the Burgess Shale fauna and a rudist reef association.

rudite ('ru:daɪt). *Geol.* Also **rudyte**. [f. L. *rūd-us* broken stone, rubble + -ITE¹.] Any consolidated breccia or conglomerate consisting of particles larger than sand grains; = PSEPHITE.

1904 A. W. GRABAU in *Amer. Geologist* XXXIII. 242 The consolidated rock whether conglomerate or breccia may be called a rudyte. 1920 —— *Gen. Geol.* xviii. 569 Three textural types of rock may be recognized: (1) the rubble-rock or rubble-stone, or rudyte, which when the fragments are rounded is a conglomerate and when angular a breccia; (2) the sand-rock or sandstone or arenyte; and (3) the mud-rock or mud-stone or lutyte. 1935 *Bull. Nat. Res. Council* (U.S.) XCVIII. 239 Rudite. This is a general term.. for fragmental sedimentary rocks coarser than sand grains. 1959 W. W. MOORHOUSE *Study of Rocks in Thin Section* xviii. 334 The clastic sediments are classified according to size as rudytes (rudaceous), which are conglomerates, arenytes (arenaceous).. and lutytes (lutaceous). 1966 B. SIMPSON *Rocks & Minerals* xvii. 174 The quartz-rich rudites are quartz conglomerates and quartz breccias. 1971 I. G. GASS et al. *Understanding Earth* i. 31/1 The rudites are represented by such rock types as conglomerate.

† **'rudity**. *Obs. rare.* [ad. obs. F. *rudité* or late L. *ruditas*: see RUDE *a.* and -ITY.] Rudeness.

1592 NASHE *Four Lett. Confut.* Wks. (Grosart) II. 236 Yea, rather than faile, Maister Bird shall.. meeter it mischieuously in maintenance of their scurrilitish and ruditie. 1609 T. BELL *Dial. Theoph. & Remigius* 51 Such things as he had reserued by reason of their rudity and imperfection in conceiuing heauenly doctrine.

rudle, obs. and dial. f. RUDDLE *sb.*

rudli(che, etc., obs. forms of RUDELY.

rudnin, -nyng: see RUDDEN *v.*

rudock, obs. form of RUDDOCK.

Rudolphine (ru:'dɒlfaɪn), *a.* [f. the name *Rudolph* (see def.) + -INE¹.] ***Rudolphine tables (numbers)***, a series of astronomical calculations published by Kepler in 1627 and named after his patron the Emperor Rudolph II.

1656 tr. *Hobbes' Elem. Philos.* (1839) 292 The strait line.. is found.. to be somewhat greater than that which is exhibited by the Rudolphine numbers. 1728 CHAMBERS *Cycl.* s.v. *Table*, And Kepler, likewise,.. in 1627, publish'd the Rudolphine Tables, which are now much esteem'd. 1761 *Ann. Reg.* 192 The imperfect state of the Rudolphine tables was the cause that the transit was expected in 1631. 1839 *Penny Cycl.* XIII. 201/1. 1882 *Encycl. Brit.* XIV. 47/2.

† **'rudstay**. *Obs.*⁻¹ [? for *rudge-stay*, f. *rudge* RIDGE *sb.*¹] (See quot.)

1688 HOLME *Armoury* III. xviii. (Roxb.) 139/1 The thill hookes, to this is fastned the rudstay which goes ouer the horse back.

rudyr, obs. form of RUDDER *sb.*

rue (ru:), *sb.*¹ Chiefly *dial.* or *arch.* Forms: 1 **hreow**, 3 **reowe**, 4–6 **rewe**, 5–6 *Sc.* **rew**, 7– **rue**. [OE. *hréow*, = Fris. *rou*, MDu. *rou(w)*, *rouwe*, *rauwe* (Du. *rouw*), MLG. *rouwe*, *ruwe* (LG. *rou*, *rau*, *ro*, etc.), OHG. *(h)riuwa* (MHG. *riuwe*, G. *reue*), related to OE. *hréowan* RUE *v.*¹]

1. a. Sorrow, distress; repentance; regret.

Beowulf 2130 þæt wæs Hroðgare hreowa tornost. c 897 K. ÆLFRED *Gregory's Past. C.* liii. 415 Ðæt beswicene mod.. wyrð.. amierred from ðære incundan hreowe. a 900 CYNEWULF *Christ* 1674 Eart nu tidfara to þam halᵹan ham þær næfre hreow cymeð. 971 *Blickl. Hom.* 35 Don we urum Drihtne soþe hreowe & bote. c 1400 *Song Roland* 555 He may walk homward with hert-rew. c 1440 *Partonope* 3052** Allas he thought I am but rewe To hur that is my soverayne lady. 1581 *Satir. Poems Reform.* xliii. 211 Of rasche decreitis cums rew and may not mend it. 1628 WITHER *Brit. Rememb.* II. 1142 His Physicke must be Rue (ev'n Rue for Sinne). 1848 LONGSTREET *Georgia Scenes* 29 I'm a man that, when he makes a bad trade, makes the most of it... I'm for no rues and after-claps. 1893 LESLIE KEITH *'Lisbeth* xxii, The heart's rue for that which it had scarce possessed, and yet had lost. 1896 HOUSMAN *Shropshire Lad* liv, With rue my heart is laden For golden friends I had. 1959 *Listener* 31 Dec. 1174/2 The nature and the mixture of the ingredients in the poetry—nostalgia, bathos, irony, rue, and religious fervour. 1976 *Publishers Weekly* 8 Mar. 64/2 A mix of rue and wit that is vintage [Mort] Sahl.

b. *Sc.* In phr. ***to take the rue***, to repent.

1789 *Shepherd's Wedding* 10 (E.D.D.), I own, indeed, I've ta'en the rue, My mind is fairly alter'd. 1816 SCOTT *Old Mort.* xxviii, Tam Halliday took the rue, and tauld me a' about it. 18.. in Nimmo *Songs Clydesdale* (1882) 145 She wanted him to break the marriage, for she had ta'en the rue.

2. Pity, compassion.

a 1250 *Owl & Night.* 1445 Ne mai ich for reowe lete,.. þat ich of murᵹþe him ne singe. c 1300 *Beket* 1051 Nou God beo this holi manes help, for he hadde ther lute Rewe.

1867 JEAN INGELOW *Story of Doom* v. 102, I was good—Had rue on thee a tender sucking child. 1900 ELLIS *Rom. Rose* I. 12 Till every eye that saw her grew Bedewed with tears of pitying rue.

rue (ru:), *sb.*² Forms: 4–5 **ruwe**, 5–6 **rewe**, 5–7 **rew**, 6 *Sc.* **reu**; 4– **rue** (5 **rwe**). [a. F. *rue*, for earlier *rude* (cf. OE. *rúde*), = Prov., Sp., Pg. *ruda*, It. *ruta*:—L. *rūta*, ad. Gr. ῥυτή, orig. a Peloponnesian word.]

1. A perennial evergreen shrub of the genus *Ruta*, esp. *Ruta graveolens*, having bitter, strong-scented leaves which were formerly much used for medicinal purposes.

α. 1382 WYCLIF *Luke* xi. 42 Woo to ȝou, Pharisees, that tythen mynte, and ruwe. a 1400 *Pistill of Susan* 112 With Ruwe and Rubarbe, Ragget ariht. c 1440 *Promp. Parv.* 438/2 Ruwe, herbe, *ruta*.

β. a 1400 *Stockholm Med. MS.* ii. 846 in *Anglia* XVIII. 328 Rewe bitter, a worthy gres, Mekyl of myth & vertu is. c 1450 *M.E. Med. Bk.* (Heinrich) 198 Tak & grynde fenel & rewe, & boyle hem in water. 1533 ELYOT *Cast. Helthe* (1539) 21 Two drye huttes, as many fygges, and .xx. leaues of Rewe. 1570 *Satir. Poems Reform.* xv. 25 Cum, Nettillis, thornie breiris, & rew, With all foull filthie weid. 1617 *Salerne's Regiment* 46 From Garlicke, Nuttes, Hearb-grace, or Rew.

γ. c 1400 *Lanfranc's Cirurg.* 104 Anoynte his nolle & his necke wiþ.. oile of rue. c 1450 METHAM *Wks.* 49 Modyrwort, rwe, red malwys. 1562 TURNER *Herbal* II. (1568) 123 The iuice of Rue.. is good for the ake of the eares. 1578 LYTE *Dodoens* 260 There be two sortes of Rue, that is garden Rue, and wilde Rue. 1608 SYLVESTER *Du Bartas* II. iv. *Decay* 425 As one same ground indifferently doth breed ..The fragrant Rose, and the strong-senting Rue. 1667 MILTON *P.L.* XI. 414 Then purg'd with Euphrasie and Rue The visual Nerve, for he had much to see. 1712 tr. *Pomet's Hist. Drugs* I. 189 A Shrub whose Leaves have a great resemblance to those of Rue. 1789 MRS. PIOZZI *Journ. France* I. 417, I perceived all the company.. stop their noses with rue. 1813 SCOTT *Rokeby* v. xiii, When villagers my shroud bestrew With pansies, rosemary, and rue. 1846 LINDLEY *Veget. Kingd.* 470 Common Rue, and another species, are said to be emmenagogue, anthelmintic, and sudorific. 1875 H. C. WOOD *Therap.* (1879) 537 The influence of rue upon the system is similar to, but less decided than that of savine.

fig. 1830 SCOTT *Demonol.* vi. 186 Persons who, upon this subject, purged their eyes with rue and euphrasie. 1862 WHITTIER *Waiting* v, For one shall.. drink life's rue, and one its wine.

b. With punning allusion to RUE *sb.*¹

1500–20 DUNBAR *Poems* lxiv. 10 Leif nor flour fynd could I nane of rew. 1583 GREENE *Mamillia* II. Wks. (Grosart) II. 297 Least time and triall make thee account Rue a most bitter hearbe. 1606 J. DAVIES (Heref.) *Select Sec. Husband*

Wks. (Grosart) II. 8/1 So shalt thou But beare thine own Harts-ease, and neuer Rue. **1721** Kelly *Scot. Prov.* 284 Rue in Thyme should be a Maiden's Posie. **1825** Waterton *Wand. S. Amer.* III. 238 They did all in their power to procure balm for me instead of rue. But it would not answer.

2. a. With qualifying word prefixed, applied to various plants:

Aleppo rue, a species of *Ruta*. **black rue** (see quot.). **dog's rue**, figwort, *Scrophularia*. **goat's rue** (see goat 4 c). **meadow rue** (see meadow *sb.* 4 c). **Syrian rue** (see Syrian *a.*). Also wall-rue.

1731 Miller *Gard. Dict.* s.v. *Ruta*, The two Aleppo Rues and the Wild Rue are somewhat tenderer than the common Sort. *Ibid.* s.v. *Scrophularia*, Figwort, commonly called Dogs Rue. **1874** *Treas. Bot.* Suppl. s.v., Rue, Black (N. Zeal.), *Podocarpus spicata*.

b. With *pl.* A species of rue.

1731 Miller *Gard. Dict.* s.v. *Thalictrum*, Some Botanists have classed this Plant with Rues. **1753** *Chambers' Cycl.* Suppl. s.v. *Ruta*, The rues would seem to belong properly to the plants, with cruciform not rosaceous flowers. **1842** *Penny Cycl.* XXIV. 278/1 Herbs which have .. a fetid smell like rue, and hence are called meadow rues.

3. *attrib.* and *Comb.*, as *rue-juice*, *-leaf*, *-oil*, *-water*; *rue-like* adj.

1558 Warde tr. *Alexis' Secr.* 37 Rue water, Rose water. **1617** *Salerne's Regiment* 133 Rew-water sprinckled in the house, kils all the fleas. **1681** Grew *Musæum* II. v. ii. 248 Of a russet colour, and as it were all over pounced, somewhat after the manner of a Rue-Leaf. **1725** *Fam. Dict.* s.v. *Ranunculus*, The Yellow Ranunculus, with Rue-like Flowers. **1799** G. Smith *Laboratory* II. 449 Put into very strong vinegar, verdigrise, rue-juice. **1863** Prior *Brit. Pl.* 193 Its rue-like much divided leaves. **1866** *Treas. Bot.* 807/2, *Rue oil*, a volatile stimulant oil obtained from the shoots of *Ruta graveolens*.

b. In plant-names, as **rue anemone**, an American species of *Thalictrum*; †**rue maiden-hair**, wall-rue; **rue-weed** (see quot. 1796).

1611 Cotgr., *Rue de muraille*, wall rue, Rue Maiden haire. **1796** Withering *Brit. Pl.* (ed. 3) II. 501 *Thalictrum alpinum*, Mountain Rue-weed. *T. flavum*, Meadow Rue-weed. *T. minus*, Lesser Rue-weed. **1802** Willich *Domest. Encycl.* s.v., Common Meadow-rue, Spurious Rhubarb, or Rue-weed. **1846–50** A. Wood *Class-bk. Bot.* 148 *Thalictrum anemonoides*, .. Rue Anemone. **1884** *Harper's Mag.* May 934/2 Burt now appeared with a handful of rue-anemones.

c. *rue family*, *order*, *-worts*, the natural order *Rutaceæ*.

1846 Lindley *Veget. Kingd.* 470 The Cneoreæ .. seem to be a form of this Order of Rueworts. **1849** Balfour *Man. Bot.* §827 *Rutaceæ*, the Rue Family. **1857** Henfrey *Bot.* 266 *Rutaceæ*, the Rue order. **1875** *Encycl. Brit.* III. 111/1 A sub-order of the Rutaceæ or rue family.

†**rue**, var. of (or error for) ree *sb.*², reeve *sb.*²

1696 *Phil. Trans.* XIX. 349 We have Ruff and Rue, the former being the Cock, the other the Hen.

rue, dial. variant of rew *sb.*¹

rue (ruː), *v.*¹ Forms: *Inf.* 1 hreowan, 2 reouwen, reuwe, rowe, 2–4 reowe; 2–4 rewen, 3–6 rewe (4 riewe), 4–7 rew (6 reew); 3–4 ruwe (5 ruwyn), 4 rywe; 4–5 reue, 4 reu, ru, rwe, 4– rue; also 3 *sing. pres.* 1 hriwð, 2 reouð, rieweð. *Pret.* 1 hreaw, 2–3 ræw, reu, 3 rew, rev, 4 rewe; 4 reud(e, reued, rwed, 4–6 rewed; 5–6 *Sc.* rewit, 5 ruet, ruit, rwyt, etc. [OE. *hréowan* (a strong vb. with pa. t. *hréaw*), = OFris. *riowa* (Fris. *rouwe*, *rouje*), MDu. and Du. *rouwen* (†*rauwen*, *ruwen*), OS. *hrewan*, pa. t. *hrau* (MLG. *rouwen*, *ruwen*, *ruen*, LG. *rouen*, *rauen*, *roen*, etc.), OHG. (*h*)*riuwan*, pa. t. *hrau*, *rou*, pl. *ruwun* (MHG. *riuwen*, *ruwen*, G. *reuen*), related to OE. *hréow* rue *sb.*¹ and to the adj. OE. *hréowe*, OS. *hriwi* sad, sorrowful. There are also slight traces of an OE. weak vb. *hréowian*, = OS. *hriwôn*, *hreuuôn*, OHG. (*h*)*riuwôn*. Related forms in ON. are *hryggr* (stem *hryggv-*, for earlier **hriww-*) adj., *hryggva*, *hryggja* weak vb., *hryggð* fem., sorrow.]

†**I.** *trans.* With dat. (or acc.) of the person, and usually with impersonal subject. *Obs.*

The various constructions illustrated under sense 2 occur also with senses 1, 3, and 4.

1. To affect (a person) with penitence or contrition (for sins or offences committed).

c **888** K. Ælfred *Boeth.* xxxvi. §7 Ne bið se cwuca ðonne nyttra ðe se deada, ȝif him his yfel ne hreowð. *c* **1000** in Thorpe *Laws* II. 260 Ȝif þu onȝite þæt him his synna hreowen. *c* **1200** Ormin 3976 Ȝiff .. þat he missdoþ Onn aniȝ kinne wise, Itt reoweþþ himm. *a* **1300** *Cursor M.* 28676 þis man sais .. þat him reuys his sinnes sare. *c* **1375** *Lay Folks Mass-Bk.* (MS. B) 359 Gyue me grace for to etchewe to do þat þing þat me shulde rewe.

2. To affect with regret (for some act); to make (one) wish one had acted otherwise.

c **897** K. Ælfred *Gregory's Past. C.* xxxix. 286 Ne do ðu nan wuht butan ȝeðeahte, ðonne ne hriwð hit ðe, ðonne hit ȝedon bið. *c* **1250** *Prov. Alfred A.* 111 Þe þat nule one youhþe yeorne leorny, .. þat him schal on elde sore rewe. *a* **1300** *Cursor M.* 16465 Þan him reued of his res, and went him-self [to] wrei. **1338** R. Brunne *Chron.* (1810) 237 Þe Walssh wer alle day slayn, now rewes þam þer res. *c* **1420** *Avow. Arth.* xxii, Ȝette Menealfe, or the mydnyȝte, Him ruet alle his rees. *c* **1440** *York Myst.* xiii. 36 Þe bargayne I made þare, þat rewes me nowe full sare.

b. With clause as subject, usually *me* (or *him*) *rues that*, etc.

a **1000** *Genesis* 1276 Hreaw hine swiðe, þæt he folcmæȝþa fruman aweahte. *a* **1300** *Cursor M.* 1602 Me reus þat euer made i man. *c* **1386** Chaucer *Epil. Merch. T.* 14 Me rewith sore I am unto hir teyd. *c* **1440** *York Myst.* xlviii. 8 Þerfore me rewis þat I þe worlde began.

c. With *it* as subject (also followed by *that*).

a **1200** *Moral Ode* 354 Þe ðe blisse for ðos for-lat, it him mai reuwe sore. **13..** *E.E. Allit. P.* B. 290 Sore hit me rwez þat euer I made hem my self. **1382** Wyclif *2 Cor.* vii. 8 If I made ȝou sori in a pistle, now it rewith me not. *c* **1412** Hoccleve *De Reg. Princ.* 754 It rewiþ me if I yow haue disesyd.

3. To affect with sorrow; to distress, grieve.

In some cases with approximation to sense 2 or 4.

a **900** Cynewulf *Christ* 1414 Ða mec ongon hreowan þæt min hondȝeweorc on feonda ȝeweald feran sceolde. *a* **1000** *Genesis* 819 Me nu hreowan mæȝ æfre to aldre, þæt ic þe minum eaȝum ȝeseah. *c* **1175** *Lamb. Hom.* 149 If he ne mei .. his neode ibete, þet him sare roweþ. *c* **1200** Ormin 5576 Himm reoweþþ þatt he dwelleþþ her Swa swiþe lange onn eorþe. **13..** *Sir Beues* 1220 Wel sore me reweþ þat tiding. *a* **1450** *Le Morte Arth.* 1029 Me Rewith the deth of hyr for his sake. **1548** Patten *Exped. Scotl.* B v b, It would haue rued any good huswiues heart, to haue beholden ye .. murder.

4. To affect with pity or compassion.

c **1200** Ormin 5592 Himm reoweþþ ec of alle þa þatt follȝhenn deofless lare. *c* **1320** *Cast. Loue* 540–1 Ful sore þe prisun reweþ me: For-þi he reweþ me wel þe more, For Merci euere clepeþ þin ore. *c* **1400** *Laud Troy Bk.* 3367 Alas, me rewes of Priamus. *c* **1555** Harpsfield *Divorce Hen. VIII* (Camden) 136 It pitieth and rueth every good man .. to remember the same. **1590** Spenser *F.Q.* I. ii. 21 Deare dame, your suddein overthrow Much rueth me.

II. *trans.* With personal subject.

5. To repent of (wrongdoing); to feel penitence, remorse, or contrition for (sin, etc.).

c **1200** *Trin. Coll. Hom.* 95 Armheorted is þe man þe swiðere reoweð his sinne. *a* **1300** *Cursor M.* 7965 In takening sare he reud his sake, An orisun sun can he make. *a* **1450** Myrc 2016 Ȝef þow hyt fynde no wey myȝte, Þrytty dayes þow rewe hyt ryȝte. **1596** Drayton *Legends* ii. 549 Ruing the spoile done by his fatall hand. **1628** Wither *Brit. Rememb.* 240 Nor shall I live to view Thy sorrows ended, if thou do not rue Thy sins with speed. **1771** Beattie *Minstr.* II. xiv, But now, with pangs of keen remorse, I rue Those years of trouble and debasement vile. **1813** Scott *Rokeby* I. ii, Conscience, anticipating time, Already rues the enacted crime. **1846** Keble *Lyra Innoc.* (1873) 139 Lest thou in sevenfold guilt thy heart's back-sliding rue.

6. To repent of (some act or course of action); to regret and wish undone or altered, on account of the consequences.

Frequently with implication of suffering or punishment following upon the act.

a **1300** *Cursor M.* 4138 Þat Baret rede i noght yee bru, þat yow mai euer after ru. *c* **1375** *Sc. Leg. Saints* xxvii. (*Machor*) 972 Bot he in þame ruit his teching, For .. þai na tyme for to scorne hym fane. *c* **1470** Henry *Wallace* VIII. 857 The layff raturnyt .. And rwyt full sar that euyr thai furth coud found. *a* **1548** Hall *Chron., Edw. IV*, 201 b, Whiche vnmercifull acte, the Welshemen sore ruied the next daie or night. **1611** Sir W. Mure *Misc. Poems* ii. 51 Too lait, I feir, thow rew thou did espy him. **1726** Pope *Odyss.* xix. 371 Whoe'er neglects to pay distinction due, The breach of hospitable right may rue. **1828** Scott *F.M. Perth* ii, Well, my princess .., I will teach you to rue this. **1874** Deutsch *Rem.* 248 Rome has had to rue many a too hasty step. **1885–94** R. Bridges *Eros & Psyche* May xxviii, And yet .. no sooner was alone, Than she for loneliness her promise rued.

b. Freq. in phr. *to rue it.*

a **1300** *Sarmun* xxxvii. in *E.E.P.* (1862) 5 Bot þou nelt þench her apan, .. þou salt hit rew bitter and sore. *a* **1400–50** *Alexander* (Dubl.) 1975 Remefe agayn to þi realm or þow sall it rewe. **1593** Shaks. *3 Hen. VI*, I. i. 94, I remember it to my griefe, And by his Soule, thou and thy House shall rue it. **1642** Rogers *Naaman* 160 Examine thy selfe about this now, one day thou wilt else rue it. **1795** Burke *Corr.* Wks. 1842 II. 459 Admitting .. the enormous and unpardonable magnitude of this their crime, they rued it in their persons. **1841** James *Brigand* xliii, If they hurt a hair of his head they shall rue it. **1871** B. Taylor *Faust* (1875) I. xxv. 210 If longer here thou stayest, We shall be made to dearly rue it.

c. In phr. *to rue the day*, *hour*, etc.

Differing from 7 b only by referring to some act committed by the party rueing.

1595 Shaks. *John* III. i. 325 France, thou shalt rue this houre within this houre. **1708** *Bickerstaff detected* in *Swift's Wks.* (1751) IV. 205, I am alive .. to make him rue the hour he ever affronted a man of Science and Resentment. **1782** Eliz. Blower *G. Bateman* II. 170 Ye shall rue the day ye took it. **1818** Scott *Br. Lamm.* ii, You'll rue the day that clogs me with this answer. **1881** 'Rita' *My Lady Coquette* ii, It will go hard with me if I don't make you rue the day you wrote or said it.

7. To regard or think of (an event, fact, etc.) with sorrow or regret; to wish that (something) had never taken place or existed.

1297 R. Glouc. (Rolls) 10127 So þat hii ne com nammore To þe croune of engelond, and þat was to rewe sore. **1390** Gower *Conf.* Prol. 164 To make of thilke werre an ende, Which every day now groweth newe, And that is gretly forto rewe. *c* **1430** *Hymns Virgin* (1867) 47 Oonys he bad me 'go, foule sathan!' Euere-more þat repreef y rewe. **1557** *Tottel's Misc.* (Arb.) 230 It was the day on which the sunne .. To rew Christ's death amid his course gaue place vnto ye night. **1648** J. Beaumont *Psyche* XII. cxlviii, Both Sence and Reason rue that tyranny. **1796** Burke *Regic. Peace* iii. Wks. VIII. 223 The world will have cause to rue this iniquitous measure. **1813** Scott *Rokeby* IV. xiv, Redmond now alone must rue The love he never can subdue. **1826** Hood *Last Man* xii, I promis'd myself an hour should come To make him rue his birth.

b. In phr. *to rue the day*, *hour*, etc. (Cf. 6 c.)

1593 Shaks. *3 Hen. VI*, v. vi. 43 Orphans, for their Parents timeles death, Shall rue the houre that euer thou was't borne. **1714** Gay *Sheph. Week* Thursday 5, I rue the day, a rueful day I trow, .. When Lubberkin to Town his cattle drove. **1807** J. Barlow *Columb.* IV. 389 Nor think the native tribes shall rue the day That leads our heroes o'er the watery way. **1887** Hall Caine *Son of Hagar* III. vi, Take him away, before I rue the day I saw him.

†**8.** To regard with pity or compassion; to feel sorry for (a person, etc.). *Obs.*

c **1200** *Trin. Coll. Hom.* 95 Mildheorted beð þe man þe reouð his nehgebures unselðe. **1375** Barbour *Bruce* XVI. 280, I trow thar is na man That he ne will rew a woman than. *c* **1400** *Pilgr. Sowle* (Caxton, 1483) IV. xx. 68 That ye ne reweth hym myn herte it sleeth. **1555** Phaer *Æneid* II. 43 Mine own hand shall my deth obteyn, my foo will rue my plight. **1590** Spenser *F.Q.* I. i. 51 Die is my dew; yet rew my wretched state. *c* **1611** Chapman *Iliad* XXI. 72, I kiss thy knees, divine Æacides! Respect me, and my fortunes rue.

III. *intr.* **9.** To be penitent or contrite; to feel repentance or remorse. Also const. *for.*

[*c* **950** *Lindisf. Gosp.* Mark i. 15 Hreowiȝas & ȝelefes to godspell.]

13.. *Cursor M.* 19014 (Gött.), Þair hert gan tru, And als for þair misdedis þai ru. *c* **1430** *Hymns Virgin* (1867) 69, I wole biþinke me on my werkis biforn, Do almes dede, praie, & rewe. **1500–20** Dunbar *Poems* lxxiii. 5 O wreche, be war! .. Remeid in tyme, and rew nocht all to lait. **1580** Gifford *Poems* (1870) 75 Ah! Jesus! how then my heart did rue Because I had folowed them, as true! **1768–74** Tucker *Lt. Nat.* (1834) I. 219, I shall find perpetual cause, if not to repent, at least to rue sufficiently for my misconduct. **1871** R. Ellis tr. *Catullus* xxx. 12 Hereafter again honour awakes, causeth a wretch to rue.

10. To be repentant, or full of regret and dissatisfaction, in respect of some act (in mod. Sc. use *esp.* of a bargain or promise, and freq. with implication of consequent withdrawing from it).

c **1374** Chaucer *Troylus* v. 1070 (Harl.), Syn I se .. þat to late is now for me to rewe To dyomede algate I wol be trewe. **1390** Gower *Conf.* I. 334 Men sen alday that rape reweth. **1426** Audelay *Poems* 42 After here werkus worche ȝe never a dele, Ellus schul ȝe reue. *a* **1586** Sidney *Ps.* XVIII. xii, They do faile, and in their mazed corners rue. **1603** J. Davies (Heref.) *Microcosmos* Wks. (Grosart) I. 41/1 Thus when our Teares doe testifie our ruth, We neede not rue, or of them be asham'd. *c* **1706** in Calderwood *Dying Testimonies* (1806) 186 That none may think .. I am rueing. **1790** Shirrefs *Poems* 87 Aft has he promis'd, that he wad be true; But, now, I find my lad begins to rue. **1830** Gen. P. Thompson *Exerc.* (1842) I. 235 The caution of the nurse is, 'Avoid green gooseberries, or you will have cause to rue'. **1884** *Harper's Mag.* Mar. 655/1 B— issued a license for the marriage of John Murphy and Mary Manning... But the intended bride 'rued'.

†**b.** Const. *of* (the act). *Obs. rare.*

a **1400–50** *Alexander* (Dubl. MS.) 871 Then rewys hym þe riche kyng of hys vnrode werkez. *Ibid.* (Ashm. MS.) 1975 Remowe agayne to þi rewme, & rew of þi werkis. **1631** Rutherford *Lett.* (1862) I. xix. 79 Do ye believe that our Lord will .. rue of the bargain and change His mind?

11. To feel sorrow or grief, *esp.* by reason of suffering from some fact or event; to lament.

13.. *K. Alis.* 3944 (Laud MS.), Þer miȝth man in herte rewe, Hou noble kniȝttes ouer þrewe. *c* **1400** *Melayne* 197 Bot þe peris take a concelle newe That made alle fraunce ful sore to rewe. *a* **1548** Hall *Chron., Rich. III*, 9 b, I remembred an olde prouerbe .., that often ruithe the realme, where chyldren rule, and woman gouerne. **1643** Trapp *Comm. Gen.* ix. 22 The whole race of Religious persons must rue for it. **1663** Butler *Hud.* I. i. 252 Like Sampson's Heart-breakers, it grew In time to make a Nation rue.

†**b.** To be sorry, feel reluctant, *to* do something.

1583 Babington *Commandm.* To Gentl., I rew to thinke it, there are witnesses moe, than I would there were, that know it. **1607** in *Harington's Nugæ Ant.* (1804) II. 138 This church, the ruins whereof I rue to behold even in wryting theis lynes. **1630** *R. Johnson's Kingd. & Commw.* 559 How long every particular Prince reigned .. I rue to record, and meane not to relate.

12. To have, take, or feel pity or compassion: †**a.** With *of.*

c **1200** Ormin 14782 Moysæs ræw off þatt follc þatt swa wass haldenn harrde. **1297** R. Glouc. (Rolls) 6747 Louerd, wiþ draw þin hond, .. and reu of engelond. *c* **1374** Chaucer *Anel. & Arc.* 287 God so wissely of my soule ruwe As verrayly ye slen me with þe peyne. *c* **1475** *Babees Bk.* 54 (1868) 3 Off myn vnkunnynge, swete lady, now Rewe. **1578** Whetstone *Promos & Cass.* II. v. iii, Rue of my teares from true intent which flowe.

b. With *on* or *upon.* Now *arch.*

1297 R. Glouc. (Rolls) 9229 He wep & cride on is men, þat hii ssolde on him rewe. **13..** *Cursor M.* 4738 (Gött.), To ioseph went þai criand þan, 'þu reu on vs, þu blisful man'. **1423** Jas. I *Kingis Q.* ci, Haue pitee now .. Off ȝour pure man, and rew on his distresse. *a* **1547** Surrey *Æneid* IV. 410 Rue on this realme, whoes ruine is at hand. **1579** W. Wilkinson *Confut. Fam. Love* 53 b, As many as rue upon the state of the poore seduced soules. **1632** Rutherford *Lett.* (1862) I. xxi. 85 Till your Dear Lord come and loose the pawn, and rue upon you. **1788** Burns *Turn again* i, Rue on thy despairing lover! Canst thou break his faithfu' heart? **1865** Swinburne *Poems & Ball.*, *Masque of Q. Bersabe* 365 Lord, thou rue on me.

†**c.** Without const. Also with *inf.*, to spare.

a **1300** *Cursor M.* 6784 Qua þat anurs godds neu, Him to sla sal naman reu. *a* **1300** *E.E. Ps.* xxxvi. 27 Alle daie he rewes, and lenes his þinge. *c* **1430** *Pol., Rel., & L. Poems* (1903) 177 Þouȝ he me wraþþe in diuerse wise, .. Ȝit muste y rue til þat he rise. **1530** Palsgr. 690/2, I rewe, I pytie or have compassion of one. *c* **1560** A. Scott *Poems* (S.T.S.) ix. 30 It is ane hairt .. set in to sabill, Ane wofull hairt, bot gif ȝe rew.

†**rue**, *v.*² *Obs. rare.* Also 6 rewe. [ad. L. *ruĕre.*] *intr.* To fall, decline. Hence **rueing** *ppl. a.*

1557 *Tottel's Misc.* (Arb.) 256 Of lofty ruing towers the fals the feller be. **1576** Gascoigne *Steele Gl.* (Arb.) 54 This is the cause (beleve me now, my Lorde) That Realmes do rewe from high prosperity. *a* **1591** H. Smith *Wks.* (1867) II. 477 So, lowly rest; so, lofty rues.

rue, to sift: see REE *v.*

rue-bargain. Chiefly *dial.* [RUE *v.*[1]] A bargain one repents of or breaks; also, the forfeit paid for withdrawing from a bargain.
1649 G. DANIEL *Trinarch., Hen. IV*, cclxxii, The King.. could haue beene well-pleas'd To quitt, if a Rue bargaine may be put In state. **1814-** in northern dial. glossaries. **1818** SCOTT *Rob Roy* xxvii, He said it would cost him a guinea of rue-bargain to the man who had bought his pony, before he could get it back again. **1844** BAMFORD *Traveller* 150 (E.D.D.), Give him a shilling or two for a rue-bargain.

rued, obs. form of REED.

rueful ('ruːfʊl), *a.* Forms: 3 reowful, 3–5 rewful(l, 4–5 reweful; 3–4 reufol, 4–5 -ful(l, 5 rouful; 4–8 ruful(l, 5 rufol, 6 ruifull, 7– rueful. [f. RUE *sb.*[1] + -FUL.]
1. Exciting sorrow or compassion; pitiable, lamentable; doleful, dismal.
In the contexts illustrated under b, c, d, the sense passes into 'expressive of sorrow or dejection'.
a **1240** *Ureisun* in *O.E. Hom.* I. 187 Bitweone þine rewfulle earmes on þe rode. **1297** R. GLOUC. *Chron.* (Rolls) 6709 þe erl godwine.. let smite of hor alre heued, & made a reufol dom. *c* **1330** *Arth. & Merl.* 6232 (Kölbing), þe kniȝtes of þe rounde table.. Com to þis reweful bataile. *c* **1385** CHAUCER *L.G.W.* 1838 *Lucrece*, She hem tolde This rewful case. *c* **1449** PECOCK *Repr.* I. xvi. 86 In this wise.. bifille the rewful and wepeable destruccioun of the worthi citee and vniuersite of Prage. **1470–85** MALORY *Morte Arth.* x. viii. 425 Hit is an honderd parte more reufullyr than my herte can vtter. **1559** *Mirr. Mag., Jack Cade* xxi, All men reioicing at the rufull sight. **1582** STANYHURST *Æneis* II. (Arb.) 55 Euery house, eech temple with ruful slaughter aboundeth. **1613** PURCHAS *Pilgr.* (1614) 546 Grinding the face of their poore tenants in ruefull manner. **1687** *Death's Vision* ix, The Rufull Ills and World from whence I Came! **1742** BLAIR *Grave* 12 How dark Thy long-extended realms, and rueful wastes! **1797** MME. D'ARBLAY *Let.* 8 Jan., Our adventures in coming back.. were rather rueful. **1812** J. WILSON *Isle of Palms* II. 90 Not even one rueful plank is seen, To tell that a vessel hath ever been. **1885** *Manch. Weekly Times* 20 June 5/5 The Conservative Opposition.. was in a rueful plight, crushed by a great defeat.
b. Of cries or utterance.
a **1225** *Leg. Kath.* 162 þeotinde unþuldeliche wið reowfule reames. *a* **1300** *Cursor M.* 20129 Til him scho cald wit reufull steuen. **1387** TREVISA *Higden* (Rolls) I. 317 In þat place beeþ.. i-herd reweful voys and gronynge. *c* **1400** *Pilgr. Sowle* (Caxton, 1483) III. iii. 52 Myn Aungell speke to these spirites that maden this reuful crye. **1572** BOSSEWELL *Armorie* II. 56b, [The cat] maketh a rufull noyse, and a gastefull, when one profereth to fighte with another. **1593** BRETON *Daff. & Prim., Asp.* Wks. (Grosart) I. 21/1 But yow that rede this ruifull verse, consider of his care. **1648** J. BEAUMONT *Psyche* VIII. ccli, In vain the skies And stones they rent with ruful Exclamations. **1671** MILTON *Samson* 1553 The accident was loud, & here before thee With rueful cry. **1748** THOMSON *Cast. Indol.* II. xliv, Alarm'd, the inferior demons of the place Rais'd rueful shrieks and hideous yells around.
c. Of looks, features, or actions.
a **1300** *Cursor M.* 14301 Lazar freindes.. cried and mad a reuful chere. *c* **1400** *Beryn* 3525 He stode al abasshid,.. And lokid oppon the Steward with a reweful cher. *a* **1547** SURREY *Æneid* II. B ij, Before mine eies, me thought, With rufull chere I sawe where Hector stood. **1636** E. DACRES tr. *Machiavel's Disc., Livy* II. 492 They usd to accompany them in a rufull manner, clad in blacke, and all sorrowfull. **1684** OTWAY *Atheist* II, That face.. o'er grown with rueful beard. **1728** POPE *Dunc.* II. 142 Piteous of his case, Yet smiling at his ruful length of face. **1781** MME. D'ARBLAY *Diary* 2 June, He suddenly called out, and with a most rueful face,—'Oh, certainly' [etc.]. **1806** J. BERESFORD *Miseries Hum. Life* v. i, As you had augured from the rueful bow of the speaker. **1835** W. IRVING *Tour Prairies* 136, I looked after him with a rueful eye as he limped off. **1877** BLACK *Green Past.* xliii, With a rueful smile.
d. Of persons.
c **1386** CHAUCER *Knt.'s T.* 2028 Of wepyng Emelye, The rewfullest of al the companye. **14..** *Pistill of Susan* 341 (I.), þen þat rewful charle began for to rore. *c* **1440** *Promp. Parv.* 439/1 Rufulle, and fulle of peyne and desese, *Anglice*, a caytyf,.. *dolorosus, penosus.* **1526** *Pilgr. Perf.* (W. de W. 1531) 306b, Now may I take and drawe out of thy moost rewfull brest the paynfull drynke of sorowe. **1650** MILTON *Eikon.* (ed. 2) 14 Those ruefull Preists whom Eliah mock'd. **1692** WALKER tr. *Epictetus* lv, Joy in a nimble moment ends its Race And rueful, pale Repentance takes its Place. **1742** YOUNG *Nt. Th.* II. 144 And all mankind,.. Rueful, aghast! cry out at his career. **1759** GOLDSM. *Bee* No. 8 ¶16 This rueful figure frightens a child into the palpitation of the heart. **1807** WORDSW. *White Doe* II. 23 Full soon to be uplifted high, And float in rueful company. **1855** MOTLEY *Dutch Rep.* v. v. (1866) 752 'Take them away; take them home again' said the rueful burgomaster. **1863** KINGSLEY *Water Bab.* v, Very rueful they looked.
transf. **1697** DAMPIER *Voy.* (1699) 415 The Sky looked very black and rueful.
Comb. **1844** KINGLAKE *Eothen* iii, Some rueful-looking fellows came rapidly shambling down the steps.
†**2.** Full of pity or compassion. *Obs.*
a **1300** *E.E. Psalter* cxi[i]. 4 [God is] Mildeherte and rewfulle and rightwis. *a* **1325** *Prose Psalter* cxl[i]v. 8 Our Lord is rewful and merciable. **1377** LANGL. *P. Pl.* B. XIV. 148 Criste.. shal.. rewarde alle dowble ricchesse, þat reuful hertes habbeth. *a* **1400** *Cast. Love* 378 (H.), Mercies herte so rufull is. *c* **1440** *Promp. Parv.* 439/1 Ruful, or ful of ruthe and pyte, *pieticus, compassivus.*
Hence †**ruefulhead**, compassion. *Obs.*[−1]
1338 R. BRUNNE *Chron.* (1810) 263 þorgh pite mykelle he les, & reufulhed of herte.

ruefully ('ruːfʊlɪ), *adv.* Forms: 3 reufulike; 4 rew-, reu-, rufullich(e, -ych); 4 rew-, reufully, 4–5 reufulli, 5–7 rufully (6 -lie), 6– ruefully. [f. RUEFUL *a.* + -LY[2].]
1. In a doleful or dismal manner; sorrowfully, dejectedly, regretfully.
c **1220** *Bestiary* 652 [The elephant] remeð reufulike on his wise. **13..** *E.E. Allit. P.* A. 1180 Rewfully þenne I con to reme. **1377** LANGL. *P. Pl.* B. XVII. 235 So wole þe fader forȝif folke.. þat reufulliche [*v.r.* rufulliche] repenten. *a* **1400–50** *Alexander* 3083 With þat reufully [*v.r.* rewfully] he rase & renkis out he sendis. *a* **1450** *Le Morte Arth.* 3423 To the kynge spake he full styll, Rewffully as he myght than Rowne. **1509** HAWES *Past. Pleas.* XIV. (Percy Soc.) 54 Of the fall of prynces.. He did endyte.., Folowynge his auctoure Bocas rufully. **1581** MULCASTER *Positions* iii. (1887) 14 She would oftimes be brought into a miserable plighte, and looke rufully vpon it. **1657** REEVE *God's Plea* 4 Would it not grieve thee.. that they should cry rufully in a sad desolation, which have cryed mightily unto their God? **1809** W. IRVING *Knickerb.* (1861) 105 It was a piteous sight to behold the late valiant burgomasters.. peeping ruefully out of their hiding-places. **1850** THACKERAY *Pendennis* i, He.. ruefully wrote off refusals to.. all his entertainers. **1888** FERGUS HUME *Madame Midas* I. ii, Slivers looked ruefully at the bottle.
†**2.** In a pitiable or lamentable fashion. *Obs.*
a **1300** *Cursor M.* 1825 Noe.. praid to godd for þam alsua.. Sin þai ware ded sua reufulli, þe saulus he wald haf of merci. **1377** LANGL. *P. Pl.* B. XII. 48 Rosamounde riȝt so reufully bysette, þe bewte of hir body in badnesse she dispended. *c* **1450** *St. Cuthbert* (Surtees) 4692 þou ert reufully fra vs reft. *c* **1485** *Digby Myst.* (1882) IV. 71 How rewfully he hinges here, That set you first in ceile! **1526** *Pilgr. Perf.* (W. de W. 1531) 254 Se there the sone of god so rewfully and piteously deformed and arayed for thy saluacion. **1590** SPENSER *F.Q.* III. viii. 30 Those pittifull outcries he heard Through all the seas so ruefully resownd. **1634** SIR T. HERBERT *Trav.* 199 All the wounded body.. rots and consumes most rufully.

ruefulness ('ruːfʊlnɪs). Also 3 reou-, reow-, 5 rew-, 7 rufulnesse. [f. RUEFUL *a.* + -NESS.]
†**1.** Compassionateness, pitifulness. *Obs.*
a **1225** *Ancr. R.* 368 þet oðer þing is heorte þeauwes, deuociun, reoufulnesse, merci, pite of heorte. *c* **1230** *Hali Meid.* 41 þolemodnesse & reowfulnesse of euch monnes sorhe. *c* **1440** *Rel. Pieces Thornton MS.* (1867) 51 Rewfulnes sall make the fermorye. *c* **1557** ABP. PARKER *Ps.* cxxx. 383 Let Jacob wayt the Lord so gent, Because with God is rufulnes.
2. Dismalness, dolefulness, dejection.
1590 SPENSER *F.Q.* I. iv. 25 He.. well could daunce; and sing with ruefulnesse. **1595** HUBBOCKE *Apol. Infants Unbaptized* 26 Haue we so learned Christ? are his lawes so ful of rufulnes? **1613** PURCHAS *Pilgrimage* IV. xv. (1614) 420 The rufulnesse of this sight was seconded with a more dismall euent. **1751** SMOLLETT *Per. Pic.* lvi. (1779) II. 152 He could not.. vanquish the ruefulness of his countenance. **1842** DICKENS *Amer. Notes* (1868) 131 Some, growing bold in ruefulness, predicted that we should land about the middle of July. **1894** MRS. DYAN *Man's Keeping* (1899) 299 'Not exactly,' said Lanyon, with hesitating ruefulness.

rueing ('ruːɪŋ), *vbl. sb.* [f. RUE *v.*[1] + -ING[1].] Repentance, sorrow, regret.
a **1300** *Cursor M.* 27341 Wit suet and luueli sermoning, He lede penant to half-reuing. *c* **1440** *Promp. Parv.* 439/1 Ruynge, for a thynge, *penitudo, penitencia.* **1559** ASCHAM in *Babees Bk.* (1868) 361 Cause of greife and sorrowe to your selfe, of chideing and rueing to your lord. **1611** SIR W. MURE *Misc. Poems* i. 106 þe poysonous potioune of late rewing. *a* **1618** SYLVESTER *Woodman's Bear* xii. Wks. (Grosart) II. 308 Who the eager game pursuing, Lost her Ladies in the chase, Till shee heard the wretche's ruing. **1730** T. BOSTON *Mem.* App. 35 Stand to the bargain and check yourselves for any semblance of rueing. **1844** *Cath. Weekly Instructor* 42 Weep, sire, with shame and ruing! Weep for thy child's undoing! **1844** MRS. BROWNING *Lost Bower* xxxii, Did she pause in tender rueing Here of all her sylvan scorn? **1891** T. HARDY *Tess* xxviii, A step which might afterwards cause bitter rueing to her husband.

'**rueing**, *ppl. a. rare.* [-ING[2].] **a.** Penitent. **b.** Compassionate, pitying.
c **950** *Lindisf. Gosp.* Luke *Intr.* 9/4 Đeæm hræwende broðer.. heht þætte were forȝefen. *a* **1300** *Cursor M.* 27153 Preist agh be skilwis, soft, and meke, Reuand, right-wis, luuelili speke. **1637** RUTHERFORD *Lett.* ccvii. (1675) 387 Christ's love.. must be a ruing, a pitiful, a melting-hearted love. *a* **1814** *Witness* II. i. in *New Brit. Theatre* I. 16 Like the ruing prodigal reclaim'd.

†**ruel**, *sb. Obs. rare.* In 4 ruwal. [a. AF. *roal*, Norman *rohal*, *rochal* (Godef.), Latinized as *rohallum*, *rohaulum* (Du Cange), in all probability a Scandinavian word of which the second element is *hval* whale.] = RUEL-BONE.
[*a* **1250** *Vie St. Auban* 3 De peres preciuses, de ivoire ne roal.] *c* **1314** *Reinbrun* lxxix. in *Guy Warw.* (1891) 657 þe walles were of cristal, þe heling was of fin ruwal þat schon swiþe briȝte.

†**ruel**, *v. Obs.*[−1] [perh. a. OF. *rueler*, *roeler*, *rouler* to roll.] *intr.* To fall.
13.. *E.E. Allit. P.* B. 953 þe rayn rueled adoun, ridlande þikke, Of felle flaunkes of fyr.

ruel, obs. form of ROWEL *sb.*, RUELLE.

†**ruelberd.** *Obs.*[−1] (Meaning doubtful.)
Perh. f. OF. *ruel(e* wheel: cf. BEARD *sb.* and BRED.
1414 *Court Roll Grt. Waltham* 18 Dec., Rota dicti molendini indiget *ruelberd* et molendinum vocatum *Champeneys mell* indiget quoddam instrumentum vocatum *le Nedele.*

†**ruel-bone.** *Obs.* Forms: 4–5 rouwel, rowel, roelle, ruel(l, rewel(l, reuyll bone (boon). [f. RUEL *sb.* + BONE *sb.*] Ivory (possibly that of the narwhal).
13.. *Leg. Pope Gregory* (Schulz) 994 Briȝter þan þe rouwel-boon. *c* **1350** *Ipomadon* 6456 A sadull all off sylke, The sege off rewell bone. *c* **1386** CHAUCER *Sir Thopas* 167 His sadel was of rowel [*varr.* rewel, ruel] boon. *a* **1400** *Sir Degrev.* 1429 [The chamber] was buskyd above With besauntus ful bryȝth All off ruel bon. *a* **1400** *Tourn. Tottenham* 83 in Hazl. *E.P.P.* III. 86 A garland on hir hed full of ruell bones. *c* **1425** *Thomas of Erceld.* (Thornton) 49 Hir selle it was of roelle bone [*Camb.* reuyll bone].

ruele, obs. form of RULE *sb.*

rue-leaved, *a.* [f. RUE *sb.*[2]] Having leaves similar to, or resembling, those of the common rue.
1744 T. BIRCH *Life of Boyle* B.'s Wks. 1772 I. p. cxlvii, Rue-leaved whitlow grass. **1777** JACOB *Catal. Plants* 102 *Saxifraga tridactylites*.., Rue-leaved Saxifrage, or Whitlow-grass. **1822** *Hortus Anglicus* II. 46, *I. Thalictroides.* Meadow Rue-leaved Isopyrum. *Ibid.* 52 *A. Thalictroides.* Meadow Rue-leaved Anemone. **1862** ANSTED *Channel Isl.* II. viii. 183 The rue-leaved spleen-wort (*A. ruta muraria*), grows abundantly in both islands on walls and churches.

ruell(e, obs. forms of ROWEL, RULE.

‖**ruelle** (rɥɛl). Also 4, 7–8 ruel. [F. *ruelle*, dim. of *rue* street, passage.]
1. The space between a bed and the wall; the part of a bed next the wall.
1393 LANGL. *P. Pl.* C. x. 79 Wo in winter-tyme, with wakynge a nyghtes To ryse to þe ruel to rocke þe cradel. **1688** *Engl. Prot. Mem. to Prince & P'cess of Orange* 21 There was a private door within the ruel of the bed into a room. **1751** ELIZA HEYWOOD *Betsy Thoughtless* II. 173 Miss Flora had thrown herself on a carpet by the bedside, her head leaning on the ruëlle. **1824** tr. *Duchesse d'Orleans' Mem. Crt. Louis XIV* 273 A number of plates were found in the ruelle of his bed.
2. A bedroom, where ladies of fashion in the seventeenth and eighteenth centuries, especially in France, held a morning reception of persons of distinction; hence, a reception of this kind.
1676 ETHEREDGE *Man of Mode* IV. ii, I have his own fault, a weak voice, and care not to sing out of a ruelle. **1697** DRYDEN *Ded. Æneid* Ess. (ed. Ker) II. 161 The poet who flourished in the scene is damned in the ruelle. **1704** SWIFT *T. Tub* ii, No approaching the Ladies Ruelles without the Quota of Shoulder-Knots. **1749** BOLINGBROKE *Lett. on Patriotism* 221 The forms of a drawing room, the regulation of a ruelle, the decoration of a ball. **1763** C. JOHNSTONE *Reverie* II. 16 How can you intrude so rudely into a lady's ruelle? You see I have set out my toilet. **1812** SCOTT *Let.* in *Lockhart* (1837) II. xii. 390 Acquainted with all the intrigues and tracasseries of the cabinets and *ruelles* of foreign courts.
3. In France, a small street; a lane, alley.
1908 T. E. LAWRENCE *Let.* 9 Aug. (1938) 59 Streets—mostly stairs, irregular and broken, running under archways and tunnels... Cover these ruelles with grass, heap them with refuse. **1911** O. ONIONS *Widdershins* vii. 242 He took us back along a plantain-groved street, and suddenly turned up an alley... It was a dilapidated, deserted *ruelle.*

‖**Ru'ellia.** *Bot.* [mod.Latin: named after the French botanist Jean *Ruel* (1479–1539).] A genus of acanthaceous plants, chiefly tropical, natives of Asia and America.
1753 in *Chambers' Cycl.* Suppl. **1846** LINDLEY *Veget. Kingd.* 679 Plants of great beauty, especially the species of Justicia, Aphelandra, and Ruellia. **1848** *Chambers' Inform.* I. 106/2 A valuable deep blue dye is said to be obtained from one of the East Indian Ruellias.

†**ruen.** *Obs.* Also 6 rewene, rowen, 7 ruin. [Of obscure origin: cf. RUENING.]
1. = RENNET *sb.*[1] 1.
1558 WARDE *Alexis' Secr.* I. I. (1568) 28b, Take the ruen of a Hare, and having frayed and consumed it in hote water, give it the woman to drinke. **1565** COOPER *Thesaurus, Coagulum*, a curde or creame: the ruen of a beast that turneth milke. **1609** BIBLE (Douay) *Ps.* lxvii. comm., Ruen turneth liquide milke into curde, and so into cheese.
2. *ruen cheese*, a soft kind of cheese.
1539 ELYOT *Cast. Helthe* (1541) 67b, Mylke hot from the udder,.. ruen chese, sweete almondes. **1542** BOORDE *Dyetary* xii. (1870) 266 Yet besyde these .iiii. natures of chese, there is a chese called a rewene chese. **1565** COOPER *Thesaurus, Caseus musteus*, greene cheese, or softe & rowen cheese. **1655** MOUFET & BENNET *Health's Improv.* 131 We may feed liberally of ruin Cheese.

†'**rueness.** *Obs.* Forms: 1 hreo(w)nis, -nys, hreu(w)nis, hreawnis, 3–4 reunes(se. [f. OE. *hréowe* adj. (see RUE *v.*[1]).]
1. Repentance.
c **950** *Lindisf. Gosp.* Matt. iii. 11 Ic fulwa iuih in wætre in hreonisse [*Rushw.* hreunisse]. *Ibid.* xxi. 29 Æfter ðon.. mid hreawnise ȝecerred [he] ȝe-eade. *c* **1000** in Thorpe *Laws* II. 170 Æfter his dædbote hreownysse.
2. Pity, compassion.
a **1300** *Cursor M.* 3134 Moght na reunes do him reu, þat he ne wald leuer his child cole þan of his lauerd wrath to thole. *c* **1300** *Havelok* 2227 God him wolde wel haue saue, He hauede reunesse of þe knaue.

†'**ruening.** *Obs. rare.* = RUEN 1.
1398 TREVISA *Barth. De P.R.* XVIII. lviii. (Bodl. MS.), His ruennynge is cheife medicine in venyms. *Ibid.* XVIII. lxvii, In no beeste wiþ teeþ in aiþer iowe is ruennynge ifounde but in þe hare.

Rueping process ('ryːpɪŋ). Also Rüping, (*erron.*) Ruping. [Named after Max *Rüping* (fl. 1902), German timber engineer, its inventor.] An economical method of preserving wood by applying creosote to it after subjecting it to high air pressure so that the cells are permeated but not filled.

1904 S. M. Rowe *Handbk. Timber Preservation* (rev. ed.) 129 In the new Ruping process the seasoned wood is for some time (from about a half hour to an hour) exposed to a pressure of 5 atmospheres in the boiler.. so that all the cells must be filled with air. 1917 A. J. Wallis-Tayler *Preservation of Wood* vii. 200 The Rueping Process has been patented in Great Britain... It was primarily devised with the object of reducing the cost of creosoting by preventing the heavy loss occasioned by dripping when the wood is treated by the ordinary process. 1930 H. Fergusson in H. Boulton *Century of Wood-Preserving* 66 The British Post Office for some little time has had all its poles done by the Rueping process. 1968 [see *empty-cell* s.v. empty *a.* and *sb.* C.].

'ruer. *rare.* Also 4 rewer(e, reewer. [f. rue *v.*^{1} + -er^{1}.]

1. One who pities or feels compassion.

*a*1300 *E.E. Psalter* lxxxv. 14 þou, laverd, rewer and milde-herted. 1382 Wyclif *Isaiah* xlix. 10 The rewere of them shal gouerne them. *Ibid.* liv. 10 The bond of my pes shal not be moued, seide the Lord, thi reewer.

2. One who repents.

1721 Kelly *Scot. Prov.* 284 Reavers should not be Ruers.

rue-raddy, *sb.* [Of obscure origin.]

1. A belt or rope passed over the shoulder in order to drag something by it.

1856 Kane *Arct. Expl.* I. 112 Each man had his own shoulder-belt or rue-raddy as we used to call it, and his own track line. 1880 *Standard* 20 May 3 One section of the men are armed.. with long knives and a 'rue raddy', or drag rope, slung across the shoulders.

2. *transf.* One who drags by means of a belt or rope passing over the shoulder.

1856 Kane *Arct. Expl.* II. xix. 190 An additional burden, but a necessary one, for our weary rue-raddies.

Hence **rue-raddy** *v.*, to attach by means of a shoulder rope.

1856 Kane *Arct. Expl.* I. xv. 181 Five men were then rue-raddied to the track-lines.

†**'ruesomeness.** *Obs.*$^{-1}$ In 2 reowsum-. [f. rue *sb.*^{1} Cf. mod. Yorks. dial. *ruesome* 'sorrowful, pitiable'.] Repentance.

*c*1175 *Lamb. Hom.* 21 Bute he hine driue a-wei mid soðe dedbote his sunne bi reowsumnesse.

†**ruet.** *Obs.* Also 5 ruett; 4 ruwet, rewet, ryuet, 6 rivette. [Of obscure origin.] A small horn or trumpet. Also *fig.*

13.. *K. Alis.* 1638 (Laud MS.), A-rovme he drouȝ quyk iwys And sett a Ruet to his mouþe. *Ibid.* 3699 A litel ruet [*v.r.* ruwet] a loude he blewe. 1362 Langl. *P. Pl.* A. v. 193 Gloten.. bleuh the ronde ruwet [*varr.* rewet, ryuet] atte rugge-bones ende. *c*1400 *Laud Troy Bk.* 5987 Ector bar a litel ruet, Vnto his mouth his horn he set. *c*1410 *Master of Game* (MS. Digby 182) xxi, Ther beth dyueres maneres of hornes, þat is to say: buglys,.. ruetes, smale forsters hornes. 1483 *Cath. Angl.* 313/2 A Ruett, *lituus.* *c*1580 Jefferies *Bugbears* I. ii, Stope downe a low & kisse my round rivette.

ruet, obs. variant of rowet *dial.*

rueth, obs. form of ruth.

ruf, obs. form of roof, rough, ruff.

ruf(e, Sc. variants of ro, rest. *Obs.*

Rufai (ruːˈfɑːiː). Also †Rifa'ee, †Rufaee, Rufa'i. Pl. as sing. or -s. [Turk. *Rufai*, ad. Arab. *rifāʿī*, f. the name of Aḥmad al-*Rifāʿī* (d. 1183), the founder of this order.] A howling dervish (see quot. 1877 and dervish), one of an order of Muslim friars pledged to poverty and self-mortification.

1832 G. A. Herklots tr. *Jaffur Shurreef's Qanoon-e-Islam* xxviii. 291 *Rufaee* or *Goorz-mar*, they originate from Syed Ahmud Kubeer, whose *fuqeers* strike the point of the *goorz* against their breasts, or into their eyes, level blows at their backs with the sword, thrust a spit through their sides, or into their eyes. 1836 E. W. Lane *Acct. Manners & Customs Mod. Egyptians* I. x. 310 The Rifa"ee durwee'shes are celebrated for the performance of many wonderful feats. 1868 J. P. Brown *Dervishes* ii. 51 *Ahmed Sa'eed Rufâ'ee* was the founder of the Order of the *Rufâ'ees*, generally known among European travellers as the 'Howling Dervishes', from their peculiar mode of worship. 1877 *Encycl. Brit.* VII. 114/1 This leads to the Devr, or rotation, in which the Rufai, or Howling Dervishes, stand in a circle, shoulder to shoulder, each on his right foot, and swaying the body and the left leg backwards and forwards or from side to side. 1885 T. P. Hughes *Dict. Islam* 120/1 Some.. wear tall caps called *kulāhs*, made also of felt; and others, such as the Rufāʿīs, use short caps called Tāqīyah, to which is added a coarse cloth. 1900 'Odysseus' *Turkey in Europe* v. 192 There are several orders.. the most important being the Bektashis, the Mevlevis, and the Rufais (the two latter commonly known to Europeans as dancing and howling dervishes). 1928 W. B. Seabrook *Adventures in Arabia* xiii. 251 The objective of our pilgrimage was a monastery of the Rufai, or Howling Dervishes—a sect fundamentally different from the Whirling Melewi—in the mountains between Hama and Aleppo. 1965 *Encycl. Islam* (rev. ed.) II. 164/2 The Sa'dis, Rifāʿīs and Aḥmadīs have particular feats, peculiar to each *tarīḳa*, of eating glowing embers and live serpents or scorpions and glass, or passing needles through their bodies and spikes into their eyes.

†**rufe,** *sb. Obs.*$^{-1}$ [ad. L. *rūfus.*] Rufous.

1477 Norton *Ordin. Alch.* v. in Ashm. (1652) 56 Theis two Colours Rufe and Citrine, Be meane Colours betweene White and Red.

†**rufe,** *a. Sc. Obs. rare.* Also 6 ruf. (Of doubtful origin and meaning; identity with OE. *róf* valiant, stout, strong, is phonetically possible.)

*c*1475 *Rauf Coilȝear* 109 Ane Ryall rufe het fyre war my desyre. 15.. *Peebles to Play* vi. in Sibbald *Chron. Sc. Poet.* (1802) I. 131 He cleikit up ane hie ruf sang.

rufe, obs. or dial. form of roof.

ru'fescence. *rare*$^{-1}$. [See next and -ence.] Tendency to rufous or reddish colour.

1874 Coues *Birds N.W.* 478 A slight rufescence of the under plumage, may frequently be observed until October.

rufescent (ruːˈfɛsənt), *a.* and *sb.* [ad. L. *rūfescent-*, *rūfescens*, pres. pple. of *rūfescĕre*, f. *rūfus* reddish.] Of a colour tending to reddish; somewhat rufous.

1817 Kirby & Sp. *Entomol.* xvii. (1818) II. 77 The rufescent ants do not leave their nests to go upon these expeditions.. till [etc.]. 1823 W. Scoresby *Jrnl.* 417 Back grey,.. lower parts rufescent. 1874 Coues *Birds N.W.* 304 The same rufescent phase occurs in other species of Owls.

b. *ellipt.* as *sb.* An ant of this colour.

1817 Kirby & Sp. *Entomol.* xvii. (1818) II. 81 When the rufescents, laden with pillage, retire, they do it in close order.

ruff (rʌf), *sb.*^{1} Forms: 5 rowe, roffe, ruf, 5–9 ruffe, 7– ruff; 7 rough. [Possibly f. rough *a.* Cf. the mod.L. name *aspredo* given to the freshwater fish by Dr. Caius, who drew attention to it about the middle of the 16th cent.]

†1. A sea-bream or other sparoid fish. *Obs.* (Cf. ruffle *sb.*^{3})

14.. *Lat.-Eng. Voc.* in Wr.-Wülcker 612 *Sparrus*, a rowe. *c*1440 *Promp. Parv.* 438/2 Ruffe, fysche, *sparrus.* 1647 Hexham I. (Fishes), A Ruffe or a Sea Breame, *een Zee-braessem.* 1668 Charleton *Onomast.* 140 *Synodon*.. Ruff, with dogs Teeth.

2. A small freshwater fish (*Acerina cernua*) of the perch family, of olive-brown colour with brown and black spots, and having rough prickly scales.

*a*1450 *Fysshynge w. Angle* (E.D.S.) 15 The bleke and the gogyn & þe Roffe. 1496 *Ibid.* 29 The ruf is ryght an holsome fysshe: And ye shall angle to him.. in the same wise as I haue tolde you of the perche. 1538 Elyot Additions, *Melanurus*, a kynde of perches, callydde Ruffes. 1577 B. Googe *Heresbach's Husb.* iv. (1586) 173 b, Some sorts.. delighting onely in Grauellie, Stonie, and Sandie Waters, as.. Gudgins, Bulheads, Ruffes, Trowtes. 1608 Sylvester *Du Bartas* ii. iv. *Schisme* 1010 Like as a Roach, or Ruff, or Gudgeon, born By some swift stream into a Weer.. Frisks to and fro. 1653 Walton *Angler* xi. 204 There is also another fish called a Pope, and by some a Ruffe;.. it is much like the Pearch for his shape, but will not grow to be bigger than a Gudgion. 1740 R. Brookes *Art of Angling* i. xv. 44 The Ruff or Pope.. is found in most of the large Rivers in England. 1797 *Encycl. Brit.* (ed. 3) XIII. 102/1 The Yare has a fish peculiar to it called the ruffe. 1836 Yarrell *Brit. Fishes* I. 18 The Ruffe is common to almost all the canals and rivers of England, particularly the Thames, the Isis, and the Cam. 1882 *Blackw. Mag.* Jan. 105 Great quantities of ruffs are caught at times, and the men's fingers get pricked with their sharp spines.

†3. A sea-urchin. *Obs.*$^{-0}$

1591 Percivall *Sp. Dict.*, *Erizo*, an hedgehog,.. also a fish called a Ruffe. 1706 Stevens *Span. Dict.*, *Erizo de mar*, a deform'd Shell-fish call'd a Ruff.

ruff (rʌf), *sb.*^{2} Also 6–7 ruffe; 6 rouffe, *Sc.* ruiff, 7 rooffe. [? f. rough *a.* Cf. ruffle *sb.*^{1} and *v.*^{1}]

†1. A circular outstanding frill on the sleeve of a garment; a ruffle. *Obs.*

1523 Fitzherb. *Husb.* §151 They haue suche pleytes vpon theyr brestes & ruffes vppon theyr sleues, aboue theyr elbowes. 1591 [see hand-ruff 1]. 1607 Heywood *Fayre Mayde Exch.* F j, Ruffes for your hands, wast-cotes wrought with silke. 1647 Hexham I, Full of ruffes and foldes, *vol rimpelen, ployen ofte vouwen.*

2. An article of neck-wear, usually consisting of starched linen or muslin arranged in horizontal flutings and standing out all round the neck, worn especially in the reigns of Elizabeth and James I.

1555 Eden *Decades* (Arb.) 320 The collars and ruffes bysette with lyttle rounde baules lyke beades. 1583 Stubbes *Anat. Abus.* ii. (1882) 35 They not onely continue their great ruffes still, but also vse them bigger than euer they did. *c*1618 Moryson *Itin.* iv. 418 They desyre to haue.. falling bands rather then Rooffes, Caps of taffety rather then hatts. 1644 Quarles *Sheph. Orac.* viii. 47 That heath'nish Ruffe of thine, that perks Upon thy stiffe-neckt coller. 1728 Young *Love of Fame* iv. 122 He shews on holidays a sacred pin, That touch'd the ruff, that touch'd queen Bess's chin. 1752 Hume *Ess. & Treat.* (1777) I. 263 Must we throw aside the pictures of our ancestors, because of their ruffs and fardingales? 1822 Scott *Nigel* x, My grey beard falls on a cambric ruff, and a silken doublet. 1880 'Ouida' *Moths* II. 375 She wore black velvet with a high ruff of old Flemish lace.

transf. 1633 P. Fletcher *Purple Isl.* xxx, As a virgin Rose.. Whom too hot scorching beams quite disarayes Down flags her double ruffe.

b. (See quot.)

1858 J. Purchas *Direct. Anglic.* 21/1 Under this 'tippet' is worn what is called by University robe-makers 'the Ruff'. *Note.* This ruff is simply a breadth of silk of about two yards long... It is *gathered* round the neck.

3. A collar of projecting or distinctively coloured feathers or hair round the neck of various birds and animals.

1698 Fryer *Acc. E. India & P.* 56 Monkeys with white Ruffs, and black shagged Bodies. 1760–72 tr. *Juan & Ulloa's Voy.* (ed. 3) I. 58 A little aboue the beginning of the crop, they haue a ruff of white feathers. 1781 [see 6 below]. 1802 Bingley *Anim. Biogr.* (1805) II. 475 The male bird does not acquire his ruff till the second season. 1856 Bryant *Old Man's Counsel* 49 The grouse that wears A sable ruff around his mottled neck. 1871 Darwin *Desc. Man* II. xvii. 267 The broad ruff round the throat and chin of the Canadian lynx is much longer in the male than in the female. 1887 *Standard* 28 May 1/2 Lost, a black and Tan Colley Dog, with white ruff.

b. An artificial variety of the domestic pigeon resembling the jacobin.

1735 J. Moore *Columbarium* 49 The Strain of Jacobines has been much vitiated.. in Order to improve their Chain by the Length of the Ruff's Feathers. 1765 *Treat. Domest. Pigeons* 119 The ruff, if attentively examined, will be found larger than the jack, with a longer beak, and a larger head. 1854 Meall *Moubray's Poultry* 285 The similarity between the Ruff and the Jacobine obviates the necessity for describing it. 1881 J. C. Lyell *Fancy Pigeons* 199 Moore describes a pigeon known as a ruff.

†4. ***the wooden ruff***, the pillory. *Cant. Obs.*

1685 *Roxb. Ball.* (1885) V. 605 The Tories to spight us,.. With a damn'd Wooden-Ruff will bedeck our Friend Titus. *a*1700 B. E. *Dict. Cant. Crew* s.v. *Wooden, He wore the Wooden-ruff*, he stood in the Pillory.

5. A circular object resembling a ruff.

1693 Evelyn *De la Quint. Compl. Gard.* II. 107 You must raise small Shavings out of the Wood of the Branch.. and make them hang like a kind of Ruff on the Extremity of that Bark. 1742 Pope *Dunciad* iv. 407 Soft on the paper ruff its leaves I spread. 1864 Webster, *Ruff*,.. an annular ridge formed on a shaft, or other piece, to prevent it from moving endwise. Ruffs are also sometimes loose rings.

6. *attrib.* and *Comb.*, as ***ruff band, sleeve***; ***ruff-like, -necked*** adjs.

1558 in Feuillerat *Revels Q. Eliz.* (1908) 28 Imployed whoolye in to twoo greate gounes with Ruff Sleves. 1591 Florio *2nd Fruites* 9 Eight ruffe bands with their hand cuffs wrought with silke. 1639 *Knaresb. Wills* (Surtees) II. 167 To Sibbill Hudsonne one ruffe band. 1781 Latham *Gen. Synop. Birds* I. i. 269 Ruff-necked Parrot... When it erects the neck feathers, it makes the appearance of a ruff round the head. 1782 *Ibid.* ii. 785 Ruff-necked Humming Bird. 1838 Audubon *Ornith. Biog.* IV. 555 Ruff-Necked Humming Bird. *Trochilus Rufus.* 1854 Meall *Moubray's Poultry* 286 A compact mass of ruff-like feathers.

ruff (rʌf), *sb.*^{3} Also 6–7 ruffe. [ad. OF. *roffle*, *rouffle*, earlier *romfle*, *ronfle* (1414), = It. *ronfa* (Florio), a certain card-game, perh. a popular corruption of F. *triomphe*, It. *trionfo*: see trump.

Godefroy also cites a F. dial. *roufe* as meaning 'the highest of two cards which one returns along with the trump-card in the game of quarante'. Pg. *rufa* and *rifa* denote a set of cards of one suit.]

†1. A former card-game. Also ***ruff and honours.***

Literary allusions occur chiefly between 1590 and 1630.

1589 Nashe *Martin Marprelate* Wks. (Grosart) I. 161 Leauing the auncient game of England (Trumpe) where euerie coate and sute are sorted in their degree, [they] are running to their Ruffe where the greatest sorte of the sute carrieth away the game. 1600 Rowlands *Lett. Humours Blood* iv. 64 At Ticktacke, Irish, Noddie, Maw, and Ruffe. 1611 Davis *Panegyrick Verses* in *Coryat's Crudities*, Of that tongue he so hath got the Body That he sports with it at Ruffe, Gleeke, or Noddy. 1674 Cotton *Compl. Gamester* (1680) 81 Ruff and Honours (alias Slamm) and Whist, are Games.. commonly known in England in all parts thereof. 1688 Holme *Armoury* iii. xvi. (Roxb.) 72/1 Ruffe and Honors and Whisk, which are generally among the Vulgar termed Trump.

†2. (See later quots.) *Obs.*

1611 Cotgr., *Triomphe*, the Card-game called Ruffe, or Trump; also, the Ruffe, or trump at it. 1651 *Royal Game of Picquet* 11 After they have done discarding,.. they then begin to look after the Ruffe, and to see how much each of them can make of a suit. 1674 Cotton *Compl. Gamester* (1680) 66 Next you speak for the Ruff, and he that hath most of a suit in his hand wins it, unless some of the Gamesters have four Aces, and then he gains the Ruff.

3. a. [f. ruff *v.*^{2} 2.] The act of trumping at cards, esp. in whist, when one cannot follow suit.

1856 *Handbk. Games* (Bohn) 176 You may suspect the lead was from a single card, and with a view to a ruff. 1856 Lt.-Col. B. *Whist-player* (1858) 31 You obtain the desired ruff to a certainty.

b. *Comb.* **ruff and discard** *Bridge*, an opportunity (usu. for declarer) to win a trick by ruffing in one hand while discarding a loser from the other.

1939 N. de V. Hart *Bridge Players' Bedside Bk.* xxxix. 120 If West leads a Heart, then declarer gets a ruff-and-discard which enables him to ruff the third round of either minor suit. 1972 R. Markus *Common-Sense Bridge* iii. 102 A ruff and discard disposed of a losing club. 1977 *Bridge Mag.* July 34/2 Aunt Agatha now played the king of clubs, giving West the option of conceding a ruff and discard or leading away from his king of spades.

ruff (rʌf), *sb.*^{4} [Perh. from ruff *sb.*^{2} 3, but this leaves the similarity to reeve *sb.*^{2} unexplained.] The male of a bird of the sandpiper family (*Tringa* or *Machetes pugnax*), distinguished during the breeding-season by a ruff and ear-tufts.

1634, 1648 [see REEVE *sb.*^{2}]. **1663** DRYDEN *Wild Gallant* I. iii, I have a delicate dish of ruffs to dinner. **1752** HILL *Hist. Anim.* 475 We call the male the ruff and the female the reeve. **1768** PENNANT *Brit. Zool.* II. 363 The males or Ruffs assume such variety of colors in several parts of their plumage, that it is scarce possible to see two alike. **1839** STONEHOUSE *Isle of Axholme* 66 Those very curious and beautiful birds, the ruffs, are now seldom to be met with. **1843** YARRELL *Brit. Birds* II. 574 The Ruff..may be considered only as a summer visiter to this country. **1863** *Sat. Rev.* 284 The extension of drainage has banished the avoset, and the ruff, and the godwit from our eastern marshes.

ruff (rʌf), *sb.*^{5} Also 7 roofe. [? Imitative.]

1. = RUFFLE *sb.*^{4} (Hence perh. Pg. *rufo.*)

1688 [see ROLL *sb.*^{2} 2]. **1706** FARQUHAR *Recruiting Officer* V. ii, The drum beats a ruff, and so to bed. **1726** SHELVOCKE *Voy. round World* 137 At the turning of every glass during the night we beat 3 ruffs on the drum. **1811** BOSWELL *Sir Albon* Poet. Wks. (1871) 102 Quicker than the drum-boy's ruff His horse hoofs clatter'd hard and tough. **1927** *Melody Maker* Aug. 804/3 All the various beats used in military drumming. The stroke-and-drag paradiddle and the four-stroke ruff, for instance, are not essential. **1957** A. A. SHIVAS *Art of Tympanist & Drummer* i. 30 *Embellishments.* These are very important and much used in side drumming... The three important ones are the flam, the drag and the ruff.

2. *Sc.* An expression of applause by making a noise with the feet.

1801– in *Eng. Dial. Dict.*

†**ruff**, *sb.*^{6} *Obs.* Also 6–7 ruffe. [Of obscure origin. Cf. Sw. *ruff* spirit, go.]

1. The highest pitch or fullest degree *of* some exalted or excited condition. Usu. ***in the ruff of.***

1549 LATIMER *2nd Serm. bef. Edw. VI* (Arb.) 49 Wher is all thy ruffe of thy gloriousnes become? **1592** G. HARVEY *Four Lett.* Wks. (Grosart) I. 199 He, which in the ruffe of his freshest iollity, was faine to cry [etc.]. **1622** FOTHERBY *Atheom.* II. vii. §1. 261 When they view themselues in the ruffe of their greatnes, they are vtterly ashamed, to thinke of their first littlenesse. **1692** L'ESTRANGE *Fables* (1694) 39 How many Emperours and Princes..in the Ruff of all their glory have been taken down.

2. An exalted or elated state; elation, pride, vainglory: **a.** With possessive pronouns, esp. in phr. ***in his*** (or ***their***) ***ruff.*** (Very common from *c* 1570 to 1675).

a **1548** HALL *Chron., Hen. IV*, 30 The duke of Burgoyn beyng now in his ruffe..toke upon him the hole rule and governance of the realme. **1568** V. SKINNER tr. *Montanus' Inquisit.* 46 b, Such is their ruffe in that triumph. **1581** J. BELL *Haddon's Answ. Osorius* 319 Which would undertake so weerysome a course for his Rhetoricall ruffe. **1615** W. HULL *Mirr. Maiestie* 51 What came ye out to see? a meere mortall man in the huffe of his ruffe? **1653** J. CARTER *Tombstone* 107 They think in their ruffe and gallantry that none can pluck them down; they vaunt, who shall us controule? *a* **1679** GOODWIN *Creatures* II. x. Wks. 1683 II. 96 When the Saints shall be in their ruff and glory.

b. Without article, esp. in phr. ***in*** (***great, jolly, rash,*** etc.) ***ruff.***

1555 J. PROCTOR *Hist. Wyat's Rebellion* 30 Where thei.. displaied their Ensignes brauelie: seeming to be in great ruffe. **1556** J. HEYWOOD *Spider & Fly* lvii, Who that (in rash roofe) beginneth to contende, He repenth beginning, ere he cum to ende. **1567** GOLDING tr. *Ovid's Met.* XII. 318 In jolly ruffe he passed straight. **1581** MULCASTER *Positions* xiv. (1887) 68 Against all..with whom all vertues be voluntarie, when reason is in ruffe. **1600** W. WATSON *Decacordon* (1602) 34 He tooke vpon him the defence of the Sea Apostolike in managing with huffe and ruffe this foisted in authoritie. [**1624** J. GEE *Hold fast* 50 A vigorous Iesuite..attired like a Gallant of none of the lowest ruffe.]

c. In phr. ***in the*** (***high***) ***ruff.***

1600 HOLLAND *Livy* XXVIII. xxviii. 690 Being in the ruffe and jolitie upon their fresh and late victorie. **1607** R. C[AREW] tr. *Estienne's World of Wonders* 352 Whilest the folly of the former abuses was in the ruffe. **1690** *Andros Tracts* II. 64 Methods that must be taken to unite England, ..and subdue France, (now in the high Ruff).

3. *Her.* Of a ship: ***in her ruff***, in full course.

1562 LEGH *Armory* 178 b, He beareth Or, a Shippe vnder Saile in her ruffe Sable. **1586** FERNE *Blaz. Gentrie* 38 You haue heard of two thinges, a ship in her ruffe and a fayre lady ..most worthye of sight. **1610** GUILLIM *Heraldry* III. xxii, The Dolphin..outstrippeth a Ship under sayle, in her greatest ruffe and merriest winde, in swiftness of course. **1688** HOLME *Armoury* III. xv. (Roxb.) 33/1 He beareth Argent, a Ship in her Ruffe, vnder full Saile and Streamers flying, all proper.

4. Excitement, passion, fury. Freq. ***in a ruff.***

1567 GOLDING *Ovid's Met.* XIII. (1593) 296 In the mids of all His bloodie ruffe I coupt with him. **1604** PARSONS *3rd Pt. Three Convers. Eng.* 112 All ignorant Craftesmen of Kent, but yet sett in such a ruffe with the heate of new opinions. **1611** J. DAVIES (Heref.) *Scourge Folly* Wks. (Grosart) II. 76 Such Stuffe (As might put plainest Pacience in a Ruffe). **1641** HINDE *J. Bruen* lii. 173 There was a Gentleman, who ..in his heat and ruffe sent his man to this Gentleman with this message, &c.

†**ruff**, *sb.*^{7} *Obs.*$^{-0}$ [Of obscure origin.] A candle or candle-wick.

c **1440** *Promp. Parv.* 439/1 Ruffe candel, *hirsepa, funale.* **1570** LEVINS *Manip.* 183 Yᵉ Ruffe of a candle, *finale.*

†**ruff**, *sb.*^{8} *Obs.*$^{-1}$ (See quot.)

1601 HOLLAND *Pliny* I. 243 Moreover in the river Donow, there is taken the Mario, a fish much like to a Ruffe or Porpuis [L. *porculo marino simillimus*].

†**ruff**, *sb.*^{9} *Obs. rare.* A blockhead.

1606 *Choice, Chance & Change* (1881) 66 The next was on a fool, on a swaggering ruffe. **1674** N. FAIRFAX *Bulk & Selv.* Ep. Ded., Though it may seem but a wooden come off, and like that of the sorry numb-skull'd Ruffes.

Ruff (rʌf), *sb.*^{10} [f. the name of W. *Ruff*, founder editor of *Guide to the Turf or Pocket racing Companion* (1842–53), a twice-yearly compendium of horse-racing information, subsequently published as *Ruff's Guide to the Turf* and since 1869 incorporating various other racing periodicals.] A colloq. abbreviation of *Ruff's Guide to the Turf.*

1854 *Sporting Rev.* Jan. 63 The racing world have in Ruff and the Book Calendar two very competent expounders of the 'forms' in which thorough-breds have 'gone' this season. **1902** in Farmer & Henley *Slang* VI. I. 70/1. **1918** G. FRANKAU *One of Them* xxi. 159 Weep for a Shrunken Ruff, a tipless tout.

ruff, var. ROUGH *sb.*^{1}; Sc. var. RO, rest. *Obs.*

†**ruff**, *a. Obs. rare.* (Meaning not clear, but perh. only a variant spelling of ROUGH *a.*)

1651 T. BARKER *Art of Angling* (1653) 15 When your grid-iron is hot you must coole it with ruff suet. **1676** WORLIDGE *Cyder* (1691) 161 Let your murc or chaff..abide in the must ..more or less ruff or tinctured.

ruff, obs. f. ROUGH *a.* and *adv.*

ruff (rʌf), *v.*^{1} Now *rare.* Forms: 6–7 ruf, ruffe, 6– ruff. [? f. RUFF *sb.*^{2} Cf. RUFFLE *v.*^{1}]

1. *trans.* To form into a ruff or ruffs; to provide with a ruff or ruffs. Also with *up.*

Chiefly in pa. pple.; cf. RUFFED *ppl. a.*^{1} 3.

a **1548** HALL *Chron., Hen. VIII*, 134 b, His base and bard wer cloth of siluer, and blacke veluet ruffed and not plain. **1571** A. JENKINSON *Voy. & Trav.* (Hakl. Soc.) I. 39 The sleeues thereof very long, which he weareth on his arme ruffed up. **1592** GREENE *Def. Conny Catch.* Wks. (Grosart) XI. 95 The round hose bumbasted close to the breech, and ruft aboue the necke with a curle. **1647** HEXHAM I, To ruffe, or gather into a ruffe, *rimpelen ofte fronsen vergaderen.* **1834** PLANCHÉ *Hist. Brit. Cost.* 238 The sleeves were also ruffed or ruffled at the hand.

2. †**a.** Of a bird: To ruffle (the feathers). *Obs.*

1590 SPENSER *F.Q.* III. ii. 27 Thenceforth the fether in her lofty crest, Ruffed of love, gan lowly to availe. *Ibid.* xi. 32 The proud Bird, ruffing his fethers wyde. **1597** DRAYTON *Heroical Ep.* 67 b, The siluer swannes..Ruffing theyr plumes, come glyding on the lake.

b. To make rough; to disorder. *rare.*

1817–8 COBBETT *Resid. U.S.* (1822) 338 To return to the thatching: Straw.., in very high winds,..is liable, if not reeded, to be ruffed a good deal.

†**3.** *Falconry.* Of a hawk: To strike (the quarry) without securing it. *Obs.*

1575 TURBERV. *Falconry* 122 Your Falcon wyll stowpe hir and ruffe hir, vntyll the dogges maye take hir. **1620–6** QUARLES *Feast for Wormes* 103 If in her downy Soreage, she but ruffe So strong a Doue, may it be thought enough. **1646** G. DANIEL *Poems* Wks. (Grosart) I. 97 Give her way to kill The Harpie She has ruff't; for I dare say She has earn'd her Bells, to bring downe such a prey.

ruff (rʌf), *v.*^{2} Forms: 6– ruff, 7 ruffe, 8–9 rough. [Related to RUFF *sb.*^{3}]

†**1.** *intr.* (See quot. 1674.) *Obs. rare.*

1598 FLORIO, *Ronfare*,..also to ruff or trump at cards. **1674** COTTON *Compl. Gamester* (1680) 82 He that hath the Ace of that [i.e. trumps], Ruffs; that is, he takes in those four Cards, and lays out four others in their lieu.

2. **a.** *trans.* To trump (a card, etc.) when unable to follow suit. Freq. *absol.*

1760 MURPHY *Way to Keep Him* III. i, Sir George, why did not you rough the spade? **1813** *Hoyle's Games of Whist & Quadrille* 50 *Ruff*, and *over-ruff*, to trump a suit led, second or third hand. **1837** DICKENS *Pickw.* xxxv, Why Mr. Pickwick had not..roughed the spade, or finessed the heart. **1856** LT.-COL. B. *Whist-player* (1858) 36 A suit being so frequently ruffed third round. **1885** PROCTOR *Whist* 49 The state of the score might render it advisable to take the trick lest second round should be ruffed.

absol. **1781** HUTTON *Tour to Caves* Gloss. (ed. 2) 95 *Rough*, to renounce at cards. **1865** LOWELL *Thoreau* Prose Wks. 1890 I. 372 He wishes always to trump your suit and to ruff when you least expect it. **1885** PROCTOR *Whist* 71 Ruff at every opportunity if so weak in trumps that you cannot hope to disarm the enemy.

b. Const. *out.* To defeat (a card, etc.) by ruffing, so as to establish master cards in the suit led; also, with suit as object.

1927 M. C. WORK *Contract Bridge* 141 *Ruffing out*, trumping the low cards of a suit before playing its high cards. **1939** N. DE V. HART *Bridge Players' Bedside Bk.* 22, I laid down dummy's Ace and King of Hearts, and then tried to ruff out the suit. **1960** T. REESE *Play Bridge with Reese* 23 If the spades are breaking as well, I can play Ace and another spade, ruff out the King of clubs and enter dummy to make two long clubs. **1967** P. ANDERTON *Play Bridge* xi. 88 South covers with his A...and West trumps. This procedure is known as ruffing out a suit and East now holds the master cards in the Spade suit. **1972** *Times* 20 May 13/3 She ruffed out the clubs ruffing the third round with the ♡10.

ruff (rʌf), *v.*^{3} *Sc.* [f. RUFF *sb.*^{5} Cf. Pg. *rufar.*]

1. *trans.* To beat a ruff or ruffle upon (a drum). Also *intr.* of a drum: To be thus beaten.

1827 W. TAYLOR *Poems* 65 (E.D.D.), He..ruff'd the drum at ilka door. **1828** MOIR *Mansie Wauch* xiv. 206 The drum ruffed, and off set four of them.

2. *trans.* and *intr.* To applaud by making a noise with the feet.

1826 WILSON *Noct. Ambr.* Wks. 1855 I. 243 A' the crowd ruffin the exploit. **1842** VEDDER *Poems* 104 They ruffed, and for the ditty clamoured. **1877** in J. A. Chalmers *Tiyo Soga* 419 He was..heartily *ruffed* by his fellow-students.

†**ruff**, *v.*^{4} *Obs.* Also 7 ruffe, ruf. [f. RUFF *sb.*^{6}]

1. *intr.* To swagger, bluster, domineer. Also with *it* and *out.*

1600 W. WATSON *Decacordon* (1602) 65 This foundation thus laid, then to huffe and ruffe it out, a Councell of women must be called to set cocke ahoope. **1612** T. JAMES *Jesuits Downefall* 65 He is now become that learned counseller, that must rule, ruffe, and range through every estate. **1683** *Songs Lond. Prentices* (Percy Soc.) 77 Rufing thus, They gave him words opprobrious.

2. To brag or boast *of* a thing.

1600 W. WATSON *Decacordon* (1602) 107 [A letter] to be huffed, ruffed and vanted of.

ruff (rʌf), *v.*^{5} [var. of ROUGH *v.*^{1}]

1. *trans.* To heckle (flax) with a ruffer.

1853 URE *Dict. Arts* (ed. 4) I. 741 He seizes the ruffed part of the strick.., and proceeds by similar treatment to 'ruff' the top end.

2. To work the beaver felt into (a hat-body).

1845 [see RUFFING *vbl. sb.*^{3}]. **1868** J. THOMSON *Hat-making & Felting* 37 The known impossibility of napping or ruffing a hat by any means with machinery.

ˈ**ruff-coat.** ? *Obs.* [prob. f. *ruff* ROUGH *a.*] The caddis-worm.

1653 WALTON *Angler* xii. 232 There is also another Cadis called by some a Straw-worm, and by some a Ruffe-coate. **1787** BEST *Angling* (ed. 2) 20 Another sort..is found..in rushes, water-weeds, straw, &c. called ruff Coats, or straw worms. **1833** J. RENNIE *Alph. Angling* 34 The grubs which are known by the name of caddis-worms, case-worms, cad or cod bait and ruff coats.

ruffe, obs. form of ROOF, ROUGH, RUFF.

ruffed (rʌft), *ppl. a.*^{1} Also 6 ruft. [f. RUFF *sb.*^{2} or *v.*^{1}]

1. Wrinkled, curled. *rare.*

1578 LYTE *Dodoens* V. vi. 553 Ruffed, or curled Colewurtes. *Ibid.* 554 The fourth kind of red Cole, is called ..in Englishe Wrinckled or ruffed Cole.

2. Ruffled. *rare*$^{-1}$.

1591 SPENSER *Teares Muses* 402 Thy gay Sonne, that winged God of Love, May now goe prune his plumes like ruffed Dove.

3. Wearing a ruff; provided with ruffs.

1586 T. B. *La Primaud. Fr. Acad.* I. (1589) 207 What would he have said of our Courtiers, so finely curled, ruft, and perfumed? **1810** CRABBE *Borough* ii. 98 That marble arch, our sexton's favourite show, With all those ruff'd and painted pairs below. **1859** KINGSLEY *Misc.* II. 134 If we met such a ruffed and ruffled worthy as used to swagger by hundreds up and down Paul's Walk.

b. In names of birds and animals: Having a ruff-like collar or markings, as ***ruffed bustard, grouse, heathcock, pigeon; ruffed lemur, macaco.***

1783 LATHAM *Gen. Synop. Birds* II. II. 805 *Ruffed Bustard. **1819** STEPHENS in *Shaw's Gen. Zool.* XI. 448 Ruffed bustard..inhabits Arabia and the northern parts of Africa. **1782** *Phil. Trans.* LXII. 397 *Ruffed Grous, *T. Umbellus.* **1785** PENNANT *Arct. Zool.* II. 301 *Ruffed Grous*, Grous with a great ruff on the hind part of the neck. **1812** A. WILSON *Amer. Ornith.* VI. 45 The Pinnated Grous was seen in great numbers, but none of the Ruffed. **1872** COUES *N. Amer. Birds* 235 *Ruffed Grouse...* Sides of the neck with a tuft of numerous..broad, soft, glossy-black feathers. **1752** EDWARDS *Glean. Nat. Hist.* I. 79 The *Ruffed Heath-cock, or Grous. **1840** *Cuvier's Anim. Kingd.* 63 One beautiful species, the *Ruffed Lemur (*L. macaco*, Lin.), is varied with large patches of black on a pure white ground. **1897** H. O. FORBES *Hand-bk. Primates* I. 69 The Ruffed or Variable Lemur [*Lemur Varius*]. **1771** PENNANT *Syn. Quadrup.* 138 *Ruffed maucauco. **1797** *Encycl. Brit.* (ed. 3) IX. 785/2 The ..ruffed maucauco, (the *Vari* of Buffon), is also an inhabitant of Madagascar. **1611** COTGR., *Pigeon chaperonné*, a *ruffed, or copped, Pigeon.

ruffed (rʌft), *ppl. a.*^{2} [f. RUFF *v.*^{5}] **a.** Covered with beaver felt. **b.** Heckled with a ruffer.

1846 MᶜCULLOCH *Acc. Brit. Empire* (1854) I. 763 Few beaver or ruffed hats meet the English manufacturer in the markets referred to. **1853** URE *Dict. Arts* (ed. 4) I. 741 When this is finished the 'ruffed' work is taken to the tool called a 'common 8'. *Ibid.* [see RUFF *v.*^{5} 1].

ˈ**ruffer**^{1}. [f. RUFF *v.*^{2}] **a.** = *ruffing trick* s.v. RUFFING *vbl. sb.*^{1} **b.** A card that ruffs or trumps another (see also quot. 1611).

1611 FLORIO, *Ronfatóre*,..a ruffer or trumper at cardes. **1936** E. CULBERTSON *Contract Bridge Compl.* xxxix. 435 A trick made by ruffing a losing card with an otherwise worthless card of the trump suit is called a ruffer. **1974** *Country Life* 28 Feb. 453/3 This not only deprives South of a diamond ruff, but the trump trick comes back if South uses dummy's Ten as a ruffer. **1975** *Ibid.* 30 Jan. 289/3 The right way is to use his own trumps as ruffers.

ˈ**ruffer**^{2}. [f. RUFF *v.*^{5}] = ROUGHER 3.

1853 URE *Dict. Arts* (ed. 4) I. 741 The pins..are much closer placed than those of the ruffer. **1882** [see ROUGHER 3].

ruffet, variant of ROUGHET.

ruffian (ˈrʌfɪən), *sb.* and *a.* Forms: α. 6 rufian, ruffyan(e, ruffiane, -ion, 6– ruffian. β. 6 rouffyn, ruffyne, 6–7 ruffin, ruffen, 7 ruffon. [a. OF. *rufyen*, *-ien*, *ruffien*, *ruffian* (mod.F. *rufien*, *rufian*), = Prov. *rufian*, *rofian*, Catal. *rufia*, Sp. *rufian*, Pg. *rufião* (*rafião*), It. *ruffiano*, med.L. *ruffianus*: the ultimate origin of these forms is obscure, there being no evidence to support any of the conjectures which have been offered. French is also the source of MDu. *roff-*, *ruffiaen* (Du. *roffiaan*), MLG., MHG., and mod.G. *ruffian*.]

1. A man of a low and brutal character; one habitually given to acts of violence or crime; a cut-throat villain.

α. **1531** ELYOT *Gov.* II. xii. (1880) II. 156 A commune and notable rufian or thefe, whiche had robbed and slayne a man. **1568** GRAFTON *Chron.* II. 119 Assemblyng together a greate rowte of Ruffians and Robbers. **1633** G. HERBERT *Church Militant* 163 The old debauched ruffian would turn writer. **1664** H. MORE *Myst. Iniq.* 413 Their beginnings being helped on by a rabble of Ruffians and Robbers. **1727–46** THOMSON *Summer* 274 Near the dire cell the dreadless wanderer oft Passes, as oft the ruffian shows his front. **1752** YOUNG *Brothers* IV. i, Stab me yourself, nor give me to the knife Of midnight ruffians. **1820** BYRON *Mar. Fal.* I. ii, With common ruffians leagued to ruin states! **1848** MRS. JAMIESON *Sacr. & Leg. Art* (1850) 64 It is not a fiend, but a degraded prosaic human ruffian. **1868** FREEMAN *Norm. Conq.* (1877) II. 68 The courts of ruffians like Harold and Harthacnut.

β. **1553** T. WILSON *Rhet.* 99 Not a common ruffin, but a most cruell cut throte. **1576** BP. WOOLTON *Chr. Man.* I v b, Some tyme lyke Routters, some tyme lyke Rouffyns, but seldome like honest folckes. **1608** SYLVESTER *Du Bartas* II. IV. *Decay* 1077 The louzie Couch Of some base Ruffon, or some beastly Slouch. **1616** R. C. *Times' Whistle* (1871) 48 Taurus, that ruffen, in his drunken fit, An execrable murder did committe. **1686** PLOT *Staffordsh.* 291 Inticed hither in a dismall stormy night by a bloody Ruffin. **1716** T. WARD *Eng. Reform.* 365 A Red-Nos'd Ruffin, called Noll.

†**b.** ***ruffian's hall***: (see quot. 1674). *Obs.*

1592 NASHE *P. Penilesse* Wks. (Grosart) II. 53 As if men will needs carouse, conspire, and quarrell, that they may make Ruffians hall of Hell. **1605** CHAPMAN, etc. *Eastw. Hoe* I. i, Heyday, Ruffins hal. Sword, pumps, heers a Racket indeed. **1632** MASSINGER *City Madam* I. ii, Beat down their weapons! My gate Ruffian's Hall! What insolence is this? **1674** BLOUNT, *Ruffians Hall*, so that part of Smithfield was antiently called, which is now the Horse-market, where Trials of Skill were plaid by ordinary Ruffianly people, with Sword and Buckler.

c. *Pugilism.* (See quot. 1823.)

1810 *Sporting Mag.* XXXVI. 125 Ballards is a game little ruffian, and has won by strength. **1823** EGAN *Grose's Dict. Vulgar T.*, *Ruffian*, in the pugilistic cant, is a fellow regardless of a knowledge of the science; one who hits away right or wrong, so that he can only obtain conquest.

†**d.** A rowdy coxcomb. *Obs.*

1820 CAPT. F. MACDONOGH *Hermit in London* V. 36 We have also a new genus of males ycleped *ruffians*, far differing from our bucks or sporting gentlemen of old. **1836** E. HOWARD *R. Reefer* lxiii, It was in the reign of the 'bloods' and the 'ruffians', more ferocious species of coxcombs than our dandies.

†**2.** One distinguished as a swaggering bully or dissolute person by his dress or appearance (esp. by wearing the hair long). *Obs.*

1560 PILKINGTON *Aggeus* H ij b, A Ruffin wil haue more in a ruffe and hys hose, than he should spend in a yeare. **1583** *Exec. for Treason* (1675) 39 All in their apparel, as Roisters or Ruffins. **1603** in Brand *Newcastle* (1789) II. 232 [Apprentices shall not] weare their haire longe nor locks at their ears like ruffians. **1623** R. CARPENTER *Conscionable Christian* 54 A feast in sicknesse when worldlings hopes.. lag like a Ruffians starcht Ruffe in a storme of raine. **1675** BAXTER *Cath. Theol.* II. I. 298, I can remember since among the Religious stricter party, it was abominable to wear long hair, even to cover the ears, and now these twenty years they many of them exceed those that then were accounted Ruffians.

†**3.** A protector or confederate of courtesans. *Obs.* Cf. BULLY *sb.*[1] 4.

A common sense in the Romance languages.

c **1618** MORYSON *Itin.* IV. 412 The Common sorte lodge with Baudes called Ruffians, to whome in Venice they pay of their gayne the fifth parte. **1632** *Holland's Leaguer* D 2, The first, a stout Ruffian to guard her. **1648** HEXHAM II, *Een hoeren-voerder*, a Ruffin, or a keeper of Whores.

4. *attrib.* or as *adj.* **a.** Characteristic of, appropriate to, ruffians.

1553 T. WILSON *Rhet.* 75 b, To eschue all folishe talke & ruffin maners. **1590** SPENSER *F.Q.* I. iv. 34 His ruffin raiment all was staind with blood. **1597** SHAKS. *2 Hen. VI*, V. ii. 49 Was't thou ordain'd thus To die in Ruffian battell? **1725** POPE *Odyss.* IV. 977 Experienc'd age May timely intercept the ruffian rage. **1746** THOMSON *Cast. Indol.* II. xv, Guile and ruffian force were all their trade. **1814** SCOTT *Ld. of Isles* VI. xxvi, Some fought from ruffian thirst of blood. *c* **1840** DE QUINCEY *War* Wks. 1862 IV. 273 A predatory and ruffian war.

b. Having the manners, behaviour, or appearance of ruffians. Also *fig.* of things.

1597 SHAKS. *2 Hen. IV*, III. i. 22 The Windes, Who take the Ruffian Billowes by the top. **1605** *1st Pt. Ieronimo* III. ii, As sithmen trim the long haird Ruffian fields. **1632** LITHGOW *Trav.* I. 2 Ruffian Pandors, by hopefull youth and prodigall gallants, are now.. richly rewarded. **1694** MOTTEUX *Rabelais* V. (1737) 217 Rovers, Ruffian-Rogues, and Hedge-Creepers; Female Chamberlains. **1728–46** THOMSON *Spring* 12 See where surly Winter.. calls his ruffian blasts. **1821** SOUTHEY *Exped. Orsua* 212 *note*, A hero of the ruffian breed. **1871** KINGSLEY *At Last* vi, The ruffian army, which is the usual curse of a Spanish American republic.

c. Relating to ruffians.

1842 BORROW *Bible in Spain* xii, One.. whose name will live for many a year in the ruffian histories of Madrid.

5. *Comb.*, as ***ruffian-faced, -looking***.

1794 MRS. RADCLIFFE *Myst. Udolpho* xxvi, Followed by a number of ruffian-faced fellows. **1824** *John Bull Mag.* I. 133 One debauched ruffian-looking scarecrow.

Ruffian, the devil: see RUFFIN[1].

ruffian (ˈrʌfɪən), *v.* Also 6 **ruffin.** [f. the sb. Cf. Sp. *rufianar*, It. *ruffianare*.]

1. *intr.* To play the ruffian; *esp.* of wind, etc., to rage, bluster. Also const. *it* and *out*.

1594 O. B. *Quest. Profit. Concern.* 12 b, What would haue serued their turnes fiue yeares at home,.. must be spent in one yeare on proud ragges, to ruffin it out in the companie of their betters. **1604** SHAKS. *Oth.* II. i. 7 Me thinks, the wind hath spoke aloud at Land,.. If it hath ruffiand so vpon the Sea [etc.]. **1822** W. TENNANT *Thane of Fife* i. 9 Their foam-becrested heads that rowl and ruffian on!

2. *Pugilism.* **a.** *trans.* To strike (one) without regard to the rules of sport; to maul, hammer.

1808 *Sporting Mag.* XXXII. 77 Gully.. kept him from falling until he had ruffianed him into an apparent senseless state. **1819** *Blackw. Mag.* IV. 728[He] ruffian'd the reeling youngster round the Ring.

b. *intr.* (Cf. RUFFIAN *sb.* 1 c.) Also *fig.*

1820 *Blackwood's Mag.* VII. 190 Even I,.. who never 'ruffian'd' in the ring, Nor know of 'challenge'. **1828** *Ibid.* XXIII. 843 [Brougham] is not particularly conscientious about a foul blow.. and he is too much given to ruffianing it.

ruffianage (ˈrʌfɪənɪdʒ). [f. RUFFIAN *sb.*] Ruffianism; ruffians collectively.

1852 *Blackw. Mag.* LXXII. 278 So long as the ruffianage of our great towns exists, so long must war continue. **1874** E. PEACOCK *J. Markenfield* III. 25 He was well known to nearly every unit of the ruffianage that was gathered together.

ˈ**ruffiandom.** [f. RUFFIAN *sb.*] The domain of ruffians; ruffians collectively; ruffianism.

1882 SALA *Amer. Revis.* (1885) 160 Some of the most amazing ruffians that the whole world of ruffiandom probably could furnish. **1886** G. GISSING *Isabel Clarendon* II. v. 109 He never sank to sheer ruffiandom.

ˈ**ruffianhood.** *rare.* [f. RUFFIAN *sb.*] The quality of a ruffian; ruffians collectively.

1856 *Titan Mag.* July 53/1 Nothing thick-lipped or wolf-eyed: no defiant ruffianhood about the men. **1884** A. FORBES *Chinese Gordon* ii. 29 The peaceful fled shudderingly before this wave of fierce stalwart ruffianhood.

ˈ**ruffianing,** *vbl. sb.* [f. RUFFIAN *sb.*]

1. Dissolute or riotous conduct. ? *Obs.*

1549 COVERDALE, etc. *Erasm. Par. Thess.* 1 That the vnlearned might.. repent of light ruffianyng and blasphemous carnal Gospelling. **1556** OLDE *Antichrist* 94 Their intemperaunce, ruffionyng, glotonie.

2. Brutal unscientific boxing.

1829 P. EGAN *Boxiana* 2nd. Ser. II. 446 Ruffianing was all *the go* at Moulsey Hurst so slippery, Till Science took the cause in hand. **1896** A. MORRISON *Child of the Jago* 131 The sparring was not long..; the main hits and guards, with much rushing and ruffianing.

ˈ**ruffianish,** *a.* *rare.* [f. RUFFIAN *sb.*] Characteristic of a ruffian; ruffianly.

1593 G. HARVEY *Pierce's Super.* Wks. (Grosart) II. 221 They that affect such ruffianish braueryes.. may bestow the reading. **1611** FLORIO, *Ruffianesco*, ruffianish. **1824** *Spirit Publ. Jrnls.* (1825) 511 The complaining coachman—a stout.., large-lipped, young, ruffianish sort of a subject.

ruffianism (ˈrʌfɪənɪz(ə)m). [f. RUFFIAN *sb.*] Conduct or manners befitting a ruffian; violence, brutality; ruffianly character; ruffians collectively.

1593 G. HARVEY *Pierce's Super.* Wks. (Grosart) II. 218 The stately Tragedie scorneth the trifling Comedie: and the trifling Comedie floweth the new Ruffianisme. **1596** NASHE *Saffron Walden* Wks. (Grosart) III. 111 Betwixt a kinde of carelesse rude ruffianisme, and curious finicall complement. **1656** BLOUNT *Glossogr.*, *Ribauldry*, Roguery, Ruffianism, Whoredom.

1839 DE QUINCEY *Murder* Wks. 1854 IV. 87 He was aware of.. the ruffianism of this whole neighbourhood. **1873** BURTON *Hist. Scot.* VI. lxv. 20 At the end of the Thirty Year's War.. there was much turbulence and ruffianism. **1890** 'R. BOLDREWOOD' *Col. Reformer* (1891) 289 This vast concourse of people, containing presumably the ruffianism of all lands under the sun.

ˈ**ruffianize,** *v.* [f. RUFFIAN *sb.*]

†**1.** *intr.* To play the ruffian or pander. *Obs.*$^{-0}$

1611 COTGR., *Ruffienner*, to Ruffianize, to pandarize it; make or set leacherous matches.

2. *trans.* To render ruffianly in character.

1833 SOUTHEY in *Life* (1850) VI. 220 The portrait prefixed to this book seems intentionally to have radicalised, or rather ruffianised, a countenance which had no cut-throat expression at that time. **1872** W. MINTO *Eng. Prose Lit.* I. i. 55 He objected to the Reform Bill of 1832, that it had ruffianised Parliament.

ˈ**ruffian-like,** *a.* and *adv.* Also 6–7 **ruffin-.** [f. RUFFIAN *sb.*]

A. *adj.* Befitting, appropriate to, a ruffian; resembling, having the qualities or manners of, a ruffian.

α. **1598** FLORIO, *Roffianamenti*, bawdries or ruffianlike tricks, ruflings. *a* **1627** HAYWARD *Edw. VI* (1630) 142 His bold answeres termed rude and ruffianlike.. only caused or much furthered his condemnation. **1657** W. COLES *Adam in Eden* xviii. 38 The late Witch of Salisbury, who sent her Ruffian-like spirits to gather Vervein and Dill. **1767** WILKES *Corr.* (1805) III. 104 A good deal of humanity, and some share of timidity, prevented the execution of such ruffian-like commands. **1818** COBBETT *Pol. Reg.* XXXIII. 242 The despots, bold and ruffian-like as they are, dare not go to war against the Patriots of Spanish America.

β. **1580** FULKE *Answ. P. Frarine* 54 To omit his ruffin-like railing, and whorish scoulding. **1581** STYWARD *Mart. Discipl.* I. 51 No souldier shall be suffered to be of a ruffin-like behauiour, either to prouoke or to giue anie blow or thrust. **1655** FULLER *Ch. Hist.* III. 18 Which Ruffin-like custom of long hair now used by the Normans, was here justly restrained.

B. *adv.* In the manner of a ruffian. *rare.*

1600 BRETON *Pasquils Fooles-cappe* Wks. (Grosart) I. 21/2 Shee that is giuen to Pride and Brauery, And Ruffin-like, will sweare, and swash it out. **1657** BUNYAN *Vind. Gosp. Truths* Wks. 1853 II. 193 Ruffian-like they will wear long hair, which nature itself forbiddeth.

ruffianly (ˈrʌfɪənlɪ), *a.* Also 6 **ruffianlie,** 7 **rufeaniely;** 6 **ruffyn-, ruffin-, ruffenly.** [f. RUFFIAN *sb.* + -LY[1].]

1. Having the character, appearance, or demeanour of a ruffian.

1570 FOXE *A. & M.* (ed. 2) 1359/1 A certeine seruyng man of the lyke ruffynly order. **1593** NASHE *Christ's T.* Wks. (Grosart) IV. 224 No Smithfield ruffianly Swash-buckler will come of with such harshe hell-raking othes as they. **1612** T. TAYLOR *Comm. Titus* iii. 3 Many ruffianly Protestants, who strengthen themselues in their sinnes. **1633** PRYNNE *Histriom.* 210 Love-lockes, growne now too much in fashion with comly Pages, Youthes, and lewd effeminate ruffianly persons. **1674** BLOUNT, s.v. *Ruffians Hall*, Where Trials of Skill were plaid by ordinary Ruffianly people. **1835** JAMES *Gipsy* xiii, I found him consorting with a gang of as ruffianly fellows as ever I beheld. **1856** R. A. VAUGHAN *Mystics* (1860) I. VI. viii. 266 He sits himself down to table with a ruffianly set of drovers and traders.

Comb. **1822** SCOTT *Peveril* xxiii, Two ruffianly-looking men, apparently his guards, had hold of his doublet. **1882** W. D. HAY *Brighter Britain!* I. xi. 301 A line of nine ruffianly-looking scarecrows, under review by.. head-master of the ceremonies.

2. Characteristic of, appropriate to, ruffians.

α. **1579** NORTHBROOKE *Dicing* (1843) 168 By the worde (dauncing) there is not ment euery maner of wanton or ruffianly leaping and frisking. **1592** G. HARVEY *Four Letters* Wks. (Grosart) I. 168 With ruffianly haire, vnseemely apparell, and more vnseemelye Company. **1603** *Lismore Papers* Ser. II. (1887) I. 44 He marvauled that he would.. breake owt into such passion in that rufeaniely sorte. **1691** T. H[ALE] *Acc. New Invent.* p. cx, He.. had from him instead of thanks a ruffianly Answer. **1750** in Dodsley *Fug. Pieces* (1761) I. 147 For daring to asperse her Daughter's Reputation in that wicked ruffianly Manner. **1821** SCOTT *Kenilw.* i, The mercer there.. affects a ruffianly vapouring humour. **1874** MOTLEY *John of Barneveld* II. xxi. 386 Two common soldiers of ruffianly aspect.

β. **1586** B. YOUNG *Guazzo's Civ. Conv.* IV. 221 b, In so ruffenly and unseemlie a sort. **1600** W. WATSON *Decacordon* (1602) 244 A new and ruffinly course.

‖**ruffiano.** *Obs.* Also pl. **ruffiani.** [a. It. *ruffiano*.] = RUFFIAN *sb.*

1611 CORYAT *Crudities* 268 Shee will either cause thy throate to be cut by her Ruffiano.. or procure thee to be arrested. **1618** *Hist. Perkin Warbeck* 15 So the Zaffi, or other desperate Ruffiani obtaine many preies and booties. **1709** *Brit. Apollo* No. 73. 3/1 And Ruffiano thou by Nature art. **1819** 'RABELAIS' *Abeillard & Heloisa* 317 Reader! hast seen a ruffiano! Stealing towards ye near the Arno?

ruffiaˈnosity. *nonce-wd.* [f. RUFFIAN *sb.*] Ruffianism (in boxing).

1823 *Blackw. Mag.* XIV. 72 No ruffianosity can ever beat science.

†ˈ**ruffianous,** *a.* *Obs.* Also 7 **ruffinous.** [f. RUFFIAN *sb.*] Ruffianly.

1555 *Instr. Gentleman* C iij, Hortentius Corbio, a man of most noughty and Ruffianous life. *c* **1611** CHAPMAN *Iliad* VI. 457 To shelter the sad Monument from all the ruffinous pride Of stormes and tempests.

ˈ**ruffianry.** *rare.* [f. RUFFIAN *sb.* Cf. obs. F. *ruffiennerie*, Sp. *ruf-*, It. *ruffianeria*.] Ruffianism; ruffians collectively.

1583 GOLDING *Calvin on Deut.* cii. 631 Though a man cast himselfe into all manner of leawdnes and ruffianry. **1891** *Cornh. Mag.* Jan. 80 Shetanpara begins to pour forth all its ruffianry.

ˈ**ruffianship.** *rare*$^{-0}$. (See quot.)

1648 HEXHAM II, *Roffiaenschap*, Ruffianship, or Bawdienesse.

ruffie, variant of RUFFY[1] *Obs.*

†ˈ**Ruffin**[1]. *Obs.* Forms: 3, 6–7 **ruffin,** 4–6 **ruffyn(e,** 5 **rofyn;** 6–7 **ruffian.** [Of obscure origin; perh. related to RUFFIAN *sb.*, but recorded much earlier than that word. See also RUFFY[1].]

1. The name of a fiend.

a **1225** *St. Marher.* 13 þou.. art mi broðeres bone, ruffines of helle. *c* **1250** *Meid. Maregrete* l, Ruffin was my broþer, þat tou here sclowe. **1426** AUDELAY *Poems* 77 So hard Rofyn rogud his roll, That he smot with his choule, Aȝayns the marbystone. *a* **1500** *Chester Plays* V. 166*, I have godis wonder fell; both ruffin and ragnell will work right as I them tell.

2. *Cant.* The Devil.

It is doubtful whether this is a continuation of the old name, or a new application of RUFFIAN *sb.* In the Chester Plays I. 239 the Harl. MS. has *Ruffian* in place of *Ruffin* of the other copies.

1567 HARMAN *Caveat* (1869) 84 *To the ruffian*, to the deuell. *The ruffian cly the*, the deuyll take thee. **1608** DEKKER *Lanth. & Candle Lt.* C iij b, The Ruffin cly the nab of the Harman beck. *a* **1625** FLETCHER *Beggar's Bush* III. iii, And let the Quire Cuffin, And Hermanbecks trine, and trine to the Ruffin. **1641** BROME *Joviall Crew* II. Wks. 1873 III. 389, I sweare by the Ruffin, That we are assaulted by a quire Cuffin.

† **'ruffin**[2]. *Obs. rare.* [f. RUFF *sb.*[1] 2, with obscure ending.] The ruff, *Acerina cernua.*

1596 SPENSER *F.Q.* IV. xi. 33 Yar.. brought a present joyfully Of his owne fish.. Whose like none else could shew, the which they Ruffins call. **1610** W. FOLKINGHAM *Art Survey* IV. iii. 83 Dace, Roach, Ruffin, Eeles.

'ruffing, *vbl. sb.*[1] [f. RUFF *v.*[2]] The action of making a ruff at cards. Also *attrib.*, as ***ruffing element, trick, value***.

1611 FLORIO, *Ronfamenti*,.. also ruffings at cardes. **1850** *Handbk. of Games* (Bohn) 162 *Ruffing*, playing a trump to any other suit. **1885** PROCTOR *Whist* 76 A trump lead may be purely defensive, made simply to prevent ruffing. **1930** E. CULBERTSON *Contract Bridge Blue Bk.* iv. 60 The.. characteristic of the Supporting Hand lies in the use of ruffing tricks. **1936** 'LUCIAN' *Straight Bid* xii. 126 In actual play the result is materially affected by.. ruffing values, etc. **1950** *Bridge from 'Times'* ii. 63 This is a pretty example of the use of the long trump hand to make ruffing tricks. **1952** I. MACLEOD *Bridge* xii. 143 The introduction of the ruffing element, and the problems of trump management make the play in a suit contract far more difficult and intricate. **1971** *Country Life* 22 Apr. 973/1 The ruffing element which obtains in a suit contract. **1977** *Bridge Mag.* Sept. 153/2 His ruffing values being distinctly unimpressive he quickly converted to seven no-trumps.

'ruffing, *vbl. sb.*[2] *Sc.* [f. RUFF *v.*[3]] The action of applauding with the feet.

1836 *Dundee Advertiser* 25 Nov., On reading the minutes, there was some ruffing. **1843** CARLYLE in Froude *1st 40 Yrs.* (1882) I. 313 Ruffing of applausive barristers over table oratory heard at a distance. **1869** A. MACDONALD *Settlement* (1877) 87 (E.D.D.), Great ruffing in the gallery.

'ruffing, *vbl. sb.*[3] [See RUFF *v.*[5] 2, and ROUGHING *vbl. sb.* 2.] The process of working beaver felt into a hat-body. Also *concr.* the felt used for this purpose.

1845 G. DODD *Brit. Manuf.* V. 165 This layer, which is called a 'ruffing', or 'roughing', is a little larger than the cap body. *Ibid.* 166 In the process of 'ruffing', each fibre of fur ..enters the substance of the felt cap. **1886** HOLLAND *Cheshire Gloss.* s.v.

'ruffing, *ppl. a.*[1] [f. RUFF *v.*[4]] Blustering.

1628 FORD *Lover's Mel.* v. i, Like ruffing winds lock'd up in caves.

'ruffing, *ppl. a.*[2] [f. RUFF *v.*[1]] That forms or rises in ruffs.

1865 R. D. BLACKMORE in *Macm. Mag.* XII. 33/1 The blackcocks.. swell their ruffing breasts, and crow for their rivals to spar with them.

Ruffini (rʊ'fi:nɪ). *Anat.* The name of Angelo *Ruffini* (1864–1929), Italian anatomist, used *attrib.* and with *of* to designate certain dermal sensory organs.

1900 HUBER & DEWITT in *Jrnl. Compar. Neurol.* X. 175 The author [*sc.* Ruffini] thus distinguishes this spindle, which may bear his name, from the neuro-tendinous end-organs of Golgi... The Ruffini organ is composed of connective and elastic tissue. **1928** *Amer. Jrnl. Psychol.* XL. 357 No Golgi-Màzzoni, Krause or Ruffini end-organs were discovered in the hairy parts of the human skin. **1974** D. & M. WEBSTER *Compar. Vertebr. Morphol.* x. 200 On the other hand, the end bulbs of Ruffini—flattened, bulblike endings within a fine, connective tissue network—respond to temperature increases. **1981** A. BRODAL *Neurol. Anat.* (ed. 3) ii. 51 Another type of slowly adapting receptor.. has a resting discharge that increases when a mechanical stimulus is applied to the skin. These receptors.. are found in the dermis and appear to be Ruffini endings.

ruffle ('rʌf(ə)l), *sb.*[1] Also 6 *Sc.* ruffill. [f. RUFFLE *v.*[1] Cf. Kilian's '*ruyffel*, ruga' (not otherwise known), and LG. *ruffel* goffering-iron.]

I. † **1.** Impairment *of* one's reputation. *Obs.*$^{-1}$

1508 DUNBAR *Tua Mariit Wemen* 332, I wald haif ridden him to Rome, with ane raip in his heid, Wer not ruffill of my renovne, & rumour of pepill.

† **2.** Disorder, confusion. *Obs.*

It is possible that these quots. may belong to RUFFLE *sb.*[2]

1533 MORE *Answ. Poysoned Bk.* Wks. 1087/2 When ye see the thynges in suche wyse before you withoute inter-lacinge, ruffle, and confusion. **1712** BLACKMORE *Creation* 252 The elements distinct might keep their seat, Elude the ruffle, and your scheme defeat.

3. a. A disturbed state (of the mind); disturbance, perturbation, excitement.

1704 M. HENRY *Commun. Comp.* Wks. 1853 I. 340/2 Free from the disorders and ruffles of passion. **1748** J. NORTON *Redeemed Captive* (1870) 21 This put them into a considerable ruffle, fearing that there might be an army after them. **1767** T. HUTCHINSON *Hist. Mass.* II. iii. 221 An administration.. calm and without ruffle. **1878** ELWIN in *Life & Lett. Pennefather* xxi. 515 To carry out innumerable details without ruffle or excitement.

b. A disturbing or annoying experience or encounter; annoyance, vexation.

1718 *Entertainer* No. 21. 138 To keep the Soul steady under the severest Pressures and Ruffles of Fortune, is a Magnanimity few Hero's can arrive at. **1735** SWIFT *Corr.* Wks. 1841 II. 757 Taking a secret pleasure in all the little ruffles you meet with in the country. **1741** MIDDLETON *Cicero* I. v. 332 As this unexpected opposition gave some little ruffle to the Triumvirate. **1878** HARE *Walks Lond.* I. iv. 136 In his after work he met with so many rubs and ruffles.

4. A break or alteration in the evenness or placidity of some surface: **a.** Of the features.

1713 *Guardian* No. 29, She.. is never seen.. to disorder her Countenance with the Ruffle of a Smile. **1895** MEREDITH *Amazing Marriage* xv, A ruffle of sourness shot over the features of the earl.

b. Of water, the sky, etc.

1750 BEAWES *Lex Mercat.* (1752) 47 The frowns and ruffles of a lowering sky. **1793** SMEATON *Edystone L.* 197 The water is generally so clear as to see the bottom; and in case of any ruffle by the wind [etc.]. **1855** GUTHRIE *Gospel in Ezekiel* (1856) 317 The cripple.. sat uncured by Bethesda's pool, nor took his anxious eye off the water as he waited for its first stir and ruffle. **1894** JESSOPP *Rand. Roam.* i. 37 In that delicious.. sunshine, with never.. a ruffle on the gently heaving water.

5. The act of ruffling cards.

1872 *Routledge's Ev. Boy's Ann.* June 435/1 The ruffle is a mere flourish.

II. † **6.** The loose turned-over portion or flap of a top-boot. *Obs.*$^{-1}$

1599 B. JONSON *Ev. Man out of Hum.* IV. vi, One of the Rowels catcht hold of the Ruffle of my Boot, and being Spanish leather, and subject to tear, overthrows me.

7. a. A strip of lace or other fine material, gathered on one edge and used as an ornamental frill on a garment, esp. at the wrist, breast, or neck.

Ruffles at the wrists were formerly an ordinary appendage of male costume.

1707 LD. RABY in Hearne *Collect.* (O.H.S.) II. 43 He wears no Ruffles. **1747** *Gent. Mag.* 541/2 He has desired the officers of the army to leave off ruffles, and sets the example himself. **1778** MISS BURNEY *Evelina* lxxii, He was very soon engaged.. in looking at lace ruffles. **1850** D. G. MITCHELL *Rev. Bachelor* 87 A little bit of lace ruffle is gathered about the neck by a blue ribbon. **1881** BESANT & RICE *Chapl. of Fleet* I. 142 He would go with waistcoat unbuttoned,.. neck-cloth loose, and ruffles limp.

transf. **1825** T. HOOK *Sayings* Ser. II. *Man of Many Fr.* 176 A haunch of mutton,.. decorated with a paper ruffle,.. to look.. like venison.

† **b.** *pl.* Handcuffs. *slang* (? *Obs.*).

1785 GROSE *Dict. Vulgar T.* **1839** W. H. AINSWORTH *Jack Sheppard* I. II. ix. 305 'I'll accommodate you with a pair of ruffles.' And he proceeded to handcuff his captive. **1840** H. COCKTON *Life Valentine Vox* xiv. 109 'Sam! here, where are the ruffles?' and the fellow addressed instantly produced a pair of handcuffs. **1912** A. H. LEWIS *Apaches of N.Y.* viii. 179 Outside they found Cohen.. with the ruffles on the Ghost.

c. An object resembling a ruffle; *esp.* the ruff of a bird.

1862 AGASSIZ *Contrib. Nat. Hist. U.S.* IV. 88 Adorned.. with waving ruffles projecting in large clusters, which are alternately pressed forward and withdrawn. **1872** COUES *N. Amer. Birds* 18 The condor has a singular ruffle all around the neck, of close, downy feathers.

8. *attrib.* and *Comb.* as ***ruffle collar, lace***; ***ruffle cuffed, headed*** adjs.; **ruffle shirt** *N. Amer.*, (*a*) a shirt decorated with ruffles; (*b*) *transf.*, an aristocrat, a person of means; hence **ruffle-shirted** *a.*, **ruffle-shirter**.

1968 J. IRONSIDE *Fashion Alphabet* 52 *Ruffle collar*, a collar cut on the bias or circular so that it falls in a fluted ruffle round the neck. **1880** 'MARK TWAIN' *Tramp Abroad* 399, I did not get back the same drawers I sent down... I got a pair on a new plan. They were merely a pair of white ruffle-cuffed absurdities. **1927** W. DEEPING *Kitty* xxix. 370 The ruffle-headed pianist bumping up and down on his chair. **1682** J. PINNEY *Let.* 4 Sept. (1939) 15 The remnant you sent downe shall speadily be cut & sent & a ruffel lace of 2 nailes broad. **1830** *Amer. Sentinel* (Philadelphia) 27 Aug. 2/2 Where a dinner is to be got up, a few mechanics are procured to take the first rank, and the ruffle shirts fall into the rear. **1831** *American* (Harrodsburg, Kentucky) 22 July 3/1 General Jackson and his friends are lessening the burthens of the people by.. placing the Tax, on Wines, Rum,.. and fine cloth such as the *Rufle* [*sic*] *shirt* gentry wear. **1838** B. DRAKE *Tales & Sk.* 64 The colonists presented, indeed, a curiously grotesque appearance, loitering about the station in ruffle shirts and coon-skin caps. **1840** J. P. KENNEDY *Quodlibet* xii. 158 If he does get on with his business, and makes a little fortune, we can call him a.. Ruffle Shirt. **1848** *Knickerbocker* XVIII. 520 It was asserted.. that he wore a ruffle-shirt and overshoes. **1835** A. B. LONGSTREET *Georgia Scenes* 85 The *ruffle-shirted* little darlings of the present day. *a* **1864** HAWTHORNE *Dr. Grimshawe* v, A decorous, powdered, ruffle-shirted dignitary. **1876** *Harper's Weekly* 26 Aug. 691/1 They belonged to the class which the ward politicians of to-day sneer at as ruffle-shirted and silk-stockinged. **1842** *Knickerbocker* XIX. 305 Many a taunt, hitherto repressed, was thrown at the ruffle-shirters, as the town boys called them.

'ruffle, *sb.*[2] Forms: 5–6 ruffull, ruffill, 6 ruffell, 6– ruffle. [f. RUFFLE *v.*[2], but in later use perh. not clearly distinguished from RUFFLE *sb.*[1] 3 (see also *sb.*[1] 2).]

1. A riotous disturbance or tumult; a hostile encounter or skirmish; a contention, dispute.

1534 MORE *Treat. Passion* Wks. 1292/1 They sayde therfore.., Not on the holy day, lest there aryse some sedicious ruffle among the people. **1559** BALDWIN in *Mirr. Magistr.* To Rdr. A ij, Omytting the ruffle made by Jacke Strawe and his meyny. **1567** DRANT *Horace, Ep.* II. i. G vj, Such rule and ruffle make the rowte that cum to see our geare.

1700 STRYPE *Life Aylmer* (1821) 97 In April 1588, he happened to have a ruffle with a mad blade named Maddocks. **1710** PALMER *Proverbs* 329 In the ruffle between two pretenders, the right owner often finds the possession. **1779** JOHNSON *Wks.* (1787) IV. 504 Calamy only says he had a ruffle with bishop Laud, while at his height. **1826** SCOTT *Woodst.* viii, That last ruffle which we had with him at Worcester. **1858** FROUDE *Hist. Eng.* IV. 34 When the ruffle of the Reformation arose in England, James inclined to the Papacy. **1890** 'R. BOLDREWOOD' *Miner's Right* (1899) 82/1, I wouldn't mind a ruffle with some of your volunteers.

† **b.** Without article. *Obs.*

a **1557** MRS. M. BASSETT tr. *More's Treat. Passion* M.'s Wks. 1357/1 Wherby raised they many yeares together, muche busines & ruffle in the church. **1571** CAMPION *Hist. Irel.* II. ix. (1633) 106 Causes of much ruffle and unquietnes in the Realme.

† **2. a.** *Sc.* A check or defeat. *Obs.*

a **1578** LINDESAY (Pitscottie) *Chron. Scot.* (S.T.S.) II. 201 That was the grettest ruffell that evir the thives of liddisdaill sufferit. **1679** *Lauderdale Papers* (Camden) III. 169 Should I have hazarded these few forces that were there and got the least ruffle, the consequences of it might have been of too great Importance to Scotland. **1721** WODROW *Ch. Hist.* (1828) III. 70 They knew well their persecutor's rage would be sharpened by this ruffle [*viz.* the defeat at Drumclog].

† **b.** A disturbing cause or event; a disturbance of peace or tranquillity; a commotion. *Obs.*

1667 WATERHOUSE *Fire of London* 169 Turned out of their callings, and unstocked by the loss of that ruffle. **1672** OWEN *Disc. Christian Love* v. Wks. 1852 XV. 155 This rule of church communion furnished Christians with peace and amity for many ages, setting aside the ruffle given them in the rashness of Victor before mentioned. **1716** BP. KENNETT in Ellis *Orig. Lett.* Ser. II. IV. 302 The Princess is in a very safe condition; the long depending labour, and the loss of a fine Prince upon it, made a great ruffle at Court.

† **3.** Ostentatious bustle or display. *Obs. rare.*

1597 SHAKS. *Lover's Compl.* ix, A reuerend man.. Sometime a blusterer that the ruffle knew Of Court, of Cittie. *a* **1694** TILLOTSON *Serm.* clxxv. Wks. 1743 IX. 4091 Wickedness is many times exalted to high places and makes a great noise and ruffle in the world.

† **4.** = RUFF *sb.*[6] *Obs.*

1647 N. BACON *Disc. Govt. Eng.* I. lxvii. 279 Though the Clergy were now in their ruffle, and felt themselves in their full strength. **1688** HOLME *Armoury* IV. (Roxb.) 403/1 Barry wavey of 6, A. and B. an English ship, O. in full ruffle with sailes A. garnished with red crosses. *Ibid.*, A ship in his full ruffle vnder full saile.

'ruffle, *sb.*[3] *rare.* [Cf. RUFF *sb.*[1] I.] The sea-bream.

1601 HOLLAND *Pliny* II. 429 The blacke-tailed ruffles or sea-breames, which the Greekes name Melanuri. **1883** *Fisheries Exhib. Catal.* 352 Oil extracted from Liver of the Ruffle, Canary Islands.

'ruffle, *sb.*[4] *Mil.* [Cf. RUFF *sb.*[5] and Pg. *rufla* in the same sense.] (See quot. 1802.)

1802 JAMES *Milit. Dict.*, *Ruffle*, a term used among the drummers of a British regiment, to signify a sort of vibrating sound, which is made upon a drum, and is less loud than the roll. **1844** *Regul. & Ord. Army* 29 A Lieutenant-General is to be received,—By Infantry, with three Ruffles. **1868** *Ibid.* §74 The trumpets sounding and the drums beating a ruffle. **1890** *Cent. Mag.* Feb. 570/1 The very drums and fifes that played the ruffles as each battalion passed the President.

'ruffle, *v.*[1] Forms: 4–5 ruffel (5 -lyn, -lone), 6 ruffill, -yll, rofel, 7 ruffell; 6–7 rufle, 5– ruffle. [Of doubtful origin. Similar forms in the related languages are LG. *ruffelen*, *rüffelen* to crumple, curl, goffer (cf. Kilian's '*ruyffelen*, rugare, striare') and ON. *hrufla* to scratch. Sense 9 is also similar to that of Du. *roffelen*, LG. *ruffelen*, to work roughly.]

I. 1. *trans.* To destroy the smoothness or evenness of, to spoil the regular or neat arrangement of (cloth, the skin, etc.).

a **1300** *Cursor M.* 26391 þai leue þe grettes plight be-hind, Bileues þe heui, and sceues þe light þat ruffeld es for to ma slight. **1530** PALSGR. 695/1, I ruffle clothe or sylkes, I bring them out of their playne foldynge, *je plionne.* Se howe this lawne is ruffylled. **1599** B. JONSON *Ev. Man out of Hum.* I. ii, Ruffle your brow like a new boot. **1607** DEKKER & MARSTON *Westw. Hoe* I. i, Pray thee looke the gowne be not rufled. **1657** in Thurloe *State P.* VI. 317 The paper being loose and ruffled up, the titles of the said books were very visible. **1700** T. BROWN tr. *Fresny's Amusem.* 49 There sits a Beau.. that dares not stir his head nor move his Body, for fear of.. ruffling his Cravat. **1711** ADDISON *Spect.* No. 42 ¶ 1 A little Boy taking care all the while that they do not ruffle the Tail of her Gown. **1833** HT. MARTINEAU *Three Ages* I. 6 The elder dame smoothed a brow which was evidently too apt to be ruffled.

b. To roughen, raise, or abrade (the skin, etc.) as by rubbing or grazing upon.

1615 G. SANDYS *Trav.* 67 They be women of elegant beauties,.. smooth as the polished iuory; being neuer ruffled by the weather. **1654** WHITLOCK *Zootomia* 327 Ruffling her incomparable Beauty with Hardships of Weather. **1727** A. HAMILTON *New Acc. E. Ind.* II. 11, I could give many Instances.., but am loth to ruffle the skin of old sores. **1730** *Phil. Trans.* XXXVI. 341 The Sword had slanted.. along the *Omentum*, grazing slightly upon it, which was superficially ruffled, but so as to be hardly perceivable. **1883** S. C. HALL *Retrospect* I. 123 A ball from the pistol of Maginn ruffled the coat-collar of Berkeley.

c. To draw together in a ruffle or ruffles; to trim with ruffles. (Usu. in pa. pple.)

1653 GREAVES *Seraglio* 62 A pair of Chackshirs, or breeches, after their fashion down to the heels, and ruffled in the small of the leg, as our boots are. **1666** PEPYS *Diary* 15 Oct., The legs ruffled with black riband like a pigeon's leg. **1711** ADDISON *Spect.* No. 129 ¶ 9 That he had a clean Shirt on, which was ruffled down to his middle. **1784** COWPER *Task* IV. 545 Her elbows ruffled, and her tott'ring form Ill propp'd upon French heels. **1869** BLACKMORE *Lorna D.* xxi, He was.. tasselled and ruffled with a mint of bravery. **1891** *Truth* 10 Dec. 1240/2 With fichu and sash ruffled with quantities of lace.

2. To disorder, disarrange (hair or feathers); to cause to stick up or out irregularly.

1490 CAXTON *Eneydos* ii. 15 Hir heyr.. hangynge indyfferently and alle rufflyd on alle partyes. **1538** LELAND *Itin.* (1768) II. 65 Then I saw to antique Heddes with Heere as rofelid yn Lokkes. **1582** STANYHURST *Æneis* II. (Arb.) 65 Heer with al in trembling with speede wee ruffled his heare-bush. **1608** WILLET *Hexapla Exod.* 32 A bird cannot enter without the rufling and pulling off her feathers. **1634** MILTON *Comus* 380 She..lets grow her wings That in the various bussle of resort Were all to ruffl'd. **1864** TENNYSON *Aylmer's F.* 660 Not a hair Ruffled upon the scarfskin. **1887** BOWEN *Æneid* III. 241 Not one feather is ruffled, the spears from their bodies glance. **1897** W. H. THORNTON *Rem. West-Co. Clergyman* 250 She..went after the other bird and brought it to me without ruffling a feather.

transf. **1703** ROWE *Fair Penit.* I. i, Enthusiastick Passion swell'd her Breast, Enlarg'd her Voice, and ruffled all her Form.

b. Of a bird: To set *up*, stiffen (the feathers), esp. as a sign of anger. Also in fig. context.

a **1643** W. CARTWRIGHT *Lesbia on her Sparrow* Comedies, etc. (1651) 225 He would..now ruffle all His Feathers o'er, now let 'em fall. **1828** SCOTT *F.M. Perth* xvi, No dung-hill cock..would ruffle his feathers at such a craven as thee! **1859** FARRAR *J. Home* xxviii, The Dean ruffled his plumage, and said with asperity. **1870** ROCK *Text. Fabr.* I. 232 A swan ruffling up its feathers at the presence of an eagle.

3. In general use: To disorder, to render uneven or irregular, in some manner. Also *refl.*

1528 *Lett. & P. Hen. VIII*, IV. II. 2233 [The jury] have viewed both the east and west jetty, and find..parts of the same greatly frusshid and ruffild, so that part must be made new. **1633** G. HERBERT *Temple, Affliction* iv, While blustring windes destroy the wanton bowres, And ruffle all their curious knots and store. **1692** BENTLEY *Boyle Lect.* iv. (1693) 117 Shocks that would ruffle and break all the little Stamina of the Embryon. **1708** *Phil. Trans.* XXVI. 37 The Shingles on the Roof adjoyning thereto..were raised or ruffled. **1784** MME. D'ARBLAY *Diary* 3 Nov., Not a particle of our whole frames seems ruffled or discomposed. **1803** WORDSW. *Airey-Force Valley* 2 Not a breath of air Ruffles the bosom of this leafy glen. **1841** CAPT. B. HALL *Patchwork* III. 17 The cool sea-breeze..ruffling the surface of the water. **1883** SYMONDS *Ital. Byways* i. 3 A hurricane blew upward from the pass.., ruffling the lake. **1889** PATER *G. de Latour* 75 The plain of La Beauce had ruffled itself into low green hills and gently winding valleys.

transf. **1722** DE FOE *Moll Flanders* 105 We had an indifferent good Voyage, till we came just upon the Coast of England,..but were then ruffled with two or three Storms.

b. In fig. contexts.

1834 GREVILLE *Mem.* 13 Nov. (1875) III. 139 Several disagreeable occurrences have ruffled the stream of my life. **1848** DICKENS *Dombey* l, To think that she..ruffled, by a breath, the harmless current of his life.

c. To blot *out* by ruffling. *rare*$^{-1}$.

a **1680** CHARNOCK *Attrib. God* (1834) I. 441 Levity of spirit..scatters our thoughts..; whatsoever we hear is like words written in sand ruffled out in the next gale.

4. a. To stir *up* to indignation. *rare*$^{-1}$.

1601 SHAKS. *Jul. C.* III. ii. 232 But were I Brutus, And Brutus Antony, there were an Antony Would ruffle vp your Spirits.

b. To annoy, irritate, vex, discompose (a person, the mind, etc.).

1658–9 *Burton's Diary* (1828) IV. 222 The member that ruffled Sir Arthur Haslerigge thus, was of no great quality. **1695** J. EDWARDS *Perfect. Script.* 26 Those murmurings and discontents which ruffle and imbroil the soul. **1710** STEELE *Tatler* No. 176 ¶6 He is sensible of every Passion, but ruffled by none. **1782** MISS BURNEY *Cecilia* VIII. i, At last,.. and evidently much ruffled in his temper, he came. **1839** ADM. PAGET *Autobiog.* (1896) ii. 55, I could not resist asking the unlucky man whether this did not ruffle his temper. **1888** BURGON *Lives 12 Gd. Men* II. xii. 413 Always equable in his temper,..nothing ever seemed to ruffle him.

c. To trouble, disturb (a state of mind, etc.).

1701 STANHOPE *S. Augustine's Medit.* 78 The love of the World and the Flesh is ruffled with anxious Fears. **1769** ROBERTSON *Chas. V*, IX. Wks. 1813 III. 143 The insult..did not even ruffle the wonted tranquillity and composure of his mind. **1788** GIBBON *Decl. & F.* l. V. 227 The concord was slightly ruffled by an accidental quarrel. **1815** MME. D'ARBLAY *Diary* (1876) IV. 286 This serenity was somewhat ruffled by the arrival of the commander of the forces. **1858** FROUDE *Hist. Eng.* III. xvii. 499 From that moment no ..violent words or actions ruffled his relations with England. **1874** GREEN *Short Hist.* vii. §3. 368 Her good humour was never ruffled by the charges.

5. To turn over (the leaves of a book) hurriedly; to slip (cards) rapidly through the fingers.

1621 DONNE *Serm.* cxvii. Wks. 1839 V. 65 It is not to be able to repeat any history of the Bible without book, it is not to Ruffle a Bible, and upon any word to turn to the chapter and to the Verse. **1826** SCOTT *Woodst.* iii, It is a mercy our good knight did not see him ruffle the book at that rate. **1872** *Routledge's Ev. Boy's Ann.* June 435/1 He ostentatiously ruffles the cards.

6. *intr.* To rise unevenly or irregularly; to form small folds or bends; to flutter in this manner.

1577 B. GOOGE *Heresbach's Husb.* IV. (1586) 158 The necke feathers of colour diuers,..which must hang rufling from his necke, to his shoulders. **1607** MARKHAM *Caval.* II. (1617) 255 About your necke you shall weare..no Ruffe whose depth or thicknes may either with the winde, or motions of your Horse, ruffell about your face. **1666** DRYDEN *Ann. Mirab.* clii, Her flag aloft, spread ruffling to the wind, And sanguine streamers seem the flood to fire. **1728–46** THOMSON *Spring* 718 Her pinions ruffle, and, low-drooping, scarce Can bear the mourner to the poplar shade. **1887** J. KER *Serm.* Ser. II. IV. 57 It [the sea] ruffles to the breeze and swells into the storm.

b. To stir with anger or impatience.

1719 YOUNG *Busiris* I. i, Ruffles your temper at offences past? **1891** *Eng. Illustr. Mag.* June 662 Whose phlegmatic calm did not ruffle for one instant under his conductor's impatient temper.

II. †**7.** *trans.* To put into disarray or confusion; to tangle, ravel. *Obs.*

c **1440** *Promp. Parv.* 439/1 Ruffelyn, or snarlyn,..*innodo. Ibid.*, Rufflyd, or snarlyd, *innodatus, illaqueatus.* **1529** MORE *Dyaloge* IV. Wks. 274/2 The world once ruffled and fallen in a wildenes, how long would it be..ere the waye were founden to set the worlde in order and peace againe. **1580** BARET *Alv.* C, After the rude vandals..had by tumult of warre, ruffled all learning out of order. **1638** RAWLEY tr. *Bacon's Life & Death* (1650) 8 Things which by that, are not onely wrinkled, but ruffled and plighted, and as it were rowled together.

†**b.** To involve in obscurity or perplexity; to confuse or bewilder (a person). *Obs.*

c **1480** HENRYSON *Poems* (S.T.S.) III. 150 ȝe wald deir me, I trow, becaus I am dottit, To ruffill me with a ryme. **1530** TINDALE *Answ. More* xi. Wks. (1573) 330 But I will declare in light that which M. More ruffeleth vp in darkenesse. **1662** GURNALL *Chr. in Arm.* (1669) 503/2 The Schoolmen.. ruffled and ensnarled the plainest Truths of the Gospel with their harsh terms. **1679** C. NESS *Antichrist* 178 This prophecy..hath been so ruffled with variety of interpretations.

†**8.** To fold, wrap, heap, rattle *up*, in a rough or careless manner. *Obs.*

1533 MORE *Answ. Poysoned Bk.* Wks. 1088/2 He ruffleth vp all the matter shortelye in a fewe words. **1587** FLEMING *Contn. Holinshed* III. 1348/2 Five webs of lead were ruffled up together, like as they had beene clouts of linnen cloth. **1615** CHAPMAN *Odyss.* VII. 396, I ruffld vp falne leaues in heape. **1658** tr. *Porta's Nat. Magick* III. i. 60, I have neither time nor leisure.., seeing this work is ruffled up in haste.

†**b.** To furl (a sail). *Obs. rare.*

1622 MABBE tr. *Aleman's Guzman d'Alf.* 191 Inforced to let fall their maine sayle, which when they had ruffled [etc.]. *Ibid.* 355 It was put to my account to tye vp the Yards, to ruffle the Sayle.

†**9.** To make a stir or search; to poke *up*. *Obs.*

c **1440** *Promp. Parv.* 437/1 Rooryn, or ruffelyn amonge dyuerse thyngys, *manumitto.* **1574** WHITGIFT *Def. Aunsw.* 114 Being faine to ransacke, and ruffle vp euery darke corner.

ruffle ('rʌf(ə)l), *v.*^{2} Forms: 5 ruffelyn, ruffule, 5–7 rufle (6 rofle), 6 ruffil(l, ruffel, 6– ruffle (7 roughle). [Of obscure origin. In senses 1 and 2 app. obsolete from before 1700 until revived by Scott.]

1. *intr.* To contend or struggle *with*, to do battle *for*, a person or thing. Now *arch.*

c **1440** *Promp. Parv.* 439/1 Ruffelyn, or debatyn (*K.P.* or discordyn), *discordo.* **1527** *State Papers Hen. VIII*, IV. 471, I haue ruffelde with the Warden, and also with the Cardinall, and truste to pluk him by the noose. **1606** G. W[OODCOCK] *Lives Emperors* in *Hist. Ivstine* Hh iv, Hee ouerthrew Iouius Maximus, and Sebastianus, ruffling for the succession in Gallia. **1630** *R. Johnson's Kingd. & Commw.* 284 If they be displeased, they are strong enough to ruffle with him. *c* **1660** PETTY in Ld. E. Fitzmaurice *Life* (1895) 50 Men of activity that could..ruffle with the several rude persons in the country. **1820** SCOTT *Abbot* xxvi, She had lords and lairds that would ruffle for her.

2. To make a great stir or display; to hector, swagger, bear oneself proudly or arrogantly. Now *arch.* (very common *c* 1540–1650).

1484 CAXTON *Fables of Avian* xxi, The evylle, cursyd & rebelles, whiche doo no thynge but playe with dees and cardes and to ruffule. **1532** MORE *Confut. Tindale* Wks. 570/2 The Lutheranes & Zwinglianes haue begunne to ryse & ruffle in rebellion in soondry partes of Almayne. **1549** LATIMER *Ploughers* (Arb.) 26 They are so troubeled wyth Lordelye lyuynge,..ruffelynge in theyr rentes,..that they canne not attende it. **1605** CAMDEN *Rem.* (1623) 248 There was a Noble man..that hauing lately sold a Mannor of an hundred tenements, came ruffling into the Court, in a new sute. **1640** BP. HALL *Episc.* II. xvii. 109 Pampering his Appetite,..or ruffling in proud and costly attyres. **1692** R. L'ESTRANGE *Josephus* (1733) 679 All his Companions..came ruffling up to him with clamorous Invectives. **1865** KINGSLEY *Herew.* xix, [He] gets drunk, ruffles, and roysters. **1894** MRS. OLIPHANT *Q. Anne* vii. 354 A man about town ruffling at the coffee-houses.

b. Const. with *it* and *out*.

(*a*) **1560** BP. PILKINGTON *Aggeus* (1562) 268 It becometh a gentleman, to make merye and ruffle it. **1594** *1st Pt. Contention* (1843) 13 His proud wife..That ruffles it with such a troupe of Ladies. **1643** TRAPP *Comm. Gen.* xlvi. 32 Chusing rather a poor shepherds life in Gods service, then to ruffle it, as Courtiers. *a* **1659** BP. BROWNRIG *Serm.* (1674) II. x. 122 Themselves ruffled it in mirth and jollity. **1821** SCOTT *Kenilw.* iv, He must ruffle it in another sort that would walk to court in a nobleman's train. **1895** MRS. OLIPHANT *Makers Mod. Rome* II. i. 105 He must no doubt have ruffled it with the best among the officials.

(*b*) **1574** GOLDING *Calvin on Job* 364 True it is that the wicked ruffle it out in this worlde. **1596** NASHE *Saffron Walden* Wks. (Grosart) III. 106 Gabriell..came ruffling it out, huffty tuffty, in his suite of veluet. *a* **1646** J. BURROUGHES *Exp. Hosea* vii. (1652) 132 The men of the world..have their day in which they ruffle it out. **1673** *Lady's Calling* II. ii. §52 But however they may ruffle it out with men, it will one day arraign them before God. **1826** SCOTT *Woodst.* xxvii, I..would willingly ruffle it out once more in the King's cause.

†**c.** *trans.* To brazen or face *out*. *Obs.*$^{-1}$

1612 W. PARKES *Curtaine-Dr.* (1876) 24 The poore harlot must be stript & whipt for the crime that the Courtly-wanton and ye Citie-sinner ruffle out,..and glory in.

3. Of winds, etc.: To be turbulent, rage, bluster.

The latest quot. perhaps belongs to RUFFLE *v.*^{1}

1579 TWYNE *Phis. agst. Fortune* II. xxv. 200 b, Whyle the windes ruffle rounde about thee, returne thou into the Hauen. **1582** STANYHURST *Æneis* I. (Arb.) 20 The east west contrarie doe struggle And southwind ruffling. *Ibid.* III. 88 Fierce the waters ruffle, thee sands with wrought flud ar hoysed. **1624** CAPT. SMITH *Virginia* V. 181 Such an extreme gust of wind and weather so ruffled in the trees and Church. **1790** A. WILSON *Th. Churchyard* Poet. Wks. 13 The chilly breeze bleak ruffles o'er the lawn.

†**4.** *trans.* To handle roughly; to set upon with violence; to bully. *Obs.*

1489 *Barbour's Bruce* IV. 145 Thai within..Sa gret defence and worthy mad, That thai full oft thair fayis ruflyt. *c* **1610** SIR J. MELVIL *Mem.* (1735) 324 They were mishandled, ruffled and delayed here the Space of.. Months. **1641** MILTON *Reform.* I. Wks. 1851 I. 17 But now ..a true Bishop of his fold shall be revil'd, and ruffl'd by an insulting..Prelate. **1673** *Remarques Humours Town* 129 You will be strangely ruffled if you are found ignorant in the nicest points. *a* **1721** SHEFFIELD (Dk. Buckhm.) *Wks.* (1753) II. 102 He was not to be ruffled out of his care for the City by any subject whatsoever.

†**b.** To handle (a woman) with rude familiarity; to touzle. *Obs.*

1607 *Barley-Breakes* (1877) 8, I tell thee, Chuck, thy Father doth disdaine To see his child so ruffled by a knaue. **1667** DRYDEN & DK. NEWCASTLE *Sir M. Mar-all* I. i, You must not suffer him to ruffle you, or steal a kiss. *a* **1704** T. BROWN *Praise of Drunkenness* Wks. 1730 I. 35 If an honest gentleman is a little too much heated with the fumes of wine and..ruffles the women. **1720** MRS. MANLEY tr. *Power Love* (1741) 323 He..came, without any Forms, to ruffle and kiss the lovely Rustic.

†**5.** To take or snatch rudely. *Obs.*

1605 SHAKS. *Lear* III. vii. 41, I am your Host, With Robbers hands my hospitable fauours You should not ruffle thus. **1715** *Town-Talk* No. 9 (1790) 109, I have..given imagination so much liberty as to fancy I ruffled a kiss from you when a country girl.

†**6.** To brandish vigorously. *Obs.*$^{-1}$

a **1537** *Thersytes* 300, I wyll ruffle this clubbe aboute my hedde.

'ruffle, *v.*^{3} *Sc.* [Cf. RUFFLE *sb.*^{4}] *intr.* Of a drum: To beat a ruffle. Also **'ruffling** *vbl. sb.*

1721 WODROW *Hist. Suff. Ch. Scot.* (1830) III. 409 Two drums were ready on each hand to ruffle as major White should order them. *Ibid.* 415 He was interrupted by the ruffling of the drums.

ruffled ('rʌf(ə)ld), *a.* [f. RUFFLE *sb.*^{1}] **a.** Having a ruffle or ruffles; adorned with ruffles. ***ruffled shirt***, a shirt decorated with ruffles; also *transf.*, = *ruffle shirt* (*b*) s.v. RUFFLE *sb.*^{1} 8.

1609 DEKKER *Gull's Horn-bk.* Proem. 2 A thousand lame Heteroclites..that cozen the world with a guilt spurre and a ruffled boote. *a* **1643** CARTWRIGHT *Ordinary* I. ii, Now it looks just like A ruffled boot. **17..** RAMSAY *Tartana* 190 Between the ruffl'd lawn and envious glove. **1754** *Calendar Virginia State Papers* (1875) I. 249, 2 fine Ruffled shirts and 2 plain shirts for themselves..sent by the Governor to them. **1768–74** TUCKER *Lt. Nat.* (1834) II. 595 The French carpenter can-not saw his boards without a long pig-tail and ruffled shirt. **1801** FUSELI *Lect. Art* (1848) 393 A mob of shepherds and shepherdesses in flowing wigs and dressed curls, ruffled Endymions, humble Junos. **1860** O. W. HOLMES *Prof. at Breakfast-Table* i. 19 Joe Warren, the first bloody ruffled-shirt of the Revolution, was as good as born here. **1868** BROWNING *Ring & Bk.* I. 932 Powdered peruke on nose, and bag at back And cane dependent from the ruffled wrist. **1894** BANKS *Camp. Curiosity* 191 Five pence for the doing up of a ruffled blouse. **1905** A. H. RICE *Sandy* 271 A few feet farther away hung a portrait of her grandfather, brave in a high stock and ruffled shirt. **1974** J. AIKEN *Midnight is Place* iv. 120 He wore black buckled shoes and a ruffled shirt.

b. *transf.* in names of plants and birds. ***ruffled grouse***, the ruffed grouse (GROUSE *sb.*^{1} 1).

1777 LIGHTFOOT *Flora Scotica* II. 1025 *Agaricus anulatus*, Ruffled Agaric. **1850** *Rep. Comm. Patents: Agric. 1849* (U.S.) 289 The ruffled oat is very much cultivated, and highly esteemed. **1878** N. H. BISHOP *Voy. Paper Canoe* 134 The Ruffled Grouse (*Bonasa umbellus*), so abundant in New Jersey, is not a resident of the peninsula. **1941** J. STEINBECK *Sea of Cortez* xvii. 170 There were many of the ruffled clams with hard, thick, wavy shells.

ruffled ('rʌf(ə)ld), *ppl. a.* [f. RUFFLE *v.*^{1}]

1. Disordered, disarranged; rendered uneven or irregular; crumpled.

1577 HARRISON *England* II. xxiii. (1877) 351 Sundrie antike heads, with ruffeled haire. **1590** SPENSER *F.Q.* I. vi. 9 The wyld woodgods..find the virgin..With ruffled rayments, and fayre blubbred face. **1638** QUARLES *Elegy upon Dr. Wilson* Wks. (Grosart) III. 19 No farre-fetch'd Metaphor shall smooth or slick My ruffled straine. **1671** MILTON *Samson* 1138 Bristles..like those that ridge the back Of chaf't wild Boars, or ruffl'd Porcupines. **1755** GRAY *Progr. Poesy* 22 With ruffled plumes and flagging wing. **1793** COWPER *Beau's Reply* 19, I only kiss'd his ruffled wing.

2. Of the sea, etc.: Agitated, disturbed.

1659 T. PECKE *Parnassi Puerp.* 156 In a black Storm, when ..Boreas chas'd the ruffled clouds. **1705** ADDISON *Italy* 6 While black with Storms the ruffled Ocean rolls. **1815** SHELLEY *Alastor* 319 Along the dark and ruffled waters. **1871** R. ELLIS tr. *Catullus* lxiv. 205 With that dreadful motion..the ruffled Ocean shook.

3. Of the mind, etc.: Discomposed, irritated.

1741 MIDDLETON *Cicero* I. v. 344 In this ruffled and querulous state of his mind. **1812** CRABBE *Tales* xvi. 550 Gentler movements soothed his ruffled mind. **1849** C. BRONTE *Shirley* vi, All-powerful in soothing her most ruffled moods. **1891** BARING-GOULD *In Troubadour Land* ii, He.. endeavoured by every means to allay her ruffled temper.

'ruffleless, *a. rare*$^{-0}$. [f. RUFFLE *sb.*^{1} + -LESS.] 'Having no ruffles.'

1860 in WORCESTER (citing Mellen).

'rufflement. *rare*$^{-0}$. The act of ruffling.

1850 in OGILVIE.

ruffler[1] (ˈrʌflə(r)). [f. RUFFLE *v.*[1]] An attachment to a sewing-machine, for making ruffles.

1875 KNIGHT *Dict. Mech.* 1999 In the Johnston ruffler, a sliding-plate is secured to the bed-plate of the machine [etc.]. **1908** *Sears, Roebuck Catal.* 41/1 The set of attachments..consists of one ruffler, one shirring plate, one tucker. **1964** *McCall's Sewing* x. 144/2 The ruffler attachment is also capable of gathering large sections of fabric.

ruffler[2] (ˈrʌflə(r)). Now *arch.* Also 6 ruffeler, -ar; rufflar, -leer; rufler. [f. RUFFLE *v.*[2]]

†**1.** One of a class of vagabonds prevalent in the 16th century. *Obs.*

1535 *Act 27 Hen. VIII*, c. 25 Idell..persons, ruffelers, callynge them selues saruing men. *c* **1540** COPLAND *Hye Way to Spyttel Ho.* 675 Rufflers and masterles men, that cannot werke, And slepeth by day, and walketh in the derke. **1561** AWDELAY *Frat. Vacab.* 3 A Ruffeler goeth wyth a weapon to seeke seruice, saying he hath bene a Seruitor in the wars, and beggeth for his reliefe. **1567** HARMAN *Caveat* (1869) 29. [**1608** DEKKER *Belman of London* Wks. (Grosart) III. 94 The next in degree to him is cald a Ruffler. **1673** R. HEAD *Canting Acad.* 65 A Ruffler..goes under the pretence of a maimed Soldier. **1796** *Grose's Dict. Vulgar T.* (ed. 3), *Rufflers,* the first rank of canters; also notorious rogues pretending to be maimed soldiers or sailors. **1818** SCOTT *Hrt. Midl.* xxv, A..fellow that has been but a twelvemonth on the lay, be he ruffler or padder.]

2. One who makes much stir or display; a proud swaggering or arrogant fellow.

1536 *Rem. Sedition* 14 The mayster gyuen to ryot, the servant must nedes thynke, that there is no thriuing for him, excepte he shewe himselfe a ruffler. **1593** G. HARVEY *Pierce's Super.* Wks. (Grosart) II. 127 In the whole, a notable ruffler, and in euery part a dowty braggard. **1631** *High Commission Cases* (Camden) 186 He was commanded in all his visitation to make knowen to all ministers that they bee more carefull in their habits not to goe like rufflers. **1649** MILTON *Eikon.* 36 The Parlament demanded justice for those assaults don at his own dores, by that crew of Rufflers. **1821** SCOTT *Kenilw.* i, Is he, too, such a would-be ruffler as the rest of them? **1881** BESANT & RICE *Chapl. Fl.* I. x, There came in an old ruffler of fifty, who..tugged out his purse.

†ˈ**ruffiered**, *a. Obs.*$^{-1}$ [irreg. f. RUFFLE *v.*[2], perh. after prec.] Boisterous.

1582 STANYHURST *Æneis* VIII. (Arb.) 137 Three wheru's fyerd glystring, with Sout[h]wynds rufflered huffling.

†ˈ**ruffiery**. *Obs.*$^{-1}$ [f. RUFFLE *v.*[2]] Uproar.

1582 STANYHURST *Æneis* III. (Arb.) 88 But neere ioynctlye brayeth with rufflerye rumboled Ætna.

ˈ**rufflesome**, *a.* [f. RUFFLE *sb.*[1] or *v.*[1]] Somewhat ruffled or disordered.

1868 HOLME LEE *B. Godfrey* v, Her hair..had a rufflesome look.

Rufflette (ˈrʌflɪt, rʌˈflɛt). [f. RUFFLE *sb.*[1] + -ETTE.] A proprietary name for a kind of tape that can be sewn to the top edge of a curtain, having slits at regular intervals by which curtain-hooks may be attached, and cords threaded through that enable the tape and curtain to be gathered or 'ruffled'.

1931 *Trade Marks Jrnl.* 18 Nov. 1533 The Rufflette. Use claimed from 28th September, 1922... Cotton curtain heading tapes included in Class 25. **1947** *Radio Times* 18 Apr. 22/2 (Advt.), There's more than material in curtains.. there's the art of making them drape beautifully—how simple that is with 'Rufflette' curtain tape with hooks and rings. **1964** *McCall's Sewing* xvi. 280 Two types of Rufflette are available giving gathered or pleated effects. In both cases first form hem..then baste Rufflette tape to this. **1973** *Guardian* 28 Feb. 11/3 Curtains, with Rufflette tape topping, are in two sizes.

ˈ**ruffling**, *vbl. sb.*[1] [f. RUFFLE *v.*[1]]

1. The action (or result) of making uneven, irregular, disordered, †or entangled; also, slight agitation, †rustling.

c **1440** *Promp. Parv.* 439/1 Rufflynge, or snarlynge, *illaqueacio, innodacio.* *c* **1460** J. RUSSELL *Bk. Nurture* 250 Then must ye draw & reyse þe vpper parte of þe towelle, Ley it with-out ruffelynge streiȝt to þat oþer side. **1582** STANYHURST *Æneis* II. (Arb.) 59 Not so great a ruffling the riuer strong flasshye reteyneth. **1611** COTGR., *Grippets*,.. the rufflings, or snarles of ouer-twisted thread. **1652** H. MORE *Antid. Ath.* 162 The ruffling of silks, as of a woman walking. **1733** SWIFT *Apology* Wks. 1751 X. 232 She,..Tho' seeming pleas'd at all she sees, Starts at the Ruffling of the Trees. *a* **1754** FIELDING *J. Wild* II. x, The storm was now entirely ceased, and nothing remained but the usual ruffling of the sea after it. **1853** G. JOHNSTON *Nat. Hist. E. Borders* I. 10 The little ruffling scarcely dims the beauty that ever waits upon her course. **1877** T. A. TROLLOPE *Life Pius IX*, I. 132 A small ruffling of the flowing stream of popularity.

b. The action of making ruffles; also, material forming, or in the form of, a ruffle.

1760–72 H. BROOKE *Fool of Qual.* (1809) I. 25 There is not a bit of all this lace and ruffling, that is not full of rank poisons. *Ibid.* 26 The lady had covered his coat, all over, with laces, and with rufflings. **1766** GOLDSM. *Vic. W.* iv, These rufflings, and pinkings, and patchings will only make us hated by all the wives of our neighbours. **1869** MRS. WHITNEY *We Girls* ii, A great..toilet-cushion..edged with magic ruffling. **1902** *Daily Chron.* 20 Feb. 8/7 Machinists wanted at once, used to ruffling.

2. The action of disturbing, troubling, annoying, or irritating.

1647 HEXHAM I, A Ruffling or stirring on a suddaine. **1733** CHEYNE *Eng. Malady* III. iv. (1734) 354 Vomits were the first Evacuations that.., without infinite Ruffling, I could bear. **1805** SAUNDERS *Min. Waters* 320 As a cathartic, the Caroline waters operate without ruffling. **1862** MRS. FRESHFIELD *Tour Grisons* ix. 149 His temper would not bear ruffling. **1889** JESSOPP *Coming of Friars* iii. 151 Such ruffling of the peace and quiet of conventual life was..not uncommon.

ˈ**ruffling**, *vbl. sb.*[2] [f. RUFFLE *v.*[2]]

†**1.** Dissension, disturbance, tumult. *Obs.*

c **1440** *Promp. Parv.* 439/1 Rufflynge, or debate, *discencio, discordia.* **1541** PAYNELL *Catiline* xxv. 45 By the reason that Fraunce should be in an vprore and ruffeling. *a* **1548** HALL *Chron., Hen. VII*, 55 b, Capitaynes and prouokers of trayterous rufflinges. **1577–87** HOLINSHED *Chron.* III. 842/1 Whilest the hottest of this ruffling lasted, the cardinall was aduertised thereof by sir Thomas Parre. **1611** COTGR., *Mutinerie*,..a stirre, trouble, businesse, ruffling, hurlyburly.

†**b.** The action of contending *with* some one or *against* something. *Obs.*

1570 FOXE *A. & M.* (ed. 2) 247/1 Uppon this ruffelyng of Anselme with maryed priests, were riming verses made. **1570–6** LAMBARDE *Peramb. Kent* (1826) 74 For recompence of the good service that hee had done, in ruffling against Priests wives.

2. Proud or haughty carriage; swaggering conduct or actions.

1538 LELAND *Itin.* (1769) IV. 53 Sum say that it longgid ons to Payne caullid for his Ruffeling there Diable. *a* **1591** H. SMITH *Serm.* (1637) 180 Like a Banner of his pride, which sheweth him in his ruffling.., before he knew God or himselfe. **1644** QUARLES *Sheph. Orac.* vi. 46 O Swain, me thinks these rufflings ill befit A Shepheard's cloth. **1667** DRYDEN & DK. NEWCASTLE *Sir M. Mar-all* I. i, His lordship then will find the prologue of his trouble, doubting I have told you of his ruffling.

ˈ**ruffling**, *ppl. a.*[1] [f. RUFFLE *v.*[1]]

1. Forming, or rising in, ruffles.

1596 SHAKS. *Tam. Shr.* IV. iii. 60 The Tailor staies thy leasure, To decke thy bodie with his ruffling treasure. **1607** TOPSELL *Serpents* (1658) 613 His rufling mane is discouraged by the extolled head of the Serpent. **1682** N. O. *Boileau's Lutrin* III. 86 Out flies the broad-fac'd Chorister of the Night, And with her ruffling wings strikes out the Light. *a* **1718** PARNELL *Hermit* 17 If a Stone the gentle Scene divide, Swift ruffling Circles curl on ev'ry side.

2. Producing or raising ruffles; making disordered, irregular, or uneven. Also *fig.*

1606 S. GARDINER *Bk. Angling* 98 The water of a spacious and deepe Lake..by ruffling windes is moued and disquieted. **1648** J. BEAUMONT *Psyche* VI. ccxxiii, The rival Winds..rais'd a ruffling tempest of Delight. **1702** ROWE *Tamerlane* v. i, Thus Stars shine bright,.. Tho' ruffling Winds deform this lower World. **1781** G. WHITE *Selborne* xcix, Those insects which love to haunt a spot so secure from ruffling winds. **1817** SHELLEY *Pr. Athan.* II. 87 O'er the visage wan Of Athanase, a ruffling atmosphere Of dark emotion..ran. **1858** KINGSLEY *Misc.* (1859) I. 200 A ruffling south-west breeze.

3. Causing irritation or annoyance.

1708 *Bickerstaff Detected* in *Swift's Wks.* (1751) IV. 209, I..prepared for bed, in hopes of a little Repose after so many ruffling adventures. **1746** HERVEY *Medit.* (1818) 271 Soon a ruffling accident intervenes and turns our composure into a fretful disquietude.

Hence ˈ**rufflingly** *adv.*[1] *rare*$^{-1}$.

1611 COTGR., *Frezé*,..set rufflingly, after the manner of the (thicke) French ruffe.

ˈ**ruffling**, *ppl. a.*[2] [f. RUFFLE *v.*[2]]

1. Of conduct, etc.: Characterized by ruffling.

1532 MORE *Confut. Tindale* Wks. 414/2 The fashion is more ruffeling and in lesse moderacion and sobernesse, then were conuenient for mouing men to deuocion. **1577** tr. *Bullinger's Decades* (1592) 281 Laie downe thy pride, and forsake thy ruffling riot. **1612** T. TAYLOR *Comm. Titus* i. 6 The ruffling, and roysting life of a number of our gallants, and lustie bloods. **1682** BUNYAN *Holy War* 59 He therefore with big and ruffling words demanded of the Trumpeter who he was? **1826** SCOTT *Woodst.* viii, That ruffling look of thine. **1870** THORNBURY *Tour rd. Eng.* II. xx. 52 There are still traces of the ruffling days of the brave Sir John.

2. Of persons: Given to ruffling.

1549 COVERDALE, etc. *Erasm. Par. Ephes.* Prol. C iij, Yf a man..marke the maners of this roiall rufflynge worlde. **1599** NASHE *Lenten Stuffe* Wks. (Grosart) V. 230 With any of these swaggering captaines..or hufti-tuftie youthfull ruffling comrades. **1635** PAGITT *Christianogr.* 46 Temporall power claymed and violently carried by this ruffling Prelate. **1653** A. WILSON *Jas. I*, 103 The Marquesse..came to the Court in a full career, with a ruffling Retinue at his heels. **1704** ROWE *Ulysses* I. i, The ruffling Train of Suiters are at hand. **1820** SCOTT *Monast.* xvi, For the rest, he is one of the ruffling gallants of the time. **1840** DICKENS *Barn. Rudge* viii, Sim Tappertit laid aside his cautious manner,..assuming in its stead that of a ruffling swaggering, roving blade. **1881** LARWOOD *Lond. Parks* xiii. 272 The company..were a wild ruffling set.

Hence ˈ**rufflingly** *adv.*[2] *rare*$^{-1}$.

1581 J. BELL *Haddon's Answ. Osorius* 258 What glorious Thraso..could ever have handled hys part uppon a stage more rufflingly.

ˈ**ruffly**, *a. rare.* Also **ruffley**. [f. RUFFLE *v.*[1]] Slightly ruffled or curled; characterized by ruffles.

1883 K. S. MACQUOID *Her Sailor Love* II. III. iii. 6 Her soft, shining, light brown hair..grew ruffly about her temples. **1909** [see HATTY *a.*]. **1980** M. G. EBERHART *Casa Madrone* ii. 30 A ruffly blouse.

ruffly, obs. form of ROUGHLY *adv.*

†ˈ**ruffmans**. *Cant. Obs.* [prob. f. ROUGH *a.* Cf. DARKMANS.] (See quots.)

1567 HARMAN *Caveat* (1869) 84 *The ruffmans*, the wodes or bushes. **1622** FLETCHER *Beggar's Bush* III. iii, To Mill from the Ruffmans, commission and slates...[i.e.] To steal from the hedge, both the shirt and the sheets.

†**ruff-peck**. *Cant. Obs.* [? f. ROUGH *a.* See PECK *sb.*[3] 3.] Bacon.

1567 HARMAN *Caveat* (1869) 83 *Ruff pek*, baken. **1609** DEKKER *Lanth. & Candle Lt.* C iij b, If we mawn'd Pannam lap or Ruff-peck. **1641** BROME *Joviall Crew* II. Wks. 1873 III. 388 Here's Ruffpeck and Casson and all of the best. *a* **1700** B. E. *Dict. Cant. Crew, Rum-ruff peck*, Westphalia-Ham.

†**ruff-raff**. *Obs.* [Imitative.] *attrib.* Noisy.

1582 STANYHURST *Æneis* VIII. (Arb.) 138 Now doe they rayse gastly lyghtnings, now grislye reboundings Of ruffe raffe roaring. **1589** NASHE in Greene *Menaphon* (Arb.) 13 Then did he make heauens vault to rebounde, with rounce robble hobble Of ruffe raffe roaring.

ruff-scuff. Alteration of *rough-scuff* s.v. ROUGH *a.* 21. (In quot. 1902, = poor fodder.)

1902 H. F. DAY *Pine Tree Ballads* 4 Drat the man who feeds out ruff-scuff, wood and wire from the swale. **1936** *N.Y. American* 13 Aug. 17/1 There is a snug harbor.. chivvied out of a city's ruff-scuff for dreamers.

†**ruff-tree**: see ROOF-TREE 2 and ROUGH-TREE.

c **1635** CAPT. BOTELER *Dial. Sea Services* (1685) 132 Roof-trees, or as they are vulgarly called, Ruff-trees, are those Timbers which go from the Half-deck to the Fore-castle, and serve to bear up the Gratings, and Ledges where the Nettings are fastned. **1789** *Trans. Soc. Arts* VII. 217 In a merchant-man, her ruff-tree.

†ˈ**ruffy**[1]. *Obs.* Chiefly *Sc.* Also 6 **ruffie, roofye**, *pl.* ruffeis. [var. of RUFFIN[1], and of *ruffin* RUFFIAN *sb.*]

1. A devil or fiend. Cf. RUFFIN[1] 1.

? *a* **1500** *Rowlis Cursing* 133 Ruffy Tasker with his flaill Sall beit thame all fra top to taill. [See also RAGMAN[1] 1.] **1528** LYNDESAY *Dreme* 285 Sum repentit neuer in thare lyue: Quhairfor, but reuth tha ruffeis did thame ryue. **1599** HARSNET *Discoverie* 308 One of them saying his name was Roofye—'Thou lyest,' quoth M. Darrell, 'that name is common to all spirits'.

b. One impersonating a fiend.

1502 *Acc. Ld. High Treas. Scot.* II. 350 Item, be the Kingis command, to Sanct Nicholais beschop, iij Franch crounis... Item, to the deblatis and ruffyis, vij s. **1507** *Ibid.* IV. 87 To Sanct Nicholais..xxviij s. To his ruffyis, ix s.

2. A ruffian.

1500–20 DUNBAR *Poems* lx. 42 Bot quhow is he content, or nocht,..Wpone this ruffie to remord? **1570** *Sat. Poems Reform.* xxi. 23 Thay Ruffyis, be thay neuer sa ryfe, Thay get na helpe of France. **1572** *Ibid.* xxxii. 81 Thay reuthles Ruffeis but reuth with crueltie Did slay my husband.

ˈ**ruffy**[2]. *Sc. rare.* [Cf. RUFF *sb.*[7] and ROUGHY[1].] (See quots. 1808 and 1825.)

1793 *Stat. Acc. Scotl.* IX. 328 When the goodman of the house made family worship, they lighted a ruffy, to enable him to read the psalm..before he prayed. **1808** JAMIESON, *Ruffy*, a wick clogged with tallow, instead of being dipped. **1825** —— *Suppl., Ruffy*,..the blaze or torch used in fishing by night with the Lister.

ruffy, variant of ROUGHY[2].

ruffy-tuffy, *a.* ? *nonce-wd.* Dishevelled.

a **1821** KEATS *Cap & Bells* lxxxvi, Powder'd bag-wigs and ruffy-tuffy heads Of cinder wenches meet and soil each other.

rufi- (ˈruːfɪ), comb. form of L. *rūfus* red, used in some terms of *Bot.*, *Ent.*, *Ornith.*, etc., as ***ruficarpous*** having red fruit, ***ruficaudate*** red-tailed, ***ruficornate***, ***-gastrate***, ***-labrate***, etc. (Mayne *Expos. Lex.* 1858), and *Chem.*, as ***ruficarmin***, ***-coccin***, ***-gallic***, ***-moric***, etc. (Watts *Dict. Chem.* 1868–1875).

rufo- (ˈruːfəʊ), comb. form (on Greek types) of L. *rūfus* red, in some adjs. denoting colour, with sense 'rufous', as ***rufo-fulvous***, ***-piceous***, ***-testaceous***; also ***rufo-catechuic acid***, rubinic acid.

1809 SHAW *Gen. Zool.* VII. II. 303 The wing-feathers are brown, but rufo-testaceous at their base. **1817** KIRBY & SP. *Introd. Entom.* (1818) II. xix. 126 The..scales that defend the base of the wings are rufo-piceous. *Ibid.*, The *tarsi* and the apex of the *tibiæ* are rufo-fulvous. **1842** *Penny Cycl.* XXII. 53/1 Shell..painted with small, rufo-fuscous,.. subfasciculated lines. **1847** *Proc. Berw. Nat. Club* II. 244 Legs, mouth, and palpi rufo-ferruginous. **1868** WATTS *Dict. Chem., Rubinic Acid*, also called Rufocatechuic acid.

rufous (ˈruːfəs), *a.* [f. L. *rūfus*: see -OUS.]

1. a. Of a brownish-red colour; reddish; ferruginous.

1782 LATHAM *Gen. Synop. Birds* I. II. 594 The whole bird is of a rufous colour on the upper parts. **1800** *Gentl. Mag.* I. 151 Colours are expressed in the French term, as *gridelin* and *rufous*, p. 200, when it would seem *greyish* and *reddish* were English words competent to convey the same idea. **1847** *Proc. Berw. Nat. Club* II. 236 Elytra and legs rufous. **1872** R. F. BURTON *Zanzibar* II. 69 Beyond it are detached hills of gneiss and grey and rufous granite. **1897** MRS. RAYNER *Type-Writer Girl* vi, He had rufous hair, a nose without a bridge. **1922** JOYCE *Ulysses* 182 Glittereyed, his rufous skull close to his greencapped desk-lamp sought the face. **1977** *Time* 3 Jan. 21/1 The flat kindly face of Mr. Earl's photographs has made no print on any of them except the rufous Billy, a wily jester.

b. In names of birds, as ***rufous fly-catcher***, ***goatsucker***, ***heron***, ***swallow***, etc.

1782 LATHAM *Gen. Synop. Birds* I. II. 594 Rufous Woodpecker. **1783** *Ibid.* II. I. 362 Rufous Fly Catcher. **1784** *Ibid.* II. II. 597 Rufous Goatsucker. **1785** *Ibid.* III. I. 99 Rufous Heron. **1815** STEPHENS in *Shaw's Gen. Zool.* IX. I. 44

Rufous Coucal. (*Polophilus rufus*.) This very rare species of Coucal was discovered by Le Vaillant. **1842** *Penny Cycl.* XXIII. 363/1 The Rufous Swallow (*Hirundo rufula*, Temm.). **1862** Johns *Brit. Birds* 128 The Rufous Sedge warbler, *Curruca Galactodes*. **1874** *Ibis* July 236 A Rufous Warbler..was taken alive on the 23rd May 1873.

c. In names of moths, as ***rufous arch***, ***carpet***, etc., or of animals, as ***rufous lemur***; ***rufous bee***, a solitary bee, *Andrena fulva*; ***rufous rat-kangaroo***, a small marsupial, *Æpyprymnus rufescens*, found in south-eastern parts of Australia.

1832 J. Rennie *Consp. Butterfl. & M.* 117 The Rufous Carpet (*Cidaria munitata*, Stephens) appears the end of June. *Ibid.* 169 The Rufous Arch (*Semasia rufana*, Stephens). **1897** H. O. Forbes *Hand-bk. Primates* I. 73 The Rufous Lemur..has a yellowish-white frontal band. **1926** Le Souef & Burrell *Wild Animals Australasia* 234 Rufous Rat-kangaroo... General colour above coarsely grizzled rufescent grey. **1928** *Observer* 17 June 24/3 That queen of burrowers,..the rufous bee, Andrena. **1972** *Sunday Mail Mag.* (Brisbane) 3 Sept. 4 The rufous rat-kangaroo..occurs in many parts of central and south Queensland, particularly in open forest.

2. *Comb.* with other names of colours, as ***rufous-brown***, ***-buff***, ***-white***.

1782 Latham *Gen. Synop. Birds* I. ii. 517 The upper parts of the body..spotted with rufous yellow. **1813** Bingley *Anim. Biogr.* (ed. 4) II. 165 Its colour is rufous-brown above, and beneath yellowish. **1838** *Penny Cycl.* X. 187/2 Under tail-coverts plain rufous-white. **1896** *Lloyd's Nat. Hist.* 73 The fore-neck and breast..tinged with rufous-buff. **1953** D. A. Bannerman *Birds Brit. Isles* I. 300 The black crown feathers are then mostly obscured by buff or rufous-brown tips to the feathers. **1968** B. Hines *Kestrel for Knave* 26 On a shelf behind the bars stood a kestrel hawk: Rufous brown. Flecked breast, dark bars across her back and wings.

3. *Comb.* with adjs. or pa. pples., as ***rufous-coloured***, ***-edged***, ***-tinged***.

1797 *Encycl. Brit.* (ed. 3) I. 661/2 It lays 10 or 12 rufous-coloured eggs. **1866** Newall *Eastern Hunters* 30 Norman's quick eye lighted for a single second on a rufous coloured mass. **1872** Coues *N. Amer. Birds* 171 The quills and tail feathers are more extensively rufous-edged. *Ibid.* 215 Upper tail coverts white, rufous-tinged.

b. In specific names of birds, etc. (see quots.).

1784 Latham *Gen. Synop. Birds* II. ii. 371 *Rufous-backed Lark. **1843** Yarrell *Brit. Birds* II. 462 *Ardea russata*, Rufous-backed Egret. **1872** Coues *N. Amer. Birds* 185 Rufous-backed Hummingbird..chiefly cinnamon-rufous above. **1803** Shaw *Gen. Zool.* IV. ii. 416 *Rufous-banded sparus, *Sparus Hurta*. **1782** Latham *Gen. Synop. Birds* I. ii. 760 *Rufous-bellied Humming Bird... Inhabits Brasil. **1784** *Ibid.* II. ii. 566 Rufous-bellied Swallow. **1877** *Nature* 15 Mar. 441/2 Two Rufous-bellied Bulbuls (*Hypsipetes Mclellandi*). **1784** Latham *Gen. Synop. Birds* II. ii. 771 *Rufous-breasted Partridge. **1783** *Ibid.* II. i. 267 *Rufous-chinned Finch, *Fringilla noctis*. **1872** Coues *N. Amer. Birds* 140 *Rufous-crowned Finch..; crown uniform chestnut. **1784** Latham *Gen. Synop. Birds* II. ii. 571 *Rufous-headed Swallow. **1823** —— *Gen. Hist. Birds* VI. 297 Rufous-headed Lark. This is the smallest of African Larks. **1898** Morris *Austral English* 56/2 Rufous-headed Bristle-bird, *Sphenura broadbentii*. **1823** Latham *Gen. Hist. Birds* VI. 297 *Rufous-hooded Lark. **1783** —— *Gen. Synop. Birds* II. i. 85 *Rufous-naped thrush. **1865** *Chambers's Encycl.* VII. 362/1 The *Rufous-necked Pelican (*P. fuscus*) abounds in the West Indies and in many parts of America. **1784** Latham *Gen. Synop. Birds* II. ii. 582 *Rufous-rumped Swallow. **1782** *Ibid.* I. ii. 517 *Rufous-spotted cuckow, *Cuculus punctatus*. **1783** *Ibid.* II. i. 30 *Rufous-tailed Thrush. **1809** Shaw *Gen. Zool.* VII. ii. 311 Rufous-tailed Shrike, *Lanius phoenicurus*. **1884** Coues *N. Amer. Birds* 434 *Myiarchus*,..Rufous-Tailed Flycatchers. **1783** Latham *Gen. Synop. Birds* II. i. 334 *Rufous-vented flycatcher. **1877** *Nature* 15 Mar. 441/2 A Rufous-vented Guan (*Penelope cristata*) from Central America. **1783** Latham *Gen. Synop. Birds* II. i. 55 *Rufous-winged Thrush.

4. *ellipt.* as *sb.* **a.** A brownish-red colour.

1783 Latham *Gen. Synop. Birds* II. 362 The under parts wholly white, with a tinge of rufous. **1817** Stephens in *Shaw's Gen. Zool.* X. i. 265 The rest of it..blackish, variegated with grey blue and rufous. **1860** Russell *Diary India* I. 66 Peaked mountains of rich rufous and Vandyck brown. **1872** Coues *N. Amer. Birds* 171 Wing coverts..as well as the primaries edged with rufous.

b. A rufous-coloured moth.

1832 J. Rennie *Consp. Butterfl. & M.* 143 The Slender Striped Rufous (*M. subrufata*, Stephens). **1907** R. South *Moths Brit. Isles* 1st Ser. 299 The Small Rufous..varies from pale ochreous white, through reddish shades, to a greyish brown. **1958** W. J. Stokoe *Caterpillars Brit. Moths* (new ed.) I. 281 The Small Rufous..occurring in fens and marshes.

'rufter-hood. *Hawking.* [Of obscure origin.] A form of hood used for a newly-taken hawk.

1575 Turberv. *Faulconrie* 141 Having a greate and easie rufterhood you muste hoode and unhoode hir oftentymes. **1614** Latham *Falconry* i. iii. 9 Let her sit where she may rest quietly for the first night, either seeled, or in a rufter hood. [**1678** in Phillips, and in later Dicts.] **1828** Sir J. S. Sebright *Obs. Hawking* 35 A rufter hood is put upon the hawk the moment he is taken. It is lighter than the common one. **1856** 'Stonehenge' *Brit. Rur. Sports* 220 The Rufter-Hood..is made in two pieces, having a neat seam down the centre, and, like the hood-proper, has a hole for the beak, and also a slit at the back with a brace.

†**rufty-tufty,** *a.* and *int.* *Obs.* [A fanciful formation. See also rifty-tufty.] **a.** *adj.* Rude, rough. **b.** *int.* Hey-day, hoity-toity.

1606 Chapman *Gentl. Usher* v. i, Were I as Vince is, I would handle you In ruftie tuftie wise, in your right kinde. **1606** *Wily Beguild* (1623) B ij, *Lelia*. Ile pranke my selfe with flowers of the prime, And thus ile spend away my Primerose time. *Nurse*. Rufty, tufty, are you so frolike?

'rufulous, *a.* *rare*$^{-1}$. [f. L. *rūfulus*: cf. rufous *a.*] Slightly rufous.

1883 *Jrnl. of Botany* XXI. 214 One or two of the younger plants (which had not acquired a rufulous tinge).

‖**'rufus,** *a.* and *sb.* [L. *rūfus*.]

A. *adj.* = rufous *a.*

1884 *Harper's Mag.* Mar. 622/1 The red-tailed hawk, so named from the deep rufus color of its tail feathers. **1887** Phillips *Brit. Discomyc.* 261 Cups..externally rufus-brown..; hymenium concave, pale rufus.

B. *sb.* (Also with capital initial.) **1.** *U.S. slang.* A countryman. **2.** *colloq.* A nickname for a red-haired person.

1955 D. W. Maurer in *Publ. Amer. Dial. Soc.* xxiv. 106 A farmer or yokel is called by old-timers a *rufus* (obsolescent) or a *hoosier*. **1959** I. & P. Opie *Lore & Lang. Schoolch.* ix. 170 Red heads attract a barrage of nicknames:..reddy, red kipper, red mop, red thatch, red paint brush, Rufus, and Rusty.

rug (rʌg), *sb.*[1] *Sc.* Also 5 **ruge.** [f. rug *v.*[1]]

1. A pull, a tug.

c **1425** Wyntoun *Cron.* iii. ii. 367 Wiþe a ruge þe rapis al He crakkyt in to pecis smalle. **1500-20** Dunbar *Poems* lxxii. 60 The claith that claif to his clere hyde, Thai raif away with ruggis rude. **1719** Ramsay *To Arbuckle* 23, I ga'e the muse a rug, Then bate my nails and claw'd my lug. **1826** J. Wilson *Noct. Ambr.* Wks. 1855 I. 228 The least rug will bring down the squash. **1861** G. H. Kingsley *Sp. & Trav.* (1900) 253 When one caught the ither by the pow, and gied him a rug. **1894** *Blackw. Mag.* July 67 An unexpected ..'rug' by a brace of pounders.

2. A torn-off portion, a 'haul', *of* something; a catch or acquisition.

c **1450** Holland *Howlat* 797 Raike hir a rug of the rost, or scho sall ryiue the. *c* **1480** Henryson *Poems* (S.T.S.) III. 151 Recipe, thre ruggis of the reid ruke.

1808 Jamieson s.v., When one purchases any thing under its common price, it is said that he has got *a rug of it*. **1824** Scott *Redgauntlet* let. xi, Sir John..voted for the Union, having gotten, it was thought, a rug of the compensations. **1875** W. Alexander *Ain Folk* iii, They agreed that the farrow cow was a great 'rug'.

rug (rʌg), *sb.*[2] Also 6-7 **rugge**, 7-8 **rugg.** [perh. of Scand. origin: cf. Norw. dial. *rugga*, *rogga* coarse coverlet (also *skinnrugga* skin-rug; *ruggefeld* shaggy cloak), Sw. *rugg* ruffled or coarse hair, frizz, *rugge* tuft, etc. These are app. related to ON. *rǫgg*: see rag *sb.*[1]]

†**1. a.** A rough woollen material, a sort of coarse frieze, in common use in the 16-17th cent. *Obs.*

1558 *Lanc. Wills* (Chetham Soc.) II. 114 Unto the poore people xij peces of gray rugge. **1592** Chettle *Kind Harts Dr.* (1841) 45 In a gown of rugge, rent on the left shoulder. **1611** Speed *Hist. Gt. Brit.* ix. xv. §46. 794 A man bare-headed, and bare-legged, attired in a coat of white rugge. **1622** Peacham *Gentl. Exerc.* ii. vii. (1634) 126 December must be..clad in Irish rugge, or coorse freeze. **1664** Power *Exp. Philos.* i. 50 A Sage Leaf looks like a white Rugge, or Shagge, full of knots, tassel'd all with white silver Thrums. **1711** *Countrey Man's Let. to Curate* 95 He goes Generally in Winter in good thick Rug, and in Summer most part in a Highland Plaid.

†**b.** With *pl.* A kind or make of frieze; also, a frieze cloak or mantle. *Obs.*

1551-2 *Act 5 & 6 Edw. VI*, c. 6 §1 All Clothes called Manchester Rugges, otherwise named Frices. *Ibid.* §24 Any of the Clothes, Karseys, Frices, Rugges or Cottons aforesaide. **1599** Hakluyt *Voy.* II. ii. 87 The townes built of stone, the people rude in conditions, apparelled in diuers coloured rugs. **1610** Holland *Camden's Brit.*, *Ireland* 63 Which [sheep] they sheare twice a yeere, and make of their course wool rugges or shagge mantles. **1657** R. Ligon *Barbadoes* (1673) 109 Forty pound I think fit to bestow on Irish Ruggs such as are made at Kilkennie, and Irish stockings. **1680** Morden *Geog. Rect.* (1685) 39 Several Manufactures as Freezes, Ruggs, Mantles, &c.

†**c.** ? One who wears a frieze cloak. *Obs.*$^{-1}$

1638 Shirley *Mart. Soldier* ii. iii, I am..Lord over these Larroones, Regent of these Rugs, Viceroy over these Vagabonds.

2. A large piece of thick woollen stuff (freq. of various colours) used as a coverlet or as a wrap in driving, railway-travelling, etc.

1591 Percivall *Sp. Dict.*, *Alcatifa*, a rug for a bed. **1625** Fletcher & Shirley *Nt. Walker* v. i, I wished 'em then get him to bed, they did so, And almost smothr'd him with rugges and pillowes. **1667** Pepys *Diary* 13 July, Mighty hot weather; I lying this night..with only a rugg and a sheet upon me. **1687** B. Randolph *Archipelago* 101 We were not free from fears least the seas should wash away those ruggs which we had stopped in between the timbers. **1731** Swift *Cassinus & Peter* Wks. 1751 X. 191 A Rug was o'er his Shoulders thrown; A Rug; for Night-gown he had none. **1778** *Eng. Gazetteer* (ed. 2) s.v. *Wigan*, Lancaster, famous for the manufacture of coverlets, rugs, blankets, and other sorts of bedding. **1862** *Macm. Mag.* June 125 The child can scarcely be too soon accustomed to be laid on its back on a mattress or rug on the floor. **1871** Carlyle in *Mrs. Carlyle's Lett.* III. 247 We had to wrap our invalid in quite a heap of rugs and shawls. **1875** Knight *Dict. Mech.* 1999/2 A railway-rug is a coarse shawl for wrapping the legs or for use as a blanket.

fig. **1626** Donne *Serm.* 817 In that Green bed whose covering is but a Yarde and a half of Turf and a Rugge of Grass.

phr. **1769** *Stratford Jubilee* ii. i, If she has the mopus's, I'll have her, as snug as a bug in a rug. **1798** W. Hutton *Life* (1816) 137 The doctor..said, 'You are as safe as a bug in a rug'.

3. a. A mat for the floor, usually of thick or shaggy stuff. Cf. hearth-rug. ***to cut a*** (or ***the***) ***rug***: to dance (esp. to jazz music); ***to pull the rug out from under someone***: see pull *v.* 20 j; ***to sweep*** (or ***kick***) (something) ***under the rug***: to conceal (something difficult, embarrassing, or unpleasant) in the hope that it will go unnoticed or be forgotten (cf. carpet *sb.* 2 e).

1808 Jane Austen *Let.* 1 Oct. (1952) 212 She does not doubt your making out the Star pattern very well, as you have the Breakfast-room-rug to look at. **1810** Knox & Jebb *Corr.* II. 5 You shall have a sofa in your bed-chamber.., and a little rug for your hearthstone. **1847** C. Brontë *J. Eyre* xix, I stood on the rug and warmed my hands. **1902** Buchan *Watcher by the Threshold* 287 The fire-lit hall, with its rugs and little tables. **1930** *Heal's Catal.: Furnit.* 9 Knotted Axminster Circular Rug, designed by the late Noel Simmons, 5 ft. in diameter. **1942** *Harper's Bazaar* July 21/3 Let's dance, wanta cut a rug. **1943** *N.Y. Times* 9 May ii. 5/4 Why, brother, all the cats cut a mean rug to that music. **1945** T. Williams *Glass Menagerie* vii. 107 'How about cutting the rug a little, Miss Wingfield?' 'Oh, I—' 'Or is your program filled up? Let me have a look at it. Why, every dance is taken!' **1961** D. M. Disney *Mrs Meeker's Money* vii. 77 The whole thing..was so far outside the normal routine..that it practically demanded being swept under the rug. **1973** *Times* 1 Dec. 20/8 Those who used to look for reds under the beds now fear bugs under the rugs. **1976** *National Observer* (U.S.) 25 Sept. 12/4, I can see numerous problems that were rather swept under the rug in the article. **1978** M. Puzo *Fools Die* xvi. 174 Unless the government covers the whole thing up, you know, kicks it under the rug.

b. *U.S. slang.* A wig.

1940 J. O'Hara *Pal Joey* 190, I even wear a little rug up front. **1967** W. & M. Morris *Dict. Word & Phr. Origins* II. 75 Advertisements for men's wigs invariably refer to them as *hair pieces*, but in the trade a wig may be a *doily*, a *divot* or a *rug*. *Ibid.*, And a *rug*? Well, that's the works—a wig to conceal over-all baldness. **1978** *Telegraph* (Brisbane) 18 Feb. 8/2 'Now, in fact, I do wear a hairpiece in the film I'm making.'..The film for which he has donned a 'rug' as they are called, is Meteor.

†**4.** ? A shaggy breed of dog (see water-rug).

5. *U.S.* (See quot.) ? *Obs.*

1792 Belknap *Hist. New-Hampsh.* III. 129 There is a natural tough sward commonly called a rug, which must either rot or be burned before any cultivation can be made.

6. *attrib.* and *Comb.* **a.** In sense 1, as ***rug-cloak***, ***-doublet***, etc.; ***rug-like*** adj. See also rug-gown.

1592 Nashe *P. Pennilesse* A iv b, Dame Niggardize his wife, in a sedge rugge kirtle. **1611** Speed *Theat. Gt. Brit.* (1614) 138/2 Over their side garments the shagge rugge mantles. **1634-5** Brereton *Trav.* (Chetham) 156 Much more comely than the rug short cloaks used by the women. **1686** *Lond. Gaz.* No. 2152/4 An Apprentice,..in a gray Coat, and white rug Doublet. **1725** De Foe *Voy. round World* (1840) 276 Colchester baize, a coarse rug-like manufacture. **1786** Mrs. Delany *Life & Corr.* (1861) III. 339, I who only go out..when the sun shines, in a rugg great coat and boot-stockings. **1796** *Plain Sense* (ed. 2) III. 190 A rug-cloak..covered her warmly over at night. **1800** Coleridge *Let. to Wedgewood* Jan., I am sitting by a fire in a rug greatcoat.

b. In senses 2 and 3. ***rug-chest***, ***-fringe***, ***-hook***, ***-hooking***, ***-making***, ***-peddler***, ***-wool***, ***-work***, ***-yarn***; **rug brick**, a rough-surfaced brick; **rug-cutter** *U.S. slang*, an enthusiastic or expert dancer; also *transf.*; so **rug-cutting**, dancing; **rug-ranking** *Canad.*, the system of determining the salary of a secretary in federal employment by the status of the person for whom she works; so **rug-rank** *v.*; **rug-rat** *U.S. slang*, a child.

[**1952** *Bricklaying* (Structural Clay Products Inst.) I. ii. 28 Types and Colors of Brick... The Matt faces and Rug faces can almost be placed in the same family. The degree of smoothness or roughness is almost unlimited.] **1961** Webster, *Rug brick. **1968** *Globe & Mail* (Toronto) 3 Feb. 43/1 (Advt.), 3 bedroom rug brick home. **1972** *Times* 19 Sept. 9/5 (Advt.), Partners desk; *rug chests. **1976** *Leicester Trader* 24 Nov. 19/2 (Advt.), Rug chests... £25. **1938** *N.Y. Amsterdam News* 2 Apr. 17/1 The thousands of ..*rugcutters..that are being hatched daily..are a peril. **1941** W. C. Handy *Father of Blues* (1957) i. 6 Country gals and their..suitors got as much enjoyment..as jitterbugs or rug-cutters get nowadays from a swing band. **1942** Z. N. Hurston in *Amer. Mercury* July 96/1 *Rug-cutter*, originally a person frequenting house-rent parties, cutting up the rugs of the host with his feet; a person too cheap or poor to patronize regular dance halls; now means a good dancer. **1959** N. Mailer *Advts. for Myself* (1961) 107 He seemed full of strength and merriment. He would clap two geishas to him, and call across..to another soldier. 'Hey, Brown,' he would shout, 'ain't this a rug-cutter?' **1940** *Amer. Speech* XV. 205/1 **Rug-cutting*, violent, eccentric dancing. **1942** *Chatelaine* Apr. 54/2 The rug-cutting addicts discovered an older form of swing. **1947** S. Lewis *Kingsblood Royal* 21 As I say: we don't know where Belfreda goes or what she does —rug-cutting or witchcraft or maybe she belongs to some coloured left-wing political gang. **1981** 'S. Caudwell' *Thus was Adonis Murdered* ix. 114 He raised again the matter of the rug-cutting expedition... The only places..where there might be dancing..looked to me formidably expensive. **1897** *Sears, Roebuck Catal.* 298/3 Wool *Rug Fringe, with gimp heading 3 inches deep. **1922** Joyce *Ulysses* 691 The upturned rugfringe. **1966** *Olney Amsden & Sons Ltd. Price List* 35 Latchet *Rug Hooks... 16/- Dozen. **1967** *House & Garden* June 19/1 *Hooked rugs*... You need open-mesh canvas and a rug hooking tool which is a metal hook fitted into a wooden handle. It has a hinged metal shank at the hook end which will open and close automatically to prevent the hook getting caught in the canvas. **1974** *Aiken* (S. Carolina) *Standard* 22 Apr. 2-A/6 *Rug Hooking, 9:30 a.m.-2:30 p.m., Recreation Center, North Augusta. **1822** Miss Edgeworth in *Life & Letters* (1894) II. 70 We went through the female wards.., and saw the women at various works,—knitting, *rug-making, &c. **1976** N. Roberts *Face of France* iii. 39 Shops with displays of equipment for tapestry work and rug-making. **1916** J. London *Let.* 12 Oct. (1966) 473 'Uncle Charley'..then proceeded to shake you down in proper money-lender,..*rug-peddler fashion. **1977** *Kingston* (Ontario) *Whig-Standard* 9 Feb. 7/2 Her abilities caught the eye of some of the rising lights of her time, and the story has it that she '*rug-ranked' her way up out of the secretarial classifications. **1973** *Globe & Mail* (Toronto) 21 July 1/1 *Rug-ranking..refers to the Government's method of establishing the pay-level of secretaries in the same way the quality of the manager's rug is determined. It goes with the title on the door. *Ibid.*, While Mr. Drury says 'there isn't much possibility' of replacing the rug-ranking system with a point-rating system, he expresses sympathy for the problems faced by the secretaries. **1968–70** *Current Slang* (Univ. S. Dakota) III–IV. 104 **Rug rat*, a small child. **1976** *Daily Tel.* (Colour Suppl.) 16 July 10/1 He is without children; he has rug-rats instead. **1891** *Anthony's Phot. Bulletin* IV. 159 The only unattached part being the *rug strap for camera. **1926** S. T. Warner *Lolly Willowes* II. 114 She bought an extensive parcel..of variously coloured *rug-wools. **1967** E. Short *Embroidery & Fabric Collage* iii. 83 A soft Persian rug wool is the easiest to sew with. **1823** E. Weeton *Let.* 21 Nov. (1969) II. 243 She is fond of *rug work, and has done a great deal in a superior and beautiful manner. **1843** *Penny Cycl.* XXVII. 180/1 Another kind of weaving..is that which relates to rug-work and tapestry. **1895** *Montgomery Ward Catal.* 124/3 Colored Rug Yarn... ingrain carpet yarn, assorted colors, 4 skeins to pound. **1932** D. C. Minter *Mod. Needlecraft* 224/2 The thinner qualities of *rug yarn—such as Persian, Straight, Shetland and various Thrums yarns.

rug, *sb.*[3] *dial. rare.* [Of Scand. origin: cf. Swed. dial. *rugg* in the same sense (Rietz). Prob. related to *rag* mist, rime, common in northern Eng. dialects.] Drizzling rain.

c **1400** *Destr. Troy* 9652 Thurgh the rug, & the rayn, þat raiked aboue, All wery for wete. **1622** Drayton *Poly-Olbion* II. xxvi. 124 Thicke Vapours, that like Rugs still hang the troubled ayre. **1866** Edmondston *Gloss. Shetl. & Orkney*, *Rug*, small rain. **1969** G. M. Brown *Orkney Tapestry* 29 The old Orkneymen had a range of words for every kind and intensity of rain—a driv, a rug, a murr..a hellyiefer.

†**rug**, *sb.*[4] *Obs. rare.* Some kind of strong liquor.

1653 J. Taylor (Water P.) *Cert. Trav. Uncert. Journey* 16 Of all the drinks potable Rug is most puisant, potent, notable. Rug was the Capitall Commander there.

rug, obs. f. ridge *sb.*; see also Rugbeian.

†**rug**, *a. Obs.* [Gaming slang, of unknown origin.] Safe, secure: **a.** In gambling.

a **1700** B. E. *Dict. Cant. Crew* s.v., *It's all Rug*, the Game is secured. **1709** Steele *Tatler* No. 39 ¶36 If one has it all Rug, as the Gamesters say, when they have a Trick to make the Game secure. **1714** T. Lucas *Mem. Gamesters* (ed. 2) 104 His great Dexterity of making all Rugg at Dice, as the Cant is for securing a Die between two Fingers.

b. *transf.* In general use.

1705 Rowe *Biter* I. i, Fear nothing, Sir; Rug's the Word, all's safe. **1721** Cibber *Refusal* I, And does this Contract secure the Lady's Fortune to you too?..O! Pox! I knew that was all Rug before. **1735** Pope *Donne Sat.* IV. 134 Who got his Pension rug, Or quicken'd a Reversion by a drug? **1797** Brydges *Hom. Trav.* II. 251 We'll here lie snug, Let him but pass, we have him rug.

c. With adverbial force.

1714 *Wentworth Papers* (1883) 394 The changes at Court does not go so rug as some people expected.

rug, obs. form of rough *a.*

rug (rʌg), *v.*[1] *Sc.* and *north. dial.* Also 4–8 **rugge**, 5–6 **ruge** (5 **ruk**); 4–5 **rogg(e**. [prob. of Scand. origin: cf. Icel., Fær., and Norw. *rugga*, obs. Da. *rugge*, to rock (a cradle), to swing backwards and forwards, to sway. The original sense was prob. 'to pull'.]

1. a. *trans.* To pull forcibly, violently, or roughly; to tear, tug.

a **1300** *Cursor M.* 15825 For[þ] þai his maister drogh, And rugged him vn-rekenli bath ouer hill and [h]ogh. *Ibid.* 21920 Ded sal rug us til his rape. *c* **1340** Hampole *Pr. Consc.* 1230 Lyons, libardes and wolwes kene, þat wald worow men bylyve, And rogg þam in sonder and ryve. *a* **1400** in *Minor Poems Vernon MS.* II. 501 Wiþ his teeþ he gon hit togge, And so radli he gon hit Rogge, þat al þe Rolle gon race. *c* **1440** *Alph. Tales* 446 Oft tymys sho was enforcid to be drawen oute, bod it was in vayn bod if þai wuld hafe rugid hur in sonder. *c* **1450** Holland *Howlat* 822 In come twa flyrand fulis,..Ruschit baith to the bard, and ruggit his hair. **1500–20** Dunbar *Poems* lxxii. 106 Than rudelie come Rememberance Ay rugging me, withoutin rest. **1570** *Satir. Poems Reform.* xxii. 51 God nor ȝe gleddis ȝe get, Or Rauinnis the rug with bludie beik in bittis. **1572** *Ibid.* xxxii. 67 We commounis all,..now, allace! ar rugit, reuin, and rent. **17..** Ramsay *To Starrat* 21 Rug frae its roots the craig of Edinburgh castle. **1795** Macneill *Scotland's Skaith* lvi, Jean..Flyt's, and storms, and rug's Will's hair. **1835** Hogg in *Fraser's Mag.* XI. 358 The Hunter he rugged his old grey hair. **1871** W. Alexander *Johnny Gibb* (1873) 20 I'se rug yer lugs t'ye gin ye dinna gae this minit. **1930** Kipling *Limits & Renewals* (1932) 234 Old dry bites—when they get good hold and rugg you. That showed he must have dealt with the Beasts.

b. Const. *down*, †*forth*, *off*, *out* (*of*), *up*.

c **1375** *Sc. Leg. Saints* xxvi. (*Nicholas*) 689 He hynt þe prioure be þe hare, & rukyt hyme of his bed in hy. *c* **1450** *Mirour Saluacioun* (Roxb.) 83 The whilk festnyng his fete thai ruggid out semblably. **1456** Sir G. Haye *Law Arms* (S.T.S.) 162 The evill herbis may nocht be gudely ruggit up be the rutis, bot..gude herbis that ar nere thaim..be ruggit up with thame. *c* **1508** Dunbar *Poems* xxxiii. 83 The pyot furth his pennis did rug. *c* **1560** A. Scott *Poems* (S.T.S.) i. 125 Ruging and raifand vp kirk rentis lyke ruikis. **1637–50** Row *Hist. Kirk* (Wodrow Soc.) 12 In taking away bells, and rugging doun..ornaments. **1738** *Scotch Presbyterian Eloquence* 43 The Devil rugg their Hearts out of their Sides. *a* **1774** Fergusson *Plainstanes & Cawsey* Poems (1845) 46 Owre me the muckle horses gallop, Eneugh to rug my very saul up. **1825** J. Wilson *Noct. Ambr.* Wks. 1855 I. 9 Can an idea..rug out a handfu' o' hair out of the head o' him?

2. a. *intr.* To pull, tear, or tug (*at* something). Also, to struggle.

In mod. dial. use freq. combined with *rive*.

c **1350** *St. Andrew* 225 in Horstm. *Altengl. Leg.* (1881) 7 þai rugget at him with ful grete bir. ? *c* **1400** *Tourn. Tottenham* 199 in Hazl. *E.P.P.* III. 91 Thus thai tuggut and thei ruggut til hit was ny nyȝt. *c* **1425** Wyntoun *Cron.* III. ii. 472 Abowt twa pillaris..He kest his armys hastely, And ruggit at þaim doggitly. **1530** Lyndesay *Test. Papyngo* 1148 The Rauin began rudely to ruge and ryue. *a* **1585** Montgomerie *Flyting* 288 The Weird Sisters..Saw reavens rugand at that ratton. **1722** Ramsay *Three Bonnets* III. 29 Jouk three times rugged at his [brother's] shoulder. **1724** —— *Tea T. Misc.* (1871) II. 129 Hunger rugg'd at Watty's breast. **1812** W. Tennant *Anster F.* IV, Each..A good Crail's capon holds, at which he rugs and gnaws. **1832** *Chambers's Edin. Jrnl.* I. 225/1 The gilly,..who comes into the town,..rugging and riving for a place in some writer's office. **1872** C. Gibbon *For the King* xvii, You'll wring my arm out o' the socket if you keep rugging at it that way. **1901** R. Anderson *Hist. of Kilsyth* xiii. 111 That night the razor was bad. It rugged and he had to stop. **1951** R. Rendall *Orkney Variants* 24 Their lowan e'en are taakan tent O'chiels like Mansie o' the Bu Whose days upon the land are spent Ruggan wi' Taurus and the Pleugh.

†**b.** *rug and reave*, to practise robbery. *Obs.*

1508 Kennedie *Flyting w. Dunbar* 404 It cumis of kynde to the to be a traytoure, To ryde on nycht, to rug, to reue, and stele. **1513** Douglas *Æneis* IX. x. 53 Best likis ws all tyme to rug and reyf, To drive away the spreith, and tharon leyf. **1596** Dalrymple tr. *Leslie's Hist. Scot.* I. 323 Thay began to rug and reiue, stryk and stick ilk vther.

†**rug**, *v.*[2] *Obs.* [Of obscure origin.] *intr.* To fish with a rug-net. Hence †'**rugging** *vbl. sb.*

1630 in Binnell *Thames* (1758) 65 No Fisherman or other shall be suffered to rug for Flounders..between London Bridge..and Westminster. *Ibid.* 79 That no Peter-man do rug from London Bridge to Blackwall. **1758** Binnell *ibid.*, Rules to be observed in Rugging.

rug, *v.*[3] [f. rug *sb.*[2]] *trans.* To cover with a rug. Freq. with *up*.

1818 M. Edgeworth *Let.* 15 Oct. (1971) 126 He hopes to have the rooms carpetted and rugged by tuesday. **1936** F. Clune *Roaming round Darling* iii. 26 Many sharp turns and wattle-trees. The latter, droopy after being out all night, should be rugged up this weather. **1961** C. H. D. Todd *Popular Whippet* iii. 39 Kennels of greyhounds usually have the inmates 'rugged up' at night. **1968** E. R. Buckler *Ox Bells & Fireflies* vi. 93 You rugged the oxen and took the double-bitted ax from its leather fastener. **1975** D. Francis *High Stakes* i. 18 He was a great horse..he would soon be rugged up nice and quiet in a stable.

‖**ruga** ('ruːgə). *Bot.*, *Zool.*, etc. Pl. **rugæ** ('ruːdʒiː). [L. *rūga*.] A wrinkle, fold, or ridge.

1775 J. Jenkinson tr. *Linnæus' Brit. Pl.* Gloss. 256 *Rugose*, full of *rugæ* or wrinkles. **1797** *Encycl. Brit.* (ed. 3) II. 387/2 The vermicularis, with faint annular rugæ. **1821** W. P. C. Barton *Flora N. Amer.* I. 125 An oblong or barrel-shaped bulb, marked by circular lines or rugæ. **1879** *St. George's Hosp. Rep.* IX. 435 Its mucous membrane was drawn up into thick dark-brown rugæ. **1913** *Cunningham's Text-bk. Anat.* (ed. 4) 1298 When this muscular layer is contracted, the scrotum becomes smaller..and the skin is thrown into folds or wrinkles called rugæ. **1962** *Gray's Anat.* (ed. 33) 1514 The loose texture of the mucous layer allows the mucous coat to be thrown into folds or rugae when the bladder is empty. **1963** J. Osborne *Dental Mech.* (ed. 5) ii. 40 The rugae may be accentuated with blue inlay wax. **1969** *Gloss. Terms Dentistry* (*B.S.I.*) 107 *Rugae*, the irregular ridges of the mucous membrane covering the anterior part of the hard palate.

Hence '**rugal** *a.*

1936 Kantner & West *Phonetics* (ed. 3) I. iii. 48 Attention should be drawn to the alveolar or rugal ridge which is the raised line of flesh found at the point where the teeth emerge from the gums.

rugate ('ruːgət), *a. Zool.* [ad. pa. pple. of L. *rūgāre*, f. *rūga*.] Having rugæ; wrinkled.

1846 Dana *Zooph.* (1848) 196 Disk brown,..rugate. **1852** —— *Crust.* I. 425 Either part is rugate or pseudo-squamate.

Hence '**rugately** *adv.*

1846 Dana *Zooph.* (1848) 200 Corallum..rugately striate and denticulate.

Rugbeian (rʌg'biːən). Also 9 **Rugbæan**, 20 **Rugboean**. [f. Rugby (see next), on Latin types.] A former or present pupil of Rugby school. (Sometimes abbreviated to *Rug.*)

1714 T. Cave *Let.* 16 June in M. M. Verney *Verney Lett.* (1930) I. xiii. 249 We also favoured this day our two young Rugbeians and found Em well. **1825** *Sporting Mag.* XVII. 2 A Rugbæan is a Rugbæan all the world over. **1845** *Rules Footb. Rugby School* 6 That Old Rugbæans shall be allowed to play at the matches of Football. **1869** *Daily News* 10 Dec., A meeting of old Rugbeians was held yesterday. **1971** *Times* 18 Dec. 13/7 He had, in the opinion of many people with whom I have spoken (including one eminent old Rugboean), fully captured Hughes's message.

Rugby ('rʌgbi). Also with lower-case initial.

a. The name of the public school at Rugby in Warwickshire, used *attrib.* or *absol.* to designate one of the leading forms of the game of football, played with an oval ball which may be kicked or handled: points are obtained by scoring tries and kicking goals (see quot. 1975). Also *Comb.*, as **Rugby League**, an association of Rugby football clubs formed in 1922 (previously the 'Northern Union'), having rules differing from those of the Rugby Union; Rugby played according to these rules; **rugby tackle**, a tackle in which the arms are used to bring an opposing player down, as in Rugby football; **Rugby Union**, an association of Rugby football clubs formed in 1871; Rugby played according to its rules. Cf. rugger[2].

1864 *Field* 446/2 The Rugby Game. Will a good Rugby authority settle the following points in their game? **1871** *Field* 22 July 82/2 (*heading*) *The Rugby Union.* A special general meeting of the Rugby Football Union will be held at the Arundel Hotel, Arundel Street, Strand, on Monday evening. **1874** G. H. West *Rugby Union Football Ann.* 2 The following clubs have now enrolled themselves under the Rugby Union. *Ibid.* 11 Since the formation of the Rugby Union, the rules of football have been somewhat modified and altered... A few hints, therefore, on the general style of play in the Rugby Union game, and also an explanation of those rules which most affect it may not be out of place. **1879** *Encycl. Brit.* IX. 367/2 The tumbles and scrimmages incidental to the Rugby code. **1885** [see association 11]. **1897** Mrs. Rayner *Type-writer Girl* iii. 31 Their discourse ..circled chiefly round the noble quadruped, with divergences on Rugby and Association football. **1906** Gallaher & Stead *Compl. Rugby Footballer* xix. 265 There were fifty thousand people present—by far the biggest attendance of spectators we had ever seen at a Rugby match. **1923** *Whitaker's Almanack* 474/2 *Northern Union in 1921–22* This body is now called the Rugby League. **1926–7** *Army & Navy Stores Catal.* 721/2 Rugby jerseys (to order only). **1929** R. Harding *Rugby* 142 It was said that a certain Rugby League Club was prepared to give me £750 to become a professional Rugby player. *Ibid.* 144 The system of professionalism which obtains in the Rugby League is the best. **1931** R. Campbell *Georgiad* I. 18 Jack Squire..who.. makes a funeral of a Rugby Match. **1959** *Times* 21 Sept. 3/6 In this community of Rugby-minded souls every man.. could readily appreciate the virtues of an attacking as against a defensive policy. **1959** F. Guest *Indian Cavalryman* viii. 97 The subaltern, who was an athletic young man, immediately dived at the men in a Rugby tackle. **1960** T. McLean *Kings of Rugby* viii. 57 His Rugby-playing days were over. **1961** *Times* 7 Apr. 20/7 In the matter of crowd behaviour, in fact, the Rugby-watching public can in no way afford to be smug. **1963** *Listener* 14 Feb. 300/1 David Storey's *This Sporting Life* is a *bildungsroman* of an unusual sort. Machin, its central character, is a miner turned Rugby League player. **1969** [see league *sb.*[2] 1 c]. **1969** *Listener* 20 Mar. 384/3 The 'sheer disorder' of the broken field of your Rugby Union game. **1975** *Oxf. Illustr. Dict.*, *Rugby football*, one of the two main types of football (the other being Association football), played with 15 players a side (in Rugby Union) or 13 (in Rugby League), with an elliptical football punted, dropped, or passed from hand to hand, the object being to touch down behind the opponents' line and score a try, and to kick the ball over the crossbar of the H-shaped goal. **1976** J. McClure *Rogue Eagle* ii. 30 Hulk's Airtex shirt and ridiculous rugby shorts. **1976** *Western Mail* (Cardiff) 27 Nov., Mid-Wales Howells Cup first round rugby tie with Mid-Glamorgan..has been postponed. **1976** *Alyn & Deeside Observer* 10 Dec. 3/7 In the second half.. Chester played some excellent rugby. **1978** *Rugby World* Apr. 45 (Advt.), The *original* long playing records of Rugby Songs in the *Jock Strapp Series*. *Ibid.* 51 (Advt.), Top quality rugby jerseys.

b. Rugby fives, the leading form of fives: see fives[2].

1897 *Encycl. Sport* I. 398/2 In the Eton court..the presence of the pepper-box, the hole, and the step, make the game in practice as different from Rugby Fives as in theory it is similar. **1935** *Encycl. Sports* 270/1 A Rugby fives court, called after the school of that name, is a covered four-walled building. The walls are all plain, except that on the front wall there is a ledge or board, above which the ball must be struck to be in play. **1958** *Times* 16 Dec. 4/6 Old Oundelians ..beat Rugby Fives Association..by 121 points to 70. **1975** *Oxf. Compan. Sports & Games* 870/1 Rugby fives is mainly a school, old boys', and university game.

†**ruge**, *sb.*[1] *Obs. rare.* [ad. L. *rūga* ruga.] A wrinkle or fold.

c **1440** *Pallad. on Husb.* IV. 724 A ferdful face, his necke in many a ruge Yfretted grete. *Ibid.* XII. 569 Olyues that me fyndeth lying crispe, With rugis drawe. **1791** A. Graham in *Publ. Hudson's Bay Rec. Soc.* (1969) XXVII. IV. 117 [The tusk of the unicorn fish] is quite straight, and has a double spiral ruge on its surface.

†**ruge**, *sb.*[2] *Obs.*—[1] [f. L. *rugīre* to roar.] Roaring.

1500–20 Dunbar *Poems* lxxii. 19 As lyonis with awfull ruge, In yre thai hurlit him heir and thair.

†**ruge**, *v. Obs.*—[1] [ad. L. *rūgāre*, f. *rūga* ruga.] *trans.* To wrinkle.

1681 Grew *Musæum* I. v. iii. 115 On his Forehead and Chaps before, where his Skin is only ruged as you draw your Finger downward.

ruge, obs. f. rug.

rugement: see rugine *v.*

ruget, obs. f. rochet *sb.*[2]

rugg, var. rug *a. Obs.*

rugge, obs. f. ridge, rug.

rugged ('rʌgɪd), *a.*[1] (and *adv.*) Also 5–6 **rogged**, **roggyd**, 7 **rugg'd**, 7–8 **ruggid**. [prob. of Scand. origin: cf. the forms cited under rug *sb.*[2], and Sw. *rugga* to roughen, put a nap on, *ruggig* rough, shaggy. The precise relationship to *ragged* is not quite clear, but the stem is no doubt ultimately the same.]

†**1. a.** Rough with hair; hirsute, shaggy; also of horses, rough-coated. *Obs.* Cf. RAGGED *a.*[1] 1.

c1330 *Arth. & Merl.* 1501 (Kölbing), Clowes he hadde qued,..A rugged taile so a fende. c1386 CHAUCER *Knt.'s T.* 2025 (Ellesm. MS.), This woful Theban Palamon With flotery berd and rugged asshy heeres. c1440 *Promp. Parv.* 439/1 Roggyd, or rowghe,..*hispidus, hirsutus.* 1447 BOKENHAM *Seyntys* (Roxb.) 46 It signifyeth that oure lord jhesu Supplanted the deuyl oure ruggyd enmy. 1530 PALSGR. 322/2 Rogged with heare, *poillu.* a1548 HALL *Chron., Hen. IV,* 9 Experience teacheth, that of a rugged colte, commeth a good horse. 1590 SPENSER *F.Q.* I. vi. 27 The Lyon whelpes she saw how he did beare, And lull in rugged armes. 1605 SHAKS. *Macb.* III. iv. 100 Approach thou like the rugged Russian Beare. 1697 DRYDEN *Virg. Georg.* III. 751 Parch'd is his Hide, and rugged are his Hairs. 1726 LEONI *Alberti's Archit.* I. 96/1 If horses see the fire, they are prodigiously frightened and will grow rugged.

†**b.** Of cloth or garments: Hairy, coarse, rough.

1558 *Richmond Wills* (Surtees) 126, ij turfill hatts, ij ruggid hatts. 1613 PURCHAS *Pilgrimage* II. vii. (1614) 136 Prophetes..whose ordinarie habite seemes to be a rugged hairie garment. 1663 BUTLER *Hud.* I. i. 307 His Breeches were of rugged Woollen. 1687 TAUBMAN *London's Triumph* 8 The rest of the Mariners in Indian stripes and ruggid Yarn Caps. 1826 HOOD *Irish Schoolm.* xx, Like tears dried up with rugged huckaback.

†**c.** Of leaves: Covered with hairs. *Obs.*

1676 *Phil. Trans.* II. 630 The leaves are rugg'd like to a Borage leaf.

2. a. Having small rough projections; broken into irregular prominences; rough, uneven.

1548 ELYOT, *Scabratus*, made rough or rugged, as it were a thyng that is scalde. 1577 B. GOOGE *Heresbach's Husb.* II. (1586) 104 The blacke hath the ruggedder bark. 1601 HOLLAND *Pliny* II. 393 If the nailes be ragged and rugged, it is not amisse to apply [etc.]. 1642 H. MORE *Song of Soul* II. II. iii. I He much perplexed is..Where to make choice to enter his rugg'd saw. 1681 GREW *Musæum* I. VI. ii. 146 The Rugged-Oyster..is of a dull ash-colour. 1750 GRAY *Elegy* 13 Beneath those rugged elms. a1787 G. WHITE *Selborne* iv, This rag is rugged and stubborn, and will not hew to a smooth face. 1816 SCOTT *Old Mort.* xliii, The little bare feet which caught..hold of the rugged side of the oak. 1839 KEMBLE *Resid. in Georgia* (1863) 18 The rice-fields, all clothed in their rugged stubble.

fig. 1859 HELPS *Friends in C.* Ser. II. II. iii. 66 Smooths everything that would otherwise be rugged in domestic life.

b. Of ground: Broken, uneven; full of stones, rocks, abrupt rises or declivities, etc.

1656 COWLEY *Anacreontiques* ix, The Wheel of Life no less will stay In a smooth then Rugged way. 1687 A. LOVELL tr. *Thevenot's Trav.* I. 14 Hills that were so high and rugged ..that our hands were as well employed as our feet. 1717 BERKELEY *Journ. Tour Italy* Wks. 1871 IV. 543 The road very rugged with stones. 1769 ROBERTSON *Chas. V*, x. III. 243 Clambering up the rugged track with infinite fatigue as well as danger. 1820 KEATS *Lamia* I. 176 At the foot of those wild hills, The rugged founts of the Peræan rills. 1841 ELPHINSTONE *Hist. Ind.* II. 181 The Bahmani kings..had suffered severe losses in that rugged and woody country. 1875 JOWETT *Plato* (ed. 2) V. 30 Our island home is rugged, and does not admit of cavalry.

fig. 1673 *Humours Town* A3b, Men generally arrive at Wisdom by such rugged steps of self-experience. 1780 COWPER *Progr. Error* 71 Is this the rugged path, the steep ascent, That virtue points to?

3. a. Of features: Wrinkled, furrowed; irregular; strongly marked.

1596 SPENSER *F.Q.* IV. Prol. I The rugged forhead, that with grave foresight Welds kingdomes causes and affaires of state. 1617 MIDDLETON & ROWLEY *Fair Quarrel* III. ii, You have a good face now, but 'twill grow rugged. 1621 BURTON *Anat. Mel.* III. ii. VI. iii. (1651) 561 Her soft corall lips will be pale, her skin rugged. 1697 DRYDEN *Virg. Georg.* IV. 146 Like their Prince appears his gloomy Race: Grim, ghastly, rugged. 1782 MISS BURNEY *Cecilia* x. viii, Tears running quick down his rugged cheeks. a1817 JANE AUSTEN *Persuasion* iii, His face the colour of mahogany, rough and rugged to the last degree, all lines and wrinkles. 1863 GEO. ELIOT *Romola* II. vii, There seemed the very opposite testimony in the rugged face. 1890 CONAN DOYLE *White Company* xxxv, A dry-wood fire had been lit,..the glare beating upon their rugged faces.

b. Wrinkled with care or displeasure; frowning.

1605 SHAKS. *Macb.* III. ii. 27 Sleeke o're your rugged Lookes, Be bright and Iouiall. 1671 MILTON *P.R.* II. 164 Such object hath the power to soft'n and tame Severest temper, smooth the rugged'st brow. 1848 DICKENS *Dombey* xv, His eyebrows..smoothed their rugged bristling aspect, and became serene.

4. a. Of weather, etc.: Rough, stormy, tempestuous. Now *rare*.

1549 COVERDALE, etc. *Erasm. Par. Tim.* Ded., There is none so rugged a wynter, but some profyte aryseth of the feldes. 1622 MALYNES *Anc. Law-Merch.* 231 Serue them in hard and rugged weather, whereby they are hindred to be abroad. 1637 MILTON *Lycidas* 93 He..question'd every gust of rugged wings That blows from off each beaked Promontory. 1773 *Life N. Frowde* 25 He was..of the most inviting Carriage that ever I observed upon the rugged Element he was employed in. 1850 W. SCORESBY *Cheever's Whalem. Adv.* iv. (1858) 58 The Commodore Preble lost.. seven whales by sinking after they were 'turned up', and three from alongside in rugged weather. 1874 SCAMMON *Marine Mammals* 311 A rough sea, accompanied with blowing weather, is termed by whalers 'rugged weather'.

b. Involving hardships or severe toil. Also *colloq.* in weakened sense: tough, difficult.

1730–46 THOMSON *Autumn* 289 Then throw that shameful pittance from thy hand, But ill apply'd to such a rugged task. 1820 KEATS *Isabella* xli, Thinking on rugged hours and fruitless toil. 1838 EMERSON *Wks.* (Bohn) II. 203 So it is in rugged crises, in unweariable endurance..that the angel is shown. 1889 JESSOPP *Coming of Friars* vi. 295 It must have been hard for the weak and sickly..to stand that rugged old Cambridge life. 1942 *Yank* 7 Oct. 7 'Rugged' the Destroyers call the Tank Hunting Course. 1943 *Newsweek* 27 Sept. 23/1 The war here is still pretty rugged, as the boys say. 1946 *News Chron.* 30 Aug. 3/8 The first night was a bit rugged, in a way (George said). There being no bed, Mrs Cain made up the bedclothes on the concrete floor. 1953 *Manch. Guardian* 31 July 4/6 They thought it not too strenuous: it had not been easy but had been 'rugged'. 1973 J. PATTINSON *Search Warrant* v. 81 If things get really rugged I just put the bite on my old man.

5. Rough to the ear; harsh; unpolished.

1590 SPENSER *F.Q.* III. ii. 3 But ah! my rymes too rude and rugged arre. 1642 MILTON *Apol. Smect.* Wks. 1851 III. 309 Declaming in rugged and miscellaneous geare blown together by the foure winds. c1645 —— *Sonn.* xi, Those rugged names to our like mouths grow sleek. 1697 DRYDEN *Ded. Æneis* Ess. (ed. Ker) II. 227 It seldom happens but a monosyllable line turns verse to prose; and even that prose is rugged and unharmonious. 1710 PHILIPS *Pastorals* iv. 21 So sweet a Scene ill Suits my ruggid Lay. 1763 J. BROWN *Poetry & Mus.* vi. 111 Eschylus is uneven, concise, abrupt, and rugged. 1841 ELPHINSTONE *Hist. Ind.* I. 427 Most of the hymns composing the Védas are in a language so rugged as to prove [etc.].

6. Austere, harsh, severe, ungentle.

1597 HOOKER *Eccl. Pol.* v. lxv. §6 Take Cato, or if he be too harsh and rugged, choose some other of a softer metal. 1621 FLETCHER *Pilgrim* I. i, Signior Alphonso, ye are too rugged to her, Believe, too full of harshness. 1682 BUNYAN *Holy War* (1905) 279 My Lord Mayor said, That the answer did not look with a rugged face. 1773 *Life N. Frowde* 25, I began to be reconciled both to him and his looks, Which at first seem'd so rugged and unsociable. 1796 BURNEY *Mem. Metastasio* I. 21 The first breach of contract with the rugged advocate was in the beginning of 1721. 1817 BONAR *Serm.* II. xix. 423 We..dislike those rugged pastors who will make no allowance for the follies of the age. 1836 THIRLWALL *Greece* II. 267 Characters like that of Aristides, even when there is nothing rugged and forbidding in their exterior, are seldom loved.

7. Lacking in culture and refinement; rude, uncultivated; also, rough and hardy (cf. next).

a1625 FLETCHER *Wife for Month* v. i, Though he be stubborn, And of a rugged nature, yet he is honest. 1665 SIR T. HERBERT *Trav.* (1677) 301 They are very humane and noble in their natures; differing..very much from the Turks, who are rugged and barbarous. a1680 BUTLER *Rem.* (1759) I. 96 Force is a rugged Way of making Love. 1732 BERKELEY *Alciphr.* v. §11 The rugged manners of northern boors. 1748 *Anson's Voy.* II. xiv. 284 Its inhabitants are a luxurious and effeminate race,..incapable..of giving any opposition to this rugged enemy. 1799 HAN. MORE *Fem. Educ.* (ed. 4) I. 119 It drives the gentle spirit to artifice, and the rugged to despair. 1826 SCOTT *Woodst.* ii, We have still about us some rugged foresters of the old Woodstock breed. 1849 M. ARNOLD *World & Quietist* 21 The rugged Labourer Caught not till then a sense..Of his omnipotence.

Comb. 1888 FENN *Dick o' the Fens* 11 A tall rugged-looking man..came slouching up.

8. Of a rough but strong or sturdy character.

1827 CARLYLE *Misc.* (1857) I. 11 He has an intellect vehement, rugged, irresistible. 1852 TENNYSON *Ode Wellington* 184 Whose life was work, whose language rife With rugged maxims hewn from life. 1853 HUMPHREYS *Coin Coll. Man.* xxvi. 397 There is a fine rugged grandeur about the great copper pieces of this latter epoch. 1873 SYMONDS *Grk. Poets* v. 150 In his style Simonides has none of Pindar's rugged majesty. 1931 *Amer. Speech* VI. 185 Frequent adjectives of encomium in book reviews are.. romantic, rugged, ruthless. 1966 *Listener* 10 Mar. 363/2 Nicholas Maw's..string quartet, a closely-knit, rugged work, product of a rich and fertile imagination. 1976 *Gramophone* Dec. 1057/2 Jochum's reading has a rugged truth combined with poetic sensibility.

9. a. *U.S.* Strong, robust, vigorous; *spec.* in phr. ***rugged individualism***. So ***rugged individualist, individuality***.

1848 BARTLETT *Dict. Amer.* 280 *Rugged*, hardy; robust; healthy. 1858 HAWTHORNE *Fr. & It. Note-bks.* I. 271 Dirty little imps,..rugged and healthy enough, nevertheless, and sufficiently intelligent. 1872 O. W. HOLMES *Poet Breakf.-t.* xii. 358 I'm getting along in life, and I ain't quite so rugged as I used to be. 1928 H. HOOVER *New Day* 154 We were challenged with a peace-time choice between the American system of rugged individualism and a European philosophy of diametrically opposed doctrines—doctrines of paternalism and state socialism. 1937 [see DELIQUESCENT *a.* 3]. 1937 *Education* Nov. 186/1 Each of them..is a rugged individualist doing everything to satisfy his own personal desire. 1946 G. B. SHAW *Geneva* III. 76 Your pose is that of the rugged individualist, the isolationist. 1962 [see SAME B. 2d]. 1973 *Guardian* 18 June 4/4 The apolitical frame of mind which is summed up in the cliche 'rugged individualism'. 1974 *Encycl. Brit. Macropædia* V. 403/1 Cypriots are a people of rugged individuality.

b. orig. *U.S.* Of a manufactured object: strongly constructed, capable of withstanding rough usage. Also *transf.*

1921 *Wireless World* 29 Oct. 477/2 The whole design has been made robust, or, as our American friends would say, 'rugged'. 1960 *Practical Wireless* XXXVI. 302/1 The mains transformer should be a rugged component capable of secure attachment to the chassis to survive the hazards of transport. 1975 J. WYLLIE *Butterfly Flood* xxvii. 128 Everybody uses Land Rovers. Good cars, too. Rugged. 1978 *Detroit Free Press* 16 Apr. (Gardening Guide) 6 (Advt.), This 19.9 hp grounds maintenance tractor is specially designed for big jobs where you need rugged, dependable power.

10. As *adv.* Ruggedly.

1661 J. DAVIES *Civil Warres* 344 Finding how rugged they moved as to his interest. 1678 BUTLER *Hud.* III. i. 374 For those that doe his business best, In Hell are us'd the ruggedest.

Hence '**ruggedish** *a.*, somewhat rugged.

1787 *Linnæus' Families of Plants* I. 78 Seed..ruggedish.

rugged (rʌgd), *a.*[2] [f. RUG *sb.*[2]] Provided or covered with a rug or rugs.

1888 *Pall Mall G.* 11 Jan. 5/1 The snugly-cushioned, hot-bottled, rugged, and scented votaries of fashion. 1899 SOMERVILLE & ROSS *Irish R.M.* 275 Two horses, carefully rugged, were in it.

†**rugged**, *v.* *Obs.*[−1] [f. RUGGED *a.*[1]] *trans.* To make rugged.

1628 FELTHAM *Resolves* II. xxix. 91 'Tis the World, that choaking vp the way, does rugged that which is naturally smoother.

ruggedize ('rʌgɪdaɪz), *v.* orig. *U.S.* [f. RUGGED *a.*[1] + -IZE.] *trans.* To make rugged; to produce in a version designed to withstand rough usage. So '**ruggedized** *ppl. a.*; **ruggedi'zation**.

1954 *Electronic Engin.* XXVI. 255 The recent introduction of 'ruggedized' valves. 1958 C. C. ADAMS *Space Flight* 198 Automatic-control mechanisms must be added to the ship so that maneuvers can be programmed into them while the men are lying all but helpless on their contour chairs. And these equipments themselves must be 'ruggedized' to withstand the very accelerations they are compensating for. 1959 *Wall St. Jrnl.* (Eastern ed.) 18 May 13/3 There are no two ways about it. Ruggedization is costly. 1962 *Daily Tel.* 21 May 10/8 A leaflet..from a New York electrical equipment firm..describes a 'ruggedised weather-proofed instrument'. 1969 *IEEE Trans. Nuclear Sci.* XVI. 314/1 An electronic subsystem packaged in a compact and ruggedized fashion suitable for operation in outer space. 1971 *Daily Tel.* (Colour Suppl.) 10 Dec. 31/4 The tubes were used extensively in the Korean War. Since then they have been miniaturised and protected—or 'ruggedised'—against the rough treatment they can expect on active service, and have spawned many instruments. 1977 *Sci. Amer.* Oct. 140/1 (Advt.), When the frequency, sinusoidal amplitude and sweep rate of the vibration levels demand the ultimate in ruggedization, consider Questar.

ruggedly ('rʌgɪdlɪ), *adv.* [f. RUGGED *a.*[1] + -LY[2].] In a rugged or rough manner.

1382 WYCLIF *Prov.* xviii. 23 With obsecraciouns speketh the pore man; and a riche man shal speke out ruggidli. 1607 BEAUM. & FL. *Woman-Hater* v. iii, Nay, look not ruggedly upon me, I am made up too strong to fear such looks. 1660 W. SECKER *Nonsuch Prof.* 156 The nettle.. stings when its gently touched, but doth not hurt when its ruggedly handled. 1668 HOPKINS *Serm.* (1685) 78 Moving upon these four sides, it must of necessity move very ruggedly, by jolts and jerks. 1701 COLLIER *M. Aurel.* (1726), Alexander the grammarian taught me not to be ruggedly critical about Words. 1737 BRACKEN *Farriery Impr.* (1757) II. 82 He play'd his Horse-play too ruggedly. a1851 ROBERTSON in *Four C. Eng. Lett.* 565, I have spoken ruggedly but not rudely. 1895 *Pop. Sci. Monthly* Sept. 718 The new land is described as ruggedly barren.

ruggedness ('rʌgɪdnɪs). [f. as prec. + -NESS.]

1. a. The state or character of being rugged; roughness, unevenness.

1530 PALSGR. 264/1 Ruggydnesse, *pellure.* 1544 PHAER *Regim. Lyfe* (1553) B v, These thinges are good for Tetters, and other ruggednesse of the skinne. 1601 HOLLAND *Pliny* II. 321 As for the ruggednesse of any blade, it will take it away more effectually..than the very file. 1674 N. FAIRFAX *Bulk & Selv.* 86 The utmost smoothness we can come at.. is full of.. little ruggednesses. 1719 DE FOE *Crusoe* II. (Globe) 585 You know not a Man from a Woman, neither by the Ruggedness of their Countenances or their Clothes. 1751 JOHNSON *Rambler* No. 88 ¶11 Our language, of which the chief defect is ruggedness and asperity. 1797 MRS. RADCLIFFE *Italian* vii, It was merely a ruggedness in the stones..that had excited his curiosity. 1871 PALGRAVE *Lyr. Poems* 127 Features by keen mountain air Moulded to solemn ruggedness.

b. Of roads, mountains, etc.

1648 WILKINS *Math. Magic* II. ii. 161 Every little ruggednesse or unevennes of the ground. 1698 FRYER *Acc. E. India & P.* A4b, Where the Ruggedness of the Ways interpose. 1774 GOLDSM. *Nat. Hist.* (1776) I. 149 The ruggedness of the road,..leading up the mountain, is not easily described. 1814 SCOTT *Diary* 30 Aug., The grounds around have been dressed, so as to smooth their ruggedness. 1836 W. IRVING *Astoria* II. 215 All the discouraging accounts of the ruggedness of the mountains lower down the river. 1875 JOWETT *Plato* (ed. 2) V. 277 The country.., owing to the ruggedness of the soil, not providing anything in great abundance.

fig. 1825 LAMB *Elia* II. *The Superannuated Man*, The faithful partners of my toils..that smoothed for me..the ruggedness of my professional road. 1862 GOULBURN *Pers. Relig.* IV. i. (1873) 253 Crosses, ruggednesses, unpleasant collisions in one day's walk.

2. Harshness or roughness of character, etc.

1647 J. MAYNE *Answ. Cheynell* 27 All they of that soft Sex, with whom I have converst, have accused me of too great severity, and ruggedness, towards them. 1676 HALE *Contempl., Medit. Lord's Prayer* 145 The Pardon that I give, is mingled with ruggedness, with revenge. 1751 JOHNSON *Rambler* No. 115 ¶7 A wife who had the ruggedness of a man without his force. 1794 GODWIN *Caleb Williams* 19 It was in vain that Mr. Tyrrel endeavoured to restrain the ruggedness of his character. 1830 CUNNINGHAM *Brit. Painters* II. 203 The habitual ruggedness of his personal manners.

3. Of manufactured objects: robustness, durability. Cf. RUGGED *a.*[1] 9b.

1936 *Physics* VII. 75/1 The ruggedness of the simplified extrusion plastometer has been established by over two years of practically uninterrupted service. 1971 *Physics Bull.* Nov. 644/1 (Advt.), Designed to provide the versatility required for laboratory use with the ruggedness of production line equipment.

ˈrugger^1. *Obs.* exc. *arch.* [f. RUG *v.*^{1} 2 b.] A plunderer, depredator, robber.

1570 *Satir. Poems Reform.* xxi. 3 Ruggars, Reifars, Rome-raikars. **1596** DALRYMPLE tr. *Leslie's Hist. Scot.* II. 130 Manifest ruggers and reiuers on the Sey. **1860** *Wills & Inv. N.C.* (Surtees) 99 *note*, The lawless propensities of the ruggers and rievers of that wild district.

ˈrugger^2, slang or colloquial alteration of RUGBY (in the sense of 'Rugby football'). Freq. *attrib.* **rugger-tackle** *v. trans.* = TACKLE *v.* 5 (*a*).

1893 *Westm. Gaz.* 17 Oct. 5/3 W. Neilson was elected captain of 'rugger' and T. N. Perkins of 'socker'. **1895** *19th Cent.* Nov. 865 He would find that a 'Rugger' blue commanded vastly more admiration. **1914** 'BARTIMEUS' *Naval Occasions* ix. 64 They earned their 'Rugger' colours together as scrum and stand-off halves. **1927** *Granta* 14 Oct. 9/1 He has had to be content with four years and a captaincy in the Magdalene Rugger side. **1929** *Mercury Story Bk.* 162 'Rubbish' I heard an eupeptic Rugger man protesting. **1930** R. CAMPBELL *Poems* 10 Nor at his Rugger-Match is Squire more gay. **1937** F. SMYTHE *Camp Six* v. 65 The football was also very popular and Nursang did his best to form the Sherpas into a rugger scrum. **1951** M. MCLUHAN *Mech. Bride* (1967) 137/1 The same contrast may be seen between the rugger crowd and the soccer crowd. **1955** *Times* 3 Aug. 7/4 Gradually strength and energy returned, and in two days the Sherpas produced the expedition rugger ball. **1967** D. PINNER *Ritual* xii. 119 He rugger-tackled the policeman. **1973** D. LEES *Rape of Quiet Town* vii. 111 It was all in the spirit of a rugger club frolic.

ruggerite (ˈrʌgəraɪt). *rare.* [f. RUGGER^2 + -ITE^1.] One who plays Rugby football.

1951 R. CAMPBELL *Light on Dark Horse* iv. 75 In the end his school of 'scruffy soccerites' defeated Langley's ruggerites at their own rugger.

ruggery (ˈrʌgərɪ), *a. rare.* [f. RUGGER^2 + -Y^1.] Being or resembling a typical Rugby player.

1961 A. COMFORT *Come out to Play* ii. 136 Gaudeamus was a large, ruggery man.

ˈrugging, *sb.* [f. RUG *sb.*^{2}] (See quot. 1858.)

1858 SIMMONDS *Dict. Trade, Rugging,* a coarse wrapping or blanket cloth. **1939** *Country Life* 11 Feb. p. xxxiii/2 (Advt.), Cheaper quality in rugging, 27/6, 25/- & 20/-. **1963** E. H. EDWARDS *Saddlery* xx. 149 The most simple of all is the Yorkshire boot, which consists of an oblong of stout rugging with a tape sewn along the centre.

ˈrugging, *vbl. sb.* [f. RUG *v.*^{1}] Pulling, tugging; seizing for oneself.

a **1578** LINDESAY (Pitscottie) *Chron. Scot.* (S.T.S.) II. 273 Thair was nathing bot rwgging and raveing of the puir laubouraris. **1581** N. BURNE in *Cath. Tract.* (S.T.S.) 167 Be rugging doun of kirkis, be spuleying of Abbayis. **1596** DALRYMPLE tr. *Leslie's Hist. Scot.* I. 187 Trubling the west seyes in thift, ruging, and reiueng. **1644** BAILLIE *Lett. & Jrnls.* (1841) II. 232 We have strange rugging with the Independents. **1814** SCOTT *Wav.* xlii, The gude auld times of rugging and riving..are come back again. **1846** G. S. FABER *Lett. Tract. Secession* 51 In the midst of this awful *rugging and riving* [etc.].

attrib. **1836** W. ARNOT *Autobiog.* (1877) 107, I do feel a tearing, rugging process going on.

b. *fig.* (See quot.)

1814 *Saxon & Gael* I. 153 The craving or rugging at the heart, i.e., hunger, is a disease but too frequent among the Highlanders.

†**ˈruggish,** *a. Obs.* [Cf. RUGGY *a.*] Rough, stubborn. So †**ˈruggishness,** roughness.

1541 COPLAND *Guydon's Quest. Chirurg.* Rj, The .ix. [sign of leprosy] is ruggyshnes of the skynne in maner of a goos. **1688** PENTON *Guardian's Instruction* (1897) 31 If he found a Boy ruggish and untractable.

†**ˈruggle.** *Obs.* [Of obscure origin.]

1. A plaything, toy.

1598 BARCKLEY *Felic. Man* III. (1603) 146 Humane power and riches, which may be likened to the ruggles and toyes which children use to play with. *Ibid.* (1631) 503 Honour, and glory,..he esteemeth as the frumps of fortune, and ruggles for children to play with.

2. A species of shell.

c **1711** PETIVER *Gazophyl.* vi. §52 Small Gibraltar Ruggle ..are also found on the Adriatick and French Mediterranean Shores.

†**rug gown.** *Obs.* [f. RUG *sb.*^{2}]

1. A gown made of rug.

1558 *Lanc. Wills* (Chetham Soc.) II. 114 That six poor men..shall have every of theme a black rugge gowne. **1591** FLORIO *2nd Fruites* 7 A night gown of chamlet, a rugge gown. **1611** TOURNEUR *Ath. Trag.* II. v, The Gentleman tooke the dog in shagge-haire to be some Watch-man in a rugge gowne. **1639** HORN & ROB. *Gate Lang. Unl.* xlvii. §517 Cloakes, rug-gownes, and the like outermost garments, we put on uppermost. **1657** R. LIGON *Barbadoes* (1673) 44 Rug Gowns, such as poor people wear in Hospitals.

2. One wearing a rug gown; *spec.* a watchman.

1619 FLETCHER *Mons. Thomas* IV. ii, Down comes a Constable, and the Sow... A whole stand of rug gowns rowted manly And the Kings peace put to flight. **1646** J. HALL *Horæ Vac.* 9 What a grand ornament our Gentry would Soon loose, if every rug-gown might be bold To rail at such Heroick feats?

Hence †**ˈrug-gowned** *a. Obs.*

1622 FLETCHER *Prophetess* II. ii, I had rather meet An enemy in the field, than stand thus nodding Like to a rug-gown'd Watch-man. **1624** MASSINGER *Renegado* v. ii, With as much ease..As ever gallants..Have set upon a drunken constable, And bore him from a sleepy rug-gown'd watch.

transf. **1630** J. TAYLOR (Water P.) *Wks.* II. 259/2 The Peare, the Apple, and the rug-gown'd Peache.

ruggy (ˈrʌgɪ), *a.* Now *dial.* Also 5 rogi, roggy, 6 ruggie. [Related to RUGGED *a.*^{1} Cf. Sw. *ruggig* in similar senses.]

1. Rugged, in various senses; rough; †shaggy; †wild, stormy.

c **1386** CHAUCER *Knt.'s T.* 2025 Tho cam this woful Theban Palamon, With flotry berd, and ruggy [*v.r.* rogi] asshy heerys. *c* **1440** *Pallad. on Husb.* VII. 188 The ruggy lordis Of broun colour be slayn for this discordis. *Ibid.* XI. 86 Threste in a braunche of roggy wilde olyue. **1577–87** HOLINSHED *Chron.* III. 61 A sore, ruggie, and tempestuous day, with wind, snow, and sleet. **1598** YONG *Diana* 171 There was seene the deadly Cypresse,..the blacke and ruggie Elme. **1615** BRATHWAIT *Strappado* (1878) 319 Leaue off to wash those cliues and ruggy caues, and now repaire to monumentall graues. **1634–5** BRERETON *Trav.* (Chetham Soc.) 155 This ruggy fringe is joined to a garment which.. reacheth to the very ground. **1849** in De Vere *Americanisms* (1872) 536 It's a mighty ruggy trail..up the Shasta Mountain.

2. (See quots. Perhaps a different word.)

1850 *Jrnl. R. Agric. Soc.* XI. II. 733 The sainfoin becomes 'ruggy', as it is called, in about 4 years, and then it is changed to another piece of land. **1860** *Slang Dict.* (ed. 2) 203 *Ruggy*, fusty, frowsy.

rugh, obs. variant of ROVE (nail).

rugh(e, obs. forms of ROUGH *a.*

ruȝ(e, ruȝhe, obs. forms of ROUGH *a.*

rug-headed, *a. rare*$^{-1}$. [f. RUG *sb.*^{2}] Shock-headed.

1593 SHAKS. *Rich. II*, II. i. 156 We must supplant those rough rug-headed Kernes.

rughh, rught, obs. forms of ROUGH *a.*

Rugian (ˈruːdʒɪən), *sb.* and *a.* [f. L. *Rugii* pl., Rugians + -IAN.] **A.** *sb.* A member of an ancient Germanic tribe; the East Germanic language of this tribe. **B.** *adj.* Of or pertaining to the Rugians.

1611 CORYAT *Crudities* 106 Odoacer the Rugian that vsurped the Kingdome of Italy..by expelling Augustulus the last Emperour of Rome. **1845** *Encycl. Metrop.* XI. 268/1 Those united bands the Heruli, the Alani, the Scyrri, and the Rugians..constituted the military force of Italy. **1884** *Encycl. Brit.* XVII. 727/1 This Rugian war was probably an indirect cause of the fall of Odoacer. **1934** PRIEBSCH & COLLINSON *German Lang.* 25 A few other Germanic languages, e.g. Skirian, Rugian, [etc.]. **1935** H. A. L. FISHER *Hist. Europe* I. x. 120 There was a bigness of scale about Theodoric which redeemed many of the grosser vices... After three years' hard fighting he eliminated from Italy the Rugian army of Odovacar, and thereafter gave thirty-six years of golden peace to that much harassed land.

†**ˈrugible,** *a. Obs.*$^{-1}$ [f. L. *rugīre* to roar.] Capable of roaring. Hence †**rugiˈbility.** *Obs.*

1620 T. GRANGER *Div. Logike* 108 Risibilitie, Rugibilitie, &c. Powers of the forme, immediatly issuing therefrom. *Ibid.* 218 A Lion is a fore-footed Beast rugible.

†**rugine,** *sb. Obs.* [a. F. *rugine*, ad. med.L. *rugina*, prob. an alteration of L. *runcīna* plane.] A surgeon's rasp.

1676 WISEMAN *Surg. Treat.* v. ix. 392, I open'd the Fissure with my Rugines, scraping away its edges that no Sanies or Matter might be detain'd. **1739** S. SHARPE *Surg.* Introd. p. xlvii, In these cases it is proper to scrape the Bone with a Rugine.

†**rugine,** *v. Obs. rare.* [ad. F. *ruginer*, or med.L. *ruginare*: see prec.] *trans.* To rasp or scrape with a rugine. Hence †**rugining** *vbl. sb.*

c **1400** *Lanfranc's Cirurg.* 132 (Add. MS.), þenne y remeffe hym aweye wiþ rugenynge [*v.r.* rugement] from þe partye þat halt. **1676** WISEMAN *Surg. Treat.* II. v. ix. 130 (R.), The next day, where you shall find it moist, there you are to rugine it.

†**ˈrugling,** *adv. Obs.* [f. *rug* RIDGE *sb.*^{1} Cf. Du. *ruggelings*, G. *rückling(s)*.] Backwards.

c **1100** in *Fragm. Ælfric's Grammar* 6 þu scalt nu ruglunge ridæn to þære eorþe. *a* **1225** *St. Marher.* 17 He rarinde rad ruglinge into helle. *a* **1225** *Juliana* 48 Ha..hef him up ant dushe him adun ruglunge.

†**rug-net.** *Obs.* [Cf. RUG *v.*^{2}] Some kind of fishing-net formerly used on the Thames.

1630 in Binnell *Descr. Thames* (1758) 66 Any Bley-Net, Rug-Net, or Smelt-Net. *Ibid.* 79 Every Rug-Net is to contain two Inches three Quarters in the Meish wet and dry.

rugorosyte: see RIGOROSITY.

rugosa (ruːˈgəʊzə). [L., fem. of *rūgōsus* (see RUGOSE *a.*) and the specific epithet of *Rosa rugosa* (C. P. Thunberg *Flora Japonica* (1784) 213).] A hardy shrub rose belonging to the species *Rosa rugosa*, or one of its varieties or hybrids, distinguished by dark green, wrinkled leaves and large, globular, orange-red hips. Also *attrib.*

1892 W. PAUL *Contrib. Hort. Lit.* 189 The Rugosa Rose. Where large showy Roses are valued these flowers will not fail to please. **1899** T. W. SANDERS *Cultivated Roses* 33 Madame Georges Bruant (hybrid rugosa). **1906** *Roses* 121 Rugosas, owing to their very bushy growth, should be in separate beds. **1920** *19th Cent.* July 174 Roses innumerable —teas, chinas, rugosas, briars, and their hybrids—are asserting their decorative uses. **1943** T. C. MANSFIELD *Roses* ii. 18 The rugosa hybrids make exceptionally fine hedges. **1962** R. PAGE *Educ. of Gardener* vii. 209 The rugosa rose 'Blanc Double de Coubert' goes into every garden I make. **1977** *Vole* No. 1. 34/3 The rugosas flower for weeks and have lovely hips.

rugose (ruːˈgəʊs), *a.* [ad. L. *rūgōs-us*, f. *rūga* wrinkle, RUGA.] Marked by rugæ or wrinkles; wrinkled, corrugated, ridgy: **a.** *Bot.* Also in combs., as *rugose-leaved* adj.; *rugose mosaic*, a mosaic disease of potatoes characterized by a marked wrinkling of the leaves and increased chlorosis and dwarfing compared with other mosaics.

1703 *Phil. Trans.* XXIII. 1424 The Fruit grows in clusters, each husk rugose. **1753** *Chambers' Cycl.* Suppl. s.v. *Leaf, Rugose Leaf*, that whose veins are sunk deep, and between which the membranous and fleshy part of the leaf rises in irregular forms, so as to give upon the whole a wrinkled surface. **1825** *Greenhouse Comp.* I. 92 A rugose-leaved branchy shrub of the easiest culture. **1831** DAVIES *Mat. Med.* 97 This bark is generally..covered with a rugose epidermis with irregular fissures. **1872** OLIVER *Elem. Bot.* App. 307 Leaves radical, tufted,..rugose. **1923** SCHULTZ & FOLSOM in *Jrnl. Agric. Res.* XXV. 52 The writers believe that most of Murphy's crinkle..is identical with the type here designated as 'rugose mosaic' with some leaf-rolling mosaic symptoms. **1967** A. E. COX *Potato* iv. 93 The two most serious of the virus diseases, leaf roll and rugose mosaic, are transmitted from infected to healthy plants by aphids.

b. *Anat., Zool.*, etc.

1752 HILL *Hist. Anim.* 144 The rugose Murex, with an expanded lip. **1769** E. BANCROFT *Guiana* 383 The voice becomes hoarse, and the nails rugose and scabrous. **1805** WEAVER tr. *Werner's Fossils* 151 A rugose surface is that which consists of several very slight linear elevations, forming different irregular curves. **1834** MCMURTRIE *Cuvier's Anim. Kingd.* 387 The sides of the thorax are sometimes tuberculous or rugose and sometimes spinous. **1872** COUES *N. Amer. Birds* 46 The plates become elevated into little tubercles, roughened or not. Such a leg is said to be granulated or rugose.

c. [a. mod.L. order name *Rugosa* (Milne-Edwards & Haime *Monogr. Brit. Fossil Corals* (1850) I. p. lxiv.] Of a fossil coral: belonging to the extinct order Rugosa (or Tetracoralla), which includes horn-shaped corals with ridged surfaces.

1872 H. A. NICHOLSON *Man. Palæont.* I. viii. 99 It has been shown that some..abnormal Rugose corals were provided with a lid. **1935** *Geol. Mag.* LXXII. 482 The rugose corals..are a group of Palaeozoic corals. **1972** *Sci. Amer.* June 61/2 The conical or cylindrical stone tube that sheltered the second type has conspicuous external growth wrinkles on its surface; these corals are called rugose.

d. *fig.*

1942 A. L. ROWSE *Cornish Childhood* vi. 133 Old Sidney was a rugose personality... I am bound to say that, rough-edged as he was with everybody, he was always very kind to me.

Hence **ruˈgosely** *adv.*

1847 DARLINGTON *Amer. Weeds* (1860) 260 Seeds rugosely pitted, under a lens.

rugosity (ruːˈgɒsɪtɪ). [ad. L. *rūgōsitas* or F. *rugosité* (16th c.): see RUGOSE *a.* and -ITY.]

1. The state of being rugose or wrinkled.

1599 A. M. tr. *Gabelhouer's Bk. Physicke* 265/1 This pomado maketh softe and whyte handes, and driveth away all rugositye therof. **1666** J. SMITH *Old Age* (1676) 63 Weaknesses..whether they be outward, as stiffness, contraction, rugosity; or inward. **1677** PLOT *Oxfordsh.* 130 Having upon it both the rugosity, and suture of the Scrotum. *a* **1788** POTT *Chirurg. Wks.* II. 236 If the quantity of water be not large, nor the distension great, the skin preserves some degree of rugosity. **1866** R. TATE *British Mollusks* iv. 194 The degree of rugosity or smoothness. **1876** SPENCER *Princ. Sociol.* (1877) I. 126 Exactly like in colour and rugosity to a piece of the bark.

2. With *a* and *pl.* A corrugation or wrinkle; a slight roughness or inequality.

1664 POWER *Exp. Philos.* 5 Little clea's or tallons..by which she [the fly] layes hold on the rugosities and asperities of all bodies she walks over. **1674** *Phil. Trans.* IX. 10 Viewed in a Microscope, they appeared very polished, and without any rugosities. **1709** *Ibid.* XXVII. 131 At the lower part of this rugosity the Bone is 13½ Inches in Circumference. **1796** KIRWAN *Elem. Min.* (ed. 2) I. 155 The folia exceedingly thin, discovering rugosities. **1835** URE *Philos. Manuf.* 127 The fibres of wool..are covered with little rugosities, like pig's skin. **1887** FERGUSON *Ogham Inscriptions* 122 The surface, with its natural pittings and rugosities.

fig. **1830** LYTTON *Paul Clifford* xiv, There is something so graceful..in her manner of smoothing down the little rugosities of Warlock House. **1900** MORLEY *O. Cromwell* v. ix. 457 History is apt to smooth out these rugosities. **1969** T. E. B. HOWARTH *Culture, Anarchy & Public Schools* iii. 54 It may..be doubted if the new sixth-former..will take kindly to the traditionally rigorous system of the old type of sixth form. He will expect his teachers to spare him the sterner rugosities.

†**ruˈgosous,** *a. Obs.*$^{-0}$ = next.

1656 BLOUNT *Glossogr., Rugosous*,..full of wrinckles, crumples, or plaits, rough, riveled, withered.

rugous (ˈruːgəs), *a.* [ad. L. *rūgōsus*: see RUGOSE and -OUS, and cf. F. *rugueux, -euse*.] = RUGOSE *a.*

1615 CROOKE *Body Man* 374 When they are contracted then they appeare..rugous and wrinkled. **1676** WISEMAN *Surg. Treat.* III. ii. 219 The internall rugous Coat of the Intestine. **1709** *Phil. Trans.* XXVII. 130 'Tis very rugous and convex before. **1753** N. TORRIANO *Midwifery* 38 Wears smooth by Labours, tho' rugous at first. **1828** STARK *Elem. Nat. Hist.* I. 140 Skin rugous, covered with thinly scattered brown hairs. **1872** COUES *N. Amer. Birds* 208 The horny covering takes the form of scutella, or reticulations, or rugous granulations.

†**rug-saw.** *Obs.*$^{-1}$ *Sc.* [? f. RUG *v.*[1]] 'Said to be a wide-toothed saw' (Jamieson).

1797 *Stat. Acc. Scotl.* XIX. 135 The spears were of such a size that a *rugg* saw was made out of each.

rugulose (ruːgjuː'ləʊs), *a. Ent., Bot.*, etc. [f. **rūgula*, dim. of L. *rūga* + -OSE.] Having small wrinkles; slightly rugose.

1819 SAMOUELLE *Entomol. Compend.* 145. **1828** KIRBY & SP. *Entom.* II. xxi. 255 *note*, The front is not rugulose, the vertex is channeled. **1852** DANA *Crust.* I. 418 The carapax is slightly granulous or rugulose near the lateral margin. **1887** W. PHILLIPS *Brit. Discomycetes* 19 Pileus campanulate, finger-shaped, rugulose.

Hence **rugu'losity**.

1874 MOGGRIDGE *Suppl. Harvesting Ants* 255 The surface of the thorax.. appeared under a lens to be covered with fine rugulosities.

'rugulous, *a. rare*$^{-1}$. = RUGULOSE *a.*

1852 DANA *Crust.* I. 235 It agrees with the *inornatus* in.. rugulous carpus, and in the posterior legs.

†**rugwort.** Perh. an error for RAGWORT.

1592 GREENE *Philomela* Wks. (Grosart) XI. 126 Such as are poisoned with rugwort count it fatal; yet such as haue the plurisie drinke it in potions.

ruh(e, ruhh, obs. forms of ROUGH.

Ruhmkorff ('ruːmkɔːf). *Physics. Obs.* except *Hist.* The name of Heinrich Daniel *Ruhmkorff* (1803–77), German-born inventor, used *attrib.*, *absol.* and in the possessive to designate a powerful type of induction coil first made by him.

[**1852** W. R. GROVE in *Phil. Mag.* IV. 500, I procured one of these apparatus from M. Ruhmkorff: the size of the coil portion of the apparatus is 6·5 inches long, 4 inches diameter.] **1855** —— in *Ibid.* IX. 1 If a small Leyden phial have its coatings connected respectively with the extremities of the secondary wire of a Ruhmkorff coil (the primary being, as usual, connected with the condenser of M. Fizean, and two wires being attached to the terminals and brought within striking distance), the noise and brilliancy of the discharges are greatly increased. **1878** *Encycl. Brit.* VIII. 103/1 The type of these is the induction coil or inductorium, sometimes called Ruhmcorff's coil, after the great Parisian instrument-maker who first brought the instrument to perfection. **1908** *Rep. Brit. Assoc. Adv. Sci. 1907* 621 The aërials connected through the secondary of a peculiarly made Ruhmkorff coil constitute one oscillating system of a low frequency. *Ibid.* 622 When the swing is worked up they burst through the spark gap, short-circuiting out the Ruhmkorff. **1971** *Sci. Amer.* May 82/2 The final phase of the coil's development was reached during the 1850's. Heinrich Daniel Ruhmkorff, a German instrument maker living in Paris, turned his attention in 1851 to the construction of better and more powerful coils... The quality of his products quickly brought him fame, and such coils soon became known as Ruhmkorff coils.

ruid, ruif, etc., Sc. ff. ROOD, RUDE, ROOF, etc.

ruin ('ruːɪn), *sb.* Forms: 4–6 ruyne (6 *Sc.* royne, rewyne), 4–8 ruine (6 *Sc.* rewvine, 7 rwine), 6 ruwyn, rwyn, 7– ruin. [a. OF. *ruyne*, *ruine* (mod.F. *ruine*), = Prov. *roina*, *ruina*, Sp. and Pg. *ruina*, It. *rovina*, *ruina*, repr. L. *ruīna*, f. *ruĕre* to fall: see RUE *v.*[2]]

I. 1. a. The act of giving way and falling down, on the part of some fabric or structure, *esp.* a building. Now *rare*.

c **1375** *Sc. Leg. Saints* xv. (*Barnabas*) 163 A part of it fel done,..& þai þat chapit þat ruyne, fled to þe tempil apolyne. *c* **1386** CHAUCER *Knt.'s T.* 1605 Myn is the ruen of the hihe halles, The fallyng of the toures and of the walles. **1535** COVERDALE *Isaiah* xxiv. 19 The earth shal geue a greate crack, it shal haue a sore ruyne, and take an horrible fall. **1560** DAUS tr. *Sleidane's Comm.* 255 b, Partly by the ruine and fall of houses. **1590** SPENSER *F.Q.* II. vii. 28 An huge cave.. From whose rough vaut the ragged breaches hong.. That heavy ruine they did seeme to threatt. **1632** SIR T. HAWKINS tr. *Mathieu's Unhappy Prosperitie* II. 246 The death of the Duke of Britaine, slaine by the ruine of a wall. **1700** ROWE *Amb. Step-Moth.* II. i, My devoted fabrick May in the universal ruine burn. **1746** FRANCIS tr. *Hor., Sat.* II. viii. 72 The canopy, that o'er us spreads, Tumbled, in hideous ruin, on our heads. **1793** WORDSW. *Descr. Sketches among Alps* 580 From age to age, throughout his lonely bounds The crash of ruin fitfully resounds.

b. The act of (a person) falling to the ground or from a height. *rare*.

1483 CAXTON *Gold. Leg.* 68 b/2, I thenne stondyng on hym slewe hym, knowyng wel that he myght not lyue after the ruyne. **1700** PRIOR *Carmen Sec.* xxiii, She, from the noble Precipices thrown, Comes rushing with uncommon Ruin down.

2. a. The state consequent upon giving way and falling down; a ruinous condition.

1390 GOWER *Conf.* I. 32 The wall and al the Cit withinne Stant in ruine and in decas. **1526** *Pilgr. Perf.* (W. de W. 1531) 62 The temple.. in thy soule wyll soone decay, and fall to moost depe ruyne. **1582** STANYHURST *Æneis* II. (Arb.) 55 The old towne fals to ruin. **1604** E. GRIMSTONE *Hist. Siege Ostend* 98 The enemie shott much vpon the towne, and battered it in ruine. **1697** DRYDEN *Virg. Georg.* I. 377 Thrice his Lightning.. their demolish'd Works in Ruin laid. **1718** LADY M. W. MONTAGU *Lett.* II. xlviii. 49 In a few years they all fall to ruin. **1820** SHELLEY *Sensit. Plant* iii. 49 The leafless network of parasite bowers Massed into ruin.

b. That which remains after decay and fall; ruins (see 3). *rare*.

1460 CAPGR. *Chron.* (Rolls) 28 In Seynt Ierom tyme men mith se be ruyne of the wall, who grete a lord he was. **1511** *Guylforde's Pilgr.* (Camden) 16 This Jaffe was somtyme a grete Cytie, as apperyth by the ruyne of the same. **1596** SHAKS. *Merch. V.* II. ix. 48 Honor Pickt from the chaffe and ruine of the times. **1607** —— *Cor.* III. i. 207 That is the way to lay the Citie flat,.. And burie all.. In heapes, and piles of Ruine. **1704** ADDISON *Campaign* Misc. Wks. 1726 I. 71 Whilst here the Vine o'er hills of ruine climbs.

†**c.** In predicative use: Ruinous. *Obs.*$^{-1}$

1467 in *Eng. Gilds* (1870) 397 So that it may be remedyed and holpen when that it ys ruyn.

3. a. *pl.* The remains of a decayed and fallen building, town, etc.

1454 *Anc. Rec. Dublin* (1889) I. 282 The wych mese ys olde ruynes and waste. **1585** T. WASHINGTON tr. *Nicholay's Voy.* II. iii. 33 Certaine ruines.., said too be of the sayde temple. *Ibid.* xi. 45 b, The promontory is ful of ruines vnhabited. **1600** J. PORY tr. *Leo's Africa* IV. 231 Now there are a few ruines onely of this towne to be seene. **1662** J. DAVIES tr. *Olearius' Voy. Ambass.* 40 There are still to be seen the ruins of a fair Monastery. **1712** ADDISON *Spect.* No. 421 ¶6 Babylon in Ruins is not so melancholy a Spectacle. **1726** LEONI *Alberti's Archit.* I. 68/2 Those walls.. may.. so be kept from filling up the ditch with their ruines. **1856** STANLEY *Sinai & Pal.* iii. (1858) 183 Palestine is a land of ruins..; Jerusalem is a city of ruins. **1886** PASCOE *Lond. of To-day* xxxiv. (ed. 3) 307 The Lycian cities, some most valuable ruins of which were removed to London.. between 1842 and 1846.

b. *fig.* Of persons, features, etc.

1590 SHAKS. *Com. Err.* II. i. 96 What ruines are in me.. By him not ruin'd? Then is he the ground Of my defeatures. **1601** —— *Jul. C.* III. i. 256 Thou art the Ruines of the Noblest man That euer liued in the Tide of Times. **1676** ETHEREDGE *Man of Mode* III. iii, A fellow beauty of the last King's time, though by the Ruines you would hardly guess it. **1700** DRYDEN *Ovid's Met.* xv. 355 So Helen wept, when her too faithful glass Reflected to her eyes the ruins of her face. **1781** COWPER *Ep. Protestant Lady in France* 24 In pity to the sinners he design'd To rescue from the ruins of mankind. **1823** LAMB *Elia* II. *Conf. Drunkard*, Trample not on the ruins of a man. **1842** TENNYSON *Love & Duty* 12 Shall.. he.. year by year alone Sit brooding in the ruins of a life?

c. *fig.* Of institutions, states, etc.

1613 SHAKS. *Hen. VIII*, II. i. 114 [He] restor'd me to my Honours: and out of ruines Made my Name once more Noble. **1695** LD. PRESTON *Boeth.* Pref. 5 Arts and Civility were buried in their own Ruines. **1788** GIBBON *Decl. & F.* xlix. V. 156 Amidst the ruins of Italy, the famous Marozia invited one of the usurpers to assume the character of her third husband. **1821** SHELLEY *Hellas* 888 Islam must fall but we will reign together Over its ruins. **1849** MACAULAY *Hist. Eng.* i. I. 5 The continental kingdoms which had risen on the ruins of the Western Empire. **1864** BRYCE *Holy Rom. Emp.* iv. (1875) 34 Of the new monarchies that had risen on the ruins of Rome, that of the Franks was far the greatest.

d. *transf.* Of material things.

1597 SHAKS. *2 Hen. IV*, II. ii. 27 God knows, whether those that bawl out the ruins of thy linen shall inherit his kingdom. **1632** LITHGOW *Trav.* x. 479 Christ forbid, that euery Shippe which coasteth the rockey shoare, should leaue her ruines there. **1719** DE FOE *Crusoe* I. (Globe) 226, I shew'd him the Ruins of our Boat. **1898** G. B. SHAW *Plays, Arms & Man* I. 8 His belt.. keeping together the ruins of the blue tunic.

4. A ruined or ruinous building, town, etc. Also *fig.* of a person.

1606 SHAKS. *Ant. & Cl.* III. x. 19 The Noble ruine of her Magicke, Anthony,.. Leauing the Fight in heighth [etc.]. **1611** BIBLE *Isaiah* xxv. 2 Thou hast made of a citie, an heape; of a defenced city, a ruine. **1780** COWPER *Progr. Error* 286 As creeping ivy clings to wood or stone, And hides the ruin that it feeds upon. **1816** J. WILSON *City of Plague* I. i. 34 There it stands, like a majestic ruin Mouldering in a desert. **1838** *Murray's Handbk. N. Germ.* 256 One of these ruins has recently been restored as far as possible to its original condition. **1884** R. PATON *Scott. Church* vii. 70 He fixed his residence in an old ruin on the top of a hill. **1946** B. MARSHALL *George Brown's Schooldays* ii. 7 Hullo, here's Abinger. He looks a fearful ruin, doesn't he? *Ibid.* xxiv. 102 A ruin's a chap who's a swot and a punk and who's rotten at games.

5. *pl.* Damage, injury, done to anything.

c **1592** MARLOWE *Jew of Malta* v. iv, Till thy father hath made good The ruins done to Malta and to us. **1631** WEEVER *Anc. Funeral Mon.* To Rdr., This worthy repairer of eating-times ruines. **1657** W. RAND tr. *Gassendi's Life Peiresc* I. 216 Designing how to repair those remarkable ruines, which had happened to the Monastery in the civill wars. **1691** RAY *Creation* (1714) 191 The Earth.. ought to be firm and stable and solid and.. secured from all Ruins and Concussions. **1727** SWIFT *To a Young Lady* Wks. 1751 V. 70 Vain endeavours to repair by Art and Dress the Ruins of time. **1731** —— *Nymph going to Bed* ibid. X. 176 Corinna wakes. A dreadful Sight! Behold the Ruins of the Night!

II. 6. a. The downfall or decay of a person or society; utter loss of means, position, or rank.

c **1374** CHAUCER *Troylus* IV. 387 There is no creature.. that evere saugh ruyne Straunger than this, thorowgh cas or aventure. *c* **1420** HOCCLEVE *Minor Poems* xviii. 73 Lady, wardeyn of peple fro ruyne, þat sauedest Theoffe and many mo! *c* **1450** HOLLAND *Howlat* 910 He bad tham rebaldis orere, With a ruyne. **1513** DOUGLAS *Æneis* III. vii. 10 O thou Anchises, that.. twise eschapit of Troy the sair rewyne. *a* **1578** LINDESAY (Pitscottie) *Chron. Scot.* (S.T.S.) I. 51 Wirkand all to thair confutioun and wtter rewvine. **1600** E. BLOUNT tr. *Conestaggio* 10 To the fatall ruine of his subiects. **1665** MANLEY *Grotius' Low-C. Wars* 235 To perfect their Ruine, there hapned another fatal Mischance to them. **1750** GRAY *Elegy* 62 Threats of pain and ruin to despise. **1788** GIBBON *Decl. & F.* xlix. V. 128 Irene more seriously undertook the ruin of the Iconoclasts. **1838** DE MORGAN *Ess. Probab.* 110 In the long run, only 170 out of 421 such banks would avoid ruin. **1874** GREEN *Short Hist.* viii. §5. 500 The ruin that James had wrought was suddenly averted. *pl.* **1621** BURTON *Anat. Mel.* I. ii. III. vii. (1651) 101 Nothing fats him but other mens ruines.

b. Dishonour of a woman; degradation resulting from this.

1624 QUARLES *Sion's Sonn.* VIII. vi, Shield my simple Love, From those that seeke her ruine. **1706** ADDISON *Rosamond* I. iv, Every charm, and every grace, That to thy ruin made their way. **1780** MADAN (*title*), Thelyphthora, or a Treatise on Female Ruin. **1848** DICKENS *Dombey* liii, Wretched marriages don't come of that, in our degree; only wretchedness and ruin.

c. Complete destruction *of* anything.

1673 *Remarques Humours Town* 64 The ruine of those excellent principles which so many Ages have honoured and revered. **1863** W. C. BALDWIN *Afr. Hunting* iv. 96, I.. escaped with no further injury than the ruin of my shirt. **1871** MACDUFF *Mem. of Patmos* ix. 113 Mourning over the apparent ruin and frustration of her fondest hopes. **1899** *Allbutt's Syst. Med.* VI. 359 Laceration, amounting to ruin and all but complete detachment of the heart.

7. The condition of being ruined, of having been reduced to an abject or hopeless state.

For examples of *rack and ruin*, see RACK *sb.*[5]

1390 GOWER *Conf.* II. 184 And for that he.. wolde noght to trouthe encline, He fell for evere into ruine. **1423** JAS. I *Kingis Q.* xxviii, Quhat was the cause that he me more comprisit Than othir folk to lyve in suich ruyne? **1502** ATKYNSON tr. *De Imitatione* I. xxv. 177 That relygyous persone that lyueth without discyplyne is redye to fall to ruyne. *a* **1513** FABYAN *Chron.* VI. (1811) 204 By which vngracious meane, he brought this lande in such ruyne. **1596** SHAKS. *Merch. V.* IV. i. 142 Repaire thy wit, good youth, or it will fall To endlesse ruine. **1667** MILTON *P.L.* II. 305 Princely counsel in his face yet shon, Majestick though in ruin. **1697** DRYDEN *Virg. Georg.* IV. 311 The great Monarch's Death dissolves the Government. All goes to Ruin. **1778** PITT in Almon *Anecd.* (1810) II. 338 A cloud, that may crush this nation,.. is ready to burst and overwhelm us in ruin. **1831** SIR J. SINCLAIR *Corr.* II. 159, I am shocked with the idea, that many.. should have perhaps .. been reduced to beggary and ruin. **1886** *Contemp. Rev.* Aug. 285 It was the Conservative.. party which brought this Bill to ruin.

8. That which causes destruction or downfall; a ruining influence or agent.

c **1425** *Engl. Conq. Irel.* 90 He graunted the kynge that he shold ynto Irland wend.. for to wythstond & lete the ruyne of syn. **1533** BELLENDEN *Livy* II. (S.T.S.) I. 205 Civil seditioun is þe onelie poisson and rewyne of all riche cieteis. **1611** BIBLE *2 Chron.* xxviii. 23 They were the ruine of him, and of all Israel. **1678** BUNYAN *Pilgr.* I. (1900) 74 He has.. caused many to stumble and fall; and will be, if God prevent not, the ruine of many more. **1781** COWPER *Heroism* 76 The sad lesson.. That wealth within is ruin at the door. **1822** SCOTT *Nigel* iv, By a quarrel you would become the ruin of me your informer. **1852** MUNDY *Antipodes* (1857) 87 Drink is the ruin, body and soul, of the people of this country. **1889** M. ARNOLD *Disc. Amer.* i. 56 The unsoundness of the majority, if it is not withstood and remedied, must be their ruin.

9. In general use: Destruction, complete overthrow or devastation. Freq. personified.

a **1586** SIDNEY *Arcadia* II. (1605) 225 This still should be my case, Ruines relique, cares web, and sorrowes food. **1593** SHAKS. *Rich. II*, III. ii. 102 Cry Woe, Destruction, Ruine, Losse, Decay. **1746** FRANCIS tr. *Hor., Sat.* I. ix. 65 Nor poison fell, with ruin stored, Nor horrid point of hostile sword. **1757** GRAY *Bard* 1 Ruin seize thee, ruthless King! **1816** SHELLEY *Mt. Blanc* 73 Is this the scene Where the old Earthquake-daemon taught her young Ruin? **1818** —— *Prometh. Unb.* I. 780 Though Ruin now Love's shadow be, Following him, destroyingly. **1859** TENNYSON *Guinevere* 423 The children born of thee are sword and fire, Red ruin, and the breaking up of laws.

10. *slang.* Gin of a poor quality. Usually ***blue ruin*** (see BLUE *a.* 13).

c **1817** KEATS in Rossetti *Life* i, He sipped no olden Tom or ruin blue. **1820** J. H. REYNOLDS *Fancy* (1906) 23 The ruin you've drawn down upon your lips Has made it rather foggy. *c* **1845** HOOD *Drop of Gin* 71 Happy the wretch that it does not win To change the black hue Of his ruin to blue.

III. 11. a. *Comb.*, as ***ruin-breathing***, ***-loving***; ***ruin-crowned***, ***-heaped***, ***-hurled***; ***ruin-like***, ***-proof*** adjs.; ***ruin-mark*** vb.; ***ruinward*** adv.

1811 MARIANA STARKE *Beauties of Carlo-Maria Maggi* 16 The *ruin-breathing tempest seems to burst. *a* **1849** MANGAN *Poems* (1859) 354 The hill, now, alas! *ruin-crowned. *a* **1878** W. CARLETON *Farm Ballads* (1893) 112 The ragged and *ruin-heaped city. **1820** T. MITCHELL *Aristoph.* I. 232 With a fleet *ruin-hurl'd, They took rank in the world. **1684** T. BURNET *Theory of E.* I. 142 There are some regions of it strangely rude and *ruine-like. **1830** N. S. WHEATON *Jrnl.* 499 The ruins.. almost covered with wild briars and the *ruin-loving ivy. **1876** LOWELL *Ode 4th July* II. i, She also hath her monuments; Not such as stand decrepitly resigned To *ruin-mark the path of dead events. **1593** NASHE *Christ's Teares* (1613) 39 Had you rested them on the true Rock they had been *ruine-proof.

1936 A. E. HOUSMAN *More Poems* 61 And on through night to morning The world runs *ruinward.

b. *attrib.*, as **ruin agate, jasper, marble** (so called from the markings they exhibit); **ruin-mound** = TELL *sb.*[2]

1823 W. PHILLIPS *Min.* (ed. 3) 20 Ruin-Jasper.. is commonly known by the name of Ruin Agate, but its opacity .. evinces that it ought to be classed with jaspers. **1883** *Encycl. Brit.* XVI. 397/2 Ruin Marble shows irregular markings like ruins. **1911** *Encycl. Brit.* XIV. 741/2 There are in Irak hundreds of ruin mounds, some of them of considerable size, covering ancient Babylonian cities. **1939** P. CARLETON *Buried Empires* i. 23 Attracted by the numerous *tells*, or ruin-mounds, in his district, he set workmen to dig.

ruin ('ruːɪn), *v.* Also 6–8 ruine. [ad. F. *ruiner* (14th c., = Sp. and Pg. *ruinar*, It. *rovinare*, *ruinare*), or med.L. *ruīnāre*, f. *ruīna* RUIN *sb.*]

I. 1. a. *trans.* To reduce (a place, etc.) to ruins.

1585 T. Washington tr. *Nicholay's Voy.* II. xii. 47b, [They] ruined and cast down to the ground the wals of the city. 1601 R. Johnson *Kingd. & Commw.* (1603) 114 From thence alongst the shore lieth Cæsaria, now ruined by them of Gallipoli. 1686 tr. *Chardin's Trav. Persia* 410 An Inundation of Waters ruin'd a thousand Houses. 1830 *Examiner* 455/1 Our batteries continued to ruin the works. 1849–50 Alison *Hist. Europe* VIII. xlix. §87. 92 The wall, which was of tough mud, was imperfectly ruined.

fig. 1590 Shaks. *Com. Err.* II. i. 97 What ruines are in me ..By him not ruin'd? 1606 —— *Ant. & Cl.* v. ii. 51 This mortall house Ile ruine, Do Cæsar what he can.

b. *fig.* To overthrow, destroy (a kingdom, etc.).

1585 T. Washington tr. *Nicholay's Voy.* II. xiii. 49 After hee hadde ruined the Empyre of Constantinople. 1671 Milton *P.R.* IV. 363 In them is plainest taught..What ruins Kingdoms, and lays Cities flat. 1743 Pitt in Almon *Anecd.* (1810) I. 107 France had a mind to have the power of that House reduced, but not to be absolutely ruined. 1856 Froude *Hist. Eng.* (1858) I. ii. 146 Charles..was not ruining the papacy, and had no intention of ruining it.

†**2.** To destroy, extirpate, eradicate; to do away with, get rid of, by a destructive process. *Obs.*

1581 Sidney *Apol. Poetrie* (Arb.) 22 Some of whom did seeke to ruine all memory of learning from among them. 1621 Burton *Anat. Mel.* II. iii. VII. (1651) 356 He fell down dead upon the Dragon, and killed him with the fall, so both were ruin'd. 1645 Symonds *Diary* (Camden) 163 Cromwell's horse and dragoons ruined some of our horse that quartered about Islip. 1658 Evelyn *Fr. Gard.* (1675) 255 You shall every year renew some of your beds, ruining such as are about four, or five years old. 1712 J. James tr. *Le Blond's Gardening* 175 Dip it into Water and drown them;.. and by doing thus, you entirely ruin them. 1725 De Foe *Voy. round World* (1840) 314 Our men were not ruined, as they certainly would have been, if the mountaineers had taken the alarm.

3. a. To inflict or bring great and irretrievable disaster upon (a person or community).

1613 Shaks. *Hen. VIII*, III. ii. 439 Marke but my Fall, and that that Ruin'd me. 1660 R. Coke *Power & Subj.* 264 At this time it ruins him, which otherwhile was of much advantage to him. 1702 Rowe *Amb. Step-Moth.* I. i, The shallow Fraud Will ruine him for ever with my Enemies. 1781 Cowper *Table Talk* 60 The diadem, with mighty projects lin'd, To catch renown by ruining mankind. 1852 Mrs. Stowe *Uncle Tom's C.* xxxiv. 311 In the judgement-day I will stand up before God, a witness against those that have ruined me and my children. 1869 Tozer *Highl. Turkey* II. 309 An obdurate lady, who is charged with ruining her lover.

absol. 1613 Shaks. *Hen. VIII*, IV. ii. 40 He was neuer (But where he meant to Ruine) pittifull.

b. To bring to financial ruin; to reduce to a state of poverty.

1660 F. Brooke tr. *Le Blanc's Trav.* 366 Having consum'd all he had gotten, besides what his sister had, and other friends whom he quite ruined. 1732 Berkeley *Alciphr.* II. §2 Many gentlemen and ladies are ruined by play. 1776 Adam Smith *W.N.* IV. i. (1900) II. 13 Though a particular merchant..may sometimes be ruined by not being able to sell them in time. 1849 Lytton *Caxtons* XI. v, A London daily paper might ruin a man in a few weeks. 1874 Stubbs *Const. Hist.* I. xii. 575 The freeman is not to be amerced in a way that will ruin him.

absol. 1810 Crabbe *Borough* vii. 72 But now our quacks are gamesters, and they play With craft and skill to ruin and betray.

c. *refl.* To bring (oneself) to ruin.

c 1588 in J. Morris *Troubles Cath. Foref.* Ser. II. (1875) 311 When the one [Judas] would fall and ruin himself wilfully. 1653 Holcroft tr. *Procopius* II. 44 Do not you by contending with us ruin your selves. 1712 Steele *Spect.* No. 278 ¶1, I am afraid I shall be obliged to ruin my self to procure her a Settlement. 1837 Carlyle *Fr. Rev.* III. II. v, The Mother-Society, so far as natural reason can predict, seems ruining herself. 1865 Ruskin *Sesame* i. §32 You never call any one a horse-maniac, though men ruin themselves every day by their horses.

d. To dishonour (a woman).

c 1679 C. Davenant *Love's Conquest*, At last, come, ruine me! she said, And then there fell a tear. 1727 Gay *Begg. Op.* I, Tell me, hussy, are you ruin'd or no? 1893 Leland *Mem.* I. 164 She replied, 'Please sir, I don't live anywhere now; I've been ruined'. 1929 E. O'Neill *Dynamo* I. ii. 28 Pa and Ma warned me linesmen were no good...they just ruined you and went their way. 1955 *Radio Times* 22 Apr. 4/3 The sentimental blatherings of Mrs. Arbuthnot who was 'ruined' by Lord Illingworth twenty years before. 1962 E. Bentley tr. *Brecht's Mother Courage* vi. 51 She's not so pretty anyone would want to ruin her.

e. To demoralize completely.

1832 Disraeli *Contarini Fleming* I. viii, It was universally agreed that college had ruined me.

4. a. To spoil, damage, injure, in a complete or destructive manner.

1656 Earl Monm. tr. *Boccalini's Advts. fr. Parnass.* I. XII. (1674) 15 They break them, and quite ruine the Lutes. 1697 Dryden *Virg. Georg.* IV. 469 Root up my Trees,..My Vineyards ruin, and my Sheepfolds burn. 1767 A. Young *Farmer's Lett. to People* 152 These destructive practices of ruining young trees. 1774 Bryant *Mythol.* I. 332 Their learning was greatly impaired, and their ancient theology ruined. 1824–9 Landor *Imag. Conv.* Wks. 1846 II. 8, I have ruined the way through my estate by the carriage of supplementary loads. 1867 Lady Herbert *Cradle L.* ix. 245 The contents of his pack, though recovered, were irretrievably ruined. 1889 A. Lang *Lett. on Lit.* vii. 87 He rides..till the thorns have ruined his silken surcoat.

b. To involve in disaster or failure; to make entirely abortive.

1596 Shaks. *1 Hen. IV*, III. ii. 37 The hope and expectation of thy time Is ruin'd. *a* 1680 Butler *Rem.* (1759) I. 208 Scholars by preposterous over-doing, And under-judging, all their Projects ruin. 1719 W. Wood *Surv. Trade* 285 This *Assiento* Contract..may be of the most dangerous Consequence to it, by ruining its Trade. 1736 Butler *Anal.* II. v. Wks. 1874 I. 211 People ruin their fortunes by extravagance. 1781 Cowper *Conversat.* 368 Our self importance ruins its own scheme. 1848 Dickens *Dombey* xlv, The reflection that you had injured her position and ruined her future hopes. 1858 Froude *Hist. Eng.* III. xii. 23 Many times a good cause has been ruined by the over-zeal of its friends. 1872 Black *Adv. Phaeton* xxvi. 357 He pretty nearly ruined his prospects in life.

c. To overturn, invalidate completely.

1665 J. Webb *Stone-Heng* (1725) 68 Whatever else he could invent to ruin Mr. Jones his Opinion. 1693 J. Edwards *Author. O. & N. Test.* 314 It ruines his hypothesis.

II. 5. *intr.* To fall into ruins; to fall headlong; to go down with a crash. Also with *in.*

1604 E. Grimstone *Hist. Siege Ostend* 202 They.. suffered it to burne and ruine. 1638 G. Sandys *Paraphr. Job* xxvii, Though he his House of polisht Marble build,..Yet shall it ruine like the Moth's fraile cell. 1667 Milton *P.L.* VI. 868 Hell saw Heav'n ruining from Heav'n. 1793 Wordsw. *Sketches Among the Alps* 203 (ed. 1), Ruining from the cliffs, the deafening load Tumbles. 1820 Shelley *Vision of Sea* 6 She sees the black trunks of the waterspouts spin And bend, as if Heaven was ruining in. 1847 Tennyson *Princ.* II. 320 Let not your prudence, dearest, drowse,..for fear This whole foundation ruin. 1872 Howells *Wedding Journ.* (1892) 177 The road..is unguarded by any sort of parapet.., and carriages go ruining over the brink from time to time.

6. To come to ruin; to be brought to poverty; to be overwhelmed by failure.

1596 Warner *Alb. Eng.* XII. lxxiii. (1602) 303 Religion, Realmes, and all haue ruin'd then. 1627 E. F. *Hist. Edw. II* (1686) 151, I yield, and will sit still and ruine. 1659 Milton *Rupt. of Commonw.* Wks. 1851 V. 404 Unless these things.. be once settl'd, in my fear, which God avert, we instantly ruin. 1691 Locke *Money* Wks. 1727 II. 11 We may Trade, ..and grow poor by it..; if to this we are idle,..we shall ruin the faster.

'ruinable, *a. rare.* [f. prec. + -ABLE.] That may be ruined; perishable.

1706 I. Watts *Horæ Lyricæ* I. 31 Above these ruinable skies They make their last retreat. 1707 —— *Hymn, 'Praise, everlasting praise be paid'* viii, Our everlasting hopes arise Above the ruinable skies.

ruinate ('ruːɪneɪt), *ppl. a.* (*sb.*) [ad. med.L. *ruīnātus*, pa. pple. of *ruīnāre*: see RUIN *v.*]

1. a. Of buildings, etc.: Ruined, ruinous. (Common *c* 1550–1680; now somewhat rare.)

1538 Starkey *England* I. iii. 70 Our cytes, castellys, and townys, of late days ruynate and fallen downe. 1555 Eden *Decades* (Arb.) 188 They found there the foundations of certeyne owlde towres ruinate. 1596 Spenser *F.Q.* v. x. 26 That same citie, so now ruinate, Had bene the keye of all that kingdomes crowne. 1627 Speed *England* xxv. §9 Castles for defence built in this County, ruinate or in strength. *a* 1674 Milton *Hist. Mosc.* Wks. 1851 VIII. 475 They who travail from Mosco to the Caspian, go..by certain Castles to Rezan, a famous Citie now ruinate. 1726 Leoni *Alberti's Archit.* II. 60/2 Those sacred Structures are now ruinate. 1868 Kingsley *Hermits* 324 The place is all ruinate now; the memory of St. Godric gone. 1901 'Lucas Malet' *Sir Richard Calmady* v. i, The house..had become rather dilapidated and ruinate.

b. Used attributively.

1596 Harington *Metam. Ajax* (1814) 85, I would not doubt, of a ruinate church to make a reverent church. 1624 Heywood *Gunaik.* III. 128 He came to a certain ruinate cottage, where he desired bread and water. 1649 J. Ellistone *Behmen's Epist.* iv. §3 The time is at hand.. that the ruinate Jerusalem shall againe be built up. 1791 Mrs. Inchbald *Simple Story* III. vi. 68 The dreary, ruinate place where her deceased mother had chosen her residence.

c. *Jamaica.* Of land: exhausted, abandoned. Hence as *sb.*, land which has reverted to the wild, scrubland, 'bush'.

1835 B. M. Senior *Jamaica* 54 Lands termed 'ruinate', which means such as have been used till worn out, and then allowed to grow up in bushes and weeds. *Ibid.* 55 In three or four years after the ruinate is cleared up, the pimento begins to bear. 1847 P. H. Gosse *Birds of Jamaica* 11 We see it [*sc.* the Red-tailed Buzzard] all the year round, sailing deliberately in wide circles over the pastures and ruinates. 1894 R. T. Banbury *Jamaica Superstitions* 30 We would advise parents never to allow their little ones to wander about near woods, or ruinates by themselves.

2. Involved in ruin or disaster. Now *rare.*

1591 Spenser *M. Hubberd* 1040 Government of state Will without wisedome soone be ruinate. 1600 Holland *Livy* VIII. vii. 285 The militarie discipline which this day by thy default is fallen downe and ruinate. 1603 Harsnet *Popish Impost.* 12 One Edward Peckham.., one of a very Ruinate estate. 1637 Sir C. Gardiner in T. Morton *New Eng. Canaan* (1883) 112 Plotting mischeife gainst the innocent, Burning their houses, as if ordained by fate, In spight of Lawe, to be made ruinate. 1868 Kingsley in *Good Words* Dec. 732 The whole character [had] been warped and ruinate from childhood. 1871 —— *At Last* II. xvi. 287 A system which..was ruinate before emancipation.

3. Used transitively as *pa. pple. rare*⁻¹.

1591 Sylvester *Du Bartas* I. i. 319 This furious debate, Even in the birth, this Ball had ruinate.

ruinate ('ruːɪneɪt), *v.* Also 6 ruynate. [f. ppl. stem of med.L. *ruīnāre*: see prec. In very common use from *c* 1550 to 1700; now rare.]

1. a. *trans.* To reduce to ruins; = RUIN *v.* 1.

a 1548 Hall *Chron., Hen. VIII*, 258 It was determined.. vtterly to ruinate and destroy the saied toune with fire. 1577–87 Holinshed *Chron.* III. 1214/2 The armie marched toward a faire proper house,..which was blowne up with powder and utterlie ruinated. 1601 R. Johnson *Kingd. & Commw.* (1603) 148 There are foure meanes to ruinate a fortresse, Ordinance, mining, fire and digging. 1640 Wilkins *New Planet* viii. (1707) 223 High Buildings, which by this would quickly be ruinated. 1726 Leoni *Alberti's Archit.* Pref. 4 Cities which..have fallen..into the Power of new Masters, who..ruinated them. 1818 G. S. Faber *Horæ Mosaicæ* I. 164 The professed iconoclast Xerxes.. ruinated, or rather defaced, the edifice itself.

absol. 1603 J. Davies (Heref.) *Microcosmos* Wks. (Grosart) I. 27/2 The Hart, the Lunges,..In region of the Brest, doe hold their States, Whose Bulke them Bulwarkes from what ruynates. 1616 J. Hayward *Sanct. Troub. Soul* II. ix. (1620) 227 Experience teacheth vs, that it is more easie to ruinate, then to repaire.

b. In fig. contexts. Now only *arch.*

1593 Shaks. *3 Hen. VI*, v. i. 83, I will not ruinate my Fathers House, Who gaue his blood to lyme the stones together. *c* 1600 —— *Sonn.* x, Seeking that beautious roofe to ruinate, Which to repaire should be thy chiefe desire. *a* 1625 Boys *Wks.* (1629) 264 The Deuil ruinates every tenement in which he dwells. *a* 1670 Hacket *Cent. Serm.* (1675) 549 You ruinate the whole tower of Faith, and demolish it to nothing. 1922 E. R. Eddison *Worm Ouroboros* xviii. 253 If I do not..remedy for you our fortunes which this bloody fool hath laboured to ruinate, spit in my face. 1935 G. Barker *Poems* 55 Time, though slowly, ruinates Love, with which it arbitrates.

2. To bring destruction or ruin upon, to overthrow, destroy (a kingdom, state, etc.).

1574 Hellowes *Gueuara's Fam. Ep.* (1584) 243 There is to be found a M. Hagbuts within youre house to ruinate this Realme. 1588 Shaks. *Tit. A.* v. iii. 204 Then afterwards, to Order well the State, That like Euents may ne're it Ruinate. 1610 Willet *Daniel* 64 Alexander the great, who ruinated the Persian monarchie. 1642 R. Carpenter *Experience* v. vii. 244 For the safety of your poore Country, which..you take paines to ruinate.

3. To ruin or impoverish (a person). Cf. RUIN *v.* 3.

a 1577 Sir T. Smith *Commw. Eng.* (1609) 17 The rest conspiring together would soone be Maisters of them, and ruinate them wholly. 1584 *Leycesters Commonw.* (1641) 76 You shall scarce find a man that..feeleth not the smart thereof: being either impoverished, beggered, or ruinated thereby. 1640 Habington *Edw. IV*, 118 To desire the Commonaltie to contribute with their purses that many of his best friends might not be ruinated. 1674 *Plymouth Col. Rec.* (1857) VII. 189 The said Barker hath said and threatened that hee would ruinate them. 1797 Mrs. A. M. Bennett *Beggar Girl* (1813) IV. 211 Mastur said he wud be ruinated, so left him at boarding school hard by. 1819 'R. Rabelais' *Abeillard & Heloisa* 172 She was indeed thus ruinated. 1860 Dickens *Uncomm. Trav.* iii, It wasn't their faults..if I warn't made bad and ruinated.

refl. 1547 J. Harrison *Exhort. Scottes* h ij, What folye, or rather what fury is this, thus to ruynate your selfes. *a* 1647 Habington *Surv. Worcs.* (Worcs. Hist. Soc.) III. 395 He deposed Kinges and disposed the kingdome till hee ruinated himselfe.

†**4. a.** To demolish or destroy; to lay waste. *Obs.*

1564–78 Bullein *Dial. agst. Pest.* (1888) 139 So for synne the bodie is ruinated and shalbe in dust until the resurrection. *c* 1590 Greene *Fr. Bacon* ix, [I have] Rais'd Hercules to ruinate that tree That Bungay mounted by his magic spells. 1609 Holland *Amm. Marcell.* 404 A strange and unknowne kind of people.., readie to ruinate and destroy all before them. 1693 Morden *Geog. Rect.* (ed. 3) 129 This Countrey (before those unhappy Wars..whereby it was much ruinated) was accounted the most fruitful and pleasant of all Germany. 1740 *New Hist. Jamaica* 221 Any Person may ruinate and destroy any Plantation deserted for the Space of 2 Months.

†**b.** With *life, health*, etc. as object. *Obs.*

c 1586 C'tess Pembroke *Ps.* LXIII. iv, Such as seeke my life to ruinate. 1621 Burton *Anat. Mel.* To Rdr. 25 Men alwaies ruinating thereby the health of their bodies. 1645 Pagitt *Heresiogr.* (1661) 28 Preserving our lives, which bloody men would soon ruinate.

†**5.** To overthrow, overturn, subvert utterly: **a.** an institution, practice, etc. *Obs.*

1585–7 T. Rogers *39 Art.* Pref. 18 They ruinate, and at one blow beat down all times and days, by just authority destined to religious and holy uses. 1590 Swinburne *Testaments* 27 Without whose ministery christianity would quickly be ruinated and subuerted. 1604 Hieron *Wks.* I. 576 Truth they haue sought to propagate, And heresies to ruinate. 1635 Pagitt *Christianogr.* I. iii. (1636) 180 These Churches not ruinating anie fundamentall Article of saving truth.

†**b.** a project, design, hope, etc. *Obs.*

1595 Daniel *Civ. Wars* v. xxx, Now at this Point t' attempt to ruinate So glorious a Design. 1639 S. Du Verger tr. *Camus' Admir. Events* 339 It had been the way wholy to ruinate his project if hee had vexed this man. 1695 Ld. Preston *Boeth.* IV. 178 The great Hopes and subtle Machinations of ill Men are by a sudden and unforeseen End ruinated and destroyed.

6. *intr.* To go or fall to ruin. Cf. RUIN *v.* 5.

1560 Whitehorne tr. *Machiavelli's Arte Warre* (1588) 9 If a king take not order in such wise,..it will follow of necessitie, that he ruinate. *Ibid.* 65 Infinite tymes there growe thynges, where by an armie ruinateth. 1642 Rogers *Naaman* 186 Neither stormes, nor tempests, nor any assaults shall ever cause thy building to ruinate. 1726 Leoni *Alberti's Archit.* I. 48/1 The Wall..is more apt to ruinate in this part than in any other. 1853 S. H. Cox *Interviews Mem. & Usef.* 115 (Cent.), We see others ruinating for want of our incomparable system of constitutional government.

†**7.** To fall with a crash. *Obs.*⁻¹

1590 Spenser *F.Q.* II. xii. 7 On thother side they saw that perilous Rocke, Threatning it selfe on them to ruinate.

ruinated ('ruːɪneɪtɪd), *ppl. a.* [f. prec. + -ED.]

1. Ruined, ruinous, in ruins. (Common *c* 1580–1780, now somewhat rare.)

attrib. 1555 Spurge in Strype *Eccl. Mem.* III. App. xl. 111 Build up again the decayed walls of thy ruinated Jerusalem. *c* 1586 C'tess Pembroke *Ps.* CXLVII. i, The Lord againe to forme doth bring Jerusalems long ruinated walls. 1603

Knolles *Hist. Turks* (1621) 943 To fortifie both with wals and ditches that ruinated citie. **1683** Cave *Ecclesiastici* Introd. p. lxiii, These ruinated Temples were generally turn'd into Churches. **1705** tr. *Bosman's Guinea* 51 The Houses are in a ruinated Condition. **1792** S. Ireland *Views Thames* I. 150 The castle probably remained in a ruinated state. **1812** Combe *Syntax, Picturesque* ix, But this fine building long has been A sad and ruinated scene. **1894** *Trans. Devon. Assoc.* XXVI. 302 The original character of this much ruinated monument.

pred. **1577** Hellowes *Gueuara's Chron.* 107 The authoritie of a common wealth is impayred, when the buildings be ruinated. **1603** Owen *Pembrokeshire* (1892) 76 Most of the Castells are ruinated and remayne vncovered. **1643** Trapp *Comm. Gen.* xxxv. 14 He repairs the pillar now ruinated, and new consecrates it. **1735** J. Price *Stone-Br. Thames* 13 That of Avignon..is ruinated, and has nothing left but some Arches. **1779** R. Graves *Columella* I. 48 On the brow of one hill appeared the Sibyl's temple, ruinated like that at Tivoli. **1847** H. Miller *First Impr. Eng.* viii. (1857) 136 They are all ruinated now.

†**2.** Brought to ruin or decay. *Obs.*

1601 R. Johnson *Kingd. & Commw.* (1603) 57 The means to prouide for decayed or ruinated prouinces. **1638** Junius *Paint. Ancients* 71 Content..to die in the revenge of their ruinated country. **1652-62** Heylin *Cosmogr.* I. (1682) 227 A sad presage of a ruinated and expiring Empire.

'ruinater. *rare*$^{-1}$. = ruinator.

1608 Crakanthorpe *Serm. 24 Mar.* C iij, That blessing and happinesse, which God hath promised..to the ruinaters and destroyers thereof.

'ruinating, *vbl. sb.* [f. ruinate *v.* + -ing^1.] The action of ruining.

1594 Plat *Jewell-ho.* iii. 4 The principall meanes of the ruinating of all mortall bodies. **1614** Camden *Rem.* 199 The sodaine ruinating of Townes by the Saxons. **1642** in J. B. Williams *Eng. Journalism* (1908) 34 This was the first step to the ruinating of the tribe of clerks.

'ruinating, *ppl. a.* [f. as prec. + -ing^2.]

1. That ruins; destructive, destroying.

1608 Dekker *Dead Tearme* Wks. (Grosart) IV. 46 Free from the mallice..of ruinating Time and the enuious blasts of Fortune. **1688** S. Sewall *Diary* 10 Jan., Not abiding in, or apostatizing from Christ, is a ruinating evil. **1720** T. Boston *Fourfold State* iv. ii, It is not the venomed ruinating thing wrapt up in the sanction of the first covenant. **1799** J. Scott *Bahar-Danush* II. xxvi. 307 The ruinating hailstones beat upon the garden.

2. Falling to ruin; decaying.

1634-5 Brereton *Trav.* (Chetham Soc.) 173 Small parcels of the walls..continue, surviving monuments of that ruinating, large, and stately fabric.

ruination (ruːɪ'neɪʃən). [f. ruinate *v.*: see -ation.] The action of ruining; the fact or state of being ruined.

1664 *Rhode Island Col. Rec.* (1857) II. 34 To ye terrour, damage, and ruination of the complaynants. **1786** Mrs. A. M. Bennett *Juvenile Indiscr.* III. 142 It may be the ruination of you, besides costing a power of money. **1802** H. Martin *Helen of Glenross* II. 232, I began to feel a few very conscientious qualms, for having abetted and countenanced such ruination. **1852** Reade *Peg Woff.* (1889) 82 Strong versatility is a very doubtful good, and weak versatility ruination. **1885** Dixon *Hist. Ch. Eng.* III. 417 It was left for posterity..to meet public necessity by private ruination.

attrib. **1850** Smedley *F. Fairleigh* xlvii, You'll have a wife to keep soon, and that isn't done for nothing..—pin-money, ruination-shops [etc.]. **1870** Miss Bridgman *R. Lynne* II. xiv. 302 He said it was ruination work.

rui'natious, *a.* *U.S.* [Cf. prec. and -ous.] Ruinous.

1845 S. Judd *Margaret* 210 (Bartlett), The war was very ruinatious to our profession. **1872** De Vere *Americanisms* 629 *Ruinatious*, an enlarged and intensified form of ruinous, frequently used in the West and South.

'ruinator. *rare.* [Agent-noun, on L. types, f. ruinate *v.*] One who ruins.

1658 Bromhall *Treat. Specters* I. 156 [It] was much feared, lest that they should..break all the necks of the ruinators. **1830** *Fraser's Mag.* II. 171 He threatened his ruinator with the High Court of Justiciary.

ruined ('ruːɪnd), *ppl. a.* [f. ruin *v.* + -ed^1.]

1. Reduced to ruins; fallen into ruin.

1585 T. Washington tr. *Nicholay's Voy.* I. xii. 14 An old ruined Church. **1590** Spenser *F.Q.* II. x. 46 The ruin'd wals he did reædifye Of Troynovant. **1613** Shaks. *Hen. VIII*, III. ii. 382 The King has..from these shoulders These ruin'd Pillers out of pitty, taken A load. **1687** A. Lovell tr. *Thevenot's Trav.* I. 121 There is nothing to be seen in it but ruined Houses. **1738** De Foe *Tour Gt. Brit.* (ed. 2) III. 62 Doncaster (so called from the River on which it stands, and the Castle which is now ruined). **1743** Francis tr. *Hor., Odes* IV. xv. 23 The rage, That..ruin'd cities fills with hostile woes. **1837** Lockhart *Scott* I. vii. 195 Exploring..every ruined peel from foundation to battlement. **1863** Lyell *Antiq. Man* 35 Some ruined towns, now half under water.

absol. **1873** Leland *Egypt. Sketch Bk.* 295 Sometimes the unfinished looks like the ruined.

†**b.** *transf.* Almost obliterated or erased. *Obs.*

1585 T. Washington tr. *Nicholay's Voy.* I. xxi. 26 b, About the edge were written diuers romaine letters, but were so ruined, that scarce they were too be known.

2. Brought to financial, social, or moral ruin.

1596 Spenser *F.Q.* V. iv. 34 Wend with me, that ye may see and know How Fortune will your ruin'd name repaire. **1615** G. Sandys *Trav.* 46 Selymus..conquered all Syria and Ægypt from the ruined Mamalucks. **1746** Francis tr. *Hor., Sat.* II. iii. 420 So may better bargains raise Your ruin'd fortune. **1770** Goldsm. *Des. Vill.* 153 The ruined spend-thrift, now no longer proud, Claimed kindred there. **1803** H. K. White *Contemplation* Wks. (1856) 134 We'll hold communion with the shade Of some deep wailing, ruin'd maid. **1848** Thackeray *Van. Fair* xl, A countess living at an inn is a ruined woman. **1855** Macaulay *Hist. Eng.* xx. IV. 384 The bigots..refused to the ruined and expatriated Protestant Lord the means of subsistence.

3. Destroyed; entirely spoiled.

1605 Shaks. *Lear* IV. vi. 137 O ruin'd peece of Nature. **1757** W. Wilkie *Epigoniad* VII. 206, I never will forsake thee, but remain While struggling life these ruin'd limbs retain. **1810** Crabbe *Borough* xix. 273 The strong yearnings of a ruin'd mind. **1822** Lamb *Elia* I. *Compl. Decay of Beggars*, Blind Tobits..casting up their ruined orbs to catch a ray of pity. **1848** Dickens *Dombey* liii, The fire shining on her ruined beauty and her wild black hair.

4. Devastated, laid waste.

1724 De Foe *Mem. Cavalier* (1840) 151 The ruined country..clamoured. **1781** Gibbon *Decl. & F.* xxx. III. 136 Alaric disdained to trample any longer on the prostrate and ruined countries of Thrace and Dacia. **1800** Campbell *Poems, Ode to Winter* 42 Sullen Winter, hear my prayer, And gently rule the ruined year. **1821** Shelley *Adonais* x, Lost Angel of a ruined Paradise!

ruiner ('ruːɪnə(r)). [f. ruin *v.* + -er^1.] One who or that which ruins.

1581 Mulcaster *Positions* xliv. (1887) 286 Great hinderers to good schooling: nay extreame ruiners in cases aboue schooling. **1595** B. Barnes *Cent. Spir. Sonn.* li. (1815) 26 The bodie's ruiner and soule's disease. **1610** Bp. Hall *Apol. Brownists* 116, I had thought you had held vs all ruiners, not builders. **1648** Boyle *Seraph. Love* xvi. (1700) 98 Absence and Rivals, those frequent Ruiners of other Lovers happiness. **1711** Steele *Spect.* No. 156 ⁋3 But commend me above all others to those who are known for your Ruiners of Ladies. **1773** Goldsm. *Song* Wks. (Globe) 688 But I will rally, and combat the ruiner; Not a look nor a smile shall my passion discover. **1814** Shelley *Ess. & Lett.* (1852) I. 163 His path..marked with the blood of the oppressor and the ruiner. **1878** *N. Amer. Rev.* CXXVI. 489 A protest against the rule of the ruiners is the dictate of prudence.

rui'niferous, *a.* *nonce-word.* Rich in ruins.

1854 *Blackw. Mag.* LXXV. 531 An antiquarian rummage in ancient and ruiniferous Cashel.

ru'iniform, *a.* *Min. rare.* [? ad. F. *ruiniforme.*] Presenting the appearance of ruins.

1805-17 R. Jameson *Char. Min.* 77 *Ruiniform.* Resembles ruins of buildings. It occurs in Florentine marble, which is from this circumstance called Landscape marble.

'ruining, *vbl. sb.* [f. ruin *v.* + -ing^1.] The action of bringing to ruin; the result of this.

1603 Drayton *Bar. Wars* I. liv, The Marchers..now perceiue their dilatory stay To be the causer of their ruining. **1660** R. Coke *Power & Subj.* 71 They must..dispose their own subjects to the ruining and destroying of one another. **1820** Shelley *Witch Atl.* lxx, She Restored the embalmers' ruining. **1891** Scrivener *Fields & Cities* 133 Large holdings have been the ruining of Italy and her provinces.

'ruining, *ppl. a.* [f. ruin *v.* + -ing^2.]

1. Productive of ruin; destructive.

c **1611** Chapman *Iliad* v. 103 When Pandarus..beheld his ruining hand..make lanes through every band. **1667** Flavel *Saint Indeed* (1754) 36 God will preserve your souls from the ruining power of temptation. **1693** R. Fleming *Disc. of Earthq.* 100 An Adversary who..hath had such prevailing Successes, to carry on a ruining and judicial work. *a* **1732** T. Boston *Crook in Lot* (1805) 124, I fear a ruining design of providence against me therein. **1733** E. Erskine *Serm.* Wks. 1871 II. 162 Ruining judgments are deferred or removed. **189.** L. Johnson *In Falmouth Harbour* 24 Far From this pure rest, the Land's drear End, And ruining waters, are.

2. Falling into ruin.

1844 Mrs. Browning *Drama of Exile* 1939 The avalanches of the ruining worlds. **1896** Swinburne *Tale of Balen* IV. vii, Like jarring steel on ruining walls, So rang their meeting then.

rui'nosity. *rare*$^{-1}$. [ad. med.L. *ruīnōsitas.*] A ruinous condition or part.

1908 J. T. Fowler *Memorials of Ripon* (Surtees) IV. p. xxxiv, He..finds terrible ruinosities.

ruinous ('ruːɪnəs), *a.* Forms: 4-6 ruynouse (5 ruynowse), 5-6 ruynous (5 roynows, 6 *Sc.* rwynus); 5 ruynose, 5-6 ruinose; 6 ruinus, 6-7 -ouse, 6- ruinous; *Sc.* 6 rewyn-, rewinus (-is). [ad. F. *ruineux, -euse* (OF. also *ruyneux*, = Sp. and Pg. *ruinoso*, It. *rovinoso, ruinoso*), or L. *ruīnōs-us*: see ruin *sb.* and -ous.]

1. a. Falling or fallen into ruin; decayed, dilapidated, broken down.

1382 Wyclif *Ezek.* xxxvi. 33, Y..shal make citees for to be enhabitid, and shal repareyle ruynouse thingis. **1432-50** tr. *Higden* (Rolls) III. 217 Whiche towne was ruinose and nye to Athenes. **1467-8** *Rolls of Parlt.* V. 591/2 Two ruynouse Tenementes, sette in the parissh of Seint Benett. **1543-4** *Act 35 Hen. VIII*, c. 4 The chiefe lorde..of whom suche..decayed and ruinous houses be holden. **1577** B. Googe *Heresbach's Husb.* I. (1586) 9 b, Some part of it, being ruinous, I built after my fancie. **1615** G. Sandys *Trav.* 154 The much raine enforced us to flie for shelter vnto a ruinous chappell. **1660** F. Brooke tr. *Le Blanc's Trav.* 5 The Town ..is very ruinous, nothing left entire, save the Market, and exchange. **1728** Morgan *Algiers* II. i. 214 The same authority proves Cesaria to have been erected on the ruinous Foundations of the most ancient Jol. **1796** Morse *Amer. Geogr.* II. 686 The palace of the Thuilleries, an old and ruinous place. **1859** Tennyson *Marr. Geraint* 462 [He] Built that new fort..And keeps me in this ruinous castle here. **1860** Tyndall *Glac.* I. iii. 27 The weather had broken up the mountains into ruinous heaps.

fig. *c* **1430** Lydg. *Min. Poems* (Percy Soc.) 252, I feele myn herte brotel and ruynous. **1661** Boyle *Style of Script.* (1675) 138 As long as we continue in these ruinous cottages of clay.

Comb. **1848** tr. *Hoffmeister's Trav. Ceylon* xi. 403 Cold, naked, ruinous-looking rocks.

†**b.** Almost obliterated. *Obs.*$^{-1}$

1624 Quarles *Sion's Elegies* To Reader, Some ruinous Accents, here and there discouered, makes them imagin, they writ some things in verse.

2. Brought to, sunk into, ruin or decay. *rare.*

1587 Collingwood in *Border Papers* (1894) I. 259 The pitefull complaynt..of this ruinose and waysted cuntre. **1605** Camden *Rem., Epitaphs* 31 The valerous vpholder of the ruinous state of Britaine against the Saxons. **1607** Shaks. *Timon* IV. iii. 465 Is yon'd despis'd and ruinous man my Lord? **1655** Fuller *Ch. Hist.* I. v. 32 The Roman Empire now grown Ruinous, could not repair it's out-Rooms.

3. Bringing or tending to bring ruin; disastrous, destructive, pernicious. Also *transf.*, excessively expensive.

1526 *Pilgr. Perf.* (W. de W. 1531) 20 b, All yᵉ worlde (as saynt Austyn sayth) is ruynous and bytter falsenes. **1605** Shaks. *Lear* I. ii. 123 Machinations, hollownesse, treacherie, and all ruinous disorders follow vs disquietly to our Graues. **1667** Milton *P.L.* VI. 216 So..together rush'd Both Battels maine, with ruinous assault And inextinguishable rage. **1736** Butler *Anal.* II. v. Wks. 1874 I. 209 Provision might be made..for preventing those ruinous consequences. **1784** Cowper *Task* IV. 460 'Tis quenchless thirst Of ruinous ebriety that prompts His ev'ry action. **1817** J. Scott *Paris Revisit.* (1819) 59 It was the ruinous imposts levied by these Sovereigns that did the most harm to the Flemish cities. **1842** Bischoff *Woollen Manuf.* II. 251 Any attempts to raise its price by artificial means.. would be ruinous to the wool trade. **1874** Green *Short Hist.* vi. §2. 275 The ruinous issue of the great struggle with France roused England to a burst of fury. **1897** A. Beardsley *Let.* 27-28 Feb. (1970) 260 If the hotel turns out too ruinous, and our expenditure in these matters could not be controlled, then we will decide for lodgings.

4. Pertaining to a fall or crash. *rare*$^{-1}$.

1667 Milton *P.L.* II. 921 Nor was his eare less peal'd With noises loud and ruinous..then when Bellona storms.

'ruinously, *adv.* [f. prec. + -ly^2.] In a ruinous manner or degree; in a way, or to an extent, which leads to ruin.

1550 Bale *Image Both Ch.* II. b v, Egipte is ruynously decayed. **1628** Wither *Brit. Rememb.* VI. 852 Gods Temples being ruinously old. **1659** *Gentl. Calling* (1696) 17 You cast away Estate..and..imploy yourselves the most ruinously, rather than endure to be Idle. **1768** *Woman of Honor* I. 34 Nothing..is easier..than to ruinously confound a true good with a false one. **1832** Babbage *Econ. Manuf.* xxiv. (ed. 3) 234 Whilst the manufacturers are complaining of the ruinously low price of their produce. **1864** *Englishw. in India* 24 Table ornaments are ruinously dear out here. **1897** Mary Kingsley *W. Africa* 542 A curse or evil disease, curable only by ruinously expensive process.

'ruinousness. [f. as prec. + -ness.]

1. The quality of bringing ruin.

1659 *Gentl. Calling* (1696) 43 The ruinousness of a perverse will is so generally understood. **1835** *Taits Mag.* II. 407 The ruinousness of a Chancery suit. **1879** M. Arnold *Mixed Ess.* 309 The ruinousness, to a poet, of symbols, hieroglyphics, mystifications.

2. The condition of being in ruins.

1665 Manley *Grotius' Low C. Wars* 78 The Ruinousness of their Walls, which to other Cities is a great Evil, was an Advantage to this. **1843** Ruskin *Mod. Paint.* I. II. vii. §26. 104 When the artist suffers the mere love of ruinousness to interfere with his perception of the art of the building,..he has lost the end of his own art.

†**ruin-tail, -tailed:** see rowen 3.

1678 Dryden *Kind Keeper* IV. i, Whores of all sorts; forkers and ruintailed. **1686** Blome *Gentl. Recreat.* II. 37/1 There are several names or distinctions of Partridges;..the fourth [are called] Ruintayles, and then they are full summed and hard set.

ruisse, obs. form of roose *sb.*

†**ruissel.** *Obs.* Forms: 5 ruys(s)el, ruiss(h)eaul. [a. OF. *ruisel, ruisseaul*, etc. (mod.F. *ruisseau*), a dim. of L. *rīvus* stream.] A rivulet, brook. (In Caxton only.)

c **1477** Caxton *Jason* 119 Two ruisseauls or two springes of a fountayne. **1481** —— *Godf.* 273 The canellys and ruissheauls ronne alle of blood. **1483** —— *Gold. Leg.* 422/1 As they came to a ruysel or chanel and wold haue passyd it.

†**ruit.** *Obs.*$^{-1}$ [a. OF. *ruit, ruyt*, in the same sense.] Noise, disorder.

a **1400** *Minor Poems fr. Vernon MS.* II. 613 Wiþ þeues þat loueden ryot and ruit, Whi schal my sone be nayled?

†**ruiter.** *Obs.* Also 6, 8 ruyter, 7 ruytter. [a. Du. *ruiter.*] = rutter^1.

In quot. 1702 used to render med.L. *ruttarii*.

1579 Digges *Stratiot.* 111 Sometimes also the Ruyters vse to wheele about with their whole Troupe. **1591** *W. Garrard's Art Warre* 242 To euerie 12 Ruiters commonly there is allowed a wagon with 4 horses. **1604** Digges *Foure Paradoxes* II. 63 Ruytters with their Pistolles, and Argoletires with their Pettronels. **1702** *Vind. Magna Charta* 8 The Flanders Ruyters, or Cavaliers, who now by Magna Charta were expressly..order'd to be expelled the Kingdom.

ruk(e, obs. forms of rook, ruck.

†**'rukel.** *Obs. rare.* Also 5 rukul, rucul. [ad. med.L. *rucula*, for *erucula, dim. of L. *ērūca*: see

ERUCA and ERUKE.] **a.** The rocket (*Eruca sativa*). **b.** The cankerworm.

c **1440** *Pallad. on Husb.* I. 853-5 Thy seed with Iuce of rukel or syngrene To wete, vp sleeth the rukel, as men wene. Eek figtre askis oon on rukul throwith.

rukelen, obs. f. RUCKLE *v.*[1]

‖**rukh** (rʊk). Also ruk. [a. Hindi *rūkh*, f. Prakrit *rukkha-* tree.] In India: a forest; a forest reserve.

1893 KIPLING *Many Inventions* 191 He made no pretence at keeping a garden, for the *rukh* swept up to his door. **1928** *Blackw. Mag.* Apr. 443/1 It was a week or two before General Devi Deen came again for our ride through the *ruk*.

rukh, variant of ROC.

rukk(e, obs. ff. RUCK *sb.*[1]

rukus, var. RUCKUS.

rulable (ˈruːləb(ə)l), *a.* Also 5 reule-, 7 ruleable. [f. RULE *v.* and *sb.* + -ABLE.]

1. Capable of being ruled; governable. ? *Obs.*

c **1449** PECOCK *Repr.* II. xvi. 242 Therfore thei helden.. that the bodili heuen and hise seid parties reuliden al that was reuleable here bynethe. **1596** BACON *Let. to Essex* Oct. (1671) 89 For the removing the Impression of your Nature to be Opiniastre and not Rulable. **1607** TOPSELL *Four-f. Beasts* (1658) 251 They make the Horses.. tractable, and rulable, to be turned, restrained, or put forward. **1680** H. DODWELL *Two Lett.* i. Contents, Some general Rules in managing a Parochial Cure for bringing the People to a Ruleable temper.

2. Admissible as a rule. *rare*⁻¹.

1624 BP. MOUNTAGU *Gagg* 201 But.. I will take no such exception: I admit it ruleable every way.

3. *U.S. colloq.* Allowable by rule; permissible.

1888-9 in *Century Dict.* s.v., It shall be rulable to reject any.. packages varying widely in color or quality from the bulk of the lot. **1890** L. C. D'OYLE *Notches* 170 He would take a cigar—not considered exactly fair, perhaps, but 'rulable' (occasionally) according to the standard of the country.

rule (ruːl), *sb.* Forms: 3 riwle, 3-4 riule; 3 revle, 4-6 reule; 4-5 reul, 6-7 reull; 4 reuel(e, 5 reuyl, 6 reuyll; 4 rewel, 4-5 rewele, 4-6 rewil (5 rewile, rewyll(e, 5-6 rewill), 4-7 rewle (5 rewlle, 5-6 rewl, 6 rewll); 3 ruyle, 4 ruiele, ruyl; 4 ruele, 6 ruell(e; 4- rule, 5 rwle, rull, 6 rulle; 6 roule. [a. OF. *riule*, *reule*, *ruile*, *rule*, etc. (see Littré and Godefroy):—L. *rēgula* straight stick, bar, ruler, pattern, etc. (cf. REGULA), which is also represented by OF. *regle* (F. *règle*) REGLE *sb.*

The development of the leading senses took place in Latin, and does not correspond to the order of their appearance in English.]

I. 1. a. A principle, regulation, or maxim governing individual conduct.

a **1225** *Ancr. R.* 2 Þeos riwle is euere wiðinnen & rihteð þe heorte... Þeos riwle is cherite. **1340** *Ayenb.* 97 Þise byeþ þe zeue ruieles of holy lyf þet þe zoþe salomon tekþ to his children. **1382** WYCLIF *Gal.* vi. 16 And who euere schulen suwe this rewle, pees vpon hem. **1451** CAPGR. *Life St. Aug.* Prol., A grete reule to all lerned men was sette be Seint Paule in þe first capitle Ad Romanos. **1542** UDALL *Erasm. Apoph.* 237 The Jewes of a great conscience & of a rewle dooen abstain from eatyng of allmaner swynes fleashe. **1617** MORYSON *Itin.* I. 26 It is a rule here to shun all sadnes. **1667** MILTON *P.L.* XI. 528 If thou well observe The rule of not too much, by temperance taught. **1706** E. WARD *Wooden World Diss.* (1708) 45 Tho' he guide others to Heaven by the plain-sailing Rules of the Gospel. **1784** COWPER *Task* II. 523 Their rules of life Defective and unsanction'd, prov'd too weak To bind the roving appetite. **1809** WORDSW. *Sonnets Indep. & Liberty* II. xii, A few strong instincts and a few plain rules. **1860** RUSKIN *Unto this Last* i. §7 All endeavour to deduce rules of action from balance of expediency is in vain.

b. Const. *of* some quality or principle.

a **1300** *Cursor M.* 17454 Quen giftes has for-don þe sight, Qua mai þan folu þe reul o right. **1535** COVERDALE *Isaiah* xxxii. 1 The kinge shal gouerne after yᵉ rule of rightuousnes. **1591** SPENSER *M. Hubberd* 1131 No care of justice, nor no rule of reason,.. Did thenceforth ever enter in his minde. **1726** SWIFT *Gulliver* I. i, I could not forbear shewing my Impatience (perhaps against the strict Rules of Decency) by putting my Finger frequently to my Mouth. **1780** *Mirror* No. 79, A scrupulous observance of certain rules of decorum. **1840** KINGSLEY *Lett.* (1878) I. 49, I had no rule of morality, felt and believed. **1859** GEO. ELIOT *A. Bede* xx, Mrs. Poyser was strict in adherence to her own rules of propriety.

c. *transf.* Applied to a person or thing.

c **1375** *Sc. Leg. Saints* xxxvi. (*Baptist*) 614 Sancte Iohnne þe scole of uertuise wes,.. & reule of rychtwisnes but wen. **1639** N. N. tr. *Du Bosq's Compl. Woman* I. 22 If they but cast their eyes on her who should be the rule of all their sex, as shee is the ornament. **1818** SHELLEY *Rev. Islam* IX. xxviii. 9 They leave All hope, or love, or truth, or liberty,.. To be a rule and law to ages that survive.

2. The code of discipline or body of regulations observed by a religious order or congregation; hence *occas.*, the order or congregation itself.

a **1225** *Ancr. R.* 4 Nu aski ȝe hwat riwle ȝe ancren schullen holden? *c* **1290** *S. Eng. Leg.* I. 59/196 Þat he scholde is ordre preouen, and is Revle al-so, Þoruȝ þe godspel of godes word. *c* **1325** *Metr. Hom.* 32 That was the reuel of sain Benet. **1377** LANGL. *P. Pl.* B. xx. 246 Haueth none envye To lered ne to lewed, but lyueth after ȝowre rewle. **1422** tr. *Secreta Secret., Priv. Priv.* 193 Seint benet ordeyned the monken rull, and Seinte Austeyn chanoun Rull in erth. **1444** *Rolls of Parlt.* V. 74/2 Professid yn the rule of Seint Austyn. **1526** *Pilgr. Perf.* (W. de W. 1531) 18 b, As our holy father Saynt Austyn sayth in his rule. **1617** MORYSON *Itin.* I. 168 A begging Friar of the Order of Saint Francis.. gave me to eat, but would receive no money for it; saying, it was against their rule to handle any money. **1631** WEEVER *Anc. Funeral Mon.* 130 There are foure rules, or religious Orders. **1738** CHAMBERS *Cycl.* s.v. *Carthusians*, Their rule.. obliges them to.. a total abstinence from flesh. **1771** *Encycl. Brit.* II. 630/1 The rule of the Franciscans.. is briefly this. **1848** J. H. NEWMAN *Loss & Gain* III. x, It was indeed but ten years.. since the severest of modern rules had been introduced into England. **1890** MEYNELL *Newman* iv. 55 Next month Father Newman, with Stanton and St. John,.. formally received Faber.. into the rule of St. Philip Neri.

transf. **1340-70** *Alex. & Dind.* 507 Sire emperour alixandre, þis arn oure lawes, Boþe oure reule & oure riht þat we þe rede holde. **1613** PURCHAS *Pilgrimage* III. vii. (1614) 276 An excellent Doctor, named Boni, framed their [Caballists] rule and prayers. **1846** KEBLE *Lyra Innoc.* (1873) 7 Angels with us rehearse their own majestic rule.

attrib. *c* **1450** in Aungier *Syon* (1840) 262 Sche schal put from her her.. cowle, mantel, crown, and veyle, and remayne in her rewle cote. *Ibid.* 264 The abbes schal ȝeue her holy water and a rewle cote.

3. a. A principle regulating practice or procedure; a fixed and dominating custom or habit.

rule of the road: see ROAD *sb.* 5 e. Similarly ***rule(s) of the sea*** (Smyth, 1867).

1387 TREVISA *Higden* (Rolls) VII. 451 Þe pope.. forsook þe reule of þe olde tyme, and sacrede Thurstyn and ȝaf hym the pal. **1470-85** MALORY *Arthur* x. lv. 505 Is þᵗ the rule of yow arraunt knyghtes for to make a knyght to Iuste will he or nyll? **1572** *Satir. Poems Reform.* xxxiv. 60 In Scotland had not bene sic tuill, Gif this had bene þe common reull. **1596** SHAKS. *Merch. V.* IV. i. 178 Of a strange nature is the sute you follow, Yet in such rule, that the Venetian Law Cannot impugne you. **1768** STERNE *Sent. Journ.*, *Case of Conscience*, 'Twas against the rules of his house. **1849** MACAULAY *Hist. Eng.* ix. II. 432 It had long been the rule at Rome that no officer of justice or finance could enter the dwelling inhabited by the minister who represented a Catholic state. **1893** GEE *Auscultation & Percussion* (ed. 4) 92 Let mediate auscultation ever be considered the rule of practice.

b. A regulation determining the methods or course of a game or the like. ***rules of the game*** *transf.*, conventions in political or social relations or the like.

1697 DRYDEN *Virg. Georg.* III. 183 The Lapithæ.. taught the Steed.. the Rules of War to know. **1778** C. JONES *Hoyle's Games Impr.* 189 The game of billiards, with the rules and odds. **1831** SCOTT *Ct. Robt.* xxxii, The rules of fair battle will be punctually observed. **1837** *Penny Cycl.* VIII. 158/1 The rules [of cricket] are at once too well known and too complicated to be here explained. **1895** *Outing* XXVII. 250/2 The off-side rule should be clearly understood. **1910** S. E. WHITE *Rules of Game* xli. 644 Things change; and a man is foolish to act as though they didn't. He's just got to keep playing along according to the rules of the game. And they keep changing too. **1936** M. MITCHELL *Gone with Wind* xxxi. 521 The rules of the game had been changed and.. honest labor could no longer earn its just reward. **1964** ROUSSEAS & FARGANIS in I. L. Horowitz *New Sociol.* 287 Operating within the rules-of-the-game of institutionalized conflict. **1974** *Daily Tel.* 15 Oct. 18/2 As leader of the Opposition Mr Heath, under the rules of the game, has the right of reply tonight to Mr Wilson's Ministerial broadcast last night.

c. Without article: Rigid system or routine. ***out of rule***, contrary to custom.

1796 CHARLOTTE SMITH *Marchmont* I. 141 Lady Dacres either did not or would not see how very much the conduct of her visitor was out of rule. **1820** IRVING *Sketch Bk.* II. 219 No being acts more rigidly from rule than the Indian.

4. *Law.* **a.** An order made by a judge or court, the application of which is limited to the case in connexion with which it is granted. Also called a ***particular rule*** or ***rule of court***.

rule absolute, an order following a rule nisi and changing a conditional direction into a peremptory command. ***rule nisi***: see NISI.

1447-8 J. SHILLINGFORD *Lett.* (Camden) 41 That matier, whiche longe tyme hath abiden yn travers bitwixte yow,.. was commytted.. to the rule of the two chief Justises and me. **1474** *Rolls of Parlt.* VI. 118/2 Like Processe, Rule, Jugement and Execution be had theryn, as usuelly is used in Writtes of Dette. **1612** BACON *Ess.*, *Of Judicature*, The partes of a Iudge are.. to giue the rule or sentence. **1768** BLACKSTONE *Comm.* III. 203 Upon this condition, that he enter into a rule of court to confess, at the trial of the cause, three of the four requisites for the maintenance of the plaintiff's action. **1771** *Junius Lett.* lxvii. (1788) 342 The rule against him was made absolute. **1841** *Penny Cycl.* XX. 220/2 Rules not general are such as are confined to the particular case in reference to which they have been granted.

transf. **1853** MISS MULOCK *Agatha's Husb.* II. 38 She thought the rule absolute was painfully prevalent in the Harper family.

b. A formal order or regulation governing the procedure or decisions of a court of law; an enunciation or doctrine forming part of the common law, or having the force of law. Also called a (***standing***) ***rule of court***. ***rules of evidence***, the legal rules that apply to the giving of evidence.

1530 PALSGR. 264/2 Rule of cannon lawe, *canon*. **1609** SKENE *Reg. Maj.* 100 Many profitable principals, and rewles of the lawes of this Realme, worthie to be remembred. **1699** LUTTRELL *Brief Rel.* (1857) IV. 541 Mr. Pugh, clerk of the rules in the kings bench court. **1756** *J. Gilbert's Law of Evidence* (rev. ed.) 8 The Rule of Evidence commands no farther than to produce the best that the Nature of the Thing is capable of. **1768** BLACKSTONE *Comm.* III. 64 The temporal courts adhering to the former, and the spiritual adopting the latter as their rule of proceeding. **1779** *Mirror* No. 6, He felt no great inclination to load his memory with the rules of our municipal law. **1801** T. PEAKE *Law of Evidence* p. v, The chapter on Parol Testimony, also is in a great measure new; for the rules of evidence in this respect have been so much altered, and so much light has been thrown on them by modern decisions, that, comparatively, little is to be collected from ancient books. **1818** CRUISE *Digest* (ed. 2) IV. 523 Lord Thurlow said, that.. the rule was such, and so many estates stood upon it, that it could not be shaken. **1841** *Penny Cycl.* XIX. 379/2 Either according to the rules of the common law, or by the operation of the Statute of Uses. **1882** *Encycl. Brit.* XIV. 358/1 The rule that every will must be in writing is a mere fragment—only the limb of a law. **1892** S. L. PHIPSON *Law of Evidence* p. v, I have.. adhered to one uniform method of arrangement throughout—that of stating: (1) The rules of evidence ..[etc.]. **1908** J. H. WIGMORE in *Sel. Ess. Anglo-Amer. Legal Hist.* II. xl. 691 (*heading*) A general survey of the history of the rules of evidence. **1942** E. M. MORGAN in *Model Code of Evidence* (Amer. Law Inst.) 5 The rules of evidence have been developed in myriads of cases. *Ibid.* 34 This has led to the invention of the hypothetical question, which, as Mr. Wigmore says, 'is one of the truly scientific features of the rules of Evidence'. **1956** E. C. CONRAD *Mod. Trial Evidence* I. i. 15 No exceptions to the general applicability of the rules of evidence as a broad proposition has been noted. **1973** *N.Y. Law Jrnl.* 4 Sept. 3/4 This committee was not bound by the rules of evidence. It was not constrained to follow courtroom procedures.

c. ***rule of law***: (*a*) with *a* and *pl.*: a valid legal proposition; (*b*) with *the*: a doctrine, deriving from theories of natural law, that in order to control the exercise of arbitrary power, the latter must be subordinated to impartial and well-defined principles of law; (*c*) with *the*: spec. in English law, the concept that the day-to-day exercise of executive power must conform to general principles as administered by the ordinary courts.

(*a*) *a* **1634** E. COKE *Third Part Institutes Lawes Eng.* (1644) vii. 53 In case of life the rule of law ought to be certain. **1756** *J. Gilbert's Law of Evidence* (rev. ed.) 16 The Rule of Law that requires the greatest Evidence that the Nature of the Thing is capable of. **1768** BLACKSTONE *Comm.* III. xxiii. 383 If a whole county is interested in the question to be tried, the trial by the rule of law must be in some adjoining county. **1969** *Columbia Law Rev.* LXIX. 1168 It is clear that those rules of precedent which are binding as 'rules of practice' are also rules of law.

(*b*) **1883** J. E. C. WELLDON tr. *Aristotle's Politics* iii. §16. 154 The rule of law then.. is preferable to the rule of an individual citizen. **1929** LD. HEWART *New Despotism* ii. 23 What is meant here by the 'Rule of Law' is the supremacy or the predominance of law, as distinguished from mere arbitrariness, or from some alternative mode, which is not law, or determining or disposing of the rights of individuals. **1936** F. G. WILSON *Elem. Mod. Politics* viii. 207 It is of historic importance that the rule of law in the medieval and early modern sense was the rule of superearthly law..—eternal law, divine law, natural law, and human law. **1953** T. D. WELDON *Vocab. Politics* iii. 69 Strictly speaking there is nothing difficult or impressive about 'the Rule of Law'. It is merely a convenient way of referring to the fact that associations have rules and unless those rules are pretty generally kept and enforced the association breaks down and the activity which it was designed to promote becomes impracticable. **1959** E. C. S. WADE in A. V. Dicey *Law of Constitution* (ed. 10) p. xcvii, In another sense the rule of law means the recognition of certain fundamental obligations as binding upon States in their dealings with one another... The United Nations.. claims to give effect to the rule of law. *Ibid.* p. cvii, The International Commission of Jurists considers that the basic idea uniting lawyers in many different legal systems is a conception of the rule of law. **1971** *Engineering* Apr. 54/1 Industry-wide negotiations, ending in a kind of rule-of-law. **1974** J. LAPALOMBARA *Politics within Nations* iii. 106 But the difference between the *Rechtsstaat* and constitutionalism is that the rule of law in the former is based on a concession from the ruler. **1977** *Rolling Stone* 24 Mar. 31/2 Those senators.. knew of the need to continue redeeming the rule of law that Edward Levi had begun.

(*c*) **1885** A. V. DICEY *Law of Constitution* v. 172 When we say that the supremacy or the rule of law is a characteristic of the English constitution, we generally include under one expression at least three distinct though kindred conceptions. We mean, in the first place, that no man is punishable or can be made to suffer in body or goods except for a distinct breach of law established in the ordinary legal manner before the ordinary courts of the land. **1923** W. S. HOLDSWORTH *Hist. Eng. Law* (rev. ed.) iv. 405 The precocious development of our common law has.. given.. the opportunity for the development of those two fundamental characteristics of our English constitution—the system of self-government and the rule of law. **1933** W. I. JENNINGS *Law & Constitution* 256 The 'rule of law' in this sense means that public authorities ought not to have large powers. **1959** *Polit. Stud.* VII. 114 He [*sc.* Dicey] would not have admitted for one moment that a Rule of Law followed from the mere fact that the conduct of government had a legal basis. **1971** S. A. DE SMITH *Constitutional & Admin. Law* ii. 40 Nor would it be justifiable to examine the general concept of the rule of law at length... The concept is usually intended to imply (i) that the powers exercised by politicians and officials must have a legitimate foundation.. and (ii) that the law should conform to certain minimum standards of justice. **1975** LD. HAILSHAM *Door wherein I Went* xxxvi. 253 The rule of law, an increasingly sophisticated idea.. is essentially a province for an official with a foot in both camps, a sworn judge as well as a sworn Privy Councillor, with an independent duty towards the judiciary and the legal profession.

5. a. A regulation framed or adopted by a corporate body, public or private, for governing its conduct and that of its members; also *attrib.*, as in ***rule-book*** (*lit.* and *fig.*). ***to bend*** or ***stretch the rules***: to interpret the rules leniently, to overlook or allow an infringement of the rules; hence ***rule-bender***.

joint rule, one observed by both branches of a legislature of two houses. *standing rule*, a permanent regulation of a corporate body governing its ordinary procedure.

1558 Q. MARY *Will* in J. M. Stone *Life* (1901) 510 To keep and observe the ancient rewles and statuts of the said hows [Savoy Hospital]. **1659** HEYLIN *Certamen Epist.* 89 Their Decretals were made by them intentionally to serve for a rule and a reiglement of the Church in general. **1706** E. WARD *Wooden World Diss.* (1708) 90 To walk the Quarter-Deck in Quirpo is to walk against the Rules of the Navy. **1802** JAMES *Milit. Dict.*, *Rules and Articles*. Under this term may be considered the military code of the British army. **1847** TENNYSON *Princ.* I. 176 Averring it was clear against the rules For any man to go. **1882** *Encycl. Brit.* XIV. 356/1 The rules set by a club or society, and enforced upon its members by exclusion from the society,.. are laws, but not positive laws. **1973** *Times* 2 Nov. 5/7 Trying to get other members of the European Community to 'bend the rules' so that exports can be resumed. **1977** 'O. JACKS' *Autumn Heroes* ii. 37 He bent over backwards to be straight in all his dealings... He wouldn't stretch the rules.

attrib. and *Comb.* **1857** [see RUBRICIST 1]. **1897** *Westm. Gaz.* 6 Apr. 9/3 The rule book of the Old English Sheep-dog Club. **1898** *Ibid.* 19 Oct. 6/1 The compounding parties bring themselves under the charge of rule-breaking. **1910** W. M. RAINE *Bucky O'Connor* 13 The situation was one not covered in the company's rule book. **1945** F. H. HUBBARD *Railroad Avenue* ii. 10 Casey was never the type known as a 'rule-book engineer'. **1954** W. FAULKNER *Fable* 113 Germans fight wars by the rule-books. **1959** M. GILBERT *Blood & Judgement* xiv. 151 Some stuffy old Chief Superintendent, who's lived with one finger in the Rule Book. **1968** *Punch* 20 Mar. 417/3 Despite some fierce and not altogether rulebook tackling by their opponents, the Students were..taking the game right into the Police half. **1973** M. WOODHOUSE *Blue Bone* iv. 36 The Communists.. were bound to loathe the guts of the big old families since that was what the rule book said. **1978** S. BRILL *Teamsters* vii. 272 They were rule-benders (or perhaps sometimes lawbreakers) in a rule-benders and lawbreakers' world.

b. (Also with lower-case initials.) **Rules Committee**, a committee of a house of a U.S. federal or state legislature responsible for expediting the passage of bills.

1918 H. W. DODDS *Procedure in State Legislatures* (Annals Amer. Acad. Polit. & Social Sci. Suppl. No. 1) iv. 60 Enjoying as much parliamentary power as the English cabinet, the rules committee [of the New York Assembly] nevertheless escapes any measure of responsibility before the people. **1976** *National Observer* (U.S.) 12 June 5/2 Lobbying..was so intense the Rules Committee wouldn't release the legislation.

c. Followed by a number or letter: a particular regulation imposed by an institution (see quots.).

1929 *Bookman* (U.S.) July 527/2 *Rule G*, in all railroad rule books, prohibiting the use of intoxicants. **1932** *Santa Fé Mag.* Jan. 34/2 Getting drunk is *Rule b*, failing to protect your train or to flag it is 99, attending an investigation is *going on the carpet*. **1974** *Guidelines to Volunteer Services* (N.Y. State Dept. Correctional Services) 43 *Rule 5*, when a parolee must abstain from alcohol. **1976** A. MILLER *Inside Outside* 6, I would also call on those men under Rule 43 (the segregation rule), and chat with them for a while. **1977** *Times* 11 Apr. 7/7 Over 60 prisoners are in segregation 'for the maintenance of good order or discipline' under rule 43 on any one day.

6. a. *the rules*, a defined area in the neighbourhood of certain prisons, *esp.* those of the Fleet and King's Bench, within which certain prisoners, esp. debtors, were permitted to live on giving proper security. (Cf. LIBERTY *sb.*[1] 7 c.) †See also quot. 1662.

1662 *Virginia Stat.* (1823) II. 77 If the sherriffe shall permitt any person dwelling within the rules of a prison..to walke abroad out of prison though with a keeper, and to have the benefitt of the rules or to lodge in his own house; the said sherriffe..shalbe ordered to pay the debt. **1786** MRS. A. M. BENNETT *Juvenile Indiscr.* V. 42 They live every bit as grand, and keep a mort of company in the rules. **1812** *Examiner* 5 Oct. 639/2 He was permitted to live in the Rules—consequently his punishment was merely nominal. **1847** MRS. GORE *Cast. in Air* xxxv. (1857) 349, I took him out of the Rules of the Bench, and brought him home to my poor chimney-corner. **1883** ASHTON *Soc. Life Q. Anne* II. 247 To aid these, the prisoners took it in turns to perambulate the rules, and solicit help in money or kind.

b. The freedom of these bounds or 'rules'. *on rule*, allowed to live in the rules.

1766 ENTICK *London* IV. 265 Any prisoner for debt may.. enjoy the rules [of the Fleet], or liberty to walk abroad, and to keep a house within the liberties of this prison, provided he can give security to the warden for his forthcoming. **1790** *Ann. Reg., Hist.* 97 This bill therefore had contained clauses ..abolishing an indulgence at present existing, commonly called rules, by which a prisoner is permitted to go out of his confinement to a certain distance. **1841** THACKERAY *Gt. Hoggarty Diamond* viii, Her lodgers used commonly to be prisoners on rule from that place [*sc.* the Fleet]. **1888** SIR W. BESANT *50 Yrs. Ago* 77 Both at the King's Bench and the Fleet debtors were allowed to purchase what were called the Rules, which enabled them to live within a certain area outside the prison, and practically left them free.

II. 7. a. A principle regulating the procedure or method necessary to be observed in the pursuit or study of some art or science. (See also RULE OF THUMB.) Also, *rule-of-brain* (nonce-wd., after RULE OF THUMB).

1387 TREVISA *Higden* (Rolls) III. 251 Plato afterward made þat art [*sc.* Logic] more, and fonde þerynne meny principles and rules. *c* **1400** tr. *Secreta Secret., Gov. Lordsh.* 113 Now y stable to þe reules of þis science of Phisonomy & constituciouns suffyceantz abbreggyd, þat shal be greet profyt to þe. **1573** *Cath. Tract.* (S.T.S.) 14 Schir Iohne Knox hes nocht weill considderit the rewlis of Dialectik. **1620** T. GRANGER *Div. Logike* 258 The consequence, formall consecution or sequell agreeable to the rules of a Syllogisme. **1695** DRYDEN *Parallel Poet. & Paint.* Ess. (ed. Ker) II. 115 One who perfectly understood the rules of painting. **1725** WATTS *Logic* (1736) 105 These two Rules being observed will always render a Definition reciprocal with the Thing defined. **1781** COWPER *Conversation* 869 [This] May prove, though much beside the rules of art, Best for the public. **1828** WHATELY *Rhetoric* in *Encycl. Metrop.* (1845) I. 263 Hence arises another Rule,..that in order effectually to excite feelings of any kind, it is necessary to employ some copiousness of detail. **1866** *Chambers's Encycl.* VIII. 365/2 *Rule of the Octave*, a well-known formula.. which shews the method of accompanying or harmonising the ascending and descending scale. **1948** L. MACNEICE *Holes in Sky* 25 Tom and Tessy..of themselves significant, To rule-of-brain recalcitrant.

b. Coupled with the name of the discoverer or expounder.

1644 MILTON *Educ.* 6 Ornate Rhetorick taught out of the rule of Plato, Aristotle [etc.]. **1780** *Mirror* No. 80, This.., if examined by the rules of Aristotle, will be found to contain all the requisites of the best dramatic composition. **1818** BYRON *Juan* I. cxx, I have a high sense Of Aristotle and the Rules. **1872** RUSKIN *Eagle's Nest* §93 We now build in our villages, by the rules of the Academy of London.

c. *Grammar.* A principle regulating or determining the form or position of words in a sentence. In modern Linguistics, usu. applied to any one of a system of rules that can be formulated in such a way that together they describe all the features of a language. Freq. *Comb.*

1495 *Trevisa's Barth. De P.R.* XVII. iii. 604 Holy wrytte wol not al way be subget to yᵉ rules of Gramer. **1530** PALSGR. 304 Here endeth the rules of the nowne adjectyve. **1581** PETTIE *Guazzo's Civ. Conv.* II. (1586) 97 An Emperor.. being reproued for that he spake contrarie to the rules of Grammer. **1636** B. JONSON *Eng. Gram.* xiv, We say not *childen*, which, according to the rule given before, is the right formation, but *children*. **1693** C. DRYDEN *Juvenal* vii. (1726) 104 Be sure he knows exactly Grammar-Rules. **1737** *Gentl. Mag.* VII. 329 The Translators had more regard to St. Stephen's Words,..than to any Grammar Rule. **1878** *Encycl. Brit.* VIII. 397/1 Confusion and loss of old inflexions, and their replacement by prepositions, auxiliary verbs, and rules of position. **1953** [see *morpheme-sequence* s.v. MORPHEME c]. **1957** N. CHOMSKY *Syntactic Struct.* x. 107 A grammar has a sequence of rules from which phrase structure can be reconstructed and a sequence of morphophonemic rules that convert strings of morphemes into strings of phonemes. Connecting these sequences, there is a sequence of transformational rules. **1965** *Language* XLI. 548 Language is rule-governed behavior, and learning a language involves internalizing the rules. **1968** J. LYONS *Introd. Theoret. Linguistics* i. 48 Learning the language 'naturally' as children, they [*sc.* the speakers of a language] come to speak it according to certain systematic principles, or 'rules', 'immanent' in the utterances they hear about them. It is the task of synchronic linguistic description to formulate these systematic 'rules' as they operate in the language at a particular time. **1968** *Language* XLIV. 735 It follows from premise 1 that from proto-language *L there will be *n* rule sequences into each of *n* daughter languages. **1971** P. KIPARSKY in W. O. Dingwall *Survey Linguistic Sci.* 612 The concept of *rule opacity*..has an important role to play elsewhere in linguistic theory. **1972** *Language* XLVIII. 83 There is every reason to believe that they will allow one to get rid of the unprincipled blocking device of extrinsic rule-ordering. **1974** G. M. GREEN *Semantics & Syntactic Regularity* vi. 194 The notions of redundancy rule, structural description feature, and deep-structure constraint were necessitated by the concepts of rule government. **1976** [see *phrase-structure* s.v. PHRASE *sb.* 7]. **1978** *Language* LIV. 41 These features trigger rules that apply only to forms bearing the corresponding rule feature. .. We can call this device the 'rule-feature' theory. **1979** *Trans. Philol. Soc.* 18 The rule-environment is *arbitrary*—why not a rule deleting *no* only when it is *followed* by N we might ask?

8. *Math.* **a.** A prescribed method or process for finding unknown numbers or values, or solving particular problems.

rule of alligation, coss, fellowship, practice, proportion: see those words. *rule of (false) position, falsehood*, etc.: see POSITION *sb.* 3.

1542 [see PROPORTION *sb.* 9 b]. **1561** [see FELLOWSHIP 9]. **1594** BLUNDEVIL *Exerc.* I. xi. (1636) 32 You must worke the first or second Question sometimes by the Rule Reverse. **1652** *News Lowe-Co.* 8 The Rules of Fellowship, of Three, And more to him familiar be. **1695** [see ALLIGATION 2]. **1706** E. WARD *Wooden World Diss.* (1708) 89 He can compose a Bowl of Punch by the Rules of Trigonometry. **1753** *Chambers's Cycl.* Suppl. *App.* s.v., Rule of five, or, Compound Rule of Three. *Ibid.* s.v. *Whist*, By Mr. de Moivre's rules it will be found, that the total of the chances for the dealer = 92770723800. **1826** in *Encycl. Metrop.* (1845) I. 456/1 There are different methods of solving questions included under the rule of five or more terms. **1867** BRANDE & COX *Dict. Sci.*, etc. III. 320/2 The rule known in the theory of equations as Descartes' Rule of Signs.

Comb. **1847** DE MORGAN *Arith. Bks.* Introd. p. xxii, I speak to the teacher, not the rule-driller.

b. *rule of three*, a method of finding a fourth number from three given numbers, of which the first is in the same proportion to the second as the third is to the unknown fourth. Also called *the golden rule* (see GOLDEN *a.* 5 b), *rule of proportion*.

The ordinary form, called the *common* or *direct rule of three*, is distinguished from the *indirect, inverse, reverse*, †*back* or *backward*: see INVERSE *a.* 3 a.

1594 BLUNDEVIL *Exerc.* I. vi. (1636) 20 And this is the common kind of working by the Rule of three, whereof it is called the common Rule of Three. **1650** RUDD *Geom. Quest.* 23 This is your first number in the Rule of Three. **1669** STURMY *Mariner's Mag.* II. iv. 62 This must be done by the back Rule of Three. **1692** *Capt. Smith's Seaman's Gram.* II. ii. 91 The Rule of Three (or Golden Rule) both Direct and Reverse. **1706** W. JONES *Syn. Palmar. Matheseos* 140 When the Rule of Three Direct has 1 for the 1st Term, 'tis usually called the Rule of Practice. **1828** MOORE *Pract. Navig.* p. xv, Rule of Three in Decimals is worked in the same manner as common Arithmetic. **1844** DICKENS *Mart. Chuzz.* xx, Working it by the rule of three direct and inversed.

attrib. **1891** MRS. RIDDELL *Mad Tour* 213 Doing a rapid rule-of-three sum.

9. Without article in preceding senses, esp. in phr. *by rule*. *work to rule*: see WORK *v.* and *sb.*

1362 LANGL. *P. Pl.* A. I. 22 Heore nomes beþ neodful and nempnen I þenke, Bi rule and bi resun. *c* **1400** *Destr. Troy* 10316 How be reason, or right, or rewle, may þou preue To deme hym so doghty in dedis of armys? **1667** MILTON *P.L.* v. 297 Nature here Wantond as in her prime,..Wilde above rule or art. *c* **1718** PRIOR *P. Purganti* 16 The picture wrought exact to rule, exempt from fault. **1780** COWPER *Progr. Error* 189 Rufillus, exquisitely form'd by rule,..Wonders at Clodio's follies. **1831** SCOTT *Ct. Robt.* xxviii, More modern taste.., by mixing the various orders, had produced such as were either composite, or totally out of rule. **1859** SEELEY *Ecce Homo* iii. (1865) 19 A certain skill in quarrelling by rule. **1870** J. H. NEWMAN *Gram. Assent* II. viii. 279 They speak by rule and by book, though they judge and determine by common-sense.

III. 10. A standard of discrimination or estimation; a criterion, test, canon.

1382 WYCLIF *2 Cor.* x. 13 Sothli we schulden not glorie into ful moche, but vp the mesure of reule, bi which God mesuride to vs. *c* **1440** *Promp. Parv.* 432/1 Rewle, of techynge, *regula, norma*. **1526** *Pilgr. Perf.* (W. de W. 1531) 279 b, It descerneth or iudgeth, not onely..temporall thynges, but also yᵉ eternall,..and that by the rules of grace, ferre aboue all naturall reason. **1580** G. HARVEY *Three Lett.* Wks. (Grosart) I. 103 We are..authorised by the..Maiestie of our speach: which I accounte the only infallible and souueraine Rule of all Rules. **1638** RAWLEY tr. *Bacon's Life & Death* (1650) 11 To finde out a Rule touching Length and Shortnesse of Life in Living Creatures is very difficult. **1681** FLAVEL *Method of Grace* xxviii. 498 If the workman's hand were the rule of his work, it were impossible he should ever err in working. **1710** J. CLARKE tr. *Rohault's Nat. Philos.* (1729) I. 253 Having often observed, that an Object appears more confused the further it is distant from us, we make this a Rule of determining the Distances of Bodies. **1781** COWPER *Hope* 566 A knave, when tried on honesty's plain rule. **1820** SOUTHEY *Life Wesley* I. 265 A determination to allow no other rule of faith or practice than the Scriptures. **1850** J. H. NEWMAN *Difficulties Anglicans* I. v. (1891) I. 138 By what rule will you determine what divines are authoritative, and what are not? **1884** *Law Times Rep.* L. 196/2 There can be no hard and fast rule by which to construe..commercial agreements.

Comb. **1577** FULKE *Two Treat. agst. Papists* 413 You are a rule giuer.

11. a. A fact (or the statement of one) which holds generally good; that which is normally the case.

On (*the*) *exception proves the rule* see EXCEPTION 1 ¶.

a **1300** *Cursor M.* 29177 Als for a reule þis sal þou take, þat for spusbreking and manath,..þat sal haue scrifte of seuen yere. *c* **1398** CHAUCER *Fortune* 56 Wikke appetyt comth ay before sykenesse; In general this rewle may nat fayle. *c* **1460** METHAM *Wks.* (E.E.T.S.) 92 And this ys a general rwle, that yff a lyne be ryght depe and wele colouryd yt sygnyfyith gode dysposycion off that membyr to the qwyche yt ys corespondent. **1508** FISHER *7 Penit. Ps.* Wks. (1876) 202 Truly it is a generall rule whan a synne ones purposed by consent in our mynde is deedly, what soeuer we do for the accomplysshement of the same is also deedly synne. **1560** DAUS tr. *Sleidane's Comm.* 333 They place this as a generall Rule, that all rites and ceremonies..be no longer meane thynges. **1639** FULLER *Holy War* III. xxiv. (1840) 162 Egypt was an exception from the rules of all other Countries. **1780** *Mirror* No. 82, They consider..that their virtues and good qualities are only exceptions from the general rule. **1805** *Med. Jrnl.* XIV. 410 Some degree of hesitation,..whether the rule is so general as has been supposed. **1862** STANLEY *Jew. Ch.* (1877) I. xix. 366 The possession of the gift throughout the Christian community was the rule and not the exception. **1883** MORFILL *Slavonic Lit.* i. 15 As we might expect, from the rule that the dialects of a language are truer to its spirit than the literary form.

Comb. **1895** RASHDALL *Univ. Mid. Ages* II. 622 The earliest exceptions are of the rule-proving order.

b. *as a* (or *the*) *rule*, normally, generally.

1842 CHRISTIE in *Fleury's Eccl. Hist.* I. 137 *note*, The Oblation was, as the rule, made in the morning. **1845** *Encycl. Metrop.* II. 818/2 Where two decisions [are] of equal value,..as a rule, the second usually prevails. **1878** HUXLEY *Physiography* 5 As a rule, hail falls in summer.

IV. † **12. a.** *good* (or *right*) *rule*, good order and discipline; a settled, well-regulated state or condition. *Obs.*

c **1305** *St. Dunstan* 46 in *E.E.P.* (1862) 35 Of þe hous of Glastnebure a gret ordeynour he was, And makede moche of gode reule, þat neuer er among hem nas. *c* **1340** HAMPOLE *Pr. Consc.* 162 Prelates and prestes [shall yield account] of ilka suggette, þat þai wald noght in right rewel sette. *c* **1400** *Rom. Rose* 4958 But Elde can..set men, by hir ordinaunce, In good reule and in governaunce. **1458** *Paston Lett.* I. 422 If he wyll take up on hym to brynge hym in to good rewyll and lernyng. **1513** T. MORE in Grafton *Chron.* (1568) II. 761 Wales..was begonne to be farre out of good rule and waxen wylde. **1570** *Satir. Poems Reform.* xii. 19 To keip gude reule he raid, and tuke na rest.

† **b.** So without adjective, esp. in phr. *to set* (or *put*) *in rule, to set a rule in*. *Obs.*

c **1450** *Brut* ccxlv. (1908) 391 þe King..restyd hym yn the Castell tylle þe toun was sette yn rewle and gouernawnce. **1467** *Paston Lett.* II. 308, I have ben abought my liffelode to set a rewle ther in. **1490** CAXTON *Eneydos* xii. 44 Folke without Rule and without mesure. *c* **1560** A. SCOTT *Poems* (S.T.S.) v. 21 Abbotis by rewll, and Lorde but ressone. **1605** SHAKS. *Macb.* v. ii. 16 He cannot buckle his distemper'd cause Within the belt of Rule.

†**c.** *out of rule*, in an irregular or disordered state. *Obs.*

1387 TREVISA *Higden* (Rolls) III. 191 þanne he torned to þe citee þat hatte ciuitas Crotoniorum, þat was al out of rule. **1390** GOWER *Conf.* I. 30 Thei hemself divide And stonden out of reule unevene. **1596** SHAKS. *1 Hen. IV*, IV. iii. 39 So long as out of Limit, and true Rule, You stand against anoynted Maiestie.

†**13. a.** Conduct, behaviour, manner of acting. *Obs.*

c **1440** *York Myst.* xxvi. 34 Þer is a ranke swayne Whos rule is no3t right. **1472** *Presentmts. Juries* in *Surtees Misc.* (1890) 24 It is necessary to charge hym to be of gode reule. **1508** KENNEDIE *Flyting w. Dunbar* 381 Sic reule gerris the be seruit wyth cald rost. **1535** in Strype *Ann. Ref.* (1824) VI. 2 It is not meet for a child of her age to keep such rule yet. **1601** SHAKS. *Twel. N.* II. iii. 132 If you priz'd my Ladies fauour.., you would not giue meanes for this vnciuill rule.

†**b.** Breeding, upbringing. *Obs.*[−1]

1469 *10th Rep. Hist. MSS. Comm.* App. V. 307 There sholde be no gentleman [h]is child of Irishe ruele..fusterid nor kepte in sojorne within the saide citie.

†**c.** Misrule, disorder, stir, riot. *Obs.*

1567 DRANT *Horace, Ep.* II. i. Gvj, Such rule and ruffle make the rowte that cum to see our geare. **1581** RICH *Farewell to Mil. Prof.* Ddj, I doubte not, but to take suche order, as there shall no more any suche rule happen betweene you. **1593** *Passionate Morrice* (1876) 79 No less rule than is in a taverne of great resort. **1622** DRAYTON *Poly-olb.* xxvii. 251 Was never seen such rule In any place but here, at Boon fire, or at Yule. **1677** COLES *Eng.-Lat. Dict.* I. s.v., Now I will go see what rule they keep, *nunc in tumultum ibo.* **1690** W. WALKER *Idiomat. Anglo-Lat.* 381 'What a rule is there?' *Quid turbæ est?* **1703** THORESBY *Let. to Ray*, 'What a reul's here! You make a nise reul'; i.e. work, mad work.

14. a. Control, government, sway, dominion.

c **1386** CHAUCER *Pars. T.* ¶217 Iob seith that in helle is noon ordre of rule. *c* **1400** *Apol. Loll.* (Camden) 73 Law canoun is callid law ordeynid of prelats of þe kirk,..to constreyn rebell bi holy rewl. *c* **1450** HOLLAND *Howlat* 968 Fra rule, ressoun and richt redless I ran. *a* **1533** LD. BERNERS *Huon* xx. 58, I pray and commaund that ye take in rule all my affayres. **1557** *Anc. Rec. Dublin* (1889) I. 466 In all places of cyvile rule and regiment. **1655** STANLEY *Hist. Philos.* (1701) 47/1 Enough has been said to deter any Man of sound Judgment from Rule. **1667** MILTON *P.L.* IV. 301 His fair large Front and Eye sublime declar'd Absolute rule. **1727** DYER *Grougar Hill* 89 A little rule, a little sway,..Is all the proud and mighty have Between the cradle and the grave. **1808** SCOTT *Marm.* VI. Introd. 40 Power laid his rod of rule aside. **1832** TENNYSON *Love thou thy land* xv, Phantoms of other forms of rule, New Majesties of mighty States. **1865** RUSKIN *Sesame* ii. §68 The woman's power is for rule, not for battle.

Comb. **1556** OLDE *Antichrist* 175 b, Their ambicion and desire of rule bearing.

b. With *a*, *the*, *that*, etc.

c **1420** LYDG. *Assembly of Gods* 1275 A rewle haue I must Withyn Macrocosme. **1462** *Paston Lett.* II. 83 Suche extorsyon..as hathe be do by suche as hathe had the rewyll. **1513** MORE in Grafton *Chron.* (1568) II. 778 He trusted by his death to obtayne much of the rule which the Lorde Hastinges bare in his countrie. **1562** TURNER *Baths* I Brimstone beareth the chefe rule. **1602** SHAKS. *Ham.* III. iv. 99 A Cutpurse of the Empire and the Rule. **1653** GATAKER *Vind. Annot. Jer.* 116 To exercise and execute that rule or regiment, whereunto they have assigned them. **1667** MILTON *P.L.* XII. 581 Though..thou..all the riches of this World enjoydst, And all the rule, one Empire.

15. a. The control or government *of* (= exercised by) a person or thing.

a **1340** HAMPOLE *Psalter* xi. 4 What is he til whas rewle & connersacioun we sall be vndirloute? **1390** GOWER *Conf.* I. 7 The people stod in obeissance Under the reule of governance. **1444** *Coventry Leet Bk.* I. 205 The for-namyd felauship..compromytted hem to abyde the Rule and ordynaunce of þe meire and his councell. **1538** STARKEY *England* I. ii. 53 Some pepul ther be to whome the rule of a prynce more agreth then a commyn counseyl. **1545** ASCHAM *Toxoph.* (Arb.) 150 Greter matters than shotynge are vnder the rule and wyll of the wether. **1681** DRYDEN *Abs. & Achit.* 333 If David's rule Jerusalem displease, The dog-star heats their brains to this disease. **1700** PRIOR *Carm. Sec.* xxv, Lead forth the Years for Peace and Plenty fam'd, From Saturn's Rule, and better Metal nam'd. **1758** BINNELL *Descr. Thames* 104 All Fishers, &c.,..coming to the City of London, shall be in the Rule of the Lord Mayor and Aldermen. **1818** SHELLEY *Rosalind* 934 Their jailors rule, they thought, Grew merciful. **1844** H. H. WILSON *Brit. India* III. 272 Ill-disposed and intriguing individuals, inimical to British rule. **1879** FROUDE *Cæsar* v. 46 The rule of an organised force was becoming the only possible protection against the rule of mobs.

†**b.** *to have one's own rule*, to be one's own master, to have one's way. *Obs.*

1390 GOWER *Conf.* I. 318 If that he mote His oghne rewle have upon honde, Ther schal no witt ben understonde. **1556** *Chron. Grey Friars* (Camden) 11 He wolde not be governyd by the bargemen, but to have hys owne rewle.

16. The control, management, government, etc. *of* (= exercised over or in) something.

1390 GOWER *Conf.* III. 161 The londes reule upon him stod. **1432** *Paston Lett.* I. 31 For the goode reule, demesnyng and seuretee of the Kynges persone. **1470–85** MALORY *Arthur* X. xxix. 460, I praye yow gyue me leue to haue the rule of the bataill. **1503–4** *Act 19 Hen. VII*, c. 27 §11 Havyng wythin the seid Towne of Calays the rule & guydyng of his maisters goodes and marchaundyse. **1598** SHAKS. *Merry W.* I. iii. 59 The report goes, she has all the rule of her husbands Purse. **1634** MILTON *Comus* 21 Neptune..Took in by lot..Imperial rule of all the Sea-girt Iles. **1667** —— *P.L.* X. 582 The Serpent, whom they calld Ophion with Eurynome,..had first the rule Of high Olympus. **1758** BINNELL *Descr. Thames* 106 In the Year 1448, an Act..was made, whereby the Mayor of London was to have the Rule of the River of Thames. **1790** BURKE *Fr. Rev.* 70 They aimed at the rule, not at the destruction of their country. **1876** FREEMAN *Norm. Conq.* IV. 69 The rule of the conquered land was entrusted to William Fitz-Osbern.

V. 17. a. A graduated strip of metal or wood (marked with feet, inches, etc.) used for measuring length, esp. by carpenters and masons.

1340 *Ayenb.* 150 Þes yefþe is þe maister of workes,..uor he deþ al to wylle and to þe line and to þe reule and to þe leade and to þe leuele. *c* **1391** CHAUCER *Astrol.* I. §13 Thanne hastow a brod Rewle, þat hath on either ende a Square plate perced with a certein holes. **1412** *York Fabric Rolls* (Surtees) 351/1 Pro levells, Squares, et reules, 20d. *c* **1440** *Promp. Parv.* 432/1 Rewle, ynstrument, *regula.* **1513** DOUGLAS *Æneis* VI. xv. 9 Sum bene mair crafty..With rewlis and with mesouris..For til excers the art of geometry. **1553** T. WILSON *Rhet.* 83 b, The carpenter hath his squyre, his rule, and his plummet. **1601** SHAKS. *Jul. C.* I. i. 7 Where is thy Leather Apron, and thy Rule? **1667** PRIMATT *City & C. Build.* 50 Such a Workman will afford to do his work cheaper, than others who walk with their Rules by their sides. **1708** SWIFT *Proc. Bickerstaff* Wks. 1751 IV. 207, I..was surprized to find my Gentleman..with a two-foot Rule in his hand, measuring my Walls. **1788** *Trans. Soc. Arts* VI. 191 A small Brass Rule..divided into quarters of an inch. **1833** HT. MARTINEAU *Vanderput & S.* ii. 25 You see that short man smoking with the rule in his hand. **1896** WOOLCOMBE *Pract. Work Physics* III. 69 Attach ..a strip of cardboard so that we may rest a rule upon them.

fig. **1606** SHAKS. *Ant. & Cl.* II. iii. 7, I haue not kept my square, but that to come Shall all be done by th' Rule. **1606** —— *Tr. & Cr.* V. ii. 133 Stubborne Criticks, apt..to square the generall sex By Cressids rule. **1622** MALYNES *Anc. Law-Merch.* 59 Moneys were inuented and made by common consent to be the rule and square to set a price vnto all things.

b. Without article, freq. coupled with *line* or *measure*. Chiefly *fig.*

1611 COTGR., *Reigleure*,..a proceeding by rule and line. **1634** SIR T. HERBERT *Trav.* 21 A Sharke..nine Foot long and a halfe by rule. **1638** R. BAKER tr. *Balzac's Lett.* (vol. II.) 72 With those that are deare to me, I neither observe Rule nor Measure. **1706** E. WARD *Wooden World Diss.* (1708) 72 He..professes to do every Thing by Rule and Measure. **1797** *Encycl. Brit.* (ed. 3) II. 248/1 Whether we take this method, or begin upon the naked floor, all must be laid with the most exact truth by rule and line. **1864** NEWMAN *Apol.* i. (1904) 17/2 The process of change had been slow; it had been done not rashly, but by rule and measure.

attrib. **1887** SAINTSBURY *Elizab. Lit.* xi. (1890) 409 He showed..a tendency towards a severe rule-and-line form both of tragic scheme and of tragic versification.

c. *to run the rule over* (one): (*a*) *Cant* see quot. 1874; (*b*) of police: to interrogate (a suspected criminal); (*c*) of a doctor of medicine: to examine (a patient).

1874 *Slang Dict.* 273 'To run the rule over,' is, among thieves, to try all a person's pockets quietly, as done by themselves, or to search any one thoroughly, as at the police-station. **1948** *Free-Lance Writer & Photographer* Apr. 54/2 When a P.C. stops a suspect in the street and interrogates him, he 'runs the rule over him'. **1953** *Times* 21 Oct. 1/5 Good afternoon, doctor, I don't suppose it's anything really, just a bit off-colour..thought you'd better run the—er—rule over me.

18. †**a.** A bar (of gold). *Obs.*

1382 WYCLIF *Josh.* vii. 21 Among the spuylis..two hundreth siclis of siluer, and a goldun rewle [L. *regula*] of fifti siclis. *c* **1425** WYNTOUN *Cron.* II. xii. 1082 Achor als þe mantil stal, þe siluir and þe rewel wiþe all.

†**b.** *Arch.* = REGLET 2. *Obs.*

1563 SHUTE *Archit.* Dj, Astragalus & his rule occupieth .I. part, the which rule is half the height of Astragalus.

c. *poet.* A shaft or beam *of* light.

1634 MILTON *Comus* 340 Som gentle taper..visit us With thy long levell'd rule of streaming light. **1745** WARTON in *Dodsley's Collect. Poems* (1782) IV. 225 The pale moon Pours her long-levell'd rule of streaming light.

d. *Plastering.* = SCREED.

1838 *Encycl. Metrop.* (1845) XXV. 176/1 The second coat ..is laid on..with the floting trowel, and floted to a straight, level surface, with rules of various lengths.

†**19. a.** Array, marshalled order or line. *Obs.*

1390 GOWER *Conf.* III. 120 Cancer after the reule and space Of Signes halt the ferthe place. *c* **1400** *Destr. Troy* 5678 Out of rule or aray raungit on lenght. **1470–85** MALORY *Arthur* XX. xii. 818 Thus they came in ordre & rule as ful noble knyghtes. **1513** DOUGLAS *Æneis* III. vi. 176 Thai leifis remainis onsterit of thair place, Ne partis nocht furth of reule.

†**b.** A line or row of figures, etc. *Obs.*

c **1425** *Crafte of Nombrynge* 4 Euery of þese figuris bitokens hym selfe & no more, yf he stonde in þe first place of þe rewele... If it stonde in the secunde place of þe rewle, he betokens tene tymes hym selfe. *c* **1440** *Pallad. on Husb.* IV. 526 Suspence in rewle, hem kepe with pusk condite Ypuld in myddis of a day serene.

†**20.** A straight line drawn on paper, *esp.* for the writing of music. *Obs.*

1597 T. MORLEY *Introd. Mus.* 3 A Cliefe is a charecter set on a rule at the beginning of a verse. *Ibid.*, Assigning to euerie space and rule a seuerall Keye. **1612** BRINSLEY *Lud. Lit.* 33 Cause them to haue each his ruling pen,..that they may rule their rules meete of the same compasse with their copies. **1662** PLAYFORD *Skill Mus.* I. i. (1674) 2 Seven Letters of the Alphabet, which are set in the first Column, at the beginning of each Rule and Space.

21. = RULER *sb.*[1] 3 b.

1703 MOXON *Mech. Exerc.* 281 Keeping one end of the Rule close to the Centre.., lay the other end of the Rule close to the Prick that you made on the line CD. **1826** SOUTHEY *Vind. Eccl. Angl.* 150 St. Fursey..happened to have in his hand a writer's rule, which he cast into the sea. **1860** J. SHERMAN in *Mem.* (1863) 23 The birch, the rule, the cane, were unsparingly used.

22. *Typog.* **a.** A thin slip of metal (usually brass) used for separating headings, columns of type, articles, etc., and in ornamental work; also a dash short or long in type-metal, thus - (en rule) or thus — (em rule), used in punctuation, etc.

1683 MOXON *Mech. Exerc., Printing* 18 He also provides Brass Rules of about Sixteen Inches long, that the Compositor may cut them into such Lengths as his Work requires. **1771** LUCKOMBE *Hist. Print.* 268 Full-points serve instead of Rules, in work of Accounts, to..connect the posted Article with its contingent valuation. **1824** J. JOHNSON *Typogr.* II. 67 Rules are of three descriptions, viz. brass, metal, or space rules. **1855** A. WYNTER *Curios. Civiliz.* 48 The partition of a thin rule suffices to separate a call for the loan of millions from the..cry of the destitute gentlewoman. **1892** A. OLDFIELD *Man. Typogr.* i, If rules are kept in standard sizes,..very little rule-cutting need be done.

b. Without article (*brass rule*), as a material.

1771 LUCKOMBE *Hist. Print.* 282 They may be counted valuable Sorts.., considering that they..save Brass rule. **1880** *Paper & Print. Trades Jrnl.* No. 32. 40 The groundwork of the design is a fan, made up in brass rule to the correct shape. **1892** A. OLDFIELD *Man. Typogr.* i, The cases of brass rule,..&c., are best kept mounted.

c. A composing- or setting-rule.

1683 MOXON *Mech. Exerc., Printing* 214 This Rule is very commodious to Work with, because the Letter slides easier. **1728** CHAMBERS *Cycl.* s.v. *Printing*, Taking the Rule from behind the last Line, he places it before it. **1892** A. OLDFIELD *Man. Typogr.* i, The notch at the back part of the rule allows of its being drawn out without so much being cut away at the fore edge of the rule.

23. *attrib.* and *Comb.* **a.** In sense 17, as ***rule-framer***, ***-staff***, ***-stone***, ***-trade***.

14.. *Deb. Carpenter's Tools* 171 in Hazlitt *E.P.P.* I. 85 Than seyd the rewle-stone, Mayster hath many fone. **1846** A. YOUNG *Naut. Dict.*, *Rule-staff*, a lath about four inches in breadth; used, in ship-building, for measuring the curve of a plank's edge in order to fay another plank to it. **1884** *B'ham Daily Post* 28 July 3/4 Rule framer..used to jointed, folding, and slipping work. **1892** *Pall Mall G.* 3 Oct. 7/2 He ..applied himself with..zeal to the rule trade.

b. In sense 22, as ***rule-border***, ***-cutter***, ***-cutting***, ***-ornament***, ***-work***.

1808 STOWER *Printer's Grammar* 94 Space rules..are, in intricate rule work,..neater than brass rule [etc.]. **1818** *Brathwait's Barnabees Jrnl.* Notes 85 All the capitals and rule ornaments used in the first edition. **1858** SIMMONDS *Dict. Trade*, *Rule-cutter*, a printers'-smith who prepares brass column and page-rules for printers. **1884** KNIGHT *Dict. Mech.* Suppl. 772/1 *Rule cutter*, a machine for cutting to lengths rules and leads. **1888** JACOBI *Printers' Vocab.* 116 *Rule borders*, a frame, usually of brass rule, fitted round a page. **1892** [see sense 22].

c. In sense 3, as ***rule formulation***, ***system***; ***rule-bound*** (hence ***-boundedness***), ***-giving***, ***-governed*** adjs.

1905 W. JAMES *Mem. & Stud.* (1911) v. 89 You ask for a free man, and these utopias give you an 'interchangeable part', with a fixed number, in a rule-bound organism. **1950** *Mind* LIX. 391 Why not say 'rule-giving' method? **1968** *Listener* 29 Aug. 266/2 Societies have defined and structured rule systems of reward and punishment. **1977** J. D. DOUGLAS in Douglas & Johnson *Existential Sociol.* i. 39 As Becker realized, there is almost always conflict over such presentations of rule-boundedness. **1977** A. GIDDENS *Stud. in Social & Polit. Theory* iii. 144 Universal pragmatics.. attempts to reconstruct the rule systems which allow actors to communicate in any type of context. **1978** C. HOOKWAY in Hookway & Pettit *Action & Interpretation* 27 If indeterminacy obtains it is likely to infect the translation of the object language into a meta-language involved in the rule-formulation. **1978** *Listener* 30 Mar. 396/2 To try to explain how the speaker's intentions, his rule-governed intentional behaviour, relates language to the world. **1979** *Dædalus* Summer 9 Rule-bound, conventional, and traditional ethics continue to hold their own. *Ibid.* 20 It remains a normal, rule-governed collective activity.

d. rule-box, a rectangle formed by ruled or printed lines.

1928 *Publishers' Weekly* 30 June 2605 Above the stamp.. must be *printed* the words..enclosed in a rule box.

e. *pl.* used *Comb.*, chiefly in senses 3 b and 5, as ***rulesmaker***, ***rulespeople***.

1963 *Punch* 20 Mar. 416/1 Does anyone ever know the order of the draw? Yes, the rulespeople. **1974** *Sunday* (Charleston, S. Carolina) 21 Apr. 3-A/3 Rulesmakers said politicians were put in a class by themselves, 'because they get to practice all year in their daily work'. **1978** *Detroit Free Press* 2 Apr. 6E/3 Whatever the coach can do for them, Bolinger-Boden-Markovich and all the other offensive linemen around have received very big help recently from the rulesmakers in their game.

rule (ruːl), *v.* Forms: 3 riwlen; 4–6 rewle (5 rewlen, -yn), 6 rewl(l; 4–5 rewele (4 -ely, reuw-, ruwele), 6 rewill, rewall; 4–5 reulen, 4–7 reule, 5–7 reull (5 reuyll); 4 ruelie, 4, 6 ruele, 7 ruil; 4 rulen, rulye, 5 rulyn, roul(e, 6 *Sc.* rull, 4– rule. [ad. OF. *riuler*, *rieuler*, *reuler*, *ruler*, etc. (see Godefroy):—L. *rēgulāre* to regulate, of which OF. *regler* (mod.F. *régler*) is a more learned adoption.]

I. 1. a. *trans.* To control, guide, direct, exercise sway or influence over (a person, his actions, life, etc.). †Also with inf.

a **1225** *Ancr. R.* 2 Moni cunne riwle beoð... þe on riwleð þe heorte. *a* **1340** HAMPOLE *Psalter* xxvi. 16 He takis me to norysch and to rewle, as fadire & modire. **1387** TREVISA *Higden* (Rolls) IV. 393 He was al i-ruled and i-ladde by ledynge and counsaille of mynstralles. **1422** tr. *Secreta Secret., Priv. Priv.* 136 Al this he didde for wrethe that this nobyll lordis hym roulide..in his tendyr age. **1447–8** J. SHILLINGFORD *Letters* (Camden) 47 That my lord of Exceter were avysed and ruled so to come. **1500–20** Dunbar *Poems* xx. 7 Trubill nevir thy self..Vthiris to rewill, that will not rewlit be. **1576** Fleming *Panopl. Epist.* 123 Your wisedome must so moderate and rule you. **1604** Shaks. *Oth.* ii. iii. 205 Now by Heauen, My blood begins my safer Guides to rule. **1638** Junius *Paint. Ancients* 166 Mercury..was esteemed to rule both our sleepe and our dreames. **1746** Francis tr. *Horace, Ep.* i. i. 35 But meaner precepts now my life must rule. **1812** Crabbe *Tales* ii. 406 Thus the frenzy ruled him. **1833** I. Taylor *Fanat.* i. 7 The very same spirit of kindness which should rule us in the performance of a task such as the one now in hand. **1871** R. Ellis tr. *Catullus* xlv. 15 So may he that is in this hour ascendant Rule us ever.

b. ***to be ruled***, to submit to counsel, guidance, or authority; to listen to reason. Also const. *by*.

c **1400** *Brut* lxxxii. 83 And when þe Emperour..saw þat Arthure wolde nouȝt bene rewelede by him, he lete assemble ..an huge hoste. **1470–85** Malory *Arthur* vi. iv. 187 And ye wylle be reulyd by me, I shal help you out of this distresse. **1500–20** Dunbar *Poems* xli. 7 Be rewlit rycht and keip this doctring. *a* **1616** Beaum. & Fl. *Little French Lawyer* iii. ii, 'Pray be rul'd Sir, This is the maddest thing. **1680** C. Ness *Church Hist.* 263 Be ruled, or you will rue it. **1731** Swift *On his Death* Wks. 1751 VII. 248 He would never take Advice: Had he been rul'd,..He might have liv'd these twenty Years. **1859** Tennyson *Enid* 1472 But listen to me, and by me be ruled. *c* **1921** D. H. Lawrence *Mr. Noon* viii, in *Mod. Lover* (1934) 266 It's just like him—but there you are. Those that won't be ruled can't be schooled.

2. a. To moderate, restrain, curb (one's appetites, etc.) by the exercise of self-control.

c **1380** Wyclif *Sel. Wks.* III. 107 þat alle þyne fyve wyttes scholde be yreuled after him. *c* **1400** tr. *Secreta Secret., Gov. Lordsh.* 70 In þy etynge þow shalt reule þy hond. **1579** Gosson *Sch. Abuse* (Arb.) 63 Though my selfe haue learned to rule mine owne talke, I can not snaffle the tounge of a Carper. **1611** Bible *Prov.* xvi. 32 He that ruleth his spirit [is better] then he that taketh a citie. **1820** Scott *Monast.* xix, The good Abbot..commanded Halbert to rule his temper.

refl. **1535** Coverdale *Prov.* xvi. 32 He that can rule him selfe, is more worth then he yᵗ wynneth a cite. **1855** Mrs. Gaskell *North & South* i. x. 126 Every one who rules himself to decency and sobriety of conduct. **1866** G. Macdonald *Ann. Q. Neighb.* xi. (1878) 225, I wanted chiefly to set forth the men that could rule themselves.

†**b.** *refl.* To conduct oneself, behave, act, in a certain way. *Obs.*

13.. *E.E. Allit. P.* B. 294 Þenne in worlde was a wyȝe.. Ful redy & ful ryȝtwys, & rewled hym fayre. *c* **1374** Chaucer *Troylus* v. 758 Who so wold..rewelyn hym by euery wightes wit shal he neuere þryue. **1470–85** Malory *Arthur* vii. xxvii. 254 Now auyse me..what shalle I saye and in what manere I shal rule me. **1500–20** Dunbar *Poems* xix. 1 How sowld I rewill me,..I wald sum wyisman wald dewyiss.

†**c.** *intr.* in the same sense. *Obs.*⁻¹

1399 Langl. *Rich. Redeles* iii. 272 To put hem in preson, a peere þouȝ he were; And not to rewle as reremys, and rest on þe daies.

†**d.** *dial.* To be unruly. *Obs.*⁻⁰

1691 Ray *N.C. Words, Reul*, to be rude, to behave ones self unmannerly, to rig.

3. †**a.** To exercise, administer, wield (some power or authority). *Obs.*

1390 Gower *Conf.* I. 12 But whil the lawe is reuled so,.. I not how that thei scholde amende The woful world. *a* **1450** *Cursor M.* 9549 (Laud), Wyth-out thise þe kyng had no myȝt For to rule his kynghed. *c* **1500** *Lancelot* 1971 His ministeris that shuld the Iustice reull. **1570** *Satir. Poems Reform.* xii. 34 Think ȝe with ressoun thay suld reule the rod.

b. To direct, guide, manage (a thing); to have under one's control.

1398 Trevisa *Barth. De P.R.* xii. ii. (Tollemache MS.), In swymmynge he [the swan] useþ þat on foot in stede of an ore, and þe oþer in stede of a roþer, and reuleþ him selfe þerwith. *a* **1400–50** *Alexander* 5542 [He] raȝt to þaim þire rekenthis to rewle & to hald. **1447–8** J. Shillingford *Lett.* (Camden) 36 Y most doe as y se the mater woll be ruled. **1526** Skelton *Magnyf.* 1460, I shall of Fortune rule the reyne. *a* **1578** Lindesay (Pitscottie) *Chron. Scot.* (S.T.S.) I. 8 Ane new courteour that rullit so the ruddar. **1630** Capt. Smith *Trav. & Adv.* 13 Being not able to rule his horse and defend himselfe, he was throwne to the ground. **1818** Shelley *Rev. Islam* iii. xxxi, I..dared not look upon the shape Of him who ruled the helm.

†**c.** *Sc.* To have charge or supervision of; to make (good) use of; to regulate (a clock). *Obs.*

1500–20 Dunbar *Poems* lii. 11 Ȝour Hienes can nocht gett ane meter..To rule ȝour robbis, and dress the sam. **1535** Lyndesay *Satyre* 2189 Sir, will ȝe reull this relict weill, All the wyfis will baith kis and kneill. **1595** *Extr. Aberd. Reg.* (1848) II. 114 To cause mend and rewll the knok within the said Gray Freiris Kirk.

4. a. To govern, to exercise sovereign power over, to control with authority.

1362 Langl. *P. Pl.* A. iv. 9 He schal reule my Reame and Rede me þe beste. **1387** Trevisa *Higden* (Rolls) III. 175 Oon of þe seuene wise men þat rulede þe kyngdom of Perses. *c* **1450** *Godstow Reg.* 13 There god reulith both angel and man. **1486** *Henry VII at York* in *Surtees Misc.* (1890) 54, I was regent and rewlid this rigion. **1535** Coverdale *Rev.* ii. 27 He shal rule them with a rodde of yron. **1593** Shaks. *2 Hen. VI*, v. i. 95 Thou art..Not fit to gouerne and rule multitudes. **1610** Healey *St. Aug. Citie of God* 720 Christ was assumed into heaven, and by him is the Church ruled. **1697** Dryden *Virg. Georg.* i. 8 Ye Deities..Who rule the Seasons, and the Year direct. **1735** Pope *Ep. Lady* 261 She, who ne'er answers till a Husband cools, Or, if she rules him, never shews she rules. **1764** Goldsm. *Traveller* 386 Laws grind the poor, and rich men rule the law. **1816** Scott *Antiq.* xxvi, Them that guide the purse rule the house. **1826** Disraeli *V. Grey* i. viii, To rule men, we must be men. **1879** Jefferies *Wild Life* vi, The belief in the power of certain persons to 'rule the planets' is profound.

b. *transf.* of things.

c **1449** Pecock *Repr.* ii. xvi. 242 These men aspieden weel ..that the seid parties of heuen reuliden ful myche the worchingis of bodies here binethe in the louȝer world. **1535** Coverdale *Gen.* i. 16 God made two greate lightes: one greater light to rule the daye, and a lesse light to rule the night. *c* **1640** Sir W. Mure *Ps.* cxxxvi. 8 The sunne to reull the day..Who did apoynt. **1697** Dryden *Virg. Georg.* iv. 530 Where Po first issues..And, awful in his Cradle, rules the Floods. **1726–46** Thomson *Winter* 1 See, Winter comes, to rule the varied year. **1748** Gray *Alliance* 80 Suspends th' inferior laws that rule our clay. **1822** Shelley *Triumph of Life* 256 The star that ruled his doom was far too fair. **1860** Tyndall *Glac.* i. xi. 79, I now found that mechanical laws rule man in the long run.

c. *Eccl.* To lead (a choir) in singing.

1898 Frere *Use of Sarum* I. 306 The rules for the days when the choir was ruled.

d. To dominate, prevail in.

1874 Symonds *Sk. Italy & Greece* (1879) 59 Soft undulating lines rule the composition.

5. *absol.* To exercise sovereignty, to govern; to hold supreme command or sway.

1509 Hawes *Past. Pleas.* i. (Percy Soc.) 7 The head must rule, it cannot be denied. **1562** J. Heywood *Prov. & Epigr.* (1867) 142 Better rule, then be rulde. **1616** Jonson *Epigr.* i. xxxv, T' obey A prince that rules by example, more than sway. **1667** Milton *P.L.* xii. 226 There they shall..thir great Senate choose Through the twelve Tribes, to rule by Laws ordaind. **1735** Pope *Prol. Sat.* 197 Such a man, too fond to rule alone. **1770** Goldsm. *Des. Vill.* 195 There, in his noisy mansion, skill'd to rule, The village master taught his little school. **1842** Tennyson *Godiva* 12 Godiva, wife to that grim Earl, who ruled In Coventry. **1865** Ruskin *Sesame* ii. §51 Substituting their own will for the law of justice and love by which all true kings rule.

(*b*) ***Rule, Britannia***: the usual name for a patriotic song sometimes sung on public occasions in Britain. Also as *attrib. phr.* Hence **Rule-Bri'tanniaism** chauvinism (*nonce-wd.*).

[**1740** Thomson & Mallett *Alfred* ii. v. 42 *Ode*... Rule, Britannia, rule the waves; Britons never will be slaves.] **1806** [see buff *sb.*² 6]. *a* **1888** *N.E.D.* s.v. *Briton*, The 'Rule Britania' period. **1898** *Academy* 8 Oct. 25/1 A preference for accuracy above Rule-Britanniaism. **1899** Kipling *Absent-Minded Beggar* 1 When you've shouted 'Rule Britannia', When you've sung 'God save the Queen'. **1918** *Daily Mirror* 12 Nov. 2/1 When the strains of 'Rule, Britannia!' rang out his Majesty raised his naval cap. **1936** G. B. Shaw *Simpleton* i. 24 Let the whole earth be England; and let Englishmen rule it. (Singing) Rule Britannia: Britannia rules the wa— He blows his brains out. **1941** 'G. Orwell' *Lion & Unicorn* 19 In England all the boasting and flag-wagging, the 'Rule Britannia' stuff, is done by small minorities. **1968** *Listener* 18 July 86/2 Judges are good at making grand Rule Britannia statements, like Judge Salmon's in 1958... 'Everyone..is entitled to walk the streets in peace,..and free from fear.'

b. Const. *over*, †*upon*.

1530 Palsgr. 695/2 This emperour ruleth upon mo regyons than any one man hath done in our tyme. **1611** Bible *Judges* viii. 23, I will not rule ouer you, neither shall my sonne rule ouer you: the Lord shall rule ouer you. **1691** Ray *Creation* i. (1692) 152 One..which by their help is enabled to rule over and subdue all inferiour Creatures. **1746** Francis tr. *Horace, Sat.* i. vii. 24 What time o'er Asia with pretorial sway Great Brutus ruled. **1812** Crabbe *Tales* xviii. 90 Better a woman o'er her house to rule, Than a poor child. **1841** Lane *Arab. Nts.* I. 2 Each of them ruling over his subjects with justice.

c. *transf.* of things.

a **1529** Skelton *Speke, Parrot* 415 Frantiknes dothe rule, and all thyng commaunde. **1591** Shaks. *1 Hen. VI*, iv. i. 111 What madnesse rules in braine-sicke men. **1657** Austen *Fruit Trees* ii. 120 Although the Graft be predominant and rule in bringing forth good fruits. **1667** Milton *P.L.* vi. 848 One Spirit in them rul'd, and every eye Glar'd lightning. **1746** Francis tr. *Horace, Sat.* i. iii. 106 Yet while Reason rules, Let it hold forth its scales with equal hand. **1810** Crabbe *Borough* vii. 128 This love of life, which in our nature rules, To vile imposture makes us dupes and tools. **1865** Mozley *Miracles* vii. 290 In matters of ordinary life common sense of itself rules.

d. Slang phr. —— ***rule(s), O.K.***, used orig. in wall graffiti to affirm the superiority of a gang, football team, etc. Freq. in *transf.* use.

1975 S. Jacobson in *New Society* 27 Mar. 780 (*title*) Chelsea rule—okay. **1976**, etc. [see O.K. A. a]. **1981** *Times* 31 June 1/1 It is a case of the tobacco industry rules, OK.

6. *Comm.* **a.** Of prices: To be at a certain rate; to be current or prevalent.

1629 *Reg. Privy Counc. Scotl.* Ser. ii. III. 11 Till they be trewlie informed how the pryces of the said victuall rules in suche parts of the countrie. **1653** Urquhart *Rabelais* i. xxv, The shepherds courteously intreated them to give them some for their money, as the price then ruled in the market. **1822–56** De Quincey *Confess.* Wks. 1862 I. 138 Which same prices..ruled..among the same kind of scenery. **1889** *Daily News* 28 May 2/8 Sales dragged somewhat, prices ruling about the same as on Monday last. **1964** *Financial Times* 3 Mar. 2/3 Prices yesterday ruled fully firm for all descriptions of merino fleece and skirtings.

b. Of commodities or trade: To bear a (specified) current price or value; to maintain a (given) average or quality. Also *transf.*

1690 W. Walker *Idiomat. Anglo-Lat.* 381 How rule swine here? **1859** Reade *Love me little* I. xii. 312 The Greek stock ruled from 56½–59. **1881** *Daily News* 17 Jan. 3/4 Trade ruled dull at barely late rates. **1887** W. Rye *Norf. Broads* 77 Things rule at starvation prices here. **1909** *Chambers's Jrnl.* June 409/1 During the past year the longest period when the wind velocity ruled below five miles per hour was only seven days. **1979** *Morning News* (Karachi) 24 May 7/1 In the jutes section Indus and Pak Jute ruled firm. Sugar shares were irregular.

c. To go in a certain way; to have a certain character, place, or quality.

a **1676** Bp. Guthrie *Mem.* (1702) 28 The Commissioners ..sent privately to him his Neighbour my Lord Cranston, to bring them intelligence how Matters ruled above. **1890** *John Bull* 5 Apr. 222/3 If these opinions..rule uppermost in the minds of the other eleven members of the Committee. **1891** *Daily News* 30 Sept. 4/6 Fields ruled good, and some interesting racing was witnessed.

II. 7. To bring *into* a certain state by laying down a rule; also ***to rule into***, to confine within (school bounds).

c **1449** Pecock *Repr.* iii. iv. 297 Therfore it [*sc.* the text] reulith no more prelatis into pouerte than ech lay persoon into pouerte. **1893** Leland *Mem.* I. 91 Freedom from bad marks, and being ruled into bounds, and sent to bed at early hours.

8. a. To lay down judicially or authoritatively; to decide, determine, declare formally. In later use const. *that*, or with *out of*. Also with object and complement.

1425 *Rolls of Parlt.* IV. 267 Howe þat courte had ruled his presence to been absent. **1642** C. Vernon *Consid. Exch.* 26 The..Remembrancer is not to rule any such petition for an absolute *exon.* [etc.]. **1818** Cruise *Digest* (ed. 2) VI. 356 This case was heard before the Privy Council in 1730, when it was ruled that Lucretia took an estate tail. **1850** J. H. Newman *Difficulties of Anglicans* (1891) I. i. i. 15 Public opinion.. rules that every conclusion is absurd..except such as it recognizes itself. **1885** *Manch. Exam.* 16 May 6/1 Mr. O'Brien..was ruled out of order on an attempt to discuss the political bearings of the recent visit to Ireland. **1928** H. G. Wells *Mr. Blettsworthy* iii. 154 He it was had first ruled me insane and immune from Reproof.

ellipt. **1884** *Law Rep. 26 Chanc. Div.* 650 The sheriff was ruled for not returning an attachment against Briggs.

†**b.** To appoint or order (a person) *to* receive or do something. *Obs.*

1463 *Bury Wills* (Camden) 24 And though William rewle hym to haue it and his yssew male, for defawte of hem I wille yᵉ seid John meryte next. **1473–5** in *Cal. Proc. Chanc. Q. Eliz.* (1830) II. Pref. 58 Which John Saunder, by auctorite of this court, is ruled to enterplede with the seide Johan.

c. To decide, settle; to decree.

1843 J. H. Newman *Eccl. Miracles* 105 Without ruling open questions this way or that. **1850** Thackeray *Pendennis* liv, This most complaisant of men would have seen no harm, ..if Pendennis the elder had so ruled it. **1873** Mrs. H. King *Disciples, Ugo Bassi* vii. (1877) 252 An order came To set us free; the statesmen having ruled Our ransom.

d. To shut or put *out* by formal decision. Also, more generally: to eliminate as a possibility; to make impossible; to decide against. orig. *U.S.*

1869 'Mark Twain' *Innoc. Abr.* li. 539 Though they have been ruled out of our modern Bible, it is claimed that they were accepted gospel twelve or fifteen centuries ago. **1883** —— *Life on Mississippi* xlv. 413 One of these [mules] had to be ruled out, because he was so fast that he turned the thing into a one-mule contest. **1890** *Spectator* 7 May, Resolved not to see expressions ruled out of the language merely because they are new. **1893** *Times* 6 May 13/4 Four instructions were ruled out..as capable of being dealt with in Committee. **1903** J. St. L. Strachey in 'Vigilans sed Æquus' *German Ambitions* p. vii, To rule out the writings of the men on whom 'Vigilans sed Æquus' has based his Letters because they are obscure..is to misunderstand the evolution of public affairs in Germany. **1925** N. E. Odell in E. F. Norton *Fight for Everest: 1924* 335 The disadvantage of the North Col is the fact that the camp here must be pitched on snow, though under all but the worst conditions this need not rule it out. **1928** *Daily Tel.* 12 June 13/4 The possibility of a battle between the rival Southern commanders cannot be ruled out. **1966** C. Mackenzie *Paper Lives* vi. 85 The Right Honourable Henry Upjohn thought for a moment about trying that joke at the next political meeting in his constituency but ruled it out at once. **1971** I. Butykai tr. *Lukovich's Electric Foil Fencing* ii. 84 Certain parts should be ruled out as being compulsory so that the combined movement should present an acceptable, applicable and expedient picture. **1976** *National Observer* (U.S.) 13 Nov. 5/2 Nothing in the group's by-laws rules out inmates, officials said, so the invitations stand. The prisoners said they were 'very pleasantly surprised' to find they could join Phi Kappa Phi.

e. With *in*, used in opposition to sense 8 d above.

1904 G. B. Shaw *Let.* 6 Dec. (1972) II. 471 It is just this personality that rules her out, whereas if we had a scrap of originality it would rule her in. **1973** *Observer* 17 June 1/1, I haven't ruled it out and I haven't ruled it in.

III. †**9.** To arrange or set in order. *Obs.*

c **1475** *Rauf Coilȝear* 466 Dyamountis and Sapheir, Riche Rubeis in feir, Reulit full richt. *Ibid.* 670 The rufe reulit about in reuall of Reid, Rose reulit ryally [etc.].

10. a. To mark (paper, etc.) with parallel straight lines drawn with a ruler or by a machine.

c **1440** *Promp. Parv.* 432/1 Rewlyn, wythe instrument, *regulo*. **1530** Palsgr. 695/2 This paper is nat well ruled, I can nat pricke upon it. **1565** Cooper *Thesaurus* s.v. *Linea*, To rule a booke. **1611** Cotgr. s.v. *Rosette*, Red Inke to rule bookes with. **1669** Sturmy *Mariner's Mag.* v. iv. 16 You must rule your Paper or Parchment with..Merid. Lines, and Parallel Lines. **1798** Hutton *Course Math.* II. 54 Some sort of a field-book must be used... This book every one contrives and rules as he thinks fittest for himself. **1865** Dickens *Mut. Fr.* i. iii, He finished ruling the work he had in hand in a very neat and methodical manner. **1872** Hardy *Under Greenw. Tree* Pref., Just enough..to pay for their fiddle-strings, rosin, and music-paper (which they mostly ruled themselves).

b. *Comm.* With *off*: to close (the books) for the day. Also *absol.*

1977 *Times* 17 Sept. 20/4 Books were eventually ruled off within a band of 5¾–6¼ per cent. **1978** *Times* 15 Aug. 18/8 Closing balances were being found at sharply lower levels, so that books were eventually ruled off within a band of 4½ per cent to 6¾ per cent. *Ibid.* 17 Aug. 21/3 Houses ruled off anywhere between 2 per cent and 4 per cent.

11. To form or mark out (a line) with or as with a ruler.

1599 Drayton *Idea* xliii, Age rules my lines with wrinkles in my face. **1819** *Pantologia, Ruled-paper*, paper on which the staves are ruled for receiving the written notes of any musical composition. **1875** KNIGHT *Dict. Mech.* 2001/1 The round form [of ruler] is very convenient for ruling parallel lines by one accustomed to its use.

fig. **1634** FORD *Perk. Warbeck* III. ii, What our destinies Have ruled out in their books, we must not search, But kneel to. **1820** LAMB *Elia* I. *South-sea House*, His actions seemed ruled with a ruler. **1860** TYNDALL *Glac.* I. xxvii. 206 The sunbeams..ruled a beam of light across the glacier. **1924** R. CAMPBELL *Flaming Terrapin* i. 18 As he rose up, the moon with slanted ray Ruled for those rapid hoofs a shining way.

ruled (ru:ld), *ppl. a.* [f. RULE *v.*]

1. †**a.** Subjected to control, guidance, or discipline. Also ***well-ruled***, well-conducted. *Obs.*

c **1385** CHAUCER *L.G.W.* Prol. 163 Pitee..mad mercy passen ryght Thurgh Innocence and ruled curtesye. **1406** HOCCLEVE *La Male Regle* 70 Why wilt thow nat enclyne, And vn-to reuled reform bowe thee? **1453** *Rolls of Parlt.* V. 267/2 Diverse and many well ruled persones. **1526** *Coventry Leet Bk.* (E.E.T.S.) 692 Euery aldemman..shall elect & chose onest & well ruled persones within his warde to be constables. **1556** [see RULELESS *a.* 1]. **1736** AINSWORTH *Eng.-Lat. Dict.* s.v., A well-ruled city, *civitas bene morata.*

b. Governed; subject. In quots. *absol.*

1847 TENNYSON *Princ.* Concl. 53 God bless the narrow sea which..keeps our Britain, whole within herself, A nation yet, the rulers and the ruled. **1875** HOPPS *Princ. Relig.* x. 32 He may become a hero, and, though punished by the rulers, may be rewarded by the ruled.

†**2.** According to rule; regular. *Obs.*

1551 RECORDE *Pathw. Knowl.* I. Defin., Cinkangles, whose sydes partlye are all equall.., and those are counted ruled cinkeangles, and partlye unequall.., and they are called unruled.

3. Judicially or authoritatively determined. ***ruled case***, an established decision or ruling.

1567–9 JEWEL *Def. Apol.* (1611) 453 This Decree in old times stood as a ruled case. **1611** SPEED *Hist. Gt. Brit.* IX. viii. §20. 544/1 When the will of a Ruler, is a rule, or ruled-case to his Iudges. **1681** FLAVEL *Meth. of Grace* xxviii. 498 The wisest and holiest among men may pretend no higher than a ruled rule. **1714** R. FIDDES *Pract. Disc.* II. 6 We have both precept, Col. 2. 18, and what amounts in effect to a ruled case to the contrary, Rev. 22. 9. *a* **1740** WATERLAND *Arg. a Priori* Wks. 1823 IV. 407 This author looked upon it as a ruled point, a thing universally agreed to.

4. Marked with parallel straight lines.

1691 WOOD *Ath. Oxon.* I. 756 Desiring the use of Ink and rul'd paper (such as we call Musical Paper). **1758** L. TEMPLE *Sketches* (ed. 2) 34 He writes but like a School-boy, who keeps in the Line only with the Help of ruled Paper. **1817** MRS. SHELLEY in Dowden *Life Shelley* (1887) II. 148 Remember..to bring me a good thick book to write extracts in, ruled. **1855** MACAULAY *Hist. Eng.* xxii. IV. 700 The neatly ruled pages of the subscription book..were still blank. **1892** *Photogr. Ann.* II. 178 A good ruled screen is obtained on development.

5. Formed with, or as with, a ruler.

1843 RUSKIN *Mod. Paint.* (1897) I. II. i. §7. 118 A violent, black, sharp, ruled penmanlike line. **1898** *Allbutt's Syst. Med.* V. 446 The number of red corpuscles in it will be.. crowded over the surface of the ruled squares.

b. *Geom.* ***ruled surface*** (see quot.).

1862 SALMON *Anal. Geom. Three Dim.* 75 A surface generated by the motion of a right line is called a ruled surface.

6. Measured with the rule.

1823 P. NICHOLSON *Pract. Build.* 345 The fine red cutting bricks are used for ruled and gauged work.

†**'ruledom.** *Obs.* [f. RULE *sb.* + -DOM.] Rule, sovereignty, sway.

1581 DERRICKE *Image Irel.* II. E iv, The hautie hartes of Woodkarne desire ruledome, but they shall haue a rope. **1612** R. CARPENTER *Soule's Sent.* 13 Where is that..happy estate of ruledome and renowne, which..time hath not ruinated? **1690** C. NESSE *Hist. O. & N. Test.* I. 218 The priviledge of primogeniture..gave him a ruledom over his younger brother.

†**'rulefully,** *adv.* *Obs.*⁻¹ [f. RULE *sb.*] According to rule; regularly.

a **1400** in Halliwell *Rara Mathem.* (1841) 65 Þe side of þe quadrat bitwene A and B mote be persede reulefully.

rule-joint. [RULE *sb.* 17.] A movable joint such as is used for measuring-rules. Also *attrib.*

1782 *Phil. Trans.* LXXII. 385 In this arm..is a kind of rule joint at *d*, that the arm may give way easily if wanted. **1825** J. NICHOLSON *Operat. Mechanic* 592 To make a rule joint for a window-shutter, or other folding flap. **1833** LOUDON *Encycl. Archit.* §84 To put inch clamped..folding shutters, with rule joints (joints like those of the common foot rule). **1875** KNIGHT *Dict. Mech.* 1927/1 A bit having a rule joint. **1966** A. W. LEWIS *Gloss. Woodworking Terms* 47 *Rule-joint hinge*, brass hinge with one long and one short leaf and with the countersinking for the screw heads on the opposite side to the knuckle. *Ibid.* 95 *Stay*, metal fitting which limits the movement of a door or lid, e.g. a shad stay, or a rule-joint stay.

ruleless ('ru:llɪs), *a.* Forms: 5 **rewleless**, 6 **rew-, rulesse**, 7 **rulelesse, rule-less**, 7, 9 **ruleless.** [f. RULE *sb.* + -LESS.]

1. Ungoverned; lawless, unruly, unrestrained; not subject to rule or order.

1443 *Pol. Poems* (Rolls) II. 212 [The] Queene of hevene lay in a symple hous, A poore stable, mong beestys rewleless. **1556** J. HEYWOOD *Spider & Fly* xcii. 115 Let rewld lords rewle rewlesse losels, when they crake. **1587** *Mirr. Mag., Morindus* x, Three yeares I ruled had this Ile Without all rule, as was my rulesse life. **1642** FULLER *Answ. Ferne* 13 How injurious doth he..labour to make the King to his posterity, as well as rulelesse in himselfe? **1689** E. HOWARD *Caroloiades* 273 Some Man, By drink made ruleless.

1837 CARLYLE *Fr. Rev.* II. I. i, Man indeed..lives in this world to make rule out of the ruleless. **1858** —— *Fredk. Gt.* III. i. (1872) I. 138 He came as the representative of law and rule; and there had been many helping themselves by a ruleless life, of late.

2. Devoid of rules, irregular.

1867 *Macm. Mag.* Apr. 521/2 This [i.e. English] seemed an altogether ruleless and unruly language.

Hence **'rulelessness.**

1879 *Academy* July 43/3 Its rulelessness, or want of rules that can be comprehended, is curiously illustrated here. **1969** P. ANDERSON in Cockburn & Blackburn *Student Power* 222 Durkheim's account..produced the concept of anomie —the unceasing reproduction of subjective rulelessness by a society that is defined by its ensemble of objective rules.

†**'rulely,** *adv.* *Obs.*⁻¹ In 4 **reweleliche.** [irreg. f. RULE *sb.* + -LY².] Regularly.

c **1380** WYCLIF *Wks.* (1880) 317 Þei maken hem a rewele to ryse reweleliche at mydnyȝt.

'rule-maker. [RULE *sb.*]

1. One who frames a rule or rules; a maker of regulations. Hence **'rule-making** *sb.*

1680 V. ALSOP *Mischief Impos.* iv. 21 There are very crooked rules in the world; and who must be the Rule-maker, for there are many pretenders? **1879** P. BROOKS *Influence of Jesus* 121 A mere rule-maker can have no personal considerations. **1893** *Westm. Gaz.* 26 Apr. 1/3 It behoves the rule-makers to be..scrupulously particular as to fairness and equity. **1926** *Amer. Bar Assoc. Jrnl.* XII. 599 Study..of rule-making in action in those states where the courts still retain much of their rule-making powers. **1946** *Nature* 21 Dec. 894/1 In Africa the rule-making power of native authorities can have a significant influence on future developments in this field. **1964** GOULD & KOLB *Dict. Social Sci.* 385/2 In sociology and related fields, *legislation* is sometimes applied to the function and products of rule-making by any agency, governmental or private, the rules of which are normally accepted by the persons to whom they apply. **1979** *Railway Age* 31 Dec. 14/2 The ICC Bureau of Operations agreed with the proposal to institute a rulemaking, but was less eager than the OPA to see IPD eliminated.

2. A maker of measuring-rules.

1723 *Lond. Gaz.* No. 6170/8 James Watson,..Rulemaker. **1845** *Penny Cycl.* Suppl. I. 198/1 Ring makers and turners, 40; rule-makers, 174.

rule of thumb. Also hyphened. [RULE *sb.*]

1. A method or procedure derived entirely from practice or experience, without any basis in scientific knowledge; a roughly practical method. Also, a particular stated rule that is based on practice or experience.

1692 SIR W. HOPE *Fencing-Master* 157 What he doth, he doth by rule of Thumb, and not by Art. **1721** KELLY *Scot. Prov.* 257 No Rule so good as Rule of Thumb, if it hit. **1785** GROSE *Dict. Vulgar T.*, *Thumb*, by rule of thumb, to do a thing by dint of practice. **1802** *Sporting Mag.* XX. 17 Too often did she apportion the drugs by the rule of thumb. **1865** M. ARNOLD *Ess. Crit.* v. 159 The English..have in all their changes proceeded, to use a familiar expression, by the rule of thumb. **1887** BESANT *World Went* xxv, [He] knew nothing save by rule of thumb of navigation. **1906** [see *drill book* s.v. DRILL *sb.*² 7 b]. **1965** C. D. EBY *Siege of Alcázar* (1966) vii. 135 In doubtful cases a rule of thumb applied: if the prisoner employed one servant in his household or two workers in his business, then he was a Fascist. **1967** G. F. FIENNES *I tried to run a Railway* ii. 14 George Jackson who timed by rule of thumb faster and as accurately as any Grapher. **1976** *Inorg. Chem.* XV. 1032/2 The i.r. spectra..show no apparent deviation from the rule of thumb that vibrational spectra of mixed-valence compounds are approximate superpositions of the single-valence spectra. **1976** *Southern Even. Echo* (Southampton) 11 Nov. 3/7 The rule of thumb over the tenancy of a council home should be 'follow the children'. **1977** *National Observer* (U.S.) 1 Jan. 7/2 The usual rule of thumb in the real-estate business is that a family can afford a house 2 to 2½ times its income. **1980** *Jrnl. R. Soc. Arts* Feb. 166/2 By day that same boy's master, and overlooker, and fellow-workmen, are all teaching him..that rule of thumb is the only safe guide.

transf. **1773** GOLDSM. *Stoops to Conquer* III, Ask me no questions and I'll tell you no fibs. I procured them by the rule of thumb.

2. *attrib.* **a.** Of methods, etc.: Based merely upon practice or experience. Also in predicative use.

1837 LOCKHART *Scott* (1839) VIII. 92 Beyond this rule of thumb calculation, no experience could bring him to penetrate his mystery. **1861** HUGHES *Tom Brown at Oxf.* xxi. (1889) 196 We never learnt anything..except a little rule-of-thumb mathematics. **1878** ABNEY *Photogr.* Pref., Though rapid advance has been made of late years in rule of thumb photography. **1935** E. WAUGH *Edmund Campion* ii. 55 Old-fashioned priests..came to him when they found their simple, rule-of-thumb dialectics insufficient to cope with their trained opponents. **1947** E. M. FORSTER in *Harper's Mag.* July 15/2 Virginia Woolf..believed in reading a book twice. The first time she abandoned herself to the author unreservedly. The second time she treated him with severity and allowed him to get away with nothing he could not justify. After these two readings she felt qualified to discuss the book. Here is good rule of thumb advice. **1962** W. NOWOTTNY *Lang. Poets Use* iii. 53 This attitude..however rule-of-thumb it may be, is reasonable enough. **1977** *N.Y. Rev. Bks.* 24 Nov. 16/1 Ridiculing the 'rule of thumb' methods used in the household.

b. Of persons: Working only by methods derived from practice.

1841 B. HALL *Patchwork* III. 83 Unlooked-for results often occur to distract the mere rule-of-thumb navigator. **1878** ABNEY *Photogr.* (1890) 10 A great difficulty to the beginner or to the rule-of-thumb photographer. **1947** [see NOMOGRAPHER].

Hence **rule-of-'thumbite**, a person who works by rule of thumb (*nonce-wd.*).

1916 H. G. WELLS *Mr. Britling* I. i. 16 Ruskin and Morris ..were as reactionary and anti-scientific as the dukes and the bishops. Machine haters. Science haters. Rule of Thumbites to the bone.

ruler ('ru:lə(r)), *sb.*¹ Forms: 4–6 **rewler**, 5–6 **rewlar**; 4 **reulor**, 4–6 **reuler**, 5 **reulure**, 6 **reular**; 6 **rueler, -ar**; 4–5 **rulere**, 5–7 **rular**, 5– **ruler.** [f. RULE *v.* + -ER¹.]

1. One who, or that which, exercises rule, command, or authority, *esp.* of a supreme or sovereign kind: **a.** Const. *of*, *over*, †*upon*.

c **1375** *Cursor M.* 4643 (Fairf.), He sal be rewler of al my lande. **1382** WYCLIF *Exod.* xviii. 21 Ordeyne of hem rewlers vpon thowsaundes, and rewlers vpon hundrethes, and rewlers vpon fifti. *c* **1420** LYDG. *Assembly of Gods* 995 The Lord of Macrocosme and rewler of that fee. **1470–85** MALORY *Arthur* XXI. i. 839 As syr Mordred was rular of alle englond. **1526** *Pilgr. Perf.* (W. de W. 1531) 224 b, Labourynge to..withdrawe yᵉ people..from the dominyon of kynges, lordes, and rulers of the temporalty. **1591** SHAKS. *1 Hen. VI*, III. ii. 11 We be Lords and Rulers ouer Roan. **1611** BIBLE *Gen.* xli. 43 He made him ruler ouer all the land of Egypt. **1757** W. WILKIE *Epigoniad* II. 49 Stern ruler of the sky! Whose sport is man, and human misery. **1784** COWPER *Task* IV. 120 Winter, ruler of th' inverted year. **1845** S. AUSTEN *Ranke's Hist. Ref.* II. 233 The Roman emperor.. was in future to be the sole protector and ruler of the country. **1875** JOWETT *Plato* (ed. 2) IV. 22 Men of old, who affirmed mind to be the ruler of the universe.

b. Without const.

1526 TINDALE *Acts* vii. 27 Who made the a ruelar and a iudge amonge vs? **1593** SHAKS. *2 Hen. VI*, V. i. 105 By heauen thou shalt rule no more O're him, whom heauen created for thy Ruler. **1641** THORNDIKE *Govt. Churches* 92 Rulers or Helps in the government, Elders of the people. **1665** BOYLE *Occas. Refl.* IV. xi. (1848) 231 Whereas..other Artificers work upon inanimate Materials, a Ruler must manage free Agents. **1717** POPE *Iliad* X. 473 Other Rulers those proud Steeds demand. **1781** COWPER *Retirem.* 104 Compar'd with this sublimest life below, Ye kings and rulers, what have courts to show? **1821** BYRON *Sardanap.* II. i, 'Tis thy natal ruler—thy birth planet. **1878** GLADSTONE *Primer Homer* 113 The absurd idea that the nation exists for the rulers, and not the rulers for the nation.

2. a. One who has control, management, or headship within some limited sphere. Now *Obs.* or *arch.* except with suggestion of sense 1.

c **1380** WYCLIF *Wks.* (1880) 242 Lordis..maken summe prestis stiwardis of here housholde..& summe conseileris & reuleris of here worldly plees. **1387** TREVISA *Higden* (Rolls) VIII. 259 Þe popes legat þat was rulere of pilgremages in þe Holy Lond. **1466** in *Archaeologia* (1887) L. I. 50 We beyng Rewlers and gouernerse of the parissch of seynt Stephan in Colmanstrete. **1480** *Bury Wills* (Camden) 65 The maister, precedent, or othir reuler of the colage of preestes. **1511–2** *Act 3 Hen. VIII*, c. 3 §1 The father, governours and rulers of such as be of tendre age. **1526** TINDALE *Mark* v. 22 There cam vnto hym won of the rulers of the sinagogge. **1555** *Act 2 & 3 Phil. & Mary* c. 7 §2 The said Ruler or Keeper of the said Fair or Market. **1766** *Ann. Reg.* 134 The Rulers of the Watermens company attended. **1864** *Reader* 21 May 652/1 The rulers of the British Museum are an irresponsible corporation.

transf. **1562** TURNER *Baths* 13 Savonarola..telleth that the chefe ruler is alume.

b. ***ruler of the choir***, a cantor. Now only *arch.*

1485 *Rutland Papers* (Camden) 21 Thoffice of the masse.. shalbe begon of the rulers of the quere with the *Kyrie* [etc.]. *a* **1538** *Acc. St. Michael Cornhill* (1871) 208 One discrete preste shalbe chosen by the Parson..to be a Ruler or Deane of the quyre in executing and seying the dyvyne servyce. **1853** ROCK *Ch. of Fathers* IV. xii. 136 The rulers of the choir, or..chanters, were arrayed in silken copes. **1877** J. D. CHAMBERS *Divine Worship* 146 Let this be sung by Rulers, Clerk, Choir, and people together.

3. †**a.** = RULE *sb.* 17. *Obs.* **b.** A straight-edged strip or cylinder, usually of wood or ivory, used for guiding a pen, pencil, or marking-instrument in forming straight lines upon paper, etc.

parallel ruler(s): see PARALLEL *a.* 1 b.

a **1400** in Halliwell *Rara Mathem.* (1841) 68 Biholde þe ende of þat oþer side þe ryver by a reulure vpon þe table.. And drawe a lyne by þe reulure on þe table. **14..** *Nom.* in Wr.-Wülcker 682 *Hoc regulare*, a rewler. **1530** PALSGR. 264/2 Ruler for a carpentar, *nieuau.* **1551** RECORDE *Pathw. Knowl.* I. 24 More easyly..may you fynde and make any suche line with a true ruler, layinge the edge of the ruler to the edge of the circle. **1634** WITHER *Embl.* 164 A Ruler or a square Or such like instruments, as usefull are In forming other things. **1656** H. PHILLIPS *Purch. Patt.* (1676) 142 Divide your ruler first into Inches, and then each inch into 10 or 100 parts. **1709** BERKELEY *Ess. Vision* §61 Take an inch marked upon a ruler. *c* **1790** IMISON *Sch. Arts* II. 17 Their use is first to measure (by help of a scale of equal parts upon the edge of your ruler) your proportions. **1834–6** *Encycl. Metrop.* (1845) VIII. 663/1 Hammering out a bar of the best iron into the form of a flat ruler. **1893** VIZETELLY *Glances Back* I. ii. 33 Pounding away at their knuckles with an ebony ruler.

c. (See quots.)

1728 CHAMBERS *Cycl.* s.v. *Glass*, To form the Thickness of a Glass, there are two iron Rulers, or Rims, placed around the edge of the Table. **1866** BRANDE & COX *Dict. Sci.* II. 737/2 The holes of each row [of organ pipes] are opened and shut by a register or ruler pierced with holes equal in number to the keys.

4. A workman who rules straight lines in account-books, etc. Also in comb. ***paper-ruler***.

1858 SIMMONDS *Dict. Trade*, *Paper-ruler*, a workman who lines paper by hand.

†**5.** (See quot.) *Obs.*

1820 F. MacDonogh *Hermit in London* IV. 122 Another class of men is what we call 'rulers'. These are men who bear a dollar's worth of liberty in their pocket, namely a four and sixpenny day rule, under pretence of settling with their creditors, or of attending to their affairs.

6. *Comb.* (sense 3 b) ***ruler-straight*** adj.; (sense 1) **ruler-cult** *Antiq.*, worship offered to a hereditary ruler; also *transf.*

1928 A. D. Nock in *Jrnl. Hellenic Stud.* XLVIII. (*title*) Notes on ruler-cult. **1951** M. P. Nilsson *Cults, Myths, Oracles, & Politics in Anc. Greece* iii. 108 The ruler cult was from the age of the Epigoni the state religion of the Hellenistic monarchies in the East. **1958** *Times* 15 Nov. 9/7 Revolutionary and critical times may produce the phenomenon we call ruler-cult. **1960** *Lebende Sprachen* V. 35/3 Ruler-straight seam, schnurgerade Naht. **1963** A. Lubbock *Austral. Roundabout* 14 The horizon meets the sky in a ruler-straight line.

†**'ruler,** *a.* and *sb.*[2] *Obs.* In 4 ruleer, reuleer, reweler. [ad. OF. *reuler*, *riuler*, etc.:—L. *rēgulāris* regular.]

1. = regular A. 1 and D. 2.

a **1380** *St. Bernard* 466 in Horstm. *Altengl. Leg.* (1878) 49 A chanoun ruleer to him com. **1399** *Rolls of Parlt.* III. 424/1 Abbotes and Priours, and all other men of holy Chirche Seculers and Rewelers.

2. = canonical *a.* 2.

a **1390** *Wycliffite Bible, Prol. Prov.*, Redeth hem..the chirche, but among the reuleer scripturis resceyueth not.

'ruler, *v. colloq.* [f. ruler *sb.*[1] 3 b.] *trans.* To beat or rap with a ruler.

1850 Dickens *Dav. Copp.* vii, I think he was caned every day that half-year, except on holiday Monday, when he was only ruler'd on both hands. **1894** N. Brooks *Tales Maine Coast* 22 Girls were not 'rulered' in that school.

'rulered, *ppl. a. poet.* [f. ruler *sb.*[1] (sense 3 b) + -ed[1].] = ruled *ppl. a.* 4.

1952 L. MacNeice *Ten Burnt Offerings* 50 Steam is a dry word; the best word is water... Best in the East..on the rulered page of a Moghul garden—Cool marrow of marble spines.

'ruleress. *rare.* A female ruler.

1648 Hexham ii, s.v. *Regeerster.* **1937** G. Frankau *More of Us* xii. 125 Was this The ruleress of waves, R.N., all-British, Who stooped to plant the Cytherean Kiss?

rule-right, *a.* and *adv.* [f. rule *sb.*]

†**1.** *Sc.* As straight or exact as a rule; exactly, precisely. *Obs. rare.*

1587 *Sc. Acts Parl.* (1814) III. 522/1 To be maid inwith plane and iust rewll richt. *Ibid.*, A plane syde Q[uhi]lk sall gang rewll richt w^t^ the edge of þe firlot.

2. According to rule; regular. *rare.*

1882 Rhŷs *Celtic Britain* 292 [This] would be the rule-right equivalent of the Latin genitive *lateris*.

'rulering, *vbl. sb. rare.* [f. ruler *v.* + -ing[1].] The action of ruler *v.*; a beating with a ruler.

1849 Dickens *Dav. Copp.* (1850) vii. 77 Tear-blotted copy-books, canings, rulerings.

'rulership. [f. ruler *sb.*[1] + -ship.]

1. a. The position, office, or quality of a ruler; sovereignty, rule.

1648 Hexham ii, *Drossaertschap*, Rulership, Presidencie over a Country, Jurisdiction, or Shriefship. **1975** F. Heer *Charlemagne* xv. 225 The Emperor dreamed that a man came to him with a present from God, a sword symbolising rulership.

1863 Hawthorne *Our Old Home* (1883) I. 37 They were ..wholly destitute of..law or rulership of any description. **1889** H. Drummond *Trop. Africa* iv. 74 One of their own number was elevated to the rulership.

b. The reign *of* a person.

1890 Talmage *From Manger to Throne* 116 The disputes and bloody events which had distinguished the rulership of Herod.

c. Rulers collectively.

1964 *Listener* 11 June 945/2 The emergence of a professional Civil Service alongside an increasingly amateur political rulership.

2. A province; a government.

1893 *Edin. Rev.* Apr. 370 There were some minor rulerships over which China exercised a disputable jurisdiction. **1894** Sir A. C. Lyall *Brit. Domin. India* x. 170 Fragmentary states..trampled under the feet of hardier rulerships.

Rules (ruːlz). [pl. of rule *sb.*]

1. *Racing.* (*a*) Jockey Club Rules (the Rules of Racing). (*b*) National Hunt Rules.

1898 A. E. T. Watson *Turf* vi. 128 Unauthorised meetings—that is to say, meetings not under Rules. **1976** *Horse & Hound* 3 Dec. 10/4 He is one of twin brothers who have both ridden several winners under Rules.

2. = *Australian rules* s.v. Australian *a.* b.

1946 D. Stivens *Courtship of Uncle Henry* 18 In those days..they played Rules in long pants that reached below the knee. **1965** *Austral. Encycl.* IV. 134/2 It is known as the Australian Game, National Football, or Australian Rules. In some parts it becomes merely 'Rules. **1967** *Canberra Times* 17 June 27 Victoria expects to win over W.A. in Rules. **1976** *Sydney Morning Herald* 27 May 22 Rules penalty upsets Saints.

†**'ruleship.** *Obs. rare.* [rule *sb.*] = prec. 1.

1654 Vilvain *Epit. Ess.* ii. xxiii, Romulus for ruleship did Remus slay. **1677** W. Hughes *Man of Sin* ii. 192 A man would think by this, that Scriptures and Traditions.. equally shared the Ruleship in the Popish World betwixt them.

rulesse, obs. form of ruleless.

rulȝeande: see note to roil *v.*[1]

ruling (ˈruːlɪŋ), *vbl. sb.* [f. rule *v.*]

1. The action of governing; exercise of authority, government, rule.

a **1225** *Ancr. R.* 8 Þeos riwleð þe horte, & of hire riwlunge is al mest þet ich riwle. **1377** Langl. *P. Pl.* B. Prol. 127 So leute þe louye, And for þi riȝtful rewlyng be rewarded in heuene! **1408** *E.E. Wills* 15 My wyll ys, that..hys Executours..haue gouernans & rewlyng of my obytis. *c* **1450** *Myrr. Our Lady* 115 Knowynge of trouthe, and ryghte rewlynge of the wylle, maye not be, but in a restfull soulle. **1561** Winȝet *Wks.* (S.T.S.) I. 4 Tyme and..deth.. manassing alrady destruction of ȝour reuling. **1590** Stockwood *Rules Constr.* 1 The concord and agreeing of words togither; and the gouerning or ruling one word of another. **1611** Bible *1 Macc.* vi. 56 Hee sought to take vnto him the ruling of the affaires. **1865** Ruskin *Sesame* i. §43 The true kings..hate ruling. **1894** *Athenæum* 22 Dec. 856/3 He was the last English Churchman who played a decisive part in the political ruling of our nation.

2. A judicial decision; also *gen.* an authoritative pronouncement.

c **1560** Stoddard in Hall *Elizab. Age* (1886) 179 Three rulings with extras, 15^s^. **1875** Maine *Hist. Inst.* ii. 45 Some extremely sensible rulings on the difficult subject of the Measure of Damages. **1883** *Law Rep. 11 Q.B.D.* 595, I.. think the ruling of the learned judge at the trial was correct.

3. a. The action of using a ruler; the action of drawing, marking, or printing parallel straight lines on paper or on textile fabrics. Also *attrib.*, as ***ruling-machine***, ***-pen***, ***-work***; **ruling engine**, a machine for engraving equally spaced parallel straight lines on a surface.

1611 Cotgr., *Reigleure*,..a ruling, or drawing by lines. **1612** Brinsley *Lud. Lit.* 33 Cause them to haue each his ruling pen, made of a quill. **1666** Pepys *Diary* 2 Mar., Setting my wife..to worke upon the ruling of some paper for the making of books. *Ibid.* 28 Apr., My wife to her father's, to carry him some ruling work. **1858** Simmonds *Dict. Trade, Ruling and Dotting Pens*, a kind of metal pen for writing music. **1865** Brande & Cox *Dict. Sci.*, etc. s.v. *Engraving*, An ingenious machine..invented by the late Mr. Wilson Lowry, called a ruling machine. **1892** *Photogr. Ann.* II. 178 He describes a kind of optical ruling on the sensitive plate itself, a system for which [etc.]. **1901** *Physical Rev.* XII. 9 It is generally assumed in treating the grating that the lines of the ruling are of equal width and are separated by equal spaces... This cannot be the case in view of..the almost inconceivable rigidity of the ruling engine which would be necessary. **1969** D. Richardson in R. Kingslake *Appl. Optics & Optical Engin.* V. ii. 28 Most ruling engines use screws as the basic indexing means. **1980** *Sci. Amer.* May 126/3 A narrow strip of phosphorescent paint was applied down the middle of this detector, which could be moved along the support with the screw of a ruling engine.

b. *concr.* A ruled line, or lines. *spec.* in *Palæography*, the lines ruled by the scribe on a page or throughout a manuscript.

1890 in *Cent. Dict.* **1893** Sir R. Ball *Story of Sun* 111 The way in which certain of the lines are grouped in pairs, somewhat suggesting the rulings of a copy-book. **1944** P. Hodgson *Cloud of Unknowing* (E.E.T.S.) p. x, Single columns of text, usually 34 lines to a page; vertical and horizontal rulings; [etc.]. **1958** *Scriptorium* XII. 51 (*title*) The ruling of the *Exeter Book*. **1963** N. R. Ker *Owl & Nightingale* (E.E.T.S.) p. xii, The pencil ruling is often indistinct. **1976** *Codicologica* I. 78 Other aspects of the medieval book: the nature of parchment, ink, pricking, and ruling.

ruling (ˈruːlɪŋ), *ppl. a.* [f. rule *v.*]

1. a. Exercising rule or authority; governing, reigning.

1648 *Canterburie March* B iij b, This unity is held by none That have more Ruling-Heads than one. **1655** *Nicholas Papers* (Camden) II. 203 The interests of the ruling party have a great connexion with Cromwell. **1704** Trapp *Abra-Mule* ii. i, The ruling part of the Divan. **1786** Burke *Art. agst. W. Hastings* Wks. 1842 II. 140 This plan, which appears to be most connected with the rights of the ruling family. *a* **1832** Bentham *Wks.* (1843) X. 571/2 He hates the ruling few; but he does not love the subject many. **1849** Macaulay *Hist. Eng.* vi. II. 133 He belonged half to the ruling and half to the subject caste. **1862** R. Cobden *Let.* in W. L. Burn *Age of Equipoise* (1964) ii. 69 There has been a great reaction..among that which I call the ruling class, against..humanitarianism. **1871** Freeman *Norm. Conq.* (1876) IV. 152 The act of the ruling body was not confirmed by the general feeling of the citizens. **1943** J. B. Priestley *Daylight on Saturday* ii. 5 Cheviot..was a good engineer... He belonged to tomorrow's ruling class. **1952** D. Kelly (*title*) The ruling few. **1955** T. H. Pear *Eng. Social Differences* i. 15 An undiscriminating ear mistakes for 'ruling-class speech' a synthetic approximation to it. **1962** L. Davidson *Rose of Tibet* xv. 280 The ex-enemy was now treating quite amiably with 'ruling circles' exiled in Chumbi. **1964** T. B. Bottomore *Elites & Society* i. 6 Mosca's 'political class' is nothing but the intellectual section of the ruling group. *Ibid.* iv. 71 A second group which has attracted attention as a potential ruling elite is that constituted by the managers of industry. **1972** 'R. Crawford' *Whip Hand* ii. i. 58 Neville, for all his blue blood, was closer to the breadline than he was... How could a ruling class produce such examples of weakness? **1979** *Dædalus* Summer 2 They are the very models of ruling-class incompetence.

transf. **1818** Scott *Hrt. Midl.* xlvii[i], She has been the ruling belle.., the universal toast of the winter.

b. ***Ruling Elder***: see elder *sb.*[3] 4. So ***Ruling Eldership***.

1593 [Bancroft] *Survey Pret. Holy Disc.* 158 That ruling elders are not comprehended vnder the name of Bischop. **1641** (*title*), An Assertion of the Government of the Church of Scotland in the Points of Ruling-Elders, and of the Authority of Presbyteries and Synods. **1641** Baillie *Lett. & Jrnls.* (1841) I. 370 In the voyceing..some borrowes two ruleing-elders getts voyce. **1736** *Gentl. Mag.* VI. 342/1 A few ignorant Artificers in Market-Towns, or Farmers in Country-Parishes,..under the Character of Ruling Elders. **1784** Burns (*title*), On a celebrated ruling Elder. **1808** Jamieson Addit., [The] *Session*..consists of the minister,.. of the Ruling Elders; and of Deacons. **1871** Carlyle in *Mrs. Carlyle's Lett.* I. 142 Thrice-great as a ruling-elder (indeed, a very long-headed, strictly orthodox man). **1891** *Presbyterian Forms of Service* (1894) 145 The Sermon..may have for its subject the scriptural warrant for the Ruling Eldership. **1945** J. T. Cox *Practice Church of Scotland* 104 All are elders—ministers being teaching or preaching as well as ruling elders, and the others 'ruling elders' only. In practice the terms 'elder' and 'ruling elder' are restricted to such as are members of a Kirk Session, exclusive of the minister or ministers of the charge. **1974** *Marlboro Herald-Advocate* (Bennettsville, S. Carolina) 18 Apr. 8/3 A congregational meeting has been called..for the purpose of electing one Ruling Elder to serve on the session.

†**c.** *dial.* Disorderly. *Obs.*$^{-0}$ (Cf. rule *v.* 2 d.)

1691 Ray *N.C. Words* s.v. *Reul*, 'A reuling lad,' a rigsby.

2. Predominating, dominant, prevalent: **a.** Of passions.

1732 Pope *Ep. Bathurst* 154 The ruling Passion conquers Reason still. **1761** Hume *Hist. Eng.* III. liv. 174 The two ruling passions of this parliament were, zeal for liberty, and an aversion to the church. **1830** D'Israeli *Chas. I*, III. v. 75 A worldly ambition was the ruling passion of this man. **1849** Macaulay *Hist. Eng.* ii. I. 230 That hatred had become one of the ruling passions of the community.

b. Of opinions, ideas, etc.

1780 *Mirror* No. 77, Mr. Addison..justifies, against the ruling opinion at that time, the practice of those writers of tragedy. **1782** Miss Burney *Cecilia* viii. vi, [This was] the ruling subject of her thoughts and meditation. **1835** I. Taylor *Spir. Despot.* iii. 92 The security..of every son of Abraham was the ruling intention of every enactment. **1873** Symonds *Grk. Poets* vii. 190 Not Fate, but Nemesis, was the ruling notion in Greek tragedy.

3. Of prices, etc.: Current, general; average.

1861 Goschen *For. Exch.* 120 There was an indication of demand for bills on England, as a means of placing capital here, to take advantage of the ruling rate. **1877** Raymond *Statist. Mines & Mining* 267 The ruling prices..were not too high to leave a small margin of profit. **1900** *Engineering Mag.* XIX. 683 The best road the Spaniards built..has a ruling grade of 7 per cent.

Hence **'rulingly** *adv.* (Webster, 1847).

ruller (ˈrʌlə(r)). *Mining.* [f. dial. *rull* to wheel, prob. a var. of roll *v.*[2]] (See quot.)

1860 *Eng. & For. Mining Gloss.* (ed. 2) 21 *Rullers*, the persons who work the wheelbarrows underground.

rulley (ˈrʌlɪ). *local.* Also **rully.** [Of doubtful origin: cf. rolley 2.] A flat four-wheeled wagon, used for conveyance of goods; a lorry.

1866 Brogden *Prov. Lincs.*, *Rully*, a low kind of goods wagon. **1886** *Leeds Mercury* 1 May, The North-Eastern Railway Company will collect and deliver goods..by Rulleys of their own. **1887** Mrs. Stannard *Siege Baby* 62 Before the baker's cart had disgorged itself, a rully appeared upon the scene. **1977** *Times* 14 Oct. 16/6 East Yorkshire's College of Agriculture has reverted to a strong cob, Folly, and four-wheel rulley to assist their shepherd on his rounds. **1979** *Bull. Yorks. Dial. Soc.* Summer 9 When the tide rose again they sailed away to Hull where they [*sc.* the goods] were transferred on rullies to the station and entrained to Hornsea.

Comb. **1806** W. Shout in *N. & Q.* (1963) Apr. 136/1, 6 rulley load of stone—7,, 6. **1857** *P.O. Directory Yorksh.* 1292/3 (Hull), Rulley-man & carrier. **1897** *Daily News* 27 Feb. 5/1 The sudden removal of seven 'rulleymen' or checkers at the Forth goods station. **1978** J. Cummings *Railway Motor Buses* I. 40 The third Stirling, fitted with a rulley body, found a home with the Mechanical Engineers Department at Hull.

rullion[1] (ˈrʌlɪən). *Sc.* [var. of rilling *sb.*[1], riveling[1].] A shoe made of undressed hide.

Also applied in various senses to persons or animals: see *Eng. Dial. Dict.*

1644 D. Hume *Hist. House Douglas* 45 Highland showes called rullions, made of raw and untand leather. **1768** Ross *Helenore, The Rock and the wee pickle Tow*, With a pair of rough rullions to scuff thro' the dew. **1820** Scott *Monast.* xxix, He had..deer-skin rullions or sandals. **1890** Lowson *Guidfollow* 70 A pleasant recreation to the fashioners of 'brogues' and 'rullions' in their hours of relaxation.

†**'rullion**[2]. *Sc. Obs.* [Of obscure origin.] Some form of ornament in metal-work.

1707 *Invent. R. Wardr.* App. (1815) 339 Antique Medusa's heads and rullion foliages. *Ibid.*, Betwixt each statue arises a rullion in forme of a dolphine, very distinct.

rullock, variant of rowlock.

†**ruly,** *a.*[1] *Obs.* Forms: α. 1 hreow- (hryw-), 1–2 reow-, 3 reolic; 3 reo(u)-, reu-, rou-, 4 rewelich(e; 4 ru-, 4–5 rewlyche. β. 3–4 reu-, 5 rew-, 5–6 ruli; 4 rewe-, 4–5 rew-, reu-, ruly. [OE. *hréowlic* (f. *hréow* rue *sb.*[1]), = MDu. *rouwelijc.*] Rueful, pitiable, pitiful, woful.

α. *c* **1000** *Ags. Ps.* (Th.) cviii. 9 His wif wyrðe wydewe hreowlic. *c* **1100** *O.E. Chron.* (MS. D) an. 1057, þæt wæs hreowlic sið & hearmlic eallre þissere þeode. *a* **1122** *Ibid.* (Laud MS.) an. 1086, Reowlic þing he dyde, & reowlicor him ȝelamp. *c* **1200** *Trin. Coll. Hom.* 147 Swiche teares shedden hie on þis reuliche wei..of reuðe of here agene sinnes. **1303** R. Brunne *Handl. Synne* 730 So rulyche makyst þou hym to be. *c* **1374** Chaucer *Boeth.* ii. pr. ii. (1868) 35 Þis rewlyche Cresus was cauȝt of Cirus and lad to þe fijr to be brent.

β. *c* **1250** *Gen. & Ex.* 1162 Abraham up on morgen stod, Wið reuli lote and frigti mod. *a* **1300** *Cursor M.* 4930 Þai fel don þan at ioseph fete And merci soght, wit reuli grette. **13..** *K. Alis.* 6485 (Laud MS.), þan hij maken a reuly cry. *a* **1400** *Sowdone* 1624 What be ye, That make here this ruly moone? *c* **1460** *Bury Wills* (Camden) 234 Wrappid in a selure as a ful rewli wrecche. **1573** G. HARVEY *Letter-bk.* (Camden) 18, I douht not but I shal finde your wurship.. favorable and gud unto me in this ruli and miserable case.

ruly ('ru:lɪ), *a.*[2] Also 5 **rewly, reulie, reuly.** [orig. f. RULE *sb.* + -Y; but in mod. use prob. a back-formation from UNRULY.]

1. Observing or amenable to rule or good order; law-abiding, disciplined, orderly.

c **1400** *Destr. Troy* 3888 Ruly & rightwise,.. He spake neuer dispituosly, ne spiset no man. *c* **1440** *York Myst.* xxvi. 38 Bees rewly, and ray fourth your reasoune. *c* **1480** HENRYSON *Fables, Fox & Wolf* iv, The oxin waxit mair reulie at the last. **1596** WARNER *Alb. Eng.* (1602) 216 It was objected, though untruely, That they were ydle, Hell lacked Guests, and men on earth waxt ruly.

1837 DISRAELI *Venetia* I. xv, 'Soldiers ruly?'.. 'Yes, your worship; quite ruly.' **1892** *Black & White* 6 Aug. 155/1 Students are an important element, and not always a ruly one, in Edinburgh life. **1952** DYLAN THOMAS *Coll. Poems* 165 And truly he Flows to the strand of flowers like the dew's ruly sea.

†**2.** = REGULAR *a.* I. *Obs.*—[1]

c **1450** *St. Cuthbert* (Surtees) 4606 Some of þaim sone were boune, Reuly men of religioune, forthe with þaim to fare.

† **'ruly**, *adv.* Forms: α. 1 **hreowlice**; 2–3 **reow-**, 3 **reo(u)-**; **rou-**, 3–4 **reu-**, **rew-**, 4 **reweliche**; 4 **rewlik.** β. 4 **reuli**; 3 **rev-**, 3–5 **reu-**, 5 **rew(e)ly**; 4 **rwly**, 5–6 **rulye, ruly.** [OE. *hréowlíce* (see RULY *a.*[1] and -LY[2]), = OS. *(h)riulîko*, MDu. *rouwelike.*]

1. Ruefully, pitifully, wretchedly.

α. *c* **893** K. ÆLFRED *Oros.* III. vii. 120 Maȝon hie swa hreowlice wepan swa ȝe maȝon þara oþra bliþeliche hlihhan. *c* **1050** *O.E. Chron.* (MS. C) an. 1036, Sume hi man wið feo sealde, sume hreowlice acwealde. *c* **1175** *Lamb. Hom.* 43 Summe þer reowliche gneȝeð his aȝene tunge. *c* **1205** LAY. 27497 þer weoren Romleoden reouliche [*c* **1275** rouliche] iladde. *c* **1330** *Arth. & Merl.* 788 (Kölbing), Hir moder was ded acurssedliche, & hir fader starf reuliche.

β. *c* **1275** *XI Pains of Hell* 192 in *O.E. Misc.* 152 Four deofle heom stondeþ bi þat pyneþ heom ful revly. *a* **1300** *Cursor M.* 12530 For he was hurt ful selli sare, Reuli can he cri and rare. **13..** *E.E. Allit. P.* C. 96 þaȝ I be.. On rode rwly to-rent, with rybaudes mony. *c* **1400** *St. Alexius* 236 Alexius þus his leue tooke; Rewely his wijf gan on hym loke. *a* **1529** SKELTON *Sp. Parrot* 116 Sion is in sadnes, Rachell ruly doth loke. **1573** TUSSER *Husb.* (1878) 122 No tempest, good Julie, Least corne lookes rulie.

2. With pity or compassion.

13.. *Cursor M.* 24115 (Edin.), Mi son þat hang apon þat croice Rewlik on me biheld.

rum (rʌm), *sb.*[1] Also 7 **rumme**, 7–8 **rhum.** [Of obscure origin: perhaps an abbreviation of the longer forms RUMBULLION or RUMBUSTION, which are found a little earlier. English is the source of Du. and G. *rum*, Da. and Sw. *rum*, *rom*, Russ. *rum'*, *rom'*; F. *rhum*, *rum*, Sp. and Pg. *ron*, etc.]

1. a. A spirit distilled from various products of the sugar-cane (esp. molasses and dunder), and prepared chiefly in the West Indies and Guyana.

The name has also been improperly applied to spirits made in imitation of this from beet-roots or other materials.

1654 [see KILL-DEVIL *sb.* 2]. **1661** *Cal. State Papers* Col. Ser. (1661–8) 42 That the former orders concerning rum, sugar, and hammocks be still in force. **1667** WARREN *Descr. Surinam* vi. 17 Rum is a Spirit extracted from the Juice of Sugar-Canes, commonly, twice as strong as Brandy. *a* **1700** B. E. *Dict. Cant. Crew, Rum*,..a West-Indian Drink stronger than Brandy, drawn from Dreggs of Sugar for the most part, yet sometimes from Fruits, and Rows of Fish. **1719** DE FOE *Crusoe* I. (Globe) 56, I found..three large Runlets of Rum or Spirits. **1776** ABIGAIL ADAMS in *Fam. Lett.* (1876) 220 Our New England rum is four shillings per gallon. **1819** BYRON *Juan* II. xxxiv, There's nought, no doubt, so much the spirit calms As rum and true religion. **1835** SIR J. ROSS *Narr. 2nd Voy.* xlv. 585 We had sold them no rum. **1890** *Standard* 21 Apr. 3/6 The stuff he calls Rum is not Rum at all. It consists of raw spirit expressed from the beetroot and other roots..mixed with a small quantity of genuine Rum.

b. *rum-and-water*, a drink prepared from these ingredients. Also *Comb.*

1779 J. WOODFORDE *Diary* 12 Aug. (1924) I. 258 At the 3 Innes for some Rum and water pd. 0.0.3. **1836–7** DICKENS *Sk. Boz, Scenes* xvi, A stout man, who had a glass of rum-and-water, warm,..at every place where we changed horses. **1848** THACKERAY *Van. Fair* xxxiii, Sir Pitt..drank rum-and-water with the farmers at Mudbury. **1850** —— *Pendennis* viii, Rum-and-water-drinking gentlemen-farmers.

c. *N. Amer.* Used generically as a hostile name for intoxicating liquors.

1800 *Upper Canada Gaz.* (York, Ontario) 5 Apr. 3/2 Many have labored to calumniate Rum, and render it unpopular, by dwelling on some of its supposed bad effects. **1851** *Voice of Fugitive* (Windsor, Ontario) 5 Nov. 2/5 Rum and Negro hate [are] the two great public evils of our time. **1858** O. W. HOLMES *Aut. Breakf-t.* viii. (1859) 184 Rum I take to be the name which unwashed moralists apply alike to the product distilled from molasses and the noblest juices of the vineyard. **1918** W. A. MACKAY *By Trench & Trail* 15 No one will rejoice more than Oscar Dhu to see the demon rum utterly destroyed in Canada ere many moons. **1933** E. O'NEILL *Ah, Wilderness!* II. 74 'Never marry a woman who drinks! Lips that touch liquor shall never touch yours!'.. Too bad! So fine a woman once—and now such a slave to rum! **1957** *Prairie Overcomer* (Three Hills, Alberta) Dec. 444/2 Of these two foes we cannot say whether *Rome* or *rum* is the greater adversary of the pure Gospel.

2. *attrib.* and *Comb.* **a.** Attrib., as ***rum-bottle, distillery, -flavour, -puncheon, ration, still, -works; rum-bathed, -brave*** adjs.

1897 G. B. SHAW *Let.* 13 May (1965) I. 762 His *rum bathed hair. **1702** C. MATHER *Magn. Chr.* vi. 36 Wo to him that gives his Neighbour drink; that puttest thy Bottle (thy *Rhum-Bottle) to him, and makest him drunken also. **1847** THACKERAY *Van. Fair* (1848) xxxix. 359 The three tumblers and the empty rum-bottle. **1967** A. LICHINE *Encycl. Wines & Spirits* 464/2, 7 francs..gave a customer the sugar-syrup bottle, the rum bottle, a tumbler, and left him to himself. **1934** E. HEMINGWAY in *Cosmopolitan* Apr. 119/2, I know you haven't got any guts unless you've got rum... I want you *rum-brave. I don't want you useless. **1774** N. CRESSWELL *Jrnl.* 4 Sept. (1925) 34 In the evening went with Mr. Perkins to see Mr. Kid's Plantation. The Sugar works and *Rum distilleries are very extensive. **1816** *Mass. Hist. Soc. Coll.* 2nd Ser. IV. 124 A rum distillery was established in 1738. **1968** *Spirits* ('Know the Drink' Ser.) 32/2 Sugar factories and rum distilleries are much larger and more efficient than they were. **1886** *Encycl. Brit.* XXI. 58/2 The spirit..has only a faint *rum flavour. **1857** KINGSLEY *Two Y. Ago* I. 201 She'd sooner have you than that old *rum-puncheon Heale. **1923** KIPLING *Irish Guards in Gt. War* I. ii. 89 Their bivouacs..where a hot meal..and a *rum-ration awaited them. **1977** *Amer. N. & Q.* XV. 135/2 Temperance campaigns, reduced rum rations, more leave, recreational programs, recruitment of higher caliber personnel, all helped to reduce alcoholism. **1914** F. C. GLASS *With Bible in Brazil* iv. 45, I recalled the big *rum-still in the back-yard. **1968** *Spirits* ('Know the Drink' Ser.) 32/1 Rum stills are often fitted with 'rectifiers' which allow the least volatile elements to return to the pot. **1825** *Gentl. Mag.* XCV. I. 214 The furnaces of the sugar and *rum works.

b. Objective, as ***rum-distiller, -drinker, -maker, -seller; rum-producing*** adj.

1839 URE *Dict. Arts* 397 So sensible are the *rum distillers of the advantage of such a plan. **1834** *Tait's Mag.* I. 412/2 Dr. Lang anticipates a moral regeneration from the *rum-drinkers being converted into wine-bibbers. **1926** J. MASEFIELD *Odtaa* i. 4 The northward provinces became sparsely inhabited by..sugar-growers, *rum-makers, and copper-miners. **1876** HAM *Rev. & Mercantile Vade-M.* 569 Australia is recognized as a *rum-producing country. **1781** J. GREENWOOD in *Maryland Hist. Mag.* (1910) V. 125 We.. took in..seven passengers, who were sutlers or *rum-sellers to Gen. Washington's army. **1828** P. CUNNINGHAM *N.S. Wales* (ed. 3) II. 181 Guarding against its sliding quietly.. into the possession of the rum-seller. **1900** *Congress. Rec.* 25 Jan. 1200/2 A rumseller is as bad as a polygamist. **1973** H. ROBERTSON *Grass Roots* iv. 76 There seems to be no limit to the number of offences these licenced rumsellers can commit.

c. Instrumental, as ***rum-bred, -crazed, -smelling.***

1866 *Evening Star* 19 Mar., He had better have been a dead man than have emitted from his mouth..such a rum-bred pestilence of breath. **1893** *Arena* April 637 The uneducated, rum-crazed negro. **1900** H. LAWSON *Over Sliprails* 30 Danny..finally collapsed into a shapeless rum-smelling heap and slept once more.

3. Special combs.: **rum baba**: see BABA[2]; **rum baron**, a magnate in illegal liquor traffic; **rum-bud** (see quots.); **rum butter**, a hard sauce made from rum and butter; **rum chaser** *U.S.*, during the Prohibition era, a coast-guard speedboat for pursuing rum-runners; **rum-cherry** *U.S.*, the wild black cherry, *Padus serotina*, or the tree bearing this fruit; **rum cocktail**, a cocktail in which rum is the principal ingredient; **rum essence** (see quot.); **rum fleet** *U.S.*, during the Prohibition era, a 'fleet' of ships engaged in rum-running; **rum-hitting** [cf. HIT *v.* 23 b] *vbl. sb.*, excessive drinking of rum; **rum-hole** (see quots.); **rum-hound** *slang*, (*a*) = *rumpot*; (*b*) a prohibition agent (*U.S.*); **rum-jar** *slang*, a type of German trench-mortar shell; **rum jelly**, a concentrated form of rum; **rum-joint** *U.S.*, formerly, a place where illicit liquor was sold; **rum-mill** *U.S.*, a tavern or liquor shop; **rum-nose** (see quot.); **rumpot** *N. Amer. slang*, a habitual heavy drinker; **rum punch, shrub, toddy**, beverages in which rum is the principal ingredient; **Rum Rebellion** *Austral. Hist.*, the rebellion against Governor William Bligh by officers of the New South Wales Corps (noted for trafficking in rum) in 1809; **Rum Row** *U.S.* (see quot. 1927); **rum-runner**, (*a*) one who smuggles or lands illicit liquor; (*b*) = *rum ship*; **rum-running** [RUN *v.* 45 c] *vbl. sb.*, smuggling or landing prohibited liquor; also as *ppl. adj.*; **rum ship**, a ship engaged in rum-running; **rum shop** *U.S.* and *Caribbean*, a shop or tavern selling rum and other liquor; a saloon; **rum-sucker**, *U.S.*, a hard drinker.

1923 *Westm. Gaz.* 4 Apr. 8/5 Reminiscences are inevitable in any gathering of *rum barons. **1975** H. WHITE *Raincoast Chron.* (1976) 12/1 A few 'rum barons' could be apprehended in the United States. **1848** BARTLETT *Dict. Amer.*, **Rum-bud*, a redness occasioned by the detestable practice of excessive drinking. Rum-buds usually appear first on the nose, and..extend over the face. **1873** LELAND *Egypt. Sk. Bk.* 120 All European travellers accuse Cophts of being rare old toss-pots, steady drinkers, regular rum-buds. **1889** A. B. MARSHALL *Cookery Bk.* ii. 38 **Rum Butter*... Prepare as in foregoing recipe, using Liquid Sunshine rum instead of brandy. **1939** [see *brandy-butter* s.v. BRANDY *sb.* 2]. **1967** 'J. MUNRO' *Money that Money can't Buy* i. 8 Shops that sold Lakeland jet, woollens and rum butter. **1972** *Country Life* 26 Oct. 1041/1 Butter was..taken to Wigton market.. with a special delicacy called rum-butter. **1924** *Rudder* Jan. 40 Congress will be asked to appropriate many millions of dollars for a fleet of *rum chasers. **1931** D. RUNYON in *Hearst's Internat.* May 64/2 She is riding in a big foreign automobile the size of a rum-chaser. **1829** A. H. LINCOLN *Familiar Lect. Bot.* 301 Wild-cherry, *rum-cherry, cabinet cherry... In dense forests, it grows to a very great height. **1843** *Knickerbocker* XXI. 585 They had been feeding him upon that inebriating article of food, rum-cherries. **1908** N. L. BRITTON *N. Amer. Trees* 506 This well-known tree, also called the Black, Cabinet, or Rum cherry, is abundant in mixed forests and neglected clearings, from Nova Scotia.. southward to Florida. **1949** COLLINGWOOD & BRUSH *Knowing your Trees* 256 They have a pleasant, slightly bitter taste and are sometimes used in a beverage called 'cherry bounce' hence the name 'Rum Cherry'. **1861** *Harper's Mag.* Jan. 150/2 Measures of the most vital importance are first introduced in *rum-cocktails, then steeped in whisky, after which they are engrossed in gin for a third reading. **1936** A. THIRKELL *August Folly* vi. 181 Richard..had made and drunk two rum cocktails. **1976** J. VAN DE WETERING *Tumbleweed* x. 93 The iced rum cocktail went down well. **1886** *Encycl. Brit.* XXI. 58/2 A fictitious rum, the flavour of which is due to '*rum essence'—a mixture of artificial ether, birch bark oil, and other substances. **1923** *Westm. Gaz.* 4 Apr. 8/5 Off-shore is the *rum fleet. **1975** J. GORES *Hammett* xvi. 113 Dom brings in most of the real Canadian from the rum fleet these days. **1910** J. MASEFIELD *Ballads & Poems* 34 There's..Stabbing, of course, and *rum-hitting, Dirt, and drink, and stink, and crime. **1859** BARTLETT *Dict. Amer.* (ed. 2) 181 A place where spirituous liquors are sold and drank; a grog-shop. In the West, often called a Doggery or Dog-hole, and in New York a *Rum-hole. **1872** DE VERE *Americanisms* 216 The State of New York alone, we believe, uses the term rum-holes for its smaller grog-shops. **1918** L. E. RUGGLES *Navy Explained* 120 **Rum Hound*, a boozer, or a man who likes his oil. **1920** ADE *Hand-Made Fables* 5 Just as the western Sun was ducking behind the Hills, the amateur Rum-Hounds piled out. **1951** E. PAUL *Springtime in Paris* xi. 192 What he resented was the insinuation that he was a chronic rumhound. **1916** P. MCGREGOR *Let.* 29 June in M. Moynihan *Greater Love* (1980) 21 A '*Rum Jar', the largest Hun shell known on our front, can knock in yards of trenches. **1923** KIPLING *Irish Guards in Gt. War* I. 252 Rum-jar by rum-jar, borne joyously through the dark streets. **1964** *Listener* 17 Sept. 431/1 The Germans also stepped up their mortar fire on our frontline trenches—the fearful 'rum jars'. **1976** J. VAN DE WETERING *Tumbleweed* x. 93 The rum comes from Jamaica, packed in drums, *rum jelly. We mix it with water in a little factory. **1928** *Sunday Express* 24 June 8/4 One of our men started a row with one of these birds... They fought in a *rum-joint and everyone joined in. **1853** *Yankee Humour & Uncle Sam's Fun* 87 Every *rum-mill, groggery and tippling-shop..is a trap set by the devil to catch those who are guilty of not having over three cents. **1867** [see DEADFALL 2 c]. **1889** BARRÈRE & LELAND *Dict. Slang* I. 238/1 *Charter the bar, charter the grocery, to* (American), to buy all the liquor in a groggery or 'rum-mill' and give it away freely to all comers. **1891** SAJOUR *Ann. Univ. Med. Sci.* 59 An aggravated case of acne rosacea (*rum-nose). **1930** D. RUNYON in *Collier's* 1 Feb. 12/1 All he sees..is this *rumpot ham. **1941** *Sun* (Baltimore) 17 Feb. 18/3 He admires good food and good whisky. 'All cooks,' he said, 'I mean, all good cooks, is rumpots.' **1966** T. H. RADDALL *Hangman's Beach* IV. xxii. 345, I had him moved in there as soon as that rumpot of a doctor was off tae the toon. **1737** *Gentl. Mag.* VII. 36/1 Plenty of small *Rum-Punch, well soured with Juice of Limon or Orange. **1824** *John Bull* I. 132 We understand that rum punch has lately become so great a favourite in high quarters. **1855** W. HOWITT *Land, Labour & Gold* ii. 118 From the date of this '*rum rebellion', and the forcible deposition of poor Bligh..the system of political grants went on swimmingly. **1938** H. V. EVATT (*title*) Rum Rebellion. **1966** G. W. TURNER *Eng. Lang. in Austral. & N.Z.* i. 8 The opposition of the Corps to authority culminated in a rebellion (the 'Rum Rebellion') against Governor William Bligh. **1923** *Lit. Digest* 26 May 52/2 Small consignments are carried from there down to the '*Rum Row' of ships anchored beyond the three-mile limit of the Long Island and New Jersey shores. **1927** W. E. COLLINSON *Contemp. Eng.* 81 We all know..about..Rum Row (where the liquor ships gather outside the prohibited area). **1949** IREY & SLOCUM *Tax Dodgers* i. 26 There were three Rum Rows, one on each coast and a smaller one working in the Gulf of Mexico. **1920** *N.Y. Times* 19 Sept. 6/1 The Detroit *rum runners have had a good deal of notoriety. **1925** H. L. FOSTER *Trop. Tramp with Tourists* 7 Is that a rum-runner? **1941** B. SCHULBERG *What makes Sammy Run?* xii. 291 We discovered one solitary light moving slowly along the horizon... It was a rum runner. **1980** *Smithsonian* Aug. 45 The match became known as 'the rum-runners' paradise' because so many Coast Guard patrol boats had to be diverted to control the spectator fleet. **1924** *Lit. Digest* 31 May 38/1 *Rum-running in New York has received at least a temporary setback. **1926** *Scribner's Mag.* Aug. 166/2 Tully—an old friend of mine, in the rum-running game now—will get you over the line into Canada. **1930** *Aberdeen Press & Jrnl.* 1 Feb. 7/5 Grey Ghost, one of the fastest rum-running craft on Lake Erie, has been sighted locked in the ice. **1959** N. MAILER *Advts. for Myself* (1961) 65 With the things he'd done, the Marines in Nicaragua,.. rumrunning in New Orleans, somehow he'd kinda forgotten that you stood a chance of dying too. **1924** *Rum-ship [see HIJACKING *vbl. sb.* and *ppl. a.*]. **1931** F. L. ALLEN *Only Yesterday* x. 245 Rum-ships rolling in the sea outside the twelve-mile limit. **1738** W. STEPHENS *Jrnl.* 10 Apr. in *Colonial Rec. Georgia* (1906) IV. 122 Those private *Rum-Shops were become as common among the People, in Proportion, as Gin-Shops formerly at London. **1873** 'MARK TWAIN' *Gilded Age* xxxiii. 302 Industry and economy soon enabled him to start a low rum shop in a foul locality. **1953** S. M. SADEEK *Windswept & Other Stories* (1969) 17 Den e lead me in the rumshop. **1974** *Sunday Advocate-News* (Barbados) 24 Feb. 17/1 Well populated with rum shops and nightclubs and most recently a horse racing betting shop, the area has become the noisiest in the country. **1808** *Sporting Mag.* XXX. 99, 38 gallons of *rum shrub. **1864** TOVEY *Brit. & For. Spirits* 283 Rum Shrub should be made with the freshest lemon juice, and a portion of Seville orange juice, the finest Jamaica Rum, and sweets from good loaf sugar. **1858** *N.Y. Tribune* 9 July, An acquired appetite as strong as that of a *rum-sucker. **1820** SCOTT *Monast.* Introd. Ep., To keep company with ony bit English rider, that sups on toasted cheese, and a cheerer of *rum-toddy.

† **rum**, *sb.*² *slang. Obs.* [In senses 2 and 3 from RUM *a.*²]

1. A poor country clergyman in Ireland.

1720 SWIFT *Wks.* (1841) II. 75/1 As if..it were fit..to give the civility of the hat or wall to any rusty rum in the street. **1729** —— *Grand Question Deb.* Wks. 1751 X. 124 No Company comes, But a Rabble of Tenants, and rusty dull Rums.

2. Ellipt. for *rum customer*.

c **1803** C. K. SHARPE *New Oxford Guide* in *Mem.* (1888) I. 18 They were angry with rums, they were troubl'd with bores. *a* **1845** BARHAM *Cousin Nicholas* xxiii, Von [= one] of the hold boy's country rums.

3. An old or unsaleable book.

1812 in Nichols *Lit. Anec. 18th C.* V. 471 *note*, The books, which booksellers call rums, appear to be very numerous... The French have *bouquins* for rums, and *bouquiniste* for the seller.

† **rum**, *sb.*³ *Obs.*⁻¹ (Meaning obscure.)

1640 SHIRLEY *St. Patrick for Ireland* IV. i, There's to show I am a linguist, with a rum in the rhyme, consisting of two several languages.

rum, *sb.*⁴ *U.S.* Also **rhum**. [Origin uncertain.] A form of rummy (RUMMY *sb.*²).

1910 [see RUMMY *sb.*²]. **1912** *Official Rules of Card Games* (U.S. Playing Card Co.) 15 Rum. (This is a combination of Conquian and Whiskey Poker.)..Objects of the Game.—To get rid of the cards dealt to the player by laying them out in triplets or fours, or in sequence and suit of three or more. **1913** *Chicago Record-Herald* 2 Mar. v. 6/1, I never found on one of them The kale I lose at rhum. **1921** M. C. WORK *Auction for Two or Three* 79 The modern game of Rum resembles Conquian in many respects and was at first called 'Coon Can'. **1974** *Encycl. Brit. Macropædia* XVI. 25/1 Among the most widely played Rummy games is 500 Rum, ..and its variants including Michigan Rum.

rum (rʌm), *a.*¹ *Cant.* Now *rare* or *Obs.* Forms: 6, 8 rome, 7 room(e, 7–9 rum. [One of the canting terms originating in the 16th cent.]

1. Good, fine, excellent; great.

The exact sense varies with the sb.; for a list of the commonest phrases, as *rum beck*, *bob*, *cull*, etc. see the *Dict. Cant. Crew* (*a* 1700).

1567 HARMAN *Caveat* (1869) 84 *Rome vyle*, London. *Ibid.*, *Rome mort*, the Quene. **1621** B. JONSON *Gipsies Metam.* (Rtldg.) 619/2 For the roome-morts, I know by their ports ..They are of the sorts That love the true sports. *a* **1700** B. E. *Dict. Cant. Crew*, *Rum*, gallant, Fine, Rich, best or excellent. *Ibid.*, *Bub*, Drink. *Rum-bub*, very good Tip. *Ibid.* s.v. *Joseph*, *A Rum Joseph*, a good Cloak or Coat. **1812** J. H. VAUX *Flash Dict.* s.v. *Chaunt*, To throw off a rum chaunt, is to sing a good song. **1847** *Simmond's Colonial Mag.* July 409 Bricks..out here [Ceylon] signifies slap-up chaps, fast goers, trumps, rum spirits, crack hands. **1859** *Slang Dict.* 83 *Rum Mizzlers*, persons who are clever in making their escape, or getting out of a difficulty. **1867** SMYTH *Sailor's Word-bk.*, *Rum-Gagger*, a cheat who tells wonderful stories of his sufferings at sea to obtain money.

2. ***rum bouse***, ***booze***, etc., good liquor, wine.

1567 HARMAN *Caveat* (1869) 83 *Rome bouse*, wyne. *Ibid.* 86 This bouse is as benshyp as rome bouse. **1641** BROME *Joviall Crew* II. Wks. 1873 III. 391 This Bowse is better then Rum-bowse. **1654** GAYTON *Pleas. Notes* IV. ix. 233 A goodly Rumbouze of Canary. **1834** *Fraser's Mag.* X. 224 The Duchess loves Nantz,..Tom Campbell rumbooze.

b. Hence ***rum-boozing*** (see quot.).

a **1700** B. E. *Dict. Cant. Crew*, *Rum-boozing-Welts*, bunches of Grapes.

3. ***rum duke*** (see first quot.).

a **1700** B. E. *Dict. Cant. Crew*, *Rum-duke*, a jolly handsom Man. **1706** FARQUHAR *Recruiting Officer* II. iii, You are a justice of peace, and you are a king, and I am a duke; and a rum duke, an't I? **1763** [see DUKE *sb.* 3 b].

4. ***rum-pad***, the highway; also *erron.*, a highwayman.

a **1700** B. E. *Dict. Cant. Crew*, *Rum-pad*, the Highway. **1707** J. SHIRLEY *Triumph of Wit* (1724) 164 By the Rum-Pad Maundeth none, Like my Clapperdogeon. **1819** MOORE *Tom Crib's Mem.* 76 The brandy and tea, rather thinnish, That Knights of the Rumpad so rurally sip.

b. Hence ***rum-padder*** (see quot.); also ***rum-pad*** vb., to attack or rob on the highway.

a **1700** B. E. *Dict. Cant. Crew*, *Rum-padders*, the better sort of Highway-men well Mounted and Armed. **1895** H. WATSON in *Chap-Book* III. 484 To be rumpadded, there, almost within the precincts of London,..could not have been greatly to his taste.

rum (rʌm), *a.*² *slang.* [perh. due to some special application of prec., such as *rum cove*, 'a great rogue'. In common use from *c* 1800.] Odd, strange, queer. Also, bad, spurious.

1774 H. KELLY *School for Wives* III. ix, Its a little rum tongue, that we understand among von another. **1777** *Monthly Rev.* LVI. 137 We have sometimes amused ourselves by dipping into honest Isaac Walton's Complete Angler, merely as a rum book. **1783** *Session Paper Cent. Criminal Court* Oct. 952 By God, this is a rum go. **1800** LD. MELBOURNE *Papers* 7, I hope you will contrive..to rub off a few rum ideas which he contracted in these philosophical colleges. *c* **1803** G. COLMAN in M. R. Booth *Eng. Plays of 19th Cent.* (1973) III. 70 Dang me, but he's a rum customer! **1837** DICKENS *Pickw.* xiv, There's rummer things than women in this world though, mind you. **1847** G. W. M. REYNOLDS *Mysteries of London* III. xxv. 71/2 Work the bulls and couters rum. **1850** THACKERAY *Pendennis* xxxviii, This was the rummest go he ever saw. **1870** D. J. KIRWAN *Palace & Hovel* xxxii. 483 'Ah! that's a rum customer,' said the policeman; 'she's fly to hevery-think.' **1887** FENN *Master of Cerem.* iv, Rum thing I should drift into being the Major's servant, isn't it? **1895** *Wales* July 323/2 What's rum is that he is one of the best 'uns in chapel. **1930** G. B. SHAW *Apple Cart* I. 3 *Pamphilius.* He must have been a rum old bird. *Sempronius.* Not rum enough to be noticed. There are millions like him. **1942** *Gen* 1 Sept. 13/1 Anything that is good in the navy is 'scran' and if it's bad it's 'rum'. **1955** J. THOMAS *No Banners* vii. 61 'This is a rum go,' Alfred said. **1971** H. A. SMITH *View from Chivo* xix. 192 A rum cove if ever I met up with one. **1977** J. I. M. STEWART *Madonna of Astrolabe* xi. 153 Some Scottish names are distinctly rum. Yours is.

Comb. **1833** M. SCOTT *Tom Cringle* (1862) 245 Like a charity school of a Sunday, led by a rum-looking beadle. **1955** *Times* 16 Aug. 10/5 That's a rum looking swallow.

† **rum**, *v. slang. Obs.* [? from prec.] *trans.* To cheat.

1811 *Spirit Publ. Jrnls.* XV. 326 When I found out how he had rummed me, I thought it was but fair to dash him.

'rumacin. [irreg. f. L. *rumex* sorrel, dock: cf. RUMICIN.] (See quot.)

1863 *Lancet* I. 337/2 Rumacin. This is another of the concentrated American remedies... It purports to be the active principle of the root of a species of Dock.

rumage, obs. f. RUMMAGE.

‖**rumaki** (ruːˈmɑːkɪ). [Perh. altered f. Jap. *harumaki* spring roll.] An appetizer, of Oriental origin, consisting chiefly of chicken livers, water chestnuts, and bacon, marinated and broiled.

1965 R. CARRIER *Cookbk.* iii. 96 To make 24 *rumaki* (Japanese hot canapés), you will need ¾ pound chicken livers, 24 half-slices of bacon, 8 water chestnuts and 24 cocktail sticks. **1972** *Village Voice* (N.Y.) 1 June 74/1 (Advt.), Chicken Liver Rumaki. **1978** *Chicago* June 221/1 Delicious Cantonese-style appetizers include superlative king crab egg rolls and the best rumaki we've ever tasted.

rumal, var. ROMAL.

Ruman, var. ROUMAN *sb.* and *a.*

rumance, obs. form of ROMANCE.

Rumanian: see ROMANIAN *sb.* and *a.*³

rumänite (ruːˈmeɪnaɪt, ˈruːmənaɪt). *Min.* Also r(o)umanite. [ad. G. *rumänit* (O. Helm 1891, in *Schr. d. Natürforsch. Ges. in Danzig* VII. IV. 186), f. *Rumänia* Romania: see -ITE¹.] A variety of amber containing sulphur and succinic acid and found in Romania.

1892 E. S. DANA *Dana's Syst. Min.* (ed. 6) 1004 *Rumänite.* .. A yellow amber-like resin obtained from different points in Rumania, as in sandstone in the Buseo district, at Telage in the Bohosa district, etc. **1904** L. J. SPENCER tr. *M. Bauer's Precious Stones* II. 554 Roumanite, or Roumanian amber, is rarely yellow, but is usually brownish-yellow to brown. **1932** G. C. WILLIAMSON *Bk. Amber* 214 The ordinary phrase of Black Amber applied by dealers to Rumanite is misleading, because its colour value is a very high one, and many examples are amongst the most lovely coloured pieces of Amber that have ever been found. **1962** R. WEBSTER *Gems* I. xxiii. 442 At several places in Romania is found an amber, named appropriately roumanite, which is said to contain less succinic acid and more hydrogen sulphide.

Rumans(c)h, varr. ROMANSH.

rumatise, obs. f. RHEUMATIZE.

rumb(e, obs. ff. RHUMB.

rumba (ˈrʌmbə), *sb.* Also **rhumba**. [Amer. Sp.] An Afro-Cuban dance; a ballroom dance imitative of this, danced on the spot with a pronounced movement of the hips. Also, the dance rhythm of the rumba; a musical composition with this rhythm. Also *transf.*

1922 J. HERGESHEIMER *Bright Shawl* 112 Her life..was incredibly, wildly, debauched. Among other things, she danced, as the mulata, the rumba, an indescribable affair. **1926** *Nation* 15 Sept. 242/1 A half-dressed couple behind a slide window dancing the rumba. **1932** *New Yorker* 9 Apr. 39/2 Ceruse's tango band reminds you of every illicit Paris bender you ever had. Rumbas and tangos abound. **1934** H. MICHAEL *Peace without Honour* in J. W. Marriott *Best One-Act Plays of 1933* 135 Put on a dance record... It's a rumba. Will that do? **1939** [see BEGUINE²]. **1950** A. LOMAX *Mister Jelly Roll* (1952) ii. 79 Time seemed to flow like a dreamy rhumba. **1956** M. STEARNS *Story of Jazz* iii. 26 The rhumba, which is by far the most popular outside of Cuba, is consistently diluted for Western ears and has become a fixture at fashionable American night clubs. **1958** E. BORNEMAN in P. Gammond *Decca Bk. Jazz* xxi. 264 Ellington..started it all in 1930 with his jazz rumba *Maori*. **1974** *Encycl. Brit. Micropædia* VIII. 716/1 Best known for the dancers' subtle side to side hip movements with the torso erect, the rumba is danced with a basic pattern of two quick side steps and a slow forward step. **1980** *Tablet* 26 Jan. 84/2 A group of liturgical dancers swathed in white, practising the Our Father dance. No doubt this particular excursion into religious rumba was absurd.

b. *slang.* A spree.

Perhaps an erroneous use.

1934 E. HEMINGWAY in *Cosmopolitan* Apr. 108/3 He'd been giving the nigger a dollar a day and the nigger had been on a rumba every night. I could see him getting sleepy already.

2. *attrib.* and *Comb.*, as ***rumba band***, ***competition***, ***dancer***, ***orchestra***, ***record***, ***rhythm***; **rumba-box** (see quot. 1961).

1944 H. MCCLOY *Panic* 110 The swish of a sand-filled gourd in a *rhumba band. **1967** O. LANCASTER *With an Eye to Future* v. 119 The strains of 'Peanut Vendor' played by one of the newly fashionable rumba bands. **1976** *Islander* (Victoria, B.C.) 4 Jan. 2/2 As far as we know the African Bongo Tribe made the first bongo drums for the latter use in the modern rhumba band. **1961** F. G. CASSIDY *Jamaica Talk* xii. 266 As for the **rumba-box*..it is a recent invention or importation which simulates the tones of the bass viol by means of four pieces of metal of different gauges attached to a box (the resonance chamber), which vibrate when they are plucked with the fingers, and are tuned to correspond to the strings. **1976** G. SIMS *End of Web* x. 69 The Rastafarians with their home-made drums and rumba-boxes. **1944** M. SHARP *Cluny Brown* xix. 130 She entered for a *Rumba competition. **1973** *Black World* Sept. 12/2 Giullén captured the vitality of Afro-Cuban life in a series of 'sones' (songs) which deal with cane cutters, *rumba dancers, and folk types. **1941** B. SCHULBERG *What makes Sammy Run?* xi. 271 He was..dancing with her out on the patio to the *rhumba orchestra. **1972** J. MCCLURE *Caterpillar Cop* viii. 118 Lisbet had to raise her voice..above the *rhumba record to catch his attention. **1932** *Radio Times* 8 Apr. 129 There is Southern glamour in the *Rumba Rhythm of a tango tune. **1957** *Encycl. Brit.* VII. 23/2 The Rumba rhythm: one, two, three, pause; one, two, three, pause. **1970** W. APEL *Harvard Dict. Mus.* (ed. 2) 744/1 After 1930 rumba rhythms were incorporated into jazz.

'rumba, *v.* Also **rhumba**. [f. the sb.] *intr.* To dance the rumba. Also, to move as though dancing the rumba.

1938 G. GREENE *Brighton Rock* II. i. 66 The tune the band was playing, the crowd on the floor trying to rumba. **1944** M. SHARP *Cluny Brown* xxiv. 156 Belinski at once rose, grasped the girl round the waist, and then began to rumba. **1951** E. TAYLOR *Game of Hide-&-Seek* II. i. 120 'Englishwomen should never rumba,' he told her. **1961** G. DURRELL *Whispering Land* iii. 85 He [*sc.* a fur seal] decided that the seagull should be taught a lesson, so he humped himself up indignantly and rumbaed towards it ferociously. **1970** V. CANNING *Great Affair* vii. 111 You once taught two boys to rhumba.

rumbelow (ˈrʌmbələʊ). Now *rare*. Forms: 4–5 romby-, rumbylogh; 5 romelowe, -ylawe; 5 rom-, 6 rumbelowe, 5 rumbeloo (6 -belo, -bolo); 6 rom- (*Sc.* rohum-), 7 room-, 6, 9 **rumbelow**; 7 rumbillow. [See sense 1; in some later uses associated with RUMBLE *v.*¹]

1. A meaningless combination of syllables serving as a refrain, orig. sung by sailors when rowing. (Cf. HEAVE HO and HEY-HO.)

13.. *Coer de L.* 2522 They rowede hard, and sungge ther too, With heuelow and rumbeloo. *c* **1315** in *Brut* (1906) clxxxviii. 208 [Foralsemiche as he louede forto go by watere, ..maidenes made a songe þerof,..] What wende þe Kyng of Engeland haue ygete Scotlande wiþ Rombylogh. *a* **1400** *Sqr. lowe Degre* 824 Your maryners shall synge arowe Hey how and rumby lowe. *c* **1515** *Cocke Lorell's B.* C j, Some songe heue and howe rombelowe. *a* **1529** SKELTON *Bowge of Courte* 252 Heue and how rombelow, row the bote, Norman, rowe! **1579** LOUTH in *Narr. Reform.* (Camden) 29 At one pulle all the golden godes came downe with heyho Rombelo. **1600** W. WATSON *Decacordon* (1602) 95 Haue at him..with heaue and hoe rumbelow.

1790 *Gentl. Mag.* LX. II. 1100, I have recollected the first verse of the song used on that day [*i.e.* Flora Day at Helston, Cornwall]... Hel-an-tow, Rum-be-low.

†**2.** A blow, a stroke. *Obs.* Cf. RUMBLE *sb.* 3.

c **1400** *Laud Troy Bk.* 14005 He ȝaff him suche a romelowe, That he went ouer his sadil-bowe.

†**3.** Used as a place-name. *Obs.*

1530 *Hickscorner* (E.E.D.S.) 137, I have ben in Gene and in Cowe, Also in the londe of Rumbelowe, Thre myle out of hell. **1549** *Compl. Scot.* vi. 65 Sal i go vitht ȝou to rumbelo fayr.

†**4.** *attrib.* Rumbling, resounding. *Obs.*

1582 STANYHURST *Æneis* I. (Arb.) 24 Through Sicil his raging wyld frets and rumbolo rustling On peeres you sayled. *Ibid.* IV. 101 Thee whilst in the skye seat great bouncing rumbelo thundring Ratleth.

†**5.** A woman of light behaviour. *Obs.*

1611 J. DAVIES (Heref.) *Commend. Poems* 67 Wks. (Grosart) II. 13 Then yee descend, where he sits in a Gondolow With Egs throwne at him by a wanton Room-be-low. **16..** *Roxb. Ball.* II. 257 In wine we call for bawdy jiggs, Catzoes, rumbillows, whirligigs.

6. A kind of carriage.

1881 BLACKMORE *Christowell* (1891) 183 Let the other flys, and rumbelows, come down first.

rumber, obs. form of RUMOUR.

rum'blante. *nonce-word.* [f. RUMBLE *v.*, after *andante*, etc.] Rumbling notes.

1775 SHERIDAN *Rivals* II. i, Such a mistress of flat and sharp, squallante, rumblante, and quiverante!

rumble (ˈrʌmb(ə)l), *sb.* Forms: α. 4–5 rombel, 4–6 romble, 5 rombul, rowmble; 5 rumbil, 6 -byll, 5– rumble. β. *Sc.* 6 rummill, -yll, 9 rummel, rummle. [f. RUMBLE *v.*¹ Cf. G. and Da. *rummel*, Norw. dial. *ruml*, Du. *gerommel.*]

1. a. A low, continuous, murmuring, grumbling, or growling sound, as that of thunder, distant cannon, heavy vehicles, etc.

c **1386** CHAUCER *Knt.'s T.* 1121 A foreste,..In which ther ran a rumbel and a swough. As though a storm sholde bresten euery bough. **1412–20** LYDG. *Troy Bk.* (E.E.T.S) 638 With rowmble and swowe resownyng vnto dethe—Swiche a noise Grekis made þere. **1513** DOUGLAS *Æneis* v.

xii. 54 Hillis and valis trymblit of thondir rummyll. **1577–87** HOLINSHED *Chron.* III. 921/2 Which [guns] made such a rumble in the aire, that it was like thunder. **1728** *Phil. Trans.* XXXVI. 126 These..Rumbles and Tremblings, were louder and greater at Newbury..than with us. **1817** J. SCOTT *Paris Revisit.* (ed. 4) 122 It was the rumble of cannon. **1842** DICKENS *Amer. Notes* (1850) 57/1 The deep rumble of carts and waggons. **1859** FITZGERALD *Omar Khayyám* xiii, The rumble of a distant Drum. **1897** *Allbutt's Syst. Med.* III. 43 The development of a true presystolic rumble.

b. Applied to language or utterance.

a **1680** BUTLER *Rem.* (1759) I. 110 You wisely scorn your Stile to humble, Or for the Sense's Sake to wave the Rumble. **1711** tr. *Werenfels' Meteors of Stile* 218 Admirable Words to fill the Mouth, and make a graceful Rumble. **1897** P. WARUNG *Tales Old Regime* 164 The rumble gave place to a strange pleading. **1902** 'LINESMAN' *Words Eyewitness* 217 As he talks in his jerky rumble.

c. In sound reproduction, low-frequency noise originating as mechanical vibration in a turntable. Also *attrib.* and *Comb.*

1949 FRAYNE & WOLFE *Elem. of Sound Recording* xiv. 271 An additional factor that must be considered in noise measurements is the vibration or 'rumble' of the turntable. **1968** *Times* 29 Nov. (Sound of Leisure Suppl.) p. vii/1 Background noise while a record is playing can be very disturbing and it is the elimination of this noise, appropriately called rumble, which is the main concern of the manufacturers of gramophone records and record playing units. **1970** J. EARL *Tuners & Amplifiers* i. 19 Sometimes the high-pass filter is referred to as the rumble filter, since its bass attenuation characteristic significantly reduces the amplifier's response to low-frequency noises generated by the turntable unit and passed on via the disc and pickup. **1971** *Hi-Fi Sound* Feb. 67/2 With a rumble-free turntable, a player may cost as much as an entire low-budget sound system. **1977** *Time* 10 Oct. 43/1 (Advt.), There is rumble from the cutting machine in most record grooves.

d. A rumour. *U.S. colloq.*

1961 P. A. BRODEUR in *Webster* s.v., Picked up the rumble ..and thought he'd pass it on just in case. **1966** 'E. MCBAIN' *Eighty Million Eyes* iv. 67 The neighbourhood rumble is that he was fooling around with one of their wives. **1974** E. MCGIRR *Murderous Journey* 63 The rumble is that he works for Marcello.

2. †**a.** Commotion, bustle, tumult, uproar. *Obs.*

c **1386** CHAUCER *Clerk's T.* 941 A stormy peple,.. Delitynge euere in rumbul that is newe. **1513** MORE *Chron.* Wks. 43 Aboute whome he found muche heauinesse, rumble, haste and businesse. **1533** —— *Apol.* xxii. ibid. 885/1 In the time of..Henry the fourth, aboute the time of a great rumble that the heretiques made. **1577** HELLOWES *Gueuara's Chron.* 425 The fighte and slaughter was so great, and the confusion, rumble, and crie of people so extreeme. **1675** COTTON *Burlesque upon B.* 101 And no more such a rumble keep. **1682** W. ROGERS *7th Pt. Christian-Quaker* 36 We see no real Cause..for the great noise and rumble he makes about Outward Laws.

b. A street-fight between rival gangs. Also *fig. slang* (chiefly *U.S.*).

1946 *Amer. Mercury* Apr. 480 We're going to have a rumble with the Happy Gents tonight. Gang kids call these fights rumbles. **1953** KRAMER & KARR *Teen-Age Gangs* p. v, A 'rumble'—a wild group fight—which gang youths consider the glamorous high point of their existence. *Ibid.* i. 4 A leader naturally headed his followers in a rumble with another gang. **1958** H. SALISBURY *Shook-Up Generation* (1959) iv. 64 He would do things no other boy would dare. He would sound a cop on the beat and run away laughing. In a rumble he was like a wild-cat. **1969** C. BURKE *God is Beautiful, Man* (1970) 38 By the time they got the drink there was a big rumble brewin'. The Israelites set up a big crash pad and there was another gang that didn't like it and they decided they would have a real big rumble with these Moses people. **1971** P. L. CAVE *Chopper* iv. 28 So I missed out on a rumble tonight. **1977** *Time* 31 Oct. 55/1 Singer Frank Sinatra seldom ducks a rumble with a reporter.

†**3.** *Sc.* A severe blow. *Obs.*

1375 BARBOUR *Bruce* XII. 557 Thar mycht men se..mony a reale romble [*v.r.* rymmyll] rid Be roucht, thar apon aythir sid. **1434** *Bk. Alexander Gt.* 57 Mony ruid rummill thay gaif.

4. The hind part of a carriage when so arranged as to provide sitting accommodation (usually assigned to servants or attendants), or to carry luggage. Cf. RUMBLER 2, and RUMBLE-TUMBLE 1. Hence in a motor vehicle, = *rumble seat. U.S.*

1808 MRS. GRANT *Mem. & Corr.* (1844) I. 162 Miss D. and Isabella go in the rumble, as it is called, behind. **1811** *Sporting Mag.* XXXVII. 128 Alterations and extras..were made, among others, a rumble, with trunks. **1854** THACKERAY *Newcomes* xxvii, Carriages which..from interior, box, and rumble discharge a dozen English people at hotel gates. **1884** Q. VICTORIA *More Leaves* 281, I got into a hired..open landau (on the rumble of which Brown sat, as in crowds it is much safer to have a person close behind you). **1929** W. FAULKNER *Sanctuary; Orig. Text* (1981) vii. 82 The car drew up... The ones in the rumble said nothing. **1939** —— *Wild Palms* 90 McCord drove them up to the lake on the Saturday night before Labor Day, the hundred dollars worth of food—the tins, the beans and rice..—in the rumble. **1941** B. SCHULBERG *What makes Sammy Run?* viii. 189 I'll look in the rumble... I think I have some.

5. A rotating box or cask in which iron articles are shaken and cleaned by friction.

1843 HOLTZAPFFEL *Turning* I. 346 Small works are additionally cleaned in a rumble, or revolving cask, where they soon scrub each other clean.

6. [Perhaps a different word.] An interruption in the course of a crime; an alarm; a tip-off. *Criminals' slang.*

1911 C. G. ROE *Horrors of White Slave Trade* iv. 80, I posed as a theatrical manager..and caught many an unwary stage struck girl... I was taking small chances of being caught and in fact did not have a 'rumble' during all the time I was there. **1913** A. STRINGER *Shadow* v. 93 'But he blew out for 'Frisco this morning,' contended the puzzled Sheiner. 'Shot through as though he had just had a rumble!' **1914** JACKSON & HELLYER *Vocab. Criminal Slang* 73 If you walk on the main stem you'll get a rumble. **1927** D. HAMMETT in *Black Mask* Feb. 17/2 The neighbors give us the rumble. **1949** A. HYND *We are Public Enemy* i. 21 The cops had gotten a rumble that..gangsters were holed up. **1949** in Wentworth & Flexner *Dict. Amer. Slang* (1960) 437/1 If there's a rumble, we do the time. **1957** *Life* 9 Dec. 57 The boys slip into town. You wouldn't think they would be noticed. But some busybody catches on and puts in a rumble.

7. *attrib.* and *Comb.*, as **rumble seat** *N. Amer.* = DICKY, DICKEY *sb.* 9 c; **rumble strip** (see quots. 1962 and 1975).

1912 *Collier's* 23 Mar. 20/3 She's burnin' the wind out of town in a college boy's car with big May on the rumble seat behind. **1929** M. LIEF *Hangover* 301 The next morning she packed a small bag of necessaries, stowed it in the rumble seat, and drove off. **1951** T. CAPOTE *Grass Harp* iv. 95 They'd stuffed her into the rumble-seat of Big Eddie's old coupé and driven straight to the jail. **1972** *Evening Telegram* (St. John's, Newfoundland) 5 Aug. 15/1 Three old-fashioned things you seldom see on the roads these days... Running boards, rumble seats and courtesy. **1962** *Punch* 27 June 960/2 American towns have been experimenting with 'rumble strips'—coarse-textured expanses of road surface just before cross-roads. **1974** *Oxford Times* 12 July 15/3 Rumble strips put down in the road to slow traffic had no effect. **1975** *Daily Mail* 3 Jan. 11/4 *Rumble strips*: These are tiny ridges on a road surface which cause a high-pitched whine as the car tyres pass over them... They indicate a hazard ahead.

rumble ('rʌmb(ə)l), *v.*[1] Forms: α. 4 romblen, 5–7 romble, 6 rombel-, roomble, roumble; 4 rumbelyn, 5–6 rumbel-, 6 rumbil(l, -byl, rumbol, 4– rumble. β. (Chiefly *Sc.*) 5 romel-, rummelon(e, rum(me)lyn, 6 rumil, -yl, rummel, -ill, -yl(l, 9 rummle. [ME. *romblen, rumblen*, = MDu. *rommelen, rummelen* (Du. *rommelen*, Fris. *rommelje*), G. *rummeln*, †*rumeln* (15th c.), MSw. *rumbla*, Da. *rumle*, Norw. *rumla*, of onomatopœic origin, and perhaps properly a LG. word.]

1. *intr.* To make a low, heavy, continuous sound: **a.** Of thunder or other natural causes.

c **1385** CHAUCER *L.G.W.* 1218 *Dido*, Among al this to rumbelyn [*v.r.* romblen] gan the heuene. **1480** *Robt. Devyll* 42 All the grounde of the noyse rombled. **1513** DOUGLAS *Æneis* IV. iv. 63 In the meyn quhile, the hevinnis all about With fellon noyis, gan to rummyll and rowt. **1582** STANYHURST *Æneis* II. (Arb.) 65 A thundring In the skye dyd rumble. **1602** DEKKER *Honest Wh.* Wks. 1873 II. 82 Romble, romble goe the waters. *a* **1680** BUTLER *Rem.* (1759) I. 198 The Thunder And Lightning loud did rumble. **1756** P. BROWNE *Jamaica* 7 The mountains rumbled, cracked, and opened in several places. **1798** COLERIDGE *Anc. Mar.* VII. viii, A sound was heard. Under the water it rumbled on. **1832** W. IRVING *Alhambra* II. 235 A large stone.. rebounded from side to side, rumbling and tumbling, with a noise like thunder. **1851** HAWTHORNE *Snow Image*, etc. (1879) 80 An earthquake rumbled through the town. **1872** JENKINSON *Guide Eng. Lakes* (1879) 148 The waves are distinctly heard.., rumbling in a narrow and distant part. *fig.* **1647** N. BACON *Disc. Govt. Eng.* I. xlvii. (1739) 77 The Canon-Law, that ever since Austin's coming, like Thunder, rumbled in the Clouds. **1655** FULLER *Ch. Hist.* III. xii. 34 That thunder which long before rumbled in his threatnings, now gave the crack.

b. Of the bowels, or the air in them.

1535 COVERDALE *Isaiah* xvi. 11 Wherfore my bely rombled (as it had bene a lute) for Moabs sake. **1572** *Satir. Poems Reform.* xxxiii. 92 My bowells Rumbills as thay wald vther eit. **1602** MARSTON *Ant. & Mel.* I. Wks. 1856 I. 16 His bowels rumbling with winde passion. **1684** tr. *Bonet's Merc. Compit.* VIII. 311 When the Belly rumbles without any swelling. **1721** MORTIMER *Husb.* (ed. 3) I. 236 And when behind he will be very stiff, and his Guts rumble. **1797** J. DOWNING *Disord. Horned Cattle* 72 The wind rumbleth in its bowels.

c. In miscellaneous uses.

1483 CAXTON *Gold. Leg.* 367/2 His thye beganne romble and made soo grete a noyse that it semed that the bone brake. **1596** SPENSER *F.Q.* v. ii. 50 His timbered bones all broken rudely rumbled. **1638** JUNIUS *Paint. Ancients* 41 When the wind-shaken ropes rumble and rustle. **1683** MOXON *Mech. Exerc., Printing* xi. ¶ 15 Irregularities will both Mount and Sink the Cramp-Irons, and make them Run rumbling upon the Ribs. **1848** DICKENS *Dombey* lvi, The organ rumbled and rolled as if the church had got the colic. **1874** LISLE CARR *J. Gwynne* I. i. 20 Those words of comfortable wisdom, which rumbled sonorously overhead.

fig. *a* **1652** BROME *Queenes Exch.* II. i, A wild confusion rumbles in my brain. **1700** DRYDEN *Wife of Bath's T.* 178 The counsel rumbled till it found a vent.

2. a. To move or travel with a continuous murmuring, or low, rolling sound. Const. *up, down, round, back, by*, etc.

c **1384** CHAUCER *Ho. Fame* II. 1026 The grete soun..that rumbleth vp and doun In fames house. ? **1569** SPENSER *Vis. Petrarch* 44 A Spring of water mildely romblyng downe. **1591** SYLVESTER *Du Bartas* I. ii. 712 It rouls, and roars, and round-round-round it rumbles. **1774** GOLDSM. *Nat. Hist.* (1776) I. 69 Stones..rumbling along the sides of the descent for some time. **1840** DICKENS *Old C. Shop* xv, Some straggling carts and coaches rumbling by. **1893** H. VIZETELLY *Glances back* II. xxiv. 47 The cab rumbled back to town.

fig. **1861** *Sat. Rev.* Nov. 539 The story would rumble on in all its dreary integrity. **1862** S. LUCAS *Secularia* 89 The war that was rumbling past them was no business of theirs.

b. *transf.* Of persons: To be conveyed in a rumbling vehicle.

1803 G. COLMAN *John Bull* II. ii. 19 I've rumbled on the road, all night, Frank; my bones ache. **1832** W. IRVING *Alhambra* II. 182 He ordered out his carriage of state, and.. rumbled down the avenue of the Alhambra. **1864** G. MUSGRAVE *Ten Days in Fr. Parsonage* I. iv. 120 We rumbled over the stones. **1883** *Harper's Mag.* Feb. 395/1 We rumbled away in a sort of mourning-coach.

3. Of persons: †**a.** To make a noise, disturbance, or tumult. *Obs.*

c **1386** CHAUCER *Monk's T.* 555 The peple cride, and rombled vp and doun, That with his erys herde he how they seyde. *c* **1412** HOCCLEVE *De Reg. Princ.* 2754 þe peple gan to rumble, & clappe & crye. **1441** *Plumpton Corr.* (Camden) p. lv, And they went ro[m]bling up the said towne & downe; they said openly [etc.].

†**b.** To mutter or murmur. *Obs.*

c **1440** *Promp. Parv.* 439/2 Rummelon or prively mystron, *mussito.*

c. To utter rumbling sounds or tones.

1755 H. WALPOLE *Let. to Conway* 15 Nov., Nugent roared, and Sir Thomas rumbled.

d. To have a gang fight. *slang* (chiefly *U.S.*).

1959 *Listener* 29 Jan. 201/2 Do you know why a 'diddley bop' should put on a 'stenjar' to 'go down' to 'rumble' at a 'jitterbug'... That is the language of the teenage gangs of New York. **1969** S. GREENLEE *Spook who sat by Door* xiv. 121 The teenage gangs..haven't been rumbling and so they have a lot of latent hostility to get rid of. **1977** 'E. MCBAIN' *Long Time no See* viii. 116 We *was* tired, man. We been rumblin all the past month..gang-busting.

4. a. To produce a rumbling noise by agitating or moving something. *rare.*

c **1386** CHAUCER *Can. Yeom. Prol. & T.* 769 He..in the water rombled to and fro. And wonder pryuely took vp also The coper teyne. **1530** PALSGR. 693/1, I romble, I make noyse in a house with remevyng of heavy thynges, *je charpente.* **17..** RAMSAY *Wyfe of Auchtermuchty* xi, Quhen he had rumblit a full lang hour, The sorrow crap of butter he gat.

†**b.** To toss about in bed or on the ground. *Obs.*

15.. *How a Serjeaunt wolde be a Frere* 247 in Hazl. *E.P.P.* III. 128 They roule and romble, they turne and tumble, as pygges do in a poke. **1520** *Calisto & Melib.* in Hazl. *Dodsley* I. 66 Crito..I think lay nat easily, and began to rumble. **1581** RICH *Farew.* N j b, Lucilla rumblyng from one side of the bedde vnto the other, had rolled of all the clothes.

†**c.** To move boisterously or noisily. *Obs.*

1553 *Respublica* I. iii. 263, I wolde fayne be shouldering & rumboling emonge them. *c* **1560** A. SCOTT *Poems* (S.T.S.) ii. 175 Sum ruscht, sum rummyld, and sum reild.

5. *trans.* **a.** To cause to move or travel (also *dial.* to stir about, agitate) with a rumbling sound. †Also *fig.* to revolve.

1519 HORMAN *Vulgaria* 196 b, Whan they had longe roumbled this treson in theyr mynde. **1614** RICH *Honestie of Age* (1844) 8 Diogenes beganne to rolle and rumble his Tubb. **1632** LITHGOW *Trav.* x. 467 So caused he euery morning..his Coach to be rumbled at his gate. **1825** JAMIESON *Suppl.*, To *Rummle*, to stir about; as, 'to rummle potatoes', when mixed with any liquid. **1867–** in *Eng. Dial. Dict.*

b. To utter, run *over*, drone *out*, give *forth*, send *down*, with a rumbling sound.

15.. *Parl. Byrdes* 63 in Hazl. *E.P.P.* III. 170 Than rombled the Doue for her lot, Folke may be mery and syng not. **1601** DENT *Pathway to Heaven* (1603) 196 Then will they rumble over their praies, or be pattering some pater nosters. **1686** G. STUART *Joco-Ser. Disc.* 23 Sometimes having tane a fresh-cup, He'll rumble you out, 'down drops the Bishop'. **1858** HAWTHORNE *Fr. & It. Note-bks.* (1872) I. 18 The organ was rumbling forth a deep, lugubrious bass. **1892** ZANGWILL *Childr. Ghetto* xii. I. 255 They rumbled and roared and chorused prayers with a zeal that shook the window-panes. **1898** KIPLING *Fleet in Being* 3 The Officer of the Bridge rumbled requests down the speaking-tube to the engine-room.

†**c.** ? To shake or furbish *up*. *Obs.*[−1]

1621 LADY M. WROTH *Urania* 476 Those that were of the age before, which hauing young minds rumbled vp their old carcases, and rubd ouer their wrinckling faces.

d. *slang.* To put *out*, rule *out*, unceremoniously; to handle roughly.

1811 *Sporting Mag.* XXXVII. 128 Mr. Jekyll..was afraid that his client must consent to be rumbled out of Court. **1815** *Ibid.* XLVI. 65 Croxey rumbled his antagonist in the first five rounds of the combat. **1963** *Times* 28 Jan. 9/5 Many people who even want Britain to enter the Common Market express a little joy in seeing de Gaulle rumbling your people. **1976** LD. ANNAN in *Ann. Rep. Univ. Coll. (London)* 1975–76 7 It looks..as if the Department of Education and Science has rumbled the Schools Council plan for a common system of school leaving examinations, a proposal which the universities regarded with the deepest suspicion.

e. To clean in a rumble.

1904 HARBORD & HALL *Metall. of Steel* xxxiv. 532 Small forged or stamped and malleable cast articles, which can be 'rumbled' bright in a shaking barrel, take the metal fairly well. **1957** *New Scientist* 7 Nov. 23/3 The thin parting bridges [of ball-bearings] are automatically severed and, after cooling, the balls are rumbled to remove the burr.

6. [Perhaps a different word.] *trans.* To get to the bottom of; to see through, understand, grasp; to recognize; to detect, discover, disturb. *slang.*

1886–96 in Farmer & Henley *Slang* (1903) VI. 75/2, I rumbled the tip as a matter of course. **1898** A. M. BINSTEAD *Pink 'Un & Pelican* ix. 209, I soon rumbled he was in it, when I heard Ball givin' him the 'me lord' for it. **1912** C. MACKENZIE *Carnival* (ed. 5) x. 126 I've properly rumbled your friends. **1925** N. VENNER *Imperfect Imposter* iii. 30 He'd have rumbled me. He can't rumble me now. **1928** E. WALLACE *More Educated Evans* iii. 69, I rumbled you as soon as I took a screw through the winder. **1930** P. MACDONALD *Link* 74 If I hadn't had so many queer things happen to me in such a short time.. I'd never have rumbled him. **1939** *Almanac for New Yorkers* 125 Some mugs rumbled us. **1956** 'A. GILBERT' *Riddle of Lady* viii. 115 The tobacconist.. had been rumbled and compelled to give evidence. *Ibid.* xi. 178, I might have guessed you'd rumble me. **1959** *Encounter* Aug. 29/2 He evidently didn't rumble anything was at all unusual. **1966** J. BINGHAM *Double Agent* iii. 43 You've been rumbled. What's the use of a gun? **1979** E. NEWMAN *Sunday Punch* xvi. 145 'Have you any influence with him?' 'He'd rumble that. He'd think I was your agent.'

†**'rumble**, *v.*[2] *Obs.* [ME. *romble*, app. f. *rome* ROAM *v.*] *intr.* To ramble.

1393 LANGL. *P. Pl.* C. VI. 11 Romynge [*v.r.* romblynge] in remembraunce thus reson me aratede. **1477** NORTON *Ordin. Alch.* iii. in Ashm. (1652) 39 This Science thei never founde, .. But rumbled foorth, and evermore they sought. **1677** *Compl. Servant-Maid* 62 A rouling stone never getteth moss, .. so if you rumble up and down you will gain but little credit. **1722** RAMSAY *Three Bonnets* 85 (1877) II. 380 [She would] Rumble to ilka market-town.

'rumbled, *ppl. a.* [f. RUMBLE *v.*[1]]

1. Emitted as, given with, a rumbling sound.

1582 STANYHURST *Æneis* III. (Arb.) 88 But neere ioynctlye brayeth with ruffleryе rumbled Ætna. **1898** KIPLING *Fleet in Being* 75 Try now to.. find a meaning in the rumbled signals from the bridge.

2. Mumbled, scrambled; mashed. Also *fig.*

1879 *B'ham Weekly Post* 24 May 1/4 Rumbled eggs we had particularly nice. **1879** *Cumb. Gloss.* Suppl., *Rummel't 'taties*, boiled potatoes mashed and mixed with milk and butter. **1930** R. CAMPBELL *Adamastor* 67 Nature.. Admits no vegetable green... But with snarled gold and rumbled blue Must disinfect the sight.

'rumbleful. [f. RUMBLE *sb.* 4.] The contents of a rumble.

1859 *Chamb. Journ.* XI. 349 Pa is kept in agitated action between his quiverful of arrows and his rumbleful of baggage.

rumble'garie, *a. Sc.* Also **-gairie.** [prob. based on RUMBLE *v.*[1]] 'Disorderly, having a forward and confused manner' (Jam.).

1722 RAMSAY *Three Bonnets* IV, Jouk and his rumblegarie wife Drive on a drunken gaming life. **1795** BURNS *Let. to G. Thompson* May, The little one.. is the most striking likeness of an ill-deedie,.. rumblegairie urchin of mine.

rumble'gumption. *Sc.* Also **rum(m)el-, rum(m)le-.** [Cf. RUMGUMPTION and GUMPTION.] Common sense.

1787 BURNS *Let. to W. Nicol* 1 June, Onie ane o' them had as muckle smeddum and rumblegumtion as the half o' some presbytries that you and I baith ken. **1791** LEARMONT *Poems* 147 Without ae spark o' rumelgumphtion. **1868** *Academia* Apr. 377 Who, devoid of rummelgumption, Courts dyspepsy and consumption. **1890** BARRIE *Little Minister* (1892) 79 That's just what I am telling you, only you hinna the rumelgumption to see it.

'rumble-'jumble, *adv.* [Cf. RUMBLE-TUMBLE and JUMBLE *v.*] In a rumbling, jumbling manner.

1887 JEFFERIES *Amaryllis* ix, So our lives go on, rumble-jumble, like a carrier's cart over ruts and stones.

'rumblement. *rare.* = RUMBLING *vbl. sb.*

1719 D'URFEY *Pills* V. 2 Her Master heard a Rumblement. **1844** MRS. CARLYLE *Lett.* I. 282, I slept much better.. in spite of.. a considerable rumblement of carts.

rumbler ('rʌmblə(r)). [f. RUMBLE *v.* + -ER[1].]

1. a. One who, or that which, rumbles or makes a rumbling noise; *spec.* a resounding line of poetry; a cart or carriage.

1611 FLORIO, *Romoreggiatore*, a noiser, a rumbler. **1670** EACHARD *Cont. Clergy* 6 Being bound to get.. two or three hundred rumblers out of Homer. **1706** BAYNARD *Cold Baths* II. 425, I only trull 'em a couple of Rumblers. **1748** RICHARDSON *Clarissa* IV. 206 The trisyllables, and the rumblers of syllables more than three. **1836** MAHONY *Reliq. Father Prout* ix. *Songs France* 269 The rumbler jugged off from his feet. **1874** *Slang Dict.* 273 *Rumbler*, a four-wheeled cab.

b. A type of round bell on a harness, etc. Also *attrib.*

1953 A. JOBSON *Household & Country Crafts* xii. 130 But at Chichester the first horse had three bells, the second four and the third five. In the case of round bells they were known as rumblers. **1961** *Countryman* LVIII. III. 596 Some early ones had round 'rumbler' bells. **1971** *Country Life* 8 Apr. 839/2 Rumblers were another type of bell, circular with a ball inside to give them their characteristic sound. This type was quite common for cart horses or pack horses, but never used on a sheep as that animal did not give the bell the right kind of motion to make it rumble properly.

†**2.** = RUMBLE *sb.* 4. *Obs.*[−1]

1801 [see RUMBLE-TUMBLE 1].

3. A machine for peeling potatoes.

1976 *Star* (Sheffield) 20 Nov. (Advt.), One 56 lb Triumph Superb Potato Rumbler, fully reconditioned, £300. **1977** *Grimsby Even. Tel.* 24 May 4/9 (Advt.), Potato room with an imperial rumbler and a Crypto chipper.

'rumble-'tumble. [f. RUMBLE *v.* + TUMBLE *v.*]

1. = RUMBLE *sb.* 4. ? *Obs.*

1801 W. FELTON *Carriages* II. App. 40 The rumbler, or rumble-tumble is a convenience fixed to the hind end of the carriage, and made to carry luggage. **1817** KEATINGE *Trav.* II. 159 The important point whether the dicky or the rumble-tumble were the more honourable place. **1858** LYTTON *What will He do* I. xv, From the dusty height of a rumble-tumble.. Vance caught sight of Lionel and Sophy.

2. A rumbling coach, carriage, or cart.

1806 J. BERESFORD *Miseries Hum. Life* VI. (ed. 3) I. 118 A name for a stage-coach which beats rumble-tumble, caterpillar, and every other English nick-name, out of the field. **1829** W. IRVING *Life & Lett.* (1864) II. 406, I leave Granada this afternoon at five o'clock in a kind of rumble tumble, called a Tartana, on two wheels. **1854** MISS BAKER *Northampt. Gloss.*, *Rumble-Tumble*, a large, old-fashioned unwieldy carriage.

3. A rough or tumbling motion.

1878 BROWNING *Poets Croisic* xxii, Suiting, to rumble-tumble of the seas, The songs forbidden a serener clime.

4. Scrambled eggs. *Anglo-Indian.*

1879 [see MUMBLED 2]. **1882** *Indian Outfits*, etc. 77 Buttered eggs, commonly called by the natives 'rumble-tumble'. **1956** D. WALKER *Harry Black* xiii. 192 'What's for breakfast?' 'Keventer's sausages and rumble-tumble,' Christian said... She went off to feed the family.. on sausages and scrambled eggs. **1966** J. & R. GODDEN *Two under Indian Sun* iii. 54 Rumble tumble, the Indian name for scrambled eggs. **1980** D. HART-DAVIS *Heights of Rimring* vii. 74 The rumble-tumble was a mighty omelette with strips of onion in it, accompanied by fried potatoes.

rumblifi'cation. *nonce-word.* Rumbling.

1835 M. SCOTT *Cruise Midge* xiv, He treated us with an extra rumblification in his gizzard.

'rumbling, *vbl. sb.* [f. RUMBLE *v.*[1] Cf. MDu. *rommelinge.*]

1. a. The action of making a rumble; an instance of this; a rumbling noise.

c **1386** CHAUCER *Sompn. T.* 525 The rumblynge [*v.r.* romblyng] of a fart, and euery soun, Nis but of Eir reuerberacioun. **1533** BELLENDEN *Livy* I. xii. (S.T.S.) I. 69 þan was herd þe huge rummylling and sound of brokin housis & wallis in all partis þareof. **1584** R. SCOT *Discov. Witchcr.* xv. xxii. (1886) 365 To find out the cause of noise and spirituall rumbling in houses. **1615** G. SANDYS *Trav.* 243 A continuall winde that keepeth a horrible rumbling. **1678** OTWAY *Friendship in F.* III. i, I can act.. any thing, I can act the rumbling of a wheelbarrow. *c* **1738** SWIFT *On his Deafness* Wks. 1751 XIV. 252 At Thunder now no more I start, Than at the Rumbling of a Cart. **1756–7** tr. *Keysler's Trav.* (1760) III. 28 In the city of Naples were heard subterraneous rumblings. **1851** D. JERROLD *St. Giles* xxviii. 291 His heart throbbing to the rumbling of his coach wheels. **1880** GEIKIE *Phys. Geog.* IV. xxii. 202 Rumblings are heard like the mutterings of distant thunder.

b. With reference to the bowels.

1544 PHAER *Regim. Lyfe* (1553) G vj b, Colica passio.. is knowen also by the rumblyng, which is a noise in the bowels. **1602** *2nd Pt. Return fr. Parnass.* III. III. 1298 Tell the meridian howre by rumbling of his panch. **1684** tr. *Bonet's Merc. Compit.* VIII. 311 If the rumbling be caused by Bile.. it may be good to give Milk. **1733** CHEYNE *Eng. Malady* II. ix. §6 (1734) 213 Inflation of the Bowels with Rumbling and Noise. **1822** GOOD *Study Med.* (1829) I. 171 Borborygmus. With frequent rumbling of the bowels. **1897** *Allbutt's Syst. Med.* III. 734 As shewn by the gurgling and rumbling in the bowels.

†**2.** Disturbance, tumult, stir. *Obs.*

c **1471** *Pol. Poems* (Rolls) II. 276 Ther was rennyng for the sovereynte, There was roryngе and rumbelynge, pete to here. *c* **1510** MORE *Picus* Wks. 15/1, I maie.. be tossed in the flode & rombeling of your worldly businesse. **1587** FLEMING *Contn. Holinshed* III. 1537/1 The time of queene Marie; in the beginning of whose reigne.. there was some rumbling thereabout.

†**3.** Muttering, murmuring. *Obs.*[−0]

c **1440** *Promp. Parv.* 436/2 Romelynge, or privy mysterynge, *ruminacio, mussitacio.*

4. Cleaning in a rumble. Also *attrib.*

1888 in *Lockwood's Dict. Mech. Engin.* 295. **1924** *Jrnl. Inst. Metals* XXXII. 294 Small articles, such as may be treated in rumbling barrels. **1965** G. J. WILLIAMS *Econ. Geol. N.Z.* xiv. 217/1 The relatively unaltered phenocrysts were experimentally removed by screening, cleaned by washing and rumbling, and analysed. **1976** *Western Mail* (Cardiff) 27 Nov., Further ancillary machines are available for drilling, tapping, rumbling and welding.

'rumbling, *ppl. a.* [f. RUMBLE *v.*[1]]

1. That rumbles, in senses of the verb.

1575 GASCOIGNE *Certayne Notes Instruct.* Wks. T iv, Rather searche the bottome of your braynes for apte wordes, than chaunge good reason for rumbling rime. **1601** B. JONSON *Poetaster* III. iv, Now, thunder, sirrah, you, the rumbling plaier. **1631** P. FLETCHER *Pisc. Eclog.* ii. 3 His songs more please my ravisht eare, Then rumbling brooks that with the pebles play. **1710** STEELE *Tatler* No. 137 ⁋4 A few rumbling Words and Consonants clapped together, without any Sense. **1788** WESLEY *Wks.* (1872) VII. 27 Of no more value.. than sounding brass or a rumbling cymbal. **1813** LADY GRANVILLE *Lett.* (1894) I. 47 We.. walked up and down the road listening to every rumbling cart. **1847** YEOWELL *Anc. Brit. Church* x. 104 A style at once rumbling, rough, and fierce. **1873** W. BLACK *Pr. Thule* vi. 87 He had driven down.. in a rumbling old trap.

b. Of a road: Causing carriages to rumble.

? **1756** H. WALPOLE *Let. to Bentley* Aug., The great road as far as Stamford is superb... It is continued much farther, but is more rumbling.

c. Of a drain: Formed of loose stones.

App. in allusion to the noise made by the water; but cf. RUMMEL 2.

1799 J. ROBERTSON *Agric. Perth* 270 In the upland where round stones are at hand, rumbling drains are most in use. **1894** HESLOP *Northumb. Gloss.*, *Rummlin-cundy*, a drain.. filled up to the surface with loose stones.

2. Of the nature of a rumble.

1635 SWAN *Spec. M.* v. §2 (1643) 116 The rumbling noise which we call Thunder. **1750** *Phil. Trans.* XLVI. 679 The hollow rumbling Noise, which is usually heard in Earthquakes. **1756** C. LUCAS *Ess. Waters* II. 124 A variety of rumbling, humming and whistling sounds. **1857** W. COLLINS *Dead Secret* III. i, The low rumbling tones of his voice ceased altogether. **1898** *Allbutt's Syst. Med.* V. 794 A kind of rumbling presystolic murmur is sometimes heard at the apex.

3. *slang.* Rough-and-tumble.

1815 *Sporting Mag.* XLVI. 129 A sort of rumbling rally followed.

Hence **'rumblingly** *adv.* (Webster, 1847).

rumbly ('rʌmblɪ), *a.* [f. RUMBLE *sb.* + -Y.] Of a rumbling character.

1874 L. TROUBRIDGE *Jrnl.* 3 Sept. in J. Hope-Nicholson *Life amongst Troubridges* (1966) 92 We.. had the usual stuffy, rumbly drive. **1881** MRS. MOLESWORTH *Adv. Herr Baby* 73 Baby was very pleased to get.. out of the rumbly, rattly noise. **1894** KIPLING *1st Jungle Bk.* 199 A gurgly rumbly voice, called out of the darkness to the right.

rumbo[1] ('rʌmbəʊ). Now *arch.* [? f. RUM *sb.*[1]] A kind of strong punch, made chiefly of rum.

1751 SMOLLETT *Per. Pickle* ix, He had provided vast quantities of strong beer, flip, rumbo, and burnt brandy. **1767** *Cries of Blood* 68 Having called for some rumbo,.. was stirring it with a spoon. **1821** SCOTT *Pirate* xxxix, Hawkins .. and Derrick.. were regaling themselves with a can of rumbo. **1824** —— *Redgauntlet* ch. xiii, Will you have.. a jorum of hot rumbo? **1889** CONAN DOYLE *Micah Clarke* 106 He found a hogshead of rumbo which was thrown up from a wreck.

attrib. **1798** O'KEEFFE *Wild Oats* II. iii, You know that her ladyship, no more than myself, has set eyes upon you since you was the bigness of a rumbo canakin.

†**rumbo**[2]. *Cant. Obs.* (See quot.)

1725 *New Cant. Dict.*, *Rumbo*, a Prison or Gaol.

rumbo[3]. *Naut. slang.* Also **rumbow.** (See quot.)

1846 *Swell's Night Guide* 130/2 *Rum bow*, rope stolen from any of the king's dock-yards. **1867** SMYTH *Sailor's Word-bk.* 585 *Rumbo*, rope stolen from a royal dockyard.

†**rumbo-ken.** *Cant. Obs.* A pawn-shop.

c **1700** *Street Robberies Consider'd*, *Rumbo ken*, Pawnbrokers. **1724** J. THURMOND in *Bacchus & Venus* (1737) N j b, Filing of a Rumbo-Ken, My Bowman is snabbled again.

rum booze, bouse: see RUM *a.*[1] 2.

rumbostan, obs. form of RAMBUTAN.

rum'bowling. *slang.* [? var. of ROMBOWLINE.] (See quots.)

1874 *Slang Dict.* 273 *Rumbowling*, anything inferior or adulterated. **1885** N. D. DAVIS in *Academy* 5 Sept. 155 Our word rum, and the longer name rumbowling, which sailors give to their grog.

†**rum'bullion**[1]. *Obs.* except *Hist.* Also **rombullion, rumbullian.** [Of obscure origin: cf. RUMBUSTION. In mod. Devon dial. *rumbullion* is used in the sense of 'tumult, uproar', but evidence of connexion is wanting.] Rum. Also, a glass or drink of rum.

c **1651** in N. D. Davis *Cavaliers & Roundheads Barbados* (1887) 112 The chiefe fudling they make in the Island is Rumbullion, alias Kill-Devill, and this is made of suggar canes distilled, a hott, hellish and terrible liquor. **1660** LEFROY *Mem. of Bermudas* (1879) II. 139 An Irishman haueing.. vndertaken to deliuer a caske of Rumbullian to the Gouernors Negroe woman. **1672** HUGHES *Amer. Physitian* 34 They.. make a sort of Strong-Water, they call Rum or Rumbullion, stronger than Spirit of Wine. **1972** F. VAN W. MASON *Roads to Liberty* 19 Katie! A brace of rumbullions. Fast as you can brew 'em!

rum'bullion[2]. Now *rare* or *Obs.* Also 8 **rumbillion, rombullion.** [Alteration of F. *Rambouillet*, the name of a town about midway between Paris and Chartres.]

1. A variety of peach.

1725 *Fam. Dict.* s.v. *Peach-tree*, The Rumbillion is the noblest and fairest of all the yellow Peaches. **1731** MILLER *Gard. Dict.* s.v. *Persica*, The Rumbullion is a middle-siz'd Fruit. **1802** FORSYTH *Fruit Trees* 25 The Rambouillet (commonly called the Rumbullion) is pretty large. **1824** LOUDON *Encycl. Gard.* 714 Rambouillet, Rumbullion.

2. A variety of gooseberry.

1786 ABERCROMBIE *Arr.* in *Gard. Assist.* 16 Gooseberries: .. Rombullion. **1835** *Trans. Hortic. Soc.* Ser. II. I. 231 Rumbullion.. is a great favourite in the gardens round London, where it has been grown upwards of forty years. **1860** HOGG *Fruit Man.* 87 Gooseberries. Rumbullion.. much grown for bottling.

rumbunctious, var. RAMBUNCTIOUS *a.*

rum'bustical, *a. dial.* and *colloq.* Also **rombustical.** [prob. an alteration of ROBUSTIC *a.* + -AL[1].] = RUMBUSTIOUS.

1795 *Spirit Publ. Jrnls.* IV. 221 If she's rumbustical By Jove we must invade her. **1825** C. WESTMACOTT *Eng. Spy* II. 248 *note*, A rumbustical green one. **1840** HOOD *Up the Rhine* 319 Frederic the Great and his rumbustical father. **1881** *Athenæum* 20 Aug. 253/2 The whole performance is robust and, if the use of such a term may be pardoned, a trifle 'rumbustical'.

†**rum'bustion.** *Obs.*[−1] In 7 **rombostion.** [Cf. RUMBULLION[1].] Rum.

1652 *Mercurius Politicus* No. 90. 1435 Partly [through] the Brandewin wherewith we have furnisht him, the spirits of Rombostion, which our men there make him, and other good hopes we give him, he becomes very valiant.

rumbustious (rʌm'bʌstɪəs), *a. colloq.* Also **rambustious, rombustious.** [prob. an alteration of

ROBUSTIOUS *a.* Cf. RUMBUSTICAL.] Boisterous, turbulent, unruly, uproarious.

1778 FOOTE *Trip to Calais* I, The sea has been rather rumbustious, I own. **1797** MRS. A. M. BENNETT *Beggar Girl* (1813) V. 156 Miss Elinor is in one of her rumbustious fits; I must fetch the doctor. **1833** L. RITCHIE *Wand. by Loire* 40 The only rumbustious individual in the whole crowd was an itinerant tooth-drawer. **1853** LYTTON *My Novel* III. XI. xix. 364 That black-whiskered alligator, the Baron,..those rambustious, unchristian filbert-shaped claws of his. **1863** KINGSLEY *Water-Babies* vii, The sperm whales are such raging, ramping, roaring, rumbustious fellows. **1894** MRS. H. WARD *Marcella* III. 105 Do you think I want to look as rumbustious as you?

rumbustiously (rʌmˈbʌstɪəslɪ), *adv.* [f. RUMBUSTIOUS *a.* + -LY².] In a rumbustious manner.

1966 *Listener* 10 Feb. 217/2 In *Horseman, Pass By!* we had a fair share of both, as well as poetry read rumbustiously by Mr O'Connor and grimly by Mr Kennelly. **1977** *Time* 5 Dec. 49/2 Lampie, the hard-drinking light-house keeper (played rumbustiously by Mickey Rooney), tells everyone that he has seen a dragon.

rumbustiousness (rʌmˈbʌstɪəsnɪs). [f. as prec. + -NESS.] Rumbustious character; boisterous behaviour.

1926 C. L. GRAVES *Hubert Parry* II. 106 In spite of his occasional exuberance and 'rumbustiousness' (a favourite word of his) he could, when the need arose, assume a wonderful dignity of demeanour. **1959** *Times Lit. Suppl.* 2 Oct. 556/4 More than one old White Russian..has felt his exiled convictions wavering a little before the rockets and rumbustiousness of the new Russia. **1977** *Gramophone* Jan. 1141/1 This come-to-the-fair rumbustiousness is well caught in the Scherzo.

rumbylow, obs. form of RUMBELOW.

rumdum, rumdumb (ˈrʌmdʌm), *a.* and *sb. N. Amer. slang.* Also **rumdumm** and with hyphen. [f. RUM *sb.*¹ + DUMB *a.* (*sb.*).] **A.** *adj.* **a.** Stupefied through drink; unconscious; incapacitated; stupid. **b.** Humdrum.

1891 *Brooklyn Eagle* 11 Sept. 2/4 *Rum-dumb*,..stupid with continual drinking. **1922** S. LEWIS *Babbitt* vii. 99 Don't faint with surprise if some of those rum-dumm liars get one good swift poke from Mike. **1936** J. STEINBECK *In Dubious Battle* i. 15. Cop slugged me from behind, right in the back of the neck... I was rumdum for a long time. **1939** — *Grapes of Wrath* xv. 215 He jus' stan's there lookin' at that dead kid. Can't get a word of 'im. Jus' rum-dumb. **1973** *Newsweek* 12 Mar. 96 Ponicsan finds surprising depth and touching delicacy in the rumdum lives he weaves together—dime-store and dinner women, odd-job truckers and coal-mine cripples. **1975** *Islander* (Victoria, B.C.) 14 Sept. 6/1 Mr. Brown had gone on a humdinger of a toot after a lucky find and wound up in bed rumdumb with no fire in his cabin.

B. *sb.* **a.** A habitual drunkard; a stupid person. **b.** Someone of ordinary ability.

1891 *Brooklyn Eagle* 11 Sept. 2/4 *Rum-dumb*,..an habitual soak. **1916** G. A. ENGLAND *Pod, Bender & Co.* 8 Why don't we lure in some rumdum of an ex-heavy-weight. **1949** N. ALGREN *Man with Golden Arm* I. 16 The cell was full of a drifting flesh-coloured light and the murmuring rumdums were being let out of the cells to wash. **1960** C. HAMBLETT in J. Pudney *Pick of Today's Short Stories* XI. 137 Other drinkers..mocked at him and called him cloth-head, or rumdum, or plain moron. **1976** *Harper's Mag.* July 72/2, I beat the rum-dums but go down before quality players.

rume, obs. form of ROOM.

rumege, obs. form of RUMMAGE.

Rumelian, var. ROUMELIAN *a.* (*sb.*).

Rumeliot, var. ROUMELIOTE.

rumen (ˈruːmɛn). [a. L. *rūmen* the throat, gullet.] The first stomach of a ruminant animal.

1728 CHAMBERS *Cycl.* s.v., In the *Rumen*, or first Ventricle of Camels, are found divers Sacculi, which contain a considerable Quantity of Water. **1834** YOUATT *Cattle* 427 (L.U.K.), There are two openings into the rumen. **1846** J. BAXTER *Libr. Pract. Agric.* (ed. 4) II. 143 All seems to go into the rumen, and has for awhile no power on the cuticular coat of that stomach. **1874** T. HARDY *Far fr. Mad. Crowd* xxi. I. 236 He punctured the skin and rumen with the lance.

rumenal, var. RUMINAL *a.*

rumenitis (ruːməˈnaɪtɪs). *Vet. Sci.* [f. RUMEN + -ITIS.] Inflammation of an animal's rumen.

1905 [see RETICULITIS]. **1963** JUBB & KENNEDY *Path. Domestic Animals* II. i. 51/1 A more common form of acute rumenitis, presumably chemical, develops after overeating on rapidly fermentable carbohydrate, usually grain. **1973** *Vet. Ann.* 1972 19 A deep haemorrhagic and necrotizing rumenitis.

rumenotomy (ruːməˈnɒtəmɪ). *Vet. Med.* [f. RUMEN + -O + -TOMY.] Incision into an animal's rumen.

1882 J. W. HILL *Bovine Med. & Surg.* xxiv. 587 Rumenotomy consists in removing the contents of the viscus through an artificial opening. **1973** [see RUMINAL *a.* 2].

rumeth, obs. form of ROOMTH.

‖**rumex** (ˈruːmɛks). *Bot.* [L. *rumex* sorrel.] A genus of plants which includes the sorrel and dock; a plant of this genus.

1771 *Encycl. Brit.* III. 557/2 *Rumex*, in botany, a genus of the hexandria trigynia class. **1786** ABERCROMBIE *Arr.* in *Gard. Assist.* 65 Tuberous rooted rumex. **1838** T. THOMSON *Chem. Org. Bodies* 584 Opium comes to this country from the Levant in rounded masses. Its surface is covered with the seeds of a species of rumex. **1874** GARROD & BAXTER *Mat. Med.* 190 Smyrna opium occurs in masses..covered externally with the capsules of a species of rumex.

rumfle, *v.* App. a var. of RUMPLE *v.*

1825 J. NEAL *Bro. Jonathan* I. 181 It's no frolick for me to be rumffled, or slobbered. **1904** in *Eng. Dial. Dict.*

Rumford (ˈrʌmfəd). *Obs.* except *Hist.* The name of Count (von) Rumford (see RUMFORDIZE *v.*) used *attrib.* to designate kitchen articles or fireplaces designed by him or improved according to systems devised by him. Also *ellipt.* as *sb.*

1810 *Agric. Museum* (U.S.) I. 42 The dinner was principally prepared hot on the ground, by means of a portable Rumford kitchen... The utility of the portable Rumford had not probably been experienced on the field on any previous occasion in New England. *a* **1817** JANE AUSTEN *Northanger Abbey* (1818) II. v. 87 The fire-place..was contracted to a Rumford. **1831** R. COX *Adventures Columbia River* II. xiv. 322 A bright brass footman..was suspended from the shining bars of a Rumford grate. **1854** THOREAU *Walden* 34 Spacious apartments, clean paint and paper, Rumford fire-place. **1937** M. LANSING *Mary Lyon through her Lett.* 230 All marveled at the Rumford oven, given by Deacon Safford... This Rumford oven was a sheet iron box with a compartment beneath in which the fire was built. **1951** *Dict. Americanisms* II. 1428/2 (*caption*) Rumford oven beside a fireplace.

†ˈ**Rumfordize**, *v. Obs.* [f. the name of Sir Benjamin Thompson, Count (von) *Rumford* (1753–1814), who invented a system for curing smoky chimneys.] *trans.* To improve (a chimney) on Count Rumford's system.

1796 COLERIDGE *Lett.* (1895) I. 209, I should think we might Rumfordize one of the chimneys. **1798** — in *Biog. Lit.* (1872) II. 741 The landlord..has promised me to Rumfordize the chimneys. **1809** *European Mag.* LV. 21 Persons may have..their kitchen fire places..Rumfordized. *fig.* **1801** *Spirit Publ. Jrnls.* V. 353 It is only now wanted that we should..Rumfordize our feelings in such a manner as to be able to vie with our wooden-fuelled neighbours in sensibility.

rumˈfustian. (See quots.)

1829 HONE *Year Bk.* 62 Rum fustian is a 'night cap', made precisely in the same way [as egg-flip]. **1862** JERRY THOMAS *How to mix Drinks* (New York) 72 *Rumfustian*,..a drink very much in vogue with English sportsmen, after their return from a day's shooting. **1900** A. M. EARLE *Stage-Coach & Tavern Days* v. 101 Rumfustian was made of a quart of strong beer, a bottle of wine or sherry, half a pint of gin, the yolk of twelve eggs, orange peel, nutmeg, spices, and sugar.

rumˈfustianish, *a.* (See quot.)

1833 *Fraser's Mag.* VII. 706 The round-about, hubble-bubble, rumfustianish,..roly-poly growlery of [Carlyle's] style, so Germanically set forth.

rumgumption (rʌmˈgʌmʃən). Chiefly *Sc.* and *north.* [Cf. GUMPTION and RUMBLEGUMPTION.] Common sense.

c **1770** BEATTIE *To Alex. Ross* xv, They need nae try thy jokes to fathom; They want rumgumption. **1785** SHIRREFS *Poems* (1790) 321 But sure it wad be gryte presumption, In ane wha has sae sma' rumgumption. **1860** *Slang Dict.* (ed. 2) 203 *Rumgumption*, or gumption, knowledge, capacity, capability. **1872** DE VERE *Americanisms* 484 There is no excuse, as there is no need, for the corruption rumgumption, common in England.

rumˈgumptious, *a. dial.* Also 8 **-gumshaws**, 20 **rumgumshus.** [Cf. prec.] (See quots.)

1781 HUTTON *Tour to Caves* Gloss. (ed. 2) 95 *Rumgumshaws*, violent, bold, and rash. *a* **1825** FORBY *Voc. E. Anglia*, *Rumgumptious*, sturdy in opinion; rough and surly in asserting it. **1828** CARR *Craven Gloss.*, *Rum-Gumptious*, forward and queer. **1962** A. JOBSON *Window in Suffolk* vi. 96 A quarrelsome person was *rumgumshus*.

Rumi, var. ROUMI.

ˈ**rumicin.** *Chem.* Also **-ine.** [f. L. *rumic-*, *rumex* sorrel + -IN.] (See quots.)

1864 WATTS tr. *Gmelin's Hand-Bk. Chem.* XVI. 172 The lapathin obtained from the root of *Rumex Hydrolapathum*.. which was prepared by Geiger..and Riegel..in a state of greater purity as rumicin. **1887** T. L. BRUNTON *Pharmacology* (ed. 3) 1011 It [the yellow dock] contains tannic acid and rumicine, which is identical with chrysophanic acid.

rumidge, obs. form of RUMMAGE.

ˈ**ruminal**, *a.* Also **rumenal.** [f. L. *rūmin-*, *rūmen* RUMEN + -AL¹.] **1.** 'Ruminant' (Webster, 1864).

2. Of or pertaining to the rumen of an animal.

1923 [see RETICULAR *a.* 4]. **1963** JUBB & KENNEDY *Path. Domestic Animals* II. i. 52/1 The ruminal environment is, except immediately after eating, anaerobic. **1973** HICKMAN & WALKER *Atlas Vet. Surg.* iii. 70 Rumenotomy is indicated ..for the relief of rumenal impaction.

ruminant (ˈruːmɪnənt), *sb.* and *a.* [ad. L. *rūminant-*, pr. pple. of *rūminārī* or *rūmināre* to RUMINATE. Cf. F. *ruminant*, Pg. and It. *ruminante*, Sp. *rumiante*.]

A. *sb.* **a.** An animal that chews the cud; one of the *Ruminantia*.

1661 LOVELL *Hist. Anim. & Min.* Isagoge a 3 b, Four-footed beasts which..are either cornigerous ruminants..or ruminants without hornes, as the Camel, dromedary. **1714** DERHAM *Phys.-Theol.* IV. xi. (1739) 635 The Description these give of the muscular Part of the Gullet..is very exact in Ruminants. **1806** *Phil. Trans.* XCVI. 370 The ruminants with horns..have two preparatory stomachs for the food previous to rumination. **1847** W. C. L. MARTIN *The Ox* 31/1 Peculiarities which distinguish between the ruminants and all other herbivorous quadrupeds. **1879** tr. *Semper's Anim. Life* 32 No one will expect to find..buffaloes, stags, and other Ruminants in Australia.

Comb. **1883** *Encycl. Brit.* XV. 417 The complex ruminant-like organ of the Lemming.

b. A contemplative person. *rare.*

1940 C. S. LEWIS *Let.* 22 Mar. (1966) 179 Why should quiet ruminants like you and I have been born in such a ghastly age?

B. *adj.* **1. a.** Chewing the cud, ruminating.

1691 RAY *Creation* II. (1692) 125 They [*sc.* camels] are Ruminant Creatures, and have four Stomacks. **1774** GOLDSM. *Nat. Hist.* (1824) I. 337 Of all ruminant animals, those of the Cow kind deserve the first rank. **1822** GOOD *Study Med.* (1829) I. 4 In the ruminant animals..the alimentary canal is twenty-seven times the length of the body. **1882** *Knowledge* Aug. 159 A curious mixture of the characters of Pigs and Ruminant animals.

†**b.** *Astr.* Represented by ruminant animals.

1679 MOXON *Math. Dict.* 133 *Ruminant Signs*, are those Signs of the Zodiack represented by Creatures that use that Quality, viz. Aries, Taurus, and Capricorn.

2. Contemplative, meditative.

1849 THOREAU *Week Concord Riv.* Monday 131 Arabia, Persia, and Hindostan, the lands of contemplation and dwelling places of the ruminant nations. **1860** RUSKIN *Mod. Paint.* V. IX. v. §10 He enjoys a quiet misty afternoon in a ruminant sort of way. **1883** *Cent. Mag.* Sept. 746 One of the long-haired ruminant men stood up.

Hence ˈ**ruminantly** *adv.*

1847 WEBSTER, *Ruminantly*, by chewing. **1893** *Scribner's Mag.* June 787/1 'You are an angel, Fred,' she repeated, ruminantly.

‖**Ruminantia** (ruːmɪˈnænʃ(ɪ)ə). [L., neut. pl. of the pres. pple. of *rūminārī* or *rūmināre* to RUMINATE.] The class of ruminant animals.

1830 R. KNOX *Béclard's Anat.* 325 In the carnivora, the ruminantia,..the hemispheres..cover a part of the cerebellum. **1870** FLOWER *Osteol. Mamm.* (1876) 77 In the *Ruminantia* there are usually seven segments altogether in the sternum.

ˈ**ruminate**, *a. Bot. rare.* [ad. L. *rūminātus*, pa. pple. of *rūminārī*: see next.] = RUMINATED *ppl. a.* 2.

1830 LINDLEY *Nat. Syst. Bot.* 280 Albumen..either ruminate, or furnished with a central or ventral cavity. **1835** — *Introd. Bot.* (1839) 466 *Ruminate*, when a hard body is pierced in various directions by narrow cavities filled with dry cellular matter.

ruminate (ˈruːmɪneɪt), *v.* [f. ppl. stem of L. *rūminārī* or *rūmināre*, f. *rūmen* RUMEN.]

1. a. *trans.* To revolve, turn over and over in the mind; to meditate deeply upon.

1533 ELYOT *Cast. Helthe* III. xi. 65 Let him..accustome him selfe to behold, and marke well them that be angry, with the successe of that anger, and ruminate it in his mynde a good space after. **1591** SHAKS. *1 Hen. VI*, v. v. 101 Conduct me, where from company, I may reuolue and ruminate my greefe. **1607** J. CARPENTER *Plaine Mans Plough* 151 In this circulatory motion, wee shuld ruminate Pauls wheele of fourteen spokes. **1642** H. MORE *Song of Soul* II. i. III. viii, While I in sullen rage did ruminate The Creatures vanity and wofull state. **1726** SHELVOCKE *Voy. round World* 240, I had a damp upon my spirits, when I ruminated within myself the certain and unavoidable difficulty. **1791** BURKE *Let. Member of Nat. Assembly* Wks. 1842 I. 481 When the guilty themselves do not choose..by ruminating their offences, [to] nourish themselves..to the perpetration of future crimes. **1928** *Oxford Poetry* 7 About your poorly-mounted majesty Stand cow-faced women ruminating sales. *a* **1961** A. HUXLEY in *Webster* (1961) s.v., Ruminating the contents of that last batch of letters she had received. **1975** *N.Y. Times* 26 Sept. 35/2 Mr. Rodgers has lived long, created much and filled an age with the sound of his music. Perhaps he has earned the right to ruminate..the art of autobiography.

b. To meditate, consider (a design, etc.) with a view to subsequent action.

1588 SHAKS. *Tit. A.* v. ii. 6 To ruminate strange plots of dire Reuenge. **1590** GREENE *Orl. Fur.* (Rtldg.) 93 Thou that ruminatest to thyself a catalogue of privy conspiracies. **1638** SIR T. HERBERT *Trav.* (ed. 2) 101 Shee ruminates a thousand severall sorts of revenge. **1655** MILTON *2nd Def. Eng. People* Wks. 1851 VIII. 251 When Salmasius was anxiously ruminating how he might reestablish his ruined character. **1725** POPE *Odyss.* xx. 8 Ruminating wrath, he scorns repose. **1740–1** RICHARDSON *Pamela* (1824) I. xii. 23, I went in, and began to ruminate with myself what I had best to do.

†**c.** With personal object. *Obs.*⁻¹

1606 SHAKS. *Tr. & Cr.* II. iii. 198 The proud Lord, That ..neuer suffers matter of the world Enter his thoughts: saue such as doe reuolue And ruminate himselfe.

2. a. To chew, turn over in the mouth, again.

1609 BIBLE (Douay) *Song Sol.* vii. 9 Like the best wine worthy for my beloved to drink, and for his lips and his teeth to ruminate. **1806** *Phil. Trans.* XCVI. 364 That liquor, which does not require to be ruminated, is conveyed directly to the fourth stomach.

b. In fig. contexts, approximating to sense 1.
1617 COLLINS *Def. Bp. of Ely* II. x. 529 Thus does he ruminate and re-ruminate his cud againe. *a* **1635** CORBETT *Iter Boreale* 43 Because he neede but ruminate that ore Which he had chew'd the Sabbath-day before. **1849** MACAULAY *Hist. Eng.* iii. I. 393 Literature which could be carried by the post bag..formed the greater part of the intellectual nutriment ruminated by the country divines and country justices. **1884** R. PATON *Scott. Church* xiv. 148 Like a clean animal, ruminating it, he turned it into most sweet verse.

3. *intr.* To chew the cud. Also *fig.*
1547 *Homilies* I. *Holy Script.*, Let vs ruminat, and (as it were) chewe the cudde, that we may haue the swete Joyse, ..taste,..and consolacion of them. **1579–80** NORTH *Plutarch* (1612) 21 The beasts feeding there, were wont to come under the same [tree].., and there did ruminate. **1661** LOVELL *Hist. of Anim. & Min.* Isagoge a 3 b, Cornigerous ruminants.., or not ruminating; as the Hogge. **1676** GREW *Musæum, Anat. Stomach & Guts* vi. 26 Of divers Beasts which Ruminate, thus much is true. **1712** ADDISON *Spect.* No. 471 ¶2 Those Repositories in several Animals, that are filled with Stores of their former Food, on which they may ruminate. **1791** BOSWELL *Johnson* (1831) I. 498 He made various sounds with his mouth; sometimes as if ruminating, or what is called chewing the cud. **1806** *Phil. Trans.* XCVI. 370 It is stated by authors that hares, rabbits, and even some men ruminate. **1881** *Nature* XXIV. 453 An animal which had two complete toes on each foot, and ruminated.
transf. **1638** RAWLEY tr. *Bacon's Life & Death* (1650) 41 That the Spirits of the Wine may have whereupon to ruminate and feed.

4. a. To muse, meditate, ponder.
1575 LANEHAM *Let.* (1871) 43 If I dyd but ruminate [for] the dayz I haue spoken of, I shall bring oout yet sumwhat more. **1606** SHAKS. *Tr. & Cr.* III. iii. 252 He..ruminates like an hostesse, that hath no Arithmatique but her braine to set downe her reckoning. **1659** *Burton's Diary* (1828) III. 217, I shall not ruminate, but look forward. **1712** ADDISON *Spect.* No. 403 ¶8 After having taken a Pipe of Tobacco, and ruminated for some time. **1785** MME. D'ARBLAY *Let.* 17 Dec., The blossom of an idea..came out into full blow as I ruminated upon my pillow. **1828** D'ISRAELI *Chas. I*, I. v. 112 The news startled the Cardinal, and he ruminated. **1876** MOZLEY *Univ. Serm.* vi. (ed. 2) 137 The glorified saint of Scripture is especially a beholder;..he does not merely ruminate within.

b. Const. *about, of, on, upon, over.*
1574 HELLOWES *Gueuara's Fam. Epist.* (1577) 108 That text of the Psalmist, about the whiche..my soule may alwayes ruminate. *c* **1590** MARLOWE *Faust.* I. i. 102 For my head But ruminates on necromantic skill. Philosophy is odious and obscure. **1612** WOODALL *Surg. Mate* Wks. (1653) 317 To ruminate of the things that most conduced to the mischief. **1682** SIR T. BROWNE *Chr. Mor.* (1756) 105 To ruminate upon evils..is to add unto our own tortures. **1722** DE FOE *Col. Jack* (1840) 30, I ruminated very much about it. **1778** MISS BURNEY *Evelina* lxxv, Ruminating very unpleasantly upon my future prospects. **1867** BURTON *Hist. Scot.* I. i. 11 Those noble lines in which Byron makes the dying gladiator ruminate over the coming vengeance for his fate. **1874** SYMONDS *Sk. Italy & Greece* (1898) I. xvi. 348 He ruminated on his melancholy.

†**5.** *refl.* To take counsel. *Obs.*
?*c* **1600** *Distr. Emperor* v. iv. in Bullen *O. Pl.*, Let us withdrawe and in pryvate rumynat our selves together.

Hence ˈ**ruminating** *vbl. sb.*
1598 FLORIO, *Ruminamento*, a ruminating, a chewing of the cudde. **1668** STEELE *Husbandm. Calling* v. (1672) 113 The reading and ruminating of it, might be as much worth as heaven to them. **1774** GOLDSM. *Nat. Hist.* (1862) I. 336 His ruminating after a full meal generally lasted about an hour and a half. **1955** *Sci. News Let.* 16 July 36/2 Grazing animals frequently chew their cud for about nine hours out of every 24, and this ruminating is somewhat concentrated at night, Dr. Balch suggested.

ˈ**ruminated,** *ppl. a.* [f. RUMINATE *v.*]
1. Meditated, considered, digested.
1605 BACON *Adv. Learn.* II. ii. §12 Which kind of Ruminated History I thinke..fit to place amongst Bookes of policie. *c* **1630** DONNE *Serm.* ix. 83 It is a second, a Ruminated, a reflected Knowledge.

2. *Bot.* Presenting a chewed appearance; permeated by striæ; striated, marbled.
1835 LINDLEY *Introd. Bot.* (1839) I. ii. 249 It is perforated in every direction by dry cellular tissue..: in this state it is said to be ruminated. **1849** BALFOUR *Man. Bot.* 281 The albumen may..present a mottled appearance, as in the Nutmeg,..and some Palms.., where it is called *ruminated*. **1874** GARROD & BAXTER *Mat. Med.* 387 When split open, the albumen is seen to be ruminated; the cut surface resembling that of a nutmeg.

3. Subjected to rumination or re-chewing.
1859 *Todd's Cycl. Anat.* V. 303/1 A muscular fold forms a direct pathway for the ruminated food.

ˈ**ruminating,** *ppl. a.* [f. RUMINATE *v.*]
1. Chewing the cud; ruminant.
1646 SIR T. BROWNE *Pseud. Ep.* 141 Some have foure stomacks, as horned and ruminating animals. **1688** BOYLE *Final Causes* IV. 191 Oxen and sheep, and many other ruminating beasts. **1713** DERHAM *Phys.-Theol.* IV. xi. (1739) 638 The curious Contrivance and Fabrick of the several Ventricles of ruminating Creatures. **1774** GOLDSM. *Nat. Hist.* (1776) III. 3 The bowels of a ruminating animal may be considered as an elaboratory. **1806** *Phil. Trans.* XCVI. 370 The following gradation of ruminating stomachs is established. **1870** GILLMORE tr. *Figuier's Reptiles & Birds* ii. 42 Various ruminating quadrupeds, as Deer and Goats.

2. Contemplative, meditative.
a **1704** LOCKE *Conduct of the Understanding* xx, We are of the ruminating kind. **1780** COWPER *Progr. Error* 24 From thoughtless youth to ruminating age. **1842** LOVER *Handy Andy* ii, He then took a ruminating walk. **1848** DICKENS *Dombey* xlix, A ruminating tone of sympathy. **1865** *Pall Mall G.* 19 May 11 The peculiarity of Tocqueville's intellect was its ruminating character.

Hence ˈ**ruminatingly** *adv.*
1872 GEO. ELIOT *Middlem.* IV. 260 She did not answer at once, but after looking down ruminatingly she said [etc.]. **1886** *Temple Bar Mag.* LXXVI. 550 He gazed ruminatingly at the view.

rumination (ruːmɪˈneɪʃən). [ad. L. *rūminātio*: see RUMINATE *v.* and -ATION. So F. *rumination*, It. *ruminazione.*]
1. Contemplation, meditation.
1600 SHAKS. *A.Y.L.* IV. i. 19 In which my often rumination wraps me in a most humorous sadnesse. **1658** J. ROBINSON *Endoxa* iii. 26 If at any times..we sin, by rumination on the foregoing signs, we may draw fresh solace. **1740** CIBBER *Apol.* (1756) I. 267 Like the ideas of a delightful spring in a winter's rumination. **1744** THOMSON *Autumn* 574 From his bury'd Flock Retiring, full of Rumination sad. **1840** THIRLWALL *Greece* liii. VII. 15 To throw away life..in frivolous amusements, or useless austerities, or indolent rumination. **1864** G. MUSGRAVE *Ten Days in Fr. Parsonage* II. ii. 42 The mind wanders into endless rumination.

b. *pl.* Meditations, thoughts, reflections.
1638 RAWLEY tr. *Bacon's Life & Death* (1651) 33 Ruminations of joy in the Memory..are good. **1797–1805** S. & HT. LEE *Canterb. T.* II. 540 In my lonely ruminations I called to mind a coffer. **1816** SCOTT *Antiq.* xxiii, Each being wrapped in his own unpleasant ruminations. **1876** GEO. ELIOT *Dan. Der.* ix, If the Arrowpoints had such ruminations.

2. The action of chewing the cud.
1658 in PHILLIPS. **1676** GREW *Musæum, Anat. Stomach & Guts* vi. 25 The Voluntary Motion of the Stomach, is that only which accompanies Rumination. **1713** DERHAM *Phys.-Theol.* IV. xi. (1739) 638 The very Act itself of Rumination is an excellent Provision for the compleat Mastication of the Food. **1800** SHAW *Gen. Zool.* I. I. Pref. p. vi, They [the *Pecora*] possess the remarkable power of rumination. **1846** J. BAXTER *Libr. Pract. Agric.* (ed. 4) II. 151 When rumination ceases..this is a most serious business. **1897** *Allbutt's Syst. Med.* III. 473 Regurgitation and even rumination of the upcast food are curious features of some cases of nervously irritable stomach.

ruminative (ˈruːmɪnətɪv), *a.* [f. RUMINATE *v.* + -IVE.] Contemplative, meditative.
1841 HOR. SMITH *Moneyed Man* III. xi. 305 Our minds becoming ruminative, we find a calm delight in chewing the cud of memory. **1855** A. MANNING *O. Chelsea Bun-ho.* xii. 207 [She] was a ruminative woman of few words. **1881** *Harper's Monthly* LXIII. 353 The flabby judge sat awhile ruminative.

Hence ˈ**ruminatively** *adv.*
1888 FARJEON *Miser Farebrother* II. xix. 253 'A long way off,' said Jeremiah ruminatively. **1893** F. ADAMS *New Egypt* 173 Nubar reposes ruminatively on the shelf.

ruminator (ˈruːmɪneɪtə(r)). [a. L. *rūminātor*, agent-noun f. *rūminārī* to RUMINATE. Cf. It. *ruminatore.*] One who ruminates.
1598 FLORIO, *Ruminatore*, a ruminator, a chewer of the cud. **1611** COTGR., *Remascheur*, a ruminator.
1813 SIR E. BRYDGES (*title*), The Ruminator, containing a Series of Moral, Critical, and Sentimental Essays. **1827** SOUTHEY *Hist. Penins. War* II. 440 At all hours of the day, some idlers or ruminators were seen on the marble benches. **1849** QUINTON *Heaven's Antidote* 44 The dominant mood of the ruminator.

†**rumine,** *v. Obs. rare.* [ad. F. *ruminer* or L. *rūminārī.*] To ruminate.
1591 SYLVESTER *Du Bartas* I. vi. 44 As studious Scholar he self-rumineth His lessons given. *a* **1618** —— *Maiden's Blush* 421 Inlie reioycing, deepely rumining, All in his minde maturely pondering.

rumis(h, variants of RUMMISH *v. Obs.*

ˈ**rumkin**[1]. Now *arch.* Also 7 romekin, rumken. [app. of LG. origin.] Some kind of drinking-vessel.
α. **1636** DAVENANT *Wits* IV. H iv b, Wine, ever flowing in large Saxon Romekins About my board. **1668** —— *News from Plimouth* III. i, I'll come, e're you can pledge Two Romekins of Wine!
β. **1656** in *Festive Songs* (Percy Soc.) 68 Ale in Saxon rumken then, Such as will make grim Malkin prate. **1664** COTTON *Scarron.* 108 With that she set it to her nose And off at once the Rumkin goes. **1801** LAMB *John Woodvil* II, Ale in a Saxon rumkin then, makes valour burgeon in tall men. **1823** *Blackw. Mag.* XIV. 521 Put it not into bottle or jug, Cannikin, rumkin, flagon, or mug.

ˈ**rumkin**[2]. [app. f. RUMP *sb.*[1] + -KIN.] The Persian rumpless or tailless cock or hen.
a **1672** WILLUGHBY *Ornith.* II. x. (1676) 110 Gallum Persicum..Hoc genus etiam à nostratibus alitur, & nonnullis Rumkins dicitur. *Ibid.* Pl. 26 Gallus ex Persia, a Rumkin. **1688** HOLME *Armoury* II. 251/2 The Persian Cock ..wants a rump and tail;..with us they are generally called Rumkines. **1776** A. RUSSELL *Aleppo* 63 The rumkin, or cock and hen without rumps. **1840** *Penny Cycl.* XVIII. 65/1 The Rumpless or Persian Cock, or 'Rumkin', as it was formerly termed, is tailless. **1849** D. J. BROWNE *Amer. Poultry Yd.* (1865) 282 The feathers of the variety of fowls called 'rumkins'..are as much proof against rain as those of other fowls.

ˈ**rumlar.** *rare*$^{-1}$. [app. f. RUMMEL, after *ashlar.*] Rough stone.
1829 J. HODGSON in Raine *Mem.* (1858) II. 161 Layers of basaltic rumlar work between each flatting of the mortar.

ˈ**rumless,** *a.* [f. RUM *sb.*[1] + -LESS.] Destitute of rum.
1882 *Pall Mall G.* 25 Nov. 4 The men not unreasonably refused point blank to navigate the Kara Sea in a rumless *Ibis*.

ˈ**rumly,** *adv. slang.* [f. RUM *a.*[1] and *a.*[2] + -LY[2].]
a. Bravely, finely. **b.** Oddly, strangely.
1673 R. HEAD *Cant. Acad.* 29 We concluded to booz it rumly. *a* **1700** B. E. *Dict. Cant. Crew*, *Rumly*, bravely, cleaverly, delicately, &c. **1819** *Blackw. Mag.* IV. 727 Touch'd with grief to see His pal..Thus rumly floor'd.

rummadan, obs. form of RAMADAN.

rummage (ˈrʌmɪdʒ), *sb.* Forms: 6–7 **romage, roomage,** 7 **rommage, rumidg,** 8, 9 **rummage.** [Orig. an aphetic adoption of older F. (also Sp.) *arrumage* (mod. *arrimage*), f. *arrumer* (mod. *arrimer*), = Sp. and Pg. *arrumar*, of doubtful origin. In later use f. the verb.]
1. †**a.** *Naut.* The arranging of casks, etc., in the hold of a vessel. *Obs.*
1526 in *Househ. Ord.* (1790) 195 Cellaridge, Cranage, Sponage, Romage, and Carridge of Wine, £100 0s. 0d. **1688** HOLME *Armoury* III. xv. (Roxb.) 40/1 The Quarter Maister hath the charg of the hould for stowage, rommage, and trimming the ship.

b. Miscellaneous articles, lumber; rubbish.
1598 W. PHILLIP tr. *Linschoten* 151 Among other romage that stood vpon the hatches, there were certaine hennes cages. *Ibid.* 168 All chestes, pottes, fattes, and other roomage that are not stowed vnder hatches, being throwne ouer borde into the sea. **1847** HALLIW., *Rummage*, lumber, rubbish. *West.* **1880** *Cornwall Gloss.*, *Rummage*, rubbish. 'A good riddance to bad rummage.'

†**c.** Place of stowage or storage; storage capacity. *Obs.*
1598 W. PHILLIP tr. *Linschoten* 164 They likewise haue a Chest in the roomage, free of fraight. *a* **1639** WOTTON *Surv. Educ.* in *Reliq.* (1672) 81 In the Oeconomical Providence of Nature, (as I may term it,) there is good store of roomage and receipt where those powers are stowed.

2. Bustle, commotion, turmoil. *Obs.* exc. *Sc.*
1575 *Durh. Deposit.* (Surtees) 304 Ther was such a dyn and rom[a]ge in the streit emangest neighbours. **1602** SHAKS. *Ham.* I. i. 107 This (I take it) Is..the cheefe head Of this post-hast, and Romage in the Land. **1882** *Jamieson's Sc. Dict.* IV. 77/1 *Rummage*, an obstreperous din.

3. a. An overhauling search.
1753 H. WALPOLE *Lett.* (1846) II. 476 A general rummage and reform in the office of matrimony. **1786** MME. D'ARBLAY *Diary* 29 July, My rummages and business sometimes occupy me uninterruptedly to those hours. **1813** MOORE *Mem.* (1853) I. 364, I took the opportunity of a lift to come on here for a last rummage of the library before the bad weather sets in. **1833** T. HOOK *Love & Pride, Snowdon* v, Which were now, after the general rummage, returned to their lawful owner. **1873** C. KEENE *Let.* in *Life* vii. (1892) 148, I shall have a rummage for it among the old music-book shops.

b. *spec.* A thorough search of a vessel by a Customs examining officer. Also *attrib.*
1867 SMYTH *Sailor's Word-bk.* 585. **1876** G. D. HAM *Rev. & Mercantile Vade-M.* 274 The Examining Officer and the waterman is to..make a strict rummage in all parts of the vessel. *Ibid.* 635 To make a memorandum to that effect at the foot of the rummage account.

4. Special combs.: **rummage goods** (see quot. 1871); **rummage sale,** (*a*) (see quot. 1858); (*b*) a kind of charity bazaar; also *attrib.* and *fig.*
1871 *Echo* 25 Jan., Seizures made for smuggling and *rummage goods—that is, goods out of date in warehouse. **1893** *Daily News* 24 June 8/1 Sale of Rummage Goods from Red Lion and other wharves, and Salvage ex-Hispania s.s. **1858** SIMMONDS *Dict. Trade*, **Rummage-sale*, a clearance sale of unclaimed goods at the docks, or of odds and ends left in a warehouse. **1887** *Times* 30 Nov. 1 Rummage Sale, by order of the proprietors of Wilson's Wharf. **1890** *Stratford on Avon Herald* 19 Dec. 3/1 A novel but most successful experiment was tried by way of what was termed a 'rummage sale'. **1895** *N. & Q.* 8th Ser. VIII. 308 It is almost impossible to dispose of gentlemen's hats at rummage sales. **1910** M. BEERBOHM *Let.* 15 Nov. (1964) 192 It will be a different sort of exhibition..: a *retrospective* and rummage-sale affair. **1912** *Strand Mag.* Aug. 155 Good wickets at rummage-sale prices. **1922** JOYCE *Ulysses* 737 Rummage sale a lot of trash. **1973** *Black World* Sept. 62 Your black skin Loose as a rummage sale coat. **1977** *Time* 24 Oct. 48/3 The *Road* shows were rummage sales of stuff out of vaudeville, burlesque—marvelously shoddy masterpieces of farce and fantasy, stitched together with clichés and ad libs.

rummage (ˈrʌmɪdʒ), *v.* Forms: 6 **roomage,** 7 **roome(d)ge;** 6–7 **romege,** 6–9 **romage,** 7 **rommage, -idge;** 6–7 **rummidge,** 7 **-ige, rumidg(e,** 7–8 **rumage,** 7– **rummage.** [f. the sb.]
I. *trans.* †**1.** *Naut.* **a.** To arrange, or rearrange (goods) in the hold of a ship. Also generally, to arrange, put in order. *Obs.*
1544 *Admiralty Court Libels* No. 55, The romeger whiche they appoynted..to romege caske wares in the said shipp did romege at the same tyme the said annyse sed. **1598** HAKLUYT *Voy.* I. 300 To give the master..a good reward for his labour to see the goods well romaged. **1622** MARKHAM *Decades Warre* III. vi. 103 Hee is continually to haue attending on him..Porters and luggage Carriers, to rummage and order things according to his directions. **1725** DE FOE *Voy. round World* (1840) 103 We careened our ships,

..rummaged our gold, and repacked some of our provisions.

†**b.** To set in order, put straight (a ship, the hold) by rearranging the cargo. *Obs.*

1577 TOWRSON in *Hakluyt* (1599) II. II. 46 The 14 day we sent in our boats to take water, and romaged our shippes. **1622** R. HAWKINS *Voy. S. Sea* (1847) 86 The most of those which had health, occupied themselves in romeging our ship. **1625** in J. S. Corbett *Fighting Instr.* (1905) 69 The hold in every ship should be rummaged and made predy, especially by the ship's sides.

2. *Naut.* **a.** To search thoroughly, ransack (the hold of a vessel, etc.).

1628–9 DIGBY *Voy. Medit.* (Camden) 4 An other English man of warre that had detained him all night and rummiged his hold and opened his letters. **1697** DAMPIER *Voy.* (1699) 174 We rummaged our Prize, and found a few Boxes of Marmalade. **1719** DE FOE *Crusoe* I. 64 Tho' I thought I had rumag'd the Cabin so effectually, as that nothing more could be found, yet I discover'd a Locker with Drawers in it. **1739** LABELYE *Piers Westm. Bridge* 19 By means of these Booms we could inclose the..Boats and Vessels from being damaged or rumaged, either by Day or Night. **1849** MACAULAY *Hist. Eng.* x. II. 561 A set of pirates who, under pretence of searching for arms or delinquents, rummaged every boat that passed. **1876** SMILES *Sc. Natur.* v. (ed. 4) 82 They are about to rummage the ship from stem to stern for runaways.

b. *spec.* of Customs officers in discharge of their duty.

1763 *Ann. Reg.* 112 The powers of the officers of the customs to rummage ships with lights. **1812** J. SMYTH *Pract. Customs* 1 The Tide-surveyor is to rummage the Ship, in order to detect the concealment of any small packages of Goods, which are liable to Duty, or are prohibited to be imported. **1863** A. YOUNG *Naut. Dict.* (ed. 2) s.v., When rummaging a ship, they have a long steel spear to pierce any soft articles. **1876** G. D. HAM *Rev. & Mercantile Vade-M.* 267 When the import cargo is discharged the Examining Officer finally rummages the vessel.

3. a. To make a search in or among; to overhaul in order to find something. Also in fig. context.

a **1616** BEAUM. & FL. *Wit without M.* II. i, Why does she not go romage all the prisons? **1677** R. CARY *Palæol. Chron.* II. I. ix. 118 Ransacking and rummaging those obscure Cells and Vaults of Antiquity. **1758** GOLDSM. *Mem. Protestant* (1895) I. 110 Before we entered this Prison, the Gaoler rummaged us from Head to Foot. **1797–1805** S. & HT. LEE *Canterb. T.* II. 550 They saw that everything had been rummaged, and all the chests and lockers were wide open. **1833** L. RITCHIE *Wand. by Loire* 57 We rummaged our pockets in vain for the required passport. **1886** G. R. SIMS *Ring o' Bells* 136, I rummaged the house from top to bottom ..; but in vain.

fig. **1621** MOLLE *Camerarius' Liv. Libr.* III. v. 162 She roomedging her past evils. **1657** W. RUMSEY *Organ. Sal.* Ep. Ded. (1659) 16 Your Instrument serves to take away the grounds of these distempers, by rummaging and scouring the stomach.

b. With *over*, *out*, *up*.

1623 G. HERBERT *Let.*, Rummage out your book-shelves. **1807** SOUTHEY *Lett.* (1856) II. 38 Pray rummage up your memory for the new volumes. **1826** LAMB *The Months* Misc. Wks. (1871) 395 Rummaging over the contents of an old stall. **1835** *Court Mag.* VI. 112/2, I only grieve for the trouble I have taken in rummaging over my musty shelves. **1889** J. K. JEROME *Three Men in Boat* iv. 57, I rummaged the things up into much the same state that they must have been before the world was created, and when chaos reigned.

4. a. To scrutinize, examine minutely, investigate.

1704 SWIFT *T. Tub* ii. 68 Upon this; they fell again to romage the Will. **1728** MORGAN *Algiers* I. vi. 185, I yet never met with the least mention of any thing like it, in all the multitude of authors I have rummaged. **1845** *Encycl. Metrop.* II. 755/1 They have rummaged the oldest monuments. **1864** BURTON *Scot Abr.* I. v. 305, I am inclined to concur in Pasquier's silence, having rummaged his 'Recherches de la France'.

b. Const. *over.*

1725 WATTS *Logic* 304 To direct their disciples..to rummage over the definitions, divisions, and canons that belong to each topic. **1741** tr. *D'Argens' Chinese Lett.* xxxviii. 287, I have rumaged over all the Authors of the Library of our Friends the Missionaries. **1825** JEFFERSON *Autobiog.* Wks. 1859 I. 6 With the help..of Rushworth, whom we rummaged over for the revolutionary precedents.

5. a. To disarrange or disorder; to knock, stir, or drive about; to force or rout out by searching or making a stir. Somewhat *rare.*

1591 RALEIGH *Last Fight Revenge* 18 Our Ships being all pestered and romaging euerie thing out of order. **1598** SYLVESTER *Du Bartas* II. i. III. *Furies* 422 Even as the matter ..Is rommidged with motions slowe or quick In feeble bodies of the Ague-sick. **1736** N. BAILEY *Househ. Dict.* 242 Add about two drams of crude alum..; rummage this well in it. **1840** MRS. TROLLOPE *Widow Married* v, I shall find all the things rummaged about. **1878** FR. A. KEMBLE *Rec. Girlhood* I. ii. 49 The wild rabbits..hunted and rummaged from their burrows.

b. To bring *out* by searching; to fish *out* or *up*.

1715 M. DAVIES *Athen. Brit.* I. Pref. 45 The Benedictin Monks..set themselves to rummage up old Manuscripts for Printing. **1786** COWPER *Let. to Lady Hesketh* 12 June, She has also rummaged up a coop that will hold six chickens. **1803** *Lett. Miss Riversdale* II. 303 In rummaging out the contents of a *secrétaire*,..[she] had discovered a private drawer. **1824** DIBDIN *Libr. Comp.* 755, I had the good fortune to rummage out another copy. **1830** D'ISRAELI *Chas. I*, III. vi. 108 The writer..has rummaged out many state secrets, which he turns to his own purpose. **1847** ALB. SMITH *Chr. Tadpole* vii. (1879) 71 An ancient spangled jacket..was rummaged out of the property box.

c. To collect by searching.

1820 BYRON *Morg. Maggiore* lxxxiv, Morgante rummaged piecemeal from the dust The whole.

6. To employ in searching or ransacking.

1825 *New Monthly Mag.* XIV. 257 A man might rummage his hands among his pockets with comfort.

II. *intr.* **7.** *Naut.* To make search (†arrange or rearrange cargo, etc.) in a vessel.

c **1595** CAPT. WYATT *R. Dudley's Voy. W. Ind.* (Hakl. Soc.) 59 They weare not idle,..but still rummidginge, as it seemeth, provided well for theire defence. **1598** HAKLUYT *Voy.* I. 300 The master or Boatswaine, or him that will take vpon him to romage. **1607** B. BARNES *Divils Charter* v. ii. K 4, Now *Signor currigantino* will I romage in the worme eaten keele of your rotten hulke. *a* **1692** POLLEXFEN *Disc. Trade* (1697) 117 They..have been actually on Board the said Ship, and have begun to rummage there, pretending to remove the Goods in order to their Inspection and Appraisment. **1728** CHAMBERS *Cycl.* s.v. *Quartermaster*, Their Business is to rummage in the Hold on all Occasions.

8. a. To engage in a search, make an investigation, of any kind.

1666 BOYLE *Orig. of Formes & Qual.* To Rdr. A 7 b, I rumag'd among my Loose papers. **1692** R. L'ESTRANGE *Fables* I. xxxii, As a Fox was Rumidging among a great many Carv'd Figures. **1726** SHELVOCKE *Voy. round World* 89 They have been ashore at some Indian houses, and have rummaged and taken several things of small value. **1789** MME. D'ARBLAY *Diary* 2 Feb., He pulled out a pocket-book, and rummaged some time, but to no purpose. **1802–12** BENTHAM *Ration. Judic. Evid.* (1827) IV. 365 *note*, I should rummage to see whether a case could be found in which [etc.]. **1852** DICKENS *Bleak Ho.* lix, This gentleman, when he comes into the property, naturally begins to rummage. **1875** MRS. TROLLOPE *A Charming Fellow* III. xvii. 220 She ..began to rummage among its contents.

b. Const. *about, around.*

1867 TROLLOPE *Chron. Barset* I. xlii. 367 In preparing a defence we have to rummage about and get up what we can. **1883** 'MARK TWAIN' *Life on Mississippi* iii. 36 He come rummaging around in the dark amongst the shingle bundles. **1885** *Manch. Exam.* 29 June 5/2 He took the keys and began to rummage about for spoil.

c. Said of mice or rats.

1842 TENNYSON *Walk to Mail* 30 A jolly ghost, that..tapt at doors, And rummaged like a rat. **1863** LONGF. *Wayside Inn, Student's Sec. T.*, So silent you can hear the mouse Run and rummage along the beams.

9. To turn or move restlessly. *rare*$^{-1}$.

1755 CROKER tr. *Orl. Fur.* XXIII. cxxii, He..wheels round to and fro, This side and that, rummaging o'er his bed.

Hence **'rummaging** *ppl. a.*

1847 C. BRONTE *J. Eyre* vii, They..had been conducting a rummaging scrutiny of the rooms upstairs. **1887** J. ASHBY STERRY *Lazy Minstrel* (1892) 161 What display, both of quantity and quality, These rummaging *douaniers* oft bring to light.

rummager ('rʌmɪdʒə(r)). Also 6 **romeger.** [f. RUMMAGE *v.* + -ER[1].]

†**1.** One who arranges cargo in a ship. *Obs.*

1544 *Admiralty Court Libels* No. 55, The romeger whiche they appoynted..to romege caske wares in the said shipp. **1600** HAKLUYT *Voy.* III. 862 The Master must prouide a perfect mariner called a Romager, to romege and bestow all marchandize in such place as is conuenient.

2. One who makes a search or overhaul.

1769 BARETTI *Mann. & Customs Italy* II. xxxix. 328 Many amongst our rummagers of libraries have occasionally quoted passages [etc.]. **1836** W. IRVING *Astoria* III. 58 There was no likelihood that the caches would escape the search of such keen eyes, and experienced rummagers. **1856** E. G. PARKER *Lesson of '76* 9 Layard, the great rummager of Nineveh. **1935** L. LUARD *Conquering Seas* iii. 44 Next time I'll let the rummagers put a stop to their nonsense.

rummaging ('rʌmɪdʒɪŋ), *vbl. sb.* [f. as prec.]

†**1.** The arranging or rearranging of cargo. *Obs.*

1553 in Hakluyt *Voy.* (1589) 267 In charging, discharging, loding againe, and roomaging of the same shippe. **1560** *Ibid.* (1903) II. 409 The masters of the ships..might bring away a great deal more than they doe if they would take paine in the romaging. **1622** R. HAWKINS *Voy. S. Sea* (1847) 44 The other [days] for roomeging, making of sayles [etc.]. **1626** CAPT. SMITH *Accid. Yng. Seamen* 5 The quarter Maisters hath the charge of the hold for stowage, rommageing, and trimming the shippe.

2. The action of searching or overhauling.

1664 BUTLER *Hud.* II. iii. 1086 This said in haste, in haste he fell To romaging of Sidrophel. **1720** DE FOE *Capt. Singleton* xiii. (1840) 231 The sloop's men took her, and had the rummaging of her, before we came up. **1768** J. BYRON *Narr. Patagonia* (ed. 2) 26 This rummaging of the shore was now becoming extremely irksome. **1838** DICKENS *Nickleby* viii, A vast deal of searching and rummaging ensued, and it proving fruitless [etc.]. **1859** W. COLLINS *Queen of Hearts* (1875) 32, I would rather have the rummaging of your memory than the rummaging of this box.

attrib. **1876** G. D. HAM *Rev. & Mercantile Vade-M.* 635 Stores to be reported and an account to be taken by the Rummaging Officers. **1891** MAYSTON *Customs Gen. Orders* 206 Extramen not to be employed on rummaging duty.

rummagy ('rʌmɪdʒɪ), *a. colloq.* [f. RUMMAGE *sb.* + -Y.] Such as may be got by rummaging about among old rubbish.

1899 BARING-GOULD *Bk. of West* I. 18 The 'rummagy' faces, with no defined shape. **1901** in *N. & Q.* 9th Ser. VIII. 522/2 He had gone and fetched the rummagy old thing, which..wasn't no good to nobody.

'rummel. *dial.* Also **rummle.** [variant of RAMMEL *sb.*[1]]

1. (See quot. and RAMMEL *sb.*[1] 4.)

c **1850** J. GIBBS in Ure *Dict. Arts* (1853) I. 393 The materials which I extract from the lias formation, locally called 'rummell'..at Barrow-on-Soar, in Leicestershire, is an especial bed of marly limestone, found above and separated from all the lias beds of limestone in that district.

2. ***rummel-cundy, -drain*** (see quots.).

1853 *Jrnl. R. Agric. Soc.* XIV. II. 314 [He] drained at first with stones, these drains being what are termed *Scottice* rummle drains. **1894** *Hetten-le-hole* (Durh.) *Gloss., Rummle cundy*, a ditch filled up with loose stones, for water to drain through.

rummer ('rʌmə(r)). Also 7–8 **romer**, 7 **rummar.** [Of Continental origin, and representing WFlem. *rummer, rommer*, or Du. *romer, roemer*, Fris. *romer*, LG. *römer* (hence Da. *rømer*, †*rømmer*), G. *römer* (†*roemer*, 1589); the original meaning is perh. 'Roman glass'.]

1. A kind of large drinking-glass. Also const. *of* (the contained liquor).

1654 GAYTON *Pleas. Notes* IV. 234 Dispatching a lusty Rummer of Rhenish to little Periwig. **1668** DAVENANT *Man's the Master* I. i, Then give him but a rummer,..and he will drink so kindly, as if he had the heart of a whale. **1673** DRYDEN *Amboyna* I. i, Whilst in full Romers we our Friendship Crown. **1706** E. WARD *Wooden World Diss.* (1708) 103 A large Rummer of Rhenish and Sugar. **1788** V. KNOX *Winter Even.* II. v. xii. 199 A real cup in the form of a common drinking glass or rummer. **1811** SIR A. FERGUSSON in Lockhart *Scott* (1869) III. 325 Many a nice slice of ham, and rummer of hot punch. **1864** C. KNIGHT *Passages Work. Life* I. vi. 246 The bottle circulates briskly or the rummers are replenished. **1886** T. HARDY *Mayor Casterbr.* v, A row of ancient rummers with ground figures on their sides.

2. *attrib.*, as ***rummer-cup, -glass.***

1728 CHAMBERS *Cycl.* s.v. *Music*, A Dutch man, who could break Rummer-Glasses with the Tone of his Voice. **1797** S. JAMES *Narr. Voyage* 49 The mate took with him some rummer glasses. **1828** SCOTT *F.M. Perth* iii, Dorothy appeared bearing three large rummer cups. **1880** BROWNING *Dram. Idyls, Clive* 16, I slap the table till no rummer-glass but shakes.

†**'rummery**[1]. *Obs.*$^{-1}$ = ROOMERY.

1638 SIR T. HERBERT *Trav.* (ed. 2) 58 In the habit of Kalenders or Friers, as if they were upon a Rummery or pilgrimage.

'rummery[2]. *U.S.* A rum-store, liquor-shop.

1898 *Advance* (Chicago) 12 Nov., His re-election does not prove that the people of the state are going to sell out to the rummeries.

rummi(d)ge, -mill, obs. ff. RUMMAGE, RUMBLE.

rummily, -ness: see RUMMY *a.*[1]

†**'rumming,** *vbl. sb. Obs.* Used in allusion to Skelton's 'Elynour Rummynge'.

1600 NASHE *Summer's Last Will* 643 The Poet is bribde.. to hold him halfe the night with riffe, raffe, of the rumming of Elanor.

'rummish, *a. slang.* [f. RUM *a.*[2]] Somewhat odd or peculiar; rather rummy.

1760 DUCHESS OF NORTHUMBERLAND *Diary* 17 Aug. (1926) 26 Ld Dumfries very drunk, talk'd of being frisky & rummish. **1826** *Sporting Mag.* XVIII. 285 Galloping them round a corner, with a rummish team. **1837** T. HOOK *Jack Brag* xiv, 'That's a rummish cut of a toggery,' said Jack. **1848** THACKERAY *Bk. Snobs, Milit. Snobs*, His little box near Epsom..: where..many 'rummish plants' are concocted.

†**'rummish,** *v. Sc. Obs.* Forms: 6 **rumb-, rummisch, rum(m)is, -ys, -e(i)s,** 7 **rumish.** [See ROMY *v.* Perhaps partly represented by later Sc. *rumish, reemish* (see *Eng. Dial. Dict.*).]

1. *intr.* To roar, bellow.

15.. *Clariodus* i. 970 He rumbischit whill rared everie roch. **1513** DOUGLAS *Æneis* III. x. 17 The hird Poliphemus ..Grassilland his teth, and rummesand full hie. *Ibid.* 36 How cavernis or furnys of Ethna round Rummist and lowit. **1552** LYNDESAY *Monarche* 5468 Gret Quhalis sall rummeis, rowte, and rair.

2. To protest loudly, make uproar.

1533 BELLENDEN *Livy* III. xiii. (S.T.S.) I. 299 þan þe small pepill began to rummys. *Ibid.* IV. xviii. II. 118 Incontinent þe hale senate began to rummys.

Hence †**'rummishing** *vbl. sb.* and *ppl. a. Obs.*

c **1480** HENRYSON *Fables, Lion & Mouse* xxx, [The lion] Welterand about with hiddious rummissing. **1533** BELLENDEN *Livy* IV. xix. (S.T.S.) II. 121 Incontinent rais ane huge rummyssing throw all the tentis. **1653** CHISENHALE *Cath. Hist.* 144 The battering shot of the Rummishing Canon.

rummle, Sc. variant of RUMBLE.

'rummy, *sb.*[1] [f. RUM *sb.*[1] + -Y.] **1.** (See quot. 1890.) *U.S.*

1860 EMERSON *Cond. Life, Power*, He led the 'rummies' and radicals in town-meeting with a speech. **1890** C. L. NORTON *Political Amer.* 96 *Rummies*, a local name for the political opponents of the temperance party in Maine.

2. a. A habitual drunkard; an alcoholic. *slang* (chiefly *U.S.*).

1851 J. H. GREEN *Twelve Days in Tombs* 55 The learned counsel of the rummies opened his defence...the court adjourned, and the rummies repaired to *another bar* to congratulate each other upon the success of the morning. **1907** G. B. SHAW *Major Barbara* 170 Your Rummies of the tamest respectability pretending to a past of reckless and dazzling vice. **1939** [see *nut factory* s.v. NUT *sb.*[1] 23]. **1962** E. LACY *Freeloaders* vi. 124 You'd go to pieces, become a rummy. **1975** *Publishers Weekly* 20 Jan. 67/1 A salty old rummy who specializes in pious letters pleading for help.

b. A stupid person; a blockhead; a sucker. *U.S. slang.*

1912 ADE *Knocking Neighbors* 108 She extracted a promise from Cousin and several other Desperate Characters that they would come out into the wilderness and give the Rummies a Touch of High Life. **1913** J. LONDON *Valley of Moon* 59 You'd better tell the rummy to beat it. **1937** *Reader's Digest* Oct. 36/2 Most rummies never discover they have been rooked.

rummy, *sb.*² orig. *U.S.* Also rumme. [Origin uncertain.] Any of a group of card games, similar to coon-can, the main object of which is to acquire runs or flushes of three or more cards. Also *attrib.* See also *gin rummy* s.v. GIN *sb.*² 2 b, OKLAHOMA.

1910 *Sun* (N.Y.) 10 Sept. II. 3/1 The leader this season seems to be a new round game that is called rum. Some persons have it rhum, rhummy and even rhumston. **1913** *Official Gaz.* (U.S. Patent Office) 13 May 536/2 Milton Bradley Company, Springfield, Mass. Filed Mar. 20, 1913. Rumme. **1915** *Chicago Herald* 30 Nov. 15/4 This gave him the idea the game was rummy and he spread the nines on the table. **1919** S. LEWIS *Free Air* xix. 202 He takes some kind of dope, and he cheats at rummy. **1928** L. NORTH *Parasites* 285 Sometimes they played écarté..or Rummy. **1934** W. SAROYAN *Daring Young Man* 213, I would sneak out of the bookie joint and run across the street to a rummy parlour and get into a game. **1964** A. WYKES *Gambling* vii. 164 Games of the rummy series appear to be the oldest. **1974** *Harrods Gift Catal.* 60/1 Packs of cards to play Bingo, Crosswords, Rummy and a variety of games.

rummy ('rʌmɪ), *a.*¹ (*sb.*³) *slang* or *colloq.* [f. RUM *a.*² + -Y.] **A.** *adj.* Odd, queer, singular. Also *Comb.*

1828 *Sporting Mag.* XXIII. 19 A neat, but rather rummy looking blue pony. **1867** TROLLOPE *Chron. Barset* II. 355 They're a rummy couple if what I hear is true. **1892** *Spectator* 13 Feb. 223/2 The 'rummy' names people give their houses in the suburbs.

B. as *sb.* An odd or unconventional person.

1975 G. V. HIGGINS *City on Hill* iv. 117 At least the rummies that swing it in Dorchester're *alive.* **1977** J. WAMBAUGH *Black Marble* (1978) vi. 72 She always had to look at the rummy to see if he was putting her on. *Ibid.*, It must be dope... This rummy's a doper!

Hence **'rummily** *adv.*; **'rumminess.**

1827 SCOTT *Jrnl.* 5 Apr., I know..it has been a rummily written work. **1899** E. PHILLPOTTS *Human Boy* 172 This story shows the rumminess of Nubby Tomkins.

'rummy, *a.*² [f. RUM *sb.*¹ + -Y.] Of or pertaining to, suggestive of, rum. Also, drunken.

1834 *Jamestown* (N.Y.) *Jrnl.* 29 Jan. 1/5 The Massachusetts Masons,..like the rummy deacon, who fell from his horse—have merely 'got off to get on better'. **1843** *Amer. Pioneer* II. 372 He departed, muttering curses loud and deep, and in a voice peculiarly rummy. **1864** WEBSTER s.v., A rummy flavour. **1961** W. A. WHITE in *Webster* s.v., His face was blotched..his eyes were rummy, his jaw was uncertain.

rummy, *v.* [f. RUMMY *sb.*²] *intr.* To obtain a hand that can be laid down at rummy; to say 'rummy' signifying this. Also const. *out.*

1929 *Encycl. Brit.* XIX. 658/2 Directly a player rummies that deal is finished, and all the hands are exposed and added up. **1966** L. DAVIDSON *Long Way to Shiloh* x. 144 'What about a game of cards?'.. She played with immense concentration and rummied out in about five minutes.

rummyll, obs. form of RUMBLE.

'rumness. [f. RUM *a.*² + -NESS.] Singularity, oddness, oddity.

1865 DICKENS *Mut. Fr.* III. iii, The Fates ordered him into it again. Which is rumness: ain't it? **1892** STEVENSON & OSBOURNE *Wrecker* (ed. 2) 220 You see something of the rumness of this job, but not the whole.

†**'rumney.** *Obs.* Forms: α. 4 **romon(e)ye, romanye**, 6 **-ny**; 5 **romenay**, 5–6 **-ney**, 6 **-nei**; 5 **rommenei**. β. 5 **rompney, romnay**, 6 **-neye, -nie, -ny**, 5–7 **romney**. γ. 4 **rumnay**, 5 **-neye**, 4, 6 **rumney**, 7 **-ny**. [a. OF. *rom(m)enie*, = obs. It. and med.L. *romania*, from the proper name *Romania*, used to designate Greece. OF. is also the source of MDu. *romanie, romenie*, MLG. *romenie, rumenie*, MDa. *rommenie, rumeni.*]

1. A sweet wine of Greek origin, much used in England during the 15th and 16th centuries. Also *attrib.*

α. **1393** *Earl Derby's Exped.* (Camden) 209 Item pro j paruo cade de Romoneye, vj *li* di. **1421** *Coventry Leet Bk.* I. 24 And that thei sell.. maluesey & romeney for xvj d. a galon and no derre. **1469** in *Househ. Ord.* (1790) 101 Item, in tyre malvesie, romenay, osey,..and other sweete wynes, by the yere..£20. **1531–2** *Act 23 Hen. VIII*, c. 7 No Malmeseis, Romeneis, Sakkes nor other swete Wynes..shal-be retailed aboue xij. d. the galon. **1546–7** *Extr. Rec. Stirling* (1887) 47 That na claret..be sald of derrer price nor xiiij d., nor Romany derrer nor xviij d. the point.

β. *a* **1460** *Play Sacrament* 340 Syr, here ys a drawte of Romney Red. **1482** *Cely Papers* (Camden) 103, I sent to them a pottell of white romnay and thai toke it thankefully. **1508** *Bk. Keruynge* in *Babees Bk.* (1868) 267 Also yf your swete wyne pale, drawe it in to a romney vessell for lessynge. **1542** BOORDE *Dyetary* x. Fij, These hote wynes as malmesye, wyne course, wyne greke, romanysk, romny. **1612** in *Halyburton's Ledger* (1867) 335 Canareis, Malagas, Maderais, Romneyis.

γ. *a* **1400** *Sqr. Lowe Degre* 753 Ye shall have rumney and malmesyne. **1414** *Maldon Court-Rolls* (Bundle 9, No. 6), ii pipas vini albi et ii botys [= butts] de Rumneye. *c* **1440** *Promp. Parv.* 439/2 Rumneye, wyne. **1519** *Interl. Four Elements* (Percy Soc.) 22 Ye shall have Spayneshe wyne and Gascoyn, Sak, raspyce, alycaunt, rumney. **1584** COGAN *Haven Health* 210 Spaine bringeth foorth wines of white colour.., as Sacke, Rumney and Bastard. **1621** BURTON *Anat. Mel.* I. ii. II. i. 93 All black Wines..: Malmesie, Allegant,..Rumny, Browne bastard, Metheglen.

b. ***rumney (of) Modon***, rumney made at Modon (the ancient Methone) in the Morea.

c **1460** J. RUSSELL *Bk. Nurture* 96 in *Babees Bk.*, þerfore ete hard chese aftir..and drynk romney modoun. *Ibid.* 119 The namys of swete wynes y wold þat ye them knewe:.. Rompney of modon.

2. A rumney cask or vessel. (Cf. 1 β, quot. 1508.)

c **1460** J. RUSSELL *Bk. Nurture* 116 in *Babees Bk.*, ȝiff swete wyne be seeke or pallid put in a Rompney for lesynge.

rumorous ('ruːmərəs), *a.* Also 6 **rumerous, rumorus, -ouse.** [f. RUMOUR *sb.* + -OUS.]

1. Making a loud confused sound; resounding. Now *arch.*

1550 SIR T. HOBY *Trav.* (Camden) 38 A river..makethe a great rumerous noise untill he cumethe into the middes of the vale. **1556** J. HEYWOOD *Spider & Fly* lx. 4 Take peace with flies they cride. At which rumorus rore [etc.]. **1604** DRAYTON *Moses Map Miracles* 62 b, The rumorous sound Of the sterne billowes. **1869** LOWELL *Cathedral* 208 Bygone grandeurs, faintly rumorous now Upon the mind's horizon, as of storm Brooding its dreamy thunders far aloof. **1889** W. B. YEATS *Wanderings of Oisin* 68 Wandering of yore in forests rumorous, Beneath the flaming eyeballs of the night. **1897** F. THOMPSON *New Poems* 52 In days whose feet are rumorous on the air. **1926** GALSWORTHY *Silver Spoon* I. xii. 89 The rumorous town still hummed; the sky was faintly coloured. **1970** I. MURDOCH *Fairly Honourable Defeat* II. xix. 371 It was dark outside, windy rainy rumorous darkness coming from far away.

2. Of the nature of rumour; rumoured. *rare.*

1605 STOW *Ann.* 1401 The Lorde Keeper, and other Lordes of the Counsell,..perswaded against rumorous talke of the Earle of Essex. *a* **1639** WOTTON *Reliq.* (1672) 377 This Bearer will tell you what we hear of certain rumorous Surmises.

3. Full of rumours or reports. *rare*$^{-1}$.

1641 T. JORDAN *Walks of Islington* v. i, Your husband.. Shall..to the bold ears of the rumorous world, Declare his errour, and your innocence.

Hence **rumo'rosity**, stir, public outcry. *rare.*

1906 JOYCE *Let.* 25 Sept. (1966) II. 166 Ibsen..seems to have disclaimed some of the rumorosity attaching to *A Doll's House.*

rumour ('ruːmə(r)), *sb.* Also α. 5 **rumur, rom-, revmour, rwmor, rumore**, 5–6 **roumoure** (6 **-ure**), 5–8, 9– (chiefly *U.S.*) **rumor.** β. 5 **rumber, romber.** γ. 5 **rymour.** [a. OF. *rumur, rumour, rumor* (mod.F. *rumeur*), and *rimur*, = Prov. *rumor, rimor*, Sp. and Pg. *rumor*, It. *rumore, romore, rimore*:—L. *rūmōr-em*, acc. of *rūmor* noise, din, etc. From OF. are also MDu. and Du. *rumoer*, MLG., MHG., and G. *rumor.*]

1. †**a.** A (wide-spread) report of a favourable or laudatory nature. *Obs.*

c **1374** CHAUCER *Boeth.* II. pr. vii. (1868) 59 ȝe men certys ne konne don no þing aryȝt, but ȝif it be for þe audience of poeple, and for ydel rumours. **1387** TREVISA *Higden* (Rolls) VII. 37 þere God for hym wrouȝte meny myracles and grete. .. By þat rumour sche þat slouȝ him was i-meoved.

b. Talk or report *of* a person or thing in some way noted or distinguished. Now *arch.*

c **1440** *York Myst.* xxvi. 34 Thurgh his romour in þis reme Hath raysede mekill reke. **1526** TINDALE *Luke* vii. 17 Thys rumor off hym went forthe throughout all Jewry. **1535** COVERDALE *1 Macc.* iii. 26 All the Heithen..were afrayed for Iudas and his brethren: so yᵗ the rumoure of him came vnto the kynges eares. **1591** SHAKS. *1 Hen. VI*, II. iii. 7 Great is the rumour of this dreadfull Knight, And his atchieuements of no lesse account.

1853 M. ARNOLD *Sohrab & Rustum* 60 Dim is the rumour of a common fight, Where host meets host, and many names are sunk: But of a single combat Fame speaks clear.

†**c.** The fact of being generally talked about; reputation, renown. *Obs.*

1637 MILTON *Lycidas* 80 Fame..Nor in the glistering foil Set off to th' world, nor in broad rumour lies.

2. a. General talk, report, or hearsay, not based upon definite knowledge. Also phr. ***rumour has it.***

1382 WYCLIF *2 Macc.* v. 5 When fals rumour, or tithing, wente out, as Antiochus hadde gon out of lijf, Jason sodeynly assailide the citee. **1579–80** NORTH *Plutarch* (1595) 94 Thus brought he common rumor to taber on his head. **1597** SHAKS. *2 Hen. IV*, Ind. 15 Rumour is a Pipe Blowne by Surmises, Ielousies, Coniectures. **1610** HEYWOOD *Gold. Age* I. i, To stop all rumour that may fil the world. *c* **1640** ROWLEY *Birth of Merlin* I. i, The court 's all filled with rumour, the city with news, and the country with wonder. **1750** GRAY *Long Story* 73 So Rumor says. (Who will, believe.) **1781** COWPER *Expost.* 357 His stamm'ring tongue With doleful rumour and sad presage hung. **1819** SHELLEY *Cenci* I. iii. 16 You seem..Too sprightly and companionable a man, To act the deeds that rumour pins on you. **1852** TENNYSON *Ode Wellington* 181 Who let the turbid streams of rumour flow Thro' either babbling world of high and low. **1869** FREEMAN *Norm. Conq.* (1875) III. 160 The mysterious power of rumour which seems to travel faster than any post. **1912** J. N. MCILWRAITH *Diana of Quebec* xviii. 276 Rumour had it they were engaged. **1922** JOYCE *Ulysses* 190 Mr. Russell, rumour has it, is gathering together a sheaf of our younger poets' verses. **1957** D. ROBINS *Noble One* xi. 111 Rumour has it that when Brett went off on his trip, he was asked to give the pretty Juliet a lift..and they've *neither* of them come back. **1961** B. N. CARDOZO in *Webster* s.v., We make our blunders..as rumour has it that you make your own.

b. Personified.

1595 SHAKS. *John* IV. ii. 123 This from Rumors tongue I idely heard. **1630** DEKKER *2nd Pt. Honest Wh.* Wks. 1873 II. 154 'Gainst me swolne Rumor hoisted euery saile. **1667** MILTON *P.L.* II. 965 Rumor next and Chance, And Tumult and Confusion all imbroild. **1736** *Gentl. Mag.* VI. 613/1 If the gossip, Rumour, truth declares. **1837** CARLYLE *Fr. Rev.* I. II. i, It is thus everywhere that foolish Rumour babbles not of what was done, but of what was misdone or undone.

c. Const. *of* (the thing spoken about).

1622 WITHERS *Philarete* (1633) 592 Where never came Report of Pan,..Nor rumor of the Muses, till of late. **1784** COWPER *Task* II. 3 Oh for a lodge in some vast wilderness, ..Where rumour of oppression and deceit..Might never reach me more. **1847** TENNYSON *Princ.* v. 108 Inward raced the scouts With rumour of Prince Arac hard at hand. **1855** PRESCOTT *Philip II*, II. xii. I. 280 The preparations..had not been conducted so secretly but that some rumor of them had taken wind.

3. a. A statement or report circulating in a community, of the truth of which there is no clear evidence. Comb., as ***rumour-factory, -mill, -monger, -mongering*** etc.; ***rumour-ridden*** adj.

c **1400** MAUNDEV. (1839) v. 52 Alle the comoun rymour and speche is of alle the peple there,..that thei ben the Garneres of Joseph. *c* **1430** LYDG. *Min. Poems* (Percy Soc.) 167 He is a foole that yevithe also credence To newe rumours and every foltisshe fable. **1533** MORE *Debell. Salem* ii. Wks. 936/1 So a rumour ones begonne and spread abrode, is not after soone remoued. **1576** FLEMING *Panopl. Ep.* 18 Why you ought not to haue beleeued such rumors, I wil say something. **1607** SHAKS. *Timon* V. i. 4 Does the Rumor hold for true, That hee's so full of Gold? **1661** BRAMHALL *Just Vind.* 285 This not by uncertain rumours, but by the Acts and Instruments themselves. **1705** PRIDEAUX *Lett.* (Camden) 197 A rumour hath been here for some time that you have of late been under some trouble. **1759** ROBERTSON *Hist. Scot.* IV. I. 303 The authors of these rumours did not confine their attention to Bothwell alone. **1832** LYTTON *E. Aram* I. ix, False rumours often beget truths. **1877** FROUDE *Short Stud.* (1883) IV. I. xi. 129 Rumours flew abroad that miracles had already begun.

Comb. **1647** HEXHAM I, A rumour spreader. **1736** AINSWORTH *Eng.-Lat. Dict.*, A rumour-bearer. **1884** *Sat. Rev.* 7 June 731/2 The rumourmongers have seen what Mr. Gladstone had not seen. **1933** DYLAN THOMAS *Let.* 11 Nov. (1966) 63 Every country in this rumour-ridden world..is branded like Cain across the forehead. **1935** Rumour-monger [see NON-ARYAN *sb.*]. **1953** in P. C. Berg *Dict. New Words* 138/2 A sincere and humble apology printed by the paper in response to charges of rumour-mongering. **1953** J. MASTERS *Lotus & Wind* vi. 76 He must come quickly for her sake—and for his own, to confront the rumourmongers and force them to eat their vile words. **1967** *Economist* 25 Mar. 1131/3 One decree, so far unused, imposing fierce penalties for rumour-mongering and another providing for custody without trial. **1973** *New Journalist* (Australia) July–Aug. 2/3 If there's any truth at all in what's been processed through the industry rumour mills, the..journalists..might well be coming from the Sydney production lines. **1977** *Private Eye* 1 Apr. 18/3 The peculiar recent gyrations in the shares.. may owe as much to the ambitious designs of certain mysterious figures..as to the myriad stories poured out by the well-primed City rumour factory. **1977** *China Now* July/Aug. 18/2 In rebellion against the People's Government, one of the..Grand Lamas went on a rumour-mongering rampage. **1979** *Time* 8 Jan. 28/1 Communications in Iran are unreliable, with the result that the country has become a vast rumor mill. **1979** *Railway Age* Nov. 34/1 Rumormongers have ranged from the *Des Moines Register*, the major newspaper of a major ICG state, to a federal official.

b. Const. *of.*

1525 ABP. WARHAM in Ellis *Orig. Lett.* Ser. III. I. 374 The first rumor and brute of this matier. **1557** N. T. (Genev.) *Matt.* xxiv. 6 Ye shal heare of warres, & of the rumors of warres. **1617** MORYSON *Itin.* I. 181 The Citie..upon the least rumour of building them, armeth their Gallies to burne the same. **1665** TEMPLE *Let. to Ld. Arlington* Wks. 1720 II. 6 Twenty Rumours more we have of his Successes, but I will not yet credit them. **1769** BURKE *Corr.* (1844) I. 217 Many rumours of war here; but I know not well how they are founded. **1840** THIRLWALL *Hist. Greece* lvi. VII. 153 It is probable that the rumour of his approach reached Athens at least some days before him. **1853** C. BRONTE *Villette* xxxviii, Rumours of wars there had been, if not wars themselves.

†**4.** Loud expression or manifestation of disapproval or protest. *Obs.*

c **1400** *Destr. Troy* 2668 þe pepull made noise, Myche Rumur & rud speche at his red sonne. *c* **1440** *Generydes* 1377 To eschew the Rumber and the crye, his purpose..he chaungyd. *a* **1513** FABYAN *Chron.* v. (1811) 87 Amonge yᵉ Knyghtys of Sygebert was spronge a great rumoure, saying that they were not contente. **1568** GRAFTON *Chron.* II. 430, I may not staye him for the rumour of the people.

5. Clamour, outcry; noise, din. Now *arch.*

c **1440** *Alph. Tales* 65 With a grete rumor & a cry he come vnto the pope, & bad hym giff hym his xij d agayn. **1481** CAXTON *Reynard* (Arb.) 15 [He] made suche a noyse and rumour, that lantfert cam out hastely. **1525** LD. BERNERS *Froissart* II. xxvii. 32 He wolde make suche a noyse and rumoure, as though all the deuylles of helle had ben in his chambre. **1581** STYWARD *Mart. Discipl.* II. 134 It is sometimes requisite that thy battailes goe forwardes with rumours and showtings. **1612** DRAYTON *Poly-olb.* xix. 79 From whose vast beechy banks a rumor straight resounds. **1747** *Gentl. Mag.* 208/2 A very particular quality is observable in this creature, of listening to any noise or rumour in the street. **1786** tr. *Beckford's Vathek* 82 The rumour every instant increased. **1851** LONGF. *Gold. Leg.*, *Nativity* v, Here a great rumour of trumpets and horses. **1885** R. L. & F. STEVENSON *Dynamiter* 97 The rumour of the wind among the garden trees. **1889** W. B. YEATS *Let.* 3 Feb. (1954) I. 110 They always long for rest and to get away from the noise and rumour of the world. **1922** JOYCE *Ulysses* 388 His heart shook within the cage of his breast as he tasted the rumour of that storm. **1927** F. B. YOUNG *Portrait of Clare* 624 Her ears became aware of an unusual sound. At first she thought it was only the wind-swept rumour of one of the great munition trains. *a* **1973** J. R. R. TOLKIEN *Silmarillion*

(1977) iii. 52 But many refused the summons, preferring the starlight and the wide spaces of Middle-earth to the rumour of the Trees.

†6. Uproar, tumult, disturbance. *Obs.*

1462 *Paston Lett.* II. 82 Swyche talkynge comyth of false screwys that wold mak a rwmor in this contre. **1483** *Cely Papers* (Camden) 132 Ther ys grett rombor in the reme. **1503** *Act 19 Hen. VII*, c. 5 Great Rumour and Variance daily increaseth among his Subjects for taking and refusing of the same [coin]. **1541** BARNES *Wks.* (1573) 219/2 Wee must geue ouer this matter for the uniuersitie is in a rumour. **1581** LAMBARDE *Eiren.* II. v. (1588) 184 Assemblies agaynst the law . . are therfore also somtimes called Rumors. **1639** S. DU VERGER tr. *Camus' Admir. Events* 130 The bawling woman began to raise a rumour about her gate by the complaints which she made unto her neighbours.

rumour ('ruːmə(r)), *v.* Also 6, 9- *U.S.* **rumor.** [f. the sb.]

1. *intr.* †**a.** To resound with disapproval. *Obs.*

1422 tr. *Secreta Secret., Priv. Priv.* 136 Than regnyde avoutry and lechurie in hym and his howse-maynage, that al the roialme thanne rumourt and lothit for that rousty Synne.

b. To invent or circulate rumours.

1858 CARLYLE *Fredk. Gt.* XI. ix. (1862) IV. 146 Diplomatic shadows fencing, Gazetteer shadows rumouring.

2. a. *trans.* To circulate by way of rumour.

1594 SHAKS. *Rich. III*, IV. ii. 51 Come hither Catesby, rumor it abroad, That Anne my Wife is very grieuous sicke. **1597** —— *2 Hen. IV*, Ind. 33 This haue I rumour'd through the peasant-Townes. **1612** BREREWOOD *Lang. & Relig.* 86 Unskilful men may rumour what they will. **1649** ROBERTS *Clavis Bibl.* 556 By the chiefe Author thereof, the Lord, rumouring it. **1735** BOLINGBROKE *Study Hist.* iv. (1777) 96 Those wretched Christians who returned from those wars . . rumoured these stories about the West. **1773-83** HOOLE *Orl. Fur.* XXIX. 40 Various tales are rumour'd of his fate.

b. In passive with dependent clause.

1607 SHAKS. *Cor.* I. ii. 11 It is rumour'd . . These three leade on this Preparation Whether 'tis bent. **1671** MILTON *Samson* 1600 All abroad was rumour'd that this day Samson should be brought forth. **1831** MACKINTOSH *Hist. Eng.* II. 73 It had been industriously rumoured . . that Richard duke of York had escaped from the assassins. **1863** LONGF. *Wayside Inn* I. Prol. 203 It was rumoured he could say The Parables of Sandabar.

c. With personal object and complement.

1602 MARSTON *Antonio's Rev.* IV. i, See you streight rumour me dead. **1833-6** H. COLERIDGE *Northern Worthies* (1852) I. 64 He [Blood] was rumoured . . to be a creature of Buckingham. **1849** M. ARNOLD *Strayed Reveller* 109 Art thou not he, whom fame This long time rumours The favour'd guest of Circe?

d. To force through rumour *into* (an action, etc.). *rare.*

1925 F. SCOTT FITZGERALD *Great Gatsby* i. 25, I had no intention of being rumored into marriage.

3. a. To transmit with a murmuring sound.

1887 HALL CAINE *Deemster* xxxix, Hearing voices of men or the sound of laughter rumoured over the quiet waters.

b. *intr.* To make a murmuring noise.

1900 *Blackw. Mag.* Oct. 474/2 The lullaby aid of the sea that rumoured light and soothingly round the rock of Doom.

Hence '**rumouring** *vbl. sb.* and *ppl. a.*

c **1563** *Jack Juggler* in Hazl. *Dodsley* II. 128 Yea, dost thou make a rumouring yet again? **1842** SYMMONS *Agamemnon* 4 Swifter than noisy fame of rumouring tongues. **1858** CARLYLE *Fredk. Gt.* IV. vi. (1872) I. 444 Such a marching and rumouring going on all round him. **1895** W. WATSON *Father of Forest* 4 Mourned not the rumouring winds? **1957** T. HUGHES *Hawk in Rain* 54 You hear . . through all The leafy valley a rumouring of air go.

rumoured ('ruːməd), *ppl. a.* [f. RUMOUR *v.*] Announced by rumour; commonly reported.

1667 MILTON *P.L.* IV. 817 Som Magazin to store Against a rumord Warr. **1751** YOUNG *Nt. Th.* II. 27 As rumour'd robberies endear our gold. **1807** J. BARLOW *Columb.* III. 50 From far The rumor'd leagues proclaim approaching war. **1868** E. EDWARDS *Ralegh* I. xii. 231 He discusses both the probability of the rumoured invasion, and the best means of defending the coasts.

'**rumourer.** *rare.* Also 7 **rumorer.** [f. RUMOUR *v.* + -ER[1].] One who disseminates rumours.

1607 SHAKS. *Cor.* IV. vi. 47 Go see this Rumorer whipt. **1886** T. HARDY *Mayor Casterbr.* xliii, When all had been said about busy rumourers.

So '**rumourist.** *rare*$^{-1}$.

1887 *L'pool Mercury* 19 Oct. 5 The Cabinet council which the rumourists with one accord had fixed for Thursday.

rump (rʌmp), *sb.*[1] Also 5-7 **rumpe,** 6 **rompe,** 7 **rumpt, rompt.** [ME. *rumpe, rompe*, prob. of Scand. origin: cf. MDa. *rumpe, rompe* (Da. *rumpe*), MSw. *rumpa, rompa* (Sw. *rumpa*), tail, posteriors, Norw. *rumpa* tail, *rump* posteriors, Icel. *rumpr.* The corresponding MDu. *romp(e), rump* (Du. and Fris. *romp*), MLG. and LG. *rump*, OHG. and G. *rumpf* mean 'trunk' of the body.]

1. a. That part of the body (of an animal or bird) from which the tail springs; †the tail; hence by extension, the hind-quarters, posteriors, buttocks.

c **1440** *Promp. Parv.* 439/2 Rumpe, tayle, *cauda.* **1530** PALSGR. 263/2 Rompe of a beest, *poiltron, croupe.* **1577** B. GOOGE *Heresbach's Husb.* IV. (1586) 158 Their Tailes dubled and flagging, their rumpes and thyes full of feathers. **1590** SPENSER *F.Q.* I. viii. 48 At her rompe she growing had behind A foxes taile. **1606** SHAKS. *Tr. & Cr.* V. ii. 56 The diuell Luxury with his fat rumpe and potato finger. **1617** MORYSON *Itin.* IV. (1903) 214 They fasten them . . to the tayles of theire horses and to the Rompts when the tayles be puld off. **1668** CULPEPPER & COLE tr. *Barthol. Anat.* IV. xv. 351 That Danish Boy, who had a Tail growing out at his Rump. **1740** SOMERVILLE *Hobbinol* I. 307 He on his Hams, or on his brawny Rump Sliding secure, derides their vain Distress. **1774** GOLDSM. *Nat. Hist.* (1776) VI. 108 The marks of the goose are, a bigger body, . . a white ring about the rump. **1826** SCOTT *Jrnl.* 2 Nov., I saw the scoundrels jumping the windows, with the bayonets at their rumps. **1846** J. BAXTER *Libr. Pract. Agric.* (ed. 4) II. 261 Sheep . . high on the loins, down on the rumps. **1884** COUES *N. Amer. Birds* 94 In general, we should call the anterior two-thirds or three-fourths of notæum 'back', and the rest 'rump'.

†**b.** That part *of* a tail which is next to the body; the stump. Also *transf. Obs.*

1608 TOPSELL *Serpents* (1658) 674 The length of it from the tip of the nose to the rump of the tail is seven or eight fingers. **1676** MOXON *Print Letters* 34 Q hath its Body made like O. The Rump of the Tail is made by drawing a straight line from Parallel 12½. **1745** P. THOMAS *Jrnl. Anson's Voy.* 40 Two [fins] . . with a small Rump of a Tail between them.

c. A part resembling a rump. *rare*$^{-1}$.

1852 BADGER *Nestorians* I. 254 We left Amedia at 7 a.m., and . . made the western rump of Jebel Gara about noon.

d. A type of bustle. *Obs.*

1786 E. SHERIDAN *Jrnl.* 22 Jan. (1960) iii. 79 However you may tell her as a friend gradually to reduce her Stuffing as Rumps are quite out in France and are decreasing here but can not be quite given up 'till the weather grows warmer. **1807** R. SOUTHEY *Lett. from England* II. xlix. 335 There were protruberances on the hips called bustlers, another behind which was called in plain language a rump.

2. a. This part of an animal or fowl as cut off and used for food.

1486 *Bk. St. Albans* C viij, She tyrith vppon Rumppys, she fedith on all maner of flesh. **1567** TURBERV. *Epit.*, etc. 111 When my back is turnde and gon, Another giues thee rumpes to tyre vpon. **1611** COTGR., *Cimier*, the vpper part of a rumpe of Beefe, &c., next, or neere, vnto the chine. **1688** PENTON *Guardian's Instruct.* (1897) 47 Treated at an Ale-house with a Rump of Beef. **1710** ADDISON *Tatler* No. 148 ¶1 The Maids of Honour in Queen Elizabeth's Time were allowed Three Rumps of Beef for their Breakfast. **1796** BURKE *Lett. Noble Lord* Wks. VIII. 63 The poor ox . . is divided into rumps, and sirloins, and briskets, and into all sorts of pieces. **1837** M. DONOVAN *Dom. Econ.* II. 237, I caused a rump of beef . . to be immersed in . . cold water for three hours. **1884** GILMOUR *Mongols* 122 To present the rump and tail was the highest honour that a host could offer a guest at a feast.

Comb. a **1700** B. E. *Dict. Cant. Crew, Rump-and-Kidney Men*, Fidlers that Play at Feasts, Fairs, . . &c. And Live chiefly on the Remnants of Victuals.

†**b.** Used with allusion to sense 3 b. *Obs.*

1660 PEPYS *Diary* 11 Feb., In King-street seven or eight [bonfires]; and all along burning, and roasting, and drinking for rumps. *c* **1665** MRS. HUTCHINSON *Mem. Col. Hutchinson* (1838) 116/1 When the youths were gathering together to make bonfires to burn the Rump, as the custom of those mad days [1660] was. **1680** *Lond. Gaz.* No. 1497/4 Several Apprentices . . had formed a design . . to come together in a considerable number on the Kings Birth-day, as they pretended, To Burn the Rump.

†**c.** ***rump and dozen***: (see quot. 1796). Also, corporal punishment administered on the buttocks. *Obs.* exc. *arch.*

1796 *Grose's Dict. Vulgar T.* (ed. 3), *Rump and dozen*, a rump of beef and a dozen of claret. **1812** *Sporting Mag.* XXXIX. 112 A bet of a rump and dozen was laid of this important point. **1827** SIR J. BARRINGTON *Pers. Sk.* 296 I'll lay you a rump and a dozen . . on the matter. **1833** J. ROMILLY *Diary* 20 Mar. (1967) 31 The original bet was 1 G[ui]n[e]a, but Sedgwick proposed a rump & dozen. **1922** JOYCE *Ulysses* 323 A rump and dozen says the citizen, was what that old ruffian sir John Beresford called it but the modern God's Englishman calls it caning on the breech.

3. a. *fig.* A small, unimportant, or contemptible remnant or remainder of a body of persons (esp. of a Parliament: cf. next).

1649 WALKER *Hist. Independency* II. 32 This fagge end, this Rump of a Parliament with corrupt Maggots in it. **1659** *Engl. Conf.* 22 This Rumpe of a casheered House of Commons. **1730** T. BOSTON *Mem.* (1899) 286 The people running away into it, so that the rump of the meeting seemed only to remain. **1795** BURKE *Corr.* (1844) IV. 318 My business with the House of Lords is over for the present; for they have, or a rump of them, done their own business pretty handsomely. **1818** COBBETT *Pol. Reg.* XXXIII. 8 What remains of it, is the Rump of the old Committee. **1849** MACAULAY *Hist. Eng.* i. I. 131 The few members who made up what was contemptuously called the Rump of the House of Commons. **1877** W. MORRIS in Mackail *Life* (1899) I. 349 The Tory Rump that we fools chose at the last election to represent us.

transf. **1708** *Brit. Apollo* No. 83. 2/1 You are . . the Rump of the Athenian Oracle.

b. *Hist.* The remnant of the Long Parliament (restored in May, 1659) which was dissolved by Monk in Feb. 1660; also (esp. in later use) the earlier remnant of the same Parliament from the time of Pride's Purge (Dec. 1648) to its dissolution by Cromwell in April, 1653.

[As to the origin of the name, cf. the following statements:—**1662** *Rump Songs* To Rdr., Now if you ask who nam'd it Rump, know 'twas so stil'd in an honest Sheet of Paper (call'd The Bloody Rump) written before the Tryal of our late Soveraign of Glorious Memory: but the Word obtain'd not universal notice till it flew from the mouth of Major General Brown at a Publick Assembly in the daies of Richard Cromwell. **1709** HEARNE *Collect.* (O.H.S.) II. 329 Which word *Rump* had it's name first from Mr. Clem. Walker in his History of Independency printed in 1648 and was given to those . . members that strenuously oppos'd the King.]

1659 C. HATTON *Let. to Hyde* 23 Dec. in *Clarendon MSS.*, The Rump, as we now call them. **1660** PEPYS *Diary* 22 Feb., Major General Brown, who had a long time been banished by the Rump. **1660** in Wood *Life* (O.H.S.) I. 363 *note*, The oath . . taken by every member of both houses of Parliament, Rumpt and all. **1681** *Trial of S. Colledge* 117 It was the Garbage of that Parliament I am sure, that is the Rump, but they called themselves the Parliament of England. **1725** B. HIGGONS *Rem. Burnet* I. Wks. 1736 II. 64 His Quarrel to Cromwell, was his having depos'd the Rump, and usurp'd the Power in a single Person. **1757** HUME *Hist. Eng.*, *Commw.* iii. IV. 97 It was agreed, that, laying aside former enmities, all efforts should be used for the overthrow of the Rump; For so they called the Parliament. **1849** MACAULAY *Hist. Eng.* i. I. 147 The Rump and the soldiers were still hostile to the House of Stuart. But the Rump was universally detested and despised. **1878** *N. Amer. Rev.* CXXVI. 538 This office he [Milton] held during the Rump, under five successive councils of state.

c. So ***Rump Parliament.***

1670 CLARENDON *Hist. Reb.* XVI. §208 Upon the recalling . . of Harry Cromwell to the rump Parliament as soon as his brother Richard was deposed. **1671** GLANVILL *Further Disc. Stubbe* 31 Styling me Chaplain to M. Rous, a Member of the Rump-Parliament. **1725** B. HIGGONS *Rem. Burnet* I. Wks. 1736 II. 48 Is it possible to conceive that the Rump Parliament, and afterward Cromwell, would have let my Lord Antrim have sat quiet for twelve Years? *Ibid.* 69 His [Monk's] Address . . in perswading the Rump Parliament to dislodge the disaffected Troops at London. **1845** CARLYLE *Cromwell* (1871) III. 196 Such was the destructive wrath of my Lord General Cromwell against the Nominal Rump Parliament of England.

4. In phrases ***rump and rig, rump and stump***, through and through; completely, entirely. *dial.* or *colloq.* (See also STUMP *sb.*)

Cf. G. *mit rumpf und stumpf* in the same sense.

1824 MACTAGGART *Gallovid. Encycl.* 499 Up rump and stump did Auchen burn. **18..** *Sk. Broad Yks.* 54 (E.D.D.), They say they're Britons rump an' rig. **1892** J. E. MUDDOCK *Detective's Triumphs* 55 My man . . bought the place. Bought it! Yes. Rump and stump.

5. *attrib.* and *Comb.* **a.** In sense 1 or 2, as ***rump-beef, -end, -feather, -gland, -patch, roast, -steak***; also ***rump-fed, -galled, -spotted*** adjs.

1605 SHAKS. *Macb.* I. iii. 6 Aroynt thee, Witch, the rumpe-fed Ronyon cryes. **1614** B. JONSON *Bart. Fair* II. ii, You'll neuer thinke of any thing, till your dame be rumpgall'd. **1675** HAN. WOOLLEY *Gentlew. Comp.* 114 Then take the rump-end of the Backbone. **1689** *Muses Farew. to Popery* 18 A lazy Mass of damn'd Rump Beef. **1747** H. GLASSE *Art of Cookery* i. 6 *To Broil* Steaks . . take fine Rump Steaks about Half an Inch thick. **1765** STERNE *Tr. Shandy* VII. xxi, The gardener . . led out the two old mules, to clip the hair from the rump-ends of their tails. **1765** GOLDSM. *Ess.* vi. Wks. (Globe) 302/2 Bad as it was, it seemed a rump-steak to me. **1834** MUDIE *Brit. Birds* (1841) I. 10 The rump feathers and upper tail coverts. **1849** D. J. BROWNE *Amer. Poultry Yd.* (1855) 282 The rump gland frequently becomes obstructed. **1886** C. E. PASCOE *London of To-day* ii. (ed. 3) 40 A mutton-chop or rump-steak may be readily got from the nearest butcher's. **1897** FORBES *Hand-bk. Primates* II. 72 Rump-spotted Guenon, *cercopithecus opisthostictus.* **1902** *Nature* 14 Aug. 375/2 The author states that the gaur and the gayal have a white rump-patch. **1926** *Daily Colonist* (Victoria, B.C.) 6 July 6/1 (Advt.), Small Rump Roasts, per lb. 23c. **1948** A. L. RAND *Mammals Eastern Rockies* 206 Elk . . Sides of body yellowish brown, rump patch lighter. **1976** *National Observer* (U.S.) 22 May 20/4 Right in the Rump Roast.

b. In sense 3 or 3 b, as ***rump caucus, -general, government, -groat, -junta, -man, meeting, -member, parliament*** (see also sense 3 c), ***party, -senate, state, -time.***

1659-60 *Hist. 2nd Death Rump* 1/2 Some Packs he inveagles, O' th' blood-coated Beagles, To's partie; the Rump-men did so too. **1663** DRYDEN *Wild Gallant* III. i, When the keys of the Exchequer were lost in the Rump-time. **1670** CLARENDON *Hist. Reb.* XVI. §144 They made no doubt but the rump members would again resume the government. **1716** HEARNE *Collect.* (O.H.S.) V. 296 Of whose being sequestred in the Rump-Time I have heard much. **1731** *Gentl. Mag.* I. 537 A Silver pair of Breeches neatly wrought, (Such as you see upon an old Rump Groat). **1826** W. E. ANDREWS *Crit. Rev. Fox's Bk. Mart.* II. 27 A rump-general, namely, John Lambert. **1838** *Ibid.* 17 Feb. 764/1 What prevents Congress from declaring itself perpetual—a rump Parliament? **1861** *Richmond* (Va.) *Examiner* 4 Dec. 3/3 It may very reasonably be doubted how far General Sherman or his officers would suffer schemes so vitally important to the Rump Government to leak out through the indiscretions of loquacious volunteers. **1861** J. E. B. MAYOR *Introd. Cicero, Philipp. ii.* (1881) p. xvii, The rump senate, thus brought together, was convened by Antonius and Cassius. **1933** *Sun* (Baltimore) 19 Apr. 1/7 The incipient revolt as reflected in the rump caucus of Democratic inflationists. **1935** *Times* 19 June 2/2 The Westminster Rump-juntas of our own day. **1935** *Sun* (Baltimore) 10 Dec. 2/7 Mr. Berry . . declared the meeting adjourned, and Dr. Haake and his confreres edged their way out to the sidewalk, where they threatened for a time to hold a 'rump meeting'. **1937** *Nation* 6 Nov. 419/1 The Franco rump government in Spain. **1938** *Sun* (Baltimore) 31 Oct. 8/3 Germany and Italy have consented to serve as arbiters in the dispute between Hungary and the rump Czechoslovakian state. **1940** *Tablet* 4 May 422/1 Herr Joseph Bühler . . is at present a sort of head of the Governor-General's Government in the rump-State of Poland. **1959** *Ann. Reg. 1958* 121 Rump parties would continue to exist and split the anti-P.A.P. vote. **1963** *Times* 23 May 13/4 This move is a direct reversal of the proposal, threatened by the Governor of the Gambia, that the remaining validly elected members of the House of Representatives constituted a 'rump parliament', capable of curing this difficulty. **1976** *New Yorker* 22 Mar. 98/2 Krishnan Kant recently made an eloquent and wide-ranging indictment of the emergency, a sort of *cri de cœur*, in what could properly be called the rump Parliament, inasmuch as so many of both its opposition and its Congress members have been jailed. **1977** *New Yorker* 10 Oct. 50/3 On the eve of Eaton's ninetieth birthday . . he was summarily booted upstairs to chairman emeritus by his own board of directors at a rump meeting. **1977** *Time* 15 Aug. 15/2 In 1975 the Turks declared their own Turkish Federated State of Cyprus; last week the only notice this rump government took of Makarios' passing was to announce flatly that it would not recognize his successor as the leader of a united Cyprus.

c. rumpsprung *a.*, sprung or become baggy in the seat; also *fig.*; hence **rumpspringing** *vbl. sb.*

1939 C. MORLEY *Kitty Foyle* xiii. 131 Pop creaking in his rumpsprung wicker chair. **1954** *Publ. Amer. Dial. Soc.* XXI. 35 *Rumpspringing*: *pres. part.*, *n.*, of a skirt, the act of bagging in the seat, caused by sitting. An inner lining is sometimes used to prevent *rumpspringing*... *Rumpsprung*: *adj.* **1970** D. WATERFIELD *Continental Waterboy* ii. 11 'In my opinion,' Mrs. Neuberger told the reporters, 'Vancouver women are rump-sprung.' **1975** *Weekend Mag.* (Montreal) 31 May 9/1 In the hallway, his rumpsprung wife is making a blasé remark about the new labor code.

6. Special combs., as **rump-band**, a leather band passing over the rump of a horse to support the trace-chains; †**rump-evil**, a disease affecting the rump; †**rump-jewel** (?); **rump-poke** (see quot.); **rump-post**, the pygostyle of a bird; †**rump-roll**, = BUSTLE *sb.*[2]; **rump-rope** (see quot.); **rump-strap**, a strap serving the same purpose as a rump-band.

1844 H. STEPHENS *Bk. Farm* III. 1192 The *rump-band is hooked on to the trace-chains. **1611** COTGR., *Mal de cropion*, the *rumpe-euill; a disease wherewith all birds..are sometimes troubled. **1710** STEELE *Tatler* No. 245 ⁋2 A Crochet of 122 Diamonds,..with a *Rump Jewel after the same Fashion. **1821** A. WELBY *Visit N. Amer.* 8 We also saw yesterday a large brown bird pursuing a Gull, and understood its name to be *Rump-poke. An appropriate appellation, as it pursues other birds for their droppings. **1890** COUES *Ornith.* II. iv. 210 That extraordinary affair called the *rump-post or pygostyle. **1707** J. STEVENS tr. *Quevedo's Com. Wks.* (1709) 403 A vast Fardel of Rags.. composed a *Rump-rowl. **1820** W. SCORESBY *Acc. Arctic Reg.* II. 296 The rump then, supported by a tackle, is drawn forward by means of a stout rope, called the *rump-rope. **1844** H. STEPHENS *Bk. Farm* III. 1192 The trace-horse is harnessed with back-strap, *rump-strap, and crupper.

†**rump**, *sb.*[2] *Obs. rare.* [= Du. *romp* 'pieces of cloves and nutmeg', in Kilian *rompe* 'nux myristica vilior, cassa, inanis', MLG. *rumpe*.] Refuse of nutmegs.

1602 in Sir G. Birdwood & W. Foster *Reg. Lett. E. India Co.* (1893) 41 To clense them & free them..from dust & the nutmegges from Rumps. **1610** *Rates of Marchandizes* F vij, Garble and Rumpes of Nutmegs the pound, xij.d.

rump (rʌmp), *v.* Chiefly *slang.* [f. RUMP *sb.*[1]]

1. *trans.* To turn one's back upon (a person), esp. as a mode of snubbing. Now *rare* or *Obs.*

1737 *Common Sense* I. 52 Whoever envies me, or whoever is not on my Side, let him be Rumped. **1790** LADY S. LENNOX *Life & Lett.* (1901) II. 76 Mr. Conolly was at Court in London, and H. M. rump'd him,..so that he did not go to the Queen's drawing-room. **1809** MALKIN *Gil Blas* IX. ii. ⁋5 Other people who attempted to speak to him, were rumped in exact proportion with the blandishments of his face towards me. **1841** BARHAM *Ingol. Leg.* Ser. II. *Old Wom. in Grey*, His Holiness not only gets the 'cold shoulder' But Nick rumps him completely. **1845** *Blackw. Mag.* LVII. 375 We believe it is an established rule, not to turn your back on —or in playhouse phrase—not to rump your audience.

2. *absol.* Of pigeons: To set up the tail feathers.

1765 *Treat. Dom. Pigeons* 106 It was apt to make them rump.

3. *trans.* To flog or scourge. *rare*$^{-0}$.

1812 J. H. VAUX *Flash Dict.*, *Rump'd*, flogged or scourged.

4. *Sc.* To plunder completely; to clean (one) of money. (Cf. RUMP *sb.*[1] 4.)

1815 SCOTT *Let.* in *Lockhart* (1837) III. xi. 366 Most of the châteaux, where the Prussians are quartered, are what is technically called *rumped*, that is to say, plundered out and out. **1825** JAMIESON *Suppl.* s.v., A phrase often applied to a losing gamester; as, 'I'm quite rumpit'.

Hence **'rumping** *vbl. sb.*

1765 *Treat. Dom. Pigeons* 96 Setting the feathers upon the rump, (which is called rumping).

rum-pad, -padder: see RUM *a.*[1] 4.

†**'rumpant**, *ppl. a. Obs.*$^{-1}$ [a. AF. *rumpant*, = F. *rompant*, pres. pple. of *rompre* to break.] Breaking the law, offending.

1621 *Irish Act 5 Edw. IV* in R. Bolton *Stat. Irel.* 38 Persons..that finde or impeach any of the said vessels Rumpants or forfeits against this Act.

'rump-bone. Now *rare* or *Obs.* [RUMP *sb.*[1]] The bone of the rump; the coccyx.

1615 [see COCCYX]. *a***1661** HOLYDAY *Juvenal* 149 An extraordinary excrescency of bones below the os coccygis, the rump bone. **1678** BUTLER *Hud.* III. ii. 1626 Then what can better represent, Than this Rump-bone, the Parliament? **1741** A. MONRO *Anat. Nerves* (ed. 3) 198 Os Coccygis, or Rump-bone. **1802** *Med. Jrnl.* VIII. 278 So, we have the terms, sacred bone, rump bone, nameless bones, boot-like bones, &c.

rumped (rʌmpt), *a.* [f. RUMP *sb.*[1]]

†**1.** Having a bustle or false rump. *Obs.*

1707 MRS. CENTLIVRE *Platonick Love* Epil. 190 Then a West-country damsel trots to Town, And talks of paint, false hair, and rumpt-up gown. **1771** SMOLLETT *Humph. Cl.* 31 May, She, to be sure, was so particular with her rumpt gown and petticoat,..that every body looked at her with surprise.

2. Having a rump of a specified form, colour, etc. Chiefly *Zool.*

1721 *Lond. Gaz.* No. 5972/3 A..Mare,..square Rumpt. **1783** LATHAM *Gen. Synop. Birds* II. I. 74 Ash-rumped Thrush. **1876** *Nature* 23 Nov. 90/1 A Hairy-rumped Agouti. **1899** W. T. GREENE *Cage-birds* 20 The Twite, or Red-Rumped Linnet. *Ibid.* 49 Yellow-rumped Finch.

Rumpelstiltskin (ˌrʌmpəlˈstɪltskɪn). [ad. G. *Rumpelstilzchen.*] The name of a vindictive dwarf in German folk-tale, used allusively.

1949 G. ORWELL *Nineteen Eighty-Four* II. 181 A little Rumpelstiltskin figure, contorted with hatred. **1976** *National Observer* (U.S.) 21 Feb. 5/2 A hunch that computerized direct marketing would become the Rumpelstiltskin of American politics in the 1970s.

†**'rumpent.** *Obs.*$^{-1}$ [ad. pres. pple. of L. *rumpĕre* to break.] An application for breaking a swelling.

1661 LOVELL *Hist. Anim. & Min.* 363 Inflammation..; it's cured by..emollients, maturants, rumpents, sternutation [etc.].

Rumper (ˈrʌmpə(r)). *Hist.* [f. RUMP *sb.*[1] 3 b.] A member or supporter of the Rump Parliament.

1660 PEPYS *Diary* 7 March, There was all the Rumpers almost come to the House to-day. **1665** WINSTANLEY *Loy. Martyrology* 152 A great Rumper, and Enemy to Royal Government. **1706** E. WARD *Hud. Rediv.* (1707) II. xii. 8 'Cause the Rumpers were about, Thro' Jealousy, to turn him out. **1731-8** SWIFT *Pol. Conv.* Introd. 34 Blasphemy, or Free-Thinking..[was] after the Restoration, carried to Whitehall by the converted Rumpers. **1826** SCOTT *Woodst.* xxvi, The possession of such a prize..might obtain from the Rumpers..a reward. **1887** J. WESTBY-GIBSON in *Dict. Nat. Biog.* IX. 460 Chaloner, being elected..for Scarborough, became a zealous 'rumper'.

So †**'Rumpier.** *Obs.*$^{-1}$

1665 J. FRASER *Polichron.* (S.H.S.) 349 Alderman Hoyle of York, a great Rumpier.

Rumpety, var. RUMPTY *sb.*[2]

'Rumpish, *a. rare.* [f. RUMP *sb.*[1] 3 b.] Of or belonging to the Rump Parliament.

1660 [T. WIDDOWES] *title*, The just Devil of Woodstock; or..the Frights and Punishments inflicted upon the Rumpish Commissioners sent thither..in the Year 1649. **1904** LANG *Hist. Scot.* III. ix. 278 The Covenants were revived by the Rumpish Parliament restored by Monk.

rumple (ˈrʌmp(ə)l), *sb.*[1] *Sc.* (and *north.*). [f. RUMP *sb.*[1] + -LE[1].]

1. A tail or rump.

? *a***1500** *Rowlis Cursing* 117 Sum with rumpillis lyk a skait. **1508** DUNBAR *Flyting* 125 He that dang sanct Augustine with ane rumple, Thy fowll front had. *c***1560** A. SCOTT *Poems* (S.T.S.) ii. 148 Thocht I had rycht nocht bot a rok To gar ȝour rumpill reik Behynd. **1721** KELLY *Scot. Prov.* 365 You ride so near the Rumple, you'll let none get on behind. **1788** PICKEN *Poems* 130 He shook his tail, an' rumple blue. *a***1878** AINSLIE *Land of Burns* (1892) 310 Your rumples to the sun, Your digits diggin' in the dirt. **1898** *Shetland News* 30 April (E.D.D.), Black wi' a white bit apo' da rumple.

Comb. **1776** HERD *Collect. Sc. Songs* II. 229 She's fa'n o'er the buffet-stool And brake her rumple-bane. **1824** CHAMBERS *Traditions of Edinb.* (1847) 195 The rumple-knot was a large bunch of ribbons worn at the peak of the waist behind.

†**2.** The Rump Parliament. *Obs.*$^{-1}$

1725 RAMSAY *Gentl. Sheph.* II. i, Monk..plaid the Rumple a right slee begunk.

rumple (ˈrʌmp(ə)l), *sb.*[2] Now *rare.* Also 6 *Sc.* rumpil. [ad. MDu. (also Du.) *rompel* or MLG. *rumpel(e*, derivatives of MDu. *rompe*, MLG. *rumpe* (G. dial. *rümpf*) wrinkle. Cf. RIMPLE *sb.*] A wrinkle, fold, crease. (See also quot. 1778.)

1500-20 DUNBAR *Poems* xxvi. 20 Round abowt him.. Hang all in rumpillis to the heill His kethat [? *read* rechat] for the nanis. **1611** COTGR., *Grippets*, the rumples of an ouerlong, or ill-made garment. **1693** DRYDEN *Juvenal* (1697) 268 Fair Virginia wou'd..change her Faultless Make For the foul Rumple of her Camel-back. **1701** FARQUHAR *Sir H. Wildair* II. i, How..could you two contrive to make a bed as mine was last night? a wrinkle on one side, and a rumple on t'other. **1778** *Exmoor Scolding* Gloss. (E.D.S.) 151 Rumple in Devon means..a Thing ruffled and drawn up together. **1834** M. SCOTT *Cruise Midge* (1863) 183 It..lay flat on the table as if unused to the rumples and creases.

†**'rumple**, *sb.*[3] *dial. Obs.* (See quot. 1778.)

1746 *Exmoor Scolding* (E.D.S.) 288 Go pey tha Score... There's a Rumple. **1778** *Ibid.* Gloss., *A Rumple*, a large Debt contracted by little and little.

†**'rumple**, *sb.*[4] *dial. Obs.* (See quot.)

1778 *Exmoor Scolding* Gloss. (E.D.S.) 151 Somerset, 'Twill come to a Rumple, or breaking, at last.

rumple (ˈrʌmp(ə)l), *v.* [f. RUMPLE *sb.*[2], or ad. MDu. *rompelen*, MLG. *rumpelen* (G. dial. *rümpflen*), f. MLG. *rumpen* (MHG. *rümphen*, G. *rümpfen*) to wrinkle, etc. Cf. RIMPLE *v.*]

1. *trans.* To wrinkle, crease, draw into wrinkles or small folds, render uneven or irregular.

In early use only in pa. pple. *rumpled.*

1603 *Mirr. Worldly Fame* in *Harl. Misc.* (Malh.) II. 521 Thy cheeks and fair forehead shall be full of wrinkles;..thy throat shall be rumpled. **1694** *Martens' Voy.* in *Acc. Sev. Late Voy.* II. 63 The Leaves are not quite plain, but somewhat rumpled at the brims. **1758** *Phil. Trans.* L. 589 They are wrinkled or rumpled over one another. **1796** H. HUNTER tr. *St.-Pierre's Stud. Nat.* (1799) II. 81 Nature employs several species of white..by dotting, rumpling, radiating, varnishing it. **1844** MRS. BROWNING *Vision of Poets* ccix, One, his smooth Pink cheeks, did rumple passionate, Like Aeschylus. **1893** H. M. DOUGHTY *Our Wherry in Wendish Lands* 18 Beds of bogbean foliage, rumpling the green floating carpet of lily leaves.

b. *refl.* or *intr.* To form into folds. *rare*$^{-1}$.

1631 MABBE *Celestina* v. (1894) 101 A pocks upon these long and large playtings in my Petticoates; Fie how they rumple and fold themselves about my legges.

2. To touzle, disorder, crumple. Also with *up*.

16.. *Collier of Croydon* in Hazl. *Dodsley* VIII. 389 He will not rumple Peg, nor Joan, nor Nan. **1672** DAVENANT *To Dk. Richmond* Wks. (1673) 294 Strait I beheld..The Sheets all rumpled and the Cordage slack. **1712-4** POPE *Rape Lock* IV. 72, I..rumpled petticoats, or tumbled beds. **1773** GOLDSM. *Stoops to Conquer* v, Though girls like to be play'd with, and rumpled a little too sometimes. **1798** MME. D'ARBLAY *Let.* 28 Aug., He seized the letter..and rumpling it up in his little hands, poked it under the cushions. **1851** D. JERROLD *St. Giles* xxviii, Taking off his hat and rumpling up his hair. **1880** MISS BRADDON *Just as I am* xix, I know I'm rumpling your collar, but I can't help it.

fig. **1641** MILTON *Animadv.* Wks. 1851 III. 191 To unpinne your spruce fastidious oratory, to rumple her laces. **1713** C'TESS WINCHILSEA *Misc. Poems* 262 By Age too, rumpl'd and undrest, We gladly sinking down to rest, Leave following Crouds behind. **1871** B. TAYLOR *Faust* (1875) II. i. 28 Though my wife assailed me loudly, Rumpled me through thick and thin.

†**3.** To squeeze together, distort. *Obs.*

1636 DAVENANT *Wits* Wks. (1673) 204 A fine young Gentleman; Only a little rumpl'd in the Womb. *a***1661** FULLER *Worthies*, *Northampton.* II. (1662) 282 He was somewhat rumpled in his Mothers womb, (which caused his crooked back). **1687** *Renowned Hist. Sir J. Hawkwood* iv. 6 Nature had been unkind, in rumpling and distorting his Body in a disorderly Form.

Hence **'rumpling** *vbl. sb.*

1736 AINSWORTH *Lat. Dict.*, A rumpling, *corrugatio.* **1839** W. IRVING *Chronicles of Wolfert's Roost* (1855) 11 The heroine of the Roost escaped with a mere rumpling of the feathers. **1842** *Penny Cycl.* XXIV. 30/2 Such surfaces..are developable, or can be unrolled without any overlapping, rumpling, or tearing. **1843** *Ibid.* XXVII. 477/1 These rods were further reduced in thickness..by a coarse kind of drawing, called ripping or rumpling.

'rumpled, *ppl. a.* [f. RUMPLE *v.* + -ED[1].]

1. Wrinkled, crumpled, creased; touzled.

1712 BLACKMORE *Creation* VI. 282 Each vital speck, in which remains Th'entire, but rumpled, animal. **1743** FIELDING *J. Wild* I. ix, A thin covering of a rumpled muslin hand-kerchief. **1802** MAR. EDGEWORTH *Moral T.* (1816) I. xix. 170 Little rumpled bits of paper, in which the fossils had ..been contained. **1840** DICKENS *Barn. Rudge* lxxiii, Smoothing the bird's rumpled feathers with his hand. **1880** 'OUIDA' *Moths* I. 35 The dreadful rumpled brown holland.

2. Of eggs: = RUMBLED *ppl. a.* 2.

1896 *Westm. Gaz.* 29 Jan. 3/1 The adjutant prepared some rumpled eggs in a manner he had learnt on service.

rumpless (ˈrʌmplɪs), *a.* [f. RUMP *sb.*[1] + -LESS.] Having no rump or tail; tailless. Hence **'rumplessness**, the state of being without a rump.

1668 CHARLETON *Onomast.* 79 *Indicus Sine Uropygio*, Rumpless. **1746** FRANCIS tr. *Hor.*, *Sat.* II. viii. 114 Then saw we blackbirds with o'er-roasted breast, Laid on the board, and ringdoves rumpless dress'd! **1783** LATHAM *Gen. Synop. Birds* II. II. 705 Rumpless Cock. This odd variety.. wants even the rudiment of a tail. **1850** *Fraser's Mag.* XLI. 656 Those who delight in oddities know how to secure a breed of rumpless fowls and tailless cats. **1885** *Encycl. Brit.* XIX. 646/1 Rumpless fowls are those in which the coccygeal vertebræ are absent; there is consequently no tail. **1945** *Jrnl. Exper. Zool.* XCVIII. 65 The injection of solutions of certain chemicals into unincubated chicken eggs led to the appearance of increased numbers of rumpless embryos and chicks. *Ibid.* 67 Insulin produced a high degree of rumplessness. **1971** *N.Z. Med. Jrnl.* LXXIII. 340 (*heading*) Lumbo-sacral agenesis or rumplessness [in humans].

'rumply, *a. rare.* [f. RUMPLE *sb.*[2] Cf. Du. *rompelig.*] Full of rumples, uneven.

1833 CARLYLE *Misc. Ess.*, *Cagliostro*, They spin out, better or worse, their rumply, infirm thread of Existence. **1961** *Guardian* 21 Jan. 1/1 The rumply 35 White House staff members who had been marooned. **1967** E. B. NICKERSON *Kayaks to Arctic* xviii. 176 But the water was only slightly rumply, our boat moved easily along.

†**Rumpship.** *Obs.* [f. RUMP *sb.*[1] 3 b.] A contemptuous title applied to members, or to the rule, of the Rump Parliament.

1659 R. WILD *Poems* (1870) 12 Well, let it be; Your Rumpship wants a scouring too, thinks he. **1660** *No Blind Guides* 3 And thus I'll Instance: Kingship, is your old Bondage; Rumpship, ours. **1663** J. H. *Hist. Cromwell* ix, Cromwell..sent Major General Harrison on the 20th of Aprill, 1653, to out their Rump-ships.

rump-te, -ti, -ty: see RUMTI-.

'rumption. *colloq.* or *dial.* = RUMPUS *sb.*

1802 *Sporting Mag.* XX. 312 We had like to have had another rumption. **1825** in JAMIESON *Suppl.* **1842-** in northern dial. gloss. (Northumb., Lanc., Linc.).

'rumpty, *sb.*[1] *Stock Exchange.* (See quot.)

1887 ATKIN *House Scraps* 12, A Rumpty or a Tooth, a $\frac{1}{32}$ part of £1.

Rumpty (ˈrʌmptɪ), *sb.*[2] *Air Force slang.* Also Rumpety. [f. RUMP *sb.*[1], after BUMPETY, BUMPITY *adv.*] A Farman training aeroplane, used esp. during the war of 1914–18.

1917 A. S. G. LEE *Let.* 31 Aug. in *No Parachute* (1968) vi. 103 The Maurice Farman Rumpety I learned to fly on. **1917** in *Liberty* (1926) 28 Aug. 14/1 We are going to start on Rumptys as these Henry Farman planes are called. **1934** V. M. YEATES *Winged Victory* I. x. 83 Tom told them the first time he went up was in a Rumpty, that was to say, a Maurice Farman Shorthorn, a queer sort of bus like an assemblage of birdcages. *Ibid.* 86 After Rumpties he had gone on to Avros which really were aeroplanes, and quite different to fly. **1968** J. J. HUDSON *Hostile Skies* iii. 33 The 'Rumpty', the famous Farman primary trainer.

†**rumpty**, *sb.*[3] and *a.* *Obs.* *Austral.* and *N.Z. slang.* [Origin uncertain.] (Something) excellent. Also ˌ**rumpty'dooler**.

1941 BAKER *N.Z. Slang* vi. 51 Expressions..in constant use by our youngsters..rorter, rumpty, rumptydooler, [etc.]. **1945** *2nd N.Z. Expeditionary Force Times* 29 Jan., What a rumpty. *Ibid.* 5 Feb. 45/4 It's a rumpty. **1945** BAKER *Austral. Lang.* vi. 126 Here are some of the many synonyms for *bonzer* (it should be noted that most of them are interchangeable as nouns and adjectives)..*rumptydooler.* **1946** E. G. WEBBER *Johnny Enzed in Italy* 45 What a rumpty.

rum-punch: see RUM *sb.*[1]

†**rumpure.** *Obs.*$^{-1}$ [a. OF. *rumpure, rompure,* f. *rompre* to break.] Rupture.

1491 CAXTON *Vitas Patr.* (W. de W. 1495) I. xlviii. 94/2 By the moyen of the sayde rumpure and brekynge..He sawe the sonne clerely shyne.

rumpus ('rʌmpəs), *sb. colloq.* [prob. a fanciful formation.] **a.** A riot, uproar, disturbance, row.

1764 FOOTE *Mayor of G.* II. i, Oh, Major! such a riot and rumpus! **1796** MRS. M. ROBINSON *Angelina* I. 188 'So! Miss Clarendon,' said he, 'you have made a fine rumpus in the family!' **1824** SCOTT in *Lockhart* (1839) VII. 281 You incur my serious displeasure if you move one inch in this contemptible rumpus. **1847** LYTTON *Lucretia* (1853) 186 Don't make such a rumpus, or No. 7 will be at you. **1894** J. KNIGHT *Garrick* ix. 153 The mock quarrel..seems almost to have ended in a real rumpus.

b. Used without article.

1768 *Boston Gaz.* 21 Mar. 3/1 The Evening concluded without Riot, or Rumpus. **1800** *Spirit Publ. Jrnls.* IV. 115 Musical rumpus; or more than was promised in the bills. **1844** *Civil Eng. & Arch. Jrnl.* VII. 82/2 The unlucky one..which caused at the time such ire and so much rumpus. **1894** *Idler* Sept. 171 It is of no use to quarrel with him. He lives on rumpus.

c. *Comb.*, as **rumpus room** orig. *N. Amer.*, a room set aside for recreation, which does not need to be kept tidy.

1940 *Chatelaine* July 37/2 Off through a double-doored hallway can be seen the 'rumpus room', that dennish haunt of Priscilla and Rosemary. **1945** NELSON & WRIGHT *Tomorrow's House* ii. 14/2 Their daughter took over the rumpus room in the basement. **1958** J. K. GALBRAITH *Affluent Society* xiii. 151 In the more censorious social levels of American society there is already a well-developed..aversion to gadgetry... In such circles shiny rumpus rooms, imaginative barbecue pits,..and magnificent cars no longer win acclaim. **1959** *Encounter* Sept. 50/2 Retreating to a rumpus room with ping-pong tables and do-it-yourself work-benches. **1960** *News Chron.* 30 June 6/4 How things start out on their journey to the rumpus room. **1970** J. BLACKBURN *Land of Promise* xvii. 222 Betty brought university friends home for many good sing-songs and games in the rumpus room which we fixed up in the basement. **1977** J. I. M. STEWART *Madonna of Astrolabe* i. 7 The festivity..became more and more of a romp. Indeed, not so much a romp as a rumpus. But this too was in order. The room was called the rumpus room.

Hence '**rumpus** *v.*, to make a disturbance.

1839 HOOD *Smithfield Market* ix, We don't want oxen at our doors to *rump-us!* **1850** LOWELL *Mr. Knott* I. 286 All night, as wide awake as gnats, The terriers rumpused after rats. **1852** MRS. STOWE *Uncle Tom's C.* xxiv. 232 Marie..rumpussed and scolded with more energy than ever all day, on the strength of this new misery.

rumpy ('rʌmpɪ). Also **rumpee.** [f. RUMP *sb.*[1] + -Y.] **1.** A Manx cat. Also *attrib.*

c **1856** *Denham Tracts* (1892) I. 199 The only animal peculiar to the island is the tailless cat, called in Manks 'stubbin', in English 'rumpy'. **1894** *Contemp. Rev.* LXVI. 642 The Isle of Man,..the native seat of fresh herrings and rumpy cats.

2. A chicken without a tail. Also *attrib.*

[**1885** L. WRIGHT *Bk. Poultry* 448 It is the Rumpless or Persian Cock of Latham, and the Rumpkin of others.] **1895** *Funk's Stand. Dict.* II. 1561/3 Rumpy... 2. A variety of domestic fowl in the Isle of Man and the Hebrides. **1972** *Nat. Geographic* Sept. 438/2 We used to have a number of animals that were special to the Isle of Man... There are still some hens without tails—'rumpy hens' we call them.

rum-shrub: see RUM *sb.*[1]

rum-strum, variant of RAM-STAM *adv.*

1827 C. G. in *Friendships of Miss Mitford* (1882) I. 180, I have gone on rum-strum, and find myself at the bottom.

'**rum-strum**, *v.* [Echoic.] *intr.* To strum.

1872 HARDY *Under Greenw. Tree* II. ii. viii. 23 [He'd] want to see her young figure sitting up at that quare instrume't, and her young fingers rum-strumming upon the keys.

rum-swizzle. *rare*$^{-0}$. (See quot.)

1858 SIMMONDS *Dict. Trade, Rum-swizzle,* the name given to a fabric made in Dublin from undyed foreign wool, which, while preserving its natural property of resisting wet, possesses the qualities of common cloth.

rumti- (also **rum-ti-**, **rumty-**; **rumpti-**, **rumpty-**, **rump-te-**), a meaningless combination of syllables used in refrains or imitations of sounds. Also, used in comb. with adjs.; ***rumti-too*** adj., commonplace.

(*a*) **1820** SCOTT *Let.* 30 Nov. in *Lockhart* (1845) 442/1 The *Rumti-iddity* chorus in Tom Thumb. **1834** *Tait's Mag.* I. 738/1 Luckily, Old Sparks hadn't christened him with any of his ridiculous rumfoozles, or rumptyiddities. **1848** DICKENS *Dombey & Son* ii, The..unmeaning and unfeeling remark of rump-te-iddity, bow-wow-wow.

(*b*) **1817** KEATS *Let.* 15 Apr. (1958) I. 129, I hope one of you will be competent to take part in a Trio..when you have said Rum-ti-ti you must not rum any more. **1834** M. SCOTT *Cruise Midge* xviii, The tabor was fiercely beaten, rumpti, tumpti. **1897** *Star* 20 Apr. 3/4 The music..is of the commonplace rum-ti-tum order. **1898** G. B. SHAW *Perfect Wagnerite* 109 A little rum-ti-tum triplet. **1901** *Pall Mall Mag.* Feb. 265 If you were to put in a little less rumty-tumty language, I'm not sure that I shouldn't agree with you. **1912** *World* 7 May 690/2 Mr. Cyril Maude makes a rather rumtifootling bishop amusing and forgivable even in his most flagrant lapses from clerical circumspection. **1974** *Listener* 31 Jan. 131/1 Try translating Goethe's *Faust* with the same metre..it's apt to sound fatally rum-ti-tum. **1976** G. EWART *No Fool* I. 31 This is a convention, we know, of course, and a wistfulness in the rum-ti-tum might be detected.

(*c*) **1906** GALSWORTHY *Man of Property* I. i. 22 Did you ever see such a collection of rumty-too people? **1920** —— *In Chancery* I. i. 9 He was feeling more strongly than ever that Timothy's was hopelessly 'rum-ti-too', and the souls of his aunts dismally mid-Victorian.

rum-tum. [A fanciful formation.]

1. *dial.* A jovial diversion or prank.

1876 BLACKMORE *Cripps* liv, The Lord only knows what a fool I be, to carry on with such rum-tums now.

2. *Boating.* A form of light racing-boat for one sculler, with outriggers and sliding seat, used on the lower Thames. Also *attrib.*

First built and named at Putney about 1888. The rum-tum is shorter and broader than the gig, and was originally an open boat, but is now canvassed in fore and aft. (N.E.D.)

1891 *Lock-to-Lock Times* 24 Oct. 6/2 May I ask why a new class of boat has sprung up, bearing the inelegant name of 'Rum-Tum'? Why 'Rum-Tum'? **1898** ANSTED *Dict. Sea Terms, Rum-tum race,* a race among Thames rowing men in boats supplied to them by the clubs to which they belong... The practice of rum-tum racing has only been instituted within the last few years.

3. Used in imitation of a regular rhythmic sound; also *attrib.*

1898 G. B. SHAW *Perfect Wagnerite* 139 The strings play a rum-tum accompaniment. **1917** —— *London Music in 1888–89* (1937) 380 The accompaniments are a derisive rum-tum. **1922** JOYCE *Ulysses* 51 Of all the glad new year, mother, the rum tum tiddledy tum. **1958** *Times* 28 Nov. 8/4 The rum-tum bars in Malcolm Arnold's *United Nations* tone-poem. **1963** *Times* 14 May 15/1 Mr. Charles Groves..brought out the rum-tum rhythms more successfully than the great arches of melody they support.

'**rumule.** *Ent. rare*$^{-0}$. [ad. L. *rumula,* dim. of *ruma,* var. of *rumis* teat.] (See quot.)

1826 KIRBY & SP. *Entomol.* IV. xlvi. 353 *Rumules* (*Rumulæ*), teat-like fleshy protuberances observable on the bodies of various larvæ.

rumy, variant of ROMY *v. Obs.*

rumyll, obs. form of RUMBLE.

run (rʌn), *sb.*[1] Forms: α. 5 **rune**, 7 **runne**, 6– **run**. β. *north.* and *Sc.* 6–7 **ryn**, 6– **rin**. See also REN *sb.* [f. RUN *v.* The verbal stem is similarly employed in Fris. *rin*, Du. *ren*, G. *renn.*]

I. 1. a. A single act or spell of running. † ***a near run***, a narrow escape, a close shave.

c **1450** *Mankind* 603 (Brandl), I was twychyde by þe neke;..þe halter brast a sondre;..The halff ys a bowte my neke; we hade a nere rune. **1638** JUNIUS *Paint. Ancients* 207 They who leape for strife use to goe backe a great way, and fetch a runne. **1692** R. L'ESTRANGE *Fables* I. cccxcvi, The Ass..fetches a Run at them Open Mouth. **1768** ROSS *Helenore* II. 89 Ralph, mean time, to the door comes wi' a rin. **1837** DICKENS *Pickw.* xxx, Mr. Pickwick..took two or three short runs..and went slowly and gravely down the slide. **1860** TYNDALL *Glac.* I. xxii. 152 A deep wide channel..; with the aid of a run I cleared it and went on. **1892** *Longman's Mag.* Nov. 87 The fish appear very fastidious in choosing their time for a big 'run'.

fig. **1713** ARBUTHNOT *John Bull* II. vi, I wish you would talk of some other subject; the thoughts of it makes me mad; our family must have their run. **1844** DICKENS *Mart. Chuz.* xxx, I think of giving her a run in London for a change. **1886** STEVENSON *Kidnapped* xxx, My eye would take a glad bit of a run over the prospect.

b. A distance covered, or taking a certain time to cover, by running.

1596 SHAKS. *Tam. Shrew* IV. i. 16 *Curtis.* Who is that calls so coldly? *Gru.* A piece of Ice:..if thou doubt it, thou maist slide from my shoulder to my heele, with no greater a run but my head and my necke. **1841** LANE *Arab. Nts.* I. 126 The run seldom exceeds three or four miles. **1872** *Routledge's Ev. Boy's Ann.* 114/2 Within a few seconds' run of the station.

c. A running away, a bolt.

1848 DICKENS *Dombey* iv, If I didn't know he was too fond of me to make a run of it, and..enter himself aboard ship.

d. ***to have a run for one's money***, to have some kind of return or satisfaction for one's expenditure or exertions (orig. racing slang). ***to give*** (someone) ***a run for his money*** (colloq.), to give (that person) satisfaction or a good return for trouble taken; to offer (him) a strong challenge.

1874 *Slang Dict.* 274 To have a run for one's money is also to have a good determined struggle for anything. **1883** *Daily Telegr.* 28 Aug. 5/1 It does not always follow that the silly backers get a run for their money. The horse may..be scratched a few hours before the race. **1889** *Pall Mall G.* 19 Jan. 1/1 So far the Macmillans have had what is called in some circles a good run for their money. **1905** *Athenæum* 1 Apr. 397 We do not get the proper run for our money, if we may put it in sporting lingo. **1908** CHESTERTON *Man who was Thursday* xiii. 277 Since the beginning of the world all men have hunted me like a wolf... I have given them a good run for their money, and I will now. **1914** G. B. SHAW *Dark Lady of Sonnets* Pref. 108 If I had been born in 1556 instead of in 1856, I should have taken to blank verse and given Shakespear a harder run for his money than all the other Elizabethans put together. **1916** 'TAFFRAIL' *Pincher Martin* ix. 160 Most of them longed for run for their money... The graver possibilities of war did not intrude themselves upon their minds until long afterwards. **1920** A. HUXLEY *Limbo* 83 'We'll give you a good run for your money,' said Hyman. 'I hope they'll be feeling a little uncomfortable by the time they have done with you, Greenow.' **1948** *Sun* (Baltimore) 26 Nov. 17/1 Backers of..Egretta, a stakes-winning filly, in the Endurance 'Cap did not get a run for their money. **1952** E. O'NEILL *Moon for Misbegotten* I. 14 You're a wonderful fighter. Sure, you could give Jack Dempsey himself a run for his money. **1955** *Times* 27 Aug. 6/1 Pickering said that he was going..'simply to satisfy the people of Bloxwich. They demand a run for their money and I will give it to them.' **1976** J. WAINWRIGHT *Bastard* i. 13 The old Beetle punches the rear wheels into the softness and with good tyres..this bus could give a snow-cat a run for its money.

e. *Cricket.* The act of running by the bowler to the bowling crease in delivering the ball; a run-up.

1836 *New Sporting Mag.* Oct. 358 The only fault is in his taking too long a run before he delivers the ball. **1891** W. G. GRACE *Cricket* ix. 240 When Smith begins his run he is behind the umpire and out of sight of the batsman... It is rather startling when he suddenly appears at the bowling crease. **1904** P. F. WARNER *How We recovered Ashes* i. 22 With a short run Relf bowls a fast medium ball. **1976** J. SNOW *Cricket Rebel* 77, I finished the match with ten wickets—the five in the second innings off a short run—for 80 runs.

f. *U.S.* A movement of settlers to new land; = RUSH *sb.*[2] 4 a.

1894 *Daily Ardmoreite* (Ardmore, Okla.) 30 Apr. 2/1 Buckskin Joe and his followers are camped at Marlow preparatory to making a run on the Fort Sill country tomorrow. **1901** *World's Work* June 894/1 Hitherto the settlers made a 'run' for the homesteads. **1930** *Publishers' Weekly* 8 Feb. 697 On April 22, 1889, this strip was opened up with the land rush known as the famous Oklahoma Run. **1948** *Daily Oklahoman* (Okla. City) 16 May E 3/2 The nine great land openings began in 1889 with the 'run' into the area now occupied by Oklahoma City, Guthrie, Norman, Stillwater and other cities.

2. a. *Cricket.* An act of running successfully from one popping-crease to the other by both batsmen, counting as an addition of one to the score.

1746 in 'Bat' *Cricket Man.* (1850) 80 Runs..40. **1772** in Waghorn *Cricket Scores* 87 Last Thursday Dartford headed Chatham just the same number of runs... Bell and Twinkler made many runs. **1843** *Blackw. Mag.* LIV. 171 In spite of Hanmer's steady bowling, they got runs pretty fast. **1859** *All Year Round* No. 13. 306 We had made our 80 runs in less than two hours.

Comb. **1853** F. LILLYWHITE *Guide to Cricketers* 32 He is a splendid field anywhere, and one of the most sure run getters to be met with. **1867** *Baily's Monthly Mag.* July 250 The wickets good, and the ground in splendid order for run-getting. *Ibid.* Dec. 137 Harrow had not a great run-getting Eleven this year. **1877** *London Society* May 416/2 The run-stealer's heart would surely be broken in his first innings. **1881** *Standard* 14 June 3/8 Such a breakdown on a run-getting wicket was without excuse. **1884** *Lillywhite's Cricket Ann.* 25 Neither of them quite as reliable run-getters. *Ibid.* 65 A match evenly drawn, after some heavy run-getting. *a* **1907** F. THOMPSON *Sel. Poems* (1908) p. viii, And I look through my tears on a soundless-clapping host As the run-stealers flicker to and fro. **1921** G. R. C. HARRIS *Few Short Runs* iv. 95 We..got two of their best bats caught..by George Remnant—one of the finest fields I ever saw, and in second-class matches a wonderful run-getter. **1934** BLUNDEN *Mind's Eye* 186 The pair amuse themselves and astonish us with slogging and run-stealing. **1950** *Sport* 7–11 Apr. 11/3 Our batsmen will find run-getting more easy. **1963** *Times* 17 Apr. 3/1 P. K. Thomas, a consistent run-scorer in the Colts, is expected to mature with the first XI experience. **1965** G. MCINNES *Road to Gundagai* xii. 209 It was an era of run-getters. **1976** *0–10 Cricket Scene* (Austral.) 7/1 His career Test aggregate of 5187 leaves him fourth on the Australian run-gathering list, among the elite. **1977** *Sunday Times* 2 Jan. 28/3 Australia's reaction..was to score at a run-a-minute rate.

b. *Baseball.* (See quots.) Also *Comb.*

1856 *Spirit of Times* 6 Sept. 13/3 At the time of the adjournment the score stood fifteen runs in favor of the Union, and twelve runs for the Baltic. **1858** *By-Laws Knickerbocker Base-Ball Club of N.Y.* 20 The game shall consist of nine innings to each side, when, should the number of runs be equal, the play shall be continued until a majority of runs, upon an equal number of innings, shall be declared, which shall conclude the game. **1875** *Encycl. Brit.* III. 407/1 A run is scored when any base-runner reaches the home base again, after touching all the other bases in proper succession, and provided three players are not put out. **1886** MRS. BURNETT *Ld. Fauntleroy* vi, Once round the field is a home run and counts one. **1891** *Harper's Weekly* 23 May 391/4 As for Poole, he is the same 'run-getter' that he was last year. **1970** *Washington Post* 30 Sept. D1/2 But the Twins came back to tie it 11–11 in their half on run-scoring singles by Cardenas and Chuck Manuel.

c. *Croquet.* The passage of a ball under a bridge or hoop. Cf. RUN *v.* 37 d.

1863 MAYNE REID *Croquet* 34 If a ball, after running a bridge, strike an obstacle, and recoil back through the bridge, the run remains good.

3. a. A spell of riding after hounds or in a race.

1812 *Sporting Mag.* XXXIX. 56 A real Lincolnshire run at a good hunting pace. **1856** 'STONEHENGE' *Brit. Rur. Sports* II. II. ii. 383/2 To guard against this, the owner of the colt should always be ready to sacrifice his own place in the run [steeplechase]. **1875** W. S. HAYWARD *Love agst. World* 2 You could never show me your horse's heels in a run yet.

b. A round of running at hare-and-hounds. Also, the course taken by the harriers.

1857 HUGHES *Tom Brown* I. vii, Which run is it?.. The Barby run,..nine miles at least, and hard ground. **1897** *Academy* 30 Oct. 348/1, I cut football,..and said I had a sore heel so as not to be run in for Tuesday's run.

4. a. A spell of sailing, esp. between two ports. Also in *Comb.*, as **run-boat** *U.S.*, a boat which collects or transports the catch made by marine fishing vessels; also *transf.*

1712 W. ROGERS *Voy. round World* Introd. (1718) 10 The general Distemper in such long Runs is the Scurvy. **1745** P. THOMAS *Jrnl. Anson's Voy.* 26 We made pretty good Runs under an easy Sail. **1851** MELVILLE *Whale* xiv. 69 After a fine run we safely arrived in Nantucket. **1890** 'R. BOLDREWOOD' *Col. Reformer* (1891) 171 After a first-class run, poor Grant made the light, sometime after nightfall. **1911** *Rudder* Aug. 49/2 The run-boats, in the local vernacular, are schooners mostly, about 60 to 70 feet on deck, and merely run back and forth between the dredging fleet and Baltimore. **1935** *Sun* (Baltimore) 6 Feb. 13/6 Most of the catch is brought to Crisfield in large run-boats, sent to the fishing grounds by fish dealers here. **1941** *Ibid.* 17 Mar. 11/3 Large dealers here go down the bay in run-boats to buy from the catchers. **1967** *Washington Star* (Sunday Mag.) 25 June 11 The Jessie Taylor out of Smith Island, Md., is typical of the 'runboats' that bring the seafood to town. **1974** *News & Observer* (Raleigh, N. Carolina) 11. 13/2 He told me he'd run aground in his private 'run boat'.

b. In phr. ***by the run*** (see quots.).

1758 J. BLAKE *Mar. Syst.* 44 It is customary in the West-Indies..to hire mariners by the run-home. *Ibid.* 46 It is proposed that all contracts and bargains by the run be made illegal. **1808** T. CLARKSON *Abol. Slave Trade* I. xv. 327 The seamen belonging to them were to be permitted to come home by what is usually called the run. **1846** A. YOUNG *Naut. Dict.* s.v., Seamen are said to be engaged by the run, when they ship with the intention of leaving the vessel at a certain port of destination.

c. An excursion, trip; a rapid journey accompanied by a short stay at a place. Now freq. an excursion or drive by car or bicycle. Also in phr. ***run ashore*** (Naut.), a brief period of shore leave; also (with hyphen) *attrib.*

1819 H. COCKBURN *Let.* 8 Oct. (1932) 18, I also took a run t'other day to Blair Adam. **1854** GREENWOOD *Haps & Mishaps* 89 After a short run on the rail we took a stage-coach. **1881** *Sportsman's Year-bk.* 199 Bicycle Touring Club... The members..enjoy Club runs or tours without the heavy outlay attendant on forming a small local Club. **1886** C. E. PASCOE *London of To-day* vii. (ed. 3) 86 Other garrisons generally manage during those weeks to get a day or two's leave for 'a run up to town'. **1902** C. L. FREESTON in Harmsworth *Motors & Motor-Driving* xxi. 388 Several tours and runs also took place, the anniversary run to Southsea..being an enormous undertaking. **1912** *Motor Man.* (ed. 14) v. 163 Never start on a run without being assured that there is ample oil. **1948** PARTRIDGE *Dict. Forces' Slang* 159 *Run ashore*, a short evening's shore leave. **1959** *Motor Man.* (ed. 36) xii. 259 A party in an ordinary family car..can count its daily run, including stops, at a kilometre a minute. **1977** *Navy News* June 8/2 It was certainly a good run ashore for the ship's company, with the Principality of Monaco granting free admission to many places of interest. *Ibid.* Aug. 31/2 Also 'out of this world' are the run-ashore opportunities.

d. A single journey made by a locomotive engine; the distance thus traversed.

1857 *Lawrence* (Kansas) *Republican* 4 June 2 The train.. made a quick and pleasant run, arriving in Jefferson City promptly in time. **1870** in De Vere *Americanisms* 360 Engineers and firemen often arrive at the end of their run somewhere among the small hours of night. **1872** *Ibid.*, The railway officials..state that the run will be made in so many hours. **1889** *Spectator* 12 Oct., The Great Northern can claim..the fastest run.

e. A brisk walk or perambulation. Now usu., a dog's exercise walk.

1837 W. TAYLER in J. Burnett *Useful Toil* (1974) II. 178, I am obliged to stay within to help the sick. This is what I don't like as I like to get a run everyday when I can. **1871** 'L. CARROLL' *Through Looking-Glass* iv. 79 'O Oysters,' said the Carpenter, 'You've had a pleasant run! Shall we be trotting home again?' **1967** P. MOYES *Murder Fantastical* viii. 106 'What on earth made you go off down to the river on your own?' 'I was only giving Tinker her run... There was no need to come after me.' **1977** 'J. BELL' *Such Nice Client* viii. 83, I was giving Caesar a very short run on the lead.

f. A single trip on a toboggan, sleigh, etc., down a slope or course. Cf. sense 23 d below.

1898 *Encycl. Sport* II. 473/2 A good average run down the Cresta course takes 75 seconds. **1919** [see LUGE *sb.*]. **1935** *Encycl. Sports* 178/2 The art of making good time on a run is acquired by long study of the ten banked turns. **1956** *Ski-ing* ('Know the Game' Ser.) 22/1 If the run is made too early, the snow will be as hard as iron. **1976** F. RAPHAEL *Glittering Prizes* 57 I'll make the first run. You grab the stop watch and bugger off down to the bottom of the hill, OK?

g. *Mil.* An offensive operation, *spec.* an attack by sea or air. See also *bomb run* s.v. BOMB *sb.* 6, *dummy run* s.v. DUMMY *sb.* 7 b. Also *transf.*

1916, etc. [see *dummy run* s.v. DUMMY *sb.* 7 b]. **1941** *Flight* 13 Mar. 204/2 The bomber had successfully bombed its target on the first run; another run was then made and incendiaries started small fires. **1944** *Hutchinson's Pict. Hist. War* 12 Apr.–26 Sept. 43 (*caption*) The aircraft is seen making its second run over the target. **1948** AUDEN *Age of Anxiety* i. 18 We began our run; Death and damage darted at our will. **1963** *Listener* 4 Apr. 585/2 Our patrol car got the call as 'shots fired', with the address given. My partner and I responded. In such radio 'runs' you never know what to expect. **1975** J. GRADY *Shadow of Condor* vi. 109 The CIA agent..tips us to another run, which we intercept. **1977** *Time* 30 May 46/3 For the climactic battle sequence, which includes dogfights in space and missile runs on the Death Star, Lucas gathered all the old war movies he could find and spliced together their aerial-combat footage.

h. A single or regular journey made by an aircraft; the distance thus travelled.

1912 KIPLING *Diversity of Creatures* (1917) 4 DeForest, whose business it is to know the out districts, told us that it ..was about half an hour's run from end to end. **1944** [see *milk-run* s.v. MILK *sb.* 10]. **1958** 'N. SHUTE' *Rainbow & Rose* i. 3, I was on the Sydney-Melbourne run. **1976** *Daily Mirror* 16 July 2/1 President Amin's jet airliner was poised last night to take off for Uganda..on a whisky run.

i. A regular round (freq. one accomplished by means of a vehicle). Also in phrases *mail-run* s.v. MAIL *sb.*³ 4 b, *milk-run* s.v. MILK *sb.* 10, *paper run* s.v. PAPER *sb.* 12.

1925 *N. & Q.* 21 Mar. 208/1 In the dairy trade phrases such as 'He has a milk-run' or, 'he has a milk-walk' or 'he has a milk-round' are common. **1946** [see *mail-run* s.v. MAIL *sb.*³ 4 b]. **1968** K. WEATHERLY *Roo Shooter* 38 At night when they had done the evening run on their traps they would return home. **1978** *Oxf. Diocesan Mag.* July 16/3 A Soup run was established, operating four nights a week, and we have made contact with up to forty people in derelict property in and around the town centre.

5. †**a.** The total amount of the cargo carried by a vessel on a single voyage. *Obs.*

1795 *Scots Mag.* LVII. 132/1 His Lordship's enquiry into the monopolizing arts of buying bread-corn out of coasting vessels, by what is called the run.

b. A landing of smuggled goods.

1832 *Times* 30 Oct. 2/6 A run of illicit goods having been effected near Bexhill on Monday night. **1895** STOKER *Watter's Mou'* 4 Keep careful watch to-night; run expected.

6. a. A rapid course; esp. ***with a run***, rapidly, with a rapid fall. (Cf. 29 d.)

1822 J. FLINT *Lett. fr. Amer.* 86 On the 11th we went down Letart's rapids, a very violent run. **1840** MARRYAT *Poor Jack* i, The lanyard of the cot gave way, and she came down with a run by the head. **1866** MRS. GASKELL *Wives & Daughters* xxi, I shall go down in your opinion with a run.., like the hall clock..when the spring broke. **1895** *Daily News* 13 Sept. 2/6 Cheese fell slowly last year, but this year values have come down with a run.

b. *Mining.* (See quots.)

1881 RAYMOND *Mining Gloss.*, *Run*, certain accidents to the winding apparatus. **1883** GRESLEY *Gloss. Terms Coal-mining*, *Run*,..a breakaway upon an inclined-plane.

7. a. *Skating.* (See quot.)

1856 'STONEHENGE' *Brit. Rur. Sports* 523/1 This is the most simple form of skating, and is called the ordinary run, or inside edge forward.

b. *Golf.* A stroke in which the ball is made to run along the ground.

1901 *Scotsman* 5 Sept. 7/3 He followed up by a fine run to within a yard of the pin.

8. With advs., as RUN-IN, RUN-OFF, RUN-OUT, RUN-OVER, RUN-UP.

II. 9. a. A small stream, brook, rivulet, or watercourse; a channel or overflow. Chiefly *U.S.* and *north. dial.*

β. **1581** *Rec. Burgh Edinb.* (1882) 557 Edward Galbrayth having oft tymes desyrit ane tak of the commodity of the rin of the said loch. **1643** *Rec. Elgin* (New Spalding Cl.) I. 276 The counsell appoyntis theis that castis the ryn of Lossie to haue for ilk ruid thairof that thai cast 26s. 8d. **1808** JAMIESON, *Rin*,..a stream. *Ibid.*, *A rin of watter*, a waterfall.

α. **1605** ROSIER *Waymouth's Voy.* (Coll. Mass. Hist. Soc.) 146 Searching up in the island, we saw it [a pond] fed with a strong run. **1652** *Virginia St. Papers* (1875) I. 1 On the Eastward side of a Runne, which falles into ye head of Ware River. **1703** DAMPIER *Voy.* III. I. 31 There is..a Run of Water in the bottom, which empties it self into a fine small Cove or sandy Bay. **1768** BOSWELL *Corsica* 36, I remember on the road between Rome and Naples, a run from a sulphureous spring. **1808** PIKE *Sources of Mississ.* (1810) II. 191 We struck on a brook which led west,..and shortly came to a small run, running west. **1863** KINGSLEY *Water-Bab.* 132 He swam to the shore and met the light as it stopped over a shallow run at the edge of a low rock. **1877** MARCUS CLARKE *Australia & Tasm.* 24 This interesting exploration discovered several 'runs' of fresh water around the bays.

b. A flow or current of water; a strong rush or sweep of the tide, etc.

1814 SCOTT *Diary* 2 Sept. in *Lockhart*, In the passage or sound between Scarba and the extremity of Jura, is a terrible run of tide. **1856** *Jrnl. R. Agric. Soc.* XVII. II. 404 This will only happen where there is a summer run of water. **1887** STEVENSON *Merry Men* iii, Already along the curve of Sandag Bay there was a splashing run of sea.

c. A flow of sand; a slip, slide, sudden fall of earth. Chiefly *Mining.*

1854 *Jrnl. R. Agric. Soc.* XV. II. 426 [He] stopped the mischief with thin parings of turf placed over the joints where the run of sand was found. **1875** *Ure's Dict. Arts* III. 294 The working..has opened up enormous excavations; whence disastrous 'runs' have taken place in the mines. **1897** *Archæol. Jrnl.* Dec. 375 There are conditions where the flints are buried in the 'head' or 'rain wash', or 'run o' th' hill'.

d. A downward flow or trickle of paint when applied too thickly; the action of paint in 'running'. Cf. RUN *v.* 22 b.

1935 J. LAWRENCE *Painting A to Z* xi. 103 Don't leave the quirks swimming in paint, or it will wrinkle, or perhaps even run down into the lower mouldings, and leave a 'run'. **1951**, **1958** [see CURTAIN *sb.*¹ 1 e]. **1975** *Amer. Speech 1969* XLIV. 24 *Run*, n., the action of paint when it is applied too heavily; it can't adhere to the wall surface and begins to stream down the wall.

†**10.** A running sore. *Obs.*$^{-0}$

1648 HEXHAM II, *Een loopende gat, ofte Fistel*, a Fistula or a Run.

11. †**a.** A rhythmical flow *of* verse. *Obs. rare.* (Cf. 29 b.)

1693 DRYDEN *Exam. Poet.* Ess. (ed. Ker) II. 10 To give my poetry a kind of cadence, and, as we call it, a run of verse. — *Disc. Satire* ibid. 85 Lucilius..minded neither his style, nor his numbers, nor his purity of words, nor his run of verse.

b. (After Gael. *ruith.*) A rapidly recited passage of measured and alliterative prose, characteristic of Gaelic folk-tales.

1891 MACDOUGALL *Folk & Hero Tales* 260 Both terms convey the same meaning, and either..preserves the alliteration and rhythm of the run well enough.

12. *Mus.* **a.** A roulade.

1835 *Penny Cycl.* III. 527/1 Purcell,..in a wretched endeavour to express descent, writes for the base a run of notes from D above to D below the staff. **1876** STAINER & BARRETT *Dict. Mus. Terms* s.v., Except for the purpose of training the voice, runs may be said to be out of fashion. **1878** MRS. HUNGERFORD *Molly Bawn* xiii, I like something I can understand, and I hate your runs and trills.

b. (See quot.)

1895 *Funk's Standard Dict.*, *Run*,..the sound of an organ-pipe caused by leakage of air into the pipe.

III. 13. a. A continuous stretch *of* something.

1674 N. FAIRFAX *Bulk & Selv.* Contents, Shewing there would be no run of unmade time between two worlds, nor formerness nor afterness. **1719** W. WOOD *Survey Trade* 139 Some of our Colonies..suffer particular Planters to keep great Runs of Land in their Possession uncultivated, on purpose to prevent New Settlements. **1825** J. NICHOLSON *Operat. Mechanic* 555 All angles within the building, if oblique,..are allowed for, under the head of *run of cut splay*. **1837** *Civil Eng. & Arch. Jrnl.* I. 24/2 During last winter I made use of this boiler; it heated 448 feet run of 3 and 4 inch iron-pipe. **1867** F. FRANCIS *Angling* i. (1880) 50, I was fishing a very promising run of trout and grayling water.

b. A continued spell or course *of* some condition or state of things.

1714 R. FIDDES *Pract. Disc.* II. 195 Men of the slowest parts..have very often..a smooth run of business. *Ibid.* 280 Wicked men have..a continu'd run of success. **1732** *Acc. Workhouses* 111 A run of the small-pox through the town in 1725, and an epidemical disease in..1727 and 1728. **1858** HAWTHORNE *Fr. & It. Note-bks.* (1871) IV. 284 They had a fine run of custom. **1863** W. C. BALDWIN *Afr. Hunting* vii. 269 We have had a long-continued run of the loveliest weather that ever poor mortal was blessed with. **1884** MCCARTHY *Four Georges* I. xiv. 294 Hardly ever since Walpole's time, has a minister had so long a run of power.

c. A course or spell of (good or ill) fortune, *esp.* in games of chance.

1697 VANBRUGH *Æsop* IV. ii, Forced to cut down his Timber, which he would willingly preserve against an ill run at dice. **1759** STERNE *Tr. Shandy* II. v, As the dice took a run against him. **1782** MISS BURNEY *Cecilia* IV. iii, He had had the preceding night an uncommon run of luck. **1824** SCOTT *St. Roman's* x, I believe in luck myself—in a good or bad run of luck at cards. **1855** MACAULAY *Hist. Eng.* xx. IV. 517 The smallest gain was welcome to those whom a long run of evil fortune had discouraged. **1884** RUSKIN *Wks.* (1908) XXXIV. 654 They have had a run of ill-luck since.

d. *Mining* and *Geol.* A continuous vein of rock or ore; (see also quot. 1747).

1747 HOOSON *Miner's Dict.* s.v., A *Run*..is always a Branch that flies out of a Vein or Pipe, or lies near to it on one side. **1839** DE LA BECHE *Rep. Geol. Cornwall*, etc. iii. 88 Taking general lines of lamination and runs of greenstone as guides. **1865** J. T. F. TURNER *Slate Quarries* 18 The various 'runs' have each their characteristics, and an observant quarrier will tell immediately whence a given slate came; naming the run [etc.]. **1882** *U.S. Rep. Prec. Met.* 636 Between walls of true country rock, termed the 'runs'.

Comb. **1877** RAYMOND *Statist. Mines & Mining* 93 This run washing was chiefly up Hilder Ravine, where bank had very little of top or poorest gravel.

e. *Oil Industry.* (A distance drilled during) a spell of drilling with a particular bit.

1880 J. F. CARLL *Geol. Oil Regions* xxviii. 310 The engineer examines the steam and the water gauges and the fire, and then proceeds to sharpen the tool required for the next 'run'. **1946** M. C. SEAMARK in *Mod. Petroleum Technol.* (Inst. Petroleum) 94 Cores of 10–20 feet can be taken at one 'run'. **1974** R. D. GRACE in P. L. Moore et al. *Drilling Practices Man.* xiv. 354 Bit records of that time [*sc.* the late 1940s] were filled with typical runs of only five to ten feet in four to five hours at depths below 10,000 feet.

f. A length of electric wiring; a distance covered by uninterrupted cable.

1905 C. C. METCALFE *Pract. Electr. Wiring* i. 5 If the run is this length..a conductor of greater sectional area, with a negligible resistance, should be used. **1938** J. W. SIMS *Elect. Installations* vii. 128 Special care should be taken to avoid metallic obstructions inside the conduit..and bushes should be fitted at the end of a run. **1957** A. L. OSBORNE *Elect. in Building* ii. 20 By eliminating long unbroken cable runs, voltage drop within the building is not likely to occur. **1970** J. EARL *Tuners & Amplifiers* iv. 94 Use 15-ampere cables for runs in excess of 10 ft.

g. A tear in a knitted garment or stocking; = LADDER *sb.* 3 b. Also *attrib.* and *Comb.* Cf. RUNNER 9 d.

1922 M. B. HOUSTON *Witch Man* xii. 146 She looked the suit over, darned a tiny run in the tights, [etc.]. **1933** *Radio Times* 14 Apr. 95, I had an awful ladder in my stocking... I scarcely ever have a run now. **1936** G. G. DENNY *Fabrics* (ed. 3) i. 104 *Run resist*, knitting process which locks stitches to reduce runs in hosiery and under-wear. **1938** O. NASH *I'm Stranger here Myself* 173 She stopped to moisten her finger on account of a run in her stocking. **1938** 'E. QUEEN' *Four of Hearts* iv. 67 You've got a run in your stocking. **1938** *Knit Goods Weekly* 15 Aug. 11 These hosiery finishes bind fibre to fibre..strengthen the fabric..make it snag-resistant, run-resistant..add miles more wear. **1939** *Business Week* 27 May 32/1 Merchants..seem not at all worried about the inroads that this really run-resistant hosiery might make in total sales volume. **1951** in M. McLuhan *Mech. Bride* (1967) 95 Ivory Flakes care helps safeguard sheerest nylons from embarrassing, eye-catching runs. **1957** M. B. Picken *Fashion Dict.* 279/2 *Run-proof*, a knitted construction where locked loops prevent a run. *Run resist*, a type of knitting with loops so constructed as to resist the tendency to run. **1969** *Sears Catal.* Spring/Summer 409 Run-resistant mesh-knit seamless stretch nylons. **1970** *Focus* June 15/2 The term run-resist is used on the advice of hosiery trade associations, as an 'out' under the Trade Descriptions Act, 1968. **1973** 'E. McBain' *Let's hear It* x. 146 She's noisy and vulgar; there are runs in her nylons. **1974** H. L. Foster *Ribbin'* v. 186 A female student may have a run in her stockings and will be ribbed about it.

14. a. A continuous series or succession. Also *spec.* (see quot. 1870).

1709 *Tatler* No. 86 ⁋4 When we came to Temple-bar, Sir Harry and Sir Giles got over; but a Run of the Coaches kept the rest of us on this Side the Street. **1740** Cibber *Apol.* (1756) I. 310, I could never hear that upon an ill run of audiences they had ever returned or brought in a single shilling. **1774** G. White *Selborne* lviii, Such a run of wet seasons, a century or two ago, would, I am persuaded, have occasioned a famine. **1870** Hardy & Ware *Mod. Hoyle, Cribbage* 78 Sequences or 'Runs' consist of three or more cards following in consecutive order. **1897** *Allbutt's Syst. Med.* III. 26 The cases are apt to occur, as it were, in runs.

b. A shoal of fish in motion, *esp.* ascending a river from the sea for spawning.

1820 W. Scoresby *Acc. Arctic Reg.* II. 214 A large tribe passing from one place to another..is denominated a 'run of fish'. **1873–86** S. F. Baird in Goode *Amer. Fishes* (1888) 94 [The scuppaug] arrives in successive detachments or 'runs' differing in size, the smallest fish coming last.

c. A set or series of consecutive numbers of a periodical publication.

1889 *J. Parker & Co.'s List of Books wanted*, Mind, A Set, or Runs. **1898** *Author's Circular* 10 Mar. 2/3 Wanted, a run of the *Field* Newspaper from 1885.

d. *U.S.* Of millstones: (see quot. 1848).

1798 *Rec. Smithtown, N.Y.* (1898) 351 The grist mill house..[will] carry three run of stones with three Bolting mills. **1815** *Niles' Weekly Reg.* IX. 187/1 The whole expense in generating steam sufficient to drive two run of stones upon this principle will not exceed two hundred and twenty dollars. **1828–32** in Webster. **1848** Bartlett *Dict. Amer.* 281 A pair of mill-stones is called a *run of stones* when in operation or placed in a mill. The Rochester flouring mills have ten or twenty run of stones. **1885** U. S. Grant *Mem.* I. 493 Every plantation..had a run of stone, propelled by mule power, to grind corn for the owners and their slaves.

e. *Mining.* A train or set of trams in a pit.

1883 Gresley *Gloss. Terms Coal-Mining.*

f. *pl.* with *the.* An attack of diarrhoea. *colloq.*

1962 E. Lacy *Freeloaders* vii. 147 I'd picked up a touch of '*la tourism*' or in basic English, the runs, from..the unwashed fruit. **1966** 'L. Lane' *ABZ of Scouse* 91 *Go like a bookie wit' ther runs*, to move very fast. **1971** B. Malamud *Tenants* 214 Sam Clemence, a witness from Harlem U.S.A., despite a bad case of the runs.., stands up for his friend Willie. **1976** U. Holden *String Horses* ix. 112 'What can she do Lil? Please help.' 'There's nothing. Pills will only give her the runs. I don't hold with that abortion lark.'

15. a. A series or rush of sudden and pressing demands made upon a bank or treasury for immediate payment. Also *spec.* a sudden movement on the part of foreign depositors to withdraw their holdings of a nation's currency by exchanging them for equivalent sums in other currencies. Freq. const. *on.*

a **1692** Pollexfen *Disc. Trade* (1697) 73 Any jealousie or suspicion that they shall not have Money for such Bills on Demand, will occasion a general run. **1727** Pope & Gay *What passed in London* Swift's Wks. 1751 VI. 265 The Tories and Jacobites, to whom he imputed that sudden Run upon the Bank, which happened on this occasion. **1776** Adam Smith *W.N.* I. v. (1904) I. 49 When a run comes upon them, they sometimes endeavour to gain time by paying in sixpences. **1802** *Edinb. Rev.* I. 193 A more permanent cause of a run upon the Bank of England for specie. **1834** Gilbert *Hist. Banking* 24 In the year 1667 occurred the first run of which we have any account in the history of banking. **1880** *Fraser's Mag.* May 679 If a run set in, no bank in the world could escape stoppage, no reserve could face it. **1891** G. Clare *Money-Market Primer* vii. 59 Country bankers,.. fearing that the shock to confidence may cause a 'run' on the part of their depositors, telegraph to London for more notes. **1932** P. Einzig *Tragedy of Pound* vii. 65 In July [1931] the failure of the Nordwolle and other commercial firms resulted in a run on several German banks. **1955** H. Wilson in *Hansard Commons* 10 June 148 More confidence has been given to the speculators, and therefore the run on sterling has temporarily stopped. **1964** S. Brittan *Treasury under Tories* vi. 189 Mr Thorneycroft responded to the run on the pound with his famous deflationary package. **1976** *Economist* 16 Oct. 23/3 The Bank of England reacted to the March run on sterling by using up reserves and borrowing money to try to check the exchange rate collapse.

transf. **1833** J. H. Newman *Arians* I. ii. (1876) 26 Causing a sudden run upon his resources, which the circumstances of time and place do not allow him to meet.

b. An extensive or well-sustained demand for something. Const. *on.*

1816 Jane Austen *Emma* II. vi. 97 A couple of pair of post-horses were kept, more for the convenience of the neighbourhood than from any run on the road. **1818** Scott *Hrt. Midl.* xxviii [xxix], Some accidental circumstances had occasioned what is called a run upon the road, and the landlord could not accommodate her with a guide and horses. **1846** Dickens *Cricket* i. 32 'Busy just now, Caleb?' asked the Carrier. 'Why, pretty well, John... There's rather a run on Noah's Arks at present.' **1888** Jacobi *Printers' Vocab., Run on sorts*, an extraordinary demand for any particular letter or letters in composing.

c. *Gaming.* A continued spell of chance falling *on* a particular colour, etc.

1826 Disraeli *Viv. Grey* v. vi, There has been a run on the red. **1850** Thackeray *Pendennis* xxxviii, A confounded run on the red had finished him, he said, at Baden Baden.

d. A concourse or resort of customers, etc.

1844 W. Cross *Disruption* xviii. (E.D.D.), The meal ye sent me wasna according to sample;..it has done my run mair ill than it was worth. **1850** Thackeray *Pendennis* xxiii, There was such a run to see the new folks, that the Low Church was deserted.

†**16.** A persistent set *against*, or attack *upon*, some thing or person. *Obs.*

1719 Swift *Lett. to Young Clergyman* Wks. 1751 V. 26 You cannot but have..observed, what a violent Run there is among too many weak People against University Education. *a* **1763** Earl Waldegrave *Mem.* (1821) 121 At the late change of administration, when there was a violent run against him. *a* **1779** Warburton *Notes on Pope* (Todd), He bade him not be discouraged at this run upon him; for.. mere wit and raillery could not hold it out long against a work of so much learning.

17. a. A success with the public, so as to be extensively bought or run after.

a **1719** Addison (J.), It is impossible for detached papers to have a general run or long continuance, if not diversified with humour. **1749** Chetwood *Gen. Hist. Stage* 19 This double Play was performed on two succeeding Nights, and had a very great Run (a Theatrical Term). **1771** Luckombe *Hist. Print.* 227 Among the Irregular Bodied sorts of Letter, none has taken so great a run as Small Pica. **1818** Cobbett *Pol. Reg.* XXX. 9 If you were to go to London,..and become a seller of glass, do you not think that your glass would have a run? **1855** Macaulay *Hist. Eng.* xix. IV. 351 A History of the Bloody Assizes..was expected to have as great a run as the Pilgrim's Progress. **1885** 'F. Anstey' *Tinted Venus* 67 I've been thinking out a machine..that ought to have an extensive run.

†**b.** Amount of export *from* a place. *Obs.*

1789 J. Williams *Min. Kingd.* I. 167 The run of coals from Newcastle and Sunderland has been..very great for above fifty years.

18. a. A continuous period of being represented on the stage. (Cf. 26 b.)

1714 Addison *Spect.* No. 592 ⁋2 Several of them lay it down as a Maxim, That whatever Dramatick Performance has a long Run, must of Necessity be good for nothing. **1756** C. Smart tr. *Horace, Sat.* I. x. (1826) II. 83 These satires, which can neither be recited in the temple of Apollo.., nor can have a run over and over again represented in the theatre. **1837** Lockhart *Scott* IV. vii. 228 The *Rob Roy* had a continued run of forty-one nights. **1857** Mrs. Mathews *Tea-Table T.* I. 38 This comedy..had a lengthened run. **1896** Mary Anderson *Few Mem.* vi. (ed. 2) 89 Each week brought..a round of new plays to these companies (long runs were almost unheard-of then).

b. *transf.* A period of continuing in favour with, or remaining open to, the public.

1884 *Manch. Guard.* 22 Sept. 5/4 The International Textile Exhibition..closed yesterday..after a run of something like six weeks. **1885** *Manch. Exam.* 11 Nov. 3/2 A work which after a few weeks' run at the circulating libraries is ignored and forgotten.

19. a. A spell of making or allowing something liquid to run; the amount run off at one time; *spec.* the amount of sap drawn off when sugar maples are tapped; the amount of maple sugar produced at one time. Also (*Oil Industry*), the action of transferring a quantity of oil through a pipeline, or of subjecting it to a process such as distillation; the amount of oil so treated.

(*a*) **1710** Whitworth *Acc. Russia* (1758) 77 And being seldom tryed when melted, their coins are of different value, as the run happens to be good or bad, Plate, Dollars, and old Copeeks, being all melted together. **1711** Addison *Spect.* No. 72 ⁋8 Sometimes they speak in Raptures of a Run of Ale in King Charles's Reign. **1838** Morewood *Hist. Inebriating Liquors* 283 The second run of the still..is of a strength from 23° to 26°. **1877** Raymond *Statist. Mines & Mining* 212 A run of this ore made in November yielded at the rate of $80 per ton. **1822** *Farmer's Diary 1823* (U.S.) sig. C 3, Sugar makers may venture to set seven or eight hundred pails to one of these pans,..in case of extra ordinary runs, which, however, do not often happen. **1890–3** E. M. Taber *Stowe Notes, Lett. & Verses* (1913) 40 The early runs are not so sweet as the later; the trees being full of frost. **1949** *Highway Traveler* Feb. 17/2 In the average season of a month..sap can be expected to run on about half of the days, while on two to five days there will be 'good runs'. **1978** N. Perrin *First Person Rural* 84 It was no hard run—but my 104 buckets would probably yield 40 or 50 gallons [of maple sap] today.

(*b*) **1883** *Cent. Mag.* July 332/2 He shuts off the flow, measures what remains in the tank, and makes out a triplicate certificate, showing depth of oil at the beginning and at the end of the run. **1888** *Science* 12 Oct. 172/2 This past spring an oil-man..was suffocated in one of these tank-sheds while making a run of oil; viz., running the oil from the receiving-tank to the transportation or pipe-line company's tanks. **1898** *19th Ann. Rep. U.S. Geol. Survey* VI contd. 29 Usually the terms 'production' and 'pipe-line runs' are considered as synonymous, but production is always slightly in excess of runs. The expression 'pipe-line runs' means the amount of oil the pipe lines have received from the wells, and as the pipe lines do not run all the oil in the tanks at the wells, it would be remarkable if the same amount remained in the tanks at the wells at the close of each year. **1914** *Chem. Abstr.* VIII. 2247 Flushing out the vapors remaining in the still with steam so that they will not mix with the vapors from the next run. **1931** *Economist* 14 Feb. 361/1 Crude oil 'runs' to refinery stills have, therefore, been restricted to about 10 per cent. below last year's level.

b. A measure of yarn for spinning: (see quots.).

1734 *Conn. Col. Rec.* (1873) VII. 512 For every yard that is well spun, wove and whitned, and is a yard wide and made of yarn that is eight runs to the pound, two shillings per yard. **1875** Temple & Sheldon *Hist. Northfield, Mass.* 161 Spinning was commonly done by the run. A run of yarn consisted of twenty knots, a knot was composed of forty threads, and a thread was seventy-four inches in length, or once round the reel. **1878** A. Barlow *Weaving* 330 Woollen yarns are weighed in lengths or 'runs' of 1600 yards.

c. A spell of making or allowing machinery to run or continue to work. Also, a spell of manufacturing some product; an instance or a spell of carrying out an experimental procedure, esp. one involving automatic equipment.

1875 Martin *Winding Mach.* 49 Its wear..is reduced as much as possible—as, also, are the number of turns of the engine in each run. **1877** Raymond *Statist. Mines & Mining* 319 The Sukey Mill made a short run in the summer, but was unsuccessful. **1882** *U.S. Rep. Prec. Met.* 473 Only one experimental run to test the machinery..has been made. **1931** *Anatomical Rec.* XLIX. 180 In an original trial run on five albino rats..three became pseudopregnant. **1935** *Industrial & Engin. Chem.* Sept. 1074/2 In one run,..the temperature began to rise and continued to rise after the heat input to the bomb was stopped. **1951** S. Jennett *Making of Bks.* vi. 106 When the make-ready is completed and the machine is ready to start its run the hand-feeder takes her place at the feeding board. *Ibid.* 107 The run then commences. **1971** J. E. Harry *Plastics Fabrication & Electrotechnol.* v. 38 Preformed materials such as sheet or tube..are sometimes used instead of moulding processes for short runs of large components. **1972** *Nature* 18 Feb. 397/1 The difference observed was found consistently in different electrophoretic runs. **1972** *National Observer* (U.S.) 27 May 11/2 At first he intended to fake the run, using plain creek water in the barrels with..foam rubber pellets floating on top to simulate the head on the fermenting mash.

d. A spell of sheep-shearing. *Austral.* and *N.Z.*

a **1910** G. Meek in A. E. Woodhouse *N.Z. Farm & Station Verse* (1950) 59 The record shearing run of nineteen-nothing nine. **1933** L. G. D. Acland in *Press* (Christchurch, N.Z.) 18 Nov. 15/7 *Run*,..stretch of work. Shearers work for an hour before breakfast, two stretches in the morning and three in the afternoon. The stretches are divided by meal-times and *smokos*. **1956** G. Bowen *Wool Away!* (ed. 2) 157 *Run*, the shearing time worked between official stops, smokos, or meals. *a* **1964** H. P. Tritton in *Penguin Bk. Austral. Ballads* (1964) 227 My shearing days are over, though I never was a gun: I could always count my twenty at the end of every run.

e. *Computers.* An instance of the execution of a program or other task by a computer.

1946 *Math. Tables & Other Aids to Computation* II. 151 From a series of positive values of *x* and *y*, it could form Σx, Σy, Σx^2, Σxy, Σy^2 and check them in one run. **1952** *Rev. Electronic Digital Computers* (Amer. Inst. Electr. Engineers) 17/2 The chance that the machine would get through any particular 20-minute run was independent of its chances of getting through any other 20-minute run. **1964** F. L. Westwater *Electronic Computers* ix. 144 It requires two runs on the computer..to solve the problem. **1971** J. B. Carroll et al. *Word Frequency Bk.* p. xxxvi, In the particular computer run that produced this table, the number turned out to be 609,798. **1977** *Sci. Amer.* Oct. 116/2 The program and certain aspects of the discharging procedure had to be modified to overcome the problems indicated by the first computer runs.

20. a. ***common, general, normal*** or ***ordinary run***, the usual, ordinary, average type or class; the generality or great majority. Also without adj.

1712 Addison *Spect.* No. 287 ⁋6 In the common Run of Mankind, for one that is Wise and Good you find ten of a contrary Character. **1747** Gray *Lett.* (Bohn) I. 165 The ordinary run of Readers. **1765** Blackstone *Comm.* I. 101 The general run of laws, enacted by the superior state, are supposed to be calculated for it's own internal government. **1809** Malkin *Gil Blas* IV. viii. ⁋7 To lead such a life would be..penance to the common run of ladies. **1875** Helps *Soc. Press.* vii. 92 They furnish very bad examples for dealing with the ordinary run of human beings. **1957** G. Ryle in C. A. Mace *Brit. Philos. Mid-Century* 257 This question did not begin seriously to worry the general run of philosophers until..sixty years ago. **1965** G. McInnes *Road to Gundagai* v. 87 What..set our tannings aside from the normal run.. was the deliberation and the ritual. **1970** *Incorporated Linguist* IX. IV. 111 This is a book which should be of interest to the scholar and the linguistic specialist, less so to the general run of professional translators.

ellipt. **1838** J. H. Newman *Let. to Faussett* 25 Would it not offend the run of religious men? **1839–52** Bailey *Festus* 320 A man of mind, above the run of men.

b. A number of animals born or reared at the same time; a batch or drove.

1847 *Jrnl. R. Agric. Soc.* VIII. I. 10 It is not uncommon to suckle the next run of lambs upon the ewes that have had their lambs taken off. **1848** *Ibid.* IX. I. 3 After the first run of oxen have been sent to market,..these pastures are cleaned up.

c. A line or class of goods.

1883 *Daily News* 23 Jan. 2/7 Makers of the ordinary runs of cloth being fully employed. **1886** *Ibid.* 20 Oct. 2/5 The best runs of English and foreign [wheat] sell at full prices.

d. *Printing.* The total number of copies of a book, newspaper, etc., printed during a single period of press-work. Cf. *press-run* s.v. press *sb.*[1] 17 b and *print run* s.v. print *sb.* 16 a.

1909 Webster *s.v. Run* n., A run of 3,000 copies on a press. **1936** *Penrose Ann.* XXXVIII. 146 Rotary printing will master any long runs. **1951** S. Jennett *Making of Bks.* ix. 138 The film assists in the retention of moisture, and longer runs can be printed at greater speed [by collography]. **1976** *Penrose Ann.* LXIX. 132 Over half of all printing jobs involve runs under 10,000 sheets.

e. ***run of the mill*** (also ***the mine***, etc.), the material yielded by a mill, mine, etc., as it emerges from the production process and before being sorted or inspected for quality; also ***run-of-mine***, etc. Hence *fig.*, the ordinary, average, undistinguished, or mediocre type (cf. *mill run* (*d*) s.v. MILL *sb.*[1] 12). Also in various extended and nonce-uses. Freq. as *adj.* or *attrib.* phrase.

1909 *Cent. Dict.* Suppl., *Run of the kiln*, bricks of all kinds and qualities just as they happen to come from the kiln. *Ibid.*, *Run of the mine*, coal just as it comes from the mine, large and small sizes and all qualities together. **1930** *Daily News Record* (U.S.) 17 Mar. 19/4 Suspicion has attached to the yarn producers' definition of 'inferior'. Leading users of these yarns say they interpret the word to mean 'run of the mill'. A purchase of such yarns may include various percentages of first, second and sub-qualities of yarn, in fact all that 'run of the mill' suggests—but the grading is done by the cloth mill. **1930** *Engineering* 20 June 811/2 This machine is intended to reduce run-of-mine coal to any size between 6in. and $1\frac{1}{4}$in. cube, in one operation. **1930** *Hearst's Internat.* Sept. 37/2 But level-headed as a wife and a darned sight better-looking than the run of the mill of wives. **1933** *Sun* (Baltimore) 14 Oct. 4/3 An ordinary, run-of-the-mill gravy. *Ibid.* 23 Dec. 8/7 The attitude of run-of-the-mine citizens on lynching. **1938** K. A. PORTER in *Southern Rev.* Winter 429 I've got a special job beside my usual run of the mill. **1939** EVANS & MCGOWAN *Guide to Textiles* 66 Run-of-the-mill is a term which in general means that the merchandise has not been inspected... Sheets and pillowcases are frequently sold as run-of-the-mill. **1940** O. NASH *Face is Familiar* 118 And in celestial circles all the run-of-the-mill angels would rather be archangels or at least cherubim and seraphim. **1941** *Sun* (Baltimore) 30 July 10/1 The balance is composed of items which, in the main, are run-of-the-mine budget pruning. **1943** B. A. DE VOTO in *Harper's Mag.* May 645/1 But what they have to say is mostly run of the mill. **1944** *Sun* (Baltimore) 17 Feb. 17/1 The growers want 25 cents a pound for wrapper leaf.. and 15 cents for 'run of the crop' as against the OPA set prices of 21 for wrapper.. and 10 for ungraded. **1945** 'L. LEWIS' *Birthday Murder* (1951) i. 13 Hime.. has managed out of.. a run-of-the-mill story, something.. unusual in its effects. **1946** *Richmond* (Va.) *News Leader* 29 Nov. 15/1 That's about 80 times the cost of a hide from a 'run-of-the-mine' cow. **1950** *Engineering* 11 Aug. 131/3 The.. washery will treat 750 tons of run-of-mine coal per hour. **1951** *News Chron.* 12 Dec. 4 To the ordinary run-of-the-mill bank customer these may perhaps seem lordly examples of living on overdrafts. **1952** [see IMPERFECT *sb.* 3]. **1952** *Amer. Speech* XXVII. 264 Fabric which is shipped to a buyer just as it comes from the loom without inspection and without elimination of weaving defects is referred to as run-of-the loom. **1953** A. UPFIELD *Murder must Wait* x. 95 Her taste wasn't the usual run of the mill. **1960** E. DELAVENAY *Introd. Machine Transl.* vii. 106 It should free intellectual ability for more productive work than that of run-of-the-mill translations. **1967** *Gloss. Mining Terms* (*B.S.I.*) VIII. 23 *Run of mine* (R.O.M.), the product of a mine before sorting or cleaning. **1969** *Daily Tel.* 21 Apr. 17/7 No hard boundaries exist to separate jazz singers from run-of-the-mill night club performers. **1975** 'D. JORDAN' *Black Account* xii. 60 The difference between run-of-mine ores and washed fines. **1975** *Publishers Weekly* 9 June 52/1 Taylor's thoughtfully written, low-keyed text proves far superior to most run-of-the-battlefield 'popular' histories. **1977** *Amer. N. & Q.* XV. 117/1 Prices of run-of-the-mine books are often more difficult to ascertain than those of $500-plus items. **1978** R. LUDLUM *Holcroft Covenant* iii. 35 Althene was not your run-of-the-mill mother, as mothers were understood by this particular son. **1980** *Times Lit. Suppl.* 31 Oct. 1240/2 We are left with a pretty run-of-the-mill thriller.

IV. 21. a. A regular track made by certain animals; the 'bower' of a bower-bird, etc.

1821 LIDDLE *Poems* 116 (E.D.D.), I'll gar her keep the run, If deils waur on't. **1838** *Encycl. Metrop.* (1845) XXV. 430/2 The burrows which the Mole forms.. are divided into several parts, its *lodge* and *runs*. **1845** *Zoologist* III. 1083 The 'run', as it is termed, of a tench is different to that of a bream or rud. **1861** *Chambers's Encycl.* II. 287/2 Their habit of making bower-like erections, called *runs* by the colonists of New South Wales. **1878** JEFFERIES *Gamekeeper at H.* 149 Hares have their regular highways or 'runs'.

b. An enclosure for domestic animals or fowls to range or take exercise in.

1856 'STONEHENGE' *Brit. Rur. Sports* II. I. vii. 339/1 Dividing off the field into the four separate runs for the mares and foals. *c* **1858** ELIZ. WATTS *Poultry Yard* 3 It is very advantageous that those who intend to rear fowls should have a large run,.. perfectly sheltered.. and supplied with gravel. **1884** E. P. ROE *Nat. Ser. Story* ii, Fowls are restricted to a narrow yard or run.

22. A large open stretch of land occupied by a settler for pasturage; an extensive range of pasture- or grazing-land; a sheep station. *Austral.* and *N.Z.* Also *attrib.*, as ***run cattle, sheep.***

The early Amer. usage in quot. 1658 is not supported by further evidence.

1658 *Rec. Brookhaven, N.Y.* (1880) 3 This land and the grass thereof for a range, or run, for to feed horses and cattle on.. I have sold. **1804** *Sydney Gaz.* 12 Feb., A commodious dwelling-house [with] an extensive run for stock. **1826** GOLDIE in Bischoff *Van Diemen's Land* (1832) 157 It is, generally speaking, a good sheep run. **1840** G. ARDEN *Aust. Felix* 109 The squatter is protected in the exclusive use of the run. **1847** A. HARRIS *Settlers & Convicts* xvi. 330 If the shepherd suffers the flock to spread, in these mountainous runs especially, they get into creeks and hollows. **1858** *Richmond-Atkinson Papers* (1960) I. vii. 421, I found that Elliot's run.. was in a capital position.. in a finely grassed country. **1889** 'R. BOLDREWOOD' *Robbery under Arms* i. (1890) 2 The.. steers have never done anything but ramble off the run now and again. **1911** C. E. W. BEAN '*Dreadnought' of Darling* i. 12 Huge 1,000,000-acre runs or little 20,000 acre homestead leases. **1930** L. G. D. ACLAND *Early Canterbury Runs* 1st Ser. i. 2 A number.. sold or abandoned their runs, and came to New Zealand early in 1851. *Ibid.* 7 All run sheep had been Merinos in the old days. **1933** —— in *Press* (Christchurch, N.Z.) 18 Nov. 15/7 *Run* sheep, *run*-cattle, as opposed to paddock sheep or milking cows and hand-reared calves. **1936** F. CLUNE *Roaming round Darling* xviii. 178 Toorale.., headquarters of a run of 1,000,000 acres. **1950** *N.Z. Jrnl. Agric.* Sept. 215/1 With fertility declining pastures are becoming more difficult to control for sheep, and because of this, run cattle numbers are being increased. **1963** *Weekly News* (Auckland) 10 July 38/3 Run cattle.. can be moved on a mob basis from one paddock to another. **1966** G. W. TURNER *Eng. Lang. Austral. & N.Z.* iii. 50 A *run* is a parcel of land as leased. A sheepfarmer might own several adjacent runs of land, in this sense, and the whole 'station' so formed might also be termed a run.

Comb. **1859** F. FULLER *Five Yrs. Residence N.Z.* ix. 162 The Runholder kept the remaining portion as the payment for his trouble and expense in looking after the sheep. **1864** *Sunday at Home* 17 Dec. 811/1 A small chapel has been built for the use of the inhabitants by a runholder near. **1872** *Routledge's Ev. Boy's Ann.* 83/1 Your New Zealand runholder only thinks.. of what sort of sheep country he is riding so gaily through. **1890** 'R. BOLDREWOOD' *Squatter's Dream* xix. 238 What do you say if I go run-hunting with you? **1911** W. H. KOEBEL *In Maoriland Bush* xxii. 284 His career as a run-holder is usually a fleeting one with an abrupt termination. **1930** L. G. D. ACLAND *Early Canterbury Runs* 1st Ser. 8 On the whole, runholding has not been much of a business in Canterbury. **1940** W. G. MCCLYMONT *Explor. N.Z.* xii. 130 The country they contained had been granted to run-holders in order of application.

23. a. An inclined slope on a tramway or railway, down which a wagon runs by impetus. ? *Obs.*

1834–6 *Encycl. Metrop.* (1845) VIII. 240/1 On these rails a single horse could readily draw three tons of coal from the pits to the river. Where any steep declivity occurred on the road, this was termed a *run*, or an inclined plane. **1838** WOOD *Pract. Treat. Railroads* (ed. 3) 229 In wet weather, boys and men were employed, strewing ashes upon the rails down the steep declivities, or, as they were termed, 'runs', to cause the brake to take effect.

b. A track or support along or on which something may run or move.

1887 *Cassell's Encycl. Dict.*, *Run*.., a plank laid down to support rollers in moving buildings and other heavy objects; also as a track for wheelbarrows. **1899** *Westm. Gaz.* 17 June 7/2 When the stableman discovered the fire, he endeavoured to induce the horses to descend the slanting run into safety. **1900** H. LAWSON *Over Sliprails* 47 To paint the runs of the sash.

c. *pl.* A place at which wagons may be loaded or unloaded. *U.S.*

1870 *Huntington* (N.Y.) *Town Rec.* (1889) III. 585 The said land.. [is] sufficient.. to build two runs, so called, or three runs.. to load brick at. **1923** C. R. COOPER *Under Big Top* 226 Many a man [is saved] from injury at the unloading runs. **1931** *Amer. Mercury* Nov. 354/1 *Runs*, the unloading place at the railroad.

d. A slope of snow on which tobogganing, skiing, etc., are carried out. Also *transf.* Cf. sense 4 f above.

1874 [see TOBOGGAN *v.*]. **1898** *Encycl. Sport* II. 470/2 The English and American visitors to St. Moritz and Davos introduced tobogganing as a sport, and set to work to construct both toboggans and runs. **1910** [see BOB-SLED, -SLEIGH]. **1935** *Encycl. Sports* 178/2 The most famous toboggan run in the world, the Cresta is rebuilt every year under expert supervision. **1956** *Ski-ing* ('Know the Game' Ser.) 22/1 The *piste* is artificial and either made by a large number of skiers ski-ing down a run, or [etc.]. **1961** [see MOGUL *sb.*[2]]. **1972** 'M. YORKE' *Silent Witness* vi. 137 She took off her skis at the bottom of the run. **1974** *Rules of Game* 253/3 The brake [on a bobsleigh] is used only in emergencies, as its serrated edge damages the surface of the run. **1976** F. RAPHAEL *Glittering Prizes* 58 As he reached the top of the run, he was conscious that someone was standing there.

24. a. A pipe or trough along or down which water may run.

1833 *Act 3 & 4 Will. IV*, c. 46 §114 The water from the roofs.. shall be conveyed by.. proper pipes or runs, to be brought down the walls of such houses. **1844** H. STEPHENS *Bk. Farm* I. 199 Rain-water spouts, or *runs* as they are technically termed. **1881** RAYMOND *Mining Gloss.*, *Run*.., a long deep Trough in which slimes settle. **1890** *Cent. Dict.*, *Run*.., a trough for water that is caught by a coaming, built across the forecastle of a steamer.

b. *Mining.* An airway.

1867 W. W. SMYTH *Coal & Coalmining* 218 But the balancing of these splits requires nice management, or the air would tend to desert the longer for the shorter runs.

V. 25. *Naut.* **a.** That part of a ship's bottom which rises from the keel and bilge, and narrows toward the stern (†or bows).

a **1618** RALEIGH *Royal Navy* 10 To make her sayle well is to give a long run forward. **1627** CAPT. SMITH *Seaman's Gram.* ii. 3 The run of the ship.. is that part of the ship vnder water which comes narrower by degrees from the floore timbers along to the sterne post, called the ships way aftward. **1711** SUTHERLAND *Shipbuild. Assist.* 29 Three or four Strakes of Elm to raise up the Run of the Ship. **1781** NELSON 24 Aug. in Nicolas *Disp.* (1845) I. 43 The Albemarle is in Dock... She has a bold entrance, and clean run. **1831** *Examiner* 740/2 A rakish.. craft,.. with a deep keel and sharp run. **1900** SIR W. KENNEDY *Life of a Sailor* 241 Having a coarse run, she carried a huge body of water in her wake, in which the rudder was useless.

†**b.** The course of a ship. *Obs.*

1688 MIÈGE *Grt. Fr. Dict.*, *Sillage*,.. Course, the Rake or Run of a Ship, her Way forward on. **1712** DESAGULIERS tr. *Ozanam's Curs. Math.* V. 114 The Line describ'd by a Ship, which is call'd the Run, or Rake of a Ship,.. still cuts all the Meridians at Right-Angles.

26. †**a.** The vogue *of* a practice. *Obs.*

1658 SIR T. BROWNE *Hydriot.* i. 3 The prevalent Practice, Not totally pursued in the highest Run of Cremation.

b. The time during which a dramatic work holds the stage continuously. (Cf. 18.)

1705 FARQUHAR *Twin Rivals* Pref., One reason that the galleries were so thin during the run of this play. **1779** JOHNSON *L.P.*, *Philips*, [The epilogue] continued to be demanded through the run, as it is termed, of the play. **1810** SCOTT *Fam. Lett.* (1894) I. 175 As for the prologue and epilogue,.. it is the rule of the stage not to resume them after the first run of the play is over. **1826** MISS MITFORD *Village* Ser. II. (1863) 269 It was as dull as a lesson, and the run would have been short. **1885** *Bath Herald* 17 Jan. 3/2 The usage was to engage stars for the run of the piece.

c. The progress or prevalence *of* a disease.

1717 J. KEILL *Anim. Œcon.* (1738) 18 During the run of that distemper now for two years thro' our town. **1828–32** WEBSTER s.v., A disease has its run.

†**27.** ***in the run***, in the long run (see LONG RUN). *Obs.*

1645 PAGITT *Heresiogr.* (1661) 245 Which we shall find in the run, slighted and scorned by them, made meerly a footstool upon which their spirit shall raise it self into her Throne. **1760–72** H. BROOKE *Fool of Qual.* (1809) I. 105, I trust that, in the run, I shall not be a loser.

28. a. The act of running, esp. in rapid retreat or flight. Chiefly in phr. ***to*** or ***on the run*** (chiefly in sense 'fleeing' or 'escaping' from justice).

1660–1 PEPYS *Diary* 10 Jan., These Fanatiques that have ..put the King's Life-Guards to the run. **1680** C. NESSE *Church Hist.* 133 He had bereaved himself.. by putting Abiathar to the run. **1830** tr. *Aristoph.*, *Birds* 227 Here comes some one on the run. **1840** R. H. DANA *Bef. Mast* xxv, The captains came hurrying down, on the run. **1900** *Westm. Gaz.* 23 Feb. 5/1 It was impossible to get in with the bayonet or to start the enemy on the run again.

fig. **1885** *Punch* 3 Jan. 4/1 But 'Arry, for once in the way, 's a stone-broker and not in the run. **1887** *Times* (weekly ed.) 25 Nov. 10/3 Every Irish member 'on the run' who gathers a dozen people together.. commits [an] offence against the law. **1909** J. B. ATLAY *Ld. Haliburton* 184 There was a widespread impression that the assailants had got the Government 'on the run', and that a vigorous campaign would show further concessions when Parliament met. **1932** *Week-End Rev.* 9 Apr. 456/2 In 'Secret Sentence' she explores another world—the world of political assassination, of criminal investigation departments, of men on the run. **1954** X. FIELDING *Hide & Seek* xi. 139 They were fugitives from justice and had been on the run in this area for over a year. **1955** *Times* 30 June 10/7 The President strongly resisted the suggestion that, as Russia was now 'on the run' it might be possible to reduce American expenditure on foreign aid. **1957** *Times* 31 Oct. 3/1 The gangster, the No. 1 Public Enemy, on the run. **1963** T. TULLETT *Inside Interpol* i. 17 If it had not been for the men in the Rue Paul Valéry he might still be 'on the run'.

b. A running pace.

1840 R. H. DANA *Bef. Mast* xvi, We returned to the village, going nearly all the way on a full run. **1856** KANE *Arctic Explor.* I. xii. 128 We started at a run, men and dogs, for the solid ice. **1901** *Munsey's Mag.* XXV. 721/2, I put the horse to his run.

c. Capacity for, or power of, running.

1857 HUGHES *Tom Brown* I. vii. 166 They have too little run left in themselves to pull up for their own brothers. **1902** *Westm. Gaz.* 17 Oct. 4/2 Another golf ball is shortly to be placed on the market;.. it is claimed for this latest production that it flies far and truly, [and] has more 'run' than other golf balls.

d. ***to get the run upon***: (see quots.). *U.S. colloq.*

1848 BARTLETT *Dict. Amer.* s.v., 'To get the run upon one, is to make a butt of him; turn him into ridicule. **1859** *Slang Dict.* s.v., 'To get the run upon any person,' to have the upper hand, or be able to laugh at them.

e. ***to get the run***: to be dismissed from one's employment. *slang* (chiefly *Austral.*).

1889 BARRÈRE & LELAND *Dict. Slang* I. 403/2 *Get the run, to*, (English and Australian), to be discharged. **1941** [see *running shoe* s.v. RUNNING *vbl. sb.* 17 a]. **1959** BAKER *Drum* (1960) II. 141 *Run, get the*, to be dismissed from employment.

29. a. The rush, flow, or onward movement *of* water, air, etc.

1626 BACON *Sylva* §344 Want of Motion, or Stoppings, (whereby the Runne of Humours or the Motion of Perspiration, is stayed,) furthers Putrefaction. *a* **1691** FLAVEL *Sea-Deliverances* (1754) 163 Keeping our boat's head to the windward, which was then at the North, as well as we could guess by the run of the sea. **1836** MARRYAT *Pirate* iv, The sea,.. which at the change of wind had been cross, appeared to have recovered its regular run. **1851** GREENWELL *Coal-trade Terms, Northumb. & Durh.* 17 By shortening the run of the air,.. a larger quantity is brought into the mine. **1862** THORNBURY *Turner* I. 360 The run of the waves and their sweeping leaps are beautifully given in these sketches. **1898** *Allbutt's Syst. Med.* V. 847 An important factor in the blood-pressure, and in the run of the circulation.

b. The flow or melody *of* verse. (Cf. 11 a.) Also, a flow *of* speech.

1725 BROOME *Notes Pope's Odyssey* VI. xvi, This verse in particular has something horrible in the very run of it. **1749** *Power of Numbers in Poet. Composit.* 83 An Iambic.. having a direct contrary Movement, interrupts the Run of the Verse very disagreeably. **1884** *Athenæum* 20 Dec. 802/1 The metre is neither quantitative nor strictly accentual, nor, when the reader has got the run of it, is it very melodious. *a* **1915** JOYCE *Giacomo Joyce* (1968) 12 She stands black-robed at the telephone. Little timid laughs, little cries, timid runs of speech suddenly broken.

c. Rapid movement *of* the eye.

1879 DOWDEN *Southey* ii. 20 A mediæval Latin chronicle he could follow with the run of the eye.

d. ***by the run***, = with a run (see 6).

1800 *Gymnastics for Youth* 277 Sailors.. will descend from considerable heights in this way [sliding down by the hands], which they call coming down by the run. **1834** *Blackw. Mag.* XXXVI. 309 See all clear to let go every-thing by the run. **1843** *Ibid.* LIII. 81 The night cab comes down by the run, the night cabman tumbles off. **1886** STEVENSON *Treas. Isl.* III. xiii, If I risk another order, the whole ship'll come about our ears by the run.

e. ***run-of-river*** adj. phr. (usu. *attrib.*), denoting (an installation employing) a water supply taken directly from a river, esp. for generating hydroelectricity, with no major attempt to store water or regulate flow.

1943 STEINBERG & SMITH *Economy Loading* v. 169 In a run-of-river plant, the flow of the river must be utilized as it comes, so that this plant would normally supply the system base load. **1956** V. A. THIEMANN in B. G. A. Skrotzki *Electric Generation* v. 228 Hydro stations may be classified as either peaking or run-of-river. **1964** LINSLEY & FRANZINI *Water Resources Engin.* xvi. 453 Some run-of-river plants have enough storage..to permit storing water during off-peak hours for use during peak hours of the same day. **1965** R. G. KAZMANN *Mod. Hydrol.* iv. 89 The raw water obtained from an impounded supply is generally better than that obtained from a run-of-river water source.

30. a. The course, direction, or tendency *of* something immaterial.

1730 T. BOSTON *Mem.* xi. (1899) 348 This run of affairs quickly issued in the General Assembly's condemning of 'The Marrow of Modern Divinity'. **1766** FORDYCE *Serm. Yng. Wom.* (1767) I. v. 193 In the run of her discourse [she might] hurt them all. **1783** JUSTAMOND tr. *Raynal's Hist. Indies* VI. 31 There is no such thing as selling, without complying with the general run of the market. **1809** MALKIN *Gil Blas* v. i. ¶20 The run of luck is against us. **1864** NEWMAN *Apol.* v. (1904) 166/2 We shall find, I think, the general run of things to be such as I have represented it. **1880** EARLE *Engl. Plant N.* p. xlviii, The place of these lists in the run of that history.

b. ***to keep the run of***, to keep in touch with, to keep oneself informed about. Also, ***to lose (the) run of***. *U.S.* Now *rare*.

1859 J. W. PALMER *New & Old* ii 62, Even if I had time to follow his fortunes, it was not possible to keep the run of him. **1862** MAURY in Corbin *Life* (1888) 212, I shall..very much wish to keep the run of public sentiment. **1872** MRS STOWE *Oldtown Fireside Stories* 29 She hed the in and out o' the Sullivan house, and kind o' kept the run o' how things went and came in it. **1893** 'THANET' *Stories of Western Town* 145 I've been in this block, Mrs Carleton and me, ever since it was built; and, some way, between us we've managed to keep the run of all the folks in it. **1893** 'MARK TWAIN' *£1,000,000 Bank-Note* 29 You couldn't afford to lose the run of business and be no end of time getting the hang of things again when you get back home. **1918** J. C. LINCOLN *Shavings* xix. 320, I kind of lost run of the time.

31. a. The direction, line, or lie *of* anything.

1748 *Anson's Voy.* III. v. 340 Her small breadth, and the straight run of her leeward-side. **1778** W. PRYCE *Min. Cornub.* 127 A valley may happen to lie at the feet of three several hills... This is also termed the Run of the country. **1848** RUXTON *Far West* v. 155 From the 'run' of the hills, there must be plenty of water. **1851** STERNBERG *Dial. & Flk. Lore Northants* 88 *Run*, the 'grain' of stone, the direction in which it most easily cleaves. **1873** *Routledge's Ev. Boy's Ann.* 73/2 Pay..attention to the run of the grain of the wood.

b. *Mining.* (See quot.)

1864 WEBSTER, *Run*, the horizontal distance to which a drift may be carried.

32. a. The freedom or range *of* a house, etc.; the privilege of free resort, access, or use.

1755 *Connoisseur* No. 76 ¶4 The curate..and the town apothecary, whom he indulges with the run of his table. **1763-5** CHURCHILL *Independence* Poems (1767) II. 21 He may obtain a patent for the run Of his Lords Kitchen. **1809** MALKIN *Gil Blas* XII. vii. ¶5, I have the run of two good houses. **1847** L. HUNT *Men, Women, & B.* II. xii. 308 She had the wholesome run of her good uncle's books. **1884** G. ALLEN *Philistia* I. 104 Then I have the run of the place entirely to myself.

transf. **1850** THACKERAY *Pendennis* xli[i], It was as good as most books of the kind that had the run of circulating libraries and the career of the season.

b. ***the run of one's teeth, knife***, free board, usually in return for work done; maintenance, support. Also *transf.*, complete freedom of action.

1807 in *N. & Q.* (1904) 11 June 478/1 And it suits to a T, To receive as your fee, The run of your teeth And five guineas a day. **1841** HARTSHORNE *Shropshire Gloss.* 552. **1879** MISS BRADDON *Cloven Foot* xxviii, It was an understood thing that he was to have the run of his teeth at Hazelhurst. **1889** R. S. FERGUSON *Carlisle* 181 The subscribers frequently in turn provided the curate with ..'the run of his teeth'. **1927** *Daily Mirror* 10 Dec. 9/1 Sir Granville Ryrie..began work as a cattle driver at £30 a year and the 'run of his knife', which means his food. **1974** *Broadcast* 2 Dec. 16/3 Hugh Carleton Green..allowed—nay! encouraged a group of bright and irresponsible young men and women to have the run of their teeth in the so-called 'satire' programmes.

c. The pasture of an animal for a certain period.

1854 *Jrnl. R. Agric. Soc.* XV. II. 418 The summer run of a beast should pay the grazier 1 *l.* a-month. **1857** G. A. LAWRENCE *Guy Liv.* viii, She ought to be in great condition now, with a summer's run.

33. (See quot.)

1887 *Encycl. Brit.* XXII. 718/1 The value of a division of the scale [on a level], in seconds of arc, is usually called the 'run'.

34. Special Comb.: **run time** *Computers*, (*a*) the time at or during which a program or other task is executed; (*b*) the length of time taken by the execution of a particular task.

1965 MITCHELL & WILLMOTT *Programming Computer in Atlas Autocode* viii. 51 Each routine or block is associated with a serial number for use in tracing faults found at run time. **1968** M. V. WILKES *Time-Sharing Computer Syst.* iv. 37 At run time, the segment number is used to enter the segment table belonging to the user whose program is running at that instant. **1972** [see OVERLAY *sb.* 6]. **1974** ADBY & DEMPSTER *Introd. Optimization Methods* v. 178 Colville found that the number of function evaluations proved a totally unreliable guide to run time.

†**run**, *sb.*[2] *Obs.*$^{-0}$ [Cf. RIN.] Brine.

c **1440** *Promp. Parv.* 439/2 Run, or bryyn.

run, obs. form of ROUN.

run (rʌn), *v.* Forms: (see below). Pa. t. **ran**. Pa. pple. **run**. [A verb of complicated history in Eng., representing two forms originally distinct (a strong intransitive and a weak transitive), each of which was subject to metathesis; the forms are thus to some extent parallel to those of BURN *v.*[1] The strong intr. verb is represented by OE. *rinnan* (*ran*, **runnon*, [*ȝerunnen*]), = OFris. *rinna*, *renna*, *runna* (*ran*, pa. pple. *runnen*, *ronnen*), mod.WFris. *rinne*, *ronne* (*roan*, pa. pple. *roun*), NFris. *ren* (*ruan*, *ronen*), *ran*, etc.; MDu. *rinnen* (*ran*, *geronnen*); OS. *rinnan* (*ran*, *runnun*, ——), MLG. *rinnen* (*ran*); OHG. *rinnan* (*ran*, *runnun*, *girunnan*), G. *rinnen* (*rann*, *rannen*, *geronnen*); ON. *rinna*, later (also mod.Icel., Fær., Norw.) *renna* (*rann*, *runnu*, *runninn*), MSw. *rinna* (also mod.Sw.), *rynna* (*ran*, *runno*, *runnin*), MDa. *rinde* (*rand*, *runde*, *runden*), Da. *rinde* (*randt*); Goth. *rinnan* (*rann*, *runnun*, *runnans*). Of this type, however, very few examples occur in OE. texts (four or five in all of the simple verb, chiefly in verse, and a similar number of the pa. pple. from the compound **ȝerinnan*). The prevailing form in all dialects appears to have been that with metathesis, *irnan*, *iẹrnan*, *yrnan* (*arn* or *orn*, *urnon*, *urnen*): for the later history of this see the forms below. The weak causative verb, of which the original form was **rannjan*, is represented in the cognate languages by OFris. *renna* (p. p. *rent*), MDu. *rennen* (*rende*, *rande*, *gerent*, *gerant*; Du. *rennen*), OS. *rennian*, MLG. *rennen* (*rende*, *rande*, etc.), OHG. *rennan*, (*ranta*, *girant*), MHG. and G. *rennen* (*rannte*, *gerannt* and *rennte*, *gerennt*), ON. (also Icel., Fær., Norw.) *renna* (*renndi*, *renndr*), MSw. and Sw. *ränna* (*rände*, *ränt*), MDa. and Da. *rende* (*rende*, *rendt*). In OE. it appears only in the metathetic form *ærnan*, *earnan* (usually in the sense of 'to ride').

The extreme rarity of OE. *rinnan*, and the entire absence of an OE. **rẹnnan*, render it probable that ME. *rinne*(*n* and *renne*(*n* are mainly, if not entirely, due to the influence of ON. *rinna* and *renna*. To a great extent they first appear in texts where Scand. influence is prominent.

The different OE. and ME. types, partly by natural development of the vowels and partly by interaction of the various tenses of the strong verb, gave rise to a large number of variations, for which see the forms below. The weak conjugation, properly belonging to the causative but soon extended to the intransitive verb, remained fairly common until *c* 1400, and still survives to some extent in dialects.

In the sense 'to curdle' the causative form exists in mod. dialects as EARN *v.*[2] For the ME. forms representing the OE. compound *ȝe-yrnan*, see YERN *v.*]

A. Inflexional forms.

I. Forms with metathesis.

1. *Infinitive.* α. **irnan, iernan,** 1–2 **yrnan,** 2 **yrnen,** 3 **irne(n),** 9 *dial.* **hirn.**

c **888** K. ÆLFRED *Boeth.* xxxv. §7 Wildu dior ðær woldon to irnan. *c* **897** —— *Gregory's Past. C.* xvi. 103 Ðæt hi mæȝen iernan & fleon. *c* **900** WÆRFERTH tr. *Gregory's Dial.* 118 Se hræfn..ongan yrnan ymb þone ylcan hlaf. *c* **1205** LAY. 19750 He..hahte hine..irne to þere welle. *Ibid.* 21229 His hors he lette irnen. **1825** JENNINGS *Obs. Dial. W. Eng.* 180 I'll hirn auver an zee where I can't help 'em.

β. 1 **iornan, [eornan],** 3 **eornen(n),** 3–4 **eorne** (3 **heorne).**

a **900** in *O.E. Texts* 178 Ðæt ða wildan hors scealden iornan. *c* **1200** ORMIN 1336 He..let itt eornenn forþwiþþ. *c* **1275** LAY. 19750 [He] hehte him..heorne to þare wille. *c* **1400** *Trevisa's Higden* (Rolls) VIII. 61 Swyn were i-seie.. renne [*v.r.* eorne] up and doun.

γ. 3 **urnen,** 3–4 **urne, vrne,** 9 *dial.* **(h)urn.**

c **1205** LAY. 24696 Summe heo gunnen urnen. *a* **1250** *Owl & Night.* 638 þat node makeþ old wif urne. *a* **1300** *K. Horn* 936 Hi gunne awei vrne. **1886** ELWORTHY *W. Somerset Wd.-bk.* 635, I zeed the stoat urn 'long the wheel-ruck. **1894** BLACKMORE *Perlycross* 257 Zippy..hath orders to hurn for her life.

δ. 1 **ærnan** (*dat.* **ærnenne, earnenne),** 3 **ærne(n), eærne, earn(n)e, earnee, hearn,** 4 (9 *dial.*) **arn;** 3–4 **ernen, ernyn, erne,** 3 **ernne,** 5 **eerne.**

These are properly forms of the causative verb.

c **825** *Vesp. Ps.* xviii. 6 He..ȝefaeh swe swe ȝiȝent to earnenne on weȝ. *c* **900** tr. *Baeda's Hist.* v. vi. 400 þæt hio ærnan moste. *Ibid.*, To ærnenne & to flitenne. *c* **1205** LAY. 1638 3eond þat lond he gon ernen. *Ibid.* 8542 þa com an gume ærnen. *c* **1275** *Ibid.* 21229 His hors he makede earnee. *a* **1300** in *E.E.P.* (1862) 9 As bestis þat wer wode a-ȝe oþir to erne her and þare. *c* **1330** *Arth. & Merl.* 1228 (Kölbing), He oȝaines hem fast gan erne. *c* **1440** *Promp. Parv.* 142/2 Ernyn, as horse (*P.* eerne), *cursito.* **1876** *Mid. Yorks. Gloss.* 163 *Arn*, to run, or walk hastily.

2. *Present Participle.* α. 1 **irn-,** 1–2 **yrnende.**

c **893** K. ÆLFRED *Oros.* I. i. 8 Seo is irnende of norþdæle. *c* **1000** *Sax. Leechd.* III. 234 Æfre heo byð yrnende ymbe ðas eorðan. *a* **1100** in Napier *O.E. Glosses* 5/2 *Uagans*, i. *circumiens*, yrnende.

β. 1 **eorn-, iornende,** 4 **eornynge.**

c **825** *Vesp. Ps.* lvii. 8 Swe swe weter eornende. *c* **950** *Lindisf. Gosp.* Matt. xxvii. 48 Hræðe iornende an of hiora ȝenom spync. *c* **1320** *Cast. Love* 728 A welle þat euere is eornynge.

γ. 2 **ernende,** 4 **erninde, ernyng(e.**

a **1100** in Napier *O.E. Glosses* 12/2 *Labentibus*,.. ernendum. **13..** *Guy Warw.* 719 Riche stedes..erninde. **1377** LANGL. *P. Pl.* B. XIX. 376 Water..ernynge out of mennes eyen.

δ. 4 **arnand, arnyng,** 5 **arnende.**

13.. *K. Alis.* 2098 (Laud MS.), Ac a kniȝth þer comeþ arnyng. *c* **1330** *Arth. & Merl.* 8404 (Kölbing), Arnand wiþ al his miȝt. **14..** *Sir Beues* (E) 1679 He prekyd hys hors al arnende.

3. *Present Indicative: 3rd pers. sing. and pl.* α. 1 **irn(e)ð, yrn(e)ð,** *pl.* **irnað, yrnað,** 3 **irneð.**

c **888** K. ÆLFRED *Boeth.* xxxvi. §6 Ða dyseȝan..irnað hidres ðidres. *c* **893** —— *Oros.* I. i. 8 Seo ea..irnð þonan suðryhte. *c* **1000** *Ags. Gosp.* Luke xxii. 10 Eow aȝen yrnð an man. *c* **1000** *Ags. Ps.* (Thorpe) cxlvii. 4 His word yrneð wundrum sniome. *c* **1205** LAY. 29664 þe ueȝereste welles stæm þe irneð on uolden.

β. 1 **iorn(e)ð,** 2 **eornð,** 1, 3 **eorneð,** 3 *Orm.* **eorneþþ,** 4 **eorneþ, -eth.**

c **825** *Vesp. Ps.* cxlvii. 15 Hreðlice eorneð word his. *c* **950** *Lindisf. Gosp.* Luke xxii. 10 To-gæȝne iorneð iuh monn. *c* **1050** *Voc.* in Wr.-Wülcker 378 *Cursat*, iornð. *c* **1160** *Hatton Gosp.* Luke xxii. 10 Eow an-ȝen eornð an man. *c* **1200** ORMIN 8832 All þiss weorrldess ald Bi seoffne daȝhess eorneþþ. *a* **1225** *Juliana* 74 As weter þat eorneð. *c* **1400** *Trevisa's Higden* (Rolls) I. 115 þe brook..corneth in to þe valey of Iosephat.

pl. *a* **1225** *Ancr. R.* 80 Heo eorneð boðe togederes. *a* **1250** *Owl & Night.* (J.) 375 If hundes eorneþ to him ward. *a* **1400** *Trevisa's Higden* (Rolls) I. 59 þe strong stremes þat renneþ [*v.r.* eorneþ] þat course.

γ. 3 *pl.* **urneþ,** 4 **urn-, vrneþ,** 9 *dial.* **urnth,** *pl.* **hurneth.**

a **1250** *Owl & Night.* (C.) 375 ȝif hundes urneþ to him ward. *a* **1300** *Floris & Bl.* 225 He vrneþ in o pipe of bras. *c* **1400** *Trevisa's Higden* (Rolls) V. 329 þat ryver renneþ [*v.r.* urneþ] under..Wygan. **1881** BLACKMORE *Christowell* ii, They little holes hurneth all round 'em. **1886** ELWORTHY *W. Somerset Word-bk.* 50 The water..urnth down his ditch.

δ. *pl.* 1 **ærnað,** 3 **ærneð, erneþ,** 4 **erniþ;** *sing.* 3 **erneþ** (*Orm.* **-eþþ**), 4 **ernnes.** Also *2nd sing.* 3 **ernst.**

c **893** K. ÆLFRED *Oros.* I. i. 20 þonne ærnað hy ealle toweard þæm feo. *c* **1200** ORMIN 13183 Ure wukedaȝȝ Bi twellfe timess erneþþ. *c* **1205** LAY. 13999 þurh þi lond heo ærneð [*c* **1275** erneþ]. **1297** R. GLOUC. (Rolls) 6570 þat lond vp wan þou ernst. *a* **1300** in *E.E.P.* (1862) 20 Be-hold..how þe stremis erniþ of is swet blode. **13..** *Guy Warw.* (A) 6730 He ouer-ernnes dounes & cuntre. *c* **1400** *Trevisa's Higden* (Rolls) V. 329 þat ryver renneþ [*v.r.* erneþ] under þe citee of Wygan.

4. *Present Subjunctive.* 1 **irne** (*pl.* **irnen**), **yrne, ierne,** 3 **vrne.**

c **888** K. ÆLFRED *Boeth.* xi. §1 þæt he irne [*v.r.* ierne] on his willan. *Ibid.* xxxiv. §1 Swa swa..irnen mæneȝe brocas & riða of. *a* **1000** in Grein *Bibl. Ags. P.* I. 352 Nefne he under seȝle yrne. *a* **1225** *Ancr. R.* 164 ȝif a wode liun vrne ȝeont þe strete.

5. *Imperative. sing.* 1 **yrn, irnn, eorn,** 9 *dial.* **(h)urn;** *pl.* 3 **ierneð, ærneð, herneþ, eærne.**

c **850** *Kentish Gloss.* in Wr.-Wülcker 59 *Discurre*, irnn. *c* **900** WÆRFERTH tr. *Gregory's Dial.* 115 Broðor Maurus! yrn hraðe. *Ibid.* 325 Eorn la, Maxime, eorn, & onfoh me! *a* **1200** *Vices & Virtues* 51 Alle ȝe Adames children,..ierneð to ȝe trewe. *c* **1205** LAY. 6138 Eorneð and eærne [*c* **1275** herneþ]. *Ibid.* 16441 Ærneð æuere vorð & vorð. **1867** ROCK *Jim an' Nell* li. (E.D.S.), Well, Jim, how be? Urn in, man, urn! **1886** ELWORTHY *W. Somerset Word-bk.* 359 Hurn cheel! and vetch the tay-run.

6. *Past Indicative: 1st and 3rd pers.* α. *sing.* 1–2 **arn** (1 **arun**), 3 **earn, ærne,** 4 **ernne, arne.** Also *2nd pers.* 1 **urne.**

c **825** *Vesp. Ps.* xlix. 18 ðif ðu ȝeseȝe ðeof, somud ðu urne mid hine. *c* **850** *O.E. Martyrol.* 26 Dec., An pleȝende cild arn under wænes hweowol. *c* **1000** *Lambeth Ps.* cxviii. 32 Weȝ beboda þinra ic arn. *c* **1160** *Hatton Gosp.* Luke xv. 20 [He] aȝen hine earn..& cyste hine. *c* **1205** LAY. 4536 Scip ærne to-ȝen scip. *c* **1315** SHOREHAM II. 84 Hys bare flesche.. arne alle a blode. *c* **1330** *Arth. & Merl.* 5984 (Kölbing), His hors..erne forþ.

β. *sing.* 1–4 **orn,** 3 **eorn,** 4 **orne,** 5 **ourne,** 9 *dial.* **uurn.**

c **825** *Vesp. Ps.* cxviii. 32 On weȝ biboda ðinra ic orn. *c* **897** K. ÆLFRED *Gregory's Past. C.* xvi. 103 Ðonne orn he eft innto ðæm temple. *c* **1205** LAY. 18806 He orn him to-ȝænes. *c* **1290** *S. Eng. Leg.* I. 43/312 To toune he orn with Ioye i-nouȝ. *a* **1310** in Wright *Lyric P.* xviii. 58 Out of thin huerte orn the flod. *c* **1380** *Sir Ferumb.* 3893 Quiklich in-to a tour he orn. *a* **1400** LANGL. *P. Pl.* C. XIII. 13 Til ich..ȝorn [*v.r.* ourne] in-to elde. **1886** ELWORTHY *W. Somerset Word-bk.* 74 Aay uurn [= I ran].

γ. *pl.* 1–2 **urnon** (1 **wurnon**), 1–3 **urnen,** 3 **hurnen;** 3 **vrne, yrne,** 4 **urne, hurne, vrn.**

c **888** K. ÆLFRED *Boeth.* xxxv. §7 Him urnon ealle hellwaran onȝean. *a* **1122** *O.E. Chron.* (Laud MS.) an. 1083, Sume urnon in to cyrcean. *c* **1175** *Lamb. Hom.* 41 Alle hire stremes urnen fur berninde. *c* **1275** LAY. 1349 þe sipes hurnen swiþe. *c* **1300** *St. Margaret* 28/137 Olibrius.. bihuld, hou hure lymes yrne ablode. *a* **1320** *Pol., Rel., & L. Poems* (1903) 243 In fif steden..Stremes hurne of blode. *c* **1330** *Arth. & Merl.* 6797 Man & woman vrn so dere.

δ. *pl.* 3 **arne,** 3–4 **orne, ourne.**

c **1275** LAY. 11977 Waȝes þar arne, streme þar vrne. *Ibid.* 27720 Ourne grete stremes of Romanisse blodes. **1297** R. GLOUC. (Rolls) 8371 Wepinde hii armed hom, þe teres orne [*v.r.* ourne] adoun.

7. *Past Participle.* 1 (ȝe)urnen, 1, 4 vrnen, 4 y-orne, i-orne.

a 1000 *Phœnix* 364 Opþæt wintra bið þusend urnen. *c* 1000 *Sax. Leechd.* III. 278 Ær þan he to dropum ȝeurnen sy. *a* 1300 *K. Horn* (C.) 1146 Feor ihc am iorne [*v.r.* yorne]. *a* 1325 *Prose Psalter* cxviii. 32 Ichaue vrnen þe wai of þy comaundementz.

8. *Weak conj.* **a.** *Past Indicative* (and *Subj.*). 3 ærnde, 3–4 arnde 3 h(e)arnde, 4 arnede; 3 hern(e)de, 4 ernde; 5 ornd, 9 *dial.* urned, (h)urn'd, hirn'd. Also *pl.* 3–4 arnden, 3 hernde.

c 1205 LAY. 9296 Hamun arnde [*c* 1275 hernede] upwarð. *c* 1275 *Ibid.* 9934 þorh þat lond he hearnde. *c* 1290 *S. Eng. Leg.* I. 48/52 His Men..Arnden bi þe weie. 1297 R. GLOUC. (Rolls) 6202 He arnde [*v.r.* harnde] vpe a lute hul. *c* 1300 *K. Horn* (L.) 1239 Efter horn he [Aþulf] ernde. 13.. *Sir Beues* (MS. A) 2021 Þe hors..arnede awai wiþ þe king. *c* 1390–1400 *R. Gloucester's Chron.* (Rolls) 11228 Hii caste awei þe dosils þat win ornd abrod so. 1825 JENNINGS *Obs. Dial. W. Eng.* 45 *Hirnd*, pret[erite]. 1842 PULMAN *Rustic Sketches* 73 Then all th' cows hurn'd back agen. 1847 H. BAIRD *Nathan Hogg's Lett.* 37 A yung humman urn'd by. 1890 *Glouc. Gloss.* 169 *Urned*, ran.

b. *Past Participle.* 4 y-eornd, y-arned, arnd, 9 *dial.* (u-)urned, a-urn'd, hirn'd.

13.. *K. Alis.* 896 (Laud MS.), Quyk away he is yarned. *Ibid.* 4357 Þe gregeys..beþ..away arnd [W. y-eornd]. 1825 JENNINGS *Obs. Dial. W. Eng.* 45 *Hirnd*,..part[iciple]. 1886 ELWORTHY *W. Somerset Word-bk.* 793 They cowcumber vines be proper a-urn'd out.

II. Forms without metathesis.

9. *Infinitive.* α. (Chiefly *north.* and *Sc.*) 1 rinnan, 4 rinn(e, 4–6 rynne, 5 rynn; 4 rinin, rine, 6 ryne; 4–7 ryn (5 reyn), 4, 6– rin.

a 900 CYNEWULF *Christ* 1114 Þær blod & wæter..ut bicwoman..rinnan fore rincum. *a* 1300 *Cursor M.* 23729 All sal we rin into his rape. *c* 1340 HAMPOLE *Pr. Consc.* 471 A best when it es born, may..ryn to and fra. 1375 BARBOUR *Bruce* I. 103 That thai..Suld ryn on fute. *c* 1450 *St. Cuthbert* (Surtees) 6217 He streynd his hors to rynn. 1483 *Cath. Angl.* 309/1 To Rynne as water dos. 1526 SKELTON *Magnyf.* 795 He that hath nede, man, let hym rynne. 1566 KNOX *Hist. Ref.* Wks. (Wodrow Soc.) I. 186 He wold nott ryne whare God had nott called him. 1603 J. DAVIES (Heref.) *Microcosmos* Wks. (Grosart) I. 29/1 Through those passages it first doth rin. 1794 BURNS *Philly & W.* ix, Let fortune's wheel at random rin. 1813 HOGG *Queen's Wake* 83 Let never an auld man..Rin post to the diel for wyne.

β. 3–4 rennen (5 rennyn), 4–6 renne, 6 rene(n); 3–7 ren.

c 1220 *Bestiary* 340 Bihoueð us to rennen to cristes quike welle. *a* 1300 in *E.E.P.* (1862) 4 Is fete sul ren of blode. *c* 1300 *Havelok* 1161 Or þou shal to þe galwes renne. 1377 LANGL. *P. Pl.* B. xv. 220, I haue seyne charite..rennen in ragged wedes. 14.. in Wr.-Wülcker 589 *Incurro*, to ren yn. *c* 1440 *Promp. Parv.* 429/2 Rennyn, or lepyn, *curro*. *a* 1529 SKELTON *Sp. Parrot* 142 Honowre..wyll ren on that syde. 1550 CROWLEY *Last Trumpet* 563 To play tenise..or to rene base. 1565 COOPER *Thes.* s.v. *Cursus*, To renne to a place.

γ. 4 run-, 6– run (7 runn); 6–7 runne, rune.

c 1325 [see the pres. pple.]. 1525 in Turner *Select. Rec. Oxford* 55, 1s...to rune..to thuse of the reparacon. 1545 ASCHAM *Toxoph.* (Arb.) 25 Lest your boke shoulde runne awaye with you. 1562 PILKINGTON *Expos. Abdias* 67 To run under some greate mans winge. 1658–9 in *Hatton Corr.* (Camden) 18 Mrs. Crue is like to rune quite mad. 1674 *Boston Rec.* (1881) VII. 89 A high way..to runn..betweene his other lands. 1683 D. GRANVILLE *Lett.* (Surtees Soc.) 163, I did..runne of halfe a sermon.

δ. 5–6 ronne, 5–7 ron; 6 rowne, roon(e.

1482 *Cely Papers* (Camden) 122 Lette hym [a horse] ron in a parke. 1523 LD. BERNERS *Froiss.* I. cxv. 137 They..began to ron togyder thre heedes in one hood. 1557 *Tottel's Misc.* (Arb.) 233, I thinke that sigh doth roon From me to you. 1592 UNTON *Corr.* (Roxb.) 271 Intendinge he shall first ronne fortune. 1667 in *Cath. Rec. Soc. Publ.* III. 64 To make him ron through fier and water.

10. *Present Participle.* α. 4–6 rynnand (4 -ande, rynand), 5–6 ryn(n)yng; 4, 6 rinnand (4 -ande, rinand), 8– rinnan, -in, -in', -ing.

a 1300 *Cursor M.* 5793 A land rinnand bath honi and milk. 1375 BARBOUR *Bruce* v. 648 His boy com fast rynand. *c* 1425 WYNTOUN *Cron.* I. 1026 A wattyr gret on hewide rynnande. *c* 1450 *Godstow Reg.* 370 Vsuell money rynnyng in Inglond. *c* 1500 *Lancelot* 2952 The stedis Rynyng with the sadillis bare. 1567 *Gude & Godlie B.* (S.T.S.) 174 O fulis,.. Rinnand fra Christ. 1785 BURNS *Halloween* xx, Young an' auld come rinnan out. 1867 *Goodwife at Home* xlix. (E.D.D.), The road's rinnin noo.

β. 4 rennand(e, 5 -ende, -onde; 4 rennenge, 4–6 rennyng (5 -ying), 5–6 rennynge; 4 renand, -yng.

a 1300 *Cursor M.* 14283 Rennand [*v.r.* renand] forth als sco war wod. *c* 1320 R. BRUNNE *Medit.* 839 Faste þese houndes come rennyng ryue. 1377 LANGL. *P. Pl.* B. xv. 453 Wilde bestes..rennenge with-out croperes. 1412–20 LYDG. *Troy Bk.* II. 656 Vynnettis rennynge in þe casementis. 1565 COOPER *Thesaurus* s.v. *Flumen*, Cocytus rennyng with a slow course.

γ. 4 runnande; 6 runnyng(e, 6–7 runninge, 6– running (7 runing).

c 1325 *Metr. Hom.* 114 He..fled fra him ful fast runnande. 1526 TINDALE *Luke* vi. 38 Good measure,..shaken to gedder, and runnynge over. 1585 T. WASHINGTON tr. *Nicholay's Voy.* IV. xxix. 151 b, A promontorie..running along by the sea side. *c* 1610 SPEED in *Lett. Lit. Men* (Camden) 108 My thoughts runnyng upon..this worke. *a* 1639 WOTTON *Reliq.* (1651) 9 Runing..as smoothly as a numerous verse.

δ. 6 ronnyng, ronning.

1530 PALSGR. 693/1 It is fayre ronnyng here by this waters syde. 1571 GOLDING *Calvin on Ps.* lvii. 2 If wee come not ronning a pace. 1590 SPENSER *F.Q.* III. x. 23 Trompart ronning hastily, him did stay.

11. *Present Indicative.* α. *1st pers. sing.* 1 rinne, 4 ryn, 6 rin; *2nd pers.* 6 rynis; *3rd pers.* 3 rinneð, 5 rynnyth, -ethe, 6 -eth, rinneth, 9 *dial.* rin'th, rinth; 4–6 rynnis, 5 rynnys, ryn(n)es, 6 rinnis, 7 rinnes, 8– rins. *Pl.* 4, 6 rinne, 5–6 rynne (5 -en), 5, 7 ryn, 4, 6– rin; 4, 6 rinnis, -es, 4 rynnys, -es, 5 rynes, 6 ryn(n)is.

c 1000 *Ags. Ps.* (Thorpe) cxviii. 32 Ic on wisne weȝ worda þinra reðne rinne. *a* 1225 *Leg. Kath.* 2477 Þat ter rinneð aa mare eoile iliche riue. *c* 1375 *Cursor M.* 26642 (Fairf.), [A] wound þat..rynnis, & rotis ay. *c* 1385 CHAUCER *L.G.W.* 60 *Prol.*, Quhen þat it is eue, I ryn belyfe. *c* 1400 MAUNDEV. (Roxb.) i. 4 It rynnes thurgh Hungary. 1422 *Secreta Secret.*, *Priv. Priv.* 151 His gladnys rynnyth al-way into worse. 1462 in *Finchale Priory* (Surtees) 95 A burn that rynes betwx the said lewod [etc.]. 1508 DUNBAR *Flyting* 225 Than rynis thow doun the gait. 1562 TURNER *Baths* 3 The..mater that thys water rynneth thorow. 1567 *Gude & Godlie B.* (S.T.S.) 127 Efter the I rin. 1609 SKENE *Reg. Maj.* Table 62 Prescription rinnes not..agains him quha is absent. *c* 1730 RAMSAY *Fable, Miser & Minos* 48 To fill the tub that ay rins out. 1825 JAMIESON *Suppl.*, It rins i' my head. 1867 ROCK *Jim an' Nell* xxxvii. (E.D.S.), Away Dick rin'th.

pl. *a* 1300 *E.E. Psalter* lvii. 7 Als watres rinnes ai. *a* 1340 HAMPOLE *Psalter* xxiii. 2 As flodes rynnys in till þe see. *c* 1400 *Secreta Secret.* 73 Waters rynnen among hilles. *c* 1460 *Towneley Myst.* iii. 277 Thise nayles so thay ryn. 1523 SKELTON *Garl. Laurel* 196 They ryde and rinne. *c* 1560 A. SCOTT *Poems* (S.T.S.) xxx. 11 Thay rin lyk wyld..horss. 1572 *Satir. Poems Reform.* xxxi. 50 Thay and ye Papists rynis togidder. 1603 J. DAVIES (Heref.) *Microcosmos* Wks. (Grosart) I. 32 Lakes that never ryn. *a* 1886 A. BURGESS *Poute* 67 [Two streams] rin below..Richt throo the Floor.

β. *1st pers. sing.* 5–6 renne; *2nd pers.* 5 rennest; *3rd pers.* 2–3 renneð (2 reonneð), 4–5 renneþ, 4–6 renneth, 4–5 -yth, 5 -ethe; 4–5 rennes, 4 rennez, ren(n)is, renes. *Pl.* 4 renis, rennys; 5–6 renneth (5 renneþ); 4–5 rennen (5 -yn, -un), 4–6 renne, 5 ren.

a 1122 *O.E. Chron.* (Laud MS.) an. 656, Swa swa þæt wæter renneð to..Norðburh. *Ibid.* an. 963, Swa swa þæt wæter reonneð to Crulande. *c* 1220 *Bestiary* 240 In ðe heruest [the ant]..renneð rapelike. *a* 1300 *E.E. Psalter* cxlvii. 15 Swiftli rennes saghe hisse. 13.. *Gaw. & Gr. Knt.* 731 Fro þe crest þe colde borne rennez. *c* 1385 CHAUCER *L.G.W.* 491 *Cleopatra*, Pete rennyth [*v.r.* renneth] sone in gentil herte. 1400–21 *26 Pol. Poems* 43 Wiþ theues..þou delest and rennest. 1433 *Rolls of Parlt.* IV. 439/1, I renne in grete indignation of my Lordes. *a* 1529 SKELTON *Bowge of Courte* 399, I renne ay on the losse. 1565 COOPER *Thesaurus* s.v. *Exeo*, The riuer..renneth into the sea.

pl. 13.. *Cursor M.* 9937 (Gött.), Þar-fra rennys [*Trin.* renneþ] four stremes. 1362 LANGL. *P. Pl.* A. II. 157 Faytours þat on Fote rennen. 1387 TREVISA *Higden* (Rolls) I. 359 Ofte grehoundes renneþ after hem. *c* 1400 *Apol. Loll.* 75 Þei ren in þe curse of God. 1449 PECOCK *Repr.* I. xvi. 90 Without him..prechingis rennen arere. 1526 SKELTON *Magnyf.* 1241 Some..renneth strayght to the stuse. 1549–62 STERNHOLD & H. *Ps.* lix. 140 From place to place they renne.

γ. *1 pers. sing.* 6–7 runne (7 rune), 7– run; *2nd pers.* 6– runnest, run'st; *3rd pers.* 6 runth, 6– runneth; 6–7 runnes (6 *Sc.* runis), 6– runs. *Pl.* 6 runnes, 6–7 runne, 6– run (6 runn).

1530 PALSGR. 695/2, I runne upon one. 1535 COVERDALE *Prov.* iv. 12 When thou runnest. 1539 TAVERNER *Erasm. Prov.* (1552) 28 He runneth farre, that neuer commeth agayne. *a* 1586 SIDNEY *Astr. & Stella* Sonn. ci, [It] runs vp and downe. 1590 SHAKS. *Com. Err.* III. ii. 72 Where run'st thou so fast? 1625 GILL *Sacr. Philos.* i. 46, I runne not with that opinion. 1644 JESSOP *Angel of Ch. of Ephesus* 22 The Phrase runnes in the plurall number. 1704 STEELE *Lying Lover* v. i, This unhappy Tongue..That still run'st on.

pl. 1551 ROBINSON tr. *More's Utopia* II. (1895) 284 They runne in verye great infamy. 1579 GOSSON *Sch. Abuse* (Arb.) 21 Curst sores..run the longer without healing. *a* 1586 SIDNEY *Ps.* XVII. iv, How fleshly fancies runn. 1611 BIBLE *Gen.* xlix. 22 Whose branches runne ouer the wall.

δ. *1st pers. sing.* 6 ronne; *2nd pers.* 6 ronnes; *3rd pers.* 6 ronneth, 7 rons. *Pl.* 4, 6–7 ronne.

1399 LANGL. *Rich. Redeles* II. 5 As þey ronne ȝoure rewme þoru-oute. 1525 tr. *Jerome of Brunswick's Surg.* Bj b/2 Circles yt ronne about the iye. 1530 PALSGR. 693/2, I ronne hastely to a..place. *Ibid.*, The potte ronneth over. 1603 OWEN *Pembrokesh.* (1892) 193 That tyme of the yeare.. when all the neighbours cattle ronne together. 1667 in *Cath. Rec. Soc. Publ.* III. 73 A vertuous youth rons great hazard [etc.].

12. *Present Subjunctive.* α. 4 ronne. β. 4–6 renne. γ. *Sc.* 6 ryn, 6– rin. δ. 6 runne, 6– run.

α. *a* 1310 in Wright *Lyric P.* v. 26 Whose ryht redeth ronne to Johon.

β. *c* 1380 WYCLIF *Sel. Wks.* II. 231 God..helpe þat Goddis word renne. 1393 LANGL. *P. Pl.* C. XIV. 32 Þauh thei renne at ones. *c* 1430 *Two Cookery-bks.* 11 Let renne.. throgh, tyl it renne clere. 1470–85 MALORY *Arthur* I. xxiii. 71 It is fayrer..that we tweyne renne more to gyders. 1544 tr. *Littleton's Tenures* (1574) 21 If escuage renne by auctoritie of parliament [etc.].

γ. 1546 *Sc. Acts Parl.* (1814) II. 465 That þis present parliament Ryn still our. *a* 1585 MONTGOMERIE *Cherrie & Slae* 1528 Quhyle that this bend of craigs rin out. 1721 RAMSAY *Prosp. Plenty* 152 If ye rin on, heav'n kens [etc.].

δ. 1575 TURBERV. *Venerie* 162 If the houndes runne him. 1577 B. GOOGE *Heresbach's Husb.* III. (1586) 146 b, If the drop runne abroade. 1611 BIBLE *Levit.* xv. 3 Whether his flesh run with his issue. ? 1630 MILTON *Time* 1 Fly envious Time, till thou run out thy race.

13. *Imperative.* α. 4–6 renne, 5 ren. β. *north.* or *Sc.* rynne, 6– rin. γ. 6–7 runne, 6– run.

α. 1382 WYCLIF *Zech.* ii. 4 Renne thou, spek to this chijld. —— *1 Cor.* ix. 24 So renne ȝe, that ȝe catche. 14.. *Pol., Rel., & L. Poems* (1903) 142 Ren to scole. 1565 COOPER *Thesaurus* s.v. *Curriculo*, Renne ouer quickly to our house.

β. *c* 1450 *St. Cuthbert* (Surtees) 1813 Rynne, gude sonn, and se ȝone thing. *c* 1560 A. SCOTT *Poems* (S.T.S.) xxx. 54 Rin not reklesly to rew. 1818 SCOTT *Hrt. Midl.* vii, Rin for it,..the road's clear.

γ. 1535 COVERDALE *2 Kings* iv. 26 Runne now & mete her. 1594 MARLOWE & NASHE *Dido* III. i, Run for Aeneas, or I'll fly to him. 1615 BEDWELL *Moham. Impost.* I. §28 Run not out..into speeches. 1633 G. HERBERT *Temple, Ch. Porch* xxx, By no means runne in debt.

14. *Past Indicative.* α. 1, 3– ran, 3 *Orm.* rann, 4–7 ranne, 4, 5–6 *Sc.*, rane, 5 raane. *Pl.* 4 rannen, 5–7 ranne, 4–5, 7 rane, 4– ran.

a 1000 *Saturn* (Thorpe) 712 Satan seolua ran and on susle feoll. *c* 1200 ORMIN 1364 An bucc rann þær aweȝȝ. *c* 1250 *Gen. & Ex.* 1009 Abraham hem ran wel swiðe agon. *a* 1300 *E.E. Psalter* lviii. 4 With-outen wiknes I ran. *a* 1325 *Prose Psalter* xlix. 19 Ȝyf þou sest a þef, þou ran wyþ hym. *c* 1375 *Cursor M.* 3322 (Fairf.), Þe maydyn ranne hame. 1422 tr. *Secreta Secret.* 153 He raane to a stake. *c* 1489 SKELTON *Death Earl Northumbld.* 124 Vpon this erle thou ran. 1500–20 DUNBAR *Poems* lxxvii. 58 At thair croce aboundantlie rane wyne. 1535 LYNDESAY *Satyre* 3061, I ran to the Consistorie. 1639 FULLER *Holy War* II. xl. (1647) 97 Now it ranne dregs.

pl. *a* 1300 *Cursor M.* 15756 All on bak þai ran. 13.. *K. Alis.* 565 (W.), They rannen thorughout the contray. *c* 1420 *Anturs of Arth.* 81 Thay rane faste to the roches. 1535 COVERDALE *Jer.* xxiii. 21, I haue not sent these prophetes,.. and yet they ranne. 1582 N. LICHEFIELD tr. *Castanheda's Conq. E. Ind.* I. xviii. 46 Ye streets ran full therof. 1635 HEYLIN *Sabbath* II. (1636) 149 They..ranne upon the spurre to their recreations.

β. 3–7 ron, 4, 6 ronne. *Pl.* 4 ronnen, -on, 5 ronen; 3–6 ronne, 4–6 ron.

a 1225 *Leg. Kath.* 203–205 Euch waried weoued..ron of þat balefule blod. 13.. *R. Gloucester's Chron.* (Rolls) App. G. 1 Blod þer ron &..muche folc þer deiȝede. *a* 1340 HAMPOLE *Psalter* xxvi. 5, I ronne til my hiler. *c* 1420 *Chron. Vilod.* 3755 Towarde þat broke..he ron. 1577–82 BRETON *Floorish upon Fancies* Wks. (Grosart) I. 8/1 Out of dores I ronne. *c* 1611 CHAPMAN *Iliad* VI. 38 The horse..ron The same way other flyers fled.

pl. 1297 R. GLOUC. (Rolls) 800** Þe terus ronne doun. 13.. *K. Alis.* 1252 (W.), The stedes ronnon with slak bridel. *c* 1369 CHAUCER *Dethe Blaunche* 163 A few wellys..ronnen doun. *c* 1400 *Destr. Troy* 9209 Terys on his chekes Ronen full rifely. *c* 1450 *Merlin* xiii. 197 Thanne thei..ronne to armes thourgh the town.

γ. 4 (*2nd pers.*), 6–7 runne, 6– run. *Pl.* 3–5 runnen (5 runnun), 4 runne, 7 (9 *dial.*) run.

1382 WYCLIF *Ps.* xlix. 18 If thou seȝe a thef, thou runne with hym. 1566 *Pasquine in Traunce* 44 b, I saw euery man run & I runne for company. *c* 1592 MARLOWE *Jew of Malta* IV. v, You run swifter when you threw [etc.]. 1641 EARL MONM. tr. *Biondi's Civil Warres* II. 87 He runne so hard away. 1655 STANLEY *Hist. Philos.* (1701) 86/4 Theramenes run to the Altar. 1705 tr. *Bosman's Guinea* 316 He immediately run away. 1831 LOVER *Leg. Irel.* Ser. I. 189 She run rootin' into every corner. 1869 TENNYSON *North. Farmer, N.S.* xiv, Feythur run oop to the farm.

pl. *a* 1300 *Cursor M.* 18952 Þai runnen til þe apostel hus. *c* 1380 *Sir Ferumb.* 2438 Þan runne þai away & saide alas. *c* 1420 *Avow. Arth.* xxv, So runnun thay to-gedur. 1670 NARBOROUGH in *Acc. Sev. Late Voy.* I. (1694) 7 [They] snatch'd some of our mens Hats off, and run away.

δ. 5 renne, ren.

14.. *R. Gloucester's Chron.* 573 (MS. Digby 205), He name his douȝty ax..& toward him renne. 1491 *Cal. Rec. Dubl.* (1889) I. 373 Part thereof ren out of his cowyres.

15. *Past Participle.* α. (1 ȝerunnen,) 4 runnen, -yn, -un, 6 *Sc.* -yne; 4–7 runne, 4–5, 7 rune; 6– run (6 *Sc.* rvn, 7 runn).

[*c* 725 *Corpus Gloss.* C 862 *Concretum*, ȝerunnen. *c* 1000 *Ags. Ps.* (Thorpe) cxviii. 70 Swa meoluc..ȝerunnen.]

a 1300 *Cursor M.* 22224 Þat es bot-if discord and strijf Ouer al þis werld be runnun rijf. *c* 1375 *Sc. Leg. Saints* xviii. (*Mary Egypt*) 1314 A place, quhare a burne had runnyn. 1390 GOWER *Conf.* II. 332 He telth..hou his houndes have wel runne. 1500–20 DUNBAR *Poems* lxix. 25 Quhill that hir glas be run and past. 1514 *Aberd. Reg.* (1848) I. 88 And the said yeir be runnyne and compleit. 1588 SHAKS. *L.L.L.* v. ii. 233 Well runne dice. 1646 H. HAMMOND in Ld. Falkland *Infallibility* 116 When our Queene had runne so many dangers. 1653 HOLCROFT *Procopius, Goth. Wars* II. 53 When five and thirty dayes are runn out.

β. 4 y-ronnen, 4–5 ronnen (-yn, -on), 5 *Sc.* ronnyne, ronnyng, rownyn.

1362 LANGL. *P. Pl.* A. IX. 82 He..is Ronnen in-to Religiun. *c* 1386 CHAUCER *Knt.'s T.* 1835 So was the blood yronnen in his face. 1399 *Pol. Poems* (Rolls) I. 364 The stedes colt is ronnon away. *c* 1425 *Cursor M.* 1548 (Trin.), Þe mychel spire is ronnen aboute. *c* 1440 *Promp. Parv.* 436/2 Ronnon, as mylke (*K.P.* ronnyn as mylke..), *coagulatus*. *c* 1470 HENRY *Wallace* IX. 1779 Mony hors, at ronnyng had so lang. 1483 CAXTON *Gold. Leg.* 273/4 The voyses haue ronnen in myn eres.

γ. 4 i-, 4–5 y-ronne, 4–6 ronne (*Sc.* 5 roune, 6 rone), 6 ronn (*Sc.* roun), 5–6, 9 *dial.* ron.

13.. *K. Alis.* 896 (W.), Quyk away he is ronne. *Ibid.* 2704 Forth he is with that y-ronne. *c* 1384 CHAUCER *H. Fame* III. 1644 Whan fire is in the poudre ronne. *c* 1407 LYDG. *Reson & Sens.* 336 Ful fer y-ronne in age. 1470–85 MALORY *Arthur* IX. xx. 368 She wold haue ronne vpon the swerd. 1513 DOUGLAS *Æneis* II. viii. 61 Hir slydry body in hankis round all roun. 1562 in *Archaeologia* XLVII. 231 Wee have rone on pillgrimage. *a* 1596 *Sir T. More* III. ii. 75 It was broacht and half ronn out. 1869 A. C. GIBSON *Folk-Sp. Cumberld.* 12 I'd ron me-sel' varra nar oot o' winnd.

δ. 4–6 renne, 5 *arch.* i-ren.

c 1350 *Ipomadon* 4141 My houndes hath renne right wele. 1426 *Pol. Poems* (Rolls) II. 132 Henry the sext, of age ny fyve yere renne. 14.. *Sir Beues* 3544 For he hadde so wel igo [*M.* iren]. 1502 ARNOLDE *Chron.* (1811) 44 Yf they be attaynted be the said peyne renne and leuyd of a M marc.

ε. 5 i-ranne, 7 ranne; 6–9 ran.

1430–40 LYDG. *Bochas* I. i, The progenitours, Of all mankynd farre I-ranne in age. 1594 O. B. *Quest. Profit. Concern.* 31 She had rather her husband had ran out. 1656 EARL MONM. tr. *Boccalini's Advts. fr. Parnass.* II. lxi, Those mischiefs into which we are ran. 1669 *Cosin's Corr.* (Surtees) II. 231 Swinbourne is ranne away 5 or 6000 *li.* in the King's debt. 1729 T. COOKE *Tales*, etc. 36 He always thinks..his Race not ran. 1827 D. JOHNSON *Ind. Field*

Sports 116 He had been..ran over by a..tiger. **1874** Dasent *Half a Life* III. 258 As though she had ran a match.

16. *Weak conj.* **a.** *Past Indicative.* α. 4 **rende**, 4–5 **rennede**, 5 **rennyd**, 8 *dial.* **renn'd**. β. 3 *pl.* **runden**, 6, 9 *dial.* **runned**. γ. 9 *dial.* **rinn'd**.

c **1205** Lay. 1349 His scipen runden swiðe. *c* **1300** *K. Horn* (O.) 1319 Faste after horn he rende. **1382** Wyclif *Gen.* xxiv. 20 She..rennede aȝen to the pit. **1388** —— *Isaiah* i. 23 *marg.*, If thou suest a theef, thou rennedist with him. **1586** D. Rowland *Lazarillo* ii. (1672) M 3, The one runned to one place, the other to another. **1795** Pindar *Royal Visit* ii. ix, Now to the tavern renn'd 'Squire Rolle. **1844** W. Barnes *Poems Rur. Life* 102 Two tears rinn'd down Ant's fiace. **1859** Hughes *Scour. White Horse* vi. 140, I..runned and hollered all I knowed. **1873** Spilling *Molly Miggs*, etc. (1903) 22, I turned round and runned away.

b. *Past Participle.* 5 **renned, ronned,** 6–9 (now *dial.*) **runned**, 8 **runn'd**.

1382 Wyclif *Ps.* xviii. 6 He ful out gladide..to be runne [*v.r.* renned, ronned] the weie. **1604** Hieron *Wks.* I. 485 He had euen runned on to his owne destruction. **1634** *Malory's Arthur* (1816) II. 187 He..would have runned through sir Tristram. **1751** C. Labelye *Piers Westm. Bridge* 20 Iron Cramps, let into the Stones, and runn'd in with melted Lead. **1887** *S. Cheshire Gloss.* 322 I'm welly runned off my legs.

B. Signification.

I. Intransitive senses.

The conjugation of the perfect and pluperfect tenses with *be* instead of *have* (as *is run, was run*, etc.) is occasionally found in literary use down to the end of the 18th century.

* *Of persons and animals, in literal or fig. senses.*

1. a. To move the legs quickly (the one foot being lifted before the other is set down) so as to go at a faster pace than walking; to cover the ground, make one's way, rapidly in this manner.

Run may be construed with a large number of preps. and advs., as *about, after, against, at*, etc. Some idiomatic uses arising from such phrases are treated under III and IV, and others will be found under some other distinctive word in the phrase (as random *sb.* 3).

c **888** K. Ælfred *Boeth.* xxxvii. §2 Færð ðonne micel folc to, & yrnað ealle endemes. *c* **950** *Lindisf. Gosp.* Matt. xxviii. 8 [Hia] eodun hreconlice from byrȝenne..iornende. *c* **1000** *Ags. Ps.* (Thorpe) xviii. 6 Swa swa ȝiȝant yrnð on his weȝ. *c* **1175** *Lamb. Hom.* 3 Heo urnen on-ȝein him al þa hebreisce men. *c* **1200** *Trin. Coll. Hom.* 39 þe swin urnen alse deulen hem driuen into þe sæ. *c* **1290** *Beket* 692 in *S. Eng. Leg.* I. 126 He orn and tolde his maister fore. *c* **1330** *Arth. & Merl.* 7002 (Kölbing), Segremor hem asked, whi þai vrn & made swiche cri. **1377** Langl. *P. Pl.* B. xvii. 83, I soiourned nouȝte, but shope me to renne, And suwed þat samaritan. **1400–10** Clanvowe *Cuckoo & Night.* 217 To the broke I ran, and gat a stoon. *c* **1470** Henry *Wallace* vi. 628 Full law thai crap, quhill thai war out off sicht; Eftir the ost syne rane in all thair mycht. **1523** Skelton *Garl. Laurel* 632 Masid as a marche hare, he ran lyke a scut. **1560** Daus tr. *Sleidane's Comm.* 116 Many were drowned in the Ryver of Neccar, wher into they ran headlong. **1592** Shaks. *Ven. & Ad.* 871 As she runs, the bushes in the way Some catch her by the neck. **1613** Purchas *Pilgrimage* (1614) 184 It is unlawfull [on the Sabbath]..to Runne, Leape, or tell Tales. **1659** Pell *Impr. Sea* 300 As soon as hee saw the ship, hee ran down to the Sea side unto her. **1760** Sterne *Tr. Shandy* iv. xvi, She is run upstairs, answered Obadiah, this very instant. **1774** Goldsm. *Nat. Hist.* (1776) V. 197 The young ones run about as soon as they are out of the shell. **1833** T. Hook *Parson's Dau.* i. iii, Here, boy.., run and ask Jenkinson for the key of the coach-house. **1863** Reade *Hard Cash* I. 21 A hundred..men, ready to run..with the boats all the way. **1871** Kingsley *At Last* x, The Coolie butler's child..ran in and out with the dogs.

b. In various fig. contexts.

c **888** K. Ælfred *Boeth.* xli. §2 þa þe..æfter hiora lichoman luste irnað. *a* **1225** *Ancr. R.* 332 þe vuere ston bitocneð hope þet eorneð & stureð hire euer ine gode werkes. *a* **1300** *Cursor M.* 17251 Fra blis to blis mai þou noght rin. **1387** Trevisa *Higden* (Rolls) V. 195 þese beeþ my synnes þat renneþ after me. *a* **1400–50** *Alexander* 3383 Out of þe rake of riȝtwysnes ren suld he neuire. *c* **1460** *Towneley Myst.* vii. 25 All that will in trowth ren shall he saue. **1530** Palsgr. 696/1 He ronneth aheed as his fantasye leadeth hym. **1579** Gosson *Sch. Abuse* (Arb.) 75, I beseech them to looke to their footing, that run ouershooes in al these vanities. **1628** Gaule *Pract. The.* 19 They..that follow their owne fancie, that run on their owne head. **1681** Flavel *Meth. Grace* xxx. 517 We must not run so far from an error, as to lose a precious truth. **1737** Whiston *Josephus* (1834) 830/1 He appears to have been so affected..as to run, as it were, in a sort of a middle way. **1821** *Examiner* 42/1 We must not..run too swiftly to our conclusions. **1868** [see harness *sb.* 4 b].

c. *Sc.* Contrasted with *ride*. (Cf. go *v.* 1.)

1375 Barbour *Bruce* i. 103 That thai, that war off hey parage, Suld ryn on fute, as rebaldaill. *c* **1450** Holland *Howlat* 647 Robyn Redbrest nocht ran, Bot raid as a hensman. *a* **1700** *Gaberlunzie-Man* vii, O fy gar ride, and fy gar rin, And haste ye [etc.]. *a* **1802** *Jamie Telfer* xxviii, The Scotts they rade, the Scotts they ran.

d. Used to denote (hurried) travelling or going about, esp. to distant places.

a **1300** *K. Horn* (C.) 1146 Drink to horn of horne, Feor ihc am iorne. *c* **1380** Wyclif *Wks.* (1880) 22 Oþere prestis rennen out of oure lond ouer grete sees. **1535** Lyndesay *Satyre* 2862 For ane vnworthie Vickarage Ane Preist will rin to Rome, in Pilgramage. **1555** *Inv. Ch. Goods* (Surtees) 156 My charges in runnyng from Duresme to Yorke. **1791** Boswell *Johnson* Advt., I have sometimes been obliged to run half over London, in order to fix a date correctly. **1870** Lowell *Study Wind., Condesc. Foreigners*, I remembered people who..must run to Italy before [etc.].

e. In proverbs and proverbial phrases.

that he who runs may read is an alteration of *Habakkuk* ii. 2, 'That he may run that readeth it'.

1523 Skelton *Garl. Laurel* 1434 Nedes must he rin that the deuyll dryuith. **1539** Taverner *Erasm. Prov.* (1552) 28 He runneth farre, that neuer commeth agayne. **1562** J. Heywood *Prov. & Epigr.* (1867) 47 He runth far, that neuer turnth againe. *Ibid.* 77 Men saie he maie yll renne, that can not go. *Ibid.* 137 Holde with the hare and run with the hounde. **1672** *Essex Papers* (Camden) 6 That what euer Rules are made,..maybe soe Plainly..worded, That he that Runs may Read & understand them. **1687** T. Brown in *Dk. Buckingham's Wks.* (1705) II. 129 If you don't like me rough, as I run, fare you well, Madam. **1784** Cowper *Tiroc.* 80 But truths..Shine..With such a lustre, he that runs may read. **1821** Scott *Kenilw.* xviii, Which..extends a lesson so clear, that he who runs may read.

f. Used allusively, with reference to the legs (in contrast to the wings) of game or poultry.

1591 Florio *2nd Fruites* 57 Shall I give you some of this capon?.. Will you flie or run? **1824** Miss Ferrier *Inher.* xiv, It's the fashion now, when you help game or poultry, to ask —Pray do you run or fly?

g. *to run counter* (*to*): see counter *adv.* 1 and 3.

h. *Cricket.* To act as a runner (runner 1 f) *for* (a disabled batsman).

1855 F. Lillywhite *Guide to Cricketers* 7 No substitute shall in any case be allowed to stand out or run between wickets for another person without the consent of the opposite party. **1900** W. A. Bettesworth *Walkers of Southgate* xi. 290 Mr Rutter..was..standing behind the wicket in the usual place of a man who is running for another. **1908** W. E. W. Collins *Leaves from Old Country Cricketer's Diary* xiii. 223 Once only in more than forty years, when I was hit badly on the knee-cap, I had a man to run for me.

i. *colloq.* To suffer pressingly from diarrhoea. Cf. run *sb.*[1] 14 f.

1966 A. E. Lindop *I start Counting* vi. 92 'I said to her .."if you lie down on that wet grass you'll come down with the running trots"—' 'And did she?'.. 'She was run, run, run, *run*! All the time.' **1967** A. Wilson *No Laughing Matter* iii. 188 Suddenly she knew by sensation the meaning of that unattractive expression 'it kept me running all night'... She was indeed kept 'running all night'.

2. a. To go about freely, without being restrained or checked in any way. Freq. with *about*; also const. *with*, and with adjs. as *wild*.

c **825** *Vesp. Psalter* xlix. 18 ðif ðu ȝeseȝe ðeof, somud ðu urne mid hine. *c* **888** K. Ælfred *Boeth.* xxxvi. §6 Ða dyseȝan..irnað hidres ðidres dwoliȝende under þæm hrofe eallra ȝesceafta. **1377** Langl. *P. Pl.* B. xv. 220, I haue seyne charite..Ryden and rennen in ragged wedes. **1402** *Pol. Poems* (Rolls) II. 79, I trowe thou menys the pardonystres.. that rennen so fast aboute. **1470–85** Malory *Arthur* ix. xx. 369 This meane whyle ranne sir Tristram naked in the forest. **1535** Coverdale *1 Tim.* v. 13 They are ydell, and lerne to runne aboute from house to house. **1542** Udall *Erasm. Apoph.* 64 b, He did..cast of, and leat renne at all auentures his soonne. **1611** Cotgr., *Rodeur*, a vagabond,.. highway-beater; a rolling stone, one that does nought but runne here and there. **1722** De Foe *Plague* (1754) 265 People..run all together promiscuously, sick and well. **1782** Miss Burney *Cecilia* viii. iv, Run about and divert yourself, 'tis all you have for it. **1855** Kingsley *Westw. Ho!* xxix, She runs about all day long after Mrs. Leigh. **1875** Jowett *Plato* (ed. 2) I. 79 We are resolved..not to let them run about as they like.

b. Of animals. Also with *in*.

1377 Langl. *P. Pl.* B. xv. 453 As in wilde wildernesse, wexeth wilde bestes,..rennenge with-out croperes. **1482** *Cely Papers* (Camden) 122 Lette hym ron in a parke. *a* **1529** Skelton *E. Rummyng* 190 The hennes ron in the mashfat. **1549–62** Sternhold & H. *Ps.* l, Neat and kyne, that runne wylde in the hils. **1607** Markham *Caval.* i. 25 They let their Colts runne with their Mares, till they couer their Dammes. **1712** J. James tr. *Le Blond's Gardening* 176 Worms.. running betwixt the Bark and the Stem. **1774** Goldsm. *Nat. Hist.* (1776) II. 343 In those boundless tracts,..where he [*sc.* the horse] runs at liberty. **1838** *Encycl. Metrop.* (1845) XXV. 1421/1 Large quantities of black cattle run wild among the hills. **1856** *Jrnl. R. Agric. Soc.* XVII. ii. 485 The flock runs, through the summer, on the seeds and grass. **1890** 'R. Boldrewood' *Col. Reformer* (1891) 263 The station..where the cattle were running. **1960** G. E. Evans *Horse in Furrow* xi. 151 But the danger of undersized or ill-bred stallions 'running in' with the mares on communal.. pastures had become considerably less. **1972** *Country Life* 3 Feb. 288/3 The heifers..run with the Hereford bull to produce their first calf.

c. *to run* (*a*)*round*: to associate or consort *with* (someone, esp. of the opposite sex); to court, have an affair with; similarly with *together*. Also in general sense, to go about hurriedly with no fixed goal; to go from one place or person to another. Also *transf.* ***to run* (*a*)*round in circles***: see circle *sb.* 1 c.

1887 in *Amer. Speech* (1950) XXV. 37/1 She used to run around with Jim Reiley. **1891** J. H. Pearce *Esther Pentreath* iii. v. 194 The speaker, a big awkward slattern, had been long trying hard..to get Casy to 'run around' with her. **1920** H. Crane *Let.* 24 Sept. (1965) 42 I've been running around talking, talking, talking and waiting for the proper persons to arrive at their offices. **1925** F. Scott Fitzgerald *Great Gatsby* vi. 125, I may be old-fashioned in my ideas, but women run around too much these days to suit me. **1929** D. Runyon in *Hearst's Internat.* July 56/1 He writes about.. who is running around with who, including guys and dolls. **1940** M. Allingham *Black Plumes* iii. 19 He and Phillida ran round together quite a bit. **1940** F. & R. Lockridge *Norths meet Murder* viii. 129 You could tell me about it, and why you didn't like Brent, if it wasn't because he was running around with your wife. **1952** M. Laski *Village* xi. 161 They've been running around together for some time... She's certainly a lovely girl. **1962** [see cruddy *a.* 2]. **1969** in Halpert & Story *Christmas Mumming in Newfoundland* 213 Since people know who the uncovered janney 'runs around with' (i.e., his friends), they will have a clue to the probable identity of the others.

3. a. To hasten *to* some end or object, or *to* do something; to make haste, be active.

Sometimes with implication of the literal sense.

c **897** K. Ælfred *Gregory's Past. C.* xvi. 103 Ðæt hi mæȝen iernan & fleon to ðæs lareowes mode him to ondettunge. *c* **1200** Ormin 14115 þe waterr tacneþþ uss mannkinn þat erneþþ till hiss ende. *a* **1300** *Cursor M.* 21563 þe Iuus to þe baptim ran, Ful fain þai war þai þider wan. **13..** *K. Alis.* 849 (W.), Theo stronge knytis of the halle, Anon ronnon to heore armes alle. **1408–9** *26 Pol. Poems* 32 So fele as shulde renne hedlyng to helle. **1526** Skelton *Magnyf.* 2070 By robbynge they rynne to *in manus tuas* quecke. **1589** Nashe *Martin Marprelate* Wks. (Grosart) I. 161 Leauing the auncient game of England (Trumpe),..[they] are running to their Ruffe. **1634** Milton *Comus* 363 What need a man..run to meet what he would most avoid? **1654** Earl Monm. tr. *Bentivoglio's Wars Flanders* 89 The people..run almost from all places to assist his cause. **1702** Steele *Grief A-la-Mode* Pref., 'Tis Habitual to 'em to run to the Succour of those they see in Danger. **1852** Mrs. Stowe *Uncle Tom's C.* xi. 91 'Boys,' says I, '*run* now! dig! put! jest when ye want to!'

†**b.** To have recourse *to* a practice. *Obs.*

a **1352** Minot *Poems* viii. 6 Whilum war ȝe wight in wede To robbing rathly for to ren. *a* **1400** *Minor Poems fr. Vernon MS.* 612/24 For grete Iewes, galwes weire greiþed, þat euer to Robbyng Ronne ryf.

c. To go or resort *to* a person, etc., *esp.* for help or guidance.

a **1340** Hampole *Psalter* xxvi. 5 Bot my hert shal not drede, for i ronne til my hiler, not to þo kastels, to seke help. **1509** Fisher *7 Penit. Ps.* xxxviii. Wks. (1876) 69 Let vs therfore renne to..Marye the moder of god. **1597** Morley *Introd. Mus.* Pref., Then was I forced to runne to the workes of manie. **1603** Parsons *Let.* in *Cath. Rec. Soc. Publ.* (1906) II. 217 In such case..the English Cath. shalbe forced to runne to the K[ing] of France for assistance. **1860** Reade *Cloister & H.* lv, That day first I did seem to glimpse why folk in trouble run to drink so. **1864** Lowell *Study Wind., Gt. Public Char.*, Even Mommsen himself..cannot get or give a lively notion of ancient Rome, without running to the comic poets.

4. a. To retire or retreat rapidly; to take to flight; to abscond or desert. Also const. *from* a place, person, etc. Also ***to run out on*** (someone), to abandon, desert.

c **1205** Lay. 29298 Bruttes for-burnen; Bruttes gunnen irnen. *c* **1450** *Myrr. our Ladye* 31 They shall not knowe whither to fle ne ren from them. **1567** *Gude & Godlie Ball.* (S.T.S.) 174 O fulis, quhairfoir tak ȝe flycht, Rinnand fra Christ? **1673** *Hatton Corr.* (Camden) 111 The souldiers in very considerable numbers dayly run from their colours. **1758** J. Blake *Mar. Syst.* 20 The time and place when, and where he entered, died, run, or was discharged. **1781** Jefferson *Corr.* Wks. 1859 I. 306 They broke twice and run like sheep. **1845** *Narr. U.S. Explor. Exped.* I. Introd. 38 Robert Boyle, Seaman, Joined in the United States; run at Sydney. **1848** Thackeray *Van. Fair* xxxii, He did not care to face Mrs. O'Dowd and Amelia, and own to them that he was about to run. **1893** *Chamb. Jrnl.* 1 July 414/1 He..had been forced to cut and run. **1920** H. C. Witwer in *Collier's* 15 May 57/1 Kin you imagine him runnin' out on me too? **1934** Ade *Let.* 8 Mar. (1973) 180, I received no invitation or notification and neither did John Golden and so we must not be accused of running out on our little pop-eyed friend. **1942** T. Rattigan *Flare Path* i. 25 You *were* a fool to run out on me, weren't you? **1951** M. McLuhan *Mech. Bride* (1967) 60/2 Some of the fellows were sneering that her husband was running out on her. **1962** H. Hood in R. Weaver *Canad. Short Stories* 2nd Ser. (1968) 210 I'm not running out on you. **1973** 'D. Halliday' *Dolly & Starry Bird* xv. 221, I decided I was going back to Rome... Johnson, on whom I was running out, listened to me with patience.

b. So *to run for it*.

1642 W. Mountagu in *Buccleuch MSS.* (Hist. MSS. Comm.) I. 306 My Lord of Stamford..made them run for it, and took their arms away. **1692** Hickeringill *Good Old Cause* Wks. 1716 II. 537 We hear the good News, that the Idolaters are run for it, the Syrians before Joab. **1725** De Foe *Voy. round World* (1840) 119 Once or twice they were ready to lay down all their loads, and run for it. **1855** Kingsley *Westw. Ho!* xviii, He fairly clapped his hands to his ears and ran for it. **1883** Stevenson *Treas. Isl.* xxx, We'll run for it like antelopes.

†**c.** To deviate or diverge *from* a standard.

1765 *Treat. Dom. Pigeons* 57 Rejecting those that ran from the feather, and judiciously matching the good coloured ones together.

d. To draw back *from* a pledge, etc.

1824 *Examiner* 57/2 Mr. D...ran from his wager. **1858** *Jrnl. R. Agric. Soc.* XIX. i. 124 The contracting party may be inclined to run from his word.

e. In weakened sense, to leave, depart (freq. with an implication of haste). Also with *along, away*. ***run along*** (***with you***)***!*** imp., used esp. to children or inferiors (cf. *get along!* s.v. along *adv.* 2).

1816 Jane Austen *Emma* II. i. 18 'I am afraid we must be running away,' said Emma..beginning to rise... 'I, had no intention..of staying more than five minutes.' **1890** O. Wilde *Pict. Dorian Gray* i, in *Lippincott's Monthly Mag.* July 7 You are not going to run away so soon, Mr. Hallward? **1902** B. Potter *Tale of Peter Rabbit* 15 Now run along, and don't get into mischief. **1927** A. A. Milne *Now We are Six* 57 But every one says, 'Run along!' (Run along, run along!) All of them say 'Run along! I'm busy as can be.' **1933** M. Lowry *Ultramarine* ii. 62 Oh well, I'll have to put up with you. Run away and play. **1934** E. Bowen *Cat Jumps* 242 'Yes, run along with you,' she said. 'And don't be so silly again.' **1935** N. Mitchison *We have been Warned* ii. 202, I must run or the garden party will miss me. **1952** E. O'Neill *Moon for Misbegotten* i. 56 So run along now and play with your horse, and don't bother me. **1962** I. Murdoch *Unofficial Rose* vi. 62 Douglas Swann rose again, accepting his dismissal. 'No thank you, Ann, I must run.' **1965** G. McInnes *Road to Gundagai* xii. 211 Tell your Mother we're going to the flicks and I'll be back about eleven. Better run along now. **1975** A. Bergman *Hollywood & Levine* xi. 164 'Helen, we'll be running, said Wohl... There was a final chorus of good-byes.

5. a. To rush *at*, *on*, or *upon* a person with hostile intention; to make an attack *on*. Also *fig.*

a **1300** *Cursor M.* 15786 Þai him vmsett on ilk side,.. Wit maces and wit neues smert vnrekenli on him þai ran. **1470–85** MALORY *Arthur* IX. xli. 407 The knyght was..in wille sodenly to haue ronne vpon syr Tristram with a swerd. *a* **1533** LD. BERNERS *Huon* xxxviii. 123 All the sarasins at ones ran vpon Huon, & tooke hym. *Ibid.* lix. 205 Huon ranne at hym.., & strake him with his spere. **1602** MARSTON *Antonio's Rev.* V. v, They run all at Piero with their Rapiers. **1662** J. DAVIES tr. *Mandelslo's Trav.* 95 He run upon him and cut off his head. **1781** D. WILLIAMS tr. *Voltaire* II. 301 He pierced the furious boar who was running at him. **1835** I. TAYLOR *Spir. Despot.* I. 17 The..popery that was furiously run upon by the sceptics of the last age. **1889** DOYLE *Micah Clarke* xxiii. 232 He ran at me and kicked me.

†**b.** To move rapidly *through* or *over* a country with hostile intent. (Cf. OVERRUN *v.* 4.) *Obs.*

1338 R. BRUNNE *Chron.* (1810) 1 Þorgh out Chestreschire werre gan thei dryue. Had þei no styntyng, bot þorgh alle þei ran. **1648** HEXHAM II, *Rotteynen*, to Roade, or Run through a Countrie. **1693** *Mem. Ct. Teckely* I. 42 Having gain'd the Fort, they could safely run over all the Peninsula that lies between the Mure and the Drave.

†**6. a.** To ride on horseback at a quick pace; *spec.* to ride in a tournament, to tilt or joust. *Obs.*

1297 R. GLOUC. (Rolls) 11078 In a foul plodde..me him slong, & orne on him mid hor hors. **1535** COVERDALE *2 Macc.* v. 2 Then were there sene..horsmen runninge to and fro in the ayre. *a* **1548** HALL *Chron., Hen. VIII*, 6 The kyng ranne neuer openly before, and there were broken many staues. **1596** SHAKS. *1 Hen. IV*, II. iv. 377 The sprightly..Dowglas, that runnes a Horse-backe vp a Hill perpendicular. **1652** COTTERELL tr. *Calprenède's Cassandra* I. 3 There appeared ten or twelve fresh well mounted Knights, running towards them at full speed.

b. In tilting, to charge with a lance or spear *at* a mark or object.

Now usually in phrase *to run (full) tilt at* or *against*: see TILT *sb.*, and cf. A-TILT *adv.*

c **1530** [see QUINTAIN *a*]. **1550** *Rutland MSS.* IV. 359 (Hist. MSS. Comm.), For a spere wyche he lent to runne at the glove with, and was broken, iij s. **1632** LITHGOW *Trav.* IV. 156 To run at the Gloue in a open place before all the people. **1686** [see RING *sb.*[1] 4].

7. a. To compete, or take part, in a race (*for* a prize). Occas. with compl. denoting final position in the race. Also in fig. context. ***to run to*** (also ***true to, up to***) ***form***: of a horse, to perform in a race consistently with its previous record; freq. *transf.* and *fig.*

c **1205** LAY. 24696 Summe heo gunnen urnen, summe heo gunnen lepen,..summe heo wræstleden. *c* **1290** *S. Eng. Leg.* I. 48/52 His Men pleiden and Arnden bi þe weie. **1382** WYCLIF *Gal.* ii. 2 Lest perauenture I schulde renne in veyn, or hadde runne. **1545** ASCHAM *Toxoph.* I. (Arb.) 103 Yf the game be onse wonne, no man wyl set forth hys foote to ronne. **1565** COOPER *Thesaurus*, *Celes*, a horse runnyng for a price or game. **1653** BINNING *Serm.* (1845) 156 Think it strange that thou runnest so slowly, when so great a prize is to be obtained. **1713** *Lond. Gaz.* No. 5151/4 A Plate of 40*l.* Value was to be run for. **1725** *Fam. Dict.* s.v. *Horse-racing*, We will only here suppose a Horse set to run for a Plate. *a* **1837** [APPERLEY] *Turf* (1851) 127 He runs in front, it is true, for he can run to win. **1863** *Sat. Rev.* 8 Aug. 189 Before running this week for the Brighton Stakes, he was led..with a chain attached to his bit. **1886** *St. Stephen's Rev.* 13 Mar. 11/2 Ironclad ran a good horse considering that he was evidently very short of work. **1891** *Sat. Rev.* 26 Sept. 358/2 Gossoon..had run second to her for the Champagne Stakes. **1891** G. CHETWYND *Racing Reminisc.* I. 85 The result of the Prince of Wales' Stakes was interesting, as it afforded a striking proof of the way in which horses sometimes consistently run up to their form.

transf. and *fig.* **1881** MRS. LYNN LINTON *My Love* III. xii. 214 She tried it on with Val, who hated her... But Val said that didn't run! **1934** WEBSTER, *Run true to form, or type*, to operate as might be expected by its inherent nature. **1960** *Bedside 'Guardian'* IX. 178 This [canvassing] ran true to form until one young woman reddened and said: 'I don't think you should accost mothers on a playground.' **1970** G. F. NEWMAN *Sir, You Bastard* viii. 253 It was simply Paul running to form, never arriving anywhere on time. **1973** D. LESSING *Summer before Dark* 227 I'd be running true to form wouldn't I? A few years in the wide world and then back to the home paddock.

b. To compete, stand as a candidate, *for* a position, seat, etc. Also, to stand as a candidate for office *on* a specific issue or policy. Orig. and chiefly *U.S.*

1826 *Virginia Herald* (Fredericksburg) 22 Nov. 3/1 Mr. Pitcher is elected Lt. Governor, by a large majority over Mr. Huntington, who ran on the same ticket with Mr. Clinton. **1851** J. A. QUITMAN in J. F. H. Claiborne *Life & Corr. J. A. Quitman* (1860) II. xvi. 147 A majority of the people have declared against the course of policy..upon which alone I had consented to run as a candidate. **1859** *Knickerbocker* Oct. 372 We have never had the misfortune to run (or 'be run', as the phrase is) for Congress. **1861** *Temple Bar* II. 353 [He] might..stand a chance of running for Congress. **1870** *Standard* 12 Nov., If he naturalised himself in the United States and ran for President. **1912** M. NICHOLSON *Hoosier Chron.* 54 I'd go into their counties and spend every cent I've got fighting 'em if they ever ran for office again. **1929** W. FAULKNER *Sartoris* II. 67, I know what I'll do: I'll run for Congress. **1950** *Manch. Guardian Weekly* 24 Aug. 15 Mr. Dewey has sworn not to run again for the Governorship. **1964** GOULD & KOLB *Dict. Social Sci.* 484/2 The Democratic candidate..ran instead on the issue, among others, that the Eighteenth Amendment should be repealed. **1967** G. F. FIENNES *I tried to run Railway* iii. 16 There's a job going as Assistant District Superintendent at Burntisland. Do you want to run for it? **1968** *Globe & Mail* (Toronto) 3 Feb. 3/8 Mr. Woodcock, who says he is running on a youth ticket, joins two other fringe candidates. **1978** *Detroit Free Press* 5 Mar. A 14/1 President Carter says he does not know whether he will run for re-election in 1980 or whether he will win if he does.

c. ***to run for luck***, to take one's chance. *U.S.*

1841 LONGF. in *Life* (1891) I. 391, I have to run for luck as to horses, which is not so agreeable.

d. *U.S.* To tout *for* a boarding-house, etc.

1891 C. ROBERTS *Adrift America* 228, I went with him to the house he was running for.

e. ***to run scared***: in *U.S.* political terminology, to compete for office in a manner indicating or suggesting a fear of losing, esp. to avoid over-confidence. Also in generalized and weakened senses, to be frightened, to panic. Usu. as *pres. pple.*

1960 *Newsweek* 19 Sept. 39/1 Confident as he is of winning, Nixon intends to run hard and scared until the very last minute. **1964** G. MCDONALD (*title*) Running scared. **1968** W. SAFIRE *New Lang. Politics* 389/2 The phrase is directed..to the candidate who is in the position of Thomas E. Dewey in 1948, considered a 'shoo-in'... Hindsighted politicians now say Dewey should have 'run scared'—conducted a more aggressive, fighting campaign. **1969** P. F. SIMON *The Boxer* (song) 3 In the quiet rail-way sta-tion run-ning scared. **1976** *Times* 1 Mar. 7/4 President Ford..has been running scared against Reagan for many months. **1976** J. PHILIPS *Backlash* III. i. 116 He's big, but running very scared. **1978** *Time* 1 May 24/2 'People are running scared,' says..a Boston drug-abuse expert. 'A situation exists which borders on hysteria,' agrees the deputy director of the Illinois dangerous-drugs commission. **1978** *Washington Post* 12 June C2/1 Members of Congress who are already running scared (this is an election year).

8. *transf.* Of fish: **a.** To swim rapidly.

c **1520** L. ANDREW *Noble Lyfe* in *Babees Book* (1868) 236 Percus is of diuers colours, & swift in ronnynge in the water. **1688** HOLME *Armoury* III. 104/1 When Fish run away with the Bait in his Mouth. **1726** *Gentleman Angler* 155 *To Run*, this is properly applied to a Jack or Pike in Trowling, who, when he has seized the Bait, runs to his Harbour to pouch it; after which he runs again. **1820** SCORESBY *Acc. Arc. Reg.* I. 465 Whales..blow strongest, densest, and loudest, when 'running'. **1867** FRANCIS *Angling* IV. (1880) 103 The pike made a splendid fight, often running to weed. **1891** *Field* 19 Dec. 948/1 This salmon showed no desire to run up stream.

b. *spec.* To pass to or from the sea; to migrate.

1743 M. CATESBY *Nat. Hist. Carolina* II. p. xxxiii, Herrings in March leave the salt waters, and run up the rivers. **1806** LEWIS & CLARK *Orig. Jrnls. Lewis & Clark Exped.* (1905) IV. 95 These women informed us that the small fish began to run which we suppose to be herring from their description. **1884** G. B. GOODE *Fisheries U.S.: Nat. Hist. Aquatic Animals* 376 [Kingfish] occasionally run to a considerable distance up the rivers. **1887** *Fortn. Rev.* Mar. 406 Immense numbers of salmon 'run' early in the year. **1892** *Longman's Mag.* Nov. 88 The season when the eels are 'running'.

*** Of inanimate things in rapid motion.*

9. a. Of things, esp. the heavenly bodies: To move rapidly through space.

c **825** *Vesp. Psalter* xviii. 6 [The sun] ȝefeah swe swe ȝiȝent to earnenne on weȝ. *a* **1000** *Genesis* 138 Him arn on last þrang þystre ȝenip. *c* **1000** *Saxon Leechdoms* III. 234 Æfre heo [the sun] byð yrnende ymbe ðas eorðan. *a* **1300** *Cursor M.* 22695 Þe cludes to þe se sal rin For to hid þam þarin. *a* **1425** *Ibid.* 23590 (Trin.), Sonne, mone, watir, & stern, þat now renneþ in cours ȝern. **1513** BRADSHAW *St. Werburge* II. 118 Sterres..Rennynge in the ayre dredfull to beholde. **1530** RASTELL *Bk. Purgat.* III. ix. 1 Where the sonne and the other sterres renne in theyr speres. **1692** DRYDEN *Eleonora* 150 Though 'tis a train of stars that, rolling on, Rise in their turn and in the Zodiac run. **1732** POPE *Ess. Man* II. 21 Instruct the planets in what orbs to run. **1754** GRAY *Progr. Poesy* 118 Oft before his infant eyes would run Such forms as glitter in the Muse's ray. **1864** TENNYSON *Voyage* iv, Far ran the naked moon across The houseless ocean's heaving field.

b. Of vehicles, etc.: To move easily or rapidly by reason of being set on wheels. Also *fig.* ***to run off the rails***: see RAIL *sb.*[2] 4 a, b.

1375 BARBOUR *Bruce* XVII. 609 Ane cren thai haf gert dres vp hey Rynand on quhelis. **1562** J. HEYWOOD *Prov. & Epigr.* (1867) 64 The world runth on wheeles. **1611** BIBLE *Nahum* ii. 4 The charets shall rage in the streets,..they shall seeme like torches, they shall runne like the lightnings. **1675** HOBBES *Odyssey* (1677) 213 Sit quietly And eat..; your tongue so runs on wheels. *a* **1774** GOLDSM. *Surv. Exp. Philos.* (1776) I. 267 A machine..that run upon wheels. **1843** *Penny Cycl.* XXVII. 551/2 A moveable carriage.. running on lower side-rails. **1863** W. C. BALDWIN *Afr. Hunting* ix. 432 The wagon runs heavily.

10. a. Of a vessel (or those on board): To sail swiftly or easily. Also in fig. context. Also of a torpedo: to pass through the water.

Used with many advs. and preps., as *adrift*, *at large*, *free*, *in*, *out*, etc.; *before* (the wind), *down* (a coast), *into* (a haven), *up* (an inlet), etc. *to cut and run* (see CUT *v.* 41).

a **1000** *Ags. Proverbs* 186 (Gr.), Seldan in sidum ceole, nefne he under seȝle yrne, weriȝ scealc wiþ winde roweþ. *a* **1122** *O.E. Chron.* (Laud MS.) an. 1046, Hi..tuȝon þa up heora seȝel, & urnon west to Axamuðan. *c* **1205** LAY. 11981 Þa scipen þa urnen bi-uoren. **1382** WYCLIF *Acts* xxvii. 16 We rennynge into sum yle..vnnethe myȝte gete a litil boot. **1390** GOWER *Conf.* I. 160 The Schip which on the wawes renneth. *c* **1450** *Myrr. our Ladye* 307 Hauen of the see, to whyche the gylty renne with truste. *c* **1595** CAPT. WYATT *R. Dudley's Voy. W. Ind.* (Hakl. Soc.) 6 The next day,.. runninge to make the lande, wee founde it to be the Groyne. **1639** S. DU VERGER tr. *Camus' Admir. Events* Pref., As in a full sea, I hoyse up sayles, and run at large. **1687** A. LOVELL tr. *Thevenot's Trav.* I. 12 The Currents of the Gulf of Venice made us run a head a pace. **1722** DE FOE *Col. Jack* xi, We were obliged to run away afore the wind as the seamen call it. **1745** P. THOMAS *Jrnl. Anson's Voy.* 121 We kept running along-shore, with an easy Sail. **1827** ROBERTS *Voy. Centr. Amer.* 34 We..got under weigh and ran down the inner passage. **1856** *Leisure Hour* V. 334/2 With a fair wind we ran past the Bird rocks. **1885** *Law Rep. 10 App. Cases* 411 On that day she deviated from the course of the voyage and ran for Mauritius. **1914** F. T. JANE *Navy as Fighting Machine* xiii. 100 The 'balance chamber'. This regulates the depth at which the torpedo will run. **1942** *R.A.F. Jrnl.* 16 May 21 They dived and dropped their torpedoes, all of which ran satisfactorily.

b. To sail or be driven *on* or *upon* the shore, rocks, etc.; to come *aground* or *ashore*. Also *fig.* Also in phr. ***to run into the sand(s)***, to peter out; to come to nothing.

c **1205** LAY. 11710 Þa scipen urnen a ðen lond. **1540–1** ELYOT *Image Gov.* (1549) 118 They be..by contrarie wyndes constreigned to renne on quicke sandes or rockes. **1579** GOSSON *Sch. Abuse* (Arb.) 24 Least I chaunce to.. runne a grounde in those Coasts. **1600** HAKLUYT *Voy.* (1810) III. 436 The ship..returned to the coast, where it ran on ground. **1656** EARL MONM. tr. *Boccalini's Advts. fr. Parnass.* I. xxix. (1674) 33 My inordinate desire..which hath made me run upon the Rock which you see. **1731** *Gentl. Mag.* I. 32/2 The *Samuel*..ran ashore on the Coast of New England. **1856** *Leisure Hour* V. 349/1 A West Indiaman had run on the rocks. **1877** MISS YONGE *Cameos* Ser. III. xv. 133 They had no escape but to run aground. **1931** E. WILSON *Axel's Castle* iv. 112 We may put it down to an academic assumption that English drama ended when the blank verse of the Elizabethans ran into the sands. **1956** A. L. ROWSE *Early Churchills* xvii. 378 A naturally clever woman with genuine interests of the mind that ran into the sand.

c. ***run foul of***, †***on***, to collide or become entangled with (another vessel, etc.); to foul. Also *fig.*

1698 FRYER *Acc. E. India & P.* 13 As long as we spooned before the Sea, and kept from running foul of one the other. **1748** *Anson's Voy.* I. i. 15 Two of the transports,..in tacking, ran foul of each other. **1767** J. BYRON *Voy. r. World* 177 We were alarmed by the ship's running foul of a whale. **1820** W. SCORESBY *Acc. Arctic Reg.* II. 477 The *John*, running foul of a piece of ice. **1867** SMYTH *Sailor's Wordbk.* 319 'A ship ran foul of us,' that is, entangled herself among our rigging.

transf. and *fig.* **1686** GOAD *Celest. Bodies* I. xvi. 101 Yet at no hand do we run foul..on uncertainties. **1786** tr. *Beckford's Vathek* (1868) 103 Plunging, kicking, and running foul of each other in the most ludicrous manner. **1830** MISS MITFORD *Village* Ser. IV. (1863) 215 The Frenchman can't drive..; he'd as nearly as possible run foul of my pigs. **1918** *Dialect Notes* V. 21 *Run foul of*, to meet. **1932** *Times Lit. Suppl.* 27 Oct. 792/4 He ran foul of the most powerful gang in New York and the police at the same time. **1971** *New Scientist* 27 May 533/1 Tamplin originally ran foul of the AEC when he was asked to demolish Ernest Sternglass's case.

d. ***run aboard, on board*** (***of***): (see ABOARD *prep.* and BOARD *sb.* 12 c).

1725 HEARNE *R. Brunne's Chron.* Gloss. s.v. *Berd*, Readily ran aboard him. **1796** NELSON 16 Apr. in Nicolas *Disp.* (1845) II. 154 Royal Sovereign put back much damaged; a Transport run on board her. **1829** MARRYAT *F. Mildmay* iii, A large..frigate ran on board of us.

11. a. To take a (hurried) journey for the purpose of making a short stay at or visit to a place. Chiefly with *down*, *over*, *up*.

1798 PITT in G. Rose *Diaries* (1860) I. 216, I have a scheme of running down..to Somersetshire. **1831** LADY GRANVILLE *Lett.* (1894) II. 115, I wish you could have run over for a week. **1841** CDL. WISEMAN in Purcell *Life & Lett. A. P. de Lisle* (1900) I. xi. 255 But I forsee that it will be necessary for me during the vacation to run to Rome. **1860** TROLLOPE *Framley P.* xxxviii, No poor lad that ever ran up from Oxford for a spree in town got so lectured. **1861** J. A. SYMONDS *Let.* 30 Apr. (1967) I. 287 This is just the time that I sd like to be at home... If I can, I shall run down for a day this Term. *Ibid.* 28 Oct. 314 Do you not think you cd persuade Papa to run up with me one night this week to see it? **1866** G. MEREDITH *Let.* 14 Jan. (1970) I. 356 A..letter disarranged the plan, which would have left me free of conscience to run down to you. **1866** TROLLOPE *Belton Estate* xxxii, in *Fortn. Rev.* 1 Jan. 429 I'll..just run over once or twice in the year. It would not be a nice place for you to live at long. **1871** J. BLACKWOOD *Let.* 31 Dec. in *Geo. Eliot Lett.* (1956) 230 Hamley only ran up for an afternoon and could not get to the Priory. **1885** C. M. YONGE *Two Sides of Shield* I. x. 168 He says he would run over to see me if it were not for the dragons. **1898** G. B. SHAW *Let.* 18 Oct. (1972) II. 68 Our visitors here are..Strandring and Pease, who run down occasionally, or at least intend to do so. **1902** E. NESBIT *Five Children & It* ix. 237 I'll run up to town and have some lunch at club. **1921** G. B. SHAW *Back to Methuselah* III. 136 Why not run over and join me for the afternoon? **1972** D. SUTTON in *Lett. R. Fry* I. 53 During the 1910s Fry had formed the habit of running over to Paris.

b. Of a conveyance, vessel, etc.: To ply between (two) places. Also const. †*it*. Also of a company, to schedule journeys *over* a given route. Now freq. with qualifying advb., as ***to run late***, (of a transport service) to be behind schedule; also *transf.* of persons.

a **1817** JANE AUSTEN *Northanger Abbey* (1818) I. vii. 84 How long do you think we have been running it from Tetbury, Miss Morland? **1825** *New Monthly Mag.* XV. 20 Steam-boats will run from Toulouse..in 32 hours. **1830** FR. IGNATIUS in Purcell *Life & Lett. A. P. de Lisle* (1900) I. iv. 82, I cannot just now tell how the coaches run between Northampton and Loughborough. **1869** *Bradshaw's Railway Man.* XXI. 177 The company authorized to run over the Mid-Kent, the West End of London and Crystal Palace,..and the West London Extension. **1886** PASCOE *Lond. of To-day* xliii. (ed. 3) 378 Steamboats run between London Bridge and Chelsea on week-days every ten minutes. **1954** L. MACNEICE *Autumn Sequel* 161, I today, equally undefended, Not knowing if we are running fast or late, Walk through this empty train. **1956** N. MARSH *Off with his Head* (1957) vi. 113, I got called out on an urgent case and found myself running late. **1973** *Daily Tel.* 3 Feb. 14 Any attempt to discover by telephone whether an incoming flight is running late is futile. **1977** N. MARSH *Last*

Ditch vi. 176 Alleyn looked at his watch. 'I'm running shamefully late,' he said.

c. To slide or travel on a sleigh or toboggan or on skis.

1887 [see COAST *v.* 13]. **1898** *Encycl. Sport* II. 472/1 Now, as each competitor is obliged to run three times, .. and as the course varies, not only day by day, but hour by hour, .. a great deal of judgment is required on the part of the rider. **1935** *Encycl. Sports* 562/2 The attitudes of skiers in running vary from an almost upright one to a very low crouch. *Ibid.* 563/1 Having acquired confidence, the ability to go fairly fast, and to run straight over moderate slopes without falling, the novice can now tackle the turns. **1956** *Ski-ing* ('Know the Game' Ser.) 13/2 The fastest method of ski-ing down a slope is naturally by running straight (*schussing*).

12. a. To spread, pass, or move quickly from point to point. Usu. const. with preps.

c **825** *Vesp. Psalter* cxlvii. 15 [= 4] Se utsendeð ȝesprec his eorðan; hreðlice eorneð word his. *a* **1300** *Cursor M.* 22224 Bot-if discord and strijf Ouer al þis werld be runnun rijf. *a* **1325** *Prose Psalter* cxlvii. 4 Þe which sendeþ his worde to þe erþe; hys worde erneþ swiftlich. *c* **1384** CHAUCER *H. Fame* III. 1644 As swift as pelet.. Whan fire is in the poudre ronne. *Ibid.* 1651 A smoke gan out wende; .. the ferther that hit ran, The gretter wexen hit began. **1451** CAPGRAVE *Life St. Aug.* xxxi. 41 This ensaumple ran oute þorw þe lond of Affrik, þat þo prestes.. had leue to preche. **1590** SPENSER *F.Q.* I. vi. 37 That cruell word her tender hart so thrild, That suddein cold did runne through euery vaine. **1655** CULPEPPER, etc. *Riverius* I. xi. 38 We say that the understanding doth run from one thing to another. **1748** *Anson's Voy.* III. x. 404 [The fire] was running along a wooden cornish, which would soon communicate it to a great distance. **1789** *Ann. Reg., Hist.* 6 The new doctrine ran like wild-fire through the nation. **1843** R. J. GRAVES *Syst. Clin. Med.* xxx. 416 Numbness.. followed by tingling pains running along the course of the nerves. **1855** M. ARNOLD *Balder Dead* iii. 183 Squalls Ran black o'er the sea's face. **1893** SIR R. BALL *Story of Sun* 302 The temperature of Chicago has been known to run through a range of 80 degrees in twenty-four hours.

b. Of sounds: To spread or pass rapidly (*along, down, through* a place, company, etc.); to be caught up or repeated in quick succession.

c **1384** CHAUCER *H. Fame* III. 1683 As lowde as any thunder That euery wight hath of hit wonder So brode hyt ran. **1629** MILTON *Hymn Nativ.* xix, No voice or hideous humm Runs through the arched roof in words deceiving. **1697** DRYDEN *Virg. Georg.* I. 491 Soft Whispers run along the leafy Woods. *a* **1744** POPE (J.), And a low murmur runs along the field. **1856** STANLEY *Sinai & Pal.* i. (1858) 103 There was a shout which ran down the long file of horsemen. **1868** MISS YONGE *Pupils of St. John* xvi, A whisper ran through the congregation. **1888** MRS NOTLEY *Power of Hand* I. vi. 67 A general assent ran from lip to lip.

c. Of statements, reports, etc.: To spread abroad rapidly; to pass quickly from mouth to mouth; to be or become widely current.

13.. *Gaw. & Gr. Knt.* 310 'Is þis Arþures hous,' quod þe haþel.., 'þat al þe rous rennes of, þurȝ ryalmes so mony?' *c* **1450** *Merlin* xv. 236 The tidinges ran so thourgh the contrey that the kynge aguysanx it herde. **1490** CAXTON *Eneydos* xxxviii. 127 Duryinge that these wordes ranne, Eneas and his people wroughte stylle to make vp theyr fortresse. *a* **1540** BARNES *Wks.* (1573) 330 There runneth a greate voyce of mee, that I haue maried a wife. **1605** SHAKS. *Macb.* IV. iii. 182 There ran a Rumour Of many worthy Fellowes, that were out. *c* **1676** *12th Rep. Hist. MSS. Comm.* App. V. 33 The niewse runs as if the Dolphin should marry the Ellector of Bavaria's daughter. **1722** DE FOE *Plague* (1754) 261 This Notion run like Lightening thro' the City. **1779** HAMILTON *Wks.* (1886) VII. 578 In haste I snatch up my pen.. to give you the news as it runs. **1853** M. ARNOLD *Scholar Gipsy* xiv, Two hundred years are flown Since first thy story ran through Oxford halls. **1858** CARLYLE *Fredk. Gt.* XVIII. vii. (1872) V. 224 There run reports that make me shudder.

d. Of plants: To creep or climb.

1565 COOPER *Thesaurus, Salicastrum*, a kynde of wylde vyne runnyng vpon willow trees. **1568** TURNER *Herbal* III. 2 The herbe groweth about ditches.. and rinneth after the maner of a vyne alonge. **1611** BIBLE *Gen.* xlix. 22 A fruitfull bough by a well, whose branches runne ouer the wall. **1725** *Fam. Dict.* s.v. *July*, Vines.. that run high, and bear chiefly out of the Knots of the old Wood. **1838** *Penny Cycl.* XII. 96/1 There is a kind [of ivy] which never runs or creeps upon other plants.

13. a. Of thoughts: To come suddenly *into* (or †*in*), to course or pass *through*, the mind.

1303 R. BRUNNE *Handl. Synne* 8536 Hyt ran hym weyl yn þoȝt þat þe abbot had inspyracyun. **1426** LYDG. *De Guil. Pilgr.* 10308 In my mynde a-noon yt ran, To calle memoyre vn-to me. **1542** UDALL *Erasm. Apoph.* 297 Par aventure this ranne in Phocions hedde, yᵗ menne ought not to.. put assured truste.. in luckie chaunces. **1662** J. DAVIES tr. *Olearius' Voy. Ambass.* 181 Upon the first sight thereof, it run into our imagination, that they were the Cosaques. **1862** TYNDALL *Mountaineer.* vi. 47 The extravagant analogies which then ran through my brain.

b. *Mus.* To sing quickly. Also with *down*.

1613 W. BROWNE *Brit. Past.* I. v, When she should run, she rests; rests, when should run. **1812** *Examiner* 14 Sept. 590/1 She ran down her notes with.. correctness.

c. Of the eye: To glance, look quickly. Also of persons, to give a rapid glance (*with* the eye).

1611 BIBLE *2 Chron.* xvi. 9 The eyes of the Lord run to and fro throughout the whole earth. **1669** STURMY *Mariner's Mag.* II. vi. 66 Run with your Eye along the Parallel Lines. **1878** *Scribner's Mag.* XV. 800/2 She ran down the first page of her letter. **1890** CLARK RUSSELL *Ocean Trag.* II. 248 His eye swiftly ran from line to line.

d. To go *back* in retrospect.

1702 ROWE *Tamerl.* Ded., I hardly have patience to run back to his having saved his own Country. **1702** STEELE *Funeral* IV. (1723) 53 How many Thousand things does my Head run back to? **1889** PHILIPS & WILLS *Fatal Phryne* II. 49 She ran back over the pages of her memory.

14. a. Of a weapon, etc.: To pass easily and quickly *through* something, *to* a certain point, etc.

13.. *Cursor M.* 16838 (Gött.), A spere.. Thoru his side vnrekenli apon his herte it rane. *c* **1330** *Arth. & Merl.* 3459 (Kölbing), A dint he ȝaf him so hard, Þe launce ran þe brini þurch. ? *a* **1400** *Morte Arth.* 2793 The rosselde spere to his herte rynnes. *c* **1460** *Towneley Myst.* iii. 277 Thise nayles so thay ryn Thoro.. Thise bordis ichon. *a* **1533** LD. BERNERS *Huon* viii. 21 [He] strake hym.. with such force that the spere ran throw parte of hys body. **1561** *Burning S. Paul's* in Arber *Garner* VIII. 111 They saw a long and spear-pointed flame of fire, as it were, run through the top of.. Paul's Steeple. **1601** SHAKS. *Jul. C.* III. ii. 178 Looke, in this place ran Cassius Dagger through.

b. *fig.* Of qualities, impressions, etc.

13.. *E.E. Allit. P.* A. 26 Þer such rychez to rot is runnen. *c* **1386** CHAUCER *Clerk's T.* 158 No likerous lust was thurgh hire herte yronne. —— *Merch. T.* 742 Lo pitee renneth soone in gentil herte. *a* **1631** DONNE *Poems* (1650) 91 Straight her beauty to my sense shall runne.

15. a. To slide, slip, or move easily or freely. Freq. with preps. or advs., as *in, off, on, through*.

13.. *Gaw. & Gr. Knt.* 857 Rudelez rennande on ropez. **1391** CHAUCER *Astrol.* I. §2 This ring rennyth in a Maner turet, fast to the Moder of thyn Astrelabie. **1481** CAXTON *Reynard* xxxiii. (Arb.) 96 Where the two bokettys henge by one corde rennyng thurgh one polley. **1552** HULOET s.v. *Knot*, Knotte whiche runneth to, called a rydynge knotte, *capulum*. **1608** WILLET *Hexapla Exod.* 605 To shoot the boords together.. that one might runne within another. **1687** A. LOVELL tr. *Thevenot's Trav.* I. 170 A Basket which they let down by a Rope that runs in a Pully. **1748** *Anson's Voy.* III. x. 415 The sails are made of matt..; they run upon the mast with hoops. **1834-6** *Encycl. Metrop.* (1845) VIII. 666/1 These variations will be more frequent.. when the ball runs very loose in the piece. **1858** CARLYLE *Fredk. Gt.* VIII. iv. (1872) III. 23 Actual neck-halter, but it seems to have been tarry, and did not run. **1875** KNIGHT *Dict. Mech.* 1819/1 Having no cheeks, the line may get out of its groove and cease to *run*.

fig. **1589** PUTTENHAM *Eng. Poesie* (Arb.) 262 Such composition makes the meetre runne away smoother. **1594, 1627** [see GLIB *adv.* 1]. *a* **1639** WOTTON *Reliquiæ* (1651) 9 Runing.. as smoothly as a numerous verse. **1712** ADDISON *Spect.* No. 405 ⁋3 The Hebrew Idioms run into the English Tongue with a particular Grace and Beauty. **1754** COWPER *Ep. to R. Lloyd* 67 That Matthew's numbers run with ease Each man of common-sense agrees. **1879** 'ANNIE THOMAS' *London Season* II. 79 [The verses] 'go' easily enough, .. but that sort of thing runs off by the yard. **1889** MRS. ALEXANDER *Crooked Path* II. x. 280 Life ran smoothly in its ordinary grooves.

b. Of the tongue: To wag freely.

a **1553** UDALL *Royster D.* I. iii, Though your teeth be gone, .. Yet your tongue can renne on patins as well as mine. **1593** SHAKS. *Rich. II*, II. i. 122 This tongue that runs so roundly in thy head. **1676** HOBBES *Iliad* II. 223 Else 'gainst the king thy tongue would not so run. *a* **1770** JORTIN *Serm.* (1771) II. xi. 217 Vanity sets the tongue running faster then is decent. **1849** JAMES *Woodman* viii, 'How your little tongue runs,' said her cousin. **1860** [see NINETEEN 2b]. **1891** MEREDITH *One of our Conquerors* II. ix. 225 Her father let his tongue run.

c. Of plants: To shoot up or grow quickly, so as to produce their seed. Cf. 81 a.

1725 *Fam. Dict.* s.v. *July*, For if the first [cauliflowers] run, they will not be quite unfit for Use. **1812** SIR J. SINCLAIR *Syst. Husb. Scot.* I. Add. 17 As soon as the turnips or ruta baga begin to run or shoot in spring. **1894** *Times* 23 April 12/2 Too large a proportion of the plants show a tendency to 'run'.

d. Of bark: To peel off easily from a tree.

1731 D. EATON *Let.* 2 May (1971) 135 We shall view the saplins at Oakly Wood on Wednesday and have the sale day on Saturday, bycause the bark runns very well. **1784** G. WHITE *Selborne* ix, These trees.. were winter-cut.. before the bark would run. **1805** R. W. DICKSON *Pract. Agric.* II. 1096 Where the wood is to be barked, .. the beginning of May may be the most proper, as it will then generally run the best.

e. To unravel, come undone.

1878 A. BARLOW *Weaving* 360 Lace made without this traversing motion would, in case a thread was broken, 'run' or become undone.

f. To slip, diverge, go awry.

1846 HOLTZAPFFEL *Turning* II. 549 The single chamfered drill.. is also more disposed of the two, to swerve or run from its intended position. **1885** FARROW *Mil. Encycl.* III. 524 A common drill may run, as it is usually termed, and produce a hole which is anything but straight.

16. a. Of a ball, etc.: To roll forward on a surface. Said also of dice when thrown.

c **1386** CHAUCER *Man of Law's T.* Prol. 27 Youre bagges been nat fild with ambes as But with sys cynk, that renneth for youre chaunce. **1412-20** LYDG. *Troy Bk.* II. 838 Ȝif on haue Ioye, anoþer suffereþ wo, Liche as þe bonys renne to and fro. **1509** BARCLAY *Shyp of Folys* (1874) I. 295 The dyse oft renneth upon the chaunce of thre. *a* **1548** HALL *Chron., Hen. V*, 56b, When Kyng Henry perceiued that the dice ranne not to his purpose, he abstained from the assault. **1588** SHAKS. *L.L.L.* v. ii. 233 Nay then two treyes..; well runne dice! **1611** MIDDLETON & DEKKER *Roaring Girl* III. ii, His bowls run with a wrong bias. *a* **1680** BUTLER *Characters* (1908) 199 He uses all manner of conjurations, to make his bowl rub or run. **1824** SCOTT *St. Ronan's* xxvi, I will fancy the dice have run wrong. **1850** *Bohn's Handbk. Games* (1867) 564 He who blows upon a ball when running makes the stroke foul. **1875** *Encycl. Brit.* III. 675/2 When the player's ball runs into a pocket without striking a ball.

fig. **1693** DRYDEN *Pref. Ovid's Met.*, Andromache.. runs off her bias, to tell him a story of her pedigree.

b. *transf.* Of a player at billiards: To make the ball roll. Cf. *run-through* in 82.

1875 *Encycl. Brit.* III. 676/1 When balls touch, the player may either run into a pocket, or play on to a third ball. **1885** *Billiards Simplified* (1889) 122 The proper way to play the stroke is to run through the red.

17. a. To revolve or turn round on or as on an axis.

a **1300** *Cursor M.* 1548 Quen sa fele yeier ar wroken oute, Þe mikel spere es rune aboute. *c* **1425** AUDELAY *XI Pains of Hell* 49 in *O.E. Misc.* 212 Þer is a brenyng wel, A þosand tymys an our about doþ ren. *c* **1500** *World & Child* 93 A newe game haue I founde! Se this gynne, it renneth rounde. **1535** LYNDESAY *Satyre* 824 Me think the warld rinnis round about. **1658** tr. *Porta's Nat. Magic* VII. xxxii. 206 There is made a rundle, with a Latin-navel upon a point, .. that it may run round freely. **1771** *Encycl. Brit.* III. 935/2 The balance-wheel G, whose pivot runs in the pieces A. **1825** J. NICHOLSON *Operat. Mechanic* 509 In which case the wheel will have liberty to run. **1851-4** TOMLINSON *Cycl. Arts* (1867) I. 485/1 Hollow centres for the spindle to run in.

b. Of machinery or mechanical devices: To go; to continue operating. Also with compl.

1562 J. HEYWOOD *Prov. & Epigr.* (1867) 112 It might ren .. and strike er the time. **1625** N. CARPENTER *Geogr. Del.* I. xi. (1635) 242 You must get you a watch or clocke, apt to runne (if you can) 24 houres. **1737** BRACKEN *Farriery Impr.* (1756) I. 184 A Stop-watch which runs Seconds. **1872** RAYMOND *Statist. Mines & Mining* 332 A 15-stamp water-power mill, which was running last summer. **1879** *Paper & Printing Trades Jrnl.* XXVI. 25 One of these little engines recently ran forty-seven days and nights without stoppage. **1912** *Motor Man.* (ed. 14) vi. 174 When a car is running badly the owner very often comes to the conclusion, [etc.]. **1939** G. B. SHAW *Geneva* III. 110 It's no use going on making motor cars that you know will never run. **1952** *Chambers's Jrnl.* Apr. 208/1 With the port outer-diesel running the exciter and the other diesels cut to no load. **1959** E. K. WENLOCK *Kitchin's Road Transport Law* (ed. 12) 112/1 The petrol tank must not be filled.. while the engine is running.

c. *transf.* Of a business, household, etc.: to function or operate.

1927 E. O'NEILL *Marco Millions* II. iii. 141 Sound common sense and a home where everything runs smooth. **1939** J. B. PRIESTLEY *Let People Sing* xiv. 416 I've got this place. It's doin' well, makin' money. But I don't want it all the time, an' now it's running easily it doesn't need me all the time. **1969** J. BARZUN (*title*) The American university: how it runs, where it is going. **1974** N. FREELING *Dressing of Diamond* 84 Meals were always on time... The 'house' ran like silk.

d. Of a cinematographic film, recording tape, etc.: to pass between spools, to (continue to) be in motion; to be shown or played.

1931 *Discovery* Dec. 386/1 The speed at which the film was running, ninety feet per minute, made it necessary that statements should be brief. **1969** 'A. GILBERT' *Missing from her Home* vi. 84 I'd been to see a film in the afternoon, and it ran longer than I expected. **1972** *Listener* 21 Dec. 852/1 Production Assistant: 'Quiet. Going for a take. Standing by.' Director: 'Right.' Sound: 'Sound running.' Director: 'Turn over.' **1973** V. CANNING *Finger of Saturn* i. 8 The film began to run... I just watched. **1976** *Oxf. Compan. Film* 743/1 The first part, running about $3\frac{1}{4}$ hours, was released as *The Wedding March*.

18. a. Of thoughts, etc.: To revolve *in* the mind, to occur or return persistently to the memory.

1601 B. JONSON *Poetaster* II. i, These courtiers runne in my minde still. **1670** G. H. tr. *Hist. Cardinals* I. III. 74 A point that was alwayes running in my head. **1719** DE FOE *Crusoe* I. (Globe) 102 This Thought run long in my Head. **1810** SCOTT *Let.* in *Lockhart* II. ix. 326, I have not the least doubt that several of the passages must have been running in my head. **1899** *Allbutt's Syst. Med.* VIII. 288 The annoyance of having a tune, a line of poetry, or a phrase 'running in the head'.

b. To form, be present as, an impression or indistinct recollection.

1798 in Dallas *Amer. Law Rep.* II. 356 Another says, 'it runs in his head that he also saw the prisoner there'. **1854** MISS BAKER *Northampt. Gloss.* s.v. *To run in one's head*, It runs in my head that I've heard something about it.

******* *Of liquids, sand, etc.* (*or vessels containing these*).

19. a. Of milk, etc.: To coagulate, curdle, form a curd. Now *dial.*

[*c* **725** *Corpus Gloss.* C 862 *Concretum*, ȝerunnen. *c* **825** *Vesp. Ps.* cxviii. 70 Ðerunnen is swe swe milc heorte heara. *c* **1000** *Saxon Leechd.* II. 230 Swa lange seoð on cetele & wylle oþ þæt hio sie eal tosoden & þicge ȝeurnen.] **1398** TREVISA *Barth. De P.R.* v. lxiii. (MS. Bodl.), Talowȝ renneþ anon whanne hit is take oute of þe bodye and isette in cold ayer. *c* **1420** *Liber Cocorum* (1862) 15 Take thykke mylke of almondes clere, .. Do hit soþenne in a canvas þenne, In soþun gar hit on hepe to renne. **1674** RAY *N.C. Wds.* 16 To *Earn*, to run as cheese doth. **1737** BRACKEN *Farriery Impr.* (1757) II. 177 It will run into Lumps and curdle like Yolks of Eggs. **1808** JAMIESON s.v. *Yyrne*, Milk is still said to *rin* .. when it breaks and forms into knots, in making of pottage, puddings, &c. **1861** *Jrnl. R. Agric. Soc.* XXII. I. 49 The temperature at which the milk is 'set', or 'run', as it is called in Gloucestershire. **1888** *Sheffield Gloss.* s.v., This pudding's all run; it's all gone to whey and cruds.

b. To unite, combine (*into one*), esp. in a moist or melted state.

a **1715** BURNET *Own Time* III. (1724) I. 373 The Church party and the Dissenters were now run into one. **1848** *Jrnl. R. Agric. Soc.* IX. I. 558 It is the nature of these soils.. to run like lime with the first little shower. **1850** *Ibid.* XI. I. 146 Its liability to run and cake together after heavy rains. **1868** HERSCHEL in *People's Mag.* 63 By this the wax on both runs into one.

20. a. Of liquids: To flow.

Freq. with advs. or preps., as *down, in, into*, etc.

c **825** *Vesp. Ps.* lvii. 8 To nowihte [hie] bicumað swe swe weter eornende. *c* **893** K. ÆLFRED *Oros.* I. i. 8 Seo [ea] is irnende of norþdæle. *a* **1000** *Boeth. Metr.* v. 15 Swa oft æspringe ut awealleð of clife harum.. & ȝereclice.. floweð, irneð wið his eardes [etc.]. *a* **1122** *O.E. Chron.* (Laud MS.) an. 963, Swa swa þæt wæter reonneð to Crulande. *c* **1205** LAY. 5075 Vrnen [h]ire teares ouer hires leores. *Ibid.* 23973 þat blod orn a-dun ouer al his breoste. **1297** R. GLOUC. (Rolls) 11228 Hii caste awei þe dosils, þat win orn abrod so. **1387** TREVISA *Higden* (Rolls) V. 207 A candlestikke i-made ..so þat þe oyle schulde renne in to þe crislere. *c* **1400** tr. *Secreta Secret., Gov. Lordsh.* 70 Þanne..þe blood for gladnesse rynnys yn þe veynys. **1523** FITZHERB. *Husb.* §54 All maner of grasse, that the lande-floudde renneth ouer, is verye ylle for shepe. **1582** N. LICHEFIELD tr. *Castanheda's Disc. E. Ind.* xvii. 40 b, Part of the water..did runne downe uppon theyr breasts. **1610** HOLLAND *Camden's Brit.* (1637) 258 The rivers that runne into the Ocean. **1639** T. DE GRAY *Compleat Horseman & Ferrier* 90 It begetteth a fluxible humour, which..falleth to running. **1720** DE FOE *Capt. Singleton* xi. (1840) 197 The flesh began to heal, and matter to run. **1779** *Mirror* No. 37, The brook which runs through my garden retires into a hollow dell. **1833** TENNYSON *Lady of Shalott* i. 12 Little breezes dusk and shiver Thro' the wave that runs for ever. **1862** *Temple Bar* VI. 402 He thrashed his naked back, until the blood ran. **1897** *Allbutt's Syst. Med.* IV. 518 The pulp is sometimes so diffluent as to run away.

b. *fig.* (See also BLOOD *sb.* 10 c.)

13.. *E.E. Allit. P.* A. 874 A hue fro heuen I herde þoo, Lyk flodez fele laden, runnen on resse. **1565** COOPER *Thesaurus* s.v. *Fluens*, A style runnyng copiously. **1583** STUBBES *Anat. Abus.* II. (1882) 52 As long as moneye runneth, they will applye gentle and easie potions. **1628** EARLE *Microcosm.* xxiv. (Arb.) 45 His Verses run like the Tap. **1647** N. BACON *Disc. Govt. Eng.* I. xvi. (1739) 30 It seemeth to run in the blood of an Englishman..to be as brave under a single Queen, as under the most valiant King. *a* **1770** JORTIN *Serm.* (1771) III. i. 7 When the thoughts have been long used to run in another course. **1868** J. H. NEWMAN *Verses Var. Occas.* 145 Who lets his feelings run In soft luxurious flow. **1881** GARDINER & MULLINGER *Study Eng. Hist.* I. iii. 49 Thought still ran in very definite channels.

c. With various complements. Also in *fig.* phr. ***to run hot***: of persons, to become angry (cf. HOT *a.* 6 b).

c **1205** LAY. 30411 Urnen þa brockes of reden blodes. *c* **1400** MAUNDEV. (Roxb.) xxx. 137 Ane of þir wellez ran of wyne, anoþer of mylke. *c* **1430** *Two Cookery-bks.* 26 Lat it renne þorw þe cloþe so ofte tylle it renne clere. **1513** DOUGLAS *Æneis* VII. Prol. 19 Reveris ran reid on spait with watteir broune. **1623** MASSINGER *Dk. Milan* v. ii, I'll make her veins run high too, As if they had true motion. **1726** LEONI *Alberti's Archit.* II. 102 b, It is not all Waters..that are good..; some running partly clear, and partly foul. **1727** GAY *Begg. Op.* I. x, The blood runs cold at my heart with the very thought of it. **1818** KEATS *Endymion* II. 544 Who Look full upon it feel anon the blue Of his fair eyes run liquid through their souls. **1893** LIDDON *Life Pusey* I. xiii. 299 Time had allowed the lecturer's thoughts to run clear, or at least comparatively clear. **1924** A. D. SEDGWICK *Little French Girl* I. iv. 31 We have our baths in the morning, and the water doesn't run very hot then. **1941** *Sun* (Baltimore) 29 July 10/7, I seen him reading across the table and called him down. He run hot and so I told him to git his money. *Ibid.*, He was so pleased with the phrase 'run hot' that he regarded himself as the gainer on balance. **1976** K. BENTON *Single Monstrous Act* v. 166 The Detective Chief Superintendent's waiting for us, and beginning to run hot, too. He's got a lot on his mind.

†**d.** To come or descend *of* (some one). *Obs.*$^{-1}$

c **1330** R. BRUNNE *Chron. Wace* (Rolls) 420 Erector cam of kynge Dardan, Dardanus of Iubiter ran.

†**e.** Of a flood: To subside, go down. *Obs.*$^{-1}$

c **1430** *Freemasonry* (ed. Halliw.) 537 Mony ȝeres after.. That Noees flod wes alle y-ronne, The tower of Babylowne was begonne.

21. a. Of the sea, tides, etc.: To course or flow, esp. in an impetuous manner. Also with compl., esp. ***to run high*** (see HIGH *adv.* 9) or ***mountain(s) high*** (see MOUNTAIN 1 f).

c **1205** LAY. 11977 Vðen þer urnen, tunes swulche þer burnen [*c* **1275** Waȝes þar arne, streme þar vrne]. *c* **1375** *Cursor M.* 6269 (Fairf.), þe king..sagh þe see ranne in twyn. **1458** in *Archaeol.* XXIX. 327 Wawes boþe wild and wode, That rynnethe on euery syde. **1694** *Martens' Voy. Spitzbergen* in *Acc. Several Late Voy.* II. 32 Here the Waves of the Sea run longer. **1694** MOTTEUX *Rabelais* IV. xxi. (1737) 92 What a devilish Sea there runs? **1793** SMEATON *Edystone L.* §259 The tides ran so remarkably short at this time, that our buss did not float at high water. *c* **1804** P. GASS *Jrnl.* (1807) v. 61 The ice began to run in the river. **1814** SCOTT *Diary* 28 Aug., The surf running heavy up between the island and the adjacent rock. **1865** GOSSE *Land & Sea* (1874) 5 A pretty heavy sea running outside. **1867** A. D. RICHARDSON *Beyond Mississippi* xi. 145 Reaching the Missouri again, I found the ice running so heavily, that it was impossible to cross. **1884** E. P. ROE *Nat. Ser. Story* vi, Don't go out again when the ice is running.

b. *fig.* With complements, as *cross*, *strong*. (See also HIGH *adv.* 9.)

1636 SANDERSON *Serm.* (1681) II. 50 Nor did his Will run cross to his Judgment but was led by it. **1657–61** HEYLIN *Hist. Ref.* II. i. 53 It..seemeth also to run cross to the holy Scriptures. **1785** CRABBE *Newspaper* 3 Unheard we sing, when party-rage runs strong. **1887** STEVENSON *Merry Men* III. 131 Evil and good run strong in me.

22. a. To flow as the result of melting; to melt and flow. Also *fig.*

c **1425** WYNTOUN *Cron.* IV. xxi. 1896 All the metall moltynnyd than In tyll a qwerne togydder ran. **1670** DRYDEN *Conq. Granada* IV. i, 'Twas long before my stubborn Mind was won; But, melting once, I on the sudden run. **1677** MOXON *Mech. Exerc.* I. 10 When your two ends are through-out of a good Heat, and that the inside of the Iron be almost ready to run. **1729** SWIFT *Direct. Serv., Footman*, You ought also to snuff them close to the Tallow, which will make them run. **1758** REID tr. *Macquer's Chym.* I. 62 If Sulphur be applied to Copper made perfectly red-hot, the metal immediately runs. **1852** *Jrnl. R. Agric. Soc.* XIII. II. 284 It forms a varnish..not liable to run in hot seasons. **1884** C. G. W. LOCK *Workshop Rec.* Ser. III. 206/2 The enamel melts; or, to speak technically, it 'runs'.

b. To spread on being applied to, or poured upon, a surface. †Also with *abroad*.

1612 BRINSLEY *Lud. Lit.* iv. 29 The like care must be, that their inke..wil not run abroad, nor blot. **1633** BP. HALL *Hard Texts, N.T.* 40 Thou art runne abroad like water that is spilt. **1725** *Fam. Dict.* s.v. *Pears*, You may know..by the drops of Syrup you shall put on a Plate, if they do not run. **1764** ELIZ. MOXON *Eng. Housew.* (ed. 9) 88 This is a paste that seldom runs if it be even roll'd. **1899** *Allbutt's Syst. Med.* VIII. 937 Outlying spots..may be observed where the fluid has 'run' during its application.

c. Of colours: To spread in a fabric when immersed in water or exposed to moisture.

1771 MRS. HAYWOOD *New Present for Maid* 268 When the colours, with bad former washings, are run into the white ground. **1782** LADY LLANOVER in *Mrs. Delany's Life & Corr.* (1861) III. 97 Pieces of paper in which the colours had run and produced extraordinary and unusual tints. **1867** LOWELL *Lett.* I. 427 Beg her not to wash them too hard, or they may run. **1889** MRS. LYNN LINTON *Thro' the Long Night* I. xvii, Here and there, when the colours were not quite fast, there were blotches as if the thread had 'run' and stained the cloth.

23. a. Of the sands of an hour-glass: To pass from one compartment into the other. Chiefly *fig.*

1557 *Tottel's Misc.* (Arb.) 138, I saw, my tyme how it did runne, as sand out of the glasse. **1608** SHAKS. *Per.* v. ii. 1 Now our sands are almost run. *a* **1796** BURNS *Red, Red Rose* iii, While the sands o' life shall run. **1821** SCOTT *Pirate* xl, The hour-glass is turned for us,..our sand is running fast. **1891** F. W. ROBINSON *Her Love & His Life* VII. v, The sands of life had run very low in the glass.

b. Of loose earth: To slip or fall in.

1799 W. NICOL *Pract. Planter* 164 The mold adheres not to the spade, nor does it run in. **1802** MAWE *Min.* Gloss. s.v., When the earth falls, and fills up shafts or works, it is said to *run*. **1860** *Eng. & For. Min. Gloss.* (ed. 2) 21 *Run*—When excavations fall together.

24. To flow, stream, be wet, *with* (†*a*, *o*, *on*, *of*) a liquid. Also with adjs., as ***run red***.

c **1205** LAY. 26703 Vrnen þa streten, mid blode stræmen. *c* **1290** *St. Edmund* 382 in *S. Eng. Leg.* I. 442 Þat al þe stret a-watere orn, ase it were a gret flod. *c* **1330** *Arth. & Merl.* 9018 (Kölbing), Mouþe & nose him ran a blod. *a* **1400** *Prymer* (1891) 38 His bodi ran al on blode. *a* **1533** LD. BERNERS *Huon* lix. 206 Þe place ran lyke a ryuer of blode. **1611** BIBLE *Lam.* i. 16 Mine eye runneth downe with water. **1664** H. MORE *Myst. Iniq.* 425 Those fat and fair Objects that make their mouths run a-water so. **1728** CHAMBERS *Cycl.* s.v. *Foundering*, [The horse] has a dry Cough..; his Nose runs with white phlegmatic Matter. **1797** *Encycl. Brit.* (ed. 3) III. 74/2 The body of the patient, which is running with sweat. **1834** T. MEDWIN *Angler in Wales* I. 77 The mud walls ran down with damp. **1884** MRS. F. E. PIRKIS *J. Wynne* II. xviii. 225 Her veins run with water, not blood. **1889** RANDOLPH *New Eve* I. iii. 107 The glass of the great conservatory is running with dew.

25. a. To discharge (or carry off) a liquid. Also in fig. context.

c **1205** LAY. 12774 Him gunnen glide teores, & urnen his æȝene. *c* **1340** HAMPOLE *Pr. Consc.* 781 His haire moutes, his eghen rynnes. *c* **1386** CHAUCER *Reeve's T.* Prol. 36 Syn that my tappe of lif bigan to renne. *c* **1450** *Trevelyan Papers* (Camden) 67 The Coundite rennyth not as I wene. **1530** PALSGR. 696/1, I lyke hym nat, his eyes be ever ronning. **1579** GOSSON *Sch. Abuse* (Arb.) 70 Launce the sore frendly and let it runne. **1602** MARSTON *Antonio's Rev.* III. iv, I have taken a murre, which makes my nose run most patheticallie. **1662** R. MATHEW *Unl. Alch.* 94 One of her leggs grew as big as three leggs, and did also break and run. **1683–4** WOOD *Life* 24 Jan., Very cold, the quil would not run. **1710** *Lond. Gaz.* No. 4777/4 The other a black Mare..., runs at the near Nostril. **1737** BRACKEN *Farriery Impr.* (1757) II. 262 [It] causes the Nose to run like a Tap. *a* **1744** LUCAS in *Trans. Cumb. & West. Archaeol. Soc.* VIII. 38 When the Furnace is fit to run..they make a long Furrow through..a level Bed of Sand. **1845** *Jrnl. R. Agric. Soc.* VI. II. 573 The drains.. were running very fast yesterday morning, and have continued running ever since. **1854** *Ibid.* XV. II. 267 Some land has been thus drained more than twenty years ago, and still runs well. *c* **1865** MRS. GASKELL *Let.* 6 Oct. (1966) 777 Still the scullery tap *did not run*; & until it does that smell will go on.

b. Of a vessel: To overflow; to leak.

Usually with *out* or *over*: see 77 b (*b*) and 78 a.

c **1230** *Hali Meid.* 39 þe croh eorneð i þe fur, & te cheorl chideð. **1390** GOWER *Conf.* I. 20 A Tonne, whanne his lye arist, Tobrekth and renneth al aboute. **1613** PURCHAS *Pilgrimage* (1614) 502 [He] carries it to the river..to see if it would hold water, and finding it to runne, came backe. **1834–6** *Encycl. Metrop.* (1845) VIII. 816/1 The risk of the still boiling over, or *running foul*, as the distillers term it. **1875** KNIGHT *Dict. Mech.* 1464/1 *Run*; said of a mold if the metal insinuates itself along the parting or otherwise leaks out.

c. Of an hour-glass: To allow the sand to pass from one compartment to the other. Freq. *fig.*

1500–20 DUNBAR *Poems* lxix. 25 And lat Fortoun wirke furthe hir rage,..Quhill that hir glas be run and past. **1596** SHAKS. *Merch. V.* I. i. 25, I should not see the sandie houre-glasse runne, But I should thinke of shallows, and of flats. **1650** BAXTER *Saints' R.* IV. v. (1654) 131 Look on thy glass, see how it runs. **1756** C. LUCAS *Ess. Waters* I. 196 They are rendered..decrepid and old before half their glass is run. **1779** [see SAND-GLASS]. **1874** MICKLETHWAITE *Mod. Par. Ch.* 179 The sand-glass..has only one fixed time to run.

d. Of a bath: to be in the process of being filled with water.

1936 J. BUCHAN *Island of Sheep* vi. 117 He's back now, for I heard his bath running. **1946** J. B. PRIESTLEY *Bright Day* x. 298 She popped her head round the door..to tell me that a bath was running for me. **1973** 'P. REID' *Harris in Wonderland* xiv. 103 Mayer woke me at nine with a mug of tea. He was fully dressed. 'The bath's running for you,' he said. **1977** 'A. YORK' *Tallant for Trouble* xii. 184 I've a bath running.

**** *Of time, money, practices, or other things having course, continuance, or extension.*

26. a. Of a period of time: To come to an end, be complete, expire. Only in pa. pple.

a **1000** *Phœnix* 364 Oþ þæt wintra bið þusend urnen. *a* **1300** *Cursor M.* 10927 Fiue thusand yeir was runnun Efter þis werld it was bigunnen. *c* **1375** *Sc. Leg. Saints* x. (*Matthew*) 497 Of his elde quhene rownyn war be reknyne fyfe & thretty ȝere. *c* **1400** *Sc. Trojan War* I. 150 Sene he has this debate bygonnyne, Per awenture, or it all be ronnyne, Als gret defoule may fall hyme till. **1486** *Rec. St. Mary at Hill* (1905) 7 After that the said xv daies be past & ronne. **1539** in *Vicary's Anat.* (1888) App. II. 105 The somme of vli, for ij quarters fully ronne at the natiuitie of saint Iohn Baptiste. **1610** WILLET *Daniel* 283 From Daniels time vntill now there are not aboue 2200 yeares runne. **1722** DE FOE *Col. Jack* (1840) 320 The night was almost run. **1884** *Law Rep.* 27 *Chanc. Div.* 530 Delay is no bar to our enforcing it, as the Statute of Limitations has not run.

transf. **1546** J. HEYWOOD *Prov. & Epigr.* (1867) 37 A bed were we er the clocke had nine runne.

†**b.** Of persons: To become advanced *in* years.

c **1400** *Rom. Rose* 4495 A rympled vekke, fer ronne in age, Frownyng and yelowe in hir visage. **1430–40** LYDG. *Bochas* I. i, The progenitours, Of all mankynd farre I-ranne in age. **1533** BELLENDEN *Livy* II. ix. (S.T.S.) I. 161 Howbeit he was waik, and fer rvn in ȝeris. *c* **1550** H. LLOYD *Treas. Health* G ij. Youre grace beyng nowe sumwhat runne in yeares.

27. a. Of time: To pass or go by; to elapse; also, to be passing or current.

c **1200** ORMIN 11251 All þiss middell ærdess ald Eorneþþ aȝȝ forþ wiþþ ȝeress. *a* **1300** *Cursor M.* 11178 Þe tide þat bringes al to fine, Ran wit þis to monet nine. **1423** JAS. I *Kingis Q.* clxxi, Thy tyme, Ane houre and more It rynnis ouer prime. **1447** BOKENHAM *Seyntys* viii. 1318 Long tyme aftyr, whan þe yere of grace On seuen hundryd ran & fourty & nyne. **1559** W. CUNNINGHAM *Cosmogr. Glasse* 40 Because the tyme doth so faste ronne, and I have also other matters to intreate on. **1581** MULCASTER *Positions* xxxvii. (1887) 148 The time to preuent it, is almost runne to farre. **1604** E. G[RIMSTONE] *D'Acosta's Hist. Indies* VI. ii. 435 Noting by those figures the yeare that did runne. **1634** FORD *Perk. Warbeck* III. i, How runs the time of day? Past ten, my lord. **1726** AYLIFFE *Parergon* 154 The Time of Instance shall not commence or run until after Contestation of Suit.

b. To continue, go on, last; to remain existent or operative.

a **1300** *Cursor M.* 24897 For to halu þis ilk fest dai,..In hali kirc rinnand bi yer. **1384** CHAUCER *L.G.W.* 1943 *Ariadne*, This wekede custome is so longe I-ronne. *c* **1460** FORTESCUE *Of Abs. & Lim. Mon.* xiv. (1885) 143 In the arrerages off such livelod..wich shall renne aftir þat resumpcion. **1558** WARDE tr. *Alexis' Secr.* 24 b, If..the disease bee olde or hath runne longe, giue the pacient..this glister. **1573** *Reg. Privy Council Scot.* II. 226 And swa hes ordanit the said Parliament to ryn and be continewit quhill the last day of August. **1677** YARRANTON *Eng. Improv.* 20 Their way of Dealing I knew, and what Security they took, which was impossible should run long. **1843** *Jrnl. R. Agric. Soc.* IV. II. 299 Leases run in general for nineteen years. **1850** *Tait's Mag.* XVII. 4/1 Must his exclusion run only during the currency of other parts of his sentence? **1893** *Strand Mag.* VI. 217/1 Her contract..had two years more to run.

c. Of a play: To keep the stage or be played continuously (for a specified time). Also of a cinematographic film: (to continue) to be shown to the public.

1808 MRS. INCHBALD *Brit. Theatre* 4 Having, on its first appearance, run, in the theatrical term, near thirty nights. **1828** *Examiner* 85/2 The piece..will run the season. **1890** *Sat. Rev.* 22 Nov. 574/2 The play now running at the Lyceum. **1923** H. CRANE *Let.* 5 Oct. (1965) 149 Charlie [Chaplin]..is here in New York at present to see that the first film he has produced in it gets over profitably... It's running now for just a week or so more at the 'Lyric' theatre. **1940** G. MARX *Let.* 5 Sept. (1967) 25 He also hates Noel Coward and even refuses to see his playlets, which are now running at El Capitan. **1976** *Oxf. Compan. Film* 646/1 Rodgers and Hammerstein's stage musical, which opened in New York in 1959 and ran for four years.

28. a. Of money: To have currency; to be in circulation; to go, pass current.

a **1300** *Cursor M.* 14038 Þis riche man lent to þat tan An hundreth penis, suilk als ran. *c* **1400** MAUNDEV. (1839) xxii. 239 Whan that Money hathe ronne so longe, that it begynnethe to waste. **1444** *Rolls of Parlt.* V. 109 That Half penyes and Ferthinges renne..in paiement in grete sommes amonge the peple. **1626** SIR R. COTTON in *Posthuma* (1651) 297 The said Royall of Eight runnes in account of Trade at 5.s. of..English money. **1662** in J. SIMON *Ess. Irish Coins* (1749) 130 All sorts of small silver moneys of the denominations of or running for groates..or under. **1888** *N. & Q.* 7th Ser. VI. 338 Are not these the Spanish 'pillar dollars'; and did they not run current in England as crown pieces?

b. Of a writ, proclamation, etc.: To issue; to have legal course or effect; to operate.

c **1400** *Apol. Loll.* 7 Þat..silk indulgencis rennun not forþ aȝen þe ordinaunce of God. **1436** *Rolls of Parlt.* IV. 497/2 Countrees where the Kynges Writt renneth noght. **1610** HOLLAND *Camden's Brit.* (1637) 589 That Writs out of the Kings Courts, should in certain cases have no place nor runne among them. **1689** T. R. *View Govt. Europe* 51 The Process and Decrees of the Court ran in the Emperor's name. **1768** BLACKSTONE *Comm.* III. 78 In all these..the king's ordinary writs..do not run; that is, they are of no force. **1852** LEVER *Daltons* xiii, Not knowing that they were in another land where the King's writ never ran. **1890** LANE-POOLE *Barbary Corsairs* I. viii. 86 It may be doubted whether the Sultan's writ would have run in either of his new provinces.

c. Of payments, practices, etc.: To be current or generally prevalent.

1429 *Rolls of Parlt.* IV. 252/1 At alle tymes when poundage hath ronne. *c* **1460** *Reg. Oseney Abbey* 126 Whenne scutage renneth generally thorowgh all Inglonde.

1599 SANDYS *Europæ Spec.* (1632) 138 Their Annates and tenths doe stille runne current. **1605** VERSTEGAN *Dec. Intell.* viii. (1628) 241 Some Names deriued from the Hebrew.. doe now run generally in common vse among al. **1656** in Picton *L'pool Munic. Rec.* (1883) I. 214 Parliam^t hath setled upon the Minist^r of this place all the tythes running within the Liberties. **1892** *Sat. Rev.* 17 Sept. 340/1 A standard authority in every country where the English language runs.

29. a. To have course or continuance, to go on, to go, proceed, etc., in various fig. uses.

a **1225** *Ancr. R.* 42 Alle þeos vreisuns eorneð bi ðeos fiue [letters]. *c* **1374** CHAUCER *Troylus* II. 1754 Ryght now renneth my sort Fully to dye or han a-noon comfort. *c* **1380** WYCLIF *Sel. Wks.* II. 231 God bringe doun þis fendis pryde, and helpe þat Goddis word renne. *c* **1400** *Rom. Rose* 6282 If god nyl done it socour, But lat renne in this colour. **1460** CAPGRAVE *Chron.* (Rolls) 2 Whan the tyme of Crist is come, than renne to noumberes togidir. **1525** in Turner *Select. Rec. Oxford* 55 [Money] to rune and to be ymployde to thuse of the reparacon of the said myllys. **1551** ROBINSON tr. *More's Utop.* II. (1895) 274 The worlde runneth at al auentures. **1587** TURBERV. *Trag. Tales* (1837) 160 A Sonne, Gerbino namde, of whom this tale Especially doth runne. **1603** SHAKS. *Meas. for M.* III. ii. 242 Much vpon this riddle runs the wisedome of the world. **1628** PEMBLE *Worthy Rec. Lord's Supper* 43 Like desperate Bankrouts to let all things runne at adventure. **1705** tr. *Bosman's Guinea* 31 After this all our Affairs run at random. *Ibid.* 420 Thus far runs our above-mentioned Relation. **1837** *Penny Cycl.* VIII. 116/2 The covenant will not run, that is, it will not bind the assignee, nor pass to him. **1840** G. DARLEY *Beaum. & Fl. Wks.* I. Introd. p. xvi, To complete a parallel which runs so far of itself. **1863** *Sat. Rev.* 8 Aug. 18/1 Those whose feelings run furthest in one direction.

b. Of qualities, etc.: To be persistent or common *in* a family.

1777 SHERIDAN *Sch. Scand.* III. iii, Learning that had run in the family like an heir-loom! **1832** L. HUNT *Gentle Armour* Poems 125 Talk of tricks that run in families. **1866** SIMPSON *Life Campion* ix. (1907) 261 The way in which fidelity and faithlessness ran in families. **1928** R. A. KNOX *Footsteps at Lock* ix. 87 These things do run in families... In *our* family, we're always appearing when we're not wanted to. **1966** A. E. LINDOP *I start Counting* xx. 259 Runs in the family, doesn't it. Goddam bossy, both of you. You're a real little chip off the brotherly block. **1971** 'H. CALVIN' *Poison Chasers* x. 137 Curiosity.. runs in the family.. like wooden legs. **1973** [see *military policeman* s.v. MILITARY *a.* 3 b].

c. Of a newspaper or magazine article: to be printed or published, to appear; to be printed without abridgement.

1928 *Amer. Speech* IV. 135 If news is 'heavy' on a 'tight day' and is permitted to 'run' in length practically as written, [etc.]. *Ibid.* The copy reader now knows whether he is to let 'copy', news articles, 'run' or must 'cut'. **1974** *Publishers Weekly* 18 Nov. 12/3 Janet Flanner's introduction to 'London Was Yesterday'.. will run in the February issue of *Travel & Leisure*.

30. a. To extend or stretch; to form a continuous line or boundary.

Usually const. with advs. or preps. of direction.

c **1391** CHAUCER *Astrol.* II. §3 The degree of the sonne rennyth so longe consentrik vpon the almykanteras, þat sothly thow shalt erre [etc.]. *c* **1400** MAUNDEV. (1839) xxvi. 266 That See of Caspye.. rennethe be the Desert. **1525** tr. *Jerome of Brunswick's Surg.* B j b/2 There be iij, materyall circles y^t ronne about the iye. **1582** STANYHURST *Æneis* III. (Arb.) 87 Two peers loftye run vpward From stoans lyke turrets. **1630** *R. Johnson's Kingd. & Commw.* 494 Tartaria.. runneth along without controll by the high looking walls of China. **1658** A. FOX tr. *Würtz' Surg.* II. xi. 88 Those Wounds, which deeply run into the body, are very dangerous. **1703** MAUNDRELL *Journ. Jerus.* (1732) 142 A very deep rupture in the side of Libanus, running at least seven hours travel. **1790** MME. D'ARBLAY *Diary* Aug., A band of musicians were stationed in a long bower running across the garden. **1834** L. RITCHIE *Wand. by Seine* 86 A balustrade runs round the building. **1861** M. PATTISON *Ess.* (1889) I. 45 On the.. northern side.. ran a lofty, massive front. **1892** *Speaker* 3 Sept. 289/2 The high road.. runs at right-angles to.. the lane.

b. In fig. contexts.

1682 in *Harl. Misc.* (1809) II. 407 The privilege ran as well to the printing it in Italian as French. **1701** W. WOTTON *Hist. Rome* 389 A vein of Superstition ran through all his Actions. **1766** BLACKSTONE *Comm.* (ed. 2) I. 98 Though certain of the king's writs.. do not usually run into Berwick. **1815** W. H. IRELAND *Scribbleomania* 99 The vein of ill-nature that ran thro' your tale. **1879** HUXLEY *Hume* i. 2 The paternal line running back to Lord Home of Douglas. **1890** *Temple Bar* Sept. 64 His patriotism very often runs far.. into the region of prejudice. **1914** G. B. SHAW *Parents & Children* p. xi, The something unpleasant may be only a look of suffering.. or it may run to forcible expulsion from the room. **1939** —— *In Good King Charles's Golden Days* I. 45 Mr. Newton: your privilege with me does not run to the length of knocking my brother down. **1967** 'S. WOODS' *And shame Devil* 222 He was brilliantly attired in crimson pyjamas... Who would have thought his taste would run to the exotic?

c. *Law.* Of recollection, memory, etc.: To extend or go back in time.

1447 SHILLINGFORD *Lett.* (Camden) 76 *note*, The Maier and Citeseyns.. have ben seised of all maner jurisdiccion.. of tyme that no mynde renneth. **1531** *Dial. on Laws Eng.* I. viii. 16 The limitacion of a prescription generally taken, is from the tyme that no mannes mind renneth to the contrarye. **1765** BLACKSTONE *Comm.* I. Introd. 76 That it [a custom] have been used so long, that the memory of man runneth not to the contrary. **1861** *Temple Bar* II. 299 The memory of Puffin ran not to the contrary.

******** *Of things passing into, assuming, or maintaining a certain condition or quality.***

31. a. To pass into or out of a certain state. Const. with various preps.

? *a* **1366** CHAUCER *Rom. Rose* 320 So depe was hir wo bigonnen, And eek hir herte in angre ronnen. **1535** COVERDALE *1 Esdras* iv. 26 Many one there be, that renne out of their wyttes.. for their wyues sakes. **1572** *Satir. Poems Reform.* xxxi. 58 Þai suld all rin by þair mynd. **1597** BEARD *Theatre God's Judgem.* (1612) 420 Like as these cursed monsters ran too much out of frame in their vn-bridled lusts. **1639** HORN & ROB. *Gate Lang. Unl.* xvii. §188 A bitch useth to runne a salt (goe proud). **1680** W. ALLEN *Persuasive Peace* Pref. p. xxvi, What.. should have been done to have kept things from running to so great an extream. **1731** *Gentl. Mag.* I. 438 Having bad Luck [she] lost all her ready Money, and run 200*l.* on Tick.

b. With adj. or other complement: To become, end in being, turn, grow, fall, etc.

See also AMOK 2, MAD *a.* 1 b, and RIOT *sb.* 3 and 3 b.

1449 PECOCK *Repr.* I. xvi. 90 For without him.. prechingis rennen arere. *a* **1553** UDALL *Royster Doyster* III. ii. (Arb.) 41 Lest ye for lesing of him perchaunce might runne mad. *a* **1586** MONTGOMERIE *Misc. Poems* xl. 57 Let Weirds rin wod; let furious Faits be fearce. **1589** —— [see MAD *a.* 1 b.] **1602** MARSTON *Antonio's Rev.* II. iv, I am not mad—I run not frantic. **1612** BRINSLEY *Lud. Lit.* 306 They will run behind with me two or three Quarters, and then they will seek some occasion to take away their children. **1764** *Ann. Reg., Chron.* 129/1 Great expectations from lord Shelburn's colt, but he ran rusty. **1794** [see RESTY *a.*[1] 1 b]. **1803** *Censor* 1 Feb. 24 Is it any wonder.. that this gentleman and many others are running behind hand? **1869** TOZER *Highl. Turkey* II. 192 The boats.. are built of thin planks, running very fine fore and aft. **1890** *Longman's Mag.* Oct. 659 The fortresses were destroyed; the roads ran wild.

c. ***run dry***, to cease to yield water or milk; hence *fig.*, to become exhausted or spent.

1637 RUTHERFORD *Lett.* I. clxxiii. (1664) 337, I am run dry of loving.. that greatest and most admirable one! **1768–74** TUCKER *Lt. Nat.* (1834) II. 390 The stream of living waters.. will never run dry. **1827** *Examiner* 152/2 The Waverley novels ran dry at last. **1863** *Jrnl. R. Agric. Soc.* XXIV. II. 301 Most cows run dry in about ten months. **1879** LUBBOCK *Addr. Pol. & Educ.* ii. 28 In 1797 the bullion in the Bank of England had almost run dry.

d. ***run low***, to be nearly exhausted, to become scanty.

1712 ARBUTHNOT *John Bull* I. xv, I am afraid our Credit will run low. **1722** DE FOE *Col. Jack* (1840) 110, I was.. anxious about my money running low. **1789** MRS. PIOZZI *Journ. France* I. 22 Recollection tires, and chat runs low. **1855** MACAULAY *Hist. Eng.* xvii. IV. 101 The stock of provisions within Limerick was already running low. **1891** *Chamb. Jrnl.* 21 Mar. 189/2 Funds began to run very low.

e. ***run short***: see SHORT *a.*

32. a. To have a given tenor or purport; to be worded or expressed in a specified manner.

c **1586** C'TESS PEMBROKE *Ps.* CV. iii, I give in fee (for soe the graunt did runne), Thee and thine heirs the Cananean ground. **1624** *Doc. Illustr. Impeachment Dk. Buckingham* (Camden) 136 It was thought fitt the acquittance runnes in these wordes. **1681** H. MORE *Exp. Dan.* 72 The sense may run thus, An Host shall be given [etc.]. *a* **1744** POPE *Hor. Sat.* II. vi. 157 Once on a time (so runs the Fable) A Country Mouse [etc.]. **1746** HERVEY *Medit.* (1818) 250 Surely it brought a message to surviving mortals, and thus the tidings ran, [etc.]. **1827** POLLOK *Course T.* I I, Thus the prohibition ran,.. in terms of plainest truth. **1862** *Temple Bar* V. 164, I know not how his proper official title ran.

b. To be constituted or conditioned.

1724 SWIFT *Drapier's Lett.* v. Wks. 1751 XII. 15 As Politicks run, I do not know a Person of more exceptionable Principles than yourself. **1764** FOOTE *Mayor of G.* I. i, We must take things rough and smooth as they run. **1864** J. H. NEWMAN *Apol.* ii. (1904) 47/1 However judgments might run as to the prudence of publishing it. **1875** *Ure's Dict. Arts* III. 106 Then the numbers run 14, 30.

33. a. To have a specified character, quality, arrangement, form, etc. Const. with preps. and adjs.

1658 SIR T. BROWNE *Hydriot.* 22 Nor onely these concealed peeces, but the open magnificence of Antiquity, ran much in the Artifice of Clay. *a* **1722** LISLE *Husb.* I. 239 Wheat and barley that is then to fill must run thin. **1789** MRS. PIOZZI *Journ. France* I. 283 The apartments.. run in suits like Wanstead house. **1821** *Examiner* 473/1 His hair was brown, with a tendency to run in ringlets. **1854** *Jrnl. R. Agric. Soc.* XV. I. 228 They are apt to run hairy in the wool, big in the bone. **1890** *Graphic* 20 Sept. 314/1 German traditions of obedience run on different lines entirely.

b. To be of a specified (average or maximum) size, price, etc. Also const. *at*, and with a specified amount.

1762 LD. RADNOR in *Priv. Lett. Ld. Malmesbury* (1870) I. 85 There are very few of them, consequently they run very dear. **1836** F. SYKES *Scraps fr. Jrnl.* 71 Large Wenner trout, running as large as twenty-six pounds. **1890** CRAWFURD *Round Calendar in Portugal* 26 The trout run to a good size in Portugal where the river-pools are deep. **1924** *Sci. Amer.* Sept. 213/1 This means that the ore runs approximately four and one-half tons per gram of radium. **1940** G. MARX *Let.* 5 Sept. (1967) 24 He ran it [*sc.* a film] yesterday for the Breen office—it runs over 13,000 feet. **1960** *Beside 'Guardian'* IX. 216 The original operetta, which runs to a bothersome two and a half hours, was compressed.. into a tight, not to say breathless, hour. **1971** *Daily Tel.* 26 Oct. 1/8 Unemployment benefit is running at about £6,900,000 a week. **1973** *Country Life* 14 June 1712/2 The Historic Buildings Council grants are now running at a rate of £1½ million a year. **1978** *Nat. Geographic* Nov. 623/1 Last autumn arrests [of illegal immigrants] were running 80 a week.

c. To be in the (average) proportion of.

1849 *Jrnl. R. Agric. Soc.* X. II. 425 It ran eleven and a half fleeces to the tod all the way through. **1892** *Field* 2 Apr. 469/3 His oats run 44 lb. to the bushel.

II. Transitive senses.

** To traverse, accomplish, aim at or avoid, etc., by running.*

34. a. (*a*) To pursue or follow (a certain way or course) in running, sailing, etc. † ***to run one's way***, to run away, make off hurriedly.

c **888** K. ÆLFRED *Boeth.* xxi, þæt hie ne moton toslupan, ac bioð ʒehwerfde eft to þam ilcan ryne þe hie ær urnon. *a* **1300** *E.E. Psalter* xviii. 6 He gladed als yhoten to renne his wai. **1375** BARBOUR *Bruce* xx. 558 At myday to turne agane The sone, that rynnis his cours all playn. **1480** *Robt. Devyll* 488 in Hazl. *E.P.P.* I. 238 Yt was no hede to bydde hym begone. He ranne hys waye. **1535** COVERDALE *Job* i. 14, I onely ranne my waye, to tell the. **1562** *Child-Marriages* 72 Wher-of Richard Pierson was so ashamid, that he wold have runne his way. **1600** SHAKS. *A.Y.L.* III. ii. 138 How briefe the Life of man runs his erring pilgrimage. **1669** STURMY *Mariner's Mag.* IV. iii. 148 You are more Easterly or Westerly, by running or sailing that Course and Distance. **1775** BURKE *On Conciliation with America* Sel. Wks. 1897 I. 176 Others run the longitude, and pursue their gigantic game along the coast of Brazil. **1814** *Sporting Mag.* XLIV. 87 Being headed on the Ipswich road, he again ran the same cover, on his way to Somes-Wood. **1892** *Field* 20 Feb. 245/3 Our fox.. did not run the chain of woodlands, but held on southwards.

(*b*) In figurative contexts.

c **1000** *Lambeth Ps.* cxviii. 32 Weʒ beboda þinra ic arn. *a* **1300** *E.E. Psalter* cxviii. 32 Wai ofe þi bodes ran i. **1572** in *Buccleuch MSS.* (Hist. MSS. Comm.) 23 Erle of Lenox.. wes persuaditt.. to rin a cours with England, attempting mony things innaturallie agains his native realme. **1622** MABBE tr. *Aleman's Guzman d'Alf.* II. 330 Wee were fellowes and Companions in one Prison, and.. had runne both of vs one and the same Carreere. **1881** GARDINER & MULLINGER *Study Eng. Hist.* I. vii. 148 The members encouraged one another in running the Christian course.

b. *Hunting.* To pursue, follow up (a scent). Also † ***to run one's country*** (see quots. 1611).

1607 MARKHAM *Caval.* III. (1617) 10 Then laying on fresh dogges,.. make your Horse run the traine with good courage and liuelinesse. **1611** COTGR., *Fendre le vent*, to runne his countrey. *Ibid.*, *Tirer pais*, (in hunting) to runne his countrey; or, to flye directly forward. **1826** SCOTT *Woodst.* iv, Hunting counter, or running a false scent. **1890** *Blackw. Mag.* CXLVIII. 548/1 Hounds are running a high scent through a stiff country.

fig. **1857** WHEWELL in Todhunter *Acc. W.'s Wks.* (1876) II. 411 The dynamical-heat men are running their scent very eagerly.

c. *transf.* Of immaterial things.

1864 W. T. FOX *Skin Dis.* 11 It is not associated with any special form of ill health, is non-contagious,.. runs a definite course [etc.]. **1881** GARDINER & MULLINGER *Study Eng. Hist.* I. v. 97 Lollardism, too, ran much the same course. **1889** TRAILL *Strafford* xiii. 169 Affairs ran their fated course.

35. To traverse or cover by running, sailing, etc.: **a.** a specified distance. Also *fig.* in colloq. phr. ***to run a mile***, to seek safety in flight; to evade through fear, reluctance, etc.

c **1200** ORMIN 6969 þatt follc rideþþ onn a der.. þatt onn a daʒʒ.. Ernеþþ an hunndredd mile. *c* **1300** *Havelok* 1831 He was ded on lesse hwile, Þan men mouthe renne a mile. *c* **1380** WYCLIF *Wks.* (1880) 30 Prelatis schulden not.. make a pore man to renne two or þre þousand myles [etc.]. **1555** EDEN *Decades* (Arb.) 379 Runnynge southwest in the sea, [we] dydde runne .xii. leagues. **1669** STURMY *Mariner's Mag.* IV. ii. 146 So many Knots as the Ship runs in half a Minute, so many Miles she saileth in an Hour. **1728** CHAMBERS *Cycl.* s.v. *Courier*, Pliny,.. and Cæsar, mention some of these, who would run 20, 30, 36.. Leagues per Day. **1748** *Anson's Voy.* III. vi. 345 We had a.. gale blowing right upon our stern: So that we generally run from forty to fifty leagues a day. **1812** *Sporting Mag.* XXXIX. 53 Flying Childers.. once run four miles in six minutes and forty seconds. **1846** A. YOUNG *Naut. Dict.*, With reference to the ship's progress.. we say she has run so many knots in an hour and so forth. **1861** *Temple Bar* I. 345 The engine had run more than 10,000 miles. **1949** D. SMITH *I capture Castle* v. 64 Men.. run a mile from obvious fascination. **1952** 'R. GORDON' *Doctor in House* xvii. 188 The ones that run a mile if they see a nurse and talk big about staying single. **1963** A. HERON *Towards Quaker View of Sex* 67 Were a woman to whom he exposed himself to respond sexually, the average exhibitionist would run a mile. **1969** H. E. BATES *Vanished World* x. 98, I run a mile from intellectual swank words such as 'esoteric' and 'proliferate'. **1973** J. WILSON *Truth or Dare* iv. 44 Full of talk—yet if Betty gave any of them the come-on they'd run a mile. **1977** *Gay News* 7–20 Apr. 29/1 Whenever anything reasonably likely appears on the scene Cole runs a mile and wallows in neo-platonic discussions on the.. differences between lust and love.

b. a defined stretch or space.

1596 SHAKS. *Merch. V.* II. ii. 110 Well, well, but for mine owne part,.. I will not rest till I haue run some ground. **1600** E. BLOUNT tr. *Conestaggio* 183 Hauing run all the coast of Algarues. **1690** LUTTRELL *Brief Rel.* (1857) II. 98 Mr. Peregrine Bertie,.. upon a wager, run the mall in St. James Park 11 times in lesse then an hour. **1715** tr. *Gregory's Astron.* (1726) I. 97 The Spaces run by a heavy Body, in its fall, are as the Squares of the Times. **1766** PENNANT *Brit. Zool.* (1776) I. 2 The same horse has also run the round course at Newmarket.. in six minutes and forty seconds. **1836** MACGILLIVRAY *Humboldt's Trav.* xxii. 312 While they were running short tacks, a false manœuvre.. exposed them.. to imminent danger. **1847** L. HUNT *Men, Women, & B.* I. x. 178 Our companion, who had run the round of the great world.

fig. **1892** *Sat. Rev.* 29 Oct. 507/2 [His] perfect elocutionary style held flexibility enough to enable him to run the whole gamut with ease.

c. To scour, run about in (a place).

1648 GAGE *West Ind.* 32 The next day in the morning Cortez went forth to run the fields. **1820** SCOTT *Monast.* xxiv, I will not see a proper lad so misleard as to run the country with an old knave, like Simmie and his brother. **1861** *Temple Bar* III. 334 Many.. would sooner let their children run the streets than pay a penny.

d. To slip or shoot down (a rope, river, etc.). *esp.* to navigate (a stream, esp. a dangerous stretch of one) in a small boat.

1805 LEWIS & CLARK *Orig. Jrnls. Lewis & Clark Exped.* (1905) III. 23 There were five shoals neither of which could be passed with loaded canoes nor even run with empty ones. **1839** J. K. TOWNSEND in R. G. Thwaites *Early Western*

Trav. (1905) XXI. xv. 358 Here Mr. M'Leod and myself debarked, and the men ran the dall. **1875** 'MARK TWAIN' *Old Times on Mississippi* ii. 37 Each of our pilots ran such portions of the river as he had run when coming up-stream. **1883** GRESLEY *Gloss. Coal-mining* 209 Running the tow is a common practice in shallow mines. **1889** *Scribner's Mag.* May 532 Two bits of rapid are run in a flash. **1892** *Field* 28 May 783 We have run most parts of the Wye in a coracle.

36. To perform or accomplish by running or riding: **a.** a course (on horseback or foot), career, etc. Freq. in fig. contexts.

to run the gantlope or *gauntlet*: see GANTLOPE, GAUNTLET *sb.*[2] b.

1494 in *Lett. Rich. III & Hen. VII* (Rolls) I. 394 Thenne therll of Suffolke and Sir Edward A Borough ran the vi. furst courses. **1551-2** EDW. VI in Halliw. *Lett. Kings Eng.* (1846) II. 53 Afterward there was run a match at tilt, six to six, which was very well run. **1568** GRAFTON *Chron.* II. 292 Eyther of them set hys speare in the rest to haue runne the first course. **1667** MILTON *P.L.* VIII. 88 By thy reasoning this I guess, Who..supposest That..Heav'n such journies [should not] run, Earth sitting still. **1725** *Fam. Dict.* s.v. *Horse-racing*, There being but a single Course to be run, you must push for all at that one Time. **1743** FRANCIS tr. *Hor., Odes* IV. xiv. 38 When thrice five times the circling sun His annual course of light had run. *a* **1827** WORDSW. *Somnambulist* 116 When a circuit has been run Of valour, truth, and love. **1854** DOBELL *Balder* Wks. (1887) 204 The doom has run its course, the hour is here! **1891** *Field* 7 Mar. 347/2 Johnny Moor practically ran a single-handed course, as Brave Briton was unable to raise a gallop.

b. a race, chase, etc. Freq. in fig. contexts (cf. RACE *sb.*[1] 1 c).

a **1557** *Tottel's Misc.* (Arb.) 153 The restlesse race that he full oft hath runne. **1592** SHAKS. *Rom. & Jul.* II. iv. 75 If our wits run the Wild-Goose chase, I am done. **1610** *Reg. Privy Counc. Scotl.* IX. 91 Upoun occasioun of ane horse race whiche wes then run at Cumnoke. **1628** EARLE *Microcosm.* xvii. (Arb.) 39 Commonly his race is quickely runne. **1729** T. COOKE *Tales*, etc. 36 He always thinks..his Race not ran; But Death, tho long delay'd, confutes the Man. **1789** BURNEY *Hist. Mus.* III. 534 The comparative speed of two coursers is best known by their running a trial. **1856** *Leisure Hour* V. 803/2 She flew along the green sward and ran races with Harry. **1873** SPENCER *Sociology* ii. 39 The Derby has been run in a snowstorm.

c. *Cricket.* To score (a run or bye). Also to score from (a stroke) by running; cf. sense 77 i (*d*).

1744 *Laws* [of Cricket] in *New & Compl. Dict. Arts & Sci.* (1755) IV. 3459/2 If in running a notch, the wicket is struck down by a throw [etc.]. **1816** W. LAMBERT *Instr. & Rules Cricket* 35 The Striker should be careful and attentive in running both his own and partner's hits. **1849** in 'Bat' *Cricket Man.* (1850) 56 The striker shall have all [the runs] which have been run. **1878** *Sussex Archaeol. Coll.* XXVIII. 80 Cricket grounds are not larger now than then, and yet the batsmen *ran* their hits. **1881** *Standard* 28 June 3/1 Three byes were now run.

d. *to run* (a thing) *fine*, to leave a very slight margin (*esp.* of time). *colloq.*

1890 W. E. NORRIS *Misadventure* II. ii. 18 On consulting his watch, he found he had run things rather fine. **1892** *Eng. Illustr. Mag.* IX. 800 One cart-load was run so fine that partner and superintendent were constrained to lend a hand to finish the packing.

e. *to run rings round*: see RING *sb.*[1] 15 d.

f. *to run interference*: in *U.S. Football*, to move in such a way as to cause interference (cf. INTERFERENCE 1 c). Also *fig.*

1929 JONES & WESSON *Football for Fan* ii. 23 Whether he is to charge straight ahead, cross check, pull out to run interference or to protect a pass..he must always look the same to his rivals before the ball is snapped. **1932** F. OAKES *Football Line Play* xi. 135 The most difficult block the center must make occurs when both linemen on each side of him drop back to run interference. **1947** *Partisan Rev.* May–June 236 The official liberal runs interference for the Communist with a system of intellectual evasion. **1972** J. MOSEDALE *Football* iii. 39 Nagurski was described as a 'man who runs his own interference'. **1976** *National Observer* (U.S.) 1 May 5/3 He said he wasn't going to allow *his* police to run interference for employees trying to get through a union picket line.

37. a. To go upon (an errand or message).

1500-20 DUNBAR *Poems* lx. 44 His erandis for to ryne and red. **1848** THACKERAY *Van. Fair* lxiv, The Prince's grandfather..ran errands for gentlemen, and lent money. **1859** JEPHSON *Brittany* xviii. 300 Idle hangers-on, who subsist upon the casual profits of..carrying luggage, or running messages.

b. *run descant, division*(*s*): see DESCANT *sb.* 6, 7, and DIVISION *sb.* 7. Now only *arch.*

1579 W. WILKINSON *Confut. Fam. of Love* 26 b, He might runne descant at will. **1602** MARSTON *Ant. & Mel.* II. Wks. 1856 I. 25 Beautie and youth run descant on loves ground. **1607** HEYWOOD *Wom. killed w. Kindn.* Wks. 1874 II. 148 Vpon this instrument Her fingers haue run quicke diuision. **1737** BRACKEN *Farriery Impr.* (1757) II. 274, I might yet run several Divisions upon this Topic. **1821** *Examiner* 300/1 The gentle lady [may] run divisions on roses and myrtle-bowers.

c. *Billiards.* (See COUP *sb.*[3] 3.)

1850 *Bohn's Handbk. Games* (1867) 608 The player may lose a life..by running a coup. **1861** *Chambers's Encycl.* II. 98/2 The points of the game are..1 for a miss,..and 3 for 'running a coo'.

d. *Croquet.* To play through (a hoop) or up to (a peg).

1874 HEATH *Croquet Player* 63 It is true that every foot nearer to the hoop makes it easier to get into position and run it. **1877** *Encycl. Brit.* VI. 608/2 In match play the hoops and pegs are set and run as in the diagram.

38. a. To flee or escape from (a place, country, etc.); to desert from (a ship).

1608 CHAPMAN *Byron's Consp.* Plays 1873 II. 235 A lusty courser..when (his headstall broken) Hee runnes his prison. **1611** COTGR. s.v. *Saut, Faire le saut*, to breake, fall bank-rupt, runne his countrey for debt. **1727** A. HAMILTON *New Acc. E. Ind.* I. x. 113 Some..were lawfully murdered, or obliged to run their Country. **1888** *Roots* 62 He had come out to New Zealand, as a sailor boy, had run his ship [etc.]. **1889** W. WESTALL *Birch Dene* III. ii. 38, I should have to run the country if he wor to dee.

b. *U.S.* To depart surreptitiously without paying for (one's board).

1898 HOWELLS *Open-eyed Conspiracy* 73 If they run their board I shall have to pay it.

39. † **a.** *to run..fortune*(s), in various phrases denoting voluntary sharing of another's lot. *Obs.*

(*a*) **1567** THROGMORTON in Robertson *Hist. Scotl.* (1759) II. App. 38 The queen will leave them in the bryers if they run her fortoun. **1670** CLARENDON *Hist. Reb.* XIII. §20 The King desired that he might command this Army, at least run the fortune of it. **1713** STEELE *Guardian* No. 19 ¶8 My Fellow-soldiers, said he, as you run my Fortune, so do I yours.

(*b*) **1610** J. MORE in *Buccleuch MSS.* (Hist. MSS. Comm.) 87, I presume you will be content to run the same fortune with him. **1676** WOOD *Jrnl.* in *Acc. Sev. Late Voy.* I. (1694) 191 Some holding Consultation to stave the Boat, and all to run the like Fortune.

(*c*) **1674** CLARENDON (J.), He would himself be in the Highlands to receive them, and run his fortune with them. *a* **1713** BURNET *Own Time* (1734) II. 376 If he thought it could do him any service, he would come in, and run fortunes with him.

b. To expose oneself, or be exposed, to (a chance, danger, etc.).

See also RISCO, RISGO(E, and RISK *sb.* 1 b.

1592 UNTON *Corr.* (Roxb.) 271 He comandeth Monsr. de Maine to take the vantgard, intendinge he shall first ronne fortune. **1642** C. VERNON *Consid. Exch.* 89, I was resolved..to runne all the hazards of envy. **1675** TEMPLE *Wks.* (1720) II. 333 He who goes to Sea, or to War, runs a Venture. **1719** DE FOE *Crusoe* I. (Globe) 143, I had run so much Hazard.., nor had I any Mind to run any more Ventures. **1847** C. BRONTË *J. Eyre* xvii, We run a chance of being busy enough now. **1860** JOWETT in *Ess. & Rev.* 392 We run a danger..of wasting time.

c. To incur, meet with, encounter.

1624 BARGRAVE *Serm.* 23 S. Paul himselfe hath runne the censure of being too much a Lutheran. **1665** J. WEBB *Stone-Heng* (1725) 4 The most remarkable Stone-Heng hath sadly run the same Fate. **1683** MOXON *Mech. Exerc.*, *Printing* xxii. ¶4 The Compositer..runs different fortunes, either of good or bad Copy, viz. well or ill writ. *a* **1822** SHELLEY *With Guitar, to Jane* 31 Many changes have been run Since Ferdinand and you begun Your course of love.

40. a. *run it*, or *a voyage* (see quot. 1838).

1787 *Minor* II. x, We resolved to run it, even without convoy. **1804** NELSON 20 Mar. in Nicolas *Disp.* (1845) V. 469 The only merchant-ship bound to England..is so well armed as to be able to run it. **1826** G. J. BELL *Comm. Law Scot.* (ed. 5) I. 620 It is important to know whether a ship is to wait for convoy, or to *run* the voyage. **1838** W. BELL *Dict. Law Scot.* 871 A vessel which in time of war does not sail with convoy, is technically said to *run* the voyage.

b. *run the* (or *a*) *blockade*: (see BLOCKADE *sb.* 1 b).

1869 *Overland Monthly* 47 How we ran the blockade. **1893** PEEL *Spen Valley* 331 If they were only lucky enough to run the blockades.

c. *run the cutter*: (see quot. 1882).

1882 *Jamieson's Sc. Dict.* IV. 33 *To rin the cutter*, i.e., to evade the revenue cutter, hence, to smuggle. **1892** H. NISBET *Bushranger's Sweetheart* iii. 22 Sailors, as a rule, are not friends of bailiffs or custom house officers, and thus appreciate 'running the cutter'.

d. *slang* (orig. and chiefly *N. Amer.*). To drive past (a traffic signal showing red). Cf. JUMP *v.* 10 b.

1935 *Harper's Mag.* June 60/2 Perhaps we even 'ran' a light, relying on the waiting cars to continue to wait until we were out of their way. **1951** *Tuscaloosa* (Alabama) *News* 28 Jan. 1/7 Mitchell..had been arrested on charges of reckless driving and running a stop sign. **1953** *Birmingham* (Alabama) *News* 8 Aug. 1/8 Wilson told officers the brakes of his..truck failed, causing him to run a red light at the intersection. **1967** *Boston Traveler* 1 June 5/6 Policeman Howard Park stopped a minister for passing a red light... 'He who runs red light gets ticket.' **1972** *Even. Telegram* (St. John's, Newfoundland) 27 June 14/4 Guy forgot to turn on his lights. And ran a stop sign. A policeman pulled him over. **1978** *Guardian Weekly* 15 Jan. 13/2 Cairo drivers run red lights and drive the wrong way down one-way streets.

41. a. To sew slightly and quickly, usually by taking a number of stitches on the needle at a time. Also const. *with.*

1708 *Mrs. Centlivre's Busie Body* Prol. 29 The Fleet-street Sempstress.., That runs spruce Neckcloths for Attorney's Clerks. **1721** AMHERST *Terræ Fil.* No. 46 (1726) 257 Long muslin neckcloths run with red at the bottom. **1815** KIRBY & SP. *Entom.* (1818) I. xiv. 461 They..*run* (as a sempstress would call it) loosely together..the two membranes on that side. **1875** *Plain Hints Needlework* 22 Take a needle and cotton and run it once round.

b. To darn (the heel of a stocking) before wearing in order to strengthen it.

1802 D. WORDSWORTH *Jrnl.* 24 Dec. (1941) I. 186, I have been..running the heel of a stocking. **1844** S. S. ARNOLD in *Proc. Vermont Hist. Soc.* (1940) VIII. 170 Paid Mrs. Wales for knitting silk stockings and running the heels 67 cents. **1904** *Eng. Dial. Dict.* V. 186/1 It is common to run the heels of stockings with cotton before wearing them.

c. To attach (a ribbon or similar decoration) to cloth by passing it through a series of holes in the material.

1872 *Young Englishwoman* Nov. 607/2 Run a braid or ribbon through the open row. **1908** M. MORGAN *How to dress Doll* v. 48 Ribbon is run through neck and sleeves.

42. a. To pursue, chase, hunt (game, etc.). *spec.*, to chase or hunt animals (e.g. buffalo) on horseback or (occas.) with a vehicle (chiefly *N. Amer.*).

Partaking, to some extent, of the causal sense.

1484 CAXTON *Fables of Æsop* II. vii, Dogges..haue grete luste to renne and take the wyld beestes. **1576** TURBERV. *Venerie* 35 The first is that he neuer accustome his houndes to runne a Hinde. **1674** N. COX *Gentl. Recr.* (1677) 17 When Deer, after being hard run, turn head against the Hounds, we say, they Bay. **1812** *Sporting Mag.* XXXIX. 185 A fox was run on Saturday..by Sir W. W. Wynne's hounds, for upwards of one hour. **1841** G. CATLIN *Lett. on N. Amer. Indians* I. 219 On this journey we saw immense herds of buffaloes; and although we had no horses to *run* them, we successfully *approached* them on foot. **1844** H. STEPHENS *Bk. Farm* III. 878 Pointers are very apt to run sheep when hunting. **1849** F. PARKMAN *Calif. & Oregon Trail* xxiv. 386 The chief difficulty in running buffalo..is that of loading the gun or pistol at full gallop. **1891** *Field* 7 Nov. 693/1 Hounds won't leave the fox they are running. **1900** W. F. DRANNAN *31 Yrs. on Plains* (1901) xxi. 300, I met about thirty Kiowa Indians going out to run the buffalo near there. **1949** L. NORDYKE *Cattle Empire* 264 Horses are furnished for the care of the cattle and for other useful purposes, and they must not be used to run wild horses, or buffalo, or antelope. **1963** G. F. G. STANLEY *Louis Riel* 5 There could be no room for selfish individualism when the métis ran the buffalo. **1968** K. WEATHERLY *Roo Shooter* 130 Hunter would have to run the little doe with the Land-Rover.

fig. **1764** *Low Life* 70 Tallow-Chandlers who do Business privately in Back Cellars..to evade the King's Duty..make Mould Candles, known by the Name of *Running the Buck.* **1841** LEVER *C. O'Malley* x, The various modes of 'running a buck' (Anglicè substituting a vote). **1876** A. S. PALMER *Leaves fr. Notebk.* Pref. p. viii, I have run it [a word] to earth in a Sanscrit root.

b. To contend with (a person, etc.) in a race.

1786 BURNS *Farmer's New Year Salutation* vii, An' ran them till they a' did wauble, Far, far behin'. **1822** SCOTT *Nigel* xxiii, Perhaps you will like to..leap a flea—run a snail. **1859** CAPERN *Ball. & Songs* 125 If..he beats me there, then I'll run him a mile. **1891** *Sat. Rev.* 25 July 107/1 Desdemona ..gave her 5 lbs. and ran her to a neck.

c. To press (one) *hard* or *close*, so as to inconvenience in some way. Also without adv.

1767 J. WEDGWOOD *Let.* 27 May (1965) 54 The Ministry were run very hard yesterday in the House of Lords. They carried their point by a Majority of three only. **1790** *Bystander* 159 My associates have run me so hard this week, as to room, that I cannot go on. **1798** CHARLOTTE SMITH *Yng. Philos.* III. 96 He never was so hard run for money. **1821** SCOTT *Pirate* xxxii, Bryce..now saw himself run so close, that pleading to the charge became inevitable. **1824** —— *St. Ronan's* xi, I shall be hard run unless I can get a certain sum of money. **1828-32** WEBSTER, *To run hard*, to press with jokes, sarcasm or ridicule. **1892** *Temple Bar* Sept. 53 Both author and artist were notoriously always run for time.

d. To press (a person or thing) *close* or *hard*, in competition or rivalry.

1806 J. BERESFORD *Miseries of Human Life* II. 40 Your quagmire-scene runs it very close. **1850** THACKERAY *Pendennis* xx[i]x, Warrington and Paley had been competitors,..and had run each other hard. **1892** *Eng. Illustr. Mag.* IX. 830 The *Gloriana* would run her very close on the score of beauty.

e. *run* (a thing) *into the ground*, to carry to excess, to overdo; to exhaust or defeat by constant pursuit or pressure; to destroy by excessive use. orig. *U.S.*

1836 W. T. PORTER in *Spirit of Times* 9 July 162/1 It's no use to run the thing into the ground. *a* **1859** in Bartlett *Dict. Amer.* (ed. 2) 374 The advocates of temperance have run it into the ground by their extreme measures. **1884** GRONLUND *Co-oper. Commw.* iii. 74 After having run this Social 'Order' into the ground, it will be supplanted by a new principle. **1947** J. STEINBECK *Wayward Bus* viii. 135 Well, start feeling good, then, and don't run it into the ground. Nobody likes sick people very long. **1955** *Times* 3 Aug. 3/7 Close marking, hard tackling, and shrewd tactical kicking, until the opposition has been 'run into the ground'. **1977** *N.Y. Rev. Bks.* 31 Mar. 21/1 Crossman during his brief tenure as editor..just about ran the paper into the ground.

*** To cause to run, move rapidly, or extend.*

43. a. To cause or force (a horse or other animal) to go rapidly, esp. when riding it. †Also *absol.* to ride. Also *transf.*, esp. in political use.

In early use only with the transitive form of the vb., and usually without object.

c **893** K. ÆLFRED *Oros.* I. i. 20 þonne ærnað hy ealle toweard þæm feo; ðonne cymeð se man se þæt swiftoste hors hafað [etc.]. *c* **900** tr. *Baeda's Hist.* v. vi. (1890) 400 þæt hio ærnan moste & gecunnian, hwelc heora swiftost hors hæfde. *c* **1205** LAY. 6752 þe king..lette enne cniht særne after an oðer eorle. *c* **1275** *Ibid.* 24696 Somme gon hors earne, somme afote eorne. *a* **1300** *K. Horn* 1319 After horn he arnde anon, Also þat hors miȝte gon. *c* **1330** *Arth. & Merl.* 8404 (Kölbing), So þai wenten, þai metten a kniȝt Arnand wiþ al his miȝt.

1504 *Acc. Ld. High Treas. Scot.* II. 428 Item,..and to the boy ran the Kingis hors, xxviij. s. **1568** GRAFTON *Chron.* II. 169 Alexander.., as he was runnyng his horse, fell horse and man to the grounde. **1647** TRAPP *Comm. Rom.* xiii. 11 As they that run their horses for a wager, spur hardest at the races end. **1725** *Fam. Dict.* s.v. *Horse-racing*, Start him off roundly, and run him to the very Top of what he can do, during the whole Course or Heat. **1797** *Encycl. Brit.* (ed. 3) VIII. 659/1 The place where they ran or breathed their coursers was called *hippodromus.* **1840** DICKENS *Old C. Shop* xlvi, Men running horses up and down the street for sale. **1880** E. W. HAMILTON *Diary* 2 Dec. (1972) I. 83 He expressed his belief that the suspension of the Habeas Corpus a month or two ago would have arrested the evil, and as things now are the only course to take is to 'run' two measures side by side the moment Parliament meets. **1883** *Harper's Mag.* Dec. 147/1, I forged on, fairly running the dogs. **1890** *Lippincott's Mag.* Mar. 372 The horses were run rapidly forward to the skirmish-line. **1898** W. S. CHURCHILL *Let.* 5 Jan. in R. S. Churchill *Winston S. Churchill* (1967) I. Compan. II. 854 We can run Tirah and Egypt in double harness.

b. *Racing.* To enter (a horse, etc.) for a race; also *fig.* to pit (lives) against each other.

1750 F. COVENTRY *Hist. Pompey* I. xiv. (1785) 35/2 Nothing is esteemed a more laudable topick of wagering than the lives of eminent men; which, in the language of Newmarket, is called running lives. **1797** *Encycl. Brit.* (ed. 3) V. 499/2 For this reason, no gre-hound of any value should be run at this course. **1812** *Sporting Mag.* XXXIX. 287 Who, to use the jockey phrase, run the lives of their respective fathers against each other. **1856** 'STONEHENGE' *Brit. Rural Sports* 364 No Person can Run More than one horse for any plate. **1892** *Pictorial World* 16 Apr. 695/1 An owner runs his horse ostensibly to win.

c. To allow to run or feed at large, to graze (cattle, sheep, etc.). Chiefly *Austral.*

1812 SIR J. SINCLAIR *Syst. Husb. Scot.* I. 343 A few farmers..still think it beneficial to run their horses in an inclosed field through the night. **1862** R. HENNING *Let.* 28 Aug. (1966) 95 He is going to run some sheep on the station, and I dare say will do very well. **1880** *Victorian Rev.* I. 630 If one man can only make a living by running his sheep in large flocks. **1892** *Cornh. Mag.* Oct. 384 A large number of milch-cows were run in the woods. **1901** M. FRANKLIN *My Brilliant Career* ii. 10 Mother felt dubious of her husband's ability to make a living off a thousand acres, half of which were fit to run nothing but wallabies. **1930** L. G. D. ACLAND *Early Canterbury Runs* 1st Ser. x. 241 The dry cattle were run further out than the sheep. **1966** G. W. TURNER *Eng. Lang. Austral. & N.Z.* iii. 50 The word might be used as a transitive verb. 'He runs merinos' i.e. has merino sheep as his stock.

d. To send (a ferret) *through* a hole.

1892 *Black & White* 5 Nov. 518/2 The common way..has hitherto been for the keeper to run a ferret through the burrows at night.

44. a. To bring into a certain state, affect in a certain way, by running. Chiefly *refl.* and in phrases (see quots.). Also *to run* (one) *off one's feet*, to occupy or overwork to the point of exhaustion (usu. *pass.*). *to run* (one) *ragged*: see RAGGED *a.*[1] 6.

1548 PATTEN *Exped. Scotl.* I v, Sum also [were] seen in this race all breathles to fal flat doun, and haue run themselues to death. **1648** WINYARD *Midsummer-Moon* 3 He runs himselfe off his legs the first daies journey. **1850** *Jrnl. R. Agric. Soc.* XI. II. 600 To use the ordinary phrase used by farmers, 'they run all the flesh off their bones'. **1891** *Field* 7 Nov. 693/1 It's hot till we are close to Garthorpe where our fox runs us out of scent. **1892** *Ibid.* 19 Nov. 786/1 He had almost run himself to a standstill.

fig. **1590** SHAKS. *Com. Err.* IV. i. 57 Fie, now you run this humor out of breath. **1637** SHIRLEY *Gamester* 111, His lordship's bones are not well set;..they will run him quite out of all. **1679** DRYDEN *Pref. Troil. & Cress.* Ess. (ed. Ker) I. 221 His inborn vehemence and force of spirit will only run him out of breath the sooner. **1716** M. DAVIES *Athen. Brit.* II. 111 To foresee that Warwick by running so a-Head, would at last run himself out of Breath. **1857** C. M. YONGE *Dynevor Terrace* II. xv. 235 Charlotte was what Martha expressively called 'fairly run off her feet'. **1937** M. ALLINGHAM *Dancers in Mourning* xxii. 279 Run off his feet, poor lad. Don't know when he sleeps. **1949** N. MITFORD *Love in Cold Climate* I. x. 107 You'd never believe that woman was nearly eighty, she could run us all off our feet. **1970** W. J. BURLEY *To kill Cat* i. 7 'I expect you've got enough to do at this time of year.' 'Run off our feet, sir.'

b. To bring, lead, drag, or force (one) *into* (†*upon*, †*to*) some state, action, etc.; †to drive or make (one) *mad*. Also, to drive (one) *crazy*, *out of one's head* (*U.S. dial.*).

1621 FLETCHER *Pilgrim* III. iii, These wild woods, and the fancies I have in me, Will run me mad. **1633** BP. HALL *Hard Texts, New Test.* 50 When he hath omitted his good services and runne himself into judgement. **1662** STILLINGFL. *Orig. Sacræ* II. iii. §7 For whatever is required as a duty, is such as the neglect of it runs men upon damnation. **1682** BUNYAN *Holy War* 91 Attempted to run the town into acts of Rebellion against our Prince. *a* **1715** BURNET *Own Time* III. (1724) I. 356 He run me into a long discourse about the authority of the Church. **1747** CHESTERF. *Lett.* I. cxxxii. 355, I should have avoided many follies and inconveniencies, which undirected youth run me into. **1820** SCOTT *Monast.* xxv, What need to run myself into trouble for a fool's word? **1828** *Examiner* 701/1 She had been running him into debt. **1889** W. WESTALL *Birch Dene* II. iii. 32 It might have run us into a loss of four or five pounds. **1924** L. VOLLMER *Sun-Up* I. 13 Neither one of us is got 'nough [learning] to run us crazy. **1928** J. PETERKIN *Scarlet Sister Mary* xxv. 288 It'll run you crazy if it don' kill you. **1940** J. STUART *Trees of Heaven* I. ii. 20 Some say whiskey will run a man crazy. **1942** L. VOLLMER in *Sat. Even. Post* 22 Aug. 12/3 Fink's meanness had run his wife out of her head.

c. To force, drive (a person or thing) *out of*, or *off*, some place. Also with advbs.

1727 A. HAMILTON *New Acc. E. Ind.* II. xlvii. 169 Who.. had rioted away a great Part of his Masters Goods and Money, and had run his own Credit out of Doors. **1822** J. FLINT *Lett. fr. Amer.* 309 Arresting a free negro, with a view to run him out of the State. *a* **1861** T. WINTHROP *John Brent* (1876) xvi. 183 But then he knows ther ain't no Utes round here to stampede his animals or run off any of his gals. **1890** *Lippincott's Mag.* Mar. 312 He ran two men out of the regiment. **1891** *Sat. Rev.* 22 Aug. 216/1 The railways had been running the travelling carriages..off the roads. **1901** W. N. HARBEN *Westerfelt* xvi. 220 He was here the night they run him off. **1911** T. DREISER *Jennie Gerhardt* i. 10 A man run us away. **1924** H. CROY *R.F.D. No. 3* xi. 189 He's got to be run out. **1946** G. FOREMAN *Last Trek of Indians* x. 195 The agent announced his intention of running out of the country any such preacher who might appear. **1949** W. GANN *Tread of Longhorns* v. 57 The city rulers felt that the marshal should have stopped the jail delivery, and for his failure to do so, he was run off the job. **1967** *Boston Sunday Globe* 23 Apr. 4/6 Something most 17-year-old girls seldom mention..rats. 'They're bad and they'd run you right out of the cellar,' she said. **1976** C. EGLETON *State Visit* xiii. 120 Some cowboy of a truck driver ran us off the road. **1977** 'E. ANTHONY' *Silver Falcon* ii. 44 Get out of Beaumont!.. There's enough of us here who loved your father to run you out.

d. To describe, put down (a person), as having deserted. Cf. RUN *ppl. a.* 2.

1797 NELSON 29 Mar. in Nicolas *Disp.* (1845) III. 7 Five or six men absent without leave, who can not be 'Run' on the Ship's books, not having been absent three musters. **1810** *Sporting Mag.* XXXV. 291, I told him I had run him on the books; he said that I ought to have discharged him to Sombrero.

45. a. To cause (a boat or ship) to move rapidly or easily forwards, esp. towards or against the land.

a **1548** HALL *Chron., Hen. VIII*, 94 The Scottes ran their shippes on land, and the Englishmen folowed wyth boates and landed. **1611** BIBLE *Acts* xxvii. 41 Falling into a place where two seas met, they ranne the shippe a ground. **1632** LITHGOW *Trav.* III. 127 [They] cut their Cables, and runne the Galley a shoare. **1775** ROMANS *Hist. Florida* App. 7 The stream will run you out in such a manner [etc.]. **1816** KEATINGE *Trav.* (1817) II. 168 Our Palinurus now ran us ashore. **1855** [J. D. BURN] *Autobiog. Beggar boy* 92 Our jolly old captain ran the *Fame* foul of a brig. **1873** W. BLACK *Pr. Thule* xxii. 356 The boat was run in to her moorings. **1889** DOYLE *Micah Clarke* xxiv. 246 The lugger had been run into a narrow creek.

refl. **1610** SHAKS. *Temp.* I. i. 4 Speake to th' Mariners: fall too't yarely, or we run our selues a ground.

fig. **1603** DRAYTON *Bar. Wars* I. lv, [They] some vnknowne Harbor suddenly must sound, Or runne their Fortunes desp'rately on ground. **1901** M. FRANKLIN *My Brilliant Career* xxiv. 207 The recent 'going bung' of a building society—his sole remaining prop—had run him entirely ashore.

b. To bring, convey, transport, in a vessel, down a stream, along rails, etc. Also *spec.*, to convey (someone) in a motor vehicle to a particular destination.

1700 LAW *Counc. Trade* (1751) 255 As much as we are obliged to pay to them for running the real species, when it is found necessary to carry it out. **1864** *Laws of Michigan* 23 The logs, timber, or other floatables, driven, boomed, rafted, or run. **1884** *Graphic* 20 Nov. 534/2 The engine runs trucks to and from the piers on the island. **1890** *Illustr. Lond. News* 1 Nov. 562 The steam-trawler has replaced the sailing-smack, and the former runs home her own cargo. **1909** W. J. LOCKE *Septimus* iv. 57 The chauffeur touched his cap. 'I'll run you both over to Nice,' said Clem Sypher... 'I'll run you back again.' **1924** KIPLING *Debits & Credits* (1926) 326 I'll run you out home before sun-up. I'm a haulage contractor now. **1936** L. A. G. STRONG *Last Enemy* ix. 274 'I must go over and see him.'.. 'I can't run you over to-day, I'm afraid.' **1939** A. THIRKELL *Before Lunch* v. 126 'Shall I run you home?' he asked. Daphne said her bicycle was in the bottle room. **1952** 'M. INNES' *Private View* iii. 60 Better run you home first... It will save you five minutes. **1958** 'A. BRIDGE' *Portuguese Escape* viii. 128 A taxi..will take aeons. I'll run you out when it's all fixed. **1971** 'D. HALLIDAY' *Dolly & Doctor Bird* iv. 58, I ran Johnson back to my house. **1976** M. BIRMINGHAM *Heat of Sun* ix. 152 I'll run you over later... You stay and have some tea now.

c. To land, smuggle (contraband goods).

1706 PHILLIPS (ed. Kersey), *To Smuggle Goods*, to run them ashore, or bring them in by stealth, without paying the Custom. **1710** *Lond. Gaz.* No. 4737/3 Goods run from on Board one of the East-India Company's Ships. **1837** R. ELLIS *Laws & Reg. Customs* I. 199 The vessel or boat, adapted for the purpose of running goods. **1887** G. M. FENN *Devon Boys* xxxi. 269 It was a smuggler running a cargo.

d. To sail (a vessel) in time of war without a convoy.

1813 in G. J. BELL *Comm. Law Scot.* (1826) I. 621 *note*, We have determined on running the Nancy.

†**e.** *run..out of sight*, to outsail (a vessel) quickly and lose sight of it. *Obs.*

1748 *Anson's Voy.* II. v. 177 The Centurion so much outsailed the two prizes, that we soon ran them out of sight. **1797** S. JAMES *Narr. Voy.* 217 The Hound then ran us out of sight in the space of four glasses.

f. To get (something) hastily carried through.

1891 *Daily News* 15 July 3/1 He said that was the time when the Tories took the opportunity of running their jobs.

46. a. To throw (oneself) *upon* or *among* something.

a **1300** *Cursor M.* 7770 Þan drogh saul self his suord And ran him-self a-pon þe ord. **1639** S. DU VERGER tr. *Camus' Admir. Events* 23 Like a furious Tigres, who runnes herselfe amongst the weapons of the hunters.

b. To drive or cause (one's head, etc.) to strike forcibly *against* (a person or thing).

1589 ? LYLY *Pappe w. Hatchet* D iij b, All the desperate & discontented persons were readie to runne their heads against their head. **1611** COTGR. s.v. *Heurter*, To runne his head against the doore. **1712** STEELE *Spect.* No. 268 ¶6, I.. chanced to run my Nose directly against a Post. **1887** MISS SERGEANT *Jacobi's Wife* I. i. 66 If we run our heads against walls we're safe to hurt ourselves.

c. To thrust, esp. to dash or force, (one's head, etc.) *into* or *through* something.

1523 LD. BERNERS *Froiss.* I. cxv. 137 They began to murmure, and began to ron togyder thre heedes in one hood. **1667** PEPYS *Diary* 23 Sept., The glass was so clear that she thought it had been open, and so ran her head through the glass! *a* **1719** ADDISON (J.), Some English speakers run their hands into their pockets. **1748** SMOLLETT *Rod. Random* xlvii, I would not have you..run your head precipitately into a noose. **1794** MRS. RADCLIFFE *Myst. Udolpho* I, Many an honest fellow has run his head into the noose that way.

47. a. To drive by violent impact. *rare*$^{-1}$.

a **1533** LD. BERNERS *Huon* cix. 372 It ranne vnder the water .iii. or .iiii. of the other old shippes.

b. To drive (a vehicle, etc.) *into*, *against*, or *through* something. Also *fig.* (see COACH *sb.* 4).

1663 *Aron-bimn.* 93 Aspiring Novices will run it into bogs and precipices. **1793** *Regal Rambler* 64 [He] ran one of the wheels foul of a garden wall. **1849** HT. MARTINEAU *Hist. Peace* I. v. 53 The mob..running the chariot against a wall, they all got out and walked. **1872** BLACK *Adv. Phaeton* iv. 46 He once or twice..pretty nearly ran us into a cart. **1888** *Times* (weekly ed.) 30 Mar. 7/4 To show..how very easily they could run a coach and four through their proclamations whenever they chose to do it.

fig. **1751** CHESTERF. *Lett.* (1792) III. cclix. 189 Another point is,..not to run your own present humour and disposition indiscriminately against every body.

c. To dash (a thing) forcibly *upon* one.

1700 T. BROWN tr. *Fresny's Amusem.* 21 There a Fat Greasie Porter runs a Trunk full Butt upon you.

d. *run..aboard*, to collide with.

1821 SCOTT *Pirate* xl, They miss stays, and the frigate runs them aboard!

48. a. To thrust or force (a weapon or the like) *through* or *into* (†*in*) a person, etc.

1480 *Robt. Devyll* 463 in Hazl. *E.P.P.* I. 237 So throughe one of theyr bodyes hys sworde [he] dyd runne. **1674** J. WRIGHT *Mock-Thyestes* 99 Faith I'le run this Pin i' your bum. **1734** tr. *Rollin's Rom. Hist.* (1827) II. 335 He drew out his dagger and run it into the thigh of the beast. **1786** BURNS *Earnest Cry* xvii, She'll..rin her whittle to the hilt, I' th' first she meets! **1820** SCOTT *Monast.* xxxvii, If you had run a poniard into him. **1892** A. OLDFIELD *Man. Typogr.* xxi, To do this, run four pins from the back of the tympan right through.

b. To pierce or stab (a person). Usually with *through* or †*into* (a specified part).

a **1533** LD. BERNERS *Huon* lix. 205 He ranne hym clene throw the body with his spere. **1599** SHAKS. *Hen. V*, II. i. 68 Ile run him vp to the hilts, as I am a soldier. **1611** BEAUM. & FL. *King & No King* II. i, I was run twice through the body, and shot i' th' head with a cross-arrow. *c* **1670** WOOD *Life* (1848) 27 Col. Greaves escaped very narrowly, being run into the body. **1712** ADDISON *Spect.* No. 475 ¶1 The next Morning he received a Challenge..and before Twelve a Clock was run through the Body. **1760–72** H. BROOKE *Fool of Qual.* (1809) IV. 94 One of the ruffians..came behind, and run me through the back. **1809** ROLAND *Fencing* 114 With as great propriety you might run him through the body before he is on the position of the guard. **1890** *Sat. Rev.* 23 Aug. 227/1 Ormonde..ran two of the cowards through the body.

49. a. To cause to roll quickly; to cause (a ball) to move rapidly in a specified direction; spec. in *Bowling*, to drive away (the jack).

1593 SHAKS. *Rich. II*, II. i. 123 This tongue that runs so roundly in thy head, Should run thy head from thy vnreuerent shoulders. **1861** *Chambers's Encycl.* II. 289/1 The last player frequently endeavours to *run* the jack [etc.]. **1889** W. T. LINSKILL *Golf* iv. 32 In 'running' the ball with the iron..keep the hands forward in advance of the club head. **1971** *Times* 15 Feb. 9/4 He ran the ball strongly 30ft. past the hole. **1977** *Observer* 30 Jan. 24/8 Tueart made ground on the left before passing to Power, who struck a low centre and David Craig ran the ball past his own keeper.

b. To cast or pass (the eye, hand, etc.) rapidly *along*, *down*, *over* (etc.) something.

1728 CHAMBERS *Cycl.* s.v. *Printing*, By running his Eye along both, he easily spies where Corrections are to be made. **1775** C. JOHNSTON *Pilgrim* 253 Having ran his eye over the letter, he desired my friend to stay there. **1828** *Examiner* 37/1 The reader runs his eye down a couple of columns. **1890** CLARK RUSSELL *Ocean Tragedy* I. iii. 53, I..caught myself running my glance round. **1890** *Chamb. Jrnl.* 1 Nov. 694/2 Running the fingers along the keys of a piano.

c. *Sc. Law.* (See LETTER *sb.*[1] 4 c.)

1818 SCOTT *Hrt. Midl.* xvi, They'll run their letters, and be adrift again, before ye ken where ye are. **1846** MCCULLOCH *Acc. Brit. Emp.* (1854) II. 224 A prisoner.. may protect himself from undue delay of trial by the remedy called 'running his letters'; a process in force since 1701.

d. To allow (bills or accounts) to accumulate for a certain time before paying.

1861 *Temple Bar* I. 277 A lady-customer who ran such heavy bills. **1874** J. S. BLACKIE *Self-Culture* 87 It is found a great safeguard against debt..not to run long accounts. **1887** RUSKIN *Præterita* II. 25 At Oxford I ran what accounts with the tradesmen I liked.

50. a. To cause to move, slide, pass, etc., in a quick or easy manner. Usually with advs. or preps. denoting direction. Also *spec.* to pass (a duster, etc.) hurriedly *over* (a surface) or *under* (furniture).

1683 MOXON *Mech. Exerc., Printing* xxiv. ¶7 He Runs the Carriage under the Plattin..: Then he Runs in the Carriage again... Then he Runs out the Carriage. **1747–96** MRS. GLASSE *Cookery* xiv. 236 Run a red-hot fire-shovel over it, to brown it. **1765** *Museum Rust.* III. 242 The poles thus prepared, the handfuls of teazels must be put on them, by running the small end through the handful. **1849** *Jrnl. R. Agric. Soc.* X. I. 272 The smaller cord to be run through a noose at the free end. **1879** *Man. Artill. Exerc.* 254 To fill the cylinder with oil, run the carriage up to the stops. **1891** *Eng. Illustr. Mag.* Oct. 69 Studding sails were run aloft. **1948** A. CHRISTIE *Taken at Flood* I. xvi. 95, I know service isn't up to much nowadays—but I still think they run a mop under the furniture. **1952** M. ALLINGHAM *Tiger in Smoke* xii. 190, I ought just to run a tape over the place. **1975** W. J. BURLEY *Wycliffe & Pea-Green Boat* viii. 115, I cook a meal for him occasionally and I run a vacuum over the place. **1977** J. R. L. ANDERSON *Death in City* i. 10 Emptying waste-paper baskets, running a duster over desks, and vacuum-cleaning floors.

transf. **1771** LUCKOMBE *Hist. Print.* 388 It is not improper to use a Comma..where figures are put after the matter, instead of running them to the end of a line. **1861** *Temple*

Bar I. 475 It was not possible.. to stifle thought, or run it in governmental grooves. 1892 *Idler* Sept. 162 Mr. Chatto.. ran *Philistia* through the pages of *The Gentleman's*.

b. To carry, pass, or suspend (a line or rope) between two points.

1769 FALCONER *Dict. Marine* (1780), *Running-out a warp*, the act of carrying the end of a rope out from the ship, in a boat. 1840 R. H. DANA *Bef. Mast* xxvi. 85 In all directions athwart-ships, tricing-lines were run, and strung with hides. 1890 S. L. POOLE *Barbary Corsairs* II. xx. 286 Some of the Intrepid's crew leisurely ran a fast to the frigate's fore-chains.

c. ***run the stage, a ship*** (see quots.).

1888 *Scribner's Mag.* Oct. 444 Before the scene can be set it is necessary to 'run the stage', that is, to get everything in the line of properties.. ready to be put in place. 1893 *Labour Comm. Gloss., Running a ship on end*, placing a ship's masts, yards, and rigging in their proper positions ready for sea again, after such ships have been stripped or dismantled.

d. *Theatr.* To move or carry (scenery) about the stage; to shift (a 'flat') along a groove. Freq. with advs., as *on, off*.

1831 J. BOADEN *Life Mrs. Jordan* I. ix. 201 English play and farce, demanding a constant succession of scenes called flats, run on suddenly for the frequent changes of place. 1889 *N.Y. Tribune* 14 July 10/5 Nearly all scenes.. are mounted on wheels which enable them to be easily moved upon the stage, hence the compound verbs 'run-on' and 'run-off', which are in universal use in the theatre. The word 'move' is scarcely ever heard. 1921 G. C. D. ODELL *Shakes. from Betterton to Irving* I. iii. 99 A Shutter is the modern 'flat', run—in two pieces— on grooves from opposite wings and clamping together when they meet midway of the stage. *Ibid.* iv. 109 The second scene is 'Ambrosio's House', and may with equal certainty be attributed to a second 'flat' scene run in, on the second groove, behind the first... The next act begins again with 'the Street', which I am convinced was run on immediately at the end of the first act. 1959 W. C. LOUNSBURY *Backstage from A to Z* 102 *Running a flat*, carrying a flat.

e. ***to run the rule over***: see RULE *sb.* 17c

51. a. To cause (a conveyance, vehicle, vessel, etc.) to ply from place to place, or between two places, or to move in a particular direction, or to a specified destination.

1764 *Jackson's Oxf. Jrnl.* 31 Mar., Samuel Borton.. Runs Neat Four-Wheeled Post-Chaises.. at Seven-Pence a Mile. 1859 *Jrnl. R. Agric. Soc.* XX. II. 314 Cheap trains had been run. 1891 *Murray's Mag.* Mar. 401 They no longer run steamers there. 1902 J. H. A. MACDONALD in A. C. Harmsworth *Motors & Motor-Driving* xix. 373 On this run he on one occasion got down for a moment, asking his friend to steer, which the friend did by promptly running the car off the road. 1913 *Autocar Handbk.* (ed. 5) xxi. 228 The car may be run in one way and out the other. 1970 J. PORTER *Rather Common Sort of Crime* iv. 42 She got back to Shangrila and ran the car into the garage.

b. To keep (a mechanical contrivance, etc.) moving or working. *spec.* to keep, use, and maintain (a road vehicle).

a1817 JANE AUSTEN *Northanger Abbey* (1818) I. vii. 86 What do you think of my gig, Miss Morland?.. A friend of mine.. ran it a few weeks, till.. it was convenient to have done with it. 1849 C. BRONTË *Shirley* ii, The hands we can't employ, the mills we can't run. a1877 KNIGHT *Dict. Mech.* II. 1346/1 Attempts are being made.. to run locomotives by means of liquid fuel. 1880 *Encycl. Brit.* XI. 203/2 Such wheels are not capable of being run at the high rate of speed which is a first essential to their efficiency. 1892 *Standard* 7 Nov. 4/7 The owners of cotton mills.. have.. been running their spindles unprofitably. 1902 A. C. HARMSWORTH *Motors & Motor-Driving* iii. 38, I am running at present four cars of French construction. 1912 *Motor Manual* (ed. 14) vi. 174 A car owner had, for a long time, been running his car with a very defective lubricator. 1924 *Discovery* June 98/1 Simple.. apparatus of this kind can be run off an ordinary lighting circuit. 1939 G. B. SHAW *Geneva* II. 45 No No: motor oil. The stuff you run your aeroplanes on. 1959 E. K. WENLOCK *Kitchin's Road Transport Law* (ed. 12) 78/2 The driver of every vehicle run under an A, special A, B or C license. 1973 'D. JORDAN' *Nile Green* xxii. 87, I can't collect you. I don't run a car.

c. To direct, conduct, carry on (a business, etc.). Orig. *U.S.* Also in various extended uses. In *transf.* sense *esp.* to look after, manage, or control (someone, *spec.* a spy). Also *refl.* (said of a business or other organization): to function smoothly, to require little administrative interference. ***to run the show***: see SHOW *sb.*[1] 16.

1861 O. J. VICTOR *Hist. Southern Rebellion* I. xvii. 252/2, I suppose I will have to run the machine as I find it. 1864 G. A. SALA in *Daily Telegr.* 23 Dec. 5/5 'To run' is a term which is so purely a modern American locution, that I cannot let it pass without brief comment... You may 'run' anything—a railroad, a bank, a school, a newspaper,..or an administration. 1866 *Harper's Mag.* Mar. 539/1 The real owner of a grocery.., which was 'run' nominally by another individual. 1883 *Referee* 29 Apr. 7/2 American evangelists and speculators who run salvation on much the same lines as Barnum runs his menagerie. 1884 J. QUINCY *Figures of Past* 370 A world which is run by steam, electricity, and newspaper extras. 1888 J. BRYCE *Amer. Commonwealth* II. lxii. 446 The primaries have almost always been so carefully packed, and so skilfully 'run', that a majority of trusty delegates has been secured. 1891 *Blackw. Mag.* CL. 788/2 He made a contract.. to run the catering department at so much per head. 1899 R. WHITEING *No. 5 John Street* i. 4 A ..coral island..'run' on principles of almost primitive Christianity. 1911 G. B. SHAW *Doctor's Dilemma* p. xxvii, He may make considerable profits at the same time by running what is the most expensive kind of hotel. 1928 E. O'NEILL *Strange Interlude* VII. 235 Why couldn't Mother let me run my own birthday? 1932 E. WAUGH *Black Mischief* viii. 295 Can't think what you see in revolutions... I suppose you ran the whole country. 1956 H. L. MENCKEN *Minority Rep.* 206 Why assume so glibly that the God who presumably created the universe is still running it? 1959 *Motor Manual* (ed. 36) xii. 265 One way of running a trial of this sort is to give each competitor a list of places. 1972 *Jrnl. Social Psychol.* Dec. 180 As a result of unexpected difficulties (early summer vacation at Patna University) only 26 groups could be run. 1974 J. MANN *Sticking Place* i. 14 He was as helpful as could be, the members always said.. though of course the place pretty well ran itself. 1977 J. AIKEN *Last Movement* iv. 76 Our staff are highly efficient; the place runs itself almost without our interference.

transf. 1888 BRYCE *Amer. Commw.* I. I. ix. 115 It is often said of the President that he is ruled, or as the Americans express it, 'run,' by his secretary. 1890 S. HALE *Let.* 2 May (1919) viii. 242 Cornelia is running me, and she is really just the right sort. 1904 CONRAD *Nostromo* I. vi. 67 He was not running a great enterprise there... He was running a man! 1931 E. F. BENSON *Mapp & Lucia* iii. 67 She wanted to run her, to sponsor her, to arrange little parties for her. 1949 *Sat. Even. Post* 23 Apr. 130/4 You're my father and all that, but I'll be damned if you run me any more. 1961 'J. LE CARRÉ' *Call for Dead* ix. 91 The East Germans.. run their agents direct from Germany. 1967 A. CHRISTIE *Endless Night* x. 89, I felt that Ellie was dependent on Greta.. that she let Greta run her. 1972 D. BLOODWORTH *Any Number can Play* xx. 206 The central Chinese department.. were running you for all you were worth. 1976 SCOTT & KOSKI *Walk-In* (1977) xv. 94 Major Ch'en was running this agent.

d. To introduce or push (a person) in society.

1897 'OUIDA' *Massarenes* ix. 98 'Everybody does [know them] through you, or rather through your wife.'.. 'Oh, we run 'em, yes.' 1900 ELINOR GLYN *Visits Elizabeth* (1906) 101, I asked her why she had invited her, then. And she said her sister-in-law.. made a point of it, as she was running them.

e. *U.S.* To support or provide for (a person or family).

1871 'MARK TWAIN' in *Galaxy* Apr. 616/1 Turnips enough to run the family for two years! 1880 —— *Tramp Abroad* 225 'Pap's so po' he cain't run me no mo', so I want to git a show somers if I kin, 'tain't no diffunce what.. I don't turn my back on no kind of work.' 1909 R. A. WASON *Happy Hawkins* 280 She was in the habit of estimatin' just how little nourishment it would take to run her to the next feed.

f. orig. *U.S.* To publish or print in a newspaper or magazine; *spec.* to publish repeatedly or successively (an advertisement, article, etc., or a series of such items). Also *transf.* of broadcast items.

1884 E. W. NYE *Baled Hay* 202 The business manager.. hated to lose old Balshazzar's whole trade, for he wouldn't run any of his ads unless he would take them all according to his contract. 1912 G. M. HYDE *Newspaper Reporting* iii. 30 If.. the editor decides not to print the story, he *kills* it; otherwise he *runs* it. 1916 J. LONDON *Let.* 31 Oct. (1966) 479 Please send me as many prints or proofs.. of this letter of mine (if you run it). 1930 *Publishers' Weekly* 8 Feb. 667/2 The full page advertisement we ran in the New York Times ..brought in more business than any advertisement we have ever run. 1950 *Time* 16 Jan. 65/3 With his vigorous news pages, Dana ran blistering editorials against Boss Tweed, the Credit Mobilier and the Whisky Ring. 1966 *Listener* 12 May 699/1 For Mr Allsop to say that the film would be shown next week was like a newspaper editor saying that he would postpone the headline of today's news to run it the following day. 1973 *N.Y. Law Jrnl.* 20 July 4/3 During the last gubernatorial election campaign in New York State, the incumbent ran some 3,000 television commercials on twenty-two different television stations. 1976 N. THORNBURG *Cutter & Bone* iii. 62 The lady who ran the ad ..evidently had liked his voice.

g. To be suffering from (a fever or high temperature).

1918 A. WOOLLCOTT *Let.* 6 July (1944) 64 Baldridge.. was running a fever which worried me a little. 1926 I. MACKAY *Blencarrow* xxxii. 273, I don't like her running this temperature. 1956 A. H. COMPTON *Atomic Quest* ii. 82 The following morning, still running a low fever, I cleared these moves with Vice President Filbey. 1961 P. DOUGHERTY *Mother Mary Potter* xxviii. 245 All through Lent Mother Potter was running a high temperature and suffering greatly. 1963 'E. MCBAIN' *Ten plus One* viii. 107, I had a little virus, I was running a small fever. 1967 C. POTOK *Chosen* xi. 189, I came home from school with a fever... I was running 103·6. 1970 D. UHNAK *Ledger* i. 17 You're warm, Christie. You must be running about a hundred and one.

h. ***to run a book*** [BOOK *sb.* 11], to take bets; also *transf.*

1931 *Economist* 10 Oct. 642/1 The discount market has been inactive, and many brokers are running narrow books, and so are needing less money than usual. 1955 *Times* 12 Aug. 5/4 Powell, who explained that he had been 'running a book' in the prison.

i. To show (a film or television recording); to set (a film camera) in action. Also with *through*.

1940 [see sense 33b above]. 1953 E. SIMON *Past Masters* III. 196 'Have you ever thought of doing anything, with that Mexican film of yours, Hamish?'.. 'If I coold have it run through somewhere and have another luke at it.' 1956 H. KURNITZ *Invasion of Privacy* viii. 64 'Your film.. unmistakably duplicates a heartbreaking episode experienced by my client.'.. 'We'll run the picture for your client and guarantee to substantially change any objectionable portion.' 1973 V. CANNING *Finger of Saturn* i. 8 I'll run them [*sc.* films] straight through. 1974 I. MURDOCH *Sacred & Profane Love Machine* 125 Harriet felt giddy and exposed as if very quietly, as in a silent film run in slow motion, the house had been hit by a bomb. 1974 *Daily Tel.* 2 May 3/4 Using a friend's projector and screen, he ran a short colour film taken at the wedding.

j. To perform (a test, analysis, experiment, or the like); to subject (something) to, or measure (a property) by means of, an experimental procedure.

1947 *Jrnl. Biol. Chem.* CLXVII. 553 Assays run in replicate of course give narrow limits of confidence, the limits decreasing with increasing replication. 1961 *Lancet* 5 Aug. 291/2 The mobility of the abnormal screen-globulin did not correspond with that of the Bence Jones protein when both were run in a starch gel containing 2-mercaptoethanol. 1964 ROBERTS & CASERIO *Basic Princ. Org. Chem.* ii. 29 Solids are often run as finely ground suspensions. 1970 H. MCLEAVE *Question of Negligence* (1973) xxi. 167 Could Cameron have some sort of brain lesion?.. It was imperative to run those tests. 1976 M. MACHLIN *Pipeline* lviii. 588 In a test he ran, oil soaked ice disintegrated and sank within five days, while adjacent ice did not melt at all. 1978 *Nature* 8 June 456/2 Curie temperatures were run for seven specimens, and they ranged from 222 to 272 °C, with an average of 248 °C.

k. *Computers.* To perform (a computation), execute (a program or other task), investigate (a problem), etc., on a computer.

1952 *Rev. Electronic Digital Computers* (Amer. Inst. Electr. Engineers) 12/3 The last problem in this field has not yet been run, but the study has shown that the entire gamut of stock control for a large supply office can be covered by the computer in approximately 3 weeks time. 1968 E. O. JOSLIN *Computer Selection* iv. 70 One should examine each class of programs to determine the equipment required to run that class of program through the computer. 1973 *Computers & Humanities* VII. 225 Instructors considering adopting this text can be assured that the programs accompanying the flowcharts do work since all solutions have been run. 1977 [see *program library* s.v. PROGRAM, PROGRAMME *sb.* 4].

52. a. ***run one's face for***, to get (an article) on credit. *U.S.* See also FACE *sb.* 7b.

a1848 in Bartlett *Dict. Amer.* 281 Any one who can run his face for a card of pens, a quire of paper, and a pair of scissors, may set up for an editor.

b. To put or set up as a candidate. Orig. *U.S.*

1789 *Maryland Jrnl.* 2 Jan. 3/2 It was agreed to run the following ticket in their respective Districts. 1792 A. HAMILTON *Let.* 10 Oct. in *Wks.* (1886) VIII. 286 Either Governor Clinton, or Mr. Burr,.. is to be run in this quarter as Vice-President, in opposition to Mr. Adams. 1825 J. K. PAULDING *John Bull in Amer.* v. 85 [They] talk of running him for the next governor. 1862 H. KINGSLEY *Ravenshoe* xxxvii, He.. might have been run for M.L.C., or possibly for Congress in a year or two. 1879 T. P. O'CONNOR *Beaconsfield* 46 The Reformers ran a candidate of their own colour.

c. *U.S.* and *Austral.* To tease, nag, or vex. Characterized by Webster (1879) as 'Colloq. or low'.

1835 P. HONE *Diary* 16 Mar. (1889) I. 134 This is a club ..where they sup, drink champagne and whiskey punch, talk as well as they know how, and run each other good-humouredly. 1860 J. G. HOLLAND *Miss Gilbert's Career* 349 Now what's the use of running a feller? 1879 WEBSTER *Suppl.* s.v. 1888 'R. BOLDREWOOD' *Robbery under Arms* xix, He thought I wanted to have my own way, and he made it up to take it out of me, and run me every way he could.

d. To prosecute (a person); to bring (one) in *for* damages.

1891 'ANNIE THOMAS' *That Affair* II. viii. 138, I shall run that woman for infringement of literary rights. 1892 *Sat. Rev.* 22 Oct. 481/2 Such a proceeding would ruin him.. and 'run' him 'for hideous damages'.

e. *slang.* To report or hand over (someone) to the police, etc. *spec.* in *Mil.* use, to bring a charge against (someone).

1909 E. WYRALL *Spike* iii. 17 In tramp language, to be 'run' is to be handed over to the police. 1919 *Athenæum* 18 July 632/2 'Running a man' means bringing a charge against him for orderly room. 1925 FRASER & GIBBONS *Soldier & Sailor Words* 247 *Run, to*, to report or charge anyone with an offence. 1930 BROPHY & PARTRIDGE *Songs & Slang 1914–1918* 157 Let them spades alone or I'll run yer. 1933 'G. INGRAM' *Stir* xii. 188 Was any of you monkeying with the cocoa last night?.. If I find out who it was, I'll run 'im and make it 'ot for him. a1935 T. E. LAWRENCE *Mint* (1955) II. iii. 107 We are supposed to have a flight-lieutenant over us. I saw one, when the Sergeant Major ran me.

f. To manipulate or falsify, esp. in phr. ***to run the odds***.

1922 JOYCE *Ulysses* 312, I heard So and So made a cool hundred quid over it, says Alf... He let out that Myler was on the beer to run the odds and he swatting all the time.

g. ***to run one's mouth***, to talk profusely or excessively, to chatter; to complain. Cf. *to shoot (off) one's mouth* s.v. SHOOT *v.* 23g. *U.S.* and *Black slang*.

1940 W. FAULKNER *Tomorrow* in *Sat. Even. Post* 23 Nov. 39/1 Drunk still & running his mouth. 1954 in CASSIDY & LE PAGE *Dict. Jamaican Eng.* (1967) 388/1 Yu run yu mout fe not a ting, all de talk yu talk fe nutten. 1970 C. MAJOR *Dict. Afro-Amer. Slang* 98 *Run (one's) mouth*, to talk excessively; to complain. 1973 *Black Panther* 24 Mar. 14/3 Maybe you call working running your mouth on these TV programs. 1977 *Time* 13 June 50/1 All there is to real estate is running your mouth a bit, knocking on doors and asking people if they want to sell their house.

h. ***to run a game***: to obtain money by deceit or trickery; freq. const. *on*. *U.S. Blacks*.

1967 J. HORTON in *Trans-Action* Apr. 6/2 Their reasons for disapproving of hustling were not moral. Hustling meant trouble... Others said there was not enough money on the street or that it was too difficult to 'run a game' on people. 1973 T. KOCHMAN *Rappin' & Stylin' Out* 162 Other operators on the street who are looking for a chance to 'whup' (Chicago) or 'run' (Los Angeles, New York) 'a game' (trick someone out of some money) are known as 'slicks' or 'slicksters'. 1974 H. L. FOSTER *Ribbin'* ii. 30 This is.. the behavior that urban blacks use to 'run a game on the man'. *Ibid.* iv. 160 He knows how to 'run a game' to get what he desires from people. 1975 *Language* LI. 246 If we look at a number of Los Angeles examples of black 'put down' terms (e.g... *to run a game on someone*..) and K's example *to mount someone*, we can see that such expressions.. are positive and kinetic.

53. †**a.** To prolong (a note) in singing. *Obs.*⁻¹

1602 MARSTON *Ant. & Mel.* IV. Wks. 1856 I. 49 The Boy runnes a note, Antonio breakes it.

b. ***run the line***(*s*, to determine, fix, or mark off a boundary-line. *U.S.*

1641 *Rhode Island Col. Rec.* (1856) I. 114 It is ordered, that Mr. Porter..and Mr. Jeoffreys shall runn the line between the Touns. **1708** S. SEWALL *Diary* 28 Mar., I agreed with Major Thaxter to run the Line of my 300 Acres of Land. **1764** T. HUTCHINSON *Hist. Mass.* i. (1765) 208 The lines between..the governments..have been run. **1809** KENDALL *Trav.* I. ii. 15 The boundaries are usually determined, or in the technical phrase, the lines run, by a land-surveyor. **1892** GUNTER *Miss Dividends* (1893) 63 Ever since he ran the lines in Nebraska when that State was a howling wilderness.

c. To cut (a mark), draw or trace (a line), on a surface.

1680 MOXON *Mech. Exerc.* xii. 214 The quick coming about of the Work may draw the edge of the Chissel into it inwards, and run a dawk on the Cilinder, like the Groove of a Screw. **1838** *Encycl. Metrop.* (1845) XXV. 301/1 It is requisite to..determine the position of the ship before running a new base. *c* **1850** *Rudim. Nav.* (Weale) 144 The running or drawing of a line on the ship, or mould-loft floor; as 'to *run* the wale line', or deck line, &c. **1895** E. ROWE *Chip-Carving* 27 This is best obtained by running lines and bevelling edges on a waste bit of wood before commencing to carve.

d. To trace or pursue (a parallel, resemblance, etc.); to draw (a distinction).

a **1716** SOUTH (J.), To run the world back to its first original..is a research too great for mortal enquiry. *a* **1768** STERNE *Serm.* (1773) I. 180 One might run the parallel much farther. **1794** PALEY *Evid.* II. iii. (1817) 96 The lawyer's subtilty in running a distinction upon the word neighbour. **1824** *Examiner* 8/1 It has been..the fashion to run comparisons between this cathedral church and that of St. Peter's. *Ibid.* 194/1, I am running my..simile too far. **1866** *Ecclesiologist* XXVII. 234 There is the danger of mistaking it by running the resemblance too far.

e. To lead, take, extend, carry (a thing) in a certain direction, or to a certain length.

1713 ADDISON *Guardian* No. 100, A slip of fine Linnen, run in a small kind of Ruffle round the uppermost Verge of Women's Stays. **1736** T. LEDIARD *Marlborough* III. 82 A Trench of Fascines and Earth being run thro' the Morass. **1832** AUSTIN *Jurispr.* (1879) II. liii. 887 A road or canal is run by authority of parliament through the lands of private persons. **1869** SIR E. REED *Shipbuild.* vi. 100 An intermediate frame..is run down from the upper deck to the third longitudinal. **1891** *Cosmopolitan* XII. 88/2 Lines of stake are run in various directions.

transf. **1849** *Tait's Mag.* XVI. 196/1 The narrative is run into three volumes, when it should have been one only. **1890** W. C. RUSSELL *Ocean Tragedy* III. xxx. 137 The work ran us deep into the afternoon.

f. *Plastering.* To form (a cornice, etc.); also, to cover (a space) with plaster.

1823 *Practical Builder* ix. 376 When the mould is ready, the process of running the cornice begins. **1825** J. NICHOLSON *Operat. Mech.* 616 In running cornices which are to be enriched, the plasterer takes care to have proper projections in the running-mould. **1849** *Jrnl. R. Agric. Soc.* X. I. 238 A chamfered skirting..to be run in cement round the living rooms. *Ibid.*, The floors of the chamber story to be run with plaster on laths. **1893** J. P. ALLEN *Pract. Building Construction* xxi. 337 Cornices, and other ornamental mouldings,..are 'run' in plaster by means of 'horsed mouldings', running on a wood ground fixed on the wall, truly horizontal, the required depth of the cornice. **1966** C. LLOYD *Building Construction* 115 (*caption*) Cornice mould run in situ in coarse plaster, using a sheet zinc profile.

g. *Bridge.* To take an uninterrupted succession of tricks in (a particular suit), to take (a number of tricks) in that way, to play (one's cards in a suit) in that way.

1929 M. C. WORK *Compl. Contract Bridge* iv. 21 The bidder..is insured against having his adversaries open and 'run' that particular suit. **1976** *Country Life* 29 Jan. 250/1 South drew trumps..then ran three Club tricks.

*** *To cause to flow or come together.*

54. a. To give forth, to flow with (a specified kind of liquid).

a **1300** *Cursor M.* 5793 A land rinnand bath honi and milk. *c* **1400** MAUNDEV. (1839) xxvii. 278 So that [of] the 3 Welles ..on scholde renne Milk, another Wyn, and another Hony. **1593** SHAKS. *2 Hen. VI*, IV. vi. 4, I..command, that of the Cities cost The..Conduit run nothing but Clarret Wine. **1601** —— *Jul. C.* III. ii. 193 At the Base of Pompeyes Statue (Which all the while ran blood). **1639** FULLER *Holy War* v. xiii. (1647) 252 They ranne dregs when first they were broched in Syria. **1684** WOOD *Life* 2 Oct., At the same time the conduit ran clarret. **1737** BRACKEN *Farriery Impr.* (1756) I. 97 To make the Nose run a thin Lymph or watery Humour. **1766** *Compl. Farmer* s.v. *Purging*, Horses.. subject to swelled legs, that run a sharp briny ichor. **1811** W. R. SPENCER *Poems* 81 His lips, his fangs, ran blood. **1835** S. SMITH *Mem.* (1855) II. 381 Rivers are said to run blood after an engagement. **1896** A. E. HOUSMAN *Shropshire Lad* xlii, All the brooks ran gold.

transf. **1858** KINGSLEY *Sappho* 17 Till all her veins ran fever.

b. To discharge; to convey (water) *out of* land.

1705 tr. *Bosman's Guinea* 286 When it hath almost run its last, they kindle a fire at bottom. **1844** *Jrnl. R. Agric. Soc.* V. I. 154 A drain, 4 feet deep, ran 8 pints of water in the same time that another 3 feet deep ran 5 pints. **1845** *Ibid.* VI. II. 574 The drains..will run the water out of the land.

c. With *out*: To exhaust (oneself) *of* something.

1889 A. E. BARR *Feet of Clay* iii. 45 You have run yourself out of threats, you have not one left that I fear.

55. a. To cause to coagulate, or to unite in a viscid mass. Also const. *to*.

1398 TREVISA *Barth. De P.R.* XVII. cxxxviii. (Bodl. MS.), Suche humoure is strongeliche ifastened & ronne bi vertu and myȝt of hete. *c* **1590** GREENE *Fr. Bacon* i, She turned her smocke ouer her lilly armes, And diued them into milke to run her cheese. **1736** PEGGE *Kenticisms* (E.D.S.) 44 Runnet, the herb *gallium*,..runs the milk together, i.e. makes it curdle. **1778** [W. H. MARSHALL] *Minutes Agric.* 29 Nov. 1774, Now, the frost, snow, and rains, having run the soil to mortar, it slides. **1848** *Jrnl. R. Agric. Soc.* IX. II. 548 They are filled up with fine soil from the surface which has been run with the frost.

b. To unite or combine. Const. *into*, *together*.

1781 H. DOWNMAN tr. *Voltaire* I. 215 Our verses cannot be run into one another. **1849** *Tait's Mag.* XVI. 202/2 The parties named have run their contributions together to form one small volume. **1868** FREEMAN *Norm. Conq.* (1877) II. 648 The events of two days have been run into one.

c. To convert *into* a certain form.

1700 DRYDEN *Pref. Fables* Ess. (ed. Ker) II. 249 To run them into verse, or to give them the other harmony of prose. *a* **1704** LOCKE (J.), Others..run natural philosophy into metaphysical notions. **1884** W. E. HENLEY in Ward *Eng. Poets* III. 230 Some of whose discourse he was at the pains of running into English verse.

56. a. To smelt (metal); to form into sheets, bars, etc., by allowing to flow into moulds.

1663 GERBIER *Counsel* 87 Lead run thin, to serve for gutters. **1699** DAMPIER *Voy.* (1729) II. I. 70 The Tonquinese understand how to run Metals. **1727** in *6th Rep. Deputy Kpr.* App. II. 118 A new way of Calcining, Melting, and Running Copper Ores. **1873** E. SPON *Workshop Rec.* Ser. I. 12/2 It should be first run into ingots, then melted. **1884** C. G. W. LOCK *Ibid.* Ser. III. 356/1 Until the crystals ..are fit to be melted, and run into pigs for market.

b. = CAST *v.* 51. Also *refl.* and *transf.*

1690 W. WALKER *Idiomat. Anglo-Lat.* 384 He run himself in brass. *a* **1744** LUCAS in *Trans. Cumb. & Westm. Archæol. Soc.* VIII. 35 The Fire will be so intense that they can run a Sow and Pigs once in about twelve hours. **1778** *England's Gaz.* (ed. 2), *Buckstead*,..where were run the first pieces of cast iron that were ever made in England. **1868** *U.S. Rep. Munitions War* 119 The quantum necessary for running a cannon of certain dimensions. **1886** CAROLINE HAZARD *Mem. J. L. Diman* ii. 40 He seems, least of all men, run in the mould of any particular school.

c. To cause (a liquid) to flow *into* a vessel, *through* a strainer, etc. Also *spec.* without *const.*, to cause water to flow into (a bathtub); to pour out water for (a bath).

1728 CHAMBERS *Cycl.* s.v. *Copper*, The melted Matter [is] run into a kind of Molds. **1838** *Penny Cycl.* X. 386/1 Instead of melting and running the metal at once from a large furnace, earthen crucibles are used. **1857** MILLER *Elem. Chem., Org.* ii. §3 (1862) 101 A small portion of water, run through a fine sieve, to keep back any portions of sand. **1879** *Man. Artill. Exerc.* 254 Repeat the operation until the quantity [of oil] required is run in. **1933** R. HICHENS *Paradine Case* xxvi. 277 His valet was running the bath. **1955** W. GADDIS *Recognitions* II. i. 341 When Basil Valentine got home, he ran his bath immediately. **1958** OSBORNE & CREIGHTON *Epitaph for George Dillon* I. 20 I'll go and run myself a bath. **1971** *Ink* 12 June 15/1 Anna..asks if she should run her bath. **1974** 'M. ALLEN' *Super Tour* vi. 225 Be a good boy. You can begin by running me a hot bath.

fig. **1844** MRS. BROWNING *Wine of Cyprus* xx, Yet that shadow..ran Both our spirits to one level.

d. *Sc.* To draw (liquor). *rare*⁻¹.

1717 RAMSAY *Elegy on L. Wood* vi, She ne'er ran sour jute.

e. To spread by allowing to flow.

1855 BREWSTER *Newton* I. vii. 158 If we take any glutinous substance, and run it exceedingly thin upon the surface of a smooth glass.

f. To wash (colour) *from* (something).

1850 MRS. BROWNING *Sonn. fr. Portuguese* viii, Frequent tears have run The colours from my life.

g. To cause water to flow over (something) held *under* a tap.

1921 in *Sc. Nat. Dict.* (1968) VII. 448/2 To run one's hands under the tap. **1972** *Guardian* 18 Aug. 11/3 Boil the pasta..then drain and run under the cold tap. **1979** *Daily Tel.* 24 Aug. 14 One wine expert commented: 'This is just the same as running a bottle under the tap. It would ruin any decent wine.'

57. †**a.** To overflow *with* tears, etc. *Obs.*

1423 JAS. I *Kingis Q.* lv, Quhen thy brestis wete Were with the teres of thyne eyen clere, All bludy ronne.

b. To fill up or fasten *together* with molten metal, etc.

1657–8 in Willis & Clark *Cambridge* (1886) II. 97 New running and repairing the leads in the new building. **1696** DE LA PRYME *Diary* (Surtees) 100 It [a glass coffin] was excellently well soldered or run together. **1735** J. PRICE *Stone-Br. Thames* 5 The Stones well cramp'd..together, run with Lead. **1793** SMEATON *Edystone L.* §274 It is.. impracticable..that the whole of the circle could be run at once. **1837** *Civil Eng. & Arch. Jrnl.* I. 12/2 [They] are to be connected by spigot and faucet joints run with lead. **1869** PHILLIPS *Vesuv.* ii. 34 The stone being set and run together by a liquid mortar.

58. To let water escape through or from (a sluice, pool, etc.); esp. ***run dry*** (also *refl.* and *fig.*).

1839 *Civil Eng. & Arch. Jrnl.* II. 76/2 The sluices have been run to night. **1891** *Blackw. Mag.* CXLIX. 782/1 The only thing to be done is to..run the pool dry and clean it. **1891** *Harper's Mag.* July 166/2 My artistic vein had run itself dry. **1892** *Argosy* Apr. 287 The old gentleman had run his subject dry.

III. With prepositions, in specialized uses.

In all of these the verb is intransitive; for prepositions following the transitive verb, see senses 43 to 56.

59. run across ——, to meet or fall in with.

1880 'MARK TWAIN' *Tramp Abroad* xxi. 202 If I don't run across you in Italy, you hunt me up in London before you sail. **1887** J. HAWTHORNE *Tragic Myst.* viii, The young man who happens to run across one of them and to make a good impression on her, may be accounted lucky. **1903** 'C. E. MERRIMAN' *Letters from Son* 151, I keep running across Job Withers. **1930** D. RUNYON in *Collier's* 20 Dec. 32/3 Now in the summer of 1928 I am in Halifax.., when I run across Louie the Lug.

60. run after ——.

a. To endeavour to gain the companionship or society of; to pursue with admiration or attentions.

1526 SKELTON *Magnyf.* 2172, I am so lusty to loke on,.. That nonnes wyll leue theyr holynes and ryn after me. **1603** PARSONS *Let.* 6 July in *Cath. Rec. Soc. Publ.* (1906) II. 214 All this courte rane after him. **1781** D. WILLIAMS tr. *Voltaire* II. 32 Many fine women have run after me. **1802** MARY CHARLTON tr. *La Fontaine's Reprobate* II. 156 When she found that her daughter was being run after by all our idle young men, she..went away. **1890** 'R. BOLDREWOOD' *Col. Reformer* (1891) 164 Every one runs after him—men, women, and children.

b. To follow, take up with, eagerly.

1611 BIBLE *Jude* 11 Wo vnto them, for they..ranne greedily after the errour of Balaam for reward, and perished. **1656** F. HAWKINS *Youth's Behaviour* (1663) 54 That English itch of running after fashions. **1751** F. COVENTRY *Pompey the Little* 154 [Her] thoughts ran wholly after..operas, Masquerades, Ridottas, and the like. **1823** KEBLE *Serm.* iii. (1848) 44 To prevent their running blindly after any doctrine, which might please their ear. **1890** TOUT *Hist. Eng. fr. 1689* 109 Frederick and the whole nobility ran after the poorer operas of the fashionable favourite.

61. run against ——.

a. To act, operate, take effect, be directed, against (one).

1375 BARBOUR *Bruce* II. 434 Sen it is swa That vre rynnys agane ws her. *c* **1489** SKELTON *Death Earl Northumbld.* 140 Tyll the chaunce ran agayne hym of Fortunes duble dyse. **1538** in R. G. Marsden *Sel. Pl. Crt. Adm.* (Selden Soc.) II. 66 The xxiiij houres beyng paste the sayed assurauns dothe rone ageynst me..and my goodes. **1624** LUSHINGTON *Resurrection* (1659) 30 Things running as they did against our Saviour. **1789** MRS. PIOZZI *Journ. France* I. 104 If conjugal disputes arise,..the public voice is sure to run against the husband. **1818** CRUISE *Digest* (ed. 2) II. 153 Where twenty years have elapsed..and the time has begun to run against the ancestor. **1891** *Law Times Rep.* LXIII. 693/2 The statute began to run when the lease was wrongfully deposited..and has never ceased to run against the plaintiff.

b. To dash rapidly and forcibly against (a person or thing); to encounter suddenly or casually. Also ***to run up against*** (fig.), to meet with difficulty, obstruction, or opposition from (a person or thing).

c **1386** CHAUCER *Can. Yeom. T.* 404 He is as bold to renne agayn a stoon, As for to go bysides in the wey. **1485** CAXTON *Paris & V.* (1868) 85, I shal rather renne wyth my hede ayenst the walle. **1575** in W. H. Turner *Select. Rec. Oxford* (1880) 359 His companye..did ronne against and break downe the dore. **1821** P. EGAN *Life in London* II. v. 285 Such is the *hypocrisy* displayed on the one side, and the saucy low independence exhibited on the other, which are to be *run against* every day in 'Life in London'! **1825** *New Monthly Mag.* XVI. 182 How can he tell that he will not run bolt against his own divorced wife? **1886** BEATRICE BUTT *Lesterre Durant* I. xv. 222 The very man I have been hoping I'd run up against one of these days. **1886** [see *up against* s.v. UP *adv.*[1] 24]. **1914** 'HIGH JINKS, JR.' *Choice Slang* 23 Running up against a stone wall. **1924** *Truth* (Sydney) 27 Apr. 6 *Run against*, to meet. **1960** A. MUNRO in R. Weaver *Canad. Short Stories* (1968) 2nd Ser. 278, I had run up against the simple unprepossessing materialism which was the rock of their lives.

62. run before ——, to keep ahead of, to anticipate (a time, subject, etc.).

1596 SHAKS. *Merch. V.* II. vi. 4 It is meruaile he out-dwels his houre, For louers euer run before the clocke. **1601** B. JONSON *Poetaster* v. iii, Let your matter runne before your words. **1732** SWIFT *Let.* 20 Mar., Wks. 1778 XVI. 366, I mean, that my heart runs before my pen. **1821** *Examiner* 762/1 Imagination will run before any power of fulfilment. **1859** HAWTHORNE *Marble Faun* xx, An impulse ran before his thoughts.

63. run in ——.

†**a.** To incur, involve oneself in (blame, penalties, loss, danger, etc.). *Obs.*

c **1386** CHAUCER *Can. Yeom. Prol. & T.* 352 Ful oft he renneth in a blame. *c* **1400** *Apol. Loll.* 75 Men..schuld tak hed how in þis same þei ren in þe curse of God. **1444** *Rolls of Parlt.* V. 113/1 That the yevers of excessyff Salaryes.. renne in the same payne. **1579** GOSSON *Sch. Abuse* (Arb.) 71 Hee forbiddeth the one too runne in daunger of the wolfe. **1613** SHAKS. *Hen. VIII*, I. ii. 110, I am sorry, that the Duke of Buckingham Is run in your displeasure. **1637** EARL MONM. tr. *Malvezzi's Romulus & Tarquin* 297 He goes himselfe in person, and runs in danger of those who stay behinde.

b. To lapse or fall into arrears of (payment, debt, etc.).

1377 LANGL. *P. Pl.* B. XI. 124 He may renne in arrerage and rowme so fro home. *c* **1380** WYCLIF *Sel. Wks.* III. 158 þus þei rennen in dette, and wasten hor godes. **1433** *Rolls of Parlt.* IV. 439/1 Yhe yeerly moste renne in much gretter Dette. **1555–6** *Cal. Anc. Rec. Dublin* (1889) I. 453 Whereas the cittie..dyd ronne in entrest due to the said Mr. Umfrey. **1605** BP. HALL *Medit. & Vows* II. §4, I haue seene many prodigall wasters runne so farre in bookes that they cannot abide to heare of reckoning. **1729** SWIFT *Direct. Servants, Waiting-Maid*, Therefore, I fear you must be forced, like the rest of your Sisters, to run in Trust, and pay for it out of your wages. **1749** FIELDING *Tom Jones* XVIII. xiii, She spends three times the income of her fortune, without running in debt. **1765–8** ERSKINE *Inst. Law Scot.* II. vi. §44 (1773) 270 The tenant running two full years rent in arrear. **1861** *Temple Bar* III. 449 He had allowed the Goldthorpe family to run in his debt. **1891** *Blackw. Mag.* CXLIX. 508/2 [They] drew usurious bills on the wages that ran for five weeks in arrear.

†**c.** To go astray in error, etc. *Obs.*

1471 RIPLEY *Comp. Alch.* v. xli. in Ashm. (1652) 158 Rennying in errors more and more, For lac of trew understandyng. **1497** BP. ALCOK *Mons Perfect.* B iij, He caused them to renne in apostacye.

64. run into ——.

For trans. uses, see various senses from 44 b to 56 c.

a. To incur (blame, displeasure, loss, etc.); to involve oneself in (debt, expenses, etc.).

c **1400** *Apol. Loll.* 42 And so many wyse to renne in to þe wrat of God. *c* **1450** *Godstow Reg.* 104 Leste that the same Rauf or his heires shold rynne into harme thereof afterwarde. **1474** *Rolls of Parlt.* VI. 108/2 Wherby he ranne into the payne conteigned in the same Acte. **1530** PALSGR. 696/1, I runne in to a daunger, or to an inconvenyence, or in the displeasure of a persone, *je encours.* **1614** J. COOKE *Greene's Tu Quoque* C j b, When the harlotries Doe pine and runne into diseases. **1678** BUNYAN *Pilgr.* I. (1900) 128, I have by my sins run a great way into God's Book. **1736** LEDIARD *Marlborough* III. 300 The Tradesmen were let run into an Arrear of 30,000*l.* *a* **1770** JORTIN *Serm.* (1771) II. xvii. 342 To run into expenses they cannot afford.

b. To rush headlong, fall, into (some practice).

c **1380** WYCLIF *Wks.* (1880) 120 Bi ypocrisie þei rennen into pride. **1628** EARLE *Microcosm., Alderman,* Hee is one that will not hastily runne into error. **1692** JAS. II in T. Longueville *Adv. Jas. II* (1904) xxviii. 478, I..would have you avoyd those faults I have run into. **1711** ADDISON *Spect.* No. 64 ¶2 The general Affectation..makes the whole World run into the Habit of the Court. **1729** BUTLER *Serm.* Wks. 1874 II. 5 These are the absurdities which even men of capacity run into.

c. To go on, advance, into (something); to mount up or amount to. Also, ***to run into money*** (see quot. 1934). *U.S. colloq.*

1679 MOXON *Mech. Exerc.* VII. 134, I shall run no further into this Argument. **1749** FIELDING *Tom Jones* Ded., I have run into a preface, while I proferred to write a dedication. **1754** CHATHAM *Lett. Nephew* iii. 13, I find my letter has run into some length. **1890** *Leisure Hour* Dec. 92/2 Railway takings run into large sums. **1893** *National Obs.* 1 July 168/1 A thesis which ran into five editions. **1934** WEBSTER s.v., *Run into money,* to amount to a considerable sum; to cost a considerable amount. **1973** N. MEYER *Target Practice* (1975) ii. 20 You realize this could run into money?.. I generally get a hundred dollars a day plus expenses.

d. To pass by change or transformation, to develop, into (something).

1422 tr. *Secreta Secret., Priv. Priv.* 151 His gladnys rynnyth al-way into worse.

1707 MORTIMER *Husb.* (1721) I. 382 A piece of flat Stone two Inches thick, will run perhaps into twenty Slates. **1792** *Ann. Reg., Hist.* 10 Anarchy, according to the nature of extremes, ran into despotism. **1855** MACAULAY *Hist. Eng.* xi. III. 30 That profound reverence for law and prescription which..runs sometimes into pedantry. **1890** *Longman's Mag.* Dec. 181 Every sermon..ran into a scathing denunciation of the new Poor Law.

e. To merge into; to blend or coalesce with. (Cf. also *run into one* under 19 b.)

1699 T. BAKER *Refl. Learning* 206 The rest of that MS. is writ in long Lines, and the Words run into one another. **1726** LEONI *Alberti's Archit.* I. 65/1 The Hills that lie beneath them all running one into another with..little Vallies between. **1849** *Jrnl. R. Agric. Soc.* X. II. 606 These patches quickly increase in size so as to run into each other. **1879** *How to teach History* ii. 29 History proper is continuous. One year runs into another.

f. To fall into; to tend towards; to be displayed in.

1721 BRADLEY *Philos. Acc. Wks. Nat.* 175 Being Subject.. to have the Benefit run only into a few Hands. **1753** *Chambers' Cycl.* Suppl. s.v. *Plastering,* The modern taste runs greatly into plastering. **1821** SCOTT *Pirate* xii, I run into rhyme when I so much as think upon them. **1890** H. S. MERRIMAN *Suspense* II. xiii. 300 [Their] talents ran more into words than into action.

g. To dash into or collide with, esp. by accident. Also of dogs, to close with (an animal).

1812 *Sporting Mag.* XXXIX. 232 The hounds ran into him [a fox] a few fields distance from the wood. **1850** R. G. CUMMING *Hunter's Life S. Afr.* (ed. 2) I. 84 One of my greyhounds..at once ran into him and pulled him down. **1885** *Law Rep. 10 Probate Div.* 101 A large steamer..ran into her, doing considerable damage. **1895** *Law Times Rep.* LXXIII. 623/1 To try and prevent the train from running into the children.

h. orig. *U.S.* To encounter, meet by chance.

1902 G. H. LORIMER in *Sat. Even. Post* 22 Feb. 11/1 You're just about due now to run into a smart Aleck buyer. **1926** E. O'NEILL *Great God Brown* I. ii. 35 The one time I ran into him, I thought he told me he'd destroyed all his pictures. **1934** 'A. BRIDGE' *Peking Picnic* vi. 60 Mrs. Leroy and the Kuniangs, walking with Derek Fitzmaurice on the City Wall, ran into Miss Ingersoll and Henri Delache. **1954** KOESTLER *Invisible Writing* xv. 164, I ran into Hahn as I was getting off the Number Eleven tram. **1977** A. MORICE *Scared to Death* iii. 21, I expect she's run into one or two acquaintances.

65. run on ——.

a. To discourse on; to refer or relate to.

1472 *Paston Lett.* III. 57 My modyr hathe herd of that mater by the reporte of old Wayte, whyche rennyth on it with opyn mowthe in hys werst wyse. **1549** CHALONER *Erasm. on Folly* N iij, Admitte theyr theme renne on charitee. **1711** ADDISON *Spect.* No. 99 ¶5 The whole Story runs on Chastity and Courage. **1892** STEVENSON & L. OSBOURNE *Wrecker* xx, The talk ran endlessly on the great house.

b. Of the mind: To be engrossed or occupied with (a subject). †Also with *of.*

[**1504** ATKYNSON tr. *De Imitatione* II. i. 179 Theyr myndes renne moost of the ende of theyr iourney.] *a* **1529** SKELTON *Bowge of Courte* 399, I haue no coyne nor crosse! I am not happy, I renne ay on the losse. *a* **1593** MARLOWE *Edw. II,* II. ii, Still his mind runs on his minion. **1602** *Narcissus* (1893) 181 Your heads may runne on crotchett..to know what manner wight..I am. **1709** STEELE *Tatler* No. 33 ¶6 My Head ran all that Day and Night on the exemplary Carriage of this Woman. **1819** SCOTT *Let.* in *Lockhart* (1837) IV. vii. 219 His mind running entirely on mathematics and fortification. **1889** M. E. CARTER *Mrs. Severn* III. III. iii. 100 Her thoughts had run on illness and death.

c. To show a marked demand or preference for (some particular thing).

1683 MOXON *Mech. Exerc., Printing* 389 When Matter runs much on some few Sorts of Letters, they say, it Runs on Sorts. **1895** *Westm. Gaz.* 22 Apr. 1/2 Colour seemed chiefly to run on that blending of purple and geranium.

d. *U.S.* (See quot. and cf. *run upon.*)

1847 WEBSTER, *Run on,* .. to press with jokes or ridicule; to abuse with sarcasms; to bear hard on.

66. run out of ——.

†**a.** To run through or squander (property). *Obs.*

1710 *Tatler* No. 221 ¶2 Having excused himself for running out of his Estate. **1747** MRS. S. FIELDING *Lett. David Simple* I. 137 This Gentleman had run out of a good Fortune when young.

b. To come to the end of, to exhaust, one's supply of (something). Also with inanimate subject.

1713 *Guardian* No. 141 ¶6 When we had run out of Mony, we had no living Soul to befriend us. **1858** CARLYLE *Fredk. Gt.* XIX. ix. (1872) VIII. 271 In the end, he must run-out of men. **1893** *Scribner's Mag.* Feb. 259/2 The British ran out of ammunition. **1929** D. MACKAIL *How Amusing!* 244 He had run out of tobacco the night before. **1938** MRS. BELLOC LOWNDES *Diary* 29 Sept. (1971) 165, I ran out of methylated in the last war. **1966** *New Statesman* 14 Oct. 546/2 There was a popular line about the Tories running into Europe because they had run out of ideas. **1970** *Amer. Speech 1968* XLIII. 59 Those who participated were asked to fill their cars with a small amount of gasoline and then have the cars run out of gas on one of the highways leading to the New York World's Fair. **1971** [see LET *v.*[1] 32 b]. **1973** J. PORTER *It's Murder with Dover* viii. 71 Do you mind just hanging on for a second, sir? I've-er-run out of cigarettes.

c. In various colloq. phrases, as ***to run out of road***: to approach the end of the roadway (usu. on failing to turn into a bend); also *transf.* and *fig.*; hence ***to run out of track,*** etc.; ***to run out of steam***: of persons, to exhaust one's energy, ideas, etc.; also of things.

1961 Run out of steam [see *post-Christmas* s.v. POST- B. 1 a]. **1961** *Sunday Tel.* 9 July 6/3 When he [*sc.* the motorist] 'runs out of road', he gets severely 'bent'. **1965** PRIESTLEY & WISDOM *Good Driving* xii. 83 'Coming unstuck' or 'running out of road' are the light-hearted expressions used by the motor racing fraternity for an experience which can be the far-from-amusing result of attempting to take a bend with the 'wrong' camber at too great a speed. **1968** *Times* 29 Nov. 13/4 It is losing energy more rapidly than other slower pulsars, and is likely to 'run out of steam' soonest. **1969** R. V. BESTE *Next Time I'll Pay* xv. 235 If Sequierez's appearance had meant anything, it was that the Cultural Attaché to Her Britannic Majesty's Embassy in Madrid had run out of rope. **1970** *Listener* 19 Nov. 710/3 The real-life situation of the superstar simply running out of road gives the work a clearly recognisable integrity of plot. **1973** D. FRANCIS *Slay-Ride* vii. 78 When I'd run out of steam, they would begin to nod while they listened. **1974** *Country Life* 26 Dec. 2009/2 At Zahedan in southern Iran I ran out of railway. **1975** I. S. BLACK *Man on Bridge* xii. 170 Munro.. drove till he ran out of track. **1977** *Times* 11 June 11/3, I chose not to hire one [*sc.* a motor-bike], having run out of road on a 350 some years back. **1977** *Gramophone* Dec. 1191/1 The disc input..tends to run out of steam at the low frequency end.

67. run over ——.

a. To take a mental review of; to think over.

1565 COOPER *Thesaurus,* s.v. *Cogitatio,* To runne ouer many thynges in mynde and cogitacion. **1727** SWIFT *On Dreams* Wks. 1755 III. II. 234 The busy head..runs o'er The scenes and actions of the day before. **1741** WATTS *Improv. Mind* I. i. §9 The Pythagoreans..every evening thrice run over the actions and affairs of the day.

b. To glance or look over; to survey, scan, peruse or read, rapidly.

1573 G. HARVEY *Lett.-bk.* (Camden) 51 If he wuld but.. take the pains to run over the title concerning the Proctor's office. **1613** SHAKS. *Hen. VIII,* III. ii. 139 You..beare the Inuentory Of your best Graces, in your minde: the which You were now running o're. **1711** STEELE *Spect.* No. 91 ¶4 He ran over, with a laughing Eye, Crastin's thin Legs, meagre Looks, and spare Body. **1789** MME. D'ARBLAY *Diary* 6 Sept., I was finishing a charming sermon of Blair, while she was running over some old newspapers. **1824** SCOTT *Redgauntlet* ch. xxi, 'Look at it yourself..' Fairford ran over the affidavit and the warrant. **1850** THACKERAY *Pendennis* xlii, As he now ran over his early performance, he was pleased to find..passages exhibiting both fancy and vigour.

c. To repeat or recite quickly; to tell over again; to recapitulate.

1563 *Satir. Poems Reform.* xlii. 536 Quhen thay haue run ouir with ane reill Thair sairles Sermone. **1625–8** tr. *Camden's Hist. Eliz.* III. (1688) 368 Not to give any Answer till he had run over the Letters of the whole Alphabet. **1742** RICHARDSON *Pamela* III. 88 As we are always running over old Stories, when we are alone. **1793** *Trial of Fyshe Palmer* 83 Mr. Burnet next proceeded to run over the evidence. **1833** HOWITT *Hist. Priestcraft* 59 Let us now briefly run over the great features of priestcraft in Greece.

d. To treat, perform, enjoy, etc., in a slight or hasty manner.

1577 HANMER *Anc. Eccl. Hist.* (1619) 512 If I have omitted ought.., or lightly runne over any matter. **1611** BIBLE Pref. ¶14 Neither did we run ouer the worke with that posting haste that the Septuagint did. **1847** L. HUNT *Men, Women, & B.* I. iv. 65 When a pleasure is great and multitudinous, one is apt to run it all over hastily in the first instance.

e. To go over *again* with some process, in a slight or rapid manner.

1607 MIDDLETON *Five Gallants* II. i, The pictures are all new run over again. **1843** *Jrnl. R. Agric. Soc.* IV. I. 70 If.. the turnips have been well hoed once, it is of comparatively little importance whether they are 'run over' again.

f. To go over with the hand or with a machine; to execute (music) rapidly. Also in fig. context. Cf. sense 50 a above.

1641 MILTON *Animadv.* Wks. 1851 III. 209 Varietie.. erects and rouses an Auditory, like the masterfull running over many Cords and divisions. **1667** PEPYS *Diary* 24 Dec., That they do run over their beads with one hand and..make signs with the other. **1825** *New Monthly Mag.* XIV. 314 He hastily ran over the beads of a rosary. *Ibid.* XVI. 409 He amuses himself in his solitude, by running over the keys of a piano. **1881** GARDINER & MULLINGER *Study Eng. Hist.* I. vi. 109 The whole gamut of human passion and feeling was run over. **1969** *Guardian* 17 July 11/5 When you've.. hoovered the landing..you could just run over Mr Neville's carpet.

g. Of vehicles: To pass over (a person, etc., knocked down or lying in the way). (Cf. sense 78 i below.)

1794 J. WOODFORDE *Diary* 15 Feb. (1929) IV. 96 A very young Man coming back from Norwich to day with an empty Waggon, falling under it was run over by it. **1811** *Ora & Juliet* III. 30 The alarm of Mr. Belford's being ran over the night before. **1856** *Titan Mag.* Dec. 516/2 He has been thrown down, and run over. **1872** *Punch* 2 Mar. 88/2 Omnibuses which..are pleasing objects to behold, except when they are going to run over you.

h. *U.S. colloq.* To impose upon, treat with contempt; to push (someone) around.

1836 *Spirit of Times* 9 July 162/2, I would not advise any man to run over me, for I ask no man any odds further than civility. **1914** B. TARKINGTON *Penrod* xxv. 264 I've stood enough around here for one day, and you can't run over *me,* Georgie Bassett. **1929** W. FAULKNER *Sound & Fury* 227 You may think you can run over me like you do your grandmother and everybody else.

68. run through ——.

See also senses 12–15, and cf. 43 d, 46 c, 47 b, 48, 56 c.

a. To examine, inspect, peruse, treat of or deal with, rapidly.

c **1449** PECOCK *Repr.* I. viii. 41 Lete a man renne thoruȝ alle the..pointis. **1581** MULCASTER *Positions* xxxix. (1887) 196, I meane briefly to runne through this title of nobilitie. **1604** SHAKS. *Oth.* I. iii. 132 Her Father..Still question'd me the storie of my life..; I ran it through. **1695** DRYDEN *Parallel Poet. & Paint.* Ess. (ed. Ker) II. 149, I have not leisure to run through the whole comparison of lights and shadows with tropes and figures. **1788** MME. D'ARBLAY *Diary* 13 Feb., He laughed, but told me they were then running through the charges. **1843** *Fraser's Mag.* XXVIII. 273, I had run through the lions of the place. **1861** *Temple Bar* II. 32 She..ran through her collection of salmon flies. **1888** FLOR. WARDEN *Woman's Face* I. viii. 196 It is only a pamphlet, and will not take you long to run through.

b. To pass or go through, in the way of trial or experience.

1602 *2nd Pt. Return fr. Parnass.* v. iv. 2132 We haue run through many trades, yet thriue by none. **1686** tr. *Chardin's Coronat. Solyman* 121 Never had any man run through so many strange adventures. **1748** *Anson's Voy.* II. iii. 148 The distresses and dangers they had already run through. **1784** COWPER *Task* II. 607 We had run Through ev'ry change that fancy..has had genius to supply.

c. To wear out, consume, spend, waste, in a rapid or reckless manner.

? *c* **1600** *Distr. Emperor* I. i, Full twoe and twentye severall liverye coatts..Have I runne throughe in your most faythfull service. **1772** T. SIMPSON *Vermin-Killer* 25 The stoat..will run through a whole brood of chickens in a little time. **1781** D. WILLIAMS tr. *Voltaire* II. 308 He ran through all he had, and left nothing for you. **1848** J. H. NEWMAN *Loss & Gain* III. ix, It might have been worse; you might have run through your money. **1863** W. C. BALDWIN *Afr. Hunting* i. 24 Oceans of milk, most of which the Kaffirs and dogs ran through. **1880** L. STEPHEN *Pope* vi. 139 He managed to run through a splendid fortune.

d. To be or continue present in; to pervade.

1710 STEELE *Tatler* No. 124 ¶2, I have received several Letters upon this Subject, but find one common Error running through them all. **1729** LAW *Serious C.* x, If anything of this kind runs through the course of our whole life. **1815** W. H. IRELAND *Scribbleomania* 20 One unvarying predeliction for the wonderful runs through the whole series of his poems. **1855** BAIN *Senses & Int.* III. ii. §47 The law of gravitation runs through all Astronomy. **1890** TOUT *Hist. Eng. fr. 1689* 178 The royal influence continued to run through every branch of the State.

e. To pass or go through, in various senses.

1709 BAGFORD in *MS. Rawl. Lett. 21,* fol. 8 All of them from y[e] Bookes themselues which haue run throw my handes. **1833** *New Monthly Mag.* XXXVIII. 142 The novels..would have run through half a dozen editions in a year. **1850** *Tait's Mag.* XVII. 623/2 A paragraph which ran through all the newspapers.

f. To rehearse, repeat, go over (a procedure, role, or the like).

1975 COWIE & MACKIN *Oxf. Dict. Current Idiomatic English* 269/2, I think I've grasped your main proposals, but would you mind running through them once again? **1980** K. HAGENBACH *Fox Potential* xvi. 157, I ran through it for her without the grim details... When I had finished the story, Frankie put her hand on my thigh.

69. run to ——. (See also 3 and 30 c.)

†**a.** Of loss, etc.: To fall upon (a person). *Obs.*

a **1513** FABYAN *Chron.* (1533) 155 b, The losse ran to theym of the castell. **1555** in *Rep. Hist. MSS. Comm.* Var. Coll. IV. (1907) 283 Also the leke paines and penalties shall ronne and be unto all those free Burgesses.

b. (*a*) To come, amount in numbers, extend in size or depth, to (a specified quantity, etc.).

1544 tr. *Littleton's Tenures* (1574) 21 If escuage renne by auctoritie of parliament to anye summe of moneye. **1601** SHAKS. *Jul. C.* II. i. 31 Fashion it thus; that what he is, augmented, Would runne to these, and these extremities. **1787** G. WHITE *Selborne* i, Our wells, at an average, run to about sixty-three feet. **1850** *Jrnl. R. Agric. Soc.* XI. I. 143 The average number.. will run to about a sheep to an acre. **1879** *Encycl. Brit.* IX. 645/1 The morality [play] might run to at least 1000 verses. **1892** *Sat. Rev.* 7 May 554/1 The Supplement will run to eight or nine numbers.

(*b*) To be able for (*esp.* capable of purchasing). Now freq. const. *can*, *could*, etc.

1859 *Slang Dict.* 84 'I don't run to it,' i.e. I can't do it,.. or I have not money enough. **1892** *St. James's Gaz.* 8 Feb. 5/2 On week-days workmen.. do not run to more than fourpenny ale. **1924** H. DE SÉLINCOURT *Cricket Match* iii. 76 [He] only gave it me.. because he knows I couldn't run to one of my own. **1931** T. R. G. LYELL *Slang, Phrase & Idiom* 653 *B.* 'How much do they want for it?' *A.* 'Five hundred pounds.' *B.* 'I'm afraid I can't possibly run to that.' **1953** E. SIMON *Past Masters* III. 156 Bits and pieces in the press, posters if we can run to them. **1970** *Alberta Hist. Rev.* Summer 1/1 Frame houses.. needed to be heated and insulated with something of the modern thoroughness to be at all tolerable; and few men could run to it.

(*c*) To cover the expense of, be sufficient for.

1883 *Daily Tel.* 4 Oct. 3/2 What I *should* like is a nice pair of spectacles, and, as far as my money would run to it, everything else accordin', sir. **1888** MCCARTHY & PRAED *Ladies' Gallery* I. vi. 145 The Unknown's cheque wouldn't have run to that landau and pair. **1891** *Longman's Mag.* June 155 My money wouldn't run to it any further: so I had to go back. **1900** P. WHITE *West End* v. 40, I always had an idea that the guv'nor had some money, but I didn't imagine it would 'run' to this. **1931** T. R. G. LYELL *Slang, Phrase & Idiom* 653 I've only got ten shillings, and.. it certainly won't run to twenty-four!

(*d*) To manage to provide, go so far as to have.

1880 *Punch* 25 Dec. 298/2 A red 'un [*sc.* button-hole] with maiden'air trimmings is what I consider O.K. Suits my style and complexion, yer know, so I runs to it once in a way. **1934** G. B. SHAW *On Rocks* I. 208 Weve got nothing out of this. We dont run to Spanish in the Isle. **1960** *Bedside 'Guardian'* IX. 215 Some of the others [*sc.* theatres] run to 1930-ish chrome and glass fittings. **1973** 'M. INNES' *Appleby's Answer* xv. 128 Am I right.. in remembering that Gibber [*sc.* a village] runs to a tea-shop?

c. To lapse or fall to (waste, ruin, etc.).

1593 SHAKS. *2 Hen. VI*, I. iii. 127 The Common-wealth hath dayly run to wrack, The Dolphin hath preuayl'd. **1601** R. JOHNSON *Kingd. & Commw.* (1603) 153 It were to be feared, least.. the other part opposite would run to ruine and decaie. **1789** MRS. PIOZZI *Journ. France* I. 177 The school.. is running to ruin apace. **1856** *Leisure Hour* V, 419/2 The estate had run to ruin by neglect. **1874** BURNAND *My Time* xxxiii. 346 His academicals.. run to.. utter rack and ruin.

d. Of land: To produce naturally. Also *fig.*

1625 BACON *Ess.*, *Of Nature in Men* (Arb.) 365 A Mans Nature runnes either to Herbes, or Weeds. **1660** SHARROCK *Vegetables* 97 When any land runs to fearn, heath, or ant-hills. **1762** MILLS *Syst. Pract. Husb.* I. 152 They.. sow it with rye and hay-seed the first year; after which they let it run to grass. **1835** BROWNING *Paracelsus* II. 317 A birth-place Where the richness ran to flowers. **1892** *Chamb. Jrnl.* 17 Sept. 604/2 He preferred to let everything run to grass.

e. Of plants: To tend to the development of (seed, straw, etc.). Now usu. ***to run to seed.***

1664 EVELYN *Kal. Hort.* July, Let such olitory-herbs run to seed as you would save. **1765** *Museum Rust.* III. 157 If they are sown late,.. they will be apt to run all to straw. **1825** *New Monthly Mag.* XV. 215 They seldom bear at all, but run entirely to leaf. **1847** *Jrnl. R. Agric. Soc.* VIII. I. 215 [Beet,] when transplanted, run much to top. **1847** EMERSON *Poems* (1857) 29 Lemons run to leaves and rind. **1893** *Burpee's Farm Ann.* 65/1 It comes early and stands a long while before running to seed.

transf. **1740** FIELDING *Champion* 15 Mar., For Virtue itself by growing too exuberant, and (if I may be allowed the Metaphor) by running to Seed changes its very Nature, and becomes a most pernicious Weed of a most beautiful Flower. **1819** SHELLEY *Peter Bell 3rd* VI. xviii, Now Peter ran to seed in soul Into a walking paradox. **1832** *Blackw. Mag.* XXXII. 506 A race notoriously said like cucumbers to run more to belly than head. **1861** *N.Y. Herald* 23 Nov. 4/5 Can such a country be.. permitted to run to seed? **1873** *Amer. Jrnl. Insanity* Apr. 559 We believe somewhat in moral depravity and in accepting the results of our father's sins, but carried to the extent advocated by the Doctor, it is Calvinism run to seed. **1873** SPENCER *Study of Sociology* viii. 189 The vital energies of this nation run mainly to teeth and claws. **1924** A. HUXLEY *Little Mexican* 249 He pictured a large, blonde, barmaidish personage, thirty-one and not yet married, running a bit to seed. **1953** J. WAIN *Hurry on Down* iv. 66 He was plump, but not yet running to seed; aged about forty-five to fifty. **1956** G. DURRELL *Drunken Forest* iii. 62 At one time she must have been a handsome woman, but now she had run slightly to seed. **1976** *National Observer* (U.S.) 27 Nov. II. 2/3 Today there is a striking resemblance among many of the 1,000 or so residents, and most of the youngsters run to tow-head.

f. To pass or develop into (some excess).

1850 *Tait's Mag.* XVII. 747/1 His historical sketches have a tendency to run to some exaggeration. **1881** W. BLACK *Beautiful Wretch* I. 226 Her kindness.. ran to extravagance. **1890** *Chamb. Jrnl.* 6 Dec. 783/2 This last fashion ran so much to the opposite extreme as to impede walking.

g. *U.S.* Of persons: to have a preference for or a leaning towards (something); to favour.

1873 'MARK TWAIN' *Gilded Age* xxxiii. 307 We had Dr. Spooner a good while, but he runs so much to emetics.. that we changed off and took Dr. Leathers. **1896** —— in *Harper's Mag.* Aug. 346/2 In my nature I have always run to pie, whilst in his nature he has always run to mystery.

70. run upon ——. (See also 5 and 10 b.)

†**a.** To come or fall upon (a person). *Obs.*

a **1300** *Cursor M.* 3556 Sir Ysaac þat dughti man, Vnfere and eld apon him ran. **1390** GOWER *Conf.* III. 255 Arrons was so wo besein With thoghtes whiche upon him runne. **1423** *Rolls of Parlt.* IV. 257 The grete disavauntage that shulde renne upon hym. **1487** *Act 3 Hen. VII*, vi. §3 The same forfeiture to renne upon the Seller or lener therof.

b. To have a tendency to, or a favour or fancy for, to seek much after (something).

1550 CROWLEY *Langland's Pierce Plowman* To Rdr., The firste two verses of the book renne vpon .S... The next [line] runneth vpon .H. **1681** H. MORE *Exp. Daniel* 110 This sense generally Interpreters run upon, and it is most congruous and coherent. **1737** BRACKEN *Farriery Improved* (1757) II. 104 Mankind run upon Horses with great Appetites. **1762** MILLS *Syst. Pract. Husb.* I. 39 A great deal of the marle in the north country runs much upon the loam; but that in Sussex is more like fuller's earth. **1878** *Graphic* 28 Sept. 315/3 The Agricultural Gazette.. thinks that the Oxfords are run upon too much.

c. To dwell upon, be occupied with (a subject) in thought or discourse.

1577–87 HOLINSHED *Chron.* I. 104/1 A late chronographer running upon this matter.. saith that [etc.]. *c* **1610** SPEED in *Lett. Lit. Men* (Camden) 108 My thoughts runnyng upon the well performance of this worke. **1698** KEILL *Exam. Th. Earth* (1734) 203 [He] asserts, that my arguments run upon impossibilities. **1719** DE FOE *Crusoe* II. (Globe) 362 His Mind run upon Men fighting and killing of one another. **1775** JOHNSON *Let. to Mrs. Thrale* 17 June, Write to me something every post, for on the stated day my head runs upon a letter. **1856** *Titan Mag.* Dec. 542/2 The conversation never ceased running upon the healing art. **1889** ADELINE SERGEANT *Deveril's Diamond* III. vii. 128 It does not do to let one's mind run too much upon these things.

d. To engage in, enter upon (some action, etc.).

1581 PETTIE *Guazzo's Civ. Conv.* I. (1586) 29 b, For.. we naturallie runne upon things which are forbidden us. **1676** TOWERSON *Decalogue* 525 They may tempt unwary Men to .. run upon any Falsity. **1696** DE LA PRYME *Diary* (Surtees) 110 Every one now runs upon tick. **1719** DE FOE *Crusoe* II. (Globe) 508 That I might not be said to run rashly upon any Thing, I stay'd here above nine Months.

e. To incur, bring on oneself, fall into.

1633 BP. HALL *Hard Texts, N.T.* 298 They.. have runne very deep upon the displeasure of God. **1656** *Nicholas Papers* (Camden Soc.) III. 258 To make there peace, least otherwise they should runne vppon there owne future ruine. **1754** CHATHAM *Lett. Nephew* vi. 40 The inconveniences, dangers, and evils, which they themselves have run upon.

f. To make a sudden demand upon (a bank) for the purpose of withdrawing deposits, etc.

1828 *Examiner* 842/1 The house was.. very severely run upon. **1892** *Daily News* 14 Sept. 5/2 These persons.. were infected by panic... They 'ran' upon the bank.

g. To come upon, encounter, suddenly.

1857 T. HUGHES *Tom Brown* I. ix, [They] run plump upon one of the masters as they emerge into the High Street.

h. *U.S.* To quiz, make a butt of (one). Cf. 65 d.

a **1859** in Bartlett *Dict. Amer.* (ed. 2) 374 He is a quiet, good-natured.. chap, and will stand running upon as long as most men.

71. run with ——.

a. To go along with; to accompany, keep pace with; to march with.

c **1380** WYCLIF *Wks.* (1880) 100 But goddis curs renneþ many þousand tyme wiþ al þis. **1609** DANIEL *Civil Wars* V. cxii, With such as with the time did run, In most vpright opinion he doth stand. **1678** H. VAUGHAN *Thalia Rediv.* in *Silex Scint.* (1900) 233 A fatal sadness, such as.. runs along with public plagues and woes, Lies heavy on us. **1837** *Penny Cycl.* VIII. 117/1 It has been contended that a covenant by the owner of land respecting the land should always run with the land; but this doctrine has not been established. **1893** *Chamb. Jrnl.* 1 Apr. 203/1 [He] offered to buy the Fairfield Farm.. which ran with his own little estate.

b. To concur, accord, or agree with.

1625 GILL *Sacr. Philos.* i. 46, I runne not with that opinion. **1662** LD. ORRERY *State Lett.* (1743) II. 429 Nor does this instruction run with the introductive words of the former. **1866** R. SIMPSON *Life Campion* xiv. (1907) 382 Public opinion did not altogether run with the statute.

c. orig. and chiefly *U.S.* Of persons: to associate with (a person or group), to befriend.

1909 *Dialect Notes* III. 365 *Run with*.., to associate with, go in the company of. **1914** B. TARKINGTON *Penrod* xiv. 126 You fellers have treated me nice—and some day you come over to my yard; I'd like to run with you fellers. You're the kind of fellers I like. **1922** E. O'NEILL *Hairy Ape* vi. 64 If I can't find her I'll take it out on de gang she runs wit. **1946** MEZZROW & WOLFE *Really Blues* (1957) 378 *Run with*, associate with. **1969** G. DONALDSON *Fifteen Men* xiv. 240 He ran with a crowd of kids known as 'Les Snobs'. **1975** *New Review* May 70/1 Hunter Thompson, who ran with the Hell's Angels for eighteen months to write *The Hell's Angels*.

IV. With adverbs, in specialized uses.

In most of these both intransitive and transitive uses are very fully represented.

72. run away.

a. To make off, retreat hurriedly, flee, in the face of danger or opposition.

c **1380** *Sir Ferumb.* 2438 þan runne þai away & saide alas. **1530** PALSGR. 695/2, I runne awaye from myne enemye, or any daunger. **1542** UDALL *Erasm. Apoph.* 335 b, That same manne, that renneth awaye, May again fight, an other day. **1642–4** VICARS *God in Mount* 164 The present was the season, else the enemy would bee run away. **1724** DE FOE *Mem. Cavalier* I. 94 The King.. rated them for running away, as he called it, though they really retreated in good Order. **1804–5** NELSON in *Sotheby's Catal.* 15 June (1897) 17 That gentleman has thought proper to write a letter stating that the fleet under my command ran away. **1848** THACKERAY *Van. Fair* xxxii, This.. Belgian hussar.. was too good a soldier to disobey his Colonel's orders to run away.

b. To abscond; to depart surreptitiously *from* or *to* a person; to elope *with* some one. Also *transf.* Freq. used jocularly in the negative (as, ***it won't run away***) to give assurance of the permanence or fixity of something or someone.

c **1460** *Towneley Myst.* iv. 227 'Where is he,'.. will she spyr; If I tell her, 'ron away', hir answere bese.. 'nay, sir!' **1530** PALSGR. 695/2 He was aboute to ronne awaye, and he had done it in dede if I had nat taken the better hede. *a* **1568** ASCHAM *Scholem.* Pref. (Arb.) 18 Scholers.. be runne awaie from the Schole. **1614** J. COOKE *Greene's Tu Quoque* C ij b, Doe not I know that thou wilt run away with the Gentleman? **1632** LITHGOW *Trav.* III. 127 There were foure-score Christian slaues, who hauing cut their Captaines throat.., runne away from Constantinople. **1754** RICHARDSON *Grandison* IV. xiv. 105 The next girl that run away to a dancing master, or an ensign. **1793** 'A. PASQUIN' *Life Earl of Barrymore* (ed. 3) 13 Mr. Stone had a tenant run away. **1892** *Daily News* 8 Jan. 3/6 It was true that the land could not run away, but they knew that rent could run away. **1882** C. M. GASKELL in *Nineteenth Cent.* Sept. 460 The landowner has been credited with the.. most valuable form of security;.. it could not 'run away'. **1888** C. M. YONGE *Beechcroft at Rockstone* II. xxi. 191 The charms of 'the halls of Ivor'.. which, after all, would not run away. **1908** A. BENNETT *Old Wives' Tale* IV. iii. 515 There's no earthly reason why you should go back... The house won't run away. **1928** A. M. M. DOUTON *Bk. with Seven Seals* 21 Sunday will be round again in a week, and Park Chapel won't run away. **1942** A. E. W. MASON *Musk & Amber* i. 15 'What of Grest [*sc.* an estate] meanwhile?' 'Grest won't run away, Sir.' **1973** J. PORTER *It's Murder with Dover* vii. 65 What's your sweat? This Tiffin bird's not going to run away.

transf. **1920** E. O'NEILL *Beyond Horizon* III. i. 152 You've spent eight years running away from yourself. **1934** —— *Days without End* I. 36 It's a rocky road.. this running away from truth in order to find it? **1944** B. HUTCHISON *Hollow Men* vi. 79 It's his mask. It fools nearly everybody. He's always running away from himself. **1966** *Listener* 17 Nov. 718/2 The whole of the world ran away from the pound, and if this doesn't reveal an inflationary situation, what does?

c. ***run away with***: (*a*) To depart surreptitiously with, to carry off (something).

1624 *Capt. Smith's Virginia* Wks. II. 401 The strongest preparing once more to run away with the Pinnace. **1660** F. BROOKE tr. *Le Blanc's Trav.* 12 The rest of the Jewes gave their seeming assistance.. whilst he run away with coat and doublet. **1719** DE FOE *Crusoe* II. (Globe) 507 That they would.. set Sail, and run away with the Ship. **1807–8** W. IRVING *Salmag.* xiv. (1860) 331 At that time ladies were not quite so easily run away with as Columbine.

(*b*) To take up with, accept, believe (an idea, etc.), hurriedly, without due reflection.

1621 BP. MOUNTAGU *Diatribæ* 186 It is great wonder that Iosephus, and Philo,.. runne away with the common acceptation. **1727** BOYER *Dict. Royal* II. s.v., To run away with (to fancy, or imagine) a thing. **1844** DICKENS *Mart. Chuz.* x, Don't run away with that opinion, sir! **1890** *Sat. Rev.* 29 Nov. 610/1 To let Dr. Barnardo run away with the notion that [etc.].

(*c*) To carry off, gain; †to carry (a point).

1698 in *Harl. Misc.* (1809) III. 343 The marshals du camp ran away with it clearly to raise the siege. **1736** AINSWORTH *Eng.-Lat. Dict.* s.v., To run away with the praise of a thing. **1822–34** *Good's Study Med.* (ed. 4) III. 303 Any prescribed medicine.. will seem to have effected the cure, and will run away with the credit of having done so.

(*d*) To consume or exhaust.

1687 MIÉGE *Gt. Fr. Dict.* II. s.v., The Collectors run away with a good Part of the Revenue. **1862** *Jrnl. R. Agric. Soc.* XXIII. 221 The cost of gathering runs away with much of the saving effected in cutting. **1890** MRS. H. WOOD *House of Halliwell* II. vii. 175 Caroline's illness.. had run away with all the ready money.

(*e*) *Naut.* (See quot.)

1867 SMYTH *Sailor's Word-bk.* 585 *Run away with it!* the order to men on a tackle fall, when light goods are being hoisted in, or in hoisting.. sails.

d. Of a horse, etc.: To rush off ungovernably, to bolt (*with* a person). Also *transf.*

13.. *Sir Beues* 2021 þe hors.. arnede awai wiþ þe king þourȝ felde & wode,.. And in a mure don him cast. **1677** MIÉGE *Fr. Dict.* II. s.v., That horse will run away with you. **1787** 'G. GAMBADO' *Acad. Horsem.* 41 It is far from improbable, that he may run away with you. **1791** —— *Ann. Horsem.* iii. (1809) 81 When a horse has run away. **1825** *New Monthly Mag.* XV. 451 The horse ran away with him. **1867** SMYTH *Sailor's Word-bk.* 585 *Run away with her Anchor*, said of a ship when she drags or 'shoulders' her anchor. **1885** *Standard* 9 Mar. 3/5 The winding engine 'ran away', owing to the sudden loss of weight upon the drum. **1891** G. D. GALTON *La Fenton* I. xi. 255 Your dog-cart ran away and you were thrown out.

transf. and *fig.* **1545** ASCHAM *Toxoph.* (Arb.) 25, I thought to come and holde you.., lest your boke shoulde runne awaye with you. **1709** STEELE *Tatler* No. 27 ¶2 His desires run away with him. **1727** GAY *Begg. Op.* I. ix, Don't let your passion run away with your senses. **1822** HAZLITT *Table-talk* II. vii. 152 Our anger runs away with our reason. **1862** *Temple Bar* IV. 560 Annoyed at having allowed his imagination to run away with him. **1898** *Allbutt's Syst. Med.* V. 812 The accelerating nerves often.. run away with the heart. **1935** *Industrial & Engin. Chem.* Sept. 1074/2 'Ethylene at a temperature above 350°C. and under a pressure of 175 kg. per sq. cm... decomposes with explosive violence.' Fortunately, this was not found to be the case, but in many experiments the temperature 'ran away'. **1945** *Rev. Mod. Physics* XVII. 482 If the reaction was not to 'run away', it was essential to make use of neutrons of very low energy in the individual steps of the chain process. **1946** [see *oil operated* s.v. OIL *sb.*[1] 6]. **1953** *Times* 31 Oct. 2/7 We have no practical experience of what happens if a reactor runs away. **1959** C. HODDER-WILLIAMS *Chain Reaction* xviii. 198 When the pile 'ran away', one of the heat-exchangers burst with the increased steam pressure.

e. To get away *from*, to outdistance completely, in running or racing.

1825 W. COBBETT *Rur. Rides* (1885) II. 52 When the dog, or dogs, never get near enough to the hare to induce her to turn, she is said, and very justly, to 'run away' from them.

1890 *Cent. Mag.* June 208/2 Our men.. have run away from all their Champions in actual races.

f. To grow rank or luxuriant.

1848 *Jrnl. R. Agric. Soc.* IX. I. 11 While other parts of the field may be found to have 'run away' in abundant seasons, these parts are always found fed down to the very roots. **1906** WOODRUFFE-PEACOCK *Ideal Thoroughbred Stud* 15 Under no circumstances should the grass be allowed to run away from the animals, and get into flower and seed.

73. run down. (See also 11 a.)

* *intr.* **a.** Of a clock, etc.: To become completely unwound; to cease to go.

1761 *Phil. Trans.* LII. 203 During my illness, my clock was run down, and stopt. **1771** *Encycl. Brit.* III. 934/2 When the cord.. is entirely run down from off the barrel, it is wound up again by means of a key. **1846** DICKENS *Cricket on Hearth* ii, The toys that had been set in motion for the Baby, had all stopped and run down long ago. **1891** F. W. ROBINSON *Her Love & His Life* III. iv, The clock-work had got out of order and run down.

fig. **1869** MARTINEAU *Ess.* II. 40 They.. run down with the time-piece that measures mortal things. **1889** PHILIPS & WILLS *Fatal Phryne* I. iii. 73 Madame burst into a flood of compliments. The doctor allowed her to run down.

b. To decline, fall off, in vigour or health: (*a*) of the system, etc.; (*b*) of persons.

(*a*) **1828** *Examiner* 678/1 The extraordinary elasticity of his spirit is somewhat weakened;—the wonder is, that long ago it did not snap and run down. **1883** HOLME LEE *Loving & Serving* III. xi. 240 His strength ran down. **1890** *Sunday Mag.* Dec. 802/2 His system seems to have run down.
(*b*) **1846** D. WEBSTER *Letters* (1902) 325, I am really 'rundown' with calls and visits. **1881** MRS. LYNN LINTON *My Love* II. x. 186 Was it to be wondered at if Stella looked worn-out and run down? **1888** LADY DUFFUS HARDY *Dangerous Experiment* II. viii. 156 She had run down.. both mentally and physically, and was in a generally unstrung condition. **1897** A. BEARDSLEY *Let.* 22 Nov. (1970) 396, I am abominably ill; I ran down at Paris quite alarmingly. *Ibid.* 22 Dec. 410, I had run down terribly before I came here and was quite shattered by the journey.

c. To diminish or decrease.

1889 C. D. WARNER *Little Journ.* x, Then they absorb its surplus; they let it run down so that it pays no dividends. **1893** *National Obs.* 5 Aug. 293/1 The value of their live stock has been steadily running down. **1901** *Scotsman* 11 Mar. 7/5 The attendance of the Nationalists is already running down.

d. To deteriorate; to fall into disuse or decay.

1844 *Jrnl. R. Agric. Soc.* V. I. 113 It [a farm] had been allowed to run down a few years before I entered upon it. **1893** *Harper's Mag.* Feb. 439/2 [She] had let everything run down. She had, in truth, no money for repairs.

e. Of a river: To settle down or subside after a flood; to diminish in volume.

1882 *Daily Telegr.* 28 Oct. 2/4 Both rivers are running down nicely. **1892** *Illustr. Sporting & Dram. News* 13 Aug. 810/2 We realise.. how very low the river has run down during the drought.

f. Of pneumatic tyres: To become deflated.

1901 *Wide World Mag.* VIII. 142 The tyres have a tendency to run down, owing to innumerable small thorn-pricks.

** *trans.* **g.** To knock down or overthrow (a person); to dash into, collide with, and sink (a vessel).

a **1578** LINDESAY (Pitscottie) *Chron. Scot.* (S.T.S.) II. 39 Quhene they iunit witht the Inglischemen they had thame all run doune ore ever the Inglische speirs might tuiche thame. **1659** D. PELL *Impr. Sea* 137 There is a great care taken on both sides who should run down one another by the board first. **1779** *Ann. Reg.* 222 Capt. Drew, from London to Quebec, was run down by the Russell man of war. **1823** *Examiner* 754/2 The Captain.. attempted to run the boat down. **1856** *Titan Mag.* Dec. 531/2 We stand a good chance of being run down by a tram. **1885** *Law Times Rep.* LIII. 60/2 The *Chusan* ran down a smack on the morning of the 24th Dec.

h. To pursue (game) until caught or killed; to hunt down. Also *transf.*

1669 HACKE *Collect. Voy.* III. (1699) 69 We should have made a better hand of them, had we had but Dogs to run them down. **1748** *Anson's Voy.* III. ii. 309 The fowls.. were likewise run down with little trouble; for they could scarce fly further than an hundred yards. **1806** J. BERESFORD *Mis. Hum. Life* XX. xlii. 259 After dropping a wash-ball,.. bestirring yourself to run it down, by following its doublings, as it rapidly rolls about the room. **1876** A. S. PALMER *Leaves fr. Notebk.* Pref. p. viii, I have been successful in running down my quarry. **1891** *Cornhill Mag.* Mar. 300 A weasel will occasionally run down the strongest hare.

i. To put down, overcome, overwhelm (a person, etc.) by superior force, argument, talk, etc.

1674 *Essex Papers* (Camden) I. 233 That he may not be run down by a Vote of ye House of Commons. **1695** J. EDWARDS *Perfect. H. Script.* 367 This good man.. in.. his.. calamities was never quite run down by them. **1719** DE FOE *Crusoe* I. (Globe) 222, I was run down again by him to the last Degree. **1766** GOLDSM. *Vic. W.* vi, Here comes our good friend.. that run you down fairly in the argument. **1779** *Mirror* No. 5, Talk.. of painting, he runs you down with a description of the gallery at Florence.

j. To disparage, defame, or vilify.

1668 DRYDEN *Even. Love* I. i, I am revenged on you, for running down my poor old master. **1689** N. LEE *Princ. Cleve* II. iii, After all this they'll run you down, and say your Grace is no Scholar. **1710** ADDISON *Tatler* No. 226 ¶4 He found himself run down as a superficial prating Quack. **1791** BOSWELL *Johnson* (Oxf. ed.) II. 342 A gentleman present.. had been running down Ode-writing in general, as a bad species of poetry. **1844** SYD. SMITH *Wks.* (1867) II. 337, I do not mean by this, unjustly and cowardly to run down O'Connell. **1889** F. C. PHILIPS *Ainslie's Courtship* I. xii. 161 You need not run down the education we received.

k. To melt (plate, etc.).

1684 BURNET tr. *More's Utopia* 104 The People might.. be unwilling to let the Plate be run down, if a War made it necessary to pay their Souldiers with it. **1895** *Daily News* 15 Nov. 7/2 The parcel was one of scrap silver, which he wanted 'run down'.

l. To bring to a stop.

1697 VANBRUGH *Æsop* III. Wks. 1893 I. 200 Has thy eternal tongue run down its larum yet?

m. To cause to sink or fall.

1737 *London Mag.* Oct. 542/1 Our directing the next Payment to be made to the Bank would, I believe, possess the Generality of Mankind with an Opinion that we were resolved to abolish the Company.., which would of course run the Price of their Stock down to very near Par. **1866** *Shareholder's Guardian* 16 May 385/1 They began by 'bearing' its shares until they run them down to a discount.

n. To reduce or bring (an activity, operation, organization, etc.) to a halt gradually or progressively.

1861 C. M. YONGE *Young Step-Mother* vii. 74 Miss Meadows began one of her tangled skeins of words.. and Mr. Kendal, knowing.. that the only chance of a conclusion was to let her run herself down, held his tongue. **1976** A. PRICE *War Game* I. vi. 118 We're running down the Incident Room, it's true. But we're not giving up. **1977** *Times* 18 Aug. 15/8 Over the past few years, Volkswagen has been progressively running down its 'beetle' production in Germany... Only 100 cars a day are at present produced.

o. *U.S. slang.* To rehearse or perform (a piece of music); to recite (verse).

1948 *Down Beat* 1 Dec. 10 We ran down three new instrumentals and a vocal for Baubles Buxon! **1959** G. KANIN *Blow up Storm* 19, I distributed the parts and we ran it down. **1960** *Jazz News* Nov. 12 When we rehearsed an arrangement that no one had seen before, we'd run it down once or twice. **1961** R. RUSSELL *Sound* i. 10 Bernie struck off a rich chord and began running the tune down in his immaculate post-Teddy Wilson style. **1969** H. R. BROWN in T. Kochman *Rappin' & Stylin' Out* (1972) 205 The teacher expected me to sit up in class and study poetry after I could run down shit like that. **1975** R. S. GOLD *Jazz Talk* 228 *Run down*,.. to perform, usually in rehearsal, a piece of written music.

p. ***to run it down***: to describe or explain a situation in full; to tell the whole truth about a subject. *U.S. slang.* (Freq. in Black English.)

1964 T. CADE in *Massachusetts Rev.* Summer 622, I tried to figure out the best way to run it down to this girl right quick that they didn't have to live in this town. **1967** J. HORTON in T. Kochman *Rappin' & Stylin' Out* (1972) 22 Street repartee at its best is a lively way of 'running it down', or of 'jiving'. **1970** G. JACKSON *Let.* 17 Mar. in *Soledad Brother* (1971) 236 Write me a letter.. and run it down; school, politics, futurities. I want to know it all. **1972** B. G. COOKE in T. Kochman *Rappin' & Stylin' Out* 48 This gesture of lowering the lip is a result of the emphatic manner in which they are 'running it down'.

74. run in.

* *intr.* **a.** To concur, agree, fall in, *with* a person, opinion, etc.

1699 BAKER *Refl. Learning* 58 Tho' Ramus run in with them.. in his opposition to Aristotle, yet he has out-done them in this, that [etc.]. **1737** BRACKEN *Farriery Impr.* (1757) II. 154 He need not.. run in with the vulgar Notion. **1892** ABP. BENSON in *Life* (1899) II. 430 Unless convocation 'runs in' with a Canon in this way, the whole liberty of the Church of England is at an end.

b. To rush in, close with, in attacking or assailing.

1815 SCOTT *Guy M.* liii, Then rin in on him, take his arms, and bind him. **1847** MARRYAT *Childr. New Forest* xi, Edward.. ordered Smoker [the dog] to run in to the bull. **1890** W. MORRIS in *Eng. Illustr. Mag.* Sept. 889 He lept aside nimbly and ran in on Hallblithe and caught his sword-arm.

c. *Rugby football.* (See quot. 1867.)

1867 *Routledge's Hdbk. Football* 31 Any player who catches the ball.. may run with it.. till he gets behind his adversary's line of goal, where he will touch it down... This feat is called 'running in'. **1889** *Field* 19 Jan. 89/3 Within ten minutes of time E. Hancock succeeded in running in, and S. Escott kicked a goal.

d. To pay a short or passing visit (occas. *to*) a person. ***to run in and out*** (*of* one another's homes, etc.): to make frequent informal visits (to one another).

1857 [see GET *v.* 24¶]. **1876** C. M. YONGE *Womankind* xi. 81 A little croquet, a great deal of chatter; and worse than all, much running in and out among near neighbours. **1892** MRS. OLIPHANT *Marriage of Elinor* II. xvii. 37 It might be a relief to her to run in to me whenever she pleased. **1952** M. LASKI *Village* iv. 77 It's lucky it's so far away; at least they can't be running in and out of each other's homes every minute. **1958** A. WHITE tr. *Colette's Claudine in Paris* iv. 30 Just a few yards from here, there's a delightful flat, and we'd be practically on each other's doorsteps... We could be always running in and out... it would be nice for Claudine and for you too.

e. *Printing.* (See quot.)

1888 JACOBI *Printers' Vocab.* 117 Matter is said to 'run in' when it 'gets in', or makes less than an anticipated quantity.

** *trans.* **f.** To fix, fill in, *with* (melted lead, etc.).

1751 C. LABELYE *Piers Westm. Bridge* 20 Iron Cramps, let into the Stones, and runn'd in with melted Lead. **1865** BRANDE & COX *Dict. Sci.*, etc. I. 782/1 Designs.. engraved with the burin, and run in, while hot, with a composition called *niello*. **1900** *Yorks. Arch. Jrnl.* XV. 322 An iron pin run in with lead.

g. To arrest and convey (a person) to prison. Also in *Naval* use (see quot. 1962).

1859 G. W. MATSELL *Vocabulum* 76 *Run in*, arrested. **1872** *Routledge's Ev. Boy's Ann.* 376/2 I'll run you in. **1874** *Slang Dict.* 274 The police are very fond of threatening to run-in any person to whom they may take exception. **1889** *N. & Q.* 20 July 49/1 The respectable gentleman who.. takes my part if I get 'run in' by the police. **1909** J. R. WARE *Passing Eng.* 212/1 Thus hooked he is 'run in', where.. he is treated for 'D.T.'s'—the origin of most amok—when he either recovers or is passed into an asylum. **1933** J. CARY *Amer. Visitor* 35 Cottee was over the boundary, so I'm going to run him in. **1938** [see FOWL *sb.* 1 d]. **1948** PARTRIDGE *Dict. Forces' Slang* 159 I've warned you, the next time you are adrift I'll run you in to the First Lootenant. **1951** *New Yorker* 15 Dec. 94 'Am I going to have to run you in?' the policeman asked. **1962** GRANVILLE *Dict. Sailors' Slang* 98/2 *Run in*, place a man in the Commander's report or bring him before the Officer-of-the-watch.

h. *Austr.* To drive (cattle or horses) into a place where they may be captured or handled.

1885 MRS. CAMPBELL-PRAED *Head Station* 45, I have had no end of sport.. in shooting wild horses and running in scrubbers. **1890** 'R. BOLDREWOOD' *Col. Reformer* (1891) 315 Their time was spent in running in these.. mustangs.

i. To insert, slip in.

1817 *Ackermann's Repository* Jan. 53/1 A row of straw-colour ribbon is run in next to the border. **1883** *Standard* 26 June 3/3 A finer thread, not drawn in with the tambour, but run in with a point needle. **1884** F. J. BRITTEN *Watch & Clockm.* 75 Many different methods of procedure are adopted for running in a cylinder. **1900** F. M. FORD *Let.* Oct. (1965) 13, I took hold of that young woman and ran in every bit of her charm I could think of and then smashed in all the repulsion I could think of.

j. To enter and secure the election of (a person).

1892 *Black & White* 6 Feb. 168/1 A compact and consistent body.. tried to run Mr. Swan in for each of the three events.

k. To operate (new machinery, esp. a motor vehicle or its engine) at reduced speed or load unti it has reached a normal working condition. Also *refl.*, said of the machinery. Also *fig.*

1919 W. H. BERRY *New Traffic (Aircraft)* xv. 86 Some engineers suggested that the flight should be used to 'run in' the engines. **1925** *Morris Owner's Manual* xvi. 103 It must, of course, clearly be understood that when an engine is new and stiff much more heat is developed than is the case when it has run itself in. **1934** *Punch* 6 June 629/1 Never start a new engine on the self-starter. The battery and dynamo need running-in before you use them. **1939** N. MONSARRAT *This is Schoolroom* III. xvii. 390 Anthea bought a car, we ran it in. **1953** A. WHITE tr. *Colette's Cat* iv. 109 We're going out to Rambouillet for lunch in the forest. I've got to run the car in. **1959** *Listener* 2 Apr. 603/1 If you are running-in a new car, and conscientiously keeping down to a maximum of thirty miles an hour, [etc.]. **1961** H. NICHOLSON *Let.* 1 June (1968) 395 Kennedy 'must run himself in' before he can inspire confidence. **1972** *Guardian* 18 Sept. 11/4 My car offers its apologies for curious behaviour: 'Running In' is plastered across its back. **1973** A. BEHREND *Samarai Affair* iii. 31 Having thus ticked over gently during the previous ten minutes, the committee had now run itself in for the major business of the afternoon.

75. run off.

* *intr.* **a.** To take to flight; to abscond or elope (*with* a person or thing).

1760–72 H. BROOKE *Fool of Qual.* (1809) II. 93 They cast their arms to the ground, and run off.. as fast as they could. **1781** *Mirror* No. 81, Hardships from which, at last, she freed herself, by running off with a recruiting serjeant. **1805** *Miniature* No. 32 (1806) II. 151 My first observation.. was, that Paris forgot to say 'What next' when he run off with Helen. **1849** MACAULAY *Hist. Eng.* vi. II. 57 The servant was taught how he might, without sin, run off with his master's plate.

b. Of water, etc.: To flow off or away.

1707 MORTIMER *Husb.* (1721) II. 322 Let it stand half an Hour undisturbed, that it may run off clear. **1797** *Encycl. Brit.* (ed. 3) IX. 512/1 The water will run off and leave the yellow matter behind. **1861** *Jrnl. R. Agric. Soc.* XXII. I. 66 When put to press the white whey runs off freely. **1869** A. W. WARD tr. *Curtius' Hist. Greece* II. II. iv. 58 Allowing the rain-water to run off on an incline.

c. To become smaller, diminish.

1765 *Treat. Dom. Pigeons* 94 It should have an hollow back, running off taper from the shoulders. **1890** *Sat. Rev.* 15 Nov. 557/1 Those who held upon borrowed money, finding margins running off and differences increasing against them, have been obliged to sell. **1925** *Daily Tel.* 13 May 4/3 On purchasing that company it was decided to allow its marine business to run off. **1955** *Times* 3 May 15/1 In the first quarter of this year the surplus has tended to run off.

d. To go off, digress, in talk. Also ***to run off at the mouth***: to talk excessively; to talk nonsense. Cf. sense 52 g above. *U.S. slang.*

1861 *Temple Bar* III. 552 Then my lady ran off to tell us how dull Fernwood was. **1889** PHILIPS & WILLS *Fatal Phryne* II. ii. 33 The sick man ran off into unintelligible mutterings. **1909** *Dialect Notes* III. 403 *Runnin' off at the mouth*,.. loquacity; talking too much. Used of one excessively loquacious. 'He's got a bad case of runnin' off at the mouth.' **1942** BERREY & VAN DEN BARK *Amer. Thes. Slang* §151/6 *Talk nonsense*... go *or* run off at the mouth. *Ibid.* §189/3 *Be talkative*... run (off) at the mouth. **1951** *Rochester* (N.Y.) *Democrat & Chron.* 12 Sept. 14/6 Culio... A run-of-the-mob gunsel—till he runs off at the mouth! **1962** A. LURIE *Love & Friendship* xi. 223 I'm a pig coming over here and running off at the mouth, probably boring you to hell. **1976** *National Observer* (U.S.) 28 Aug 1/1 The man they simply ran off at the mouth about here, Jimmy Carter.

e. To diverge, alter.

1871 EARLE *Philol. Eng. Tongue* 142 It [*whole*] has since run off from sense of *hale, sound*.., into that of *complete.*

** *trans.* **f.** To dash or rattle off; to write or recite rapidly.

1683 D. GRANVILLE *Letters* (Surtees Soc.) 163, [I] did.. on a new text.. runne of halfe a sermon at leisure hours. **1809** SCOTT *Let.* in *Lockhart* (1837) II. vi. 232 You can so easily run off an article.., that it would be inexcusable not to afford us your assistance. **1861** *Temple Bar* III. 123 [He] ran off glibly..a list of all that was entertaining and interesting in the neighbourhood. **1891** Miss Dowie *Girl in Karp.* xxi. 296 A curious specimen of beadledom who ran off long unintelligible histories in atrocious Viennese patois.

g. To allow to flow out; to draw or drain off (a liquid).

1737 Bracken *Farriery Impr.* (1756) I. 92 A Supply will be wanted in the Vessel, which is running off its Contents. **1771** *Encycl. Brit.* II. 601/2 Until the former water be run off, and the canal cleaned. **1837** *Penny Cycl.* IX. 25/2 They derived a profit proportionable to the quantity of spirits they could run off in a given time. **1853** *Jrnl. R. Agric. Soc.* XIV. I. 140 Three days will now run off the highest floods. **1890** *Chamb. Jrnl.* 30 Aug. 557/1 The clear portion..is run off into another vessel.

transf. **1820** in Bischoff *Woollen Manuf.* (1862) II. 13 The stocks of woollen goods in the United States of America were then run off, and they must require fresh supplies.

h. To cart off, remove.

1864 *Jrnl. R. Agric. Soc.* XXV. II. 528 We generally preserve a portion of mangold on the land... But we always run off sufficient to secure us in the long spring.

i. *U.S.* To steal.

1864 G. A. Sala in *Daily Telegr.* 23 Aug., The negroes his agents have bought in North Carolina, or 'run off', i.e. stolen, in Kentucky. **1882** B. Harte *Flip* ii, He's down on tramps ever since they ran off his chickens.

j. *Sport.* To decide (a race) finally.

1881 *Eagle Mag.* XI. 353 The remaining two events being run off on the following Tuesday. **1892** *Field* 17 Sept. 446/3 It was a big order to have to run off eighty courses in the day.

absol. **1892** *Illustr. Sport. & Dram. News* 23 Apr. 209/3 In running off for second place in the sprint hurdles he succeeded in running the distance in 16 sec.

k. To produce or turn out (duplicated copies, etc.).

1889 *Cent. Dict.* 5271/2 *To run off*,.. In printing, to take impressions of; print: as, this press will run off ten thousand every hour; to run off an edition. **1901** Merwin & Webster *Calumet 'K'* vi. 106 Now, we'll write to Mr. Brown—no,.. I'll do that one myself. You might run off the other and I'll sign it. **1932** A. J. Worrall *Eng. Idioms* 78 This machine will run off eighty copies per minute. **1970** H. McLeave *Question of Negligence* xxvii. 229 They had trundled in a portable X-ray machine... They ran off six plates.

l. *Austral.* and *N.Z.* (See quots.)

1933 L. G. D. Acland in *Press* (Christchurch, N.Z.) 25 Nov. 15/7 *Run off*,..(3) To separate: e.g., 'I will *run off* the strangers when we draft the mob'. **1965** J. S. Gunn *Terminol. Shearing Industry* II. 15 *Run-off*, to take a group of sheep from the flock without necessarily 'cutting out' all of this group or 'drafting' them into special lots, for example 'I'll run off some fats'.

76. run on.

* *intr.* **a.** To continue running or going on, in various lit. and fig. senses.

1595 Shaks. *John* v. vii. 67 Euen so must I run on, and euen so stop. **1621** Bp. Mountagu *Diatribæ* 138 The multitude of those that haue runne on amayne vnto this Sinne. **1740** Cibber *Apol.* (1756) I. 144 A new comedy of Mr. Congreve's..which ran on with..extraordinary success. **1779** *Mirror* No. 67, Having run on in the usual career, I became tired with the sameness..of the scenes. **1833** *Penny Cycl.* I. 384/2 What are called the cursive letters, which run on in continuous succession. **1866** *Jrnl. R. Agric. Soc.* II. I. 54 The pen learning to run on and to print each idea as it occurs. **1971** *Rand Daily Mail* 4 Sept. 23/4 Fighting Heart was running on when he beat Desert Oil over 1000 metres. **1977** *Field* 13 Jan. 56/1 Trainers had no way of knowing whether their fastest puppies had that ability to 'run on', an endowment with stamina so essential for Altcar honours.

b. To continue in operation, effect, etc. Also const. *to* (a certain point).

(*a*) **1622** Mabbe tr. *Aleman's Guzman d'Alf.* I. 240, I was willing to let the bond runne on, till the time it was due. **1736** Lediard *Marlborough* III. 120 It was judg'd more convenient, and conducive to the Publick Good, to let the Navy-Debt run on. **1843** R. J. Graves *Syst. Clin. Med.* xxix. 366 A case of this kind, which has been allowed to run on unchecked. **1892** *Black & White* Xmas No. 33/1 You have ..let the engagement run on without a word of protest.

(*b*) **1847** W. C. L. Martin *The Ox* 128/1 This disease may run on to a horrible extent before it destroys life. **1851** *Jrnl. R. Agric. Soc.* XII. II. 538 Wounds..often run on to suppuration.

c. Of time: To pass or elapse.

1593 Shaks. *Rich. II*, v. v. 59 But my Time Runs poasting on. **1611** —— *Cymb.* v. v. 128 Since she is liuing, let the time run on, To good, or bad. **1736** Ainsworth *Eng.-Lat. Dict.* s.v., The time runneth on. **1855** Tennyson *Maud* III. iii, As months ran on and rumour of battle grew. **1869** Hughes *Alfred the Gt.* iv. 45 New shapes, and ever more vile, as the years run on.

d. To continue speaking; to speak volubly; also in recent use, to chatter.

1704 Steele *Lying Lover* v. i, This unhappy Tongue.. That still run'st on. **1713** —— *Englishman* No. 1. 4 He ran on in a Way which he could never learn at any Place but one. **1762** *Ann. Reg., Acct. of Books* 232/2 Let him talk, ask questions, and run on at pleasure. **1824** Scott *St. Ronan's* xxvii, But I must not run on in a manner which..cannot be very pleasant to you. **1856** *Titan Mag.* Nov. 444/2 Thus did the little fellow run on, nor did I care to interrupt him. **1891** F. W. Robinson *Her Love & His Life* VII. v, 'I'm a fool—I always was,' he ran on, hurriedly.

e. To expand or develop *into*.

1886 Ruskin *Præterita* I. 395 The proposed six lessons ran on into perhaps eight or nine.

f. *Printing.* (See quot.)

1892 A. Oldfield *Man. Typogr.* iii, When two paragraphs are required to be made into one, or, in technical language, 'to run on'.

** *trans.* **g.** To continue to narrate (a story).

1749 Fielding *Tom Jones* XVI. iv, He ran on a long, unintelligible story about his wife.

h. *Printing.* (See quots. 1888, 1892.) Also, to set (an advertisement) as continuous text rather than displayed matter.

1888 Jacobi *Printers' Vocab.* 116 *Run on chapters*, an intimation that the commencement of chapters in a work are not necessarily to begin on a fresh page. **1892** A. Oldfield *Man. Typogr.* iv, The Synopsis of Chapters should be 'set out and run on'; that is, the first line full out at both ends, and the rest indented an em. **1951** S. Jennett *Making of Bks.* xv. 256 Some manuscripts and some of the early printed books avoided paragraph divisions and ran all paragraphs on, indicating the commencement of each by means of a paragraph mark. **1973** F. Jefkins *Advertising made Simple* I. i. 17 By classified we mean not only that the advertisements are small and run-on but that they are grouped together under identifying headings. *Ibid.* III. xvii. 200 *Displayed classified*, or *semi-display*—advertisements in the classified section which are not merely run on, but set out and possibly illustrated.

i. *Cutlery.* (See quot.)

1893 *Labour Comm. Gloss.*, *Run on*, the process of placing imitation or spelter bolsters on common table knife blades.

77. run out.

* *intr.* **a.** Of a period of time, etc.: To expire, terminate, come to an end.

a **1300** *Cursor M.* 15177 Þe thre dais was runnen vte, And þe ferth on hand. **1535** Coverdale *Ezek.* vii. 10 Beholde,.. the daye is come, the houre is runne out. **1601** J. Wheeler *Treat. Comm.* 99 When the ten yeares were almost complete and run out. **1660** tr. *Amyraldus' Treat. Relig.* III. v. 389 Two thousand years pass'd before the Law,..and two thousand more shall run out under the reign of the Messias. **1826** *Examiner* 585/1 The time allowed by law..was fast running out. **1879** Froude *Cæsar* xx. 337 He was to remain with his troops till his term had run out. **1894** *Cornhill Mag.* Feb. 168 The lease of the inn was running out.

b. (*a*) Of water, etc.: To escape from the containing vessel, part, etc. Also *fig.*

a **1325** *Prose Psalter* civ. 39 God brake þe stone, and waters ran out. *c* **1400** Love *Bonavent. Mirror* (1908) 20 [Grace] abideþ nouȝt in þe soule bot renneþ out as water. **1565** Cooper *Thesaurus, Transfluo*, to leake or renne out. **1611** Bible *Matt.* ix. 17 The bottels breake, and the wine runneth out. **1725** *Fam. Dict.* s.v. *Honey*, Scrape them a little, that so the Honey may the more freely run out. **1803** *Med. Jrnl.* X. 564 It may be opened with a lancet or a needle, when the fluid will run out. **1861** *Temple Bar* II. 563 A retired London physician whose sands of life had nearly run out. **1890** W. F. Rae *Maygrove* II. i. 2 An aged parent whose sands are running out.

(*b*) Of vessels, etc.: To allow the contained liquid to escape; to leak.

1530 Palsgr. 693/2 This tubbe runneth out, let it be had to the coupers. **1625** Massinger *New Way* III. ii, The baked meats are run out, the roast turned powder. **1727** *Philip Quarll* (1816) 52 The runlet..being unstopped, ran all out. **1768–74** Tucker *Lt. Nat.* (1834) II. 645 Whenever we find the glass run out, we may rest contented [etc.]. **1800** *Monthly Mag.* IX. I. 322 The tub runs out.

c. (*a*) To come to the end of one's resources or stock; to spend all one's means.

1692 *15th Rep. Hist. MSS. Comm.* App. II. 21 'Tis supposed he ran out by liveing above his fortune. **1720** Swift *Stella's Birthday* Wks. 1751 VII. 119 Had her Stock been less, no doubt, She must have long ago run out. **1781** Johnson *Let. to Mrs. Thrale* 23 Oct., I sincerely applaud your resolution not to run out, and wish you always to save something. *a* **1809** Mrs. Cowley *Who's the Dupe?* I. i, I was obliged to listen to some very wise dissertation about running out, as he calls it. **1965** A. Nicol *Truly Married Woman* 103 'Oxygen,' Doc said. 'We ran out last week, sir, I forgot to tell you,' the nurse said. **1972** J. Wilson *Hide & Seek* vi. 106 'Haven't you got any?' asked Alice. 'No—no, I've run out,' he said.

(*b*) To become expended or exhausted; to come to an end.

a **1700** Dryden (J.), Th' estate runs out, and mortgages are made. **1836** Haliburton *Clockm.* (1862) 192 The land gets run out in his hands, and is no good for ever after. **1864** Lowell *Study Wind., Gt. Public Char.*, The New England breed is running out, we are told! **1889** J. Masterman *Scotts of Bestminster* II. xi. 217 The stock of ready-made clothing had run out.

(*c*) Of a crop variety: to lose its distinguishing characteristics in successive generations.

1890 *Bull. Cornell Agric. Exper. Station* XXI. 88 We are still confirmed in our belief that varieties of tomatoes are unstable and that they soon 'run out'. **1901** I. P. Roberts in L. H. Bailey *Cycl. Amer. Hort.* III. 1418/1 Old varieties [of potatoes] which have 'run out' often find their way into a locality where conditions are superior. **1957** Duncan & Ross *Growing Field Crops* 10 Sometimes disease and insect invasions reverse the process of plant improvement by adjustment. When this happens, varieties are said to run out.

†**d.** (*a*) To launch out into bold or profuse speech; to expatiate. *Obs.*

1554 in Strype *Eccl. Mem.* (1824) III. App. xx. 56 Then he ran out against the late government. **1615** Bedwell *Mohamm. Impostura* I. §28 Run not out..into speeches to say, That God cannot do all things. **1712** Arbuthnot *John Bull* I. viii, Upon all Occasions she run out extravagantly on the praise of Hocus. **1728** Wodrow *Corr.* (1843) III. 358 Then he run out on the iniquity of the late times. **1779** *Mirror* No. 4, They ran out in praise of French cookery.

(*b*) To break out, find vent.

1719 De Foe *Crusoe* II. (Globe) 346 To see how the next Day his Passion run out another way.

(*c*) *Cricket.* To move out rapidly from the block to hit the ball.

1875 *Baily's Mag.* July 162 Mr Greenfield in particular running out almost to every ball and driving it along the ground. **1882** *Daily Telegr.* 27 May, Bannerman only made one hit before running out to hit Barratt and getting disposed of. **1883** *Ibid.* 15 May 2/7 Hill ran out to the.. bowler, and was..stumped.

†(*d*) *Cricket.* To be run out. Cf. sense 77 m below. *Obs.*

1828 *Boy's Own Bk.* 22 When a striker has run out, the notch they were running for shall not be reckoned. **1860** F. Lillywhite *Eng. Cricketers' Trip to Canada & U.S.* 20 Hayward contrived to run out. **1876** *Haygarth's Cricket Scores 1855–75* V. 368 Five ran out on the Bradford side.

e. (*a*) To continue running.

1589 Puttenham *Arte Eng. Poesie* II. iv. (Arb.) 89 Our auncient rymers..let their rymes runne out at length, and neuer stayd till they came to the end.

(*b*) Of a rope: To pass out in continuous length; to be paid out.

1730 A. Gordon *Maffei's Amphith.* 349 Nor did they run out in the same way that the small Cords did. **1753** *Chambers' Cycl.* Suppl. s.v. *Stopper*, It serves, when they are hoising the main-yard, to stop it, that it don't run out too fast. **1867** Smyth *Sailor's Word bk.* 103 A ship is 'brought up to a bitter' when the cable is allowed to run out to that stop. **1890** *Cornhill Mag.* Sept. 271 The object of these breaks is to prevent the cable running out too quickly.

f. To extend or project; to protrude, jut out.

1565 Cooper *Thesaurus, Peninsula excurrit*, the countrey lieth, or renneth out in length. **1604** E. G[rimstone] tr. *D'Acosta's Hist. Indies* I. xx. 67 Many hold, that above Florida, the Land runnes out very large towards the North. **1705** Addison *Italy* 8 The chief of 'em is situate on a Rock that runs out into the Sea. **1780** W. Coxe *Russ. Disc.* 166 It is divided..into three promontories, one of which runs out in a Westerly direction. **1816** Scott *Let.* in *Lockhart* (1837) IV. i. 30, I have now several hundred acres thereof, running out as far as beyond the lake. **1869** Tozer *Highl. Turkey* II. 106 A projection, running out at an angle to the main chain. **1883** *Eng. Illustr. Mag.* Nov. 82/1 At right angles to the façade a row of buildings ran out to Whitehall Gate.

g. To shoot out (*into* excrescences, etc.); to go on *to* something.

1646 Hammond *Tracts* 119 The want of blood was the cause that they ran out into so many legs. **1650** Jer. Taylor *Holy Living* III. iv. 256 The zeal of love which runs out into excresences and suckers, like a fruitful and pleasant tree. **1727** De Foe *Hist. Appar.* iv. 26 Others run out to an imaginary Scheme of Guardian Angels. **1790** W. H. Marshall *Rur. Econ. Midl. Co.* Gloss., To *run* out; to grow or sprout as corn in harvest.

h. To emerge from or come out of (a contest) in a specified manner or position. Also without complement, to win.

1885 *Field* 4 Apr. 436/3 Roberts..eventually ran out a winner by 92 points. **1897** *Daily News* 20 Apr. 3/5 Dundee ..ran out winners with 392 points. **1928** *Daily Tel.* 26 June 11/7 He went on to lead 4–2 in the third set, and then at 5–4, had three set balls before running out. **1941** G. Heyer *Envious Casca* xii. 219 [She] miscued... 'You'll run out now.' **1959** *Times* 19 Mar. 17/5 Then Borch began to smash brilliantly and ran out for the game. **1960** E. S. & W. J. Higham *High Speed Rugby* xxi. 289 In ninety-nine cases out of a hundred, a fitter team will run out winners. **1976** *Bridgwater Mercury* 21 Dec., British Cellophane's second team ran out 4–1 winners against Bridgwater Police in the fourth division of the Somerset Squash League.

** *trans.* **i.** (*a*) To finish or complete (a race, or period of time). Freq. in fig. contexts.

1557 *Tottel's Misc.* (Arb.) 167 When Audley had runne out his race and ended wer his days. **1571** N. Boweman in Farr *S.P. Eliz.* (1845) II. 555 Houres, dayes, and yeeres, runne out their course at last. ? **1630** Milton *Time* I Fly envious Time, till thou run out thy race. **1710** Addison *Tatler* No. 154 ⁋5 Not having run out the whole Thread of their Days. **1850** Tennyson *In Mem.* cv. vii, Run out your measured arcs, and lead The closing cycle rich in good. **1861** *Temple Bar* II. 242 Ere its sands of life had run out the boiling of an egg. **1892** *Illustr. Sport. & Dram. News* 23 July 691/3 He didn't run his race out gamely and do his very best.

†(*b*) To fulfil (an engagement). *Obs.*

a **1837** [Apperley] *Turf* (1851) 11 [He] continued it [horse-racing] for a short time after his brother's death to run out his engagements.

(*c*) *Sport.* To bring (a race, etc.) to a conclusive result; to determine or decide.

1891 *Field* 7 Nov. 711/3 The Tenant Farmers' Cup was, of course, run out, and was won by..Lavender Green. *Ibid.* 712/1 Had the stake been run out he would have taken a deal of beating. **1977** *New Yorker* 10 Oct. 152/2 He then dropped service again, after which Connors ran out the set, 6–2.

(*d*) *Cricket.* To score from (a hit) by running. Freq. *imp.*

1856 *Househ. Words* 2 Feb. 60/2 When you holloa out... 'Run it out!' **1886** J. Pycroft *Oxf. Memories* II. xxi. 89 There were no bounds, all hits were run out. **1898** J. A. Gibbs *Cotswold Village* xi. 234 'Come six, Podder!' I shouted, amid cries of 'Keep on running!' 'Run it out!' etc., from spectators and scouts alike. **1908** W. E. W. Collins *Leaves from Old Country Cricketer's Diary* xi. 180 Run it out, sir, run it out. I hope you'll get six.

j. (*a*) To go through, spend, squander (money or property). ? *Obs.*

1632 Massinger *City Madam* v. ii, Your bonds lie For your sons' truth; and they shall answer all They have run out. **1693** S. Harvey in *Dryden's Juvenal* (1697) 241 A Fop in Rome, that had run out his Estate. **1712** Steele *Spect.* No. 264 ⁋2 At which Age he ran out a small Patrimony. **1809** Malkin *Gil Blas* III. iv. ⁋7 He..taught them..to squander their substance: he had no qualms as to running out his own, for the deed was done.

(*b*) *Agric.* To impoverish, exhaust (land).

1799 J. Robertson *Agric. Perth* 139 By this management however, it is impossible they can run out the land. **1901** *Contemp. Rev.* Mar. 443 The law, as it now stands, encourages the Irish farmer to run out his farm.

(*c*) Of expenses: To amount to, equal, or be as much as (the profit).

1740 Tull *Horse-hoeing Husb.* (ed. 2) 269 The Expence doth not run out the Profit of them.

k. (*a*) To advance (a gun) so that the muzzle projects from the port-hole (or embrasure).

1669 STURMY *Mariner's Mag.* I. ii. 19 That we may be ready to run out our Guns when the Word is given. **1748** *Anson's Voy.* III. viii. 378 Men..were constantly moving about the decks, to run out and fire such guns as were loaded. **1805** BERRY in Nicolas *Disp. Nelson* (1846) VII. 118, I ordered the quarter-boat to be cut away, and ran out the stern chasers. **1840** R. H. DANA *Bef. Mast* xxix, Our bow gun had been loaded and run out. **1862** *Temple Bar* VI. 148 Cannon were run out; matches kept lighted.

(*b*) To expand, extend, or fill out; spec. in *Printing* (see quots.).

1683 MOXON *Mech. Exerc., Printing* xxiii. 375 When a Compositor Sets Wide, he is said to Drive out or Run out. **1716** ADDISON *Freeholder* No. 30 ¶10 Having already run my paper out to its usual length. **1888** JACOBI *Printers' Vocab.* 117 To fill up or 'run out' a line with quadrats or full points.

(*c*) To drive out (horses or cattle), *esp.* to pasture.

1851 MAYNE REID *Scalp Hunt.* xviii. 130 We ran our animals out on their trail-ropes to feed. **1890** 'T. BOLDREWOOD' *Col. Reformer* (1891) 241 First, Jack..ran out half a dozen quiet cattle. **1893** [see 81 i (*d*)].

(*d*) To allow or cause (a line) to be drawn or carried out.

1863 KINGLAKE *Crimea* (1877) I. ii. 162 The Prince declared that he had run out the whole line of his moderation. **1892** *Illust. Lond. News* 9 April 455/2 The salmon..runs out some yards of line.

l. (*a*) *U.S.* To mark off, define. Cf. 53 b.

1719 *New Hampshire Prov. Papers* (1868) II. 726 The above boundaries when so run out..is the bounds of said Parish. **1763** CROGHAN in *Gist's Jrnls.* (1893) 194, I am sorry the Col. John Armstrong has not returned yᵉ four Tracts run out for you last fall.

(*b*) To enumerate, detail.

1878 CAYLER *Pointed Papers* 253 It would be easy to run out the points of resemblance.

(*c*) To turn out, produce.

1877 RAYMOND *Statist. Mines & Min.* 19 The Sunderland, with a furnace of 15 tons of daily capacity, ran out 1,500 flasks last year. **1911** *Chambers's Jrnl.* Sept. 596/2 When you have read it over, I will run out another copy.

m. *Cricket.* To put out (a batsman) while running between the popping-creases. Also *refl.* Also, of a batsman: to cause one's partner to be run out.

1750 in H. T. Waghorn *Cricket Scores 1730–73* (1899) 47 Tom Bell (run out) 0. **1803** *Laws of Cricket* 8 When a striker is run out, the notch they were running for is not to be reckoned. **1823** M. R. MITFORD in *Lady's Mag.* July 391/1 Joel Brent..ran out his mate, Samuel Long. **1825** C. WESTMACOTT *Eng. Spy* II. 89 Bacelli run him out. **1860** *Baily's Monthly Mag.* Aug. 364 His only perceptible fault was his tendency to run himself and others out. **1891** *Sat. Rev.* 18 July 81/2 In attempting an ill-judged run, Crabtree ..was run out at 122. **1892** *Ibid.* 16 July 71/1 With the score at 5, Studd foolishly ran himself out. **1900** P. F. WARNER *Cricket in Many Climes* I. iv. 59 Dick Berens ran me out when I was well on my way to a hundred. **1912** —— *England v. Australia* xii. 134 Hitch and Strudwick between them ran out Tumilty. **1933** M. LOWRY *Ultramarine* ii. 80 You go in first and run out the chief steward. **1974** *Times* 4 Feb. 1/1 A decision whereby Kallicharan..was given run out for 142 off the last ball of the day..was later reversed.

n. *refl.* To exhaust (oneself) by running; to come to an end, exhaust one's means, etc.

1836–7 DICKENS *Sk. Boz, Tales* x, He ran himself out..as regularly as an eight-day clock. **1845–6** TRENCH *Hulsean Lectures* Ser. I. i. 10 Controversies which..have not yet run themselves out. **1891** *Black & White* 24 Oct. 569/1 The Beaufort line..would on the morrow run itself miserably out in muddy lees upon the scaffold. **1892** *Eng. Illustr. Mag.* IX. 451 It is not an uncommon thing to see the two last men running themselves out in order to beat each other.

78. run over. (See also 11 a.)

* *intr.* **a.** Of a vessel, etc.: To overflow. (Cf. OVERRUN *v.* 7.) Also *fig.* and *transf.*

1530 PALSGR. 693 The potte ronneth over, *le pot sen fuyt.* **1539** ELYOT *Image Gov.* (1541) 59 The stinkynge Canelles of vice, whiche beyng ones brimme full, sodeinly renneth ouer through the Citee. **1602** MARSTON *Ant. & Mel.* v. Wks. 1856 I. 56 Boy, keele your mouth, it runnes over. **1678** BUNYAN *Pilgr.* I. (1900) 131 Now was my heart full of joy,.. and mine affections running over with love. **1737** BRACKEN *Farriery Impr.* (1757) II. 160, I shall not look for the Ladle till the Pot runs over. **1838** LYTTON *Alice* 13 When the heart is full of affection, the eyes easily run over. **1850** *Tait's Mag.* XVII. 23/2 His coffers were running over with gold. **1879** TROLLOPE *Thackeray* ii. 76 His mind was running over with the idea.

b. Of liquid (or grain): To flow over the side of a vessel. Also *fig.*

1526 TINDALE *Luke* vi. 38 Good measure, pressed doune, shaken to gedder, and runnynge over, shall men geve. **1611** COTGR. s.v. *s'Enfuir*, The wine spils, or runnes ouer, at the top of. **1729** SWIFT *Direct. Servants, Footman*, Carry up your Coffee boldly, and when your Lady..examines you whether it has not run over, deny the Fact absolutely. **1758** REID tr. *Macquer's Chym.* I. 247 Its contents swell, and might run over without this precaution. *c* **1820** S. ROGERS *Italy, Venice* 17 As though the wealth within them had run o'er.

c. = GO *v.* 89 d.

1642 NEWCOMEN *Craft & Cruelty of Church's Advers.* (1643) 8 The Iesuites have a practice of running over to the Lutheran Church, pretending to be converts. **1700** S. L. tr. *Fryke's Voy. E. Ind.* 227 Running over from the Christians to some Heathenish King.

** (*passing into*) *trans.* **d.** To recount, relate, or repeat rapidly or succinctly.

1610 HOLLAND *Camden's Brit.* (1637) 471, I will..runne over briefly those which are more memorable. **1695** ADDISON *To the King* 117 But who can run the British Triumphs o'er, And count the Flames disperst on ev'ry Shore? **1762–71** H. WALPOLE *Vertue's Anecd. Paint.* (1786) II. 260 The particulars of his life have been often written, and therefore I shall run them over very briefly. **1852** DICKENS *Bleak Ho.* xxii, Will you run over, once again, what the boy said?

e. To review rapidly. Usu. *in* the mind, etc.

1710 ADDISON *Tatler* No. 157 ¶3, I ran over in my Thoughts the several Characters. **1798** CHARLOTTE SMITH *Yng. Philos.* IV. 336 Running over in his mind all the distress that at once awaited his Medora. **1851** MAYHEW *Lond. Labour* IV. 226/1 A man who knew..a great many regular scavagers,..'ran them over', and came to the conclusion [etc.]. **1871** *Routledge's Ev. Boy's Ann.* 371 Hilton had already run over in his own mind the probable consequences.

f. To glance over, read hurriedly.

1677 MIÉGE *Fr. Dict.* II. s.v., To run over a writing. **1719** SWIFT *Let. to Yng. Clergyman* Wks. 1751 V. 16 On Sunday Morning [he] took care to run it [his sermon] over five or six times. **1796** NELSON 1 Dec. in Nicolas *Disp.* (1845) II. 307, I send you some papers of Troubridge. You will like to run them over.

g. To retouch slightly or quickly.

1677 MIÉGE *Fr. Dict.* II. s.v., To run over his work again.

h. *Sc.* To rub (a horse) over *with* something.

1815 SCOTT *Guy M.* lv, Just to rin the beast ower wi' a dry wisp o' strae.

i. Of a vehicle, etc.: to knock down and pass over (someone); to injure or kill by knocking down. Also *transf.* Freq. in *pass.*

The passive use is indistinguishable from that of sense 67 g.

1932 L. GOLDING *Magnolia St.* I. vii. 114 He is so small the driver hardly notices him till he has very nearly run him over. **1954** T. S. ELIOT *Confid. Clerk* III. 109 *Eggerson*: .. Unfortunately, the father died suddenly.. *Lady Elizabeth*: He was run over. By a rhinoceros In Tanganyika. **1970** [see ROAR *v.* 3 e]. **1978** *Daily Tel.* 1 Nov. 19/6 Mann appeared to be more concerned about the damage to his motor-cycle than the youth he had run over.

79. run through.

a. To pierce or stab through the body with a weapon, etc.

[*c* **1400** *Song of Roland* 936 He..with a scherp sper rann throughe his hert. *c* **1450** *St. Cuthbert* (Surtees) 821 Ilk ane of þaim thurgh othir rann; þai were sone deed ilk a mann.] **1470–85** MALORY *Arthur* XII. ii. 595 He gat a spere..& wold haue ronne syr launcelot thurgh. **1560** DAUS tr. *Sleidane's Comm.* 130 A souldiour encountred with him & ran him through. **1609** HOLLAND *Amm. Marcell.* XXX. i. 380 In menacing wise readie to run the young prince through. **1663** R. BOYLE *Usef. Exp. Nat. Philos.* II. i. 22 Flying insects may have their colour and shape preserved..by running them through in some convenient part with pins. **1727** SWIFT *City Shower* Wks. 1751 VII. 39 Those Bully Greeks, who, as the Moderns do, Instead of paying Chair-men, run them thro'. **1878** BOSW. SMITH *Carthage* 233 Rushing at him, [he] ran him through with his spear. **1890** G. M. FENN *Double Knot* I. ii. 102, I shall shoot that fellow, or run him through.

fig. **1592** SHAKS. *Rom. & Jul.* II. iv. 14 He is already dead .., runne through the eare with a Loue song.

b. To read over rapidly. †*run the chapter through*, to go over an old quarrel again. *Obs.*

1673 WOOD *Life* 17 Mar., I told him I..would not come, or run the chapter through, as uncivil people. **1727** BOYER *Dict. Royal* II. s.v., To run through a Book (*or* to read it over).

c. To strike out, draw a line through (words).

1817 *Statutes Realm* II. 2 *note*, Which latter Words are run through with a Pen.

d. *Founding.* (See quot.)

1875 KNIGHT *Dict. Mech.* 2004/2 A mold is said to be *run through* when a quantity of metal is made to enter at one gate and out at another, to remove sullage, air, etc.

80. run together. (See also 55 b, 57 b.)

†**a.** To fall together; to coincide. *Obs. rare.*

a **1225** *Ancr. R.* 80 Of silence & of speche nis bute a lore, & forði, ine writunge, heo eorneð boðe togederes. *c* **1374** CHAUCER *Boeth.* v. pr. i. (1868) 151 It bytidde and ran togidre þat he dalf þere as þat oþer hadde hidd þe golde.

b. To combine, coalesce, unite, *esp.* in a moist or melted state.

c **1374** CHAUCER *Boeth.* v. pr. i. (1868) 151 Þilke ordre.. makeþ þat þe causes rennen and assemblen to-gidre. *c* **1430** *Two Cookery-bks.* 44 Lat þin bature renne dowun,..& whan it is ronne to-gedere on þe chafere [etc.]. **1610** B. JONSON *Alchemist* II. v, The Aqueitie, Terreitie, and Sulphureitie Shall runne together againe. *a* **1713** BURNET *Own Time* (1724) II. 229 They had time enough to run together and form themselves. **1818–20** E. THOMPSON *Cullen's Nosologia* (ed. 3) 207 They are whitish, sometimes distinct, often running together. **1823** P. NICHOLSON *Pract. Builder* 344 Burrs or Clinkers are such as are so much over-burnt as to vitrify, and run two or three together. **1861** *Jrnl. R. Agric. Soc.* XXII. II. 357 This land, though apt to run together, breaks again with comparative ease.

†**c.** To join in combat, engage in fight; *esp.* to tilt or joust. *Obs.*

1387 TREVISA *Higden* (Rolls) VII. 103 Þerfore þese kynges rennynge to gidres in myddes of þe ile [etc.]. *c* **1400** MAUNDEV. (1839) xxii. 238 Thei rennen to gidre a gret randoum;..and they breken here speres so rudely. **1470–85** MALORY *Arthur* I. xxiii. 71 Therwith they ranne to gyders that Arthurs spere al to sheuered. **1565** COOPER *Thesaurus, Acies incurrunt*, the armies incounter or runne together. *Ibid.*, *Decurrere dicuntur milites*, to iust or renne together with speares.

81. run up. (See also 11 a.)

* *intr.* **a.** (*a*) To shoot up; to grow rapidly.

1390 GOWER *Conf.* I. 173 As the Netle which up renneth The freisshe rede Roses brenneth. **1664** EVELYN *Kal. Hort.* Aug., If plants run up to seed over-hastily..pull their roots a little out of the ground. **1731** MILLER *Gard. Dict.* s.v. *June*, Which will cause them [*sc.* lettuce] to run up, and not cabbage. **1821** SCOTT *Kenilworth* iii, But these [hedges], having been untrimmed for many years, had run up into great bushes. **1847** *Jrnl. R. Agric. Soc.* VIII. II. 577 The grass is again running up for a second crop of seed. **1873** M. COLLINS *Squire Silchester* I. ix. 126 Silvester was a tall fellow for his age; had run up a little too fast.

(*b*) To grow up *to*, arrive at, manhood.

17.. RAMSAY *Birth of Drumlanrig* vii, Your Prince, who late Up to the state of manhood run.

(*c*) To increase, mount up.

1677 MIÉGE *Fr. Dict.* II. s.v., Why did you let your score run up thus? **1828–32** WEBSTER s.v., Accounts of goods credited run up very fast.

†**b.** To land; to arrive on shore. *Obs.*

c **1450** *St. Cuthbert* (Surtees) 802 With Cuthbert and his moder þen Rane vp þar bot thre men. *Ibid.* 4732 Þa rane vp at þe hauen agayne.

c. To go back in time or memory.

1662 STILLINGFL. *Orig. Sacræ* III. i. §12 If it had no beginning, it could be no tradition; for that must run up to some persons from whom it first came. **1698** J. COLLIER *Short View* vi (1730) 166 He exhorts them to refresh their Memories, to run up to their Baptism. **1851** NEWMAN *Lect. Pres. Posit. Cath.* ii. (1904) 5 A general belief or impression ..running up beyond the memory of man.

d. (*a*) To rise *to* a high price or value.

1793 JEFFERSON *Writ.* (1830) IV. 482 Money being so flush, the six per cents run up to twenty-one and twenty-two shillings. **1870** [see BREAK *v.* 8 c].

(*b*) To amount *to* a large sum.

1884 *Manch. Exam.* 17 Mar. 5/1 They anticipate that the costs..will run up to something like £100,000. **1891** *Chamb. Jrnl.* 26 Sept. 622/2 Its price ran up to a fabulous amount.

(*c*) To attain *to* a certain weight, size, etc.

1892 *Field* 2 Apr. 490/2 The trout run up to about 3 lb.

e. Of cloth, etc.: To shorten, shrink, or contract after wetting.

1855 *Jrnl. R. Agric. Soc.* XVI. I. 242 They do not 'shrink' or 'run up' in the washing. **1884** W. S. B. MᶜLAREN *Spinning* (ed. 2) 12 The fibre becomes thicker and shorter, and the cloth 'runs up' to an indefinite extent.

f. *Sporting.* To be runner-up in a race, etc.

1842 THACKER *Courser's Ann.* 10 The winner to receive £220..; the dog running up, a bonus of £50. **1890** *Field* 8 Nov. 709/3 Mr. Chambers, who ran up, also played an excellent game [of golf]. **1970** *Field* 16 Apr. 703/1 Stanley and Michael Lunt, father and son who between them won three amateur championships and ran up in a fourth.

** *trans.* **g.** (*a*) To make up (a sum or number); to increase or augment (one's fortune).

1583 STUBBES *Anat. Abus.* II. (1882) 32 Promising them.. that they shall pay no more rent yeerelie, till the same be runne vp. *a* **1700** B. E. *Dict. Cant. Crew*, *To Push on one's Fortune*, to advance, or run it up. **1891** *Sat. Rev.* 19 Sept. 332/2 What was surprising was to see them..run up 117 for the loss of a wicket. **1955** *Times* 25 Aug. 3/3 The South Africans ran up 467 runs for the loss of eight wickets. **1977** *Sunday Times* 2 Jan. 28/3 They ran up 322 for four wickets despite a rain-soaked outfield.

(*b*) To accumulate (a bill, debt, etc.) against oneself or another.

1736 AINSWORTH *Eng.-Lat. Dict.* s.v., To run up a score. **1768** FOOTE *Devil on Two Sticks* II, *Julep.* Dr. Linctus..run me up a bill of thirty odd pounds. **1780** MME. D'ARBLAY *Diary* Apr., He would be rather pleased than surprised if I should run him up a new bill. **1824** *Examiner* 541/1 An account to a large amount had been run up. **1844** J. T. HEWLETT *Parsons & Widows* vi, I was running up fresh bills with my tradesmen. **1887** *Contemp. Rev.* July 13 A public debt, very heavy in proportion to..the wealth of the country, has been rapidly run up.

(*c*) To bid against (a person) at an auction in order to compel him to pay more.

1862 *Temple Bar* VI. 419, I..suffered myself to be induced to bid.., and then to be 'run up' by the..wealthy broker. **1881** A. LANG *Library* i. 19 By bidding for a book.., and by then leaving in the lurch the professionals who combine to 'run him up'.

(*d*) To cause (prices) to rise; to force (a thing) up to a higher price.

1870 W. W. FOWLER *Ten Yrs. in Wall St.* xxiv. 394 They stepped into the gap, and ran up the price again. **1885** *Money Market Rev.* 29 Aug. (Cassell), Engaged in running up the prices of the Southern Lines. **1890** *Sat. Rev.* 18 Oct. 451/1 Mexican Railway stocks..were run up partly because of the rise in silver.

h. To trace or follow up in some way.

1657 OWEN *Commun. w. Father, Son & H. Ghost* III. iii, I cannot intend to run this expression up into its rise and original. **1662** STILLINGFL. *Orig. Sacræ* II. ii. §9 In Moses his time it was a very easie matter to run up their lineall descent as far as the flood. **1740** CHEYNE *Regimen* 186, I might..run this analogy up to all the Qualities and Attributes [etc.]. **1815** SCOTT *Guy M.* xxxiii, He would run the scent up like a blood-hound, and surprise us. **1873** M. ARNOLD *Lit. & Dogma* (1876) 201 We can run up nearly all faults of conduct into two classes.

i. (*a*) To cause to ascend or rise, to lead, bring, or force up, *to* some point.

1658 SIR T. BROWNE *Hydriot.* To T. Le Gros, And so run up your thoughts upon the ancient of dayes. **1711** *Fingall MSS.* in *10th Rep. Hist. MSS. Comm.* App. V. 188 There is nothing which runs a man sooner up to holyness than a perfect patience in affliction. **1825** T. HOOK *Sayings* Ser. II. *Man of Many Fr.* (Colburn) 130 Sheriff's officers, I mean; who sometimes are left in possession, when any man in a hurry runs us up to execution.

(*b*) To build, erect, set up (a wall, etc.).

1726 LEONI *Alberti's Archit.* I. 68 From the bottom of the ditch a wall shou'd be run up, thick and strong. **1772** C. HUTTON *Bridges* 97 If the middle of the pier be run up to its full height. **1828–32** WEBSTER, *To run up*,..to thrust up, as any thing long and slender.

(*c*) To bring (a gun) up to the firing position.

1828 J. M. SPEARMAN *Brit. Gunner* (ed. 2) 180 Number 1 [detachment]..assists to run the gun up; 2, sponges, runs up, and elevates. **1879** *Man. Artill. Exerc.* 317 Under the muzzle of the gun when run up.

(*d*) *Austral.* To fetch or bring (a horse) from pasture, etc.

1888 'R. BOLDREWOOD' *Robbery under Arms* (1890) 350 Run up the horses..; they're in the little horse paddock. **1893** *Pall Mall Mag.* II. 78, I used to run up the horses at five o'clock in the morning, and run 'em out again..at night.

(*e*) To raise (a flag) to the top of a mast, etc. Also *fig.* (see quot. 1962).

1901 G. B. SHAW *Devil's Disciple* I. 28 Run up the American flag on the devil's house. **1930** E. M. BRENT-DYER *Chalet Girls in Camp* v. 76 Nearer the lake were the two flag-poles, and the flags would be run up at six o'clock the next morning. **1938** A. J. LIEBLING *Back where I came From* 27 He run up the American flag. **1962** S. STRAND *Marketing Dict.* 639 *Run it up the flag pole*, a Madison Avenue jargon for trying out any idea. Full expression: 'Let's run it up the flag pole and see who salutes it.' **1964** MRS L. B. JOHNSON *White House Diary* 21 May (1970) 143 They had already provided a flag pole and we ran up the flag while they all gave the Pledge of Allegiance. **1966** *New Statesman* 25 Mar. 409/2 The decision was made—in the admen's jargon that comes naturally to Tory strategists—to run it up the flagpole and see if anyone saluted.

(*f*) To run (an aircraft engine) quickly while it is out of gear in order to warm it up. Also *intr.*

1938 W. O. MANNING *Flight Handbk.* iii. 77 These [wheel brakes] are used..for holding the aeroplane while the engine is being 'run up'. **1942** *R.A.F. Jrnl.* 3 Oct. 26 Intermittently, the sound of engines running up over-comes the wind. **1958** 'N. SHUTE' *Rainbow & Rose* i. 33 Billy Monkhouse had got the Auster out and was running it up outside the hangar. **1976** *Farnborough* 76 (Soc. Brit. Aerospace Companies) 11/1 Inboard engines '2' and '3' are run up first, then the outboards '1' and '4' follow.

j. (*a*) To build or construct rapidly or hurriedly (and unsubstantially).

1687 MIÈGE *Gt. Fr. Dict.* II. s.v., To run up..a Wall. **1726** LEONI *Alberti's Archit.* II. 95 To run up any thing that is immediately necessary for any particular purpose. **1779** SWINBURNE *Trav. Spain* xliv. 412 Valladolid has the appearance of having been run up in a hurry to receive the court. **1820** *Examiner* 474/2 He ran them up a fine new opera-house. **1890** TOUT *Hist. Eng. fr. 1689* 108 Many hideous and formless brick buildings were run up.

transf. **1815** SCOTT *Guy M.* (1862) 85 You have a genius for friendship, that is, for running up intimacies which you call such. **1821** LAMB *Elia* I. *My Relations*, Nature never ran up in her haste a more restless piece of workmanship. **1965** *New Statesman* 19 Mar. 458/3 Were one to ask a computer to run up a composite 18th-century man, the result would be remarkably like Dr Burney. **1974** 'J. LE CARRÉ' *Tinker, Tailor* ix. 68 In KL I had them run me up a British passport.

(*b*) To add up (a column of figures, etc.) rapidly.

1830 *Examiner* 436/2 The worthy Member has characteristically amused himself with running up a calculation. **1854** H. MILLER *Sch. & Schm.* (1858) 512, I never acquired the facility, in running up columns of summations, of the early-taught accountant.

transf. **1852** MRS. STOWE *Uncle Tom's C.* i. 4 The quick eye of the trader, well used to run up at a glance the points of a fine female article.

(*c*) To sew quickly (and loosely). Now usu. to make (a garment, etc.) by sewing quickly or simply.

1859 READE *Love Me Little* xiv. I. 47, I want you to run up a tear in my flounce. **1883** MRS. BANKS *Forbidden to Marry* II. i. 9 To keep the raw apprentice for a whole year running up the seams of gown-skirts. **1977** *Lancashire Life* Nov. 74/1 The women keep it clean, scrubbing floors, washing curtains, running up new ones on the machine [etc.]. **1979** P. DRISCOLL *Pangolin* iii. 38 The tailors who ran up suits in twenty-four hours.

k. To cut up (a tree) as sound wood.

1890 W. J. GORDON *Foundry* 116 The pine lies prostrate. Then comes the question, how far can it be 'run up' into the branches? A cut is made in it, and if the wood is not sound a lower cut is made.

l. *Printing.* (See quot.)

1888 JACOBI *Printers' Vocab.* 117 *Run up colour*, to distribute ink and to prepare for printing.

V. 82. In various collocations used attributively or as sbs., as **run and fell** *Needlework* (see quot. 1968); also *attrib.*; **run-and-read**, given to hasty reading (see 1 e); **run-flat** *a.*, applied to a kind of tyre on which a vehicle may run after a puncture has occurred; **run-over**, due to being run over by a vehicle; **run-sheep(y)-run** *N. Amer.* and *Sc.*, a children's hiding game (see quot. 1909); **run-the-hedge**, a vagabond; **runther(e)out** (only in Sc. form *rin-*), a vagabond, roving person; also *attrib.*; **run-through**, applied to a particular stroke in billiards.

1882 CAUFEILD & SAWARD *Dict. Needlework* 428/1 **Run and fell*..is a method sometimes adopted in lieu of Over-sewing, and employed in making seams, either in underlinen, or in the skirts and sleeves of dresses. **1961** M. SPARK *Prime of Miss Jean Brodie* iii. 69 In the worst cases they unstitched what had been done and did it again, saying 'This'll not do', or 'That's never a run and fell seam'. **1968** J. IRONSIDE *Fashion Alphabet* 99 *Run-and-fell*, a seam similar to a flat-fell but only one row of machining shows. The two edges are seamed together, one is trimmed close to stitching and the other turned under and then laid flat against the main part of garment and machined. **1976** P. CLABBURN *Needleworker's Dict.* 230 *Run and fell seam*,..type of seam worked on fairly light fabrics, commonly used for children's garments and undergarments, but now often superseded by other varieties. **1890** *Pall Mall G.* 24 June 2/3 The ordinary *run-and-read public. **1895** J. HOLLINGSHEAD *My Lifetime* I. 142 In the hands of every run-and-read book-buyer. **1946** R. STORRS *Dunlop in War & Peace* xi. 61 As the name **Run Flat* (*Bullet-proof*) *Tyre* suggests, a bullet may penetrate this tyre, but there is no immediate deflation. **1958** A. G. DONNITHORNE *Brit. Rubber Manuf.* iv. 39 New kinds of tyres were produced to meet service demands in the two World Wars, such, for example, as Dunlop's 'run-flat' tyre. **1973** *Guardian* 30 May 9/3 The Dunlop Denovo 'run-flat' tyre, designed to end the dangers of punctures at high speed, and to enable the motorist to continue his journey without changing the wheel, will be available in October. **1899** CHEYNE & BURGHARD *Man. Surg. Treat.* I. ix. 189 Contused wounds are caused by crushes, *run-over accidents, bites, gun-shot injuries, and the like. **1905** *Dialect Notes* III. 93 **Run, sheep, run*,..a kind of hide and seek in which the participants hide together. **1909** J. H. BANCROFT *Games* 6 The author found a good example of folklore-in-the-making in the game usually known as 'Run, Sheep, Run!' in which a band of hidden players seek the goal under the guidance of signals shouted by a leader. **1949** M. MEAD *Male & Female* 456, I set myself to study changing patterns of run, sheepy, run or prisoner's base. **1962** W. STEGNER *Wolf Willow* I. i. 15 The open field beside Down's where we used to play run-sheep-run in the evenings. **1968** *Sc. Nat. Dict.* VII. 447/1 Rin-sheep-rin. **1969** I. & P. OPIE *Children's Games* iv. 173 'Run, Sheepie, Run' (Cumnock [in Scotland]). **1975** *Islander* (Victoria, B.C.) 4 May 2/1 It seems to me I played run-sheep-run there. **1882** STEVENSON *New Arab. Nts.* (1884) 108 Perhaps you think I don't know a gentleman when I see one, from a common *run-the-hedge like you? **1814** SCOTT *Waverley* lviii, The ne'er be in me, sir, if I think you're safe amang thae Highland *rinthereouts. **1818** —— *Hrt. Midl.* v, Ye little rinthere-out deil that ye are. **1863** H. KINGSLEY *Austin Elliott* I. 193 The daft rintherout callant. **1873** BENNETT & CAVENDISH *Billiards* 231 A winning hazard or possibly a *run-through stroke will be left for the adversary.

run (rʌn), *ppl. a.* [f. RUN *v.*]

I. 1. Of liquor: That has run out or leaked.

1669-70 MARVELL *Corr.* Wks. (Grosart) II. 306 Also the clauses subsequent of abatement to the merchant for leakage, run, and decayed wines.

2. *Naut.* That has deserted. ***run man***, a deserter. Hence ***run-money*** (see quot. 1867).

1702 *Lond. Gaz.* No. 3874/4 Otherwise they will either be made Run, or stay for the Recals of the said Ships, before they receive their Wages. **1758** J. BLAKE *Plan Mar. Syst.* 45 It is proposed that every deserter from a merchant ship be marked *Run* upon the muster-roll. **1823** CRABB *Technol. Dict.*, *Run-man* (Mar.), a runaway or deserter from a ship of war. **1867** SMYTH *Sailor's Word-bk.* 660 If a man be absent from his duty without leave, but not absent long enough to be logged as *run. Ibid.* 586 *Run-money*, the money paid for apprehending a deserter, and charged against his wages.

3. *Sc.* Thorough-going, complete.

1786 BURNS *Twa Dogs* 222 But hear their absent thoughts o' ither They're a' run deils an' jads thegither.

4. Of a fish: That has made a migration up a freshwater stream from the sea (also *dial.* from a stream to the sea).

1828 DAVY *Salmonia* (1840) 50 *Salmo fario*, which in colour and appearance is like a fresh run salmon. **1863** [see FRESH *adv.* 2]. **1881** *Daily Telegr.* 17 Oct., It was..impossible to tell the cutlets or..'head and shoulders' thus obtained from [those of] the freshest and cleanest run fish.

5. *Sc.* Of a knot: (see quot.).

1887 *Jamieson's Scot. Dict.* Suppl., A *run*-knot, a complete knot, one that is tightly drawn.

6. *Hort.* (See quot. 1852.)

1851 *Beck's Florist* 75 In some summers the complaint of an unusual number of run flowers will be pretty general in a particular district. **1852** G. W. JOHNSON *Cottage Gard. Dict.* 794/1 When the dark colouring of a carnation, or other flower, becomes confused or clouded with its lighter ground colour, they say it is *a run flower*.

7. a. *Mining.* (See quots.)

1730 DALE *Taylor's Hist. Harwich & Dovercourt* 454 Whence the Miners call them Run-Lime-Stone; they supposing these Figures to be produced by a more than ordinary Heat. **1789** J. WILLIAMS *Min. Kingd.* I. 246 One variety of this coal [stone or splent coal] is by Scots colliers very properly called run splent. **1864** W. W. SMYTH *Cat. Min. Coll.* 11 (E.D.D.), Copper pyrites, botryoidal ('run' or 'blister ore' of the miners). **1883** GRESLEY *Gloss. Coal-mining* 208 *Run Coal*, soft bituminous coal.

b. *dial.* Of milk: Coagulated, clotted.

Cf. '*Viscum*, ȝerunnen blod' in Ælfric's Gloss.

1866 T. EDMONSTON *Shetl. & Orkney Gloss.*, *Run-milk*, milk coagulated by the heat of the weather. **1888** EDMONDSTON & SAXBY *Home Naturalist* 100 Delicate people who dare not for their lives drink a cupful of sweet cream, can devour that quantity of 'run' cream with impunity.

II. 8. Of goods: Illicitly landed or imported; smuggled.

1714 *French Book of Rates* 123 All the said Silk Stockings and Stirrups which..shall by them be exposed to Sale, not having the said Mark, shall be reputed as run and concealed. **1754** SHEBBEARE *Matrimony* (1766) I. 227 Buying great quantities of run Claret and Coniac Brandy whenever he could. **1837** LOCKHART *Scott* I. vii. 199 In quest of a supply of run brandy from the Solway Frith. **1853** HAWKER *Prose Wks.* (1893) 126 It was a very guilty practice in the authorities to demand taxes for what he called run goods.

transf. **1854** *Pereira's Polarized Light* (ed. 2) 151 The reason why run glass (that is, glass made without paying the duty) is very apt to crack.

9. a. Poured in or out in a melted state; caused to flow out. ***run butter***: see BUTTER *sb.*[1] 1 d.

1774 T. PENNANT *Tour in Scotl.* (ed. 3) 287 Some of the walls, all of run lime, do as yet remain. **1806** FORSYTH *Beauties Scotl.* IV. 430 A wall..cemented with lime after the manner of what is commonly called run-lime. **1866** BRANDE & COX *Dict. Sci.*, etc. II. 135/1 Pure white honeycomb, free from bee-bread or brood, and worth from four to five times the value of ordinary run honey, obtained on the single hive system. **1885** W. L. CARPENTER *Soap & Candles* 188 This kind, technically known as 'run soap', was at one time largely made in America.

b. ***run metal, steel***, a form of cast iron.

1833 J. HOLLAND *Manuf. Metal* II. 39 Run, or virgin steel.., in the proper sense of the term, is no steel at all, but rather good cast metal. **1851-4** *Tomlinson's Cycl. Useful Arts* (1867) I. 483/2 The best description of iron scissors are falsely named *run* or *virgin steel*. **1887** *Jamieson's Scot. Dict.* Suppl., *Run-metal*, cast-iron: metal that has been run into a mould, as opposed to that which has been forged.

10. Of a race, etc.: That has been run or raced. Usually with prefixed adverb.

1822 T. CREEVEY in *Creevey Papers* (1903) I. x. 236, I met ..the Duke [of Wellington]... 'It has been a damned serious business,' he said... 'It has been a damned nice thing—the nearest run thing you ever saw in your life.' **1856** 'STONEHENGE' *Brit. Rur. Sports* 337/2 Nothing differs more from a true-run race than the ordinary careful gallop used in training. **1863** TREVELYAN *Compet. Wallah* (1866) 180 The scars which testify to their prowess on more than one hard-run day of battle.

11. Hunted, chased. Also, exhausted by running; worn out.

1876 *Coursing Calendar* 147 Troapham proved herself a rare stayer, for she was fearfully run in her first course. **1892** *Field* 2 Apr. 472 They left their run fox for dead beat. **1917** G. BELL *Let.* 13 Jan. (1927) I. xv. 393, I wonder you have time to write me such splendid long letters! You really must not do it when you feel dreadfully run.

12. a. Carried on, continuous; running.

1811 *Agric. Surv. Aberdeen* (Jam.), 129 Strong spars, called run joists, were laid along side of the roof. **1833** LOUDON *Encycl. Archit.* §1103 The back posts of the trivesses to be..mortised into a run-tree (a rail fixed along the tie-joists) at top. *Ibid.* §1214 The mangers..to have a run-beam (front rail) rounded on the top,..fixed along the top of the racks. **1844** H. STEPHENS *Bk. Farm* I. 219 Plain cornices, runbeads, and arises, 12-inch girth and under. **1879** *Cassell's Techn. Educ.* II. 366/2 The measurements..are taken by the lineal inch, foot, or yard, and are then said to be 'run'.

b. ***run line***: (see quots.). *Sc.*

1873 MACKELVIE *Ann. & Stat. U.P. Church* 16 'The run-line,' as it was popularly called, (that is, singing continuously, instead of singing and reading alternately) was then introduced. **1888** BARRIE *Auld Licht Idylls* iii, The old, reverent custom in the kirk was for the precentor to read out the psalm a line at a time... Where run line holds, however, the psalm is read out first, and forthwith sung.

13. a. ***run lace***: (see quots.).

1865 F. B. PALLISER *Hist. Lace* xxxvi. 424 To France must be assigned the application of the Jacquard system to the net-frame, and consequently the invention of machinery lace. Shawls and large pieces in 'run lace', as it is termed, had previously been made after this manner. **1882** CAULFEILD & SAWARD *Dict. Needlewk.* 428/2 *Run Lace.* During the eighteenth century this description of lace was made in Northamptonshire... The lace ground..was made upon the Pillow, and the design embroidered or run upon it afterwards with the needle. **1883** *Standard* 26 June 3/3 The well-known Limerick production is of four kinds: Tambour, the simplest and commonest; 'Run,' finer and lighter, the pattern formed in the net with a finer thread, not drawn in with the tambour, but run in with a point needle.

b. ***run stitch***, a running stitch. Also as *vb.*

1880 *Plain Hints Needlework* 23 The run-stitch should be placed under the tuck or fold. *Ibid.*, Where the material has been joined by run-stitching the breadths. *Ibid.* 107 Run-stitch..is the only term which can with any propriety be used for the actual stitch as used in plain-work.

14. With adverbs, as ***run-after***, sought after; popular; ***run-in***, inserted; ***run-off***, = sense 6; ***run-on***, continued into the next line, couplet, etc.; ***run-out***, exhausted; ***run-over***, (*a*) of (the heels of) shoes: worn down on one side; (*b*) = ***run-on***.

1810 CRABBE *Borough* viii. 102 This is no shaded, run-off, pin-eyed thing, A king of flowers. **1877** DOWDEN *Shaks. Primer* vi. 82 The proportion of the run-on lines in Lucrece is 1 in 10·81. **1878** *Trans. Illinois Dept. Agric.* XIV. 144 The long, lank hog of the old, run-out breed has given place to the improved Poland China. **1880** *Rep. Vermont Board Agric.* VI. 28 The first condition of fertility we have, even in these run-out pastures. **1882** G. M. HOPKINS *Lett. to R. Bridges* (1955) 158 The question of what they call run-on lines and the rhymes or other final words belonging is difficult. **1893** *Jrnl. R. Agric. Soc.* Dec. 801 A field of run-out inferior pasture. **1897** MISS KINGSLEY *W. Africa* 110 These garments have a band that consists of a run-in string. **1906** 'O. HENRY' in *N.Y. World Mag.* 8 July 8/1 'Smoky' was dressed in..run-over shoes, and trousers of the 'serviceable' brand. **1908** R. W. CHAMBERS *Firing Line* vi. 75 I've heard that you are the most assiduously run-after girl at Palm Beach. **1919** *Ladies' Home Jrnl.* Mar. 89/4 '*Why* do my heels run-over?' Run-over shoe heels are more than unsightly. They are warning of incipient foot trouble. They are usually due to a weakness of the foot structure which permits the foot to 'give' outwardly or inwardly in walking. **1931** *Times Lit. Suppl.* 15 Jan. 43/2 His rules about mid-verse pause and run-over lines. **1946** B. MACDONALD *Egg & I* xvi. 175 Reddish cotton stockings, run-over shoes. **1955** *Ess. & Stud.* VIII. 61 The madcap movement of the run-on lines perfectly parallels the hither-thithering of the trapped mind. **1965** R. E. LONGACRE in *Language* XLI. 74 Such imbedding of sentence within a phrase has special phonological characteristics (level, run-on intonation, and lack of pause before termination of the imbedding phrase). **1978** J. A. MICHENER *Chesapeake* 667 He wore run-over shoes, baggy trousers, torn shirt and smashed hat, items which he rarely changed. **1979** *Dictionaries* I. 15 The question arises of whether run-on entries will be defined or not.

'run-about. Also runabout.

1. a. One who runs about from place to place; a roving or strolling person; *dial.* a pedlar. Also, an assistant, a dogsbody.

[**1377** Langl. *P. Pl.* B. vi. 150 Robert renne-aboute shal now3te haue of myne.] **1549** in Tytler *Edw. VI* (1839) I. 187 Let one of those Runabouts come,..straight they call up their neighbours. **1607** Marston *What you Will* iii. i, A runne-about, a skipping French-man. **1685** R. Dunning *Plain Method* 11 Not..of the better sort of Workmen, but equal with the Scotchmen, the most genteel sort of Run-abouts. **1820** *Blackw. Mag.* May 163 Some handy rin-about had emptied our laird's hen-bawks. **1886** Elworthy *W. Somerset Word-bk.* s.v., A hawker or pedlar is often called a run-about. **1957** [see garde champêtre]. **1959** M. Summerton *Small Wilderness* i. 15 He hadn't relished my taking a job as a tea-maker and general runabout on a ritzy household magazine. **1976** J. Fraser *Who steals my Name?* xv. 186 A constable was kept on duty as a part-time secretary to the chief superintendent, a run-about, a screen protecting his privacy.

b. *attrib.* Given to wandering or roving.

1775 J. Woodforde *Diary* 13 June (1924) I. 163 His whole Face..was uncommonly ugly, not unlike one of the runabout gipsies. **1788** Wesley *Wks.* (1872) VII. 210 Begging that he would please to 'take a course to stop these run-about Preachers'. **1884** *Folk Lore Jrnl.* II. 6, I am not one of those runabout doctors. **1899** Raymond *No Soul above Money* ii. ii, You fortune-telling, thieving, runabout rogue!

2. A plant inclined to straggle or stray.

1882 *Garden* 15 July 52/1 The plant is not quite such a run-about.

3. *Austral.* (See quot. 1898.)

1890 'R. Boldrewood' *Col. Reformer* xviii. 218 'Open that gate, Piambook,' said Ernest.., pointing to the one which led into the 'run-about' yard. **1898** Morris *Austral Eng.* 397/2 Runabouts are cattle left to graze at will, and the runabout-yard is the enclosure for homing them.

4. A small light horse-vehicle or motor-car. Also *attrib.* with *car*.

1890 in *Cent. Dict.* **1900** Ade *Fables in Slang* 155 He took her riding in his new Runabout every Evening. **1900** *Motor-Car World* I. 130/2 A new small car... It is known as the University Runabout. **1901** *Munsey's Mag.* XXIV. 835/1 The horses high of action,..the runabout rolling dreamily on its cushion tires. **1902** *Westm. Gaz.* 30 May 5/1 The battery..propelled a 'runabout' car sixty-two miles over roads of varying quality. **1912** *Chambers's Jrnl.* Feb. 144/1 The 'auto-carrier'..gives everything that the small runabout motor-car can offer. **1930** *Punch* 2 Apr. 374/1 Just ahead of us was a small runabout car. **1949** *Chicago Tribune* 18 Sept. 34/2 Among some 70 old-time cars will be a one cylinder 1904 Cadillac runabout, [etc.]. **1956** *News Chron.* 1 Nov. 8/5 It is the latest in a line of economy runabouts—the Mark E Bond Minicar. **1968** 'J. Le Carré' *Small Town in Germany* ii. 24 The pavements are obstructed by the runabout cars of British Counsellors' wives. **1980** *Times* 7 Mar. 25 Whereas the Mini is really a Town runabout, the Metro is conceived as a family car that will be more comfortable for longer runs.

5. A light aircraft.

1904 A. Santos-Dumont *My Airships* xxii. 282, I determined to build a small air-ship runabout for my pleasure and convenience only. **1922** *Westm. Gaz.* 14 Nov. 3/6 Arrangements are being made..to launch the first power-driven runabout of the air. **1932** *Flight* 13 Oct. 952 The machines would have been the forerunners of cheap aerial runabouts. **1959** *Economist* 3 Jan. 58/2 A small aircraft need not be barred from using a big airport provided that it carries radio. But many of the smallest runabouts have no radio. **1966** P. O'Donnell *Sabre-Tooth* vi. 87 The twin-engined de Haviland Dove, the six-passenger aircraft which plied as a runabout from the valley..to Kabul. **1977** 'J. Le Carré' *Hon. Schoolboy* xii. 273 'Is that a single-engine plane?'.. 'Kind of executive runabout kind of thing.'

6. orig. and chiefly *U.S.* A small motor-boat.

1932 *Daily Progress* (Charlottesville, Va.) 7 Sept. 10/3 This event will be followed by..two free-for-all outboard races and a race for runabouts not over 50 horsepower. **1946** *Sun* (Baltimore) 16 Sept. 12 (*caption*) The D, E, F and G Class service and racing runabouts leave the starting line in the second heat. **1966** T. Pynchon *Crying of Lot 49* iii. 64 'Help,' said Di Presso, looking back..across the lake. Another runabout had appeared and was headed toward them. **1970** J. Cleary *Helga's Web* xv. 274 He had started up the motor of the runabout and cruised quietly back to the yacht. **1975** B. Garfield *Hopscotch* ii. 27 A little motor runabout zipped past the barge.

† **'runagade.** *Obs. rare.* Also **runn-.** [var. of renegade *sb.* Cf. next.] = runagate *sb.*

a **1604** Hanmer *Chron. Irel.* (1809) 338 By their runnagades they summoned..all the Chieftaines of Irish birth to a parlee. **1693** *Mem. Cnt. Teckely* ii. 146 The Turks having only some Runagades for Engineers.

† **runa'gado.** *Obs.* Also 7 **runna-, runnegado.** [Alteration of renegado, after next.]

1. = renegade *sb.* 1.

1614 W. Davies *Trav.* B iij b, He is Circumcised.. denying his Christian name, so that euer after he is called a Runagado. **1629** *Capt. Smith's Wks.* (Arb.) II. 915 Many an accursed runnagado or Christian turned Turke.

2. = renegade *sb.* 2.

1624 Capt. Smith *Virginia* iv. 143 A few of the Westerly Runnagados had conspired against the..King. **1652** A. Ross *Hist. World* i. ii. 8 One Cleon of Cilicia gathered together 70000 runnegadoes; these overthrew the Roman Pretors. **1699** Dampier *Voy.* (1729) II. i. 138 On what Score the two English Runagadoes turn'd here, I know not.

attrib. **1628** Prynne *Love-lockes* 40 That which euery Runnagado, Light-footed, or False-handed Irish-boy weares. **1688** Holme *Armoury* iii. 407/2 Used in the hand of a Runagado Rogue.

runagate ('rʌnəgeɪt), *sb.* (and *a.*). Now *arch.* Forms: 6 ron(ne)agate, 7 ronnagat; 6 runne-, 6–9 runn-, 6– runagate; 6–8 runne-, 7 runni-, 8 runegate. [Alteration of *renna-, rennegate,* renegate, by association with *ren(ne* run *v.* and agate *adv.* In common use from *c* 1550 to 1700, sometimes as a vague term of abuse.]

† **1.** An apostate. *Obs.* = renegade *sb.* 1.

c **1530** *Exam. W. Thorpe* (Tindale) G iij, The lustie lyuyng and the slyding fro the treuth of these runagates shall be to me..an example [etc.]. **1554** *Lydgate's Bochas* viii. xiii. 185 An Idolater and runneagate in dede. **1589** Nashe *Martin Marprelate* Wks. (Grosart) I. 156 Lucian the Atheist, was neuer so irreligious; nor euer Iulian the runnagate so blasphemous. **1632** Lithgow *Trav.* iii. 90 There arriued from Tunnis in Barbary, an English Runagate. **1692** Washington *Milton's Def. People* M.'s Wks. 1851 VIII. 31 Meddle with your own matters, you Runagate, and be asham'd of your actions, since the Church is asham'd of you.

2. A deserter, fugitive, runaway.

a **1548** Hall *Chron., Rich. III,* 54 b, A compaigne of traytors, thefes, outlawes and ronneagates. **1576** Fleming *Panopl. Epist.* 128 It is reported to me, that your clearke or Secretarie, hath plaide the fugitiue or runnagate. **1600** Holland *Livy* xxiii. 480 If he went to Rome,..he should bee sooner lodged there in prison like a fugitive runagate, than intertained..for a friend. **1674** Milton *Hist. Moscovia* Wks. 1851 VIII. 498 Many Letters and Messengers therupon were sent from Boris into Poland..to acquaint them who the Runnagate was. **1737** Whiston *Josephus, Hist.* ii. xxi. §7 John.., together with his two thousand Syrian runagates. **1778** Foote *Trip Calais* ii. Wks. 1799 II. 345 What news from the runagate? have you seen her? **1824** W. Irving *T. Trav.* II. 241 Crews of these desperadoes,..the runagates of every country and every clime. **1866** Brogden *Prov. Lincs., Runnagate,* a runnaway. **1890** Conan Doyle *White Company* xxxiv, I shall leave my Winchester runagates to the care of the provost-marshal.

fig. **1641** Milton *Reform.* ii. Wks. 1851 III. 55 Commit securely to true wisdome the vanquishing and uncasing of craft and suttletie, which are but her two runnagates. **1746** Hervey *Medit.* II. 17 Our Moments slip away silently and insensibly—and will the Runagates never stop?

Comb. **1648** Gage *West Ind.* 3 Whosoever..runagate-like shall return, may be constrained to return again to the India's.

3. A vagabond, wanderer; a run-about.

1547 Boorde *Brev. Health* Pref. 6 b, Let al men beware of vagabundes and ronagates that wyl smatter with phisicke. **1594** Nashe *Unfort. Trav.* Wks. (Grosart) V. 141 The first traueller was Cayn, and hee was called a vagabond runnagate on the face of the earth. **1634** Ford *Perk. Warbeck* v. iii, You are known For Osbeck's son of Tournay a loose runagate, A Land-loper. *a* **1677** Barrow *Serm.* (1683) II. 201 A crew of wild thieves and runnagates. **1822** Galt *Sir A. Wylie* xii, Get twa shillings frae that flea-luggit rinnagate Charlie Pierston. **1881** Besant & Rice *Chapl. of Fleet* I. 181 We have been kept in scarceness among runnagates and spendthrifts.

4. *attrib.* or as *adj.*

1563 Foxe *A. & M.* 985/2 A runnagate Scot dyd take away the adoration..of Christe in that sacrament. **1579** W. Wilkinson *Confut. Fam. Love* 10 Lyke a runnagate Apostata..ye betray his Saints to Sathan. **1612** T. Taylor *Comm. Titus* ii. 9 Paul hauing conuerted Onesimus a runnagate seruant.., sent him to Philemon againe. **1653** R. Sanders *Physiogn., Moles* 25 He is a runnagate fugitive, and wanders out of his native country. **1737** Whiston *Josephus, Antiq.* xii. vii. §3 There came also to them..many of the runagate Jews. **1810** *Q. Rev.* Nov. 458 We have seen..how much harm has been done by the runagate sailors in Polynesia. **1851** G. H. Kingsley *Sp. & Trav.* (1900) 335 The beach-comber, a runagate rogue without property, position, or influence.

So **'runagates.** *rare*$^{-1}$.

1865 W. G. Palgrave *Arabia* II. 366 Much as a well-trained schoolboy does a runagates street urchin.

‖**runanga** ('runaŋa). *N.Z.* Also with capital initial. [Maori.] In Maori society, an assembly or council. (See also *whare runanga* s.v. whare.)

1858 J. Morgan *Let.* 21 June in *Richmond-Atkinson Papers* (1960) I. 411 This arrangement was proposed by Potatau's *runanga.* **1861** A. S. Atkinson *Jrnl.* 18 Nov. in *Ibid.* 727 The King party will not..accept the new runanga system. **1862** —— *Jrnl.* 5 Feb. in *Ibid.* 744 One man, the head of the Runanga, shall have £100 a year, 7 Runanga men £70 each, [etc.]. **1905** W. Baucke *Where White Man Treads* 33 He..carves effigies of his tribe-founders and heroes on the memorial posts of his runanga house, that when the elders meet to discuss matters of state, the presence of his dear dead may preside, and guide the thoughts of the council. **1946** *Jrnl. Polynesian Soc.* June 157 *Runanga,* assembly; council; so, *whare-runanga,* meeting-house. **1967** J. Metge *Maoris of N.Z.* ii. 33 As a group, the kaumātua formed a community council (*runanga*) which advised and could influence the chief. **1975** D. Scott *Ask that Mountain* (1976) ii. 41 Discussion and debate was reserved for the *runanga,* the council of leaders and elders.

run-around. Also as one word. [f. run *v.*]

1. A felon or whitlow. Also called ***run-round.*** *U.S. colloq.*

1857 *Knickerbocker* XLIX. 97 There comes us a 'run-round' on the end of our pen-finger. **1872** Talmage *Serm.* 224 Some hypochondriac with a 'run-around' or a 'hang-nail'. **1913** J. London *Valley of Moon* iii. iv. 352 His finger was hurting too much, he said... 'It might be a run-around,' Saxon hazarded. **1968** Leider & Rosenblum *Dict. Dermatol. Words* 364 *Run(-)around..,* is colloquial for inflammatory conditions of the soft parts about nails and conveys the idea of tendency to extend circularly.

2. *colloq.* (orig. *U.S.*). Deceit, evasion; behaviour likely to mislead or cause inconvenience, esp. in phr. *to give* (someone) ***the run-around.***

1915 *Chicago Herald* 2 Dec. 13/4 Pitts is satisfied that he is the victim of the grandest run-around ever put over on a boxing promoter. **1924** H. C. Witwer in *Cosmopolitan* Jan. 84/2 If you wanted to give William a run around why not say we were Cleopatra and Salome and be done with it? **1929** J. P. McEvoy *Hollywood Girl* i. 3 All I get is the run around —that nothing today, my dear, but keep in touch with us, you never know what is liable to turn up. **1933** *Sun* (Baltimore) 24 Nov. 20/4 The fans were given the runaround in the third race here yesterday. **1934** E. S. Gardner *Case of Lucky Legs* xiii. 191 A small-town dentist.., and you think that fits you to give me a run-around in a murder case. **1938** O. Nash *I'm Stranger here Myself* 115 Humanity must continue to follow the sun around And accept the eternal run-around. **1944** 'N. Shute' *Pastoral* ii. 27 Perhaps her boy friend was giving her the run around. **1950** 'S. Ransome' *Deadly Miss Ashley* ix. 109 He had already taken more than enough of a run-around from her. **1960** W. Haggard *Closed Circuit* iv. 43 My instructions are to..give him the runaround and soften him up. **1973** J. Wainwright *Devil You Don't* 176, I don't trust you... It could be a runaround. **1979** E. Newman *Sunday Punch* xix. 164 We were seeing a deliberate run-around by Smith.

3. *Printing.* Type set in shorter measure so as to fit at the side of an illustration.

[**1934** V. Steer *Printing Design & Layout* 327/2 *Run Round Block,* type set to surround a block.] **1949** Melcher & Larrick *Printing & Promotion Handbk.* 260/2 The use of run-arounds increases the cost of type composition and is often avoided on that account. **1978** *Verbatim* May 7/1 It is extremely difficult (and expensive) to program a computer to set run-arounds.

4. *colloq.* (orig. *U.S.*). A short journey or excursion. Also *attrib.* and *fig.*

1954 *Ties* (U.S.) Dec. 14/2 Steve operates the Little Southern's passenger train and local freight on regular-style train orders, with 'meets' and 'runarounds' carefully scheduled. **1976** *Broadcast* 29 Nov. 7/3 Over 1600 [people] have said they would become 'runaround drivers', ferrying around the elderly and infirm. **1977** *Time Out* 28 Jan.–3 Feb. 15/3 LBC's runaround with Alexander Walker on the week's new films.

'runaway, *sb.* (and *a.*). Also 6 **renawaye,** 6–7 **runne away, run(n)awaie** (7 **-waye**). [f. run *v.* + away *adv.*]

I. 1. a. One who runs away; a fugitive, a deserter.

[*c* **1515** *Cocke Lorell's B.* 5 Her husbonde dwelleth.. Nexte house to Robyn renawaye.] **1547** *Act 1 Edw. VI,* c. 3 §2 The same Iustices..shall adiudge the loyterer and run away to be the said masters slaue for euer. **1589** Greene *Menaphon* (Arb.) 57 What are you, sir,..that deale thus with me by interrogatories, as if I were some runne away? **1617** Moryson *Itin.* ii. 78 Private Captaines gave pasportes to run awaies. **1665** Manley *Grotius' Low-C. Wars* 614 Many Runaways from them affirmed, They had not tasted a bit of Bread in five days. **1712** *Perquisite Monger* 17 A general Defection ensu'd upon this Run-aways Example. **1758** J. Blake *Plan Mar. Syst.* 22 Half the gross wages of such run-aways from the ship, shall be deposited..in the Pay-office. **1833** Ht. Martineau *Briery Creek* ii. 29 This lad is a notorious runaway: he has escaped three times. **1897** Mary Kingsley *W. Africa* 344 One of those miscreant boys was a runaway from a Fan village.

fig. **1612** J. Davies (Heref.) *Muse's Sacrifice* Wks. (Grosart) II. 50/2 Riches, but Runnawayes; Fauours, but lyes. *a* **1616** Beaum. & Fl. *Queen of Corinth* v. ii, A Slave To beastly passions, a Fugitive, And run away from virtue.

† **b.** An apostate, a renegade. *Obs.*

1561 T. Norton *Calvin's Inst.* iv. 5 He compteth him for a traiterous runne away and forsaker of Religion. **1583** Babington *Commandm.* (1590) 103 An heretike hee is, a runne-away from the church. **1606** Dekker *Double P.P.* Wks. (Grosart) II. 175 A Papist Volant, or The Run-away. **1647** Trapp *Comm. 1 Cor.* i. 13 Those then that will needs be called Franciscans, Lutherans, &c...become run awaies from Christ.

c. A horse which runs away or bolts while being ridden or driven. Also *transf.* of (part of) a railway train.

1607 Markham *Caval.* ii. (1617) 67 For run awaies and mad Iades, I haue known him haue seauen or eight in his charge at an instant. **1619** Bert *Hawkes* (1891) 56 If a horse prooue hard-mouthed, a run-away, carry an vnsteady head [etc.]. **1856** 'Stonehenge' *Brit. Rural Sports* 536/1 In such a case it is better to do anything than to persevere in the course which the runaway is taking. **1870** *Field* 2 Apr. 200/3, I have not had an opportunity of seeing one tried on a regular runaway, such animals being luckily not very common. **1945** G. B. Grundy *55 Yrs. at Oxf.* i. 17 The eight trucks of a luggage train which I had seen were runaways.

2. a. An act of running away; *spec.* an elopement, a runaway match (see 3 b); (*U.S.*) of horses: an act of bolting. Also *transf.* of a railway train or wagons.

1724 De Foe *Mem. Cavalier* 278 We..forced them at last to a down right Run-away, on Foot. **1830–2** Carleton *Traits* (1843) I. 349 Many of the young people made, on these occasions, what is called 'a runaway'. **1845** Jane Robinson *Whitehall* v, He would have made another run-away of it. **1850** L. H. Garrard *Wah-to-Yah* xxi. 291 Three of the muleteams, made handsome runaways. **1872** *Court Jrnl.* 2 Mar. 244/1 It is not generally the young lady who takes the lead in an elopement,..but when she does, the runaway is pretty sure to prove a success. **1898** *Kansas City* (Missouri) *Star* 18 Dec. 1/5 Miss Agnes Peterson was hurt in a runaway caused by the driver of an express wagon. **1967** G. F. Fiennes *I tried to run Railway* iv. 32 We never had a runaway. **1971** *Leader* (Durban) 7 May 16/4 Occasional runaways by Derrick Norris and Elijah Adams looked dangerous at times, but failed to bring home any goals. **1975** *Budget* (Sugarcreek, Ohio) 20 Mar. 7/8 Jacob D. Shetler had a runaway recently. He wanted to haul wood to saw, when the horses took off.

b. = runway 1 a. *colloq.* (chiefly *U.S.*).

1868 *Fur, Fin, & Feather* 205 After a hard pull after a deer, or a long and tiresome vigil on a 'run-away', nothing is so vexatious as a miss-fire. **1944** *Living off Land* ii. 32 Carry a few snares..set them on the runaways through the grass or bushes... Set the noose in a spot where the runaway is narrow.

c. *transf.* (*ellipt.* uses of senses 4 and 6.)

1947 *Sun* (Baltimore) 8 Jan. 18/1 The [stock-market] ticker tape frequently was idle until the final hour when sufficient offerings arrived to quicken the pace. There was nothing like a run-away, however. **1967** *Boston Sunday Herald* 14 May 2-5/2 Nineteen hits, 14 walks and three big innings added up to a 26–4 runaway for Bates over Brandeis Saturday. **1976** 'G. BLACK' *Moon for Killers* ii. 23 That book didn't need promoting. It was a runaway.

d. *Science.* Uncontrolled departure of a system from its usual or intended equilibrium.

1955 *Sci. Amer.* Oct. 60/3 Although reactors are designed so that there is a built-in tendency to overcome runaways automatically, accidents are always possible. **1957** *Practical Wireless* XXXIII. 684/1 Damage might result due to the heating effect of the lamp raising the temperature of the junction causing a 'run away', irreparably damaging the photo-transistor. **1973** *Physics Bull.* July 411/2 The danger of runaway of a fusion reactor is minimal, for the total deuterium and tritium in the reactive zone would be only about 0·25 g per 1000 MW of output power. **1974** *Nature* 29 Mar. 399/1 When the mass accreted exceeds $\sim 10^{-5} M_\odot$ nuclear energy generation becomes violent enough to drive a thermal runaway typical of novae.

II. *attrib.* or as *adj.*

3. a. Of persons: Having run away; given to running away; fugitive; *spec.* (*U.S.*) of slaves. Also *fig.*

1548 PATTEN *Exped. Scotl.* M iiij, A Syllogisim thus formed of such a theuing maior, a runaway minor, and a trayterous consequent. **1632** *Star Chamber Cases* (Camden) 111 One of them is an Irish runne away footman. **1676** *Life Father Sarpi* in *Brent's Counc. Trent* 34, I have seen many of that run-away Race, who..would give a leap into such a compendious way of life. **1699** *N. Carolina Colonial Rec.* (1886) I. 514 A particular law..injoyns all persons on a penalty to apprehend runaway Negroes. **1724** DE FOE *Mem. Cavalier* I. 135 They were driven upon their own Friends, who..were trodden down by their own run-away Brethren. **1784** J. F. D. SMYTH *Tour U.S.A.* II. 102 Run-away Negroes have resided in these places for twelve, twenty, or thirty years and upwards. **1804** R. SUTCLIFF *Trav. N. Amer.* (1811) iii. 58 Whenever he saw a Negro whom he judged to be a runaway slave, he would..jump from his work-board. **1824** CAROLINE BOWLES in *Corr. w. Southey* (1881) 48 The magistrates..have secured the runaway ringleader of the gang that robbed me. **1845** DARWIN *Voy. Nat.* ix. (1879) 188 A population, of which rather more than half were runaway rebels and murderers. **1852** *Morning Courier* (N.Y.) 8 Oct. 2/2 She causes a reward to be offered for the recovery of a runaway slave 'dead or alive', when no reward with such an alternative was ever heard or dreamed of south of Mason and Dixon's line. **1876** BLACK *Madcap Violet* vii. 59 If she was a runaway school-girl, there was little fear about her. **1885** 'MARK TWAIN' *Huck. Finn* xxxviii. 325 On the scutcheon we'll have a..crest, a runaway nigger, *sable*, with his bundle over his shoulder. **1977** *Time* 30 May 14/2 Rhodesian officials shrugged off Kaunda's declaration as the diplomatic equivalent of a mosquito bite, but the brutal civil war in the runaway British colony continues.

b. Pertaining to, connected with, accompanied by, running away or elopement. In later use esp. ***runaway match*** or ***marriage***.

1748 RICHARDSON *Clarissa* (1811) III. 173 That I might not make such a giddy and runaway appearance to any of his relations. **1775** SHERIDAN *St. Patrick's Day* II. iv, But I always knew Lauretta was a runaway name. **1809** MALKIN *Gil Blas* III. ii. ¶6, I will not say a word about the run-away trick. **1838** MRS. GASKELL *Let.* 17 Aug. (1966) 27 Wm has promised..to marry you if it comes to a runaway match. **1842** LEVER *J. Hinton* xi, All the dinners and duels of the capital, all its rows and run-away matches, were there discussed. **1871** MISS BRADDON *R. Godwin* i, No one knew the real story of that runaway marriage. **1921** Runaway marriage [see *film actress* s.v. FILM *sb.* 7 c].

c. ***runaway knock, ring***, one given at a door as a trick or joke, and followed by the rapid flight of the giver.

1840 BARHAM *Ingol. Leg.* Ser. I. *Lady Rohesia*, St. Peter.. went back to his lodge, grumbling at being hoaxed by a runaway ring. **1844** DICKENS *Mart. Chuz.* ii, 'I see you,' cried Miss Pecksniff, to the ideal inflictor of a runaway knock.

4. a. Of horses, etc.: Escaped, or given to escaping, from the control of the rider or driver.

1607 MARKHAM *Caval.* II. (1617) 103 This manner of reclaiming a runne away horse. **1692** SIR W. HOPE *Fencing-Master* 130 Your Horse, if he be not a Runn-away-jade. **1768–74** TUCKER *Lt. Nat.* (1834) II. 151 It carries us like a runaway horse, so much wider out of our way. **1775** J. JEKYLL *Corr.* (1894) 2 We had a runaway mare in the shafts from Croydon. **1833** HT. MARTINEAU *Tale of Tyne* ii. 31 Mr. Milford was..anxious about his runaway pony. **1865** MRS. CARLYLE *Lett.* III. 295 My black mare..got her foot hurt by a run-away cart. **1957** [see *hair-raising* adj. s.v. HAIR *sb.* 10]. **1958** HAYWARD & HARARI tr. *Pasternak's Dr. Zhivago* II. ix. 268 Revolutionaries who take the law into their own hands are horrifying, not as criminals, but as machines that have got out of control, like a run-away train.

fig. **1822** BYRON *Vis. Judgem.* ii, To wind up the sun and moon, Or curb a runaway young star or two. **1853** LYTTON *My Novel* III. xxix, Others have..a runaway hobby that there's no stopping. **1897** *Allbutt's Syst. Med.* III. 160 The cardiac pulsations become extremely rapid; and a condition is produced which may be termed a 'runaway heart'. **1960** *New Left Rev.* Sept.–Oct. 40/1 More important than sympathy actions for and with Negroes, the sit-ins stimulated a similar burst, a run-away brush fire of activity for all sorts of other aims. **1971** *Fremdsprachen* XV. 45 The site of an oil tanker wreck and a runaway underwater oil well. **1973** *N.Y. Law Jrnl.* 1 Aug. 4/7 The third occurrence of pacemaker failure involved the supplying of an accelerated beat by the second pacemaker. This is a situation commonly known as a 'run-away' pacemaker.

b. In general use, of economic, natural, etc., conditions: thoroughly out of control, developing at an ever-increasing rate; unrestrained, rampant.

1925 *Scribner's Mag.* July 59 All of them expressed relief that predictions of a 'runaway market' for staple products had not been fulfilled. **1936** *Sun* (Baltimore) 23 Nov. 2/4 Because such an oversupply of excess funds might provide the basis for 'runaway' credit expansion, the board is considering increasing reserve requirements. **1949** *Ibid.* 3 Mar. 2/7 Representative Eberharter..warned against making the home relief program 'too attractive', pointedly asserting that some states already were showing a 'runaway' tendency. **1967** *Listener* 21 Dec. 807/2 Lots of aspects of the world..are..'in a runaway condition'; population growth, technological growth, the destruction of Nature, to name only three. **1974** *Ibid.* 21 Feb. 235/2 If the miners' dispute is settled on very inflationary terms..it's going to be runaway inflation in Britain. **1980** *Times* 9 Jan. 12 The private pocket, not the public purse, is the best defence against runaway inflation.

c. Of commercial sales, etc.: immeasurable, overwhelming. *spec.* in phrases ***runaway best seller, success***. Also *fig.*

1953 L. Z. HOBSON *Celebrity* iii. 31 If *The Good World* should develop a runaway sale in bookstores, this windfall might reach a *hundred* and fifty-two thousand. *Ibid.* xii. 180 So this was what a 'run-away best seller' meant. **1960** *Harper's Bazaar* July 18/2 The season's runaway best-seller. **1968** M. JONES *Survivor* ii. 27 *Down in Flames* had been such a runaway best-seller in 1946 that there were bound to be people who remembered it. **1971** *Sunday Times* (Johannesburg) 28 Mar. 6/5 This film was a runaway box-office success. **1976** BOTHAM & DONNELLY *Valentino* ix. 71 His plan was a runaway success.

5. Of a chin: Receding.

1891 CONST. MACEWEN *Three Women One Boat* 100 He has cut off his beard! Heavens! he's got a runaway chin! **1894** A. MORRISON *Mean Streets* 256 He was a small shabby man with a runaway chin.

6. *Sporting.* Easily won; one-sided.

1877 *Illust. London News* 2 June 515/3 The only other noteworthy feature..was the runaway victory of Lady Lumley in the Stanley Stakes. **1895** *Daily News* 29 May 3/5 Mr. J. Best's representative, who scored a run-away victory from Sancho Panza. **1900** *Westm. Gaz.* 8 Jan. 9/3 The game was a thoroughly good one from start to finish, there was nothing of a runaway character about it.

7. In U.S. industrial terminology, designating a plant which is transferred from one location to another in order to prevent trade-union activity or evade labour regulations. Also applied *transf.* to a ship sailing under a *flag of convenience* (see FLAG *sb.*[4] 1 f).

1949 *Dict. Labor Law Terms* 71 *Runaway shop*, a plant transferred to destroy union effectiveness and to evade bargaining duties. **1952** J. A. MORRIS *Woolen & Worsted Manuf. Southern Piedmont* iv. 118 Even though few 'runaway plants' are involved in the southern woolen and worsted movement, the effect of unions is nevertheless felt. **1954** *West Coast Sailors* 1 Oct. 4/1 Why has Mr. Rothschild started this program to assist operations of runaway foreign flags? **1957** CLARK & GOTTFRIED *Dict. Business & Finance* 308/1 In the textile and apparel industries, especially, many such runaway shops have left the New England and Middle Atlantic states over a period of years, and relocated in the South. **1960** *Wall St. Jrnl.* 15 Mar. 14 On the high seas, according to the maritime unions, are 1,695 'runaway' flag ships which have owners of one nationality and registry of another... Registered in Panama, Liberia and Honduras.. these ships are described as flying 'flags of necessity' by operators and 'flags of convenience' by seamen. *Ibid.*, The union claimed that the use of foreign technicians was the equivalent of a 'runaway shop'. **1967** *Ibid.* 12 Dec. 1 Runaway plants set up by U.S. companies just inside Mexico to utilize cheap labour will come under increasing attack from the AFL-CIO.

run-back. [f. RUN *v.*] **1.** The action or fact of running backwards.

1926 *Gloss. Terms Electr. Engin.* (Brit. Engin. Stand. Assoc.) 140 *Runback preventer*, a system of connection in a tramcar controller such that, in the event of the car running backwards, the motors act as short-circuited generators and thus exert a braking action. **1929** A. T. DOVER *Electric Traction* (ed. 2) viii. 183 Where the motors are cross-connected for braking..the braking positions of the controller are effective for both directions of motion of the car, and may, therefore, be used for preventing a run-back. **1973** P. DICKINSON *Green Gene* ii. 41 He wanted to see whether any usable figures were available for..the mid-nineteenth century, enough at least for him to construct a crude model and attempt a run-back.

2. The additional space located at either end of a lawn tennis court.

1908 A. W. MYERS *Compl. Lawn Tennis Player* 213 At Auteuil..the run-back is inadequate and the timbered roof too low. **1927** *Daily Express* 30 May 3/5 The proper run-back for a court should be 21 ft. from the base-line to the stop-netting. **1977** *Club Tennis* Mar. 15 Where economy of space and/or money are important considerations a size of 33.53m × 16.46m (110ft × 54ft) which gives a 4.88m (16ft) run back is entirely adequate for the average home player.

3. *Amer. Football.* (See quot. 1976.)

1944 *Sun* (Baltimore) 6 Oct. 14/1 The 'one-man gang's' total net gain was 275 yards, 243 yards gained in 22 times carrying the ball from scrimmage, and 37 yards gained in two kickoff runbacks. **1949** *Lafayette Alumnus* (Lafayette Coll., Easton, Pa.) 24 Oct. 1/2 Winston Williams was outkicking Delaware's Smith and the Maroon had a slight edge on runbacks. **1971** L. KOPPETT *Guide to Spectator Sports* ii. 59 The receiving team can attempt a 'runback' at any time, even after a fumble. **1976** *Webster's Sports Dict.* 364/1 *Runback*,..a run made to advance the ball after catching a kick or punt or after intercepting a forward pass.

†**run'cation.** *Obs.* [ad. L. *runcātio*, f. *runcāre* to weed.] The action of weeding.

1664 EVELYN *Sylva* (1679) 10 For the more commodious runcation, hawing, and dressing the trees. *a* **1722** LISLE *Husb.* (1752) 80 They pulled up by hand the weeds..; this they termed runcation. **1733** TULL *Horse-hoeing Husb.* 93 After a few Days when it began to spring, they repeated their Runcation.

runch (rʌnʃ). *Sc.* and *north.* [Orig. obscure.] **a.** Charlock or wild mustard, *Brassica Sinapistrum.* **b.** Wild radish, *Raphanus Raphanistrum.*

a **1585** POLWART *Flyting w. Montgomerie* 181 On ruites and runches in the fielde, With nolt thou nurishde was a ȝeir. **1691** RAY *N.C. Words* 59 *Runches* and *Runchballs*, carlock when it is dry and withered. **1743** MAXWELL *Sel. Trans.* 80 This Ground, if it is much dunged, runs excessively to Runches, Skellochs, etc. **1788** W. H. MARSHALL *Rur. Econ. Yorks.* Gloss., Runsh, *sinapis arvensis*; wild mustard; catlock. **1817** *Blackw. Mag.* II. 235 He sows his barley early, and it is choked by runches and skelloch. **1848** *Proc. Berw. Nat. Club.* II. 318 *Raphanus Raphanistrum*, (the Runch or Jointed Charlock). **1896** P. A. GRAHAM *Red Scaur* iii. 35 The wheat-field where they have been pulling runches or charlock.

attrib. **1552** HULOET, Runchball herbe or wylde rapes, *Campestre rapistrum.* **1691** [see above]. **1891** ATKINSON *Moorland Parish* 346 Two tablespoonfuls of 'runch' seed.

'runchie. *Sc.* (See quots. and compare prec.)

1715 A. PENNECUIK *Tweeddale* 6 There are amongst them, that will not suffer the Wrack to be taken of their Land..till the first Week of May be over, which they call Runchie Week. **1807** G. CHALMERS *Caledonia* II. 936 The word runchies, for weeds, is generally known to rurigenous people.

runcible ('rʌnsɪb(ə)l), *a.* [Prob. a fanciful alteration of ROUNCIVAL.] A nonsense word used by Edward Lear in ***runcible cat, hat***, etc., and esp. in **runcible spoon**, in later use applied to a kind of fork used for pickles, etc., curved like a spoon and having three broad prongs of which one has a sharp edge.

The illustrations provided by Lear himself for his books of verse give no warrant for this later interpretation.

1871 E. LEAR *Owl & Pussy-Cat* in *Nonsense Songs*, They dinèd on mince, and slices of quince, Which they ate with a runcible spoon. **1872** —— *More Nonsense* 235 The Dolomphious Duck, who caught Spotted Frogs for her dinner with a Runcible Spoon. **1877** —— *Laughable Lyrics* 24 He has gone to fish, for his Aunt Jobiska's Runcible Cat with crimson whiskers! **1888** —— *Nonsense Songs & Stories* (ed. 6) 8 His body is perfectly spherical, He weareth a runcible hat. **1895** —— *Ibid.* (new ed.) 76 What a runcible goose you are! *Ibid.* 77 We shall presently all be dead, On this ancient runcible wall. **1926** *N. & Q.* 11 Dec. 430/2 A runcible spoon is a kind of fork with three broad prongs or tines, one having a sharp edge, curved like a spoon, used with pickles, etc. Its origin is in jocose allusion to the slaughter at the Battle of Roncevaux, because it has a cutting edge. *Ibid.*, Does a 'runcible' hat mean one of the sort called a trilby? In that case a 'runcible' spoon may be one with prongs or teeth. **1949** PARTRIDGE *Name into Word* 373 'He weareth a runcible hat.' Thus Edward Lear in 'Self-Portrait', where the hat is a 'topper' with a sharp rim. Now, a *runcible spoon* (Lear, 1871) is not a spoon at all but a pickle fork, broadly and triply tined, one tine being sharp-edged and curved like a spoon... The word *runcible* has been built in the architectural style of fencible; indeed, it may constitute a blend of Roncevaux and fencible (capable of defending). **1969** R. & D. DE SOLA *Dict. Cooking* 195/2 *Runcible spoon*, not a spoon but a fork with three broad curved prongs, used for serving appetizers. **1979** *Washington Post* 25 Mar. N6/2 A runcible spoon..is a large, slotted spoon with three thick, modified fork prongs at the bowl's end, and a cutting edge on the side.

runcinate ('rʌnsɪnət), *a. Bot.* (and *Ent.*). [f. L. *runcīna* a plane (formerly taken to mean a saw).] Irregularly saw-toothed, with the lobes or teeth curved toward the base.

1776 J. LEE *Introd. Bot.* 383 *Runcinatum*, runcinate, like the Teeth of a great Saw whose Serratures are bent downwards. **1785** MARTYN *Rousseau's Bot.* xxvi. (1794) 382 Wild Succory has runcinate leaves. **1835** LINDLEY *Introd. Bot.* (1848) I. 261 The runcinate blade of Taraxacum. **1861** BENTLEY *Man. Bot.* 161 When the terminal lobe is triangular..it is said to be runcinate. **1877–85** HULME *Wild Flowers* p. viii, Leaves obovate,..deeply pinnatifid, runcinate.

Comb. **1822** *Hortus Anglicus* II. 170 *Brassica Erucastrum.* Runcinate-leaved Cabbage. **1847** W. E. STEELE *Field Bot.* 11 Leaves runcinate-pinnatifid, with unequal teeth. **1870** HOOKER *Stud. Flora* 27 Leaves runcinate-toothed.

So **'runcinated** *a.* Also **'runcinato-**, used as comb. form of RUNCINATE.

(*a*) **1797** *Encycl. Brit.* (ed. 3) III. 442/2 *Runcinated*, pinnatifid.., in such sort that the segments are convex on the fore-side and transverse behind. **1853** G. MACDONALD & J. ALLEN *Botanist's Word-bk.* 28/2 *Runcinated*, a term applied to leaves, the margin of which is cut into very large teeth.

(*b*) **1829** LOUDON *Encycl. Plants* 671 Leaves glab[rous] runcinato-dentate. **1887** *Encycl. Dict.* s.v., Runcinato-laciniate.

runcival, obs. form of ROUNCIVAL.

†**'runcle.** *Obs. rare.* [ad. G. *runkel*, also *runkelrübe*, of obscure origin.] A variety of beet.

1784–1815 in Britten *Old Country Wds.* (1880) 108.

runcle, -cul: see RUNKLE *sb.* and *a.*

rund (rənd). *Sc.* and *north.* Also **ruind, rind**, etc. [Of obscure origin.] = ROON.

1661 *Sc. Acts Chas. II* (1820) VII. 253/2 Runds of cloath, ilk three thousand ells. **1808** in JAMIESON. **1816** SCOTT *Antiq.* xxiv, That's no lists or tailor's runds and selvedges o' claith. **1828** MOIR *Mansie Wauch* xx, Asking me as a favour for a yard or two of spare runds, or selvages. **1846** *Brockett's N.C. Gloss.*, *Run* or *Rund*, the selvage of woollen cloth, list.

rundale ('rʌndeɪl). Also 6 ryndale, rindaill, 8 rendal, rennal, -el. [f. RUN *v.* + DALE² 1.]

1. A form of joint occupation of land, characterized by dividing it into small strips or patches, a number of which, not contiguous to each other, are occupied and cultivated by each of the joint holders. Freq. in phrase *in rundale*.

Used esp. to designate this mode of occupation as practised in Ireland; in Scotland, to which the earliest quots. refer (with the word used adverbially), the current term is RUNRIG.

α. **1545** *Reg. Mag. Sig.* II. 747 Et lie Fieldland jacentem ryndale in territorio de Cottis. **1593** *Burgh Rec. Lanark* (1893) 110 The balleis and cunsall hes vottet that the toun muir be delt amang the..induelleris in this brught..rindaill amang thaim. **1793** *Stat. Acc. Scotl.* VII. 398 (Shetland), The small farms..are parcelled out in discontiguous plots and run-rigg, termed here *rigg* and *rendal*. **1794** *Ibid.* X. 26 (Caithness), Possessing land in what is called *rig and rennal*, or run-rig.

β. **1780** YOUNG *Tour Irel.* I. 213 There is a custom here called rundale, which is a division of their farms into spaces by balks, without fences, which they take here and there exactly like the common fields of England. **1816** MASON *Survey Ireland* II. 163 The custom of holding farms in rundale, is alone sufficient to impede agricultural improvement. **1848** *Edin. Rev.* LXXXVII. 240 In Mayo and other western counties the old barbarous Irish tenure called *Rundale* (Scotch *runrigg*) still prevails. **1888** *Pall Mall G.* 29 Nov. 3/1 The third improvement was the squaring of the holdings; they had formerly been held in rundale.

b. *attrib.*, as *rundale holdings*, *lands*, etc.

1780 YOUNG *Tour Irel.* I. *215 There is some land yet in the rundale way. **1846** MᶜCULLOCH *Acc. Brit. Empire* (1854) I. 525 A large extent of land is leased to several persons jointly, according to the village or run-dale system. **1875** MAINE *Hist. Inst.* iv. 101 The extensive prevalence of rundale holdings in parts of the country. **1884** *Times* (weekly ed.) 19 Sept. 5/2 When he sub-divided the rundale lands in lots distributed round the dwellings.

2. Land occupied in this manner, or a share in such land.

1819 MASON *Survey Ireland* III. 17 Each tenant takes a share of those divisions, commonly called a rundale. **1843** S. C. HALL *Ireland* III. 261 The tenants had divided and subdivided the small portions of arable land into Rundale. **1895** *Times* 21 Sept. 8/4 Scattered scraps of rundale ranged over by the cattle and sheep.

Hence **'rundaled** *ppl. a.*, divided out on the rundale system.

1884 MARY HICKSON *Irel. in 17th C.* I. 32 Owners of rundaled scraps of pasturage. *Ibid.* 34 Mere shreds, or scraps of land, rundaled through different farms.

rundeau, rundelaye, rundelet, obs. ff. RONDEAU, ROUNDELAY, RUNLET.

rundelis, rennet: see RUNDLE³.

rundle¹ ('rʌnd(ə)l). Also 4–7 (9 *dial.*) rundel, 6–7 rundell, 9 *dial.* -all. [var. of ROUNDLE. In senses 1 and 2 very common in the 17th cent.]

†**1.** A circle; a circular or annular form, appearance, or arrangement; a round. *Obs.*

In some cases approximating to sense 2.

c **1305** *Pop. Treat. Sci.* (Camden) 133 As me mai the mone i-seo while heo is nue riȝt, A lute rundel, as a sikel, me siȝth therof that liȝt. **1523** [COVERDALE] *Old God* (1534) O j b, Your hedde is well nere altogether shauen & smothe, a lytell garlonde & rundell onely beynge left. **1597** LYLY *Wom. in Moon* I. i, Lastly the rundle of this Massiue earth, From vtmost face vnto the Centers point. **1611** SPEED *Hist. Gt. Brit.* IX. xxiv. §210 Which forced them..to gather themselues close into a rundell, their best and greatest Ships standing without. **1690** LEYBOURN *Curs. Math.* 450 b, Saturn [is]..at other times represented with two Rundles adhering to each side. *a* **1722** LISLE *Husb.* (1752) 322 At the root of her horn she will put forth a rundle like a curled ring. *a* **1843** SOUTHEY *Comm.-pl. Bk.* Ser. II. (1849) 474 The flat side [of the lute], where we use to carve a rose, or a rundle, to let the sound go inward.

Comb. **1581** T. NUCE *Seneca's Octavia* 175 The cyrcled world in rundel wyse ydight.

†**b.** A circular orbit. *Obs.*⁻¹

1574 EDEN tr. *Taisner's De Nat. Magnetis* Ded., Euery of the Planettes are carried in their rundels or circles by course.

†**c.** A coil, curve, spiral. *Obs.*

1565 COOPER *Thesaurus* s.v. *Turbo*, The rundell or windinge of a serpent. **1631** WIDDOWES *Nat. Philos.* 63 The Jejunum beginneth where the Duodenum beginneth to turne into rundells.

†**2.** An object of a circular (or spherical) form.

1388 WYCLIF *Exod.* xxv. 33 Thre cuppis at the licnesse of a note..and litle rundelis togidere. **1611** COTGR., *Tournet*, a small turning rundle, or ring, in the mouth of a Bit, &c. **1669** STURMY *Mariner's Mag.* II. vi. 67 This Instrument contains two Parts or Rundles..moving one upon the other. **1680** MACKENZIE *Her.* 99 The Collar..having thereunto pendent on a blew Rundle, the image of St. Andrew.

†**b.** = ROUNDEL 2 b. *Obs.*

1565 COOPER *Thesaurus*, *Orbis*, a rundel to set dishes on for soilyng the table cloathe. **1611** COTGR., *Esclisse*, the Rundle, or Circlet put vnder a dish at Table.

†**c.** A round slice or paring; a small round cake. *Obs.*

1607 TOPSELL *Four-f. Beasts* (1658) 326 Take a good great dock-root clean scraped, and cut thereof five little rundles or cakes to be used as followeth. **1611** COTGR., *Trochisque*, a little rundle, or cake, whereinto diuers medicinable things be reduced. *c* **1700** KENNETT in *MS. Lansd. 1033* fol. 331 *Rundels*, round pieces or parings, as the *rundels* of an apple or an onion, &c.

d. A circular enclosure or field. Now *dial.*

1577–87 HOLINSHED *Chron.* I. 22/1 The maior bestoweth a costlie dinner within a mote or a rundell, and both the shiriffs within another. **1895** RYE *E. Angl. Gloss.*, *Rundle*, *Rundall*, or *Roundle*, a round field or marsh, or a field that lies round..a person's property or house.

3. = ROUNDEL 3.

1591 *Garrard's Art Warre* 210 Carrying light Venetian rundels and targets on their backes.

4. *Her.* = ROUNDEL 5 b.

1562 LEGH *Armory* (1597) 86 Whether are Rundels of all such colours, as ye haue spoken of here before? or shal they be named Rundels of those colours? **1592** WYRLEY *Armorie, Ld. Chandos* 86 Those rundels in the loftie chiefe do stand In sable bordure deepely ingreled. **1661** MORGAN *Sph. Gentry* I. ii. 17 As the Ring hath no end, no more hath the Ball or Rundle. **1704** J. HARRIS *Lex. Techn.* I, *Rundles*,..a Word used in Heraldry.

†**5.** *Bot.* A whorl, verticil, umbel. *Obs.*

1578 LYTE *Dodoens* 269 The floures..do grow in spokie tuffets or rundels at the top of the stalkes. **1597** GERARDE *Herbal* 914 There stande at the top tufts or spoked rundles. **1676** RAY *Flora* 41 The Verginian Martagon..hath stalks set with small sharp-pointed whitish-green leaves in rundles. **1682** WHELER *Journ. Greece* VI. 452 The Branches also grow at small distances in rundles, round the Body, like the Fir-Trees. *c* **1700** *Dampier's Voy.* (1729) III. 438 Its Burs grow in Rundles. **1784** TWAMLEY *Dairying Exemp.* 116 Water-hemlock—with rundles or flower branches opposite the leaves. **1807** J. E. SMITH *Phys. Bot.* 236 An Umbel, for which some authors retain the obsolete..name of Rundle.

attrib. *c* **1700** *Dampier's Voy.* (1729) III. 455 Rundle Plantain. Because it bears its Flowers in Whorles.

6. a. A rung of a ladder. Now *rare* or *Obs.*

1565 COOPER *Thesaurus* s.v. *Scala*, To beare a ladder on his shoulders and put out his heade betweene the rundels. **1686** W. DE BRITAINE *Hum. Prud.* 200 Confidence..is the Scale and Rundle by which many climb up to the Pinnacle. **1856** BOKER *Anne Boleyn* III. ii, You and I..Had climbed the rundles of a slippery ladder.

b. A cylinder or roller of wood; *spec.* one of the bars in a lantern-wheel.

1565 COOPER *Thesaurus*, *Magis*, a kneadinge trough; also a rundell that they vse to kneade with. **1611** FLORIO, *Rotoloni*, rundles or rowlers of wood. **1875** KNIGHT *Dict. Mech.* 2634 *Trundle*, a pair of round disks united by round bars or rundles which act as teeth. *Ibid.* 1252.

c. A solid wheel or barrel.

1611 FLORIO, *Raggij*, the shiuers or rundles of a pullie. **1615** BRATHWAIT *Strappado* (1878) 64 He had a wit at will: Running like the rundell of a blind horse-mill. **1648** WILKINS *Math. Magic* I. vi. 37 It consists of an axis or cylinder, having a rundle about it, wherein there are fastned divers spokes. **1728** CHAMBERS *Cycl.*, *Pulley*,..a little Wheel, or Rundle, having a Channel around it, and turning on an Axis. **1867** SMYTH *Sailor's Word-bk.* 586 *Rundle*, that part of a capstan round which the messenger is wound, including the drum-head.

†**7.** An umbrella; = ROUNDEL 3 c. *Obs.*

1677–8 in J. T. Wheeler *Madras* III. 438 Rundells shall not be worne by any men in this Towne, without the Governours permission. **1680** in Yule & Burnell *Hobson-Jobson* (1886) 850 A Rundell to be carried over him, in respect to the memory of Verona.

8. *dial.* A pollard tree.

Possibly an alteration of RUNNEL *sb.*²

a **1697** AUBREY *Wilts.* (Halliw.), The little rundels in shrowdes, which are come to their full growth (which will be about eighteen yeares). **1839** SIR G. C. LEWIS *Gloss. Hereford*, *Rundle*, a hollow pollard tree. **1879** MISS JACKSON *Skropsh. Word-bk.* s.v., These pollards are usually spoken of as 'old rundels', because for many years oaks have not been polled.

'rundle². Now *dial.* Also 6–7 rundel. [var. RUNNEL *sb.*¹ For the intrusive *d* cf. RINDLE *sb.*] A small stream or rivulet.

1587 HARRISON *Descr. Brit.* xi. in *Holinshed* 45 An infinit sort of small streames, brookes, beckes, waters, and rundels. **1600** SURFLET *Countrie Farme* II. lxi. 403 Let their place of abode be neere some small brooke.., and this rundle must haue by the edges stones or boughes of trees for the bees to light vpon. **1650** in *Trans. R. Hist. Soc.* (N.S.) XIV. 32 A great dike..with a little rundle of water running in the middle of it. **1651** tr. *De-las-Coveras' Don Fenise* 58 There was a little rundle betwixt them which stayed the course of Marcell. **1877–86** in Cheshire glossaries.

†**'rundle³**. *Obs. rare.* Also 5 roundeles, rundelis, 6 ronnelles, 7 runnell. [var. of RENDLES.] Rennet. Also *attrib.*

c **1400** *Lanfranc's Cirurg.* 21 Riȝt as þe roundeles of chese haþ bi him-silf wei of worchinge.., & riȝt as þe rundelis & þe mylk maken a chese. **1530** PALSGR. 177 The ronnelles suche as chese is made with. **1611** COTGR., *Gallion*,..also, the hearbe Cheese-runnell. **1758** MRS. DELANY *Life & Corr.* (1861) III. 474 The plant you call Runnet or Rundle grass... She thinks it is the jagged spearwort.

†**'rundled**, *ppl. a.* *Obs.*⁻¹ [f. RUNDLE¹.] Rounded, circular.

c **1611** CHAPMAN *Iliad* VII. 239 The round stone broke within His rundled target.

'rundlet. *rare.* [dim. of RUNDLE¹, or var. of ROUNDLET.]

†**1.** *Her.* = ROUNDLET 2 c. *Obs.*

1688 HOLME *Armoury* I. vi. 60/2 It is not requisite in Blason, to name the colloars of these nine Rundlets, except they be counter changed.

2. *Bot.* An umbellule. Cf. RUNDLE¹ 5.

1858 MAYNE *Expos. Lex.*

3. *dial.* A small circle.

1875 W. D. PARISH *Sussex Dialect.*

rundlet, var. RUNLET¹.

run-down, *ppl. a.* [RUN *v.*]

1. Downtrodden, oppressed. *rare*⁻¹.

1683 O. HEYWOOD *Diaries* (1883) III. 340 That lost oppertunity of clearing..the run-down truth.

2. Of watch-plates: Faced with only one coat of enamel.

1834–6 *Encycl. Metrop.* (1845) VIII. 490 The coarser description of watch plates are made rather differently, and are termed run-down plates, and run-down one coats.

3. Completely unwound. Also *transf.* of appliances not run by clock-work. Cf. also quot. 1866 at sense 5 below.

1894 A. ROBERTSON *Nuggets* 9 Bill..put his finger on the dead man's pulse, and placed his hand over the heart. They were both still as a run-down clock. **1974** A. GODDARD *Vienna Pursuit* iv. 141 As though a run-down gramophone had been rewound, he went on. **1977** E. AMBLER *Send no more Roses* x. 231 On the bench was a trickle charger with spring-clip connectors on long leads for attaching the thing to a run-down battery.

4. Tumble-down, dilapidated. *spec.* of districts, etc.: decayed, shabby, seedy.

1896 *Boston* (Mass.) *Youth's Comp.* 10 Dec. 659/4 He lived in a little old run-down place. **1929** T. WOLFE *Look Homeward, Angel* xxxix. 612 He was offered employment.. on the teaching staff of the run-down military academy. **1938** M. BRINIG *May Flavin* iv. 369 The particular district was one of cheap run-down rooming houses. **1948** H. LAWRENCE *Death of Doll* iv. 75 Run-down neighbourhood but respectable; rooming houses and railroad flats. **1953** K. TENNANT *Joyful Condemned* xxxii. 309 A run-down little suburban house with..a broken wooden verandah. **1962** A. LURIE *Love & Friendship* iv. 71 The streets of run-down two- or four-family frame houses. **1977** *New Yorker* 27 June 24/3 The church, a structure in American-Gothic style.. dominates a run-down neighborhood.

5. In a low state of health.

1866 GEO. ELIOT *Let.* 12 Feb. (1956) IV. 232 George.. was a little benefited, but only a little. He is too far 'run down' to be wound up in a very short time. **1889** *Jrnl. Mental Sci.* XXXV. 200 Her general appearance gave the idea of being 'run down' in bodily health. **1901** *Westm. Gaz.* 6 Sept. 1/2 Tasmania has, for many years past, been the happy holiday-ground of run-down Indian officers and officials. **1916** [see NERVY *a.* 5]. **1927** C. CONNOLLY *Let.* *c* 24 Jan. in *Romantic Friendship* (1975) 219, I am sorry you are run down. **1938** E. WAUGH *Scoop* I. ii. 32 Once or twice when Mrs. Salter complained of being run down, they had visited prosperous resorts on the East Coast.

Hence **run-'downable** *a.*; **run-'downness.**

1859 SALA *Tw. round Clock* (1861) 373 Of all things huntable, chaseable, rundownable, I doubt if there be one that can equal a Fire. **1902** *Brit. Med. Jrnl.* 12 Apr. 923 If consumption is nothing more than 'an aggravated attack of run-downness' how is it that an elaborate training is required for its treatment?

'rundown, *sb.* Also run-down and as two words. [f. RUN *v.*] **1.** *U.S. Baseball.* An action whereby defensive players attempt to tag out a runner caught off base between them. Also *attrib.*, as *rundown play*.

1908 *Spalding's Base Ball Guide* 69 Chance forced Tinker and then working the steal stunt for a run down was put out. **1946** *Sun* (Baltimore) 27 May 15 (*caption*) Charlie Keller, the Yankee's slugger, is shown being caught in a rundown in the ninth inning of the first game. **1971** L. KOPPETT *N.Y. Times Guide Spectator Sports* i. 30 Less reprehensible mixups occur on rundown plays. **1978** *Detroit Free Press* 5 Mar. c 3/1 Chilly, wet weather prevented the pirates from a scheduled workout on pickoffs, rundowns and cutoff throws.

2. *U.S. horse-racing slang.* A list of entries and betting odds. Chiefly *attrib.* (see quot. 1942).

1935 *Sun* (Baltimore) 12 Jan. 7/8 Sergt. Ignatius Benesch, who led the raiders, said the bookmaking activities were being carried out on the second floor... Sergeant Benesch and his squad took several telephones and a quantity of run-down sheets to the station as evidence. **1942** BERREY & VAN DEN BARK *Amer. Thes. Slang* 102 733/2 *Rundown board*, the bookmaker's board on which is posted the sheet of entries and odds; *rundown sheet*, *slate*, a list of entries and betting odds posted by a bookmaker. **1948** *Sun* (Baltimore) 17 Dec. 12/5 He observed Yateman making off with a board containing run-down sheets, while Hoffman was attempting to flee with a money bag and race-bet slips. **1951** *Publ. Amer. Dial. Soc.* XVI. 55 *Run down*,..the current change of odds in a booking establishment, caused by fluctuations of opinion or by a flurry of betting. *Ibid.* 56 *Run down sheet*,..a printed list provided for the patrons of the book. It contains the day's entries and the morning line odds and is used by the gambler to keep track of the fluctuations in odds.

3. *slang* (orig. *U.S.*) A (usu. verbal) listing of items of information; a summary or brief account of pertinent facts; a short description.

1945 *Sun* (Baltimore) 21 Feb. 7/4 In between taking care of the general's two uniforms..Orderly Powder gave inquiring correspondents a short rundown. **1949** *Tuscaloosa* (Alabama) *News* 8 Oct. 1/8 Here's a quick run-down of major disputes which already have made idle more than a million workers. **1953** *N.Y. Times* 29 June 29/1 A run-down on market conditions for various steel products follows. **1960** *Guardian* 21 Sept. 6/2 The movie guide provides a brief run-down on each film and assesses its suitability for children. **1966** T. PYNCHON *Crying of Lot 49* v. 105 John Nefastis..brought out his Machine... 'You know how this works?' 'Stanley gave me a kind of rundown.' **1971** *Farmer & Stockbreeder* 23 Feb. 8/2 He gave a strangely fragmented rundown of British Rail policy as it affected horticulture in the West. **1977** I. SHAW *Beggarman, Thief* III. i. 184 I'm going to tell them they got to give me a complete rundown on the family.

4. A gradual and sustained reduction in the size or scope of an organization, enterprise, or activity.

1948 *Hansard Commons* 8 Mar. 931, I feel that the timing of the run-down [of the Navy] has not been very satisfactory. **1955** *Times* 5 Aug. 7/1 A few minor financial worries have also intruded. So far all have been surmounted, and the 'run down' of British forces is proceeding swiftly and smoothly. **1957** *Economist* 21 Dec. 1068/2 If informal agreements can be reached with newly independent Commonwealth countries about the pace of the run-down of their balances, so be it. **1960** *Guardian* 10 Nov. 3/3 The telegraph service again showed a deficit, but the rate of run-down in the traffic has been checked. **1973** *Listener* 14 June 785/3 By attracting people away from the city centre, they [*sc.* ringways] generate the run-down of the city centre. **1978** *Daily Mirror* 12 Jan. 2/2 They produced a report which could lead to an even swifter and more drastic rundown in the industry than has been planned.

† **rune**, *sb.*[1] *Obs.* Forms: 1, 4 **ryne, rene, 2 rine, 3 rune.** [OE. *ryne, rene,* = OFris. *rene,* f. *run-* the weak grade of the stem *rin-* RUN *v.*]

1. Course, onward movement, *esp.* of the heavenly bodies; running (of persons).

c **825** *Vesp. Hymns* xi. 13 Deȝred ryne forðweȝeð [L. *Aurora cursus provehit*]. *c* **888** K. ÆLFRED *Boeth.* xxi, Hie.. bioð ȝehwerfde eft to þam ilcan ryne þe hie ær urnon. *c* **1000** ÆLFRIC *Saint's Lives* iv. 352 þæt ic moste þone ryne mines lifes werlice ȝeendian. *c* **1055** *Byrhtferth's Handboc* in *Anglia* VIII. 305 Æfter sunnan ryne & æfter þæs monan ryne. *a* **1225** *St. Marher.* 9 þe sunne recched hire rune euch buten reste. *a* **1225** *Ancr. R.* 74 þer is mest neod hold hwon þe tunge is o rune, & ivollen on to eornen. *a* **1250** *Owl & Night.* 1156 Oþer þu bodest huses brune Oþer ferde of manne oþer þeues rune. *c* **1330** *Arth. & Merl.* 8386 On Arundels wal þai gun lene, A kniȝt com arnand wiþ gret rene.

2. A flow *of* blood.

c **1000** *Ags. Gosp.* Luke viii. 44 Ða æt-stod sona þæs blodes ryne [*c* **1160** *Hatton Gosp.* þas blodes rine]. *c* **1225** *Leg. Kath.* 1398 Ʒe schulen.. beteh alle þe bruchen þet ȝe ibroken habbeð in ower blodes rune. *a* **1240** *Lofsong* in *O.E. Hom.* I. 207 Ich bide þe.. bi his blodi Rune þet ron inne monie studen.

3. A watercourse. Cf. REEN and RHINE[1].

c **1330** *Florice & Bl.* (1857) 307 Thilke that beth maidenes clene Thai mai hem wassche of the rene. **1706** PHILLIPS (ed. Kersey), *Rune,* a Water-course, so call'd in the Marshes of Somerset-shire.

rune (ruːn), *sb.*[2] [In origin the same word as ROUN, mystery, etc., but in sense 1 adopted in the 17th cent. (through Danish writers on Northern antiquities) from ON. and Icel. *rún,* pl. *rúnar,* later *rúnir* (Da. *rune,* pl. *runer;* Sw. *runa,* pl. *runor*). Hence also G. and Du. *rune,* pl. *runen,* F. *rune,* pl. *runes,* etc. In sense 2 the immediate source is the Finnish *runo,* itself an adoption of the ON. word.]

1. A letter or character of the earliest Teutonic alphabet, which was most extensively used (in various forms) by the Scandinavians and Anglo-Saxons. Also, a similar character or mark having mysterious or magical powers attributed to it; applied to a letter or character of a non-Germanic alphabet (esp. in fictional writings) having a resemblance to the Germanic runes.

The original runic alphabet dates from at least the second or third century, and was formed by modifying the letters of the Roman or Greek alphabet so as to facilitate cutting them upon wood or stone.

[**1685** W. NICOLSON in *Phil. Trans.* XV. 1293 We are sufficiently assured, that the Heathen Saxons did also make use of these Runæ. **1686** [see RIMESTOCK].] **1690** TEMPLE *Ess., Poetry* 37 Runes, was properly the Name of the antient Gothick Letters or Characters. **1705** *Phil. Trans.* XXV. 2058 He thinks it remarkable, that Magog is there mention'd Inventer of the Runes. **1770** PERCY *Mallet's Northern Antiq.* I. 375 The noxious, or as they called them, the bitter runes, were employed to bring various evils on their enemies. **1848** LYTTON *Harold* I. i, Her pale hand seemed tracing letters, like runes, in the air. **1851** D. WILSON *Preh. Ann.* (1863) I. 4 Intelligible inscriptions engraven in Anglo Saxon Runes. **1851** D. WILSON *Preh. Ann.* (1863) II. IV. ii. 238 The inscriptions on the sculptured or Memorial Stones.. include.. the Ogham or Celtic Runes. **1883** I. TAYLOR *Alphabet* 201 An adaptation or survival of the 'Slavonic Runes', the existence of which is however entirely hypothetical. **1883** MORFILL *Slavonic Lit.* i. 23 The view that the Slavs had runes is based upon a passage in the writings of the Monk Khrabr. **1937** J. R. R. TOLKIEN *Hobbit* i. 30 Look at the map.. and you will see there the runes in red. **1948** D. DIRINGER *Alphabet* II. v. 314 The monumental inscriptions are written in a runic character, termed Kök Turki runes. **1954** J. R. R. TOLKIEN *Fellowship of Ring* v. 339 They were written by many different hands, in runes, both of Moria and of Dale, and here and there in Elvish script. **1958** *Everyman's Encycl.* (ed. 4) IX. 461/1 Orkhon Inscriptions (also known as Siberian, Early Turki, Pre-Islamic Turki or Kök Turki Runes) are the earliest epigraphical monuments written in Turki. **1961** M. SAVILL tr. *E. Doblhoffer's Voices in Stone* ix. 289 Babinger sent a photograph.. to the decipherer of the Old Turkish runes, Vilhelm Thomsen. **1968** U. K. LE GUIN *Wizard of Earthsea* iv. 67 He studied the Further Runes and the Runes of Éa, which are used in the Great Spells. *a* **1973** J. R. R. TOLKIEN *Silmarillion* (1977) 322 *Cirth,* the Runes, first devised by Daeron of Doriath.

2. † **a.** An incantation or charm denoted by magic signs. *Obs.*

1796 MORSE *Amer. Geogr.* II. 35 [The Laplanders] have neither writing or letters,.. but a number of hieroglyphics which they make use of in their Rounes.

b. A Finnish poem, or division of a poem, *esp.* one of the separate songs of the Kalevala. Also incorrectly applied to old Scandinavian poems.

1854 LATHAM *Native Races Russian Emp.* 73 There is Heathenism, and plenty of it, in the Fin poems—the Runes, as they are called. **1863** LONGF. *Wayside Inn* I. Interlude iv, Fragments of old Norwegian tunes That bound in one the separate runes. *Ibid., K. Olaf* IV. vii, One was singing the ancient rune Of Brynhilda's love. **1879** *Encycl. Brit.* IX. 220/1 He [Lönnrot] was successful in collecting 12,000 lines. These he arranged as methodically as he could into thirty-two runes or cantos.

c. *transf.* Any song, poem, or verse. *spec.* a cryptic or magic verse, an incantation; a lament.

1847 EMERSON *Poems, Woodnotes* 11 But the runes that I rehearse Understand the universe. **1860** SANGSTER *Hesperus* 128 My heart would sit and sing Shrillest runes of wintry cold. **1870** D. G. ROSSETTI *I saw Sibyl at Cumæ* in *Coll. Wks.* (1886) I. VI. 378 'I saw the Sibyl at Cumæ' (One said).. 'She hung in a cage, and read her rune.' **1889** FRANON A. KNIGHT *By Leafy Ways* 9 The light-hearted and irrepressible starling.. crooning his own quaint runes. **1900** A. CARMICHAEL *Carmina Gadelica* I. p. xx, The wife knew many secular runes, sacred hymns, and fairy songs. **1908** SOMERVILLE & 'ROSS' *Further Experiences Irish R.M.* viii. 211 She chanted.. words in measured cadence.. By the time this rune had been repeated three times she was in the hall. **1922** JOYCE *Ulysses* 203 There he keened a wailing rune.—*Pogue mahone! Acushla machree!* **1936** W. HOLTBY *South Riding* I. i. 20 Curses could be lifted by spells. Midge was always trying them, inventing her own runes and incantations. **1949** *New Yorker* 22 Oct. 38/2 (*title*) Runes for an old believer. **1973** G. M. BROWN *Magnus* i. 23 Tana repeats a small bridal rhyme, a rune of fertility, the meaning of which is not at all clear but she has learned it from her grandmother. **1977** P. FITZGERALD *Knox Brothers* i. 32 Eddie had begun on Kennedy's Latin Grammar; there were more inexplicable runes for Wilfred to repeat in the nursery: 'Caesar adsum jam forte—Cæsar had some jam for tea.'

3. *attrib.* and *Comb.* **a.** Objective, as ***rune-bearer, -carver, -collector, -cutter, -rister*** (= cutter), ***-singer, -writer; rune-bearing*** adj.

1851 D. WILSON *Preh. Ann.* (1863) II. IV. iv. 287 To this, subsequent Rune-writers have made additions. *Ibid.* 294 The Rune-carver by whom many of these Memorial Stones were executed. *c* **1865** E. CHARLTON in *Archæologia Æliana* VI. 131 The ignorance of the Rune cutter has transposed one or two of the letters. **1866** G. STEPHENS *Runic Mon.* I. p. ix, Till these rune-bearers gradually disappeared before Roman-lettered pieces. *Ibid.* 199 Only one can have been the real meaning of the rune-rister. **1872** *Archaeol. Cant.* VIII. 223 The rune-bearing boss at Thorsbjerg. **1883** VIGFUSSON & POWELL *Corpus Poeticum Boreale* I. 571 Bali, a Swedish Rune carver from Upland, appears to have lived about the end or middle of the eleventh century. **1898** I. M. ANDERTON tr. *Comparetti's Trad. Poetry of Finns* I. i. 5 The first rune collectors.. only considered and published detached songs, and did not think of classifying them. **1904** *Saga-Bk. of Viking Club* III. III. 320 The.. uniformity can only be explained by supposing that there were professional rune-writers, travelling over the country and inscribing stones. **1908** *Ibid.* V. II. 258 To the right of the stem is an inequality in the stone, which the rune-cutter (*rune-rister*) apparently wished to avoid. **1927** E. V. GORDON tr. runic inscription in *Introd. Old Norse* 170 Biari has the temple, a wise rune-carver. **1962** C. L. WRENN in Davis & Wrenn *Eng. & Medieval Stud. presented to J. R. R. Tolkien* 316 If the 'first fronting' had in fact not yet been completed in the dialect of the rune-cutter. **1963** S. B. F. JANSSON in Browne & Foote *Early Eng. & Norse Stud.* ix. 112 In all probability the rune-carver wished his rune-ribbon to start and end at the same level on the stone. **1972** *Funk's Stand. Dict. Folklore* 382/1 Lönnrot himself said, 'Because I am sure that not one of the rune-singers could surpass me in the knowledge of the runes, I used my right to put together the songs as it seemed best.'

b. Attrib., in sense 'inscribed with runes', as ***rune-clog, font, -stick, -stone.*** Also RUNE-STAFF a.

1851 D. WILSON *Preh. Ann.* (1863) II. IV. iv. 294 The Rune Stones of the Norse fatherland. **1857** BORROW *Romany Rye* iv, I have, what some people would dread much more, an Armenian rune-stick. **1866** G. STEPHENS *Runic Mon.* I. p. ix, Rune-clogs of all sorts of material and of every size. **1883** VIGFUSSON & POWELL *Corpus Poeticum Boreale* II. 589 A Swedish Rune-stone has the roasting-scene of l. 4 carved upon it. **1931** *Times Lit. Suppl.* 9 July 548/1 The discovery of the Eggjum rune-stone in 1917. **1962** P. G. FOOTE tr. *S. V. B. Jansson's Runes of Sweden* 163 The finest of the rune fonts is the one.. carved by the Gotlander Sigraf. **1980** K. RANDSBORG *Viking Age in Denmark* 32 The persons mentioned on the early rune-stones were connected with royal power.

c. Misc., as ***rune-craft, -folk, -inscription, -letter, -lore, -magic, -maiden, -master, -name, -poem, -smith, -song, -word, -worship; rune-blazoned, -inscribed, -less, -like*** adjs.; **rune-ribbon**, the carved scroll on a runic stone in which the runes are engraved; **rune-row**, a runic alphabet; **rune-tree**, (*a*) = *tree-rune* s.v. TREE *sb.* 10 c; (*b*) (see quot. 1899).

1938 W. DE LA MARE *Memory* 76 A subtle Serpent.. Raised its *rune-blazoned head. **1871** G. STEPHENS in *Archaeologia* XLIII. 98 Modern Swedish *runecraft largely depends upon his many and valuable publications. **1866** —— *Runic Mon.* I. p. xi, There is therefore neither time nor place for a certain *Runefolk to carry its letters from land to land. **1872** *Archaeol. Cant.* VIII. 266 The *rune-inscribed horn was found in 1734. **1898** *Saga-Bk. of Viking Club* II. II. 337 Asfrid.. raised a.. gravehaugh over the body of her husband, whereon she set up a rune-inscribed stone in his honour. **1931** C. L. EWEN *Hist. Surnames* iii. 65 The rune-inscribed crosses. **1925** *Saga-Book of Viking Soc.* IX. II. 272 The *rune-inscriptions.. must be assigned to the first part of the 11th century. **1866** G. STEPHENS *Runic Mon.* I. p. x, The *runeless bronze-wielding populations they found in Scandinavia. **1937** J. R. R. TOLKIEN *Hobbit* iii. 64 'What are moon-letters?'.. 'Moon-letters are *rune-letters.' **1877** *Rep. Brit. Assoc., Trans.* 117 Some *Rune-like Characters on Chalk. **1965** C. L. WRENN in Bessinger & Creed *Medieval & Linguistic Stud.* 50 The seven rune-like symbols just mentioned. **1868** G. STEPHENS *Runic Mon.* I. 94 (*heading*) *Rune-lore. **1959** R. W. V. ELLIOTT *Runes* iii. 30 Other pagan rites and customs that went hand in hand with rune-lore. **1877** SKEAT *Will. Palerne* Pref. p. xxix, This might be classed amongst the instances of *Rune-magic. **1906** C. M. DOUGHTY *Dawn in Britain* I. II. 80 Her covert image.. and holy cart Shall her *rune-maiden ministers, in the lake, Wash. **1965** R. DEROLEZ in Bessinger & Creed *Medieval & Linguistic Stud.* 33 A simple formula such as.. 'unknown Danish *runemaster > Hrabanus Maurus', is tempting but dangerous. *Ibid.* 34 One might.. suppose that a 'rune master'.. would resort to runes if asked to write the names in full. **1970** FOOTE & WILSON *Viking Achievement* ix. 312 Once the act of carving stone had developed in southern Scandinavia, Swedish sculptors and rune-masters experimented to bring it to fruition. **1879** I. TAYLOR *Greeks & Goths* xviii. 117 Let us compare these.. Ogham names with the corresponding *rune names. **1927** E. V. GORDON *Introd. Old Norse* 161 The first letter of each rune-name gives the value of the rune. **1974** *Eng. Stud.* LV. 512 The inscriber of the Franks Casket normally represented the voiceless dorsal fricative by 'g', so that for him the rune-name would have been *eg.* **1861** D. H. HAIGH *Anglo-Saxon Sagas* 16 In the Anglo-Saxon *rune-poem, the following stanza occurs:- Ing wæs ærest, mid East-Denum, (etc.). **1879** VIGFUSSON & POWELL *Icelandic Prose Reader* 457 The idea is.. possibly taken from some such English poem as the Exeter Codex Rune Poem. **1962** C. L. WRENN in Davis & Wrenn *Eng. & Medieval Stud. presented to J. R. R. Tolkien* 316 The Old English, Old Norse, and Icelandic rune-poems. **1963** S. B. F. JANSSON in Browne & Foote *Early Eng. & Norse Stud.* ix. 111 All that was visible.. was a short section of the *rune ribbon, with some carved lines above it. **1868** G. STEPHENS *Runic Mon.* I. 105 All the *oldest written *Runerows are Futhorcs.* **1955** J. R. R. TOLKIEN *Return of King* 397 It was often called *Angerthas Moria* or the Long Rune-rows of Moria. **1973** R. I. PAGE *Introd. Eng. Runes* xii. 190 The common English rune-row had twenty-eight [characters] or more to the Germanic twenty-four. **1866** G. STEPHENS *Runic Mon.* I. p. vi, The later or Scandinavian Runic Monuments, which.. are now being gradually collected and publisht by competent *runesmiths. **1868** G. STEPHENS *Runic Mon.* I. 105 As for there being any 'German' people whatsoever.. who.. practist heathen rites and used *Rune-songs and Rune-books and Rune-carvings in incantations and divinations—why the thing is ridiculous. **1892** S. A. BROOKE *Hist. Early Eng. Lit.* I. 192 These phrases are from the *Rune Song.* **1927** E. V. GORDON *Introd. Old Norse* 161 The usual forms of this fuþark.. are given in the Rune-Song. **1863** J. M. MITCHELL tr. runic inscription in *Mesehowe* 51 Cut to our late Father these *Rune Trees, (He was a) leader on the West Sea. **1879** I. TAYLOR *Greeks & Goths* xviii. 129 The characteristic of the five classes of the rune trees would be (1) branches; (2) forks; (3) loops; (4) crooks; (5) roots. **1899** A. H. KEANE *Man, Past & Present* ix. 341 A great feature of the system were the 'rune-trees', made of pine or birch bark, inscribed with figures of gods, men, or animals, which were consulted on all important occasions. **1883** G. STEPHENS *Bugge's Stud. North. Mythol.* 67 The principal *runewords on this Bewcastle Cross are plain enough. **1940** F. SCOTT FITZGERALD *Let.* Dec. (1964) 100 But be sweet to your mother at Xmas despite her early Chaldean *rune-worship which she will undoubtedly inflict on you.

Hence **runed** (ruːnd) *a.*, inscribed with runes.

1886 *N. & Q.* 7th Ser. II. 50 A leaden *bulla* of Archdeacon Boniface and a runed ivory comb.

rune (ruːn), *v. rare.* [f. RUNE[2].] *intr.* To compose or perform poetry or songs; to lament.

1936 M. FRANKLIN *All that Swagger* i. 7 He was wont to rune to himself as he sat alone, thrust aside by his sons as childish. **1964** AUDEN in *Listener* 1 Oct. 575/2 Our handful Of clients at least can rune.

rune, obs. form of ROUN.

† '**runer.** *Obs.* [An erroneous use (due to Olaus Wormius) of Da. *runer,* pl. of *rune* RUNE *sb.*[2]] A writer of runes.

1690 TEMPLE *Ess., Poetry* 37 The Writers or Composers of them were called Runers or Rymers. *Ibid.* 40 This made the Runers among the Goths, as much.. admired as any of the ancient and most celebrated Poets.

rune-staff. Also 8 runstaff. [a. Sw. *run-staf,* f. *run* RUNE *sb.*[2] + *staf* STAFF.] **a.** A magic wand inscribed with runes. **b.** A runic calendar or clog-almanac.

1705 *Phil. Trans.* XXV. 2029 He tells us of wonderful performances, said to have been wrought by the means of their *Scipio Runicus,* or Runstaff. **1753** *Chambers's Cycl.* Suppl. s.v. *Almanac,* Almanacs of this kind are known by various names.., as rimstocks,.. runstaffs,.. clogs, &c. **1851** *N. & Q.* 1st Ser. III. 53/1 The ancient Clog or Rune-staff.. has been extirpated by the printed calendar. **1862** H. MARRYAT *Year Sweden* II. 359 *n.,* Then the victor gave a rune-staff to the shepherd.

rune-stave. Now only *arch.* [OE. *rún-stæf,* f. *rún* ROUN (RUNE[2]) + *stæf* STAFF, STAVE; cf. OHG. *rûnstab,* OIcel. *rúnastafr.*] A runic letter or symbol.

Beowulf 1695 Swa wæs.. þurh run-stafas rihte ȝemearcod. *c* **1000** ÆLFRIC *Homilies* (Thorpe) II. 358 Ðurh drycræft oððe ðurh runstafum. *c* **1205** LAY. 9961 He lette þer on grauen sælcuðe run-stauen. **1884** *Athenæum* 30 Aug. 271 In a chapter upon runes he [Stephens] gives it as his opinion that rune-staves were an independent offshoot from the old Greek alphabet in Scythia.

rung (rʌŋ), *sb.* Forms: 1 **hrung, 5- rung** (7 **rungg, wrung**); 3 **roungue,** 4, 6 **roung,** 6 **rounge;** 4-7 **ronge,** 7 **rongue, rong, roonge.** [OE. *hrung,* = Fris. *ronge,* MDu. *rong(h)e* (Du. *rong*), MLG. *runge* (LG. *runge, rung*), OHG. *runga* (MHG. and G. *runge*), Goth. *hrugga* (rendering Gr. *ῥάβδος*), not traceable outside of Teutonic.]

1. A stout stick of a rounded form, *esp.* one used as a rail (in a cart, etc.), cross-bar, or spoke.

The precise sense in the first quot. is not clear.

a **1000** *Riddles* xxiii. 10 Ongunnon stigan þa on wæȝn weras & hyra wicȝ somod hlodan under hrunge. **13..** W. DE

Bibbesworth in Wright *Vocab.* (1857) I. 168 [Checune charette ke meyne blés Deyt aver redeles, *glossed*] rayes, ronges [au coustés]. **1481-2** *Durh. Acc. Rolls* (Surtees) 322 Pro prostracione del rongez in Acleywod. **1483** *Cath. Angl.* 311/2 A Ronge of a carte, *epiridium, limo.* **1591** *Mem. St. Giles's Durh.* (Surtees) 16 Paid..for a burthen of rounges to the Yeate, 7*d.* **1641** Best *Farm. Bks.* (Surtees) 107 These rammers are made of..such like thinges as have holes; they putte into the holes two rungs to hold by. **1656** Tucker in *Misc. Sc. Burgh Rec. Soc.* 26 Whence [Ireland] they bring hoopes, ronges, barrell staves, meale, oates, and butter. **1762** *Information for Anne Inch agst. J. Bruce* 2 He, the said Bruce,..beat her with the Rungs of a broken Sledge. **1765** A. Dickson *Treat. Agric.* (ed. 2) 192 Fig. 9. represents the two handles fixed together by the two rungs. **1833** Loudon *Encycl. Archit.* §990 The hay-racks to be made 2 feet and a half wide; the rungs (spokes) of 1 inch and a half deal. **1864** *Morn. Star* 7 Dec., The chair had no rung on which to rest them. **1873** Miss Broughton *Nancy* I. 20 Algernon has thrust his head far out between the rungs of his chair-back.

†**b.** ***cogs and rungs***: (see cog *sb.*[2] 1). Also as the name of a dance-tune (quot. 1621). *Obs.*

1477 in *24th Rep. Deputy Kpr. Irel.* 107 The miller to provide cogges and ronges for the mill wheels. **1483-4** *Durh. Acc. Rolls* (Surtees) 249 Pro adquisicione de le cogges et ronges pro molendino de Milburne, viij *d.* **1523** Fitzherb. *Husb.* §134 To sell..the crabbe-trees to myllers, to make cogges and ronges. **1621** Brathwait *Nat. Embassie*, etc. (1877) 259, I am sure thou there shalt find, Measures store to please thy mind; Roundelayes, Irish-hayes, Cogs and rongs and Peggie Ramsie.

2. A round or stave of a ladder.

c **1290** *S. Eng. Leg.* I. 287/332 Ase he sat on þis laddre lowe on þe neþemeste roungue. *c* **1386** Chaucer *Miller's T.* 439 His owne honde than made he laddres thre, To clymben by the ronges and the stalkes Unto the tubbes. **1439** *Tintinhull Churchw. Acc.* (Som. Rec. Soc.) 180 Pro j scala xiij rongarum empta pro le belfray, xx *d.* **1483** *Cath. Angl.* 311/2 A Ronge of a stee, *scalare.* **1611** Coryat *Crudities* 488 A ladder which containe[s] seuen and twenty steps or rungs as we call them in Somersetshire. **1694** *Phil. Trans.* XVIII. 71 Three Ladders differently Runged, that is, the Rungs or steps placed at several distances. **1781** Hutton *Tour to Caves* Gloss. (ed. 2) 95 *Rungs*, the steps in a ladder. **1802** Mar. Edgeworth *Moral Tales* (1806) I. vi. 38 Henry saw his friend reach the last rung of the ladder. **1860** Wynter *Curios. Civiliz.* II. 402 Will the nimble figure gain the topmost rung ere nature fails? **1887** Besant *World Went* xv. 122 A young man got upon a ladder..and sat upon the topmost rung.

b. *fig.*, or in fig. context.

1377 Langl. *P. Pl.* B. xvi. 44 And [the fiend] leith a laddre þere-to, of lesynges aren þe ronges. *c* **1380** Wyclif *Sel. Wks.* II. 379 Þus þe ladder þat men shulden come to heven by, eiþer wantiþ roungis, or ellis it is not rerid. **1635** J. Hayward tr. *Biondi's Banish'd Virg.* 21 The religious Founder thereof hath fashioned out the rongues of a ladder to heaven. **1670** Clarendon *Tracts* (1727) 176 It is a vow of obedience.., as the upper and highest wrung of the ladder, to the pope. **1865** *Sat. Rev.* 16 Dec. 766 On the lowest rung of the Christmas ladder stand the Infant Books. **1883** S. C. Hall *Retrospect* I. 1 One of the lowest rungs of Memory's ladder.

3. *Sc.* and *north.* A cudgel; a stout staff or walking-stick.

1540 *Rec. of Elgin* (New Spald. Cl.) I. 49 For the manessing of the saidis Katerine with ane rung. **1588** *Reg. Privy Council Scot.* IV. 270 The said Robert Lekky.. maliciouslie straik and dang thame with rungis and treis. **1678** Sir G. Mackenzie *Crim. Laws Scot.* II. (1699) 235 With a great Batton, or Rung in his hand, and with Knives and other invasive Weapons. **1721** Kelly *Scot. Prov.* 396 I'll take a Rung, and rizle your Rigging with it. **1795** Burns *Dumfries Volunteers* ii, Till slap!—come in an unco loon, And wi' a rung decide it. **1838** J. Grant *Sketches London* 296 The Scotchman threw his 'rung', as he called it, and sure enough he hit the stick. **1893** Crockett *Stickit Minister* 195 The sound of the watchman's oak 'rung' had been too much for them.

b. *fig.* or in fig. context.

1711 Ramsay *On Maggy Johnstoun* vii, Death wi' his rung rax'd her a yowff, And sae she died. **1805-6** J. Nicol *Poems* I. 120 (Jam.), An' as for Poortith,..Aft hae I..felt her rung. **1858** M. Porteous *Souter Johnny* 32 Yet there ye sang, though neth the dred O' poortith's rung.

4. *Shipbuilding.* A floor-timber. Now *rare.*

a **1625** *Nomenclator Navalis* (Harl. MS. 2301), Rungs are the Timbers which doe give the flower of ye Shipp, and theise are bolted to the Keele. **1627** Capt. Smith *Seaman's Gram.* ii. 2 They lay the Rungs, called floore timbers, or ground timbers, thwart the keele. **1688** Holme *Armoury* III. xv. (Roxb.) 37/1 The Runges or Rung heads, the same to hooks and futtocks. **1875** Knight *Dict. Mech.* 2003/1 The spaces between the rungs are spirkets.

5. *attrib.*, as ***rung-cart***, †***-staff***, †***-stower***, ***-wheel***.

13.. W. de Bibbesworth in Wright *Vocab.* (1857) I. 168 [En les reideles vount les rolous, *glossed*] ronge-stafs. **1389-90** *Durh. Acc. Rolls* (Surtees) 596 Pro lucracione xx. gang de rungstoures pro carectis, xviij *d.* **1612** Sturtevant *Metallica* (1854) 106 The Water Plegnick which mooueth either invisibly and secretly under the water and by the water with one rong wheel. **1825** Jamieson *Suppl.* s.v. *Rung-wheel*, In a corn-mill..the one which has cogs drives the other, and is called the cog-wheel; the other, from its having spokes or rungs, is called the rung-wheel. **1854** H. Miller *Sch. & Schm.* (1858) 122, I was..so greatly recruited..as to be fit..to be removed, in the old man's rung-cart. **1882** *Jamieson's Sc. Dict.*, *Rung-Cairt*, a cart with open sides, i.e., made with rungs or spars of wood.

Hence **runged** *ppl. a.*; **'runging** *vbl. sb.* Also **'rungless** *a.*

1523 *Acc. Ld. High Treas. Scot.* V. 220 Item, for sawing of ane tre to be an leddir, and for runggging and making of the samyn, ij *s.* **1554** *Extr. Burgh Rec. Edinb.* (1871) 350 Item for runging of the kirk ledder, xxx[d]. **1694** *Phil. Trans.* XVIII. 71 Three Ladders differently Runged. **1875** *Contemp. Rev.* XXV. 563 Four rungless chairs are solemnly watching the operation. **1886** Macleod *Clyde District Dumbarton.* 160 The ladder by which he climbed to fame and fortune was runged by indomitable perseverance.

rung, *ppl. a.*[1] [f. ring *v.*[1]] **a.** Having a ring inserted in the nose. **b.** Ring-barked.

a. *c* **1630** B. Jonson *Underwoods* lxxvi, Like those, That hang their richest jewels in their nose: Like a rung bear or swine. **1778** [W. H. Marshall] *Minutes Agric.* 7 Feb. 1775, The rung ox is as passive as a spaniel.

b. **1901** *Sword & Trowel* Jan. 24 The white skeletons of the rung trees.

rung, *ppl. a.*[2] [f. ring *v.*[2]] Made to ring or resound.

1860 Dobell in *Macm. Mag.* Aug. 327 Tho'..the encountered shock Of your clashing battles jar The rung heav'ns.

rung, obs. pa. pple. reign *v.*, ring *v.*[1]

runge (rʌndʒ), *sb. dial.* Also 9 **runze.** [Of obscure origin.] A kind of tub (cf. ringe *sb.*[2] and flasket 1 d).

1574 *Ludlow Churchw. Acc.* (Camden) 161 Item, for a runge of lyme, v *d.* **1674** Ray *N.C. Words*, A *Runge*, a flasket. **1688** Holme *Armoury* III. xiv. (Roxb.) 11/2 A Runge or Soe: which is a kind of vessell that Tanners, Glouers, and Beere-brewers use to carry water in. **1814** Pegge *Suppl. Grose*, *Runze*, a long tub. **1886** Holland *Cheshire Gloss.* 295 *Runge*, salt-mining term, a large tub or bucket used for drawing water or brine out of a rock-salt mine.

†**runge**, *v. Obs. rare.* [Of obscure origin.] *intr.* To rise *up.*

a **1225** *Ancr. R.* 22 Ȝe schulen..euer et Gloria Patri arisen up [*C.* rungen vp] & buwen. *Ibid.* 290 Þet is to siggen, rung up & sture þe; hef up on heie eien & honden touward heouene.

Runge-Kutta ('rʊŋgə 'kʊta). *Math.* The names of Carl David Tolme *Runge* (1856-1927) and Martin Wilhelm *Kutta* (1867-1944), German mathematicians, used *attrib.* to designate a method of approximating to solutions of differential equations.

1930 J. B. Scarborough *Numerical Math. Analysis* xiii. 274 In the special case where dy/dx is a function of x alone the Runge-Kutta method reduces to Simpson's rule. **1950** *High-Speed Computing Devices* (Engin. Res. Associates) vii. 128 By the Runge-Kutta method, the formulas which are applied are given below. **1975** *Nature* 9 Oct 516/2 Membrane action potentials were computed with Hodgkin-Huxley equations, modified for *Myxicola*, using a modified fourth-order Runge-Kutta algorithm, and the six-parameter model. **1980** *Daily Tel.* 16 Sept. 2 (Advt.), It has 128 program steps that fulfil practically every function a mathematician needs. From setting a program for the definite integral by the Simpson's rule..to the Runge-Kutta method.

†**rung-head.** *Shipbuilding. Obs.* [f. rung *sb.* 4 + head *sb.*[1]] (See quots.)

a **1625** *Nomenclator Navalis* (Harl. MS. 2301), Rungheads are the heads or endes of the Rungs... Also more generally, the outward ends of Hooks which are in the same manner compassing are called Rungheads; for the Sleeper which is boulted into the other Rungheads is also boulted into theise, and they saie it is bolted fore and aft to the Rungheads. **1691** T. H[ale] *Acc. New Invent.* 48 The reaching of the Ship crackt every seam of her from the rung-heads upwards. **1769** Falconer *Dict. Marine* (1780), *Rung-heads*, a name sometimes given by shipwrights to the upper ends of the floor-timbers, which are otherwise more properly called floor-heads. **1863** A. Young *Naut. Dict.* (ed. 2), *Rung-heads*, ..a name formerly given to the floor-heads.

†**'runging**, *ppl. a. Obs.*[-0] [? f. rung *sb.* or runge *sb.*] ***runging adze***, a cooper's tool.

1688 Holme *Armoury* III. 318/2 The Runging Addice: This is in all respects like an Hatchet, save the edge part stands cross to that of the Hatchet.

†**'runian.** *Obs. rare.* (See quot.)

1665 J. Webb *Stone-Heng* (1725) 86 From these [Runæ] the Characters called Runick took Name, and the Cimbrians, Dacians and Goths are stiled Runians.

runic ('ruːnɪk), *a.* and *sb.* Also 7, 8 **runick.** [ad. mod.L. *runicus*, f. ON. *rún* rune *sb.*[2] So F. *runique.*]

A. *adj.* **1. a.** Consisting of runes.

1662 Evelyn *Chalcogr.* iii, Lyons, bears,..&c. wrought on the hardest rocks, together with Runic characters. **1686** Plot *Staffordsh.* 432 [A stone] with Runic characters still remaining upon it. **1763** Percy *Five Pieces Runic Poet.* Pref., The Characters in which this language was originally written, were called Runic. **1789** Sir W. Jones *Wks.* (1799) I. 86 Many of the Runick letters appear to have been formed of similar elements. **1851** D. Wilson *Preh. Ann.* (1863) II. IV. iv. 273 The Manx Runic alphabet. **1870** Farrar *Fam. Speech* ii. (1873) 74 Instead of the old linear runic characters, he introduced an alphabet founded on the Greek. **1948** [see rune[2] 1]. **1962** G. Clauson *Turkish & Mongolian Stud.* v. 72 The Runic alphabet is in a class by itself. **1968** W. S. Allen *Vox Graeca* i. 37 Special symbols are found only in the Old Germanic Runic and Old Celtic Ogham systems of writing. **1973** *Cassell's Encycl. World Lit.* i. 412/1 *Orhon Inscriptions*, the most important of the oldest surviving specimens of the Turkish language... They are inscribed in the Turkish runic alphabet.

b. Carved or written in runes; expressed by means of runes.

1685 W. Nicolson in *Phil. Trans.* XV. 1287 Giving you a more perfect Account of our two Runic Inscriptions at Beau-Castle and Bridekirk. **1775** Warton *Hist. Eng. Poetry* I. 25 Modern travellers report, that there are Runic inscriptions now existing in the deserts of Tartary. **1840** Carlyle *Heroes* i. (1904) 28 Snorro tells us..that Odin invented Poetry; the music of human speech, as well as that miraculous runic marking of it. **1865** Lubbock *Preh. Times* i. (1878) 11 A short Runic inscription. **1890** *Murray's Lincolnshire* 195 A scarcely decipherable Runic legend.

c. Inscribed with runes.

1728 Chambers *Cyclopædia* s.v., There are some Runic Medals in the Closets of the Curious. **1756-7** tr. *Keysler's Trav.* (1760) IV. 284 The ridiculous superstitions with which the Runic calendars abound beyond all others. **1825** Fosbrooke *Encycl. Antiq.* 87 To this period [16th cent.] we may assign the first Runic Obelisks. **1851** D. Wilson *Preh. Ann.* (1863) II. IV. iv. 267 The most remarkable relic..is the beautiful Runic-brooch. **1855** M. Arnold *Stanzas fr. Grande Chartreuse* 83 As..a Greek In pity and mournful awe might stand Before some fallen Runic stone.

d. Of or pertaining to runes; concerned with runes.

1861 J. Farrer *Let.* 28 Sept. in J. M. Mitchell *Mesehowe* (1863) p. viii, I shall send one to an English Runic scholar. **1862** P. A. Munch in J. Farrer *Notice Runic Inscr. Orkneys* 29 In the later times of the Runic period. **1868** G. Stephens *Runic Mon.* I. 94 The 'Scandinavian Futhork' is..a peculiar modification and compendium of the common Runic traditions. *Ibid.* 410 This runic drama was not yet ended. **1881** *Yorkshire Archæol. & Topogr. Jrnl.* *1879-80* 54 His learning was of a very varied character. 'Anglo-Saxon' and Runic lore was that by which he was best known. **1953** *Saga-bk. Viking Soc.* XIII. 281 Random runic studies in the eighteenth century. **1973** R. I. Page *Introd. Eng. Runes* i. 3 It was the scholars of the late seventeenth and early eighteenth centuries who put English runic studies on a sound basis. *Ibid.* 4 His [*sc.* George Hickes's] *Thesaurus* contained a large amount of runic material. *Ibid.*, Runic knowledge. *Ibid.* viii. 113 A living runic tradition there.

2. a. Of poetry, etc.: Such as might be written in runes; belonging to the peoples or the age which made use of runes; *esp.* ancient Scandinavian or Icelandic. Now *rare.*

This use of the word (cf. B. 1) is mainly due to Olaus Wormius, who used *Literatura Runica* as a name for ancient Scandinavian literature, and in 1650 published an Icelandic dictionary (compiled by Magnús Ólafsson) under the title of *Specimen Lexici Runici.*

1690 Temple *Ess.*, *Poetry* 25 Among the antient Western Goths.. the Runick Poetry seems to have been as old as their letters. **1699** Garth *Dispens.* IV. (1730) 123 Up these Walls much Gothick Lumber climbs, With Swiss Philosophy and Runick Rhymes. **1726** Bolingbroke *Study Hist.* ii. (1752) 12 The triumphs of Odin were celebrated in runic Songs. **1763** Percy (*title*), Five Pieces of Runic Poetry, translated from the Islandic Language. **1828** Scott *F.M. Perth* vi, I told him that his runic rhymes were no proof against the weapons which fought at Loncarty. **1851** D. Wilson *Preh. Ann.* (1863) I. II. i. 330 In Iceland where the language of their runic literature is still a living tongue.

b. *transf.* Applied to ancient Scottish poetry or poets.

a **1759** Collins *Ode Superst. Highl. Scot.* 41 At every pause before the mind possest Old Runick bards shall seem to rise around. **1762** Foote *Orator* I. Wks. 1799 I. 205 Gentlemen who have..rummaged the Highlands of Scotland and Ireland for the remains of Runic poetry. **1813** Hogg *Queen's Wake* 12 She heard the Caledonian lyre Pour forth its notes of runic fire.

3. a. Belonging to ancient Scandinavia or the ancient North.

1665 J. Webb *Stone-Heng* (1725) 192 These Places of Election..have been from all Antiquity proper to the old Runick Kingdoms. **1762** Falconer *Shipwr.* I. 814 The hardy offspring of some Runic dame. **1786** Polwhele tr. *Theocritus*, etc. (1792) II. 52 We recollect the Scythian or Runic mythology. **1813** Scott *Rokeby* IV. i, [They] Fix'd on each vale a Runic name. **1822** Byron *Juan* VIII. xxiii, Time, Which settles all things, Roman, Greek, or Runic.

b. Of ornament: Of the interlacing type (originally Celtic) which is characteristic of rune-bearing monuments, metal-work, etc.

1838 Britton *Dict. Archit. & Archæol.* 404 Runic-Knot, Danish Knot, a twisted ornament common on buildings of the Anglo-Saxon, or Danish era. **1848** Rickman *Archit.* 73 Amongst these ornaments the interlaced figures called Runic are of frequent occurrence. **1872** Ellacombe *Bells of Ch.* in *Ch. Bells Devon* vii. 360 The upper part is.. beautifully inlaid with interlaced ribbon patterns, or runic knots of gold, silver, [etc.].

B. *sb.* †**1.** The ancient Scandinavian tongue. *Obs.*

1665 J. Webb *Stone-Heng* (1725) 85 The Teutonick and Runick were one and the same Language. *a* **1682** Sir T. Browne *Tracts* (1683) 146 The Danes can continue such a series of sense out of their present language and the old Runick. **1690** Temple *Ess.*, *Poetry* 44 *Mara* in old Runick was a Goblin that seized upon Men asleep.

2. a. A runic inscription.

1866 G. Stephens *Runic Mon.* I. p. xxvii, We have this formula also in Scandinavian-runics.

b. One of the runic alphabets. Also in *pl.*, runic characters collectively (*rare*).

1863 J. M. Mitchell *Mesehowe* 32 It is probable that only one or two of the best educated in each ship could write or read the Runic. **1868** G. Stephens *Runic Mon.* I. 94, 4 of these [letters] (the h—for which the Runic prefers the Phœnician mark for ch—, the z, the gh and the sh) are more or less wanting in the Runic. *Ibid.* 157 In Scandinavian-runics, when the w had quite died out. *Ibid.* 159 In Scandinavian-runics the old rune for y lingers on for a time. **1886** T. Le Marchant Douse *Introd. Gothic of Ulfilas* I. 16 Of the foregoing letters, *urus* and *faíhu* are runes..*baírka*, *eis*, *ôthal*, and perhaps, *quaírthr*, common to runic and Greek. **1961** M. Savill tr. *E. Doblhoffer's Voices in Stone* ix. 280 The traveller discovered an impressive granite monument engraved with three inscriptions:..the third in 'Siberian' runic. **1963** *Times* 4 June 14/6 And after thousands and thousands and thousands of years, and after Hieroglyphics, and Demotics, and Nilotics, and Cryptics, and Cufics, and Runics, and Dorics, and Ionics, and all sorts of other ricks and tricks..the fine old easy, understandable

Alphabet—A, B, C, D, E, and the rest of 'em—got back into its proper shape again for all the Best Beloveds to learn when they are old enough.

3. *Ent.* A name given to certain moths.

1832 J. RENNIE *Consp. Butterfl. & M.* 81 The Runic (*Diphthera runica*..) appears the beginning of June. *Ibid.* 221 The Small Runic (*Ypsolophus sequellus*..) appears in August, on hedges.

4. *Typog.* A style of display lettering (in the Roman alphabet) having a thickened face and often of a condensed form.

1873 *Specimen of Printing Types* (Reed & Fox), Eight lines Pica Runic,.. Two lines Double Pica Runic. **1900** DE VINNE *Typog.* 327 Another style of runic is made with all lower-case characters, but of slightly expanded form.

Hence **runic-like** *a.*

1665 J. WEBB *Stone-Heng* (1725) 69 That Runick-like nothing might in it chance, Art's self, and all her Strength consulted was.

'runically, *adv.* [f. RUNIC *a.* + -AL + -LY[2].] In a runic manner; with runes.

1920 *Times Lit. Suppl.* 28 Nov. 779/3 Runically inscribed objects contained in.. better known public collections.

run-in. Also run in.

1. An act of running in; *spec.* in Rugby football, an act of running over the touch-line of the opposite side with the ball; also, the home stretch in a run at hare-and-hounds, or in a race.

1857 G. A. LAWRENCE *Guy Liv.* ix, The down-hill run-in favours his vast stride. **1857** HUGHES *Tom Brown* I. vii, I know we're close to the run in. **1864** *Field* 403/2 After several severe scrimmages.. a run-in was obtained. **1895** J. G. MILLAIS *Breath fr. Veldt* (1899) 220 [He] had got first run-in at the big herd of buffaloes.. and killed nine.

2. *colloq.* (chiefly *U.S.*). A quarrel, argument, or row; a clash or fight. Usu. in phr. ***to have a run-in*** (***with*** someone).

1905 'H. MCHUGH' *You can search Me* 82 Sorry we had the run in but it was all my fault. **1912** C. MATHEWSON *Pitching in a Pinch* viii. 180 Fred Tenny has said for a long time that Mr. Klem gives him a shade the worst of it on all close ones because he had a run in with that umpire one day when they came to blows. **1920** I. OSTRANDER *How Many Cards?* xii. 145 The cook at the de Forests' two doors away had a run-in with that Sarah, the butler's wife, and she won't speak to any of them. **1930** D. RUNYON in *Collier's* 20 Dec. 32/3, I am all tired out.. from getting a slug in my chest in the run-in with Jerk Donovan's mob in Jersey. **1945** G. MARX *Let.* 16 Feb. (1967) 50 Your father and I have many run-ins these days... He can't get it into his thick skull that I have come of age. **1952** A. BARIN *With Hope, Farewell* 44, I 'ad a run-in with the caterers, too. **1962** A. LURIE *Love & Friendship* ii. 31, I had a run-in with the Administration about it last spring. **1979** 'A. HAILEY' *Overload* I. iii. 19, I hear you had a run-in with Nancy Molineaux.

3. The approach of an aircraft to a dropping point or landing place; = RUN-UP I d.

1943 *Combined Operations* (Min. of Information) ii. 19 Two lights—a red switched on when the pilot is beginning his run-in to the dropping zone and a green indicating that the moment to jump has arrived. **1944** *Hutchinson's Pict. Hist. of War* 27 Oct. 1943–11 Apr. 1944. 366/2 An aircraft would be mortally wounded during its attacking run in but would not crash until after that attack had been well and truly pressed home. **1958** 'CASTLE' & 'HAILEY' *Flight into Danger* x. 137 We must have plenty [of fuel] in hand for a long run-in over the ocean, if I decide.. to ditch. **1958** P. KEMP *No Colours or Crest* (1960) v. 88 On the first run-in the aircraft would loose the containers and the 'free drops'. **1971** R. DENTRY *Encounter at Kharmel* ix. 158 Alden reached his bedroom window in time to see the Cherokee.. lose height for its run-in on to the strip.

4. An introductory statement or event; an approach (to a subject).

1961 *Clergy Rev.* Oct. 627 Mr Derrick provides a run-in to Fr Brown's story in the form of a Prologue. **1962** A. NISBETT *Technique Sound Studio* viii. 140 Remember not to start fading up until the run-in is complete. **1966** 'A. HALL' *9th Directive* i. 13 He sensed I would try to refuse the mission... He poured some more lime to give himself a last chance of planning his run-in. 'This is a special job,' he began.

5. *Criminals' slang.* A place to which stolen goods are driven and in which they are concealed.

1959 J. GOSLING *Ghost Squad* iii. 43 He tipped us off to the whole plot, gave the address of the 'run-in'—the place where the stolen goods were cached—and the names of the thieves. *Ibid.* x. 130 The normal method was to hire a van from a small lorry-owner, run the van to the warehouse, break in, load the van, take the contents to a 'run-in'—usually a shed or garage in the central London area—and return the van. **1962** D. WARNER *Death of Bogey* IV. v. 163 Just waiting to hear that the lorry reached the run-in. It's late. *Ibid.* 170 Sapper Neal and a bunch of the Sparrow boys been seen cruising around this manor in a car like they was looking for something. Is the run-in round here? **1970** P. LAURIE *Scotland Yard* vi. 129 It's a run-in for stolen lorries.

6. *Comb.*, as **run-in groove**, on a gramophone record, the blank groove traversing the annular area outside the grooves carrying the recording; **run-in shed** *U.S.*, an open-fronted shelter in which horses are housed.

1962 A. NISBETT *Technique Sound Studio* viii. 146 If the disc is being played from the start, or if there is no sound definite enough to be used as a cue, it will be necessary to count the revolutions from the run-in groove. **1976** *Gramophone* Sept. 510/1 It.. moves the stylus to the run-in groove of the record. **1964** *Blood-Horse* 26 Dec. 1874/1 Kelly has built a pair of L-shaped run-in sheds... The run-in sheds—unlike three sided Madden sheds used on many Blue Grass horse farms—are closed on only two sides, the north and west. **1977** J. W. EVANS et al. *Horse* xxiii. 723 Flies, hot weather, cold rains, and strong, cold winds seem to bother horses, and run-in sheds provide adequate protection from these conditions.

runish ('ruːnɪʃ), *a.*[1] *rare.* [f. RUNE *sb.*[2] + -ISH. Cf. G. *runisch*, Sw. *runisk.*] Runic.

1883 *Yorks. Arch. & Topogr. Jrnl.* VIII. 55 The lithograph in Sjöborg is useless for minute runish purposes. **1884** G. STEPHENS *Old-North. Runic Mon.* III. 15 A 'new' O.N. runish risting.

†'runish, *a.*[2] *Obs. rare.* [var. RENISH *a.*] Fierce, violent, rough.

13.. *Gaw. & Gr. Knt.* 457 With a runisch rout þe raynez he tornez. **13..** *E.E. Allit. P.* B. 1545 Ay biholdand þe honde til hit hade al grauen, & rasped on þe roȝ woȝe runisch sauez.

Hence **†'runishly** *adv.*, fiercely, roughly. *Obs.*

13.. *Gaw. & Gr. Knt.* 304 Runischly his rede yȝen he reled aboute. **13..** *E.E. Allit. P.* C. 191 He.. Arayned hym ful runyschly what raysoun he hade In such slaȝtes of sorȝe to slepe so faste.

†runk, *v. Obs.*[−1] [Cf. Flem. *ronken* to mutter, speak covertly about one.] *intr.* To whisper, murmur. Hence **†'runker**, a whisperer.

The more usual phrase is *rouk and rown*: see ROUK *v.*

c **1460** *Towneley Myst.* ix. 118 If I here any runk or rowne, I shall fownd to crak thare crowne: Ouer all, in ylk a stede. *Ibid.* xxx. 298 Here ar a menee.. Of runkers and rowners, God castys thaym out, trulee, From his temple.

runkle ('rʌŋk(ə)l), *sb. Sc.* and *†north.* Forms: 4 runkel, 4, 6 -il, 5 -ylle, 6 -ill; 4 roncle, 6, 9 runcle, 8– runkle. [prob. of Scand. origin: cf. Norw. dial. *rukla* (for **rukkla*), dim. of *rukka*, ON. *hrukka* (see RUCK *sb.*[2]), related to MSw. *rynkia*, Sw. *rynka*, Da. *rynke.*] A wrinkle, crease.

a **1300** *Cursor M.* 18840 His for-hed [was] fair, wemless to sight, Wit-vten ani runkel slight. **1483** *Cath. Angl.* 313/2 A Runkylle, *ruga.* **1513** DOUGLAS *Æneis* VII. viii. 26 Hir forryt scoryt wyth runclys and mony rat. **1581** J. HAMILTON in *Cath. Tract.* (S.T.S.) 99 Not haifing ony spot, runkill or ony vthir sic blot. **1721** RAMSAY *Prospect of Plenty* 201 "Till age and runkles shaw Their canker'd spirit's good for nought at a'. **1737** —— *Sc. Prov.* (1750) 107 We may ken your eild by the runkles of your horn. **1808** in JAMIESON.

†'runkle, *a. Obs.*[−1] In 5 runcul, runcle. [Cf. prec.] Wrinkled.

c **1440** *Pallad. on Husb.* IV. 699 Compact a runcul [*v.r.* runcle] nek, dewlapped side Vnto the kne.

'runkle, *v. Sc.* and *†north.* (also rarely *colloq.*). Also 4 rouncle, 5 runkylle. [Related to RUNKLE *sb.*] *intr.* and *trans.* To wrinkle, rumple. Also with *up.*

c **1340** HAMPOLE *Pr. Consc.* 773 Þan waxes his gaste seke and sare, And his face rouncles, ay mare and mare. **1483** *Cath. Angl.* 313/2 To Runkylle, *rugare, conrugare.* **1721** RAMSAY *Elegy on Patie Birnie* xii, He catch'd a crishy webster loun At runkling o' his deary's gown. **1808** JAMIESON, *Runkle*,.. to crease, to crumple. **1827** J. WILSON *Noct. Ambr.* Wks. 1855 I. 307 Ilka ane by itsel in far awa spats, whare the grass runkled only to the shepherd's foot. **1929** E. BOWEN *Joining Charles* 188 She.. pulled down the sofa loose-cover where it had 'runkled' up. **1958** M. ALLINGHAM *Hide my Eyes* viii. 85 He looked so neglected with his green tights runkled round his ankles.

runkled ('rʌŋk(ə)ld), *ppl. a. Sc.* and *†north.* Also 4 ronkled, 5 rouncled, runkillit, runklet, 8 runckled. [f. prec. + -ED[1].] Wrinkled, rumpled.

13.. *Gaw. & Gr. Knt.* 953 Riche red on þat on rayled ay quere, Rugh ronkled chekez þat oþer on rolled. *c* **1430** *Pilgr. Lyf. Manhode* in *Cath. Angl.* 313 When I am elded and bycomen rouncled and frounced and discolowred. *c* **1480** HENRYSON *Fables, Frog & Mouse* vii, The mous beheld vnto hir fronsit face, Hir runkillit cheikis. **1596** DALRYMPLE tr. *Leslie's Hist. Scotl.* I. 287 His hyd al contracted and runklet. **1718** RAMSAY *Christ's Kirk Gr.* III. v, A moupin runkled granny. **1785** BURNS *Holy Fair* v, Gin ye'll go there, yon runkl'd pair, We will get famous laughin At them this day. **1810** R. TANNAHILL in *Harp of Renfrewshire* (1819) 240 Runkled hags and warlock men. **1894** LATTO *Tam. Bodkin* iv, Thae runkled bits o' paper.

'runkly, *a. Sc.* Also 8 runkley. [f. RUNKLE *sb.* + -Y.] Full of wrinkles; wrinkled.

1790 A. WILSON *Poet. Wks.* (*c* 1846) 179 Auld, runkley-faced, and brown. **1807–10** R. TANNAHILL *Poems* (1846) 99 Wealthy pride but ill can hide Your runkly measled shins.

runless ('rʌnlɪs), *a.* [f. RUN *sb.*[1] + -LESS.] In *Baseball* and *Cricket*: devoid of runs; unable to score.

1921 *Daily Colonist* (Victoria, B.C.) 7 Oct. 11/4 The New York Americans made world's series history today.. leaving the New York Nationals runless. **1963** *Times* 30 May 4/7 Devereux, a left-hander of medium pace, rendered the patient Tebay runless and strokeless for lengthy periods by the simple expedient of bowling a shade short of a good length.

runlet[1] ('rʌnlɪt). Now only *arch.* or *Hist.* Forms: α. 4–6 rondelet, 6–7 rondlet. β. 6 rundelet, 6–7 rundlett, 6–9 rundlet. γ. 5 ronlett, 6 ronelete, runlett, 7 ronlet, 7– 9 runlet. δ. 7 renlet(t. [a. OF. *rondelet*, dim. of *rondelle*, f. *ronde* ROUND *a.* Cf. ROUNDLET.] A cask or vessel of varying capacity; the quantity of liquor contained in this.

Large runlets appear usually to have varied between 12 and 18½ gallons, small ones between a pint or quart and 3 or 4 gallons.

α. **1394** in Wylie *Hist. Hen. IV*, IV. 179 A Rondelet of Rumney. **1483** *Act 1 Rich. III*, c. 13 §1 Every Rondelet to holde xviij galons and an half. **1531–2** *Act 23 Hen. VIII*, c. 7 §4 The prices of.. the butt, tonne, pype,.. teers, barrell, or rondlett. **1593** G. HARVEY *New Letter* Wks. (Grosart) I. 280 Her beginning [is] like the purest Oyle in the crowne of the rondelet. **1605** H. PLAT *Delightes for Ladies* II. xiv, I haue knowne Roseleaues kept well in Rondlets. **1618** DALTON *Countr. Just.* lxv. (1630) 144 Sixteene gallons maketh the Rondlet. **1674** S. JEAKE *Arith.* (1696) 72, 1 Rundlet or Rondlet = 18½ Gallons.

β. **1542** *Rutland MSS.* IV. 324 (Hist. MSS. Comm.), For the carege off a rwndlett off Mus[c]adene, viij d. **1588** LAMBARDE *Eiren.* IV. iv. 457 Any kilderkins, tertian, firkins or rundlets. **1600** NASHE *Summer's Last Will* 486 Wks. (Grosart) VI. 105 Actors, bring now a black Iack, and a rundlet of Renish wine. **1674** S. JEAKE *Arith.* (1696) 72 Rundlet is now grown a general name to any small Cask not gage. **1703** DAMPIER *Voy.* III. I. 150 My Men came aboard and brought a Rundlet of brackish Water. **1725** DE FOE *Voy. r. World* (1840) 6 One hundred and twenty two small ankers or rundlets of brandy. **1814** CARY *Dante, Inf.* XXVIII. 21 A rundlet, that hath lost Its middle or side stave, gapes not so wide. **1822** SCOTT *Nigel* xvii, I will presently order you a rundlet of Rhenish. **1873** *Atlantic Monthly* Jan. 48 He set out for the wreck, bringing back a boat which was given to them, with butter, sugar, a rundlet of wine, and chocolate.

fig. **1594** LYLY *Mother Bombie* III. ii, My bodie being the rundlet, and my mouth the vent. **1607** MIDDLETON *Family of Love* II. iii, Lets pierce the rundlets of our running heads. **1651** CLEVELAND *Poems* 11 When we have fil'd the Rundlets of our eyes, We'll issue't forth.

attrib. **1837** WHITTOCK *Bk. Trades* (1842) 161 (*Cooper*), The 'Rundlet-cooper' works principally for distillers and makers of various cordials.

γ. **1491–2** *Rec. St. Mary at Hill* 179 For a ronlett of malvinseyn gevyn vnto master plomere. **1530** *Nottingham Rec.* III. 184 Quatuor roneletes vini dulcis vocati Malvesy. **1579** in W. H. Turner *Select. Rec. Oxford* (1880) 401 Bruers measures, as barells,.. firkins, runletts, ladlemeales. **1612** T. TAYLOR *Titus* i. 7 They make their bodies like runlets or wine caskes. **1667** DAVENANT & DRYDEN *Tempest* II. i, The runlet of brandy was a loving runlet, and floated after us out of pure pity. **1727** *Philip Quarll* (1816) 50 At the bottom of the chest lay a runlet of brandy. **1741** *Compl. Fam.-Piece* I. v. 274 Then strain it out, and put it in a Runlet. **1814** SOUTHEY *Carmina Aulica* Poet. Wks. III. 314 Many a runlet of right Nantes, I ween, Hath suffer'd percolation through that trunk. **1851** TURNER *Dom. Archit.* I. iii. 124Æneas [Sylvius] had received at a certain monastery a few loaves and a runlet of red wine. **1882** *Good Words* 606 Who brought him venison pasties and apple turnovers and runlets of ale.

δ. **1616** *Lismore Papers* Ser. I. (1886) I. 112, I sent my lord Careie a Renlett of choice aquavite. **1641** BROME *Joviall Crew* v. Wks. 1873 III. 437 And perhaps save me the expence of a Renlet of sack the while.

runlet[2] ('rʌnlɪt). [f. RUN *sb.*[1] + -LET.] A little run or stream; a runnel; †a channel.

1755 in *Rutland Gloss.* (1891) s.v., Paid.. for two days Work at scowring Wire Lane Runlett, 20 June,.. 1*s.* 6*d.* **1801** WOLCOT (P. Pindar) *Tears & Smiles* Wks. 1812 V. 69 The runlet that murmurs away [seems] To wind with a murmur of woe. **1853** G. JOHNSTON *Nat. Hist. E. Borders* I. 18 It receives many little livelier runlets that brattle down the green hills on each side. **1874** SYMONDS *Sk. Italy & Greece* (1898) I. v. 84 We found a well,.. a runlet flowing from it down the rocky steps.

†runlong. *nonce-word.* Course.

1674 N. FAIRFAX *Bulk & Selv.* 26 The understanding cannot take it, how one now should hold on with the whole runlong of all ages.

'runnable, *a.* [f. RUN *v.* + -ABLE.] Of deer: Proper for the chase; warrantable.

1884 FORTESCUE in *Longm. Mag.* Sept. 491 Two tines on the top of one horn.. was in itself judged sufficient to make a warrantable or runable deer. **1884** JEFFERIES *Red Deer* ii. 33 His coat was in perfect condition,.. and he was a runnable deer, that is, of age and size sufficient for the chase.

runnable, -ably, dial. ff. RENABLE, -ABLY.

runnagado, -gate, varr. RUNAGADO, -GATE.

'runnage. *rare*[−1]. [f. RUN *v.* + -AGE.] Flow or quantity of water in a river.

1864 *Standard* 15 Jan., During the late frost the water in the Ettrick and Yarrow had gradually lessened, until the runnage became insufficient to admit of the large numbers of spawning fish leaving the pools.

runnawaie, -waye, obs. ff. RUNAWAY.

†runned, *ppl. a. Obs.*[−1] In 6 ronned. [obs. pa. pple. RUN *v.*] Coagulated, curdled.

1527 ANDREW *Brunswyke's Distyll. Waters* Mj, [It] causeth the ronned and congeled mylke to be.. dyssolved frome the ronnynge togyder.

runnegade, -gate: see RUNAGADE, -GATE.

runnel ('rʌn(ə)l), *sb.*[1] Also 6–7, 9 *dial.* runnell, 7 runnil(l. [Later form (after RUN *v.*) of *rinel* RINDLE *sb.* See also RUNDLE[2].]

1. A small stream of water; a brooklet, rivulet, rill, or trickle.

1577 in Hakluyt *Voy.* (1904) VII. 229 The water.. sinketh into the earth and so vanisheth away, without any runnell above the earth. **1600** FAIRFAX *Tasso* XII. lxvii, With murmur lowd downe from the mountaines side A little runnell tumbled neere the place. **1656** *Rec. Braintree, Mass.* (1886) 7 This way.. formerly going up the rockes straight from the runnill of water in the country highway. **1747** COLLINS *Passions* 63 Dashing soft from rocks around, Bubbling runnels join'd the sound. **1784** tr. *Beckford's Vathek* (1868) 51 Vathek applied his ear with the hope of catching the sound of some latent runnel. **1817** SCOTT *Harold* VI. xvii, He placed her on a bank of moss, A silver runnel bubbled by. **1856** VAUGHAN *Mystics* (1860) I. 110 The groves of the orchard, watered by crossing runnels from the river. **1883** C. DAVIES *Norfolk Broads* xxvi. 198 Herons stand in the little runnels which trickle over the flats.

fig. **1827** HALLAM *Const. Hist.* (1876) I. vi. 322 The wickedness of mankind..confused the pure stream of the fountain with its muddy runnels. **1865** A. SMITH *Summer in Skye* I. 243 Ossian drew into himself every lyrical runnel.

2. A small watercourse or channel; a gutter.

1669 W. SIMPSON *Hydrol. Chym.* 296 The rain..is carryed away by runnels. **1863** MARY HOWITT tr. *Bremer's Greece* II. xiv. 102 A clear stream of water flowed..into a stone runnel along the floor. **1883** *Fortn. Rev.* July 144 Small runnels are generally chiselled for the purpose of conducting the water into the cistern.

3. *dial.* A funnel.

1868- in Yorkshire glossaries.

Hence **'runnelling** *a.*, forming a runnel.

1849 SYMINGTON *Harebell Chimes* 140 A little mountain girl..Sings to the runneling brook, alone.

'runnel, *sb.*[2] *dial.* Also 8-9 runnell. [Of doubtful origin: cf. RUNDLE[1] 8.] Pollard wood, or a shoot of this; a pollard or stunted tree.

1674 RAY *N.C. Words, Runnel*, pollard wood, from running up apace. **1829** BROCKETT *N.C. Gloss.* (ed. 2) 252 *Runnel*, pollard wood. **1861** W. BARNES in *Macm. Mag.* June 127 If an ash-tree is polled, there grow out of its head.. young runnells. **1879** MISS JACKSON *Shropsh. Word-Bk.*, *Runnel*, an old stunted tree, usually a pollard, and hollow.

runnel ('rʌn(ə)l), *v.* [f. RUNNEL[1].] *trans.* To form streams or channels in (a surface); to channel or furrow. Hence **'runnelled** *ppl. a.* Cf. RUNNELLING *a.*

1933 G. BARKER *Thirty Preliminary Poems* 13 And sparkling veins Escape in dark wooded places Runnelling like willow trees The lachrymose moist soil. **1947** *New Writing* XXXI. 164 Their faces were black with coal dust, runnelled with sweat. **1970** R. J. SMALL *Study of Landforms* ix. 309 These pediments were..usually 'runnelled', and dissections of up to 15-20 ft in depth were not uncommon. **1977** P. SCUPHAM *Hinterland* 19 A disenfranchised demon wears His runnelled face in sour grotesque, A conduit for the tumbling skies.

runner ('rʌnə(r)). Forms: 1 -iornere, -irnere; 4 urnare; 4 rener, 4-5 rennere (5 -are), 4-6, 9 *dial.* renner (5 -ar); 5 rynner, 5-7 rynnar, 6, 9 *Sc.* and *dial.* rinner; 6 ronner, rouner, runnor, 7 runer, 6- runner. [f. RUN *v.* + -ER[1]. Cf. Fris. *rinner, rinder*, MDu. *renner, runner* (Du. *renner*), MLG. *renner, ronner*, G. *renner*, MSw. *rennare, rinnare*, ON. *rennari*. In OE. recorded only in *fore-iornere* fore-runner.]

I. 1. a. One who runs; a racer.

c **1325** *Chron. Eng.* 900 in Ritson *Metr. Rom.* II. 307 He wes cleped Harefot, For he wes urnare god. **1382** WYCLIF *2 Sam.* ii. 18 Ceertis Asahel was a moost swift renner. *c* **1400** *Poem on ix Commandm.* (MS. Laud 416 fol. 3), Fle farre from besy tungges as bytter as gall, And rynnars to howsis where good ale is. *c* **1440** *Promp. Parv.* 297/1 Lepare, or rennare, *cursor*. **1593** SHAKS. *3 Hen. VI*, II. iii. 1 Fore-spent with Toile, as Runners with a Race. **1671** MILTON *Samson* 1324 Have they not..ev'ry sort Of Gymnic Artists, Wrestlers, Riders, Runners? **1792** BROOK *Precious Remedies* 165 God loves the runner, not the questioner. **1833** NYREN *Cricketer's Tutor* 80 He was a fine batter, a fine field, and the swiftest runner I ever remember. **1868** MORRIS *Earthly Par.* (1870) I. I. 110 And there two runners did the sign abide Foot set to foot.

b. With advs., as ***runner-about, -away***.

1362 LANGL. *P. Pl.* A. XI. 199 None renneris aboute, Ne no leperis ouer lond. *c* **1386** CHAUCER *Friar's T.* Prol. 19 A sompnour is a renner up and doun With maundementz for fornicacioun. *c* **1440** *Promp. Parv.* 297/1 Lepare, or rennar a-wey, *fugax, fugitivus*. **1451** CAPGRAVE *Life St. Aug.* (E.E.T.S.) 38 Ȝe be renners a-boute þe cyte; and þei fle þe sith of men. *a* **1548** HALL *Chron., Hen. VI*, 83 b, The Frenchmen knowyng by these good runners away of ye erles approchyng. **1574** G. BAKER *Compos. Oleum Magistrale* fol. 43 Among the common Runners about (which use to cut for the stone and Ruptures) is used a great abuse. **1647** HEXHAM I, A runner after, *een na-looper*. **1736** AINSWORTH *Eng.-Lat. Dict.*, A runner forth, *excursor*. **1848** DICKENS *Dombey* xxxii, You conspirators, and hiders, and runners-away, should know better than that.

†**c.** A wandering person; a vagabond. *Obs.*

1574 G. BAKER *Compos. Oleum Magistrale* fol. 44 Such is the covetouse desire of these Runners. **1575-6** *Durh. Deposit.* (Surtees) 270 As for Lawson he is but a runner, of no honestie or credit, being a maker of strawe hatts, seves, and riddles, goinge frome town to town.

d. *N. Amer.* One who chases or hunts buffalo. Now *Hist.* Cf. RUN *v.* 42 a.

1837 W. IRVING *Captain Bonneville* I. xvii. 286 'It was a beautiful sight,' says the captain, 'to see the runners, as they are called, advancing in column, at a slow trot, until within two hundred and fifty yards of the outskirts of the herd, then dashing on at full speed, until lost in the immense multitude of buffaloes.' *Ibid.* II. xi. 173 The 'runners', then, as they are called, mounted on fleet horses, and armed with bows and arrows, moved slowly and cautiously toward the buffalo. **1974** *Publishers Weekly* 11 Mar. 46/2 The early buffalo runners (hunters).

e. *Baseball.* = *base runner* s.v. BASE *sb.*[1] 20 b.

1845 [see BALK *sb.*[1] 5 b]. **1857** *Spirit of Times* 7 Feb. 372/3 Mr. Thos. Leavy..mans the first base, and rare it is, that a runner reaches the first base, if the ball is passed up quickly. **1948** *Lawton* (Oklahoma) *Constitution* 4 July 12/2 If the pitcher doesn't keep the runners close to base, the best catcher in baseball can't throw them out.

f. *Cricket.* One who runs on behalf of a disabled batsman. (Cf. RUN *v.* 1 h.)

1862 J. PYCROFT *Cricket Tutor* 4 Having the luck to be lamed by a sprain, I was allowed a runner. **1908** W. E. W. COLLINS *Leaves from Old Country Cricketer's Diary* xiii. 219 Once, then, only in my life have I acted as runner for another batsman. **1971** *Times* 16 Feb. 7/6 His knee is stiff..and unless it improves he may need the help of a runner.

g. *N. Amer.* One who runs ahead of a dog-sledge in order to find or clear a path in snow.

1867 *Ann. Rept. Smithsonian Inst. 1866* 309 The man was a famous runner, and despite the disadvantage of small tripping snow-shoes..he would have reached the houses before them had not the line that confined the snow-shoe on his foot broken. **1921** *Beaver* (Winnipeg) June 27/2 The 'runner's' duty is to travel in front of the dogs picking out and breaking the trail. It is also his duty to clear away with an axe any trees which may have been blown across the road. **1930** L. MUNDAY *Mounty's Wife* iv. 60 [We] were making a trip..without a runner (that is, an Indian guide who goes ahead of the dogs to break trail). **1971** T. BOULANGER *Indian Remembers* 62 From Norway House..the runner was Old John Clark... In Berens River..the runner was Donald Bittern.

†**2.** A fugitive; a deserter. *Obs.*

c **1440** *Promp. Parv.* 429/2 Rennare, or vnstable a-bydare, *fugitivus, fugitiva*. **1606** SHAKS. *Ant. & Cl.* IV. vii. 14 Let vs score their backes,..'Tis sport to maul a Runner. *c* **1624** in *Capt. Smith's Wks.* (Arb.) II. 473 If I finde any more runners for Newfoundland with the Pinnace, let him assuredly looke to arriue at the Gallows.

3. a. One who carries messages on foot or horseback; a messenger, courier, errand-bearer; a scout. Also used to designate one whose employment also involves the fetching and carrying of articles; an assistant; *spec.* in *U.S.* prison terminology, a prisoner entrusted with special duties; *Mil.* an orderly; a soldier who carries messages, esp. along the front line.

a **1300** *Cursor M.* 7679 Son to þe king tald was it sua, And his reners he þeder send For to rauis dauid he wend. **1382** WYCLIF *Ezek.* vii. 22 Foule men, or renners [L. *emissarii*], shulen entre in to it, and shulen defoule it. **1511-2** *Acc. Ld. High Treas. Scot.* IV. 262 To Finlay, rynnar, to by him sarkis..xiiij *s.* **1517** *Love's Bonavent. Mirr.* (W. de W.) x, The space of xiiij or xv dayes iourney of a comyn renner. **1611** BIBLE *1 Kings* xiv. 27 Rehoboam..committed them vnto the hands of the chiefe of the guard [*margin* runners]. **1686** tr. *Chardin's Trav. Persia* 258 They generally send a Runner along with 'em to bring the Horses back. **1727** SWIFT *Wks.* (1841) II. 609 It would have been wiser to direct it to Tonson or Lintot, to whom I believe his lodgings are better known than to the runners of the post-office. **1800** WELLINGTON in Gurw. *Desp.* (1837) I. 105, I have..ordered Colonel Torfrey, fourthly, to post runners from his camp to Oustara. **1830** *5th Ann. Rep. Boston Prison Discipline Soc.* 7 [At the Charlestown prison] there is, however, a class of men, consisting of ten or twelve, called *runners* and *lumpers*, whose duty consists in moving about the yard. **1850** THACKERAY *Pendennis* xxxii, The same little runner who had brought Shandon's note. **1877** A. B. EDWARDS *Up Nile* viii. 214 The Egyptian and Nubian mails are carried by runners stationed at distances of four miles all along the route. **1912** T. DREISER *Financier* lxvi. 679 Some of the prisoners, after long service were used as 'trusties' or 'runners', as they were locally called; but not many. **1917** G. S. GORDON *Let.* 13 Feb. (1943) 69, I was searching for the Hqs. of a Battn. and there wasn't a living soul above ground to ask except myself and my runner. **1929** R. C. SHERRIFF *Journey's End* III. iii. 116 Stanhope sits at the table and begins to write a short report... Stanhope calls 'Runner!' as he writes. A soldier comes from the servants' dug-out. **1933** *Sun* (Baltimore) 17 Apr. 14/4 Clifton had been assigned to the odd-jobs duties of a 'runner' on the first floor of the south wing, where both his and Kellam's cells were located. **1960** J. GRANT *Come again, Nurse* xxvii. 180 The theatre runner opened the doors and said quietly: 'Mr. Spindells has arrived, sir.' **1974** *Guidelines to Volunteer Services* (N.Y. State Dept. Correctional Services) 43 *Runner*, inmate whose job is to deliver things around the prison. **1976** F. WARNER *Killing Time* I. i. 6 I'd sooner be in the assembly trench waiting to go over the top than a runner. **1976** 'W. TREVOR' *Children of Dynmouth* v. 100 Mrs Abigail took round Meals on Wheels with Miss Poraway as her assistant, or runner, as the title officially was.

†**b.** One employed as spy to a gambling-den, band of thieves, etc. *Obs.*

1726 BAILEY, *Runner* (of a Gaming House), one who is to get Intelligence of the Meetings of the Justices, and when the Constables are out. **1762** FOOTE *Liar* I, Runner to a gaming-table and bully to a bawdy-house. **1776** *Ann. Reg.* 178 The runner to a set of sharpers..was convicted..at Westminster... The rest of the gang were lucky enough to escape.

c. One employed or acting as a collector, agent, or intelligencer for a bank, broker, †government, †newspaper, bookmaker, etc. (Cf. quots.)

(*a*) **1768-74** TUCKER *Lt. Nat.* (1834) I. 621 The directors of the bank above have constant intelligence from all parts of the universe, and their runners traversing to and fro among their customers. **1834** *Laws of Alabama* 46 The following salaries shall be paid to the officers in the bank of the State of Alabama and its several branches, to wit:..to the runner of the branch at Mobile, six hundred dollars per annum. **1884** *Pall Mall G.* 17 June 5/1 Bill-brokers complain that their runners are unable to obtain bills from the merchants as freely as usual. **1894** *Daily News* 29 Oct. 7/7 A 'runner' was a person who, not being himself upon the Stock Exchange, introduced business into the office of a member of that body for the sake of himself getting a share in the commission earned.

(*b*) **1777** BURKE *Corr.* (1844) II. 205 One of the runners of government in the city,—a tool of Harley. **1810** *Ann. Reg.* 3 In spite of all the runners and dependents of administration, that general would be always revered. **1824** SYD. SMITH *Wks.* (1859) II. 52 The pitiful propensity which exists among Government runners to vent their small spite.

(*c*) **1785** CRABBE *Newspaper* 291 For this their runners ramble day and night, To drag each lurking deed to open light. **1833** *Fraser's Mag.* VIII. 471 In one man we recognise a sub-editor of the *Globe*,..in another the runner of one of the *Times* reporters.

(*d*) **1902** *Scotsman* 21 Jan. 8/3 Stiles..was in the employment of..a bookmaker...Stiles acted as his 'runner'. That was to say, he went about to find out what the betting was.

d. A police officer. Also ***Bow-street runner*** (see BOW-STREET) and ***police-runner*** (see POLICE *sb.* 6). Now only *Hist.*

1771 *Gentl. Mag.* XLI. 230 Peter Murphy and Silas Goddard were tried for the wilful murder of John Atwood, one of the Runners of Clerkenwell Bridewell. **1838** [see BOW-STREET]. **1848** KINGSLEY *Yeast* iii, I'd sooner be a sheriff's runner, or a negro slave. **1877** E. LEIGH *Chesh. Gloss.* s.v., The runners want him.

e. One whose business it is to solicit custom for a hotel, tradesman, etc.; a tout. Also *spec.* one who provides custom for a lawyer. Orig. *U.S.*

1824 *Microscope* (Albany, N.Y.) 21 Feb. 183/3 Our wholesale property-speculators and their gentry in livery, called *runners*. **1836** C. R. GILMAN *Life on Lakes* I. 31 [At Oswego] a struggle began between the runners of the two boats. **1840** R. H. DANA *Bef. Mast* xxxvi, The landlords, runners, and sharks in Ann Street learned that there was a rich prize for them down in the bay. **1883** *Harper's Mag.* Nov. 814/1 The runners for several livery-stables offered to provide special transportation. **1899** F. T. BULLEN *Log Sea-waif* 337 The enterprising boatman was the runner for a Falmouth tailor. **1948** *Chelsea* (Massachusetts) *Record* 30 Nov. 8/7 Unethical lawyers, plus their hired 'runners', probation officers, jail attaches and police officers were 'selling' justice in the courthouse corridors to ignorant criminal defendants. **1951** *Life* 25 June 119/1[They] employed 15 runners to give school children free samples of heroin and ridicule those who wouldn't try it as 'squares'. **1974** *Times* 21 Jan. 6/6 If there is a car crash, one of the first people on the scene is likely to be a 'runner', who has heard about it by tuning in to police radio frequencies. He will point out that the victim needs a lawyer immediately, and will sign him up with one on the spot.

f. A freelance antique dealer.

1969 R. QUEST *Cerberus Murders* xxviii. 153 He was a free-lance—the trade term is 'runner'—picking up antiquities here and there and selling them at a profit. **1976** G. SIMS *End of Web.* xii. 86 Klein is a sort of runner..buys things in the country and sells them to West End dealers. **1978** *Observer* 16 Apr. 38/3 There are 'runners' going from shop to shop, detecting the margin of a bargain and taking the merchandise one step nearer to Bond Street.

4. a. A horse capable of running well; a good roadster or racer; a horse taking part in a race.

1582 N. LICHEFIELD tr. *Castanheda's Conq. E. Ind.* I. lxiii. 129 b, Alonso de Alburquerque, and Antonio del Campo,.. presented him with..two horses out of Persia, the which were great runners. **1655** L. THETFORD *Perfect Horseman* 24 Every horse for the wars may be train'd for a Runner or Hunter at pleasure. **1697** VANBRUGH *Æsop* I. IV. ii, Your worship has six coach-horses (cut and long tail), two runners, half-a-dozen hunters. **1815** *Sporting Mag.* XLVI. 118, I knew in their day, runners of fair repute, and as well bred as any horses upon earth. **1887** *Daily News* 8 July 6/2 Half a dozen runners only contested the Chesterfield Stakes.

b. *N. Amer.* A horse trained for hunting buffalo. Now *Hist.* (Cf. sense 1 d above.)

1858 J. PALLISER *Jrnl.* 31 July (1863) 90 Breakfast finished, our 'runners' saddled and mounted, the whole party moved slowly on... Having ascended the slightly elevated ridge we then beheld our game, four or five thousand buffalo. **1971** J. MCDOUGALL *Parsons on Plains* viii. 63 From all parts of the camp riders came forth, many of them leading their runners, so as to have them as fresh as possible for the coming race.

c. *transf.* A roadworthy motor vehicle; phr. ***good runner***, a motor vehicle which runs well.

1948 PARTRIDGE *Dict. Forces' Slang 1939-1945* 159 *Runner*, a vehicle that was in running order, as opposed to one that was off the road. **1972** *Fairbanks* (Alaska) *Daily News-Miner* 3 Nov. 23/7 (Advt.), '67 Chrysler Newport, stick shift, winterized, a good runner. $750. **1975** *Drive* Spring 40/2 We were asked to collect a car from a chap who had stripped it to service an identical second car... We found a car standing in the drive. So naturally we took it. But it was the runner we towed away. The wreck was in the garage. **1978** *Cornish Guardian* 27 Apr. 22 (Advt.), Peugeot 204 Saloon. Sun roof. Good runner.

5. †**a.** A domestic fowl allowed to range freely.

c **1540** *Househ. Ordin.* (1790) 221 Prices of all kindes of Poultry-stuff—Ronners, the piece, 2d. **1601** HOLLAND *Pliny* I. 297 That no man should haue his table serued with any foule, vnlesse it were one hen, and no more, and the same a runner only, and not fed vp and crammed fat.

b. The water-rail, *Rallus aquaticus*; also *dial.* the land-rail; †(see also quots. 1668 and 1774).

1668 CHARLETON *Onomast.* 97 *Trochilus*,..the Trochilus, or fin-footed Runner. *Ibid.* 107 *Erythropus, Ralla Aquatica*, the Runner. **1678** RAY *Willughby's Ornith.* 315 The Velvet Runner, *Gallinula Serica*. Perchance the same with the precedent [i.e. the water-rail]. **1774** GOLDSM. *Nat. Hist.* (1824) II. 375 To this bird of the crane kind so little known, I will add another still less known—the Corrira, or Runner of Aldrovandus. **1862** JOHNS *Brit. Birds* Index, *Runner*, the Water Rail. **1893** in Cozens-Hardy *Broad Norf.* 46 *Runners*, Land and Water Rails.

c. A bird belonging to the order *Cursores*.

1870 H. A. NICHOLSON *Man. Zool.* lxviii. (1875) 530 The third order of Birds is that of the *Cursores*, or Runners.

d. *Ent.* A member of the sub-order *Cursoria* of orthopterous insects.

1840 *Penny Cycl.* XVII. 43/2 Latreille divides the order *Orthoptera* into two sections, to which he applies the names *Cursoria* and *Saltatoria*, or runners and jumpers. **1882** *Cassell's Nat. Hist.* VI. 121 These true Orthoptera may be readily divided into three tribes.., namely, the Leapers, or Saltatoria; the Runners, or Cursoria; and the Earwigs, or Euplexoptera.

e. Any of several carangid fishes found in tropical or temperate seas, esp. *Elagatis pinnulatus*, *Caranx crysos* (= HARDTAIL a), or *C. ruber*.

1876 GOODE *Fishes of Bermudas* 15 Subjoined is a list of names in use among the fishermen, to the application of which I can give no clew:—..Runner. **1884** [see SHOEMAKER 2a]. **1888** GOODE *Amer. Fishes* 234 The Runner, *Elagatis pinnulatus*, known at Key West as 'Skipjack' or 'Runner', and at Pensacola as 'Yellow-tail' or 'Shoemaker'. **1902** [see HARDTAIL a]. **1905** D. S. JORDAN *Guide Study of Fishes* II. xvii. 272 Most like the true mackerel are the 'leather-jackets', or 'runners', forming the genera *Scomberoides* and *Oligoplites*. **1913** C. F. HOLDER *Game Fishes of World* xxii. 211 There are a number of smaller allied fishes which are game in every sense, if taken with appropriate tackle, as the Runner (*Caranx crysos*). **1952** L. L. MOWBRAY in J. O. La Gorce *Bk. Fishes* (rev. ed.) 210 The runner (bottom—*Caranx ruber*) ranges throughout the West Indies and Florida, and strays northward along the southern United States. *Ibid.*, The runner and other jacks are the terror of small fishes. **1966** LEIM & SCOTT *Fishes Atlantic Coast of Canada* 247 Blue runner. *Caranx crysos* (Mitchill). *Ibid.* 248 Although there are few actual records it is believed that the blue runner occurs sparingly along the Nova Scotian coast in the late summer months. **1975** J. G. WALLS *Fishes Northern Gulf of Mexico* 201 Rainbow runner. *Elagatis bipinnulata* (Quoy & Gaimard)... A popular sportfish which is not uncommon offshore.

f. *U.S.* A black snake, the racer, *Coluber constrictor*.

1795 T. TODD *Let.* Feb. in S. Williams *Nat. & Civil Hist. Vermont* (1809) I. 485 In a field in Connecticut..I approached with caution within twenty feet of a black snake, about seven feet long, having a white throat, and of the kind which the people there call runners. **1855** W. G. SIMMS *Forayers* xxxix. 456 Push forward, quick as a runner (black snake).

g. In full, ***runner duck***. A small white or fawn duck belonging to the breed so called and distinguished by an erect posture.

1895 W. COOK *Ducks* (rev. ed.) 96 Many cross-bred Indian Runner ducks have been sold as pure. **1900** *Reliable Poultry Jrnl.* Apr. 207/2 The Runners are particularly adapted to the market poultry man's needs. **1918** E. A. TAYLOR *Runner Ducks* ii. 15 The Runner Duck differs from all other breeds in that it has an upright carriage, which ensures the running gait. **1921** *Daily Colonist* (Victoria, B.C.) 29 Oct. 4/3 Anyone who has used runner ducks' eggs can hardly discern in cooking the difference between these and hens' eggs. **1937** [see KERRY[2]]. **1960** L. BONNET *Pract. Duck-Keeping* xiii. 116 The Indian Runner was the prolific layer of the duck world.

6. A fast-sailing ship; †*esp.* one for the carrying of dispatches without convoy in war time. Also *spec.* = *run-boat* s.v. RUN *sb.*[1] 4a (*U.S.*).

a **1700** B. E. *Dict. Cant. Crew*, *Runner*,..a Galley, or nimble Vessel, to make quick Voyages, as also to escape Privateers, Pirates, &c. **1705** *Lond. Gaz.* No. 4164/3 By the Opportunity of a Runner, called the Neptune Galley,..we have..received Letters from the..Fleet. **1799** NELSON 20 Aug. in Nicolas *Disp.* (1845) III. 454 The St. Vincent Cutter shall be a runner between us, as she sails very fast. **1804** *Ibid.* 17 Apr. V. 501 Three French Privateers..have taken their Station off Tunis for the purpose of intercepting stragglers from Convoys or Runners. **1881** E. INGERSOLL *Oyster Industry* 164 Another branch of the trade conducted by vessels, generally known as runners... The runner will anchor near some tonging-ground, and an empty basket or a small flag will be hoisted to the masthead as a signal that she is ready to receive oysters. **1890** *Cent. Dict.*, *Runner*,.. a market-vessel for the transportation of fish, oysters, etc.

7. a. One engaged in running contraband goods; a smuggler; also, a smuggling vessel. Now chiefly with qualifying sb.: see *gun-runner* s.v. GUN *sb.* 17, *rum-runner* s.v. RUM *sb.*[1] 3, etc. Also *slang* (chiefly *U.S.*), one engaged in conveying prohibited goods (as drugs, liquor) secretly.

(*a*) **1721** *Lond. Gaz.* No. 5978/1 A Gang of Runners of Goods from France..were..met. *a* **1734** NORTH *Lives* (1742) I. 254 The unfair Traders and Runners, and such as come in before the Duties are recharged, will undersell us. **1870** E. PEACOCK *Ralf Skirl.* II. 148 Tha've ta'en five and twenty hogsheads of gin and shot three o' th' runners.

(*b*) **1731** *Gentl. Mag.* I. 78 Lately a small runner put into Marazion in Cornwal, which had on board about 3 or 4 score anchors of brandy, some tobacco and soap.

(*c*) **1930** *Amer. Mercury* Dec. 457/2 *Runner*, one who transports liquor from the border to inland towns. 'He's a torpedo for a big runner.' **1963** T. TULLETT *Interpol* v. 65 Members of the gang, known as 'runners', were sent to Paris, or Marseilles, to pick up the drug. **1963** *Amer. Speech* XXXVIII. 276 A student is not permitted to buy liquor; hence, should he want some, he must find someone to obtain it for him. Such an intermediary is termed a *runner*. **1971** E. E. LANDY *Underground Dict.* 163 *Runner*,..person carrying a drug between buyer and seller.

b. A blockade-runner. (See BLOCKADE *sb.* 4.)

1867 SMYTH *Sailor's Word-bk.* 586 *Runners*, ships which risk every impediment as to privateers or blockade, to get a profitable market. **1897** *Westm. Gaz.* 6 Apr. 2/1 From a blockader's point of view, this precaution is absolutely necessary, as no 'runner' worthy of the name would attempt a venture during the day-time.

c. A sailor engaged for a short single voyage.

1878 *Daily News* 26 Sept. 2/3 One of the two men at the wheel on Tuesday was an A.B.,..and the other was a 'runner' engaged to take the ship down to Newcastle.

8. †**a.** *Sc.* A tapster. *Obs.*⁻¹

1610 *Rec. Privy Council Scot.* (1893) 286 The ventennar & rynnar of the said beir micht accordinglie sell the same.

b. *Shoemaking.* One who inserts a piece of leather between the sole and uppers.

1866 *Lond. Rev.* 27 Oct. 459/2 There are welters, repairers, clobberers, clickers, blockers, runners, closers, and cleaners.

c. One who manages or 'runs' a machine, institution, etc.; *spec.* an engine-driver. Chiefly *U.S.* Also, the leader of a (freq. Black) street gang.

1874 M. N. FORNEY *Catechism of Locomotive* 547 Every locomotive runner should..have an exact knowledge of the engine intrusted to him. *a* **1890** *Engineer* LXVIII. 349 (Cent.), There are two classes of runners, and a second-class man must run an engine two years before he can be promoted to first-class. **1893** M. HOLLEY *Samantha at World's Fair* i. 4 His parents..[were] good respectable.. people..and runners of a cheese factory. **1901** *Munsey's Mag.* XXV. 699/1 A new express..glided up to the platform under the hand of..one of the most experienced runners on the road. **1945** F. H. HUBBARD *Railroad Avenue* ii. 9 Dispatchers regarded him as a 'fast roller', a runner who could be depended upon to get his train over the road 'on the card'. **1962** *Amer. Speech* XXXVII. 135 *Runner*,..a locomotive engineer. **1972** C. H. FULLER in W. King *Black Short Story Anthol.* 142 'He coulda' done you in,' Rosalee enjoined... 'He's the *runner* of Tenth and Montgomery—Reuben is 'Little Blood', girl!' *Ibid.* 145 'Durango,' the *runner*, stood to the rear of his troops and when they were ready nodded to 'Cornbread' the warlord, who moved to the center of the street screaming challenges. **1973** *Philadelphia Inquirer* (Today Suppl.) 14 Oct. 29/1 Often nobody even knows who the runner (gang leader) is.

d. *Mining.* (See quot.)

1883 GRESLEY *Gloss. Coal-mining* 208 *Runner On*,..the person who loads the cages at the pit bottom, and gives the signals to bank.

II. 9. †**a.** A strainer. *Obs. rare.*

c **1460** J. RUSSELL *Bk. Nurture* 127 To iij. basouns ye must haue iij bagges renners, so clepe ham we, & hange þem on a perche. **1513** *Bk. Keruynge* in *Babees Bk.* (1868) 269 Loke ye haue fyue or syxe bagges for your ypocras to renne in, & a perche that your renners may ren on. **1516** in *3rd Rep. Hist. MSS. Comm.* 418/2 A irne brander, twa rynnars, a irne chimney.

b. *north.* A small stream; a brooklet, runnel.

1789 BRAND *Newcastle* II. 684 A little runner or feeder to supply the reservoir with water, is necessary. **1805** *Trans. Soc. Arts* XXIII. 59 To prevent a runner of water overflowing several acres of flat land. **1893** J. WATSON *Confess. Poacher* 91 A sea-salmon is in the domain of the whole world one day; in a trickling runner among the hills the next.

c. *Founding.* A channel along which molten metal runs from the furnace to the mould.

1843 HOLTZAPFFEL *Turning* I. 295 In casting large masses of gun-metal, it frequently happens that little hard lumps.. work up to the surface of the runners or pouring places. *Ibid.* 350 The flasks require to be poured through a hole in the upper half..., which is formed by placing a wooden runner stick in the top part. **1873** E. SPON *Workshop Rec.* Ser. I. 361/2 Holding the ladle at least 1 ft. above the runner so as to give weight and force to the burning metal.

d. = RUN *sb.*[1] 13g.

1928 L. NORTH *Parasites* 42 His quick eye detected a neatly darned spot near the heel of one, and a laboriously-checked runner in the other. **1931** M. DE LA ROCHE *Finch's Fortune* xvii. 257 Alayne noticed a long 'runner' on the shoulder of her knitted jumper. **1942** in H. Wentworth *Amer. Dial. Dict.* (1944) 525/1 She wears my finest evening gowns, gets runners in my hose.

10. a. A horizontal millstone capable of revolution, being usually the upper one of a pair.

1533 J. HEYWOOD *Weather* 743 (Brandl), Fere not the lyder, be ware your ronner. **1591** SYLVESTER *Du Bartas* I. ii. 648 Somtimes whirling..The round-flat Runner in a roaring Mill. **1611** COTGR., *Courant*,..also, an vpper Mill-stone, called (also by our Millers) the runner. **1686** PLOT *Staffordsh.* 337 Two wheels, whereof one was fastened to the runner of the first Mill, and the second to the runner of the grinding-Mill. **1702** *Phil. Trans.* XXIII. 1287 This being heavier,..I suppose might be the Runner. **1805** R. W. DICKSON *Pract. Agric.* I. Pl. 24 An iron pin or pivot, which runs through the centre of the bed-stone, into a socket in the bridge of the upper stone or runner. **1853** GLYNN *Treat. Power Water* 143 Nether stone (runner) of the lower pair... Hollow spindle on which the runners or revolving millstones are hung. **1875** KNIGHT *Dict. Mech.* 2003/1 Sometimes both stones..are driven, and thus become the upper and lower runner, respectively.

b. A vertical millstone, or a disk of stone, metal, etc., employed in the same manner.

1707 MORTIMER *Husb.* (1721) II. 387 A Mill may probably be so contriv'd, that the Grinding-stone or Runner may be vertical. **1759** *Phil. Trans.* LI. 168 In a mill..applied to the crushing of rape seed, by means of two runners upon the edge. **1824** *Encycl. Metrop.* (1845) XVI. 672/1 The Cider-mill consists of a stone wheel, provincially a 'runner', somewhat in the shape of a corn-mill-stone, running on its edge in a circular stone trough, provincially 'the chase'. **1875** *Popular Sci. Rev.* 46 Each mill consists of a pair of runners coupled together by a strong axle.

attrib. **1825** J. NICHOLSON *Operat. Mechanic* 451 The first part of the process is bruising the seed under the runner-stones. **1875** KNIGHT *Dict. Mech.* 2004/1 *Runner-ball*, (Gunpowder) a wooden disk which crushes the mill-cake through the meshes of the sieves in granulating gunpowder.

c. A slab of stone or (rarely) iron, used in polishing stone surfaces.

1850 HOLTZAPFFEL *Turning* III. 1196 The size of the grinder or, as it is called, the runner, depends upon the size and condition of the work to be ground. **1875** KNIGHT *Dict. Mech.* 2003 *Runner*..(Stone-working), the upper, moving slab..in the process of grinding and polishing stone.

d. A cast-iron support to which lenses are cemented while being ground or polished.

1850 HOLTZAPFFEL *Turning* III. 1263 For common glasses, that are ground several together, a convex tool of cast iron, called a runner, of about half an inch less radius than the templates, is also required.

e. A tool used in decorating pottery (see quots.).

1893 E. A. BARBER *Pottery & Porcelain of U.S.* i. 9 Incised ornamentation is sometimes added by the use of a small wheel, bearing an engraved device on the edge, called the 'runner', which is held in a frame. **1974** SAVAGE & NEWMAN *Illustr. Dict. Ceramics* 250 *Runner*, a pointed tool used to decorate the body of a piece of pottery while it is cheese-hard and revolving on the potter's wheel.

f. The rotor or wheel of a turbine.

1908 S. F. WALKER *Steam Boilers, Engines & Turbines* v. 317 The moving wheels or runners consist of wrought-steel discs. **1916** R. L. DAUGHERTY *Hydraulics* xi. 179 The part of the turbine upon which the water does its work is called the runner. **1947** G. F. WISLICENUS *Fluid Mech. Turbomachinery* i. 1 The most essential part of all types of turbomachinery is a vane-carrying rotating element, the 'runner', operating inside a stream of fluid or under its influence. **1972** J. M. K. DAKE *Essent. Engin. Hydraulics* vi. 172 These concepts are applied to the runner of reaction pumps.

11. *Naut.* **a.** A stout rope rove through a single block, with one end passed round a tackle-block and the other having a hook attached to it. Often coupled with *tackle*.

(*a*) *a* **1625** *Nomenclator Navalis* (Harl. MS. 2301), Runner is a roape..that doth belong to the Garnett and the two boate Tackles... It is reeued in a single block [etc.]. **1644** MANWARING *Seaman's Dict.* 87 Over-hale the Runner, that is, pull down that end which hath the hook in it, to hitch it into the slings, or the like. **1688** HOLME *Armoury* III. xv. (Roxb.) 50/1 The Runner is generally taken for any rope, running through a block which is called a running rope. **1769** FALCONER *Dict. Marine* (1780), *Runner*, a thick rope used to increase the mechanical powers of a tackle. **1841** R. H. DANA *Seaman's Man.* 29 Rack the runner to the topmast backstay or after shroud. **1875** BEDFORD *Sailor's Pocket Bk.* vi. 214 Haul the runners hand taut before hoisting.

(*b*) **1728** CHAMBERS *Cycl.* s.v. *Ship* Pl., 39. Runners & Tackles. **1789** G. KEATE *Pelew Isl.* 231 They..carried out an anchor and hawser a-head, and got a runner and tackle purchase upon it. **1805** *Log Victory* 21 Oct. in Nicolas *Disp.* VII. 153 Got up runners and tackles to secure lower masts. *c* **1860** H. STUART *Seaman's Catech.* 36 Runners and tackles, for staying the masts and for securing them, in the event of the standing rigging having been shot or carried away.

b. *attrib.*, as ***runner-block***, ***-purchase***, ***-tackle***.

1793 SMEATON *Edystone L.* 198 The runner block K will only rise..through half that space. **1841** R. H. DANA *Seaman's Man.* 46 A Runner-Tackle is a luff applied to a runner. **1867** SMYTH *Sailor's Word-bk.* 586 *Runner-purchase*, the addition of a tackle to a single rope, then termed a pendant, passing through a block applied to the object to be moved.

c. A single movable block in a system of pulleys.

1829 *Hand-bk. Nat. Philos., Mechanics* II. viii. 33 (U.K.S.), The single moveable pulley, sometimes called a runner.

12. a. A naked creeping stem thrown out from the base of the main stem of the strawberry and certain other plants, and itself taking root.

1664 EVELYN *Kal. Hort.* Aug., Pluck up strawberry runners, extirpate the tall stalks [etc.]. **1763** MILLS *Syst. Pract. Husb.* IV. 180 Their runners cannot supply the fruit with due nourishment, if they themselves have not proper strength. **1786** ABERCROMBIE *Arr.* in *Gard. Assist.* 84 Propagate by runner young plants produced in summer. **1837** *Trans. Hortic. Soc.* (1842) II. 176 The runners.. having taken root, the old plants must be destroyed. **1882** *Garden* 25 Mar. 205/1 The single sorts..are best grown from runners every year.

attrib. **1786** ABERCROMBIE *Gard. Assist.* 80 Plant strawberries..by young runner-plants of last year.

†**b.** A plant which sends out creeping stems or runners. *Obs.*

1731 MILLER *Gard. Dict.* s.v. *Acetosa*, It is a great Runner at the Root, by which Means it is easily propagated. *Ibid.* s.v. *Circea*, They are both great Runners in a Garden.

c. One of several cultivated varieties of beans which twine round stakes for support, esp. the scarlet runner (see SCARLET *a.* 4c). Also *attrib.* with (*kidney*) *bean*.

1786 ABERCROMBIE *Gard. Assist.* 203 Runner kidney beans—may also be sowed now. *c* **1820** *Edin. Encycl.* (1830) XI. 252/2 There are many varieties, both of what are called dwarfs, and of runners. *Ibid.*, Runners..have long climbing stems, and..require stakes. **1882** *Garden* 11 Mar. 164/3 Early Peas..might be cleared off in time for a crop of dwarf French or Runner Beans.

d. *dial.* (See quot.)

1889 *N.W. Linc. Gloss.* 630 *Runner*, a turnip or mangel-wurzel which, in autumn, instead of forming a fleshy root shoots up a flowering stalk.

13. †**a.** Some kind of firework running mechanically upon a line. *Obs.*⁻¹

1688 *Lond. Gaz.* No. 2362/3 Rockets, Runers on the Line, Wheels, Reporters, Hercules Club, and great Guns, with all manner of other Fire-works were discharged.

b. A ring or other device capable of slipping or sliding along a strap, rod, etc., or through which something may readily be passed or drawn; *spec.* in *Mountaineering* = *running belay* s.v. RUNNING *ppl. a.* 23c. Also *attrib.*, as ***runner-ring***, ***-staple***.

1688 HOLME *Armoury* III. 325/2 Two other Kinds of Barnacles..hath a Runner or Ring to make it wider or closer together, as the Runner is drawn up it. *Ibid.* (Roxb.) 126/1 Parts and appurtenances belonging to a sword and belt... The Buckle. The Runner. **1793** SMEATON *Edystone L.* §259 They had secured the sweep rope by letting drop a Runner-Ring. **1844** H. STEPHENS *Bk. Farm* III. 1176 It consists of the runner-staple, *b*, which is from 8 to 10 inches in length. **1875** KNIGHT *Dict. Mech.* 934/2 *Gag-rein*, a rein which passes over runners attached to the throat-latch, so as to draw the bit up into the corners of the horse's mouth when pulled upon. *Ibid.* 2003 *Runner*, .. the slider of an umbrella to which the spreaders are pivoted. **1956** C. EVANS *Kanchenjunga* xii. 126 Runner—a 'running belay' made by threading the climber's rope through a ring fixed to the mountain. **1956** [see CHOCK *sb.*[1] 8]. **1971** D. HASTON in C. Bonington *Annapurna South Face* xvii. 206 The rope ran out so I tied all my aid slings and runners together. **1973** C. BONINGTON *Next Horizon* xii. 179 I'm thirty feet above my last runner, time for another but the skin of ice is too thin to take ice screws.

c. *Mining.* A device by which the loose end of the pulley-rope is connected with the boring-rods.

1839 URE *Dict. Arts* 966 The runner, for taking hold of the topit. **1869** GREENWELL *Mine Engin.* 137 A runner attached to the rope from the jack-roll is passed over the top of the rods.

d. *dial.* A jack-towel, round towel.

1882 JAGO *Dial. Cornw.*, *Runner*, a round towel on a roller. **1891** J. H. PEARCE *Esther Pentreath* I. v, The stalwart great miller.. was busily drying his hands on the *runner* that hung against the wall.

14. a. A long piece of wood or metal, curved at the ends, supporting the body of a sledge, toboggan, or the like, esp. for travel over snow or ice.

1747 [see *sleigh runner* s.v. SLEIGH *sb.* 4]. **1765** *Boston Gaz.* 22 July 4/1 To be sold, a light fashionable four wheeler Carriage, with Runners to the same. **1789** ANBUREY *Trav.* I. 142 Those [carioles] of their superiors are raised upon what are called runners, which elevate them about two feet. **1837** MACDOUGALL tr. *Graah's E. Coast Greenl.* 118 Its very bones serve to tip his darts, and shoe the runners of his sledge. **1859** F. A. GRIFFITHS *Artil. Man.* (1862) 63 The recoil may be.. lessened by placing a small chain round each of the runners. **1881** *Scribner's Mag.* XXII. 535/2 [The ice-yacht] is then backed farther, till the runners are also raised on the farther edge of the ice.

attrib. **1897** *Outing* XXIX. 341/1 The runner-board of a careening, unruly ice-boat.

b. The blade of a skate; a skate with a blade curving up at the toe.

1860 WORCESTER, *Skate*, a sort of shoe.. furnished with an iron runner, used to slide or travel on the ice. **1875** KNIGHT *Dict. Mech.* 2192/2 In an in-door sport suggested by skating, the sole has rollers instead of a runner. **1893** *Daily News* 5 Jan. 7/1 The beautifully-made modern runner, the narrow blade of which is prolonged a prodigious distance beyond the toe and finished with a curious up-turned boss.

c. orig. *U.S.* A long narrow strip of (freq. embroidered) cloth, usu. placed along or across a table as an ornament.

1889 *Harper's Bazar* 20 Apr. 284/2 (*caption*) Embroidered table runner. *Ibid.* (Suppl.) 2/4 The cream-colored canvas grenadine centre of this table runner is a yard and three quarters long and twelve inches wide. **1904** *Buffalo Commercial* 2 June 6 Two long linen runners, one each way of the table, are now used in preference to the whole cloth or doilies. **1922** *Daily Mail* 11 Dec. 14 The illustrated table runner.. was decorated at each end with a simple design. **1932** *Modern Weekly* 5 Mar. 997 Such a lovely runner to add a freshening touch to your dining-table. **1974** M. INGATE *Sound of Weir* ii. 11 On the lace runner on the dressing table was a photograph.

d. A long narrow rug or strip of carpet, used esp. in a hall or on a staircase.

1901 J. K. MUMFORD *Oriental Rugs* vii. 95 *Makatlik*, or 'runners'.—These are what we know as 'hall' or 'stair' rugs. **1910** S. HUMPHRIES *Oriental Carpets, Runners & Rugs* 251, I have used the term 'runners', instead of 'strips' (as some call them), because the latter description might lead one to suppose that only a fragment of a carpet was intended, whereas the runner is distinct and complete in itself... Runners are, in fact, very long rugs. **1918** V. O. FREEBURG *Art of Photoplay Making* 236 He tries the stairs vaguely again, and, losing his balance at the top, grasps the 'runner' which pulls loose and wraps itself around him as he rolls down. **1937** M. ALLINGHAM *Dancers in Mourning* xvi. 200 Petals lay on the imitation parquet.. and on the imitation Persian runner in the hall. **1947** [see *body carpet* s.v. BODY *sb.* 30]. **1955** C. SMITH *Speaking Eye* xiii. 140 The corridor was yellow with a pale green runner. **1960** *News Chron.* 12 Sept. 6/4 A good buy in Oriental carpeting is the.. runner. **1972** 'H. CARMICHAEL' *Naked to Grave* i. 8 The entrance hall had a runner of royal-blue carpet down the centre with parquet flooring on either side. **1977** *Times* 9 Sept. 16/3 In the carpet section a rare pair of Shiraz runners were bought.. for £1,500.

15. a. A support or groove along, on, or in which anything slides; a roller.

1815 *Niles' Reg.* IX. 201/2 [We] moved the one-half of the arch off sideways, forty-six feet, on to the runners one hundred and eighty-five feet long. **1833** LOUDON *Encycl. Archit.* §1585 Proper framed legs, rails, and runners (pieces of wood for the drawers to slide on, and to guide them). **1871** *Scribner's Mag.* Nov. 46 The barn or house was pried up, and great runners, cut in the woods, placed under it, and under the runners were placed skids. **1891** C. ROBERTS *Adrift Amer.* 57 Taking a fish-plate he uses it as a lever to shift the door from its runners, and crawls in. **1939–40** *Army & Navy Stores Catal.* 1077/2 Curtain fittings... 'Huntband' Glide... 4 Runners to the foot. **1952** GRANVILLE *Dict. Theatrical Terms* 155 *Runner*,.. a curtain track. **1960** *Practical Wireless* XXXVI. 328/2, 1 nylon ball-bearing curtain runner.

b. A long horizontal beam, girder, or other member (see quots.).

1891 *Notes on Building Constr.* (new ed.) II. x. 216 The capsills or 'runners' [of a gantry].. are supported by struts. **1932** DOWSETT & BARTLE *Pract. Formwork & Shuttering* i. 1 Propped shuttering [for floors] consists, generally, of 'sheeting' or 'decking' laid on joists.. supported by heavier timbers, called 'binders' or 'runners', resting on upright 'props'. **1960** O. SKILBECK *ABC of Film & TV* 112 *Runners*, overhead girders with their depending tackle, from which, on modern stages, lamps and even complete prefabricated sets are hung. **1968** *Gloss. Formwork Terms* (*B.S.I.*) 21 *Runner*. 1. A longitudinal member spanning across a number of support members to lace them together. 2. One of a pair of supports running parallel to the axis of the centering for a deep arch or tunnel. One runner is above the other and they are separated by folding wedges. 3. See 'ledger' [= a horizontal timber supported on posts or hangers and carrying joists].

c. (See quot. 1940.)

1891 *Notes on Building Constr.* (new ed.) II. x. 209 Sometimes in very bad soil long planks called 'runners', having sharp ends shod with iron, are substituted for the poling boards. **1928** W. SIMPSON *Foundations* vii. 176 When test pits are of considerable depth, say, 40 ft., it is necessary to 'double set' the timbers, in which case two, or more sets of runners are used to reach the bottom. **1940** *Chambers's Techn. Dict.* 734/2 *Runners*, a form of sheet pile much used for timbering wide excavations. It consists of short planks shaped to a chisel point at one end and usually shod with thin steel strip, so that as each runner is driven in, it wedges up against its neighbour. **1963** M. J. TOMLINSON *Foundation Design & Construction* ix. 538 In water-bearing sands and silts continuous support will have to be given to the face by means of timber runners or poling boards or by steel trench sheets or sheet piling.

16. *Bookbinding.* (See quot. 1818.)

1818 *Art Book-binding* 2 *Runner*, a smooth-faced board placed on the right hand of the book when cutting. **1885** C. G. W. LOCK *Workshop Rec.* Ser. IV. 240/2 The book being lowered into the press, the runner is put flush with the cheek of the press.

17. A wagon or trolley: (see quots.).

1853 URE *Dict. Arts* (ed. 4) II. 224 When every skip arrives at the top of the shaft, a carriage, boarded over, called the 'runner', is wheeled over the mouth of the pit whilst the coal is landed. **1893** *Labour Comm. Gloss.*, *Runner*, a small iron trolley used in the printing industry for shifting stones about. **1898** *Standard* 20 Oct., The timber in each load came within the compass of the three waggons and.. no 'runner' was necessary. The 'runner'.. was an extra waggon coupled on to cover the projecting ends of the timber.

18. *Sc.* (See quot. 1825).

1825 JAMIESON *Suppl.*, *Runner*, in cutting up of beeves, the slice which extends across the fore-part of the carcase under the breast. **1842** J. AITON *Domest. Econ.* (1857) 98 For boiling-pieces of beef, the runner, the nineholes and the breast are the best.

19. *Typogr.* (See quot. 1956.)

1888 C. T. JACOBI *Printers' Vocab.* 117 *Runners*, figures or letters placed down the length of a page to indicate the particular number or position of any given line. **1926** W. H. SLATER *What Compositor should Know* III. 16 Runners are generally used in translations, and then only when the author has written a running commentary on the peculiarities of the original. **1956** *Bookman's Conc. Dict.* 259/2 *Runners*, letters or figures placed in the margin of a page opposite lines at regular intervals for assistance in reference (especially in poetry).

20. In various technical and specific senses: (see quots.).

1688 HOLME *Armoury* III. xxii. (Roxb.) 274/2 Instruments belonging to the Cook. The first is termed a Runner with Twichers... The second is called a Runner with an Halfe Round... These are to cut through past, or make veriaty of marks and indents. **1788** W. H. MARSHALL *Rur. Econ. Yorks.* I. 269 A simple improvement of the Wheel-washer —provincially 'Runner'. **1836** YARRELL *Brit. Fishes* I. 3 A Perch of eight pounds taken.. by a runner, or night-line, baited with a roach. **1839** URE *Dict. Arts* 348 [In a cotton-card] *h*' is the small runner or urchin, and *i*' the large runner. **1843** HOLTZAPFFEL *Turning* I. 324 The breaks, or the runners, of the types are first broken off [etc.]. **1875** KNIGHT *Dict. Mech.* 1275/1 Green-salted hides and skins.. if thin and poor are called runners or murrains, and are sold at two thirds the price of good kip. **1877** *Encycl. Brit.* VI. 32/2 (*Clocks*), The points of the driven wheel or *runner* (as it may be called, more appropriately than the usual term *follower*). **1882** CAULFEILD & SAWARD *Dict. Needlewk.* 428/2 *Runners*, the name by which the Bobbins that work across a pattern in Pillow Lace making are known. **1884** F. J. BRITTEN *Watch & Clockm.* 230 An idle wheel is also sometimes called a runner. **1892** JACOBI *Some Notes on Books* 47 *Runners*, figures or letters placed down the length of a page to indicate the particular number or position of any given line.

Hence **'runnered** *a.*, furnished with runners.

1887 *Cornh. Mag.* March 270 The small, runnered sleigh is used.

runnerless ('rʌnəlɪs), *a.* [f. RUNNER 12 + -LESS.] Of a strawberry plant, esp. an alpine one: not producing runners.

1956 *Dict. Gardening* (R. Hort. Soc.) *Suppl.* 118/2 Baron Solemacher. (Alpine.) This is runnerless and makes large plants. **1957** E. HYAMS *Speaking Garden* ix. 114 The most useful of these [mutants].. was a runnerless strawberry. **1981** *Country Life* 25 June 1846/2 The new French Bordurella perpetual [strawberry], virtually runnerless, and therefore a suitable plant for flower borders.

runner-up. Also **runnerup**; pl. **runners-up, runner-ups.**

1. a. *Coursing.* A dog that takes the second prize, losing only the final course to the winner.

1842 THACKER *Courser's Ann.* 210 Dividers or runners up for stakes of only four dogs. **1853** 'STONEHENGE' *Greyhound* xi, The Ages of.. the Winners and Runners up. **1856** —— *Brit. Rural Sports* II. III. viii. 207/1 The dog beaten by the runner-up in the last tie but one. **1890** A. R. STARR in *Upland Shooting* 471 The dog last running with the winner is called the runner up, because he ran through the races up to the last race without being defeated once.

b. *gen.* A competitor or competing team that comes in second or takes the second place, *esp.* one defeated only in the final heat or tie of a series of matches or races.

1886 *Pall Mall G.* 2 Aug. 3/2 Now Bird is nowhere, while Brown is the runner-up for the first place. **1887** IRVINE *Football* 113 In 1873 the Wanderers again won the cup, the runners-up being Oxford University. **1949** *Cavalier Daily* (Univ. of Virginia) 22 Oct. 1/3 The last issue of the magazine will announce the award winner and the runner-ups. **1955** *Times* 16 May 13/4 Miss Garvey, twice runner-up was unable to play. **1976** *Burnham-on-Sea Gaz.* 20 Apr., Highbridge soccer team Bristol Bridge look like losing their chance of finishing runners-up in the second division of the Bridgwater and District Sunday Football League. **1976** *Billings* (Montana) *Gaz.* 27 June 8-F/6 Other accomplished cowboys attending the rodeo include Royce Smith.. who was runnerup for the world title twice.

c. *transf.* and *fig.*

1932 *New Yorker* 11 June 24/3 Blyth Daly is the horsy young lady who serves as runner-up to the Brat in offensiveness. **1949** *Sat. Rev. Lit.* (U.S.) 11 June 38/2 It was a 'runner-up' for the *Herald Tribune* award. **1974** *Times* 9 Nov. 10/5 Shirley Gee's *Stones* was runner up in the *Radio Times* play competition.

2. One who 'runs up' bids at an auction.

1905 *Daily Chron.* 9 Aug. 6/4 Some of the functions of a professional 'runner up' of bids.

3. *attrib.*, as ***runner-up list, prize***.

1925 *Scribner's Mag.* Oct. 384/1 At the tournament dance ..he was called out for the runner-up prize in the fourth division. **1976** *National Observer* (U.S.) 18 Dec. 6/4 Britain's Queen Elizabeth II and Prince Philip made the runner-up list, as did Alistair Cooke, Shirley MacLaine, [etc.].

'runnet[1]. Now *dial.* Also 5–6 **runnett**, 9 **urnet**, *Sc.* **ronnet**. [var. of RENNET *sb.*[1], with the vowel of RUN *v.*]

1. = RENNET *sb.*[1] 1. ? *Obs.*

1471 RIPLEY *Comp. Alch.* II. ix. in Ashm. (1652) 137 So doth our Runnett by kynde curd our Mylke. **1563** T. HYLL *Art Garden.* (1593) 80 The mints put into milke, will not suffer the milke to curd, although the runnet bee put into it. **1600** SURFLET *Countrie Farme* I. xiv. 91 The way to curdle it [milk], is to mingle therewith of the runnet, of a lambe, kidde, or hare. **1686** PLOT *Staffordsh.* 388 The Runnet of Ranton.. made of the innermost membran of a Calves Stomack or Mawe. **1741** *Comp. Fam.-Piece* I. ii. 124 Cool it till 'tis but Blood-warm, and then put in a Spoonful of Runnet. **1784** TWAMLEY *Dairying Exemp.* 15 Many a Dairy-maid.. has no consistent idea how the Runnet operates, or perhaps of the different states of the Curd. **1808** MITCHILL & MILLER *Med. Repository* V. 140 The runnet, or gastric ferment taken from the stomach of a calf,.. will assist in restoring it. **1867** ROCK *Jim an' Nell* xi, Laist Zinday wi' a drap o' runnet I jist a junket made.

fig. *a* **1661** FULLER *Worthies, Somerset* III. (1662) 17 The Unity and Amity of those Female Neighbours.. giveth the better Runnet and Relish to their handiwork.

2. = RENNET *sb.*[1] 2. ? *Obs.*

1678 SALMON *Pharm. Lond.* 59 Gallium.. is used for Rennet or Runnet to make cheese with. **1736** PEGGE *Kenticisms* (E.D.S.) 44 *Runnet*, the herb *gallium*; called in Derb. 'erning'; anglicè cheese-runnet. **1758** MRS. DELANY *Life & Lett.* (1861) III. 474 The plant you call Runnet or Rundle grass,.. she thinks it is the jagged spearwort.

3. *attrib.*, as ***runnet-bag, -plant, -pot***.

1686 PLOT *Staffordsh.* 95 The Women also put it in their Runnet pots, it makeing (as they say) the best Cheese. **1707** MORTIMER *Husb.* (1721) I. 248 Give her to eat some Oats.. or the small End of the Runnet-Bag. **1784** TWAMLEY *Dairying Exemp.* 104, I have heard of a Plant called the Runnet-plant;.. I am informed the Jews make all their Cheese with it. **1824** MACTAGGART *Gallovid. Encycl.*, *Ronnet Bags*, the rennets for coagulating milk.

†**'runnet**[2]. *Obs. rare.* Also **-ett**. [f. RUN *v.*] A stream or small river; a runnel.

1601 WEEVER *Mirr. Mart.* I. ii, This crawling runnet, hony-bubbling fountaine.., Descending from the Diamond-rockie mountaine. **1646** *Providence Rec.* (1892) I. 80 The Runnett called Papaquinapauge River. **1704** *Ibid.* (1894) V. 184 A small Walnut tree neare a small Runnett comeing downe the hill.

runnet, obs. variant of RENNET *sb.*[2]

running ('rʌnɪŋ), *vbl. sb.* [f. RUN *v.* + -ING[1].]

I. 1. a. The action of the vb. RUN (in sense 1); rapid motion on foot; racing; an instance of this. *spec.* in *Cricket*, the action of making runs; also in phr. ***running between*** (***the***) ***wickets***.

c **888** K. ÆLFRED *Boeth.* xxxvii. §2 Færð ðonne micel folc to, & yrnað ealle endemes, ða ðe hiora ærninge trewað. *c* **1386** CHAUCER *Prol.* 551 Ther nas no dore þat he nolde heue of harre, Or breke it, at a rennyng, with his heed. **1387** TREVISA *Higden* (Rolls) IV. 167 þere ofte he travaylede wylde bestes, and took hem wiþ swifte rennynge. *c* **1449** PECOCK *Repr.* I. xx. 120 That men.. schulden pleie.. by rennyng or leping or schuting. **1509** HAWES *Past. Pleas.* II. (Percy Soc.) 38 The gentyll beast they wyll regarde nothyng, But to the swyne take course of rennyng. **1591** COKAINE *Treat. Hunting* B 3, Their hardie fighting and swift running. **1664** PEPYS *Diary* 30 Jan., I home.. and, in great fear, to bed, thinking every running of a mouse really a thiefe. **1728** CHAMBERS *Cycl.* s.v. *Gymnic*, Gymnic Games.. are those wherein the Body is exercised; such are Wrestling, Running, Dancing. **1744** *Laws* [of Cricket] in *New & Compl. Dict. Arts & Sci.* (1755) IV. 3460/1 They [*sc.* the Umpires] are sole judges of all hindrances, crossing the players in running, and standing unfair to strike. **1801** STRUTT *Sports & Past.* II. ii. 70 There is no kind of exercise that has more uniformly met the approbation of authors in general than Running. **1833** *New Sporting Mag.* V. *Cricketers' Reg.* 12 The steady manner in which Pilch bowled rendered the running very difficult throughout. **1869** TOZER *Highl. Turkey* II. 310 In order to be less impeded in running and jumping. **1877** *Encycl. Brit.* VI. 580/1, 21 Or if in running the wicket be struck down by a throw.. before his bat (in hand) or some part of his person be grounded over the popping crease. **1897** *Encycl. Sport* I. 225/2 The art of running between wickets, without coming to a misunderstanding with one's partner, is indispensable. *Ibid.* 226/1 Every information should be given to one's partner that may help him in running. **1906** A. E. Knight *Compl. Cricketer* ii. 87 Some of the best running between wickets ever witnessed has been shown by Australian teams, who rarely miss a possible run. **1963** A. Ross *Australia 63* vii. 151 Catching and running between the wickets apart, England had at least given as good as they had got. **1976** *Milton Keynes Express* 23 July 39/3 David Berrill and Finch with some firm strokes and quick running between the wickets took the score to 61 all out after 17.3 overs.

transf. **1633** P. Fletcher *Poet. Misc.* 91 Jerusalem, thy burning If I forget; Forget thy running My hand, and all thy cunning To th' harp to set. **1672** Eachard *Lett.* 1 A friend had promised me the running of two or three letters. *a* **1761** Law *Comf. Weary Pilgr.* (1809) 39 That vanity and emptiness, burden and deceit must follow us in every course we take, till we have done with all our own running.

†**b.** The action of moving rapidly with hostile intent; raiding; a raid or inroad. *Obs.*

1297 R. Glouc. (Rolls) 11060 In þis manere þe barons bigonne hor vrning. **1387** Trevisa *Higden* (Rolls) VI. 13 Þe province was swiþe destourbed by rennynge [*v.r.* ȝurnyng, ernyng] of reses of straungers. **1489** *Barbour's Bruce* xii. 754 Thai Suld hald thair fayis all that day Doand.. With thair rounnyngis that thai suld ma. **1596** Dalrymple tr. *Leslie's Hist. Scot.* (S.T.S.) II. 165 Tha war the only authoris of thift, rubrie, and rinning of forrayis.

c. *local.* Rapid skating in a direct line.

1878 Miller & Skertchly *Fenland* vi. 163 Here some of the fastest 'running' in the world might be seen. **1893** *Eng. Illustr. Mag.* X. 303/1 Fen skating, or, as it is locally called, 'running', is distinct from figure skating.

d. Rapid surface-swimming on the part of a harpooned whale.

1890 in *Cent. Dict.*

2. a. The action, on the part of a horse, of going at (great) speed, *esp.* in a race; racing; †a race. Also *fig.* of a person, the action of standing as a candidate or competing (*for* an office); cf. run *v.* 7 b. (orig. *U.S.*).

c **900** Wærferth tr. *Gregory's Dial.* 38 On dæȝred com ærendraca..mid swiðe ȝeswenctan horse for ærninge. *c* **1400** *Destr. Troy* 2365, I..Beheld to my horse, þat hote was of Rennyng. **1509** Fisher 7 *Penit. Ps.* xxxviii. Wks. (1876) 58 By his boldnes & rennynge to moche vpon his owne brydell. **1577** in Picton *L'pool Munic. Rec.* (1883) I. 119 There was a running of horses..for a silver bell. **1704** *Lond. Gaz.* No. 4000/4, Galloways..to be entred at the White-Horse Inn..14 days before the day of Running. **1830** *Wiscasett* (Maine) *Citizen* 20 Aug. 3/2 Such politicians..bet on a candidate's running for the Chief Magistracy of the Union or of a single State, precisely as they would bet on the running of a race horse. *a* **1837** [Apperley] *Turf* (1851) 128 Many of them [*sc.* colts] die before the day of running. **1863** *Sat. Rev.* 23 May 656 Lord Clifden, on the strength of his good two-year-old running,..had been made first favourite for more than twelve months. **1870** *Nation* (N.Y.) 7 July 1/1 He has never failed in getting such offices as he wanted, the record of his 'running' being about as good as that of any man in the country. **1910** *Sat. Even. Post* 24 Dec. 16/2 There was less excuse for his running on the liquor ticket. **1961** T. H. White *Making of President 1960* iv. 86 Kennedy ..felt that running for the Presidency was his most important full-time business and Senate attendance took second place.

†**b.** The action of riding or racing upon horseback, esp. *at* the ring; an instance of this. *Obs.*

c **1480** *Robt. Devyll* 13 Lordes came fro many a farre lande And Ladyes also that runnynge to see. **1563** in Robertson *Hist. Scot.* (1759) II. App. 14 We..pass our time in feasts, banquetting, masking, and running at the ring, and such like. *c* **1618** Moryson *Itin.* iv. v. i. 465 They haue Tiltings, Runnings with lances against a Post Armed like a man at all peeces. **1670** Cotton *Espernon* ii. v. 211 The Duke..had invited all the Nobility and Gentry of the Country to Bordeaux to a publick running at the Ring.

c. In phrases with *make*, as *to make* (*strong*, etc.) *running*, *to make the running*.

Chiefly denoting good or successful racing, and often used *fig.* In (*d*) the meaning is 'to set the pace'.

(*a*) *a* **1837** [Apperley] *Turf* (1851) 33 He is averse to making running, sometimes even to a fault. **1855** Thackeray *Newcomes* II. 50 We fancy we've been making running, and suddenly we find ourselves nowhere.

(*b*) **1862** *Cornh. Mag.* Sept. 371 The world had esteemed him when he first made good his running with the Lady Fanny. **1902** Annie F. Hector *Stronger than Love* vi, Hubert Denham was making no end of running. He was.. everything to the forsaken lady.

(*c*) **1865** Dickens *Mut. Fr.* i. xiii, He may make the running and come in first. **1886** D. C. Murray *First Person Singular* xxi, He had not made the running so fast as he might have done.

(*d*) **1861** *Macm. Mag.* Oct. 429 Ben Caunt was to make the running for Haphazard. **1884** *Illustr. Lond. News* 29 Nov. 522/1 The owner whose horse is employed 'to make the running'. **1923** Galsworthy *Captures* 161 Dinner was certainly a disharmonic feast: little Mrs. Weymouth..and the Countess subdued, Radolin artificial, our scoundrel and myself had to make the running. **1954** I. Murdoch *Under Net* v. 80 'Where did you meet Madge?' I asked. I wasn't going to let him make all the running. **1958** *Times* 13 Sept. 7/2 First Russia turns on the heat in the Middle East and then it is China's turn to make the running. **1971** *Sunday Nation* (Nairobi) 11 Apr. 18/1 When he begins courting, he is unsure of himself, half-frightened of the girl, so she has to make the running. **1977** B. Freemantle *Charlie Muffin* vi. 65 You'll have to be bloody careful. Let Kalenin make the running.

d. *to take up the running*, to take the lead. Often *fig.*

1858 Trollope *Dr. Thorne* v, But silence was not dear to the heart of the Honourable John, and so he took up the running. **1868** Helps *Realmah* xvii. (1876) 484 Sir John will be very much obliged to me if I take up the running in his stead. **1894** *Times* 25 May 11/1 Totley waited on his field until nearing the distance, when he took up the running and eventually won by two lengths.

e. *out of the running*, having no place among the leading competitors in a race. Similarly, *in the running*. Usually *fig.* Also const. *for* (some prize or objective).

(*a*) **1863** Kingsley *Water Bab.* 31 Which quite put her out of the running, so that she came in nowhere and is consequently not placed. **1885** W. E. Norris *A. Vidal* xxi, Heriot doesn't count, does he? He is something like me, out of the running? **1906** *Dialect Notes* III. 149 'Isn't Jack sweet on the girl I saw with that fellow?' 'No, he's out of the running.' **1918** Galsworthy *Five Tales* 304 When a man is very old and quite out of the running, he loves to feel secure from the rivalries of youth, for he would still be first in the heart of beauty. **1930** G. B. Shaw *Apple Cart* i. 34, I think I am in the running. That is why I do not feel bound to accept this ultimatum. By signing it I put myself out of the running. **1949** M. Mead *Male & Female* xvi. 341 His married daughter, who with each step that she takes towards maturity puts him more definitely out of the running.

(*b*) **1886** H. Baumann *Londinismen* 162/2. *c* **1926** 'Mixer' *Transport Workers' Song Bk.* 65 And I never strike a top-job That the other fellows get, For I'm out upon my 'lonesome', And not in the running yet. **1930** W. S. Maugham *Cakes & Ale* xi. 120 It may be that posterity will scrap all the best-sellers of our day, but it is among them that it must choose. At all events Edward Driffield is in the running. **1950** W. Cooper *Scenes from Provincial Life* iv. ii. 235 It was one of the events in which Frank was hoping to shine, since he was in the running for victor ludorum. **1975** N. Blakiston in C. Connolly *Romantic Friendship* 5, I was in the running for playing in the school eleven.

3. a. With prepositional complements, as *about* (a place), *against* (a person), etc. Also *fig.*

c **1380** Wyclif *Wks.* (1880) 31 Siþ prechynge of þe gospel is betere þan bodely rennynge so to ferre placis. *c* **1500** *God Speed the Plough* 69 (Skeat), With ronnyng in reragis it doth vs sorowe Inough. **1565** Cooper *Thesaurus, Occursus*, a runnyng agaynst one: a meetyng: an incountrynge. **1566** in *Harington's Nugæ Ant.* (1804) I. 89 The lief of man..is called a ronninge for the best game. **1722** De Foe *Plague* (Rtldg.) 209 This running of distemper'd People about the Streets was very dismal. **1735** Sir J. Chardin in *Buccleuch MSS.* (Hist. MSS. Comm.) I. 386 Your running towards me.

b. With adverbial complements, as *abroad*, *amuck*, *astray*, *away*, etc.

1719 De Foe *Crusoe* i. (Globe) 310 For almost seven Years she prevented my *running Abroad. **1858** *Sat. Rev.* 6 Nov. 438/1 The furious unpatriotic *running-a-muck on all our institutions. **1526** Skelton *Magnyf.* 2458 Cyrcumspeccyon inhateth all *rennynge astray. **1560** Daus tr. *Sleidane's Comm.* 36 Lest they should call his journey a *runnynge awaye. **1618** Bolton tr. *Florus* (1636) 275 Runnings away of Beasts ordained for sacrifice. **1856** 'Stonehenge' *Brit. Rur. Sports* 535/2 *Running Away* is only an extreme form of pulling in the gallop. **1675** T. Brooks *Gold. Key* Wks. 1867 V. 572 A willing, wilful, presumptuous *running cross to divine commands. **1591** Percival *Sp. Dict.*, *Aventamiento*, the *running headlong. *a* **1548** Hall *Chron., Hen. VI*, 125 To..stop thenglishmen to make sodain *runnynges in or rodes into the countrey of Beauvoys. **1845** *Rules Footb. Rugby School* §8 Running in is allowed to any player on his side, provided he does not take the ball off the ground, or take it through touch. **1565** Cooper *Thesaurus, Procursus*,.. a course or *runnyng oute of souldiours to skyrmyshe with their enemies. **1681** H. More *Exp. Daniel* 226 As it is usual with the Prophets, there is a running out from the Temporal deliverance of the Jews to the Spiritual deliverance. **1382** Wyclif *Acts* xix. 40 No man is gilty, of whom we mown ȝelde resoun of this *rennyng to gidere. **1580** Hollyband *Treas. Fr. Tong* s.v. *Accourement*, A running togither, or assemblie of men.

4. Capacity for, or power of, running or racing.

1842 Lever *J. Hinton* xxv, Although the ground was trying, his breeding began to tell, and I could feel that he had plenty of running still in him. **1891** Nat. Gould *Double Event* 205 He glanced at Caloola, and saw the horse seemed full of running.

5. a. Ranging or pasturage of animals. ? *Obs.* Cf. also *running-season*, *-time* in 17 below.

1695 Kennett *Paroch. Antiq.* Gloss. s.v. *Porcus*, To grant pannage or free running of hogs in such a wood. **1725** Berkeley in Fraser *Life* iv. (1871) 117 You will also inform yourself whether Coll. Maceasland demands any thing for the running of my horse. **1754** Bartlet *Gentl. Farriery* (ed. 2) 4 A summer's grass is often necessary; more particularly to horses..who use little exercise, but a month or two's running is proper for most.

b. The action of forming a 'run' or burrow.

1712 J. James tr. *Le Blond's Gardening* 44 To hinder the running of Moles.

6. a. Of a ship or other vessel: The action of sailing, *esp.* of sailing close-hauled before the wind; also, speed of sailing.

1687 A. Lovell tr. *Thevenot's Trav.* i. 118 We reckoned our running to be ten miles an hour, though we carried only our Mainsail. **1748** *Anson's Voy.* ii. i. 295 A few days after our running off the coast of Mexico. **1875** Bedford *Sailor's Pocket Bk.* vi. 215 Running dead before the wind in a gig is very dangerous. **1884** *Sat. Rev.* 14 June 784/1 In running a cutter has, so far as sails go, a very obvious advantage over the two-masted vessel.

b. Movement from place to place of wheeled vehicles; performance of a journey.

1776 G. Semple *Building in Water* 41 Notwithstanding the almost constant running of Carriages,..there did not fall one Handful of it. **1884** *G.W.R. Time Tables* July 90 The running of these Trains is dependent upon the arrival of the Boats.

c. With *on.* (Cf. run *v.* 10 b.)

1832 J. Hall *Leg. of West* 153 More than once he lost both boat and cargo by runnings on the snags and the sawyers of the Mississippi.

7. a. The action of rapid moving or sliding, *esp.* by mechanical propulsion or by gravitation. Also with advs., as *about*, *amain*, *down*, and in fig. use.

1530 Palsgr. 264/2 Runnyng of a whele, *peau.* **1680** Moxon *Mech. Exerc.* x. 187 The springing up of the Pole makes an intermission in the running about of the Work. **1850** *Bohn's Handbk. Games* (1867) 564 If, after the striker has played, the adversary should obstruct or accelerate the running of the balls [etc.]. **1883** Gresley *Gloss. Coal-mining* 208 *Running Amain*, the breaking and running of a winding rope down into the pit-shaft. **1890** *Longm. Mag.* Oct. 620 The running down, if I may so call it, of the powers of the body.

b. Shooting up of a plant into stalk.

1847 *Jrnl. R. Agric. Soc.* VIII. i. 15 The feeding qualities of the root are thereby preserved, the land is not drawn by running up [etc.].

c. Slipping of a thread in a woven fabric.

1878 A. Barlow *Weaving* 360 On the breaking of a thread the 'running' would be stopped by the repeated twistings in a diagonal direction.

d. With *out.* The disappearance of the characteristics of a particular variety of a crop.

1891 *Proc. Western N.Y. Hort. Soc.* 86 By 'running out' is meant the disappearance of the characteristics of any variety... Running out, therefore, is not necessarily deterioration. **1918** Babcock & Clausen *Genetics in Relation to Agric.* xviii. 340 The so-called 'running-out' of varieties can be prevented by reasonable care to avoid mixing seed and by occasional mass selection from the field. **1949** C. C. Lindegren *Yeast Cell* xxvii. 2 The degeneration or 'running out' of hybrids showing heterosis has been one of the principal problems of hybrid vigor. **1952** tr. *Gram & Weber's Plant Dis.* 361/2 (*heading*) 'Running out' or 'decline' of strawberry crops.

e. With *off.* = run-off 4.

1921 *Jrnl. Pomol.* II. 160 Investigations relating to the 'Running off' or dropping of Black Currant Fruits before they are ripe. **1939** H. Wormald *Dis. Fruits & Hops* ix. 181 Running off is not caused by a parasite, but is a result of defective pollination.

II. 8. The flowing or discharge of blood or humours from the body; a sore which discharges matter. †*running of the reins*, gonorrhœa.

c **950** *Lindisf. Gosp.* Matt. ix. 20 [An] wif ðiu blodes flouing *vel* iorning ȝeðolade..tuelf ȝer ȝeneolecde. **1388** Wyclif *Lev.* xv. 2 A man that suffrith the rennyng out of seed, schal be vncleene. **1398** Trevisa *Barth. De P.R.* v. xxxix. (Bodl. MS.), Also by-passing rennyng oute of blood..comeþ of openyng of veynes þat springen oute of þe lyuour. **1569** R. Ambrose tr. *Secrets of Alexis* iv. ii. 32 To remedie the running of the reynes occasioned by a sharpe cause. **1579** Langham *Gard. Health* (1633) 55 Barley..stoppeth the running of the belly. **1607** Topsell *Four-f. Beasts* (1658) 346 A very good and effectual remedy against..the running of the reins. **1705** tr. *Bosman's Guinea* 110 The Wound gangrenes, and at best turns to a running, which continues the whole Life. **1804** Abernethy *Surg. Obs.* 165 A running came on from the urethra. **1898** *J. Hutchinson's Arch. Surgery* IX. 121 Until lately I have always had a slight thin running from the nose.

fig. **1704** Swift *Tale of Tub* x, Since my Vein is once opened, I am content to exhaust it all at a Running. **1839** (*title*), Hood's Own, or Laughter from Year to Year, being former runnings of his comic vein.

9. a. A channel or watercourse; a stream or rivulet. Somewhat *rare.*

a **1325** *Prose Ps.* i. 3 He schal be as þe tre, þat hijs sett by þe ernynges [**1388** Wyclif rennyngis] of waters. *a* **1425** *Cursor M.* 11942 (Trin.), Wiþ erþe & wiþ euel witt þe watir rennyng gon he dit þat watir to þe takes brouȝt. **1648** Gage *West Ind.* 172 We presently met with a deep Barranca, or bottome, where was a running. **1650** *Boston Rec.* (1877) II. 101 The Bounds betwixt both is the naturall Passage of the Water in a small Running. **1890** Clark Russell *Ocean Trag.* I. viii. 160 Each broad soft brow was alive with runnings of flaming oil.

b. The action or condition of flowing on the part of water, sand, etc.; an instance of this.

1398 Trevisa *Barth. De P.R.* xiii. iii. (Bodl. MS.), A ryuer is euerlastinge rennynge. *c* **1440** *Promp. Parv.* 429/2 Rennynge, of water, or oþer lycure, *manacio.* **1656** Harrington *Oceana* (1658) 179 An hour-glasse,..such an one as is to be of an houre and an halfe's running. **1712** J. James tr. *Le Blond's Gardening* 168 To facilitate the Running of the Water. **1750** tr. *Leonardus' Mirr. Stones* 150 If carried in the left hand, it stops the running of tears of aged people. **1823** J. Badcock *Dom. Amusem.* 151 Flour, being..exposed to the constant running of water, until it comes off colourless, the gluten will remain. **1883** Stevenson *Treas. Isl.* xxiv, The difficulty of the shore, and the high running of the surf.

10. Rhythmical flow of verse. *rare*$^{-1}$.

1589 Puttenham *Eng. Poesie* ii. iii. (Arb.) 83 Take this away from them, I meane the running of their feete, there is nothing of curiositie among them more then with vs.

11. a. The flow of liquor during the process of wine-making, brewing, or distillation; the liquor obtained at a specified stage of the process.

1601 Holland *Pliny* I. 411 The right keeping of grapes, is in a small thinne wine of the second running. **1616** Surfl. & Markh. *Country Farme* v. xxiii. 589 The second running of this beere (for it will beare but one besides the best). **1707** Mortimer *Husb.* (1721) II. 338, I should propose..to take only the first running of your Spirits to mix with your Cyder. **1770** *New Dispens.* 471/1 It is not necessary to.. throw away the first runnings in the distillation. **1830** M. Donovan *Dom. Econ.* I. 363 The juice that exudes last will be of a lively acid sweet; the first portion, a heavy sweet without acidity; and the middle runnings will be intermediate. **1900** *Jrnl. Soc. Dyers* XVI. 2 The 'first runnings' is washed firstly with conc. sulphuric acid.

fig. **1676** Dryden *Aureng-zebe* iv. i, From the Dregs of Life, think to receive What the first sprightly running could not give. **1748** Richardson *Clarissa* (1811) IV. 282 This, Jack, is my scheme, at the first running.

b. The result of smelting metals; the process of melting and flowing.

1666 *Phil. Trans.* I. 376 The first running of the Stone is Sulphur. **1719** De Foe *Crusoe* I. (Globe) 122, I had..two other Earthen Pots, as hard burnt as cou'd be desir'd; and one of them..glaz'd with the Running of the Sand. *a* **1744** Lucas in *Trans. Cumb. & Westm. Archæol. Soc.* VIII. 38 The Hearth [of a blast furnace] grows wider by using, so that their Runnings are much larger at the latter End than at the Beginning. **1793** Smeaton *Edystone L.* §307 To give much trouble by the running of the candles.

c. Exudation of sap from a tree.

1753 *Chambers' Cycl.* Suppl. s.v. *Resin*, Theophrastus.. observes, that a good pine might be made to yield resin every year,..and that three runnings were as much as a tree could bear. **1832** D. J. Browne *Sylva Amer.* 232 The scraping is a coating of sap which becomes solid before it reaches the boxes, and which is taken off in the fall and added to the last runnings. **1872** *Trans. Dept. Agric. Illinois* IX. 73, I have a plantation five or six years old, parts of which still grow fine fruit, with two runnings annually.

d. The spreading of ink or colour in a porous material; clouding in a flower.

1781 Cowper *Wks.* (1837) XV. 71 My paper is so intolerably bad, as you may perceive by the running of the ink, that it has quite worn out my patience. **1851** *Beck's Florist* Apr. 75 The propensity to sport observable in the Carnation, which we term 'running'. [Cf. run *ppl. a.* 6.]

12. Leakage of air: (see quots.).

1781 *Phil. Trans.* LXXI. 264 A very easy and effectual remedy for that defect so long complained of in all kinds of brass ordnance, the running of the vent. **1855** Hopkins *Organ* 34 Sometimes a little air will escape through a groove-hole, and make its way up to some pipe, and cause it to produce a low, disagreeable, and continuous humming. This is called a 'running'. **1881** Dickson *Pract. Organbuild.* iv. 50 The gluing on of these latter must..be very sound.. in every part, or a running of wind might ensue.

III. 13. a. Rennet. Now *dial.*

c **1000** Ælfric *Gloss.* in Wr.-Wülcker 128 *Coagulum*, rynning. **1530** Palsgr. 263/2 Ronnyng of chese, *maisgre.* **1562** Turner *Herbal* II. 2 As runnynge or chese lope maketh mylke runne together into cruddes. **1635** J. Swan *Spec. M.* vi. §4 (1643) 249 Mints put into milk will not suffer the milk to curd, although the runnet or running (as they call it) be put into it. **1789** W. H. Marshall *Rur. Econ. Glouc.* I. 331 *Running*, rennet; the coagulum in chees-making. **1825** Hone *Every-day Bk.* I. 561 Rennet, or running, as it is.. called [at Penzance]. **1854** Miss Baker *Northampt. Gloss.* **1890** *Glouc. Gloss.*

†**b.** With *together*: Coagulation. *Obs.*

1398 Trevisa *Barth. De P.R.* xvii. lxi. (Tollemache MS.), The milke of þe fige tre haþ vertu of rennynge to geder to make chese. **1527** Andrew *Brunswyke's Distyll. Waters* M j, [It] causeth the ronned and congeled mylke to be well and dyssolved frome the ronnynge togyder.

IV. 14. †**a.** *at long running*, in the long run.

c **1412** Hoccleve *De Reg. Princ.* 1630 At longe rennyng, loue beste schal preue. **1528–1670** [see long-running]. **1674** *Govt. Tongue* 141 Wisdom is commonly at long running justified even of her despisers.

b. Course; direction; career (of life). *rare.*

1530 Palsgr. 263/2 Ronnyng or course of any thynge, *decours.* *a* **1618** Raleigh *Hist. World* Pref. (1634) B 6, All the Rivers in the world, though they have divers risings, and divers runnings,..doe at last find, and fall into the great Ocean. **1870** *Nation* XI. 1 He has never failed in getting such offices as he wanted, the record of his 'running' being about as good as that of any man in the country.

c. Constant succession; continuance. *rare.*

1662 Stillingfl. *Orig. Sacræ* III. ii. §7 What ever is moved, must bee moved by something else, and consequently there must bee a running in Infinitum. **1674** N. Fairfax *Bulk & Selv.* 42 God does as truly abide, after the way of his everlasting nowness, as other things do after the guise of their timesom running on and on, without being himself timesom, like them.

d. The fact of being current. *rare*$^{-1}$.

1788 Priestley *Lect. Hist.* III. xvi. 137 Which value (by the running of guineas as they now do for twenty one shillings each) is yet further advanced.

V. 15. a. The action of the vb. run in various transitive senses. Chiefly with advs., as *in*, *off*, *together*, *up*.

(*a*) **1683** Moxon *Mech. Exerc.*, *Printing* xxiv. ¶7 The too short or too far Running in of the Carriage. **1706** E. Ward *Wooden World Diss.* (1708) 33 He lays far more Stress upon the running up of Yards and Top-masts well after a Storm. **1774** *Ann. Reg.*, *Projects* 105/2 We are at a great remove from the Greeks and Romans, with respect to the running up of buildings with the degree of rapidity they used to do. **1809** W. Irving *Knickerb.* vi. v. (1849) 342 The Van Winkles,.. noted for running of horses, and running up of scores at taverns. **1871** Lowell *Study Wind.* (1886) 243 Slurrings-over and runnings-together of syllables.

(*b*) **1844** G. Dodd *Textile Manuf.* vii. 225 This working round of the outline is called 'running', while the filling-up of the interior parts is termed either 'fining' or 'open-working'. *c* **1850** *Rudim. Navig.* (Weale) 144 This term is.. used to signify the running or drawing of a line on the ship. **1876** Preece & Sivewright *Telegr.* 217 The poles having been properly fitted up, stayed or strutted,..and raised, the running of the wire is then proceeded with.

b. A line of running stitches.

1845 Mrs. M. J. Howell *Hand-bk. Dressmaking* 46 As many runnings as you choose to introduce will each form a distinct puffing. **1900** *Daily News* 28 July 6/6 Then come the gathers which have to be done with three runnings and very neatly finished off.

c. *U.S. colloq.* Teasing; scolding. Cf. run *v.* 52 c.

1832 S. Smith *Life & Writings Major Jack Downing* (1833) 158, I feel a little put out with Dr Burnham for an unhansome running he gave me 'tother day. **1902** J. Corbin *Amer. at Oxford* ii. 16 The freshman breakfast is nothing in the world but a variation of the 'running' that is given newcomers in those American colleges where fraternity life is strong. **1936** *Nat. Geogr. Mag.* LXIX. 799/1 Much of this 'running', or badgering, is in the spirit of fun.

d. ***running in***, the process of operating a new machine (*spec.* the engine of a motor vehicle) at reduced power in order to establish proper working.

1935 *Jrnl. R. Aeronaut. Soc.* XXXIX. 159 Tapered piston rings reduce the running-in period considerably. **1963** R. F. Webb *Motorists' Dict.* 189 The object of running-in is to enable microscopic irregularities in the working surfaces to become burnished. **1968** 'M. Finch' *Eye with Mascara* viii. 80 A little rev-up from time to time is good for running-in.

16. a. Illegal landing *of* goods; smuggling.

1699 Luttrell *Brief Rel.* (1857) IV. 518 One Stapleton and Basse, sea captains, were tryed..for smugling and running of prize goods in time of war. **1718–9** *Act 5 Geo. I*, c. 11 Title, An Act against clandestine running of uncustomed Goods. **1766** *Museum Rusticum* VI. 420 The clothiers attributed it to the running of wool. **1884** Dowell *Taxes in Eng.* IV. 216 Heavy penalties..were now imposed upon customhouse officers for neglect of duty in preventing the running of brandy.

b. Conveyance or carriage *of* anything. ***log running***: see log *sb.*[1] 9.

1880 *Michigan Rep.* XXXVIII. 603 [He] was to manage the logging in the woods and running of the logs to the mill.

VI. 17. a. *attrib.* and *Comb.*, as ***running clothes***, ***contest***, ***costume***, ***costs***, ***drawers***, ***expenses***, ***game***, ***ground***, ***pants***, ***path***, ***place***, ***shorts***, ***suit***, ***track***, ***vest***, etc.; also **running brand** *U.S.*, a cattle brand made with a running iron; also = *running iron*; **running business**, smuggling; **running iron** *U.S.*, a straight branding iron used (freq. illegally) for altering cattle brands; also *fig.*; **running light**, (*a*) *Naut.* = *navigation light* s.v. navigation 8; (*b*) one of a set of small lights located on the front, rear, or sides of a motor vehicle that remain illuminated during the running of the vehicle (see quots.); **running order**, (*a*) a condition in which a machine, etc., will function; (also qualified by *well*, *badly*, etc.); the condition in which a road, etc. is fit to be used (cf. *working order* s.v. working *vbl. sb.* 16 b; (*b*) *Theatre* and *Broadcasting*, the sequence in which scenes or parts of a programme are presented; **running powers**, permission granted to a railway company to run trains over the lines of another company; **running road** (see quot.); †**running-saddle**, a small saddle with round skirts; **running season**, *U.S.*, the season at which certain animals move from one district to another; **running shoe**, a (freq. spiked) shoe for running (usu. *pl.*); also *fig.*, esp. in (orig. *N.Z.*) phr. ***to give*** (one) ***his running shoes*** (see quots.); **running time**, (*a*) = *running season* above; (*b*) the time occupied by the running of a machine, performance, etc.; so, a schedule; †**running woodness**, a kind of madness in dogs, characterized by aimless wandering. Also running board.

1884 Sweet & Knox *On Mexican Mustang through Texas* xii. 160 The other, called a *running brand, is a long piece of iron curved at the end. **1934** *Denver* (Colo.) *Post* 4 Aug. 10/3 A running brand..[is] a brand made with a straight poker called a 'running iron', and used like a pencil. **1809** Kendall *Trav.* III. 296 On the Province Point..I was taught to expect to find a store, inhabited, and in the bustle of the *running business. *a* **1727** in *Gentl. Mag.* (1791) LXI. I. 199 No money allowed when I run any way under twenty miles. To find my own stockings and pumps, and to have my *running clothes washed in the house. **1916** W. Owen *Let.* 14 Mar. (1967) 385, I shall consider my running clothes as my Birthday Present. **1886** *Encycl. Brit.* XXI. 61/1 Nearly all *running contests now take place on prepared cinder paths. **1907** *Sports Trades Jrnl.* X. 25 (Advt.), *Running costumes. **1913** *Autocar Handbk.* (ed. 5) i. 14 Depreciation is a large item generally included amongst *running costs. **1979** *Homes & Gardens* June 153/2 Keep running costs to a minimum by placing the freezer in a cool, well ventilated room and ensuring that it is full. **1903** *Sports Trades Jrnl.* III. 101 (Advt.), *Running drawers, running vests. **1904** *N.Y. World Mag.* 1 May 6/6 This does not include *running expenses. *c* **1440** *Promp. Parv.* 430/1 *Rennynge game, *bravium.* **1876** Morris *Æneid* XII. 765 There they strive in running-game for Turnus' life and blood. **1744** *Laws* [of Cricket] in *New Dict. Arts & Sci.* (1755) IV. 3459/2 When the ball is hit up, either of the strikers may hinder the catch in his *running ground. **1787** in Waghorn *Cricket Scores* (1899) p. xii, When the ball is struck up in the running-ground between the wickets. **1863** *Sat. Rev.* 23 May 656 A few hours' dry weather would have brought the running-ground into first-rate order. **1927** E. V. Gordon *Introd. Old Norse* 196 Let the adventurous steed of the sand's heaven explore the broad running-ground of ships. **1894** *McClure's Mag.* July 101/2 The *running-irons, or *guachos*,..are now considered bad form by progressive cattlemen. **1913** L. V. Kelly *Range Men* 16 But the running or round iron was most favored, as it was easily and secretly made by cutting a wagon-iron in two and using the rounded end. **1945** *Everybody's Digest* Aug. 89 Of a dying man, the puncher might say: 'Death's got the runnin' iron on him brandin' him for the Eternal Range.' **1968** R. F. Adams *Western Words* 261/1 *Running iron*, a branding iron made in the form of a straight poker or a rod curved at the end... In the 1870's a law was passed in Texas forbidding the use of this iron in branding. This was a blow aimed at the brand blotter, whose innocent single iron would tell no tales. **1881** *Naval Encycl.* 439/2 *Light*,..the term for all lamps or lanterns used on ship-board; as, **running lights, signal-lights, mast-head lights*, etc. **1948** R. de Kerchove *Internat. Maritime Dict.* 613/1 *Running lights*, a general term applied to the various lights carried from sunset to sunrise by different classes of vessels when under way. **1971** M. Tak *Truck Talk* 135 *Running lights*, a tractor-trailer's clearance lights. **1975** *Times* 21 Aug. 3/2 Volvo cars..are to be fitted with 'running lights', special side lights switched on automatically with the ignition. **1977** *Observer* 3 Apr. 37/8 The working group appointed by the Nordic Road Safety Council has proposed that the use of running lights be made mandatory in daytime all year round in Denmark, Finland, Sweden and Norway. **1978** H. Wouk *War & Remembrance* xx. 192 Unescorted, floodlights on a white hull, brilliant running lights, huge red cross painted on her side. **1850** N. Kingsley *Diary* 4 Mar. (1914) 112 Got up steam again today and tried the larboard engine and have got both in *running order. **1860** A. Sherwood *Gazetteer of State of Georgia* (ed. 4) 152 Soon, say in summer of 1861, much will be in running order. **1875** *General Statutes of State of Michigan* I. (1882) 829 Every corporation owning a road in use shall..draw over the same the merchandise and cars of any other corporation..: Provided, such cars are of the proper gauge, are in good running order, and properly loaded. **1902** 'O. Henry' in *Ainslee's Mag.* Apr. 209/2 The running order of the bank was smooth and clean, and that had facilitated his work. **1939** N. Coward *Play Parade* II. p. x, *Running order*, a list of the Scenes in their correct order. **1948** [see runner 4 c]. **1961** G. Millerson *Technique Television Production* x. 186 A running order, prepared from this script after the technical planning meeting, will contain a breakdown of the entire studio operations throughout the show. **1977** B. Langley *Death Stalk* ii. 21 If you're editing a programme and you're not prepared for it [*sc.* an item], it can knock hell out of your running order. **1930** L. W. Olds *Track Athletics* i. 4 The *running pants should have plenty of room in the hips. **1889** *Boy's Own Paper* 14 Sept. 794/3 All the records are held by one man,..the amateur who turned professional in his last years on the *running path. **1539** Taverner *Gard. Wysed.* I. 39 If I ran in a *runnynge place for the mastrye. **1727** Boyer *Dict. Royal* II. s.v., A fine running place. **1868** Morris *Earthly Par.* (1870) I. II. 533 Within the running place at home I played. **1865** *Railw. News* Dec., The agreement with the Erie and Niagara Railway Company for *running powers over that company's line. **1865** J. T. F. Turner *Slate Quarries* 8 When the distance is great, by an admirable system of '*running roads', which fall one foot per 100 feet, the wagons are impelled by their own weight. **1688** R. Holme *Armoury* III. 345/1 *Running Saddle. **1841** Catlin *N. Amer. Ind.* (1844) II. xxxii. 13 It was in the midst of the *running season, and we had heard the roaring of the herd. **1884** *Spectator* 26 July 975/2 The *running-shoes must be doffed for good and all. **1913** C. Mackenzie *Sinister St.* I. I. vii. 107 Every evening there was steady practice.. in spiked running-shoes on the grass-track. **1941** Baker *N.Z. Slang* vi. 53 *To give a person his running shoes*, to dismiss a person from office.., which is an extension of the phrase *to get the run*, to be dismissed or fired. **1943** J. A. W. Bennett in *Amer. Speech* XVIII. 92 Only a few current phrases can be traced to their creators. One of these is 'to give a man his running shoes', coined by a New Zealand Minister of the Crown as a vivid substitute for the English 'sack' or the American 'fire'. **1960** Wentworth & Flexner *Dict. Amer. Slang* 438/1 *Running shoes, give someone his*, to dismiss someone, as a suitor or an employee; to terminate a personal or business relationship, usu. in anger. **1963** B. Pearson *Coal Flat* vi. 111 Like Bob Semple used to say about hit-and-run drivers— give them their running shoes. **1979** *Tucson* (Arizona) *Citizen* 20 Sept. 6A/1 President Carter is losing ground by waiting to put on his official re-election running shoes. **1912** E. W. Hjertberg *Athletics in Theory & Practice* xii. 54 The *running shorts should be wide and should not sit tightly anywhere, whatever movement one happens to make. **1974** *Times* 10 Apr. 13/2 A lifelessly wordless eccentric in running shorts. **1905** Graham & Clark *Pract. Track & Field Athletics* 9 Sufficient capital to purchase a *running suit and a pair of spiked shoes,..and a spare hour somewhere in the course of the day are all that are required to give any one a chance to develop his latent possibilities. **1806** W. Clark in *Lewis & Clark Exped.* (1905) V. 294 Emence herds of Buffalow about ..as it is now *running time with those animals. **1890** L. C. D'Oyle *Notches* 60 The loud, shrill, snorting whistle peculiar to the buck in 'running' time. **1897** Kipling *Capt. Cour.* ix. 195 Our runnin' time from San Diego to Chicago was 57.54. **1911** H. S. Harrison *Queed* xii. 143 Queed.. pulled into supper only three minutes behind running-time. **1952** Granville *Dict. Theatrical Terms* 156 *Running time*, the actual time the play takes in performance, act by act, excluding intervals and final curtain calls, which are logged separately. **1962** D. R. Cox *Renewal Theory* vii. 80 Suppose that a machine is subject to stoppages and call the time necessary to restart a stopped machine a repair-time. There is thus an alternating sequence of running-times and repair-times. **1977** A. Morice *Murder in Mimicry* II. x. 176 Even in normal running time my first entrance did not come for ten minutes. Nevertheless..I got to the theatre with two hours to spare. **1883** *Harper's Mag.* Oct. 416/2 The *running track, commonly used for trotting as well, has.. seen some notable achievements. **1907** *St. Nicholas* June 694/1 'And a new running track', added Dick. **1903** *Running vest [see *running drawers* above]. *c* **1410** *Master of Game* (MS. Digby 182) xii, þis wodenesse is ycleped *rennynge wodenesse.

b. With advs., as *about*, *back*, *down*, *in*, *out* (see quots.).

1966 J. Derrick *Teaching Eng. to Immigrants* iv. 155 Traditional children's games..are mainly *running-about games which are probably more suited to the playground.. than to the classroom. **1879** *Man. Artill. Exerc.* 254 The *running-back gear consists of part of the traversing gear. **1825** *Spirit of Public Jrnls. 1823* 315 Mr. Joseph Arnold being thus foiled in his *running-down scheme, placed his jarvey right across the road. **1856** Dickens in *Househ. Words* XIII. 554/2 The landsman was relating his experience..of a fearful running-down case in the Channel. **1867** Smyth *Sailor's Word-bk.* 586 *Running-Down Clause*, a special admission into policies of marine insurance, to include the risk of..the collision of the ship insured with other vessels. **1931** *Times* 16 Jan. 14/2 He acquired a large practice, esp. in running-down cases. **1968** *Times* 29 Nov. 13/3 The running-down rate of the pulsar implies that it has a lifetime of the same order as the Crab nebula. **1930** *Engineering* 4

Apr. 439/1 In the *running-in process, it has usually been necessary for the engine to be carefully watched..to prevent damage from over heating or seizing. **1957** *Railway Mag.* June 438/1 This is part of a regular two-day running-in roster from Crewe Works. **1973** 'J. ASHFORD' *Double Run* iii. 18 The driver ignored both the fifteen m.p.h. factory speed limit and the forty-five running-in limit. **1839** URE *Dict. Arts* 699 The finery furnace, or *running out fire.., is a smelting hearth, in which..gray cast iron..is converted into white cast iron. **1879** *Man. Artill. Exerc.* 326 He..gives 'run up', when the handspikes are applied under the *running up bolts.

running (ˈrʌnɪŋ), *ppl. a.* [f. RUN *v.* + -ING^{2}.]

I. 1. a. Of water, streams, etc.: Flowing.

[*c* **825** *Vesp. Psalter* lvii. 8 To nowihte bicumað swe swe weter eornende. *c* **1200** *Trin. Coll. Hom.* 177 Ac alle woreld þing ben fletende, alse water erninde.] **1297** R. GLOUC. (Rolls) 1796 Ac ladde him to londone & is men echon To an vrninde water. **1382** WYCLIF *Bible, Pref. Ep. St. Jerome* vii, Bi alle cytees, villagis, hillis, and flodis, rennynge watres, and the nyȝ coostis. **14..** *Siege Jerus.* 226 (E.E.T.S.), He.. Receyued hit wyd reuerence & rennande teris. *a* **1548** HALL *Chron., Edw. IV*, 26 b, As a runnyng ryuer by goyng more & more augmenteth. **1667** *Phil. Trans.* II. 527 Then wash it clean in a running stream. **1719** DE FOE *Crusoe* I. 115 It was no more than a little Brook of running Water. **1845** FORD *Handbk. Spain* I. 55 The Spaniards allow their horses, when on a journey, to drink very freely at all running streams. **1878** HUXLEY *Physiogr.* 135 To understand how running water usually effects denudation.

b. ***running water***, water taken straight from a running stream; river-water. Also, a constant supply of water from a tap, main, or the like.

1523 FITZHERB. *Husb.* §44 Than sethe them in a pan of .xx. gallons with rennynge water. **1545** RAYNOLD *Byrth Mankynde* 116 Take of the same sede brused fyrst: and then sethe it in fayre runnyn water. **1609** SKENE *Reg. Maj.* 57 Of sea water, foure pound: of Rynnand water, foure pound: and of standand water in stankis foure pound. **1759** BROWN *Compl. Farmer* 13 Boil all together..in three pints of running water. **1912** M. L. FULLER *Domestic Water Supplies for Farm* xx. 151 In very few ways, if any, may the drudgery be so readily lessened or the pleasures and comforts of rural life so increased as by the installation of running water in the houses & barns. **1936** G. MITCHELL *Dead Men's Morris* i. 16 We got no runnen water endoors round this part. **1946** A. HUXLEY *Let.* 21 Apr. (1969) 543 There is running water, electric light and bottled gas, so that the fundamentals are all right. **1961** L. MUMFORD *City in History* xv. 466 A collective water system with running water available for every house. **1974** O. MANNING *Rain Forest* I. iii. 52 There's no running water, the sani-cans stink.

c. ***running ice***, ice which moves downstream in blocks and sheets. *N. Amer.*

1913 W. OGILVIE *Early Days on Yukon* iii. 44 In this it satisfactorily succeeded, when running ice put a stop to further mining operations. **1922** H. A. CODY *King's Arrow* xii. 101 The bark canoe seemed like a thing of life as it cut through the water... It had battled with running ice; it had been borne over innumerable portages. **1959** M. SHAND *Summit & Beyond* iv. 65 The Mounted Police sent out warnings that no more small boats could be used on lakes and rivers on account of the running ice. **1968** [see CEILING *vbl. sb.* 6 c].

2. a. Fluid, liquid; melting readily.

1398 TREVISA *Barth. De P.R.* XVII. cxiv. (Bodl. MS.), Þe wose and juse þerof is rennynge and somtyme clensinge and druyinge. *c* **1430** *Two Cookery-bks.* 44 So þat it be renneng & not to styf. **1603** OWEN *Pembrokeshire* (1892) 88 Called the runinge Coale; for that when it first kindleth it melteth and runeth as wax, and groweth into one Clod. **1666** BOYLE *Orig. Forms & Qual.* 210, I obtain'd a considerable quantity of good running Mercury. **1829** R. CHRISTISON *Treat. Poisons* xiii. (1832) 380 The blue ointment, which is made with running quicksilver, will act as a mercurial when rubbed upon the skin. **1868** JOYNSON *Metals* 31 Where an easily running metal adds to the sharpness of the casting.

b. Of sand, soil, etc.: Having no coherence, so as readily to slip or fall.

1833 N. ARNOTT *Physics* (ed. 5) I. 453 The common hour-glass of running sand is..of the same principle. **1882** JAGO *Dial. Cornw.*, *Running ground*, loose, sandy, or soft ground which falls in just as fast as it is excavated. **1892** *Daily News* 23 Mar. 2/7 The bed of the river consisted of running sand instead of boulder clay as anticipated.

3. †**a.** Of a vessel: Leaking. *Obs.*$^{-0}$

1483 *Cath. Angl.* 309/2 Rynnynge as a wesselle, *futilis.*

†**b.** ***running glass***, a sand-glass, hour-glass. *Obs.*

1485 *Naval Accs. Hen. VII* (1896) 51 Rennyng glasses.. j, leede lynes..j. **1497** *Ibid.* 241 Compasses & Rynnyng glasses for the seid ship. **1599** HAKLUYT *Voy.* II. II. 45 Their men..tooke out their compasses, and running glasses. **1632-3** *Woodbury Churchw. Accs.* (E.D.D.), Paied for a Runninge Glasse, 00. 00. 08.

c. Allowing water to pass through.

1839 URE *Dict. Arts* 749 The apparatus subservient to the first objects are sieves, running buddles, and gratings. *Ibid.*, The running buddle serves at once to sort and cleanse the ore. **1884** KNIGHT *Dict. Mech.* Suppl. 772/2 *Running Trap*, a depressed bow-shaped section in a pipe..through which water passes freely. **1975** *Times* 4 Sept. 19/3 If the water is very hot it stops people washing things under a running tap.

4. Of sores, etc.: Discharging matter; suppurating. Also of the eyes or nose. ***running sore*** *fig.*, a constant nuisance or irritation; a long-lasting trouble or problem.

1535 COVERDALE *2 Sam.* iii. 29 In the house of Ioab there ceasse not one to haue a rennynge yssue and a leprosy. **1590** SPENSER *F.Q.* III. ii. 39 Ne can my running sore find remedie. **1611** BIBLE *Lev.* xv. 2 When any man hath a running issue out of his flesh. **1753** J. BARTLET *Gentl. Farriery* 297 Of the Running Thrush. **1807** E. WEETON *Let.* 18 Nov. (1969) I. 50 As to the running eyes and noses of which you request me to give you the exact number. **1843** R. J. GRAVES *Syst. Clin. Med.* xxix. 368 Few are exempted from the misfortune of a running eruption or the like. **1882** JAGO *Dial. Cornw.*, *Running-wound*, a wound discharging matter. **1961** C. COCKBURN *View from West* ix. 117 At that time the National Union of Journalists was as a running sore to the anti-Communists of the T.U.C. **1964** J. P. CLARK *Three Plays* 82 Do forgive my running nose. **1973** *Times* 21 Nov. 6 Running sore of London staff shortages may defy short-term cure.

†**5.** Coagulating. *Obs.*$^{-1}$

1495 *Trevisa's Barth. De P.R.* XIX. lxxvi, Rennynge mylke is made thycke in the mawes of certen beestes.

II. 6. a. Passing rapidly from place to place.

1382 WYCLIF *Exod.* ix. 23 And the Lord ȝaf thundres, and hawle, and dyuersly rennynge leytis vpon the erthe.

b. Of diseases, etc.: Passing from one part of the body to another; *esp.* spreading over the skin.

1382 WYCLIF *Lev.* xiii. 12 If forsothe out flow[r]e the rennynge lepre in the skynne, and couer al the flesh. *c* **1450** *Mankind* 616 (Brandl), I haue a lytyll dyshes [= disease].. Wyth a runnynge rynge-worme. **1562** TURNER *Baths* List of Authors, etc., The rinnyng gout which rynneth from one joynte to an other. **1585** HIGINS *Junius' Nomencl.* 441 *Herpes*, Some call it the shingles, some y^{e} running worme, some wild fire. **1671** SALMON *Syn. Med.* I. xiv. 33 Running pains in all the Extream parts of the Body. **1697** HEADRICH *Arcana Philos.* 40 In Wounds, in the Wolfe, in the Cruent, and running Herpes. **1818-20** E. THOMPSON tr. *Cullen's Nosologia* 329 *Impetigo*, Running Tetter.

7. †**a.** ***running hound***, a hunting dog employed to run down game. *Obs.*

c **1410** *Master of Game* (MS. Digby 182) ii, In Englond þei be not slayne, but with houndes, or with shote, or with strength of rennynge houndes. **1470-85** MALORY *Arthur* III. v. 104, xxx couple of black rennyng houndes cam after with a greete crye. **1513** DOUGLAS *Æneis* IV. iv. 46 The ryning hundis of cuplis sone thai kest.

†**b.** ***running-horse, -nag***, a race-horse. *Obs.*

1608 DEKKER *Lanth. & Candle Lt.* Wks. (Grosart) III. 284 A race of fiue myles by a couple of Running-Horses. **1664** BUTLER *Hud.* II. III. 935 Some calculate the hidden fates Of..Running-Nags, and Fighting-Cocks. **1777** SHERIDAN *Trip Scarb.* III. i, A running horse does require more attendance than a coach-horse. *a* **1837** [APPERLEY] *Turf* (1851) 6 In John's reign, running-horses are frequently mentioned in the register of royal expenditure. *Ibid.* 117 In the United States, breeding and running-horses are advancing with rapid strides.

c. In names of animals or classes of animals.

1766 tr. *Hasselquist's Voy. & Trav. Levant* 238 *Cancer cursor*, the Running Crab. This lives in the sea, and on the coasts about Egypt and Syria. **1868** *Mus. Nat. Hist.* II. 172/3 A New-Zealand species, seen by Cook, obtained from that navigator's companions the appellation of the 'running-fish'. **1882** *Cassell's Nat. Hist.* VI. 104 Tribe *Geocores*, or Land Bugs. The term 'Running Bugs' would, perhaps, better express the habits of the insects of this tribe, as some of them frequent the water and even run briskly over its surface. **1895** P. H. EMERSON *Birds*, etc. *Norf. Broads* 392 The Running Toad..has a yellow stripe down his back.

d. ***running dog***: (see quot.). *local.*

1628 *Orkney & Shetland Acts* in *Misc. Maitland Cl.* 203 That no man sall keip running doggis that runnes fra hous to hous or throw the cuntrie slaeing thair nychtbouris sheip.

e. ***running mate***, a horse entered in a race in order to set the pace for another horse from the same stable which is intended to win. Also in *transf.* use, a fellow candidate (*of* someone), usu. one standing for a subordinate office, and *spec.* the vice-presidential candidate in U.S. presidential elections; *gen.*, a partner, colleague, spouse, etc. orig. and chiefly *U.S.*

1868 H. W. WOODRUFF *Trotting Horse of Amer.* xxxvi. 284 He has been..especially great for his knack at going with a running-mate. **1883** *Illustr. Sporting & Dramatic News* 30 June 399/2 'How fast do you think she can trot with a running-mate?' the reporter asked; a 'running-mate' it is, perhaps, unnecessary to explain, being a horse harnessed to a pole, which gallops or 'runs' while the other trots. **1900** *Rev. of Reviews* Jan. 7/2 A better man could hardly be selected as Mr. McKinley's 'running mate'. **1902** B. WHITLOCK *13th District* 61 There were..pictures of the candidate himself,..and pictures, too, of his 'running mate', the candidate for vice-president. **1911** *Munsey's Mag.* Mar. 865/2 His running-mate, Elizabeth Brice, in spite of the eyes she makes, also inspires liking. **1935** *N. Amer. Rev.* Mar. 275 Nast's representation of a running-mate by a tag on the coat-tail of the head of the ticket is a fair indication of popular interest and respect. **1944** *Newsweek* 31 July 25/1 The substitution of Sen. Harry S. Truman of Missouri for Vice President Henry A. Wallace as Mr. Roosevelt's running mate. **1953** *Economist* 25 July 258/1 Eisenhower and his running-mate, Senator Nixon, spoke in stern criticism. **1958** *Listener* 21 Aug. 255/1 From President Nasser's point of view, the Sudan would be a far more desirable running-mate in the United Arab Republic than Syria. **1968** R. F. ADAMS *Western Words* 261/1 *Running mate*, a cowboy's term for his pal or his wife. **1968** W. SAFIRE *New Lang. Politics* 389/1 In horseracing, a single stable will often enter two horses in a race, the lesser horse used as a pacesetter and called a running mate. This second horse usually vanishes into obscurity. **1972** D. H. LAURENCE *Bernard Shaw: Coll. Lett. 1898-1910* 188 A similar letter had been posted..to women voters, appealing to them to vote for Shaw and his five Progressive running-mates to protect women's rights in the Borough. **1973** 'D. HALLIDAY' *Dolly & Starry Bird* i. 2, I..shared digs with my running mate, a photographer. **1977** *Irish Times* 8 June 8/6 His running-mate, Alice Glenn, received 1,240 first preferences in Dublin North-Central in 1973.

8. a. Of persons: Cursory, hasty. *rare*$^{-1}$.

1588 LAMBARDE *Eiren.* IV. xiv. 553 Howsoeuer the booke ..or the Statute..may seeme (to a running Reader).

†**b.** *Mil.* = FLYING *ppl. a.* 4 d. *Obs.*

1591 UNTON *Corr.* (Roxb.) 255, I respecte not the dangers soe much as I doe the discommodities of a runinge campe, wherin we have neither lodginge nor good victualls. **1624** CAPT. SMITH *Virginia* 152 That they should be as a running Army till this were effected. ? **1630** SIR R. GORDON *Hist. Earldom Sutherland* (1813) 198 Earle Alexander, to prevent such suddent incursions thereefter, did alwayes manteyn a cursarie and runing guard. **1652-66** in Gilbert *Contemp. Hist. Ireland* I. 41 A runinge armie consisting of 4,000 foote and 400 horse.

c. Employed to run as a messenger, etc.

1604 in Peacock *Rom. Cath. Yorks.* (1872) 23 Running Recusant or Messanger among [them]. **1689** *Lond. Gaz.* No. 2446/4 One George Tough, a Scotch Running Footman, of short Stature. **1721** RAMSAY *Content* 276 No broken China-bowls disturb the joy Of waiting handmaid, or the running-boy. **1791-1856** [see FOOTMAN 3].

transf. **1825** DANNELEY *Dict. Music*, *Laufer*, or Running Footman, groups of ascending or descending notes.

d. Moving rapidly about, esp. in the course of one's business or profession. Also *transf.*

1611 COTGR., *Coureur*,..also, a roamer, or wanderer abroad; one whose shooes are made of running leather; one that neuer keepes at home, or where he should be. *a* **1700** B. E. *Dict. Cant. Crew*, *Running-stationers*, Hawkers, or those that cry News and Books about the Streets. **1845** CARLYLE *Cromwell* (1871) I. i. 93 He might be a 'Running Lecturer', not tied to one locality. **1851** MAYHEW *Lond. Lab.* I. 214 That order or species of the pattering genus known as 'running patterers', or 'flying stationers'.

e. Taking to flight.

1897 SIR G. T. GOLDIE in *Times* 23 Jan. 13/1 It is more humane to shoot down promptly a few running carriers than to sacrifice the lives of some 2,000 men of a column.

f. ***running dog*** [tr. Chinese *zǒugǒu*, f. *zǒu* to run + *gǒu* dog]: in communist terminology, one who is subservient to counter-revolutionary interests; a lackey (see LACKEY *sb.* 1 c). Also in generalized use.

1937 E. SNOW *Red Star over China* IX. iv. 325 Vanguards of young Moslems were..urging the overthrow of the 'Kuomintang running-dog'. **1961** tr. *Mao Tsetung's Sel. Works* IV. 284 Without a revolutionary party,..it is impossible to lead the working class and the broad masses of the people in defeating imperialism and its running dogs. **1968** *Guardian* 13 July 9/5 The Kremlin's fears that the Czechoslovak revolution has become a treacherous running dog of the West. **1969** R. QUEST *Cerberus Murders* xxi. 119 This is how we worked—we were not a team and I was certainly not his running-dog. **1970** [see *housenigger* s.v. HOUSE *sb.*^{1} 24]. **1977** 'E. CRISPIN' *Glimpses of Moon* xi. 226 'Imperialist running-dogs,' said the hunt saboteuse. **1978** J. UPDIKE *Coup* (1979) iii. 98 He admired the French, he admires the polluting Americans and their new running dogs the Chinese.

g. ***running back***: in American football, a back whose function is to run carrying the ball.

1924 *Collier's* 20 Dec. 38/4 There has been no running back in football history who had these baffling, bewildering qualities to such an extent. **1962** R. WALKER *Compl. Bk. Backfield Play* ii. 28 What distinguishes a back from a linesman? Many ends would make outstanding running backs. **1967** R. GRAVES *Guide to Mod. Football Offense* vi. 47 In discussing techniques and drills involved in backfield play, we will place the position of fullback and tailback under the classification *running backs*... Since the play of the quarterback is uniquely different from that of running backs, the fundamental requirements of his position will be discussed separately. **1971** L. KOPPETT *Guide to Spectator Sports* ii. 50 And the halfback and fullback are simply 'running backs'. **1979** *Arizona Daily Star* 5 Aug. (Parade Suppl.) 6/1 Susie Forton played running back and middle linebacker for the Vikings.

9. Of plants: Creeping, climbing, or spreading rapidly; sending out many runners. Also in specific names, as ***running thyme***, ***twitch***, etc. ***running moss*** = CLUB-MOSS; ***running postman*** = *coral-pea* s.v. CORAL *sb.*^{1} 9.

1548 TURNER *Names Herbes* (E.D.S.) 35 Elatine.. groweth amonge the corne and in hedges; it maye be named in englishe running Buckwheate or bynde corne. *Ibid.* 72 Serpyllum..is of .ij. sortes. The one is called..in englishe runnyng tyme. **1615** W. LAWSON *Country Housew. Gard.* (1626) 16 There is another way..to get not onely Plants for graffing, but Sets to remaine for Trees, which I call a Running Plant. **1634** FORD *Perkin Warbeck* I. i, He's but a running weed, At pleasure to be pluck'd up by the roots. **1786** ABERCROMBIE *Gard. Assist.* 72 Beds of close running plants, as mint, &c. **1790** W. H. MARSHALL *Rural Econ. Midland* I. 211 Running Twitch, *agrostis alba*, creeping bentgrass. **1845** Running moss [see MOUNTAIN LAUREL]. **1855** *Jrnl. R. Agric. Soc.* XVI. I. 111 Running weeds..being spudded up. **1876** BRITTEN & HOLLAND *Dict. Eng. Plant-n.*, Running Moss, *Lycopodium clavatum*. **1898** E. E. MORRIS *Austral Eng.* 247/1 *K[ennedya] prostrata* is called the Coral Pea..or Running Postman. **1917** H. H. RICHARDSON *Fortunes R. Mahoney* I. ix. 87 The short-lived grass was picked out into patterns by the scarlet of the Running Postman. **1945** E. STEP *Wayside & Woodland Ferns* (ed. 2) 129 These local names [for common club-moss] are.. numerous... Others are..Lamb's-tail, Running Moss, Robin Hood's Hatband, [etc.]. **1962** Running postman [see *coral-pea* s.v. CORAL *sb.*^{1} 9].

†**10.** Volatile, flighty, giddy. *Obs.*

1571 in S. H. Sole *Jesu's Psalter* (1888) 90 The mocyons of my renninge mind. **1579** GOSSON *Sch. Abuse* (Arb.) 70 Newe cuttes are the paternes of running heads. **1603** KNOLLES *Hist. Turkes* (1621) 920 Of Maximillian the emperour, or of the duke of Muscovie, both men of running wits. **1653** R. SANDERS *Physiogn.* 104 A Vagabond, one of an unsetled Running head.

Comb. **1599** *Broughton's Lett.* v. 17 A paradoxicall expositor,..a forlorne Pharisee, a running-headed fugitiue.

11. a. Of metre, music, etc.: Of a smooth, easy, or rapid character. Also in phr. ***running rhythm***, used by G. M. Hopkins to denote common English metre.

1589 PUTTENHAM *Eng. Poesie* I. v. (Arb.) 26 It appeareth, that our vulgar running Poesie was common to all the nations of the world besides. **1593** NASHE *Christ's T.* Wks.

(Grosart) IV. 109 The younge men in their merry-running Madrigals..for thee, should haue honoured mee. **1608** WILLET *Hexapla Exod.* 231 So should church musike..be.. not with diuisions and running catches. **1673** *True Notion Worship of God* 56 Without this all other Sermons are but empty sounds..; they are running divisions upon Religion to them that have not yet perceived the grounds. **1743–4** MRS. DELANY *Life & Lett.* (1861) II. 262 Her notes are more distinct, and there is something in her running-divisions that is quite surprising. **1789** TWINING tr. *Aristotle's Poet.* 72 *note*, The Trochaic or running metre here spoken of. *c* **1883** G. M. HOPKINS in *Poems* (1967) 45 The poems in this book are written some in Running Rhythm, the common rhythm in English use, some in Sprung Rhythm, and some in a mixture of the two. Common English rhythm, called Running Rhythm above, is measured by feet of either two or three syllables. **1957** N. FRYE *Anatomy of Criticism* 263 The sixteenth century was a period of experiment, mainly in verse *epos* or running rhythm, to use Hopkin's term. **1970** J. T. SHIPLEY *Dict. World Lit. Terms* (ed. 3) 284/2 *Running rhythm*, the common Eng[lish] rhythm, measured by feet of 2 or 3 syllables... Opp[osed] by G. M. Hopkins to sprung rhythm.

†**b.** Of persons: Fluent. *Obs.*$^{-1}$

1628 FELTHAM *Resolves* II. lix, The running Montaigne speaks of such another.

12. Of a ship: Sailing in time of war without a convoy.

1816 G. J. BELL *Comm. Law Scot.* (1826) I. 621 *note*, 1. That this was a prize; 2. That it was a running ship: both of which facts, though material, were concealed. **1834** MARRYAT *P. Simple* lx, I was sent home..in a running vessel.

13. *Med.* Of the pulse: (see quot. 1901).

1898 P. MANSON *Tropical Diseases* xviii. 291 The pulse becomes small and running. **1901** W. OSLER *Princ. & Pract. Med.* I. (ed. 4) 19 In the extreme prostration of severe cases it may reach 150 or more and is a mere undulation—the so-called running pulse.

III. 14. a. Performed with, or accompanied by, a run; hence, rapid, hasty. Also in various (chiefly *U.S. Sporting*) phrases, as ***running attack, game, start*** (see quots.).

a **1300** *Cursor M.* 26732 Qua will yeild a-cuntes right He agh it for-wit for to dight, Ne tell noght ouer wit renand ras. *c* **1450** *Fencing w. two-handed Sword* in *Rel. Ant.* I. 308 Smyte a rennyng quarter sory owte of thy honde. *c* **1470** *Golagros & Gaw.* 910 Twa rynnyng renkis raith the riolyse has tane, Ilk freik to his feir. **1639** FULLER *Holy War* III. viii. (1840) 128 Though the French king thought with a running pull to bear the city away. **1670** MILTON *Hist. Eng.* II. 72 The fourth Summer..he spent in settling and confirming what the year before he had travail'd over with a running Conquest. **1720** DE FOE *Capt. Singleton* (1907) 115 He had taken a running leap, I suppose, and with all his might had thrown himself clear over our palisades. **1775** ADAIR *Hist. Amer. Ind.* 396 He was obliged to support nature with such herbs, roots, and nuts, as his sharp eyes, with a running glance, directed him to snatch up in his course. **1838** *Encycl. Metrop.* (1845) XXV. 301/1 Nautical surveys are sometimes conducted under canvass when a landing cannot be effected, which is termed a *running survey*. **1841** R. H. DANA *Seaman's Man.* 84 A Flying Moor, sometimes called a Running Moor. **1892** *Daily News* 12 July 2/7 A clever running catch by Newham at third man got rid of the Yorkshiremen. **1910** W. CAMP *Bk. Foot-Ball* viii. 306 Probably there is greater fascination in the running game than in any other department of foot-ball... There is no play that brings the spectators to their feet to such wild enthusiasm as a good run. **1929** D. RUNYON in *Hearst's Internat.* July 125/1 Dave the Dude is more corned than anybody else, because he has two or three days running start on everybody. **1961** J. S. SALAK *Dict. Amer. Sports* 375 *Running play*,..a play during which there is a runner and which is not followed by a kick or forward pass from behind scrimmage line. **1971** L. KOPPETT *Guide to Spectator Sports* ii. 56 To stop a running attack, a defensive line must hold its ground. **1976** *Webster's Sports Dict.* 160/2 *Flying start*, auto racing, a start of a race in which the competitors are already moving as they cross the starting line or receive the starting signal (also called *running start*). **1977** *New Yorker* 10 Oct. 177/1 Princeton, which has another useful quota of real heavyweights..has as well a sturdy running attack, now that Isom is paced by Larson.

†**b.** Of a banquet, collation, etc.: Taken hurriedly; slight. Also *fig.* of a whipping. *Obs.*

1613 SHAKS. *Hen. VIII*, I. iv. 12 Some of these Should finde a running Banket, ere they rested, I thinke would better please 'em. *Ibid.* v. iv. 69 Besides the running Banquet of two Beadles, that is to come. *a* **1661** FULLER *Worthies* (1840) III. 2136 A running collation to stay his stomach—no set meal to satisfy his hunger. *c* **1728** EARL OF AILESBURY *Mem.* (Roxb.) 575 The evening of the birthday I gave a great ball and a running collation. [**1734** WATTS *Reliq. Juv.* 49 When persons, each for themselves, took a slight repast, in a running manner.]

c. ***running fire***, a rapid successive discharge of firearms by each of the men forming a rank or ranks; a rapid and continuous fire. Also *transf.*

1629 *Descr. S'hertogenbosh* 27 They followed Eastward the one after the other, round about the Leager, as a running Fire. **1702** *Lond. Gaz.* No. 3838/1 Her Majesty's Companies of Foot, with the Militia.., in two Lines, made as many running Fires. **1822** *Creevey Papers* (1904) II. 36, I kept up a kind of running fire upon Coke. **1854** R. MONCKTON MILNES in *Life* (1891) I. xi. 497 The Duke and Sir Robert keep up a running fire of banter, accusing one another reciprocally. **1860** W. G. CLARK *Vac. Tour* 22 The crowd kept up a running fire of vivas to pass the time.

d. ***running battle, running fight***, a naval engagement carried on during a retreat or flight; any military engagement which constantly changes its location. Also *transf.* and *fig.* (in later use, perh. influenced by sense 17 a).

1690 *Lond. Gaz.* No. 2595/3 The *Grafton* Sloop has brought into Dartmouth a French Privateer.., which she took the 18th instant, after a running fight of 3 hours. **1707** *Ibid.* No. 4386/2, 3 French Privateers..attack'd a Dutch Ship.., who maintain'd a running Fight. **1760–72** H. BROOKE *Fool of Qual.* (1809) III. 83 They crouded away.., maintaining a running fight with their stern-chace. **1823** BYRON *Island* II. xxi, We'll make no running fight, for that were base. **1846** DICKENS *Battle of Life* II, It could hardly be said of these conflicts that they were running fights. **1916** 'TAFFRAIL' *Pincher Martin* xvii. 317 The *Mariner* and various other destroyers were present with the battle-cruisers throughout the first shock of the engagement and the running fight which ensued. **1928** G. B. GRINNELL *Two Great Scouts* iv. 65 The Pawnee warriors sprang on their horses and set out in pursuit of the enemy. During a running fight, the Pawnees killed a number of Sioux. **1945** *Ann. Reg. 1944* I. 2 The raiders..carried on a running fight with German fighter planes. **1967** in G. Marx *Groucho Lett.* 13 (*heading*) Running battle with Warner Brothers. **1974** [see MOTOR-CYCLE *sb.*].

e. ***running repairs***, hurried, minor, or temporary repairs made to machinery, equipment, etc., while in service. Also *transf.*

1913 *Autocar Handbk.* (ed. 5) i. 16 He [*sc.* the chauffeur] should do most of the running repairs, such as tyre repairs. **1924** KIPLING *Debits & Credits* (1926) 166 We'd been sent back for rest an' runnin'-repairs, back pretty near our base. **1951** N. MARSH *Opening Night* vi. 134 He..effected a number of what he called running repairs to her make-up and hair. **1957** *Encycl. Brit.* XVIII. 935/2 Most yards of any considerable size also include, or have adjacent, facilities for servicing of, and running repairs to, cars and locomotives. **1971** D. J. SMITH *Discovering Railwayana* x. 59 *Running repairs*, small scale repairs carried out in a 'running' or engine shed. **1973** K. BENTON *Craig & Jaguar* vii. 89 Your nose is shiny..Make some running repairs while we leave you for a moment.

f. ***running jump***, a jump preceded and augmented by a run. Usu. *fig.*, esp. in phr. ***to take a running jump (at oneself)***, freq. used colloq. as an expression of hostility, contempt, or indifference to someone.

1914 E. A. POWELL *Fighting in Flanders* i. 18 Thompson took a running jump. **1920** S. LEWIS *Main Street* xxxv. 415 There aint a town..got a better chance to take a running jump..right up into the two-hundred-thousand class. **1933** M. LOWRY *Ultramarine* ii. 76 You go and take a running jump at yourself. **1953** A. UPFIELD *Murder must Wait* xi. 104 Tell your Chief Commissioner to take a running jump at himself. **1954** J. B. PRIESTLEY *Magicians* vi. 120 The public can take a running jump at itself. I stopped liking people a long time since. **1959** 'R. MACDONALD' *Galton Case* xii. 97 Tell him to take a running jump in the Truckee River and do us all a favor. **1968** *Landfall* XXII. 22 If you think I'm subsidizing you..you can take a running jump at yourself. **1972** M. GILBERT *Body of Girl* xx. 180, I told her to take a running jump at herself. The only person who could make trouble for *me* would be old Henry Prior.

g. ***running fix***, a fix obtained by determining bearings at different times and making allowance for the distance covered by the observer in the interval.

1916 S. F. CARD *Navigation Notes & Examples* vii. 32 A running fix is the position obtained from two position lines by observations at different times, allowing for the run in the interval. **1942** *Tee Emm* (Air Ministry) II. 82 Here's a good tip to save yourself a running fix. **1974** K. WILKES *Pract. Yacht Navigator* (ed. 2), ix. 119 The accuracy of the running fix depends on the correctness of the direction and distance travelled over the ground between the two bearings.

15. ***running hand***, a cursive form of script.

1648 HEXHAM II. s.v. *Loopen*, To write with a Running hand. **1685** J. MATLOCK *Fax Nova Artis Scribendi* 22 The Running-Hand begets a great freeness and readiness in those Letters, in which it is composed. **1763** MASSEY *Orig. & Progr. Lett.* ii. 26 A neat and expeditious running-hand, so necessary in every business. **1815** SCOTT *Guy M.* xx, He entered them in the catalogue in his best running hand. **1900** SAYCE *Babylonians & Assyrians* x. 209 In Egypt the.. running-hand of the scribe developed out of the primitive pictographs.

attrib. **1784** ASTLE *Orig. & Progr. Writing* 106 The running hand Saxon letters are more like the pure or elegant Saxon which succeeded them.

IV. 16. a. Carried on or extending continuously. Used *esp.* of architectural or decorative ornament. Also with advs., as ***running-around***.

1390–1 *Durham Acc. Rolls* (Surtees) 391 Freyns, tays, et rynnyng orfrays. **1776** G. SEMPLE *Building in Water* 139 The first Course of the Grating is to be let in by a running Mortice. **1849** GREENWELL *Coal-Trade Terms*, *Running Balk*, a balk set in the direction of a drift, at its side, instead of across it, to form a support for the cross balks. **1861** SIR C. BARRY in *Life* (1867) vi. 186 The ground..of a warm yellowish tint, covered with a running foliage. **1870** E. PEACOCK *Ralf Skirl.* I. 136 A running pattern composed of peonies and sun-flowers. **1901** *Westm. Gaz.* 11 July 3/2 A running-around insertion of either guipure or Valenciennes.

b. ***running title, head(line)***, a short title or headline placed at the top of the page, sometimes restricted to one which is continued throughout the whole of a book.

1668 WALLIS in *Corr. Sci. Men* (1841) II. 492 The running title on the several heads is easily added, being the same with that of each chapter. **1691** MIÉGE *Eng. Gram.* (ed. 2) 130 Besides this general Title, there is commonly at the head of every Page a Title expressed in few Words, called the Running Title. **1756** C. LUCAS *Ess. Waters* II. 60 The running titule over every following page is De Uso Aquæ Marinæ. **1816** *2nd Rep. Comm. Public Rec.* App. ¶11, The Collection now technically called The Fœdera, from the First Word of its Running-title. **1839** HANSARD *Treat. Printing* (1841) 85 He..places at the top..the running head, or line which indicates the title of the work or the subject of the page or chapter. **1888** JACOBI *Printers' Vocab.* 117 *Running headline*, the fixed or general title of the volume as distinct from the chapter or section headline.

c. Of measurements: Linear.

1663 GERBIER *Counsel* 48 Work rated on running measure. **1703** R. NEVE *City & C. Purchaser* 121 Some Cornishes.. are measur'd, and rated by the Foot Running-measure, i.e. by the number of Feet in length only. **1797** BILLINGSLEY *Agric. Somerset* 79 The expence of a list-wall may be thus calculated per rope of twenty feet running length. **1812** J. SMYTH *Pract. of Customs* (1821) 14 Linens particularly..are generally measured by running measure, being no more than taking the length of the piece from one end to the other. **1889** WELCH *Text Bk. Naval Archit.* iv. 73 It is usual to state the weight per square foot of material in the former case, and per running foot in the latter.

17. a. Continuous, sustained; going on, carried on, right through or continuously; also, continually produced or maintained; constantly repeated or recurring.

1492 in *Somerset Med. Wills* (1901) 300 That..there be in the church of the seid priory euery day whiles the wordle standeth a rennyng masse ther seyd. **1622** MALYNES *Anc. Law-Merch.* 207 There are two manner of Lotaries, namely Standing Lotaries, and Running Lotaries:..the latter to bee drawne daily and at all conuenient houres. **1629** H. BURTON *Truth's Triumph* 352 If it bee but a running lottery, wherein the whole countrey is coosened. **1707** HEARNE *Coll.* (O.H.S.) II. 68 He has put out short running Notes upon Ovid's Epistles. **1793** BURKE *Corr.* (1844) IV. 159 There is a perpetual running allusion to events and actions, as well as new laws and customs. **1822** HAZLITT *Table-t.* Ser. II. ix. (1869) 188 His face is the running comment on his acting. **1865** TYLOR *Early Hist. Man.* iii. 36 With a running accompaniment of grunts. **1888** BRYCE *Amer. Commw.* III. 603 The apparent coldness of the audience, which..refuses him the running encouragement of cheers. **1966** *This is Bill-Broking* (Allen, Harvey & Ross Ltd.) 34 *Running yield*, the interest rate on an investment, expressed in terms of a percentage on the capital invested. **1966** *Listener* 17 Nov. 732/1 A series of comic set-pieces linked into a wildly slapstick context by carefully contrived running gags. **1973** *Daily Tel.* 7 Mar 21 At the issue price of £99½ the 1980 stock will give a running yield of 9·05 p.c. and a gross redemption yield of 9·10 p.c. to 1980. **1973** *Times* 30 Oct. 4/6 As he walked the Dalai Lama gave a running audience.

b. Of accounts, etc.: Allowed to run on for a certain (specified or indefinite) time.

1742 RICHARDSON *Pamela* III. 250 Makes up his running Accounts to Mr. Longman. **1853** LYTTON *My Novel* I. ix, The Squire..gave him a running lease of seven, fourteen, or twenty-one years, at a rent merely nominal. **1891** C. ROBERTS *Adrift Amer.* 40, I had a running order on the store.

c. ***running days***: (see quots.).

1816 G. J. BELL *Comm. Law Scot.* (1826) I. 577 In settling the lay-days, or the days of demurrage, the contract generally specifies 'working days', or 'running days'... Under the latter, the days are reckoned like the days in a bill of exchange. **1849** FREESE *Comm. Class-bk.* 41 'Lay-days'.. are either running-days, or working-days, as may be agreed upon; the former including Sundays and holidays, the latter excluding them.

d. (See quot.)

1886 C. SCOTT *Sheep Farming* 28 By a running ewe stock is understood the practice of buying-in ewe lambs to maintain the flock, and selling all the produce.

e. ***running commentary***, a sustained series of comments on events, actions, utterances, etc., as they occur; a continuous description of an event in progress, *spec.* a broadcast report of a game, contest, or race.

1811 C. LAMB in *Reflector* IV. 342 The writings of Fuller are usually designated by the title of quaint... But..his way of telling a story, for its eager liveliness, and perpetual running commentary of the narrator happily blended into the narration, is perhaps unequalled. **1824** *Mirror of Literature* 17 Jan. 44/2 The Count's running commentary upon these evolutions, too, is a *chef d'oevre* in the art of reasoning. **1853** R. S. SURTEES *Mr. Sponge's Sporting Tour* lxi. 348 His pleasure was, perhaps, damped by a running commentary he overheard through the lattice-window of the stable. **1858** *Chambers's Jrnl.* 4 Dec. 359/1 (*heading*) Bill Fustian's running commentary on the doings of the respectable classes. **1883** J. M. BARRIE *Auld Licht Idylls* xii. 239 He loved to recite long screeds from Spenser, with a running commentary on the versification and the luxuriance of the diction. **1905** *Pall Mall Mag.* July 40/2 She gasped and..trembled out her tale of horrors, while..her daughter, ..in the exasperating fashion of the chorus in a Greek play, kept up a running commentary, emphasising the points. **1927** *B.B.C. Hand-bk. 1928* 140/1 Running commentaries fall easily under two different headings—Sporting and purely Descriptive. **1929** *B.B.C. Year-Bk. 1930* 146 Tennis ..provides excellent material for a running commentary, although the commentators find the strain of following the strokes..with an instantaneous spoken description very great. **1931** *Discovery* Dec. 386/1 This was the first scientific film of its kind to be synchronized with the running commentary. **1946** G. N. M. TYRRELL *Personality of Man* VI. xviii. 158 Then there is Mrs. Willett's running commentary. She is always there, interjecting her own comments. **1966** B. JOHNSTON *Armchair Cricket* 26 He has to comment rather than give a *running* commentary which is basically what happens with football or racing on television. **1969** M. PUGH *Last Place Left* xvii. 124, I drank tea with my back to the floor but Katriona gave me a running commentary until Nell rejoined me. **1977** D. BENNETT *Jigsaw Man* iv. 71 I'll give you a sort of running commentary... Reorient you... The village is on the right.

f. ***running set*** (see SET *sb.*[2] 14), a country dance, originating in the Appalachian Mountains, in which the dancers perform a number of figures in quick succession.

1918 C. SHARP *Country Dance Book* v. 9 The Running Set ..differs materially from any other known form of the Country-dance. **1927** *Observer* 27 Nov. 14/5 He got..from elsewhere in that district, the 'running set'—a fine dance which has been received here with outspoken enthusiasm. **1938** *Times* 10 Jan. 10/4 Two American dances, the Running Set and the Big Set, were shown. **1964** W. G. RAFFÉ *Dict.*

Dance 431/2 *Running set*, an English square dance in quick time, preserved in villages of the Appalachian Mountains, in North America. *Ibid.*, Danced by four couples (sometimes more), the *Running Set* consists of an Introduction and some fourteen figures, which follow each other without pause. **1974** *Encycl. Brit. Micropædia* IX. 501/2 Historians trace the square dance to two derivatives of English country dance: the Kentucky running set, a rhythmic, complicated figure dance derived from pre-17th-century English round dances; and the cotillon.

18. (Placed after the sb.) Following each other; successive, in succession.

1719 Ramsay *To Arbuckle* 76 To be a dummie ten years' running. **1758** L. Temple *Sketches* (ed. 2) 34 It does not require a very exquisite Ear to write two smooth or even harmonious Lines running. **1848** J. H. Newman *Loss & Gain* iv. viii, He can speak seven hours running without fatigue. **1881** Mrs. Craik *Sydney* I. viii. 201 This is the third Sunday running that I have [etc.].

V. 19. Current, prevalent, general.

c **1449** Pecock *Repr.* iii. xi. 346 Bi his natural condicion and bi the rennyng condicioun of the world. **1530–1** *Durh. Househ. Bk.* (Surtees) 5, 2 qu. frumenti, rynnynge measour ad 9d. bus. **1570** Foxe *A. & M.* (ed. 2) 1050/1 To stoppe the running brutes of their holy assemblies, they should write Apologies. **1627** *Rep. Parishes Scotl.* (Bann. Cl.) 3 We walow it to be worth sex bollis..off rining wictuall. **1851** Mayhew *Lond. Lab.* (1861) III. 145, I generally get my 25*s.*, that's my running price, though I try for my 30*s.* **1865** Mozley *Mirac.* (1883) 166 Hence the confession of inferiority when this running supernaturalism was confronted by real miracles.

20. a. That is in progress, going on, or existing, at the present time.

1584 *Reg. Privy Council Scot.* III. 666 This present rynnand Parliament. **1688** Dryden *Britannia Rediv.* 49 That James this running century may view, And give his son an auspice to the new. **1726** Berkeley *Wks.* (1871) IV. 134 They might have been paid the subsequent years out of the running income. **1861** Mrs. H. Wood *E. Lynne* I. xv. 222 To make me forfeit my running quarter's salary.

†**b.** Of cash: Available for use. *Obs.*

1679 Dryden *Limberham* iv. ii, I have at present, no running cash to throw away. **1727** Swift *State Irel.* Wks. 1751 IX. 139 The running Cash of the Nation, which was about Five Hundred Thousand Pounds, is now less than Two, and must daily diminish.

†**c.** Of trade: Giving a certain turnover. *Obs.*

1706–7 Farquhar *Beaux' Strat.* i. i, I have a good running trade. **1736** *Gentl. Mag.* VI. 458/2 There are Multitudes of People in this Kingdom, who..just make a Shift to rub on, from Year to Year, upon Credit and a running Trade.

21. Temporary; †transitory. *rare.*

1632 J. Hayward tr. *Biondi's Eromena* 49 To prefix and give himselfe a law for his life, founded upon a running griefe, imagining it to be everlasting. **1851** *Jrnl. R. Agric. Soc.* XII. ii. 365 Occasionally..there is sown a 'running' crop of beans or seeds.

VI. 22. a. Moving easily or rapidly by mechanical means or as a piece of mechanism; easily moved, slid along, shifted, etc.

c **1425** *Cast. Persev.* 1076 in *Macro Plays*, Whyl I reste on my rennynge whel, I schal not suffre, if þat I may. **1459** *Paston Lett.* I. 482 Item, j. rynnyng bedde with a materas. *c* **1535** in *Yorks. Archæol. Jrnl.* (1886) IV. 323 Wt ij ronnyng dores and a shittynge dore. **1558** *Wills & Inv. N.C.* (Surtees, 1835) 163, ij fether bedds, a trussinge bed, a ronnyng bedd. **1603** Owen *Pembrokeshire* (1892) 62 But use for the most part a runinge fold of hurdels of cloven oake about foure foote heighe. **1648** Hexham ii, *Een Looperken*, a Running Pullie or Windlase. **1764** J. Ferguson *Lect.* 48 When the furrows become blunt and shallow by wearing, the running stone must be taken up. **1799** G. Smith *Laboratory* I. 19 The decorations that are usually fixed to these running rockets. **1851–4** *Tomlinson's Cycl. Useful Arts* (1867) II. 461/2 In the manufacture of plate glass a thick cylinder of cast brass, called a running roll, is used for spreading the glass over the casting table.

b. ***running mould*** (Plastering), a pattern moving on fixed guides and used to shape cornices and other mouldings.

1825 [see run *v.* 53 f]. **1911** *Encycl. Brit.* XXI. 786/1 Plain, or unenriched, mouldings are formed with a running mould of zinc cut to the required profile. **1955** N. W. Kay et al. *Mod Building Encycl.* 483/2 Solid cornices are..formed in the position they are to occupy, by a running mould, called a horse, which runs along guides fixed to the walls.

23. a. Of ropes, etc.: Capable of moving when pulled or hauled; *esp.* moving or passing through a block, ring, etc. Chiefly *Naut.*

a **1625** *Nomenclator Navalis* (Harl. MS. 2301), Running Roapes..are taken generally for all roapes that doth not stand fast to the Masts without veering or haveing [etc.]. **1632** Lithgow *Trav.* iv. 153 They drawe in his middle together so small with running cords, that they strike his body a two with one blow. **1688** Holme *Armoury* iii. xv. (Roxb.) 50/1 The Runner is generally taken for any rope running through a block which is called the running rope. **1753** Hanway *Trav.* (1762) I. ii. xvi. 72 Our boat had no keel, nor any running tackle. **1797** *Encycl. Brit.* (ed. 3) VIII. 669/1 For horses..who poke out their noses, a running snaffle is of excellent use. **1841** R. H. Dana *Seaman's Man.* 45 The parts of all tackles between the fasts and a sheave, are called the standing parts; the parts between sheaves are called running parts. **1885** C. F. Holder *Marvels Anim. Life* 67 A running bow-line [was] passed around the fish's tail.

Comb. **1740** Brookes *Art of Angling* 17 Running-Line-Angling is with one or two small Pellets of Lead to your Line without a Float.

b. ***running rigging***: (see rigging *sb.*² 2 a).

1667 *Lond. Gaz.* No. 159/4 We likewise Anchoring within a mile of them, to repair our running Rigging, and main shrowds. **1748** *Anson's Voy.* ii. ii. 135 To unlay a cable to work into running rigging. **1840** R. H. Dana *Bef. Mast* xxiii, He had got rid of all the useless blocks and running rigging. **1890** *All Year Round* 29 Mar. 304 The guide-ropes, the halliards, the running-rigging of the scenic show beneath [*sc.* in a theatre].

c. ***running belay*** (Mountaineering), a belay (see belay *sb.*) through which the climbing rope runs freely, and which acts as a pulley if the climber falls.

1941 T. A. H. Peacocke *Mountaineering* ii. 26 Without the use of slings, running belays are unsatisfactory. **1946** Leonard & Wexler in *Sierra Club Bull.* Dec. 91 He [*sc.* G. W. Young] is fully aware of the dynamic belay, referring to it as the 'running belay', one of the 'expert belays' that only great skill and strength can hope to regulate. **1956** C. Evans *On Climbing* iii. 52 When negotiating a difficult pitch, the leader will, if possible, arrange running belays at intervals. .. He..drives a piton into a crack, and runs his rope through a snap-link clipped to the..piton. **1968** P. Crew *Encycl. Dict. Mountaineering* 87/1 Apart from the ease of carrying, the fact that the sling goes *through* a nut, instead of *round* a chockstone, often makes the running belay more mechanically sound. **1973** C. Bonington *Next Horizon* xx. 274 Don went up..quickly and smoothly without bothering to protect himself with running belays.

24. a. Of knots, etc.: Slipping or sliding easily, esp. so as to catch something tightly.

1648 Hexham ii, *Gestrickt*, Laced, or Tyed in a running knot. **1687** A. Lovell tr. *Thevenot's Trav.* iii. 41 They use a certain Slip with a running-noose, which they can cast.. about a Mans Neck, when they are within reach of him. **1726** [see knot *sb.*¹ 1 b]. **1748** *Anson's Voy.* i. vi. 65 A thong of several fathoms in length,..with a running noose at one end of it. **1821** Scott *Pirate* xxxi, In your..profession [piracy]..every man speaks under correction of the yard-arm and a running noose. **1855** *Orr's Circle Sci., Organ. Nat.* III. 306 In the middle of the chamber a small upright stick is placed supporting two running loops of horse-hair. *c* **1860** H. Stuart *Seaman's Catech.* 24 A running eye is then spliced in the end.

b. ***running bowline*** (†***knot***), a bowline adapted to form a noose.

1726 Defoe *Four Years Voyages of Capt. George Roberts* 110, I got ready another Rope, at the end of which I made a running bowling knot, and the Noose so as to keep it open with one Hand. **1823** [see bowline¹ 2]. **1883** *Man. Seamanship* (Admiralty) 89 *Q.* What is a running bowline used for..? *A.* It is used for throwing over anything out of reach, or anything under water. **1911** *Encycl. Brit.* XV. 872/1 Running bowlines are formed by making a bowline round its own standing part... It is the most common and convenient temporary running noose. **1932** E. M. Brent-Dyer *Chalet Girls in Camp* vii. 111 The rope was swung down, and as it stopped swinging, Miss Wilson knew that Jo had it safely. 'Running bowline!' she called down. **1968** E. Franklin *Dict. Knots* 24 *Running bowline*, the knot which was universally used at sea whenever a noose was needed. Useful for commencing to tie a parcel.

25. a. ***running stitch***, a loose, open stitch.

1848 E. C. P. in C. H. Hartshorne *Eng. Medieval Embroidery* 128 An inner line of yellow floss silk in a running stitch. **1850** *Mech. Mag.* Feb. 99 A Machine for Sewing Cloth of all kinds with a Running Stitch. **1899** Miss Masters *Bk. Stitches* 5 A successful outlining, and one that is not so often used as it might be, is obtained by running stitch. **1967** E. Short *Embroidery & Fabric Collage* iii. 86 Although traditionally carried out by hand in running or back stitch, the quilting can be done on the sewing machine.

b. ***running string***, a drawing string.

1882 Caulfeild & Saward *Dict. Needlewk.* 428/2 *Running String*..denotes the ribbon, tape, braid, or Bobbin which is passed through a Hem, or double Running, by means of a bodkin.

26. a. Of a machine: In operation; working.

1896 *Law Times* C. 360/1, Sect. 9 does not prevent the cleaning of a fixed part of a running machine.

b. With advbs., as ***running-down*** (in sense 73 a of the vb.).

1968 *Times* 29 Nov. 13/7 A running-down pulsar might be found. **1973** L. Cooper *Tea on Sunday* xxiv. 177 For what was supposed to be a running-down business it all looked remarkably active.

27. ***running fit***: (see quots.).

1908 S. H. Moore *Mech. Engin. & Machine Shop Practice* vii. 184 A running fit is designed to allow the surfaces in contact to move or revolve freely over each other. *Ibid.*, Two formulas are given for running fits; one for close running fits, to be used in ordinary work.., and the other for free running fits, to be used for high-speeds, heavy pressures, rocker shafts, etc. **1953** W. H. Armstrong *Mech. Inspection* iv. 51 A running fit is one in which an allowance is made so that a shaft will be free to rotate in a bearing. **1964** S. Crawford *Basic Engin. Processes* xiv. 290 Running fits.., tolerances which allow the shaft to rotate freely in the hole.

Hence **ˈrunningly** *adv.* † (*a*) concurrently *with* something (*Obs.*) (*b*) rapidly, readily.

c **1449** Pecock *Repr.* v. iii. 499 The sect of Ebionytis.. helden the riȝtis and obseruauncis of the Iewis rennyngli with lawe of kinde. **1580** Hollyband *Treas. Fr. Tong*, *Couramment*,..runningly, swiftly, redily. **1736** Ainsworth *Eng.-Lat. Dict.*, Runningly, *cursim.* **1855** Browning *Men & Women, Master Hugues of Saxe-Gotha* vii, Played I not off-hand and runningly, Just now, your masterpiece?

ˈrunning-board. Also running board. [f. running *vbl. sb.*] †**1.** A narrow gangway on either side of a keel-boat. *U.S. Obs.*

1817 *Essex Inst. Hist. Coll.* (1866) VIII. 240 Our boat being very deep..[we] were obliged to give up after being at the expense of putting on running boards. **1834** H. Brackenridge *Recoll.* iv. 37 One night..I..lay.. on the running board (a plank at the edge of the boat, on which the men walk in pushing with the pole). **1843** *Amer. Pioneer* II. 271 Keel-boats..were provided with running boards, extending from bow to stern, on each side of the boat... The crew, divided equally on each side, set their poles near the head of the boat, and bringing the end of the pole to their shoulders, with their bodies bent, walked slowly down the running board to the stern.

2. a. A foot-board extending along the side of a locomotive, railway wagon, or tram, or one extending along the roof of a railway wagon. orig. and chiefly *U.S.*

1860 Clark & Colburn *Recent Practice Locomotive Engine* 51/2 The cab, domes, 'running-board', and other matters of external finish, are very much the same on most American engines. **1874** M. N. Forney *Catechism of Locomotive* 337 The running-boards are planks..placed on each side of the boiler to enable the locomotive runner or fireman to go from the cab to the front end of the engine when it is running. **1889** *Cent. Dict.*, *Running board*,..(*a*) A narrow platform extending along the side of a locomotive. (*b*) A horizontal board along the ridge of a box freight-car or the side of an oil-car, to form a passage for the trainmen. **1903** *Electrical World & Engin.* 14 Nov. 795/2 The 'mule' has two large hooks for the towropes and has also a running board and guard hand rail. **1917** C. Mathewson *Second Base Sloan* 284 The cars that buzzed and clanged their way past Wayne were filled to the running-boards. **1930** *Amer. Speech* V. 277 *Running-board* is a bit puzzling, but the speculation that it was derived from the old summer trolleys, now almost extinct in the north, is at least permissible. **1940** *Life* 4 Mar. 50/2 The rear-end brakeman ..makes an inspection tour along the 'running board', looking for loose brake beams or hot boxes. *a* **1966** 'M. na Gopaleen' *Best of Myles* (1968) 187 Particularly if the running board of the tram was already crowded with fat women.

b. A foot-board located on either side of a motor vehicle between the front and rear mudguards.

1907 S. Krausz *Practical Automobile Dict.* 26 *Running-board*, s., marchepied, s.m. **1910** *Sears, Roebuck Motor Buggy Booklet* 28 With the addition of running boards connecting front and rear fenders, convenient for shopping or business where frequent getting in and out is necessary. **1914** E. A. Powell *Fighting in Flanders* vii. 169 A big grey car shot down the road... Clinging to the running-board was her English chauffeur. **1927** M. de la Roche *Jalna* xii. 136 Wakefield mounted the running board and held the Michaelmas daisies out to her. **1929** *Daily Express* 14 Jan. 6/3 Heath, leaning over the running-board, shouted some unintelligible words. **1932** Kipling *Limits & Renewals* 139 Phil sat down on the running-board of Mr. Haman's car. **1959** *Motor* 7 Oct. 246/2 The body sides have now been carried out towards the rear to narrow down the running boards and reduce the protruding width of the rear wings. **1965** M. Bradbury *Stepping Westward* viii. 380 They sat on the running-board of the car. **1974** *Country Life* 17 Oct. 1104/1 There is the Volkswagen Beetle... Here in the 1970s we still have a car with very rounded lines, small windows, a very cramped interior and outside running boards.

3. A device used in positioning overhead power lines which enables several conductors to be pulled simultaneously using a single pulling line.

1898 E. J. Houston *Dict. Electr. Words* (ed. 4) 911/1 *Running-board*, a device employed in the construction of a heavy overhead line, consisting in placing a number of reels of wire, usually ten or more, on a spindle, and arranging a piece of wood as a cross-arm to which ten or more wires are attached, harnessing horses to the cross-piece, and then dragging the running board away as the wires are paid out from the reels, and passing them over their appropriate cross-arms, where they are at once secured to the insulators by line-men. **1964** E. B. Kurtz *Lineman's & Cableman's Handbk.* (ed. 4) xiv. 7 Tension stringing of bundled conductors. Usually two or three conductors are pulled simultaneously by one pulling line with the use of a unidirectional articulated running board.

running gear. orig. and chiefly *U.S.* Also **running-gear.** [f. running *ppl. a.*; in senses 1 and 3 a the plural form is used interchangeably with the singular.] **1.** The moving parts of a mill or other large machine.

1662 *Rec. East-Hampton, N.Y.* (1887) I. 201 Mr Backer shall have seven pounds for this year for tendinge the mill and maintayninge the runninge geares that is coggs and rounds. **1725** *New England Courant* 18–25 Jan. 2/2 The Wind...carry'd off the Top of the Mill, with the Shaft, Vanes, and running Geer, and brake them to Pieces. **1834** in J. S. Bassett *Southern Plantation Overseer* (1925) vi. 73 The runinge geares that is hear I cant under take to pick a crop with them. **1901** Merwin & Webster *Calumet 'K'* xiv. 262 Down in the cellar putting in the running gear for the 'cross-the-house conveyors'.

2. The rope and tackle used in handling (part of) a boat; = *running rigging.*

1838 J. F. Cooper *Homeward Bound* II. iii. 55 The standing rigging are the bones and gristle; the running gear the veins in which her life circulates. **1856** E. K. Kane *Arctic Explorations* II. iii. 48 We can burn hemp cable and cast-off running-gear. **1911** J. Barten *Compl. Naut. Pocket Dict.* 165/1 Running gear. **1962** A. G. Course *Dict. Naut. Terms* 163 *Running gear*, ropes, tackles, etc., that move in the course of ship handling or cargo working.

3. a. The wheels and axles of a cart or carriage. Also *transf.* and *fig.*

1857 D. H. Strother *Virginia Illustrated* 230 A shadowy group was dimly visible, a carriage mounted on the running-gear of a wagon, and drawn by four horses. **1876** *Encycl. Brit.* IV. 704/2 There is no wood on the Pacific coast from which any part of the running-gear of a good waggon can be made. **1904** *N.Y. World* (Mag. Sect.) 1 May 6/1 The running gear is dark red and the upholstering is drab. **1916** *Dialect Notes* IV. 348 *Running gear*, the remnants or 'carcass' of a fowl served up cold. **1923** *Ibid.* V. 208 *Runnin' gears*, Those portions of a wagon other than the box or bed. **1924** F. R. Bechdolt *Tales of Old-Timers* 363 The boy was driving a span of horses hitched to the running-gear of a lumber-wagon. **1941** *Amer. Speech* XVI. 24/1 Of a skinny person. 'He's got the running-gears of a katydid.' **1948** E. N. Dick *Dixie Frontier* xix. 208 The driver..fastened a big deep box on the axle or the front wheels of a wagon running-gear. **1953** Randolph & Wilson *Down in Holler* viii. 184

When an airplane crashed and burned, my neighbor viewed the wreckage. 'It looks *like the runnin'-gears of a grasshopper*,' said he. **1972** J. S. HALL *Sayings from Old Smoky* 53 (Someone or something) 'looks like the runnin' gears of a crow's nest'.

b. The wheels, axles, and suspension of a railway locomotive, carriage, or wagon; the steering, suspension, and wheel systems of a motor vehicle.

1853 *Ann. Rep. U.S. Commissioners of Patents* 64 Cars, railroad, running gear of. Henry D. Taylor. Newark, N.J. Feb. 3, 1852. **1877** *11th Ann. Rep. Proc. Master Car-Builders Assoc.* 57 Probably every one of us who has experience in handling foreign cars can fully realize the importance of our draw bars and oil-boxes, and, in fact, of all the running gear of the car. **1889** *Nat. Car & Locomotive Builder* Mar. 35/1, I have always believed that the running gear of railway rolling stock should be constructed of such strength and with such intelligence as to give it a high factor of safety. **1900** *Motor World* 8 Nov. 100/1 The motor is located centrally of the vehicle, and is hung on the upper section of the running frame, which is spring supported from the main tubular running gear. **1905** *Motor Man.* (ed. 7) v. 85 Periodical cleaning and inspection of all the running gear is..the best possible insurance against breakdowns. **1919** FRASER & JONES *Motor Vehicles* xxvi. 270 The parts of a motor vehicle not included in developing and transmitting power are classified under the general heading of running gear. This includes such parts as frames, springs, axles, wheels, brakes, steering gear, etc. **1932** *New Yorker* 14 May 32/2 It was a club-sedan,..with red running gear. **1957** *Encycl. Brit.* XIV. 284/1 The mechanical parts include those portions of the locomotive which make it suitable as a vehicle, *i.e.*, the running gear, and the cab or superstructure. **1959** *Motor Man.* (ed. 36) v. 99 What is often referred to as the running gear comprises the steering system, the springing or suspension, the brakes and the wheels and tyres. **1969** *Northern Territory News* (Darwin) *Focus '69* 13/2 (Advt.), Semi-trailer tippers. Tough structural design, coupled with the best hoist and running gear available, assures down time reduced to periodic servicing.

†**'runnion.** *Obs.* Also 7 **ronyon, runnyon.** [Of obscure origin.]

1. An abusive term applied to a woman.

The usual explanation 'a mangy creature' (after F. *rogne*) is due to Johnson s.v. *Runnion*, but under *Ronion* he defines it as 'a fat bulky woman'.

1598 SHAKS. *Merry W.* IV. ii. 195 Out of my doore, you Witch, you Ragge, you Baggage, you Poulcat, you Runnion, out, out. **1605** —— *Macb.* I. iii. 6 Aroynt thee, Witch, the rumpe-fed Ronyon cryes.

2. The male organ.

The piece is written in imitation of Chaucer.

1655 MENNIS & SMITH *Mus. Deliciæ* 86 He faire could gloze among the Country Wives, A lusty Runnyon ware he in his hose.

runny ('rʌnɪ), *a.* [f. RUN *v.* + -Y[1].] **a.** Tending to run or flow; having the consistency of liquid, fluid, not set; soft, melting, watery; (of eggs, etc.) soft-centred.

1817 *Niles' Reg.* XII. 165/2 This flour would prove similar to a previous baking of new flour (which was *runny*). **1904** *Eng. Dial. Dict.* V. 185/2 *Runny*,..inclined to liquefy. **1913** G. STRATTON-PORTER *Laddie* vii. 210 He slid in a whole plateful of bread, another of cake... Then we took some of every thing that wasn't too runny. **1935** M. MORPHY *Recipes of All Nations* 73 A well-made purée should be almost 'runny'—only just sufficiently thick to be eaten with a fork. **1937** *Evening News* 23 Mar. 15/5 (Advt.), No runny butter or sour milk: no more waste. **1951** *Good Housek. Home Encycl.* 524/1 A 'runny' jelly is very difficult to manipulate. **1957** J. FRAME *Owls do Cry* (1958) II. 103 Haven't I told you ..to leave the egg till it's..hard, that I don't like them runny? **1972** K. LO *Chinese Food* I. 43 Eggs are sometimes scrambled with minced meat, mushrooms, onions, lard and some good broth. The dish is called Runny Yellow Egg (*Liu Huang Ts'ai*), and is another good runny dish to eat with rice.

b. Of the nose: running, discharging mucus.

1951 J. STEINBECK *Log from 'Sea of Cortez'* p. xxxii, She was a red-eyed..woman with a runny nose. **1969** A. LURIE *Real People* (1970) 85 All he had produced so far was a slow pathetic drip and trickle, as if the fat marble cherub poised above the marble bowl had a bad runny nose.

Hence **'runny-,nosed** *a.*

1972 J. WILSON *Hide & Seek* ii. 32 A couple of runny-nosed children..tried to get on [the roundabout] too. **1976** M. HARTMANN *Leap for Sun* i. 28 Big-arsed nannies squatting on the pavements surrounded by runny-nosed kids.

‖**runo** ('ruːnəʊ). Also Runo; pl. **runot, runos.** [Finnish: cf. RUNE[2].] In Finland, a short poem or song on an epic or legendary subject; *spec*: one of the songs which together constitute the Kalevala, = RUNE[2] 2 b.

[**1802** J. ACERBI *Travels* I. xxiii. 301 The species of verse is called *runic*, from the ancient Gothic word *runoot*. *Ibid.* 317 These songs, called *jauho runot* or *mill-songs*, are..sung to a slow plaintive air.] **1895** *Oracle Encycl.* II. 653/1 It was long known that there lived amongst the Finns a great number of lyrics known as *Runot* ('Runic songs'). *Ibid.*, The discovery that many of these *Runot* could be dovetailed into a true and noble epic, based on the old myths. **1898** I. M. ANDERTON tr. *Comparetti's Tradit. Poetry of Finns* I. i. 3 There is one word, *runo*, which characterises and distinguishes the traditional poetry of the Finns. **1944** W. APEL *Harvard Dict. Music.* 266/2 Next follow the *runos* (sung to the traditional poems of epic characters, called 'runes'), which are melodic and rhythmically vigorous. **1954** *Grove's Dict. Mus.* (ed. 5) III. 238/1 The ancient melodies of the period following are the beautiful *runo* tunes mentioned above. *Ibid.*, Sibelius..has a distinctive *runo* style of his own. **1963** B. J. TIMMER tr. *De Vries's Heroic Song & Heroic Legend* vii. 143 Lönnrot was a folklorist, who set himself the task of collecting the older poetry of the Finns, in particular the epic songs or *runot*. **1974** *Encycl. Brit. Macropædia* VI. 910/2 Elias Lönnrot.., who composed this master-piece [*sc.* the *Kalevala*] by combining short popular songs (*runot*) collected by himself among the Finns, had absorbed his material so well, and identified himself so completely with the *runo* singers.

runo-, comb. form of mod.L. *runa* RUNE *sb.*[2], used in a few forms, as **runo'graphic** *a.*, pertaining to runic writing; **runo'logical** *a.*, pertaining to runes or runology; **ru'nologist**, one who studies or is skilled in runes; **ru'nology**, the study or science of runes.

1868 G. STEPHENS *Runic Mon.* II. 630 This, united to certain unusual *Runographic forms and to an archaism in the last word, has hitherto prevented its being correctly read. **1962** *N. & Q.* Dec. 451/2 Values he could have taken from contemporary *runological works. **1965** R. DEROLEZ in Bessinger & Creed *Medieval & Linguistic Stud.* 31 No satisfactory explanation has been offered for this runological revolution. **1977** *Ann. Bibliogr. Eng. Lang. & Lit. 1974* 214 The runological placing of the Caistor-by-Norwich inscription. **1847** I. A. BLACKWELL in M. Mallet *Northern Antiquities* (ed. 2) i. 247 These celebrated *Runologists.. arrived at the same interpretation of the characters. **1866** G. STEPHENS *Runic Mon.* I. 178 John Bure was a good runologist. **1894** *Academy* Oct. 258/3 The veteran runologist has here given a..catalogue of the more important runic inscriptions. **1971** S. E. MORISON *European Discovery Amer.: Northern Voy.* iii. 76 Every leading runologist of Scandinavia and Germany who has deigned to examine the inscription has called it a clumsy forgery. **1862** J. FARRER *Notice Runic Inscr. Orkneys* p. ix, My very imperfect acquaintance with *Runology. **1871** G. STEPHENS in *Archaeologia* XLIII. 98 Of late..great progress has been made in runology. **1887** *Athenæum* 17 Sept. 368/3 By this work the science of runology has been placed on a sound scientific basis.

run-off. Also **runoff.** Pl. **run-offs.** [f. RUN *v.*]

1. a. The amount of water that is carried off an area by streams and rivers after having fallen as precipitation; the water itself; also, water that runs straight off the ground without first soaking into it.

1892-3 *14th Rep. U.S. Geol. Surv.* 149 The run-off, that is, the quantity of water flowing from the land. **1895** J. W. POWELL in *Nat. Geogr. Monogr.* I. 6 The mean run-off by streams is more than half the run-off. **1910** *Westm. Gaz.* 19 Feb. 2/2 Iron ore, which stains all the other streams..and the run-off of the night's rain to the colour of tanyard. **1929** WEAVER & CLEMENTS *Plant Ecol.* ix. 190 It [*sc.* rainfall] may be of such a torrential nature that only part of it can be absorbed and the rest is lost as run-off. **1957** G. E. HUTCHINSON *Treat. Limnol.* I. iv. 229 A number of independent estimates of total runoff have been made by attempting to sum the rate of discharge of the rivers of the world. **1959** *Listener* 10 Sept. 378/2 The run-off from the winter snowfields of the Australian Alps. **1969** *Physics Bull.* Oct. 410/1 Calculated by subtracting runoff from rainfall, annual evaporation ranges from about 16 in per year in the north of England to 19 in per year in the Thames valley. **1970** T. HILLERMAN *Blessing Way* xiii. 109 He stopped at a pool where runoff had been trapped in a pocket of rocks. **1978** J. IRVING *World according to Garp* iv. 81 The runoff from the rain—washing over the Steering School, rinsing everything clean.

b. The process or fact of water, or what the water contains, running off from an area; an instance of this; (*N. Amer.*) the period when such a process occurs, esp. the spring thaw.

1935 *Discovery* Aug. 219/2 The rapid run-off causes disastrous floods at lower levels. **1944** F. CLUNE *Red Heart* 6 West of the Darling..the thirsty red soil soaks every particle of rain that falls, with no surplus for a run-off. **1949** W. VOGT *Road to Survival* v. 104 The rate of runoff can be reduced on even the steepest land. **1962** W. O. MITCHELL *Kite* iii. 25 As soon as the sky is blue and the run-off starts—down town every Saturday morning. **1972** *Times* 26 June 12/2 Sewage and run-off of fertilizer from agricultural land is eliminating desirable fish. **1980** *Beautiful British Columbia* Summer 4 This bucolic alternative becomes impossible when the snow flies and during spring runoff, as Duffey Lake Road then becomes impassable.

c. *attrib.*, as ***run-off map, rate, water.***

14th Rep. U.S. Geol. Surv. 150 For comparison with this run-off map a similar map showing the mean annual precipitation is introduced. **1937** *Sun* (Baltimore) 1 July 24/3 Slowing up the run-off rate of heavy rainfall. **1939** C. W. TOWNE *Her Majesty Montana* 95 Our farmers are fortified by thousands of dams for the storage of run-off waters for livestock needs and to supply irrigation for feed and hay crops. **1979** A. HAILEY *Overload* III. viii. 229 Hydroelectric power next year might be reduced by twenty-five percent because of the lack of runoff water.

2. a. A final deciding race held after a dead heat. Also in other kinds of contest.

1873 *Carthusian* June 56 Hanson and Jeaffreson ran a dead heat for second place... The run-off for the second prize was won by Hanson. **1893** *Outing* XXII. 155/1 In the run-off Harding had the best of the start. **1894** *Daily News* 13 Sept. 3/2 The former easily defeated his opponent in the run-off. **1963** H. GARNER in R. Weaver *Canad. Short Stories* (1968) 2nd Ser. 49 'You tryin' out for the bowling team, Eric?' he asked. 'Sure thing. You?' 'May as well. Run-offs are on Thursday night.' **1973** *Shooting Times & Country Mag.* 7 July 19/3 If the judges have difficulty in arriving at a result, they can arrange a more difficult 'run-off' for the top dogs.

b. Chiefly *U.S.* An election held to decide the issue between the two candidates who gained the largest number of votes in a previous indecisive election. Freq. *attrib.* or as *adj.*, esp. in ***run-off primary*** (see PRIMARY *sb.* 6).

1924 *Lit. Digest* 6 Sept. 8/2 Texas..has a double primary. If no one has a majority in the first primary election, a later 'run-off' primary is held, in which the voters choose between the two candidates receiving the highest number of votes at the first balloting. **1933** *Sun* (Baltimore) 15 Sept. 3/4 A. H. Carmichael, of Tuscumbia, and B. L. Malone, of Decatur, will face each other in a run-off primary October 3 for the Democratic nomination to Congress from the Eighth Alabama district. **1944** *Ibid.* 31 May 7/1 (*heading*) Alabama run-offs watched for clue to group's strength. **1954** *Economist* 31 July 365/2 In Oklahoma Senator Kerr failed to gain the necessary clear majority of the votes cast, and was threatened with having to fight a 'run-off' election against a rival millionaire, Mr Roy Turner. **1959** B. & R. NORTH tr. *M. Duverger's Polit. Parties* (ed. 2) II. i. 220 In primaries in the South where the nomination is conducted at a single ballot the Democratic party generally divides into two factions;..in the system with two successive primaries..the second or run-off primary operating in the event of no candidate securing an absolute majority at the first primary—the factions tend to increase in number. **1965** *N.Y. Times* 7 Dec. 4/2 (*heading*) De Gaulle silent on whether he will enter runoff. **1966** MRS. L. B. JOHNSON *White House Diary* 4 June (1970) 386 Today is the Democratic primary runoff and we had come home to vote. **1968** *Listener* 27 June 826/1 If General de Gaulle's victory at the polls is confirmed by the run-off vote next Sunday, he may well see this as a mandate for his projected social reforms. **1973** *Times* 31 Mar. 5/4 His nearest rival, Señor Ricardo Balbin, announced he would not contest a runoff. **1977** *Time* 21 Nov. 29/1 The gloves are expected to come off when Briscoe faces former City Councilman Jim McConn, a Houston developer, in a run-off next week.

3. a. The action or process of running off a person or thing in other senses of the vb.; a quantity run off or removed; *spec.* the material run off or produced by a mechanical process; a print run.

1843 J. H. GREEN *Exposure of Gambling* 96 The adversary, fearing that his hand is really the better hand, will, in preference to risking more, throw up his own hand, and forfeit what has already been bet. This is a run-off, as well as in cases where he has no money enough to meet the proposed bet. *a***1948** L. G. D. ACLAND *Early Canterbury Runs* (1951) 393 *Run off*,..sheep counted out from a mob without being drafted; e.g., 'I cannot buy the whole line. I will take a run off of 300.' Usually *fair r.o.* **1952** *Bull. Poetry Soc. Amer.* Oct. 4 An impromptu and rather novel program was offered: a run-off of a phonograph recording of a broadcast made in 1948 of poems from the PSA *Anthology*. **1967** A. L. LLOYD *Folk Song in England* i. 27 Several of these [broadsides] were produced in massive run-offs. **1972** *Times* 30 Oct. 19/4 Insurance companies are seldom capable of an accurate assessment of the outstanding liabilities on their current portfolio of business (a 'run-off'). **1979** *Church Times* 26 Oct. 7/3 The low price for such a well-produced volume must indicate a large run-off.

b. An instance of running off a railway or road.

1855 *Chicago Western Times* 9 Aug. 1/8 The frequency of these run-offs demands the special attention of all railroad directors. **1872** W. S. HUNTINGTON *Road-Master's Assistant* 87 It is best always to keep spare [switch] rods on hand, to be used in case of a run-off. **1970** *Courier-Mail* (Brisbane) 19 Mar. 6/2 An invitation..to the Transport Minister..to discuss whether runoff roads could be a means of preventing semi-trailer accidents in the Adelaide hills.

4. The dropping of fruit before it is ready for picking; = ***running off*** s.v. RUNNING *vbl. sb.* 7 e.

1921 *Jrnl. Pomol.* II. 170 If frost caused the 'Run off' on half the bush, why did it not do so on the other? **1974** *Daily Tel.* 6 June 6/4 A grower at Cropthorne, Worcestershire, said the level of fruit 'run-off'—unformed fruit shrivelling and falling from trees—was much higher than usual through lack of moisture.

5. *N.Z.* Also ***run-off paddock.*** (See quot. 1933.)

1933 *Press* (Christchurch, N.Z.) 25 Nov., *Run off*, paddock used with turnips or green feed on which the sheep may camp and get what extra feed they can. **1950** *N.Z. Jrnl. Agric.* Apr. 366/3 Utilisation of the heavier pockets [of coastal land] and sand dunes is complementary, the latter being used mainly as a winter run-off. *Ibid.* 389/1 During early winter they [*sc.* ewes] are rationed turnips, fed good hay, and driven off their turnip break on to a large run-off paddock daily.

6. *slang.* An act of urination.

1961 PARTRIDGE *Dict. Slang* Suppl. 1255/2 *Run off, have a*, to urinate. **1967** H. W. SUTHERLAND *Magnie* ix. 117 What with the cold and the beer she was bursting for a run off again... The nearest ladies she knew was at Pier Head.

'run-out. Also **run out, runout.** [f. RUN *v.*]

1. *Founding.* †**a.** (See quots.) *Obs.*

1825 J. NICHOLSON *Operat. Mechanic* 334 Releasing the pig-iron of its carbon..by placing it in an open furnace, termed a refinery, and by some a run-out furnace. **1881** RAYMOND *Mining Gloss.*, *Run-out fire*, a forge in which cast-iron is refined.

b. Leakage of molten metal from a cupola or a mould.

1888 *Lockwood's Dict. Mech. Engin.* 296 *Run out*, the escape of metal from a mould during the act of pouring, due to open joints somewhere. **1901** *Shop & Foundry Practice* (Colliery Engineer Co.) IV. xxxv. 20 If there is any breaking of joints by drawing the pattern or from a straining of the cope, allowing large fins or a run out, the metal will run into the vent channels..and fill them with iron. **1928** *Proc. Inst. Brit. Foundrymen* XX. 366 In Fig. 1—an ordinary scullery copper—it is quite obvious that if there be a runout there is little chance of saving the casting. **1960** R. LISTER *Decorative Cast Ironwork in Gt. Brit.* ii. 56 Possible defects in castings are manifold, and may be in the form of blow holes, unfused chaplets, wrong grain-structure, fractures, distortions, runouts, [etc.].

2. *Cricket.* An instance of a batsman being put out while trying to make a run.

1851 *Bell's Life* 21 Sept. 6/5 (*heading*) The 'runs out' and 'runs lost' at cricket. **1867** G. H. SELKIRK *Guide to Cricket Ground* vii. 122 Never run past the wicket, unless to save a run out, when you can stop yourself. **1891** [see RETURN *sb.*

12 e]. **1892** *Longman's Mag.* Aug. 440 Oxford began with a duck and a run out. **1930** *Morning Post* 16 July 11/6 Only once..during their many long partnerships has a run-out been recorded. **1950** W. HAMMOND *Cricketers' School* xv. 140 He broke the wicket from 30 yards away in one of the most startling run-outs I have ever seen. **1976** *Milton Keynes Express* 2 July 41/6 If it had not been for three run-outs they might have got nearer their mammoth target.

3. *Mountaineering.* The length of rope required to climb a single pitch; also *transf.*, a pitch climbed by means of a single length of rope.

1920 [see BELAYING *vbl. sb.* 2]. **1965** A. BLACKSHAW *Mountaineering* vii. 195 There are exceptions such as the routes on the Idwal Slabs in North Wales where many pitches involve run-outs of eighty feet or more. **1971** D. HASTON in C. Bonington *Annapurna South Face* xvii. 206 It was a long and tortuous pitch done in one run-out on one of our big ropes. *Ibid.* 214 My immediate prospect was a three hundred foot run-out to the top of the gully. **1972** —— *In High Places* ii. 28 It's slightly awkward to do full run-outs with three people on the rope.

4. An act or instance of running out, fleeing, or escaping; also *attrib.*, esp. in U.S. slang phr. ***to take a run-out powder***, to withdraw; to leave, abscond; cf. POWDER *sb.*[1] 2 h.

1920 *Our Navy* Aug. 33/1 The 'Wilmington' challenged us to a boat race, but when we slapped up a sack of good Chinese taels to back our team the 'Wily Willie' took a run-out powder and called off the race. **1928** *Amer. Mercury* May 80/1 The fair charmer has taken 'a run-out with the bank roll.' **1933** D. RUNYON in *Collier's* 28 Jan. 7/4 Well, The Sky says he sees no way of meeting these obligations and he is figuring the only thing he can do is to take a run-out powder. **1943** *Richmond* (Va.) *Times-Dispatch* 23 Aug. 2/1 (*heading*) Kiska forces disappointed by run-out. **1952** POHL & KORNBLATH in *Galaxy Sci. Fiction* July 147/2 You crossed us up with that cowardly run-out. *a* **1953** E. O'NEILL *Hughie* (1959) 14, I stuck it till I was eighteen before I took a run-out powder. **1968** 'E. PETERS' *Grass Widow's Tale* viii. 114 They came back for their money, just when she had everything planned for her run-out.

5. A mock auction. Cf. MOCK *a.* 2. Usu. with def. article or *attrib.*

1934 P. ALLINGHAM *Cheapjack* vii. 72 The London Mob were working the R.O. This is short for the 'Run Out'. **1938** F. D. SHARPE *Sharpe of Flying Squad* xv. 171 'Run out' shops disposing of valueless jewellery worked in conjunction with the pickpockets. *Ibid.* xxvii. 280 Run Out Shops have given me a good deal of work. Many of the methods of the Run Out Mob and their premises on which they hold their mock auctions of worthless junk range from small and cheap set-ups on the race-courses..to elaborate dens of swindle in the West End. **1939** J. B. PRIESTLEY *Let People Sing* x. 258 He told me his old partner, Charlie, had left him to join the run-out boys from Brum—that is, the gang from Birmingham running a fake auction—and, by the way, if anybody wants to see me lose my temper just let 'em talk as if I was on the run-out game. **1943** *Police Jrnl.* Mar. 69 *Run-out mob*, a gang that conducts mock auctions. **1959** *News Chron.* 16 Nov. 5 The run-out men..are mock auctioneers who draw large crowds with their showman's patter... As well as in Petticoat Lane, they operate in many of the seaside towns during the summer.

6. *Engin.* Deviation of a wheel, drill, etc., from its proper course; the extent of this.

1946 W. H. CROUSE *Automotive Mech.* xxiv. 512 Wobble or 'run-out' of the wheels can be checked by spinning the front wheels and holding a piece of chalk against the rim or side wall of the tire. **1951** C. W. KENNEDY *Inspection & Gaging* ii. 28 Common terms..are squareness, parallelism, waviness,..eccentric, run-out and out-of-line. **1975** BRAM & DOWNS *Manuf. Technol.* vii. 194 An important point of design is to reduce end thrust, to prevent bowing and flexing, producing as a consequence hole run-out and short drill-life. **1977** *Hot Car* Oct. 58/1 Subsequent to machining the wheels undergo a rigorous testing programme checking for run-out and wobble.

7. *Skiing.* = OUTRUN *sb.* 4.

1956 *Ski-ing* ('Know the Game' Series) 13/2 These [nursery slopes] should be of average steepness at the top, have a gentle gradient in the middle and a long flat run out so that the ski will come to a stop naturally if the skier is unable to control them. **1974** *Rules of Game* 239/1 There must be a wide, gently sloping, and unobstructed run-out at the finish [of a ski-slope].

8. On a gramophone record, (the blank groove traversing) the annular area between the label and the grooves carrying the recording. Freq. *attrib.* as ***run-out groove***.

1962 A. NISBETT *Technique Sound Studio* viii. 150 If the surface noise on the run in and run out of the two records is not sufficient..a 'blank'..record can be used to lend continuity of background. **1975** *Gramophone* May 2048/3 A new TD 145 turntable..has an automatic lift and shut-off device relying on electronic sensing of the run-out groove. **1976** *Ibid.* Nov. 768/2 What puzzles me is that both these discs do in fact bear the re-make matrix numbers on both label and needle run-out.

9. Special Comb.: **run-out table** (see quot. 1948).

1948 T. LYMAN *Metals Handbk.* 12/2 *Runout table*, in a rolling mill a plane area at the receiving end, for holding rolled metal. **1973** J. G. TWEEDDALE *Materials Technol.* II. 99 Most commonly, a hot semicontinuous extrusion press..is placed horizontally so that the extruded product can be discharged straight on to a 'run-out' table and never has to carry its own weight in tension whilst in its weakened hot state.

'run-over. Also runover. [f. RUN *v.*]

1. An act of running over, esp. with the eyes; a hasty perusal. Also, an instance of overrunning a time limit.

a **1814** *Intrigues of Day* II. i. in *New Brit. Theatre* I. 97 The newspapers are probably arrived, and I'll just give them a run-over. **1937** *Printers' Ink Monthly* May 42/1 Runovers, occasions when the [radio] program itself overruns its allotted time. **1947** J. BERTRAM *Shadow of War* VI. 203 The shifts of the P.O.W. in stowing his loot, and..the *amount* that can be carried by one man on his own person, even through a 'run-over' and a 'strip-search'. **1963** *Times* 27 Sept. 12/4 Lord Home, the Foreign Secretary, today met Mr. Dean Rusk, the American Secretary of State, for nearly three hours and had what was called 'a very full runover' of matters of mutual concern.

2. In *Printing*, etc., the action or an instance of continuing matter into a margin, or on to a subsequent line or page.

1934 WEBSTER, *Run-over*, an extension, as of printed matter, beyond the space allotted; overmatter; also, U.S., the part of an article continued from a preceding page. **1956** N. R. KER *Pastoral Care* 21 The runover to avoid breaking a word at the end of the last line on fos. 49v, 50v, 68r, marked by a dot at the end of the line and another before the runover itself. **1969** in Halpert & Story *Christmas Mumming in Newfoundland* 192 The placing of the speech designations has been regularized, the run-over of lines in narrow newspaper columns abandoned, [etc.]. **1976** H. MACINNES *Agent in Place* ix. 96 The typescript finished each line neatly —no runovers onto the right-hand margin.

run-ridge, anglicized form of next.

1805 R. W. DICKSON *Pract. Agric.* I. 404 When the lands were generally cultivated in the open field, or run-ridge state. **1826** MORISON *Dict. Dec.* XVIII. 1365 Lands lying mixed in larger parcels are not divisible as run-ridge.

runrig ('rʌnrɪg). *Sc.* Also 5 rynryg, -rig, 6 rinrig, 8–9 runrigg. [f. RUN *v.* + RIG *sb.*[1] 3. Cf. RUNDALE.]

1. A ridge of land lying among others held by joint tenure. *rare.*

1437 in *Reg. Dunfermline* (Bann. Cl.) 285 Ten fute of þe rynryg of þe Abbot..& tuenti fute of þe rynrig of þe said Dauid. **1585** in *Liber Eccl. Scone* (Bann. Cl.) 230 The landis callit the fourt rinrig of the Sandy hill. **1875** *Sc. Acts* XII. Index s.v., The heritors may apply..for division of the run-rigs according to their respective interests.

2. A form of land-tenure, = RUNDALE 1.

a **1583** SIR J. BALFOUR *Practicks* (1754) 536 Landis lyand togidder in rin-rig, and swa pertenand and occupyit be divers and sindrie persounis. **1733** P. LINDSAY *Interest Scot.* 47 The arable Land or Grounds for Tillage are divided by Runrig equally amongst them. **1791** NEWTE *Tour Eng. & Scot.* 239 Every tenant should have his farm, not in the way of runrigg, but by itself. **1845** MᶜCULLOCH *Acc. Brit. Empire* (1854) I. 287 Several of the landlords..having..divided the lands held in common, or in run-rig, into separate possessions. **1880** CARMICHAEL in Skene *Celtic Scotl.* III. 379 In Uist and Barra the arable land is divided, in part into crofts, and in part worked in runrig.

3. As *adv.* In separate ridges cultivated by different occupiers.

1695 *Sc. Acts* IX. 421/1 Act anent Lands lying Run-rig. **1751** MᶜDOUALL *Inst. Laws Scot.* I. 220 The possession of lands lying run-rig..is most prejudicial to the policy of the nation. **1814** SCOTT *Diary* 4 Aug., There are several obstacles to improvement, chiefly the undivided state of the properties, which lie run-rig.

4. *attrib.* Held or characterized by this mode of tenure.

1751 MᶜDOUALL *Inst. Laws Scot.* I. 220 Lands are run-rig, where one heritor has one ridge or rig, and another the second, and so on interchangeably over the whole parcel of land. **1765–8** ERSKINE *Inst. Law Scot.* III. iii. §59 The division competent to landholders..is not in practice confined to runrig lands in a strict sense of the word. **1792** *Stat. Acc. Scot.* III. 217 This runrig disposition of lands in Scotland. **1805** BARRY *Orkney* (1808) 356 Unless these commons be divided, and runrig possessions abolished, agricultural improvements are impracticable. **1874** *Act 37 & 38 Vict.* c. 94 §35 A decree of division of commonty or of common property or runrig lands. **1880** CARMICHAEL in Skene *Celtic Scotl.* III. 380 A wet or a dry season affects.. the tenant of the combined system more than the tenant of the runrig system.

Hence **'runrigged** *ppl. a.*, portioned out on the runrig system.

1683 M. MACKAIL *Orkney* in MacFarlane *Geogr. Collect.* (S.H.S.) III. 1 The Earles and Bishops lands were runrig'd through Orkney and Shetland. **1765** *Forfeited Est. Papers* (S.H.S.) 71 To measuring the runrigged lands on the Lovat estate. **1805** FORSYTH *Beauties Scotl.* II. 443 [The land] was often run-rigged or mixed property.

runsh, obs. variant of RUNCH.

†**runsik**, obs. form of RANSACK *v.*

c **1470** HENRY *Wallace* VII. 120 My witt vnabill is To runsik [*v.r.* ransik] sic, for dreid I say off myss.

runsy, obs. form of ROUNCY.

runt (rʌnt), *sb.* Also 6 ront(e, 7 runte. [Of obscure origin. It seems unlikely that sense 2 is at all connected with MDu. *runt* (Du. *rund*) ox.]

1. a. An old or decayed stump of a tree. Also *attrib.*, as ***runt-tree***, ***-wood***, and *fig.* (quot. *a* 1585). Now *dial.*

1501 DOUGLAS *Pal. Hon.* I. iii, Not throw the soyl bot muskane treis sproutit,..Auld rottin runtis quhairin na sap was leifit. *a* **1585** POLWART *Flyting w. Montgomerie* 789 Iock Blunt, deid runt! I sall dunt whill I slay thee. **1601** HOLLAND *Pliny* XVI. xxxix. I. 480 Neither yong poles nor old runts are fit for durable building. **1603** —— *Plutarch* 399 Like unto old runt-trees or dodils, which repining as it were at others, do manifestly hinder and take away the spring and growth of yoong poles and plants which come up under them, or grow neere about them. **1710** *Tusser Redivivus* in *Tusser's Husb.* (1878) 78 Few Pollards perish for want of it [lopping], but Runt-wood will. **1841** HARTSHORNE *Shropsh. Gloss.* 552 *Runts*, decayed stumps of trees.

b. *Sc.* and *north.* A hardened stem or stalk of a plant, *esp.* of a cabbage (cf. *kale-runt*, KALE 4).

1785 BURNS *Halloween* iv, Poor hav'rel Will..pow't, for want o' better shift, A runt was like a sow-tail Sae bow't that night. **1786** —— *Ordination* vi, Lapfu's large o' gospel kail ..An' runts o' grace. **1807–10** TANNAHILL *Poems* (1846) 117 They got naething for crowdy, but runts boiled to sowdie. **1829** BROCKETT *N.C. Gloss.* **1928** R. CAMPBELL *Wayzgoose* ii. 58 The Sacred Carrot with the golden rind, Whose magic runt..The more one nibbled it, the larger grew.

2. a. An ox or cow of a small breed or size, esp. one belonging to the small breeds characteristic of Wales and the Highlands of Scotland.

1549 *Act 3 & 4 Edw. VI*, c. 19 §1 Any manner of Oxen, Steres, Rontes, Kyen, Heighfers or Calves. **1579** SPENSER *Sheph. Cal.* Feb. 5 My ragged rontes all shiver and shake, As doen high Towers in an earthquake. **1620** MIDDLETON *Chaste Maid* IV. i, She's full of cattle, some two thousand runts. **1649** BLITHE *Eng. Improv. Impr.* (1652) 184 That year may put up three midling Runts upon an Acre and feed them up. **1700** J. BROME *Trav.* I. (1707) 23 Multitudes of Oxen, which they call Runts. **1768** PENNANT *Brit. Zool.* I. 18 The Welsh runts are much larger: the black cattle of Cornwall are of the same size with the last. **1825** COBBET *Rur. Rides* 253 The cattle here are chiefly Welsh, black and called runts. **1847** W. C. L. MARTIN *Ox* 100/1 From the midland and western counties, 230 Herefords, runts, Devons, &c. **1886** *Daily News* 14 Dec. 2/5 Welsh Runts were in good force, and maintained a prominent rank in the exhibition.

attrib. **1884** *W. Sussex Gaz.* 25 Sept., 25 Scotch Cows and Heifers, 16 Runt Steers. **1886** *Daily News* 15 Sept. 2/4 Prime sides of English runt beef.

b. An old cow or ox. Now *dial.*

1638 LAUD *Wks.* (1857) VI. 538 Your hung beef..was.. as hard as the very horn the old runt wore when she lived. **1808** JAMIESON. **1823** E. MOOR *Suffolk Wds.* **1877** *Cumb. Gloss.*

c. A small or inferior horse.

1725 *Portland Papers* (Hist. MSS. Comm.) VI. 90 We met a parcel of Scots horses... I should let them pass unremembered but for the extravagant value I thought they set upon one of their runts. **1895** *Westm. Gaz.* 7 Sept. 2/1 He ..drove a little ole runt that couldn't go seven mile a hour.

d. (*a*) A small pig, esp. the smallest in a litter. *dial.* and *U.S.* (*b*) In *gen.* use, a small pig that is weakly or undernourished.

1841 HARTSHORNE *Shropsh. Gloss.* 552 *Runt*, *Runtling*, the smallest in a litter of pigs. **1886** *Cent. Mag.* XXXII. 107 While the runt is the weakest and most forlorn of pigs [etc.]. **1887** in *Kent. Gloss.* **1939** V. C. FISHWICK *Pigs* I. i. 19 Such piglings grow well and are a sound proposition. They are not regarded as 'runts', a term which is here used to describe a pig that is in poor condition. **1939** *Nature* 23 Sept. 552/2 Radiographic examination of a 'runt', the small starveling pig, shows evidence of arrested growth in the skeleton. **1977** P. R. ENGLISH et al. *Sow* viii. 163 One can have a litter in which most piglets are thriving well but in which one or two are obviously suffering from malnutrition and are in danger of becoming nutritional 'runts'.

3. *transf.* **a.** An ignorant, uncouth, or uncultivated person.

1614 B. JONSON *Barth. Fair* IV. vi, Sir, you are a welsh Cuckold, and a prating Runt, and no Constable. *a* **1658** CLEVELAND *Sir J. Presbyter* 24 Reforming Tweed Hath sent us Runts even of her Churches breed. **1719** D'URFEY *Pills* II. 77 Shone a Welch Runt, and Hans a Dutch Boor. **1723** MRS. CENTLIVRE *Artifice* III. i, This City spoils all Servants. I took a Welsh Runt last Spring. **1830** GLEIG *Country Curate* II. iii. 62 Things have come to a pretty pass, when a set of beggarly Welsh runts use threats to their betters.

b. An old woman, esp. an ill-favoured or ill-conditioned one; a hag. Now *Sc.* or *dial.*

a **1652** BROME *Eng. Moor* III. iii, Sure some old runt with a splay-foot hath crost him. **1676** COLES *Eng.-Lat. Dict.*, An old runt, *vetula*. **1769** *Herd's Songs* (1904) 159, I think the auld runt be gone mad. **1787** W. TAYLOR *Scot. Poems* 26 At last brave Jess..Did had Dad's hands, till the auld runt, Wi' boilin broe, John Ploughman brunt. **1823** E. MOOR *Suffolk Wds.*, *Runt*,..an ill-conditioned woman. *a* **1856** G. OUTRAM *Annuity* in *Lyrics* (1874), Catch the doited runt forget To ca' for her annuity. **1899** S. R. CROCKETT *Kit Kennedy* 40 The auld runt Babby is fell fond o' ye.

c. A person of low but thick-set build; a stunted or undersized person; a dwarf. Also used in weakened sense as a term of abuse.

a **1700** *Dict. Cant. Crew*, *Runt*, a little, short, truss Man. **1828** CARR *Craven Gloss.*, *Runt*, a person of a strong though low stature. **1854** MISS BAKER *Northampt. Gloss.*, *Runt* or *Runty*, a dwarfish person; particularly a child stunted in its growth by short food or over work. **1890** L. C. D. D'OYLE *Notches* 65 My brother Bill..was a fine, tall fellow—not a little bit of a 'runt' like me. **1896** *Dialect Notes* I. 423 *Runt*, worthless fellow. (Cowboys.) *c* **1926** 'MIXER' *Transport Workers' Song Bk.* 52 As a slimy runt, I'm it! **1930** *Amer. Speech* V. 119 The expression 'little runt' was merely contemptuous. **1936** *Nat. Geogr. Mag.* June 787/2 A cadet's height determines his assignment, the tall men going to the 'flanker' companies, A and M, the 'runts' to companies F and G in the center. **1956** J. CANNON *Who struck John?* 228 You're Conn McCreary, a fat runt. You're tiny. **1958** *Chicago Tribune* 9 Feb. (Comics Feature Mag.) 9 'Anyhow, who'd ever think of connecting that runt with *this* deal?' 'Maybe you're right! But just the same I'm going to keep my beady eye on young Mister Dondi.' **1969** I. & P. OPIE *Children's Games* viii. 234 'Come on you miserable runts,' we say, and one of the runts runs up the steps, only to be thrown over the side of the railing.

d. A dwarfish or diminutive object.

1819 M. WILMOT *Let.* 8 Dec. (1935) 32 What think you of my *deeply* regretting not having brought a white Tabinet gown. 'Tis admired here beyond satin, and my old *runt* has in consequence been jinkumbobbed out of Mamselle and white satin till the poor dear old dress..is become the most admired thing I have. **1845** *Punch* VIII. 224 You work in that little runt of a garden of yours for half-an-hour or so before breakfast. **1873** CARLETON *Farm Ball.* 43 Takin' all the biggest apples, leavin' all the littlest runts. **1900** R. Barr *Unchanging East* 258 This insignificant runt of a Turkish steamer. **1973** *Amer. Speech 1969* XLIV. 249 In official terminology, ground signals are referred to as *dwarf* signals, but railroad men call them *pots*, because they are round and silver, or *runts*, because they are small in comparison with the signals on bridges that span the tracks.

attrib. **1874** Coues *Birds N.W.* 36 In a large number examined, little 'runt' eggs are sometimes found.

4. a. A domestic pigeon of a breed characterized by size and stoutness of build, of which there are a number of varieties.

1661 Walton *Angler* (ed. 3) iv. 73 Of the tame [pigeons] there be Cropers, Carryers, Runts. **1668** Charleton *Onomast.* 77 *Columbæ Russicæ*, Runts. **1725** *Fam. Dict.* s.v. *Pigeon*, Of Runts are different Sorts, one called Spanish Runts, generally of a Blood Red, or Mottled Colour. **1735** Moore *Columb.* 44 There are other Sorts of Runts, as the Roman Runt.., and the Smyrna Runt. **1840** Dickens *Barn. Rudge* i, The wheeling and circling flights of runts, fantails, tumblers, and pouters, were perhaps not quite consistent with the grave and sober character of the building. **1881** J. C. Lyell *Fancy Pigeons* 104 In appearance runts are like huge common pigeons.

attrib. and *Comb.* **1688** Holme *Armoury* ii. 244/1 The Runt Pigeon, or Russian Dove,..are large Pigeons as big as young Hens. **1854** Meall *Moubray's Poultry* 249 In the head and bill the Archangel is very Runt-like. *Ibid.* 252 In size it would seem to be the smallest of the Runt family.

†**b.** A canary-bird over three years old. *Obs.*

a **1700** B. E. *Dict. Cant. Crew.* **1704** *Dict. Rust.* (1726) s.v. *Canary-birds*, The several Names of these Birds at different Times and Ages: Such as are above 3 years old are called Runts.

†**runt**, *v.* *Obs.*⁻¹ In 5 runte, ront. [Cf. arunt *v.*] *trans.* To reprove, rate.

c **1440** Capgr. *Life St. Kath.* iii. 96 Euyr hys body wold he chyde & runte [*v.r.* ront]: 'What eylyth þe now?'

'**runted**, *a.* [f. runt *sb.* + -ed².] Stunted in growth, undersized, dwarfish.

1681 *Lond. Gaz.* No. 1651/4 The other is a middle aged Runted Ox, all Black, his Horns turn a little round. **1783** Burns *Mailie's Elegy* vi. (orig. text), She was nae get o' runted rams. **1879** Miss Jackson *Shropsh. Wd.-Bk.* **1951** E. Paul *Springtime in Paris* iii. 50 The myriads of chimney pots and vents are like runted gargoyles which look up toward scudding clouds and mackerel skies instead of downward. **1961** R. P. Hobson *Rancher takes Wife* ii. 38 Two runted pearl-gray kittens purred and rubbed themselves against Rich's legs. **1976** T. Heald *Let Sleeping Dogs Die* v. 87 Runted little dogs hers are. No wind and dreadful temperaments.

'**run-through.** Also runthrough. Pl. run-throughs, runs-through. [f. run *v.*] **1.** A (freq. hasty or cursory) rehearsal of a play, a radio or television programme, etc. Also *gen.* a performance or showing (of a play, film, etc.), esp. a preview.

1923 Wodehouse *Inimitable Jeeves* x. 104 It must have been about a week after this rummy little episode that George Caffyn called me up and asked me if I would care to go and see a run-through of his show. **1930** J. Dos Passos *42nd Parallel* iv. 287 She felt it in her bones that the play would be a hit..and Mr Freelby said Ike Gold..had sat through the runthrough with the tears running down his cheeks. **1946** *Life* 2 Dec. 51 The director, handsomely played by Sam Wanamaker, talks of his theatrical troubles until the star, Mary Grey, appears. There begins a run-through of a play about Joan of Arc, with Mary in the lead. **1952** S. Kauffmann *Philanderer* (1953) xiii. 217 She had to go back for the final run-through. **1957** Duncan & Bone *Oxf. Pkt. Bk. Athletic Training* (ed. 2) v. 71 Minor adjustments being made before competition after practice runs-through. **1959** *Times* 10 July 9/1 The two gentlemen were felicitously played at this public *première* (as at the private run-through half a year ago) by Mr. Stephen Manton and Mr. Bruce Boyce. **1963** *Ann. Reg. 1962* 421 *Christopher Sly*, a chamber opera by Thomas Eastwood, heard in Britain only in a public run-through in 1960, was given its first staging at Pforzheim. **1973** *Times* 17 Oct. 11/2, I..immediately asked about rehearsals. I was told there would be run-throughs with a full orchestra but without the chorus and other principals. **1973** E. Lemarchand *Let or Hindrance* xiv. 177 The film..has been very recently edited. .. Like a run-through of this last part? **1977** S. Brett *Star Trap* v. 53 The..cast assembled for a pre-tour run-through.

2. A brief survey (of facts); a summary, a concise account.

1947 *Sun* (Baltimore) 20 Mar. 1/6 The Big Four conference which, at the conclusion of the ninth session tonight, had accomplished little more than a run-through of German issues on which the Council is split. **1957** [see fado]. **1963** *Listener* 7 Mar. 432/2, I gave a group of young Russians a quick run-through of Eng. Lit. from Hopkins and Hardy to Amis and Osborne. **1973** A. Hunter *Gently French* iv. 36 Tell me about Quarles... Give me a quick run through.

3. The fact or an instance of running trains through intermediate points without stopping for crew changing, loading, etc.

1964 *Canad. Labour* Dec. 31/3 Representatives of the non-operating railway unions met in Montreal with officials of the running trades to work out a common policy on rail abandonments, runthroughs and other technological changes. **1967** *Canad. Ann. Rev. 1966* 29 The implementation of the Freedman report on railway run-throughs. **1969** *Jane's Freight Containers 1968–69* 125/3 To improve interline service, the Frisco is co-operating with connecting rail carriers to pre-block traffic in run-through trains—avoiding intermediate terminal switching operations.

runting ('rʌntɪŋ), *vbl. sb.* [f. runt *sb.* + -ing¹.]

1. The birth or development of (laboratory) animals that are small for their kind.

1959 *Jrnl. Exper. Med.* CX. 522 Runting is the result of an immunological reaction of foreign cells against a tolerant host. **1974** *Nature* 11 Oct. 548/2 In some litters all rats grew normally and there was no runting. **1978** *Ibid.* 27 July 365/2 In the colony described here there has been no evidence of the runting syndrome frequently seen in conventional nude mice.

2. (See quot.) *slang.*

1976 *Drive* July–Aug. 37/2 In the [ice-cream] trade, giving kids small portions when no parents are about is called 'runting'.

'**runtish**, *a.* [f. runt *sb.* + -ish.]

1. Of animals: Stunted; dwarfish. Also, of human beings.

1641 Best *Farm. Bks.* (Surtees) 5 These usually that fall to grasse over soone, proove short runtish sheepe. **1738** *Briton Described* 60 The Cattle, we saw most legible on their Mountains, were Goats and Heifers, a runtish Sort of Animals. **1805** R. W. Dickson *Pract. Agric.* II. 1124 This same kind of runtish coarse breed continues all the way to the Frith of Forth. **1969** N. Cohn *AWopBopaLooBop* (1970) x. 89 He grew up small, runtish, with bad hair and unhealthy skin. **1974** 'R. Tate' *Birds of Bloodied Feather* ii. 30 The child..was about thirteen, runtish and not very clean.

†**2.** Like a runt (pigeon).

1765 *Treat. Dom. Pigeons* 137 It is of a runtish make, and has a gravel eye.

Hence †'**runtishly** *adv.* *Obs.*

1735 J. Moore *Columb.* 45 The Trumpeter is a bird much about the size of a Laugher, and very runtishly made.

'**runty**, *a.* *U.S.* and *dial.* [f. runt *sb.*]

1. Dwarfish, undersized; small and ill-made; of low, thick-set build. Also *Comb.*

1807 W. Irving *Salmagundi* (1824) 86 A trio of as odd, runty, mummy-looking originals as ever Hogarth fancied in his most happy moments. **1834** Burgon in Goulburn *Life* (1892) I. 81 These runty little thick-set Yorkshire men seem to consider me as a wild beast escaped from some show. **1848** in Farmer & Henley *Slang* (1903) VI. 84/2 'No indeed,' ses another little runty-lookin' feller—we've got enuff to do to take care of our own babys in these diggins. **1891** T. N. Page *Ole Virginia* 42 Sometimes you see a weevly runty pig in a right good litter. **1903** J. London *People of Abyss* xii. 143 We cannot understand the starved and runty toiler of the East End..till we look at the strapping Life Guardsmen of the West End. **1938** M. K. Rawlings *Yearling* xiv. 156 Us Baxters is all runty and tough. **1972** *New Yorker* 22 Jan. 100/2 A young English mother..gets herself sexually awakened by a runty Italian actor... If Miranda were more intelligent and Oreste less swinish, their obsessive affair might touch us deeply. **1974** *Sci. Amer.* Nov. 61/1 The treated birds were runty and deficient in lymphocytes; all cell-mediated immune functions were suppressed.

2. *dial.* Surly, ill-tempered, obstinate.

a **1825–66** in dial. glossaries (E. Anglia, Linc., Northampt.).

run-up. Also run up, runup. [f. run *v.*]

1. The act of running up to a certain point; esp.

a. *Coursing.* The race between two greyhounds up to the first turn or wrench of the hare.

1834 Thacker *Courser's Comp.* I. 134 One dog is sometimes behind the other in the first run up to the hare. **1853** 'Stonehenge' *Greyhound* 358 The first cote constitutes what is sometimes called the run up, or speed to the hare. **1884** *Field* 6 Dec. (Cassell's), Pious Fraud scored the run-up from Alone.

b. The act of taking or sending a ball up to the goal or into a position for final play. Also *attrib.* Chiefly in *Golf.*

1897 *Outing* XXX. 484/1 Foster.., after a clean run from 'way down the field, puts the ball through the uprights... The excitement of the run-up has been intense. **1901** *Scotsman* 9 Sept. 4/7 Vardon, after being short in his run up, missed the hole for a 3. **1907** 'I. Hay' *Pip* iii. xi. 339 Anything in the shape of a run-up ball would be trapped. **1931** *Daily Express* 31 Jan. 9/5 Compston, playing a run-up shot to the first green, shouted after the ball, 'Hit the stick.' **1955** *Times* 2 May 4/1 On most of Friday he putted well, and his run-ups were often in the highest class. **1963** *Times* 14 Jan. 3/7 Agate won back the 13th, where he played a run-up to the hole.

c. A run made in preparation for jumping, throwing, etc., in *Athletics*; in *Cricket*, the bowler's approach to the bowling crease before delivery.

1897 *Encycl. Sport* I. 52/2 Pace in the run-up supplies the impetus; spring enables the jumper to lift himself into the air. **1919** F. A. M. Webster et al. *Success in Athletics* x. 83 The last stride must be a short one, so that the jumping leg may be gathered well under the body for the spring. This accounts for the run-up, which must be most assiduously practised. **1929** G. M. Butler *Mod. Athletics* ix. 120 *The run-up.* The first essential of successful long jumping is speed in the approach. *Ibid.* 122 Should the run-up be inaccurate, there will be a loss of at least a foot. **1948** K. S. Duncan *Oxf. Pkt. Bk. Athletic Training* iv. 62 Practise and standardize the run-up, cross step and throwing stance. **1959** *Times* 17 June 6/6 Horner, with his upright stance and utter immobility during the bowler's run-up. *Ibid.* 24 Aug. 4/2 She was handicapped..in the long jump by a crumbling run-up. **1966** B. Johnston *Armchair Cricket 1966* 97 If the batsmen attempt to steal a run during the bowler's run-up [etc.]. **1974** *Rules of Game* 18/3 The parallel lines may be crossed during run-up, but the competitor must be between them when the javelin is released. **1977** J. Laker *One-Day Cricket* 48 The length of a bowler's run-up is limited to 15 yards.

d. = run-in 3.

1942 *R.A.F. Jrnl.* 27 June 8 Another Stirling and a Wellington adopted almost identically the same run-up as ourselves. **1958** 'N. Shute' *Rainbow & Rose* ii. 43, I went up again and circled round... 'I'm going to do a dummy run.' .. I took a longer run-up this time. **1976** 'G. Black' *Moon for Killers* vii. 99 A small, single-prop job was coming in for a landing..its turn completed, the run-up going to be towards us.

e. A period of time or series of occurrences leading up *to* some important (freq. political) event; an action which prepares the way for one on a larger scale.

1966 *Sunday Times* 20 Nov. 48/2 The Petit Palais show offers, also, invaluable evidence in its drawing section of the ways in which Picasso manoeuvred during the crucial run-up to the 'Demoiselles d'Avignon'. **1968** *Listener* 5 Dec. 761/1 The run-up to the election of Oxford's new Poetry Professor has aroused a good deal of mirthful interest. **1970** *Daily Tel.* 2 Jan. 14 The 1970s open, with the approach and run-up to the most critical General Election in a generation. **1975** M. Kenyon *Mr. Big.* v. 47 Heathrow was the run-up to the train job because there had to be capital. **1976** *Nature* 29 July 344/2 Remaining hitches in reactor technology can, it is argued, be straightened out during the 20-year run-up to a commercial FBR network. **1977** *Film & Television Technician* Jan. 1/2 During the run-up to the overtime ban ..the Trade Press was uniformly critical of the employers.

2. *Bookbinding.* (See quot. 1875.) Also *attrib.*

1875 Knight *Dict. Mech.* 2004/2 *Run-up*, a fillet-mark which runs from head to tail on the back, without mitering with the horizontal cross fillets on the panels. **1880** Zaehnsdorf *Bookbinding* 131 With a 'run-up' back, the edge of the leather round the end papers is to..have a roll run round it in gold.

3. On the *U.S. Stock Market*, a rapid increase in the price or value of a commodity. Now also in *gen.* use.

1935 *Sun* (Baltimore) 13 Apr. 17/8 Corn advanced to 1 to 1⅜ cents a bushel, but cotton was reactionary after Thursday's run-up. **1942** *Ibid.* 1 Oct. 21 Laclede gas preferred had a runup of 6½ points. **1953** *Ibid.* 30 Oct. B-28/1 A fast runup in the final dealings gave the stock market one of its sharpest boosts of the year yesterday. **1958** *Wall St. Jrnl.* 3 Dec. 27/4 Referring to the recent sharp run-up and activity in Walworth Co. stock, amid talk of merger possibilities, Fred W. Belz, president, said [etc.]. **1976** *National Observer* (U.S.) 6 Mar. 4/3 The price scare and runup in the futures prices in recent weeks 'says to me that farmers deep down inside know that this crop is not lost'. **1978** *Daily Tel.* 15 Sept. 21/4 Money market analysts have been watching a rapid run-up in short-term, negotiable bank certificates of deposit and commercial paper traded by corporations. **1979** *Time* 13 Aug. 26/3 The industry most severely dented by the oil run-up is auto manufacturing.

4. The running of a motor or mechanical device until it attains normal working or speed; warming up.

1943 *Yank* 26 Feb. 6 Last summer the intensive heat raised hell with us AMs in making engine run-ups for regulation check on props, [etc.]. **1946** *Happy Landings* July 3/1 Correct use of air filters and observing precautions against dust during run up are matters for the pilot to remember. **1958** 'Castle' & 'Hailey' *Flight into Danger* i. 16 In the run-up each engine in turn is opened to full throttle and each of the mags tested separately. **1959** W. S. Sharps *Dict. Cinematogr.* 126/2 *Run up*, the term given to the passage of film or a magnetic recording medium through a camera or recorder before the correct recording speed is obtained; or through a projector or other machine before the first subject image or sound is reached. **1962** A. Nisbett *Technique Sound Studio* viii. 139 The reproducer may take as much as a second or so to run up... Check this run-up time by using a recording of pure tone.

runway ('rʌnweɪ). Also run-way. Orig. *U.S.* [f. run *v.*]

1. a. The customary track or run of an animal (*esp.* of deer) or a fish.

1833 C. F. Hoffman *Winter in West* (1835) I. 202 The numerous deer-runways,..and innumerable tracks of rackoons, wolves, and bears, showed us that we were upon a favourite hunting ground of the Pottawattamies. **1855** *Knickerbocker* XLV. 193 The sound of the rifle has by this time brought the other hunters from their run-ways. **1873** *Forest & Stream* I. 178/2 We crossed the runway where the deer and pack had passed. **1894** *Outing* XXIV. 186/2 Sometimes we followed a 'runway' or deer's path for a distance, and then it was mostly easy going. *Ibid.* 453/1 After a minute's rest, to let him settle in his runway, I made a cast. **1908** A. J. Dawson *Finn* x. 168 Reynard picked up the dead rabbit and..trotted leisurely down the run-way towards his own earth. **1948** A. L. Rand *Mammals Eastern Rockies* 45 Four of them [*sc.* species of shrews] are terrestrial animals, often making little runways through the moss. **1953** P. Provencher *I live in Woods* xii. 117 In winter the rabbit runway is easily distinguished in the snow. **1977** *Sci. Amer.* May 106/2 Rats in the laboratory have logged endless miles in runways, mazes and activity wheels.

b. A place for fowls to run in.

1871 W. M. Lewis *People's Pract. Poultry Bk.* 8 The hennery should be placed in a warm, dry location..with runways ample to allow of plenty of exercise. **1886** *Pall Mall G.* 27 Aug. 14/1 The incubators, hatching houses, brooding houses and runways have a capacity to keep 5,000 eggs in process of hatching all the time. **1913** J. London *Valley of Moon* xiv. 459 A goodly portion was devoted to white-washed henhouses and wired runways wherein hundreds of chickens were to be seen. **1949** *Sat. Even. Post* 9 Apr. 59/2 He even had a plan for one in his desk; the runways were to be painted green outside and whitewashed inside.

c. A running-path.

1889 *Pall Mall G.* 19 Jan. 7/1 The field [in baseball] consists of a continuous runway of clay-covered paths.

2. a. Any artificial (sloping or horizontal) track or gangway made for convenience of passage or carriage. *spec.* in *Theatr.* use (see quot. 1926);

also in *Fashion*, a raised gangway on which models parade when exhibiting clothes.

1883 E. W. HOWE *Country Town* iv. 20 Pushing this into my wagon with the assistance of his wife, after we had first made a run-way of boards, I hauled him to Fairview. **1888** *Scribner's Mag.* Oct. 444 If there is a 'runway', which is an elevation like the rocky ascent in the second act of Die Walküre.., it is 'built' by the stage-carpenters. **1901** MERWIN & WEBSTER *Calumet 'K'* xiii. 246 A runway from the hoist to the end of the building. **1912** 'W. LAWTON' *Boy Aviators' Flight for Fortune* ix. 102 The rolling glide down the runway was made..and at last the bow of the *Sea Eagle's* hull struck the water. **1926** *Amer. Speech* I. 437/2 *Runway*, a platform built at stage level and extending part way down the center aisle of the theater. Used in burlesque and musical comedy for the presentation of chorus numbers. **1929** *Variety* 11 Sept. 54 Muggs still going for burlesque want that close-up of flesh which the runway provides or they won't give the teasers a tumble. **1941** B. SCHULBERG *What makes Sammy Run?* xii. 287 The solid glass desk looked like a burlesque runway. **1961** *Sunday Times* 3 Dec. 29/2 Advertising is the next fattener of bank accounts, then fashion photography and finally live modelling on the runways at fashion shows. **1971** C. FICK *Danziger Transcript* 95 Fourteen skinny models rehearsing on a runway. **1979** *Tucson Mag.* Mar. 12/3 Producer Spots Baxter's lifeless body stretched out on the runway of his great stage.

b. A specially prepared surface on an airfield for the taking off and landing of aircraft.

1923 *Aviation* 8 Oct. 445/1 (*caption*) A wonderful landmark—Boston Airport with its T type runways. **1926** *Nat. Geogr. Mag.* Sept. 363/2 We got off the end of the runway at a terrific speed. **1930** *Flight* 7 Feb. 194/1 To make it usable for aircraft, cinders have been laid to form three runways and these are raised above the rest of the unprepared ground. **1943** *Times* 16 Dec. 3/4 In northern Burma the U.S. Air Forces destroyed runways and dumps and burned barrack areas. **1957** *Economist* 21 Sept. 922/2 The sprawling Tachikawa airfield on the northern fringes of Tokyo is regularly the scene of 'anti-base' demonstrations by Japanese who uproot boundary fences, plant flagpoles on the runways and skirmish with the police. **1977** *Whitaker's Almanack 1978* 572 There was an official death toll of 576 when two Boeing 747 jumbo jets..collided on the runway at Santa Cruz airport.

3. A groove in which anything slides, *esp.* one of the grooves in the casing of a sash-window.

1890 in *Cent. Dict.* **1900** R. BARR *Unchanging East* 309 Its runway was so smooth..that a man of ordinary strength could roll it backward and forward.

4. The bed or channel in which a stream runs.

1874 B. F. TAYLOR *World on Wheels* II. vii. 250 Like the dusty 'run-ways' of thy brooks, soft pulses have grown dry and dumb. **1879** in WEBSTER *Suppl.*

5. *attrib.* and *Comb.*, as (sense 2 b) ***runway aerodrome, marker, strip***; **runway light**, each of a series of lights marking the course of a runway.

1933 *Jrnl. R. Aeronaut. Soc.* XXXVII. 3 Detroit, where a purely runway aerodrome has been developed. **1951** *Gloss. Aeronaut. Terms (B.S.I.)* III. 24 *Runway lights*, lights defining a runway to indicate the area of taking-off and landing. **1958** 'CASTLE' & 'HAILEY' *Flight into Danger* xi. 154 Put out your runway lights, except zero-eight. **1976** 'A. HALL' *Kobra Manifesto* xv. 200 The flick-flick-flick of the runway lights, falling away. **1939** *Air Ann. Brit. Empire* 65 A new metal runway marker has been introduced in order to improve the safety of aeroplane landings. **1937** *Sun* (Baltimore) 21 Apr. 9/6 The field should be equipped with boundary and beacon lights and the area of the runway strips outside of the paved portion should be sod.

Hence **'runwayed** *a.*, provided with a runway; consisting of runways.

1948 *Hansard Commons* 15 Mar. 1806 Two-fifths of a runwayed airfield is covered with concrete runways. **1949** *Jrnl. R. Aeronaut. Soc.* LIII. 903/1 Large grass areas on runwayed aerodromes are a liability in upkeep, except insofar as grass drying is a revenue-earning aspect.

†**runy**, *a. Obs. rare.* [Of doubtful origin: cf. RUNISH *a.*^{2}] Fierce, furious.

c **1205** LAY. 1545 Corineus heom rasde to, swa þe runie [*c* 1275 wilde] wulf. *Ibid.* 20123 Arður..gon to rusien swa þe runie [*c* 1275 wode] wulf.

Runyonesque (ˌrʌnjəˈnɛsk), *a.* [f. the name *Runyon* (see below) + -ESQUE.] Characteristic of or resembling Alfred Damon *Runyon* (1884–1946), U.S. journalist and author, or his writings. Also **Runyonese** (-ˈiːz), slang or underworld jargon characteristic or suggestive of that used in the short stories of Runyon.

1938 *Times Lit. Suppl.* 22 Jan. 59/2 A good many people appear to think that 'runyonese'..is not only vulgar but also pernicious. **1938** *N.Y. Times* 28 Feb. 19/1 For a Runyonesque panel the casting director had the marvelous good fortune to find Edward G. Robinson and Ruth Donnelly to play Mr. and Mrs. **1950** *Observer* 22 Oct. 7/4 It is hard to comment on the quality of translation without seeing the original, and Mr. Maclaren-Ross had had to cope with that appallingly difficult problem of specialised slang. Mr. Maclaren-Ross's solution is Runyonesque, probably the most suitable, but still inevitably tending to denationalise the book. **1953** P. BONNER *SPQR* xvii. 150 Runyonese..is the patois which best illustrates the swath which this character is cutting. **1955** *Time* 6 June 109/1 Ruth was singing in obscure Chicago nightclubs when she first encountered a Runyonesque character who called himself Colonel Martin Snyder. **1964** *Amer. Speech* XXXIX. 304 He gives details of murders, gang wars, robberies, and the activities and special talents of such Runyonesque members of Costa Nostra as Vincent 'Jimmy Blue Eyes' Alo, [etc.]. **1964** E. P. HOYT *Gentleman of Broadway* xvi. 249 Librarians were surprised that Runyon continued to be popular long after his style of slang and much of the language which was called 'Runyonese' had been thoroughly absorbed in American English. **1980** *Jewish Chron.* 4 Jan. 15/5 Its characters are a little self-consciously drawn, notably a pair of Runyonesque policemen.

†**ruoken**, *v. Obs.*$^{-1}$ [Cf. note to ROCK *v.*^{1} 5 b.] *trans.* ? To clean by rubbing.

c **1205** LAY. 22287 Heo ruokeden burnen [*c* 1275 hii rollede wepne]; bonneden helmes.

rupee (ruːˈpiː). Forms: *α.* 7 **rupia**, 7–8 **ropia**, 8 **roupia**; 7 (9) **rupeia**. *β.* 7 **roopee, rowpee, roupy**, 7–8 **roupie**; 7 **rupeye, rupie**, 7– **rupee**. [ad. Urdū *rūpiyah*, f. Skr. *rūpya* wrought silver.] The monetary unit of India, represented by a cupro-nickel (formerly silver) coin and equivalent to 100 paise (see PAISA). Also, the monetary unit of Pakistan, Sri Lanka, and a number of other countries.

The silver rupee was introduced by Shir Shah in 1542, and varied in weight at different times and places between 170 and 192 grains; from 1836 the weight in British India was 180 grains, but the value diminished considerably after 1875. A slightly heavier rupee was in use in Bengal: see SICCA^1. The gold rupee mentioned in quot. 1678 is properly called a MOHUR.

α. **1612** N. WITHINGTON *Trav.* (1735) 289 Givinge mee 200 Rupeias, everye Rupie containinge 2*s.* 6*d.* **1613** PURCHAS *Pilgrimage* v. xvii. (1614) 544 The Kings reuenue of his Crown-land is fiftie Crou of Rupias. **1665** *Phil. Trans.* I. 104 They now sell us a Maon of 6 pounds for two Rupias. **1704** *Collect. Voy.* (Churchill) III. 578/2, 1000 of them weigh not above 20 Ropias, and cost about 60 Ropias. **1728** CHAMBERS *Cycl.* s.v. *Money*, A Lacre of Roupias is a hundred thousand Roupias. [**1841** ELPHINSTONE *Hist. Ind.* II. 245 Shir Sháh changed the name of tankha to that of rupeia, or rupee, which was adopted by Akber.]

β. **1615** SIR T. ROE *Jrnl.* (Hakl. Soc.) I. 95 *note*, A rupee is 2*s.* 3*d.* starling. **1638** SIR T. HERBERT *Trav.* (ed. 2) 62 Thirty, sometime twenty tack make one roopee; a roopee is two shillings three pence. **1678** J. PHILLIPS tr. *Tavernier's Trav.* II. 2 The Roupy of Gold weighs 2 Drams and a half, and 11 Grains, and is valued..at 14 Roupies of Silver. **1712** E. COOKE *Voy. S. Sea* 164 Forty Roupies to be allow'd James Stretton in India, as Smart-Money. **1761** *Ann. Reg., Hist.* 55 Sixteen roupies (half-crowns) had been paid for the flesh of a dog. **1842** BISCHOFF *Woollen Manuf.* II. 312 The usual price demanded for such a pair of shawls is 3000 rupees. **1893** SIR W. HUNTER *Ind. Empire* (ed. 3) 506 The rupee, which formerly was nearly equal to two shillings, has fallen to nearly fourteen pence.

attrib. **1727** A. HAMILTON *New Acc. E. Ind.* II. 42 Rupee Silver, which has no Alloy in it, will bear twenty eight per Cent. of Copper-alloy. **1884** *St. James's Gaz.* 10 May 7/2 There was a sharp rise yesterday in rupee paper. **1887** *Pall Mall G.* 7 Nov. 11/1 The rupee prices in India of commodities exported to..England.

Rupelian (ruːˈpiːlɪən), *a. Geol.* [a. F. *Rupelien*, f. *Rupel*, the name of a small tributary of the river Scheldt.] A division of the oligocene of Belgium, lying above the tongrian.

1852 *Jrnl. Geol. Soc.* VIII. 296 They [shells] are referred by M. Dumont to part of his Rupelian system. **1883** *Science* II. 16/1 The oligocene system shows two principal divisions (tongrian, rupelian), which stretch across the lower part of the river Escaut.

†**rupellary**, *a. Obs.*$^{-1}$ [irreg. f. L. *rūpes* rock.] Rocky.

a **1700** EVELYN *Diary* 27 Feb. 1644, In this rupellary nidary do the fowle lay eggs and breede.

rupert's drop, metal: see DROP *sb.* 10 h, and PRINCE *sb.* 12.

rupestral (ruːˈpɛstrəl), *a.* and *sb.* [f. mod.L. *rupestris*, f. L. *rūpes* rock + -AL^1.] Growing on rocks. Also as *sb.*, a rupestral plant.

1847 H. C. WATSON *Cybele Brit.* I. 340 Native. Rupestral and Pascual. Frequent on the Highland mountains. **1854** J. H. BALFOUR *Outl. Bot.* 527 Rupestral and mural plants are those found on rocks and walls, such as species of Saxifrage, Sedum, Draba,..Lichens and Mosses. **1926** J. J. WALKER *Nat. Hist. Oxford Distr.* 104 Many of these [alpine species] are rupestrals. **1932** G. C. DRUCE *Comital Flora Brit. Isles* p. xiii, A 'rupestral' may also be a wet or a dry lover. **1970** *Watsonia* VIII. 115 Unlike most species of *Hieracium* it is usually a soil plant rather than rupestral.

So **ru'pestrean, ru'pestrine**, *adjs.*; **ru'pestrian** *a.*, done on rock or cave walls.

1786 ABERCROMBIE *Arr.* in *Gard. Assist.* 66 Rupestrean or rock stone-crop sedum. **1890** *Cent. Dict.*, *Rupestrine*, rock-inhabiting; living or growing on or among rocks. **1896** A. H. KEANE *Ethnology* 137 The carvings on the dolmen *des marchands*, Brittany, are almost identical with those of the so-called 'rupestrian inscriptions' of Tunisia and South Algeria. **1934** 'H. MACDIARMID' *Stony Limits & Other Poems* 52 Look over this beach. What ruderal and rupestrine growth is here? **1952** O. R. GURNEY *Hittites* 215 The powerful rupestrian art of the later [Hittite] empire was probably stimulated by the rulers. **1967** M. BULLOCK tr. *Lommel's World of Early Hunters* iv. 127 The influence of rupestrian art on Negro art, particularly Negro sculpture, has not been elucidated. When we speak of African art we have grown accustomed to thinking only of Negro art, ignoring the rock-paintings or referring to them only marginally.

‖**rupia** (ˈruːpɪə). *Path.* [mod.L. (Bateman), f. Gr. ῥύπος dirt, filth.] A skin disease characterized by an eruption of broad, flattish, scattered vesicles, succeeded by thick ulcerating scabs.

Good *Study Med.* (1822) points out that the spelling *rhypia* would have been more in accordance with analogy.

1815 BATEMAN *Delin. Cutaneous Dis.* Pref. p. v, With the exception of the representations of Impetigo, Porrigo,.. Rupia [etc.]. **1834** *Cycl. Pract. Med.* III. 632 Rupia may be considered as altogether a constitutional affection, being only seen in the aged, or..debilitated. **1878** T. BRYANT *Pract. Surg.* I. 27 Constitutional sores..originating in some ulcerating skin eruption, such as ecthyma or rupia.

Hence **'rupial** *a.*, pertaining to, of the nature of, affected with, rupia.

1861 BUMSTEAD *Ven. Dis.* (1879) 541 The small rupial eruption begins either about the face or on the inner and outer surface of the forearms. **1879** *St. George's Hosp. Rep.* IX. 608 On the left shin he had a rupial sore.

rupiah (ruːˈpiːə). [Indonesian, f. Hind. *rūpiyah*: see RUPEE.] The basic monetary unit of Indonesia, equal to 100 sen.

1947 *Encycl. Brit. Bk. of Year* 307/2 The new Indonesian republic on Oct. 30 [1946] began the issue of its own currency, the rupiah, and on Dec. 1 declared its value to be 1·9 per U.S. dollar. **1952** *Ann. Reg. 1951* III. 335 The estimated deficit in the Budget was reduced to Rupiahs 987 million. **1959** 'M. DERBY' *Tigress* iv. 154 Traders.. preferred to sell..in free markets for honest currency instead of government controlled prices in semi-worthless Indonesian *rupiahs*. **1964** *Asia Mag.* 27 Sept. 17/2 A fantastic rise in the rupiah costs of Indonesian projects. **1973** D. MAY *Laughter in Djakarta* ii. 33 He gave her a hundred rupiah note. **1977** *Time* 16 May 14/1 You start dropping in 10,000-rupiah ($24) notes until he says that's enough and closes the drawer.

‖**rupi'capra**. *Zool.* [L., f. *rūpes* rock + *capra* she-goat.] The chamois (*Rupicapra tragus*).

1693 SIR T. P. BLOUNT *Nat. Hist.* 385 Some beasts and birds we find live upon the highest tops of the Alps,..as the Ibex, and Rupicapra, or Chamois. **1728** CHAMBERS *Cycl.*, *Chamois Leather*..is prepar'd from the Skin of the Chamois, a kind of Rupi-Capra, or wild Goat.

Hence **rupi'caprine** *a.*

1827 GRIFFITH tr. *Cuvier* IV. 281 The Rupicaprine Group. **1876** *Encycl. Brit.* V. 384/1 The only Antelope found in Western Europe, and..the type of the Rupicaprine or goat-like group of that family. **1891** FLOWER & LYDEKKER *Mamm.* 349 Rupicaprine section [of the Bovidæ].

ru'picoline, -colous, *adjs.* (See quots.)

1858 MAYNE *Expos. Lex.*, *Rupicolus*, living in or among rocks..: rupicolous. **1890** *Cent. Dict.*, *Rupicoline*,..rock-inhabiting; growing on rocks; living among rocks.

ru'pitic, *a. Path. rare*$^{-1}$. [irreg. f. RUPIA.] Pertaining to, characterized by, rupia.

1878 HAMILTON *Nerv. Dis.* 38 There were three rupitic phlegma on the head, each of which contained a little pus.

ru'pography. *rare.* [f. G. ῥύπος sealing-wax: see -GRAPHY.] The art of taking an impression of a coin or medal upon sealing-wax. Hence **rupo'graphical** *a.*

1838 *Jrnl. Asiat. Soc. Bengal* VII. 415 As a first specimen, then, of the capabilities of this art of rupography I select a coin, or rather medal [etc.]. *Ibid.*, The rupographical process may be safely confined to the first stage, or simple impression on sealing-wax.

rupontike, obs. form of RHAPONTIC.

rupt, obs. form of RUT *sb.*^{2}

†**rupt**, *v. Obs.*$^{-1}$ [f. L. *rupt-*, ppl. stem of *rumpĕre* to break.] *trans.* To break, nullify.

1726 AYLIFFE *Parergon* 32 When the Will which he has made is rupted and made void by the Birth of a Posthumous Issue.

rupt (rʌpt), *a. rare.* [f. as RUPT *v.*] Broken, craggy.

1916 BLUNDEN *Harbingers* 66 Run, echo, up the tarn's rupt wall.

†**'ruptic**, *a. Obs.*$^{-1}$ [f. as RUPT *v.* + -IC.] Breaking; causing (a sore) to break.

1541 R. COPLAND *Guydon's Quest. Chirurg.* O iij b, Whose operacions..appereth afterward as they that be made with brenning or ruptycke medecines.

'ruptile, *a.* Now *Bot.* [ad. mod.L. *ruptilis* or F. *ruptile*: cf. prec. and -ILE.] (See quots.)

1721 BAILEY, *Ruptile*, easy to be broken. **1858** MAYNE *Expos. Lex.*, *Ruptilis*, applied to an organ that..opens in an irregular manner by the enlargement of the parts it contains ..: ruptile. **1866** *Treas. Bot.* 999/1 *Ruptile*, bursting irregularly, not in the line of union of parts in cohesion.

ruption (ˈrʌpʃən). Now *rare.* Also 5 **rupcioun**, 6 **-cyon, -tioun**. [ad. obs. F. *ruption*, or late L. *ruptio*, noun of action f. *rumpĕre* to break.]

1. Breach of the peace; disturbance. *rare.*

1483 in *Lett. Rich. III & Hen. VII* (Rolls) I. 51 How beit that oft tyme afore certain rupcioun, breke and distrublaunce, has been betwixt the realmes of Ingland and Scotland. **1893** HESLOP *Northumbld. Gloss.* s.v. *Ruction*, *Ruption*, a turmoil, as in cleaning; a disturbance, a row.

2. Breaking or rupture of some membrane or tissue of the animal body.

1541 R. COPLAND *Galyen's Terap.* 2 A ij b, The solution of contynuyte..commeth most often with concussyon and ruption. **1578** BANISTER *Hist. Man* v. 80 Membrans, and Fibers, toughe..and able, not in prompt to euery ruption. **1655** CULPEPPER, etc. *Riverius* II. v. 74 The Tunicle..is obnoxious to divers diseases, and especially to Ruption, Distortion, Dilatation, and Constriction. **1676** *Phil. Trans.* XI. 607, I found..I could easily enough unravel that cluster to a considerable length,..before ruption. **1855** HALIBURTON *Nature & Human Nat.* (1902) 218 You can't cure it, for it's a ruption of an air vessel, and you can't get at it to sew it up.

fig. **1650** ELDERFIELD *Civ. Right Tythes* 343 When mens greedy affections are also checked, their lusts crossed, and their tender ruptions touched to danger of offence.

'ruptive, *a. rare.* [f. L. *rupt-* (cf. next) + -IVE.] Causing, or tending to cause, breaking.

c **1425** tr. *Arderne's Surgery* (E.E.T.S.) 83 Witte þou þat auripigment is desiccatyue,.. ruptyue and cauteriatyue. *a* **1890** *Engineer* LXIX. 492 (Cent.), The action of a torsional ruptive force on rounding curves.

†'ruptor. *Obs. rare.* [a. L. *ruptor*, agent-noun f. *rumpĕre* to break.] (See quot.)

1656 BLOUNT *Glossogr.*, *Ruptor*, a breaker or tearer in peeces, a destroyer, he that violates.

†'ruptory, *sb. Med. Obs.* [ad. med.L. *ruptōrium*: cf. prec. and -ORY. So obs. F. *ruptoire*, Sp. and Pg. *ruptorio*, It. *rottorio*.] An application which causes a swelling to come to a head and break.

c **1400** *Lanfranc's Cirurg.* 292 Manye lewid lechis haue I seen þat coude on ruptorie, & þei supposide..bi þis maner ruptorie for to surmounte Galien in worchinge. *c* **1425** tr. *Arderne's Surgery* (E.E.T.S.) 14 Þer shewed ane bolnyng vndernepe,.. whiche I opned wiþ a ruptorie. **1544** PHAER *Pestilence* (1553) Pj, Some..breake the forsaid botche with a strong ruptorie. **1597** A. M. tr. *Guillemeau's Fr. Chirurg.* 42/1 To prævent that the *Escara* of the cauteryes or ruptoryes be not to harde. **1603** LODGE *Treat. Plague* (Hunterian Cl.) 68 Insteed of the actuall cautery..you must proceede with familiar ruptories, of which the best is that which is made of ashes and quicke lime boyled together. **1684** tr. *Bonet's Merc. Compit.* XII. 388 Then apply the Ruptory..till all the superfluous flesh be consumed. *c* **1720** W. GIBSON *Farrier's Guide* II. (1738) 121 The same author also recommends the use of *Retoires* or Ruptories.

So **†'ruptory** *a. Obs. rare.* [Cf. obs. F. *oingnement ruptoire*.]

c **1425** tr. *Arderne's Surgery* (E.E.T.S.) 14, I putte on his testiculez oon oyntement ruptorye. *c* **1720** W. GIBSON *Farrier's Dispens.* II. (1734) 91 It has the effect of a..Ruptory plaister without any considerable swelling.

'rupturable, *a.* [f. RUPTURE *v.* + -ABLE.] Capable of being ruptured or broken.

1898 W. JAMES *Human Immortality* 35 The veil of nature can grow thin and rupturable enough for such effects to occur.

rupture ('rʌptjʊə(r)), *sb.* Also 5 **ruptur**, 6 *Sc.* **ruptor**. [a. F. *rupture*, or ad. L. *ruptūra*, f. *rupt-*, ppl. stem of *rumpĕre* to break: see -URE.]

1. † **a.** Breach *of* a covenant, intercourse, or the peace. *Obs.*

1481 *Coventry Leet Bk.* 475 Wherby the seid trewes & other conuencions..myght fall in vyolacion or Ruptur in any wyse. **1496** *11th Rep. Hist. MSS. Comm.* App. III. 13 His requeste for to have..entrecours of merchandise..is gretly to our honour seing that the ruptur and discontinuaunce therof hathe not stand by us. **1535** *Act 27 Hen. VIII* c. 5 §1 Manifolde robberies,..ruptures of his peace & many other malfaites. **1551** *Reg. Privy Council Scot.* I. 118 Provyding alwayis that the said Lord do, nor procure to be done,..that may tend to the ruptor of the peace. *c* **1645** HOWELL *Lett.* I. IV. xxvii, Which was promis'd upon the rupture of the Treaties with Spain.

b. A breach of harmony or friendly relations between two persons or parties.

1583 STUBBES *Anat. Abus.* II. (1882) 115 Making schismes, ruptures, breaches, and factions in the church of God. *c* **1645** HOWELL *Lett.* I. III. xxvii, For we that have business to negotiate here are like to suffer much by this rupture. **1674** *Essex Papers* (Camden) I. 286 Who have declared a war..by open Acts of Hostilitie; and also those of Algier, Tripoly, and Tunis have offered faire for a Rupture. **1759** ROBERTSON *Hist. Scot.* VI. Wks. 1813 I. 461 This rupture contributed..to render the Duke still more odious to the nation. **1788** H. WALPOLE *Reminis.* vii. (1818) 50 She was safe while under the royal roof, even after the rupture between the king and prince. **1838** PRESCOTT *Ferd. & Is.* (1846) II. xviii. 164 He at first threw out hints of an immediate rupture. *a* **1862** BUCKLE *Civiliz.* (1869) III. ii. 93 The rupture between Church and State was now complete.

Comb. **1810** CRABBE *Borough* VI. 90 The litigious rupture-stirring race; Who to contention as to trade are led.

†c. Breach of continuity; interruption. *Obs.*

1639 FULLER *Holy War* I. xxiii, Some eminent particulars ..which constant tradition without rupture hath entailed on Posteritie. **1640** LD. DIGBY in Rushw. *Hist. Coll.* (1692) I. III. 147 A truer cause than the Ruptures and Intermission of Parliaments.

†d. The act of breaking out *into* arms. *Obs.*

1647 CLARENDON *Hist. Reb.* V. §91 [He] believed..that the preserving that Magazine..would likewise prevent any possible rupture into Armes.

2. *Path.* Abdominal hernia; a case of this.

1539 ELYOT *Cast. Helthe* 49b, Than shal ensue to hym that exerciseth, no peryll of obstruction or rupture. **1581** MULCASTER *Positions* xv. (1887) 69 The holding of ones breath vnadvisedly and with to much strayning causeth ruptures. **1615** CROOKE *Body of Man* 79 Which inward membrane if it be broken, and the externall dilated,.. causeth the one kinde of rupture or the other. **1662** R. MATHEW *Unl. Alch.* 126 Who said, that he had been troubled with a Rupture for ten or eleven years. **1706–7** FARQUHAR *Beaux' Strat.* I. i, She cures rheumatisms, ruptures, and broken shins in men. **1796** STEDMAN *Surinam* (1813) II. xviii. 63 Two fine young officers arrived, unfit for service by ruptures. **1818** CANNING *Sp. Indemnity Bill* Speeches (1838) VI. 33 That he had been cured of a rupture at the public expense. **1880** *Encycl. Brit.* XI. 752/2 Rupture is either congenital or acquired. *Ibid.*, Ruptures are most frequent at the extremes of life.

b. *attrib.* and *Comb.*, as ***rupture-cutter***, ***-doctor***, ***-quack***, ***-surgeon***.

1654 WHITLOCK *Zootomia* 436 A rare Oculist, Operator, Stone, or Broke, or Rupture-cutter, &c. **1763** *Ann. Reg.* 57 Another trial..wherein a rupture surgeon was plaintiff. **1783** POTT *Chirurg. Wks.* II. 48 That positive assertion which all rupture-quacks make use of. *Ibid.* 65 *note*, Some of these rupture-doctors have been largely rewarded. *a* **1843** SOUTHEY *Comm.-pl. Bk.* (1851) IV. 589 There were itinerant rupture-surgeons.

3. † **a.** A break in a surface or substance, such as the skin, flesh, etc. *Obs.*

c **1550** H. LLOYD *Treas. Health* R iij, Agaynst the chopping or ruptures. The Causes. Muche goynge in cold wyndes and drynesse. **1607** ROWLANDS *Earl of Warwick* (Hunterian Cl.) 78 He lent him such a powerful stroke It made wide ruptures in the Giant's flesh. **1673–4** GREW *Anat. Pl.*, *Trunks* I. iii. 120 The Pith,..as the Plant grows up,..hath divers openings or Ruptures made in it.

b. A break in the surface of the earth, etc.; a ravine, chasm, gorge, rift.

1555 EDEN *Decades* (Arb.) 212 In the riuers or ruptures or breaches of water. **1594** GREENE & LODGE *Looking Gl.* G.'s Wks. (Rtldg.) 132 What..malevolent Conspiring power.. Hath made the concave of the earth unclose, And shut in ruptures lovely Radagon? **1609** BIBLE (Douay) *Zech.* xiv. 4 The mount of olives shal be cloven..with a stiepe rupture exceding great. **1684** T. BURNET *Theory Earth* II. 50 At this chasm or rupture we suppose the fire wou'd gush out. **1703** MAUNDRELL *Journ. Jerus.* (1732) 142 There is a very great rupture in the side of Libanus. **1853** KANE *Grinnell Exp.* xxxvii. (1856) 344 The sea has dwindled to a narrow lane, flanked by the heavy hummocks, whose rupture formed the sides.

4. The act of breaking or bursting; the fact of being broken or burst.

1647 LILLY *Chr. Astrol.* xxxvi. 215 It's probable..your Water-course will be subject to ruptures or breaking downe of the Banks. **1667** MILTON *P.L.* VII. 419 The Egg that soon Bursting with kindly rupture forth disclos'd Thir callow young. **1731** ARBUTHNOT *Nat. of Aliments* (1735) 157 A Lute-string will bear a hundred Weight without Rupture. **1739** S. SHARPE *Surg.* 137 The Rupture of the Vessels of the Brain. **1799** KIRWAN *Geol. Ess.* 97 The rupture of the isthmus that joined Calais and Dover was probably effected by an earthquake at a later period. **1839** G. BIRD *Nat. Philos.* 276 A rapid succession of powerful currents being at each rupture of contact sent through the long coil. **1860** TYNDALL *Glac.* I. vi. 44 The rupture of the ice by the expansion of the air-bubbles. **1878** T. BRYANT *Pract. Surg.* I. 607 Rupture of the diaphragm is an accident that occurs in practice, but difficult to diagnose.

fig. **1642** FULLER *Holy & Prof. St.* III. i. 153 If with feasting him thou breakest thyself, he will not cure thy rupture. **1648** BOYLE *Seraph. Love* xi. (1700) 63 The glad Heart..to make room for such Guests, would stretch into a Rupture. **1745** *De Foe's Eng. Tradesm.* (1841) I. vii. 46 Nor can a man be supposed, in the rupture of his affairs, to receive any comfort.

rupture ('rʌptjʊə(r)), *v.* [f. prec.]

1. *trans.* **a.** To break, burst (a vessel, membrane, etc.).

1739 S. SHARPE *Surg.* 136 [If] the Vessels of the Brain and Membranes..are ruptur'd, they absorb the extravasated Blood again. **1797** M. BAILLIE *Morb. Anat.* (1807) 446 The vessels of the brain under such circumstances of disease, are much more liable to be ruptured than in a healthy state. **1834** J. FORBES *Laennec's Dis. Chest* (ed. 4) 143 We observe ..that some of the cells are simply dilated, while others are ruptured. **1875** DARWIN *Insectiv. Pl.* iii. 57 Here and there a few cells both in the glands and in the pedicels had escaped being ruptured.

b. To cause a breach of; to sever.

1854 MRS. JAMESON *Comm. Pl. Book* 256 The first [marriage], though perhaps unhappy or early ruptured. **1869** GOULBOURN *Purs. Holiness* vi. 53 My filial relationship to Him cannot be ruptured by my sin.

c. To affect (a person) with hernia.

1818 [see RUPTURED *ppl. a.* 2]. **1907** *Westm. Gaz.* 15 July 3/2 A printer..stated that he had been put in irons and had been thereby ruptured.

2. *intr.* To suffer a break or rupture.

1863 SPENCER *Ess.* II. 25 *note*, Instead of a nebulous ring rupturing at one point and collapsing into a single mass. **1876** BRISTOWE *Theory & Pract. Med.* (1878) 556 Aneurysms..are very apt to rupture at an early period into the pericardial cavity.

'ruptured, *ppl. a.* [f. prec. + -ED¹.]

1. Broken, burst.

1747 tr. *Astruc's Fevers* 292 The heat may be so great, as to..form a scab or crust on these ruptured pustules. **1813** J. THOMSON *Lect. Inflam.* 209 Fractured, torn, or ruptured surfaces. **1860** MOTLEY *Netherl.* V. I. 163 The patriots.. now erected a sconce..upon the ruptured dyke of Borght. **1887** D. MAGUIRE *Art Massage* iii. (ed. 4) 44, I will treat of ruptured tumours while on therapeutics.

2. Affected with rupture or hernia.

1818 CANNING *Sp. Indemnity Bill* Speeches (1838) VI. 32 With all the pomp of eloquence..was introduced, the revered and ruptured Ogden.

3. ruptured duck *U.S. Forces' slang*, (*a*) a damaged aircraft; (*b*) the discharge button given to ex-service men, with reference to its eagle motif.

1930 'W. W. WINDSTAFF' in S. Longstreet *Canvas Falcons* (1970) xvii. 291, I began to look for a place to bring down my ruptured duck, oil spitting in my face. **1945** *Time* 29 Oct. 11/1 The design of the present discharge button is not popular (G.I.s know it as the 'ruptured duck'). **1953** R. CHANDLER *Long Goodbye* xxxiii. 202 He was wearing a British Army Service badge. Their version of the ruptured duck. **1955** A. MORGAN *Great Man* 34 Just another guy in a sailor suit with a ruptured duck and a set of discharge papers. **1959** W. FAULKNER *Mansion* xii. 333 The ex-soldier or -sailor or -marine with his ruptured duck pushing the perambulator with one hand.

'rupturewort. *Bot.* [f. RUPTURE *sb.* 2.]

1. A plant of the genus *Herniaria*, esp. *Herniaria glabra*, formerly supposed to be efficacious in curing rupture or hernia.

1597 GERARDE *Herbal* II. clxxii. 569 A kind of knot grasse called Rupture Woorte. **1611** COTGR., *Boutonnet*, Rupture-wort, Burstwort. **1671** SALMON *Syn. Med.* III. xxii. 403 *Herniaria Millegrana*, Rupture-wort,..cures Ruptures, the Jaundies, Fluxes. **1713** *Phil. Trans.* XXVIII. 35 This seems to differ from the common hairy Rupture-wort, in having more twiggy Branches. **1775** J. JENKINSON tr. *Linnæus' Brit. Pl.* 38 Smooth Rupturewort. Found in gravelly places. *Ibid.*, Rough or hairy Rupturewort. In gravelly places, but not common. **1828** SIR J. E. SMITH *Eng. Flora* II. 8–9. **1848** JOHNS *Week at Lizard* 304 *Herniaria glabra*, variety *subciliata*, Fringed Rupture-wort,..is a plant peculiar to the district. **1866** *Treas. Bot.*

2. (See quots.)

1760 J. LEE *Introd. Bot.* App. 325 Rupture-wort, Least, *Linum*. **1777** JACOB *Catal. Plants* 92 *Linum Radiola*... The least Rupture-wort, or All-seed.

3. A West Indian plant (see quot.).

1864 GRISEBACH *Flora Brit. W. Ind.*, Colonial Names 787/1 Rupture-wort, *Alternanthera polygonoides*.

'rupturing, *vbl. sb.* [f. RUPTURE *v.* + -ING¹.]

1. *Bot.* (See quot. 1839.)

1839 LINDLEY *Introd. Bot.* 226 Rupturing consists in a spontaneous contraction of a portion of the pericarp, by which its texture is broken through. **1862** DARWIN *Orchids* i. 12, I will not affirm that the rupturing of the exterior membrane of the rostellum takes place spontaneously.

2. *attrib.* **rupturing capacity** *Electr. Engin.*, a measure of the ability of a circuit-breaker to withstand the surge produced by its operation.

1916 C. C. GARRARD *Electr. Switch & Controlling Gear* ii. 54 The remaining considerations which determine the rupturing capacity of an oil circuit breaker apart from size, robustness, quickness of break and, of course, the quality of the oil used, are length and number of breaks under oil, or speaking generally the capability of the switch to bring a large quantity of oil into intimate contact with the arc so as to smother the same as effectively as possible. **1930** *Engineering* 24 Jan. 97/3 These circuit breakers were designed for a rupturing capacity of 1,000,000 kva. **1970** J. SHEPHERD et al. *Higher Electr. Engin.* (ed. 2) xvii. 560 It is normal practice to specify the rupturing capacity of circuit breakers in kilovolt-amperes or megavolt-amperes. This practice is well established but may be criticized as not being logical, since the breaking capacity in megavolt-amperes is obtained from the product of short-circuit current and recovery voltage.

rural ('rʊərəl), *a.* and *sb.* Also 5 **rurale**, 5–7 **rurall**, 6 **-ell**. [a. F. *rural*, *-ale* (14th cent.), or ad. L. *rūrāl-is*, f. *rūr-*, *rūs* country: cf. RUSTIC *a.*]

In early examples there is usually little or no difference between the meanings of *rural* and *rustic*, but in later use the tendency is to employ *rural* when the idea of locality (country scenes, etc.) is prominent, and *rustic* when there is a suggestion of the more primitive qualities or manners naturally attaching to country life.

A. *adj.* **1. a.** Of persons: Living in the country; having the standing, qualities, or manners of peasants or country-folk; engaged in country occupations; agricultural or pastoral.

1412–20 LYDG. *Chron. Troy* (E.E.T.S.) 618 Ful likly is þat al þe gentil blood þoruȝ-out þe world shal distroied be; And rural folke..Shal han lordshipe & holy gouernaunce. **1430–40** —— *Bochas* IV. xv. (MS. Bodl. 263), Agothodus of berthe ful rurall Promooted was vnto estat roiall. *c* **1480** *St. Ursula* (Roxb.) A vij, The rurall rebelles aspyed her with her spouse. **1509** BARCLAY *Shyp of Folys* (1570) 152 A rurall man, rude and of simplicitie. **1547** BOORDE *Introd. Knowl.* v. (1870) 140 They do dyffer..as well in theyr apparel as in theyr maners, for they be rurall and rusticall. **1606** SHAKS. *Ant. & Cl.* V. ii. 233 Heere is a rurall Fellow, That will not be deny'de your Highnesse presence. **1697** DRYDEN *Virg. Georg.* I. 11 Ye Fawns, propitious to the rural Swains,..Join in my Work. **1784** COWPER *Task* I. 281 Not all its pride secures The grand retreat from injuries impress'd By rural carvers. **1837** LOCKHART *Scott* I. ii. 76 It was a system which bound together the various classes of the rural population in bonds of mutual love and confidence. **1876** MISS BRADDON *J. Haggard's Dau.* II. 16 Perhaps to keep company—odious phrase—with some rural swain.

absol. **1611** SPEED *Hist. Gt. Brit.* IX. xix. (1632) 931 Hee lulled the rural to thinke that his like had neuer raigned in England.

b. Presiding over, haunting, the country. *rare*⁻¹.

1582 STANYHURST *Æneis* III. (Arb.) 71 Thee sweete Nymphs rural I woorshipt.

c. Applied to a moth (see quot.).

1832 J. RENNIE *Butterfl. & M.* 53 The Rural Dart.. appears in August... Huntingdonshire and Kent.

2. a. ***rural dean***, ***deanery***: (see DEAN¹ 5).

c **1450** HOLLAND *Howlat* 809 The dene rurale, the Ravyn, reprovit him than. **1534** *Const. Provinc.* 2, 3 deanes rurall. *c* **1628** in Foley *Rec. Eng. Prov. S.J.* I. I. 137 Vicaires Generalls,..deanes, archdeacons, rurall deanes. **1642** SIR E. DERING *Sp. on Relig.* 91 The rurall Deanery. **1697–1765** [see DEAN¹ 5]. **1867** TROLLOPE *Chron. Barset* xlvii, Such a preliminary inquiry..need not be done by the rural dean at all. *Ibid.*, You will select two [clergymen] yourself out of your rural deanery.

b. Employed or stationed in country districts.

1840 BARHAM *Ingol. Leg.* Ser. I. *Bagman's Dog*, It's your uncle, or one of the 'Rural Policemen'. **1870** E. PEACOCK *Ralf Skirl.* III. 142 There were no rural messengers in those days.

3. a. Of or pertaining to, characteristic of, peasants or country-folk; rustic.

1513 DOUGLAS *Æneis* I. Prol. 316 And ȝit persaif I wele, be my consait, The king of poetis ganis nocht for rurale estait. **1617** MORYSON *Itin.* III. 100 The inhabitants [of Jutland] keeping their enemies out, long preserved a rude or rurall liberty. **1634** MILTON *Comus* 952 All the Swains that there abide, With Jiggs, and rural dance resort. **1770** GOLDSM. *Des. Vill.* 398, I see the rural virtues leave the land. **1784** COWPER *Task* IV. 557 Scenes rarely grac'd with rural manners now! **1874** GEO. ELIOT *Coll. Breakf.-P.* 368 In a sleek and rural apathy.

†**b.** = RUSTIC *a.* 1 c. *Obs.*$^{-1}$

1560 DAUS tr. *Sleidane's Comm.* 99 The state of christendom was troublesome..for the late sedition and rurall warre, and for disobedience within the Empyre.

4. a. Of poetry, music, etc.: Natural or appropriate to the country or to country-people; unpolished, plain, simple.

c **1470** HENRY *Wallace* XI. 1431 All worthi men at redys this rurall dyt, Blaym nocht the buk. **1552** LYNDESAY *Monarche* 6335 All gentyll Redaris hertlye I Implore For tyll excuse my rurall rude Indyte. **1579** SPENSER *Sheph. Cal.* Jan. 64 Shee deignes not my good will, but doth reprove, And of my rurall musicke holdeth scorne. **1634** MILTON *Comus* 547, I..began..To meditate my rural minstrelsie. **1738** *Gentl. Mag.* VIII. 152/1 The Stile [of Comus], as it is rural, is more simple and plain than that of his Paradise Lost.

b. Similarly of musical instruments.

1610 WILLET *Daniel* 96 It was a kind of rurall harpe [sackbut]. **1717** LADY M. W. MONTAGU *Let. to Pope* 1 Apr., I have often seen them..playing on a rural instrument, perfectly answering the description of the ancient fistula, being composed of unequal reeds. **1797** MRS. RADCLIFFE *Italian* xiii, They were amusing themselves by playing upon these rural instruments.

5. a. Of, pertaining to, or characteristic of the country or country life as opposed to the town.

1590 SPENSER *F.Q.* III. vi. 15 In the countrey she abroad him sought, And in the rurall cottages inquired. **1611** SHAKS. *Wint. T.* IV. iv. 449 If euer henceforth, thou These rurall Latches to his entrance open. **1638** R. BAKER tr. *Balzac's Lett.* (vol. II.) 129, I see..that our rural pleasures are not worthy so much as to amuse so great a spirit. **1667** MILTON *P.L.* IX. 451 Each rural sight, each rural sound. **1746** FRANCIS tr. *Horace, Ep.* I. xvii. 12 By my advice retreat To the calm raptures of a rural seat. **1784** COWPER *Task* III. 625 So manifold,..All healthful, are th' employs of rural life. **1810** *Sporting Mag.* XXXVI. 167 Innocent country amusements called Rural Sports. **1841** W. SPALDING *Italy & It. Isl.* II. 32 Where a rural lane strikes off from the Appian Way towards the Grotto of Egeria. **1884** *Standard* 29 Feb. 2/4 The smaller tradesmen scattered throughout our rural towns.

b. Of occupations, labour, etc.

1608 WILLET *Hexapla Exod.* 11 They wrought..in all manner of rurall workes. **1667** MILTON *P.L.* V. 211 On to thir mornings rural work they haste Among sweet dewes and flours. **1725** POPE *Odyss.* XIV. 28 Of four assistants who his labour share, Three now were absent on the rural care. **1835** THIRLWALL *Greece* I. 405 To force a part of the population to quit the capital, and seek subsistence in rural occupations. **1875** RUSKIN *Fors Clav.* lviii, They can work..better than their labourers at all rural labour.

transf. **1774** GOLDSM. *Nat. Hist.* (1776) VIII. 87 How they are treated..belongs rather to the rural œconomist, than the natural historian.

c. Of a rustic form or make. *rare.*

1624 WOTTON *Architecture* in *Reliq.* (1672) 23 The Tuscan is a plain, massie, rural Pillar, resembling some sturdy well-limb'd Labourer, homely clad. **1875** KNIGHT *Dict. Mech.* 2004/2 *Rural Lock*, a cheap kind of lock with a wooden case. **1885** R. BUCHANAN *Annan Water* xi, She came to the rural bridge above Annan Water.

6. Special collocations, as ***rural district council***, the local council of a rural district (see DISTRICT *sb.* 3 b); abbrev. *R.D.C.*; ***rural free delivery*** (U.S.), the free delivery of mail to a rural area with limited local postal services; ***rural industry***, an industry or manufacture carried out in the country; (***Women's***) ***Rural Institute*** (Sc.), a Women's Institute (see quot. 1958); ***rural municipality*** (Canad.), an administrative division of a province; ***rural route*** (N. Amer.), a rural mail-delivery route; ***rural science***, the study of rural concerns, esp. agriculture; ***rural slum***, a country dwelling in disrepair; ***rural-urban*** adj., designating comparison or interchange between country and town; ***rural urbanization***, the investment of the country with an urban character.

1894, **1895** Rural district council [see *district-council* s.v. DISTRICT *sb.* 6]. **1929** [see COUNCIL-HOUSE 2]. **1974** *Times* 1 Apr. 14/1 In all, 422 authorities take over the functions of the 1,385 existing authorities—counties, boroughs, urban and rural district councils. **1893** M. H. CUSHING *Story of our Post Office* 1006 A very important effect of the rural free delivery has been to increase the pay of postmasters where it has been tried. **1900** *Congress. Rec.* 16 Jan. 873/1 The rural free delivery service has come to stay. **1930** J. M. STAHL *Growing with West* viii. 109, I talked upon rural free delivery to many thousands. **1944** *N.Y. Times* 19 Oct. 23/2 Mr. Stahl first proposed the establishment of the rural free delivery service in 1879. **1892** *Pall Mall Gaz.* 23 June 2/1 There is little hope of the general establishment of rural industries as long as the Post Office treats country districts with such scant consideration. **1949** 'J. TEY' *Brat Farrar* xxiv. 219 Mrs Stack,..being interested solely in rural industries, represented a Fixed Point in the flux of an agricultural show. **1958** *Listener* 6 Nov. 746/3 Are the efforts of the Rural Industries Organization being bent in the right direction? **1973** *Country Life* 28 June 1904/2 Twenty-seven small rural industries serving agriculture will be represented. **1922** *Scottish Women's Rural Institutes Handbk. 1921* 24 The Badge of the Scottish Women's Rural Institutes may be obtained from..London. **1932** 'O. DOUGLAS' *Priorsford* xxvii. 242 'Have you heard how many teams are going in for the Festival?'.. 'Seven. Three of them Rural Institutes.' 'The Rurals are very good as a rule.' **1958** *Everyman's Encycl.* XII. 637/1 In Scotland there is a similar [to the Women's Institutes] but quite independent organisation, and the title 'Rural Institutes' is used. **1861** *Nor' Wester* (Red River Settlement, Canada) 15 Aug. 1/4 Such was the state of things in Canada until 1847, when the Canadian Legislature passed an act (4 & 3 Vic. cap 10) to extend the municipal system to districts (now counties) and other rural municipalities. **1904** *Univ. Toronto Stud. Hist. & Econ.* II. 140 The council of a rural municipality is made up of a reeve and not less than four nor more than six councillors, the number being fixed by by-law. **1945** G. W. BROWN *Canad. Democracy in Action* (1947) vii. 84 One of the reasons for the apparent confusion is that rural municipalities go by different names in different provinces. **1964** *Naicam* (Sask.) *Sentinel* 26 Mar. 2/3 A meeting of the council of the Rural Municipality of Pleasantdale No. 398 was held in the R.M. office Wednesday. **1898** *Ann. Rep.* (U.S. Post Office Dept.) 163 Nine rural routes were carefully laid out by special agents of the free delivery service. **1956** *Chatham* (Ont.) *Daily News* 14 June 2/6 Entrants will be accepted from Thamesville and surrounding rural routes. **1965** *Globe & Mail* (Toronto) 15 Oct. 7/1 George Harris Hees of Bay Street, Toronto, St. James Street, Montreal, and, within the last month, of Rural Route 5, Cobourg. **1914** Rural science [see HOUSECRAFT]. **1939** *Nature* 18 Feb. 305 (*heading*) Training teachers of rural science. **1976** *Daily Times* (Lagos) 24 May 13/3 In order to promote sufficent interest in the tillage of the land subjects like nature study and rural science should be made compulsory in all primary schools. **1958** P. POLLACK *Picture Hist. Photogr.* III. 350/2 The somber, seamy existence endured by Americans living in rural slums. **1972** L. LAMB *Picture Frame* i. 13 Why.. should an extremely sophisticated exponent of abstract expressionism decide to set up his easel in..this rural slum? **1975** *Times* 10 Sept. 18/3 The site enveloped a rural slum community. **1957** R. K. MERTON *Soc. Theory & Soc. Structure* (1962) xviii. 592 Differences in rural-urban distribution of the two religions..may be seen. **1970** B. ROBERTS in I. L. Horowitz *Masses in Lat. Amer.* x. 346 The career experiences of low-income families, such as rural-urban and intra-urban migration. **1974** tr. *Wertheim's Evolution & Revolution* 198 Intensified rural-urban relationships might equally increase the revolutionary potential while..facilitating communication lines for revolutionaries. **1970** J. COTLER in I. L. Horowitz *Masses in Lat. Amer.* xii. 436 As a result of the confluence of urban ruralization and of rural urbanization, there has been a change in the patterns of social stratification of Mancha India.

B. *sb.* **1. a.** An inhabitant of the country; a countryman, rustic. Now *rare*.

a **1513** FABYAN *Chron.* VII. (1811) 497 Sir Thomas punysshed the sayd vyllages and rurallis by greuous fynes. *a* **1575** tr. *Pol. Vergil's Eng. Hist.* (Camden No. 36) 41 Theruralls and common people bie the entercourse..are made verie civill. **1602** J. DAVIES (Heref.) *Mirum in Modum* ccxlii, The Cittizens the outward Sences bee, The Ruralls be the Bodies rare. **1657** G. THORNLEY *Daphnis & Chloe* 47 Every rural began to be busie in the fields. **1831** *John Bull* Aug. 250 This delightful place continues the resort of the *élite* of the town; nor are the 'rurals' less liberal in their patronage.

b. A rural policeman.

1860 *Illustr. Lond. News* 26 May 506/2 Sir Richard Mayne's picked A's, and the ever-meddling Surrey 'rurals'.

†**2.** *pl.* = GEORGIC B. 2 b. *Obs.*

1589 A. FLEMING *Virg. Georg.* 3 First beginning with his Bucoliks or Pastoralls,..then his Georgiks or ruralls went in hand, as he fell in loue with good husbandrie.

3. ellipt. for: (*a*) (*Women's*) *Rural Institute*; (*b*) *Rural District Council* (rare); see A 6 above.

1932 [see (*Women's*) *Rural Institute*, sense A. 6 above]. **1940** 'O. DOUGLAS' *House that is our Own* viii. 82 'She takes to do wi' the Nursing and the Rural.' 'The Rural?' 'Aye, ye ken, Women's Rural Institute.' **1952** M. LASKI *Village* iv. 71 The new Housing Estate..the Walbridge Rural is going to put down at the bottom of Archery Lane. **1967** I. TAIN *Cherrycake Death* ii. 15 The Rurals were generally held to fulfil a need in the district. **1973** A. MACVICAR *Painted Doll Affair.* x. 113 Jessie's out at a Women's Rural and Moira's at night school.

'ruralism. [f. prec. + -ISM.]

1. Rural quality or character; country life.

1864 WEBSTER, *Ruralism*, the state of being rural; ruralness. **1879** MRS. HUNGERFORD *Airy Fairy Lilian* II. 208 Addicted to City pursuits and holding country life and ruralism generally in abhorrence. **1894** MRS. H. WARD *Marcella* I. 51 The agricultural world as it is,—no stage ruralism, but the bare fact.

2. A country idiom or expression; a rusticism.

1882 *Ogilvie's Imp. Dict.* (Annandale).

'ruralist. [f. as prec. + -IST.]

1. A countryman, peasant.

1739 H. COVENTRY *Philemon to Hydaspes* III. 66 An Image, which must have pleaded so strongly with our Egyptian Ruralists for a direct and unqualified Adoration of the solar Orb. **1756** AMORY *Buncle* (1770) II. 172 The Egyptian ruralists, without a creed and without a philosophy. **1822** LAMB *Elia* I, *Distant Correspondents*, Four poor elms, from whose smoke-dyed barks, the theme of jesting ruralists, I picked my first lady-birds. **1892** *Temple Bar* June 176 His childish faith..and absence of all hypocrisy make him [the Russian peasant] one of the most interesting ruralists in Europe.

2. An advocate of country as opposed to town life; one who leaves the town for the country.

1828 *Blackw. Mag.* XXIV. 326 The London season is over. Spite of the showery weather, the ruralists carry the day. **1889** WHITTIER *Prose Wks.* II. 248 The mere dilettante and the amateur ruralist may as well keep their hands off.

rurality (rʊ'rælɪtɪ). [f. RURAL *a.* + -ITY, perh. after F. *ruralité* (med.L. *ruralitas*).]

1. Rural quality or character, rusticity; country life, manners, or scenery.

1730 BAILEY (folio), *Rurality*, Ruralness, Country-likeness, Clownishness. **1778** [W. H. MARSHALL] *Minutes Agric., Digest* 1 A few years acquaintance with the World had convinced him, that Nature, Rurality, Contemplation and Happiness, are nearly allied. **1809** PINKNEY *Trav. France* 236 It has..an animation, an air of cleanness and rurality which seldom belong to a populous city. **1853** SURTEES *Sponge's Sp. Tour* (1893) 11 The full rurality of grass country, sprinkled with fallows and turnip-fields. **1883** W. BESANT *All in Garden Fair* I. ii, The rurality of the place, to one fresh from town, seems overdone.

2. With *a* and pl. A rural characteristic, feature, or topic; a rural object, locality, landscape, etc.

1823 SCOTT *Fam. Lett.* (1894) II. xix. 171 The 12th of July dismisses me to my ruralities for four months. **1844** R. P. WARD *Chatsworth* I. 17 The Regent's Park ruralities of Marienbad; the Primrose-hill prettiness of Kissingen. **1893** *Athenæum* 9 Dec. 813/2 Spottiness and..slight opacity.. have long beset his pleasant ruralities.

rurali'zation. [f. next + -ATION.] Going into, transference to, the country.

1859 SALA *Tw. round Clock* (1861) 198 Turnham Green and Kew were places where citizens took their wives to enjoy the perfection of ruralisation. **1892** *Standard* 10 June 5/2 This ruralisation of the great Metropolitan schools.

ruralize ('rʊərəlaɪz), *v.* [f. RURAL *a.* + -IZE.]

1. *trans.* To render rural or rustic in character.

1805 WORDSW. *Prel.* I. 89 Casting then A backward glance upon the curling cloud Of city smoke, by distance ruralised. **1883** STEVENSON *Silverado Sq.* 29 This tardy favourite of fortune..—thoroughly ruralized from head to foot.

2. *intr.* To go into the country; to sojourn in the country, to rusticate.

1822 MRS. E. NATHAN *Langreath* I. 15 A large party, whom he intended bringing from London to ruralize during the autumn. **1843** F. E. PAGET *Warden of Berkingholt* 139 It will be found that they have been ruralizing with Dr. Wiseman at Oscott. **1866** *Lond. Rev.* 23 June 697/2 In these days a man won't ruralize without publishing.

Hence **'ruralizing** *vbl. sb.*

1837 *New Monthly Mag.* LI. 341 A few days' ruralizing in the forest on such primitive fare. **1895** *Daily News* 4 June 3/5 The ruralising of parts of the metropolis through opening new grounds.

rurally ('rʊərəlɪ), *adv.* [-LY^{2}.] In a rural or country-like manner.

1792 WAKEFIELD *Mem.* (1804) I. 80 Jesus College is rurally situated at some distance from the body of the town. **1799** J. ROBERTSON *Agric. Perth* 476 In a situation warmly sheltered and rurally picturesque. **1845** J. COULTER *Adv. Pacific* xvii. 267 The houses are all so rurally concealed, that [etc.]. **1871** B. TAYLOR *Faust* II. III. (Chandos) 299 Rurally quiet [do thou] Brighten the plain.

'ruralness. *rare*$^{-0}$. [-NESS.] 'Country-likeness, clownishness' (Bailey, 1730).

†**'ruralty.** *Obs.*$^{-1}$ [-TY.] Agricultural or country population.

c **1640** J. SMYTH *Lives Berkeleys* (1883) II. 287 None other guests but the gentlemen and ruralty of the County.

†**'rurate.** *Obs.*$^{-1}$ (Apparently f. *rur-al*, after *curate*; but perh. an error for *jurate*.)

c **1560** *Phylogamus* in *Skelton's Wks.* (1843) I. p. cxvi, O poet rare and recent.., Sparyng no priest or curate, Cyuylyan or rurate.

rurban ('rɜːbən), *a.* [f. R(URAL *a.* + URBAN *a.*] Combining the characteristics of country and town; designating an area sharing rural and urban ways of life.

1918 C. J. GALPIN *Rural Life* iii. 64 The word *rurban* is formed by blending *rural* into *urban*. **1932** *Times Lit. Suppl.* 11 Feb. 86/2 The science of towns..shows itself a science with technical terms, such as 'conurbation' and 'rurban'. **1939** O. E. BAKER in *Agric. in Mod. Life* I. ix. 165 Should.. rural and urban merge in what has been called a 'rurban' civilization the cultural consequences would also be profound. **1945** H. H. BALK in *Econ. Geogr.* XXI. 108/2 A rurban area has very definite advantages over a strictly agricultural or rural area from the farmer's point of view. **1961** *New Yorker* 28 Oct. 43/3 In an article about the spread of highways and housing developments from cities to former farmland, we came upon a reference to 'the rurban explosion'. **1981** *Country Life* 2 July 7 To draw attention to his unsatisfactory rural-urban development, the Second Land Utilisation Survey has given it a distinctive name: rurban fringe.

Hence **'rurbanism**, the properties of town and country life regarded as interacting and inseparable; **'rurbanist**, an advocate of rurbanism; **rurbani'zation** the susceptibility of town life to rural influences.

1918 C. J. GALPIN *Rural Life* iii. 64 The idea of rurbanism is that..the open country is an element in the clustered town, and the town is a factor of the land, and the civilization, culture, and development of rural people are to be found in conjunction with town and small city, and not apart. *Ibid.*, The rurbanist boldly attempts to adjust anew the malrelations of the farm to the cluster. **1931** N. CARPENTER *Sociol. City Life* xiv. 453 Urbanized societies are those in which the cultural effects of 'rurbanization' are to be found. **1943** C. L. WHITE *Regional Geogr. Anglo-America* xiii. 403 Rather than have three fourths to four fifths of our population reside in great cities, O. E. Baker recommends rurbanism. **1959** *Economist* 30 May 850/1 Millions of city dwellers have swarmed into the countryside to set a new and increasingly widespread pattern of life which is sometimes called 'rurbanisation', sometimes 'urbiculture'. **1976** *National Observer* (U.S.) 10 July 6/4 He calls the young back-to-the-landers the 'vanguard of a new ruralism'. Another way to look at it is the 'rurbanization' of America, he says.

rurd(e, obs. variants of RERD(E.

† **rure.** *Obs.* Forms: 1 hryre, 2 rere, 3 rure. [OE. *hryre*, f. *hrur-, hrus-*, weak grade of *hréosan* REOSE *v.*] Fall; ruin.

Beowulf 1681 Hit on æht ȝehwearf æfter deofla hryre. *c* **888** K. ÆLFRED *Boeth.* xvi. §4 We witon.. hwilce hryras.. se unrihtwisa kasere Neron weorhte. *c* **1000** ÆLFRIC *Hom.* I. 144 Þis cild is ȝesett maneȝum mannum to hryre. *c* **1160** *Hatton Gosp.* Mark v. 13 On mycelen rere se heord warð on sæ bescofen. *a* **1250** *Owl & Night.* 1154 Þu singst aȝen eiȝte lure, Oþer of summe frondes rure.

† **'ruric,** *a. Obs.*$^{-1}$ In 5 ruryk. [Cf. med.L. *ruricus* (Du Cange).] Rustic.

c **1470** HENRY *Wallace* VII. 398 Thocht ruryk folk tharoff haff litill feill, Na deyme na lord, bot landis be thair part.

ru'ricolist. *rare*$^{-0}$. [f. L. *rūricola*.] A husbandman (Bailey, 1730). So **ru'ricolous** *a.*, 'living in the country or fields' (Mayne, 1858).

ruridecanal (rʊərɪ'dɛkənəl, -dɪ'keɪnəl), *a.* [f. L. *rūri-*, combining form of *rūs* country, + DECANAL.] Of or pertaining to a rural dean or deanery.

1861 J. A. PHILLIPS *Missionary Pupils* 10 Members of each Ruri-decanal chapter should find a Missionary-candidate and raise funds for his education. **1888** BURGON *Lives 12 Gd. Men* II. x. 280 A revival of Ruridecanal action throughout the diocese had preceded.

† **'rurify,** *v. Obs.*$^{-1}$ [See prec. and -FY.] *trans.* To countrify.

1593 R. HARVEY *Philad.* 77 His grace is lost, his maiestie diminished, and hee euen rurified like a priuate subiect.

† **'rurigene.** *Obs.*$^{-0}$ (See quot. and next.)

1656 BLOUNT *Glossogr.*, *Rurigene*, born in, dwelling or abiding in the Country; country people. [Hence in Phillips, Bailey, etc.]

ru'rigenous, *a. rare.* [f. L. *rūrigen-a* + -OUS.] Born or dwelling in the country; rustic.

1730 in BAILEY (folio). **1799** E. DU BOIS *Piece Family Biog.* II. 119 Rurigenous cook-maids, and automatical bankers' clerks may take care of their autography. **1807** G. CHALMERS *Caledonia* II. 936 The word runchies, for weeds, is generally known to rurigenous people.

Ruritania (rʊərɪ'teɪnɪə). [Name of the scene of Anthony Hope's novels *The Prisoner of Zenda* (1894) and *Rupert of Hentzau* (1898); f. L. *rūri-s*, *rūs* country + *-tania* as in *Lusitania*.] An imaginary kingdom of Central Europe: used allusively for a scene of court romance and intrigue in a modern setting, or for a petty state; more generally, any imaginary country.

[**1894** 'A. HOPE' *Prisoner of Zenda* i. 9 There came on a visit to the English Court a certain prince, who was afterwards known to history as Rudolf the Third of Ruritania.] **1897** G. B. SHAW in *Sat. Rev.* 30 Jan. 115/2 If Mr Alexander.. had produced it and Sodom's Ende and so forth at a series of *matinées* of the 'Saturday Pop' class, financing them from the exchequer of the Kingdom of Ruritania [etc.]. **1929** —— *League of Nations* 8 Let us suppose that Ruritania is given a mandate to govern Lilliput provisionally for Lilliput's good. **1939** *Flight* 21 Sept. 249/1 One cannot expect every Ruritania to maintain an air arm equal to that of the Germans. **1956** A. WILSON *Anglo-Saxon Attitudes* 154 Inge.. looked like the queen of some Northern Ruritania at the novel's happy ending. **1965** *New Statesman* 23 Apr. 638/1 Britain is being slowly pushed out of the main manufacturing export markets, and is taking refuge in the luxury trades... I suppose if we can't make our living in any other way, it will have to do. But let's not kid ourselves about a renaissance. This is national senescence, the Road to Ruritania. **1976** *Times* 9 Mar. 17/2 The right tactics.. are to let the central bank of Ruritania drive the price of sterling down against itself.

Ruritanian (rʊərɪ'teɪnɪən), *a.* (*sb.*) [f. prec. + -AN.] Of, pertaining to, or characteristic of Ruritania, esp. with reference to the romantic or fanciful associations of the name; hence used with reference to any imaginary country. Also as *sb.*, an inhabitant or supporter of a Ruritania, or a person endowed with Ruritanian attributes or characteristics; more generally, an imaginary inhabitant of a country.

1894 'A. HOPE' *Prisoner of Zenda* i. 9 Prince Rudolf.. was adroitly smuggled off by the Ruritanian ambassador. *Ibid.* ii. 24 Every Ruritanian knows Duke Michael. **1896** G. B. SHAW in *Sat. Rev.* 11 Jan. 39/1 Our common sense which, if aroused, must immediately put a summary stop to the somewhat silly Ruritanian gambols of our imagination. **1902** *Daily Chron.* 21 Nov. 5/4 'The Traitors' is a spirited example of what may be called Ruritanian romance. **1920** H. G. WELLS *Outl. Hist.* xxxvii. 601 He [*sc.* Mirabeau] had.. indulged in a sort of Ruritanian flirtation with the queen. **1935** *Punch* 20 Mar. 335/1 The third volume of *The Story of My Life* by Marie, Queen of Roumania.. consists almost entirely of entries in the author's diaries. A book for Ruritanians and royalists. **1944** H. G. WELLS *'42 to '44* II. 52 The planners count noses and claim this or that district because there are 59 per cent. alleged Ruritanians here, or because 42 per cent. of the people there belong to the Lutheran Church. **1950** 'P. WOODRUFF' *Island of Chamba* v. 71, I do enjoy it,.. the alternations between rich farce, charming comedy and Ruritanian politics. **1958** *Times* 20 May 10/5 In the Ruritanian world of mountain Lebanon almost anything can happen. **1969** G. GREENE *Travels with my Aunt* I. xii. 113 The Montreux Palace in baroque Edwardian like the home of a Ruritanian King. **1977** *Times* 5 Nov. 15/3 The modern world.. invaded the 'ruritanian charm' of the travel writers.

rurp (rɜːp). *Mountaineering.* [f. initial letters of *r*ealized *u*ltimate *r*eality *p*iton.] A type of very small piton.

1968 P. CREW *Encycl. Dict. Mountaineering* 104/2 *Rurp*,.. a very small American chrome-molybdenum piton, designed for use in hair-line cracks. **1972** D. HASTON *In High Places* ix. 104 A rurp—the smallest piton, about the size of a postage stamp. **1976** *Times* 13 Nov. 12/6 A curious armoury of pegs, rurps, sky hooks, bolts, and bongs now form the armoury of the modern [rock] climber.

ruru ('ruːruː). *N.Z.* [Maori.] The morepork, *Ninox novæseelandiæ*; = MOPOKE, MOREPORK 1.

1859 A. S. THOMSON *Story of N.Z.* I. i. 25 The natives call the owl Kou-Kou or Ru-ru. **1862** A. S. ATKINSON *Jrnl.* 22 Aug. in *Richmond-Atkinson Papers* (1960) I. xiii. 782 Old Potatau had likened himself to a ruru mobbed by a flock of popokateas. **1905** W. BAUCKE *Where White Man Treads* 48, I.. heard snatches of an ancient witch karakia being muttered round the corner, wherein a ruru.. is the medium of destruction.

Rus (rʌs, ruːs). Also 9 **Russ.** [Russ. *Rus'* (see RUSS *sb.* and *a.*), Arab. *Rūs*; cf. medieval Gr. *οἱ 'Pῶς*.] The name of a group of Swedish merchant warriors who established themselves around Kiev and the Dnieper in the ninth century, whose settlements gave rise to the later Russian principalities.

1845 *Encycl. Metrop.* XXIV. 225/1 The Vareghi (*conquering*) Russ, one of the enterprising Tribes of Scandinavia, whose fleets had appeared in the Bosphorus during the first half of the IXth Century. **1876** V. THOMSEN *Relations betw. Anc. Russia & Scandinavia* II. 37, I am going to.. corroborate.. the Scandinavian origin of the Russ. **1918** R. BEAZLEY et al. *From Varangians to Bolsheviks* I. i. 3 Both the name of *Rus* and the fact of a Russian people and Russian States are due to them [*sc.* the Scandinavians]. **1927** E. V. GORDON *Introd. Old Norse* p. xxi, From the Swedish founders of this kingdom.. Russia takes its name, for the Swedes were known in the east as Rus. The population of the kingdom of the Rus was.. mainly Slavonic, and the Rus themselves gradually lost their traditions and language. **1948** G. VERNADSKY *Kievan Russia* vi. 138 In Kiev the prince's retinue.. consisted of the Swedish Rus. **1965** H. M. SMYSER in Bessinger & Creed *Medieval & Linguistic Studies* 92 In 921, Ibn Faḍlān.. described.. a tribe of Swedish Rūs Vikings, or, more accurately, Rūs armed merchants, and.. a funeral which these Rūs accorded one of their chief men. **1976** H. R. ELLIS DAVIDSON *Viking Road to Byzantium* I. iv. 56 It is in the ninth century that we first hear of the Rus, who were well known to Arab geographers, and whom the Byzantine Greeks called *Rhos*... For most western scholars, the name *Rus* is taken primarily to denote the Scandinavian settlers in Russia, particularly those established at Kiev in the ninth century. *Ibid.* 62 There is.. general agreement that in the ninth century the important Rus state on the Dnieper around Kiev was formed.

rus, abbrev. of RUSTICATION 3.

a **1890** SIR R. F. BURTON in Lady Burton *Life* (1893) I. 90 I was singled out.. by an especial recommendation not to return to Oxford from a Rus.

rusa ('ruːsə). [mod.L. (C. Hamilton Smith, 1827), a. Malay *rūsa*: cf. BABIROUSSA.] Either of two deer, *Cervus equinus* or *C. unicolor*, native to southern Asia. Cf. SAMBUR.

1783 W. MARSDEN *Hist. Sumatra* 94 Deer: *rooso*: *keejang*. There are variety of the deer species; of which some are very large. **1827** C. H. SMITH in Griffith tr. *Cuvier* IV. 104 The Rusa Group. This group consisting of Stags entirely Asiatic, is distinguished from all other Deer, by having round horns with a brow antler, but no median or bezantler. *Ibid.* 105 The Great Rusa (*Cervus Hippelaphus*). *Ibid.* 116 Although the true Axines have horns of similar form with the Rusas, their structure is more slender. **1839** T. J. NEWBOLD *Straits of Malacca* I. vii. 436 Of the genus Cervus, are the Kijang.., the Rúsa or Cervus Hippelaphus. **1862** BEVERIDGE *Hist. India* I. Introd. 11 The Saumer, or black rusa of Bengal. *Ibid.*, The great rusa stag, nearly as large as a horse. **1877** *Nature* 26 Apr. 562/1 The additions.. during the past week include a Rusa Deer (*Cervus rusa*) from Java. **1958** J. SLIMMING *Temiar Jungle* ii. 23 A few yards away were the tracks of a *Rusa*, a Malayan deer.

rusa, variant of ROOSA.

† **Rusband.** *Obs.*$^{-1}$ [Perhaps a misprint for *Rusland* Russia.] Some kind of hemp.

1641 S. SMITH *Herring Buss Trade* 13 The best Rine and Rusband are these, Hempe brought in by the Eastland Merchants from the parts of Leiffeland and Prusia.

rusbank ('røsbaŋk). *S. Afr.* Also **rus-bank, rustbank,** etc. *Pl.* **rusbanks, rusbanke, rust banken.** [Afrikaans, f. *rus(t)* rest + *bank* bench.] A wooden settle or couch, usu. with a seat of woven leather thongs or riempies. Also *attrib.*

1880 J. NIXON *Among Boers* 216 Hans was seated on the 'rustbank', smoking a short wooden pipe. **1902** W. DOWER *Early Annals of Kokstad* 25 The few very rough seats and the rust banken.. were occupied by the men, the women sat on the floor. **1910** D. FAIRBRIDGE *That which hath Been* xxiii. 277 The baas and huisvrouw.. came out on their stoeps and sank into the capacious chairs and rust-banks. **1935** P. SMITH *Platkops Children* 76 After that was a long white house with a big stoep an' rus'-banks at each end. **1939** S. CLOETE *Watch for Dawn* 29 How alike all these Boer houses were. Each had the same rough, home-made riempie-seated rus-banks. **1947** *Cape Times* 5 Feb. 14 The farm-house has a huge dining-room with a massive centre table and, along one wall, the district's longest rustbank. **1965** M. G. ATMORE *Cape Furniture* 77 At all times the rustbank has been a 'multiple chair' in which the form was copied from the single chair of the time. **1971** *Evening Post* (Port Elizabeth) 8 May 20 The Furniture: Round Hand-made Stinkwood and Yellowwood Table on Pedestal Leg: three Yellowwood and Stinkwood Rusbanke. **1971** *Daily Dispatch* (East London) 8 Sept. 18 Old Rusbank-type Lounge Suite. **1972** *Grocott's Mail* (Grahamstown) 22 Feb. 1 Rusbank with riempie seat.

ruscan, variant of RUSKIN^{2} *Obs.*

rusche, obs. form of RUSH *sb.* and *v.*

ruschew, variant of RISHEW *Obs.*

† **'ruscled,** *a. Obs.*$^{-1}$ [Of obscure origin.] ? Wrinkled, rugged.

? *a* **1400** *Morte Arth.* 1096 Bullenekkyde was þat bierne, and brade in the scholders,.. Ruyd armes as an ake with rusclede sydes.

‖ **ruscus** ('rʌskəs). [med.L., for class. L. *ruscum*.] The plant butcher's broom or knee-holly.

1578 [see BUTCHER'S BROOM]. **1753** *Chambers' Cycl.* Suppl. s.v. *Bonifacia*, The broad-leaved ruscus, or butcher's-broom, commonly called the Alexandrian bay. **1882** 'OUIDA' *Maremma* I. 250 Where the tombs of the Tyrrhenes were hidden away behind the fence of thorny ruscus. **1899** *Allbutt's Syst. Med.* VIII. 517 Birch tar (often sold as oleum rusci, but not made from the ruscus).

ruse ('ruːz), *sb.* [a. F. *ruse* (14th c.), vbl. sb. from *ruser*: see next.]

† **1.** *Hunting.* A detour; a doubling or turning of a hunted animal to elude the dogs. *Obs.*

c **1410** *Master of Game* (MS. Digby 182) ii, Somtyme he goth away with hem and þen he maketh a ruse in some side. *Ibid.* xxx, Alle his blenches and his ruses beforeseyde.

2. A trick, stratagem, artifice, 'dodge'.

1625 in *Buccleuch MSS.* (Hist. MSS. Comm.) I. 261 The ruse of the bill of plague will start men to come up that are in the country. **1670** *Ibid.* 473 This might have been a ruse of the French. **1692** RAY *Creation* (ed. 2) 128 The wiles and ruses, which these timid creatures [hares] make use of to save themselves. **1746** G. TURNBULL tr. *Justin* XXI. iii, When there was no more opportunity for rapine, he out-reached the whole city by this cunning ruse. **1823** J. BADCOCK *Domestic Amusem.* 33 The double ruse of decyphering the despatches, and then forwarding them by another hand. **1845** M. PATTISON *Ess.* (1889) I. 14 They.. endeavoured by some clumsy expedient, or grotesque ruse, to evade it. **1879** FARRAR *St. Paul* (1883) 173 The asserted conversion might be only a ruse to enable Saul to learn their secrets.

b. Without article.

1815 W. H. IRELAND *Scribbleomania* 120 Ruse ever ranks with the Cloth as Fair Game. **1863** *Sat. Rev.* 4 Apr. 447 Seizing by ruse the game that evaded other snares.

† **ruse,** *v.*^{1} *Obs.* Also 4 **ruyse,** 5 *Sc.* **rus.** [a. OF. *ruser, ruiser* (mod.F. *ruser*): see RUSH *v.*^{2}]

1. a. *trans.* To drive back in battle.

c **1330** R. BRUNNE *Chron. Wace* 4658 Þeyr egre comyng þe Romayns a-boden,.. & ruysed þe Brutons abak in feld. **1375** BARBOUR *Bruce* XII. 527 The Scottis men fast can thame payne Thair fais mekill mycht to rus. I trow thai sall no payne refus [etc.].

b. *intr.* To give way, retreat.

c **1450** *Merlin* xviii. 288 As soone as Gawein was come he be-gan to do so well that the saisnes rused and lefte place.

2. Of a hunted animal: To make a detour or other movement in order to escape from the dogs.

c **1369** CHAUCER *Dethe Blaunche* 381 So at þe last This hert rused & stale away Fro al þe houndis a prive way. *c* **1410** *Master of Game* (MS. Digby 182) ii, Þenne he begynneth to shewe his wiles and ruseith to and fro. *Ibid.*, Þen he shall ruse oute of þe wey for to stalle or qwatte to rest hym.

Hence † **'rusing** *vbl. sb. Obs.*

c **1410** *Master of Game* (MS. Digby 182) xxxiii, He seeth þat betynge vppe þe ryueres and brokes,.. nor rusyng to and froo vpon hymselfe.., ne may not helpe.

ruse, *v.*^{2} *dial.* Variant of ROSE *v.*^{2}

1847 HALLIW., *Ruse*, to slide down a declivity with a rustling noise. *Devon.* **1874** MRS. WHITCOMBE *Bygone Days Devon & Cornw.* 91 Hold up your mare, for just here the cliff roozed down last week. **1888** ELWORTHY *W. Som. Word-bk.* s.v. *Ruse* and *Rusement*.

ruse, obs. form of ROOSE *sb.* and *v.*

‖ **rusé** (ryze), *a.* Also fem. **rusée,** Pl. **rusés.** [Fr.] Given to ruses, sly, cunning; deceitful, deceptive. Also as *sb.*

1761 G. COLMAN *Jealous Wife* III. 45 Your Ladyship, I hope, has no Objections to my being a little *rusé*, for I must have Her, 'pon Honour. **1847** DISRAELI *Tancred* II. iv. iii. 189 Aberdeen and Sir Peel will never give her this advice; their habits are formed. They are too old, too *rusés*. **1889** G. MEREDITH *Let.* 20 Sept. (1970) II. 980 *Rusée* that you are! **1903** A. BENNETT *Truth about Author* i. 8, I.. ordered the old rusé self to exploit the self just born. **1923** G. ATHERTON *Black Oxen* viii. 33 She was certainly *rusée*. **1938** H. G. WELLS *Apropos of Dolores* ii. 31 We hunted for five of the most rusé tennis balls I have ever known... They changed colour according to their surroundings. **1940** G. ARTHUR *Concerning Winston Spencer Churchill* 143 It was a most successful, if rather rusé, coup, but when anyone spoke of it as a military measure Kitchener would always say that Winston Churchill must have a large share of the credit. **1955** A. L. ROWSE *Expansion of Elizabethan England* x. 399

As a commander, he [*sc.* Sir Francis Vere] was exceedingly *rusé*. **1968** *Listener* 13 June 779/1 The values are unsurprising—the baby, the reliable if *rusé* Italian director, the true choice at the end. **1973** C. M. Woodhouse *Capodistria* v. 110 They constantly used of him [*sc.* Capodistria] the conventional epithets which seemed to fit his nationality—wily, *rusé*, supple, crafty.

‖**ruse de guerre** (ryz də gɛr). Pl. **ruses de guerre**. [Fr., lit. 'ruse of war': see RUSE *sb.*] A course of action intended to deceive an enemy in war; a stratagem. So, in extended uses, a justifiable trick.

1807 *Naval Anecdotes* vii. 185 We consider the whole of this singular passage as a kind of *ruse de guerre* to divert the public censure from Lord St. Vincent's Admiralty in regard to the supply of stores. **1814** M. Edgeworth *Patronage* III. xxxii. 302, I..thought even your praises of Rosamond's disposition..might only be *ruse de guerre*, or *ruse d'amour*. **1888** *Academy* 10 Nov. 300/2 Stubborn party duels, *ruses de guerre*, and all the heiving and hacking of the parliamentary fray. **1915** F. Piggott *Neutral Merchant* i. 11 By a *ruse de guerre*, or stratagem of war, I understand the adoption of some means of deceiving the enemy in war, some device out of the ordinary course of fighting. **1919** G. B. Shaw *Peace Conference Hints* vii. 99 These deceptions are necessary as *ruses de guerre*. **1922** J. Buchan *Huntingtower* v. 84 'It was an abominable lie.'..'Not at all. It was a necessary and proper *ruse de guerre*.' **1938** C. S. Forester *Flying Colours* i. 8 That had been a legitimate *ruse de guerre* for which historical precedents..could be quoted. **1962** *Times* 24 Apr. 12/6 It [*sc.* martial music] was no longer used as a *ruse de guerre*.

ruset-offal: see RUSSET *sb.* 5.

rusewale, variant of RUSSWALE *Obs.*

rush (rʌʃ), *sb.*[1] Forms: α. 1 risc (hrisc), risce, 3 riges (?), 4–5 rische (5 rissche), 4–6 risshe, 4–7 rishe (5 riche), 4–7 (9 *dial.*) rish; 4–5 rysche (5 rysch, ryche), 5–6 rys(s)he, rysse (5 ryse), 6 ryessh, rysh; also 1 (8– 9 *dial.*) rix, 1 rixe. β. 1 (h)rysc-, 2 rysse-, russe-, 4 rusche, ruysshe, 4–6 russhe (5 russh), 6 rushe, 5– rush; 5 roysche, rossh, 6 roche. γ. 1 resce, 4 ress(e, resshe, reisshe, reysshe, 5 resch(e, ressch, 5–6 (9 *dial.*) resh (6 reshe), 9 *dial.* reish; also 8–9 *dial.* rex (rexen). δ. 6 *north.* and *Sc.* rasch, rashe, raiche, 8– rash. [The remarkable variations in the vowel of this word make its precise history far from clear. The OE. *risc* (*rix*) and *risce* (*rixe*) correspond to MDu. *risch*, MLG. *risch(e*, *rysse*, and *risk*, *rysk*, LG. *risch(e*, *risk(e*, WFris. *risk*, and it is no doubt these forms, rather than *rysc*, which are represented by ME. *risch(e*. The evidence for OE. *rysc* is very slight, but is strengthened by the existence of continental forms with *u*, as Du. *rusch* (16th cent.), MLG. *rusch*, MHG. *rusch(e*, G. *rusch*, LG. and WFris. *rusk* (LG. also *rüsschen*, *rüsken*, etc.); whether ME. *rusch(e* is merely a dialectal representative of OE. *rysc*, or is due to foreign influence, is not clear. The continental forms, however, are prob. the source of OF. *rusche*, *rousche*, *rouche* (mod.F. dial. *rouche*, *rouce*), rush, reed, or sedge, which may have had some effect in ME. The OE. *resce* (found only once) appears to have no parallel in the cognate languages; the northern and Scottish *rash* is probably a variant of this, as in the case of *nash* for NESH *a.*

All the forms might have arisen as natural variants from an ablaut series *resc-, rasc-, rusc-, but the disturbing effect of both *r* and *sh* on adjacent vowels makes it uncertain how far this is really the case. The German adj. *rasch* has an almost parallel series of variants, and some ultimate connexion between this and the sb. is not impossible. The suggestion that the Teutonic word is an early adoption, with complete change of meaning, of L. *ruscum*, butcher's broom, is in the highest degree improbable.]

1. a. A plant of the order *Juncaceæ*, having straight naked stems or stalks (properly leaves) and growing in marshy ground, or on the borders of rivers or ponds; a single stem or stalk of this, either as growing, or as cut and used for some purpose.

Down to the 17th century green rushes were commonly employed for strewing on the floors of apartments.

α. *c* **725** *Corpus Gloss.* I. 530 *Juncus*, risc. *c* **900** tr. *Baeda's Hist.* III. xxiii, In þæm cleofum..wære upyrnende grownes hreodes & rixa. *c* **1000** Ælfric *Hom.* II. 402 Spyrte bið..of rixum ȝebroden. *Ibid.*, Rixe weaxst ȝewunelice on wæteriȝum stowum. *c* **1250** *Gen. & Ex.* 2595 In an fetles, of rigesses wrogt,..ðis child wunden ghe wulde don. **13..** *Coer de L.* 6038 Kyng Richard garte al the Ynglys Schere rysches in the marys. ? *a* **1366** Chaucer *Rom. Rose* 1701 The stalke was as risshe right, And theron stood the knoppe upright. *c* **1400** *S. Eng. Leg.* (MS. Bodl. 779) in Herrig's *Archiv* LXXXII. 335 Vppon a bed of risschen..his body he gan reste. **1483** *Act 1 Rich. III*, c. viii. §4 The seid Diers.. upon the lystes of the same Clothes festen and sowe great Risshes called Bull Risshes. **1529** More *Dyaloge* IV. Wks. 286/1, I haue laid you the places ready with ryshes betwene the leaues. **1562** Turner *Herbal* II. (1568) 104 It hath leues lyke succory and stalkes lyke rysshes. **1601** Holland *Pliny* XIX. ii, The Greekes in old time emploied their rishes in drawing of ropes. **1778** *Exmoor Scolding* Gloss. (E.D.S.), *Rex* or rather *Rix*, a Rush; *Rixen*, Rushes. **1828** Carr *Craven Gloss.*, *Rish*, rush. **1831** Lover *Leg.* 182, I..was peepin' out iv a turf o' rishes.

β. ? *c* **1000**, *a* **1200** [see 5 a]. **1393** Langl. *P. Pl.* C. x. 81 To rubbe and to rely, russhes to pilie. **1426** Lydg. *De Guil. Pilgr.* 14673 And placys ful off old ordure, I kan strowhe with Rosshys grene, That ther ys no Felthe sene. *c* **1475** in Wr.-Wülcker 786 *Hic cirpus*, a roysche. **1513** T. More in Grafton *Chron.* (1568) II. 765 The Queene..sate alone alowe on the rushes all desolate. **1561** in *Record of Caernarvon* (1838) 298 Permitting the rushes..and the roots of the same to stand and growe. **1635–56** Cowley *Davideis* I. 696 The Scholars far below upon the Ground, On fresh-strew'd Rushes place themselves around. **1697** Dryden *Virg. Past.* I. 66 Tho' Rushes over-spread the Neighb'ring Plains. **1756–7** tr. *Keysler's Trav.* (1760) I. 379 A wretched country, all overgrown with heath and rushes. **1796** H. Hunter tr. *St.-Pierre's Stud. Nat.* (1799) III. 416 It was lighted by a window shut by a texture of rushes. **1839** Ure *Dict. Arts* 836 The miner requires a powder-horn, rushes to be filled with gunpowder. **1848** *Jrnl. R. Agric. Soc.* IX. II. 556 The rush should at all times be tied only in a slip knot. **1869** Ruskin *Queen of Air* §79 The rushes differ wholly from the sedge and grass in their blossom structure.

γ. *a* **1100** in Wr.-Wülcker 324 *Juncus, uel scyrpus*, resce. *a* **1300** [see 2 a]. **1340** *Ayenb.* 253 Þet byeþ ylich þan þet zekþ þe crammeles ine þe russoles..oþer þane knotte ine þe resse. **1382** Wyclif *Job* viii. 11 Whether a resshe may liuen withoute humour? *a* **1400–50** *Alexander* 4126 Þare fand þai bernys & bridis..resild as a resch & roghe as a bere. **1489** *Accs. Ld. High Treas. Scotl.* I. 118 For resschis to the Haw off Lythqow the tyme of the Imbassatouris. **1570** Levins *Manip.* 91 A Resh, *iuncus.* **1778** [see α]. **1855** [Robinson] *Whitby Gloss.*, *Reshes*, the wire rush, the seaves of the moors and wastes. **1886** Elworthy *W. Somerset Wd.-Bk.*, *Rexen*, rushes. One of the very few words which retain the *en* plural.

δ. ? **15..** *Song* in *Compl. Scot.* (1872) vi. 64 Cou thou me the raschis grene. **1548** Turner *Names Herbes* (E.D.S.) 71 Scirpus..is called..in english a rishe or a rashe. **1554** *Extr. Burgh Rec. Edinb.* (1871) 283 For beireing of burds and trestis to the Queenis luging..and for flouris and raichis. ? *a* **1700** *Bessy Bell & Mary Gray* i. in Child *Ballads* IV. 76/2 They bigget a bower..And theekit it oer wi rashes. **1795** Macneill *Scotland's Skaith* I. viii, Light he bare her,.. Plac'd her on the new-mawn rashes. **1827** *Peril & Captivity* (Constable's Misc.) 133 See these hurdles of reeds.., this bed of rashes.

b. Used for burning; also *ellipt.*, a rush-light.

14.. in Wr.-Wülcker 722 *Hic lichinus*, a weke... *Hec secula*, a rysch. **1499** *Promp. Parv.* 456/2 Synke, of a lampe (*P.* holdinge the risshe), *mergulus.* **1572** Baret *Alv.*, The rushe, weeke, or match, that mainteyneth the light in the lampe. **1775** G. White *Selborne* lxviii, A good rush, which measured in length two feet four inches and a half, being minuted, burnt only three minutes short of an hour. **1840** Hood *Up Rhine* 206 Without the glimmer of a farthing rush! **1884** *Leisure Hour* Feb. 79/2 A long tallowed rush, which preserved an economical flame.

†**c.** Used for making a finger-ring: cf. RUSH-RING. *Obs.*

c **1449** Pecock *Repr.* II. v. 166 It is weel allowid..that he make a ring of a rische and putte it on his fynger. **1589** Greene *Menaphon* (Arb.) 88 Twas a good world..when a ring of a rush woulde tye as much Loue together as a Gimmon of golde. **1601** Shaks. *All's Well* II. ii. 24 As fit.. as Tibs rush for Toms fore-finger.

†**d.** In reference or with allusion to the practice of strewing fresh rushes for visitors. *Obs.*

1562 J. Heywood *Prov. & Epigr.* (1867) 48 Greene rushes for this straunger, strawe here. **1589** Greene *Menaphon* (Arb.) 85 When you come you shall haue greene rushes, you are such a straunger. **1602** Breton *Wonders worth Hearing* Wks. (Grosart) II. 5 Greene rushes, M. Francisco, it is a wonder to see you heere in this Country. **1617** Fletcher *Valentinian* II. iv, Rushes, Ladys, rushes, Rushes as green as Summer for this stranger. **1731–8** Swift *Pol. Conv.* 7 If we had known of your Coming, we would have strown Rushes for you.

e. Without article, as a material or species of plant.

1728 Chambers *Cycl.* s.v. *Shuttle*, A little Tube of Paper, Rush, or other Matter. **1847** C. Brontë *J. Eyre* xxviii, It showed no variation but of tint: green, where rush and moss overgrew the marshes. **1879** Tennyson *Lover's T.* IV. 141 A flat malarian world of reed and rush! **1907** *Athenæum* 14 Dec. 772/2 The body should be wrapped in rush, or bast, or grass, or hemp, and placed in a cage.

2. a. Used as a type of something of no value or importance, esp. in negative phrases as ***not to care a rush, not worth a rush.***

(*a*) *a* **1300** *Cursor M.* 21441 O ranscun namar þan a ress Wald he of her [= hear] bot of his flesche. *c* **1374** Chaucer *Troylus* III. 1161 He seide,..Not I not what, al dere ynow a rische. **1390** Gower *Conf.* II. 284 Only the value of a reysshe Of good in helpinge of an other. *a* **1450** *St. Cuthbert* (Surtees) 6077 Noȝt harmed þe valu of a resch. *a* **1568** Ascham *Scholem.* (Arb.) 54 To be able to raise taulke, and make discourse of euerie rishe. **1581** J. Bell *Haddon's Answ. Osor.* 423 It forceth not of a rush what you do there. **1841** Miall in *Nonconformist* I. 17 It matters not a rush. **1884** *Western Daily Press* 11 July 8/1 It does not signify a rush whether they can find..a precedent for what they ask.

(*b*) **1362** Langl. *P. Pl.* A. III. 137 Heo þat ben curset in constorie counteþ hit not at a russche. **1390** Gower *Conf.* II. 97 For til I se the daies spring, I sette slep noght at a risshe. *c* **1440** *Generydes* 1680 Of all his payne he wold not sett a rissh. **1543** Grafton *Contn. Harding* 533 He should then bee hable to matche with theim well ynough, and not to care a rushe for theim. **1584** R. Scot *Discov. Witchcr.* VI. iii. (1886) 93 Night-walking sprites..Esteeme them not twoo rushes. **1622** Massinger & Dekker *Virg. Martyr* II. iii, I weigh thee not a rush. **1658** Bramhall *Consecr. Bps.* viii. 194 Whose unjust Iudgement we doe not value a rush. **1712–3** Swift *Jrnl. to Stella* 9 Mar., People will grumble; but Lord Treasurer cares not a rush. **1759** Sterne *Tr. Shandy* I. xvi, He did not mind it a rush. **1848** J. Grant *Aide-de-C.* xxiv, He would not value his ducats..a rush. **1883** F. M. Crawford *Dr. Claudius* vii, Claudius did not care a rush whether the night were beautiful or otherwise.

(*c*) *c* **1422** Hoccleve *Min. Poems* xxiv. 193 They can nat keepe conseil worth a risshe. **1577** B. Googe *Heresbach's Husb.* I. (1586) 14 Without whiche, he is not woorth a rushe. **1627** Hakewill *Apol.* (1630) 296 They esteem not worth a rush any of our actions or manners. **1674** W. Pope in *Flatman's Poems* 2 Friends Applauses are not worth a Rush. **1768** Goldsm. *Good-n. Man* IV, My master's bill upon the city is not worth a rush. **1858** Lincoln in Herndon *Life* (1892) II. 116 Not one of them is worth a rush if you deny it.

(*d*) **1563** Foxe *A. & M.* 1367/2 Tush! a rushe for holy bread! *c* **1610** Rowlands *Terrible Battell* (Hunterian Cl.) 38 A figge for the whole world. A rush for thee. **1632** Vicars *Virgil* XI. 335 Brave sirs, our main work done,..A rush for what remains.

b. In various fig. or allusive phrases.

With quot. 1649 cf. the phrase *to seek a knot in a rush*, s.v. KNOT *sb.*[1] 14 b.

1525 Ld. Berners *Froiss.* II. lviii. 198 They..were redy for waggyng of a rysshe to make debate and stryfe. **1579** Fulke *Heskins' Parl.* 289 It hangeth on a rush that M. Hes. concludeth. **1611** Bible *Isaiah* ix. 14 The Lord will cut off from Israel head and taile, branch and rush in one day. **1629** H. Burton *Babel no Bethel* 103 They are all head and taile, branch and rush, one intire Papall faction. **1649** Jer. Taylor *Gt. Exemp.* iii. §14 The Lawyer being captious made a scruple in a smooth rush, asking what is meant by Neighbour. **1844** H. Stephens *Bk. Farm* I. 191 The larch.. shoots up, as straight as a rush, to a great height. **1889** 'R. Boldrewood' *Robbery under Arms* xiii, She was always as straight as a rush.

3. †**a.** One of the branchlets springing from the stem of Equisetum. *Obs.*

1578 Lyte *Dodoens* 100 The stemmes..do bringe forth rounde about every knot or joynt divers little, small, slender, and knottie rushes.

b. *U.S.* The horsetail. (Cf. DUTCH *a.* 3 c.)

1817 J. Bradbury *Trav.* 15 On the islands which we passed there is abundance of *Equisetum hyemale*, called by the settlers *rushes*.

4. With specific epithets:

a. Denoting various species of *Juncus*.

See also *moss-* (MOSS *sb.*[1] 6 b), *sea-*, *toad-*, and *wood-rush*.

1753 *Chambers' Cycl.* Suppl. s.v. *Juncus*, The species of rush, enumerated by Mr. Tournefort, are these: The sharp or pointed Rush... The smooth or soft Rush [etc.]. **1796** Withering *Brit. Pl.* (ed. 3) II. 345 Trifid Rush... Round-headed Rush... Soft Rush. Common Rush [etc.]. **1855** Miss Pratt *Flower. Pl.* V. 295 Lesser Bog Rush, or Little Bulbous Rush. *Ibid.* 296 Clustered Alpine Rush, or Black-spiked Rush.

b. ***flowering rush***: (see quots.).

1731 Miller *Gard. Dict.*, *Butomus*,..the Flowering Rush or Water Gladiole. **1760** J. Lee *Introd. Bot.* App. 325 Rush, Lesser flowering, *Scheuchzeria*. **1858** Baird *Cycl. Nat. Sci.*, *Butomus umbellatus*, the flowering rush, is considered the handsomest herbaceous plant of the British flora.

c. Applied to many plants of different genera more or less resembling the rush, as ***bog-, club-, Dutch, hare's-tail-, nut-, paper-, scouring, shave-, sweet, twig-, wood-rush*** (see these words).

5. *attrib.* **a.** Denoting the growth or prevalence of rushes, as ***rush-bed, -bottom, -drain, -land, -plat, -tuft.***

The second element in *rush-aisle* and *-hylle* appears to be the Lanc. dial. *hile* a cluster.

956 in Earle *Land Charters* 192 Of ðam broce..on þæt riscbed; of ðam riscbedde on ðone weȝ. ? *c* **1000** in Birch *Cartul. Sax.* I. 183 Of þam streame on ryscealas middewearde. *a* **1200** *Ibid.* III. 189 Fram gryndeles sylle to russemere, fram ryssemere to bælȝenham. **1483** *Cath. Angl.* 309/2 A Rysche hylle, *cirpetum.* **1736** Ainsworth *Eng.-Lat. Dict.*, A rush bed, *juncetum.* **1800** Bewick *Hist. Quad.* 354 A Hound bitch..pupped four whelps during a hard chase, which she carefully covered in a rush aisle. **1821** Clare *Vill. Minstr.* I. 58 The rush-tuft gone that hid the skylark's nest. *Ibid.* 105 Swamps of wild rush-beds. **1831** J. M. Peck *Guide for Emigrants* II. 105 In all the rush bottoms they [*sc.* cattle] fatten during the severe weather on rushes. **1855** Singleton *Virgil* I. 15 You skulked Behind the rush-plats. **1878** H. M. Stanley *Dark Cont.* I. xvi. 425 River-like marshes or broad rush-drains, choked with spear-grass. **1886** *All Year Round* 14 Aug. 36 Rush-land letting at four pounds an acre.

b. In sense 'made of rushes', as ***rush-bag, -basket, -boat, -bottom*** (also as *adj.*), ***-cap, -house, -mat, -matting, -mill, -rope, -seat*** (also as *adj.*), ***-work***, etc.

1896 A. Morrison *Child Jago* 185 Dicky, zealous at rush-bag-making. **1681** Grew *Musæum* IV. §iii. 372 A Rush Basket..very prettily woven together. **1605** Sylvester *Du Bartas* II. iii. III. *Lawe* 166 At length she layes it forth; in Rush-boat weaves it. **1792** A. Young *Trav. France* I. 24 Oak chairs with rush bottoms. **1809** 'D. Knickerbocker' *Hist. N.Y.* I. III. iii. 258 The young ladies seated themselves demurely in their rush-bottom chairs. **1866** D. G. Rossetti *Let.* 20 May (1965) II. 598 If there is anything besides rush-bottoms and ascetic glasses on which I should be glad to offer a fundamental remark..it is this. **1923** W. Deeping *Secret Sanctuary* xiii. 138 He made a move to sit down, and she saw him take one of the straight-backed rush-bottoms. **1960** J. Stroud *Shorn Lamb* iii. 27 Facing the magistrates.. was a single rush-bottom chair. **1842** *Dumfries Herald* Oct., The rush-cap on his head nodding like a mandarin's. **1835** Rush-house [see RAUPO]. **1797** *Encycl. Brit.* (ed. 3) XI. 638/1 A parcel of miserable rush huts. **1726** Swift *Gulliver* IV. x, The Sides and Floors..I..covered with Rush-matts of my own contriving. **1869** Tozer *Highl. Turkey* I. 337 Rooms.. furnished..with the usual rush mats. **1926–7** *Army & Navy Stores Catal.* 1103/4 Rush matting, 36 in. wide — per yard. 4/9. **1942** E. Waugh *Put out More Flags* ii. 108 The floor was covered in coarse rush matting and in places by bright Balkan rugs. **1964** *New Statesman* 14 Feb. 271/4 (Advt.), Rush-matting made-to-measure 2s. sq. ft. Rush-seated Italian chairs 9 gns a pair. **1804** Tarras *Poems* I We see.. Him near the burn..Dammin the gush, to gar his rash-mill rin. **1395** in *East Anglian* (1871) IV. 86 For ij bunches of Russherope, iij*d.* **1922** Joyce *Ulysses* 508 Woman undoing with sweet pudor her belt of rushrope, offers her allmoist yoni to man's lingam. 1896 *Heal & Son Catal.* 156 Ebonised Rush-Seat Chair—£0 4 9 Ebonised Chair, Rush Seat £0 6 3. 1918 *Ibid.* 25 Dark Oak Rush-seat Arm chair, 35/-. 1949 R. Harvey *Curtain Time* i. 6 And soon the audience would begin to gather, first for the rush seats in the gallery, then for the balcony and the main floor. 1971 *Country Life* 18 Feb. 366/3 The square drop-in rush seat was originally upholstered. 1687 Norris *Coll. Misc.* (1699) 38 If Tears in Rush-work may decipher'd be. 1934 E. Bowen *Cat Jumps & Other Stories* 190 She had discovered that Miss Weekes morris-danced, that she did rush-work. 1959 *Observer* 15 Mar. 14/5, I have just had a rustic chair reseated... Very neat rushwork. 1977 *Vogue* Feb. 115/2 A Connemara Craft Centre with ceramics, rushwork, tweeds.

c. In sense 'made of, consisting of, a rush', as ***rush-dip***, ***-lance***, ***-tube***, ***-wick***.

1673 Dryden *Epil. Univ. Oxford* 15 Stout Scaramoucha with rush lance rode in. 1725 *Fam. Dict.* s.v. *Candle*, Put.. in a small Rush-wick. 1780 Coxe *Russ. Disc.* 150 Hollowing out a stone, into which they put a rush-wick, and burn train oil. 1839 Ure *Dict. Arts* 836 A paper smift.. is then fixed to the top of the rush-tube. 1861 Reade *Cloister & H.* lvii, I'll not give him a rush dip.

d. In sense 'of or belonging to a rush', as ***rush-bent***, ***-pith***, ***-root***.

c1420 *Anturs of Arth.* 553 No more for þe faire fole þene for a risshe rote. 1801 *Encycl. Brit.* Suppl. I. 574/1 A rush-pith electrometer. 1821 Clare *Vill. Minstr.* I. 137 Quick the rush-bent fann'd away, As they danc'd and bounded through. 1862 H. Marryat *Year in Sweden* II. 419 A better light than the rush-pith burnt by English peasants twenty of thirty years since.

6. *Comb.* **a.** Objective, as ***rush-bearer***, ***-cutter***, ***-cutting***, ***-dealer***, ***-peeler***, ***-reaper***, ***-worker***.

c1552 in Strype *Cranmer* (1694) II. 137 A rope is a fytt reward for such ryshe repers As have strowed this church ageinst the Kings prechers. 1595 in Hanshall *Hist. Cheshire* (1817) 581 For wine to the Rushbearers. 1607 *Ibid.*, To the Rushbearers, wine, ale [etc.]. 1851 in *Illustr. Lond. News* 5 Aug. (1854) 119/3 Rush-manufacture, dealer. 1885 *Census Instructions* Index, Rush Peeler (for Rushlights). 1888 *Carlisle Patriot* 17 Aug. (E.D.D.), Service over, each rushbearer received the customary present. 1889 *Pall Mall G.* 17 Aug. 3/1 Fishing in the river, chatting with the rush-cutters. *Ibid.*, Rush cutting.

b. Instrumental, as ***rush-bordered***, ***-bottomed***, ***-floored***, ***-fringed***, ***-girt***, ***-matted***, ***-plaited***, ***-seated***, ***-seating***, ***-strewn***, ***-wove***.

a1847 Eliza Cook *Winter is here* v, The rush-bordered rills. 1912 W. de la Mare *Child's Day* 26 A green, rush-bordered pool. 1753 S. Fielding *Adv. David Simple* (ed. 2) V. vii. ii. 178 His Candle falling off the Table, set fire to a Rush-bottomed Chair. 1759 *Phil. Trans.* LI. 287 Several rush-bottomed chairs were burnt. 1840 C. F. Hoffman *Greyslaer* II. iii. i. 96 The apartment.. was large and rudely furnished, containing only.. a small cherry-wood table and a few rush-bottomed chairs. 1867 A. D. Richardson *Beyond Mississippi* xi. 131 The adjacent settlers came.. in heavy ox-wagons sitting upon rush-bottomed chairs. 1902 *Chambers's Jrnl.* July 471/2 Here were.. ancient rush-bottomed chairs, an old corner-cupboard with glass doors [etc.]. 1918 *Heal & Son Catal.* 2 Rush-bottomed Chair. 1976 'D. Halliday' *Dolly & Nanny Bird* v. 60 A creak from the stairs.. or the sounds of the rushbottomed chair I had used when feeding Benedict. 1741 Richardson *Pamela* III. 118 We went to bed,.. I to my Loft, and they to their Rush-floor'd cleanly Bedroom. 1881 Taunt *Map Thames* 60/2 The picturesque farm with its rush-fringed river's bank. 1836–48 B. D. Walsh *Aristoph., Acharnians* II. vi, In the rush-girt flask.. Mix the greasy Thasian soy. 1960 C. Day Lewis *Buried Day* x. 226 Our stone-floored, rush-matted living-room.. felt at first like an Aeolus' cave of draughts. 1939 F. Thompson *Lark Rise* xv. 273 His wide, rush-plaited hat. 1868 *Lessons of Middle Age* 273 The congregation sit on rush-seated chairs in the nave. 1952 M. Laski *Village* viii. 135 A long rush-seated oak stool. 1977 *Times* 3 Sept. 11/3 Rush-seated chairs and homely local service. 1926 *Daily Colonist* (Victoria, B.C.) 14 July 5/1 We do old-fashioned rush seating also chair recaning... The Red Cross Workshop. 1979 *Jrnl. R. Soc. Arts* CXXVII. 453/2 The pieces to be shown will demonstrate the variety of the skills learned by the students..—rush-seating, marquetry, turning, [etc.]. 1861 W. F. Collier *Hist. Eng. Lit.* 106 The gallants, who paid sixpence apiece for stools upon the rush-strewn stage. 1789 E. Darwin *Bot. Gard.* II. 38 With rush-wove crowns in sad procession move.

c. Similative, as ***rush-leaved***, ***-stemmed***; ***rush-looking***. Also rush-like.

1753 *Chambers' Cycl.* Suppl. s.v. *Narcissus*, The.. rush-leaved narcissus. 1855 Miss Pratt *Flower. Pl.* V. 269 Chive Garlic, or Rush-leaved Onion. 1871 M. C. Cooke *Hdbk. Fungi* 102 Rush-stemmed Nolanea. 1889 Westgarth *Austral. Progr.* 273 It has no grass, but in its stead some green rush-looking tufts, pleasant to our eyes.

7. Special combs., as **rush-broom**, (*a*) Spanish broom; (*b*) a yellow-flowered Australian shrub, *Viminaria denudata* (Morris, 1898); **rush-cart**, a cart piled with rushes at a rush-bearing; †**rush chicory**, = *rush succory*; †**rush cress** (?); **rush family**, the natural order *Juncaceæ*; †**rush garlic**, chives (cf. *rush leek*, *rush onion*); **rush-grass**, a species of grass having a rush-like appearance; **rush-holder**, a device for holding a rushlight; †**rush leek**, = *rush garlic*; **rush-man**, one who supplies or deals in rushes; **rush-nut** (see quot. 1819); †**rush onion**, = *rush garlic*; †**rush-pin** (?); **rush-sad** (?); †**rush succory**, the plant *Chondrilla juncea*; †**rush-tail**, a bird having a long slender tail; **rush-toad**, the natterjack; **rush veneer**, a species of moth; **rush wheat**, a species of wild wheat (*Triticum junceum*) growing on sandy shores.

1713 *Phil. Trans.* XXVIII. 219 Common Spanish *Rush-Broom. 1848 Ainsworth *Lancs. Witches* I. 148 In the rear of the performers in the pageant came the *rush-cart drawn by a team of eight stout horses. 1860 Kay-Shuttleworth *Scarsdale* I. 202 To assemble at its rushbearing.. at least eight, and sometimes a dozen, rush-carts. 1611 Cotgr., *Lettron*, Gumme Cichorie, *rush Cichorie. c1710 Petiver *Catal. Ray's Eng. Herbal* xlviii, Irish *Rush Cress. 1849 Balfour *Man. Bot.* §1084 *Juncaceæ*, the *Rush Family. 1578 Lyte *Dodoens* 643 This kinde is called in French, *des Oignoncettes*.., that is to say, *Rushe Garlike. 1753 *Chambers' Cycl.* Suppl. s.v. *Plantago*, The *gramen junceum* or *rush-grass. 1796 Withering *Brit. Pl.* (ed. 3) II. 76 Small Plymouth Rush-grass. 1820 Shelley *Hymn Merc.* xvii, With rushgrass tall, Lotus, and all sweet herbage. 1857 Thoreau *Maine W.* (1894) 36 Cutting the native grass—rush-grass and meadow-clover, as he called it. 1578 Lyte *Dodoens* 643 In Latine [it is called] *Scœnoprasum*, which may be Englished, *Rushe Leekes. 1606 Chapman *Gentleman Usher* II. i, Here is one That was a *Rush-mans jerkin, Wer't not absurd a Broome-man should weare it? 1819 *Pantologia* X, **Rush nut*, the root of the cyperus esculentus.., a native of Italy, where it is collected and eaten. 1887 Moloney *Forestry W. Afr.* 445 Chefa, Chufa or Earth Almond, Tiger or Rush Nut (*Cyperus esculentus*, L.)... The tubers, which are about the size of an ordinary bean, may be eaten either raw or cooked. 1578 Lyte *Dodoens* 642 Cyues or *Rushe Onyons, in the steede of leaues haue litle, smal, holowe.. blades, lyke to smal Rushes. 1673 *Maldon Borough Deeds* (Bundle 98, fol. 1), [Innkeepers fined] vis. viiid. a peece,.. for using *rushpinns in their severall yards. 1811 *Sporting Mag.* XXXVII. 34 The flag-sads cut too much, *rush-sads too little. 1548 Turner *Names Herbes* (E.D.S.) 26 Chondrilla.. maye be named in englishe *Ryshe Succory or gum Succory. 1598 Hakluyt *Voy.* II. ii. 100 The Portugals haue named them all according to some propriety which they haue; some they call *rushtailes, because their tailes be ..long and small like a rush. 1880 *Cassell's Nat. Hist.* IV. 360 The Natter-Jack, or *Rush Toad, is not common. 1819 Samouelle *Entomol. Compend.* 425 *Botys hybridalis*, the *rush Veneer. 1832 J. Rennie *Butterfl. & M.* 151 The Rush Veneer (*Nymphula hybridalis*, Schrank) appears in July. 1796 Withering *Brit. Plants* II. 173 *Triticum junceum.* Sea Wheat-grass. *Rush Wheat.

rush (rʌʃ), *sb.*² Also 4 russche, 5–6 rusche, 6 russhe, rushe. [f. rush *v.*²]

1. The act, or an act, of rushing; a sudden violent or tumultuous movement; a charge, an onslaught: **a.** Of persons or animals. *Esp.*, the movement of large numbers of people at a specified time or season to or from work, recreation, shops, etc.; *gen.*, haste, urgency; excessive activity.

c1380 *Sir Ferumb.* 2888 þan schullaþ our men.. be-trappe hem þar & take hem at one russche. c1470 Henry *Wallace* IV. 450 At the fyrst rusche feill Inglismen war slayne. a1639 Wotton *Life Dk. Buckhm.* in *Reliq.* (1651) 111 A Gentleman of his train.. spurred up his Horse, and with a violent rush severed him from the Duke. 1813 Shelley *Q. Mab* IV. 44 The ceaseless clangour, and the rush of men Inebriate with rage. 1885 *Sat. Rev.* 21 Feb. 235/2 Preparing their young horses for the wild rush of the hunting-field. 1924 G. B. Shaw *Saint Joan* p. vii, His accuser.. might have been picked out of any first class carriage on a suburban railway during the evening or morning rush from or to the City. 1925 H. Crane *Let.* 1 Dec. (1965) 220 Selling books in stores during the Christmas rush. 1931 H. Nicolson *Diary* 22 Aug. (1966) 88, I have learnt that rapidity, hustle and rush are the allies of superficiality. 1932 E. Bowen *To the North* vi. 51 She had not come down all this way.. in the middle of what she and Peter considered the Whitsun rush. 1939 [see after- I. 1]. 1943 E. B. White *Let.* 13 Aug. (1976) 243, I would like to discuss my publishing life with you some time. .. There is no rush about it, however, as I have no book ready to go. 1951 E. Paul *Springtime in Paris* ix. 157 The easter rush of tourists.. had crowded the St. Sulpice district to overflowing. 1973 [see *office worker* s.v. office *sb.* 12].

b. Of material things. Also, a rushing sound; a rushing sensation in the body; a thrill (of fear, pleasure, etc.); a drug-induced euphoria, = flash *sb.*² 1 h (*colloq.*).

c1425 Wyntoun *Cron.* IV. vii. 724 þar men mycht here bot dusche for dusche, Rappis ruyde withe mony a rusche. *Ibid.* IV. xxv. 2384 þat al þe wyndois in a rusche Off his chawmyr qwhar he laye Brak wp. 1535 Coverdale *2 Esdras* xiii. 11 The blast of fyre.. fell with a russhe vpon yᵉ people. 1541 Paynell *Catiline* xiv. 20 b, Whatsoeuer noise or rushe they hard, they fered it was Catiline and Manlius. 1648 Crashaw *Delights of the Muses* Poems (1904) 143 The rush of Death's unruly wave, Swept him off into his Grave. 1751 Johnson *Rambler* No. 126 ¶2 Overset by.. the rush of a larger vessel. 1789 J. Williams *Min. Kingd.* II. 148 Some mighty current, rush, or eddy of the tide. 1817 Shelley *Rev. Islam* v. xxix, Like the rush of showers Of hail in spring, pattering along the ground. 1848 Dickens *Dombey* xxvi, There was a sudden rush of blood to Mr. Dombey's face. 1873 'Ouida' *Pascarèl* I. 120 My eyes grew wet with a rush of tears. 1916 'Boyd Cable' *Action Front* 113 At nine, sharp to the tick of the clock, the rush, rush, rush of a field battery's shells passed overhead. 1922 Joyce *Ulysses* 509 He couldn't get a connection. Only, you know, sensation. A dry rush. 1971 *Frendz* 21 May 11/1 When you start smoking one type of Hash, the best rushes come during the first day of smoking. (Assuming the Hash is good). 1976 *National Observer* (U.S.) 23 Oct. 6 Methadone is addictive, too, but it doesn't give the pleasurable 'rush' that heroin addicts speak of. 1979 *Washington Post* 25 Mar. N5 Never again was there anything quite like the rush we got from the simple fact of spring.

c. *fig.* Of immaterial things.

1849 Macaulay *Hist. Eng.* viii. II. 336 In a ferment with the sudden rush of business from all corners of the kingdom. 1868 Dickens *Let. to M. de Cerjat* 26 Aug., To this hour I have sudden vague rushes of terror. 1883 F. M. Peard *Contrad.* xi, She.. gave the girl time to recover from her first rush of shyness.

d. *pl.* *Cinemat.* The first prints of film resulting from a period of shooting; the preliminary showing of such film; = daily *sb.* 4.

1924 G. R. Chester *On Set & Off* xvii. 206 Isidor Iskovitch sat very cockily exhibiting to his friend and boss.. some thousands of feet of 'rushes' on his pet picture, 'the Woman's Half'. 1927 L. Fawcett *Films Facts & Forecasts* xiv. 130 A good many pictures are entirely remade, and sometimes sequences are ordered to be reconstructed when the 'rushes' (short lengths of film) are seen during actual production. 1934 [see daily *sb.* 4]. 1940 *Manch. Guardian Weekly* 15 Nov. 355 We were shown 'stills' of Mr. Gielgud's Disraeli and.. in a private theatre we saw 'rushes' of the previous day's work. 1952 [see daily *sb.* 4]. 1956 B. Holiday *Lady sings Blues* (1973) xv. 126 Every night after we'd finished work at six o'clock, Blondie would rush to the projection room to see the rushes. 1962 *Movie* Sept. 31/2 For Rouch, the ideal film of this title would be the four hours of 'rushes', without cuts or montage. 1969 *New Yorker* 29 Nov. 160/2 Nothing makes us more aware of staginess than actors reciting poetry outdoors—as directors of Shakespearean movies discover when they look at their first day's rushes. 1976 C. Bermant *Coming Home* II. iv. 160 My function was to write the outline script as a rough guide for the film crew. Then, when the rushes were available, I re-wrote to fit the pictures.

e. Used *fig.* in phrs. ***bum's rush***, see bum *sb.*⁴ 1 b; ***to get a rush***, of a girl or woman: to be the recipient of frequent attentions from men; ***to give*** (someone, *spec.* a girl or woman) ***a rush***: to lavish attention on (that person) in the form of social engagements and entertainment. *colloq.*

1928 *Amer. Speech* III. 221 To say that a girl 'certainly gets a big rush' means that she has many desirable dates, and is 'cut' a lot at dances. 1934 J. O'Hara *Appointment in Samarra* (1935) i. 20 Wilhelmina Hall.. was still the best dancer in the club, and was getting the best rush. 1938 E. Bowen *Death of Heart* II. iv. 249, I don't think most girls appreciate friendship; all they want is to be given a rush. 1940 Wodehouse *Eggs, Beans & Crumpets* 93 He's been giving me the rush of a lifetime. 1953 H. Waugh *Last seen Wearing* 71 She goes round with another guy.. and I think he was giving her pretty much of a rush. 1956 W. H. Whyte *Organization Man* (1957) 252 An actor.. comes to town from the city for a short stay. He gives her a mild rush, and she dreams of a glamorous life with him. 1969 A. Lurie *Real People* 18 She certainly wasn't prepared for the rush she got, probably for the first time in her life... You've got to admit she's not madly attractive.

f. In *attrib.* use passing into *adj.*, denoting rapidity of movement, haste, or urgency. Also *ellipt.* as quasi-*adv.*

1879 W. Whitman *Daybooks & Notebooks* (1978) I. 145, I am told that Saturday is a real rush day. 1896 Rush order [in sense 9 below]. 1900 J. London *Let.* 15 Mar. (1966) 102 This isn't sharpshooting, but repelling a rush attack of a body of men. 1901 C. Moffett *Careers of Danger* 381 Already the mail clerks are swarming at the pouches, like printers on a rush edition. 1901 Merwin & Webster *Calumet 'K'* vii. 126 But if you ever try to put me on a rush job, I'll quit and buy a small farm. 1904 *N.Y. Herald* 17 Sept. 1 He stated that six weeks' rush work would be required to repair the boilers to make them serviceable and the ship seaworthy. 1929 T. H. Burnham *Engin. Econ.* xv. 199 Rush orders are difficult to put through, even in well-organized works. 1933 D. L. Sayers *Murder must Advertise* viii. 126 Mr. Copley.. was left working overtime upon a rush series of cut-price advertisements for Jamboree Jellies. 1933 Balmer & Wylie *When Worlds Collide* i. 24 You see, Tony, some—some things were being sent rush, by airplane. 1939 C. Day Lewis *Child of Misfortune* II. vi. 241 Christmas was a rush-time of services, visits to the sick, parties for the children and old people of the parish. 1946 *Ann. Reg. 1945* 40 There should be a three weeks' interval.. so as to avoid a rush election. 1955 'A. Gilbert' *Is she Dead Too?* viii. 151 She was gone before he arrived on the scene. It was a rush job. 1958 [see one *numeral a.* 30 b]. 1965 Mrs L. B. Johnson *White House Diary* 2 July (1970) 292 So I got a rush appointment with Mr. Per and went over for a permanent. 1968 *Listener* 8 Aug. 176/3 It was an odd life at Oxford at the time because most people had just come out of the army and were going in for quick degrees, sort of rush degrees. a1974 R. Crossman *Diaries* (1975) I. 238 They are horrifyingly superficial—merely a collection of the facts available to central government with one or two rush-job social surveys and some very hasty conclusions. 1977 R. V. Hudson in Bond & McLeod *Newslett. to Newspapers* II. 123 His expertise earned him an assignment to rush work and the highest wage among some fifty printers.

2. †**a.** *slang.* (See quots.) *Obs.*

1785 *Gentl. Mag.* LV. I. 485 Patroles have been productive of a new species of robbery called the *Rush*; that is, a number of villains assemble at the door of a house, and as soon as opened rush in, bind the family, and plunder the house. 1812 J. H. Vaux *Flash Dict.* s.v., A rush may signify a forcible entry by several men into a detached dwelling house for the purpose of robbing its owners.

b. *dial.* (See quots.)

1788 W. H. Marshall *Rur. Econ. Yorks.* Gloss., *Rush*, a feast; a merry-making; a rout. 1855 [Robinson] *Whitby Gloss.* s.v., A merry-making is often spoken of as 'the grand rush' that is going to be held.

3. a. *Rugby* and *N.Amer. Football.* An attempt by one or more players, *esp.* the forwards, to force the ball through the opponents' line and towards their goal. Also, a player who is skilled in this.

1857 Hughes *Tom Brown* I. v, Then follows rush upon rush, and scrummage upon scrummage. *Ibid.*, Don't give the rush a chance of reaching you! 1897 *Sportsman* 16 Dec., The Dark Blues broke away, but the rush was well saved by Black. 1903 *Westm. Gaz.* 13 Jan. 5/2 He.. had the reputation of being the best centre rush that the university [of Harvard] ever had. 1970 *Globe & Mail* (Toronto) 28 Sept. 18/6 Fleming was Hamilton's leading ground gainer with four catches for 66 yards and nine rushes for 42 more.

1979 *Honolulu Advertiser* 8 Jan. C-1/1 Larry's strong rush helped keep pressure on Ram quarterback Pat Haden.

b. *Croquet.* (See quot. 1874.)

1874 HEATH *Croquet Player* 14 *Rush*, a shot or roquet played so hard as to send the object ball to some spot where the striker desires to place it. **1877** *Encycl. Brit.* VI. 609/1 The learner should next practise.. *cutting*, which is a rush played fine instead of full.

c. *Amer.* A scrimmage or struggle between first and second year students.

1860 *Yale Lit. Mag.* XXVI. 22 As a basis, a Rush tacitly assumes that it is promoting a rivalry that is proper and praiseworthy. **1871** G. R. CUTTING *Stud. Life Amherst Coll.* 128 Participants will, however, readily recall the..'rush' of '67 and '68, in Athenæ Hall;..and..the 'rushes' of '71 with '72. **1905** *Dundee Advt.* 5 Dec. 4 What is known in Canadian academic life as 'rush', that is, a trial of strength between the freshmen and the second year students. **1916** C. A. EASTMAN *From Deep Woods to Civilization* 68 The two classes met in a first 'rush'. **1937** *Amer. Speech* XII. 156 *Cane rushes*, or encounters between freshmen carrying canes and sophomores seeking to break them were an institution at the University of Nebraska in the late '80's of the last century. They were vigorous affairs and fraternity rushing may well have had name from them.

d. *U.S.* A round of entertainment in which candidates for admission to a fraternity or a sorority participate. Also *attrib.*, as ***rush party, week***, etc.

1899 A. H. QUINN *Pennsylvania Stories* 60 It was not long before Theta Chi gave him a bid to a rush smoker. **1918** *Dialect Notes* V. 27 The object of the many attentions of a frat-rush. **1931** *Kansas City Times* 24 Sept. 20/6 Aunt Phoebe Tilden read where so many colleges are having rush parties. **1940** *Sun* (Baltimore) 16 Sept. 2/8 (*heading*) Rush week for C. of C. **1944** *Greeley* (Colo.) *Daily Tribune* 24 Sept. 3/5 Formal rush week for all sororities on the campus will be Oct. 1 to Oct. 6. **1964** Rush week [see *pledge week* s.v. PLEDGE *sb.* 7]. **1970** *Guardian* 23 Apr. 11/4 What is called the Rush Programme. Girls who want to be 'rushed', i.e. who want to join a sorority, put their names down for sororities (the screening process) and 'rush' to about 30 or 40 parties. **1979** *Arizona Daily Star* 19 Apr. 6/2 Jennifer Johnston.. was elected assistant rush chairman.

4. a. A sudden migration of numbers of people to a certain place, *esp.* to a new goldfield.

1848 *Morning Courier & New-York Enquirer* 11 Dec. 2/1 There is a general rush for the new found *Dorado*. **1849** *Merchant's Mag.* XX. 60 In May, the gold itself began to come into the town. And then began the rising and the rush. **1850** R. MONCKTON MILNES in *Life* (1891) I. x. 444 The rush of English to those parts is so great that there is hardly a bed to be had. **1861** T. M'COMBIE *Austral. Sk.* 86 We had a long conversation on the 'rush', as it was termed. **1890** 'R. BOLDREWOOD' *Col. Reformer* (1891) 289 A large proportion had been lured to Turonia by the golden possibilities of the great rush. **1893** [see *gold-rush* s.v. GOLD[1] 10 a]. **1897** *Boston Globe* 29 Aug. 6/6 There are only about 1600 new Americans in the mines... There are plenty of supplies there for those already in but not for any big rush late in the fall. **1908** E. J. BANFIELD *Confessions of Beachcomber* II. ii. 288 A party of bushmen, fresh from the excitement and weariness of the Gilbert rush. **1911** C. E. W. BEAN '*Dreadnought' of Darling* xxxv. 306 A friend of the writer's, who was in Coolgardie from the time when the rush there first started, tells of how first the waistcoat came onto the mining field. **1935** *Chambers's Encycl.* VI. 459/2 Only in 1896 was gold found in such abundance as to create a rush [to the Klondike]. **1947** R. PEATTIE *Sierra Nevada* 60 The discovery in 1859 of a glittering silver bonanza in Washoe County, Nevada, started a frantic rush over the mountains to Virginia City. **1955** *Bull. Atomic Sci.* Mar. 88/2 Thus the uranium boom began. The rush has grown rather than quieted, but there are healthy signs of stabilization. **1966** 'J. HACKSTON' *Father clears Out* 104 Following on this 'rich' find, the big Red Range rush set in. **1972** *Standard Encycl. Southern Africa* V. 227/1 By then [*sc.* 8 Sept. 1886] the rush of diggers had already set in, so that fully 3 000 people were estimated to be scattered along the Rand by this time.

b. *transf.* The scene of such a migration; *spec.* a new goldfield.

1855 W. HOWITT *Land, Lab., & Gold* I. 172 It is a common practice for them to mark out one or more claims in each new rush. **1885** FORBES *Souvenirs* (1894) 272 When he migrates to a new rush, he takes live belongings with him. **1900** H. LAWSON *Story of Oracle* in *Stories* (1964) I. 435 My Uncle Bob was mates with him on one of those rushes along there—the Pipeclay, I think it was, or the Log Paddock. **1966** 'J. HACKSTON' *Father clears Out* 52 Why is he so poor now, after finding all the rich reefs and rushes?

5. a. An eager demand *for*, a strong run *on*, something.

1856 R. MONCKTON MILNES in *Life* (1891) II. xii. 10 There is such a rush for places I shall probably not see it. **1884** *19th Cent.* Nov. (1889) 854 There was a slight boom in the mining market, and a bit of a rush on American rails.

b. ***with a rush***, with a sudden onset; in a sweeping or rapid manner.

1841 *Daily Picayune* (New Orleans) 10 Dec. 2/2 They all travel round to the old brushing ground where they 'go it with a rush'. **1846** S. F. SMITH *Theatrical Apprenticeship & Anecdotal Recollections* 152 When you find yourself in possession of *four aces*, go it with a perfect rush. **1859** BARTLETT *Dict. Amer.* (ed. 2) s.v., 'To go it with a rush, or with a perfect rush,' is to do a thing energetically, with spirit. **1861** *Times* 6 June, Already the Confederate States perceive that they cannot carry all before them with a rush. **1898** *McClure's Mag.* X. 352 The gray-backs came through with a rush. **1903** G. B. SHAW *Man & Superman* III. 138 The complete reality comes back with a rush. **1914** T. DREISER *Titan* i. 3 Chicago, when it finally dawned on him, came with a rush on the second morning. He had spent two nights in the gaudy Pullman..when the first lone outposts of the prairie metropolis began to appear. **1934** A. CHRISTIE *Parker Pyne Investigates* 53 She stared at Mr Parker Pyne with a desperate intentness. Suddenly she spoke with a rush.

c. ***(all) in a rush*** (and variants): phrs. denoting rapidity, liveliness, briskness, suddenness, or haste.

1859 HOTTEN *Dict. Slang* 84 *Doing it on the rush*, running away, or making off. **1876** 'MARK TWAIN' *Tom Sawyer* xviii. 149 He is always in such a rush that he never thinks of anything. **1877** G. M. HOPKINS *Spring* in *Poems* (1967) 67 That blue is all in a rush With richness. **1890** KIPLING *Barrack-Room Ballads* (1892) 11 An 'appy day with Fuzzy on the rush Will last an 'ealthy Tommy for a year. **1901** H. JAMES *Sacred Fount* iv. 75 Last night she was on the rush. **1916** 'TAFFRAIL' *Pincher Martin* i. 11 Take a pride in yourself, an' obey all orders at the rush. **1938** *Sun* (Baltimore) 8 June 8/8 Later in the season they [*sc.* soft crabs] drop off almost altogether until late July or in August, when they seem to come back all of a rush. **1962** E. B. ATWOOD *Regional Vocab. Texas* iii. 71 *To leave in a rush.* The most common single expression for hurried departure is *light a shuck*. **1971** *Cassell's Mod. Guide to Synonyms* 502 The slow, jolting pace of one who is in no rush.

6. a. A (migratory) flock or flight of birds.

1875 'STONEHENGE' *Brit. Rur. Sports* I. ix. 118 A 'flight' or 'rush' of dunbirds. **1901** *Scotsman* 10 Sept. 7/1 The greater number of birds in the autumn rushes.

b. *Austr.* A stampede of horses or cattle.

1881 A. C. GRANT *Bush Life* (1882) 298 A confused whirl of dark forms swept before him... It was 'a rush', a stampede.

7. Dysentery in cattle.

1799 *Prize Ess. Highland Soc.* III. 407 Purging or Rush. **1838** in W. C. L. Martin *Ox* (1847) 18/2 They are bad breeders, and much subject to the rush, a complaint common to animals bred in and in.

8. *Mining.* (See quot.)

1883 GRESLEY *Gloss. Coal-mining* 209 *Rush*, the sudden weighting of the roof when robbing the pillars begins, and the roof is a strong one.

9. *Comb.*, as **rush dodge**, the act of overcoming or disarming a person by means of a rush; **rush line** (see sense 3 a); also *fig.*; **rush order**, an order for goods required in a hurry; **rush-release**, the action or an instance of producing and marketing a gramophone record in the shortest possible time; so ***rush-release*** vb. trans. Also RUSH HOUR.

1888 'R. BOLDREWOOD' *Robbery under Arms* II. ii. 19 It's no use trying the rush dodge with them. **1887** *Century Mag.* XXXIV. 891/2 Across the field stretch the football infantry, the 'rush-line' or 'rushers'. **1891** *Harper's Weekly* 19 Sept. 715/3 Princeton's rush line is where she needs material and plenty of it. **1906** *Life* 4 Oct. 366 We hear of a surprising prevalence among the young men..of the disposition to get into the political rush-line. **1923** R. D. PAINE *Comr. Rolling Ocean* i. 3 The unlucky young men who were left in his wake when he tore through a rush-line. **1976** *Webster's Sports Dict.* 365/1 *Rush line*, the defensive line of a football team. **1896** *Daily News* 28 Dec. 3/7 Makers..have so much work on hand that they are neglecting rush orders. **1966** *Melody Maker* 16 July 4 The group's 'Pet Sounds' LP—rush-released by EMI—entered the MM's best-selling LPs chart this week at number nine. **1968** *Ibid.* 22 June 2 The Regal Zonophone label is rush-releasing the new Move E.P. **1978** *New Musical Express* 11 Feb. 4/2 Radiators From Space have just finished recording their new single..and Chiswick hope to have it ready for rush release on February 17.

rush, *sb.*[3] *north. dial.* [Of obscure origin.] A thick growth of plants or shrubs; a brake.

1796 W. H. MARSHALL *Rur. Econ. Yorks.* (ed. 2) II. 340 *Rush* (of grass or corn); a tuft, knot, cluster, or crowd of plants. **1822** BEWICK *Mem.* 39 In the midst of a 'whin rush'—that is, a great extent of old whins. **1844** M. A. RICHARDSON *Historian's Table-bk., Leg. Div.* II. 43 Through a rush of briars and nettles. **1892** M. C. F. MORRIS *Yorks. Folk-Talk* 155 A field..has a 'rush' or narrow strip of wood or rough ground at one end of it.

Rush, obs. form of RUSS *sb.*

rush (rʌʃ), *v.*[1] Also 5 **russhe**, 6 **rysshe**. [f. RUSH *sb.*[1]]

1. *trans.* **a.** To strew with rushes.

1422 *Secreta Secret., Priv. Priv.* 242 Noght vpon harde erthe ne Pament, but vpon erthe nesshly y-strawet or russhet. *c* **1430** *Pilgr. Lyf Manhode* II. cxxvi. (1869) 142, I can wel russhe a dungy place. *a* **1851** [see RUSHED *ppl. a.*]. **1895** ELLWOOD *Lakeland Gloss.* 78 In some parishes, rushing the church in this way was paid for.

b. To tie up, work or make, with rushes.

1848 *Jrnl. R. Agric. Soc.* IX. II. 556 Keep them [i.e. hop-bines] well rushed around at the bottom. **1885** *Leisure Hour* Jan. 47/1 Women and children..caning or rushing the 'bottoms' [of chairs].

2. *intr.* To gather rushes. *rare.*

1530 PALSGR. 692/2, I rysshe, I gather russhes, *je cueils des joncs. Ibid.*, Go no more a rysshynge Malyn. **1896** BARING-GOULD *Dartmoor Idylls* 234 Don't y' go a-rushing, maids, in May.

rush (rʌʃ), *v.*[2] Forms: 4 **russchen**, 4–6 **rusche** (5 **russch-**, **ruyssch-**, *Sc.* **rousch-**); 4–6 **russhe** (5 **rosshe**, 6 **russzh-**); 4–6 **rushe**, 6– **rush**. [a. AF. *russher*, var. of *russer*, = OF. *re(h)usser*, *re(h)user*, *ruser*, etc. (mod.F. *ruser*: see RUSE *v.*[1]). The forms with *s* would normally represent a pop.L. **refūsāre*, f. ppl. stem of L. *refundĕre* to cause to flow back, but it is difficult to regard those in *ss* and *ssh* as having this origin.

The development of some of the senses may have been helped by a feeling of phonetic appropriateness: cf. the similar uses of MHG. *rûschen, riuschen* (G. *rauschen*), which is quite unconnected in origin.]

I. *trans.* † **1. a.** To force out of place or position by violent impact; to drive back, down, etc. *Obs.*

1375 BARBOUR *Bruce* II. 404 In the stour sa hardyly He ruschyt with hys chewalry, That he ruschyt his fayis ilkane. *c* **1420** *Avow. Arth.* iv, He betus on the busshes; Alle he riues and he russhes, That the rote is vnryȝte.

† **b.** Const. *down*, *up*; *to* (the ground), *under* (foot), etc. *Obs.*

c **1375** *Sc. Leg. Saints* i. (*Peter*) 527 þe hound..schot on symeon..and to þe ȝerde hym vndirnethe Ruschit. ? *a* **1400** *Morte Arth.* 1339 Of alle his ryche castelles [I will] rusche doune the walles. *c* **1425** WYNTOUN *Cron.* III. ii. 333 Conȝhe and rabit bathe he brak, And ruschit wp þe ȝhettis þar. *c* **1470** HENRY *Wallace* III. 193 Hors..rouschede frekis wndir feit. *c* **1530** LD. BERNERS *Arth. Lyt. Bryt.* (1814) 192 A tempest of winde..rusht downe standerdes, and tare downe lodgynges. *a* **1578** LINDESAY (Pitscottie) *Chron. Scot.* (S.T.S.) II. 39 They ruschit thame rouchlie to the earth. **1635** SWAN *Spec. M.* vi. §2 (1643) 225 Many hills and buildings have been rushed down by this kind of earthquake. **1678** SIR G. MACKENZIE *Crim. Laws Scot.* II. (1699) 235 He thereupon ran and rushed the said Main..to the ground under his Feet.

fig. **1592** SHAKS. *Rom. & Jul.* III. iii. 26 The kind Prince Taking thy part, hath rusht aside the Law.

† **c.** To smash, shatter. *Obs.*$^{-1}$

1470–85 MALORY *Arthur* V. x. 176 He smote thurgh shelde ..and al to russhed and brake the precious stones.

2. a. To cause to move with great speed and force; to send or impel violently. Chiefly with preps.

1382 WYCLIF *2 Macc.* iii. 25 He with feersnesse..rushide the former feet to Heleodore. *c* **1430** *Syr Gener.* (Roxb.) 8931 He armed him, and russhed his stede, And forto Ioust fast he yede. **1470–85** MALORY *Arthur* VI. ii. 185 He russhed his hors on syre Ector and..bare hym clene out of the sadel. **1592** tr. *Junius on Rev.* xii. 18 A most mighty tempest that he rushed upon the whole world. *c* **1611** CHAPMAN *Iliad* v. 18 Then rush'd he out a lance at him. **1654** I. AMBROSE *Ultima* 18 Into what a sea of misery have I now rushed saile! **1730** T. BOSTON *Mem.* vii. (1899) 153 There was a spit sticking in the wall of the house... I rushed inadvertently my face on it. **1858** *Times* 30 Nov., How skilfully these young creatures managed their frail tiny barks! They rush them through the fiercest rapids.

† **b.** To pull *out* hastily, drag *off* violently. *Obs.*

? *a* **1400** *Morte Arth.* 2550 Redely theis rathe mene rusches owtte swerdes. **1470–85** MALORY *Arthur* IV. x. 132 Syr Arthur..pulled hym to the erthe, and thenne russhed of his helme. *a* **1600** *Sir Lancelot du Lake* 120 in Percy *Reliques* (1765) I. 186 He pull'd him downe upon his knee, And rushing off his helm [etc.].

3. a. *refl.* To move with speed and force (*obs.*); to impel (oneself) heedlessly, violently, or hurriedly *upon* or *on* something. ? *Obs.*

c **1400** *Song Roland* 589 'Lordingis,' said Roulond, 'rusche you be-dene'. *c* **1470** HENRY *Wallace* VII. 819 Rudly till ray thai ruschit thaim agayne. **1642** ROGERS *Naaman* 47 To have made him desperate, and to have rusht himselfe upon vile courses. **1659** *Gentl. Calling* 448 Men, that can thus knowingly and consideringly rush themselves upon such unspeakable mischiefs.

b. *trans.* To drag, force, or carry rapidly; (*orig.* rapidly and violently); to convey (someone or something) rapidly or urgently. Chiefly const. *into*, *to*, *out of*.

1577 *Reg. Privy Council Scot.* II. 627 The said Thesaurare ..put violent handis on the said complenar, ruschit him to the Tolbuith. **1632** J. FEATLY *Hon. Chast.* 15 His will rushes him headlong to the whirlepoole of destruction. **1658** *Whole Duty Man* vi. §21 Consideration..we owe to our Souls. For without it, we shall..rush them into infinite perils. **1721** YOUNG *Revenge* IV. i, O, how like innocence she looks! what, stab her, And rush her into blood? **1740–1** RICHARDSON *Pamela* II. 30 Tell me you forgive me for rushing you into so much Danger and Distress. **1897** *Sportsman* 16 Dec., From a line out here the leather was finely rushed up. **1898** G. B. SHAW *You never can tell* Plays II. 294 They rush him out of the room between them. **1914** S. LEWIS *Our Mr. Wrenn* 214 I'll make Tom rush us a growler of beer. **1927** U. SINCLAIR *Oil!* 264 It was our job to rush them supplies. **1935** in A. P. Herbert *What a Word!* v. 143 She was rushed to Alton Hospital, where her condition is critical. **1947** *Milwaukee Jrnl.* 29 Oct. 2 Uncle Tom doesn't scurry around to rush us a loan. **1958** [see JERRICAN, JERRYCAN]. **1966** L. COHEN *Beautiful Losers* I. 107 Rush to me the *free* book on the Home Method of Slenderizing Heavy Legs. **1971** *Sunday Express* (Johannesburg) 28 Mar. 7/5 (Advt.), Rush me my..illustrated Guide. **1976** *Star* (Sheffield) 3 Dec. 10/7 My husband to be was rushed into hospital for a serious operation.

c. *transf.* To get or bring *out*, carry *through*, push on, etc., in an unusually rapid manner.

1830 SCOTT *Jrnl.* II. 106 Cadell rather wished to rush it out by employing these different presses. **1864** *Daily Tel.* 21 Sept., When his name was proposed they rushed it through with a will. **1890** *Standard* 20 Feb., All we desire is that the measure shall not be rushed through the House. **1893** *Daily News* 14 Apr. 2/6 There is no disposition to rush business, and caution is being manifested by dealers.

d. To make (one's way) with a rush.

1896 BADEN-POWELL *Matabele Campaign* xii, This morning by dawn we were rushing our way along the Uvunkwe.

4. a. To force at an unusual or excessive pace or speed. Also with *off*, *on*, *through*, *up*. Also, in weakened senses, to accomplish or produce rapidly; to expedite; to hurry or hustle.

1850 R. G. CUMMING *Hunter's Life S. Afr.* (1902) 39/1 This Bushboy..would never rush his horse to overtake any antelope if the ground were at all rough. **1883** 'MARK TWAIN' *Life on Mississippi* li. 452 Since there was so much time to spare that nineteen years of it could be devoted to the construction of a mere towhead, where was the use, originally, in rushing this whole globe through in six days? **1887** SMILES *Life & Labour* 355 While the country boy is allowed to grow up, the city boy is rushed up. **1892** *Garden* 27 Aug. 184 There is no doubt that Cucumbers can be rushed on with heat and moisture. **1894** [GODLEY] *Aspects Mod. Oxford* 43 Nor will he..allow himself to be 'rushed' through the various objects of interest. **1901** *Chambers's Jrnl.* Apr. 210/1 Candida rushed her news. **1918** W. OWEN *Let.* 19 Aug. (1967) 569 I rushed off a note in time for this evening's post. **1938** *Amer. Speech* XIII. 156/1 *Bootleg 'em,* to rush a special order through outside of regular channels. **1946** *R.A.F. Jrnl.* May 161 Do not through nervousness rush your replies. **1947** *Sun* (Baltimore) 8 Nov. 6/2 Representative Knutson..announced his intention of rushing the special session with a 'quickie' bill for income-tax reduction. **1949** SHURR & YOCOM *Mod. Dance* 5 Head of Developing and Printing at Willoughby's Camera Stores, Inc., who rushed prints and supplies through in record time. **1974** *Times* 1 Feb. 2/8 Nevertheless, Mr Campbell Adamson, director general, emphasized that the CBI was 'rushing' a council meeting, a somewhat unprecedented action, to consider Mr Heath's letter. **1976** M. MACHLIN *Pipeline* lxi. 517 If you ask me..he's rushing the whole thing and I think that these ULCC'S—these ultra-big tankers—are a mistake.

b. *colloq.* To defraud or cheat, to 'do', *out of.* Also *ellipt.*

1887 J. PAYN *Glow-Worm Tales* II. 44 That a fraud had been committed on us was certain, and a fraud of a very clumsy kind... He had 'rushed us' as, the phrase goes. **1891** *L'pool Mercury* 26 May 5/4 With an added 2^{d} it is equivalent in value to the dollar, and..much good sport is to be obtained in America in trying to rush the natives out of that 2^{d}. **1930** BROPHY & PARTRIDGE *Songs & Slang 1914–1918* 158 *How much did they rush you?* meant 'How much did you have to pay?' **1931** T. R. G. LYELL *Slang, Phrase & Idiom* 655 *Rush a person,*..to overcharge a person; to make him pay an exorbitant price. *A.* 'How much d'you say you paid for this car?' *B.* 'Two hundred and fifty pounds.' *A.* 'My word! they rushed you, all right! It's not worth a penny more than £120.' **1973** N. W. SCHUR *British Self-Taught* 340 *Rush,*.. soak. For instance: 'How much did they rush you for that sherry?' To rush is to charge, with the distinct implication that the price was too high.

c. To hurry or pressure (a person); now freq. *pass.* (passing into *ppl. a.*), of a person: to have much to do in a limited time, to be hard-pressed by shortage of time (also with the activity or the period of time as subject). Hence in colloq. phrases ***to be rushed around, to be rushed off one's feet*** (or *legs*) (cf. *run off one's feet* s.v. RUN *v.* 44 a).

a **1890** *Elect. Rev.* XV. xiv. 10 (Cent.), Nearly all [telegraph operators] are ambitious to send faster than the operator at the receiving station can write it down, or in other words to rush him. **1902** W. N. HARBEN *Abner Daniel* 268 Wish I had more time at my disposal..but I really am rushed, to-day particularly. **1911** M. BEERBOHM *Let.* 2 Oct. (1964) 204, I wish you would tell Sister Loveridge..that I was so 'rushed' that I had not time to go and see anybody. **1916** E. FENWICK *Diary* 14 Feb. (1981) 111 Just rushed off my legs the whole day long. **1923** H. CRANE *Let.* 6 Feb. (1965) 118, I have been so rushed around with too much society that I have not yet got at the review for your study. **1924** *Ibid.* 5 Mar. (1965) 177 What with one's work, one's friends, books, writing, eating and sleeping, things are certainly rushed! **1937** W. H. SAUMAREZ SMITH *Let.* 20 Sept. in *Young Man's Country* (1977) ii. 91 I've been so rushed off my feet that I've not had a moment to do anything except work. **1943** D. POWELL *Time to be Born* x. 225 Amanda's too rushed right now to attend to these details. **1944** C. HIMES *Black on Black* (1973) 196 'State yo' plan, Charlie Chan—then scram!' 'Don't rush me, don't rush me.' **1947** M. MORRIS in B. James *Austral. Short Stories* (1963) 345 She.. waited on the tables in Gleeson's dining-room when they were rushed. **1963** *Listener* 31 Jan. 223/2 Lentil soup requires little preparation, and, on a rushed day, takes kindly to the pressure cooker. **1965** *Listener* 4 Nov. 724/2 The elegant Harley Street Consultants, the fatherly GPs, the harassed hospital house surgeons,..those 'you can talk to' and those who are 'rushed off their feet'. **1966** 'J. HACKSTON' *Father clears Out* 203 In fact, I rushed her so, that I flabbergasted her, got her rattled. **1977** *Oxford Star* 22 Dec. 1/1 Shopkeepers have been rushed off their feet rolling out the barrel at Sainsburys, the Co-op, [etc.].

d. *U.S.* Of fraternity or sorority members: to entertain (a new student) in order to assess his or her suitability for membership, or to offer him or her membership.

1896 W. C. GORE in *Inlander* Jan. 149 *Rush,*..to entertain a student in various ways, with the view of inducing him to join a fraternity. **1922** S. LEWIS *Babbitt* xxvi. 309 He was on the committee for the Freshman Hop, and..he was being 'rushed' by two fraternities. **1924** P. MARKS *Plastic Age* vii. 62 He ought to be a good man for the fraternity... We've got to rush him sure. **1946** E. B. THOMPSON *Amer. Daughter* x. 173 There were a lot of students who weren't rushed or pledged who found solace in the Y, in literary or musical clubs, but not Dora. **1970** [see RUSH *sb.*[2] 3 d].

e. To court the affection of (a girl or woman) by means of frequent entertainment, 'dating', etc. orig. and chiefly *U.S.*

1899 F. NORRIS *McTeague* xi. 226 Marcus had 'taken up with' Salna a little after Trina had married, and had been 'rushing' her ever since. **1922** F. SCOTT FITZGERALD *Beautiful & Damned* II. i. 144 With one she had gone to New Haven..she had been flattered because 'Touch down' Michaud had 'rushed' her all evening. **1932** 'B. ROSS' *Tragedy of X* 71 He had 'rushed' her, she said, for several months, and they had decided to announce their engagement. **1938** E. BOWEN *Death of Heart* II. iv. 249 That may be because you are so young that no fellow has started to rush you yet. **1955** F. A. COLLYMORE *Barbadian Dialect* 73 Who's the girl your brother's rushing now?

5. a. *Austr.* (See quot.)

1852 G. C. MUNDY *Our Antipodes* I. 313 Sometimes at night this animal will leap into the fold amongst the timid animals and so 'rush' them—that is, cause them to break out and disperse through the bush.

b. *Mil.* To overcome, take, capture, carry, by means of a sudden rush. Also, in extended uses, to attack (someone) by means of a sudden rush; to 'go for' (a person).

1863 A. S. ATKINSON *Jrnl.* 29 May in *Richmond-Atkinson Papers* (1960) II. 47 There were two sets of pits (called *rifle* pits by courtesy) the first were rushed but the Maoris ran & got all away. **1865** *Cornh. Mag.* Oct. 498 They break from our Christianity and 'rush' our pickets. **1884** *Pall Mall G.* 4 July 1/2 The Arabs 'rushed' the town, putting every man to the sword. **1888** BESANT *50 Yrs. Ago* 137 Peeresses.. occupied every seat, and even 'rushed' the reporters' gallery. **1889** 'R. BOLDREWOOD' *Robbery under Arms* xxiii, A single bushranger was rushed by a couple of determined men. **1896** BADEN-POWELL *Matabele Campaign* ii, The town was to be rushed in the night, and the whites to be slaughtered without quarter to any. **1930** L. G. D. ACLAND *Early Canterbury Runs* viii. 196 The cook took up his gun and ordered him off, but the man rushed him and the cook shot him dead. **1934** WODEHOUSE *Right Ho, Jeeves* xvi. 197 Damn it, they'd rush the platform. **1937** C. HIMES *Nigger* in *Black on Black* (1973) 131 He tried to shift the wire to his right hand so he could flay her with it, but she rushed him, clawing and biting. **1939** *Sun* (Baltimore) 23 Aug. 1/2 The shots were fired by Gerald Blowers..after about fifty pickets rushed a milk truck on which he was riding. **1962** WODEHOUSE *Service with Smile* iii. 42 'Your sermon was a success, I trust?' 'Well, they didn't rush the pulpit.'

c. To cross, penetrate, traverse, negotiate (or endeavour to do so) with a rush. ***to rush one's fences***: see FENCE *sb.* 5 c.

1884 *Graphic* 29 Nov. 166/2 In 'rushing' the hurdles, men are stationed..to prevent the horses swerving. **1893** EARL DUNMORE *Pamirs* II. 298 The next one [snow-drift] we came to, the driver thought he could 'rush' it. **1897** MARY KINGSLEY *W. Africa* 280, I rushed it, and reached the other side in safety.

fig. **1888** BESANT *Eulogy of R. Jefferies* vii. 188 Most readers like to rush a volume. You cannot rush Jefferies.

d. To occupy by a rush (of gold-miners).

1862 *Otago: Goldfields & Resources* 26 The Highlay [goldfield]..has been rushed, condemned, almost deserted, and yet survives. **1872** *Daily Tel.* 9 Feb. 3/3 The place was 'rushed'—an expressive word,..which signifies that the diggers swarmed to the spot in such crowds as to render merely foolish any resistance which an owner might be inclined to make. **1878** I. L. BIRD in *Leisure Hour* 5 Oct. 635/2 Even their [*sc.* Indians'] 'reservations' do not escape seizure practically; for if gold should 'break out' on them, they are 'rushed'. **1879** ATCHERLEY *Trip to Boerland* 171 The locality was 'rushed' for gold. **1887** HAYTER *Xmas Adv.* 3 The Bald Hill had just been rushed, and therefore I decided..a claim to take up. **1973** *Nation Rev.* (Melbourne) 31 Aug. (Suppl.) 1/1 It was first explored by Hume and Hovell, then opened up by cattlemen, rushed by gold seekers, and finally developed as a prosperous agricultural area.

e. *Croquet.* To roquet (a ball) with considerable force. Also *absol.*

1874 HEATH *Croquet Player* 14 It is rushed at an angle, instead of in a direct line. **1877** *Encycl. Brit.* VI. 609/2 When able to rush, the strokes made in taking croquet..should be practised.

II. *intr.* **6. a.** Of persons or animals: To run, dash, or charge with violence or impetuous rapidity. Usually const. with advs. or preps.

1375 BARBOUR *Bruce* II. 380 In the stour sa hardyly He ruschyt, that all the semble schuk. *c* **1386** CHAUCER *Knt.'s T.* 783 The hunters..hereth hym come russhyng in the greues. ? *a* **1400** *Morte Arth.* 2880 So raythely thay rusche with roselde speris, That the raskaille was rade. *c* **1470** HENRY *Wallace* IX. 1049 The worthi Scottis ruschyt on thaim, in gret ire. **1526** SKELTON *Magnyf.* 1910, I rushe at them rughly, and make them ly full lowe. **1590** SHAKS. *Com. Err.* v. i. 143 Doing displeasure to the Citizens, By rushing in their houses. **1617** MORYSON *Itin.* I. 151 The wilde Boare rushed upon one of these frames wheeling towards him. **1680** OTWAY *Orphan* I. ii, The desperate savage rusht within my Force. **1748** GRAY *Alliance* 93 To brave the savage rushing from the wood. **1797–1805** S. & HT. LEE *Canterb. T.* II. 198 Strangely departing from all the civilities of life ..[he] would rush from the room. **1862** H. KINGSLEY *Ravenshoe* I. 110 Then the colt rushed by them..hard held. **1880** MRS. FORRESTER *Roy & V.* I. 79 A few minutes later Madame de Férias rushed into her husband's room.

b. *fig.* To press, make an attack or descent, *on* or *upon* one.

1535 COVERDALE *Bel & Dragon* 30 Now whan ye kynge sawe, that they russhed in so sore vpon him,..he deliuered Daniel vnto them. **1592** NASHE *Four Lett. Confut.* Wks. (Grosart) II. 274 For with none but clownish and roynish ieasts dost thou rush vppon vs. **1848** THACKERAY *Van. Fair* xvii, All his creditors would have come rushing on him in a body.

c. *fig.*, denoting precipitate, rash, or unconsidered action. Freq. const. *into.*

1560 DAUS tr. *Sleidane's Comm.* 62 You rushe forth headlong unadvisedly. **1563** WINȜET *Wks.* (S.T.S.) II. 13 Rinnand and ruscheand without knaulege quhat thai othir do or say. **1630** PRYNNE *Anti-Armin.* 159 Restraine and keepe backe men from rushing presumptuously..in their sinnes. **1729** BUTLER *Serm.* Wks. 1874 II. 7 One man rushes upon certain ruin for the gratification of a present desire. **1781** COWPER *Conversat.* 185 To rush into a fixt eternal state Out of the very flames of rage and hate. **1846** J. BAXTER *Libr. Pract. Agric.* (ed. 4) I. 252 The inquiring reader..rushes blindly to the experiment, indifferent to the nature of his soil. **1872** O. W. HOLMES *Poet. Breakf.-t.* vi, So many foolish persons are rushing into print. **1873** MRS. BROOKFIELD *Not a Heroine* II. 268 He always rushes into extremes.

d. To go *on* hurriedly in speaking.

1850 THACKERAY *Pendennis* xvi[i], 'My means,' rushed on Smirke, 'are at present limited, I own'.

e. To pass or travel rapidly. Also, to hurry, to hasten. Freq. with *(a)round* (hence ***rush-round*** attrib. phr.); ***to rush round in circles***: see CIRCLE *sb.* 1 c.

1852 M. ARNOLD *Human Life* 17 We rush by coasts where we had lief remain. **1897** *Windsor Mag.* Jan. 250/2 It might be done by leaving the ship at Plymouth, and rushing up to London by the first train. **1914** 'HIGH JINKS, JR.' *Choice Slang* 22 We rush off shopping. **1916** W. OWEN *Let.* 18 Mar. (1967) 386, I am obliged to rush into Romford for Running Clothes for a Run announced for the 17th. **1923** H. CRANE *Let.* 9 May (1965) 134 Of course I have been rushing around to a lot of other agencies. **1958** *Spectator* 20 June 807/2 Young Asia and young Africa delight to pull the legs of rush-round correspondents. **1965** G. MCINNES *Road to Gundagai* xii. 216, I..tore out of the room and rushed off to school. **1973** [see NOSE-BAG 3]. **1976** F. RAPHAEL *Glittering Prizes* 23 'It's C7, Third Court, St John's. Only I've got to rush.' 'I shall be there.'

f. With *it* and *out.*

1526 SKELTON *Magnyf.* 856 Properly drest..To russhe it oute In euery route. **1856** in B. H. Hall *College Words & Customs* (rev. ed.) 365 Leg it, put it, rush it, streak it, *Run* and worship God. **1859** BARTLETT *Dict. Amer.* (ed. 2), *To Rush it,* to do a thing with spirit; as, 'The old negro is rushing it with his fiddle'. **1976** L. SANDERS *Hamlet Warning* (1977) ix. 79 She laughed and looked up at him. 'Well, let's not rush it, Loomis.'

g. In American football, to run carrying the ball; to gain ground by running with the ball.

1949 *Lafayette Alumnus* (Lafayette College, Easton, Pa.) 24 Oct. 1/1 The Maroon had made 9 first downs rushing, three by passing and one by penalty. **1974** *Cleveland* (Ohio) *Plain Dealer* 13 Oct. c. 1/3 The Buckeyes rushed for 359 yards as quarterback Cornelius Greene and wingback Brian Baschnagel each scored twice. **1979** *Tucson* (Arizona) *Citizen* 20 Sept. 10 D/7 The Warrior running game hasn't been as effective as McKee would like, having rushed for only 133 yards in the first two games.

7. a. Of things: To move, flow, fall, etc., with great speed or impetuosity.

13.. *E.E. Allit. P.* B. 368 Mony clustered clowde clef alle in clowtez, To-rent vch a rayn-ryfte & rusched to þe vrþe. *c* **1380** *Sir Ferumb.* 497 He..lokede on þe kniȝte, & saw þe red blod russchen out. **1460** in *Pol., Rel., & L. Poems* (1866) 206 The elementes gonne to rusche & rappe. *c* **1470** HENRY *Wallace* VI. 553 The noyis rouschit throuch straikis that thai dang. **1513** DOUGLAS *Æneis* XII. i. 125 Of our wondis the red blude ruschis owt. **1582** STANYHURST *Æneis* I. (Arb.) 20 Rush do the winds forward... They skud too the seaward. **1610** HOLLAND *Camden's Brit.* (1637) 730 Swale rusheth rather than runneth..with foaming waters. **1671** MILTON *P.R.* IV. 414 Nor slept the winds Within thir stony caves, but rush'd abroad. **1757** W. WILKIE *Epigoniad* II. 46 Beyond the hostile ranks the weapon drove; The warriors stooping as it rush'd above. **1819** SCOTT *Ivanhoe* xlii, The blood rushed in anger to the countenance of Richard. **1860** TYNDALL *Glac.* I. ii. 13 A dozen avalanches rushed downwards from its summit. **1884** W. C. SMITH *Kildrostan* 45 When you..hear the water rushing Around you, and beneath.

b. *fig.* Of immaterial things.

1596 SHAKS. *Merch. V.* IV. i. 222 Many an error by the same example, Will rush into the state. **1671** MILTON *Samson* 21 Restless thoughts, that..rush upon me thronging, and present Times past. **1778** MISS BURNEY *Evelina* xl, Almost instantly the whole truth of the transaction seemed to rush upon her mind. **1850** THACKERAY *Pendennis* x[i]x, A dreadful rumour rushed through the University. **1863** GEO. ELIOT *Romola* I. xvi, His mind rushed over all the circumstances of his departure from Florence.

c. To come suddenly into view.

1798 COLERIDGE *Anc. Mar.* III. xiii, The Sun's rim dips; the stars rush out. **1879** MRS. A. E. JAMES *Ind. Househ. Managem.* 65 In India that luminary does not 'peep up', he rushes up.

d. To grow or shoot *up* rapidly.

1819 SCOTT *Ivanhoe* xl, The weeds have rushed up, and conspired to choke the fair and wholesome blossom.

†8. To fall quickly or violently. *Obs.*

Now only contextually, as in sense 7.

1375 BARBOUR *Bruce* III. 139 He rouschit doun off blud all rede. ? *a* **1400** *Morte Arth.* 120 The Romaynes for radnesse ruschte to the erthe. **1470–85** MALORY *Arthur* IV. xviii. 142 Therwith syre Gawayne and his hors russhed doune to the erthe. **1533** BELLENDEN *Livy* I. xxi. (S.T.S.) I. 121 Brutus.. ruschit (as It had bene aganis his wil) to þe ground and kissit þe erde.

'rush-ˌbearing. [RUSH *sb.*[1]] An annual ceremony in northern districts of carrying rushes and garlands to the church and strewing the floor or decorating the walls with them; usually made the occasion of a general holiday.

1617 ASSHETON *Jrnl.* (Chetham Soc.) 29 At Whalley: ther a rushbearing, but much less solemnitie then formerlie. **1654** GATAKER *Disc. Apol.* 20 May-games, Whitsun-Ales, Morrice-dances, Rush-bearings,..and other sports. *c* **1700** KENNETT in *MS. Lansd. 1033* fol. 331 b, The wake or day of a Churches dedication in West Riding of Yorksh. is calld the rush-bearing of such a Parish. **1781** J. HUTTON *Tour to Caves* Gloss. (ed. 2) 95 *Rush-bearing,* a ceremony of carrying garlands or rushes to the church. **1810** *Ann. Reg., Antiq.* 672/1 Rush bearing..was a custom which formerly prevailed generally in Cheshire. **1841** HAMPSON *Medii Ævi Cal.* I. 341 The festival of Rush-bearing does not always coincide with the feast of the dedication. **1894** *Times* 21 Aug. 11/3 Rochdale, Aug. 20.—Rushbearing, the local holidays, commenced to-day.

attrib. **1649** in *N. & Q.* 9th Ser. VII. 294/1 Ringinge on the Rushbering Day. **1889** *Graphic* 22 June 682/2 On rush-bearing evening the churchyard wall is crowded with childish figures.

†rush-buckler. *Obs.*[-1] [? f. RUSH *v.*[2]] A swashbuckler.

1551 ROBINSON tr. *More's Utop.* II. (1895) 146 Take into this numbre also their seruauntes; I mean, all that flocke of stout bragging russhe bucklers [L. *cetratorum nebulonum*].

rush-bush. Also 5 reschebusk, 6 resche-bush, 8–9 *dial.* rex-bush; *Sc.* 6 rysche-, rasch(e)-bus(s),

8–9 **rash-buss, -bush.** [f. RUSH *sb.*[1] Cf. G. *ruschbusch*.] A tuft of rushes.

In early Scottish use common in a proverbial expression denoting the strict suppression of cattle-lifting.

c **1425** in Wr.-Wülcker 645 *Hec papirio*, reschebusk. **1529** LYNDESAY *Compl.* 408, Ihone Upeland bene full blyith, I trow, Because the rysche bus kepis his kow. **1596** DALRYMPLE tr. *Leslie's Hist. Scot.* II. 77 This prouerb of him [James II] in the cuntrie was commoun: He garis the rasche bus keip the kow. *a* **1649** DRUMM. OF HAWTH. *Hist. Jas. V*, Wks. (1711) 114 The Poor Man loved him, the Great feared him: He made the Rush-Bushes keep the Herds of Cattel. **1746** *Exmoor Scolding* (E.D.S.) 38 Rex-bush!—Fath! tell me o' tha Rexbush. **1785** BURNS *Address to Deil* vii, Ye, like a rash-buss, stood in sight. **1833** CARLYLE in *Froude* (1882) II. 387 Remember always what you said of the rush-bush here at Puttock on the wayside. **1898** J. MACMANUS *Bend of Road* 149 All who are..on the Ocean with no rush-bush to hould by when the storms come up.

rush-candle. [RUSH *sb.*[1]] A candle of feeble power made by dipping the pith of a rush in tallow or other grease; a rushlight.

1591 NASHE *Pref. to Sidney's Astr. & Stella*, Put out your rush candles, you Poets and Rymers. **1634** MILTON *Comus* 338 A rush Candle from the wicker hole Of som clay habitation. **1677** HORNECK *Gt. Law Consid.* vi. (1704) 321 What is all the light our eyes behold, but a rush-candle to him that is the father of lights? **1753** *Chambers' Cycl.* Suppl. s.v. *Candle*, Rush Candles, used in divers parts of England, are made of the pith of a sort of rushes, peeled, or stripped of the skin, except in one side, and dipt in melted grease. **1816** A. C. HUTCHISON *Pract. Obs. Surg.* (1826) 165 There being only the usual light in the ward, a common rush-candle. **1895** 'G. MORTIMER' *Tales Western Moors* 119 He pictured her knitting placidly by the light of a rush candle.

rushed, *ppl. a.* [f. RUSH *sb.*[1] or *v.*[1]] Overgrown or strewn with rushes. Also, made of rushes.

1753 T. WARTON *Ode Approach of Summer*, As slow he winds in museful mood, Near the rush'd marge of Cherwell's flood. *a* **1851** JOANNA BAILLIE (Cent.), Rushed floors, whereon our children play'd. **1918** *Heal & Son Catal.: Cottage Furnit.* 31 Jacobean Chair, in Dark Oak with rushed seat. **1957** A. CLARKE *Later Poems* (1961) 67, I think of rushed bones, Bogland, in furnaces, grown greener.

rushee (rʌ'ʃiː). *U.S. College slang.* [f. RUSH *v.*[2] + -EE[1].] One who is 'rushed' (see RUSH *v.*[2] 4 d); a candidate for membership of a fraternity or sorority.

1916 *Dialect Notes* IV. 279 *Rushee*,..a girl being 'rushed' for a college fraternity. 'The chapter has some good-looking rushees this year.' Widespread at Nebraska University. **1928** *Amer. Speech* III. 220 *Rushee*,..an individual who is being rushed by fraternities or sororities. **1940** *Sun* (Baltimore) 16 Sept. 2/8 It [*sc.* a telegram] requested a report on the character, family and scholarship of a rushee. **1942** *College Topics* (Univ. Virginia) 12 Oct. 1/2 (*heading*) Rushees navigate to houses by maps. **1960** *Amer. Speech* XXXV. 104 The girl rushee who does not have 'tights-omania' will be blackballed in short order.

rushen ('rʌʃ(ə)n), *a.* Also 1 riscen, 4 russchen, 8–9 *Sc.* rashen. [OE. *riscen*, f. *risc* RUSH *sb.*[1] Cf. LG. *rüsken*.] Made of rushes, or of a rush.

c **1000** ÆLFRIC *Exod.* ii. 3 þa nam heo anne riscenne windel on scipwisan ȝesceapenne. **1398** TREVISA *Barth. De P.R.* XVII. cxxvi. (Bodl. MS.), Of russches beþ russchen vessels made. **1676** *Doctrine of Devils* 39 Tom Thumb with his Rushen Spear. *Ibid.*, Can a Crismer..bind Behemoth with a rushen cord? **1738** CHAMBERS *Cycl.* s.v. *Bridge*, Rushen Bridge, *pont de jonc*, is made of large sheaves of rushes growing in marshy grounds. **1792** *Statist. Acc. Scotl.* IV. 395 The straw brechem is now supplanted by the leather collar, the rashen theets by the iron traces. **1833** HT. MARTINEAU *Loom & Lugger* II. v. 87 Allowed to pull rushen seats to pieces. **1864** DASENT *Jest & Earnest* (1873) II. 215 He..held out to him two fair rushen wands.

†**'rusher**[1]. *Obs.*$^{-1}$ [f. RUSH *sb.*[1]] One who strews rushes on a floor.

1630 B. JONSON *New Inn* v. i, Pipers, fidlers, rushers, puppet-masters, Jugglers, and gipsies.

rusher[2] ('rʌʃə(r)). [f. RUSH *v.*[2] + -ER[1].]

1. One who or that which rushes; one who acts precipitately or without deliberation.

With quot. 1796 cf. RUSH *sb.*[2] 2 a.

1654 WHITLOCK *Zootomia* 148 Remit such Rushers not into the Church onely, but Pulpit, to the Philosophy Schoole to be shamed. **1796** *Grose's Dict. Vulgar T.* (ed. 3), *Rushers*, thieves who knock at the doors of great houses in London,..and on the door being opened by a woman, rush in and rob the house; also housebreakers who enter lone houses by force. **1861** HUGHES *Tom Brown at Oxf.* III. 148 We always thought a rusher [in a fight] no good at school. **1876** MISS BRADDON *J. Haggard's Dau.* I. 82 He..was a rusher across country. **1887** *Cyclist* 11 May 739/1 This irrepressible writer and rusher to conclusions.

2. *U.S.* One who takes part in a rush to a new gold-field or to new territory.

1872 DE VERE *Americanisms* 629 *Rushers*, in California and all the gold-bearing districts of the West, is the comprehensive name of persons going to the mines. **1892** *Current History* I. 433 As many of the 'rushers' are very poor, there is sure to be great suffering in the territory.

3. *U.S. Football.* A forward; any player who rushes (see RUSH *v.*[2] 6 g).

1883 *Atlantic Monthly* May 682/1 An attempt to break through the line of rushers, in a scrimmage. **1894** *Outing* XXIV. 215/2 Putting the goalkeepers..in the front and placing the tired rushers at the goals. **1969** *Internat. Herald Tribune* 6 Nov. 13/6 Floyd Little, leading rusher in the American Football League, suffered a sprained right knee. **1974** *Cleveland* (Ohio) *Plain Dealer* 13 Oct. c. 6/2 Wellington carried 12 times for 129 yards to lead all rushers. **1979** *Tucson* (Arizona) *Citizen* 3 Oct. 1D/4 The seventh-leading rusher in the city.

4. *colloq.* A 'go-ahead' person.

1889 *Century Mag.* Oct. 874/1 The pretty girl from the East is hardly enough of a 'rusher' to please the young Western masculine taste.

rushet, obs. or erron. form of RUSSET.

rush-grown, *a.* [RUSH *sb.*[1]]

1. Having the slender tapering form of a rush.

1545 ASCHAM *Toxoph.* (Arb.) 126 Those [shafts] that be lytle brested and big toward the hede called by theyr lyke-nesse taperfashion, reshe growne, and of some merrye fellowes bobtayles. **1615** MARKHAM *Country Contentm.* I. i, His tail long, and rush grown, that is big at the setting on, and small downward. *Ibid.* I. x, An excellent streight and well grown Ground Hazel, being from the bottome to the top finely Rush-grown. **1664** POWER *Exp. Philos.* I. 27 With an Annular body like a Wasp,..and conical or rush-grown towards the tayl. **1735** SOMERVILLE *Chase* I. 247 His Rush-grown Tail O'er his broad Back bends in an ample Arch. **1828** CARR *Craven Gloss.*, *Rush-grown*, tapering like a rush.

2. Overgrown with rushes.

1777 T. WARTON *Suicide* ii, By the brook, that ling'ring laves Yon rush-grown moor with sable waves. **1777** MASON *Eng. Garden* II. 342 Oft too the coward hare, then only bold .., Will quit her rush-grown form. **1886** W. J. TUCKER *E. Europe* 213 The vast rush-grown swamps and verdant pastures of the lordly Theiss.

rush hour. Also rush-hour. [f. RUSH *sb.*[2] + HOUR.] A period of the day during which the movement of people is at its height, esp. one during which large numbers of people are travelling to or from work. Also *attrib.*

1898 *Westm. Gaz.* 28 Oct. 8/3 Trailer cars can be put on during the 'rush hours', mornings and evenings. **1907** 'O. HENRY' *Trimmed Lamp* 233 As solid as granite in the 'rush-hour' tide of humanity, stood the Man from Nome. **1926** *Daily Graphic* 13 May 1 (*caption*) The 'rush hour' at Earl's Court yesterday. Travelling discomforts are mitigated by much good humour and politeness. **1931** *Morn. Post* 18 Aug. 6/4 Rush-hour trains held up. **1932** D. L. SAYERS *Have his Carcase* iv. 50 The place is like the Corner House in the rush hour. **1955** *Times* 17 June 9/4 Even now, great congestion is caused by traffic entering and leaving the park, particularly in the rush hours. **1961** I. MURDOCH *Severed Head* xxvii. 221 Through the rush-hour traffic the god that protects drunken men protected me. **1973** 'M. INNES' *Appleby's Answer* iii. 32 It was the first of London's evening rush-hours, and their taxi made only a tedious stop-go progress. **1977** B. PYM *Quartet in Autumn* ii. 17 A woman, slumped on a seat on the Underground platform while the rush hour crowds hurried past her.

'rushiness. *rare*$^{-0}$. [f. RUSHY *a.*[1]] 'A being full of or having Rushes' (Bailey, 1730).

'rushing, *vbl. sb.* [f. RUSH *v.*[2]] **a.** The action of running or moving with great speed or force; the noise produced by some rapid or violent movement. Also in fig. uses.

c **1340** HAMPOLE *Pr. Consc.* 7350 þare salle be swilk rareyng and ruschyng And raumpyng of devels. **1398** TREVISA *Barth. De P. R.* XVIII. lxiv. (Bodl. MS.), [A lion] dredeþ noise and russchinge of wheles. *c* **1430** *Syr Gener.* 5921 The hors he held for al his russhing. **1535** COVERDALE *Judith* xiv. 13 They..made a greate russzhinge to wake him vp, because they thought with the noyse to haue raised him. *a* **1548** HALL *Chron.*, *Hen. VIII* 79 b, The two kynges had their speres ready, then began the rushyng of speres. **1611** BIBLE *Isaiah* xvii. 12 The rushing of nations, that make a rushing, like the rushing of mighty waters. *a* **1680** CHARNOCK *Attrib. God* (1834) II. 682 Our..careless rushings into his presence in worship. **1753** *Chambers' Cycl.* Suppl. s.v. *Sea*, The rushing up continually of such a body of water makes a roundish cavity. **1817** SHELLEY *Rev. Islam* I. iii, Hark! 'tis the rushing of a wind that sweeps Earth and the ocean. **1898** *Q. Rev.* Apr. 429 We buried those whom the ..brute had slain in his rushings.

b. *spec.* in croquet, North American Football, etc. (see quots.). Cf. RUSH. *v.*[2] 5 e, 6 g.

1877 *Encycl. Brit.* VI. 609/1 The learner should next practise *rushing, i.e.*, roqueting with such force as to move the ball aimed at some distance. **1883** *Atlantic Monthly* May 681/2 Avoirdupois and strength are at a premium for rushing, blocking and tackling. **1966** ROTE & WINTER *Lang. Pro Football* III. 134/2 *Rushing*,..offensive yardage gained by running with ball. **1970** *Globe & Mail* (Toronto) 26 Sept. 36/5 Raimey..is leading the Eastern Football Conference in rushing. **1972** J. MOSEDALE *Football* x. 143 He led the league in rushing in 1942 and 1946.

c. *U.S. Univ. slang.* (See quot. 1888.)

1878 *N. Amer. Rev.* CXXVI. 236 'Hazing,' 'rushing,' secret societies.., are unknown at Oxford and Cambridge. **1888** BRYCE *Amer. Commw.* VI. cii. III. 454 *n.*, Sophomores and freshmen have a whimsical habit of meeting one another in dense masses and trying which can push the other aside on the stairs or path. This is called 'rushing'.

d. *rushing bases*, a children's game, = *King Cæsar* s.v. KING *sb.* 5.

1849, 1969 [see KING *sb.* 5].

e. *U.S.* The process of entertaining candidates for fraternities and sororities and of selecting those who are suitable (see RUSH *v.*[2] 4 d). Also *attrib.*

1901 *Independent* (N.Y.) 15 Feb. 392/1 The inter-fraternity contract..limited the 'spiking' or 'rushing' (terms covering all methods of competing for desirable members) to ten days. **1910** *Collier's* 23 July 16/3 My four friends.. admitted that during this so-called 'rushing' for new members there was considerable rivalry among sororities. **1929** *Daily Maroon* (Chicago) 8 Oct. 2/1 No pledges are made until the fourth day of rushing week. **1931** *Kansas City Star* 10 Oct., Fraternity rushing is entirely over and the freshmen have been told their place in life. **1942** *College Topics* (Univ. Virginia) 12 Oct. 1/2 Rushing got underway and first year-men sought in the darkness for the various fraternity houses. **1946** *Life* 18 Nov. 114/2 Howard has a normally lively interest in extracurricular activities like football, swimming, college dances..fraternity and sorority rushing. **1957** *Encycl. Brit.* IX. 701/2 All of the fraternities aim to be select and to choose their members carefully from the mass of incoming students, the rushing, as the process of selection is called, being well organized and supervised by the older members. **1972** C. S. OGILVY *Tomorrow's Math.* (ed. 2) ii. 37 On college campuses where the fraternity system flourished, it was customary to allow each fraternity to choose..whom it should invite to become members. There were rules and 'codes of rushing', but even so..many undergraduates never had a chance to get into any fraternity.

'rushing, *ppl. a.* [f. RUSH *v.*[2]] That rushes; moving or acting with rapidity or impetuosity. Also *fig.*

1557 N. T. (Geneva) *Acts* ii. 2 And sodenly there came a sounde from heauen, as it had bene of a russhing and mighty winde. **1605** DANIEL *Queen's Arcadia* Wks. (1717) 177 Here by the Murmurs of this rushing Spring, She sweetly lay. **1667** MILTON *P.L.* VI. 97 Rushing sound Of onset ended soon each milder thought. **1743** FRANCIS tr. *Horace*, *Odes* I. xiv. 8 Nor without ropes thy keel can longer brave The rushing fury of th' imperious wave. **1805** SOUTHEY *Madoc* II. xxv, Around the rushing keel The waters sing. **1848** DICKENS *Dombey* xx, Tortured by these thoughts he carried monotony with him, through the rushing landscape. **1881** W. G. MARSHALL *Through America* (1882) 93 Each and all of these have done a 'rushing' business during the past year. **1897** VOYNICH *Gadfly* (1904) 24/2 The blackness seemed to fall away from him in pieces with a rushing noise. **1915** *N. Y. World* 7 Aug. 1/3 All this time the soda-water stands were doing a rushing business.

'rushingly, *adv.* [f. prec. + -LY[2].] In a rushing manner; rapidly or impetuously.

1388 WYCLIF *Job* vi. 15 My britheren passiden me, as a stronde doith, that passith ruschyngli [L. *raptim*] in grete valeis. **1598** FLORIO, *Prorotto*,..lept or gone out rushinglie or running swiftlie. **1837** *Tait's Mag.* IV. 168, I beheld a dark shadow come rushingly forth. **1870** DISRAELI *Lothair* lxvii, All his life during the last year passed rushingly across his mind.

'rushingness. *rare*$^{-1}$. [f. as prec. + -NESS.] The fact of making a rushing sound.

1833 *New Monthly Mag.* XXXVIII. 436 Aloft, with its peculiar rushingness of wing, you heard the flight of the scarce-seen ring-dove.

†**'rushle,** *v. Obs. rare.* [perh. f. RUSH *v.*[2] + -LE, but cf. RUSTLE *v.* 2.] *intr.* To rush. Hence †**'rushling** *ppl. a. Obs.*

1553 BALE *Vocacyon* 39 b, Than was all the rable of the shippe..called to the reckeninge, rushelinge together as they had bene the cookes of helle. **1632** LITHGOW *Trav.* VI. 262 As I was placing his feete in the holes, distempred feare brought him downe upon me with a rushling hurle.

rushle, obs. variant of RUSTLE *v.*

'rushlight. Also rush-light. [RUSH *sb.*[1]]

1. a. = RUSH-CANDLE.

1710 *Lond. Gaz.* No. 4673/2 Small Rush Lights once dipped or drawn through Grease, or Kitchin Stuff. *a* **1764** LLOYD *Tale* Poet. Wks. 1774 I. 78 As rushlights in a spacious room, Just burn enough to form a gloom. **1817** KIRBY & SP. *Entomol.* xxv. (1818) II. 409 A single candle, not more vivid than the rush-light which glimmers in the peasant's cottage. **1856** *Orr's Circ. Sci., Pract. Chem.* 451 The rush-lights that are sold in London vary from ten to eighteen in the pound. **1889** JESSOPP *Coming of Friars* ii. 89 Why should he burn a rushlight when there was nothing to look at?

b. Without article: The light of a rush-candle.

1827 G. GRIFFIN *Holland-Tide* 326 It was neither like sun-light, nor moonlight, nor the light of the stars, nor fire, nor rush light. **1847** C. BRONTË *J. Eyre* vi, The next day commenced as before, getting up and dressing by rushlight.

c. *fig.*, denoting something insignificant or of little account; a glimmer. Also of persons.

1829 CARLYLE *Misc.* (1857) II. 1 A lamp or rushlight of understanding. *Ibid.* 112 A dwelling in the rush-light of 'closet-logic'. **1866** *Yale Lit. Mag.* Apr. 229 Peters told him that good scholars were looked upon here as mere rush-lights. **1893** F. F. MOORE *I Forbid Banns* xxxiv, You have spoken according to your lights, I daresay; but such lights as yours are rush-lights, Mr. Hardy.

2. *attrib.*, as ***rushlight box, candle, holder, life, love, shade.***

1721 AMHERST *Terræ Fil.* No. 13 (1726) 64 The late bishop of Bristol..found him in his lodgings by a little starving fire, with a rush-light candle before him. **1838** DICKENS *O. Twist* xii, The little circles of light, which the reflection of the rushlight-shade threw upon the ceiling. **1863** W. CORY *Lett. & Jrnls.* (1897) 104 It was a great day in my rushlight life. **1934** L. B. LYON *White Hare* 34 And dowsed in dark Their little rush-light love. **1937** *Discovery* Jan. 12/1 Rushlight holders (examples of which date from the 15th century onwards but are commonly of the 18th or early 19th) are generally in iron but might be..merely split sticks. **1955** G. STEVENS *In Canadian Attic* 23 Light for domestic purposes was first supplied by the campfires; next came the rushlight holder. **1969** E. H. PINTO *Treen* 123 Rush-light boxes. These containers..usually of oak or mahogany and mostly dating from the 18th century, are rare and seldom identified correctly. **1969** *Canadian Antiques Collector* Jan. 19/2 An interesting item you may be able to pick up is a 'Rushlight-holder'.

Hence **'rushlighted** *a.*

1866 RUSKIN *Crown Wild Olive* §154 As many candles.. as would comfort the old eyes..of a whole rushlighted country village.

'rush-like, *a.* [f. RUSH *sb.*[1]] Resembling a rush or rushes.

1578 LYTE *Dodoens* 642 Amongst the Rushlyke leaues growe smal rounde stemmes. **1610** NICCOLS *Englands Eliza* xxvi, Ne yet did seeke their glorie to advance, By only tilting with a rush-like lance. **1688** HOLME *Armoury* III. 55/2 The Spanish Silver-cupped Moly hath a Stalk proceeding from 2 or 3 rush like leaves. **1753** *Chambers' Cycl.* Suppl. s.v. *Equisetum*, The rush-like naked, or not branched Horsetail. **1833** *Penny Cycl.* I. 187/1 The plains are permanently clothed with patches of a rush-like plant called *Restio*. **1859** R. F. BURTON *Centr. Afr.* in *Jrnl. Geog. Soc.* XXIX. 105 Their profuse herbage of reeds and rush-like grass.

'rush-ring. [RUSH *sb.*[1]] A ring made of a rush or rushes.

1579 SPENSER *Sheph. Cal.* Nov. 116 The knotted rush-ringes, and gilte Rosemaree. **1593** B. BARNES *Parthenopil* viii, The meanwhile The Shepherd sate, but did compile Green-knotted rush[r]ings. **1617** in Birch *Crt. & Times Jas. I* (1848) II. 35 Ned Wymarke, for all the ancient acquaintance between them, hath not so much as a rush-ring for remembrance. **1646** QUARLES *Sheph. Oracles* VI, The Love-sick Swains Compose Rush-rings and Myrtleberry Chains.

b. Used as a wedding-ring.

1668 DAVENANT *Rivals* v, I'l Crown thee with a Garland of straw then, and I'le Marry thee with a Rush ring. **1813** ELLIS *Brand's Pop. Antiq.* II. 38 A custom.. appears antiently to have prevailed,.. of marrying with a Rush Ring; chiefly practised, however, by designing men. **1877** W. JONES *Finger-ring* 284 The abuse of the rush ring led to the practice being strictly prohibited.

rushy ('rʌʃɪ), *a.*[1] Also 4 resshi, 5-6 russhy, 8- *Sc.* rashy. [f. RUSH *sb.*[1] + -Y[1].]

1. Made or consisting of rushes; rushen.

1382 WYCLIF *Isaiah* xviii. 2 Wo to the lond.. that sendeth in the se messageres, and in resshi vesseles vp on watris. *c* **1440** *Pallad. on Husb.* XI. 494 A multitude of reysouns puld they take, And into russhy frayels rare hem gete. **1613** W. BROWNE *Brit. Past.* I. i, His spring should [not].. drive the rushy-mils, that in his way The shepheard's made. **1728** SWIFT *Pastoral Dial.* Wks. 1751 VII. 204 Sharp are the Stones, take thou this rushy Matt. **1766** GOLDSM. *Vic. W.* viii, Then turn to-night, and freely share.. My rushy couch and frugal fare. **1821** CLARE *Vill. Minstr.* II. 131, I.. bound my posies up with rushy ties. **1842** F. E. PAGET *M. Malvoisin* 94 She laid her head on her rushy pillow.

fig. **1579** FULKE *Heskins' Parl.* 121 Beside this rushie cheine of M. Heskins necessitie you shall heare matter of congruitie. **1617** HIERON *Wks.* II. 362 Surely this rushie religion.. will but help to make more fuell for those eternal flames. **1659** C. NOBLE *Mod. Answ. Immod. Queries* To Rdr., These rushy and sedgy expressions that are set down in this Paper.

2. Producing, full of, covered with, rushes.

c **1586** C'TESS PEMBROKE *Ps.* CXXXVI. vii, [God] cutt in two the russhy sea,.. And made the middest Jacobs way. **1590** SHAKS. *Mids. N.* II. i. 84 By paued fountaine, or by rushie brooke. **1610** FLETCHER *Faithf. Sheph.* I. i, Sit Down on this rushy Bank. *a* **1683** SCROGGS *Courts-Leet* (1714) 210 Whereby the Land is overflowed, so that it becomes rushy and unprofitable. *c* **1750** SHENSTONE *Ode to Sir R. Lyttleton* 20 Where coots in rushy dingles hide. **1794** COWPER *Needless Alarm* 9 A narrow brook, by rushy banks conceal'd. **1805** R. W. DICKSON *Pract. Agric.* II. 952 Coarse rushy lands may.. be converted into good pastures. **1899** BARING-GOULD *Bk. of West* II. 141 All the land except the combes was a great furzy and rushy waste.

3. Resembling a rush or rushes; rush-like.

1597 GERARDE *Herbal* 3 Many sower, rushie leaves. *Ibid.* 11 Rushie Water grasse hath his rootes.. with many fibres or strings hanging at them. **1617** DRUMM. OF HAWTH. *Poems* Wks. (1711) 36/1 The snaky Dun, the Ore with rushy Hair. **1695** J. EDWARDS *Perfect. Script.* 170 The former was of that rushy plant. **1821** WELBY *Visit N. Amer.* 151 The effect upon the long rushy grass as the fire reaches it, is frightfully grand. **1843** *Penny Cycl.* XXV. 262/2 *Triticum junceum*, Sea Rushy Wheat-grass. **1870** HOOKER *Stud. Flora* p. xix, *Junceæ*,.. Rushy herbs.

4. *Comb.*, as *rushy-fringed*, *-leaved*, *-margined*.

1634 MILTON *Comus* 890 By the rushy-fringed bank, Where grows the Willow and the Osier dank. **1753** *Chambers' Cycl.* Suppl. s.v. *Narcissus*, The smallest, white, mountain, rushy-leaved narcissus. **1786** ABERCROMBIE *Arr. in Gard. Assist.* 26 Broom,.. Rushy twigged, or Spanish. **1890** *Spectator* 7 June, A particular roadside, along which there was a rushy-margined pool.

rushy ('rʌʃɪ), *a.*[2] [f. RUSH *sb.*[2] + -Y[1].] Quick, hurried. Also as *adv.*, in a rush, hurriedly.

1908 H. G. WELLS *War in Air* iv. 153 Too soon, Bert my boy—too soon and too rushy. **1976** W. TREVOR *Children of Dynmouth* i. 34 It was all half joking, all quick and rushy, his mother laughing her shrill staccato laugh, Rose-Ann laughing also, neither of them listening to him.

Rushy, variant of RUSSIE *Obs.*

rusien, obs. form of RESE *v.*[2]

'rusiform, *a.* [f. RUSA.] (See quot.)

1877 *Proc. Zool. Soc.* 7 When it [the Spigelian lobe] is pedunculate, as is generally the case in the genus *Rusa*, it may be termed *rusiform*.

rusine ('ru:saɪn), *a. Zool.* [See RUSA and -INE[1].] Of, belonging to, or characteristic of the cervine genus *Rusa*.

1852 J. E. GRAY *Catal. Mamm. Brit. Mus.* III. 186 The Rusine Deer have a distinct, anterior basal snag to the horns, the muffle very high and not separated from the edge of the lips. **1882** *Jrnl. R. Soc. Bengal* LI. II. 45 The Rusine type of antler prevailed in Pliocene times.

‖**rus in urbe** ('ru:s ɪn ˌɜ:beɪ), *phr.* [a. L. *rūs in urbe* country in city.] The creating of an illusion of the countryside in a city; an urban building, garden, prospect, etc., which suggests the countryside. Also *attrib.* So **rus-in-'urbe-ish** *a.*

1759 GRAY *Let.* 24 July (1827) II. 40, I am now settled in my new territories commanding Bedford gardens, and all the fields as far as Highgate and Hampstead..; so *rus-in-urbe-ish*, that I believe I shall stay here. **1795** tr. *C. P. Moritz's Travels* 68 In Grosvenor-square.. there is a little circular wood, intended, no doubt, to give one the idea of *rus in urbe*. **1804** A. SEWARD *Life of Dr. Darwin* i. 16 To this *rus in urbe*.. resorted.. a knot of philosophic friends. **1841** W. M. THACKERAY in *Fraser's Mag.* XXIV. 393/2 A very handsome country place.. a first-rate *rus in urbe*, as the great auctioneer called it when he hammered it down. **1873** A. J. MUNBY *Diary* 21 May in D. Hudson *Munby* (1972) 330 P. A. Taylor is going to sell this charming rus in urbe; ample widespreading old country house, with timbered lawns, and acres of garden. **1939** 'N. BLAKE' *Smiler with Knife* ii. 33 This.. is a remarkably non-committal room. Not so much *rus in urbe* as *surburbia in rure*. **1963** *Times* 6 Apr. 11/3 The Rumanian passion for *rus in urbe* exceeds even the English. **1968** *Times* 15 Oct. 7/1 It is a natural progression of the rus in urbe feeling of fashion this autumn. **1976** *Times* 9 Aug. 10/8 Two foxes.. live in a corner of the allotments—which seems to be taking *rus in urbe* too far.

†**rusk**, *sb.*[1] *Obs.*[−1] [Related to RUSK *v.*[1] Cf. Icel., Norw., and MSw. *rusk*.] A blow.

c **1425** WYNTOUN *Cron.* I. v. 206 To þat boy he gef a rusk, .. He dang him with his bow to deid.

rusk (rʌsk), *sb.*[2] Also 6-7 ruske. [a. Sp. or Pg. *rosca* a twist, turn, coil, screw, and spec. a twisted roll of bread (Sp. *rosca de mar* sea-rusk).]

1. Bread in the form of small pieces which have been re-fired so as to render them hard and crisp; formerly much used on board ships.

1595 *Drake's Voy.* (Hakl. Soc.) 15 The provision.. was seven or eight cakes of bisked or rusk for a man. **1617** MORYSON *Itin.* II. 192 His new men grew weake with feeding onely upon ruske. **1639** LECHFORD *Note-Bk.* (1885) 113 You must.. have some refreshments besides the ships provisions,.. that is, some suger and fine ruske or bisket. **1719** DE FOE *Crusoe* I. (Globe) 20 A large Basket of Rusk or Bisket of their kind. **1789** G. KEATE *Pelew Isl.* 31 A canister of tea, a canister of sugar-candy, and a jar of rusk. **1821** SCOTT *Pirate* xxx, Naething to eat but a mouthful of Norway rusk.

attrib. **1794** STEDMAN *Surinam* (1813) I. x. 254 This rusk biscuit is made of a coarse rye loaf cut in two and baked as hard as a stone.

b. *U.S.* 'Bread or cake dried and browned in the oven, and reduced to crumbs by pounding.'

1890 in *Century Dict.*

2. A piece of bread hardened or browned by re-firing and sometimes sweetened.

1759 W. VERRAL *Cookery* 25 Putting on it some rusks or toasts of French bread. **1767** S. PATERSON *Another Trav.* I. 454 Some of the best rusks I ever eat in my life. **1799** UNDERWOOD *Dis. Child.* (ed. 4) I. 135 Rusks and biscuit-powder are more suitable than bread. **1835** *Court Mag.* VI. 144/2 Breakfast.. consists of warm *café-au-lait* and a rusk. **1883** GILMOUR *Mongols* xviii. 217 Crows perch themselves on the top of loaded camels, and deliberately steal Chinamen's rusks and Mongols' mutton.

rusk, *sb.*[3] (See quot.)

1883 GRESLEY *Gloss. Coal-mining* 209 *Rusks*, small slack, or that next larger than dust or dead small.

rusk, *v.*[1] *rare.* [Of Scand. origin: cf. Icel., Fær., Norw., MSw. *ruska*, Da. *ruske*, in the same or related senses.]

†**1.** *trans.* To disturb violently; to shake; to tear or tug *up*. *Obs.*

c **1275** *Serving Christ* 71 in *O.E. Misc.* 92 Ne geyneþ vs .. þe ronke racches þat ruskit þe ron [= roe-deer]. *c* **1400** *Sege Jerus.* 727 (E.E.T.S.), Foules fallen to fote & her feþres rusken. *c* **1420** *Avow. Arth.* xii, He ruskes vppe mony a rote, With tusshes of iij. fote.

2. *intr.* To pluck roughly; to scratch, claw. *Sc.*

1880 *Jamieson's Sc. Dict.* s.v., When a horse tears hay from a stack, he is said to be *ruskin'* at it.

rusk, *v.*[2] *rare*[−0]. [f. RUSK *sb.*[2]] *trans.* To convert (bread or cake) into rusk (*Cent. Dict.*).

Ruski, var. RUSSKI *a.* and *sb.*

ruskie, variant of RUSKY.

†**'ruskin**[1]. *Obs.* In 5-6 ruskyn. Some kind of fur. Also *attrib.*

[**1287** in Rogers *Agric. & Prices* (1866) I. xxii. 583 In the year 1287 the fur is called 'squirrel and ruskin'.] **1427** *Will M. Colbroke, Comm. Ct. London* (MS.), Unam togam de blod furratam cum Ruskyn wombes. *a* **1550** *Treat. Galaunt* (1860) 17 Thou ruskyn galaunt, that pouerte doth menace For all thy warrocked hoode, and thy proude araye.

†**'ruskin**[2]. *Obs.* Also 8 ruscan, rouskin. [a. Ir. *rusgán*, f. *rusg* bark: cf. RUSKY.] **a.** A vessel made of bark or roots. **b.** Butter preserved in a vessel of this kind.

1679 BLOUNT *Anc. Tenures* 80 A Tub of Butter, in Ireland still called a Ruskin [*printed* Rushin] of Butter. **1710** *Phil. Trans.* XXVII. 305 They at several Feet deep cut thro' what the Irish call a Ruskin of Butter (which was a Firkin, or Vessel, made of the Barks of Trees..). **1719** D'URFEY *Pills* IV. 325, I have.. Ruscan and Cream joy, Wherewith you may slabber you. **1797** *Encycl. Brit.* (ed. 3) IX. 344/1 Butter, called *rouskin*, hath been found in hollowed trunks of trees..; that the length of time it had been buried was very great, we learn from the depth of the bog.. that had grown over it.

†**'ruskin**[3]. *Obs.*[−1] ? A rusk.

c **1803** C. K. SHARPE *New Oxford Guide* ii. in *Mem.* (1888) I. 15 Cakes, ruskins, prunelloes, and sweet damson cheese.

Ruskin[4] ('rʌskɪn). The surname of John Ruskin (1819–1900), distinguished as a writer on art and social subjects, used *attrib.* in ***Ruskin linen***, a kind of hand-woven linen produced near Keswick in Cumbria; ***Ruskin ware***, a kind of pottery with leadless glaze produced at Birmingham; ***Ruskin work*** = *Ruskin linen*. Also the base of various nouns, adjs., etc., as **'Ruskinade**, a discourse in Ruskin's manner; **Ruski'nese** *sb.*, the language or style of Ruskin; *a.*, = next; **Ruski'nesque** *a.*, characteristic of Ruskin; *sb.*, the style of art or architecture favoured by Ruskin; **Ru'skinian** *a.*, = prec. *a.*; *sb.*, a follower of Ruskin; **Ruskini'ana**, memorabilia of Ruskin; **Ru'skinianly** *adv.*, in a Ruskinian manner; **'Ruskinish** *a.*, suggestive of Ruskin; **'Ruskinism**, the principles of Ruskin; **'Ruskinist** = RUSKINIAN *sb.*; **'Ruskinite** *sb.* and *a.* = RUSKINIAN *sb.* and *a.*; **'Ruskinize** *v.*, *trans.* to bring to views like those of Ruskin; *intr.* to advocate or adopt Ruskinian principles; **'Ruskiny** *a.*, designating the style admired by Ruskin.

1865 *Sat. Rev.* 30 Dec. 820 For the purpose of delivering hortatory *Ruskinades, in the fashion of the nineteenth century. **1863** G. M. HOPKINS *Let.* 10 July (1938) 55, I.. hope you will approve some of the sketches in a *Ruskinese point of view. **1863** *Macmillan's Mag.* Nov. 67/2 'Laying by', therefore, in Ruskinese, can only mean simple hoarding. **1869** *Times* 11 June 4/2 Some.. will be formally incorporated into the language.., while others may remain emblems of Ruskinese and Carlylism. **1884** *Spectator* 23 Aug. 1093/2 Almost with a Ruskinese eloquence and discrimination. **1933** *Scrutiny* II. 1/2 Almost every page is littered with clichés, floating in Ruskinese, and quotations from Horace are liberally applied. **1853** R. H. PATTERSON *Ess. Hist. & Art* (1862) 339 The true *Ruskinesque style of criticism. **1873** FREEMAN in W. R. W. Stephens *Life* (1895) II. 76 One would welcome a bit of Ruskinesque in the dull modern streets of Rome. **1876** GROSART *Wks. A. Wilson* II. Pref. p. xxv, A *Ruskinian denunciation of falsehood and sham. **1876** RUSKIN *St. Mark's Rest* xi. §209 So that no true disciple of mine will ever be a 'Ruskinian'! **1931** *Times Lit. Suppl.* 18 June 492/2 Every scrap of *Ruskiniana is now scattered to all quarters. **1978** *Lancashire Life* July 50/4 It was the Severns' ill-luck to preside over the gradual running-down of Brantwood after 1918, a process completed after Arthur's death in 1931, in his ninetieth year, by the sale of household effects and Ruskiniana. **1974** SHERWOOD & PEVSNER *Buildings of England: Oxfordshire* 325 Capitals of the French Early Gothic foliage type but also *Ruskinianly naturalistic. **1884** *Bookseller* 6 Nov. 1187/2 There is a *Ruskinish colouring about her style. **1851** 'AN ARCHITECT' *Something on Ruskinism* p. iv, These few pages do not pretend to exhibit a portraiture of *Ruskinism, or anything like one. **1853** R. H. PATTERSON *Ess. Hist. & Art* (1862) 336 If he be not previously inoculated with Ruskinism. **1940** E. GILL *Autobiogr.* vii. 277 Anything that looks like Ruskinism in my subsequent development is chiefly due to the fact that we both accepted the same first principles. **1969** *Daily Tel.* 8 Feb. 15/4 For long there have been a few devoted *Ruskinists in this country and America. **1889** *St. James's Gaz.* 31 July 9/1 (*heading*) The travels of a *Ruskinite's letter. **1899** G. B. SHAW *Let.* 17 Oct. (1972) II. 113 On the whole, the wooden figures [in the Alhambra], which classical & Ruskinite tourists alike disdain, are the things best worth looking at. **1975** *Maclean's Mag.* May (B.C. Suppl.) 6 As far back as 1890, a utopian community of Ruskinites had set up shop in the Fraser Valley. **1880** *Athenæum* 18 Dec. 808/1 If we are so minded we may *Ruskinize ourselves in all seriousness. **1882** *Ibid.* 1 Apr. 82 Mr. Ruskin has not Ruskinized in vain. **1892** *Pall Mall G.* 12 Oct. 5/2 It is made of home-spun '*Ruskin' flax linen. **1963** *Bookseller* 20 July 248/1 It was Ruskin who introduced linen cut-work to England and it is sometimes called *Ruskin work, but.. the proper name [is].. *Linen Cut-Work.* **1977** M. GREEN *Children of Sun* (rev. ed.) iii. 135 Harold [Acton] liked the Brighton Pavilion, but not the grey Gothicism, nor the *Ruskiny ruins.

†**'ruskle**, *v. Obs.*[−0] (Cf. RASKLE *v.*)

1570 LEVINS *Manip.* 194 To Ruskle, *pandiculari.*

'rusky. *Sc.* Also ruskie, -key. [ad. Gael. *rusgan*: see RUSKIN[2].] A basket for holding meal or seed-corn, made of twigs and straw; a bee-hive of straw or rushes; a coarse straw-hat.

1721 KELLY *Scot. Prov.* 395 You are as small as the Twitter of a twin'd Rusky, a Taunt to a Maid, that would gladly be esteem'd neat, and small. **1810** THOMSON *Poems* 143 (E.D.D.), A rusky fu' o' seed. **1844** H. STEPHENS *Bk. Farm* II. 374 Bee-hives and ruskies.. are beautifully and lightly made of rye-straw.

Rusky, var. RUSSKI *a.* and *sb.*

rusle, obs. form of RUSTLE.

rusma ('rʌzmə). Also 9 rhusma. [app. ad. Turk. *khirisma*, ad. Gr. χρῖσμα ointment (see CHRISM).] A depilatory composed of lime and orpiment, now chiefly used in tanning.

1615 G. SANDYS *Trav.* (1637) 69 [They] take away the haire with a composition of rusma (a minerall of Cyprus) and unsleakt lime. **1681** GREW *Musæum* III. §ii. ii. 332 A Piece of Rusma or crude Zernick. **1797** *Encycl. Brit.* (ed. 3) III. 75/1 It is composed of a mineral called *rusma*, which is of a deep brown. **1839** URE *Dict. Arts* 387 The rusma should never be applied but to a small surface at a time. **1872** CROOKES tr. *Wagner's Handbk. Chem. Technol.* 87 Orpiment is used..to prepare what is called rusma, a paste applied in dressing skins in order to remove the hair.

Rusnak, Rusniac, Rusniak, varr. RUSSNIAK *sb.* and *a.*

†'**ruspicer.** *Obs.*$^{-1}$ [f. L. (*h*)*aruspic-*, stem of (*h*)*aruspex* + -ER[1].] A diviner.

c **1400** *Apol. Loll.* 95 Ruspiceris are þoo þat loken to horis or tymis,..or wen þat þei may bowe God to do þing in on houre, þat he wil not do in an oþer.

Russ (rʌs), *sb.* and *a.* Forms: 6 **Rows(s)e, Rousse, 6–8 Russe, 7 Rush, 7– Russ.** [ad. Russ. *Rusĭ*, native name of the people and country. Cf. Sw. *Ryss*, Du. *Rus*, G. and F. *Russe.*]

A. *sb.* **1.** A Russian. Now *rare.*

1567 JENKINSON in Tolstoy *40 Yrs. Intercourse Eng. & Russia* (1875) 38 To assist and ayde such Russes as be my freinds. **1574** in Hakluyt *Voy.* (1598) I. I. 396 They..slew divers of the Russes that were of the ship. **1600** G. ABBOT *Jonah* 450 In our age there is not the Russe but hath his solemne Senate. **1655** J. COTGRAVE *Wits Interpr.* (1662) 270 The Rush, Turk,..and Grecian. *Ibid.*, The Rush with sable furrs his cap. **1667** PEPYS *Diary* 8 Sept., Here were some Russes come to see the King at dinner. **1709** MRS. MANLEY *Secret Mem.* (1720) III. 303 A Party of the Goths and wild Russes came down to seek for Booty. **1784** COWPER *Task* v. 129 Imperial mistress of the fur-clad Russ! **1822** BYRON *Juan* VIII. cxx, Some twenty times he made the Russ retire. **1897** 'OUIDA' *Massarenes* xxxix, There are [at Cannes] no end of Germans and Russes to play with.

Comb. **1882** *Times* 10 Apr. 7/1 [Bismarck] annihilated the old Conventional, Russ-ridden Bund.

†**b.** An adherent of the Russian Church. *Obs.*

1607 T. ROGERS *39 Art.* (1853) 278 We also condemn the opinion of the Russes, that there is such necessity of baptism. **1635** PAGITT *Christianogr.* 66 The Russes and the Greeks do not elevate the consecrated Bread to be worshipped at the Altar.

2. The Russian language.

1571 A. JENKINSON *Voy. & Trav.* (Hakl. Soc.) II. 285 When the said lettre shalbe translated into rowse. **1753** HANWAY *Trav.* (1762) II. III. xxxii. 144 With the assistance of the tartar boy, who spoke turkish and russ, I found my way to the sea-coast. **1851** *Proc. Philol. Soc.* V. 27 The Ruthenian dialect..partakes of the character both of the Polish and Russ. **1882** SALA *Amer. Revis.* (1885) 31, I tried my hardest..to learn a little Russ.

B. *adj.* Russian.

1574 in Hakluyt *Voy.* (1598) I. I. 396 Certaine Russe Cassaks, which are outlawes or banished men. *a* **1618** RALEIGH *Rem.* (1661) 7 As in the Russe and Turkish Government. **1716** J. PERRY *State of Russia* 7 *note*, A Ruble is 100 Russ Copecks. **1745** H. WALPOLE *Corr.* (1846) II. 12 The Russ tongue. **1822** BYRON *Juan* VII. xxix, The Russ flotilla getting under way.

Russ, var. RUS.

russed, obs. form of RUSSET.

†'**russel**[1]. *Obs. rare.* Also 5 **russall.** [a. OF. *russel, roussel* (mod.F. *rousseau*) reddish, red-haired, also used as sb.] A reddish thing or animal.

a **1450** *Tourn. Tottenham, Feest* vii. in Hazl. *E.P.P.* III. 95 Ther come in iordans in iussall Als red as any russall. *c* **1480** HENRYSON *Fables, Fox, Wolf, & Cadger* ii, Swa happinnit him..To meit ane Foxe... 'Welcum to me', quod he, 'thow Russell gray'.

†'**russel**[2]. *Obs.* Forms: α. 5–6 *Sc.* **ryssil(l)is, rissillis, ristlis;** 6 **ryssel,** *Sc.* **ryssill.** β. 6 **russelles,** 6–7 **russells, -els;** 6 **ross-, russell,** 7 **rustell,** 7–8 **russel.** [Of obscure origin; possibly from *Rijssel*, the Flemish name of Lille. The early forms, and the fact that black and other colours occur earlier and more frequently than red, are against connexion with prec.]

1. A kind of woollen fabric formerly used for articles of attire, esp. in the 16th century.

α. **1488** *Acc. Ld. High Treas. Scot.* I. 159 For ij elne and j quartar of grene Ryssillis for a gowne and a coyt. *Ibid.*, For v quartaris of browne Ryssillis for a gowne til him.

β. **1541** *Act 33 Hen. VIII*, c. 16 Straungers..doe make and weave sayes, russelles, worstedes, and diverse..other clothes. **1545** *Fabric Rolls York Minster* (Surtees) 136 For a ȝerde and a quarter of red russell, 2s. 6d. **1587** FLEMING *Contn. Holinshed* III. 1290/1 Over the first loome was written, the weaving of worsted; over the second, the weaving of russels.

2. *attrib.* **a.** In names of stuffs, as ***russel(s) black, cloth, satin, silk, worsted.***

α. **1493** HALYBURTON *Ledger* (1867) 30, 3 stekis of ryssillis clath, an blak, an bron, and an grey. **1494** *Acc. Ld. High Treas. Scot.* I. 224, ij ellis of Rissillis blak, to be a coit aboune his Jak. **1542** *Inv. R. Wardr.* (1815) 86 Item, ane coit of rissillis blak. **1550** J. COKE *Eng. & Fr. Heralds* §212 Sayes, tapisterie, ryssel worstedes, cloth, carpettes.

β. **1552** in J. C. Jeaffreson *Middlesex County Rec.* I. (1886) 8 A womans kertyll of Russell worsted. **1554** *Act 1 & 2 Phil. & Mary*, c. 14 §1 Russels called Russelles Sattens and Satten Reverses. **1606** in *Lismore Papers* Ser. II. (1887) I. 110, iij dosson of rustell silkes & silver longe buttens. **1653** *Acts of Parlt.* (1658) 270 The Wardens and Fellowship of the Mystery of Russel-Sattins, Sattins-Reverses, and Fustian of Norwich making.

b. Denoting 'made of russel(s)'.

1567 *Richmond Wills* (Surtees) 149 My sarcenet typpet, my best russelles typpet, and my best cappe. **1703** *Lond. Gaz.* No. 3915/4 Stolen..., a black Russel Petticoat flower'd.

†'**russelet.** *Obs.* Also 8 **russelette.** [ad. F. *rousselet*, f. OF. *roussel*: see RUSSEL[1]. The French form of the name is still in use.] One of several varieties of pear, distinguished by their reddish-brown colour or by russet specks.

1693 EVELYN *De la Quint. Compl. Gard.* I. 91 This Russelet-pear..is a Pear of a midling bigness,..of a grey Colour, reddish on one side, and of a dark red on the other, with some greenish Parts interlac'd. **1706** LONDON & WISE *Retir'd Gard.* I. vii. 29 The Russelet of Reims is esteem'd one of the best Pears that grows. *Ibid.*, There is another Sort of Russelet, which is smaller than that last mention'd. **1786** ABERCROMBIE *Arr.* in *Gard. Assist.* p. xii, Pears...Principal Varieties,..Great russelette. *c* **1820** *Edin. Encycl.* XI. 212/1 The Great Russelet..is a large oblong fruit, of a brownish colour, becoming dark red next the sun.

Russell[1] ('rʌsəl). A ribbed or corded fabric, usually made with a cotton warp and woollen weft. Commonly called ***Russell cord.***

1868 *Chambers's Encycl.* X. 268/1 Some Coburgs, Orleans, Russells, and Damasks are likewise made with silk warps. **1873** [see *Persian cord* s.v. PERSIAN *a.* 2]. **1882** CAULFEILD & SAWARD *Dict. Needlewk.* 429/1 *Russell Cord*, a kind of corded Rep, employed for making summer coats, scholastic gowns, lawyers' bags, etc. **1888** *Encycl. Brit.* XXIV. 662/1 The variety of worsted cloths is still greater, embracing says, serges,..Russell cords, coburgs,..and Orleans cloth. **1896** *Woman's Life* 11 July 179/2, I cannot say that the coarse blue alpaca in various shades of navy blue and prune finds favour in my eyes... It reminds me too much of the fearsome fabric known as Russell cord, that in the far-off days of my childhood constituted my school dresses. **1940** *Chambers's Techn. Dict.* 735/1 *Russel cord* (textiles), a dress fabric of plain weave, with a cord effect; made from cotton warp and worsted or mohair weft, the warp being in tapes. **1966** *Guardian* 25 Apr. 7/2 Russell cord is the right stuff for stuff wearers.

Russell[2] ('rʌsəl). The name of Patrick *Russell* (1727–1805), Scottish physician and naturalist, used *attrib.* and in the possessive in **Russell('s) viper** to designate a venomous snake, *Vipera russellii*, found in India, Burma, and Thailand, distinguished by a yellowish-brown skin marked with black rings or spots, and first named *Coluber russellii* in his honour by G. Shaw in 1797.

[**1797** G. SHAW *Naturalist's Miscellany* VIII. pl. ccxci (*caption*) The Russelian Snake. *Ibid.*, Dr. Patrick Russel.. presented the elegant specimen here figured to the British Museum.] **1908** E. P. STEBBING *Man. Elem. Forest Zool. India* xii. 182 The Russell's Viper is one of the most deadly of all snakes. **1937** L. BROMFIELD *Rains Came* I. i. 7 With the first splattering drop of rain they would come swarming out of old roots and crannies in the wall—the cobras, the Russell's vipers, the fierce little kraits. **1940** *Lancet* 17 Aug. 195/1 It was decided to determine how far commercial preparations of Russell-viper venom would meet these requirements. **1961** *Listener* 2 Nov. 735/2 Russell's Vipers, when I have caught them, were always very sluggish. **1972** M. RICHARDSON *Fascination of Reptiles* xv. 158 Another snake which Indian snake charmers sometimes carry around in their baskets is Russell's viper.

Russell[3] ('rʌsəl). The name of Bertrand Arthur William *Russell*, 3rd Earl Russell (1872–1970), mathematician and philosopher, used *attrib.* and in the possessive in connection with a paradox concerning the set of all sets that do not contain themselves as members: the condition for it to contain itself is that it should not contain itself.

1922 tr. *Wittgenstein's Tractatus* 57 Herewith Russell's paradox vanishes. **1937** *Jrnl. Symb. Logic* II. 31 This contradiction corresponds to Russell's paradox. **1950** W. V. QUINE *Methods of Logic* (1952) §42. 249 This difficulty is called *Russell's paradox*, for its discoverer (1901). **1963** G. T. KNEEBONE *Math. Logic* iv. 127 Russell's antinomy..this is the paradox of the class $\{x/x\notin x\}$. **1967** *Encycl. Philos.* V. 46/1 *Russell's Paradox*,..Russell..came upon a new paradox, that of the set of all sets that do not contain themselves as elements. A set *r*, the 'Russell set', is defined by the following condition: for every x, $x\notin r$ if and only if $x\in x$. By substitution we obtain: $r\notin r$ if and only if $r\notin r$. **1977** BELL & MACHOVER *Course in Math. Logic* x. 462 Unfortunately ..(1.2) is untenable even when $k = 0$, because it leads to the well-known Russell paradox.

Russell[4] ('rʌsəl). The name of George *Russell* (1857–1951), English gardener, used *attrib.*, esp. in **Russell lupin,** to designate a large perennial lupin belonging to a variety of *Lupinus polyphyllus* developed by him, introduced in 1937, and distinguished by long racemes of papilionaceous flowers in one or two of a wide range of colours.

1937 *My Garden* XI. 332 The 'Russell Lupins'..would be more correctly described as a new 'race' rather than an improvement of an old. **1957** A. BLOOM *Hardy Perennials* 229 The famous Russell strain..has superseded all others in recent years. *Ibid.* 230 Russell Lupins..have few dislikes other than over-rich or limy soils. **1974** *Country Life* 17 Jan. 72/3 George Russell, a Yorkshire gardener, was attempting to improve the perennial lupin and found..one that had sported to a new shape of flower... Virtually all subsequent lupins have been of the 'Russell' type. **1979** *Guardian* 25 Aug. 9/6 We grow Russell lupins as a hobby.

Russell body ('rʌsəl). *Path.* [Named after William *Russell* (1852–1940), Scottish pathologist, who described it in 1890 (*Brit. Med. Jrnl.* 13 Dec. 1356–60).] A hyaline mass of immunoglobulin produced in numbers in, and sometimes extruded by, plasma cells in excessive response to challenge by antibodies.

1913 O. C. GRUNER *Biol. of Blood-Cells* vi. 276 The intracellular Russell bodies are considered the result of myelin degeneration of the cell-substance. **1970** PASSMORE & ROBSON *Compan. Med. Stud.* II. xxv. 39/2 Sometimes the fabrication of antibody within plasma cells is so excessive that hyaline masses of protein (Russell bodies) are deposited in their cytoplasm. **1977** R. B. THOMPSON *Disorders of Blood* xxxii. 508/2 Occasionally Russell bodies are present. .. They are intra-cellular acidophil hyaline bodies which can be produced in animal cells by injections of bacteria and can be found in many organs and tissues.

Russell fence ('rʌsəl). *Canada.* Also **Russel fence, rustle fence.** [Said to derive from the name of Mr. *Russell*, its inventor.] A fence in which the top rail lies in the crux of crossed posts and the lower rails hang suspended from it by looped wires.

1932 N. M. JAMIESON *Cattle in Stall* 75 There was the rustle fence, with boom on top and centre. **1953** *Canad. Geogr. Jrnl.* Dec. 226/2 The Russell fence has..been patented and Russell, the inventor, succeeded..in collecting royalties from people who built fences on his model. It consists of pairs of crossed posts,..but the rails are hung from the crotches and from each other in wire loops. **1962** A. FRY *Ranch on Cariboo* i. 4 It was Russel fence, an ingenious stake and rail structure held together by heavy wire and named, I'm told, after the man who invented it. **1968** *Islander* (Victoria, B.C.) 29 Dec. 16/4 The contract price for a log fence would be around $400 a mile while a Russel fence of the same length could be had for $150. **1971** W. HILLEN *Blackwater River* xiii. 122 This..falcon would have been seen sitting on nearly any Russell fence..a few years back. **1972** R. WRIGHT *Cariboo Mileposts* 14 (*caption*) A typical Cariboo scene of a Russell fence, cattle and pine trees.

Russellian (rʌ'sɛlıən), *a.* and *sb.* [f. the name *Russell* (see RUSSELL[3]) + -IAN.] **A.** *adj.* Designating the mathematical or philosophical ideas of Bertrand Russell; characteristic of or pertaining to Russell (in quot. 1956, *spec.* of *Russell's paradox*: see RUSSELL[3]). **B.** *sb.* An adherent of Russell's ideas. Hence '**Russellism,** the system of Russell's thought and practice.

1923 C. D. BROAD *Sci. Thought* xiii. 534 Physical objects in the Russellian sense. **1934** R. CAMPBELL *Broken Record* 145 Russellism and Waughism seem to me to be as tyrannical and brutal..as Arnold-of-Rugby-ism. **1937** *Discovery* Feb. 61/1 The Russellian 'calculus of propositions'. **1950** *Mind* LIX. 344 Neither Aristotelian nor Russellian rules give the exact logic of any expression of ordinary language. **1954** R. WELLS in *Word* X. 235 Thus Wittgenstein has played a major part in all three branches of the Russellian movement. *Ibid.* 245 Examples..have been separately discussed by various Russellians and Wittgensteinians. **1956** G. E. M. ANSCOMBE tr. *Wittgenstein's Remarks on Found. of Math.* v. 166 The Russellian contradiction is disquieting, not because it is a contradiction, but because the whole growth culminating in it is a cancerous growth. **1972** *Listener* 27 Jan. 119/1 His interest is the more Russellian one of getting the system to work. **1977** *Language* LIII. 74 Perhaps he is taking a Russellian view of definite descriptions.

russellite ('rʌsəlaıt). *Min.* [f. the name of Arthur E. I. M. *Russell* (1878–1964), English mineralogist + -ITE[1].] A tetragonal mixed oxide of bismuth and tungsten, $Bi_2O_3.WO_3$, found as pale yellow or green fine-grained masses.

1938 HEY & BANNISTER in *Mineral. Mag.* XXV. 42 We propose for the mineral the name russellite, in honour of Mr. Arthur Russell. *Ibid.* 49 Russellite..occurs at the Castle-an-Dinas wolfram mine, St. Columb Major, Cornwall, as pale yellow fragments. **1944** *Ibid.* XXVII. 2 Two pellets of comparatively pure russellite about the size of split peas were found to show on their rounded surfaces blebs of bright gold easily visible to the naked eye. **1970** *Ibid.* XXXVII. 705 Russellite $Bi_2O_3.WO_3$ occurs in a small pegmatite near Poona, Western Australia.

Russell-Saunders ('rʌsəl 'sɔːndəz). *Physics.* [The names of Henry Norris *Russell* (1877–1957), U.S. astrophysicist, and Frederick Albert *Saunders* (1875–1963), U.S. physicist; they first described the scheme in *Astrophys. Jrnl.* (1925) LXI. 38.] ***Russell-Saunders coupling***, an approximation employed in a procedure for describing the possible energy states which can be adopted by a set of electrons in an atom; = *LS-coupling* (s.v. L II. 7); also ***Russell-Saunders scheme, state,*** etc.

[**1927** *Zeitschr. f. Physik* XL. 532 Im Russell-Saunderschen Schema.] **1928** *Physical Rev.* XXXI. 957 In most spectra there is a different coupling of the quantum vectors, the Russell-Saunders coupling, which is responsible for normal multiplets. **1935** CONDON & SHORTLEY *Theory of Atomic Spectra* vii. 208 The Russell-Saunders terms corresponding to the configurations s^x and p^x. **1961** WALKER & STRAW *Spectroscopy* I. i. 87 It will be assumed..that Russell-Saunders coupling applies to the individual momentum vectors associated with the electrons. **1962** COTTON & WILKINSON *Adv. Inorg. Chem.* xxvi. 574 Just as the set of five *d* orbitals is split apart by the electrostatic field of surrounding ligands to give two or more sets of lower degeneracy, so also are the various Russell-Saunders states of a d^n configuration. **1966** D. H. WHIFFEN *Spectroscopy* xi. 141 Weak transitions disobeying these selection rules..are not at all uncommon and their existence implies that the Russell-Saunders scheme is not accurately applicable. **1967**

W. R. HINDMARSH *Atomic Spectra* iii. 27 The assumption of negligible spin-orbit interaction on which the Russell-Saunders coupling scheme is based.

Russenorsk ('ruːsənɔːsk). [Norw.] A pidgin of Russian and Norwegian used by fishermen.

1964 E. PALMER tr. *Martinet's Elem. General Linguistics* v. 155 *Russenorsk*, the product of contacts between Russian and Norwegian fishermen on the shores of the Arctic Ocean, which had an ephemeral existence but has been adequately described. **1974** L. TODD *Pidgins & Creoles* i. 6 Russenorsk, a pidgin now almost extinct, arose from the contact of two Indo-European languages, Russian and Norwegian, as a means of facilitating communication between Russian and Norwegian fishermen. **1974** *Encycl. Brit. Macropædia* VI. 1063/2 Pidgins..are not true languages since they are derivations from two or more parent tongues. An example is Russenorsk (from Russian and Norwegian), used by Norwegian fishermen with Russian traders.

†**russerine.** *Obs.*⁻¹ Some kind of fabric.

1710 *Lond. Gaz.* No. 4706/4 For Sale.., black Prenels [= prunellas] and Russerines.

russet ('rʌsɪt), *sb.* and *a.* Also 4–6, 9 **russett** (6 **-ette**), 5–6 **russat**, 7 **russed**, **rushet**; 5 **rousset**, **-at**, 6 **-ett**; 5 **rosset(e**, **roset(t)e**, 5–6 **roset**, 6 **rosat**. [a. OF. *rousset*, *rosset*, *roset*, etc., dim. of *rous* (mod.F. *roux*) red: see ROUSE *a.* Cf. also F. *roussette* sb. fem.]

A. *sb.* **1. a.** A coarse homespun woollen cloth of a reddish-brown, grey or neutral colour, formerly used for the dress of peasants and country-folk; also with *a* and pl., a kind or make of this.

c **1275** *Serving Christ* 70 in *O.E. Misc.* 92 Ne geyneþ vs ..þe robes of russet ne of rencyan. **1362** LANGL. *P. Pl.* A. IX. 1 Thus i-robed in russet, romed I a-boute. **1377** *Ibid.* B. XV. 162 Charite..is as gladde of a goune of a graye russet As of a tunicle of tarse or of tyre scarlet. **1417** *E.E. Wills* 27, xiij. poure men clothed in Russett ylyned witt white. *c* **1489** CAXTON *Sonnes of Aymon* xxvi. 571 Thenne reynaude..toke a cote of sory russet vpon his flesshe. **1541** *Act 33 Hen. VIII*, c. 3 A certayne kinde and sorte of walshe clothes called whytes, russettes, and kenettes. **1561** in *Vicary's Anat.* (1888) App. VI. 190 My gowne of london russet, furred with black. **1615** G. SANDYS *Trav.* 109 Ouer their shashes the men weare rounds of stiffened russet; to defend their braines from the piercing feruor. **1685** DRYDEN *Pref. to Sylvæ* Ess. (Ker) I. 265 Like a fair shepherdess in her country russet, talking in a Yorkshire tone. **1730–46** THOMSON *Autumn* 353 Be mindful of those limbs in russet clad. *a* **1763** SHENSTONE *Elegies* x. 52 Yet sure on Delia seems the russet fair. **1819** SCOTT *Ivanhoe* xxvi, I wore russet before I wore motley. **1866** ROGERS *Agric. & Prices* I. 576 Russet was the dress affected by the Lollards.

fig. *c* **1430** LYDG. *Min. Poems* (Percy Soc.) 24 Constreynt of colde makith floures dare With winter frostes,..All clad in russet, the soil of grene is bare. **1762** CHURCHILL *Prophecy of Famine* Wks. 1767 I. 89 Far as the eye could reach, no tree was seen, Earth, clad in russet, scorn'd the lively green.

†**b.** *pl.* Garments of such cloth. *Obs.*

1586 WARNER *Alb. Eng.* IV. xx. (1602) 95 He borrowed on the working daies his holy russets oft. **1627** S. WARD *Life of Faith* 112 See whether hee will cry when you bid him lay off his russets? *a* **1645** HEYWOOD *Fortune by Land & Sea* II. i, And so you were..forc'd to put on these russets and sheepskins.

2. A reddish-brown colour; a shade of this.

1532–3 *Act 24 Hen. VIII*, c. 13 Veluette, satten, and damaske, being of the colours of blacke, tawny, or russet. **1573** *Art of Limming* p. viii, If you will mingle a litle portion of white with a good quantitie of redde, you may make thereof a Russet, or a sadde Browne, at your discretion. **1624** MIDDLETON *Game at Chess* II. i, Take these papers, Scorch me 'em soundly, burn 'em to French russet, And put 'em in again. **1688** HOLME *Armoury* III. 344/2 With..an Hand Brush..Plasterers..lay Whiting and Russet within their own compass or reaching. **1719** LONDON & WISE *Compl. Gard.* 90 'Tis Gray, over-cast with something of a Russet, coming near the Colour of the Belly of a Doe. **1834** MUDIE *Brit. Birds* (1841) I. 172 There is russet in the spots of the starling. **1875** STEVENSON *Ess. Trav., Autumn Effect* (1905) 119 The sky was an opal-gray, touched here and there.. with certain faint russets that looked as if they were reflections of the colour of the autumnal woods below.

3. a. A variety of eating apple, of a reddish or yellowish brown colour, or marked with brownish spots, and having a rough skin; an apple of this kind. (Cf. the earlier RUSSETING *sb.* 3.)

1708 J. PHILIPS *Cyder* I. 30 Of pimpled Coat The Russet, or the Cats-Head's weighty Orb. **1741** *Compl. Fam. Piece* II. iii. 352 Apples...Winter Pearmain, Aromatick Russet, Pear Russet. **1843** J. SMITH *Forest Trees* 156 Golden russet will do ordinarily well as a standard. **1846** J. BAXTER *Libr. Pract. Agric.* (ed. 4) I. 59 Golden pippins, Golden russet. *a* **1898** MRS. LYNN LINTON in Layard *Life* (1901) ii. 26 He filled my pockets with golden russets.

attrib. **1887** JEFFERIES *Amaryllis* xii, Iden junior sent in the best apples for sauce from his favourite russet trees.

†**b.** A variety of pear. [F. *roussette.*] *Obs.*

1725 *Fam. Dict.* s.v. *Pears*, Skinless Pear, is a Russet in Shape and Taste.

4. A species of noctuid moth.

1832 J. RENNIE *Butterfl. & M.* 72 The Russet..appears in August.

5. (See quots. and cf. B. 5.) Also *attrib.*

1851–3 *Tomlinson's Cycl. Useful Arts* (1867) II. 35/2 At this part of the process, the currier stores his skins, because they are brought to that state (technically called *finished russet*) in which they can be best preserved. **1858** SIMMONDS *Dict. Trade*, *Rus[s]et-offal*,..kip or calf curried leather.

B. *adj.* **1. a.** Of a reddish-brown colour.

In the 15th and 16th cent. usually of cloth.

? *a* **1400** *Morte Arth.* 237 Maluesye and muskadelle, þase meruelyous drynkes, Raykede fulle rathely in rossette cowpes. *c* **1420** LYDG. *Assembly of Gods* 325 The rewde god Pan,..Clad in russet frese. **1465** *Paston Lett.* II. 232, ij peyir hose, j peyir blak and an othyr payir roset. **1562** LEGH *Armorie* (1597) 116 Some part of them of colour Russet, which is somewhat lighter then blacke. **1594** *Warres of Cyrus* 226 The woods Where first the hounds put vp a russet beare. **1632** MILTON *L'Allegro* 71 Russet Lawns, and Fallows Gray, Where the nibling flocks do stray. **1668** WILKINS *Real Char.* 127 Either that of a russet colour,..or that of a shining green. **1704** POPE *Windsor Forest* I. 23 In full light the russet plains extend. **1755** J. SHEBBEARE *Lydia* (1769) II. 273 Sir Simon..beheld one blue stocking peeping above the boot, the other russet. **1820** SCOTT *Monast.* viii, The oak-trees only retained that pallid green that precedes their russet hue. **1848** DICKENS *Dombey* lix, Objects began to take a bleared and russet colour in his eyes. **1877** W. BLACK *Green Past.* xxxiv, We saw an eagle slowly sailing over the russet woods.

b. Applied to varieties of apples (†or pears).

1629 J. PARKINSON *Parad.* III. xix. 587 The Russet pippin is as good an apple as most of the other sorts of pippins. *Ibid.* xxi. 592 The russet Catherine is a very good middle sized peare. **1664** EVELYN *Kal. Hort.* Oct., *Pears.*—The caw-pear .., clove-pear, roussel-pear,..russet-pear. *Ibid.* (1729) 191 *Apples*, Kentish Pippin, Russet Pippin, Golden Pippin [etc.]. **1731** MILLER *Gard. Dict.* s.v. *Leaves*, On the sixth of August, he cut off a large Russet-Pippin. **1887** BESANT *World Went* i. 3 Creased and lined like a russet apple. **1929** M. DE LA ROCHE *Whiteoaks* vii. 99 'H'm,' grunted Finch, tearing a bite from a russet apple. **1970** *Globe & Mail* (Toronto) 28 Sept. 5/1 (*caption*) Seventy-eight acres of.. Russet and Tolman Sweet apple trees, all of them laden with ripe fruit.

c. In names of birds, as ***russet kingfisher***, ***starling***, ***wheatear***; or plants, as ***russet sedge***.

c **1700** in Dampier *Voyages* (1729) III. 403 Russet King's Fisher. Is known by a white Ring about his neck. **1783** LATHAM *Gen. Synop. Birds* II. II. 468 Russet Wheat Ear. **1859** MISS PRATT *Brit. Grasses* VI. 34 Russet Sedge. Fertile spikelets ovate, obtuse, the lower one stalked. **1883** *19th Cent.* Aug. 302 The russet-starling seems possessed with an insatiable desire to kill insects.

d. Qualifying adjs. and sbs. denoting colour.

1676 *Phil. Trans.* XI. 585 Some kinds of those black and russet-tawny Plums may be dried in a kind of Solar stove. **1731** MILLER *Gard. Dict.* s.v. *Pyrus*, The Skin is..of a Russet-green Colour. **1748** THOMSON *Cast. Indol.* II. xxxiii. In russet brown bedight,..He crept along. **1821** CLARE *Vill. Minstr.* I. 92 A russet red the hazels gain. **1861** J. G. WHITTIER *Cobbler Keezar* in *Poet. Wks.* (1898) 84/2 Yellow and red were the apples, And the ripe pears russet-brown. **1873** LONGF. *Wayside Inn* III. *Emma & Eginhard* 87 The leaves fell, russet-golden and blood-red. **1959** E. POUND *Thrones* cii. 82 The colour..As lacquer in sunlight haliporphuros, russet-gold In the air.

e. *Comb.*, as ***russet-backed***, ***-bearded***, ***-clad***, ***-coloured***, ***-faced***, ***-haired***, ***-pated***, ***-roofed***, ***-skinned***. Also RUSSET-COATED.

1590 SHAKS. *Mids. N.* III. ii. 21 As Wilde-geese, that the creeping Fowler eye, Or russet-pated choughes. **1704** *Dict. Rust.*, *Pear-skinless*..is longish shaped, and Russet-colour'd. **1743** G. EDWARDS *Nat. Hist. Birds* I. 31 The Red or Russet-colour'd Wheat-Ear. **1849** THOREAU *Week Concord Riv.* 19 It may be many russet-clad children lurking in those broad meadows. **1854** WHYTE MELVILLE *Gen. Bounce* i, Those gaunt, grim, russet-bearded giants that made the despot of the Lower Empire quake upon his throne. **1878** G. M. HOPKINS *Lett. to R. Bridges* (1955) 48 He [*sc.* a seaman]..is..russet-of-morning-skinned With the sun, salt, and whirling wind. **1884** COUES *N. Amer. Birds* 247 *T[urdus] ustulatus*... Russet-Backed Thrush. **1897** W. B. YEATS *Secret Rose* 80 A russet-faced boy..sat..watching the swallows. **1898** *The Month* Nov. 487 Its clustering, russet-roofed hamlets. **1936** M. H. BRADLEY *Five-Minute Girl* ix. 159 A small girl of eight, hazel-eyed, russet-haired.

2. a. Of garments, etc.: Made of russet cloth.

c **1440** *Pallad. on Husb.* I. 830 Eek as for hail a russet weede is To kest vpon the querne. **1459** *Paston Lett.* I. 476 Item, iij. quarters of a russet gowne withought slevys. **1509** HAWES *Past. Pleas.* xxxv. (Percy Soc.) 180 In a russet banner on the sixt heade There was wrytten this worde, Detraction. **1514** BARCLAY *Cyt. & Uplondyshm.* (Percy Soc.) 21 And we poore herdes in russet cloke and hode, It is not clothynge can make a man be good. **1602** SHAKS. *Ham.* I. i. 166 But looke, the Morne in Russet mantle clad, Walkes o're the dew of yon high Easterne Hill. **1642** FULLER *Holy & Prof. St.* II. xviii. 116 He weares russet clothes, but makes golden payment. **1742** SHENSTONE *Schoolmistr.* 64 A russet stole was o'er her shoulders thrown. **1788** BURNS *Written in Friars-Carse Hermitage* 2 Be thou clad in russet weed, Be thou deckt in silken stole. **1826** HOOD *A Fairy Tale* viii, Weary of sitting on her russet clothing. **1828** MACAULAY *Ess., Milton* (1851) I. 8 His muse had no objection to a russet attire. **1883** *Fisheries Exhib. Catal.* (ed. 4) 133 One Pair 'Russett' Woollen Trousers, undyed, handspun, and woven.

†**b.** ***russet gown***, a country girl. *Obs.*⁻¹

1703 in Ashton *Soc. Life Q. Anne* II. 112 Squires come to Court to some fine Town Lady, and Town Sparks to pick up a Russet Gown.

3. Clad in russet or homespun cloth.

c **1613** MIDDLETON *No Wit like a Woman's* IV. ii, I've given welcome To forty russet yeomen at a time. **1635** TAYLOR *Parr* in *Harl. Misc.* (Malh.) IV. 209 From the emp'ror to the russet clown, All states, each sex, from cottage to the crown. **1642** H. MORE *Song of Soul* II. xlii, He pincht his hat, and from his horses side Stretcht forth his russet legs.

4. Rustic, homely, simple.

1588 SHAKS. *L.L.L.* V. ii. 413 Henceforth my woing minde shall be exprest In russet yeas, and honest kersie noes. **1603** DEKKER & CHETTLE *Grissil* 935 This is thy russet gentrie, coate and crest: Thy earthen honors I will neuer hide. **1652** BENLOWES *Theoph.* XII. ii, Ill suits it with a Russet Life, to write Court-Tissue. **1882** PEBODY *Eng. Journalism* xii. 88 That terse and epigrammatic style..which, with its russet Saxon, has since given him one of the highest positions in the Parliamentary arena.

5. Of boots or shoes: Made of leather which has not been blackened; tan, brown.

1667 WOOD *Life* (O.H.S.) II. 102 To Rich for blacking my russet shoes. **1838** DICKENS *Nickleby* vi, With russet boots on his feet. **1851** MAYHEW *Lond. Labour* I. 274 The minstrel's garb..was not always the short laced tunic, tight trousers, and russet boots. **1893** ASHBY STERRY *Naughty Girl* vi, Their print frocks, their pinafores, their russet shoes were gone.

Hence '**russetly** *adv.*, with a russet colour; in a russet state. *poet.*

c **1864** E. DICKINSON *Poems* (1955) II. 687 Though Pyramids decay And Kingdoms, like the Orchard Flit Russetly away.

russet ('rʌsɪt), *v.* [f. the adj.]

1. *trans.* To render russet in colour; †to scorch or parch to a russet colour.

a **1592** GREENE *Vision* Wks. (Grosart) XII. 224 His doublet was of leather, russeted after the best fashion. **1628** FELTHAM *Resolves* II. xviii, If the Land be russeted with a bloudlesse Famine, are not the poore the first that sacrifice their liues to Hunger? **1688** HOLME *Armoury* III. 396/1 Plasterers..may..Whitten, Russet, or Black any Posts, or parts of an House. **1730** THOMSON *Hymn Seasons* 96 The Summer ray Russets the plain, inspiring Autumn gleams. **1903** *Daily Chron.* 28 May 7/3 The whole surface [of a sword] russeted, and encrusted with cherubs' heads.

2. *intr.* To become russet in colour.

1678 VAUGHAN *Silex Scint.* III. *Thalia Rediv.* 245 Our grass straight russets, and each scorching day Drinks up our brooks. **1891** [see the *ppl. a.*].

Hence '**russeting** *ppl. a.*

1891 *Daily News* 23 Sept. 3/1 Under the russeting boughs of the trees.

russet, obs. form of ROSET *a.*

russet coat. [RUSSET *a.*]

1. A coat of russet cloth or colour, typical of a humble or rustic condition.

1552 LATIMER *Serm.* (1584) 231 Though we bee very poore, and haue but a Russet coate. **1594** NASHE *Terrors of Night* Wks. (Grosart) III. 279 Yet bow your knees to their leathern bagges and russet coates, that they may blesse you from the ambition of Tiburne.

attrib. **1553** M. WOOD tr. *Gardiner's True Obedience* 59 b, His first wife, olde plaine russet cote Ione of the countri, good wife truth.

†**2.** A peasant, rustic; a homely person. *Obs.*

1568 SKINNER tr. *Montanus' Sp. Inquisit.* 86 Being but a plaine fellow and as a man would say a very Russet-cote. **1580** LYLY *Euphues* (Arb.) 443 Disdaine not those that are base, thinke with your selues that russet coates haue their Christendome. **1597** *Pilgr. Parnass.* III. 277 Each earth-creepinge peasant russet-coate Is in request for his well-lined pouche.

3. A russet apple. Also *attrib.*

1602 LYLY *Wks.* (1902) I. 492 Wee haue jenitings, paremayns, russet coates, pippines, able-johns. **1860** HOGG *Fruit Manual* 21 Pitmaston Nonpareil (Russet Coat Nonpareil)... Skin dull green, covered with a thin yellow russet.

russet-coated, *a.* [RUSSET *a.* 1 e. Cf. also prec.] Wearing a russet coat; rustic, homely.

1596 R. LINCHE *Diella* (1877) 69 With this, hee seekes a russet-coated Tree, and straight disclothes him of his long-worne weed. **1643** CROMWELL *Let.* Sept. in *Carlyle*, A plain russet-coated Captain who knows what he fights for. **1683** TRYON *Way to Health* 394 As great content and satisfaction with his poor Russet-Coated Wife, as the greatest Prince with his Gayest Bride. **1867** CARLYLE *Reminis.* (1881) II. 31 It looks to me now like a kind of humble russet-coated epic.

'**russeted**, *ppl. a.* [f. RUSSET *v.*] Russet in colour; also *spec.* (of fruit and vegetables) rough-skinned; (of their skin) rough.

1885–94 R. BRIDGES *Eros & Psyche* Aug. viii, Entering 'neath the shade Of cedar old and russeted tall pine. **1917** [see RUSSETING *vbl. sb.*] **1930** *Jrnl. Pomology & Hort. Sci.* VIII. 299 Examination of the russeted fruit revealed the presence of the fungus already mentioned. **1950** SMOCK & NEUBERT *Apples & Apple Products* iii. 29 This periderm is a cork cambium and is capable of forming cork-like cells which result in the russetted appearance of some fruits. **1978** *Sci. Amer.* June 64/3 The 'Idaho' potato..is the most prized of the North American varieties because of its large size, pulpy interior,..and russeted (textured) skin.

russeting ('rʌsɪtɪŋ), *sb.* Also 6–7 **russetting**, 7 **rousset(t)ing**; 7 **russeten**, 7–9 **russetin**, 8–9 **russetine**. [f. RUSSET *sb.* or *a.* + -ING³.]

†**1. a.** Russet clothing. *Obs.*⁻¹

a **1588** TARLTON in *T.'s Jests* (Shaks. Soc.) p. xxv, He must chaunge his russetting For satin and silke.

†**b.** A boot of russet leather. *Obs.*⁻¹

c **1613** ROWLANDS *Paire of Spy-Knaves* (Hunterian Cl.) 16 Yet still in Russettings he will appeare, Although with Shoomaker he neuer cleere.

†**2.** A peasant, rustic; a simple fellow. *Obs.*

1597 BP. HALL *Sat.* I. iii, A goodly hoch-poch, when vile Russettings Are match't with monarchs, and with mighty kings. **1605** *Tryall Chevalr.* IV. i. in Bullen *Old Pl.*, Away, ye russeting. **1632** CHAPMAN & SHIRLEY *Ball* II. i, Farewell, russeting; Thou art not worth my spleen.

3. A russet apple. Cf. RUSSET *sb.* 3.

1607 HEYWOOD *Fair Maid Exch.* G iv, *Fid.* You are a pippinmonger to call me Russetting or apple Iohn. *Bow.* Sirra Russetting, ile pare your head off. **1664** EVELYN *Kal. Hort.* Dec., *Apples.* Roussetting, Leather-coat, Winter Reed, Chess-nut apple. **1707** MORTIMER *Husb.* (1721) II. 286 The Aromatick or Golden-Russeting hath no compare. **1745** *Phil. Trans.* XLIII. 525, I have sent you some Russetings changed by the Farina of a next-door Neighbour. **1824** MISS MITFORD *Village* Ser. I. (1866) 47

The brown rough fruitage of the golden-rennet's next neighbour the russeting.

b. *attrib.* with *apple, face.*

1605 *Tryall Chevalr.* II. i. in Bullen *Old Pl.*, Leere not, Lobster, lest I thump that russeting face of yours with my sword hilt. **1611** COTGR., *Roussette*, a russetin Apple. **1725** SLOANE *Jamaica* II. 197 A fruit.. as big as a large Russeting apple. **1861** T. L. PEACOCK *Gryll Gr.* vi, The tears in his eyes and the passionate utterances of his voice, contrasted strangely with a round russetin face.

'russeting, *vbl. sb.* [f. RUSSET *v.*] Becoming russet in colour; *spec.* the roughening of the skin of normally smooth-skinned fruit, esp. apples.

1576-7 in Feuillerat *Revels Q. Eliz.* (1908) 262 For xij sheepe skynnes vj^s. For paring and russeting of them ij^s. **1917** *32nd Ann. Rep. Maine Agric. Experiment Station* 86 These plots have been introduced solely.. as a basis of comparison with other sprays.. with respect to scab control and the production of fruit russetting and foliage injury... This treatment has increased the number of russetted apples from 5 to 10 per cent. **1928** C. E. OWENS *Princ. Plant Path.* xxv. 609 Bordeaux is apt to cause leaf injury and russeting of fruit.. in moist weather. **1974** *Nature* 8 Feb. 337/3 The most insidious type of damage is russeting, and fruit skins are sensitive to certain fungicides in May and June.

'russetish, *a. rare.* [f. RUSSET *a.* + -ISH.] Somewhat of a russet colour.

1600 SURFLET *Countrie Farme* II. xxiii. 230 White ones [onions] are a great deale better then those of a russettish or reddish colour. **1640** PARKINSON *Theatr. Bot.* 247 Of a pale russettish colour.

russety ('rʌsɪtɪ), *a.* [f. RUSSET *a.* + -Y.] Inclining to, approaching, a russet colour.

1778 [W. H. MARSHALL] *Minutes Agric., Observ.* 167 Hedges look russetty in June. **1812** H. & J. SMITH *Rej. Addr.* vii. (1873) 61 And Yamen's cheek is a russety brown. **1860** HOGG *Fruit Manual* 190 Skin.. thickly covered with grey russety dots. **1890** H. M. STANLEY *Darkest Africa* I. xi. 250 Rich russety circles of leaves.

russewale, variant of RUSSWALE *Obs.*

Russia ('rʌʃə). [med.L., f. *Russi* the Russians: see RUSS. The Russian form *Rossiya* appears to have been adopted from Byzantine Gr. 'Ρωσία.] The name of the country in the east of Europe, used attributively.

1. a. ***Russia leather***, a very durable leather made of skins impregnated with oil distilled from birch-bark, extensively used in book-binding.

1658 SIR T. BROWNE *Gard. Cyrus* iii. 147 The like Reticulate grain is observable in some Russia Leather. **1662** J. DAVIES tr. *Olearius' Voy. Ambass.* 76 Their boots.. are made of Russia leather, or Goats skin. **1716** HEARNE *Collect.* (O.H.S.) V. 365 He hath bound it in Russia Leather. **1740** WOODROOFE in Hanway *Trav.* (1762) I. II. xvii. 74 Casan.. has several manufactures of red russia leather. **1852** MORFIT *Tanning & Currying* (1853) 372 Russia leather consists of calf, sheep, and goat skins, dyed generally of a red color. **1871** M. COLLINS *Marq. & Merch.* II. viii. 227 Russia leather odorous with the aroma of silver birch-rind.

attrib. **1656** in Willis & Clark *Cambridge* (1886) III. 383 For 2 dozen of Russ. Leather chayres at 7^s. 6^d. **1676** *Ibid.*, 18 Russia leather Chayres for the Parlor. **1704** *Lond. Gaz.* No. 4027/4 With a new Russia Leather Saddle and Bridle.

b. *ellipt.* in this sense.

1818 *Art Bk.-binding* 45 Mark the paper into squares from point to point each way, and then lay it exactly on the russia. **1862** BURTON *Bk. Hunter* I. 27 No one likes sheep's clothing for his literature, even if he should not aspire to russia or morocco. **1876** GEO. ELIOT *Dan. Der.* xxxvi, The scent of russia from the books.

attrib. and *Comb.* **1817** DIBDIN *Bibliogr. Decam.* II. 510 Specimens of his own russia-bindings. **1818** *Art Bk.-binding* 45 When the lacing is complete, put a piece of paper on the russia bands. **1846** G. DODD *Brit. Manuf.* VI. 103 An elegant morocco or russia-bound book.

2. a. In the specific names of various articles, chiefly made in, or imported from, Russia, as ***Russia ashes, braid, crash, drab, duck***, etc. (see quots.).

1819 *Pantologia*, **Russia ashes*, the impure potash, as imported from Russia. **1847** *Lady's Newspaper* 11 Dec. 566 Gentleman's waist-coat. Material—blue.. cloth, and green or amber *Russia braid. **1873** *Young Englishwoman* Nov. 572/1 Travelling toilet of brown cashmere, braided with brown of a darker-shade in Russia and Breton braid. **1882** CAULFEILD & SAWARD *Dict. Needlewk.* 429/1 *Russia Braids.* These are made respectively in two materials—Mohair and Silk. *Ibid.*, **Russia Crash*, a coarse linen, or hempen textile, derived from Russia, or made of Russian hemp. **1780** J. HOWARD *Prisons* 299 The men have a *Russia-drab coat and breeches. **1761** *Essex Inst. Hist. Coll.* (1912) XLVIII. 95 Best prime *Russia Duck. **1822** M. EDGEWORTH *Let.* 6 Feb. (1971) 344 His Russia duck jacket and trowzers. **1858** SIMMONDS *Dict. Trade*, *Russia-duck*, a white linen fine canvas. **1882** CAULFEILD & SAWARD *Dict. Needlewk.* 429/2 *Russia Duck*, this is a description of strong coarse linen Jean, made for trouserings, and having its origin in Russia. **1663** PEPYS *Diary* 6 June, To see the orders about the *Russia hemp that is to be fetched from Archangel. **1897** *Sears, Roebuck Catal.* 127 We make it [*sc.* a stove] lined and unlined, and in smooth steel and planished iron (usually called *Russia iron). **1901** *Daily Colonist* (Victoria, B.C.) 12 Oct. 8/7 (Advt.), 'Famous' Air-Tights [*sc.* stoves]. Built for light service. Will burn rough blocks of wood. Made of Russia iron. **1839** J. J. AUDUBON *Ornithol. Biogr.* V. 504 The nest.. has uniformly been built of *Russia matting. **1875** KNIGHT *Dict. Mech.* 2005/2 *Russia-matting*, matting manufactured in Russia from the inner bark of the linden. **1882** CAULFEILD & SAWARD *Dict. Needlewk.* 429/2 *Russia Musquash (*Fiber zibethicus*), this animal is also known as the Perewiaska. **1773** *Russia oil [see RUSSIAN B. 2 c]. **1764** *Phil. Trans.* LIV. 5 The uppermost fillets.. were woven something after the manner of *Russia-sheeting. **1859** *Rep. Comm. Patents 1858* (U.S.) I. 530 The process of manufacturing sheet-iron, to possess most of the qualifications of 'polished *Russia sheet-iron'. **1875** KNIGHT *Dict. Mech.* 2005/2 *Russia Sheet-iron*, sheet-iron made in Russia, and having a smooth, glossy surface of a purplish color, sometimes mottled.

b. *ellipt.* for ***Russia iron, linen.***

1798 *Monthly Mag.* June 481 Irish linens are becoming exceedingly scarce... Russias are also very scarce at present. **1884** KNIGHT *Dict. Mech.* Suppl. 772/2 s.v. *Russian Iron*, The American product, or 'imitation Russia'.

Russian ('rʌʃən), *sb.* and *a.* Also 9- *colloq.* **Rhoosian, Roos(h)ian,** etc.: see RHOOSIAN *sb.* and *a.* [ad. med.L. *Russiān-us*, f. *Russia*: see prec. So F. *Russien*, Sp. *Rusiano.*]

A. *sb.* **1. a.** A native or inhabitant of Russia. Also with distinguishing adjs., as ***Great, Little, White Russians*** (see quot. 1866). See also WHITE *a.* 11 e.

1538 ELYOT s.v. *Scytæ*, They be nowe called Russyans, Moscouites, and Tartariens. **1588** SHAKS. *L.L.L.* v. ii. 443 What did the Russian whisper in your eare? **1606** DEKKER *Seuen Deadly Sinnes* Wks. (Grosart) II. 28 The Russians haue an excellent custome; they beate them on the shinnes, that haue mony, and will not pay their debts. **1716** LADY M. W. MONTAGU *Lett.* xlv[i]. II. 28 My grooms are Arabs;.. my housemaids Russians. **1831** SINCLAIR *Corr.* II. 248 The Russians are so fond of a country life.. that almost all of them who have estates, quit the army and navy as soon as they can. **1845** *Encycl. Metrop.* XXIV. 225/1 Two principal branches are distinguished, rivals of each other, and still cherishing the bitterest animosity—the Russians *great* and *little*, and the Poles. **1854** J. S. MAXWELL *Czar & his People* xxiii. 125 The Great Russian is predominant among the various peoples of the empire. **1866** *Chambers's Encycl.* VIII. 380/2 The 50,500,000 Russians.. are divisible into ——1. Great Russians.. 2. Little Russians.. 3. White Russians. **1886** *Encycl. Brit.* XXI. 79/1 Three different branches.. can be distinguished among the Russians since the dawn of their history:—the Great Russians, the Little Russians.., and the White Russians.

b. A member of the Russian church.

1585-7 T. ROGERS *39 Art.* (1607) 74 Which hold and affirm that.. the Holy Ghost proceedeth from the Father, but not from the Son; as at this day.. the Russians.. maintain. **1866** *Chambers's Encycl.* VIII. 388/2 The Russians adopt the same expedient with the Greeks, viz., of selecting the bishops from among the monks. **1963** T. WARE *Orthodox Church* viii. 165 It is not without reason that the expressions 'Soviet Church' and 'Soviet Patriarch' have now become common in the mouth of Russians.

c. *Austr.* An unruly animal.

1845 D. MACKENZIE *Emigrant's Guide* 118 These wild *Russians*, as they are here called, will.. clear at the first leap a stockyard six feet in height. **1848** H. W. HAYGARTH *Recoll. Bush Life Austral.* xii. 135 Though he had been among horses since he was a child, his present lot were a set of the veriest 'Russians' (Anglicè, wild things) *he* ever had anything to do with. **1945** BAKER *Austral. Lang.* iii. 68 An old term worth noting, since it has been obsolete for half a century or more, is *Russians* for wild stock.

2. The language of Russia; also (with distinguishing adjs.), a form or dialect of this. Also *Comb.*, as ***Russian-speaking.***

1716 LADY M. W. MONTAGU *Lett.* xlv[i]. II. 28 In Pera they speak Turkish, Greek, Hebrew, Armenian, Arabic, Persian, Russian. **1842** *Penny Cycl.* XXII. 106/2 There have been several translations of it into the present Russian. **1883** MORFILL *Slavonic Lit.* i. 6 The Little Russian is spoken in all the southern governments of Russia. **1960** *Amer. Speech* XXXV. 163 The material.. was gathered among the Russian-speaking population. **1976** 'M. BARAK' *Secret List of Heinrich Roehm* vii. 77 You need Russian-speaking agents to infiltrate Russian circles.

3. *ellipt.* for ***Russian cigarette, hemp, iron, leather, wheat.***

1862 BURTON *Bk. Hunter* I. 41 The plebeian sheepskin and the aristocratic russian. **1892** [see EGYPTIAN *sb.* 5 b]. **1893** *Daily News* 5 June 2/8 Italian hemps are very scarce... Russians are also advancing. **1897** *Ibid.* 9 Dec. 11/4 The cargo market for wheat is still very quiet... Russians are still held far above the market value. **1937** R. CHANDLER in *Dime Detective Mag.* Nov. 43/2 There were three long cigarettes .... Russians, with hollow mouthpieces. **1963** N. FREELING *Because of Cats* x. 163 He had juju cigarettes too; like Russians, with a big mouth piece, and pretty loose.

B. *adj.* **1. a.** Of or pertaining to Russia or its people; inhabiting, native to, characteristic of, Russia. Also with distinguishing adjs., as ***Great, Little, White Russian*** (see sense A. 1 a and WHITE *a.* 11 e).

1588 SHAKS. *L.L.L.* v. ii. 401, I will wish thee neuer more to dance, Nor neuer more in Russian habit waite. **1601** R. JOHNSON *Kingd. & Commw.* (1603) 155 Horsemen with all necessaries meete for the warre after the Russian manner. **1653** H. COGAN tr. *Pinto's Trav.* xxvii. 104 There we happened to meet with a Russian prisoner, that received us very charitably. **1728-46** THOMSON *Spring* 113 If, brush'd from Russian wilds, a cutting gale Rise not. **1797** *Encycl. Brit.* (ed. 3) I. 659/2 The great goose.., weighing near 25 or 30 Russian pounds. **1838** *Penny Cycl.* XI. 436/1 The Russian church, which now constitutes the most important branch of the Greek church. **1842** PRICHARD *Nat. Hist. Man* 198 The Russian peasantry have often light-brown, or flaxen, or red hair. **1883** MORFILL *Slavonic Lit.* iii. 49 Kiev .... was the first seat of the Russian nationality. **1911** C. J. HOGARTH tr. *V. O. Kluchevsky's Hist. Russia* I. xiii. 203 The Great Russian stock stands to the Little Russian in the proportion of three to one, and the Little Russian to the White Russian in a similar ratio. **1918** R. BEAZLEY et al. *Russia, from Varangians to Bolsheviks* I. iii. 79 The principality of Moscow had become a Great Russian nation, the Prince of Moscow a Great Russian sovereign. **1942** L. B. NAMIER *Conflicts* 8 The conflict with Russia turned on Poland's dominion over vast stretches of land inhabited by White Russian and Little Russian peasantries. **1963** *Times Lit. Suppl.* 31 May 388/4 The growth of Great-Russian jingoism.

Comb. **1868** *Rep. U.S. Commiss. Agric.* (1869) 175 The Russian-born inhabitants were.. almost without exception convicts from Siberia or elsewhere. **1900** *Westm. Gaz.* 22 Nov. 11/1 In future only Russian-made goods are to be used in the department. **1963** R. I. MCDAVID *Mencken's Amer. Lang.* v. v. 265 *Nudnik*.. is widely used by Russian-Jewish immigrants. **1976** *Times* 15 May 14/8 Sholem Aleichem came from a middle class Russian-Jewish background.

b. Trading with Russia or in Russian goods.

1885 *Census Instruct.* Index, Russian Merchant.

2. In specific names or designations: **a.** Of animals, etc., as ***Russian bear*** (often *fig.*), ***dove, eagle, gadus. Russian Blue***, a lightly built short-haired cat belonging to the breed so called, distinguished by greyish-blue fur, green eyes, and large pointed ears; ***Russian long-hair(ed) (cat)***, a stocky, long-coated cat with a relatively short tail, belonging to a breed once so called but no longer a distinct group; ***Russian pony***, a small, hardy, roan pony belonging to a breed originally developed in Russia; cf. COSSACK 2 b; ***Russian sable***, the heavy dark fur of the sable, *Martes zibellina*; cf. SABLE *sb.*[1] 1 a; ***Russian wolfhound*** = BORZOI.

1599 SHAKS. *Hen. V*, III. vii. 154 Foolish Curres, that runne winking into the mouth of a Russian Beare. **1605** —— *Macb.* III. iv. 100 Approach thou like the rugged Russian Beare. **1737** POPE *1st Epistle 2nd Bk. Horace Imitated* 22 No Lord's Anointed, but a Russian Bear. **1806** M. EDGEWORTH *Leonora* II. lxix. 121 It would really be pleasant to have a Czar at one's feet... The ancients represent Cupid riding the Numidian lion, and why should he not tame the Russian bear? **1972** C. SHORT *Naked Skier* xxvi. 147 All the gay, waltzing and slightly frenetic set-up [of Vienna] can be shattered at an instant by the roar of a Russian bear. **1977** W. FEAVER *When We were Young* 19 The political cartoon figures—British lion, Russian bear, German eagle. **1889** H. WEIR *Our Cats* 66 The Blue Cat was at first shown as the Archangel cat, then Russian blue, Spanish blue, Chartreuse blue, and.. the American blue. **1933** E. BUCKWORTH-HERNE-SOAME *Cats* xxxvii. 164 Russian Blues, so called because they were originally brought from Russia, are now known as 'Foreign Blues'. **1953** A. WHITE tr. *Colette's Cat* viii. 191 I'll withdraw.. into my cold room.. under the protection of.. a Russian Blue cat. **1971** W. J. BURLEY *Guilt Edged* viii. 132 Trotsky is our cat—a Russian blue. **1976** *Loughborough Monitor* 26 Nov. 2/3 (Advt.), Ready for Christmas.. Russian Blue Kittens. **1688** HOLME *Armoury* II. 244/1 The Runt Pigeon or Russian Dove.. are large Pigeons as big as young Hens. **1781** LATHAM *Gen. Synop. Birds* I. I. 43 Russian Eagle. **1803** SHAW *Gen. Zool.* IV. I. 158 *Russian Gadus*, a third variety of the Weesle Gadus, under the above title is described by Mr. Walbaum. **1889** H. WEIR *Our Cats* 30 The Russian long-haired cat.. differed from the Angora and the Persian in many respects. **1939** [see *Burmese cat* s.v. BURMESE *a.* b]. **1972** ING & POND *Champion Cats of World* 72 The Russian Longhair.. apparently had an even more woolly coat, and a shorter tail. **1842** YOUATT *Dog* 144 The Russian pointer is a rough, ill-tempered animal. **1898** J. D. BRAYSHAW *Slum Silhouettes* 151 I'm off the the Cattle Market to buy one o' those little Rooshian ponies. **1903** A. BENNETT *Truth about Author* xvi. 214 Arrival of the second post on a Russian pony that cost fifty shillings. **1936** A. W. SEABY *Brit. Ponies* 144, I stopped before a strange looking old light roan pony between the shafts of a sweep's cart. It was a Russian pony the owner averred. **1871** Russian sable [see *doll-land* s.v. DOLL *sb.*[1] 5]. **1930** M. BACHRACH *Fur* xxi. 322 There probably has never been a peltry that has enjoyed such popularity.. for so long a period of time as the Russian Sable. **1952** 'M. COST' *Hour Awaits* 152 The fur was sable, and Russian sable. **1973** D. ORGILL *Jasius Pursuit* x. 99 He took one of the fur coats... It was a magnificent garment ——Russian sables. **1872** G. H. LEWES *Jrnl.* 28 Dec. in *Geo. Eliot Lett.* (1956) V. 352 He took us up to Lady Paget to see a superb Russian Wolf-hound. **1922** R. LEIGHTON *Compl. Bk. Dog* ix. 141 There is not a more elegant and graceful dog than the Borzoi or Russian Wolfhound... The wearer of a lovely silky coat, he is essentially a spectacular animal. **1941** B. SCHULBERG *What makes Sammy Run?* viii. 157 She walked.. with a haughty pride, the way one does with Russian wolfhounds. **1976** BOTHAM & DONNELLY *Valentino* viii. 59 He bought a pair of Russian wolfhounds (white).

b. Of fruits or plants, as ***Russian apple, birch, cabbage, fenugreek, maple, rhubarb. Russian olive*** (U.S.), the oleaster, *Elæagnus angustifolia*, a spiny shrub with silvery leaves belonging to the family Elæagnaceæ, native to Europe and western Asia, and naturalized in parts of western North America; ***Russian poplar*** (Canada), a poplar native to north-east Asia, *Populus maximowiczii*, which has leathery leaves with whitish undersides; ***Russian thistle*** (U.S.), a tumbleweed, *Salsola kali*, a creeping prickly herb belonging to the family Chenopodiaceæ; = SALTWORT 1; ***Russian vine***, a fast-growing deciduous climbing plant, *Polygonum baldschuanicum*, of the family Polygonaceæ, native to southern Turkestan and bearing clusters of white or pink flowers.

1797 *Encycl. Brit.* (ed. 3) III. 520/2 The Russian cabbage was formerly in much greater esteem than at present. **1882** *Garden* 9 Dec. 507/2 The name Russian is broadly applied to all apples developed from the Russian or Astrachan Crab wherever they may have originated. **1822** *Hortus Anglicus*

II. 285 *Trigonella Ruthenica.* Small or Russian Fenugreek. **1843** HOLTZAPFFEL *Turning* I. 74 Some of the Russian birch (called Russian maple) is very beautiful and of a full yellow colour. **1938** W. R. VAN DERSAL *Native Woody Plants U.S.* 119 Russian olive... A large shrub to small tree; introduced from Europe and Western Asia. **1951** T. H. KEARNEY et al. *Arizona Flora* 586 Russian-olive, native of the Old World, often cultivated as an ornamental in the United States. **1972** W. A. WEBER *Rocky Mt. Flora* 173 The Russian Olive.. is cultivated throughout the region at lower elevations. **1950** E. A. MCCOURT *Home is the Stranger* ii. 19 Around the farmyard ran a stunted, ill-kempt wind-break of Russian poplar. **1965** I. REEKIE *Melita Trail* ii. 6 He planted the first grove of trees in the community—ash, cottonwood, Russian poplar, and Manitoba maples. **1861** BENTLEY *Man. Bot.* 621 The principal kinds of Rhubarb are Russian or Turkey, Chinese or East Indian, Himalayan, and English. **1894** *Amer. Folk-Lore* VII. 97 *Salsola Kali*, var. *Tragus*, Moguin, Russian thistle, Russian cactus. **1898** *Monthly S. Dakotan* I. 103 Only tiny triangular spots remained dry in the lee of broken corn-stalks and scattered Russian thistles. **1939** *Nat. Geogr. Mag.* Aug. 262/2 The Russian thistle.. is a relative of beets and spinach in the family of the 'goosefoots'. **1971** *Country Life* 2 Sept 583/1 In autumn the Russian Thistles.. ran freely before the wind at thirty miles an hour. **1948** N. CATCHPOLE *Flowering Shrubs & Small Trees* vii. 156 A vigorous climber, and the quickest growing one known in our gardens.. is commonly called the Russian vine. **1963** *Oxf. Bk. Garden Flowers* 164/2 Russian Vine.. is, in fact, a native of Bokhara, and is a rampant twining plant which will quickly smother any unsightly object in one season. **1977** K. O'HARA *Ghost of T. Penry* iv. 25 The stone arch.. was half-blocked by the ruins of a ramshackle gate overgrown with Russian vine.

c. Of economic products, as ***Russian deal, iron, leather*** (cf. RUSSIA 1), ***mat, rope.***

1773 tr. *De La Lande's Art of Tanning* 198 The Russian leather being thus printed, is smeared with Russia oil. **1839** Russian iron [see SABLE *sb.*[1] 3]. **1846** LINDLEY *Veget. Kingd.* 372 The Russian mats of commerce are manufactured from the Tilia. **1861** BENTLEY *Man. Bot.* 659 *Pinus sylvestris* the Scotch Fir, which yields the timber known as Dantzic or Riga Fir, and Russian Deal. **1874** in Ruskin *Fors Clav.* xlvi. IV. 242 On the relative strength of hand-spun yarn rope.. and Russian yarn rope.

d. Miscellaneous uses, as ***Russian bagatelle, blouse, braid, chess, crash, diaper, embroidery, poker, stitch.***

1850, etc. Russian bagatelle [see COCKAMAROO]. **1898** *Pall Mall G.* 10 Feb. 3/2 A hope.. that the days of the Russian blouse are numbered. **1953** R. SENHOUSE tr. *Colette's Gigi* 25 The Russian braid of her nightdress. **1973** *Country Life* 15 Feb. 425/1 Black wool suit, the jacket.. trimmed with Russian braid. **1871** *Routledge's Ev. Boy's Ann.* 181 Who's for a game at Russian chess? **1932** Russian crash [see *nurse cloth* s.v. NURSE *sb.*[1] 8]. **1827** *Hallowell* (Maine) *Gaz.* 20 June 4/4 (Advt.), Received.. Russian Diaper. **1957** SIMPSON & WEIR *Weaver's Craft* (ed. 8) xiii. 165 *Russian diaper.*—This has a total of 26 threads to each pattern,.. and it can also be used quite successfully as a border to some of the other patterns, for curtains, covers, etc. **1882** CAULFEILD & SAWARD *Dict. Needlewk.* 429/2 Russian Embroidery.. is worked either upon hollands and washing materials.. or upon cloth. **1970** T. LILLEY *Projects Section* x. 121 He plays Russian poker in the mess. *Ibid.* xvii. 232 In Russian Poker there are four players: each has thirteen cards which he arranges in three hands—two of five cards and one of three. These hands are each arranged in poker fashion... Three players play against the fourth—the banker—and the bank changes after every fourth deal. **1882** CAULFEILD & SAWARD *Dict. Needlewk.* 125/1 Ribbed Stitch.. is also called Russian stitch. It is much used for babies' socks and muffatees.

e. Special collocations: **Russian ballet**, a style of ballet developed at the Russian Imperial Ballet Academy and popularized in the West by Sergei Diaghilev's Ballet Russe from 1909; also a group of dancers trained in this style; **Russian Bank (Banker, banque)**, a card game similar to solitaire but played by two persons; **Russian bath** = *Turkish bath* s.v. TURKISH *a.* 2a; also *fig.*; **Russian boot**, a leather boot that extends to the calf, usu. with a wide cuff; **Russian cigarette**, a cigarette with a hollow pasteboard filter; **Russian dancer**, one who performs a Russian folk-dance; **Russian dinner**, a style of dinner in which fruit and wine are placed at the centre of a table and courses are served from a sideboard; **Russian doll**, any of a set of hollow wooden dolls, the smallest of which fits inside the next smallest, and so up to the largest; **Russian dressing**, a savoury dressing with a mayonnaise base; **Russian Easter egg**, an artificial egg shell designed as a container for presents given at Easter; **Russian egg**, a poached egg served on a lettuce leaf with mayonnaise; **Russian (spring-summer, etc.) encephalitis**, a viral encephalitis transmitted by wood ticks; **Russian Revolution**, the overthrow of the Tsar and the eventual establishment of the Bolshevik form of government in Russia between February and October (Old Style) 1917; cf. *October Revolution* s.v. OCTOBER 3 and REVOLUTION *sb.* 11; **Russian roulette**, an act of bravado in which a person loads (usu.) one chamber of a revolver, spins the cylinder, holds the barrel to his head, and pulls the trigger; also *fig.*; **Russian salad**, a salad of vegetables with mayonnaise; **Russian scandal**, (*a*) a game in which a whispered message, after being passed from player to player, is contrasted in its original and final versions; (*b*) gossip inaccurately transmitted; **Russian tea**, (*a*) tea grown in the Caucasus or a drink made from this; (*b*) any tea laced with lemon or rum.

1911 *Westm. Gaz.* 3 June 2/3 She disapproved of early morning tea and auction bridge, of ski-ing and the two-step, of the Russian ballet and the Chelsea Arts Club ball. **1928** A. CHRISTIE *Mystery of Blue Train* xxxi. 261, I never saw anything in this Russian ballet... Too highbrow for me. **1937** J. LAVER *Taste & Fashion* viii. 110 The overwhelming wave of Orientalism which swept over Parisian society.. was due to.. Paul Poiret and the Russian ballet. **1947** *Ballet Ann.* I. 68 Diaghileff, in search of inspiration, made straight for Paris, *chic* and *chi-chi*, and so Russian ballet became *Ballet Russe.* **1973** W. TUTE *Resident* ii. 36 As you know the Russian ballet is the best in the world. **1915** W. DEL MAR *Rules of Russian Bank* 1 The game of Russian Bank is played by two persons each with a pack of fifty-two cards. The object of the game is to dispose of the cards. **1930** A. WOOLLCOTT *Let.* 26 Apr. (1944) iv. 85 We played backgammon or Russian Bank all the way over [the Atlantic]. **1930** 'E. QUEEN' *French Powder Mystery* xv. 118 Not many people know how to play Russian banque. **1970** R. LOWELL *Notebk.* 121 Ford, playing Russian Banker. **1804** M. WILMOT *Let.* 24 Apr. in *Russ. Jrnls.* (1934) I. 94 The true Russian Bath admits a Vapour which I cou'd not support. **1863** C. LEVER *Day's Ride* in *All Year Round* 16 Feb. 455/1 It is a sort of intellectual Russian bath, in which the luxury consists in the exaggerated alternative between being scalded first and rolled in the snow afterwards. **1961** L. MUMFORD *City in Hist.* xiii. 386 In the seventeenth century.. the bath was reintroduced as a foreign importation, a luxury..: the so-called Turkish or Russian bath. **1975** A. HAILEY *Moneychangers* II. vi. 193 Mr Quartermain likes either a sauna or a Russian bath wherever he is. **1915** in C. Willett Cunnington *Eng. Women's Clothing* (1952) iv. 132 The fashionable side-lacing Russian boots with fawn cloth tops and patent leather fronts, 21/- a pair. **1926** WODEHOUSE *Heart of Goof* iii. 108 You bet your Russian boots I was! **1977** V. S. PRITCHETT *Gentle Barbarian* xiii. 212 Turgenev.. wandered about in heavy Russian boots. **1905** C. MACKENZIE *Diary* 30 Mar. in *My Life & Times* (1964) III. 222 A lazy young man.. who used to smoke Bobbie's Russian cigarettes. **1926** C. BEATON *Diary* 24 Apr. in *Wandering Yrs.* (1961) 87 Smoking Russian cigarette after Russian cigarette. **1940** E. HEMINGWAY *For whom Bell Tolls* ii. 20 Robert Jordan.. brought out one of the flat boxes of Russian cigarettes... They were long narrow cigarettes with pasteboard cylinders for mouth pieces. **1972** J. WAINWRIGHT *Requiem for Loser* iii. 52 They sipped tea, smoked Russian cigarettes and discussed this and that. **1913** MRS. P. CAMPBELL *Let.* 25 Mar. in *B. Shaw & Mrs. Campbell* (1952) 102 Russian dancers were imitated —shoes kicked off—hair came down. **1931** C. REMFRY-KIDD tr. *Colette's Renée Néré* I. i. 9 The Russian dancers are trying to get warm... They shout 'Yonk!' all together. **1851** *London at Table* I. 26 We have already alluded to a Russian dinner, which is the best and most economical. It is always served hot from the kitchen, and as the entrées are not exposed to the public gaze, there may be fewer of them; the joints served at the side-board by an experienced artist, are more palatable and tempting than when carved on the table. **1868** M. JEWRY *Warne's Model Cookery* 56 The present fashion of Russian dinners is fast banishing the necessity for promiscuous carving. **1937** K. BLIXEN *Out of Afr.* ii. 135 Those Russian wooden dolls which will unscrew, and have then got another doll inside them, and another inside that, and which are sold under the name of Katinka. **1967** C. FREMLIN *Prisoner's Base* xvi. 114 Each item in the dream was fitting into her interpretation like a set of Russian dolls. **1922** *Hotel World* 15 Apr. 15/1 Russian Dressing. **1938** L. BEMELMANS *Life Class* II. ii. 127 The salad, covered with Russian dressing, is a mixture of endives.. pineapple.. cream cheese with chopped chives. **1976** *Billings* (Montana) *Gaz.* 1 July, In medium bowl, thoroughly combine ¼ cup Russian dressing, ground beef, and breadcrumbs. **1949** H. C. BAINBRIDGE *P. C. Fabergé* iv. 67 (*heading*) The Imperial Russian Easter Eggs. **1955** W. GADDIS *Recognitions* III. v. 903 Like a Russian Easter Egg, this Thing had a tiny window in one end. **1932** M. F. DANIELS tr. *F. Nietlispach's Cold Dishes & Hors-D'œuvre* I. 16 *Russian Eggs.* Poach the eggs, strain and cool. Arrange on a lettuce leaf.. cover with mayonnaise and sprinkle with.. minced ham and a little chopped parsley. **1969** G. LYALL *Venus with Pistol* vii. 39, I yelled an order for.. Russian eggs... It comes up a salad the size of the Garden of Eden. **1943** *Science* 12 Mar. 246/1 (*heading*) Close relation between Russian spring-summer encephalitis and louping-ill viruses. **1948** OLITSKY & CASALS in T. M. Rivers *Viral & Rickettsial Infections of Man* viii. 192/1 Russian Far East encephalitis (Synonyms: Russian spring-summer encephalitis; Russian spring or summer encephalitis; Russian forest-spring encephalitis; Russian tick-borne encephalitis; Russian endemic encephalitis). *Ibid.*, Russian Far East encephalitis is a disease occurring in spring and early summer, mainly in the Far East provinces of the Soviet Union and less frequently in European and Siberian Russia. **1976** W. L. DREW *Viral Infections* i. 7 Group B [*sc.* arboviruses] includes the viruses of St. Louis encephalitis, yellow fever, and dengue, as well as the viruses of Russian encephalitis and hemorrhagic fever found in Europe and Russia. [**1805** C. WILMOT *Let.* 7 Dec. in *Russ. Jrnls.* (1934) II. 208 The famous 28th of June 1762, the day of the Russian Revolution. **1907** I. ZANGWILL *Ghetto Comedies* 399 We are a Labour party... We have the whole Russian Revolution on our shoulders.] **1917** C. P. SCOTT *Let.* 25 Mar. in D. Ayerst *Guardian* (1971) xxvii. 403 Don't you feel the Russian revolution rather stirring in your bones? **1919** *Mr. Punch's Hist. Great War* 176 A 'History of the Russian Revolution' has already been published. **1922** *Encycl. Brit.* XXXII. 319/2 The history of the Russian Revolution starts with the gradual dissolution of all fundamental institutions and notions. **1945** 'G. ORWELL' in *Common Wealth Rev.* Nov. 12/1 The failure of the Russian Revolution—failure, that is, in the sense that the Revolution has not fulfilled the hopes that it aroused twenty-five years ago. **1977** *Times* 26 Mar. 12/4 A history-teaching colleague suggested that it might have been better if the Russian Revolution had never taken place. **1937** G. SURDEZ in *Collier's* 30 Jan. 16 'Did you ever hear of Russian Roulette?' .. With the Russian army in Rumania, around 1917,.. some officer would suddenly pull out his revolver,.. remove a cartridge from the cylinder, spin the cylinder, snap it back in place, put it to his head and pull the trigger. **1946** *N.Y. Post* 23 Oct. 5/2 The game was 'Russian Roulette', and the odds were 5-1. **1956** 'M. INNES' *Appleby plays Chicken* I. ii. 18 'Is it done with a revolver.. with one of the six chambers loaded?' 'No. That's Russian roulette.' **1960** *Guardian* 27 July 16/4 This party.. had 'played Russian roulette with American strength and American progress'. **1976** *Lancet* 9 Oct. 776/2 Abusive parents are often the scarred survivors of generations of reproductive russian roulette. **1879** M. JEWRY *Warne's Model Cookery* (new ed.) 456/2 *Russian Salad...* Cold boiled beetroot; cold carrots [etc.].. smoked salmon, or white meat of chicken and tongue. Cut the vegetables into pieces all of one size, add the salmon.. mix with Mayonnaise sauce. Garnish with anchovies. **1940** M. DICKENS *Mariana* iii. 64 'I'll tell you something, Tich,' said Uncle Geoffrey beginning on his Russian salad. **1973** 'S. HARVESTER' *Corner of Playground* I. viii. 70 He had carved the cold roast chicken and served it with Russian salad. **1873** L. TROUBRIDGE *Jrnl.* 28 Aug. in J. Hope-Nicholson *Life amongst Troubridges* (1966) vi. 50 We played Russian Scandal in the train, which was very jolly. **1873** C. M. YONGE *Pillars of House* IV. xxxviii. 126 Susie has been well lectured on Russian scandal! **1893** —— *Girl's Little Bk.* 17 Do not repeat it [*sc.* gossip]. You will probably make Russian scandal of it, and the next person will add to it. **1929** H. G. WELLS *King who was King* ii. 59 '*We used to play a game called Russian scandal*'... The screen shows a row of young people... The first whispers to the second, who whispers to the third, and so on. **1953** 'P. WENTWORTH' *Ivory Dagger* lxii. 209 There used to be a game called Russian scandal. Something was whispered from one to another, and you have no idea what it would come out like by the time even a few people had had the handling of it. **1960** G. E. EVANS *Horse in Furrow* xiii. 177 Stories passed from one to another are proverbially incorrect as 'Russian scandal'. **1862** M. B. CHESNUT *Diary* 25 in C. V. Woodward *M. Chesnut's Civil War* (1981) 395 They had Russian tea, champagne, a samovar. **1884** G. MEREDITH *Let.* 24 Mar. (1970) II. 732 Bid him arrive by half-past five, that the thirsty troop may be refreshed by Russian tea. **1930** L. G. D. ACLAND *Early Canterbury Runs* v. 111 The publican offered to make him some 'Russian tea'... 'Russian tea' turned out to be ordinary tea well laced with rum. **1952** 'R. CROMPTON' *William & Tramp* vii. 217 She said he had lemon in his tea 'stead of milk an' I know that's called Russian tea. **1975** *Times* 1 May 15/3 There is Russian tea, a long leaf variety grown in the foothills of the Caucasian mountains. **1976** *Eastern Even. News* (Norwich) 9 Dec. 8/1 Tins of Russian, Formosa or Jasmine tea are about 68p for half a pound.

3. Of or pertaining to, concerned with, the Russian language or literature.

1797 *Encycl. Brit.* (ed. 3) XIV. 567/1 The Russian letters. *Ibid.* 567/2 The Russian grammar above-mentioned. **1842** *Penny Cycl.* XXII. 127 Some works.. printed in the Russian character. **1888** JACOBI *Printers' Vocab.* 117 *Russian cases*, cases of special lay for type used in composing that language.

Hence **'Russian** *v.*, to force by Russian influence or pressure. *nonce-word.*

1756 H. WALPOLE *Let. to Mann* 25 Jan., The King of Prussia has been Russianed out of their [the French] alliance.

Russianism ('rʌʃənɪz(ə)m). [f. RUSSIAN *a.*]

1. Tendency to favour Russia.

1855 *Fraser's Mag.* LI. 240 Lord John Russell, who will hardly be suspected of Russianism, distinctly disclaimed any such view.

2. a. Prevalence of Russian ideas or spirit.

1864 *Daily Telegr.* 26 May, If you walk through the streets of Warsaw with a hat, which is considered a symbol of Russianism. **1878** SEELEY *Stein* III. 15 'If only,' he writes, 'there were common sense in Kutusoff's army instead of Russianism.'

b. Soviet communism as practised by the Russians.

1933 *Catholic Times* 21 Apr. 5/1 One of the reasons for the great success of Russianism was the austerity of many of its leaders and the complete self-sacrifice of many of its rank and file.

c. A Russian custom.

1957 V. NABOKOV *Pnin* iii. 71 Shy graduate students would be taught vodka-drinking rites and other stale Russianisms.

3. a. Adoption of Russian idioms.

1886 *American* XII. 219 The translation.. is free from.. excessive Russianism.

b. A Russian idiom.

1957 V. NABOKOV *Pnin* iii. 87 Her fluent and flashy New York English, with.. soft lapses into furry Russianisms. **1962** *Amer. Speech* XXXVII. 279 (*title*) Russianisms in the American press. *Ibid.*, Russianisms are divided here into three main groups: loanwords, foreignisms, and calques. **1967** *Listener* 19 Jan. 99/3 Professor Markov allows the occasional Russianism to show through in his introduction, which isn't perfectly idiomatic.

Russianist ('rʌʃənɪst). [f. RUSSIAN *sb.* + -IST.] A student of Russian language and literature.

1976 *Times Lit. Suppl.* 23 Jan. 79/4 The occupational obsessions of Russianists writing on Chekhov. **1980** *Ibid.* 19 Sept. 1018/4 Joe Andrew will be known to most British Russianists as a co-chairman of the Neo-Formalist circle.

,Russiani'zation. [f. next + -ATION.] The action or process of Russianizing.

1891 *Daily News* 10 Nov. 5/6 With the object of encouraging Russians to settle in Poland, and of thus contributing to the more rapid Russianisation of that country.

Russianize ('rʌʃənaɪz), *v.* [f. RUSSIAN *a.* + -IZE. Cf. F. *russianiser.*] *trans.* To render Russian in character; to Russify.

1831 PALGRAVE *Hist. Anglo-Saxons* i. 11 A 'Diet', formed, in part, out of the original legislature possessed by the country when independent—but Russianized, re-modelled,

..and re-formed. **1865** *Chambers's Encycl.* VII. 634/1 The most severe and arbitrary measures [were] taken to Russianise the people [of Poland]. **1873** *New Monthly Mag.* IV. 98 A Kabardian prince whose name was Russianised into Bekewitch Tcherkasky.

absol. **1883** *Athenæum* 8 Dec. 734 The aim of the former is only to Russianize.

Hence '**Russianized** *ppl. a.*, '**Russianizing** *vbl. sb.*

1849 *Athenæum* Aug. 857/2 His most intimate friend,..a Russianized Englishman in the service of the Empress. **1886** *Pall Mall G.* 30 Sept. 8/1 The Russianizing of Bulgaria and Servia.

Russianness ('rʌʃənnɪs). [f. RUSSIAN *a.* + -NESS.] The quality or state of being Russian.

1937 *Sunday Times* 21 Nov. 9/2 His [*sc.* Lenin's] essential Russianness had not been weakened by culture; it had not been Westernised by foreign contacts. **1954** U. WEINREICH in Saporta & Bastian *Psycholinguistics* (1961) 382/2 We may characterize the utterance by the feature of 'Russianness' or 'Englishness'. **1968** *Economist* 9 Nov. p. x/2 This book is an account of the author's life-long love affair with Russianness: not with Russia, past or present, but with a Russianness conceived in the nursery as a daydream of the trans-Siberian railway. **1973** *Observer* 4 Feb. 37/3 Wilson is worrying away about the peculiarities of the Russian language and the astonishing Russianness of Russians. **1977** V. S. PRITCHETT *Gentle Barbarian* ii. 27 The Russian disease ..the ever shadowy figure of Russianness.

† '**Russic,** *a. Obs.* In 7 Russick. [f. RUSS *sb.* + -IC.] Russian.

1670 RAY *Prov.* 57 It is a Russick Proverb and of frequent use in that nation. **1757** J. DYER *Fleece* IV. 399 Culder's woofs, and those of Exe and Frome,.. Thither by Russic caravans are brought.

† '**Russie.** *Obs.* Also 7 **Rushy.** [var. of RUSS *sb.* or RUSSIA, perh. after F. *Russie.*]

1. *attrib.* = RUSSIAN *a.*

1601 R. JOHNSON *Kingd. & Commw.* (1603) 142 The residue with a greate parte of Siberia,.. though they speak not the Russie language, yet obey they the Emperour. **1696** J. F. *Merch. Wareho. laid open* 35 Rushy cloth,.. although it is a coarse cloth, is of much use with us;.. of this there is two sorts, Hempen and Flaxen.

2. = RUSSIAN *sb.* 1 b.

1607 T. ROGERS *39 Art.* (1853) 240 Causes, which indeed are none, to debar men from the ecclesiastical function; as if men have been twice married (an error of the Russies).

,**Russifi'cation.** [See -FICATION.] The action or process of Russifying or of being Russified.

1842 J. G. KOHL *Russia* 333 The good old German city is undoubtedly undergoing a rapid Russification. **1877** WALLACE *Russia* x. 151 During my wanderings in these northern provinces I have found villages in every stage of Russification. **1936** *Discovery* Feb. 50/1 The education provided by the Russian authorities was..entirely subordinated to the policy of 'Russification' uncompromisingly adopted since the suppression of the Polish rebellion in 1863. **1972** *Times* 15 May 14/4 In the non-Russian republics one can get a 'feel' for the way people react to russification. **1976** A. POWELL *Infants of Spring* x. 173 An increasing policy of Russification resulted in much unrest there [*sc.* in Finland]. **1976** *Survey* Spring 188 Ukrainians, Byelorussians, Lithuanians and Latvians..are exposed to intensive Russification. **1979** *Daily Tel.* 29 Nov. 18 The policy of the Soviet Union in the Baltic countries is to annihilate their peoples by enforced Russification and deportation.

'**Russificator.** [Cf. prec.] = next.

1895 *Daily News* 6 Mar. 5/6 The lower Russian officials in Poland.. for a time gave up the part of zealous Russificators, but now..go on with the same malpractices.

'**Russifier.** [f. next.] One who Russifies.

1895 *19th Cent.* May 833 The best and most enlightened people..view with disgust the lawless and capricious behaviour of the Russifiers.

Russify ('rʌsɪfaɪ), *v.* [f. RUSS *a.* + -IFY. Cf. F. *russifier.*] *trans.* To Russianize. Hence '**Russifying** *ppl. a.*

1865 QUEEN VICTORIA *Let.* 23 May in R. Fulford *Your Dear Letter* (1971) 27 Good Alice seems quite Russified. **1868** G. DUFF *Glance over Eur.* 41 The attempts of the ultra-Muscovite party to Russify the Baltic provinces. **1877** WALLACE *Russia* x. 153 In the districts not completely Russified. **1924** [See PRUSSIFICATION]. **1954** KOESTLER *Invisible Writing* x. 110 The natives were drawn into the towns, educated, Russified and Stalinised. **1960** E. R. GOODMAN in J. A. Fishman *Readings Sociol. of Lang.* (1968) 731 The..denigration of Stalin left the Russifying impact of Stalin's linguistic policy intact. **1973** *Listener* 5 Apr. 444/2 The Party instructions were to Russify the *Moscow News.* **1974** *Encycl. Brit. Macropædia* XVI. 47/1 His [*sc.* Ivan III's] churches, the original aspect of which has been altered by successive russifying restorations, were clearly in the Italian style.

'**Russism.** [f. RUSS *a.* + -ISM.]

1. = RUSSIANISM 2.

1868 G. DUFF *Pol. Surv.* 41 The wreck of the empire would throw them headlong into the gulf of Russism.

2. A Russian idiom.

1883 MORFILL *Slavonic Lit.* 16 From the thirteenth to the sixteenth century is the middle age of the Slavonic language, as altered gradually by Russian copyists, and full of Russisms.

'**Russki,** *a.* and *sb. slang* or *colloq.* Also **Roosky, Ruski, Rusky, Russky.** [ad. Russ. *Russkiy.*] = RUSSIAN *a.* and *sb.* Hence '**Russki-land,** Russia.

1858 F. DUBERLY *Let.* July in E. E. P. Tisdall *Mrs Duberly's Campaigns* (1963) vi. 197 Was I the Englishwoman who had gone with the armies to make war against the Ruski? **1859** *All Year Round* No. 36. 220 The rough warrior, whose keen shaska had lopped off Rusky heads like radishes. **1894** ASTLEY *50 Yrs. Life* I. 212 As they advanced, the Ruskies let drive with their big guns. **1919** *Amer. Legion Weekly* 22 Aug. 22/1 Large numbers of lowly 'Rooskies' plodded through the weary days. **1919** *Our Navy* (U.S.) Nov. 15/1 The Russkis were friendly to us because we had a lot of rubles. **1920** *Amer. Legion Weekly* 12 Mar. 5 A.E.F. Siberia..en route to Russki-land. **1923** D. YORK *Company A* 50 A little Russki at one side drew our attention. **1937** G. FRANKAU *More of Us* xiii. 135 To Mussolini's braves and Hitler's huskies Left we the task of tackling Stalin's Russkies. **1948** M. LASKI *Tory Heaven* i. 14 People like the Russkis and the Yanks like dealing with gentlemen. **1957** V. NABOKOV *Pnin* 71 He and Serafima, his large, cheerful, Moscow-born wife.. would throw Russki parties every now and then, with Russki hors d'oeuvres. **1959** C. MACINNES *Absolute Beginners* 55 We've got to produce our own variety, and not imitate the Americans—or the Ruskis, or anybody. **1961** *Even. Bull.* (Philadelphia) 29 Mar. 22/3 *(caption)* Keeping up with the (Russki) Joneses. **1978** I. B. SINGER *Shosha* ii. 38 A Russky with all these qualities is awaiting you there.

russle, obs. form of RUSTLE.

Russniak (rʊs'njæk), *sb.* and *a.* Also **Russniac, Rousniak, Rusnak, Rusniac, Rusniak.** [a. the native name *Rusnyák, Rusnák.* So Hung. *Rusznyák*, G. *Russniak.*] **a.** *sb.* A member of the Ukrainian people inhabiting Galicia; also, the language of this people. **b.** *adj.* Of or pertaining to this people.

c **1829** *Encycl. Metrop.* (1845) XX. 397 In the North-Eastern Carpathians the Russniacs, or Red Russians, extend to the County of Marmaros. *Ibid.*, Wherever they settle, the Russniac and Servian population is sure to become extinct. **1862** [see RUTHENIAN *sb.* 2]. **1883** *19th Cent.* Nov. 754 Two-thirds of its population..belonging to the Reformed Church, the remaining third being mainly Russniaks or Ruthenes. **1894** A. LEFÈVRE *Race & Lang.* 239 Little Russian, Rusniac, or Ruthene. **1955** R. JAKOBSON *Slavic Lang.* (ed. 2) 4 Ukrainian dialects are classified into Northern, Southeastern, Southwestern, and Carpathian groups; the marginal dialects (called Rusnak) of the latter group are Slovak-influenced.

Russo- ('rʌsəʊ), combining form (on Greek analogies) of RUSS: **a.** Used parasynthetically with terms denoting other peoples or countries, as ***Russo-American, -Byzantine, -Caucasian, -Chinese, -Czech, -French, -German, -Greek, -Japanese, -Persian, -Polish, -Slavonic, -Swedish, -Turkish,*** etc.

1814 tr. *G. H. von Langsdorff's Voyages & Travels* II. 99 At our arrival, we found this new settlement of the Russio-American [*sic*] Company in want of almost all the necessaries of life. **1977** *Gramophone* June 56/3 A Russian conductor..and a Russo-American concerto which I haven't heard him play before. **1889** *Cent. Dict.*, Russo-Byzantine. **1973** *Country Life* 6 Dec. 1913/1 Russo-Byzantine work in purple and gold. **1857** T. MOORE *Handbk. Brit. Ferns* (ed. 3) 222 In Asia it is found in the Russo-Caucasian provinces. **1903** G. BELL *Let.* 20 May (1927) I. viii. 162 We had to go to the renowned Russo-Chinese bank to change our notes. **1949** I. DEUTSCHER *Stalin* 418 The Russo-French and the Russo-Czech alliances were concluded. **1897** E. A. BARTLETT *Battlefields of Turkey* ii. 39 Two such evenly poised camps as the Russo-French League and the German monarchies. **1928** L. ROBINSON *Let.* in *Lett. S. O'Casey* (1975) I. 266 The second act in the modern Russo-German manner is very fine. **1775** *Ann. Reg., Chron.* 135/1 The exercise of the Russo-Greek religion. **1972** D. DAKIN *Unification of Greece* ix. 126 Phillipon..was sent to.. Athens in the hope of improving Russo-Greek relations. **1906** A. BENNETT *Let.* 6 Mar. (1966) I. 70 The last trick of bringing the Russo-Japanese war into the story. **1953** A. SMITH *Blind White Fish in Persia* iii. 50 Further along the coast there was a Russo-Persian Caviare industry but their fleet was not visible. **1838** *Penny Cycl.* XI. 436/1 In Polish and in Russo-Polish. *Ibid.*, In the same Russo-Polish dialect. **1926** Russo-Polish [see EXPRESSIONISM]. **1959** G. NANDRIŞ *Handbk. Old Ch. Slavonic* I. 20 In the later period Russo-Slavonic, Old Serbian, and Old Croatian texts show a regular epenthetic *l.* **1974** *Encycl. Brit. Macropædia* XVI. 60/2 Russo-Swedish relations were settled during the Napoleonic era. **1878** *N. Amer. Rev.* CXXVII. 393 [Disraeli's] policy would have..prevented the Russo-Turkish War.

b. Objective, in adjs. or sbs. denoting tendency to admire or favour Russia, Russian methods, policy, etc., as **Ru'ssolatrous, Russo'maniac(al, 'Russophil(e, Ru'ssophilism**; or morbid dread of these, as **'Russophobe, -'phobia, -'phobian, -'phobism, -'phobist.**

1880 SWINBURNE *Stud. Shaks.* 195 Anti-Gallican and *Russolatrous insanities of perverse and morbid eloquence. **1882** MORLEY *Cobden* iv. (1902) 12/1 The *Russo-maniac ideas of Russian power are demonstrably absurd. **1892** *Pall Mall G.* 31 Mar. 1/2 Since all things Russian are fashionable, the Russo-maniacs should take care [etc.]. **1891** *Times* 15 Aug. 5/3 The Russophil or *Russomaniacal demonstrations in France. **1882** MARVIN *Russian Adv. towards India* i. 6, I am both a *Russophil and a Russophobe. **1885** —— *The Russians at Gates of Herat* viii. 167 The offer ..cannot be accepted, even by the most willing Russophile. **1887** *Spectator* 17 Sept. 1235 The Russophil party in Sofia. **1897** E. A. BARTLETT *Battlefields of Thessaly* ii. 38 There was a curious outburst of Russophile writing in a portion of the English Press. *Ibid.* iii. 46 One great factor in the game..is also ignored by our English Russophiles. **1946** R. CAPELL *Simiomata* III. 153 The new Foreign Minister..is a socialist and Russophil. **1967** C. SETON-WATSON *Italy from Liberalism to Fascism* ix. 342 Aehrenthal..had the reputation of an extreme conservative and Russophil. **1971** *Daily Tel.* 11 May 9/4 It is true that as a result of our history we have been and still are Russophile. **1893** *Current Hist.* III. 385 The tendency..to rash legislation and unreflecting *Russophilism. **1868** G. DUFF *Pol. Surv.* 67 A *Russophobe preaching an aggressive movement in the north-west. **1887** *Pall Mall G.* 14 Feb. 1/2 India, they say, is 'Russophobe'. **1946** G. STIMPSON *Thousand Things* 250 The war party, the Russophobes, who urged Prime Minister Disraeli to side with the Turks, against the Russians, became known as jingoes. **1966** R. BLAKE *Disraeli* xxvi. 607 The more Turcophobe Gladstone became, the more Russophobe was Disraeli. **1836** J. S. MILL in *Westm. Rev.* XXV. 276 Ministers are smitten with the epidemic disease of *Russophobia. **1844** DISRAELI *Coningsby* IV. ix, Materials for a 'slashing' article against the Russophobia. **1980** *Daily Tel.* 8 July 14, I fear that it might only serve to conceal the ever lurking presence of good old 19th-century British Russophobia. **1885** *Daily News* 22 June 5/5 A *Russophobian Opposition speaker is not necessarily a Russophobian Minister. **1880** E. W. HAMILTON *Diary* 25 Aug. (1972) I. 37 It is extraordinary what amount of *Russophobism pervades the royal mind. **1881** *Times* 3 Jan. 5/5 The Russophobism of many Englishmen. **1877** WALLACE *Russia* xxxiv. 596 'Where, then,' asks the alarmed *Russophobist, 'is the aggression of Russia to stop'? **1882** E. W. HAMILTON *Diary* 4 June (1972) I. 284 She may have the Russophobist and anti-Russian party in power again in this country. **1886** *Pall Mall G.* 27 July 3/2 Last week the Russophobist watchdogs began to bay as is their wont.

Russonorsk ('rʌsəʊnɔːsk). [f. RUSSO- + Norw. *norsk* Norwegian.] = RUSSENORSK.

1966 R. A. HALL *Pidgin & Creole Lang.* I. i. 12 On a basis of Russian and Norwegian, there grew up a pidgin known as Russonorsk, which was used..between Russian and Norwegian fishermen along the Arctic coast of Norway. **1977** C. F. & F. M. VOEGELIN *Classification & Index World's Lang.* 311 Russonorsk can be said to be a Russian-based pidgin-creole, but might just as well be said to be Norwegian-based.

† **russwale.** *Obs.* Forms: 4 **russhewale,** 4–5 **russe-,** 5 **rusewale.** [Ultimately ad. Icel. *hrosshvalr* 'horse-whale': see WALRUS.] Walrus hide.

1336 in Nicolas *Hist. Royal Navy* (1847) II. 471 Cords of russhewale [with] schivis and trussis. *Ibid.*, Russewale, shives [and] polives. **1485** *Naval Accs. Hen. VII* (1896) 38 Stroppes of Russewale, ij. **1486** *Ibid.* 45 Stroppes of Rusewale, ij.

rust (rʌst), *sb.*[1] Forms: *α.* 1– rust, 4–6 ruste, 6 rost. *β.* 4, 6 roust, 5–6 rouste; 5 rowste, 6 rowst. [OE. *rúst* (? and *rust*), = Fris. *rûst, rust, roast*, MDu. and Du. *roest*, OS. *rost* (MLG. *rost, rust*, LG. *rust, rüst*), OHG. and G. *rost*; also (from MLG.) MDa. *rost, røst*, MSw. and Sw. *rost*, Da., Norw., and Fær. *rust.* The pre-Teutonic **rudhs-to-* is based upon the stem **rudh-* (see RUD *sb.*[1] and RED *a.* and *sb.*[1]), whence ON. *ryð* (and *ryðr*) rust; a different grade of this is represented by L. *rōbīgo, rūbīgo.*

The length of the vowel in OE., in whatever way it may have originated, is proved by the mod. dial. forms *roust, rowst* (*rāst, raist*) and Sc. *roost*, but the form with short *u* may also have existed at an early date. The vowel of Du. *roest* has not been satisfactorily accounted for.]

1. a. A red, orange, or tawny coating formed upon the surface of iron or steel by oxidation, esp. through the action of air or moisture; also, by extension, a similar coating formed upon any other metal by oxidation or corrosion.

α. *c* **725** *Corpus Gloss.* E 297 *Erugo*, rust. *c* **950** *Lindisf. Gosp.* Matt. vi. 19 In eorðo ðer..rust & mohða..ȝespilled bið [*sic*]. ? *a* **1030** *Rule St. Benet* (Logeman, 1888) 108 þæt he na to swiðe ne ȝewilniȝe upawyrtlian rust oððe om. *a* **1225** *Ancr. R.* 160 Ne beo neuer so briht..iren, ne stel þet hit ne schal drawen rust. *c* **1325** *Metr. Hom.* (1862) 105 It clenses man of sinful lust, Als fire clenses iren of rust. **1382** WYCLIF *Ezek.* xxiv. 6 Woo..to the pot whos rust is in it, and the rust therof wente not out of it. *c* **1400** *Pilgr. Sowle* (Caxton, 1483) IV. xxxiv. 83 Bras draweth soone ruste yf it be not clensid. *c* **1450** tr. *De Imitatione* II. iv. 44 Like as yren put in þe fire lesiþ his rust, & shal be made briȝt. **1530** PALSGR. 264/2 Rust of yron or any other metall, *enrovillevre.* **1593** SHAKS. *Rich. II*, III. iii. 116 His glittering Armes he will commend to Rust, His barbed Steedes to Stables. **1668** CHARLETON *Onomast.* 302 *Coeruleum*, the Blew Rust of Silver. **1676** D'URFEY *Mme. Fickle* III. i, We..can by the Rust on a Sword tell how long it has been durable. **1756** C. LUCAS *Ess. Waters* III. 297 The iron begins to separate, and falls like rust to the bottom. **1789** MRS. PIOZZI *Journ. France* I. 224 The tomb of Antenor..venerable with rust. **1819** SHELLEY *Cenci* II. i. 70 When the rust Of heavy chains has gangrened his sweet limbs. **1853** SIR H. DOUGLAS *Milit. Bridges* (ed. 3) 380 Some of the iron wires..had become corroded by rust.

β. **13..** *Gaw. & Gr. Knt.* 2018 þe rynges rokked of þe roust, of his riche bruny. **1387** TREVISA *Higden* (Rolls) III. 445 Roust destroyeþ iren. **14..** *Pol., Rel., & L. Poems* (1903) 257 Ase þe worm on þe treo,..and roust on þe knife. **1549** *Compl. Scot.* vii. 70 The glaspis var fast lokkyt vitht rouste. **1595** DUNCAN *App. Etym.* (E.D.S.), *Rubigo*, rowst.

b. In fig. uses or contexts.

1600 SHAKS. *2 Hen. IV*, I. ii. 246, I were better to be eaten to death with a rust, than to be scoured to nothing with perpetuall motion. **1615** BRATHWAIT *Strappado* (1878) 36 A miser loues not him that craues his due:..such men..loue their Conscience rest lesse then their rust. **1737** POPE *Hor. Epist.* II. i. 36 Authors, like coins, grow dear as they grow old; It is the rust we value, not the gold. **1752** HUME *Polit. Disc.* xii. 204 Perhaps rust may grow to the springs of the most accurate political machine, and disorder its motions. **1812** *Examiner* 9 Nov. 716/1 His voice would perhaps have been a..good one, had it not been prematurely exerted:—as it is, there is a general rust about it. **1863** TYNDALL *Heat* iii.

55 Carbon acid may be regarded as the rust of the body, which is continually cleared away by the lungs.

c. *ellipt.* Rust-cement (Ogilvie *Suppl.* 1855).

d. *slang.* Money.

1858 MAYHEW *Paved with Gold* III. v, There's no chance of nabbing any rust (taking any money).

e. A period of rusting. *rare*$^{-1}$.

1865 DICKENS *Mut. Fr.* IV. xiii, As if his money had turned bright again, after a long long rust in the dark.

2. a. Moral corrosion or canker; corruption.

c **897** K. ÆLFRED *Gregory's Past. C.* xxxvii. 268 Ne meahte mon him of animan ðone miclan rust. **1435** MISYN *Fire of Love* 99 Þe sawle þat it takis with blyst fyre is purgyd, & in it bidys no rust ne fylþ. *c* **1440** *Pol., Rel., & L. Poems* (1903) 218 Thowȝe I have been oniust,.. I hope to Rube A-waye the Ruste, with penaunce, frome my gostely syhte. **1577** *St. Aug. Manual* E ij b, From canckred rust Christ shall make iust. **1611** SHAKS. *Wint. T.* III. ii. 172 How he glisters Through my Rust? and how his Pietie Do's my deeds make the blacker?

b. With defining word or phrase.

c **897** K. ÆLFRED *Gregory's Past. C.* xxxvii. 268 He wolde from us adon ðone rust urra unðeawa, ac we.. nyllað alætan from us ðæt rust ðara unnyttra weorca. *c* **1400** LOVE *Bonavent. Mirr.* (1908) 274 He.. enflawmeth her hertes goostly, consumynge al the rouste of mysbyleue. *c* **1440** *Jacob's Well* 234 Do oute þe ruste of ydell thouȝtys fro ȝoure herte. **1513** DOUGLAS *Æneis* IV. Prol. 166 Out on the, ald trat,.. Eschamis na thing in roust of syn to ly! **1581** G. PETTIE tr. *Guazzo's Civ. Conv.* (1586) II. 117 Their mindes .. are thereby.. eaten as it were with the rust of idlenesse. **1621** BRATHWAIT *Nat. Embassie* (1877) 126 Worse to the state then rust of flatterie. **1746** FRANCIS tr. *Horace, Art Poet.* 369 When the rust of wealth pollutes the soul.

†**3.** *Sc.* Cankered malice; rancour. *Obs.*

1508 DUNBAR *Tua Mariit Wemen* 163, I sall a ragment reveil fra the rute of my hert, A roust that is sa rankild quhill risis my stomok. **1533** BELLENDEN *Livy* I. xii. (S.T.S.) I. 71 All wayis þe sabinis persuadit mony of þe said pepill with small lauboure to assist to þare opinioun, throw roust and auld haterent of weris.

†**4.** The effacing effects *of* time. *Obs.*

1533 BELLENDEN *Livy* I. ix. (S.T.S.) I. 52 At last þe memorye þareof perist be roust of ȝeris. *Ibid.* II. ii. 134 Þare names be roust of ȝeris Is perist. **1577–87** HOLINSHED *Chron.* I. 157/1 Which lawes with diuers other of like antiquitie are forgot and blotted out by rust of time.

5. a. Any deteriorating or impairing effect or influence upon character, abilities, etc., especially as the result of inactivity.

c **1000** *Ags. Hom.* (Assmann) xviii. 135 Ærest ic wille beon ȝefremed in littlum weorce, þæt ic mæȝe sum rust on weȝ adrifan of minre tungan.

a **1676** HALE *Prim. Orig. Man.* (1677) 3 A Man hath this advantage by the exercise of this Faculty about it, that it keeps it from Rust and torpidness. **1711** ADDISON *Spect.* No. 112 ¶1 Sunday clears away the Rust of the whole Week. **1732** BERKELEY *Alciphr.* I. §11 In rubbing off the rust and pedantry of a college education. **1796** W. H. MARSHALL *W. Eng.* II. 142 The rust of prejudice may not yet be sufficiently worn away. **1855** C. BRONTE *Villette* vi, The eating rust of obscurity. **1868** BROWNING *Ring & Bk.* VIII. 54 Just so much work as keeps the brain from rust.

fig. **1836–40** HALIBURTON *Clockm.* (1862) 251 It took the rust off of him pretty slick, you may depend.

b. *in rust*: (see quot.).

1889 *Pall Mall G.* 15 Jan. 5/1 If you are bent on looking out for actors 'in rust'—namely, out of engagements.

6. a. A disease in plants marked by ferruginous spots and caused by uredinous fungi; also loosely, any plant-disease presenting a similar appearance.

a **1340** HAMPOLE *Psalter* lxxvii. 51 And he gaf til rust þe froitis of þaim, and þaire trauails til þe locust. **1563** HYLL *Art Garden.* (1593) 28 When rust is falling on the hearbes, then Beritius in his husbandry instructions, willeth.. to make a great smoake forthwith round about the garden. **1591** PERCIVALL *Sp. Dict.*, *Añublo de trigo*, rust of wheate, *rubigo.* **1759** MILLS tr. *Duhamel's Husb.* I. xvi. 79 If rust attacks the corn whilst young.., the hurt is less. *Ibid.*, If the infected wheat is washed by a plentiful rain, the rust disappears almost entirely. **1813** VANCOUVER *Agric. Devon* 156 The early wheats.. are generally found free from the rust. *a* **1817** T. DWIGHT *Trav. New Eng.*, etc. (1821) II. 341 A rust (as it is commonly called), of a brown hue, and an offensive smell. **1852** G. W. JOHNSON *Cottage Gard. Dict.* 794/1 *Rust*, a disease of the berries of the grape. It appears in the form of a rough, rusty appearance of their skins. **1876** *Nature* 28 Dec. 189/1 The disease known as 'rust' which has been causing great havoc among the sugar-canes in Queensland.

b. One or other of the uredinous fungi producing 'rust' in plants.

Also used with adjs., as *black, brown, red, white rust.*

1813 SIR H. DAVY *Agric. Chem.* (1814) 267 The propagation of mildew, funguses, rust, and the small parasitical vegetables. **1857** HENFREY *Elem. Bot.* 460 Species of *Uredo*, constituting the 'blights', 'rusts', &c., of corn and other cultivated plants. **1881** WHITEHEAD *Hops* 58 There are special forms of these fungi, known as rust or brand.

7. A coating or stain resembling rust.

1684 R. WALLER *Nat. Exper.* 130 This stupifying of its force proceeds.. rather from some fine Rust, or hoariness, as it were, contracted by the Amber, from the Salt. **1859** TENNYSON *Guinevere* 73 The rust of murder on the walls.

8. The colour of rust.

1716 GAY *Trivia* III. 379 When the sun veil'd in rust his mourning head. **1893** *Daily News* 25 Mar. 6/1 The sky had turned from grey to a deep, malignant rust.

9. *Comb.* **a.** Instrumental, objective, etc., as ***rust-cankered, -eaten, -free,*** †***-fretten, -stained, -worn; rust-preventing; rust-bearded, -complexioned.***

c **1440** *Jacob's Well* 121 Pore men.. þat myȝte haue be releuyd wyth þi rust-fretyn monye. **1601** R. CHESTER *Love's Martyr* cxvi, Time that rust-cankard wretch. **1742** JARVIS *Quix.* I. i, A suit of armour, which.. being mouldy and rust-eaten, had lain by, many long years, forgotten in a corner. **1744** J. ARMSTRONG *Art Pres. Health* I. 180 The rust-complexion'd man.. whose blood is dry. **1804** J. GRAHAME *Sabbath* (1808) 21 The blossoming pea, That climbs the rust-worn bars. **1868** JOYNSON *Metals* 124 There are still some rust-preventing substances which cannot well be included amongst the coatings. **1890** CONAN DOYLE *White Company* xix, The dark hard-faced cavalier in the rust-stained jupon. **1922** JOYCE *Ulysses* 238 A sailorman, rustbearded, sips from a beaker. **1951** WHITBY & HYNES *Med. Bacteriol.* (ed. 5) iii. 30 Iron in the form of rust-free filings.. reduces the oxidation-reduction potential of liquid media.

b. With other names of colours, as ***rustblack, -brown, -red, -yellow.***

a **1915** JOYCE *Giacomo Joyce* (1968) 15, I kissed her stocking and the hem of her rustblack dusty skirt. **1811** A. T. THOMSON *Lond. Disp.* (1818) 105 It is a very beautiful animal,.. of a rust-brown colour on the upper part of the body. **1977** *Lancashire Life* Nov. 56/2 By May 19 these were six [eggs]—tiny, white and rust-brown speckled. **1832** J. RENNIE *Butterfl. & M.* 84 Wings one inch one-fourth,.. first pair yellowish, with rust-red bands. **1937** V. WOOLF *Years* 297 The down was soft rust-red on its wings. *a* **1963** S. PLATH *Ariel* (1965) 21 A sunken rust-red engine. **1875** W. MORRIS in Mackail *Life* (1899) I. 313 A shade or two of rust-yellows or buffs.

c. Special Combs.: **rust-resistant, -resisting** *adjs.*, (of a metal) made so as not to rust; (of a plant) not liable to rust disease; so **rust-resistance.**

1911 *Jrnl. Agric. Sci.* IV. 99 Have any results of a definite progressive nature in the physiology of rust-resistance been yet obtained? **1940** J. C. HUDSON *Corrosion Iron & Steel* ii. 10 The use of rust-resisting steels has hitherto.. been confined to definite fields of service, in which rust resistance is of primary importance. **1947** *Ann. Rev. Microbiol.* I. 78 The population shifts of physiologic races show the practical need for extensive replication in time and space in testing varieties for stem rust resistance. **1907** *Jrnl. Agric. Sci.* II. 127 In some countries a careful search has already been made for rust-resistant varieties, but on the whole, with comparatively little success from the economic point of view. **1930** H. GOLDSCHMIDT tr. *Müller-Hauff & Stein's Automobile Steels* iv. 142 Krupp was the first to use rust-resistant steel. **1947** *Ann. Rev. Microbiol.* I. 78 The case of Ceres wheat.. illustrates this point. This rust-resistant variety was distributed in 1926, and by 1934 was grown on more than four million acres. **1964** *Abraham & Straus Catal.* Jan. 29 Rust-resistant, lightweight, aluminium ladder. **1891** R. WALLACE *Rural Econ. Austral. & N.Z.* iv. 72 A sample of rust-resisting wheat from Queensland. **1909** *Chambers's Jrnl.* Nov. 766/1 The steel used is a special light, thin, rust-resisting, seamless metal. **1962** *Sci. Survey* XXI. 332 'Stainless steel' (more correctly 'rust-resisting steel') is now familiar in both domestic and industrial applications.

10. *attrib.*, as ***rust-colour, -ground, -test, -tint;*** **rust-ball** (see quot.); **Rust Belt** *U.S.* [BELT *sb.*[1] 5 a], the declining industrial heartland of Mid-West and North-East America, *spec.* the area around Pittsburgh and other steel-producing towns; **rust bucket** *N. Amer. colloq.*, an old and rusty ship; also *Austral. colloq.*, a rusty old car; **rust-cement**, a composition for joints which oxidizes on exposure to the air; **rust disease** = sense 6 a; **rust-finish**, a process in lacquering (see quot.); **rust-fungus** = sense 6 b; **rust hypha**, a hypha of a rust fungus; **rust-joint**, a joint made with rust-cement; **rust-mite**, a gall-mite producing rust-like excrescences on plants.

1787 G. WHITE *Selborne* iv, Among the blue rags turn up .. every now and then balls of a friable substance, like rust of iron, called *rust balls. [**1984** W. MONDALE in *Cleveland (Ohio) Plain Dealer* 18 Sept. 1/1 Mondale pointed to Reagan as the culprit. 'His.. policies are turning our great industrial Midwest and the industrial base of this.. country.. into a rust bowl.'] **1984** *Times* 2 Nov. 7/1 Mr Mondale's nightmare is inspired by the once great but now decaying cities of the Frost Belt—or *Rust Belt, as he describes the old industrial heartland of the Mid-West and North-East. **1985** *Harper's Mag.* Jan. 62/1 In Pittsburgh, the capital of the Rust Belt, the battle for Gulf was the biggest story in town. **1945** *Seafarers' Log* 8 June 2/2 C. M. Chaney, J. D. Riffle and R. R. Ullan were dispatched to one of the more notorious *rust buckets as Quartermaster and AB's respectively. **1959** *Wall St. Jrnl.* 13 Oct. (Eastern ed.) 1/6 To try to get the jump on the weather, ore carriers.. 'will put every rust bucket that floats into the ore trade'. **1969** *Sunday Mail* (Brisbane) 9 Nov. 15/4 (*heading*) Car trade-ins fit for scrap. Dealers stuck with 'rust-buckets'. **1979** F. FORSYTH *Devil's Alternative* 7 The *Garibaldi* an amiable old rust-bucket out of Brindisi. **1839** URE *Dict. Arts* 552 Cast-iron plates bolted together, and made tight with *rust-cement. **1753** *Chambers' Cycl. Suppl.* s.v., Their stalks.. seem burnt up, and appear of a sort of *rust colour. **1865** M. ARNOLD *Ess. Crit.* iii. 88 It looks desolate just now that all is bare and the woods are rust-colour. **1902** W. WATSON *Thompson's Gardener's Assistant* (rev. ed.) II. 600/1 (Index), *Rust disease on vines —cause and treatment. **1975** *Times* 30 May 16/5 A team of scientists at Wye College has discovered in the tobacco plant a naturally produced fungicide effective against the 'rust' diseases which are commonly destructive to important food crops, vegetables and garden flowers. **1884** C. G. W. LOCK *Workshop Rec.* Ser. III. 326/2 '*Rust finish' is the name given to the operation which produces the relief work for the figures. **1883** *Science* I. 369/2 The relations between the *rust-fungi and certain insects which visit their spermogonia. **1853** URE *Dict. Arts* (ed. 4) I. 345 [Calico] Goods padded in iron liquor, dried, and then padded in a solution of chlorine containing a little free-lime, acquire a good *rust ground. **1909** W. BATESON *Mendel's Princ. Heredity* 25 Miss Marryat found that the *rust-hyphae are checked before entering the stomata of the resistant plants. **1839** *Civil Eng. & Arch. Jrnl.* II. 436/1 The joints made with the basement plate in the usual way, either with a *rust joint, or lead, or other jointing. **1865** GESNER *Treat. Coal, Petroleum*, etc. (ed. 2) 173 In making rust-joints, as the iron cementing is called. **1887** *Pall Mall G.* 7 Mar. 5/1 These guns were all exposed to the sand and *rust tests which in no way affected their efficiency. **1897** *Allbutt's Syst. Med.* II. 254 Elevated nodules of a salmon or *rust tint.

rust, *sb.*[2] *rare*$^{-1}$. [Back-formation from RUSTY *a.*[2]] Rusty or reasty bacon.

1845 DISRAELI *Sybil* (1863) 129 There's a very nice flitch hanging up in the engine-room; the men wanted some rust for the machinery.

rust, *sb.*[3] *colloq.* [Back-formation from RUSTY *a.*[3]] ***to take*** (or ***nab***) ***the rust***, of a horse: To become restive.

1775 COLMAN *Prose Sev. Occas.* (1787) I. 201 On the second day his brown horse, Orator, took rust, ran out of the course, and was distanced. **1801** *Sporting Mag.* XVIII. 101 To nab the rust; a jockey term for a horse that is restive. **1837** COL. HAWKER *Diary* (1893) II. 127 My horse.. shied at a road waggon, and then 'took the rust', which I fetched out of him instanter. **1895** RYE *E. Angl. Gloss.* s.v. *Reast*, Some talk of a horse 'taking reast or rust',.. meaning that he becomes restive.

transf. **1860** *Slang Dict.* (ed. 2) 204 'To nab the rust,' to take offence.

rust (rʌst), *v.*[1] Forms: *α.* 3 **rusten**, 5 **ruston**, 5–6 **ruste**, 4– **rust**; 5–6 **rost(e**. *β.* 3–6 **rouste**; *Sc.* 6 **rowst**, 8 **roust**. [ME. *rusten, rouste(n)*, f. RUST *sb.*[1]: cf. Fris. *rûst-, rust-, roastsje*, MDu. and Du. *roesten*, MLG. *rusten* (LG. *rüsten*), OHG. *rostên* (G. *rosten*); also (from G.), MDa. and Da. *ruste*, Norw. *rusta*, MSw. and Sw. *rosta.*]

I. *intr.* **1.** Of iron or other metals: To contract rust, grow rusty; to undergo oxidation.

a **1225** *Ancr. R.* 344 [To] leten þinges muwlen oðer rusten, oðer uorrotien. *c* **1290** *S. Eng. Leg.* I. 370/120 Ake þat tresor þat ich of telle, þat is heouene riche, þat ne roustez ne a-peirez nouȝt. **1382** WYCLIF *Jas.* v. 3 Ȝoure gold and siluer hath rustid. *c* **1400** *Laud Troy Bk.* 8182, I trowe that roste schal oure knyues, When we haue no bred for to kerue. **1426** LYDG. *De Guil. Pilgr.* 11427 What ys the cause.. That a swerd burnysshed cler, Somwhyle rusteth? **1509** BARCLAY *Shyp of Folys* (1570) 28 Were not proude clothing and also fleshely lust, All the fetters and gives of England should rust. **1530** PALSGR. 696/1 Your knyfe wyll ruste, and you wyppe it nat after salte meates. **1601** SHAKS. *All's Well* IV. iii. 373 Rust sword, coole blushes, and Parrolles liue Safest in shame. *a* **1774** GOLDSM. *Surv. Exp. Philos.* (1776) II. 35 In these places gold is actually found to rust. **1793** COWPER *To Mary* 11 Thy needles.. Now rust disus'd, and shine no more. **1855** TENNYSON *Maud* III. vi. 26 No more shall.. the cannon-bullet rust on a slothful shore. **1878** HUXLEY *Physiogr.* 75 Although they do not rust at ordinary temperatures, they may be caused to rust more or less rapidly.

b. To form a rust. *rare*$^{-1}$.

1593 SHAKS. *3 Hen. VI*, I. iii. 49 And this thy Sonnes blood cleauing to my Blade Shall rust vpon my Weapon.

2. To deteriorate, degenerate, spoil, *esp.* through inactivity or want of use. Also with *out.*

a **1300** *Cursor M.* 1568 Al þair luf þai gaue to lust, Þai did þair sauls all to rust. *c* **1386** CHAUCER *Prol.* 502 If a preest be foul, on whom we truste, No wonder is a lewed man to ruste. *c* **1425** *Cast. Persev.* 527 Who-so wyl drawe to Lykynge & Luste, & as a fole, in foly ruste. **1557** EDGEWORTH *Serm. Repert.*, Better it is to shine with laboure, then to rouste for idlenes. **1629** DAVENANT *Albovine* I. i, Let now the knotty Laborer rust with ease. **1692** DRYDEN *Cleomenes* I. i, Then must I rust in Ægypt, never more Appear in Arms? **1768–74** A. TUCKER *Lt. Nat.* (1834) II. 303 When people come into a situation of perfect ease and security, with nothing ever to vex or ruffle them, they quickly rust in idleness. **1781** COWPER *Table-T.* 546 Neglected talents rust into decay. **1840** *Chamb. Jrnl.* 4 Apr. 88/1 Better to 'wear out' than to 'rust out' has been truly said. **1849** MACAULAY *Hist. Eng.* iv. I. 518 Most men would, in such a situation, have allowed their faculties to rust. **1885** *Law Times* LXXIX. 68/2 His fine abilities rusting from disuse.

3. To become rust-coloured.

1541 HYRDE tr. *Vives' Instruct. Chr. Wom.* 22 b, All the fauour of the face waxeth olde, and the breth stynketh, and the tethe rusten. *c* **1586** C'TESS PEMBROKE *Ps.* XC. iv, The hearb that early growethe,.. Eu'ning change with ruine moweth, And laies to rost in withering aire. **1842** TENNYSON *E. Morris* 100 When the bracken rusted on their crags. **1882** 'OUIDA' *Maremma* viii. I. 191 The gold of the sun-flower wanes and rusts.

4. Of wheat, etc.: To become affected with rust or blight.

1868 *Rep. U.S. Commiss. Agric.* (1869) 415 The wheat rusted badly on the blade and slightly on the stalk.

II. *trans.* **5.** To affect with rust; to oxidize.

1596 SPENSER *F.Q.* V. ix. 30 But at her feet her sword was likewise layde, Whose long rest rusted the bright steely brand. **1604** SHAKS. *Oth.* I. ii. 59 Keepe vp your bright Swords, for the dew will rust them. **1644** DIGBY *Nat. Bodies* XV. (1658) 170 Brass and iron.. are easily rusted by salts dissolving upon them. **1728** CHAMBERS *Cycl.* s.v., The Air apparently rusts Bodies, but 'tis only in Virtue of the Water it contains. **1815** J. SMITH *Panorama Sci. & Art* II. 350 This gas.. is evolved in every instance in which metals are tarnished or rusted by moisture. **1879** PROCTOR *Pleas. Ways Sci.* xv. 348 Its power of oxidizing or rusting metals.. is much greater than that which oxygen possesses.

b. *fig.* To render antiquated or obsolete.

1694 ADDISON *Acc. Greatest Eng. Poets* 13 Age has rusted what the Poet writ, Worn out his language, and obscured his wit.

6. To corrupt or corrode morally or physically.

1697 DRYDEN *Virg. Georg.* I. 190 The Sire of Gods and Men.. Himself did Handy-Crafts and Arts ordain, Nor suffer'd Sloath to rust his active Reign. *c* **1770** BEATTIE *To Alex. Ross* iii, Oh may the roupe ne'er roust thy weason. **1839** J. H. NEWMAN *Par. Serm.* IV. xxii. 374 The breath of the world has a peculiar power in.. rusting the soul.

7. To affect (corn, etc.) with rust or blight.
1759 Mills tr. *Duhamel's Husb.* I. 85 Bad effects from feeding cattle with fodder which has been rusted. **1763** —— *Syst. Pract. Husb.* II. 409 When a hot sun has succeeded such dry hazy weather, the corn was rusted within a few days after. **1861** *Times* 24 Sept., Three-fourths of the crop [of hops] will be of the best quality; the remainder was rusted by spiders towards the end of last month.
8. To make rust-coloured.
1801 Southey *Thalaba* viii. ii, The sun, and the wind, and the rain, Had rusted his raven locks.
9. To waste *away* by idling. Also *refl.*
1853 W. Jerdan *Autobiog.* III. vi. 67 [He] appeared..to be rusting away a life which might be serviceable to his country. **1887** Miss Braddon *Like & Unl.* xii, We must not rust away our lives here. **1894** G. M. Fenn *In Alpine Valley* I. 36 I'm not going to rust myself away.

†**rust**, *v.*[2] *Obs.*$^{-1}$ [ME. *rüsten*, repr. OE. *hrystan*, var. of *hyrstan*.] *trans.* To ornament.
c **1205** Lay. 25812 He bar..ænne sceld on his rugge irust al mid golde.

rustbank, var. rusbank.

† **rust-cock**, obs. variant of roost-cock.
1610 Guillim *Heraldry* vi. v. 404 The Carians had Rust-cocks for their crests.

rust-coloured, *a.* [rust *sb.* 9a.] Having the reddish colour of rust.
1692 Boyle *Hist. of Air* 227 These stones, which when the ground was newly turned up, were rust-coloured. **1753** *Chambers' Cycl.* Suppl. s.v. *Passer*, The..field sparrow of Aldrovand..is of a dusky rust-coloured brown. **1826** Miss Mitford *Village* Ser. ii. (1863) 408 Beside another streamlet, whose deep rust-coloured scum gives token of a chalybeate spring. **1870** Rolleston *Anim. Life* 128 Intervals in the rust-coloured line on the dorsal.

ruste, obs. or dial. var. rest *sb.*[1] and *v.*[1]

rusted (ˈrʌstɪd), *ppl. a.* [f. rust *v.*[1]] Affected or covered with rust; stuck or lodged as a result of rusting; made rusty in colour. Also in *transf.* and *fig.* uses, and with *in* and *up*.
pred. *a* **1225** *Ancr. R.* 160 þet hit..schal drawen rust of on þet is irusted, uor hwon þet heo longe liggen togederes. *c* **1412–20** Lydg. *Chron. Troy* ii. 1072 O rancour rustid of inpacience! **1535** Stewart *Cron. Scot.* II. 33 That rancour is so rowstit in thair hart..That force it is it man out at the last. **1549** *Compl. Scot.* vii. 69 Ane vthir part of the schieldis & harnes var brokyn ande roustit. **1604** E. Grimstone tr. *D'Acosta's Hist. Indies* iii. ix. 144, I have seene grates of yron..so rusted and consumed, that pressing it betwixt your fingers, it dissolved into powder. **1670** Narborough *Jrnl.* in *Acc. Sev. Late Voy.* i. (1694) 45 The Salt-pond, which is rusted all over like a Pavement, with very white and good Salt. **1725** Ramsay *Gentle Sheph.* iii. ii, Rousted with eild, a wee piece gate seems lang. **1742** Young *Nt. Th.* ii. 483 What numbers, sheath'd in erudition, lie Plung'd to the hilts in venerable tomes, And rusted in. **1816** Byron *Chillon* i, My limbs are..rusted with a vile repose, For they have been a dungeon's spoil. **1859** W. Collins *Queen of Hearts* (1875) 18 My wits had become sadly rusted by long seclusion from society. **1924** J. Masefield *Sard Harker* ii. 82 The catch of this beastly revolver seems to have jammed. .. I'm afraid it's rusted-in, or something. **1972** *Guardian* 15 Mar. 10/2, I don't ever feel that I get rusted-up. I don't think I could have done this play if I'd been rusted-up.
attrib. **1726** Pope *Odyss.* xxiv. 575 Old Dolius too his rusted arms put on. **1763** Mills *Syst. Pract. Husb.* II. 413 The straw of smutty, mildewed or rusted corn. **1810** Scott *Lady of L.* vi. xii, Then, from a rusted iron hook, A bunch of ponderous keys he took. **1865** Swinburne *Ballad of Death* 102 Many rusted sheaves Rain-rotten in rank lands. **1873** W. Black *Pr. Thule* xxiii. 376 The hills are red and brown with rusted bracken and heather. **1929** J. M. Ross in *Oxford Poetry* 36 The Purple Beech..brandishing aloft his burnt, dark, rusted leaves. **1967** E. Short *Embroidery & Fabric Collage* i. 18 A piece of rusted up metal..could be noted in a sketch-book.

†**ˈrustful**, *a.* *Obs.*$^{-1}$ [f. rust *sb.*[1]] Rusty.
1635 Quarles *Embl.* i. vii. 29 Why dost thou suffer rustful sloth to creep into thy wanton brows?

rustic (ˈrʌstɪk), *a.* and *sb.* Forms: 5 **rustyk**, 6 **rustike**, 6–7 **rusticke**, **rustique**, 6–8 **rustick**, 7– **rustic**. [ad. L. *rūstic-us*, f. *rūs* country. So F. *rustique* (14th c.).]
A. *adj.* **1.** Of or pertaining to the country (as opposed to the town); found in the country.
c **1440** *Pallad. on Husb.* i. 1027 Aftir hem is best Of rosemary, and sauery; thenne is noon So good as they but rustyk swete vchoon. **1578** Timme *Calvin on Gen.* 127 The whole life rustike is hurtless, simple, and most of all framed to the true order of Nature. **1611** Shaks. *Wint. T.* iv. iv. 84 Of that kind Our rusticke Garden's barren. **1767** A. Young *Farmer's Lett. to People* 104, I think it is of vast consequence both to the farmer and the public to extend the use of oxen for all rustic business. **1794** Mrs. Radcliffe *Myst. Udolpho* i, A rustic hall and two excellent sitting-rooms. **1815** Scott *Ld. of Isles* iv. xxx, The spot where his bold train Held rustic camp upon the plain. **1838** Dickens *Nickleby* iv, Something like this..must be the prevalent notion of Snow Hill in those remote and rustic parts. **1877** Talmage *Serm.* 370 So we all understand rustic allusions.
b. In names of plants, animals, insects, etc.
1601 Holland *Pliny* II. 85 Bacchar is named by some Rustick-Nard. **1620** Venner *Via Recta* iii. 63 Woodcocks... Some iudge them to approch somewhat neere vnto the nature of the Partridge, and therefore is of them called the rusticke Partridge. **1781** Barbut *Insects* Index, Ord. ii. Gen. 8, *Cimex Campestris*, the rustic-cimex. **1781** Pennant *Hist. Quadrup.* II. 448 Rustic Rat, *Mus Agrarius*. **1832** J. Rennie *Butterfl. & M.* 71 The Rustic Shoulder Knot..appears the beginning of June. *Ibid.* 72 The Rustic Mourner..appears in August.
†**c.** ***Rustic war***, the peasant war of 1525 in Germany. *Obs.*$^{-1}$ (Cf. rustical A. 3b.)
1732 Neal *Hist. Purit.* (1822) I. 48 Among others that fled out of Germany into England, from the Rustic war, there were some that went by the name of Anabaptists.
2. Of persons: Living in the country as opposed to the town; following country occupations; of peasant or agricultural stock or condition.
1601 R. Johnson *Kingd. & Commw.* (1603) 16 The abundance of people and plenty of vittailes are the strongest sinewes of all kingdomes, and therefore the Romaines highly prized the rusticke diuision for their numbers and prouision. **1620** Venner *Via Recta* i. 19 It is most meete for rusticke labourers. **1681** H. Nevile *Plato Rediv.* 61 The Rustick Tribes being twenty seven, and the vrbane Tribes nine. **1750** Gray *Elegy* xxi, And many a holy text around she strews, That teach the rustic moralist to die. **1784** Cowper *Task* iv. 708 Assembling..The rustic throng beneath his fav'rite beech. **1821** Shelley *Epipsych.* 485 A lone dwelling, built by whom or how None of the rustic island-people know. **1849** Macaulay *Hist. Eng.* v. I. 596 If Beaufort and his rustic followers could be overpowered before the regular troops arrived. **1883** 'Ouida' *Wanda* I. 295 We are only rustic people.
†**b.** = rustical *a.* 2b. *Obs.*$^{-1}$
1643 tr. *Hildanus' Exper. Chyrurg.* ii. 4 Those of a hard and rustique flesh, and which are strong men, require more stronger Remedies.
3. Of persons: Having the appearance or manners of country people; lacking in elegance, refinement, or education; sometimes, devoid of good-breeding, clownish, boorish.
1585 T. Washington tr. *Nicholay's Voy.* iii. ii. 71 After they haue put the..pretiest of them into the Sarail of the great Turke, send the other being the most rustique..to labour and till the ground. **1590** Spenser *F.Q.* iii. Introd. v, But let that same delitious Poet lend A little leaue vnto a rusticke Muse To sing his mistresse prayse. **1642** Milton *Apol. Smect.* Wks. 1851 III. 306, I am not altogether so rustick, and nothing so irreligious. **1688** Holme *Armoury* iii. 72/1 A Rustick Fellow, one without City or School breeding, without cleanliness, and of a slovenly Speech. *a* **1720** Sewel *Hist. Quakers* (1795) II. vii. 53 G. Croese, who writ the pretended history of the Quakers, calls him a rustick fellow. **1743** H. Walpole *Lett. to Mann* (1834) I. xcii. 322 You see how rustic I am grown again. **1847** Yeowell *Anc. Brit. Church* iv. 173, I Patrick a sinner, the most rustic, and the least of all the faithful.
absol. **1841** Emerson *Ess., Love*, It [love] is the dawn of civility and grace in the coarse and rustic.
4. Characteristic or typical of countryfolk or peasants; *esp.* unmannerly, unrefined; rough.
1589 Greene *Tullies Loue* Wks. (Grosart) VII. 215 Fabius ..as famous for his rusticke and vnciuile life, as now he is woondred at for his braue and courtly behauiour. **1628** Feltham *Resolves* i. viii. 20 Sores are not to bee anguish't with a rusticke pressure. **1637** R. Humfrey tr. *St. Ambrose* i. 126, I doe not approve..of unmannerly and rusticke behaviour. **1761** Hume *Hist. Eng.* (1806) IV. lii. 82 That rustic contempt for the fair sex, which James affected. **1784** Cowper *Task* ii. 457 This is fulsome; and offends me more Than..rustic coarseness would. **1815** Elphinstone *Acc. Caubul* (1842) II. 133 The rustic customs of the Afghauns are also in a great measure laid aside. **1873** Hale *In His Name* viii. 71 That dialect of rustic Latin.
b. Plain and simple; unsophisticated; having the charm of the country.
1600 Shaks. *A.Y.L.* v. iv. 183 Meane time, forget this new-falne dignitie, And fall into our Rusticke Reuelrie. **1634** Milton *Comus* 849 For which the Shepherds at their festivals Carrol her goodnes lowd in rustick layes. **1700** Dryden *Ovid's Art of Love* i. 685 Lay bashfulness, that rustic virtue, by. **1738** Johnson *London* 79 [My] rustick tongue Ne'er knew to puzzle right, or varnish wrong. **1855** Brimley *Ess.* 48 The rustic grace and sweetness of the *May Queen*. **1860** Ruskin *Mod. Paint.* V. i. i. 4 Another use of words may be forced upon us by a new aspect of facts, so that we may find ourselves saying: 'Such and such a person is very gentle and kind—he is quite rustic'.
5. Of rude or country workmanship; of a plain or simple form or structure; *spec.* constructed of undressed branches or roots of trees.
1594 Nashe *Unfort. Trav.* Wks. (Grosart) V. 19 He rose and put his rustic ring on my finger. **1667** Milton *P.L.* xi. 433 Ith' midst an Altar as the Land-mark stood Rustic, of grassie sord. **1752** Mrs. Delany *Life & Corr.* (1861) III. 89 Three rustick arches, set off with ivy, moss, icicles, and all the rocky appurtenances. **1784** Cowper *Task* i. 267 Descending now..upon a rustic bridge We pass a gulph. **1826** Scott *Woodst.* ii, The gentleman and lady continued to advance, directing their course to a rustic seat. **1834** L. Ritchie *Wand. by Seine* 73 The court..paved in rustic mosaic, is precious in the eyes of antiquaries. **1872** Jenkinson *Guide Eng. Lakes* (1879) 30 Two rustic bridges span the chasm.
b. Of letters: Having a free or negligent form; applied *spec.* to one of the styles employed in early Latin manuscripts (in contrast to *square*).
1784 T. Astle *Orig. & Progr. Writing* 79 The Rustic capitals were bold, negligent, unequal, composed of strokes, generally oblique, sometimes extravagant, and always inelegant. **1873** E. Spon *Workshop Rec.* Ser. i. 4/2 Vaguely formed 'rustic' or other free-hand letters are in bad taste on such drawings. **1883** I. Taylor *Alphabet* II. 163 The earliest codices..are usually written in Capitals. There are two types, 'Square' and 'Rustic'.
6. *Arch.* Characterized by a surface artificially roughened or left rough-hewn, or by having the joints (esp. the horizontal ones) deeply sunk or chamfered; also, †of or pertaining to the Tuscan order.
1563 Shute *Archit.* E iiij b, Rusticke or Rughe hewed stone. **1663** Gerbier *Counsel* 29 The Tuscan Column, or Rustick, Base and Capital. **1697** Evelyn *Architects & Archit.* Misc. Wks. (1825) 405 Tuscan, Rustic, or by whatever name dignified, or disgrac'd. **1730** A. Gordon *Maffei's Amphith.* 400 The Work is rustic, made with Knobs or Protuberances..without being smoothed. **1766** Entick *London* IV. 11 The present structure [is made] of brick, strengthened by rustic quoins of stone at the corners. **1841** *Penny Cycl.* XX. 272/1 Some tasteful specimens of rustic quoining. **1842** Gwilt *Encycl. Arch.* 1027 *Rustic Order*, a species of building wherein the faces of the stones are hatched or picked with the point of a hammer. **1875** Knight *Dict. Mech.* 2007/2.
b. ***rustic work***, masonry of this type.
1715 Leoni *Palladio's Archit.* (1742) I. 33 Rustick-work ..does not look well, unless..in a very large Building. **1811** *Self Instructor* 140 Bricklayers' work,..piers, pilasters, rustic work. **1841** *Penny Cycl.* XX. 272 Of this kind is the rustic work of the Königsbau at Munich. **1859** Turner *Dom. Archit.* III. ii. 391 The front to the courtyard is faced with that peculiar kind of masonry called rustic-work.
7. *Comb.*, as ***rustic-like*** adj. and adv.
1558 Phaer *Virgil, Life* (1584) A vj b, This Poet..seemeth to doubt least that Ecloge which is intituled Pollio, will not appeare rustickelike enough. **1683** D. A. *Art of Converse* 19 Telling you more rustick-like yet to be silent, and let them speak.
B. *sb.* **1.** A countryman, a peasant.
c **1550** in Duncumb *Hereford* (1804) I. 339 There are other markett-townes..wherein are both natives and rusticks of auncient tyme. **1585** T. Washington tr. *Nicholay's Voy.* iii. ii. 71 b, The figure following..is of the Azamoglan Rustique. **1611** Shaks. *Wint. T.* iv. iv. 735 How now (Rustiques); whither are you bound? **1650** Bulwer *Anthropomet.* 173 Your Rustics and Handicraft-men never pare their Nails. **1722** Wollaston *Relig. Nat.* ix. 178 In how many countrey affairs must the scholar take the rustic for his master? **1782** Cowper *Let. to J. Hill* 7 Dec., For instance, here are two rustics and your humble servant in company. **1828** Carlyle *Misc.* (1857) I. 196 Strange and half unwarrantable that he should do such honour to a rustic. **1862** Miss Braddon *Aurora Floyd* i, The Kentish rustics know very little of this City banking-house.
b. A boorish or rude person. *rare.*
1706 Addison *Rosamond* i. iii, Thou art a rustick to call me so; I'm not ugly nor old. **1770** Langhorne *Plutarch* (1879) II. 766/2 He who finds fault with any rusticity, is himself a rustic.
c. One of several species of noctuid moths, as the ***garden***, ***grey***, ***mottled*** (etc.) ***rustic***.
1819 G. Samouelle *Entom. Comp.* 420. **1832** J. Rennie *Butterfl. & M.* 50, etc.
2. *Arch.* Rustic work. (Cf. A. 6.)
1731 Pope *Ep. Burlington* 34 Then clap four slices of Pilaster on't, That, lac'd with bits of rustic, makes a Front. **1796** Morse *Amer. Geogr.* I. 489 The lower part is of a light rustic. **1817** D. Hughson *Walks thro' London* 216 Rock-work, or rustic, can never be better introduced than in buildings by the side of water. **1842** Gwilt *Encycl. Arch.* §2669 We now return to the subject of the rock-worked rustic, whereof, above, some notice was promised.
Comb. **1762–71** Walpole *Vertue's Anecd. Paint.* (1786) IV. 96 His arched windows, his rustic-laced windows,..are striking proofs of his want of taste.
b. A stone (†or joint) of the kind employed in rustic work. Usually in *pl.*
1728 R. Morris *Anc. Archit.* 76 An uniform Disposition of equidistant Cavities, term'd Rusticks. **1797** *Encycl. Brit.* (ed. 3) II. 242 The rustics may either be plain, hatched, or vermiculated. **1813** *Gentl. Mag.* LXXXIII. i. 37/2 A sort of rock-work, giving birth to that species of masonry termed 'Rough Rustics'. **1839** *Civil Eng. & Arch. Jrnl.* II. 357/1 The principal front is faced with red kiln-burnt bricks, with bath-stone rustics to the quoins. **1842** Gwilt *Encycl. Arch.* §2666 When square joints are used, they should not be wider than one eighth part of the height of the rustic itself.
3. Country dialect.
1841 *Penny Cycl.* XX. 84/1 Sardinian Rustic.

rustical (ˈrʌstɪkəl), *a.* and *sb.* Also 5–6 **rusticalle**, 6–7 **-all**; 6 **rustycal**. [ad. OF. *rustical*, or med.L. *rusticāl-is*: see prec. and -al[1].]
A. *adj.* **1.** = rustic *a.* 2. Now *arch.*
1432–50 tr. *Higden* (Rolls) II. 345 He was trowede to haue bene a godde of the rusticalle peple. **1531** Elyot *Gov.* iii. xxii. (1880) II. 340 The Lacedemones somtyme purposely caused their rusticall seruauntes to be made very dronke. **1577** Vautrouillier *Luther on Ep. Gal.* 170 Stirring vp the rusticall people to sedition. **1606** J. Carpenter *Solomon's Solace* xxiv. 97 The ordinary matters..much ruminated among the very rusticall and Countrey people. **1649** Roberts *Clavis Bibl.* 549 God purposely raised up Amos of Judah, and a poor rusticall Herdman of Tekoa. **1714** Gay *Sheph. Week* Proeme, The manners also meetly copied from the rustical folk therein.
2. = rustic *a.* 3.
1513 More *Rich. III* (1641) 218 To bridle and rule the rude rusticall and blustering bold people of that region. **1542** Udall *Erasm. Apoph.* 167 Feloes of no fyne witte.., but alltogether grosse, clubbyshe, and rusticall. **1609** Bible (Douay) *Gen.* xxi. *comm.*, The spiritual never persecuteth the carnal; but spareth him as his rustical brother. *a* **1661** Fuller *Worthies, Oxf.* II. 327 Whose inhabitants..were so rustical in their behaviour, that boarish and clownish people are said born at Hogs-Norton. **1706** *Reflex. upon Ridicule* 38 Theodemus is..rustical and unpolite. **1820** Scott *Monast.* xv, This rustical and mistaught juvenal. **1844** Thackeray *Crit. Rev.* Wks. 1886 XXIII. 46 A rustical boy, hired at twopence per week. **1877** Besant & Rice *Golden Butterfly* vii, He thought she must be some shy maiden from the country—a little 'rustical' perhaps.
†**b.** Physically strong; robust. *Obs.*
1575 Banister *Chyrurg.* (1585) i. 43 That you wisely make choyse of your medicynes,..knowing that the rusticall body maye endure fittest, the stronger sorte. **1620** Venner *Via Recta* iv. 76 They may in want of better meat, serue for Mariners, and rusticall bodies. **1693** Evelyn *De la Quint.*

Compl. Gard. II. 168 More tender and less able to resist the Frost.. than the others which are more rustical and hardy.

3. Pertaining to, connected with, the country or life in the country; rural. = RUSTIC *a.* 1.

1546 LANGLEY tr. *Pol. Verg. de Invent.* III. i. 64 b, Without doubt y^e Hebrues dyd fyrst finde out the way of tilling corne, grinding, with other rusticall instrumentes. **1549** *Compl. Scot.* vi. 43 In ald tymis pastoral and rustical ocupatione vas of ane excellent reputatione. **1601** HOLLAND *Pliny* I. 320 There is a kind of rusticall and wild Bee. **1654** GAYTON *Pleas. Notes* IV. iv. 193 Such plaine and easie proverbs learned in his rusticall life. **1693** DRYDEN *Persius* (1697) 420 He makes a digression to Romulus the first King of Rome, who had a Rustical Education. **1707** *Curiosities in Husb. & Gard.* 121 Such as are capable of so rustical an Occupation.

†**b.** = RUSTIC *a.* 1 c. *Obs.*

1560 DAUS tr. *Sleidane's Comm.* 93 b, Their preachers were a great occasion of the commotion and rusticall warre. **1599** A. M. tr. *Gabelhouer's Bk. Physicke* 329/2 An other [prescription for gunshot wounds] which in the Rusticalle warres hath oftentimes binne tryed.

4. = RUSTIC *a.* 4.

1550 J. COKE *Eng. & Fr. Heralds* § 102 The rustycall and myserable estate of the French courte. **1579** SPENSER *Sheph. Cal.* Ded., Thinking them fittest for such rusticall rudenesse of shepheards,.. for that theyr rough sounde would make his rymes more ragged and rustical. **1615** BRIGHTMAN *Revelation* 790 Neither will we be inueigled any more with her rustical roundelayes. **1695** MOTTEUX tr. *St. Olon's Morocco* 37 Their native rustical Temper, and wilful Ignorance. **1698** FARQUHAR *Love & a Bottle* II, O fie, Mr. Mockmode! what a rustical Expression that is! **1850** L. HUNT *Autobiog.* II. xi. 55 An extraordinary mixture.. of rustical, mechanical tastes.., with the most exalted ideas of authority. **1874** M. COLLINS *Transmigr.* I. ix. 164, I.. was awakened by sounds of rustical music.

†**b.** Roughly approximate; unscientific, rude.

1662 CHANDLER *Van Helmont's Oriat.* 108 Let us measure these things in a rusticall sense.

5. Of a kind, make, or fashion appropriate to the country; *esp.* plain or simple.

1483 CAXTON *Gold. Leg.* 428/2 His breed was rustical broun, made of barleye or ootes. **1591** FRAUNCE *C'tess of Pembroke's Yuychurch* IV. Prol., Leaving Christall throanes for bowres and rustical harbors. **1610** WILLET *Daniel* 96 Such rusticall oaten pipes. **1610** HOLLAND *Camden's Brit.* (1637) 43 Compassed about with a rude and rusticall rampire. **1665** J. WEBB *Stone-Heng* (1725) 89 They wrought only the.. Cornices, and left the rest rude or rustical. **1864** CHRISTINA ROSSETTI *Poems* (1904) 365/2 [She] sang a country ditty.., Pathetically rustical, Too pointless for the city. **1871** M. COLLINS *Marq. & Merch.* III. xiii. 301 A jolly rough honeymoon,.. with everything simple and rustical.

B. *sb.* A countryman, peasant, rustic. Now *arch.*

1555 EDEN *Decades* (Arb.) 81 The inhabitantes of these mountaynes differ no lesse.. then among vs the rusticalles of the countrey from gentylmen of the courte. **1579** NORTHBROOKE *Dicing* (1843) 165 If thou doe not kiss hir.., then thou shalt be taken for a rusticall. **1600** HEYWOOD *1st Pt. Edw. IV*, II. ii, Falconbridge, what are these rusticals? **1820** SCOTT *Monast.* xix, Let me entreat you not to be wroth with this rustical. **1861** C. READE *Cloister & H.* lv. (1896) 163, I to be rid of roaring rusticalls, and mindless jests,.. drew on the table a great watery circle; whereat the rusticalls did look askant.

Hence **rusti'cality**, rusticity. *rare*$^{-1}$.

1576 FLEMING *Panopl. Epist.* 372 Ignoraunce is suche an impediment in man,.. it ingendreth in him rusticalitie or clownishnesse.

rustically ('rʌstɪkəlɪ), *adv.* [f. RUSTICAL *a.*]

1. In a rude or uncultured style (of speech or diction).

a **1548** HALL *Chron., Hen. VII*, 48 b, The Scottes.. aunswered theim proudly & rustically with many disdeinfull woordes. **1583** FULKE *Def. Tr. Script.* i. 46 You haue no skill.., that speake so barbarously and rustically of Greeke elegancies. **1634** in *4th Rep. Hist. MSS. Comm.* 135/2 Dr. Osberne.. did very licentiously and rustically reproache me in very base and opprobrious termes. *a* **1652** J. SMITH *Sel. Disc.* iv. 74 Lest they should speak too rudely and rustically of it by calling it matter. **1828** *Blackw. Mag.* XXIV. 904 The pulpit style has been always either rustically negligent, or bristling with pedantry.

b. In a country dialect; dialectally. *rare.*

1611 COTGR., *Mortau*, as *Mortel* (rustically).

2. After the manner of country-folk or peasants; in a countrified condition or fashion.

1579 J. JONES *Preserv. Bodie & Soul* I. xxvi. 50 That the infant be neyther too delicately brought vp, nor too rustically. **1600** SHAKS. *A.Y.L.* I. i. 7 For my part, he keepes me rustically at home, or (to speak more properly) staies me heere at home vnkept. **1693** DRYDEN *Persius* (1697) 412 Returning home, And Rustically Joy'd, as Chief of Rome. **1826** SCOTT *Woodst.* ii, I am but a rude man, and rustically brought up to arms and hunting. **1883** STEVENSON *Silverado Squatters* 2 Life in its shadow goes rustically forward. *Ibid.* 129 Rustically ignorant, but with a touch of wood-lore.

†'**rusticalness.** *Obs.* [f. as prec. + -NESS.] Rusticity.

a **1603** T. CARTWRIGHT *Confut. Rhem. N.T.* (1618) Pref. p. xv, Auoiding as well barbarousnesse and rusticalnesse of the one side, as curiositie and affectation of the other. *a* **1661** FULLER *Worthies, Hertfordshire* II. 18 Some will wonder how this Shire, lying so near to London,.. should be guiltie of so much Rusticalness.

†'**rustican.** *Obs. rare.* [a. L. *rusticān-us.*] A countryman, rustic.

1570 LEVINS *Manip.* 19/27 A Rusticane, *rusticus.* **1579** TWYNE *Phis. agst. Fortune* II. v. 167 b, Marius was also a rusticane of the countrey.

rusticate ('rʌstɪkeɪt), *v.* [f. L. *rusticāt-*, ppl. stem of *rusticārī* to live in the country, etc., f. *rustic-us* RUSTIC *a.* Cf. F. *rustiquer.*]

1. *intr.* To go or retire into the country; to stay or sojourn in the country; to assume rural manners, to live a country life.

1660 GAUDEN *Brownrig* 159 To rusticate (as Elisha sometimes did) among plain people that follow the Plough. **1698** FRYER *E. India & Persia* 259 In the Afternoon.. we went to Mirge,.. to an old lonely Inn, where was the last place we rusticated. **1789** *Triumphs Fortitude* I. 22 Wherever those of the fashionable world assemble, in spite of all they can do to rusticate, Art will generally appear to prevail over Nature. **1804** *Something Odd* II. 163 Sir Christopher.. thought it his duty to attend the House for the present rather than rusticate. **1838** LYTTON *Alice* I. ix, Lady Elizabeth is not going there this year; so I am compelled to rusticate. **1886** C. KEENE in *Life* (1892) 358, I.. heard.. that you were going to rusticate on some riverside.

transf. **1829** MARRYAT *F. Mildmay* ii, Murphy was dismissed in disgrace, and ordered to rusticate on board till his eye was bright.

2. *trans.* **a.** To dismiss or 'send down' from a university for a specified time, as a punishment.

1714 *Spect.* No. 596 ¶3, I was sent away, or in the University Phrase, Rusticated for ever. **1734** in Peirce *Hist. Harvard Univ.* (1833) App. 140 If.. it be denied him, such Undergraduate shall be degraded, rusticated, or expelled. **1766** CLAP *Hist. Yale College* 86 If they do persist, and are guilty of some greater Crime, they are publickly admonished or rusticated, for some Months. **1825** C. WESTMACOTT *English Spy* I. 171 Rattle was rusticated for a term. **1858** TROLLOPE *Dr. Thorne* ii, This son had been first rusticated from Oxford and then expelled. **1868** H. LEE *B. Godfrey* xxxi, I was rusticated for.. painting the college pump scarlet.

b. To remove or send (one) into, settle (one) in, the country. Also *refl.*

1733 CHEYNE *Eng. Malady* I. vi. § 6 Seldom any lasting.. Cure is perform'd till the Diseased be rusticated and purified. **1749** FIELDING *Tom Jones* I. x, From which time he had entirely rusticated himself.

3. To imbue with rural manners; to countrify.

a **1766** MRS. SHERIDAN *Sidney Bidulph* IV. 157 The poor creatures are absolutely rusticated. **1794** MARY WOLLSTONECR. *Hist. View Fr. Rev.* I. 503 They did not inhabit the homely recesses of indigence, rusticating their manners as they cultivated their understandings. **1824** *Examiner* 170/2 Our thoughts, environed by the rural objects of the picture, are happily rusticated in the mimic country.

4. To mark masonry by sunk joints or roughened surfaces. Also rarely *absol.*

1715 LEONI *Palladio's Archit.* (1742) I. 10 Brick-walls ought not to be rusticated. **1839** *Civil Eng. & Arch. Jrnl.* II. 319/1 A ground story, rusticated and terminated by an enriched lace band or string course. **1851** RUSKIN *Stones Ven.* I. xxvi. § 6 Do not think that Nature rusticates her foundations... She does rusticate sometimes. **1901** *J. Black's Carp. & Build.* 56 The concrete forming the steps is rusticated with shells and pebbles, &c., on the fronts, and clean coarse gravel on the top faces or treads.

Hence '**rusticating** *vbl. sb.* and *ppl. a.* Also '**rusticater**, one who is rusticating.

1801 W. TAYLOR in *Monthly Mag.* XII. 579 A rustic and rusticating fashion for farmery. **1823** P. NICHOLSON *Pract. Builder* 311 Rusticating, in architecture and masonry, consists in forming horizontal sinkings, or grooves. **1834** DE QUINCEY *Autobiogr. Sk.* Wks. 1853 I. 101 At these rusticating seasons, he had often much further to come than ourselves. **1878** *Tinsley's Mag.* XXIII. 112 A 'rusticater' (please excuse the noun) Exploring leisurely a spot in Surrey.

'**rusticated,** *ppl. a.* [f. prec. + -ED^1.]

1. Relegated to the country; temporarily dismissed from a university.

1759 JOHNSON *Idler* No. 80 ¶2 The time is now come when the town is again beginning to be full, and the rusticated beauty sees an end of her banishment. **1873** W. S. TYLER *Hist. Amherst College* 49 Rev. Timothy M. Cooley.., afterwards so famous as a teacher of rusticated students.

2. a. Rendered rustic in manners; countrified.

1754 H. WALPOLE *Lett.* (1846) III. 48 Are you such a rusticated animal as to suppose that the Duke is dismissed for inability? **1798** *Geraldina* I. 30 You see how rusticated I am, by writing on such uninteresting subjects. **1822** W. IRVING *Braceb. Hall* (1823) I. 14 The squire is.. rusticated a little by living almost entirely on his estate.

b. Settled in the country; leading a country life.

1764 *Museum Rust.* III. 238 Extracts from approved modern authors, of which many of the rusticated readers of this work would have remained ignorant. **1809** MALKIN *Gil Blas* X. i, Scipio.. would have liked better to see me once more blazing at court, than either cloistered or rusticated. **1826** R. POLWHELE *Trad. & Recoll.* II. ix. 605 In the last age some of the rusticated clergy used to favour the popular superstition.

3. a. Of masonry, parts of buildings, etc.: Rendered rustic in appearance.

1743 POCOCKE *Descr. East* I. 23 To the south of the west entrance.. I saw a rusticated wall three feet.. thick. **1775** WASHINGTON *Let.* Writ. 1893 XIV. 315, I wish you had done the end of the New Kitchen next the Garden as also the Old Kitchen with rusticated Boards. **1783** W. F. MARTYN *Geogr. Mag.* II. 129 The lower story is of rusticated architecture. **1843** *Penny Cycl.* XXVI. 270/2 Rusticated Doric and Corinthian, some of the columns of the latter fluted spirally. **1872** RUSKIN *Fors Clav.* xxi, An immense mass of merely squared or rusticated stones.

b. Of pottery: (see quot. 1936).

1936 *Proc. Prehistoric Soc.* II. 19 Rusticated pottery, *i.e.* pottery of which the surface has been roughened all over as a method of decoration. **1939** V. G. CHILDE *Dawn Europ. Civilization* (ed. 3) 338 Definitions of certain terms, descriptive of *ceramic decoration*, here used in a special or restricted sense... Rusticated—by roughening the surface, generally covered with a thick slip, by pinching with the fingers, brushing, etc. ('barbotine'). **1967** *Antiquaries Jrnl.* XLVII. 202 Somersham.. is further known for its imposing 'pot-beaker', with rusticated finger-decoration. **1977** G. CLARK *World Prehistory* (ed. 3) x. 448 Impressed and rusticated pottery was supplemented by polychrome painted Tupiguarini ware.

rustication (rʌstɪ'keɪʃən). [ad. L. *rusticātio*, noun of action f. *rusticārī*: see RUSTICATE *v.*]

1. The action of retiring to, or living in, the country; a spell of residence in the country; †a rural pursuit or occupation.

1623 COCKERAM, *Rustication*, a dwelling in the Countrey. **1696** EVELYN *Mem.* (1857) III. 366, I confess I am foolishly fond of these and other rustications. **1783** JOHNSON *Let. to Mrs. Thrale* 23 July, Whether this short rustication has done me any good I cannot tell. **1805** LAMB *Let. to Wordsw.* in *Final Mem.* iv. 228 We have been two tiny excursions this summer for three or four days each..: and this is the total history of our rustications this year. **1823** SYD. SMITH *Wks.* (1859) II. 29/1 How absurd it would be to offer to the higher orders the exclusive use of peaches, nectarines, and apricots, as the premium of rustication. **1890** J. DICKIE *Words of Faith*, etc. (1893) 342, I hope that your rustications, at this time, may set up your bodily vigour a little.

b. The condition naturally attaching to life in the country.

1771 SMOLLETT *Humph. Cl.* 18 Apr., I am here in a state of absolute rustication. **1809** MALKIN *Gil Blas* IV. iv. ¶12 A young person brought up in a state of rustication, and.. unacquainted with the manners of a court.

2. Temporary dismissal from a university; an instance or period of this.

1734 in Peirce *Hist. Harvard Univ.* (1833) App. 142 All public admonitions, rustications, and degradations,.. shall be by the President and Tutors. **1779** JOHNSON *L.P., Milton*, It seems plain from his own verses to Diodati, that he had incurred *rustication*, a temporary dismission into the country, with perhaps the loss of a term. **1825** C. WESTMACOTT *English Spy* I. 129 A severe imposition and sometimes rustication. **1854** 'C. BEDE' *Verdant Green* II. vi, A humorous series of plucks, rustications, and heavy debts. **1887** DOWDEN *Life Shelley* I. iii. 122 A sentence of rustication might have sufficed for an offence against discipline.

3. The action of banishing, or the state of being banished, into the country.

1751 JOHNSON *Rambler* No. 195 ¶12 His father, after some threats of rustication.., reduced the allowance of his pocket. **1806** *Col. Hutchinson's Mem.* 56 *note*, From the moment of Cardinal Richlieu's coming into power under Louis the XIIIth to Neckar's return to power after his rustication under Louis XVIth. **1818** SCOTT *Rob Roy* ii, I persuaded myself, that all I had to apprehend was some temporary alienation of affection—perhaps a rustication of a few weeks. **1869** TOZER *Highl. Turkey* I. 62 Athos.. is used as a place of rustication for refractory prelates.

4. *Arch.* The action or practice of rusticating masonry; the style of masonry produced by this.

1815 J. SMITH *Panorama Sci. & Art* I. 174 An ornament.. of large square blocks as parts of the shaft, which are called rustication, and are sometimes roughened. **1841** *Penny Cycl.* XX. 272/1 Rustication.. is now almost entirely banished from architectural design. **1895** *Times* 14 Jan. 14/2 A good building.. spoilt by an abuse of 'rustication', which deprives it of all dignity.

b. A rustic feature or part.

1839 *Civil Eng. & Arch. Jrnl.* II. 381/1 The destruction of the form of the columns, rustications, &c. **1848** RICKMAN *Archit.* 17 Many architects have given to this order.. large square blocks, as parts of the shaft, which are called rustications.

rusti'catory, *a. nonce-wd.* [f. RUSTICATE *v.* + -ORY^2.] Pertaining to rustication.

1823 *Spirit Publ. Jrnls.* 523 St. George's Day does not interfere with the rusticatory arrangements of the fashionable hemisphere folks.

ru'sticial, *a. pseudo-arch.* = RUSTICAL *a.* 4.

1820 SCOTT *Monast.* xiv, Our English courtiers of the hodiernal strain.. have infinitely refined upon the plain and rusticial discourse of our fathers.

'**rusticism.** *rare*$^{-1}$. [f. RUSTIC *a.* + -ISM.] A rustic idiom or expression.

1882 GOSSE in *Grosart's Spenser* III. p. xvi, Extravagant and almost laughable rusticisms.

rusticity (rʌ'stɪsɪtɪ). Also 6 rustycyte, 6–7 rusticitie. [ad. F. *rusticité* (1460) or L. *rusticitas*: see RUSTIC *a.* and -ITY.]

1. Lack of breeding, culture, or refinement; clownishness, awkwardness.

1531 ELYOT *Governor* III. xvii. (1880) II. 309 Which in them was neyther folisshenes nor yet rusticitie, but of a prudent consideracion. **1590** SPENSER *F.Q.* III. vi. 1 Seemeth that such wilde woodes should far expell All civile usage and gentility, And gentle sprite deforme with rude rusticity. **1643** SIR T. BROWNE *Relig. Med.* I. § 13 The wisedome of God receives small honour from those vulgar heads that rudely stare about, and with a grosse rusticity admire his workes. **1691** HARTCLIFFE *Virtues* 185 Rusticity.. is nothing but a stupid Sullenness, that makes men appear Ill-bred, and unfit for Company. **1760** *Phil. Trans.* LII. 68 The aukward rusticity of a stranger, introduced the first time to your presence. **1820** SCOTT *Abbot* xxiv, Yet these high accomplishments were mixed with an air of rusticity and harebrained vivacity. **1880** 'OUIDA' *Moths* II. 253 Ischl has a little rusticity still in her elegant manners.

b. An instance of this.

1803 MAR. EDGEWORTH *Manufacturer* Wks. 1832 I. 62 You must not think ill of my cousin, notwithstanding his little rusticities. **1814** JANE AUSTEN *Mansf. Park* ii, The little rusticities and awkwardnesses..necessarily wore away.

2. Lack of intellectual culture; ignorance.

1583 FULKE *Def. Tr. Script.* i. 51 To condemne all men,.. out of your readers chaire at Rhemes, of ignorance,.. barbarusnes, rusticity. **1695** WOODWARD *Nat. Hist. Earth* II. 95 An universal Rusticity presently took place... Those first Ages of the new World were simple, and illiterate to Admiration. **1809** MALKIN *Gil Blas* VII. xiii, He began laughing at my rusticity. Well,..replied he,..this sonnet would confuse clearer heads than thine.

3. Of language, composition, etc.: Lack of polish or refinement; uncouthness, inelegance.

1565 COOPER *Thesaurus* s.v. *Sal*, Pleasant sayinges without rusticitie. **1589** PUTTENHAM *Eng. Poesie* III. xxi. (Arb.) 256 Some manner of speaches are alwayes intollerable,..namely barbarousnesse, incongruitie,.. rusticitie, and all extreme darknesse. **1697** DRYDEN *Virgil, Ded. to Ld. Chudleigh*, There is a kind of Rusticity in all those pompous Verses. **1741** MIDDLETON *Cicero* (1742) III. xii. 318 It was in Cicero's time, that the old rusticity of the Latin muse first began to be polished. **1839** HALLAM *Hist. Lit.* II. v. §61 Praises which we cannot bestow on the uncouth provincial rusticity of Spenser. **1858** MARTINEAU *Stud. Chr.* 303 A taste formed from the Study of Plato and Seneca may be offended by the rusticity of Mark.

b. A rustic expression.

1711 ADDISON *Spect.* No. 59 ¶3 Obsolete Words and Phrases, unusual Barbarisms and Rusticities. **1871** R. ELLIS *Catullus* xxxvi. 19 But ye verses,..Rank rusticities, empty vapid annals Of Volusius.

4. Rustic or rural life, quality, or character.

1638 JUNIUS *Paint. Ancients* 183 He was a man that might seeme to be more given to rusticitie than to such kinde of delicacies. **1713** *Guardian* No. 30 ¶10, I may be allowed, for the Honour of our Language, to suppose it more capable of that pretty Rusticity than the Latin. **1785** WALPOLE *Let. to J. Pinkerton* 26 June, He..could captivate a lord of Augustus's bed-chamber, and tempt him to listen to themes of rusticity. **1809** PINKNEY *Trav. France* 276 The town.. had an air of rusticity and recluseness which might have delighted a romantic imagination. **1883** *Harper's Mag.* July 165/1 There is little left of the sweet rusticity of Dulwich.

b. A rural feature or characteristic; a rural thing or object.

1662 EVELYN *Chalcogr.* 68 What they graved after Mich. de Vos, and others whose Rusticities they set forth. **1669** WORLIDGE *Syst. Agric.* Pref., These Rusticities..supply us for our Necessities and advantages; for without this Art none in City or Country could subsist. **1873** BROWNING *Red Cott. Nt.-cap* 114 Nought you missed Of one and all the sweet rusticities!

†**5.** Rusticated style (of masonry). *Obs.*$^{-1}$

1730 A. GORDON *Maffei's Amphith.* 212 The Rusticity of the Work..seems to contribute towards Grandeur and Strength.

6. *collect.* Country persons.

1831 CARLYLE *Sart. Res.* I. iii. (1902) 16 A thousand carriages, and wains, and cars, come tumbling-in with Food, with young Rusticity, and other Raw Produce.

rusticize (ˈrʌstɪsaɪz), *v.* [f. RUSTIC *a.* + -IZE.]

1. *intr.* To speak in a country dialect.

1822 *New Monthly Mag.* V. 244 Our farmers neither wear cowskin waistcoats, nor rusticise like Hobbinol and Diggon Davy.

2. *trans.* To relegate to the country.

1841 *Blackw. Mag.* XLIX. 488 What can interest you or me, Eusebius, rusticized in this odious February?

3. To render rustic in appearance.

1868 BROWNING *Ring & Bk.* viii. 1309 We changed our garb And rusticized ourselves with uncouth hat [etc.].

ˈ**rusticly**, *adv.* Now *rare.* [f. RUSTIC *a.* + -LY².] In a rustic manner; rustically.

c **1611** CHAPMAN *Iliad* XXIII. 416 'To you it seems so,' rusticly Ajax Oileus said. **1620** VENNER *Via Recta* viii. 168 If..the appetite be..yeelded unto, and the body not rusticly strong. *a* **1700** EVELYN *Diary* 1646 (Switzerland), The people very clownish and rusticly clad, after a very odd fashion. **1813** J. C. HOBHOUSE *Journ.* App. Albanian Lang. (ed. 2) 1142 *Katundsisct*, rusticly.

ˈ**rusticness.** *rare.* [f. RUSTIC *a.* + -NESS.] Rustic quality; rusticity.

1684 tr. *Agrippa's Van. Arts* iii. 20 Lucilius is damn'd for the rustickness of his hobling Verse. **1838** CARLYLE *Lect. Hist. Lit.* (1892) 145 There is in him [Knox] a genuine, natural rusticness—a decided earnestness of purpose.

rusticoat: see RUSTY *a.*¹ 10 c.

rustily (ˈrʌstɪlɪ), *adv.* [f. RUSTY *a.*¹ + -LY².] In a rusty manner.

a **1586** SIDNEY *Arcadia* I. (1622) 21 Their armour they should as well as might be, couer, or at least make them looke so rustilie, and ill fauouredly as might well become such wearers. **1609** W. M. *Man in Moone* D 3 b, His spurres haue scaped a scouring, they looke so rustily. **1663** COWLEY *Cutter Colman St.* Wks. (Grosart) I. 200/2 Nay, if thou do'st begin but to look rustily—I'l ha' thee Paint thy self. **1865** DICKENS *Mut. Fr.* II. xvi, Other joints working rustily in the morning.

Comb. **1837** DICKENS *Pickw.* xxx, In conversation with a rustily-clad, miserable-looking man.

rustiness (ˈrʌstɪnɪs). [f. RUSTY *a.*¹ and *a.*³]

1. The state of being rusty; rusty condition or quality; rust. Freq. *fig.*

1398 TREVISA *Barth. De P.R.* XVI. ii. (Bodl. MS.), [Gravel] haþ vertu to clense metal and to waste þe rustynes of metal bi frotinge..þereof. *c* **1450** *Cov. Myst.* (Shaks. Soc.) 47 Rustynes of synne is cawse of these wawys. **1491** CAXTON *Vitas Patr.* (W. de W. 1495) II. 205/1 Yf thou be harde as is the yron thou shalt lese thy Rustynes by fyre. **1547–64** BALDWIN *Mor. Phil.* (Palfr.) 333 Idlenesse..is a thing like a cankering rustinesse both to the body and to the soule. **1576** FLEMING *Panopl. Epist.* 357 Let us rub off the rustinesse of our tongues. **1601** LYLY *Love's Metam.* II. i, Her teeth hollow and red with rustinesse. **1679** C. NESS *Antichrist* Pref., If the rustiness of gold witness against men at the last day. **1851** HAWTHORNE *Ho. Sev. Gables* i, The rustiness and infirmity of age gathered over the venerable house itself. **1882** *Garden* 3 June 389/1 This rustiness [in strawberries] is caused by the sun.

2. *slang.* Irritableness, bad temper.

1860 WHYTE MELVILLE *Mkt. Harb.* 104 Old Isaac,.. subject to occasional 'rustiness', and imbued with a strong aversion to what he called being 'put upon'. **1900** G. B. SHAW *Let.* 14 Mar. (1972) II. 156 In the old days I was always standing between Bland and the rustinesses that used to come from his Tory imperviousness to the Radical notions with which Socialism was adulterated.

ˈ**rusting,** *vbl. sb.* [f. RUST *v.*¹ + -ING¹.] The fact or process of developing rust or of becoming rusty: **a.** Of metals.

1398 TREVISA *Barth. De P.R.* XVII. cxii. (Bodl. MS.), Clene oile kepiþ briȝt yren fro rustinge. **1562** J. HEYWOOD *Prov. & Epigr.* (1867) 210 Great diffrence betweene rubbyng and rustyng. **1633** P. FLETCHER *Purple Isl.* VIII. xxiv. In an iron grave Himself protects his god [gold] from noysome rusting. **1667** *Phil. Trans.* II. 494 The rusting of Iron, in such houses as front the Sea. **1728** CHAMBERS *Cycl.* s.v. *Printing*, They rub it over with Oil of Olives, to prevent its rusting. **1792** W. H. MARSHALL *W. England* (1796) II. 320 These fractures are occasioned by the rusting of the iron. **1844** H. STEPHENS *Bk. Farm* I. 182 These parts are all made of copper, to withstand rusting from the water. **1878** HUXLEY *Physiogr.* 75 The air must be..connected with the phenomenon of rusting.

fig. **1597** in Ellis *Orig. Lett.* Ser. I. III. 41, I have been enforced this day to scour up my old Latin that hath lain long in rusting. **1887** MISS BRADDON *Like & Unl.* vii, 'Do you call this rusting,' he asked tenderly.

b. Of grain.

1398 TREVISA *Barth. De P.R.* XVII. cxv. (Bodl. MS.), Barlich..is ripe & igadered ere corupcionne oþer rostinge falle vpon whete. **1674** FLAVEL *Husbandry Sp.* xiii. 118 Sad relapses like blasts and rustings do often fade it, when it's even ready for the harvest.

ˈ**rusting,** *ppl. a.* [f. RUST *v.*¹ + -ING².]

1. Causing rust. In quot. *fig.*

1749 CHESTERF. *Lett.* (1792) II. 167 Sottish drinking,.. rusting sports, such as fox-chases, horse-races, &c.

2. Becoming rusty, developing rust.

1884 *Harper's Mag.* Oct. 754/2 The long grass..hides their rusting forms. **1888** *Pall Mall G.* 7 May 5/2 The degenerate cattle-lifters..still nurse their rusting swords in their arms.

rustique, obs. form of RUSTIC.

rustle (ˈrʌs(ə)l), *sb.* [f. the vb.]

1. A continuous succession of light crisp sounds produced by some kind of movement.

1759 JOHNSON *Idler* No. 44 ¶4 When the noise of a torrent, the rustle of a wood, the song of birds, or the play of lambs, had power to fill the attention. **1820** KEATS *Fancy* 41 Thou shalt hear..Rustle of the reaped corn. **1841** B. HALL *Patchwork* III. x. 196 The rustle of bank-notes could also just be heard. **1877** MRS. OLIPHANT *Makers Flor.* xii. 300 For half an hour there was silence, except from the rustle of the multitude which knelt around.

2. *U.S. colloq.* Bustle, hustle.

1899 'R. CONNOR' *Sky Pilot* xxi, It's about time for me to get a rustle on.

rustle (ˈrʌs(ə)l), *v.* Forms: 4 rouschel-, 6–7 rushle; 5 rousle, rossle, 6–7 russel (6 *Sc.* russil), 7 russle; 5 roustle, rustel (-ely), 5– rustle. [Imitative: cf. older Flem. *ruysselen*, *rijsselen*, Fris. *risselje*, *russelje*, Du. *ridselen*, *ritselen* in the same sense.]

1. a. *intr.* Of things: To give forth a continuous succession of light, rapid, crisp sounds, as the result of some kind of movement.

1398 TREVISA *Barth. De P.R.* XVI. i. (Tollemache MS.), Yf it were þruste and brosid to gederes in a mannis honde, hit schulde rustel [*v.r.* rustely] and make noyse for drynesse and hardnesse. *c* **1400** *Siege of Troy* 136 (MS. Harl. 525) in *Archiv neu. Spr.* LXXII. 15 There were..baners rustland with þe wynde. **1565** COOPER *Thesaurus*, *Strepito*, to make noyse often: to make a great noyse: to rustle. **1603** SHAKS. *Meas. for M.* IV. iii. 38 He is comming Sir,..I heare his Straw russle. **1638** JUNIUS *Paint. Ancients* 41 When the wind-shaken ropes rumble and rustle. **1791** BURNS *Tam O' Shanter* 51 The storm without might rair and rustle, Tam did na mind the storm a whistle. **1815** SHELLEY *Alastor* 104 The dry leaf rustles in the brake. **1843** CARLYLE *Past & Pres.* (1858) 146 Scotland itself still rustled shaggy and leafy. **1897** W. H. THORNTON *Rem. W.-Co. Clergyman* vi. 177 A person had been terrified by hearing the curtains of the bed rustle.

b. Of persons or animals: To cause sounds of this nature to be produced.

1560 ROLLAND *Seven Sages* 54 The Falcon this behalding ..With hir wingis scho russillit & rang hir bellis. **1560** DAUS tr. *Sleidane's Comm.* 114 b, Beynge charged to make a signe, ..he rustleth and maketh a noyse agayne. **1603** KNOLLES *Hist. Turkes* (1621) 1158 Which caused them..to russle with their armes, to keepe a stir with their souldiours. **1627** E. F. *Hist. Edw. II* (1680) 110 To russle boysterously, or grumbling murmur some unsavoury Prayers. **1700** DRYDEN *Pal. & Arcite* II. 183 So stands the Thracian herdsman.. and hopes the hunted bear, And hears him rustling in the wood. **1735** SOMERVILLE *Chase* IV. 421 Thro' reedy Pools Rustling they work their Way. **1819** S. ROGERS *Human Life* 382 The otter rustling in the sedgy mere. **1845** MRS. S. C. HALL *Whiteboy* xi, She rustled at an old cabinet, which she unlocked and locked, as if placing the papers therein. **1892** E. REEVES *Homeward Bd.* 18 Woman rustles, and bustles, and creaks, and fusses.

2. With advs. or preps.: **a.** To come, go, move, etc., with a rustling sound.

In the earliest quots. the prominent idea appears to be that of rapid motion, and this may be the origin of the special development in sense 4.

a **1586** SIDNEY *Arcadia* I. (1605) 63 As he let his sword fall vpon it, another knight all in blacke came rustling in. **1594** LYLY *Mother Bombie* v. iii, These minstrelles..rustle into euery place. **1607** TOPSELL *Four-f. Beasts* (1658) 372 Four strong men, armed with shields,..rustle in upon the lion lying in his den. He..with such celerity rustleth upon them as if it were some storm or tempest. **1728–46** THOMSON *Spring* 93 Where the deer rustle through the twining brake. **1840** CARLYLE *Lect. Heroes* i. ¶27 All Life is figured by them as a Tree... It grows there, the breath of Human Passion rustling through it. **1896** A. E. HOUSMAN *Shropshire Lad* xli, In the woodland brown I heard the beechnut rustle down.

b. To go about, be finely dressed, *in* some material which rustles.

1598 SHAKS. *Merry W.* II. ii. 68 All Muske, and so rushling, I warrant you, in silke and golde. **1611** —— *Cymb.* III. iii. 24 This life Is..Prouder, then rustling in unpayd-for Silke. **1691** *The Weesils* ii. 7 His Wife too, in..richest Silks, can rustle with the best. **1750** GRAY *Long Story* vi, A brace of Warriors, not in buff, But rustling in their silks and tissues. **1788** [see BUSTLE *sb.*²]. **1816** SCOTT *Antiq.* vi, The elderly lady rustled in silks and satins. **1847** TENNYSON *Princ.* i. 200 He..holp To lace us up, till, each, in maiden plumes We rustled.

3. *trans.* **a.** To cause to move in some way with a rustling sound. Const. with advs. and preps.

1648 J. BEAUMONT *Psyche* XIV. ccx, And many sleeping Saints by it awaked, Russled their Dust together and gat up. **1853** M. ARNOLD *Scholar Gypsy* iii, Air-swept lindens.. rustle down their perfum'd showers Of bloom on the bent grass. **1870** LOWELL *Study Wind.*, *Gd. Word Winter*, Euroclydon..rustles snowflakes against the pane.

refl. **1892** *Cornhill Mag.* May 547 Mrs. Aylmer rose horrified, and rustled herself out of the room.

b. To shake or stir with a rustling sound.

a **1821** [see RUSTLED]. **1838** LYTTON *Leila* I. iii, Nor was the stillness broken, save as an occasional breeze..rustled the fragrant leaves of the citron and pomegranate. **1856** EMERSON *Eng. Traits, Religion*, They who come to the old shrines find apes and players rustling the old garments. **1868** MORRIS *Earthly Par.* (1870) I. II. 619 From off the sea a little west-wind blew, Rustling the garden leaves like sudden rain.

4. orig. *U.S. colloq.* **a.** *intr.* To bestir oneself or move about vigorously; to work with strenuous energy; to hustle, push one's way.

1872 R. B. JOHNSON *Very Far West* xiv. 195 I've rustled upwards from a picayune printin' office down to New Orleans. **1883** *Advance* (Chicago) 31 May, A man who earns his livelihood by exposure and hard riding is said to 'rustle'. **1891** C. ROBERTS *Adrift Amer.* 52, I rustled round but could not get a job, as things were very slack.

b. *trans.* To shift, deal with, rapidly; to pick up, acquire, or get together by one's own exertions. Now usu. with *up*.

1844 *Spirit of Times* 14 Sept. 343/3 He nailed my thumb in his jaws, and rostled up a handful of dirt & throwed it in my eyes. **1882** *Cent. Mag.* XXIV. 508/2 'Rustle the things off that table,' means clear the table in a hurry. **1890** L. C. D'OYLE *Notches* 45, I was out one day after antelope (I 'rustled' all my meat, except a ham now and then as a luxury). **1891** *Advance* 29 Jan. 101/2 Some of the members have arranged..to go out on the hills and 'rustle up' wood. **1894** *Harper's Mag.* Jan. 299. I'll sure buy Pedro back off him just as soon as ever I rustle some cash. **1903** A. ADAMS *Log of Cowboy* xxi. 332 Honeyman being excused on agreeing to rustle the wood and water. **1919** *Punch* 29 Jan. 87/1 All George's performances in the art of rustling bivvies rank as star. **1931** 'DEAN STIFF' *Milk & Honey Route* viii. 81 Kid, you go out and rustle some breakfast and meet us at the water tank. **1944** M. LASKI *Love on Supertax* iii. 45 Do you think you can rustle me up something to eat? **1959** *Spectator* 11 Sept. 331/1 They put on their programme with such costumes as they could rustle up from Edinburgh's shops. **1978** G. GREENE *Human Factor* v. ii. 243 We may not be able to rustle up more than an omelette, Muller. Pot luck.

c. Of animals: to forage (for). Also *absol.* and *transf.*

1881 *N.Y. Times* 18 Dec. 4/3 Cattle, in winter, 'rustle' for food by nosing through the snow to the dried grass beneath. **1913** L. V. KELLY *Range Men* 109 The [Red River] settlement took up the ranching of cattle, the turning out of herds to rustle their own living. **1916** 'B. M. BOWER' *Phantom Herd* xiv. 243 He turns you out thinking he'll let you rustle for yourself awhile. **1924** R. CAMPBELL *Flaming Terrapin* iv. 61 As shepherd winds drove forth their foamy sheep To rustle through the verdure of the deep. **1925** *Chambers's Jrnl.* Mar. 168/1 It is accustomed to rustle its living through the long severe winters of its habitat. **1955** J. C. EWERS in *Bull. U.S. Bureau Amer. Ethnol.* No. 159. 42 Unless the snow was too deep..(i.e. over ca. 2 feet) they [*sc.* horses] generally could rustle enough food..to gain a meagre subsistence. **1961** R. P. HOBSON *Rancher takes Wife* vii. 111 The range horses never had to be fed hay, but rustled all year round. **1966** H. MARRIOTT *Cariboo Cowboy* ii. 32 One year with another most of the cattle, except the calves, bulls, and thin cows, all rustled out in most of these ranges for most of, if not all, the winter.

d. To gather, round *up*; also with *in* and *out*.

1896 G. W. DICE *Life* vi. 30, I was more fortunate than ever this time, and..'rustled up' a good big herd of cattle, which we shipped to Kansas City. **1903** A. ADAMS *Log of Cowboy* iv. 53 Our foreman..sent Honeyman to rustle in the horses. **1924** A. J. SMALL *Frozen Gold* iii. 81 Why ain't you rustlin' a crowd of the boys up to corral the swabs? **1947** 'N. BLAKE' *Minute for Murder* v. 101 He's to rustle out all his men..and post them round the building. **1965** G. MCINNES *Road to Gundagai* x. 183 Well, go and rustle up the rest of them.

e. To steal (cattle, horses, etc.) by rounding them up. Also *transf.* and *absol.*

1902 A. H. LEWIS *Wolfville Nights* xv. 234, I claims that this Bowlaig b'ar is guilty of rustlin' the mails an' must.. be hanged. **1910** W. M. RAINE *B. O'Connor* xix. 299 We're after them for rustling a bunch of Circle 33 cows. **1916** 'B. M. BOWER' *Phantom Herd* xiv. 243 You hold a grudge against your dad, and you rustle from him mostly. **1948** *Range Riders Western* May 30/1, I ain't ever rustled a cow in my life. **1951** L. MACNEICE tr. *Goethe's Faust* 163 One rustles cattle, one a wife.

Hence **'rustled** *ppl. a.*

a **1821** KEATS *Hyperion* II. 2 Hyperion slid into the rustled air. **1876** BROWNING *Forgiveness* 208 And turning, saw whose rustled gown Had told me my wife followed.

rustler ('rʌslə(r)). [f. RUSTLE *v.* + -ER[1].]

1. One who or that which rustles; a rustling leaf, bird, etc.

1820 SCOTT *Monast.* viii, The fairy hopes of my youth I have trodden under foot like those neglected rustlers [leaves]. **1838** *Fraser's Mag.* XVIII. 559 Not a rustler in the thicket moved, But he could name it.

2. a. An energetic or bustling man. *U.S.*

1872 R. B. JOHNSON *Very Far West* xiv. 191 There is the middle-class rustler, who starts a store.. upon credit. **1885** *Milnor* (Dakota) *Teller* 24 Apr. 2/6 One of the Lisbon rustlers lately sold one of his farms.. for $18 an acre. **1887** M. ROBERTS *Western Avernus* 183 He does not know much about saw-mills, but I just tell you he is a rustler.

b. A cattle-thief; also in extended and *transf.* uses. orig. *U.S.*

1882 *Blackw. Mag.* Mar. 273 A gang of 'rustlers'—as the lawless desperadoes who abound in Arizona, New Mexico and Texas are called. **1885** *Harper's Mag.* May 826/1 We could hear the stealthy tread of rustlers and Indians and murderous Mexicans. **1908** J. M. SULLIVAN *Criminal Slang* 20 *Rustler*, a horse thief. **1964** *Wall St. Jrnl* 9 Jan. 1/4 He covered the orange rustlers with a double-barreled shotgun. **1971** *Daily Tel.* 19 Apr. 2/1 East Anglian farmers were warned to beware of pig rustlers after 15 sows and five pigs .. were stolen. **1977** *Oxford Times* 16 Sept. 5/5 Police trying to round up horse rustlers in Oxfordshire have admitted the efforts often prove futile.

rustless ('rʌstlɪs), *a.* [f. RUST *sb.*[1] + -LESS.]

1. Free from rust; characterized by the absence of rust. Also *fig.*

1845 FORD *Handbk. Spain* II. 786 Mistaking the dry rustless climate of Castile for her own.. damp land. **1853** C. BRONTE *Villette* viii, When once a bloodless and rustless instrument was found, she was careful of the prize. **1880** BARING-GOULD *Mehalah* xxvi, The married life of some is smooth and shining and rustless like the gold.

2. Not liable to be rusted.

1856 RUSKIN *Mod. Paint.* IV. v. xvi. §17 A strength as of imperishable iron, rustless by the air. **1884** *Health Exhib. Catal.* 57/2 Soil Pipe Traps in rustless iron and stoneware.

rustling ('rʌslɪŋ), *vbl. sb.* [f. RUSTLE *v.*]

1. The action of the vb., in literal senses; an instance of this; a rustling sound.

1387 TREVISA *Higden* (Rolls) VI. 93 Wiþ som manere rouschelynge þat he made.. his felowe awook. **1565** COOPER *Thesaurus* s.v. *Crepitus*, The rustlyng or noyse of feete goyng. **1579** SPENSER *Sheph. Cal.* Mar. 72, I.. then heard no more rustling. **1603** HOLLAND *Plutarch's Mor.* 437 The great rustling and clattering that harneis and armor made. **1641** MILTON *Reform.* II. Wks. 1851 I. 67 They would request us to indure still the russling of their Silken Cassocks. **1706** FARQUHAR *Recruiting Officer* IV. iii, I hear the rustling of silks. Fly, sir! tis madam Melinda. **1797** MRS. RADCLIFFE *Italian* i, They heard a sudden rustling of the branches. **1848** DICKENS *Dombey* i, His meditations.. were soon interrupted.. by the rustling of garments on the staircase. **1875** WHITNEY *Life Lang.* iv. 64 Containing a rustling or friction of the breath through a narrowed aperture.

2. *U.S. colloq.* Energetic, bustling activity.

1872 R. B. JOHNSON *Very far West* 191 'Rustling' is an Americanism, denoting the process of fighting against odds for a living. **1886** *Milnor* (Dakota) *Teller* 2 July 4/1 It may be expected that some tall rustling will be indulged in during the next few weeks.

3. Stealing (esp. cattle) from farms, ranches, etc. Also *transf.* and *attrib.*

1893 *Aberdeen* (S. Dak.) *Sun* 5 Jan. 7/4 Rustling cattle is an exciting trade and very profitable, but extremely hazardous. **1907** [see *cattle-rustling* s.v. CATTLE 8 a]. **1924** C. E. MULFORD *Rustlers' Valley* x. 118 There had been no signs of rustling for months. **1937** *Sun* (Baltimore) 23 Oct. 3/2 Battle front of the cotton-rustling racket.. is the Fabens Island area.. comprising 3,000 acres of rich cotton land. **1942** E. PAUL *Narrow St.* ix. 69 These crows had learned that living in Paris, near the central markets.., was easier than rustling in the country, exposed to the farmers' shotguns. **1963** *Wall St. Jrnl.* 11 Oct. 9 Add 'orange rustling' to the list of crimes against society. **1976** *Evening Post* (Nottingham) 14 Dec. 6/2 It's the peak of the shoplifting season.. a time for turkey rustling and Christmas tree thefts.

rustling ('rʌslɪŋ), *ppl. a.* [f. RUSTLE *v.*]

1. Producing or giving out a series of light crisp sounds.

1565 COOPER *Thesaurus, Squamæ crepitantes*, rustlyng scales. **1632** J. HAYWARD tr. *Biondi's Eromena* 60 They danced at the sound of the rustling waves. **1667** MILTON *P.L.* I. 768 The spacious Hall.. Thick swarm'd,.. Brusht with the hiss of russling wings. **1735** SOMERVILLE *Chase* II. 257 The rustling Stubbles bend Beneath the driving Storm. **1778** J. SCOTT *Mor. Ecl.* iii. 9 The bending osier, and the rustling reed. **1813** BYRON *Corsair* I. iv, Hoarse o'er her side the rustling cable rings. **1850** THACKERAY *Pendennis* lxvi, Under the dark arcades of the rustling limes. **1871** PALGRAVE *Lyr. Poems* 96 The rustling pine-tree-tops.

2. Of the nature of a rustle.

1565 COOPER *Thesaurus, Strepitus arboris*, the rustlinge noyse of a tree. **1611** COTGR., *Vacarme*,.. the rustling noyse made by armor, or armed men, in a battaile. **1755** *Phil. Trans.* XLIX. 22 Warts.. so stiff and elastic, that, when the hand is drawn over them, they make a rust[l]ing noise. **1835** J. DUNCAN *Beetles* (Nat. Lib.) 252 A rustling sound accompanies its flight. **1870** MORRIS *Earthly Par.* III. IV. 383 And therewithal a rustling noise he heard.

3. *U.S. colloq.* Bustling, energetic, active.

1882 *Cent. Mag.* XXIV. 508/2 To do a rustling business is to carry on an active trade. **1884** *Milnor* (Dakota) *Teller* 17 Oct. 8/1 A rustling real estate dealer of Forman.. was in the city most of the week.

Hence **'rustlingly** *adv.*, with a rustling noise; so as to rustle.

1778 [W. H. MARSHALL] *Minutes Agric., Digest* 67 Do not put Hay into Stack before it be rustlingly dry. **1834** MEDWIN *Angler in Wales* II. 243 The blasts.. howled rustlingly over the dry heather and withered grass. **1887** *Old Man's Favour* III. ii, Rustlingly she rose, and majestically advanced with outstretched hands.

rustly ('rʌslɪ), *a. rare.* [f. RUSTLE *sb.* + -Y.] Given to rustling.

1513 DOUGLAS *Æneis* VIII. i. 75 Russly reidis dekis weill hys haris. **1886** RANDOLPH *Mostly Fools* II. xi. 295 She was very red, very rustly, very strainy in the seams. **1936** M. MITCHELL *Gone with Wind* xlviii. 851 She wanted a tafetta petticoat.. so rustly that the Lord God would think it was made of angels' wings. **1959** *N.Z. Listener* 13 Mar. 5/4, I always wrapped my sandwiches in cloth rather than rustly paper.

'rustproof, *a.* [See PROOF *a.* 1 b.] **a.** Of metal: not susceptible to corrosion by rust; rust-resistant.

1691 T. H[ALE] *Acc. New Invent.* 21 Being so Rust-proof in themselves. **1907** *T. Eaton & Co. Catal.* Spring & Summer 215/3 Three large cupboards.. each one has metal rust proof bottom. **1931** *Chambers's Jrnl.* June 414/1 (*caption*) A new rust-proof coating. **1960** *Farmer & Stockbreeder* 19 Jan. 45/2 Rust-proof heavy gauge pressed steel bowl. **1972** *Sat. Rev.* (U.S.) 27 May 4/2 The early safety-razor blades rusted, so I had to dry them... But soon came rustproof steel.

b. Of a plant: resistant to infection by rust.

1931 J. S. HUXLEY *What dare I Think?* i. 36 We can now produce relatively rust-proof wheat.

rustproof ('rʌstpruːf), *v.* [f. the adj.] *trans.* To make rustproof.

1910 *Cycling* 2 Feb. 95 (*heading*) Rust-proofing the bicycle. **1953** *Archit. Rev.* CXIV. 393 Before despatch each link was tested for size and strength and 'rust-proofed' by immersing it, when hot, in an oil bath and heating it again on removal until the oil dried on the surface. **1977** 'E. CRISPIN' *Glimpses of Moon* xii. 252 Was it practicable to rustproof metallic structures, as one did cars?

Hence **'rustproofed** *ppl. a.* Also **'rustproofer**, one who makes something rustproof.

1925 *Morris Owner's Man.* 83 The K.L.G. is a detachable plug consisting of three parts—a rustproofed steel body and gland nut and an insulated central electrode. **1960** *Farmer & Stockbreeder* 22 Mar. 138/2 (Advt.), Storage Bin. Substantially made from rust-proofed steel. **1976** *Globe & Mail* (Toronto) 4 Dec. 1/2 Car dealers were often able to avoid liability in those situations by saying that the customer's contract was with the rustproofer alone.

'rustproofing, *vbl. sb.* [f. prec. + -ING[1].]

1. The action or process of making something rustproof. Also *attrib.*

1918 *Aviation* 1 Aug. 40/2 The increased cost of.. processes of rust-proofing.. has turned attention to the safety transparent, rust-proof and acid-proof finish. **1931** *Machinery* Oct. 111/2 News comes from England of the development of a new process known as the 'thermo-zinc' rust-proofing method. **1941** STEINBECK & RICKETTS *Sea of Cortez* xiv. 135 The eventual disintegration of a stick of wood or a piece of iron.. is assured, even though it may be delayed by such protection.. as is afforded by painting and rustproofing. **1980** *Times* 29 Feb. 19 Rust-proofing methods are available which can delay by about five years the onset of corrosion.

2. A substance with which something is made rustproof.

1976 *Time* 20 Dec. 57/2 (Advt.), Each car receives 2 separate coats of rustproofing.

‖**'rustre.** Also 8 roustrie. [F. *rustre*, †*ruste* (? *rute*), of obscure history.]

1. *Her.* A charge having the form of a lozenge, with a round hole in the middle through which the field appears.

[**1680** MACKENZIE *Herauldry* 48 The English call their Figures Macles..; but if they be pierc'd round, the French call them *rustres*.] **1722** A. NISBET *Syst. Her.* I. 171 The Sub-Ordinaries... Fusils, Lozenge, Mascle, Roustrie, Frett [etc.]. *Ibid.* 211 Of the Rustre. **1762** tr. *Busching's Syst. Geogr.* V. 480 A lion crowned Or in a field sable, and below it eight black rustres in a field Or. **1838** *Penny Cycl.* XII. 141/2 The subordinate ordinaries,.. the Lozenge, the Fusil, the Mascle, and the Rustre. **1868** CUSSANS *Her.* (1893) 71 Some Armorists blazon a Rustre as a Mascle pierced round. **1880** *Encycl. Brit.* XI. 697/1 The lozenge, the mascle, and the rustre are all derived from the fret or fretty.

¶**2.** (See quot. 1824.)

This is due to a mere inference by Meyrick as to the origin of the heraldic charge. Cf. MASCLE *sb.*[1] 4.

1824 MEYRICK *Anc. Armour* III. Glossary, *Rustre*, a ring, or rather open scale, of a number of which hauberks were formed in the twelfth century. **1847** PARKER *Gloss. Her.* 270 Some ancient armour was composed of rustres sewn upon cloth.

Hence **'rustred** *ppl. a.*, furnished with rustres.

1818 MEYRICK in *Archaeol.* (1821) XIX. 126 Such an expression, seems more suitable to the rustred [mail]. **1824** —— *Anc. Armour* I. 27 The form of the rustred armour seems.. to have grown out of the ringed. **1877** DEMMIN *Arms & Armour* 310 The 'rustred' hauberk.. was protected by oval flattened rings, overlapping each other half way.

rusty ('rʌstɪ), *a.*[1] Forms: α. 1 rustiȝ, 4–6 rustye, 6–7 rustie, 4– rusty. β. (Chiefly *north.* and *Sc.*) 4 rousti, 5–6 roustie, 5–6, 8–9 rousty; 7 rowstie, 7–8 rowsty; 9 roosty. [OE. *rústiȝ* (f. *rúst* RUST *sb.*[1]), = Fris. *rûst-*, *roastich*, MDu. *roestich* (*rostich*; Du. *roestig*), OHG. *rostag* (MHG. *rostic*, G. *rostig*); also MDa. *rustich*, later *rustig*, *røstig*.]

In the 16th and 17th centuries frequently used as a term of general disparagement.

I. 1. Covered or affected with rust or red oxide of iron; rusted.

α. *c* **893** K. ÆLFRED *Oros.* V. xv. 250 þa wurdon Ianes dura fæste betyned, & his loca rusteȝa. *c* **1386** CHAUCER *Prol.* 618 By his syde he bar a rusty blade. **1390** GOWER *Conf.* III. 321 He out breide A rusti swerd. *c* **1440** *Jacob's Well* 233 þou.. seruyst, & worschepyst.. þe world, þi rusty monye, þi rotyn muk. **1481** CAXTON *Godfrey* cxxvii. 191 Their swerdes rusty, their gownes.. were old and roten. *a* **1533** LD. BERNERS *Huon* liv. 182 He.. toke out of his cofer an olde rusty swerde.. & spere with a rusty hed. **1590** SPENSER *F.Q.* I. v. 20 Coleblacke steedes.. That on their rustie bits did champ, as they were wood. **1614** RALEIGH *Hist. World* I. (1634) 167 The rustie Axe or other Instrument of a Carpenter or Carver. **1663** BUTLER *Hud.* I. i. 358 The trenchant blade, Toledo trusty, For want of fighting was grown rusty. **1719** DE FOE *Crusoe* I. 330 The Money.. had lain by me so long useless, that it was grown rusty, or tarnish'd, and could hardly pass for Silver. **1784** COWPER *Task* II. 746 Bars and bolts Grew rusty by disuse. **1824** W. IRVING *Tales Trav.* I. 48 The steward had a rusty blunderbuss; the coachman a loaded whip. **1877** BESANT & RICE *Harp & Crown* xxxiv. 328 A rusty spur, and one or two fragments of pottery.

β. *a* **1400** *Octavian* (Percy Soc.) 32 Rowsty were the naylys. *c* **1489** CAXTON *Sonnes of Aymon* 117 Theyr harneys was all rousty, and theyr sadylles and brydelles all roten. **1639** in *Glouc. Gloss.* (1890) 197 For dust, wee say, doust: rowsty, for rusty. **1789** ROSS *Helenore* (ed. 3) 64 To air his rousty coin. **1828** CARR *Craven Gloss.*, *Rousty*, rusty.

†**2.** Morally foul or corrupt. *Obs.*

1362 LANGL. *P. Pl.* A. VII. 66, I schal fynden hem heore fode.. Saue.. Robert þe Ribaudour, for his rousti wordes. *c* **1412** HOCCLEVE *De Reg. Princ.* 1428 He rekkeþ neuer how rusty ben his schepe. **1422** tr. *Secreta Secret., Priv. Priv.* 136 Al the roialme thanne.. lothit for that rousty Synne. **1579** TOMSON *Calvin's Serm. Tim.* 208/1 He.. sheweth that his soule is very roustie, & full of filthe. *c* **1586** C'TESS PEMBROKE *Ps.* CXL. i, Men.. Whose rusty lipps enclose A pois'nous sword.

3. Of persons: Presenting an appearance suggestive of something old and rusted.

? *a* **1366** CHAUCER *Rom. Rose* 159 Ful hidous was she for to sene, Ful foul and rusty was she. *a* **1529** SKELTON *Bouge of Court* 345 Wyth that came Ryotte,.. A rusty gallande, to-ragged and to-rente. **1570** FOXE *A. & M.* (ed. 2) 1592/2 Cranmer.. was brought to them with a great number of rusty bilmen. **1688** EARL CLARENDON *Diary* 11 Dec., There was a guard by St. Giles's of rusty ruffians, kept by Lord Lovelace's order. **1721** N. AMHERST *Terræ Fil.* No. 46 (1726) 247 A great many of these transitory foplings, who came to the university with their fathers, rusty old country farmers. **1730** SWIFT *Panegyr. on the Dean* Wks. 1751 X. 165 What can my Lady mean, Conversing with that rusty D.. n! **1824** W. IRVING *T. Trav.* II. viii. 86 A little rusty, musty old fellow, always groping among ruins. **1850** DICKENS *Dav. Copp.* xxii, You never saw such a rusty Prince. **1882** F. MONTGOMERY *Misunderstood* v, He looked like a being of another sphere, among the rusty old gentlemen congregated in the room.

4. a. Lacking polish or refinement; rough, rude, or rugged in manner or behaviour; surly, morose, churlish.

a **1500** in Ashm. *Theatr. Chem.* (1658) 208 Therefor make no Man of thy Councell rude nor rustie. *a* **1529** SKELTON *Magnyfycence* 768 Cankard Jacke Hare, loke thou be not rusty. **1594** NASHE *Unfort. Trav.* Wks. (Grosart) V. 54 Diogenes was one of the first and formost of the ring-leaders of this rustie morosotie. **1651** FIRMIN *Serious Quest.* 36 There are companies of rusty, rugged, rich fellowes in our Parishes. *a* **1700** B. E. *Dict. Cant. Crew*, *Rusty-gutts*, an old blunt Fellow. *c* **1720** PRIOR *Daphne & Apollo* 12 Nor ill bred swain, nor rusty clown, am I. **1740** SOMERVILLE *Hobbinol* II. 180 But hostile Rage Inquisitive found out the rusty Swain. **1833** F. & A. TENNYSON *Poems* 153 You did mingle blame with praise, Rusty Christopher.

†**b.** *Sc.* Of a rime or verse: Rough, rugged, unpolished. *Obs.*

1501 DOUGLAS *Pal. Hon.* Concl. 8 Ressaue this roustie rurall rebaldrie, Laikand cunning, fra thy pure leige vnleird. **1560** ROLLAND *Seven Sages* To Rdr., Ye may persaue that be this roustie ryme. *a* **1585** POLWART *Flyting* 146 Roustie ratrimes.

c. Hoarse, raucous, harsh, grating. Also *transf.*

1570 B. GOOGE *Pop. Kingd.* IV. (1880) 50 b, Straight the Priest with rustie throte, alowde begins to cry. **1606** HOLLAND *Sueton.* 18 A smal and rusty [*margin* Or hoarse] voice though he had. **1697** COLLIER *Ess. Mor. Subj.* (1709) I. 243 If any of the Council or Witnesses happen to have a Rusty Voice, or a Fantastical Face. **1728** SWIFT *Mullinix & Timothy* Wks. 1751 VII. 211 When they hear his rusty Voice, With what Impatience they rejoice. **1787** TAYLOR *Sc. Poems* 4 (E.D.D.), Upo' that hint I scour'd my rusty throat. **1868** ALEX. SMITH *Last Leaves* 72 The rusty caw of the homeward-sliding rook. **1924** R. CAMPBELL *Flaming Terrapin* iii. 47 Huge carrion crows came rasping rusty jaws. **1936** J. B. PRIESTLEY *They walk in City* vii. 192 All the time his rusty voice went on and on, half jeering at himself, half mocking the audience. **1938** M. K. RAWLINGS *Yearling* x. 95 They [*sc.* cranes] made a great circle against the sunset, whooping their strange rusty cry that sounded only in their flight. **1967** G. F. FIENNES *I tried to run Railway* ii. 14 At 87 [he] talked in his slow, rusty voice as if he were still on the job.

5. a. Stiff, lacking in alertness or activity (of body or mind), through want of exercise or old age.

1508 DUNBAR *Tua Mariit Wemen* 141, I haue conditioun of.. A ring with a ryall stane, or other riche iowell, Or rest of his rousty raid. **1537** *Thersytes* in Pollard *Miracle Plays* 129 My body so lusty, Whiche for lacke of exercise is nowe almost rustye. **1606** SHAKS. *Tr. & Cr.* I. iii. 263 A Prince calld Hector.. Who in this dull and long-continew'd Truce Is rusty growne. **1673** TEMPLE *Let. to Sir J. Temple* Wks. 1720 II. 294, I went to the King, and said.. that I would serve Him, as well as I could, though I doubted I was grown a little rusty, by lying still so long. **1768** WASHINGTON *Let.* Writ. 1889 II. 258, I presume, he has grown a little rusty in both [Latin and Greek], having had no benefit of his tutor since Christmas. **1854** EMERSON *Lett. & Soc. Aims, Immortality* Wks. (Bohn) III. 283 It is a perception that comes by the activity of the intellect; never to the lazy or rusty mind. **1861** *Times* 25 Sept., An artillery driver.. would, unless in constant exercise, get rusty. **1890** HUXLEY in *Life* (1900) II. xvi. 269, I am getting rusty in science—from disuse.

b. Of knowledge, accomplishments, etc.: Impaired by neglect; requiring to be revived or polished up.

1796 PORSON in Watson *Life* 134 For the benefit of those whose Greek is rather rusty with disuse, I have added a Latin version. **1873** HAMERTON *Intell. Life* III. ii. 82 Neglected pursuits become rusty. **1888** J. PAYN *Myst. of Mirbridge* x, To have to admit that her French was a little rusty.

6. That has fallen out of use or lost its freshness; old, antiquated, obsolete.

1551 ROBINSON tr. *More's Utopia* To P. Giles (1895) 10 Some there be that haue pleasure onely in olde rustie antiquities. **1601** CORNWALLIS *Ess.* I. vii, Come then, put away your rustie tradition all you that think not thus. **1678** BUNYAN *Pilgr.* II. (1900) 185 That Prayer.. has lain by till 'tis almost rusty. **1693** J. EDWARDS *Auth. O. & N. Test.* 315 The rusty and antique fragments of the primitive times. **1732** BERKELEY *Alciphr.* III. §7 Rusty declaimers upon the necessity and usefulness of the great points of Faith. **1842** LOVER *Handy Andy* xiii, 'Lord Bacon's sayings—' ''Pon my conscience,' said Murphy, 'both himself and his sayings are very *rusty* by this time'.

II. 7. Of plants: Affected with rust or mildew.

[**1398** TREVISA *Barth. De P.R.* XVII. lxv. (Bodl. MS.), Corupt dew þat comeþ.. in corne & makeþ as it were rede oþer rustye.] **1502** ARNOLDE *Chron.* (1811) 165 Yf an appyl tree begynne to roten or yf the aplys begynne to wex rusty, than ye barke of hym is syke. **1591** PERCIVALL *Sp. Dict., Añublado,* rustie wheate, *Rubiginosus.* **1865** *Chambers's Encycl.* VII. 301/2 The parsnip.. is apt to become *rusty*, if allowed to remain too long in the ground. **1880** DISRAELI *Endym.* 291 The spring corn had never grown, and the wheat was rusty.

8. a. Having the colour of rust; of a (disagreeable) light reddish brown; rubiginous, ferruginous; *spec.* in *Path.*, of sputa.

Frequently implying some impairment of the proper or original colour of the thing.

1528 PAYNELL *Salerne's Regim.* b iiij b, The other is called rusty coler, lyke to rusty iron. **1565** COOPER *Thesaurus*, s.v. *Dens*, Rough and rustie teeth. **1589** GREENE *Menaphon* (Arb.) 66 And send foorth Winter in hir rustie weede. **1607** TOPSELL *Four-f. Beasts* (1658) 205 His feet and nails be most sharp, his skin rusty, the hair very sharp. **1646** BP. HALL *Poems* 22 Here maist thou shame The rusty Violets, with the Crimson flame Of either cheek. **1763** MILLS *Syst. Pract. Husb.* II. 411 That thick substance which is red on garden-beans, [and] of a rusty colour on all kinds of corn. **1817** SCOTT *Ivanhoe* i, His own thick hair,.. scorched by the influence of the sun into a rusty dark-red colour. **1849** MURCHISON *Siluria* iii. 42 Associated above and below with black and rusty slates. **1882** *Garden* 18 Feb. 111/3 A cool dusky green, with rusty shadows.

absol. **1872** COUES *N. Amer. Birds* 172 Very young birds have some feathers skirted with rusty.

b. Of (dark) clothes: Showing signs of age or use; shabby, worn, or faded.

1709 *Tatler* No. 68 ¶7 A Poor Fellow.. with a rusty Coat. **1776** MME. D'ARBLAY *Early Diary*, *Let.* 5 Apr., Her cloak which was rusty and powdered, was flung half on and half off. **1818** LADY MORGAN *Autobiog.* (1859) 76 It was driven by a little dumpy coachman, in a livery.. old and rusty. **1848** DICKENS *Dombey* iii, They began to think their mourning was wearing rusty too. **1892** W. S. GILBERT *Foggerty's Fairy* 117 His rusty old suit of clothes was the cast-off of a waiter.

c. Of colours: Inclining towards, modified by, the colour of rust. (Cf. 10.)

1791 HAMILTON tr. *Berthollet's Dyeing* II. II. I. ii. 31 The processes employed for dyeing wool would only give a rusty black to silk. **1817** STEPHENS in *Shaw's Gen. Zool.* X. II. 472 The breast, belly, and vent, rusty red. **1822–34** *Good's Study Med.* (ed. 4) IV. 526 In this case the hair is directly hoary or of a yellowish or rusty white. **1882** *Garden* 1 Apr. 218/3 The Carrots.. turn a rusty yellow colour.

9. In special applications:

a. With names of birds, fishes, etc., as ***rusty bunting, flycatcher, grackle, oriole***; ***rusty dab, flat-fish, flounder***, etc.

Also in names of moths or butterflies, as ***rusty button, dot, mitre***, etc.; see Rennie *Butterfl. & M.* (1832).

1784 PENNANT *Arct. Zool.* II. 364 **Rusty Bunting* with head, neck, breast, and sides, rust-colored. **1839** STORER *Fishes Massach.* 141 The *Rusty Dab.. is occasionally brought to our market in the winter season only. **1848** BARTLETT *Dict. Amer.* 375 *Rusty Dab*.., the popular name of the Rusty Flat-fish, a fish found on the coast of Massachusetts and New York in deep water. **1888** GOODE *Amer. Fishes* 326 The Sand Dab, or rough Dab, *Hippoglossoides platessoides*, also sometimes known as the *Rusty Flounder. **1811** WILSON *Amer. Ornith.* III. Pref. p. xiii, *Rusty Fly-catcher, wings and tail black; plumage above brown; inhabits the southern states. *Ibid.* III. 41 *Rusty Grakle, *Gracula Ferruginea*. **1872** COUES *N. Amer. Birds* 159 Rusty Grackle,.. nearly all the feathers skirted with warm brown above, and brownish-yellow below. *c* **1700** in *Dampier's Voy.* (1729) III. 428 The *Rusty Mantiss. Resembles a dead Leaf. **1787** LATHAM *Gen. Syn. Birds* Suppl. I. 89 *Rusty Oriole... The edges of the feathers are rust-coloured.

b. With names of plants, as ***rusty fern, fig, gum, inga***.

c **1711** PETIVER *Gazophyl.* viii. 73 Small, round wing'd, Smyrna *Rusty Fern. **1889** MAIDEN *Useful Native Pl.* 538 *Ficus rubiginosa*,.. *Rusty Fig. **1847** LEICHHARDT *Jrnl.* II. 48 The range was openly timbered with white-gum, spotted-gum, Ironbark, *rusty-gum and the cypress-pine. **1889** MAIDEN *Useful Native Pl.* 236 *Angophora lanceolata*,.. Rusty Gum. *c* **1700** in *Dampier's Voy.* (1729) III. 434 *Rusty Inga. The Pods of this are flat and covered with a rusty coloured Hair.

c. ***rusty coal, crown bark, gold, gravel*** (see quots.).

1830 *Cumbld. Farm Rep.* 49 in *Husb.* III. (L.U.K.), Gravelly soil, on an open bottom of gravel, technically called a rusty gravel. **1860** *Eng. & Foreign Mining Gloss.* (ed. 2) 62 *Rusty coals*, coals discoloured by water or exposure to air. **1880** MARKHAM *Peruv. Bark* 40 The *C[hinchona] Chahuarguera* is the rusty crown bark of commerce... With this rusty crown bark are mixed larger quills particularly rich in the alkaloid called chinchonidine. **1881** RAYMOND *Mining Gloss., Rusty gold*,.. free gold, which does not easily amalgamate, the particles being coated, as is supposed, with oxide of iron.

d. ***rusty spot*** = RED SPOT 2.

1900 *Bull N.Y. Agric. Exper. Station* No. 183. 188 'Rusty Spot' is the name given to small yellowish-red points or patches scattered quite evenly throughout the mass of the cheese and having the general appearance of iron rust. *Ibid.* 189 Connell.. isolated from a rusty spot cheese an organism which he called *Bacillus rudensis*. **1958** E. M. FOSTER et al. *Dairy Microbiol.* ii. 20 *Lactobacillus plantarum* var. *rudensis* and *Lactobacillus brevis* var. *rudensis* have been implicated as causes of rusty spot defect in Cheddar cheese.

10. *Comb.* **a.** Qualifying adjs. and sbs. of colour, as ***rusty-brown, -brownish, -red***. (Cf. 8 c.)

1596 SPENSER *F.Q.* V. xii. 14 On his head a steele cap he did weare Of colour rustie browne, but sure and strong. **1758** G. EDWARDS *Glean. Nat. Hist.* II. 209 The whole bird ..is covered with feathers of a rusty-brownish or black colour. **1832** W. IRVING *Alhambra* I. 48 A tall meagre varlet, whose rusty-brown cloak [etc.]. **1863** *N. Brit. Rev.* May 375 A disease called rust,.. from the rusty-red or yellowish patches which it forms. **1872** COUES *N. Amer. Birds* 206 Upper parts ranging from the color of *gnoma* to a rusty-red.

b. ***rusty-dusty, rusty-fusty***, characterized by rust and dust or fustiness. Also *fig.* Also ***rusty-dusty*** *sb.*, the buttocks (*Black English*).

1593 G. HARVEY *Pierce's Superer.* Wks. (Grosart) II. 246 All the rusty-dusty iestes in a country. *Ibid.* 289 To how many rusty-dusty Waines was braue Liuy beholding? **1630** J. TAYLOR (Water P.) *Wks.* II. 24 Our cottage, that for want of use was musty, And most extremely rusty-fusty-dusty. **1849** in D. J. Browne *American Poultry Yd.* (1855) 47 None but the brave.. are likely to enjoy any favor from the present class of rusty-fusty colored beauties. **1864** *Daily Telegr.* 13 Oct., All your rusty-fusty British notions about comfort, civility, privacy, and the like. **1953** W. BURROUGHS *Junkie* iv. 42 A negro voice was singing, 'Get up, get up, woman, off your big fat rusty-dusty.' **1970** C. MAJOR *Dict. Afro-Amer. Slang* 99 *Rusty dusty*, the buttocks.

c. With sbs., as ***rusty-coat*** (attrib.), ***rusty-stove***; **rusty-back (fern)**, the scale fern, *Ceterach officinarum*

1782 J. ADAMS in *Fam. Lett.* (1876) 404 But how much more luxurious it would be to me to dine.. upon rusticoat potatoes with Portia! **1797** *Encycl. Brit.* (ed. 3) I. 96/2 *Acrosticum*, Rustyback, Wall rue, or Fork-fern. **1873** LELAND *Egypt. Sketch-Bk.* 118 There were many other shades besides anthracite, ranging from rusty-stove to sole-leather,.. old or new ivory, and so on. **1874** *Treas. Bot.* Suppl., *Rusty-Back*, a provincial name for *Blechnum Spicant*, and, according to other authorities, also for *Ceterach officinarum*. **1908** E. STEP *Wayside & Woodland Ferns* 50 The development of the sori gives a distinctly red hue to the underside and justifies the name Rustyback. **1945** A. B. JACKSON *Step's Wayside & Woodland Ferns* (ed. 2) 57 The Rusty-back Fern is pretty generally distributed in England. **1960** P. TAYLOR *Brit. Ferns & Mosses* 120 The Rusty-back Fern is mainly confined in Europe to the Mediterranean region, extending northwards up the Atlantic coast to Great Britain. **1976** *Westmorland Gaz.* 10 Sept. 10/2 Interest was aroused.. by seeing the Rusty-back and Wall-rue ferns on a wall.

11. a. Parasynthetic and other combs., as ***rusty-coated, -coloured, -rested, -voiced; rusty-looking, -old***, etc.

1615 CHAPMAN *Odyss.* XXII. 223 A broad and ancient rusty-rested shield. **1700** in *Dampier's Voy.* (1729) III. 434 The Pods.. are flat and covered with a rusty coloured Hair. **1820** SCOTT *Monast.* xvi, This rugged and decayed dungeon of rusty-coloured stone. **1837** P. KEITH *Bot. Lex.* 312 A number of rusty-looking spots or patches dispersed over the surface of the leaf. **1874** GARROD & BAXTER *Mat. Med.* 415 Marked with six rusty-coloured longitudinal stripes. **1883** *Cent. Mag.* Oct. 925/2 The snipe is certainly much better able to take care of himself than his rusty-coated cousin. **1912** W. OWEN *Let.* 2 July (1967) 148 A taciturn, rusty-voiced man. **1917** —— *Poems* (1963) 57 Finished fields, and wire-scrags rusty-old.

b. In the specific names of birds, plants, etc.

(*a*) **1784** PENNANT *Arct. Zool.* (1792) II. 153 Rusty-crowned Heron. Crest and hind part of the neck of a deep ferruginous color. **1787** LATHAM *Gen. Syn. Birds* Suppl. I. 170 Rusty-Collared Finch.. inhabits Terra del Fuego. **1817** STEPHENS in *Shaw's Gen. Zool.* X. II. 392 Rusty-throated Flycatcher (*Muscicapa gularis*). **1872** COUES *N. Amer. Birds* 214 Rusty-crowned Falcon... Crown ashy-blue, with a chestnut patch. **1880** *Cassell's Nat. Hist.* II. 57 The Rusty-spotted Cat,.. *Felis rubiginosa*.

(*b*) **1855** MISS PRATT *Flower. Pl.* V. 89 Don's Willow, or Rusty branched Willow. **1889** *Cent. Mag.* Aug. 553 *Olea ferruginea*, the rusty-leaved olive of the country between the upper Indus and the Suleiman mountains.

rusty ('rʌstɪ), *a.*[2] [var. of RESTY *a.*[2], perhaps by association with prec.] Reasty, rancid.

Very common in the 17th and 18th centuries, and still wide-spread in dialect use.

1515 BARCLAY *Egloges* iv. (1570) C iv b/2 Such rusty meates inblindeth so our brayne, That of our fauour the muses haue disdayne. **1577** B. GOOGE *Heresbach's Husb.* III. (1586) 152 b, The Bacon..; if you hang it in grete smoke at the first, it will be rustie. **1648** GAGE *West Ind.* 93 Though it were but to help him scrape rusty gammons of bacon. **1690** STRUTTON *Relat. Cruelties French* 15 An Ounce of rusty Pork with Bread and Beverage. **1745** W. THOMPSON *R.N. Adv.* (1757) 8 The Wind and Sun more forcibly convey themselves into the Flesh, which dries up its Juices, and makes it rusty. **1792** *Trans. Soc. Arts* X. 345 Preserving salted provisions from becoming rancid or rusty. **1847** C. BRONTË *J. Eyre* v, Indifferent potatoes and strange shreds of rusty meat, mixed and cooked together. **1898** BESANT *Orange Girl* II. xxvi, The beef may have been tough and the pork rusty.

rusty ('rʌstɪ), *a.*[3] Also 9 *dial.* rousty. [var. of RESTY *a.*[1], perhaps influenced by RUSTY *a.*[1]]

1. Of horses: Restive.

1562 J. HEYWOOD *Prov. & Epigr.* (1867) 142 This rude rustie, bolde blinde bayerd of mine.. chopt foorth. **1594** ? GREENE *Selimus* Wks. (Grosart) XIV. 213 Thinks he to stop my mouth with gold or pearle? Or rustie iades fet from Barbaria? **1787** 'G. GAMBADO' *Acad. Horsem.* (1809) 38 It is extremely wrong to put a gentleman on a restive horse. [*Foot-note.* A strange epithet this, and I wonder who coined it; tell me of a rusty horse, and I shall know what it means.] **1828–** in dial. glossaries (Cumb., Yks., Northampt., Heref.).

b. In phr. ***to ride***, or ***run, rusty***. Freq. of persons: To become intractable or obstinate; to be angry or annoyed; to take offence (cf. 3).

(*a*) **1709** *Brit. Apollo* No. 32. 3/2 How is't Apollo rides so rusty, Why so Grum, and why so Crusty? **1785** GROSE *Dict. Vulgar T.* s.v. *Rusty*, To ride rusty, to be sullen. **1821** SCOTT *Pirate* xxxix, How the devil am I to get the crew to obey me? Why, even Dick Fletcher rides rusty on me now and then. **1837** DICKENS *Pickw.* xli, 'Rides rather rusty,' said Mr. Roker, with a smile.

(*b*) **1764** *Ann. Reg., Chron.* 129/1 Great expectations from lord Shelburn's colt, but he ran rusty. **1855** LAWRENCE in Bosw. Smith *Life* (1883) I. 469 To add to my misery Neville Chamberlain has again run rusty. **1863** READE *Hard Cash* III. 199 They.. watched the yard till dusk, when its proprietor ran rusty and turned them out.

†**2.** *transf.* Of things. (Cf. RESTY *a.*[1] 2.)

1625 in Birch *Crt. & Times Chas. I* (1846) I. 36 There is much urging and spurring the parliament for supply and expedition, in both which they will prove somewhat rusty. **1656** OWEN *Mortif. Sin* vi, Indwelling distempers grow rusty and stubborn by continuance in ease and quiet.

3. *colloq.* Ill-tempered, cross, nasty. Chiefly in phr. ***to turn rusty*** (cf. 1 b).

1815 SCOTT *Guy M.* xxviii, The people got rusty about it. **1843** THACKERAY *Mr. & Mrs. Frank Berry* ii, You.. turn rusty because he forgets your last message. **1876** FARJEON *Love's Victory* xi, He never said a word to make the governor turn rusty. **1889** D. C. MURRAY *Dangerous Catspaw* 186 He was a bit rusty at first.

†'**rusty**, *v. Obs. rare.* [f. RUSTY *a.*[1]] *intr.* and *trans.* To become or make rusty.

1567 MAPLET *Greene Forest* 20 b, It.. rustieth; but being newe rubbed ouer with Sande and Salte, commeth to his olde colour againe. **1608** SYLVESTER *Du Bartas* II. iv. iii. *Schisme* 186 God so rustied every joynt, that there.. it could not stir. *a* **1618** RALEIGH *Rem.* (1661) 156 As the bonds of Reason and Love are immortal, so do all other chains.. both rustie and rot Noble parts.

'**rustyish**, *a. rare*[−1]. [f. RUSTY *a.*[1]] Somewhat rusty.

1803 MARY CHARLTON *Wife & Mistr.* IV. 22 If they gets ever so rustyish in the country, they always brightens up in Lunnon!

rut (rʌt), *sb.*[1] Forms: 5–6 rutte (5 ruthe), 5, 7 rutt, 7 rute; 6– rut. [a. OF. *rut*, var. of *ruit*:—pop. L. **rugīt-um* for L. *rugītum*, acc. of *rugītus*, f. *rugīre* to roar.]

1. The annually recurring sexual excitement of male deer; also, by extension, periodic sexual excitement in other animals, as goats, sheep, etc.

c **1410** *Master of Game* (MS. Digby 182) ii, þei [*sc.* harts] be in hir loue, þe whiche men calleth Rutte, aboute þe tyme of holy rode in Septembre. **1576** TURBERV. *Venerie* xvii. 45 During the time of their Rut, they [*sc.* harts] lyue with small sustenance. **1600** SURFLET *Countrie Farme* VII. xxiv. 845 Thus also they passe and spende both day and night, being so enraged and feruently caried away with the rut.. (alwaies following the steps and footings of the Hinde). **1646** SIR T. BROWNE *Pseud. Ep.* 127 This part in Deere.., about the end of their Rutt,.. sometimes becomes.. relaxed and pendulous. **1774** GOLDSM. *Nat. Hist.* (1824) I. 379 A short time after they [*sc.* stags] have furnished their horns, they begin to feel the impressions of the rut. *Ibid.* 381 In the time of rut it [the stag's voice] is even terrible. **1860** TANNER *Pregnancy* 49 During the rut or heat of animals. **1861** G. F. BERKELEY *Eng. Sportsman* iii. 41 They kill the bucks too late or when the 'rut' is coming on.

b. In phr. ***at*** or †***in (the) rut, to go to (the) rut***.

(*a*) *c* **1410** *Master of Game* (MS. Digby 182) ii, They sle.. eyther oþer, whann þei be in Rutte, þat is to say in þer loue. **1422** tr. *Secreta Secret., Priv. Priv.* 225 Of suche lokynge bene bestis in ruthe. **1575** LANEHAM *Let.* (1871) 31 Az ramz at their rut. **1576** TURBERV. *Venerie* xliv. 141 When a Hart hath bene .xiiii. dayes at Rut, then the Bucke doth but scarcely beginne. *a* **1653** G. DANIEL *Idyll* iii. 88 Antler'd and

Palmed now,..he goares them out Stand in his way, now rageing at the Rutt. **1714** GAY *Sheph. Week* Proeme, He [Theocritus] rightly, throughout his fifth Idyll, maketh his Louts..behold their Goats at Rut in all Simplicity. **1796** W. H. MARSHALL *W. England* II. 7 The Ewes are now at rut.
(*b*) *c* **1410** *Master of Game* (MS. Digby 182) iii, þe herte goth raþer to þe Rutte [than the buck]. **1523** FITZHERB. *Husb.* §37 Than the bucke goth to the rut, and so wolde the ramme. **1577** B. GOOGE *Heresbach's Husb.* III. (1586) 144 b, The time when you shall suffer them to go to rutte, is in Autume. **1626** BACON *Sylva* §758 We finde, that the Time of Going to Rut of Deere is in September.
transf. **1648** WINYARD *Midsummer-Moon* 1 He was begot ith' Dog-dayes, or at Michaelmas when his Dam went to Rut.

†**2.** The company of deer among which a stag goes to rut. *Obs.*
c **1410** *Master of Game* (MS. Digby 182) ii, Communlich the grettest hert..holdeth þe rutte and is maistre þerof. *Ibid.*, Also þer is diueres ruttes in þe forest. **1621** BURTON *Anat. Mel.* III. ii. I. i. (1651) 436 Lions and Harts, which.. many times kill each other, or compell them to abandon the rut, that they may remain masters in their places. **1640** EARL OF CORK in *Lismore Papers* 1st Ser. (1886) V. 162 One live Buck, to beat the Rutt withall.

3. *attrib.*, as ***rut-time***.
1598 SHAKS. *Merry W.* v. v. 15, I am heere a Windsor Stagge, and the fattest (I thinke) i'th Forrest. Send me a coole rut-time (loue). **1611** COTGR., *Ruité*, thats killed, or gotten, in rut-time. **1889** WESTERMARCK *Orig. Marriage* 36 Dr. Mohnike..mentions the occurrence of a rut-time with the Orang-utan.

rut (rʌt), *sb.*[2] Forms: *α.* 6- rut, 6 rupt, 7 rutt. *β.* 6 rotte, 7-8 rote, 7 -root(e. [Of obscure origin.
Usually regarded as a variant of ROUTE *sb.*, but the difference in vowel, and the rarity of *route* in the 16th cent., make this improbable. The spelling *rupt* suggests possible connexion with OF. *rupt, rut* stream, but the English sense is app. unknown in French. The question is also complicated by the variants *rote, root(e, rit(t*, occurring chiefly in the combs. *cart-rote, -root(e*, and *cart-ritt* (1649): cf. also RUCK *sb.*[3]]

1. A (deep) furrow or track made in the ground, esp. in a soft road, by the passage of a wheeled vehicle or vehicles.
1580 HOLLYBAND *Treas. Fr. Tong, Vne Ornière*, the rut or tracke of a wheele. **1600** SURFLET *Countrie Farme* v. vii. 668 The furrowes and rupts of carts. **1658-9** in *Burton's Diary* (1828) IV. 5, I desired them, as the course is, to put on, or to let me have one of the ruts. **1794** GIBBON in *Misc. Wks.* (1796) I. 296, I was almost killed..by hard, frozen, long, and cross ruts, that would disgrace the approach of an Indian wig wam. **1806** J. BERESFORD *Miseries Hum. Life* II. v, When you have trusted your foot on a frozen rut. **1864** TENNYSON *Aylmer's F.* 34 A sleepy land, where under the same wheel The same old rut would deepen year by year. **1883** S. C. HALL *Retrospect* II. 304 We had to leave the car ..while peasants helped it over the ruts.

b. *fig.* and in fig. context.
1608 SYLVESTER *Du Bartas* II. iv. III. *Schisme* 624 A long-tail'd squib, a flaming ridge, for rut Seems seen a while, where the bright Coach hath cut. **1705** *Pennsylvania Hist. Soc. Mem.* X. 32 He might prove such a rut in his way as might render his journey very fruitless. **1768-74** TUCKER *Lt. Nat.* (1834) I. 455 The goddess..drives so eagerly as not to heed the rotes in her way. **1892** STEVENSON *Across the Plains* 213 It had worn a rut in the commerce of Great Britain.

c. *fig.* A settled or established habit or mode of procedure; a narrow, undeviating course of life or action; a groove.
1839 CARLYLE *Chartism* 112 Parliaments, lumbering along in their deep ruts of commonplace. **1865** SKELTON *Campaigner at Home* iv. 71 On his return to civilised life, he will settle at once into the rut. **1874** L. STEPHEN *Hours Libr.* (1892) II. iii. 95 A man whose conversation runs in ruts.

2. A track or passage hollowed out, cut, or excavated in the ground. *rare.*
c **1611** CHAPMAN *Iliad* IV. 479 As from hils, raine waters headlong fall, That all waies eate huge Ruts, which, met in one bed [etc.]. **1787** WINTER *Syst. Husb.* 326 The soil lying hollow with the mole's ruts. **1844** H. STEPHENS *Bk. Farm* I. 405 It is of course worked by the hand alone, and makes simply a rut in the ground. **1884** T. SPEEDY *Sport Highl.* xix. 374 As daylight began to close, the ravens appeared and settled in the 'rut' [a gully].

3. *transf.* A deep mark or depression on the skin, some part of the body, etc.
1623 WEBSTER *Duchess Malfi* II. i, From your scuruy face-physicke, To behold thee not painted enclines somewhat neere A miracle: These in thy face here, were deepe rutts. *a* **1635** RANDOLPH *Hey for Honesty* IV. iii, These many ruts and furrows in thy cheeks Proves thy old face to be but champion-ground, Till'd with the plough of age. **1863** tr. *Waitz' Introd. Anthrop.* 95 The negro has no inter-maxillary bone, but only..a rut which marks it. **1899** *Allbutt's Syst. Med.* VIII. 897 The groove [of ainhum] always begins as a shallow transverse crack or rut, at the inner angle of the digito-plantar fold.

4. *attrib.* and *Comb.*, as ***rut-gulled, -rifted, -way***; **rut scraper**, *U.S.*, a machine for filling up cart-ruts by scraping in the displaced material.
1611 COTGR., *Charrau*, a Cart-way; Rutt-way. **1821** CLARE *Vill. Minstr.* I. 111 When thy rut-gull'd lanes Run little brooks with hasty rains. *Ibid.* II. 33 We turned up the rut-rifted lane. **1868** *Rep. U.S. Comm. Agric.* (1869) 361 Prevention [of mud-holes] can be effected..by the use of the rut scraper.

rut (rʌt), *sb.*[3] Now *U.S.* and *dial.* Also 7 rutt(e. [Of doubtful origin: cf. the variant ROTE *sb.*[6] There is connexion of sense with ROUT *sb.*[5] and *v.*[2], and with ON. *rót* (whence Gael. *rot*) breaking of waves, but the vowels of these do not agree with either *rut* or *rote*.] The roaring of the sea, *esp.* in breaking on the shore. Freq. ***rut of the sea***.
1633 T. JAMES *Voy.* 8 We heard the rutt of the shoare, as we thought: but it prooued to be the rutt against a banke of Ice. **1694** MOTTEUX *Rabelais* IV. xviii, The Rut of the Sea was great, the Waves breaking upon our Ships Quarter. **1820** WILBRAHAM *Cheshire Gloss.* 55 The rut of the sea is the dashing of the waves against any thing. **1847** D. WEBSTER *Priv. Corr.* (1857) II. 262, I hear the sea very strong and loud at the north... They call this the rote or rut of the sea. *a* **1862** THOREAU *Cape Cod* v. (1894) 115 The old man said that this was what they called the 'rut', a peculiar roar of the sea before the wind changes.

†**rut**, *sb.*[4] *Obs. rare.* [Of doubtful origin: cf. prec. and ROUT *sb.*[1] 8.] Noise, disturbance.
1612 DRAYTON *Poly-olb.* ii. Argt., To see the rutte the Sea-gods keepe: There swaggering in the Solent deepe. *Ibid.* ii. 446 There arose such rut th' unrulie rout among That soone the noyse thereof through all the ocean rong. **1630** J. TAYLOR (Water P.) *Praise Hempseed* Wks. III. 62 One with the Grasshopper doth keepe a rut, Another rimes vpon a Hazell nut. *c* **1700** KENNETT in *MS. Lansd. 1033* s.v., To keep a rut; i.e. to be meddling and doing mischief. *Kent.*

rut, *sb.*[5] *Sc. rare.* [f. RUT *v.*[2] Cf. RIT *sb.*[1]] A cut or incision.
1805 R. W. DICKSON *Pract. Agric.* I. Pl. xxix, A long rut ..is made with the spade along each side,..so as to form the cut of the turf slanting outward.

rut: see ROOT *sb.*[1]

†**rut**, *v.*[1] *Obs.* [app. related to ROUT *v.*[6]]
1. *trans.* To fling, cast, or throw.
1375 *Creation* 301 in Horstm. *Altengl. Leg.* (1878) 128 Whanne we were þus fro blesse rut, And þow in þat blisse put, þo hadde y to þe enuye. *c* **1400** *Destr. Troy* 3695 The wyndes..Rut vp the rughe se on rokkes aboute. *c* **1440** *Promp. Parv.* 439/2 Rutton, or throwyn (*K.* rwtyn,..*P.* ruttyn..), *projicio*.
2. *intr.* To dash, move with violence.
c **1400** *Destr. Troy* 5699 His shippes..Gird on the ground ..Till þai rut on a Rocke, & rent all to peses. *Ibid.* 12691 Barges & othir..Rut euyn to þe rokkis with a rank will.

rut, *v.*[2] Now *Sc.* [var. of RIT *v.*[1]]
†**1.** To cut, pierce, thrust, with a weapon. *Obs.*
c **1400** *Destr. Troy* 6977 þen Paris,..with a pile sharp, Rut hym in thurgh þe rybbis. *Ibid.* 10704 He pairet his armur, Rut þurgh his rybbes, rent hym with in.
2. *spec.* To cut or make a furrow through (turf) with a spade, etc. Cf. RIT *v.*[1] 1 b.
1805 R. W. DICKSON *Pract. Agric.* I. Pl. xxix, The work is to proceed in this manner, always rutting the through band rows of turf in both ends. **1844** H. STEPHENS *Bk. Farm* I. 374 With the common spade then cut, or, as it is technically termed, *rut* the line of hedge-bed behind the cord. *Ibid.* 503 The upper rough turf is rutted in a perpendicular direction.
b. To cut *off* (earth) with a spade; to take *off* or remove by rutting.
1844 H. STEPHENS *Bk. Farm* I. 507 The principal workman is rutting off the second side of the top of the drain with the common spade.

rut (rʌt), *v.*[3] [f. RUT *sb.*[1], or ad. obs. F. *rutter, ruter* (Godef.).]
1. *intr.* To be under the influence of (periodic) sexual excitement.
a **1625** FLETCHER *Elder Brother* v. ii, That is your penance, you know for what, and see you rut no more; you understand me. **1663** DRYDEN *Wild Gallant* II. ii, I am just in the condition of an out-lying deer, that's beaten from his walk for offering to rut. **1884** *Pall Mall G.* 12 Aug. 4/1 As for stags ..they are rutting in October. **1889** WESTERMARCK *Orig. Marriage* 49 The buck and the ass in southern countries.. rut throughout the whole year.
2. *trans.* To mount or cover (the female). *rare*$^{-1}$.
1700 DRYDEN tr. *Ovid's Cinyras & Myrrha* 46 What piety forbids the lusty ram, Or more salacious goat, to rut their dam?

rut (rʌt), *v.*[4] [f. RUT *sb.*[2]]
In quots. 1822 and 1647 (sense 2) there may be some connexion with ROOT *v.*[2] and ROUT *v.*[8]
1. *trans.* To mark (a road or the ground) with ruts; to furrow. (Chiefly in *pa. pple.*)
1607 MARKHAM *Caval.* IV. (1617) 54 Some high way which in the winter time hauing been rutted [etc.]. **1815** SCOTT *Paul's Lett.* (1839) 152 The ground was..strangely broken up and rutted by the wheels of the artillery. **1822** J. FLINT *Lett. fr. Amer.* 205 The adjoining grounds perhaps.. overgrown with rank weeds, or rutted by hogs. **1884** SALA *Journ. South* I. xxiv. (1887) 313 One street [in Pompeii] with ..its pavement rutted by chariot-wheels.
fig. **1819** SCOTT *Let.* in *Lockhart* xlvi. (1837) IV. 336, I certainly studied..to get out of the old beaten track, leaving those who like to keep the road, which I have rutted pretty well. **1844** KINGLAKE *Eothen* xvi, I saw how deeply it was rutted with the ruts of age and misery.
†**2.** *intr.* Of a stag: (see quot.). *Obs.*$^{-1}$
1647 HEXHAM I. *Hunting-terms*, The Stagg ruts with his hornes in the earth.

†**rut**, *v.*[5] *Obs.*$^{-1}$ [app. for *route*: see ROUTE *sb.* 1, quots. 1568-1594.] *intr.* To keep a course.
1588 PARKE tr. *Mendoza's Hist. China* 305 From whence vnto the..Canarias is two hundred and thirtie leagues, and [the ships] alwayes doo Rut to the southwest.

rutabaga (ˌruːtəˈbeɪgə). *U.S.* Also 9 roota, ruta baga, ruta-baga. [ad. Swed. dial. (W. Götland) *rotabagge*. So G. *ruta-, rota-baga*, F. *rutabaga*.] The Swedish turnip, *Brassica napus* var. *napobrassica*. = SWEDE 3. Also *attrib.*
1799 J. B. BORDLEY *Essays & Notes on Husbandry* 30 The new turnip, called roota baga, is likely to stand our winters. **1800** TUKE *Agric. N. Riding* 157 The ruta-baga has been sown in small quantities by a few individuals, most of whom approve of it. **1820** SHELLEY *Œd. Tyr.* I. 47 Hog-wash or grains, or ruta-baga, none Has yet been ours since your reign begun. **1833** W. SEWALL *Jrnl.* 20 June (1930) 149/2 Finished planting potatoes. Sowed rutabaga turnips. **1865** E. BURRITT *Walk to Land's End* 376 The great landlake.. rimmed with the green and purple verdure of the turnip and ruta-baga. **1916** *Yukon Territory* (Canada Dept. Interior) 213 The type shape is similar to a rutabaga, but the roots are smooth without laterals. **1951** O. NASH *Family Reunion* 107 We gobbled like pigs On rutabagas and salted figs. **1975** *New Yorker* 10 Nov. 176/2 Pertly written by pertly pretty housewives who have discovered organic gardening and how to rub two rutabagas together to feed four happy, whimsical tots—such books glut the shelves. **1976** [see *oyster plant* s.v. OYSTER 7 d].

rutaceous (ruːˈteɪʃəs), *a.* [f. mod.L. *Rutaceæ* the rue family, f. L. *rūta* rue. Cf. L. *rūtāceus* made from rue.] Of or belonging to the order *Rutaceæ*; resembling rue; rue-like.
1830 LINDLEY *Nat. Syst. Bot.* 132 Thus far the structure of Diosmeæ is little different from that of other Rutaceous plants. **1866** *Treas. Bot.* 1015/1 A rutaceous shrub from Western Australia. **1881** *Encycl. Brit.* XII. 289/2 *Ruta graveolens*.—A hardy evergreen rutaceous undershrub.

†**rutar**. *Obs.*$^{-1}$ [ad. med.L. *rutar-ius*, ad. OF. *routier*: see ROUTER[1] and RUITER.] = RUTTER[1].
1610 HOLLAND *Camden's Brit.* I. 812 Which King Iohn and his Rutars set on fire. *Ibid.*, That age called forraine and willing Souldiours, Rutars.

ˈ**rutate**. *Chem. rare.* [f. RUT-IC + -ATE.] A salt due to the action of rutic acid.
1873 *Fownes' Chem.* (ed. 11) 689 The metallic rutates are mostly sparingly soluble in water.

†**rute**, *sb. Obs.*$^{-0}$ (See quot.)
1747 HOOSON *Miner's Dict.* R iv, A small thread of Ore, and those that are of the least Size of all, such are called *Rutes* when they are under a finger thick, even to the smallest Size.

rute, *v. dial. rare*$^{-0}$. (See quot.)
1674 RAY *N.C. Gloss.* 39 He Rutes it: *Chesh.* spoken of a Child, he cries fiercely.

rute, obs. f. ROOT *sb.*[1] and *v.*[1]; obs. f. ROUT and ROUTE *sb.*

ruter, var. RUTTER[1], RUTTIER.

†ˈ**rutey**, *sb. Obs.*$^{-1}$ In 5 rotey. [f. next.] = RUT *sb.*[1] 1. ***rutey-time***, rutting-time.
1377 LANGL. *P. Pl.* B. XI. 329 After course of concepcioun, none toke kepe of other. As whan þei hadde ryde in rotey tyme, anon riȝte þer-after, Males drowen hem to males.

†ˈ**rutey**, *v. Obs.*$^{-1}$ Also 5 rotey, rot(e)i-. [? ad. AF. **rutei-er*, f. *rut* RUT *sb.*[1] Cf. *ruteison* RUTSON.] *intr.* = RUT *v.*[3] 1.
1393 LANGL. *P. Pl.* C. XIV. 146 After cours of concepcioun, non tok kepe of oþer; As when þei hadde ruteyed, anon þei resten after.

†**rut-goose**. *Obs.*$^{-1}$ (Cf. ROUT *sb.*[7])
1531 *Durh. Household Bk.* (Surtees) 327, 1 rutgoys, 3*d.* —1 mawlert, 2*d.*—6 dunlyngs, 2*d.*

ruth[1] (ruːθ). Now *arch.* Forms: *α.* 2-5 **reuþe**, 3 **reu(h)ðe, ræuðe**, 4-5 **reuthe** (5 **-þthe, -thþe**), **reuþ** (4 **reut**), 4-6 **reuth** (5 **reutht**); 3 **rewðe, -de**, 3, 5 **reweþe**, 4-5 **rewþe**, 4-6 **rewthe**, 4-7 **rewth** (5 **-eth**). *β.* 3 **reo(w)ðe, reoþe**; 3 **reouþe, -ðe, -de**, 4-5 **reouþ, -th.** *γ.* 2-5 **rouþe**, 4-5 **routhe**, 5, 7 **routh** (5 **rought**); 2 **rowðe**, 4-5 **rowthe**, 5 **rowith**; 4 **rau-, rawþe**, 4-5 **raw-**, 5 **rauthe, roth.** *δ.* 4-5 **ruþe**, 4-6 **ruthe**; 4 **ruþ**, 5- **ruth**, 6-7 **rueth.** [Early ME. *reuðe, rewðe*, etc., f. *rewen* RUE *v.*[1] Cf. OE. *hreow* RUE *sb.*[1], and for the ending, ON. *hryggð*.]

1. The quality of being compassionate; pitifulness; the feeling of sorrow for another; compassion, pity.
c **1175** *Lamb. Hom.* 149 Heorte sar for þe monnes aȝene sunne, and rowðe for his emcristenes wawe. *c* **1200** *Vices & Virtues* 63 Pietas hatte on of ðese hali mihtes, þat is, reuhðe on engelisc. *c* **1250** *Gen. & Ex.* 2339 Ðo cam iosep swilc rewðe up-on, he dede halle ut ðe toðere gon. **13..** *E.E. Allit. P.* A. 858 Al-þaȝ..ȝe remen for rauþe wythouten reste. *c* **1374** CHAUCER *Troylus* II. 349 If therewith-al in you ther be no routhe, Than is it harm ye liven. *c* **1440** *Jacob's Well* 310 ȝyue þe poore ruthe & compassioun of þin herte. *c* **1470** *Gol. & Gaw.* 966 Knichtis ramyt for reuth, schir Gawyne thai rew. **1508** DUNBAR *Tua Mariit Wemen* 316 For neuer bot in a gentill hert is generit ony ruth. **1576** TURBERV. *Venerie* lxii. 177 And yet can man..Vse wracke for rewth? can murder like him best? *c* **1614** SIR W. MURE *Dido & Æneas* III. 413 With dying groanes..For rewth would rent a flinty heart a sunder. **1637** MILTON *Lycidas* 163 Look homeward Angel now, and melt with ruth. **1748** THOMSON *Cast. Indol.* I. lii, Oft they snatch the pen, As if inspir'd,..Then write, and blot, as would your ruth engage. **1774** BEATTIE *Minstr.* II. xxx, If my desultory strain with ruth And indignation makes thine eyes o'erflow. **1808** SCOTT *Marm.* II. xix, Upon whose wrinkled brow alone, Nor ruth, nor mercy's trace, is shown. **1861** HUGHES *Tom Brown at Oxf.* xvi, He..was filled with ruth for the poor wrong-headed youngster. **1878** S. COX *Salv. Mundi* i. (ed. 3) 6 Another slight but significant indication of this mood of ruth and pity.

Comb. **1603** FLORIO *Montaigne* III. iv. (1632) 467 All with an eager continuall ruth mooving motion.

b. Frequent in phr. *to have ruth*, usually const. †*of*, *on*, or *upon*. Now *arch.*

c **1175** *Lamb. Hom.* 79 þa com þer an helendis Mon, and heuede rouþe of him. *a* **1225** *Ancr. R.* 32 Habbeð reouþe of þeo þet beoð ine stronge temptaciuns. *c* **1275** *Passion our Lord* 322 in *O.E. Misc.* 46 He is wrþe to beo ded... Of þe kynge of heuene none reuþe hi nedde. *c* **1300** *Beket* 808 Somme gode men that ther stode hadde of him Ruthe ynouȝ. **13..** *E.E. Allit. P.* B. 972 Þer-of clatered þe cloudes þat kryst myȝt haf rawþe. *c* **1384** CHAUCER *Ho. Fame* I. 332 Allas that euer had routhe Any woman on any man. *c* **1400** *Destr. Troy* 8511 He hade no ruthe of hor remyng. *a* **1450** MYRC 1361 Hast þou in herte rowþe I-had, Of hem þat were nede be-stad? **1509** FISHER *Serm.* Wks. (1876) 281 These two persones had so grete ruthe and compassyon of theyr maysters. **1567** *Gude & Godlie B.* (S.T.S.) 170 O Lord,.. Haif reuth on me thy Creature. **1819** SCOTT *Ivanhoe* xxxiii, Have ruth on me, and let me go! **1860** PUSEY *Min. Proph.* 191 She has no one to raise her up; none to have ruth upon her. **1890** CONAN DOYLE *White Company* xiv, Methinks that I should have ruth upon you.

c. So *to take ruth*.

1540–54 J. CROKE *13 Ps.* (Percy Soc.) 8 Vppon me then thou wolt take ruthe. **1577–87** HOLINSHED *Chron.* III. 1220/1 Taking ruth of their miserable estates. *c* **1586** C'TESS PEMBROKE *Ps.* LXXVII. v, Will God no more take ruth?

2. Contrition, repentance; remorse. Now *rare*.

c **1200** *Trin. Coll. Hom.* 49 Vte we.. habben on ure heorte sorinesse and reuðe of ure synnes. *a* **1300** *Cursor M.* 25749 [To] mak to preist his costes cuth, Wit reuth of hert and scrifte o mouth. *a* **1603** ELIZ. GRYMESTON *Misc.* (1604) F4b, Thou pardon promisest, where hearts true ruth is showne. **1603** J. DAVIES (Heref.) *Microcosmos* Wks. (Grosart) I. 41/1 Thus when our Teares doe testifie our ruth, We neede not.. of them be asham'd. **1855** M. ARNOLD *Stanzas Grande Chartreuse* 77, I seek these Anchorites, not in ruth, To curse and to deny your truth.

3. Sorrow, grief, distress; †lamentation.

c **1205** LAY. 12970 þat word com to herede, hu þe king iuaren hafde; þa wes muchel reoðe. *a* **1225** *Leg. Kath.* 2340 Nalde ȝe neauer.. makien reowðe for me, þe fare to eche reste. *a* **1300** *Cursor M.* 24054 Moder, traistnes of vr trewþe, Don vs to rewen wit þi rewþe. *c* **1384** CHAUCER *L.G.W.* 669 *Cleopatra*, This woful Cleopatrie hath made swich routhe That ther nys tonge noon that may yt telle. *a* **1400–50** *Alexander* 2813, I may noȝt ryde ȝow to reschow, my reuthe is þe mare. **1562** LEGH *Armory* 209 Where-fore, leaue of this rewthe, and seke to liue by Hope. **1591** SPENSER *Vis. Petrarch* 25 O, how great ruth, and sorrowfull assay, Doth vex my spirite with perplexitie. **1616** B. JONSON *Epigr.* I. xxii, Here lies, to each her Parents ruth, Mary, the Daughter of their youth. **1654** E. JOHNSON *Wonder-w. Provid.* 116 The supreame judge of all the World.. stood not as an idle spectator beholding his peoples Ruth. *c* **1800** H. K. WHITE *Childhood* II. 4 That every age and rank is born to ruth. **1841–6** LONGF. *Maidenhood* xiv, Bear through sorrow, wrong, and ruth, In thy heart the dew of youth. **1868** KIRK *Chas. the Bold* v. iii. III. 441 Flanders and Hainault had their share of ruth for gallant sons and stalwart sires.

†**4. a.** Matter or occasion of sorrow or regret. *Obs.*

c **1200** *Trin. Coll. Hom.* 219 Acke nu is reweþe, for nu is euerihc man ifo þare he solde fren be. **1297** R. GLOUC. (Rolls) 2258 þe brutons.. bigonne vaste to fle, Some in roches, some in wodes, þat reuþe it was to se. *c* **1330** *Arth. & Merl.* 94 (Kölbing), Sone þat traitour.. brak his treuþe & dede hem wrong, & þat was reuþe. **1377** LANGL. *P. Pl.* B. xv. 501 Now is routhe to rede, how þe red noble Is reuerenced. *c* **1412** HOCCLEVE *De Reg. Princ.* 330 The more routhe is, allas! *c* **1470** *Gol. & Gaw.* 1129 The roy ramand ful raith, that reuth wes to se. **1500–20** DUNBAR *Poems* iv. 91 Gret reuth it wer that so suld be. **1590** SPENSER *F.Q.* III. v. 6 That is great woe, And wondrous ruth to all, that shall it heare. *a* **1626** BP. ANDREWES *96 Serm.* (1661) 223 If he were not a man, but some other unreasonable creature, it were great ruth to see him so handled.

†**b.** Mischief; calamity; ruin. *Obs.*

c **1205** LAY. 20169 Hundes in þam reode mid reouðe hine imeteð. *Ibid.* 21764 þenne is þat folc buten wene þat reouðe heom is to cumene of summes cunnes leoden. *c* **1330** *Arth. & Merl.* 7693 (Kölbing), He dede ribaudes ten þousinde Bren þat þai miȝtten finde; So he dede michel rewþe. *a* **1400–50** *Alexander* 4010 It is better for to bate & on þe bent faile, þan se þis rewthe on ȝour renkis. **1584–7** GREENE *Carde of Fancie* Wks. (Grosart) IV. 22 Thou shalt finde.. lusting Loue the load-stone to ruth and ruine. **1594** NASHE & MARLOWE *Dido* 111, Yet now I doe repent me of his ruth, And wish that I had neuer wrongd him so. **1615** BRATHWAIT *Strappado* (1878) 48 See here the fall of youth, Begun in pleasure, but wouen vp in rueth. **1647** TRAPP *Marrow Gd. Authors* in *Comm. Ep.* 670 Cholerike kings and persons of great note.. hereby have wrought their own ruth and ruine.

†**5.** With *a* and pl. in senses 3 and 4. *Obs.*

c **1205** LAY. 25506 þis lond heo for-radden mid ræuðen uniuoȝen. *a* **1225** *Ancr. R.* 54 Biginnunge & rote of þis ilke reouðe was a liht sihðe. *c* **1386** CHAUCER *Clerk's T.* 562, I trowe that to a norice in this cas It had ben hard this rewthe for to se. **1390** GOWER *Conf.* I. 333 And thanne I scholde in such a wise In rewardinge of my servise Be ded; me thenkth it were a rowthe. **1412–20** LYDG. *Chron. Troy* II. 1450 For sothfastly it is to gret a routhe To recorde how ȝe haue hir vsed. *c* **1489** CAXTON *Blanchardyn* iv. 20 After the rewthes and lamentacions of the kynge. *Ibid.* xlv. 174 She lened vpon a wyndowe that loked vpon the see, makyng full pyteouse rewthes for her loue that she sawe. **1589** PUTTENHAM *Eng. Poesie* III. xix. (Arb.) 227 They say it is a ruth to see thy louer neede.

ruth[2] (rʌt). *Anglo-Ind.* Also rut, rutt. [a. Hindī *rath* (rʌth), a car, carriage, coach, etc.] A native vehicle or carriage.

α. **1813** MRS. SHERWOOD in *Life* xxv. (1847) 422 When these girls travel, they generally go hidden by crimson curtains in a rutt or car drawn by bullocks. **1829** JOHN SHIPP *Mem.* II. 183, I took the liberty of taking the rut and horse to camp as prize property.

β. **1834** [A. PRINSEP] *Baboo* II. ix. 176 The driver of the ruth had been found. **1866** SIR T. SEATON *Cadet to Colonel* xvii. 364 Hodson stopped the ruth.., and made the three prisoners descend. **1901** KIPLING *Kim* iv, Kim marked down a gaily ornamented ruth or family bullock-cart.

ruth, variant of ROUTH *a. Sc.*

ruthe, obs. variant of RUT *sb.*[1]

†**ruthe**, *v. Obs. rare.* [Of obscure origin.] *trans.* To awaken, rouse.

13.. *E.E. Allit. P.* B. 895 Ful erly þose aungelez þis haþel þay ruþen & glopnedly on godez halue gart hym vpryse. *Ibid.* 1208 Ryche, ruþed of her rest, ran to here wedes.

ruthenate (ˈruːθənət). *Chem.* [f. RUTHENIUM + -ATE[1] 1 c.] A salt formed by the action of ruthenic acid.

1879 ROSCOE & SCHORLEMMER *Treat. Chem.* II. II. 452 The blackish-green solution.. giving rise to potassium ruthenate. **1887** *Cassell's Encycl. Dict.* s.v. *Ruthenium*, The former [is] converted into ruthenate of potassium by fusion with potash. **1894** MORLEY & MUIR *Watts' Dict. Chem.* IV. 417/2 Ruthenates in solution are easily reduced.

Ruthene (ruːˈθiːn), *sb.* and *a.* Also 6 Ruthen, Rutene. [ad. med.L. *Rut(h)eni* (pl.), related to *Ruzi*, *Russi* Russians, as *Prut(h)eni* to *Pruzi*, *Prussi*: see note to PRUSSIAN.]

A. *sb.* **1.** A former name for a member of the Ukrainian people; freq. in restricted sense = RUSSNIAK.

1548 PATTEN *Exped. Scotl.* cij b, Neyther the Grekes, the Ruthens nor many nations in theast partes besides. **1560** BECON *New Catech.* v. Wks. 1564 I. 446 The churches of the Grekes, of the Ethiopes, of the Rutenes, of the Bohems, &c. **1838** *Penny Cycl.* XI. 42/2 Of the inhabitants.. 1,900,000 are Ruthenes or Russniaks,.. who have spread into the centre of Russia, and are also numerous on the Hungarian side of the Carpathians. **1883** *19th Cent.* Nov. 754 Two-thirds of its population.. belonging to the Reformed Church, the remaining third being mainly Russniaks or Ruthenes.

2. The language of the Ruthenes.

1891 MISS DOWIE *Girl in Karp.* 195, I am inclined to think that.. the language.. is by no means pure Ruthene.

B. *adj.* = RUTHENIAN *a.*

1849 *Blackw. Mag.* May 627/2 The revolt of the Ruthene peasants.. in 1846. **1891** [see RUTHENIAN B.].

Ruthenian (ruːˈθiːnɪən), *sb.* and *a.* [See prec.]

A. *sb.* **1.** A Ruthene; a member of the Ruthenian church.

1863 *Chambers's Encycl.* V. 88/1 The union of the Galician Greeks or Ruthenians is of much later date. **1886** *Encycl. Brit.* XX. 631/1 The Ruthenians attribute their conversion to Christianity to St. Methodius.

2. The language of the Ruthenes.

1862 LATHAM *Elem. Compar. Philol.* 627 With the exception.. of the Malo-Russian, Ruthenian, Russinian, Rusniak, or Little Russian,.. none of the dialects of Russia have commanded much attention. **1902** MERRIMAN *Vultures* xxiv, Galician, Ruthenian, Polish,.. would be required.

B. *adj.* Of or pertaining to the Ruthenes, their liturgy, language, etc.

1850 *Proc. Philol. Soc.* V. 27 The Ukraine.. is the land of the Kosaks; they speak the Ruthenian dialect. **1885** *Catholic Dict.* 803 There were in 1865 about 250,000 Catholics of the Ruthenian rite in Russian Poland. **1891** MISS DOWIE *Girl in Karp.* 195 Throughout this book the Ruthenian spelling has been given when the word has been traced to be Ruthene.

rutheniate (ruːˈθiːnɪət). *Chem.* [f. RUTHENIUM + -ATE[1] 1 c.] = RUTHENATE.

1849 D. CAMPBELL *Inorg. Chem.* 255 The mass dissolved affords a solution of rutheniate of potash with an excess of potash. **1877** *Nature* 28 June 167/1 Saturating the rutheniate of potash with chlorine.

ruthenic (ruːˈθɛnɪk), *a. Chem.* [f. RUTHENIUM + -IC 1 b.] Pertaining to or derived from ruthenium; containing ruthenium.

1849 D. CAMPBELL *Inorg. Chem.* 255 When an excess of an acid is added to this alkaline solution, an oxide of ruthenium is said to precipitate along with ruthenic acid. **1868** *Fownes' Chem.* (ed. 10) 440 The tetrachloride or Ruthenic chloride, $RuCl_4$, is known only in its double salts. *Ibid.*, Ruthenic oxide, RuO_2. **1881** WATTS *Dict. Chem.* 3rd Suppl. II. 1768 Ruthenic anhydride being perhaps temporarily formed.

ru'thenio-, combining form of RUTHENIUM, as in ***ruthenio-chloride***, ***-cyanide***.

1862 MILLER *Elem. Chem.*, *Org.* x. §1. 692 Ruthenio-cyanides may.. be obtained, corresponding in composition to the ferrocyanides. **1876** *Encycl. Brit.* V. 537/2 The chlorides of ruthenium and osmium form numerous double salts, but the most important are the ruthenio- and osmio-chlorides.

ru'thenious, *a. Chem.* [f. RUTHENI-UM.] (See RUTHENIC *a.* and -OUS c.)

1868 *Fownes' Chem.* (ed. 10) 440 The trichloride or Ruthenious chloride, Ru_2Cl_6,.. is a yellow-brown, crystalline, very deliquescent mass. *Ibid.*, The sesquioxide, or Ruthenious oxide, Ru_2O_3.

ruthenite (ˈruːθənaɪt). *Chem.* [f. RUTHENIUM + -ITE[1] 4.] (See quot.)

1894 MORLEY & MUIR *Watts' Dict. Chem.* IV. 413 Ruthenites,.. salts of oxyacids of Ruthenium.

ruthenium (ruːˈθiːnɪəm). [f. med.L. *Ruthenia* Russia (having been first noticed in platinum ores from the Ural Mountains) + -IUM.]

a. A metal of the platinum group, discovered and named by Osann in 1828, but first isolated by Claus in 1845. Chem. symbol Ru.

1848 FOWNES *Chem.* (ed. 2) 343 Ruthenium. M. Claus has described under this name a new metal contained in the residue from crude platinum. **1854** *Orr's Circ. Sci.*, *Chem.* 516 Ruthenium very much resembles iridium. **1880** CLEMINSHAW *Wurtz' Atom. The.* 222 The compounds which are called sesquichloride of osmium and ruthenium.

attrib. **1849** D. CAMPBELL *Inorg. Chem.* 252 The residue contains the ruthenium compound. *Ibid.* 257 While the ruthenium salt is in the retort. **1876** *Encycl. Brit.* V. 537/1 Ruthenium tetroxide, RuO_4, is a golden-yellow crystalline substance, sparingly soluble in water.

b. ruthenium red, an intensely coloured red mixed-valence complex salt of ruthenium, $[(NH_3)_5Ru^{III}ORu^{IV}(NH_3)_4ORu^{III}(NH_3)_5]Cl_6$, obtained by air oxidation of a solution containing ammonia and ruthenium (III) chloride, and employed as a microscopic strain.

1912 *Chem. Abstr.* VI. 297 (*heading*) Differentiation of natural textiles and artificial silks by means of ruthenium red. **1950** N. V. SIDGWICK *Chem. Elements* II. 1472 The colour of ruthenium red itself can be detected in solutions more dilute than one in a million. **1978** *Sci. Amer.* Jan. 86 (*caption*) In both preparations the cells were stained with ruthenium red, which is taken up by any polysaccharide glycocalyx fibers that are present.

ruther (ˈrʌðə(r)), *adv.* [Repr. a U.S. colloq. or dial. pronunc. of RATHER.] = RATHER *adv.*

1872 [see HOLD *v.* 42 c]. **1929** *Amer. Mercury* Sept. 47 Ruther be in cornfield workin' hard, Than be buck private in National Guard. **1938** M. K. RAWLINGS *Yearling* viii. 71 I'd ruther they hunted their way and leave me hunt mine. **1942** W. FAULKNER *Go down, Moses* 59, I ruther never to know than to find out later I have been fooled. **1970** M. CHISHOLM *McAllister says No* vi. 48 I'd ruther have him in front of me than behind.

ruther, variant of RATHER *sb.*, RIDDER *sb.*[1], RUDDER *sb.*

Rutherford (ˈrʌðəfəd). *Physics.* [The name of Ernest *Rutherford* (1871–1937), New Zealand-born English physicist.]

1. Used *attrib.* and in the possessive to designate concepts developed by him, as **Rutherford('s) (scattering) formula** or **law**, a mathematical expression of Rutherford scattering; **Rutherford model**, a model of the atomic nucleus devised to account for Rutherford scattering; **Rutherford scattering**, elastic scattering of charged particles by the electric fields of atomic nuclei; = *Coulomb scattering*; hence **Rutherford-scatter** *v. trans.*

1931 G. GAMOW *Constitution of Atomic Nuclei* iv. 85 The ratio of the observed scattering to that given by Rutherford's formula for a given angle falls to a minimum and then rises again. **1961** POWELL & CRASEMANN *Quantum Mechanics* xii. 465 Coulomb scattering of low-energy protons, for which the classical cross section is given by the Rutherford formula. **1931** G. GAMOW *Constitution of Atomic Nuclei* iv. 84 If.. the potential barrier is high enough compared with the energy of the α-particle.. deviations from Rutherford's law will be small. **1970** I. E. MCCARTHY *Nuclear Reactions* I. i. 8 The first example of nuclear information being obtained from measurements of the differential cross-section as a function of momentum transfer is the Rutherford law for elastic scattering. **1930** J. BUCKINGHAM *Matter & Radiation* iii. 59 The Rutherford model. **1968** M. S. LIVINGSTON *Particle Physics* ii. 17 The nucleus of the Rutherford model must have a diameter of less than 10^{-12} cm. **1974** G. REECE tr. *Hund's Hist. Quantum Theory* iv. 62 The formula remains true in Bohr's theory, while (4) is also valid for the Rutherford model of the atom. **1977** *Nature* 6 Jan. 35/2 A beam of ^{32}S ions is Rutherford scattered backwards from the sample and the energies of the scattered ions are measured. **1928** *Proc. R. Soc.* A CXVIII. 548 This gives the Rutherford scattering formula exactly for all velocities of the incident particles. **1935** J. DOUGALL tr. *Born's Atomic Physics* v. 126 It can actually be proved that Rutherford's scattering formula is strictly valid in wave mechanics also. **1977** *Nature* 6 Jan. 36/1 The Z^2 dependence of the Rutherford scattering cross section has been taken into account.

2. (Usu. written **rutherford**.) A unit of radioactivity orig. equal to one million disintegrations per second; later defined as the quantity of any particular nuclide exhibiting this degree of activity.

The curie is the more usual unit; one rutherford is approximately $2{\cdot}7 \times 10^{-5}$ curie.

1946 CONDON & CURTISS in *Physical Rev.* LXIX. 673/1 Since the curie was named in honor of M. and Mme. Curie, the co-discoverers of radium, it is natural to select the name 'rutherford' for the new unit. The appropriate abbreviation is 'rd' which conflicts with the abbreviation of no other well-accepted physical unit. The micro-rutherford would become one disintegration per second. **1947** *Nucleonics* Oct. 34/2 A carefully defined new unit, the rutherford (rd), has been proposed for general use. Ambiguities as a result of choice of numerical values, failure to distinguish between beta rays per sec and disintegrations per sec, and extensions to arbitrary and undefined gamma-ray intensities, can then be avoided. **1958** S. GLASSTONE *Sourcebk. Atomic Energy* (ed. 2) xvii. 521 In 1948, the Committee on Standards and Units of Radioactivity of the National Research Council (United States).. favored the adoption of the proposal.. that the term 'rutherford' be used to designate a quantity of radio-active material giving 10^6 disintegrations per second. **1962** H. D. BUSH *Atomic & Nuclear Physics* iv. 84 The standard unit adopted is the curie... Another unit, which has not achieved universal acceptance, is the rutherford.

rutherfordine ('rʌðəfədiːn). *Min.* [ad. G. *rutherfordin* (W. Marckwald 1906, in *Centralbl. f. Mineral.* 763); see RUTHERFORD + -INE[5].] An orthorhombic uranyl carbonate, $UO_2.CO_3$, found as yellow fibrous masses, esp. in association with uraninite in East Africa.

1907 *Mineral Mag.* XIV. 409 *Rutherfordine*, a yellow uranyl carbonate, $UO_2.CO_3$, resembling uranochre in appearance and resulting by the alteration of uraninite. **1955** *Science* 1 Apr. 473/1 In actual crystals of rutherfordine, faults occur in the stacking of layers; regions in which the sequence of layers corresponds to structure A are occasionally terminated by regions in which the layers follow the sequence of structure B. **1959** HOGAN & GILBERT in G. J. Williams *Econ. Geol. N.Z.* (1965) xiii. 206/2 The yellow uranium mineral is rutherfordine which is consistent with the carbonate cement in the rock.

rutherfordite[1] ('rʌðəfədaɪt). *Min.* [f. the name *Rutherford* (see below) + -ITE[1].] A name given to a poorly characterized yellow-brown form of fergusonite found in gold mines in Rutherford County, North Carolina.

1851 C. U. SHEPARD in *Proc. Amer. Assoc. Adv. Sci.* IV. 312 *(heading)* Rutherfordite. **1852** *Amer. Jrnl. Sci.* LXIV. 344 By its translucency, rutherfordite is readily distinguished from samarskite, which it otherwise closely resembles. **1880** *Ibid.* CXX. 57, I have detected along with the samarskite of this locality a few very small crystals.. nearly identical with those found in the sands from the gold washings of Rutherford, N.C., named by me as rutherfordite, and which I now consider as belonging to the species fergusonite. **1966** Z. LERMAN tr. *Vlasov's Geochem. & Mineral. Rare Elem.* II. xi. 430 Synonyms of fergusonite: rutherfordite.., bragite.., tyrite.., arrhenite..and sipylite.

'rutherfordite[2]. *Min.* [f. as RUTHERFORDINE: see -ITE[1].] Used as a synonym of RUTHERFORDINE.

1922 N. H. & A. N. WINCHELL *Elem. Optical Mineral.* II. v. 88 Rutherfordite (UO_2CO_3) is orthorhombic (?), finely fibrous. Soft... Color yellow, earthy. An alteration product of uraninite. Rare. **1971** *Mineral. Mag.* XXXVIII. 104 Recommendations of the Commission on minerals for which more than one name is in common use... Rutherfordine, not rutherfordite.

rutherfordium (rʌðə'fɔədɪəm). *Chem.* [f. RUTHERFORD + -IUM.] (A name proposed for) an artificially produced transuranic element, atomic number 104. Symbol Rf. Cf. KURCHATOVIUM.

1969 *Science* 5 Dec. 1254/1 Scientists from the Lawrence Radiation Laboratory of the University of California announced results of chemical experiments on element 104 and used the occasion [*sc.* 17–19 Nov. 1969] to propose a new name. Albert Ghiorso..suggested that the element be called rutherfordium for Lord Rutherford 'the great pioneer of nuclear science'. **1970** A. GHIORSO et al. in *Physics Lett.* XXXII. B. 95/1 We have proposed that the element 104 be named rutherfordium. **1971** *Inorg. & Nuclear Chem. Lett.* VII. 1115 As not until 1969 did the American researchers at Berkeley also succeed in obtaining element 104..there is no ground to use the name rutherfordium proposed by them. **1971** *Nature* 26 Feb. 603/1 Certain questions have been raised regarding the validity of our work on the discovery of two alpha-emitting isotopes of element 104 (rutherfordium). **1975** [see NIELSBOHRIUM].

ruthful ('ruːθfʊl), *a.* Now *arch.* [f. RUTH *sb.*[1]]

1. Full of compassion or pity; compassionate.

a **1225** *Ancr. R.* 222 He bihalt on oðre þet he ne mei nones weis makien vuele iðoncked, so lufful & so reouðful is hire heorte. **1340** *Ayenb.* 198 Þe rewþeuolle, and þo þet doþ ham to þe poure and to þe workes of merci,..ssolle by do in-to sayzine of þe riche of heuene. **14..** *Pol., Rel., & L. Poems* 254 Biholt, þou man wiþ routhful herte, Þe sharpe scourge wiþ knottes smerte. **1500–20** DUNBAR *Poems* xlvii. 74 Ane lufe..So riche, so rewthfull and discreit,..Nevir moir salbe nor ȝit hes bene. **1595** BARNFIELD *Cassandra* (1841) 31 It mou'd compassion in this ruthfull Dame. **1628** WITHER *Brit. Rememb.* iv. 1029 Who on me cast A ruthfull eye. **1827** HOOD *Hero & Leander* xxvi, Let ruthful dolphins rest him on their back.

Comb. *c* **1560** A. SCOTT *Poems* (S.T.S.) xxxiv. 52 Ȝe rame as ȝe wer rent, And thay ar rewthfull hairtit.

2. That excites compassion or pity; lamentable, piteous, rueful.

a **1225** *Ancr. R.* 326 Þet oðer þing is þe muchele & þe reouðfule lure þet he uorleoseð. *a* **1240** *Sawles Warde* in *O.E. Hom.* I. 253 Swa is þe sihðe grislich ant reowðful to bihalden. *c* **1320** *Cast. Love* 197 Þus Adam þorw reuþful rage Was cast out of his heritage. *c* **1440** *Pallad. on Husb.* IX. 9 In Aust ek, yf the vyneyerd be lene And she, thy vyne, a ruthful thing to se. **1513** DOUGLAS *Æneis* IV. Prol. 71 The reuthfull smert and lamentable cace..of Leander ȝing. **1588** SHAKS. *Tit. A.* v. i. 66 Complots of Mischiefe, Treason, Villanies Ruthfull to heare. **1607** MILWARDE *Jacobs Gt. Day* (1610) I 3 b, Jeremy..makes a description of a sad and ruthfull day.., a day of sorrow. **1655** J. OWEN *Vind. Evang.* Wks. 1853 XII. 460 Astonishment arising from the contemplation of some ruthful spectacle. **1703** ROWE *Ulysses* III. i, It is a heavy and a ruthful Tale. **1808** SCOTT *Marm.* IV. xvi, When last this ruthful month was come. **1840** BROWNING *Sordello* I. 687 Or say a ruthful chance broke woof and warp.

b. Of sounds, actions, etc. (passing into the sense 'expressive of grief or sorrow').

13.. *K. Alis.* 6501 (W.), And thanne they maken a reouthful crye. *c* **1330** *King of Tars* 267 Merci heo criyede.. With a reuthful stevene. *a* **1425** *Cursor M.* 14301 (Trin.), Lazares frendes. Cryed & made reuþeful chere. **1495** *Trevisa's De P.R.* XVIII. lxxvi. 830 He [the cat] makyth a ruthefull noyse and gastfull whan one profryth to fyghte wyth a nother. **1579** SPENSER *Sheph. Cal.* Aug. 150 And tune your pypes as ruthful as may. **1598** YONG *Diana* 400 My ruthfull song and verse shall not intreate..Of any flames. **1604** T. WRIGHT *Passions* v. 181 The voyce ought sometimes to bee interrupted with wofull exclamations and ruthfull repetitions. **1663** SPARKE *Prim. Devot.* (ed. 3) 218 Wheresoever is this man of sorrows, there is likewise the same Ruthfull Ecce! Behold the man! **1861** LYTTON & FANE *Tannhäuser* 67 To do this desperate wrong in sight of all The ruthful faces of the Saints in Heaven.

c. Of persons or feelings (passing into the sense 'sad, dejected, doleful').

1513 DOUGLAS *Æneis* XII. xiii. 209 Thir sa gret dolouris mycht I end in hy, And with my reuthfull brother go. **1568** T. HOWELL *Arb. Amitie* (1879) 37 Most greedy gripes with plunging paines, do pierce my ruthfull hart. **1584–7** GREENE *Carde of Fancie* Wks. (Grosart) IV. 168 She who of late was a royall Princesse, was now a ruthfull prisoner. **1831** PALGRAVE *Hist. Anglo-Sax.* 352 Sad and ruthful were the forebodings of the English.

'ruthfully, *adv.* Now *rare.* [-LY[2].]

1. In a pitiable or lamentable fashion; piteously, dolefully, dismally, ruefully.

a **1225** *St. Marher.* 4 Leuestu ant luuest him the reowðfulliche deide ant dreorliche on rode? *c* **1400** *Arth. & Merl.* 1067 (Kölbing), Reouþfully heo gan to grete. **1483** CAXTON *Gold. Leg.* 397/4 Thenne Judas thanked sannt brandon soo ruthefully that it was pyte to see. **1533** BELLENDEN *Livy* III. xii. (S.T.S.) I. 296 The small pepill, opprest with mony harmes, beheld reuthfully þe visage of þe faderis. **1579** SPENSER *Sheph. Cal.* Aug. 175 Helpe me..my deadly cryes Most ruthfully to tune. **1611** COTGR., *Miserablement*,..ruthfully, distressefully. **1661** R. L'ESTRANGE *Interest Mistaken* 118 The Sisters Groan so ruthfully, you'd swear Five hundred Women were in Labour. **1936** 'M. INNES' *Death at President's Lodging* xv. 246 No change, he reflected ruthfully a moment later, was to be got from Empson that way.

2. Compassionately. *Obs.*

1642 HOWELL *For. Trav.* 83 He may ruthfully observe how that Countrey.. is now ore whelm'd with barbarisme and ignorance. **1668** HOPKINS *Serm.* (1685) 62 All things will stare ruthfully upon thee, and..confess their impotency to rescue thee from the gripe of death.

'ruthfulness. *rare.* [-NESS.]

1. Sorrowfulness, grief. = RUEFULNESS 2.

1596 LODGE *Marg. Amer.* 118 Neither Fawniaes words, nor the hope she had to revisit her beloved, could rid her of ruthfulnesse.

2. Compassionateness. = RUEFULNESS 1.

1674 N. FAIRFAX *Bulk & Selv.* 191 Boundless good will and ruthfulness in sparing some from everlasting burnings. **1730** BAILEY (folio), *Ruthfulness*, compassionateness.

ruthle, variant of RUTTLE *v.*

ruthless ('ruːθlɪs), *a.* [f. RUTH *sb.*[1] + -LESS.] Devoid of pity or compassion; pitiless, unsparing, merciless.

c **1327** *Pol. Songs* (Camden) 255 For wel is wo. the lond is reutheles. *c* **1374** CHAUCER *Anel. & Arc.* 230 Of my woo he is so rewthelesse. *c* **1386** —— *Man of Law's T.* 765 Sche loketh bak-ward to the lond, And seyde, 'Farwel, housbond rewtheles!' **1412–20** LYDG. *Chron. Troy* II. 8593 Achilles.. Routheles in his malencolye. **1513** DOUGLAS *Æneis* IV. Prol. 145 Thus thou prayis, 'Haif mercy, lady, haif reuth and sum piete!' And scho, reuthles, agane rewis on the. **1593** SHAKS. *2 Hen. VI*, II. iv. 34 The ruthlesse Flint doth cut my tender feet. **1598** SYLVESTER *Du Bartas* II. i. II. 482 Till ruth-less Death..Thy dust-born body turn to dust again. **1603** SHAKS. *Meas. for M.* III. ii. 121 Why, what a ruthlesse thing is this.., to take away the life of a man? **1717** POPE *Iliad* IX. 585 The vengeful Fiends below, And ruthless Proserpine, confirm'd his Vow. **1762** FALCONER *Shipwr.* II. 345 Ye who, unmov'd, can brave the ruthless storm. **1791** COWPER *Odyss.* XVIII. 105 He shall despoil thee with his ruthless steel. **1830** D'ISRAELI *Chas. I*, III. xii. 264 Ruthless and inexorable, when his theological empire was in peril. **1879** GEO. ELIOT *Theo. Such* xii. 219 He was..defended against a ten years siege from ruthless facts. **1890** 'R. BOLDREWOOD' *Col. Reformer* (1891) 217 The unsparing use of the ruthless stockwhip.

'ruthlessly, *adv.* [-LY[2].] In a ruthless or remorseless manner; pitilessly.

1586 MARLOWE *1st Pt. Tamburl.* v. ii, And let not Conquest, ruthlessly pursu'd, Be equally against his life incens'd. **1755** in JOHNSON. **1809** W. IRVING *Knickerb.* (1861) 107 It came ruthlessly home to those sweet affections that grow close around the heart. **1849** J. H. PARKER *Introd. Gothic Archit.* i. 8 These buildings..were ruthlessly destroyed by the barbarians who succeeded them. **1879** FROUDE *Cæsar* xvi. 261 In this case the limits had been ruthlessly exceeded.

'ruthlessness. [-NESS.] Ruthless quality or character; pitilessness.

1777 POTTER *Æschylus, Prometheus Chain'd* 10 Yet upbraid not My ruder and unpitying ruthlessness. **1855** SINGLETON *Virgil* I. 150 A crabbed eld And toil, and ruthlessness of rigorous death. **1874** GREEN *Short Hist.* iv. §3. 175 He had inherited the fierce ruthlessness of the Angevins.

†'ruthly, *a.* and *adv.* *Obs. rare.* [f. RUTH *sb.*[1]]

a. *adj.* Sorrowful, piteous. **b.** *adv.* Sorrowfully.

c **1275** LAY. 13638 Ich ȝou telle rouþliche spelles of mochele sorinesse. **14..** *Sir Beues* 1578 (S.), To Iesu Crist ..& to his moder, mylde Marie, Wel rewthelych he gan crie.

†'ruthness. *Obs.* [f. RUTH *sb.*[1]] Compassion.

a **1300** *Cursor M.* 9680 All was right in sothfastnes, Witvten merci and reuthnes. *Ibid.* 14299 Iesus biheild þan hir a-stert, And had gret reuthnes in his hert.

ruthyr, obs. Sc. variant of RUDDER *sb.*

†rutic ('ruːtɪk), *a.* *Chem. Obs.* [f. L. *rūta* rue + -IC.] ***rutic acid,*** *(a)* = RUTIN; *(b)* capric acid.

1857 SCHUNCK in *Manch. Mem.* Ser. II. XV. (1860) 128 A comparison of the properties and composition of this substance with those of Rutine or Rutic Acid..leads to the conclusion that they are identical. **1876** HARLEY *Mat. Med.* (ed. 6) 680 Rutic acid crystallises in colourless needles.

ruticilline (ruːtɪ'sɪlaɪn), *a.* *Ornith.* [f. mod.L. *ruticilla.*] Pertaining to, or forming, the genus *Ruticilla* (the Redstarts).

1893 NEWTON *Dict. Birds* 277 These [genera] are adopted by Mr. Oates, who..refers all to the Ruticilline group (Redstart) of *Turdidæ.* **1899** A. H. EVANS *Birds* 516 As regards the Saxicoline and Ruticilline forms attention should be drawn to the jerky, flitting flight.

rutilant ('ruːtɪlənt), *a.* Also 5 **rutilaunt,** 6 *Sc.* **ruteland.** [ad. L. *rutilant-, rutilans*, pres. pple. of *rutilāre*: see next.] Glowing, shining, gleaming, glittering, with either a ruddy or golden light. Also *fig.*

In quot. 1868 used participially with object.

1497 BP. ALCOCK *Mons Perf.* E ii/2 Lykned to the rose rutilaunt and the whyte lely. **1513** BRADSHAW *St. Werburge* I. 3456 This rutilant gemme and specious floure. **1542** BECON *Christm. Banq.* iii, O repentance, more rutilant & shining than gold. **1599** NASHE *Lenten Stuffe* 36 The lordly sonne the most rutilant planet of the seuen. **1684** tr. *Bonet's Merc. Compit.* XIX. 808 The florid and rutilant part in the coagulated Blood. *a* **1706** EVELYN *Silva* (1776) 385 This cheerful green and Rutilant berries. **1868** BROWNING *Ring & Bk.* III. 359 The Abate's guardian eye—Scintillant, rutilant, fraternal fire. **1884** G. MOORE *Mummer's Wife* (1892) 285 Show-rooms..rutilant with gas and electric light. **1917** A. HUXLEY *Let.* 30 Sept. (1969) 135 Behemoth His eyes are little rutilant stones Sunk in black basalt. **1944** S. PUTNAM tr. *E. da Cunha's Rebellion in Backlands* i. §4. 35 Diminutive-leafed opuntias,..bordered with rutilant flowers. **1954** *Times Lit. Suppl.* 2 July 425/4 There are certain magical elements constantly working against the proof-corrector—a being less rutilant, but not less vulnerable, than Tchaikovsky's Prince. **1956** K. WATSON *Source* 46 Rutilant the trail in space Of some recurrent meteor.

Hence **'rutilance** [-ANCE], rutilant quality (*rare*).

1922 JOYCE *Ulysses* 691 He..ignited it in the candle-flame, applied it when ignited to the apex of the cone till the latter reached the stage of rutilance.

†'rutilate, *v.* *Obs. rare.* [f. ppl. stem of L. *rutilāre*, f. *rutilus* reddish, golden, shining, etc.] (See quots. and cf. prec.)

1623 COCKERAM, *Rutilate*, to shine, to make to glister. **1656** BLOUNT, *Rutilate*,..to shine or glare, to make to shine or glister like Gold, to make bright, yellow. **1669** *Addr. Yng. Gentry Eng.* 77 Our painter may fear to begin a face so full of life, as all his skill and oyl will be too little to rarifie and air, to brisk and rutilate.

So **†ruti'lation.**

1658 PHILLIPS, *Rutilation*, a shining, glistring, or glaring.

rutilated ('ruːtɪleɪtɪd), *a.* *Min.* [f. RUTIL(E + -ATE[2] + -ED[2].] Of quartz: containing needles of rutile. Cf. SAGENITE.

1889 in *Rep. Min. Ind. U.S.* (1892) 675 Smoky quartz, Gold quartz, Rutilated quartz. **1977** A. HALLAM *Planet Earth* 136 Rutilated quartz contains orientated needles of rutile.

rutile ('ruːtɪl). *Min.* [a. F. *rutile* or G. *rutil* (Werner, 1803), f. L. *rutilus* red.] An ore of titanium (a form of titanium dioxide).

1803 in *Trans. R. Irish Acad.* (1806) X. 14 Rutile is generally of cotemporaneous formation with its associated fossils. **1836** MACGILLIVRAY *Trav. Humboldt* xx. 295 The formation..contained cyanite, rutile, and garnets. **1888** RUTLEY *Rock-Forming Min.* 136 The crystals of rutile met with in rocks are usually of exceedingly small dimensions. **1951** *Chambers's Jrnl.* Sept. 568/2 Both the principal titanium minerals, ilmenite and rutile, are present in the black sands of streams and beaches in many parts of the world. **1965** *Sunday Mail Mag.* (Brisbane) 17 Jan. 11 Rutile was also needed as a flux for electric welding rods, armaments, ship building, tanks, etc. **1971** *Materials & Technol.* II. viii. 502 Still more spectacular fire is seen in synthetic rutile (titanium oxide) which can also be made by flame-fusion.

attrib. **1836** MACGILLIVRAY *Trav. Humboldt* xi. 142 Veins of quartz, containing rutile titanite. **1888** RUTLEY *Rock-Forming Min.* 136 This grouping of rutile crystals may sometimes be found forming intergrowths with specular iron. **1971** *Jrnl. Oil & Colour Chemists' Assoc.* LIV. 849 Film volume measurements..showed a shrinkage of 6 per cent during six weeks of ageing at 25°C in the laboratory, for unpigmented and rutile titanium dioxide pigmented alkyd films.

rutilite ('ruːtɪlaɪt). *Min.* [f. RUTILE + -ITE[1] 2 b. Cf. F. *rutilite.*] = RUTILE.

1803 in *Trans. R. Irish Acad.* (1806) X. 17 Rutilite. Calcareo-siliceous titan ore of Kirwan. *Ibid.* 20 [The] very compounded nature of hornblende and rutilite. **1815** AIKIN *Man. Min.* (ed. 2) 137 Rutilite... Colour redish, yellowish, greyish, and blackish brown.

rutilous ('ruːtɪləs), *a.* *rare.* [f. L. *rutilus* red.]

a. Shining with a ruddy hue. **b.** Reddish.

1657 TOMLINSON *Renou's Disp.* 630 The Female [viper] should be.. with a fiery aspect, rutilous and red eyes. **1829** T. PRICE *Physiogn. & Physiol.* 113 In Burgundy, the light brown hair, and gray eye, have succeeded to the asserted rutilous character of its ancient conquerors. *Ibid.* 120 The German states, the real seats of the ancient rutilous fiery Goths of Cæsar and Tacitus.

rutin ('ru:tɪn). *Chem.* Also †-ine. [a. G. *rutin* (A. Weiss 1842, in *Pharm. Centralbl.* XIII. 903), f. L. *rūta* RUE *sb.*[2]: see -IN[1].] A yellow crystalline phenolic glycoside, $C_{27}H_{30}O_{16}$, found in several plant species (notably common rue, buckwheat, and capers) which possesses vasopressor properties and is taken to reduce blood pressure.

1857 [see RUTIC *a.*]. **1868** WATTS *Dict. Chem.* V. 139 According to Stein, safflower yellow is uncrystallisable rutin. **1895** *Naturalist* 24 The leaves contain a considerable quantity of a tannin which.. seems associated with rutin. **1967** *Times Rev. Industry* Feb. 118/1 (Advt.), High blood pressure? Rutin, the natural product, has helped thousands of sufferers. **1977** *Martindale's Extra Pharmacopoeia* (ed. 27) 1697/2 Rutin was formerly used in the treatment of disease states characterised by capillary bleeding associated with increased capillary fragility but evidence of its value is inconclusive.

attrib. **1868** WATTS *Dict. Chem.* V. 141 Rutin sugar.. isomeric with glucose.. is not fermentable.

rutl, variant of ROTL.

Rutland ('rʌtlənd). [Trade-name, first used in 1889.] A superior roan leather used in bookbinding. (Orig. called ***Rutland morocco.***)

1894-5 *Oxf.* (*Clar. Press*) *Trade Catal.*, etc. 18 Rutland Morocco, limp,.. gilt roll. **1903** *Ibid.* 36 Also in straight grain roan, rutland, half-calf,.. and turkey morocco.

rutle, obs. form of RUTTLE *v.*

rutour, -owr, Sc. variants of ROUTER *sb.*[1] *Obs.*

†'**rutsel**, *v. Obs.*[−1] [ad. MDu. *rutselen*, freq. of *rutsen*, *rotsen* to slide.] *intr.* To slide.

1481 CAXTON *Reynard* (Arb.) 18 He satte vpon his hammes, and began to rutsele ouer his tayl.

†'**rutson.** *Obs. rare.* In 5 rot-, rutsonn, rutteson. [ad. AF. *ruteison* (Bozon): cf RUTEY *v.* and RUT *sb.*[1]] Rutting. Chiefly *attrib.*

c **1410** *Master of Game* (MS. Digby 182) ii, Alle þe tyme fro þe Rutteson into whitsonday into Rutteson tyme men shall fynde but fewe gret dere, saue vpon þe hilles. *Ibid.* xiii, None of alle þise iii. manere of houndes hunteth not at þe herte in rotsonn tyme.

rutt, obs. f. RUT *sb.*; var. RUTH[2].

rutte: see ROUT *v.*[4] *Obs.*

rutted ('rʌtɪd), *ppl. a.* [f. RUT *v.*[4] or *sb.*[2] + -ED[1].] Of roads, etc.: Broken, cut up, or marked, with ruts. Also *fig.*

1823 MOIR in *Blackw. Mag.* XIII. 647 Over the rutted road the empty wane Homewards is driven. **1846** RUSKIN *Mod. Painters* I. II. I. vii. §22 The painter is evidently embarassed without his rutted road.. and his boggy pool. **1861** GEO. ELIOT *Silas M.* iii, Raveloe lay low among the bushy trees and the rutted lanes. **1913** [see ROUTINED *ppl. a.*]. **1957** G. RYLE in C. A. Mace *Brit. Philos. in Mid-Cent.* 259 Equations are not mere records of deeply rutted associations of ideas.

‖**ruttee** ('rʌti:). Also 7 rotti, 7, 9 rati. [ad. Hindī *rattī*, the seed of a leguminous creeper, *Abrus precatorius.*] A small Indian weight (about 1.75 grs. Troy) used for weighing gems.

1625 PURCHAS *Pilgrims* I. III. 223 Yet could he find neuer any one [diamond] for his purpose, but one of fiue Rotties, which was not very foule neither. **1678** J. PHILLIPS *Tavernier's Trav.* II. 140 At the Mine of Soumelpour in Bengala, they weigh by Rati's, and the Rati is seven eighths of a Carat, or three Grains and a half. **1698** FRYER *Acc. E. India & P.* 206, 8 Ruttees is 7 Carracks. **1753** *Chambers' Cycl.* Suppl. s.v. *Caract*, Eighty eight caracts make an hundred ruttees. **1866** *Treas. Bot.* s.v. *Abrus*, These seeds.. are employed in India as a standard of weight under the name of Rati. **1901** KIPLING *Kim* ix, There is one ruby of Burma, of two ruttees without a flaw.

rutter[1] ('rʌtə(r)). Also 6 ruter, 9 ruttier. [a. MDu. *rutter*, var. of *ruter*, *ruyter* (Du. *ruiter* RUITER, whence G. *reuter*), ad. OF. *routier*, *routeur*: see ROUTER *sb.*[1] Cf. med.L. *rut(t)arius* RUTAR, and (M)Sw. *ryttare*, Da. *rytter*.]

1. A cavalry soldier (*esp.* a German one), of the kind employed in the wars of the 16th and 17th centuries. Now *arch.*

1506 *Paston Lett.* III. 405 Thyse to the rutters of the spers. **1523** LD. BERNERS tr. *Froiss.* I. cccxlvii. 551 There he assembled a great nombre of such rutters, englisshe, gascons, bretons, almayns. **1592** KYD *Sol. & Pers.* I. iii, You are a Rutter borne in Germanie. **1630** *R. Johnson's Kingd. & Commw.* 148 An Army.. amounting all to ten thousand horse. To which he might adde three or foure thousand German Rutters. **1654** EARL MONM. tr. *Bentivoglio's Wars Flanders* 206 Mustering a considerable strength of Foot.. together with a good number of Rutters. **1865** KINGSLEY *Herew.* xxi, He and his troop of Angevine ruttiers had fought like tigers by William's side at Hastings.

†**b.** Used with allusion to the dress or manners of such persons; hence, a gay cavalier, a dashing gallant. Cf. ROUTER *sb.*[1] 2. *Obs.*

a **1500** MEDWALL *Nature* (Brandl) I. 1078 Whan he is in suche aray, There goth a rutter, men wyll say, a rutter huf a galand. **1526** SKELTON *Magnyf.* 762 Howe sayst thou, man? am not I a ioly rutter? **1567-9** JEWEL *Def. Apol.* (1611) 360 Zuinglius was a godly Preacher, and no Rutter.

comb. **1603** KNOLLES *Hist. Turks* (1621) 832 The high Dutch attired in blacke, with.. long breeches little lesse than Rutter wise.

†**2.** One of a party of swindlers (see quot.). *Obs.*

1591 GREENE *Conny Catch.* To Rdr., Four persons were required to perfourm their coosning commodity. The taker-vp, the Verser, the Barnard and the Rutter. *Ibid.*, Then standeth the Rutter at the doore.

'**rutter**[2]. Also ritter. [f. RUT *v.*[2], RIT *v.*[1] + -ER[1].] A spade for cutting or slitting peat turf.

1877 [see RIT *v.*[1] 1 b]. **1923** *Chambers's Jrnl.* 12 May 370/1 The rutter is a two-handed spade, the blade heart-shaped and sharp. **1975** *Times* 27 Aug. 8/5 A curved rutter is used for cutting the [peat] turf, a long-handled spade or flaughter for removing it.

'**rutter**[3]. *N. Amer.* [f. RUT *sb.*[2] or RUT *v.*[4] + -ER[1].] A kind of plough used by lumberjacks for making tracks for sleighs.

1969 L. G. SORDEN *Lumberjack Lingo* 100 *Rutter*, a form of plow for cutting ruts in an iced logging road for the runners of a sleigh. It was often combined with a snowplow. The roads were sprinkled with water from the water tank and frozen to make ice roads. **1972** *Islander* (Victoria, B.C.) 19 Nov. 4/3 The lumbermen had a unique system of hauling logs. In early fall, while the ground was still soft, they would build a rutter. Using the front bob of a wide logging sleigh, a small V-shaped plow was welded to the point of each sleigh runner. Then the sleigh bob was taken to the top of the proposed logging road, turned around, and twin tracks were then plowed eight inches deep and six inches wide down to the main camp.

rutter, obs. form of RUTTIER.

†'**rutterkin.** *Obs.* Also 6 -kyn(e, -kine, -king. [f. RUTTER[1] + -KIN.] A swaggering gallant or bully.

1526 SKELTON *Magnyf.* 757 Rutty bully, ioly rutterkyn. **1530** *Songs* in *Anglia* XII. 593 When all is done this mynyon ys A rutterkyn. **1556** OLDE *Antichrist* 82 Those noble rutterkines of the churche, dyd more cruell feates than these. **1581** J. BELL *Haddon's Answ. Osorius* 397 The Romish Rutterkyne must call us backe to his filthy Cesternes.

attrib. **1594** O. B. *Quest. Profit. Concern.* 2 b, The Rutterking Tailors of the old stampe.

†'**ruttery.** *Sc. Obs. rare*[−1]. [f. RUT *sb.*[1] + -ERY.] Lust, lechery.

1567 *Satir. Poems Reform.* vii. 117 Bothwell.. the Quene syne rauyssit to him sell, In fylthie lust..; Thocht sho, bewitcheit, wald in ruttery ring [etc.].

rutteson, variant of RUTSON *Obs.*

'**ruttier.** Now *arch.* Also 5- rutter, 6 ruter. [ad. F. *routier*, f. *route* ROUTE *sb.*] A set of instructions for finding one's course at sea; a marine guide to the routes, tides, etc. Cf. ROUTIER.

α. *a* **1500** (*title*), The Booke of the Sea Carte called the Rutter, which sheweth ye tydes, courses, kennynges,.. aboute the whole Ile of Brytanye. **1561** EDEN *Arte Nauig.* Pref. ¶ ¶ i, Without any Rutter or Carde of Nauigation. **1594** BLUNDEVIL *Exerc.*, *Art Navig.* lv. (1597) 353 Whose Tables touching the tydes are called Rutters. *Ibid.*, I would wish such general Rutter to be made in maner of an Alphabet. **1937** *Geogr. Jrnl.* XC. 386 It appears that there were existing rutters up to this point. **1962** [see ROUTIER[1]]. **1971** S. E. MORISON *European Discovery Amer.*: *Northern Voy.* v. 138 The rutters (*routiers*), unofficial coast pilots of the period [*sc.* the sixteenth century], were written primarily for finding one's way along European shores. **1973** D. DIVINE *Opening of World* v. 85 An English Rutter, the northern and slightly less refined version of the *portolano*, describing a harbour entrance in 1295.

β. **1600** HAKLUYT *Voy.* III. 719 A ruttier or course to be kept for him that will sayle from Cabo Verde to the coast of Brasil. **1611** COTGR., *Routier*,.. a Ruttier; a directorie for the knowledge, or finding out of courses, whether by sea or land. **1802** in JAMES *Milit. Dict.* **1855** KINGSLEY *Westw. Ho!* i, See if he don't tell you over the ruttier as well as Drake himself.

ruttier: see RUTTER[1].

'**rutting,** *vbl. sb.* [f. RUT *v.*[3]]

a. The fact of being in, or passing into, a state of (periodic) sexual excitement. Also *fig.*

1607 TOPSELL *Four-f. Beasts* (1658) 101 At the time of their lust or rutting, they are above measure fierce. **1608** SHAKS. *Per.* IV. v. 9, I'll do any thing now that is virtuous; but I am out of the road of rutting for ever. **1681** T. FLATMAN *Heraclitus Ridens* No. 37 (1713) I. 244 Have you heard how the Whigs go a Rutting in the Country, as well as a Bulling in the City? **1749** FIELDING *Tom Jones* v. xi, Rutting (an uncouth phrase, by which the vulgar denote that gentle dalliance which.. passes between lovers of the ferine kind). **1772** *Ann. Reg.* II. 100 Several people.. make use of them for hunting wild deer, or for decoying them home, especially in the time of their rutting. **1847-9** TODD *Cycl. Anat.* IV. 473/2 The period of rutting among most animals .. is associated with the commencement of the warmer season. **1861** BONER *Forest Creatures* 42 This.. was merely a preparation for a later rutting, which took place in December.

b. *attrib.*, as ***rutting call, -part, -season, -sport, -state, -time, -wrath***; **rutting-angles** (see quot. 1834).

1576 TURBERV. *Venerie* 147 Then you may hunte them [*sc.* goats] vntill theyr Rutting time come. **1600** BRETON *Pasquils Fooles-cappe* Wks. (Grosart) I. 21/1 And cares not how, nor where she leaue the Ramme, When she hath gotten once the rutting parte. **1675** COTTON *Burlesque upon B.* 61 With some Goddess hee would be at the Rutting sport. **1706-7** FARQUHAR *Beaux' Strat.* v. iii, Ha! the very timorous stag will kill in rutting time. **1774** GOLDSM. *Nat. Hist.* (1824) I. 383 Its excessive viciousness during the rutting season. **1825** JAMIESON *Suppl.* s.v. *Ruttery*, As brute animals, in the rutting state, run from place to place. **1834** JESSE *Glean. Nat. Hist.* Ser. II. 25 During a particular season the male mole makes what mole catchers call the rutting-angles. These are much larger than the usual runs. **1877** J. A. ALLEN *Amer. Bison* 463 During the rutting season, the bulls often wage fierce battles. **1893** KIPLING *Seven Seas* (1896) 59 And when the first September gales have slaked their rutting-wrath, The great man-seal haul back to the sea. **1937** *Discovery* Oct. 314/1 The rutting call of the stag.

'**rutting,** *ppl. a.* [f. RUT *v.*[3]] Given to rutting; in a state of rut.

1624 MASSINGER *Parl. of Love* IV. v, Fie! you shame yourself, And the profession of your rutting gallants. **1891** *Athenæum* 7 Feb. 186/3 A man pursued by a rutting elephant. **1896** NEIL MUNRO *Lost Pibroch* (1902) 11 The rutting deer bellowed with loud throats.

†'**ruttingly,** *adv. Obs.*[−1] [irreg. f. RUTTER[1] 1 b.] Dashingly; so as to make a gallant show.

1526 SKELTON *Magnyf.* 847 My robe russheth So ruttyngly, Me seme I flye.

†'**ruttish,** *a. rare.* [f. RUT *v.*[3] + -ISH.] Lewd, lustful, lascivious; of or pertaining to sexual excitement.

1601 SHAKS. *All's Well* IV. iii. 243 A foolish idle boy: but for all that very ruttish. **1602** MIDDLETON *Phœnix* I. ii, He was too ruttish himself to let me thrive under him. **1938** R. GRAVES *Coll. Poems* 158 A score of bats bewitched By the ruttish odour Swoop singing at his head. **1977** *Daily Tel.* 2 Dec. 15/5 He returns to ogling the field with his ruttish chum.

Hence '**ruttishness.** *rare*[−0]. (Webster, 1847.)

ruttle ('rʌt(ə)l), *sb.*[1] Now *dial.* [f. RUTTLE *v.*] A rattling noise in the throat.

1713 BURNET *Serm.* 175 The last Agonies, the fixed Eyes, and the dismal Ruttle,.. tell all those about the Dying-Bed, that he.. is now going to his Home. **1838** HOLLOWAY *Prov. Dict.*, *Ruttles*, a noise, occasioned by a difficulty of breathing. **1862** C. C. ROBINSON *Dial. Leeds* Gloss. 396 Persons are said to have the 'death-rattle' or 'ruttle' in their dying moments.

'**ruttle,** *sb.*[2] (See quot. 1876.)

1876 A. H. GREEN *Phys. Geol.* ix. 363 Cracks roughly parallel to the plane of the fault, which are sometimes called 'Ruttles' by quarrymen. **1883** GRESLEY *Gloss. Coal-mining* 209.

ruttle ('rʌt(ə)l), *v.* Now *dial.* Forms: 4 rutele, 5 ruthle, 5-6 rutill, rutle, 7, 9 ruttle. [= MLG. *rutelen*, prob. of imitative origin: cf. ROTTLE *v.* and RATTLE *v.*] *intr.* To rattle; to make a rattling noise in the throat.

a **1400** *Pol., Rel., & L. Poems* 250 þin teth ratilet.., and þi þrote rutelet3. **14..** in *Reliq. Antiq.* I. 54 If he rutills: this er the takenynges of dethe. *c* **1425** *Eng. Conq. Irel.* 16 With wepne ryngynge, speres and sparthes ruthlynge [*v.r.* rutlynge] to-geddre. **1566** DRANT *Horace, Sat.* II. v. H v, If one of thy cooparteners gin to rutle in the throte. **1651** R. WATKINS *Newes fr. Dead* 2 The Coffin being opened, she was observed to breath, and in breathing.. obscurely to ruttle. *Ibid.* 3 Shee ruttled more than before, and seemed obscurely to cough. **1828-** in dial. glossaries (E. Anglia, Linc., Craven, Leeds).

Hence '**ruttling** *vbl. sb.* and *ppl. a.*

c **1400** *MS. Cott. Calig. A* ii. fol. 113 Then was rutlynge in Rome, and rubbynge of helmes. **1530** LYNDESAY *Test. Papyngo* 668, I am ane blak Monk, said the rutlande [1592 rutilland] Ravin. **1857** BORROW *Romany Rye* xl, Little or no ruttling having been heard in the tube. **1862** —— *Wales* III. viii. 75 The ruttling of the smoker's pipe in the chimney-corner.

†'**ruttock.** *Obs. rare.* A stick or staff.

1542 UDALL *Erasm. Apoph.* 154 Laie me a litle ruttocke hard beside me, wher with to beate theim awaye. *Ibid.* 214 b, He putte abrode the louvres of the tente with a ruttocke that he had in his hande.

rutty ('rʌtɪ), *a.* [f. RUT *sb.*[2] + -Y.]

1. Marked by, full of, abounding in, ruts.

1596 SPENSER *Prothalamion* 12 Themmes, Whose rutty Bancke.. Was paynted all with variable flowers. **1610** G. FLETCHER *Christ's Triumph* ii, That heav'nly voice I more delight to heare, Then.. whistling reeds, that rutty Jordan laves. **1767** G. S. CAREY *Hills of Hybla* 14 Some long and rutty lane. **1810** *Splendid Follies* I. 156 A dirty narrow rutty green. **1865** KNIGHT *Passages Work. Life* II. xiii. 264 No sound of wheels was heard but that of the cart labouring through the rutty ways. **1891** MISS DOWIE *Girl in Karp.* 7 We dashed down the rutty road.

transf. **1892** *Temple Bar* Nov. 374 There is too much rutty conventionality about.

2. Of a drive: Performed on a rutted road.

1883 LD. R. GOWER *Rem.* II. xxi. 61 After a rough and rutty drive, Bolsover Castle.. was reached.

3. Deeply sunk or furrowed.

1894 K. GRAHAME *Pagan P.* 108 Mud is muddier now than heretofore; and ruts are ruttier.

†'**rutty** (also roty), used in refrains. *Obs.*

1526 SKELTON *Magnyf.* 757 Rutty bully, ioly rutterkyn, heyda! *a* **1529** —— *Agst. comely Coystrowne* 29 He lumbryth on a lewde lewte, Roty bully joyse,.. hey go, now, now!

rutyl ('ru:tɪl). *Chem.* [f. as RUTIC *a.* + -YL.] (See quots.)

1868 WATTS *Dict. Chem.* V. 141 *Rutyl*, syn. with Capryl, $C^{10}H^{19}O$, the radicle of rutic or capric acid. **1894** MORLEY

& MUIR *Watts' Dict. Chem.* IV. 419/2 *Rutyl*, a name sometimes used for decoyl $C_{10}H_{19}O$ or decyl $C_{10}H_{21}$.

'rutylene. *Chem.* [f. prec. + -ENE.] (See quots.)
1868 WATTS *Dict. Chem.* V. 141 *Rutylene*,..a hydrocarbon polymeric with acetylene... Rutylene is a colourless liquid, lighter than water, and having an agreeable odour, somewhat like that of turpentine-oil. **1873** *Fownes' Chem.* (ed. 11) 561 Decine, or Rutylene, is obtained by the action of alcoholic potash on diamylene dibromide.

ruve, Sc. variant of RO, rest. *Obs.*

†**ruvell.** *Sc. Obs.*$^{-1}$ (Meaning obscure.)
1538 *Acc. Ld. High Treas. Scot.* VII. 87 For nyne quhynȝearis ouregilt, and twa of thame with schethis of welvot, all furnist chaip and ruvell witht silver werk.

ruvid ('ruːvɪd), *a. rare.* [ad. It. *ruvido*, app. repr. L. *ruidus* (Pliny).]
†**1.** Rude, barbarous. *Obs.*
1632 LITHGOW *Trav.* VI. 291 The ruvid Cittizens, being Turkes, Moores, Iewes,..and Nostranes. *Ibid.* 296 Their food also [is] semblable, to their ruvid condition.
2. Rough, rugged. *rare*$^{-1}$.
1837 A. B. GRANVILLE *Spas of Germany* I. 322 On passing my hand all over the body..it felt ruvid, and the two surfaces seemed to meet with resistance.
So †'**ruvidous** *a. Obs.*$^{-1}$
1632 LITHGOW *Trav.* IX. 421 Polland is..charged with a proud Nobility, a familiar and manly Gentry, and a ruvidous vulgarity.

Ruwala, var. RUALLA.

ruwe, obs. form of ROW *a.*[1], RUE *sb.*[2]

ruwet, variant of RUET *Obs.*

ruwyn, obs. form of RUIN *sb.*

†**rux**[1]. *Obs.*$^{-1}$ (See quot.)
1739 TONKIN *Carew's Cornwall* (1811) 23 *note*, An account of a gentleman that..took up out of the heap of tin certain glorious corns (which they call rux), which he affirmed to be pure gold.

rux[2] (rʌks). *Naut. slang.* [Origin unknown: cf. RUCK *v.*[6] and RUCKUS.] Disturbance, uproar.
1918 *Blackw. Mag.* CCIV. 68/1 Harker, who for fifteen months had haunted the shadows on the look-out for just such a 'rux', whose ear caught every illicit sound. **1931** KIPLING *Limits & Renewals* (1932) 196 The nastiest rux I ever saw, when a boy, began with 'All hands to skylark.' *I* don't hold with it. *Ibid.* 200 I've seen worse ruxes in my time, but a quicker breeze-up—never!

rux, var. RUCK *v.*[6]

ruyd(e, ruyd(e)ly(che, obs. ff. RUDE *a.*, RUDELY *adv.*

ruyghe, obs. f. ROUGH *a.*

ruyl, obs. f. RULE *sb.*

Ruy Lopez ('ruːiː 'ləʊpɛz). *Chess.* [The name of *Ruy López* de Segura (fl. 1560), Spanish bishop and writer on chess, who developed this opening.] A chess opening characterized by the moves 1 P-K4, P-K4; 2 Kt-KB3, Kt-QB3; 3 B-Kt5.
1876 *Encycl. Brit.* V. 594/2 The following are given as indicative illustrations of certain of the leading openings... Ruy Lopez. **1894** *Yale Wit & Humor* 49/1 Our [chess] team appears to have executed a masterly flank movement in 'retaking the exchanged Pawn in the Ruy Lopez'. **1958** [see NIMZO-INDIAN *a.*]. **1976** *Milton Keynes Express* 2 July 40/5 He opened with the Ruy Lopez and won in 20 moves.

ruynat(e, ruyne, ruynose, etc.: see RUINATE, RUIN (and RYNE[1]), RUINOUS.

Rwanda ('rwændə, ruː'ændə). Also **Ruanda**.
a. A Bantu language of East Africa. **b.** An East African people; the inhabitants of the country of Rwanda. **c.** An East African republic (founded 1961), formerly kingdom. Also *attrib.* Hence **Rwandan** *sb.* and *a.*, **Rwan'dese** *a.*
1902 H. H. JOHNSTON *Uganda Protectorate* II. 969 Urunyaruanda is spoken in Ruanda, or Bunya-ruanda, south of Ankole... English, *ant*... Ruanda, *entωzi*. **1924** SMITH & SHARP *Ruanda's Redemption* 18 (*heading*) Receipts for Kigezi and Ruanda work 1920–23. *Ibid.* 22 The only literature in the Ruanda language is a translation of the four Gospels. **1939** L. H. GRAY *Foundations of Lang.* 405 Homburger's classification [of Bantu languages] is as follows:..(2) *Ruanda*, north-east of Tanganyika. **1959** *Listener* 29 Oct. 740/1 The Ruanda and Urundi of that trusteeship territory, the Belgian Congo, Uganda and Tanganyika. **1969** J. C. KING *Evangelicals* vii. 60 A similar tight-knit group within Church of England Evangelicalism is the Ruanda movement. This consists of people influenced by the East African revival movement, through the Ruanda Mission. **1973** *Times* 11 Dec. (Zaire Suppl.) p. vii/9 On our return to Goma we passed a memorial to 23 wardens killed while defending the park against Zairian, Ugandan and Rwandese poachers. **1974** *Encycl. Brit. Micropædia* VIII. 737/3 In 1969, an estimated 3,600,000 Rwanda occupied an area of roughly 10,000 square miles. **1974** *Encycl. Brit. Macropædia* XVI. 109/1 The first impression given by the Rwandan landscape is that it resembles an immense green park dominated by banana plantations. *Ibid.* 109/2 Traditionally, Rwandans believe in a supreme being called Imana. **1979** *Brit. Med. Jrnl.* 15 Dec. 1560/1 We slowly came to appreciate the fabric of a Rwandan home, from the mud walls without to the complex and supportive family within.

rwch, rwd, rwik, rwine, obs. Sc. ff. ROUGH *a.*, ROOD *sb.*, ROOK *sb.*[1], RUIN *sb.*

rwly, rwmor, obs. ff. RULY *adv.*, RUMOUR.

rwtowr, Sc. var. ROUTER *sb.*[1] *Obs.*

rwyn, rwynus, obs. ff. RUIN, RUINOUS.

ry-, a common ME. spelling in all words beginning with RI-, as *ryal* RIAL *a.*, *ryb* RIB *sb.*, *rybald* RIBALD, *ryband* RIBAND, etc. For variants not entered below, see the corresponding forms with RI-.

-ry, *suffix*, a reduced form of -ERY, occurring chiefly after an unstressed syllable ending in *d*, *t*, *l*, *n*, or *sh* (the usual type being words of three syllables with the stress on the first), but also in a few cases after stressed vowels or diphthongs. The older examples sometimes represent OF. forms in *-rie*, with variants in *-erie*, but the great majority are comparatively late English formations. Examples of the various types are *heraldry*, *husbandry*, *ribaldry*, *wizardry*; *casuistry*, *dentistry*, *harlotry*, *infantry*, *papistry*, *peasantry*, *tenantry*; *chivalry*, *devilry*, *rivalry*; *blazonry*, *yeomanry*; *Englishry*, *Irishry*; *avowry*, *Jewry*. In some cases both *-ery* and *-ry* are in use, as *baptist(e)ry*, *command(e)ry*, *jewel(le)ry*.

rya ('riːə). Also **ryiji, ryijy**. [Sw. *rya* in same sense; cf. Finnish *ryijy*.] A Scandinavian type of knotted pile rug. Also *attrib.*
1957 B. PEPIS *Guide Interior Decorating* iv. 124 The only remotely luxurious note is the small, brightly colored heavily piled 'rya' rug, an adaptation of a Finnish design. **1960** *Guardian* 20 July 4/6 Rya rugs are a very old form of Finnish folk art. *Ibid.* 4/7 Ryas..were used in everyday life up to the sixteenth century. **1960** H. HAYWARD *Antique Coll.* 245/2 *Ryijy rugs*, Finnish rugs made in the old Norse tradition of knotted pile technique, which may go back to the Danish Bronze Age. **1964** G. LYALL *Most Dangerous Game* xviii. 139 The only shot I fired hit the ryiji on the floor. **1972** *Homes & Gardens* Aug. 28/2 The choice of rugs ranges from Axminster..to the wildest, woolliest rya imaginable. **1975** 'E. LATHEN' *By Hook or by Crook* vi. 55 When rya rugs first came into fashion..she had..become a trend setter.

ryacolite, ryakolite, varr. RHYACOLITE.

ryakonite, erroneous f. RHYACOLITE.
1837 DANA *Syst. Min.* 293 Feldspar. *Spatum orthotomum.* .. Ice spar. Ryakonite.

rya(u)t, obs. ff. RIOT.

rybadous, var. RIBALDOUS *a.*

ryban(n)e, obs. ff. RIBAND.

rybat ('raɪbət). *Sc.* Forms: 6 rebatt, 9 ribet, rybet, rybat; 8–9 ribbet, 9 ribbit, rebbit. [prob. a variant of RABBET *sb.*, REBATE *sb.*[2], but used in the same sense as REVEAL *sb.*[2]] A polished stone reveal (side-piece) for windows, doors, etc. Also *attrib.*
α. **1554** *Extr. Rec. Burgh Edinb.* (1871) 302 Item, for twa greit rebatt stanis and leidin of thame fra the said querrell to the abbay, iij[s] iiij[d]. Item, to ane masoun to hew the saids rebatts and lintale and to reforme the said yett, xviij[s]. **1789** J. WILLIAMS *Nat. Hist. Mineral Kingd.* I. 76 Some of the thickest of them produce good cutting stones for ribbets. **1808** JAMIESON, *Rebbits*, polished stones for windows. **1833** LOUDON *Encycl. Archit.* §1170 The corners, ribbits (reveals), arches, and skews are supposed to be of hewn stone. **1844** H. STEPHENS *Bk. Farm* I. 118, *d* is the giblet-check in the lintel, and *e* that in the ribbets, into which the door shuts flush.
β. **1833** LOUDON *Encycl. Archit.* §911 The whole of the window rybets (reveals), sills, and lintels..are to be of neatly polished freestonework. **1844** J. BALLANTINE *Deanhaugh* iv. 77 The door-piece, the window rybats, were all kept..clean and bright. **1885** BLACKLAW *Quarry Price List*, Rybats 2 ft. by 12 in. by 6 in. to 8 in. on head 9½d. each.

ryb(b)aud-, rybawd-: see RIBALD-.

rybben, obs. f. RIBBON.

rybe, obs. f. RIB, RUBY.

rybeck. *slang.* (See quot.)
1851 MAYHEW *Lond. Labour* II. 120 This the old Jew agrees to do upon the understanding that he is to have 'half Rybeck', that is, a moiety of the profit. *Ibid.* 121.

rybee, rybwe, obs. varr. RUBY.

rybende, obs. f. RIBAND.

rybod(r)y, obs. ff. RIBALD(R)Y.

rybuck, var. RYEBUCK *a.* (*adv.*) and *int.*

rych(e, obs. forms of RUSH *sb.*[1]

rychellys, rychels, varr. *rechels* REKELS, incense.

rydal, obs. f. RIDEL.

Rydberg ('rɪdbɜːg). *Physics.* The name of Johannes Robert *Rydberg* (1854–1919), Swedish physicist.
1. Used *attrib.* and in the possessive to designate various concepts developed by him, as **Rydberg('s) constant**, an atomic constant, evaluated from several of the fundamental constants of physics, which appears in the formulae for the wave numbers of lines in all atomic spectra (in the case of a hypothetical atom whose nucleus has infinite mass, equal to $2\pi^2me^4/ch^3$, where *m* and *e* are the rest mass and charge of the electron, *c* is the speed of light, and *h* is Planck's constant); see also R III. 4; **Rydberg correction**, a correction term appearing in the formula for the energy of the single electron in the outermost shell of hydrogen-like atoms, arising because the inner shells do not screen the electron completely from the nucleus; **Rydberg('s) formula**, an empirical formula giving the wave numbers of frequencies of the lines in the spectral series of atoms and simple molecules.
1913 *Phil. Mag.* XXVI. 489 An attempt to explain the appearance of Rydberg's constant in the formula for the line-spectrum of any element. **1920**, etc. [see R III. 4]. **1937** *Ann. Reg. 1936* II. 61 Birge..pointed out that the substitution of well-established values for e/m and h/e in the Bohr formula for the Rydberg constant gives a value for *e* nearly half of 1 per cent less than the others. **1955** C. G. DARWIN in W. Pauli *Niels Bohr* 7 There can be few other cases in science where a theory has been made which succeeds in yielding a particular number—here Rydberg's constant—from quantities all of which are known, without the admissibility of any adjustable constant to help in doing so. **1979** *Sci. Amer.* Mar. 74/3 Later refinements have complicated Rydberg's empirical formula for the wavelengths of spectral lines, and so the Rydberg constant is now defined as this combination of *m*, *e* and *h*. **1927** J. W. FISHER tr. *Born's Mechanics of Atom* iii. 160 Rydberg was the first to suggest this form and verified it by measurements of numerous spectra. We shall therefore denote the quantity δ as the Rydberg correction. **1936** *Discovery* Jan. 28/1 The quantisation of the Rydberg correction into multiples of a fundamental unit. **1974** G. REECE tr. *Hund's Hist. Quantum Theory* vii. 95 Schroedinger in 1921 realized that the essential point for the interpretation of the large 'Rydberg corrections' was that the s orbits dipped deep into the atom. **1913** *Phil. Mag.* XXVI. 12 The constant K entering in Rydberg's formula is the same for all substances. **1974** G. REECE tr. *Hund's Hist. Quantum Theory* vii. 97 In 1914 A. Fowler, inspired by Bohr's theory of the He^+ lines, showed that for the doublet series of these elements Rydberg formulae held with $4R$ and that they therefore belonged to Mg^+ and Ca^+.
2. (Also written **rydberg**.) **a.** A unit of energy given by $e^2/2a_0$ (approximately $2{\cdot}425 \times 10^{-18}$ joule), where *e* is the electronic charge and a_0 is the radius of the first Bohr orbit for a nucleus of infinite mass. Freq. *attrib.* as ***Rydberg unit***.
1935 *Jrnl. Chem. Physics* III. 563/2 The first choice would lower all [energy] values by 2·3 Rydberg units. **1944** *Physical Rev.* LVI. 336/1 The energy difference of curves III and IV is 0·44 Rydberg units more in Fig. 5 than it is in Fig. 4. **1954** *Ibid.* XCIV. 1519/2 (*caption*) Energy integrals (in Rydbergs) for diamond. **1975** *Nature* 27 Mar. 297/2 If gas accretion by this object produces all the ionising radiation required to maintain the H II region at the galactic centre, the luminosity of this radiation is $L_i = 1{\cdot}9 \times 10^8 L_0$ ..if the energy per photon is 2 rydberg.
b. A name proposed for the unit of wave number, cm^{-1}; = KAYSER.
1951 C. CANDLER in *Nature* 21 Apr. 649 Call 'cm.$^{-1}$' by some new name, such as 'Rydberg', however, and the difficulty disappears. Absorptions can be conveniently recorded in 'kilo-rydbergs'... The name 'Rydberg' was suggested to me many years ago by Prof. H. Dingle.

ryddel, rydelle, etc., obs. ff. RIDEL, RIDDLE.

ryddylled, rydelid, etc., varr. RIDELED *Obs.*

rydelles, rydlesse, obs. varr. REDELESS *a.*

rydels, obs. f. RIDDLE *sb.*[1]

rydilich, var. REDILY *adv. Obs.*

rydoun: see RIDDER *sb.*[1]

rydowre, var. REDDOUR *Obs.*

rydy, obs. f. READY *a.*

rye (raɪ), *sb.*[1] Forms: 1 ryʒi, ryʒe, 4 ruȝe, reye, 4–6 ry, 5–8 rie, 5– rye (7 rey, rhie). [OE. *ryʒe*, = ON. *rug-r* (Fær. *rug-ur*, Norw. *rug*; MSw. *rugh*, *rogh*, *rygh*, Sw. *råg*; MDa. *rugh*, *roug*, *roff*, Da. *rug*):—original **rugiz*. (The long vowel of mod.Icel. *rúgur*, Norw. dial. *ruug*, is of later origin.) Forms corresponding to **rugiz* are found in the Balto-Slavic languages, as OPruss. *rugis*, Lith. *rugỹs* (a single grain; pl. *rugieĩ* rye), Lett. *rudsis* (pl. *rudsi*), Russ. *rozhĭ*; also Esthonian *rukis*, *ru'is*, Finnish *ru'is* (gen. *rukiin*); it is probable that the original home of the word was in eastern Europe. Outside of OE. and ON., the Teutonic languages exhibit derivative forms which represent an earlier **ruggn-* (with normal doubling of *g* before *n*), as OS. *roggo* (MLG. *rogge*, MDu. *rogge*, *rugge*, etc.; LG., Du., WFris. *rogge*, NFris. *rog*, *răg*, *ruag*, etc.), OHG. *roggo* (MHG. *rogge*, G. *roggen*) and *rocco*, *rocko* (MHG. *rocke*, G. *rocken*, now rare).]

1. A food-grain obtained from the plant *Secale cereale*, extensively used in northern Europe.

c **725** *Corpus Gloss.* S 339 *Sicalia*, ryȝe [*Epinal* ryȝi]. *a* **1327** *Pol. Songs* (Camden) 152 Ruls [*sic*] ys oure ruȝe ant roted in the stre. *a* **1352** MINOT *Poems* (ed. Hall) i. 20 þai sent þaire schippes on ilka side With flesch and wine and whete & rye. **1430–1** *Rolls of Parlt.* IV. 369/1 Whete and Rye, and Floure. *a* **1470** *Brut* ccli. (1908) 507 Stephen Brown,.. Mair of London,.. brought to London certeyn shippes laden with Rye. **1540** *Act 32 Hen. VIII*, c. 14 For euerye last of wheat and rie, xxvi.*s.* viii. **1577** HARRISON *England* II. vi. (1877) I. 153 Wheate and rie will be no graine for poore men to feed on. **1624** CAPT. SMITH *Virginia* II. 26 The seed is not much vnlike to Rie, though much smaller. **1676** *Phil. Trans.* XI. 761 The Company gave order to make bread both of this Rey alone, and of the same Rey mingled in different proportions with good Rey. **1707** MORTIMER *Husb.* (1721) I. 125 They sow it.. in the driest time they can, according to the old Saying of Sowing, Rye in the Dust, and Wheat in the Dirt. **1767** A. YOUNG *Farmer's Lett. to People* 266, I have generally, at Michaelmas, sown a few acres of rye for feed in the following spring. **1825** J. NICHOLSON *Operat. Mechanic* 149 The power.. would grind one boll of good rye in one hour. **1864** LONGF. *Wayside Inn* 214 A scant handful.. of wheat, Or rye, or barley, or some other grain.

2. a. The plant *Secale cereale*, which has some resemblance to wheat, but flourishes in poorer soils; the principal cereal of northern Europe, but in Great Britain now chiefly cultivated as a forage crop. Also *collect.*, a number of growing plants of this kind (in a field).

c **1440** tr. *Pallad. on Husb.* I. 165 Thy whete.. In lond to faat wol turne into other corn, And rie of whete ysowen wul vp growe. **1500–20** DUNBAR *Poems* liii. 17 Lyk a stirk stackarand in the ry. **1562** *Child-Marriages* 107 [He] was ware also of John Leigh ronnynge further into the Ry, belike to hide hym-self. **1610** SHAKS. *Temp.* IV. i. 61 Thy rich Leas Of Wheate, Rye, Barley, Fetches, Oates and Pease. **1676** *Phil. Trans.* XI. 758 A strange sort of Rey, growing sometimes in certain parts of France. **1762** MILLS *Syst. Pract. Husb.* I. 373 Both wheat and rye may be cut somewhat before they are thoroughly ripe. **1785** MARTYN *Rousseau's Bot.* xiii. (1794) 143 In Rie, the exterior valve or chaff of the corolla ends in a long beard or awn. **1833** TENNYSON *Lady of Shalott* i. 2 Long fields of barley and of rye. **1872** OLIVER *Elem. Bot.* II. 276 The spikelets in Rye.. are arranged singly upon the rachis, as in Wheat.

b. *pl.* Rye-crops.

1795 *Scots Mag.* LVII. 273/1 The Ryes are in general healthy and vigorous.

c. ***wild rye***: (see quots.).

c **1475** *Pict. Voc.* in Wr.-Wülcker 787 *Hec silago*, wyld rye. **1760** J. LEE *Introd. Bot.* App. 325 Rye, Wild, *Hordeum.* **1796** WITHERING *Brit. Pl.* (ed. 3) II. 171 *Hordeum murinum.* Wall Barley, Way Bennet, Wild Rye. **1846–50** A. WOOD *Class-Bk. Bot.* 620 *Elymus Virginicus.* Lime Grass. Wild Rye.

3. *ellipt.* **a.** Rye-whisky. *U.S.* and *Canad. colloq.*

1835 J. H. INGRAHAM *South-West* II. 56 The painful effects of 'old rye' in the abstract upon the body. **1860** *Grumbler* (Toronto) 19 May 3/3 And, tho' the crowd may smile at me, I'll take some neat 'old rye'. **1873** G. W. PERRIE *Buckskin Mose* xvii. 248 But for the quantity of rye we had all of us been swallowing, the others must have seen through this impudent operation as I had done. **1894** *Outing* XXIV. 60/1, I knew better than to put straight rye on top of it [cider]. **1913** J. LONDON *Valley of Moon* 392 Some drink rain and some champagne..; But I will try a little rye. **1930** D. RUNYON in *Collier's* 1 Feb. 12/3 Wilbur is a great hand for drinking Scotch, or rye. **1945** P. CHEYNEY *I'll say she Does!* iii. 66, I.. finish off my rye an' pour myself another four fingers. **1974** E. MCGIRR *Murderous Journey* 31 He slopped along.. towards the living-room bar. I took a straight rye.

b. *Comb.* in the names of drinks, as ***rye-and-dry*** (see DRY *sb.* 2 c), ***rye-and-ginger***, ***rye-and-orange***, ***rye-and-soda***, ***rye-on-the-rocks***.

1909 G. ADE *Let.* 24 Mar. (1973) 45, I have just had a rye & soda. **1942** *Tee Emm* (Air Ministry) II. 127 Say? What's mine? A Rye and dry. **1956** 'N. SHUTE' *Beyond Black Stump* 5 'What's it to be?' 'Orange juice,' said the young man. Mr Johnson ordered it, with rye on the rocks for himself. **1963** R. I. MCDAVID *Mencken's Amer. Lang.* 168 Canadian topers have an array of combinations.. as *rye and orange* (Canadian whiskey and orange pop). **1964** *Time* (Canada ed.) 31 Jan. 7/1 Accepting a rye and ginger, Mike Pearson then went back to writing out a personal report.

4. *ellipt.* Rye-bread.

1941 [see PASTRAMI]. **1969** [see MAYO]. **1971** 'O. BLEECK' *Procane Chron.* xiv. 123 A Danish sardine sandwich.. between two thick slices of German rye. **1976** H. MACINNES *Agent in Place* v. 48 A ham on rye with a gallon of coffee.

5. *attrib.* **a.** In sense 'made, prepared, or derived from rye', as ***rye-beer***, ***-cake***, ***-dough***, ***-loaf***, ***-mush***, ***-paste***, ***-whisky***.

1861 BENTLEY *Man. Bot.* 699 Quass or *Rye Beer is a favourite drink in Russia. **1549** *Compl. of Scot.* vi. 43 Thai hed na breyd bot *ry caikis. **1875** *Encycl. Brit.* III. 250/2 In the country part of Sweden no bread is made but rye-cakes. **1600** BRETON *Pasquils Fooles-cappe* Wks. (Grosart) I. 20/2 As though she were an Image of *Rie Dowe. *c* **1440** *Jacob's Well* 192 Þe aungelys seyden to him, 'Perys, make þis *rye-loof heuyere in almes-dede, ellys þe feendys schal haue þis soule'. *a* **1652** BROME *Eng. Moor* IV. iv, He keeps this Rie-loaf for his own white tooth. **1897** VOYNICH *Gadfly* (1904) 91/1 Cutting off a chunk from the rye-loaf on the table. **1872** DE VERE *Americanisms* 41 In some parts of the West, another mush is frequently used, but as it is made of rye after the manner of a Hasty Pudding, it is called *Rye Mush. **1615** MARKHAM *Eng. Housew.* II. ii. (1668) 74 *Rye-paste would be kneaded only with hot water, and a little butter. **1897** FLANDRAU *Harvard Episodes* 328, I think I should like a little, a very little, *rye whiskey and water.

b. Miscellaneous, as ***ryebloom***, ***-crop***, ***-ear***, ***-field***, ***-grain***, ***-ground***, ***-grower***, ***-harvest***, ***-hay***, ***-seed***, ***-seedtime***, ***-sheaf***, ***-stalk***, ***-stubble***; ***ryehigh*** adj.

1922 JOYCE *Ulysses* 261 The bag of Goulding, Collis, Ward led Bloom by *ryebloom flowered tables. **1764** *Museum Rust.* IV. 223 We depend much on our *rye-crops, which are very valuable. **1855** *Househ. Words* XI. 129/1 Ophthalmoxystic as a name for a little *rye-ear brush used to smooth the eyebrows. **1762** MILLS *Syst. Pract. Husb.* I. 373 It certainly is extremely wrong ever to turn cattle of any kind into a *rye-field, to feed there. *c* **1841** LONGF. *Frithiof's Saga* Poems (1855) 223 Man-high was waving the rye-field. **1881** WATTS *Dict. Chem.* 3rd Suppl. II. 1768 A. Muntz.. has found in unripe *rye-grain a peculiar substance called synanthrose. **1523** FITZHERB. *Husb.* §18 To set out the shepefolde.. vppon the *rye-grounde, if he haue any. **1764** *Museum Rust.* IV. 348, I own the rye-ground more advantageous to the farmer. *Ibid.* 350 Any balance.. would fall considerably on the side of the *rye-growers. **1577** GOOGE *Heresbach's Husb.* 41 *Rye and Wheate haruest. **1801** *Farmer's Mag.* Aug. 312 The whole to be laid off in *rye hay, (not rye grass hay, but hay made from rye cut green). **1922** JOYCE *Ulysses* 282 O'er *ryehigh blue. Bloom stood up. **1838** T. THOMSON *Chem. Org. Bodies* 878 The grey-coloured substance.. was separated into.. gluten, starch, and the coats of the *rye-seeds. **1611** COTGR., *Semailles de seigles*, *rye-seed-time. **1587** MASCALL *Govt. Cattle, Horses* 188 Some giue a *Rie-sheafe. **1859** MISS CARY *Country Life* (1876) 127 She leaped fences and divided hedges and underbrush as lightly as *rye-stalks. **1707** MORTIMER *Husb.* (1721) I. 135 'Tis good to plow the Wheat or *Rye-stubble up in November.

6. Special combs., as **rye and Indian** (also **Injun**) **(bread)** *U.S.*, bread made from a mixture of rye and (Indian) cornmeal; **rye-asthma** (see quot.); **rye brome (grass)**, a variety of brome, *Bromus secalinus*, with rye-like seeds, occurring as a weed in wheat-fields; **rye coffee** *U.S.*, a drink resembling coffee, made from roasted rye; **rye-crake**, *Sc.*, the corn-crake; **rye-land**, land, usually of a light or inferior quality, suitable for the cultivation of rye; **rye-moth**, (see quot.); **rye waltz** *N. Amer.* (see quot.); **rye-worm** (see quot. 1856).

1840 *Knickerbocker* XVI. 18 There were eggs and fried ham,.. *rye-and-Indian bread. **1887** A. W. TOURGÉE *Button's Inn* 224 She passed around a hot plateful of toasted slices of 'rye and Indian'. **1932** L. I. WILDER *Little House in Big Woods* iv. 45 She baked salt-rising bread and rye 'n' Injun bread and Swedish crackers. **1875** tr. *von Ziemssen's Cycl. Med.* II. 540 In England it is called Hay Fever, or Hay Asthma. It is also called June cold, *Rye asthma. **1812** W. WITHERING JR. *Withering's Brit. Plants* (ed. 5) II. 210 Smooth *Rye Brome-grass... In corn-fields. **1844** H. STEPHENS *Bk. Farm* III. 942 Smooth rye-brome grass, *Bromus secalinus.* **1954** C. E. HUBBARD *Grasses* 67 'Rye Brome' was no doubt introduced into the British Isles long ago with the seeds of cereals. **1769** *Boston Gaz.* 16 Oct. 1/3 And as true Daughters of Liberty, they made their Breakfast upon *Rye Coffee, and their Dinner was partly made of that sort of Venison called Bear. **1877** H. RUEDE *Jrnl.* 13 June in *Sod-House Days* (1937) 99 Most people out here don't drink real coffee, because it is too expensive... So rye coffee is used a great deal—parched brown or black according to whether the users like a strong or mild drink. **1951** L. CRAIG *Singing Hills* iv. 31 Every one had coffee... When I tasted mine I thought, for a moment, that poison had been put in it; it certainly was not like anything I had ever tasted before, for never before had I drunk rye coffee. **1807–10** TANNAHILL *Poems* (1846) 128 The *rye-craik rispt his clamorous throat. **1676** *Phil. Trans.* II. 797 The.. Improvement of the greatest part of Worcester, Gloucester,.. Stafford and Shropshire, in all their *Ryelands. **1707** MORTIMER *Husb.* (1721) I. 125 A little sprinkling of Dung or Mud upon Rye-Land will mightily advance a Crop. **1764** *Museum Rust.* IV. 349 Rye-land is lighter.. than wheat-land. **1856** MORTON *Cycl. Agric.* II. 779/2 The caterpillars.. of the *rye-moth (*Pyralis Secalis*) live within the spathe. **1941** W. C. HANDY *Father of Blues* ii. 16 The waltz was popular, as was also the *rye waltz, a combination of three-four and two-four tempos. **1856** MORTON *Cycl. Agric.* II. 779/2 The *rye-worms.. are the larvæ of little flies called *Oscinis pumilionis.* **1891** *Pall Mall G.* 7 Oct. 5/2 The appearance of the rye-worm is notified over several hundreds of acres.

†**rye**, *sb.*[2] *Obs.* Also 5 ree, rey, ry, 7 rie. [prob. of AF. origin.] A disease in hawks.

c **1450** in *Reliq. Antiq.* I. 295 The Ree cometh in faute of hote mete, of colde, other of smoke, other els of grete fervent hete in the neste. *a* **1450** *Treat. Fishing w. Angle* (1883) 3 Þen schall sche haue the frounce, þe Rey [1496 Rye], þe Cray, and mony oþer seknes. **1485** *Bk. S. Albans* a iiij, For defawte of hoote meete this sekenese the Ry commyth. *c* **1575** *Bk. Sparhawkes* (1886) 27 Rye is a Stuffinge or Swellinge of the head growinge by colde or euell dyet. **1618** LATHAM *Falconry* (1633) 129 Of all the diseases that belongs to these Hawkes, there bee onely three that they bee most subiect vnto, which is the Rye, the Crampe, and the Craye. **1725** *Family Dict.* s.v. *Rye*, The Cold or Rye in her Head, being apt, in time, to fall into her Eyes.

transf. **1759** BROWN *Compl. Farmer* 78 [It] will preserve them [hens] from the rye and other diseases in the head.

rye (raɪ), *sb.*[3] *slang.* [ad. Romany *rai* gentleman; cf. Skr. *rāj* to rule.] A man, gentleman. Also *Comb.*, as **rye mort**, a lady (in quot., *attrib.*); **rye mush**, a gentleman. See also *Romany rye* s.v. ROMANY[3] 3 b.

1851 BORROW *Lavengro* II. xxvi. 242, I had always.. been a great favourite with Mrs. Petulengro, who had frequently been loud in her commendation of the young rye, as she called me. **1857** —— *Romany Rye* I. vi. 74 Gentility will carry the day, madam, even with the young rye. He will ask words of the black lass, but beg the words of the fair. **1936** J. CURTIS *Gilt Kid* 55 He did not feel choosey; why, he could be a rye mush himself for one night. *Ibid.* 232 Anyone taking a quick look at her might think she was on the up-and-up. She would give that impression too, to anyone who heard her talk and saw her act. Though.. she would have to give up that rye mort touch. **1939** —— *What Immortal Hand* xiv. 151 If she's gone and got herself tangled up with a lot of rye mushes she don't want to have nothing to do with a gaol-bird like me.

†**rye**, *v. Obs.*[−1] [Of obscure origin.] *intr.* To fish in some special manner.

1496 *Treat. Fishing w. Angle* (1883) 11 Lynes for the dubbyd hoke to fysshe for the trought and graylynge: and.. smalle lynes for to rye for the roche and the darse.

rye: see REE *v.* and RIE.

ryeall, variant of RIAL *a. Obs.*

rye-bread. [RYE *sb.*[1] Cf. MSw. *roghbrödh*, Sw. *rågbröd*, Da. *rugbrød*, Icel. *rúgbrauð*; WFris. *roggenbrea*, MDu. *rogge*(*n*)-, *ruggenbroot*, Du. *roggebrood*, G. (*rocken-*,) *roggenbrot*.] Bread made from rye-flour.

1579 LANGHAM *Gard. Health* (1633) 528 Rye bread is heauy and hard to digest. **1580** HOLLYBAND *Treas. Fr. Tong*, *Du pain de seigle*, Rie bread. **1638** RAWLEY tr. *Bacon's Life & Death* (1650) 40 Rye bread, or Barly bread, are more solid than Wheat Bread. **1676** *Phil. Trans.* XI. 761 If this gangren seiseth only on those that eat Rey-bread [etc.]. **1766** *Compl. Farmer* s.v. *Rye*, Nor can this be practised where the people are not accustomed to eat rye-bread. **1814** SCOTT *Diary* 11 Aug., I got and cut a crust of it; it was rye-bread. **1875** *Encycl. Brit.* III. 251/1 Rye bread.. is largely consumed by the inhabitants of the northern parts of Europe.

ryebuck (ˈraɪbʌk), *a.* (*adv.*) and *int. slang* (chiefly *Austral.*). Now *obsolescent.* Also **ribuck**, **rybuck**, **rye buck**, etc. [Origin uncertain: perh. ad. G. *reibach*, var. of *rebbach* profit, ad. Yiddish (Heb.) *revaḥ*: cf. RYBECK.]

A. *adj.* Good, excellent; genuine; ***ryebuck shearer***, an expert or 'gun' shearer (see GUN *sb.* 14). Also as *adv.*

1859 G. W. MATSELL *Vocabulum* 55 My pals have got up a bene moey to send to the head bloke, and if it comes off rye buck, I shall soon vamose from the stir. **1895** *Bulletin* (Sydney) 9 Feb. 15 I'm ryebuck and the girl's okay. **1906** E. DYSON *Fact'ry 'Ands* x. 132 'It's rybuck, girls,' said Feathers. 'Yer on velvet. Ther firm's willin' t' accept responsibility fer ther actions iv it's dooly accredited cat, 'n' pays compensation.' **1916** C. J. DENNIS *Moods of Ginger Mick* 92 But the reel, ribuck Australia's 'ere among the fightin' men. **1918** R. H. KNYVETT *Over There* viii. 82 They even knew our slang, for here was 'The Fair Dinkum' Store', and across the way 'Ribuck Goods'. *a* **1957** in Stewart & Keesing *Old Bush Songs* (1957) 267 There's a bloke on the board and I heard him say I couldn't shear a hundred sheep a day, But some fine day I'll show him the way And prove I'm a ryebuck shearer. **1965** J. S. GUNN *Terminol. Shearing Industry* II. 16 *Ryebuck shearer*, see *gun*. *Ibid.* I. 30 *Gun*, a really fast shearer, also known as a 'ryeback [*sic*] shearer', but not the same as the fastest in the shed (see *ringer*).

B. *int.* An expression of agreement or assent.

1859 G. W. MATSELL *Vocabulum* 76 *Rybuck*, all right; straight, it will do; I am satisfied. **1898** *Bulletin* (Sydney) 17 Dec. (Red Page), *Rye-buck* (all right) is no doubt an abbreviation of 'all right, my buck'. **1911** L. STONE *Jonah* i. 11 'Oh! I don't suppose you'll be missed,' replied Chook, graciously. 'Rye buck!' cried Jonah. **1916** C. J. DENNIS *Songs of Sentimental Bloke* 21 We kin get an intro, if we've luck. 'E sez, 'Ribuck'. *Ibid.* 72 'E'en in the days when she's no longer fair She's still yer wife,' 'e sez. 'Ribuck,' sez I. **1933** *Bulletin* (Sydney) 27 Sept. 42/2 'We'll meet you at the yards.' 'Ryebuck, Boss,' said The Gov'ner civilly.

ryede, obs. form of RIDE *v.*

rye-flour. [RYE *sb.*[1]] Flour made from rye.

a **1400** *Stockh. Medical MS.* i. 237 in *Anglia* XVIII. 301 Of cler hony & rye-flour late bake a kake. *a* **1513** FABYAN *Chron.* (1516) 171 The prouycyon of Marchauntes that brought Rye and Rye floure out of Spruce. **1620** VENNER *Via Recta* i. 18 If a quantity of Rie flower be added to it, there will be made of them both an yeoman-bread. **1753** J. BARTLET *Gentl. Farriery* (1754) 297 A handful of linseed powdered; or oatmeal and rye flower. **1868** WATTS *Dict. Chem.* V. 141 Ergot may be detected in rye-flour by first boiling the flour twice with alcohol [etc.]. **1899** *Allbutt's Syst. Med.* VI. 590 In two of his clinical cases rye-flour had been used for a time in the diet.

rye-grass (ˈraɪgrɑːs, -æ-). Also 8 **rie-**. [In sense 1 an alteration of RAY-GRASS. In sense 2 perh. directly f. RYE *sb.*[1]]

1. One or other of several species of *Lolium*, esp. *L. perenne* (common rye-grass) and *L. italicum* (Italian rye-grass), extensively cultivated as forage and fodder grasses.

A large number of varieties of the common species are described by Morton *Cycl. Agric.* II. 279–281.

1712 J. MORTON *Nat. Hist. Northants.* ix. 482 Rye-grass is with us accounted the best thing in the World for Woodland in Enclosures. **1753** *Chambers' Cycl.* Suppl. *App.*, Rye-Grass, in botany, the same with what is otherwise called Rey-grass. **1766** *Museum Rust.* VI. 196 The Red Darnel-grass, which has been so much cultivated, under the name of Ray-grass, or vulgarly Rie-grass. **1795** BURKE *Thoughts Scarcity* Wks. VII. 406 The rye-grass, or coarse bent, suffered more than the clover. **1814** SCOTT *Ld. Isles* III. i, The rye-grass shakes not on the sod-built fold. **1834** *Brit. Husb.* (L.U.K.) I. 515 Another species of this plant.. has been lately introduced from the continent under the name of

Italian rye-grass. **1871** KINGSLEY *At Last* v, The ground on the opposite slope..is covered with a grass like tall rye-grass, but growing in tufts. **1961** R. M. PATTERSON *Buffalo Head* vi. 216 The rocks were all hidden and a magnificent growth of rye-grass was swaying in the wind. **1979** *Buffalo* (N.Y.) *Evening News* 18 May II. 22/2 The new turf-type perennial rye-grasses available today are real beauties.

attrib. **1747** FRANKLIN *Let.* Wks. 1887 II. 81, I sowed an acre more with two bushels of rye-grass seed. **1801** *Farmer's Mag.* Aug. 312 Not rye grass hay, but hay made from rye cut green. **1890** SERVICE *Notandums* 5 Shall I reprint the roup bills o' my ryegrass parks? **1931** R. BEALE *Bk. Lawn* iv. 48 Rye grass mixtures..are recommended for heavy soils.

2. = *wild rye* (see quots. and RYE *sb.*[1] 2 c).

1760 J. LEE *Introd. Bot.* App. 325 Rye-grass, *Hordeum.* **1794** MARTYN *Fl. Rustica* III. 108 Rie-grass [*Hordeum pratense*] is not uncommon in good meadows. **1796** WITHERING *Brit. Pl.* (ed. 3) II. 171 *Hordeum murinum*... Wild Rye. Rye-grass. **1846–50** A. WOOD *Class-Bk. Bot.* 621 *Elymus villosus.* Rye Grass.

Ryeland (ˈraɪlənd). The name of a district in Hereford & Worcester, where the breed was first developed, used *attrib.* and *absol.* to designate a sheep belonging to the small, hornless breed so called, which is a good producer of both wool and meat.

[**1801** J. POWELL *Let.* in *Ann. Agric.* (1808) XLV. 6 The hardiness of the Ryelanders..is proverbial, as milkers.] **1802** J. SOMERVILLE *Let.* 12 Nov. in *Facts & Observations relative to Sheep* (1803) 10 The same land, which carried forty-five breeding ewes, was immediately stocked with 150 Ryelands in their stead. *Ibid.* 12 We..sent this Ryeland mutton to market. **1837** W. YOUATT *Sheep* vii. 258 The distinguishing breed of sheep in Herefordshire is the Ryeland, so called from a district in the southern part of the county. *Ibid.* 260 The Ryeland sheep.. quickly fattens. **1861** MRS. BEETON *Bk. Househ. Managem.* xiv. 323 Eleven varieties have been reared in this country of the domesticated sheep..embracing..the Ryeland; South-Down; the Merino. **1912** R. LYDEKKER *Sheep & its Cousins* v. 101 The modern Ryeland..retained the diminutive proportions of the ancestral breed. *Ibid.*, Ryeland wool was formerly regarded as the finest produced in the British Islands. **1929** W. C. COFFEY *Productive Sheep Husbandry* (ed. 2) xxi. 173 The Ryeland originated in Herefordshire, early in the nineteenth century. **1971** *Farmers Weekly* 19 Mar. 83/1 Both Suffolk and Ryland [*sic*] rams have been used this season.

ryell, variant of RIAL *a. Obs.*

rye-meal. [RYE *sb.*[1] Cf. MSw. *roghmiöl*, Sw. *rågmjöl*, Icel. *rúgmjöl*, Norw. *rugmjøl*, Da. *rugmel*, Du. *roggemeel*, G. (*rocken-*,) *roggenmehl.*] Meal made from rye.

a **1400** *Stockh. Med. MS.* i. 245 in *Anglia* XVIII. 301 A porcyoun of rye-mele. **1662** CHANDLER *Van Helmont's Oriatrike* xxxii. 247 Suppose though Rie meal doth not become a Stone. **1767** *Ann. Reg.* I. 126 The free importation ..of..rye or rye-meal..is permitted. **1818** COLEBROOKE *Import Col. Corn* 71 Many of these numerous sorts can..be afforded much cheaper than..rye meal. **1844** H. STEPHENS *Bk. Farm* II. 367 The grains of the fecula of rye-meal are peculiarly shaped.

ryemele, variant of RIMEL *Obs.*

rye-mouse, dial. variant of REARMOUSE.

†**ˈryen**, *a. Obs. rare.* Also 1 riȝen, 5 ryene, reone. [f. RYE *sb.*[1] + -EN[4]. Cf. MDu. *rogghen*, *rugghen*, Du. *roggen*; MHG. *ruggîn*, *ruckîn*, *rockîn*, obs. G. *rocken*, *roggen.*] Made from rye.

c **1000** *Sax. Leechd.* (Rolls) II. 236 Sume of riȝenum melwe wyrceað briwas. *c* **1450** *M.E. Med. Bk.* (Heinrich) 140 Medle hem wyþ hony & ryen mele and flowre of whete. *Ibid.* 201 Þe croste of reone bred. *Ibid.* 216 Mak pappe of ryene flour.

ryepeck (ˈraɪpɛk). Also rypeck, ripeck. [Of obscure origin.] An iron-shod pole used for mooring a punt, or serving as a mark for competitors in aquatic sports.

α. **1857** F. T. BUCKLAND *Curios. Nat. Hist.* (1859) 227 The boat is pushed out into the middle of the river, the two rypecks are fixed firmly into the ground at the bottom, and the boat is fastened to them across the stream. **1862** H. KINGSLEY *Ravenshoe* lxiv, He ordered the fisherman to take up the rypecks, and he floated away down stream. **1881** LESLIE *Our River* 230 A couple of ripecks are also necessary for mooring the punt.

β. **1891** *Lock to Lock Times* 1 Aug. 979 He being the first to get round the ryepeck. **1898** GRENFELL *Rowing* ix. 74 In amateur races it is usual..to have a separate turning ryepeck for each competitor.

ryese, obs. form of RISE *sb.*

ryessh, obs. form of RUSH *sb.*[1]

rye-straw. [RYE *sb.*[1] Cf. MDu. *rogghestro*, Du. *roggestroo*, G. *rock(en)-*, *rogg(en)stroh*, WFris. *rog(ge)strie.*] **a.** The dried haulm of rye. **b.** A single straw of this; also *fig.* a weak insignificant person.

1523 FITZHERB. *Husb.* § 122 Than to make a couerynge of wheate-strawe or rye-strawe, to couer and house the hyue aboute. **1615** HEYWOOD *Foure Prent.* I. F j. Think'st thou this rye-strew can ore-rule my arme? **1686** PLOT *Staffordsh.* 156 A firm pebble..having a smooth hole through it about the bigness of a Rye-straw. **1763** MILLS *Syst. Pract. Husb.* I. 187, I gave my oxen hay mixed with an equal quantity of rye-straw. **1805** R. W. DICKSON *Pract. Agric.* II. 799 When this cannot be had in sufficient quantity, rye-straw may be substituted. **1857** MILLER *Elem. Chem.*, *Org.* xiii. § 1 (1862) 833 One ton of..rye straw contains 60 lb. of ash.

attrib. **1610** SHAKS. *Temp.* IV. i. 136 You Sun-burn'd Sicklemen.., Make holly day: your Rye-straw hats put on.

ryet, obs. form of RIOT, RYOT.

ryf(e, ryff(e, obs. ff. RIFE, RIVE.

†**ryfant**, *a. Obs.*[−1] [Origin obscure.]

The glossary explains *ryfant gablet* as 'a small gable, the outline of which is an ogee arch'.

1512–3 in Willis & Clark *Cambridge* (1886) I. 610 Fynyalles, ryfant gablettes, Batelmentes,..and euery other thyng belongyng to the same.

ryfel, ryffle, ryffyl, etc., obs. ff. RIFLE.

ryffen, obs. f. RIVEN *ppl. a.*

ryfly, obs. f. RIFELY.

ryft(e, obs. ff. REEF *sb.*[1], RIFT.

rygalte, rygolte, obs. ff. REGALTY.

ryg(g)e, obs. ff. RIDGE, RIG *sb.*[2]

†**ryghtmathy.** *Obs.*[−1] [ad. med.L. *rithmachia*, for *arithmomachia*, ad. Gr. **ἀριθμομαχία.*] The philosophers' game (see PHILOSOPHER 5 b).

c **1407** LYDG. *Reson & Sens.* 2414 The play he kan of Ryghtmathye, Which dulle wittis doth encombre, For thys play stant al by novmbre.

ryhchesse, variant of RICHESSE *Obs.*

ryiche, ryif, obs. ff. RICH, RIFE.

ryiji, ryijy, vars. RYA.

ryim, obs. f. RIME.

rying-sieve: see REEING *vbl. sb.*

ryip, ryis, ryiue, obs. ff. RIPE, RISE, RIVE.

ryke, Sc. var. REACH *v.*[1]

Rylean (ˈraɪliːən), *a. Philos.* [f. the name of Gilbert *Ryle* (1900–76), English philosopher + -AN.] Of, pertaining to, or characteristic of Ryle's theories or his approach to linguistic philosophy or philosophical behaviourism.

1958 *Times Lit. Suppl.* 10 Oct. 581/1 The first part of this book gives an account, in roughly Rylean terms, of different senses of 'know', and of the relations between 'knowing that' and 'knowing how'. **1963** W. SELLARS *Sci., Perception & Reality* v. 178 What I shall call a Rylean language, a language of which the fundamental descriptive vocabulary speaks of public properties of public objects located in Space and enduring through Time. **1966** *Philos. Rev.* LXXV. 99 Farrer shrinks..from the Hobbist mortalism that would naturally go with this Rylean view of body and mind. **1971** G. J. WARNOCK in Wood & Pitcher *Ryle* 273 It was the answer which his very Rylean proforma of a solution temptingly left room for.

rym, obs. f. REAM, RIM, RIME.

rymare, obs. f. RIMER.

ryme (of the water): see RIM *sb.*[1]

rymer[1] (ˈraɪmə(r)). Also rimer. [Of obscure origin.] A post in a weir or lock, in or on which a paddle works up and down.

α. **1794** VANDERSTEGEN *Pres. St. Thames* 16 Weirs.., made open at pleasure, by taking up the rimers. **1805** ALLNUTT *Navig. Thames* 22 When the moveable Gates, Overfalls and Rimers are taken away. **1857** P. COLQUHOUN *Comp. Oarsman's Guide* 19 Into these notches, timbers termed rimers are fitted.

β. **1823** *Examiner* 384/2 The musicians saved themselves by clinging to the rymers of the lock. **1872** TAUNT *Map Thames* 7 Weirs..are generally composed of three different parts, viz. the bridge, the rymers, and the paddles.

ˈRymer[2]. A variety of apple. Also *attrib.*

1820 J. TURNER in *Hortic. Trans.* III. 314 The most remarkable of which [sorts] was the Rymer apple. **1846** J. BAXTER *Libr. Pract. Agric.* (ed. 4) I. 59 Ribston pippin, Rymer,..Salopian pippin. **1860** HOGG *Fruit Manual* 24 *Rymer*... Large, roundish, regularly formed, and angular. Skin pale yellow, tinged all over with delicate rose.

rymer, var. RIMER.

rymour, var. RIMER *sb.*[1], RUMOUR.

ry-mouse, dial. var. REARMOUSE.

ryn, obs. f. RUN *v.*

rynde, obs. variant of RINE *v.*[1]

†**ˈryndle**, variant of RENDLES, rennet.

1546 PHAER *Bk. Childr.* (1553) T vj, The ryndle mawe of a younge sucking kydde.

†**Ryne**[1] (also ruyne), obs. f. RHINE[3], used *absol.* for 'Rhenish wine'.

a **1400** *Sir Degrevant* 1414 (Linc. MS.), Ever scho drewe thame the wyne, Bathe the Roche and the Ryne. *c* **1400** *Beryn* 280 For spycys & eke wyne Went round aboute, þe gascoyn, & eke the ruyne.

†**ryne**[2]. *Obs.*[−1] (Meaning obscure.)

c **1470** *Gol. & Gaw.* 225 The roy with his Round Tabill, richest of ryne.

ryne, obs. f. REIGN *v.*, RIND, RINE, RUN *v.*

rynesh, obs. f. RINSE.

ryng(e, obs. Sc. ff. REIGN.

†**rynmart.** *Sc. Obs.* [f. MART *sb.*[2], with obscure first element.] An ox or cow paid as part of a rent in kind. (Cf. RHIND-MART.)

1433 *Liber S. Thome de Aberbrothoc* (1856) II. 62 Reddendo..quadraginta solidos..ad duos anni terminos cum rynmart et vethyr et oneribus husbandalibus debitis et consuetis. **1458** *Exch. Rolls Scotl.* VI. 481 Pro octo martis qui dicuntur rynmartis. **1483** *Liber S. Thome de Aberbrothoc* (1856) II. 190 Vna cum rynmart wethir et aliis husbandorum oneribus. **1496** *Ibid.* 301 Cum rynmartis, vethiris, caponibus, [et] aliis husbandorum oneribus.

So †**ryn-mutton.** *Obs. rare*[−1].

1473 *Exch. Rolls Scotl.* VIII. 149 Idem onerat se de xiiij rynmartis xiiij rynmutone vicecomitatuum de Elgin et Fores de anno computi.

rynn(e, obs. forms of RUN *v.*

rynnet, rennet: see RINNET.

rynt (raɪnt), *v. north.* Also 8 rynd-, 9 rhint, roint, roynt. [Of unknown origin: cf. AROINT.] *refl.* To make way, give place, stand aside.

1674 RAY *N.C. Words* 39 *Rynt ye*: By your leave, stand handsomly. As Rynt you witch, quoth Besse Locket to her Mother; Proverb. Chesh. **1703** THORESBY *Let. to Ray*, *Ryndta*, used to cows to make them give way, and stand in their stalls or booyses. **1820** WILBRAHAM *Chesh. Gloss.* s.v., *Rynt thee*, is an expression used by milk-maids to a cow when she has been milked, to bid her get out of the way. **1845** THORNBER *Penny Stone* (1886) 13 Rhint ye, Bess, a place for the gentle on the lang-settle.

‖**ryo** (rjoː). Also 9 rio, riyo. [Jap.] A former Japanese monetary unit (see quots.).

1871 A. B. MITFORD *Tales of Old Japan* I. 70 A Japanese noble will sometimes be found girding on a sword, the blade of which unmounted is worth from six hundred to a thousand riyos, say from £200 to £300. **1876** W. E. GRIFFIS *Mikado's Empire* (1877) II. 610 In popular language, the terms *hiyaku* (hundred), *fun*, *mommé*, and even *riō* (4 mommé, 5 fun), do not represent any coin, but are used to denote values. They are expressions belonging to the period when money was computed by weight only. **1899** L. HEARN *In Ghostly Japan* vi. 103 The sum of a hundred ryō in gold. **1915** F. BRINKLEY *Hist. Jap. People* xxxi. 438 The gold *ryō* represented 2 *koku*, or 30 *yen* of modern currency, the silver *ryō* representing 3 yen. *Ibid.* xxxii. 444 Gold..was much more valuable in China than in Japan. Ten *ryō* of the yellow metal could be obtained in Japan for from twenty to thirty *kwan-mon* and sold in China for 130. **1938** D. T. SUZUKI *Zen Buddhism & its Influence on Japanese Culture* I. vii. 160 Two loads of gold were equivalent in the currency of the time to 12,000 *ryo*. **1964** *Japan* (Unesco) (rev. ed.) i. 45/2 It is said that between 1601 and 1647 about 4,800,000 *ryō* (one *ryō* contained four *me* of pure gold) of gold and 750,000 *kan* of silver were paid to foreign countries. **1972** *Mainichi Daily News* (Japan) 6 Nov. 7/4, I will kill anyone or accept a mission of the sword for five hundred ryo in gold.

‖**ryokan** (ˈrjokan). [Jap.] A traditional Japanese inn or hostelry.

1963 *Maclean's Mag.* 9 Mar. 37 The most charming hotel I ever stayed at was a Japanese ryokan in the mountain spa of Kinugawa north of Tokyo. **1968** *Sat. Rev.* (U.S.) 23 Dec. 57/2 Stay in a 17th-century *ryokan*—inn. **1970** *Guardian* 12 Dec. 6/6 The *ryokans*, country inns, are worth the slight additional expense over Westernized hotels. **1972** *Times* 8 May (Japan Suppl.) p. viii/2 The site..contains a magnificent temple and several *ryokan*—traditional Japanese inns. **1979** *Amer. Poetry Rev.* Mar./Apr. 45/2 Several ferries, sighted from the small balcony of our private Ryokan overlooking the beach, circle Dogashima Bay from dawn to dusk.

ryot (ˈraɪət). Forms: 7 riat, 8 reiot, 9 riot; 8–9 ryott, 8– ryot, 9 ryat(t, ryet. [Urdū *raʿīyat*, *raiyat*, ultimately of Arabic origin: see RAYAT and RAYAH.] An Indian peasant, husbandman, or cultivating tenant.

1625 PURCHAS *Pilgrims* I. III. 223 His poore Riats or Clownes. **1776** *Trial J. Fowke*, *Deposit.* 18/1 Such oppressions as produced complaints..against him from great numbers of the Reiots. **1788** GLADWIN tr. *Mem. Khojeh Abdulkurreem* 150 An army of these free-booters [Mahrattas], who distressed the ryotts. **1800** WELLESLEY in Owen *Desp.* (1877) 192 A systematic settlement..for promoting the security and ease of the ryots. **1844** H. H. WILSON *Brit. India* II. 488 To make advances to the Ryots, in order to restore to them the means of cultivating the lands which had fallen into neglect. **1879** H. GEORGE *Progr. & Pov.* II. ii. (1881) 106 The actual slavery to which the ryots are reduced.

attrib. **1802** JAMES *Milit. Dict.*, *Ryot Lands*, lands farmed out and cultivated by the tenant.

‖**ryotti**, *a.* Also 8 ryotty. [Urdū (Bengālī) *raiyati*, adj. f. *raiyat* RYOT.] Of land in Bengal: Held on a permanent tenure in return for the payment of a certain rent.

1772 H. VERELST *View Eng. Gov. Bengal* 69 Those [lands] called ryotty are possessed by tenants resident on the spot, who by their grants ought to be continued as long as they paid their rents. **1883** *19th Cent.* Sept. 425 Persons holding ryotti lands.., the immediate cultivators of the soil.

‖**ryotwar** (ˈraɪətwɑːr), *a.* Also rayetwar. [Urdū *raiyatwār*, f. *raiyat* RYOT + *-wār* pertaining to, etc.] = RYOTWARY *a.* (Chiefly in ***ryotwar system.***)

a **1827** SIR T. MUNRO in Gleig *Life* (1830) III. 353 Our revenue system..cannot, consistently with usage, be other than Rayetwar. **1844** H. H. WILSON *Brit. Ind.* I. 445 The

Government of Madras was induced to entertain a doubt whether it was not desirable to relinquish the Ryotwar system. **1858** in J. B. Norton *Topics* 163 Meet a ryotwar Collector in his own house,..he will admit [etc.]. **1863** *Chambers's Encycl.* V. 546 Under Sir Thomas Monro, the ryotwar system was introduced. *Ibid.*, Ryotwar Settlements.

‖**ryotwary** (ˈraɪətwɑːrɪ), *a.* and *sb.* Also **ryotwarree, -warry, -wari (rayatwari).** [Urdū *raiyatwārī*, f. *raiyatwār*: see prec.]

A. *adj.* Of land-tenure in India: Characterized by direct settlement between the government and the cultivators, without the intervention of a zemindar or landlord.

1834 [A. PRINSEP] *Baboo* I. v. 71 By your ryotwary system, you would elevate the peasant and the labourer. **1861** *All Year Round* 13 July 376 There are two ways of raising indigo: one by 'neez or private cultivation; the other by the ryotwarree system. **1902** S. SMITH *My Life Work* xxii. 211 Two great systems of land tenure divide the soil of India —the Zemindary or landlord type and the Ryotwary or peasant type.

B. *sb.* The ryotwary system.

1858 J. B. NORTON *Topics* 189 The tendency of all village systems is to crumble to pieces, and revert to ryotwarry. **1867** R. A. DALYELL *Mem. Madras Famine* 67 The 'annual settlements' under ryotwary are often misunderstood.

ryparographer, var. of RHYPAROGRAPHER.

‖**rype** (ˈryːpə). Pl. ryper. [a. Norw. *rype*, var. of *rjupe*, *rjupa*, ON. and Icel. *rjúpa*. See also RIPA[1].] The ptarmigan. Also *Comb.*

The sing. and pl. forms are often confused by English writers.

1743 *Phil. Trans.* XLII. 611 Their Birds are the Ryper, or Wood-Partridge, Ravens,..Goldfinches, &c. **1881** *Three in Norway* 194 The skipper put up a large brood of ryper. **1894** *Fortn. Rev.* June 749 All Englishmen may be credited with the knowledge that the rype is a grouse. *Ibid.*, Rype-shooting in Norway without dogs. **1896** *Blackw. Mag.* July 87 The reindeer-stalker and the ryper-shooter..exchange ideas.

rypereue: see REAPREEVE.

rypophagy, var. RHYPOPHAGY.

†**ryptage.** *Obs.*$^{-1}$ A Portuguese wine.

c **1451** FORTESCUE *Wks.* (1869) 554 Owte of the Kynges londe of Portyngale & Algarbe cummythe..4 Osseye, 5 Ryptage, 6 Bascarde.

rys, obs. form of RICE, RISE *v.*

rysagon, var. RISAGON.

rysimeter, var. RHYSIMETER.

ryssavour, obs. f. RECEIVER.

rysschew: see RISHEW.

rysse, obs. f. RICE *sb.*, RISE *v.*, RUSH *sb.*[1]

rythful, obs. f. RIGHTFUL.

rytina, variant of RHYTINA.

rytt(e, obs. ff. RIT *v.*[1]

ryuaye, var. REVAY *v. Obs.*

ryue(ly, obs. forms of RIFE(LY.

ryuet(te, obs. ff. RIVET.

ryuilde, ryuyled, obs. ff. RIVELLED.

ryuir, ryuyre, obs. ff. RIVER.

ryvaille, -aylle, obs. ff. RIVAL.

ryvaye, var. REVAY *v. Obs.*

†**ryveling**, app. a var. of RIFLING *vbl. sb.*[1]

1460 CAPGRAVE *Chron.* (Rolls) 236 Thei of Portingale were eke wery of hem for ryveling and oppression.

ryvilde, ryvill, obs. ff. RIVELLED, RIVEL.

†**ryving.** *Obs.*$^{-1}$ [Cf. *rye* REE *v.* and REEVE *v.*[2]] *pl.* Siftings.

c **1600** in *Househ. Ord.* (1790) 283 The Yeoman Garnetor hath..for his fee the ryvinges and outcast of the corne when it is cleansed.

Ryvita (raɪˈviːtə). Also **ryvita.** [f. RYE *sb.*[1] + L. *vīta* life.] The proprietary name of a type of crispbread.

1925 *Trade Marks Jrnl.* 18 Feb. 385 Ryvita..Bread. John Edwin Garrat, 96 Southwark Street, London SE1 Manufacturer. **1926–7** [see CRISPBREAD]. **1930** A. BENNETT *Imperial Palace* xxii. 142 Oldham softly entered with the tea-tray... 'I've brought you some hot ryvita in case you should fancy it, sir.' **1937** 'G. ORWELL' *Road to Wigan Pier* vi. 95 A millionaire may enjoy breakfasting off orange juice and Ryvita biscuits. **1953** R. FULLER *Second Curtain* v. 79 A girl..carrying a plate of Ryvita spread with paste. **1967** *Trade Marks Jrnl.* 22 Mar. 368/1 Ryvita..Bread, crispbread and biscuits (other than biscuits for animals). The Ryvita Company Limited..London. **1974** *Times* 19 Oct. 6/6 He had inadvertently eaten the toast (possibly Ryvita).

ryvullyng, ryvyled, obs. ff. RIVELING, RIVELLED.

ryvyn, obs. f. RIVE *v.*[1] and *v.*[2]

rywe, obs. Sc. f. RIVE *v.*[1], *v.*[2]; obs. f. RUE *v.*[1]

rywen, rywine, obs. Sc. pa. pple. of RIVE *v.*[1]

rywere, rywir, obs. Sc. ff. RIVER *sb.*[1]

ryyf, ryynse, ryyt, obs. ff. RIFE, RINSE, RITE.

ryze, dial. form of RICE *sb.*

S

S (ɛs), the nineteenth letter of the English and other modern alphabets, and the eighteenth of the ancient Roman alphabet, derives its form (through the ≶ and Σ, ≷ of early Latin and Greek inscriptions) from the Phœnician **W** (Hebrew ש *shīn*), which represented a voiceless sibilant: in some of the Semitic langs. (s), in others (ʃ). (Each of these phonetic symbols is intended to represent a class of sounds the articulatory positions of which vary considerably; the difference between the two classes is acoustically very recognizable, but the nature of the essential difference in formation is still obscure.) In ancient Greek and Latin the value of the letter is believed to have been always (s). In late L. *s* between vowels was in most instances pronounced (z), a sound which was not separately represented in the Latin alphabet. Hence when the Roman letters were adopted in OE., the letter S was used to represent both the unaltered Germanic (s), and the (z) which had been developed from that sound in certain positions.

In OE. *s* was pronounced (s) initially and finally, and medially when it was either contiguous with a voiceless consonant or began the second element of a compound; medially between voiced sounds it was pronounced (z). The southern dialect had in ME., and possibly in late OE., the peculiarity of voicing the initial *s* (in native words) as well as the initial *f* and *þ*. This phonetic habit extended to Kent as late as 1340, as is shown by spellings like *zenne* (OE. *synn*, sin) in the *Ayenbite of Inwyt*; it is now confined to the south-western dialects.

In mod. English the general rule is that *s* is pronounced (s) at the beginning of a word or of the second element of a compound, and when doubled or in contact with a voiceless consonant. Between vowels, and when phonetically final, a single *s* is mostly (z). But there are many anomalies and uncertainties, especially in classical derivatives: cf., e.g., *absurd* (æb'sɜːd), *observe* (əbz-); with regard to some words usage is divided, as in *absolve* (æbs-, æbz-), and the words in *-ive*, e.g. *effusive*, *evasive*. Even *ss* is in some words sounded (z), as in *dissolve* (against *dissent*, *dissect*, etc.), *dessert*, *possess*.

The phonetic combinations (sj), (zj), when rapidly pronounced, are very similar in acoustic effect to the simple consonants (ʃ), (ʒ), the position of the tongue for these being intermediate between the positions for (s) or (z) and (j). Hence in some words where earlier Eng. had (sj) or (zj), written either as *s* (before diphthongal *u*) or as *si*, the modern language has (ʃ) or (ʒ), so that the letter has acquired these two new values. Examples are *sure*, *sugar*, *censure*, *mission* ('mɪʃən), *Asia* ('eɪʃə), *treasure* (-ʒə(r)), *evasion* (-ʒən). In some varieties of vulgar speech this tendency is carried much further, as in the pronunciations (ʃuː), (prɪ'ʒuːm) for *sue*, *presume*.

S is silent in a few words adopted from Old French, as in *aisle*, *isle* (hence also pseudo-etymologically in *island*); in the Law French *mesne*, *demesne*, a silent *s* was inserted by false analogy.

I. 1. a. The letter and its sound.

c **1000** ÆLFRIC *Gram.* ii. (Z.) 6 *Semivocales* syndon seofan: *f, l, m, n, r, s, x.* *c* **1460** *Pol. Rel. & L. Poems* 2 An S. for Salisbery, without any avision. **1709** STEELE *Tatler* No. 77 ¶1 Some [lispers] never uttered the letter H; and others had as mortal an Aversion for S. **1842** *Gentl. Mag.* May 480/2 The letter S was the device of Henry of Lancaster.

b. ***s-aorist*** (Philol.), in certain Indo-European languages, an aorist formed from the verbal stem by adding *s* and the ending; a sigmatic aorist.

1895 CONWAY & ROUSE tr. *Brugmann's Compar. Gram. Indo-Gmc. Lang.* IV. 371 Special vowel-grades for the root-syllable, as in the *s*-aorist.., cannot be made out for the parent language. **1933** C. D. BUCK *Compar. Gram. Greek & Latin* 281 The distinctive IE aorist is the *s*-aorist formed from the root by the addition of *s* and the secondary endings. **1962** C. W. WATKINS *Indo-Europ. Orig. Celtic Verb* I. 55 The more common situation in Vedic is one where a root athematic present has an s-aorist associated with it.

2. a. The shape of the letter; an object having this shape.

1426 LYDG. *De Guil. Pilgr.* 17952 Every .s. y-crokyd is, lyche a crose highe in the top. **1614** B. JONSON *Barth. Fair* II. ii, I doe water the ground in knots, as I goe like a great Garden-pot, you may follow me by the S.S.[s.] I make. **1688** R. HOLME *Armoury* III. xvi. (Roxb.) 58/1 The seuerall parts of a Viol... The S'es of the belly or round holes. **1894** *Outing* (U.S.) XXIII. 407/1 Make an S of wire, sharpened at one end. **1898** HAWEIS *Old Violins* 77 One 'ʃ' is a shade lower than the other, a practice so common with Strad.. that it must have been intentional. **1899** *Blackw. Mag.* 331/2 Round the great S the river made She battled her blind way.

b. ***collar of S, S's, SS.***, or ***Esses***: see COLLAR *sb.* 3 c.

c. *attrib.* and *Comb.*, as ***S-curved***, ***-decorated***, ***-necked***, ***-scrolled***, ***-shaped*** adjs.; ***S-bend***, ***-curve***, ***-hook***, ***-ornament***, ***-perforation***, ***-piece***, ***-rope***, ***-scroll***, ***-sofa***, ***-trap***, ***-turn***.

1930 *Motor* 10 June 892/2 We were negotiating an *S bend on the proper side of the line on a main road. **1931** D. L. SAYERS *Five Red Herrings* xi. 115 The road makes a very sharp and dangerous S-bend. **1975** R. BROWNING *Emperor Julian* x. 187 The northern section of the frontier formed a great S-bend. **1839** *Civil Eng. & Arch. Jrnl.* II. 139/1 He is compelled to connect by a *S curve. **1977** R. E. HARRINGTON *Quintain* xii. 109 Fronck negotiated an s-curve, and..pulled the Ford out onto a straight stretch. **1940** *Burlington Mag.* Mar. 81/2 The wings with their *S-curved shape. **1961** M. W. BARLEY *Eng. Farmhouse & Cottage* IV. i. 189 An English boat came into Boston in 1628 with 3,500 tiles aboard, and the earliest references to pantiles, the S-curved roofing tile, occur in the 1630s. **1963** G. DANIEL in Foster & Alcock *Culture & Environment* ii. 21 The *S-decorated pottery which may be a degeneration of the duck motifs found on Early Iron Age pottery in Brittany and north Spain. **1844** *Civil Eng. & Arch. Jrnl.* VII. 152/1 An *S hook of iron must be fitted into the eye of the valve. **1896** *Royal Nat. Hist.* V. 89 The foregoing assemblage of *S-necked or Cryptodiran tortoises. **1934** *Burlington Mag.* Sept. 120/2 A finely-carved double-headed eagle, resting on a symmetrical *S-ornament at the bottom. **1851** D. WILSON *Prehist. Ann.* (1863) I. II. iv. 391 Produce the appearance of an *S or Ogee perforation. **1891** KIPLING *Light that Failed* viii, Uncouth brick and zinc mysteries supported by iron stanchions and clamped by *S-pieces. **1883** W. S. GRESLEY *Gloss. Coal-Mining* 234 **S-rope*, the winding rope which passes round the under side of the drum from or to the pulley; so called because it takes the form of the letter S. **1934** *Burlington Mag.* Sept. 120/2 The symmetrically inverted *S-scroll. **1956** G. TAYLOR *Silver* vii. 143 The graceful and irregular S- and C-scrolls that are the chief ingredient of the style in its linear form. **1934** *Burlington Mag.* Sept. 125/2 The lambrequin 'apron' and the *S-scrolled legs both, I would suggest, came to Europe from India. **1955** R. FASTNEDGE *Eng. Furnit. Styles* iii. 77 Early examples with S-scrolled legs and bun feet were frequently decorated with floral, or later, seaweed, marquetry. **1837** KIRBY *Richardson's Fauna Bor.-Amer.* IV. 8 The third becoming a broken or *S-shaped band. **1937** T. RATTIGAN *French without Tears* II. ii. 57 From sideways on it's a bit S-shaped, if you know what I mean. **1966** *Publ. Amer. Dial. Soc.* XLII. 3 *Chicane*,..an S-shaped curve of a race track. **1906** W. DE MORGAN *Joseph Vance* xxvi. 211, I found myself sitting beside Miss Spencer on a thing like an S in the back drawing-room... As I sat by Miss Spencer on the *S-sofa. [**1882** S. HELLYER *Lect. Sci. & Art Sanitary Plumbing* iii. 108 About the first form of trap used for fixing under water-closets was the syphon or round-pipe trap, *i.e.*, a pipe bent and recurved in the shape of the letter ∽.] **1885**, **1976** *S trap [see *P trap* s.v. P III. 1]. **1920** A. J. L. SCOTT *Sixty Squad* 56 Putting in a couple of '*S' turns, he made a good slow landing. **1973** *Times* 3 Mar. 15/2 The Labour Party has done an S-turn when the Government has merely done a U-turn.

3. Used like the other letters of the alphabet to denote serial order; applied e.g. to the nineteenth (or more usually the eighteenth, either I or J being omitted) group or section in classification, to the eighteenth sheet of a book or quire of a MS., etc.

4. Abbreviations. **a. S.** = various proper names, as Samuel, Sarah, etc.; **S.** *Her.* (also *l.c.*) = Sable; **S.** *Anat.* and *Zool.* = sacral (vertebra); **S** = Saint; so **SS.** = Saints; **S.** † = Sir (prefixed to the name of a knight or a priest); **S** *Bacteriol.* = SMOOTH *a.*; **S.** = snow (in ship's log-book); **S.** = Society (L. *societas*), as in *F.R.S.*, Fellow of the Royal Society, *F.S.A.*, Fellow of the Society of Antiquaries; **S.** *Mus.* = Solo; **S.**, strain (of virus etc.), *spec.* in *S.19, S19 = strain 19* s.v. STRAIN *sb.*[1]; **S.** *Chem.* = Sulphur; **S.A.**, **s.a.**, sex appeal; **S.A.**, **S-A** (*Med.*), sino-auricular or -atrial; **S.A.**, small arms; **S.A.**, **S/A** [F. *société anonyme*; also It. *società anonima*, Sp. *sociedad anónima*], in France, Italy, etc., a limited or joint-stock company; **S.A.** = STURMABTEILUNG; **S.A.A.**, small arm(s) ammunition; **S.A.C.**, senior aircraftman; **SAC** (*U.S.*), Strategic Air Command; **S.A.C.EUR.**, **SACEUR**, **Saceur** (also with pronunc. 'sækjʊə(r)), Supreme Allied Commander Europe; **S.A.C.W.**, senior aircraftwoman; **S.A.E.**, Society of Automotive Engineers (used *spec.* to designate a scale of viscosity used for lubrication oils); **S.A.E.**, **s.a.e.**, stamped addressed envelope; **S.A.L.**, South Arabian League; **SAM**, surface-to-air missile; **S & L** (*U.S.*), savings and loan (association); **S and M**, **S–M**, sadism and masochism, sado-masochism; **SAR**, search and rescue; **S.A.S.**, Special Air Service; **SAT** (*U.S.*), scholastic aptitude test; **S.B.**, simultaneous broadcast; **S.B.** = smooth bore (gun); **S.B.**, Special Branch; **S.B.**, stretcher bearer; **S.B.A.**, sick-berth attendant; **SBA** (*U.S.*), Small Business Administration; **S.B.A.C.**, Society of British Aerospace Companies (formerly Society of British Aircraft Constructors); **SBM**, **sbm**, single buoy moor(ing); **SBN**, Standard Book Number (now *ISBN*: see I 3); **SBR**, styrene-butadiene rubber; **S.C.**, **s.c.**, self-contained; **SC**, structural change (in Transformational Grammar); **SCAP** (also with pronunc. skæp), Supreme Commander Allied Powers (in Japan); also used *transf.* of the Command Headquarters; **Sc.D.** [L. *Scientiæ Doctor*], Doctor of Science; **S.C.F.**, Save the Children Fund; **scf**, standard cubic feet (i.e. cubic feet of gas at standard temperature and pressure); **SCLC** (*U.S.*), Southern Christian Leadership Conference; **S.C.M.**, State Certified Midwife; **S.C.M.**, Student Christian Movement; **SCP**, single-cell protein; **S.C.R.**, senior common room (orig. and chiefly in the University of Oxford); **SCR** (*Electronics*), silicon-controlled rectifier; **S.C.U.A.**, Suez Canal Users' Association; **S.D.**, **s.d.**, semi-detached (house); **S.D.**, sequence date; **S.D.** = SICHERHEITSDIENST; **s.d.**, **S.D.** (*Statistics*), standard deviation; **SD**, structural description (in Transformational Grammar); **S.D.A.**, Scottish Development Agency; **S.D.E.C.E.** [F. *Service de documentation étrangère et de contre-espionnage*], the official counter-intelligence agency in France; **S.D.F.**, Social Democratic Federation; hence *S.D.F.er*; **S.D.I.** (*U.S.*), Strategic Defence Initiative (see *Star Wars* s.v. STAR *sb.*[1] 20); **S.D.L.P.**, Social Democratic and Labour Party; **S.D.O.**, Subdivisional Officer; **S.D.P.**, Social Democratic Party; **S.D.R.**, special drawing right (usu. *pl.*); **S.D.S.** [G. *Sozialistischer Deutscher Studentenbund*], the Federation of Socialist Students (in West Germany); **SDS** (*U.S.*), Students for a Democratic Society; **s.e.(m.)**, **S.E.(M.)** (*Statistics*), standard error (of the mean); **S.E.**, **S/E**, Stock Exchange; **S.E.A.C.** (also with pronunc. 'siːæk), South East Asia Command; **SEC** (*U.S.*), Securities and Exchange Commission; **SECAM** [F. *séquentiel couleur à mémoire* colour sequence by memory], a colour television system developed in France and widely used; **SEM**, scanning electron microscope, microscopy; **S.E.N.**, State Enrolled Nurse; **SERPS**, **Serps** (sɜːps), State earnings-related pension scheme; **S.E.T.** (also with pronunc. sɛt), selective employment tax; **S.F.**, San Francisco; **S.F.**, **s.f.**, science fiction; **S.F.** = SINN FEIN; **S.F.A.**, Scottish Football Association (cf. *F.A.* s.v. F III. 3); **S.F.A.**, Sweet Fanny Adams (cf. *F.A.* s.v. F III. 3, FANNY ADAMS 2); **S.F.I.O.** [F. *Section française de l'Internationale ouvrière*, French section of the workers' International], the French socialist party, known since 1969 as the *Parti Socialiste*; **s.h.**, shit-house; **S.H.F.**, **s.h.f.** (*Radio*), superhigh frequency; **S.H.O.**, Senior House Officer; **s.h.p.**, **S.H.P.**, shaft horsepower; **SI** [F. *système international (d'unités)*], International System of Units (see SYSTÈME INTERNATIONAL and INTERNATIONAL *a.* 1 c); **S.I.D.**, **s.i.d.** (*Radio*), sudden ionospheric disturbance; **SIDS**, sudden infant death syndrome; **S.I.N.S.**, ship's inertial navigation system; **S.I.S.**, Secret Intelligence Service; **S.I.W.**, self-inflicted wound (see also quot. 1929); **S.J.**, Society of Jesus (cf. JESUIT *sb.*); **S.L.A.**, Symbionese Liberation Army; **SLBM**, submarine-launched ballistic missile; **SLCM**, submarine-launched cruise missile;

SLE (*Med.*), systemic lupus erythematosus; **S level**, Scholarship (also, Special) level (of the General Certificate of Education examination); **S.L.P.**, Scottish Labour Party; **SLR** (*Photogr.*), single-lens reflex (camera); **S-M**: see *S and M* above; **S.M.**, sergeant-major; **S.M.**, short metre (cf. SHORT *a.*, *sb.* and *adv.* 26); **S.M.** = Silver Medallist (in shooting competition); **S.M., s.m.**, stage manager; **S.M.L.E.**, short magazine Lee-Enfield (rifle); **S.M.M.T.**, Society of Motor Manufacturers and Traders; **S.M.O.N.** (see SMON as main entry); **SMP**, statutory maternity pay (payable in the U.K. by an employer to an employee on maternity leave, and recoverable from the government Department of Health and Social Security); **SMPTE** (*U.S.*), Society of Motion Picture and Television Engineers; **SNCC** (*U.S.*), Student Nonviolent Co-ordinating Committee; **S.N.C.F.** [F. *Société Nationale des Chemins de Fer*], the French State railway authority, also used for the railway system itself; **S.N.F., s.n.f.**, solids, non-fat; **SNG**, simulated, substitute, or synthetic natural gas; **S.N.O.**, Senior Naval Officer (cf. *N.O.* s.v. N II. 1); **S.N.P.**, Scottish National Party; **SNU** (snju:) *Astr.*, solar neutrino unit (see quot. 1970); **S.O.**, standing order; **S.O.B., s.o.b.** (chiefly *U.S.*), son of a bitch, also silly old bastard, etc.; **S.O.E.**, Special Operations Executive; **S. of S.**, Secretary of State; **S.O.L., s.o.l.**, soldier (also strictly, shit, surely: see quot. 1917) out of luck (*U.S.*); **SOP**, standard operating procedure (*U.S.*, orig. *Mil.*); **S.P., s.p.**, starting price; **S.P.A.B.**, Society for the Protection of Ancient Buildings; **S.P.C.K.**, Society for the Promotion of Christian Knowledge; **S.P.D.** [G. *Sozialdemokratische Partei Deutschlands*], the Social Democratic Party in West Germany; **S.P.E.**, Society for Pure English; **S.P.G.**, Society for the Propagation of the Gospel, etc.; **S.P.Q.R.** [L. *Senatus Populusque Romanus*], the Senate and People of Rome; also in joc. adaptations, esp. = small profits, quick returns; **S.P.R.**, Society for Psychical Research; **SQ** [f. *s*tereophonic-*q*uadraphonic], a designation (proprietary in the U.S.) of audio equipment used with reference to a system of quadraphonic recording and reproduction; **S.R.**, Socialist Revolutionary (Party); **S.R.**, Southern Railway; **S.R.**, Special Reserve; **sr**, steradian; **S–R**, stimulus–response *adj.* (in Psychol.); **SRBC** (*Med.*), sheep red blood cell(s); **S.R.M.N.**, State Registered Mental Nurse; **S.R.N.**, State Registered Nurse; **sRNA** († **S-RNA**) (*Biol.*), soluble RNA; **SRO** (*U.S.*), single-room occupancy; **S.R.O.** (orig. *U.S.*), standing room only; **SRS(-A)** (*Med.*), slow-reacting substance (of anaphylaxis); **S.S.** = SCHUTZSTAFFEL; **S.S.**, secret service, security service; **SS**, social security (benefit); **S.S., s.s., ss.**, steam-ship; **SSB, ssb** (*Radio*), single side-band (transmission); **SSBN** [Submarine (symbol SS), Ballistic, Nuclear], a nuclear-powered ballistic missile submarine; **S.S.N.**, severely subnormal; **SSP**, statutory sick pay (payable in the U.K. by an employer to a sick employee and recoverable from the government Department of Health and Social Security); **SSPE** (*Path.*) subacute sclerosing panencephalitis; **SSR**, secondary surveillance radar; **S.S.R.** [Russ. *Sovétskaya Sotsialisticheskaya Respúblika*], Soviet Socialist Republic (cf. U.S.S.R.); **SSRC**, Social Science Research Council; **S.S.S.I.**, site of special scientific interest (so designated by the Nature Conservancy Council); cf. *A.O.N.B.* s.v. A III; **SST**, supersonic transport; **S.T.C.**, short-title catalogue, esp. *A Short-Title Catalogue of Books Printed in England, Scotland, and Ireland 1475–1640*, by A. W. Pollard and G. R. Redgrave, first published in 1926; **STD** (*Teleph.*), subscriber trunk dialling; **STOL, stol.**, short take-off and landing; **S.T.V.**, single transferable vote; **SU** (*Physics*), special unitary (*sc.* group): used with following numeral denoting the number of rows and of columns in the matrices that can be used to represent it, as *SU*(3): cf. SPECIAL *a.*; **SV** (*Med.*), Simian virus: used, freq. with following numeral to identify the strain, as the designation of various viruses isolated from monkeys or cultures of monkey cells; **s.v.** = *sub verbo*, *sub voce* s.v. SUB *Latin prep.*; also **s.vv.**, *sub verbis* (followed by more than one citation); **SVD**, swine vesicular disease; **S.W.**, small women('s size); **S.W.A.(L.)K.**, **SWA(L)K**, sealed with a (loving) kiss; **SWAT** (*U.S.*), Special Weapons and Tactics; **s.w.g., S.W.G.**, standard wire gauge; **SWP**, Socialist Workers' Party; **S.W.R., s.w.r.**, standing-wave ratio. See also (as main entries) SAGE, SALT, SAVAK, SEATO, SHAEF, SHAPE, SNAFU, SOGAT, S.O.S., STP, SWANU, SWAPO.

1828–40 BERRY *Encycl. Herald.* I, *S. This letter.. signifies sable, or black. *a* **1400** *Wyclif's Bible* IV. 690 *S. Lucie virgyn. **1535** JOYE *Apol. Tindale* (Arb.) 4 His felowe called Hijpinus pastour of .s. nicholas parisshe in Hambourg. **1549** LATIMER *6th Serm. bef. Edw. VI* (Arb.) 166, I am goynge to S. Tomas of Acres to the sermon. **1648** HERRICK *Hesper.* 172 (*title*), To his Valentine, on S. Valentines day. **1591** HARINGTON *Orl. Fur.*, *Apol. Poetrie* ¶vij b, If *S. Philip Sidney had counted this a fault. **1628** SIR J. CAMPBELL in *Thanes of Cawdor* (Spalding Cl.) 271, I rest, your loueing father S. J. Campbell of Calder. **1920** J. A. ARKWRIGHT in *Jrnl. Path. & Bacteriol.* XXIII. 359 The appearance of colonies on agar of the two forms is different. The *S form makes smooth, round, domed, shiny, translucent colonies; the R form grows in colonies which have a more or less jagged outline. **1974** [see ROUGH *a.* 1 e]. **1724** *Explic. Foreign Words Mus.* 66 The letter **S* is used as an Abbreviation of the Word Solo. **1949** *Vet. Rec.* LXI. 318/1 Each animal was inoculated intravenously with approximately 20 times the recommended vaccine dose of *S.19 in a volume of 50 ml. **1960** *Farmer & Stockbreeder* 26 Jan. 89/1 As the animals are ready to go out on the early spring grazing they are collected together on the farms for vaccination with S19. **1978** *Amer. Jrnl. Vet. Res.* XXXIX. 884/1 Lymphocyte stimulation..was detected in 3 steers which had been vaccinated with S19 but not with lymphocytes from 5 nonvaccinated heifers. **1926** *Amer. Mercury* Dec. 465 The girl is a looker with an armful of *S.A. (sex appeal). **1932** P. MACDONALD *Maze* 216 A Gallic young woman with apparently some looks and, let us say, 98 per cent. vigorous S.A. **1961** *John o' London's* 6 July 57/2 Surely one of Hollywood's finest character actresses—all this and blonde S.A. too. **1974** E. MCGIRR *Murderous Journey* 96, I saw you and the dame go into her apartment. .. I expected you to take longer. Losing the old s.a., Piron? [**1907** *Jrnl. Anat. & Physiol.* XLI. 175 (*caption*) **s.a.j.*, sino-auricular junction.] **1908** J. MACKENZIE *Dis. Heart* p. xix, Sino-auricular node (s.-a. node.) **1910** *Jrnl. Physiol.* XLI. 69 This observer finds no altered rhythm as the result of destruction of the S-A node by burning. **1944** C. P. ANTHONY *Textbk. Anat. & Physiol.* v. 177 It is named the sinoatrial node but is usually referred to simply as the S.A. node... It is also called the 'pacemaker' of the heart. **1974** M. C. GERALD *Pharmacol.* xxi. 386 Digitalis directly depresses the conducting tissues responsible for carrying the excitatory impulse from the S.A. node pacemaker. **1876** VOYLE & STEVENSON *Mil. Dict.* (ed. 3) p. x, **S.A.*, small-arms. **1888** *Man. Field Service—Army Signallers* (War Office) 12 Pins, linch, 3rd class (or 2nd class, steel, if for cart, ammunition, S.A.). **1924** *Regulations Equipment of Army (Provisional)* (War Office) II. i. 4 Eyepieces, rubber, sights, telescopic, S.A., No. 2. **1921** *London Directory* 1707/1 Geneva, Switzerland. Mondiale Express Transports *S/A. **1938** E. AMBLER *Cause for Alarm* v. 83 There it was in black and white—Società Anonima Braganzetta, Torino. I had found S.A. Braga of Turin! **1977** 'J. LE CARRÉ' *Hon. Schoolboy* iv. 80 Indocharter, Vientiane SA..was an overseas Chinese company. **1931** W. LEWIS *Hitler* II. 60 The abovementioned defence-service..received the name of *Storm-detachments*—**S.A.*, in memory of the 'heroic onset of the at that time mere handful'. **1934** *Ann. Reg. 1933* 168 On February 22 Goering incorporated picked S.A. men as auxiliary Police Corps. **1955** *Times* 15 Aug. 4/4 A picture of him..wearing S.A. uniform and with his right arm raised. **1968** *Listener* 19 Sept. 358/3, I do not even know the difference between the SA and the SS, so how can I make such a film. **1977** *Daily Tel.* 17 Nov. 36/7 The SS (Schutzstaffel) emerged as a powerful force after the 1934 purge which eliminated the SA (Sturmabteilung), the brown-shirted thugs who helped bring Hitler to political prominence. **1876** VOYLE & STEVENSON *Mil. Dict.* (ed. 3) p. xi, **S.A.A.*, small-arm ammunition. **1907** *Field Service Pocket Bk.* ii. 50 A total of 500 rounds S.A.A. will be maintained in the field..for every man, whether combatant or not, included in an expeditionary force. **1954** J. MASTERS *Bhowani Junction* I. xi. 95, I rummaged in the table drawers and found a list:..1,000 feet of slow-burning fuse; 12,000 rounds of SAA .303 Mark VIII Z. **1952** *R.A.F. Rev.* Jan. 11/1 Under the New Trade Structure I am now expected to pass a *SAC board to qualify as a Corporal and gain the increase in pay. **1970** *Athanian* 1 Apr. 31/1 The club is an 'All Ranks' affair ranging from an S.A.C. to a Sqn Ldr. **1947** *Army & Navy Bull.* 1 Feb. 8/3 General St. Clair Streett, *SAC Deputy Commander since its activation last March, received a new assignment in the War Department. **1958** *Times* 8 May 11/6 Right now, therefore, the S.A.C. crew in a S.A.C. plane is the west's number one deterrent to the Kremlin. **1974** *Publishers Weekly* 16 Dec. 22 (Advt.), H. Bruce Franklin, Melville Scholar, former SAC officer, and tugboat mate. **1951** *Army Information Digest* July 27 Supreme Allied Commander Europe (**SACEUR*). **1953** *Britannica Bk. of Year* 752/2 Saceur, Supreme Allied Commander, Europe. **1958** *Economist* 1 Feb. 393/1 Its [*sc.* Britain's] dwindling proportion of the forces at Saceur's disposal. **1959** *Times Lit. Suppl.* 13 Feb. 79/2 Proposals for placing the missile bases under the command of S.A.C.EUR... do not, as Mr. Moore says, really change the situation. **1964** *Ann. Reg. 1963* 162 Approval was given to the assignment of the British V-bomber force..to the Supreme Allied Commander Europe (SACEUR). **1979** *Observer* 25 Nov. 34/3 SACEUR, Supreme Allied Commander Europe, the military head of NATO; currently the American General Bernard W. Rogers. **1951** *R.A.F. Rev.* Sept. 34/3 The R.A.F.'s qualifying trade test leads to promotion to Senior Aircraftsman or *SACW. **1977** *R.A.F. News* 30 Mar.–12 Apr. 18/1 The only WRAF rider, SACW Jennie Hye of West Drayton, put up a plucky 44·42. **1924** *Jrnl. Soc. Automotive Engineers* XV. 31/1 The fact that the present *S.A.E. numbers for crankcase lubricating oil specifications were used..is of interest. **1966** *McGraw-Hill Encycl. Sci. & Technol.* XIII. 313/1 The carburizing steels ..which have the greatest ability to harden..are SAE 3310 and 4320. **1967** KARCH & BUBER *Offset Processes* x. 475 The pump oiler should be filled every 25 to 50 hours of running time with ≠ 105SAE or equivalent pure mineral oil. **1974** *Encycl. Brit. Macropædia* XIV. 188/2 In the U.S., the Society of Automotive Engineers established a system of SAE numbers to indicate the viscosity at a particular temperature, 0°F (– 18°C). Oils in common use have SAE numbers varying from 5 to 50. *Ibid.*, An oil designated 10W/40 has the viscosity of an SAE 10W oil at 0°F.., and of an SAE 40 oil at 210°F... Such an oil will help start an engine in winter (hence the suffix W) and will lubricate well under running conditions in summer. **1939** 'F. O'BRIEN' *At Swim-two-Birds* i. 15 To all my friends forwarding 6d. and two *S.A.E.'s I will present this three-star cast-iron plunger. **1962** *Woman's Own* 15 Sept. 69/3, I will send you a leaflet on this subject on request (s.a.e., please). **1966** *Punch* 26 Jan. 116/3 That stream of SAEs for the free, illustrated brochure. **1977** *Vogue* Dec. 90/2 Send a SAE for the catalogue. **1966** *Economist* 29 Oct. 457/3 The much publicised series of talks between federal ministers, *SAL leaders and a couple of dissident sheikhs..has come to nothing. **1970** H. TREVELYAN *Middle East in Revolution* 218 The original Nationalist party, the South Arabian League, known as SAL, were in decline. **1958** *Chambers's Techn. Dict.* 983/2 *SAM. **1975** R. JACKSON *South Asian Crisis* v. 107 The Indian SAM missile systems were improved. **1979** P. NIESEWAND *Member of Club* xv. 122 Tanks, armoured cars, SAM missiles..are being landed at Beira. **1951** *Business Week* 22 Sept. 152/2 (*heading*) 'Thin Ice' for *S & L's. **1967** *Economist* 25 Mar. 1145/2 Some Californian S & Ls suffered near runs on their accounts as savers began to doubt their solvency. **1976** *National Observer* (U.S.) 25 Dec. 7/1 The result is that institutions that finance a large volume of home purchases, as S&Ls do, may not be able to afford to be as generous on longer-term deposit rates. **1965** *Acronyms & Initialisms Dict.* (Gale Research Co.) 645 **S & M*,.. sadism and masochism (generic term). **1966** *Realist* May 19/3 Remember the S–M ads: 'seeks discipline', 'seeks uniforms', 'seeks leather and rubber'. **1975** *New Yorker* 26 May 32/2 Death is by far the most controversial and hottest subject in America, ranking twenty-five shock points above transsexuality, school busing, S & M, and interracial cloning. **1977** *Time* 15 Aug. 31/1 The streets teemed with whores, transvestites and the S–M crowd dangling slave bracelets and chains. **1955** R. J. SCHWARTZ *Compl. Dict. Abbrev.* 159/1 **SAR*,..search and rescue. **1958** *Oxf. Mail* 1 Aug. 6/6 SAR..has two squadrons situated at ten stations mainly around the south and east coasts. **1977** *R.A.F. News* 5–18 Jan. 3/1 An SAR Wessex was scrambled from Manston the following morning. **1945** M. JAMES *Born of Desert* xxi. 319 As the continental offensive developed and gained weight, so the *S.A.S. probed deeper and deeper into the enemy lines. **1960** B. A. YOUNG *Artists & S.A.S.* xix. 46 The S.A.S. first went into action on November 16, 1941, when their target was the enemy airfields at Gazala and Tmimi, and their object to cripple the enemy's air before General Auchinleck launched his attack a few days later. **1976** G. SEYMOUR *Glory Boys* xvi. 221 The SAS anti-hi-jack force had been lifted by Wessex helicopter from their base camp. **1961** A. ANASTASI *Psychol. Testing* (ed. 2) ix. 226 A number of tests have been specially developed for use in the admission, placement, and counseling of college students. An outstanding example is the Scholastic Aptitude Test (*SAT) of the College Entrance Examination Board. **1971** E. ASHBY *Any Person, Any Study* ii. 59 Taken together with SAT scores the information is as good as any measure yet devised to predict academic performance in college examinations. **1974** A. LURIE *War between Tates* ii. 39 Until very recently, girls like her, whatever their SAT scores, didn't usually go to graduate school. **1923** J. REITH *Diary* 29 Aug. (1975) ii. 132, I read the News Bulletin at 7.00 p.m. —the first real *SB. **1929** *B.B.C. Year-Bk. 1930* 310 One or two transmissions are, perhaps, being sent to the provinces via the S.B. lines... Tests are being taken of outside broadcasts or incoming S.B. **1903** SIR M. G. GERARD *Leaves fr. Diaries* iv. 104 In 1870 our armament was still the old 12-pr. *S.B. gun and 24-pr. howitzer. **1964** L. DEIGHTON *Funeral in Berlin* xxxvii. 228 'Makes me curious about the locked room,' said the young *S.B. man. **1975** O. SELA *Bengali Inheritance* iv. 34 Special Branch won't like it... But you will need some assistance from SB—the files at least. **1917** A. G. EMPEY *Over Top* 307 *S.B., stretcher bearer. The motive power of a stretcher. He is generally looking the other way when a fourteen-stone Tommy gets hit. **1919** W. DEEPING *Second Youth* xix. 168 'Ere, you blitherin' S.B.'s, get a move on. **1942** PARTRIDGE *Dict. Abbrev.* 87/2 **S.B.A.*, Sick-Bay Attendant. **1964** J. HALE *Grudge Fight* iii. 44 'Got a nice new one for you,' said the sick bay attendant to Adams, meaning the needle which glittered in space for a moment before the S.B.A. rammed it into his arm and pressed the plunger. **1953** *Newsweek* 24 Aug. 62/3 The new Small Business Administration whirled into rapid action... *SBA..will keep some functions formerly performed by the ..Small Defense Plants Administration. **1976** *Billings* (Montana) *Gaz.* 27 June 2-D/8 They file for Small Business Administration (SBA) loans and get on the long HUD list for trailers. **1932** *Flight* 1 July 601 The Flying Display arranged by the *S.B.A.C., with the co-operation of the Air Ministry, at Hendon last Monday must be counted a success. **1951** *R.A.F. Rev.* Oct. 13/2 It flew faster than any aircraft has ever flown before in an S.B.A.C. show. **1968** C. SIMS *Royal Air Force* xi. 174 An item in the S.B.A.C. show. **1973** HOBSON & POHL *Mod. Petroleum Technol.* xxix. 945 A development during recent years has been the so-called Single Buoy Mooring (*SBM) which may be either a fixed tower or a large buoy to which the ship is moored bow on. **1975** *Offshore Engineer* Sept. 33 (*heading*) Pioneering new sbm system off coast of Anglesey. **1975** *Petroleum Rev.* XXIX. 324/1 Floating hose conveys the crude from the SBM into a tanker. **1967** *Standard Book Numbering* (S.B.N. Agency) 7/3 Each edition *must* have a different *SBN. **1969** *Publishers' Weekly* 27 Jan. 72/1 The *Bookseller* list of publications for the first week of 1969 carries SBNs for 71% of the titles. **1979** SBN [see *ISBN* s.v. I III]. **1956** *Rubber World* May 239/2 The use of the term 'butadiene-styrene rubber' and the coding '*SBR'. **1971** G. J. VAN DER BIE et al. in C. M. Blow *Rubber Technol. & Manuf.* iv. B. 84 Emulsion SBR, for long the only synthetic general purpose rubber, has blossomed from the few 'hot' types produced during World War II into the multiplicity of grades now available in 'cold' types. **1920** *Dalton's Weekly Advertiser* 10 Jan. 3/2 (Advt.), House or *S.C. Flat wanted by married couple. **1975** *Irish Independent* 27 May 18/1 (Advt.), Newly furnished hall flat, completely s.c., own door, double bedroom. **1977** *Weekly Times* (Melbourne) 19 Jan. 58/7 (Advt.), Clean, SC, ground level flats, acc. 2 to 6. **1964** E. BACH *Introd. Transformational Gram.* iv. 61 The second part of the rule specifies the *structural change* (*SC) by means of variable signs. **1966** A. KOUTSOUDAS *Writing Transformational Gram.* i. 24 There are different notational conventions for writing a T-rule; rule (8) above can also be written.. SC: $x_1-x_2-x_3 \rightarrow x_3-x_1-x_2$. **1946** *Newsweek* 12 Aug. 43/3 Again *SCAP (Supreme Commander for the Allied Powers, the official designation of the occupation) left the implementation up to the Japanese. **1978** C. HUMPHREYS *Both Sides of Circle* xii. 131 The formal opening took place of our own Empire Building near that of S.C.A.P. (headquarters of the American army). **1885** *Ordinances Univ. Cambr.* p. viii, *Students in Science and Letters.* Proceeding to the Degrees of *Sc.D. and Litt.D. **1917** J. R. TANNER *Hist. Register Univ. Cambr.* 195 Sc.D. Robes and hood of scarlet cloth, both lined with silk shot with pink and light blue. **1979** *Oxford Univ. Gaz.* 1 Mar. 554/2 University Preachers... Sunday, 11 March, at 10.15 a.m. D. E. Broadbent, C.B.E., M.A., D.Sc. (M.A., Sc.D. Cambridge, Hon. D.Sc. Southampton). **1921** *Ann. Rep. Save the Children Fund* 4/1 During the year under review, the *S.C.F. has succeeded in making the needs of the children widely known throughout the United Kingdom and the British Empire. **1967** *Punch* 1 Mar. 292/2 'A simple pleasure,' said the SCF supervisor, 'but one that flat-dwelling kids just don't have.' **1974** *Petroleum Rev.* XXVIII. 794/2 The combined recoverable reserves of the field are estimated to be in the order of 1·5 to 2·0 × 10⁹ barrels of oil, with some 3·0 × 10¹² *scf of associated gas. **1959** L. D. REDDICK *Crusader without Violence* xii. 205 There was so much..rumor about friction between the *SCLC and NAACP that King scampered up to New York. **1968** L. LOKOS *House Divided* x. 375 SCLC called upon the President to de-escalate the war unilaterally. **1973** *Freedomways* XIII. 8 Recent action taken by the leaders of ..SCLC..is a most welcome development. **1935** *Nursing Mirror & Midwives' Jrnl.* 2 Feb. p. xx/3 (Advt.), *S.C.M. required... General training not essential. **1955** *Times* 8 July 2/5 Candidates must be S.R.N., S.C.M., and should preferably have had similar experience in a Teaching Hospital. **1924** *Fellowship of Students* (Student Christian Movement) 49 The work of the *S.C.M. must be closely related to the developing work of the Churches. **1948** H. G. G. HERKLOTS in M. Warren *Triumph of God* vii. 180 Now it was men and women who had been schooled in the S.C.M., who accepted its 'interdenominational position', who were planning the Edinburgh Conference. **1976** A. LOCKLEY *Christian Communes* vi. 55 The SCM headquarters were moved out of London in 1974 to Wick Court, a Jacobean mansion near Bristol, where the central staff attempted to live communally. **1971** *Nature* 16 Apr. 430/1 The big attraction of *SCP is the possibility of utilizing cheap raw materials as fermentation substrates. **1976** *Jrnl. R. Soc. Arts* CXXIV. 580/2 It might be more economical to convert part of our oil supplies into food by using it as a substrate for micro-organisms, to produce 'Single Cell Protein' (SCP) that could be used as the raw material for the textured meat substitutes that were referred to earlier. **1923** D. K. HORNE in G. Bailey *Lady Margaret Hall* v. 94 Each student..is placed under a tutor, who is almost invariably one of the resident members of the *S.C.R. **1964** M. HUTT in D. Daiches *Idea of New Univ.* iii. 49 Falmer House belongs neither to the Union nor the SCR. **1965** *New Statesman* 7 May 734/1 Mr Soyinka..knows the SCRs of Ibadan and Ife. **1976** A. CROSS *Question of Max* vi. 73 If..I had one wish right now, it would be to be connected for a time with an Oxford college and dine at the high table, chat in the SCR. **1963** *New Scientist* 13 June 600/1 The *SCR, at the outset, is basically an 'insulator'. It does not allow current to pass. **1975** D. G. FINK *Electronics Engineers' Handbk.* VII. 52 During forward-bias operation.., the *pnpn* structure of the SCR is electrically bistable and may exhibit either a very high impedance (OFF state) or a very low impedance (ON state). **1956** *Times* 22 Sept. 10/4 The members of the Suez Canal Users' Association (*S.C.U.A.) shall be those nations which have participated in the second London Suez conference and which subscribe to the present declaration, and any other adhering nations. **1970** H. TREVELYAN *Middle East in Revolution* 100 The Menzies Mission..was followed by the second conference of the 'users', the formation of the 'users'' association and the realisation that the S.C.U.A., the skewer as we called it, had a blunt point. **1939** *London Weekly Advertiser* 7 June 6/4 £70 Exclusive.—*S.D. Modern House, three beds, etc., near Dyke Road Park. **1975** *Evening Herald* (Dublin) 8 May 10/2 (Advt.), Very unusual 4 bedroomed s.d. in cul de sac. **1901** W. M. F. PETRIE *Diospolis Parva* i. 6 We now make a first division into fifty equal stages, numbered 30 to 80, termed *sequence dates* or *S.D. **1939** —— *Making of Egypt* vii. 55 This period (S.D. 60–75) has no generally distinctive culture. **1944** *Jrnl. Near Eastern Stud.* III. 110 Petrie distinguished it from Gerzean by naming it the Third Predynastic of Semainean, ranging from Sequence Dates 60/63 to S.D. 76. **1950** G. E. DANIEL *Hundred Yrs. of Archaeol.* v. 176 He started his sequence with S.D. 30,..and carried on to dynastic times at S.D. 80. [**1940** H. KOEHLER *Inside Gestapo* ii. 30 Heydrich's power is much more founded on the Security Service of the Reich Fuehrer S.S. (shortened *SD. RFSS.) than on the Gestapo.] **1947** H. TREVOR-ROPER *Last Days of Hitler* i. 28 Otto Ohlendorf was head of *R.S.H.A. Amt III* (also called S.D. or *Sicherheitsdienst*). **1968** *Listener* 8 Aug. 174/3, I was wearing my old SD cap which I'd brought through the whole war. **1974** A. WILLIAMS *Gentleman Traitor* xiii. 212 The father had returned to Germany in 1938..and had served in the SD, the civil arm of the S.S. **1902** *Biometrika* I. 206, σ_1 is the *S.D. of the organ. **1973** *Nature* 31 Aug. 587/2 The mean (±s.d.) IQ then was 98·7 (±7·1) with no precocity. **1978** *Jrnl. R. Soc. Med.* LXXI. 659 Twin, malformed or grossly autolysed fetuses, and any which were ⩾ 2 s.d. below the mean for the gestational age group, were excluded. **1964** E. BACH *Introd. Transformational Gram.* iv. 61 The first part of the rule is a *structural description* (*SD ..) specifying the class of strings (in the terms of their analysis by P markers) to which the rule applies. **1975** *Studies in Eng. Lit.: Eng. Number* (Tokyo) 170 The term 'obligatory'..has generally been understood to mean that an obligatory rule must apply to a phrase-maker which meets the SD of that rule. **1975** *Glasgow Herald* 17 Dec. 1 (*heading*) *S.D.A. pledge quick action. **1976** *Scotsman* 15 Dec. 5/1 Capital restructuring..will give the SDA one-third of the shares at a cost of £60,000. **1966** *Economist* 22 Jan. 301/2 His superior in *SDECE admitted last week that this was true. **1966** M. WOODHOUSE *Tree Frog* viii. 58 There is Defensive Intelligence and Active Intelligence... In France, the Ministry of the Interior and S.D.E.C.E. **1972** K. BENTON *Spy in Chancery* xvii. 193 They have a..gentleman's agreement..with both MI6 and CIA—and with the French SDECE, too, I think. **1893** G. B. SHAW *Let.* 24 Apr. (1965) I. 390 My remarks..were not levelled at the I.L.P., but at the *S.D.F. **1910** CHESTERTON *George Bernard Shaw* 68 Bernard Shaw was thrown early into what may be called the cosmopolitan club of revolution. The Socialists of the S.D.F. call it 'l'Internationale'. **1957** R. HOGGART *Uses of Literacy* xi. 261 They worked for Hyndman's S.D.F. in the 'eighties, and for the I.L.P. in the 'nineties. **1980** 'FIRST' & SCOTT *Olive Schreiner* iv. 109 The Democratic Federation [of 1881] became the Social Democratic Federation (SDF) in 1883. **1936** *S.D.F.er [see MORRISITE]. **1984** *N.Y. Times* 10 Apr. I. 28/1 The [Defense and Administration] officials.. are now referring to the President's plan as '*S.D.I.', for 'strategic defense initiative'. **1985** *Ann. Reg. 1984* 70 The US Government sought to win the agreement of its European allies to its Star Wars programme, properly known as the Strategic Defence Initiative (SDI), which was a research project into the practicalities of space weaponry, including the use of laser beams and other non-nuclear ways of destroying incoming missiles. **1985** *Daily Tel.* 27 Nov. 36/4 Gen Chervov, a Soviet arms control spokesman, had suggested that if Russia decided to counter SDI, it would not attempt to match it but would seek a lower cost solution. **1970** *Times* 22 Aug. 3/1 'The *S.D.L.P. is the only institution that can bring about reform in Northern Ireland,' he said. **1974** *Freedom* 25 May 8/1 Willing followers of the power seekers of the IRA, SDLP and all the 'loyalist' organisations. **1978** D. MURPHY *Place Apart* vi. 117 An elderly woman then observed, 'What we need is a sort of cross between the Provos and Stickies and SDLP.' **1936** W. H. S. SMITH *Let.* 21 June in *Young Man's Country* (1977) i. 9 I've been in correspondence with the present *S.D.O. **1947** *Civil & Milit. Gaz.* 9 Apr. 2/4 'Youngsters are attached to S.D.O.s to learn their jobs. **1977** W. H. S. SMITH *Young Man's Country* iii. 103, I was welcomed by several clerks in the S.D.O.'s office. **1908** *Times* 18 Apr. 10/1 The delegate..declared that as a militant force the *S.D.P. could desire no more suitable antagonist than the scion of the aristocracy who represented Rossendale. **1912** R. MACAULAY *Views & Vagabonds* ii. 24 We stand for all the principles of the Fabian Society, the S.D.P., and..so forth. **1961** C. TSUZUKI *H. M. Hyndman & Brit. Socialism* viii. 164 In October 1907 this progress and the desire to emulate the Labour Party encouraged the executive to change the name of the Federation to the Social Democratic Party (S.D.P.). **1981** *Times* 27 Mar. 1/1 (*heading*) SDP launched with aim of 'reconciling the nation'. *Ibid.* 3 (Advt.), If you share our aims you can join the *SDP* by filling in the application and returning it with a subscription. **1967** *Guardian* 28 Aug. 1/7 It will be up to the managing director of the IMF..to initiate and suggest the size of any proposed allotment of special drawing rights (*SDRs). **1972** *Penguin Dict. Econ.* 382 The S.D.R...is an entry in a member country's bank balance with the I.M.F. **1976** 'J. DAVEY' *Treasury Alarm* iii. 43, I happened to hear some Treasury folk gossiping..and I find that SDRs, which baffled me, are Special Drawing Rights. **1968** *Times* 19 Apr. 10/4 The extreme left-wing Federation of German Socialist Students (*S.D.S.). **1977** in R. Crossman *Diaries* III. 77 In West Berlin on April 11th there was an attempt to assassinate Rudi Dütschke, left-wing leader of the militant Socialist Students' League (S.D.S.). **1961** *Mademoiselle* Aug. 335/2 'Students have a mystique about action,' says Al Haber, president of the nationwide Students for a Democratic Society... Haber.. has traveled to many campuses this year to establish new *S.D.S. groups. **1965** *Moderator* Winter 14/2 SDS was re-formed in 1962, at which time the Port Huron statement defined its purposes. **1974** H. L. FOSTER *Ribbin'* iii. 92 The SDS and some third world groups sold drugs to college students to earn money and keep their cause going a few years ago. **1946** C. E. WEATHERBURN *Math. Statistics* vi. 110 This S.D. is usually called the standard error (*S.E.) of the number of successes in a sample of size *n*. *Ibid.* 111 A deviation from the mean less than twice the S.E. is regarded as not significant. **1964** F. N. KERLINGER *Foundations Behavioral Res.* ix. 167 $SE_M = 2{\cdot}73$. **1971** *Nature* 1 Jan. 62/1 On these assumptions, the mean number (± s.e.) of skeletomotor nerve fibres in normal nerves was 191 ± 26. **1974** *Ibid.* 23 Aug. 654/1 The mean concentration of prolactin in the peripheral blood of women during the cycle is 15± 1 (± s.e.m.). **1927** *Financial Times* 7 May 6/5 (*heading*) *S.E. Clerks' Provident Fund. **1942** PATRIDGE *Dict. Abbrev.* 88/2 *S/E*, Stock Exchange. **1978** *Times* 23 Jan. 15/1 A Stock Exchange investigation..is now awaiting examination by the SE Council. **1944** *SEAC: Daily Newspaper of South East Asia Command* (Calcutta) 10 Jan. 1/1 First light is breaking over this awakening city as the birthday issue of *SEAC (pronounce it See-ack) comes flying off the presses. **1945** *Daily Mirror* 15 Aug. 1/1 There is an Army warning against expecting the quick homecoming of SEAC troops. **1971** R. RUSSELL tr. *Ahmad's Shore & Wave* xv. 159 In those days he [*sc.* Lord Mountbatten] was the head of S.E.A.C., and was there on leave. **1934** *Time* 16 July 46/1 The *S.E.C. will take over enforcement of the Securities Act of 1933. **1955** *Times* 29 Aug. 11/3 Banks..have indicated an interest if the S.E.C. provides a means of registering them. **1966** *Economist* 1 Oct. 46/3 The SEC has steadfastly opposed the exchange's efforts to limit trading in listed stocks to members only. **1978** *Financial Times* 3 Mar. 18/2 The setting-up of a body like the SEC is a last resort. **1962** *Rep. Comm. Broadcasting 1960* 218 in *Parl Papers 1961–2* (Cmnd. 1753) IX. 259 Our attention has..been drawn to another system of colour-transmission, the '*SECAM' system. This might..prove a serious rival to the NTSC system. **1968** [see *PAL* s.v. P II]. **1978** *Gramophone* Aug. 391/1 All the major video protagonists have mounted elaborate press launches of their systems, suitably adapted to the PAL TV format commonly used in Europe instead of the SECAM standard employed elsewhere. **1968** *Proc. Symp. Scanning Electron Microscope* 3/1 The scanning electron microscope, or *SEM, as I shall henceforth call it. **1974** SEM [see MACERATE *sb.*]. **1961** *Nursing Mirror & Midwives' Jrnl.* 26 May 760/1 Male *S.E.N. or Nursing Auxiliaries required for duties in acute wards & departments. **1964** G. L. COHEN *What's Wrong with Hospitals?* ix. 192 Negro domestics abounded, but the S.E.N. school was conspicuously white. **1977** *R.A.F. News* 22 June–5 July 13 (*caption*) SACW Margie Lee, an SEN, nursing a premature baby in the maternity unit at RAF Hospital Wegberg. **1983** *Economist* 1 Oct. 23 *Serps is a two-tier system that provides a universal flat-rate pension [etc.]. **1984** *Ibid.* 19 May 22/1 Introduced in 1978, Serps gives extra benefits to those who choose not to 'contract out' of the state system. **1985** *Daily Tel.* 10 May 1/2 Labour's leader Mr Kinnock said his party would press ahead with its 'Save Serps' campaign. **1985** *Listener* 16 May 5/1 A young Tory MP..shook his head grimly over the proposed abolition of SERPS (state earnings-related pension scheme). **1966** *Financial Times* 4 May 1/1 Most Fleet Street papers seized on the payroll tax (*SET) as the Budget's main news point. **1966** *Observer* 8 May 9/1 The main virtue of S.E.T. is that it is indirect. *a* **1974** R. CROSSMAN *Diaries* (1975) I. 508 My first reaction to S.E.T. was that in terms of farming at Prescote Manor as well as in terms of building it was absolutely unbearable. *c* **1875** *Pocket Exchange Guide San Francisco* 178 *S.F. Ten-Cent Parcel Delivery Co.—16 Post. **1975** B. MEGGS *Matter of Paradise* IX. iii. 267 One year at the University of Wisconsin, then moved to S.F. with her boyfriend, drummer in a rock-band. **1929** *Sci. Wonder Stories* June 92/3 The *S.F. Magazine. (Science-Fiction). **1948** G. CONKLIN *Treas. Sci. Fiction* p. ix, Many SF writers are feeling the urgent need for social controls over our physical powers. **1954** I. ASIMOV in *Mag. Fantasy & Sci. Fiction* Oct. 69 (*title*) The foundation of S.F. success. **1959** *Times Lit. Suppl.* 20 Mar. 166/2 Both are by O.K.-names in the s.f. world. **1968** *Punch* 10 Jan. 69/3 Let's take a step *beyond* in the company of Ray Bradbury..and other (mainly *sf*) bloodcurdlists. **1969** *Daily Tel.* 16 Oct. 22/7 Two regular themes in S.F. are the world dominated by a, usually evil, visionary and the world run by a Great Computer. **1973** 'D. HALLIDAY' *Dolly & Starry Bird* viii. 108 Johnson..was looking as everybody looks when they first step into an electronic workshop. That is blasé. This is the fault of the S.F. kiddie shows on the telly. **1975** FELTON & FOWLER *Best, Worst & most Unusual* 44 Arguably, it is the peak of sf film in its long history. **1980** *Times Lit. Suppl.* 7 Nov. 1263/1 The reason for preferring the old established and unpretentious 'sf' need not baffle us. The use of 'sci-fi' was clearly intended to imply a jaunty insider's knowledge coupled with a modern..demonstration of slick neologism. **1922** LADY LESLIE *Let.* 17 Mar. in M. Gilbert *Winston S. Churchill* (1977) IV. Compan. III. 1809 The Union Jacks are being silently stored away—the *SF flag floats on the orange Hall. **1973** *Irish Times* 2 Mar. 8/3 Sherlock J. (S.F.)... 2,488. **1882** *Football* 4 Oct. 4/1 The match would be played under the supervision of the *S.F.A. **1974** *Evening News* (Edinburgh) 9 Apr. 18/8 The SFA stipulated that no game could be cancelled at such an early hour on the strength of a weather forecast. **1933** *Bulletin* (Sydney) 14 June 12/3 Ask any modern sailor who has been refused an issue of pay or rations 'What luck?' and he will be apt to reply 'Sweet Fanny Adams', or just '*S.F.A.', meaning that he received nothing. **1935** *Ann. Reg. 1934* I. 172 Thus at Toulouse the *S.F.I.O. (the French section of the Workers' International) sought.. to form an entente with the Communists against Fascism. **1977** *Compar. Politics* IX. 364 The Popular Front, with its broad policies of alliance extending past the SFIO to the radical party..responded to Soviet and Comintern demands. **1949** E. POUND *Pisan Cantos* lxxvii. 52, I heard it in the *s.h. a suitable place To hear that the war was over. **1948** *Prof. Papers Inst. Post Office Electr. Engineers* No. 197. 3/1 *S.H.F. systems are those operating in the range 3,000 to 30,000 Mc/s, 10 to 1 cm. wavelength. **1958** *Electronic Engin.* XXX. 276/1 The radio repeater design is based on the principle of amplification at intermediate-frequency with reconversion to s.h.f. and the use of a travelling-wave amplifier to deliver the final output power. **1965** *Acronyms & Initialisms Dict.* (Gale Research Co.) 638 **SHO*,.. Senior House Officer. **1976** *Proc. R. Soc. Med.* LXIX. 818/1 A hypothetical increase in the number of graduates to over 5000 by 1980 would require about 18 000 SHO and registrar posts in 1982. **1931** *Times Trade & Engin. Suppl.* 24 Jan. p. iv/3 Six vessels, of 10,500 *s.h.p. **1972** C. MUDIE *Motor Boats & Boating* 28 The most important is SHP which is Shaft Horse Power or power delivered to the propeller shaft. **1961** *SI [see INTERNATIONAL *a.* 1 c]. **1970** *Nature* 2 May 473/2 Editors of scientific journals have been recently accused of forcing some unwilling scientists to adopt SI units. **1971** *Inside Kenya Today* Mar. 30/1 The Engineering and Construction Industries can go ahead with the change-over to the Metric System, but in particular in its modernized version called the 'Système International d'Unités' or the SI as it is popularly known in all languages. **1973** tr. *Internat. System of Units* 1 The 11th CGPM [*sc.* General Conference of Weights and Measures] (1960), by its Resolution 12, adopted the name *International System of Units*, with the international abbreviation SI, for this practical system of units of measurement. **1977** *Westworld* (Vancouver, B.C.) May–June 34/1 Canada..is one of the last major countries still using the imperial system of measurements instead of the International System of Units —universally known as SI. **1955** *Sci. News Let.* 29 Jan. 72/2 Polarized radio waves may also be a solution to the problem caused by '*SID's', or sudden ionospheric disturbances, when the sun may hurl out a great tongue of flame from which hydrogen atoms bombard the earth about 20 hours later. **1968** *Radio Communication Handbk.* (ed. 4) xii. 8/2 Ionospheric storms are often preceded (by approximately two days) by what are called sudden ionospheric disturbances (s.i.d.). **1970** J. B. BECKWITH in A. B. Bergman et al. *Sudden Infant Death Syndrome* 15, I personally feel the term 'Sudden Death Syndrome' should at least be amplified to include the word 'infant'... I should like, therefore, to cast my vote for the term 'Sudden Infant Death Syndrome' (*SIDS). **1980** *Sci. Amer.* Apr. 52/1 The phenomenon, which is also known by its initials SIDS (pronounced as letters rather than as a word), is defined clinically as the sudden, unexpected death of an apparently healthy infant for whom a routine autopsy fails to identify the cause of death. **1958** *Listener* 13 Nov. 779/2 The 'Nautilus' used a fully integrated apparatus of this kind called the Ship's Inertial Navigation System—inevitably contracted into its initials, '*S.I.N.S.' **1979** A. FOX *Threat Warning Red* i. 2 He could check those latitude and longitude figures against the readings on the SINS dials on the bulkhead. **1939** J. REITH *Diary* 21 Apr. (1975) iv. 227 Meeting in the foreign secretary's room, where I have never been before. Present: Halifax, Chatfield, Hoare, Cadogan, Leeper, CID secretary and Admiral Sinclair, the hush-hush *SIS chief. **1964** G. LYALL *Most Dangerous Game* xiii. 91 You're SIS—one of the

Foreign Office boys. What the mob would call The Secret Service. **1978** R. V. Jones *Most Secret War* vii. 63 While my evenings were spent discussing cryptography, my days went in perusing the S.I.S. files. *a* **1918** W. Owen *Coll. Poems* (1963) 74 (*title*) *S.I.W. **1929** *London Mag.* Dec. 629/2 'What really coopered him, was being in charge of an S.I.W. just before Armistice.' 'What is an S.I.W.?' I said. 'A hospital for self-inflicted wounds.' **1975** P. Fussell *Gt. War & Mod. Memory* viii. 294 The final two lines of 'S.I.W.' tell us how the victim of the self-inflicted wound was buried. **1822** *Catholic Miscellany* May 208 H. More Hist. Prov. Ang. *S.J. p. 467. **1916** Joyce *Portrait of Artist* iv. 187 The Reverend Stephen Dedalus, S.J. His name in that new life leaped into characters before his eyes. **1967** *Cath. Dict. Theol.* II. 1/2 J. A. Jungmann SJ, *Handing on the Faith*.. contains much recent information. **1974** *Time* 18 Feb. 16/1 The *S.L.A. emblem is a seven-headed cobra. **1978** *Maledicta 1977* I. 123 Terrorists have come to rely on the press to deliver their graphic messages to the world—the Hanafi Muslims in Washington, the PLO at the Munich Olympics, the SLA in Oakland. **1967** *New Scientist* 9 Feb. 340/2 To achieve overwhelmingness, especially in the face of Russia's ABM effort, Mr. McNamara proposes to produce and deploy the Poseidon *SLBM. **1973** *Sci. Amer.* Feb. 14/2 The primary SALT I restrictions..impose numerical ceilings on both land-based intercontinental ballistic missiles (ICBM's) and submarine-launched ballistic missiles (SLBM's). **1979** *Financial Rev.* 28 Sept. 10/3 The strategic deterrent is conceived as a triad consisting of bombers armed with nuclear weapons, submarine-launched ballistic missiles (SLBMs) and land-based intercontinental ballistic missiles (ICBMs). **1972** *Time* 19 June 17/3 The Pentagon is also asking for $20 million to get started on another submarine-based missile, the *SLCM (Submarine-Launched Cruise Missile). **1975** *Bull. Atomic Sci.* XXXI. 13 *SLCM*, submarine-launched cruise missile. **1979** *Observer* 25 Nov. 34/1 *Cruise Missile*... Can be ground-launched (GLCMs, known as Glickums).. or launched from submarines (SLCMs). **1958** *Jrnl. Clin. Invest.* XXXVII. 876/1 The serum of patients with systemic lupus erythematosus (*SLE) has been shown to contain factor(s) with a special affinity for nucleohistone (NH). **1978** *Jrnl. R. Soc. Med.* LXXI. 149 This is..the first case in which SLE has been reported in a patient with Hashimoto's thyroiditis and pernicious anaemia. **1951** *Times Educ. Suppl.* 8 June 466/1 (Advt.), Wanted for January, 1952, Senior English Mistress. The work includes G.C.E. at O., A., and *S. levels. **1973** *Guardian* 28 June 13/3 Jonathan Mestel is 16 and has just finished his A and S level maths and physics exams. **1975** *Glasgow Herald* 23 Dec. 4/2 Mr Sillars said the *SLP did not believe oil was a Scottish resource, but something to be used for the benefit of the entire United Kingdom. **1976** *Times* 23 Jan. 14/3 The new threat which the SLP presents..is untimely. **1964** *Colour Photogr.* Mar.–Apr. 68/3 With one manufacturer recently introducing a half-frame *SLR, I wondered if this type of instrument would replace its larger brother. **1971** *Amateur Photographer* 13 Jan. 80/3 (Advt.), Nikkorex F, f2 Nikkor, w/meter, S.L.R...£69. **1977** J. Hedgecoe *Photographer's Handbk.* 14 Because of the SLR's world-wide popularity the newest and most advanced electronic and optical technology tends to be designed to suit this camera before the others. **1890** Webster 1923/2 **S.M.*,..sergeant major. **1953** J. Masters *Lotus & Wind* v. 70 It wouldn't affect his chances of promotion to S.M. **1973** J. Wood *North Beat* xiii. 163 He had been the first company S.M. to earn a Bar to the decoration in the division. **1764** A. Williams *Universal Psalmodist* (ed. 2) 57 [Tune] Southwell. Psalm 90th Dr W. *S.M. **1832** J. Jowett *Man. Parochial Psalmody* 12 St. Bride's. S.M. **1909** W. H. Frere in *Hymns Anc. & Mod.* p. lvi/2 The whole musical balance was now altered [by the influence of T. Ravenscroft's *Psalmes* of 1621]: the D.C.M. and P.M. tunes had hitherto formed the bulk of the collection, with a few C.M. and S.M. tunes to supplement them. **1899** *Daily News* 21 July 11/1 Who..was to have the honour of figuring in future records, with the letters '*S.M.' attached to his name. **1909** J. R. Ware *Passing Eng.* 212/2 *S.M. (*Theatrical*), stage manager. **1952** Granville *Dict. Theatr. Terms* 172 When artistes have settled into their parts, the S.M. (as he is known) may hand over the book to his assistant. **1972** V. C. Clinton-Baddeley *To study Long Silence* II. viii. 82, I was still in the theatre when the S.M. found him. **1909** *Army & Navy Gaz.* 27 Mar. 297/3 (*heading*) *S.M.L.E. Rifle. **1958** J. A. Barlow *Elem. Rifle Shooting* (ed. 5) p. xii, The S.M.L.E...will shortly be replaced by a self-loading rifle. **1914** *Autocar* 2 May 817/1 The R.A.C., the A.A. and M.U., and the *S.M.M.T. **1958** *Economist* 1 Nov. 435/2 If it were desired to try to stop the rush at some point there is no salient that looks capable of being held and no one body that could do it—not the Finance Houses' Association, not the Industrial Bankers, not the SMMT nor the Hire Purchase Trade Association. **1978** *Dumfries & Galloway Standard* 21 Oct. 7/6 Although organising international motor shows is but one function of the SMMT, it is best known for this role. **1986** *Guardian* 11 Oct. 29/1 The lower rate of *SMP is to be set at the same rate as the *lowest* level of Statutory Sick Pay.., currently £31·60. **1950** *Jrnl. Soc. Motion Pict. & Television Engin.* Mar. 389 *SMPTE Officers and Committees..are published annually in the April issue of the Journal. **1959** W. S. Sharps *Dict. Cinematogr.* 11. 129/2 In Britain, the *British Kinematograph Society* was created originally as the British branch of the S.M.P.T.E. **1975** G. J. King *Audio Handbk.* viii. 191 The l.f. bands adhere to the SMPTE (Society of Motion Picture and Television Engineers) requirements for IMD analysis. **1960** *Atlanta Daily World* 18 Oct. 1/3 There was no announcement of formal action on *SNCC's proposed march on the polls on election day. **1961** *Commonweal* 15 Dec. 311/1 This fall the S.N.C.C. has been concentrating on recruitment on white campuses. **1971** J. Bishop *Days of M. Luther King* iv. 369 The Student Nonviolent Coordinating Committee had been in that part of Selma for eighteen months... SNCC was in Marion too. **1949** *Progress French Nat. Railways Oct. 1948* 28 (*colophon*) *S.N.C.F. 1949. **1963** *Times* 23 May 13/6 French Railways (SNCF) most closely resemble B.R. in size. **1976** A. White *Long Silence* vi. 46 The S.N.C.F. did not permit the express trains to stop at Colauvin. **1944** *Jrnl. Dairy Res.* XIII. 53 Milk has been deteriorating in quality (*s.n.f. content) during the last two or three years. *Ibid.*, This extra labour would detect adulterated samples which yet had over 8·5% s.n.f. **1960** *Farmer & Stockbreeder* 16 Feb. 66/3 A Milk Marketing Board survey..had shown an average of 3·7 per cent butter-fat and 8·75 s.n.f. for the breed. **1976** *Burnham-on-Sea Gaz.* 20 Apr. (Advt.), Butterfats 4%. S.N.F. 8·83%. Total 12·83%. The cows have not been prepared for sale in any way. **1972** E. N. Tiratsoo *Natural Gas* (ed. 2) i. 15 The incipient shortage of natural gas..led to the adoption of the CRG process..as the basis of what is planned to be the world's largest reforming plant producing *SNG ('substitute natural gas'). *Ibid.* viii. 149 Simulated natural gas (SNG)..has been extensively used as an intermediate fuel to facilitate the changeover of industrial plants from manufactured town gas to full-scale natural gas supply. **1974** *Natural Gas* (Shell Internat. Petroleum Co.) 11 Apart from LNG, which is natural gas cooled to the liquid state, there are three main possible supplementary sources of supply, namely low-calorific-value gas from coal, synthetic natural gas (SNG) from oil or coal, and methanol derived from natural gas. **1977** K. A. D. Inglis in P. A. Stockil *Our Industry Petroleum* (Brit. Petroleum Co.) (ed. 5) 26 As supplies of natural gas run short..systems for the manufacture of substitute (or synthetic) natural gas (SNG) are being developed. **1914** A. B. Milne in *Publ. Navy Rec. Soc.* (1970) CXV. 146 Have requested *S.N.O., Gibraltar, to keep special look-out for *Strassburg*. **1955** C. S. Forester *Good Shepherd* II. 264 SNO meant senior naval officer in accordance with British usage, not one of those odd collections of letters like DSO or MBE which merely meant a decoration. **1970** A. J. Marder *From Dreadnought to Scapa Flow* V. I. ii. 17 The S.N.O. on the spot..would not allow him to have a go at the *Goeben* as soon as it was known that she was aground. **1935** *Glasgow Herald Index 1934* 231/1 Compton Mackenzie addresses first *S.N.P. mtg. in Edin., 21 Ap. **1977** M. Walker *National Front* viii. 215 It may have been, as the SNP posters said 'Scotland's Oil' but a goodly portion of it had already been used by British Governments to guarantee foreign loans. **1970** Bahcall & Ulrich in *Astrophysical Jrnl.* CLX. L58 We have expressed the counting rate in solar-neutrino units: 1 *SNU $\equiv 10^{-36}$ capture per target atom per second. **1972** *Ann. Rev. Astron. & Astrophysics* X. 28 The best present estimates suggest.. that the ultimate sensitivity of the current 10^5-gallon experiment will be set by the cosmic-ray background at $\sim$ 0·4 SNU. **1976** J. Kleczek *Universe* ii. 78 It is usual to specify the rate of the neutrino capture reactions..in terms of so-called solar neutrino units (SNU or 'snew') which are such that 1 SNU corresponds to 10^{-36} captures per target Cl atom per second. **1844** T. E. May *Treat. Parliament* xii. 215 A division is effected in the lords by the not-contents remaining within the bar, and the contents going below the bar. [note] Lords' *S.O. No. 22. **1929** G. F. M. Campion *Introd. Procedure House of Commons* iv. 136 S.O. No. 11 of 1888 (the so-called 'Ten Minutes Rule'). **1976** in R. Crossman *Diaries* II. 75 It was only when the S.O. was redrafted in 1967 that M.P.s could make full use of its possibilities. **1918** H. V. O'Brien *Wine, Women & War* (1926) 286 What an *S.O.B. that fellow is! **1930** E. Pound *XXX Cantos* x. 45 That monstrous swollen, swelling s.o.b. Papa Pio Secundo. **1934** C. Stead *Seven Poor Men of Sydney* iv. 120 That s.o.b. Montagu got me the job 'ere, you know. **1955** Auden *Shield of Achilles* iii. 79 And all poor s-o-b's who never Do anything properly. **1962** L. Deighton *Ipcress File* xxxii. 211 Just a simple case of a couple of well-informed S.O.B.s. **1975** 'E. Lathen' *By Hook or by Crook* xvi. 154 A stubborn SOB who doesn't give a damn. **1948** *Jrnl. R. United Service Inst.* XCIII. 212 An *S.O.E. base was established alongside General Eisenhower's Headquarters in Algiers from the outset, primarily for work into France. **1968** D. Lampe *Last Ditch* xi. 113 SOE, the most special of the Special Forces, had just been set up under the cover of the Ministry of Economic Warfare. **1978** G. Greene *Human Factor* III. i. 104 Over his head were a retired businessman who had once been connected with the rival wartime service SOE, and a retired general who had fought in the Western Desert. **1905** W. S. Churchill *Let.* 28 Oct. in R. S. Churchill *Winston S. Churchill* (1969) II. Compan. I. 402 Of course the *S of S must always control the Viceroy. **1922** G. Bell *Let.* 4 Dec. (1927) II. xxii. 658, I sent you by post the yearly report to the S. of S., a very silly sort of Xmas present. **1958** L. Durrell *Mountolive* iv. 92 My dear chap..if you propose to make an issue of it with the S. of S. I can't help it. **1917** R. Lord *Captain Boyd's Battery A.E.F.* (1920) ii. 24 *S.O.L. —Payroll abbreviation for Soldier, adapted to mean Soldier Out 'a Luck or Certainly Out 'a Luck, according to the way you spell it. Applicable to everything from death to being late for mess. **1921** J. Dos Passos *Three Soldiers* II. iii. 99 'We shall have to put him down A.W.O.L. You know what that means?'..'I guess he's S.O.L.'; this from someone behind Fuselli. **1946** B. C. Bowker *Out of Uniform* iii. 48 As the phrase went, they were 'SOL' ('surely' out of luck). **1942** *Yank* 2 Sept. 14/2 Our regimental *SOP in reference to any MP reports on enlisted men. **1961** B. Fergusson *Watery Maze* x. 248 The Americans had evolved what they call a Standard Operating Procedure, or S.O.P., which was thoroughly unsatisfactory. **1980** S. King *Firestarter* 335 There will be two Shop men along, partly to act as stewards and partly to keep an eye on you. SOP, you know. **1911** *s.p. [see job *sb.*[2] 4 e]. **1928** E. Wallace *More Educ. Evans* ix. 201 You backed that horse s.p. with every unfortunate bookmaker in England. **1974** G. F. Newman *Price* ii. 60 What's the full SP, Trevor? **1937** *Q. Rep. Soc. Protection Anc. Buildings* I. 1. 4 From that moment almost it can be said that the *S.P.A.B. was born. **1943** J. Lees-Milne *Ancestral Voices* (1975) 234 At an S.P.A.B. meeting I found a small attendance considering a matter of the first importance, whether or not to protest in the press against the night bombing of historic German cities. **1978** *Jrnl. R. Soc. Arts* CXXVI. 477/1 The Canterbury Cloisters have been discussed by the SPAB recently as being a *bad* example of restoration. **1861** *Sat. Rev.* 23 Nov. 535/2 Strong in S.P.G. and *S.P.C.K. **1892** C. M. Yonge *Old Woman's Outlook* x. 240 A charming book of my childhood, which I rather believe belonged to the S.P.C.K. **1939** J. Cary *Mr. Johnson* 10 Johnson's idea of a civilized marriage, founded on..a few novels approved by the S.P.C.K., is a compound of romantic sentiment and embroidered underclothes. **1969** *Listener* 24 Apr. 586/2 Judas looking for all the world like an SPCK Jesus, all gently waving locks and sad benevolence. **1921** *Labour Monthly* Oct. 344 We may say, without presumption, that the *S.P.D. (German Social-Democratic Party) is the party which deserves above all others the title of Republican Party. **1947** *Partisan Rev.* Mar.–Apr. 143 The arduous theorists of the SPD were steeped in German pedantry. **1976** T. Allbeury *Only Good German* ix. 58 Both the SPD and the CDU had offered him party seats in the Bundestat. **1913** R. Bridges (*title*) *S.P.E. [manifesto of the Society for Pure English]. **1919** —— *Let.* 22 June (1940) 147 Is there any reason for delay about the S.P.E. **1923** J. M. Murry *Pencillings* 268 Such is the appearance—neat, decorous, small, discreet—of an S.P.E. tract. **1948** *S.P.E. Tract* LXVI. 177 When I addressed myself to the honourable, melancholy task of writing the obsequy of S.P.E., I revived fond memories by turning over my file. **1839** C. Fox *Jrnl.* 22 Aug. (1883) v. 53 Mary Coleridge..read a letter from Macaulay describing the state of feeling into which one of Samuel Wilberforce's sermons had thrown him, who is now on a tour westward for the *S.P.G. **1854** V. Lush *Jrnl.* 16 Feb. (1971) 153 We settled to write to the Bishop and request him in conjunction with the Revd Mr Venn and Revd Mr Hawkins, secretaries of C.M.S. and S.P.G.—to select a master for us. **1885** *Daily News* 12 May 5/1 The Society for the Propagation of the Gospel, familiarly known as the S.P.G. **1565** J. Jewel *Replie M. Hardinges Answeare* 294 Beda..expounded these foure solemne letters **S.P.Q.R.* in this wise. *Stultus populus quærit Romam. Foolishe Folke Flee to Rome.* **1621** I. Sylvester *Lacrymæ Lacrymarum* in *Du Bartas, His Diuine Weekes*, This loss (alas!) which unto All belongs!.. To all the world; except S.P.Q.R. **1881** *N. & Q.* 8 Jan. 34/2 S.P.Q.R... The following interpretation of these letters may amuse your readers. They form part of the decoration of the Adam ceiling of the Court Room of the Bank of England, and on a remark by a visitor that they seemed very incongruous in such a place, 'Not at all,' said one of my colleagues; 'they stand for small profits and quick returns.' **1927** E. J. P. Benn *Trade* iii. 52 Our grandfathers used to talk of small profits and quick returns. 'S.P.Q.R.', which most schoolboys of my time imagined had something to do with the early Romans, was a very favourite shop sign. **1977** L. Meynell *Hooky gets Wooden Spoon* xiv. 180 'So far he seems to have steered clear of anything big.' 'Wise man. S.P.Q.R. Small profits quick returns.' **1978** P. Finney *Crow Goddess* 112 'What does that say?' he asked, pointing at the label. 'S.P.Q.R.—the Senate and People of Rome.' **1883** *Proc. Soc. Psychical Res.* p. i, The Council of the *S.P.R. have from time to time received letters from Members and Associates. **1926** A. Conan Doyle *Hist. Spiritualism* I. viii. 185 No serious attempt of any sort, up to the formation of the S.P.R., was made to understand or explain a matter which was engaging the attention of millions of minds. **1937** A. Huxley *Let.* 17 Feb. (1969) 415 Broad's presidential address to the SPR is interesting in this context. **1968** M. Collis *Somerville & Ross* xiv. 157 Arthur Balfour, who for a time was President of the S.P.R. **1971** B. Bauer et al. in *Jrnl. Audio Engin. Soc.* XIX. 639/1 We..'encode' (combine) the four channels into two by using a special 'matrix', or linear additive circuit.., which we called the *SQ (for stereophonic-quadraphonic) matrix encoder. **1973** *Official Gaz.* (U.S. Patent Office) 20 Nov. TM 138/2 Columbia Broadcasting System, Inc., New York, N.Y. Filed Dec. 6, 1971... The mark represents the stylized lettering 'SQ'. For pre-recorded phonograph records, and pre-recorded tapes... First use June 10, 1971. **1976** *Listener* 23 Dec. 846/1 Discs in compatible quadraphonic/stereo pressings utilising the SQ system. **1919** *Round Table* IX. 286 The British Labour Party is described as 'worse than the right *S.R.'s'. **1967** *Soviet Stud.* XVIII. 449 The SR's were able to obtain absolute majorities even in Petrograd and Moscow. **1974** T. P. Whitney tr. *Solzhenitsyn's Gulag Archipel.* I. I. ii. 30 The Left SR's had been cleverer and had gone on pretending longer that they were allies of the one and only consistent party of the proletariat. **1923** *Southern Railway Mag.* Sept. p. xvi (Advt.), For All Southern Railway Staff..Halden Estates Co., Ltd. (*S.R. Proposition). **1959** *Chambers's Encycl.* XI. 490/1 Subsequently S.R. lines west of Exeter were transferred to the Western region. **1967** J. Joyce *Story Passenger Transport in Britain* vii. 186 Nationalisation came in 1948 when the 'Big Four'—the LMS, LNER, GWR and SR..became the all-embracing 'British Railways'. **1908** *Army & Navy Gaz.* 26 Dec. 1241/3 The latter officer joins the 3rd (*S.R.) Batn. **1919** W. S. Churchill in M. Gilbert *Winston S. Churchill* (1977) IV. Compan. I. 466 The Regular Army and such SR & TF officers and men as must be retained. **1923** Kipling *Irish Guards in Gt. War* I. 44 Major Webber, 'S.R.' (this is the first time that the Diary makes mention of the Special Reserve), arrived the day before. **1963** *Recommendations for Letter Symbols, Signs & Abbreviations* (*B.S.I.*) VI. 26 Steradian... sr. **1977** J. Narlikar *Struct. Universe* vii. 223 The survey is over 3 sr.. in the sky. **1935** C. L. Hull in *Psychol. Rev.* XLII. 502 A trace conditioned reaction in an *S $\rightarrow$ R relationship. **1948** E. R. Hilgard *Theories of Learning* xii. 349 Woodworth gradually shifted from his *S-R* motto. **1967** [see *neo-behaviourism* s.v. neo- 1 a]. **1977** *Dædalus* Fall 120 When Chomsky demonstrated that the simple application of S-R learning theory to chained responses is inadequate in principle as an account of grammar, he could not be ignored. **1971** *Nature* 23 Apr. 531/1 While investigating the interaction between antigen-antibody-complement complexes and lymphoid cells, we have noticed that sheep red blood cells (*SRBC) adhered to a surprisingly large proportion of human peripheral blood lymphocytes forming clusters ('rosettes'). **1977** *Lancet* 19 Feb. 394/2 These eight dilutions and two control tubes..were tested for the formation of rosettes between human lymphocytes and S.R.B.C. **1946** *Nursing Times* 11 May p. ix/1 Mental Ward Sisters..required, *S.R.M.N., or holding R.M.P.A. Certificate. **1965** *Nursing Mirror & Midwives' Jrnl.* 2 Apr. (Suppl.) 18/1 (Advt.), Applicants must be S.R.N., S.R.M.N. **1922** *Ibid.* 1 July 261/1 The Scottish General Nursing Council..'unanimously adopted' the resolution as to the undermentioned initials..General Trained ..[England] *S.R.N...[Scotland] R.G.N. **1926** *Ibid.* 25 Dec. p. x/3 (Advt.), General, S.R.N., fever, and mental nurses Wanted for private work. **1974** R. Ingham *Yoris* ii. 5 She was wearing her stiff white nurse's uniform with..the small brooch on her left breast bearing the initials SRN. **1957** M. B. Hoagland et al. in *Biochim. & Biophys. Acta* XXIV. 216 This is apparently a low molecular weight RNA (*S-RNA) with different metabolic properties from the high molecular weight RNA of the ribonucleoprotein of the microsomes. **1963** F. H. C. Crick in *Progr. in Nucleic Acid Res.* I. 196 Holley and his collaborators fractionated yeast sRNA by countercurrent distribution. **1971** D. J. Cove *Genetics* x. 146 If the sRNAs act as adoptor molecules, recognising the codon of the amino acid they carry, then it is to be expected that they will have somewhere in their sequence, three adjacent bases which are complementary to that codon, and able therefore to specifically hydrogen bond to it. In all the sRNAs whose sequence has been analysed, this has been found to be true. **1941** *SRO [see PALSY *sb.*[2]]. **1966** *Social Work* Oct. 32/1 The clustering of unattached individuals, many of whom are economically dependent and chronically ill, in licensed SRO buildings is a recognizable pattern. **1977** *New Yorker* 27 June 85/3 Queens has only nine of New York's several hundred S.R.O. buildings (the letters stand for 'single-room occupancy', and the tenants.. are often present or former drug addicts). **1890** *Texas Siftings* 15 Nov. 13/1 At the Grand Opera House Bobby Gaylor, in the Irish Arab, called out the *S.R.O. sign. **1903** 'O. HENRY' in *McClure's Mag.* July 333/1 After one reading of the Declaration of Independence in New York I've known the S.R.O. sign to be hung out at all the hospitals and police stations. **1970** *Islander* (Victoria, B.C.) 5 Apr. 16/2 The 1970 edition [of an annual concert], held on March 3, ..was an SRO success. **1939** *SRS [see *slow-reacting substance* s.v. SLOW *adv.* 2 a]. **1955** W. E. BROCKLEHURST in *Jrnl. Physiol.* CXXVIII. 1 ¶ The occurrence of a slow-reacting substance together with histamine, in the perfusate coming from the isolated lung of a guinea-pig during anaphylactic shock, has been reported previously... The substance has been provisionally named 'SRS-A' (slow-reacting substance in anaphylaxis) to differentiate it from the considerable number of ill-defined gut-contracting substances to which the term 'SRS' has been applied. **1958** *Pharmacol. Rev.* X. 422 When egg yolk is incubated with cobra venom a slow reacting substance (SRS-C) is formed. **1964** W. G. SMITH *Allergy & Tissue Metabolism* i. 14 Evidence for the existence of chemical mediators of anaphylaxis other than histamine has existed since 1940. Recent work on one of these, the slow reacting substance of anaphylaxis (SRS-A), led to the discovery that the hypersensitive state exerts a profound influence on tissue metabolism. **1979** *Nature* 6 Sept. 14/2 SRS has now been identified as a novel cysteinyl derivative of arachidonic acid. **1932** H. NICOLSON *Diary* 5 Jan. (1966) 105 The former would correspond to the *S.S. or *Schutzstaffel* organisation of the Nazis. **1938** *Encycl. Brit. Bk. of Year* 125/1 They are known as the 'SS'..or Élite Hitler Protective Guard, now under the command of Heinrich Himmler. **1945** *Daily Mirror* 8 May 3/2 S.S. men went through the streets driving people out of their homes. **1958** *New Statesman* 19 Apr. 505/2 The nature of his work compelled him to form intimate relationships with members of two rival German organisations, the *Abwehr*, or Counter-Intelligence, and the SS. **1968** *Listener* 19 Sept. 359/1, I myself had only one sound-camera, and just before the opening of the Games a squad of SS men tried to take it away from me by force. **1975** W. CRAIG *Strasbourg Legacy* i. 4 A short, red-faced officer, resplendent in his black SS uniform, read from a memorandum. **1933** C. MACKENZIE *Water on Brain* xviii. 276 Katzenschlosser, the American *S.S. man. **1969** *Sun* 12 Feb. 5/5 An advance party of 60 State Department men arrived from Washington on Monday. Probably 20 of them were SS men. (They do actually call them that in the U.S.). **1979** *Maclean's Mag.* 9 Apr. 29/1 The Trudeau government was pressuring the SS for better intelligence..about suspected FLQ cells in Quebec. **1963** F. D. FAWCETT *Cycl. Init. & Abbrev.* 140/1 *SS*,..Social Security. **1973** *Freedom* 21 July 5/2 Hardly any squatter draws SS and parasites on society. **1975** *New Society* 20 Nov. 412/3 Tez thinks he'll be a rock star..tomorrow. Meanwhile he's having trouble getting it together and lives off the SS. **1980** L. CODY *Dupe* xxiii. 168 The father was knocked off in a pub bombing.. and..the family's been on the SS ever since. **1868** *Times* 1 July 2/2 (Advt.), To sail 9th of July, the Liverpool and Australian Navigation Company's *s.s. *Great Britain.* **1870** *Weekly Standard* (Buenos Aires) 12 Jan. 7/5 Departures. Per ss. Flamsteed on the 9th Jan. **1876** W. S. LINDSAY *Hist. Merchant Shipping* IV. xv. 558 (*caption*) S.S. 'Victoria'. **1907** *Shipping World* 16 Jan. 111 (Advt.), S.S. 'Lusitania' is being fitted with Passenger Lifts. **1955** *Times* 5 July 11/3 Things have gone very wrong indeed when British vessels suffer the treatment received by the ss. Anshun. **1956** *SSB [see *PEP* s.v. P II]. **1976** *S9* (N.Y.) May/June 5/2 If, however, you don't want to go for ssb, then by all means buy the best radio you can find with the largest number of features. **1969** *New Acronyms & Initialisms* (Gale Research Co.) 389 *SSBN, Fleet Ballistic Missile Submarine (Nuclear powered). **1973** *Washington Post* 13 Jan. A23/3 Gormley's proposals..stem from his realization that SSBN's are the only survivable, non-provocative, anti-proliferative nuclear deterrent forces, existing or planned. **1961** *Forward Trends* V. IV. 47 The Guild Art Exhibition was in two main parts. All of it, naturally, dealing with the use of art with *S.S.N., E.S.N., and backward children. **1967** *Punch* 19 Apr. 557/1 Down below the plimsoll line of an IQ of fifty are the erstwhile imbeciles and idiots, now classed as SSN—severely subnormal. **1972** *Observer* 20 Aug. 7/8 A sixth of the children in the SSN (severely subnormal) department of this school are boys like these. **1982** *Financial Times* 26 Oct. 17/6 The Government's Statutory Sick Pay (*SSP) proposals, due to come into effect next April... Each piece of information..can..be transferred onto the SSP Assessment and Payment form to calculate the employee's entitlement. **1986** *Guardian* 15 Nov. 28/5 SSP is not considered to be a social security benefit but is regarded as 'earnings'. **1968** *Neurology* XVIII. II. 48/2 Our data suggest that *SSPE is caused by the measles virus, or a virus immunologically indistinguishable from the measles virus. **1974** SSPE [see *panencephalitis* s.v. PAN- 2]. **1962** *Aeroplane* 21 June 6/3 Secondary surveillance radar (*SSR), the so-called answer to the air traffic controller's prayer, does not appear to be so near, or as technically perfect, as one is led to believe. **1977** *R.A.F. News* 22 June–5 July 9 (Advt.), Experience is required of approach and long range surveillance equipment plus SSR, HF, VHF and UHF radio equipments. **1926** *Encycl. Brit.* III. 429 The population of the Union of Socialist Soviet Republics and its principal parts was, in 1924... Ukraine *S.S.R... 27,700,000. **1947** *Whitaker's Almanack* 972/1 Uzbekistan comprises the former feudal states of Bokhara and Khiva and the Kara Kalpak S.S.R. **1977** R. PERRY *Dead End* vi. 77 He elected to resume his studies in the Turkmen SSR. **1967** *Economist* 11 Feb. 501/1 Under the direction of Dr Michael Young, the *SSRC has begun to deliver the goods. **1975** M. BRADBURY *History Man* ii. 20 He was now..a research student, with an SSRC grant. **1977** *Dædalus* Summer 62 The major funding agencies, the NSF, NIMH, SSRC, Ford Foundation, etc., should be approached to provide the basis for a series of 'summit' meetings among the leaders of the various modes of 'anthropologizing'. **1962** (*title*) Notifications under the National Parks..Act, 1949 in East Riding, Yorkshire. Sites of Special Scientific Interest (*S.S.S.I.) notified under Section 23. **1984** *National Trust* Spring 11/3 SSSIs of considerable importance, particularly small, isolated, herb-rich meadows becoming increasingly rare with the decline in traditional farming systems. **1961** *Fortune* June 161/1 Now in the preliminary design stage is the supersonic transport, or *SST. **1969** *Listener* 6 Mar. 313/2 Russia is talking about getting her SST into passenger use before the end of 1970. **1977** *New Yorker* 27 June 86/3 The Concorde's sponsors believe that if the plane doesn't get New York landing rights the SST enterprise will end in financial disaster. **1932** *N. & Q.* 16 July 45/2 He published seven books of airs, of which the above is the sixth, at various dates between 1604 and 1638 (*S.T.C. 7460–67). **1952** J. CARTER *ABC for Bk.-Collectors* 164 STC, a landmark in enumerative bibliography and one of the most frequently quoted of reference books, has recently been reprinted. **1962** DAVIS & WRENN *Eng. & Medieval Stud.* 270 The edition is attributed to 1550 in *S.T.C.* under no. 4817. **1958** *New Scientist* 4 Dec. 1421/1 In planning a scheme for *STD it is very desirable that the dialling procedure should be simple and easy to understand. **1963** *Engineering* 25 Jan. 176 STD is not limited to the United Kingdom—it exists on both the Continent and America. **1973** J. WAINWRIGHT *Pride of Pigs* 169 She..picked up the receiver, waited for the S.T.D. pips to stop, said 'Hello?' **1977** P. STREVENS *New Orientations Teaching Eng.* viii. 105 STD code, oh-three-one. **1956** *Aeronaut. Engin. Rev.* Mar. 48 This type, or types, of airplane can..be called Short Take-Off and Landing, or *STOL, airplanes. **1959** *Times Rev. Industry* July 80/1 Any s.t.o.l. aircraft can use quite short airstrips. **1974** *Sci. Amer.* Mar. 83/3 If STOL and VTOL aircraft, including helicopters, become accepted as a major means of intercity transport, traffic density will increase substantially. **1975** E. HILLARY *Nothing venture, Nothing Win* xvi. 260 The answer was to build an airfield and use STOL. **1953** BATHAM & THORPE *To All who are interested in Democracy* 14 The National Union of Teachers elects its officers and executive by the *S.T.V. **1974** *Times* 12 Mar. 15/4 This is the single transferable vote (STV). Its effect is to ensure that every vote is of equal value, and that nearly every voter has an MP of his choice. **1955** B. HIGMAN *Appl. Group-Theoretic & Matrix Methods* xii. 175 (*table*) Special unitary [matrix group] **SU(n)*. **1967** G. G. HALL *Appl. Group Theory* vi. 84 *SU(n)*. The special unitary group is the subgroup of *U(n)* whose matrices have a determinant of unity. **1977** *Nature* 4 Aug. 469/1 It provides a classification of a totally different nature to the canonical isospin, strangeness (SU(2) and SU(3)), beloved of group theorists which classifies objects of the same spin. **1956** R. N. HULL et al. in *Amer. Jrnl. Hygiene* LXIII. 205/1 The agents isolated will be referred to as 'Simian viruses' (*S.V.) until such time as a definite association with some other host or identification can be established. *Ibid.* 214/1 A large number of production samples has not been studied for S.V. contamination but of those that have been assayed a few have been found to contain S.V.$_2$ only. **1957** *Ann. N.Y. Acad. Sci.* LXVII. 414 (*caption*) Agents received from other laboratories and temporarily classified as SV's. **1967**, etc. [see POLYOMA]. **1970** *New Scientist* 29 Jan. 194/1, SV40 occurred as a contaminant in many of the earlier batches of polio vaccine.., but has had no discernible effect on Man. **1977** *Time* 18 Apr. 48/2 He hoped to insert a monkey virus, SV40, into *E. coli.* **1864** *N. & Q.* 12 Mar. 211/2 See Richardson *On the Study of Words*, and *Dict.*, *s.vv. 'Lord', 'Lady'. **1962** *Ibid.* Aug. 304/2 *Lotus-eating* (O.E.D. s.v. *Lotus-eater*). **1976** *Classical Q.* XXVI. 310 For this incorrect form of the name of the elder Suetonius, cf. *OCD* s.v. Suetonius. **1981** *Times Lit. Suppl.* 2 Jan. 6/2 One receives no help if one tries to check it sv, 'music'. **1973** *Vet. Rec.* 3 Mar. 234/1 On occasion some pigs have shown no abnormal behaviour although they had widespread lesions of *SVD. **1975** G. P. WEST *Black's Vet. Dict.* (ed. 11) 747/1 SVD has been transmitted to laboratory workers. **1980** *Times* 15 Sept. 14/4 SVD cannot be distinguished from foot-and-mouth disease (FMD) on the farm. [**1917** *Harrod's Gen. Catal.* 1385/2 S. Wm's... Wm's... O.S. Wm's.] **1926–7** *Army & Navy Stores Catal.* 674/3 White drill coat... Sizes *S.W., W. and O.S. **1974** *Harrods Xmas Catal.* 7 Sophisticated wrap... SW, W, or WX. **1925** FRASER & GIBBONS *Soldier & Sailor Words* 274 *SWAK*, from the initials *S.W.A.K.—i.e., Sealed with a Kiss. A common superscription on the envelopes of letters to sweethearts from sailors and soldiers. **1948** PARTRIDGE *Dict. Forces' Slang* 185 *S.W.A.K.* was the commonest (Sealed With a Kiss), with the variant *S.W.A.L.K.*, the *L* in this case standing for 'Loving'. **1952** E. WAUGH *Men at Arms* III. viii. 312 The old soldiers wrote SWALK on the envelope, meaning 'sealed with a loving kiss'. **1971** R. QUEST *Death of Sinner* xvi. 154 They [*sc.* the letters] might represent a sentence like S.W.A.K... Girls at school sometimes wrote it on the backs of envelopes. It means 'sealed with a kiss'. **1973** 'D. HALLIDAY' *Dolly & Starry Bird* xi. 164, I posted him a long letter with SWALK on it to make him laugh. **1968** *Time* 19 July 18/3 Two hundred marksmen have been assigned to a squad named *S.W.A.T. (Special Weapons and Tactics), designed to pick off snipers and to eliminate..the need for indiscriminate police gunfire. **1979** *Tucson* (Arizona) *Citizen* 28 Apr. 1A/1 Police said a SWAT team bombarded the vehicle with tear gas and gun blasts. **1911** *Motor Manual* (ed. 13) ii. 50 The 'secondary' winding, composed of many turns of fine wire (42 or 44 *s.w.g.). **1953** *Electronic Engin.* XXV. 66, 1200 turns 36 S.W.G. enamelled copper. *a* **1977** *Harrison Mayer Ltd. Catal.* 50/1 The working ends are fabricated from 15swg stainless steel which will not rust. **1938** *Socialist Appeal* 22 Jan. 2/4 The *S.W.P. will advocate the continuance of the cass struggle. **1943** *Fourth International* Aug. 234/1 The new movement of the masses was developing outside the SWP. **1977** *Times* 8 Sept. 12/3 In true Marxist fashion, the SWP looks forward to the withering away of the state. **1961** *Amateur Radio Handbk.* (ed. 3) xiii. 358 The ratio of maximum to minimum voltage at the crest and trough of the standing wave, is called the voltage standing wave ratio (v.s.w.r., often abbreviated to *s.w.r.). **1976** *S9* (N.Y.) Feb. 62/2 The column will also contain useful information about adjusting antennas, dope about SWR (standing-wave-ratio) measurements, and all that good stuff.

b. S. = South; also **S.E., SE., S.W.,** South-east, South-west, etc.; also used to designate a London postal district. Also **S.A.,** South Africa(n), South America(n), South Australia(n); **S.A.P., Sap,** South African Party; †**S.S.** = South Sea (Company).

1708 *Lond. Gaz.* No. 4418/3 The Wind was, this Morning ..at 10, at S. and S.S.E. **1720** DE FOE *Capt. Singleton* xvi. (1840) 273 After that it blew..S.W. by S. then S.W. by W. **1840** MARRYAT *Olla Podr.* III. 10 [The wind] is S.W. and by W. ¾ W. **1857** *Punch* 7 Feb. 51/2 Rowland Hill has just divided London's waste of brick by ten... Pimlico is in S.W., Brompton fast, and Chelsea mild. *Ibid.*, Yonder dismal hole S.E., Southwark. **1884** H. A. MORIARTY in *Encycl. Brit.* XVII. 277/1 A point of destination bore W.S.W. 10 miles; a current ran S.E. by S. 4 miles an hour. **1885** *List of Subscribers, Classified* (United Telephone Co.) (ed. 6) 62 Atkinson & Co, Westminster Bridge Road, S.E. **1934** DYLAN THOMAS *Let.* Dec. (1966) 147, 5 Redcliffe Street, London, S.W.10... Dear Bert. **1968** *Listener* 19 Dec. 810/2 In between the bombing raids, the doodle-bugs and the V2s they'd improvised a splendid life in SE20.

1864 *N. & Q.* 6 Feb. 117/1 Cape Town, S.A. **1891** W. S. CHURCHILL *Let.* 27 Sept. in R. S. Churchill *Winston S. Churchill* (1967) I. Compan. I. v. 270 Mama has got a big map of S.A. on which she follows your route. **1933** J. CARY *Amer. Visitor* iv. 39 We were in S.A. together—the yeomanry. **1967** L. MEYNELL *Mauve Front Door* xv. 214 A bottle of S.A. sherry. **1890** WEBSTER, *S.A.*, South America. **1930** E. POUND *XXX Cantos* xii. 55 And the bust-up of Brazilian securities (S.A. securities). **1864** *South Austral. Advertiser* 17 Oct. 2/4 Share List... S.A. Insurance... S.A. Gas. **1944** *Living off Land* iv. 82 The S.A. family..could have been saved had they carried sufficient drinking water. **1971** *Sunday Australian* 8 Aug. 11/2 Senator Hannaford of SA suffered a heart attack. **1920** S. BLACK *Dorp* 9 The scornful word 'Sappers', which he knew to be a term of contempt applied by members of Hertzog's Party (the Nationalists) to all those of the Botha-Smuts element or 'SAP'. **1933** J. C. SMUTS *Let.* 7 Oct. in *Sel. Smuts Papers* (1973) V. 567 It may be a case of Sap predominance, with a Nat prime minister with a small following of his own. **1935** *Ann. Reg. 1934* I. 132 Around him rallied those S.A.P. men who vowed with him that a surrender of principles was too heavy a price to pay. **1972** *Sunday Times* (Johannesburg) 3 Sept. 2 Nats, Progs, Saps all climb in to make mischief. **1977** *Jrnl. Commonwealth & Compar. Politics* XV. 7 The networks of rural and provincial notables originally fused together by the South African Party (SAP) gave it majorities in the Cape, Transvaal, and Orange Free State. **1768** *Ann. Reg.* 178 Transferring 50*l.* new S.S. annuities,..at the S.S. house, as if it had been his own.

c. s. = L. *solidus* and so used for shilling(s; † = SCILICET; = second (of time).

1387 *E.E. Wills* (1882) 1 Also y be-quethe genet my dowter xl. s. *a* **1450** MYRC *Festial* lxxiv. 300 Ther was a man on a time þat lant to anothur man iiii s of money to an certeyn day. **1540** PALSGR. *Acolastus* Prol. B iij b, Suche as opteyne vyctory (.s. in some great enterpryse). *a* **1548** HALL *Chron.*, *Hen. VIII* 241 b, A Subsedy, of twoo .s. of landes. **1579** E. K. *Gloss. Spenser's Sheph. Cal.* July 33 Lurdanes s. Lord Danes. **1664** PEPYS *Diary* 4 July, My wife..have lain out 25s. upon a pair of pendantes for her eares. **1702** DE FOE *Shortest Way w. Dissenters* 21 To talk of 5*s.* a Month for not coming to the Sacrament, and 1*s.* per Week for not coming to Church, this is such a way of converting People as never was known. **1848** THACKERAY *Van. Fair* xxxviii, The best coals at —— *s.* per chaldron. **1884** H. A. MORIARTY in *Encycl. Brit.* XVII. 274/1 The chronometer showed 9[h] 43[m] 15[s]·5 as a mean. **1884** F. J. BRITTEN *Watch & Clockm.* 24 It [*sc.* a watch] is found to have lost 8 s.

d. In *Biol.* S or *S* (also **s**) = Svedberg unit: used after a number to denote the (often characteristic) sedimentation coefficient of a subcellular body.

1942 [see SVEDBERG]. **1942** W. B. BRIDGMAN in *Jrnl. Amer. Chem. Soc.* LXIV. 2350/2 The average values of s_{20}.. varied from 60 to 70 *S* (one Svedberg unit, $S_1 = 1 \times 10^{-13}$ c.g.s. units). **1944** *Jrnl. Exper. Med.* LXXIX. 310 Its sedimentation constant of approximately 800 S is higher than either of those associated with A virus. **1977** M. W. BERNS *Cells* iv. 71 In the eukaryotic organism, it appears that 18s and 28s cytoplasmic ribosomal RNAs are produced from a larger 45s ribosomal RNA molecule that is cleaved in a stepwise sequence that produces several intermediate size RNA molecules. **1978** *Nature* 5 Oct. 461/1 Both reconstituted 30S and reconstituted 50S particles containing mutant 16S and (23 + 5S) RNA, respectively, could form 70S couples with their complementary native subunits only in the presence of higher Mg^{2+} concentration.

II. Symbolic uses. **5.** *s* or *S* (*Physics* and *Chem.*) = sharp: orig. used to designate one of the four main series of lines in atomic spectra, but now more frequently applied to electronic orbitals, states, etc., possessing zero angular momentum and total symmetry.

1890 J. R. RYDBERG in *Phil. Mag.* XXIX. 335 Mg (S_2) [denotes] the (whole) second sharp series of Mg. **1922** A. D. UDDEN tr. *Bohr's Theory of Spectra* III. iii. 97 He [*sc.* Schrödinger] assumes that the 'outer' electron in the states corresponding to the *S* terms—in contrast to those corresponding to the *P* and *D* terms—penetrates partly into the region of the orbits of the inner electrons during the course of its revolution. **1926**, etc. [see L 7 b]. **1930** [see K 3 f]. **1935** PAULING & WILSON *Introd. Quantum Mech.* v. 142 Only for *S* states (with $l = 0$) is the wave function different from zero at $r = 0$. **1963** F. A. COTTON *Chem. Applic. Group Theory* viii. 193 An *s* orbital is totally symmetric in the O_h environment. **1978** P. W. ATKINS *Physical Chem.* xiv. 433 Whereas the s-orbitals all have non-zero values at the nucleus, the p-orbitals vanish there.

6. [Initial letter of *secondary.*] Used, chiefly in *S wave*, to denote an earthquake wave which oscillates transversely to the direction of propagation, a shear wave; so named because secondary waves arrive at a given place later than primary waves. (See also P III. 3.)

1908, etc. [see P III. 3]. **1913** G. W. WALKER *Mod. Seismol.* vi. 39 A pronounced movement corresponding to the arrival of the longitudinal disturbance, and..a pronounced movement when the transversal disturbance arrives, both of which have travelled by the brachistochronic path... These are..identified with the beginning of the first phase P and the second phase S of a seismogram. **1937** WOOLDRIDGE & MORGAN *Physical Basis Geogr.* ii. 16 The velocities of both P and S waves increase with depth, to a depth of approximately three-tenths of the radius. **1955** *Sci. Amer.* Sept. 57/1 S waves travel at about two thirds of the speed of P waves. **1971** I. G. GASS et al. *Understanding Earth* iii. 54/1 The core is liquid..as can be shown from its inability to transmit shear waves, the *S* waves of earthquakes.

7. In *Physics*, *s* and *S* denote the quantum numbers of spin angular momentum of one electron and a group of electrons, respectively. [Introduced by F. Hund 1926, in *Zeitschr. f. Physik* XXXVI. 658.]

1926 *Bull. Nat. Res. Council* (U.S.) No. 57. 5 Electronic angular momentum in units of $h/2\pi$... *s*. **1932** BACHER & GOUDSMIT *Atomic Energy States* 6 The spin moments *s* of the individual electrons form, together, a definite resultant spin moment *S*. **1966** D. H. WHIFFEN *Spectroscopy* xi. 134 One must be careful not to confuse *S* meaning a state with $L = 0$, with *S* the value of the total electron spin. **1970** G. K. WOODGATE *Elem. Atomic Struct.* iv. 57 There is no integration in the normalization condition.., and there is no approach to the classical limit in the sense that $s \to \infty$ because *s* is confined to the value ½ only.

8. S is used to denote one of the two directions of twist (see quot. 1935); so ***S-spun***, etc.

1935 *Proc. Amer. Soc. for Testing Materials* XXXV. I. 448 A yard or cord has 'S' twist if, when held in a vertical position, the spirals conform in slope to the central portion of the letter 'S', and 'Z' twist if the spirals conform in slope to the central portion of the letter 'Z'. **1950** A. V. PRINGLE *Theory of Flax Spinning* xiii. 45 Because the outer fibrils in flax ultimates are arranged in 'S' twist spirals it is considered that a stronger yarn or thread can be spun when the final twist is inserted 'Z'-wise. Hence yarns for weaving are always spun Z-wise, but yarns for twisting are commonly spun S-wise. **1964** H. HODGES *Artifacts* ix. 129 Thus, if the threads are S-spun the ply will normally be Z-spun.

9. [Initial letter of *slow*.] ***s-process*** (Astr.): a process thought to occur in giant stars by which heavy atomic nuclei are produced from other nuclei over a long time scale by a combination of neutron captures and more rapid beta decays.

1956 [see R III. 7]. **1971** *New Scientist* 27 Apr. 248/2 The solar-system proportions of many heavy elements reflect the results expected from the s-process, but the lighter elements defy quantitative explanation. **1977** [see R III. 7].

10. ***S meter***: a meter on a radio that indicates the strength of a received signal.

1939 *A.W.A. Technical Rev.* IV. 187 It is preferable that the S-meter be available for signal strength comparisons when the receiver gain is manually controlled. **1962** *B.B.C. Handbk.* 130 The more expensive short-wave receivers include such additional features as..'comprehensive bandspread' and 'S' meter or magic eye, which facilitate accurate tuning. **1976** PERKOWSKI & STRAL *Joy of CB* ix. 96 The output is about four times the talk power (6 dB) of AM, equivalent to a difference of one 'S' meter unit, or slightly better.

11. ***S-matrix*** (Physics): a scattering matrix, i.e. a matrix of probability amplitudes that occurs in the expression of the initial wave functions in a scattering process in terms of all the possible final wave functions. [After G. *matrix S* (W. Heisenberg 1943, in *Zeitschr. f. Physik* CXX. 521).]

1945 C. MØLLER in *Matematisk-Fysiske Meddelelser* XXIII. I. 18 The discrete energy values are completely independent of the form of the *S*-matrix. **1964** W. K. HEISENBERG in *Cambr. Rev.* 24 Oct. 47/1 The S-matrix elements for complicated processes will be functions of many variables. **1974** *Nature* 15 Mar. 265/1 He begins by developing the mathematical description starting from the Minkowski formalism of space-time, passing briefly through field theory, finally arriving at the S-matrix formalism which is to form the basis for the rest of the investigation.

12. ***S-band***: the range of microwave frequencies between 1550 and 5200 megahertz, used for radio communication and radar.

1946 *Radar: Summary Rep. & Harp Project* (U.S. Nat. Defense Res. Comm.) 143/2 *S-band*. Refers to wave-lengths of the order of 10 cm. **1952** REINTJES & COATE *Princ. Radar* (ed. 3) i. 33 Radar equipment operating..in the S, X, and K bands is called microwave radar. **1965** FILIPOWSKY & MUEHLDORF *Space Communications Techniques* ii. 111 S-band high power transmitters in the 2000 to 2400 Mc range are being provided for future Earth to spacecraft deep-space communications, with power ratings from 10 KW to 100 KW. **1970** N. ARMSTRONG et al. *First on Moon* xi. 257, I haven't heard a word from those guys, and I thought I'd be hearing them on your S-band relay. **1974** *Encycl. Brit. Macropædia* XV. 370/1 Early in the war, the British had developed an airborne S-band..radar for bombing, called the H2S.

13. *Chem.* [Abbrev. of L. *sinister* left.] *S* is used to designate (compounds having) a configuration about an asymmetric carbon atom in which the substituents, placed in order according to certain rules, form an anticlockwise sequence when viewed from a particular direction. Opp. R III. 6.

1956, **1971** [see R III. 6]. **1973** *Nature* 6 Apr. 367/3 In these experiments, the R(−) isomers..were considerably more active than the alternate S(+) configuration.

14. *S* denotes the strangeness quantum number of sub-atomic particles.

1956 M. GELL-MANN in *Nuovo Cimento* IV. Suppl. 852 Since we have $S = 0$ for ordinary particles and $S \neq 0$ for 'strange' ones we shall refer to *S* as 'strangeness'. **1965** C. M. H. SMITH *Nuclear Physics* xi. 734 In the final state the total strangeness is zero as Λ^0 and K^+ have *S*-values of −1 and +1 respectively. **1973** L. J. TASSIE *Physics of Elem. Particles* vi. 54 The K^- is the antiparticle of the K^+, and has $S = -1$.

15. *Particle Physics.* [Repr. *strange*; also understood as = *singlet* or *sideways*.

'The letters u and d stood for "up" and "down" (that is to say, isotopic spin projection up and down) and s stood for "strange", with "singlet" (isotopic spin singlet) as a supplementary meaning. "Sideways" was a joke that I used from time to time.'—M. Gell-Mann, let. to R.W.B.]

s is used to designate one of the three quarks originally postulated by Gell-Mann, viz. the 'strange' quark, which has zero isospin and charge $-\frac{1}{3}$.

1964 [see QUARK *sb.*]. **1964** *Physics* I. 74 There is a triplet *t* of fermion fields corresponding to three spin ½ quarks: the isotopic doublet *u* and *d*, with charges ⅔ and −⅓ respectively, and the isotopic singlet *s*, with charge −⅓. **1973** *Physics Lett.* XLVII. B. 365/2 Even if there is a fourth 'charmed' quark u' in addition to the usual u, d, and s, there are still three colors. **1975** *Physics Bull.* Apr. 177/1 There are two nonstrange quarks, u and d, a doublet under SU(2), and a strange quark s which is a singlet under SU(2). **1975** L. H. RYDER *Elem. Particles & Symmetries* xi. 192 Let us..take up the suggestion of Gell-Mann in 1964 that the three basic particles, which he called quarks, do not have the same hypercharge *Y* as *p*, *n* and *Λ*, but are as shown in Figure 2. (*u* and *d* stand for isospin up and down, *s* for singlet.) **1975** *Sci. Amer.* Oct. 43/1 The third quark, *s*, is needed only to construct strange particles, and indeed it provides an explicit definition of strangeness: A strange particle is one that contains at least one *s* quark or $\bar{s}$ antiquark. **1977** *Nature* 21 July 204/1 Quark model enthusiasts have been having a field day predicting..the properties of new 'charmed' hadrons composed of c-quarks together with the old u, d and s-quarks. *Ibid.* 204/2 Each flavour of quark (u, d, s or c) comes in each of the three colours, but hadrons are always combinations of quarks with no net colour.

'S, a euphemistic shortening of *God's* in certain oaths (now *Obs.* or *arch.*); written continuously with the following word, as in 'SBLOOD, 'SDEATH, 'SFAX, 'SLIFE, etc.

s'. 1. A colloquial shortening of *sal*, northern dialect form of SHALL *v.* when occurring in unstressed positions. Written continuously with the preceding noun or pronoun, usually in the incorrect form 's.

2. = SO *adv.* Now *colloq.* (Written continuously with the succeeding word.) Cf. S'ELP.

1607 SHAKES. *Cor.* IV. vi. 120 You have brought A trembling vpon Rome, such as was neuer S'incapeable of helpe. **1930** M. ALLINGHAM *Mystery Mile* xxi. 200 'It anythink yer see, and 'it like 'ell—s'long as it ain't me. **1947** K. TENNANT *Lost Haven* i. 20 Man brings his own booze, and gets shot out without s'much as one drink of it.

's, representing a shortened pronunciation of various monosyllables when unstressed. (Written continuously with the preceding word, except in 1 b, 1 c.)

1. a. = *is*: see BE *v.* Now only *colloq.* and *poet.*

1584 LYLY *Sappho* III. ii. 75 Whats he so swaggers in the Van? O! thats a roring Englishman. **1611** BEAUM. & FL. *Philaster* I. i, But I'le suppress him, he's a factious spirit. **1699** DAMPIER *Voy.* (1729) II. I. 19 In some Places there's very strong Clay. **1741** RICHARDSON *Pamela* II. 356 The Devil's in't if we are not agreed in so clear a case. **1821** BYRON *Sardan.* III. i. 401 Again the love-fit's on him.

b. = *it is.* Chiefly *poet.* or (in imitation of informal or careless speech) *colloq.*

1599 SHAKES. *Much Ado* III. iv. 9 By my troth's not so good, and I warrant your cosin will say so. **1933** H. C. BAILEY *Mr. Fortune Wonders* 98 You wouldn't blame your dear boy! Your only one! 's too bad. **1951** J. WYNDHAM *Day of Triffids* i. 25 'S that bloody comet, b—— it! Thash what done it.

c. = *that's*, esp. in phr. ***'sright*** (and varr.) = *that's right* (see RIGHT *a.* 7 e). *colloq.*

In some uses represented erron. by *s'*.

1939 M. HARRISON *What are we waiting For?* 99 'It was two years last August: wasn't it, Fred?' 'Sri,' said Fred. **1958** C. WATSON *Coffin, scarcely Used* xix. 174 'I thought he had only one funeral today.' 'S'right.' **1968** S. WOODS *Past Praying For* III. 245 'Wednesday, the twenty-second of September?' ''sright.' **1969** N. FREELING *Tsing-Boum* x. 64 'Man to see you, chief. Says you're expecting him.' ''s right.' **1977** 'M. UNDERWOOD' *Fatal Trip* xxv. 153 'Did they all leave together?' ''Sright.' 'By car?' ''Sright.'

2. = *has*: see HAVE *v.* *colloq.*

a **1845** HOOD *Parental Ode* 38 He's got a knife!

3. = US *pron.* Now *dial.* exc. in ***let's*** = let us (*colloq.*).

1588 SHAKS. *L.L.L.* v. ii. 228 If you desire to dance, let's hold more chat. **1634** MILTON *Comus* 599 But com let's on. **1662** COKAINE *Trag. Ovid* v. v, Let us go home, send for a Priest of Hymens, And presently each Couple on's be married. **1741** RICHARDSON *Pamela* II. 300 But come, I must love him! Let's find him out. **1893** CROCKETT *Stickit Minister* 100 What'll ye gie's?

4. = HIS *poss. pron.*, q.v. *Obs.* exc. *dial.*

5. = AS. orig. *Sc.* and *north. dial.* Now also *colloq.*, esp. in phr. *so's* = *so as* (see SO *adv.* and *conj.* 29; AS *adv.* 21 a).

1718 RAMSAY *Christ's Kirk* III. 49 I've done my best..As well's I may. **1786** BURNS *To a Haggis* i, A grace As lang's my arm. **1861** QUINN *Heather Lintie* (1863) 85 Let us crack the news As soon's we greet. **1867** J. T. TROWBRIDGE in *Our Young Folks* Mar. 133 Soon's I've got the hang o' the thing, ..I'll astonish the nation. **1942** *R.A.F. Jrnl.* 16 May 2 We heave sandbags and pull ropes and tie knots..till we get so's we don't notice the weather. **1948** D. BALLANTYNE *Cunninghams* I. 5 He had a system for using up the day so's time didn't drag too much. **1955** W. MOORE *Bring Jubilee* iii. 28 You're a gloomy gus, Hodge. Tain't's bad's that. **1970** 'R. LLEWELLYN' *But we didn't get Fox* ii. 22 I'm sore's hell, but that's the situation!

6. = *does*: see DO *v.* A. 2 c. *colloq.*

1934 N. BELL *Winding Road* xxii. 611 When's Parliament reassemble, Stephen? **1938** N. MARSH *Artists in Crime* xvii. 253 What's he know about it? **1966** J. HACKSTON *Father clears Out* 22 That fellow was most disheartening. What's he know about gold! **1980** 'M. UNDERWOOD' *Crime upon Crime* i. 7 What's he do?.. I wondered if he belonged to one of those hush-hush outfits?

-s, *suffix*[1], forming adverbs, was originally *-es*, identical with the suffix of the genitive singular of many neuter and masculine sbs. and adjs. Several of the adverbs in *-es* that existed in OE. are genitives either of sbs. (neut. or masc.) as *dæʒes* by day, *nédes* NEEDS, *þances* voluntarily, or of neuter adjs., as *sóðes* truly; on the analogy of these, *-es* was added, with adv.-forming function, to feminine nouns, as in *nihtes* by night, *endebyrdes* in order. OE. had also advs. compounded of *tó* prep. and a genitive governed by it, as *tó-ʒeʒnes* (see TO-GAINS), *tó-middes* (see TO-MIDS); side by side with these there existed parallel and synonymous advs. like *on-ʒeʒn* AGAIN, *on-middan* AMID, in which the dat. or accus. was governed by a prep. Hence there arose in early ME. mixed forms such as *aȝeines*, *amiddes*; and the frequent coexistence of the two forms of the same adv., one with and the other without *s*, led to the addition of *s* to many advs. as a sign of their function. In some instances the extended form prevailed, as in *eftsoons*; in others it survived only in dialects, as in *oftens*, *gaylies* (Sc.). See also the articles -LING[2], -LI(N)GS, -WARD, -WARDS, -WAY, -WAYS.

In *once*, *twice*, *thrice*, *hence*, *since*, etc., the suffix is written differently. In AGAINST, ALONGST, AMONGST, AMIDST, and the dialectal *onst* (see ONCE), the original *-es*, *-s* has become *-st*.

-s, *suffix*[2]. A shortened form of the hypocoristic dim. suffix -SY, added to the same classes of words, as *Babs*, *Toots*; *ducks* (see DUCK *sb.*[1] 3 c), *moms*.

sa, obs. f. SEE *v.*, SOE *sb.*; obs. or dial. f. SO.

sa', obs. var. of SAVE *v.* in ***God sa' me*** and similar phrases.

1604 DEKKER *Honest Wh.* A 4, Yet so god sa mee shees mine owne sister. *Ibid.* G 3 b, Thats all so god sa me, I thirst after. **1668** SHADWELL *Sullen Lovers* IV. 61 As Gad shall sa'me, she is a very ingenious Woman. **1819** SCOTT *Ivanhoe* xxxiv, Friend Isaac, will you pleasure us in this matter, and our day shall be truly kept, so God sa' me?

sa. *Her.* Abbreviation of SABLE *sb.*[2]

1780 EDMONDSON *Heraldry* I. *Arms Abbies* etc., Augustine's [St.] Monastery, Canterbury. Sa. a cross ar. **1828–40** BERRY *Encycl. Herald.* II, *Abberbury*..or, a fesse embattled sa. **1871** BURKE *Peerage*, etc. 195/2 Sa., a naked man, ppr.

saa(e, obs. f. SOE.

saab, sa'ab, varr. SAHIB.

saac(ke, obs. f. SAKE.

saad(e, obs. forms of SAD; pa. t. of SAY *v.*, q.v.

Saadian ('sɑːdɪən), *a.* Also **Sadian**, **Sa'dian**. [f. Arab. *Sâadi*, *Sa'dī*, the name of a 16th- and 17th-cent. dynasty of sharīfs in Morocco + -AN.] Of or belonging to the Sa'dī dynasty.

[**1899** B. MEAKIN *Moorish Empire* vii. 116 In consequence of..the assertion that this family only belonged to the Beni Sâad, it was contemptuously known as the Sâadi dynasty.] **1951** W. BLUNT *Black Sunrise* iv. 40 In the sixteenth century ..Marrakesh had risen again under the Sadian kings. **1963** *Guardian* 27 Feb. 15/3 There are two marvellous things to see [in Marrakesh]—the Saadian tombs, and the Souks, or covered bazaars. **1971** J. M. ABUN-NASR *Hist. Maghrib* viii. 205 The Sa'dian *Sharifs* were able to organize a religio-political movement which eventually unified Morocco.

saaf(e, saaff, obs. ff. SAFE and SAVE *prep.*

saage, obs. f. SAGE *a.*

‖**saaidam** ('saɪdam). *S. Afr.* Also **zaai-** and with capital initial; pl. **-damme, -dams.** [Afrikaans, f. *saai* to sow + *dam* DAM *sb.*[1]] A basin of land enclosed by artificial earthen walls, designed to receive flood-water for its irrigation. Also *attrib.*

1925 R. DEAKIN *Southward Ho!* vii. 79 The raising of crops with the help of *saaidams*..would transform the scene. **1937** MARAIS & SIM in D. J. Seymore *Handbk. for Farmers in S. Afr.* (S. Afr. Dept. Agric. & Forestry) 704 The so-called 'saaidam' system is practised. **1947** *S. & E. Afr. Year Bk. & Guide* 551 From Kotjeskolk to Sak River the branch line runs through the fertile Fish River valley along which large 'Zaaidams' have been made. Cultivation by zaaidams is carried out by diverting the flood water..into extensive areas enclosed by dams. **1953** *Cape Argus Mag.* 2 June 1/6 'Koos Nel' constructed the first large 'Saaidam' in the North-West. **1955** J. H. WELLINGTON *S. Afr.* I. 385 Saaidam irrigation is practised along the Sak river... The sowing 'dam' is a basin bordered by low earthen walls into which the flood waters are diverted. **1972** *Stand. Encycl. S. Afr.* V. 445/1 There is considerable irrigation, including the unique system whereby flood-water is diverted into shallow basins, known as 'saaidamme'. **1975** *Ibid.* XI. 422/2 In the North-Western Cape wheat is grown on saaidams.

saake, obs. f. SACK *sb.*

‖**saal** (zɑːl). *rare.* Also **Saal**. [Ger.; cf. SALLE.] A large room or hall. (Used with reference to European countries, esp. Germany.)

1855 GEO. ELIOT in *Fraser's Mag.* LI. 702/1 A more interesting place to visitors is the library, which occupies a large building not far from the Schloss. The principal *Saal* ..is ornamented with some very excellent busts. **1876** —— *Dan. Der.* I. II. xv. 291 Sir Hugo saying as they entered the large *saal*—'Did you play much at Baden, Grandcourt?' **1978** *Chicago* June 52/1 The Chicago Public Library offers tours of this splendid building—it ranks with the best of the European saals.

saald, obs. pa. t. of SELL *v.*

Saale (ˈzɑːlə). *Geol.* The name of a river in E. Germany used *attrib.* with reference to the third (penultimate) glaciation of the Pleistocene epoch in northern Europe, equivalent to the Riss glaciation in the Alps.

1937 W. B. WRIGHT *Quaternary Ice Age* (ed. 2) x. 136 In several places two deposits of loess are separated from one another by glacial formations, indicating that loess formation preceded the advance of the Saale Ice-sheet. **1945** F. E. ZEUNER *Pleistocene Period* iii. 76 The most remarkable feature of the Ukrainian succession is the moraine of the Dnjepr lobe of the Saale glaciation. **1959** WELLS & KIRKALDY *Outl. Hist. Geol.* (ed. 4) xix. 368 The Gipping and Lowestoft Boulder Clays must be correlated with the Saale and Elster glaciations respectively. **1971** R. F. FLINT *Glacial & Quaternary Geol.* xxiv. 628 The distribution of the extensive Saale drift is generally well defined, though in places it is not differentiated clearly from the Elster. **1979** *Nature* 18 Jan. 172/1 It lies between Saale glacial deposits and the sands of the Last (Weichselian) Glaciation (isotope stages 2, 3, 4 and 5a–5d).

saale, obs. f. SALE *sb.*

Saalian (ˈzɑːlɪən), *a.* (*sb.*) *Geol.* [ad. G. *saalisch* (H. Stille 1920, in *Nachr. v.d. K. Ges. d. Wissensch. z. Göttingen* (Math.-phys. Kl.) 219), f. *Saale* (q.v.): see -IAN).] Designating, or pertaining to, a minor orogenic episode in Europe which is believed to have occurred in the Permian period. Also *ellipt.* as *sb.* Also **'Saalic** *a.*

1931 GREGORY & BARRETT *Gen. Stratigr.* 19 The Saalian is represented in England by the Armorican which is earlier than Middle Permian. **1933** *Proc. Leeds Philos. & Lit. Soc.* (*Sci. Sect.*) II. 456 (*table*) Saalian folding. **1937** A. L. DU TOIT *Our Wandering Continents* vii. 156 The relatively weak Saalian and Pfalzian Phases marked out the end of the Lower and Upper Permian respectively in the central Variscan zone. *Ibid.* xvi. 309 The Saalian was weak in Europe and the Urals, but strong in both west and east—in the Caribbean and Appalachians and along the southern margin of Asia. **1969** BENNISON & WRIGHT *Geol. Hist. Brit. Isles* x. 244 The pre-Permian unconformity of north-east England may be due to the Asturic Phase or to the (later) Saalic Phase. **1973** P. J. BUREK in Tarling & Runcorn *Implications Continental Drift to Earth Sci.* II. 822 The closing of the Ural trough along with the formation of the Uralides (Saalian orogenic phase). **1974** *Encycl. Brit. Macropædia* XIV. 99/1 In Europe, orogenic and igneous activities were on a much smaller scale than they had been in the Carboniferous. Here, two minor orogenies..are generally named Pfälzian (post-Early Permian) and Saalian (Late Permian).

Saam(e, var. SAMI.

Saan, var. SAN².

saand, obs. f. SAND *sb.*

Saanen (ˈsɑːnən). The name of a small town in the canton of Berne, Switzerland, used *attrib.* and *absol.* to designate (a member of) a breed of white goats which was first developed in the region.

1908 'HOME COUNTIES' *Case for Goat* iii. 26 Something is now heard of the white Saanen. **1909** G. J. G. JENSEN *Goat-Keeping for All* ii. 7 Saanen Goats.—Some two or three specimens of this breed were recently imported by Mr. H. E. Hughes, of Broxbourne. **1920** C. J. DAVIES *Goat-Keeping for Milk Production* i. 14 The white breed of Switzerland takes its name from Gessenay in Berne... In England the variety is usually known as the Saanen. **1948** A. HUXLEY *Ape & Essence* (1949) 125 Three-horned and robed impressively in a white Saanen soutane the great man is sitting with a couple of two-horned Familiars at a large table. **1976** *Denbighshire Free Press* 8 Dec. 17/6 (Advt.), Territone goats, Anglo Nubian British Saanen.

saap(pe, obs. forms of SAP *sb.*

Saar (zɑː(r)). The name of a river in West Germany, a tributary of the Moselle, used *attrib.* and *absol.* to designate a white wine produced in this region.

1905 G. MEREDITH *Let.* 1 Mar. (1970) III. 1515 Can it be a Moselle? Or a Saar wine. **1967** A. LICHINE *Encycl. Wines* 474/1 The Saars can outclass the Moselles in the best years. .. Saar wines..are always classed with the Moselles. *Ibid., Kauzem.* Very delicious wines, heavier, fuller, rounder than most Saars.

saar, Saara, obs. forms of SORE *adv.*, SAHARA.

saarce, -cyn, obs. forms of SEARCE, -CING.

Saarlander (ˈzɑːlændə(r)). [Ger., f. *Saarland*, the name of a West German *Land*; cf. SAAR] An inhabitant of Saarland. Also *attrib.* or as *adj.*

1955 *Times* 4 May 10/1 A Gaullist senator complained that the Government, in accepting the Franco-German consortium, had excluded the Saarlanders. **1975** *Times* 18 June 25/3 The iron and steel works..were returned to German control at the request of the Saarlanders. **1980** E. LEATHER *Duveen Let.* xv. 175 He was a Saarlander, and a dedicated Nazi. *Ibid.* 178 His ancestors had been.. Saarlander plumbers.

saat(e, obs. forms of pa. t. of SIT *v.*

saater, var. SAETER, SETTER.

†**sab.** *Her. Obs.* Abbreviation of SABLE *sb.*²

1660 M. CARTER *Honor rediv.* 249 Bernards Inne Beareth party per pale indented Ermin and Sab. a Cheveron Gul. fretty.

sab, obs. form of SAHIB.

sabadilla (sæbəˈdɪlə). [a. Sp. *cebadilla*, dim. of *cebada* barley.] = CEVADILLA; a preparation of this for medicinal or agricultural use. Also *attrib.*

1812 J. SMYTH *Pract. of Customs* (1821) 208 Sabadilla seed, Indian Caustic Barley, very useful in Medicine. **1836** J. M. GULLY *Magendie's Formul.* (ed. 2) 71 Boil the seeds of the sabadilla with alcohol. **1876** DUHRING *Dis. Skin* 596 Powdered sabadilla..may be sprinkled throughout the hair with good result. **1890** HUGHES & DAKE *Cycl. Drug Pathogenesy* III. 759 We have thought it better to omit the symptoms belonging to them, lest they should prove as worthless as those..which were observed in a boy suffering from tape-worm before he took Sabadilla 30, and which (naturally) disappeared after 46 ells of the worm had been passed. **1907** *Brit. Pharmaceutical Codex* 241 Sabadilla consists of the dried ripe seeds of *Schoenocaulon officinale*,.. a tall herbaceous plant growing on the low mountain slopes in Mexico, Guatemala, and Venezuela. **1946** *Richmond* (Va.) *Times-Dispatch* 4 Feb. 4/1 A powerful new insecticide has been developed from a long-known plant... The new bug killer is known as sabadilla. **1977** *Martindale's Extra Pharmacopoeia* (ed. 27) 796/2 Sabadilla was formerly used as a parasiticide, especially for pediculosis capitis, in the form of ointment..or vinegar.

Hence **saba'dillia, saba'dilline**, *Chem.*, an alkaloid obtained from sabadilla seeds.

1836 J. M. GULLY *Magendie's Formul.* (ed. 2) 70 M. Couerbe..has severally named them [*i.e.* the principles in sabadilla] sabadilline, veratrin [etc.]. **1857** MILLER *Elem. Chem.* (1892) III. 503 Three other poisonous bases, sabadillia, colchinia, and jervia, are found, along with veratria, in the *Veratrum album.* **1887** A. M. BROWN *Anim. Alkaloids* 29 Anemonine, peltierine, sabadilline.

sabadine (ˈsæbədiːn). *Biochem.* Also †**sabatine**. [ad. G. *sabadin* (E. Merck 1891, in *Arch. der Pharm.* CCXXIX. 164): see SABADILLA and -INE⁵.] A veratrum alkaloid ester, $C_{29}H_{47}NO_8$, present in sabadilla seeds.

1891 *Jrnl. Chem. Soc.* LX. II. 844 The author has isolated two alkaloïds from sabadilla seeds, *Asagræa officinalis*. Sabadine is best separated as the nitrate. **1951** A. J. HENNIG et al. in *Jrnl. Amer. Pharmaceut. Assoc.: Sci. Ed.* XL. 168 Evidence has been obtained of at least five additional alkaloids in the water-soluble portion, crude fraction D..of sabadilla alkaloids. One of the new alkaloids has been obtained in crystalline state and given the name 'sabatine'. **1962** *Jrnl. Med. & Pharmaceut. Chem.* V. 693 Sabatine was found to be identical with sabadine... On historical grounds, the names sabadine and sabine (for the ester and alkamine respectively) deserve preference. **1976** *Jrnl. Neurochem.* XXVII. 1271/2 Veratrine sulfate consisted of the alkaloids veratridine, cevadilline, sabadine and cevadine.

Sabæan, Sabean (sæˈbiːən), *a.* and *sb.* Also **Sabaean.** [f. L. *Sabæ-us*, Gr. *Σαβαῖ-ος* (f. *Saba*, *Σάβα*, Arabic *Saba'* = Heb. *Shᵉbā*, the ancient name of the people of Yemen; by Gr. and Roman writers imagined to be the name of the capital city) + -AN.

In one passage (Isa. xlv. 14) the Eng. Bible, following the LXX and the Vulgate, uses *Sabeans* for the quite different tribal name *Sᵉbāīm*. Another instance of this is in Ezek. xxiii. 42, but the marginal reading in 1611 is *drunkards*, which the Revised Version (1884) adopts in the text.]

A. *adj.* Of or belonging to the ancient population of Yemen in Arabia. In poetic use, often with allusion to the ancient renown of the spices brought from Yemen. Also, of or pertaining to the language of the Sabæans (see below B. b).

a **1586** SIDNEY *Ps.* XLV. iv, The fragrant riches of Sabean grove, Mirrh, Aloes, Cassia. **1623** MASSINGER *Bondman* IV. iii, Whole Hecatombes or Sabæan Gums. **1698** FRYER *Acc. E. India & P.* 115 Two skins of Sabæan Asses. **1700** DRYDEN *Cinyras & Myrrha* 323 Sabæan Fields afford her needful Rest. **1830** TENNYSON *Adeline* v, Dripping with Sabæan spice On thy pillow. **1883** I. TAYLOR *Alphabet* I. 345 The Himyaritic or Sabean Alphabet. **1886, 1902** [see MINÆAN *sb.* and *a.*]. **1968** [see LIHYANIC *sb.*]. **1974** *Encycl. Brit. Macropædia* I. 620/1 The Sabaean offshoot, a graceful and elegant script consisting of 29 letters, spread into Africa, where it became the progenitor of the Ethiopic alphabet.

B. *sb.* **a.** One of the ancient inhabitants of Yemen.

1607 TOPSELL *Four-f. Beasts* 239 The Sabeans by reason of continual vse of Mirrhe and Frankinsens, grow to a loathing of that sauour. **1611** BIBLE *Joel* iii. 8 They shall sell them to the Sabeans, to a people farre off.

b. The language of the Sabæans, a dialect of Old South Arabic.

1905 G. BELL *Let.* 23 Feb. (1927) I. 196 A mass of rocks all covered with inscriptions..one..very like the oldest script of Yemen Sabaean. **1910** J. BUCHAN *Prester John* xi. 183 It must have been some old sacred language—Phoenician, Sabæan, I know not what—which had survived in the rite. **1951** [see MINÆAN *sb.* and *a.*]

Sabæan, erroneous form of SABIAN.

sabahdaur, variant of SUBAHDAR.

Sabaism (ˈseɪbeɪɪz(ə)m). Also 8–9 **Zabaism**, 9 **Sabeism, Sabiism, Sabism, Tsabaism, Sabæism.** [f. Heb. *çābā* host (after the presumed etymology of SABIAN) + -ISM. Cf. F. *sabéisme, sabaïsme, sabisme.*] The worship of 'the host of heaven'; star-worship. Also sometimes used for SABIANISM in its various historical applications.

1727–41 CHAMBERS *Cycl.* s.v., *Sabaism* consisted in the worship and adoration of the stars. **1794** SULLIVAN *View Nat.* II. xliv. 281 The first variation from the purer zabaism consisted in the ophilatreia, or worship of the serpent. **1839** YEOWELL *Anc. Brit. Ch.* xiii. (1847) 148 The worship of the celestial bodies, or Sabæism, as it is termed. **1841** *Penny Cycl.* XX. 295/2 The religious books of Tsabaism were written in Syriac. **1859** J. M. ARNOLD *Ishmael* 36 The more corrupt form of superstition, which in a measure co-existed with Sabeism. **1878** A. FORNANDER *Polynesian Race* I. 36 Glimpses of Cushite Zabaism.

sabal (ˈseɪbəl). [Generic name (M. Adanson *Familles des Plantes* (1763) II. 495), perh. a. S. Amer. native name.] A fan palm of the genus so called, or a related fossil plant, belonging to the family Palmaceæ and native to tropical America. Cf. PALMETTO.

1812 *Curtis's Bot. Mag.* XXXV. 1434 (*heading*) Dwarf Sabal, or Swamp Palmetto. **1902** L. H. BAILEY *Cycl. Amer. Hort.* IV. 1593/1 The Sabals have proved a great success. **1975** *Islander* (Victoria, B.C.) 20 Apr. 14/2 Leaves from sabal have been found around Nanaimo.

sabalo (ˈsæbələʊ). *U.S.* [a. Sp. *sábalo* shad.] The tarpon, *Megalops atlanticus.*

1889 in *Cent. Dict.* [**1904** W. M. GALLICHAN *Fishing & Trav. Spain* xvi. 161 These traps were set for the sábalos, or shad.] **1938** V. HEILNER *Salt Water Fishing* xii. 195 Look at all the big marlin Hemingway has taken. And of course sabalo. **1965** A. J. MCCLANE *Stand. Fishing Encycl.* 924/2 Tarpon... Also known as the *sabalo* (Spanish), this species is considered by many anglers as the king of gamefishes.

‖**Sabaoth** (ˈsæbeɪɒθ, ˈsæbeɪɒθ, sæˈbeɪɒθ). Also 6 **sabbaoth.** [L. *Sabaōth* (Vulg.), a. Gr. *Σαβαώθ* (LXX and New Testament), a. Heb. *çᵉbāōth* pl. of *çābā* army.] A Hebrew word (lit. 'armies', 'hosts'), retained untranslated in the English New Testament (as in the original Greek and in the Vulgate) and the *Te Deum*, in the designation ***the Lord of Sabaoth***, for which in the original Old Testament passages the English versions have the rendering 'The Lord of Hosts'.

The Gr. and L. forms being indeclinable, and therefore not easily recognizable as genitives, a frequent early form in Eng. was *the Lord Sabaoth*.

a **1325** *Prose Psalter, Te Deum* 6 Holy! holy! holy! Lord God Sabaoth. **1398** TREVISA *Barth. De P.R.* IX. xxviii. (1495) 364 On the saterdaye in Albis..in the gospell we ben taughte to traueylle in the vyneyerde of our lorde Sabaoth. **1535** COVERDALE *Rom.* ix. 29 The Lorde of Sabbaoth [**1611** Sabaoth]. —— *Jas.* v. 4 The cryes of them which haue reped, are entred in to the eares of the Lorde Sabaoth [**1611** the Lord of Sabaoth].

¶ Confused with *sabbath*. (See also SABBATH β.)

1596 SPENSER *F.Q.* VII. viii. 2 But thence-forth all shall rest eternally With Him that is the God of Sabaoth hight: O! that great Sabaoth God, grant me that Sabaoths sight.

sabarcane, variant of SARBACANE.

sabat(e, obs. f. SABBATH.

sabatia, var. SABBATIA.

Sabatier (sabatje). *Photogr.* Also (*erron.* but more commonly) **Sabattier**. The name of Armand *Sabatier* (1834–1910), French physician and scientist, used *attrib.* and in the possessive to designate a process and an effect developed by him, as †**Sabatier's amphipositive process**, the process of image-reversal giving rise to the Sabatier effect; **Sabatier effect**, partial or complete reversal of an image on film or paper, resulting from exposure to unsafe light after partial development. Cf. SOLARIZATION 1, PSEUDO-SOLARIZATION.

1894 E. L. WILSON *Cyclopædic Photogr.* 329/1 Sabatier's Amphi-Positive Process. The peculiarity of this process consists in the pictures being the result of a superposition, or entangling of two images, one negative, the other positive. **1930** tr. *L. P. Clerc's Photogr.* xvi. 138/1 A similar phenomenon is observed when white light is momentarily admitted to the room while the normal image is still weak. (Sabatier effect.) **1939** M. NATKIN *Fascinating Fakes in Photogr.* 58 Solarisation, sometimes called Sabatier effect, has been known for a very long time. **1956** [see SOLARIZATION 1 a]. **1970** C. B. NEBLETTE *Fund. Photogr.* v. 52 If a photographic material is exposed, developed, washed but not fixed and then exposed to diffused light and again developed, a positive image or a combination of a positive and a negative image is obtained... This is known as the Sabattier effect (Sabatier, 1850). **1970** M. J. SETHNA *Photography* xii. 180 Actually producing the Sabatier effect is not an easy matter. **1976** K. I. & R. E. JACOBSON *Imaging Syst.* v. 105 Although the Sabattier effect has been ascribed to the screening effect of the negative image produced by the first exposure and development on the printing by the second exposure onto the underlying emulsion, desensitization by the products of development is a more likely explanation.

sabatille, obs. f. SAPODILLA.

†**'sabatine.** *Obs.* In quots. sab(b)atyne. [a. Pr. *sabatina*, dim. of *sabata*: see SABATON and -INE.] A kind of buskin.

c **1460** in *Archæologia* XVII. 295 First ye must set on sabatynes and tye them upon the shoo. *c* **1538** *Ibid.* XLIII. 248 A payr of sabbatynes; and a payre of syndalls.

sabatine, obs. var. SABADINE, SABBATINE.

†**sabaton.** *Obs.* Also 4–5 **sabatoun**, 5 **sabatton**, 9 **sabbaton.** [a. Pr. *sabató* (mod.Pr. *sabatoun* shoe), augmentative of *sabata* = F. *savate*, Sp. *zapata* boot (also *zapato* shoe), Pg. *sapata*, It. *ciabatta* shoe. Cf. med.L. *sabbatum*.

The ultimate origin of the Rom. word is obscure. It exists in Arabic (*sabbāt*, *ṣabbāt*, etc., Dozy II. 626), in Berber (*sappāt*, ibid.), and in Basque (*zapata*), but is prob. in all these a loan-word from Spanish.]

A broad-toed armed foot-covering worn by warriors in armour.

c **1330** R. BRUNNE *Chron. Wace* (Rolls) 10026 Hym self was armed fynly wel Wyþ sabatons [Wace *cauces de fer*], & spores, & iaumbers of stel. **13..** *Gaw. & Gr. Knt.* 574 Þenne set þay þe sabatounz vpon þe segge fotez. *c* **1420** ? LYDG. *Assembly of Gods* 346 Gauntlettes on hyr handys, & sabatouns on hyr fete. *c* **1450** J. METHAM *Wks.* (E.E.T.S.) 36 This forsayd knyght Blak sabatouns weryd. **1485** *Materials Reign Hen. VII* (Rolls) II. 21 For making of a paire of sabatons of clothe of golde IIII s. **1543** GRAFTON *Contn. Harding* 594 The hernayes.. was all ouer gylte frome the heade peece to the sabattons. **1869** BOUTELL *Arms & Arm.* x. (1874) 206 At the commencement of the 16th century, the pointed sollerets were succeeded by broad sabbatons, cut off square or rounded at the toes.

‖**sabayon** (sabajɔ̃). [Fr., ad. It. *zabaione* zabaglione.] A dessert or sauce made with egg yolks, sugar, and white wine, whipped together, thickened over a slow heat, and served hot or cold. Also *attrib.* and *Comb.*

1906 *Mrs. Beeton's Bk. Househ. Managem.* lxii. 1669 (*heading*) Sabayon.. Pudding sauce, composed of cream or milk, sugar, white wine, and eggs. **1939** A. SIMON *Conc. Encycl. Gastron.* I. 46/2 (*heading*) Sabayon sauce. 4 egg yolks. 1½ oz. sifted sugar. 2 gills Marsala wine. **1960** V. NABOKOV *Invitation to Beheading* I. 13 Excellent sabayon! Should still like to know if it will be long now. **1973** *Sat. Rev. World* (U.S.) 18 Dec. 48/3 *Sabayon* reeling from an overdose of Grand Marnier. **1975** *Times* 31 May 7/4 There were.. triumphs:.. the white wine sauce for sole paillard, and the sabayon au kummel.

Sabba-day. Now *rare.* Also **Sabber-day**, etc. U.S. colloq. var. of SABBATH-DAY. Also *Comb.*, as **Sabba-day house**, a house used for rest in the interval between church services; = *noon-house* s.v. NOON *sb.* 6 b.

c **1772** T. BURBANK in *Essex Inst. Hist. Coll.* (1920) LVI. 292 Thare was in the yeare 1738 a great athcak one sabbady. **1858** *Harper's Mag.* Nov. 856/2 A thousand terrible thoughts rushed into her mind;.. above all, the loss of her 'Sabber-day' dinner. **1868** H. W. BEECHER *Norwood* 47 Duties never conflict, you said, only Sabby-day morning last. **1876** J. E. TODD *John Todd* 40 Near by were a number of rough, stone-built 'Sabba'-day houses, where they flocked at noon, for warmth in winter (they had chimneys), and coolness in summer. **1891** [see *noon-house* s.v. NOON *sb.* 6 b]. **1935** J. C. LINCOLN *Cape Cod Yesterdays* 5, I knew that, when I next dressed, it would be in the prim and stiff and spotless garments befitting what Grandmother often said her mother used to call 'Sabba' Day'.

‖**Sabbat** (saba). In 7–8 sabat. [Fr.; a special application of *sabbat* SABBATH.] A 'witches' sabbath'; see SABBATH 3. Also *attrib.*, and *fig.*

1652 J. WRIGHT tr. *Camus' Nat. Paradox* VII. 153 In this Desart corner, which.. seemeth onely fit for a Sabat or Assembly of Sorcerers. **1658** tr. *Bergerac's Satyr. Char.* xiii. 54 As to the sabat-voyages, this is my beliefe; they noint themselves with some somniferous oyles, and as while they wake they easily fancy to be carried astride upon a broome through the chimny, into a Hall, where is feasting, dancing, and where they kisse the Goate's brich. **1763** H. WALPOLE *Let. to Montagu* 15 Aug., My youthfullity, which bears me out even at a sabat. I dined last week at Lady Blandford's, with her, the old Denbigh, the old Litchfield, and Methuselah knows who. **1861** LYTTON *Str. Story* xxvi, I could have fancied myself at a witch's sabbat. **1893** LELAND *Mem.* I. 75 The book was a perfect Sabbat of deviltry and dramatic horrors.

sabbatarial (sæbə'tɛərɪəl), *a. rare*⁻¹. [f. L. *sabbatāri-us* (see SABBATARIAN *a.* and *sb.*) + -AL¹.] Favouring or tending to the observance of the Sabbath.

1867 TROLLOPE *Last Chron. Barset* II. lxxiii. 294 The archdeacon had been very stoutly anti-sabbatarial when the question of stopping the Sunday post to Plumstead had been mooted in the village.

Sabbatarian (sæbə'tɛərɪən), *a.* and *sb.* [a. L. *sabbatāri-us* (Sp. *sabatario*, Pg. *sabbatario*), f. *sabbatum* SABBATH: see -ARIAN.]

A. *adj.* †**a.** Of or pertaining to the Sabbath or its observance. *Obs.* **b.** Having relation to the tenets of the Sabbatarians.

a **1631** DONNE in *Select.* (1840) 105 A sabbatarian righteousness is no righteousness. **1654** H. L'ESTRANGE *Chas. I* (1655) 129 The rigour and strictnesse of Sabbatarian Ministers, in denying People recreations on the Sunday. **1668** WELLS (*title*) The Practical Sabbatarian or Sabbath Holiness crowned with Superlative Happiness. **1733** NEAL *Hist. Purit.* II. 250 These Divines, instead of softening some excesses in Bradbourne's Sabbatarian strictness, ran into the contrary extreme. **1796** MORSE *Amer. Geog.* I. 436 These are called Sabbatarian, or Seventh day Baptists. **1837** WHEWELL *Hist. Induct. Sci.* (1857) I. 224 With references to Jewish Sabbatarian notions. **1859** MILL *Liberty* 161 Another important example of illegitimate interference with the rightful liberty of the individual.. is sabbatarian legislation. **1863** A. BLOMFIELD *Mem. Bp. Blomfield* I. vi. 154 He entertained rather strict, or what would now be called 'Sabbatarian' notions.

B. *sb.*

1. A Jewish observer of the (Saturday) Sabbath.

1613 PURCHAS *Pilgrimage* (1614) 149 The word *Masbothæi*, Scaliger saith, signifieth Sabbatists or Sabbatarians, because they professed to haue learned the obseruation of the Sabbath from Christ, and therein differed from the other Iewes. *a* **1641** BP. MOUNTAGU *Acts & Mon.* (1642) 454 These Esseni were yet further, more, and most rigid Sabbatarians, beyond all other sects and schismes amongst the Jewes. **1830** D'ISRAELI *Chas. I*, III. xv. 330 Sabbatarians, became a term of reproach for the Jews with the Polytheists.

2. A Christian who regards the Lord's Day as a Sabbath, deducing its obligation from the Fourth Commandment. Also, and more commonly, one whose opinion and practice with regard to Sunday observance are unusually strict.

1620 J. DYKE *Counter-poyson* 15 He is none of your precise Sabbatarians. **1656** HEYLIN *Extraneus Vapulans* 110 We are now come unto the business of the Lords day, in which our Author sheweth himself a stiffe Sabbatarian. **1718** HICKES & NELSON *J. Kettlewell* III. xxiv. 237, I don't know whether you are a Strict Sabbatarian. **1864** EASTWICK *3 Years in Persia* I. 4, I am not a Sabbatarian, I showed it by travelling on Sunday.

3. A member of a Christian sect founded towards the close of the sixteenth century, the members of which maintained that the Sabbath should be observed on the seventh and not on the first day of the week; a Seventh-day Baptist. Cf. SABBATARY *sb.*, SABBATHARIAN.

1645 PAGITT *Heresiogr.* (1647) Bj, The Sabbatarians affirme the old Jewish Sabbath to be kept, and not the Lords day. **1710** STEELE & ADDISON *Tatler* No. 257 ¶12 Præ-Adamites, Sabbatarians, Cameronians, Muggletonians ..and the like. **1820** *Trav. Cosmo III* 445 Robert Dogs, a coal-man in London, was the first founder of the sect of Sabbatarians.

Sabbatarianism (sæbə'tɛərɪənɪz(ə)m). [f. prec. + -ISM.] Sabbatarian principles or practice.

1673-4 BP. WARD *Case of Joram* 34 [Laws] against Prophanation of the Lord's Day (I do not mean tending to Judaism or Sabbatarianism). **1876** GLADSTONE *Glean.* (1879) II. 360 The rather judaical Sabbatarianism of Scotland.. was simply a form of Protestant tradition. **1894** MAX O'RELL *J. Bull & Co.* 54 Narrow Sabbatarianism is neither Protestant nor Christian: it is a Jewish institution.

†**'Sabbatary**, *a.* and *sb. Obs.* Also 6–7 **sabbatharie.** [ad. L. *sabbatārius*, f. *sabbatum* SABBATH: see -ARY. Cf. F. *sabbataire*.]

A. *adj.* Pertaining to the Sabbath.

1613 PURCHAS *Pilgrimage* (1614) 204 They are of opinion, that themselues haue a superfluous Sabbatharie soule, which on that day is plentifully sent in to them, to inlarge their heart. **1635** HEYLIN *Sabbath* II. (1636) To Rdr., This sabbatarie soule, may be a Pythagoricall μετεμψύχωσις. **1641** H. L'ESTRANGE *God's Sabbath* Pref., Had they left us no other demonstrations of their excellency that way then their Sabbatary Tracts, they should never have attained so high a repute amongst us. **1674** JEAKE *Arith.* (1696) 663 Seven.. is sometime called the Sacred and Quiet, or Sabbatory [*sic*] Number.

B. *sb.* A Christian who observes the Jewish (seventh-day) Sabbath.

1596 BELL *Surv. Popery* I. III. v. 112 The sabbatharies contend with tothe and nail. **1621** *Three Quest. Answ. conc. 4th Commandm.* 3 The Sabbatharies, which heretofore would haue vs Christians obserue the Iewes Sabbath.

Sabbath, sabbath ('sæbəθ). Forms: α. 1, 3–5 **sabat**, (3 *pl.* **sabaz**), 3 **sabadt**, 4 **sabath, -aat**, 4–5 **sabate**, 4–6 **sab(b)ot**, 4–7 **saboth**, 5 **sabott(e, sabbate, -atte, -ott**, 5–6 **sabote**, 5–7 **sabboth**, 6 **sabett, -att, -otte, othe**, *Sc.* **sabbuth**, 6– **sabbath**; β. (*erron.*, by confusion with SABAOTH) 4–8 **sabaoth**, 6 **sabaothe, sabbaoth.** See also SABBAT. [ad. L. *sabbatum* (partly through OF. *sabbat*, *sabat*, mod.F. *sabbat* = Pr. *sabbat*, Sp. *sábado*, Pg. *sabado*, It. *sabbato*), Gr. σάββατον, ad. Heb. *shabbāth*, f. root *shābath* to rest. Cf. Goth. *sabbatus, -o*, MDu. *sabaet, sabbet, sabbot*, Du. and G. *sabbat*.

The Sp., Pg., and It. forms are the ordinary names in those langs. for Saturday; but Pr. used *dis-sapte* (:—L. *diēs sabbatī*) in that sense. A popular Latin nasalized form **sambatum* (of oriental origin) appears in F. *samedi* (:—**sambatī diēs*), OHG. *sambaztac* (mod.G. *samstag*) Saturday.

The confusion with SABAOTH was not peculiar to England; it occurs in MHG. and in med.Latin.]

1. a. In the original use: The seventh day of the week (Saturday) considered as the day of religious rest enjoined on the Israelites by the fourth (or in mediæval reckoning the third) commandment of the Decalogue. Phrases, ***to keep, break the Sabbath.***

The word was never in England, as in some continental countries, a vernacular synonym for Saturday, though English writers of med.Latin used *dies Sabbati* as frequently as *dies Saturni*.

α. *c* **950** *Lindisf. Gosp.* Matt. Capitula Lectionum §87 From efernes sabates [L. *a vespere sabbati*]. *c* **1230** *Hali Meid.* 17 Low, godd him seolf seið þurh þe prophete: 'þeo þe habbeð from ham forcoruen flesches lustes, & haldeð mine sabaz'. **13..** *Cursor M.* 11987 (Cott.) And o lame o þaa lakes selue Wit handes made he sparus tuelue, Apon þair sabadt þus he did. **1340** *Ayenb.* 7 Þe þridde heste is þellich: 'Loke þet þou halȝi þane day of þe sabat (Zeterday)'... Þis word, zeterday, þet þe iurie clepeþ sabat, is ase moche worþ ase reste... And ine þe stede of þe sabat.. zet holi chereche þane sonday to loky ine þe newe laȝe. *c* **1380** WYCLIF *Serm.* Sel. Wks. I. 41 And Jesus spake to wyse men of þe lawe, and to Pharisees where it were leveful to hele in þe Sabot. **1382** —— *Acts* i. 12 Thanne thei turneden aȝen to Jerusalem, fro the hil that is clepid Olyuete, the which is bisydis Jerusalem, hauynge the iurney of a saboth. **1432-50** tr. *Higden* (Rolls) IV. 267 Oure Savioure Criste was borne.. in the nyȝhte of the holy Sabotte [orig. *sancti Sabbati*]. **1596** SHAKS. *Merch. V.* IV. i. 36 By our holy Sabbath haue I sworne To haue the due and forfeit of my bond. **1649** JER. TAYLOR *Gt. Exemp.* II. Disc. ix. 119 The Primitive Church kept both the Sabbath and the Lords day. **1727-41** CHAMBERS *Cycl.* s.v. *Week*, The Days of the Week were denominated by the Jews, from the order of their succession from the sabbath. **1871** R. W. DALE *Commandm.* iv. 106 The Christian Sunday and the Jewish Sabbath are absolutely different institutions.

β. **13..** *Cursor M.* 11987 (Gött.) Apon þar sabaoth þus he did. *c* **1520** NISBET *N. Test. in Scots* (S.T.S.) I. 11[Jesus] Healith the ydropysie vponn the sabaothe. *c* **1610** *Women Saints* 171 Of the Iewes, hating Circumcision, yet with them keeping their Sabaoth. **1658** PHILLIPS, *Sabaoth*,.. a celebration of the seventh day of the week.

b. Since the Reformation, often applied to 'the Lord's day', i.e. the first day of the week (Sunday) observed by Christians in commemoration of the resurrection of Christ. This use was originally connected with the opinion that the sabbatic law of the Decalogue remains in force under the Christian dispensation, the date of the 'Sabbath' having by Divine appointment been changed from Saturday to Sunday; but it occasionally appears in writers who did not hold this view. In Scotland it is still very common. (Phrases as in 1 a.)

The notion that the Lord's day is a 'Christian Sabbath', or, more commonly (as in quot. 1340 under a) a substitute for the Sabbath, occurs in theological writings from the 4th c. onwards, but was not popularly current before the Reformation. In English, *Sabbath* as a synonym for 'Sunday' did not become common till the 17th century.

[*c* **1440**: see SABBATH-DAY.]

α. **1509** BARCLAY *Ship of Fools* (1874) II. 175 Amonge the whiche preceptis this was one The sabbot to Worshyp and sanctyfy alway The seuenth day of the weke called the sonday. **1594** SHAKS. *Rich. III*, III. ii. 113 *Hast.*... Come the next Sabboth, and I will content you. *Priest.* Ile wait vpon your Lordship. **1607** HIERON *Wks.* I. 150 Thou art laboured with from sabboth to sabboth.. that thou maist be prepared for Christ. **1654** TRAPP *Comm. Ps.* xxiv. Introd., The first day of the week.. which is now the Christian Sabboth. **1717** *Wodrow Corr.* (1843) II. 237 Mr. John Adamson, Sabbath was fortnight, intruded on the ministry. **1809** SYD. SMITH *Serm.* I. 74 Prayer should be offered up eminently, and emphatically.. on the Sabbath. **1863** HAWTHORNE *Our Old Home* II. 100 Severe and sunless remembrances of the Sabbaths of childhood. **1888** *Ch. Times* 9 Nov. 977/2 The British Sabbath is now-a-days always on its trial. **1897** *Q. Rev.* Jan. 66 The term Sabbath as applied to the Lord's Day is unknown to the Articles, the Canons, and the Prayer-book of the Church of England.

β. **1583** STUBBES *Anat. Abus.* I. Pref. (1879) 11 To the prophanation of the Lord his sabaoth. **1591** SYLVESTER *Du Bartas* I. ii. 940 Common Blaspheming of God's Name in Oaths: Usuall profaning of his Sabbaoths. **1621** ELSING *Debates Ho. Lords* (Camden) 3 The Bill for Sabaoth.

c. *gen.* Applied occas. to the day of the week set apart for rest or worship by any religious body, e.g. to the Friday as observed by Muslims.

1613 PURCHAS *Pilgrimage* (1614) Table, Sabath.. of Saracens on Friday..; of Peguans on Monday. **1704** J. PITTS *Acc. Mohammetans* 42 Friday is their Sabbath, or Gemahgune.

d. Applied to the sabbatical year of the Israelites.

1382 Wyclif *Lev.* xxv. 4 The seuenthe forsothe ȝeer of the loond shal be the saboth of the restynge of the Lord. [So in later versions.]

2. *transf.* and *fig.* A time or period of rest; a cessation from labour, trouble, pain and the like.

α. **1591** Sylvester *Du Bartas* i. vii. 446 He would, this Sabbath should a figure be Of the blest Sabbath of Eternity. **1611** Bible *Heb.* iv. 9 There remaineth therefore a rest [*marg.* keeping of a Sabbath] to the people of God. **1681** Dryden *Abs. & Achit.* 913 He..safe enjoys the Sabbath of his Toils. **1737** Pope *Hor. Ep.* i. i. 3 Why will you break the Sabbath of my days? **1795** Southey *Pauper's Funeral* 8 Yes, I will weep; but not that thou art come To the cold sabbath of the silent tomb. **1854** Neale *Hymn*, '*Oh, what the joy*', Those endless Sabbaths the blessed ones see. **1860** Tyndall *Glac.* i. ii. 20 It was Sunday, and the scene was itself a Sabbath, with no sound to disturb its perfect rest.

β. **1398** Trevisa *Barth. De P.R.* ix. xxviii. (1495) 364 Whan we come to the Sabaoth of endles rest thenne we shall haue joye. **1598** Sylvester *Du Bartas* ii. ii. iv. *Columnes* 132 Th'eternall sacred Sabbaoth. **1610** G. Fletcher *Christ's Vict.* i. vi, To keep an everlasting Sabbaoths rest.

3. A midnight meeting of demons, sorcerers and witches, presided over by the Devil, supposed in mediæval times to have been held annually as an orgy or festival. Often more explicitly ***witches' sabbath***. Also Sabbat.

α. **1660** F. Brooke tr. *Le Blanc's Trav.* 312 Divers Sorcerers..have confessed that in their Sabbaths,..they feed on such fare. **1735** Pope *Ep. Lady* 239 As Hags hold Sabbaths, less for joy than spite, So these their merry, miserable Night. **1860** J. A. Hessey *Bampton Lect.* 399 Here malignant spirits have held their sabbath or hellish revelries. **1883** *Harper's Mag.* 831/2 It might have been..a veritable Witches' Sabbath.

β. **1857** B. Taylor *North. Trav.* xi. 115 It would be far more picturesque to describe a sabaoth of Lapland witches than a prayer-meeting of shouting converts.

4. *attrib.* and *Comb.*: simple attrib., as ***Sabbath devotion, dress, evening, morning, music, rite, season, service, sound, tide, work***; ***Sabbath-dark, Sabbath-like*** adjs.; objective and objective genitive, as ***Sabbath-breach*** (*rare*$^{-1}$), ***-breaker, -breaking*** sb. and adj., ***-keeper, -keeping*** sb. and adj. Also **Sabbath candle**, a candle lit shortly before dusk on the eve of the Jewish Sabbath; †**Sabbath-ceased** *a.*, discontinued during the Sabbath; **Sabbath goy** [goy], a Gentile who performs for Orthodox Jews tasks forbidden to the latter on the Sabbath; = *Shabbos-goy* s.v. Shabbos b; **Sabbath lamp**, a lamp lit on the eve of the Jewish Sabbath; **Sabbath loaf**, a plaited loaf eaten on the eve of the Jewish Sabbath; **Sabbath school**, (*a*) = Sunday-school; (*b*) a Jewish school held on the Saturday for giving religious instruction to children.

1784 Cowper *Task* iv. 653 To show at home By lewdness, idleness, and *sabbath-breach, The great proficiency he made abroad. **1607** Hieron *Wks.* I. 234 It cutteth the *sabboth-breaker, to heare his prophanenesse still cried out vpon. **1738** *Gentl. Mag.* VIII. 658/2 The excellent Laws against Tippling Houses, Tipplers, Sabbath-Breakers, &c. **1853** Card. Wiseman *Ess.* I. 636 They tax Papists..with being habitual Sabbath-breakers. **1651** *Petition* in *Proc. Parl.* No. 85. 1304 Acts past against Blasphemies, prophan cursing and swearing, *Sabbath breaking, &c. **1714** Mandeville *Fab. Bees* (1733) I. 92 In the commission of the peace,..he becomes.. the..constant plague to sabbath-breaking butchers. **1769** Blackstone *Comm.* IV. 63 Profanation of the lord's day, or sabbath-breaking. **1815** Mills & Smith *Rep. Missionary Tour* 29 Sabbath-breaking, profanity and intemperance prevail [in New Orleans] to a fearful extent. **1918** H. G. Wells *Joan & Peter* v. 96 Secularists and socialists..planned..to..plunge the whole world into vice and rapine and Sabbath-breaking. **1958** B. Hamilton *Too Much of Water* iii. 59 Charity can do without help from the proceeds of vice and Sabbath-breaking. **1978** P. Bailey *Leisure & Class in Victorian Eng.* ii. 39 Certain magistrates..prosecuted sabbath-breaking cricket players. **1892** I. Zangwill *Children of Ghetto* I. viii. 191 She, at least, would never fail to light the *Sabbath candles. **1967** *Listener* 20 July 83/3 My mother..stopped lighting the Sabbath candles..but still spoke as constantly to God. **1593** Nashe *Christ's T.* 30 Theyr vnrespited, and not so much as *Saboth-ceased blood-shed. **1945** Dylan Thomas *Let.* 30 July (1966) 280, I went to the Edwinsford Arms, a *sabbath-dark bar. **1613** Zouch *Dove* To Rdr. E6b, Poetry..in which diuers haue shewed their thoughts not vnfit for solemne, yea *Sabaoth deuotions. **1825** J. Wilson *Poems* II. 94 Smiling in their *Sabbath-dress. **1977** H. Kaplan *Damascus Cover* (1978) iv. 35 Girls in white Sabbath dresses laced with colored embroidery. **1820** Southey *Wesley* II. 87 Having..spent a *sabbath evening at an inn. **1977** *Listener* 24 Mar. 382/3, I was a *Sabbath *goy*; that is, for a penny or two, I lighted fires and performed other chores forbidden to orthodox Jews on Saturday, or Friday evening. **1977** *Times* 8 June 4/3 My host had been a sabbath *goy*, that is he had lighted fires for the orthodox on the sabbath. **1854** Neale *Hymn*, '*Oh, what the joy*', There dawns no Sabbath,—no Sabbath is o'er; These *Sabbath-keepers have one, and no more. **1643** W. Walwyn *Power of Love* 32 Men are not pleased except salvation be proved to be very difficult to bee obtained, it must still depend either on our beleeving.., or repenting,..or *Sabbath-keeping,..or else man is not pleased. **1832** F. Trollope *Domestic Manners of Americans* I. xviii. 284 The waiving the sabbath-keeping by the proprietor, was for his own convenience. **1897** Mary Kingsley *W. Africa* 403 His rigid Sabbath-keeping. **1850** G. Aguilar *Vale of Cedars* xxxiv. 281 It was..the Sabbath eve... The *Sabbath lamps were lighted. **1892** I. Zangwill *Children of Ghetto* I. v. 139 For three things a woman dies in childbirth, for not separating the dough, for not lighting the Sabbath lamps, for not ——. **1824** Miss Mitford *Village* Ser. i. 28 A *sabbath-like pause of work and play, rare on a work-day. **1878** B. Harte *Man on Beach* 74 An almost Sabbath-like stillness prevailed. **1892** I. Zangwill *Children of Ghetto* II. xviii. 79 The *Sabbath loaves shaped like boys' tip-cats—with a curious plait of crust from point to point, and thickly sprinkled with a drift of poppy-seed, and covered with a velvet cloth embroidered with Hebrew words. **1951** L. W. Leonard *Jewish Cookery* v. 26 *Challah*, in twist form or Biblical beehive coil, is the Sabbath loaf of white bread. It is customary to place two *challas* under a special napkin... The two loaves are symbolic of the 'two portions of manna' which fell for the Sabbath. **1972** H. Kemelman *Monday Rabbi took Off* xlvii. 271 The candles were already lit and the table set with the two braided Sabbath loaves. **1863** Geo. Eliot in Cross *Life* (1885) II. 355 Your letter was a welcome addition to our sunshine this *Sabbath morning. **1807** Wordsw. *White Doe* vii. 1761 When the bells of Rylstone played Their *sabbath music—'*God us ayde*'. **1784** Cowper *Task* i. 746 Till *sabbath-rites Have dwindled into unrespected forms. **1820** *Rec. Early Hist. Boston* (1909) XXXIX. 131 The application for liberty to use the Boylston school house on Fort hill for a *Sabbath school..was granted. **1832** W. D. Williamson *Hist. State of Maine* III. 688 *Sabbath-schools*..[were established] in Philadelphia, about 1811, and have since spread over the United States. **1845** R. W. Hamilton *Pop. Educ.* vi. (ed. 2) 133 The Sabbath school generally supplies the sanctuary with its most intelligent hearers. **1866** J. C. Gregg *Life in Army* 209 It was sung by the colored Sabbath School children. **1900** *Congress. Rec.* 23 Jan. 1104/2 A wonderful petition is rolled in..from Sabbath schools, sectarian churches, and societies. **1864** Skeat *Uhland's Poems* 14 Nature's *Sabbath-season reigns. **1617** Hieron *Wks.* II. 365 John..neglected not the spirituall part of the *sabbath-seruice, though hee was restrained from the outward. **1855** Longf. *My Lost Youth* 49 The early loves Come back with a *sabbath sound. **1945** J. Betjeman *New Bats in Old Belfries* 48 And so my thoughts this happy *Sabbathtide. **1625** Bacon *Ess.*, *Truth* (Arb.) 500 His *Sabbath Worke, euer since, is the Illumination of his Spirit.

Sabbathaism (sæbə'θeɪɪz(ə)m). [f. *Sabbathai* + -ism.] The doctrines of Sabbathai Zebi (Heb. *Shabbᵉthai Çᵉbī*), a false Messiah born at Smyrna A.D. 1626.

1882-3 *Schaff's Encycl. Relig. Knowl.* II. 1129 Two Polish rabbis, who travelled extensively to propagate Sabbathaism.

Sabbatharian (ˌsæbə'θɛərɪən). *Hist.* [f. Sabbath + -arian. Cf. Sabbatarian.]

a. = Sabbatarian *sb.* 3. **b.** A member of the religious sect founded by Joanna Southcott in 1801–14.

1719 Ozell tr. *Misson's Mem. & Observ.* 235 These Sabbatharians are so call'd because they will not remove the Day of Rest from Saturday to Sunday. **1882-3** *Schaff's Encycl. Relig. Knowl.* III. 2089 Sabbatharians or New Israelites,..a religious sect founded by Joanna Southcott.

Sabbatharie, -y, variant forms of Sabbatary.

ˌSabbath-'day. Forms: (see Sabbath).

1. a. = Sabbath 1 a.

a **1300-1400** *Cursor M.* 17355 (Laud) After that sabot-day was gon Thedir come they euery-chon. *c* **1380** Wyclif *Wks.* (1880) 58 He helid a sik man vpon þe sabaat day. **1432-50** tr. *Higden* (Rolls) IV. 327 Whiche peple keped theire Sabbatte day [orig. *Sabbatum*], and hade hyt in so grete veneracion, that thei wolde not ordeyne meyte þat day. **1534** More *Treat. Passion* Wks. 1308/1 So do..their sabbot dayes begynne in the euenyng, and endure to the euenynge folowynge. **1562** Cooper *Answ. Def. Truth* ix. 75 By necessitie of their enemies constreined they [*sc.* the Jews].. fought on the Sabboth day. *c* **1610** *Women Saints* 156 He.. with the Iewes kept the Saboth day,..yet refused Circumcision. **1709** J. Johnson *Clergym. Vade M.* ii. 104 Christians must not Judaize and rest on the Sabbath-day; but work on that very day; and give the preference to the Lord's day. **1726** J. Henley *Prim. Liturgy* 10 Feasts, are all Lords-days, all Sabbath-days, or Saturdays [etc.].

b. ***Sabbath day's journey***: the distance (2,000 *ammōth* or 'ells' = 1225 yards) which (according to Rabbinical prescription in the time of Christ) was the utmost limit of permitted travel on the Sabbath.

1526 Tindale *Acts* i. 12 Mount olivete which is neye to Jerusalem..conteynynge a saboth dayes iorney. **1628** Earle *Microcosm.*, *Shee Precise Hypocr.* (Arb.) 63 Her oftest Gossipings are Sabaoth-dayes iourneyes.

2. = Sabbath 1 b.

The first two quots. may perhaps not be rightly placed here, as it was the common view that the commandment 'to keep holy the Sabbath-day', in its Christian interpretation, related to the festivals of the Church in general, and not to Sunday only or eminently.

c **1440** *Gesta Rom.* x. 30 (Harl. MS.) Hope we hit is our lord ihesu crist, þe which hath ordeyned for lawe, þat ech man shold kepe þe saboth day. **1513** Bradshaw *St. Werburge* ii. 879 A woman which brake the commaundement Of god and holy churche hye sabbot-day dyd violate Vnlaufully wurkynge. **1575** Laneham *Let.* (1871) 12 On sunday: the forenoon occupied (az for the Sabot day) in quiet and vacation from woork, & in diuine seruis. **1605** *Vestry Bks.* (Surtees) 284 There shall be no meetinge as concerning any business about upon the Sabbath day. **1651** *St. Andrews, Newcastle-on-Tyne Par. Reg.* in *N. & Q.* 8th Ser. I. 223 Robard Fenwick..which was drowned in the Bares myll dam wher he went to swim on the Saboth day. **1715** De Foe *Fam. Instruct.* i. iii. (1841) I. 63 As soon as they come home next Sabbath-day from the sermon. **1810** Wordsw. *Prose Wks.* (1876) II. 33 The sensations of pious cheerfulness, which attend the celebration of the sabbath-day in rural places. **1830-2** Carleton *Traits Irish Peasantry* (1860) I. 146 (*Priest*) On the Sabbath day too, without my leave!

3. = Sabbath 1 c.

1704 J. Pitts *Acc. Mohammetans* 42 The *Hattech*, i.e. a Priest which is above the *Emaum*, officiates on their Sabbath-day.

4. *gen.* A Sabbath, day of sacred rest.

1755 Pope *Prol. Sat.* 12 No place is sacred, not the Church is free; Ev'n Sunday shines no Sabbath-day to me.

Sabbathine ('sæbəθaɪn), *a.* [f. Sabbath + -ine¹.] Affecting or pertaining to the Sabbath.

1850 T. M'Crie *Mem. Sir A. Agnew* viii. (1852) 194 The Sabbathine rules enjoin the Sons of Abraham to prepare for the Feast, by laying in a stock of provisions the day before.

sabbathize ('sæbəθaɪz), *v.* [Altered form of sabbatize after Sabbath.] *intr.* To observe or keep a Sabbath or period of rest.

1609 Bible (Douay) *1 Esdras* i. 58 The land quietly kept her sabbathes, al the time of her desolation she sabbathized in the application of seventie yeares. **1621** Ainsworth *Annot. Pentat.* Gen. ii. 2 Rested: or Sabbathised, that is, kept Sabbath. **1633** W. Struther *True Happiness* 75 This dwelling in God is our spiritual sabbathizing, the type of the eternall. **1705** Hickeringill *Priest-cr.* i. Wks. 1716 III. 52 The Solemn League and Covenant..Mr. Knox did..bring into Scotland, where it is rampant to this day, and more rigid than the Inquisition in Spain, with the additional Bigotism of Sabbathising.

Sabbathless ('sæbəθlɪs), *a.* [f. Sabbath + -less.] Observing no Sabbath.

1605 Bacon *Adv. Learn.* ii. xxiii. §46 This incessant and Sabbathlesse pursuite of a mans fortune leaueth not tribute which we owe to God of our time. *a* **1656** Hales *Gold. Rem.* (1688) 178 Prayer itself is Sabbathless, and admits no rest, no intermission at all. **1820** Lamb *Sonn.*, '*Who first invented work*', Sabbathless Satan! he who his unglad Task ever plies. **1888** *Pall Mall G.* 31 Oct. 2/2 In 1885 Austria-Hungary in response to the bitter cry of Sabbathless toilers enacted a stringent Sunday law.

Sabbathly ('sæbəθlɪ), *a.* [f. Sabbath + -ly¹.] Recurring every Sabbath.

1822 Galt *Sir A. Wylie* III. xvii. 139 It was a Sabbathly theme of regret.

'Sabbathly, *adv.* [f. Sabbath + -ly².]

1. Every Sabbath; Sabbath by Sabbath. *Sc.*

1627 in Cramond *Ann. Banff* (1893) II. 34 Their absenceis fra the Kirk Sabbothlie at the direction of the bailyies and elderis. **1671** *Rec. Presbyt. Inverness* 29 Mar. (S.H.S. 1896) 9 They were refreshed very much by him Sabbathly. **1820** *Blackw. Mag.* VII. 467 As the Rev. Mr. F——..Sabbathly says, in the peroration of his sermons.

2. In a manner befitting the Sabbath.

1891 C. James *Rom. Rigmarole* 110 The Squire was Sabbathly solemn and imposing.

sabbatia (sæ'beɪʃɪə). Also **sabatia**. [mod.L. (M. Adanson *Familles des Plantes* (1763) II. 503 as *Sabatia*), f. the name of Constantino and Liberato Sabbati, 18th-cent. Italian botanists + -ia¹.] An annual or perennial herb of the genus so called, belonging to the family Gentianaceæ, native to eastern North America, and bearing clusters of pink or white flowers.

1814 *Curtis's Bot. Mag.* XXXIX. 1600 (*heading*) Dichotomous sabbatia. **1847** W. Darlington *Agric. Bot.* 260 Angular sabbatia. Centaury. **1902** L. H. Bailey *Cycl. Amer. Hort.* IV. 1594/2 Sabbatias require a light, sweet soil. **1949** *Natural Hist.* June 278/3 On grassy, pine-sprinkled savannas, in the company of gaudy sabbatias, insignificant burmannias, and orange habenarias. **1972** F. Perry *Flowers of World* 123/1 *Sabatia* (*Sabbatia*) are annual or biennial [*sic*] plants from North America with erect branching stems. .. The plants contain a bitter principle and when dried are used as a tonic.

Sabbatian (sæ'beɪʃɪən), *sb.*¹ [f. *Sabbati-us* (see below) + -an.] A member of a sect founded by Sabbatius (originally a convert from Judaism), who seceded from the Novatianists before 380, having adopted Quartodeciman views.

1708-22 Bingham *Orig. Eccles.* xx. iii. §5 The Marcianists ..kept the Sabbath also a fast. So did also the Sabbatians, Lampetians [etc.]. **1727-41** Chambers *Cycl.* s.v., The Sabbatians are recorded by ecclesiastical historians, as having a great abhorrence of the left-hand. **1882-3** *Schaff's Encycl. Relig. Knowl.* III. 2090 By his followers, the Sabbatians, he was honored as a martyr.

Sabbatian (sæ'beɪʃɪən), *a.* and *sb.*² [f. **Sabbatius* (mod.L. form of *Shabbethai*: see Sabbathaism) + -an.]

A. *adj.* Pertaining to Sabbathaism.

1892 tr. *Grätz's Hist. Jews* V. 151 The Sabbatian mystics. **1941** G. G. Scholem *Major Trends in Jewish Mysticism* viii. 284 The swift rise and the sudden collapse of the Sabbatian movement in 1665 and 1666, from Sabbatai Zevi's proclamation of his messianic mission to his renunciation of Judaism. **1974** *Times Lit. Suppl.* 20 Sept. 1024/5 The seventeenth-century mystical Messiah, Sabbatai Sevi (1626–1676), and the Sabbatian heresy named after him.

B. *sb.* A believer in Sabbathaism.

1892 tr. *Grätz's Hist. Jews* V. 159 At Venice..a quarrel broke out between the Sabbatians and their opponents. **1974** *Encycl. Brit. Micropædia* IX. 99/1 A sect of Muslim Sabbatians—the Dönme of Salonika—survived him [*sc.* Shabbetai Tzevi]. **1977** *N.Y. Rev. Bks.* 14 Apr. 27/1 The antinomian energies of the Sabbatians..did in fact feed the subsequent currents of enlightenment and reform in Western Europe.

Hence **Sa'bbatianism** = Sabbathaism.

1892 tr. *Grätz's Hist. Jews* V. Index, Sabbatianism, revival of, v. 219. **1898** Zangwill *Dreamers Ghetto* vi. 205 Sabbatianism did not play much part in my early life. **1941**

G. G. SCHOLEM *Major Trends in Jewish Mysticism* viii. 297 Sabbatianism as a movement was long identified with its more extreme, antinomian and nihilistic aspects. **1977** *N.Y. Rev. Bks.* 14 Apr. 28/1 The way was thus prepared for the mighty swell of Sabbatianism.

sabbatic (sæˈbætɪk), *a.* and *sb.* Also **Sabbatic.** [ad. F. *sabbatique* (= Sp. *sabático*, Pg., It. *sabbatico*), ad. med.L. **sabbaticus*, a. Gr. σαββατικός, f. σάββατ-ον SABBATH: see -IC.] **A.** *adj.* **a.** Of or pertaining to the Sabbath; resembling or appropriate to the Sabbath. ***sabbatic year*** = *sabbatical year* (SABBATICAL *a.* 2 a).

1649 JER. TAYLOR *Gt. Exemp.* II. Disc. ix. 119 Strict and necessary rest..was one great part of the Sabbatick rites. **1650** *Vind. Hammond's Addr.* §16. 6 The servant..is to be set free from that servitude..in the seventh, or sabbatick year. **1660** JER. TAYLOR *Duct. Dubit.* II. ii. rule vi. §46 They kept their first Sabbatick rest upon the very day in which their redemption was completed. *a* **1711** KEN *Preparatives* Poet. Wks. 1721 IV. 30 Sabbatick Dawn, a Priest of old, By sound of Trumpet told. **1737** WHISTON *Josephus, War* VII. v. §1 They call it the sabbatick river. **1861** LEWIN *Jerusalem* 87 Provisions in the little garrison from the effect of the sabbatic year, began to run short. **1882** J. PARKER *Apost. Life* I. 99 Grant Sabbatic peace to every soul.

b. = SABBATICAL *a.* 2 c. *rare.*

1905 *N.Y. Even. Post* 23 Sept. 8 Professors Hull and Durham are spending their sabbatic year in Europe. **1970** *Newslet. Amer. Dial. Soc.* Nov. 7 Budget requests may include..up to two-thirds of sabbatic, academic, or other leave pay offered by an applicant's institution.

†**B.** *sb.* A sabbatic year. *Obs.*

1650 *Vind. Hammond's Addr.* §16. 6 The Jubilee, which is the great Sabbatick (made up of seven times seven).

sabbatical (sæˈbætɪkəl), *a.* and *sb.* Also with cap. initial and 8 **sabbathical.** [f. mod.L. **sabbatic-us* (see SABBATIC *a.* and *sb.*) + -AL[1].]

A. *adj.* **1.** Pertaining to or appropriate to the Sabbath.

1645 *City Alarum* 20 The formerly mentioned are but our working dayes abuses, now followes our seventh and Sabbaticall errour, wherein we seeme to rest. **1799** CORRY *Sat. Lond.* (1803) 94 The Curate is so far from being prepared for his sabbatical avocation, that he is engaged during the week in some worldly pursuit. **1849** H. MILLER *Footpr. Creat.* xv. (1874) 295 It seems, besides, to throw light on the prominence of the Sabbatical command. **1877** MRS. OLIPHANT *Carita* II. xxxi. 291 This, too, was a kind of solemn sabbatical exercise. **1892** A. BIRRELL *Res Judic.* ii. 38 A sabbatical calm results from the contemplation of his labours.

b. ***Sabbatical river***: an imaginary river celebrated in Jewish legend, which was said to observe the Sabbath. Similarly ***Sabbatical pool***: see quot. 1649.

The legend of the 'sabbatical river' existed in two discrepant forms: cf. quots. 1671 (after Josephus) and 1849.

1613 PURCHAS *Pilgrimage* (1614) 519 This was the issue of their Pilgrimage to the Sabbaticall streame, which they supposed to finde in this Persian Gulfe. **1649** JER. TAYLOR *Gt. Exemp.* III. xiv. 51 The sabbaticall pool in Judea, which was dry six dayes, but gushed out in a full stream upon the sabbath. **1671** STILLINGFL. *Serm.* viii. (1673) 151 The famous Sabbatical River..which for 6. days bear's all before it..: the admirable nature of that River is, that it keeps the Sabbath and rests all that day. **1849** LONGF. *Kavanagh* XI. (1857) 221 And must my life, then, be always like the Sabbatical river of the Jews, flowing in full stream only on the seventh day?

c. Of the nature of a Sabbath or period of rest.

1836 SIR H. TAYLOR *Statesman* xi. 79 It were to be wished that he should set apart from business, not only a sabbatical day in each week, but if it be possible a sabbatical hour in each day!

2. a. ***sabbatical year***: the seventh year, prescribed by the Mosaic law to be observed as a 'Sabbath' in which the land was to remain untilled and all debtors and Israelitish slaves were to be released. Also *allusively*.

1599 PONT *Right Reckoning of Years* 2 These Sabbaticall yeares. **1635–56** COWLEY *Davideis* II. Note 8 From hence contracts, and the account of Sabbatical years and Jubilees bare date. **1705** HICKERINGILL *Priest-cr.* I. Wks. 1716 III. 24 Neither Seventh Days..nor Sabbath Days, nor Sabbathical Years..is now any more obligatory to us. **1828** E. IRVING *Last Days* p. viii, May it prove unto us as a sabbatical year of rest!

b. ***sabbatical millenary, millennium***: the last of the seven thousands of years which (on the analogy of the seven days of the creation) were supposed to form the destined term of the world's existence.

1646 SIR T. BROWNE *Pseud. Ep.* VI. i. 278 He conceaveth the Elementall frame shall end in the seventh or Sabbaticall millenary. **1814** J. CHRISTIE *Ess. Early Idol.* 11 The supposed continuance of this earth as many thousand years, the last thousand of which, it was reported, would be a Sabbatical Millenium.

c. orig. *U.S.* Designating a period of leave from duty granted to university teachers at certain intervals (orig. every seven years) for the purposes of study and travel; *spec.* in ***sabbatical year*** (cf. sense 2 a). Now freq. used *transf.* of rest or absence from other occupations, professions, or activities. Also ***sabbatical officer***, one granted sabbatical leave (from work or study) for the performance of a certain office.

[**1880** *Ann. Rep. Pres. & Treas. of Harvard Coll.* *1879–1880* 19 The Corporation adopted, on the 31st of May, 1880, new rules with regard to leave of absence for professors and assistant professors... The Corporation have decided that they will grant occasional leave of absence for one year on half-pay, provided that no professor have such leave oftener than once in seven years.] **1886** E. N. HORSFORD *Scheme adopted by Trustees, Wellesley Coll.* 8 To each of the heads of the above departments the Sabbatical Grant contemplates that every seventh year of her academic service from a given date, she shall be eligible to have..a year's leave of absence, to be passed in Europe, and with it her half-yearly salary. If for any reason an eligible officer declines the Sabbatical Year, the grant in her case may be offered to another equally eligible. **1892** W. JAMES *Let.* 13 July (1920) I. 321 Only why talk of 'sabbatical' years? **1905** *N.Y. Even. Post* 23 Sept. 8 Professors Allinson, Sears and Hill are spending their sabbatical year of absence in foreign travel and study. **1926** B. RUSSELL *On Education* III. xviii. 242 Every university teacher ought to have a Sabbatical year (one in every seven) to be spent in foreign universities or in otherwise acquiring knowledge of what is being done abroad. **1949** *Time* 18 Dec. 12/2 Kennan announced that he was leaving the State Department 'on sabbatical leave'. **1962** *Times* 12 Apr. 18/2 The break-up of his subsequent marriage impels him to escape from England and to spend a 'sabbatical year' in travel. **1972** *Nature* 4 Feb. 277/2 On sabbatical leave from the Department of Therapeutic Research, University of Pennsylvania School of Medicine. **1976** *Postmaster* (Merton Coll., Oxf.) 30 A union of university students, with clearly defined objectives, and with no sabbatical officers. **1976** *Gramophone* Apr. 1575/3 I'm doing it on May 9th with Rostropovich in the last concert before I take off a sabbatical year, promised to my wife when I reached sixty.

B. *sb.* A period of sabbatical leave; a sabbatical year (cf. sense 2 c above). Freq. in phr. ***on (a) sabbatical.***

1934 in WEBSTER. **1946** H. HOWE *We Happy Few* 18 Then when Papa had his sabbatical, we went to Paris. **1958** *Manch. Guardian* 7 June 1/6 Parliament will be reconstituted after a six-month sabbatical. **1961** *Harper's Bazaar* Dec. 47/2 The ultimate in holidays is the 'sabbatical', a term which business is taking over from the academic world. **1978** L. HEREN *Growing up on The Times* iii. 102 Pat found a furnished flat, which belonged to an academic on a sabbatical in the United States.

Hence **saˈbbatically** *adv.*, **saˈbbaticalness.**

1727 BAILEY vol. II., *Sabbaticalness*, the Being of the Nature or Quality of a Sabbath. **1847** DISRAELI *Tancred* II. xv, He sabbatically abstains from the debate or the rubber.

Sabbatine (ˈsæbətaɪn), *a. Hist.* [ad. med.L. *sabbatīn-us* (and Sp. *sabatino*), f. *sabbat-um* SABBATH, Saturday.]

a. ***Sabbatine preacher***: one appointed to preach on Saturdays. **b.** ***Sabbatine bull***: a bull of Pope John XXII, proclaiming, as a reward for the wearing of the scapular, a plenary indulgence available on the first Saturday after the death of him who gains it. So ***Sabbatine indulgence.***

1674 BREVINT *Saul & Sam.* xiii. 281 Sabbatine bull. **1772** NUGENT tr. *Hist. Fr. Gerund* I. 437 Friar Gerund appeared a Priest *in facie ecclesiæ*, and Sabatine Preacher in full form. **1826** T. COLEMAN *Indulgences*, etc., *Order Mt. Carmel* 15 That the so celebrated name of the Sabbatine Bull might not be forgotten. **1886** *Month* Dec. 473 The second of these privileges..is..the Sabbatine Indulgence. It is a plenary.. Indulgence..available on the first Saturday after the death of him who gains it, releasing him then and there from Purgatory and admitting him straightway to the joys of Heaven.

Sabbatism (ˈsæbətɪz(ə)m). *rare.* [ad. late L. *sabbatismus*, Gr. σαββατισμός, n. of action f. σαββατίζειν to keep the Sabbath, f. σάββατ-ον SABBATH: see -ISM.]

1. A sabbatical rest: in allusions to Heb. iv. 9.

1582 N.T. (Rhem.) *Heb.* iv. 9 Therefore there is left a sabbatisme [Vulg. *sabbatismus*, Gr. σαββατισμός; *Wycl.* 1382 a saboth halowynge; 1611 a rest; 1881 *Revised* a sabbath rest] for the people of God. **1647** J. COTTON *Sing. Ps.* iii. 11 There is now remaining to us another Sabbatisme, or day of rest, now in the dayes of the Gospel, different from the seventh day of rest. **1886** S. COX *Expositions* II. xxvii. 376 This Divine sabbatism, this pure eternal rest.

2. The formal observance of the Sabbath.

1611 BROUGHTON *Require of Agreement* 13 In the Iubilee the Maiestie of God will be a remission, and redemption, and ending of Sabbatisme to Israell. *a* **1711** KEN *Preparatives* Poet. Wks. 1721 IV. 29 Sabbatism. To a Seventh Day God Jews restrain'd, For Joy, Rest, Praise ordain'd. **1879** FARRAR *St. Paul* (1883) 117 Sabbatism had been elevated above faith and purity.

Hence **Sabbaˈtismal** *a.*, characterized by holy rest.

1881 J. C. BURNS in *I. Bruce's Serm.* Biog. 102 Very peaceful, Sabbatismal, these years were.

Sabbatist (ˈsæbətɪst). [f. L. *sabbat-um* SABBATH + -IST.] = SABBATARIAN.

1857 BADEN POWELL *Chr. without Judaism* 161 Some Sabbatists..keep holy the seventh day of the week. **1865** J. GILL tr. *Bovet's Banished Count* xxi. 222 The Sabbatists observed the Seventh day of the week instead of the first.

sabbatization (sæbətaɪˈzeɪʃən). [f. next + -ATION.] The action of sabbatizing:

a. Observance of the Sabbath, Sabbath-keeping. **b.** The conversion (of Sunday) into a Sabbath.

1644 LAUD *Troub. & Tryal* xxxv. (1695) 345 Those Men who stand so strictly upon the Morality of the Sabbath, do by a gross and carnal Sabbatization, three times out-go the Superstition of the Jew. **1827** G. S. FABER *Orig. Expiat. Sacr.* 202 He actually mentions the non-sabbatisation of the patriarchal religionists as a circumstance quite indisputable. **1882** *Ch. Times* 11 Aug. 544 The Sabbatization of Sunday came in comparatively late.

sabbatize (ˈsæbətaɪz), *v.* Also SABBATHIZE. [ad. L. *sabbatīz-āre*, ad. Gr. σαββατίζειν, f. σάββατον SABBATH: see -IZE. Cf. F. *sabbatiser.*]

1. *intr.* To keep the Sabbath; to observe a specified day as a day of rest.

1608 WILLET *Hexapla Exod.* 247 They are also commanded to keepe the Sabbaths rest, to Sabbatize. *a* **1716** BLACKALL *Wks.* (1723) I. 214 We do not so Sabbatise as we should do, if we give only one Day of the Week to God, and the other six Days to the Devil. **1881** BLACKIE *Lay Serm.* ii. 105 A Samaritan..made it a point..in whatever attitude the first moment of the day had found him, in that position to remain..: if sitting, then to Sabbatise in the sitting attitude.

b. *fig.* To enjoy or undergo a period of rest analogous to a Sabbath.

1382 WYCLIF *1 Esdras* i. 58 Al the time of ther forsaking he [*i.e.* the land] sabatisede, in the apliyng of seuenti ȝer. **1596** BELL *Surv. Popery* I. III. v. 109 Although the minde regenerate do sabbatize in the Lord. **1625** GILL *Sacr. Philos.* II. 140 But if there were no incarnation..neither our understanding, nor our sences could have any object wherein to rest and sabbatize. *a* **1711** KEN *Edmund* Poet. Wks. 1721 II. 89 It was the Day which Jesus canoniz'd, When he from all his Dolours sabbatiz'd.

2. *trans.* To observe or keep as a Sabbath; to assimilate to a Sabbath.

1609 BIBLE (Douay) *Lev.* xxv. 2 Thou shalt sabbatize the sabbath to the Lord. **1880** *W. Smith's Dict. Chr. Antiq.* II. 1052/2 The tendency to sabbatize the Lord's day is due chiefly to the necessities of legal enforcement. **1906** H. BEGBIE *Priest* xvi. 256 Silvia is inclined to Sabbatize the week-days.

†**3.** To give sabbatical rest to. *Obs. rare*[−1].

1701 BEVERLEY *Apoc. Quest.* 8 For the Type is Sacrifice Honourably Sabbatiz'd, and at Rest in the Antitype, Our Lord Jesus Christ, our great Sacrifice Sabbatizing All Sacrifice by the sacrifice of Himself.

Hence **ˈsabbatizing** *vbl. sb.* Also **ˈsabbatizer,** in quot. one who observes the Jewish Sabbath.

1613 PURCHAS *Pilgrimage* (1614) 122 The Jewes on their Sabbaths..did vse..to drink somwhat more largely (a Sabbatising too much, by too many Christians imitated). **1683** HICKES *Case Inf. Bapt.* 61 Let the Adversaries of Infant-Baptism consider..Whether rejecting of it..they do not teach others, especially Atheists, pure Deists, and Sabbatizers..a way to deny all the rest. *a* **1711** KEN *Preparatives* Poet. Wks. 1721 IV. 20 Wear Jesus Yoke, ..'Twill prove a Sabbatising to your Mind. **1742** J. GLAS *Lord's Supper* ii. (1883) 76 Our sabbatizing, or resting from our own works on the first day of the week is a sign of the truth of the promise of entering into his rest. **1855** *People's Sunday* 5, I shall, therefore, further show the complete absence of scripture authority for the doctrines of our Sabbatizing brethren.

sabbaton, -tyne: see SABATON, SABATINE.

‖**saˈbbeka.** *Antiq. rare*[−1]. [Biblical Aramaic *sabbᵉkā.*] An ancient musical instrument mentioned in the Book of Daniel; in the English Bible erroneously called SACKBUT, q.v.

1844 WHITTIER *Ezekiel* ix, They listen, as in Babel's throng The Chaldeans to the dancer's song, Or wild sabbeka's nightly play.

Sabber-day, var. SABBA-DAY.

‖**sabdariffa** (sæbdəˈrɪfə). [mod.L.; in Lobel *Plantarum Hist.* (1576) 375; of obscure origin.] An East Indian rose-mallow, *Hibiscus Sabdariffa* (Linnæus 1759), cultivated for its acidulous calyxes.

1866 *Treas. Bot.* 1002/2 Sabdariffa. *Hibiscus Sabdariffa*, called Red Sorrel in the West and Rozelle in the East Indies, where it is used in tarts, jellies and salads, and to form a cooling drink.

sabe (ˈsɑːbeɪ, ˈsɑːveɪ), *v. slang* (orig. *U.S.*). Also 9 sabee. [Re-formation after, or re-borrowing of, Sp. *sabe*: see SAVVY *v.*] = SAVVY *v.* Cf. QUIEN SABE.

1850 *California Courier* (San Francisco) 6 Sept. 2/3 Ha! *Sabe* that? **1865** NIXON *Peter Perfume* 58 The 'no sabee' dodge to try they'd fain. **1874** B. HARTE *Wan Lee*, I asked if the juggler was the father of the baby. 'No sabe!' said the imperturbable Hop Sing, taking refuge in that Spanish form of non-committalism so common in California. **1903** A. ADAMS *Log of Cowboy* vi. 37 Girls, you know, sabe each other that way. **1907** S. E. WHITE *Arizona Nights* i. 9, I sabed that they'd seen the original exhibit your Uncle Jim was making of himself.

sabe (ˈsɑːbeɪ, ˈsɑːveɪ), *sb. slang* (orig. *U.S.*). [See prec.] = SAVVY *sb.*

1872 B. HARTE in *Atlantic Monthly* Mar. 352/2 Did n't hev no more *sabe* than to come round yar with sickness in the house and no provision. **1892** KIPLING & BALESTIER *Naulahka* 273 You have been romping around for six months after something you hadn't the sabe to hold when you'd got. **1913** J. LONDON *Valley of Moon* 311 We ain't got the *sabe*, or the knack, or something or other. **1931** *Lariat* Apr. 53 You ain't got much sabe.

Sabean: see SABÆAN.

Sabei, var. SEBEI.

Sabeism: var. SABAISM.

sabel, obs. form of SABLE.

†**sabeline**, *sb. Obs.* Also 3 **sablyne**, 7 **sabelline**. [a. OF. *sabeline* (12th c. in Godef.), ad. med.L. *sabelīna* (*pellis*), sable (fur), f. *sabellum* SABLE *sb.*[1] Cf. ZIBELINE.] The fur of the sable.

a **1200** *Moral Ode* 364 (Egerton MS.) Ne scal þer beo fou ne grei ne cunig ne ermine ne ocquerne ne martres cheole ne beuer ne sabeline [*c* **1275** *Jesus MS.* sablyne]. ? **1700** *Cruel Mother* in Child *Ballads* (1882) I. 221/2 We neither wore the silks nor the sabelline. **1876** PLANCHÉ *Cycl. Costume* I. 439 *Sable, sabelline*, the skin of an animal of the weasel or marten kind.

sabeline: see SABELLINE *a.*[1]

‖**sabella** (səˈbɛlə). *Zool.* [mod.L. (Gmelin *Linnæus Syst. Nat.*, ed. 12, 1788), perh. f. *sabulum* sand.] A tubicolous annelid of the family *Sabellidæ*.

a **1851** DALYELL *Powers Creator* (1853) II. 175 Different species or varieties of the Sabella are found on the shores and in the seas of Scotland. *Ibid.*, *Sabella alveolaria*.—The Honeycomb Sabella. **1851** MEDLOCK tr. *Schoedler's Bk. Nature* II. 530 There are besides, the Sabellas, or *pencil*, *fan*, and *comb-worms* (Sabella). **1863** WOOD *Illustr. Nat. Hist.* III. 699 We now come to another pretty tube-inhabiting annelid, which is called Sabella, because it lives in the sand and forms its tube of that substance. Several species of Sabella are found on the British coasts, the most common of which is the Shore Sabella (*Sabella alveolaria*).

Sabellian (səˈbɛlɪən), *a.*[1] and *sb.*[1] *Theol.* [ad. eccl. L. *Sabelliān-us*, f. *Sabelli-us* (see B): see -AN.]

A. *adj.* Pertaining to the Sabellians (see B) or their doctrine.

1577 HANMER *Anc. Eccl. Hist.* VII. v. 126 Of the Sabellian heresie... The Sabellian heretickes. **1720** WATERLAND *Eight Serm.* 4 Under the Sabellian Interpretation I include all that belongs to Men of Sabellian Principles. **1848** R. I. WILBERFORCE *Doctr. Incarnation* ix. 259 The Sabellian theory is, that there exists no real diversity of Persons in the Ever-Blessed Trinity.

B. *sb.* One who accepts the view of Sabellius (an African heresiarch of the third century) that the Father, Son, and Holy Spirit are merely different aspects or modes of manifestation of one Divine person. Cf. MODALIST.

1402 *Pol. Poems* (Rolls) II. 92 He is callid an heretike that heresies sowith, as Arrians, Wyclyfanes, Sabellyanes, and other. **1556** CLEMENT in Strype *Eccl. Mem.* III. App. lxi. 214 From all Arians, Eutichians, Manichians, Sabellians.. and all other heretikes. **1685** RYCAUT tr. *Platina's Lives Popes* 52 The Sabellians.. asserted that the Father, Son, and holy Ghost were but one Person. **1702** ECHARD *Eccl. Hist.* (1710) 619 Tho' those who then held this opinion were call'd Sabellians, yet the heresie itself was more ancient than Sabellius. **1850** ROBERTSON *Serm.* Ser. III. iv. (1872) 45 Sabellians, or worshippers of one person under three different manifestations.

Sabellian (səˈbɛlɪən), *a.*[2] and *sb.*[2] *Hist.* [f. L. *Sabell-us* + -IAN.]

a. *adj.* Pertaining to a group of related peoples who inhabited certain parts of ancient Italy, comprising the Sabines, Samnites, Campanians, and others. Also, of or pertaining to the language of the Sabellians. **b.** *sb.* A person belonging to any of these peoples. Also, any of the numerous dialects of Italic spoken by the Sabellians.

In Latin poetry *Sabellī* is commonly used as a synonym of *Sabīnī*. The use of *Sabellian* by modern writers is somewhat arbitrary.

1601 HOLLAND *Pliny* I. 64 Of Samnites, whom the Greekes called Sabellians and Saunites, The Colonie Bouianum, the old. **1841** W. SPALDING *Italy & It. Isl.* I. 277 The territory of those Sabellian tribes [*sc.* the Sabines, Marsians, Pelignians, Vestinians, and Samnites], which are here classed together, includes the central heights and valleys of the Apennines. **1880** *Encycl. Brit.* XIII. 445/2 Oscan is.. a useful term to designate the nation or group of tribes composed of the Samnites, together with their descendants or offshoots, the Campanians, Lucanians, and Bruttians. The name Sabellians, used by the Roman poets, has been employed by some modern writers in much the same signification. **1904** C. D. BUCK *Gram. Oscan & Umbrian* 3 The Oscan-Umbrian group.. includes also the dialects of most of the minor tribes of central Italy, which may be conveniently designated as Sabellian. *Ibid.*, Strictly speaking the Samnite tribes were Sabellian, and their language, the Oscan, a Sabellian dialect. **1939** [see *Latino-Faliscan* s.v. LATINO-]. **1939** [see MARSIAN *sb.* and *a.*]. **1972** W. B. LOCKWOOD *Panorama Indo-Europ. Lang.* 58 A few early inscriptions characterised as Sabellian show that this dialect was closely akin to Oscan.

Sabellianism (səˈbɛlɪənɪz(ə)m). [f. SABELLIAN *a.*[1] and *sb.*[1] + -ISM.] The doctrinal conception of the Trinity as held by the followers of Sabellius; belief in the Sabellian doctrine of the Trinity.

1668 H. MORE *Div. Dial.* Schol. (1713) 549 Sabellianism, which allows the Consubstantiality or Coequality in the Trinity. **1852** ROBERTSON *Serm.* Ser. IV. xi. (1876) 104 A heresy known by the name of Sabellianism or Modal Trinity. **1907** ILLINGWORTH *Doctr. Trin.* vii. 127 To avoid Tritheism on the one hand,.. and Sabellianism on the other.

Sabellianize (səˈbɛlɪənaɪz), *v.* [f. SABELLIAN + -IZE.] *intr.* To adopt Sabellian views.

1833–40 J. H. NEWMAN *Church of Fathers* (1842) 171 We have bid farewell to contentious deviations of doctrine,.. neither Sabellianizing nor Arianising. **1833** —— *Arians* V. i. (1876) 356 Not only did he [Athanasius] reluctantly abandon his associate, the unfortunate Marcellus, on his Sabellianizing but [etc.].

Sabellic (səˈbɛlɪk), *a.* [f. L. *Sabellus* SABELLIAN *a.*[2] + -IC.] Pertaining to the language or the nationality of the Sabellians.

1880 *Encycl. Brit.* XIII. 126/1 The Sabellic inscriptions. **1902** GILES in *Encycl. Brit.* XXXIII. 898/2 The Sabellic alphabet,.. found in a few inscriptions.

sabellid (səˈbɛlɪd), *a.* and *sb.* *Zool.* [f. SABELLA + -ID.] **A.** *adj.* Pertaining to or connected with the family *Sabellidæ*, of which the genus *Sabella* is the type.

1900 *Nature* 6 Dec. 140/1 A paper.. on the sabellid worms collectively designated as Polychætes.

B. *sb.* An individual of the family *Sabellidæ*.

1893 *Jrnl. Mar. Zool.* Nov. 13 On the method of dispersion and fertilization of ova in some sabellids. **1896** BENHAM in *Camb. Nat. Hist.* II. 286 The beautiful branchial crowns of various Sabellids.

sabelline (səˈbɛlaɪn), *a.*[1] Also (in Dicts.) sabeline. [ad. med.L. *sabellīnus*, f. *sabellum* SABLE *sb.*[1]] Of the colour of sable fur.

1888 *Longm. Mag.* July 297 Bird and beast must assume alike the uniform grey sabelline tint of external nature.

sabelline (səˈbɛlaɪn), *a.*[2] *Zool.* [f. SABELLA + -INE[1].] Pertaining to the genus *Sabella* or to the family *Sabellidæ* (Cent. Dict. 1891).

sabelline, variant of SABELINE *Obs.*

sabellite (sæˈbɛlaɪt). *Zool.* [f. SABELLA + -ITE[1].] A fossil sabella, or some similar worm (*Cent. Dict.* 1891).

sabelloid (səˈbɛlɔɪd), *a.* and *sb.* *Zool.* [f. SABELLA + -OID.] **a.** *adj.* Of or resembling the annelidan *Sabellidæ* (Cent. Dict. 1891). **b.** *sb.* One of the *Sabellidæ* (ibid.).

saber, obs. or U.S. form of SABRE.

‖**sabha** (səˈbɑː). [Hind. *sabhā* assembly.] In India, an assembly; a council or society (see quots.). Cf. LOK SABHA, RAJYA SABHA.

1922 A. B. KEITH in *Cambr. Hist. India* I. iv. 96 The power of the king [in Vedic India] cannot have been in normal circumstances arbitrary or probably very great. There stood beside him as the mode of expression of the will of the people the assembly, which is denoted by the terms *samiti* and *sabha* in the Saṃhitā. **1936** J. NEHRU *Autobiogr.* xli. 323 All manner of allied or sympathetic or advanced organisations had been declared unlawful—kisan sabhas and peasant unions. **1950** M. MASANI *Our Growing Human Family* vii. 66 Some of these ancient Indian republics were extremely democratic... They had popular assemblies of all the people called the samiti and a parliament elected by the people called the sabha. **1968** *Jrnl. Mus. Acad. Madras* XXXIX. 119 Hardly 250 to 300 kritis are sung in the concerts of today—in spite of the availability of Music Sabhas. **1974** *Encycl. Brit. Micropædia* VIII. 747/3 *Sabhā* .., an important unit of self-government in Hindu society. It is basically an association of persons who have common interests, such as members of the same endogamous groups, but may also be an intercaste group (*e.g.*, a *mazdūr sabhā*, or association of labourers). The *sabhā* differs from the *pañcāyat* (caste or subcaste council) in that its scope is much larger.

‖**sabi** (ˈsɑːbi). [Jap.] In Zen Buddhist philosophy, a quality of simple, restrained, and mellowed beauty.

1932 B. L. SUZUKI *Nōgaku* 15 The feeling of *sabi* or *shibumi* is the essence of the art of Nō. **1938** D. T. SUZUKI *Zen Buddhism* I. ii. 17 *Sabi* consists in rustic unpretentiousness or archaic imperfection, apparent simplicity or effortlessness in execution, and richness in historical associations. **1948** *Introd. Classic Jap. Lit.* (Kokusai Bunka Shinkōkai) p. vi, This new spirit was restrained by the persistence of traditional ideas as.. in the appreciation and cultivation of 'mellowness' (*sabi*, patina) in literature. **1965** W. SWAAN *Jap. Lantern* xvi. 184 A quality most valued in architecture and art connected with the tea-ceremony is that of *sabi* or *wabi*. **1979** S. COE in I. Webb *Compl. Guide Flower Arrangement* xvii. 227/3 The first [mood] is *sabi*, a sense of loneliness which comes from being completely detached, and seeing things as if they are happening by themselves.

Sabian (ˈseɪbɪən), *sb.* and *a.* Also 7–8 **Zabian**, 7–8 **Sabean**, 8 **Zabæan**, **Tsabæan**, 8–9 **Sabæan**, **Tsabian**. [f. Arab. *çābi'* + -AN.

According to Nöldeke, the word represents the pr. pple. of the Aramaic *ç'ba*ʻ to baptize (the ע being changed into א as is usual in the Mandæan and cognate dialects). In the actual form in which the word occurs in Arabic, it has the appearance of being derived from the same root as the Hebrew *çābā* host (see SABAOTH); hence, as certain sects claiming the name of Sabians were alleged to be worshippers of the stars, the name was (already by Maimonides in the 12th c.) interpreted as referring to 'the host of heaven'.]

A. *sb.*

1. a. An adherent of a religious sect mentioned in three passages of the Koran (ii. 40, v. 73, xxii. 17), and by later Arabian writers.

In the Koran the Sabians are classed with Muslims, Jews, and Christians, as believers in the true God. On account of the toleration extended by Muslims to them, the name of Sabians was, some centuries after Muhammad, assumed not only by the Gnostic half-Christian Mandæans (whose religion is perhaps akin to that of the true Sabians), but also by certain actual polytheists. The statement of some Arabic writers is that the Sabians were professedly Christian, but secretly worshippers of the stars. (Cf. SABAISM.)

1614 PURCHAS *Pilgrimage* I. xii. (ed. 2) 63 These Zabians thought whatsoeuer went from their bodies was vncleane. **1661** BOYLE *Style of Script.* (1675) 35 For want of knowing the Religion of the antient Zabians... Of those Zabiists.. I find a deep and general silence in Classick Authors. **1797** *Encycl. Brit.* (ed. 3) X. 462/1 The fourth [*sc.* apartment of hell] named *al Sair*, [Mohammedans assign] to the Sabians. **1841** *Penny Cycl.* XX. 295/2 That the unity of the Deity was however still acknowledged in the religious system of the Tsabians is manifest from the way in which this religion is spoken of in the Korán.

b. Used for MANDÆAN (see quot. 1883).

1797 *Encycl. Brit.* (ed. 3) X. 458/2 The Sabians have several books which they attribute to some of the antediluvian prophets. **1883** K. KESSLER *ibid.* (ed. 9) XV. 467/2 *note*, In their dealings with members of other communions the designation they [*i.e.* the Mandæans] take is Sabians.

2. In erroneous use: A worshipper of 'the host of heaven'; a star-worshipper.

1716 PRIDEAUX *O. & N. Test. Connected* I. III. (1718) I. 140 The remainder of this sect still subsists in the east under the same name of Sabians... That which hath given them the greatest credit among the people of the east is, that the best of their astronomers have been of this sect... For the stars being the gods they worshipped, they made them the chief subject of their studies. **1864** COL. GREENWOOD in *Athenæum* 23 July 115/3 Bishop Cumberland and Bishop Warburton.. agree that Cain.. and his descendants were Sabæans. Abraham and Moses were Sabæans till Jehovah revealed himself to them.

B. *adj.* Pertaining to the Sabians (in the various applications of the name: see A).

1748 T. BLACKWELL *Lett. conc. Mythol.* 369 This Zabian Principle of the Worship of one God by Prayer and Incense. **1787** W. JONES in *Asiatick Researches* (1790) II. 8 It is generally asserted, that the old religion of the Arabs was entirely Sabian; but I can offer so little accurate information concerning the Sabian faith, or even the meaning of the word, that I dare not yet speak on the subject with confidence. **1796** MORSE *Amer. Geog.* II. 571 The Sabean Christians have, in their religion, a mixture of Judaism and Mahometanism. **1859** J. M. ARNOLD *Ishmael* 35 In a Sabian Almanac.. it is stated: 'They fast in it seven days.. in honour of the great Lord, the Sun, the Lord of all Good.' **1886** *Encycl. Brit.* XXI. 128/1 It is quite inappropriate to call star-worshippers in general Sabians or Zabians or to speak of a distinct Sabian religion, as older writers do.

Sabianism (ˈseɪbɪənɪz(ə)m). Also 9 **sabæanism**, **Zabianism**. [f. prec. + -ISM.] The religion of the Sabians; chiefly in erroneous use, worship of 'the host of heaven', star-worship. Cf. SABAISM.

1788 GIBBON *Decl. & F.* V. l. 194 Sabianism was diffused over Asia by the science of the Chaldæans and the arms of the Assyrians. **1816** G. S. FABER *Orig. Pagan Idol.* I. 31 Astrolatry or Sabianism; that is to say, the worship of the Sun, the Moon, and the Host of Heaven. **1845** *Vulgar & Common Err.* 74 Zabianism, or star worship. **1871** PROCTOR *Light Sci.* 333 Sabæanism, or star-worship.

sabicu (sæbɪˈkuː). A timber tree, *Lysiloma Sabicu*, native of Cuba, the wood of which is greatly valued for its hardness and durability; the wood of this tree. Also *attrib.*

1866 *Treas. Bot.* 704/1 The valuable hard timber known as Sabicù, Savacù or Savicò wood. *Ibid.*, Sabicu timber is imported.. from Cuba. **1875** *Encycl. Brit.* I. 68/2 *Acacia formosa* supplies the valuable Cuba timber called sabicu. **1879** *Man. Artillery Exerc.* 588 A number of 5-in. sabicu shifting rollers.

Sabiism: see SABAISM.

sabill, obs. f. SABLE.

sabin (ˈseɪbɪn). *Acoustics.* Also **sabine** and with capital initial. [f. the name of Wallace Clement *Sabine* (1868–1919), U.S. physicist.] A unit of sound absorption equal to the absorbing power of one square foot of perfectly absorbing surface; = *open window unit* s.v. OPEN *a.* (*adv.*) 22 c.

1934 *Jrnl. Acoustical Soc. Amer.* VI. 101 Total absorption —600 units (Sabine—0·50 sec.). **1936** *Gloss. Acoustical Terms* (*B.S.I.*) 22 The unit of equivalent absorption is termed an absorption unit. When the unit of area is a square foot, this unit is called a sabin. **1956** *IRE Trans. Audio* IV. 21 *A* is the absorption of the room in sabins. **1968** [see *open window unit* s.v. OPEN *a.* (*adv.*) 22 c]. **1969** *Daily Tel.* 5 Nov. 5/1 The Professor assembled 10 miniskirted secretaries in a physics department's reverberation chamber... The 10 girls averaged a sabine count of 2·5 each, whereas a similar test in 1964, when skirts were longer, produced an average sabine count of 4·6. Twice as much sound was therefore absorbed in 1964. **1975** G. J. KING *Audio Handbk.* i. 23 A room of total surface area 111·45 m² (1200 ft²),.. and 0·2 coefficient of absorbency, signifying that 20% of the sound is absorbed.., would have a total absorbency of almost 240 sabins.

sabin(e, var. ff. SAVIN.

Sabine ('sæbaɪn), *a.* and *sb.*[1] *Hist.* [ad. L. *Sabīn-us* adj. and sb.] **A.** *adj.* **a.** Of or pertaining to the Sabines: see B.

1600 HOLLAND tr. *Livy's Romane Hist.* I. 8 And the youth of Rome upon a token and watch-word given, fell on every side to carrie away the Sabine maidens. **1606** JONSON *Hymenaei* sig. Cv, The Speare, which (in the Sabine tongue) was called Curis. **1697** DRYDEN *Æneid* VIII. 842 Sabine dames. **1756** C. SMART tr. *Horace, Sat.* I. ix. (1826) II. 75 An old Sabine sorceress. **1784** COWPER *Let.* 3 July (1904) II. 219, I may..refresh my spirits by a little intercourse with the Mantuan and the Sabine bard. **1822** M. WILMOT *Jrnl.* 19 Apr. in *More Lett.* (1935) 165 We set out..to seek for Horace's Sabine Farm at the back of Mt Lucretiles. **1823** BYRON *Don Juan* IX. vii. 8 You, my Lord Duke!..half a million for your Sabine farm Is rather dear! **1841** W. SPALDING *Italy & It. Isl.* I. 220 The..valley of the Hernici ..separates the Sabine heights from the group of mountains anciently inhabited by the Volscians. **1908** O. CRAWFORD in *19th Cent.* Jan. 69 Liquor that Horace drank and sang of on his Sabine farm.

b. Of or pertaining to the Sabine language.

1888 [see MARRUCINIAN *sb.* and *a.*]. **1977** *Word 1972* XXVIII. 7 They are obviously Italic (Sabine), not really Latin words.

B. *sb.*[1] **a.** One of a race of ancient Italy who inhabited the central region of the Apennines.

1387 TREVISA *Higden* (Rolls) III. 61 Tacius kyng of Sabyns was i-slawe by assent of Romulus. **1533** BELLENDEN *Livy* I. iv. (S.T.S.) I. 29 Ane huge nowmer of Sabinis with þare wyiffis, barnis, & servandis. **1601** HOLLAND *Pliny* I. 65 The Sabines..dwell hard by the Veline lakes. **1783** W. GORDON tr. *Livy's Rom. Hist.* (1823) I. xxxviii. 70 The Sabines fled to the Mountains. **1841** W. SPALDING *Italy & It. Isl.* I. 46 The Sabines, as it is..conjectured, had a settlement covering the Capitoline and Quirinal Hills.

b. *transf.* in allusion to the proverb *Sabini quod volunt somniant*, 'the Sabines dream what they will' (Festus).

1610 HOLLAND *Camden's Brit.* 542 Grimsby, which our Sabins, or conceited persons dreaming what they list, and following their owne fansies, will have to be so called of one Grime a merchant.

c. The Italic language of the Sabines.

1834 W. GELL *Topogr. Rome* II. 381 Cata, in Sabine, says Varro, means pointed. **1933, 1939** [see MARSIAN *sb.* and *a.*]. **1974** [see MARRUCINIAN *sb.* and *a.*].

d. Sabine wine. *rare.*

1863 WHYTE-MELVILLE *Gladiators* x. 153, I talked myself well-nigh hoarse, and stayed out the drinking of two flagons of sour Sabine to boot.

Sabine ('sæbaɪn), *sb.*[2] The name of Sir Edward *Sabine* (1788–1883), British explorer, soldier, and President of the Royal Society, used *absol.*, *attrib.*, or in the possessive in **Sabine('s) gull** to designate *Xema sabinii*, an Arctic gull with a forked tail, grey head, and black collar, first named *Larus sabini* in his honour by his brother Joseph Sabine in 1818 (*Trans. Linn. Soc.* XII. 522).

1852 P. C. SUTHERLAND *Jrnl. Voy. Baffin's Bay* II. 88 Sabine and ivory gulls, and other birds,..were on their flight up the Channel. **1886** *Code Nomencl. & Check-list N. Amer. Birds* (Amer. Ornithologists' Union) 91 (*heading*) Sabine's Gull. **1958** *Evening Telegram* (St. John's, Newfoundland) 6 May 30/5 Few people have the opportunity to see Sabine's gulls as they rarely come south. **1972** S. BURNFORD *One Woman's Arctic* ii. 43 Once only I saw a solitary sabine.

sabine, var. SABIN.

sabinene ('seɪbɪniːn). *Chem.* [ad. G. *sabinen* (F. W. Semmler 1900, in *Ber. d. Deut. chem. Ges.* XXXIII. 1464), f. L. (*Juniperus*) *sabin-a* (see SAVIN, SAVINE) + *-en* -ENE.] A colourless liquid bicyclic terpene, $C_{10}H_{16}$, found in a number of essential oils, notably oil of savin.

1900 *Jrnl. Chem. Soc.* LXXVIII. I. 454 When oil of savin is distilled, a fraction, forming 30 per cent. of the whole, boils between 162° and 170°, and consists principally of a terpene, $C_{10}H_{16}$, which the author terms sabinene. **1942** *Jrnl. Org. Chem.* VII. 399 The presence of α-terpinene in this case, is due probably to isomerization of sabinene under the conditions of the experiment. **1976** *Nature* 22 Apr. 726/2 Terpenes with an exomethylene bond (for example, sabinene, nopinene and camphene) show three strong peaks in the Raman spectrum around 920, 877 and 856 cm^{-1}.

Sabinian (sə'bɪnɪən), *sb.* and *a.*[1] *Roman Law.* [ad. L. *Sabinianus*, f. *Sabinus* (see below).]

A. *sb.* A follower of Massurius Sabinus, a celebrated jurist in the time of the emperor Tiberius. **B.** *adj.* Of or pertaining to Massurius Sabinus or his views.

1862 T. MACKENZIE *Stud. in Roman Law* 13 Capito..was the chief of the rival sect, called after two of his followers Sabinians or Cassians. **1886** E. E. WHITFIELD tr. *Salkowski's Inst. & Hist. Roman Law* 47 The opposition..arises between the two schools of Law..the Proculians and Sabinians. **1903** F. P. WALTON *Hist. Introd. Roman Law* xvii. 137 We frequently read that the Proculian view upon some question was so and so, and that the Sabinian view differed from it. **1907** S. L. PHIPSON *Law of Evidence* (ed. 4) xlvi. 558 The old controversy between the Proculians and the Sabinians, between the logical, inferential or liberal school of interpreters, and the grammatical or literal. **1953** A. BERGER *Encycl. Dict. Roman Law* 687/1 Among the prominent Sabinians after Sabinus and Cassius were Lavolenus, Gaius, and Julian. **1977** A. WATSON *Nature of Law* vii. 102 Even in the second century A.D. one of the two famous schools of jurists, the Sabinian, argued that barter should be included within the contract of sale.

Sa'binian, *a.*[2] *rare.* [f. SABINE *a.* and *sb.*[1] + -IAN.] = SABINE *a.*

1902 BELLOC *Path to Rome* 432 Rome was hidden by the low Sabinian hills.

sabino (sə'biːnəʊ). [app. altered form of Sp. *sabina* SAVIN.] **a.** The bald or deciduous cypress, *Taxodium distichum* (Treas. Bot., Suppl., 1874). **b.** The Mexican swamp cypress, *Taxodium mucronatum* (Webster Suppl., 1902). **c.** The wood of a species of *Talauma* (Encycl. Brit. XIX. 532/2, 1885).

Sabin vaccine ('seɪbɪn). *Med.* [Named after Albert Bruce *Sabin* (b. 1906), Russian-born U.S. microbiologist who developed the vaccine in 1955.] A vaccine against poliomyelitis made from attenuated viruses of the three serological types and administered orally.

1955 *Brit. Med. Jrnl.* I. 24/1 (Index), Vaccination; human trial of Sabin (live) vaccine. **1961** *Lancet* 30 Sept. 756/2 Administration of candied live Sabin vaccine led to a sharp reduction in poliomyelitis incidence and complete prevention of a seasonal rise in incidence during summer and autumn months. **1978** *Daily Tel.* 13 June 16 The production of anti-polio vaccine in America is being imperilled because India has stopped the export of rhesus monkeys, needed for processing Salk and Sabin vaccines, in the past few months.

Sabiny, var. SAPINY.

Sabir (sə'bɪə(r), ‖sabir). Also (in *transf.* sense) sabir. [Fr., a. *sabir* 'to know' in the language invented by Molière for a song in *Le bourgeois gentilhomme* (1670), prob. ad. Sp. *saber* to know.] A French-based pidgin language used in parts of North Africa; also, = *lingua franca*; also *transf.* and *attrib.*

1867 'OUIDA' *Under Two Flags* III. i. 18 'You are great warriors,' he cried, in the Sabir tongue. **1939** L. H. GRAY *Foundations of Lang.* 37 *Sabir*, a mixture of French, Spanish, Italian, Greek, and Arabic, which serves as a *lingua franca* for the Mediterranean ports. **1964** E. PALMER tr. *Martinet's Elem. Gen. Linguistics* v. 155 These somewhat sketchy tools of communication are often called *sabirs* after the language which long flourished in the Mediterranean ports and is also known as the *lingua franca*. **1972** R. MAYNE *Europeans* iv. 58 The multinational institutions of the Common Market are gradually developing a modern administrative *sabir* compounded from French, German, Italian, and even English. **1974** *Florida FL Reporter* XIII. 17/1, I cannot agree that the 'Sabir Pidgins'..at least are special formations. Rather, they were transmitted by maritime routes—and in some frontier situations. **1978** *Language* LIV. 338 It seems clear that temporal priority must be granted to the contact system used with North Africans of the western Mediterranean ('Sabir') over that used with Black Africans (the reconnaissance language). *Ibid.*, Eastern Sabir, the pidgin used by pilgrims and merchants in the eastern Mediterranean, was, however, much more destructured than the Western Sabir recorded in the Portuguese documents.

sabir: see SAMBUR.

sabji, var. SUBJEE.

sabkha ('sæbxə, 'sæbkə). *Geogr.* Also **sabquha, sebk(h)a**. Pl. **sabkha(s), sebakh.** [ad. Arab. *sabḵah* a saline infiltration, salt flat.] A flat, salt-encrusted depression, usu. just above the water-table, that is subject to periodic flooding and evaporation, resulting in accumulation of alternating layers of æolian clays and salts, and is found esp. in N. Africa and Arabia. Cf. CHOTT, KAVIR, PLAYA 1, SHOTT.

1878 [see SHOTT]. **1891** [see CHOTT]. **1909** GROOM & BALFOUR tr. *E. Warming's Œcol. of Plants* lviii. 233 Here also may be placed the *shotts* and *sebakh* of North Africa, depressions which contain salt water during the rainy season, but many of which are dry and covered with incrustations of salt in summer. **1911** G. BELL *Let.* 23 Feb. (1927) I. xii. 280 The ground here is what the Arabs called 'sabkha', soft, crumbly salt marsh, sandy when it is dry and ready at a moment's notice to turn into a world of glutinous paste. **1937** *Trans. Connecticut Acad. Arts & Sci.* XXXIII. 110 In the smaller sebkas, comparable in dimensions to Carson Lake, the water is less salt, and supports a more varied fauna. **1957** R. J. H. CHURCH *W. Afr.* xiv. 231 There is, in the north, a succession of salt encrusted mud-flats (sebkhas), marshy only after rare rains, which are remnants of former lagoons. **1963** [see KAVIR]. **1964** *Nature* 23 May 759/1 The coast of the Sheikdom of Abu Dhabi, Trucial States,..is bordered for most of its length by low coastal flats which stand just above normal high-tide level. These flats are known locally as sabkha. **1972** *Sci. Amer.* Dec. 29/3 Sabkhas became an object of considerable interest to geologists soon after it was realized that certain types of ancient rock formation are practically identical with the sabkha sediments; both are characterized by the presence of nodular anhydrite and stromatolitic dolomite. **1973** *Nature* 20 July 145/1 The Triassic sabkhas were not all coastal sabkhas, or tidal flats, some may have been continental sabkhas, or playa flats. *Ibid.* 7 Sept. 29/2 The cores..show microalternations of organic matter and carbonate (sometimes replaced by chert) which closely resemble Recent supratidal deposits in the Persian Gulf (sabquha),.. which are a product of a hot dry climate and hypersaline marine conditions with frequent drying out of the sediment. **1977** A. HALLAM *Planet Earth* 157 Many modern desert coasts are bordered by salt marshes, usually known as sabkhas. **1980** D. CREED *Scarab* v. 39 The long flat distances of the sabkha..the time-worn cliffs, the unbroken blue of the sky.

sable ('seɪb(ə)l), *sb.*[1] Forms: α. 4 **sabylle**, 5 **sabulle**, 5–6 **sabill**, 5–7 **sabel**, 6 **sabil(le**, 7 **sabell**, 4– **sable**. β. 7 **cebal**. [a. OF. *sable*, *saible* sable fur, also quasi-*adj.* in *martre sable* ('sable marten') as the name of the animal and its fur, med.L. *sabelum*, *sabellum* sable fur, Icel. *safal*, *safali* sable (the animal), sable-fur, Du. *sabel* sable-fur. The OF. word was prob. adopted from Slavonic: cf. Russian *sobol'*, Polish, Czech *sobol* (whence G. *zobel*, Da., Sw. *sobel*), Lith. *sabalas*, Hung. *czoboly*, the sable. See also ZIBELINE, which represents a Romanic derivative from the same Slavonic word.

The rare 17th c. form *cebal* is of obscure origin; it may possibly be a shortening of one of the Rom. forms cited s.v. ZIBELINE.]

1. a. A small carnivorous quadruped, *Mustela zibellina*, nearly allied to the martens, and native of the arctic and sub-arctic regions of Europe and Asia. Also ***Russian, Siberian sable***. In ME. the animal and its fur are called also *martrix sable*, *martryn sable*, after OF. *martre sable*.

The American sable, *Mustela Americana*, native of the arctic and sub-arctic regions of North America, is now regarded as a geographical variety of the Old World species. The ***red*** or ***Tatar sable*** is the Siberian mink, *Putorius sibiricus*.

1423 JAS. I *Kingis Q.* clvii, The bugill, draware by his hornis grete; The martrik sable, the foynȝee, and mony mo. **1463–4** *Rolls of Parlt.* V. 504/2 That noo Knyght..nor noo Wyf of eny such Knyght..were eny manere Cloth of Gold ..or eny Furre of Sables. **1585** T. WASHINGTON tr. *Nicholay's Voy.* II. xxiii. 62 Furres of martirs, Zebelins, Sables,..and other fine skins. **1668** CHARLETON *Onomast.* 19 *Mustela Zibellina*,..the Cebal, or Sable. **1719** DE FOE *Crusoe* (1840) II. xvi. 326 They..catch sables and foxes. **1877** COUES *Fur Anim.* iii. 95 The Sable is principally trapped during the colder months.

b. *Painting.* A brush made of the sable's hair. Cf. KOLINSKY.

1891 in *Cent. Dict.* **1899** [see *red sable* s.v. RED *a.* 19 a]. **1958** M. L. WOLF *Dict. Painting* 41 Modern painters' brushes are in two general types: bristle, or coarse hair, usually that of the pig; and fine hair, made of sable, or so-called 'camel hair'. **1973** F. TAUBES *Painter's Dict.* 207 Sables are standard painting tools for all water-based mediums—watercolor, acrylic, casein, gouache, etc.—which require large, thin passages of fluid color.

2. a. The skin or fur of the sable.

14.. LYDG. *Life Our Lady* (MS. Bodl. 75, fol. 72 b) Ne martres sable [*Caxton and other texts* Ne martyrn ne sabyl] ..Was noon founde in her garment. **1508** *Acc. Ld. High Treas. Scot.* IV. 20 Item, put in the samyn [goun] sevin score of mertrikis of the Kingis and pair of sabilles. **1553** EDEN *Treat. Newe Ind.* (Arb.) 20 The riche furres called *Zibellini*, which we call Sables. **1638** SIR T. HERBERT *Trav.* (ed. 2) 180 Raw silks, exchang'd for sables. **1717** LADY M. W. MONTAGU *Let. to C'tess Mar* 30 Jan., This lady was in a gown..lined and faced with sables. **1835** *Court Mag.* VI. p. vi/2 When we say furs, we should rather say fur, for sable is the only one adopted by ladies of high fashion. **1893** F. F. MOORE *Gray Eye or So* III. 211 Mrs. Mowbray's set of sables had cost..seven hundred guineas.

b. Short for *sable coat*.

1975 R. STOUT *Family Affair* xiv. 123, I..went to the hall with Mrs Bassett's mink or sable or sea otter and held it for her. **1977** J. CROSBY *Company of Friends* xvi. 105 She eyed the sable some more... In a few more years they would be hanging that coat on the wall..like a painting.

3. A superior quality of Russian iron, so called from being originally stamped with a sable.

1785 *Daily Universal Reg.* 1 Jan. 4/3 About 140 tons of old Sable and Gurioff's iron saved out of the Westmoreland. **1815** J. SMITH *Panorama Sci. & Art* I. 12 That kind [of iron] called old sable. **1839** URE *Dict. Arts* 462 Those [files] made from the Russian iron, known by the name of old sable, called from its mark CCND, are excellent.

4. *attrib.* and *Comb.* **a.** simple attrib., as ***sable-skin***; (made of the hairs of the sable) ***sable-brush***, ***-pencil***; (used for taking the sable) ***sable-trap***; (made of the fur of sable) ***sable-coat***, (hence ***-coated*** adj.), ***muff***, ***tippet***; ***sable-trimmed*** adj. Also objective, as ***sable-hunter***.

1873 E. SPON *Workshop Receipts* Ser. I. 2/1 Chinese white ..may be applied with a fine *sable-brush. **1753** HANWAY *Trav.* (1762) I. III. l. 228 It is common to see a great man sit in his *sable-coat in the height of summer. **1928** Sable coat [see ASK *v.* 5 d]. **1978** F. MACLEAN *Take Nine Spies* 336 The seductive, *sable-coated countess..on the Orient Express. **1719** DE FOE *Crusoe* (1840) II. xvi. 335 They were the *sable-hunters of Siberia. **1784** KING *Cook's 3rd Voy.* VI. ii. III. 220, I had a present..of a handsome *sable muff. **1811** *Self Instructor* 518 The latter kind are called *sable pencils. **1719** DE FOE *Crusoe* (1840) II. xv. 316, I was curious to see the *sable-skins. **1882** H. LANSDELL *Through Siberia* I. 208 A good sable skin fetches from 50s. to £10. **1686** *Lond. Gaz.* No. 2202/4 Lost.., a *Sable Typpet. **1784** J. BELKNAP in *B. Papers* (1877) II. 188 We saw..abundance of *sable-traps, and one bear-trap. **1922** JOYCE *Ulysses* 457 A *sabletrimmed brick quilted dolman.

b. sable-mouse [= Ger. *zobelmaus*] = LEMMING.

1699 SIR P. RYCAUT in *Phil. Trans.* XXI. 110 In the Year 1697, these Sable-Mice were first observ'd. **1700** W. KING *Transactioneer* 81 Sable-Mice..are so fierce and angry that if a stick be held out at them, they will bite it.

sable ('seɪb(ə)l), *sb.*[2] and *a.* Also 4–5 **sabyll(e**, 5–6 **sabill**. [a. F. *sable* sable (as heraldic term: in

Godef. cited only from 15th c.), whence Sp., Pg. *sable*, MDu., Du. *sabel*. The identity of the word with SABLE *sb.*[1] is commonly assumed, though some difficulty is presented by the fact that the fur of the sable, as now known, is not black but brown.

Some have conjectured that it may have been customary to dye sable-fur black (as is now often done with sealskin), perh. in order to heighten its contrast with ermine, with which it was often worn.

The development by which the heraldic term has become a general (poetical or rhetorical) synonym for 'black' is peculiar to English.]

A. *sb.*

1. *Her.* Black, as one of the heraldic colours; in engraving represented by horizontal and vertical lines crossing each other. Abbreviated *S* (also *s*), *sa.*, †*sab.*

1352 *Wynnere & Wastoure* 157 The thirde banere one bent as of blee whitte With sexe galeys I see of sable with inn. ? *a* **1400** *Morte Arth.* 771 His hede and hys hals ware.. Oundyde of azure,.. Hys feete ware floreschede alle in fyne sabylle. **1470–85** MALORY *Arthur* XII. vi. 601 A shelde alle of Sabel. **1489** CAXTON *Faytes of A.* IV. xvii. 280 That other colour is blak that men calle in armoyrie sable. **1562** LEIGH *Armorie* (1597) 87 b, These [Ogresses] are Pellets of guns, and are neuer of other colour, then Sable. **1611** COTGR., *Sable*,.. the colour sables, or blacke, in Blason. **1864** BOUTELL *Her. Hist. & Pop.* xv. 175 Changing the tincture of the field of his shield from sable to azure.

2. a. The colour black; black clothing, also, esp. as a symbol of mourning. *poet.* and *rhetorical.*

c **1374** CHAUCER *Compl. Mars* 284 Now haue ye cause to clothe yow in sable. **1390** GOWER *Conf.* III. 372 A Peire of Bedes blak as Sable Sche tok and heng my necke aboute. *c* **1470** *Gol. & Gaw.* 20 Thair baneris schane with the sone, of siluer and sabill. **1508** DUNBAR *Gold. Targe* 126 Thare was Pluto.. In cloke of grene, his court usit no sable. **1602** SHAKS. *Ham.* I. ii. 242 *Ham.* His Beard was grisly? No. *Hor.* It was, as I haue seene it in his life, A Sable Siluer'd. **1728** POPE *Dunc.* II. 262 The King of dykes! than whom no sluice of mud With deeper sable blots the silver flood. **1855** LONGF. *Hiaw.* VIII. 38 Painted was he with his war-paints,.. Spots of brown and spots of sable.

†**b.** Blackness, darkness. *Obs.*

1503 DUNBAR *Thistle & Rose* 56 The purpour sone,.. Doing all sable fro the hevynnis chace. **1774** tr. *Helvetius' Child of Nature* II. 336 The sable of death was spread upon his face. **1781** COWPER *Conversat.* 872 Let no man charge me that I mean To clothe in sable every social scene.

3. *pl.* **a.** Mourning garments; a suit of black worn as an emblem of grief. *poet.* or *rhetorical.*

1602 SHAKS. *Ham.* III. ii. 138 Nay then let the Diuel weare blacke, for Ile haue a suite of Sables. **1676** OTWAY *Don Carlos* V. i, You'll find her all in rueful Sables clad. **1795** WOLCOT (P. Pindar) *Pindariana* Wks. 1812 IV. 164 Her gloomy sables change to pink and gold. **1848** THACKERAY *Van. Fair* lvii, Her little boy sate by her side in pompous new sables. **1867** 'OUIDA' *C. Castlemaine* (1879) 18 The sables she wore were not solely for the dead Earl.

b. *fig.*

1655 tr. *Com. Hist. Francion* I. 1 Already had the Night worn out neare half her Sables. *a* **1708** BEVERIDGE *Priv. Th.* I. 101 This Hatred.. puts on the mournful Sables of Grief and Sorrow. **1746** HERVEY *Medit.* (1818) 162 Then the earth, disrobed of all her gay attire, must sit in sables, like a disconsolate widow. **1882** MRS. OLIPHANT *Lit. Hist. Eng.* I. 58 Thus Cowper kept on his sables, his melancholy countenance [etc.].

4. A book-name of several species of pyralid moths, esp. of the genera *Botys* and *Ennychia*.

1832 RENNIE *Conspect. Butterfl. & M.* 149 The Wavy-barred Sable (*Ennychia anguinalis*). *Ibid.* The Silver-barred Sable (*E. cingulata*).

5. In full ***sable antelope***. A large stout-horned antelope, *Hippotragus* (*Ægocerus*) *niger*, native of South and East Africa, the male of which is of a deep black colour.

1850 R. G. CUMMING *Hunter's Life S. Afr.* (1902) 95/1 An old buck of the sable antelope, the rarest and most beautiful animal in South Africa. **1895** J. G. MILLAIS *Breath fr. Veldt* (1899) 294, I saw the head and horns of a grand sable, looking straight at me. **1900** GROGAN & SHARP *Cape to Cairo* v. 49, I saw two grand bull sable browsing.

6. *Comb.*, parasynthetic and instrumental, as ***sable-bordered, -cinctured, -coloured, -gowned, -hooded, -lettered, -robed, -spotted, -stoled, -suited, -tinted, -vested, visaged*** adjs.

a **1758** RAMSAY *Death R. Alexander* i, Thou *sable-border'd sheet begone! **1744** AKENSIDE *Pleas. Imag.* III. 97 Learning's garb, With formal band, and *sable-cinctur'd gown. **1588** SHAKS. *L.L.L.* I. i. 233 It is besieged with *sable coloured melancholie. **1596** R. L[INCHE] *Diella* (1877) 75 Night puts on her mistie sable-coloured vayle. **1848** J. G. WHITTIER in *National Era* 14 Dec. 198/5 The *sable-gowned divine.. shall prove Their trade accordant with the Law of Love. **1770** W. HODSON *Ded. Temple Solomon* 13 The dreary Realms Of *sable-hooded Night. **1810** SCOTT *Lady of L.* III. vi, In vain, the learning of the age Unclasp'd the *sable-letter'd page. **1599** T. M[OUFET] *Silkwormes* 54 Like *sable-robed Ants. **1857** RUSKIN *Pol. Econ. Art* ii. (1868) 104 Walled towers.. *sable-spotted with cannon-courses. **1629** MILTON *Hymn Nativity* xxiv, The *sable-stoled Sorcerers bear his worship Ark. **1590** GREENE *Orl. Fur.* (1599) G 3 b, Phœbus, put out thy *sable suted wreathe. **1918** G. FRANKAU *One of Them* II. xvi. 121 Hat thrown aside from tresses *sable-tinted. **1667** MILTON *P.L.* II. 962 With him Enthron'd Sat *Sable-vested Night. **1608** *Merry Devil of Edmonton* Prol. 24 The silent *sable visagde night.

B. *adj.* In 6–7 also **sables**.

1. *Her.* Of a black colour; black.

1470–85 MALORY *Arthur* v. ix. 176 The knyght bare in his sheld thre gryffons of gold in sable charbuncle. **1610** HOLLAND *Camden's Brit.* 193 In a shield sables, they beare for their armes six Swallowes argent. **1875** FORTNUM *Maiolica* ix. 79 Paly gules and or, on a fess argent a dog in the act of bounding sable.

2. *gen.* Black. Chiefly *poet.* and *rhetorical.*

a. Of material objects, persons, animals, etc. At one time applied *joc.* to Black people. ***his sable majesty*** (also, ***excellency***): applied to a dark-complexioned potentate; *spec.* the Devil.

1485–1509 in Grose *Antiq. Rep.* (1809) IV. 408 The margent sylver and the notis sabill. **1508** DUNBAR *Tua Mariit Wemen* 447 According to my sable weid I mon haif sad maneris. **1589** GREENE *Menaphon* (Arb. 81) He apparailed himselfe in armour, colour sables, as mourning for his Mistres. **1595** R. JOHNSON *7 Champions* (1608) 72 The walles [were] behung with sable mourning cloth. **1655** FULLER *Ch. Hist.* II. iii. §29 This Year the English have cause to write with Sable letters in their Almanack,.. that [etc.]. *a* **1700** DRYDEN *Theodore & Honoria* 272 Last came the Fellon on the Sable Steed. **1769** SIR W. JONES *Palace Fortune* Poems (1777) 22 His few gray locks a sable fillet bound. **1815** *Ann. Reg., Chron.* 63 The ceremonies were performed by a sable archbishop. **1822** SOUTHEY *Vis. Judgm.* VIII. Poet. Wks. 1838 X. 232 He of the sable mail, the hero of Cressy. **1867** G. H. LEWES *Let.* 8 Aug. in *Geo. Eliot Lett.* (1956) IV. 384 Here he translated the Bible, and here he wrestled with Satan, flinging (like a true literary antagonist) his ink-stand at his sable majesty's head, and staining the whitewashed wall. **1875** J. D. LANG *Hist. Acct. New South Wales* (ed. 4) I. xi. 393 If Her Majesty could have commissioned the Prince of Darkness to represent her in the Colony.., I doubt not but his sable Excellency would have received a Farewell Address of respect. **1881** [see MAJESTY 2]. **1890** 'R. BOLDREWOOD' *Miner's Right* (1899) 56/1 When the middle passage is safely passed and the death-scared sable crowd 'sold and delivered'. **1895** *Photos* 8 June 10 His sable majesty.. is a man of great force of character.

b. Of sky, sea, land, night, and the like.

1500–20 DUNBAR *Poems* xlvi. 2 Aurora did vpspring, With cristall ene chasing the cluddis sable. *c* **1586** C'TESS PEMBROKE *Ps.* CXXXIX. vi, Doe thou thy best, O secret night, In sable vaile to cover me. **1615** BRATHWAIT *Strappado* (1878) 15 Whose storie, Shall.. shew it selfe.. more bright, Then chast Latona on the sablest night. **1633** P. FLETCHER *Purple Isl.* VII. xxxii, So when the South (dipping his sablest wings In humid Ocean) sweeps.. Th' aire, earth, and seas. **1634** MILTON *Comus* 221 Was I deceiv'd, or did a sable cloud Turn forth her silver lining on the night? **1735** SOMERVILLE *Chase* II. 415 The Night Wrapt in her sable Veil forbids the Chace. **1810** SCOTT *Lady of L.* II. xxxiv, As flashes flame through sable smoke. **1853** C. BRONTE *Villette* vi, Down the sable flood we glided.

c. Of agencies personified.

1726 POPE *Odyss.* XX. 308 Your future thought let sable Fate employ. **1749** SMOLLETT *Regicide* IV. ii, Ha! Did'st thou say, revenge? Hail, sable pow'r.

d. Of dark-coloured liquids. *rare.*

1791 COWPER *Iliad* IV. 58 Quick flowed a sable current from the wound. *Ibid.* XXI. 200 The other as it flew Grazed his right elbow: sprang the sable blood. **1808** SCOTT *Marm.* VI. Introd. 13 They.. Caroused in seas of sable beer.

†**3.** Mournful. *Obs.*

1603 CHETTLE *Eng. Mourn. Garm.* D 3, Nor doth the siluer tonged Melicert, Drop from his honied muse one sable teare. **1613** R. CAWDREY *Table Alph.* (ed. 3), *Sable*,.. mournefull. **1708** *Repl. to Swift's Bickerstaff detected* S.'s Wks. 1755 II. I. 167 A long sable elegy. **1780** COWPER *Lett.* 6 Apr., Such a sable state of mind as I labour under.

†**'sable**, *sb.*[3] *Obs.* Also 7 **zable**, 7–8 **sabel**; and see SHABLE. [Prob. a. Du. or early mod.Ger. *sabel* (later Ger. *säbel*): see SABRE.] = SABRE *sb.*

1617 J. TAYLOR (Water P.) *Fight at Sea* Wks. (1630) III. 34/1 Some with Sabels, which we call Fauchions.. and some with Half pikes. **1652** J. WRIGHT tr. *Camus' Nat. Paradox* III. 50 Stanislas.. came with his Sable in his Hand. **1674** *Phil. Trans.* IX. 184 They use Musquets, Bows and Arrows, Zables, Javelins; and for their Trumpets they employ great Elefants-teeth. **1682** *Lond. Gaz.* No. 1765/1 The Moneys.. has on one side a Hand with a naked Sable in it. **1706** PHILLIPS (ed. Kersey), *Sable*, or *Sabre*.

sable ('seɪb(ə)l), *sb.*[4] [ad. Pg. *savel*.] An Indian fish; = HILSA. Usually ***sable-fish***.

1810 T. WILLIAMSON *East India Vade M.* II. 154 The *hilsah*, (or sable fish,) which seems to be mid-way between a mackarel and a salmon,.. is, perhaps, the richest fish with which any cook is acquainted. **1846** J. T. THOMPSON *Hindu Dict.*, *Ilëesh*.. the Hilsa or Sable. **1883** F. DAY *Indian Fish* 34 (Fish. Exhib. Publ.) An anadromous shad termed 'Pulla' in the Indus,.. 'Sable-fish' by the Madrassees,.. [and] 'Hilsa' or 'ilisha' in Bengal.

sable ('seɪb(ə)l), *v.* Chiefly *poet.* [f. SABLE *a.*] *trans.* To blacken or darken. Also, to clothe in 'sables'. Now *rare.*

1610 G. FLETCHER *Christ's Tri.* I. xxxvi, And sabled all in blacke the shadie skie. **1640** FULLER *Joseph's Coat, David's Sin* xxxii. (1867) 213 Sepian juice did sink Into his spongy paper, sabling o'er The same. **1726** POPE *Odyss.* XX. 103 Airy terrors sable ev'ry dream. **1800** MOORE *Anacreon* lix, Sabled by the solar beam, Now the fiery clusters teem. **1890** *Temple Bar* Sept. 14 She is probably no longer sobbing and sabled.

Hence **'sabled** *ppl. a.*, clad in black.

1804 *Something Odd* II. 88 The sabled gentleman fancies himself struck with the sublimities of Miss Gervaise.

sablefish ('seɪb(ə)lfɪʃ). *N. Amer.* [f. SABLE *a.* + FISH *sb.*[1]] A grey- or black-skinned fish of the family Anoplopomatidæ, esp. *Anoplopoma fimbria*, found in the Pacific off the western coast of North America.

1936 P. S. BARNHART *Marine Fishes S. Calif.* 61 Family Anoplopomatidae. Sablefishes... *Anoplopoma fimbria* (Pallas). Sablefish... In northern waters this fish becomes very fat and is much valued for food. **1964** G. C. CARL *Some Common Marine Fishes Brit. Columbia* 48 The sablefish.. is smoked and sold under the name of 'black cod'. **1972** *Islander* (Victoria, B.C.) 16 Apr. 13/3 Should black cod, or sablefish, prove to be unrewarding, she is designed to convert easily for tuna fishing. **1975** *Sci. Amer.* Oct. 88/3 The flatnose codling, the sablefish and the arctic sleeper shark are common inhabitants of the bottom off the coast of southern California and Lower California.

†**sableize** ('seɪb(ə)laɪz), *v. Obs. rare*$^{-1}$. [f. SABLE *a.* + -IZE.] *trans.* To make black.

1611 DAVIES *Sco. Folly*, etc. 237 Some Chroniclers that write of Kingdomes States Do so absurdly sableize my White With Maskes and Enterludes by Day and Night.

sableness ('seɪb(ə)lnɪs). [f. SABLE *a.* + -NESS.] Blackness; †mournfulness, gloom.

1607 *Schol. Disc. agst. Antichr.* I. iii. 128 This was a signe of some sablenes, of some saddnes. **1839** *Fraser's Mag.* XX. 63 The funereal sableness of the far-stretching forests. **1884** G. P. LATHROP *True* xi. 117 The sable driver subsided completely into the depths of his sableness.

†**sabliere**[1]. *Arch. Obs.* [a. F. *sablière*, of obscure origin.] 'A piece of wood as long as a beam but not so thick' (Phillips 1696).

1800 HENRY & THOMPSON *Jrnl.* 23 Oct. in E. Coues *New Light Early Hist. Greater Northwest* (1897) I. iii. 123 Oak logs.. contg. 100 ft. for the sableries. **1809** D. THOMPSON *Jrnl.* 18 Nov. (1950) 64 Men put up the partition Wall of my Room & finished the Walls the Sablier Beams Roof Beams &c which ended the Day.

†**sabliere**[2]. *Obs.* [a. F. *sablière* sand-pit, f. *sable* sand:—L. *sabulum*.] A sand-pit or gravel-pit.

1706 in PHILLIPS.

sably ('seɪblɪ), *adv.* [f. SABLE *a.* + -LY[2].] Darkly, blackly.

1831 *Fraser's Mag.* III. 336 The sably snowy swan. **1887** MRS. C. READE *Maid o' Mill* II. xxxviii. 285 A funeral train streams sably down Ewshot Hill.

sablyne, variant of SABELINE *Obs.*

Sabme, var. SAMI.

‖**sabot** (sabo). [F. *sabot* (OF. in 13th c. *çabot*, mod.Picard *chabot*) prob. related in some way to *savate* shoe, Pr. *sabata*: see SABATON.]

1. a. A wooden shoe made of a single piece of wood shaped and hollowed out to fit the foot.

1607 R. C[AREW] tr. *Estienne's World of Wonders* 299 Wodden shoes properly called sabots. **1673** C. HATTON in *H. Corr.* (Camden) 118 A sabot having a great bracelet of beades passed through yᵉ heel. **1765** H. WALPOLE *Let. to J. Chute* 3 Oct., Two fellows were sweeping it [*sc.* the Dauphin's bedchamber] and dancing about in sabots to rub the floor. **1792** A. YOUNG *Trav. France* 18 The ploughmen ..have neither sabots nor feet to their stockings. **1846** CHURCH *Misc. Writ.* (1891) I. 92 Captains in the imperial armies.. resumed their sabots and baggy breeches. **1888** MISS BRADDON *Fatal Three* I. iv, Two boys in blouses and sabots.

attrib. **1800** WEEMS *Washington* viii. (1877) 62 The Sabot or wooden shoed nation, the French.

b. A kind of shoe having a thick wooden sole and 'uppers' of coarse leather.

1840 BARHAM *Ingol. Leg.* Ser. I. *Bagman's Dog*, He'd a 'dreadnought' coat, and heavy *sabots* With thick wooden soles turn'd up at the toes. **1879** BEERBOHM *Patagonia* iii. 43 [He] would now and then wear a pair of sabots made with the skin of the hind legs of the guanacho.

2. *Mil.* **a.** A wooden disc attached to a spherical projectile by means of a copper rivet for the purpose of keeping it evenly in place in the bore of the piece when discharged. **b.** A metal cup fixed by means of metal straps to a conical projectile, to cause it to 'take' the rifling of the gun.

1855 NORTON in *Mech. Mag.* LXII. 88 Expanding self-cleansing sabot for rifle-shot. **1859** F. A. GRIFFITHS *Artill. Man.* (ed. 8) 86 The 'bottoms' or 'sabots' of all naval shells are hollowed out. *Ibid.* 97 Wooden Bottoms, or Sabots. **1860** TENNENT *Story Guns* (1864) 209 The shot, unprotected by a sabot, may have shifted its place. **1866** *Cornh. Mag.* Sept. 355 An egg-shaped bullet, its base embedded in a *papier mâché* sabot. **1868** *Rep. to Govt. U.S. Munitions of War* 63 The fulminate which is put in a card-board *sabot* next the charge.

c. Any device fitted inside the muzzle of a gun to hold or support the projectile to be fired (as when they are of different calibres).

1950 SCOTT & RICHARDSON *Fin Stabilized Projectile Devel. for 3 inch/70 Gun* (NAVORD Rep. 1537: AD 857–242) 3 Removal of the sabot by spin can be disregarded as the projectile acquires little, if any, spin in the smooth bore tube... The type of sabot developed by the Germans during World War II, and operating primarily by muzzle blast with the assistance of the air stream, is the simplest in design. **1954** K. W. GATLAND *Devel. Guided Missile* (ed. 2) ii. 47 Models launched from guns in the new supersonic free-flight wind-tunnel are protected in the gun barrel by plastic 'sabots' which keep the models correctly aligned and act as pistons. **1957** E. BURGESS *Guided Weapons* iv. 100 The models.. which are being tested are launched through a smooth-bore gun by means of a discarding sabot. **1963** *Dict. U.S. Mil. Terms* (U.S. Dept. Defense) 188 *Sabot*, lightweight carrier in which a subcaliber projectile is centered to permit firing the projectile in the larger caliber weapon. The carrier fills the bore of the weapon from which the projectile is fired; it is normally discarded a short distance from the muzzle. **1975** I. V. HOGG *German Artillery of World War Two* 267 An enormous range of sabot shells was developed in Germany with the intention of either increasing the range of field guns or reducing the time of flight of anti-aircraft shells.

3. *Mech.* The iron shoe or point of a pile (Knight *Dict. Mech.* Suppl., 1884); an iron shoe used to protect the end of a file for working metal (*Cent. Dict.* 1891); a cutting armature at the end of a tubular boring-rod.

1884 *Public Opinion* 3 Oct. 432 The system of sinking shafts..by means of hollow iron tubes with cutting sabots.

4. A brace connected with the pedal of a harp and used for shortening the string.

1891 in *Century Dict.*

5. (See quot. 1966.)

1962 *Internat. Art Treasures Exhib., Victoria & Albert Mus.* 20/2 A Louis XV parquetry table à écrire..raised on cabriole legs with gilt bronze sabots. **1966** M. M. Pegler *Dict. Interior Design* (1967) 383 *Sabots*... Decorative metal coverings for the feet of wood furniture..appeared in the 18th century, and were made of bronze doré, bronze, brass, etc. **1980** *Country Life* 3 July 11/2 A ravishing writing desk. .. The cabriole legs are framed by moulded ormolu borders reaching down to pierced sabots.

6. In baccarat and chemin de fer, a shoe: see shoe *sb.* 5.

[**1963** C. Graves *None but the Rich* 3 Baccarat, in fact, is chemin-de-fer played with a fixed bank, chemin-de-fer taking its name from the fact that the 'shoe' (in French, *sabot*), as the deal box is known, moves like a toy railway train round the table each time the dealer loses.] **1964** A. Wykes *Gambling* vii. 177 (*caption*) The *sabot* from which the 'chemmy' cards are dealt. **1966** P. O'Donnell *Sabre-Tooth* vi. 93 The sabot containing the six packs of cards, recently shuffled and stacked by the croupier. **1977** X. Fielding *Money Spinner* 162 Finally they are placed in the 'shoe' or *sabot*, from which the banker deals them one by one.

Hence 'saboted *ppl. a.*, shod with sabots.

1862 Simeon in *Macm. Mag.* Mar. 421 The bloused and saboted driver. **1885** *Pall Mall G.* 28 Aug. 11/2 Colonies of greasy, sabotted Frenchmen. **1905** *Daily Chron.* 27 Mar. 4/5 His blue-bloused and sabotted gardeners.

sabotage ('sæbətɑːʒ, ‖sabɔtaʒ), *sb.* [Fr., f. *saboter* to make a noise with sabots, to perform or execute badly, e.g. to 'murder' (a piece of music), to destroy wilfully (tools, machinery, etc.), f. *sabot*: see sabot and -age.] The malicious damaging or destruction of an employer's property by workmen during a strike or the like; hence *gen.* any disabling damage deliberately inflicted, esp. that carried out clandestinely in order to disrupt the economic or military resources of an enemy. Also *transf.*, *fig.*, and *attrib.*

1910 *Church Times* 11 Nov. 631/2 We have lately been busy in deploring the *sabotage* of the French railway strikers. **1916** *Sydney Morning Herald* 18 Oct., A shearing rouseabout,..charged..with having written a letter to Senator Lynch, threatening him and certain other Labour politicians and employers of Australia with acts of sabotage. **1918** E. S. Farrow *Dict. Mil. Terms* 528 *Sabotage*, wanton destruction of property to embarrass or injure an enemy; such as the smashing of machinery, flooding of mines, burning of wheat and grain, destroying fruit and provisions, dynamiting reservoirs and aqueducts, tying up railroads, etc. **1920** *Glasgow Herald* 26 June 7 Forces are at work in Germany for the sabotage of the Treaty. **1931** W. Martyn *Scarlett Murder* iv. 53 He was in that mood of smouldering rage which only sabotage would slake. **1948** *N.Y. Jrnl. American* (Sunday Mail ed.) 9 May 1/5 Berger and Dasch gave..'full and complete' identification of all connected with the sabotage plot. **1955** *Times* 27 Aug. 6/7 These were the most considerable sabotages of telephone lines which have yet occurred in this area. **1958** *Spectator* 20 June 791/3 The most recent attack on him has been for cultural sabotage. **1977** *South China Morning Post* (Hong Kong) 22 July 1/4 The border flare-up began on July 12, the radio said, when a four-man Libyan sabotage squad was arrested after crossing the border armed with machineguns and explosives. **1978** T. Allbeury *Lantern Network* vii. 86 Langlois had led six-man teams on fifteen sabotage missions. **1979** *Tucson* (Arizona) *Citizen* 20 Sept. 11A/5 The PLO has provided guns and sabotage devices to its IRA friends.

Hence 'sabotage *v. trans.*, to ruin, destroy, or disable deliberately and maliciously (freq. by indirect means); 'sabotaging *vbl. sb.*

1918 *New Appeal* 7 Dec. 1/2 Testimony..that the companies are sabotaging the government. **1920** *Glasgow Herald* 20 Aug. 7 When the miners threaten to sabotage the commerce of the country struggling to get back to pre-war prosperity. **1923** *Ibid.* 4 Jan. 4 The sabotaging of the Dual Monarchy, the revolt of the Yugoslav troops, [etc.]. **1934** C. Lambert *Music Ho!* v. 303 Technically speaking it [*sc.* the atonal school] sabotaged the moribund romantic tradition. **1941** *Sun* (Baltimore) 22 Mar. 24/1 The fireworks bill..was passed by the Senate tonight..despite eleventh-hour attempts to sabotage it or delay enactment. **1975** *Times* 14 Jan. 14/3 [Michael Foot] defended the social contract and weighed into the press for sabotaging it.

sabota lark (sə'bəʊtə lɑːk). [f. *sabota*, native name of the bird adopted as its specific name (A. Smith *Rep. Exped. for Exploring Central Africa* (1836) 47) + lark *sb.*[1]] A buff-coloured lark, *Mirafra sabota* or *M. nævius*, of the family Alaudidæ, found in southern Africa.

1884 R. B. Sharpe *Layard's Birds S. Afr.* (rev. ed.) 526 Sabota Lark... Sir Andrew Smith procured this lark on the arid plains north of Latakoo. **1896** H. A. Bryden *Tales S. Afr.* v. 109 There, too, are the thick-billed lark, the Sabota lark, with its clear ringing call, and a few other—but not many—small birds. **1948** C. D. Priest *Eggs of Birds breeding in S. Afr.* 67 Sabota Lark... In grass on the ground, at times the cup-shaped nest not being well concealed. **1964** P. A. Clancey *Birds Natal & Zululand* 293 The sabota lark commences to breed in October.

saboteur ('sæbətɜː(r), ‖sabɔtœr). Also fem. **saboteuse**. [Fr.] One who commits sabotage.

1921 tr. *W. Rathenau's New Society* 125 The *saboteurs* of labour. **1931** *Observer* 11 Jan. 20/2 Two managers of a dairy were dubbed saboteurs and sentenced to..imprisonment for letting two hundred tons of butter spoil. **1947** J. Mulgan *Report on Experience* xii. 148 The men who were killed had been *saboteurs*, or gleaners of information for the Allies, patriots in their own quiet and dangerous way. **1973** E. Pace *Any War will Do* iii. 199 They're too chicken to send in their paratroopers, and they're not smart enough to send in saboteurs. **1977** Saboteuse [see pig *sb.*[1] 6 b]. **1977** *South China Morning Post* (Hong Kong) 22 July 1/3, 12 members of the 9th Libyan Armoured Division were taken prisoner along with 30 saboteurs. **1980** *Daily Tel.* 20 Mar. 1/5 Two fox-hunt saboteurs who had appeared as prosecution witnesses against hunt followers.

sabquha, var. sabkha.

Sabra ('sæbrə). [ad. mod.Heb. *ṣābrāh* prickly pear.] **1.** (Also with small initial.) A Jew born in Palestine (see Palestinian *a.* and *sb.*) or, after 1948, in Israel (see Israel 3). Also *attrib.*

1945 *Zionist Rev.* 16 Nov. 8/2 Of course I was born here. No, I am not a new immigrant, not even an old one; I am a *sabra*. **1946** Koestler *Thieves in Night* i. ii. 9 They were Sabras—nicknamed after the thorny, rather tasteless fruit of the cactus, grown on arid earth, tough, hard-living, scant. *Ibid.* ii. ii. 95 These Sabra-boys regard a glass of wine as something like opium or hashish. **1949** —— *Promise & Fulfilment* 222 He is a *sabra*, with a pleasant open face and good physique. **1958** M. E. Spiro *Children of Kibbutz* p. x, My research problem, therefore, was restricted to the relationships between kibbutz child training and *sabra* (one born and raised in a kibbutz) personality. **1971** *Times* 28 Sept. (Israel Suppl.) p. iv/4 Only two of the 18 Ministers in Israel's Government are *sabras*, native Israel Jews... There is no *sabra* university president. **1977** *Time* 4 July 16/1 Begin's predecessor, Yitzhak Rabin, was a nonobservant Sabra who often seemed uncomfortable wearing a yarmulke and unfamiliar with the words of daily prayers.

2. (See quots.)

1970 *House & Garden* Nov. 139/1 Sabra is a new liqueur from Israel..a blend of Jaffa orange and chocolate. **1975** *Times* 11 Jan. 11/5 Sabra, the Israel liqueur made with bitter oranges and a very bitter Swiss chocolate.

†**sabras.** *Obs.* Also 3 **sabraz**, 5 **saberas, saberace**. [? a. Pr. *saboratz*, pa. pple. of *saborar* to season.] A decoction or infusion.

a **1225** *Ancr. R.* 364 þe on uorgeð al þet he luued of metes & of drunches, & drinkeð bitter sabraz uorto akoueren his heale. *c* **1440** *Promp. Parv.* 440/1 Sabrace, *sabracia*. *c* **1480** *Sloane MS.* 73, lf. 211 Tak thi lether and basche it wel in this sabras. *Ibid.*, That that saberas be wel drunken up in to the lether. *Ibid.*, Poure thi sabrace al aboven the lether.

sabre ('seɪbə(r)), *sb.* Also 8 sabir, 9- *U.S.* saber. [a. F. *sabre* (17th c.), an unexplained alteration of *sable* (Oudin 1640: cf. Sp. *sable*) a. G. *sabel* (now *säbel*), whence sable *sb.*[3] The ultimate source is prob. to be sought in some Oriental language; forms with initial (ʃ) are found in Hungarian *szablya* (whence perh. It. *sciabla*, shable) and Polish *szabla*; the Russian *sablya* may be from German.]

1. a. A cavalry sword having a curved blade specially adapted for cutting.

1680 Otway *Orphan* ii. iii. 514 With my good Sabir drawn..I..clove the Rebel to the Chine. **1697** *Lond. Gaz.* No. 3291/1 The Chief Officers..came with their Sabres in their Hands. **1791** Mrs. Radcliffe *Rom. Forest* xii, He received himself the stroke of a sabre on his head. **1845** Darwin *Voy. Nat.* iii. (1879) 41 My companions were well armed with pistols and sabres. **1889** Gunter *That Frenchman* x, Several pairs of foils, and sabers.

b. Put for: Military force; esp. in phr. *to rattle the sabre*.

1851 Gallenga *Italy* 91 The Milanese were long since under the rule of the sabre. **1922**, etc. [see *sabre-rattling* vbl. sb. and ppl. adj., sense 4 a below]. **1928**, etc. [see *sabre-rattler*, sense 4 a below]. **1949** *Western Folklore* VIII. 112 To rattle the saber. To threaten military action. **1968** *Listener* 29 Aug. 259/2 The antique apparatus of Soviet diplomacy complete with rattling sabres and dutiful crowd noises from the Warsaw satellites, was mobilised in the hope of strengthening the Old Guard in the Czechoslovak party. **1976** *Times* 27 Jan. 1/3 At least a few Conservatives..doubt whether Mrs Thatcher was prudent to appear to rattle sabres and remind electors that women national leaders.. have sometimes looked more warlike than men. **1978** J. A. Michener *Chesapeake* 704 Orators from many southern states came north to excite voters against the dangers of black franchise, and sabers rattled as ancient battles were recalled.

c. In Fencing, a weapon with a flattened blade and blunted cutting edge, either curved or straight, lighter than the épée; the exercise of fencing with sabres.

[**1880** J. M. Waite *Lessons in Sabre* p. xi, I have had the honour of instructing the following Clubs in both Fencing and Sabre:—The London Fencing Club [etc.].] **1910** *Encycl. Brit.* X. 252/1 Just as the practice of the 'small' or thrusting sword gave rise to two rival schools, the French and the Italian, that of the sabre or cutting sword..became split up into two main systems, Italian and German. **1927** L. Bertrand *Cut & Thrust* vi. 75 He was..a resplendent figure..waving..a light and fragile silver-plated sabre. **1935** *Encycl. Sports* 531/1 In fencing with the sabre, the upper part of the body is the sole target, and the hits are made by cuts. **1952** *Fencing* ('Know the Game' Ser.) 5 To hit at foil, épée and sabre, is to strike the opponent with the point of the sword so that it fixes clearly and distinctly and has a character of penetration. **1954** R. Crosnier *Fencing with Sabre* i. 22 At sabre, the distance between two fencers is such that body or head cannot be hit when the opponent lunges fully. **1971** I. Butykai tr. *Lukovich's Electric Foil Fencing* ii. 166 This is also in support of what is described above about the application in sabre of feints with the body. **1978** G. Wright *Illustr. Handbk. Sporting Terms* 32 If, in foil and sabre, hits are equal, the bout continues until a deciding hit is landed. *Ibid.* 33 The ancestors of the sabre include the eastern sabre, the English broadsword, and the cavalry sabre.

2. A cavalry 'unit'; a soldier armed with a sabre.

1829 Napier *Penins. War* (1878) II. 484 General total,.. 56,239 sabres and bayonets in the field. **1895** Sir E. Wood *Cavalry in Waterloo Camp.* v. 120 Somerset's Heavy Brigade:—..Total paper strength 1,220 sabres.

3. An implement used for removing scum from the surface of molten glass.

1832 G. R. Porter *Porcelain & Gl.* 202 Removing with a broad copper sabre any scum that may have formed on the surface of the glass. **1839** Ure *Dict. Arts* 590 The bucket is skimmed by means of a copper tool called a sabre.

4. a. *attrib.* and *Comb.*, as *sabre-fencer*, *-fencing*, *-play*, *-player*, *-stroke*; *sabre-cut*, *-like*, *-shaped* adjs.; **sabre-bayonet**, a weapon which can be used either as a sabre or a bayonet; **sabre-bill**, a South American dendrocolaptine bird of the genus *Xiphorhynchus*; **sabre-cut**, (*a*) a blow with a sabre; (*b*) a cut or scar left by the stroke of a sabre; **sabre-fish**, *U.S.*, the cutlass-fish, *Trichiurus lepturus*; **sabre leg** (see quot. 1952); also *attrib.*; **sabre-rattler**, a reckless militarist; one who threatens violent action; **sabre-rattling** vbl. sb., military aggression; threatening violent action; aggressive blustering; also as *ppl. adj.*; **sabre saw**, a portable electric saw with a narrow reciprocating blade, used for cutting curves; **sabre-wing**, a humming-bird of the genus *Campylopterus* (and related genera).

1863 T. E. C. *Battlefields of the South* I. 252 Many more were destroyed with the *sabre-bayonet when our men closed in upon them. **1859-62** Sir J. Richardson, etc. *Mus. Nat. Hist.* 319 The Brazilian *Sabre-bill (*Xiphorhynchus procurvus*). *c* **1820** S. Rogers *Italy* (1839) 216 On his wan cheek a *sabre-cut. **1828** Miss Mitford *Village* Ser. iii. 49 Against Justice and Constable, treadmill and stocks, the sabre-cut was a protection. **1883** Stevenson *Treas. Isl.* ii. vii, The captain..with his..sabre-cut cheek. **1952** *Fencing* ('Know the Game Ser.) 26 Modern *sabre fencers..have developed a technique when attacking, of directing the blade, changing its direction, and striking, by means of wrist actions and finger manipulation. **1954** R. Crosnier *Fencing with Sabre* i. 28 Sabre fencers who have progressed in technique and sword control, acquire the ability to change their grip, slightly, when attacking or defending. **1927** L. Bertrand *Cut & Thrust* vi. 77 The rules of *sabre-fencing are eminently practical. **1954** R. Crosnier *Fencing with Sabre* 14 When reading this text-book, some may accuse me of having approached the subject of sabre fencing with the mind of a confirmed foilist. **1975** *Oxf. Compan. Sports & Games* 304/2 It is..necessary to have..a president to control the bout and award hits according to the rules and conventions applicable to sabre fencing. **1863** *Chamb. Encycl.* V. 192/2 The Silvery Hair-tail..is called *Sabre-fish in Cuba. **1888** Goode *Amer. Fishes* 255 The Cutlass-fish ..is known..on the coast of Texas as 'Sabre-fish'. **1952** J. Gloag *Short Dict. Furnit.* 404 *Sabre leg, a hollow curved leg of rectangular section, so called because of its resemblance to the curve of a cavalry sabre. It was copied from the seats and thrones depicted on Greek and Roman vases, and was introduced towards the end of the 18th century. After 1815, it was sometimes called a Waterloo leg. In chairs of cheap quality the front edge is usually rounded. **1963** *Times* 2 Mar. 5/4 A small walnut kneehole desk made £220 (Quinney's), six sabre-leg Regency dining chairs £160. **1974** *Country Life* 5 Dec. (Suppl.) 78/2 A George III Sofa Table..with swept sabre legs. **1934** Webster, *Saber-like. **1962** D. Nichols *Echinoderms* i. 20 *Machaeridia*, bilaterally symmetrical worm-like remains with a skeleton of imbricating plates. Greek: 'sabre-like'. **1880** J. M. Waite *Lessons in Sabre* p. vi, The English method of *sabre play.. could be considerably improved. **1927** L. Bertrand *Cut & Thrust* vi. 81 In..observance of this maxim [*sc. sciabola in mano*] lies the *alpha and omega* of all sabre-play. **1954** R. Crosnier *Fencing with Sabre* i. v. 26 The Hungarian principle..maintained that sabre play was a combination of finger-play and wrist work, conducive to light, rapid, and precise blade actions. **1880** J. M. Waite *Lessons in Sabre* p. vi, *Sabre players, as a rule, have not been fencers, or at least have been fencers with trifling skill. **1928** *Daily Express* 6 Dec. 5/2 There is no reason for supposing that the child Napoleon will grow up a *sabre-rattler. **1975** *Times Lit. Suppl.* 6 June 625/4 When he [*sc.* Churchill] came to the rescue of Montagu in the stormy Amritsar debate, he incurred the disgust of the sabre-rattlers. **1922** *Weekly Dispatch* 19 Nov. 8 A policy of adventure, *sabre-rattling, and reckless expenditure. **1928** *Observer* 26 Feb. 16/4 A sabre-rattling gesture against a nation with whom we have been at peace for more than a hundred years. **1958** Hayward & Harari tr. *Pasternak's Dr. Zhivago* i. iv. 105 You have to swagger about in an officer's uniform too, you have to do your own bit of sabre-rattling. **1973** 'I. Drummond' *Jaws of Watchdog* x. 136 A sabre-rattling pink-hating American. **1977** C. McCullough *Thorn Birds* ii. 40 Look at the way that saber-rattling Churchill sent our men into something as useless as Gallipoli! **1977** *Time* 24 Oct. 8/1 Despite saber-rattling rhetoric, a steel war is far from inevitable. **1953** R. J. De Cristoforo *Power Tool Woodworking for Everyone* v. 179 *Saber saws are usually confined to heavy cutting when curves are not too severe. **1976** M. Machlin *Pipeline* xxviii. 334 The group carried two battery operated saber-saws with hacksaw blades in their chucks. **1980** *Sci. Amer.* Mar. 29/2 A big saber saw, its diamond blade able to cut a four-foot slab at one pass (beyond the two-foot reach of the biggest rotary blades), requires some 25 horsepower, delivered by hydraulic flow from its engine trailer nearby. **1796** *Encycl. Brit.* (ed. 3) III. 442/2 [Of a part of a plant.] *Sabre-shaped. **1841** *Penny Cycl.* XXI. 423/1 The rostrum [of *Rhynchocinetes*]..is very large, sabre-shaped, and dentilated on both edges. **1895** A. H. COOKE *Molluscs* (Camb. Nat. Hist. III.) 236 Laterals simple, sabre-shaped. **1854** TENNYSON *Charge of Light Brigade* in *Wks.* (1896) 222/2 Cossack and Russian Reel'd from the *sabre-stroke Shatter'd and sunder'd. **1861** GOULD *Humming-B.* II. pl. 43 *Campylopterus pampa*, Wedge-tailed *Sabre-wing. **1893** NEWTON *Dict. Birds* 446 The group known as 'Sabre-wings'.

b. sabre-toothed, *a.*, designating extinct animals, see below; also *fig.*, ferocious; **sabre-tooth(ed) cat** = *sabre-toothed lion, tiger*; **sabre-toothed lion** or **tiger**, a large extinct feline mammal of the subfamily Machærodontinæ, with long sabre-shaped upper canines. Also **sabre-tooth** *a.* and *sb.*

1849 *Todd's Cycl. Anat.* IV. 909/2 The great extinct sabre-toothed tiger. **1880** DAWKINS *Early Man Britain* iii. 57 The great sabre-toothed lion, *Machairodus*. **1896** KIPLING *Seven Seas, Ung* iii, He..pictured the sabre-tooth tiger dragging a man to his lair. *Ibid.* v, Hath he..followed the Sabre-tooth home? **1906** E. INGERSOLL *Life Animals: Mammals* 86 A divergent branch..developed amazingly throughout most of the Tertiary period,..to which Cuvier gave the name of 'saber-tooth cats'. **1933** A. S. ROMER *Vertebr. Paleont.* xv. 294 In sharp contrast are the saber-toothed 'cats', Machaerodontinae... In the saber-tooths the upper canines were exceedingly long stabbing and slicing structures. **1968** *Times* 21 Dec. 2/3 There was a sabre-toothed scrummage of photographers. **1973** Sabretooth cat [see MACHÆRODONT *a.*]. **1975** J. G. EVANS *Environment Early Man Brit. Isles* i. 21 Three species of mammal considered to have become extinct prior to the Hoxnian..a sabre-toothed cat (*Homotherium latidens*) and two voles. **1977** *Times* 14 Mar. 5/3 Henry Howard, Earl of Surrey..fell in the sabre-toothed power struggle for the succession when Henry VIII was dying.

sabre ('seɪbə(r)), *v.* [f. SABRE *sb.* Cf. F. *sabrer*.] *trans.* To strike, cut, or wound with a sabre.

1790 BURKE *Fr. Rev.* Wks. V. 399 And now you send troops to sabre and to bayonet us into a submission to fear and force. **1845** DISRAELI *Sybil* VI. xii, The people were fired on and sabred. **1875** CLERY *Min. Tact.* x. (1877) 123 Ponsonby's cavalry..sabred the gunners and stabbed the horses.

absol. **1865** CARLYLE *Fredk. Gt.* XVIII. xiii. (1872) VIII. 50 The Seidlitz cavalry went sabring till, for very fatigue, they gave it up.

Hence **'sabrer** [cf. F. *sabreur*], one who cuts down with a sabre.

1831 GEN. P. THOMPSON *Exerc.* (1842) I. 416 When men and women were massacred at Manchester..did they dream it was love for the sabrers, that produced an after compliance with their mandates?

sabre, obs. f. SAMBUR, Indian elk.

sabred ('seɪbəd), *a.* [f. SABRE *sb.* + -ED[2].] Furnished or armed with a sabre.

1760–72 H. BROOKE *Fool of Quality* (1792) IV. 162 An arrangement of sabred Hussars with their fierce-looking mustachoes. **1866** *Daily Tel.* 16 Jan. 7/4 There were the Guardsmen, whiskered, mustachio'd, padded, epauletted, sabred. **1883** E. F. KNIGHT *Cruise Falcon* (1887) 61 A gentleman most gorgeously uniformed and sabred.

sabretache ('sæbətɑːʃ, -æ-). Also **sabretasch(e, -tash.** [a. F. *sabretache*, ad. G. *säbeltasche*, f. *säbel* sabre, SABLE *sb.*[2] + *tasche* pocket.] A leather satchel suspended on the left side by long straps from the sword-belt of a cavalry officer.

A MS. letter of 1812 has the word in the corrupt form *zappadash*. The Dicts. incorrectly give ('seɪbətɑːʃ, -æ-).

1812 *Sporting Mag.* XXXIX. 167 A pouch belt and a sabre-tache. **1841** LEVER *C. O'Malley* xv, As strapping a fellow as ever carried a sabretasch. **1858** SIR E. CUST *Ann. Wars* p. viii, The Volume has been so managed that it may not be too much for the pocket, or the sabretash. **1858** CARLYLE *Fredk. Gt.* VII. i. (1872) II. 237 He is withal a kind of soldier..a man of many sabre-tashes. **1901** *Scotsman* 7 Nov. 5/8 The King has been graciously pleased to approve the abolition of the sabre tache.

‖**sabreur** (sabrœr). [Fr.; agent-n., f. *sabrer* to SABRE.]

a. One who fights with a sabre; usually applied to a cavalry soldier distinguished rather for bravery than for skill in war. See also BEAU SABREUR.

1845 W. H. MAXWELL *Hints to Soldier* 77 The humbler but no less gallant sabreur of New Ross. **1854** BADHAM *Halieut.* 418 Our expert sabreur rushes to the conflict, and, carefully avoiding the sweep of his opponent's tremendous tail, soon effects his purpose, by stabbing the luckless leviathan at all points. **1969** N. FREELING *Tsing Boum* ix. 59 Castries the cavalryman, swaggering sabreur.

b. A sabre-fencer.

1927 L. BERTRAND *Cut & Thrust* vi. 81 How to acquire this touch is a question the would-be sabreur has to answer. **1952** *Fencing* ('Know the Game' Ser.) 26 Sabreurs attack more often by means of a 'Flèche', than by means of a lunge. **1958** *Oxf. Mag.* 13 Mar. 377/1 The Cambridge sabreurs challenged our supposed superiority in the sabre. **1978** G. WRIGHT *Illustr. Handbk. Sporting Terms* 35 (*caption*) The flèche attack demonstrated by a sabreur.

sabrina neckline (səˈbriːnə). *U.S.* Also with capital initial. [f. *Sabrina*, the title of a film (1954), in which the actress Audrey Hepburn appeared wearing a dress with such a neckline.] A neckline with ties at the shoulders.

1959 E. HEAD *Dress Doctor* ix. 119, I had to console myself with the dress, whose boat neckline was tied on each shoulder—widely known and copied as 'the *Sabrina* neckline'. **1967** *Boston Sunday Herald* 30 Apr. v. 4/2 The bride wore an 18th century gown of white satin sabrina neckline with a long bodice trimmed with pearls and crystals and a train fastened at the shoulders with bows. **1976** *Columbus* (Montana) *News* 3 June 2/4 The bride's gown fashioned with chantilly lace basque bodice with long fitted sleeves and sabrina neckline, had a full skirt with petal overskirt of organza.

sabugalite (səˈbjuːgəlaɪt). *Min.* [f. *Sabugal*, name of a town in Beira Province, Portugal + -ITE[1].] A mineral of the autunite group, $HAl(UO_2)_2(PO_4)_4.16\text{-}24H_2O$, first found as yellow crystals in a number of mines in Portugal, and also prepared artificially.

1951 C. FRONDEL in *Amer. Mineralogist* XXXVI. 671 Sabugalite is a new member of the autunite group with the composition $HAl(UO_2)_4(PO_4)_4.16H_2O$. **1959** *Ibid.* XLIV. 420 The average index of refraction of the synthetic product indicated a value of about 1·57, which is within the range of indices given by Frondel for natural sabugalite. **1959** [see SALÉEITE].

sabuline ('sæbjuːlaɪn), *a.* [f. L. *sabul-um* sand: see -INE[2].] = SABULOUS.

In recent Dicts.

sabulite ('sæbjuːlaɪt). *Mil.* [f. L. *sabul-um* sand + -ITE[1].] A high explosive consisting of ammonium nitrate with some TNT and calcium silicide.

1914 *Daily Consular & Trade Rep.* 17 June 1641 Tests were recently made..of a new explosive called sabulite, which will be manufactured at Coguitlam, British Columbia. **1914** *Mining & Engin. World* XLI. 676/1 Sabulite, a recent invention by a Belgian explosive expert, had a thorough and satisfactory test..a few days ago. **1919** E. DE B. BARNETT *Explosives* IV. 114 Very similar explosives in which calcium silicide is used in place of aluminium are also manufactured, Sabulite being an explosive of this class. **1940** *Thorpe's Dict. Appl. Chem.* (ed. 4) IV. 464/1 Military sabulite contained ammonium nitrate 78%, trinitrotoluene 8% and calcium silicide 14%, the latter constituent increasing the heat of explosion.

sabull, obs. form of SABLE.

sabulose ('sæbjuːləʊs), *a.* [ad. L. *sabulōsus*: see SABULOUS and -OSE.]

1. *Bot.* (See quot.)

1866 *Treas. Bot.* 1003/1 *Sabulose*, growing in sandy places.

2. = SABULOUS.

In mod. Dicts.

†**sabu'losity.** *Obs.* [ad. L. type **sabulōsitātem*: see next and -ITY.] Sandiness.

1721 in BAILEY; and in later Dicts.

sabulous ('sæbjʊləs), *a.* [ad. L. *sabulōs-us*, f. *sabul-um* sand: see -OUS.] Sandy; consisting of or abounding in sand; arenaceous.

1632 LITHGOW *Trav.* (1906) 226 The austiere conspicuosity of the sabulous and stony Desarts. **1670** R. WITTIE in *Phil. Trans.* V. 1076 Water..strained from all sabulous mixture. **1793** SMEATON *Edystone L.* §193 The quantity and species of sabulous matter that entered into the texture of the lime-stone. **1822** G. WOODLEY *Scilly Isl.* II. iii. 289 This part of the Island..appears rather to have gained from the sea by these sabulous accumulations. **1881** *Academy* 1 Oct. 252 The author [E. W. White] is terribly fond of long words. To him..plains are sabulous..parrots are psittacs.

b. *Med.* Applied to a granular secretion, esp. in the urinary organs.

1670 W. SIMPSON *Hydrol. Ess.* 137 The one Water layes a stony Foundation for a Fabrick of Sabulous diseases. **1694** SALMON *Bate's Dispens.* (1713) 170/2 It..dissolves any tartarous or sabulous Coagulation in the Reins or Ureters. **1836–41** BRANDE *Chem.* (ed. 5) 1389 Sabulous depositions in the urine are of various characters. **1881** *Trans. Obstetric Soc. Lond.* XXVII. 39 Sabulous matter, mixed with mucus.

c. *Anat.*, applied to the acervulus cerebri, or gritty substance of the pineal body of the brain (*Cent. Dict.* 1891).

Hence **'sabulousness**, the state or quality of being sabulous.

1727 in BAILEY vol. II.

‖**saburra** (səˈbʌrə). *Med.* [L. *saburra* sand, cogn. w. *sabulum*: see prec.] Foul granular matter deposited in the body, esp. in the stomach.

1710 T. FULLER *Pharm. Extemp.* 316 This Medicament.. extirpates the Saburra..out of the whole Body. **1772** D. MACBRIDE *Physic* II. 93 The terms Cacochylia and Saburra are used to denote the general accumulation of offensive matters in the alimentary canal. **1822–34** *Good's Study Med.* (ed. 4) I. 644 The slaty or purplish and granular saburra thrown up from the stomach.

Hence **sa'burral** *a.* [cf. L. *saburrālis* consisting of sand], of or belonging to saburra.

1822–34 *Good's Study Med.* (ed. 4) I. 714 An inflammatory fever passing into a saburral fever. **1876** BARTHOLOW *Mat. Med.* (1879) 150 The saburral state of the mucous membrane.

†**sa'burrate**, *v. Obs. rare*$^{-0}$. [f. ppl. stem of L. *saburrāre*, f. *saburra*: see SABURRA.] To ballast a ship.

1623 in COCKERAM. **1658** in PHILLIPS.

saburration (sæbʌˈreɪʃən). *Med.* [ad. mod.L. *saburrātiōn-em* (16th c.), n. of action f. L. *saburrāre* (in mod.L. sense to treat with sand): see prec.] The application of heated sand to the body; sand-bathing, arenation.

1763 A. SUTHERLAND *Attempts Anc. Med. Doctr.* I. 48 Saburration was a species of Bathing in antient use. The body was buried in sand and exposed to the sun. **1849** PEREIRA *Elem. Mat. Med.* (ed. 3) I. 16. **1860** R. FOWLER *Med. Vocab.*, *Saburration*, the application of hot sand enclosed in a bag or bladder to a part of the body.

sabylle, obs. form of SABLE.

sabzi, var. SUBJEE.

sac[1]. *Old Eng. Law.* Forms: 1 saca, 3 sacha, sache, 3, 6 sak, 2, 4, 7 sake, 5, 7 sack, (5 saca, sacke), 7– sac. [repr. OE. *saca*, accus. and genit. pl. of *sacu* str. fem., dispute, case at law, litigation, crime (see SAKE), as occurring in the 11th c. phrases *saca and sócne habban* (*ȝifan*) 'to have (give) sac and soke', *saca and sócne wyrðe*, 'worthy of sac and soke'.

As both words occur in Scandinavian (OIcel. *sǫk, sókn*), it is not unlikely that the alliterative formula may be of Danish origin, though it has not actually been found in Scandinavian law-books.]

Properly only in *sac and soc* (or *soke*), a modernized form of the expression (see above) used in charters from the reign of Cnut onward to denote certain rights of jurisdiction which by custom belonged to the lord of a manor, and which were specified (along with others) as included in the grant of a manor by the crown.

1020–12.. [see INFANGTHIEF]. **1086** *Domesday-bk.* 280 b/1 Si tainus habens sacam et socam forisfecerit terram suam. [*Ibid.* in many other passages.] **1290** *Rolls of Parlt.* I. 15/1 Teneant predictas villas.., cum Sacha & Socha, Thol & Them [etc.]. **1387** TREVISA *Higden* (Rolls) II. 95 Sake: (a Frensche, court justice forfet ou achesoun). *c* **1460** *Oseney Regr.* 9 [tr. charter of Hen. I *c* 1130] Sake and soc, tol and teme, and infangenethefe. *Ibid.* 10 [explanation of terms] Sacke ys pleys and amendys of mysdoynges of your men in your courte, for *sacke* in Englysh is *cheson* in frensh,..and sacke also is a forfete. **1641** *Termes de la Ley* 244 The priviledge called Sake is for a man to have the amerciaments of his tenants in his owne Court. *a* **1657** [see INFANGTHIEF]. **1874** STUBBS *Const. Hist.* I. v. §47 There existed..side by side with the hundreds and wapentakes, large franchises or liberties in which the jurisdiction..was vested in private hands. The particular rights thus exercised were termed sac and soc.

sac[2] (sæk). [a. F. *sac* or ad. L. *saccus* (see SACK *sb.*[1]) in mod.L. applications.]

1. *Biol.* Any natural bag-like cavity with its membranous covering in an animal or vegetable organism. **a.** in animal bodies. ***laryngeal sacs*** [mod.L. *sacculi laryngis*], membranous pouches connected with the larynx, for the reception of air.

1741 MONRO *Anat. Nerves* (ed. 3) 77 The Lacteal Sac..is contracted into a slender..Pipe. **1780** Lachrymal sac [see LACHRYMAL *a.* 2]. **1796** MORSE *Amer. Geog.* I. 205 The castor used in medicine is found in sacs formed behind the kidneys [in the beaver]. **1844** STEPHENS *Bk. Farm* II. 725 A small spot is discernible upon the yolk, composed of a membraneous sac containing fluid matter in which the embryo of the future chick swims. **1851** RICHARDSON *Geol.* viii. 224 In the sea-star, the stomach is a capacious sac. **1854** BUSHNAN in *Orr's Circ. Sci.*, *Org. Nat.* I. 143 In the monkeys of the old continent there are also laryngeal sacs. **1875** HOUGHTON *Sk. Brit. Ins.* 140 The female beetle makes a pear-shaped flexible bag of silk, in which she encloses her eggs; the sac is attached to some water weed. **1888** ROLLESTON & JACKSON *Anim. Life* 55 The air-sacs appended to certain bronchi are nine in number. **1897** *Syd. Soc. Lex.* s.v., *Fœtal, gestation sac*,..the sac in which an embryo is enclosed in cases of extra-uterine pregnancy.

b. in plants.

1830 LINDLEY *Nat. Syst. Bot.* 173 The embryo has no kind of vascular connexion with the sac that contains it. **1879** LUBBOCK *Sci. Lect.* i. 5 Utricularia, an aquatic species [of Venus's Fly-trap *Dionæa Muscipula*], bears a number of utricles or sacs.

2. *Path.* A pouch formed by the morbid dilatation of a part, the membranous envelope of a hernia, cyst, tumour, etc.

[Cf. *hernial bag* 1736 *s.v.* HERNIAL *a.*]

1802 *Med. Jrnl.* VIII. 40 In consequence of the distension ..a sac or pouch is usually formed, in which the food lodges. **1804** ABERNETHY *Surg. Obs.* 210 It [the blood] could be entirely expressed from the aneurismal sac. **1899** *Allbutt's Syst. Med.* VII. 243 The same change follows the repeated tappings of the sacs.

¶**3.** Used *occas.* for: A bag.

1814 M. BIRKBECK *Journey through France* 18 In three days the same postillion left our sac at the hotel unopened, not an article missing. **1869** LUBBOCK *Prehist. Times* xi. 339 [Among the Hottentots] milk is kept in leathern sacs.

4. *Comb.*, as **sac-bearing**, **-like** adjs. **sac-winged bat**, a South American bat belonging to the genus *Saccopteryx* or closely related genera of the family Emballonuridæ, distinguished by the pouch-like scent gland found in the wing membrane of the males.

1888 *Cath. Househ.* 30 June 13 Sac-bearing spiders. **1849** *Sk. Nat. Hist., Mammalia* III. 186 The hood or sac-like appendage of the head. **1891** W. S. DALLAS in P. M. Duncan *Cassell's Nat. Hist.* I. v. 313 The Striped Sack-winged [*sic*] Bat is rather a small species. **1939** G. M. ALLEN *Bats* ix. 139 Still more remarkable..are the South American sac-winged bats,..in which a large pouchlike gland is present in the membrane that extends from the fore shoulder to the wrist. **1964** E. P. WALKER et al. *Mammals of World* I. 235/1 Sac-winged bats generally roost in groups of 3 to 30 individuals.

sac³, sacch (sæk). *slang.* [Abbrev. SACCHARINE *a.* and *sb.*] A saccharine tablet.

1961 PARTRIDGE *Dict. Slang* Suppl. 1257/1 *Sac*, a saccharine tablet: coll. (domestic, and small traders'): heard in 1917, but not gen. until 1942. **1968** 'E. TREVOR' *Place for Wicked* vi. 79 Sacchs. You couldn't get them down there.

sac: see SACK.

Sac, var. SAUK.

Saca, var. SAKA.

sac à commis, var. SAGAKOMI.

sac-à-lait. *U.S.* Also sacalai, sacola (*Cent. Dict.*). [Fr.: lit. 'milk bag'; perh. an etymologizing perversion of some Indian word.] A name locally applied to certain fishes of the genera *Pomoxys* and *Fundulus*.

[**1877** C. HALLOCK *Sportsman's Gazetteer* 378 Goggle-eyed Perch;..sac-a-lac (New Orleans Creoles).] **1884** GOODE *Nat. Hist. Aquatic Anim.* 407 The Crappie—*Pomoxys annularis*..is commonly called..'Sac-à-lait'..in the Lower Mississippi. *Ibid.* 466 *Fundulus grandis*, is known at Pensacola by the name of 'Sac-à-lait'. **1903** T. H. BEAN *Fishes N.Y.* 463 Still other names of local application [for the calico bass] are barfish, bitter head, tinmouth, *sac-a-lait*, lamplighter, [etc.]. **1931** W. A. READ *Louisiana-French* 67 In Louisiana the final *t* of *sacalait* is silent. **1937** *Zeitschr. für Französische Sprache & Literatur* LXI. 82 *Sacalait*, the Louisiana name for the crappie.., commonly thought to have been suggested by the beautiful white flesh or the silvery appearance of this fish. The actual source of the name is Choctaw *sakli*, 'trout', French *sac à lait* being merely a typical example of folk etymology. **1949** *New Orleans Times-Picayune Mag.* 16 Oct. 20/3 If you run out of bait while the bream, sacalait, and other fish are practically jumping into the boat, then the lily is your friend. **1973** *Trailer Travel* Jan. 73/2 You can catch large-mouth bass, channel cats, breams, and sac-a-lait or crappie.

sacaline, var. SACHALINE.

sacande, obs. pres. pple. of SHAKE *v.*

sacar, -ing, obs. ff. SAKER², SACRING.

sacate, zacate (səˈkɑːteɪ, zə-). Also Zacate. [ad. Mexican Sp. *zacate* grass, hay, ad. Nahuatl *çacatl, zacatl* grass, reed.] Any of several grasses grown in Mexico, the southern U.S.A., and the Philippines, and used for hay or fresh forage; fodder made from such a grass. Cf. next.

1848 J. W. ABERT *Rep. Exam. New Mexico 1846–'47* 29 As there were no pasture grounds near the village, I was forced to buy 'zacate' for my mules. **1891** G. VASEY *Illustr. N. Amer. Grasses* (U.S. Dept. Agric. Div. Bot.) I. II. (*facing plate* XX), [*Sporobolus wrightii* is] a tall coarse grass, growing in dense tufts, commonly called Saccaton or Zacate. **1921** *Blackw. Mag.* Nov. 659/1 The jungle almost obliterated the track. He cut it down with his *machete*.., and, pushing his tired beast through *sacate* and bamboo, emerged..on a gravelly bank. **1977** A. V. BOGDAN *Trop. Pasture & Fodder Plants* 44 *Axonopus affinis* Chase... Carpet grass;..Zacate amargo. *Ibid.* 45 *Axonopus compressus* (Swartz) Beauv. Carpet grass;..Zacate amargo. *Ibid.* 92 *Cynodon dactylon* (L.) Pers... Bermuda grass;..Zacate Bermuda.

sacaton, zacaton (ˈsækətəʊn, ˈzæ-, ‖sakaˈton). Also **sacatone, †saccato, †saccaton(e),** and with capital initial. [ad. Mexican Sp. *zacatón*, augmentative of *zacate* (see prec.).] Any of several coarse, tough grasses grown in Mexico and the southern U.S.A. and used for hay, esp. species of *Sporobolus* and *Epicampes*; ***alkali sacaton***, a tussock grass, *Sporobolus airoides*, able to survive drought and alkaline soils. Cf. prec.

1865 *Harper's Mag.* Jan. 147/1 The grass consists of three principal varieties; the sacatone, a coarse, thick, and strong variety, growing in bunches; the mesquit..and the grama. **1886** *Outing* Dec. 223/2 We came upon a caved-in well, a wide hollow with a black bottom, covered with high rank grass, the Mexican *zacaton*. **1891** G. VASEY *Illustr. N. Amer. Grasses* (U.S. Dept. Agric. Div. Bot.) I. I. (*facing plate* XXV), It [sc. *Muhlenbergia distichophylla*] is one of the grasses called saccato. *Ibid.* (*facing plate* XXVII), This [sc. *Epicampes macroura*] is another of the grasses called saccato, or saccatone. **1929** J. W. BEWS *World's Grasses* v. 201 Two species of the S.W. States are important forage grasses in the arid or semi-arid regions of Nebraska, Arizona, and Texas—*S*[*porobolus*] *wrightii* Munro, 'Saccaton', and *S. airoides* Torr., 'Alkali Saccaton' or 'Alkali Drop-seed'. **1936** J. A. MCKENNA *Black Range Tales* 177 The Indians..crept from rock to rock; they crawled like snakes from one bunch of sacatone to another. **1942** CASTETTER & BELL *Pima & Papago Indian Agric.* 22 Along the edges and in the openings of the forests of these two drainages, sacaton grass (*Sporobolus Wrightii*) thrives. **1968** F. W. GOULD *Grass Systematics* v. 265 *Sporobolus airoides* (Torr.) Torr., alkali sacaton, is a characteristic bunchgrass of alkaline areas in the western states. **1972** G. DURRELL *Catch me a Colobus* ix. 194 The zacaton grass..is tall—as much as three feet high—a very pale golden-yellow in colour, and it grows in huge tussocks all over the soft, black, volcanic soil. **1977** A. V. BOGDAN *Trop. Pasture & Fodder Plants* 181 *Panicum maximum* Jacq. Guinea grass;..Zacaton (Mexico).

sacatra (ˈsækətrə). *local U.S.* [Of obscure origin; given in Littré as French.] (See quot.)

1859 BARTLETT *Dict. Amer.*, *Sacatra*, the name given in Louisiana to the offspring of a griffe and a negress. **1894** GOULD *Dict. Med.*, *Sacatra*, a person of seven-eighths black and one-eighth white blood.

sacbrood (ˈsækbruːd). [f. SAC *sb.*² + BROOD *sb.*] A fatal viral disease of bee larvæ.

1913 G. F. WHITE in *Circular Bureau Entomol., U.S. Dept. Agric.* No. 169. 1 Sacbrood..is no new disease. *Ibid.* 3 There is, therefore, a disorder attacking the brood of bees in which [the] brood dies, but in which there has not been demonstrated any microorganism to which the cause of the trouble could be attributed. For this disease the name of 'sacbrood' is here suggested. *Ibid.*, Many larvæ dead of this disease can be removed from the cell without rupturing their body wall. When thus removed they have the appearance of a small closed sac. This character suggested the name 'sacbrood'. **1928** R. W. GLASER in T. M. Rivers *Filterable Viruses* viii. 281 The number of colonies that die as a direct result of sacbrood is comparatively small; the loss of individual bees, however, in the aggregate is enormous. **1967** K. M. SMITH *Insect Virol.* v. 95 Not much is known of the biology of sacbrood but at the moment the virus has only been recorded from the larvae of the honeybee.

sacbut, obs. form of SACKBUT.

saccacom(m)i(s), varr. SAGAKOMI.

saccade (sakad, səˈkɑːd). [Fr.]

a. A jerk or jerky movement (in various specific applications).

1727–41 CHAMBERS *Cycl.*, *Saccade*, in the manage, a jerk or violent check which the rider gives his horse, by drawing both the reins very suddenly. **1876** STAINER & BARRETT *Dict. Mus. Terms*, *Saccade* (Fr.), strong pressure of a violin bow against the strings, which by forcing them to a level enables the player to produce three or four notes simultaneously. **1897** *Syd. Soc. Lex.*, *Saccade*, the involuntary jerking movement in the act of swallowing.

b. A brief, rapid movement of the eye from one position of rest to another, whether voluntary (as in reading) or involuntary (as when a point is fixated).

1953 *Jrnl. Optical Soc. Amer.* XLIII. 495/2 These [types of eye movement] include relatively large slow waves, saccades, and slow drifts of fixation. **1962** *Ibid.* LII. 571/2 The eye does not move continuously along a line of print in reading, but executes a regular alternation of rapid jumps, called saccades, and fixational pauses. **1967** *New Scientist* 20 Apr. 156/1 Apart from a rapid trembling which plays a part in the mechanism of perception itself, there are two main types of eye-movement: slow 'drifts' away from the target image, and rapid jerks or 'saccades' tending to recentre it. **1971** *Sci. Amer.* June 35/2 Each saccade leads to a new fixation on a different point in the visual field. Typically there are two or three saccades per second. **1974** *Nature* 22 Mar. 308/3 Some observers can learn to suppress small saccades completely, without decreasing the accuracy of fixation or the visibility of the target.

saccadic (səˈkædɪk), *a.* [f. prec. + -IC.]

1. Of the nature of or pertaining to a saccade or saccades (sense b).

1916 R. DODGE in *Psychol. Bull.* XIII. 422 German and Scandinavian writers are commonly using the descriptive class term 'saccadic' to denote the rapid eye-movements for which we have only the arbitrary name of 'type 1'. I am not sure with whom the term originated, but it seems worth adopting. *Ibid.* 423 He independently rediscovers and thus confirms a number of eye-movement phenomena; such as the inability to see during saccadic movements. **1940** R. S. WOODWORTH *Psychology* (ed. 12) xiv. 478 The saccadic movement carries the eyes from one object to another, while the pursuit movement follows a moving object. **1948** *Brit. Jrnl. Psychol.* XXXVIII. 144 In a task such as reading, where we wish to observe different parts of the field successively, it can be shown by photography that the eye makes jerks, or 'saccadic movements', having a mean duration of 0·03 to 0·05 sec. **1954** *A.M.A. Arch. Ophthalm.* LII. 710 Most experimenters have found that all voluntary movements executed in the absence of a moving visual stimulus are saccadic. **1977** DELL'OSSO & TROOST in Brooks & Bajandas *Eye Movements* 52 Saccadic palsy with normal pursuit occurs in both congenital and acquired ocular motor apraxia.

2. *gen.* Jerky, discontinuous.

1937 SCOTT & VLASTOS *Towards Christian Revolution* 247 Marxists are disposed to charge Christians with..failure to appreciate the saccadic movement of history. **1951** J. S. BRUNER *Beyond Information Given* (1974) vi. 92 The reader may object that our model of the information-confirming cycle seems too saccadic, too jumpy. **1980** *Times Lit. Suppl.* 18 Jan. 54/2 From these things—parties, cafes, trips, gigs—a saccadic inconsequential life is made.

Hence **saˈccadically** *adv.*

1962 *Jrnl. Optical Soc. Amer.* LII. 572/2 One can produce conditions of stimulation under which the saccadically moving eye will not be able to see as well as the fixating eye. **1964** *Jrnl. Physiol.* CLXXIV. 259 In Fig. 11B is also shown what can never be measured in practice, the net active-state tension needed to drive the eye saccadically. **1975** *Nature* 1 May 68/2 When the cage was rotated, the bird showed the classical optomotor response of the head: alternately stabilising in visual space and saccadically moving to a new position.

saccage, saccaring: see SACKAGE, SACRING.

saccarist, var. SACRIST 2.

saccate (ˈsækeɪt), *a.* [ad. med.L. *saccātus*, f. *saccus* SAC²: see -ATE².]

1. *Bot.* Dilated into the form of a sac.

1830 LINDLEY *Nat. Syst. Bot.* 19 The constant tendency of the outer series to become saccate at the base, which is not uncommon in the calyx of Cruciferæ. **1861** BENTLEY *Man. Bot.* 237 In the Snapdragon..the lower part of the tube of the corolla becomes dilated on one side, and forms a little bag or sac, it is then termed *saccate* or *gibbous*. **1874** COOKE *Fungi* 76 In Perisporiacei..the asci are saccate.

2. = ENCYSTED. So also **ˈsaccated** *a.*

1846 SMART *Suppl.*, *Saccated*, having the water (from dropsy) encysted. **1860** MAYNE *Expos. Lex.* s.v. *Saccatus*. **1889** WAGSTAFFE *Mayne's Med. Voc.*, *Saccate*, encysted, or contained in a membranous bag: saccated.

saccato, saccaton(e, varr. SACATON, ZACATON.

saccawinkee: see SAKAWINKI.

sacch: see SAC³.

†sacchaˈraceous, *a. Obs. rare*⁻¹. [f. med.L. *sacchar-um* sugar + -ACEOUS.] Containing sugar.

1689 G. HARVEY *Curing Dis. by Expect.* vi. 42 In the Stomach the Rheum..converts..any such Saccharaceous Medicine, into a corroding Acid.

saccharase (ˈsækəreɪz). *Biochem.* [f. med.L. *sacchar-um* sugar + -ASE.] Invertase, sucrase.

1920 *Chem. Abstr.* XIV. 2344 Influence of the temperature and the acidity upon the formation of saccharase. **1930** J. B. S. HALDANE *Enzymes* ix. 168 In the case of saccharase the amount of substrate transformed is proportional over wide ranges both to the enzyme concentration and the time. **1973** *Enzyme Nomenclature* (Commission on Biochem. Nomenclature) 217/2 β-Fructofuranosidase... Other Names: Sucrase, Invertase, Invertin, Saccharase, β-*h*-Fructosidase.

saccharate (ˈsækərət), *sb. Chem.* [f. SACCHAR-IC + -ATE¹.] A salt of saccharic acid.

1815 *Ann. Philos.* V. 265 The objection that the saccharate analyzed might contain some other body besides sugar. **1897** *Allbutt's Syst. Med.* II. 948 Schobert recommended saccharate of lime as an antidote to phenol poisoning.

ˈsaccharate, *a. rare*⁻⁰. [f. med.L. *saccharum* sugar + -ATE².] = next.

1860 in MAYNE *Expos. Lex.* **1866** in *Treas. Bot.*

saccharated (ˈsækəreɪtɪd), *a.* [f. med.L. *sacchar-um* sugar + -ATE³ + -ED¹.] Containing or made with sugar; sweetened.

1784 CULLEN tr. *Bergman's Phys. & Chem. Ess.* I. 319 Saccharated Magnesia. **1791** PEARSON in *Phil. Trans.* LXXXI. 323 The saccharated soda immediately occasioned a slight precipitation. **1866** AITKEN *Pract. Med.* II. 61 For ..children the saccharated carbonate of iron is a most valuable preparation.

saccharescent (sækəˈrɛsənt), *a. rare.* [f. as SACCHARINE *a.* and *sb.* + -ESCENT.] Exuding sugar; sugary. Also *absol.* as *sb.* (In quots. *fig.*)

1930 E. POUND *XXX Cantos* xv. 65 The saccharescent, lying in glucose, the pompous in cotton wool. **1979** *Sunday Tel.* 15 July 12/7 A. C. Benson..dispensed saccharescent sweetness and cosy light through a number of best-sellers.

saccharhinoceros (sækəraɪˈnɒsərəs). *nonce-wd.* [Blend of SACCHARINE *a.* and *sb.* and RHINOCEROS.] A lumbering person with an excessively effusive or affectedly sentimental manner. So **saccharhiˈnoceroid** *a.*

1951 R. CAMPBELL *Light on Dark Horse* xvii. 240 The saccharine of false purity exuded from every pore of this saccarhinoceros advocate of virtue. *Ibid.* 241 The saccharhinoceros went off rumbling out some inarticulate phrases about 'Impertinence'. *Ibid.* 251 Sennacheribs..lost his head completely, and seemed to be about to make a sort of saccharhinoceroid charge.

saccharic (səˈkærɪk), *a.* [f. med.L. *sacchar-um* sugar + -IC. Cf. F. *saccharique*.] **1.** *Chem.* ***saccharic acid***: (*a*) a dibasic acid formed by the action of nitric acid on dextrose; oxalhydric acid; (*b*) a monobasic acid forming crystalline salts prepared by the action of bases on glucoses. ***saccharic ether***, an ether obtained from saccharic acid.

1800 *Med. Jrnl.* IV. 185 By a chemical analysis, those crystals were found to consist of saccharic acid. **1838** R. D. THOMSON in *Brit. Ann.* for 1839. 347 Saccharic Acid..was first noticed by Scheele as being obtained from the action of acids upon mucous bodies, or sugar. **1866** ROSCOE *Elem. Chem.* 325 Lactose, when oxidized, yields mucic, saccharic, tartaric, and oxalic acids. **1868** WATTS *Dict. Chem.* V. 143 Saccharic ethers.

2. Also *loosely*: sweet.

1945 R. HARGREAVES *Enemy at Gate* 138 Anything from porter and sour Crimean wine to..exalted, if saccharic champagne.

saccharide (ˈsækəraɪd). *Chem.* [f. med.L. *sacchar-um* sugar + -IDE.] **†a.** A substance formed in the fermentation of melted sugar (see quot. 1862). *Obs.* [Introduced in Fr. by A. Gélis 1859, in *Compt. Rend.* XLVIII. 1062.]

1860 *Q. Jrnl. Chem. Soc.* XII. 376 Researches on melted sugar, and on a new principle—saccharide: by A. Gélis. **1862** W. A. MILLER *Elem. Chem., Org.* (ed. 2) 78 According to Gélis, when sugar which has thus been melted is dissolved in water it furnishes a solution which when fermented with yeast yields only half the quantity of alcohol that ordinary sugar would have produced, a peculiar body to which he gives the name of saccharide ($C_{12}H_{10}O_{10}$) remaining in solution. It exerts a slight rotatory power to the right upon a beam of polarized light.

†**b.** A compound formed by the action of an acid on a sugar. *Obs.* [Introduced in Fr. by M. Berthelot 1860, in *Ann. de Chim. et de Phys.* LX. 94.]

1862 H. WATTS tr. *Gmelin's Handbk. Chem.* XV. 316 By heating dextro-glucose with (organic) acids, compounds are formed..which belong to the class of saccharides.

c. A sugar, esp. a monosaccharide; freq. used unsystematically to denote any mono- or oligosaccharide or a simple derivative of such a compound. [Introduced as G. *saccharid* by B. Tollens in *Kurzes Handb. d. Kohlenhydrate* (1888) 16.]

1895 THOMSON & BLOXAM *Bloxam's Chem.* (ed. 8) 705 The above considerations have given rise to a classification of the carbohydrates into (1) saccharides or monoses,..(2) disaccharides or bioses,..(3) polysaccharides or polyoses. **1914** *Chem. Abstr.* VIII. 2716 (*heading*) Resolution of racemic saccharides by means of optically active amyl mercaptan, and some mercaptals. **1932** *Analyst* LVII. 374 By reducing the concentration of nitric acid, it is possible to obtain a mixture which reacts rapidly with saccharides and not with polysaccharides. **1955** *Stain Technol.* XXX. 286 Methods for the demonstration of saccharide, fatty acid, amino acid, vitamin and ketosteroid were chosen for testing. **1973** *Jrnl. Biochem.* (Tokyo) LXXIV. 144/2 Changes in the CD [sc. Circular Dichroism] bands at 295 and 305 nm on adding saccharides, acetamides or alcohols were monitored to study the interaction with lysozyme. **1974** *Amer. Jrnl. Physiol.* CCXXVI. 720/1 Hyperosmolarity with these saccharides [*viz.* glucose, mannitol, raffinose] caused sustained reduction of spontaneous frequency.

sacchariferous (sækəˈrɪfərəs), *a.* [f. med.L. *sacchar-um* sugar + *-fer* bearing + -OUS.] Yielding or containing sugar.

1757 T. BIRCH *Hist. R. Soc.* IV. 380 Mr. Hooke said, that there were several sacchariferous trees mentioned by Piso and some other writers. **1799** *Nicholson's Jrnl.* III. 337 The Russian bear's-breech from Kamtschatka..has long been known among the sacchariferous plants. **1906** *Pall Mall G.* 19 Mar. 4/1 Fermentation will set in after a time in almost any sacchariferous liquid.

saccharification (ˌsækərɪfɪˈkeɪʃən). [Noun of action f. next.] The natural process by which starch and gum become converted into sugar.

1839 URE *Dict. Arts* 456 The vinous fermentation precedes the saccharification. **1883** R. HALDANE *Workshop Receipts* Ser. II. 12/2 Three principal methods of effecting the saccharification were in use.

saccharify (səˈkærɪfaɪ, ˈsækərɪfaɪ), *v.* [f. med.L. *sacchar-um* sugar + -(I)FY.] *trans.* To convert (starch) into sugar.

1839 URE *Dict. Arts* 400 The best heat for saccharifying starch. **1897** *Allbutt's Syst. Med.* IV. 273 The fluid may.. saccharify starch and digest albumin and fibrin.

Hence **saccharifying** *vbl. sb.* (in quot. *attrib.*). Also **saccharifier** (see quot.).

1839 URE *Dict. Arts* 456 This saccharifying process advances much quicker. **1884** KNIGHT *Dict. Mech.* Suppl., *Saccharifier*, an apparatus for treating grain and potatoes by steam under high pressure, for converting the starch into sugar previous to the alcoholic fermentation.

saccharilla (sækəˈrɪlə). *Disused.* [app. fancifully f. L. *sacchar-um* sugar.] A kind of muslin.

1851 *Illustr. Catal. Gt. Exhib.* III. 480/1 Saccharilla book muslin. *Ibid.*, Saccharilla mull muslin. *a* **1877** KNIGHT *Dict. Mech.* II. 1503/2 s.v. *Muslin*, Varieties are known as..lawn, saccharilla, harness. **1884** *Encycl. Brit.* XVII. 109/2 Plain, striped, and figured grenadines, and saccarillas.

saccharimeter (sækəˈrɪmɪtə(r)). [a. F. *saccharimètre*, f. Gr. σάκχαρι (= σάκχαρον) sugar + μέτρον measure: see -METER.

This form, taken from Fr., has been generally retained by English writers because the name SACCHAROMETER had been appropriated to a different instrument.]

A form of polariscope, an instrument for testing sugars by polarized light.

1874 tr. *Lommel's Light* 349 The Saccharimeter of Soleil has the previously described double plate between the two Nicol's prisms. **1883** R. HALDANE *Workshop Receipts* Ser. II. 316/2 A polarising saccharimeter.

saccharimetry (sækəˈrɪmɪtrɪ). [ad. F. *saccharimétrie*: cf. prec. and -METRY.] = SACCHAROMETRY.

1851 *F. Knapp's Chem. Technol.* III. 434. **1858** WATTS in *Graham's Elem. Chem.* (ed. 2) II. 469. **1880** *Nature* XXI. 357 Prof. Landolt's experience in saccharimetry.

Hence **sacchariˈmetric, -ˈmetrical** *a.*, pertaining to saccharimetry.

1851 *F. Knapp's Chem. Technol.* III. 435 The first saccharimetrical test was proposed by Barreswill, in the year 1844. **1876** *Jrnl. Chem. Soc.* II. 215 Influence of the Asparagine contained in the Sugar Liquors from Beets and Canes on the Saccharimetric Determination.

saccharin (ˈsækərɪn). *Chem.* [f. med.L. *sacchar-um* or Gr. σάκχαρον, σάκχαρ(ι) sugar + -IN.]

1. The anhydride of saccharic acid. (Discovered and named by Péligot 1880.)

1880 *Jrnl. Chem. Soc.* Abstr. 232 Saccharin is not a sugar; it does not ferment; it has not a sweet taste.

2. An intensely sweet substance obtained from coal tar, *o*-sulphobenzoic imide, $C_7H_5NO_3S$, used in minute quantities for sweetening the food or drink of persons to whom sugar is injurious. In non-technical use (prob. as a result of confusion with SACCHARINE *a.* and *sb.*) also **saccharine** (ˈsækəriːn).

1885 *Jrnl. Soc. Chem. Ind.* 608/1 The inventors [*sc.* Fahlberg and List] name the new substance 'Saccharine', although it is not related to the class of sugars, but is a derivative of benzoic acid. The scientific name of the substance is benzoylsulphimide. **1887** *Brit. Med. Jrnl.* 8 Jan. 93/2 Saccharine is not at present procurable. **1893**, etc. [see DULCIN b]. **1918** G. FRANKAU *One of Them* xvii. 128 Swiftly and cloying-sweet as saccharine In Governmental tea, a week had melted. **1973** J. G. TWEEDDALE *Materials Technol.* II. vii. 164 Many pharmaceutical products (including the sweetening substance saccharine) originated from coal-gas waste. **1977** *N.Y. Times Mag.* 15 May 88 It seems to strike most people as absurd, even outrageous, that saccharin has been indicted, convicted and condemned as a carcinogen. **1977** *New Yorker* 27 June 24/2 Only recently, the press has devoted acres of space to the subject of saccharin.

attrib. **1926–7** *Army & Navy Stores Catal.* 480/1 Saccharine tablets. bot. 100 -/10. **1968** *Canad. Antiques Collector* Nov. 21/2 During World War II still another use was found for these decorative little boxes..as containers for saccharin pills. **1978** G. FOX *Amok* iii. 25 Lenore took a tiny saccharin pill.., grimaced as she dropped it into her coffee. **1978** E. MALPASS *Wind brings up Rain* iv. 43 He pushed the bag of sugar into a drawer. If she wanted a cup of tea she could use her saccharine tablets.

saccharine (ˈsækəraɪn, -ɪn), *a.* and *sb.* [Formed as prec. + -INE. Cf. F. *saccharin.*]

A. *adj.*

1. a. Of, pertaining to or of the nature of sugar; characteristic of sugar; sugary.

1674 BLOUNT *Glossogr.* (ed. 4), *Saccharine*, belonging to Sugar, sweet like Sugar. **1685** BOYLE *Effects of Mot.* iv. 31 The lump [of sugar] consisted of very numerous saccharine corpuscles. **1731** ARBUTHNOT *Aliments* iii. (1735) 53 Manna, which is an essential saccharine Salt, sweating from the Leaves of most Plants. **1757** A. COOPER *Distiller* I. i. (1760) 6 The..Saccharine Sweetness of the Malt. **1841–4** EMERSON *Ess., Circles* Wks. (Bohn) I. 132, I am gladdened by seeing the predominance of the saccharine principle throughout vegetable nature. **1879** GEO. ELIOT *Theo. Such* xiii, Bovis had never said inwardly that he would take a large allowance of sugar, and..he was naturally disgusted at the saccharine excesses of Avis. **1880** BARING-GOULD *Mehalah* viii, She precipitated herself against a treacle barrel and upset it. A gush of black saccharine matter spread over the floor.

b. *saccharine fermentation* = SACCHARIFICATION.

1801 W. NICHOLSON tr. *Fourcroy's Syn. Tables Chem.* xi, The saccharine fermentation. I first described under this name the spontaneous formation of sugar in vegetable matters left to themselves. **1839** URE *Dict. Arts* 456 The saccharine fermentation, in which starch and gum are changed into sugar.

2. Composed chiefly of sugar; of a plant, containing a large proportion of sugar; also, of urine, containing sugar in excess of what is normal.

saccharine diabetes, diabetes characterized by excess of saccharine matter in the urine.

1710 T. FULLER *Pharm. Extemp.* 109 A Saccharine Draught. *a* **1793** G. WHITE *Selborne, Observ. Veget.* (1875) 359 All the maples have saccharine juices. **1845** BUDD *Dis. Liver* 257 Albuminous urine and saccharine urine. **1874** GARROD & BAXTER *Mat. Med.* (1880) 27 This salt has considerable power in checking the formation of sugar in saccharine diabetes. **1889** BARNARD *Noted Breweries* I. 16 In the mashing process the starch of the malt is converted into a saccharine liquid, called wort.

†**3.** *Chem. saccharine acid*: oxalic acid. *Obs.*

1784 CULLEN tr. *Bergman's Phys. & Chem. Ess.* I. 311 The residuum consisted of crystallized saccharine acid. **1802** T. THOMSON *Chem.* II. 103 At first, however, it was called the acid of sugar, or the saccharine acid.

4. Resembling sugar. **a.** *Geol.* Of rocks: Granular in texture = SACCHAROID *a.*

1833 [see SACCHAROID]. **1854** HOOKER *Himal. Jrnls.* I. xvii. 406 Beds of saccharine quartz. **1858** GEIKIE *Hist. Boulder* xii. 242 Where they pass through limestone, they sometimes convert it into a white saccharine marble.

b. *Bot.* Covered with shining grains like those of sugar (*Cent. Dict.* 1891).

5. *fig.* Chiefly in playful or sarcastic use: Sweet.

1841–4 EMERSON *Ess., Prudence* Wks. (Bohn) I. 95 The abundant flow of this saccharine element of pleasure in every suburb. **1858** O. W. HOLMES *Aut. Breakf.-t.* (1865) 31 You will be saccharine enough in a few years. **1863** LD. W. P. LENNOX *Biog. Remin.* I. 179 A saccharine smile beamed upon the royal countenances. **1872** M. COLLINS *Two Plunges* I. v. 98 Those sweet, soft, saccharine sylphs. **1890** *Spectator* 1 Feb. 169/2 Too saccharine, is our short judgment on these poems. **1933** *Punch* 16 Aug. 178/1 Here is actually a Viennese film based not on copious draughts of The Blue Danube (with sugar), but on the crisper life which must presumably exist in that city, even in defiance of the saccharine mirage which appears to be the fondest of Hollywood's illusions. **1934** C. LAMBERT *Music Ho!* II. 106 Such a saccharine melody as 'None but the Weary Heart'. **1951** *Essays in Crit.* I. III. 289 The saccharine honeymoon by the seaside. **1955** W. GADDIS *Recognitions* II. ii. 370 A saccharine line drawing of a woman. **1970** K. MILLETT *Sexual Politics* II. iii. 92 It was enough for him to rely on sentiment, a vague nostalgia about the heroic middle ages, and saccharine assertions about The Home. **1976** *Amer. N. & Q.* XIV. 147/2 The parable is saccharine and simplistic. Its sentimental treatment..asks for the cheap pity of melodrama and offers too easy a solution.

B. *sb.* Saccharine matter, sugar.

See also SACCHARIN 2.

1841 CATLIN *N. Amer. Ind.* (1844) II. lviii. 226 They live ..without saccharine and without salt. **1856** OLMSTED *Slave States* 670 Chemical analysis proves that a large amount of saccharine is still wasted.

Hence **ˈsaccharineish** *a.*, somewhat saccharine. **sacchaˈrinity**, sweetness.

1857 *Tait's Mag.* XXIV. 6/2 Swedish turnips..being of a saccharineish and sugarish taste. **1868** HELPS *Realmah* xii. (1876) 313 The polite stranger assiduously presents the fallacious palliative of the consequential saccharinity. **1888** *Nature* XXXVIII. 573/1 A streaky distribution of brine and water or of syrup and water, in which portions of greatest and least salinity or saccharinity are within half a millimetre of one another. **1932** B. DE VOTO *Mark Twain's Amer.* viii. 191 Similar items in saccharinity..had created a brummagem reputation. **1971** A. BURGESS *MF* i. 15 Loewe suddenly smiled with horrible saccharinity. **1977** *Times Lit. Suppl.* 18 Feb. 176/2 Juxtapositions of venom and saccharinity, iciness and boredom.

saccharined (ˈsækərɪnd), *a.* [f. SACCHARINE *a.* and *sb.* + -ED².] Excessively sweet and sugary in tone.

1962 *Punch* 13 June 916/1 The recipe here [in a BBC series] has a queasy mélange of saccharined goodies with disc jockies selecting tunes by pop composers [etc.]. **1973** O. SELA *Portuguese Fragment* (1974) xxi. 118 A saccharined voice announces that your flight will be delayed.

saccharinic (sækəˈrɪnɪk), *a.* *Chem.* [f. SACCHARIN + -IC.] = SACCHARIC.

1881 *Jrnl. Chem. Soc.* Abstr. 149 Saccharin..is the anhydride, $C_6H_{10}O_5$, of a new acid, $C_6H_{12}O_6$, which the author [*sc.* Scheibler] calls saccharinic acid. **1894** MUIR & MORLEY *Watts' Dict. Chem.* IV. 420/2 *Saccharinic acid.*

saccharinize (ˈsækərɪnaɪz), *v.* [f. SACCHARIN + -IZE.] *trans.* To sweeten by adding saccharin. Freq. *fig.*, to make agreeable; to render inoffensive. Hence **ˈsaccharinized** *ppl. a.*

1971 S. MARCUS in *Atlantic Monthly* Apr. 95 His praiseworthy intention to bring great genius before large numbers of readers comes to seem suspect in the light of the corrupt and corrupting means he employs in censoring, simplifying, and saccharinizing it. **1977** *New Scientist* 27 Oct. 208 The House..would require such a notice to be displayed only at the shop or other retail outlet where 'saccharinised' products are actually bought.

saccharite (ˈsækəraɪt). *Min.* [Named by E. F. Glocker in 1845 (G. *saccharit*), from its resemblance to sugar: f. Gr. σάκχαρ(ι, σάκχαρ-ον sugar + -ITE.] A granular, massive mineral, at first referred to andesite, but now considered a mixture.

1859 PAGE *Handbk. Geol. Terms, Saccharite*..is found in veins in serpentine, in the chrysoprase mines, near Frankenstein in Silesia. **1862** DANA *Min.* 175 Saccharite resembles a granular feldspar, of a white or greenish-white color.

ˈsaccharize, *v. rare*⁻¹. [Formed as prec. + -IZE.] *intr.* To undergo saccharine fermentation.

1764 GRAINGER *Sugar Cane* I. 179 Poor tastes the liquor; coction long demands, And highest temper 'ere it saccharize. *Note*, It is hoped the reader will pardon the introduction of the verb saccharize.

Hence **sacchariˈzation**, the conversion (of starch) into sugar.

1902 in *Cassell's Encycl. Dict.* Suppl.

saccharo- (ˈsækərəʊ), comb. form of Gr. σάκχαρο-ν sugar, forming compounds (usually written with hyphen) with the sense 'partly saccharine and partly (something else)'; 'containing sugar and (something else)'.

1839 URE *Dict. Arts* 97 Mashing is the operation by which the wort is extracted..from the malt, and whereby a saccharo-mucilaginous extract is made from it. *Ibid.* 401 The saccharo-starchy matter. **1842** R. KANE *Elem. Chem.* (1849) 818 Saccharo-humine and saccharo-humic acid. **1889** *Nature* XXXIX. 433 Saccharocolloids. **1896** *Allbutt's Syst. Med.* I. 407 Saccharo-farinaceous elements.

saccharoid (ˈsækərɔɪd), *a.* and *sb.* [f. Gr. σάκχαρ-ον sugar + -OID.]

A. *adj.* *Geol.* Having a granular texture resembling that of loaf-sugar.

1833 LYELL *Princ. Geol.* III. 11 Saccharoid gypsum. *Ibid.* 79 Saccharoid, Saccharine. When a stone has a texture resembling that of loaf-sugar. **1833–4** J. PHILLIPS in *Encycl. Metrop.* (1845) VI. 560/1 Its frequent high state of granular or saccharoid crystallization. **1865** BRISTOW tr. *Figuier's World bef. Deluge* ii. 72 Limestone becomes granular and saccharoid—it is changed into marble.

B. *sb.* *Chem.* **a.** (See quot. 1868.) **b.** A saccharine substance.

1868 WATTS *Dict. Chem.*, *Saccharoid*, a name given by Kane to a sweetish substance, probably identical with orcin, produced by the decomposition of Heeren's pseudo-erythrin (ethylic orsellinate). **1882** *Athenæum* 2 Dec. 738/2 Non-nitrogenous food (stearoids and saccharoids).

saccharoidal (sækəˈrɔɪdəl), *a.* [Formed as prec. + -AL¹.] = SACCHAROID *a.*

1838 W. F. AINSWORTH *Res. Assyria*, etc. 26 The chalk is indurated, compact, granular, or saccharoidal, at the foot of Taurus. **1852** TH. ROSS tr. *Humboldt's Trav.* I. xi. 391 We find also saccharoidal limestone in gneiss of the most ancient formation. **1863** DANA *Man. Geol.* 383 'Ferruginous' brown and red, coarse, friable sandstone, in some parts white and 'saccharoidal'.

saccharolytic (ˌsækərəʊˈlɪtɪk), *a. Biochem.* [f. SACCHARO- + -LYTIC.] Of or pertaining to the chemical breakdown of carbohydrates; able to effect this.

1908 *Jrnl. Med. Res.* XVIII. 86 Bacillus coli showed but a weak sugar-splitting power, the saccharolytic action ceasing after twenty-four and sometimes after eighteen hours. **1928** L. E. H. WHITBY *Med. Bacteriol.* xv. 154 Saccharolytic organisms are so-called on account of their marked power of producing acid and gas in a carbohydrate medium. **1975** R. R. GILLIES *Lect. Notes Med. Microbiol.* xiv. 81 The six antigenically distinct types show variation in their saccharolytic and proteolytic activities.

saccharometer (sækəˈrɒmɪtə(r)). [f. Gr. σάκχαρο-ν sugar + -METER. Cf. SACCHARIMETER.]

1. A form of hydrometer for estimating the amount of sugar in a solution by specific gravity; used esp. in brewing to ascertain the amount of saccharine or fermentable matter in wort.

1784 J. RICHARDSON (*title*) Statistical Estimates of the Materials of Brewing, showing the use of the Saccharometer. **1836-41** BRANDE *Chem.* (ed. 5) 1257 An instrument not quite correctly called a saccharometer, since it is influenced by all the contents of the wort, and not by the sugar only. **1880** *Act 43 & 44 Vict.* c. 24 §21 The gravity of the wort or wash..can be ascertained by the prescribed saccharometer.

2. Used for SACCHARIMETER. *rare.*

1866 HERSCHEL *Fam. Lect. Sci.* (1871) 392 An elegant instrument called the saccharometer, by which the quantity of sugar contained in a given solution is ascertained by simple inspection of the tint.

saccharometry (sækəˈrɒmɪtrɪ). [Formed as prec. + -METRY.] The process of determining the quantity of sugar in a solution.

1871 *Jrnl. Bot.* IX. 253 A paper on Saccharometry, giving the results of the determination of sugar in..sugar-beet.

‖**saccharomyces** (ˌsækərəʊˈmaɪsiːz). Also anglicized **-myce.** [mod.L., f. Gr. σάκχαρο-ν sugar + μύκης mushroom.] A genus of ascomycetous fungi, including the yeast-fungi; a fungus of this genus, esp. the yeast-plant. Also *attrib.*

1873 B. STEWART *Conserv. Force* vii. 185 The..yeast-plant (saccharomyce). **1879** *Encycl. Brit.* IX. 96/1 We then place the flask in a chamber kept at the particular temperature which is most favourable to the development of 'saccharomyces'. The saccharomyces-cells..will multiply at a greater rate than the foreign cells. **1882** VINES tr. *Sachs' Bot.* 249 The genus *Saccharomyces*, which causes the alcoholic fermentation in saccharine fluids, consists of separate cells of an ellipsoidal form with smooth and thin walls.

saccharomycetes (ˌsækərəʊmaɪˈsiːtiːz, -ts), *sb. pl.* [mod.L., f. generic name SACCHAROMYCES (J. Meyen 1838, in *Archiv für Naturgeschichte* IV. II. 100) + MYCETES.] A group name for yeasts, esp. those now included in the family Saccharomycetaceæ.

1884 W. B. GROVE *Synopsis Bacteria & Yeast Fungi* ii. 57 The saccharomycetes, or Yeast Fungi, are unicellular plants, which multiply themselves by budding. **1902** *Encycl. Brit.* XXVIII. 560/2 No satisfactory proof has as yet been given that Saccharomycetes are derived by culture from any higher form. **1906** G. MASSEE *Text-bk. Fungi* i. 54 In the Saccharomycetes, or Yeasts, three modes of spore-formation are known. **1958** J. LODDER et al. in A. H. Cook *Chem. & Biol. Yeasts* i. 13 The fission yeasts were placed in a subfamily of their own,..separated from the Saccharomycetes.

saccharon (ˈsækərən). *Chem.* Also **-one.** [f. Gr. σάκχαρ-ον sugar: see -ON.]

1. A white crystalline substance obtained by the oxidation of saccharin; the lactone of saccharonic acid.

1897 in *Syd. Soc. Lex.*

2. An oily liquid obtained by the reduction of saccharin.

In recent Dicts.

saccharonic (sækəˈrɒnɪk), *a. Chem.* [f. SACCHARON + -IC.] Of, pertaining to or derived from saccharon. ***saccharonic acid***, an acid formed by oxidation of saccharin by means of nitric acid.

1894 in MUIR & MORLEY *Watts' Dict. Chem.* IV. 421/1.

saccharose (ˈsækərəʊs). *Chem.* [f. Gr. σάκχαρ-ον sugar + -OSE.] **a.** = SUCROSE b.

1876 tr. *Schützenberger's Ferment.* 32 Saccharose or cane sugar is changed, when hydrated, into two isomeric molecules. **1928** A. B. CALLOW *Food & Health* i. 15 Each molecule of saccharose is composed of one atom of glucose (also called dextrose or grape sugar), and one atom of fructose (also called laevulose or fruit sugar). **1962** *Nature* 22 Sept. 1201/1, I have isolated two melibiose-fermenting yeasts,..which..are capable of fermenting maltose, but which neither ferment nor assimilate saccharose. **1979** *Digestion* XIX. 213 The jejunal absorption of either an elemental solution (amino acids, glucose and glucose oligosaccharides), or of nonelemental diet (chicken meat,..glucose, saccharose, maltose and dextrin maltose, corn and wheat oils) were compared in 25 healthy subjects.

†**b.** Any one of the group of sugars having the common formula $C_{12}H_{22}O_{11}$; = DISACCHARIDE. Now *Obs.*

1887 *Encycl. Brit.* XXII. 623/1 'Sugar' is now a collective term for two chemical genera named saccharoses (all $C_{12}H_{22}O_{11}$) and glucoses (all $C_6H_{12}O_6$). **1911** [see GLUCOSE 1 b].

saccharous (ˈsækərəs), *a. rare.* [f. med.L. *sacchar-um* sugar + -OUS.] Saccharine, sugary.

1896 *Lancet* 21 Mar. 787/2 The crisp and saccharous tartlet. **1897** in *Syd. Soc. Lex.*

saccharum (ˈsækərəm). [a. med.L. *saccharum* SUGAR.] An invert sugar prepared from cane sugar, used chiefly in brewing.

1839 URE *Dict. Arts* 397 In which mixture there is about one twelfth part of solid saccharum. **1885** *Act 48 & 49 Vict.* c. 51 §7 Saccharum, glucose, or other saccharine substance.

saccharumic (sækəˈruːmɪk), *a. Chem.* [app. f. med.L. *sacchar-um* sugar + HUMIC *a.*, a synonym of *ulmic*.] Derived from or containing sugar and ulmic acid. ***saccharumic acid***, an acid formed by the action of baryta on dextrose.

[**1842**: see SACCHARO-*humic*.] **1875** in *Watts' Dict. Chem.* 2nd Suppl.

sacche, obs. form of SACK.

†**sacchoˈlactate.** *Chem. Obs.* Also **sacco-**, and SACLACTATE. [f. SACCHOLACT-IC + -ATE[4].] A salt of saccholactic acid.

1807 J. MURRAY *Syst. Chem.* IV. 755 Index, Saccholactates. **1815** *Ann. Philos.* V. 268 Saccolactate of lead. **1826** HENRY *Elem. Chem.* II. 417 A genus of salts which are called *saccholactates* or *saclactates.*

†**sacchoˈlactic**, *a. Chem. Obs.* Also SACLACTIC. [a. F. *saccholactique*, f. *saccho-* contracted for SACCHARO- + L. *lact-*, *lac* milk: see LACTIC *a.*] ***saccholactic acid***, mucic acid (prepared from sugar of milk).

1790 KERR tr. *Lavoisier's Elem. Chem.* 281 The saccholactic acid discovered by Scheele. **1826** HENRY *Elem. Chem.* II. 191 Saccholactic or mucic acid.

†**ˈsaccholate.** *Chem. Obs.* Also **saccholat**, *erron.* saccolate. [a. F. *saccholat*, f. *sacchol(actique)*: see -ATE[1].] = SACCHOLACTATE.

1790 KERR tr. *Lavoisier's Elem. Chem.* 280 Saccholat of lime. **1802** PYE *New Chem. Nomencl.* 32 Saccholates. **1807** T. THOMSON *Chem.* (ed. 3) II. 302 The compounds which it forms with earths, alkalies, and metallic oxides, are denominated *saccolates.* **1815** *Ann. Philos.* V. 270 Saccolate of ammonia. **1819** BRANDE *Chem.* 438 Saccholates.

sacchulmic (sæˈkʌlmɪk), *a. Chem.* [f. med.L. *sacch(arum)* sugar + ULM(IN) + -IC.] ***sacchulmic acid***: an acid obtained by treating sacchulmin with alkaline solutions.

1842 [see SACCHULMIN]. **1858** *Fownes' Chem.* (ed. 7) 354 Ulmic acid, the sacchulmic acid of Liebig, dissolves freely. **1894** in MUIR & MORLEY *Watts' Dict. Chem.*

sacchulmin (sæˈkʌlmɪn). *Chem.* Also **-ine.** [f. med.L. *sacch(arum)* sugar + ULMIN.] A brown substance obtained in the decomposition of sugar by dilute acids.

1842 R. KANE *Elem. Chem.* (1849) 817 When sugar is acted upon by a very dilute acid..two brown substances are formed... For these bodies the names *sacchulmine* and *sacchulmic acid* may be retained. **1858** *Fownes' Chem.* (ed. 7) 354 By long-continued boiling with water, sacchulmic acid is converted into sacchulmin.

sacciferous (sækˈsɪfərəs), *a. Anat., Zool.* and *Bot.* [f. L. *sacc-us* SAC[2] + *fer* bearing + -OUS.] Bearing a sac.

1880 in WEBSTER *Suppl.* [Bot.].

sacciform (ˈsæksɪfɔːm), *a.* [ad. mod.L. *sacciform-is*, f. *sacc-us* SAC[2]: see -FORM.] Having the form of a sac or pouch; sac-shaped.

1836 *Penny Cycl.* V. 311/1 The sacciform branchiæ of the Ascidiæ. **1861** HULME tr. *Moquin-Tandon* II. VII. ix. 372 Another animal becomes developed, which has the form of a locomotive sac. These young sacciform larvæ..continue to live for a certain time. **1890** HUMPHRY *Old Age* 149 The calibre of the ducts..becomes increased and their terminal parts, or acini, become dilated and sacciform.

saccine (ˈsæksɪn), *a. rare*[−1]. [f. L. *sacc-us* sac + -INE[2].] Composed of sacs or air-cells.

1853 KANE *Grinnell Exp.* xl. (1856) 366 The saccine vegetation of the confervas.

‖**saccolabium** (sækəʊˈleɪbɪəm). [mod.L., f. *sacco-* (assumed combining form of *sacc-us* SAC[2]) + L. *labium* lip.] A genus of plants (N.O. *Orchidaceæ*); also a plant of this genus.

1850 in OGILVIE. **1882** *Garden* 30 Dec. 584/1 The Saccolabiums are also there in great numbers.

saccoon (səˈkuːn). *Fencing.* ? *Obs.* exc. *Hist.* Also 8 **segoon.** [Oral adoption of F. *seconde* (səgɔ̃d).] = SECONDE.

1708 in Ashton *Soc. Life Q. Anne* I. 135 [There were the lively Gauls..] ready to wound every Pillar with their Canes, as they pass'd by, either in Ters, Cart, or Saccoon. **1761** COLMAN *Jealous Wife* IV, We'll go through the whole exercise: carte, tierce, and segoon, Captain! **1889** DOYLE *Micah Clarke* 72 In quarte, tierce, or saccoon, the same holds good.

Saccopastore (ˌsækəʊpæˈstɔəreɪ). The name of a village near Rome used *attrib.* in **Saccopastore cranium, skull**, to designate the remains of a Neanderthal type of *Homo sapiens* found there in 1929.

1934 S. SERGI in *Proc. 1st Internat. Congr. Prehist. & Protohist. Stud. 1932* 50 The dimensions of the Gibraltar skull are slightly larger than those of the Saccopastore skull. *Ibid.* 51 The Saccopastore cranium does not at present permit of a complete examination. **1973** B. J. WILLIAMS *Evolution & Human Origins* xi. 181/2 In terms of dimensions and overall form the Saccopastore skull is much like the earlier Steinheim skull.

saccular (ˈsækjʊlə(r)), *a.* [f. SACCUL-US + -AR.] Of the nature of or resembling a sac.

1861 J. R. GREENE *Man. Anim. Kingd., Cœlent.* 48 The generative products are lodged in saccular processes. **1870** ROLLESTON *Anim. Life* Introd. 34 A heart of saccular shape. **1880** J. W. LEGG *Bile* 346 The ducts may show uniform or saccular dilatations.

†**saccuˈlarian.** *Obs.* [f. late L. *sacculāri-us* (f. *saccul-us* dim. of *saccus* bag) + -AN.] One of a class of jugglers mentioned in the Digest.

1652 GAULE *Magastrom.* 362 They were also called Saccularians; because..they would charm and convey the money out of others purses into their owne.

sacculate (ˈsækjʊleɪt), *a.* [f. SACCUL-US + -ATE[2].] = next.

1870 ROLLESTON *Anim. Life* 138 The sacculate character of the digestive tract.

sacculated (ˈsækjuːleɪtɪd), *a.* [Formed as prec. + -ED[1].] Composed of or divided into saccules.

1835-6 *Todd's Cycl. Anat.* I. 220/2 The circumference of each of these vessels is distended into three sacculated pouches. **1853** MARKHAM tr. *Skoda's Auscult.* 70 Patients in whom the pleuritic fluid existed in a sacculated form. **1879** WRIGHT *Anim. Life* 10 In the kangaroos the whole extent of the stomach is sacculated. **1897** *Allbutt's Syst. Med.* IV. 435 In some cases [of pyonephrosis] the kidney becomes completely sacculated.

sacculation (sækjuːˈleɪʃən). [f. SACCUL-US + -ATION.] The formation of or division into saccules; an instance of this.

1869 E. A. PARKES *Pract. Hygiene* (ed. 3) 509 Distention and sacculation of the colon. **1898** *Allbutt's Syst. Med.* V. 70 A sacculation of a small bronchus is fatally exposed to an accumulation of secretion during periods of catarrh.

saccule (ˈsækjuːl). [Anglicized form of SACCULUS.] A small sac, cyst, or bag; esp. the smaller of the two vesicles or sacs in the membranous vestibule of the internal ear.

1836-9 *Todd's Cycl. Anat.* II. 537/1 The component parts of the membraneous labyrinth [of the ear] are:—1. The common sinus. 2. The membraneous ampullæ... 3. The saccule. **1880** BASTIAN *Brain* iv. 76 In close relation with the pedal ganglia or ganglion, there are two minute saccules to which an auditory function is usually ascribed. **1888** ROLLESTON & JACKSON *Anim. Life* 464 It developes within a sac, which then bursts, disclosing a large arm with peculiar suckers, and a terminal saccule.

†**ˈsacculet.** *Obs. rare*[−1]. [f. L. *saccul-us* + -ET[1].] = SACCULUS 1.

1694 WESTMACOTT *Script. Herb.* 4 Dry Almond-Cakes..are used by some Barbers..in Sweet-waters,..Sacculets and Beautifying Medicines.

‖**sacculina** (sækjuːˈlaɪnə). *Zool.* [mod.L., f. *saccul-us*: see SACCULUS.] A genus of degenerate cirripeds parasitic on crabs; an animal of this genus.

1876 *Beneden's Anim. Parasites* 59 The most singular..of all these cirrhipedes, are the Gallæ, which appear under the tail of crabs or the abdomen of paguri, and which zoologists designate under the names Peltogaster or Sacculina. *Ibid.* 60 A curious opinion..is that the Peltogaster of the Pagurus has become a Sacculina on the crab; the host having been transformed, its acolyte has done the same thing under the same influence. **1883** H. DRUMMOND *Nat. Law in Spir. W.* (1884) 341 This simple organism is known to the naturalist as a Sacculina.

sacculine (ˈsækjʊlaɪn), *a.* [ad. mod.L. *sacculīnus*, f. *saccul-us* little bag: see SACCULUS and -INE.] Of or belonging to the genus SACCULINA.

1883 H. DRUMMOND *Nat. Law in Spir. W.* 344 But instead of rising to its opportunities, the sacculine Nauplius, having reached a certain point turned back.

‖**sacculus** (ˈsækjʊləs). Pl. **sacculi** (ˈsækjʊlaɪ). [L.; dim. of *saccus* SAC[2].]

†**1.** A small bag containing medicaments (see quot. 1693). *Obs.*

1621 BURTON *Anat. Mel.* II. iv. I. v, Sacculi or little bagges of hearbs,..and the like applied to the head. **1661** LOVELL *Hist. Anim. & Min.* 163 Applied with mints and southern-wood in a sacculus it helps..paines. **1693** tr. *Blancard's Phys. Dict.* (ed. 2), *Sacculi Medicinales*, several Simples, according to the Nature of the Disease, compounded and beaten together, and tied up in little Bags, to be applied to the part affected.

2. a. *Anat., Biol.* A small sac; a pouch-like dilatation of an organ.

1748 *Phil. Trans.* XLV. 528 A large Sacculus, formed out of the very Coats of the Intestines. **1857** MILLER *Elem. Chem.* (1862) III. 514 The oils appear to exist ready formed in the plant, being enclosed in little sacculi. **1859** HUXLEY *Oceanic Hydrozoa* 70 Sacculi without involucra, and ending in a single filament. **1877** —— *Anat. Inv. Anim.* iii. 141 In the *Calycophoridæ*..complex organs..terminate each lateral branch of a tentacle. Each consists of an elongated sacculus, terminated by two filamentous appendages. **1897**

Allbutt's Syst. Med. III. 972 Often a thin layer of muscle is spread over the whole surface of a sacculus.

b. *Microbiol.* A bag-shaped macromolecule present as a structural element in the cell walls of some bacteria.

1964 WEIDEL & PELZER in *Adv. Enzymol.* XXVI. 194 Sacculi, as we shall call bagshaped macromolecules of the kind discussed here, are objects located on that border where Organic Chemistry merges into Morphogenesis and Morphology... A sacculus is not merely a complex chemical compound; it is, in a truly biological sense, a morphological entity. **1972** *Nature* 25 Feb. 426/2 Penicillin has been shown to interfere with the biosynthesis of the structural element of the bacterial cell wall, the sacculus. **1973** R. G. KRUEGER et al. *Introd. Microbiol.* v. 189/2 The mucopeptide sacculus obtains much of its structural rigidity from the repeating β-1,4-glycosidic bonds between the polysaccharide monomers.

‖**sac de nuit** (sak də nɥi). ? *Obs.* [Fr.] A night-bag, a travelling bag.

1814 M. BIRKBECK *Journey through France* 18 An article of our baggage was missing... It was a *sac de nuit* containing sundries of some value. **1819** M. WILMOT *Let.* 3 Sept. (1935) 10 My invaluable Parisian pelisse..was only crammed, on second thoughts, to fill up a chink in my sac de nuit. **1845** R. FORD *Hand-bk. for Travellers Spain* I. i. 17 The company makes itself responsible for baggage..at relative allowances for *sacs de nuit*, portmanteaus, and trunks. **1860** *Once a Week* 8 Dec. 646/2 A little black *sac-de-nuit*.

sace, obs. Sc. form of CEASE *v.*

1572 *Satir. Poems Reform.* xxxi. 207 God will haue his will, but mair, Fulfillit or he sace.

sace, obs. form of SAUCE, SEARCE.

‖**sacellum** (sə'sɛləm). Pl. **sacella** (sə'sɛlə) [L., dim. of *sacr-um* shrine, neut. of *sacer* holy.]

1. *Eccl. Arch.* (See quot. 1842.)

1806 J. DALLAWAY *Obs. Eng. Archit.* 119 In that church [Winchester Cathedral] is an unrivalled series of sepulchral sacella. **1842** GWILT *Archit.* Gloss., *Sacellum*... In old church architecture, the term signifies a monumental chapel within a church, also a small chapel in a village. *a* **1845** BARHAM *Ingol. Leg.* Ser. III. *Ld. Thoulouse*, The sounds that were heard To proceed now and then from the father's *sacellum.* **1881** W. STEPHENS *Diocese Chichester* 167 *note*, A very beautiful sacellum, with an altar in it, on the south side of the nave.

2. *Roman Antiq.* A small, roofless temple consecrated to some deity. Also, see quot. 1842.

1832 GELL *Pompeiana* I. iv. 49 The Pantheon..may be..considered as a place of feasting..under the protection of some deity, who, from his more elevated sacellum, was supposed to..patronize the banquet. **1842** GWILT *Archit.* Gloss., s.v. *Sacellum*, Small sacella, too, were used among the Egyptians, attached frequently to the larger temples. **1848** LYTTON *Harold* I. i, A small sacellum, or fane to Bacchus.

'**sacerdoce.** *rare.* [a. F. *sacerdoce*, ad. L. *sacerdōtium*: see SACERDOCY.] = SACERDOCY.

1829 [J. R. BEST] *Pers. & Lit. Mem.* 378 In this connection, or alliance..of the sacerdoce and empire, the Church..becomes itself secularized. **1926** R. FRY *Transformations* 58 Sir Claude Phillips was a great High Priest [of art history]..and..had to the full the sense of his sacerdoce.

sacerdocy ('sæsədəʊsɪ). [ad. L. *sacerdōtium* priestly office, f. *sacerdōt-*, *sacerdōs* priest: see SACERDOTAL *a.*] **a.** The sacerdotal character, spirit, or system. **b.** A priestly function or office.

1657–83 EVELYN *Hist. Relig.* (1850) II. 21 And so it continued till the Levitical sacerdocy was fixed and confined to Aaron and his posterity. **1843** C. WORDSWORTH *Theoph. Angl.* (1850) 167 Let him [*sc.* the Bishop] make restitution.. lest under pretext of sacerdocy the pride of power should creep in. **1844** R. M. BEVERLEY *Ch. Eng. Exam.* (ed. 2) 101 He held true and real Levitical sacerdocy to be a constituent part of the clerical character. **1851** *Ecclesiologist* XII. 274 The sacerdocy of the whole machine being an emanation from the vagaries of a Presbyterian preacher. **1877** MRS. CHAPMAN *Ht. Martineau's Autobiog.* III. 78 Literature remained ever to her a Sacerdocy.

‖**sa'cerdos.** *rare.* [See SACERDOTAL.] The Latin word for 'priest'; in quot. *c* 1590 used as a plural.

c **1590** GREENE *Fr. Bacon* vii. 121 No, no, out with your blades, and hamper these Iades,..And teach these Sacerdos, that the Bocardos..are meet for themselues. **1930** E. POUND *XXX Cantos* xxix. 135 As who with four hands at the cross roads By King's hand or sacerdos' are given their freedom. **1949** —— *Pisan Cantos* lxxx. 92 Torn from the *sacerdos* hurled into unstillness.

sacer'dotage. *jocular.* [f. L. *sacerdōt-* (see next) with allusion to *dotage*. Cf. *anecdotage*.]

a. Derisively used for: The sacerdotal order, or the partisans of sacerdotalism. **b.** Sacerdotalism as characteristic of a religion in its 'dotage'.

1859 LONGSTAFFE in *Archæol. Æliana* IV. 11 (*art.*) The Hereditary Sacerdotage of Hexham. **1875** W. CORY *Lett. & Jrnls.* (1897) 382 Your representatives will have a sharper strife with the Sacerdotage. **1884** A. LANG *Custom & Myth* (1885) 27 A people fallen early into its sacerdotage and priestly second childhood.

sacerdotal (sæsə'dəʊtəl), *a.* and *sb.* Also 7 *erron.* **-ial.** [a. F. *sacerdotal*, ad. L. *sacerdōtāl-is*, *sacerdōt-*, *sacerdōs*, f. *sacri-*, *sacer* holy, sacred (neut. pl. *sacra* sacrifices) + *dō-* ablaut-var. of *da-* in *dare* to give. The etymological sense of the sb. is thus 'one who offers sacrifices'.]

A. *adj.*

1. Of or belonging to the priests or priesthood; of or pertaining to a priest; befitting or characteristic of a priest; priestly.

c **1400** MAUNDEV. (1839) vi. 66 That Cytee [*sc.* Ebron] was also Sacerdotalle, that is to seyne, seyntuarie, of the Tribe of Juda. *c* **1450** *Mirour Saluacioun* 1181 Encense is oblacionne ȝe wote is sacerdotale. **1547** *Bk. Marchauntes* c vj b, The .C vi. byshop was a woman... I would wit than if shee were chosen *Via Spiritus sancti*... Item whereby cam the sacerdotall Carecte, & many other thynges whyche for this tyme I let pas [etc.]. **1632** LITHGOW *Trav.* I. 24 Perugia, a Sacerdotall Vniuersity. **1638** JUNIUS *Paint. Ancients* 179 A consular, sacerdotal, and triumphall familie. **1654** R. CODRINGTON tr. *Justine* xx. 288 The Priestess..having on her the Sacerdotial ornaments. **1737** WATERLAND *Rev. Doctr. Eucharist* v. Wks. 1823 VII. 93 The ancient Fathers are still more particular in expounding the sacerdotal consecration, and the Divine sanctification consequent there-upon. **1739** CIBBER *Apol.* (1756) I. 110 A cholerick sacerdotal insolence. **1821** BYRON *Sardan.* II. i, That's a sacerdotal thought, And not a soldier's. **1838** PRESCOTT *Ferd. & Is.* (1846) I. Introd. 10 Priests..arrayed in their sacerdotal robes, not unfrequently led the armies to battle. **1849** MACAULAY *Hist. Eng.* iii. I. 326 Thus the sacerdotal office lost its attraction for the higher classes. **1874** GREEN *Short Hist.* viii. §3. 488 They had none of the sacerdotal independence which Rome had at any rate preserved.

Comb. **1845** S. AUSTEN *Ranke's Hist. Ref.* II. 7 The destructive forces..which this sacerdotal-military state had certainly not been able to neutralise or destroy.

b. Holding the office of a priest.

1681–6 J. SCOTT *Chr. Life* (1747) III. 223 He is a Sacerdotal King, *i.e.* a King that holds his Regal Power in the right and vertue of his Priestly intercession. **1870** DISRAELI *Lothair* xlvi, His Lordship was a sacerdotal orator of repute.

2. Now often used as the epithet of doctrines that assert the existence in the Christian church of an order of priests charged with sacrificial functions and invested with supernatural powers transmitted to them in ordination.

1871 MORLEY *Crit. Misc.* Ser. I. *Carlyle* (1878) 173 It led to the sacramental and sacerdotal developments of Anglicanism. *a* **1884** M. PATTISON *Mem.* (1885) 166 High sacerdotal doctrines were openly proclaimed.

†**B.** *sb.* [Cf. med.L. *sacerdōtāle.*] Priestly function.

a **1640** J. BALL *Answ. Canne* I. (1642) 133 Since they made their new office or sacerdotall, thus they make their catechumine.

Hence **sacer'dotally** *adv.*, †**sacer'dotalness.** Also †**sacerdo'tality**, priestly character.

1668 H. MORE *Div. Dial.* v. xi. (1713) 447 *Philoth*... That is also a farther Intimation of their Sacerdotality. **1727** BAILEY vol. II, *Sacerdotalness*, Priestliness, or Likeness to a Priest. **1836** E. HOWARD *R. Reefer* ii, He has most sacerdotally put down all the jollity. **1864** *Reader* III. 671/3 Why does not some scientific man, clothing himself for the moment sacerdotally.., heave back the charges.

sacerdotalism (sæsə'dəʊtəlɪz(ə)m). [f. SACERDOTAL *a.* + -ISM.]

1. The sacerdotal spirit or system; the principles or practice of the priesthood. Chiefly in unfavourable sense: Pursuit of the interests of the priestly order in opposition to those of the laity; undue assumption of authority on the part of the priesthood.

1847–54 WEBSTER, *Sacerdotalism*, the spirit of the priesthood. **1860** H. B. WILSON in *Ess. & Rev.* 150 A self-satisfied sacerdotalism..might succeed in keeping peace within the walls of emptied churches. **1869** *Pall Mall G.* 7 Jan. 4 A people so imbued with detestation of sacerdotalism or priestly assumption of power as are the English. **1877** FROUDE *Short Stud.* (1883) IV. I. xi. 128 In the eyes of Europe, the cause in which Becket fell was the cause of sacerdotalism. **1880** L. OLIPHANT *Gilead* xvii. 494 The influence for evil of the rival sacerdotalisms as they exist in Turkey.

2. The assertion of the existence in the Christian church of a sacerdotal order or priesthood having sacrificial functions and invested with supernatural powers.

1856 R. A. VAUGHAN *Mystics* (1860) I. 237 These sermons of Tauler assert so audaciously against sacerdotalism, the true priesthood of every Christian man. **1881** *Ch. Q. Rev.* XII. 434 Sacerdotalism, i.e. the belief in certain individuals ordained in a certain way being the exclusive instrument, in the Divine covenant, of sacramental graces. **1905** *Ch. Times* 22 Sept. 337/3 True sacerdotalism is all one with true Churchmanship.

sacerdotalist (sæsə'dəʊtəlɪst). [f. SACERDOTAL *a.* + -IST.] One who advocates or defends sacerdotalism.

1865 *Pall Mall G.* 29 Sept. 10/2 The sacerdotalists are grievously mistaken if they take all this for the proof of a latent belief in sacramental theories. **1874** H. R. REYNOLDS *John Bapt.* v. §1. 298 The awful emphasis laid by the sacerdotalist on the efficacy of that ordinance [*sc.* baptism]. **1896** BP. STUBBS *Visit. Charges* (1904) 304 The advocate of religious education, the opponent of divorce and simony, the maintainer of the sanctity of Sunday, are all alike sacerdotalists.

sacerdotalize (sæsə'dəʊtəlaɪz), *v.* [f. SACERDOTAL *a.* + -IZE.] *trans.* To make subservient to sacerdotalism. Hence **sacer'dotalized** *ppl. a.*, **sacer'dotalizing** *vbl. sb.*

1865 *Pall Mall G.* 29 Sept. 10/2 As to the sacerdotalizing of the English poor by any such means as these [etc.]. **1883** MAINE *Early Law* ii. 26 The existing very imperfectly sacerdotalised customary law of the Hindus in the Punjab. **1899** *Sp.* in *Times* 11 May 15/1 The policy of the Bishops seemed to be to sacerdotalize the Church and substitute their own authority for that of the law.

†**sacerdote.** *nonce-wd.* In 7 **sacerdott.** [ad. L. *sacerdōt-em.*] A priest.

1685 in Maidment *Bk. Sc. Pasquils* (1868) 285, I swear on word of Sacerdott.

†**sacerdotical,** *a.* *Obs. rare*$^{-1}$. [f. L. *sacerdōt-em* + -ICAL.] = SACERDOTAL.

1641 J. TRAPPE *Theol. Theol.* 69 As in the New, the Gospels are regall..the Epistles more Sacerdoticall.

‖**sacerdotium** (sæsə'dəʊʃɪəm, sækə'dəʊtɪəm). [a. L. *sacerdōtium*: see SACERDOCY.]

a. = SACERDOCY. **b.** The dominion of the Church in mediæval Europe.

1931 *Times Lit. Suppl.* 20 Aug. 628/2 The unhappy Episcopus..nearly lost his 'sacerdotium' in consequence. **1955** *Times* 2 July 7/3 When later the regular universities grew up the journey from Paris to Oxford, though arduous, was a routine event in the life of a scholar. This easy movement within the European *Studium*—as it called itself in grand contrast to the *Imperium* and *Sacerdotium*—was killed like many other good things by the rise of nationalism. **1956** *Scottish Jrnl. Theol.* IX. 174 Does the consecration of a bishop confer a new *character*? Or does it simply give him authority and grace to perform functions inherent in the *sacerdotium* or *ordo* of the presbyter, but not at present exercised by presbyters? Historically the *sacerdotium*, or ministry of the Word and Sacraments, was at one time regarded as particularly the characteristic of the bishop rather than of the presbyter.

sacha, obs. form of SAC[1].

sachaline ('sækəlɪn, -iːn). Also **sacaline.** [ad. the specific epithet of *Polygonum sachalinense* (F. Schmidt in C. J. Maximowicz *Primitiæ Floræ Amurensis* (1859) 233), f. *Sakhalin*, name of an island north of Japan.] A large perennial knotweed, *Polygonum sachalinense*, of the family Polygonaceæ, native to Japan and bearing clusters of small greenish flowers and very large oval leaves which are sometimes used as fodder.

[**1882** *Garden* 22 Apr. 280/2 (*heading*) The Sachalian knotweed.] **1901** L. H. BAILEY *Cycl. Amer. Hort.* III. 1393/2 Sacaline... Exceedingly vigorous plants, spreading rapidly from the tips of strong underground shoots. **1905** W. J. SPILLMAN *Farm Grasses U.S.* xv. 234 The two most prominent fads of this kind in recent years were sachaline, a well-nigh worthless representative of the smartweed family, and penicillaria. **1943** FERNALD & KINSEY *Edible Wild Plants* iii. 176 The leafy summits of young stems of Sachaline..cooked as a potherb..are as good as or superior to French Sorrel. **1952** L. & J. BUSH-BROWN *America's Garden Bk.* (ed. 2) xii. 535 Perennials blooming in September and October... Sacaline. **1975** *Daily Colonist* (Victoria, B.C.) 9 Oct. 6/1 A fast-growing weed threatening new growth in forests [is] sachaline, a bamboo-like weed from eastern Europe.

‖**sachamaker.** *Obs.* Also 8 **sacka-maker.** [app. a derivative or a corruption of *sachama* SACHEM.] = SACHEM, SAGAMORE.

1682 *Pennsylv. Archives* I. 47 Indyan Sachamakers. **1683** PENN *Wks.* (1782) IV. 311 Another made a speech to the Indians, in the name of all the Sachamakers or kings. **1701** C. WOLLEY *Jrnl. New York* (1860) 54 They have the greatest Sachim or Sacka-maker, i.e. King.

sache, obs. form of SAC[1], SACK *sb.*[1]

sachel, -ell, -elle, obs. forms of SATCHEL.

sachem ('seɪtʃəm, 'sætʃəm). Also 7 **sachama, sachema, sachim,** 9 **saquem.** [a. Narragansett *sachem* = Delaware *sakima*, Micmac *sakumow*, Penobscot *sagamo* (whence SAGAMORE).]

1. The supreme head or chief of some American Indian tribes.

The alleged distinction between *sachem* and *sagamore* (quot. *a* 1817) appears to be erroneous.

1622 *Relat. Plantation Plymouth, New Eng.* 49 They brought vs to their Sachim or Gouernour. **1677** W. HUBBARD *Narrative* 5 Miantonimoh the chief Sachem or Lord of the Narhagansets. **1683** PENN *Wks.* (1782) IV. 310 Their government is by kings, which they call sachama. **1685** R. BURTON *Eng. Emp. America* 117 Sachema. **1710** LUTTRELL *Brief Rel.* (1857) VI. 571 Four Indian sachems, or kings of the 5 Indian nations, lately arrived here. *a* **1817** T. DWIGHT *Trav. New Eng.*, etc. (1821) I. 119 Their principal chiefs were called Sachems; their subordinate ones, Sagamores. **1858** LONGF. *M. Standish* I. 52 Let them come, if they like, be it sagamore, sachem, or pow-wow. **1865** LEVER *Luttrell of Arran* xiii, He was a great Saquem, delivering the laws of his tribe.

2. *jocularly* applied to a prominent member of a society, etc.; a 'chief'.

1684 in *Documents Colonial Hist. New-York* (1853) I. 402 Wee have put ourselves under the Great Sachim Charles that lives over the Great Lake. **1773** J. ADAMS *Wks.* (1854) IX. 335 It is whispered that the Sachem has it in contemplation to go home soon. [*Note.* Adams refers to some one prominent in Mass. politics.] **1836** O. W. HOLMES *Song for Centennial Celebr. Harvard Coll.* in *Poems* (1849) 194 And, when at length the College rose, The sachem cocked his eye At every tutor's meagre ribs Whose coat tails whistled by. **1861** *Charleston* (S. Carolina) *Mercury* 29 Mar. 1/2 The Sachems of the Black Republican party did not appreciate the peculiarity of the times when they enacted the Morrill Tariff. **1942** E. Paul *Narrow St.* xx. 164 [André] Breton, the pontifical sachem, turned to Trotsky and became an enemy. **1972** *Science* 16 June 1222/2 Chairman of the study group was Detlev W. Bronk, former president of Rockefeller University, president of the academy from 1950 to 1962, and himself a grand sachem of the advisory system. **1973** *Caribbean Contact* Feb. 2/2 It's the customs and immigration sachems, though, who must get top billing as the real purveyors of theatre in this world within a world. **1977** *Time* 18 July 26/3 Most party sachems are lining up behind either Incumbent Abraham Beame or Governor Hugh Carey's choice.

3. *U.S. Politics.* One of a body of twelve high officials in the Tammany Society of New York. ***grand sachem***, the head of this body.

1890 *Nation* 20 Mar. 236/1 The tribulations of Tammany's former Grand Sachem, the Sheriff. **1890** *Boston* (Mass.) *Jrnl.* 23 Apr. 2/3 Among the Sachems unanimously re-elected by Tammany Hall are [etc.].

Hence **'sachemdom, 'sachemship**, the position or 'realm' of a sachem; **'sachemic** *a.*, of or pertaining to a sachem.

1765 T. Hutchinson *Hist. Mass.* I. v. 459 Two cantons or sachemdoms of the cape Indians. **1771** Smollett *Humph. Cl.* 26 Oct., A little traffic he drove in peltry during his sachemship among the Miamis. *a* **1817** T. Dwight *Trav. New Eng.*, etc. (1821) II. 18 Alexander, the eldest son of Massasoit, died..and left the Sachemdom to Philip. **1876** Bancroft *Hist. U.S.* II. xxxvi. 395 The forests beyond the Sace, New Hampshire, and the country as far as Salem, constituted the sachemship of Penacook. **1885** *Riverside Nat. Hist.* (1888) VI. 163 The sachemic office was hereditary.

sachemore, obs. form of sagamore.

‖**Sachertorte** ('zaxər,tɔrtə). Also **Sacher Torte, sachertorte.** [Ger., named after *Sacher*, proprietor of a hotel in Vienna, or the hotel itself + *torte* cake.] A rich chocolate cake of a kind orig. made in Vienna.

1906 *Mrs. Beeton's Bk. Househ. Managem.* lii. 1543 *Sacher torte.* (German chocolate tart.) **1954** 'M. Cost' *Invitation from Minerva* 133 That crowning achievement of the Viennese table: *Sachertorte.* **1961** W. Buchan *Helen All Alone* 58 Large..cups of coffee..with brioches and sachertorte. **1974** *Times* 5 Apr. 16/3 Ice-cream, butterscotch,..Sachertorte, pears, Baked Alaska. **1978** M. Dickens *Open Bk.* i. 4 A rather formal tea, with damp cucumber sandwiches and *Sachertorte.*

‖**sachet** (saʃɛ, 'sæʃeɪ). [Fr. *sachet* (from 12th c.; in ONF. *saquet*: see sacket), dim. of *sac*:—L. *saccus* bag, sack *sb.*[1] Cf. It. *sacchetto*.]

†**1.** A small bag, a wallet. *Obs. rare.*

1483 Caxton *Gold. Leg.* 224/2 He..ete..twyes a day of the same loof and alwaye on the morn he fond it hool in his sachet. **1487** —— *Bk. Gd. Manners* I. xvii. (W. de W. *c* 1515) E v b, In stede of a celyer he [*sc.* Diogenes] had but a lytell sachet.

2. A small perfumed bag or satchel.

1838 *Times* 3 July 5/6 The 'letter of felicitation' forwarded by the Sultan to her Majesty on the occasion of her coronation..was put in an envelope..and the whole enclosed in a crimson cloth sachet or bag, somewhat resembling a lady's small reticule. **1880** Disraeli *Endym.* xxi, You will not perhaps be able to find your pocket-handkerchiefs at first. They are in this sachet.

3. A dry perfume made up into a packet for placing among articles of clothing, etc. (see quot. 1892).

1855 Piesse *Perfumery* vii. 145 Besides the sachets mentioned there are many other substances applied as dry perfumes, such as scented wadding. **1856** *Athenæum* 18 Oct. 1268 He is scented like a sachet. **1892** G. W. Askinson *Perfumes* xvi. 208 Expensive sachets are sold in silk bags... Cheap sachets are sold in envelopes or in round boxes.

attrib. **1855** Piesse *Perfumery* vii. 137 Sachet Powders.

4. A small sealed bag-like container, now usu. of plastic, for holding a liquid, a powder, or air.

1917 *Harrod's Gen. Catal.* 358/3 Shampoo Sachets...box 1/0. **1941** N. Marsh *Death & Dancing Footman* (1942) ii. 42 The sachets used in permanent waving. **1970** *Which?* June 169/1 Jackets using air-filled sachets should be very safe too. **1975** C. F. Ross *Packaging of Pharmaceuticals* I. 4 *Powders* ..are sometimes presented in single-dose containers. These may include sachets, filled automatically on suitable strip-packaging machines using paper, aluminium foil, plastics films or laminations of these.

sacheverell (sə'tʃɛvərəl). ? *Obs.* or *U.S.* Also -el. [Said to have been named by the inventor on account of the popularity of Dr. Sacheverell: see next.] (See quots.)

1769 Franklin *Lett.* Wks. 1840 VI. 325 This is seen in narrow stove chimneys, when a sacheverell or blower is used. **1785** Grose *Dict. Vulg. Tongue, Sacheverel*, the iron door, or blower to the mouth of a stove, from a divine of that name, who made himself famous for blowing the coals of dissention, the latter end of the reign of Queen Ann.

Sacheverellite (sə'tʃɛvərəlaɪt). [f. *Sacheverell* (see below) + -ite.] One who adopted the extreme High Church and Tory views of Dr. Henry Sacheverell, an English clergyman whose condemnation for 'seditious libel' in 1709 excited great popular indignation. Also *attrib.* or *adj.*

1710 *Chuse which you Please* 4 A Sacheverellite swears to Her Majesty only as Queen de Facto. *Ibid.* 7 The Sacheverellite Clergy have long groan'd under this their Subjection to the State.

‖**Sachlichkeit** ('zaxlɪçkaɪt). [Ger., = 'objectivity'.] Objectivism, realism; *spec.* in the fine arts = Neue Sachlichkeit.

1930 *Times Lit. Suppl.* 24 Apr. 341/4 The prevailing note is one of indifference, of complete detachment, of *Sachlichkeit.* **1938** C. Fullman tr. *P. Thoene's Mod. German Art* 9 The general characteristics to be found in contemporary German painting..belong to the spiritual categories of a post-war world: Despair and its concomitants—satire and irony; realism, matter-of-fact-ness, *Sachlichkeit*. *Ibid.* 95 Max Beckmann has called his form 'transcendental *Sachlichkeit*'. **1968** *Listener* 3 Oct. 436/1 A generation of excellent artist-designers, such as Bruno Paul, Hans Poelzig and the brothers Taut, all worked in the spirit which was already associated with the word *Sachlichkeit*, which—taken literally—means 'thingness'; it is usually translated as 'matter-of-fact', 'realistic', 'sober', 'objective', and gained currency in matters of art and design early in this century.

‖**Sachverhalt** ('zaxfɛrhalt). *Philos.* Pl. **Sachverhalte.** [Ger., = status rerum (Grimm).] Esp. with reference to the philosophy of Wittgenstein and phenomenology, a state of affairs, an objective fact.

1922 B. Russell in *Wittgenstein's Tractatus* 9 Facts which are not compounded of other facts are what Mr Wittgenstein calls *Sachverhalte.* **1931** W. R. B. Gibson tr. *Husserl's Ideas* 461 The 'substantive' quality attaches to the 'Substrat' underlying the 'Sachverhalt', as well as to the 'Sachverhalt' itself. **1932** A. H. Gardiner *Theory of Speech & Lang.* i. 26 The unit of speech is the sentence and hence the 'thing' signified by every such unit is always of a complex kind—a state of things, as we might say, or a *Sachverhalt*, if we prefer to use the convenient German equivalent. **1950** *Mind* LIX. 266 That new type of object called the *Sachverhalt* or State of Affairs (the Meinongian 'Objective'). **1972** J. N. Findlay *Meinong's Emotional Presentation* p. xv, We become aware of what Husserl called variously states of affairs (*Sachverhalte*) or propositions.

saciate, sacietie, -ty, obs. ff. satiate, satiety.

sack (sæk), *sb.*[1] Forms: 1 sacc, sæcc, 3-4 **sac, seck(e**, (3 sec, 6 *north.* seik), 3-6 **sakke**, 3-7 **sacke**, 4-5 **sak, sekke**, 4-6 **sek**, (5 **sac, cek, sache, sake, saccke**, *Sc.* **secke**, 7 *Sc.* **seck**), 5- **sack.** [OE. *sacc* masc., ad. L. *sacc-us* bag, sack, sackcloth (F. *sac*, from 11-12th c., Pr. *sac*, Sp., Pg. *saco*, It. *sacco*), a. Gr. σάκκος, ad. Heb. (? Phœnician) *saq* = Jewish Aramaic *saq, saqqā*, Syriac *saq, saqå*, Assyrian *saqqu*. The word appears in most of the Teut. langs.: Goth. *sakkus* sackcloth is prob. from Greek, but in the other langs. the proximate source is Latin: MDu. *sak* (Du. *zak*), OHG. *sac, sach*, acc. pl. *secchi* (MHG. *sac*, mod.G. *sack* bag), ON. *sekk-r* sack (Sw. *säkk*, Da. *sæk*). The ON. and some of the OHG. forms, and perh. the OE. *sæcc* (confined to the sense 'sackcloth') indicate a prehistoric type **sakki-z*: cf. med.L. '*saccia*, σάκκος' in a Lat.-Gr. glossary.

The word is found also as Irish and Gael. *sac*, Welsh *sach*, Hungarian *zsak*, Russian *sak'*, Polish, Czech, Serbian, Albanian *sak*, which are all directly or indirectly from the Latin or Greek.]

I. 1. a. A large bag oblong in shape and open at one end, usually made of coarse flax or hemp, used for the storing and conveyance of corn, flour, fruit, potatoes, wood, coal, etc.

c **1000** Ælfric *Gen.* xlii. 25 He..bead his þegnum þæt hiȝ fyldon hira saccas mid hwæte. *c* **1250** *Gen. & Ex.* 2223 Quan men ðo seckes ðor un-bond, And in ðe coren ðo aȝtes fond. *a* **1300** *Cursor M.* 5090 Your seckes sal i fil o gift. *c* **1385** Chaucer *L.G.W.* 195 (*Dido*) Sakkes ful of gold. *c* **1440** *Promp. Parv.* 64/1 Cek, or Cekclothe, or poke, *saccus.* **14..** *Tretyce* in *W. of Henley's Husb.* (1890) 50 To kepe þe corne þat falithe when it is put into þe sekkis. *a* **1529** Skelton *Bk. 3 Foles* Wks. 1843 I. 200 Pecunyous fooles, that..weddeth these olde wyddred women, whych hath sackes full of nobles. **1573** Tusser *Husb.* (1878) 176 Good huswifes be mending and peecing their sackes. **1753** *Scots Mag.* Aug. 421/2 Five men in sacks run for a guinea. **1840** Hood *Up the Rhine* 222 What do you think, Margaret, of having your head caught in a baker's sack, hot from the oven [as a cure for a 'blight in the eyes']. **1864** Tennyson *En. Ard.* 63 The younger people.., With bag and sack and basket.., Went nutting.

b. With reference to the punishment of drowning in a sack. ***the sack***: the punishment (awarded in ancient Rome to a parricide) of being sewn in a sack and drowned.

c **1375** *Sc. Leg. Saints* iii. (*Andreas*) 211 þe Iuge..gert bynd þe ȝounge man rath, and put hym in a sek to mere. *c* **1386** Chaucer *Merch. T.* 956 And if I do that lakke Do strepe me and put me in a sakke And in the nexte ryuer do me drenche. **1500-20** Dunbar *Poems* xlii. 87 Gud Fame wes drownit in a sek. **1538** Elyot *Dict.* Add. s.v. *Culeus.* **1678** R. L'Estrange *Seneca's Mor., Clemency* (1696) 441 Caligula, in five years condemn'd more People to the Sack, then ever were before him. **1820** Scott *Monast.* x, Didst thou think me fool enough to wait till thou hadst betrayed me to the sack and the fork!

c. *transf.* and *fig.*

a **1300** *Sarmun* in *E.E.P.* (1862) 2 þi felle wiþ-oute nis bot a sakke. **1426** Lydg. *De Guil. Pilgr.* 12791 Ther Sak, ther wombe, (I vndertake,) Off hem ther goddys they do make. **1559** *Mirr. Mag., Edw. IV*, vi, A man is but a sacke of stercory. **1581** Sidney *Apol. Poetrie* (Arb.) 45 Although perchance the sack of his owne faults, lye so behinde hys back. [Cf. Sacket, quot. 1549.]

†**d.** (See quots.) Cf. woolsack. *Obs.*

1539 *Act 31 Hen. VIII*, c. 10 §8 Suche of them as shall happen to be under the saide degree of a Baron, shall sitt.. at the uppermost parte of the sakkes in the middes of the saide Parliament Chamber. **1577** Harrison *England* ii. viii. (1877) i. 174 In the middest [of the House of Lords]..lie certeine sackes stuffed with wooll or haire, whereon the judges of the realme, the master of the rols, and secretaries of estate doo sit.

†**e.** ***sack and seam***: pack-horse traffic. *Obs.*

1631 in *N. Riding Rec.* (1885) III. ii. 312 [Two yeomen presented for stopping up the King's highway for] sacke and seame. **1829** Brockett *N.C. Words* (ed. 2), *Sack-and-seam-road*, a horse road—properly a pack-horse road over moors.

f. *Criminals' slang.* A pocket.

1699 B. E. *New Dict. Canting Crew, Sack*,..a Pocket. **1858** A. S. Mayhew *Paved with Gold* iii. iii. 265 I've brought a couple of bene coves, with lots of the Queen's pictures in their sacks. **1955** *Publ. Amer. Dial. Soc.* xxiv. 125 Rarely one hears the side coat pocket called a *sack.*

g. (*a*) A hammock; a bunk; (*b*) a bed; freq. as ***the sack***; ***to hit the sack***: see hit *v.* 11 c. *slang* (chiefly *U.S.*; orig. *Naval*).

1829 *Sailors & Saints* II. iv. 92 There was no more to do, nor hand him below, and bundle him into his sack. **1883** Melton & Oliphant *Cruise of U.S.S. Galena* 48 We were congratulating ourselves that the drills were over and retired to our 'dreaming sacks'. **1942** *Chevron* 17 Jan. 4/3 *Sack*, bunk. **1943**, etc. [see hit *v.* 11 c]. **1947** *Reef Points 1947–48* (U.S. Naval Acad., Annapolis) 219 *Flake out*, to utilize one's sack between Reveille and Taps. **1950** 'D. Divine' *King of Fassarai* vi. 41 The first time I came on board you were lying in your goddam sack. **1952** in Wentworth & Flexner *Dict. Amer. Slang* (1960) 439/2 Let me stay in the sack all day. **1963** 'E. McBain' *Ten Plus One* xv. 194 Helen seems to think a little more than necking took place... She seems to think you all crawled into the sack. **1968** J. Updike *Couples* ii. 168 Women with that superheated skin are usually fantastic in the sack. **1977** I. Shaw *Beggarman, Thief* iii. x. 342 Probably in the sack, he thought, with that fellow with the beard.

h. A bag, large or small, made of paper or the like; ***paper sack***: see paper *sb.* 12. *U.S.*

1904, etc. [see paper *sb.* 12]. **1928** *Dialect Notes* VI. 60 A paper bag is always a *sack* or a *poke*, since *bag* means scrotum in the hill country. **1933** *Collier's* 28 Jan. 8/1 While he is at the ball game, he buys himself a sack of Harry Stevens' peanuts. **1956** B. Holiday *Lady Sings Blues* (1973) viii. 77, I got so tired of scenes in crummy roadside restaurants over getting served, I used to..sit in the bus and rest—and let them bring me out something in a sack. **1974** M. G. Eberhart *Danger Money* v. 56 Greg paid for the food and took the sacks to the station wagon.

i. A base in baseball. Cf. bag *sb.* 1 c. *U.S.*

1914 Lardner & Heeman *Mar. 6, 1914* 30 We've larruped out th' four-sack poke And scored among a salvo. **1922** E. J. Lanigan *Baseball Cycl.* iii. 47 Until 1920, a notable athlete ..could skip around the circuit in the ninth..and, although unmolested, receive credit for a group of stolen sacks. **1938** H. E. West *Baseball Scrap Bk.* 20 Before he reached the keystone sack the umpires flagged him down and sent him back to bat over again.

j. In American football, an act or occasion of tackling a quarter-back behind the scrimmage line before he can make a pass.

1972 S. Deluca *Football Playbk.* 370 *Sack*, when the quarterback is thrown for a loss while attempting to pass. **1974** [see *quarterback sack* s.v. quarterback *sb.* 3]. **1978** *Detroit Free Press* 2 Apr. 6E/3 Other changes have been made, this year and in recent years, to put juice into the offence, the feeling being that people come to see touchdowns and not quarterback sacks. **1980** *Washington Star* 3 Nov. D3, I would have to say the sacks were the difference in the game.

k. ***sad sack***: see as main entry.

2. A sack with its contents; also the amount usually contained in a sack; hence taken as a unit of measure or weight for corn, flour, fruit, wool, coal, etc.

1314-15 *Rolls of Parlt.* I. 313/1, li saks & x peres de leine. **1427-8** *Rec. St. Mary at Hill* 69 For iij sak lyme to þe same mason..vj d. **1479** in *Eng. Gilds* (1870) 425 That they bryng their sakkes of juste mesure. **1494** *Act 11 Hen. VII*, c. 4 §2 Be it also enacted that ther be but only..xiiij lb. to the stone of Wolle and xxj stone to the sakke. **1565** *Reg. Privy Council Scot.* I. 334 The conservatour sall haif..of euer ilk sek of gudis twa sturis. **1609** Skene *Reg. Maj., Dav. II* 44 There salbe ane maister of the Trone, quha sall receaue fra the King, ane pennie for ilk seck of woll (quhilk conteines twentie foure stanes). **1687** A. Lovell tr. *Thevenot's Trav.* i. 229 Having taken out of her ten sacks of Carobs, they..let her go. **1704** *Lond. Post* 14-17 Apr. 2/1 Last Week 6 Sacks of Cocoa-Nuts were seiz'd by a Custom-house Officer, being brought up to Town for so many sacks of Beans. **1846** J. Baxter *Libr. Pract. Agric.* (ed. 4) II. 443 Of corresponding Prices per Load, Quarter, Sack, and Bushel. **1859** Tennyson *Enid* 263 An ancient churl,..Went sweating underneath a sack of corn. **1872** Raymond *Statist. Mines & Mining* 143, 90 pounds is the weight taken per sack of interior ores.

3. a. Proverbs and proverbial phrases. †***to buy a cat in the sack*** [cf. F. *acheter chat en sac* Cotgr.]: to buy an article without first inspecting it. ***to bring, carry (more) sacks to the mill***: see mill *sb.*[1] 1 b. †***to cover oneself with a wet sack*** [= F. *se couvrir d'un sac mouillé*, 16th c.]: to make vain excuses. ***to hold the sack***: to be saddled with an unwelcome responsibility (*U.S.*).

c **1380** Wyclif *Sel. Wks.* III. 422 To bye a catte in þo sakke is bot litel charge. **1546** J. Heywood *Prov.* (1867) 47, I promise you an olde sacke axeth much patchyng. **1579** Tomson *Calvin's Serm. Tim.* 340/2 Therefore the Papists couer them selues with a wet sack, when they say [etc.]. *a* **1651** Calderwood *Hist. Kirk* (1843) II. 404 Where they alledge we sould have beene occasioun to caus our sonne follow his father hastilie, they cover themselves theranent with a wett seck. **1904** W. H. SMITH *Promoters* xxiv. 343 They are the ones that are always left to hold the sack. **1921** C. E. MULFORD *Bar-20 Three* xii. 140 Long an' Thompson are holding the sack. They're scapegoats for th' whole cussed gang. **1929** *Univ. Kansas Graduate Mag.* Apr., We will be holding the sack for an additional.. deficit of nearly $1000. **1936** E. S. GARDNER *Case of Stuttering Bishop* xii. 191 Perhaps you didn't plan to drag me into the case and leave me holding the sack, but it sure looks as though you did. **1954** W. FAULKNER *Fable* (1955) 176 You might leave your own kinfolks holding the sack, but these are the sheriff's friends.

b. in various similative phrases.

1426 LYDG. *De Guil. Pilgr.* 5127 Swych wer foul & blake of syht Lych to a colyers sak. *c* **1440** *Jacob's Well* 263 þou faryst as a saccke wyth-oute botome, þere may no-thyng abyde þer-in. **1470–85** MALORY *Arthur* x. xv. 437 Kyng Marke.. tombled adoune out of his sadel to the erthe as a sak. **1886** HALL CAINE *Son of Hagar* II. xvi, Tom was drawn wet as a sack to the opposite bank.

4. slang. ***to give*** (a person) ***the sack***: to dismiss from employment or office; *transf.* to discard, turn off (a lover). So ***to get the sack***: to receive one's dismissal.

The phrase has been current in Fr. from the 17th c.: cf. '*On luy a donné son sac*, hee hath his pasport giuen him (said of a seruant whom his master hath put away)' (Cotgr.). Cf. Du. *iemand den zak geven*, to give one the sack (already in MDu.), *den zak krijgen*, to get the sack.

1825 C. M. WESTMACOTT *Eng. Spy* I. 178 You munna split on me, or I shall get the zack for telling on ye. **1837** DICKENS *Pickw.* xx, I wonder what old Fogg 'ud say, if he knew it. I should get the sack, I s'pose—eh? **1840** THACKERAY *Shabby Genteel Story* v, The short way would have been.. to have requested him immediately to quit the house; or, as Mr. Gann said, 'to give him the sack at once'. **1902** BESANT *Five Yrs.' Tryst* 12 Frivolity and even lightness of conversation were sure to be followed by the sack. **1913** J. STEPHENS *Here are Ladies* 102 Getting the 'sack' is an experience which wearies after the first time. **1935** D. GARNETT *Beany-Eye* I. 34 If I just give him the sack he won't get another job and will get into a brawl and be sent to prison again. **1937** 'G. ORWELL' *Road to Wigan Pier* I. i. 11 If they failed to secure a minimum of twenty orders a day, they got the sack. **1958** *Times Lit. Suppl.* 16 May 274/1 Always late, crumpled and scruffy, perpetually in debt, hourly expecting the sack, Greave takes refuge from the horrid realities of life in Mittyesque fantasies, pretending he is a high-powered American salesman.

†**II. 5.** Sackcloth, esp. as the material of penitential or mourning garments. Also, a piece or a garment of sackcloth. *Obs.*

c **1000** ÆLFRIC *Saints' Lives* I. 538 He aras þa of þære flora and of þam wacan sæcce þe he lange on-uppan dreoriȝ wæs sittende. *c* **1200** *Trin. Coll. Hom.* 139 [John the Baptist chose] stiue here to shurte and gret sac to curtle. ? *a* **1366** CHAUCER *Rom. Rose* 457 She [*sc.* Poverty] nadde on but a streit old sak. **1382** WYCLIF *Dan.* ix. 3 To preye and byseche in fastyngis, sac, and ashe. **1422** tr. *Secreta Secret., Priv. Priv.* 198 This kynge Ezechie.. hym clothid in a sake, he Put hym-Selfe to Penaunce. **1483** CAXTON *Gold. Leg.* 231 b/2 His bedde was alle enuyronned with asshes and hayre and with a sacke. **1535** COVERDALE *2 Esdras* xvi. 2 Gyrde youre selues with clothes of sack & hayre. **1589** NASHE *Martins Months Mind* H 1, Away with silke, for I will mourne in sack, Martin is dead. **1594** GREENE & LODGE *Looking-gl.* (1598) H 3 b, Lords,.. see it straight proclaim'd, That man and beast.. For fortie daies in sacke and ashes fast. *c* **1620** Z. BOYD *Zion's Flowers* (1855) 35 For Silks I will with rugged Sack be clad.

†**6.** Some kind of material for ladies' dresses: = SACKING *sb.*[3] 2. *Obs.*

1595 *Acc. Bk. W. Wray* in *Antiquary* XXXII. 317, j pece stro coler seck, xxvis.; and viij yeardes checker seckynge, vjs. viijd... Ite' j pece ashe coler seckynge, xxjs.

III. *attrib.* and *Comb.*

7. a. simple attrib., as ***sack-band***, ***-barrow***, ***-cart***, ***-end***, ***-hoist***, ***-pile***, ***-pocket***, ***-weight***; (sense 1 j) ***sack pack***. **b.** objective, as ***sack-bearer***, ***-hauling***, ***-maker***, ***-making***; in names of mechanical contrivances, as ***sack-carrier***, ***sack-emptier***, ***-holder***, ***-lifter***; **c.** similative, as ***sack-formed***, ***-shaped*** adjs.; ***sack-like*** adj. and adv. ***sack-wise*** adv.

c **1460** *Towneley Myst.* xii. 167 Hold ye my mare.. Whylst I.. lawse the *sek band. **1638** PENKETHMAN *Artach.* H j, For Salt, Yeast, Candle, and Sack-bands 2*d.* **1850** OGILVIE, *Sack barrow. **1979** *Daily Tel.* 10 Nov. 10/6, I stuff the bags till I can hardly drag them, and then have to move them on a sack barrow. **1565** COOPER *Thesaurus*, *Saccarius*, a *sackebearer. **1745** W. ELLIS *Agriculture Improv'd* in *Mod. Husbandman* VII. I. 124 So.. that *Sack-carriers or Corn-porters convey the bought Wheat.. to such Loft or Granary. **1966** 'L. LANE' *ABZ of Scouse* p. iv, Merseyside's prosperity depended mainly.. upon the crate-handlers, the sack-carriers and the horse-whackers, or in the most up-to-date cliché, the 'service industries'. **1963** *Times* 14 Jan. 10/7 My duties, on the other hand, were many and varied. They included propelling a two-wheeled vehicle, known to the initiated as a *sack-cart, for long distances, delivering parcels at the houses of well-to-do customers. **1969** *Listener* 8 May 640/3, I used to have to get them [*sc.* sacks of flour] onto what we call a sack-cart, a trolley, shoot them into a bin. **1884** KNIGHT *Dict. Mech.* Suppl., **Sack Emptier*. **1937** E. MUIR *Journeys & Places* 26 Proud history has such *sackends. **1835–6** *Todd's Cycl. Anat.* I. 693/2 It is by a *sack-formed process of the mantle filled with this yellowish matter that the peduncle is first formed. **1965** A. BLACKSHAW *Mountaineering* III. xvii. 420 If *sack hauling is unavoidable use a separate rope. **1875** KNIGHT *Dict. Mech.* Suppl., **Sack-hoist*, an adaptation of the wheel and axle to form a continuous hoist for sacks. **1880** J. W. HILL *Guide Agric. Implements* 468 Combined *Sack Holder and Barrow. *Ibid.* 469 This Machine is an efficient *Sack Lifter, Loader, Unloader, and Shooter. **1826** KIRBY & SP. *Entomol.* III. XXXI. 257 The *sack-like cases in which the larva resides. **1898** G. MEREDITH *Odes Fr. Hist.* 71 Sack-like droop bronze pears. **1780** *Westm. Mag.* VIII. Suppl. 730/2 *Sack and sacking-maker. **1885** *Manch. Exam.* 10 Jan. 5/1 A young woman named Mary Dawson, sackmaker.. was found guilty of a robbery from the person. **1976** *Time* 13 Sept. 68/2 On defense, the Colts' front four is largely unknown to fans but not to opposing quarterbacks. Pittsburgh's fearsome front four has the rep, but it was the Colts' '*Sack Pack' that led the league in dumping passers last season. **1897** 'MARK TWAIN' *Following Equator* xxviii. 273 He saw a white linen figure stretched in slumber upon a pile of grain-sacks... The form whirled itself from the *sack-pile. **1938** F. D. SHARPE *Sharpe of Flying Squad* xiv. 154 Others [*sc.* shoplifters] have spacious *sack pockets underneath their skirts large enough to contain a roll of cloth, a dress, or a small suitcase. **1839** SOWERBY *Conchol. Man.* 21 The head.. is placed above a *sack-shaped body. **1429** *Rolls of Parlt.* IV. 359/2 The *sak weyght is sold for XII Marc. **1923** D. H. LAWRENCE *Birds, Beasts & Flowers* 178 And all her weight, all her blood, dripping sack-wise down towards the earth's centre.

8. Special comb.: **sack-bag** (see quot.); **sack-bearer**, the larva of an American moth of the family Lacosomidæ, which makes cases from leaves; **sack chair** (see quot. 1970); **sack coal**, screened coal for delivery in sacks; †**sack custom**, a toll on sacks of wool; **sack-doodling** *ppl. a.*, quasi-*arch.* [cf. G. *dudelsack* bagpipe], that plays on the bagpipes; **sack drill**, **duty** *U.S. Naval slang*, sleep; time spent in bed; **sack-filter**, a form of filter used in sugar-refining (Knight *Dict. Mech.* 1875); †**sack gown** *Sc.*, a sackcloth garment worn by an offender when doing public penance; **sack kraft**, a type of strong brown paper used esp. for making large paper sacks; **sack lunch** *N. Amer.*, a packed lunch; a lunch in a paper bag; **sack-pants** *U.S.*, loosely fitting trousers; **sack paper** = *sack kraft*; **sack pipe** ? *U.S.* [after G. *sackpfeife*], a bagpipe (*Cent. Dict.*); **sack race**, a race in which each competitor is enveloped in a sack, the mouth of which is secured round his neck; so ***sack racing***, ***running***; also ***sack-racer***; **sack-sailed** *a.* (nonce-word), having sails made of sackcloth; **sack ship** *Canad. Hist.*, a large vessel used for transportation in the Newfoundland fisheries; **sack-shoot**, an inclined plane or trough for delivering sacks to a lower level; **sack-shouldered** *a.* (*nonce*), carrying a sack on the shoulders; **sack-tackle**, tackle for hoisting sacks; **sack time** *slang* (orig. *U.S. Forces*'), time spent in bed; sleep; bedtime; **sack tree** (see quot. 1866); **sack-worthy** *a.*, deserving of the sack (sense 4).

1842 S. S. ARNOLD *Diary* 28 Oct. in *Proc. Vermont Hist. Soc.* (1940) VIII. 160 Mr. Gleason borrowed a *sack bag to carry up his cocoons in. **1885** WARREN & CLEVERLY *Wand. 'Beetle'* 10 The sack-bag, a sort of canvas bolster, an ever-ready receptacle for items forgotten in packing. **1842** T. W. HARRIS *Treat. Insects New Eng. Injurious to Vegetation* 298 The Germans give these insects a more characteristic name, that of *sackträger*, that is *sack-bearers. **1895** J. H. & A. B. COMSTOCK *Man. Study of Insects* xviii. 358 Melsheimer's Sack-bearer... The larva of this species feeds on oak. **1954** BORROR & DELONG *Introd. Study Insects* xxvi. 524 The Lacosomidae are called sack-bearers because the larvae make cases from leaves and carry the cases about. **1970** *Sack chair [see POLYSTYRENE]. **1976** 'Z. STONE' *Modigliani Scandal* IV. v. 188 Dee was lying in a sack chair, naked. **1898** *Westm. Gaz.* 9 June 1/3 *Sack coal.. has.. been kept up to 1*s.* 2*d.* a cwt. *a* **1513** FABYAN *Chron.* VII. 595 Y^t al straungers y^t caryed any wolles out of this londe, shuld pay xliii.s. iiii.d. for a *sakke custome. **1824** SCOTT *Redgauntlet* let. xi, Stop though, thou *sack-doudling son of a whore! **1946** *Calif. Folklore Q.* Oct. 387 The Navy Man enjoys resting or sleeping. A sailor who retires *hits the sack, sacks in, sacks out, gets in some *sack drill,.. or gets some shut-eye.* **1954** WEBSTER Add., *Sack duty. **1960** WENTWORTH & FLEXNER *Dict. Amer. Slang* 440/1 *Sack duty*, sleep; time spent sleeping. **1693** in G. Lorimer *Leaves fr. Bk. West Kirke* vi. (1885) 51 [In September 1693 Wm. MacMorran, a cobbler, confessed to a grave breach of morals. He was appointed to] buy ane *sack goun to stand in at the kirk door.. on Sabbath next. **1963** *Economist* 11 May 555/1 Reed's will take.. the paper —*sack kraft—into its own mills for conversion. **1972** *Daily Colonist* (Victoria, B.C.) 18 June 24/1 Others brought blankets and *sack lunches early Saturday and sat sprawled on the grass. **1975** J. GRADY *Shadow of Condor* (1976) v. 91 There was still enough room for the sack lunch he would buy at the restaurant and his two thermos jugs, one for coffee, one for milk. **1856** KANE *Arct. Expl.* II. x. 98 An extra jumper and *sack-pants for sleeping. **1957** V. S. SMITH *Introd. Paper & Papermaking* 125/1 (Index), *Sack paper. **1968** Sack paper [see KRAFT]. **1859** GEO. ELIOT *Adam Bede* II. xxv. 195 Here is the prize for the first *sack race. **1945** G. MILLAR *Maquis* x. 207, I got up in the sleeping-bag and crossed the floor in it like a child doing the sack-race. **1967** MRS. L. B. JOHNSON *White House Diary* 12 Sept. (1970) 568, I was wild about the sack races! **1884** *Harper's Mag.* Jan. 303/1 The champion *sack-racer of the world. **1887** *World Almanac* 103 (*heading*) *Sack-racing records. **1801** STRUTT *Sports & Past.* IV. iii. 277 *Sack Running, that is, men tied up in sacks, every part of them being enclosed except their heads. **1882** CHR. ROSSETTI *Ballad of Boding Poems* (1904) 56/2 The *sack-sailed boat. **1732** E. FALKINGHAM *Let.* 4 Oct. in *Calendar State Papers Amer. & W. Indies 1732* (1939) 225 Which fish they sell to the British *sack ships, for bills of exchange. **1907** J. G. MILLAIS *Newfoundland* viii. 160 In 1527, the little Devonshire fishing ships were unable to carry home their large catch, so 'sack ships' (large merchant vessels) were employed to carry the salt cod to Spain and Portugal. **1965** W. S. MACNUTT *Atlantic Provinces* 14 Its larger vessels, now known as 'sack ships', appeared on the scene at St. John's, taking no part in the catching of the cod, and serving primarily as freighters and transporters. **1902** *Westm. Gaz.* 5 May 7/3 A *sack-shoot at the north side of the warehouse. **1922** JOYCE *Ulysses* 429 A *sack-shouldered ragman bars his path. **1825** J. NICHOLSON *Operat. Mechanic* 140 A granary.. with.. bins.. to contain the different sorts of grain which is raised up by the *sack-tackle. **1944** *Yank* 18 Feb. 4 The biggest difference between the Scouts and other doughboys is their *sacktime conversation. **1945** *House Beautiful* Jan. 39 Sack Time means just lying on your cot doing nothing. **1949** in Wentworth & Flexner *Dict. Amer. Slang* (1960) 440/1, I didn't have any sack time. **1959** *Alfred Hitchcock's Mystery Mag.* Feb. 74/1 Last night, when I was just getting eyes for some sack time, this bear falls up to my pad, a type looking to score for free. **1974** L. DEIGHTON *Spy Story* xix. 204 I'll make sure they kick your ass from sun-up to sack-time. **1849** BALFOUR *Man. Bot.* Index, *Sack-tree. **1866** *Treas. Bot.*, *Lepurandra*, the Sack-tree of Western India, a tree.. now.. called *Antiaris saccidora*... It is a gigantic tree.. having a strong tough fibrous inner bark.. of which the natives.. make capital sacks. **1942** D. F. BRUCE *Dimsie carries On* xxi. 197, I can't just sack her for talking to a man in the road, even if he happens to be one for whom we have no great liking; there's nothing *sack-worthy in that.

sack (sæk), *sb.*[2] Forms: 6 **sak**, 6–7 **sac**, **sacke**, 6– **sack**. [a. F. *sac* (in phr. *mettre à sac*), ad. It. *sacco* (= Sp. *saco*, Pg. *saque*), of doubtful origin.

By some scholars it is regarded as identical with *sacco* bag, SACK *sb.*[1], or as a verbal noun from the derivative verb *saccare* to put in a bag, with reference to the putting up of plunder into bags or sacks. This is possible, but evidence is wanting.]

The action of SACK *v.*[2]; sackage, plundering; esp. in phr. ***to put to sack***, † ***to put to*** or ***unto the sack*** (*obs.*).

1549 *Compl. Scot.* xiv. 114 Thai gat entres victh in the toune, and pat it to sac. **1567** TURBERV. *Dispraryse of Women* in *Epitaphes*, etc. 61 b, Helen that to vtter sack, both Greece and Troie brought. **1577–87** HOLINSHED *Hist. Scot.* 246/1 The said earle of March.. comming to the said towne, tooke it, slue all the Englishmen found within it, put their goods to the sacke, and after set the towne on fire. **1581** STYWARD *Mart. Discipl.* II. 141 Graunt not license to thy souldiers to put all to sacke. **1598** BARRET *Theor. Warres* I. ii. 11 Licence graunted to fall vnto the sacke and spoile. **1610** HEALEY *St. Aug. Citie of God* III. xxviii. 147 Many also of the noblest citties and townes were put vnto the sacke. *c* **1645** HOWELL *Lett.* vi. 75 Before the Sac of Troy, 'twas said and sung up and down the streets. **1777** WATSON *Philip II* (1793) II. XIII. 136 He despaired to reduce so strong a place by sack and storm. **1808** SCOTT *Marm.* IV. xxxii, Or.. call The burghers forth to watch and ward, 'Gainst southern sack and fires to guard. **1849** MACAULAY *Hist. Eng.* v. I. 614 Those inhabitants who had favoured the insurrection expected sack and massacre. **1873** SYMONDS *Grk. Poets* vii. 191 The storm.. was a punishment for their impiety and pride during a sack of Troy. **1893** F. ADAMS *New Egypt* 40 But Memphis was gone, having suffered a hundred sacks and dilapidations.

b. *transf.* and *fig.*

a **1586** SIDNEY *Arcadia* III. (1622) 353 Alas sorrow, now thou hast the full sacke of my conquered spirits. **1590** GREENE *Neuer too late* Wks. (Grosart) VIII. 105 Hast thou had the spoile of my virginitie, and now wouldest thou haue the sacke of my substaunce?

c. Plundered goods. *rare.*

1859 TENNYSON *Enid* 694 He found the sack and plunder of our house All scatter'd thro' the houses of the town.

sack (sæk), *sb.*[3] *Obs.* exc. *Hist.* Forms: *α.* 6 *north.* **wyn seake**, *Sc.* **wyne seck**, **vyne sekk**; *β.* 6 **seck(e**; *γ.* 6 **sakke**, 6–7 **sacke**, 6– **sack**. [Early 16th c. *wyne seck*, ad. F. *vin sec*, 'dry wine'. Cf. G. *sekt*, earlier (17th c.) *sek*, Du. *sek*.

Vin sec is given by Sherwood 1632 (but not by Cotgrave 1611–32) as the Fr. equivalent of 'sacke'. According to Littré, *vin sec* meant only 'dry wine' in the current Eng. sense, i.e. wine 'free from sweetness and fruity flavour'; there appears to be no ground for the assumption made in Grimm's *Deutsches Wörterbuch*, s.v. *Sekt* (and in earlier German dictionaries from the 17th c. onwards), that it at some time meant 'wine from *dried* or partially dried grapes'. Some difficulty therefore arises from the fact that *sack* in English, as well as *sekt* in German, was often described as a sweet wine (so already in our earliest quot.), though Shakspere's mention of 'sack and sugar' shows that it was not always such even in the 16th c. It is possible that before the recorded history of the name begins it had already been extended from the 'dry' wines of a certain class to the whole class, and had afterwards come to be applied esp. to those wines of the class which were originally excluded. But evidence is wanting. The Sp. **vino seco*, It. **vino secco*, usually cited by etymologists, appear not to be recognized by the lexicographers of the respective langs.

The form *sack* is not a normal development from the original *seck*. It may perhaps be explained by the fact that in the 16th c. *seck* was a provincial form of SACK *sb.*[1]; persons who were accustomed to regard 'seck' as a mispronunciation of *sack* may have applied the supposed correction to the name of the wine. It is not, in the present state of the evidence, probable that there was ever any confusion with the OF. *vin de sac* ('Saccatum, vin de buffet, vin de sac', in a gloss quoted by Godefr.), OHG. *sacwîn* (written *saicwin*), MDu. *sacwijn*, which according to early explanations meant a beverage made by steeping the lees of wine in water, and then straining through a bag.]

1. a. A general name for a class of white wines formerly imported from Spain and the Canaries.

α. **1536–7** *Durham Acc. Rolls* (Surtees) 691 Et in vino Clareto et le Wyn seake. **1547** SALESBURY *Welsh Dict.*, Seck win, *secke*. **1558** *Aberdeen Reg.* (1844) I. 311 Ane bot of wyne seck. *a* **1578** LINDESAY (Pitscottie) *Chron. Scot.* (S.T.S.) II. 320 Burdeous vyne gave v schilling the pynt and vyne sekk vij schilling.

β, γ. 1531–2 *Act 23 Hen. VIII*, c. 7 §3 It is further enacted ..that no Malmeseis Romeneis Sakkes nor other swete Wynes..shalbe rateiled aboue .xij. d. the galon. 1542 BOORDE *Dyetary* x. (1870) 255 Also these hote wynes, as malmesye, wyne course, wyne greke, romanysk, romny, seck [etc.].. be not good to drynke with meate. 1555–6 *Rec. St. Mary at Hill* 403 Item, payde in Claret wyne, sacke and sugar..iij s. xj d. 1592 GREENE *Conny Catch.* II. Wks. (Grosart) X. 93 Haue with you for a pottle of burnt Secke. 1596 SHAKS. *1 Hen. IV* (Qo. 1598) II. iv. 516 If sacke and sugar be a fault, God helpe the wicked. 1601 —— *Twel. N.* II. iii. 206 Ile go burne some Sacke. 1607 DEKKER & WEBSTER *Northw. Hoe* I. B 1, Come weele ha some muld Sack. 1620 [see *canary wine*: CANARY *sb.* 7]. 1622 R. HAWKINS *Voy. S. Sea* xliii. 103 Since the Spanish Sacks haue beene common in our Tavernes..our Nation complaineth of Calenturas [etc.]. 1623 MARKHAM *Eng. Housew.* ii. 149 Your best Sacks are of Seres in Spaine, your smaller of Galicia and Portugall; your strong Sacks are of the Ilands of the Canaries, and of Malligo. 1663 DRYDEN *Wild Gallant* I. i, My Business is to drink my Morning's-draught in sack with you. 1686 [see MALAGA]. 1769 MRS. RAFFALD *Eng. Housekpr.* (1778) 165 Grate sugar round your dish, and serve them up with sack for sauce. 1771 MRS. HAYWOOD *New Present* 227 The racy taste of Canary, now commonly called Sack.

b. With qualifying word, chiefly with words indicating the place of production or exportation, as ***Canary***, ***Malaga***, ***Palm*** [= Palma], ***Sherris*** or ***Sherry*** [= Xeres: see SHERRY] ***sack***.

1597 SHAKS. *2 Hen. IV* (Qo. 1600) IV. iii. 104 A good sherris sacke hath a two fold operation in it. 1625 HART *Anat. Ur.* I. v. 45 A cup of good sherry Sacke, Malago, or Canary. 1632 Canary sack [see CANARY *sb.* 7]. *c*1660 *New Mad Tom* 51 in *Roxb. Ballads* II. 261 A cup of old Malaga Sack. 1680 MORDEN *Geog. Rect., Spain* (1685) 176 Hence come our Sherry-Sacks. 1735–7 BERKELEY *Querist* §151 Men of nice palates have been imposed on,..by mead for palm sack. 1756 ROLT *Dict. Trade* s.v. *Canary islands*, Palma ..is remarkable for its produce of wine, called palm-sack, or Canary.

c. The following passage is often alluded to as a proverbial type of flagrant disproportion, esp. where there is an absurd excess of what is unsubstantial or unimportant over what is solid.

1596 SHAKS. *1 Hen. IV* (Qo. 1598) II. iv. 592 O monstrous! but one halfepeniworth of bread to this intollerable deale of sack?

2. *attrib.* and *Comb.*: **a.** simple attrib., as ***sack-pot***; **b.** objective, as ***sack-guzzler***; ***sack-holding*** ppl. adj. **c.** instrumental, as ***sack-sopped*** adj.; **d.** spec. in the names of beverages, etc., made with sack, as **sack-cream**, **-mead**, **-posset**, **-whey**. Also SACK-BUTT.

1665 R. MAY *Accomplisht Cook* (ed. 2) 283 To make a *Sack Cream. 1767 *Mrs. Glasse's Cookery* 361 Sack cream like butter. 1823 BENTHAM *Mem. & Corr.* Wks. 1843 X. 536 Then came..the ultra-servile *sack-guzzler, Southey. 1858 W. BAGEHOT in *National Rev.* Oct. 474 Falstaff is a sort of *sack-holding paunch. 1769 MRS. RAFFALD *Eng. Housekpr.* (1778) 331 To make *Sack Mead. To every gallon of water pour four pounds of honey, boil it.., then put it in your cask, and to thirteen gallons of the above liquor, add a quart of brandy or sack. 1599 B. JONSON *Cynthia's Rev.* II. iv, Shee composes a *sack posset well. 1747 MRS. GLASSE *Cookery* 80 To make an Excellent Sack-Posset. Beat fifteen Eggs..; then put three quarters of a Pound of White Sugar into a Pint of Canary [etc.]. 1851 THACKERAY *Eng. Hum.* v, His genius had been nursed on sack posset, and not on dishes of tea. 1857 J. MARRYAT *Pottery & Porcelain* (ed. 2) 143 Of the *sack-pots one at Strawberry Hill was dated 1647. 1593 G. HARVEY *Lett. & Sonn.* Wks. (Grosart) II. 345 Thy Clarret spirite, And *sack-sopt miseries of thy Confutations. 1736 *Gentl. Mag.* VI. 619/2 Drink plentifully of small, warm *Sack-Whey.

sack (sæk), *sb.*[4] Also 7, 9 sac, 8– sacque. [Cf. G. *französischer sack* (Grimm), Du. *zak*, both applied in the 18th c. to a French fashion of gown then worn by ladies. This, with Pepys' spelling (quot. 1668–9), would seem to indicate adoption from F. *sac*, but the Fr. lexicographers do not recognize the word in this sense.

It is possible that both the senses below, or sense 2 only, may have originated as transferred uses of SACK *sb.*[1] To place them under that word would however be inconvenient, on account of the marked divergence of application, and the fact that the pseudo-Fr. spelling *sacque* is still frequent in both senses.

Sense 2 is given by M. Heyne (in *Grimm*) as a modern tailors' use of G. *sack* (also *sackpaletot* 'sack' overcoat); but this may possibly be from English.

In the following quot. *sackes* may denote some article of clothing, but its sense is obscure, and it is not certain that it is English:—

1390–1 *Earl Derby's Exp.* (Camden) 112 Et eiusdem pipours et thrumpours pro vj. sackes de fostyon ex precepto domini, lx s.]

1. A loose kind of gown worn by ladies. ? *Obs.* Also, from the 18th c., an appendage of silk attached to the shoulders of such a dress, and forming a train (see quot. 1882).

1599 PEELE *Sir Clyomon* xv, But there's Frumpton's wench in the frieze sack [*orig.ed.* scake], it will do thee good to see What canvosing is at the milking-time between her and me. 1601 B. JONSON *Poetaster* IV. i, This straight-bodied citty attire (I can tell you) will stirre a Courtiers blood, more, then the finest loose Sackes the Ladies vse to be put in. 1634 SIR T. HERBERT *Trav.* 199 The women [of Macassar, or the Celebes]..weare a large long cawle or sack, like net-worke, which as a garment hides them wholy. 1668–9 PEPYS *Diary* 2 Mar., My wife this day put on first her French gown, called a Sac. 1748 H. WALPOLE *Let. to Conway* 27 June, The Prince himself..leading Madame l'Ambassadrice de Venise in a green sack with a straw hat. 1762 GOLDSM. *Cit. W.* lxxvii, I can assure you, my Lady Traill has had a sacque from this piece this very morning. 1775 *Lond. Mag.* July 343/1 Flowing loosely down her back Draw with art the graceful sack. 1782 MME. D'ARBLAY *Diary* 8 Dec., I can't bear a sacque. *a*1845 BARHAM *Ingol. Leg.* Ser. III. *Wedding Day*, The flowered silk sacques, which they wore on their backs. 1852 THACKERAY *Esmond* II. xv, How am I to go trapesing to Kensington in my yellow satin sack before all the fine company? 1882 CAULFEILD & SAWARD *Dict. Needlework*, *Sac* (*Sack* or *Sacque*), an old term, still in use, denoting a superfluous, but decorative, piece of a dress material fastened to the shoulders at the back of the gown in wide, loose plaits, and descending to the ground, of such a length as to form a train. The gown itself is always complete without this appendage.

attrib. 1770 CHATTERTON *Let.* 8 July, Wks. 1803 III. 444 Direct for me at Mrs. Angel's, Sack-maker, Brooke Street, Holborn. 1896 *Daily News* 25 June 6/6 The last two, being children, were attired in pretty old-fashioned sacque frocks.

2. a. A loose-fitting coat the back of which is not shaped to the figure, but hangs more or less straight from the shoulders. Also *attrib.*

1847 LONGF. in *Life* (1891) II. 90 In fair weather he wears a brown linen sack. 1847 S. S. MAGOFFIN *Diary* 26 Aug. in *Down Santa Fé Trail* (1926) 253 The general was dressed in his famed old gray sack coat. 1869 S. BOWLES *Our New West* v. 100 My last winter's thick pantaloons and heavy sack coat ..completed my clothing. 1883 D. C. MURRAY *Hearts* I. 33 He wore a velvet sacque to paint in. 1883 C. F. WOOLSON *For the Major* v, Miss Honoria disapproved of the rector because he occasionally wore a sack-coat. 1883 HOWELLS *Woman's Reason* II. xxi. 204 The two women laughed together, and began to pull up their sacks, which had dropped from their shoulders into their chairs behind them. 1892 *Daily News* 3 May 2/4 The sack-back coat is now rapidly finding its way to the lower social strata. 1896 *Ibid.* 19 Mar. 6/5 Sacque jackets divide the honours with capes. 1903 *Westm. Gaz.* 18 June 4/2 The sac bolero..gives size to the slender and veils that of the stout.

b. sack suit, a suit with a straight, loose-fitting jacket; a lounge suit. Hence **sack-suited** *a.*

1895 *N.Y. Dramatic News* 6 July 14/4 Four button sack suit, $25. 1907 H. LAWSON in Murdoch & Drake-Brockman *Austral. Short Stories* (1951) 68 He wore a saddle-tweed sac suit two sizes too small for him. 1960 B. KEATON *Wonderful World of Slapstick* 116, I cleaned up, got into a natty sack suit, and brushed my hair. 1978 J. RAVEN *Triad Consignment* iii. 26 Those sack-suited characters in B-pictures.

3. (May belong under SACK *sb.*[1]) A cut of dress, being short, unwaisted, and usu. narrowing at the hem; a dress in this style; also ***sack dress***.

Fashionable during the second half of the 1950s.

1957 *Punch* 18 Sept. 333 After all, the *belted* sack-dress, in some form or another, is a perennial we have known all down the years, flowering chiefly in the suburbs and the provinces. 1957 *Daily Mail* 26 Sept. 4/2 The sack has swept London like a prairie fire. *Ibid.* 10 Oct. 10/3 A sack, however well cut, needs a tallish figure, and it *must* be very short and tight at the hemline. 1958 *Observer* 21 Sept. 9/3 If there's still a sack to be seen, next week it will acquire a drawstring below the bust. 1959 *Listener* 8 Jan. 56/2 The sack is out. Now, it's the Empire line. 1959 *Times* 25 July 7/4 Hence the rapid disappearance of the A line, the Z line, the *sac*, and the rest of the hideous devices for disguising the fact that women really look their best when they wear bright colours and bulge (moderately) in the proper places. 1969 *Listener* 14 Aug. 206/3 The next big fashion thing was the Sack, and after that the waist, if it was indicated at all, was round the knees or the hips or the diaphragm. 1973 *Guardian* 10 Apr. 13/3 Lagerfeld shows signs of the sack coming back. 1975 'M. FONTEYN' *Autobiogr.* II. iv. 173 Elizabeth [Taylor] was wearing a 'sack' dress, the latest fashion.

sack (sæk), *v.*[1] [f. SACK *sb.*[1]: cf. L. *saccāre* to strain through a bag (med.L. also to put into a bag), MDu. *sacken* (Du. *zakken*), G. *sacken* to put into a bag.]

1. a. *trans.* To put into a sack; to pack or store (goods) in sacks. Also with *up*.

*c*1386 CHAUCER *Reeve's T.* 150 Whan the Mele is sakked and ybounde. *c*1430 *Pilgr. Lyf Manhode* III. xl. (1869) 156, I sakke as michel sum time as tweyne or thre poore men mihten wel fille here sakkes with. 1510–20 *Everyman* (Greg) 396 In chestes I am locked so fast, Also sacked in bagges. *a*1710 BETTERTON (J.), Now..The grist is sack'd, and every sack well bound. 1772 R. GRAVES *Spir. Quixote* (1783) I. 206 The Tinker, however, sacked up his budget, and his companion her bundle. 1844 STEPHENS *Bk. Farm* II. 505 The pickled wheat is then sacked up and carried to the field in carts. 1845 *Jrnl. R. Agric. Soc.* VI. II. 321 It threshes, cleans, and finally sacks the grain. 1882 *Rep. to Ho. Repr. Prec. Met. U.S.* 321 The ore..is being sacked for shipment. 1891 ATKINSON *Moorland Par.* 65 The corn would be threshed, dressed, and sacked, nobody knew how.

b. To put (a person) in a sack to be drowned.

1425 *Rolls of Parlt.* IV. 298/2 Ye said Erle lete sakke hym forthwith, and drounyd him in Thamyse. 1530 PALSGR. 696/2 He shall nat be hanged, but he shall be sacked and throwen in to Seyne. 1823 BYRON *Juan* VI. civ, A foolish or imprudent act Would..have..ended in his being..sack'd, And thrown into the sea. 1836 WILLIS *Summer Cruise in Medit.* xliii. (1852) 257 A Turkish woman was sacked and thrown into the Bosphorus this morning.

c. *Sporting.* To 'bag' (game).

1838 COL. HAWKER *Diary* (1893) II. 140 Shot 29 geese and sacked every bird.

d. In American football, to tackle (a quarter-back) behind the scrimmage line before he can make a pass.

1969 *Internat. Herald Tribune* 6 Nov. 13/4 If you're sacked it's second and 17. 1974 *Plain Dealer* (Cleveland, Ohio) 27 Oct. 7-C/3 Despite all the problems the Buckeye defense managed to sack Anderson three times and picked off three of his passes. 1976 *Washington Post* 4 Sept. D1/5 Kilmer..was sacked hard early in the second quarter by Bears tackle Ron Rydalch.

†**2.** To heap up in or as in a sack. *Obs.*

1599 PEELE *Sir Clyom.* xv, He, whose heart more hard than flint Hath sack'd on me such hugy heaps of ceaseless sorrows here. 1612 T. JAMES *Jesuits' Downf.* 22 It was an old state principle of Machiavell, to packe and sack vp sackes of money to..binde mens tongues therewith.

3. *colloq.* To 'pocket'.

1807 E. S. BARRETT *Rising Sun* I. 59 All complained that he sacked the receipts, without letting them touch one farthing. 1830 GALT *Lawrie T.* II. ii. (1849) 47 To sack a reasonable profit. 1836 W. IRVING *Astoria* I. 213 The money advanced had already been sacked and spent. 1888 CHURCHWARD *Blackbirding* 210 We sold the oil to one of the merchants, and sacked the dollars.

4. a. To put into a case or sack-like covering. *rare.*

1880 L. WALLACE *Ben-Hur* IV. xiii. 253 At the corners they placed pillows..sacked in cloth blue and crimson.

b. *pass.* with *in*, *out*, or *up*: to be in bed or asleep. Cf. sense 8 below.

1954 BERREY & VAN DEN BARK *Amer. Thes. Slang* (ed. 2) §251/11 Asleep,..sacked out. *Ibid.* §892/3 In bed,..sacked out. 1959 W. FAULKNER *Mansion* xii. 280, I was all right. I had had it. I had it made. I was sacked up. 1965 'R. L. PIKE' *Police Blotter* iii. 56 His punk grandson took it when the old man was sacked in one night.

5. *slang.* **a.** To 'give the sack' to; to dismiss or discharge (a person) from his employment or office. Chiefly *passive*. Also *transf.* and *fig.*, esp. (*a*) to reject (a suitor), to jilt; (*b*) to expel from school.

1841 in *Cath. News* 3 June (1899) 15/5 He said he had just come from Glasgow, and had been 'sacked'. 1861 H. MAYHEW *London Labour* II. 469/1 Ah! she's a good kind creetur'; there's no pride in her whatsumever—and she never sacks her servants. 1865 *Daily Tel.* 3 Nov. 2/1 If..the solicitor by whom he was employed, had made up his books, he (the plaintiff) would have been 'sacked six months ago'. 1882 R. D. BLACKMORE *Christowell* III. xi. 160 He had never known more than one girl, worth the end of a cigar—and that one had sacked him. 1890 'R. BOLDREWOOD' *Col. Reformer* (1891) 363 The committee ought to be sacked. 1907 G. B. SHAW *Major Barbara* II. 214 When trade is bad ..and the employers az to sack arf their men, they generally start on me. 1914 'I. HAY' *Lighter Side School Life* vii. 191 Tommy..arrives home one afternoon in a taxi in the middle of term, and announces..that he has been 'sacked'. 1929 *Amer. Speech* V. 20 When a hillman announced that 'Lucy done *sacked* me' he meant that his sweetheart had refused him a date, or rejected his proposal of marriage. 1930 *Punch* 2 Apr. 376/3 If it doesn't turn out well I shall sack the lot of you. 1933 *Sun* (Baltimore) 8 May 8/2 The general contention that competition must be sacked in favor of some scheme of controlled coöperation. 1955 *Times* 21 July 13/4 The difficulties were due to the failure of nationalization and ..the remedy was to sack the Coal Board, [etc.]. 1970 G. F. NEWMAN *Sir, You Bastard* iii. 110 Scotty sacked the policemen who had arrived in the patrol car; they could add nothing. 1977 *Times Lit. Suppl.* 14 Jan. 24/1 He hated the two and a half terms he spent as a boy there before, aged twelve.., he was sacked.

b. To beat in a contest. (Cf. SACK *v.*[2])

1820–3 CARLETON *Traits Irish Peasantry* (1864) I. 275 The terms of defeat or victory..were called sacking and bogging. .. 'Twas young Brady that didn't sack him clane..and went nigh to bog the priest himself in Greek. 1841 E. FITZGERALD *Lett.* (1889) I. 71 F. Tennyson says that he and a party of Englishmen fought a cricket match with the crew of the Bellerophon..and sacked the sailors by 90 runs. 1846 in *Brasenose Ale* 80 The pluckiest crew on Isis stream..Is the one that has sacked the Christ Church Boat, And distanced all the rest.

6. *Lumber-trade.* See quot. 1860 s.v. SACKING *vbl. sb.*[1]

1860 [see SACKING *vbl. sb.*[1] 1]. 1893 *Scribner's Mag.* June 715/1 And thus, wading and 'sacking' logs, the rear crew works..from daylight to dark.

7. *intr.* To bulge or 'bag'.

1799 [implied in SACKING *vbl. sb.*[1] 1].

8. *intr.* With advbs. **a.** *to sack in*: to turn in, to go to bed; also, to lie in. *slang* (orig. *U.S.*).

1946 [see *sack drill* s.v. SACK *sb.*[1] 8]. 1951 in Wentworth & Flexner *Dict. Amer. Slang* (1960) 440/1 Shut up and sack in. 1962 'S. RANSOME' *Without Trace* x. 107 After she left I had some more drinks and sacked in. 1966 D. F. GALOUYE *Lost Perception* xvi. 168 'I let you sack in this morning,' he told Gregson, 'so you could stockpile your energy.' 1967 'T. WELLS' *What should you know of Dying?* iii. 41 Benedict's call, at about nine o'clock, woke me up... I'd planned to sack in till about eleven. 1976 N. THORNBURG *Cutter & Bone* iii. 79 Listen, pal, before I sack in..why don't you tell us.

b. *to sack out*: to go to bed, to have a sleep, to doss down. *slang* (orig. and chiefly *U.S.*).

1946 [see *sack drill* s.v. SACK *sb.*[1] 8]. 1951 *Arkansas Democrat* 3 July 14/5 Well, it's time to sack out. 1961 'E. LATHEN' *Banking on Death* viii. 66 The radio said the roads were closed, so I said the hell with it and sacked out on the couch. 1970 J. HANSEN *Fadeout* vii. 55, I was getting ready to sack out. I'd just had a shower. 1971 *Daily Tel.* 19 July 3/2 Many young travellers..are faced with the choice of curling up in a doorway or 'sacking out' in one of London's parks. 1977 *New Yorker* 9 May 46/1 One night we missed the last train. We sacked out in the waiting room in Grand Central.

c. *to sack down*: to go to bed. *slang.*

1956 F. HERBERT *Dragon in Sea* 84 Want me to bring up some sandwiches before I sack down? 1978 E. V. CUNNINGHAM *Case of Russian Diplomat* i. 11, I lost a night's sleep... How about I sack down for a few hours?

sack (sæk), *v.*[2] Also 6 *Sc.* sact. [f. SACK *sb.*[2] Cf. Pr., Sp., Pg. *saquear*, It. *saccheggiare*.]

1. *trans.* To give over (a city, town, etc.) to plunder by the soldiery of a victorious army; to strip (a person or place) of possessions or goods; to plunder, despoil.

*a*1547 SURREY *Ecclesiastes* v. Wks. 1815 I. 76 The plenteous houses sackt; the owners end with shame Their sparkled goods. *a*1548 HALL *Chron., Hen. V* 45 The toune was sacked to the greate gayne of the Englishemen. 1563 WINȜET *Vincent. Lirin.* To Marie Q. Scottis, Wks. (S.T.S.) II. 5 That al the enimeis thairof..suld nocht mak thame be force and plane violente to sact it, or onyways subdew it. 1567 *Satir. Poems Reform.* v. 52 Spair not to gif thame all ane syse, Quhome ȝe beleif the King did sact. 1574 tr. *Marlorat's Apocalips* 44 He wil be sacked of all his goods or be throwen into prison. 1634 HEYWOOD *Maidenh. Lost* I. Wks. 1874 I. 111 We sack't the Citty after nine Moneths siege. 1807 J. BARLOW *Columb.* III. 13 They sack the temples, the gay fields deface. 1840 DICKENS *Barn. Rudge* lxxi, People..are flying from the town which is sacked from end to end. 1855 MACAULAY *Hist. Eng.* xix. IV. 295 From Bow to Hyde Park..there was no parish in which some quiet dwelling had not been sacked by burglars. 1879 GREEN *Read. Eng. Hist.* xvii. 83 The monastery was sacked by the Danes.

b. said of an inanimate agent.

1571 *Satir. Poems Reform.* xxv. 119 Gif fyre may þair buildings sacke, Or bullat beat þaim downe. 1817 SHELLEY *Rev. Islam* VII. xxxviii, When I woke, the flood Whose banded waves that crystal cave had sacked Was ebbing round me.

†**2.** To take as plunder or spoil. *Obs.* *rare*$^{-1}$.

1590 tr. *P. Ubaldino's Disc. conc. Span. Invas.* 21 The Englishmen departed,..hauing sacked 22000. duckets of gold,..and 14. coffers of mooueables.

fig. 1590 GREENE *Never too late* II. Wks. (Grosart) VIII. 155 Thou seekest not only to sacke mine honour, but to suck my bloud.

sack, obs. form of SAC[1].

sackable (ˈsækəb(ə)l), *a.* [f. SACK *v.* 5 a + -ABLE.] For which one may be sacked; justifying the sack. So **sackaˈbility**, liability to be sacked.

1975 *Financial Times* 13 Jan. 25/6 Mr. Carew thinks that to-day's average British executive has had sackability built into him from childhood. 1975 *Daily Tel.* 3 Oct. 6/5, I admit I may have been impetuous in writing what I did about the school, but every word is truth. I don't consider publication of the truth to be a sackable offence.

sackage (ˈsækɪdʒ), *sb.* Now *rare*. Also 6–7 saccage. [a. F. *saccage*, according to Hatz.-Darm. a verbal noun f. *saccager*: see SACKAGE *v.*]

1. The action, or an act, of sacking (a city, etc.).

1577–87 HOLINSHED *Chron.* III. 1097/1 For the defense and safegard of this citie from spoile and saccage. 1583 BABINGTON *Commandm.* (1590) 226 In sackages of Cities. 1601 HOLLAND *Pliny* I. xv. xviii. 443 Howbeit Cato survived not the rasing and saccage of Carthage, for he died the yeare immediatly following this resolution. 1654 tr. *Martini's Conq. China* 190 The sackage endured from the 24. of November till the 5. of December. 1755 T. H. CROKER *Orl. Fur.* XXXIII. xli, Ravenna is in sackage laid. 1808 SOUTHEY *Chron. Cid* 386 Some among us, says he, in this city, count from the sackage of the Jews. 1875 TENNYSON *Q. Mary* II. ii, To guard and keep you whole and safe from all The spoil and sackage aim'd at by these rebels.

†**2.** Booty, plunder. *Obs.* *rare*$^{-1}$.

1609 HOLLAND *Amm. Marcell.* XXIV. viii. 251 When the saccage therefore was divided and dealt,..himselfe tooke for his share a dumbe boy.

†**ˈsackage, ˈsaccage**, *v.* *Obs.* [a. F. *saccager*, prob. ad. It. *sa cheggiare*, f. *sacco* SACK *sb.*[2]] *trans.* To put to sack; to plunder.

1585 T. WASHINGTON tr. *Nicholay's Voy.* I. vii. 5 b, Their intent was to..haue good means to saccage vs. *Ibid.* xii. 13 b, The houses..hauing been twise saccaged [orig. *deux fois saccagees*] and spoyled by the Spaniardes. 1628 *Priv. Mem. Sir K. Digby* (1828) 28 Before they went out of it they saccaged the town. 1662 J. BARGRAVE *Pope Alex. VII* (1867) 94 They..set upon the barch [? *read* bank] where the money was, and sackaged all. 1687 A. LOVELL tr. *Thevenot's Trav.* I. 6 It..having been..saccaged and ruined by a Roman Army.

Hence †**ˈsaccaging** *vbl. sb.*, †**ˈsaccagement**.

1585 T. WASHINGTON tr. *Nicholay's Voy.* II. xiii. 48 b, The saccaging..continued 3. daies. *Ibid.* IV. xxxvi. 160 The ruine, saccagement, & desolation of their countrey. 1654 tr. *Martini's Conq. China* 90 After the saccaging and burning of so many Provinces.

sackalever (sækəˈliːvə). Also sacoleva. [ad. It. *saccaleva*. Cf. F. *sacolève*.] A small lateen-rigged sailing vessel used in the Levant.

1819 T. HOPE *Anastasius* (1820) I. xi. 223 Meaning myself to go by land as far as Gallipoli, where the sacoleva was to ballast. 1878 TRELAWNY *Shelley* (1887) 83 A Turkish sackalever.

sackbut (ˈsækbʌt). Forms: 6–7 **sagbut, -bot,** 6 **sagbout, saggebut,** 7 **sagbutt,** 6–7 **shagbot(e,** (6 **shakbott, shagbush,** 7 **-but),** 6 **sackbot,** 7 **-butt, sacke-but,** 7 **sacbutt,** 8–9 **sacbut,** 7– **sackbut.** [a. F. *saquebute*, earlier *saqueboute*, *-botte*, etc.; not found as the name of a musical instrument earlier than the latter half of the 15th c., but presumably identical with ONF. *saqueboute*, explained in the 14th c. as a lance furnished with 'an iron hook for pulling men off their horses' ('un grau de fer pour les garchons *saquier* jus de leurs quevaulz'). In the modern Norman dialect the word means a squirt. The first element is clearly ONF. *saquier* (= Sp., Pg. *sacar*) to pull, draw (which accounts for all the senses of the compound); the etymology of the second element is obscure; some scholars connect it with *bouter* to push.

The Sp. *sacabuche* (cf. the 16th c. Eng. form *shagbushe*), sackbut, also tube used as a pump, and the Pg. *sacabucha*, *-buxa*, with the same meanings, appear to be corrupt adoptions of the Fr. word. The Pg. word is identical in form with a word meaning a hook for drawing the wad from a gun, regularly f. *saca-r* to draw + *bucha, buxa*, wad. Possibly the Fr. word may, when adopted into Pg., have undergone assimilation to the native word and then passed in the altered form into Sp.; but evidence is wanting.]

1. a. A musical instrument of the Renaissance; a bass trumpet with a slide like that of a trombone for altering the pitch. Recently revived in the performances of some early music.

The word is to many readers known only from its occurrence in Dan. iii, where it is a mistranslation of Aramaic *sabbᵉkā*, which the LXX and Vulgate render (doubtless correctly) by Gr. σαμβύκη, L. *sambūca*, the name of a stringed instrument (see SAMBUCA[1]). Coverdale 1535 (for what reason is not clear) renders the word by *shawmes*, thus taking it to denote a wind instrument; the Geneva translators, accepting this view, seem to have chosen the rendering 'sackbut' on account of its resemblance in sound to the Aramaic word. In this they have been followed by the 'Authorized' (1611) and 'Revised' (1885) Versions.

1533 ELYOT *Cast. Helthe* (1539) 51 The entrayles..be exercised by blowyng, eyther by constraint, or playeng on shaulmes, or sackbottes. 1536 WRIOTHESLEY *Chron.* (Camden) I. 44 And shalmes, sagbuttes, and dromeslawes playing also in barges going before him. 1560 BIBLE (Genev.) *Dan.* iii. 5 The cornet, trumpet, harpe, sackebut, psalteries, dulcimer, and all instruments of musicke. 1577–87 HOLINSHED *Chron.* III. 930/2 In which barge were shalmes, shagbushes, and diverse other instruments. 1638 BURTON *Anat. Mel.* II. ii. III. (ed. 5) 249 As he that playes upon a Sagbut by pulling it up and downe alters his tones and tunes. 1674 PLAYFORD *Skill Mus.* Pref. 3 The sound of a Sackbut or Trumpet, should skip from Concord to Concord. 1675 SHADWELL *Psyche* I. Wks. 1720 II. 16 Voices, Flagellets, Violins, Cornets, Sackbuts, Hautboys; all joyn in Chorus. 1797 SOUTHEY *Tri. Woman* 108 And shrill were heard the flute, The cornet, sackbut, dulcimer, and lute. 1808 SCOTT *Marm.* IV. xxxi, And sackbut deep, and psaltery. 1862 LONGF. *Wayside Inn* Prel. 213 In vision or in trance He heard the solemn sackbut play. 1972 *Register of Early Music* Autumn 19 (*heading*) People who have expressed an interest in:—Cornetts, Serpents, Sackbuts and Early Brass. 1973 *Early Music* I. 48 (Advt.), Brass Instruments... Sackbuts, Renaissance and Baroque trumpets by Meinel & Lauber. 1978 *Early Music Gaz.* Jan. p. 11/3 *Cornett and Sackbut* is a new magazine for all players of early lip-reed instruments.

†**b.** A player on the sackbut. *Obs.*

1539 *Rutland MSS.* (1905) IV. 293 To Doctre Lee's shawmes and shagboshes that playt before my Lorde of Solfolke, iijs. iiijd. 1540 in *Vicary's Anat.* (1888) App. xii. 241 Item, for Pilligrine, sagbut, wages, xls. 1647 HAWARD *Crown Rev.* 25 Six Sackbuts: Fee *le peice*, 24. 6. 8.

¶**2.** *Roman Antiq.* Used to render L. *sambuca*: see SAMBUCA[1] 2. *rare*$^{-1}$.

1756 HAMPTON *Polybius* (1773) III. 131 These vessels.. carried to the walls certain machines called Sackbuts.

Hence †**ˈsackbut(t)er**, a player on the sackbut.

1503 in *Cal. Doc. rel. Scot.* (1888) 347 [Warrant..to deliver..a banner..to..the K.'s five trumpetters, and also to Johannes and Edward], shakbotters. 1916 STANFORD & FORSYTH *Hist. Mus.* ix. 180 *Four* sackbutters were enough for her grandfather. *Ibid.* 188 The other three are playing on brass instruments with slides. One may call them simply trombones. These are the *Royal Sackbutters*.

†**ˈsack-butt.** *Obs.* [f. SACK *sb.*[3] + BUTT *sb.*[2]] A butt of sack.

1600 HEYWOOD *2nd Pt. Edw. IV*, Wks. 1874 I. 93 Will no man thrust the staue into a sack-butt? 1623 MARKHAM *Eng. Housew.* ii. 149 The depth of euery Sack-Butt is the foure pricks next to the puncheon. 1657 TRAPP *Comm. Ezra* ix. 6 But he is past grace that is past shame, and can blush no more then a sackbut.

punningly. 1623–4 MIDDLETON & ROWLEY *Sp. Gipsy* II. i, *Al*... You must not look to have your Dinner serv'd in with Trumpets. *Cor.* No, no, Sackbuts shall serve us. 1623 FLETCHER *Rule a Wife* V. v, I' th' celler..He will make dainty musick among the sack-butts.

sackcloth (ˈsækklɒθ, -ɔːθ). Forms: 4 **sekk-clathe, sekklath,** 5 **sekclath, -cloth, cekclothe, sak clothe,** 6 **sack(e)cloth(e, sacclothe, sack-cloath,** 6– **sackcloth.** [f. SACK *sb.*[1] + CLOTH.]

1. a. A coarse textile fabric (now of flax or hemp) used chiefly in the making of bags or sacks and for the wrapping up of bales, etc.; sacking.

1373–4 *Durham Acc. Rolls* (Surtees) 578 In Sekklath empt. in villa et in patria, xxvjs. iiijd. *c*1420 ? LYDG. *Assembly of Gods* 290 Ceres, the goddesse, in a garment Of sak clothe..Embrowderyd with sheues & sykelys bent. 1423 JAS. I *Kingis Q.* cix, Als like ȝe bene, as..sek-cloth is vnto fyne cremesye. *c*1440 *Promp. Parv.* 64/1 Cek, or cekclothe, or poke, *saccus*. 1484–5 *Durham Acc. Rolls* (Surtees) 415 Sol. pro ix uln. de Sekclath pro altaribus ecclesiæ, ijs. iijd. 1548 THOMAS *Ital. Dict.* (1567), *Canauaccio*, canuasse or sackeclothe. 1623 MARKHAM *Cheap Husb.* I. iv. (ed. 3) 50 Cloath him temperately, as with a single cloth, of canuase or sacke-cloth. 1896 *Daily News* 21 Apr. 6/4 The latest novelty in dress materials is sackcloth... It is common hemp sacking,..but let no one imagine for a single moment that it is cheap. The open canvas ground is intended to be lined with the richest..silks and satins, and itself forms a groundwork for elaborate embroideries.

b. As the material of mourning or penitential garb; also (in contrast with 'purple' or 'gold') as the coarsest possible clothing, indicative of extreme poverty or humility. ***in sackcloth and ashes*** (Biblical): clothed in sackcloth and having ashes sprinkled on the head as a sign of lamentation or abject penitence. †Also with *a* (cf. SACK *sb.*[1] 5).

The penitential 'sackcloth' of the Bible (Heb. *saq*, Gr. σάκκος) was a dark-coloured fabric of goats' or camels' hair.

13.. *St. Alexius* 191 in Horstm. *Altengl. Leg.* (1881) 178 All hir bodi scho made bare & did apon hir a sekk-clathe. 1526 TINDALE *Matt.* xi. 21 They had repented longe agon in sack cloth and asshes. 1535 COVERDALE *Ps.* xxxiv. 13 When they were sick, I put on a sack cloth. 1553 EDEN *Treat. Newe Ind.* (Arb.) 5 He whiche cloteth [*sic*] an ape in purple, & a king in sacke-cloth. 1575 GASCOIGNE *Flowers* Wks. 51, I was in sack-cloth I, now am I clad in gold, And weare such robes, as I my selfe take plesure to behold. 1590 SPENSER *F.Q.* I. iii. 14 And to augment her painefull penaunce more,..shee ..next her wrinkled skin rough sacke-cloth wore. 1649 JER. TAYLOR *Gt. Exemp.* I. Disc. iv. 128 S. Lewis King of France wore sack-cloth every day unless sicknesse hindred. 1726 AYLIFFE *Parergon* 47 And being clad in Sackcloth, he was to lie on the Ground, and..implore God's Mercy. 1788 GIBBON *Decl. & F.* xlviii. V. 55 While he groaned and prayed in sackcloth and ashes, his brother..smiled at his remorse. 1829 LYTTON *Devereux* IV. v, I should have gone into a convent and worn sackcloth. *a*1839 PRAED *Poems* (1864) II. 356 The low and great, Who in their sack-cloth or their purple, creep Beneath the summit of the viewless steep. 1885 'H. CONWAY' *Fam. Affair* xxvi, He knew that for all that had befallen she was mourning in mental sackcloth and ashes.

†**c.** *pl.* [See CLOTHES.] Garments of sackcloth.

1594 GREENE & LODGE *Looking-gl.* (1598) H 4, He sits him down in sack-cloathes, his hands and eyes reared to heauen.

d. *attrib.* and *Comb.*, as ***sackcloth-bag, -garb, -mourner, -prophecy***, etc.; ***sackcloth-bound, -clad***, adjs.

1679 C. NESSE *Antichrist* 127 The sackcloth-prophecy of the witnesses. *Ibid.* 221 A sackcloth-mourner. *Ibid.* 229 Italy it self had several sackcloth-witnesses. *Ibid.* 232 That famous sackcloth-prophet John Wickliffe. 1812 BYRON *Ch. Har.* II. lxxviii, Ere his sackcloth garb Repentance wear. 1843 LYTTON *Last Bar.* I. iii, It's ill-leaping now-a-days in a sackcloth-bag. 1843 J. G. WHITTIER *Lays of My Home* 14 And mate with maniac women, loose-haired and sackcloth-bound. 1855 MILMAN *Lat. Chr.* XIV. viii. (1864) IX. 287 The sackcloth-clad bare-foot friar.

†**2.** A material for ladies' dresses. Cf. SACK *sb.*[1] 6.

1571 in Feuillerat *Revels Q. Eliz.* (1908) 136 Sackclothe stripte with sylver. [1896: see 1.]

Hence **ˈsackclothed** *a. rare*, clad in sackcloth; also *fig.*

1641 BP. HALL *Mischief Faction* Rem. Wks. (1660) 69 To be joviall when God calls to mourning,..to glitter when he would have us sackcloth'd and squalid, he hates it to the death. 1829 I. TAYLOR *Enthus.* ix. 250 A healthy force of mind utterly incompatible with..the petty solicitudes of sackclothed abstinence. 1922 BLUNDEN *Shepherd* 23 And rising floods gleam silver on the verge Of sackclothed skies and melancholy grounds. 1924 R. CLEMENTS *Gipsy of Horn* ix. 169 Half-bred negroes and Indians, sackclothed and uncivilised.

sacked (sækt), *a.* *nonce-wd.* [f. SACK *sb.*[4] + -ED[2].] Wearing a sack.

1847 DISRAELI *Tancred* II. xiv, Gentlemen in wigs, and ladies powdered, patched and sacked.

sacked (sækt), *ppl. a.*[1] [f. SACK *v.*[2] + -ED[1].] That has been given up to sack; plundered, ravaged.

1593 SHAKS. *Lucr.* 1740 Who like a late sack't Iland vastlie stood Bare and vnpeopled. 1632 LITHGOW *Trav.* v. 200 Semblable to that sacked Lacedemon in Sparta. 1697 DRYDEN *Æneid* IX. 350 Two large Goblets..which, when old Priam reign'd, My conqu'ring Sire at sack'd Arisba gain'd. 1864 LOWELL *Fireside Trav.* 239 An old woman.. who looked as sacked and ruinous as everything around her.

sacked, *ppl. a.*[2] [f. SACK *v.*[1] + -ED[1].] **1.** That has been put into a sack; stored in a sack.

1895 *Funk's Stand. Dict.* s.v. sack[1] *vt.*, Sacked grain. 1937 E. HEMINGWAY *To have & have Not* II. i. 78 The man went on slowly lifting the sacked packages of liquor and dropping them over the side. 1970 D. WATERFIELD *Continental Waterboy* i. 3 The trouble with lock gates built of sacked mud is that they do not ordinarily open easily.

2. That has been 'given the sack'; dismissed, discharged (from employment or office). Also *absol.*

1934 G. B. SHAW *On Rocks* 148 The exterminated, or, as we call them, the evicted and sacked, try to avoid starvation. 1981 *Daily Tel.* 10 Sept. 8/8 (*heading*) Pay out for sacked heart man.

Sacked Friar: see SACK-FRIAR.

†**ˈsacken**, *a.* *Obs.* *rare.* [f. SACK *sb.*[1] + -EN[4].] Made of sackcloth. ***sacken gown, sark, weed*** = *sack gown*: see SACK *sb.*[1] 8.

13.. *S. Eng. Leg.* (MS. Bodl. 779) in *Archiv Stud. neu. Spr.* LXXXII. 334/47 Þat was a sakken curtil & a pilche also & a blak froccke þer-vppon. 1710 *Brit. Apollo* III. No. 20. 2/2 Sacken bottom'd Beds. 1779 D. GRAHAM *Jocky & Maggy's Courtship* Writ. 1883 II. 20 And wha can bide the shame, when every body looks to them, wi' their sacken sarks or gowns on them. 1780 W. FORBES *Dominie* 6 In case they wear the sacken-weed For fornication. *Ibid.* 13 He'll get the dud an' sacken gown.

sacker[1] (ˈsækə(r)). [f. SACK *v.*[2] + -ER[1].] One who sacks or plunders.

1589 RIDER *Bibl. Schol.*, A sacker, *populator, direptor*. 1824 J. SYMMONS tr. *Æschylus' Agam.* 71 O sacker of Troy town divine! **1907** A. Lang *Hist. Scot.* IV. xiv. 360 He made no effort to discourage the sackers of Shawfield's house.

ˈsacker^3. *U.S.* [f. sack *v.*^{1} 6 + -er^1.] One engaged in sacking logs.

1902 S. E. White *Blazed Trail* lii. 360 It was noon. The sackers looked up in surprise.

ˈsacker^3. *N. Amer.* [sack *sb.*^{1} 1 i.] A baseman in baseball. (Usu. preceded by ordinal number indicating the base position.)

1914 Lardner & Heeman *Mar. 6, 1914* 46 He once was the world's most famous first sacker. **1926** *Amer. Speech* I. 369/2 Basemen are 'sackers'. **1938** H. E. West *Baseball Scrap Bk.* 158 Wally Pipp became the Yankee first sacker in 1915, and Lou Gehrig succeeded him ten years later and is still going strong. **1944** *College Topics* (Univ. Virginia) 30 Mar. 3 Bob Bryon, first sacker from North Carolina State, seems assured of the first base position. **1958** [see home-brew 2]. **1974** *Anderson* (S. Carolina) *Independent* 22 Apr. 7A/1 As proof of his defensive prowess, Hargrove led the WCL first sackers in fielding with a .988 percentage.

sacker, variant of saker.

sacket (ˈsækɪt). Also 5 sakett, 6 sakket, 9 sackit. [a. OF. *saquet*, dim. of *sac* sack *sb.*^{1}; cf. sachet.]

1. A bag. *Obs.* exc. *dial.*

c **1440** *Alphabet of Tales* 307 A grete sakett full of mony in his hand. **1520** M. Nisbet *N.T. Scots* Luke x. 4 Tharfor will ye nocht bere a sacket [*Wycl.* sachel], nouthir scrippe, nouthir schonne. **1549** *Compl. Scot.* xvi. 138 Euerye man of this varld baris tua sakkettis vitht hym [viz., one before him containing his neighbour's faults, the other behind containing his own; see Phædrus *Fab.* iv. x]. **1632** Lithgow *Trav.* x. 449 My Linnen, Letters, and Sacket was lying in my hostery. **1741** *Compl. Fam.-Piece* i. i. 34 Fill with this Powder a little square Bag or Sacket of Sarsenet. **1834** Smart *Rhymes* 102 (E.D.D.) It was a weel-filled weighty sacket.

2. *dial.* as a term of reproach or abuse: see E.D.D. (Cf. G. *sack* in similar use.)

1868 R. M. Fergusson *Village Poet* (1897) 155 Ye needna craw, ye sneerin' sackit. **1889** Barrie *Window in Thrums* xxi, 'If he ever comes back, the sacket (rascal)', T'nowhead said to Jess, 'we'll show 'im the door gey quick'.

ˈSack-friar. Also Sacked Friar. [sack *sb.*^{1} 5. Cf. MDu. *sacbroeder*, G. *sackbruder*, OF. *frere au sac*.] A member of a mendicant order of the 13th and early 14th c., called 'Fratres de Pœnitentia Jesu Christi' or 'de Saccis' (also *Saccati*, *Saccitæ*, *Saccini*, *Sacci*), who were clothed in sackcloth.

c **1400** *Rom. Rose* 7462 So been Augustins and Cordileres, ..and eek Sakked Freres. **1553** in *Archæologia* (1775) III. 131 It. rec^t. of theyrs of Christopher Cornwall, for ferme of a parcell of grounde..sometyme parcell of the sakfryers by yere xvi. **1772** Pegge *ibid.* 125 Memoir concerning the Sac-Friars, or Fratres de Poenitentia Jesu Christi, as settled here in England. **1867** C. F. R. Palmer *Life P.T. Howard* 53 The Order of Sacked Friars was put down in 1307.

sackful (ˈsækfʊl), *sb.* [f. sack *sb.*^{1} + -ful.] As much as would fill a sack; hence, hyperbolically, a great quantity, large amount.

1484 Caxton *Fables of Æsop* v. v, I haue a sak ful of scyences and wyles. *a* **1619** Fotherby *Atheom.* ii. viii. §4 (1622) 287 Not..by the sackfull, but by the whole Barnefull. **1623–4** Middleton & Rowley *Sp. Gipsy* i. v, This little ape gets money by the sack-full. **1653** Holcroft *Procopius, Goth. Wars* iv. 127 The Enemy fortified the breach with sack-fuls of Sand. **1718** R. Frampton in T. Evans *Life* (1876) 149 A sackfull of canting books. **1724** Swift *Drapier's Lett.* Wks. 1755 V. ii. 150 Wood..goes about with his sack-fulls of dross, odiously misrepresenting his prince's countenance. **1882** *Harper's Mag.* July 200 They had there found a number of broken mummies and a large heap of papyri. Of these last they offered him a sackful.

† **ˈsackful,** *a.* *Obs. rare*$^{-1}$. [f. sack *sb.*^{2} + -ful.] Given to plundering.

c **1611** Chapman *Iliad* ii. 601 Now will I sing the sackfull troopes Pelasgian Argos held.

sackie (ˈsækɪ). [Local name in Guyana.] Any of several small parrots found in northern South America, esp. *Pionites melanocephala*, which has black, blue, and green plumage.

[**1916** C. Chubb *Birds Brit. Guiana* I. 340 The 'Macusis' call it [*sc.* the black-headed caique] *Sackuih.*] **1951** E. Mittelhölzer *Shadows move among Them* iii. ii. 260 Sackies kept up a gay twittering. **1969** S. M. Sadeek *Windswept* 3, I would..imitate the kiss-ka-dees and sackies as they sang.

sacking (ˈsækɪŋ), *vbl. sb.*^{1} [f. sack *v.*^{1} + -ing^1.]

1. The action of sack *v.*^{1}, in various senses.

1568 Grafton *Chron.* II. 362 The businesse that there was in chargyng and ladyng of shippes with haye, sackyng of Bisket [etc.]. **1799** G. Smith *Laboratory* I. 6 To prevent the sacking of the paper. **1860** *Harper's Mag.* XX. 452 Another frequent and laborious part of the drive is sacking... When the logs have been lodged upon the shore..three or four men seize each log with their cant-dogs and absolutely lift or drag it along the mud and sand a considerable distance. **1887** Raymond *Statist. Mines & Mining* 98 Sacking, 41 sacks per ton, 20 days' labor, at $3. **1958** *Daily Sketch* 2 June 1/2 This will not mean sackings as the buses are 3,000 men short now. **1970** G. F. Newman *Sir, You Bastard* vi. 183 The normal fracas following a sacking would bring too much attention to Sneed when he stepped into the vacancy.

† **2.** *cant.* The occupation of a prostitute. *Obs.*

1591 Greene *Disc. Coosnage* (1592) C 1 b, Sacking law, lecherie. *Ibid.* C 2, In sacking Law The Bawd if it be a woman [is called] a Pandar. **1592** —— *Disput.* Ded. A 2, The sacking and crosbyting lawes, which strumpets vse. *Ibid.* A 4 b, Why Nan, are you growne so stiffe, to thincke..that your sacking can gaine as much as our foysting?

sacking (ˈsækɪŋ), *vbl. sb.*^{2} [f. sack *v.*^{2} + -ing^1.] The action of plundering (a city, etc.).

1560 Daus tr. *Sleidane's Comm.* 74 Whan newes were brought into Spayn of the sacking of Rome. **1638** *Penit. Conf.* vii. (1657) 177 At the sacking of Jericho the spoils were devoted to the Lord. **1653** H. Cogan tr. *Pinto's Trav.* xlix. 192 Yet for all that he could not keep the cabbins from sacking. **1783** Justamond tr. *Raynal's Hist. Indies* IV. 184 The sacking of Panama in 1670 by John Morgan the English pirate. **1837** W. Irving *Capt. Bonneville* I. 223 Sackings, burnings, plunderings, scalpings.

sacking (ˈsækɪŋ), *sb.* Also 6 seckynge. [f. sack *sb.*^{1} + -ing^1.

OE. had *sæccing* of equivalent formation, occurring with the sense 'bed' (Vulg. *grabatum*) in Mark vi. 55.]

1. A closely woven material of flax, jute, hemp, or similar material, used chiefly in the making of sacks, bags, etc.; also, a piece of such material; *transf.* of other material used for the same purpose.

1707 Ld. Raby in Hearne *Collect.* 14 Sept. (O.H.S.) II. 42 His Horses stand with..Sackings instead of Cloaths. **1753** Hanway *Trav.* (1762) I. vii. lxxxviii. 406 Sacking of different qualities for bags..is..exported. **1810** *Hull Improv. Act* 62 Such sack shall be made of linen called Sacking. **1833** Ht. Martineau *Cinnamon & Pearls* v, If his dress has always been sacking, his ignorant choice will be of sacking still. **1843** 'R. Carlton' *New Purchase* I. xxi. 199 Next was a sacking of clapboards pinned down; and then a very thick straw bed. **1844** G. Dodd *Textile Manuf.* v. 168 The flax fabrics woven in Ireland are chiefly fine and coarse linens, canvas, sacking, and damask. *a* **1849** Poe *Murders in Rue Morgue* Wks. 1895 III. 70 They were both then lying on the sacking of the bedstead. **1881** *Daily News* 23 Aug. 3/6 There is less doing in ropes..and sackings.

† **2.** A material for ladies' dresses. (Cf. sack *sb.*^{1} 6, sackcloth 2.) *Obs. rare.*

1589 *Acc. Bk. W. Wray* in *Antiquary* XXXII. 79, iii yeards & a d. striped seckynge, iis. xjd. **1595** [see sack *sb.*^{1} 6].

3. *attrib.* and *Comb.*, as ***sacking bottom***, ***sacking-cloth***, ***goods***, ***-maker***, ***needle***; parasynthetic, as ***sacking-bottomed***, ***sacking-wrapped*** adjs.

1707 *Rec. Baron Court of Stitchill* (S.H.S.) 158 To pay..10sh. 8d...for 8 ells of sacking-cloth. *c* **1710** in Ashton *Soc. Life Q. Anne* I. v. 75 New sacking bottom'd Bedsteads at 11s. a piece. **1744** J. Hempstead *Diary* (1901) 425 [I was] fitting a new Bedstid that I Sent with Sacking Bottom. **1780** *Westm. Mag.* Suppl. 730/1 James Allen,..Wantage, Berks, sacking-maker. **1797** *Indenture Doncaster* (MS.), George Needham, sacking-manufacturer. **1841** G. Catlin *Lett. on N. Amer. Indians* I. 191 A sacking-bottom, made of the buffalo's hide. **1868** G. G. Channing *Early Recoll. Newport, R.I.* 254 Sometimes it [*sc.* the bedstead] was furnished with a 'sacking bottom'. **1881** Whitehead *Hops* 61 The hops are picked into bins, long, light, wooden frames, with sacking bottoms. **1886** *Daily News* 15 Sept. 2/4 Canvas, and sacking goods meet with a fair sale at firm prices. **1895** Mrs. B. M. Croker *Village Tales* (1896) 185 He was..put in leg-irons, and a convict sacking-coat. **1952** M. Allingham *Tiger in Smoke* viii. 129 One small sacking-wrapped bundle. **1970** A. H. Whiteford *N. Amer. Indian Arts* 67/1 Sacking needles are used to insert the final weft threads.

sackit, variant of sacket *dial.*

sackless (ˈsæklɪs), *a.* Forms: 1–2 sacléas, 2 sacclæs, saclese, 3 sac(c)les, sakelease, 4–6 sa(c)kles, 4–5 sa(c)keles, (4 saklas, 5 saklace), 6 saikles(s(e, sackelesse, 6–7 sakelesse, sacklesse, 8 saickless, 7– sakeless, 8– sackless. [Late OE. *sacléas* (see sac^1 and -less); perh. after ON. *saklauss* (Sw. *saklös*, Da. *sagløs*). Cf. MDu. *sakeloos*.

OE. *sacléas* occurs as adv. in the sense 'without cause' (*gratis*, Vulg.) in the Lindisfarne Gospels, John xv. 25. Cf. ON. *saklaust* adv. in the same sense.]

† **1.** Secure from accusation or from dispute; unchallenged, unmolested. *Obs.*

c **950** *Lindisf. Gosp.* Matt. xxviii. 14 And ʒif ðis ʒehered bið from ðen groefa we ʒe-trewað him & sac-leaso iwih we ʒedoeð [Vulg. *et securos vos faciemus*]. *a* **1067** *Charter of Eadweard* in Kemble *Cod. Dipl.* IV. 199 Ich keðe eu ðat Ælfred hauet yseld Gise biscop his land at Hlytton sacleas and clæne. *a* **1122** *O.E. Chron.* an. 1106, Eadgar æþeling þe litle ær..was ʒe faren..þone let se cyng syððan sacleas faran. *c* **1250** *Gen. & Ex.* 916 Oc al ðat euere fel him to, Sac-les he let hin welden it so. **1513** Douglas *Æneis* xii. x. 13 Turnus ..behaldis the cite, Sakles of batale, fre of all sic striffe. **1819** Scott *Ivanhoe* xxxiii, Theow and Esne art thou no longer, ..Folkfree and Sacless art thou in town and from town, in the forest as in the field.

2. Not guilty, innocent. Const. *of.* Now *arch.*

a **1000** *Laws Ethelred* iii. c. 3 (Schmid), Swerian..þæt hiʒ nellan nænne sacleasan man forsecgan ne nænne sacne forhelan. *c* **1200** Ormin Ded. 202 He ʒaff hiss aʒhenn lif.. To þolenn dæþþ o rodetre sacclæs wiþþutenn wrihhte. *a* **1300** *Cursor M.* 2440 And sco vnsoght saccles o sin. *a* **1352** Minot *Poems* (Hall) ii. 3 þare slogh ʒe many sakles, als it was sene. *c* **1450** *Mirour Saluacioun* 1286 And marye son be thaym slayne saklest y^t eure was manne. **1535** Stewart *Cron. Scot.* (Rolls) I. 73 Saikles he wes, tha wist weill, of sic thing. **1599** Nashe *Lenten Stuffe* 35 There was..a deale of whinyards drawne about him, and many sacklesse wights.. run through the tender weambs. **1632** Lithgow *Trav.* iii. 122 Curst be the hands, that sakelesse Troianes slay. **1670** *Deposit. York Castle* (Surtees) 177 As for the bewitchinge of any of his children, shee is sacklesse. **1725** Ramsay *Gentle Sheph.* v. iii, They'd smoor the sakeless orphan in her bed. **1831** *Blackw. Mag.* XXX. 386 That you are sackless of this murder who shall testify? **1882** Miss Yonge *Unknown to Hist.* I. 11 Poor Lady she is, in all sooth, if sackless: poorer still if guilty. **1897** W. Beatty *Secretar* viii. 62 My father would be sackless of all intent to make his market out of the misfortunes of his queen.

absol. *a* **1225** *Ancr. R.* 68 þe treowe is misleued, & te sakelease ofte bilowen, uor wone of witnesse. **13..** *E.E. Allit. P.* B. 716 Schal synful & saklez suffer al on payne. **14 ..** *Gosp. Nicod.* (Galba) 950 ʒe childer of irraell, listens me, þat has þis sakles slayne. *c* **1560** A. Scott *Poems* (S.T.S.) xxvi. 46 Thay sklander saikles, & thay suspectit.

b. *Sc.* and *north. dial.* Innocent of wrong intent, guileless, simple; also, of a thing, harmless. Hence, in disparaging sense, feeble-minded; lacking energy, dispirited. (Cf. innocent *a.* 3, 3 b.)

a **1600** Montgomerie *Sonn.* li, ʒit thoght thou [the nightingale] sees not, sillie, saikles thing! The piercing pykis brods at thy bony breist. **1804** R. Couper *Poetry* I. 228 Ill fated Du!..December's snaw, Fell saickless at thy side. **1847** E. Brontë *Wuthering Heights* xxii, 'It looks melancholy, does it not, Ellen?' 'Yes,' I observed, 'about as starved and sackless as you—your cheeks are bloodless.' **1862** [C. C. Robinson] *Leeds Dial.* Gloss. s.v., A poor sackless feal [= fool]. **1872** J. Hartley *Yorksh. Ditties* Ser. i. 81 Shoo'll..ax him if he knows who's writing that is? An' he'll luk at it as sackless as if he didn't know it wor his own.

† **3.** Of an accusation or penalty: Having no just cause; brought against or inflicted on an innocent person. *Obs.*

a **1300** *Cursor M.* 4625 þi saccles scam wel it is kyd. *c* **1470** Henry *Wallace* vi. 215 The saklace slauchter off hir, blith and brycht. **1513** Douglas *Æneis* vi. vii. 14 Wrangusly put to deid for cryme saikles. **1525** *St. Papers Hen. VIII*, IV. 418, I denunce..all..the committaris of the said saikles murthuris. **1572** *Satir. Poems Reform.* xxxii. 2 Quhat murther & oppressioun, Quhat saikless slauchter.

Hence † **ˈsacklessly** *adv.*, innocently, without just cause.

a **1300** *Cursor M.* 11563 And vtewit mani barntem Did he sacclesli o lijf. **1483** *Cath. Angl.* 316/2 Saklesly, *jnculpabiliter.* **1525** *St. Papers Hen. VIII*, IV. 417 How our Soverane Lordis trew liegis..ar saikleslie part murdrist, part slane. **1535** Stewart *Cron. Scot.* (Rolls) III. 201 Wallace..Quhilk saiklislie of ony gilt or cryme,..sufferit hes the deid. *a* **1578** Lindesay (Pitscottie) *Chron. Scot.* (S.T.S.) II. 211 He was bruited behind his back sacklislie. *c* **1626–7** in *Sel. Biog.* (Wodrow Soc.) I. 352 Because of my carriage towards her, who suffered sakelessly for his cause.

sacklet (ˈsæklɪt). *rare.* [f. sack *sb.*^{1} + -let.] A little sack.

1844 Tupper *Crock of G.* xxvi, Bridget..had made one of its [*sc.* a glove's] fingers into a very tidy little leather sacklet. **1847** R. Hill in Gosse *Nat. Jamaica* (1851) 466 The cutting just disclosed the uppermost of the blood-cells, but nothing of the sacklets that contained the honey.

sacky (ˈsækɪ), *a.* [f. sack *sb.*^{4} + -y.] Of a garment: Hanging more or less loosely from the shoulders; not fitted to the waist.

1891 C. James *Rom. Rigmarole* 51 A sacky frock-coat. **1906** *Daily Chron.* 25 Apr. 8/4 In the..dust coat the straighter and more sacky cuts will still predominate.

Sacky, var. Sauk.

† **saclactic** (sæˈklæktɪk), *a.* *Chem. Obs.* Also sac(c)hlactic. = saccholactic. So † **saˈclactate** = saccholactate.

1794 G. Adams *Nat. & Exp. Philos.* I. App. (Amer. ed.) 542 The saclactic and the lactic acids. **1802** Pye *New Chem. Nomencl.* 32 Sach-lactic radical. **1826** Saclactate [see saccholactate]. **1897** *Syd. Soc. Lex.*, *Sacchlactate*, *Sacchlactic acid.*

sacola, variant form of sac-à-lait. *U.S.*

sacoleva: see sackalever.

sacque: see sack *sb.*^{4}

‖ **sacra** (ˈsækrə), *sb. pl.* [ad. L. *sacr-a* sacred things, rites, etc., neut. pl. of *sacer* sacred.] Things endowed with sacred significance.

1819 S. Fleming *Sherburne's Misc. Poems* p. xiii, The poems are of a miscellaneous description: some being amatory, which the Author styles Erotica;..and others of a graver cast, to which he applies the titles of Ethica and Sacra. **1903** J. E. Harrison *Prolegomena to Study of Greek Relig.* iv. 126 Probably on this day the magical *sacra* lay upon the altars where the women placed them. *Ibid.* 132 Special cakes..were provided for them, but whether to eat or to carry as *sacra* does not appear. **1945** *Mind* LIV. 77 The contemplation of *sacra* gives rise to motor attitudes—shouting, prancing, rolling on the earth—which are no doubt in the first instance self-expressive. **1959** *Listener* 14 May 853/2 Plato..included the *sacra* in his concept of play. **1964** V. W. Turner *Forest of Symbols* (1967) iv. 102 In the Lesser Eleusinian Mysteries of Athens, *sacra* consisted of a bone, top, ball, tambourine, apples, mirror, fan, and woolly fleece.

sacra, pl. of sacrum.

sacrad (ˈseɪkræd), *adv.* [f. sacr-um + -ad: see dextrad.] Term proposed by Barclay for: Towards the sacrum, or the lower part of the body.

1803 Barclay *New Anat. Nomencl.* 166 Sacrad will signify towards the sacral aspect. **1808** —— *Muscular Motions* 315 If rotatory motions were to be admitted immediately sacrad and atlantad of the atlas. **1814** Wishart tr. *Scarpa's Treat. Hernia* i. 25 A little lower than [*note* Sacrad of] the ring it is attached to the spine.

sacrafice, -ies, -ise, obs. forms of SACRIFICE.

sacraire, variant of SACRARY *Obs.*

sacrait, obs. Sc. form of SECRET.

sacral (ˈseɪkrəl), *a.*[1] *Anat.* [ad. mod.L. *sacrālis*, f. SACR-UM: see -AL[1].] Pertaining to the sacrum.

1767 GOOCH *Treat. Wounds* I. 423 Pain in the groins, *pubes* and sacral region. **1827** ABERNETHY *Surg. Wks.* I. 111 Disease had taken place in the bone..and had affected the sacral nerves. **1872** MIVART *Elem. Anat.* 27 Five or six sacral vertebræ coalesce to form the sacrum.

b. Used by Barclay for: Belonging to the lower part of the body. (Cf. SACRAD.)

1803 BARCLAY *New Anat. Nomencl.* 120 Instead of the words *Superior* and *Inferior*, I would therefore propose *Atlantal* and *Sacral*. **1808** —— *Muscular Motions* p. xx, An aspect..towards the region where the sacrum is situated [is] *sacral*. **1814** WISHART tr. *Scarpa's Treat. Hernia* i. 20 The superior one [i.e. portion of the external oblique] is larger than the inferior [*note* Sacral] portion.

c. quasi-*sb.* = *sacral vertebra*.

1854 OWEN *Skel. & Teeth* in *Orr's Circ. Sci., Org. Nat.* I. 200 In the..iguana the pleurapophyses of the first caudal incline backwards as much as those of the second sacral do forwards. **1890** COUES *Ornith.* II. iv. 208 These sacrals proper are at or near the middle of the whole sacral mass.

sacral (ˈseɪkrəl, ˈsækrəl), *a.*[2] orig. *Anthropology.* [f. L. *sacr-um* sacred thing, rite, etc. (neut. sing. of *sacer* sacred) + -AL[1]. Cf. G. *sacral.*] Of or pertaining to sacred rites and observances; set apart for a religious purpose, sacred; pertaining to that which is sacred.

1882 A. J. EVANS in *Archæologia* XLVIII. 77 A sacrificial knife, the use of which was possibly not unconnected with the sacral functions of these Naronese Seviri. **1899** J. S. REID in *Classical Rev.* July 312/1 They found it, not in the living language,..but in sacral or legal formulæ alone. **1901** A. J. EVANS in *Jrnl. Hellen. Stud.* XXI. 181 Sacral Gateways or Portal Shrines. **1901** F. W. MAITLAND in *Soc. Eng.* (illustr. ed.) I. 415 The arms..possibly..have been in use for this sacral purpose [*sc.* trial by battle]. **1912** J. E. HARRISON *Themis* p. xi, The *dromenon* in its sacral sense is, not merely a thing done, but a thing *re*-done, or *pre*-done with magical intent. **1958** R. F. C. HULL tr. *Jung's Psychol. & Relig.* in *Coll. Wks.* XI. 350 Any sacral action, in whatever form, works like a vessel for receiving the contents of the unconscious. **1974** R. HELMS *Tolkien's World* i. 24 Tolkien's profoundly suggestive insights into the sacral nature of the human imagination parallel Blake's rather than Arnold's. **1977** *Church Times* 10 June 10/2 A kind of apostolic succession of kingship, temporal and sacral intermingled to form a regal high priesthood. **1977** J. N. M. WIJNGAARDS *Did Christ rule out Women Priests?* vii. 66 The Old Testament priests had to offer frequently at specified sacral times. **1979** *N.Y. Rev. Bks.* 25 Oct. 15/1 Moon recently announced in that sacral third person he uses in public appearances, 'he will go to Germany.'

sacralege, obs. form of SACRILEGE.

‖**sacralgia** (seɪˈkrældʒɪə). *Path.* [mod.L., f. SACR-UM + Gr. ἄλγ-ος pain.] Pain in the sacrum.

1891 in *Century Dict.*

sacrality (səˈkrælɪtɪ). Chiefly *Anthrop.* [f. SACRAL *a.*[2] + -ITY.] Sacral character.

1958 W. R. TRASK tr. *Eliade's Birth & Rebirth* iii. 59 Sacrality, spirituality, and immortality are expressed in images that, in one way or another, signify the beginning of life. **1964** R. MANHEIM tr. *Eliade's Mystery & Spiritual Regeneration* in *Papers from Eranos Yearbks.* V. 26 It is not the natural phenomenon of birth that constitutes the mystery; it is the revelation of feminine sacrality, that is, of the mystical bond between life, woman, nature, the godhead. **1977** J. N. M.. WIJNGAARDS *Did Christ rule out Women Priests?* vii. 64 Christ replaced a priesthood based on sacrality by a priesthood based on grace.

sacralization (ˌsækrəlaɪˈzeɪʃən). *Anthrop.* [f. next + -ATION.] The action or fact of endowing with sacred qualities. Also *transf.* Cf. DESACRALIZATION.

1918 *Encycl. Relig. & Ethics* X. 897/1 This 'sacralization' is not proved for sacrifice generally, either savage or civilized. **1937** C. CAUDWELL *Illusion & Reality* vi. 112 To the capitalist commodity-fetishism takes the form of sacralisation of the common market-denomination of all commodities—money. **1954** B. & R. NORTH tr. *Duverger's Pol. Parties* I. ii. 122 Totalitarian parties are in the 'sacred' category... The Party is personified (with a capital letter: a typical characteristic of 'sacralization'), the all-powerful infallible, protective, transcendent Party. **1958** G. W. BROMILEY tr. *Barth's Church Dogmatics* IV. ii. 667 It [*sc.* the Church] may fall victim either to alienation (secularisation) or self-glorification (sacralisation). **1976** *Times Higher Educ. Suppl.* 6 Aug. 7/4 [Stanley] Spencer's sacralization is often concerned with transforming profane, urban or suburban icons. **1980** *Times Lit. Suppl.* 8 Aug. 902/5 Unexpected, if partial, justifications of..boredom in church, learning by rote, the sacralization of war.

sacralize (ˈsækrəlaɪz), *v. Anthrop.* [f. SACRAL *a.*[2] + -IZE, after F. *sacraliser* (see quot. 1899).] To endow with sacred significance (freq. through ritual); to set apart from ordinary life or use as sacred.

[**1899** HUBERT & MAUSS in *l'Année Sociologique* III. 215 Pour employer la terminologie que nous voudrions faire admettre: ils se sacralisent et, en même temps, désacralisent pour les autres l'espèce totémique.] **1933** E. E. EVANS-PRITCHARD in *Ess. Social Anthropol.* (1962) vii. 134 Exchange of blood in such situations [*sc.* blood-brotherhood] sacralizes and endows with sanctions a politico-economic transaction. **1957** V. W. TURNER *Schism & Continuity in an Afr. Society* x. 294 In the past doctors drove the uninitiated away..from areas in the bush which they had sacralized for ritual purposes. **1967** *Listener* 11 May 616/3 In spite of his call to sacralize secularity, there is little expectation of transcendence here. **1972** S. TUGWELL *Did you receive Spirit?* ix. 75 It is only where action and contemplation have become secularised (or sacralised, for that matter..), that any contradiction appears.

sacrament (ˈsækrəmənt), *sb.* Forms: 3–6 sacrement, (*pl.* 2 sacramens, 3 sacra-, sacremenz, 4 sacremens), 4 sakermente, 5 sacramen, sacriment, sakyr-, sacurment, 5–6 sacramente, 2– sacrament. [a. F. *sacrement* (12th c. in Hatz.-Darm.), ad. L. *sacrāmentum* (whence the Fr. popular form *serment* oath), f. *sacrāre* to consecrate, set apart religiously, to secure by a religious sanction, f. *sacr-*, *sacer* holy, dedicated, set apart: see SACRED *a.*

In accordance with the functions of the suffix *-mentum* (see -MENT), the etymological sense of L. *sacrāmentum* would be either (1) a result of consecration, or (2) a means of consecrating, dedicating, or securing by a religious sanction. The latter of these notions is that which seems to be present in the classical uses of the word: (1) the military oath, oath or solemn engagement in general; (2) the caution-money deposited by the parties to a lawsuit; hence (3) a civil suit or process. In Christian Latin from the 3rd century the word was the accepted rendering of Gr. μυστήριον MYSTERY[1]. This use is evidently not based on either of the specific applications above mentioned, but is the result of a recourse to the etymological meaning. In early Christian language *sacramentum* and the synonymous μυστήριον were applied indiscriminately to any ritual observance of the Church, or to any spiritually symbolic act or object; but they were also often applied in an eminent sense to the two most important observances, baptism and the Lord's Supper or Eucharist. For the later history of the use, see below in sense 1.]

1. *Eccl.* Used as the common name for certain solemn ceremonies or religious acts belonging to the institutions of the Christian church.

The English use before the Reformation adopts the enumeration of seven sacraments (believed to have been first formulated by Peter Lombard in the 12th c.; the same list is recognized in the Eastern Church): viz., Baptism, Confirmation, the Eucharist, Penance, Extreme Unction, Order, Matrimony. As late as the 14th c., however, there were still traces in English of the wider application of the word formerly current; while the seven sacraments were viewed as eminently entitled to the name, it could be applied in a more general sense to certain other rites (see quot. *c*1315). From the 16th c., Protestants generally have recognized two sacraments only, viz. baptism and the Lord's Supper.

The formal definition of *sacrament* depends on the answer to the question what is the distinctive feature common to the seven or to the two 'sacraments', on account of which they form a separate class from all other observances. Those who accept the number seven, and many of those who admit only two sacraments, say that the sacraments differ from other rites in being channels by which supernatural grace is imparted. By those Protestants who deny that baptism and the Lord's Supper in themselves convey supernatural grace, the specific difference of the 'sacraments' from other observances is regarded as consisting in their paramount obligation as having been expressly commanded by Christ Himself, and in the special spiritual benefits obtainable by their faithful use.

By some of the English Puritans and Nonconformists, the word was avoided as being associated with opinions regarded by them as superstitious; the usual term applied by them to baptism and the Lord's Supper was *ordinance*.

*c***1175** *Lamb. Hom.* 51 þe halie sacramens þe me sacreð in alesnesse of alla sunfulle. *a***1225** *Ancr. R.* 268 Al þet holi chirche redeð ant singeð, ant alle hire sacramenz strencðeð ou gostliche. *a***1300** *Cursor M.* 12894 A! Ion..nan was worthier þan þou Hand to lai on suete iesu, To giue him þat hali sacrament. *c***1315** SHOREHAM I. 183 Al hit beþ cherche sacremens þet tokeneþ holi þynges, As hali water, and haly bred, Liȝt, and belryngynges To leste; And of alle oþer sacremens þes seuene beþ þe greste. **1340** *Ayenb.* 14 þe zeve sacremens þet byeþ ine holy cherche. *c***1386** CHAUCER *Merch. T.* 75 Mariage is a ful greet sacrement. *c***1460** *Wisdom* 1115 in *Macro Plays* 72 Ande now ye be reformyde by þe sakyrment of penaunce. *c***1440** *Alphabet of Tales* 186 He tuke his sacramentis of holy kurk and dyed. **1460** *Rolls of Parlt.* V. 375/2 By the sacrament of matrymonie. *c***1475** *Harl. Contin. Higden* (Rolls) VIII. 491 A pestilence.. folowede soone after at Cantebrigge, causynge moche peple to dye as sodenly as madde men withowte the sacramentes of the churche. **1509** FISHER *Hen. VII*, Wks. (1876) 273 The true byleue that he had in god, in his churche & in the sacramentes therof, whiche he receyued all with meruaylous deuocion, namely in the sacrament of penaunce, the sacrament of the auter, & the sacrament of anelynge. **1604** *Bk. Com. Prayer, Catechism, Q.* What meanest thou by this word *Sacrament*? *A.* I mean an outward and visible sign of an inward and spiritual grace given unto us [etc.]. **1647** CLARENDON *Hist. Reb.* I. §198 [They suffered] the Sacraments themselves to be administered where the people had most mind to receive them. **1657** *Penit. Conf.* iv. 49 The Sacrament of Penance will supply all other defects. **1864** J. H. NEWMAN *Apol.* 416 The fact of a parishioner dying without the Sacraments through his fault is terrible to him.

b. *in sacrament*: sacramentally. *rare.*

1628 *R. Field, Of the Church* III. App. 205 The crucified body of Christ thy sonne, which is here present in mystery, and sacrament.

2. *spec.* (with *the*). The Lord's Supper, Eucharist or Holy Communion. Often called ***the sacrament of the altar, the Blessed Sacrament***, and (esp. formerly) ***the Holy Sacrament***. Phr. ***to receive, take the sacrament***, to communicate.

*a***1225** *Ancr. R.* 268 Al þe deofles strencðe melteð þuruh þe grace of þe holi sacrament,..þet ȝe iseoð ase ofte ase þe preost messeð & sacreð þet meidenes bearn, Jesu. **1303** R. BRUNNE *Handl. Synne* 10198 þe folk þat to þe preste went For to receyue þe sacrament. *a***1340** HAMPOLE *Psalter* vi. 1 Comunynge of sacrament of þe autere. **1340** *Ayenb.* 14 þe sacrement of þe wyefde. **1387** TREVISA *Higden* (Rolls) V. 231 He ordeynede..þat þe grayel and þe offertorie schulde be i-seide to fore þe sacrement [orig. *ante sacrificium*]. *c***1440** *Alphabet of Tales* 339 He had a gude frend, a preste, þat said a mes for hym and offred þe sacrament for hym. **1500–20** DUNBAR *Poems* ix. 86 Anis in the ȝeir to tak the sacrament. **1509** FISHER *Hen. VII*, Wks. (1876) 273 The sacrament of the auter he receyued at myd-lent, & agayne vpon eester day. **1534** MORE *Treat. Passion* Wks. 1337/2 Onelye this blessed sacrament is called and knowne by the name of sacrament alone. **1610** R. FIELD *Of the Church* App. to 4 bks. I. 34 The true presence of Christs body & bloud in the blessed Sacrament. **1647** CLARENDON *Hist. Reb.* I. §199 The obliging all persons to come up to those rails to receive the Sacrament. **1712** ARBUTHNOT *John Bull* III. viii, They never had a quiet night's rest, for getting up in the morning to early sacraments. **1804** SOUTHEY in *Ann. Rev.* II. 202 They received the sacrament weekly. **1835** ALISON *Hist. Europe* (1847) IV. 136 A courageous priest..at the hazard of his life, often administered to her the Sacrament.

b. The consecrated elements, esp. the bread or Host.

*a***1225** *Ancr. R.* 68 Ut of chirche þurle ne holde ȝe none tale mid none monne, auh bereð wurðschipe þerto, uor þe holi sacrament þet ȝe iseoð þer þurh. **1395** PURVEY *Remonstr.* (1851) 40 The sacrament of the auteer, which is whight and round, visible and palpable. **1419** in S. Bentley *Excerpt. Hist.* (1831) 30 The box or vessell in the whiche the precious sacrement is in. **1548–9** (Mar.) *Bk. Com. Prayer, Communion*, Without any eleuacion, or shewing the Sacrament to the people. **1645** EVELYN *Diary* 26 Mar., The Sacrament being this day expos'd, and the reliques of the Holy Crosse. **1660** F. BROOKE tr. *Le Blanc's Trav.* 216 The people never behold the blessed Sacrament, but they bow their face to the ground.

c. ***to take*** or ***receive the sacrament*** (***to do*** something, or ***upon*** a matter): to receive Holy Communion as a confirmation of one's word.

1591 SHAKS. *1 Hen. VI*, IV. ii. 28 Ten thousand French haue tane the Sacrament, To ryue their dangerous Artillerie Vpon no Christian soule but English Talbot. **1594** —— *Rich. III*, I. iv. 208. **1601** —— *All's Well* IV. iii. 156 Ile take the Sacrament on't. **1681** *Trial S. Colledge* 65 *Mr. Lun.* I will take the Sacrament upon it, what I say is true. **1691** LUTTRELL *Brief Rel.* (1857) II. 191 The Irish under col. Clifford had took the sacrament to fight it out to the last man. **1749** FIELDING *Tom Jones* II. vi, Notwithstanding the positiveness of Mrs Partridge, who would have taken the sacrament upon the matter, there is a possibility that the schoolmaster was entirely innocent. *Ibid.* XVII. iv. **1876** TENNYSON *Harold* IV. i, *Harold.* Morcar and Edwin, will ye upon oath, Help us against the Norman? *Morcar.* With good will; Yea, take the Sacrament upon it, king.

†**d.** used in oaths. *Obs.*

1500–20 DUNBAR *Poems* xxxiv. 41 Ane fleschour swoir be the sacrament, And be Chrystis blud maist innocent, Nevir fatter flesch saw man with E. **1573** *New Custom* I. ii, Sacrament of God, who hath hearde suche a knaue? **1575** *Gamm. Gurton* I. iii. 27 Gogs sacrament, I would she had lost tharte out of her bellie!

e. ***the last sacraments***, Holy Communion and Extreme Unction administered to the dying; (see also quot. 1920); ***the sacrament of the sick***, in the Roman Catholic Church, Extreme Unction (now officially termed the Anointing of the Sick).

1760 in J. O. Payne *Old English Catholic Missions* (1889) 29 Jan. 7, William Hornby died at Middleham. He had the last sacraments. **1893** E. BELLASIS *Mem. Serjeant Bellasis* viii. 184 He left him..to go and tell the Curé..that the Serjeant ought to have the last Sacraments without delay. **1920** *Encycl. Relig. & Ethics* XI. 574/1 At Cwm Yoy, in the Black Mountain, on the way to Llanthony, the people have at a funeral what they call 'the Last Sacrament'. The coffin is brought out and placed on trestles, and beer and cake are then partaken of by the guests and persons assembled.., before the funeral procession starts. **1966** 'HAN SUYIN' *Mortal Flower* i. 41 The priest..with a Chinese choir boy holding the implements of Extreme Unction,..myself and my sisters assembled in Father's hospital room, to witness.. the last sacraments of the Church. **1972** S. TUGWELL *Did you receive Spirit?* xi. 98 It is painful,..and at times comic, to read the Fathers of Trent arguing about the sacrament of the sick. **1975** *N.Y. Times* 26 Oct. 1/5 A mass was held in the Prado Palace at which he [*sc.* Franco] took communion and received the sacrament of the sick, a religious ritual that used to be known as the last rites. **1981** *Church Times* 4 Sept. 9/4 He was the priest in the famous photograph giving the Last Sacraments (a term seldom used now) to the wounded and dying on what the Irish call 'Bloody Sunday'.

3. In widened application: **a.** Something likened to the recognized sacraments, as having a sacred character or function; a sacred seal set upon some part of man's life; the pledge of a covenant between God and man.

*a***1340** HAMPOLE *Psalter* xvii. 1 þis psalme contens þe sacrament of all chosen men. **1399** GOWER *Praise of Peace* 309 The pes is as it were a sacrement Tofore the god. **1563** *Homilies* II. *Common Prayer & Sacram.* 146 b, And so was circumcision a sacrament, whiche preached vnto the outwarde senses the inwarde cuttyng away of the foreskyn of the harte, and sealed and made sure in the hartes of the circumcised, the promise of god. **1613** PURCHAS *Pilgrimage* (1614) 42 Hereunto the Lord addeth the Rainbow, a new Sacrament, to seale his mercifull Couenant with the earth, not to drowne the same any more. **1679** CROWNE *Ambit. Statesman* IV. 65 Nature gives man a Sacrament In his own blood, never to hurt a woman. **1841** EMERSON *Lect., Man the Reformer* Wks. (Bohn) II. 243 Economy is a high, humane office, a sacrament, when its aim is grand. **1899** W. R. INGE *Chr. Myst.* vii. 258 To the true mystic, life itself is a sacrament.

b. A type, token, sign, or symbol. Const. *of.*

Derived from the accepted definition of a sacrament as a 'sign of grace'. Quot. 1660 exhibits an attempt to assign to the word a general sense in which the specific applications are included.

1534 More *Treat. Passion* Wks. 1331/1 For they make theym wene, that..it is none other but a bare sacrament onelye, that is to wytte a token, a figure, a sygne or memoriall of his bodye and hys bloude crucified and shed. **1563** *Homilies* II. *Repair. Ch.* 85 The Temple..was a figure, a Sacrament, or a signification of Christe. **1660** Jer. Taylor *Worthy Communicant* i. §3. 61 When Jonathan shot his arrows beyond the boys, he then by a sacrament sent salvation unto David. **1875** E. White *Life in Christ* IV. xxvii. (1876) 486 This second death is never set forth as a sacrament of immortality. **1904** A. R. Whitham *Epist. Consolations* vii. 87 Doubtless also those mysterious contents of the inner sanctuary..were copies of heavenly realities..; signs and sacraments they must have been of God's mercy and justice.

c. A mystery; something secret or having a secret meaning. [After L. *sacramentum*, used by Tertullian and in the Old Latin and Vulgate Bibles as a rendering of *μυστήριον*.]

1382 Wyclif *Dan.* ii. 30 This sacrament, or hid trewthe [Vulg. *sacramentum hoc*]. —— *1 Tim.* iii. 16 And opynly it is a greet sacrament of pite. **1388** —— *Rev.* i. 20 The sacrament [1382 mysterie, or priuytee] of the seuene sterris. *c* **1400** tr. *Secreta Secret., Gov. Lordsh.* 51 God..make cleer ȝoure vnderstondynge to persayue þe sacrament of þis science. *a* **1600** Hooker *Frag. on Sacraments* in *Eccl. Pol.* (1888) II. 550 In a word Sacraments are God's secrets, discovered to none but his own people. **1607** Topsell *Four-f. Beasts* Ep. Ded. A 4 b, Seeing God hath vsed them as Sacraments or Mysteries to containe his will. **1867** Manning in *Ess. Relig. & Lit.* II. 362 All the words of Scripture are so many sacraments (or mysteries).

d. ***sacrament of the present moment***, any and every moment regarded as an opportunity for the reception of divine grace.

1921 E. J. Strickland tr. *de Caussade's Abandonment to Divine Providence* I. i. 3 What treasures of grace lie concealed in these moments filled, apparently, by the most ordinary events... O Bread of Angels! heavenly manna!.. Sacrament of the present moment! **1930** J. Chapman *Spiritual Lett.* (1935) 83 The whole point of the 'Sacrament of the present moment' is that it is a..sacrament; it is God's action, God's will. **1943** O. Wyon *School of Prayer* iii. 38 God makes His will known to us through the things that happen every day... Once we see it, our whole life is lifted on to a higher plane. This way of living has been described as *The Sacrament of the Present Moment.* **1967** J. N. Ward *Use of Praying* iii. 36 There is the use of the 'Jesus Prayer'... There is the cultivation of the 'sacrament of the present moment'. **1979** *Tablet* 22/29 Dec. 1251/2 We miss the many-splendoured thing in the goings-on of daily life, but it is there, totally transforming it and bestowing the sacrament of the present moment on those who are willing to accept it.

4. An oath or solemn engagement, esp. one which is ratified by a rite. (Chiefly as a Latinism.)

1387-8 T. Usk *Test. Love* I. vi. (Skeat) l. 165 This..haue I saide for no harme, ne malyce of tho persones, but onely for trouth of my sacrement in my leigeaunce. *c* **1400** *Destr. Troy* 703 Here I aske you hertely þat ye may het here, With a solemne sacrement on þis sure gode, All þe forward to fulfille, þat ye first made. **1430-40** Lydg. *Bochas* VIII. xv[i]. (1494) D iv, He dyd varye From his promyse made by sacremente. **1461** *Rolls of Parlt.* V. 483/1 And tofore theym make ooth and Sacrament convenient, to be true and lowly Subgettes. **1596** Spenser *F.Q.* V. i. 25 This doubtfull causes right Can hardly but by Sacrament be tride, Or else by ordele, or by blooddy fight. **1611** B. Jonson *Catiline* I. i. Wks. (1616) 693 Nothing wants, then, But that we take a solemne sacrament, To strengthen our designe. **1646** Sir T. Browne *Pseud. Ep.* I. vii. 25 Nor are the deepest sacraments or desperate imprecations of any force to perswade where reason only, and necessary mediums must induce. **1752** Young *Brothers* II. i, Those whom I swore, before they parted hence, In dreadful sacraments of wine and blood, To bring back such reports, as shou'd destroy him. **1801** Eliz. Helme *St. Marg. Cave* (1819) I. 78 An infant at whose baptism she [as sponsor] had taken a sacrament to sustain and instruct in the best manner she was able. **1832** *Blackw. Mag.* XXXII. 609 Bound by no sacrament of military obedience to the state. **1890** R. Bridges *Shorter Poems* I. 7 Have not the young flowers been content, Plucked ere their buds could blow, To seal our sacrament?

5. *Roman Law.* The *sacramentum* or pledge which each of the parties deposited or became bound for before beginning a suit.

1880 Muirhead *Gaius* IV. §12 The procedure in those *legis actiones* was in one or other of five modes,—by sacrament, by petition for a judge [etc.]. **1886** —— in *Encycl. Brit.* XX. 682/1 He required sureties from the parties for the eventual payment by him who was unsuccessful of the sacrament he had offered to stake.

6. *attrib.* (sense 2), as ***sacrament-wine***; †**sacrament-box**, a pyx; †**sacrament-cloth**, a cloth or veil for covering the pyx; **sacrament day**, a day on which Holy Communion is celebrated; **sacrament house**, a tabernacle; **sacrament-money**, the alms collected at Holy Communion, formerly used as a fund for poor-relief; **sacrament Sabbath** = *Sacrament Sunday*; **Sacrament Sunday**, the Sunday on which the Lord's Supper is celebrated (in Scotland formerly only once or twice a year).

c **1440** *Alphabet of Tales* 112 On þe morn sho went vnto þe preste, and askid of hym how many hostis war in þe *sacrament-box in þe kurk. **1535-6** *Rec. St. Mary at Hill* 369 Item, ffor dressyng of ij *sacrament Clothes. **1853** Rock *Ch. of Fathers* IV. xii. 206 Over the cup itself was cast the Sacrament cloth, or piece of thin, cloud-like muslin,—*pannus nebulatus*. **1687** W. Sewall in *Mass. Hist. Soc. Coll.* (1878) 5th Ser. V. 176 May 15th was our *Sacrament-day. **1765** T. Lindsey *Let.* 1 Nov. in *N. & Q.* (1942) 1 Aug. 62/2 Being a sacrament-day, I could but barely ask the former how he did as he went out of the church. **1826** A. Constable *Let.* 10 Oct. in J. Constable *Corr.* (1962) 228 Golding din'd with me on Sunday (Sacrament day). **1551** *Inscr. in Deskford Old Ch., Banffs.*, This present loueable vark of *sacrament hous maid..the yeir of god 1551. **1876** C. Schreiber *Jrnl.* 16 July (1911) I. 464 Many objects of the rarest interest—a dance of death (1742).., a sacrament house. *Ibid.* 24 July 470, I saw a fine Sacrament house, the third I have met with. **1975** A. Maycock *Malling Abbey* (rev. ed.) 15 The nuns enter their choir from the cloister.., passing..on the right a circular sacrament house on which the light falls from a conical shaft immediately above it. **1716** *Rules Disposal Sacrament-Money* 3 In the appropriating all *Sacrament Money to the Poor only..they have the concurrent Sense of the whole Church of England..for above an 100 Years after the Reformation. **1860** Mrs. W. P. Byrne *Undercurrents* II. 77 *note*, That fund known as the 'Sacrament money' is a relic of this venerable custom. **1816** in *Sc. Nat. Dict.* (1971) VIII. 3/2 'Twas *sacrament Sabbath and much had been laid in. **1957** E. E. Evans *Irish Folk Ways* xviii. 253 The 'sacrament Sabbaths' of Presbyterian Ulster were great gatherings having something of the nature of fairs. **1768** J. Woodforde *Diary* 9 Oct. (1924) I. 80 David Maby..dined with us, being *Sacrament Sunday. **1796** C. Simeon in Carus *Life* vi. (1847) 121 Sunday, 26th.—Sacrament Sunday at Moulin. **1897** 'Ian Maclaren' *Dr. of Old School* i. 37 Black he wore once a year, on Sacrament Sunday, and, if possible, at a funeral. **1698** in *14th Rep. Hist. MSS. Comm.* App. III. 141 Theres a discovery of a designe to have poysoned his Majesty in the *sacrament wine on Christmas day.

sacrament ('sækrəmənt), *v. rare.* [ad. med.L. *sacrāment-āre* to bind by an oath, f. *sacrāmentum* SACRAMENT *sb.* Cf. Sp., Pg. *sacramentar.*]

1. *trans.* To bind by an oath or solemn engagement. Const. *to* or †*to do*, also *against*.

Frequent in Sydney Smith.

1621-31 Laud *Serm.* (1847) 55 When desperate men have sacramented themselves to destroy, God can prevent and deliver. **1804** Syd. Smith *Serm.* II. 218 A nation of free men, sacramented together. **1834** Emerson in *Corr. Carlyle & E.* (1883) I. iii. 34 A friend of mine and of yours remarked,..'that people were not here as in England sacramented to organized schools of opinion, but were a far more convertible audience'. **1860** —— *Cond. Life* vii. 160 All those who are..by many an oath of the heart, sacramented to you.

2. To make sacred, consecrate.

1829 Southey in *Q. Rev.* XLI. 212 The prince was assured, also,..that..his name was sacramented in the hearts of the people. [Literal rendering from Pg.] **1844** *N. Brit. Rev.* I. 128 Chivalry might well be engaged in the service of religion, for religion sacramented profession.

sacramental (sækrə'mɛntəl), *a.* and *sb.* [a. F. *sacramental* (now *sacramentel*) or ad. late L. *sacrāmentāl-is*, f. *sacrāment-um*: see SACRAMENT and -AL[1].] A. *adj.*

1. Pertaining to, or of the nature of, a sacrament of the Church.

c **1400** Love *Bonavent. Mirr.* (1908) 302 In this gostly mete and sacramentale commemoracioun of oure lord Jesu. **1451** Capgrave *Life St. Aug.* (E.E.T.S.) 25 In þe time of baptising, whan þe principal sacramental wordes wer said. **1526** *Pilgr. Perf.* (W. de W. 1531) 15 Penaunce, bothe sacramentall, whiche is secrete, and also solemne or open penaunce. **1532** More *Confut. Tindale* Wks. 384/1 What meaneth he other then that..we bee borne againe by the sacramentall water and the sacramentall worde? **1597** Hooker *Eccl. Pol.* v. lviii. §2 To make complete the outward substance of a sacrament, there is required an outward forme, which forme sacramentall elements receiue from sacramentall words. **1643** Milton *Divorce* Pref., Wks. 1851 IV. 16 Afterwards it was brought so Sacramentall, that no adultery or desertion could dissolve it. **1737** Waterland *Rev. Doctr. Eucharist* v. 136 But as there is a Sacramental Feeding and a Spiritual Feeding; and as the Spiritual is the nobler of the two [etc.]. **1899** W. R. Inge *Chr. Myst.* vii. 255 There are three requisites..for the validity of a sacramental act.

b. *transf.* with reference to non-Christian religious rites.

1851 D. Wilson *Archæol. Scot.* I. v. 102 The petty persecutions with which the natives sought to revenge the destruction of their sacramental stone. **1886** *Encycl. Brit.* XXI. 137/2 Mystic sacrifices of this sacramental type prevailed also among the heathen Semites.

c. *fig.*

1874 Geo. Eliot *Coll. Breakf. P.* 582 The sacramental rites of fellowship In common woe. **1877** Dowden *Stud. Lit.* (1890) 246 The little action of laying her head upon her father's knee was endowed with sacramental efficacy.

d. *spec.* Pertaining to the sacrament of the Lord's Supper.

1552 *Bk. Com. Prayer, Communion*, The Sacramentall bread or wyne. **1635** Quarles *Embl.* v. x. (1718) 285 Daily fed With sacred wine, and sacramental bread. **1704** Nelson *Fest. & Fasts* iii. II. (1739) 472 It was their Office to deliver the Sacramental Elements..to the People. **1827** in *Haggard's Eccl. Rep.* II. 32 Any the smallest portion of the sacramental alms collected at Queen Square Chapel within my parish. **1855** Macaulay *Hist. Eng.* xviii. IV. 181 The laws which instituted the Sacramental Test were passed without the smallest difficulty. **1862** H. Marryat *Year in Sweden* II. 274 Sacramental safe of Götland marble. **1863** *Chambers' Bk. Days* I. 732/1 A person came to my father (a clergyman) and asked him for a 'sacramental shilling'—i.e. one out of the alms collected at the Holy Communion, to be made into a ring and worn as a cure for epilepsy.

e. Of religious doctrine and the like: Based upon the sacraments; characterized by insistence upon the importance of the sacraments.

1871 [see SACERDOTAL *a.* 2]. **1879** R. T. Smith *Basil Gt.* x. 116 There is no doubt that he held sacramental doctrine. **1898** Illingworth *Div. Immanence* vi. 142 The religion of the Incarnation..was essentially and fundamentally sacramental.

f. Applied, in Scotland, to communicants.

1818 Chalmers in Hanna *Mem.* (1850) II. 198, I cannot leave Glasgow till Tuesday..owing to my having to meet a few more sacramental people on Monday.

2. Of the nature of, relating to, or expressed by an outward sign or symbol (see SACRAMENT 3 b).

1534 More *Treat. Passion* Wks. 1334/2 The verye naturall bodye and bloude of Christ in the forme of breade and wyne, be bothe sacramentall sygnes, because they sygnifye and also sacramental thinges because they be sygnified. **1605** Bacon *Adv. Learn.* II. xi. §3 That Ceremonies, Characters, and Charmes doe worke, not by any Tacite or Sacramentall contract with euill spirits, but [etc.]. **1653** Jer. Taylor *Serm. for Year, Winter* xii. 155 Though I cannot think that Nature was so sacramentall, as to point out the holy and mysterious Trinity by the triangle of the heart. **1664** H. More *Myst. Iniq.* 221 Their whole Camp was but one living and moving Sacramental Image of Christ and his Body. **1845** S. Austin *Ranke's Hist. Ref.* III. 307 Eck explained the sacrifice as merely a sacramental sign, in remembrance of that which was offered up on the cross. **1874** Stubbs *Const. Hist.* I. vii. 167 In a further stage the land becomes the sacramental tie of all public relations.

3. Of an oath, obligation, etc.: Peculiarly sacred; ratified by a religious sanction.

In quots. 1460 and 1644 the reference may be to an oath confirmed by the taking of the sacrament (see SACRAMENT 2 c).

1460 Capgrave *Chron.* (Rolls) 250 In this Parlement the lordes desired of the Kyng to make his sacramental oth byfore the puple. **1644** K. Chas. I in Rushw. *Hist. Coll.* III. II. 753 That holy Religion which, when We receiv'd the Crown and Scepter of this Kingdom, We took a most solemn Sacramental Oath to profess and protect. **1697** Evelyn *Numism.* iii. 78 Contrary to the most Sacramental Obligations. **1863** Geo. Eliot *Romola* xxvii, The fulfilment of her father's lifelong ambition about this library was a sacramental obligation for Romola.

†**b.** 'Sworn'; pledged as if by an oath. *Obs.*

1665 Glanvill *Def. Van. Dogm.* 79 Depriving themselves ..of their Liberty in Philosophy by a sacramental adherence to an Heathen Authority.

c. ? Bound by a soldier's oath (with secondary allusion to sense 1). *poet. nonce-use.*

1784 Cowper *Task* II. 349 He..trains, by ev'ry rule Of holy discipline, to glorious war, The sacramental host of God's elect!

4. *Roman Law.* Belonging to an action in which a *sacramentum* or pledge was deposited by each of the parties beforehand.

1861 Maine *Anc. Law* iii. 48 The alien..could not sue by the Sacramental Action. **1886** Muirhead in *Encycl. Brit.* XX. 683/1 Forfeiture of the sacramental cattle, sheep or money that would follow a verdict that an oath had been unjust.

5. *jocular.* Of a form of speech: Sacred to the occasion, 'consecrated'.

1896 *Daily News* 26 Feb. 3/3 With regard to the wager of a guinea the right hon. gentleman had not the presence of mind at the time to utter the sacramental word 'done'. **1898** *Times* 29 Oct. 11/4 As Lord Rosebery remarked last night in coyly introducing the sacramental quotation, many things besides Waterloo have been won in the playing-fields of Eton.

B. *sb.*

1. *Eccl.* A rite, ceremony, or observance analogous to a sacrament, but not reckoned among the sacraments; e.g. the use of holy water and of holy oil, the sign of the cross.

1529 *Petition of Commons* in Froude *Hist. Eng.* (1856) I. 194 To exact and take of your humble servants divers sums of money for the sacraments and sacramentals of Holy Church. **1536** Cromwell in Merriman *Life & Lett.* (1902) II. 27 That the sacramentes and sacramentalles be duely and reuerently ministred in their parishes. **1654** Jer. Taylor *Real Pres.* 77 The Eucharist it self was in the external and ritual part, an imitation of a custome and a sacramental already in use among the Jews. *a* **1662** Heylin *Laud* Introd. (1668) 10 Marriage, Orders, Confirmation, and the Visitation (though not the Extream Unction) of the Sick being retained under the name of Sacramentals. **1850** S. Wilberforce in *Life* (1886) II. ii. 65 Craving after confession and absolution, &c. as sacramentals. **1892** *Month* Nov. 440 Sacramentals are certain outward signs and usages instituted by the Church, which are the occasion of grace and blessing to those who piously use them.

†**2.** Occas. used for: Something which pertains to a sacrament; a constituent part of a sacrament.

1619 W. Sclater *Exp. 1 Thess.* i. 6 (1630) 52 Comes it [*sc.* sitting at Holy Communion] vnder the Mandate, *Hoc facite*? then is it amongst the Sacramentals of the Supper. For (*hoc facite*) comprizeth not Circumstantials, but Sacramentals. **1633** T. Morton *Discharge* 80, 81 That which wee are taught of him here, is, that these words Cup, and Testament, although they be Sacramentalls, yet are they not to be called The Sacramentals.

sacramentalism (sækrə'mɛntəlɪz(ə)m). [f. prec. + -ISM.]

1. = SACRAMENTARIANISM.

1861 Goldw. Smith *Lect. Mod. Hist.* Pref. 4 Sacerdotalism, sacramentalism [etc.]. **1881** Froude *Short Stud.* IV. 186 The revival of sacramentalism..found a voice in Keble.

2. The theory that the natural world is a reflection or imitation of an ideal, supernatural, or immaterial world.

1936 C. S. Lewis *Allegory of Love* ii. 45 The attempt..to see the archtype in the copy, is what I mean by symbolism or sacramentalism. **1963** H. Blamires *Christian Mind* II. vi. 175 A living Christian mind would elucidate for the young a finely articulated Christian sacramentalism which would make sense of, and give value to, the adolescent's cravings towards the grandeur of natural scenery, towards the potent emotionalism of music and art, and towards the opposite sex.

sacramentalist (sækrə'mɛntəlɪst). *rare.* [f. SACRAMENTAL + -IST.]

1. = SACRAMENTARIAN B. 1.

1840 tr. *Löwenberg's Persecut. Lutheran Ch. in Prussia*, In this sense I am..a Lutheran, and herein I separate myself from all sects, whether Papists, Sacramentalists, Anabaptists, or others.

2. One who holds 'high' doctrine in regard to the sacraments.

1880 SHORTHOUSE *J. Inglesant* v, [Hobbes *loq.*] We, doubtless, and not they, are the true sacramentalists, that is, the seekers for the hidden and the Divine truth. It is for this reason that I take the Sacrament in the English Church.

sacramentality (ˌsækrəmɛn'tælɪtɪ). [-ITY.] Sacramental character.

1660 JER. TAYLOR *Duct. Dubit.* II. iii. Rule 9 §31 He therefore that takes this [the wine] away, takes away the very Sacramentality of the mystery. **1843** NEALE & WEBB *Symbolism Ch.* Introd. Ess. 26 Sacramentality is that characteristic which so strikingly distinguishes ancient ecclesiastical architecture from our own. **1887** C. W. WOOD *Marriage* 31 The sacramentality of the contract depends solely on two facts.

sacramentally (ˌsækrə'mɛntəlɪ), *adv.* [f. SACRAMENTAL + -LY^{2}.]

1. In a sacramental manner; after the manner of a sacrament.

*c*1380 WYCLIF *Sel. Wks.* II. 170 þis oost is breed in his kynde, as ben oþer oostes unsacrid, and sacramentaliche Goddis bodi. *c*1422 HOCCLEVE *Learn to die* 25 How a man sacramentally Receyue me shal wel and worthyly. **1533** MORE *Answ. Poysoned Bk.* Wks. 1065/2 Thys is ment..of theym that receyue the sacrament, not onelye sacramentallye, but also effectually. **1609** DOWNAM *Chr. Liberty* 15 You haue been..by baptisme sacramentally vnited to the body of Christ. **1736** CHANDLER *Hist. Persec.* 191 The Counsellor must absolve him sacramentally. **1884** A. R. PENNINGTON *Wiclif* viii. 253 When it has come to be sacramentally the body of Christ, it is still bread substantially.

†**2.** By way of oath or solemn obligation. *Obs.*

1599 NASHE *Lenten Stuffe* 34 In generous reguerdonment whereof he sacramentally obliged himselfe, that [etc.]. **1654** 'PALAEMON' *Friendship* 26 Did not the satisfying of Curius his Lust cost him the lives of his dearest and Sacramentally-combined Partners?

sacra'mentalness. *rare.* [-NESS.] The quality of being sacramental (see the adj.).

1633 D. R[OGERS] *Treat. Sacram.* I. 66 Pollute not..the Sacramentalnesse and Symbolicalnesse of the things of God by your unsutablenesse. **1664** H. MORE *Myst. Iniq.* 222 The Sacramentalness of the Jewish Church in reference to the Christian.

sacramentarian (sækrəmən'tɛərɪən), *a.* and *sb.* [f. mod.L. *sacrāmentāri-us* SACRAMENTARY + -AN.] **A.** *adj.*

1. *Hist.* Relating to the views held by the 'Sacramentarians' in regard to the Eucharist (see B. 1).

1640 BP. HALL *Chr. Moder.* II. viii. 53 As for the Sacramentarian quarrels, Lord, how bitter have they beene. **1674** HICKMAN *Hist. Quinquart.* (ed. 2) 50 The Sacramentarian Controversie. **1837–9** HALLAM *Hist. Lit.* II. i. §24 He boasts that Luther predicted the deaths of Zwingle, Carlostadt, and Œcolampadius as the punishment of their sacramentarian hypothesis. **1845** J. H. NEWMAN *Ess. Developm.* 287 Ernesti seems to consider the [Syrian] school, in modern language, Sacramentarian.

2. *gen.* Relating to the sacraments (or to 'high' doctrine in regard to them).

1865 LECKY *Ration.* I. 287 Among the Protestants the same tendency is displayed with equal force in the rapid destruction of what is termed the sacramentarian principle. **1878** BAYNE *Purit. Rev.* iii. 85 He [Laud] does not seem to have gone much upon sacramentarian symbolism.

B. *sb.*

1. *Hist.* A name given by Luther to those Protestant theologians (esp. Zwingli and Œcolampadius) who maintained that it is merely in a 'sacramental' or metaphorical sense ('sacramentaliter sive μετωνυμικῶς', Zwingli) that the bread and wine of the Eucharist are called the body and blood of Christ. Hence used in the 16th c. (by opponents) as a general name for all deniers of the doctrine of the Real Presence.

1535 in Froude *Hist. Eng.* (1856) II. ix. 403 The anabaptists and sacramentarians. **1537** in Ellis *Orig. Lett.* Ser. III. III. 128 That the Kyng his Hyghtnes and Cownsell to be become Sacramentarians. **1624** BEDELL *Lett.* ii. 47 The vehement speeches of Luther and some of his followers against those whom they call the Sacramentarians. **1782** PRIESTLEY *Corrupt. Chr.* II. IX. 194 Cranmer, whilst he was a Lutheran, consented to the burning of John Lambert and Ann Askew..; and when he was a sacramentarian he was the cause of the death of Joan Bocher, an Arian. **1903** *Cambr. Mod. Hist.* II. x. 333 Zwingli..made this Sacrament purely symbolical... In this he was followed by the later Sacramentarians.

2. *Hist.* A nickname given to the early Methodists at Oxford. (See quot. 1733.)

1732 J. WESLEY *Let.* 18 Oct. (1931) I. 130 Some of the men of wit in Christ Church..made a pretty many reflections upon the Sacramentarians, as they were pleased to call us. **1733** *Oxf. Methodists* 7 The young Gentlemen..thought it requisite to Communicate as often as they had Opportunity; which at Oxford is once a Week; and hence their Ill-willers gave them the Name of Sacramentarians. **1797** *Encycl. Brit.* (ed. 3) XI. 623/2 To the name of *Methodists* two others were quickly added, viz. those of *Sacramentarians* and the *Godly club*.

3. One who holds 'high' doctrine as to the sacraments.

1651 BIGGS *New Disp.* ¶214 The transubstantial migration of the grapy juice of the papall Sacramentarians. **1870** SPURGEON *Treas. Dav.* Ps. l. 10 Ye Ritualists, ye Sacramentarians.

Sacramen'tarianism. [f. prec. + -ISM.] 'High' doctrine in regard to the sacraments (cf. prec. B. 3).

1882 *Athenæum* 9 Sept. 335/1 The advance of sacerdotalism and sacramentarianism. **1903** *St. George* VI. 191 The Broad-Church Sacramentarianism of Mr. Shorthouse.

sacra'mentarist. *rare*$^{-1}$. = SACRAMENTARIAN B. 1.

1828 PUSEY *Hist. Enq.* I. 16 An edict of 1534..which directed the immediate expulsion of Anabaptists and Sacramentarists from Bremen.

sacramentary (sækrə'mɛntərɪ), *a.* and *sb.* Now *rare.* Also 6 -arie, *Sc.* -aire. [ad. med. and mod.L. *sacrāmentāri-us* (= F. *sacramentaire*; as sb. = G. *sacramentirer*, *sacramenter*, both used by Luther), f. L. *sacrāmentum*: see SACRAMENT and -ARY.]

A. *adj.* Pertaining to the sacraments of the Church: **a.** *Hist.* = SACRAMENTARIAN A. 1. Of a person: Holding sacramentarian views.

1563 HARDING *Answ. to Jewel* v. vi. (1564) 98 Berengarius first beganne openly to sowe the wicked sede of the sacramentarie heresie. **1600** J. HAMILTON *Facile Traict.* 327 Thir sacramentaire Ministers, to hyde this trew worscheping of God be sacrifice..hes mutilat this passage. **1830** COLERIDGE *Table-t.* 20 May, Arnauld, and the other learned Romanists, are irresistible against the low Sacramentary doctrine.

b. Relating to 'high' doctrine in regard to the sacraments.

1561 T. NORTON *Calvin's Inst.* IV. 149 These Sacramentarie doctors [orig. *les Papistes, quant à leur nombre de sept Sacremens*]. **1884** G. SMITH *Short Hist. Chr. Missions* II. vi. 74 All missionary effort which did not proceed on sacerdotal and sacramentary lines.

c. *gen.*

1594 NASHE *Unfort. Trav.* L 1, Ile hire them that make their wafers or sacramentary gods, to minge them after the same sort. **1641** T. EDWARDS *Reas. agst. Independ.* Ep. Ded. 2 The controversie of that age was concerning the Sacrament of the Lords Supper, being generally stiled *Bellum Sacramentarium*, and the Sacramentary Controversie. **1647** TRAPP *Comm. Gal.* v. 26 It was this vice [i.e. vainglory] that..bred the Sacramentary war that is not yet ended. **1837** *Penny Cycl.* VII. 196/2 The question as to the sacramentary efficacy which has been sometimes attributed to the rite [of circumcision].

B. *sb.*

1. *Hist.* = SACRAMENTARIAN B. 1.

1538 CROMWELL in Merriman *Life & Lett.* (1902) II. 148 Certain persones denyeng the holy sacrament of Christes blessed body and blud of suche opinion as commonly they calle Sacramentaries. **1651** C. CARTWRIGHT *Cert. Relig.* I. 86 The Divisions that are between old and new Sacramentaries. **1732** NEAL *Hist. Purit.* I. 29 The king began to discover his zeal against the Sacramentaries (as those were called who denied the corporal presence of Christ in the Eucharist). **1858** FROUDE *Hist. Eng.* III. xv. 339 A few years later, a sacramentary had ceased to be a criminal.

†**2.** One who holds 'high' doctrine as to the sacraments. *Obs. rare*$^{-1}$.

1595 HUBBOCKE *Apol. Infants Unbapt.* 30 Zwinglius.. calleth them sacramentaries who attribute so much grace to the sacrament, so much vertue to Baptisme of it selfe.

3. [med.L. *sacrāmentārium.*] An early form of office-book in the Western Church, containing the rites and prayers belonging to the several sacraments.

1624 USSHER *Answ. Jesuit Irel.* 200 Such is the prayer..in Grimoldus his Sacramentarie. **1685** STILLINGFL. *Orig. Brit.* iv. 230 The Sacramentary of Gregory. **1832** W. PALMER *Orig. Liturg.* I. 308 The Sacramentary comprised the collects and the canon or prayers that never varied. **1844** LINGARD *Anglo-Sax. Ch.* (1858) I. vii. 293 *note*, The blessing..may be found in most sacramentaries.

†**sacramentated,** *ppl. a. Obs. rare*$^{-1}$. [f. med.L. *sacrāmentāt-us* (f. *sacrāmentum* SACRAMENT) + -ED.] Made into a sacrament, received in the sacrament.

1651 HOWELL *Venice* 183 Impious Priests..who ev'ry day receave the Sacramentated Redeemer, peradventure more unworthily then Judas.

sacramented, *ppl. a. rare*$^{-1}$. Consecrated, made sacred, sealed by a sacrament.

1914 R. BROOKE in *New Numbers* I. 116 They'll..sell Love's trust And sacramented covenant to the dust.

sacramenter. *rare.* Also 6 -our. [f. SACRAMENT *sb.* + -ER^{1}. In sense 2 after G. *sacramenter* (Luther).]

†**1.** ? One who is frequent in attendance at the sacrament. *Obs.*

1536 in W. A. J. Archbold *Somerset. Relig. Ho.* (1892) 63 Doctour Tregonwell sertefying cornyshemen to be very good subjectes and sacramentours.

2. = SACRAMENTARIAN B. 1.

1845 S. AUSTIN *Ranke's Hist. Ref.* III. 187 They too exhorted the council to have nothing to do with the 'Sacramenters'.

†**sacramenting,** *ppl. a. nonce-wd.* [-ING^{2}.] ? That celebrates the Mass.

1687 R. L'ESTRANGE *Brief Hist. Times* I. 15 The short-English of the Device, was, to make as Arrant, a Jugling, sacramenting Rascal of me, (saving the Then Kings Evidences) as ever Renounc'd God upon the Holy Altar.

'sacramentism. *rare*$^{-1}$. [f. SACRAMENT *sb.* + -ISM.] = SACRAMENTARIANISM.

1840 GLADSTONE *Ch. Princ.* 187 It is not any blind sacramentism..that she would inculcate.

†**'sacramentize,** *v. Obs. rare*$^{-1}$. [f. SACRAMENT *sb.* + -IZE.] *intr.* To administer the sacraments. Hence **sacramentizing** *vbl. sb.* or *ppl. a.*

1655 FULLER *Ch. Hist.* XI. v. §65 Ministers..lawfully ordained..both to Preach and Sacramentize. *Ibid.* vii. §19 That the Governing part should be in the hands of the Bishops; the Teaching and Sacramentizing in the Presbyters.

†**sacramently,** *adv. Obs. rare.* [f. SACRAMENT *sb.* + -LY^{2}.] Sacramentally.

In quot. 1624 perh. a misprint for *sacramentally*.

*c*1425 *Orolog. Sapient.* vi. in *Anglia* X. 369/8 He is..after þe manhede sacramently to me presente. *Ibid.* 377/28 þere beþ summe þatte in this borde receyue me sacramently. **1624** DARCIE *Birth of Heresies* xxi. 86 All sacred signes ordained by God in the Israelitish Church, though they really and sacramently represented that which was by them figured..yet did [etc.].

sacrarial (sə'krɛərɪəl), *a. Ornith.* [f. SACRARIUM^{2} + -AL^{1}.] Of, pertaining to, or connected with the sacrarium of birds.

1890 COUES *Ornith.* II. iv. 211.

‖**sacrarium**^{1} (sə'krɛərɪəm). Pl. sacraria (-rɪə). [L. *sacrārium*, f. *sacr-*, *sacer* sacred, holy: see -ARIUM.]

1. *Roman Antiq.* Any place in which sacred objects were deposited and kept; the adytum of a temple; also, a small apartment in a house where the images of the penates were kept.

'In the time of the emperors, the name sacrarium was sometimes applied to a place in which a statue of an emperor was erected' (*Smith's Dict. Grk. & Rom. Antiq.*, 1842, s.v.).

*a*1746 HOLDSWORTH *Rem. Virgil* (1768) 291 The Lituus and Trabea of Romulus and the Ancilia were kept in the Sacrarium of the Salii. **1842** GWILT *Archit.* §253 In more magnificent houses there were the sacrarium, the venereum, the sphæristerium [etc.].

b. *gen.* A repository for what is sacred. In quot. *fig.*

1890 J. MARTINEAU *Seat Author. Relig.* III. ii. 300 If either Church or Scripture could be constituted a *sacrarium* for secluding all that is simply divine.

2. *Eccl.* **a.** That part of a church immediately surrounding the altar or communion table; also called the sanctuary.

[**1708–22** J. BINGHAM *Orig. Eccles.* VIII. vi. §2 The Latins called it [*sc.* the chancel] *sacrarium*, 'the sanctuary': as in the first Council of Bracara, which forbids laymen to come into the sanctuary to communicate.] **1727** *Acc. Ceremonies Coronations* 31 In the midst of the Area or Sacrarium before the Altar. **1846** *Ecclesiologist* Apr. 134 By the sacrarium we mean the part of the church immediately set apart for the celebration of the highest mysteries, into which..none but the clergy would ever, under ordinary circumstances, be allowed to enter: the part, in short, which in a common English church is within the altar-rails. **1887** *Pall Mall G.* 16 Nov. 5/4 The tablet..instead of being within the sacrarium, will be at the entrance to the chancel.

attrib. **1848** B. WEBB *Cont. Ecclesiol.* 173 There are sacrarium-rails, no screen.

b. In Roman Catholic use = PISCINA 2.

1848 *Ecclesiologist* Dec. 157 *note*, Sacrarium in the present Roman ritual means exclusively the piscina. **1853** ROCK *Ch. of Fathers* IV. xii. 167 The piscina, or sacrarium.

‖**sa'crarium**^{2}. *Ornith.* [mod.L., f. SACR-UM + -ARIUM.] (See quot.)

1890 COUES *Ornith.* II. iv. 209 Such is the general character of a bird's complex sacrarium, as I name the whole mass of bones that are ankylosed together.

†**sacrary.** *Obs.* Also 4–7 sacrarie, 5 sacraire, -ayre, sacrear, sacrarye. [a. OF. *sacraire*, *-eire*, *sacrarie*, ad. L. *sacrārium* (see SACRARIUM^{1}); cf. Sp. *sagrário*, It. *sacrario.*]

1. *gen.* A place where sacred objects are kept; a sacred building or apartment; a temple, shrine, sanctuary.

1382 WYCLIF *1 Cor.* ix. 13 Thei that wirchen in the sacrarie, that is, a place where hooly thingis ben kept, eten tho thingis that ben of the sacrarie. **1412–20** LYDG. *Chron. Troy* II. 3823 þei token al þat cam to her honde,..Reliques sacrid, þe holy eke vessels,..oute of þe sacrarie. **1490** CAXTON *Eneydos* xv. 59 This Yarbas..had..made an hondred temples wythin his royalme, wyth an hondred othre sacraryes, in whiche he had consecrated the fyre brennyng without ceasse. *c*1557 ABP. PARKER *Ps.* lxxviii. 226 Hys sacrary, which once in Sylo stoode. **1620** J. KING *Serm. 24 Mar.* 27 The dilapidation of any of Gods Oratories and Sacraries, his Heauens vpon earth, goeth to his heart like swords. **1652** GAULE *Magastrom.* 256 The sacrary of Serapis, in Alexandria, was burnt.

b. *fig.*

13.. *Minor Poems fr. Vernon MS.* xxiii. 425 Heil þou holy sacrarie, Vr askynges euer heryng [*Aue secretarium* *exaudicionis*]. **14..** LYDG. *Life Our Lady* lxxvii. (1484) l v b, God chase thy wombe for his tabernacle And halowed it so clene in euery coost To make hit sacrarye for his owen ghoost. **1615** T. ADAMS *Myst. Bedlam* i. (1634) 12 The purified heart is Gods Sacrary, his Sanctuary, his House, his Heauen. **1668** M. CASAUBON *Credulity* (1670) 135 A more venerable..man..who would open all sacraries and fountains of Truth, should appear upon earth. **1676** NEEDHAM *Pacquet Adv.* 50 That draws a Reverence to the Throne itself; which should be religiously fenced about, not only as the Sacrary of Royalty, but as the Sanctuary also of other Princes.

2. *spec.* In a Christian church: = SACRARIUM 2 a.

1387 TREVISA *Higden* (Rolls) VI. 155 By schewynge of God he fonge [*read* fonde] a greet deel of þe cros in Seynt Peter his sacrarie. **14..** *Nom.* in Wr.-Wülcker 721/1 *Hoc sacrarium*, a sacrear. **1482** *Monk of Evesham* xiii. (Arb.) 35 Abowte the sacrarye of the same auter y knowe wele y left my selfe. **1560** BECON *Catech.* v. Wks. I. 455 b, The ashes to be reposed in the sacrary among the other reliques. **1727** *Acc. Ceremonies in Coronations* 22 The Bishops to their Seats on the North side of the Area or Sacrary.

†**sacrate**, *a.* (*ppl. a.*) *Obs.* Also 6 sacrat. [ad. L. *sacrāt-us*, pa. pple. of L. *sacrā-re*: see next.] Consecrated, dedicated to God or a divinity; hallowed, sacred.

1432-50 tr. *Higden* (Rolls) VI. 401 Seynte Edburga, a virgyn sacrate to God. **1513** BRADSHAW *St. Werburge* I. 2783 She..cast her sacrat vayle..to fle from the traytour. **1526** *Pilgr. Perf.* (W. de W. 1531) 264 Hauyng no reuerence to that moost blessed eyes, nor to yᵉ heuenly visage & sacrate mouth. *a* **1533** LD. BERNERS *Gold. Bk. M. Aurel.* (1546) Gg j, Thou doest complayne..of the sacrate senate. **1544** *Exhort. Praier* A iij b, The holy and sacrate cuppe of the precious and blessed blood, which was shedde for vs vppon the crosse. *a* **1572** KNOX *Hist. Ref.* Wks. 1846 I. 301 Becaus we wold attempt nothing without the knowledge of the sacrate authoritie,..it was concluded, that..we should attempt the favouris..of the Quein then Regent, to a godly Reformatioun.

†**sacrate**, *v.* *Obs. rare.* [f. L. *sacrāt-*, ppl. stem of *sacrāre*: see SACRE *v.*] *trans.* To consecrate, dedicate.

1653 WATERHOUSE *Apol. Learning* 51 His mind..called on him to write his memorial on the Marble of some Monument sacrated to Learning. **1660** —— *Arms & Arm.* 82 Some are allowed what others are not, because they are of more conspicuity then others are, and therefore sacrated and separate from vulgar familiarities. **1755** AMORY *Mem.* (1769) I. 72 By the most dreadful prophanation, she [*sc.* Rome] sacrates her temples to Satan.

†**sa'cration.** *Obs. rare.* [ad. L. *sacrātiōn-em*, n. of action f. *sacrāre*: see prec.] Consecration.

1627-77 FELTHAM *Resolves* II. xxxvi. 233 Why then should it not as well from this, be auoided as from the other find a Sacration? **1628** W. SCLATER *Three Serm.* (1629) 18 The worst mens speeches and actions receiue a kinde of sacration by their recording in holy writ.

[**sacratyle, -til**, erron. form of SERRATILE.

1541 R. COPLAND *Guydon's Quest. Chirurg.* D ij b, And other [bones] ben sacratyles [**1579** G. BAKER *Guydo's Quest.* 11 b, sacratils] or sawe wyse, as the skull of the heade.]

sacrayre, variant of SACRARY *Obs.*

†'**sacre**, *sb.*¹ *Obs.* [a. OF. *sacre*, of twofold formation: (1) in sense 1, ad. L. *sacrum*, orig. neut. of *sacer* adj., sacred; (2) in sense 2, a verbal noun from *sacre-r* to consecrate (see SACRE *v.*¹).]

1. A religious observance or festival; *pl.* rites of worship.

a **1500** *Chaucer's Dreme* 2135 Which tent was church perochiall Ordaint was in especiall For the feast and for the sacre Where archbishop, and archdiacre Song ful out the seruise. **1542** UDALL *Erasm. Apoph.* 59 b, She customably resorted to all places, where any solemnitee of sacres or martes was. *Ibid.* 340 b, The sacres of Ceres. **1548** —— *Erasm. Par. Luke* i. 17 The ministring of the sacres and holy rites in the temple.

2. Consecration. **a.** The coronation of a sovereign. **b.** The festival of Corpus Christi. *rare.*

1584 [CARD. ALLEN] *Def. Eng. Cath.* 51 They [*sc.* the bishops] doubted also lest she [*sc.* Elizabeth] would refuse in the verie time of her sacre, the solemne diuine ceremonie of vnction (accustomed in the consecration of al Christian princes). **1653** URQUHART *Rabelais* II. xxii, The next day was the great festival of Corpus Christi called the Sacre.

‖**sacré** (sakre), *sb.*² [Fr., cf. SACRÉ *v.*²] (The utterance of) the word 'sacré' as a profane imprecation.

1828 LYTTON *Pelham* I. xix. 148 He uttered a short, low, laugh..; and, pushing through the atmosphere of *sacrés* and *mille tonnerres*..strode quickly to the door.

†'**sacre**, *a.*¹ *Obs. rare.* [ad. L. *sacr-*, *sacer.*] Sacred.

1513 MORE *Rich. III* (1883) 60 The sacre magesty of a prince. *a* **1548** HALL *Chron., Hen. VIII* 199 There dyd swere that they woulde obey the sacre & holy counsels, & woulde follow the Decrees of the Fathers. **1577-87** HOLINSHED *Chron.* III. 924/2 The..decrees and constitutions of the sacre and holie church.

‖**sacré** (sakre), *a.*² [Fr.: cf. SACRÉ *v.*²] Holy, sacred, used in various French oaths, as ***sacré bleu*** (sakre blø), also ***sacre bleu, sacrebleu***, a euphemism for *sacré Dieu*; ***sacré Dieu*** (sakre djø); ***sacré nom*** (sakre nɔ̃), ***sacré tonnerre*** (sakre tɔnɛr).

1768 STERNE *Sentimental Journey* II. 134 If there is but a cap-full of wind in or about Paris, 'tis more blasphemously *sacre Dieu*'d there than in any other aperture of the whole city. **1869** 'MARK TWAIN' *Innoc. Abr.* xxvii. 294 Is, ah—is he dead?' 'Oh, *sacre bleu*, been dead three thousan' year!'. **1901** S. J. WEYMAN *Count Hannibal* i. 1 Sacré nom, am I King, or a dog of a——. **1905** BARONESS ORCZY *Scarlet Pimpernel* i. 10 '*Sacré tonnerre*,' said the captain. **1923** W. L. LOCKE *Moordius & Co.* ii. 23 *Sacrebleu!* the world had changed since 1870. **1974** K. BENTON *Craig & Tunisian Tangle* vi. 63 But *sacre bleu!* you can't depend on that.

†'**sacre**, *v.*¹ *Obs.* Forms: *Inf.* 3-7 **sacre**, (3 **sacri**, 5 **sacryn, sakyre, sakor**). *Pa. t.* and *pa. pple.* 3-4 **sacrede**, 3-5 **sacrid**, 4 **sakred**, (*Sc.*) **sacryt**, 4-5 (*Sc.*) **sacrite**, 5 **sacride, sakird, sakyrd(e, sakeret, sacryed**, (*Sc.*) **sacrit**, 5-6 **sacryd**, 6 (*Sc.*) **sacreit**, 3-7 **sacred**; also *pa. pple.* 3 **i-sacret**, 3-5 **i-sacred**, 4 **y-sacred(e**, 5 **y-, i-sacryd**. [a. F. *sacre-r* (12th c. in Hatz.-Darm.), = Pr., Pg. *sagrar*, It. *sacrare*, *sagrare*, ad. L. *sacrāre*, f. *sacr-*, *sacer* sacred.]

1. *trans.* **a.** To consecrate (the elements, or the body and blood of Christ) in the Mass.

a **1225** *Ancr. R.* 268 Ase ofte ase þe preost messeð & sacreð þet meidenes bearn, Jesu. **1297** R. GLOUC. (Rolls) 7209 Vor prustes mid vnclene honden..sacrieþ godes fless & is blod. **1340** *Ayenb.* 235 Þet bodi of our lorde Iesu crist þet þe prestes sacreþ and onderuongeþ and betakeþ oþren. **1387** TREVISA *Higden* (Rolls) VIII. 9 Anon þey brouȝte an obley þat was i-sacred. *c* **1485** *Digby Myst.* III. 2068, I sakor þe body of ower lord Iesu cryst.

absol. *a* **1225** *Ancr. R.* 34 Efter þe messecos, hwon þe preost sacreð, þer uorȝiteð al þene world, & þer beoð al vt of bodi. *c* **1400** *Apol. Loll.* 30 It semiþ hem to preche, it is profit to bles, it is congrew to sacre. *c* **1460** *Play Sacram.* 363 He hath oftyn sacred as yt ys skylle.

b. To celebrate (the Eucharist).

a **1240** *Lofsong* in *Cott. Hom.* 207 Þe holi sacrement..þet ðe preost sacreð. *c* **1450** *St. Cuthbert* (Surtees) 7038 To sacre þe haly sacrement. **1535** STEWART *Cron. Scot.* (Rolls) II. 424 King Druskene with his lordis ilkone Into the tempill present at the mes, Solempnitlie quhen it sacreit than wes.

c. To sacrifice. *rare*⁻¹.

c **1250** *Gen. & Ex.* 612 Wið-uten ilc seuend clene der ðe he sacrede on an aucter. *Ibid.* 938 Ðre der he toc, ilc ðre ȝer hold, And sacrede god on an wold.

d. ? To worship. *rare*⁻¹.

1390 GOWER *Conf.* III. 243 Hire god Moloch that with encense He sacreth, and doth reverence In such a wise as sche him bad.

2. a. To consecrate (a king, bishop, etc.) to office. Const. with compl. object (in *pass.*, subject); also *to* (an office), *to*, *into* (bishop).

c **1290** *Beket* 301 in *S. Eng. Leg.* I. 115 Þat dai of þe Trinite bischop i-sacret he was And onder-feng þis dignete. **1297** R. GLOUC. (Rolls) 10719, & maister Richard þe grant in is stede was ido & wende uorþ to rome to sacri him þer to. *a* **1375** *Joseph Arim.* 300 Ihesu..sacrede him to Bisschop wiþ boto his hondes. *c* **1420** *Chron. Vilod.* 1586 To sacre hurre abbas of þe abbay of Wynchestre. *a* **1450** MYRC *Festial* 12 And sakeret hym byschoppe. *c* **1450** *St. Cuthbert* (Surtees) 6494 Aftir warde, at ȝorke cite, Sakird solemply was he Of archebischop theodere. **1504** LADY MARGARET tr. *De Imitatione* IV. v. 267 Beholde nowe thou arte made a preste and sacreyd to doo his holye mysterye. *a* **1548** HALL *Chron., Hen. IV* 9 b, Henry Plantagenet..was at Westminster with great solemnitee and royal pompe, sacred, enoynted and crouned King by the name of Kyng Henry the fourth. **1606** G. W[OODCOCKE] tr. *Justin, Epit. Emp.* Ll 5 b, Rodolph the second, eldest son of Maximilian, was sacred Emperour in the yeare 1577. **1631** WEEVER *Anc. Funeral Mon.* 251 Petronius was sacred to this Ecclesiasticall dignitie by Archbishop Honorius. *a* **1648** LD. HERBERT *Hen. VIII* (1683) 53 This Prince was Sacred (to use the French term) at Reymes 25 of January, 1515.

arch. **1976** N. ROBERTS *Face of France* xxv. 229 French kings, with rare exceptions have been sacred in Reims Cathedral.

b. Said of the vessel used in anointing. *rare*⁻¹.

1644 EVELYN *Diary* 6 June, The Holy Ampoule, the same with that which sacres their Kings at Rhemes, this being the one which anoynted Hen. IV.

c. To unite in the sacrament of marriage; to celebrate (a marriage).

c **1425** *Brut* 365 And þere the Bischop of Worcestre wedded & sacred ham to-gedir, as holy churche it wolde. *Ibid.* 368 þere was this lady weddid and sacryd to þe King of Denmark with moche solempnite. *c* **1440** *Jacob's Well* 53 And ȝif it [an unlawful marriage] be sacryd, þer owyth be lawe to be made a deuorce. **1485** CAXTON *Chas. Gt.* 198 And the bysshop sacred and blessed them.

3. To hallow, bless, sanctify, make holy.

c **1380** WYCLIF *Wks.* (1880) 480 ȝif freris founden wordis to sacre þe armes of a prest. *c* **1394** *P. Pl. Crede* 186 Seyntes y-sacred opon erþe. **1530** TINDALE *Answ. More* Wks. (1573) 253/1 The bishop sacreth the one [oyle] as well as the other. **1545** RAYNOLD *Byrth Mankynde* Prol. C j, To sacre, halow, yea and with theyr holye poeticall spiryte to breath ouer this booke. **1601** HOLLAND *Pliny* x. vi. I. 274 They vsually lay three egs, whereof they take one of them to sacre and blesse (as it were) the other eggs and the nest, and then soon after they cast it away. **1621** BP. MOUNTAGU *Diatribæ* 251 To thinke, that God had sacred that Number [ten] above all other. **1627-77** FELTHAM *Resolves* II. lix. 283 Prayer does sacre all our Actions.

4. a. To dedicate (a person) *to* a deity; chiefly *passive.*

13.. *E.E. Allit. P.* B. 1139 For when a sawele is saȝtled & sakred to dryȝtyn, He holly haldes hit his. *c* **1450** *Godstow Reg.* 49 With hys two dowhters there I-sacryd to god. **1621** BP. MOUNTAGU *Diatribæ* 514 A yeerely Feast was there kept in honour of Diana, whereat all the young maides in the Countrey aboue fiue yeeres old, and vnder ten, were sacred, and dedicated vnto Diana. *a* **1641** —— *Acts & Mon.* (1642) 204 He promiseth forgivenesse of sins by washings, and in this sort, as yet he sacreth men to Wittnes, where he signeth his soldiers in the forehead.

b. To dedicate (something) *to* (a particular person, a deity, or some special purpose).

c **1477** CAXTON *Jason* 84 b, Whan Jason..had sacred his shyp unto the Goddesse Pallas and to the goddesse of the see. **1513** DOUGLAS *Æneis* VI. i. 160 And, O thow blissit woman, onto the Wise walit men [I] sall dedicat and sacre. **1587** A. DAY *Daphnis & Chloe* (1890) 9 Diuers flutes.. which the auncient Shepheards had often totore-time sacred vnto the Nimphes for their greatest offrings. **1591** SYLVESTER *Du Bartas* I. v. 558 Here with solemn vowes I sacre Unto thy glory..My Heart and Art, my Voyse, Hand, Harp, and all. **1608** *Ibid.* II. iv. *Schisme* Ded. 12 This Tract I sacre unto Sackvil's Name. **1620** CAPT. SMITH *New Eng. Trials* Ep. Ded., How euer you please to dispose of him, that humbly sacreth himselfe and best abilities to his Countries good.

c. To make (a class of thing, as a tribe of animals, etc.) sacred *to* a deity.

1633 BP. HALL *Occas. Medit.* §65 The ancients have sacred this Bird [the owl] to wisdome.

5. To take a solemn oath. *rare*⁻¹.

c **1380** *Sir Ferumb.* 1405 'Ȝe', said he, 'þat wil y do, do say me now þy wille'. 'Þat wil y noȝt', quaþ sche þo, 'til þou me han sakred tille'. Þan Olyuer huld vp his hant; trewely for to holde By his power þat couenant.

6. *nonce-use.* To cremate as a religious act.

1665 SIR T. HERBERT *Trav.* (1677) 46 Their Funerals are of the old stamp..sacring the Corps to Ashes in a holy fire.

sacré (sakre), *v.*² [f. F. *sacré*, lit. 'sacred', used *ellipt.* as an oath.] *intr.* To utter the French exclamation 'sacré'.

1837 CARLYLE *Fr. Rev.* I. v. iv. 248 Vengeful Gardes Françaises, *sacreing*, with knit brows, start out on him. **1856** WHYTE MELVILLE *Kate Cov.* xxiii, The Frenchman *sacréed*, and fumed, and stormed.

sacre: see SACRY, SAKER, SAKRE.

sacrear, variant of SACRARY *Obs.*

sacred ('seɪkrɪd), *a.* and *sb.* Forms: see SACRE *v.* [f. SACRE *v.*¹ + -ED¹.

The original ppl. notion has (as the pronunciation indicates) disappeared from the use of the word, which is now nearly synonymous with the L. *sacer*. A similar change of meaning has taken place in the corresponding Romanic forms, F. *sacré* (which prob. influenced the English use), Sp., Pg. *sagrado*.]

A. *adj.*

† **1.** Of the Eucharistic elements: Consecrated.

c **1380** WYCLIF *Wks.* (1880) 465 But nou in þe reume of englond stryuen manye of þe sacrid oost. *c* **1450** *Mankind* 383 in *Macro Plays* 15 By cokkys body sakyrde, I haue such a peyn in my arme. *Ibid.* 605 For Cokkes body sakyrde, make space!

2. (Followed by *to.*) **a.** Consecrated *to*; esteemed especially dear or acceptable *to* a deity.

13.. *K. Alis.* 6777 That on [tree] to the sonne..That othir..Is sakret [*MS. Laud* sacrified] in the mone vertue. *c* **1407** LYDG. *Reson & Sens.* 4408 Two tren..The ton y-sacryd to the mone, The tother halwed to Phebus. *c* **1430** —— *Min. Poems* (Percy Soc.) 214 This fowle is sacred unto Jupiter. **1719** *Free-thinker* No. 116 ¶1 The First of May has been, and will be Sacred to Love in all polite Nations. **1788** LEMPRIÈRE *Classical Dict.* (1792) s.v. *Jupiter*, The oak is sacred to him because he first taught mankind to live upon acorns. **1874** DEUTSCH *Rem.* 439 The dove sacred to Venus.

b. Dedicated, set apart, exclusively appropriated *to* some person or some special purpose.

1667 MILTON *P.L.* III. 208 To destruction sacred and devote. *Ibid.* IX. 924 Had it bin onely coveting to Eye That sacred Fruit, sacred to abstinence. **1721** in *Collect. Epitaphs* (1802) 10 Sacred to the memory of Samuel Butler. **1729** BUTLER *Serm.* Wks. 1874 II. 79 The sacrifice being over, he retires alone to a solitude sacred to these occasions. **1784** COWPER *Task* VI. 571 Scenes Sacred to neatness and repose. **1811** PINKERTON *Mod. Geog., Egypt* (abr. ed. 3) 756 The papyrus, sacred to literature. **1821** SHELLEY *Epipsych.* 492 A pleasure-house Made sacred to his sister and his spouse. **1842** GWILT *Archit.* §245 The parts [of a Roman house] which were sacred to the use of the family were the peristyle [etc.].

3. a. Of things, places, of persons and their offices, etc.: Set apart for or dedicated to some religious purpose, and hence entitled to veneration or religious respect; made holy by association with a god or other object of worship; consecrated, hallowed.

1412-20 LYDG. *Chron. Troy* II. 3822 Reliques sacrid, þe holy eke vessels. **1590** SPENSER *F.Q.* II. xii. 37 Said then the Palmer; 'Lo! where does appeare The sacred soile where all our perills grow'. **1611** SHAKS. *Wint. T.* II. i. 183, I haue dispatch'd..To sacred Delphos, to Apollo's Temple, Cleomenes and Dion. **1678** CUDWORTH *Intell. Syst.* I. iv. 510 Some pools have been made sacred for their immense profundity and opacity. *a* **1704** T. BROWN *Lond. & Lacedem. Oracles* Wks. 1709 III. III. 147 Their [the Jewish Priests'] sacred Garments were of Linnen. **1744** AKENSIDE *Ode, On Leaving Holland* 36, I trace the village and the sacred spire. **1819** SCOTT *Ivanhoe* xxxiv, Thou art..one of those disorderly men, who, taking on them the sacred character without due cause, profane the holy rites. **1820** SHELLEY *Hymn Merc.* lxxxviii, By sacred Styx a mighty oath to swear. **1839** THIRLWALL *Greece* VI. 77 A circular building, called the Philippeum,..within the sacred precincts in which the Olympic games were celebrated. **1857** WILKINSON *Egypt Time of Pharaohs* 9 The sacred boats of the dead. **1883** H. YULE in *Encycl. Brit.* XV. 330/2 Thus the Bo-tree (or pippal), so sacred among the Buddhists of Ceylon, is still cherished near mosques. **1885** J. H. MIDDLETON *ibid.* XIX. 607/2 The other [vase], from

Cyprus, has the Assyrian sacred tree, with similar guardian animals.

b. *sacred book, writing*, etc.: one of those in which the laws and teachings of a religion are embodied. *sacred history*: the history contained in the Bible. *sacred number*: a number (esp. seven) to which is attributed a peculiar depth of significance in religious symbolism. *sacred poetry*: poetry concerned with religious themes. *sacred music*: music which accompanies sacred words or which has a certain solemn character of its own. *sacred concert*: a concert of sacred music. *Sacred Blood*, the blood of Christ. *sacred orders* [eccl. L. *ordines sacri*], the holy or major orders.

1593 SHAKS. *2 Hen. VI*, I. iii. 61 His Weapons [are] holy Sawes of sacred Writ. *a* **1604** HANMER *Chron. Irel.* (1633) 59 Who for the space of certaine yeeres, brought him up in sacred letters. **1629** MILTON *Christs Nativ.* iii, Say Heav'nly Muse, shall not thy sacred vein Afford a present to the Infant God? **1697** DRYDEN *Virg. Bucol.* IV. 5 The last great age, foretold by sacred rhymes, Renews its finish'd course. **1709–29** V. MANDEY *Syst. Math., Arith.* 8 Seven is a Sacred Number, chiefly used in Holy Scripture. [**1709** J. BINGHAM *Origines Ecclesiasticæ* II. III. i. 9 The Clergy of the Superior Orders are commonly called the ἱερώμενοι Holy and Sacred, as in Socrates and others.] **1726** J. AYLIFFE *Parergon* 184 The first [*sc.* sub-deacons, deacons, and priests] the Canon Law..stiles Sacred Orders. **1781** COWPER *Hope* 449 The sacred book no longer suffers wrong, Bound in the fetters of an unknown tongue. **1784** —— *Task* VI. 634 Ten thousand sit Patiently present at a sacred song. **1832** *Rep. Sel. Comm. Dramatic Lit. with Minutes of Evidence* 50 in *Parl. Papers 1831–2* VII. 1, I thought it would be a better thing to represent plays than to give a pretended sacred concert. **1836** *Penny Cycl.* VI. 374/1 The clerical orders of the Catholic church are divided into two classes, *sacred* and *minor* orders. **1845** *Encycl. Metrop.* IX. Sub-introd. 73 Sacred History is that narrative of events, commencing from the creation of the world, which is recorded in the Bible, and is so called, because it is assumed to be written under divine superintendence, and is evidently associated with the being, perfections, and plans of Deity. **1853** (*title*) Catalogue of the Library of the Sacred Harmonic Society. *a* **1854** H. REED *Lect. Eng. Lit.* vi. (1878) 211 The relation in which sacred poetry stands to revealed teaching and Holy Writ. **1862** in N. Longmate *Hungry Mills* (1978) viii. 113 Never was so much sacred music heard upon the streets of Manchester as during the last few months. **1877** MONIER WILLIAMS *Hinduism* i. 13 India..has only one sacred language and only one sacred literature, accepted and revered by all adherents of Hinduism alike. **1884** ADDIS & ARNOLD *Cath. Dict.* 622/1 The orders of bishop, priest, deacon, and (but only since the thirteenth century) subdeacon are called sacred' or 'greater'. **1900** *Cornish Echo* 30 Mar. 4/4 Wesley Chapel Falmouth. *Sacred Concert* by Truro Wesleyan Church Choir. **1901** PROCTER & FRERE *Prayer Bk.* xvi. 650 The Sacramentary of Serapion gives forms of ordination only for the three sacred orders. **1920** WODEHOUSE *Jill the Reckless* (1922) xvi. 230 It is the custom of the dwellers in Atlantic City..to attend a species of vaudeville performances—incorrectly termed a sacred concert—on Sunday nights. **1922** CHESTERTON *Ballad of St. Barbara* p. vii, In the grey rocks the burning blossom Glowed terrible as the sacred blood. **1934** *Daily Gleaner* 5 Jan. 21/2 *Sacred Concert*..A fine programme of sacred songs, instrumental music and recitations will be presented at St. Thomas' Church, Bath, on Sunday. **1950** *Cornishman* 12 Jan. 4/2 Sacred Concert by Ludgvan Male Choir with Elise Harvey, guest soloist. **1965** *New Statesman* 19 Nov. 794/3 We are made aware of the ideas of the period—notably the Pope's own contributions to the Franciscan v. Dominican battle about the Sacred Blood. **1978** *Listener* 24 Aug. 244/4 By 1733 Bach had written the vast majority of his sacred music.

c. *rarely* of a deity: Venerable, holy.

1697 DRYDEN *Virg. Georg.* III. 461 Now, sacred Pales, in a lofty Strain I sing the Rural Honours of thy Reign.

d. Applied as a specific defining adj. to various animals and plants that are or have been considered sacred to certain deities.

1783 LATHAM *Synopsis Birds* I. II. 526 Sacred Cuckow... Inhabits Malabar, where the natives hold it sacred. **1790** J. WHITE *Jrnl. Voy. N.S. Wales* 193 We this day shot the Sacred Kings-Fisher. **1840** tr. *Cuvier's Anim. Kingd.* 243 The Sacred Ibis (*I. religiosa*). **1866** *Treas. Bot.* 120/2 Bamboo, sacred, of the Chinese, *Nandina domestica*. *Ibid.* 781/2 *Nelumbium speciosum*, the Sacred Lotus. **1870** NICHOLSON *Man. Zool.* lxxxiii. (1875) 657 The Sacred Monkey of the Hindoos (*Semnopithecus entellus*). **1877** J. GIBSON in *Encycl. Brit.* VI. 131/2 The Sacred Beetle of Egypt, *Ateuchus sacer*. **1879** C. P. JOHNSON *ibid.* IX. 154/2 The Sacred Fig, Pippul, or Bo, *Ficus religiosa*.

4. *transf.* and *fig.* Regarded with or entitled to respect or reverence similar to that which attaches to holy things.

1560 DAUS tr. *Sleidane's Comm.* 247 In so sacred a senate [*sc.* the Council of Trent: orig. *in tam augusto conventu*]. **1591** SHAKS. *1 Hen. VI*, IV. i. 40 He..Doth but vsurpe the Sacred name of Knight, Prophaning this most Honourable Order. **1596** —— *Tam. Shr.* I. i. 181 Sacred and sweet was all I saw in her. *a* **1645** WALLER *At Pens-hurst* II. 26 Goe boye and carve this passion on the barke Of yonder tree, which stands the sacred marke Of noble Sidneys birth. **1656** COWLEY *Misc., On Death of Crashaw* 2 Poet and Saint! to thee alone are giv'n The two most sacred Names of Earth and Heav'n. **1712** STEELE *Spect.* No. 456 ¶3 There is something sacred in Misery to great and good Minds. **1754** GRAY *Progr. Poesy* 94 Ope the sacred source of sympathetic Tears. **1813** SHELLEY *Q. Mab* IV. 108 Ere he can lisp his mother's sacred name. **1842** BROWNING *K. Vict. & K. Chas.* 1st Yr. 11, Ay, call this parting—death! The sacreder your memory becomes. **1853** C. BRONTE *Villette* xxi, To a feather-brained school-girl nothing is sacred. **1863** HAWTHORNE *Our Old Home* II. 114 But the most sacred objects of all [at Greenwich Hospital] are two of Nelson's coats, under separate glass cases. **1878** R. W. DALE *Lect. Preach.* ix. 292 To you America must be sacred as well as Judea.

b. *esp.* as an epithet of royalty. Now chiefly *Hist.* or *arch.*; formerly often in the phrase ***His (her, your) most Sacred Majesty***.

1590 SHAKS. *Com. Err.* v. i. 133 Iustice most sacred Duke against the Abbesse. **1599** —— *Hen. V*, I. ii. 7 God and his Angels guard your sacred Throne, And make you long become it. **1634** FORD *Perk. Warbeck* III. iv, Sacred King, Be deafe to his knowne malice! **1639** MRQ. OF HAMILTON in *H. Papers* (Camden) I. 76 Most sacred Souuraigne. *a* **1645** WALLER *Danger His Majesty Escaped* 54 Yet the bold Britans still securely row'd, Charles and his vertue was their sacred load. **1726** SWIFT *Gulliver* I. vii, That his sacred Majesty, and the Council, who are your Judges, were [etc.]. **1757** *Acts Gen. Assembly Georgia* (1881) 127 We therefore pray your most Sacred Majesty that it may be Enacted.

c. in sarcastic use.

1820 SHELLEY *Œdipus* I. 5 And these most sacred nether promontories Lie satisfied with layers of fat. *Ibid.* II. i. 107 That her most sacred Majesty should be Invited to attend the feast of Famine. **1865** M. ARNOLD *Ess. Crit.* Pref. 17 To obtain from Mr. Bentham's executors a sacred bone of his great, dissected Master.

5. a. Secured by religious sentiment, reverence, sense of justice, or the like, against violation, infringement, or encroachment.

1530 PALSGR. 696/2 Touch it nat, it is sacred. *a* **1548** HALL *Chron., Edw. V* 8 b, Syth that tyme, was neuer so vndeuoute a kynge that euer enterprised that sacred priuilege to violate. **1603** SHAKS. *Meas. for M.* IV. iii. 149, I am combined by a sacred Vow. **1667** SOUTH *Serm.* (1697) II. 29 The sacredest Bonds which the Conscience of Man can be bound with. **1682** SIR T. BROWNE *Chr. Mor.* III. §19 Let thy Oaths be sacred. **1781** COWPER *Charity* 28 The rights of man were sacred in his view. **1793** HORSLEY *Serm.* (1811) 187 Maintaining what in the new vocabulary of modern democracy is named the sacred right of insurrection. **1849** MACAULAY *Hist. Eng.* vi. II. 139 He assured them that their property would be held sacred. **1855** *Ibid.* xii. III. 210 Strong desires and resentments which he mistook for sacred duties.

transf. **1697** DRYDEN *Virg. Georg.* IV. 280 No buzzing Sounds disturb their Golden Sleep, 'Tis sacred Silence all.

b. Of a person (hence of his office): Having a religiously secured immunity from violence or attachment; sacrosanct, inviolable.

1565 COOPER *Thesaurus, Sacrosancta potestas*, the sacred and vnuiolable power of the Tribunes. **1618** BOLTON *Florus* I. v. (1636) 14 The Augurship became sacred among the Romans. **1879** FROUDE *Cæsar* v. 48 The persons of Saturninus and Glaucia were doubly sacred, for one was tribune and the other prætor.

c. With *from*: Protected by some sanction *from* injury or incursion.

1788 GIBBON *Decl. & F.* xl. IV. 63 No place was safe or sacred from their depredations. **1845** STEPHEN *Comm. Laws Eng.* (1874) II. 479 He is himself sacred from punishment of every description. **1847** TENNYSON *Princess* II. 152 Lapt In the arms of leisure, sacred from the blight Of ancient influence and scorn.

d. *fig.* Devoted to some purpose, not to be lightly intruded upon or handled.

1867 BAKER *Nile Tribut.* i. 15 Thus I had a supply when every water-skin was empty, and on the last day I divided my sacred stock amongst the men.

6. Accursed. [After L. *sacer*; freq. translating or in allusion to Virgil's *auri saca fames* (*Æn.* III. 57).] Now *rare*.

1588 SHAKS. *Tit. A.* II. i. 120 Our Empresse with her sacred wit To villainie and vengance consecrate. **1596** SPENSER *F.Q.* v. xii. 1 O sacred hunger of ambitious mindes. **1600** DEKKER *Fortunatus* Wks. 1873 I. 95 If through golds sacred hunger thou dost pine. **1615** G. SANDYS *Trav.* 122 Hither the sacred thirst of gaine..allureth the aduenturous merchant. **1700** DRYDEN *Cock & Fox* 254 For sacred hunger of my Gold I die. **1728–46** THOMSON *Spring* 124 A feeble race! yet oft The sacred sons of vengeance; on whose course Corrosive famine waits, and kills the year. **1864** BURTON *Scot. Abr.* II. i. 62 Smitten with a sacred rage for topography.

7. Special collocations. †**sacred artery** (see quot.). **sacred axe**, a mark on Chinese porcelain, supposed to designate warriors. **sacred band**, *Gr. Hist.*, a body consisting of 300 young nobles, who formed part of the permanent military force of Thebes from B.C. 379. **sacred bark** [Sp. *cáscara sagrada*], the bark of *Rhamnus Purshianus* of California, used as a tonic aperient. **sacred circle**, an exclusive company, an élite. **sacred college** (see COLLEGE *sb.* 1). **sacred egoism** = SACRO EGOISMO. †**sacred elixir** = *sacred tincture*. †**Sacred Empire**, the Holy Roman Empire. **sacred fire** [L. *sacer ignis*, see HOLY FIRE], erysipelas. **sacred malady** [L. *sacer morbus*], epilepsy (*Syd. Soc. Lex.* 1897). **sacred month, place** (see quots.). †**sacred tincture** [= mod.L. *tinctura sacra*: see Chambers *Cycl. Supp.* (1753) s.v. *Aloes*], a preparation of rhubarb and aloes. †**sacred vein** [L. *vena sacra*] (see quot.). **Sacred War** (see WAR). **sacred way**, a route used by religious processions, pilgrims, etc.

1656 BLOUNT *Glossogr.* s.v. *Artery*, **Sacred Artery*, a branch of the great Arteries descendent branch, goes to the Marrow which is in the *Os Sacrum*. **1866** CHAFFERS *Marks Pottery & Porcelain* (ed. 2) 389 The *sacred axe; a [Chinese] mark found on green porcelain. **1868** J. MARRYAT *Pottery & Porcelain* ix. (ed. 3) 274 The sacred axe is assigned to warriors. **1770** LANGHORNE *Plutarch's Lives, Pelopidas* II. 335 Gorgidas as some say, first formed the **sacred band.* **1891** *Century Dict.*, **Sacred bark.* **1897** in *Syd. Soc. Lex.* **1939** *Country Life* 11 Feb. 156/1 The courses, however, which have been admitted into this *sacred circle—Westward Ho! for the Amateur Championship, Carnoustie for the Open, and Troon and St. Anne's for both meetings, have all been of a certain ancient standing. **1928** H. W. SCHNEIDER *Making Fascist State* i. 11 Salandra's policy of '*sacred egoism', of bargaining with both sides to see who would promise Italy the most for her neutrality, is both disgraceful and useless. **1970** R. A. H. ROBINSON *Origins of Franco's Spain* iv. 186 Aguirre still pursued a policy of sacred egoism and held aloof from non-Basque causes. **1797** *Encycl. Brit.* (ed. 3) XVI. 591/1 **Sacred Elixir.* **1811** A. T. THOMSON *Lond. Disp.* (1818) 660 Tincture of Rhubarb and Aloes; formerly, Sacred Elixir. **1617** MORYSON *Itin.* I. 284 It was decreed..that hereafter in the *sacred Empire the under written pieces of money should be coyned. **1693** *Emilianne's Hist. Monast. Ord.* xiv. 127 In the year 1089.. the *Sacred Fire.., having spread it self into several parts of Europe. **1872** W. N. MOLESWORTH *Hist. Eng.* II. 361 Among the other expedients that had been suggested in this convention [of Chartist delegates, 1838] was that of observing what was called a '*sacred month', during which the working classes throughout the whole kingdom were to abstain from every kind of labour, in the hope of compelling the governing classes to concede the charter. **1727–52** CHAMBERS *Cycl.* s.v., In the civil law, **sacred* place chiefly denotes that, where a person deceased has been interred. **1797** *Encycl. Brit.* (ed. 3) XIV. 393/1 Aloetic wine, or *sacred tincture. **1656** BLOUNT *Glossogr.* s.v. *Vein*, **Sacred vein* (*vena sacra*) the second branch of the flank veine running to the *Os sacrum*, and thence getting this name. **1884** A. LANG in M. Hunt tr. *Grimm's Household Tales* I. p. xiv, Amber and jade and slaves were carried half across the world by the old trade-routes and *sacred ways. **1910** *Encycl. Brit.* II. 883/2 The chain..of Aegaleos, through a depression in which was the line of the sacred way, where the torchlight processions from Athens used to descend to the coast. **1937** G. MITCHELL *Come away, Death* i. 31 Now we go to Eleusis along the Sacred Way, to penetrate the meaning of the Mysteries. **1971** GARSIDE & WILKINS tr. *Ceram's Gods, Graves & Scholars* (ed. 2) xxiii. 292 The Sacred Way of Babylon ran..from the outer city walls to the Gate of Ishtar.

†**B.** *sb. pl.* [after L. *sacra* neut. pl.] *Obs.*

1. Sacred rites or solemnities.

1624 HEYWOOD *Gunaik.* 26 Her Sacreds and Festivalls were called Angeronalia. **1665** J. WEBB *Stone-Heng* (1725) 60 They might..also behold whatever Sacreds were solemnized within the Court of their great Jupiter Capitolinus. **1669** GALE *Crt. Gentiles* I. II. iii. 35 These Sacreds were first celebrated in the East by these She-priests of Bacchus. **1741** WATTS *Improv. Mind* I. iii. §3 By his manuscripts we are more acquainted in this last century with the Turkish sacreds than any one had ever informed us. **1749** *Phil. Trans.* XLVI. 216 The Romans became extremely fond of the Mithriac Sacreds.

2. Things consecrated or offered in sacrifice to the gods.

1608 TOPSELL *Serpents* 24 This snake the holy dishes.. Did hast to touch, like as it would the sacreds tast. **1624** HEYWOOD *Gunaik.* I. 47 The sacreds that were made to these, were by such as having escaped any dangerous desease, or pestilent sicknesse, had bin spared by the fates.

3. Sacred utensils or vessels.

1665 J. WEBB *Stone-Heng* (1725) 219 The Heads of Bulls ..have been found in and about our Antiquity, together with other Sacreds peculiarly appertaining to the Ministration of Their Idolatrous Rites. **1669** GALE *Crt. Gentiles* I. I. x. 56 Hieroglyphic Leters, i.e. Leters engraven in sacreds.

sacred cow. [f. SACRED *a.* + COW *sb.*[1]]

1. The cow as an object of veneration amongst Hindus.

1891 J. L. KIPLING *Beast & Man in India* vi. 116 The Muhammedan..creed is in opposition to theirs [*sc.* the Hindus] and there are rankling memories of a thousand insults to it wrought on the sacred cow. **1972** E. J. SHARPE in Hinnells & Sharpe *Hinduism* xxxvii. 121 As every visitor to India knows, the 'sacred cow' is not as a rule particularly well looked after. **1979** E. H. GOMBRICH *Sense of Order* vi. 167 The couch in Tutankhamun's tomb..was shaped like a sacred cow, ready to carry the pharaoh into the other life.

2. *fig.* (orig. *U.S.*). **a.** *Journalism.* (*a*) someone who must not be criticized; (*b*) copy that must not be altered or cut.

1910 *Atlantic Monthly* Mar. 308/1 In the office these corporations were jocularly referred to as 'sacred cows'. **1922** U. SINCLAIR *They call me Carpenter* xxvi. 92 It doesn't matter, because I couldn't use the story. Mr. Stebbins is one of our 'sacred cows'. **1923** O. G. VILLARD *Some Newspapers* 143 The editors gave me their word that there is..no list of men to be attacked and no 'sacred cows' (i.e., favourites to be spared) in their shop. **1936** W. E. HALL *Reporting News* 430 Sacred cow—copy which is not to be changed or cut. **1940** R. E. GARST *Headlines & Deadlines* 206 *Sacred cow*, slang for a subject or story in which the publisher or higher editors are interested and which must be printed. **1973** B. BROADFOOT *Ten Lost Years* xxxi. 351 Newspapers had a lot more sacred cows than they do now.

b. An idea, institution, etc., unreasonably held to be immune from questioning or criticism.

1936 M. MITCHELL *Gone with Wind* xiii. 240, I think of my brother, living among the sacred cows of Charleston, and most reverent towards them. **1955** *Bull. Atomic Sci.* Feb. 62/2 The need for widespread secrecy has become a sacred cow, a belief hedged by the deepest emotions and accepted without question by many Americans. **1961** L. MUMFORD *City in Hist.* vi. 182 Economic exploitation, slavery, war, specialized life-time labor... Plato's polis relied for daily meat and drink on these sacred but diseased cows. **1962** *Listener* 5 July 10/2 Business is the 'sacred cow' here. **1963** *Richmond* (Va.) *Times-Dispatch* 16 Dec. 19/1 Military bases ..are sacred cows in Congress. **1967** COULTHARD & SMITH in Wills & Yearsley *Handbk. Managem. Technol.* 207 A new movement, variously described as 'management by objectives', 'improving management performance' or 'performance planning', now promises to sweep away some of the 'sacred cows' of management development. **1971** *Country Life* 4 Nov. 1223/3 By clearing away any sacred-cow reputation clinging to the master he stirs the reader to look for himself. **1978** *Maledicta* 1977 I. 111 He has for many years attacked most of their sacred cows and revealed them to be dry and motheaten skins. **1978** L. HEREN *Growing up on The Times* iv. 152, I was not an Establishment man. I had often caused trouble for the paper because of my refusal to give proper obeisance to sacred cows.

Sacred Heart. **1.** The heart of Jesus, regarded as an object of devotion; similarly, ***Sacred Heart of Mary***. ***Feast of the Sacred Heart*** (R.C. Ch.), a festival observed on the Friday in the week following Corpus Christi; also *ellipt.*

1765 (*title*) The devotion to the Sacred Heart of Jesus. **1793** J. BERINGTON in *Panzani's Memoirs* p. xxxii, He might be busied in preparing a gay posey of devotion to the *sacred heart of Mary*. **1823** C. BUTLER *Contin. A. Butler's Lives Saints* 228 The devotion to the sacred Heart was sanctioned by all the prelates of the neighbouring country. **1833** M. ARUNDELL *Let.* 30 June (1894) vii. 47/2 You will pity me however confined to a sick bed during all my favourite feasts, Whit-Sunday, Corpus Christi, Sacred Heart! **1853** J. B. DALGAIRNS *Devotion to Heart of Jesus* i. 59 Symbols, which are also realities, as the Sacred Hearts of Jesus and Mary, the Five Wounds, or the Precious Blood of our Lord. **1881** G. M. HOPKINS *Sermons* (1959) 100 (*heading*) For Sunday June 26 1881 being the Sunday.. nearest the Feast of the Sacred Heart (which this year is to be kept on Monday the 27th). **1924** E. LEAHY tr. *Bainvel's Devotion to Sacred Heart* II. ii. 103 To St Margaret Mary and her revelations is really due the inception of the devotion to the Sacred Heart in the form that has received the Church's sanction. **1945** J. BETJEMAN *New Bats in Old Belfries* 25 As Thy Sacred Heart displays Lush Kildare of scented meadows, Roscommon, thin in ash tree shadows,.. Kneeling all in silver haze? **1967** K.-H. & B. KRUGER tr. *Rahner's Theol. Investigations* III. xxii. 331 The Sacred Heart devotion in the doctrine and practice of the Church both past and present manifests itself under many aspects and forms. **1977** B. LUCAS tr. *De Foucauld's Lett. from Desert* iv. 69, I was determined to write ..to tell you how close I shall be to you on the feast of the sacred Heart.

2. *transf.* **a.** A form of prayer used in private devotions to the Sacred Heart.

1815 J. MILNER in F. C. Husenbeth *Life J. Milner* (1862) xvi. 288 Spiritual Reading afternoon.—Grace, Rosary, Sacred Heart. **1881** G. M. HOPKINS *Sermons* (1959) 102 When we say the Sacred Heart it is of Christ himself we are thinking and not of his heart only.

b. A devotional picture of the Sacred Heart.

1931 *Jrnl. Amer. Folk-Lore* XLIV. 413 Pictures of Saints, etc., are used also [in voodoo magic in America]... Sacred Heart of Jesus. For organic diseases. **1941** A. WHITE *Let.* 22 Mar. in *Hound & Falcon* (1965) 108, I prefer the Catholic Church with all the awful Sacred Hearts and Little Flowers and the rest to the still more awful bleak 'tastefulness' of the others. **1977** M. KENYON *Rapist* iv. 40 Above the door.. hung the Sacred Heart in lurid primaries.

3. Used as (part of) the name of several religious orders and of schools run by them; freq. *attrib.* and *ellipt.*

1885 H. JAMES *Little Tour in France* iii. 22 The modern buildings (of the Sacred Heart).. are in the vulgar taste which seems doomed to stamp itself on all new Catholic work. **1907** E. WHARTON *Fruit of Tree* ii. 20 A girl who was at the Sacred Heart in Paris with me. **1919** T. S. ELIOT *Sweeney among Nightingales* in *Poems*, The nightingales are singing near The Convent of the Sacred Heart. **1965** A. WHITE *Hound & Falcon* 20 Even in my day Tunbridge Wells was always said to be much less strict... [*Note*] Another Sacred Heart convent. **1973** *Guardian* 25 Apr. 15/3 Mr Joe Faye.. of the Sacred Heart School, Redcar... The 12-man governing board of Sacred Heart (a Catholic maintained school.) **1974** V. CANNING *Mask of Memory* i. 19 Gave the sweets to the Sacred Heart children on the beach.

sacredly ('seɪkrɪdlɪ), *adv.* [-LY².]

1. With religious or strict care; inviolably; with rigid attention to the truth.

1561 T. NORTON *Calvin's Inst.* I. viii. (1634) 26 The originall booke [of the Law] itselfe was appointed to be sacredly kept in the Temple. *a* **1677** HALE *Prim. Orig. Man.* II. i. 130 Authors.. kept sacredly and inviolably in certain Archives. **1706** HEARNE *Collect.* 14 Jan. (O.H.S.) I. 163 Observing these Oaths.. sacredly. **1871** MACDUFF *Mem. Patmos* ix. 112 The sealing further implied that its contents were sacredly locked and concealed from public gaze.

2. In a sacred or religious manner.

1694 POMFRET *On Death Q. Mary* 137 Next mighty Pan, was her illustrious Lord, His high Vicegerent, sacredly ador'd. **1884** *Chr. Commw.* 20 Mar. 535/2 [Paul's] only offering was the sum total of his Gentile converts, whom he sacredly and joyfully offered unto God.

sacredness ('seɪkrɪdnɪs). [-NESS.] The condition or quality of being sacred (see the adj.).

1681–6 J. SCOTT *Chr. Life* II. vii. Wks. 1698 I. 416 When we consider how he is secluded by the infinite sacredness of his own Majesty from all immediate converse and intercourse with us. **1689** *Consid. Success. & Alleg.* 33 The Sacredness of an Oath makes it a strong Tie to bind us. **1797** MRS. RADCLIFFE *Italian* xvi, Ellena immediately admitted the sacredness of the promise which she had formerly given. **1856** FROUDE *Hist. Eng.* (1858) I. iv. 349 Such was the mystical sacredness which clung about the ordained clergy. **1868** J. S. MILL in *Morn. Star* 13 Mar., The sacredness of property is connected, in my mind, with feelings of the greatest respect. **1885** *Law Times* LXXX. 111/1 When the rule was first invented there was a sort of reason for it, as a certain sacredness attached to real estate.

sacrefice, -fis(e, -fy, obs. ff. SACRIFICE, -FY.

sacreit: see SACRE *v.* and SECRET *a.*

sacrelage, -leger, -legie, obs. ff. SACRILEGE, SACRILEGER, SACRILEGY.

sacreng, sacret, obs. ff. SACRING, SAKERET.

sacri, sacrid: see SACRE *v.*

† **sa'cricolist.** *Obs.*$^{-0}$ [f. L. *sacricol-a* sacrificer (formed as next + *col-ĕre* to tend, worship) + -IST.] (See quot.)

1727 BAILEY vol. II, *Sacricolist*, a devout Worshipper.

† **sa'criferous,** *a. Obs. rare*$^{-0}$. [f. L. *sacrifer*, f. *sacri-*, *sacer* sacred (*sacra* neut. pl., sacrifices) + *-fer*: see -FEROUS.] (See quot.)

1656 BLOUNT *Glossogr.*, *Sacriferous*, that bears holy things.

† **sacri'fiable,** *a. Obs. rare.* [a. F. *sacrifiable*, f. *sacrifier*: see SACRIFY *v.*] = SACRIFICABLE.

1603 FLORIO *Montaigne* I. xxix, For these wretched sacrifiable people.. all ful of glee, singing, and dancing with the rest, they present themselves to the slaughter.

† **sa'crific,** *a.*¹ *Obs. rare*$^{-0}$. [ad. L. *sacrificus*, f. *sacri-*, *sacer* sacred (*sacra* neut. pl., sacrifices) + *-ficus*: see -FIC.] = SACRIFICAL.

1727 BAILEY vol. II, *Sacrifick*, used in Sacrifices.

sa'crific, *a.*² *Anat. rare.* [f. mod.L. SACR-UM + -FIC.] 'Entering into the composition of the sacrum: as, a sacrific vertebra' (*Cent. Dict.* 1891).

sacrificable (stress variable), *a. rare.* [f. L. *sacrificāre* to sacrifice, f. *sacrific-us* SACRIFIC *a.*: see -ABLE.] Capable of being offered as a sacrifice; also, rightly or properly to be sacrificed.

1646 SIR T. BROWNE *Pseud. Ep.* v. xiv. (1658) 310 Yet might it [Jephthah's vow] be restrained in the sence, for whatsoever was sacrificable, and justly subject to lawfull immolation. **1973** *N.Y. Law Jrnl.* 27 Feb., No citizen's individuality is sacrificable to expediency.

† **sa'crifical,** *a. Obs.* [ad. L. *sacrificālis*, f. *sacrific-us* SACRIFIC: see -AL¹.] Pertaining to or employed in sacrifice.

1608 PANKE *Fal of Babel* 28 The blessed chalice of the aultar.. hath the verie sacrifical blood in it that was shed vpon the Crosse. **1686** WAKE *Expos. Doctr. Ch. Eng.* 65 When we examine the first Institution of this holy Communion, we cannot perceive either in the words or action of our Blessed Saviour, any Sacrifical Act or Expression. **1756** WATSON in *Phil. Trans.* XLIX. 502 A priestess of Bacchus, which in one hand holds the sacrifical knife. **1796** BURKE *Regic. Peace* iii. Wks. 1802 IV. 510 The sacrifical ministers (who were a sort of intruders in the worship of the new divinity).

sacrificant (sə'krɪfɪkənt). *rare.* [ad. L. *sacrificant-em*, pr. pple. of *sacrificāre*: see SACRIFY *v.*] One who offers up as a sacrifice.

1665 J. WEBB *Stone-Heng* (1725) 103 The Sacrificants might.. behold both the Altar and Signum. **1885** J. FITZGERALD tr. *Schultze's Fetichism* vi. §7 The sacrificant takes away the flesh of the victim.

sacrifi'cation. *rare*$^{-1}$. [ad. L. *sacrificātion-em*, n. of action of *sacrificāre*: see SACRIFY *v.*] The action of making a sacrificial offering.

1694 MOTTEUX *Rabelais* v. (1737) 232 And to kind Nature make Sacrification.

sacrificator ('sækrɪfɪkeɪtə(r)). *rare.* [a. L. *sacrificātor*, agent-n. f. *sacrificāre*: see SACRIFY *v.* Cf. F. *sacrificateur*.] One who sacrifices. Also *fig.*

? **1548** tr. *Viret's Expos. XII Art. Chr. Faith* E j b, He is called Christe bycause of the same oyntment, by the whyche he hathe ordeyned hym prophete, kynge, and sacrificatour. **1646** SIR T. BROWNE *Pseud. Ep.* v. xiv. 255 It is not probable the Priests.. would have permitted it, and that not onely in regard of the subject or sacrifice it selfe, but also the sacrificator. **1818** BENTHAM *Ch. Eng.*, *Ch. Eng. Catech. Exam.* 361 The Noble Reformer, in the character of Arch-Sacrificator. **1859** *All Year Round* No. 28. 30 Here was evidently a grand Sacrificator, and an unexceptionable Altar.

So † **'sacrificatory** *a.*, sacrificing, belonging to sacrifice. † **'sacrificature,** the office or function of sacrificing.

1581 J. BELL *Haddon's Answ. Osor.* 344 He seeth no markette of pardons,.. no sacrificatory masses. **1593** NASHE *Christ's T.* 22 The sky-perfuming prayers, & profuse sacrificatory expences of ful-hand oblationers. **1612** W. SCLATER *Minister's Portion* 9 A second sort [of tithes] which wee may call sacrificatory. **1699** BURNET 39 *Art.* vii. (1700) 99 Those Sacrificatory Phrases that they use in speaking of the Messiah. **1779** HORNE *Disc.* (1799) I. 107 Such were the ritual observances regarding sacrificature. *a* **1812** MCLEAN *Comm. Heb.* x. (1847) II. 80 The sacrifice of Christ's body once offered has for ever abrogated the whole of the Mosaic sacrificature. **1827** G. S. FABER *Orig. Expiat. Sacr.* 64 This grossly-corrupt mode of sacrificature is alluded to and justly castigated by Solomon.

sacrifice ('sækrɪfaɪs), *sb.* Forms: 3–5 sacrifise, sacrefice, -fise, 4 sacrifijs, -fies, -fys(e, sacrefis, -fyse, saker-, sacerfyse, sacrafies, -fyse, 4–5 sacrafice, 4–6 sacrifis, 5 sacrafise, sacryfyce, sacurfyce, 5–6 sacrifyce, 6 sacryfice, 4– sacrifice. [a. F. *sacrifice* (12th c. in Hatz.-Darm.) = Pr. *sacrifici*, Sp., Pg. *sacrificio*, It. *sagrifizio*, ad. L. *sacrificium*, f. *sacrific-us* SACRIFIC *a.*]

1. a. Primarily, the slaughter of an animal (often including the subsequent consumption of it by fire) as an offering to God or a deity. Hence, in wider sense, the surrender to God or a deity, for the purpose of propitiation or homage, of some object of possession. Also applied *fig.* to the offering of prayer, thanksgiving, penitence, submission, or the like. Phrases, † ***to do, make sacrifice***; also, † ***to put in sacrifice***, to devote as a sacrificial victim.

In the primary use, a 'sacrifice' implies an 'altar' on which the victim is placed. Hence the figurative uses are often associated with references to a metaphorical altar.

a **1300** *Cursor M.* 1064 And for his offrand was Rightwys, Godd tok to quen [*read* queme] his sacrifijs. *Ibid.* 3142 Bot now es he asked,.. Til godd til make of sacrifise. *c* **1300** *St. Margarete* 92 And wende to his false godes, to do sacrifise. **1340** *Ayenb.* 187 þer byeþ manie men.. makeþ sacrefices naȝt to god. **1390** GOWER *Conf.* III. 250 He let do make a riche feste With a sollempne Sacrifise In Phebus temple. *a* **1450** MYRC *Festial* 205 Then sawe Maudelen mony pepyll comyng towart þe tempyll and þe lorde of þat contre, forto haue don ofryng and sacrefise to hor mawmetys. **1471** CAXTON *Recuyell* (Sommer) I. 304 By this edicte.. many estrangers nobles and other were putte in sacrefice and had their blood shedde in egipte. **1526** *Pilgr. Perf.* (W. de W. 1531) 195 Yᵉ sayd women called & entyced the iewes to theyr sacrifices. *c* **1595** CAPT. WYATT *R. Dudley's Voy. W. Ind.* (Hakl. Soc.) 42 Wee did dailie aborde make sacrifice to God, in great devotion calling upon Him in hartie prayer for them. **1687** A. LOVELL tr. *Thevenot's Trav.* III. 65 Their Sacrifices are never bloody. **1727–41** CHAMBERS *Cycl.* s.v., Divines divide Sacrifices into bloody, such as those of the old law; and bloodless, such as those of the new law. **1774** PENNANT *Tour Scot. in 1772*, 181 An altar for sacrifices to the immortal gods. **1876** J. P. NORRIS *Rudim. Theol.* II. i. 147 Sin cannot be undone without Suffering; and we find Sacrifice instituted to give continual expression to it.

† **b.** A slaying as for a sacrifice. *Obs. rare*$^{-1}$.

1585 T. WASHINGTON tr. *Nicholay's Voy.* I. xxi. 27 b, A cruel sacryfice vppon the person of Iohn Chabas.

2. That which is offered in sacrifice; a victim immolated on the altar; anything (material or immaterial) offered to God or a deity as an act of propitiation or homage.

c **1250** *Kent. Serm.* in *O.E. Misc.* 27 Stor þet me offrede wylem be þo ialde laghe to here godes sacrefise. *a* **1325** *Prose Psalter* l. 18 [li. 17] Trubled gost is sacrifice to God. **13..** *E.E. Allit. P.* B. 507 Noe.. heuened vp an auter & halȝed hit fayre, & sette a sakerfyse þer-on of vch a ser kynde. *c* **1380** WYCLIF *Sel. Wks.* III. 517 þere sacrifises shulden not be ȝoven to him, but taken fro him,.. and anoþer trewe man.. shulde be ordeyned to resceyve siche sacrifices. *c* **1400** *Destr. Troy* 12137 My maydynhed I merk to myghtifull goddis: Accepte hit as sacrifise, & my saule to! **1456** SIR G. HAYE *Law Arms* (S.T.S.) 32 Tribulacioun is worthy sacrifice. **1594** MARLOWE & NASHE *Dido* IV. ii, Come seruants, come bring forth the Sacrifize, That I may pacifie that gloomy Ioue, Whose emptie Altars haue enlarg'd our illes. **1606** G. W[OODCOCKE] *Hist. Ivstine* XI. 46 Before any saile departed from the shore, he slue sacrifices, making his prayer for victory by battell. **1613** SHAKS. *Hen. VIII*, II. i. 77 Make of your Prayers one sweet Sacrifice. **1678** DRYDEN *All for Love* I. i, Does the mute sacrifice upbraid the priest? **1710** PRIDEAUX *Orig. Tithes* ii. 81 The Skins of the Sacrifices.. were to be given to the Priests. **1807** ROBINSON *Archæol. Græca* III. iv. 213 Only the larger sacrifices, as oxen, were thus adorned. **1845** MAURICE *Mor. & Met. Philos.* in *Encycl. Metrop.* II. 556/1 Those daily sacrifices which each man brought to the door of the tabernacle.

3. *Theol.* **a.** The offering by Christ of Himself to the Father as a propitiatory victim in his voluntary immolation upon the cross; the Crucifixion in its sacrificial character.

c **1375** *Sc. Leg. Saints* xiii. (*Marcus*) 72 þe sacrifice þat he mad for man one þe rud-tre. *a* **1450** MYRC *Festial* 261 For a calfe þat was offerd yn sacurfyce yn þe old law for synne, yn tokenyng þat Cryst schuld come, þat schuld be offurt yn sacryfyce for synne of þe pepull yn þe auter of þe crosse. **1560** DAUS tr. *Sleidane's Comm.* 313 b, Ther be in al ii sacrifices of christ, the one, blody upon the crosse, thother, wherin.. he himself offred up unto his father, his body and blud. **1681–6** J. SCOTT *Chr. Life* (1747) III. 463 In consideration of Christ's Death and Sacrifice, he would freely forgive all penitent and believing Sinners their personal Obligation to eternal Punishment. *a* **1769** RICCALTOUN *Notes Galat.* Wks. 1772 III. 127 A Sacrifice there was, and still is, the way God in his wisdom chose to condemn and put away sin and by which the pardon of sin was conveyed. **1825** J. MONTGOMERY *Hymn*, '*Go to dark Gethsemane*', Mark that miracle of Time,—God's own sacrifice complete. **1861** W. THOMSON in *Aids to Faith* viii. 337 The sacrifice of the death of Christ is a proof of Divine love, and of Divine justice.

b. Applied to the Eucharistic celebration: (*a*) in accordance with the view that regards it as a propitiatory offering of the body and blood of Christ, in perpetuation of the sacrifice offered by Him in His crucifixion; (*b*) in Protestant use, with reference to its character as an offering of thanksgiving (cf. sense 1).

1504 LADY MARGARET tr. *De Imitatione* IV. i. 262 For if the sacryfyce of this holy sacrament were done onely but in one place and but of one preest in all the worlde, with howe great desyre wene ye the people wolde go to that plase and to that preest to here the godly mysteryes done of hym. **1548** RIDLEY *Answ. Queries touching Mass* iii, The Representation and Commemoration of Christ's Death and Passion, said and done in the Mass, is called the Sacrifice, Oblation or Immolation of Christ. **1560** DAUS tr. *Sleidane's Comm.* 44 He exhorteth the people to flee from the accustomed sacrifices of the masse. **1704** NELSON *Fest. & Fasts* II. ix. (1739) 579 The Christian Sacrifice wherein Bread and Wine are offered. **1884** *Cath. Dict.* (1897) 814/1 In the sacrifice of the Mass, 'the immutatio', as the Fathers technically call the sacrificial act, is not the destruction but the production of the victim. **1899** B. J. KIDD *39 Art.* (1901) II. II. xxxi. 245 Nor does it (Art. xxxi. §2) condemn the sacrifice of the Mass but the sacrifices of Masses. **1901** GORE *Body of Christ* iii. 201 Only by communion can we in any effective sense share the eucharistic sacrifice.

c. ***sacrifice of praise*** (***and thanksgiving***): a phr. drawn from biblical sources (e.g. Lev. vii. 12, Ps. l. 14, 23 (R.V., etc.), Heb. xiii. 15) used *gen.* for an offering of praise to God, and liturgically in the anaphora of many post-Reformation Eucharistic rites, tr. *sacrificium laudis* of the Latin Canon of the Mass.

1535 COVERDALE *Heb.* xiii. 15 Let vs therfore by him offre allwayes vnto God the sacrifice of prayse. **1549** *Bk. Common Prayer* f. cxxviii^v, Entierely desiryng thy fatherly goodnes, mercifully to accepte this our Sacrifice of praise and thankes geuing. **1611** BIBLE *Jer.* xvii. 26 Bringing sacrifices of praise vnto the house of the Lord. **1864** F. PIERPOINT *For the Beauty of the Earth* (hymn) in O. Shipley *Lyra Eucharistica* (ed. 2) 340 Christ, our God, to Thee we raise This our Sacrifice of Praise. **1877** E. DANIEL *Prayer-Bk.* 296 That sacrament in which we offer our sacrifice of praise and thanksgiving for the redemption of the world. **1884** ADDIS & ARNOLD *Cath. Dict.* 564/1 The Mass is a sacrifice of adoration, of praise and thanksgiving. **1980** *Alternative Service Bk. 1980* 132 Accept through him, our great high priest, this our sacrifice of thanks and praise.

4. a. The destruction or surrender of something valued or desired for the sake of something having, or regarded as having, a higher or a more pressing claim; the loss entailed by devotion to some other interest; also, the thing so devoted or surrendered. Cf. SELF-SACRIFICE.

1592 SHAKS. *Rom. & Jul.* v. iii. 304 As rich shall Romeo by his Lady ly, Poore sacrifices to our enmity. **1601** in Moryson *Itin.* II. (1617) 151 The lively affections you beare to her person (for which you desire to bee made a Sacrifice). **1651** HOBBES *Leviath.* II. xxviii. 166 The benefit which a Soveraign bestoweth on a Subject, for fear of some power.. are not properly Rewards.. but are rather Sacrifices, which the Soveraign.. makes. **1742** GRAY *Eton* viii, To bitter Scorn a sacrifice. **1841** W. SPALDING *Italy & It. Isl.* III. 86 An eager sacrifice of means to an end. **1849** MACAULAY *Hist. Eng.* x. II. 647 Clarendon saw that he was not likely to gain anything by the sacrifice of his principles. **1868** FREEMAN *Norm. Conq.* (1877) II. x. 474 One more ecclesiastical appointment must, at some slight sacrifice of chronological order, be recorded.

b. A victim; one sacrificed to the will of another; also, a person or thing that falls into the power of an enemy or a destructive agency. Now *rare*.

1697 tr. *C'tess D'Aunoy's Trav.* (1706) 60 They are caused to make Vows, when 'tis often the Father or Mother, or some near Relation, who pronounce them for them, whilst the little Sacrifice disports herself with Sugar-plums, and lets them dress her how they will. **1732** NEAL *Hist. Purit.* I. 25 The two greatest sacrifices were John Fisher bishop of Rochester, and Sir Thomas More. **1779** *Mirror* No. 1 (1787) I. 5, I was prevented from falling a sacrifice to that languid inactivity which a depression of spirits never fails to produce. **1821** *John Bull* 15 Apr. 143/3 The organ fell a sacrifice to the devouring element. **1827** ROBERTS *Voy. Centr. Amer.* 95 On one occasion an acquaintance had.. nearly fallen a sacrifice to one of these animals.

5. a. A loss incurred in selling something below its value for the sake of getting rid of it. Hence, an article sold 'at a sacrifice'.

1844 DICKENS *Chimes* ii. (1845) 53 Its patterns were Last Year's and going at a sacrifice. **1849** THACKERAY *Pendennis* lxi, He bought a green shawl for Mrs. Bolton, and a yellow one for Fanny: the most brilliant 'sacrifices' of a Regent Street haberdasher's window. **1915** *Truth* 30 June 1068/1 Being convinced that his 'trade sacrifice' will result in increased business. **1976** *Billings* (Montana) *Gaz.* 5 July 9-c/8 (Advt.), Yaesu FT101 base, desk mike, antenna & tripod. *Sacrifice.* **1976** *Evening Advertiser* (Swindon) 31 Dec. 17/2 (Advt.), Bargain: 1971 Ford Escort 1100.. genuine sacrifice, £380 only.

b. *Baseball.* = *sacrifice hit* (see 6).

1880 *Inter-Ocean* (Chicago) 29 June 8/3 Force's winning run came off a wild throw by Ward, a sacrifice and single. **1904** R. H. BARBOUR *Bk. School & Coll. Sports* 173 When the batsman is looking for a sacrifice keep the ball high. **1912** C. MATHEWSON *Pitching in a Pinch* xii. 261 Snodgrass got a base on balls and journeyed to second on a sacrifice. **1968** *Washington Post* 4 July C2/8 Willie McCovey threw wildly trying to force the Atlanta pitcher at second on a sacrifice. **1976** *Billings* (Montana) *Gaz.* 6 July 3-C/1 Rookie Butch Hobson drove in three runs with a sacrifice and a single.

c. *Chess.* The action of SACRIFICE *v.* 3 e.

1915 J. DU MONT tr. *Lasker's Chess Strategy* I. iv. 25 White.. prefers to end up with a magnificent sacrifice. **1933** H. PHILLIPS *Week-End Problems Bk.* 310 The key-move.. offers double sacrifice with a cross-check. **1952** E. LASKER *Chess Secrets* 122 With this Bishop sacrifice Janowski tears down his opponent's defenses. **1977** *Guardian Weekly* 25 Dec. 23/5 Black took 80 minutes to decide to accept this strong pawn sacrifice.

d. *Bridge.* = *sacrifice bid(ding)*.

1952 *Bridge Mag.* Apr. 39/2 Five clubs is only two down, a good sacrifice against five spades. **1964** FREY & TRUSCOTT *Offic. Encycl. Bridge* 480/1 One will earn a fat score with one's sacrifice only when most of the field is bidding game with his opponents' cards. **1974** [see MAKE *sb.*[2] 10].

6. *attrib.* and *Comb.*, as ***sacrifice bringer***, ***-maker***, ***sale***; **sacrifice allowance** (see quot.); **sacrifice bid(ding)** *Bridge*, (making) a bid higher than the contract that one expects to be able to fulfil, in order to prevent opponents from making a score greater than the penalty one is likely to suffer; **sacrifice bunt** *Baseball*, a bunt that puts the batter out whilst allowing a base runner to advance; **sacrifice fly** *Baseball*, an outfield fly that is caught so that the batter is put out but which allows a base runner to advance after the ball is caught; **sacrifice hit** *Baseball* (see quot.); **sacrifice market**, a market in which goods are sold below cost price, a 'dumping ground'; **sacrifice meat**, meat eaten at a feast following the offering of a sacrifice to a deity; **sacrifice-offerer**, one who immolates himself (said of Christ); **sacrifice price**, a price entailing loss on the seller.

1891 *Labour Commission* Gloss., **Sacrifice Allowance*, a weekly sum paid by workmen's unions to those men who are discharged from work because they take an active part in their organisation or are too weak to make the average. These latter are called *sacrificed* men. **1932** H. PHILLIPS *One Hundred Contract Bridge Hands* 115 This is a good example of a '*sacrifice bid'... South now bids Four Hearts as probably a cheaper 'sacrifice' (even if doubled) than that of the game. **1959** *Listener* 13 Aug. 262/1 The hidden value of a part score has a bearing also on *sacrifice bidding at the game level. **1964** FREY & TRUSCOTT *Offic. Encycl. Bridge* 481/1 A hidden advantage of sacrifice bidding is the chance that the opponents will be pushed one higher and will go down. **1923** D. H. LAWRENCE *Birds, Beasts & Flowers* 149 And you, great bird... Can be put out of office as *sacrifice bringer. **1974** *Anderson* (S. Carolina) *Independent* 24 Apr. 5B/2 Jack Brohamer.. moved to second on Buddy Bell's *sacrifice bunt. **1970** *Globe & Mail* (Toronto) 25 Sept. 31/1 Roger Freed's *sacrifice fly.. helped Baltimore stretch its lead to 4-1 in the fifth. **1979** *Arizona Daily Star* 22 July C5/5 Butch Wynegar also drove in a run in the sixth with a sacrifice fly to help Goltz raise his record to 9-6. **1881** *N.Y. Herald* 21 July 8/3 The Metropolitans scored another run on two pretty singles, a passed ball and a *sacrifice hit. **1896** KNOWLES & MORTON *Baseball* Gloss., *Sacrifice-hit.*—When the batsman purposely makes a hit upon which he is retired, but which advances a base-runner. ? **1548** tr. *Viret's Expos. xii Art. Chr. Faith* E iv, He is the true.. prophete and the Soueraygne *sacrifice maker, whyche was figured by the kynges, and prophetes of Israell. **1888** *Pall Mall G.* 13 Jan. 2/1 Americans.. would make this a *sacrifice-market at first, simply to kill all our manufacturers. **1926** D. H. LAWRENCE *David* iv. 24 They be all there, waiting for the *sacrifice meat. *a* **1560** BECON *Chr. Knt.* Wks. II. 153 Our mediatour, our satissfyer or *sacrifyce offecer [? *read* offerer]. **1888** *Pall Mall G.* 12 June 11/2 A 'clearance sale', in fact, at '*sacrifice prices'. **1902** G. H. LORIMER *Lett. Self-Made Merchant* x. 129 It was the record-breaking, marked-down *sacrifice sale of the year on dogs.

sacrifice ('sækrɪfaɪs), *v.* Forms: see the sb.; also 3 **sacrefize**, 7 **sacrifize**. [f. SACRIFICE *sb.*]

1. a. *trans.* To offer as a sacrifice; to make an offering or sacrifice of. Const. *to*.

a **1300** *Cursor M.* 3262 For quas luue he wild not warn To sacrifise his auen barn. *a* **1425** *Ibid.* 3201 (Trin.) Þe sheep he sacrifised & brent. **1471** CAXTON *Recuyell* (Sommer) I. 308 The egypciens cryed vnto hercules sacrefice sacrefice hym, whan hercules cam in to the temple he sacrefised hym. **1555** EDEN *Decades* 158 When hee had fyrst sacrifyced them to his Zemes. *a* **1631** DONNE *Paradoxes* (1652) 68 Though he sacrifize Hecatombs. **1646** SIR T. BROWNE *Pseud. Ep.* v. viii. 246 The Picture of.. Abraham sacrificing his son. **1697** DAMPIER *Voy.* (1699) 485 If they Sacrifice their Enemies it is not necessary they should Eat them too. **1875** JOWETT *Plato* (ed. 2) V. 94 There are nations in which mankind still sacrifice their fellow men.

†**b.** *nonce-uses.* To slay or burn in the manner of a sacrifice; to burn in a sacrifice.

1602 in Moryson *Itin.* II. (1617) 258, I.. tooke Ocanes brother prisoner.. (whom I sacrificed in the place) and so passed by. **1634** SIR T. HERBERT *Trav.* 39 They sacrifice him [a dead man] to ashes, in costly perfumes.

2. a. *intr.* To offer up a sacrifice.

c **1290** *S. Eng. Leg.* I. 69/43 Anoure ore godes, ich rede, a-non and heom sacrefise. **1377** LANGL. *P. Pl.* B. XII. 118 Saul, for he sacrifised, sorwe hym be-tydde. *a* **1400-50** *Alexander* 1082 Þare lengis him lefe þe kynge & logis all a neuen, And sacrifyce þar efsones to many sere godis. **1484** CAXTON *Fables of Æsop* v. x, I.. toke on me for to sacryfyce and to synge before the goddes. **1628** J. HUME *Jewes Deliv.* i. 10 They were wont to immolate and sacrifice vnto their heathenish Gods. **1784** COWPER *Task* I. 411 An idol, at whose shrine Who oft'nest sacrifice are favour'd least. **1818** SHELLEY *Homer's Castor & P.* 13 The sailors.. sacrifice with snow-white lambs.

b. *Eccl.* To celebrate the Eucharist.

1661 tr. *Erasm. Life Colet* in *C.'s Serm.* 74 Whereas it is the custome in England for Priests to consecrate the host, and receive it almost every day, he was content to sacrifice on Sundays and Holi-days, or some few days beside.

3. a. *trans.* To surrender or give up (something) for the attainment of some higher advantage or dearer object. Const. *to*.

1706 PHILLIPS (ed. Kersey), *To Sacrifice*,.. to quit or leave a Thing upon some Consideration. **1710** SWIFT *Jrnl. to Stella* 23 Sept., Deuce take Lady S——; and if I know D——y, he is a rawboned-faced fellow..; she sacrifices two thousand pounds a year, and keeps only six hundred. **1720** OZELL *Vertot's Rom. Rep.* I. v. 298 The first Obligation which a Roman lay under.. was to sacrifice his Life in Defence of the Public Liberty. **1837** KEIGHTLEY *Hist. Eng.* I. 416 Henry [VIII].. was never known to sacrifice an inclination to the interest or happiness of another. **1875** JOWETT *Plato* (ed. 2) V. 126 Everything seems to have been sacrificed to a false notion of equality. **1879** HARLAN *Eyesight* vii. 97 Generally, the only men who can be persuaded to wear protecting glasses are those who have already sacrificed one eye to their objections.

b. To permit injury or ruin to the interests of (a person) for the sake of some desired object. Also *refl.* Const. *to*.

1751 JOHNSON *Rambler* No. 145 ¶13 Instead of sacrificing each other to malice and contempt. **1838** THIRLWALL *Greece* xviii. III. 49 Pericles.. was charged with sacrificing the Samians to private feelings. **1849** MACAULAY *Hist. Eng.* vii. II. 222 Could it then be doubted that, if the Churchmen would even now comply with his wishes, he would willingly sacrifice the Puritans? **1870** MOZLEY *Univ. Serm.* iv. (1876) 88 How will persons sacrifice themselves to their objects! **1873** BLACK *Pr. Thule* xviii, He is too much an artist to sacrifice himself to his clothes. **1891** KIPLING *Light that Failed* vii, It isn't got at by sacrificing other people,.. you must sacrifice yourself.

c. To sell or get rid of at a sacrifice, esp. in commercial use. Also *absol.*

1850 *Punch* XVIII. 130/2 A newspaper advertisement announces that 'A Professional gentleman is instructed to sacrifice *three* young sound *Horses* at half their cost.' We wonder what deity horses could be sacrificed to? **1903** FARMER & HENLEY *Slang* VI. 91/1 *Sacrifice*.. to sell regardless of cost. **1930** *San Antonio* (Texas) *Light* 31 Jan. 14/7 (Advt.), Owner Must Sacrifice Must sell at bargain. **1947** E. HODGINS *Mr. Blandings builds his Dream House* ii. 23 'Farm dwelling.. original beams.. will sacrifice', The *New York Times* advertisement had said.

d. *Baseball.* (*a*) *intr.* To make a hit which advances another player, the batter being put out. (*b*) *trans.* To advance (another player) in this way.

1905 *Sporting Life* 2 Sept. 4/1 Lumley's effort to sacrifice resulted in a short pop fly. **1912** C. MATHEWSON *Pitching in a Pinch* ix. 202 Brown sacrificed, sending Kling to second. **1971** L. KOPPETT *N.Y. Times Guide Spectator Sports* i. 31 When a batter walks, is hit by a pitch, sacrifices (by bunting so that other runners advance even though he is out),.. he is not charged with an official time at bat. **1974** *News & Courier* (Charleston, S. Carolina) 22 Apr. 9-A/3 Denny Doyle.. was sacrificed to second. **1975** *Verbatim* Sept. 5/1 But Joe Ferguson did something much more drastic than that: *He sacrificed Garvey home!*

e. *Chess.* To put or leave (a man) in a position where it can be captured without equivalent loss by one's opponent, in order to gain a future advantage.

1915 J. DU MONT tr. *Lasker's Chess Strategy* II. 224 White decides to sacrifice a Knight in order to open the files in the centre for his Rooks. **1952** E. LASKER *Chess Secrets* 54 White could sacrifice a piece for three Pawns. **1969** A. GLYN *Dragon Variation* vii. 193 They'd both sacrifice every piece on the board. By the middle-game they'd just have the two Kings left. *Ibid.* ix. 271 He tried to break the stranglehold by sacrificing first a Knight and then a Rook. **1974** HARTSTON & KEENE *Karpov–Korchnoi 1974* 66 Korchnoi plucks up his courage and sacrifices his K-side in order to create a passed pawn of his own.

f. *Bridge. intr.* To make a sacrifice bid.

1952 PHILLIPS & REESE *Bridge with Mr. Playbetter* xiv. 59 He must take all possible measures to prevent Hurry sacrificing in Five Clubs. **1959** *Listener* 22 Jan. 189/2 Is it possible, under the Laws, to sacrifice at the level of Eight? **1962** *Ibid.* 13 Sept. 410/3 Over Four Hearts North could raise to six. No doubt, in that event, East-West would sacrifice in Six Spades. **1964** FREY & TRUSCOTT *Offic. Encycl. Bridge* 480/2 Be alert to sacrifice against confident auctions when it appears that everyone else will be in game too.

4. To kill (an experimental animal) for scientific purposes.

1903 *Jrnl. Physiol.* XXIX. 83 The animal was sacrificed on the 315th day after the 1st lesion had been established. **1926** J. S. HUXLEY *Ess. Pop. Sci.* 282 When, after a couple of months, the dog was sacrificed, it was found.. that the histological character of the cells had changed, cross-striations arising in them. **1944** *Jrnl. Immunology* XLIX. 316 The animals were sacrificed by a blow on the head and the small intestine was immediately removed. **1971** *Sci. Amer.* July 55/1 In rats we destroyed the mitral cells in the olfactory bulb by surgical intervention and, after a survival time of from three to five days, sacrificed the animal to conduct a microscopic examination of the fibers leading from these cells.

†**sacrificeable**, *a. Obs.* Also 5 **sacrefysable**. [f. SACRIFICE *v.* + -ABLE. Cf. SACRIFIABLE, SACRIFICABLE.] Proper to be sacrificed.

1483 CAXTON *Gold. Leg.* 333/2 The oxe is a moralle beest.. and it is a best sacrefysable. **1603** HOLLAND *Plutarch's Mor.* 1299 If they[*sc.* kine and oxen] have but one haire blacke or white, they be not sacrificeable.

sacrificed ('sækrɪfaɪst), *ppl. a.* [f. SACRIFICE *v.* + -ED[1].]

†**1.** Made sacred; sanctified. *Obs.*

1504 LADY MARGARET tr. *De Imitatione* IV. i. 261 All cristen people.. kysses the sacryfyced bones [orig. *sacra ossa*] of ayntes, wrapped in clothes of Sylke and Golde.

2. Offered as a sacrifice.

1597 HOOKER *Eccl. Pol.* v. lxvii. §7 What merit force or vertue soeuer there is in his sacrificed body & bloud. **1626** BACON *Sylva* §400 It is reported by one of the Ancients, of credit, that a Sacrificed Beast hath lowed, after the Heart hath been severed. **1681-6** J. SCOTT *Chr. Life* (1747) III. 184 This Address is performed by the presenting his sacrificed Body to the Father in Heaven. **1715** LEONI *Palladio's Archit.* (1742) II. 77 The Entrails of sacrificed Beasts. **1768** S. BENTLEY *River Dove* 14 Still yearly, to popular Rage, A sacrific'd Bull is the Sport.

3. Given up or abandoned for the sake of others.

1884 M. ARNOLD in *Pall Mall G.* 1 Dec. 6/2 Those classes which, in comparison with the great possessing and trading classes—who may be called the fortunate classes—may be called the sacrificed classes. **1891** [see SACRIFICE *sb.* 6].

sacrificer (ˈsækrɪfaɪsə(r)). [f. SACRIFICE *v.* + -ER[1].]

1. One who offers up a sacrifice.

1563 WINȝET *Four Scoir Thre Quest.* §25 Wks. (S.T.S.) I. 90 Quhy teche ȝe.. that the wordis of sanctificatioun of the sacrament of our Lordis body and bluid ar nocht to be pronounceit to the end, that thair suld be ony transubstantiatioun thairby, or be the intent of the sacrificear [*Edinb. MS.* sacrifiar]? **1597** *Cert. Prayers* in *Liturg. Serv. Q. Eliz.* (Parker Soc.) 672 We.. live and die the sacrificers of our souls for such obtained favour. **1643** MILTON *Divorce* Pref. (1644) 2 A famous man in Israel could not but oblige his conscience to be the sacrificer.. of his innocent and only daughter. **1742** BLAIR *Grave* 140 Like.. victim.. That throbs beneath the sacrificer's knife. **1848** R. I. WILBERFORCE *Doctr. Incarnation* xii. (1852) 305 The earthly sacrificer truly exhibits to the Father that body of Christ which is the one only Sacrifice for sins. **1884** WHITON in *Chr. World* 4 Sept. 663/2 Paul boldly intimates, that if Christ is the only sacrificer and sufferer for humanity, then something is lacking in the saving work of the Saviour.

2. *spec.* A sacrificial priest.

1547 *Bk. of Marchauntes* e v b, It is much better to here.. Helie alone than all the sacryficers of Baal. ? **1548** tr. *Viret's Expos. xii Art. Chr. Faith* E iv, Whyche was figured by the kynges and prophetes of Israell, and by the sacrificers of the Leuites. **1605** WILLET *Hexapla Gen.* 168 The great sacrificer and high priest Melchisedech. **1693** J. EDWARDS *Author. O. & N. Test.* 385 He being a Jewish priest, a legal sacrificer. **1727** DE FOE *Hist. Appar.* iii. (1840) 24 The patriarchal heads of families, who.. were the only sacrificers at that time, as Abraham and as Job were. **1865** J. H. INGRAHAM *Pillar of Fire* (1872) 518 The chief sacrificer advanced, leading a Hebrew boy,.. whom he laid on the altar.

Hence †**ˈsacrificership**, the office of a sacrificer.

1562 T. NORTON *Calvin's Inst.* Table of Matters s.v. *Orders*, Of Priesthode or sacrificership.

sacrificial (sækrɪˈfɪʃəl), *a.* [f. L. *sacrifici-um* + -AL[1]. Cf. the older SACRIFICAL; also 16th c. F. *sacrificial*.]

1. a. Pertaining to or connected with sacrifice.

1607 SHAKS. *Timon* I. i. 81 Raine Sacrificiall whisperings in his eare. **1656** BLOUNT *Glossogr.*, *Sacrificial* (*sacrificialis*) of or belonging to a Sacrifice, Offering, or Oblation. **1737** WATERLAND *Rev. Doctr. Eucharist* i. 53 This Observation will be of use, when we come to consider the Eucharist in its Sacrificial View. **1799** GILPIN *Serm. Country Congregat.*, etc. III. xxxviii. (R.), The law may be explained as an institution.. threatening judgment on every transgression; at the same time, accepting, in mercy, certain sacrificial atonements. **1856** EMERSON *Eng. Traits, Stonehenge* Wks. (Bohn) II. 123 The *sacrificial stone*, as it is called, is the only one in all these blocks, that can resist the action of fire. **1864** MAX MÜLLER *Chips* (1867) I. 104 Innumerable sacrificial utensils. *Ibid.* 110 All this would be embodied in the sacrificial formulas known in later times principally by the name of Yagush.

b. *sacrificial mound*: a prehistoric mound built by the natives of certain parts of America and containing a hearth or altar, on which are found relics exhibiting traces of the action of fire.

1862 D. WILSON *Preh. Man* I. xii. 370 The name of sacrificial mounds has been conferred on a class of ancient monuments.. peculiar to the New World.

2. Self-sacrificing. *nonce-use.*

1890 'R. BOLDREWOOD' *Col. Reformer* (1891) 160 'That's all very well', said the sacrificial parent, 'but five or six hours are not so easy to dispose of at sixty odd'.

3. *Comm.* Involving 'sacrifice' or loss to the vendor.

1895 *Daily News* 24 Dec. 6/2 Jewelled trimmings.. will be sold at much reduced prices during next week's sacrificial sales. **1902** *Daily Chron.* 19 June 7/2 The first Monday in July, the traditional date for the opening of the summer sales, when ladies demand sacrificial prices.

4. Involving or being an anode of a metal that is used up when protecting another metal against electrolytic corrosion.

1861 *Mechanics' Mag.* 5 Apr. 229/1 A curious statement made in the House of Commons, a few days ago, induces us to offer a few remarks on what may be called, appropriately enough, 'the sacrificial function in metals'... Failing.. to achieve what was intended of it, the copper-protecting process of Davy ceased to be employed; but the failure of it is that which alone concerns us here, as illustrating what we would wish to convey by the words *sacrificial metal*. **1937** U. R. EVANS *Metallic Corrosion Passivity & Protection* xii. 531 The protection method is sacrificial, the valuable iron boiler being protected by sacrificing the easily replaceable zinc. **1949** *Jrnl. R. Soc. Arts* XCVII. 598 A sufficient cathodic current density may be impressed upon structures of iron or steel by the use of external anodes of magnesium, aluminium or zinc, the anode undergoing 'sacrificial corrosion'. **1968** *Rep. Progr. Appl. Chem.* LIII. 69 It was better to use an all-nickel coating.. rather than a copper undercoat where sacrificial corrosion resulted in complete loss of plate. **1976** *Daily Tel.* 25 Nov. 7/1 It is common practice to fit the pipes with collars of a zinc alloy, which act as 'sacrificial anodes', corroding in preference to the steel pipe. **1978** *Metals* (Shell Internat. Petroleum Co.) 7 Zinc is ideal as a sacrificial metal for the corrosion-protection of steel.

Hence **sacriˈficialness.** *rare*[−0].

1727 BAILEY vol. II, *Sacrificialness*, the being of the Nature of a Sacrifice.

sacriˈficially, *adv.* [f. SACRIFICIAL *a.* + -LY[2].] In a sacrificial manner.

1937 L. C. DOUGLAS *Forgive us our Trespasses* i. 2 'Wish you was a-goin' along'... 'No,' Martha would reply, sacrificially, 'somebody's got to stay on th' place.' **1972** *Daily Tel.* 7 Sept. 18 Our officers and staff who serve so sacrificially year in and year out.. are not men who have come to terms with squalor.

sacrificing (ˈsækrɪfaɪsɪŋ), *vbl. sb.* [f. SACRIFICE *v.* + -ING[1].] The action of the verb SACRIFICE.

1601 in Moryson *Itin.* II. (1617) 152 The uttermost of our endeuours and seruices, euen to the sacrificing of our liues. *a* **1639** W. WHATELEY *Prototypes* I. iv. (1640) 32 Sacrificing was a profession of their owne guiltinesse. **1727-41** CHAMBERS *Cycl.* s.v. *Sacrifice*, The manner of sacrificing among the ancient Hebrews, is amply described in the books of Moses. **1742** J. GLAS *Treat. Lord's Supp.* III. iv. (1883) 114 The apostle sets forth Christ's death as the truth of the sacrificing of the passover.

b. *attrib.*

c **1586** C'TESS PEMBROKE *Ps.* LXV. i, Thou my sinns.. Dost turne to smoake of sacrificing flame. **1604** E. G[RIMSTONE] *D'Acosta's Hist. Indies* v. xxx. 426 They presently tooke the sacrificing rasors, the which they washed and clensed from the blood of men. **1631** WEEVER *Anc. Funeral Mon.* 618 Two sacrificing dishes of smooth and pollished red earth. **1672** R. VEEL *New Court-Songs* 35 My winged Feet, each Sacrificing day, Lead me to gaze upon her, more than pray. **1709** HEARNE *Collect.* 2 Dec. (O.H.S.) II. 319 Roman sacrificing Axes.

sacrificing (ˈsækrɪfaɪsɪŋ), *ppl. a.* [f. SACRIFICE *v.* + -ING[2].] That offers sacrifice; that makes sacrifices.

1826 T. COLEMAN *Indulgences*, etc. *Order Mt. Carmel* 61 He.. for another Memento of the sacrificing priest, grants, to the souls in Purgatory, rest and peace in the kingdom of glory. **1848** R. I. WILBERFORCE *Doctr. Incarnation* xii. (1852) 293 He [the High Priest] was the type of Him who stretched out His sacrificing arms upon the Cross.

Hence **ˈsacrificingly** *adv.*

1601 CHESTER *Love's Mart., Dialogue* (New Shaks. Soc.) 128 And in a manner sacrificingly, Burne both our bodies to reuiue one name.

†**sacrificul(e.** *Obs. humorously pedantic.* [a. F. *sacrificule* (Rabelais), ad. L. *sacrificulus* an extension of *sacrificus* SACRIFIC *a.*] A priest.

The misapprehension in quot. 1604 is found also in a Fr. glossary to Rabelais.

1604 R. CAWDREY *Table Alph.*, *Sacrificule*, a little offering. **1653** URQUHART *Rabelais* II. vi, I mumble off little parcels of some missick precation of our sacrificuls.

†**sacriˈficulist.** *Obs.* [f. L. *sacrificul-us* (see prec.) + -IST.] A sacrificing priest.

1652 GAULE *Magastrom.* 309 This, said the soothsaying sacrificulists, presaged victory to the Bœotians. *Ibid.* 352, 365.

†**sacrificy.** *Obs. rare.* In 6 sacrificie. [ad. L. *sacrificium.*] = SACRIFICE *sb.*

c **1511** *1st Eng. Bk. Amer.* (Arb.) Introd. 36/1, I [am] preste after the outshewyng of sacrificie of the auters.

†**ˈsacrifier.** *Obs.* [f. SACRIFY *v.* + -ER[1].] A sacrificing priest.

1382 WYCLIF *Isa.* xix. 3 Thei shul aske.. ther deuel cleperes and ther deuel sacrifieres [Vulg. *ariolos*]. **1547** *Bk. of Marchauntes* e v b, The Pharisiens, sacrifiers, Scribes, and docters. **1553** BALE *Vocacyon* 7 Baals.. sorcerouse sacrifiers. **1563** [see SACRIFICER 1].

†**ˈsacrify,** *v. Obs.* [a. OF. *sacrifi-er* (12th c.), ad. L. *sacrificāre*, f. *sacrific-us*: see SACRIFIC.]

1. *trans.* To offer as a sacrifice.

a **1300** *Cursor M.* 10389 þam hale þan sacrified he, And delt þam siþen al thre. **1390** GOWER *Conf.* III. 336 And forth unto the temple he com.., Hise yiftes forto sacrifie. **1484** CAXTON *Fables of Auian* xxvii, Thow shalt be take.. and shalt be sacryfyed to theyre goddes. **1588** A. KING tr. *Canisius' Catech.* in *Cath. Tractates* (S.T.S.) 181 Melchizedec sacrifeit breid and wyne in figure of the bodie and bloud of our lord. **1590** SPENSER *F.Q.* II. xii. 49 A mightie mazer bowle of wine was set As if it had to him been sacrifide.

refl. **1490** CAXTON *Eneydos* xxiv. 87 Alwayes she doubted her self in noo wyse, that her suster wolde.. sacryfye hir self with funerailles mortalle, by fyre horrible.

2. *intr.* To offer sacrifice.

a **1325** *Prose Psalter* liii[i]. 6 Y shal sacrifye to þe wyþ gode wylle. *c* **1375** *Sc. Leg. Saints* v. (*Johannes*) 295 þa.. to þe tempil of dyane drew hym rudly, ore þai fane, for to strenȝe hym to sacrify. **1382** WYCLIF *Exod.* x. 11 Go ȝe oonly men, and sacryfye to the Lord. *c* **1425** WYNTOUN *Cron.* III. i. 120 He sulde.. Deuotly to God sacryfy. **1555** W. WATREMAN *Fardle Facions* I. v. 52 That there might be none occasion of filthinesse, when they shold ministre or sacrifie.

3. *trans.* To offer sacrifice to.

1474 CAXTON *Chesse* III. v. (1883) 124 As he sacrefyed his goddes he receyuyd lettres from the senate of rome. **1491** —— *Vitas Patr.* (W. de W. 1495) I. lv. 111 [He] was broughte.. in to a temple of ydolatrye.. for to adoure and sacrefye the ydolles.

4. *nonce-use.* To consecrate.

1819 W. TENNANT *Papistry Storm'd* (1827) 167 Whan the great Kirk was sacrify'd.

Hence †**ˈsacrifying** *vbl. sb.*

13.. *K. Alis.* 272 (Bodl. MS.) To goddes I made sacrifyeynge. *c* **1374** CHAUCER *Boeth.* IV. met. vii. 114 (Camb. MS.) The sory preest yeuith in sacryfyinge the wrechched kuttynge of throte of the douhter.

sacrilege (ˈsækrɪlɪdʒ), *sb.*[1] Forms: 3-4 sacrilage, 4 sacre-, sacrylage, sacrilegge, 4-6 sacrylege, 5 sacrilag, 6 sacrileage, *Sc.* sacralege, 6-7 sacriledge, -lidge, 7 sacrileg, 3- sacrilege. [a. OF. *sacrilege* (12th c. in Hatz.-Darm.; mod.F. *sacrilège*) = Sp., Pg., It. *sacrilegio*, ad. L. *sacrilegium*, f. *sacrileg-us* one who steals sacred things or commits sacrilege, f. *sacri-*, *sacer* sacred + *-leg-*, *legĕre* to gather, after the phrase *sacrum* or *sacra legere* to purloin sacred objects, to commit sacrilege.]

1. The crime or sin of stealing or misappropriating what is consecrated to God's service. In ecclesiastical use, extended to include any kind of outrage on consecrated persons or things, and the violation of any obligation having a sacramental character, or recognized as under the special protection of the Church. Also, an instance of this offence.

In mediæval writings the classification of 'sacrilege' as a branch of avarice, which is based on the primary meaning of the term, is somewhat inconsistently combined with an enumeration of the varieties of sacrilege implying the wider sense explained above. Cf., e.g. *Ayenbite* pp. 40-41 Chaucer's *Parson's Tale* ¶727-9.

a **1300** *Cursor M.* 27840 O couaitise.. cums.. sacrilege, to reue or stele Of halud thing. *Ibid.* 27946. **1303** R. BRUNNE *Handl. Synne* 8608 þey þat haue cherches broke, And stole þo þynges þat were þer-ynne, 'Sacrylage' men calle þat synne. **1382** WYCLIF *2 Macc.* iv. 39 Many sacrilegis don in the temple. *c* **1440** *Jacob's Well* 160 An-oþer is sacrilege, þat is, brekyng of þe sacrament of holy cherche. **1526** *Pilgr. Perf.* (W. de W. 1531) 18 Some.. for theyr pryde and sacrilege, god suffreth oftentymes to make an ende lyke as a beest. **1632** SANDERSON *Serm.* 381 The stinke of their divelish sacriledge in robbing the Church. **1649** HOWELL *Pre-em. Parl.* 9 Rufus (who came to such a disastrous end, as to be shot to death in lieu of a Buck for his sacriledges). **1734** tr. *Rollin's Anc. Hist.* XIX. (1827) VIII. 326 After this adding sacrilege to profanation he carried away the altar of incense. **1827** SOUTHEY *Hist. Penins. War* II. 239 In consideration of the sacrileges which the enemy committed ..they were enlisting the peasantry. **1838** ARNOLD *Hist. Rome* (1846) I. xxi. 457 An unscrupulous sacrilege, which appropriated the very offerings to the Gods, so made, to his own individual uses. **1875** MANNING *Mission H. Ghost* ix. 235 The very books that are used in the worship of God are Sacred. The man who steals them is guilty of sacrilege.

b. *spec.* in popular use as a name for robbery from a church or other place of worship.

The term is not technically used in Eng. Law, though formerly special penalties were imposed for the offence. From the 17th c. a robbery from a church has been regarded legally as a 'larceny' or a 'burglary' according to the circumstances.

1820 *John Bull* 17 Dec. 8/2 Norwich.—Sacrilege is now very common, the churches of Carbrook and Eaton were broken into; out of the former the thieves stole all the plate, communion cloth and surplice. *Mod. newspaper*, Sacrilege at Middleton.

2. *transf.* and *fig.* The profanation of anything held sacred.

1390 GOWER *Conf.* II. 371 The cause why that he so doth Is forto stele an herte or tuo,.. And as I seide it hier above, Al is that Sacrilege of love. **1529** MORE *Dyaloge* IV. Wks. 267/1 That it is as Luther sayth, great sinne and sacrilege to go about to please god by good woorkes, and not by onely fayth. ? **1548** tr. *Viret's Expos. XII Art. Chr. Faith* B j b, That were a greate blasphemie & sacrilege to haue suche an opinion of God as to think that [etc.]. **1623** FLETCHER *Rule a Wife* V. i, 'Tis sacrilege to violate a wed-lock, You rob two Temples. *a* **1678** MARVELL *Upon Appleton House*, 'T'were Sacrilege a man to admit To holy things, for heaven fit. **1858** FROUDE *Hist. Eng.* xix. IV. 193 To kill a herald was, by the law of arms, sacrilege. **1874** MICKLETHWAITE *Mod. Par. Churches* 204 Almost every stone.. is a historical monument, which it would be sacrilege to remove or destroy.

†**sacrilege,** *sb.*[2] *Obs.* exc. *poet.* [ad. L. *sacrileg-us*: see SACRILEGE *sb.*[1]] One who is guilty of sacrilege.

1491 CAXTON *Vitas Patr.* (W. de W. 1495) I. xl. 61 b/2 Yf ony defaylled there that hadde not ben atte theyr laste seruyce, They were reputed and holden as Sacryleges. **1556** OLDE *Antichrist* 74 They bewray themselues.. to be theues and sacrileges. **1585** T. WASHINGTON tr. *Nicholay's Voy.* IV. xxxiii. 155 He was aswel condemned to death, as if he had bin a murtherer, or sacriledge. **1802** W. S. LANDOR *Poetry* 7 Thrown prostrate on the earth, the Sacrilege Rais'd up his head astounded.

sacrilege (ˈsækrɪlɪdʒ), *v. rare.* [f. SACRILEGE *sb.*] *trans.* To commit sacrilege upon. Hence †**ˈsacrileging** *ppl. a.*

1554 LATIMER in Strype *Eccl. Mem.* (1822) III. II. 293 Wherfor stande from the aulter you sacrilegynge (I shulde have said you sacrificinge) preistes. **1578** FLORIO *1st Fruites* 73 The ende of warre is this,.. churches are profanizated and sacrileged. **1778** *Hist. Eliza Warwick* I. 10 Lord Huntley will not be tempted to sacrilege the temple—to storm a convent. **1866** J. B. ROSE tr. *Ovid's Met.* 92 Thou didst rend Pentheus, and him thy rites who sacrileged Lycurgus.

sacrileger (ˈsækrɪlɪdʒə(r)). *arch.* Also 4 sacrelegir, sacrilegeer, 5 sacrilegir, 6 sacre-, sacryleger, sacriledger, -leager. [f. SACRILEGE *sb.*[1] or *v.* + -ER[1].] One who commits sacrilege.

c **1380** WYCLIF *Sel. Wks.* III. 273 Curseden [*read* curseder] sacrelegires þan bodily þeves þat breken chirchis and stelen chalicis, vestementis, or nevere so moche gold out of hem. **1395** PURVEY *Remonstr.* (1851) 49 A sacrilegeer, that is, a theef of holi thingis. ? *a* **1500** in Becon *Reliq. Rome* (1563) 253 Al sacrilegiers, yt is to say, al yt wrongfulliche doen away any thing halowed. *a* **1500** in Arnolde *Chron.* (1811) 175 All sacrelegers whiche goodes of chirchis perteyning..aweye taken. **1614** RALEIGH *Hist. World* IV. i. §4 II. 162 [They] for refusall were exposed as Sacrilegers, and accursed to all their Neighbour-Nations. **1642** BP. MORTON *Presentm. of Schismatic* 25 Thou Sacrileger art as ill as the Idolater is. **1838** G. S. FABER *Inquiry* 444 These imposters, sacrilegers, and idolators, ought..to be removed from their degree. **1883** *Cornh. Mag.* Apr. 453 The adulterer and the sacrileger.

sacrilegious (sækrɪˈlɪdʒəs, sækrɪˈliːdʒəs), *a.* [f. L. *sacrilegi-um* SACRILEGE *sb.*[1] + -OUS.]

1. Committing sacrilege; guilty of sacrilege.

1582 N.T. (Rhem.) *Acts* xix. 37 These men being neither sacrilegious nor blaspheming your Goddess. *c* **1586** C'TESS PEMBROKE *Ps.* LXXIV. iii, Lord,..This sacrilegious seed Roote quickly out. **1610** HOLLAND *Camden's Brit.* (1637) 102 He might without processe of condemnation be killed as a sacrilegious person. **1696** DE LA PRYME *Diary* (Surtees) 319 The wicked sacrilegous, non-conformists. **1791** MRS. RADCLIFFE *Rom. Forest* ii, Reproving the sacrilegious mortal who thus dared to disturb their holy precincts. **1854** MILMAN *Lat. Chr.* IV. viii. (1864) II. 422 His conduct..contrasted..with that of the sacrilegious Iconoclast Leo. **1864** BRYCE *Holy Rom. Emp.* xix. (1875) 341 Leave the church lands in the grasp of sacrilegious spoilers.

absol. **1682** NORRIS *Hierocles* 8 The Offerings which they hang up in the Temple, serve only to enrich the Sacrilegious.

2. Involving sacrilege.

1621 BURTON *Anat. Mel.* I. ii. I. i. (1624) 35 The like happened to Brennus..vpon such a sacrilegious occasion. **1673-4** BP. WARD *Case of Joram* 1 The Sacrilegious and Bloody Martyrdom of our late most Excellent Sovereign. **1736** BOLINGBROKE *Patriot.* (1749) 11 A most sacrilegious breach of trust. **1844** THIRLWALL *Greece* VIII. lxiv. 275 He ..repeated his sacrilegious devastations in the sanctuary of Apollo. **1867** FREEMAN *Norm. Conq.* (1877) V. xxiv. 380 The practices introduced by Flambard..were deemed to be sacrilegious.

Hence **sacriˈlegiously** *adv.*, **sacriˈlegiousness**.

1609 BP. W. BARLOW *Answ. Nameless Cath.* 355 Then is he Sacrilegiously false. **1727** *Philip Quarll* (1816) 66 Those villians had most sacrilegiously rifled and ransacked his habitation. **1727** BAILEY vol. II, *Sacrilegiousness.* **1848** LYTTON *Harold* I. i, In the center of which had been sacrilegiously placed an altar to Thor.

sacrilegist (sækrɪˈliːdʒɪst). [f. SACRILEGE *sb.*[1] + -IST.] One addicted to or guilty of sacrilege.

1621 BP. MOUNTAGU *Diatribæ* 102 To the third Generation, neuer yet did prosper, nor euer shall, the Sacrilegist. **1683** O. U. *Parish Ch. no Conventicles* 6 He doth ..charge us..with being Sacrilegists, worse than the worst of Conventiclers. **1866** ANNIE HARWOOD tr. *E. de Pressensé's Jesus Christ* I. iii. 98 A sacrilegist never hesitating to elevate his creatures to the priesthood. **1898** WATTS-DUNTON *Aylwin* (1900) 109/1 Secrecy is the first thing for us sacrilegists to consider.

†**sacrilegy**. *Obs.* Forms: 4-5 sacri-, sacry-, sacrelegi(e, -legy(e, 6 sacralagie. [ad. L. *sacrilegium.*] = SACRILEGE *sb.*[1]

13.. *Ipotis* 251 (Vernon MS.) in Horstm. *Altengl. Leg.* (1881) 344 In sacrilegye he sungede sore. *c* **1380** WYCLIF *Wks.* (1880) 132 What eucre þou haldest to þe..ouer symple liflode & streit cloþing..is þefte, raueyne & sacrelegie. **1387** TREVISA *Higden* (Rolls) III. 463 ȝif ȝe despiseþ God wytyngly, þanne ȝe beeþ i-holde in þe synne of sacrelegy. *c* **1449** PECOCK *Repr.* III. xix. 409 It is raueyn, it is sacrilegi [*sacrilegium est*], that is to seie thefte of holi good. **1529** RASTELL *Pastyme, Hist. Pap.* (1811) 40 Banished for sacralagie.

sacring (ˈseɪkrɪŋ), *vbl. sb.* Now only *literary.* Also 3-6 sacringe, 4 sakryng, -ring, 4-6 sacryng(e, sakeryng(e, 5 sacryn, sacreng, sakering(e, saycrying, sac(c)aring, *Sc.* sacryne. [f. SACRE *v.*[1] + -ING[1].]

1. The consecration of the eucharistic elements in the service of the mass. Sometimes more fully, the *sacring of (the) mass.*

1297 R. GLOUC. (Rolls) 6818 Riȝt atte sacringe he stod as be lowe In þe churche at westmunstre. **13..** *Coer de L.* 222 And whene the belle began to ryng The preest scholde make the sakeryng, Out of the kyrke sche wolde away. *c* **1375** *Lay Folks Mass Bk.* (MS. B) 400 þen tyme is nere of sakring, A litel belle men oyse to ryng. *c* **1380** WYCLIF *Serm.* Sel. Wks. I. 137 Bitwene þe sacringe of þe masse and þe þridde Agnus Dei. *c* **1451** AGNES PASTON in *P. Lett.* I. 217 And on Friday after sakeryng, one come fro cherch warde, and schoffe doune all that was thereon. **1482** CAXTON *Trevisa's Higden* IV. xxxii. 222 b, The grayel and the offretory sholde be sayde to fore the sacrynge [*MSS.* sacrement; L. *sacrificium*]. **1550** CRANMER *Defence* 101 What made the people to runne.. from altar to altar, and from sakeryng (as they called it) to sakeryng? *a* **1571** JEWEL *On Thess.* iii. 5-10 (1594) 90 It is a small matter to looke vp and holde vp thy handes at the sacring. **1584** R. SCOT *Discov. Witchcr.* xv. xxvii. (1886) 376 Words..written in the canon, or rather in the saccaring of masse. **1626** *Scogin's Jests* (? 1680) 12 By and by the Bells were tolled for sacring, and Scogin hied him to Church lustily and merry. **1871** ROSSETTI *Poems*, tr. *Villon's Mother's Service to our Lady* ii, Oh help me, lest in vain for me should pass..The blessed Host and sacring of the Mass.

†**b.** *concr.* Used for: The consecrated elements.

c **1290** *S. Eng. Leg.* I. 358/105 Muche folk þare was in Rome þat in guode bi-leue nere Ne bi-lieueden nouȝt þat þe sacringe ore louerdes licame were. **1448** M. PASTON in *P. Lett.* I. 72 [The Parson of Oxened] being at messe in one Parossh Chirche, evyn at levacion of the sakeryng.

2. The ordination and consecration of persons to certain offices, as those of bishop, king, queen, etc.

1297 R. GLOUC. (Rolls) 2318 Ac him sulf him crounede & made him king so His sacringe was lute worþ & naþeles it was ydo. *c* **1380** WYCLIF *Wks.* (1880) 393 þe clerkis han many grete & smale perquisitiuys,..as..for halowynge of chapels..& for sacrynge of ordres, & fulle many mo. *c* **1450** *Merlin* vi. 105 We wolde that his sacringe and coronacion be respite to Penticoste. **1496** *Dives & Paup.* (W. de W.) VII. xviii. 305/1 Yf the offycer of ye bysshop axe of custome ony gyft..in sacrynge of bysshopes..yf they yt sholde be.. sacred gyue theym suche gyftes..is it symonye. **1672** TEMPLE *Ess., Govt.* Wks. 1731 I. 98 The Sacring of the Kings of France (as Loysel says) is the Sign of their Soveraign Priest-hood, as well as Kingdom. **1814** SOUTHEY *Roderick* XVIII. 107 For acclamation and for sacring now One form must serve. **1902** *Q. Rev.* July 356 The fullest development of the service for the sacring of the French Kings is contained in the Coronation Book of Charles V.

†**3.** *gen.* The action of consecrating. *Obs.*

1610 W. FOLKINGHAM *Art of Survey* Ep. Ded. 2, I will screw-vp this Key with the prostrate sacring of my selfe..at the Shrine of your gracious Clemencie. **1613** PURCHAS *Pilgrimage* II. viii. 136 Elias Leuita describeth the forme of sacring or hallowing their Teraphim in this sort.

4. *Comb.* as ***sacring time***, SACRING-BELL.

1482 CAXTON *Trevisa's Higden* VIII. xix. 414 The lyeutenaunt..forth with commanded that euery man shold kepe his wepen in his hond sacryng tyme and other. **1577-87** HOLINSHED *Chron.* III. 946/2 Those that..held not vp their hands at the sacring time. **1594** T. BEDINGFIELD tr. *Machiavelli's Florentine Hist.* (1595) 198 The time of the execution should be at the sacring time of Masse.

†**ˈsacring**, *a. Obs. rare.* Also 6 *Sc.* sacrand. [f. SACRE *v.*[1] + -ING[2].] In senses of the vb.

In quot. 1508 used for the vbl. sb. attrib.: see next.

1508 DUNBAR *Flyting* 160 And quhen thow heiris ane guse cry in the glennis, Thow thinkis it swetar than sacrand bell of sound. **1644** BULWER *Chirol.* 138 Because it hath a sacring and sanctifying signe.

sacring-bell. [SACRING *vbl. sb.*]

1. A small bell rung at the elevation of the host.

1395 *E.E. Wills* (1882) 5, I bequethe a chales and a paxbred,..and a sacrynge belle. **1449** *Churchw. Acc. Yatton* (Somerset Rec. Soc.) 90 For a rop for the sacryng bell, iiiid. **1502** *Acc. Ld. High Treas. Scot.* (1900) II. 343 Item, for tua small sacryne bellis, tane at ane cremar. **1584** R. SCOT *Discov. Witchcr.* v. iii. (1886) 76 He heard a little saccaring bell ring to the elevation of a morrowe masse. **1846** R. HART *Eccl. Rec.* 225 The sacring bell, which was rung at the elevation of the host. **1884** *Sunday at Home* Feb. 102/2 No latticed confessional—no sacring bell.

¶**2.** In post-Reformation times, sometimes applied to a small bell rung to summon parishioners to morning prayers, or to mark the point in the Communion Service at which the people should go up to communicate.

1598 DRAYTON *Heroic Ep.* III. 71 Who would not rise to ring the Mornings Knell, When thy sweet Lips might be the sacring Bell? **1641** I. H. *Petit. agst. Pocklington* 2 He hath caused a Bell to be hung up in his Chancell, called a Sacring Bell, which the Clarke always rings at the going up to second Service. **1766** ENTICK *London* IV. 75 A lantern, which.. incloses the sacring-bell, to call the parishioners to prayers.

ˈsacripant. *rare.* [a. F. *Sacripant*, ad. It. *Sacripante*, a character in Boiardo's *Orlando innamorato.*] A boastful pretender to valour.

1830 W. TAYLOR *Hist. Surv. Germ. Poetry* II. 320 He is surprised by a nymph..who is at length seized by the supervening Itifal, a Sacripant of knighthood.

sacrist (ˈseɪkrɪst). Also 7 sachriste, 8 saccarist. [a. OF. *sacriste* (= It. *sacrista*), ad. L. *sacrista*, f. *sacer* sacred (*sacra* neut. pl. sacred objects) + *-ista*: see -IST.]

1. An official charged with the custody of the sacred vessels, relics, vestments, etc., of a religious house or a church.

In English cathedrals the 'sacrist' (sometimes called 'sacristan') is always in orders, often a minor canon.

1577-87 HOLINSHED *Chron.* III. 1241/2 Frier Combe, a sacrist of that house of Westminster. **1635** PAGITT *Christianogr.* III. (1636) 103 Two Sacrists, carrying two silver Lanthorns. **1656-61** [See SACRISTAN 1]. **1665** S. BING in Ellis *Orig. Lett.* Ser. II. IV. 23 It is said the Sacrist [of St. Paul's] is out of town, -and there will be no Communion as customarily. **1726** AYLIFFE *Parergon* 216 A Sacrist or Treasurer which are not Dignitaries in the Church of Common Right, but only by Custom. **1883** *Daily News* 19 Sept. 1/1 [Died.] Mr. W. Sanders, for many years Sacrist and Librarian of Westminster Abbey.

2. An officer in the University of Aberdeen (formerly King's and Marischal Colleges); orig. a cleric whose responsibilities included the furnishings of the church, later a senior janitor or head porter with some ceremonial duties.

1638 *King's Coll.* (Aberdeen) *Minutes* 27 Dec., In the visitatioun of the Kinges Colledge of the Universitie of Aberdeine..convenit..Mr. Alexander Ross doctor of divinitie, principall of the said Colledge,..Mr. Gilbert Ross, cantor, and Patrick Innes, sacrist. *a* **1670** SPALDING *Troub. Chas. I* (Bannatyne Cl.) I. 111 To the which committee..was summoned..the principall of the King's Colledge of Old Aberdein, the four regents, canonist, doctor of medicine, civilist, sacrist, and cantor. **1732** in A. M. Munro *Rec. Old Aberdeen* (1899) I. 256 Robert Gordon, Saccarist in the King's College. **1792** J. SPALDING *Hist. Troubles* I. 127 Mr. David Lindsay Parson of Belhelvie, was said to be moderator of this committee, to the which committee upon the 24th of March were summoned in name of the assembly and moderator, the principal of the King's College of Old Aberdeen, the four regents, the canonist, Doctor of Medicine, civilist, sacrist, and janitor, founded members thereof. **1825** *Aberdeen Censor* Dec. 210 Enrolled as a student in divinity, by paying six shillings to the sacrist of Marischall College and a moiety to the library. **1865** G. MACDONALD *Alec Forbes* II. ii. 8 A long broom which the sacrist had been using to clear foot-paths. **1902** *Minutes Aberdeen Univ. Court* V. 250 The Joint Committee were of the opinion that appropriate costumes, including robes and hats, for the two sacrists, could be procured for £15. **1965** *Aberdeen Univ. Rev.* Autumn 70 No ceremony is complete without the presence of the sacrist (or sacrists) robed in purple, with a tricorne hat trimmed with gold upon his head, and bearing his silver, bell-headed, mace.

sacristan (ˈsækrɪstən). Also 4-5 -ane, 7 -on. See also SEXTON. [ad. med.L. *sacristānus* (whence mod.F. *sacristain*), f. *sacrista* SACRIST; see -AN.

OF. had the semi-popular forms *segrestain*, etc., whence Eng. SEXTON.]

1. a. The SEXTON of a parish church. *Obs.* or *arch.* **b.** = SACRIST.

c **1375** *Sc. Leg. Saints* xvii. (*Martha*) 245 Quhene I mad me bowne þat holy body to lay done, & to þe sacristane to kepe gafe, quhene ȝe raysit me fra slepe. **1483** *Cath. Angl.* 315/1 A Sacristane, *sacrista, edilis.* **1563** *Reg. Privy Council Scot.* I. 246 And als the Sacristanis, beand Vicaris of the said paroche kirk, wer in use..to mak and uphald the glassin windoes of the said kirk. **1608** *Vestry Bks.* (Surtees) 213 Item: that the Sacriston shall not presume to breake anye grave in the church without the consent of the Churchwardins. **1656-61** BLOUNT *Glossogr.*, *Sacrist* or *Sacristan*, a Sexten or Vestry-Keeper in a Church, or Religious house. **1763** DEL PINO *Span. Dict.*, *Escolano*, the sacristan..that has charge of the vestments and holy vessels of the church. **1800** COLERIDGE *Christabel* II. 8 The sacristan, Who duly pulls the heavy bell, Five and forty beads must tell Between each stroke. **1854** J. D. H. DALE *Sacristan's Man.* Pref. 10 The Pope's Sacristan is a Bishop. **1870** DICKENS *E. Drood* i, The Sacristan locks the iron-barred gates that divide the sanctuary from the chancel.

2. In a nunnery, a sister charged with a function corresponding to that of sacrist. Cf. SACRISTINE.

c **1440** *Alphabet of Tales* 319 Sho was sacristan of þe kurk and sho had grete deuocion vnto our Ladie. **1896** tr. *Huysman's En Route* vii. 92 A sacristan-sister, tall and pale and rather bent, entered like a shadow.

Hence ˌ**sacristaˈness** = SACRISTINE. Also *fig.*

1866 *Cornh. Mag.* XIV. 440 The sacristaness was going through the corridor..on her way to ring the bell for matins. **1924** C. C. MARTINDALE *St. Paul* xi. 141 The city of Ephesus was the sacristaness of the great Artemis and of the image that fell from heaven.

†**sacristanry.** *Obs.* [f. SACRISTAN + -RY. Cf. OF. *segrestainerie* SEXTONRY.] = SACRISTY.

1483 *Cath. Angl.* 315/1 A Sacristanry, *sacristarium.*

‖**sacristine** (ˈsækrɪstiːn). [F. *sacristine*, altered form of *sacristaine* fem. of *sacristain* SACRISTAN.] A female sacristan.

1832 MOORE in *Mem.* (1854) VI. 286 Rogers..told a story of a young girl who had been sacristine..in a convent.

sacristy (ˈsækrɪstɪ). [a. F. *sacristie*, a. med.L. *sacristia*, f. *sacrista* SACRIST.] The repository in a church in which are kept the vestments, the sacred vessels and other valuable property.

[**1630** WADSWORTH *Further Observ. Pilgr.* 6 Betweene this house and the high Altar stands the Sacristia, within which is the Custodia of the holy Eucharist (as they call it). **1644** EVELYN *Diary* 8 Nov., Through this we went into the Sacristia, where..one of the Order preach'd.] **1656** BLOUNT *Glossogr.* *a* **1668** LASSELS *Voy. Italy* (1698) II. 93 In the Sacristy of this church I saw the chains in which St. Peter was fettered. **1845** S. AUSTIN *Ranke's Hist. Ref.* III. 630 The Lübekers took the confiscated church treasures out of the sacristies. **1846** *Ecclesiologist* Jan. 5 Sacristies, or, as they are more usually called now, Vestries. *Ibid.* 6 The proper situation of a Sacristy is on the north side of the chancel, towards its eastern part.

sacrit(e, obs. Sc. pa. t. and pple. of SACRE *v.*[1]

sacro-[1] (ˈsækrəʊ, ˈseɪkrəʊ), assumed as combining form of L. *sacer* sacred, in various nonce-words, as **sacro-pictorial** *a.*, relating to sacred portraiture; **sacro-secular** *a.*, partly sacred and partly secular; **sacro-seric** *a.*, (*jocular*), sacred and silken.

1849 [K. H. DIGBY] *Compitum* II. 357 All which form a code of *sacropictorial law. **16..** DOROTHY OSBORNE *Lett. to Sir W. Temple* (1888) 18 The Priory is a low-built *sacro-secular edifice. **1772** NUGENT tr. *Hist. Fr. Gerund* II. 372 The *sacro-seric vestments which adorn the priest in the celebration of the sacrifice of the mass.

sacro-[2] (ˈseɪkrəʊ), *Anat.*, used as combining form of L. (*os*) *sacrum* SACRUM, prefixed (usually with hyphen) to various adjs., forming compounds with the sense 'pertaining jointly to the sacrum and (some other part indicated by the second element)', as in ***sacro-caudal***, ***-coccygeal***, ***-coccygean***, ***-costal***, ***-cotyloid***, ***-cotyloidean***, ***-femoral***, ***-iliac***, ***-inguinal***, ***-ischiac***, ***-ischiadic***, ***-ischiatic***, ***-lumbal***, ***-lumbar***, ***-pectineal***, ***perineal***, ***-pubic***, ***-rectal***, ***-sciatic***, ***-spinal***, ***-spinous***, ***-tuberous***, ***-uterine***, ***-vertebral*** adjs. Also ˌ**sacro-iliˈitis**, inflammation of the sacro-iliac joint. **sacro-ˈmedian** *a.*, the epithet of the artery running along the median line of the sacrum (*Cent. Dict.* 1891).

1831 R. KNOX *Cloquet's Anat.* 193 *Sacro-coccygeal Articulation. *Ibid.*, Anterior Sacro-coccygeal Ligament. **1875** SIR W. TURNER in *Encycl. Brit.* I. 822/1 At the time of birth the sacro-coccygeal part of the spine is concave forwards. **1840** E. WILSON *Anat. Vade M.* (1842) 110 The posterior *sacro-coccygean ligament. **1890** COUES *Ornith.* II. iv. 211 These 'sacral ribs' or *sacrocostals are furthermore distinguished by being devoid of the epipleural or uncinate processes, with which other true ribs are furnished. **1899** *Allbutt's Syst. Med.* VI. 865 *Sacro-femoral or 1st lumbar area. **1831** R. KNOX *Cloquet's Anat.* 193 Irregular fibres placed before the *sacro-iliac articulation. **1886** J. M. DUNCAN *Dis. Women* (ed. 3) 438 Rheum of a sacro-iliac joint. **1934** *Acta Rheumetologica* VI. XXIII. 7/1 All the cases of Spondylitis adolescens..so far examined, have radiographically shown indications of bilateral infection of both sacro-iliac joints, (*Sacro-ileitis) usually in the form of ankylosis. **1936** *Brit. Jrnl. Radiol.* IX. 127 (*caption*) Complete ankylosis of the sacro-iliac joints—the end-result of a chronic sacro-iliitis. **1977** *Lancet* 17 Sept. 591/1 Around the classic centre, rigid spine with radiographic sacro-iliitis, there is a very large fringe of milder forms of spondylitis. **1899** *Allbutt's Syst. Med.* VI. 865 *Sacro-inguinal or 12th dorsal area. **1790** R. BLAND in *Med. Commun.* II. 437 Where the *sacro-ischiatic ligaments cross. **1870** ROLLESTON *Anim. Life* 18 The sacroischiatic notch of anthropotomy. **1859** *Todd's Cycl. Anat.* V. 207/1 The bones composing the *sacro-lumbar articulations. **1876** GROSS *Dis. Bladder* 20 The pain shoots along..to the sacrolumbar region. **1899** *Allbutt's Syst. Med.* VI. 454 The *sacro-perineal region. **1841** RAMSBOTHAM *Obstet. Med.* 23 The antero-posterior, *sacro-pubic, or conjugate [diameter]. **1753** CHAMBERS *Cycl. Supp.*, *Sacro-sciatic ligaments... The small sacro-sciatic, or internal sciatic ligament. **1782** A. MONRO *Anat. Bones, Nerves*, etc. 146 Two strong ligaments which are extended to the *os ischium*; and are therefore called *sacro-sciatic*. **1893** A. S. ECCLES *Sciatica* 55 The cause of obstinate sacro-sciatic tenderness. **1910** H. W. CATTELL *Lippincott's New Med. Dict.* 845/1 **Sacrospinous ligament* = sacrosciatic ligament, lesser. **1913** *Gray's Anat.* (ed. 18) 354 The sacrospinous ligament (small sacrosciatic ligament) is thin, and triangular in form. **1967** G. M. WYBURN et al. *Conc. Anat.* vi. 163/2 The short sacrospinous ligament lies anterior to the sacrotuberous ligament and extends from the spine of the ischium to the lower part of the sacrum and coccyx. **1910** H. W. CATTELL *Lippincott's New Med. Dict.* 845/1 **Sacrotuberous ligament*, = Sacrosciatic ligament, great. **1925** *Jrnl. Amer. Med. Assoc.* 31 July 307/2 Von Meyer..described the rotary movement of the sacrum, and showed..the restraint put on this rotation by the sacrotuberous and sacrospinous ligaments. **1962** *Gray's Anat.* (ed. 33) 531 The sacrotuberous ligament..is placed at the lower and posterior part of the pelvis. **1967** Sacrotuberous [see *sacrospinous* above]. **1888** W. H. & H. T. BYFORD *Pract. Med. & Surg.* (ed. 4) ii. 83 Two fingers carried high up in the posterior fornix vaginae can usually feel the semi-circular folds of the *sacro-uterine ligament extending outward, backward and upward. **1946** R. W. TE LINDE *Operative Gynecol.* vii. 125/1 Pushing back the mucosa in the attempt to see the peritoneum exposes each sacro-uterine ligament. **1831** R. KNOX *Cloquet's Anat.* 193 *Sacro-vertebral Ligament. **1872** MIVART *Elem. Anat.* 57 The sacro-vertebral angle is generally replaced by almost a straight line.

‖**sacro egoismo** ('sakro ego'izmo). [It., 'sacred egoism': see SACRED *a.* 7.] Nationalism without scruples in relationships with other states. Also *transf.*

[**1914** A. SALANDRA in G. Fumagalli *Chi l'ha Detto?* (1958) 560 Anima sevro..da ogni sentimento che non sia quello della illimitata ed esclusiva devozione alla Patria nostra, del *sacro egoismo* per l'Italia.] **1944** *Zionist Rev.* 21 Apr. 6/3 Characteristic of our present attitude is the suggestion that my insistence on 'using every means for the pursuit of our own aims', sounds rather like the doctrine of *sacro egoismo*. **1947** 'G. ORWELL' *Eng. People* 15 Power politics, 'realism', *sacro egoismo* and the doctrine that the end justifies the means. **1981** J. SUTHERLAND *Bestsellers* xi. 126 The adolescent's values..*sacro egoismo*, refusal to form lasting relationships, machismo.

sacrosanct ('sækrəʊsæŋkt, 'seɪkrəʊ-). Also 7 **-sainct, sant, sackersaint.** [ad. L. *sacrōsanctus*, properly two words, *sacrō* abl. of *sacrum* sacred rite (neut. of *sacer* sacred) and *sanctus* pa. pple. of *sancīre* to render holy or inviolable. Cf. F. *sacrosaint*, earlier *-sainct* (whence some 17th c. Eng. forms), Sp., Pg. *sacrosanto*, It. *sacro-*, *sagrosanto*.] Of persons and things, esp. obligations, laws, etc.: Secured by a religious sanction from violation, infringement, or encroachment; inviolable, sacred.

1601 HOLLAND *Pliny* I. 178 Armed as he was with his sacrosanct and inuiolable authoritie. **1603** —— *Plutarch's Mor.* 1332 Which [Isles] he found to have very few inhabitants, and those all were by the Britaines, held for sacro-sainct and inviolable. **1637** HEYLIN *Answ. Burton* 80 Perhaps you thinke, because Mass. Prinne is of a factious Tribunitian spirit, he must be Sacrosanct and uncontrolable. **1659** H. L'ESTRANGE *Alliance Div. Off.* 291 What confederacy can be imagined more noble, more sacrosant, than that between Man and Wife? **1787** JEFFERSON *Writ.* (1859) II. 331 Let them establish your fundamental rights by a sacrosanct declaration. **1871** MORLEY *Crit. Misc.* Ser. I. 270 Truth, which alone of words is essentially divine and sacrosanct. **1891** C. E. NORTON *Dante's Purgat.* xxix. 184 O Virgins sacrosanct. **1895** SALA *Life & Adv.* II. lvi. 327 Beyond this sacrosanct city the railway was only available for about fifty miles.

transf. **1880** *World* 16 June, When the persons of hares and rabbits have ceased to be sacrosanct, what guarantee of inviolability is there for the grouse?

Hence †**sacrosanctified**, †**sacrosanctious** *adjs.* = SACROSANCT; **sacrosanctness** = next.

1621 QUARLES *Argalus & P.* (1678) 57 Where plighted faith, and Sacro-sanctious vow Hath given possession, dispossess not thou. *a* **1693** *Urquhart's Rabelais* III. ii. 28 The Sacro sanctified Domicile of your Celestial Brain. **1876** CARTWRIGHT *Jesuits* 206 The Pontifical utterances of which the dogmatic sacrosanctness is open to no doubt.

sacrosanctity (,sækrəʊ-, ,seɪkrəʊ'sæŋktɪtɪ). [f. SACROSANCT *a.*, after *sanctity*.] The condition of being sacrosanct; inviolability; sacredness.

1650 H. MORE *Observ.* in *Enthus. Tri.*, etc. (1656) 94 His bold entitling of his own writings to the Sacrosanctity of Mysteries. **1831** H. COLERIDGE in *Blackw. Mag.* XXIX. 521 Protected by the sacro-sanctity of an Ambassador. **1900** E. LUMMIS *Speaker's Chair* 34 All they did was to wrap themselves in their sacrosanctity, and 'curse for their tithes'.

sacrosant, obs. form of SACROSANCT.

sacrum ('seɪkrəm). *Anat.* Pl. **sacrums, sacra.** [Subst. use of neut. sing. of L. *sacer* sacred: see *os sacrum* s.v. OS.] A composite, symmetrical, triangular bone which articulates laterally with the ilia, forming the dorsal wall of the pelvis and resulting from the ankylosis of two or more vertebræ between the lumbar and coccygeal regions of the spinal column.

1753 CHAMBERS *Cycl. Supp.* s.v. *Sacro-sciatic*, The false transverse apophyses of the sacrum. **1797** ABERNETHY *Surg. & Physiol. Ess.* III. 137 The medulla spinalis, or a substance of an apparently similar nature, was continued into the sacrum. **1845** TODD & BOWMAN *Phys. Anat.* I. 140 The spinal column, in man,..rests upon the sacrum. **1881** *Trans. Obstet. Lond.* XXII. 74 There are [in a double-headed human monster] two well-developed sacra, placed side by side. **1886** J. M. DUNCAN *Dis. Women* (ed. 3) 438 A clergyman's wife was thrown out of a little pony phaeton, and fell on her sacrum. **1890** COUES *Ornith.* II. iii. 138 The numerous anchylosed..vertebræ compose the *sacrum*.

†'**sacry.** *Obs.* Forms: 4 **sacre, sakare, sacry.** [ME. *sa'crē*, app. due to a confusion of SECRE (the 'secret of the Mass') with F. *sacré* pa. pple. of *sacrer*: see SACRE *v.*[1]] The consecration of the Mass; = SACRING *vbl. sb.* 1.

1303 R. BRUNNE *Handl. Synne* 7297 Here ȝyt a messe, Al holy, and no lesse, And nat symple, a sakare, For hyt ys nat y-now for þe. *Ibid.* 7949 For euery prest, aftyr þe sacré, He parteþ þere Goddys body yn þre. **13..** *Metr. Hom.* (Vernon MS.) in *Archiv Stud. neu. Spr.* LVII. 282 [He said] Ihesu was not þat oble þat was raised atte sacre. **1463** *Bury Wills* (Camden) 29 To do the chymes goo at yᵉ sacry of the messe of Jhū.

b. *attrib.* **sacry bell** = SACRING-BELL.

c **1430** LYDG. *Min. Poems* (Percy Soc.) 255 Than gon to chirche or heare the sacry belle. *c* **1460** *Promp. Parv.* (Winch.) 388 Sacrybelle, *tintinabulum*.

sacryt, obs. Sc. pa. t. and pple. of SACRE *v.*[1]

sacsac ('sæksæk). [Pidgin.] A local name in Papua New Guinea for the sago palm, *Metroxylon sagu*. Also *attrib.*

1947 I. L. IDRIESS *Isles of Despair* xxiv. 163 Sago from the sac-sac palm. **1962** *Coast to Coast 1961–62* 55 We told them where they would find the sago-palms, the sacsac, to plait for walls and roof.

sact, obs. Sc. form of SACK *v.*[2]

Sacta, Sacti, varr. SAKTA, SAKTI.

sad (sæd), *a.* and *adv.* Forms: 1–3 **sæd**, 3 **sað, sead, sed,** 5–7 **sade,** 4 **saad, zed,** 4–5 **said,** 4–6 **sadd(e,** 3– **sad.** [Com. Teut.: OE. *sæd* = OS. *sad*, MDu. *sat* (Du. *zat*), OHG., MHG. *sat* (mod.G. *satt*), ON. *sað-r* (rare: superseded by *sadd-r*, pa. pple. of the derived verb *seðja* to satiate), Goth. *saþ-s* (pl. *sadai*):—OTeut. **saðo-* full, satiated:—WIndogermanic **sətó-* in **n̥-səto-s*, Gr. ἄ-ατος insatiate (cf. L. *sat*, *satis* enough, *satur* satisfied, full, OIrish *sathech* satiated); the word is a pa. pple. with suffix *-tó-* from the root **sā-* to satisfy; cf. Gr. ἄδην (:—**sə-dām*), enough. A parallel form from the strong grade of the root (with unaccented suffix) is Goth. *sōþ* (:—pre-Teut. **sā́to-m*) satisfaction, whence *gasōþjan* to satisfy.]

A. *adj.*

I. Of persons and immaterial things.

†**1.** Having had one's fill; satisfied; sated, weary or tired (of something). Const. *of* (in OE. *genitive*) or *infinitive*.

a **1000** *Riddles* vi. (Gr.), Ic eom anhaȝa iserne wund,.. beadoweorca sæd, ecȝum weriȝ. *c* **1000** *Ags. Ps.* (Th.) lxxvii. 29 Swiðe ætan, and sæde wurdan. *c* **1200** *Trin. Coll. Hom.* 75 Ich nam noht ȝiet sad of mine sinnes, and forþi ne mai ich hie noht forlete. *c* **1205** LAY. 9345 Claudien þe kæisere Sað wes of þon compe. *a* **1240** *Ureisun* 30 in *Cott. Hom.* 193 Vor heo neuer ne beoð sead þi ueir to iseonne. *a* **1250** *Owl & Night.* 452 (Jesus MS.) Ich..skente hi myd myne songe Ac noþeles nouht ouer longe; Hwenne ich iseo þat men beoþ glade, Ich nelle þat hi beon to sade. *a* **1300** *Cursor M.* 23436 þof þat þou euer apon him se, Of him sadd [*Edinb.* said] sal þou neuer be. *a* **1310** in Wright *Lyric P.* vii. 29 For selden y am sad that semly forte se. *c* **1386** CHAUCER *Can. Yeom. Prol. & T.* 324 Yet of that Art they kan nat wexen sadde ffor vn-to hem it is a bitter sweete. **1387** TREVISA *Higden* (Rolls) I. 9 Now men beþ al sad [orig. *modernorum saturitatem*]. *c* **1407** LYDG. *Reson & Sens.* 1265 Al our lyf..Ys but a maner exile here, Of which he ought[e] to be sad. *a* **1450** *Le Morte Arth.* 716 To serve hym was there no man sad.

†**2.** Settled, firmly established in purpose or condition; steadfast, firm, constant. *Obs.*

c **1315** SHOREHAM VII. 298 So þat hyt was god and sad, Al þys world, þat was ymad Of hym þat can. **1340** *Ayenb.* 83 Non ne is aryȝt preus..þet ne ys..zed and stable uor to uolȝy. *c* **1350** *St. John* 349 in Horstm. *Altengl. Leg.* (1881) 38 When saynt John herd..how sad trowth in þam was set [etc.]. *c* **1350** *Will. Palerne* 1371 Al saxoyne was set wiþ wel sadde lawes. *c* **1374** CHAUCER *Boeth.* III. pr. x. 70 (Camb. MS.) Ther may no man dowte that ther nis som blysfulnesse þat is sad [L. *solidam*] stydefast and parfyt. *c* **1375** *Sc. Leg. Saints* xlii. (*Agatha*) 36 As quincyane persawing had þat scho wes of wil sa sad. **1382** WYCLIF *2 Pet.* i. 19 We han a sadder [Vulg. *firmiorem*] word of the prophet. *c* **1412** HOCCLEVE *De Reg. Princ.* 4784 Ther may no prince in his estate endure, Ne ther-yn any while stande sad, But he be loued. *c* **1450** *St. Cuthbert* (Surtees) 234 Sho sall be to þe a sadde frende. *c* **1450** *Godstow Reg.* 64 þat her graunt shold be sure & sad, she strengthid hit with her seele. **1493** *Festivall* (W. de W. 1515) 75 b, Be ye stable & sadde in the fayth. **1553** BECON *Reliques of Rome* (1563) 175 b, All christen people that will be saued, must haue sad beliefe in the holy Sacrament. **1590** SPENSER *F.Q.* III. xi. 45 More eath to number with how many eyes High heven beholdes sad lovers nightly theeveryes. **1667** MILTON *P.L.* VI. 541 Settl'd in his face I see Sad resolution and secure.

†**3.** Strong; capable of resisting; valiant. *Obs.*

1382 WYCLIF *Rom.* xv. 1 Forsothe we saddere [Vulg. *nos firmiores*] owen for to susteyne..the feblenesse of syke men. **1388** —— *Ezek.* xxxiv. 16 Y schal make sad that that was sijk. ? *a* **1400** *Morte Arth.* 3289 The secunde sir..Was sekerare to my sighte, and saddare in armes. *c* **1400** MAUNDEV. (1839) xiv. 159 And it [the diamond] maketh a man more strong and more sad aȝenst his Enemyes. *c* **1400** *Destr. Troy* 1277 þan pollux full pertly aprochet in hast With seuyn hundrithe sad men assemblit hym with, ffrochit into þe frount & a fray made. *c* **1475** *Partenay* 4876 Noble knightes ten, Stronge, hable, and light, men sad and myghty.

4. †**a.** Orderly and regular in life; of trustworthy character and judgement; grave, serious. Often coupled with *wise* or *discreet*. *Obs.*

c **1375** *Sc. Leg. Saints* xxvi. (*Nycholas*) 175 In thewis saddare þane wes he ere. *c* **1386** CHAUCER *Man of Law's T.* 37 In Surrye whilom dwelte a compaignye Of chapmen riche and therto sadde and trewe. **1429** *Rolls of Parlt.* IV. 338/2 Ye Kyng shall..come to sadder yeres of discretion. **1440** in Glew *Hist. Walsall* (1856) 106 One of the sadest and weldesposed Prest of Saynt John's Gylde. *c* **1450** *Godstow Reg.* 98 He shold behote, afore good men and sadde in Wycombe, openly. **1486** *Act 3 Hen. VII*, c. 4 Twelve sad and discreet Persons, of the Cheque Roll of the King's honourable Houshold. **1490** CAXTON *Eneydos* xxix. 113 Sadde of behauoure, and of symple contenaunce. **1551** ROBINSON tr. *More's Utop.* II. xii. (1895) 225 A sad and an honest matrone [orig. *grauis et honesta matrona*]. **1562** in W. H. Turner *Select. Rec. Oxford* (1880) 292 The..wyseste Baylliffs and other sadd and discreate cytezens. **1579** NORTHBROOKE *Dicing* (1843) 167 What woman nowe-a-dayes (that is sadde and wyse) will be knowne to haue skill of dauncing, &c.? **1605** BACON *Adv. Learn.* II. xxiii. §5 Of this wisedome it seemeth some of the auncient Romanes in the saddest and wisest times were professors. **1632** LITHGOW *Trav.* II. 71 The solid, and sad man, is not troubled with the floods and ebbes of Fortune. **1665** POWELL in Wood *Life* (O.H.S.) II. 48 An old donation of the College to a sad priest that preaches on that day.

†**b.** Of looks, appearance: Dignified, grave, serious. *Obs.*

c **1350** *Will. Palerne* 228 Of lere ne of lykame lik him nas none, ne of so sad a semblant þat euer he say wiþ eiȝyen. **13..** *E.E. Allit. P.* A. 887, & þe alder-men so sadde of chere, Her songe þay songen neuer þe les. *c* **1369** CHAUCER *Dethe Blaunche* 860 And whiche eyen my lady had, Debonayre, good, glad, and sad. *c* **1400** *Rom. Rose* 4627 She, demurely sad of chere.

†**c.** Profoundly or solidly learned (*in*). *Obs.*

c **1400** *Destr. Troy* 1485 A philosoffer,..In þe Syense full sad of þe seuyn Artes. **1523** *Act 14 & 15 Hen. VIII*, c. 5 Those persons that be profounde, sad, & discrete, groundly lerned, and depely studied in Phisicke.

d. Of thought, consideration: Mature, serious. *Obs.* exc. *arch.* in the phrase ***in sad earnest***, which as now used belongs rather to sense 5.

1485 *Surtees Misc.* (1888) 43 The said Maire, after sad and mature examinacion of the said recordes..decreed [etc.]. *c* **1500** *Three Kings' Sons* 24 And so, aftir sad deliberacion, he answerd the messengere yn this maner. **1540** *Act 32 Hen. VIII*, c. 42 The said Maistres or Governours..aftre their sadd discretions,..shall [etc.]. **1637** RUTHERFORD *Lett.* (1862) I. xcix. 253, I wᵈ. I cᵈ. begin to be a Christian in sad earnest. **1643** J. M. *Soveraigne Salve* 38 At least they may deigne this last motive the honour of a deep and sad thought or two. **1649** BP. HALL *Confirm.* (1651) 73 They are exceeding weighty and worthy of sad consideration. **1771** SMOLLETT *Humph. Cl.* 5 May, An attack that made me shed tears in sad earnest.

5. a. Of persons, their feelings or dispositions: Sorrowful, mournful.

? *a* **1366** CHAUCER *Rom. Rose* 211 She was cleped Avarice... Full sad and caytif [orig. *megre et chetive*] was she. *c* **1450** HOLLAND *Howlat* 187 Ay sorowfull and sad at evin song and houris. *c* **1470** HENRY *Wallace* IV. 188 Malancoly he was of complexioun,..Sorouful, sadde, ay dreidfull but plesance. **1526** *Pilgr. Perf.* (W. de W. 1531) 87 Consyderyng some persones to be iocunde and mery, some sadde and heuy. *a* **1548** HALL *Chron., Hen. VII* 56 This Ambassade was sent ..to visite & comforte the kyng, beyng sorowful & sad for the death of so good a quene & spouse. *a* **1553** UDALL *Royster D.* III. iii. (Arb.) 43 But why speake ye so faintly, or why are ye so sad? *R. Royster.* Thou knowest the prouerbe, bycause I can not be had. **1611** BIBLE *Gen.* xl. 6 And Ioseph came in vnto them in the morning, and looked vpon them, and behold, they were sad. **1667** MILTON *P.L.* x. 18 Th' Angelic Guards ascended, mute and sad For man. **1678** BUNYAN *Pilgr.* I. 196, I was very sad, I think sader than at any one time in my life. **1725** POPE *Odyss.* IX. 72 With sails outspread we fly th'unequal strife, Sad for their loss, but joyful of our life. **1754** Gray *Poesy* 77 The sad Nine in Greece's evil hour. **1860** Tyndall *Glac.* i. xii. 88, I felt a little sad at the thought. *a* **1878** P'cess Alice *Mem.* (1884) 63, I ought not to make you sadder, when you are sad enough already.

absol. **1588** A. King tr. *Canisius' Catech.*, *Cert. Devout Prayers* 39 The hop and comforter of all sad, haue mercie on me. **1784** Cowper *Tiroc.* 665 Behold that figure, neat, though plainly clad; His sprightly mingled with a shade of sad.

b. *Phrase.* (Possibly suggested by the older association of *sad* and *wise*: see 4.)

1798 Coleridge *Anc. Mar.* vii. *ad fin.*, A sadder and a wiser man He rose the morrow morn. **1814** Scott *Wav.* lxiii, 'A sadder and a wiser man', he felt [etc.]. **1877** Mrs. Forrester *Mignon* I. 175 When he takes his way homewards, he is a sadder and a wiser man.

c. Of looks, tones, gestures, costume, etc.: Expressive of sorrow.

c **1386** Chaucer *Knt.'s T.* 2127 With a sad visage he siked stille. *a* **1400–50** *Alexander* 5052 With sare sighingis & sadd for sake of his wirdis. **1508** Dunbar *Tua Mariit Wemen* 447 According to my sable weid I mon haif sad maneris, Or thai will se all the suth. **1535** Coverdale *Matt.* vi. 16 When ye fast, be not sad [**1611** of a sad countenance] as ye ypocrytes are. **1634** Milton *Comus* 235 Where the love-lorn Nightingale Nightly to thee her sad Song mourneth well. **1660** F. Brooke tr. *Le Blanc's Trav.* 221 A sad pale countenance. **1671** Milton *P.R.* i. 43 Them amidst With looks agast and sad he thus bespake. **1792** S. Rogers *Pleas. Mem.* i. 320 His sad inquiring eye. **1819** Scott *Ivanhoe* xxxvi, Two halberdiers, clad in black,.. and others, in the same sad livery. **1848** Thackeray *Van. Fair* xii, Poor little Amelia, with rather a sad wistful face.

d. Of times, places, actions, etc.: Characterized by sorrow, sorrowful.

13.. *E.E. Allit. P.* B. 525 Ne þe swetnesse of somer, ne þe sadde wynter. **1617** Moryson *Itin.* i. 243 We passed a sad night in this place, and never had more need of Job his patience then heere. **1662** J. Davies tr. *Mandelslo's Trav.* 252 This was the saddest night we had in all our Voyage. **1667** Milton *P.L.* xi. 478 Immediately a place Before his eyes appeard, sad, noysom, dark, A Lazar-house it seemd. **1722** De Foe *Relig. Courtsh.* i. i. (1840) 10 'Tis a sad life, for a woman to have no help from her husband in things that are good. **1881** Lady Herbert *Edith* 201 His was one of the saddest lots I have ever known in life. **1888** Lowell *Heartsease & Rue* 149 It gives me a sad pleasure to remember that I was encouraged in this project by my friend the late Arthur Hugh Clough.

†**e.** Morose, dismal-looking. *Obs.*

1593 Shaks. *Rich. II*, v. v. 70 And how com'st thou hither? Where no man euer comes, but that sad dogge That brings me food, to make misfortune liue?

f. Causing sorrow; distressing, calamitous, lamentable. In early use partly fig. of sense 7, 'heavy'.

c **1375** *Sc. Leg. Saints* xii. (*Mathias*) 189, & [of] þat sad ded þe ranowne Sowne rane throw al þe towne. **1567** *Gude & Godlie B.* (S.T.S.) 33 Him will he scurge with plagues sad and sair. **1637** B. Jonson *Sad Sheph.* i. ii, A sadder chance hath given allay Both to the Mirth and Music of this day. **1654** Fuller *Two Serm.* 8 It is not improbable that this Psalm [xi] might be composed on the sad murther of the Priests by Saul. **1667** Milton *P.L.* i. 135 With sad overthrow and foul defeat. **1688** Penton *Guard. Instruct.* (1897) 22 It quickly appear'd how sad is the condition of a Gentleman without Learning. **1712** Addison *Spect.* No. 536 ¶2 'Tis sad so considerable a part of the Kingdom.. should be of no manner of use. **1793** Cowper *To Mary* 33 Partakers of thy sad decline, Thy hands their little force resign. **1823** Byron *Juan* xiii. ix, Of all tales 'tis the saddest—and more sad Because it makes us smile. **1859** Tennyson *Guinev.* 492 How sad it were for Arthur, should he live To sit once more within his lonely hall!

6. Deplorably bad; chiefly as an intensive qualifying terms of depreciation or censure. Often *jocular*. *sad dog*: cf. dog *sb.*1 3 b, and 5 e above.

1694 Echard *Plautus* 60, I am the saddest shiftless creature upon earth. **1697** Dampier *Voy.* (1699) 30 His French Sea-men were the saddest creatures that I was ever among; for tho we had bad weather that required many hands aloft, yet the biggest part of them never stirr'd out of their Hammocks, but to eat or ease themselves. **1706** Farquhar *Recruit. Officer* iii. ii, *Sil.* You are an ignorant, pretending, impudent Coxcomb. *Braz.* Ay, ay, a sad Dog. *c* **1710** Celia Fiennes *Diary* (1888) 71 A sad poore thatch'd place. **1727** Gay *Begg. Op.* i. viii, Our Polly is a sad slut. **1748** Smollett *Rod. Rand.* xvi, I suppose you think me a sad dog,.. and I do confess that appearances are against me. **1771** Mrs. Haywood *New Present* 252 Red brick should not be used [for scouring fire-irons] for it makes sad work. **1819** Shelley *Peter Bell 3rd* vi. xii, All Peter did on this occasion Was, writing some sad stuff in prose. **1819** Byron *Juan* ii. cxxvii, Heaven knows what cash he got or blood he spilt, A sad old fellow was he, if you please. **1835** J. MacDonald in Tweedie *Life* iii. (1849) 249, I am a sad coward. **1836–7** Dickens *Sk. Boz, Charact.* vii, The sad-dog sort of feeling came strongly upon John Dounce. **1892** *Daily News* 25 Jan. 5/3 Unpolished granite.. is a sad harbourer of soot and dust.

II. In various physical senses.

7. Of material objects. †**a.** Solid, dense, compact; massive, heavy. *Obs.* [So early mod.G. *satt.*]

13.. *K. Alis.* 5587 Two grete ymages.. of golde sad. *c* **1330** R. Brunne *Chron.* (1810) 198 With iren nayles sad.. his fete was schod. **1340** Hampole *Pr. Consc.* 3189 þe mast veniel syns sal þar bryn langly, Als wodde brinnes, þat es sadde and hevy. *c* **1350** *Will. Palerne* 1072 No strengþe him wiþstod of sad stonen walles. **1388** Wyclif *Exod.* xxxviii. 7 Forsothe thilke auter was not sad [Vulg. *solidum*], but holowe. *c* **1440** *Promp. Parv.* 440/1 Sad, or hard, *solidus*. *c* **1450** *Cov. Myst.* xxiv. (Shaks. Soc.) 236 In feyth it is an holy ston, Ryth sad of weyth and hevy of peys. **1513** Douglas *Æneis* xi. xi. 47 The schaft was sad and sound, and weill ybaik. **1587** Harrison *England* iii. i. (1878) ii. 2 The flesh of buls.. is of sadder substance and therefore much heauier as it lieth in the scale. **1611** Cotgr., *Fourmage de taulpe*, heauie or sad cheese. **1625** Lisle *Du Bartas, Noe* 29 This kind of timber.. growes so sad and hard that it cannot rot. *c* **1638** Strafford in Browning *Life* (1891) 219 To those that.. tell you.. I am but as a feather, I shall be found sadder than lead. **1641** Best *Farm. Bks.* (Surtees) 147 Short barley-strawe.. is the best for stoppinge of holes.. because it is sadder, and not soe subjeckt to blowe out with everie blast of winde, as other light and dry strawe is.

fig. *c* **1400** *Rom. Rose* 6907 For sadde burdens that men taken Make folkes shuldres aken. *c* **1400** *Apol. Loll.* 45 Wo worþ ȝow þat tiȝen mynt, aneis, & comyn, & ilke herbe, & leuen þe sadder þings of þe lawe, dome, feiþ, & mercy. *c* **1485** *Digby Myst.* (1882) iv. 1328 The wordes of Andrewe beyn sadd & ponderose. **1611** Beaum. & Fl. *Knt. Burn. Pestle* iv. i, Damsel right faire, I am on many sad adventures bound, That call me forth into the wilderness.

†**b.** Solid as opposed to liquid. *Obs.*

c **1380** Wyclif *Serm.* Sel. Wks. II. 259 þer mete was þer bileve þat þei hadden of sadde þingis, and þer drynke was þer bileve þat þei hadden of moist þingis. **1382** —— *Heb.* v. 13 To whom is nede of mylk, and not sad mete [Vulg. *solido cibo*].

†**c.** Firmly fixed. *Obs.* exc. *dial.*

1338 R. Brunne *Chron.* (1810) 305 St[r]ength suld non haf had, to perte þam þorgh oute, So wer þei set sad with poyntes rounde aboute. *a* **1375** *Joseph Arim.* 258 þenne he seos Ihesu crist in a sad Roode. **1382** Wyclif *2 Tim.* ii. 19 But the sad foundement [Vulg. *firmum fundamentum*] of God stondith. *a* **1400** *Leg. Rood* (1871) 137 Beo a staf stondeþ sad, Whon ȝe fongen flesch in godes hous, þat staf is Cristes Crouche.

d. Of soil: Stiff, heavy. ? *Obs.* exc. *dial.*

1340–70 *Alex. & Dind.* 912 For to sowe & to sette in þe sad erthe. *c* **1420** *Pallad. on Husb.* ii. 173 Vynes preueth best yf they Be sette anoon aftir the spade or plough, Er then the lond be woxen sadde or tough. **1600** Surflet *Country Farm* v. xviii. 702 Nauets and turneps delight in a light and fine mould, and not in a churlish and sad ground. **1707** Mortimer *Husb.* (1721) I. 66 Chalky Lands are naturally cold and sad. **1712** J. Morton *Nat. Hist. Northampt.* 44 The Clay-land.. is the toughest, or most tenacious, and the most dense of all our Soils; upon this Account, on the Thrapston Side, they call it Sad-land. **1889** *N.W. Linc. Gloss.* s.v., Land is *sad* when the frosts of winter have not mellowed it.

e. Of bread, pastry, etc.: That has not 'risen' properly; heavy. Now *dial.*

1688 R. Holme *Armoury* iii. 317/1 Bakers Terms in their Art... Sad, heavy, close Bread. **1747–96** Mrs. Glasse *Cookery* xiii. 191 It makes the crust sad, and is a great hazard of the pie running. **1824–9** Landor *Imag. Conv.* Wks. 1846 I. 82 Let him place the accessaries on the table lest what is insipid and clammy, and (as housewives with great propriety call it) sad, grow into duller accretion and inerter viscidity the more I masticate it. **1889** Skrine *Mem. E. Thring* 51 Of what meagre straw and doughy brick was our weekly batch! It was what bakers call 'sad'.

†**f.** Of a number of persons or things: Forming a compact body. *Obs.*

a **1400–50** *Alexander* 2614 þe multitude ware to me meruaile to reken, þat sammed was on aiþir side many sadd thousand. *Ibid.* 5559 þai sett in a sadd sowme & sailid his kniȝtis. *c* **1430** *Chev. Assigne* 119 Of sadde leues of þe wode wrowȝte he hem wedes.

8. a. Of colour: Dark, deep. In later use, influenced by sense 5: Not cheerful-looking; neutral-tinted, dull, sober.

The Ger. *satt* and MDu. *sat* (Du. *zat*) have the sense 'dark' or 'deep' as applied to colours, as a direct development from the primary sense 'full' (see sense 1 above).

c **1412** Hoccleve *De Reg. Princ.* 695 And where be my gounes of scarlet, Sanguyn, murreye, & blewes sadde & lighte. *c* **1425** *Cast. Persev.* (Stage direction) in *Macro Plays* 76 þe iiij dowteris schul be clad in mentelys;.. Trewthe in sad grene, & Pes al in blake. *c* **1483** Caxton *Dialogues* 14/38 Yelow, reed, Sad blew [Fr. *entrepers*], morreey. *a* **1539** in *Archæologia* XLVII. 53 Noo more to use rede stomachers but other sadder colers in the same. **1578** Hunnis *Hyvef. Hunnye* xxxvii. 92 Colours lyght and sad. **1600** Surflet *Country Farm* vi. xxii. 802 Russet wines: In the number wherof, are contained the red wines, or sad, and light red. **1609** C. Butler *Fem. Mon.* (1634) 105 The second Summer, this light yellow is changed to a sad. **1658** Rowland tr. *Moufet's Theat. Ins.* 936 Long and slender shanks of a very sad black colour. **1686** Plot *Staffordsh.* 201 First of a dark greenish colour, growing sadder by degrees as the plant decays, till it approaches a black. **1799** G. Smith *Laboratory* II. 311 Dubbing, of the down of a sad grey cat. **1836** *Backwoods of Canada* 241 The leaves are of a sad green, sharply notched, and divided in three lobes. **1855** Brimley *Ess., Tennyson* 99 Sad greys and browns. **1867** O. W. Holmes *Guard. Angel* iii, She had always.. been dressed in sad colors. **1883** Stevenson *Treas. Isl.* xiii, The general colouring was uniform and sad.

†**b.** Dark-coloured, sober-coloured. *Obs.*

1560 Becon *Catech.* vi. Wks. I. 536 If they be olde women and maryed: not lyght apparell, but sad raiment pleaseth a godly husband. **1590** Spenser *F.Q.* i. xii. 5 Arayd in antique robes downe to the grownd, And sad habiliments. **1668** Pepys *Diary* 24 Aug., My wife is upon hanging the long chamber.. with the sad stuff that was in the best chamber. **1711** *Lond. Gaz.* No. 4919/4 A Man.. between 20 and 30 years of Age, pale Visage and sad Hair.

†**9.** Of sleep: Sound, deep. *Obs.*

a **1350** *St. Nicholas* 329 in Horstm. *Altengl. Leg.* (1881) 15 Sodanly he fell on full sad slepe. **1377** Langl. *P. Pl.* B. v. 4 þanne waked I of my wynkynge and wo was with-alle, þat I ne hadde sleped sadder and yseiȝen more. *c* **1400** *Destr. Troy* 679 Medea.. Persauyt.. þat all sad were on slepe. *c* **1450** *Mankind* 585 in *Macro Plays* 22 ȝe may here hym snore; he ys sade a-slepe. **1485** Caxton *St. Wenefr.* 20, I couerd my hede and fylle in to a sadde slepe.

†**10. a.** Of blows: Heavy, delivered with vigour.

[So early mod.G. *satt.*]

c **1350** *Will. Palerne* 2775 He.. set hire a sad strok so sore in þe necke, þat sche top ouer tail tombled ouer þe hacches. *c* **1400** *Destr. Troy* 1263 One caupet with hym kenely,.. And set hym a sad dynt. **1470–85** Malory *Arthur* xi. iv. 576 And there they dasshed to gyders many sadde strokes. **1503** Hawes *Examp. Virt.* xi. xix, But I my swerd in my hand had Strykynge at hym with strokes sad. *a* **1578** Lindesay (Pitscottie) *Chron. Scot.* (S.T.S.) I. 222 The strampe of Mr Patrickis was so sade wpoun his brotheris footte.

b. Of a fire: Violent. *Obs.*

c **1420** *Chron. Vilod.* 1911 Hurre thouȝt þat hurre chaufere.. Was set ouer a feure bothe gret & sadde.

c. Of rain: Heavy. *Obs.*

1638 Sir T. Herbert *Trav.* (ed. 2) 30 Heaven it self at that instant weeping so abundantly, that I never saw a sadder raine and of lesse continuance. *c* **1645** Howell *Lett.* (1650) I. 184 In a sad shower of rain.

III. 11. *Comb.* in many adjs., chiefly parasynthetic, as ***sad-avised*** (quasi-*arch.* after black-a-vised), ***-coloured***, ***-eyed***, ***-faced***, ***-garbed***, ***-hearted***, ***-lidded***, ***-looking***, ***-making***, ***-natured***, ***-paced***, ***-seeming***, ***-tuned***, ***-visaged***, ***-voiced***; **sad-ass** *N. Amer. slang*, used *attrib.* as a term of abuse; also **sad-assed** *a.*; **sad-cake** *dial.* and *U.S.*, an unleavened cake.

1971 *Black World* Apr. 63 How is Philadelphia?.. Thats one *sad-ass city.. bout to sink into the ground. **1974** D. Sears *Lark in Clear Air* xiii. 158 A few general comments on sad-assed, puritanical sons-of-bitches individually and collectively. **1878** Besant & Rice *Monks Thelema* III. 124 She did not writhe as she walked; she was not *sad-avised. **1889** J. Nicholson *Folk Sp. E. Yorksh.* 79 *Sad keeaks and dip form a favourite breakfast. **1660** Blount *Boscobel* ii. (1680) 27 His Majesty.. cloathed in a short Juppa of *sad coloured cloath. **1818** Scott *Hrt. Midl.* iv, A decent suit of sad-coloured clothes. **1599** Shaks. *Hen. V*, i. ii. 202 The *sad-ey'd Iustice with his surly humme. **1588** —— *Tit. A.* v. iii. 67 You *sad facde men, people and sons of Rome. *c* **1893** A. W. Pinero in M. R. Booth *Eng. Plays of 19th Cent.* (1969) II. 285, I knew her when she was a sad-faced, pale baby. **1947** J. Mulgan *Report on Experience* xi. 126 In the streets were sad-faced men and women, still hungry and no longer happy. **1971** *Where?* Oct. 309/1 Indeed, one might argue that there is an urgent and essential need to produce this quality of communal participation and commitment if our society is to survive. Not that this means a sadfaced approach. **1848** J. R. Lowell *Poems* 2nd Ser. 167 He looks a sachem, in red blanket wrapt,.. 'mid some council of the *sad-garbed whites. **1593** Shaks. *3 Hen. VI*, ii. v. 123 *Sad-hearted-men, much ouer-gone with Care. **1952** C. Day Lewis tr. *Virgil's Aeneid* i. 16 And spoke these words of comfort to his sad-hearted friends. **1921** D. H. Lawrence *Tortoises* 35 His black, *sad-lidded eye sees but beholds not. **1961** C. McCullers *Clock without Hands* iv. 78 The red lamp with ragged fringes, two obviously broken chairs and other pieces of *sad-looking furniture. **1930** E. Waugh *Vile Bodies* xii. 208 'My dear, isn't that rather *sad-making for you?' 'I'm desperate about it.' **1955** J. D. Salinger *Franny* in *New Yorker* 29 Jan. 30/3 But just so tiny and meaningless and—sad-making. **1960** J. Stroud *Shorn Lamb* xxiii. 251 You were watching the end of an epoch; that's always rather sad-making. *a* **1568** Ascham *Scholem.* i. (Arb.) 36 This *sadde natured, and hard witted child. **1599** Marston *Sc. Villanie* i. Proem., Stay his quick iocund skips, and force him runne A *sad pas't course. *a* **1633** Austin *Medit.* (1635) 131 So all is Joy againe; till this *Sad-seeming Tydings come. **1597** Shaks. *Lover's Compl.* 4 And downe I laid to list the *sad tun'd tale. **1869** 'Mark Twain' *Innoc. Abr.* xxxiv. 370, I never saw such.. starving, *sad-visaged, broken-hearted looking curs in my life. **1844** Mrs. Browning *Wine of Cyprus* vi, I am *sad-voiced as the turtle Which Anacreon used to feed.

B. *adv.* *Obs.* exc. *poet.*

†**1.** Firmly, strongly, fixedly. *Obs.*

c **1380** *Sir Ferumb.* 353 Loke þat þou be armed sad & hele þy bare scolle. *c* **1400** *Destr. Troy* 2078 He þat set is full sad on a soile euyn,.. Hym þar not hede to be hurt with no hegh falle. *c* **1440** *Pallad. on Husb.* vii. 59 Nowe potage ware in askes mynge, & kepe In oil entrelles or salt tubbis done; Saad cleyed wel, they saaf beth leyd to slepe. *c* **1475** *Partenay* 3859 Adieu, my suete loue prented in hert sad!

†**2.** Heavily, with force. *Obs.*

? *a* **1400** *Arthur* 605 þey fowȝt euer sore & sadde; Men nyst ho þe betere hadde. *c* **1420** *Avow. Arth.* xxv, He stroke him sadde and sore. **1629** Z. Boyd *Balme of Gilead* 41 (Jam.) The longer the stroake be in comming it commeth downe the sadder. *a* **1743** Relph *Misc. Poems* (1747) 4 Up flew her hand to souse the cowren lad, But ah, I thought it fell not down owr sad.

†**3.** Steadfastly. *Obs.*

c **1440** *Partonope* 1863 These covenauntis to holde surely and sadde. *a* **1450** Myrc *Instr. Par. Priests* 260 Teche hem alle to leue sadde, þat hyt þat ys in þe awter made, Hyt ys verre goddes blode.

†**4.** Seriously, soberly, discreetly. *Obs.*

14.. *How Gd. Wyfe taught Dau.* 198 in *Q. Eliz. Acad.* (1869) 50 And þus thi frendes wylle be glade þat thou dispos þe wyslye and sade.

†**5.** Thoroughly, truly, certainly. *Obs.*

c **1380** Wyclif *Serm.* Sel. Wks. I. 56 Maister, þei seiden, we witen wel þat þou art sad trewe. *c* **1400** *Destr. Troy* 3605 In sorow may be sene who is sad wise. *c* **1475** *Partenay* 874 Ful wel thay sad knew it the fayry was. *Ibid.* 950 Merueles,.. I se ful sad; Neuer humain ey saw to it egal!

6. a. Sorrowfully.

1667 Milton *P.L.* iv. 28 Sometimes towards Eden.. his grievd look he fixes sad. **1819** Keats *Lamia* ii. 49 Why will you plead yourself so sad forlorn?

b. *Comb.* = *sadly-*.

1593 Shaks. *Lucr.* 1590 Which when her sad beholding husband saw. **1613** W. Browne *Brit. Past.* ii. iv, Their sad-sweet glance. **1909** E. Pound *Exultations* 12 Ye know somewhat the strain, the sad-sweet wonder-pain of such singing. **1925** J. Gregory *Bab of Backwoods* iii. 33 He managed to get his one free arm about her, hugging her tight while he said good-bye; Bab would never forget that terribly sad-sweet moment. **1928** Blunden *Undertones of War* 4

And there, sad-smiling,..were two or three of the convalescent squad. **1933** W. de la Mare *Fleeting* 17 How sad-serene the abandoned house. **1953** S. Kauffmann *Philanderer* xiv. 233 A lamp-lighted restaurant table, the distant sad-sweet music, all these flowed together in a comfortable alcoholic haze.

sad (sæd), *v.* Forms: see the adj. [f. sad *a.* Cf. sade *v.*]

1. *trans.* To make solid, firm, or stiff; to compress. *Obs.* exc. *dial.* Cf. sadden *v.* 1.

1382 Wyclif *Acts* iii. 7 And anoon the groundis and plauntis of him ben saddid to gidere [Vulg. *consolidatæ sunt*]. **1398** Trevisa *Barth. De. P.R.* vii. lviii. (1495) 272 The matere is thycked and sadded and not obedyente to dygestyon. **14..** *Tretyce* in *Walter of Henley's Husb.* (1890) 47 Sowe your wyntur corne tymely so þ^t your lande may be sadid & your corne rotyd afore þ^t grete wyntur com. *c* **1440** *Promp. Parv.* 440/1 Saddyn, or make sadde, *solido, consolido.* **1496** *Dives & Paup.* (W. de W.) vi. xxi. 268/2 The fende by suffraunce of god may sadde the ayer and make hym a bodye of the ayer. **1807** Hogg *Mtn. Bard, Sandy Tod* 111 Sandy.. Then the hay, sae rowed an' saddit, Towzled up that nane might ken.

†**2.** To make steadfast, establish, confirm (*in*).

1377 Langl. *P. Pl.* B. x. 242 Austyn þe olde here-of he made bokes, And hym-self ordeyned to sadde vs in bileue. *c* **1425** *Orolog. Sapient.* i. in *Anglia* X. 333/2 þe sowle þat is not ȝit fullye saddete and stablete in þe moste parfyte degre of loue. *c* **1450** tr. *De Imitatione* iii. l. 120 My mynde is saddid [orig. *solidata est*] in god, & groundid in crist.

†**3.** To darken (a colour). *Obs.*

1573 *Art of Limning* 4 Two parts azure and one of cereuse and sadded with the same azure or with blacke incke. **1634** J. B[ate] *Myst Nat.* 124 You may alay your Orpment with chalke, and sadde it with browne of Spain [etc.].

†**4.** To make sorrowful; to sadden. *Obs.*

1602 Marston *Antonio's Rev.* iv. iii, May it not sad your thoughts. **1643** Prynne *Sov. Power Parl.* i. (ed. 2) 24 The Lords hearing of these proceedings were much sadded. **1692** *Covt. Grace Conditional* 73 The Hearts of your Friends [are] exceedingly sadded. **1810** *The Age: A Poem* 3 When nature's visage sads the sight.

†**b.** To make dull or gloomy. *Obs.*

1610 G. Fletcher *Christ's Vict.* i. ix, As when a vapour.. sads the smiling orient of the springing day.

†**c.** *intr.* ***to sad it***: to talk in a sad manner.

1663 Killigrew *Parson's Wedd.* ii. v. 95 While you sad it thus to one.

sad, obs. form of said, shed.

Sadaiceus, obs. pl. of Sadducee.

†**'sadded,** *ppl. a. Obs.* [f. sad *v.* + -ed[1].] In senses of the verb: **a.** Solidified; compacted. **b.** Confirmed, strengthened. **c.** Saddened, made sorrowful.

c **1520** Nisbet *N.T. in Scots, Rom.* xv. 1 Bot we saddit men aw to sustene the febilnes of seek men, and nocht pleise to our self. **1610** G. Fletcher *Christ's Tri.* i. xxxviii, The sadded aire hung all in cheerlesse blacke. **1654–66** Earl Orrery *Parthen.* (1676) 693 The sadded Soldiers marched in the first Ranks. **1680** Lacy *Prol. to 'Love Lost in the Dark'*, Which keeps our sadded Hearts in deep suspence.

saddeli, -ly, obs. forms of sadly.

sadden ('sæd(ə)n), *v.* [f. sad *a.* + -en.]

1. *trans.* To make solid, firm, or stiff; to compress, render cohesive; to press or beat *down* into a compact mass. Now *dial.*

1600 G. Plat in Worlidge *Syst. Agric.* (1669) 44 Also the roots of the Corn will spread better..if the ground be saddned a little in the bottom of every hole. **1641** Best *Farm Bks.* (Surtees) 77 Hee woulde have the water sattle away, and the grownd somewhat saddened. **1649** Blithe *Eng. Improv.* xvii. 102 For your Lime after it is once Slacked, and Melted, it is of a very cold Nature; for it will sadden your Land exceedingly. **1688** R. Holme *Armoury* iii. 73/1 Treading it [*sc.* Hay] is to sadden it down either in the Mow or Rick, &c. **1707** Mortimer *Husb.* (1721) I. 94 If Marle sadden Land, or make it stiff or binding, you must dung it well. **1813** T. Batchelor *Gen. View Agric. Bedf.* 342 (E.D.D.), The soil below will, instead of being brought up, be trampled and saddened.

†**b.** *intr.* To become stiff or solid. *Obs.*

1641 Best *Farm. Bks.* (Surtees) 77 If there bee any winds aloft without raine, the grownd will sadden and the fields waxe dry. **1764** *Museum Rust.* I. xcii. 407 After which the ground began to sadden. **1764** Eliza Moxon *Eng. Housew.* (ed. 9) 117 Then take them off the fire and let them stand a little to sadden.

2. *trans.* To render sad or sorrowful; to depress in spirits. Also, to give a sad appearance to.

1628 Feltham *Resolves* ii. [i.] lviii. 166 He smarts, and pines, and sadneth his incumbred soule. **1717** Pope *Eloisa to Abelard* 167 Her gloomy presence saddens all the scene. **1797** Mrs. Radcliffe *Italian* i, With a heart saddened by disappointment. **1824** W. Irving *T. Trav.* I. 28 Its beauty was saddened by care and anxiety. **1863** Geo. Eliot *Romola* xx, Her round face much paled and saddened since he had parted from it. **1884** *Graphic* 4 Oct. 358/2 It saddens me to enter a Government bureau at the present day.

b. *intr.* To become sad or gloomy.

1718 Pope *Iliad* xiv. 558 Troy sadden'd at the View. **1727–46** Thomson *Summer* 979 And Mecca saddens at the long delay. **1751** Smollett *Per. Pic.* xviii, Her countenance saddened in a moment. **1818** Keats *What the Thrush said* 12 He who saddens At thought of idleness cannot be idle. **1859** FitzGerald tr. *Omar* xxxix, Better be merry with the fruitful Grape Than sadden after none, or bitter, Fruit.

fig. **1795** Coleridge *Aeolian Harp* 7 And watch the clouds, that late were rich with light, Slow saddening round.

3. *Dyeing* and *Calico-printing*. To tone down (colours) by the application of certain chemicals.

1791 Hamilton *Berthollet's Dyeing* II. ii. iii. v. 196 These substances however saddened the crimson colour and gave it less lustre than alum. **1866** *Chamb. Encycl.* VIII. 414/2 *Saddening*, a peculiar method of applying certain mordants in dyeing and printing cloths, so as to give duller shades to the colours employed. **1873** E. Spon *Workshop Receipts* Ser. i. 30/2 Winch 30 minutes, and lift for saddening. **1874** Sir W. Crookes *Handbk. Dyeing & Calico-print.* 53 For saddening olives, drabs, clarets, &c.,..it [*sc.* copperas] has been generally discarded in favour of a nitrate of iron.

saddened ('sæd(ə)nd), *ppl. a.* [f. sadden *v.* + -ed[1].] Made sad.

1700 Dryden *Iliad* i. 768 The Limping Smith observ'd the sadden'd Feast. **1842** Manning *Serm.* xi. (1848) I. 146 There is something peculiarly touching in the saddened tone of these few words. **1874** Lisle Carr *Jud. Gwynne* I. ii. 47 A bright flush swept over her..rather saddened face. **1879** Farrar *St. Paul* (1883) 58 The Resurrection of Christ had scattered every cloud from their saddened souls.

saddening ('sæd(ə)nɪŋ), *ppl. a.* [-ing[2].]

†**1.** That saddens or renders stiff. *Obs.*

1653 Blithe *Eng. Improv. Impr.* 135 In..working it [lime] into the Land..it seems & appeares to be Coldest, and most sadning of Land of any Soyl whatsoever.

2. Causing sadness.

1742 Collins *Oriental Ecl.* iv. 24 And shrieks and sorrows load the saddening wind. **1804** J. Grahame *Sabbath* 705 He never longs to read the saddening tale Of endless wars. **1856** Froude *Hist. Eng.* (1858) II. vii. 190 The circumstances under which this session opened were..grave and saddening. **1884** *Chr. Commw.* 23 Oct. 21/3 It is saddening to hear that the Sunderland engineers have been on strike for 60 weeks.

saddhu, var. sadhu.

saddil, obs. form of saddle.

†**'sadding,** *vbl. sb. Obs.* [f. sad *v.* + -ing[1].] The action of making sad.

1643 W. Greenhill *Axe at Root* 35 Those Nations are remisse in Justice: besides the sadding of those are innocent, they abound in Delinquents and dangers. **1645** Rutherford *Tryal & Tri. Faith* xxiv. 277 There is a sadding of the spirit, ..which is forbidden.

†**'sadding,** *ppl. a. Obs.* [f. sad *v.* + -ing[2].] **a.** That makes sad. **b.** Becoming sad.

1650 Baxter *Saints' R.* iv. vi. §7 (1654) 154 Are these such sadding and madding thoughts? *a* **1839** Galt *Demon Destiny* v. (1840) 34 Alas! my son, the sadding matron cried.

saddish ('sædɪʃ), *a.* [f. sad *a.* + -ish.] Somewhat sad (see the adj.). Also *Comb.*

1647 W. Browne *Polex.* ii. 265 Our Heroe..put off aswell all his saddish Ornaments, as his triumphant. **1686** *Lond. Gaz.* No. 2192/4 A saddish coloured stuff Sute. **1848** J. H. Newman *Loss & Gain* 336 His companion..in a hesitating, saddish voice, said that he was an Englishman.

saddle ('sæd(ə)l), *sb.* Forms: 1 sadol, 3–6 sadel, 4–6 sadill, 5–6 sadell, sadil, 5 saddill, sadille, -yl, -yll(e, -elle, -ul, 5, 9 *Sc.* saidle, 5–7 sadle, 6– saddle. [Com. Teut.: OE. *sadol*, *-ul* masc. = MDu. *sadel* (mod.Du. *zadel, zaal*), OHG. *satal*, *-ul* (MHG. *satel*, mod.G. *sattel*), ON. *sǫðull* (Sw., Da. *sadel*):—OTeut. **sađulo-z*.

Possibly adopted in OTeut. from some other Indogermanic language, and if so perh. a derivative of the root **sed-*, ablaut-var. of **sed-* (see sit *v.*), whence the synonymous L. *sella* (:—**sedlā*), OSl. *sedlo* (Russian *sʲedlo*, Pol. *siodlo*). No known language, however, has a corresponding derivative from the *o* grade of the root.]

I. 1. a. A seat for a rider to be used on the back of a horse or other animal; esp., a concave seat of leather having side flaps and fitted with girths and stirrups. Also an analogous kind of seat for use on a cycle.

for the saddle, for riding purposes. ***in the saddle***, on horseback. ***to lose one's saddle***, to become unhorsed.

Beowulf 1038 (Gr.) Eahta mearas..þara anum stod sadol ..þæt wæs hildesetl heahcyninges. *c* **1205** Lay. 6473 Æt his sadele an æx. *c* **1250** *Gen. & Ex.* 3949 Vp-on hise asse his sadel he dede. *c* **1330** *Arth. & Merl.* 3871 (Kölbing) Mani in sadles held hem stille, & mani al so of hors felle. *c* **1385** Chaucer *L.G.W.* 1199 Vpon a thikke palfrey paper white With sadel rede..Sitte Dido. **1484** Caxton *Chivalry* 65 Lyke as by the sadyl a knyght is sure upon his hors. **1596** Shaks. *1 Hen. IV*, ii. i. 6, I prethee Tom, beate Cuts Saddle, put a few Flockes in the point. **1640** tr. *Verdere's Rom. of Rom.* III. 182 [They] let fly..with such a force, that they had almost lost their saddles. **1650** Fuller *Pisgah* iv. v. §31. 91 Yea, such was his persevering beauty (fair in the Cradle and Saddle too)— that it lasted unto his old-age. **1672** Petty *Pol. Anat.* (1691) 56 The 16,000 Families have for the Coach and Saddle near 40 M. Horses. *a* **1745** Swift *Direct. Servants, Groom*, Contrive that the Saddle may pinch the Beast in his Withers. **1837** W. Irving *Capt. Bonneville* I. 113 Taking a couple of horses, one for the saddle, and the other as a pack-horse. **1859** Tennyson *Elaine* 96 Sir King, mine ancient wound is hardly whole, And lets me from the saddle. **1887** Bury & Hillier *Cycling* (Badm. Libr.) 340 A suitable saddle is a necessity for the comfort of the cyclist.

fig. **1630** *R. Johnson's Kingd. & Commw.* 42 Nothing awes a great River so much as a bridge;..a bridge is the saddle to ride the Sea-horse.

b. With qualifying word indicating a particular kind of saddle; esp. ***great saddle***, a saddle for the 'great horse' (see horse *sb.* 22).

For *hunting, pad, portmanteau, running, war saddle*, etc. see the first element. Also packsaddle *sb.*, side-saddle.

1508 *Acc. Ld. High Treas. Scotl.* IV. 119 Item, for v French sadilles to giff away; ilk sadill xxviij *s.* **1581** *Will of Wylteshire* (Somerset Ho.), Scottissh sadell. **1598** Florio, *Scrignuto naso*, a camoset, a flat-nose, a nose like a scotch-saddle. **1607** Markham *Cavelarice* vi. ix. 49 [*margin*] The great horse saddle. *Ibid.* 50 Next vnto this saddle is the Morocco saddle.., and these two Saddles for seruice in the warres, are..sufficient. **1644** Evelyn *Diary* 1 Apr., The designe is admirable, some keeping neere an hundred brave horses, all managed to ye greate saddle. **1665** Sir T. Herbert *Trav.* (1677) 314 Saddles..high and close, like our great Saddle. **1688** R. Holme *Armoury* iii. 345/1 A Burford Saddle, hath the Seat plain, and the Skirts plain and streight. **1701** P. Warwick *Mem. Chas. I*, 66 He rid the great horse very well; and on the little saddle he was..a laborious hunter, or field-man.

†**c.** ***saddle curule*** [nonce-use, tr. L. *sella curulis*], the curule chair.

1533 Bellenden *Livy* i. iii. (S.T.S.) I. 47 He cled him with riche & riall abilȝementis, þat he was wourthy to sett in þe sadill curall. *Ibid.* 25, 181.

d. Ellipt. for *saddle brown* in sense 12 below.

1976 *Billings* (Montana) *Gaz.* 26 June 14-a/3 (Advt.), The perfect handbag for carrying everything in Saddle, Tan or Rust. **1977** *West Briton* 25 Aug. 31/5 (Advt.), 1974 (Oct.) Lancia Fulvia 3 Coupe, finished in maroon with saddle interior.

2. Figurative phrases. **a.** ***in the saddle***, in a position of active management and guidance of affairs, in office; also, in readiness for work. Similarly ***to get into the saddle. to cast out of saddle***, to deprive of office or position.

1660 Pepys *Diary* 3 Mar., He told me he feared there was new design hatching, as if Monk had a mind to get into the saddle. **1675** tr. *Machiavelli's Prince* vii. (Rtldg. 1883) 52 Such as by the favour of fortune..have got into the saddle. **1738** Neal *Hist. Purit.* IV. 225 The Presbyterians being now again in the saddle. **1819** Scott *Ivanhoe* xxv, I have known when my bare word would have cast the best man-at-arms among ye out of saddle and out of service. **1879** *19th Cent.* 668 All the states of Italy accepted the new Pope; and Rodrigo Borgia, once in the saddle, was not a man to be easily dislodged. **1881** R. G. White *Eng. Without & Within* xiv. 323 The phrase 'in the saddle'—as an expression of readiness for work, is a peculiarly English phrase. **1891** S. C. Scrivener *Our Fields & Cities* 28 Otherwise the happy-go-lucky..system of production could not keep itself in the saddle to any durable extent.

b. †***to be beside the saddle***: to be beside the mark. (Cf. cushion *sb.* 10b.) †***to put*** or ***set beside the saddle***: to put 'out of the running', to defeat the plans or ruin the career of. (Cf. cushion *sb.* 10c.) †***to sit beside the saddle***: ? to abandon oneself to despair.

1568 Grafton *Chron.* II. 873 The French king..fearing least when he had almost runne his race, King Henry would put him beside hys sadell, whome he did halfe suspect to be a back friend of hys. **1579–80** North *Plutarch, Tiberius & Caius* (1656) 693 If he could obtain it [*sc.* the Consulship], he was fully bent to set Caius beside the saddle. *a* **1590** Greene *Metamorph.* Wks. (Grosart) IX. 81 Well, howsoeuer it be, Lucidor shall be mine, hee shall haue my heart, and I his, or else I will sit beside the saddle. **1644** Vicars *God in Mount* (1844) 19 As that no power either of Prince or Parliament, shall ever be able to set us, hereafter, beside the saddle. **1664** J. Webb *Stone-Heng* (1725) 36 This Doctor is besides the Saddle, what is now in Use is not our Enquiry.

c. (***I will***) ***either win the saddle or lose the horse*** (or vice versa): said by one engaging in an adventure of which the issue will be either highly profitable or ruinous. Hence in various similar phrases.

1579 W. Wilkinson *Confut. Fam. Love* 62b, He hath both ieoperded the horse, and lost the saddle. **1594** Nashe *Unfort. Trav.* Wks. 1883–4 V. 131 Whatsoeuer two resolute men will goe to dice for it, and win the bridle or lose the saddle. **1596** Spenser *F.Q.* iv. v. 22 But Blandamour..litle prays'd his labours evill speed, That for to winne the saddle lost the steed. **1603** Breton *Packet Mad Lett.* 7 But my state being so downe the winde..I wil..thrust my selfe into some place of seruice in the warres, where I will either winne the Horse, or lose the Saddle. **1678** Cudworth *Intell. Syst.* i. v. §42. 894 They..resolve either to 'win the saddle or loose the Horse'.

d. ***to lay*** or ***set the saddle upon the right horse*** (and similar phrases): to lay the blame on the right person.

1635 in Sainsbury *Cal. of Court Min. E.I. Co.* (1907) 15 [Resolving how they might] sett the saddle upon the right horse. **1652** Collinges *Caveat for Prof.* (1653) ii. C 1, You have laid the saddle upon the wrong Horse. *a* **1653** Gouge *Comm. Hebr.* xi. 37 To remove this scandal, the apostle setteth the saddle on the right Horse, and sheweth, that [etc.]. **1690** Wood *Life* 25 July (O.H.S.) III. 336 E. G. with child, layd on the tapster, who said that 'set the saddle on the right horse'. **1727** De Foe *Syst. Magic* i. iii. (1840) 83 But let us bring things to a right understanding, do Satan justice, and set the saddle upon the right devil. **1752** Mrs. C. Lennox *Female Quixote* (1820) II. vii. xii. 154 I'll clear myself, and put the saddle upon the right horse! **1839** Hood *Tale of a Trumpet* xlviii, And the cat at last escapes from the bag—And the saddle is placed on the proper nag.

e. ***to put*** (one) ***to every corner of*** or ***to all the seats of*** (one's) ***saddle***: to compel to try every expedient. *Sc.*

1825 Scott in Lockhart *Life* (1837) VI. 24, I have the dregs of Abbotsford House to pay for..so I must look for some months to be put to every corner of my saddle. **1825** Jamieson *Dict.* s.v., *To put one to a' the seats o' the Saddle*, to nonplus, to gravel one, S.

f. In proverbial similative phrases.

1566 Knox *Hist. Ref.* Wks. (1846) I. 242 Als seimlye a sight..as to putta a sadill upoun the back of ane unrewly kow. **1663** *Aron-bimn.* 88 But for this pretence of pulling down

Antichrist, it is a saddle that will fit any back. **1677** W. HUGHES *Man of Sin* II. xii. 215 That becometh him as handsomely (according to our Proverb) as A saddle doth a Cowes back.

3. That part of the harness of a shaft-horse which takes the bearing of the shafts (see quot. 1851); a cart- or gig-saddle.

[**1377**: see *cartsaddle* vb., CART *sb.* 6. *c* **1425** *Voc.* in Wright-Wülcker 665/33 *Hoc dorsilollum*, cartsadylle.] **1794** [see HOUSING *sb.*[2] 2 b]. **1837** MARRYAT *Olla Podr.* xxxvi, The shaft horse neither felt his saddle nor his belly-band. **1851** H. STEPHENS *Bk. of the Farm* (ed. 2) I. 430 The shaft-horse requires bridle, collar, haims, saddle, and breeching, to be fully equipped... The saddle—as saddle and breeching together are commonly called—is placed on the horse's back immediately behind the shoulder. **1856** 'STONEHENGE' *Brit. Rural Sports* III. III. iv. 543/1 The supporting and backing part [of gig harness] consists of the Pad or Saddle... This has two rings for the reins, called the Terrets, and a Hook for the bearing rein. **1875** [see PAD *sb.*[3] 2 b]. **1882** J. PHILIPSON *Harness* 25 The pad is sometimes used instead of a saddle for single harness.

II. Something resembling a saddle in shape or position.

4. *Physical Geogr.*, *Mining*, etc. **a.** A depression in a hill or line of hills [so G. *sattel*]; *spec.* in *Geol.*, a depression along the axis of an anticline, concave in longitudinal section and convex in transverse section. **b.** A long elevation of land with sloping sides; a ridge, esp. one connecting two hills; also, a similar formation of ice or snow.

1555 EDEN *Decades* 350 A lowe longe lande, and a longe poynt, with a saddle throwgh the myddeste of it. **1697** DAMPIER *Voy.* (1699) 267 A very high Hill..with a Saddle or bending on the top. **1779** FORREST *Voy. New Guinea* 159 [We] discerned other land, bearing from N.W. to W.N.W. forming in saddles and hummocs. **1833** M. SCOTT *Tom Cringle* xix, There was a long narrow saddle or ridge of limestone about five hundred feet high. **1839** MURCHISON *Silur. Syst.* I. 134 The carboniferous strata are thrown into partial saddles and curvatures. **1860** TYNDALL *Glac.* I. xvi. 108 The..glacier..being terminated by a saddle which stretches across from mountain to mountain. **1862** MERIVALE *Rom. Emp.* (1865) V. xl. 23 The Palatine is connected with the Esquiline by the low ridge or saddle of the Velia. **1871** L. STEPHEN *Playgr. Eur.* (1894) 130 We stepped at last on to the little saddle of snow. **1876** GREEN *Phys. Geol.* ix. §3. 347 When the beds have been bent into the form of arches these are called Anticlinals or Saddles. **1886** T. M. READE *Origin of Mountain Ranges* xvi. 187 (*caption*) Saddle in lower Silurian rocks between Clarach Bay and Aberystwyth, formed by the junction of anticlinal and synclinal curves. **1928** E. R. LILLEY *Geol. Petroleum & Natural Gas* xii. 293 Where the amount of oil and gas is sufficient only to fill the distinctly domed portions of the fold, the saddle is normally water-bearing. **1952** *Q. Jrnl. Geol. Soc.* CVIII. 16 Individual anticlines have lengths of up to 250 miles, following long straight courses and rising and falling into culminations and saddles. **1977** *Offshore Engineer* May 52/1 The structure is a tilted fault block with hydrocarbons trapped on the upthrown side of a normal fault in two culminations separated by a saddle.

c. *Mining.* = *saddle reef* in sense 12 below; *spec.* one that is anticlinal rather than synclinal.

1872 *Rep. Vermont Board Agric.* 630 The miners were quarreling about false and true veins, horses of rock and saddles of ore. **1908** J. M. MACLAREN *Gold* II. 368 In working the saddles, prospecting for lower saddles is effected by sinking shafts designed to strike a 'leg' of an underlying saddle, from whence stopes are carried up to the crest of the anticline. **1937** W. H. EMMONS *Gold Deposits of World* vii. 528 As many as 24 quartz saddles in an anticline have been passed through from the surface to a depth of 2,200 feet. **1950** DAVID & BROWNE *Geol. Commonwealth of Austral.* II. xxvii. 196 Inverted saddles are smaller and less common than saddles, but they have given profitable yields in several mines.

5. In mechanical uses. **a.** *Naut.* A block of wood, hollowed out above and below, fastened to a spar to take the bearing of another spar attached to it.

1512–13 *Acc. Ld. High Treas. Scot.* IV. 463 Item..for viij greit treis to mak the sadillis to the greit schip and Margret ..xlviij *s.* **1769** FALCONER *Dict. Marine* (1780), *Saddle*, a small..wooden block,..nailed on the lower yard-arms, to retain the studding-sail booms in a firm and steady position. **1882** NARES *Seamanship* (ed. 6) 178 To get the heel of the boom..down in the saddle.

b. *Bridge-construction.* (*a*) A block on the top of a pier to carry the suspension cables. (*b*) A frame used in the construction of a pontoon-bridge (see quot. 1853).

1831 J. HOLLAND *Manuf. Metal* I. 108 On the extreme height of the suspension piers are placed the cast iron blocks or saddles. **1853** SIR H. DOUGLAS *Milit. Bridges* (ed. 3) 30 The Saddle [of a pontoon bridge] is a frame of fir timber, which is placed centrally over the axis of a pontoon..and serves to receive the ends of the balks. **1868** *Daily Tel.* 14 Apr., A fresh pontoon was brought alongside, fresh saddles were lashed to it, another length of balks..was dropped into the saddle. **1876** *Encycl. Brit.* IV. 301/2 Suspension Bridges.—The chains where they pass over the piers rest on saddles.

c. A 'seat' or support on which a gun is placed for bouching.

1862 F. A. GRIFFITHS *Artil. Man.* (ed. 9) 190 Saddle [for Armstrong gun], with Tightening Screws. **1875** in KNIGHT *Dict. Mech.*

d. (See quot. 1888.)

1888 *Lockwood's Dict. Mech. Engin.* s.v., The seatings or supports which carry horizontal cylindrical boilers..are called saddles. **1899** *Daily News* 9 Mar. 5/3 The saddles that held the six thirty-ton boilers in place broke.

e. *Telegraphy.* A bracket to support the wire on the top of a pole or ridge.

1867 R. S. CULLEY *Pract. Telegr.* (ed. 2) 122 The saddle or bracket must be fixed with screws. **1885** *Ibid.* (ed. 8) 148 At the top of the pole a galvanised iron roof is fixed, and over it a cast-iron saddle, into which the insulator bolt fits. **1884** *Law Times Rep.* LI. 161/2 The attachments to buildings were made..by means of standards or ridge saddles attached to the roofs.

f. *Railways.* (? *U.S.*) (*a*) The bearing resting on the journal of an axle in the axle-box. (*b*) A chair for a rail.

1875 in KNIGHT *Dict. Mech.* 459, 2011.

g. In various machines: The base of a slide rest, drilling head, etc., which slides along its support.

1869 W. J. M. RANKINE *Cycl. Mach. & Hand-Tools* Plate H 8 The self-acting motion for the saddles is arranged as follows. **1869** *Eng. Mech.* 24 Dec. 355/1 The saddle (which carries the wood) is drawn to the hand-wheel end of the machine. **1879** *Cassell's Techn. Educ.* IV. 264/2 The lower part of the slide-rest is termed the 'saddle'. **1888** *Lockwood's Dict. Mech. Engin.*, *Saddle*, the base of a slide rest... Similarly, the sliding plate which carries the drill spindle and gear wheels of a radial drill.

h. (*a*) A saddle-shaped electrical conductor. (*b*) A concave pad to be applied to a limb that is to be electrified.

1838 FARADAY *Exper. Researches* (1844) II. 5 A plate of copper..was bent into a saddle shape,..a jacket of sheet caoutchouc was put over the saddle. **1849** NOAD *Electricity* (ed. 3) 492 If, then, we wish to administer *direct* shocks to a paralytic limb, say the leg, we apply a sponge director or saddle..to the hip.

i. In various applications: see quots.

1750 BLANCKLEY *Nav. Expositor*, *Saddles* are used by the Smiths to turn Thimbles hollow on. **1833** LOUDON *Encycl. Arch.* 492 To pebble-pave the byres..with proper cribstone and saddle (the former partitions off the crib; and the latter the gutter behind). **1856** MORTON *Cycl. Agric.*, *Provincialisms*, *Saddle*, (Fife), that part of stall between manger and grip. **1873** E. SPON *Workshop Receipts* Ser. I. 61/2 [Varnish making.] A saddle, which is a sheet of plate-iron, or tin, 12 in. broad, and turned up $1\frac{1}{2}$ in. at each side.. to prevent the spilling of the varnish during the time of taking..out. **1875** T. SEATON *Fret Cutting* 76 There are two very efficient aids to the saw... The first is the bench saddle. .. It is a piece of wood with reverse shoulders; the under shoulder hooks against the side of the bench,..the upper shoulder catches any piece of wood laid against it for sawing. **1884** W. S. B. MCLAREN *Spinning* 250 *Saddles*, the steel bars in a gill box on which the fallers travel. **1887** *Archit. Publ. Soc. Dict.*, *Saddle*, a term used in Suffolk for a thin piece of wood fixed on the floor between the jambs of a door and under it.

j. An insulating device designed to be fitted around an electrical wire or conduit to help to hold it in place.

1888 D. SALOMONS *Managem. Accumulators & Private Electr. Light Installations* (ed. 3) II. ii. 107 Leather saddles answer well to keep the wires in place. **1930** F. C. RAPHAEL *Electr. Wiring of Buildings* vi. 91 Multiple saddles are used if two or more lengths of conduit run together. **1969** H. A. MILLER *Pract. Wiring* I. v. 34 It is good practice to secure single runs by clips and multiple runs by saddles.

k. *Dentistry.* The basal part of a denture, which replaces alveolar tissue and bears the artificial teeth.

1907 H. J. GOSLEE *Princ. & Pract. Crown & Bridgework* xxiv. 443 The saddle should now be swaged of 30 to 32 gauge platinum, trimmed to the proper outline, fitted in the mouth with the caps in place, and then soldered thereto with platinum solder. **1930** I. G. NICHOLS *Prosthetic Dentistry* xli. 638 The various materials employed in rebasing saddles are: modeling compound, plaster, and wax. **1962** BLAKE & TROTT *Periodontol.* iv. 39 The free end saddle, which cannot be supported by occlusal rests, always presents a problem.

l. A fire-clay bar for supporting ceramic ware during glazing.

1911 A. B. SEARLE tr. *Bourry's Treat. Ceramic Industries* (ed. 2) xii. 399 The pieces, especially plates, may be placed upright in rectangular saggers, kept up at the bottom by rectangular saddles and at the top by a series of thimbles. **1930** —— *Encycl. Ceramic Industries* III. 74/2 *Saddle*, a type of support used for plates, etc. in a saggar. It consists of bars of triangular cross-section. Two of these are laid parallel to each other on the bottom of the saggar, and the plates are stood on end across these. **1964** H. HODGES *Artifacts* i. 39 These setters vary considerably in shape, and their names are usually adequately descriptive—saddle, stilt, spur, thimble, pin. **1967** M. CHANDLER *Ceramics in Mod. World* iii. 102 Thimbles, saddles, and stilts are made of fireclay and so designed that the weight rests only on sharp points.

6. *Cookery.* In full ***saddle of mutton***. A 'joint' of mutton, venison, etc., consisting of the two loins and conjoining vertebræ.

1747 MRS. GLASSE *Cookery* 4 The Saddle of Mutton (which is the two Loins). *Ibid.* 24 To French a Hind Saddle of Mutton. It is the two Rumps. **1789** MRS. PIOZZI *Journ. France* II. 338 A saddle of mutton, or more properly a chine. **1806** PIKE *Sources Mississ.* (1810) 75 Hams and saddles of venison. **1844** H. STEPHENS *Bk. of the Farm* II. 99 When cut double, forming the chine or saddle. **1859** *All Year Round* No. 29. 57 Nowhere can the equal of a Sussex haunch or saddle be obtained. **1890** L. C. D'OYLE *Notches* p. ix, They took merely the skins and 'saddle' of the antelope they killed.

7. Applied to certain parts of animals. **a.** A natural saddle-like marking on the back of the Harp Seal. Cf. SADDLE-BACK *sb.* 4 c.

1784 PENNANT *Arctic Zool.* I. 165 The Newfoundland Seal-hunters call it the Harp, or Heart Seal, and name the marks on the sides the saddle. **1884** GOODE, etc. *Nat. Hist. Aquatic Anim.* 62.

b. *Conchol.* †(*a*) A saddle-oyster (see 12); (*b*) see quot. 1851.

1815 S. BROOKES *Introd. Conchol.* 156 Saddle, *Anomia Sella.* **1851** WOODWARD *Mollusca* 78 The shell..is an extremely elongated cone,..divided into cells or chambers by a series of partitions (*septa*)... When they are folded, the elevations are called 'saddles'. **1894** *Geol. Mag.* Oct. 436 Shell (cast) discoidal, with somewhat inflated whorls;.. outer saddle only partly known.

c. (See quots.)

1854, etc. [see *saddle feather*, *saddle hackle* (*feather*), sense 12 below]. **1872** L. WRIGHT *Poultry* xvii. 205 *Saddle*, the posterior part of the back, reaching to the tail, in a cock, answering to the cushion in a hen; often, however, applied to both sexes, cushion being more restricted to a great development, as in Cochins, while 'saddle' may be applied to any breed. **1976** J. BATTY *Understanding Old Eng. Game* (ed. 2) 58 *Saddle*, that part of the back of a male bird nearest to the tail which includes long feathers known as saddle hackles.

8. *Bot.* A ridge separating the fovea and foveola in the leaves of *Isoetes*.

1882 VINES tr. *Sachs' Bot.* 475 Above the fovea and separated from it by the 'saddle', lies a smaller depression.

9. a. A piece of leather stitched across the instep of a shoe, often in a contrasting colour.

1930 *Footwear Organiser* Jan. 37/1 The tie shoe is a development of the one-bar, with a bar or saddle fastened in the centre by means of a fancy lace or ribbon tie through eyelets. **1948** R. T. WILCOX *Mode in Footwear* 170 (*caption*) Saddle oxford—white elk—brown calf saddle—red rubber sole—worn since the 1920's. **1972** *N.Y. Times* 3 Nov. 8/1 (Advt.), In bone leather with a blue saddle..in big girl sizes 5 to 9 medium width.

b. Ellipt. for *saddle shoe* in sense 12 below.

1972 *N.Y. Times* 3 Nov. 8/1 (Advt.), Everyone loves our bumpy, bouncy saddle—the shoe that sparks up the classics.

10. *Math.* A saddle point.

1952 W. HUME-ROTHERY el al. *Metall. Equilibrium Diagrams* xxx. 262 (*heading*) Diagrams involving intermediate compounds: saddles. *Ibid.*, The highest point in the saddle, *R*, will be a maximum in the direction of the eutectic valleys, and at this point the solidus line..touches the liquidus. **1978** *Nature* 7 Sept. 76/1 They explain.. Thom's listing of the ways in which critical points of functions (that is, maxima, minima and saddles) of *n* variables can coalesce as k parameters vary.

III. attrib. and Comb.

11. Simple attrib., as ***saddle-cover***, ***-flap***, ***-girt***, ***-girth***, ***-horn*** (HORN *sb.* 22 b), ***-lap***, ***-lashing***, ***-lining***, ***-load***, ***-nail***, ***-pad***, †***-panel*** (PANEL *sb.*[1] 1), ***-paste***, ***-place***, ***-pommel***, ***-pouch***, ***-soap***, ***-spring***, ***-strap***, ***-stuffing***, ***-tack***, ***-withers***; ***saddle-like***, ***-peaked*** adjs.; with the sense 'used for riding', as ***saddle-ass***, ***-colt***, ***mare***, ***-ox***, ***pony***, ***stock***; with the meaning 'saddle-shaped', as ***saddle flange***, ***key***; in the names of affections incident to the use of the saddle, as ***saddle boil***, ***-bruise***, ***raw***, ***sore***, ***soreness***, ***-weariness***; also appositive, as (sense 5 a) ***saddle-crutch***, (sense 4) ***-glacier***, (sense 5 g) ***-piece***; objective, as ***saddle-maker***, ***-making***, ***-stitching***.

1657 J. WATTS *Vind. Ch. Eng.* 112 God once opened the mouth of Balaams *Saddle-asse. **1816** U. BROWN *Jrnl.* 20 Aug. in *Maryland Hist. Mag.* (1916) XI. 151 Cumberland's Back is Compleatly full of *Saddle Biles & in a full fever. **1884** 'MARK TWAIN' *Huck. Finn* ii. 8 He said they rode him all over the world..and his back was all over saddle-boils. **1977** *Times Lit. Suppl.* 8 Apr. 422/1 His [*sc.* Mark Twain's] more excruciating experiences (seasickness, saddle boils, the running war against vermin). **1709** *Lond. Gaz.* No. 4523/4 He had..a white Spot on his Back, that came by a *Saddle-bruise. **1707** MORTIMER *Husb.* (1721) I. 208 The first Year *Saddle-Colts should only be walked. **1676** S. SEWALL *Diary* 27 Oct. (1878) I. 27 *Saddle Cover [was] lost. **1895** M. A. JACKSON *Mem. Stonewall Jackson* (ed. 2) xx. 403 A superb English saddle, bridle, holsters, saddle-cover. **1926** T. E. LAWRENCE *Seven Pillars* (1935) VIII. xcii. 508 Afterwards we slept on our saddle-covers, the tanned fleece hooked last of all over the saddle-load to make a slippy and sweat-proof seat for the rider. **1867** SMYTH *Sailor's Word-bk.* s.v. *Saddles*, We have a *saddle-crutch for the main or driver boom on the taffarel. **1888** *Lockwood's Dict. Mech. Engin.*, **Saddle Flange*, a curved flange hollowed out to fit a boiler, a pipe, or other cylindrical vessel. **1844** H. STEPHENS *Bk. of the Farm* II. 219 The *saddle-flaps should be sponged clean of mud. **1813** J. C. HOBHOUSE *Journey* (ed. 2) 712 We.. found the stream as high as the *saddle-girts. **1813** SCOTT *Rokeby* VI. xxxiii, And, bursting in the headlong sway, The faithless *saddle-girths gave way. **1884** *Pall Mall G.* 10 June 11/1 The summit of the [Kangla] pass..is crowned by a noble *saddle glacier. **1856** A. CARY *Married* 184 The bridle rein was twisted around the *saddle horn. **1890** L. C. D'OYLE *Notches* 73, I..threw the rein of his horse up over the saddle-horn. **1926** T. E. LAWRENCE *Seven Pillars* (1935) VII. lxxxviii. 490 She [*sc.* a camel]..was docile and smooth to ride, turning left or right if the saddle-horn were tapped on the required side. **1971** D. C. BROWN *Yukon Trophy Trails* i. 20, I hung the box by a string from the saddlehorn and climbed on. **1888** *Lockwood's Dict. Mech. Engin.*, **Saddle Key*, a key whose inner face is hollowed to fit its shaft. **1803** *Scott's Minstrelsy* III. 266 He louted owr his *saddle lap, To kiss her ere they part. **1822** A. CUNNINGHAM *Tradit. Tales, Last Ld. of Helvellyn* (1887) 217 My fathers have fought to the saddle-laps in English blood for the men of the house of Maxwell. *c* **1860** H. STUART *Seaman's Catech.* 1 The muzzle and *saddle lashings of guns. **1784** J. KING *Cook's Voy.* III. VI. iii. 238 On each side of this break the land is quite low; beyond the opening rises a remarkable *saddle-like hill. **1919** J. MASEFIELD *Reynard* I. 5 Some..Brushed at saddle-flaps or hove *Saddle-linings to the stove. **1926** *Saddle-load [see *saddle-cover* above]. *c* **1500** *Melusine* 43 Raymondyn sent for a *Sadlemaker, to whom he said: 'My frend..ye muste cutte this hyde in fourme of a thonge'. **1886** *Encycl. Brit.* XXI. 142/1 The saddle-maker has to consider the ease and comfort of both horse and rider. *Ibid.*,

*Saddle-making and the cutting and sewing of bridles. 1707 *Lond. Gaz.* No. 4312/3 Lost.., a bay *Saddle Mare. 1975 *Islander* (Victoria, B.C.) 7 Sept. 16/2 His reports usually dealt with his saddlemare, Snippet, and her unexpected foal. 1875 KNIGHT *Dict. Mech.*, **Saddle-nail*, a short nail having a large, smooth head, used in making saddles. 1824 W. J. BURCHELL *Trav. S. Africa* Index, s.v. *Oxen*, *Saddle Oxen: their rate of travelling. 1750 J. HEMPSTEAD *Diary* 30 Mar. (1901) 546, I mended my old *Sadle pad. 1971 J. MCDOUGALL *Parsons on Plains* xv. 135 Then I dressed, and putting a saddle-pad on, rode her [*sc.* a mare] all the afternoon. 1465–6 *Durh. Acc. Rolls* (Surtees) 90 Pro ij *Sadillpanell empt. pro le ffissheman, ij s. iiij d. 1725 BRADLEY *Fam. Dict.* s.v. *Saddle*, Some stuff their Saddle-Pannels with well dry'd Moss. 1917 *Harrods Gen. Catal.* 537/4 Harrods' *Saddle Paste. Per tin... 0/6. 1919 J. MASEFIELD *Reynard* I. 5 The savour Of saddle-paste and polish spirit. 1939–40 *Army & Navy Stores Catal.* 767/2 Propert's Saddle Paste.. 1/-. 1869 'MARK TWAIN' *Innoc. Abr.* xlix. 521 *Saddle-peaked Hattin, traditional 'Mount of Beatitudes'. 1825 J. NICHOLSON *Operat. Mechanic* 322 When the screw is turned round, the *saddle-piece will slide uniformly along the triangular bar. 1890 SLINGO & BROOKER *Electr. Engin.* xvii. 600 The channelling [for underground cables] consists of blocks of bituminous concrete made in six-foot lengths and jointed by a saddle-piece of the same material. 1707 MORTIMER *Husb.* (1721) I. 209 Whoever.. takes not off his [horse's] Saddle 'till he is cold, and then rubs the *Saddle-place well. 1593 MARKHAM *Horsemanship* B 3 b, Casting the raynes thereof ouer the *Saddle pomell. 1900 H. SUTCLIFFE *Shameless Wayne* xxiv. (1905) 308 His return blow.. grazing the Lean Man's saddle-pummel as it fell. 1926 T. E. LAWRENCE *Seven Pillars* (1935) VIII. xcvi. 532 We followed dragging my few things in their light *saddle-pouch. 1887 ANSTEY in *Macm. Mag.* Feb. 261/2 My riding was interrupted for a while. Brutus was discovered.. to have a *saddle-raw. 1889 *Field* 7 Dec. LXXIV. 793/2 The *saddle soap made by Messrs. B——. 1946 M. C. SELF *Horseman's Encycl.* 354 Riders with bad seats will often give a *horse saddle sores. 1962 C. STORR *Lucy runs Away* v. 26 I've ridden two miles... I've got saddle sores. 1907 *Daily Chron.* 1 Mar. 7/5 *Saddle soreness is provoked if every stroke of the pedals extends the leg to the utmost. 1887 BURY & HILLER *Cycling* (Badm. Libr.) 340 The combined *saddle-springs recently introduced. 1954 E. JENKINS *Tortoise & Hare* xii. 149 A small suitcase.. was being repaired by the local iron-monger, who did *saddle-stitching for the farmers. 1903 A. ADAMS *Log of Cowboy* 17 Then the entire *saddle stock was driven in, so as to be at hand in case a hasty change of mounts was required. 1948 F. BLAKE *Johnny Christmas* II. 75 He went directly on to the door and pushed it open, passing in among the oxen and saddle-stock of the fort. 1753 CHAMBERS *Cycl. Supp.*, **Saddle-straps*.. are used to hold the girths fast to the saddle. 1890 'R. BOLDREWOOD' *Col. Reformer* (1891) 193 Cut a straight sapling while we rouse out the saddle-straps for a splice. 1871 KINGSLEY *At Last* xiii, We saw the husk carded out.. for.. *saddle-stuffing. 1821 *Blackw. Mag.* IX. 132 Hogg should purchase a pennyworth of *saddle-tacks, and.. nail the ears of the Gude Grey Catte to his stable-door. 1909 *Chambers's Jrnl.* June 347/1 In a general way, the word Bush recalls to the writer.. the sun and dust and *saddle-weariness of the great gray inland plains. 1725 BRADLEY *Fam. Dict.* s.v. *Saddle*, The *Saddle-Withers should be low.

12. Special comb., as **saddle-band** *Sc.*, ? the band of a pedlar's pack; **saddle-bar**, (*a*) *Glazing*, each of the small horizontal iron bars (fitting over the upright stanchions) to which the lead panels are secured; (*b*) *Saddlery* (see quot. 1875); **saddle-bill** = *saddle-billed stork*; also *attrib.*; **saddle-billed** *a.*, an epithet applied to the stork *Ephippiorhynchus senegalensis*, from the recurved shape of its bill; † **saddle bitten** *a.*, galled with a saddle; **saddle-blanket** *U.S.*, a small blanket used, folded, as a saddle-cloth; **saddle block** *Obstetrics*, the technique of anæsthetizing the perineal region by a low spinal injection; freq. *attrib.*; **saddle-boiler**, a boiler of concave form for use with heating apparatus; **saddle-bracket**, (*a*) a receptacle for a saddle when not in use; (*b*) *Telegr.* = 5 e above; **saddlebred** *a.*, bred to have the gaits of an American Saddle Horse; also *ellipt.* as *sb.*; **saddle bronc** *U.S.*: in a rodeo, a bronco ridden with a saddle; freq. *attrib.* as ***saddle bronc riding*** (also *ellipt.* as ***saddle bronc***); **saddle brown**, the tan colour of saddle-leather; **saddle-burned** *a.*, chafed by a saddle; **saddle carp** (see quot.); **saddle-carpenter**, one who makes the frames or trees of saddles; **saddle-case**, † (*a*) the housing of a saddle (*obs.*); (*b*) a travelling case for a saddle; † **saddle-charge**, ? a saddle load; **saddle clip** (see quot.); **saddle club**, a riding club; **saddle-coloured** *a.*, (of complexion) saddle brown, tanned; † **saddle drum**, ? a small drum carried on the saddle; **saddle-eaves** *pl.*, jocularly used for the side of a saddle; **saddle embolus** *Med.*, an embolus straddling the fork of an artery, esp. the aorta, so as to block both branches; **saddle-fast** *a.*, firmly seated in the saddle; **saddle feather** = *saddle hackle* (*feather*) below; **saddle-gall**, a sore produced on the back of a horse by the chafing of the saddle; **saddle-galled** *a.*, chafed with the saddle; affected with saddle-gall; **saddle graft**, a graft made by saddle grafting; **saddle-grafting** (see quot.); **saddle gun** *U.S.*, a gun carried on the saddle of a horse; **saddle hackle (feather)**, any of the long feathers growing backwards from the saddle of a cock; so **saddle-hackled** *a.*; † **saddle-hill**, a saddle-back hill; **saddle horse**, (*a*) a horse which is used for riding; (*b*) (see quot. 1958); **saddle-house**, † (*a*) a saddle-cloth (*obs.*); (*b*) a building in which saddlery is kept; **saddle-iron** *Sc.*, a stirrup; **saddle-joint**, (*a*) *Mech.* (see quot. 1875); (*b*) *Building* (see quot. 1901); (*c*) *Anat.* (see quot. 1897); **saddle-leaf** *U.S.*, = TULIP-TREE 1 a; **saddle-leather**, the leather composing a saddle; also, leather specially prepared for saddle-making; **saddle mark**, (*a*) a mark or patch on a horse's back produced by the friction of a saddle; (*b*) (see quot. 1963); **saddle-mat**, a mat used in the Western U.S. as a saddle-cloth; **saddle-nose**, (*a*) a flat or snub-nose; (*b*) see quot. 1897; **saddle-nosed** *a.*, having a saddle-nose; also, of a bird 'having a soft nasal membrane saddled on the bill' (*Cent. Dict.*); **saddle-notch** (see quot. 1930); hence as *vb. trans.* and **saddle-notched** *a*; **saddle oxford**, a saddle shoe in the Oxford style; **saddle-oyster**, a name given to certain anomioid bivalves, the shape of which resembles that of a saddle; **saddle-pin**, the pin of a cycle saddle which fits into a socket on the cycle frame; **saddle pistol**, a holster pistol; **saddle-plate**, the bent plate which forms the arch of the furnace in steam boilers of the locomotive type (*Cent. Dict.*); **saddle point** *Math.*, (*a*) a point at which a curved surface is locally level but at which its curvature in two directions differs in sign, i.e. for a surface defined by a function f of x and y, a point at which $\partial f/\partial x = \partial f/\partial y = 0$ and $(\partial^2 f/\partial x^2)(\partial^2 f/\partial y^2) < 0$; (*b*) in a zero-sum game, the joint outcome of the two parties following their unmixed optimal strategies, where these exist; **saddle quern** (see quot.); **saddle-rack** = *saddle-bracket* (a); **saddle-rail, -reed** (see quots.); **saddle reef** *Mining*, a reef or vein of ore between the strata in the curve of an anticline or syncline; † **saddle-rings**, circular marks on the back of a horse caused by the abrasion of the saddle; **Saddle Rock** *local U.S.*, a large oyster; in full ***Saddle Rock oyster***; **saddle-roof**, a saddleback roof; **saddle-room**, a room in which saddlery is kept when not in use; **saddle-rug**, a saddle-cloth made of carpeting (*Cent. Dict.*); **saddle scabbard** *N. Amer.* (see quot. 1944); **saddle sealing**, hunting and catching the saddleback seal; **saddle-shaped** *a.*, (*a*) resembling a saddle in shape; (*b*) *Geol.*, anticlinal; **saddle-shell** = *saddle-oyster*; **saddle shoe**, a shoe with a saddle (sense 9 a); **saddle shoulder** *Fashion*, a square-cut shoulder on a jersey, etc., that is an extension of the sleeve; also *attrib.*; **saddle-sick** *a.*, *Sc.*, indisposed through riding; † **saddle side**, the concave lower side (of the liver); **saddle-skirts** *pl.*, the lowermost parts of a saddle; also, the part of a horse's flanks covered by these; **saddle-sore** *a.*, chafed with the saddle; † **saddle-speck**, a mark caused by the abrasion of the saddle; **saddle spot** = prec.; hence **saddle-spotted** *a.*; **saddle-stead** *poet.*, the place of the saddle; **saddle-stone**, (*a*) *Arch.*, the stone forming the angle at the summit of the coping of a gable; (*b*) 'an old name for a variety of stone containing saddle-shaped depressions' (*Cent. Dict.*); **saddle-stool** = *saddle-bracket* (a); **saddle-tank** (see quot. 1871); also *attrib.* as **saddle-tank engine** (see quot. 1888); **saddle thrombus** *Med.* = *saddle embolus* above; † **saddle tore** (see quot.); **saddle tramp** *N. Amer. slang*, a vagrant on horseback; **saddle vein** *Mining* = *saddle reef* above; **saddle wire**, (*a*) *Telegr.*, the wire running along the tops of telegraph posts. (*b*) *Bookbinding*, a wire staple passed through the back fold of a single gathering; usu. *attrib.*; hence **saddle-wired** *a.* Also SADDLE BACK, -BAG, -BOW, -CLOTH, SEAT, -TREE.

a 1604 in Row *Hist. Kirk* (1842) 463 It [*sc.* the ministrie] will die in thy hand Therefor the backe shall beare the *saddle-band. 1825 J. NICHOLSON *Operat. Mechanic* 638 Frames [in lead-work] intended to receive these lights are made with bars across, to which the lights are fastened.. called *saddle-bars. 1874 MICKLETHWAITE *Mod. Par. Churches* 293 It is now most common to place the saddle-bars outside the glass. 1875 KNIGHT *Dict. Mech.*, *Saddle-bar*, the side-bar, side-plate, or spring-bar of a saddle-tree, one on each side connecting the pommel and cantle. 1906 W. L. SCLATER *Birds S. Afr.* IV. 43 (*heading*) *Saddle-bill, or African Jabiru. *Ibid.* 44 The Saddle-bill is found all over tropical Africa. 1947 J. STEVENSON-HAMILTON *Wild Life S. Afr.* xxxiv. 289 The saddle bill or jabiru (*Ephippiorhynchus sinegalensis*)... They are striking-looking birds; the forepart of the long bill crimson, the centre black, and the saddle or shield which comes just above the nostrils, bright yellow. 1973 *Times* 11 Dec. (Zaire Suppl.) p. vii/5, I was able to identify a saddle-bill stork. 1877 *Nature* 17 May 54/1 The additions to the Zoological Society's Gardens.. include.. a *Saddle-billed Stork. 1592 GREENE *Conny Catch.* II. Wks. (Grosart) X. 80 He.. made him spotted in the backe, as if he had been *saddle bitten. 1817 E. P. FORDHAM *Let.* 26 July in *Personal Narr. Travels* (1906) 98 My cloak and *saddle-blanket, spread on the floor, form my couch. 1885 B. HARTE *Maruja* vi, His quick eye was attracted by a saddle-blanket. 1925 C. JACOBSON *Life Story Jeff Davis* xxviii. 234 When I licked that gang at Little Rock during the last campaign, they went around on the streets with their faces looking as long as a saddle blanket. 1973 A. H. WHITEFORD *N. Amer. Indian Arts* 75 Twill weaving is done by the Navajo in making saddle blankets. 1946 PARMLEY & ADRIANI in *Southern Med. Jrnl.* XXXIX. 194/2 The term '*saddle block analgesia' is well chosen inasmuch as it is not only descriptive but is also free from the word spinal which sounds very, very dangerous to most obstetric patients. 1974 PASSMORE & ROBSON *Compan. Med. Stud.* III. xl. 17/2 Low spinal anaesthesia (saddle block) involves the injection of local anaesthetic into the C[erebro] S[pinal] F[luid] of the subarachnoid space. *Ibid.*, The incidence of serious complications is low and saddle block is popular in North America. 1881 *Encycl. Brit.* XII. 228/2 The *saddle boiler is very efficient in form, steady and sure in its working. 1885 *Bazaar* 30 Mar. 1254/2 Wanted, saddle boiler.. to heat small greenhouse. 1844 H. STEPHENS *Bk. of the Farm* I. 190 The riding-horse-stable should have *saddle-brackets. 1876 PREECE & SIVEWRIGHT *Telegraphy* 210 If a wire is to be run along the top of the pole, brackets.. named saddle-brackets, or simply saddles, are.. used. 1974 *Saddlebred [see *pleasure-horse* s.v. PLEASURE *sb.* 6]. 1976 *Horse & Hound* 10 Dec. 73/1 (Advt.), 2 beautiful colts to mature 15 hands 2 in by American saddlebred Goldmount Bourbon Genius. 1977 *Islander* (Victoria, B.C.) 18 Sept. 6/1 Lancer, an American saddlebred, who is nearly eight. 1949 G. ROUNDS *Rodeo* 49 (*heading*) *Saddle Bronc Rodeo. 1956 *N.Y. Times Mag.* 23 Sept. 47/2 Rodeo people call them broncs, but never broncos if they are saddled. Otherwise, they're 'bareback horses'. Saddle broncs usually are larger. Neither are apt to be vicious. Most can be halter-led. *Ibid.*, A saddle bronc ride, which requires more skill, lasts ten [seconds]. 1973 *Houston Chron.* 14 Oct. (Suppl.) 2/3 Texas Prison Rodeo features bareback riding, saddle bronc riding, calf tussles, clowns and other events. 1976 *Columbus* (Montana) *News* 3 June 1/4 The rodeo picks up again at 1:00 p.m. Sunday. Events are saddle bronc, bull riding, steer wrestling, [etc.]. 1977 *New Yorker* 6 June 48/2 He rode dogies and then steers and saddle broncs. 1961 WEBSTER, *Saddle brown. 1975 *Cleveland* (Ohio) *Plain Dealer* 31 Mar. 24-D (Advt.), Perfectly matched Rocker-Recliner or Swivel Rocker in handsome, saddle-brown Masland Duran vinyl. 1941 J. STEINBECK *Sea of Cortez* xvi. 160, I removed the saddle to see whether he might not be *saddle-burned. 1888 G. B. GOODE *Amer. Fishes* 416 When there is a row of large scales down the back it [*sc.* the King Carp] is called the '*Saddle Carp'. *a* 1720 W. GIBSON *Dict. of Horses* viii. (ed. 3) 125 A Country where there is perhaps the most expert *Saddle-Carpenters and Sadlers in the World. 1753 CHAMBERS *Cycl. Supp.*, **Saddle-case*. See the article *Housing*. 1895 *Army & Navy Co-op. Soc. Price List* 497 Tin-lined Saddle Cases for Ladies' Saddles. *a* 1500 *Lat. & Eng. Voc.* in Wr.-Wülcker 609/35 *Sauma*, a *Sadyl-charge. 1884 KNIGHT *Dict. Mech.* Suppl., **Saddle Clip*, a clip which straddles the spring and axle. 1946 *Carleton Coll.* (Northfield, Mass.) *Bull.* Mar. 85 The *Saddle Club, open to students proficient in horsemanship. 1962 A. SAMPSON *Anat. of Britain* xvi. 258 Guards officers.. have their own club in Mayfair, their own polo club, cricket club, saddle club, flying club, shooting club. 1977 *Navy News* June 18/3 Services saddle clubs have been helped. 1854 'LOGAN' *Master's House* 260 That '*saddle-colored' nigger grinning at me.. would be all the better for about 'forty-five', well laid on. 1900 KIPLING *Land & Sea Tales* (1923) 39 The saddle-coloured sons of the soil looked down their noses. 1936 M. MITCHELL *Gone with Wind* xxxiii. 553 A saddle-colored negro of middle age. 1617 PURCHAS *Pilgrimage* (ed. 3) 593 *Saddle drummes of gold set with stones, vsed in Hawking. 1663 BUTLER *Hudibras* I. i. 412 But after many strains and heaves, He got up to the *saddle-eaves. 1937 *Ann. Surg.* CVI. 909 Incisions have been made very close to the aorta, in either one or the other iliac arteries, and successful removals of *saddle emboli accomplished. 1974 J. D. MAYNARD in R. M. Kirk et al. *Surgery* xi. 236 Retrograde catheterisation to the bifurcation of the aorta will allow dislodgement of a saddle embolus. 1805 SCOTT *Last Minstr.* III. vi, Still sate the warrior *saddle-fast. 1854 L. A. MEALL *Moubray's Treat. Poultry* 128 The hackle and *saddle feathers are straw colour. 1901 *Nature* 4 July 233/1 Manipulation of the tail-feathers.. would not account for the likewise abnormal elongation of the saddle-feathers. 1946 WINTER & FUNK *Poultry Sci. & Pract.* (ed. 2) iii. 55 Castrated males grow longer neck, saddle, and tail feathers than do cockerels. 1726 *Dict. Rust.* (ed. 3), **Saddle-gall*. 1831 YOUATT *Horse* 169 For saddle galls there is no better application than [etc.]. 1946 K. TENNANT *Lost Haven* (1947) xiv. 224 The smooth patch of grey rock that looked like a saddle gall. 1680 *Lond. Gaz.* No. 1555/4 One brown bay Nag.. having been lately *Saddle-galled. 1898 DOYLE *Trag. Korosko* i, The saddle-galled donkeys. 1951 *Dict. Gardening* (R. Hort. Soc.) II. 917/1 (*caption*) *Saddle graft. 1959 *New Biol.* XXX. 38 He.. made a saddle graft between the two plants then, when the graft had taken, he cut transversely across the graft-union so that the wound callus formed would be a mixture of tissues from the two plants. 1824 LOUDON *Encycl. Gard.* §2032 *Saddle-grafting is performed by first cutting the top of the stock into a wedge-like form, and then splitting up the end of the scion..; it is then placed on the wedge, embracing it on each side. 1886 *Outing* (U.S.) VIII. 7/1, I.. had with me the little forty-sixty Winchester *saddle gun. 1949 *10 Story Western* May 21/1 They jerked the saddle guns from their scabbards. 1854 L. A. MEALL *Moubray's Treat. Poultry* 85 The *saddle hackle and back feathers. 1855 *Poultry Chron.* III. 44/1 Should the saddle-hackle feathers of the Silver Spangled cock be spangled, or perfectly white? 1951 W. H. SILK *Bantams & Miniature Fowl* iv. 26 Neck and saddle hackle are silvery-white as free from black striping as possible... Saddles and wing-bows are rich yellow or orange, shading to silvery-white in saddle-hackle. 1976 Saddle hackle [see sense 7 c above]. 1855 *Poultry Chron.* III. 209/2, I consider the really perfect hen-feathered cocks vastly superior in plumage to the long-feathered *saddle-hackled. 1773 *Cook's 1st Voy.* II. vii. in

Hawkesworth's Voy. III. 419 There is, . . very near the shore, a remarkable *saddle-hill. **1662** GERBIER *Principles* 32 To accustome the Neapolitan great *Saddle-Horse to raise their Neck. **1867** TROLLOPE *Chron. Barset* I. xxvii. 238 He hired a saddle-horse . . and started after breakfast. **1958** J. HISLOP *From Start to Finish* viii. 67 The best way to [learn] . . is to practise on a saddle-horse (a wooden stand, upon which saddles are cleaned). **1431–2** *Durh. Acc. Rolls* (Surtees) 231 Et in j nova hakney-sadyll et j nova *Sadyllehouse. **1799** *Hull Advertiser* 12 Oct. 1/1 A very excellent Mansion House with coach house, saddle house and stabling. **1870** E. PEACOCK *Ralf Skirl.* III. 101 The Squire sought out Bob in the saddle-house. **1822** GALT *Gilhaize* i. 3 His father having a profitable traffic in *saddle-irons and bridle-rings among the gallants of the court. **1875** KNIGHT *Dict. Mech.*, **Saddle-joint*, a form of joint for sheet-metal. . . One portion overlaps and straddles the vertical edge of the next. **1897** *Syd. Soc. Lex.*, *Saddle-joint*, a joint in which the articulating bony surfaces are convex in one direction and concave in the other. **1901** R. STURGIS *Dict. Archit.* s.v. *Joint, Saddle Joint.* In a weathered course of masonry, . . a joint formed between two adjoining stones whose ends are cut higher than the surface of the weathering between. The projections at the ends are usually sloped or rounded away from the joint . . so as to shed water from the mortar. **1820** C. MATHEWS *Let.* 31 Aug. in A. Mathews *Mem. C. Mathews* (1839) III. vii. 149 If you have not got any in the grounds, a *saddle-leaf tulip is beautiful. **1931** W. N. CLUTE *Common Names of Plants* 39 The tulip-tree (*Liriodendron tulipifera*) was called saddle-leaf because the young leafblades in the bud were bent back across the petiole in such a way as to retard the growth of the tip and make it appear as if cut square across. **1832** TENNYSON *Lady of Shalott* III. iii, Thick-jewell'd shone the *saddle-leather. **1908** *Animal Managem.* (War Office) 32 *Saddle marks are extremely common, in fact it is the exception to find an old troop horse without them. **1963** BLOODGOOD & SANTINI *Horseman's Dict.* 172 *Saddle mark*, hair left unclipped on a horse's back in the shape of a saddle; usual in clipping hunters. **1976** *Horse & Hound* 10 Dec. 67/2 (Advt.), Bay mare. . . Some saddle marks. **1883** *Century Mag.* Aug. 523/1 Mats, called 'cocas', . . are much sought after by California ranchmen as *saddle-mats. **1626** BACON *Sylva* §27 The Raising gently of the Bridge of the Nose [of an infant], doth preuent the Deformity of a *Saddle Nose. **1897** *Syd. Soc. Lex.*, *Saddle-nose*, a nose the bridge of which has sunk, in consequence of necrosis of the nasal bones. **1598–9** HAKLUYT *Voy.* I. 101 His wife . . had cut and pared her nose betweene the eyes, that she might seeme to be more flat and *saddle-nosed. **1742** C. JARVIS *Quix.* I. III. ii. 86 An Asturian wench, broad-faced, flat-headed, and saddle-nosed. **1930** J. BEAMES *Army without Banners* 12 He disdained the clumsy 'squaw notch', where one log sits simply in a shallow groove cut in the one below, and fitted them neatly into place with the '*saddle notch', a triangular ridge cut to fit closely into a deep V in the log above. **1974** *Islander* (Victoria, B.C.) 8 Sept. 4/2 After the logs were peeled David . . saddle-notched each log and fitted them into place. **1976** *Amer. Speech 1973* XLVIII. 166 In the South the saddle-notch was favored, while in the Mid-Atlantic and Midwestern areas V-notching was preferred. **1967** *Dict. Canadianisms* 651/2 *Saddle notch*, a *saddle-notched joint. **1977** *New Yorker* 27 June 58/3 He and Lilly built a . . cabin of unpeeled, saddle-notched logs. **1948** R. T. WILCOX *Mode in Footwear* 165 (*caption*) *Saddle oxford of the period—black or brown and white. **1967** A. WEST in *Coast to Coast 1965–66* 212 Onto her feet she secured a pair of saddle oxfords that were too big by wrapping the laces around her ankles. **1856** WOODWARD *Mollusca* 256 *P[lacuna] sella*, called, from its shape, the '*saddle-oyster', is remarkably striated. **1896** *Westm. Gaz.* 28 Apr. 5/2 He carried the despatches in the *saddle-pin of his bicycle. **1881** GREENER *Gun* 376 The Double-grip *Saddle Pistol. Side-lever action Saddle Pistol. **1922** G. N. WATSON *Treat. Theory Bessel Functions* viii. 235 The points [$u_0, v_0, Rf(w_0)$] are *saddle points, or passes, on the surface. **1946** H. & B. S. JEFFREYS *Methods of Math. Physics* xvii. 472 Through any saddle-point it will be possible to draw at least two curves such that ϕ is constant along them. **1960** A. RAPOPORT *Fights, Games, & Debates* vii. 136 A saddle point is an entry in the game matrix which is the smallest in its row and the largest in its column. **1966** S. BEER *Decision & Control* xviii. 467 In the inadequate game-theoretic model, neither side can exploit information about the other, because the game has a fixed saddle point. **1973** *Listener* 21 June 826/2 We can conceive of a kind of space that has saddle-points in it, over which massive bodies slide in some directions more easily than in others. **1867** *Archaeol. Jrnl.* XXIV. 246 A '*saddle-quern', resembling that found at Ty Mawr, was sent to the museum of the Institute at the Hull meeting, 1867. **1872** J. EVANS *Anc. Stone Impl.* x. 226 The name of saddle-quern has been given to this form of grinding apparatus [*sc.* a bed-stone slightly hollowed on its upper surface and a large oval pebble for a muller]. **1938** *Proc. Prehist. Soc.* IV. 35 The true saddle-quern . . was a two-handed implement allowing only a to-and-fro movement of the upper stone. **1978** A. & G. RITCHIE *Anc. Monuments Orkney* 41 The original rubbing stones were found beside this massive saddle quern, together with a pile of crushed razor-shells. **1890** A. T. FISHER *Through the Stable* xii. 93 *Saddle-racks are usually fixed to the walls of a saddle-room. **1875** KNIGHT *Dict. Mech.*, **Saddle-rail*, a railway rail which has flanges straddling a longitudinal and continuous sleeper. *Ibid.*, **Saddle-reed*, small reeds used in the place of cord to form the edges of gig-saddle sides. **1860** *Mining Surveyors' Rep.* (Mining Dept., Victoria) Aug. 216 The Wellington Reef . . is what is termed by miners a *saddle reef, or, in other words, a vein of quartz branching from the cap in two distinct underlies, viz. one to the east and the other to the west. **1906** J. PARK *Text-bk. Mining Geol.* ii. 49 The gold-bearing veins at Cape Terawhiti, near Wellington, in New Zealand, are interesting examples of saddle-reefs which exhibit both an anticlinal and synclinal arrangement. **1975** E. HILLARY *Nothing venture, Nothing Win* (1977) xviii. 351 Saddle reefs of quartz in the goldfields of Victoria, Australia, and on the west coast of New Zealand. **1694** *Lond. Gaz.* No. 3017/4 Stolen . . a brown bay Mare with a bald Face, *Saddle-rings [etc.]. **1852** *Lantern* (N.Y.) II. 158/1 Oyster House sages . . acknowledge that for a consideration they will puff anything from *Saddle Rock Oysters to Fancy soap. **1865** J. H. BROWNE *Four Years in Secessia* 279 The stewing of 'Saddle-Rocks' in a chafing dish, or the preparation of a lobster salad, was as far as I had ever advanced in the mysteries of the cuisine. **1881** E. INGERSOLL *Oyster-Industry* 244 *Fancy Oysters.*—In New York, these are 'Saddle Rocks', 'Blue Points', etc. *Ibid.* 247 *Saddle Rock Oysters*, a trade name in New York for the largest and finest oysters. **1875** KNIGHT *Dict. Mech.*, **Saddle-roof*, a double gabled roof. **1883** *B'ham Weekly Post* 18 Aug. 8/6 He procured a loaded gun from the *saddle-room. **1679** *Rec. Court of New Castle on Delaware* (1904) 361, 2 *saddle Ruggs & 3 old Blancketts. **1931** A. U. DILLEY *Oriental Rugs & Carpets* Pl. 20 (*caption*) Kerman Saddle Rug. **1898** H. S. CANFIELD *Maid of Frontier* 185 His horse came up to his ranch . . with the gun still in the *saddle scabbard. **1944** R. F. ADAMS *Western Words* 137/1 *Saddle scabbard*, a heavy saddle-leather case in which to carry a rifle or Winchester when riding. The gun fits in as far as the hammer, leaving the stock exposed. **1973** R. D. SYMONS *Where Wagon Led* VI. xviii. 280 He couldn't get at his rifle which was in the saddle scabbard. **1888** *Encycl. Brit.* XXIV. 527/1 The majority of the vessels, after prosecuting the '*saddle' sealing at Newfoundland or Greenland, proceed direct to Disco. **1833–4** J. PHILLIPS *Geol.* in *Encycl. Metrop.* (1845) VI. 594/2 The limestone is uplifted into a *saddle-shaped or anticlinal ridge. **1870** ROLLESTON *Anim. Life* 17 Being concave from side to side and therefore saddle-shaped. **1900** B. D. JACKSON *Gloss. Bot. Terms*, *Saddle-shaped*, applied to such valves of Diatoms as those of *Coscinodiscus*. **1950** DAVID & BROWNE *Geol. Commonwealth of Austral.* II. xxvii. 176 A few of the ore-bodies appear to be saddle-shaped. **1863** J. G. WOOD *Nat. Hist.* III. 419 *Saddle-shell, *Anomia ephippium*. **1941** J. C. FURNASS *How Amer. Lives* 272 You could paint an accurate oil portrait from those data alone, right down to the socks and *saddle shoes. **1958** *Listener* 31 July 157/2 A young American boy and girl, dressed in teenage style of blue jeans, suede saddle shoes, and peach-coloured polo shirts. **1974** D. RAMSAY *No Cause to Kill* i. 6 Saddle shoes. Brown and white. . . Of all things! Who wore saddle shoes nowadays? **1957** M. B. PICKEN *Fashion Dict.* 280/2 **Saddle shoulder sleeve*, sleeve with shoulder extended into neckline somewhat like raglan, but square-cut in 'saddle' effect. **1969** *Sears Catal.* Spring/Summer 20 Classic Cardigan. . . Saddle shoulders add a well tailored look. **1978** *Detroit Free Press* 2 Apr. (Detroit Suppl.) 21 (Advt.), Crew neck pullover with saddle shoulder. **1823** GALT *Entail* vii, Weel do I ken what it is to be *saddle-sick mysel'. **1844** MRS. CARLYLE *Let.* 7 July, New Lett. & Mem. 1903 I. 140 The girls were dreadfully saddle sick. For me, my old habit of riding, I suppose, had saved me. **1615** CROOKE *Body of Man* I The inward face of the Liuer which is the lower, is . . hollow, vnequall, and is called the *Simus* or *saddle side, that it may giue way to the stomacke strutting . . with plenty of meat. **1610** MARKHAM *Maister-p.* II. xliv. 286 Of Wennes or Knobs growing about the *saddle skirts. *a* **1656** USSHER *Ann.* vi. (1658) 153 Pharnabazus . . rid his horse into the very sea, up to his saddle-skirts. *a* **1725** THORESBY *Diary* (1830) I. 295 We missed the deepest of the Wash . . though we rode to the saddle-skirts for a considerable way. **1907** *Daily Chron.* 22 Oct. 8/4 Nicholas *saddle-sore by this time, and the mare too weary to shy. **1956** R. BRADDON *Nancy Wake* xv. 178 It's just that damned bicycle. I'm so saddle-sore I could die. **1975** *Times* 8 Feb. 10/5 What if riding pales and saddlesore guests seek other diversions? **1685** *Lond. Gaz.* No. 2062/4 Lost a black Coach Mare . . , hath a small *Saddle-speck. **1668** *Ibid.* No. 272/4 A Baye Mare, no white, save some *Saddle spots. **1676** *Ibid.* No. 1098/4 Stolen . . , a large brown bay Coach Gelding, . . *saddle-spotted. **1876** MORRIS *Sigurd* II. 133 And his war-gear clanged and tinkled as he leapt to the *saddle-stead. **1843** *Civil Eng. & Arch. Jrnl.* VI. 320/1 Modern gables too are generally awkwardly terminated at the eaves by . . *saddle-stones. **1932** G. M. BOUMPHREY *Story of Wheel* 42 The '*saddle-stone', which had a hollow face in which a smaller stone was rubbed backwards and forwards. **1856** 'STONEHENGE' *Brit. Rural Sports* 583/2 Hooks and *saddle-stools, or brackets, for the saddles or harness. **1871** *Young Gentleman's Ann.* Dec. 28 Other engines of this class [*sc.* tank-engines], however, carry their water in a tank (called a *saddle-tank) which rests on the top of the boiler. **1888** *Lockwood's Dict. Mech. Engin.*, *Saddle Tank Engine*, a locomotive engine in which the water tank envelops the top and sides of the boiler. **1933** *Ann. Surg.* XCVIII. 262 At about the point of bifurcation of the deep and superficial femoral is a constricted portion with a *saddle thrombus which shows beginning organization. **1937** *Ibid.* CVI. 908 The . . patient was operated upon rather late, after the saddle thrombus developed, by the transabdominal route. **1681** COLVIL *Whigs' Supplic.* (1741) 13 A Pistol . . at either *Saddle tore. *Note.* Saddle tore, *Saddle Bow.* **1942** BERREY & VAN DEN BARK *Amer. Thes. Slang* §913/10 **Saddle . . tramp*, a cowboy who rides from ranch to ranch living on Western hospitality. **1962** E. LUCIA *Klondike Kate* 7 Most of them [*sc.* prostitutes] led wretched lives, . . attached to gamblers, card sharps . . saddle tramps, gun-slingers and rogues. **1979** *Radio Times* 5–11 May 23/2 Kirk Douglas back on the range for King Vidor, in the one about the saddle tramp up against the barbed wire. **1935** STOČES & WHITE *Structural Geol.* 293 Saddle *veins are filled openings . . which were similarly formed in the arches and troughs of folded beds. **1977** A. HALLAM *Planet Earth* 314/3 Saddle veins are lens-shaped, concave below and convex above. **1876** PREECE & SIVEWRIGHT *Telegraphy* 253 The most important circuit is generally worked upon the *saddle wire. **1911** WEBSTER, Saddle wire stitch. **1948** R. R. KARCH *Graphic Arts Procedures* xii. 301 Saddle-Wire bound booklets are the simplest and cheapest in form. . . The cover and pages are held by two or more stitches on saddle-wire booklets, which allows them to lie flat and open. **1967** V. STRAUSS *Printing Industry* x. 659/1 Saddle wire stitching produces a completely flat-opening book. **1967** KARCH & BUBER *Offset Processes* xii. 492 *Saddle-wired books lie flat when open, and may be folded upon themselves.

saddle ('sæd(ə)l), *v.* Forms: 1 sadolian, sadelian, 3–6 sadel, (6 -ell), 4–5 sadyl(l, (5 -ylle), 4–7 sadle, (5 sadulle, sadil, 6 -ill), 6– saddle. [OE. *sadolian*, f. *sadol* SADDLE *sb.*; cf. MLG. *sadeln*, MDu. *sadelen*, Du. *zadelen*, OHG. *satalôn* (MHG. *satelen*, mod.G. *satteln*), ON. *sǫðla* (Sw. *sadla*, Da. *sadle*).]

1. a. *trans.* To put a riding-saddle upon (a horse or other animal); also *to saddle up*. Also *absol.*

c **1000** ÆLFRIC *Gram.* xxviii. (Z.) 165 *Sterno* . . ic sadelige hors. *c* **1205** LAY. 13512 Fortiger hæhte his sweines sadeli his blonken. *a* **1300** *K. Horn* 763 (Cambr. MS.) Horn sadelede his stede. *c* **1320** *Sir Beues* 757 (MS. A.) Beues let sadlen is ronsi. **1388** WYCLIF *1 Kings* xiii. 13 And he seide to hise sones, Sadle ȝe an asse to me. And whanne thei hadden sadlid, he stiede, and ȝede after the man of God. *c* **1420** *Sir Amadace* (Camden) xxviii, Quen Sir Amadace hade etun, To sadulle his horse was noȝte forȝetun. **1485** *Rutland Papers* (Camden) 4 A spare coursar lad in hand . . sadlet with a saddell of estate. **1587** TURBERV. *Trag. T.* iv. 69 b, He sadled vp his horse, and roade in post away. **1637** J. WILLIAMS *Holy Table* 206 What needs the Writer saddle up his Horse. **1761** GRAY *Odin* 2 Uprose the king . . And saddled strait his coal-black steed. **1839–55** W. IRVING *Wolfert's Roost* 47, I almost determined . . to . . saddle my horse, and ride off. **1901** *Daily Chron.* 27 Aug. 5/5, I then asked him to saddle-up my horse while I was dressing.

†**b.** *intr.* or *absol.* To inure a colt to the saddle.

1656 *Markham's Perfect Horseman* 19 When to Saddle.

c. *to saddle and bridle* fig., to subject to control.

1864 LOWELL *Fireside Trav.* 133 The cover [of the kettle] was chattering with the escaping steam, which had thus vainly begged of all men to be saddled and bridled, till James Watt one day happened to overhear it.

d. *S. Afr. to saddle off* = OFFSADDLE, OFF-SADDLE *v.*

1835 J. W. D. MOODIE *Ten Yrs. S. Afr.* I. 65 He . . asked us if we would 'saddle off' our horses.

e. *trans.* To enter (a horse that one has trained) in a race.

1928 *Daily Mail* 25 July 14/2 Scott will not saddle Lamintone for the Church House Handicap Plate (2.30) at Liverpool. **1947** *Sun* (Baltimore) 11 June 17/4 Palmer Sowers, of Washington, saddled two winners on the program and might have made it three had not Jockey J. Keenan lost a stirrup in the final drive of the second race. **1970** *Globe & Mail* (Toronto) 25 Sept. 32/3 Trainer Glen Magnusson . . saddled three successive winners. **1976** *Southern Even. Echo* (Southampton) 13 Nov. 15/3 The Bishop Auckland trainer should start successfully by saddling Clever Prince to win the Threlkeld Handicap Chase.

†**2.** *trans.* To ride, bestride (an animal). Also *transf. Obs.*

1550 BALE *Eng. Votaries* II. 18 b, Take that benefyce to you (sayth he to the priest) but saddle nomore the nonne. **1585** JAS. I *Ess. Poesie* (Arb.) 68 Vpon Alhallow ene, Quhen our gude nichtbors rydis . . Some sadland a sho ape, . . Some hotcheand on a hemp stalk. **1598** R. DALLINGTON *Meth. Trav.* X 2 b, No maruell then, the bridle being left in their owne [French wives'] hands, though sometimes they be saddled, and their husbands know not. **1713** PETIVER in *Phil. Trans.* XXVIII. 184 Its lower Leaves are like the Garden Poppy, which higher saddle or ride the Stalk.

3. *intr.* To get into the saddle. Orig. in Colonial use, *to saddle up*.

1835 BURNES *Trav. Bokhara* (ed. 2) II. 198 We dressed ourselves . . and saddled at three P.M. **1849** E. E. NAPIER *Excurs. S. Africa* II. 12 Another term of Colonial import is that of 'saddling-up', and 'off-saddling'. **1863** W. C. BALDWIN *Afr. Hunting* ii. 33 We saddled and went in pursuit. **1865** KINGSLEY *Herew.* I. i. 61 Ay, every churl who owns a manor, must needs arm and saddle and levy war. **1890** 'R. BOLDREWOOD' *Col. Reformer* (1891) 206 Bothwell, myself, and the six troopers, saddled up and departed.

4. a. *trans.* To charge or load *with* (a burden); now only *fig.* to load *with* (something) as a burden.

1693 DRYDEN *Persius* v. 207 The Slaves thy Baggage pack, Each saddled with his Burden on his Back. **1728** VANBRUGH & CIBBER *Prov. Husb.* I, His Estate . . was left him saddled with two Joyntures, and two weighty Mortgages upon it. **1731** BAILEY vol. II. s.v., To saddle, . . to embarrass, as to saddle a Cause. **1767** A. YOUNG *Farmer's Lett. to People* 162 But Mr. Justice . . saddles the parish with whatever burthen he thinks proper. **1775** SHERIDAN *Duenna* I. iv, I'll saddle him with this scrape. **1837** LOCKHART *Scott* (1839) III. ix. 295 The earnest wish of Scott and Ballantyne to saddle the publisher of the new poem with part of their old 'quire stock'. **1858** SURTEES *Ask Mamma* xliv. 196 The chances then, are, that he is saddled with a sort of old man of the sea. **1874** L. STEPHEN *Hours in Library* (1892) I. iv. 157 We are perhaps inclined to saddle Scott unconsciously with the sins of a later generation. **1895** *Law Times Rep.* LXXIII. 691/1 Otherwise a testator would be able to saddle people with duties of an onerous description.

b. ? To secure *for* (a burdensome task). *rare*$^{-1}$.

1826 SCOTT *Jrnl.* 25 Oct., Sotheby . . endeavoured to saddle me for a review of his polyglot Virgil.

5. To put (a burden) *upon* (another's back).

1808 COBBETT *Pol. Reg.* XIV. 547 The men . . who, if they serve us but for a few years, are saddled upon our devoted ass-like backs for life. **1812** *Sporting Mag.* XL. 153, I should not wonder if that Bully Mitchell saddles this poisoning upon me. **1820** L. J. JENNINGS in *Croker Papers* I. vi. 158 The whole of the Bergami family had . . been saddled upon the Princess. **1881** BESANT & RICE *Chapl. Fleet* III. 248, I found her only too eager to marry anyone upon whom she could saddle her debts.

6. a. *Masonry.* To work (a joint) so as to form a 'saddle' projecting above the horizontal surface of the stones joined. **b.** *Carpentry.* To join or fit together by HALVING.

1823 P. NICHOLSON *Pract. Build.* 311 A process by workmen called saddling the joints. **1897** *Westm. Gaz.* 3 Sept. 2/1 These consist of one log laid upon another, saddled in at the corners.

c. To attach after the manner of a saddle.

1831 J. J. AUDUBON *Ornith. Biogr.* I. 303 The nests were fixed to a horizontal bough, but were not *saddled* upon it so deeply as those of the Wood Thrush are. **1881** *Amer. Naturalist* XV. 217 Our nest . . was saddled to a horizontal limb after the fashion of our wood pewee. **1940** *Bull. U.S.*

Nat. Museum No. 176. 321 It was about 30 feet from the ground, saddled on a horizontal branch of a maple over the trail.

7. To bend downwards in the middle.

1803 *Sporting Mag.* XXI. 327 Saddling the cards..is bending the sixes, sevens, eights, and nines, in the middle longways. **1880** *Standard* 10 Dec., Walls are cracked and roofs 'saddled' in every direction.

8. (See quot.)

1731 BAILEY vol. II. s.v., To saddle,..to furnish, as to saddle a spit.

†9. Comb.: **saddle-goose**, a nickname for a fool; **saddle-nag**, a stable-boy, groom. *Obs.*

1526 SKELTON *Magnyf.* 1834 Sym Sadylgose was my syer, and Dawcocke my dame. **1646** J. HALL *Poems* 7 Who would employ his Sadle-nagg to come And hold a trencher in the Dining-roome?

saddleback ('sæd(ə)lbæk), *sb.* and *a.* [f. SADDLE *sb.* + BACK *sb.*] **A.** *sb.*

1. †**a.** *Archery.* A saddle-backed feather. *Obs.* **b.** A saddle-backed hill. (Cf. SADDLE-BACKED *a.* 1.)

1545 ASCHAM *Toxoph.* II. (Arb.) 133 The swyne backed fashion..gathereth more ayer than the saddle backed, and therefore the saddle backe is surer for daunger of wether. **1869** E. A. PARKES *Pract. Hygiene* (ed. 3) 289 A saddleback is usually healthy..so are positions near the top of a slope. **1907** *Gentl. Mag.* Mar. 247 A regular saddleback of grey Silurian blocks the wayfarers path.

†**2.** A back (of an animal) having a depression in the middle of it. *Obs.*

1625 PURCHAS *Pilgrims* II. 1694 Certaine beasts..much like unto a Deere, hauing a Saddle-backe like unto a Camell.

3. *Arch.* A roof of a tower, having a gable at two opposite sides connected by a ridge-roof; a packsaddle roof.

1849 FREEMAN *Archit.* 238 The gabled tower..does not seem to occur; but we meet with the form usually called a saddle-back. **1861** BERESF. HOPE *Eng. Cathedr. 19th C.* 243 The due and moderate use of the gabled tower of the German style..may be adopted,..so too may the saddle-back. **1893** C. HODGES in *Reliquary* Jan. 15 The finish of the tower was what is generally known as a saddle-back, a form common in Normandy, but rare in England.

4. A name of various birds and animals etc. **a.** The Grey or Hooded Crow, *Corvus cornix*; also called ***saddleback crow***.

1864 ATKINSON *Prov. Names Birds*, Saddleback Crow.. Hooded Crow. *Corvus cornix.* **1895** P. H. EMERSON *Birds* etc. *of Norf. Broadland* xlix. 140 A useful bird is the handsome but sluggish 'saddle-back' [*i.e.* the grey crow].

b. The adult of either of the Black-backed Gulls, *Larus marinus* and *L. fuscus*; also ***saddleback gull***.

1770 G. CARTWRIGHT *Jrnl.* 2 Oct. (1792) I. 40 They returned with three shellbirds and a saddleback. **1847** COL. HAWKER *Diary* (1893) II. 275 A huge saddle-back gull. **1864** ATKINSON *Prov. Names Birds*, Saddle-back, Saddleback Gull..Great Blackbacked Gull. *Larus marinus.* **1872** *Daily News* 23 Aug., The decrease of the gulls would be attended with certain loss to fishermen who were often directed and piloted to the shoals by the keen-eyed saddle-back. **1872** COUES *Key N. Amer. Birds* 312 Great Black-backed Gull. Saddle-back. **1932** J. BARBOUR *Forty-Eight Days Adrift* vi. 61 A 'saddleback' coming towards us..was a good sign we were getting near land.

c. The male of the Greenland or Harp Seal (*Phoca grœnlandica*) when three years old; in full ***saddleback seal***.

1856 KANE *Arct. Expl.* I. ii. 22 The valued furs of the saddle-back seal. **1896** LYDEKKER *Brit. Mammals* 156 It is not till the third year that the males (then called 'Saddle-backs') assume the characteristic dark harp-shaped markings.

d. A New Zealand wattle-bird, *Creadion* (or *Philesturnus*) *carunculatus*.

1868 W. BULLER *Ess. Ornithol.* in *Trans. N.Z. Inst.* I. 5 (Morris) The Saddle-back (*Creadion carunculatus*) of the North is represented in the South by *C. Cinereus*, a closely allied species. **1966** *Weekly News* (Auckland, N.Z.) 1 June 17/1 A pair of saddlebacks point like hunting dogs... They snap from one rigid position to another, head down, tail erect, wattles a blood crimson, the fragmented sunlight burnishing the chestnut saddle on their backs.

e. A variety of the goose (see quot. 1885).

1885 *Encycl. Brit.* XIX. 647/1 The common variety [of the goose] frequently marked with dark feathers on the back, and hence termed 'saddlebacks'.

f. A kind of oyster (see quot. 1876).

1876 *Weale's Dict. Terms, Saddle-backs*, in fishery, a name given to a bastard kind of oyster by the fishers; they are considered unfit for human food.

g. The brown and green larva of the moth *Sibine stimulea*, which has stinging spiny hairs and is found in southeastern North America.

1895 J. H. & A. B. COMSTOCK *Man. Study of Insects* xviii. 225 The Saddle-back Caterpillar... Its most characteristic feature is a large green patch on the back. **1943** *Sun* (Baltimore) 9 Sept. 16/7 The Saddleback is of the family *Eucleidae.* **1954** [see 10[2]].

h. A parti-coloured black and white pig belonging to the breed so called. Also ***saddleback pig***.

1919 (*title*) The Wessex Saddleback Pig Society's herd book. **1927** *Daily Tel.* 6 Dec. 9/2 Mr. Douglas Vickers' herd of Wessex saddlebacks at Temple Dinsley, Hitchin. **1978** E. DOWNING *Keeping Pigs* iii. 25 The Large Black and the Saddleback are still hardy. **1981** *Times* 25 May 10/6 The Johnstone Cup..was won by the cider firm, Whiteways.. with British saddleback pigs.

i. The African black-backed jackal, *Canis mesomelas*.

1947 J. STEVENSON-HAMILTON *Wild Life S. Afr.* ii. 23 The side-striped jackal..began to decrease... Its place had been taken by the black-backed jackal... It may be that it contracted and died from the same disease as affected the wild dog, and from which the saddle-back..remained.. immune. **1964** D. VARADAY *Gara-Yaka* vii. 61 A pair of saddle-back jackals coming into view from the sands of an ant-bear hole.

j. The North American Arctic shrew, *Sorex arcticus*.

1948 A. L. RAND *Mammals Eastern Rockies* 51 The saddle-back shrew with is red-brown sides and tricolour pattern is the most beautiful of our shrews. **1966** R. L. PETERSON *Mammals E. Canada* 38 *Sorex arcticus* Kerr—Arctic or Saddle-back Shrew. *Ibid.* 38/1 The young do not show the distinct dorsal band or 'saddle back'.

5. a. *Coal-mining* (see quot.). **b.** *Geol.* An anticlinal (*Cassell's Encycl. Dict.* 1887).

1883 GRESLEY *Coal-mining Terms, Saddleback*, a depression or valley in strata.

B. *adj.*

1. = SADDLE-BACKED *a.*, in various senses.

1677 *Lond. Gaz.* No. 1257/4 Stolen or strayed.., one dapple gray Gelding..a little saddle-back. **1696** *Ibid.* No. 3202/4 A brown Mare,..Saddle Back, well risen on the Crest. **1862** *Ecclesiologist* XXIII. 252 Gabled or saddle-back towers. **1876** *Encycl. Brit.* IV. 472/1 [Coping] sloping to both sides from the middle..is technically termed saddle-back coping. **1897** *Daily News* 3 May 7/3 The Greek troops occupied..a saddleback hill. **1904** *Westm. Gaz.* 2 Sept. 4/1 A high saddle-back peak. **1904** M. BEERBOHM *Let.* 3 Jan. (1964) 155 There is nothing to do except to sit in the hall on a saddle-back chair. **1906** *Edin. Rev.* Jan. 114 A plain.. building..with two low gable or 'saddle-back' roofs. **1981** P. VANSITTART *Death of Robin Hood* III. iii. 142 The dulled crimson sofa and saddleback chairs.

2. ***saddleback caterpillar, crow, gull, jackal, pig, seal, shrew***: see A. 4.

3. *Mech.* (See quot.)

1844 *Civil Engin. & Arch. Jrnl.* VII. 236/2 At the bottom of the hopper there is a number of angular or 'saddle back bars', placed transversely..; the 'saddle back bars' will have the effect of dividing the ores. **1888** *Lockwood's Dict. Mech. Engin., Saddle Back Rail*, or *Barlow Rail*, a rail whose sides curve rapidly outwards and downwards.

4. *Geol.* (See quot.)

1854 PAGE *Introd. Textbk. Geol.* §31 When strata dip in opposite directions from a ridge or line of elevation..the axis is termed anticlinal or saddleback.

5. *Path.* (Cf. *saddle-nose*, SADDLE *sb.* 12.)

1897 *Allbutt's Syst. Med.* IV. 686 As a result of cicatricial contraction of the connective tissue..the so-called 'saddle-back' nose may be formed.

6. Put for 'horse-back'. Also *advb.*

1899 'ZACK' *On Trial* xiv. 124 If 'tworn't that I can trust 'ee saddle-back..I shuld hold you had done the mare a mischief. **1904** *Westm. Gaz.* 29 Feb. 1/3 His love of saddle-back exercise.

saddle-backed ('sæd(ə)lbækt), *a.*

1. a. Having the back, upper surface, or edge curved like a saddle; having a concavely curved outline; *spec.* in *Archery* (see quot. 1545).

1545 ASCHAM *Toxoph.* II. (Arb.) 129 Fourthly in couling or sheryng [the feather of a shaft],..whether somewhat swyne backed (I must vse shoters wordes) or sadle backed, whether rounde, or square shorne? **1599** HAKLUYT *Voy.* II. II. 126 It is a hill sadlebacked..: and..we saw a row of hils sadlebacked also. **1601** HOLLAND *Pliny* I. 238 They [dolphins] are saddle-backed. *Ibid.* 492 The Walnut tree wood soone bendeth, and is saddle-backt as it lieth. **1884** G. ALLEN *Philistia* I. 235 A saddle-backed hill. **1910** A. BENNETT *Clayhanger* II. xxi. 313 He would begin to establish himself in a saddle-backed, ear-flapped easy-chair.

b. Placed astride like a saddle.

1878 J. H. BEADLE *Western Wilds* xxx. 487 Colorado is divided nearly down the center by the main chain of the Rocky Mountains—or, in miner's phrase, 'saddle-backed across the range'.

2. Of a horse: see quot. 1831.

1675 *Lond. Gaz.* No. 967/4 Strayed or stolen.., a bright Bay Gelding,..a little Saddle-back'd. **1753** CHAMBERS *Cycl. Supp.* **1831** YOUATT *Horse* 166 Some horses have a very considerable hollow behind the withers. They are said to be saddle-backed. **1895** *Westm. Gaz.* 29 July 2/3 A thorough-bred Arab..should be..very slightly saddle-backed. To be 'saddle-backed' is to have a depression where the saddle would naturally come.

3. *Arch.* **a.** Of coping: see quot. 1842. **b.** Of a tower: Having a SADDLEBACK.

1842 GWILT *Archit.* s.v. *Coping*, Coping thicker in the middle than at the edges is called saddle-backed coping. **1870** F. R. WILSON *Ch. Lindisf.* 23 A small straight saddle-backed tower.

4. An epithet applied to birds and animals having saddle-like markings on the back, as ***saddle-backed crow***, the Grey Crow, *Corvus cornix*; ***saddle-backed shrew*** = SADDLE-BACK *sb.* 4 j.

1838 HOLLOWAY *Provinc., Saddle-backed crow*, the Royston, or sea-crow, so called from its mixture of black and grey feathers. *Sussex.* **1894** R. B. SHARPE *Birds Gt. Brit.* I. 12 The Hooded, or Saddle-backed Crows. **1895** J. G. MILLAIS *Breath from Veldt* vii. 142 Here also are a big flock of saddle-backed Jabiru storks (*Mycteria senegalensis*). **1927** H. H. T. JACKSON *Taxon. Rev. Amer. Long-Tailed Shrews* 69 A specimen of the American saddle-backed shrew..was mentioned as early as 1772.

'saddle-bag, *sb.*

1. A bag carried at the saddle; esp. one of a pair laid across the back of a horse, behind the saddle, or one attached behind the saddle of a bicycle.

1773 H. FINLAY *Jrnl.* (1867) 43 The rider had saddle bags quite full besides. **1780** W. FLEMING in N. D. Mereness *Trav. Amer. Colonies* (1916) 651 Capt. Pawling..had gone back for my saddlebags. **1796** MORSE *Amer. Geog.* I. 542 Manufactures of leather..holsters, saddle-bags [etc.]. **1841** LANE *Arab. Nts.* I. 43 He..put his hand into his saddle-bag, and eat a morsel of bread and a date which were among his provisions. **1856** STANLEY *Sinai & Pal.* i. (1858) 67 The great saddle bags act like sails to the camels. **1857** HUGHES *Tom Brown* I. i, A visit..which the Squire made on his horse with a pair of saddle-bags containing his wardrobe. **1901** DUNCAN & SCOTT *Allen & Woodson Counties, Kansas* 619 The doctor of 1858,..with saddle-bags like paniers to a pack mule, would make a strange comparison with the well-dressed and well-barbered M.D. of the present era. **1920** *Cycling* 12 Aug. p. xvii/3 (Advt.), Few pigskin saddle bags, 9 by 6 by 4, 17s 6d, post 9d. **1940** J. BETJEMAN *Old Lights for New Chancels* 49 Kant on the handle-bars, Marx in the saddlebag. **1965** D. MURPHY *Full Tilt* p. xi, Apart from the normal accessories—saddle-bag, bell, lamp and pump—she carried only pannier-bag holders on either side of the back wheel. **1973** R. T. WAY *Bicycle* 63/2 For normal day-to-day riding, a small saddlebag is all that is needed—it only has to take a cape, cap, tools, snack and camera.

2. *attrib.* Used to designate a fine quality of carpeting, made in sizes and designs imitating the saddle-bags carried in the East by camels; chiefly employed as a covering for cheap classes of dining-room furniture. Also *ellipt.*, a saddle-bag chair.

1882 *Daily News* 30 May 5/7 Settees and easy-chairs upholstered in what is known as the Persian saddle-bag pattern. **1900** FLO. WARDEN *Plain Miss Cray* 80 There was ..a saddle-bag couch and two big easy-chairs. **1903** MCNEILL *Egregious English* 125 A saddle-bag suite. **1919** C. DANE *Legend* 82 'There's your chair. Isn't that always your chair?'..But he did not take the saddle-bag near Anita's own seat.

'saddle-bag, *v. U.S.* Also (*rare*) **saddle-bags**. [f. the sb.] *intr.* To double round an obstruction.

1884 'MARK TWAIN' *Huck. Finn* xiii. 114 They lost their steering-oar..and saddle-baggsed on the wreck. **1898** *Derrick's Handbk. Petroleum* 32 A boat..laden with 1,500 bbls. of oil, 'saddle-bagged' on pier of Oil Creek bridge. Boat and contents a total loss. **1901** W. F. FOX in *6th Ann. Rep. N.Y. State Forest, Fish & Game Comm.* 254 Sometimes the long, floating mass [*sc.* a lumber raft] would swing in the wind and current so that it would 'saddle-bag' on the head of the bar below the dam. **1905** *Terms Forestry & Logging* (U.S. Dept. Agric. Bureau Forestry) 45 *Saddlebag*, as applied to a boom, to catch on an obstruction and double round it.

'saddle-bow. Now *arch.* or *poet.* [BOW *sb.*[1] Cf. OHG. *satilpogo* (MHG. *satelboge*, mod.G. *sattelbogen*).] The arched front part of a saddle-tree or of a saddle.

*c*725 *Ags. Voc.* in Wr.-Wülcker 11/17 *Carpella*, sadulboᵹa. *a* **1250** *Prov. Alfred* 229 in *O.E. Misc.* 116 If þu hauest seorewe, ne seye þu hit nouht þan arewe, seye hit þine sadelbowe [*a* **1275** seit þin sadilbowe] and ryd þe singinde forþ. *c* **1330** *Arth. & Merl.* 8148 (Kölbing) Wawain him ȝaue a dent of howe & cleued him to þe sadel bowe. **1470–85** MALORY *Arthur* IX. xvi, And the lady of the lake took vp her heed and henge it vp by the heyre of her sadel bowe. **1592** SHAKS. *Ven. & Ad.* 14 Vouchsafe, thou wonder, to alight thy steed, And rein his proud head to the saddle-bow. **1658** tr. *Porta's Nat. Magick* XIV. 314 We use to hang up Turkies alive by the bills, at the sadle-bow, when we ride. **1757** BURKE *Abridgm. Eng. Hist.* Wks. X. 411 The beast.. plunged, and threw his rider violently on the saddle-bow. **1805** SCOTT *Last Minstr.* I. v, Steeds..Barb'd with frontlet of steel, I trow, And with Jedwood-axe at saddlebow. **1879** 'OUIDA' *Cecil Castlemaine's Gage* 7 He lifted his hat, and bowed down to his saddle-bow as he passed her.

saddle-cloth. Forms: see SADDLE and CLOTH; also 5 **sadylclow.** A cloth placed on a horse's back beneath the saddle; †in early use = foot-cloth, housing-cloth.

1481–90 *Howard Househ. Bks.* (Roxb.) 222 Item,..paied ..for ij. yerdes and di. and. di. qrter of blak cloth, for a sadylclow for my Lord. **1523** FITZHERB. *Husb.* §142 Spere, male, hode, halter, sadelclothe, spores. **1683** *Lond. Gaz.* No. 1786/4 A bay Mare, with..a black Saddle, and a green Saddle-Cloth. **1776** BOSWELL *Johnson* II. 349, I observed them [at Lichfield] making some saddle-cloths. **1818** SCOTT *Hrt. Midl.* v, The Laird..has had his running foot-man here..to see when the broidered saddle-cloth for his sorrel horse will be ready. **1845** FORD *Handbk. Spain* I. 31 There is no bed like the saddle-cloth. **1867** S. W. BAKER *Nile Trib. Abyssinia* v. 111 We were requested to mount two superb white hygeens, with saddle-cloths of blue Persian sheep-skins.

saddled ('sæd(ə)ld), *ppl. a.* [f. SADDLE *v.* + -ED[1].]

1. Furnished with a saddle.

1002 in Kemble *Cod. Diplom.* VI. 147 Ic ᵹeann minum hlaforde..feower hors twa ᵹesadelod and twa unᵹesadelode. **1890** *Daily News* 15 Feb. 2/5 A saddled horse was seen in a field without a rider.

2. As the epithet of fishes, insects, etc., having saddle-like markings.

1803 SHAW *Zool.* IV. 467 Saddled Sparus. Sparus Ephippium. *Ibid.* 596 Saddled Mackrel. Scomber Equula. **1880** SWINTON *Insect Variety* 162 The common Saddled Leaf-cricket of the Vine (*Ephippigera vitium*) has especially thick cup-shaped elytra.

saddleless ('sæd(ə)llɪs), *a.* [f. SADDLE *sb.* + -LESS.] Without a saddle; esp. of a horse, not furnished with a saddle. Also *rarely* of a rider: †(thrown) out of the saddle.

14.. *Sir Beues* 253–8 (MS. C.) The erle, amonge them all To the grounde he ys falle And ys sadulles. *c* **1489** CAXTON *Sonnes of Aymon* 268 But he had no sadel upon his horse... Whan Reynawd sawe brayforde sadeles, he called to oger, & sayd [etc.]. *a* **1500** *Prophecy* in *Bernard. de cura rei fam.* (E.E.T.S.) 18 The Egyll and þe antelope..And Sadilles horse. **1886** G. GISSING *Isabel Clarendon* I. ii. 33 She had learned her riding on a saddleless colt.

saddler (ˈsædlə(r)). Forms: 4–5 **sadelere**, 5 **sadel(l)er**, 5–8 **sadler**, (5 **sedler**, **sadlare**), 5 **sadyllar**, **-yl(l)er**, 5–6 *Sc.* **sadillar**, 6 **sadiller**, *Sc.* **saiddlair**, **saidlar**, 7– **saddler**. [f. SADDLE *sb.* + -ER[1]. Cf. MLG. *sadeler*, *sedeler*, MDu. *sadelare*, *saellaer*, OHG. *satilari* (MHG. *sateler*, mod.G. *sattler*).]

1. One who makes or deals in saddles or saddlery.

1389 in *Eng. Gilds* (1870) 42 Yese ordenaunce of fraternyte of Sadeleres and Sporyeres. *c* **1400** *Destr. Troy* 1585 Sadlers, souters, Semsteris fyn. *c* **1500** *Melusine* 43 Raymondyn sent for a Sadlemaker, to whom he said: '..ye muste cutte this hyde in fourme of a thonge.'.. The Sedler dide cutte it. *c* **1515** *Cocke Lorell's B.* 5 Here is saunder sadeler of froge strete corner. **1590** SHAKS. *Com. Err.* I. ii. 56 Oh sixe pence that I had.. To pay the Sadler for my Mistris crupper. **1651** HOBBES *Leviath.* III. xlii. 315 One Power may be subordinate to another, as the art of a Sadler, to the art of a Rider. *a* **1745** SWIFT *Direct. Servants, Groom*, Come home by the Street Door with the same Bridle..dangling in your Hand, as if you came from the Sadler's. **1832** LYTTON *Eugene Aram* II. vi. 98 'How long have you had this whip?' said Walter to the saddler. **1887** BURY & HILLIER *Cycling* (Badm. Libr.) 166 Some of the cycling saddlers do not see that their iron-workers cut the threads far enough up the screw. **1904** *Daily Chron.* 7 Oct. 9/7 Sit[uation] wanted by first-class brown saddler.

2. *Mil.* An official who has charge of the saddlery in a cavalry regiment. Also ***saddler corporal, sergeant.***

1865 H. M. HOZIER *Equipm. Cavalry* 30 Organisation..of the Household Cavalry... Composition of a Regiment of Life Guards or Horse Guards... Non-commissioned Officers and Privates... Armourer Corporal, Saddler Corporal [etc.]. *Ibid.* 51 Cavalry of the Line... Composition of a Regiment of Cavalry... Second Class Staff Serjeants:—Armourer-serjeant, Saddler-serjeant [etc.]. *Ibid.* 152 Promotion to the superior grade of saddler-serjeant will be open to saddlers.

3. A saddle-horse. *colloq. U.S.*

1888 *Boston* (Mass.) *Jrnl.* 16 June 1/1 Another auction sale of choice family horses (including matched pairs and saddlers). **1893** *Columbus* (Ohio) *Dispatch* Apr. 9 A thoroughbred filly, which..bids fair to make a fine saddler.

4. The Saddleback Seal: see SADDLEBACK 4 c.

1873 M. CARROLL *Seal & Herring Fish. Newfoundl.* in Goode *Nat. Hist. Aquatic Anim.* (1884) 62 The reason why they are called Harp Seals, or 'Saddlers', is, [etc.].

5. *attrib.*

c **1449** PECOCK *Repr.* I. x. 49 Whanne that a point or a treuthe..of sadeler craft is affermed. **1483** *Cath. Angl.* 315 A Sadyller schoppe, *sellarium.* **1567** *Reg. Privy Council Scot.* I. 584 Ane craftisman of the saidlar craft.

saddlery (ˈsædlərɪ). [f. prec. + -Y: see -ERY.]

1. The art or occupation of a saddler.

c **1449** PECOCK *Repr.* I. x. 49 Euen as sadelarie and talarie been ij. dyuerse facultees and kunnyngis. **1872** YEATS *Techn. Hist. Comm.* 296 A new impulse was given to saddlery by the introduction of coaches.

2. *collect.* Articles made or sold by a saddler; saddles and other articles pertaining to the equipment of a horse, esp. of one used for riding.

1796 MORSE *Amer. Geog.* I. 258 Harness and saddlery of all kinds. **1833** *Reg. Instr. Cavalry* I. 77 The saddlery should be..examined. **1874** R. TYRWHITT *Sketch. Club* 156 Modern boots and saddlery are utterly intractable in a picture. **1887** BURY & HILLIER *Cycling* (Badm. Libr.) 340 A great many firms have made a speciality of cycling saddlery.

3. A place where saddles and other equipment for riding-horses are made or kept when not in use.

1841 ORDERSON *Creoleana* vi. 60 Premises..occupied as.. a saddlery. **1885** *Field* 4 Apr. 430/1 A room for drying, saddlery, &c.

saddle seat. **1.** The seat of a saddle.

1822 J. FOWLER *Jrnl.* 28 Apr. (1898) 135 We then passed threw Some low Hills a little East of South Seven miles to the River and Crossing over found the Watter up to the Saddle Sceats. **1850** *Rep. Comm. Patents* 1849 (U.S.) I. 263 The bent tension springs CC, for supporting the saddle seat. **1963** BLOODGOOD & SANTINI *Horseman's Dict.* 170 *Waist*, saddle-seat at its narrowest point.

2. *dial.* A horse used for riding.

1895 'HUGH HALIBURTON' *Dunbar* 70 Farmers that hed a saddle seat,.. Keep nae beast noo but cats an' mice.

3. a. A seat made by the crossed hands of two persons.

1913 *Amer. Jrnl. Insanity* Jan. 575 She..suggested that a couple of gentlemen..should clasp their hands so as to form a 'saddle seat' for her, and thus she rode from the platform to the car.

b. A chair seat resembling a saddle (see quot. 1960); also, a chair with such a seat.

1934 in WEBSTER. **1952** J. GLOAG *Short Dict. Furnit.* 406 *Saddle Seat*, a solid wooden seat with two shallow depressions separated by a slight central ridge, suggesting the shape of a saddle. It is used on many types of Windsor chair. **1960** H. HAYWARD *Antique Coll.* 246/1 Some late 18th cent. chairs have a gently curving seat sloping down in the centre which is described colloquially as a saddle seat. A slightly different form is found on Windsor chairs where the centre of the wooden seat is shaped to resemble a saddle. **1976** *Country Life* 27 May (Suppl.) 486/1 Late 18th century wheel-back armchairs with saddle seats and X-frame legs.

saddle stitch, *sb.* **a.** *Bookbinding.* A stitch of thread or a wire staple passed through the back fold of a booklet while it lies open on a saddle-shaped support.

1934 WEBSTER, Saddle stitch. **1956** A. WILLIAMSON *Methods Bk. Design* xix. 331 The whole is fastened together by a saddle-stitch which passes through the spine fold. **1960** G. A. GLAISTER *Gloss. Bk.* 365/1 *Saddle stitch*, a method of stitching brochures or pamphlets by placing them open astride a saddle-shaped support and stitching through the back.

b. *Needlework.* (See quot. 1964.)

1962 W. BUTLER *Dolls' Dressmaking* 92 This trim shirt has saddle-stitch outlining the cuffs, collar and front opening. **1964** *McCall's Sewing* ii. 31/2 *Saddle stitch*, a decorative top-stitch made by taking longer stitches on top and shorter ones underneath. **1974** H. MCCLOY *Sleepwalker* viii. 157 Glove seams were mended, too, with a special stitch like the saddle stitch.

Hence **'saddle-stitch** *v. trans.*; so **'saddle-stitched** *a.*; **'saddle-stitching** *vbl. sb.* (see also SADDLE *sb.* 11). Also **'saddle-stitcher**, a device that performs saddle-stitching.

1923 H. A. MADDOX *Dict. Stationery* 69 *Saddle Stitching*, the method of wire stitching pamphlets and single section books through the centre of the fold. **1933** J. MASON in W. Atkins *Art & Pract. Printing* V. viii. 193 Thread-stitching machines are widely used for pamphlets, exercise books, and note-books. They will saddle-stitch a single section. **1947** C. TALBOT *Compl. Bk. Sewing* xxi. 144/2 Saddle-stitching is a very smart..finish for tailored clothes. It can be done in self-colour or definite contrasts. **1948** *Words into Type* 546 *Saddle stitched*, stitched through the back, the thread, silk, or wire showing on the back and in the middle fold. **1958** *Times* 6 Oct. 13/1 The next figure wears a coat designed in France and made in a supple taupe-colored suède with saddle-stitching along the seams in a lighter shade. **1961** *Harper's Bazaar* Feb. 75 A short-sleeved white shirt, saddle-stitched..round the collar. **1964** *McCall's Sewing* xiii. 239/2 *Saddle stitching.* Take short stitches through the garment and facing an even distance from the edge. The stitches on the top side are longer than the stitches on the underside. **1967** V. STRAUSS *Printing Industry* x. 659/1 The cover of saddle-stitched books is usually, but not necessarily, of paper. **1973** *Country Life* 11 Oct. 1089 The suit..in 100% wool, with deep centre vent and impeccable saddle stitched lining. **1974** *McGraw-Hill Yearbk. Sci. & Technol.* 121/2 The most popular methods of binding soft-cover books are saddle stitching, side stitching, and perfect or patent binding. **1975** M. BANISTER *Bookbinding as Handcraft* xiii. 114/1 Like the Swingline Saddle Stitcher, this one also clinches its own staples. **1979** *Jrnl. R. Soc. Arts* July 485/2 The work involved..collating and folding the sheets and the covers, and saddle-stitching the copies with stainless steel staples.

'saddle-tree.

1. The framework which forms the foundation of a saddle.

1411 *Nottingham Rec.* II. 86, j. sadeltre. **1483** *Act 1 Ric. III*, c. 12 §2 No Merchant Stranger..shall bring into this Realm..Saddles, Saddle-trees, Horse-harness [etc.]. **1536–7** *Durh. Acc. Rolls* (Surtees) 697 Cum frenis, stirropleders, sadletreys, et ceteris illis pertinentibus. **1607** MARKHAM *Cavalarice* VI. ix. 54 The greatest goodness in saddles consisteth in the saddle tree. **1714** *Fr. Bk. Rates* 81 Saddle Trees per 100 Weight, 00 10. **1782** COWPER *John Gilpin* 49 For saddle-tree scarce reached had he, His journey to begin. **1877** W. MATTHEWS *Ethn. & Phil. Hidatsa Ind.* 19 They now make saddle-trees in somewhat the same way as we do.

Comb. **1619** *MS. Canterb. Marr. Licences*, John Worsiter of Challocke, saddle tree maker. **1723** *Lond. Gaz.* No. 6171/7 Joshua Tipping.., Saddletree-maker. **1865** H. M. HOZIER *Equipm. Cavalry* 152 Saddlers' and saddletree makers' tools.

2. = *saddle-rack*: see SADDLE *sb.* 12.

1864 R. KERR *Gentlem. House* 294 A row of saddle-trees from 6 to 8 feet from the floor, with hooks and brackets for the bridles, girths, and stirrups under them.

3. The North American tulip tree, *Liriodendron tulipifera.*

1866 *Treas. Bot.* 688/1 The leaves [of Liriodendron] large, ..four-lobed and somewhat like a saddle in shape; hence the tree is sometimes spoken of as the Saddle-tree.

saddling (ˈsædlɪŋ), *vbl. sb.* [f. SADDLE *v.* + -ING[1].] **1. a.** The action of the vb. SADDLE.

1483 *Cath. Angl.* 315/2 A Sadyllinge, *sellatura.*

b. *esp.* The action of putting on the saddle and other equipment of a racehorse preparatory to a race; also *attrib.* as ***saddling bell, enclosure***; **saddling paddock**, (*a*) a paddock in which horses are prepared for a race; (*b*) *spec.* (*Austral. slang*) a nickname for a bar in the Theatre Royal, Melbourne, frequented by prostitutes in the nineteenth century; also, a similar bar elsewhere; hence, a known place of rendezvous.

1844 J. T. HEWLETT *Parsons & W.* xxi, That is the saddling-bell. **1890** *Daily News* 11 Sept. 3/4 No horse could possibly have looked better..in the saddling paddock. **1876** *Argus* (Melbourne) 1 July 4/4 The stranger sees that the women, possibly picking up a male companion, all enter the apartment which was previously closed, and which is now guarded by swing doors. Curiosity will doubtless prompt him to enter, and he will find himself in the far-famed 'saddling paddock' of the Royal. *Ibid.* 4/5 The existence of the 'saddling paddocks' is a scandal established with a forethought for the courtesan's benefit which is an eternal disgrace to their promoters. **1909** J. R. WARE *Passing Eng.* 213/1 *Saddling-paddock* (*Australian*), place of amusement or rather place of assignation. **1958** G. CASEY *Snowball* iii. 29 The ribald, popular name of the enclosure round the Government Dam was 'the saddling paddock'. **1969** *Sun* (Melbourne) 12 July (Turf Guide) 4/2 The AJC new grandstand in the saddling paddock at Randwick will be open on August 4. **1969** *Sun-Herald* (Sydney) 13 July 33/1 Mr Swales told us he could not get through to the stewards on the phone and gave us permission to return to the saddling enclosure to put our case to the stewards.

†**'saddling**, *sb. Obs. rare*[−1]. [f. SADDLE *sb.* + -ING.] = SADDLE *sb.* 4.

1697 DAMPIER *Voy.* (1729) I. 112 The Land is low, making a saddling between 2 small Hills.

Sadducaic (sædjʊˈkeɪɪk), *a.* [f. Gr. *Σαδδουκαῖος* (see SADDUCEE), after PHARISAIC.] Pertaining to or characteristic of the Sadducees.

1840 MILMAN *Hist. Christianity* I. vii. I. 293 The Sadducaic party. **1883** J. M. WILSON *Theory of Inspir.* 30 It is as wrong..to have the Sadducaic pride of scepticism as the Pharisaic pride of religion.

†**Saddu'caical**, *a. Obs. rare*[−2]. Also 7 **Sadusaicall**. [Formed as prec.: see -ICAL.] = prec.

1601 DEACON & WALKER *Spirits & Divels* 11, I alowe not your pestiferous opinions, iumping so pat with the Parepateticall and Sadusaicall sort. **1702** ECHARD *Eccl. Hist.* (1710) 121 Herod's guilty conscience, notwithstanding his Sadducaical principles, made him..suspect that it was John himself risen from the dead.

Sadducean, Sadducæan (sædjuːˈsiːən), *a.* and *sb.* Also 6 **Saducian**, **Saducæan**, 6–7 **Saducean**. [f. late L. *Saddūcæ-us* SADDUCEE + -AN.]

A. *adj.* Of, belonging to, or resembling the Sadducees.

1593 NASHE *Christ's T.* 58 What are these Atheists but Saducæan sectaries that deny the resurrection? **1681** H. MORE *Exp. Dan.* ii. 26 This dull Sadducean Age. **1681** GLANVILL *Sadducismus* II. (1726) 455 There is a latent Atheism at the root of the Saducean Principle. **1840** MILMAN *Hist. Christianity* II. i. I. 392 The unpopular Sadducean party. **1861** GOLDW. SMITH *Irish Hist.* 61 It is not surprising to find Pharisaical fanaticism..linked with Sadducean depravity and worldliness. **1880** *Encycl. Brit.* XIII. 425/1 The Sadducæan aristocracy.

†**B.** *sb.* = SADDUCEE (in both senses). *Obs.*

1547 *Bk. of Marchauntes* e iij, Full simply faining a lowting countenance selling them selfe as the Essians, Saducians, or Pharisians dyd. **1597** J. PAYNE *Royal Exch.* 8 Saduceans of this age. **1678** CUDWORTH *Intell. Syst.* 6 The Sadduceans, among the Jews, have been noted for the same.

Sadducee (ˈsædjʊsiː). Forms: *pl.* 1 **sad(d)ucéas**, 3–4 **Saduceus**, 3–5 **Saduceis**, 4 **Sadaiceus**, 4–5 **Saducees**, 4–7 **Saduces**, 6–8 **Sadduces**; (also 4 **Saducey** repr. L. *Sadducæi*); *sing.* 6– **Sadducee**. [ad. late L. *Saddūcæus*, a. late Gr. *Σαδδουκαῖος*, f. late Heb. *Çaddūqī*, app. f. the personal name *Çaddūq* (LXX *Σαδδούκ*, Ezek. xl. 46), in Masoretic vocalization *Çādōq* (LXX *Σαδώκ*, 2 Sam. viii. 17, etc.; English Bible Zadok).]

The prevailing modern view is that the Zadok referred to is the high-priest of David's time, from whom the priesthood of the Captivity and later periods claimed to be descended. The late Jewish notion of a post-exilian Zadok (*Çaddūq*), the founder of the sect, is now regarded as baseless; the hypothesis that the word is directly derived from *çaddīq*, righteous, is philologically untenable.]

1. A member of one of the three 'sects' (the others being the Pharisees and Essenes) into which the Jews were divided in the time of Christ. According to the New Testament and Josephus, they denied the resurrection of the dead, the existence of angels and spirits, and the obligation of the unwritten law alleged by the Pharisees to have been handed down by tradition from Moses.

In origin the Sadducees seem to have been not so much a theological or philosophical sect or school, as a political party composed of the nobility, i.e. the members and connexions of the high-priestly family.

c **975** *Rushw. Gosp.* Matt. xvi. 1, & eodun to him fariseas & sadduceas. *a* **1300** *Cursor M.* 19123 þa saduceis [*Fairf.* sadaiceus, *Gött.* saduceus, *Trin.* saduces]..For þe vprising ner wald wede. *c* **1380** WYCLIF *Serm.* Sel. Wks. II. 36 þer weren in Cristis tyme, Essey, Saducey, and Pharisey. **1382** —— *Acts* xxiii. 8 Saducees [**1388** Saduceis, **1534** TINDALE Saduces, **1557** (Geneva) Sadduces, **1582** (Rheims) Sadducees]. **1592** SYLVESTER *Tri. Faith* II. xxxiv, In foremost rank, heer goe the Sadduces, That doe deny Angels and Resurrection. **1635** HEYWOOD *Hierarch.* I. 3 The Atheist, Sadduce, and Mahumetan. **1727–41** CHAMBERS *Cycl.*, *Sadduces*, or *Sadducees.* **1879** FARRAR *Christ* (1881) 471 This wretched, dissolute Idumæan Sadducee.

2. A person of Sadducean disposition; a materialist, a denier of the resurrection. Also as *adj.*

1680 BAXTER *Answ. Stillingfl.* xxxiv. 58 Hobbists, Infidels, Atheists, Sadduces. **1857** BAGEHOT *Lit. Stud.* (1879) II. 282 The world is Sadducee itself; it cannot be anything else.. without ceasing to be the world.

Saddu'ceeic, *a. rare*[−1]. [f. SADDUCEE + -IC.] = SADDUCEAN *a.*

1875 LE FANU *Willing to Die* xxxi, That smiling Sadduceeic world without a home..that..accepts..satire and pleasure in lieu of the affections.

Sadduceeism ('sædju:si:ɪz(ə)m). Also 7 Sadduceisme, 9 **Sadducæism.** [f. SADDUCEE + -ISM. Cf. F. *Saducéisme.*]

1. The doctrine or tenets of the Sadducees.

1845 KITTO *Cycl. Bibl. Lit.* s.v. *Sadducee*, Sadduceeism. **1886** *Encycl. Brit.* XXI. 142/1 The common view that Sadducæism was essentially a philosophico-religious school is due partly to Josephus. **1891** DRIVER *Introd. Lit. O.T.* (1892) 446 An absence of national feeling and religious enthusiasm, in which the author [of Ecclesiastes] seems to be a forerunner of the later Sadduceeism.

2. The character and spirit of the Sadducees; materialistic unbelief; denial of immortality.

1661 BAXTER *Mor. Prognost.* I. xvii. 4 When they incline to Brutishness or Sadduceisme. **1849** THACKERAY *Pendennis* lxii[i], And on this and on other matters he thought he would compromise with his conscience, and that Sadduceeism was a very convenient and good-humoured profession of faith. **1872** M. COLLINS *Two Plunges for Pearl* II. viii. 126 The subtle melancholy Sadduceeism of the 'Saturday Review' is not in the spirit of the Sermon on the Mount.

So **'Sadduceeist** [-IST], in quot. *adj.*, sceptical, indifferentist.

1888 BLACK *In Far Lochaber* viii, Your friends..are not so tolerant and Sadduceeist as some of us up here.

†**Sadducism** ('sædjʊsɪz(ə)m). *Obs.* Also 7 Sadducisme, Saducism. [ad. mod.L. *Saddūcismus*, either irreg. f. late L. *Saddūcæus*, or f. the personal name *Saddūc*: see SADDUCEE and -ISM.] = SADDUCEEISM 1 and 2.

1635 HEYWOOD *Hierarch.* I. 3 Atheisme and Sadducisme disputed; Their Tenents argued, and refuted. **1647** H. MORE *Song of Soul* To Rdr. 6/2 The best Antidotes against that earthly and cold disease of Sadducisme and Atheisme. **1681** GLANVILL *Sadducismus* II. 309 The Discourse may prove as useful for reclaiming men from Saducism. **1778** T. HARTLEY *Pref. Swedenborg's Heaven & H.* (1851) 21 A general disbelief of all things supernatural has..introduced Sadducism amongst us, to the denying of all spiritual visions and apparitions of angels as things incredible.

Sadducize ('sædjʊsaɪz), *v. rare.* [Formed as prec. + -IZE.] *intr.* To hold the doctrines of the Sadducees. Hence **'Sadducizing** *ppl. a.*

1707 ATTERBURY *Vind. Doctr. Bennet's Funeral Serm.* 31 Sadducizing Christians, I suppose they were, who said there was no Resurrection, neither Angel or Spirit, Acts 23. 8. **1854** MILMAN *Lat. Chr.* IV. viii. (1864) II. 402 His whole conduct seemed tinged with a kind of Sadducising Judaism.

sade (seɪd), *v.* Forms: 1 sadian, 5 sadde, (9 seed), 4- sade. [OE. *sadian* = MLG., MDu. *saden*, Du. *(ver)zaden*, OHG. *satôn* (MHG. *saten*):—WGer. **sadôjan*, f. **sado-* SAD *a.*]

†**1.** *intr.* To become satiated or weary. *Obs.*

c **888** K. ÆLFRED *Boeth.* xxxix. §4 Me þincð eac þæt þu sadiȝe hwæth wuȝununges, & þe ðyncen to ælenge þas langan spell. *c* **1325** *Song of Yesterday* 4 in *E.E.P.* (1862) 133 Whon men beoþ muriest at heor mele With mete and drink to maken hem glade With worschipe and with worldliche wele þei bene so sette þei conne not sade. **14..** *Pety Job* 179 in *26 Pol. Poems* 126 Although I can of synne nat sade, Yet *Parce michi, domine.* *c* **1422** HOCCLEVE *Min. Poems* xxiv. 175 Of the lake of good he felte no greef, Al whyles þat the ryng he with him hadde; But faylynge it his frendshipe gan sadde.

2. *trans.* To glut, satiate; to make weary (*of*). *Obs.* exc. *dial.* (see E.D.D.).

c **1000** *Ags. Ps.* (Th.) cxlvii. 3 He..þe ȝesadade, mid þy selestan hwæte cynnes holde lynde. **1440** in *Wars Eng. in France* (1864) II. 455 He was so sadded of the werre. **1611** COTGR., *Assouvir*,..to cloy, glut, sade. *Ibid.*, *Rassasier*, to fill, glut, sade, satiate, satisfie. **1764** *Coles' Lat. Dict.* (ed. 17), To sade (cloy), *satio.*

sade, obs. form of SAD *a.* and SAID *ppl. a.*

Sadean ('sɑːdiːən, seɪ-), *a.* Also **Sadeian, Sadian.** [f. the name of the Count de *Sade* (see SADISM) + -AN.] Of, pertaining to, or characteristic of de Sade.

1960 *20th Cent.* Mar. 206 The Sadian dream of the unleashed subconscious. **1963** N. GEAR *Divine Demon* 5 There were also many fantastic accounts of his life which obscured the facts in a mist of Sadeian mythology. **1978** R. HAYMAN *De Sade* xiv. 228 Baudelaire was the first poet to express modern alienation, but his negativity is Sadean.

sadel(l, sadely, obs. ff. SADDLE, SADLY.

'sadful, *a. rare.* [f. SAD *a.* + -FUL.] Sorrowful.

1658 MERITON *Love & War* IV. ii. H iv b, The service of a sadfull humour. **1884** 'MARK TWAIN' *Huck. Finn* xvii. 158 She could write about anything..just so it was sadful.

‖**sadhana** ('sɑːdənaː). *Indian Philos.* Also **sadhan** and with capital initial. [Skr. *sādhanā* dedication to an aim; *sādhana* means to the goal, etc., f. *sādh* to succeed, attain.] (See quots.)

1898 K. L. SARKAR *Hindu System of Relig. Sci. & Art* vii. 137 Worship and prayer (Sadhana and Upashana) are in the main of two kinds. *Ibid.* 138 Some leaders of those sects in which *sakama sadhana* (selfish prayer) prevails, are more or less driven to give preference to that blank conclusion of Rationalism called *Nirvan Mukti* (merger in the Infinite One.) **1909** S. TATTAVABHÛSHAN *Philos. of Brâhmaism* i. 2 Brâhmaism..presents itself to us in three aspects,—(1) as a creed, (2) as a system of *Sâdhan* or spiritual culture, and (3) as a scheme of social reform. **1921** C. ELIOT *Hinduism & Buddhism* II. xxxii. 282 *Siddhi* is produced by Sâdhana, or that method of training the physical and psychic faculties which realizes their potentialities... It is part of Sâdhana to arouse..energy and make it mount from the lower to the higher centres. **1932** N. K. BRAHMA *Philos. of Hindu Sādhanā* ii. 13 The term '*Sādhanā*' is a current Bengali expression... Its literal meaning is 'that by which something is performed' or more precisely 'means to an end'. In the sphere of religion, it is always used to indicate the essential preliminary discipline that leads to the attainment of the spiritual experience which is regarded as the *summum bonum*... *Sādhanā* includes all the religious practices and ceremonies that are helpful to the realisation of spiritual experience. **1941** K. G. MASHRUWALA *Practical Non-Violence* 48 Violence is born of a narrow conception of 'I' and 'Mine'. The search and discipline of non-violence (the *Sadhana of Ahimsa*) consists in a constant and progressive widening of that conception. **1958** V. RAGHAVAN in W. T. de Bary et al. *Sources of Indian Tradition* xiii. 303 As Indian philosophy aims at experiencing the Truth, all the schools include disciplines (*Sādhanas*), practical means for the attainment of the spiritual goal. **1968** *Indian Music Jrnl.* V. 33 After seven years of Sādhanā..[he] was appointed the principal teacher of Lahore branch. **1972** P. HOLROYDE *Indian Music* vii. 252 The artistic search through feeling out the sādhana of the musical art is, as a result, inward and contemplative.

sadhu ('sɑːduː). Also **saddhu** and with capital initial. [Skr. *sādhú* good, pious, holy man, saint, f. as prec.] In India, a holy man or sage.

1845 *Encycl. Metrop.* XXI. 672/2 When their [*sc.* spiritual guides'] sanctity is such, that they are believed to have the power of securing or withholding divine blessings, they are styled Sád'hú (saint). **1901** KIPLING *Kim* xi. 291 He switched out his..turban-cloth and..rolled it over and under about his loins into the intricate devices of a Saddhu's cincture. **1920** *Glasgow Herald* 25 May 9 He put on the saffron robe of the Sadhu. **1924** *Blackw. Mag.* Oct. 481/2 The temple's guest-chamber, kept for visiting *sadhus* and *sanyasis.* **1955** *Times* 10 Aug. 8/3 A procession of sadhus or 'holy men' is said to have left Pathankot on the Kashmir frontier. **1958** L. DURRELL *Balthazar* x. 208 The old man was a judge in India... He dresses like a *saddhu*... You English are eccentrics. **1968** *Indian Music Jrnl.* V. 32 The philosophical discussions which his father had with the Scholars and sādhu-s who came to see him. **1978** *Times Lit. Suppl.* 3 Feb. 145/2 The Hindu Sadhus were pythons of the psychic world, whose slumbrous coils contained, and at the same time hid, the force of a battering ram.

Hence **'sadhuism**, the principles or practices of a sadhu; **'sadhuship** [-SHIP 3 b], in ***his sadhuship***, a humourous title for a sadhu.

1903 J. C. OMAN *Mystics, Ascetics & Saints of India* xii. 278 (*heading*) The future of Sadhuism. **1914** W. G. LAWRENCE *Let.* 2 Apr. in *Home Lett. T. E. Lawrence* (1954) 519 It's wonderful to see and hear the way the students listen to him owing to their respect for his old sadhuship. **1979** F. OLBRICH *Sweet & Deadly* vii. 74 Holiness is a game to them [*sc.* hippies], a cheap thrill—instant Sadhuism.

Sadian, var. SADEAN *a.*

Sadian, Sa'dian, varr. SAADIAN *a.*

sadic ('sɑːdɪk, seɪ-), *a.* [f. the name of the Count de *Sade* (see SADISM) + -IC.] = SADEAN, SADISTIC *adjs.*

1919 R. FRY *Let.* 5 Jan. (1972) II. 443 A pretty bad melodrama..a Sadic German Jew who starts the worship of Astarte. **1926** T. E. LAWRENCE *Seven Pillars* I. i. 5 What now looks wanton or sadic seemed in the field inevitable. **1928** *Daily Tel.* 6 Nov. 10/6 The oily warder..finds a Sadic pleasure in flogging the life out of his helpless charges. **1976** *Times Lit. Suppl.* 17 Sept. 1147/4 There's a new genre coming into focus..which may illuminate thanatos, celebrate the death wish or merely exploit a sadic lechery.

Sadie Hawkins ('seɪdɪ 'hɔːkɪnz). *U.S.* The name of a character in the cartoon strip *Li'l Abner* by 'Al Capp' (Alfred Gerald Caplin, 1909–79), used *attrib.* to designate a day early in November on which, according to a 'tradition' in the cartoon series, women can propose marriage to men, demand dates with them, etc., or to designate events taking place on that day.

1939 *Daily Mirror* (N.Y.) 4 Nov. 21 Sadie Hawkins Day!! **1940** *Ibid.* 2 Nov. 12 Oh, happy Sadie Hawkins Day! Befo' the sun goes down Ah'll catch me a man, daid or alive!! *Ibid.* 8 Nov. 39 The first 'gun'! The Sadie Hawkins Day Race is on. **1941** *Sun* (Baltimore) 3 Nov. 15/2 Rulman also promised a free marriage to women who catch a man in the Sadie Hawkins footrace. **1942** *Ibid.* 27 Oct. 16 Your chances are four times as good of marrying up wid him on Sadie Hawkins Day as on Leap Year Day—Sadie Hawkins Day comes once *every year.* **1952** *Ibid.* 28 Feb. 32/2 The dean..was the only man to get away in the Sadie Hawkins Day race this afternoon. **1977** *Guardian Weekly* 20 Nov. 19/1 Much of Li'l Abner has been absorbed into American folklore—Sadie Hawkins Day, when sexual roles are reversed and girls chase and catch their men.

'sad-iron. [f. SAD *a.* or *v.*] A smoothing iron, properly a solid flat-iron, in contradistinction to a 'box-iron'.

1761 *Newport* (Rhode Island) *Mercury* 3 Nov. 4/3 To be sold by Naphtael Hart, jun...sad Irons, Tellescopes, [etc.]. **1815** *Niles' Weekly Reg.* IX. 94/2 Sad irons [were manufactured]. **1832** BABBAGE *Econ. Manuf.* xvii. (ed. 3) 153 Sad-irons and other castings. **1833** J. HOLLAND *Manuf. Metal* II. 253 Dealers commonly distinguish these useful implements by the terms 'sad-iron', 'box-iron' and 'Italian-iron'. **1899** *Daily News* 30 Oct. 2/7 Sadirons 10s. per ton [dearer]. **1936** M. MITCHELL *Gone with Wind* I. v. 84 Hands like sadirons when it comes to reins. **1964** F. O'ROURKE *Mule for Marquesa* 99 Washday smell,..don't forget to damp and starch, spit on the sadiron.

sadism ('seɪ-, 'sɑːdɪzm). [ad. F. *sadisme*, f. the name of the Count (usually called 'Marquis') de *Sade* (1740–1814; infamous for his crimes and the character of his writings): see -ISM.] A form of sexual perversion marked by a love of cruelty. Now understood as cruelty that evidences a subconscious craving and is apparently satisfied, sexually or otherwise, by the infliction of pain on another by means of aggressive or destructive behaviour or the assertion of power over that person; also *loosely*, deliberate or excessive cruelty morbidly enjoyed.

1888 *Pall Mall G.* 10 Sept. 4/2. **1897** *Lancet* 13 Nov. 1263/2 Crimes committed by people afflicted with what is technically known as 'sadism'. **1924** J. RIVIERE et al. tr. *Freud's Coll. Papers* II. xxii. 261 We should not be astonished to hear that under certain conditions the sadism or destruction instinct which has been directed outwards can be introjected. **1937** H. G. WELLS *Brynhild* vii. 116 He ..with an expression of impish sadism..prodded his sceptre into young Bates. **1943** H. READ *Politics of Unpolitical* ii. 18 Sadism is the unconscious impulse to acquire unrestricted power over another person, and to test the fullness of this power by destroying that other person. **1952** *Times Lit. Suppl.* 11 Jan. 28 Feeling [in France] had been bruised by the war [of 1914–18], but it had not been forced (as happened after the Second World War) to find.. an outlet in sadism or violence. **1965** H. DEUTSCH *Neuroses & Character Types* ix. 132 Such observations led Freud to assume that it is the same aggression whether it is attached to the libidinal impulses in the form of sadism or whether.. it is incorporated in the superego and made the expression of its severity. **1974** I. BIEBER in S. Arieti *Amer. Handbk. Psychiatry* III. xv. 318/2 In my view sadism is a maladaptive response to threat; it is a paranoid constellation in which the victim is a personified representative of a variety of irrationally perceived threats. **1979** M. GLASSER in I. Rosen *Sexual Deviation* x. 281 The distinction I am making between aggression and sadism may be illustrated by some simple examples.

sadist ('seɪ-, 'sɑːdɪst), *sb.* (and *a.*) [f. SADISM: see -IST.] 'An individual affected with sadism' (*Syd. Soc. Lex.* 1897); more generally, someone who derives satisfaction from inflicting pain or asserting his or her power over others. Also as *adj.*

1919 H. WALPOLE *Secret City* I. x. 68 There was something almost sadist..in the old gentleman's observation of Markovitch's labours. **1919** M. K. BRADBY *Psycho-Anal.* x. 133 The need for a greater outlet of emotion and energy in daily life where the sadist has capacity for ruling others by the strength..of his personality. **1920** *Glasgow Herald* 9 Sept. 6 The fatal policy which has given a handful of political cranks, aided by hired mercenaries and sadist abnormals, the right to stand for Russia. **1934** H. G. WELLS *Exper. Autobiogr.* II. ix. 760 Those mucky little sadists, Stalky and Co. **1954** B. KARPMAN *Sexual Offender* xix. 355 Every sadist possesses certain elements of masochism. **1962** C. ALLEN *Textbk. Psychosexual Disorders* vii. 105 Those who retain a sentimental view of the blue-eyed innocence of the child naturally find it difficult to imagine..that the ruthless ferocity of the sadist originates at that time. **1974** J. BANCROFT *Deviant Sexual Behaviour* v. 120 Some interesting studies of suppression of fantasy have been carried out. An example is a sadist treated by Marks.

sadistic (sə'dɪstɪk), *a.* [f. as prec.: see -STIC.] 'Related to sadism' (Dunglison *Dict. Med. Sci.* 1893); more generally, of or characteristic of a sadist. Also *Comb.*, as ***sadistic-anal*** adj., relating to sadism that is typical of the anal stage of development; ***sadistic-masochistic*** adj. = SADO-MASOCHISTIC *a.*

1892 C. G. CHADDOCK tr. *Krafft-Ebing's Psychopathia Sexualis* iii. 170 The pain of tight lacing, experienced by himself or induced in women, is a delight to him,—sadistic-masochistic element. **1897** *Lancet* 13 Nov. 1263/2 Several recent tragedies having probably had their origin in sadistic impulses. **1915** C. R. PAYNE tr. *Pfister's Psychoanal. Method.* 78 The sadistic-masochistic instinctive tendency. **1922** J. RIVIERE tr. *Freud's Introd. Lect. Psycho-Anal.* 289 Regression of..the Libido to the antecedent stage of the sadistic-anal organization. **1929** B. RUSSELL *Marriage & Morals* 98 He drowns his dissatisfaction..by the sadistic pleasure to be derived from watching prize-fights or persecuting radicals. **1936** H. G. WELLS *Anatomy of Frustration* xx. 255 He hated people who nursed 'wrongs'. The 'wrongs' of Ireland—of India—of women, roused an almost sadistic impatience in him. **1946** H. PEARSON *Life O. Wilde* xvi. 319 Like all people who believe in punishment, he [*sc.* the governor of Reading Gaol] was vindictive and sadistic by nature, modelling himself on the God of his fathers as depicted in the Old Testament. **1952** *Times Lit. Suppl.* 15 Feb. 124/3 The vicarious sadistic lust for power of a disappointed man. **1954** B. KARPMAN *Sexual Offender* ix. 101 He admits drawing pictures of a sadistic nature; the torture of females, perversion of corpses. **1973** 'E. MCBAIN' *Let's hear It* xiv. 209 Teddy normally enjoyed films, except when she was submitted to the excesses of a sadistic *nouvelle vague* camera. **1977** A. SHERIDAN tr. *Lacan's Écrits* vii. 270 Regression is no more dependent on the need in demand than sadistic desire is explained by anal demand.

sadistically (sə'dɪstɪkəlɪ), *adv.* [f. prec.: see -ICALLY.] In a sadistic manner; cruelly.

1922 G. B. SHAW in S. & B. Webb *Eng. Prisons under Local Govt.* p. ix, When such people are..sadistically excited by reports of the White Slave traffic, they clamor to have sentences of two years' hard labor supplemented by a flogging. **1936** F. M. FORD *Let.* 6 Sept. (1965) 261, I believe that publishers should be as sadistically punished as possible. **1951** M. MCLUHAN *Mech. Bride* (1967) 16/2 The rest of the program fits this pattern by allowing Charlie to ride sadistically over a number of carefully selected victims. **1963** *Times* 12 Jan. 4/1 The east wind continued to blow sadistically at Littlestone yesterday.

saditty ('sædɪtɪ), *a.* *U.S. Blacks.* Also **seditty.** [Orig. unknown.] Affecting an air of superiority.

1967 *Jet* 20 July 43 Eartha..is considered 'seditty' by many Negroes. **1971** C. Mitchell-Kernan in T. Kochman *Rappin' & Stylin' Out* (1972) 318 That's all I hear lately—soul food, soul food. If you say you don't eat it you get accused of being saditty. **1973** *Black World* Aug. 61/2 Them big man-eatin' dogs them saditty niggers had roun' the house.

Sadler ('sædlə(r)). The name of John *Sadler* (fl. 1871–80), British botanist, used *attrib.* or in the possessive in **Sadler('s) oak** to designate *Quercus sadleriana*, an evergreen shrub with serrate leaves, found in parts of western North America and named in his honour by Robert Brown in 1871 (*Ann. Mag. Nat. Hist.* 4th Ser. VII. 249).

1908 N. L. Britton *N. Amer. Trees* 338 Sadler's oak..is an interesting shrub of the high mountains of northwestern California and adjacent Oregon, with sharply serrate leaves. **1939** L. Rowntree *Flowering Shrubs Calif.* ix. 149 When the endemic..Sadler's Oak or Deer Oak, has room to do as it pleases,..it takes on the shape of an inverted pyramid. **1951** H. E. McMinn *Illustr. Man. Calif. Shrubs* 83 Deer Oak. Sadler Oak. An evergreen shrub, 2 to 8 feet high, with many slender flexible stems from the base.

sadler, obs. form of saddler.

sadly ('sædlɪ), *adv.* Forms: 4 sadd(e)li, sadlyk, saydly, 4–5 saddely, sadli, sadliche, -lyche, 4, 6 sadely, 6 sadlich, sadlie, -ye, 4 sadly. Also 4 *compar.* sadloker. [f. sad *a.* + -ly[2].]

†**1.** Heavily. *Obs.*

a **1300** *Cursor M.* 22478 Þe sterns wit þair leman leuen Ful saddli fall sal þai dun fra heuen. *c* **1400** *Rowland & O.* 1313 So sadly one his scholdire it [the blow] felle, The knyghte by-gane to knele. *c* **1435** *Torr. Portugal* 1625 Glad pluckys there he toke, Set sadly and sare. *a* **1568** *Knt. Curtesy* 77 In swoune [she] fell downe hym upon, So sadly that the Knyght awoke. *a* **1578** Lindesay (Pitscottie) *Chron. Scot.* (S.T.S.) I. 222 Mr. Patrick Lindsay..strampit sadlie on his brotheris foott to gar him wnderstand that [etc.]. **1633** Bp. Hall *Occas. Medit.* cxxxvi. 335 An empty cart runs lightly away: but if it be soundly laden, it goes sadly.

†**2.** Firmly, tightly, closely. *Obs.*

1340–70 *Alex. & Dind.* 1135 Þere his burnus he bad bulden of marbre A piler sadliche i-picht or he passe wolde. **1375** Barbour *Bruce* xiii. 374 Knyt ȝow als sadly as ȝhe may. *c* **1386** Chaucer *Knt.'s T.* 1744 In goon the speres ful sadly in arrest. **1398** Trevisa *Barth. De P.R.* xvii. ii. (1495) 597 In smale trees is more hete and drynesse that byndeth the partyes therof faste and sadly togyder. *c* **1440** *York Myst.* viii. 102 Þus sall I iune it with a gynn, And sadly sette it with symonde fyne. **1470–85** Malory *Arthur* xviii. xxiii. 768 And whan we haue delyuerd hem, lete vs thre hold vs sadly to gyders.

†**3.** Solidly, fully; (to drink) deeply; (to sleep) soundly, heavily. *Obs.*

13.. *E.E. Allit. P.* C. 442, & þer he swowed & slept sadly al nyȝt. **1362** Langl. *P. Pl.* A. v. 4 Þenne Wakede I of my wink me was wo with alle þat I nedde sadloker I-slept and I-seȝe more. *c* **1380** Wyclif *Sel. Wks.* I. 11 Þis fillyng is not voide but sadly replenchid. *c* **1386** Chaucer *Man of Law's T.* 645 This Messager drank sadly ale and wyn.

†**4.** Resolutely, vigorously, hardily. *Obs.*

c **1350** *Will. Palerne* 2751 Whan þe ludes where neiȝ lond he leped ouer borde, sadli in al here siȝt for þei him sew schold. **1375** Barbour *Bruce* xiii. 494 In Cambuskynneth the kyngis vittale He tuk, and sadly gert assale Schir Wilȝame of Herth, and him slew. *c* **1400** *Song Roland* 763 They went to sadly, And set ther dyntis. **1470** Henry *Wallace* ii. 84 The Perseys stwart sadly till him socht. **1471** Caxton *Recuyell* (Sommer) I. 269 The two champions approchid eche other and smote to gyder so sadly and sore that the place redounded of her strokes. *c* **1475** *Sqr. lowe Degre* 646 The stewarde at hym full sadly fought.

†**5.** Steadfastly, firmly, fixedly, unchangingly. *Obs.*

c **1340** Hampole *Prose Tr.* 14 Whene þe mynde es stablede sadely with-owttene changynge and vagacyone in Godd. *c* **1380** Wyclif *Wks.* (1880) 199 Þat alle brennynge charite.. be so sadly rotyd in vs. *c* **1380** *Lay Folks Catech.* (Lamb. MS.) 957 Loke þou withstande sadly þe furst begynnynge of þe temptacoun of þe fend. *c* **1386** Chaucer *Pars. T.* 124 Fro that tyme that he loueth sadly oure lord Ihesu crist [etc.]. **1493** *Festivall* (W. de W. 1515) 48 Sadly beleue the fader is full god almyghty. *c* **1530** *Crt. of Love* 877 Emprent my speche in your memorial Sadly. **1622** Bacon *Hen. VII* 133 But the King finding that he did sadly, and constantly (without hesitation or varying,..) stand to that that hee had said.

†**6.** Steadily, quietly, without excitement. *Obs.*

c **1330** R. Brunne *Chron. Wace* (Rolls) 13544 Þe batailles neyghed ney & ney, Sadly passing, and softely. *c* **1391** Chaucer *Astrol.* ii. §29 Tak thanne thyn Astrolabie with bothe handes sadly & slely. *c* **1430** *Pilgr. Lyf Manhode* i. cvi. (1869) 56 Wel ȝ telle thee that sureliche and sadliche thou miht go.

†**7.** Seriously; in earnest; gravely, soberly. *Obs.*

c **1350** *Will. Palerne* 557 What ȝif I saide him sadly þat i sek were, & told him al treuly þe entecches of myn euele? *c* **1357** *Sc. Leg. Saints* iv. (*Jacobus*) 176 Til hym þan sancte Iames prechit, and crystis law sa sadly techit. *c* **1385** Chaucer *Shipman's T.* 76 This Marchant vp ariseth, And on hise nedes sadly hym auyseth. *c* **1440** *York Myst.* xxxii. 62 Saie me sadly þe soth. **1489** Caxton *Faytes of A.* i. xv. 40 Mesurably and sadly demened. *a* **1548** Hall *Chron., Hen. VIII*, I. 69 Thei daunsed with Ladies sadly, and communed not with the ladies after the fashion of Maskers, but behaved themselves sadly. **1570** Jewel *Def. Apol.* ii. (1571) 161 This booke..was readde sadly vnto the people, and had in reuerence. **1599** Shaks. *Much Ado* ii. iii. 229 This can be no tricke, the conference was sadly borne. **1611** Chapman *Widowes T.* iii. i. (1612) F 4 b, But doe you brother sadly intend the pursuite of this triall? **1634** Milton *Comus* 509 To tell thee sadly Shepherd, without blame, Or our neglect, we lost her as we came. **1642** Jer. Taylor *Episc.* §xxxi, But this to them that consider things sadly, is true or false according as any man list. **1777** M. Morgann *Ess. Dram. Char. Falstaff* 122 As a caution to the audience not to take too sadly what was intended only..'as an argument for a week'.

8. a. Sorrowfully, mournfully.

c **1350** *Will. Palerne* 539 Sadly sikand & sore for sorwe atte here herte. *c* **1450** Holland *Howlat* 42, I herd ane petuoss appele, with ane pur mane, Solpit in sorowe, that sadly couth say [etc.]. **1535** Coverdale *Gen.* xl. 7 Why loke ye so sadly to daye? [So **1611**.] **1600** Shaks. *Sonn.* viii. 1 Musick to heare, why hear'st thou musick sadly? **1627** May *Lucan* i. 583 Sadlyer barke Scyllaes doggs then they were wont. *c* **1665** Mrs. Hutchinson *Mem. Col. Hutchinson* (1846) 13 He died in the month of May, 1630, sadly bewailed. **1697** Dryden *Virg. Georg.* iv. 505 Near his Paternal Stream he sadly stands, With down-cast Eyes, wet Cheeks, and folded Hands. **1856** Kane *Arct. Expl.* II. x. 107 He speaks sadly.. of the fortunes of the winter. **1884** W. C. Smith *Kildrostan* 43 There at the head of a late filled grave Sadly a youth and a maiden stood.

Comb. **1697** Dryden *Æneid* x. 1167 A sadly pleasing Thought. **1816** Wordsw. *Ode* 1815, 44 To..utter England's name with sadly-plausive voice.

†**b.** With regret; reluctantly. *Obs.*

1611 Beaum. & Fl. *Philaster* v. v, I must request of you One fauour, and will sadly be denyed.

9. a. In a manner to cause sadness; lamentably, grievously, deplorably, badly.

1658 *Whole Duty Man* Sund. iii. §7. 29 That have provoked so great a Majesty, who is able so sadly to revenge himself upon you. **1731–8** Swift *Pol. Conversat.* 202 Mr. Neverout we wanted you sadly. **1753** H. Walpole *Let. to Mann* 27 Mar., Drawings..which I am sure will charm you, though none of them are quite well engraved, and some sadly. **1782** Cowper *Friendsh.* 87 Authors..Are sadly prone to quarrel. **1782** Miss Burney *Cecilia* iii. viii, O, he is so ill! indeed I am sadly, sadly afraid he will never be well again! **1819** Byron *Juan* ii. lxxx, Who had already perish'd, suffering madly For having used their appetites so sadly. **1857** Ruskin *Arrows of Chace* (1880) I. 47, I have written you a sadly long letter, but I could not manage to get it shorter. **1863** W. C. Baldwin *Afr. Hunting* viii. 340 The flies torment us sadly. **1868** Freeman *Norm. Conq.* II. ix. 391 The poor girl was sadly buffeted by the indignant saint. **1879** Huxley *Hume* x. 196 Metaphysicians, as a rule, are sadly deficient in the sense of humour.

b. As a sentence adverb: regrettably, unfortunately.

1973 *Times* 16 Feb. 19/4 The Headmaster of Winchester College asks: 'Is there any other ancient cathedral city in Western Europe with so much fast, heavy, long-distance traffic planned to run so near?' Sadly, the answer is 'Yes, York'. **1974** *Times Lit. Suppl.* 7 June 607/3 No one would dispute the pointed courage of Camus's early journalistic campaigning. Sadly, though, this does not make him a great artist. **1978** *Lancashire Life* July 44/3 Sadly, his collection was sold and dispersed throughout the world after his death.

†**10.** Sombrely, in dark colours. *Obs.*

1607 B. Jonson *Entertainm. Theobalds* Wks. 1616 I. 887 A gloomie obscure place, hung all with black silkes, and in it only one light, which the Genius of the house held, sadly attir'd.

11. Used *predicatively*: In bad health, ill, 'poorly'. Now *dial.*

1711 Swift *Jrnl. to Stella* 15 May, I look better already, for faith I looked sadly. **1866** Geo. Eliot *F. Holt* xxvii, Lyddy had said, 'Miss, you look sadly; if you can't take a walk, go and lie down'. **1898** Mrs. H. Ward *Helbeck of B.* v. ii. 395 Mrs. Fountain's nobbut sadly, I unnerstan.

sadness ('sædnɪs). [-ness.] The condition or quality of being sad.

†**1.** Firmness, hardness, solidity. *Obs.*

1398 Trevisa *Barth. De P.R.* iii. xvii, The fyfþe is sadnesse and þiknesse of þe þinge þat is sen [L. *soliditas sive densitas rei visæ*]. *c* **1400** *Lanfranc's Cirurg.* 90 Þou schalt knowe by reednes & sadnesse of fleisch þat is wiþinne þe festre al aboute. *c* **1420** *Pallad. on Husb.* vi. 152 When hit [cheese] is wel confourmed to sadnesse. *c* **1485** *Cath. Angl.* 515/1 A Sadnes, *solidamen, soliditas.* **1577–87** Harrison *England* ii. xxii. 212/2 If you respect the sadnes therof, it doth proue in the end to be verie hollow & not able to hold out water. *Ibid.* 214/1 Which moulds wanting their due sadnesse are now turned into moorie plots.

†**2.** Seriousness, soberness, staidness; gravity of mind or demeanour. *Obs.*

c **1315** Shoreham 7 *Sacram.* 1428 For ȝeres Ne makeþ so nauȝt þane prest ald, Ac sadnesse of maneres. *c* **1386** Chaucer *Merch. T.* 347 Another stant so in the peples grace ffor hire sadnesse, and hire benygnytee. **1451** Capgrave *Life St. Aug.* (E.E.T.S.) 20 A bord on whech þei vsed to pleye certeyn games to refresch with þe sadnesse of her study. **1495** *N. Riding Rec.* (N.S.) I. 127 We trustyng in youre pollicie, sadness, wisdome, and discrecion. *c* **1515** *Cocke Lorelles B.* 13 They banysshed prayer, peas, and sadnes; And toke with them myrthe, sporte, and gladnes. **1593** Shaks. *3 Hen. VI*, iii. ii. 77 But mightie Lord, this merry inclination Accords not with the sadnesse of my suit. **1611** Speed *Hist. Gt. Brit.* ix. xix. (1632) 928 Other persons of approued sadnesse, prudence, pollicy and experience.

†**b.** Phr. ***in sadness, in good*** or ***sober sadness***: in earnest, not joking. *Obs.*

1544 Ascham *Toxoph.* i. (Arb.) 102 But in good sadnesse Toxophile thus you se. *a* **1553** Udall *Roister D.* iv. iii. (Arb.) 61, I haue nought to them, nor they to me in sadnesse. **1593** Nashe *Strange Newes* Wks. (Grosart) II. 245 Thou hast borrowed aboue twenty phrases and epithites from mee, which is sober sadnesse thou makst vse of as thy owne. *c* **1610** Middleton, etc. *Widow* v. i. 228 Pray, in sadness, say, that is the gentleman? **1696** S. Sewall *Diary* 13 Oct. (1878) I. 435 Seem'd to be in good sober sadness. **1705** Vanbrugh *Confederacy* iii. ii, In serious sadness. **1708** Mrs. Centlivre *Busy Body* i. i, In sober sadness she cannot abide 'em.

†**3.** Dignity, importance. *Obs.*

1494 Fabyan *Chron.* vi. clix. 149 The sayd Lewys.. causyd them to vse and were browne, and sad colours, accordynge to theyr honours and sadnes.

†**4.** Steadfastness, constancy; firmness of faith.

1377 Langl. *P. Pl.* B. vii. 150 Catoun and canonistres conceilleth vs to leue To sette sadnesse in songewarie, for *sompnia ne cures.* **1382** Wyclif *Coloss.* ii. 5 The sadnesse of that ȝoure bileue that is in Crist. —— *2 Pet.* iii. 17 Lest ȝe.. falle awey fro ȝoure owne sadnesse [Vulg. *a propria firmitate*]. **1426** Lydg. *De Guil. Pilgr.* 11177 But yiff he hadde ffeet off led, In gret sadnesse to endure. *a* **1529** Skelton *Dyuers Balettys* iii. 17 Saphyre of sadnes, enuayned wyth indy blew.

5. Sorrowfulness, mournfulness.

1500–20 Dunbar *Poems* xxiii. 13 Seik to solace quhen sadnes the assailis. **1588** Shaks. *L.L.L.* i. ii. 7 How canst thou part sadnesse and melancholy my tender Iuuenall? **1611** Bible *Eccl.* vii. 3 By the sadnesse of the countenance the heart is made better. **1667** Milton *P.L.* x. 23 Dim sadness did not spare That time Celestial visages. **1707** Floyer *Physic. Pulse-Watch* 409 In a malignant Fever from Heat, there is a Delirium, Fluxes, Sadness. **1784** Cowper *Task* v. 464 Thy clime..disposes much All hearts to sadness. **1847** Tennyson *Princess* vii. 14 Sadness on the soul of Ida fell.

b. A condition of sorrowfulness.

1602 Shaks. *Ham.* ii. ii. 147 [He] Fell into a Sadnesse. *a* **1631** Donne *Serm.* xlv. 450 To blow away and scatter these sadnesses with a false, an illusory, and a sinfull comfort. **1737** L. Clarke *Hist. Bible* (1740) II. v. 96 After this he thunders out woes and sadnesses against their impieties. **1818** Byron *Juan* i. lxxii, She look'd a sadness sweeter than her smile.

c. Gloomy appearance.

1849 Ruskin *Sev. Lamps* iii. §xii. 76 The architect not being able to secure always the same depth or decision of shadow, nor to add to its sadness by colour.

sado- ('seɪdəʊ), *Psychol.*, comb. form of sadism or sadistic *a.* Cf. also sado-masochism.

1935 [see sado-masochism]. **1954** B. Karpman *Sexual Offender* ix. 131 Alcohol is the illegitimate satiation of appetite which she fights in obsessionalism based on sado-necrophilia. **1964** *Observer* 30 Aug. 28 Client prints paperbacks for all tastes from (I think) the nasty sado-snobbism of poor Fleming to Tolstoy. **1970** *Guardian Weekly* 11 Apr. 19 A kind of all-senses collage assembled from bits of girlie photos, tropical stills, and mock-ups of sado-erotic temple carvings. **1976** *New Yorker* 26 Apr. 121/1 Given the sado-erotic content of the film...one tends to make Grace a woman. **1980** R. Ludlum *Bourne Identity* xiii. 195 The sado-romantic myth turns into a brilliant, blood-soaked monster who brokers assassination.

sado-maso (ˌseɪdəʊ'mæsəʊ), *a.* (*sb.*) Slang (chiefly *U.S.*) abbrev. of sado-masochist; sado-masochistic *a.*

1970 *Time* 23 Feb. 54/1 A gang of seminude galley slavettes..bend to the oar under a whip cracked by everyone's favorite sado-maso slave queen, Raquel Welch. **1973** *Listener* 22 Feb. 237/1 He passed..the spill-out of the sado-maso bar... At present, the sado-masos are in the ascendant. **1978** M. Puzo *Fools Die* xxiv. 277 No fantasies could be spun around them unless you were into sado-maso stuff.

sado-masochism (ˌseɪdəʊ'mæsəkɪz(ə)m). *Psychol.* Also **sadomasochism.** [f. sado- + masochism.] The co-existence of sadism and masochism in one individual; the need both to inflict and to suffer pain or to assert power over another and to be submissive combined as one psychic condition evidenced in sexual relationships (freq. in a fantasied manner) or socially, as an outlet for aggressive or destructive impulses. Also *transf.* and *fig.*

1935 L. Brink tr. *Stekel's Sadism & Masochism* I. p. v, I do not claim that I have solved the perplexing problem of sadomasochism. **1937** M. Hirschfeld *Sexual Anomalies* xvi. 302 Thus it is quite correct to speak of sado-masochism and, quite logically, many sadists are, simultaneously, also masochists. **1959** *Listener* 16 Apr. 683/3 The sado-masochism of the Christian ascetic tradition. **1963** A. Heron *Towards Quaker View of Sex* 67 Clinical instances of sado-masochism are not sufficiently numerous to constitute a threat to society. **1975** T. Allbeury *Special Collection* xvii. 114 I've been covering a vice-ring..in Mayfair... It specializes in sado-masochism..every thing from thumb-screws to a crucifix. **1977** *Early Music* July 415/3 The *Art of Fugue* is invariably presented in 'complete' performances which strike one rather as exercises in musical sado-masochism.

Hence ˌ**sado-'masochist,** one afflicted with the condition of sado-masochism; also *attrib.* or as adj.; ˌ**sado-maso'chistic** *a.*

1935 L. Brink tr. *Stekel's Sadism & Masochism* I. p. v, The literature concerning sadomasochistic disorders is extraordinarily abundant. *Ibid.* iv. 60 All sadomasochists are affect-hungry individuals. **1942** *Observer* 15 Nov. 3/6 Sado-masochistic fusions of instinct are an all-important factor in the unconscious development of character. **1951** M. McLuhan *Mech. Bride* (1967) 10/1 This sado-masochist mechanism of punch and get punched will be found everywhere. **1963** *Jrnl. Amer. Psychoanal. Assoc.* XII. 306 Abraham stressed the importance of the sadomasochistic elements in his patient. **1977** *Gay News* 24 Mar. 3/2 Study and encounter groups for sadomasochists, transvestites and Jewish homosexuals are the latest projects of Pastor Douce. **1980** *Times Lit. Suppl.* 25 Apr. 459/4 His [*sc.* Somerset

Maugham's] relationship with Haxton, the only person with whom he established intimacy, was sado-masochistic.

†**'sadore.** *Obs.* (See quot.)

1681 GREW *Musæum* App. 386 Sadore, or Bitter Wood. It hath a brownish Barque.

sad sack (sæd sæk). *slang* (chiefly *U.S.*). [The name of a cartoon character invented by G. Baker, U.S. cartoonist.] A stupid and blundering member of the armed services; an inept, ineffectual, and unfortunate person; a social or occupational misfit. Also *transf.* and *attrib.*

[**1942** *Yank* 17 June 7 (*caption*) The Sad Sack.] **1943** *Sun* (Baltimore) 28 Dec. 14/6 A forlorn look, a G.I. haircut, an oversized fatigue uniform and all the paraphernalia that goes with them branded me as a typical 'sad sack'. **1951** M. McLUHAN *Mech. Bride* (1967) 68/2 Model mother saddled with a sad sack and a dope. **1953** *Word Study* May 5/1 Everyone knows of the sensitive misfit, the 'sad sack' who suffers a good deal of spiritual depression, the result of an unfortunate maladjustment to service routine. **1967** *New Yorker* 15 Apr. 148/3 Mr. Goldman's movie sweeps up a dustpanful of young Village sad sacks and patronizes them. **1971** J. GRAY *Red Lights on Prairies* iii. 58 A sad-sack of a shack town on Pile of Bones Creek. **1973** *Observer* (Colour Suppl.) 15 July 21/4 On the whole the pre-1914 spinster had been something of a sad sack. **1974** T. P. WHITNEY tr. *Solzhenitsyn's Gulag Archipel.* I. I. v. 222 These sad-sack spies, with the milk hardly dry on their lips. **1978** *Listener* 31 Aug. 286/4 The sad sack of a hero, who speaks in the first person, is called Lewis Redfern.

'sad-tree. [f. SAD *a.* (sense 5); transl. of mod.L. *arbor tristis.*] The Night Jasmine of India, *Nyctanthes Arbor-tristis.* (Earlier called MELANCHOLY *tree.*)

1866 *Treas. Bot.* s.v. *Nyctanthes*, During the day it loses its brightness, whence its specific name *Arbor tristis* or Sad-tree. [In recent Dicts.]

Saduce(e, -ean, etc.: see SADDUCEE, -EAN, etc.

sadue, obs. form of SHADOW.

Sadusaicall: see SADDUCAICAL.

‖**sadza** ('sædzə). [Native name.] In southern and eastern Africa, a porridge made of ground maize.

1950 *Cape Times Week-end Mag.* 3 June 2/3 Manaas had gorged himself with *sadza* and his little stomach was distended. **1965** *Observer* 7 Nov. 2/3 Each family owns its few acres of land from which it produces its main diet of maize (made into a porridge called sadza) and pumpkin. **1975** M. HARTMANN *Game for Vultures* vi. 79 Marunga pecked at the greasy stew and dry sadza. **1979** P. NIESEWAND *Member of Club* xiii. 88 The sadza—thick, starchy maize meal porridge—bubbled in tins.

sae: see SAW, SAVE, SAY, SEA, SEE, SO, SOE.

sæcular: see SECULAR.

saefte, sael, obs. ff. SAFETY, SEAL *v.*

saer, obs. form of SAWYER, SEAR.

‖**saeta** (sa'eta). Also saetta. [Sp., lit. = arrow.] An unaccompanied Andalusian folk-song, sung during religious processions.

1923 *Chambers's Jrnl.* Mar. 213/1 Somewhere in the crowd a woman is singing a *saeta*, sad and undulating, like no other music on earth. **1939** SPENDER & GILI tr. *Lorca's Poems* 19 Among troubled *saetas* And stars of crystal. **1966** *New Statesman* 26 Aug. 297/1 Clusters of microtones which resemble nothing so much as the ululations of the *saeta* singers in the Easter Day procession in Seville. **1977** P. SOMERVILLE-LARGE *Eagles near Carcase* vi. 123 He hummed a high nasal tune which I recognized as a *saetta* I had last heard sung to a Seville Madonna during Holy Week.

saeter, setter ('seɪtə(r), 'sɛtə(r)). Also **saater, sæter, saether, sater, seater, seter.** [ad. ON. *sætr* mountain pasture; cf. Norw. *sæter, seter*; Sw. *säter*. In sense 2 a directly from Norw.

In sense 1, the word in some examples may represent ON. *setr* a homestead, a residence (see esp. quot. 1931). The two are common formative elements in placenames of the Northern Isles, and cannot always be distinguished (see J. Jakobsen *Etymol. Dict. Norn Lang. in Shetland* (1932), s.v. *seter*).]

1. *Shetland* and *Orkney.* A meadow associated with a dwelling; a summer pasture in the outfield.

1576 in D. Balfour *Oppressions 16th Cent. in Orkney & Zetland* (1859) 72 The said Magnus complenis upon the said Laird, that quhair he had ane steding, callit Sater, lying in Brassay, of four merk and ane half land..: nevertheless, quhen he had gottin bot ane ȝeiris crope thairoff, he put him furth of the same. *c* **1772** in A. C. O'Dell *Historical Geogr. Shetland Islands* (1939) II. xi. 239 Feued property and udal comprehend the lands of Shetland of all denominations Setter-lands excepted. **1795** *Statistical Acct. Scotl.* XIV. 321 As to our meadows, they are always called *Seaters.* Though I am little acquainted with the Norwegian language, I understand a *Seater* to be a place for maintaining milch cows; and these *Seaters* are to this moment properly adapted for it. **1822** S. HIBBERT *Descr. Shetland Isles* 427 In the ancient Shetland language, the green pasturage attached to a dwelling was named a Setter or Seater. **1931** *Proc. Orkney Antiquarian Soc.* IX. 27/2 Just beyond the Wideford Burn..lies the three-farthing land, skatland, of Grymesetter. Next adjacent lies the 'quoyland' of Grymesquoy... Both names point to an original farmer *Grimr.* He apparently settled there on a 'setter' just before skat was imposed on the Orkney lands. **1939** A. C. O'DELL *Historical Geogr. Shetland Islands* II. xi. 246 The 'Setter Lands', or areas settled since Norwegian times, as revealed by a MSS Scatt Rental of 1824 have been mapped, and the distribution reveals mainly an intensification in the Norwegian settlement [over that of the Merk Lands]. **1952** H. MARWICK *Orkney Farm-Names* III. 229 In Orkney.. there is no evidence of sæters, and accordingly in the present work no derivation [of farm-names] from *sætr* is suggested.

2. a. In Scandinavia, a mountain pasture where cattle remain during the summer months. Also *attrib.*

1799 MALTHUS *Diary* 9 July (1966) 132 His cows are now gone to pasture on the mountains—to Saaters, as they seem to call it. **1841** H. MARTINEAU *Feats on Fiord* vi. 161 The mountain pasture belonging to a farm is called its Seater. **1882** LEES & CLUTTERBUCK *Three in Norway* 56 This sæter is in a most beautiful situation, perched on a little flat bit of ground on the mountain side. **1924** *Contemp. Rev.* Feb. 236 Part of a herd of sixty or seventy..had wandered down from the *fjeld* into the *saether.* **1940** J. BUCHAN *Memory Hold-the-Door* viii. 191, I do not mean the Swiss alp or the Norwegian saeter pasture, for these are on too large a scale. **1968** G. JONES *Hist. Vikings* II. ii. 82 Increasingly the husbandman came to have his own upland grazing, his seter (*seter*, Swedish *såter*). Sometimes the seter was of a permanent nature.

b. A mountain dairy or farm on such a pasture.

1923 G. F. BARBOUR *Life Alex. Whyte* xxii. 451 He and Dr. Sutherland Black..drove seventy miles up the Saetersdal..picnicked for several days in a fishing 'saeter'. **1926** *Public Opinion* 25 June 585/2 Mountain farms were being turned into saeters. **1931** *Hardy's Anglers' Guide* 42 The angler taking up his quarters at a small farm or 'saeter'. **1955** M. E. B. BANKS *Commando Climber* vi. 106 The local farmer and his wife in a neighbouring *saeter*..always moved about their wooded farm on skis.

saetta, *var.* SAETA.

‖**saeva indignatio** ('saɪvə ɪndɪg'nɑːtɪəʊ). [L.] 'Savage indignation', an intense feeling of contemptuous anger at human folly. (Orig. and in later allusive use with reference to the epitaph of Swift: see quot. *a* 1745.)

[*a* **1745** SWIFT *Wks.* (1841) I. p. lxxi/1 (*epitaph*) Hic depositum est corpus Jonathan. Swift... Ubi saeva indignatio Ulterius cor lacerare nequit.] **1853** THACKERAY *Eng. Humourists of Eighteenth Cent.* i. 32 The 'sæva indignatio' of which he [*sc.* Swift] spoke as lacerating his heart..breaks out from him in a thousand pages of his writing, and tears and rends him. **1900** F. M. FORD *Let.* Oct. (1965) 12 You haven't enough contempt, enough of the *saeva indignatio.* **1928** W. B. YEATS in *Exile* Spring 5 Swift beating on his breast in sibylline frenzy blind Because the heart in his blood-sodden breast had dragged him down into mankind... *Saeva Indignatio* and the labourer's hire. **1957** R. SPEAIGHT *Life H. Belloc* xxi. 529 The furniture of home itself, the laughter and the love of friends—must he leave them, too? Yes, he exclaimed, with a *saeva indignatio* worthy of his master Swift, he must. **1969** *Punch* 1 Jan. 34/1 There was Solzhenitsyn's *The First Circle*..which..fell short of greatness because it was too docile. It lacked *saeva indignatio.* **1972** *Eng. Stud.* LIII. 280 It lacks the poised humour which saved Aluko's earlier characters from becoming mere sitting ducks for his *saeva indignatio.*

saf, obs. form of SAFE, SAVE.

Safaitic (sæfə'ɪtɪk), *a.* Also **Safahitic.** [f. the Arab. place-name *Safa* in Syria, SE of Damascus + -ITIC (see -ITE[1]).] Of or pertaining to an ancient Semitic language known only from inscriptions probably of the first centuries AD discovered near Safa.

1905 G. BELL *Let.* 24 Oct. (1927) I. xi. 225 I'm going to his house tomorrow to look over some Nabathean and Safaitic inscriptions and discuss what is to be found in Nejd. **1911** *Encycl. Brit.* XXIV. 626/1 To the first centuries of the Christian era belong the thousands of Arabic inscriptions, found in the wild, rocky districts south-east of Damascus, which are commonly termed Safaitic, after Safa, a locality in their neighbourhood. **1939**, etc. [see LIHYANIC *sb.*]. **1951** A. M. HONEYMAN in H. H. Rowley *Old Testament & Mod. Study* ix. 270 A new Pars Quinta has been projected to cover the Safaitic, Lihyanite, and Thamudic material. **1976** *Times* 3 Sept. (Qatar Suppl.) p. iv/9 From..the end of the first millennium BC,..a Safaitic inscription by a warrior to Du-Shara, high god of the Nabataeans.

safare, obs. Sc. form of SAVIOUR.

safari (sə'fɑːrɪ), *sb.* Also †**sefari.** [Swahili, journey, expedition, f. Arab. *safar* journey.]

1. a. A journey; a cross-country expedition, often lasting days or weeks, orig. in E. Africa and on foot, especially for hunting; now often with motorized vehicles, for tourism, adventure, or scientific investigation. Often in phr. *on safari.*

[**1860** *Harper's Mag.* Oct. 630/1 Safari! safari los! a journey, a journey to-day!] **1907** J. H. PATTERSON *Man-Eaters of Tsavo* vi. 61 [He] had left me and gone on *safari* (a caravan journey) to Uganda. *Ibid.* xi. 119 They join another caravan and begin a new *safari* to the Great Lakes. **1922** H. B. HERMON-HODGE *Up against it in Nigeria* iv. 54, I am an indifferent marksman both at range and on safari. **1928** *Daily Express* 16 Nov. 9 The royal safari—as a shooting expedition of this nature is described in Africa—is complete to the minutest detail. **1935** E. HEMINGWAY *Green Hills of Africa* II. iii. 46 We had gone on a foot safari to hunt rhino in the forest. **1958** L. VAN DER POST *Lost World of Kalahari* iv. 74 It was time we did another safari together. **1964** C. WILLOCK *Enormous Zoo* ii. 23 Justin Tokwar's account of his historic porter safari to the Nile. **1970** *Drum* (E. Afr. ed.) Feb. 27/5 The time when safari in Tanzania meant roughing it will soon be over and visitors can enjoy the awe-inspiring scenery..and the relaxation of miles of unspoiled tropical beaches in comfort and luxury. **1976** *San Francisco Examiner* 30 May (Sunday Scene) The safari is organized to be an inside view of the naturalist's Africa.

b. *transf.* and *fig.*

1958 *Spectator* 22 Aug. 249/3 The London Studio are performing for a group of ten, for each other. And as long as they pursue this safari down a cul-de-sac, this is all the audience they will either attract or deserve. **1975** T. DINESEN *My Sister, Isak Dinesen* vi. 79, I cannot help seeing it like our safari sometime in the future, in which we shall remember all the shauries as shadows and smile at them. **1977** P. HILL *Liars* viii. 105 His educated hands went on safari down her stomach.

2. A hunter's or traveller's party or caravan.

1890 F. LUGARD *Diary* 2 Feb. (1959) I. 92 A Safari is by no means an easy thing to manage, especially at first. **1892** *Daily News* 15 July 5/6 It would be a great thing if the next sefari (caravan) brought up a small Nordenfelt or Hotchkiss gun. **1901** *Ann. Rep. Board of Regents Smithsonian Inst. 1900* 433 We collected our safari of one hundred and thirty Manyema carriers. **1909** W. S. RAINSFORD *Land of Lion* vi. 141 Be always careful to look for signs of crocodiles,..and warn your safari to be careful. **1928** *Blackw. Mag.* Oct. 549/1 It is seldom indeed that a safari passes through the bush without some news of it being 'telegraphed' ahead by the natives.

3. *attrib.* and *Comb.* **a.** *gen.*, as ***safari accounts, coach, horn, lodge, path, plan, ranch, work.*** **b.** Designating articles of clothing suitable for wearing on safari, or made in a similar fashionable style, as ***safari boot, hat, jacket, kit, shirt, suit.*** **c.** Of furniture, etc. (proprietary name): designed for use whilst on safari or otherwise travelling, as ***Safari (camp) bed, chair, mattress.*** **d.** Special Combs.: **safari ant,** a nomadic, carnivorous, African ant of the subfamily Dorylinæ, esp. one belonging to the genus *Anomma*; **safari camp** *Austral.*, a camp in the outback; **safari look** (see quot. 1968); **safari park,** an area of parkland where wild animals are kept in the open and through which visitors may drive in motor vehicles.

1890 F. D. LUGARD *Diary* 30 Jan. (1959) I. ii. 89 Discussed a plan for working safari accounts &c. with Dick. **1926** D. STRICKLAND *Through Belgian Congo* vi. 94 The driver or safari ant is perhaps, from an entomological standpoint, the most interesting. **1966** B. KIMENYE *Kalasanda Revisited* 51 Safari ants..those large, shiny black insects whose jaws clamp into flesh. **1976** K. THACKERAY *Crownbird* ix. 189 A crawling mass of siafu, large safari ants with big pincers. **1945** *Trade Marks Jrnl.* 7 Mar. 123/2 *Safari*... Beds (furniture). Hounsfield Limited, 81, Morland Road, Croydon, Surrey, manufacturers. **1976** M. BIRMINGHAM *Heat of Sun* vii. 110 [We] dragged a safari bed from the bottom of the linen cupboard and set it up in..my room. **1970** *Times* 20 May 7/1 Mr. Lea was said to have been wearing..khaki trousers, and brown safari boots. **1977** H. INNES *Big Footprints* III. iii. 292 [We] took our safari boots off and dabbled our bare feet in a pool. **1969** *Northern Territory News* (Darwin) *Focus '69* 97/1 More are being encouraged here by small plane links between Darwin and Arnhem Land safari camps, as well as other outback attractions. **1972** V. CANNING *Rainbird Pattern* ii. 39 The inner room, smaller, contained a safari camp bed with the appropriate bedclothes. **1977** *Bulletin* (Sydney) 22 Jan. 65/1 One lives 48 kilometres away on the Nourlangie safari camp. **1967** H. HARRISON *Technicolor Time Machine* (1968) viii. 75 Slithey was leaning back in her safari chair while her wig was being combed. **1973** 'S. HARVESTER' *Corner of Playground* III. vii. 224 A safari coach of rich Americans drew up. **1968** J. IRONSIDE *Fashion Alphabet* 144 Topee or *Safari hat*, shaped like a pith-helmet with rounded crown and brim sloping down, slightly wider at the back and front. **1977** H. INNES *Big Footprints* II. iii. 179 Her eyes, shaded by the safari hat, were gazing towards the distant mountains. **1928** *Blackw. Mag.* Oct. 549/1 The sound of a safari horn came drifting across the bush. **1972** *Vogue* Feb. 86 Safari jacket, unlined seersucker. **1977** M. ALLEN *Spence in Petal Park* xii. 50 She was wearing a gold roll-neck sweater and a brown suede safari jacket. **1928** *Daily Express* 29 Nov. 1/1 The Prince, dressed in safari kit. **1964** C. WILLOCK *Enormous Zoo* iii. 34 The safari lodge at Mweya was unexpectedly losing money. **1975** 'D. JORDAN' *Black Account* xxxii. 163 There was a safari lodge with hot water and white sheets. [**1968** J. IRONSIDE *Fashion Alphabet* 27 *Safari.* This is a White-hunter look that has been in and out of fashion since the beginning of the twentieth century. Details such as belted and vented jackets..imitation pith helmets and epaulettes.. in both skirt and trouser suits.] **1969** *Sears Catal.* Spring/Summer 40 Cape, Top and Pants Set for the total safari look. **1974** *Times-Picayune* (New Orleans) 4 Oct. IV. 1 (Advt.), The safari look with shell and slacks in beige, belted jacket in brown. **1971** Safari mattress [see *garden umbrella* s.v. GARDEN *sb.* 4 a]. **1969** *Times* 1 Oct. 14/2 Opened early this summer Windsor Safari Park covering an area of 140 acres on the north edge of Windsor Great Park has proved very successful. **1977** B. PYM *Quartet in Autumn* v. 45 There would be visits to a safari park and to the stately homes that offered the best attractions. **1920** *Blackw. Mag.* Feb. 205/1 A good safari path winds through a deep valley in the Livingstone Mountains. **1907** F. D. LUGARD *Diary* 3 Apr. (1959) I. vi. 170 Had a long talk over Safari plans and worked out the details of my idea of food supply &c. **1975** 'D. JORDAN' *Black Account* xix. 104 Angel Engelbrecht has a safari ranch in Northern Transvaal. **1968** *Vogue* 15 Apr. 77 Safari shirt in brave bright red Linoseta over navy blue supraline trousers. **1967** *Observer* 26 Feb. 29/3 (*heading*) Safari suit. The most convincing and adaptable fashion from Paris. **1979** P. NIESEWAND *Member of Club* xv. 115 A mild-mannered American..wearing a light blue safari suit. **1890** F. D. LUGARD *Diary* 17 Jan. (1959) I. i. 75 A fine body of men..ready to take service with the Company in fort and station building, shamba making, and safari work.

Hence as *v. intr.*, to go on safari; also *transf.*

1908 *Times Lit. Suppl.* 19 Nov. 413/1 Mr. Chapman then has safaried twice for pleasure to British East Africa. **1936**

Punch 5 Aug. 164/1 I've safaried in Sahara, And I've wandered in Peru. **1971** L. GUTTERIDGE *Cold War in Country Garden* I. iii. 55 The two men went up-country and safaried around for a while. **1977** W. MCILVANNEY *Laidlaw* xxxiv. 160 The receptionist was waiting... In the time it took Harkness to safari to her desk, she didn't look up once.

Safavid ('sæfəvɪd), *a.* and *sb.* Also **Safawid.** [ad. Pers. *ṣafawī* (see SOPHY[1]) + patronymic suff. *-id.*] **A.** *adj.* Of or pertaining to a ruling dynasty in Persia (1501–1736). **B.** *sb.* A member of this dynasty.

1911 *Encycl. Brit.* XXI. 233/2 By the fall of the Safawid dynasty Persia lost her race of national monarchs. **1957** *Ibid.* XVII. 574/1 The Safawid dynasty did not actually come to an end until Nadir Shah usurped the throne in 1736. **1972** *Country Life* 20 Jan. 155/3 The numerous flasks of wine for which the Safavid Kings had such a weakness. **1975** *New Yorker* 13 Oct. 31/3 'This is not a catalogue,' Mr. Ross said, 'because many of the objects now on view will help you sort out the Timurids from the Safavids.'

safe (seɪf), *sb.* Also 5, 7 **save.** [Originally *save*, f. SAVE *v.*; later assimilated to SAFE *a.*]

1. A receptacle for the safe storage of articles: esp. **a.** A ventilated chest or cupboard for protecting provisions from insects and other noxious animals; a meat-safe (see MEAT *sb.* 6).

c **1440** *Promp. Parv.* 10/1 Almery of mete kepynge, or a saue for mete, *cibutum.* **1611** COTGR., *Chasiere*,..the great, or grated Saue hung by a pulley, to the top of a Dayriehouse, or Store-house; and seruing to keepe cheese, white-meates, and other belly-timber in. **1688** R. HOLME *Armoury* III. xiv. (Roxb.) 17/2 The Arke or Safe, is a kind of little house made of wood and couered with haire cloth, and so by two rings hung in the midle of a Rome, thereby to secure all things put therein from the cruelty of devouring Rats, mice [etc.]. **1706** PHILLIPS (ed. Kersey), *Safe*, a sort of Cup-board to keep Victuals, contrived with Holes to let in the Air. **1881** B. W. RICHARDSON in *Gd. Words* XXII. 51/2 It is good practice, whenever the air of the safe is close and tainted, to have it fumigated with antiseptic gas.

b. A fire-proof and burglar-proof receptacle for plate, money, deeds, and other valuables. Usually made of steel and iron, with one or more doors secured by elaborate locks.

1820 *Rec. Early Hist. Boston* (1909) XXXIX. 174 A fire proof safe in the Selectmens room for the security of the records. **1838** BETHUNE *Sc. Peasant's Fireside* 70 A penknife ..and a letter..were found lying near the safe, as if they had been lost by the robber. **1850** CHUBB *Locks & Keys* 17 The bank may be entered, the misnamed safe, or strong room, be entered. **1874** MICKLETHWAITE *Mod. Par. Churches* 164 An iron fire-proof safe must be built into the wall.

2. *Saddlery.* 'A piece of leather placed under a buckle, to prevent it from chafing' (Knight *Dict. Mech.* 1875).

3. A tray laid under plumbing fixtures to receive spilled water.

1862 *Illustr. Catal. Internat. Exhib., Industr. Dept., Brit. Div.* II. No. 6392 Patent Bath, sienna marbled inside, verdantique outside. Taps and safe fitted. **1896** T. E. COLEMAN *Sanitary House Drainage* xvi. 129 The floor of the bath-room should be laid with mosaic..the bath standing within a properly constructed safe, which may be made of slate, marble, glazed earthenware, or tiles. **1956** GUMBRILL & SMITH *Blake & Jenkins's Drainage & Sanitation* (ed. 11) vii. 215 The lead safe sometimes placed under the cistern must have a waste pipe which should be carried through an external wall.

4. A contraceptive sheath. *colloq.*

1897 *Science of Generation* xx. 235 The use of various mechanical contrivances, such as French Safes, Condom Sheaths, etc., is also objectionable. **1959** V. PACKARD *Status Seekers* (1960) xi. 155 Young Italian-American men..of high-school age regularly carry 'safes' or condoms. **1979** E. KOCH *Good Night Little Spy* x. 94 Just in time he remembered his safe. He took it out of his pants pocket.

5. The operative position of a firearm's safety device; the state in which a gun cannot be fired. Cf. SAFETY 8.

1920 G. BURRARD *Notes on Sporting Rifles* 71 One may.. fail to stop a dangerous charge through the rifle being at 'safe'. **1967** V. CANNING *Python Project* ii. 31, I hope you've got that damned thing on 'safe'? **1978** F. ROSS *Sleeping Dogs* 127 The safety catch was off. He clicked it to 'safe' and tossed it on the carpet.

6. *attrib.* and *Comb.* (chiefly sense 1 b): simple attrib., as ***safe-door, -key, -robbery***; objective, as ***safe burster, buster, -maker, -making, -opener, -robber***; **safe-blower** orig. *U.S.*, a safe-robber who uses explosive material to burst open safes; hence **safe-blowing** *vbl. sb.*; **safe-breaker** orig. *U.S.*, a robber who breaks open safes; hence **safe-breaking** *vbl. sb.*; **safe-cracker** orig. *U.S.* = *safe-breaker*; hence **safe-cracking** *vbl. sb.*

1873 G. LENING *Dark Side N.Y. Life* 148 Namely, first those who burst open the safe with gunpowder,—'safe blowers'. **1951** WODEHOUSE *Old Reliable* iv. 51 Are you a safeblower magically gifted with the art of buttling, or a butler who has somehow picked up the knack of blowing safes? **1972** *Times* 12 May 2/8 A former safe-blower.. claimed to have got away with a total of £10,000 at a cost of 20 years in different jails. **1928** H. ASBURY *Gangs of N.Y.* x. §2. 217 [Marm Mandelbaum] also offered advanced courses in burglary and safe-blowing. **1970** 'D. HALLIDAY' *Dolly & Cookie Bird* viii. 113 We amuse ourselves with safeblowing. **1870** M. H. SMITH *20 Yrs. Wall St.* xxv. 320 A safe-breaker from Boston, a bank-robber from Philadelphia, a New York thief, have each their own way of doing things. **1977** J. WAINWRIGHT *Nest of Rats* I. vi. 46 The genuine peterman —the safe-breaker who takes a personal pride in pitting his wits against those of the safe-makers. **1934** WEBSTER, Safebreaking. **1937** 'M. INNES' *Hamlet, Revenge!* II. ii. 115 The burglary and safe-breaking had been unsuccessful. **1981** 'M. HEBDEN' *Pel is Puzzled* vii. 61 Two years for attempted safe-breaking in Lyons. **1873** G. LENING *Dark Side N.Y. Life* 148 Then those who, not using powder, have recourse to mechanical means, these are 'safe bursters' *par excellence.* **1934** WEBSTER, Safecracker. **1960** *Times* 27 May 18/6 His hero, Bob, is an (almost) reformed safe-cracker. **1977** D. BAGLEY *Enemy* xiv. 111 The chief safe-cracker was a man I'd met before. **1934** WEBSTER, Safecracking. **1937** 'M. INNES' *Hamlet, Revenge!* II. iii. 130, I know something about this safe-cracking business. **1967** *Times* 28 Feb. (Canada Suppl.) 31 Montreal claimed that it had more.. safecrackings than any other city in the world. **1977** D. BAGLEY *Enemy* xiv. 111, I..found the safe-cracking team at work. **1894** 'MARK TWAIN' in *Century Mag.* XLVIII. 22 The safe-door was not open. **1911** *Encycl. Brit.* XXIII. 997/1 Where larger quantities of valuables had to be preserved than a safe would conveniently hold, a safe-door of larger dimensions would be made and attached to a masonry or brick room. **1894** 'MARK TWAIN' in *Century Mag.* XLVIII. 22 His plan was, to..steal the safe-key..and then go back and rob the safe. **1911** *Encycl. Brit.* XXIII. 996/2 Well-authenticated experiments performed by safe-makers on their own and other makers' productions. **1977** Safe-maker [see *safe-breaker*]. **1886** *Encycl. Brit.* XXI. 144/1 The ingenuity of inventors has..effected much in safe-making. **1970** H. TREVELYAN *Middle East in Revolution* 251 The combination lock was stuck and only the girls, who had been evacuated, could open the safe. Miraculously, an amateur safe-opener appeared and did the trick. **1873** G. LENING *Dark Side N.Y. Life* 148 The safe robber..usually obtains access to houses by means of false keys. **1959** J. CARY *Captive & Free* xxvii. 124 He might have been a test pilot, a racing motorist, an explorer, a climber of Himalayan peaks; or perhaps a cat burglar, safe-robber, or hold-up man. **1886** *Frank Leslie's Pop. Monthly* XXI. 47/2 The Egerton safe-robbery..had baffled all the detectives in town.

Hence **safed** *ppl. a.*, provided with a safe.

1881 *Blackw. Mag.* CXXIX. 176 A solidly furnished though dismal apartment, duly safed and grated.

safe (seɪf), *a.* Forms: 3–6 **sauf,** (3–4 **sauve**), 4–6 **saufe,** 5 **sauuf,** 5–6 **sauff(e;** 3–5 **saf,** 4–5 **saff(e,** 4–6 **saaf,** (5 **saafe, saaff**); 4–6 **saulf, salve,** 5–7 **salf(e,** 6–7 **salffe, saulfe;** 5–7 *Sc.* **saiff,** 6 **saif, saiv, sayfe, sailf,** 6–7 **saife,** 7 **saiffe;** 3–5 (6–7 *Sc.*) **save,** 4– **safe.** [ME. *sauf, sāf*, a. F. *sauf* (fem. *sauve*) = Pr. *salv-s, sal-s*, Sp., Pg., It. *salvo*:—L. *salvus* uninjured, entire, healthy (whence *salūt-, salūs* health, *salvē* imperative, 'hail').

The L. word corresponds in root and suffix, though prob. not in ablaut-grade, to Gr. ὅλος (Ionic οὖλος) whole, Skr. *sarva* all, whole:—Indogermanic **solwo-*. The root occurs also in Irish *slán* healthy, and in OL. *sollus* whole, Welsh *holl* all, whole:—**solno-*.

With regard to the phonology in Eng. cf. *sage* (the plant) from F. *sauge*, and *gage* (*gauge*) from ONF. *gauge*.

The forms with *v* in ME. usually represent either the plural or the definite inflexion of the adj. From the 15th to the 17th c. *save* sometimes occurs (latterly only Sc.), in most instances prob. as a mere graphical alteration of *safe*.]

I. Free from hurt or damage; unharmed.

1. a. Unhurt, uninjured, unharmed; having been preserved from or escaped some real or apprehended danger. Chiefly (now only) with quasi-advb. force after verbs of coming, going, bringing, etc.

1297 R. GLOUC. (Rolls) 6895 ȝif hire vet beþ þanne sauf wiþoute wemminge. *a* **1300** *Cursor M.* 11546 þai ferd al sauf in to þair kyth. **1340** *Ayenb.* 36 þet hi habbe, huet cas yualle, hire catel sauf. *c* **1386** CHAUCER *Can. Yeom. T.* 397 Somtyme his good is drenched in the see, And somtym comth it sauf un-to the londe. *c* **1450** *Merlin* xxvii. 559 That ye sholde yeve hym trewys saf to come and saf to go..be-twene this and yole. **1471** CAXTON *Recuyell* (Sommer) I. 217 Ye shall retorne saulf fro this entrepryse. **1513** DOUGLAS *Æneis* X. i. 104 Suffyr that ȝyng Ascanyus mot be Salf [*v.r.* sauff] fra all wapynnis [L. *ab armis incolumem*], and of perrell fre. **1538** STARKEY *England* I. ii. 67 As gud marynerys..bryng theyr schype saue out of tempestys into the sure port. **1600** in *10th Rep. Hist. MSS. Comm.* App. v. 458 To retowrn saulfe without any molestacion. *a* **1674** CLARENDON *Hist. Reb.* XV. §57 As if the principal art requisite in the captain of a ship had been to be sure to come home safe again. **1737** C. PITT in J. Duncombe *Lett.* (1773) II. 98 The papers came safe to hand. **1760–72** H. BROOKE *Fool of Qual.* (1809) III. 83 As the Moors are excellent swimmers, I suppose most of them got safe. **1785** COWPER *Let. to Lady Hesketh* Wks. 1836 V. 198 My desk..is safe arrived. **1799** T. HOLCROFT *Mem.* (1816) III. 229 [In a stiff breeze a sailor swore that] he could not keep his hair safe on his head. **1831** *Society* I. 209 He always insists on seeing us safe across the Downs. **1902** WISTER *Virginian* xix, Your..man brought us out..safe and dry.

b. Often in phr. ***safe and sound.*** Occas. † ***sound and safe;*** also ***safe and sure,*** † ***safe and sicker,*** † ***quit and safe.*** [F. *sain et sauf*; L. *sanus et salvus, salvus sanus, salvus et sospes*, etc.] Also † ***safe and soon,*** † ***soon and safe.***

a **1300** *Cursor M.* 7867 Sauf and sond ai mot þou be To all þe folk es vnder þe. *c* **1350** *Will. Palerne* 2816 þei were gretli glad..þat he sauf was & sound fro þe men a-schaped. **1390** GOWER *Conf.* I. 233 So that thei mihten sauf and sone The water passe. **1398** TREVISA *Barth. De P.R.* XVII. cii. (1495) 667 Deed bodyes ben kepte sauf and sounde whan they ben bawmyd wyth confeccyons of mirra. *c* **1440** *Promp. Parv.* 440/2 Saaf, and sekyr, *salvus.* *c* **1450** MYRC *Festial* 17 And soo he ȝede sonde and saf hys way. *c* **1489** CAXTON *Sonnes of Aymon* i. 29, I shall lete you goo quyte & sauf. **1585** T. WASHINGTON tr. *Nicholay's Voy.* II. ix. 42 b, [He] was by a Dolphin brought safe and sound to the porte. **1610** HOLLAND *Camden's Brit.* (1637) 635 *Gobanium*.., keeping the ancient name, as it were, safe and sound is tearmed Aber-Gevenny. **1590** SHAKS. *Com. Err.* I. i. 49 And soone, and safe, [she] arriued where I was. **1819–24** BYRON *Juan* IV. liv, I leave Don Juan for the present, safe—Not sound, poor fellow, but severely wounded. **1847** GROTE *Greece* II. l. (1862) IV. 353 He would again replace him 'safe and sound' in the fortification.

c. ***to be, arrive,*** etc., ***safe*** (or ***safe and sound***): often merely a colloq. or epistolary formula for 'to be duly arrived', 'to be at one's destination', etc.

1710 SWIFT *Jrnl. to Stella* 9 Sept., I send this only to tell that I am safe in London. **1882** SALA *Amer. Revis.* ii. (1885) 25, I was safe and sound in the Brevoort coach. **1887** *Century Mag.* Dec. 197/2, I promised to bring you both to lunch, safe and sound.

† **d.** (***to come***) ***to safe hand***: confusedly used for 'to come safe to hand'. *Obs.*

c **1645** HOWELL *Lett.* (1655) III. xviii. 27 Your last of the fourth current came to safe hand.

† **2.** In sound health, well, 'whole'; *usually* healed, cured, restored to health. Also ***safe and sound;*** also const. *of*. *Obs.*

c **1290** *S. Eng. Leg.* 458/51 þe Quen a-non þoruȝh is bone deliuered was of childe, In guod lif, and hire child al-so..þo þe king i-say þe Quene sauf, and þat child al-so. *a* **1300** *Cursor M.* 8170 Thoru þe, he said, sal þis mesele Be sauf and sund of al vn-hele. *c* **1350** *Will. Palerne* 868 He was al sauf & sound of alle his sor greues. **1382** WYCLIF *Luke* xviii. 42 Thi feith hath maad thee saaf [Vulg. *te salvum fecit*]. *c* **1400** *Secreta Secret., Gov. Lordsh.* 92 He þat drynkys it, with þe sauour þeroff he shall fele hele, and he shal be sauf of catarre, of Malencoly..and of many oþer syknes. *c* **1450** *St. Cuthbert* (Surtees) 3661 þe seke man with his hand he blisse; Fra he him touched safe he was. **1486** *Bk. St. Albans* c vj b, Put som in the Roofe of her mowth and she shall be saafe. **1526** TINDALE *Luke* viii. 48 Thy fayth hath made the safe.

† **3.** *Theol.* [After L. *salvus* in the Vulgate.] Delivered from sin or condemnation, saved; in a state of salvation, spiritually 'whole'. *Obs.*

a **1300** *Cursor M.* 19967 All to be sauf o sin and scam, þat wald tru in his hali nam. *a* **1300–1400** *Ibid.* 10867 (Gött.) His folk all saf [*Cott.* saued] þan sal he make, And bring þaim vte of sinne and wrake. **1340** HAMPOLE *Pr. Consc.* 2959 Bot yhit has the saul mare drede þan, Til þe dome be gyven and it may se Whether it sal dampned or saufe be. **1382** WYCLIF *Acts* xvi. 31 Bileue thou in to the Lord Jhesu and thou schalt be saf [Vulg. *salvus eris*; Gr. σωθήσῃ]. **1399** LANGL. *Rich. Redeles* Prol. 81 As my soule be saff ffrom synne at myn ende. *c* **1440** HYLTON *Scala Perf.* (W. de W. 1494) I. xli, Some by sorowe..some by prechyng & techyng..shal be saaf & come to blisse. **1562** WINȜET *Cert. Tractates* Wks. (S.T.S.) I. 81 God makis ws sauff be the lawar of regeneratioun [*Tit.* iii. 5].

† **4.** Mentally or morally sound or sane. *Obs.*

The phr. ***with*** (***a***) ***safe conscience*** was suggested by L. *salvā conscientiā* (cf. 5 below).

1390 GOWER *Conf.* II. 32, I mai wel with sauf conscience Excuse me of necgligence Towardes love in alle wise. **1492** In god mynde and saf memorye [see MEMORY 2 b]. **1549** LATIMER *1st Serm. bef. Edw. VI* D j, The which treasure, if it be not sufficiente, he maye lawfully and wyth a salue conscience, take taxis of hys subiectes. **1560** DAUS tr. *Sleidane's Comm.* 6 b, To revoke his sentence already taught and defended, he cannot with a safe conscience [orig. *cum bona conscientia*]. **1567** in F. J. Baigent *Crondal Rec.* (1891) 172 Any personne..beinge of the full age of twenty and one yeares, of saulf memorie. **1577** NORTHBROOKE *Dicing* (1843) 91 Fewe men or women come from playes, and resortes of men, with safe and chaste mindes. **1601** SHAKS. *Jul. C.* I. i. 14 A Trade Sir, that I hope I may vse with a safe Conscience. **1604** —— *Oth.* IV. i. 280 Are his wits safe? Is he not light of Braine? **1611** —— *Cymb.* IV. ii. 131 No single soule Can we set eye on: but in all safe reason He must haue some Attendants. *a* **1817** JANE AUSTEN *Northanger Abbey* (1818) I. xiii. 231 Now we may all go to-morrow with a safe conscience.

† **5.** Used in a construction corresponding to the L. ablative absolute (e.g. *salvā fide, salvo jure*; so F. *sauf votre respect*) with the sense: Keeping..safe or intact, without hurt or prejudice to.., without loss of.., making reservation of.., with due respect to... *Obs.* (See also *safe*, SAVE *prep.*)

c **1290** *S. Eng. Leg.* 120/488 Trewenesse we þe sworen ase riȝt was, and eorþelich honour al-so, Sauue ore ordre and ore riȝte, bote þat was out i-do. **1297** R. GLOUC. (Rolls) 1242, & þat he vor is neueu wolde, vorto abatie strif, Do hey amendement, sauue lume & lif. *c* **1374** CHAUCER *Troylus* II. 480 But elles wol I fonde, Myn honour sauf, plese him fro day to day. **1423** JAS. I *Kingis Q.* cxliii, Hir worschip sauf. **1470** HENRY *Wallace* XI. 1208 Tharfor till him is no comparisoun, As off a man, sauff reuerence off the croun. *c* **1483** CAXTON *Dialogues* 17 *Non feray, sauue le vostre grace*, I shall not, sauf your grace. *c* **1500** *Melusine* 3 Saaf theire juggement.

II. Free from danger; secure.

6. a. Not exposed to danger; not liable to be harmed or lost; secure.

1387 TREVISA *Higden* (Rolls) II. 227 þey bulde hem smale cootes and cabans..þat hire lyf myȝte be þe more saaf. *c* **1400** *Laud Troy Bk.* (E.E.T.S.) 18201 Off no-thing were thei a-dredde; Thei wende thei hadde ben saue & sure. *c* **1440** *Pallad. on Husb.* XII. 363 And wrie hem that noon ayer vppon hem shyne, So beth they sauf. **1447–8** *Shillingford's Lett.* (Camden) 88 To bryng yn stuf for the werre..ther to be kept stronge saf and sure. **1590** SHAKS. *Com. Err.* I. ii. 105, I greatly feare my monie is not safe. **1596** —— *Tam. Shr.* V. ii. 151 Whil'st thou ly'st warme at home, secure and safe. **1591** SPENSER *Daphn.* xx, Safe then and safest were my sillie sheepe, Ne fear'd the Wolfe. **1849** MACAULAY *Hist. Eng.* V. I. 662 No second witness could be found... Cornish thought himself safe. *Ibid.* vii. II. 190 Apprehensions that the interests of the Anglican Church might not be safe under the rule of a man bred among Dutch Presbyterians. **1852** MRS. STOWE *Uncle Tom's C.* vii. 43 No, no, Harry darling! mother can't eat till you are safe!

quasi-*adv.* 1860 *Bohn's Handbk. Games, Billiards* 572 Either decline the chance altogether, and lay the balls safe, or make that stroke which seems most sure and easy.

b. Const. *from*, †*of* (= secure against).

1390 GOWER *Conf.* III. 153 That he mesure in his expence So kepe, that of indigence He mai be sauf. *c*1440 *Pallad. on Husb.* I. 973 Al the lond that thou hast goon aboute ffro cloudis wicke is saaf [*Bodl. MS.* saue]. *Ibid.* 982 Thy seedis with cucumber rotis grounde Let stepe, and saaf of euery mys they are. 1535 COVERDALE *Job* xxi. 9 Their houses are safe from all feare. 1577 B. GOOGE *Heresbach's Husb.* I. (1586) 33 Yf they be steeped in Capons blood, they wyll be safe from all hurtful weedes. 1697 DRYDEN *Æneid* VII. 1065 Where then he liv'd obscure, but safe from Jove. 1801 *Med. Jrnl.* V. 403 That a person once infected with the small-pox is safe from having it a second time. 1866 G. MACDONALD *Ann. Q. Neighb.* v. (1878) 66, I did not feel safe from him till I was once more in my study. 1891 HELEN B. HARRIS *Apol. Aristides* ii. 14 The hermits..petitioned him to build them a house where they might be safe from the incursions of the Arabs.

7. Of a place or thing: Affording security or immunity; not exposing to danger; not likely to cause harm or injury. Also const. *for*.

1390 GOWER *Conf.* I. 165 Neptunus..kept hire in so sauf a place Fro Polipheme and his manace, That he..Ne mihte atteigne hir compaignie. 1590 SHAKS. *Com. Err.* I. ii. 78 Answer me, In what safe place you haue bestow'd my monie. 1603 OWEN *Pembrokeshire* (1891) 111 A good and salfe roade for shippinge. 1666 *Act 18 & 19 Chas. II*, c. 8 §5 The building with Bricke is not onely more comely and durable but alsoe more safe against future perills of Fire. 1680 LADY R. RUSSELL *Lett.* I. iii. 11 The Iesuits' Powder is ..held most safe to be taken by the best doctors. 1697 DRYDEN *Virg. Georg.* IV. 608 A Station safe for Ships, when Tempests roar. 1789 W. BUCHAN *Dom. Med.* (1790) 129 All kinds of linen and bedding, when not frequently used, become damp. How then is it possible that beds, which are not slept in above two or three times a year, should be safe? 1861 FLOR. NIGHTINGALE *Nursing* 14 The safest atmosphere of all for a patient is a good fire and an open window. 1866 YOUNG *Fires* 59 Staircases, to be fireproof, or at least safe under the ordinary circumstances of fire. 1870 DICKENS *E. Drood* viii, That part of the world is at a safe distance. 1917 W. WILSON in *Sel. Addresses* (1918) 195 The world must be made safe for democracy. Its peace must be planted upon the tested foundations of political liberty. 1929 H. W. NEVINSON *English* viii. 63 It was believed by some that the Great War was waged to make the world safe for democracy, and the result has been that democracy was destroyed in many European countries. 1932 J. FORTESCUE in *Eighteen-Sixties* 244 The pain of seeing the world made safe for that most unsafe and lowering of influences, vulgarity. 1932 A. P. HERBERT in *Punch* 15 June 653/2 The last few years of the War were directed by the great brains up above to thinking out new ways of making the War safe for the infantry. 1963 J. F. KENNEDY in *Evening Star* (Washington, D.C.) 10 June A-7/4 And if we cannot end now our differences, at least we can help make the world safe for diversity.

8. a. Used *transf.* in the compounds SAFE-CONDUCT, SAFEGUARD, q.v.; hence with sbs. of similar meaning, as ***safe convoy***, ***custody*** (cf. L. *tuta custodia*), † ***stowage***; also SAFE KEEPING, SAFE WARD.

1536 CROMWELL in Merriman *Life & Lett.* (1902) II. 9 To kepe the same Offeley in your salve custodye. 1547 in *Vicary's Anat.* (1888) App. III. i. 129 Which lettres were forwyth Delyuered ouer to the sauffe Custody of Master Chamberleyn. *a*1605 MONTGOMERIE *Misc. Poems* xlix. 22 Than grant thou vs..Thy saiv sure conduct [cf. OF. *salf et seur conduit*]. 1611 SHAKS. *Cymb.* I. vi. 192 And I am something curious, being strange, To haue them in safe stowage. 1634 MILTON *Comus* 81, I shoot from Heav'n to give him safe convoy. 1649 CROMWELL *Let.* 24 Nov. in Carlyle App. C. No. 14, I have by this Bearer returned a Safe-convoy, as you desire, for what Commissioners you think fit to send out to me. 1651 HOBBES *Leviathan* II. xxviii. 164 The safe custody of a man accused. 1766 BLACKSTONE *Comm.* II. 505 His only business being to keep the goods in his safe custody.

†**b.** ***safe pledge*** (see quot.). *Obs.*

1684 *Cowel's Interpr.* (ed. Manley), Safe pledge, *Salvus plegius*, is a Surety given for a Man's Appearance against a day assigned, *Bracton lib. 4. cap. 2. num. 2.* where it is also called *certus plegius*.

9. a. Of an action, procedure, undertaking, plan, etc.: Free from risk, not involving danger or mishap, guaranteed against failure. Sometimes = free from risk of error, as in *it is safe to say*...

1590 SPENSER *F.Q.* III. xi. 23 Therefore, Sir knight, Aread what course of you is safest dempt. 1605 SHAKS. *Macb.* II. iii. 148 Our safest way Is to auoid the ayme. 1624 MIDDLETON *Game at Chess* II. i. 21 What haue you there? *Bl. Bs.* A Note (Sir) of State-Policie, And one exceeding safe one. 1651 HOBBES *Leviathan* II. xxvii. 151 It is safer to erre on that hand, than on the other. 1721 DE FOE *Mem. Cavalier* (1840) 43 'Tis never safe to despise an enemy. 1728 SWIFT *Charac. Mrs. Johnson* Wks. 1824 IX. 286 Perhaps she was sometimes too severe, which is a safe and pardonable error. 1751 JOHNSON *Rambler* No. 173 ¶11 It is always safer to err in favour of others than of ourselves. 1790 COWPER *Odyss.* XXIII. 150 To me the safest counsel and the best. 1810 SCOTT *Lady of L.* II. xxxvi, Far up the lake 'twere safest land. 1854 J. B. LANGLEY *Life-Agent's Vade-mecum* 53 If an assurance company has obtained 1000 policies, it is statistically safe. 1863 W. PHILLIPS *Sp.* xi. 254 This is Choate, who made it safe to murder. 1893 *Law Times* XCIV. 454/1 It is safe to say that propositions of this kind will not figure upon the Statute-book yet awhile.

†**b.** In stronger sense: Conducive to safety. *Obs.*

1625 BACON *Ess., Seditions* (Arb.) 407 An Embleme, no doubt, to shew, how safe it is for Monarchs, to make sure of the good Will of Common People.

c. Phr. ***on the safe side*** = with a margin of security against error. Cf. *the sure(r) side* s.v. SURE *a.* 1 e.

1811 JANE AUSTEN *Sense & Sens.* III. iv. 78 Determining to be on the safe side, he made his apology in form as soon as he could say any thing. 1847 MARRYAT *Childr. N. Forest* xi, Be on the safe side, and do not trust him too far. 1858 *Merc. Mar. Mag.* V. 84 They should rather err on the safe side. 1893 SIR R. BALL *Story of Sun* 307 For the sake of being on the safe side, I have taken the lowest value.

d. applied *transf.* to the agent.

1874 HEATH *Croquet-Player* 53 Remember that the dead ball is not so safe a helper as your partner. 1884 *Liverpool Merc.* 18 Feb. 5/2 One is perfectly safe in saying that the position of the defendants has relatively improved.

10. Secured, kept in custody; unable to escape. Hence, not likely to come out, intervene, or do hurt; placed beyond the power of doing harm, not at present dangerous.

?*c*1600 *Distr. Emperor* I. i. in Bullen *Old Pl.* (1884) III. 200 What, madam? is he salve asleepe? Most soundlye, Sir. 1605 SHAKS. *Macb.* III. iv. 25 But Banquo's safe? *Mur.* I, my good Lord: safe in a ditch he bides. 1610 —— *Temp.* III. i. 21 My Father Is hard at study; pray now rest your selfe, Hee's safe for these three houres. 1613 —— *Hen. VIII*, v. iii. 97 Receiue him, And see him safe i' th' Tower. 1618 BOLTON *Florus* III. x. (1636) 204 Cæsar was at this time absent out of Gallia;..and so the wayes cloyed up, they presumed hee was fast and safe enough. 1667 MILTON *P.L.* IX. 815 And other care perhaps May have diverted from continual watch Our great Forbidder, safe with all his Spies About him. 1678 R. L'ESTRANGE *Seneca's Mor., Epist.* v. (1696) 490 When the Snake is Frozen, 'tis safe. 18.. *Nursery Rhyme, 'Three children sliding on the ice,'* Ye parents that have children dear,..If you would have them safe abroad, Pray keep them safe at home.

Prov. 1573 TUSSER *Husb.* (1878) 173 Drie sunne, drie winde, Safe binde, safe finde. [Cf. FAST *adv.* 2, quot. 1596.]

11. a. Sure in procedure; not liable to fail, mislead, or disappoint expectation; trustworthy; *spec.* in *Cricket*. **b.** Cautious, keeping to 'the safe side'. Also in proverbial phr. ***better (to be) safe than sorry***.

1604 SHAKS. *Oth.* II. iii. 205 My blood begins my safer Guides to rule. 1667 MILTON *P.L.* XI. 372 Ascend, I follow thee, safe Guide, the path Thou lead'st me. 1678 CUDWORTH *Intell. Syst.* I. iii. §37. 24 (1820) I. 367 That safe and sure-footed interpreter, Alex. Aphrodisius. 1823 *Lady's Mag.* July 387/1 Samuel Long..is..so steady a [cricket] player! so safe! 1851 J. PYCROFT *Cricket Field* x. 185 The safest pair of hands in England. 1887 A. BIRRELL *Obiter Dicta* Ser. II. 46 As a master of style and diction, Milton is as safe as Virgil. 1894 *Daily News* 3 May 5/3 The first [hymnal] is described by Canon Twells as being generally acceptable to high churches, the second to low churches, and the third to intermediate, 'sometimes called safe churches'. 1897 K. S. RANJITSINHJI *Jubilee Bk. Cricket* ii. 18 'A safe field'..signifies that the fielder may be relied upon to stop hits that come within reasonable distance of him, and to hold practically all catches. 1975 *Oxf. Compan. Sports & Games* 648/2 A bulky left-handed batsman of safe and unspectacular method.

Prov. [1837 S. LOVER *Rory O'More* II. xxi. 148 'Jist countin' them,—is there any harm in that?' said the tinker: 'it's betther be sure than sorry'.] 1933 *Radio Times* 14 Apr. 125/1 Cheap distempers very soon crack or fade. Better be safe than sorry. Ask for Hall's. 1958 [see LIGHTSHIP]. 1962 A. NISBETT *Technique Sound Studio* vii. 120 For tapes that are to be broadcast it is better to be safe than sorry. 1972 J. WILSON *Hide & Seek* vii. 128 It's not that I want to shut you in...But—well, it's better to be safe than sorry.

c. ***to play safe***: see PLAY *v.* 18f.

12. a. With *of*: Sure to obtain. ?*Obs.*

1667 PEPYS *Diary* 23 Aug., I find most people pleased with their being at ease, and safe of a peace. 1802 SOUTHEY *La Caba* 3 Here I stand, Safe of my purpose now! 1846 THACKERAY *Let.* 9 Feb. (MS.), What I meant by 'Safe' is the best word to be applied to a play I think—safe of a real agreeable—of course I don't know how permanent—success.

b. *to be safe*, followed by inf. or †const. *for*, is predicated of a person or thing to express the certainty of the fact or event involved in the predication.

Hence used *attrib.* in colloquial phrases like 'He is a safe first' = he is safe to take a first class.

1790 GROSE *Prov. Gloss.* (ed. 2) Suppl., 'He is safe enough for being hanged.' Cumb. 1852 SMEDLEY *L. Arundel* xxvii. 204 Society had better shut up shop at once, for it's safe to be 'uprooted from its very foundations'. 1860 WHYTE MELVILLE *Mkt. Harb.* 107 He'll win it, as safe as safe! 1865 F. OAKELEY *Hist. Notes* 46 If..you had happened to enter any common-room in Oxford..you would have been safe to hear some ten or twenty voices eloquent on the subject of Tract 90. 1874 WHYTE MELVILLE *Uncle John* viii. I. 225 The foreign horse was safe to win the Two Thousand. 1882 B. M. CROKER *Proper Pride* I. vii. 137, 'I am sure a man never sent it,' said Helen. 'I'm sorry to say it of my own sex, but it's safe to be a woman'. 1894 'J. S. WINTER' *Red Coats* 50 You know the Colonel is as safe as houses to come round after church parade.

†**c.** ? Certain, established as fact, not to be called in question.

1788 PRIESTLEY *Lect. Hist.* I. i. 14 For want of acquaintance with history, we are apt to pronounce *a priori* many things to be impossible, which in fact really exist, and are very safe.

†**13.** quasi-*sb.* ***in safe*** (OF. *en sauf*): in a safe place, in safety. ***with safe***: with safety, safely. *Obs. rare.*

*c*1430 *Pilgr. Lyf Manhode* I. xvii. (1869) 13 þe official turned him, and bar with him þe oynementes, and putte hem in saaf. 1569 PRESTON *Cambises* E 3 b, If I with safe may graunt this deed, I will it not refuse.

14. Special collocations. **safe area**, during the war of 1939–45, an area not liable to be attacked or invaded; **safe deposit** (orig. *U.S.*), a place in which valuables are stored; also *attrib.*; **safe edge,** (*a*) a smooth edge of a file; hence **safe-edge, -edged** *adjs.*; (*b*) *Photogr.* (see quot. 1891); **Safehand, safe(-)hand,** applied *attrib.* and *absol.* to a variety of courier services available for confidential documents; also as *adv.*; **safe hit** *Baseball* (see quot. 1895); **safe house,** a place of refuge or rendezvous for those wanted by the authorities, engaged in spying, etc.; **safe lamp, lantern, light,** †(*a*) a safety-lamp; (*b*) *Photogr.*, a translucent filter for use on a dark-room light, coloured according to the sensitivity of the materials used; also, a lamp that produces such a dim, coloured light; so **safe-lighting** *vbl. sb.*, **-lighted, -lit** *ppl. adjs.*; **safe load,** a load which leaves a required margin of security against causing breakage or injury to a structure (cf. SAFETY 6); **safe period,** the part of the menstrual cycle during which conception is least likely; **safe seat** *Pol.*, a parliamentary seat which is likely to be retained at an election with a large majority; **safe-tray** = SAFE *sb.* 3.

1944 *Ourselves in Wartime* 175 The threat of invasion, and the air-blitz of 1940–1941 over London and the provinces stimulated evacuation afresh... Many thousands of children were removed to *safe areas, and..over 620,000 children were settled in reception areas. 1944 *Daily Tel.* 11 July 2 Married couple wanted. Safe area (Alva, Scotland). 1783 J. HUNTINGTON in Sparks *Corr. Amer. Rev.* (1853) IV. 27 West Point..may be made a *safe deposit where every military article may be kept in good order and repair. 1880 W. NEWTON *Serm. Boys & Girls* (1881) 338, I went down into the vaults of one of our great safe-deposit buildings. 1882 *Century Mag.* Mar. 769/1 They did not ask for the key of the safe-deposit box, or for other evidence. 1886 *Encycl. Brit.* XXI. 145/1 The public safes or safe-deposits erected in most of the great cities of America and in London. 1970 K. ROOS *What did Hattie See?* x. 92 You don't give a dame a key to your safe deposit box. 1846 HOLTZAPFFEL *Turning* etc. II. 821 Some files have one or more edges that are left uncut, and these are known as *safe-edges, because such edges are not liable to act upon those parts of the work against which they are allowed to rub,..The safe-edge file is principally required in making a set-off, or shoulder [etc.]. 1891 *Anthony's Photogr. Bull.* IV. 66 The negative to be printed from, should have an opaque border, called a safe edge, about a quarter of an inch wide made around it. 1884 F. J. BRITTEN *Watch & Clockm.* 230 *Safe Edged File. 1947 LD. MOUNTBATTEN *Let.* 12 June in *India Office Rec.* 1450 GG 43 Coll. I. p. 31 Please follow it up with the letter, which should be sent by *safehand of pilot. 1965 'W. HAGGARD' *Hard Sell* xi. 113 The rumblings from London..had ceased with a Safehand letter from the Minister. 1975 N. LUARD *Robespierre Serial* iv. 16 Delivered safe-hand by courier eight months before, the letter stated briefly that Darley had been approached by an individual who's indicated he might be interested in political asylum. *Ibid.* 17 A second safe-hand letter had arrived. 1867 *Ball Player's Chron.* 6 June 2/3 Flagg afterward made his base by a *safe hit. 1895 G. J. MANSON *Sporting Dict.* 98 *Safe Hits*, this term is applied to high balls sent from the bat with just force enough to carry them over the head of the infields, but not far enough out for the outfielders to catch. 1897 *Encycl. Sport* I. 77/2 Immediately the batsman hits a fair ball, he endeavours to get to first base... He may get there on a safe hit made by the succeeding batsman. 1963 J. JOESTEN *They call it Intelligence* I. iv. 44 A so-called '*safe house'..is usually a piece of extra-territorial property owned by a particular embassy. 1969 H. MACINNES *Salzburg Connection* xv. 212 So that is what it was: a safe house. They could shelter several people here.. while new passports and identities were being faked. 1979 H. KISSINGER *White House Years* xxi. 889 A seedy little apartment in an old brownstone that the CIA had used as a safehouse. 1815 DAVY *Let.* 30 Oct. in Paris *Life* (1831) II. 82, I trust the *Safe lamp will answer all the objects of the collier. 1968 *Gloss. Terms Offset Lithogr. Printing* (*B.S.I.*) 11 *Safelamp*, a lamp providing light of a spectral composition to which a photographic material is relatively or completely insensitive. 1978 *Amateur Photographer* 2 Aug. 131/1 With a 150-watt enlarger lamp, two 25-watt lamps in the safelamps and a 60-watt lamp in the illuminator there is no risk of overload. 1815 DAVY in *Phil. Trans.* CVI. 12 The first *safe lantern that I had constructed, was made of tin-plate, and the light emitted through four glass plates in the sides. 1816 *Ibid.* 23, I have already had the honor of communicating to the Royal Society an account of a *safe light. 1903 A. PAYNE *Pract. Orthochrom. Photogr.* 90 Red sensitive plates..may be used with a safe light. 1932 *Discovery* Sept. 292/1 These infra-red plates are..easy to manipulate in the dark room with a lamp screened by a greenish yellow safe-light filter. 1976 J. MCCLURE *Rogue Eagle* vi. 98 If..he'd had the orange safe-light turned on.. the film would have fogged instantly. 1977 J. HEDGCOE *Photographer's Handbk.* 51 These features make the paper convenient to handle in an orange *safe-lighted darkroom. *Ibid.* 39 Printing papers and films intended for copying black and white originals have this sensitivity, allowing the use of bright orange *safe-lighting. 1979 *Amateur Photographer* 10 Jan. 75/1 Electronic timers are far more accurate than relying on peering at your watch in a *safelit darkroom. 1868 HUMBER *Strains in Girders* 67 Breaking and *Safe Loads for Bridges, Girders, etc. 1908 *Daily Tel.* 30 Jan. 15/4 This particular chain was certified..as being capable of standing a strain of three tons, so that its 'safe' load was 1½ ton. 1918 M. STOPES *Wise Parenthood* iv. 31 Some people..may find the comparative security of a '*safe period' sufficient. 1923 —— *Contraception* ii. 14 The proper form of contraceptive must be one available at *any* time by the pair: and so the 'safe period' often advocated by those who pose as moralists is not satisfactory. 1934 *Jrnl. Amer. Med. Assoc.* 10 Feb. 452/2 The woman determines her 'safe period' on the basis of her shortest cycle, and also of her longest cycle. The overlapping 'safe days' constitute her 'safe period'. **1936** C. G. Hartman *Time of Ovulation in Women* xviii. 183 There is an absolute Safe Period for the monkey female. *Ibid.* xix. 192 Announcement of failures of the Safe Period is a daily occurrence. **1956** A. Huxley *Adonis & Alphabet* 284 In the kind of society which has the most urgent need of birth control, the Safe Period Method is almost useless. **1971** *Petticoat* 17 July 6/3 The safe period should more correctly be known as the safer period. You are less likely to conceive then, but that is all. **1976** *Winter's Crimes 8* 180 The so-called safe period won only limited approval... She couldn't let herself be pregnant. **1891** W. Fraser *Disraeli & his Day* 491 A material element in the future of Constitutional Government is the non-existence of *safe seats. **1939** W. I. Jennings *Parliament* ii. 27 The influence of a great landowner... May Secure nomination by the local Conservative association and so enable the person nominated to acquire a safe seat. **1974** *Times* 13 Feb. 4/6 Redistribution can make a safe seat marginal. **1886** *Encycl. Brit.* XXI. 715/2 Under most plumbing fixtures it is usual to place a *safe-tray to receive any water accidentally spilt. **1912** G. Thomson *Mod. Sanitary Engin.* xvi. 142 When built-up baths were in use, safe trays were an indispensable part of the installation.

15. a. Comb., as †*safe-bestowing*, †*-maker*, †*-making* (where 'safe' is objective); *safe-borne*, *-buttressed*, *-enshrined*, *-going*, *-marching*, *-moored*, *-sequestered*, *-swung* ppl. adjs. (where 'safe' is quasi-adv.).

1575 in Feuillerat *Revels Q. Eliz.* (1908) 254 Putting in order and *safebestowinge of the garmentes. **1896** Kipling *Seven Seas* 38 Average fifteen hunder souls *safe-borne fra' port to port. **1918** G. Frankau *One of Them* xxxii. 249 O Empire thrice and four times blessed by Fate, *Safe-buttressed on ten thousand O.B.E.s! **1926** W. de la Mare *Memory* in Kipling & de la Mare *St. Andrews*, Keeps she for me, then, *safe-enshrined—Cold of the north—those bleached grey streets. **1874** Trollope *Way we live Now* (1875) I. xlvii. 296 In this *safe-going country young men perhaps are not their own masters till they are past thirty. **1643** Trapp *Comm. Gen.* xlix. 10 Others render *Shiloh*, *Tranquillator*, *Salvator*, The *Safe-maker, The Peace-maker. **1579** W. Wilkinson *Confut. Fam. Love* 13 Their ministration is the *safemaking ministration. **1755** J. N. Scott *Ess. Transl. Homer's Wks.* 3 *Safe-marching through the Camp. **1831** Carlyle *Sart. Res.* III. xii, *Safe-moored in some stillest obscurity. **1725** Pope *Odyss.* v. 561 Some smooth ascent, or *safe-sequester'd bay. **1930** R. Campbell *Poems* 17 Safe-sequestered in some rural glen. **1900** Kipling in *Century Mag.* Jan. 407 *Safe-swung above the glassy death.

†**b.** In verbal phrase used subst.: see quot. *Obs.*

c **1640** J. Smyth *Lives Berkeleys* (1883) I. 96 He hath letters of safe come, safe goe, and safe staye for five dayes.

¶ *vouch.. safe, safe vouch*: see VOUCHSAFE.

safe, *v.* [f. SAFE *a.*] †**a.** *trans.* To render safe or secure. Also, to conduct safely *out of*. *Obs.*

1602 Marston *Ant. & Mel.* IV. Hj b, Deare Lord, what means this rage, when lacking vse: Scarce safes your life, will you in armour rise? **1606** Shaks. *Ant. & Cl.* I. iii. 55 My more particular, And that which most with you should safe my going, Is Fuluias death. *Ibid.* IV. vi. 26 Best you saf't the bringer Out of the hoast. *c* **1611** Chapman *Iliad* v. 112 Thus he brau'd, and yet his violent shaft Strooke short with all his violence, Tydides life was saft. *Ibid.* VII. 285 At which we will erect Wals, and a raueling, that may safe, our fleet and vs protect.

b. *intr.* and *trans.* In *Mountaineering*, to belay. Also const. *up*. Hence ˈ**safing** *vbl. sb.*

1940 *Tararua Tramper* July 6 The real uses for alpine work may be divided into three: Step-cutting, 'safing' (by which I mean anchoring or belaying), and control during descent. *a* **1945** E. R. Eddison *Mezentian Gate* (1958) xxxviii. 202, I am sick..of for ever climbing mountains safed with a dozen ropes held by a dozen safe men. **1960** M. Redgrove in *Pick of Today's Short Stories* XI. 194 His mountain-sense stabbed a quick reproach and he dragged his attention back to safing Creade up. **1969** *Word Study* Apr. 6/1 To avoid having any unused explosive going off in the faces of members of the post-recovery team, the capsule must be disarmed or *safed*. **1972** *New Scientist* 14 Dec. 645 'Safing' procedures were now being carried out by the astronauts while Launch Control itself tried to identify the cause of the cut-off. **1974** 'J. le Carré' *Tinker, Tailor* xxv. 215 We tossed them agents we could do without, we gave them good communications, safed their courier links.

safe-conduct (seɪfˈkɒndʌkt), *sb.* Forms: see SAFE *a.* and CONDUCT *sb.*[1] [a. F. *sauf-conduit* (13th c.), f. *sauf* SAFE *a.* + *conduit* CONDUCT *sb.* Cf. Sp., Pg. *salvoconduto*, It. *salvocondotto*, med.L. *salvus conductus*.]

1. The privilege, granted by a sovereign or other competent authority, of being protected from arrest or molestation while making a particular journey or travelling within a certain region. Phrases, *in* or *with safe-conduct*, *under* or *upon (a) safe-conduct*.

1297 R. Glouc. (Rolls) 10226 To vinde him gode borewes, & sauf condut al so. *c* **1325** *Coer de L.* 3617 Ye schole gon in saff coundyte; No man schal do ye despyte. **1338** R. Brunne *Chron.* (1810) 260 In stede of messengeres, saue condite vs gyue, þorgh þi lond to go in þin auowrie, þat non vs robbe ne slo, for þi curteysie. **1390** Gower *Conf.* II. 160 For he anon hem wolde assaile.. His sauf conduit bot if thei hadden. **1412–20** Lydg. *Troy Bk.* I. 935 For þei of pryde, with-outen any leue Or safcondyte, han þe stronde y-take. **1433** *Rolls Parlt.* IV. 475/1 Letters of save condut. *c* **1450** *Merlin* 82 Thei hadde saf condite to returne to Tintagel. **1456** Sir G. Haye *Law Arms* (S.T.S.) 93 Gif a man be tane presonare apon ane otheris sauf condyt. **1470–85** Malory *Arthur* VIII. xxxii. 322 Thenne the Barons sente for syr Tristram vnder a sauf conduyte. *a* **1548** Hall *Chron., Hen. VIII* 34 Then the capitayne sent woorde that with saufeconduyte he would come and speke with the kynges counsayll. **1549** *Compl. Scot.* xiii. 107 Nor scottis men til entir on inglis grond vitht out the kyng of ingland saue conduct. **1568** Grafton *Chron.* II. 254 Graunting to all commers out of every Countrie safe conduyte to come and go. **1577–87** Harrison *England* II. ii. (1877) I. 53 To be short, upon safe-conduct, the bishop commeth to the king's presence. *a* **1578** Lindesay (Pitscottie) *Chron. Scot.* (S.T.S.) I. 83 The Earle gat saif cundit to come throw Ingland. **1677** *Govt. Venice* 238 Sixtus V, and Clement VIII, granted Safe-conduct to the Maranes, to remain, and traffick in the Town of Ancona, without being molested or disturbed by the Inquisitors. **1840** Dickens *Barn. Rudge* lxxi, The task of conveying one female in safety through such scenes as we must encounter..is enough... If you accept the service I tender..she shall be instantly placed in safe conduct. **1879** Froude *Cæsar* iv. 35 He had come over under a safe conduct, and he was not detained. **1887** Rider Haggard *Jess* xxi, A pass..giving you and Miss Jess Croft a safe conduct to Mooifontein.

2. A document by which this privilege is conveyed.

[**1392** *Earl Derby's Exped.* (Camd.) 179/32 Pro scriptura et sigillacione vnius saueconducti Ducis de Stulpez.] ? **1404** Skydmore *Let.* 5 July in Ellis *Orig. Lett.* Ser. II. I. 20 And ther y was and spake with hym [Owen Glendower] upon truys, and prayed of a saufconduyt under his seal to send home my wif and hir moder and thaire mayne. **1473** *Acc. Ld. High Treas. Scot.* (1877) I. 67 Traistand at the said Inglisman had na saulf conduct, and thareftir he schew a conduct. **1523** Skelton *Garl. Laurel* 503 Some shewid his salfecundight, some shewid his charter. **1620** Sir R. Naunton in *Fortescue Papers* (Camden) 115 And humbly praies his Majesties signature to this safe conduct here inclosed. **1766** Blackstone *Comm.* II. 401 Such goods as are brought into this country by an alien enemy..without a safe-conduct or passport. **1849** Macaulay *Hist. Eng.* x. II. 576 Feversham was asked for his safe conduct. He had none. **1875** Stubbs *Const. Hist.* II. xiv. 122 The safe conduct granted them on their departure is dated on the 27th of July.

3. The action of conducting or convoying in safety; safe convoy.

1338 R. Brunne *Chron.* (1810) 80 He praied þam of alle þing.. To haf saf condite, vnto þe New Kastelle. & Hugh did as he hight, led þam sauely welle. **1529** *Household Bk. Hen. VIII* in *Trevelyan Papers* (Camden) 152 For the costes of him and such other with him, as attended upon the salve conduct of the said moneye. **1577** E. Hogan in *Hakluyt's Voy.* (1589) 156 For my safe conduite to the Court he had sent foure captaines. **1652** Needham tr. *Selden's Mare Cl.* 481 And give them such safe Conduct and Convoie, as they shall reasonably require.

4. *fig.*

1426 Lydg. *De Guil. Pilgr.* 112 Vn-to synnerys, that deye repentaunt, To yive pardon off hys benynge graunt, [The] Wych ys to hem, vn-to ther refut, Proteccyon and true sauff-conduit, Hem to save, that thay be nat lorn. **1526** *Pilgr. Perf.* (W. de W. 1531) 5 b, In heuynesse, feblenes, and trouble of ennemyes, it is our conforte, our strengthe, saueconducte and peace. **1551** T. Wilson *Logike* (1580) A 3 b, This worke maie not at the first enteraunce, haue the saufe conducte and protection of your most noble roiall Maiestie. **1574** Hellowes *Gueuara's Fam. Ep.* 267 Being as we are fallen into the most grievous sinnes, we do live, and go so contented, as though we had received of God a safeconduit to be saved. **1625** tr. *Gonsalvio's Sp. Inquis.* 146 God vnder his mighty protection, and by his owne safe-conduct, brought that holy burthen thither. **1872** Lowell *Wks.* (1890) IV. 102 A great controlling reason in whose safe-conduct we trust implicitly.

†**safe-conduct**, *v. Obs.* [f. prec. sb.] *trans.* To lead, convoy, or conduct safely.

In verse stressed *safe-'conduct* as well as *safe-con'duct*.

1564 Jenkinson in *Hakluyt's Voy.* (1599) I. 346 That he would..giue me..men to safeconduct me vnto the sayd Sophy. **1567** Drant *Hor. Ep.* I. vii. D iij, If he maye be safeconducted and welcum to thy grace. **1590** Marlowe *1st Pt. Tamburl.* I. ii, Bearing his priuie signet and his hand To safe conduct vs thorow Africa. *a* **1600** (?) Hooker *Serm. Jude* ii. §22 He indeed was able to Safe-Conduct a Theefe from the Crosse to Paradise. **1600** Fairfax *Tasso* VI. xiii. 96 This Sword (I trust) shall well safeconduct mee. **1639** Ainsworth *Pentateuch* Contents 2 This Second Booke of Moses sheweth.. the bringing out of Israel..the safe-conducting of them in the Wildernesse.

safe-guard (ˈseɪfgɑːd), *sb.* For forms see SAFE *a.* and GUARD *sb.* See also SAGGAR, SEGGARD. [ME. *savegarde* (*sauf-*, *safe-*, etc.), a. F. *sauvegarde* (13th c. in Hatz.-Darm.), f. *sauve* fem. of *sauf* SAFE + *garde* GUARD *sb.* Cf. It., Sp. *salvaguardia*, Pg. *salvaguarda*, med.L. *salvagardia*.]

1. Protection, safety. Now *rare* or *Obs.* (see b).

1421 *Rolls of Parlt.* IV. 159/2 The pore Soudeors..have truly served the sauf garde of the forsaid Town. *c* **1470** Henry *Wallace* IV. 652 Saiffgarde he gat wndir a bowand tre. **1513** More *Rich. III* (1641) 450 King Richard, as the fame went, might have escaped and gotten safegard by flying. *a* **1548** Hall *Chron., Hen. IV* 8 b, Besechyng the Duke to grant to him the safegarde of his lyfe. **1555** Eden *Decades* 6 To the which they flye for safegarde if any man resorte vnto them. **1572** *Reg. Privy Council Scot.* Ser. I. II. 132 That na men..tak upoun thame the saulfgaird and protectioun of ony knawin inymeis or convoy..to thame.. ony gudis. **1598** Barckley *Felic. Man* II. (1603) 89 Preferring the savegard of his people before his owne life. **1632** Lithgow *Trav.* III. 83 A place of safeguard, called commonly the Monastery of refuge. **1634** Sir T. Herbert *Trav.* 200 The women [of Sumatra] are for courage, Amazonian, and of such account with their tyrannique Lords, that the safeguard of their bodies are committed sometimes to their care. **1736** Ainsworth *Lat. Dict.* s.v. *Attribute*, He attributeth to me the safe guard of the whole empire.

b. *for (the) safeguard of* (now *arch.*), † *to (the) safeguard of*, † *in safeguard of*: for the defence or protection of, in order to the safety of. Formerly freq. in phr. *for safeguard of one's life*.

[**1347** *Rolls of Parlt.* II. 194/1 Pur salve garde de la pees.] **1433** *Ibid.* IV. 445/1 To walle,..and fortefie, youre seid Towne and Havyn, sufficiently..for the saufgarde of alle Marchaundises and other Goodes thedir comynge. **1440** in Slew *Hist. Walsall* (1856) 107 For the more suertye and saufgard of the tresour and euydence of that Gylde. **1467** in *Eng. Gilds* (1870) 398 For savegarde of the kynges cite. *c* **1500** *Melusine* 17 And there the lady Pressyne stablysshed a strong geaunt to the sauegarde of the tresoure. **1519** *Mem. Ripon* (Surtees) I. 315 For savegard of my lyf and for savegard of my body. **1536** in W. H. Turner *Select. Rec. Oxford* (1880) 139 For safeguard of his life he was fayne to leape from ye bridge. **1538** Bale *Thre Lawes* 2039 To sauegarde of the iust & synners ponnyshment. **1571–2** in Swayne *Sarum Churchw. Acc.* (1896) 285 Boxes for the belles ropes to run in for savegard of the ropes. **1585** T. Washington tr. *Nicholay's Voy.* II. x. 43 b, The streit of Hellespont, for the safegard wherof there are 2. strong castles. **1594** Shaks. *Rich. III*, v. iii. 259 If you do fight in safegard of your wiues. **1620** J. Wilkinson *Coroners & Sherifes* 13 A. flyeth as much as he can for safeguard of his life. *a* **1625** Sir H. Finch *Law* (1636) 39 To rase ones house on fire, in safegard of the neighbours houses. **1669** Mrs. Alice Thornton *Autobiog.* (Surtees) 18 But the king, being constrained for the saveguard of his owne life, passed that fatall bill. **1727** Threlkeld *Stirpes Hibernicæ* Pref. 23 He was for the Safeguard of his Life compelled in his Age, to fly into High Germany. **1848** Arnould *Mar. Insur.* I. viii. I. 197 [Form of policy], To make every exertion in their power 'for the defence, safeguard, and recovery' of the property.

†**c.** *in safeguard*, in safety or security. *Obs.*

c **1440** *Brut* (E.E.T.S.) 468 Forto kepe the towne in saufgarde from oure enemys. **1472–3** *Rolls of Parlt.* VI. 5/2 The seid sommes of money..to be put in sauf gard. **1553** Eden *Treat. Newe Ind.* (Arb.) 30 Fortresses where his men might lye in safegarde. **1611** Bible *1 Sam.* xxii. 23 With me thou shalt bee in safegard. **1642** J. M[arsh] *Argt. conc. Militia* 4 The King ought to provide that his Subjects have their passage throughout the Realme by all high wayes in safeguard.

†**d.** Custody or safe-keeping. *Obs.*

1528 Roy *Rede me* (Arb.) 112 They put men in soche savegarde That with in a whyle afterwarde They be sure to go no forther. **1817** Sir F. Burdett in *Parl. Debates* 1693 The safeguard of the prisoners had originally belonged to the sheriff.

2. Protection or security afforded by a specified person (or thing). Phr. *in* or *under (the) safe-guard of*. Now *rare* or *Obs.*

1456 Sir G. Haye *Law Arms* (S.T.S.) 238 Thay ar all in the protectioun and salvegarde of the pape. **1484** Caxton *Æsop* II. ii. (1889) 34 Who that..submytteth hym self vnder the saue gard or protection of the euylle. *c* **1490** *Paston Lett.* III. 366 Our Lord..have you in His blissid saufegard. **1561** T. Norton *Calvin's Inst.* II. 136 Whome he..had receiued into his sauegard, custodie, and protection. **1600** Holland *Livy* XXXI. xxvii. 789 To commit themselves under the protection and savegard of the Romanes. **1632** Lithgow *Trav.* III. 84, I detained my selfe vnder safe-guard of the Cloyster. **1657** *Whole Duty of Man* v. §14 (1660) 117 [We] therefore should tremble to venture on the perils either of day or night without his safeguard. **1732** Lediard *Sethos* II. VII. 125 Under the safeguard of the colony of their nation.

†**b.** *to stand upon one's safeguard*: to stand on the defensive, to defend one's self. *Obs.*

1609 Bp. W. Barlow *Answ. Nameless Cath.* 236 If any Prince were euer forced to stand vpon his safe-guard, and fence himselfe with Lawes.

†**3.** Guarantee of safety or safe passage given by a person in authority; safe-conduct. *on safeguard*, on the strength of such guarantee. *Obs.*

c **1374** Chaucer *Troilus* IV. 111 (139) And whan Priam his saue garde sente Thembassadours to troie streught wente. *c* **1420** ? Lydg. *Assembly of Gods* 118 For where as I my sauegard grauntyd, Ay in that cost he comonly hauntyd. **1433** *Rolls of Parlt.* IV. 475/2 Letters of save conduct and save gard. **1526** in *10th Rep. Hist. MSS. Comm.* App. v. 402 If anny man..will convey him oute of the town under any Irishman [h]is salfe garde or winges. *a* **1568** Ascham *Scholem.* II. (Arb.) 154 He tooke his penne and wrote his warrant of sauegard with these most goodlie wordes, *Viuat Varro vir doctissimus*. **1594** West *2nd Pt. Symbol.* §45 For the ease, savegard, and passage of the inhabitants of the said townes, villages [etc.]. **1594** R. Ashley tr. *Loys le Roy* 81 Crassus..was slaine as he parlied on safe-guard. **1607** Shaks. *Cor.* III. i. 9 On safegard he came to me.

†**b.** *Law.* (See quot.) *Obs.*

1670 Blount *Law Dict.*, *Safe-guard*. See *Salva-guardia*. *Salva Guardia*, is a Protection given by the King to a stranger, fearing the violence of some of his Subjects, for seeking His Right by course of Law.

4. A permit for safe passage: = SAFE-CONDUCT 2. Also, a guard or escort granted for the same purpose.

1633 T. Stafford *Pac. Hib.* I. xi. 72 Whereupon second Letters together with a safe guard were dispatched unto him. **1642** *Laws of War Army Earl Essex* A 4 b, Whosoever shall presume to violate a Save-guard, shall die without mercy. *a* **1674** Clarendon *Hist. Reb.* VIII. §199 So a trumpet was sent to the earl of Essex for a safe guard or pass to those two lords. **1687** T. Brown *Saints in Uproar* Wks. 1730 I. 79 Without a farthing of money in your pockets, guides to conduct you or safeguards to protect you. **1688** *Lond. Gaz.* No. 2380/3 They..have need, for themselves and 100 Persons, of Passports and Safeguards to be sent from your Army. **1860** Woolsey *Introd. Internat. Law* § 147 (1875) 183 Passports and safeguards, or safe-conducts, are letters of protection, with or without an escort, by which the person of an enemy is rendered inviolable. **1861** W. H. Russell in *Times* 6 June, I am obliged to see all that can be seen of the South at once, and then, armed with such safeguards as I can procure, to make an effort to recover my communications.

5. A warrant granted by a military commander to protect a place from pillage. Also, a guard or detachment of soldiers sent to protect the place.
1706 PHILLIPS (ed. Kersey), *Safe-Guard*, In Military Affairs, a Protection given by a Prince or his General, to some of the Enemy's Country, to be secur'd from being ravag'd by his Men or quartering them; also Soldiers left in such Places for that Purpose. **1707** *Lond. Gaz.* No. 4377/2 The Princess was there, and had.. Safe-guards granted her for the Protection of the Place.

†**6.** A picket or outpost of soldiers. *Obs.*
1677 *Lond. Gaz.* No. 1238/4 The Mareschal d'Humieres has called in all his Safe-guards, and caused the Bridges on the Canal to be taken up. **1707** LUTTRELL *Brief Rel.* (1857) VI. 195 Vendosm has called in all the safeguards round his camp.

7. *gen.* Something that offers security from danger; a defence, protection. Now chiefly in immaterial applications: e.g. a legal proviso or a stipulation serving to prevent some encroachment; a course of action, a habit or sentiment, tending to protect the subject against some temptation; or the like. (The chief current sense.)
1471 RIPLEY *Comp. Alch., Ep. to Edw. IV* in Ashm. (1652) 109 O Honorable Lord,.. The savegard of England, & maynteyner of right. **1513** MORE *Rich. III*, Wks. 47 That sacred Sainctuary, that hath bene the safegarde of so many a good mannes life. **1523** FITZHERB. *Husb.* §18 This maner of foldynge.. shall be a greate sauegarde to the shepe for rottynge. **1573** G. HARVEY *Letter-bk.* (Camden) 32 Whitch saiing I.. do now recount a soverain save gard against all incumbrancis. **1584** R. NORMAN (*title*) The safe-gard of Sailers, or great Rutter. **1610** HOLLAND *Camden's Brit.* (1637) 701 [York] a singular safeguard and ornament both, to all the North parts. **1634** SIR T. HERBERT *Trav.* 88 His owne valour was his safeguard. **1776** GIBBON *Decl. & F.* xii. (1782) I. 393 Their poverty indeed became an additional safeguard to their innocence. **1849** MACAULAY *Hist. Eng.* i. I. 43 No new safeguards for public liberty were devised. **1868** FREEMAN *Norm. Conq.* (1877) II. ix. 425 There was a still further reason for placing some special safeguard on that border. **1874** L. STEPHEN *Hours in Library* (1892) I. vii. 251 Admirable skill of expression is.. no real safeguard against logical blunders. **1891** *Law Times* XC. 419/2 The old reticence of the Bench was a grand safeguard of its dignity.

†**8.** An outer skirt or petticoat worn by women to protect their dress when riding. (See also quot. 1706.) Also SEGGARD. *Obs.*
1585 HIGINS *Junius' Nomencl.* 167 *Limus*,.. a kind of aray or attire reaching from the nauill downe to the feete, by this description like a womans safegard, or a bakers. **1588** in Nichols *Progr. Q. Eliz.* (1823) III. 3 A safegard with a jhup or gaskyn coate of faire cullored satten. **1590** *Lanc. Wills* (Chetham Soc.) II. 23 My cloake and savegarde. **1608** *Merry Devil of Edmonton* I. i. (Stage Direct.), The gentlewomen in cloakes and safeguardes. **1611** MIDDLETON & DEKKER *Roaring Girl* II. i. D 1, Enter Mol in a freese Ierkin and a blacke sauegard. **1706** PHILLIPS (ed. Kersey) s.v., There is also a kind of Dust-gown, or upper Garment worn by Women, commonly called a *Safe-Guard*; also a coloured Stuff-Apron, and a sort of Swathing-Band for a young Child. **1789** *Append. Chron.* in *Ann. Reg.* 264 Habited in loose white gowns, with nankeen safeguards.

b. Similarly *attrib.* (see quot.).
1822 *Blackw. Mag.* XII. 69 With a safe-guard handkerchief, enveloping her turban.

†**9.** Alleged term for a 'company' of porters.
1486 *Bk. St. Albans* f vij, A Safegarde of Porteris.

10. A name for various technical contrivances for ensuring safety.
1818 *Sporting Mag.* III. 83 Purdey's Patent Safeguard, to prevent the accidental discharge of guns. **1875** KNIGHT *Dict. Mech., Safeguard* 1, *a.* A *rail-guard* at a switch or crossing. *b.* A contrivance attached to a locomotive for throwing stones and other obstructions off the track.

11. A name for the monitor lizards of America.
[After F. *sauvegarde*; for the origin of the appellation cf. MONITOR *sb.* 5. Shaw *Zool.* III. 215 (1802) gives the equivalent Sp. *salvaguarda* as the South American name.]
1831 CRAIGIE *Anat.* 160 The American safeguard. **1841** *Penny Cycl.* XX. 469–70. **1847–9** *Todd's Cycl. Anat.* IV. 288/1 Safe-guards (*Tejus*).

safeguard (ˈseɪfgɑːd), *v.* [f. prec. sb. Cf. F. *sauvegarder*, which Littré and Hatz.-Darm. call a 'néologisme'.] **a.** *trans.* To keep secure from danger or attack; to guard, protect, defend. Now chiefly with immaterial obj. (e.g. interests, rights).
1494 FABYAN *Chron.* II. xxix. 21 Brenne.. was fayne to Sauegard hymselfe by flyght. **1501** *Surtees Misc.* (1888) 51 Suche thyng as may safegard hym yt is born in England that he shall not be suspect for a Skott. **1561** *Godly Q. Hester* (1873) 17 The Quene muste sauegarde all the hole prouince. **1594** R. ASHLEY tr. *Loys le Roy* 111 b, Building in their countries fortresses thereby to safegard the trafficke of the East. **1616** SURFL. & MARKH. *Country Farm* 64 Heat doth safegard and thicken the Milke. **1617** HIERON *Wks.* (1619–20) II. 393 The walls of Iericho could not save-gard it from the invasion of Joshua. **1619** W. SCLATER *Exp. 1 Thess.* (1630) 551 By auoiding ill shewes, we safe-gard our fame. **1634** SIR T. HERBERT *Trav.* 169 The coast is safeguarded from sand and stealth by a defensive wall. **1675** BROOKS *Gold. Key* Wks. 1867 V. 489 This angel secured and safeguarded them all the way through the wilderness. **1865** *Times* 23 Jan. 9/5, I am very thankful that their [my decisions'] correctness is safeguarded. **1887** *Standard* 13 May 5/3 A compromise calculated to safeguard French interests. **1889** *Edin. Rev.* Oct. 329 Nor could the troops be safeguarded against a surprise.

†**b.** To send or conduct in safety. *Obs.*
1606 G. W[OODCOCKE] *Hist. Justine* xv. 63 b, Demetrius.. safegarded home into Egipt, Leuticke Ptolomies son, and Menelaus his brother ransomelesse. **1634** SIR T. HERBERT *Trav.* 31 With his Army to safegard him to the Kings Metropolis.

c. To 'protect' (a native manufacture or industry) against foreign imports.
1903 *Daily Mail Year Bk.* 149/1 *Protection* is the name given to the system of safe-guarding from foreign competition, native industries by the imposition.. of duties. **1926** *Encycl. Brit.* III. 445/2 (*heading*) Four classes of goods safeguarded. **1928** *Manch. Guardian Weekly* 10 Aug. 105/1 By appointing a Royal Commission to inquire into the expediency of safeguarding the iron and steel industries. **1929** *Morning Post* 5 Feb. 14/4 Safe-guarding Wool.

Hence ˈ**safeguarding** *vbl. sb.* (also *attrib.*) and *ppl. a.* Also ˈ**safeguarder**.
a **1513** FABYAN *Chron.* VII. 429 Wherfore in safe-gardynge of hym selfe, he fled with a small companye to warde Walys. **1534** MORE *Comf. agst. Trib.* II. x. (1553) G v b, My strength and my prayse is our Lorde, he hathe bene my safegarder. **1621** USSHER *Serm.* 5 The Watchmen.. who were appoynted for the safegarding of the Church. **1658** OWEN *Temptation* viii. 152 We are arrived then to the summe of this safeguarding Duty. **1862** J. SEVERN in *Atlantic Monthly* LXIX. 636 The French troops.. have been ordered to concentrate here at once, for the safeguarding of the Eternal City. **1921** *Act 11 & 12 Geo. V* c. 47 Part 1, Safeguarding of Key Industries. **1925** *Times* 10 Feb. 12/4 The idea of introducing a general Safeguarding of Industry Bill has been abandoned. **1926** H. BELL in F. W. Hirst *Safeguarding* p. vi, Protection is no longer called 'Tariff Reform'. It is called 'Safeguarding of Industries' or 'Buy British Goods' or 'Merchandise Marks'. **1932** G. D. H. COLE *Brit. Trade & Industry* 366 The McKenna and Safeguarding duties.

safeguardance (ˈseɪfˌgɑːdəns). *rare.* [f. SAFEGUARD *v.* + -ANCE.] Safeguarding, protection.
1908 HARDY *Dynasts* III. v. v. 213 To all eyes it is imperative That some mode of safeguardance be devised.

safe-hold. [f. HOLD *sb.*[1]: cf. *stronghold.*] A place of safety from attack.
1793 ANNA SEWARD *Lett.* (1811) III. 332 That misleading enthusiasm which led her.. far from the safe-holds of her native country. **1828–40** TYTLER *Hist. Scot.* (1864) II. 304 The chamberlain.. commenced the war by.. securing the strong tower of Blacater... To this safehold the queen.. now resolved to retire. **1843** BROWNING *Ret. Druses* III. Poems (1905) 238/1 From this safehold of mine Where but ten thousand Druses seek my life.

safekeep, *v. rare.* [Back-formation f. SAFEKEEPING *vbl. sb.*] *trans.* To keep safe, protect.
1966 *Anchor Bible* XVI. *Psalms* i. 6 But Yahweh shall safekeep the assembly of the just, While the assembly of the wicked shall perish. **1972** *Harper's Mag.* Oct. 80 Banking on Dictys to safekeep her, I'd set out for Samos.. to learn about life from 'art'.

safe-keeper. *rare*[−1]. [cf. next.] A protector.
1561 T. NORTON *Calvin's Inst.* I. Pref. 2 b, She assuredly trusteth that he is her safekeper and defender.

safe-keeping, *vbl. sb.* The action of keeping safe; protection, preservation; custody.
1432 *Rolls of Parlt.* IV. 390/1 For the safe kepyng of the See. **1587** in Feuillerat *Revels Q. Eliz.* (1908) 378 The Arringes, brushinges & salffe kepinge of the robes. **1721** STRYPE *Eccl. Mem.* III. xiii. 123 A number of people were in boats to see her.. heavy for her trouble, seeing her go under safe-keeping. **1884** *Manch. Exam.* 1 Dec. 5/1 He was willing to pay for the safe-keeping of his wife in Dr. W.'s asylum.

safely (ˈseɪflɪ), *adv.* Forms: 3–4 sauveli, 3–5 saveliche, 4–5 -lich, -lych(e, -like, (*compar.* saveloker, -lokr), 4–5 salvely, 4–6 savely, (5–6 -lye, 6 -lie); 3–5 saufli, 4–5 saufliche, -lych(e, -like, sauffly, sawf(f)ly, 4–6 saufly, 6 saulfly(e, saulfely; 3–6 safly, 4–5 safliche, saff(e)ly, salfly, 6 saf(f)eli, *Sc.* saifly, 5– safely. [f. SAFE *a.* + -LY[2].] In a safe manner.

1. Without harm or injury occasioned or received. Often with verbs of *coming*, *going*, *keeping*, and the like, where the adj. might be used (see SAFE *a.* 1).
a **1300** *Cursor M.* 4944 Lede þam saueli [*Gött.* safly, *Fairf.* sauely] to þair land. *c* **1330** R. BRUNNE *Chron. Wace* (Rolls) 6622 Sauelike held þey þer castels & touns. **1375** BARBOUR *Bruce* III. 359 The queyn.. sawffly come to the castell. **1418** *E.E. Wills* (1882) 44 And also that it be put in a bagge, & asselid, and safly kepid. *c* **1440** *Generydes* 6456 Ye shall savely come and savely goo. **1456** SIR G. HAYE *Law Arms* (S.T.S.) 178 How suld thai be callit sauf condytis, bot gif thai condyte thair maisteris saufly and surely? **1529** CROMWELL *Will* in Merriman *Life & Lett.* (1902) I. 58 All the which parcelles of plate and houseold stuf I will shalbe savelye kept to thuse of my saide Soonne Gregorye. *a* **1533** LD. BERNERS *Huon* xxi. 58 They aryuyd sauely at the port of Jaffe. **1613** SHAKS. *Hen. VIII*, v. i. 70 God safely quit her of her Burthen. **1635** HAKEWILL *Apol.* v–vi. 116 The earth being safely delivered from that inundation. **1765** WARBURTON in *W. & Hurd's Lett.* (1809) 365, I hope this will find you safely returned. **1853** MISS YONGE *Heir of Redclyffe* xliii, They were safely at home again the same evening. **1859** CLOUGH *Poems*, etc. (1869) I. 239 Your article.. came safely to hand. **1868** THIRLWALL *Lett.* (1881) II. 169, I send the Contemporary Review by this post. Pray let me know that it has reached you safely. **1891** *Law Times* XC. 461/2 She was in the train, lawfully.., and therefore a duty was cast upon the company of carrying her safely.

2. In a manner free from danger or hazard; securely, without risk.
1297 R. GLOUC. (Rolls) I. 347 (Harl. MS.) ȝe mowe sauflyche þet holy þyng as he dude auonge. *a* **1300** *Cursor M.* 686 Be-tuix þe wolues lai þe schepe, Saueli [*Gött.* saufli, *Fairf.* sauely] moght þai sam slepe. **1390** GOWER *Conf.* II. 248 And thanne he may saufliche ynowh His Oxen yoke into the plowh. *c* **1400** *Rowland & O.* 1362 Ther myghte no wapen his medys ryfe, So Savely was he dighte. **1597** HOOKER *Eccl. Pol.* v. lxvii. §12 Are we not hereby.. admonished which wee may safeliest cleaue vnto? **1697** DRYDEN *Virg. Georg.* III. 837 Nor safely cou'd they shear the fleecy Store. **1751** JOHNSON *Rambler* No. 162 ¶4 No man can safely do that by others, which might be done by himself. **1849** MACAULAY *Hist. Eng.* vii. II. 205 He could not safely venture to outrage all his Protestant subjects at once. **1884** *Manch. Exam.* 29 May 4/7 The demand for advances will exceed.. the sum which the State can safely or conveniently lend.

b. Without risk of error.
c **1350** *Will. Palerne* 3051 But saufly þis may [i] seye & þe soþe proue. *c* **1386** CHAUCER *Frankl. T.* 33 For o thinge, sires, saufly dar I seie. **1390** GOWER *Conf.* I. 308 Bot I dar saufly make an oth, Mi ladi was me nevere loth. **1573** T. CARTWRIGHT *Reply to Whitgift's Answ.* 17 Howe can we doe safelyer then to follow the Apostles customes? **1647** GREAVES *Roman Foot* 103 Therefore wee may the safelier give credit to them. **1710** ADDISON *Tatler* No. 250 ¶1, I can safely say, I acted according to the best of my Understanding. **1825** COLERIDGE *Aids Refl.* (1848) I. 26 Such a one (safeliest spoken of by the neuter pronoun). **1875** T. W. HIGGINSON *Hist. U.S.* xxxii. 328 We can safely assume something more than this.

†**3.** In safe confinement or custody. *Obs.*
c **1420** *Brut* 429 All his prisoneris weren.. brought into the Toure of London, to kepe hem there-ynne saufly. **1505** *Mem. Hen. VII* (Rolls) 268 That he shuld resayve and savely kepe the said rebell. **1601** SHAKS. *All's Well* IV. i. 104 Ile keepe him darke and safely lockt. **1611** BIBLE *Acts* xvi. 23 Charging the Iaylour to keepe them safely.

†**4.** With confidence or assurance. *Obs.*
1609 BIBLE (Douay) *2 Kings* xvi. Comm., King David was here abused by false information: to which he ought not so safely to have geven credite. **1674** CAMPION *Art of Descant* 38 Doing that safely and resolutely which others attempt timorously and uncertainly.

safener (ˈseɪfnə(r), -fənə(r)). [f. SAFE *a.* + -EN[5] + -ER[1].] A substance that reduces the harmfulness to plants of other substances, esp. one in an insecticide or fungicide.
1942 *Industr. & Engin. Chem.* Apr. 498/1 The principal use of zinc as a spray is for the control of peach bacterial spot and as a 'safener' for arsenate of lead sprays on peach. **1950** J. C. WALKER *Plant Path.* xvi. 647 Glyceride oils are.. good safeners for copper sprays. **1975** *Big Farm Managem.* June 61/2 George Moore considers Eradicane to be the important herbicide for the British market at present. This is the chemical which as a built-in 'safener' which protects maize from the herbicide which would otherwise kill it.

safeness (ˈseɪfnɪs). [-NESS.] The quality or state of being safe (in various senses).
a **1375** *Cursor M.* 18742 (Fairf.) þe toþer [man] vs come fra heyuen toure þat broȝt us sauenes & socoure. *c* **1440** *Promp. Parv.* 440/2 Saafnesse, or salvacyon, *salvacio*. **1530** PALSGR. 265/2 Safenesse, *saueté*. **1607** MARKHAM *Caval.* I. (1617) 69 Besides the safenesse and no danger in the cure. **1610** HOLLAND *Camden's Brit.* (1637) 651 Neither is this Haven famous for the secure safeness thereof. **1639** FULLER *Holy War* III. xiii. (1640) 130 The nearnesse of the way is to be measured not by the shortnesse but the safenesse of it. **1685** BAXTER *Paraphr. N.T.* 2 Tim. ii. 3 The Life of a Minister or Bishop is not a Life of Ease, and Idleness, and Safeness. **1688** SOUTH *Serm.* xii. (1697) I. 546 If a Man should forbear his Food,.. till he had Science and Certainty of the Safeness of what he was going about, he must starve, and die Disputing. **1889** *Spectator* 28 Dec., He must be, first of all, a man of sure judgment, or the public will not trust him long, they discerning the quality we call 'safeness' clearly enough.

safer, obs. form of SAVIOUR, SAVOUR.

safer *Sc.* = *so far* adv.: see SO *adv.* and *conj.*

safer(e, saferay, obs. ff. SAPPHIRE, SAVORY.

saferen, -erne, -ero(u)n, obs. ff. SAFFRON.

safety (ˈseɪftɪ). Forms: 3–4 **sauvete, savte,** 4–5 **savetee, sawete, savite, -yte,** 4–6 **savete,** 5 **salvetee,** 6 **savity, salvetie;** 4–5 **safte(e, sawfte,** (5 **saefte),** 4–6 **saufte,** 5 *Sc.* **saifte,** 6 **safitie, safetye, saulftie, saulfty(e, saufftye, sauftie, salf(e)ty,** *Sc.* **saiftie,** 6–7 **safetie, saftie,** 7 **safty,** 6– **safety.** [a. F. *sauveté* (11th c. *salvetet*), ad. med.L. *salvitāt-em*, f. *salv-us* SAFE. Cf. Pr. *salvetat*, *saubetat*, Sp. *salvedad*.]
Scanned by Spenser (and in Shaks. *Ham.* I. iii. 21 Qq.) as a trisyllable.

1. a. The state of being safe; exemption from hurt or injury; freedom from danger. Phr. ***in safety***.
Committee of Safety: a body of 23 members appointed in Oct. 1659 by the parliamentary army to conduct the government of England during the interregnum following the practical deposition of Richard Cromwell.
13.. *E.E. Allit. P.* B. 489 þat was þe syngne of sauyte þat sende hem oure lorde. **1375** BARBOUR *Bruce* III. 183 And he eftyr his mengȝe raid; And in-till saufte thaim led. *c* **1380** *Sir Ferumb.* 3410 þay buþ in sauete. *c* **1450** *Merlin* xvii. 272 The lorde of palerne.. shall lede the pray to saftee. **1539** BIBLE (Great) *Ps.* iv. 8 For it is thou Lorde onely, that makest me dwell in safetye. **1590** SPENSER *F.Q.* II. xii. 17 Here now behoueth vs well to auyse, And of our safetie good heede to take. **1611** BIBLE *Prov.* xi. 14 In the multitude of counsellers there is safetie. **1617** MORYSON *Itin.* I. 243 Merchants, passengers and drivers of loaded Camels, keeping together for safety against theeves. **1651** HOBBES *Leviath.* II. xvii. 87 In those things which concerne the Common Peace and Safetie. **1659** WHITELOCKE *Mem.* (1853) IV. 367. **1697** DRYDEN *Virg. Georg.* IV. 697 All Dangers past, at length the

lovely Bride In safety goes, with her Melodious Guide. **1771** *Junius Lett.* lxii. (1820) 322 It is..his duty..not to hazard the safety of the Community. **1856** C. J. ANDERSSON *Lake Ngami* 9, I arrived late in the evening at our hotel, where they had begun to entertain some doubt of my safety. **1860** TYNDALL *Glac.* I. vii. 48 The least presence of mind would be sufficient to place him in safety.

Proverb. **1816** JANE AUSTEN *Emma* II. i. 2 She determined to call upon them and seek safety in numbers. **1886** C. M. YONGE *Chantry House* II. xii. 112 They all came creeping down after her, feeling safety in numbers. **1914** T. DREISER *Titan* xvii. 140 Perhaps he was beginning to run around with other women. There was safety in numbers—that she knew. **1941** E. HOWIE *Murder for Christmas* xi. 135 The old adage—there's safety in numbers—may very well apply here. **1973** 'S. WOODS' *Yet she must Die* 115 'Lydia was flirtatious. But nobody took that seriously, least of all the men concerned.' 'Safety in numbers, in fact.'

†**b.** Salvation (of the soul). *Obs.*

a **1300** *Cursor M.* 13093 Yee ask him if he be þat gom þat for man sauuete suld com. *c* **1375** *Sc. Leg. Saints* xxii. (*Laurentius*) 376 Lord Ihesu, þat dengnit þe fore oure sawfte to mane be. *c* **1400** *Rom. Rose* 6869 For her soules savetee. **1675** M. CLIFFORD *Hum. Reason* 32 Those whose Ignorance in these matters has been invincible, they left to the hands of God, without declaring a definitive Opinion either of their safety or perdition.

†**c.** ***with (the) safety of***: without damage to, preserving..unhurt. *Obs.*

1619 in *Eng. & Germ.* (Camden) 10 The King my master professeth he could neither with the saftie of his honor or conscience leave them to be consumed by the sword. **1633** MARMION *Antiquary* III. i. (1641) E4b, I am..a kinde of lawlesse Justicer,..that will kill any man with my safety. **1640** SHIRLEY *St. Patrick* III. ii, That I with safetie of thy sence, Emeria, Might visit thee.

†**d.** Sometimes *pl.* = the safety of more than one person. (In quot. 1605 ? = occasions of safety.)

1605 SHAKS. *Macb.* IV. iii. 30 Let not my Iealousies be your Dishonors, But mine owne Safeties. **16..** *Chevy Chase* i. (Percy MS.), God prosper long our noble king, our liffes and saftyes all! **1686** PLOT *Staffordsh.* 439 To attend his or their own safeties, every one at his peril. *a* **1774** GOLDSM. tr. *Scarron's Com. Rom.* (1775) II. 55 But still a more predominant regard to their safeties, obliged him to spend all his time in spurring..his own and his mistress's beast. **1814** SCOTT *Ld. of Isles* III. xxviii, To Allan's eyes was harder task, The weary watch their safeties ask.

†**e.** Phr. ***to be safety*** = to be safe (*for*). *Obs.*

1596 SPENSER *State Irel.* Wks. (Globe) 623/1 The Irish were not ameanable to lawe, soe as it was not safetye for the townesemen to goe to them foorth to demaund theyr dett.

†**f.** A deliverance or rescue from peril. *Obs. rare.*

1657 HEYLIN *Eccl. Vind.* II. i. §10. 111 Noah..offered unto God the sacrifice of thanksgiving..for so miraculous a safety.

g. *Billiards.* See quot. 1884. Also *attrib.* ***to play for safety***: see PLAY *v.* 18 f.

1857 M. PHELAN *Game of Billiards* (ed. 2) iv. 65 Playing for safety.—When you forego a possible advantage, in order to leave the balls in such a position that your opponent can make nothing out of them. **1873** BENNETT *Billiards* 386 It is, of course, a matter of judgment, when to play for a score, and when to play for safety. **1884** W. COOK *Billiards* 12 When a player, instead of playing to score, plays to leave some position in which his opponent will be unable to score in his next stroke, he is said to play for safety. **1897** *Westm. Gaz.* 18 Feb. 9/1 By some judicious safety play [he] succeeded in reaching his points without allowing his opponent to improve his position.

†**2.** Close custody or confinement. *Obs.*

1338 R. BRUNNE *Chron.* (1810) 236 þe mayden Edward toke, als he was fulle curteys, In saufte did hir loke. **1592** SHAKS. *Rom. & Jul.* v. iii. 183 Hold him in safety, till the Prince come hither. **1595** —— *John* IV. ii. 158 Away with him! imprison him;..Deliuer him to safety.

†**3.** A means or instrument of safety; a protection, safeguard. *Obs.*

c **1375** *Sc. Leg. Saints* xxviii. (*Margaret*) 362 For þis payne þat done is to me þe saufte of my saule sal be. **1399** *Rolls of Parlt.* III. 451/2 Syche Juggement..os myght be savete and seurtee..to the Kynges hegh Estate. **1470–85** MALORY *Arthur* XIII. viii. 623 He that suffred vpon the crosse..he be vnto yow good conduyte and saufte. **1577** B. GOOGE *Heresbach's Husb.* I. (1586) 12 Beside, the pargetting or seeling, is a good safetie against fyre. ? *c* **1580** in Rye *Cromer* p. lxii, The said Peere..will..in tyme be made a very competent harborough or safetie to the Coast men..and a sound safetie to the Towne. **1689–90** TEMPLE *Pop. Discontents* Wks. 1731 I. 260 The first Safety of Princes and States, lies in avoiding all Councils or Designs of Innovation in Ancient and Establish'd Forms and Laws. **1713** STEELE *Englishm.* No. 52. 334 Political Fear and Aversion..is generally the Safety of a People. **1793** SMEATON *Edystone L.* §332 Two lights..not only of great benefit, but an absolute safety to all navigators on that coast.

†**4.** Used in active sense: The action of saving. **a.** *Sc.* Protection. ***under safety of***, under protection of. ***for the safety of***, in order to save or avert. *Obs.*

1465 in *Exch. Rolls Scotl.* VII. 321 *note*, For saufte of his lyffe. *c* **1470** HENRY *Wallace* VII. 938 To saiff his lyff thre ȝer he duelt in But;..Wndir saifte off Jamys than lord Stewart. **1504** in *Charters, etc. Edinb.* (1871) 188 For recovering, saufte, and getting of thar merchandice. *Ibid.*, Returning fra the saufte and getting of thair saidis merchandice. **1567** *Reg. Privy Council Scot.* I. 587 My Lord Regent for the sauftie of the inconvenient and danger quhilk..wes lyke to follow, enterit ane servand of his awin in Ingland.

b. Saving (of money). *Obs. rare*$^{-1}$.

1549 LATIMER *2nd Serm. bef. Edw. VI*, D iij, But I feare one thynge, and it is: lest for a salfety of a lytle money, you wyll put in chauntrye Pryestes, to saue theyr pentions.

5. a. The quality of being unlikely to cause or occasion hurt or injury; freedom from dangerousness; safeness. ***with safety***, without occasioning danger or risk.

1717 LADY M. W. MONTAGU *Let. to Miss S. Chiswell* 1 Apr., I am very well satisfied of the safety of the experiment. **1806** *Med. Jrnl.* XV. 386 If these incisions into the abdomen can be made with safety. **1816** BUDDLE *Let.* 1 June in Davy *Mem. Sir H. Davy* (1836) II. 12 The safety of the lamps is ..easily proved by taking them into any part of a mine charged with fire-damp. **1895** *Daily Tel.* 18 Sept. 4/3, I have found it necessary never to go out shooting with a miscellaneous lot of 'young men from town', until I have had a report..as to their safety in the field.

b. Sureness, steadiness. ? *nonce-use.*

1841 MISS MITFORD in L'Estrange *Life* (1870) III. viii. 119, I am, and always have been, a very active person..with great fearlessness and safety of foot and limb.

6. Engineering. ***factor*** or ***coefficient of safety***: see quots. Now usu. as ***safety factor***. (Cf. *safe load*, SAFE *a.* 14.)

1858 RANKINE *Man. Appl. Mechanics* §247. 274 Factors of Safety are of three kinds. **1868** HUMBER *Strains in Girders* 56 Coefficients of Safety are numbers representing the proportions of the ultimate strength of materials to the strains that can safely be brought upon them. **1891** ANGLIN *Design Structures* 17 The ratio of the ultimate strength to the working strength is termed the *factor of safety* of the material. **1909** WEBSTER, Safety factor. **1916** W. H. MOLESWORTH *Spons' Electr. Pocket-Bk.* 482/1 Safety factor, aerial conductors. **1971** L. PILBOROUGH *Inspection of Chem. Plant* ii. 16 Factors of safety for many metallic materials at temperatures up to 650°F may vary from 4 to 5 in the U.K. **1973** C. SAGAN *Cosmic Connection* (1975) iii. 17 Its orbit [*sc.* that of Pioneer 10] was not disturbed by an errant asteroid—the safety factor was estimated as 20 to 1.

7. ***Patent Safety (Cab)***: the original HANSOM CAB, which was furnished with a contrivance to prevent an upset if the cab tilted up or down.

1851 *Fraser's Mag.* XLIII. 308/2 Hansom's Patent Safety. **1864** F. W. ROBINSON *Mattie* II. 25 Dodging the policeman behind a Patent Safety. **1882** *Builder* 8 July 44/1 The 'Patent Safety Cab'.

8. In full ***safety-bolt***. A contrivance for locking the trigger of a gun, so as to prevent accidental discharge. Also, a gun fitted with this contrivance.

1881 GREENER *Gun* 332 The safety is fixed upon strap of break-off. *Ibid.* 344 A safety bolt is fixed to this gun, which bolts the scears to the triggers. **1884** *St. James's Gaz.* 25 Aug. 6/2 The old safety-bolts..were never very general favourites. **1892** GREENER *Breech-Loader* 36 A safety,.. which bolts the triggers effectually. **1936** HEMINGWAY in *Hearst's Internat.* Sept. 168/1 He had the safety on and..he lowered the rifle to move the safety over. **1968** K. WEATHERLY *Roo Shooter* 11 The shooter picked up the smaller rifle and brought it to his shoulder, flipping the safety off with his thumb. **1972** *Shooting Times & Country Mag.* 27 May 13/3 Never push the safety off until the moment of shooting.

9. In full ***safety bicycle***. Former name for the type of bicycle now in use, differing from the 'Ordinary' in the lower position of the saddle, whereby greater safety is afforded to the rider.

Some of the earlier 'safeties' had a geared front driving-wheel still much larger than the trailing-wheel. In the present form the driving wheel is behind, and the two wheels are equal in diameter.

1877 *Bicycle Jrnl.* 4 May 16 Advt., The 'Challenge' Bicycle, and the 'Safety' Bicycle. **1884** GRIFFIN *Bicycles of Yr.* 82 The Devon Safety Roadster... One of the oldest and simplest of safety bicycles. **1885** *Field* 31 Jan. 121/3 Advt., The Club Safety has been constructed so as to contain all the merits of existing 'Safeties'.

10. a. (*a*) *N. Amer. Football*, an act of carrying the ball into one's own end zone; a score of two points awarded against a team for this; (*b*) *Polo* (see quots. 1905).

(*a*) **1881** *Proc. Intercollegiate Conventions Conf.* in P. H. Davis *Football* (1911) 469 If the game still remains a tie the side which makes four or more safeties less than their opponents shall win the game. **1910** W. CAMP *Bk. of Foot-Ball* ii. 54 A 'safety' is made when a side are so sorely pressed that they carry the ball behind their *own goal line.* **1941** *Charlottesville* (Va.) *Daily Progress* 14 Jan. 11 If a legal forward pass is incomplete in the offensive team's end zone, it is to be ruled an incompleted pass instead of a safety. **1950** *Chicago Tribune* 26 Feb. 20/2 A blocked kick and safety can be credited against him. **1972** J. MOSEDALE *Football* iv. 48 The ball hit a goal post and was ruled a safety—the winning margin.

(*b*) **1905** T. F. DALE *Polo* xvi. 309 Whenever a player either accidentally or intentionally gives the ball an impetus with his mallet which carries the ball over the goal line he is defending, and it touches nothing except the goal-post or the ground after leaving his mallet, it shall be deemed a safety. *Ibid.* 310 A safety (an excellent word, by the way, to define what we describe as a hit behind to save their goal by the defending side) counts as $-\frac{1}{4}$. **1931** 'MARCO' *Introd. Polo* II. iv. 72 In America, hitting the ball over one's own line is called hitting a 'safety'; since it is occasionally safer to do this when one can't clear the ball, than to leave it in position for a certain goal to be scored. **1959** *Times* 3 Aug. 2/1 Lucas managed to force in a safety and this was followed by Harper's run. **1973** H. DISSTON *Beginning Polo* x. 119 'Technical' fouls, such as hitting the ball behind your own goal line (a safety).

b. *ellipt.* for *safety match.*

1900 J. VAIZEY *About Peggy Saville* v. 31, I..go in for safeties, which 'strike only on the box'. **1927** R. A. KNOX *Three Taps* iv. 39 That match worries me... Those are ordinary safeties. This is a smaller kind. **1938** S. BECKETT *Murphy* xii. 263 Whether..it was a Brymay safety that exploded the mixture, or a wax vesta.

c. *Baseball.* A safe hit.

1905 *Sporting Life* 9 Sept. 2/3 Harry whaled away at the ball and hit it on a line over short stop for a safety. **1917** C. MATHEWSON *Second Base Sloan* 105 Billy White led off with a safety to left. **1931** *Randolph Enterprise* (Elkins, W. Virginia) 9 July 5/3 The locals hammered out 15 hits on the first contest while the visitors collected eight safeties. **1968** *Washington Post* 4 July C2/8 Pappas..gave up six safeties in the seven innings he pitched. **1976** *Billings* (Montana) *Gaz.* 5 July 3-C/1 Carlos Pimental and Scott Meade led Billings' 12-hit attack with three safeties apiece.

d. *ellipt.* for ***safety razor*** in 11.

1924 KIPLING *Debits & Credits* (1926) 165 'You could with a Safety, though,' said Anthony. And, indeed..one might have shaved in it with comfort. **1925** *Punch* (Almanack No.) 2 Nov. p. iv, When you decided to use a 'safety', instead of the old solid hollow-ground razor, why did you do so? **1932** D. L. SAYERS *Have his Carcase* iv. 62 A young man who had so much difficulty with his razor would be more likely to change over to a safety and use a new blade every few days.

e. *N. Amer. Football. ellipt.* for *safety man* (b) in 11.

1931 K. K. ROCKNE *Coaching* iii. 19 The safety who always catches the punts, but never brings them back very far is more valuable than the 'flash' who brings them back quite a distance, but is inclined to fumble. **1969** *Eugene* (Oregon) *Register-Guard* 3 Dec. 1D/2 Washington State's Eric Dahl was supposed to be the top sophomore defensive back, but in retrospect, the writers should have given that nod to UCLA's 5-9 safety, Ron Carver. **1976** *Honolulu Star-Bull.* 21 Dec. H-3/1 'You can't cry over spilled milk,' said Chuck Foreman. 'We're just glad we're going to be there.' Minnesota strong safety Jeff Wright concurred.

f. *N. Amer.* A metal-ringed outlet for a stove-pipe in the roof of a tent, etc.

1962 M. E. MURIE *Two in Far North* I. iv. 40 The pipes from the many stoves went out through the roofs through galvanized-iron drums called 'safeties'. **1968** C. HELMERICKS *Down Wild River North* I. v. 83 You could hear a breeze sigh across the tent, rattling the tin safety against the little stove pipe.

11. *attrib.* Used very freely since *c* 1800 as a specific designation for contrivances for ensuring safety, or for implements, machines, etc., constructed with a view to safety in use; as ***safety arch, bar, barrier, bell, buoy, car, carabiner, cartridge, device, equipment, gun, harness, hook, inkstand, keel, line, lintel, lock, -mechanism, plug, rail, rein, rope, seat, sling, snap, spring, strap***, etc.; also designating items of protective clothing, as ***safety boot, helmet, jacket, shoe, suit***; gen., as ***safety code, margin, measure, regulation, standard; safety-conscious, -related*** adjs.; **safety belt**, a protective or restraining belt; *spec.* (*a*) a belt in an aeroplane to hold a passenger in his seat, esp. on take-off or landing; (*b*) a belt in a motor vehicle to hold the wearer in his seat in the event of a collision or emergency stop (cf. *seat belt* s.v. SEAT *sb.* 29); **safety bicycle** (see sense 9); **safety boat**, a life-boat; **safety bolt** (see sense 8); **safety box**, (*a*) a box with a surface on which safety matches can be ignited; (*b*) a safe-deposit box; **safety cab**, (*a*) (see sense 7); (*b*) a tractor cab designed with a view to safety in use; **safety cage**, (*a*) the wire guard of a safety lamp; (*b*) a miner's cage fitted with apparatus to prevent its falling if the rope breaks; **safety car** (see quots.); **safety catch**, a catch or stop attached to a mechanical contrivance as a safe-guard, esp. in hoisting apparatus or on the trigger of a gun; **safety chain**, a chain providing additional security; *spec.* (*a*) a subsidiary chain connecting railway-cars, etc., together; (*b*) a chain securing a watch or jewellery to the clothing; (*c*) (see quot. *a* 1877); (*d*) a chain on a door preventing opening beyond a certain point; **safety committee**, a committee appointed to deal with safety in a place of work, etc.; **safety curtain**: in theatres, a fire-proof curtain which can be lowered to protect the main body of the theatre from fire on or behind the stage; **safety deposit** (chiefly *attrib.*) = *safe deposit* s.v. SAFE *a.* 14; so as *v. trans.*, to place or store in a safe deposit; **safety distance**, the distance which suffices to ensure safety; **safety engineer**, a person trained in accident prevention and the organization and implementation of (esp. industrial) safety measures; hence **safety engineering**; **safety factor** (see sense 6); **safety-film**, a slow-burning film specially prepared for cinematographic work; **safety fuse**, (*a*) a fuse which can be ignited at a safe distance from the charge; (*b*) *Electr.*: see FUSE *sb.*[5]; **safety glass**, toughened or laminated glass; **safety island, isle**, a traffic island constituting a safety zone: = REFUGE *sb.* 3c; **safety lamp**, a miner's lamp the flame of which is so protected that it will not ignite fire-damp (the kind best known is that invented by Sir H. Davy); formerly also called *safe lamp* (see SAFE *a.* 14) and †**safety lantern**; **safety man**, a person responsible for safety; *spec.* (*a*) a person whose work is to guard a temporarily disused mine-shaft in readiness for the resumption of work; (*b*) *N. Amer. Football*, the defensive back who plays in the deepest position; **safety match**, one which ignites only when rubbed on a prepared surface; **safety net**: chiefly in circuses, a net to prevent injury in the event of a fall from a height; also *fig.*; **safety officer**, a person responsible for safety in a factory, etc.; **safety paper**, paper specially prepared to guard against the tampering with or counterfeiting of banknotes, etc.; **safety play**, (*a*) *Billiards* (see sense 1 g); (*b*) *Bridge* (see quots.); † **safety plug**, (*a*) a plug or stopper that allows the quick release of contents when their presence becomes unsafe, *spec.* one of fusible metal that melts when the contents become too hot; (*b*) an electrical fuse; **safety razor**, a razor in which the blade is prevented by a guard from cutting the skin during shaving; also *attrib.*; **safety representative**, a representative of the work-force on an industrial safety committee; **safety rod** *Nuclear Engin.*, a rod of a neutron-absorbing material which can be inserted into a reactor in an emergency to slow or stop the reaction; **safety switch** (see quot. 1940); **safety touch(down)** *N. Amer. Football* = sense 10 a above; **safety tube**, a tube specially contrived to furnish outlet or inlet for gases, etc; **safety vault**, a vault or strong room for the safe custody of valuables; **safety vent**, an outlet affording safety; *spec.* = sense 10 f; also *fig.*; **safety zone**, (*a*) an island or part of a road or square where pedestrians may wait in safety for buses, etc.; (*b*) an area round the Americas in which warlike activities were to be proscribed during the war of 1939–45; also *transf.* Also SAFETY FIRST, SAFETY-PIN, SAFETY-VALVE.

1850 OGILVIE, **Safety-arch*, a discharging arch. **1963** E. H. EDWARDS *Saddlery* xiv. 99 Numerous so-called '*safety bars'... These ingenious devices, which were hinged in various ways to open up and release the stirrup leather when occasion demanded, have largely disappeared. **1951** *Gloss. Aeronaut. Terms (B.S.I.)* III. 25 **Safety barrier*, a net or other contrivance by means of which an aircraft that misses the arresting gear is brought to rest. **1875** KNIGHT *Dict. Mech.* 2015–18 **Safety-beam*, etc. **1875** *Encycl. Brit.* III. 539/2 *Safety bell on swinging coil (fastened to shutters or doors). **1858** SIMMONDS *Dict. Trade*, **Safety-belt, Safety-buoy*, a swimming belt or buoy, intended as a protection from drowning. **1911** *Aero* 8 Apr. 6 Safety belt made for monoplanists. **1948** 'N. SHUTE' *No Highway* iii. 56 Then she pulled out the safety belt from behind the seat and showed him how to clasp it round his body. **1955** *Sci. News Let.* 17 Sept. 181/1 He would not drive without a safety belt. **1962** *Which?* Jan. 5/1 Safety belts should really be an integral part of car safety. **1976** S. BARSTOW *Right True End* III. xiii. 195 Now he wants to sit with his mother in front. I lengthen the safety-belt and strap them in together. **1976** P. CAVE *High Flying Birds* iii. 40 Blood pounding in my head and lungs bursting, I was only dimly aware of the safety-belt catch finally coming free to let me float gently towards the surface. **1840** *Niles' Reg.* 4 Apr. 71/2 Lake, sound and sea going steamers [are] to have an equipment of..*safety boats sufficient to carry all the passengers and crew. **1850** HT. MARTINEAU *Hist. Peace* (1877) III. IV. xiv. 155 Lionel Lukin, the inventor of the safety-boat. **1976** *Yachts & Yachting* 20 Aug. 369/1 On the first day a race was abandoned..because one safety boat was unserviceable (despite the presence of mark boats and spectator boats which could have doubled as safety boats in an emergency). **1967** *Times Rev. Industry* Mar. 16/3 Their shoe arose out of their earlier interest in the *safety boot market. **1977** *West Briton* 25 Aug. 5/2 Mr. Cock..wore safety boots, leather gloves and carried a torch as he climbed down into the tank. **1858** *Safety-buoy [see *safety-belt* above]. **1902** 'MARK TWAIN' *Double-Barrelled Detective Story* II. 131, I hold in my fingers a burnt Swedish match—the kind one rubs on a *safety-box. **1926** J. BLACK *You can't Win* x. 133 If I get snared by the bulls they won't know I've got a safety box. **1965** *Farmer & Stockbreeder* 21 Sept. 58/2 (Advt.), *Safety cab by Clydebuilt... For your positive safety Clydebuilt has enormous structural strength, N.I.A.E. tested under rigorous conditions. **1973** *Times* 17 Nov. 6/1 All new tractors sold to farmers after September 1, 1975, would have to be fitted with a safety cab in which the noise level did not exceed 90 decibels. **1839** URE *Dict. Arts* 1079 This lamp gives so little light as to tempt rash men to remove its *safety-cage. **1867** W. W. SMYTH *Coal & Coal-mining* 172 A number of inventions, to which the name of safety-cage, in French *parachute*, has been applied. **1840** TANNER *Canals & Rail Roads U.S.* 258 **Safety car*, a machine which follows or precedes rail-road cars in their passage of inclined planes, and prevents their descent in case of accident to the machinery, or otherwise. **1881** RAYMOND *Mining Gloss.*, *Safety-car*. See *Barney*. **1972** D. HASTON *In High Places* xii. 148 Sliding back down the ropes was something of a joke: you just fixed a *safety carabiner and ran down the line. **1881** GREENER *Gun* 505 *Safety cartridges. **1877** *Encycl. Brit.* VI. 75 Various forms of *safety catch and disengaging hooks. *a* **1884** KNIGHT *Dict. Mech.* Suppl. s.v. *Safety Catch*, Safety catches attached to the cage are held away from the guides while the weight of the cage hangs on the rope. **1908** *Chambers's Jrnl.* 26 Dec. 61/2 The door can be opened a few inches and yet be held by the safety-catch. **1928** *Daily Mail* 31 July 5/3 Thinking the safety-catch was fixed she handled the revolver carelessly and the trigger fell. **1962** *Daily Tel.* 6 July 1/8 An electronic 'safety catch' which could be released only by a coded radio signal from headquarters. **1970** H. TREVELYAN *Middle East in Revolution* 35 He had therefore imposed a limit on trade with the Communists: what he called his safety catch. **1973** 'R. MACLEOD' *Nest of Vultures* 8 The gun was a Mauser and the safety catch was off. **1841** C. H. GREGORY *Managem. Locom. Engine* 10 The draw-bar connecting the Engine and Tender must be secure, and the *safety-chains attached. **1845** *Business Advertiser & Gen. Directory Chicago* 122 Clocks, Jewelry, Gold Safety Chains, Gold Fob Chains. **1851** *Illustr. Catal. Gt. Exhib.* III. 674/1 Safety chain brooches, for effectually fastening a lady's dress. *a* **1877** KNIGHT *Dict. Mech.* III. 2016/1 *Safety-chain*, a slack chain which attaches a truck to a car-body and limits the excursions of the former as it slues round. **1965** D. FRANCIS *Odds Against* x. 138 A nervous grey haired elderly man opened the front door on a safety chain. **1972** M. J. BOSSE *Incident at Naha* i. 23, I called through the door, 'Who's there?' and opened it only to the length of the safety chain. **1973** J. STUBBS *Dear Laura* i. 21, I wonder whether you could not look at the safety chain of my new brooch? **1976** *Billings* (Montana) *Gaz.* 30 June 9-D/1 (Advt.), New tow bar and safety chain for pinto Datsun, Toyota, Vega, etc. **1954** (*title*) Institute of Petroleum Marketing *Safety Code. **1961** *Lancet* 12 Aug. 365/2 A safety code for workers exposed to ionising radiations in industry is laid down. **1971** *Guardian* 22 June 6/6 Moving pavements..could become a major form of city transport with the adoption of a new safety code to supersede the existing 2 mph speed limit. **1945** *Proc. Inst. Mech. Engin.* CLII. 149 Safety engineering is advancing in experience and practice, and is receiving an impetus by the appointment of safety officers and *safety committees by many important firms. **1838** MARY HOWITT *Birds & Fl.*, *House-Sparrow* iv, He knows the *safety-distance to an inch. **1906** *Westm. Gaz.* 5 May 3/1 Two motor-omnibuses require 46 ft. of street with a safety distance of 18 ft. between each of the two omnibuses. **1961** *Sunderland Echo* 14 Jan. 2/1, 120,000 miners each received a letter from the divisional chairman urging them to be more *safety conscious. **1973** C. BONINGTON *Next Horizon* xxi. 291 It seemed bitterly ironic that the person in the team who was, perhaps, the most safety-conscious should have been caught out by this cruel act of fate. **1909** *Weekly Budget* 21 Aug. 4/6 The *safety curtain at the Lyceum went on strike one evening last week. **1912** *Theatreland* 11 Oct. 4/2 It was left to his successor, Richard Brinsley Sheridan, to stand sponsor for the iron 'safety' curtain. **1974** J. GARDNER *Return of Moriarty* 303 Dr. Night had the stage cleared, the safety curtain lowered. **1891** 'MARK TWAIN' *Lett. to Publishers* (1967) 280 Yes, the statement was what I wanted... I sent it to Whitmore to be *safety-deposited. **1892** *Ibid.* 304 As fast as Halsey delivers the securities to you I want you to put them in a box in a Safety Deposit Vault, and keep the key yourself. **1936** L. C. DOUGLAS *White Banners* v. 86 She maintained a safety deposit-box there which she occasionally visited. **1978** S. SHELDON *Bloodline* xxxix. 350 A safety-deposit box in Zurich, contents unknown. **1884** *Harper's Mag.* Dec. 118/1 If the elevator has a *safety device. **1929** *Daily Express* 7 Nov. 8/4 All the latest safety devices, such as four-wheel or six-wheel brakes, and safety glass. **1971** *Reader's Digest Family Guide to Law* 580 An employee working in a place from which he could fall more than 6 ft 6 in. must be provided with a safety device, such as fencing, where this is 'reasonably practicable'. **1934** WEBSTER s.v. *Safety adj.* 2, *Safety engineers. **1945** *Proc. Inst. Mech. Engin.* CLII. 166/1 The management of a mechanical engineering works should be just as much safety engineers as those claiming to be specialists in that direction. **1974** *Encycl. Brit. Macropædia* XVI. 138/1 The safety engineer is concerned with reducing both the frequency with which accidents occur and the frequency with which they threaten. **1945** *Safety engineering [see *safety committee*]. **1977** *Jrnl. R. Soc. Arts* CXXV. 668/2 The effective application of safety engineering must go hand in hand with an understanding of management techniques. **1969** *Safety equipment [see *chastity belt* s.v. CHASTITY 6]. **1971** *Reader's Digest Family Guide to Law* 612/1 If..the employer can prove that he..provided the necessary safety equipment, he may not have to pay damages. **1928** *Daily Mail* 25 July 5/5 All the film used is *safety film. **1959** W. S. SHARPS *Dict. Cinematogr.* 84/2 *Cellulose acetate base*.., a slow burning safety film base. **1981** *Daily Tel.* 10 Feb. 12/4 We have been able to keep up to schedule because we stockpiled safety film when the price was low. **1839** DE LA BECHE *Rep. Geol. Cornwall*, etc. xv. 575 Accidents, however, are frequent..notwithstanding the invention of the *safety-fuse. **1922** *Tatler* 4 Oct. p. xii. (Advt.), Another striking testimony for the Triplex *Safety Glass. **1935** [see ARMOURED *ppl. a.* 3]. **1950** *Engineering* 10 Feb. 167/3 The cab is..fitted with safety-glass windows. **1964** L. DEIGHTON *Funeral in Berlin* xix. 111 The safety glass shattered into milky opacity. **1884** *St. James's Gaz.* 25 Aug. 6/2 *Safety-guns..have now been brought to a high pitch of perfection. **1920** *Flight* 9 Sept. 978/2 Attention is drawn to the necessity of ensuring that the fitting and maintenance of *safety belts and harness in aircraft is secure and functions properly. **1937** C. BOFF *Boys' Bk. of Flying* xvii. 185 The pupil, in the rear cockpit, held the aeroplane on its back, with the startled instructor, in the front cockpit, holding on for dear life... His safety harness should have been properly secured, but it wasn't. **1972** D. FRANCIS *Smokescreen* i. 7, I sat in the driving seat of a..sports car... [It] would not start until the safety harness was fastened. **1961** J. H. GOODIER *Dict. Painting & Decorating* 247 Modern *safety helmets are often made from resin bonded fibreglass, with a head harness of polythene. **1973** *Daily Tel.* 6 June 14/1 Britain's turbanned Sikh motor-cyclists are not alone in having problems with the new law making it compulsory for riders to wear crash helmets (sorry, *safety* helmets). **1875** R. F. MARTIN tr. *Havrez' Winding Mach.* 95 Good *safety hooks will hold up the cage, but they allow the rope to be hurt. **1869** J. C. PATTESON *Let.* 24 Nov. in C. M. Yonge *Life J.C. Patteson* (1874) II. xi. 391 Patent *safety inkstands—these things are useful on board ship. **1873** C. M. YONGE *Pillars of House* II. xx. 180 Felix..his safety ink-stand planted in the sand. **1933** *Sun* (Baltimore) 4 Apr. 3/4 A few years ago *safety islands were placed in the middle of some of Cambridge's principal thoroughfares to safeguard the lives of pedestrians. **1965** J. VON STERNBERG *Fun in Chinese Laundry* vii. 189, I met the man..on one of the safety islands for pedestrians in the middle of Piccadilly Circus. **1934** *Transit Jrnl.* Nov. 437/1 Serious accidents in which fast moving automobiles crashed into the ends of *safety isles in Baltimore. **1971** *Rand Daily Mail* (Home Owner) 27 Mar. 16/4 (Advt.), Wetlook diving suits... *Safety jackets. **1976** A. PRICE *War Game* I. 46 There was a cowman in the road ahead, bright in his orange-banded safety jacket. **1874** THEARLE *Naval Archit.* 53 The late Mr. Lang introduced what were termed '*safety keels' and are now known as 'thick garboards'. **1816** WALDIE *Let.* 25 Mar. in Paris *Life Davy* (1831) II. 110 The great and important discovery of your *Safety-lamp for exploring mines charged with inflammable gas. **1815** DAVY in *Phil. Trans.* CVI. 14 The second *safety lantern that I have had made is upon the same principle as the first. **1957** R. G. COLLOMB *Dict. Mountaineering* 134 **Safety Line*, an independent rope attached to a climber's waistline when he is making an abseil. **1973** C. BONINGTON *Next Horizon* xix. 262 Alastair Newman had swum across first and McLeod followed, after tying on a safety-line. **1850** OGILVIE, **Safety-lintel*, a name given to the wooden lintel which is placed behind a stone lintel, in the aperture of a door or window. *a* **1877** KNIGHT *Dict. Mech.* III. 2017/1 **Safety-lock*. 1. (*Lock*). A lock so contrived as not to be opened by a picklock or without the proper key... 2. (*Fire-arms.*) One provided with a stop or catch to prevent accidental discharge. **1970** *Which?* July 217/1 Most had a safety lock to prevent you exposing the film by accident. **1928** *Sunday Dispatch* 23 Dec. 3/4 These officials, known as '*safety men', will eat their dinner in semi-darkness hundreds of feet below the surface of the earth. **1929** *Daily Express* 7 Nov. 2/4 'Although,' she said, 'I am not a safety man myself, I have lived twenty-five years with a safety man, so I think I may claim to know a little how things work.' **1931** K. K. ROCKNE *Coaching* iii. 19 In catching punts the safety man stands with both feet flat on the ground. **1962** C. FORSYTE *Diving Death* xx. 161 As Left began to get into his diving things again he wished..that somebody could be left in the boat as safety man. **1972** J. MOSEDALE *Football* ix. 135 He scored from four yards out, running straight over the safety man. **1967** W. SOYINKA *Kongi's Harvest* 40 Five minutes. That's enough of a *safety margin isn't it? It had better be! **1863** ABEL in *Lond.* etc. *Philos. Mag.* Nov. 357 Varieties..of so-called '*safety matches'. **1866** BRANDE & COX *Dict. Sci.* etc. s.v. *Lucifers*, Such matches, as not being affected by accidental friction, and as being free from poison, are called safety matches. **1934** WEBSTER s.v. *Safety* adj. 2, *Safety measures. **1959** *Petroleum Handbk.* (ed. 4) 379 The safety measures at installations and depots are..based on the elimination of all possible sources of ignition from all areas where dangerous concentrations of petroleum vapours are at all likely. **1977** P. JOHNSON *Enemies of Society* xv. 197 The technique of all-purpose explanation is completed by another *safety-mechanism. **1950** P. TEMPEST *Lag's Lexicon* 183 **Safety net*, the steel nets spread across the hall, from landing to landing on the first floor, to prevent accidents, attempts at homicide, suicide, etc. **1953** *Economist* 11 July 87/1 A genuine flexibility, 'worked out' in the market, is compatible with the security of floor prices, or more accurately of 'safety net' prices that would protect the farmer against serious losses. **1958** *Spectator* 22 Aug. 249/3 Acrobatic tricks no commercial management would risk without a safety net. **1965** 'W. HAGGARD' *Hard Sell* iv. 45 The fire chief was speaking into the walkie-talkie.. and men were running with a safety net. They spread it and held it. **1971** *Guardian* 29 July 11/6 An open invitation..to let costs rise in expectation of a taxpayers' safety net. **1974** G. MITCHELL *Javelin for Jonah* xi. 137 He had been with a travelling circus ..but they dismissed him... He had begun to insist on having a safety-net for his act. **1978** D. A. STANWOOD *Memory of Eva Ryker* xxiii. 215 It'll be the first time.. without Dr. Stanford's help... A triple somersault, with no safety net. **1939** *Engineering* 18 Aug. 215/2 The Chief Inspector of Factories..was prepared to call together a committee representing makers of presses,..*safety officers, ..and factory inspectors. **1972** *Classification of Occupations* (Dept. Employment) II. 78/1 *Safety officer.* Advises on industrial safety and organises and co-ordinates accident prevention and safety measures within an organisation. **1976** *Guardian* 15 Apr. 1/4 The firm's safety officers wearing breathing apparatus went down the tunnel..to see that all the men had escaped. **1851** *Illustr. Catal. Gt. Exhib.* III. 540/1 White and coloured *safety paper for bankers' cheques. **1967** KARCH & BUBER *Offset Processes* 553 Safety Paper, paper treated usually by printing a design in a light tint which protects the sheet against forgery. **1896** *Safety play [see BALK *sb.*[1] 9]. **1959** *Listener* 3 Sept. 370/1 The safety play, properly so called, is a play that risks the loss of a trick which can be spared to guard against the possible loss of a trick which cannot be spared. **1964** *Official Encycl. Bridge* 481/2 A safety play is the play of a suit in such a manner as to protect against an abnormal or bad break in that suit, thereby either eliminating or minimizing the danger of losing the contract. **1977** *Cleethorpes News* 6 May 29/4 Sid's superb safety play in this last frame..stood him in good stead. **1837** P. NICHOLSON *Pract. Masonry* II. viii. 145 In the case..of any choking up of the connection-pipes, the stoker has merely to lift the *safety-plugs, and clear out the pipes, by introducing a rod of iron into them. **1869** *Appleby's Illustr. Handbk. Machinery & Iron Work* p. xiii/1 (Index), Safety plugs, fusible. **1882** *Engineering* 7 July 11/3 Every lamp in the electrolier has its safety plug. **1887** *Ibid.* 11 Nov. 503/2 The fusible safety plug illustrated..has been adopted by the South Wales and Monmouthshire Boiler Insurance Company. **1890** J. W. URQUHART *Electr. Light Fitting* v. 163 The usual safety plugs are marked with the number of ampères of current they can carry without fusion. **1923** *Power Engineer* XVIII. 475/2 (*heading*) Safety plug for heavy oil engines. **1828** *Lights & Shades* II. 103 The front [of the pigeon-holes in the theatre- gallery] is provided with a *safety-rail. **1940** *Chambers's Techn. Dict.* 154/2 *Check rail*.., a third rail laid on a curve alongside the inner rail and spaced a little from it, to safeguard rolling-stock against derailment due to excessive thrust on the outer rail. Also called..*safety rail.* **1964** *Eng. Stud.* XLV. 23 A pulpit is a raised safety-rail in the bows of a yacht or motor cruiser. *a* **1877** KNIGHT *Dict. Mech.* III. 2018/1 *Safety-razor. **1903** *Hardwareman* 11 July 53 (Advt.), Something new in safety razors. **1921** A. HUXLEY *Crome Yellow* xxiv. 262 The packet of safety-razor blades. **1973** 'R. MACLEOD' *Nest of Vultures* 8 The fair-haired man had shaved that morning. A safety razor shave by the smooth shine of his cheeks. **1956** A. TOYNBEE *Historian's Approach to Relig.* xviii. 238 The need for *safety-regulations would not be eliminated if atomic power were to be applied exclusively to pacific and beneficent uses. **1971** *Reader's Digest Family Guide to Law* 580/1 Employees must observe safety regulations so that they do not endanger themselves or other workers. **1976** *National Observer* (U.S.) 28 Aug. 9/1 General Motors Corp. has been ordered to..pay a $400,000 penalty to the United States for refusing to notify owners of a *safety-related defect. **1977** *Jrnl. R. Soc. Arts* CXXV. 676/2 *Safety representatives will have the legal right to paid time off from work for undertaking these functions and for undergoing training for them. **1950** *Chem. & Engin. News* 4 Dec. 4257 The Argonne heavy water reactor is equipped with two control rods, two *safety rods, and three shim rods. The safety and control rods are each formed of a 3·5-inch tubular sandwich of 1/32-inch cadmium placed between two aluminium tubes. **1971** *New Scientist* 13 May 389/1 The safety rods of a nuclear reactor are for use in emergencies when the neutron flux within the reactor core has to be immediately reduced. **1845** *Times* 31 July 1/5 Carriage for the Continent.—A Travelling Britzska, with every possible travelling appendage, namely eight trunks and imperials, two drag shoes and staff, *safety ropes, pair and four horse bars, solid flap and German shutter. **1935** *Discovery* Mar. 73/1 For the descent..it is essential..to make constant use of the safety-rope. **1975** G. Moffat *Miss Pink* xii. 168 He wouldn't have fallen backwards... The safety rope would have held him. **1966** *Observer* 17 Apr. 21/3 The most hopeful sign is the emergence of the '*safety seat',..bolted firmly to the floor, with belts built-in. **1976** *Star* (Sheffield) 26 Nov. (Advt.), K. L. Jeenay Safety Seat. £8. **1943** *Sun* (Baltimore) 31 Mar. 13/2 A worker will be required to fill in a form showing..that the employer does not furnish *safety shoes to him, that he needs the shoes to protect his health and safety [etc.]. **1974** *Encycl. Brit. Macropædia* XVI. 144/1 Safety shoes have been developed for protection in a wide variety of situations. **1974** H. MacInnes *Climb to Lost World* xi. 192, I had a karabiner and *safety sling running on the other rope. **1932** *Safety snap [see karabiner]. **1862** *Safety spring [see bradoon]. **1960** *B.S.I. News* June 8/2 Finally, Mr. NcNeill considered the question of '*safety' standards. **1976** 'R. B. Dominic' *Murder out of Commission* i. 7 You're in the Atomic Energy Commission... You can bring Ben up to date on safety standards. *a* **1877** Knight *Dict. Mech.* III. 2018/2 **Safety-strap*.., an extra back band passing over the seat of a gig-saddle..; used as a safeguard on light trotting harness. **1938** R. G. Collingwood *Princ. Art* xi. 240 The child's finding itself..wheeled about in a perambulator with a safety-strap round its waist. **1963** *Amer. Speech* XXXVIII. 207 The safety straps that are snapped or tied..from the ski to the boot to prevent run-away skis. **1917** *Chambers's Jrnl.* Oct. 702/2 A recently-invented life-saving apparatus, known as the 'ever-warm *safety-suit', goes far towards removing this danger. **1974** *Times* 21 Feb. 3/4 (Advt.), Safety suits. **1940** *Chambers's Techn. Dict.* 293/2 *Emergency stop*, a switch installed in a lift-car, or other similar piece of equipment, by means of which the power to the operating motor can be cut off. Also called a **safety switch*. **1944** *Engineering* 8 Sept. 192/3 Investigation..revealed that some time previously the safety switch had failed. **1815** Davy in *Phil. Trans.* CVI. 12, I had another chimney fitted to this lantern, furnished with a number of *safety tin-plate tubes. **1904** 'R. Connor' *Prospector* 38 With a brilliant series of passes the 'Varsity quarters and halves work the ball through the McGill twenty-five line, and by following hard a high punt, force the captain to a *safety touch. **1958** *Edmonton* (Alberta) *Jrnl.* 7 Aug. 7/2 Flying wing Jack Hill..booted three converts while guard Don Walsh picked up two points on a safety touch. **1970** *Globe & Mail* (Toronto) 25 Sept. 33/3 The Panthers conceded a safety touch for Humberside's other points. **1887** *Century Mag.* XXXIV. 889/2 A '*safety' touch-down counts two points against the side which makes it. **1957** *Encycl. Brit.* IX. 472/2 No penalty was attached to the safety touchdown until 1881. **1841** Brande *Chem.* (ed. 5) 480 The escape of any uncondensed gas [should be] provided for by a *safety-tube. **1846** T. L. McKenney *Mem.* I. 26 One set [of vouchers was] for the Treasury Department, one for my office proper, and the third for a *safety vault. **1902** A. D. McFaul *Ike Glidden* xvii. 129 The safe suddenly became the people's depository and safety vault. **1963** *Times Lit. Suppl.* 26 Apr. 297/2 Using his diary as a *safety-vent. **1968** C. Helmericks *Down Wild River North* i. vi. 86 The little stovepipe rattled and scratched against the tin safety vent of the tent. **1915** *Policeman's Monthly* Oct. 3/2 (*caption*) *Safety zone at near-side car stop, Detroit. **1921** *Daily Colonist* (Victoria, B.C.) 8 Apr. 9/4 Mr. E. S. Harris asked the board to make some provision for 'safety zones' on the busiest streets of Victoria. **1939** *Daily Tel.* 18 Dec. 7/2 The safety zone would help the Allies, by keeping German submarines out of, roughly, a third of the Atlantic. **1940** J. Betjeman *Old Lights for New Chancels* 56, I will labour for Thy Kingdom, Help our lads to win the war, Send white feathers to the cowards Join the Women's Army Corps, Then wash the Steps around Thy Throne In the Eternal Safety Zone.

safety first. A maxim or slogan inculcating the necessity of taking precautions for the avoidance of accident. Also *attrib.*; occas. applied to the safest kinds of investment.

Various safety-first campaigns (in factories, schools, etc.) were organized in Britain in the early-twentieth cent. The slogan is said to derive from the American railway industry (see *Encycl. Brit.* (1926) III. 446). It was widely used as a slogan in Conservative election posters in 1922 and (with reference to Stanley Baldwin) in 1929.

1873 *Cassell's Mag.* Nov. 71/2 A system that would go on the motto of safety first. **1914** G. M. Price *Mod. Factory* 138 Corporations which have within the last five years taken up the slogan of 'safety first' and have done great work in accident prevention. **1924** J. S. C. Bridge *Hist. France* II. 118 The so-called battles were conducted under the rules of a carefully framed code, of which 'safety first' was the unacknowledged watchword and inspiration. **1927** [see *narrow-beamed* s.v. narrow *a.* 7]. **1927** *Daily Mail* 5 Aug. 3/1 (*heading*) Rising 'Safety First' Stocks. **1931** *Daily Mirror* 27 Aug. 4 These and other safety first signs are being introduced all over the Dominion. **1932** *Daily Mail* 2 July 3/1 The volume of business transacted in 'safety-first' stocks was probably not so large as earlier in the week. **1936** A. Christie *Cards on Table* xiii. 130 The moment you begin.. adopting as your motto 'Safety First'—you might as well be dead. **1944** *Living off Land* iii. 61 Where the ground appears to be in the least unsafe, it should *always* be timbered as an essential 'safety-first' principle. **1953** Earl Winterton *Orders of Day* xi. 153 Mr Davidson was accused by many Conservatives, at least in private, of being responsible for the defeat of the Government and the invention of the Party's election slogan, 'Safety First'. **1964** S. Duke-Elder *Parsons' Dis. Eye* (ed. 14) xxvi. 377 Every attempt should be made by the provision of comfortable goggles and by educative means, such as 'Safety First' notices. **1965** A. J. P. Taylor *Eng. Hist. 1914–1945* viii. 282 The cause had a strong appeal for many Conservatives who wanted something more exciting than Baldwin's Safety First. **1977** J. Wainwright *Nest of Rats* i. ix. 64 The Koh-i-noor's twin sister... The glitter deserving of all that sophisticated safety-first garbage.

Hence **safety-ˈfirster**, a person unwilling to take risks.

1928 *Daily Express* 19 Nov. 5 Many women would dislike the uncertainty, so the safety-firster, the shy, the unadaptable, and the disliker of change should keep their permanent posts and be thankful they have them. **1929** E. Linklater *Poet's Pub.* xi. 140 You're trying to persuade me to be cowardly and middle-aged, a safety-firster.

ˈsafety-pin, *sb.*

1. A pin for fastening clothing, bent back on itself so as to form a spring, and with a guard or sheath to cover the point and prevent its accidental unfastening. In *Archæology*, a *fibula* or brooch made on the same principle.

1857 *Prov. Patent Specif.* No. 134 Imp'ts in safety pins. **1880** Dawkins *Early Man* 388 The peculiar brooch made of twisted wire, of the 'safety pin' kind, so abundant in the Etruskan tombs of Bologna. **1882** A. J. Evans in *Archæologia* XLVIII. 100 As an example of a Roman safety-pin this *fibula*, so far as I am aware, is altogether unique.

2. A pin used for fastening, locking, or securing some part of a machine.

1878 *N. Amer. Rev.* CXXVII. 387 Some say that the Russians had neglected to take out the safety-pins, thus leaving the torpedoes as it were on half-cock. **1884** F. J. Britten *Watch & Clockm.* 143 The object of the safety-pin is to prevent the wheel being unlocked except when the impulse pin is in the notch of the lever. **1884** Knight *Dict. Mech.* Suppl., *Safety Pin*, a temporary pin in a percussion fuse, to prevent the plunger from striking accidentally against the percussion powder. **1896** *Westm. Gaz.* 9 June 4/4 Lifting the cotter, or safety pin, which locked the bolt.

ˈsafety-pin, *v.* [f. the sb.] *trans.* **a.** To pin *on* or attach with a safety-pin; also *fig.* **b.** To attach a safety-pin or safety-pins to; to put a safety-pin into.

1919 'K. Mansfield' *Let.* 30 Oct. (1928) I. 270 Her ears which are neatly buttonholed on to the sides of her head and not just safety-pinned on as most babies' are. **1960** P. A. Bennett in J. Pudney *Pick of Today's Short Stories* XI. 12 The buttons on my coat will have to be sewn on..so she safety-pinned them on. **1971** *Country Life* 6 May 1087/1 Fortunately, I had sent the engineer over the side to safety-pin the bombs beforehand. **1975** *Listener* 6 Feb. 176/1 Delysia dressed me in her clothes, safety-pinned me all down the back.

ˈsafety-valve.

1. A valve in a steam-boiler which automatically opens to permit steam to escape when the pressure is becoming dangerous. Also, a similar valve opening inwards, to admit air when a partial vacuum has been formed.

1815 J. Smith *Panorama Sci. & Art* II. 134 The safety-valve..is loaded so that the steam escapes when it is stronger than the engine requires. **1832** Babbage *Econ. Manuf.* ii. (ed. 3) 26 The boiler of a steam engine some-times bursts even during the escape of steam through the safety-valve. *transf.* **1830** Lyell *Princ. Geol.* I. 371 The volcanos in different parts of this island are observed..to be in activity by turns, one vent often serving for a time as a safety-valve to the rest. **1876** C. D. Warner *Wint. Nile* i. 22 The volcanic islands which serve as chimneys and safety-valves to this part of the world.

2. *fig.* An opening or channel for 'letting off steam', giving vent to excitement, getting rid of a dangerous excess of energy, or the like. Also *attrib.*

1818 Lady Morgan *Autobiog.* (1859) 172 Our hereditary nobility have safety-valves in their rank, and in the offices of which they are the inheritors in church and state. **1825** Hone *Every-day Bk.* I. 1344 As a sort of 'safety valve',.. recourse is had..to the flinging about of..cabbage stalks. **1835** Marryat *Olla Podr.* xix, I am convinced that they [*sc.* public lotteries] were beneficial, acting as safety-valves to the gambling spirit of the nation. **1861** M. Arnold *Pop. Educ. France* 183 What a safety-valve to the high pressure of a compulsory system is here! **1878** Stubbs *Const. Hist.* III. xviii. 276 Commercial activity..was..a safety-valve for energies shut out of their proper sphere. **1925** I. A. Richards *Princ. Lit. Crit.* xxxi. 232 If we do not..try to bring under this Safety-valve heading work with which it has no concern, it may be granted that in some cases the explanation is in place. **1956** 'J. Wyndham' *Seeds of Time* 100 There had been nothing worse than safety-valve grumbling. **1964** R. Miliband in I. L. Horowitz *New Sociol.* 868 What Mills condemned in Safety-valve welfarism was not the welfare.

Hence **ˈsafety-valving** *vbl. sb.* (*nonce-use*), letting *off* or discharging as though through a safety-valve.

1965 K. Amis *James Bond Dossier* ix. 93 Violent films, TV shows and the like are useful in safety-valving off our private aggressions.

† **safe ward.** *Obs.* [ward *sb.*] Safe-guard, safe-keeping.

1398 Trevisa *Barth. De P.R.* v. viii. (Tollem. MS.), The ye liddes..reulen and hilen and gouerne þe yen in saue warde [L. *tuta custodia*]. **1414** in *Proc. Privy Council* (1834) II. 142 That..the sauf warde of alle youre [? realm] be wel and suffissantly purveied. *c* **1420** *Avow. Arth.* xxx, Inne saue-ward that pou bryȝte To Carlele to bringe. **1474** Caxton *Chesse* iii. vi. (1883) 129 To putte hyt in seure and sauf warde and kepynge.

safewr, obs. form of sapphire.

saff(e, obs. forms of safe, save.

saffage, obs. form of savage *a.*

saffer(e, obs. forms of sapphire, zaffre.

saffern, -eron, obs. and dial. forms of saffron.

saffi, variant of saphie, amulet.

saffian (ˈsæfɪən). Forms: 6 **saphian, -ion,** 8– **saffian.** [a. Russ. *saf'yan*, corruptly a. Rumanian *saftian*, a. Turkish (Persian) *saχtiyān*. Cf. Ger. *saffian.*] A leather made from goatskins or sheepskins tanned with sumach and dyed in bright colours. Also *saffian leather*.

1591 G. Fletcher *Russe Commw.* xix. 74 Whither the Russe marchants trade for raw silks, syndon, saphion, skins, and other commodities. *Ibid.* xxviii. 114 His buskins..are made of a Persian leather called Saphian. **1796** Morse *Amer. Geog.* II. 460 The skins of these sheep, and skins of goats, are used in making Saffian and Morocco leather. **1834–6** P. Barlow in *Encycl. Metrop.* (1845) VIII. 551/2 A valuable Saffian or dyed Maroquin leather, almost equal to that of Turkey, is prepared at Astracan and in other parts of Asiatic Russia. **1882** J. Paton in *Encycl. Brit.* XIV. 388/1 The Germans distinguish between saffian and morocco, including under the former term leather tanned with sumach, and dyed bright colours without previous stuffing with fats... Saffians are, according to this classification, the leathers principally used for bindings and fancy purposes.

safflor(e, obs. forms of safflower.

safflorite (ˈsæflǝraɪt). *Min.* [a. G. *safflorit* (1835), f. *safflor* safflower: see -ite[1].] An orthorhombic arsenide of cobalt and iron.

1852 Brooke & Miller *Phillips' Introd. Min.* 146. **1862** Dana *Min.* 263.

safflower (ˈsæflaʊǝ(r)). Forms: α. 6 *corruptly* **samfleure, -floure;** β. 7 **saf(f)lore,** (erron. **salfore**), 8 **saf(f)lor;** γ. 7 **safflowr, saflower,** 8 **saff-flower,** 8– **safflower;** δ. 8–9 **safflow.** [a. Du. *saffloer*(*s* = G. *safflor*, a. OF. *saffleur*, *safour*, a. early It. *saffiore*, also *asfiore*, *asfrole*, *zaffrole*, etc. (Yule). The ultimate source is obscure: the Arabic *ʿuçfur* is prob. a foreign word assimilated to *açfar* yellow.

The form has been influenced by association with the words *saffron* (F. *safran*) and *flower* (It. *fiore*, F. *fleur*); although safflower is a wholly different plant from saffron, the former was often used as a substitute for the latter in medicine, whence the name *bastard saffron.*]

1. The dried petals of the *Carthamus tinctorius* (see 2), also the (red) dye produced from these petals. Used in the preparation of rouge.

α. **1583** L. M[ascall] tr. *Bk. Dyeing* 20 Yee shall take one pound of samfleure and let it soke halfe a day [etc.]. *Ibid.*, Samfloure.

β. **1642** *Rates Merchandizes* 47 Saflore the pound oo. o1. oo. **1662** *Stat. Ireland* (1678) 658 Safflore. **1777** G. Forster *Voy. round World* II. 588 Safflor, which the Portuguese employ to colour their eatables yellow.

γ. **166.** Petty *Hist. Dyeing* in Sprat *Hist. Roy. Soc.* (1667) 298 This Mather..dyeth on Cloth a colour the neerest to our Bow-dye,..the like whereof Safflowr doth in Silk. **1799** G. Smith *Laboratory* I. 385 Then take the safflower out of the bag. **1836–41** Brande *Chem.* (ed. 5) 1113 Safflower contains two colouring matters, a yellow and a red. **1877** O'Neill in Encycl. Brit. VII. 571/2 Specimens of mummy cloth of a reddish colour appeared to have been dyed with safflower.

2. The thistle-like plant *Carthamus tinctorius*, extensively cultivated in Southern Europe, Egypt, India, and China for the dye obtained from its flowers (see 1); the seeds yield an oil used in cooking, making margarine, in lamps, etc.

β. **1762** tr. *Busching's Syst. Geog.* V. 536 Woad, saflor, or wild-saffron, and garden-fruits.

γ. **1682** S. Wilson *Acc. Carolina* 18 Sumack growes in great abundance naturally, so undoubtedly would Woad, Madder and Sa-Flower, if planted. **1756** *Compl. Body Husb.* 535 Saff-flower, or Carthamus, is cultivated for the sake of its flower, as the Saffron is. **1900** *Jrnl. Soc. Dyers* XVI. 6 Other Philippine dye plants..are the sibucao, or sapan wood, the beri, or safflower [etc.]. **1974** *Nature* 13 Dec. 519/2 No work is at present supported at international level on oil seeds such as sunflower, safflower and rapeseed, although their oils are important in the diets of many developing countries. **1980** *Holistic Health News* (Berkeley, Calif. Holistic Health Center) Sept./Oct. 8/3 Mix together: 1 cup of oil, safflower works well. 1½ teaspoons of sea salt.

δ. **1707** Mortimer *Husb.* 131 In Oxfordshire, about Norton and Ashton, grows a sort of herb that they call Safflow or Bastard Saffron, which the Dyers use for the dying of Scarlet. **1885** Stallybrass tr. *Hehn's Wand. Plants & Anim.* 201 The Safflow or Zaffer..a kind of thistle native to the East Indies.

3. *attrib.*

1812 J. Smyth *Pract. of Customs* (1821) 204 The Seeds of the Safflower Plant. **1857** E. Balfour *Cycl. India* 1631 Safflower Oil. *Ibid.*, Safflower Seed. **1968** *Globe & Mail* (Toronto) 17 Feb. B7 Safflower seed oil has especially good stability for cooking and frying oils. **1971** H. McCloy *Question of Time* i. iii. 28 Margarine made with safflower oil (butter is as bad for arteries as eggs).

‖**saffo.** *rare*[−1]. Pl. **saffi.** [It. 'a catchpole, a sergeant' (Florio, 1598).] A bailiff.

1605 B. Jonson *Volpone* iii. viii. (1607) H 4 *Volp.* Hearke, who's there? I heare some footing, Officers, the Saffi, Come to apprehend vs!

† **saffora.** *Obs. rare.* Also **saphora.** [Of unknown origin.] = BARILLA 2.

a **1618** *Rates Marchandizes* D 2, Barilia or Saphora, to make glasse. *Ibid.* K 3, Saffora to make Glasse.

safforn(e, obs. forms of SAFFRON.

saffra(a)n (sə'frɑːn). [Afrikaans, f. Du. *zaffraan* yellow.] A large evergreen forest tree, *Cassine crocea*, of the family Celastraceæ, found in coastal areas of south-eastern Africa, and bearing yellowish bark and clusters of greenish flowers followed by white plum-shaped fruit; also, the hard light brown wood of this tree. Also *attrib.*

1819 C. G. CURTIS *Acct. Colony Cape of Good Hope* 72 Saffran hout... Close and hard. **1831** G. GREIG *S. Afr. Almanac* 187 The other woods most in request, and found in Albany are.. Red and White Pear, Saffran. **1854** L. PAPPE *Silva Capensis* 11 Saffronwood; Saffraan-hout. Branches much spreading. **1950** *Cape Argus* 22 Apr. (Mag. Section) 2/3 He points to a.. saffraan, as the oldest inhabitant of the Cape Town gardens. **1953** *Ibid.* 28 Feb. (Mag. Section) 3/7 Near the fountain were some high Saffraan pear trees. **1957** *Cape Times* 26 July 11/1 Holes are being dug.. for about 80 shade trees. The species agreed upon.. are saffraan and milk-wood. **1973** *Eastern Province Herald* (Port Elizabeth) 28 May 13 A typical wagon of the Great Trek period would have had.. wheel falloes of hard pear or saffraan.

saffranon ('sæfrənən). Also 8 **saffranoune.** [App. a var. of F. *safranum* with the same meaning, a. med.L. *safranum* SAFFRON.] = SAFFLOWER 1.

1731 *Gentl. Mag.* I. 451 As the *Jacob*,.. bound from Alexandria with Hides, Coffee, Saffranon, &c. to Leghorn lay off Monte Christo, the Saffranon smothering in the Hold, on opening the Hatches the Flames burst out. **1743** R. POCOCKE *Egypt* I. iv. 39 An export of coffee, senna, saffranounes for dying, flax [etc.]. **1834** McCULLOCH *Dict. Comm.* (ed. 2) 1001 The flowers.. are sometimes sold under the name of *saffranon*.

saffre, variant of ZAFFRE.

† **'saffred,** *a.* ? *Anglo-Irish. Obs.* In 5 **saffyrred,** 6 **saufred.** [f. SAFFR(ON) + -ED[2].] = SAFFRONED.

1466 *Anc. Cal. Rec. Dublin* (1889) 326 Ne woman.. use to werre saffyrred smokes ne saffyrred kewryches. **1582** STANYHURST *Æneis* I. (Arb.) 38 The roabe pretiouse colored lyke saufred Achantus [*croceo Acantho*]. *Ibid.* 40 With roabs of saffrod [? *read* saffred] Acanthus.

saffrene, variant of SAFRENE.

saffron ('sæfrən), *sb.* and *a.* Forms: α. 3 **saffran,** 4–5 **saffroun, saf(f)run,** 4–6 **safron,** 5 **saffronn, safroun, -ryn,** 6 **saphron, saffrane, -rone, saffroune,** 7 **safran,** 5– **saffron;** β. 5 **safforn,** 6 **saf(f)orne, -erne;** γ. 5 **saferen, saferoun, saipheron, sapheron(e, saferon, saffyron,** 5–6 **safferon.** [a. F. *safran* (12th c. in Hatz.-Darm.), whence also MLG. *safferân*, MDu. *saffraen* (Du. *saffraan*), MHG. *saffrân* (mod.G. *safran*). The ultimate source is Arab. *zaʿfarān* (adopted unchanged in Turkish, Persian, and Hindustāni); also Jewish Aramaic *zaʿp[e]rānā*). The Arabic word with prefixed definite article, *azzaʿfarān*, is represented by Sp. *azafran*, Pg. *açafrão*; the word without this prefix gives rise to It. *zafferano, zaffrone*, Pr. *safran, safrá*, Cat. *safrá*, F. *safran*, med.L. *safranum*, med.Gr. ζαφρᾶς, mod.Gr. σαφράνι, Russian *shafran'*.

The origin of Arab. *zaʿfarān* is unknown; it is not connected with *ṣafrā'* fem. of *aṣfar* yellow. The Turkish synonym *ṣafrān* (Zenker; given in Redh.-Wells only as an incorrect pronunciation) may however be derived from this adj., and may be the source of some of the European forms.]

A. *sb.*

1. a. An orange-red product consisting of the dried stigmas of *Crocus sativus* (see 2). Now used chiefly for colouring confectionery, liquors, etc., and for flavouring; formerly extensively used in medicine as a cordial and sudorific.

hay saffron, cake saffron: see quot. 1849.

c **1200** *Trin. Coll. Hom.* 163 Hire winpel wit oðer maked ȝeleu mid saffran. *a* **1350** *St. Stephen* 318 in Horstm. *Altengl. Leg.* (1881) 32 The ferth [panier].. ful of safron semyd it right. *c* **1386** CHAUCER *Sir Thopas* 19 His heer, his berd was lyk saffroun. *c* **1450** *Two Cookery-bks.* 70 Cast thereto Sapheron and salt. *c* **1460** *Play Sacram.* 177 Peper and saffyron and spycis smale. **1572** in Feuillerat *Revels Q. Eliz.* (1908) 176 Cloves and saferne. **1582** N. LICHEFIELD tr. *Castanheda's Conq. E. Ind.* 91 A bason of silver to wash his hands in, full of Saforne. **1611** SHAKS. *Wint. T.* IV. iii. 48, I must haue Saffron to colour the Warden Pies. **1685** TEMPLE *Ess., Health* Wks. 1731 I. 284 Saffron is of all others the safest and most simple Cordial. **1718** PRIOR *Pleasure* 460 Saffron and myrrh are on his garments shed. **1808** *Med. Jrnl.* XIX. 118 Syrup of saffron, a sufficient quantity to form an electuary. **1840** PEREIRA *Elem. Mat. Med.* II. 674, 4,320 flowers are required to yield one ounce of saffron. **1849** BALFOUR *Man. Bot.* § 1068 These stigmata are either dried in the loose state, forming Hay Saffron, or compressed into masses, constituting Cake Saffron. **1860** TRISTRAM *Gt. Sahara* vii. 119 Saffron.. is a grateful addition to fried, boiled, or stewed.

Prov. phrase. **1778** T. HUTCHINSON *Diary* 11 Jan., Called on Bliss, who is as yellow as saffron with the jaundice.

b. *Indian saffron*: turmeric.

1727–41 CHAMBERS *Cycl.* s.v. *Turmeric*, The Indians use it to dye their rice, and other foods, of a yellow colour; whence some call it Indian saffron. **1874** *Treas. Bot.* Suppl., *Saffron, Indian*, the roots of various species of *Curcuma*.

2. a. The Autumnal Crocus, *Crocus sativus*, which produces saffron.

c **1425** *Voc.* in Wr.-Wülcker 645/18 [*Nomina herbarum*] *Hic crocus*, safurroun. **1551** TURNER *Herbal* I. L iij b, Colchicon.. bryngeth furthe a whytishe floure lyke vnto safforne in the ende of autumne. **1578** LYTE *Dodoens* II. lv. 216 Saffron.. groweth plentifully also in some places of England and Irelande. **1669** EVELYN *Kal. Hort.*, Aug. (ed. 3) 23 Note, that English Saffron may be suffered to stand for increase to the third or fourth year. **1776** WITHERING *Brit. Plants* (1796) II. 68 *Crocus officinalis sativus*... Common or autumnal Saffron. **1782** J. SCOTT *Poet. Wks.* 113 Cantabrian hills the purple saffron show.

b. ***bastard saffron*** = SAFFLOWER 2; called also ***American, dyer's,*** † ***mock saffron. meadow or wild saffron, Colchicum autumnale. spring saffron,*** † ***saffron of the spring, Crocus vernus. African*** or † ***Cape saffron, Lyperia crocea.***

1548 TURNER *Names of Herbes* 29 Cnecus.. is called.. in englishe Bastarde saffron or mocke-saffron. *Ibid.*, Cholchicum... It maye be called in englishe, wylde saffron. **1578** LYTE *Dodoens* I. xxii. 34 The seede of Bastarde Saffron .. is hoate. **1597** GERARDE *Herbal* I. lxxxi. 126 In English spring time Saffrons, and vernall Saffrons. **1599** —— *Catalogus* B 2 *Crocus vernus*.. Saffron of the spring. **1598** SYLVESTER *Du Bartas* II. i. III. *Furies* 178 Colchis' banefull Lilly, (With us Wilde-Saffron). **1664** EVELYN *Kal. Hort.* Nov. 79 Flowers in Prime... Anemonies, Meadow Saffron [etc.]. *c* **1711** PETIVER *Gazophyl.* VI. lviii, Cape saffron with a knotty stalk. **1776** WITHERING *Brit. Plants* (1796) II. 69 Spring Saffron, or Crocus. **1866** *Treas. Bot.* 1004/2 Saffron, African, *Lyperia crocea.*

3. The orange-yellow colour of saffron (sense 1).

1382 WYCLIF *Lam.* iv. 5 That weren nurshid in faire clois of saffroun [Vulg. *qui nutriebantur in croceis*]. **1601** SHAKS *All's Well* IV. v. 2 Your sonne was misled with a snipt taffata fellow there, whose villanous saffron wold haue made all the vnbak'd and dowy youth of a nation in his colour. **1712** ADDISON *Spect.* No. 265 ¶9 Aurora.. is robed in Saffron. **1798** LANDOR *Gebir* II. 212 Go early, ere the glad-some Hours Strew saffron in the path of rising Morn. **1895** YEATS *Wand. Usheen* Poems 35 When the sun once more in saffron stept.

4. *Old Chem.* = CROCUS 3.

1681 tr. *Belon's Myst. Physick* Introd. 54 Draw off the Menstruum, till the Saffron of the Gold remain almost dry. **1704** J. HARRIS *Lex. Techn.* I, *Saffron of Steel*, or *Mars.* See *Crocus Martis. Ibid., Crocus Martis Astringens, Binding Saffron of Steel.* **1727–41** CHAMBERS *Cycl.* s.v., Saffron is also a name given to several chymical preparations, from the resemblance of their colour to that of the vegetable Saffron, but more usually called *Croci*. Such are Saffron of Venus... Saffron of Mars... Saffron of Gold. **1758** REID tr. *Macquer's Chym.* I. 368 Saffron of Mars. **1842** FRANCIS *Dict. Arts, Saffron of Antimony.* Sesquisulphuret of antimony.

5. Short for *saffron butterfly, moth*: see B. b.

1829 J. F. STEPHENS *Catal. Brit. Insects* II. 171 *Lozotænia croceana*.. the Saffron. **1832** J. RENNIE *Conspect. Butterfl. & M.* 2 The Clouded Saffron (*Colias Edusa*, Fabricius).

6. *attrib.* and *Comb.* **a.** simple attrib., as ***saffron bulb, colour, flower, head, -kiln, ointment, yellow*** (adj.).

1398 TREVISA *Barth. De P.R.* XVII. xli. (1495) 626 Crocomagma is callyd the superfluyte of spycery: of the whyche saffron oynement is made. *Ibid.* XIX. xvi. 873 Saffron colour dieth and coloureth humours and lycours more thanne cytryne. *c* **1440** *Pallad. on Husb.* III. 545 Now saffron bulbes beth to sette or sowe. **1725** BRADLEY *Fam. Dict.* s.v., *Saffron-kiln*, a Kiln to dry Saffron with. **1728** DOUGLAS in *Phil. Trans.* XXXV. 572 To take up the Saffron Heads. **1832** J. RENNIE *Conspect. Butterfl. & M.* 2 Wings.. above deep saffron yellow. **1910** W. DE LA MARE *Three Mulla-Mulgars* viii. 108 A little bunch of faded saffron-flower. **1970** SIMON & HOWE *Dict. Gastron.* 332/1 The English town of Saffron Walden was an important producer [of saffron] and its town arms still have three saffron flowers pictured within the turreted walls.

b. objective, as ***saffron-gatherer***; parasynthetic and with pa. pples., as ***saffron-clad, -coloured, -flavoured, -hued, -robed, -spotted*** adjs.

1881 O. WILDE *Poems* 106 Beheld an awful image *saffron-clad. **1548** ELYOT *Dict., Crocotularius*, a dyer of *saffron coloured garmentes. *a* **1586** SIDNEY *Arcadia* II. (1622) 207 But (as the Poets say) Hymen had not there his saffron coloured coat. **1828** STARK *Elem. Nat. Hist.* II. 51 Aperture white, and throat saffron-coloured. **1931** W. FAULKNER *Sanctuary* (1981) xviii. 175 A final *saffron-colored light lay upon the ceiling. **1959** I. & P. OPIE *Lore & Lang. Schoolch.* xii. 243 Simnel Cake, a rich *saffron-flavoured fruit cake with almond icing. **1856** DELAMER *Fl. Gard.* (1861) 42 The *saffron-gatherers in the field. **1513** DOUGLAS *Æneis* VI. iii. 97 With *saffron hewit frute. **1971** *Guardian* 5 July 18/5 The *saffron-robed members of the [Hare Krishna] order. **1945** J. BETJEMAN *New Bats in Old Belfries* 26 Little fields with boulders dotted, Grey-stone shoulders *saffron-spotted.

c. Special combinations: † **saffron-bag,** ? a bag in which saffron is kept; **saffron bun,** a bun flavoured with saffron; **saffron cake,** (*a*) a cake flavoured with saffron; (*b*) (see quot. 1867, cf. *cake saffron* in sense 1); **saffron cordial,** a cordial made with marigold-flowers, nutmeg and saffron; **saffron crocus,** the *Crocus sativus* (see 2); † **saffron cut** *a.*, the designation of a kind of tobacco; **saffron milk cap,** an edible orange-coloured funnel-shaped agaric, *Lactarius deliciosus*; † **saffron noble,** ? a saffron-cake made in imitation of the coin; **saffron rice,** rice flavoured with saffron; † **saffron sauce,** ? sauce flavoured with saffron; **saffron-tea,** 'an infusion of the flowers of *Carthamus tinctoria* [SAFFLOWER 2], used as a diuretic in febrile disorders' (*Syd. Soc. Lex.* 1897); **saffron-thistle** = SAFFLOWER 2 (*Cent. Dict.* 1891); † **saffron-tree,** the American hackberry, *Celtis crassifolia*; **saffron-wood** (see quot.); = SAFFRA(A)N.

1508 DUNBAR *Flyting* 171 Thy skolderit skin, hewd lyk ane *saffrone bag. **1540** BARNES *Wks.* (1573) Life 6, I haue beene slaundered to preache that our lady was but a Saffron bagge. **1852** C. M. YONGE *Two Guardians* i. 12 A feast.. of *saffron buns, Devonshire cream, and cyder. **1922** JOYCE *Ulysses* 158 Saffron bun and milk and soda lunch in the educational dairy. **1977** *West Briton* 25 Aug. 3/4 Each child received a saffron bun and a bottle of pop. **1747** MRS. GLASSE *Cookery* 139 To make a fine Seed or *Saffron Cake. **1867** TRISTRAM *Nat. Hist. Bible* 479 These [stigmas of the saffron crocus] are pressed into small tablets before drying, when they form the saffron cake of the bazaars of the East. **1892** 'Q.' (QUILLER-COUCH) *Three Ships* v. 87 A slice o' saffern-cake, crowder, to stay ye. Don't say no. **1728** E. SMITH *Compl. Housew.* 229 The *Saffron Cordial. **1857** HENFREY *Bot.* § 588 The *Saffron Crocus, *C. sativus*. **1766** W. GORDON *Gen. Counting-ho.* 324, 10 hhds *saffron cut tobacco. **1954** E. M. WAKEFIELD *Observer's Bk. Common Fungi* 55 *Saffron Milk Cap.. is recognisable by the orange milk which quickly turns green on exposure to the air. **1972** *Times* 23 Sept. 14/5 The.. 'Saffron Milk Cap' is harmless and eagerly sought. **1593** DEE *Diary* (Camden) 45, I gave him a *saffron noble in ernest for a drinkpeny. **1926** T. E. LAWRENCE *Seven Pillars* (1935) III. xxxvii. 217 They took very long about the food and it was not till near noon that at last it came: a great bowl of *saffron-rice, with a broken lamb littered over it. **1973** R. PARKES *Guardians* ii. 42 Dan helped himself to another portion of saffron rice, annointed it with curry and tabasco. *c* **1480** HENRYSON *Test. Cress.* 421 The swete meitis servit in plaittis clene, With *saipheron sals of an gude sessoun. **1716** *Petiveriana* I. 276 *Saffron-tree, Celtis Amer. fol. Citri subtus aureo fructu rubro. **1854** *Saffron-wood [see SAFFRA(A)N]. **1862** *Chamb. Encycl.* III. 801/1 The timber of *Elæodendron croceum*, called Saffron-wood at the Cape of Good Hope, is much used there in building and cabinet-making.

B. *adj.* **a.** Resembling saffron in colour. In early use also, †Coloured with saffron.

1567 MAPLET *Gr. Forest* 35 Cammomill.. there is three kindes hereof. One which hath a Saffron flower. **1590** SHAKS. *Com. Err.* IV. iv. 64 Did this Companion with the saffron face Reuell and feast it at my house to day. **1596** SPENSER *State Irel.* Wks. (Globe) 622/1 [The law] which putteth away saffron shirtes and smockes. **1632** MILTON *L'Allegro* 126 There let Hymen oft appear In Saffron robe. **1697** DRYDEN *Æneid* IV. 840 Aurora now had left her Saffron Bed. **1716** GAY *Trivia* II. 384 Nor lazy Jaundice dulls your Saffron Eye. **1871** R. ELLIS *Catullus* lxviii. 136 Array'd in bright broidery, saffron of hue. **1873** BLACK *Pr. Thule* xxvii, The clear saffron glory of the western sky.

b. Special collocations: **saffron butterfly, moth,** collectors' names for certain lepidoptera having yellow wings; † **saffron pear,** a variety of winter pear; **saffron plum,** a West Indian and mainland sapotaceous tree (*Bumelia cuneata*) having a yellow fruit.

1704 PETIVER *Gazophyl.* II. xiv, *Papilio croceus, apicibus nigricantibus*... The *Saffron Butterfly. **1829** J. F. STEPHENS *Catal. Brit. Insects* II. 3 *Colias Edusa*... Clouded yellow or Saffron B. **1664** EVELYN *Kal. Hort.* Oct. 76 Lombart-pear, Russet-pear, *Saffron-pear. **1884** SARGENT *Rep. Forests N. Amer.* (10th Census IX.) 103 *Bumelia cuneata*... Ants' Wood. Downward Plum. *Saffron Plum.

c. *Comb.*, as ***saffron-fruited, -mantled, robed,*** adjs.

1558 PHAER *Æneid* VI. P iv b, But saffronfrutid [*orig.* 207 *croceo fetu*] bows the stubbes therof doth ouerspreede. **1791** COWPER *Iliad.* VIII. 1 The saffron-mantled morning [Ἠὼς κροκόπεπλος]. **1842–63** I. WILLIAMS *Baptistery* II. xxviii. (1874) 141 Saffron-rob'd descending Charity.

Hence **'saffronic** *a.* (*rare*) = SAFFRONY *a.*

1949 E. SITWELL *Canticle of Rose* 245 Then the King who is part of the saffronic dust.

saffron ('sæfrən), *v. rare.* Also 5 **saferon, safroun.** [f. SAFFRON *sb.* Cf. F. *safraner*, med.L. *saffranāre*, It. *zafferanare*, Sp. *azafranar.*] *trans.* **a.** To season with saffron. †Also *fig.* **b.** To dye with saffron; also, to give a saffron-yellow colour to.

c **1386** CHAUCER *Pard. T.* 17 And in Latyn I speke a wordes fewe, To saffron [*MS. Bodl.* 686 saferon] with my predicacion. *c* **1430** *Two Cookery-bks.* 32 Safroun it wel. *Ibid.* 49 Safroun þin cofynn a-boue. **1593** DRAYTON *Idea, Eglog* ii. (1870) 6 The lothlie morpheu saffroned the place. **1622** T. STOUGHTON *Chr. Sacrif.* xii. 166 In Ireland.. they saffron all their wearing linnen. **1833** *Blackw. Mag.* XXXIV. 540 She saffrons the hills, and azures the mountains, to delight him.

saffroned ('sæfrənd), *a.* Forms: 4 **saffrunde,** 5 **saffrond,** 6 **saferned,** 6–7 **safrond,** 6– **saffroned.** [f. SAFFRON *sb.* or *v.* + -ED. Cf. F. *safrané.*] Coloured with saffron, or having the colour of saffron; also, flavoured with saffron.

1303 R. BRUNNE *Handl. Synne* 3445 Wymples, kerchyues, saffrunde betyde [orig. *Les gympeus ausi safronez*]. *a* **1400–50** *Alexander* 4600 Ȝour women has.. no gay gere to glyffe in ȝour eȝen, Silke of Sipris, ne say ne saffrond kellis. **1559** W. CUNNINGHAM *Cosmogr. Glasse* 173 Their shirtes, and smokes are saffroned. **1585** T. WASHINGTON tr. *Nicholay's Voy.* IV. xxxiv. 149 b, On their head is a yelow Tulbant safrond. **1587** MASCALL *Govt. Cattle, Sheep* (1627) 199 The yellow sheepe be in Asia, the which they call red Saferned sheepe. **1621** B. JONSON *Gipsies Metam.* (1641) 51 Give us .. Ribands, bells, and Safrond lynnen. **1881** *Q. Rev.* Oct.

516, I saw seven hundred dishes served... Everything in them was saffroned and peppered. **1903** KIPLING 5 *Nations* 22 In the saffroned bridesails scenting all the seas.

†'saffronish, *a. Obs.* [+ -ISH.] = next.

1530 PALSGR. 323/1 Safronnysshe of the coloure of safrone, *saffronneux*. **1562** TURNER *Baths* 7 Thre colours one saffronish, another rede, and the thyrde grene. **1699** EVELYN *Acetaria* 44 Underneath of a pale saffronish hue.

saffrony ('sæfrənɪ), *a. rare.* [f. SAFFRON *sb.* + -Y.] Of a colour somewhat resembling saffron.

1630 LORD *Banians* 9 This woman was of complexion yealowish or Saffrony. **1688** R. HOLME *Armoury* II. 39/2 The Agate is of a Saffrony or pale yellow colour. **1725** BRADLEY *Fam. Dict.* s.v. *Jaundice*, The Yellow Jaundice is of a Saffrony, or Lemon Colour. **1838** GRANVILLE *Spas Germ.* 378 The cheeks, formerly tallowish and saffrony, became ruddy.

saffyr, saffyron, obs. ff. SAPPHIRE, SAFFRON.

safir, safitie, obs. forms of SAPPHIRE, SAFETY.

saflor, sa-flower, obs. forms of SAFFLOWER.

safour, obs. form of SAPPHIRE.

safranine ('sæfrəni:n). *Chem.* Also 9 **safranin** (-ɪn). [f. F. *safran* SAFFRON *sb.* + -IN¹.] †**a.** The yellow colouring matter of saffron. Now *Obs.* **b.** A coal-tar colour which dyes yellowish-red. Also, any of a large class of azine dyestuffs (chiefly red) related to this, which are obtained typically by coupling of diazotized aromatic monoamines with aromatic diamines. Sometimes with following letter designating particular compounds.

1868 WATTS *Dict. Chem.* V. 145 *Safranin* or *Saffron-yellow*.. a colouring matter obtained, though not in the pure state, from saffron. **1872** *Jrnl. Chem. Soc.* XXIV. 271 (*heading*) Preparation of saffranine [*sic*]. *Ibid.* 828 Safranine when treated with aniline yields a purple dye. **1875** WATTS *Dict. Chem.* 2nd Suppl. 1063 *Safranine*.. a red dye prepared commercially.. by treating aniline with nitrous acid [etc.]. **1885** GOODALE *Physiol. Bot.* 380 An alcoholic solution of safranin. **1897** *Allbutt's Syst. Med.* III. 215 Solution of safranine. **1905** CAIN & THORPE *Synthetic Dyestuffs* xviii. 134 The first technical production of Safranine under this name was carried out under the French patents of Felix Duprey in 1865, but without success. **1911** I. W. FAY *Chem. Coal-Tar Dyes* xii. 298 Mauve, the very first dye prepared by Perkin in 1856, has been shown.. to be a true safranine. **1952** K. VENKATARAMAN *Chem. Synthetic Dyes* II. xxv. 766 The simplest Safranine (Safranine B; Phenosafranine; CI 840) is obtained by oxidizing a mixture of *p*-phenylenediamine and aniline to the indamine by means of dichromate and hydrochloric acid, and boiling the solution to convert the blue indamine into the red Safranine. **1971** R. L. M. ALLEN *Colour Chem.* viii. 124 Safranine T is used for dyeing tannin-mordanted cotton, bast fibres, wool, silk, polyacrylonitrile fibres, leather and paper.

safranophile ('sæfrənəʊfɪl), *a.* [Formed as prec. + -PHILE.] 'Having an affinity for, or staining readily with, safranin' (*Syd. Soc. Lex.* 1897).

1890 in BILLINGS *Nat. Med. Dict.*

safrene ('sæfri:n). *Chem.* Also **saffrene**. [ad. G. *safren* (Grimaux and Ruotte 1869), f. (*sas*)*safr*(*as*): see SASSAFRAS and -ENE.] (See quot. 1897.)

1872 WATTS *Dict. Chem.* Suppl. 1014 The hydrocarbon, safrene, has the composition $C^{10}H^{16}$. **1897** *Syd. Soc. Lex.*, *Safrene*... A volatile compound obtained by the fractional distillation of sassafras oil.

safrole ('sæfrəʊl). *Chem.* Formerly **safrol** (-ɒl). [ad. F. *safrol* (Grimaux & Ruotte 1869, in *Compt. Rend.* LXVIII. 928) f. *sas*)*safr*(*as* SASSAFRAS: see -OL, -OLE.] A colourless, liquid, bicyclic, aromatic ether, $C_{10}H_{10}O_2$, which occurs in a number of essential oils, esp. oil of sassafras of which it is the major constituent.

1869 *Chem. News* 16 July 35/1 The oil further contains safrol, $C_{10}H_{10}O_2$, boiling at between 231° and 233°. **1884** *Jrnl. Chem. Soc.* XLVI. 1338 Safrole is the main constituent of the essential oil of sassafras. **1922** [see PINENE]. **1950** *Thorpe's Dict. Appl. Chem.* (ed. 4) X. 656/1 Oil of sassafras is obtained from *Sassafras officinale* Nees.. and contains 78% safrole... Safrole is also found as a constituent of many essential oils especially those derived from the order *Lauraceæ*. **1970** *New Scientist* 30 July 232/2 There are very many substances used as food ingredients.. which might, like the safrole in root beer, be found to be toxic. **1976** *Nature* 22 July 252/1 After many generations of people had enjoyed the natural flavour of sassafras, it turned out that safrole, the substance responsible for this, caused cancer in rats.

safron, -oun, -un, -yn, obs. ff. SAFFRON.

saft, obs. f. *saved* (see SAVE *v.*), SHAFT; Sc. var. SOFT.

safur, -yr(e, obs. forms of SAPPHIRE.

sag (sæg), *sb.*¹ Now *dial.* Also 6–7 **sagge**. [var. of SEG, SEDGE.] = SEDGE.

1531 *Lett. & Pap. Hen. VIII*, V. 184 Payment to James Hole for sagge. *Ibid.* 186 Paide to James Hole, of Collam, for saggde for the brykmakrs.. for savyng of the brykkes. Paide to Mychell Bynde for reede for the saide brykmakers. **1598** FLORIO *Sermenti*.. flags, sags, or reeds growing by the water side. **1651** T. BARKER *Art of Angling* (1653) 9 Leave about a yard, either to tye a bunch of sags or a bladder to boy up the Fish. **1688** R. HOLME *Armoury* IV. iv. (Roxb.) 299/1 A Pond or pitt of water surrounded with Reeds and Sagges Vert. **1893** P. H. EMERSON *Eng. Lagoons* 118 They say eels are hid up this weather.. but these weren't... I think they must have worked out of the sags (hovers).

b. *attrib.* and *Comb.*, as *sag-bed*, *-bottomed*, *-seated*; † **sag-spear**, ? a 'spear' or stalk of sedge.

1672 W. HUGHES *Amer. Phys.* 28 Like those Sag-beds which grow many together in some.. boggy places in England. **1688** R. HOLME *Armoury* IV. v. (Roxb.) 310/2 On a crowne three sagge-speares in Triangle O. tyed together with a Rubin G. the ends extended. **1735** SOMERVILLE *Chase* IV. 396 Ah! on that yielding Sag-bed, see, once more His Seal I view. **1890** *Gloucestersh. Gloss.*, *Sag-seated chair*, a rush-bottomed chair. **1893** *S.E. Worc. Gloss.* App., *Sags*, rushes, used for the seats of chairs, such chairs being called 'sag-bottomed chairs'.

sag (sæg), *sb.*² [f. SAG *v.*] The action of sagging.

1. *Naut.* Movement or tendency to leeward.

1580 BURROUGH in *Hakluyt's Voy.* (1599) I. 436 It is very necessary that you doe note at the ende of euery foure glasses, what way the shippe hath made,.. and howe her way hath bene through the water, considering withall for the sagge of the sea to leewards, accordingly as you shall finde it growen. **1882** *Daily Tel.* 2 Sept. (Casell), Shoving through it very slowly, with a surprising sag to leeward.

2. In a rope, wire, etc. supported at two points: The dip below the horizontal line, due to its weight; the perpendicular distance from its lowest point to the straight line between the points of support.

1861 *Ann. Reg.* 73 The 'sag' or droop of the cable from a straight line is 12 feet. **1889** PREECE & MAIER *Telephone* 136 A consideration which is of the highest importance for telephonic networks of wire is the length of the sag, or dip, of the wires between two supports. **1892** C. T. DENT *Mountaineering* iv. 104 The rope.. should stretch from one waistloop to the next without any sag at all.

3. a. A sinking or subsidence; quasi-*concr.* a place where the surface has subsided, a depression.

1727 in *Amer. Speech* (1940) XV. 387/1 Thence along the North Side of the Mountains to a Corner Several Saplins by a Sagg. **1850** *Rep. Comm. Patents 1849: Agric.* (U.S.) 443 Strawberries are met with.. on the edges of 'sloughs' or 'saggs'. **1872** C. KING *Mountain Sierra Nev.* viii. 167 A gray canopy of cloud which stretched from wall to wall, hanging down here and there in deep blue sags. **1874** RAYMOND *Statist. Mines & Mining* 324 To cross with pipes a 'sag' in the divide 280 feet deep and.. eight miles wide from one crest to the other. **1888** 'PAUL CUSHING' *Blacksmith of Voe* I. ii. 61 There was a deep sag in the seat, which, however, added to the comfort of sitting in it. **1892** C. LAPWORTH in *Proc. Geog. Soc.* 689 Where the great continental sag sinks below the ocean level.

b. *fig.*

1868 W. JAMES *Let.* 15 May in R. B. Perry *Tht. & Char. W. James* (1935) I. 512 Such an event rather dislocates my mind from its habitual 'sag' in contemplating the world. **1938** E. BOWEN *Death of Heart* III. i. 323 Behind the opaqueness of her features control permitted no sag of tiredness.

4. *Comm.* A decline in price, in a business, or in a programme of development.

1891 *Daily News* 4 Mar. 2/2 In the American market there is a slight but general 'sag'. **1897** E. HOUGH *Story of Cowboy* 334 Then in time came.. the 'sag' in the cattle business. **1946** *Sun* (Baltimore) 20 Aug. 8/2 (*heading*) The sag in the housing program. *a* **1974** R. CROSSMAN *Diaries* (1975) I. 555 The Chancellor had cut back local-authority spending on mortgages... In that case, I said, he must permit us to use public-sector building to make up for the sag.

5. *attrib.* and *Comb.*, as **Sagbag**, the proprietary name of an informal chair consisting of a large bag filled with polystyrene granules which accommodates itself to the form of the sitter; also **sagbag**; **sagbend**, the curved stretch of pipe below the point of inflexion in the S-shaped length of pipeline as it is lowered on to the sea bed from a barge (cf. OVER-BEND *sb.*); **sag pond**, a pond whose basin is the result of earth movement associated with a fault; **sag wagon** *Cycling* (see quot. 1961); also *transf.*

1974 *Observer* 13 Jan. 23/6 (*caption*) Polystyrene sagbag in various colours of canvas.. from.. Habitat. **1974** *Trade Marks Jrnl.* 18 Dec. 2520/2 *Sagbag*... Furniture; chairs and settees: seats and seating... cushions (not for medical or surgical purposes);.. Habitat Designs Limited, Hithercroft Road, Wallingford, Berkshire; Merchants. **1978** *Evening Standard* 28 Apr. 18/4 June Mendoza's picture of La Rippon, shoeless in a denim jump-suit and reclining fetchingly in a purplish sag-bag. **1969** *Preprints 1st Ann. Offshore Technol. Conf.* II. 37/2 To prevent excessive bending in the sag bend a straight stinger must discharge the pipe very near to the bottom. **1975** *Petroleum Rev.* XXIX. 309/1 A pipe tensioning system has been provided which will avoid buckles in the sagbend. **1933** *Calif. Jrnl. Mines & Geol.* XXIX. 197 Numerous little water-holding depressions known as sag ponds mark the site of local subsidences. **1974** GRIBBIN & PLAGEMANN *Jupiter Effect* x. 114 And yet in the San Francisco Peninsula, where memories of 1906 should prompt some caution, lines of so-called sag ponds, which geologists use as a clear indicator of the fault line, have been filled in to make building land! **1961** PARTRIDGE *Dict. Slang* Suppl. 1257/1 *Sag-wagon*, a van that, following a [cycle] race, picks up exhausted riders. **1963** *Times* 6 June 5/7 When, later, Selaru had gear trouble they both gave up the struggle for the solace of a sag waggon. **1977** C. MCFADDEN *Serial* (1978) xlvii. 102/2 You wanna come along in the bus in case I need a sag wagon?

†sag, *a. Obs. rare.* [f. SAG *v.*] Hanging or sagging down. Also in Comb. *sag-bellied*.

? *a* **1550** *Schole-ho. Women* 472 in Hazl. *E.P.P.* IV. 123 Put me two bones in a bag..; That doon, holde it some what sag, Shake it also, that it may wag. **1648** HERRICK *Hesper.*, *Oberon's Feast* 27 Then.. He.. eates the sagge And well bestrutted Bees sweet bagge. **1651** OGILBY *Æsop* (1665) 208 An old Sag-bellied Toad.

sag (sæg), *v.* Inflected **sagged, sagging**. Forms: 5–7 **sagge**, (6 **sacke**), 9 **sagg**, 6– **sag**; 8–9 *dial.* **seg(g** (see E.D.D.). [First recorded in the 15th c.; the meaning (as well as the 16th c. form *sacke*) appears to point to connexion of some kind with mod.Du. *zakken*, MLG. *sacken*, Sw. *sacka*, Norw. dial. *sakka* to subside, settle down (also *sakk* subsidence), Da. *sakke* to lag behind (the Du. and Sw. words have also the nautical sense below). With sense 3 cf. Norw. dial. *sagga* 'to walk heavily and slowly, as from weariness' (Ross), for which other dialects have *sigga*, *sugga*.

The Du., LG., and Sw. forms appear to admit of no etymological explanation as native words; on the other hand the Norw. dial. *sakka* may be related to *sekka* (ON. *sekkva*) to SINK. It seems possible that the word is originally WScandinavian, and has passed (? as a nautical term) into Sw., Du., LG., and (perh. through LG.) into English.

On this hypothesis the representation of the continental Teut. *kk* by *gg* would be an instance of the common uncertainty in the phonetic appreciation of foreign sounds. It is uncertain whether the Norw. dial. *sagga* abovementioned is related to the other words, and whether its resemblance in sense to the Eng. word is more than a coincidence.]

1. a. *intr.* To sink or subside gradually, by weight or pressure.

c **1425** *Cast. Persev.* 1294 in *Macro Plays* 116 Mankynne is soylyd & saggyd in synne! *c* **1440** *Promp. Parv.* 440/2 Saggyn or satlyn [? *read* satlyn] (satelyn, *P.*, stytlyn, *S.*), *basso*. **1599** A. M. tr. *Gabelhouer's Bk. Physicke* 96/1 Quilte the bagge least the herbes sacke the one vppon the other. **1601** HOLLAND *Pliny* I. 492 The Cherrie tree wood is firme and fast; the Elme and the Ash are tough; howbeit, they will soone settle downward and sag, being charged with any weight, but bend they will before they break. **1630** J. LEVETT *Ord. Bees* (1634) 19 Leaving a shoulder on the inside to stay it and this is good to keep the crowne of Hives from sagging downewards. **1881** DARWIN *Veg. Mould* iv. 215 We see in these three sections.. that the old pavements have sunk or sagged considerably. **1889** *Nature* 5 Dec. 103 The crust of the earth must have sagged foot by foot as additional feet of burdens were laid upon it.

b. Of a part of the body (occas. of a person): To droop; to sink or hang *down* loosely.

1526 *Pilgr. Perf.* (W. de W. 1531) 304 b, Thy blessed body, whiche synkynge downe, sagged & honge by yᵉ crosse. **1563–83** FOXE *A. & M.* 1114/1 At last his feruour began to grow cold and faint, & his handes sagged downward. *a* **1565** SIR T. CHALLONER tr. *Boeth.* I. metr. i. 12 in *Q. Eliz. Englishings* App. 150 My skynne do sagg in wrinkles slacke, my fflaggy lymbes do tremble. **1567** GOLDING *Ovid's Met.* XI. (1593) 263 Appollo could not suffer well his foolish eares to keepe Their human shape, but drew them wide, and made them long and deepe. And fild them full of whitish heares, and made them downe to sagge. **1592** NASHE *P. Penilesse* B 4 b, Cheeks that sag like a womans dugs ouer his chinbone. *a* **1600** DELONEY *Thomas of Reading* (1827) 73 It is, sir, your ill-favoured great nose, that hangs sagging so lothsomely to your lips. **1816** W. TAYLOR in *Monthly Mag.* XLI. 144 O could this wrinkled hand unlearn to sag I'd go; and from this crosier shake the union flag. **1849** LONGF. *Kavanagh* xxi. 132 Except little Alfred, who was tired and cross, and sat sleepy and sagging on his father's knee. **1902** *Westm. Gaz.* 5 June 2/1 The head slowly sagged down on to the cushions.

c. 'To hang down on one side' (Phillips, ed. Kersey 1706). Of a garment: To hang unevenly, to slip out of position. Now chiefly *dial.* and *U.S.* Hence occas. of a person: †To wear 'sagging' clothes, to be dressed untidily.

1592 NASHE *P. Penilesse* A 2 b, Sir Rowland Russet-coat, their dad, goes sagging euery day in his round gas-coynes of white cotton, & hath much a do.. to keepe his vnthrift elbowes in reparations. *Ibid.* A 3, A paire of trunke slops, sagging down like a Shoomaker's wallet. **1600** SURFLET *Country Farm* I. viii. 32 If the croisant or bodie of the moone hang sagging. **1611** COTGR., *Glacer*,.. to flesh-bast; or stitch downe the lyning of a garment thereby to keepe it from sagging. **1624** BP. HALL *True Peace-maker* Wks. (1625) 541 The girdle of whose equity sags downe on that side, where the purse hangs. **1703** T. N. *City & C. Purchaser* 29 To prevent a Door from sagging, or sinking at the fore corner. **1854** MISS BAKER *Northampt. Gloss.* II. 193 A load of hay or corn that is badly put on the waggon, leaning on one side, and, as it is termed, top-heavy, is said to *sag*. **1877** *N.W. Linc. Gloss.* s.v., Rebecca's made my Sunda' goun sag sorely. **1878** *Masque Poets* 156 His coat is green and sags. **1883** MRS. ROLLINS *New Eng. Bygones* 190 It [the bridge] sags to one side. **1885** *Harper's Mag.* May 867/1 The.. gates sag apart. **1903** J. FOX jun. *Little Sheph. Kingd. Come* 345 The gate sagged on its hinges.

d. To bend or curve downwards in the middle, from its own weight or superincumbent pressure. Said, e.g., of a rope supported at two points, of a beam, plank, etc. *Naut.* opposed to HOG *v.*¹

1777 W. HUTCHINSON *Pract. Seamanship* 13 And that their bottoms not only hog upwards, but sag (or curve) downwards, to dangerous and fatal degrees. **1819** RAINBIRD *Agric. Suffolk* (1849) 298 (E.D.D.). **1842** GWILT *Archit.* §2031 The beam by its own gravity.. would have a tendency to sag or bend in the middle. *Ibid.*, When the rafters are of such length that they would be liable of themselves to sag down, supports *aa* are introduced at the points where such failures would occur. **1859** WHITTIER *Proph. Sam. Sewall* 102 Great beams sag from the ceiling low. **1883** R. HALDANE *Workshop Rec.* Ser. II. 290/1 The rod will lose its straightness, first sagging in the middle, then dropping. **1886** E. S. MORSE *Jap. Homes* i. 27 One..comes to wonder why the whole ceiling does not sag.

transf. **1888** HENLEY *Bk. Verses* 152 The sky saggs low with convoluted cloud.

e. To bulge (*out*); to belly *in*. Chiefly *dial.*

1853 G. J. CAYLEY *La Alforjas* II. 151 It sagged in like a bellying sail. **1855** ROBINSON *Whitby Gloss.*, *Sagg'd out*, bulged out at the side, as a bowing wall. **1897** KIPLING *Captains Courageous* 108 The other half come up sagging full o' big uns.

2. a. To decline to a lower level, through lack of strength or effort. Chiefly *fig.* (Common in U.S.)

1508 FISHER *Seven Penit. Ps.* xxxviii. Wks. (1876) 88 Yf the helpe of his grace be not redy at all seasons we must nedes sagge & bowe. **1605** SHAKS. *Macb.* v. iii. 10 The minde I sway by, and the heart I beare, Shall neuer sagge with doubt, nor shake with feare. **1891** *Harper's Mag.* Sept. 644/1 Is she sagging towards Realism or rising towards Idealism? **1902** GILDERSLEEVE in *Amer. Jrnl. Philol.* XXIII. 137 Professor Lawton..says that Parmenides sags in his flight.

b. *dial.* 'To decline in health; to begin to show signs of old age' (E.D.D.).

1784 CULLUM *Hist. Hawsted* iii. 173 He begins to *sag*. To decline in his health. **1893** ZINCKE *Wherstead* 261 For anything to be over-poised, or metaphorically to decline in health, is to 'sag'.

c. *Comm.* To decline in price. Also with *down*, *away*, *off*.

1870 W. W. FOWLER *Ten Yrs. in Wall St.* xxv. 393 The price grew firmer when two or three men were observed selling quietly large amounts, and then the price sagged to 250. **1887** [see SAGGING *ppl. a.*]. **1892** *Daily News* 11 May 3/5 Wheat..further sagged down owing to the increase in amount on passage. **1903** *Westm. Gaz.* 29 Aug. 7/1 With lack of support the market has sagged away, and closes some 27*s.* 6*d.* below last week's values. **1905** *Ibid.* 1 June 9/1 There are appreciable advances on the share figures of three months ago on those investments which sagged through last year's bad balance-sheets.

3. To drag oneself along wearily or feebly. Also *U.S.* (see quot. 1880).

1573 TWYNE *Æneid* x. Eejb, Encounter them at land Whilest fearful they come forth, and their first steps do sag in sand. **1612** DRAYTON *Poly-olb.* xvi. 219 This said, the aged Steed sagd sadly on alone. **1880** *Webster's Suppl.*, *Sag*, to loiter in walking; to idle along; to drag or droop heavily. **1897** RHOSCOMYL *White Rose* 165 'And I am not more than a third of the way along', said he to himself, as the horse sagged slower at every stride.

4. a. *Naut.* Of a ship or boat: To drift, be carried out of the intended course. Chiefly in the phrase ***to sag to leeward***.

1633 T. JAMES *Voy.* 93 [In tacking] we did sagge upon the maine rand of Ice. **1769** [see SAGGING *vbl. sb.*]. **1794** *Rigging & Seamanship* II. 256* *To Sag to leeward*, to make considerable lee-way. **1849** *Blackw. Mag.* LXVI. 726 The want of actual headway making the Indiaman sag dead away to leeward. **1856** KANE *Arct. Expl.* II. xxix. 287 McGary hung upon his oar, and the boat, slowly but noiselessly sagging ahead. **1892** KIPLING *Barrack-r. Ballads* 206 We're sagging south on the Long Trail.

†**b.** *transf.* To drift, deviate insensibly (*into*, *from*). *Obs.*

1639 FULLER *Holy War* IV. xix. (1640) 202 We see elective States in Christendome, though bound with the straitest laws, often sagge aside into schismes and factions. **1655** —— *Ch. Hist.* IX. v. §2 Yet such [spheres] as are excentricall can never observe equall distance in their motion, but will sagg aside to grind, and grate one the other. *a* **1661** —— *Worthies* (1662) II. *Lond.* 224 No Hospital is tyed with better or stricter laws, that it may not Sagg from the intention of the Founder.

5. *trans.* in causative senses. †**a.** [From sense 4.] Of a current at sea: To cause to 'sag' or drift; to carry out of the intended course. *Obs.*

1628 DIGBY *Voy. Medit.* (Camden) 77 The current sagged me into the bay deeper towardes the eastward. **1635** *Voy. Foxe & James to North West* (Hakl. Soc.) 191 After he was loos'd he was sagged into the Bay.

b. [From sense 1 d.] To cause to bend downwards in the middle.

1755 JOHNSON, *To Sag*, *v.a.* To load; to burthen. **1777** W. HUTCHINSON *Pract. Seamanship* 13 Their bottoms were thus sagged down by the cargoes. *Ibid.*, Sagged downwards six inches by her cargo. **1869** SIR E. J. REED *Shipbuild.* v. 93 The ultimate measures of the strengths of the ships to resist a strain tending to hog or sag, or break them across is as 5 : 4. **1892** C. LAPWORTH in *Proc. Geogr. Soc.* 689 The surface of this American arch is sagged downwards in the middle into a central depression which lies between two long marginal plateaux. **1902** *Westm. Gaz.* 5 July 8/3 The vessel will first be 'sagged' by being hung by the head and the stern only from two platforms, one at each end.

6. *intr.* and *trans.* To play truant (from). *Liverpool local.*

1959 I. & P. OPIE *Lore & Lang. Schoolch.* xvii. 372 *Sagging*. This is definitely the prevailing term [for playing truant] amongst delinquents in all parts of Liverpool. **1965** *Woman* 28 Aug. 8, I re-visit childhood haunts in Liverpool, meet the next generation in the Cathedral grounds where we used to 'sag'—that is, play truant. **1966** F. SHAW et al. *Lern Yerself Scouse* 45 *I'm saggin skewl*, I am playing truant.

sag, variant of SEG (castrated bull).

saga[1] ('sɑːgə). [a. ON. and Icel. *saga* wk. fem. (Sw. *saga*) narrative, story, history; corresp. (exc. in declension) to OE. *sagu* str. fem.: see SAW *sb.*[2]]

1. a. Any of the narrative compositions in prose that were written in Iceland or Norway during the middle ages; in English use often applied *spec.* to those which embody the traditional history of Icelandic families or of the kings of Norway.

1709 HICKES in *Pepys' Diary* (1879) VI. 201 The histories of the old Northern nations, which commonly have the title of Saga, which signifies a narration of History. **1777** ROBERTSON *Hist. Amer.* (1783) I. 326 The credit of this story rests, as far as I know, on the authority of the Saga, or Chronicle of King Olaus..published by Perinskiold at Stockholm A.D. 1697. **1805** SCOTT *Last Minstr.* VI. xxii, Many a Saga's rhyme uncouth. **1897** W. P. KER *Epic & Romance* 66 The Icelandic Sagas—the prose histories of the fortunes of the great Icelandic houses.

b. *transf.* A narrative having the (real or supposed) characteristics of the Icelandic sagas; a story of heroic achievement or marvellous adventure. Also, a novel or series of novels recounting the history of a family through several generations, as *The Forsyte Saga*. Now freq. in weakened use, a long and complicated (account of a) series of more or less loosely connected events.

1857 LONGF. *Discov. North Cape* viii, For the old seafaring men Came to me now and then, With their sagas of the seas. **1862** H. MARRYAT *Year in Sweden* II. 63 With this last visit terminates my saga of Gripsholm. **1891** KIPLING *Light that Failed* v, Dick delivered himself of the saga of his own doings. [**1891** R. L. STEVENSON *Let.* 19 May (1899) II. 231 Henry Shovel has now turned into a work called 'The Shovels of Newton French'.., which work is to begin in 1664..and end about 1832... I mean to make it good; it will be more like a saga.] **1895** HALL CAINE *Bondman* (ed. 4) p. viii, I have called my story a Saga, merely because it follows the epic method. **1919** J. GALSWORTHY *Let.* 25 Nov. in H. V. Marrot *Life & Lett. J. Galsworthy* (1935) IV. i. 485, I have just finished a sequel to *The Man of Property*, and, in accordance with the scheme I broached to you..have still one story and a third novel in further sequel to write, to make the whole of *The Forsyte Saga*. **1935** D. L. SAYERS *Gaudy Night* iii. 51 She felt she would rather be tried for life over again than walk the daily treadmill of Catherine's life. It was a saga, in its way, but it was preposterous. **1942** 'M. INNES' *Daffodil Affair* II. 89 Appleby and Hudspith were scarcely in a position to give it the dispassionate appraisal of literary critics; the saga had a sort of aura of alligator which made it uncomfortable hearing. **1952** *Times Lit. Suppl.* 1 Jan. 15/3 The latest, no doubt the logical, development of the 'life with mother' saga is the chronicle of pregnancy and childbirth. **1959** *Listener* 18 June 1074/1 The Burrell Collection..is still, after a long saga of misadventures, looking for a site. **1970** *Nature* 18 Apr. 197/1 By now, the daily newspapers will tell how the saga of Apollo 13 has been finished. **1977** 'E. CRISPIN' *Glimpses of Moon* x. 190 Rousing themselves hastily from the morbid fascination induced by this saga, Thouless, Padmore and the Major all went into action. **1978** H. WOUK *War & Remembrance* xlix. 497 '*Found* her! Where?' 'In Marseilles. Told me about it for two hours over dinner. It's a saga.'

¶**2.** In incorrect uses (partly as the equivalent of the cognate Ger. *sage*): A story, popularly believed to be matter of fact, which has been developed by gradual accretions in the course of ages, and has been handed down by oral tradition; historical or heroic legend, as distinguished both from authentic history and from intentional fiction.

1845 B. THORPE in *J. M. Lappenberg's Hist. Eng.* I. 90 The poem of Beowulf.., in which the old Anglian saga is ennobled by an Anglo-Saxon of the eighth century. **1855** GEO. ELIOT in *Fraser's Mag.* July 55/1 The libretto is founded on the old German *saga* of the Venusberg and the knightly minstrel Tannhäuser. **1864** KINGSLEY *Rom. & Teut.* i. (1875) 1, I shall begin..with a saga. **1869** TOZER *Highl. Turkey* II. 265 The Popular Tale is thus.. distinguished from..the Myth, or Saga. **1873** MISS R. H. BUSK *Sagas fr. Far East* 242 While displaying the usual exaggerations common to the Sagas of all nations, these Indian Sagas have one leading peculiarity. **1881** H. MORLEY *Longer Works in Eng. Verse & Prose* I. i. 1/1 Most ancient of English poems is the old saga which tells how Beowulf rescued Hrothgar from the attacks of Grendel. **1883** KENNEDY tr. *Ten Brink's E. Eng. Lit.* 150 The Sagas of Guy of Warwick and Bevis of Hampton. **1898** T. ARNOLD *Notes on Beowulf* v. 71 Whether the Sigemund— Siegfried saga is of Scandinavian or German origin. **1903** L. F. ANDERSON *Anglo-Saxon Scop* 16 The great number of sagas learned by the scop of *Beowulf* is expressly mentioned... It was praiseworthy in a scop to have learned not only the more familiar sagas, but some not generally known. **1912** R. W. CHAMBERS *Widsith* 15 How much of this is history, and how much saga, it is not easy to say. **1960** M. B. MCNAMEE in *Jrnl. Eng. & Gmc. Philol.* LIX. 199 At least by the eleventh century, the mysterious serpent-infested mere of Anglo-Saxon saga had provided a means of making the story of Christ and Satan and Hell graphic to the Anglo-Saxon imagination.

3. *Comb.*, as ***saga-age***, ***-cycle***, ***-hero***; ***-writer***; **saga boy** *W. Indies*, [perh. f. a different word], a well-dressed lounger, a playboy; **saga-man** [= ON. *sǫgu-maðr*], a narrator of sagas, also the hero of a saga.

1897 W. P. KER *Epic & Romance* iii. 230 In the material conditions of Icelandic life in the 'Saga Age' there was all the stuff that was required for heroic narrative. **1956** PETERSON & FISHER *Wild Amer.* xxxiii. 354 The..Eskimos used to drive the geese across the tundra..and net them..a method of wildfowling known..in Iceland, where it became a great art in the Saga Age. **1949** *Human Relations* II. 358/2 This change in behaviour is clearly demonstrated by men who have been to Aruba, Curacao, Trinidad, or U.S.A., and who have acquired some money... In this group the 'Saga-Boys' are to be found—flamboyantly dressed men with exaggerated manners and mannerisms and somewhat aggressive tendencies. **1959** V. S. NAIPAUL *Miguel St.* xi. 118 Eddoes was a real 'saga-boy'. This didn't mean that he wrote epic poetry. It meant that he was a 'sweet-man', a man of leisure, well-dressed, and keen on women. **1966** P. SHERLOCK *West Indies* xi. 143 Saga boys dressed in sheath-like saga pants, 'peg-top trousers' and saga coats called Bim-Bams. **1892** S. A. BROOKE *Hist. Early Eng. Lit.* I. 104 The first saga-cycle includes the songs sung concerning the earlier deeds of Beowulf before he became king. **1899** W. H. SCHOFIELD tr. *S. Bugge's Home of Eddic Poems* 172 In the oldest reference to this saga-hero, in *Widsith*, 21, we read: *Hagena* [*wéold*] *Holmrygum*. **1823** CRABB *Technol. Dict.*, *Saga-man* (Archæol.), a tale-teller, or secret accuser. **1853** KINGSLEY *Hypatia* xxix, You are the hero! you are the Sagaman! We are not worthy. **1866** *Reader* 3 Mar. 221/3 All the skalds and sagamen of any note were Icelanders. **1866** BARING-GOULD *Myths Mid. Ages* Ser. I. 113 An arrow.. penetrated the windpipe of the king, and it is supposed to have sped, observes the Saga writer, from the bow of Hemingr.

‖**saga**[2] ('seɪgə). [L. *sāga*.] A witch.

1583 *Leg. Bp. St. Androis* 312 Thair Saga slew ane saikles beast. **1834** LYTTON *Pompeii* III. x, 'Patience', resumed the witch,..'My mother was herself a saga'.

‖**saga**, pl. of SAGUM.

sagaciate (sə'geɪʃɪeɪt, -'æʃuː-), *v.* U.S. *dial.* Also **segashuate**, etc. [App. jocularly f. SAGACI(OUS *a.* + -ATE[3].] **a.** *intr.* To thrive or prosper. (Freq. used when inquiring after one's health.)

1832 *Boston Transcript* 2 Aug. 2/3 Well, Clem, how do you sagatiate dis lubly wedder? **1842** *Literary Gaz.* 1 Jan. 6/3 How does your copperosity sagaciate this morning? **1880** J. C. HARRIS *Uncle Remus* ii. 24 'How duz yo' sym'tums seem ter segashuate?' sez Brer Rabbit, sezee. **1890**, etc. [see CORPOROSITY]. **1906** *Dialect Notes* III. 154 How are you sagashawatin'? **1976** K. BONFIGLIOLI *Something Nasty in Woodshed* xi. 131 My symptoms started to sagashuate again but Jock blocked my every move to slink back into bed.

b. *nonce-uses.*

1904 A. MORRISON *Green Eye of Goona* v. 181 The police sagaciate that Pooley must ha' gone straight to London. **1909** 'O. HENRY' *Roads of Destiny* xxii. 366, I sagatiated in your associations once, if I am not mistaken.

sagacious (sə'geɪʃəs), *a.* [f. L. *sagāc-em* (whence F. *sagace*), *sagax*, f. the root **sāg-* (= OTeut. **sōk-*, SEEK *v.*) in *sāgīre* to discern acutely.]

†**1.** Acute in perception, esp. by the sense of smell. Const. *of*. *Obs.*

1607 TOPSELL *Four-f. Beasts* Ep. Ded. A5, The Bees seeke out their King if he loose himselfe, and by a most sagacious smelling-sence, neuer cease till he be found out. **1656** BLOUNT *Glossogr.*, *Sagacious*,..quick of scent, taste or sight. **1667** MILTON *P.L.* x. 281 So sented the grim Feature, and upturn'd His Nostril wide into the murkie Air, Sagacious of his Quarry from so farr. **1700** DRYDEN *Cock & Fox* 751 With Might and Main they chas'd the murd'rous Fox,..Nor wanted Horns t' inspire sagacious Hounds. **1732** POPE *Ess. Man* I. 214 And hound sagacious on the tainted green.

2. Gifted with acuteness of mental discernment; having special aptitude for the discovery of truth; penetrating and judicious in the estimation of character and motives, and in the devising of means for the accomplishment of ends; shrewd.

1650 BULWER *Anthropomet.* 145 It would seem a wonder if sagacious Nature should faulter only in the forming of that part. **1682** SIR T. BROWNE *Chr. Mor.* I. §6 True Charity is sagacious, and will find out hints for beneficence. **1704** RAY *Creation* I. (ed. 4) 95 The Study and Endeavours of the most sagacious Naturalists. **1756** C. LUCAS *Ess. Waters* III. 125 Our very sagacious author found them in this condition. **1781** COWPER *Conversat.* 742 The world grown old, her deep discernment shows, Claps spectacles on her sagacious nose. **1794** S. WILLIAMS *Vermont* 136 He appeared to the greatest advantage, sagacious in distinguishing and observing. **1849** MACAULAY *Hist. Eng.* vii. II. 194 He had been urged by an adviser less sagacious and more impetuous than himself, to try a bolder course. **1863** GEO. ELIOT *Romola* xix, Bardi was entirely under the ascendency of his sagacious and practical friend.

b. Of observations, sayings, actions, etc.: Resulting from or exhibiting acuteness of mental discernment; characterized by sagacity.

1831 BREWSTER *Newton* ix. 108 Hence he concluded that diamond 'is an unctuous substance coagulated',—a sagacious prediction, which has been verified in the discoveries of modern chemistry. **1856** KANE *Arct. Expl.* II. xv. 161 The Esquimaux examines the track with sagacious care. **1857** MILLER *Elem. Chem.* (1862) III. 438 This sagacious conjecture has since been fully verified by the discoveries of Wurtz and Hofmann. **1876** BLACKIE *Lang. & Lit. Sc. Highl.* ii. 87 In Homer himself,..we find not a few of those sagacious, curt sentences, into which men unacquainted with books are fond of compressing their experience of human life.

3. Of animals: Intelligent.

1759 GOLDSM. *Bee* No. 4 Of all the solitary insects I have ever remarked, the spider is the most sagacious. **1819** KEATS *Eve St. Agnes* xli, The wakeful bloodhound rose, and shook his hide, But his sagacious eye an inmate owns.

Hence **sa'gaciously** *adv.*, **sa'gaciousness**.

1678 CUDWORTH *Intell. Syst.* I. i. §28. 33 Wherefore they sagaciously apprehended, that there must needs be [etc.]. *Ibid.* iv. §14. 250 Where this Love is not only called πολυμήτις, of much-counsel or sagaciousness,..but also πρεσβύτατος. *a* **1711** KEN *Edmund* Poet. Wks. 1721 II. 102 But Edmund..Sagaciously the Pageantry suspects. **1818** HALLAM *Mid. Ages* (1872) I. 64 But his measures had been so sagaciously taken, that except through that perverseness of fortune,..he could hardly fail of success. **1884** J. HAWTHORNE *A. Malmaison* iii, It is always a delicate matter to fathom the depth of a medical man's sagaciousness.

sagacity (sə'gæsɪtɪ). [ad. F. *sagacité*, ad. L. *sagācitāt-em*, f. *sagāc-em* SAGACIOUS *a.*: see -ITY.] The quality of being sagacious.

†**1.** Acute sense of smell. *Obs.*

1607 TOPSELL *Four-f. Beasts* 151 marg., What smelling or sagacity in Dogs is. *Ibid.* 451 This Beast is not onely enemy to the crocodile and Aspe, but also to their Egges, which she hunteth out by the sagacity of her nose. **1677** PLOT *Oxfordsh.* 179 Ladies, who commonly have great sagacity in smelling, may hereby be directed in the choice of their Melitæi or Lap-dogs. **1784** COWPER *Task* VI. 616 Some [animals] show that nice sagacity of smell. **1798** PENNANT *Hindoostan* II. 36 All this genus are remarkable for their voracity and their sagacity of nostril.

2. Acuteness of mental discernment; aptitude for investigation or discovery; keenness and soundness of judgement in the estimation of persons and conditions, and in the adaptation of means to ends; penetration, shrewdness.

a **1548** HALL *Chron., Hen. VII* 13 b, Both for age and prudent sagacitie, fatherly, a wyse & a grave personage, which for renuyng of the olde amitie, were commanded [etc.]. **1604** R. CAWDREY *Table Alph., Sagacitie*, sharpnes of wit; witnesse. **1647** CLARENDON *Hist. Reb.* I. §24 As he had a wonderfull Sagacity in such Reflections, a thousand Difficulties and Dangers occurred to him. **1693** J. EDWARDS *Author. O. & N. Test.* 18 Men of skill and sagacity do sometimes foretel futurities. **1743** EMERSON *Fluxions* 107 These are the general Rules, but after all, many things must be left to the Sagacity and Invention of the Artist. **1791** MRS. RADCLIFFE *Rom. Forest* x, She was somewhat surprised at Peter's sagacity. **1844** DICKENS *Mart. Chuz.* xxxviii, Relying on your advice as a man of great sagacity in money matters. **1849** MACAULAY *Hist. Eng.* ii. I. 182 He discerns the signs of the times with a sagacity which to the multitude appears miraculous. **1864** PUSEY *Lect. Daniel* (1876) 160 It was beyond human sagacity..to predict the Roman Empire.

b. *pl.* Sagacious observations.

1866 CARLYLE *Remin.* (1881) I. 103 His native sagacities.. made him the most delightful of companions. **1891** *Spectator* 13 June 829/1 Who..is always pressing her homely sagacities on the imagination of the young.

3. Of animals: Exceptional intelligence; skill in the adaptation of means to ends.

1555 EDEN *Decades* 189 Are there many of such sagacitie and industrye as the lyke is not seene in beastes of greater quantitie. **1646** SIR T. BROWNE *Pseud. Ep.* III. iv. 112 Why they placed this invention upon the Bever..might be the sagacitie and wisedome of that animall. **1725** DE FOE *Voy. round World* (1840) 337 Black cattle..by a natural sagacity, apprehensive of being swept away with the flood. **1759** GOLDSM. *Bee* No. 4 The sagacity of some insects. **1837** W. IRVING *Capt. Bonneville* II. 134 He had heard much of the sagacity of the beaver in cutting down trees.

sagakomi (sægə'kəʊmɪ). *N. Amer.* Also 8 **segockimac,** 8- **sac à commis,** 9- **saccacom(m)i(s).** [a. Ojibwa *sakākkomin* bearberry.] = BEARBERRY a, b; also, the leaves of this plant used with, or as a substitute for, tobacco.

In quot. 1934 wrongly applied to madroño, *Arbutus menziesii*, another member of the Ericaceæ.

1703 L. A. LAHONTAN *New Voy. N. Amer.* II. 53 They are forc'd to buy up Brasil Tobaco, which they mix with a certain Leaf..call'd Sagakomi. **1778** J. CARVER *Trav. Interior Parts N. Amer.* 31 A weed that grows near the great lakes..is called by the Indians Segockimac, and creeps like a vine on the ground,..bearing a leaf about the size of a silver penny, nearly round... These leaves, dried and powdered, they likewise mix with their tobacco. **1823** J. FRANKLIN *Narr. Journey to Polar Sea* 741 Jackashey-puck.. has received the name of *Sac à commis*, from the trading clerks carrying it in their smoking bags. **1836** G. BACK *Narr. Arctic Land Exped.* ix. 257 We passed many sandhills, variegated by the..plant, called..by the traders 'sac à commis'. **1837** *Trans. Lit. & Hist. Soc. Quebec* III. 91 Saccacommi [is] frequently used to smoke in lieu of tobacco, by the traders engaged in the fur countries. **1890** L. F. R. MASSON *Bourgeois de la Compagnie du Nord-Ouest* II. 102 *Graine d'ours*, bear berry, also called *sac à commis*, a creeping plant which is smoked, and which the clerks put in their sacs. **1910** F. W. HODGE *Handbk. Amer. Indians.* II. 407/2 Sagakomi. The name of a certain smoking mixture, or substitute for tobacco, applied also to the bearberry bush.. or other shrubs the leaves and bark of which are used for the same purpose. **1934** L. L. HASKIN *Wild Flowers Pacific Coast* 263 The coast Indian name for it [*sc.* madroño] seems to have been *saccacomis*, upon which the French constructed a pun, calling it *sac-a-commis*.

sagamité (sə,gɑːmɪ'teɪ). Also 8 **shaggamitie, sagamitty, sagamite,** 9 **sagamity.** [a. F. *sagamité* (Sagard, 1632), repr. Cree Indian *kisamitew*, hot drink of any kind.] **a.** A kind of gruel or porridge made from coarse hominy. †**b.** (See quot. 1748.)

c **1665** P. E. RADISSON *Voyages* (1885) 40 Then my father made a speech shewing many demonstrations of vallor, broak a kettle full of Cagamite with a hattchett. **1698** *Hennepin's Contn. New Discov. Amer.* xxviii. 106 Sagamite, or Pap made of Indian corn. **1744** J. DE CHAMPIGNY *Present State Louisiana* 22 They were employed in..making Sagamité and baking it. **1748** H. ELLIS *Voy. Hudson's Bay* 188 The broth of fish, which they call shaggamitie. **1763** tr. *Father Charlevoix' Acc. Voy. Canada* 279 (Stanf.) The women come for several days and pour Sagamitty on the place. **1796** *Hist. Ned Evans* II. 103 But they were all refreshed with as much Indian corn pounded and stewed with bear's grease as they could eat, which they call sagamity. **1807** G. HERIOT *Trav.* 586 Sagamité, pudding made of Indian corn. **1829** H. MURRAY *N. Amer.* I. vii. 375 The dishes were Sagamity or boiled Indian Corn. **1880** G. W. CABLE *Grandissimes* 26 They sat down to bear's meat, sagamite and beans. **1916** F. W. WAUGH *Iroquois Foods* 91 Probably no corn or other food is referred to so frequently as hominy, or sagamité, as it was more familiarly known to the early French. **1931** W. CATHER *Shadows on Rock* IV. iii. 193 Cécile did not want much breakfast... She had sagamite and milk. **1940** E. J. PRATT *Coll. Poems* (1958) II. 256 It was the middle room that drew the natives, Day after day, to share the sagamite And raisins, and to see the marvels brought From France. **1963** *Beaver* Autumn 17/2 Their [*sc.* the Hurons'] sagamité, a kind of corn porridge that drew excruciatingly long faces from the early Frenchmen, was, nevertheless, remarkably nourishing.

sagamore ('sægəmɔə(r)). Also 7 **sagamos, sagomo, sagomore, saggamore, segamore, sagamor,** 7-8 **sagamo,** 8 **sachemore.** [a. Penobscot *sagamo*: see SACHEM.] = SACHEM I.

1613 PURCHAS *Pilgrimage* (1614) 750 He obserued a feast made by Anadabijon the great Sagamo, in his Cabin. *Ibid.* 756 When a Sagamos dieth, they blacke themselues. **1624** CAPT. SMITH *Virginia* VI. 240 The Massachusets call..their kings there abouts Sachems: the Penobscotes..their kings Sagomos. **1642** LECHFORD *Plain Dealer* (1867) 115 They are governed by sachems, kings, and saggamores, petie lords. **1675** *Lond. Gaz.* No. 1017/1 King Philip the Indian Segamore of those parts, had raised about six hundred Men in Arms. **1751** C. GIST *Jrnls.* (1893) 72 This Beaver is the Sachemore or Chief of the Delawares. **1826** J. F. COOPER *Mohicans* xxx, Uncas,..the wisest Sagamore of the Indians! **1865** PARKMAN *Champlain* iv. (1875) 246 But the vision of the centenarian sagamore put them all to shame.

transf. **1882** DOWDEN in *Academy* 30 Dec. 464/1 But readers on this side of the Atlantic cannot be supposed to owe allegiance to every local sagamore of learning or Puritan pow-wow of the old colonial days.

†**b. sagamore's head**: ? some American tree.

1741 P. COLLINSON in *Mem. Bartram* (1849) 148 The butter-nut..with the Medlar and Sagamore's head.

Hence †**'sagamoreship.**

1674 JOSSELYN *Voy. New Eng.* 123 The three Kingdoms or Sagamoreships of the Mattachusets were very populous, having under them seven Dukedoms or petti-Sagamoreships.

‖**Sagan** ('seɪgən). *Jewish Antiq.* Also 9 **segan.** [Late (Talmudic) use of Heb. *sāgān* or *'segen* (found only in pl. *s^egānīm*), Jewish Aram. *s^egan*, a. Assyrian *shaknu* prefect (of conquered city or province). In the Bible the word denotes only a civil governor.] The deputy of the Jewish high-priest; the second highest functionary of the Temple.

In Biblical times this official seems to have been called 'second priest' (Heb. *kōhēn hammishneʰ*): see Jer. lii. 24.

1625 T. GODWIN *Moses & Aaron* I. (1641) 18 The High Priest and his Sagan, resembled our Bishop and his Suffragan. **1681** DRYDEN *Abs. & Achit.* 866 With him the Sagan of Jerusalem, Of hospitable soul and noble stem. **1877** C. GEIKIE *Christ* lx. (1879) 737 The ancient hierarchy as consisting of the high priest; his deputy, or Sagan: two suffragans of the Sagans, [etc.]. **1904** *Jewish Encycl.* VI. 390/2 Every high priest had a 'mishneh' (a second) called the Segan, or 'memunneh', to stand at his right.

†**sagapen(e.** *Obs.* Also 6 ? **sagape.** [Anglicized form of next.] = SAGAPENUM; also the plant producing sagapenum.

1548 TURNER *Names of Herbes* 37 *Ferula*... It maye be named in englishe herbe Sagapene or Fenel gyante. **1570** LEVINS *Manip.* 26/37 Herbe-sagape [rimes *ape, grape*, etc.], *ferula.* **1601** HOLLAND *Pliny* II. 67 As for our Sacopenium here in Italy, it differeth altogether from that which grows beyond sea. For the outlandish kind..is called Sagapen. **1611** COTGR., *Ferule*,..the hearbe Ferula, Sagapene, Fennell Giant. **1651** J. F[REAKE] *Agrippa's Occ. Philos.* 86 The root of the reedy Hearb Sagapen. **1712** tr. *Pomet's Hist. Drugs* I. 190 Chuse your Sagapen in fine Tears, clear and transparent, of a strong smell.

‖**sagapenum** (sægə'piːnəm). [Late L. *sagapēnum, -on*, a. Gr. σαγάπηνον a plant (prob. *Ferula persica*); also the gum obtained from it.] A gum-resin, the concrete juice of *Ferula persica*, formerly used as an antispasmodic and emmenagogue, or externally. Also ***gum sagapenum.***

1579 LANGHAM *Gard. Health* (1633) 573 Sagapenum or Serapinum..is a precious gumme, the best shineth through darke in colour yelow without and white within. **1616** BULLOKAR *Eng. Expos., Sagapenum*, the sappe or Gum of a plant growing in Media..vsed in Physicke against diuers cold diseases. **1718** QUINCY *Compl. Disp.* 125 Sagapenum.. is likewise the Tear or Gum of a Tree. **1815** KAUFFMAN *Dict. Merchandize* Gum sagapenum. **1851-9** HOOKER in *Man. Sci. Enq.* 424 Compared with assafœtida and galbanum, sagapenum is a rare and costly drug.

sagar, obs. form of CIGAR and SAKER[1].

sagaret, obs. form of SAKERET.

‖**sagaris** ('sægərɪs). *Antiq.* Also anglicized 8 **sagar.** [Gr. σάγαρις, from some Eastern language.] A single-edged battle-axe used by Scythians, Persians, Amazons, etc.

1623 BINGHAM *Xenophon* 69 A weapon called *Sagaris*, such as the Amazons beare. **1776** J. BRYANT *Mythol.* III. 140 Their chief arms were..battleaxes, and sagars. **1860** RAWLINSON *Hist. Herodotus* IV. 65 The Sacæ..carried the battleaxe, or *sagaris*.

sagarston, obs. form of SEXTON.

sagashuate, etc., varr. SAGACIATE.

sagat(e, -gates, obs. northern var. ff. SOGATE(S.

†**sagate,** *a. Her. Obs.*$^{-1}$ [ad. L. type **sagātus*, f. *sag-um* mantle.] Clothed in a mantle.

1688 R. HOLME *Armoury* IV. viii. (Roxb.) 328/2 A Head-peece..Argent..Mantled with a Rockett, or Sagate Gules, lynned with white.

sagathy ('sægəθɪ). *Obs.* exc. *Hist.* Also 8 **sagathea, saggathe, sagathee,** 8-9 **segathy,** 9 **sagathoy, -thay.** [In Fr. *sagatis* (Boiste 1840; not in Littré or Hatz.-Darm.), Sp. *sagatí*; of unknown origin.] A woollen stuff (see quot. 1727-41).

1707 *Postman* 15 Nov. in Ashton *Soc. Life Reign Q. Anne* (1882) I. 151 Broad Cloaths, Camblet, Druggits and Sagathys. **1709** *Female Tatler* No. 9/1 Any Camlets, Drugets, or Sagathies. **1710** STEELE *Tatler* No. 270 ¶4 Making a Panegyrick on Pieces of Sagathy or Scotch-Plod. **1727-41** CHAMBERS *Cycl., Sagathee*,..a slight woollen stuff; being a kind of serge, or ratteen; sometimes mixed with a little silk. **1745** *De Foe's Eng. Tradesman* xxvi. (1841) I. 261 Norwich buys..serges and segathies from Devon and Somersetshire. **1804** *Monthly Mag.* 418 Not more than three persons are engaged in making..serges, duroys, sagothoys and dimities. **1810** J. T. in *Risdon's Surv. Devon* Introd. Remarks 25 Segathies, druggets, coatings, beavers, ..found a market in Spain. **1882** J. ASHTON *Soc. Life Reign Q. Anne* I. 151 They [*sc.* clothes] were made of drugget and sagathay, camlet, but the majority of men wore cloth. **1884** BESANT *Dorothy Forster* ii, He..went about dressed in grey sagathy and woollen stockings.

b. *attrib.* or *adj.* Made of sagathy.

1711 *Lond. Gaz.* No. 4901/4 A brown-colour'd Sagathea Wastcoat and Breeches. **1712** *Ibid.* No. 5058/4 A Led-coloured Saggathe Coat and Wastecoat. **1889** DOYLE *Micah Clarke* ii. 14 Beneath my sagathy stuff jacket.

sagay, variant of ZAGAIE.

sagbo(u)t, -but(t, obs. forms of SACKBUT.

sage (seɪdʒ), *sb.*[1] Forms: 4-6 **sauge,** 4-5 **sawge, salge,** (5 **sauoge**), 6 **saulge, seage,** 5- **sage.** [ME. *sauge*, a. F. *sauge* (13th c. in Littré):—L. *salvia* (whence late OE. *saluie*, ME. SAVE *sb.*). Cf. Pr., Sp., It. *salvia*, Pg. *salva*; also MLG. *salvie, selve*, Du. *salie*, OHG. *salbeia, salveia* fem. (mod.G. *salbei* masc.). For the phonology in Eng. cf. CHAFE *v.*, GAUGE, SAFE, SAVE.]

1. A plant of the genus *Salvia*, N.O. *Labiatæ*; esp. *S. officinalis*, an aromatic culinary herb. Hence, the leaves of this plant used in Cookery.

Sage, much esteemed formerly as a medicinal herb, is not now included in the British Pharmacopœia, but in domestic medicine is still used in the preparation of sage-tea (see 6 b).

a **1310** in Wright *Lyric P.* (Percy Soc.) 26 He is blosme opon bleo brihtest under bis, With celydoyne ant sauge, as thou thi self sys. **1390** GOWER *Conf.* III. 131 Salge is his herbe appourtenant Aboven al the remenant. *c* **1420** *Liber Cocorum* (1862) 11 Do þer to sage and persely ȝoyng. **1533** ELYOT *Cast. Helthe* II. xvi. (1541) 29 Sauge. It healeth, and sommewhat byndeth. **1578** LYTE *Dodoens* II. lxxvii. 250 There be two sortes of Sage, the one is small and franke, and the other is great. The great Sage is of three sortes, that is to say, greene, white, and redde. **1584** COGAN *Haven Health* xi. 33 Sage is vsed commonly in sawces, as to stuffe veale, porke, rosting pigges, and that for good cause. **1590** SPENSER *Muiopotmos* 187 The wholesome saulge, and lavender still gray. **1610** FLETCHER *Faithf. Sheph.* II. ii, These for frenzy be A speedy and a soueraigne remedie. The bitter Wormewood, Sage and Marigold. **1714** GAY *Sheph. Week* II. 13 Marbled with Sage the hard'ning Cheese she press'd. **1766** [ANSTEY] *Bath Guide* II. (1807) 77 But what's the sage without the goose? **1881** *Encycl. Brit.* XII. 289/2 Sage, *Salvia officinalis*, a hardy evergreen undershrub, belonging to the labiates, of which there are two varieties, the green-leaved and the red-leaved.

2. *Cookery.* †**a.** A force-meat, 'pottage', or sauce in which sage is the chief ingredient. ***sage yfarced***, sage stuffing. Also quasi-*adj.* in partly anglicized names of culinary preparations containing sage, as ***fritter sage, sauce sage.*** *Obs.*

? *c* **1390** *Forme of Cury* (1780) 23 Pygges in sawse Sawge. *Ibid.* 72 Sawge yfarced. *c* **1430** *Two Cookery-bks.* 28 Sauge. Take Gyngere, Galyngale, Clowys, & grynde in a morter; þan take an handfulle of Sawge, & do þer-to [etc.]. *Ibid.* 41 Sauoge. Take Pigis fete clene y-pekyd; þan tak Freysshe broþe of Beff, & draw mylke of Almaundys, & þe Piggys þer-in; þen mence Sawge [etc.]. *c* **1450** *Ibid.* 72 Pigge or chiken in Sauge. *c* **1460** J. RUSSELL *Bk. Nurture* 501 Frutur sawge.

b. ***sage and onions***: a stuffing chiefly composed of those ingredients, used for goose, duck, pork, etc. Also ***sage-and-onion stuffing.***

1747 MRS. GLASSE *Cookery* 4 Some love the Knuckle [of pork] stuffed with Onions and Sage shred small. **1824** *New Syst. Cookery* 113 Ducks roasted. Stuff one with sage and onion,..crumbs,..and pepper and salt. **1861** MRS. BEETON *Bk. Househ. Managem.* 241 (*heading*) Sage-and-onion stuffing, for geese, ducks, and pork. **189.** *Encycl. Pract. Cookery* (ed. Garrett) s.v., Sage-and-Onion Stuffing.

3. In the names of plants of other genera. **Bengal sage,** *Meriandra bengalensis* (Treas. Bot. 1866). **bitter,** †**garlick,** †**mountain** or **wood sage,** *Teucrium Scorodonia.* **black sage,** (*a*) *Cordia cylindrostachya*; (*b*) in California, *Trichostema lanatum* (Cent. Dict. 1891). **French sage,** *Phlomis fruticosa.* †**Jerusalem sage,** also †**sage of Jerusalem** or †**Bethlehem,** (*a*) *Pulmonaria officinalis*; (*b*) *Phlomis fruticosa.*

seaside sage, *Croton balsamiferum* (Treas. Bot.). †**rock sage**, a species of *Sideritis*. **white sage**, in U.S., a woolly chenopodiaceous plant used as a febrifuge, *Eurotia lanata*; also applied to other plants of the same order, *Kochia prostrata* and *Audibertia polystachya* (Cent. Dict.). **wild sage**, (*a*) = *bitter sage*; (*b*) see quot. 1866.

a **1387** *Sinon. Barthol.* (Anecd. Oxon.) 10/2 *Ambrosia*, wild sauge. **1548** TURNER *Names of Herbs* (1881) 18 Bacchar or Baccaris is the herbe (as I thynke) that we call in english Sage of Hierusalem. **1562** Rock sage [see IRONWORT]. **1578** LYTE *Dodoens* I. lxxxv. 125 Sage of Jerusalem hath rough, hearie, and large, browne greene leaues, sprinckled with diuers white spots. **1597** GERARDE *Herbal* II. ccv. 535 Wood Sage, or Garlicke Sage. *Ibid.* ccliii. 625 Of French Sage, or woodie Mullein... They are called of the learned men of our time *Verbasca syluestria*... In English it is generally called French Sage, we may call it Sage Mullein. *Ibid.* cclxxv. 663 *Pulmonaria*,.. Sage of Ierusalem, Cowslip of Ierusalem, Sage of Bethlem. **1731** MILLER *Gard. Dict.*, *Scordium*,.. Wild Sage, *vulgo*. **1741** *Compl. Fam.-Piece* II. iii. 374 Several other.. Shrubs.. are now in Flower, as the several sorts of Jerusalem Sage. **1864** GRISEBACH *Flora W. Ind. Isl.* 787 Black sage: *Cordia cylindrostachya*. **1865** GOSSE *Land & Sea* (1874) 15 The wood germander, or bitter sage. **1866** *Treas. Bot.* s.v., Wild Sage, a name in the Cape colony for *Tarchonanthus camphoratus*.

4. = *sage-brush* (see 6 b).

1805 M. LEWIS *Jrnl.* 12 May in *Orig. Jrnls. Lewis & Clark Exped.* (1904) II. 29 The wild hysop sage.. and some other herbs also grow in the plains and hills. **1807** P. GASS *Jrnl.* 127 A kind of wild sage or hyssop, as high as a man's head, ..grows in these bottoms. **1837** W. IRVING *Capt. Bonneville* II. 206 The country, hereabout,.. producing very little grass, but a considerable quantity of sage or wormwood. **1851** MAYNE REID *Scalp Hunt.* xxvi, A desert country, here and there covered with wild sage and mezquite. **1872** C. KING *Mountain. Sierra Nev.* xiii. 265 Desert too gentle and overspread with sage to be terrible.

5. The colour of sage.

1881 C. C. HARRISON *Woman's Handiwork* I. 20 A ground of sage or of Pompeian red velvet. **1971** *Vogue* 15 Sept. 129/1 Suit.. sizes 10–16: colours: brown/white, burnt orange/white, olive/sage.

6. a. *attrib.* and *Comb.*: simple attrib., as ***sage-ash, colour, juice, leaf, oil, root, -scrub***; also in the names of preparations flavoured or medicated with sage, as ***sage ale, bread, drink, gargle, wine***; instrumental, as ***sage-covered*** adj.; similative, as ***sage-leaved*** adj.; parasynthetic, as ***sage-coloured*** adj.

1584 COGAN *Haven Health* xi. 33 Much after the same manner [as the making of sage wine] is made *Sage ale. **1597** GERARDE *Herbal* II. cclii. 624 Sage ale, being brewed as it shoulde be, with Sage, Scabious, Betonie, Spikenard, Squinanth, and Fennell seedes. **1923** D. H. LAWRENCE *Birds, Beasts & Flowers* 147 An eagle at the top of a low cedar-bush On the *sage-ash desert. **1668** R. SHARROCK *Let. to Boyle* 7 Apr., B.'s Wks. 1744 V. 4, I have known *sage bread do much good in drying up watry humours. **1596** *Acc. Bk. W. Wray* in *Antiquary* XXXII. 79 Sould him of the leight *sayge culler q' & d. *Ibid.*, iij yeardes of leight *sayge cullerd fustian. **1851** MAYNE REID *Scalp Hunt.* xlii, We passed over *sage-covered plains. **1747** MRS. GLASSE *Cookery* 121 *Sage Drink. **189.** *Encycl. Cookery* (ed. Garrett), *Sage gargle. **1755** WESLEY *Prim. Physic* cxx. 73 Hoarseness... Take a Spoonful of *Sage-juice Morning and Evening. **14..** *Med. MS.* in *Anglia* XIX. 78 Take a *sawge-leef and wryte þeron. **1661** J. CHILDREY *Brit. Baconica* 5 They have a slate of three sorts, blew, sage-leaf-coloured, and gray. **1747** WESLEY *Prim. Phys.* (1762) 88 Apply boiled Sage leaves hot. **1884** BROWNING *Ferishtah* Prol., Sage-leaf is bitter-pungent—so's a quince. **1822** *Hortus Anglicus* II. 13 *C. Salvifolius*. *Sage-leaved Cistus. **1825** *Greenhouse Comp.* I. 95 *Phlomis Lychnites*... A sage-leaved whitish rugose plant. **1888** W. T. BRANNT *Treat. Anim. & Veget. Fats* 539 *Sage oil, *oleum salviæ*, obtained by distillation from the leaves of the sage. **14..** *Stockholm Med. MS.* II. 867 in *Anglia* XVIII. 328 Rwe is eke a souereyn bote, To settyn abowtyn a *sawge-rote. **1927** D. H. LAWRENCE *Mornings in Mexico* 136 Across the grey desert.. low, grey, *sage-scrub was coming to pallid yellow. **1579** LANGHAM *Gard. Health* (1633) 575 Vse it as *Sage wine to consume flegme.

b. Special Comb.: **sage-apple**, a gall-apple formed on a species of sage, *Salvia pomifera*, eaten as a fruit in Crete; **sage-brush**, a collective name applied to various species of *Artemisia*, esp. *A. tridentata*; also *attrib.*; **Sagebrush State**, popular name of Nevada (formerly also applied to Wyoming); **sage-bush** = *sage-brush* above; **sage-cheese**, a kind of cheese which is flavoured and mottled by mixing a decoction of sage-leaves with the cheese-curd; **sage grass**, *U.S.* = *sage-brush*; **sage-green**, a shade of dull greyish green resembling that of the foliage of the sage plant *Salvia officinalis*; also as adj.; hence **sage-greeny** *a.*, of the colour of sage-green; **sage-grey** *a.* = *sage-green*; †**sage mullein** = French sage (see 3 above); **sage rose**, †(*a*) a plant of the genus *Cistus* (obs.); (*b*) a shrub, *Turnera ulmifolia*, found in the W. Indies and S. America; **sage tea**, an infusion of sage-leaves, used as a stomachic and slight stimulant; **sage tree**, (*a*) *Phlomis fruticosa*; (*b*) see quot. 1884; **sage-willow**, a dwarf grey American willow, *Salix tristis*; **sage-wood**, (*a*) = *sage-brush*; (*b*) a small tree or shrub, *Buddleia salviifolia*, of the family Loganiaceæ, found in southern Africa and bearing leaves like those of common sage and racemes of white or purple flowers; also, the hard, heavy wood of this tree.

1832 *Veg. Subst. Food* 321 *Sage-apples. **1850** K. WEBSTER *Gold Seekers of '49* (1917) iii. 84 We were compelled to tie our mules to *sage brush to keep them from straying away. **1861** 'MARK TWAIN' *Lett.* (1917) I. 54 On the plains, sage-brush and grease-wood grow about twice as large as the common geranium. **1872** COUES *Key N. Amer. Birds* 233 Confined to the sterile plains and sage-brush (*Artemisia*) tracts of Western U.S. **1888** BRYCE *Amer. Commw.* II. II. xlvii. 217 A desert.. whose lower grounds were covered with that growth of alkaline plants which the Americans call sage-brush. **1907** S. E. WHITE *Arizona Nights* 191 We began to toil in the ankle-deep sand of a little sage-brush flat. **1946** D. C. PEATTIE *Road of Naturalist* v. 53 A few forms like sage-brush or creosote bush.. repeat themselves for fifty miles on end. **1893** L. WAGNER *Significance of Names* 35 Nevada is also called.. *The *Sage-Brush State*, from the wild artemesia covering the plains. **1917** *Boston Even. Globe* 11 Apr. 16/4 Nevada has been known for many years as the Sagebrush State. **1934** G. E. SHANKLE *State Names* ii. 155 The sobriquet, the *Sagebrush State*, applied to Wyoming, refers to the fact that wild sage (*Artemisia tridentata*) grows on the desert sections of this State. **1976** *Billings* (Montana) *Gaz.* 20 June 10-c/2 Sagebrush, Silver and Battle Born State are nicknames for Nevada, first explored by the Spaniards in 1776. **1976** *Sci. Amer.* Oct. 20/3 Strong lives with his wife and 11-year-old daughter in pine and sagebrush country overlooking the Rio Grande. **1977** J. F. FIXX *Compl. Bk. Running* ii. 25 We are in a canyon surrounded by mountains, trees and sagebrush. **1807** P. GASS *Jrnl.* 204 The *sage bushes.. grow in great abundance on some parts of these plains. **1874** *Treas. Bot.* Suppl. s.v., Sage-bush, *Artemisia tridentata*. **1902** 'MARK TWAIN' in *Harper's Mag.* Jan. 269/2 He started on a run, racing in and out among the sage-bushes. **1977** J. L. HARPER *Population Biol. Plants* xx. 604 Woodland dominated by pinyon pine.. is intimately associated with *Artemisia* sage-bush communities. **1714** GAY *Sheph. Week* II. 16 But Marian now.. Nor yellow Butter nor *Sage Cheese prepares. **1852** DICKENS *Bleak Ho.* xii, It [the sea] is habitually hard upon Sir Leicester, whose countenance it greenly mottles in the manner of sage-cheese. **1893** *Scribner's Mag.* June 801/2 To inhale the odor of.. pungent aromatic things in the tall '*Sage grass'. **1810** *Repository of Arts* (Ackermann) Apr. 262/2 Light *sage green, or cream-coloured kerseymere breeches. **1825** J. NICHOLSON *Operat. Mechanic* 642 Sage-green, pea, and sea-greens. **1929** [see DEMI-SEMI]. **1976** *Star* (Sheffield) 20 Nov. 10/2 (Advt.), Bed-settee with arms. Teak frame. Sage green expanded vinyl. **1884** G. ALLEN *Philistia* I. 49 Three afternoon dresses, the grey,.. the *sage-greeny æsthetic one, and the peacock-blue. **1923** D. H. LAWRENCE *Birds, Beasts & Flowers* 190 Day has gone to dust on the *sage-grey desert. **1562** TURNER *Herbal* II. 161 The wilde one [Verbascum].. may be called in Englishe *Sage mullen. **1597** GERARDE *Herbal* Table *Sage rose and his kinds, looke *Cistus*. **1864** GRISEBACH *Flora W. Ind. Isl.* 787 Sage-rose: *Turnera ulmifolia*. **1705** HICKERINGILL *Priest-cr.* II. vi. 62 As for *Sage-Tea, it being an English Drink,.. I care not if they Drink it without the assistance of Mr. Say-Grace. **1824** LOUDON *Encycl. Gard.* (ed. 2) §4141 The decoction called sage-tea is usually made from one variety, the small-leaved green, or sage of virtue. **1741** *Compl. Fam.-Piece* II. iii, There are several other Trees.. in Flower, as.. Phlomis or *Sage Trees. **1753** CHAMBERS *Cycl. Supp.* App. s.v., Sage of Jerusalem, or Sage-tree. **1884** W. MILLER *Plant-n.*, Sage tree, Brush-land, of Australia. *Psychotria daphnoides*. **1846** G. B. EMERSON *Rep. Trees & Shrubs Mass.* 256 The *sage willow is a slender, hoary plant, or a spreading tufted bush. **1854** L. PAPPE *Silva Capensis* 31 *Sage-wood... Wood hard, tough, heavy. **1932** WATT & BREYER-BRANDWIJK *Medicinal & Poisonous Plants S. Afr.* 140 Sagewood, Saliehout,.. is possibly used medicinally by the Hottentots. **1973** *Stand. Encycl. S. Afr.* IX. 458/2 The sagewood.. belongs to the rather heterogeneous family Loganiaceæ.

c. In the names of animals and birds found chiefly in the sage-brush districts of N. America, as **sage cock, grouse**, the largest grouse found in America, *Centrocercus europhasianus*; **sage hare** = *sage rabbit*; **sage hen**, = *sage cock*; **sage rabbit**, one of several small hares of western North America, esp. *Sylvilagus nuttallii*; **sage sparrow**, each of the two fringilline birds *Amphispiza bilineata* and *A. belli*; **sage thrasher**, the mountain mocking bird, *Oreoscoptes montanus*.

1840 A. WISLIZENUS *Ausflug nach Felsen-Gebirgen 1839* ix. 49 *Sage cock, cock of the plains. **1859** S. F. BAIRD *Catal. N. Amer. Birds* (Smithsonian Misc. Coll.) 462 *Centrocercus urophasianus* Sw. Sage Cock. **1917** T. G. PEARSON *Birds Amer.* II. 30/1 The Sage Cock has a sharp cackle. **1884** COUES *Key N. Amer. Birds* (ed. 2) 580 *Sage Grouse. **1868** *Amer. Naturalist* II. 536 The *Sage Hare.. is more rare near Fort Benton. **1843** J. WILLIAMS *Jrnl.* 27 July in *Narr. Tour to Oregon* (1921) 14 The *sage hen is found here also. **1861** G. F. BERKELEY *Sportsm. W. Prairies* ii. 25 There is a certain bird of the grouse species.. called the 'sage hen'. **1917** [see COCK sb.[1] 10]. **1962** E. LUCIA *Klondike Kate* viii. 170 A great flight of sagehens darkening the sky. **1846** R. B. SAGE *Scenes Rocky Mts.* p. iv, [The] *sage rabbit.. is nearly three times the size of the common rabbit. **1859** S. F. BAIRD *Mammals N. Amer.* 602 *Lepus Artemisia*, Bachman. Sage Rabbit. **1879** GOODE etc. *Catal. Anim. Resources U.S.* 20 *Lepus sylvaticus* Bach., var. *Nuttalli*.—Sage Rabbit. **1884** COUES *Key N. Amer. Birds* (ed. 2) 375 *Amphispiza*.. *Sage Sparrows. *Ibid.* 249 *Sage Thrasher.

d. *attrib.* or as *adj.* Resembling the colour of sage (sense 1). Cf. sense 5 above.

1785 E. SHERIDAN *Jrnl.* 5 July (1960) 59, I have one [plume of feathers] for mine [*sc.* a hat] of dark sage, pink and white feathers. **1820** M. EDGEWORTH *Let.* 8 June (1979) 160 My two tabbinets, sage and fawn ditto have done excellent service, new furbished. **1904** *T. Eaton & Co. Catal.* Spring & Summer 187/1 All-wood carpet.. in red and sage colorings.

sage (seɪdʒ), *a.* and *sb.*[2] Also 6 **saage**, *Sc.* **saig(e, sauge.** [a. F. *sage* adj. and sb. (11th c. in Hatz.-Darm.; OF. had also *saige, savie*):—Com. Rom. *sabio* (Pr. *satge-s, sabi-s*, Sp., Pg. *sabio*, It. *saggio, savio*):—popular L. **sapius* (cf. L. *nesapius* ignorant) f. *sapĕre* to be wise (pr. pple. *sapiens* wise).]

A. *adj.* Now only *literary*.

1. Of a person: Wise, discreet, judicious. In ME. often *the sage* (following a proper name). In modern use in narrowed applications: Practically wise, rendered prudent or judicious by experience.

1297 R. GLOUC. (Rolls) 4069 Nou it worþ iended þat Sibile þe sage sede biuore. **13..** *E.E. Allit. P.* B. 1576 As þe sage sathrapas þat sorsory coupe. **1362** LANGL. *P. Pl.* A. XI. 257 For salamon þe sage þat sapience made. **1390** GOWER *Conf.* II. 383 This.. Is that Sibille of whom ye wite, That alle men yit clepen sage. *c* **1460** ASHBY *Dicta Philos.* 1222 To speke litil, is knowen a man sage. **1490** CAXTON *Eneydos* liii. 148 Retourne agayn towarde eneas and make peas wyth hym yf ye be sage. *a* **1533** LD. BERNERS *Huon* lxxxvi. 274 There is no clerke lyuynge so sage that can put it in wrytynge. **1545** ASCHAM *Toxoph.* (Arb.) 45 The best learned and sagest men in this Realme.. both loue shoting and vse shoting. **1562** WINȜET *Cert. Tractates* i. Wks. (S.T.S.) I. 5 Ȝour wyse, saige, and grave familiar servands. **1571** *Satir. Poems Reform.* xxvii. 11 Bot schaw thyselff both scharpe, sauge [*v.r.* saig], and sinceir. **1594** SHAKS. *Rich. III*, III. vii. 227 Cousin of Buckingham, and sage graue men, Since you will [etc.]. **1597** —— *2 Hen. IV*, IV. v. 121 All you sage Counsailors, hence. *a* **1625** SIR H. FINCH *Law* (1636) 481 The Chancellor, and Treasurer, taking to them the Iustices, and other such sage persons, as they thinke fit. *a* **1687** WALLER *Maid's Trag.* v. Wks. (1729) 348 Can you expect, that she should be so sage To rule her blood, and you not rule your rage? **1732** BERKELEY *Alciphr.* v. §35 The wise reasoning of a certain sage magistrate. **1817** BYRON *Beppo* xxvii, For most men (till by losing rendered sager) Will back their own opinions with a wager. *Ibid.* xxxv, No wonder such accomplishments should turn A female head, however sage and steady. **1833** HT. MARTINEAU *Three Ages* ii. 70 These housekeepers, made sage by circumstance, looked and spoke with something very little like mirth. **1868** MILMAN *St. Paul's* xiii. 346 But sager Juxon.. withdrew from the proud but perilous office. *a* **1872** MAURICE *Friendsh. Bks.* i. (1874) 12 If I thought of him [*sc.* Bacon], even as the sagest of book-makers and not as a human being.

b. Of advice, conduct, etc.: Characterized by profound wisdom; based on sound judgement.

1531 ELYOT *Gov.* III. xxii. (1534) 218 b, Roboaz.. comtempned the sage counsayle of auncyente men, and imbraced the lyght perswasions of yonge men. *c* **1590** MARLOWE *Faust.* I. i. 97 Come.. make me blest with your sage conference. **1601** SHAKS. *Twel. N.* III. iv. 413 Weel whisper ore a couplet or two of most sage sawes. **1641** MILTON *Reform.* II. 45 Little thought he of this sage caution. **1796** H. HUNTER tr. *St.-Pierre's Stud. Nat.* (1799) II. 380 The infinitely sage plans of Nature. **1875** JOWETT *Plato* (ed. 2) III. 176 He gives sage counsels about the nursing of children.

c. Of the countenance, bearing, etc.: Exhibiting sageness or profound wisdom. In mod. use commonly somewhat *ironical*.

1816 SCOTT *Antiq.* ix, Miss Oldbuck re-entered, with a singularly sage expression of countenance. **1849** DICKENS *Dav. Copp.* xix, Mr. Dick had regularly assisted at our councils, with a meditative and sage demeanour.

2. In phraseological combinations after Fr. use: †**a.** ***sage fool*** (also in Fr. form ***fol sage***): a jester or court fool. *Obs.* **b.** ***sage woman*** (also in AF. form †***sage feme***): a midwife. *rare.*

1377 LANGL. *P. Pl.* B. XIII. 423 Ȝe lordes and ladyes.. þat fedeth foles sages, flatereres and lyeres. *Ibid.* 444 A fol sage syttynge at the heyȝ table. ?*c* **1475** in *Q. Eliz. Acad.* 77 There was A grete lorde þat had A Sage fole, the whyche he lovyd Marvaylous well. **1672** [H. STUBBE] *Rosemary & Bayes* 2 Baptisme 'tis thought may be administred by a sage feme. **1833** DISRAELI *Cont. Flem.* III. xix, A sage woman of great reputation was at our house.

†**3.** Grave, dignified, solemn. *Obs.*

1564 *Brief Exam.* C iij b, I woulde haue the Ministers of Churches to vse sage vesture. **1592** NASHE *P. Penilesse* A iij, He wore.. a garnish of night-caps, which a sage butten cap ..ouer spread very orderly. **1602** SHAKS. *Ham.* v. i. 260 We should prophane the seruice of the dead, To sing sage Requiem, and such rest to her As to peace-parted Soules. **1632** MILTON *Penseroso* 117 And if ought els great Bards beside In sage and solemn tunes have sung, Of Turneys and of Trophies hung. **1644** —— *Judgm. Bucer* Wks. 1851 IV. 301 In a point of sagest moment.

B. *sb.*

1. A man of profound wisdom; *esp.* one of those persons of ancient history or legend who were traditionally famous as the wisest of mankind; hence, one whose exceptional wisdom entitles him to a degree of veneration like that which was accorded to these. In early use sometimes with weaker sense, a wise man.

The 'seven sages of Greece' were Thales, Solon, Periander, Cleobulus, Chilon, Bias, and Pittacus, to each of whom some wise maxim is attributed by ancient writers. The 'seven sages of Rome' are the personages of a romance, of Oriental origin, which was popular throughout Europe in the Middle Ages. 'Eastern sages': often applied in hymns (after Milton) to the 'three Magi': see MAGUS 2.

13.. *Seuyn Sag.* (W.) 4, I sal yow tel,.. Of the seuen sages of Rome. **1399** LANGL. *Rich. Redeles* III. 7 Me thynkyth, Sauynge soueraynes and sages avise, þat þe moste myscheff ..Is demed þe dede y-do aȝeins kynde. *c* **1440** *Generydes* 88 This old fader.. Of vij Saugys callid the wysest That was in Rome. **1547–64** BAULDWIN *Mor. Philos.* (Palfr.) 1 There were besides these sophistes, another kinde called sapientes, or sages, as was Thales, Solon [etc.]. **1577** tr. *Bullinger's Decades* II. x. (1592) 223 Musonius, Hierocles, and other auncient sages. **1642** tr. *Perkins' Prof. Bk.* xi. §739. 323 Master Littleton who was an honorable sage of the Law. **1667** MILTON *P.L.* XII. 362 A Starr..proclaims him com, And guides the Eastern Sages, who enquire His place. **1735** THOMSON *Liberty* II. 222 The great Athenian Sage, And Father of Philosophy [*sc.* Socrates]. **1862** STANLEY *Jew. Ch.* (1877) I. xviii. 337 He was..but as one of the old chiefs of the bygone age—half warrior, half sage.

b. In playful or ironic use.

1751 JOHNSON *Rambler* No. 120 ¶2 He called for help upon the sages of physick. **1822** W. IRVING *Braceb. Hall* xxvi. 238 In vain did the sages of the village interfere. **1893** *Times* 8 May 9/3 They have cited..some of the mustiest sages of the law in confirmation of this view.

2. *Comb.*: simple attrib., as ***sage-like*** adj.; objective, as ***sage-inspiring*** adj.; instrumental, as ***sage-exalted***, **-*instructed*** adjs.

1728–46 THOMSON *Spring* 209 The dissolving clouds..to the sage-instructed eye unfold The various twine of light. **1735** —— *Liberty* II. 197 The Sage-exalted Chief [Xenophon]. **1745** T. WARTON *Pleas. Melancholy* 256 Tho' thro' the blissful scenes Ilissus roll His sage-inspiring flood. **1879** R. H. DOUGLAS *Confucianism* iii. 72 He alone, possessing all the sage-like qualities, shows himself..fitted to exercise rule.

SAGE, Sage (seɪdʒ), *sb.*³ *Mil.* [Acronym f. the initial letters of '*s*emi-*a*utomatic *g*round *e*nvironment'.] A name given to an early warning and air defence control system covering the United States and Canada. Freq. *attrib.*

1955 *N.Y. Times* 25 Sept. IV. 2/2 Some time in 1954—the exact date has not been disclosed—the National Security Council gave the Air Force the go-ahead on a project..called Sage. **1958** *Times* 23 July 9/6 Sage is basically a computer..which will evaluate all the information received from the early warning networks, guide missiles and aircraft to their targets, and even work out which is the best weapon to use in a particular situation. **1958** *Electr. Engin.* LXXVII. 793/1 At the present time, excluding other connecting weapons systems, there are three main types of data systems used in the SAGE system. Grouped according to use, these are ground-to-ground, ground-to-air and radar data systems. **1961** *Aeroplane* C. 115/1 Construction has started on the new SAGE (semi-automatic ground environment) defence system which is to be introduced into Canada during this year. **1971** E. LUTTWAK *Dict. Mod. War* 44/2 Guidance is by command direct from the SAGE Air Defence System supplemented by radar homing for final interception.

sage, obs. f. SEDGE; var. SEG *Obs.*

†**saged**, *a. Obs. nonce-wd.* [f. SAGE *sb.*² + -ED¹.] Befitting a sage; characterized by wisdom.

1563 B. GOOGE *Eglogs* I. (Arb.) 31 And many a saged sawe lies hyd within thine aged brest. *Ibid.* 32.

sageer: see SAKIA.

sagely (ˈseɪdʒlɪ), *a. rare*⁻¹. [f. SAGE *sb.*² + -LY¹.] Belonging to or befitting a sage.

1867 LEGGE *Confucius* iv. 54 His gorgeous but unsubstantial pictures of sagely perfection.

sagely (ˈseɪdʒlɪ), *adv.* Also 5 **sagilly**. [f. SAGE *a.* + -LY².] In a sage manner.

a **1400–50** *Alexander* 3359 So bus a kyng to consaile haue a clere hert, To se at syttis him to se & sagely to wirke. *c* **1475** *Partenay* 5315 Sagilly hym ruled to intelligens. **1523** LD. BERNERS *Froiss.* I. vii. 5 The kyng..demaunding right swetely of her astate and besynesse. And she answered him ryght sagely. **1590** SPENSER *F.Q.* I. i. 29 Sober he seemde, and very sagely sad. **1671** MILTON *P.R.* IV. 285. **1714** POPE *Wife of Bath* 341 He, against this right sagely would advise. **1833** HT. MARTINEAU *Charmed Sea* v. 87 Paul explained, very sagely, how right it was. **1872** MORLEY *Voltaire* (1886) 11 If he adroitly or sagely preserved his buckler.

‖**sagene**¹ (ˈsæʒɛn). Also 8 **sajen**, 9 **sachine, sashen, sashine, sajene, sazhen.** [Russian *sazhen'*.] A measure of length formerly used in Russia, equal to seven English feet.

1737 *Phil. Trans.* XL. 29 Wersts, divided each into 500 Sagenes, and each Sagene supposed to be exactly seven Feet English. **1858** SIMMONDS *Dict. Trade*, *Sachine, Sashen*, other names for the sagene, a Russian linear-measure. **1896** REDWOOD *Petroleum* I. 285 Boring, at 75 roubles per sagene (1 sagene = about 7 feet) for the first 100 sagenes [etc.].

sagene² (səˈdʒiːn). *rare.* [ad. L. *sagēna*, a. Gr. σαγήνη.] A fishing-net. In quots. *transf.* and *fig.*, a network (of railways, etc.).

1846 RUSKIN *Mod. Paint.* II. III. I. i. 5 At this time, when the iron roads are tearing up the surface of Europe,..when their great sagene is drawing and twitching the ancient frame and strength of England together. **1871** M. COLLINS *Mrq. & Merch.* II. i. 14 Fortunate folk who live beyond the grasping reticulation of the great railway sagene.

sageness (ˈseɪdʒnɪs). [f. SAGE *a.* + -NESS.] The quality of being sage; profound wisdom.

1509 WATSON *Ship of Fools* xxxiv. (1517) H vij, He is a foole without sagenesse. **1540–1** ELYOT *Image Gov.* xiv. (1541) 24 A man..whom for his great witte and sagenes in apparance, the Emperour had in syngular fauour. **1654** GAYTON *Pleas. Notes* IV. v. 196 The sagenesse, civility, thrift, abstinence, and such like personated parts and customes at home, will be all laid aside. **1755** JOHNSON, *Sageness*, gravity, prudence. **1814** COLERIDGE *Let. to J. Kenyon* (1895) 640 Public prudence and practical sageness. **1907** *Q. Rev.* Oct. 365 If we [*sc.* Confucians] could renounce our sageness and discard our wisdom it would be better for the people a hundredfold.

sagenite (səˈdʒiːnaɪt). *Min.* [Named by H. B. de Saussure, 1796: f. Gr. σαγήνη net + -ITE.] A variety of rutile in which slender crystals are interlaced, forming a network.

1802 THOMSON *Syst. Chem.* IV. 120.

Hence **sageˈnitic** *a.*, of or belonging to sagenite (Cassell's *Encycl. Dict.*).

†**ˈsageously**, *adv. Obs. rare*⁻¹. [f. SAGE *a.* + -OUS + -LY².] Sagely.

c **1500** *Melusine* xxxvi. 259 Whan the knight herd her speke so sageously [Fr. *sagement*].

sagerston, obs. form of SEXTON.

sageship (ˈseɪdʒʃɪp). *rare.* [f. SAGE *sb.*² + -SHIP.] The personality of a sage; the quality of being a sage.

a **1832** BENTHAM *Deontol.* iii. (1834) I. 40 Men, who by whatever name they called their own sageships, were called by others wisest of men. **1887** F. H. BALFOUR *Leaves fr. Chinese Scrapbook* 110 (*title*) Confucius on Sageship.

†**sagess.** *Obs.* In 5 **sagesse.** [a. F. *sagesse*, f. *sage* SAGE *a.*] Sageness, profound wisdom.

1474 CAXTON *Chesse* III. v. (1883) 119 Yf he haue not sagesse and wysedom in hym self of dyuerce wrytynges. *c* **1475** *Partenay* 6224, I hold it no gret wisdome ne sagesse To ouermoche suffre sorew and paine. **1676** GLANVILL *Ess.* VI. 13 Thus the Sagess, and grandeur of the Prince of Darkness need not be brought in question on this Occasion.

sagewar, obs. form of SAGWIRE.

sagey, sagy (ˈseɪdʒɪ), *a. rare.* [f. SAGE *sb.*¹ + -Y.] Of, pertaining to or of the nature of sage.

1747 POSTON *Pratler* I. 134 The sagy wholsome Herb of Wisdom is more stable..than the rosy fading Flower of Beauty. **1871** MRS. WHITNEY *Real Folks* iii, How sagey and doughnutty, and good it always smelt.

sagg, variant of SAG.

saggamore, obs. form of SAGAMORE.

saggar, sagger (ˈsægə(r)), *sb.* Forms: [7 shrager], 7 segur, 8–9 saggar, seggar, 9 sagger (saggard), segger, sagre. [Prob. a contraction of SAFEGUARD *sb.*

This explanation is supported by the existence of the form SEGGARD for *safeguard* as the name of an article of dress. The earliest recorded form, *shrager* (quot. 1686 below), seems to be a corruption due to etymological association with G. *schragen* to prop up; perhaps it may have been invented by the German workmen employed in the Staffordshire potteries.]

1. a. A protecting case of baked fire-proof clay in which the finer ceramic wares are enclosed while baking in the kiln. Also, more widely, any case made of refractory material or cast or wrought iron used to protect objects while in a furnace, as during annealing of iron castings.

[**1686** PLOT *Staffordsh.* iii. 123 If they be leaded hollow-wares, they do not expose them to the naked fire, but put them in shragers, that is, in course metall'd pots, made of marle (not clay).] **1752** *Gentl. Mag.* XXII. 348 Great kiln for segurs. **1768** WEDGWOOD *Let.* 6 Nov. in *Life* (1866) II. 83, I shall..put some men into them to make Saggars, prepare Clay, build ovens, &c. **1782** *Encycl. Brit.* (ed. 2) IX. 6420 *note*, The cases are called by English potters, seggars. **1807** T. THOMSON *Chem.* (ed. 3) II. 493 Cylindrical earthen vessels, formed of pounded fire-bricks and clay, called seggars. **1847** HALLIWELL, *Saggard*, the rough vessel in which all crockery, fine or coarse, is placed when taken to the oven for firing. **1879** MISS J. J. YOUNG *Ceram. Art* 77 The Japanese do not make any extensive use of seggars. **1888** *Lockwood's Dict. Mech. Engin.* 298 *Saggers*, cast-iron boxes used for packing the castings and sifted red hæmatite, in readiness for the annealing oven, in the process of manufacture of malleable cast iron. **1928** H. M. BOYLSTON *Iron & Steel* v. 151 If the parts are small..they are packed with a mixture of rolling-mill scale or scale from saggers and brick-bats or sand. The packed pots, or saggers, are then heated in an annealing furnace. **1960** *Times Rev. Industry* July 22/1 A rich iron ore is packed, together with coke breeze (the reducing agent) and limestone, into clay containers called saggars (the term is taken from the pottery industry, and in fact the process is very similar to that used in making pottery). **1964** H. HODGES *Artifacts* i. 39 Some glazed wares need to be protected from the direct flame, and..this may be done by placing them in lidded boxes called saggars (saggers or seggers). **1967** M. CHANDLER *Ceramics in Mod. World* ii. 79 The ceramist uses saggers only when he must. **1977** R. FOURNIER *Illustr. Dict. Pract. Pottery* (rev. ed.) 196/2 With the coming of cleaner fuels, smaller kilns, and 'continuous' firing the use of the saggar has declined sharply and it is becoming difficult to purchase them.

b. *attrib.* and *Comb.*, as ***saggar-maker***; **saggar-bung**, a pile of saggars; **saggar-house**, the room where the articles to be baked are put into the saggars.

1828 *Potter's Art* II. 184 The *saggar bung Or column. **1853** URE *Dict. Arts* II. 454 When ready it is carried to the '*sagger-house'..and here it is placed in the 'saggers'. **1825** J. NICHOLSON *Operat. Mechanic* 468 The *sagger-maker is expected to know [etc.].

2. The clay of which 'saggars' are made. Also ***saggar-clay***.

1786 J. WEDGWOOD *Let.* 13 Feb. (1965) 292 With regard to Sagger clays, they cannot be judged of from their external appearance. **1839** URE *Dict. Arts* 1020 Space appointed as a depôt for the sagger fire-clay. **1842** BRANDE *Dict. Sci.* etc., *Sagger*. **1843** *Civil Eng. & Arch. Jrnl.* VI. 350/1 The sagger clay from the Staffordshire pottery was also a fire clay. **1851** GREENWELL *Coal-trade Terms Northumb. & Durh.* 45 *Sagre Clay.*—Fire-clay; a soft argillaceous shale.

saggar (ˈsægə(r)), *v.* Also **sagger.** [f. SAGGAR *sb.*] *trans.* To place in or upon a saggar. Hence **ˈsaggaring** *vbl. sb.*

1839 URE *Dict. Arts* 1023 When..any piece, a soup plate for example, is to be saggered. **1901** W. P. RIX tr. *Bourry's Treat. Ceramic Industries* xiii. 718 The great trouble of burning porcelain, looked at from all points, is saggering.

†**ˈsaggard.** *Obs. rare*⁻¹. [? f. SAG *v.* + -ARD.] ? One who 'sags' or hangs helplessly.

c **1440** *York Myst.* xxxvi. 82 þou saggard [Christ on the Cross], þi selffe gan þou saie.

saggard, variant of SAGGAR.

saggathe, var. SAGATHY.

sagge, var. SAG.

saggebut, obs. form of SACKBUT.

sagged (sægd), *ppl. a. rare.* [f. SAG *v.* + -ED¹.] That has sunk in the middle; hanging loose.

1647 R. STAPYLTON *Juvenal* 185 Sagg'd cheeks, wherein such wrinkles are descry'd, As..we see scratcht in an old she-ape. **1893** 'Q' (QUILLER-COUCH) *Delect. Duchy* 235 A sagged and lichen-covered roof.

sagging (ˈsægɪŋ), *vbl. sb.* [f. SAG *v.* + -ING¹.] The action of the verb SAG in various senses.

c **1440** *Promp. Parv.* 440/2 Saggynge, or satlynge, *bassacio, bassatura.* **1769** FALCONER *Dict. Marine* (1780), *Sagging to leeward*, the movement by which a ship makes a considerable *lee-way*, or is driven far to leeward of the course whereon she apparently sails. It is generally expressed of heavy-sailing vessels. **1797** *Encycl. Brit.* (ed. 3) XVII. 420/1 Practical observations on the hogging and sagging of ships. **1868** *Rep. U.S. Commissioner Agric.* (1869) 252 The stakes also prevent the sagging of pleached or obliquely laid saplings. **1898** F. DAVIS *Silchester* 14 The sagging of some of the tesselated pavements.

sagging (ˈsægɪŋ), *ppl. a.* [f. SAG *v.* + -ING².] That sags (in various senses of the verb).

1599 NASHE *Lenten Stuffe* 37 A sagging paire of cheekes like a sows paps that giues suck. **1650** BULWER *Anthropomet.* 178 This goodly sagging Dugs, a Pap fashion. **1859** R. F. BURTON *Centr. Afr.* in *Jrnl. Geog. Soc.* XXIX. 32 The Raz de marée, or rollers, that hurling sagging sea, so trying to small vessels upon the Mozambique coast..is here little feared. **1887** *Scott. Leader* 21 June 5 The tone on the Chicago market was dull and weak, with a 'sagging' tendency. **1897** KIPLING *Captains Courageous* 107 The long, sagging line may twitch a boat under in a flash.

†**ˈsaggish**, *a. rare*⁻¹. [f. *sag* SOG *v.*¹ + -ISH¹.] ? Somewhat moist and decayed.

a **1595** SOUTHWELL *100 Medit.* (1873) 373 As a little spark is wont to be quenched by casting wet and saggish wood upon it.

saggy (ˈsægɪ), *a.*¹ *Obs.* exc. *dial.* [f. SAG *sb.*¹ + -Y.] Sedgy, reedy.

1609 HEYWOOD *Brit. Troy* XV. xxviii. 391 Fear gave my body winges. In a deepe Saggy couert I obscure me. **1881** *Leicestersh. Gloss.*

saggy (ˈsægɪ), *a.*² *colloq.* and *dial.* [f. SAG *v.* + -Y.] Apt to 'sag' (see quots.).

1853 KANE *Grinnell Exp.* xlii. (1856) 391 The observatory of Sir James Ross at Leopold Island was moist and saggy. **1854** MISS BAKER *Northampt. Gloss.* II. 193 That gate wants knocking up at the hinges, it hangs so saggy. **1862** C. C. ROBINSON *Dial. Leeds* s.v. *Sag*, 'A saggy body,'—a very stout person, whose flesh appears to hang. **1881** *Leicestersh. Gloss.*, *Saggy, adj.* said of anything drawn or bent down by weight. **1977** 'L. EGAN' *Blind Search* ii. 30 An old saggy couch to sleep on.

sagh(e, saȝ, obs. forms of SAW.

saȝel: see SOWEL *Obs.*

saght(e, -il, etc., var. ff. SAUGHT, -LE, etc.

sagina (səˈdʒaɪnə). [a. L. *sagīna* (fatness, adopted as a generic name by Linnæus (*Systema Naturæ* (1735)).] A small annual or perennial mat-forming herb of the genus so called, belonging to the family Caryophyllaceæ, esp. *S. pilifera* or *S. procumbens*, which are sometimes used instead of grass as lawn plants; = PEARLWORT.

1962 R. PAGE *Educ. of Gardener* iv. 132 A smaller, sunken oval..set out in a chessboard design with squares of stone alternating with squares of sagina. **1972** *Country Life* 23 Mar. 676/2 During recent years continental exhibitors at flower shows have employed turves cut from prostrate, moss-like sagina, and lawns of this have met with limited success in Germany.

†**saginary.** *Obs. rare.* [ad. L. *sagīnāri-um*, f. *sagīna*: see next.] A place where animals are fattened.

1657 TRAPP *Comm. Ps.* xvii. 14 The rich Glutton (who thought this life to be his saginary or boares-frank).

saginate (ˈsædʒɪneɪt), *v. rare.* [f. L. *sagīnāt-*, ppl. stem of *sagīnāre*, f. *sagīna*, process or means of fattening.] *trans.* To fatten (animals). Also *fig.* Hence **ˈsaginated** *ppl. a.*

1623 COCKERAM, *Saginate*, to fatten a beast. *Sagination*, the fattening thereof. **1633** T. ADAMS *Exp. 2 Peter* ii. 22 At last when they are saginated and franked, their turn comes to bleed. **1650** tr. *Caussin's Ang. Peace* 45 The odious rejoycings of the unjust are saginated with the tears of the miserable. **1657** TOMLINSON *Renou's Disp.* 447 Chickens, .. when saginated and castrated, [are] fit for Courtiers. **1791** COWPER *Iliad* XXIII. 40 Many a saginated boar [θαλέθοντες ἀλοιφῇ]. **1854** LANDOR *Lett. Amer.* 78 The [French] Emperor .. has saginated the priesthood, and has winked at the miraculous apparitions that winked at him.

sagination (sædʒɪ'neɪʃən). *rare.* [ad. L. *sagīnātiōn-em*, n. of action f. *sagīnāre*: see prec.] The action of fattening animals for food.

1607 TOPSELL *Four-f. Beasts* 81 After their labour which bringeth leannesse, they vse to put them [*sc.* oxen] by for sagination, or .. for feeding. **1623** [see prec.]. **1822** *Blackw. Mag.* XII. 12 There are very many persons whose intellect will not submit to this priestly sagination. **1833** *Fraser's Mag.* VIII. 484 We see the greedy porker before us in all the glories of sagination.

sagirstane, obs. form of SEXTON.

†**sagit.** *Obs. rare*$^{-1}$. [Anglicized form of SAGITTA.] The sagittal suture.

c **1550** H. LLOYD *Treas. Health* xii. E vij, On the fore-parte of the head by the ioynte Sagit.

‖**sagitta** (sə'dʒɪtə). [L., lit. an arrow.]

1. *Astr.* A northern constellation lying between *Hercules* and *Delphinus*: = ARROW *sb.* 4.

1704 in J. HARRIS *Lex. Techn.* I. [And in mod. Dicts.]

2. *Geom.* **a.** The versed sine of an arc: = ARROW *sb.* 6.

[**1594**: see ARROW *sb.* 6.] **1704** in J. HARRIS *Lex. Techn.* I. **1726** LEONI *Alberti's Archit.* I. 9/2 The .. Line .. from the middle Point of the Chord up to the Arch, leaving equal Angles on each Side, is call'd the Sagitta. **1853** SIR H. DOUGLAS *Milit. Bridges* (ed. 3) 32 The sagitta, or versed sine, of the curvature being about one fifth of the side of the triangle.

†**b.** In extended sense: The abscissa of a curve. *Obs. rare*$^{-0}$.

1727–41 in CHAMBERS *Cycl.*

3. *Arch.* The key-stone of an arch.

1703 R. NEVE *Builder's Dict.* (1736). **1823** P. NICHOLSON *Pract. Build.* 592. **1849–50** WEALE *Dict. Terms.*

4. The middle horizontal stroke in the Greek letter ϵ. [App. an application of sense 2.]

1864 ELLICOTT *Pastoral Ep.* (ed. 3) 103 The thickened extremity of the sagitta of ϵ. **1881** *Dublin Rev.* VI. 134 The disputed line is really the sagitta of an epsilon.

5. *Anat.* 'The sagittal suture' (*Cent. Dict.* 1891).

6. *Zool.* **a.** One of the otoliths of a fish's ear.

1888 ROLLESTON & JACKSON *Anim. Life* 86 There are [in the ear of the perch] generally two large otoliths, a sagitta in the sacculus, an asteriscus in the recessus cochleae. **1897** PARKER & HASWELL *Text-bk. Zool.* II. 199.

b. One of the components of certain sponge-spicules: see quot.

1898 SEDGWICK *Text-bk. Zool.* I. 83 The Triæne consists of the rhabdome, or shaft, and the cladome, which consists of the three cladi, a straight line joining the ends of the two cladi is the chord. The sagitta is a perpendicular from the origin of the cladome to the chord.

sagittal (sə'dʒɪtəl), *a.* [ad. mod.L. *sagittālis*, f. L. *sagitta* arrow: see -AL[1]. Cf. F. *sagittal.*]

1. *Anat.* **a.** ***sagittal suture*** (†***addition***, †***commissure***): 'the median antero-posterior suture between the two parietal bones on the vertex of the skull' (*Syd. Soc. Lex.* 1891).

1541 R. COPLAND *Guydon's Quest. Chirurg.* F ij, There commeth .ix. [muscles to the tongue] that brede of the addycyon called sagitall of the bone named Lapheoides. **1597** A. M. tr. *Guillemeau's Fr. Chirurg.* 40 b/2 The sagittal suture, where she ioyneth her self with the Coronalle suture. **1653** URQUHART *Rabelais* I. xliv, The sagittal commissure or dart-like seame which distinguisheth the right side of the head from the left. **1882** WILDER & GAGE *Anat. Technol.* 183 In Human Anatomy the sagittal suture is confined to the articulation of the two parietals with each other, the two frontals uniting so early that they are considered as a single bone.

b. Pertaining to the sagittal suture; pertaining to or lying in 'the median longitudinal anteroposterior plane of the body, or to any plane parallel with this' (*Syd. Soc. Lex.* 1891).

1831 R. KNOX *Cloquet's Anat.* 57 Four Edges. The upper or sagittal (*margo sagittalis*) is the longest. **1854** OWEN *Skel. & Teeth* in *Orr's Circ. Sci., Org. Nat.* I. 250 The sagittal and occipital crests.

2. Pertaining to an arrow; resembling an arrow or an arrow-head in shape. *rare.*

1656 BLOUNT *Glossogr., Sagittal* ..; Also belonging to an Arrow. **1772** PENNANT *Genera of Birds* (1781) 16 Hoopoe... Tongue, short, sagittal. **1785** —— *Arctic Zool.* II. 207 Feathers of the thighs long, white, crossed with sagittal bars of yellow. **1886** R. F. BURTON *Arab. Nts.* (abr. ed.) I. 148 Sagittal shots from eyelids Sagittarius threw. **1887** SOLLAS in *Encycl. Brit.* XXII. 416/2 (Fig. 13) [Forms of sponge-spicules] *h*, sagittal triod.

3. *Optics.* Pertaining to or designating the plane that contains the chief ray from an off-axis point source and those rays that are brought to a point in the further (radial) line image formed by an astigmatic system (in a plane at right angles to the sagittal plane).

1902 MANN & MILLIKAN tr. *Drude's Theory of Optics* iii. 50 All the rays emitted by P .. cross the axis at the same point P_2. The beam made up of such rays is called a sagittal beam. It has a focal point at P_2. **1910** J. P. C. SOUTHALL *Geom. Optics* vii. 333 Following the usage of most modern writers, we shall call the incident and refracted rays lying in the planes $\bar{\pi}$, $\bar{\pi}'$, respectively, the Sagittal Rays. [*Note*] 'Sagittal' is a term borrowed from Anatomy... Some writers .. prefer .. the word 'equatorial' instead of sagittal. **1936** H. T. FLINT *Geom. Optics* vii. 150 This line and $P_2P_2{}^1$ are the focal lines of the astigmatic reflected pencil, .. the sagittal and tangential lines respectively. **1972** O. N. STAVROUDIS *Optics of Rays* xii. 266 These skew rays, called sagittal rays, also pass through opposite sides of both the circle on the exit pupil and the ellipse on the image plane... Any fan of sagittal rays from the fixed object point will converge to .. the sagittal focus... The tangential focus and the sagittal focus are the astigmatic foci.

Hence **sa'gittally** *adv.*, *Anat.*, 'in the direction of the sagittal plane' (*Cassell's Suppl.* 1902).

1895 in *Funk's Standard Dict.* **1950** *Jrnl. Compar. Neurol.* XCII. 142 The right postcentral sulcus .. its lower limb running almost sagitally. **1977** *Lancet* 29 Oct. 930/2 The pineals were removed, bisected sagitally, homogenised, and stored at −20°C.

†**sagittar.** *Obs. rare.* Forms: 4 **sagittaire**, 7 **sagittar**. [a. F. *sagittaire* (12th. c. in Hatz.-Darm.), ad. L. *sagittārius*.] = SAGITTARIUS 1.

1390 GOWER *Conf.* III. 123 The Sagittaire. *Ibid.* 127 Libra .. and Sagittaire. **1604–22** [see SAGITTARY A. 2 b]. **1634** T. CAREW *Cœlum Brit.* Wks. (1824) 160 The centaure the horn'd goatfish capricorne, The snake-head gorgon, and fierce sagittar.

Sagittarian (sædʒɪ'tɛərɪən), *sb.* and *a.* *Astrol.* [f. SAGITTARI(US + -AN.]

A. *sb.* A person born under Sagittarius (22 November–21 December), the ninth sign of the Zodiac. **B.** *adj.* Of, pertaining to, or characterized by Sagittarius; born under Sagittarius.

1911 I. M. PAGAN *Pioneer to Poet* ix. 126 The chief characteristic of the fully developed Sagittarian is his extraordinary power of mental activity. **1924** C. E. O. CARTER *Conc. Encycl. Pychol. Astrol.* 11 Psychologically the progressiveness of the Sign shows as Hope, reaching forward into the future... The belief in immortality is typically Sagittarian. **1940** R. GLEADOW *Astrol. in Everyday Life* ix. 210 Sagittarian luck depends very much upon Jupiter's condition. **1950** C. FRY *Venus Observed* I. 12 Your birthday? No, you're a Sagittarian. This is only October. **1964** L. MACNEICE *Astrol.* iii. 96 In music the Sagittarian type is Beethoven. **1979** J. LEASOR *Love & Land Beyond* i. 12 He enjoyed the ultimate privilege of freedom which, as a Sagittarian, he put .. beyond price.

‖**Sagittarius** (sædʒɪ'tɛərɪəs). [L. *sagittārius* archer: see SAGITTARY. Cf. F. *sagittaire.*]

1. a. *Astr.* (With capital S.) The zodiacal constellation of the Archer; hence, the ninth sign of the zodiac, which the sun enters about 22 Nov.

1390 GOWER *Conf.* III. 123 The nynthe Signe .. Is cleped Sagittarius. **1398** TREVISA *Barth. De P.R.* III. x. (1495) 313. **1591** PERCIVALL *Sp. Dict., Sagittario*, the signe Sagittarius. **1727–41** CHAMBERS *Cycl.* s.v., The constellation Sagittarius. **1868** LOCKYER *Guillemin's Heavens* (ed. 3) 382 The bifurcation continues through the Wolf, the Altar, the Scorpion, and Sagittarius, as far as the Serpent.

b. The mythic Centaur who was fabled to have been transformed into this constellation.

1590 GREENE *Orl. Fur.* (1599) E 4 b, As though that Sagitarius in his pride, Could take braue Laeda from stoute Iupiter?

2. *Her.* A bearing representing a centaur (or perh. in early use a horseman) with a drawn bow.

1619 R. BROOKE *Catal. Kings*, etc. ¶ 3 b, It is said, that King Stephen entring this Realme, the signe being in Sagittarius, and obtayning great victory by the helpe of his Archers, assumed the Sagitarius for his Arms. **1707** SANDFORD *Geneal. Hist.* 38 *marg.* **1868** CUSSANS *Her.* vi. (1893) 101 In addition to these [supporters] may be enumerated .. the Sagittarius, or Centaur.

3. *Astrol.* = SAGITTARIAN *sb.* Also without article.

1940 R. GLEADOW *Astrol. in Everyday Life* ix. 209 No one, of course, can think more quickly than Gemini; but Sagittarius can guess; he is very intuitive. **1969** 'V. PACKER' *Don't rely on Gemini* (1970) i. 3 'Was Pope John a Gemini?' 'Oh no... He was a Sagittarius.' **1970** *Guardian* 27 Apr. 1/1 The Labour member for Bebington is a Sagittarius. **1979** S. RIFKIN *McQuaid in August* (1980) vi. 35 It is clear to me you're Sagittarius. You're prompt, calm, and very reliable.

sagittary ('sædʒɪtərɪ), *sb.* and *a.* [ad. L. *sagittārius* adj., pertaining to arrows, as sb. an archer; f. *sagitta* arrow. Cf. F. *sagittaire.*]

A. *sb.*

†**1.** *Astr.* = SAGITTARIUS 1. *Obs.*

1413 *Pilgr. Sowle* (Caxton 1483) V. xi. 102 The sonne entred the sygne of Sagitary that is the Archer. *a* **1547** COPLAND *Hye Way to Spyttel Hous* 89 Scorpio, pisces or sagyttary. **1641** *Witt's Recr.* X 8 b, If thou wouldst please the lasse that thou dost marry The signe must ever be in Sagittary. **1683** TRYON *Way to Health* xxi. (1697) 445 Being under the Dominion of Jupiter and Mercury, in the Sign Sagitary. **1788** GIBBON *Decl. & F.* xliii. IV. 322 While the sun was in Capricorn, another comet appeared to follow in the Sagitary.

2. A centaur; *spec.* the centaur who according to mediæval romance fought in the Trojan army, against the Greeks.

1509 HAWES *Past. Pleas.* XI. (Percy Soc.) 40 Unto the Sagittary They feyne the Centures to be of lykenesse, As halfe man and halfe horse truely. **1589** GREENE *Tullies Love* To Rdr., Chiron the Sagitarie was but a fained conceipt. **1606** SHAKS. *Tr. & Cr.* V. v. 14 The dreadfull Sagittary Appauls our numbers. **1638** SIR T. HERBERT *Trav.* (ed. 2) 158 The Castle is .. defended by a troop of leane fac't, beardlesse, memberless Eunuchs, who like so many angry Sagittaries guard their ladies. *a* **1859** L. HUNT *Cambus Khan* Poems (1860) 165 A chief who had a mother a sea-fairy And slew a terror called the sagittary.

¶**b.** ? As the name of an inn.

For the disproof of C. Knight's conjecture that this was a name for the Arsenal at Venice, see the note on the passage in H. H. Furness *Variorum Shakspere.*

Cf. 'Centaur' as the sign of an imaginary inn at Ephesus in *Comedy of Errors* I. ii. 9.

1604 SHAKS. *Oth.* I. i. 159 Lead to the Sagitary [1st Qo., 1622 sagittar] the raised Search. *Ibid.* I. iii. 115.

3. A representation of a centaur or of a mounted archer; *spec.* in *Her.* = SAGITTARIUS 2.

1610 GUILLIM *Heraldry* I. i. (1660) 5 The Persians [bare] an Archer or Sagitary stamped on their coynes. **1849** FREEMAN *Archit.* 250 The sagittary, or mounted archer, the badge of King Stephen, is not unfrequently met with.

†**4.** A daric, because the figure of an archer was stamped on one side. *Obs. rare.*

Cf. Sir T. Herbert *Trav.* (ed. 2, 1638) 230, referring to Plutarch *Agesilaus.*

1665 SIR T. HERBERT *Trav.* (1677) 243 Timagoras .. had received a bribe of ten thousand Dariques or Sagittaries.

5. An archer.

1832–4 DE QUINCEY *Cæsars* Wks. 1859 X. 175 The imperial sagittary [Commodus], .. whose hand was so steady and whose eye so true, that he was never known to miss. **1863** *Pilgrimage over Prairies* I. 275 Seeing how certain was my fate, remaining where I was, I darted towards the bank, to engage the fell sagittary at close quarters.

†**B.** *adj.* Pertaining to arrows. *Obs.*

a **1682** SIR T. BROWNE *Tracts* i. (1683) 82 With such differences of Reeds, Vallatory, Sagittary, Scriptory, and others they might be furnished in Judæa.

sagittate ('sædʒɪteɪt), *a.* *Bot.* and *Zool.* [ad. mod.L. *sagittātus*, f. L. *sagitta* arrow: see -ATE[2].] Shaped like an arrow-head.

1760 J. LEE *Introd. Bot.* III. v. (1776) 191 *Sagittate*, Arrow-shaped; when they [*sc.* leaves] are triangular, hollowed at the Base, and furnished with Angles at the lower Part. **1785** MARTYN *Rousseau's Bot.* xxiii. (1794) 324 [Woad has] the stem-leaves sagittate or shaped like the head of an arrow. **1826** KIRBY & SP. *Entomol.* IV. 262 *Sagittate*... Arrow-shaped. Triangular, hollowed out at the base with posterior angles. **1840** SWAINSON *Malacol.* 390 Shell very much compressed, .. sagittate. **1864** GRAY in *Reader* 30 Apr. 559/2 The linear or elongated and sagittate anthers, and petals with long canaliculate claws. **1872** COUES *Key N. Amer. Birds* 195 With sagittate dusky marks on the sides.

sagittated ('sædʒɪteɪtɪd), *a.* *Bot.* and *Zool.* [f. prec. + -ED[1].] = prec.

1752 J. HILL *Hist. Anim.* 403 The tongue [of Cuculus] is entire and of a sagittated figure. **1753** CHAMBERS *Cycl. Supp.* s.v. *Leaf.* **1802** SHAW *Zool.* III. II. 526 Sagittated Snake... Brown Snake, with whitish sagittated dorsal spots edged with black. **1835–6** OWEN in *Todd's Cycl. Anat.* I. 524/2 In the Sagittated Calamary this important cartilage consists of three portions.

sagi'ttato-, used as comb. form of SAGITTATE.

1806 GALPINE *Brit. Bot.* §328 Stipulæ sagittato-cordate.

†**sagittel(le.** *Obs. rare*$^{-1}$. Also **sagytelle**. [ad. med.L. *sagittella*, dim. of L. *sagitta* arrow.] Some plant. Also *attrib.*

c **1400** *Lanfranc's Cirurg.* 91 With þe leeues of sagittel [*v.r.* sagytelle, orig. L. *sagittellæ*]. *Ibid.*, Fille it [the ulcer] ful of drie leeues of sagittelle & leie a sagittel-leef aboue.

sagittiferous (sædʒɪ'tɪfərəs), *a.* [f. L. *sagittifer*, f. *sagitta* arrow: see -FEROUS.] (See quots.)

1656 BLOUNT *Glossogr., Sagittiferous*, that bears or weares Arrowes. **1858** MAYNE *Expos. Lex., Sagittiferus*, .. *Bot., Conchol.* Applied to a plant, one of the petals of which is like an arrow, as the *Pleurothallis sagittifera*, and to a shell having arrow-like spots, as the *Trochus sagittiferus*; sagittiferous.

sagittiform (sæ'dʒɪtɪfɔːm), *a.* *rare.* [ad. L. type *sagittiformis*, f. *sagitta* arrow: see -FORM.] Having the shape of an arrow or arrow-head.

1895 in *Funk's Standard Dict.* **1900** B. D. JACKSON *Gloss. Bot. Terms, Sagittiform*, .. arrow-shaped. **1904** WINDLE *Rem. Prehist. Age Eng.* ii. 19 It is true that sagittiform chips are common enough in some parts of the country.

†**sagittipotent**, *a.* *Obs. rare*$^{-0}$. [ad. L. *sagittipotent-em*, f. *sagitta* arrow + *potent-em* POTENT *a.*] 'That can do much by shooting with Arrows, a cunning Archer' (Blount *Glossogr.* 1656).

sagitto-, used as combining form of SAGITTATE.

1852 DANA *Crust.* II. 1299 Spiculum sagitto-capitate.

sagittocyst ('sædʒɪtəsɪst). *Zool.* [irreg. f. L. *sagitta* arrow + CYST *sb.*] A structure occurring in the ectoderm of turbellarian worms (see quot.).

1888 ROLLESTON & JACKSON *Anim. Life* 667 *note*, Still more rare are the structures known as sagittocysts, i.e. capsules similar to those of the nematocysts, but inclosing a needle-like rod, which is expelled on irritation of the animal.

sago ('seɪgəʊ). Forms: 6–7 **sagu**, (7 **zago**, ? erron. **sagous**), 7–8 **sagow**, 8 **sagoe**, **-oo**, **sego**, **seago**, 7– **sago**. [a. Malay *sāgū*. Cf. F. *sagou*, Sp. *sagú*, Pg. *sagu*, *zagu*, It. *sagù*, G. *sago*.]

1. The tree from which sago (see 2) is obtained.

1555 EDEN *Decades* 229 In all the Ilandes of Molucca is founde cloues, ginger, breade of the roote of Sagu, ryse, goates [etc.]. **1783** JUSTAMOND tr. *Raynal's Hist. Indies* I. 143 Beside the cocoa tree, the Moluccas produce a singular kind of palm, which is called sago. **1820** CRAWFURD *Hist. Ind. Archipelago* I. 385 The sago, like other palms, is propagated from the seed or fruit.

2. a. A species of starch prepared from the 'pith' of the trunks of several palms and cycads, esp. *Metroxylon lævis* and *M. Rumphii*, chiefly used as an article of food.

French s., common arrowroot (*Syd. Soc. Lex.* 1897). ***Japan s.***, the sago prepared from various species of *Cycas*. ***pearl s.***, ***Portland s.***: see the epithets.

c **1580** *Sir F. Drake's Voy.* in *Hakluyt* (1600) III. 740 We receiued of them meale, which they call Sagu, made of the tops of certaine trees..whereof they make certaine cakes. *Ibid.* 742 Certaine wordes of the naturall language of Iaua... *Sagu*, bread of the Countrey. **1619** W. PHILLIP tr. *Schouten's Wonderf. Voy.* 75 Wee bartered for a great deale of Sagow and some Ryce, for Linnen, Beades [etc.]. **1688** BRAMSTON *Autobiog.* 381 She tasted and tryed all waters,.. and all the opiats, asses milk, and zago, to prevent consumption, but yet was wasted to the lowest degree. **1727** A. HAMILTON *New Acc. E. Ind.* II. xl. 94 The inland People subsist mostly on Sagow. **1747** MRS. GLASSE *Cookery* 120 To boil Sago. **1755** *Gentl. Mag.* XXV. 431 He allows chicken broth, salop, seago, milk-pottage, for breakfast. **1806** A. HUNTER *Culina* (ed. 3) 95 Have ready two ounces of sago sufficiently boiled. **1840** PEREIRA *Elem. Mat. Med.* II. 700 This fecula (Japan sago) is quite unknown to me; and I doubt whether it ever reaches this country. **1849** BALFOUR *Man. Bot.* §1048 From the stems of *Cycas revoluta* and *circinalis*, a kind of Sago is made. **1861** BENTLEY *Man. Bot.* 684 *Caryota urens*... From the trunks of the old trees a kind of Sago is obtained in Assam. **1884** MARY HARRISON *Skilful Cook* 167 Simmer the sago in the milk until it thickens.

b. A prepared food made by boiling sago in water or milk, etc. ? *Obs.*

1769 MRS. RAFFALD *Eng. Housekpr.* (1778) 309 The chief ingredients in gruels, sagos, and wheys.

fig. **1769** [E. THOMPSON] *Trinculo's Trip* 40 Yes—your pap —poetick sago, Quite a soporifick pill.

3. *attrib.* and *Comb.*: as ***sago †-bread***, ***-cake***, ***-flour***, ***-gruel***, ***milk***, ***-pudding***, ***-starch***; ***sago-like*** adj.; **sago-grain**, *transf.* a granule on the eyelid in granular ophthalmia; **sago-palm (tree)** = sense 1; **sago-spleen**, amyloid degeneration of the Malpighian corpuscles of the spleen, resembling boiled sago; **sago-tree** = sense 1.

1613 PURCHAS *Pilgrimage* v. xvi. 453 A piece of *Sagu bread. **1779** FORREST *Voy. N. Guinea* 42 A *sago cake. **1862** O'NEILL *Dict. Calico Printing* 188 Other kinds of starchy substances in occasional use for printing..as..*sago flour —which is not a flour at all, but nearly pure starch. **1873** R. B. CARTER in *Lancet* 20 Dec. 872/1 In technical nomenclature they are known as 'follicular granulations', but to-day I will call them '*sago grains'. *Ibid.*, The very existence of these 'sago grains' remained unknown until the year 1848, when they were discovered by Dr. Löffler. **1764** ELIZA MOXON *Eng. Housew.* (ed. 9) 136 To make *Sagoo Gruel. **1893** LELAND *Mem.* II. 134, I infinitely prefer the original Icelandic Saga of Frithiof to his sago-gruel imitation of strong soup. **1879** *St. George's Hosp. Rep.* IX. 159 The solitary glands of the intestine were swelled and *sago-like. **1827** *New Syst. Cookery* 287 *Sago, Rice,..or Macaroni Milks. **1769** W. STORK in J. Bartram *Jrnl.* (*Florida*) (ed. 3) p. v, *Cycas Circinalis*... *Sago Palm-tree. In Java, and the warmest parts of the East-Indies. **1820** CRAWFURD *Hist. Ind. Archipelago* I. 383 The Sago Palm (*Metroxylon sagu*). **1865** TYLOR *Early Hist. Man.* vii. 178 The art of extracting sago from their native sago-palms. **1747** MRS. GLASSE *Cookery* 106 A *Sagoe Pudding. **1764** ELIZA MOXON *Eng. Housew.* (ed. 9) 66 A Sagoo Pudding. **1973** 'D. JORDAN' *Nile Green* xxiii. 92 A notorious property developer..was spooning sago pudding into his face. **1873** T. H. GREEN *Introd. Pathol.* (ed. 2) 70 Amyloid degeneration of the spleen is met with in two forms—one in which the disease is limited to the Malpighian corpuscles ('*Sago Spleen'), and the other [etc.]. **1681** GREW *Musæum* IV. iii. 377 The *Sagous-Tree; which those that inhabit the Molucca Islands, eat instead of Bread. **1777** MILLER *Sumatra* in *Phil. Trans.* LXVIII. 162 The houses..are.. thatched with the leaves of the sago-tree. **1840** PEREIRA *Elem. Mat. Med.* II. 700 *Cycas revoluta*, or the Japan Sago tree.

sagoin (sə'gɔɪn). Forms: 7–9 **sagouin**, (8 **sangwyn**), 9 (in Dicts.) **saguin**, 7– **sagoin**. [a. F. *sagouin*, †*sagoin*, a. Pg. *saguim*, a. Guarani *sagui*, *çagui* (= Tupi *sahy*: see SAI[1]), whence by misreading the synonym CAGUI.] A small South American monkey, *esp.* one of the genus *Callithrix*.

1607 TOPSELL *Four-f. Beasts* 18 This figure of the Sagoin, I receiued of..a very learned Apothecary of Antwerpe. **1613** PURCHAS *Pilgrimage* (1614) 838 A kind of Monkey called Sagouin. **1704** *Nieuhof's East Indies* in *Churchill's Voy.* II. 362 Those [monkeys] called sangwyns. **1774** GOLDSM. *Nat. Hist.* (1776) IV. 235 Those [monkeys] with muscular holding tails, are called Sapajous; those with feeble, useless tails, are called Sagoins. **1840** *Cuvier's Anim. Kingd.* 62 The Masked Sagouin (*Callithrix personata*, Geof.), the Widow Sagouin (*C. lugens*, Humb.). **1852** TH. ROSS tr. *Humboldt's Trav.* I. viii. 279 They never play like the young sagoins.

†**'sagoize**, *v. Obs. rare*[−1]. [f. SAGO + -IZE.] *trans.* To put on a regimen of sago as diet.

1847 *Tait's Mag.* XIV. 794 The excellence of the test may recommend a course of 'sagoizing' to all those guardians who are never done with tests and testing.

sagomo(re, obs. forms of SAGAMORE.

sagoone, var. SACCOON (= SECONDE, in *Fencing*).

sagow, obs. form of SAGO.

sagre, dial. form of SAGGAR; obs. f. SAKER[1].

†**sagree**. *Obs. rare*[−1]. [? Connected with SHAGREEN.] The Picked Dogfish, *Squalus acanthias*.

1752 J. HILL *Hist. Anim.* 300 The Sagree... This is frequent in the Mediterranean... Willughby and Ray call it *Galeus acanthias sive spinax fuscus*, the brown, prickly Hound-fish. **1753** CHAMBERS *Cycl. Supp.* App.

sagu, obs. form of SAGO.

‖**saguaro** (sə'gwɑːrəʊ). Also **saguara**, **sahuaro**, **sugarro**, **suwarrow**. [? Mexican.] A large branching cactus, *Carnegiea gigantea*, found in desert regions of southwestern North America. ***saguaro woodpecker***, the Pitahaya woodpecker (*Centurus uropygialis*) usually nesting in the giant cactus.

1856 *Wild West* (San Francisco) Oct. 4/6 There are in this region a few Indian rancharies, to which the *Papagos* resort to gather the fruit of the *sugarro*. **1864** S. MOWRY *Arizona & Sonora* 161 Gradually appear..scattered saguaras. **1881** *Amer. Naturalist* XV. 982 By far the most conspicuous form is..the 'saguara' cactus. **1883** *Harper's Mag.* Mar. 502/2 We made haste..to cut down an example of the..saguaras, the organ-cactus. **1884** SARGENT *Rep. Forests N. Amer.* (10th Census IX.) 90 *Cereus giganteus*... Suwarrow. Saguaro. **1884** COUES *Key N. Amer. Birds* (ed. 2) 488 Saguaro Woodpecker. **1907** S. E. WHITE *Arizona Nights* 220 [The] snake..looked just like a sahuaro stalk. **1916** E. C. PEIXOTTO *Our Hispanic Southwest* 64 Tall saguaros reared their fluted columns like giant candelabra. **1933** *Sun* (Baltimore) 27 Sept. 15/6 The Southwest's giant tree cactus, or sahuaro, is susceptible to crown gall. **1955** [see CHOLLA]. **1968** W. GARNER *Deep, Deep Freeze* xxxii. 261 Drieter slipped behind a great saguaro with a girth matching his own. **1978** *Times* 21 Aug. 10/6 We could tell this was the real desert because we glimpsed our first saguaro cactuses—those monstrous plants, some more than 100 years old and standing up to 15 feet high. **1979** *Arizona Daily Star* 1 Apr. (Advt. Section) 16/7 This parcel [of land] is dotted with native sahuaro.

saguin, **saguire**: see SAGOIN, SAGWIRE.

‖**sagum** ('seɪgəm). *Roman Antiq.* Pl. **saga**. [L.; also *sagus*, = late Gr. σάγος: said to be of Gaulish origin.] A Roman military cloak; also, a woollen cloak worn by the ancient Gauls, Germans, and Spaniards.

1706 PHILLIPS (ed. Kersey), *Sagum*, a sort of Woollen Coat or Cassock for Soldiers, which the Greeks and Romans us'd, and was peculiar to the Gauls. **1800** J. DALLAWAY *Anecd. Arts Eng.* 399 A statue of Colonel Codrington..in a Roman military Sagum. **1851–9** PRICHARD in *Man. Sci. Enq.* 261 The Germans [were known] by their saga or military cassocks. **1879** FARRAR *St. Paul* (1883) 701 The scarlet sagum of the Procurator.

‖**sagwire** ('sægwaɪə(r)). Forms: 7 **sagewar**, 8 **saguire**, 9 **sagueir**, 9– **sagwire**. [app. ad. Pg. *sagueiro*, f. *sagu* SAGO. Cf. F. *saguier*.] The Gomuti palm, *Arenga saccharifera*, of the Indian Archipelago. Also, the toddy or palm-wine obtained from this tree.

1681 GREW *Musæum* IV. iii. 377 A Sagewar-Tree; whose Flower being cut, renders a Juyce like Wine. **1792** T. FORREST *Voy. Mergui* 73 (Y.) The natives drink much of a liquor called saguire, drawn from the palm-tree. **1820** CRAWFURD *Hist. Ind. Archipelago* I. 397 One of the most useful and abundant of all the palms is the Saguire or Gomuti (*Borassus gomutus*). **1869** A. R. WALLACE *Malay Archipelago* I. 362 His palm-trees supplied him all the year round with 'sagueir', which takes the place of beer.

sagy, variant of SAGEY.

sah (sɑː), colloq. and (U.S.) dial. var. SIR *sb.* Cf. SUH.

1893 H. A. SHANDS *Some Peculiarities of Speech in Mississippi* 54 *Sah* (sa), Negro for *sir*. **1901** W. CHURCHILL *Crisis* I. i. 5 'But, Ephum! Say, Ephum!' 'Yes *sah*.'

sah, obs. pa. t. of SEE.

sa-ha. Also 7 **sa-haw**. [? Var. of SO-HO.] A cry used in coursing.

1605 SYLVESTER *Du Bartas* II. iii. IV. *Captains* 410 With shrill *Sa-haw, here-here ho, here-again*, The Warren rings. **1885** *Sat. Rev.* 21 Feb. 235/2 We are nearly across the field when the cry of 'Sa ha' tells us that some one has seen a hare in her form.

sahab, obs. form of SAHIB.

†**sahagun**. *Obs. rare*[−1]. [? From *Sahagun*, a city in Castile.] ? A sword made at Sahagun.

a **1668** DAVENANT *Man's the Master* IV. (1669) 57 Suppose that with a Sahagun, or with a Rapier of Toledo, I were pierc'd like a Cullender.

Sahaptin (sə'hæptɪn), *sb.* and *a.* Also †**Sahapotin**, **Shahaptan**. [Southern Interior Salish *Sʔaptnx* Sahaptin, Nez Percé; of uncertain ulterior etymology.] **A.** *sb.* **a.** Formerly, a (member of an) American Indian people of the Snake River basin, also called the NEZ PERCÉ; also, any of several groupings of the Nez Percé and others believed to be linguistically related. Now applied to a number of closely related North American Indian peoples of the Columbia River basin. **b.** The language or language grouping of any of these peoples. **B.** *adj.* Of or pertaining to any of these peoples or their language.

1836 A. GALLATIN in *Trans. Amer. Antiquarian Soc.* II. 264 (*map*) Sahapotins. **1841** *Jrnl. R. Geogr. Soc.* XI. 225 The first and more northern Indians of the interior may be denominated the Shahaptan Family, and comprehends.. the Shahaptan, or *Nez Percés*..; the Kliketat..; and the Okanagan. **1846** H. HALE *U.S. Exploring Exped.: Ethnogr. & Philol.* 198 The South-Oregon division. To this belong the *Sahaptin* family (Nez-percés and Wallawallas), [etc.]. **1918** J. E. REES *Idaho Chronol.* 109 Their earliest home was upon the Columbia River and when they were pushed southward the Salish called them 'Shahaptans', meaning 'strangers from up the river'. **1918** *Internat. Jrnl. Amer. Linguistics* I. 176, I have..gathered voluminous data supporting previously expressed contentions concerning the genetic relationship between Lutuamian, Wailatpuan, and Sahaptin. **1921** E. SAPIR *Language* 222 The presence of postpositions in Upper Chinook..is clearly due to the influence of neighboring Sahaptin languages. **1940** M. W. SMITH *Puyallup-Nisqually* 22 If he spoke Sahaptin, it is also certain that he spoke Salish. **1947** B. A. DE VOTO *Across Wide Missouri* 11 Ethnologists use the name which the Flatheads bestowed on them, the Shahaptan, of uncertain meaning but perhaps a designation of the country they lived in. **1965** *Canad. Jrnl. Linguistics* X. 125 Jacobs also has published a considerable quantity of Sahaptin texts. **1971** *Language* XLVII. 840 The northernmost example, the Sahaptin and Nez Perce shift of $n > l$, is reversed in comparison to the more southern shifts.

Sahara (sə'hɑːrə). Also 7 **Sarra**, 7–9 **Za(h)ara**, 9 **Saara**, **Sahra**. [a. Arab. *çaḥrā* desert.] **1. a.** The great desert of Libya or northern Africa. (With capital S as proper name.)

1613 PURCHAS *Pilgrimage* (1614) 556 Lybia, he calleth Sarra, for so the Arabians call a desert. **1615** BEDWELL *Arab. Trudg.*, *Sahara*. The stonie countrey, the sands: the same almost that *Sarra* is. **1698** FROGER *Voy.* 13 The Deserts of Zaara. **1728** MORGAN *Algiers* II. iii. 246 He withdrew among his Arab Confederates in the Sahara, or Desert. **1812** BRACKENRIDGE *Views Louisiana* (1814) 28 Having some resemblance to the Stepps of Tartary, or the Saara's of Africa. **1819** REES *Cycl.* XXXI., *Zahara*. **1834** DE QUINCEY *Cæsars* iv. Wks. 1890 VI. 332 The..sandy Zaarras of Africa. **1849** C. BRONTE *Shirley* xxiii, The shadowless..wastes of Zahara.

b. *transf.* and *fig.* A desert, wilderness.

1855 DICKENS *Holly-Tree Inn* in *Househ. Words* Extra Christmas No. 2/2 The bleak wild solitude..was a snowy Saharah. **1862** 'SHIRLEY' [J. Skelton] *Nugæ Crit.* i. 4 During this autumnal season,..the city is a desert, a Sahara. **1865** DICKENS *Mut. Fr.* I. iv, Between Battle Bridge and that part of the Holloway district in which he dwelt, was a tract of suburban Sahara. **1893** *Lit. World* 3 Nov. 332/1 In the Sahara of contemporary verse there are sometimes..oases full of beauties and surprises.

2. A shade of brown or yellow. Also *attrib.*

1923 *Daily Mail* 9 Oct. 1/1 Colours: Lemon,..Fawn, Sahara, Mole. **1930** *Daily Express* 8 Sept. 11/5 The suit is stocked in shades of sand, Sahara Brown and Grey. **1970** 'D. HALLIDAY' *Dolly & Cookie Bird* ii. 12 He was..broad-shouldered, with that super kind of Swedish suède jacket in Sahara sand colour. **1974** *Times* 4 May 5/2 Bathroom suites in..honeysuckle, orchid, midnight blue, sahara, black. **1976** *Yorkshire Evening Press* 9 Dec. 20/2 (Advt.), 1971 Opel Rekord coupe in Sahara Gold.

Hence **Sa'harian**, **Sa'haric** *adjs.*

1892 LOUNSBURY *Stud. Chaucer* I. ii. 216 As well might one hope to squeeze rain from a Saharic sand-cloud. **1897** *Edin. Rev.* Jan. 129 The Saharian district.

Saharan (sə'hɑːrən), *a.* and *sb.* [f. SAHARA + -AN.]

A. *adj.* Of or characteristic of the Sahara.

1849 M. ARNOLD *Consolation* viii, Saharan sand-winds Sear'd his keen eyeballs. **1860** *All Year Round* No. 76. 606 We were to have one of the hottest days of a Saharan summer.

B. *sb.* **a.** One of a group of languages spoken in the eastern Saharan region. **b.** A member of a people living in the Sahara, *spec.* native to or inhabiting the former Spanish Sahara on the Atlantic coast.

1963 J. H. GREENBERG *Lang. Afr.* vi. 130 To the.. grouping which consists of Songhai, Saharan, Maban, Fur and Coman in addition to Chari-Nile, the name Nilo-Saharan is given. **1970** *Daily Tel.* 30 June 16 The men from the Spanish Sahara, known as 'Saharans', now in Egypt have two main objectives. **1975** *N.Y. Times* 8 Nov. 26/2 The referendum under international supervision, recommended by a United Nations commission, will be difficult to conduct fairly among mostly illiterate and nomadic Saharans.

Saharaui, var. SAHRAWI.

sahe, obs. form of SAW.

Sahelian (sə'hiːlɪən), *a.* [f. *Sahel*, proper name of the region + -IAN.] Of, pertaining to, or designating the belt of land in West Africa south of the Sahara desert which comprises parts of Senegal, Mauritania, Mali, Niger, and Chad and is mostly savannah.

1973 *Nature* 28 Sept. 194/2 The present drought situation and the probable long term trends now seriously threaten the economic and political viability of the Sahelian states of West Africa. **1973** *Times* 30 Oct. 16/6 The exhibition shows the effects of the drought in the Sahelian region of West Africa. **1976** *New Society* 29 Apr. 220/2 Africa's poorest region, the Sahelian 'famine belt' from the Atlantic to Lake Chad, was once a place of fabulous wealth. **1980** *Spectator* 21 June 18 Next come the even more gruesome aid donors, whose antics Markham witnessed during the terrible Sahelian drought a few years ago.

‖**sahib** (ˈsɑːɪb, sɑːb). Also 7 **sab, sahab,** 8–9 **saib,** 9 **saheb, saheeb,** 20 **saab, sa'ab.** [Urdū, use of Arab. *çāḥib*, orig. 'friend'.] **1. a.** A respectful title used by the natives of India in addressing an Englishman or other European (= 'Sir'); in native use, an Englishman, a European. Also affixed as a title (equivalent to 'Mr.' prefixed) to the name or office of a European and to Indian and Bangladeshi titles and names. (See also MEM-SAHIB.)

1696 OVINGTON *Voy. Suratt* 326 Thus the distracted Husband..often in his Indian English confest, English fashion, sab, best fashion have, one Wife best for one Husband. **1698** FRYER *Acc. E. India & P.* 417 To which the subtle Heathen replied, 'Sahab (*i.e.*) Sir, why will you do more than the Creator ever meant?' **1796** ELIZA HAMILTON *Lett. Hindoo Rajah* (1811) I. 43 This Saib..purposed returning with me. **1811** MRS. SHERWOOD *Henry & Bearer* 25, I used to be so pleased when anybody bowed to me, and said 'Sahib'. **1822** *Fifteen Yrs. in India* Gloss., *Saheeb.* **1832** in *Rep. Sel. Comm. Salt Brit. India* (1836) App. 34 If a bird flies, saheb shoots it. **1834** *Baboo* II. ii. 28 (Stanf.) These English Sahebs are white-skinned white-livered lepers. **1859** LANG *Wand. India* 323 'They are strangers to me, Sahib', said the khansamah,..'but their bearers say that they are Lord Sahibs'. **1886** KIPLING *Departmental Ditties* (ed. 2) 7 Rajah Rustum..Heaped upon the Bukshi Sahib wealth and honours manifold. **1891** KIPLING & BALESTIER *Naulahka* (1892) 201 The lady sahib kissed me on both cheeks. **1921** E. M. FORSTER *Let.* 1 Apr. in *Hill of Devi* (1953) 60 The Palace is inhabited by four chief people—me, H. H., Malarao Sahib, and Deolekr Sahib. **1971** *Shankar's Weekly* (Delhi) 4 Apr. 8/1 Here we are grappling with basic issues and our director saab is bothered about mixed metaphors and split infinitives. *Ibid.* 21/4 He then went to Lalaji's house outside which Vijay was furiously pacing up and down. 'Yes, sa'ab,' he meekly announced his arrival. **1977** 'D. MACNEIL' *Wolf in Fold* ii. 18 The native nodded. 'I understand, Ogilvie sahib. I believe also that the *risaldar* sahib will help.' **1978** F. OLBRICH *Desouza pays Price* iii. 12 A gentleman would like to see you, Inspector saab.

b. *transf.* A gentleman; someone considered socially acceptable.

1919 W. DEEPING *Second Youth* xxv. 212, I happen to know Colonel Horseley out there; he's a sahib, and quite big, one of the biggest things I've met. **1928** D. L. SAYERS *Unpleasantness at Bellona Club* ix. 102 'Is the fellow a sahib?' 'Good God, no! Looks like an attorney's clerk or something.' **1952** A. GRIMBLE *Pattern of Islands* 24 A sahib, naturally..right kind of breeding, right kind of school. **1977** *Listener* 28 July 123/1 Being a muff can be as arduous a vocation as being a sahib.

2. *Comb.*, as **sahib-log** [Urdu *log* people, caste], the European gentlefolk in India.

1848 J. H. STOCQUELER *Oriental Interpreter* 199/2 *Sahib logue*, the common appellation given to European gentlemen in India. **1927** W. H. TODD *Tiger, Tiger!* vii. 117 The 'sahib-log' were after him. **1953** P. SCOTT *Alien Sky* I. iv. 42 The *Sahib-log* lived in whitewashed bungalows. **1978** 'M. M. KAYE' *Far Pavilions* ii. 30 The troopers..asserted that all the Sahib-log in Meerut were dead.

So **ˈsahiba(h** [Arab. *çāḥibaʰ*], mistress, lady.

1849 E. B. EASTWICK *Dry Leaves* 88 What calamity is this that the Madam Sáhebah is so fond of! **1903** *Smart Set* IX. 114/2 Oh, dear Sahiba, the gods are very wise and terrible!

Sahib-dom (ˈsɑːɪbdəm). ? *Obs.* [f. SAHIB + -DOM.] The quality or condition of being a sahib.

1901 KIPLING *Kim* ix. 215 'Oah!' said Kim, firmly resolved to cling to his Sahib-dom. **1909** M. DIVER *Candles in Wind* iv. 45 A creature without either the birthright of caste, or the prestige of Sahib-dom.

sahibhood (ˈsɑːɪbhʊd). [f. as prec. + -HOOD.] = prec.

1946 [see NEGRONESS]. **1953** J. TRENCH *Docken Dead* vii. 104 He looked round for admiration..at..the evidence of sahibhood. **1977** A. WILSON *Strange Ride R. Kipling* i. 23 The need to assert his lost sahibhood.

Sahidic (səˈhɪdɪk), *a.* [f. Arab. *saʿīd*, with article *as-saʿīd*, lit. 'the Fortunate', a name for Upper Egypt + -IC.] Belonging to the dialect of Coptic spoken in Thebes and Upper Egypt, in which a version of the Bible is extant. Also quasi-*sb.*, the Sahidic language, or the Sahidic version of the Bible.

1830 TATTAM *Egypt. Gram.* 14 Sahidic words which change their termination to form the plural. *Ibid.* 49 Numbers are usually expressed in Sahidic by words. **1898** J. A. ROBINSON in *Expositor* Apr. 257 Both forms of this Version—the Bohairic (or Memphitic) and the Sahidic (or Thebaic)—take the verb in the passive sense.

‖**sahitya** (ˈsɑːhitjə). [Skr., association, agreement; composition, literature; lyrical verse.] The lyrical verse which forms part of an Indian dance-song (see quots.).

1953 F. BOWERS *Dance in India* 46 Three types of singing, determined by the nature of the dance, are performed in Bharata Natya: (1) Ordinary poetic songs with words for abhinaya portions, called *sahitya*. **1965** E. BHAVNANI *Dance in India* v. 34 Then comes the rendering in gesture language and emotional acting, the explanation of a song or *Sahitya* which are devotional sentiments in lyrical verse form and are the text to be interpreted. **1968** *Jrnl. Mus. Acad. Madras* XXXIX. 8 The Raga chosen for the song aptly conveys the sentiment expressed by the Sahitya. **1971** *Shankar's Weekly* (Delhi) 18 Apr. 24/1 One of the sisters was out to prove that they could tackle the swaraprasthara to coincide terminally with the point of commencement of the sahitya.

Sahiwal (ˈsɑːhɪvɑːl, -wɑːl). Also **Sanhiwal.** [The name of a town in the central Punjab, Pakistan.] A cow or bull belonging to the breed so called, originally native to Pakistan but now used in tropical regions elsewhere, distinguished by small horns and a hump on the back of the neck; also, the breed itself. Also *attrib.*

1916 *Rep. Agric. Research Inst. & Coll., Pusa 1914–15* 10 Two herds are now being maintained at Pusa, one of selected Sanhiwal (Montgomery) cows and their descendants, the other of cross-bred Ayrshire-Sanhiwal cattle. **1919** *Rep. Progress Agric. in India 1917–18* v. 182 Experiments with crossing the ordinary *desi* cow of good stamp with the Hissar, Sahiwal and Kosi strains are in progress. **1941** *Empire Jrnl. Exper. Agric.* IX. 11 The Sahiwal has reached in 25 years a level of milking performance which foreign breeds would have taken more than a century to attain. **1959** R. B. KELLEY *Native & Adapted Cattle* v. 71 Sahiwal cattle are also known as Montgomery cattle. *Ibid.* 75 Most Sahiwals are red. **1968** *Sunday Mail Mag.* (Brisbane) 7 July 5/1 We have 1200 head of cattle—Ayrshires; four horses and a few sahiwals. **1970** *Kenya Farmer* Feb. 13/1 The range of breeds in Kenya is now very considerable. For dairy, there are Ayrshire, Friesland, Guernsey and Jersey; for dual purpose, Brown Swiss, Red Poll and Sahiwal.

Sahli (ˈsɑːlɪ). *Med.* The name of Hermann *Sahli* (1856–1933), Swiss physician, used *attrib.* and in the possessive with reference to a method he devised for determining the hæmoglobin content of the blood by converting a sample into acid hæmatin and adding water until the colour matches a standard.

1906 R. C. CABOT *Physical Diagnosis* (ed. 3) xxiii. 465 Sahli's instrument..must be obtained from one of the firms recommended by him. *Ibid.* 569/2 (Index), Sahli's test for hæmoglobin. **1931** OSGOOD & HASKINS *Textbk. Lab. Diagnosis* II. ix. 354 The ordinary type of Sahli apparatus is worthless because the acid hematin used as the standard fades too rapidly. *Ibid.* 347 Diluted to the 100 mark in a Sahli tube. **1956** *Nature* 17 Mar. 524/1 No significant change was noted in the red-cell count; but there was a drop in the hæmoglobin-level from 81 to 70 per cent when tested by the Sahli method. **1974** PASSMORE & ROBSON *Compan. Med. Stud.* III. xxi. 2/1 The Hb of blood is measured colorimetrically after it has been converted to a stable form. The methods available use acid haematin, oxyhaemoglobin or cyanmethaemoglobin. The simplest is the Sahli method.

sahlinite (ˈsɑːlɪnaɪt). *Min.* [f. the name of Carl A. *Sahlin* (1861–1943), manager of a Swedish ironworks + -ITE[1].] A basic monoclinic arsenate and chloride of lead found as pale yellow scales in dolomite at Långban, Sweden.

1934 G. AMINOFF in *Geol. Foreningen Förhandlingar* LVI. 493 (*heading*) Note on a new mineral from Långban (Sahlinite). **1951** C. PALACHE et al. *Dana's Syst. Min.* (ed. 7) II. 775 Sahlinite... Monoclinic. In aggregates of small thin scales. **1968** I. KOSTOV *Mineral.* 467 Sahlinite has perfect cleavage on {010}.

sahlite (ˈsɑːlaɪt). *Min.* Also **salite.** [a. G. *sahlit*, named in 1800, f. *Sahla* (*Sala*) in Sweden: see -ITE.] A variety of pyroxene.

1807 AIKIN *Dict. Chem. & Min.* II. 279. **1836** T. THOMSON *Min., Geol.*, etc. I. 190 The fifth and sixth minerals [analysed above] are sahlites; so named because they occur in the lead mine of Sahla in Sweden. **1878** LAWRENCE tr. *Cotta's Rocks Class.* 16 A sahlite, termed malakolite, is found separately imbedded in granular limestone.

Saho (ˈsɑːhəʊ), *sb.* and *a.* Also †**Shiho, Shoho.** [Cushitic.] **A.** *sb.* **a.** A (member of a) Cushitic-speaking people of Eritrea. **b.** The language or dialect of this people. **B.** *adj.* Of or pertaining to this people or their language.

1790 J. BRUCE *Trav.* III. v. iii. 68 The Shiho were once very numerous; but, like all these nations having communication with Masuah, have suffered much by the ravages of the small-pox. **1831** S. GOBAT *Jrnl.* 22 May (1834) iv. 291, I have just passed three very disagreeable months, in the midst of the savage Shohos. **1842** ISENBERG & KRAPF *Jrnl.* 30 Apr. (1843) 521 The Governor promised this morning that he would send to the next Shoho village for a guide to take us to Arkeeko. *a* **1860** W. C. PLOWDEN *Trav. Abyssinia* (1868) i. 23 The Shihos, a nomad race to the southward of Massowah. *Ibid.* xviii. 360 There are two roads, through the countries of two tribes of Shihos, leading to Adowah, the one through the tribe called Asowarta, the other, Tora... These two tribes form the Shiho nation, and occupy the mountainous tracts between Massowah and Christian Abyssinia. **1883** R. N. CUST *Sk. Mod. Lang. Afr.* I. ix. 128 (*heading*) Saho *or* Shiho *or* Shoho. *Ibid.* 129 The Saho bring down their herds in the rains to graze. **1885** [see DANAKIL *sb.* and *a.*]. **1932** W. L. GRAFF *Lang.* xi. 404 The most important dialects [of Cushitic] are Bedja, Saho and Afar. **1960** E. ULLENDORFF *Ethiopians* iii. 40 The Saho tribes live in the coastal depression between Massawa in the north, the gulf of Zula in the east, and the escarpment of the Akkele Guzay in the west. **1962** G. A. LIPSKY et al. *Ethiopia* iv. 47 Almost all the Saho-speaking tribes are located in Eritrea. *Ibid.* vii. 113 The Saho and Dānākil people also are Moslem. **1968** M. ABIR *Ethiopia* vi. 132 Most of the Sahos and their Belau rulers left Arkiko and the surrounding area, and escaped into the mountains. **1972** *Language* XLVIII. 847 His list can be supplemented with examples from.. Chinantec, Saho, Slave.

sah(o)ukar, var. SOUCAR.

Sahrawi (səˈrɑːwɪ). Also **Saharaui.** [a. Arab. *ṣaḥrāwī* (whence Sp. *saharaui*) of the desert, f. *ṣaḥrāʾ* desert, SAHARA.] An inhabitant of Western (formerly Spanish) Sahara, a Saharan; also *collect.*, the people itself. Also *attrib.*

1976 *Times* 27 Feb. 14/1 Self-determination for the Sahrawi people is a prerequisite for any settlement. *Ibid.*, Polisario should be recognised as the legitimate representative of the Sahrawis. **1976** *Times Lit. Suppl.* 16 Apr. 466/2 In either case the Saharauis will hardly be the beneficiaries. *Ibid.*, The inner working and tensions of Saharaui society. **1977** *Guardian Weekly* 6 Nov. 12/4 Two French technicians..taken away along with 24 Mauritanian workers by a Sahrawi guerrilla unit... The Sahrawi are not agents of subversion, but people who want back the homeland [*sc.* Western Sahara] they were forced to quit. **1980** J. MERCER *Canary Islanders* 264 In 1975 Spain handed over the Spanish Sahara and the Saharaui people to Morocco and Mauretania, in exchange for economic and other benefits. This led to the current war between the occupying neo-colonial powers and the Saharauis (Polisario).

saht(e, sahut, etc.: see SAUGHT *Obs.*, etc.

saht-bai, var. SAT-BHAI.

sahuaro, var. SAGUARO

‖**sai**[1] (saɪ). [a. Brazilian *sahy*, *çahy*; in Fr. *saï*. Cf. SAIMIRI, SAGOIN.] A South American monkey, *Simia capucina* L.

1774 GOLDSM. *Nat. Hist.* (1776) IV. 236 The Sai..is somewhat larger than the Sajou... It is also called the Bewailer. **1859** WOOD *Illustr. Nat. Hist.* I. 92 The Weeper Monkey or Sai.

‖**sai**[2] (saɪ). A bird, *Cœreba cyanea*, inhabiting tropical America.

1869–73 T. R. JONES *Cassell's Bk. Birds* III. 3 The voice of the Sai is only capable of producing a gentle twitter.

sai, obs. form of SAY; obs. pa. t. of SEE.

saibling (ˈseɪblɪŋ). Also **sæbling.** [a. Upper German dial. *saibling* = *salbling*, *sälbling* the char.] The European char, *Salvelinus alpinus*, introduced into N. America.

1884 GOODE, etc. *Nat. Hist. Aquatic Anim.* 503 The Saibling, which through the courtesy of the German Government is now being introduced into the United States, is the European Char in its highest state of perfection. **1896** *Roy. Nat. Hist.* V. 501 The sæbling (*Salmo salvelinus*) of the mountain-lakes of Bavaria and Austria.

‖**saic** (ˈseɪk). Forms: 7 **saich, saicque,** 8 **shyke,** 7–8 **saique,** 7–9 **saic, saick.** [a. F. *saïque*, ad. Turkish *shāïqā*.] A kind of sailing vessel common in the Levant (see quot. 1769).

1667 *Lond. Gaz.* No. 119/2 Two large Saichs laden with Horses, were taken by some of our Vessels in their passage from Napoli di Romania to Canea. **1686** tr. *Chardin's Trav. Persia* 64 The Saic lay at an Anchor. **1687** A. LOVELL tr. *Thevenot's Trav.* I. 73 They build Saiques, and other Merchants Vessels pretty well. **1704** J. PITTS *Acc. Mohammetans* 63 There are many of the Turks Merchant-Men, navigated by Greeks, which are called by the name of Shykes, somewhat like our English Ketches, of Two or Three Hundred Tun. **1715** *Comm. Jrnls.* 45/1 The Fishing-Ships and Saicks employed at Newfoundland. **1769** FALCONER *Dict. Marine* (1780), *Saic*, a sort of Grecian ketch, which has no top-gallant-sail or mizen-top-sail. **1813** BYRON *Corsair* II. iv, From Scalanovo's port to Scio's isle, The Saick was bound. **1834** [MORIER] *Ayesha* III. 31 The bark ..which was called a saique, was square-rigged.

saice, variant of SYCE.

saickless, obs. form of SACKLESS.

said (sɛd), *ppl. a.* Forms: see the vb. [Pa. pple. of SAY *v.*]

1. Named or mentioned before. (Also *abovesaid, aforesaid* qq. v.)

a **1300** *Cursor M.* 14978 (Cott.) Son þar went disciplis tua Vnto þe said [*Gött.* þis said] castel. *c* **1375** *Sc. Leg. Saints* xi. (*Symon & Judas*) 16 þe sad king agabarus (L. *prædictus rex Abgarus*). **1435** *Contract Fotheringhay Ch.* (1841) 20 At my seide Lord's cost. **1457–8** *Anc. Cal. Rec. Dublin* (1889) 297 Aftyr the sayd terme to ber the saydyn v. *s.* **1486** *Bk. St. Albans* b iij b, Lay thessaid hede and the necke ther-uppon. **1548–9** (Mar.) *Bk. Com. Prayer, Collect St. Matthew*) To folowe thy sayed sonne Jesus Christ. **1568** GRAFTON *Chron.* II. 251 The King of England gaue the sayde Castell to the sayde Erle. **1716** *Lond. Gaz.* No. 5450/4 The Administratrixes of the said Wilson, do hereby give Notices. **1868** T. H. KEY *Philol. Ess.* 282 The said chapter begins with an admirable extract from a work of Dugald Stewart's. **1885** *Law Times Rep.* LIII. 51/2 The said chimney belonged to the said brewery.

absol. **1648** GAGE *West. Ind.* 186 Some English or Holland ships was abroad at sea..and the said were sometimes lurking about the Islands of St. John.

†**b.** With inflected pl. *Obs.*

Continued in Sc. until the 17th c.

1448 in Willis & Clark *Cambridge* (1886) II. 8 The Felowes of the seid college..and Thomas Sturgeon of the seides town and shire carpenter. **1527** *Lanc. Wills* (Chetham Soc.) I. 25 Tenants of the saidis landis. **1581** HAMILTON *Cert. Orth. & Cath. Conclus.* Ded. 3 And yair ye saidis ministers and ve being assemblit. **1609** SKENE *Reg. Maj., Forme Proces* 125 The officiar..may sell and assigne the saides landes.

†**2.** Spoken, uttered. In phr. (*old*) *said saw.*

1530, *c* **1570**, **1828** [see OLD E. 1 c]. *a* **1553** UDALL *Royster D.* I. i. (Arb.) 11 Therefore an other sayd sawe doth men aduise, That they be together both mery and wise. **1581** J. BELL *Haddon's Answ. Osor.* 202 b, Accordyng to the old sayd saw Quite agaynst the heare. **1659** HOWELL (*title*) Proverbs, or Old Sayed Sawes & Adages.

†**3.** quasi-*sb.* Something said or spoken. *nonce-use.*

1578 FLORIO *1st Fruites* 18 b, So say I also. But from the said vnto the deed there is a great throw.

said, obs. f. SAD, SIDE.

saie, obs. f. SAY.

saie, obs. pa. t. and pa. pple. of SEE.

saif, obs. Sc. form of SAVE.

saif(e, saiff(e, obs. Sc. forms of SAFE.

saifare, saiffer, obs. Sc. forms of SAVER.

saiffer, obs. form of SAPPHIRE.

saifte, -tie, obs. Sc. forms of SAFETY.

saiga ('seɪgə, 'saɪgə). [a. Russ. *saïga*. Cf. F. *saïga*.] A kind of antelope (*Saiga tartarica*) of the steppes of Russia. Also ***saiga-antelope***.

1801 SHAW *Zool.* II. II. 339 The Saiga, or Scythian Antelope. *Ibid.* 340 The Saigas are of a migratory disposition. **1896** LYDEKKER *Brit. Mammals* 305 The Saiga Antelope.

saige, obs. f. SIEGE.

Saigonese (saɪgɒ'ni:z), *collect. sb.* [f. *Saigon* (now Ho Chi Minh City), formerly the capital of South Vietnam + -ESE.] The people of Saigon. (No longer in official use.)

1967 [see HIGH *adv.* 9 b]. **1975** *Daily Tel.* 1 May 1 Laughing guerillas..drove through the streets exchanging waves and banter with the Saigonese.

saih, obs. pa. t. of SEE.

saik, obs. Sc. form of SAKE.

saikles(se, obs. Sc. forms of SACKLESS.

saikyr, obs. Sc. form of SAKER (cannon).

sail (seɪl), *sb.*[1] Forms: 1 **segel, segl**, 3 **sæil(e**, 3–4 **seil**, 3–5 **seile, seyle**, 3–7 **sayle**, 3–8 **saile**, 4 **seille, seyll(e**, 4–5 **seyl**, 4–7 **sayl**, 4–8 **sale**, 5 **ceyle, seylle**, 5–6 **saill(e, sayll(e**, 6 **sal, saule**, 4– **sail**. [Com. Teut.: OE. *seȝ(e)l* neut. (and masc.), corresp. to OS. *segel* (MLG. *segel*, MDu. *zeghel*, *zeil*, Du. *zeil*), OHG. *segal*, *segil* (MHG., mod.G. *segel*), ON. *segl* (Sw. *segel*, Da. *seil*):—OTeut. **seglo*[m].

The ulterior origin is obscure. No certainly equivalent form is known outside Teut., and the only known root of the form **seg-* (:—Indogermanic **segh-*) has only the senses 'to hold, have, conquer', which do not satisfactorily account for the meaning of the word. Some scholars refer the word to the root **sek-* (Teut. **seh-*), to cut, taking it to mean a piece of cloth cut to shape.]

1. a. One of the shaped pieces of canvas or other strong textile material fastened to the masts, spars or stays of a vessel, so as to catch the wind and cause it to move through the water. Also occas. a similar apparatus for propelling a wind-driven carriage.

c **888** K. ÆLFRED *Boeth.* xli. §3 Hæt fealdan þæt segl & eac hwilum lecȝan þone mæst. *a* **900** *OE. Martyrol.* 4 Mar. 34 Ferað nu swa swa eowre seȝlas sendon ȝeseted. *c* **1205** LAY. 1101 Heo rærden heora mastes heo wunden up seiles. *c* **1290** *Beket* 1803 in *S. Eng. Leg.* I. 158 In þe schipes seile an heiȝ: þis holi man let do Ane Croiz, þat Man fer isaiȝ. **1297** R. GLOUC. (Rolls) 2828 Hor seiles hii spredeþ in þe se & hider hii comeþ iwis. *a* **1300** *Cursor M.* 24829 þair sail þai sett up o þair scipp. **1375** BARBOUR *Bruce* XVI. 692 Thai rasit salys but abaid. *c* **1386** CHAUCER *Miller's T.* 346, I vndertake with-outen Mast and seyl Yet shal I sauen hire and thee and me. **1387** TREVISA *Higden* (Rolls) IV. 183 Schippes..wiþ seilles and wiþ oores. **1390** GOWER *Conf.* II. 258 Thei gon withinne schipes bord, The Sail goth up, and forth thei strauhte. *c* **1440** [see 5]. *c* **1470** HENRY *Wallace* IX. 53 The seymen than..Thair lynys kest, and waytyt well the tyd; Leyt salys fall, and has thar cours ynom. *c* **1489** CAXTON *Blauchardyn* xxxiv. 127 They made to take vp the ancres & to hale vp their saylles. **1506** *Acc. Ld. High Treas. Scot.* III. 295 Item..for j[c]xiiij elne cammes to the schip callit the Mergreit for hir sales..summa v *li.* xj *s.* viiij *d.* **1530** PALSGR. 268/2 Seyle of a shyppe, *uoille.* **1533** *Acc. Ld. High Treas. Scot.* VI. 165 For xij elnis canves to mend hir saulis. **1568** GRAFTON *Chron.* II. 242 He drew vp the sayles and came with a quarter winde to haue the vauntage of the sonne. **1611** BIBLE *Isa.* xxxiii. 23 Thy tacklings are loosed..they could not spread the saile. **1667** MILTON *P.L.* III. 439 The barren plaines Of Sericana, where Chineses drive With Sails and Wind thir canie Waggons light. **1669** STURMY *Mariner's Mag.* I. 17 Now the Sail is furled, and you have the Ship in all her low Sails. *c* **1764** GRAY *Triumphs Owen* 15 The Norman sails afar Catch the winds. **1850** TENNYSON *In Mem.* cxv, The flocks are whiter down the vale, And milkier every milky sail On winding stream or distant sea. *c* **1860** H. STUART *Seaman's Catech.* 20 What is meant by small sails? Topgallant sails and royals, topmast, topgallant, and lower studding sails. *Ibid.*, What are meant by storm sails? Fore storm staysail and trysail, main staysail and trysail, and mizen trysail.

fig. *a* **1533** LD. BERNERS *Gold. Bk. M. Aurel.* (1537) N n ij, They lacke the reyne of knowlege, & the sayles of wisedome, & the ankers of experience. *a* **1568** ASCHAM *Scholem.* II. (Arb.) 151 Where Tullie doth set vp his saile of eloquence. **1599** SHAKS. *Hen. V*, I. ii. 274 But tell the Dolphin, I will keepe my State, Be like a King, and shew my Sayle of Greatnesse, When I do rowse me in my Throne of France.

b. *transf.* Applied to the wing of a bird. *poet.* Also *techn.* in Falconry, the wing of a hawk.

1590 SPENSER *F.Q.* I. xi. 18 He, [a dragon] cutting way With his broad sayles, about him soared round. **1592** NASHE *P. Penilesse* c j b, To clippe the winges of a high towring Faulcon, who..was wont..to looke with an amiable eye vpon her gray breast, and her speckled side sayles. **1678** PHILLIPS (ed. 4), *Sails*, in Faulconry are the Wings of a Hawk. **1810** SCOTT *Lady of L.* III. iii, The mountain eagle..Spread her dark sails on the wind.

c. *transf.* Applied to something that is spread out like a sail, or that catches the wind.

1616 T. SCOT *Philomythie* (ed. 2) D 2, The Pehen drest her selfe and spred her taile, The Turky-hen aduanc'd her spotted saile. **1697** DRYDEN *Virg. Georg.* I. 246 The Fan of Bacchus, with the flying Sail. **1824** MISS FERRIER *Inher.* lxxiii, The drooping capes, arms, sails, and tails of his cloak were all in commotion.

†**d.** *Aeronaut.* Applied to a flat aerodynamically structured part of an aircraft. *Obs.*

1808 G. CAYLEY *Aeronaut. & Misc. Note-bk.* (1933) 64, I tried a small square sail in one plane, with the weight nearly in the same, & I could not perceive that the centre & resistance differed from the centre of bulk. **1817** *Phil. Mag.* L. 35 The sketch..represents a side view of the arrangement of the moving and steering sails of a balloon on the wing plan. **1837** *Mechanics' Mag.* XXVI. 421/2 From the hinder mast C a sail may be conveniently braced to either side, so as to act as a rudder, and thus preserve a steady course. **1902** F. WALKER *Aërial Navigation* viii. 118 A head sail *i* and stern sails *h*, *h*[1] had braces and halliards for steering... The sails *h*, *h*[1] acted as aëroplanes as well as for steering purposes. **1903** —— *Pract. Kites & Aëroplanes* ii. 25 The 'leeches', or free edges of the sails..are double-stitched around a leech-rope.

2. a. Sails collectively. Also *fig.* Often in phrases *to* ***carry***, ***cross***, ***crowd***, ***hoist***, ***lower***, ***make***, ***set***, ***shorten***, ***strike*** (etc.) ***sail***, for which see also those verbs.

c **1385** CHAUCER *L.G.W.* 654 (*Cleopatra*) Fleth ek the queen, withal hire porpere sayl. *c* **1435** *Torr. Portugal* 1426, I rede we take down sayle & rowe. *a* **1548** HALL *Chron., Edw. IV* 209 The kynges shyp was good with sayle. **1567** FENTON *Trag. Disc.* v. (1898) I. 232 It ought to have sufficed to have revoked, and made hym cross saile, from the pursute of so bad an adventure. **1806** A. DUNCAN *Nelson* 65 The Admiral ..carried all sail. **1831** SCOTT *Ct. Robt.* ii, Every way qualified to bear me through the cross currents of the court by main pull of oar and press of sail. **1853** M. ARNOLD *Scholar Gypsy* xxv, [He] snatched his rudder, and shook out more sail. **1893** LELAND *Mem.* I. 155 Our captain was a handsome, dissipated, and 'loud' young man, with rather more sail than ballast, but good-natured and obliging.

†**b.** *transf.* See quot. *Obs.*

1759 STILLINGFL. tr. *Riberg's Econ. Nat., note* in *Misc. Tracts* (1762) 45 As i have..weighed several kinds of birds, i shall here subjoyn a table..with the proportions of the weight to the sail. N.B. By sail i mean the extent of the wings and tail.

3. Phrases (senses 1 and 2). †**a.** ***to bear sail***: said *lit.* of a ship; hence *fig.* to be exalted, to be prosperous, also ***to bear a great, high*** or ***lofty sail***. ***to bear*** (***a***) ***low sail, to be of low sail***: to demean oneself humbly; to live at a modest rate; to cut down expenses (see BEAR *v.*[1] 3 b.). ***to live at a low sail***: to live humbly. ***to pull down one's sail*** or ***sails***: to moderate one's ambitions or one's scale of expenditure. *Obs.*

a **1300** [see BEAR *v.*[1] 3 b]. **1390** GOWER *Conf.* I. 65 Bot whanne he berth lowest the Seil, Thanne is he swiftest to beguile The womman. *a* **1548** HALL *Chron., Hen. VI* 140 Whiche maie by pinchyng and bearyng a lowe saile, Waxe riche and be set at libertie. **1548** UDALL *Erasm. Par.* Pref. 18, I was utterly myndeded to pulle downe my sayles agaiue. **1549** LATIMER *2nd Serm. bef. Edw. VI* To Rdr. (Arb.) 51 Pul downe thy sayle. **1573** TUSSER *Husb.* (1878) 211 Then waies I saught, by wisdome taught, To beare low saile, least stock should quaile. **1587** HARRISON *England* II. v. in *Holinshed* I. 164/1 How diuerse of them also coueting to beare an high saile doo insinuate themselues with yoong gentlemen and noble men newlie come to their lands. **1587** FLEMING *Concl. Holinshed* III. 1592/1 If the helpe of such as are furnished with varietie of knowledge,..had beene as forward to aduance this worke,..as some of low saile, willing to laie out their poore talent, have affoorded what furtherance they were able [etc.]. **1601** B. JONSON *Ev. Man in Hum.* (Qo. 1) I. i, Moderate your expences (now at first) As you may keepe the same proportion still. Beare a low saile. **1602** *2nd Pt. Return fr. Parnass.* IV. iii. 1941 Schollers must frame to liue at a low sayle. **1610** HEALEY *St. Aug. Citie of God* (1620) 731 If learning had many such friends as he, it would beare an higher sayle then it doth. **1665** MANLEY *Grotius' Low C. Warres* 211 They drew in their Mooned and crescent Squadrons into the Body of the Fleet, and that one might not go before another, bore less Sayl. **1733** *Oxf. Methodists* 6 Be not high-minded; but fear... Bear no more Sail than is necessary.

†**b.** ***to come to sail***: to set out on a sailing voyage; = SAIL *v.* 3. ? Also (earlier) in the same sense, ***to go*** or ***fere to*** (***the***) ***sail***. (Cf. SAIL *sb.*[2])

c **1350** *Will. Palerne* 2731 þe werwolf waited wiȝtly which schip was ȝarest, to fare forþ at þat flod & fond on sone þat was gayly greyt to go to þe seile, & feiþliche frauȝt ful of fine wines. *Ibid.* 2745 And faire at þe fulle flod þei ferden to saile. **1633** T. JAMES *Voy.* 5 Wee came to Sayle. **1712** W. ROGERS *Voy.* 3 About twelve we fir'd a Gun, and all came to sail. **1743** BULKELEY & CUMMINS *Voy. S. Seas* 6 At Eight weigh'd, and came to Sail.

c. ***full sail***: a sail (or sails collectively) filled or distended by the wind; the condition of a ship with sails so filled. ***at***, †***with full sail(s*** [= L. *pleno velo*, *plenis velis*, F. *à pleines voiles*]: (sailing) with a strong favourable wind, at full speed; *fig.* making rapid and unresisted progress; so also ***full sail*** as advb. phrase. In mod. use, ***in full sail*** is applied to describe the condition of a ship with all sails set; also *fig.*

a **1533** LD. BERNERS *Huon* lx. 208 Yonder comyth a shyppe with full sayle. **1560** DAUS tr. *Sleidane's Comm.* 134 b, Sathan..shall make towardes us with full sayle [orig. *plenis velis*]. **1564** GRINDAL *Serm. Ferdinandus* D j, The doctrine of purgatorie and praying for the dead hath gone with full saile. *c* **1600** SHAKS. *Sonn.* lxxxvi, Was it the proud full saile of his great verse. **1618** BOLTON *Florus* Ded. (1636) 2 To increase in the full saile of fortune. **1648** GAGE *West Ind.* xxi. 201 So the two ships..sailed away *con Viento en Popa*, with full Sail. **1653** H. MORE *Antid. Ath.* III. xiv. §7 Faith and Desire ought to be full-sail to make such Voyages prosperous. **1699** DAMPIER *Voy.* II. III. 39 Constant..Land-winds, by which the Wherry-men run with full sail, both to..and back again. **1715** *Lond. Gaz.* No. 5357/2 The Danish Fleet having the Wind came full sail up with the Swedes. **1758** GOLDSM. *Mem. Prot.* (1895) II. 274 Smith went full Sail to reconnoitre the Enemy. **1818** SCOTT *Hrt. Midl.* ix, Her father..often took an opportunity of going full-sail into controversial subjects. **1848** A. & H. MAYHEW *Greatest Plague of Life* xiii. 202 The stupid engravings..that had nothing at all to do with the song, for I declare if there wasn't a ship in full sail put as an illustration to 'Away, Away, to the Mountain's Brow!' **1858** W. H. HASWELL in *Merc. Marine Mag.* V. 208 The vessel was at full sail. *a* **1859** MACAULAY *Hist. Eng.* xxiii. V. 12 The Protestant wind, before which the Dutch armament had run full sail down the Channel, had driven King James's navy back into the Thames. **1864–8** BROWNING *Jas. Lee's Wife* II. iv, With whom began Love's voyage full-sail. **1867** SMYTH *Sailor's Word-bk.*, *Full sails*, the sails well set, and filled by the wind. **1887** BOWEN *Æneid* I. 400 Thy vessels..the haven have entered, or bend Now full sail for its mouth.

transf. and *fig.* **1671** MILTON *P.R.* IV. 582 So Satan fell and strait a fiery Globe Of Angels on full sail of wing flew nigh. **1893** 'MARK TWAIN' *Lett. to Publishers* (1967) 348 A well-organized business..an enterprise not experimental but under full sail.

d. ***under sail***: having the sails set.

c **893** K. ÆLFRED *Oros.* I. i. §21 þæt þæt scip wæs ealne weȝ yrnende under seȝle. **1508** KENNEDIE *Flyting w. Dunbar* 457 Quhen that the schip was saynit, et vndir saile [etc.]. **1588** SHAKS. *L.L.L.* v. ii. 549 The ship is vnder saile, and here she coms amain. **1690** LEYBOURN *Curs. Math.* 454 Suppose.. you see a Ship..under Sail, making towards the Land. **1748** *Anson's Voy.* II. iv. 162 In the afternoon [we] got under sail. **1836** MARRYAT *Midsh. Easy* xiii, About ten miles distant, followed by the Harpy, under all sail. **1857** C. GRIBBLE in *Merc. Marine Mag.* (1858) V. 1 Weighed anchor.., under all sail. **1867** SMYTH *Sailor's Word-bk.*, *Under sail*, the state of a ship when she is in motion from the action of wind on her sails.

4. a. In collective sing. (also formerly †in plural), chiefly with numeral: (So many) sailing-vessels.

1436 *Rolls of Parlt.* IV. 501/1 A Navey..to ye noumbre of xii score Sailles. **1458** *Paston Lett.* I. 428 Ther were xxviij[ie] sayle of Spaynyards on the se. **1480** CAXTON *Chron. Eng.* ccxliv. (1482) 296 The kyng ordeyned his nauye of shippes in the hauen of southampton in to the nombre of cccxx sailles. **1568** GRAFTON *Chron.* II. 237 The Frenchmen were .xiij. sayles great and small. **1590** *Disc. Sp. Fleet inv. Eng.* 4 The whole nauie was at this present about 90. saile of all sorts. **1595** SHAKS. *John* III. iv. 2 So by a roaring Tempest on the flood A whole Armado of conuicted saile Is scattered and dis-ioyn'd from fellowship. **1633** T. STAFFORD *Pac. Hib.* II. viii. (1821) 325 Of their fiue and fourtie Saile of ships, seventeene saile onely are fitted for men of warre. **1649** W. GRAY *Surv. Newcastle* 19 The Shipping which comes into this River for Coales, there being sometimes three hundred Sayles of Ships. **1743** BULKELEY & CUMMINS *Voy. S. Seas* 3 We were informed of ten Sail of Ships cruising off and on, to the Westward. **1831** BREWSTER *Optics* xxvi. 258 He saw from the mast-head eighteen sail of ships. **1863** H. COX *Instit.* III. viii. 717 The Royal navy comprised in all twenty-seven sail.

b. A ship or other vessel, esp. as descried by its sails. ***sail ho!*** 'the exclamation used when a strange ship is first discerned at sea' (Adm. Smyth).

1517 TORKINGTON *Pilgr.* (1884) 12 The Duke [Doge of Venice]..went in ther Archa triumphali, which ys in maner of a sayle of a straange facion. **1556** W. TOWRSON in Hakluyt *Voy.* (1589) 99 We spyed a saile comming towardes vs, and as soone as wee spyed him we..manned out our Skiffe. After the saile had espyed vs, he kept about. **1627** CAPT. SMITH *Seaman's Gram.* xiii. 59 A saile, how beares she or stands shee, to wind-ward or lee-ward, set him by the Compasse. **1634** SIR T. HERBERT *Trav.* 11 Our Admirall descried a Saile, and immediately made towards her. **1669** STURMY *Mariner's Mag.* I. ii. 18 A Sail, a Sail. Where? Fair by us. **1726** SWIFT *Gulliver* I. viii, I descried a Sail steering to the South-East. **1813** BYRON *Corsair* I. ii, Gaze where some distant sail a speck supplies, With all the thirsting eye of Enterprise. **1840** R. H. DANA *Bef. Mast* ii, Her decks were filled with passengers who had come up at the cry of 'Sail ho!'

5. An apparatus (consisting formerly of a sheet of canvas stretched on a frame, now usually of an arrangement of boards) attached to each of the arms of a windmill for the purpose of presenting a surface to be acted on by the wind. Also (windmill) sails collectively, surface presented by the sails.

c **1440** *Promp. Parv.* 65/1 Ceyle of a schyppe, or mylle, *velum. carbasus.* **1589** R. HARVEY *Plain Perc.* (1590) 3 The clacke of thy mill is..noisome.., thou hast wind at will to thy sailes. **1688** R. HOLME *Armoury* III. 340/2 The parts of a Wind-Mill... The Sail or Wind end. *a* **1700** B. E. *Dict. Cant. Crew*, *Sails*, Hawk's Wings; also Windmill-wings. **1759** SMEATON in *Phil. Trans.* LI. 161 The velocity of the extremities of Dutch sails,..are considerably quicker than the velocity of the wind. **1825** J. NICHOLSON *Operat. Mechanic* 122 Into these arms are mortised several small cross-bars, and to them are fastened two, three, or four, long bars,..so that the bars intersect each other, and form a kind of lattice work, on which a cloth is spread to receive the action of wind. These are called the sails. **1845** *Encycl. Metrop.* VIII. 131/2 There are usually four states in which it can be set according to the velocity of the wind .. which are termed *full sail*, *quarter reef*, *sword point*, and *dagger point*. **1868** *Chamb. Encycl.* X. 218/1 The amount of sail that a windmill can carry with advantage is limited. *a* **1887** Jefferies *Field & Hedgerow* (1889) 86 One day pussy was ingeniously examining the machinery [of a windmill], when the wind suddenly rose, the sails revolved, and she was ground up. **1888** *Encycl. Brit.* XXIV. 599/2 *American windmills*... The sails consist of narrow boards or slats arranged radially.

6. *Zool.* **a.** The large dorsal fin of the sail-fish. **b.** One of the two large tentacles of the Nautilus, formerly believed to be used as sails.

1817 Shelley *Rev. Islam* vii. xxvi, A Nautilus upon the fountain played, Spreading his azure sail. **1822** Raffles *Let.* 30 Nov. in Lady Raffles *Mem.* (1830) 526 The only amusing discovery which we have recently made is that of a sailing fish, .. I have sent a set of the sails home. **1840** *Penny Cycl.* XVII. 210/2 The first two arms [of the Argonaut] are more robust than the others, and should be so, because they serve as masts to support the sails, which, spread out, act before the wind as such. **1860** *Chamb. Encycl.* I. 390/1 The descriptions .. of argonauts .. employing six of their tentacula as oars, and spreading out two .. as sails to catch the breeze, are now regarded as entirely fabulous.

7. *S. Africa.* A tarpaulin or canvas sheet for covering a wagon.

1850 R. G. Cumming *Hunter's Life S. Afr.* (ed. 2) I. 220, I covered my waggon with new sails. **1891** Olive Schreiner *African Farm* ii. xii, He drew the sails down before and behind, and the wagon rolled away slowly.

8. *Naut.* and *Mining.* A funnel-shaped bag or orifice on the deck of a vessel or on the ground over mine-galleries, for the purpose of ventilation. Cf. wind-sail.

1874 J. H. Collins *Metal Mining* (1875) 117 In Cornwall .. the writer has seen a zinc rain-water pipe .. with a miner's jacket extended by wires at the top for a 'cap-head' or 'sail'. **1875** in Knight *Dict. Mech.*

9. The conning-tower of a submarine.

1959 *Jane's Fighting Ships* 414/1 'The sail', as the conning tower is now called on nuclear submarines. **1963** *Guardian* 1 Mar. 1 The Ethan Allen looked like any other submarine though the conning tower—which they call the sail these days—was much larger than usual. **1968** *New Scientist* 26 Dec. 704/2 Photographs of the wreckage show that the *Scorpion* split in two at the point on the hull where the 'sail' (the new name for the conning tower) is mounted near the forward end. **1974** L. Deighton *Spy Story* xviii. 190 The great submarine threaded its way out through the Sound... The skipper came down from the sail.

10. Obvious combinations. **a.** simple attrib., as ***sail area***, ***canvas***, ***drill***, ***pulley***, † ***-rope***, ***sewing-machine***, ***-spread***; **b.** objective, as ***sail-carrying***, ***furler***, ***-keeper***, ***looser***, ***-making***, ***sewer***, ***sewing***, ***trimmer***; also ***sail-bearing***, ***-filling***, ***-stiffening*** adjs.; **c.** instrumental, as ***sail-assisted***, ***-dotted***, ***-propelled***; **d.** similative, as ***sail-broad***, ***-stretched*** adjs.

1898 W. F. Jackson in W. A. Morgan *'House' on Sport* I. i. 19 Traditions are still heard of boats lurking behind barges .. to dart out at the last moment with something surprising in the way of *sail area. **1976** *Oxf. Compan. Ships & Sea* 947/2 There was no form of handicap on size or sail area. **1593** Nashe *Unfort. Trav.* (1594) G 2 b, As the Estrich hath a sharpe goad or pricke wherewith he spurreth himselfe forward in his *saile-assisted race. *c* **1595** J. Dickenson *Sheph. Compl.* (1878) 12 And *saile-bearing pine glide through thin aire. **1667** Milton *P.L.* ii. 930 At last his *Sail-broad Vannes He spreads for flight. **1482** in *Charters* etc. *Edin.* (1871) 169 Of the hundreth *sail canves ij s. **1883** *Harper's Mag.* Aug. 444/2 We believed in great beam for *sail-carrying power. **1894** *Outing* (U.S.) XXIV. 21/1 To gain stability [in a canoe] for sail-carrying. **1898** Kipling in *Morn. Post* 9 Nov. 5/1 The little strip of *sail-dotted blue. **1886** *Pall Mall G.* 17 Sept. 11/1 While at *sail drill an ordinary seaman .. fell .. on to the upper deck. **1887** Morris *Odyss.* xi. 8 A goodly breeze *sail-filling. *c* **1860** H. Stuart *Seaman's Catech.* 45 The *sailfurlers .. get the sail out of the sailroom. *c* **1440** *Promp. Parv.* 451/2 *Seyl kepare, or rewlare, *p[ro]reta*. *c* **1860** H. Stuart *Seaman's Catech.* 45 *Sail loosers will go aloft at the order 'bend sails'. **1797** *Encycl. Brit.* (ed. 3) XVII. 431/2 A few general observations on *sail-making. **1888** *Times* 14 Jan. 16/2 *Sail-propelled training ships. **1601** Holland *Pliny* I. 390 Whereof they vse to turne for curtain rings and *saile pullies. *c* **1205** Lay. 17395 ȝe mote uaste heom wriðen mid strongen *sæil-rapen. *c* **1475** *Pict. Voc.* in Wr.-Wülcker 805/7 *Hic rudens*, .. a seyllerope. **1513** *Acc. Ld. High Treas. Scot.* IV. 471 Item, to iij *saill sewaris for iij wolkis wagis. **1884** Knight *Dict. Mech.* Suppl., **Sail Sewing Machine*, a large-sized sewing machine with extensive table for sewing widths of duck to form sails. **1886** *Encycl. Brit.* XXI. 823/2 In determining what *sail-spread can be safely given to a ship. **1945** P. Larkin *North Ship* 35 Increasingly to fear *Sail-stiffening air. **1623** Massinger *Bondman* i. iii, O're our heads with *sayle stretch'd wings, Destruction houers. *c* **1810** Adm. Patton in *19th Cent.* Nov. (1899) 724 *note*, *Sail trimmers were immediately sent to clear the sail.

11. Special Comb.: **sail-arm**, (*a*) one of the radiating beams to which the sails of a windmill are attached; a 'whip'; (*b*) one of the tentacles of a nautilus which bear the 'sails'; **sail-axle**, the axle on which the sails of a windmill revolve; **sailboard** orig. *U.S.*, a surf-board or light sail-boat which is propelled by wind caught in its sail; also as *v. intr.*; hence **sailboarder**, **sailboarding** *vbl. sb.*; **sail-boat** (chiefly *N. Amer.*), a sailing-boat; † **sail-bond**, (? error for *-bonet*) = bonnet *sb.*[2] (cf. quot. 1483 there); **sail-burton** (see quot.); **sail curtain** = curtain *sb.*[1] 2 a; **sail-duck** [a. Du. *zeildoek*] = duck *sb.*[3] 1; † **sail-fan**, a species of fan used in winnowing corn; **sail-fluke**, the whiff, *Rhombus megastoma*; **sail-flying** = sailplaning *vbl. sb.*; **sail-hook**, a small hook for holding the seams of a sail while it is being sewn; **sail-hoop**, one of the wooden rings by which fore and aft sails are secured to masts and stays (Knight *Dict. Mech.* 1875); **sail-house**, a house where sails are stored; **sail-lizard** (see quot.); **sail-loft** (see quot. 1769); **sail-maker**, one whose business it is to make, repair, or alter sails; *spec.*, on board ship, a sailor (in the U.S. navy, a warrant officer) whose duty it is to take charge of and keep in repair all sails, awnings, etc.; **sail-needle**, a large needle used in sewing canvas; **sail plan** (see quot. 1961); **sail-room**, a room (in a ship) for storing sails; **sail-shell**, a name for the nautilus; **sail-ship**, a sailing-vessel; **sail-swelled** *a.*, having filled sails; **sail thread**, **twine**, thread or twine used in sewing sails; † **sail wand**, one of the rods forming the framework of a windmill sail; **sail wing**, the sail of a hang glider with its framework; (the structures described in quots. 1972, 1974 differ from one another); **sail-winged** *a.*, *poet.* [after L. *vēlivolus*], (*a*) of ships, having sails that serve as wings; (*b*) *transf.* as an epithet of the sea; (*c*) having wings like sails.

1760 J. Ferguson *Lect.* (1764) 52 The same velocity that it would move if put upon the *sail-arms. **1840** *Penny Cycl.* XVII. 210/2 In fact, the series of suckers of the sail-arms, when the membrane of the sails is wrapped about the shell, is placed exactly over the keel of it in such a manner that [etc.]. **1868** *Chamb. Encycl.* X. 218/1 A whip or radius of from 33 to 40 feet in length, firmly fastened at right angles to the *sail-axle. **1962** D. Klein *Beginning with Boats* iv. 95 Another boat that may tempt you because it can give you a great deal of fun at rather low cost is what is called a **sailboard*—that is, a sort of surfboard equipped with centerboard, rudder, and sailing rig. **1978** B. Webb tr. *Brockhaus & Stanciu's Sailboarding* 8 You can ski in any mountainous region where there is snow, just as you can sailboard on any water, whether it be an ocean or a reservoir. **1980** *Daily Tel.* 15 Sept. 2 (*caption*) A 22ft-long sailboard made for two .. being demonstrated at Southampton. **1974** A. H. Drummond *Sailboarding* 10 The surfboarder catches a wave and uses its energy to surf along. The *sailboarder does just about the same thing, except that he uses a sail to capture the energy of the wind... Thus, sailboarding is surfing using wind power. **1979** *Yachts & Yachting* 9 Nov. 1433/3 Wandering sailboarders could be pleased with a complete cover for their board. **1974** *Sailboarding [see *sailboarder* above]. **1978** *Times* 5 Apr. 8/5 Beau Vallon is the island's most visited beach... Enthusiasts use it for sail-boarding, water-skiing, para-gliding, diving and goggling. **1798** C. Williamson *Descr. Genesee Country* iii. 19 The number of *sail-boats have greatly increased on the Lake. **1831** M. Holley *Texas* (1833) 47 From Brazoria to Bolivar, I came in a sail-boat. *a* **1835** Mrs. Hemans in H. F. Chorley *Mem.* (1837) II. 17 Neither steam-packet nor sail-boat was attainable. **1888** F. M. Crawford *With Immortals* II. 129 The happiest moments of my life? I think they were spent in a sail-boat. **1911** J. C. Lincoln *Cap'n Warren's Wards* xxi. 333 He had gone to see the sail-boat man. **1956** M. Duggan *Immanuel's Land* 64 A flatbottomed sailboat on the slope shifted almost afloat, and settled again into the mud. **1977** E. Leonard *Unknown Man No. 89* xxi. 211 A painting .. of .. a sailboat with the mast broken off. *c* **1475** *Pict. Voc.* in Wr.-Wülcker 805/8 *Hec supera, -eris*, a *seyllebonde. **1867** Smyth *Sailor's Word-bk.*, **Sail burton*, a purchase extending from topmast-head to deck, for sending sails aloft ready for bending. **1941** J. Masefield *Gautama* 52 The red *sail-curtain droops. **1776** T. Pennant *Tour in Scotl. & Voy. Hebrides 1772* II. 143 At present the manufactures have risen to a great pitch: for example, that sail-cloth, or *sail-duck, as it is here called, is very considerable. **1795** *Scots Mag.* LVII. 610/1 Sail-duck manufacturer. **1812** J. Smyth *Pract. of Customs* (1812) 145 Sail Duck. **1707** Mortimer *Husb.* 112 Four Men with either the Wicker or *Sail-fan. **1882** Tenison-Woods *Fish & Fisheries N.S. Wales* 190 *Sail-fluke. **1886** R. C. Leslie *Sea-painter's Log* x. 194 It is said .. the sail-fluke gets its name from a habit of .. lifting its tail out of water like a sail, running before the wind into shallow water. **1931** A. Gymnich in V. W. Pagé *Henley's ABC of Gliding* 148 By *sailflying we understand a flight without any kind of motor or other driving power in which the energy required for the flight without loss in altitude, is taken solely from the air currents. **1944** T. Horsley *Soaring Flight* 71 The chapter on soaring sites will have given an indication of the winds used in the simplest sail-flying. **1794** *Rigging & Seamanship* I. 88 *Sail-hook. **1886** *Encycl. Brit.* XXI. 155/1 The tools .. of a sailmaker are .. fids, .. sail-hook, bobbin for twine, and sundry small articles. **1884** *St. James's Gaz.* 22 Feb. 7/1 It is apparently the inside of a *sail-house at a fishing-port. **1885** *Standard Nat. Hist.* (1888) III. 413 The *sail-lizard, *Histiurus amboinensis*, so called from the enormous perpendicular development surmounting its tail. **1769** Falconer *Dict. Marine* ii. (1780), *Voilerie*, a *sail-loft, or place where sails are constructed. **1891** *Leeds Mercury* 9 Oct. 4/4 Dr. Hurst .. traced the history of Methodism in America from the first meeting held in a sail-loft in New York in 1776 to the present day. **1596** Shaks. *Tam. Shr.* v. i. 80 He is a *saile-maker in Bergano. **1773** *Cook's 1st Voy.* iii. xii. in *Hawkesworth's Voy.* III. 722 Every individual had been sick except the sail maker. **1916** H. Barber *Aeroplane Speaks* 103 All is now ready for the sail-maker to cover the surface with fabric. **1497** *Naval Acc. Hen. VII* (1896) 297 *Sayle Nedylles price the c xij^{d}. **1769** Falconer *Dict. Marine* Uu ij b, Sail-needles, or bolt-rope needles. **1851** H. Melville *Whale* xxii, The sail-needles are in the green locker. **1953** J. Masefield *Conway* 298 As it happens, we have the *sail-plan of her sister-ship. **1961** F. H. Burgess *Dict. Sailing* 178 *Sail plan*, a diagram to show a boat's rig and measurements. **1805** *Shipwright's Vade-M.* 126 *Sail-Rooms are built between decks upon the orlop or lower deck to contain the spare sails. **1905** A. R. Wallace *My Life* I. 310 The captain then had the sail-room amid-ships cleared out for men to sleep in. *c* **1711** Petiver *Gazophyl.* x. Tab. 99 Common Indian Nautilus or *Sail-shell. *a* **1850** Marg. Fuller *At Home & Abr.* (1860) 438 It went into the mail-bag of some *sail-ship, instead of steamer. **1600** Tourneur *Transf. Metam.* lii, As *sail-swel'd barks are droue by wind. **1513** *Acc. Ld. High Treas. Scot.* IV. 471 Item, for xliiij li *saill threid .. xlviij s. **1486** *Naval Acc. Hen. VII* (1896) 13, vj skaynes of *Saile Twyne. **1497** *Ibid.* 185, c weyght seyle twyne—xxxiij^{s} iiij^{d}. *c* **1860** H. Stuart *Seaman's Catech.* 52 Sails are sewn with sail twine. **1342-3** *Durham Acc. Rolls* (Surtees) 543 In *Saylwandis emp. et aliis reparac. factis in molend. de Hesilden—xxiiij s. **1962** C. H. Gibbs-Smith *Sir George Cayley's Aeronautics 1796–1855* xlii. 129 It is interesting to find at the present time (1962) a powered aeroplane using flexible *sail-wings: this is the American Ryan 'Flex Wing' which has plastic-coated nylon wings supported in a delta plan by only three rigid spars, which meet at the front; one is central and the other two spread out to form the sides of the triangle. **1972** *Daily Tel.* (Colour Suppl.) 13 Oct. 9 A sail wing is a device shaped rather like an extremely ambitious paper dart and is made from dural aluminium and nylon. From a point at its centre hangs an 'A' frame... The pilot hangs in space upon an arrangement structurally similar to a child's swing, complete with a narrow wooden seat. **1974** *Sci. Amer.* Dec. 141/1 The sail wing consists of a tubular spar that supports the leading edge of a fabric envelope and a set of short, rigid booms at the tip and foot of the spar between which a slender cable is stretched to form the trailing edge of the wing. **1978** P. O'Donnell *Dragon's Claw* xiv. 293 The sail-wing rested on the grass... They stood surveying the wing. *c* **1586** C'tess Pembroke *Ps.* civ. xi, There the *saile-winged shipps on waves doe glide. **1641** Milton *Ch. Govt.* ii. Wks. 1851 III. 180 They should make it their Knightly adventure to .. vanquish this mighty sailewing'd monster. **1855** Singleton *Virgil* I. 236 Gazing down Upon the sail-winged ocean.

sail (seɪl), *sb.*[2] [f. sail *v.*[1]]

1. An act of sailing; a voyage or excursion in a sailing vessel.

1604 Shaks. *Oth.* v. ii. 268 Heere is my butt And verie Sea-marke of my vtmost Saile. *a* **1619** Fotherby *Atheom.* i. ii. §2 (1622) 12 Where in the Lawes broad Sea, with wind and tyde, Ther's happier saile, then any where beside. **1663** Gerbier *Counsel* 109 Six weeks sail from England. **1748** *Anson's Voy.* ii. vi. 195 We made an easy sail for the bay. **1807-8** Syd. Smith *Plymley's Lett.* Wks. 1859 II. 163/2 The nearest of these harbours is not two days' sail from the southern coast of Ireland. **1853** W. Irving in *Life & Lett.* (1864) IV. 157 We went by way of the lakes, and had a magnificent sail (if I may use the word) down Lake Champlain in a steamer to Plattsburg. **1859** Jephson *Brittany* xii. 212 We had a delightful sail among the numerous islets. **1868** G. Duff *Pol. Surv.* 99 Hiogo and Kobé .. are situated upon two bays of the inland sea, about 365 miles' sail from Yokohama. **1884** *Times* (weekly ed.) 29 Aug. 14/1 The day was beautiful and the sail was delightful.

b. *transf.* (*Sc.* and *Irish*). A ride in a vehicle of any kind.

1830 Galt *Lawrie T.* vi. viii, I thought it my duty to take a sail in our wagon with Mr. Herbert. **1902** *Ballymena Observer* (E.D.D.), Wull ye gie me a sail in the kert?

c. ***to take sail***: to embark.

1904 *Westm. Gaz.* 10 May 8/1 He took sail in the capacity of a cabin-boy in a vessel bound for New Orleans.

2. ? *nonce-uses.* A number sailing: **a.** of ships; **b.** of water-birds.

1608 Shaks. *Per.* i. iv. 61 Wee haue descryed vpon our neighbouring shore, a portlie saile of ships make hitherward. **1727** Swift *Country Post* Wks. 1755 III. i. 175 Yesterday a large sail of ducks passed by here.

3. Sailing qualities; speed in sailing.

In many contexts hardly to be distinguished from sail *sb.*[1]

1602 Mansel *True Rep. Service* 9 The Gallies being .. quicker of saile then they. **1615** G. Sandys *Trav.* 87 A ship of better defence then saile. **1622** R. Hawkins *Voy. S. Sea* li. 122 Being of better saile then we, and the night comming on, we lost sight of her. *a* **1642** Sir W. Monson *Naval Tracts* i. (1704) 179/2 Finding his Ship but ill of Sail. **1643** *Declar. Commons, Reb. Irel.* 51 [He] could not take her [the ship], because she fled away, and was more swift in sayle then he. **1667** Milton *P.L.* vi. 534 Back with speediest Sail Zophiel, of Cherubim the swiftest wing, Came flying.

4. *Comb.* † **sail-star** = lodestar; † **sail-stone** [= Du. *zeilsteen*] = loadstone.

c **1511** *1st Eng. Bk. Amer.* (Arb.) Introd. 28/1 That men the northe sayle sterre or pollumarticum, or the waghen called, no more may be seen. **1595** Duncan *App. Etym.* (E.D.S.), *Magnes*, the adamant, the saile-stone. **1683** Pettus *Fleta Min.* i. (1686) 320 The Magnet is also called the Sail stone, for the Sailors look upon it as their Chief Instructor.

sail, *sb.*[3] [app. f. sail *v.*[3] (sense 3). Cf. the synonymous F. *saillie*, f. *saillir* to project.] Amount of projection from a surface. Also Comb. ***sail-over*** = oversail *sb.*

1611 Cotgrave, s.v. *Couronne*, The Corona, crowne, or member of greatest sayle, in a Cornish. **1660** H. Bloome *Archit.* A, *Projectura*, the sayle of every moulding. **1812** P. Nicholson *Mech. Exerc.* 267 Sail over, is the overhanging of one or more courses [of bricks] beyond the naked of the wall. **1924** H. J. Butler *Motor Bodywork* xviii. 276 Some of the lighter types of delivery van are made with a recessed rocker side... The body is then built up to the seat line by means of, say, an $1\frac{1}{4}$″ hardwood rocker side lapped on vertically, or with a slight sail, into the bottom side.

sail (seɪl), *sb.*[4] *dial.* [? repr. OE. **sǽȝel* var. of *sáȝol* staff: see sowel.] (See quot.)

1813 Davis *Agric. Wilts* in *Archæol. Rev.* (1888) Mar., *Sails*, .. upright rods of hurdles used for sheep folding. **1893** Mrs. A. Kennard *Diog. Sandals* vi. 90 There are ten 'sails' to each 'wattle hurdle'.

sail (seɪl), *v.*¹ Forms: 1 **siȝlan, seȝl(i)an,** 3 **sæilien, seili(en, sayli,** 3–4 **seily, seile,** 4 **seylle, seille,** 4–6 **sale,** (5 **ceylyn, seylyn**), 5 **sayll(e,** 6 **saill,** 4–7 **sayl(e,** 3–7 **saile,** 6–7 **sail.** [OE. *siȝlan, seȝl(i)an* corresponds to MDu. *zeghelen, zeilen* (mod.Du. *zeilen*), MHG. *sigelen, segelen* (mod.G. *segeln*), ON. *sigla* (Sw. *segla*, Da. *seile*):—OTeut. type **segljan*, f. **seglom* SAIL *sb.*¹

The Teut. vb. was adopted in OF. as *sigler* to sail (whence *sigle* a sail); an altered form of the same word is believed to exist in later OF. *singler*, mod.F. *cingler* to sail (in a specified direction), whence Sp. *singlar*, Pg. *singlar*.]

I. Intransitive uses.

1. a. Of persons: To travel on water in a vessel propelled by the action of the wind upon sails; now often in extended sense, to travel on water in a vessel propelled by any means other than oars; to navigate a vessel in a specified direction.

c **893** K. ÆLFRED *Oros.* I. i. §14 He..siȝlde ða east be lande. *Ibid.* IV. x. §10 þa he hamweard seȝlde. *c* **1205** LAY. 20889 And swa heo scullen wræcchen..sæilien [*c* **1275** sayli] ouer sæ. *Ibid.* 28797 þeo comen Sexisce men seilen to londe. *c* **1320** *Sir Tristr.* 1013 þai seylden in to þe wide Wiþ her schippes tvo. **1338** R. BRUNNE *Chron.* (1810) 236 Now þei saile and rowe to Wales to Leulyns. **13..** *Cursor M.* 24833 (Gött.) Forth þai sailed [*MS. Cott.* floted] on þat flode, for all to will þe wind þaim stode. *c* **1350** *Will. Palerne* 2673 þat he may nouȝt saile swiftli as he wold. **1375** BARBOUR *Bruce* XX. 322 A lang way furthwarde salyt he. *c* **1386** CHAUCER *Prioress' Prol.* 2 Now longe moote thou saille by the cost, Sire gentil maister gentil Maryneer! **1387** TREVISA *Higden* (Rolls) VI. 163 Egbertus þe monk..hadde i-seilled about Bretayne. **1390** GOWER *Conf.* II. 26 King Demephon, whan he be Schipe To Troieward with felaschipe Sailende goth. *c* **1440** *Promp. Parv.* 65/1 Ceylyn vpon watyr, *velifico*. *c* **1470** HENRY *Wallace* x. 797 Thai saylyt furth by part of Ingland schor. **1470–85** MALORY *Arthur* X. lxi. 517 Thenne sir palomydes sailed euen longes humber to the costes of the see. **1471** CAXTON *Recuyell* (Sommer) I. 139 He sayled and rowed vnto the cyte. **1530** PALSGR. 696/2, I loue nat to sayle by see, but when I can nat chose. **1565** *Reg. Privy Council Scot.* I. 333 That nane saill in marchandice without he be honestlie abelyeit lyk ane marchand. **1585** T. WASHINGTON tr. *Nicholay's Voy.* I. ii. 2 b, We sayled along..towardes the ..cape De creo. **1590** SHAKS. *Com. Err.* I. i. 63 A league from Epidamium had we saild. *a* **1691** BOYLE *Hist. Air* (1692) 201 An observing man, that had sailed to and fro between Europe and the East Indies. **1712** ADDISON *Spect.* No. 489 ¶1 A troubled Ocean, to a Man who sails upon it, is, I think, the biggest Object that he can see in Motion. **1798** COLERIDGE *Anc. Mar.* V. xix, Till noon we quietly sailed on, Yet never a breeze did breathe. **1830** TENNYSON *Sea-Fairies* 1 Slow sail'd the weary mariners. **1836** W. IRVING *Astoria* I. 41 [They] sail down that river to its supposed exit near the straits of Annian. **1860** G. BENNETT *Gatherings Naturalist Austral.* 425 We sailed..one day 191 miles, another 225 miles.

fig. *c* **1374** CHAUCER *Troylus* I. 606 Loue..Wiþ dessespeir so sorwfully me offendeth þat streght vn-to þe deth myn herte saileth. **1551** HADDON *Exhort. Repent.* in Furniv. *Ballads fr. MSS.* I. 324 But .lv. yere after, it [the plague] sayled into Flaunders. **1623** A. TAYLOR in Farr *S.P. Jas. I* (1847) 203, I spent my dayes in sorrow for thy good, I sayl'd to th' cradle in teares, to the graue in blood.

b. *spec.* To make excursions in, or to manage, a sailing-boat: to practise the sport of yachting.

1898 *Daily News* 30 Aug. 4/5 She is devoted to sports and outdoor exercises... She boats and sails.

c. In figurative context. Chiefly in proverbial phrases: † ***to sail all in one ship***, to 'row in the same boat', to belong to one party or class; † ***to sail on another board*** (see BOARD *sb.* 15); ***to sail near*** (or ***close to***) ***the wind***, to come very near to transgression of a law or a received moral principle.

1589 R. HARVEY *Pl. Perc.* (1590) 7 You be all of one Church, saile all in one ship. **1608** D. T[UVIL] *Ess. Pol. & Mor.* 123 They will alwaies saile by the Carde and Compasse of their own mind. **1823** BYRON *Juan* IX. xxvi, My words, at least, are more sincere and hearty Than if I sought to sail before the wind. **1865** H. KINGSLEY *Hillyars & B.* iv, A certain kind of young English gentleman, who has sailed too close to the wind at home, and who comes to the colony to be whitewashed. **1883** W. E. NORRIS *Thirlby Hall* viii, With regard to Turf transactions again, he may sail very near the wind indeed, and be pardoned.

†**d.** quasi-*refl.* *Obs.*

1640 tr. *Verdere's Rom. of Rom.* III. xxviii. 116 Away they sayled them, as they hoped with a prosperous wind.

2. Of a ship or other vessel: To move or travel on water by means of sails, or (in modern use) by means of steam or any other mechanical agency.

c **1205** LAY. 25525 þer comen seilien sone ȝeond þa sæ wide scipes uniuoȝe. *c* **1350** *Will. Palerne* 567, I sayle now in þe see as schip boute mast, boute anker or ore. **1375** BARBOUR *Bruce* XIX. 193 Marchand-schippis that saland war Fra Scotland to Flandriss with war. *c* **1384** CHAUCER *H. Fame* II. 395 And behelde..shippis seyllynge in the see. *c* **1400** MAUNDEV. (1839) xxx. 305 It rennethe in so grete Wawes, that no Schipp may not rowe ne seyle azenes it. **1500–20** DUNBAR *Poems* lxxxviii. 29 Where many a barge doth saile, and row with are. **1530** PALSGR. 696/2, I sayle, as a shyppe doth in the see whan she is under sayle, *je single*... Some shyppe wyll sayle as faste with a syde wynde as some wyll with a full wynde. **1535** COVERDALE *Isa.* xxxiii. 21 In that place..shal nether Gallye rowe, ner greate shippe sale. **1606** SHAKS. *Tr. & Cr.* II. iii. 277 (Qo.) Light boates saile swift, though greater hulkes draw deepe. **1687** A. LOVELL tr. *Thevenot's Trav.* I. 110 These Saiques..carry great Cargoes of Goods, but they sail not fast, unless they be before the Wind, or rather they sail no otherwise, for they cannot go upon a Wind. **1734** POPE *Ess. Man* IV. 385 Say, shall my little bark attendant sail, Pursue the triumph, and partake the gale? **1785** J. PHILLIPS *Treat. Inland Navig.* 34 The vessels ..are built so as to sail either end foremost, by removing the rudder. **1797** *Encycl. Brit.* (ed. 3) XVII. 376/2 It would be an easy matter to determine the form of a ship intended to sail by means of oars. **1828** J. H. MOORE *Pract. Navig.* (ed. 20) 60 A ship from the Lizard, in lat. 49° 59′ N. sails S.W. by W. 488 miles. Required the latitude she is in. **1886** GLADDEN *Applied Chr.* i. 3 Steamships sail from every shore with the contributions of all the continents to the world's trade.

3. a. To begin a journey by water; to set sail, start on a voyage; to leave the port or the place of anchorage. Said both of a vessel and of the persons on board.

c **1375** *Sc. Leg. Saints* xxvi. (*Nycholas*) 235 þis done, þai sailyt but bad quhare-to þare tryst wes mad. **1387** TREVISA *Higden* (Rolls) VIII. 105 þe queen Alianore..and meny oþer compelled hym for to seille aȝen. **1493** *Ledger-bk. A. Halyburton* 2 His costis in Medilburgh bydand quhill the schip sallit. **1611** BIBLE *Acts* xxi. 2 And finding a ship sailing ouer vnto Phenicea, wee went abroad, and set foorth. **1777** *Cook's 2nd Voy.* I. i. I. 5 On the 13th, at six o'clock in the morning, I sailed from Plymouth Sound. **1802** in W. Selwyn *Law Nisi Prius* (1817) II. 932, I think the captain will sail to-morrow. **1847** C. BRONTE *J. Eyre* xxxiv, I have taken my berth in an East Indiaman which sails on the twentieth of June. **1874** WHYTE MELVILLE *Uncle John* xiii, A friend of mine..met with an accident the very night before the steamer sailed. **1891** *Law Times* XCI. 2/2 The deceased..wrote a letter..in which he stated that he ought to have made his will before sailing.

†**b.** Conjugated with *to be*. *Obs.*

1633 *Fife Witch Trial* in *Statist. Acc. Scotl.* (1796) XVIII. App. 656 Her husband being newly sailed, she craved some money of her. **1764** GOLDSM. *Hist. Eng. in Lett.* (1772) II. 84 The fleet of the prince was already sailed. **1776** T. HUTCHINSON *Diary* 20 Jan. II. 8 He says six of the seven Regiments at Corke were embarked, and he concludes the whole have been sailed some days. **1786** MRS. A. M. BENNETT *Juvenile Indiscretions* V. 111 Sir James..was sailed for India on an appointment from government. **1787** JEFFERSON *Writ.* (1859) II. 281 Should the packet be sailed, I will pray you to send my letter by the first of the vessels which you mention.

4. *transf.* **a.** To glide on the surface of water or through the air, either by the impulsion of wind or without any visible effort.

1377 LANGL. *P. Pl.* B. XVIII. 304 And now I se where a soule cometh hiderward seyllynge With glorie & with grete liȝte. **1592** SHAKS. *Rom. & Jul.* II. ii. 32 A winged messenger of heauen..When he bestrides the lazie puffing Cloudes, And sailes vpon the bosome of the ayre. **1667** MILTON *P.L.* v. 268 Down thither prone in flight He speeds, and..Sailes between worlds and worlds, with steddie wing. **1697** DRYDEN *Virg. Georg.* I. 529 Swans that sail along the Silver Flood. **1754** GRAY *Poesy* 116 Sailing with supreme dominion Thro' the azure deep of air. **1804** SCOTT *Bard's Incant.* 34 Mute are ye all? No murmurs strange Upon the midnight breeze sail by. **1820** BYRON *Mar. Fal.* IV. i. 74 The high moon sails upon her beauteous way. **1849** M. ARNOLD *Forsaken Merman* 43 Where great whales come sailing by, Sail and sail, with unshut eye, Round the world for ever and aye? **1849** THACKERAY *Pendennis* lxiii, When a man, under pecuniary difficulties,..dives out of sight, as it were, from the flock of birds in which he is accustomed to sail. **1865** MATHIAS *Sport in Himalayas* 16, I shot an immense eagle.. as he was sailing in fancied security over my head. **1884** *Manch. Exam.* 19 Feb. 5/4 The flowing clouds..sail over the scene of the hay harvest in the Welsh meadow. **1884** *Pall Mall G.* 12 Aug. 4/1 As for blackcock..the wary old birds.. sail in the open over the moor a hundred yards out of shot. **1897** [see GLIDER 2 a]. **1910** *Daily Mail Year Bk.* 149/2 The Gross was compelled to descend, after sailing above the enemy's line.

b. Of a vehicle: To move smoothly and without apparent propelling force.

1866 'MARK TWAIN' *Speeches* (1923) 13 The Kanaka, without spur or whip,..sailed by us on the old plug. **1902** C. N. & A. M. WILLIAMSON *Lightning Conductor* 26 The car.. looked so handsome as it sailed up to the hotel door that my pride in it came back.

5. Of persons, in various transferred senses.

†**a.** *slang.* To saunter, go casually. *Obs.*

a **1700** B. E. *Dict. Cant. Crew* s.v., *How you Sail about?* How you Santer about? **1700** T. BROWN *Amusem. Ser. & Com.* viii. 121 From thence I sailed into a Presbyterian Meeting near Covent-Garden.

b. To move or go in a stately or dignified manner, suggestive of the movement of a ship under sail. (Chiefly of women; also *occas.* of an animal.) Also in weakened sense, to glide over a surface; to pass rapidly or smoothly.

1819 M. R. MITFORD *Let.* 18 Mar. (1925) 161 Just as we were at our merriest, in sailed Madam J——, like a tragedy queen. **1836** W. DUNLAP *Thirty Years Ago* I. ii. 22 Mrs. Epsom sailed majestically about the house. **1841** MOTLEY *Corr.* (1889) I. iv. 84 Stately *dames de la cour* would sail into the room and sail out again with their long trains sweeping after them. **1847** C. BRONTE *J. Eyre* vii, Then all the great people sailed in state from the room. **1859** G. MEREDITH *R. Feverel* xxxviii, A rumour spread that reached Mrs. Doria's ears. She rushed to Adrian first... She sailed down upon Richard. **1860–1** THACKERAY *Lovel* iii. 110 Lady B. sailed in .., arrayed in ribbons of scarlet. **1876** 'MARK TWAIN' *Tom Sawyer* v. 58 Then there was a wild yelp of agony and the poodle went sailing up the aisle. **1885** RIDER HAGGARD *K. Solomon's Mines* iv, A troop of tall giraffes, who galloped, or rather sailed off, with their strange gait. **1909** R. A. WASON *Happy Hawkins* 10, I flopped onto a pony an' sailed out to a little glen. **1949** W. AWDRY *Tank Engine Thomas Again* 50 He remembered the Level Crossing. There was Bertie fuming at the gates while they sailed gaily through. **1979** C. EGLETON *Backfire* xii. 135 He sailed through Immigration and collected his suitcase.

c. ***to sail in*** (slang): to proceed boldly to action. Also, to launch *into* or attack; also *fig.*

1856 'Q. K. P. DOESTICKS' *Plu-ri-bus-tah* iv. 69 'Sailing in', without regard to Any of the laws of 'Fancy'. **1883** 'MARK TWAIN' *Life on Mississippi* xxvi. 246 Old General Pillow..sailed in, too, leading his troops as lively as a boy. **1889** *Harper's Mag.* Mar. 561/1 A man must dismiss all thoughts of..common-sense when it comes to masquerade dresses, and just sail in and make an unmitigated fool of himself. **1891** *Morn. Advertiser* 30 Mar. (Farmer), John Harvey called William Tillman a liar 150 times,..and offered to lick him 104 times. At the 104th William.. thrashed John. The verdict of the jury was that William ought to have sailed in an hour and a half earlier. **1894** FISKE *Holiday Stories* (1900) 164 'I'll tell you the whole affair, if you care to listen to it.' 'Sail right in, Colonel,' cried the company. **1903** A. H. LEWIS *Boss* iv. 52 Half an hour before six, blow your whistle an' sail in. **1934** R. CAMPBELL *Broken Record* ii. 33, I sailed into him with a beauty on the ear. **1936** F. CLUNE *Roaming round Darling* xvii. 173, I sailed into Mrs. O'Malley's cooked meat and damper.

II. Transitive senses.

6. a. Of persons, also of a vessel: To sail over or upon, to navigate (the sea, a river, etc.). Now somewhat *arch.*

1382 WYCLIF *Ecclus.* xliii. 26 Who seilen the see [Vulg. *qui navigant mare*; 1388 The that seilen in the see]. *c* **1500** *Priests of Peebles* 204 Then brocht he wol, and wyselie couth it wey; And efter that sone saylit he the sey. *c* **1555** LYNDESAY *Tragedy* 104 Quhowbeit his grace Had salit the sey. **1560** ROLLAND *Crt. Venus* Prol. 146 [To sum] Ingyne hes geuin to saill the see. **1604** E. G[RIMSTONE] *D'Acosta's Hist. Indies* II. vi. 92 The river of Amazons..which our Spaniards sailed in their discoveries. **1608** SHAKS. *Per.* IV. iv. 2 Thus time we waste, & long leagues make short, Saile seas in Cockles, haue and wish but fort. *a* **1700** DRYDEN *Ovid's Met.* XII. 9 A thousand Ships were man'd to sail the Sea. **1708** J. PHILIPS *Cyder* I. 459 Now turn thine Eye to view Alcinous' Groves, ..from whence, Sailing the Spaces of the boundless Deep, To Ariconium pretious Fruits arriv'd. **1725** POPE *Odyss.* v. 354 Far on the left those radiant fires to keep The Nymph directed, as he sail'd the deep. **1840** LONGF. *Wreck of Hesperus* 2 It was the schooner Hesperus That sailed the wintry sea.

†**b.** To visit (a region) by sailing; to sail along (a coast). *Obs.*

a **1548** HALL *Chron., Hen. VI* (1550) 88 This lusty Capitain saylyng al the cost of Susseix and Kent, durst not once take lande, til he arriued in the dounes. **1594** R. ASHLEY tr. *Loys le Roy* 123 b, In ancient times the North was sailed by the commandement of Avgvstvs.

7. a. With cognate object: †To perform (a voyage, etc.) by sailing (*obs.*). Also ***to sail through, out***: to continue (a sailing-match, race), to the end.

c **1386** CHAUCER *Frankl. T.* 123 Where as she many a shipe and barge seigh Seillynge his cours. **1726** SHELVOCKE *Voy. round World* Pref. 5 Such as may never have an occasion or inclination to sail such long Voyages. **1886** *Field* 4 Sept. 364/2 The match [for yachts] could not be sailed through before the close time, 6.30. **1899** *Daily News* 29 Sept. 3/2 The uninjured vessel shall sail out the race.

b. To 'sail' or glide through (the air).

1725 POPE *Odyss.* I. 126 Sublime she sails Th' aerial space, and mounts the winged gales. **1765** BEATTIE *To Churchill* 34 He soars Pindaric heights, and sails the waste of Heaven. **1899** *Daily News* 26 June 8/3 The buzzard..is a fine-looking figure, as on broad wings he slowly sails the sky.

8. a. To navigate (a ship or other vessel).

1566 *Act 8 Eliz.* in *Hakluyt's Voy.* (1599) I. 371 But onely in English ships and sailed for the most part with English Mariners. **1675** *Lond. Gaz.* No. 1024/1 She had on board about 80 or 90 Negroes, and was sailed by Greeks. **1848** J. F. COOPER *Capt. Spike* III. 207 The Poughkeepsie was admirably sailed and handled. **1888** LOWELL *Heartsease & Rue* 177 He's a Rip van Winkle skipper,..who sails his bedevilled old clipper In the wind's eye, straight as a bee. *a* **1890** R. W. CHURCH *Oxford Movement* iii. (1891) 35 He [R. H. Froude] loved the sea; he liked to sail his own boat. **1908** *Westm. Gaz.* 28 Mar. 3/1 We were rowed and sailed by an amusing..ex-sailor.

b. To put (a toy boat) on the water and direct its course.

1863 HAWTHORNE *Our Old Home* I. 270 Schoolboys sail little boats on the river or play at marbles.

†**9.** To cause to sail, carry away sailing. *Obs.*

16.. *Balow* in *Laneham's Let.* (1871) p. clxxi, Till from myne eyes a sea sall flow, To saile my soule from mortall woe To that immortall mirtall shore.

†**10.** With adv. ***to sail down***: to bring (an object) below the horizon by sailing away from it.

1847 A. M. GILLIAM *Trav. Mexico* 276 We at once determined to sit up all night, to watch that the steersman would not sail the light down. We were induced to do so for ..the night previous..he saw a light-house,..and steered from the object.

†**11.** To provide with sails. *Obs.*

1600 HAKLUYT *Voy.* III. 862 It is ordeined that the shippes haue double sailes, that is, that they bee thorowly sayled, and all newe sayles [etc.].

†**sail,** *v.*² *Obs.* Forms: 4 **sail, sayly,** 4–5 **saile, sayle,** 4–6 **saill(e, sale, saylle.** See also SAILYIE *v.* (Sc.) [Aphetic form of ASSAIL *v.*]

1. *trans.* = ASSAIL *v.* in various senses.

a **1300** *Cursor M.* 9654 Ne he mai scap, ga quar he ga, þat him ne sailles ai his fa. *Ibid.* 24846 þe see þam sailed on ilk side. **13..** *Guy Warw.* (A.) 4134 When þe dragon seye com Gij þe lyoun he forlett, & gan him sayly. *c* **1375** *Sc. Leg. Saints* xxxii. (*Iustin*) 395 þane, tholand god, hyre he can saile with felone feuere & gret trawale. *a* **1400–50** *Alexander* 5559 þai sett in a sadd sowme & salid his kniȝtes. *c* **1460** *Towneley Myst.* xx. 506 The feynd ful fast salys you, In wan-hope to gar you fall. **1535** STEWART *Cron. Scot.* (Rolls) I. 342 That cruell cald hes saillit him so soir.

2. *absol.* quasi-*intr.* To make an assault.

c **1330** R. BRUNNE *Chron. Wace* (Rolls) 4364 When alle were set in ylka bataille, & schept..whilk of þam suld formast saile. *c* **1400** *Rom. Rose* 7338 Than was ther nought, but 'Every man Now to assaut, that sailen can'. *c* **1470**

HENRY *Wallace* XI. 414 'Falowis', he said, 'agayn all at this place Thai will nocht saill'.

Hence †'**sailing** *vbl. sb.*[2]

13.. *K. Alis.* 7392 Aither gan so areche, With 'saylyng, and with smytyng. *c* **1330** *Arth. & Merl.* 8257 In þe first of þat seylinge þai slowen michel heþen genge. **1426** LYDG. *De Guil. Pilgr.* 24206, I [Sekenesse] overthrowe hir [*sc.* Helthe] ageyn,.. And, ne were that medicyne Ys cause that she doth releve, My sayllyng shold hir often greve.

†**sail**, *v.*[3] *Obs.* Forms: 3-4 **sayle**, 4 **saile**, **saille**, **sailly**; also (sense 3) 7 **sailie**. [a. OF. *saillir* to dance, also as in mod.Fr. to issue forth, sally, to project = Pr. *salir*, *salhir* to dance, issue forth, Sp. *salir*, Pg. *sahir* to go out, It. *salire* to ascend:—L. *salīre* (pres. ind. *salio*) to leap. Cf. SALLY *v.*[2]]

1. *intr.* To dance.

1297 R. GLOUC. (Rolls) 5633 Vor þe deuel com biuore him & hoppede & lou & saylede & pleyde & made ioye ynou. **1377** LANGL. *P. Pl.* B. XIII. 233, I can.. noyther sailly ne saute, ne synge with þe gyterne.

2. To issue forth, sally.

1583 STOCKER *Civ. Warres Lowe C.* III. 93 The Souldiers of the Towne, sayling out, chased the Enemy.

3. *Arch.* To project from a surface. *to sail over* = OVERSAIL *v.*

1563 SHUTE *Archit.* C iv b, The Proiectures be like vnto their heightes but that Corona, doth sayle ouer twise his height. **1664** EVELYN tr. *Freart's Archit.* 138 That part of Corona which sailies over.

sail, variant of SEAL; obs. form of SALE.

‖**sailab** ('saɪlɑːb). Also **sailaba**. [Hindi, Punjabi *sailāb(ā)* flood, torrent f. Pers. *sail* flowing + *āb* water.] A method of cultivation used in the Indus basin in Pakistan and northern India in which the land is irrigated by flood-water from the rivers.

1916 J. DOUIE *Panjab, N.W. Frontier Province & Kashmir* xiv. 142 'Unirrigated' embraces cultivation dependent on rain (*bárání*) or on flooding or percolation from rivers (*sailáb*). **1960** *Indus Basin Devel. Fund Agreement* 30 in *Parl. Papers 1961* (Cmnd. 1527) XXXVII. 501 Pakistan may also withdraw such waters from each of the following Tributaries.. for irrigation of that part of the following areas cultivated on *sailab*. **1962** *Times* 2 June 11/6 The annual migration follows a restricted round which includes short halts for cultivation by the *sailaba* method. Rough earthen bunds are built in the wadis to form a trap for the soil wash from the occasional flash floods and the sorghum and millet seeds are sown in these small patches of saturated soil. **1973** N. D. GULHATI *Indus Waters Treaty* iii. 43 The total area in the Indus basin, along different rivers, cultivated annually after inundation or *sailab*, was about 2·17 million acres... This cultivation was referred to as *sailab*.

sailable ('seɪləb(ə)l), *a.* Now *rare.* [f. SAIL *v.*[1] + -ABLE.]

1. Of a ship, etc.: That can be sailed or navigated; that is in a condition to sail. ? *Obs.*

1655 MRQ. WORCESTER *Cent. Inv.* § 16 How to make a Sea-castle or Fortification Cannon-proof yet sailable at pleasure. **1698** LANGFORD in *Phil. Trans.* XX. 410 If a Man keeps his Ship sailable.

2. Of the sea, a river, etc.: That can be sailed on, navigable.

1555 W. WATREMAN *Fardle Facions* II. ix. 196 The Gerrites.. dwell vpon the floude Boristhenes, about the place wher it becometh first saileable. **1611** COTGR., *Navigable*, nauigable, sailable, passable by shipping. **1698** FRYER *Acc. E. India & P.* 56 The River which is Sailable round to Durmapatan. **1976** *New Scientist* 16 Dec. 646/2 A sailable expanse of water.

sailage ('seɪlɪdʒ), *sb.* [f. SAIL *sb.*[1] + -AGE.]

1. The speed of a ship under sail. ? *Obs.*

1632 LITHGOW *Trav.* v. 181 Pirats.. gaue vs diuers assaults to their owne disaduantages; our saylage being swifter.

2. The sails of a ship collectively. Also *transf.*

1889 *Pall Mall G.* 20 June 3/1 The machinery will.. enable the vessel to go to sea without any sailage. **1904** *Harper's Mag.* May 907/1 The filaments that buoy her [the spider] up and give sailage surface to the wind.

sailcloth ('seɪlklɒθ, -ɔːθ). [f. SAIL *sb.*[1] + CLOTH *sb.*]

†**1.** A piece of cloth forming or designed to form part of a sail of a vessel or a windmill. *Obs.*

c **1205** LAY. 4549 Sulkene wes þat seil-clæð. **1351-2** *Durham Acc. Rolls* (Surtees) 553 Et in Saylclathis empt. pro molend. de Fery, 5*s.* **1455-6** *Ibid.* 191 In reparacionibus factis circa molend. ventriticum de Hemingb. viz. in newe sayl clas, 14*s.* 7*d.* **1562** BULLEYN *Bk. Simples* (1579) 27 The sayle clothes, the shroudes,.. can not be made without it [Hempe]. **1598** HAKLUYT *Voy.* I. 163 Whatsoeuer sale-clothes are.. to bee transported out of England into Prussia by the English marchants.. whether they be whole cloathes or halfe cloathes, they must containe both their endes. **1888** *Encycl. Brit.* XXIV. 599/1 Sometimes the sails [of a windmill] consisted of a sail-cloth spread on a framework.

2. a. Canvas or other textile material such as is used for sails.

1615 THOMAS *Lat. Dict.*, *Lintearius*,.. a maker of sale cloathes and other necessaries of linnen. **1626** CAPT. SMITH *Accid. Yng. Seamen* (Arb.) 790 The Boteswaine is to haue the charge of all the Cordage,.. sailes,.. saile-cloth [etc.]. **1691** T. H[ALE] *Acc. New Invent.* 118 Sail-Cloath, Cables, and all other sorts of Cordage. **1753** HANWAY *Trav.* (1762) I. III. xxv. 108 Sail-cloth he made of cotton.

attrib. **1806** *Gazetteer Scotl.* (ed. 2) 3 The sail-cloth manufacture produced nearly as much. **1812** *Examiner* 31 Aug. 553/2 Sail-cloth-manufacturer. **1899** *Atlantic Monthly* Aug. 197/1 There I hung up my sailcloth cap.

b. A piece of this material used as a covering.

1778 [W. MARSHALL] *Minutes Agric.* 27 July an. 1774, The Sail-cloth saved the flat stack suprisingly. **1796** MORSE *Amer. Geog.* II. 411 Protected from the sun by sail-cloths, hung across from the opposite houses. **1804** *Anna Seward's Lett.* (1811) VI. 203 The shelving roof is also painted green, the floor a mosaic sale-cloth.

3. A similar material used for ladies' dresses, other garments, upholstery, etc.

1873 *Young Englishwoman* Jan. 39/1 This hunting pouch consists of a back, front, and flap of grey sailcloth, lined with dark green American cloth. **1881** C. G. HARRISON *Woman's Handiwork* I. 48 Among other washing fabrics used in art needlework are *crash*.., *twilled cotton*, *duck*, *sail-cloth*, [etc.]. **1902** *Daily Chron.* 24 May 3/3 Optimists are ordering linen dresses now, and sail cloth is in request, a coarse flax fabric that is serviceable and smart. **1962** R. P. GILES *Fabrics for Needlework* iv. 79 Sail-cloth. A very strong, firm, canvas-type fabric made in different weights... Not originally intended for a clothing fabric but nowadays the lighter weights are used for jeans, sportswear, and even summer dresses and skirts. **1979** *Arizona Daily Star* 5 Aug. (Parade Suppl.) 14/1 (Advt.), Comfortable, carefree sailcloth casuals that go their fun-loving way on soft and springy crepe soles.

sailed (seɪld), *a.* [f. SAIL *sb.*[1] + -ED[2].

But cf. OE. *ȝeseȝled* ppl. a. in *ȝeseȝled scip* Sal. & Sat. (Gr.) 225.]

Of a vessel: Fitted with sails. Chiefly in parasynthetic derivatives, as ***full-sailed***, ***white-sailed*** adjs.

c **1611** CHAPMAN *Iliad* XIX. 335 Prostrated, in most extreme ill fare, He lies before his high-sail'd fleet, for his dead friend. *a* **1628** F. GREVIL *Sidney* (1652) 221 Her Fleet could hardly be over sailed, or under ballasted. **1725** DE FOE *Voy. round World* (1840) 100 A great heavy boat which seemed to have been a large ships longboat, built into a kind of yacht, but ill masted, and sailed heavily. **1832** TENNYSON *Eleanore* iv, How may full-sail'd verse express,.. The full-flowing harmony Of thy swan-like stateliness? **1892** *Black & White* 25 June 805/2 Sailed boats lay to be loaded. **1900** *Westm. Gaz.* 16 Aug. 3/2 White-sailed yachts.

sailer ('seɪlə(r)). Also 6 **salar**, **saler**, **sayler**. [f. SAIL *v.*[1] + -ER[1]. Cf. G. *segler* sailor, sailer, Du. *zeiler*, Sw. *seglare*, Da. *seiler*.

See SAILOR, a variant spelling of this word, now restricted to a specific application and regarded as a distinct word.]

1. a. One who sails. Now *rare.*

a **1400-50** *Alexander* 4359 We ere na sailers on þe see to sell ne to byi. *c* **1400** *Destr. Troy* 4589 All softe was the see to sailers þerin. **1513** DOUGLAS *Æneis* I. iii. 43 On the huge deip quhen [= *wheen*, few] salaris did appear [Virg. *adparent rari nantes in gurgite vasto*].

†**b.** = SAILOR 1. *Obs.*

15.. *Sir A. Barton* in *Surtees Misc.* (1888) 64 The best salers in Christentie! **1585** T. WASHINGTON tr. *Nicholay's Voy.* II. i. 31 b, Cape S. Ange, very dangerous for saylers. **1605** CAMDEN *Rem.* I Furnished with shipping and Saylers.

†**c.** The Nautilus; = SAILOR 3 a. *Obs.*

1668 CHARLETON *Onomast.* 178 *Nautilus*.. the Nautilus, or Sailer. **1713** PETIVER *Aquat. Anim. Amboinæ* Tab. x, *Nautilus tenuis & legitimus*... Great brittle Sayler.

2. a. A ship or vessel with reference to her powers of sailing.

1582 N. LICHEFIELD tr. *Castanheda's Conq. E. Ind.* I. xlix. 106 For that theyr ships were great saylers. **1624** CAPT. SMITH *Virginia* v. 185 A small Barke, but an excellent sailer. **1725** DE FOE *Voy. round World* (1840) 69 A very strong tight ship, and a pretty good sailer. **1820** SCORESBY *Acc. Arctic Reg.* II. 338 The fastest sailers lead the way. **1891** J. WINSOR *Columbus* xix. 438 His excuse was that his principal caravel was a poor sailer.

b. A sailing vessel.

1871 R. ELLIS *Catullus* lxiv. 11 That first sailer of all [i.e. Argo] burst ever on Amphitrite. **1883** *Chamb. Jrnl.* 35 A Steamer costs much more than a Sailer. **1908** *19th Cent.* Aug. 235 Wooden sailers were superseded by iron creatures of the engineer.

3. *Baseball.* (See quot. 1961.)

1937 *Sun* (Baltimore) 28 May 14/7 There were two strikes and three balls on Cochrane when Hadley threw his ill-fated 'sailer'. **1961** J. S. SALAK *Dict. Amer. Sports* 379 *Sailer* (baseball), a pitched fast ball that takes off, that is, sails. **1975** *New Yorker* 17 Nov. 158/2 The throw, however, was a horrible sailer that glanced off Burleson's glove and went on into center field.

sailf, obs. Sc. form of SAFE.

'sail-fish. A name applied to various fishes having a large dorsal fin: in the British Isles to the Basking shark, *Selachus maximus*; in the U.S. to species of *Histiophorus*, *Xiphias*, and *Carpiodes*.

1591 SYLVESTER *Du Bartas* I. v. 381 *marg.*, The sayle-Fish. **1808** FORSYTH *Beauties Scotl.* V. 356 The sail-fish, or, as it is called by the Scottish fishermen, the basking shark, frequently appears here [Northern Sea] in May or June. [**1860** G. BENNETT *Gatherings Naturalist Austral.* 24 *Histiophorus*, called.. by the Dutch *Zeyl-fish*, or 'Sail-fish', because it is said that it raises the dorsal fin like a fan and employs it as a sail.] **1879** GOODE, etc. *Catal. Anim. Resources U.S.* 39 *Histiophorus americanus*... Sail-fish. **1882** TENISON-WOODS *Fish & Fisheries N.S. Wales* 190 Sail-fish. *Carpiodes.* N. America.

†'**sailful.** *Obs. rare.* [f. SAIL *sb.*[1] + -FUL[1].] Enough of wind to fill the sails.

1650 W. BROUGH *Sacr. Princ.* (1659) 486 Some points of wind may serve to make the way, every ship hath not sail-ful.

sailie, var. SAIL *v.*[3] *Obs.*, to project.

sailing ('seɪlɪŋ), *vbl. sb.*[1] [f. SAIL *v.*[1] + -ING.]

1. a. The action of travelling on water in a ship or other vessel which is propelled by means of sails; the action or method of directing the course of such a vessel. In modern use also in wider application: the action of travelling in or of directing the course of a ship or vessel of any kind.

For *circular*, *globular*, *oblique*, *parallel sailing*, see those words. *great circle sailing*, see CIRCLE *sb.* 2 b. See also PLAIN SAILING, PLANE SAILING.

a **900** tr. *Bæda's Hist.* v. i. (Cambr. Univ. MS.), Swa reðe stormas coman þæt we [ne] mid seȝlinge ne mid rownesse [L. *neque velo neque remigio*] owiht fremian mihte. *c* **1330** R. BRUNNE *Chron.* (1810) 70 He had redy sailyng. **1387** TREVISA *Higden* (Rolls) IV. 175 þe Romayns.. hadde no siker sillynge wiþ oute oþer socour. *c* **1400** *Destr. Troy* 3678 Hor sister to sese, with sailyng þai wend. *c* **1440** *Promp. Parv.* 65/1 Ceylynge, *velificacio.* **1540** *Act 32 Hen. VIII*, c. 14 § 1 Making them expert and connyng in the arte and science of shippmen and sayling. **1599** SHAKS. *Much Ado* III. iv. 58 There's no more sayling by the starre. **1632** LITHGOW *Trav.* I. 37 After three dayes sayling.. we arriued at.. Venice. *a* **1649** DRUMM. OF HAWTH. *Fam. Ep.* Wks. (1711) 146 Of all pastimes and exercises I like sailing worst. **1671** W. PERWICH *Despatches* (1903) 136 This may not turne to their account, for want of ships and cheap sailing. **1704** J. HARRIS *Lex. Techn.* I, *Mercator's Sailing*, is the Art of finding on a Plane the Motion of a Ship upon any assign'd Course. **1748** *Anson's Voy.* III. ix. 391 Provision for their subsistence, during their sailing down the river. **1769** FALCONER *Dict. Marine* (1780) s.v., *Sailing* also implies a particular mode of navigation,.. regulated by the laws of trigonometry. **1834** *Nat. Philos.*, *Navig.* II. iv. 21 (Usef. Knowl. Soc.) This method is called middle latitude sailing. **1908** *Westm. Gaz.* 13 Aug. 5/2 The four cutters made a splendid start over a course of forty-six miles, which will provide a test on all points of sailing.

b. In particularized use: A voyage.

1535 COVERDALE *Acts* xxvii. 10, I se that this saylinge wyl be with hurte and moch dammage. **1665** MANLEY *Grotius' Low C. Warres* 413 The Frost again approaching, will not suffer any Sailings.

2. a. Progression, speed or style of progression, of a ship or other vessel (originally, of a sailing-vessel).

a **1687** PETTY *Treat. Nav. Philos.* 127 How Top-sails [etc.] .. may be fitted to promote or hinder the Sailing upon occasion. **1721** PERRY *Daggenh. Breach* 115 Ships, more especially such as are sharp and built for Sailing. **1797** *Encycl. Brit.* (ed. 3) XVII. 377/2 These are very important circumstances, and would contribute much to improve the sailing of such vessels. **1836** W. IRVING *Astoria* III. 135 A vessel.. remarkable for her fast sailing.

b. *fig.* Progress, success in some activity. Usu. with qualifying adj., as ***fair sailing***, ***smooth sailing***, etc. See also PLAIN SAILING.

1827, etc. [see PLAIN SAILING *sb.*]. **1841** LYTTON *Night & Morning* II. viii. 118 'Oh! then it's all smooth sailing,' replied the other. **1927** H. CRANE *Let.* 19 Dec. (1965) 313 After a good deal of fair 'sailing' since arriving here—I am now convinced that 'flying' is even better. Right now however.. I am 'all fives' on the ground. **1959** *Daily Tel.* 15 Oct. 12/2 Brilliant sailing in the comparatively calm waters of the Post Office.

3. Departure (of a ship) from port.

1748 *Anson's Voy.* II. xi. 253 The time fixed by the Viceroy for her sailing. **1785** T. HUTCHINSON, jun. in *T. H.'s Diary* 9 June II. 418 Hearing there is a vessel upon sailing for America [etc.]. **1855** MACAULAY *Hist. Eng.* xv. III. 601 A fleet of transports was awaiting the signal for sailing. **1887** *Daily News* 14 Dec. 2/6 London sailings... Dec. 13. Tenedos. s, Dunkirk; Cormorant, s, Boulogne [etc.].

4. *Comb.* **a.** Simple attrib., as in ***sailing club***, ***date***, ***day***, ***instructions***, ***match***. Also †**sailing cloth** = *sailing ware*; **sailing-ice** (see quot. 1820); **sailing-line**, (*a*) the line on a vessel's hull which marks the level of the water when she is ballasted and rigged for sailing, but not laden or armed; (*b*) a line (LINE *sb.*[2] 22) of sailing vessels; **sailing master**, an officer charged with the navigation of a vessel (in British use chiefly with reference to yachts; formerly in the U.S. navy, a commissioned officer, usually a lieutenant, appointed to direct the navigation of a ship of war); **sailing orders**, the directions given to the captain of a vessel with regard to time of departure, destination, etc.; also *fig.*; **sailing rule**, a rule of the sea, to prevent the collision of ships, etc.; **sailing thwart**, the thwart at or through which the mast of a sailing-boat is stepped; **sailing ton**, the 'ton' used in measuring the capacity of sailing vessels; †**sailing ware**, ? cloth suitable for wear at sea.

1593 in *3rd Rep. Hist. MSS. Comm.* 7/1 *Sailing cloths [made in Somerset]. **1810** E. WEETON *Let.* 5 Sept. in *Jrnl. of Governess* (1969) I. 293 A *sailing club consisting of four or five young men of fortune, have conducted the annual Regattas. **1973** G. MOFFAT *Lady with Cool Eye* vii. 73 The inspector, meeting the traffic superintendent in the local sailing club, chanced to mention Mrs. Wolkoff's latest protest. **1906** J. LONDON *Let.* 1 Dec. (1966) 227 All.. that you wanted answered.. was my *sailing-date. **1839** in M. Johnson *Amer. Advertising, 1800-1900* (1960), The *sailing days of the above ship have been altered. **1879** *Yachtman's Holidays* 20 Next morning promised a poor sailing day. **1890** 'R. BOLDREWOOD' *Col. Reformer* (1891) 179 When the sailing day comes.. Jack must get on board. **1820** SCORESBY *Acc. Arctic Reg.* I. 229 Open ice, or *sailing-ice, is where the pieces are so separate as to admit of a ship sailing conveniently among them. **1748** *Anson's Voy.* I. ii. 15 He delivered them their fighting and *sailing instructions.

a **1687** Petty *Treat. Naval Philos.* 125 Our second Water-line..I call the *sailing-line, as the first was called the launching-line. **1905** *Chamber's Jrnl.* May 366/1 Sailing-lines to the West Indies..give Bermuda a wide berth. **1779** in *New Hampsh. Hist. Soc. Coll.* (1863) VII. 194 Appointed—Curtis *Sailing Master of the armed ship Hampden. **1836** Marryat *Three Cutt.* i, He..is..on board as sailing-master of the yacht. **1871** W. Collins *Miss or Mrs.?* ii, On one side there were the sleeping-berths of the sailing master and his mate. **1810** E. Weeton *Let.* 15 Aug. in *Jrnl. of Governess* (1969) I. 284 You must not suppose that Mr. and Mrs. P. or myself were in the boat during the *sailing match. **1890** 'R. Boldrewood' *Col. Reformer* (1891) 130 Ernest caught the sound of some reference to a sailing match. **1692** Luttrell *Brief Rel.* (1857) II. 545 This day another express was sent to the Downes with *sailing orders. **1748** Smollett *Rod. Rand.* xxvii, About this time, Captain Oakum, having received sailing orders, came on board. **1796** W. Scott *Let.* 26 Sept. (1932) I. 56 Your sailing orders are—If the subject is casually introduced to treat it lightly. **1886** *Illustr. Lond. News* 6 Feb. 142/1 You [*sc.* a governess] told me what were your sailing orders from Mrs. Meeburn. **1877** *Regulations for Government of Navy of U.S.* 185 *Steering and *sailing rules*, ..Art. 15. If two ships, one of which is a sailing-ship, and the other a steamship, are proceeding in such directions as to involve risk of collision, the steamship shall keep out of the way of the sailing-ship. **1976** *Oxf. Compan. Ships & Sea* 954/1 The actual sailing rules embody in general the Rule of the Road as it affects sailing vessels. *c* **1860** H. Stuart *Seaman's Catech.* 7 The man on the lee side of the *sailing thwart gathers the sail forward. **1898** *Daily News* 1 Feb. 5/2 Calculating a steam ton as equal to three *sailing tons, the tonnage has increased [etc.]. **1483–4** *Act 1 Rich. III*, c. 8 (end), La feisure dascun drap lanuez appellez *Sailyngware.

b. In compounds designating vessels propelled by sails, as ***sailing-barge, -boat, dinghy, -packet, -ship, -trawler, -vessel, -yacht***; also ***sailing-car, -carriage, -chariot, -waggon***.

These combinations admit of being regarded as collocations of sailing *ppl. a.*^{1} Cf. however *rowing-boat*.

1886 C. E. Pascoe *London of To-day* xviii. (ed. 3) 176 The Thames sailing-barge match is also an event to be noticed. **1721** *New-England Courant* 14 Aug. 2/2 On the 4th Inst. at Night were drowned going to Thomsons Island in a small sailing-Boat, Mr. Heskew, [etc.]. **1797** Sailing-boat [see *sailing-chariot* below]. **1976** *Oxf. Compan. Ships & Sea* 960/2 A sailing boat with masts stepped as above but sloop-rigged on the foremast would be termed a yawl. **1884** Knight *Dict. Mech., Suppl., Sailing Car*, a car..rigged with sail..used on the railroads on the plains, by telegraph repair parties... Sailing chariots were tried in Holland..more than two hundred years since. **1759** Johnson *Rasselas* I. vi. 35 He..found the master busy in building a sailing chariot. **1797** *Encycl. Brit.* (ed. 3) X. 758/2 Another contrivance for being carried without draught, is by means of a sailing chariot or boat fixed on four wheels. **1884** Sailing-chariot [see *sailing-car* above]. **1930** A. P. Herbert *Water Gipsies* vi. 55 Sailing-dinghies, eights and single-scullers. **1975** *Oxf. Compan. Sports & Games* 1123/1 To take part, all a man needs is a yacht,..or a sailing dinghy as small as 12 ft. (3.65 m.) long. **1842** Dickens *Let.* 17 Feb. (1974) III. 66 There is a sailing-packet from here to England tomorrow. **1883** S. C. Hall *Retrospect* II. 302 [They] would be forced to cross the channel in a sailing-packet. **1871** D. G. Rossetti *Let.* July (1967) III. 959 They are coming back..by sailing-ship. **1884** *Pall Mall G.* 16 Oct. 2/1 There are still no fewer than 15,000 sailing ships registered in Great Britain. **1891** *Labour Commission* (Gloss. s.v. *Steam*, A *steam trawler* is a fishing vessel..propelled by means of steam power, in contra-distinction to a *sailing trawler* which is propelled by sails only. **1748** B. Franklin *Exper. & Observations Electricity* (1751) I. 38 In the wake of every sailing vessel. **1976** Sailing vessel [see *sailing rule*, sense 4a above]. **1707** Mortimer *Husb.* (1721) I. 362, I shall not here mention anything of the Sailing-Waggons, and several other Contrivances of that kind.

† **sailing**, *vbl. sb.*^{2}: see under sail *v.*^{2}

sailing (ˈseɪlɪŋ), *vbl. sb.*^{3} *Arch.* [f. sail *v.*^{3} + -ing^{1}.] The condition or fact of projecting from a surface; projection.

1563 Shute *Archit.* B iv b, The proiecture, or saylling out or hanging ouer of the foote of the pillor. **1664** Evelyn tr. *Freart's Archit.* ii. i. 92 The Modul upon which afterward I regulate all the Members as well for their height as sailings over and projectures of their Profiles. **1728** Chambers *Cycl.* s.v. *Projecture*, These the Greeks call *Ecphoræ*,..the French *Sailles*, our Workmen frequently *Sailings over*. **1842** in Gwilt *Archit.* Gloss.

sailing (ˈseɪlɪŋ), *ppl. a.*^{1} [f. sail *v.*^{1} + -ing^{2}.]

1. That travels on water by means of sails. (Cf. sailing *vbl. sb.* 4 b.)

1590 Spenser *F.Q.* i. i. 8 The sayling Pine; the Cedar proud and tall. **1709** *Brit. Apollo* II. No. 43. 2/1 To Persons in a Sailing Ship the Shoar seems to be in motion. **1855** Macaulay *Hist. Eng.* xx. IV. 415 A swift sailing vessel was instantly despatched to warn Rooke of his danger.

b. In names of animals.

1781 Pennant *Hist. Quadrupeds* II. 417 Sailing Squirrel. **1803** Shaw *Zool.* IV. ii. 224 Sailing Coryphene.

2. Spreading out like a full sail.

13.. *Gaw. & Gr. Knt.* 865 Ryche robes..þat sete on hym semly, wyth saylande skyrtez. **1617** Fletcher *Valentinian* ii. vi, His fame and family have growne together, And spred together like to sayling Cedars, Over the Roman Diadem.

sailing (ˈseɪlɪŋ), *ppl. a.*^{2} *Arch.* [f. sail *v.*^{3} + -ing^{2}. Cf. F. *saillant*.] Projecting. ***sailing course***: a projecting course in (usually) the upper part of a light-house or other tower-like building.

1493–4 *Rec. St. Mary at Hill* 197 Item, payd to parys for a saylyng pece for sentt stevyn ys Autyr, iiij d. **1531** *Ibid.* 37 A Rownde cobbord with a saylyng hause [? *read* hanse]. **1807** T. D. W. Dearn *Bricklayer's Guide* 50 Then proceed to take the sailing course, and the wall on either side the chimney. **1857** *Skyring's Builders' Prices* (ed. 47) 73 Sailing courses are generally measured in with the work, in which case take the length by the width, three or six inches, as it may appear square brick sailing. **1946** Holgate & McDougall *Bricklaying* v. 63 An attractive method of making an all-brick coping more effective is by first laying on top of the wall a course of three-quarter bats as headers and after completing the coping, filleting this 'sailing' course with cement mortar.

saill(e, obs. forms of sail.

sailless (ˈseɪllɪs), *a.* [f. sail *sb.*^{1} + -less.] Having no sails. **a.** Of a boat, rigging, etc.

a **1618** Sylvester *Mem. Mortal.* xxv, But, Beauty, Gracelesse, is a Saile-lesse Bark. **1837** *Fraser's Mag.* XVI. 165 Oarless and sailless sped we. **1895** Marg. Stokes *Three Months in Forests France* 230 The phantom ship, sail-less, rudderless, and unmanned.

b. Of the sea: Destitute of ships, vessels, etc. Also *fig.*

1827 Pollok *Course T.* iii. (1869) 80 What nights he spent, Of tideless, waveless, sailless, shoreless woe! **1858** Longf. *M. Standish* iii. 37 The disk of the ocean, Sailless, sombre, and cold. **1859** Whittier *Double-headed Snake* 15 On the desolate shore of a sailless sea.

† **ˈsaillie.** *Arch. Obs.* [a. F. *saillie*, f. *saillir* to project: see sail *v.*^{3} Cf. sail *sb.*^{3}, sally *sb.*^{1}] A projecting member.

1664 Evelyn tr. *Freart's Archit.* 124 Beneath the Projectures of the Stylobata Cornices and other Saillies.

saillour: see sailour *Obs.*

sailly, var. sail *v.*^{3}

sail-off. *N. Amer.* [f. sail *v.*^{1} + off *adv.*, after *play-off*, *row-off*.] **a.** An additional sailing contest to decide between tied contestants. **b.** A series of sailing contests or races held to decide a championship.

1949 *Sun* (Baltimore) 19 July 14/6 The Miller Series at Gibson Island last week end also was sail-off of the home star fleet's championship tie between Ron Blizzard, with Snowflake and Dave Dunigan who sails Lodestar. **1955** *Ibid.* 27 June 13/1 There will be two unlucky sailors next week end when the tie is broken by a sudden death sail-off. **1970** *Times* 19 Aug. 6/6 The winner of the France-Australia sail-off will meet America for the Cup. **1972** *Even. Telegram* (St. John's, Newfoundland) 5 Aug. 15/5 Small-boat sailing ..is gaining in popularity and the skippers might like to show what they can do in an annual sail-off.

sailor (ˈseɪlə(r)). Also 7 saylor. [An altered spelling of sailer, prob. assimilated to *tailor*, in order to distinguish the designation of a regular calling from the unspecialized agent-noun. The differentiation, however, does not appear in our early examples, and was not fully established before the 19th c.]

1. a. One who is professionally occupied with navigation; a seaman, mariner. Also, in narrower sense, applied (like 'seaman') to a member of a ship's company below the rank of officer.

[**15..**, **1585**, **1605**: see sailer 1 b.] *a* **1642** Sir W. Monson *Naval Tracts* i. (1704) 214, 500 Men at Sea, where-of 340 Mariners, 40 Gunners, 120 Sailors. **1697** Dryden *Virg. Georg.* i. 296 Nor must the Ploughman less observe the Skies ..Than Saylors homeward bent. **1706** E. Ward *Wooden World Diss.* (1708) 94 Let us e'en turn about, and view honest Jack the Sailor. **1769** Falconer *Dict. Marine* ii. (1780) Y y 3 b, It is..the office of the commissaire general to keep a list of the..sailors, able and ordinary. **1784** Cowper *Task* i. 541 She would sit and weep At what a sailor suffers. **1801** *Med. Jrnl.* V. 354 Nor has a single soldier or sailor been prevented from doing his ordinary duty. **1852** Tennyson *Ode Death Wellington* 86 Thine island loves thee well, thou famous man, The greatest sailor since the world began. **1857** Buckle *Civiliz.* I. vii. 344 The credulity of sailors is notorious.

transf. **1847** Emerson *The Humble Bee* 15 Sailor of the atmosphere.

b. *to be a good sailor* [= F. *être bon marin*]: to be exempt from sea-sickness.

1833 Disraeli *Cont. Fleming* iii. xvi, We were excellent sailors, and bore the voyage without inconvenience. **1870** Miss Bridgman *Rob. Lynne* II. vi. 142 He wished people who were bad sailors would not travel. *a* **1895** Ld. C. E. Paget *Autobiog.* iii. (1896) 70 He pleaded that he was a wretched sailor.

† **2.** Said of a ship; = sailer 2. *Obs.*

a **1642** Sir W. Monson *Naval Tracts* v. (1704) 492/2, 10 or 12 Ships, choice Sailors. **1710** *Lond. Gaz.* No. 4643/4 The Ship Triton,..being the best of Sailors,..is to be sold. **1775** Romans *Florida* App. 62 She was a heavy schooner of about 70 tons, and a dull sailor.

3. As a name for various animals and plants.

† **a.** Used as a vernacular rendering of nautilus.

[**1668**, **1713**: see sailer 2 c.] **1776** [see pearly *a.* 2 b]. **1815** S. Brookes *Introd. Conchol.* 156 Paper Nautilus, Paper Sailor, *Argonauta Argo.* *Ibid.*, Great Sailor, *Nautilus Pompilius.*

b. *dial.* A kind of beetle, *Cantharis fusca*; 'a child's name for any Telephorus of a bluish colour' (*Cassell's Encycl. Dict.* 1887).

1854 Miss Baker *Northampt. Gloss.*, *Sailor*,..*Cantharis fusca.* **1863** Wood *Illustr. Nat. Hist.* III. 472 The Telephoridæ..represented in England by the well known beetles, popularly called from their red or bluish colours, Soldiers and Sailors.

c. = *sailor-fish* (see 5 b).

1860 G. Bennett *Gatherings Naturalist Austral.* 24 The *Histiophori*, or 'Sailors', differ, however, from the *Tetrapturi* by the greater comparative height of the dorsal fin.

d. *West Indian.* (See quot.)

1883 A. J. Adderley *Fisheries Bahamas* 7 (Fish. Exhib. Publ.) At certain times of the year myriads of small fish, known as 'sailors', arrive at the field and stir up the muddy bottom to such an extent that not a single sponge can be seen.

e. ***blue sailors***: the flowers of the wild chicory.

1902 *Outing* (U.S.) June 272/2 The wild chicory, or blue sailors (*Cichorium intybus*).

4. Short for *sailor collar*, *hat*.

1890 *Demorest's Family Mag.* June 504/2 Boat-shaped, wide-brimmed sailors in white..are worn by either boys or girls for play-hats. **1891** *Delineator* Sept. 230/1 *Ladies' felt sailor hat*—A stylish and dressy sailor is pictured here in a dark brown felt. **1898** *Westm. Gaz.* 5 May 3/2, I have tried in many shops to get a quite round sailor. **1903** *Ibid.* 2 July 4/2 Big hats very round in shape need not be avoided, nor Breton sailors. **1922** H. Titus *Timber* xxix. 252 She pulled the straw sailor tighter over her golden hair. **1943** D. Powell *Time to be Born* x. 227 Her smart little toasted straw sailor with floating pink veil. **1968** J. Ironside *Fashion Alphabet* 52 *Sailor*, A collar cut deep and square at the back, narrowing to a '*V*' in the front. It is often trimmed with braid—as worn by sailors. **1979** D. Eden *Storrington Papers* vi. 68 Miss Featherstone had whipped off her modest sailor and arranged the light-as-air confection on her head.

5. *attrib.* and *Comb.*: **a.** simple attrib., as in ***sailor fashion, mind, phrase, soul***; ***sailor-blue, -like*** adjs.; appositive (quasi-*adj.*), 'that is a sailor', as in ***sailor-boy, fisherman, -king, -lad, -poet***; 'consisting of sailors', as in ***sailor-train***; similative, as ***sailor-looking*** adj.

1930 J. Dos Passos *42nd Parallel* i. 91 She was waiting for him..looking like a Gibson girl with her neat *sailor-blue dress. **1978** J. Krantz *Scruples* iii. 65 Perhaps his height came from his father, but the bright blond hair and sailor-blue eyes were pure Swedish Viking. **1835** J. E. Alexander *Sk. Portugal* x. 245, I..engaged a Portuguese *sailor-boy.. to accompany me to Africa. **1855** Kingsley *Heroes, Perseus* i. 4 Halcyone..loved a sailor-boy [Ceyx] and married him. **1903** C. E. Osborne *Fr. Dolling* vii, The sailor boys from the *St. Vincent.* **1848** J. F. Cooper *Capt. Spike* III. 160 Captain Mull was slow to yield his confidence, but when he did bestow it, he bestowed it *sailor-fashion, or with all his heart. **1883** Goode *Fish. Indust. U.S.* 26 (Fish. Exhib. Publ.) The 20,000 or more men who may properly be designated the '*sailor fishermen' of the United States. **1911** Fletcher & Kipling *School Hist. Eng.* 91 He [*sc.* Edward III] was merchant-king, *sailor-king, soldier-king. **1965** Finer & Savage *Sel. Lett. J. Wedgwood* i. 38 [The Royal patronage] was again extended in 1830 by William IV, the 'Sailor King'. **1975** B. Meyrick *Behind Light* xii. 149 King George, the Sailor King, because he had served at sea. **1842** Tennyson '*Break, break*' ii, O well for the *sailor lad, That he sings in his boat on the bay! **1808** Lamb *Ulysses* in *Mrs. Leicester's School* (1885) 121 With such *sailor-like sayings and mutinous arguments..they [etc.]. **1890** 'R. Boldrewood' *Col. Reformer* (1891) 168 Paul, with a couple of *sailor-looking men, was down at the jetty. **1894** Gunter *King's Stockbroker* i. 7 Wondering in his *sailor mind what the deuce the whole affair means. **1812** Sir R. Wilson *Priv. Diary* 1 June (1862) I. 69 We are now entering the Archipelago, or, according to the *sailor phrase, the Arches. **1856** Kane *Arct. Expl.* II. xvi. 169 Every bag was, in sailor-phrase, roped and becketed. **1877** Tennyson *Sir J. Franklin* 2 Thou Heroic *sailor-soul, Art passing on thine happier voyage now. **1725** Pope *Odyss.* ii. 441 Now descends the *sailor train.

b. Special combinations: **sailor collar** (see quot. 1968); **sailor-fish** = sail-fish; **sailor hat**, a hat such as is worn by sailors; hence applied to a form of hat (with flat brim of even breadth all round) worn by women, and to a different form (with turned-up brim) worn by children; hence **sailor-hatted** *a.*; **sailor knot** = *sailor's knot*; hence **sailor-knotted** *a.*; **sailor-man**, (*a*) in uneducated and jocular use = sense 1; also *occas.* an adult sailor; (*b*) a sailing-barge(man); **sailor pants** *U.S.*, flared trousers such as those worn by sailors; **sailor-plant** *U.S.*, the strawberry-geranium, *Saxifraga sarmentosa* (Cent. Dict. 1891); **sailor-shape**, the shape worn by sailors, the shape of a sailor hat (also *attrib.* as *adj.*); so **sailor-shaped** *a.*; **sailor suit**, a suit similar to that of an ordinary seaman, worn mainly by small boys; hence **sailor-suited** *a.*; **sailor top**, a jerkin similar to that worn by sailors; also applied to a ladies' blouse of this design; **sailor trousers** *U.S.* = *sailor pants*.

1895 *Montgomery Ward Catal.* 79/2 Guipure Open work *sailor collars. **1932** 'E. M. Delafield' *Thank Heaven Fasting* ii. v. 223 A grey satin blouse, with a black bow in the front of the square sailor collar. **1974** *She* Jan. 52/2 Braided jacket with square-back sailor collar, £8·50. **1980** *Times* 22 Oct. 10/7 Sailor collar, shift shape and hip belt. **1885** C. F. Holder *Marvels Anim. Life* 70 The great sail—or *sailor—fish (*Histiophorus*) of the Mediterranean and Indian Ocean. **1873** *Young Englishwoman* Mar. 131/2 Brown velvet *sailor hat of two shades. **1912** A. Bennett *Matador of Five Towns* 46 A quite little girl..with a short frock and long legs, and a sailor hat (H.M.S. *Formidable*). **1976** *Vogue* Jan. 48 White tunic..with white duck American sailor hat. **1909** E. Nesbit *Daphne in Fitzroy St.* x. 152 'It's only me, miss,' said the *sailor-hatted charwoman. **1872** 'Mark Twain' *Roughing It* lxii. 447 Black silk neck-cloth tied with a *sailor knot. **1939** T. S. Eliot *Old Possum's Bk. Pract. Cats* 14 The curtain-cord she likes to wind, and tie it into sailor-knots. **1923** W. J. Locke *Moordius & Co.* viii. 109 With deft fingers she gave his *sailor-knotted tie a twist and a pull. **1761** G. Colman *Jealous Wife* iii. 45 The Irish *Sailor-Man, for whom I prevailed on your Lordship to get the Post of a

Regulating Captain. **1790** R. TYLER *Contrast* II. ii. (1887) 39 A parcel of sailor men and boys got round me. **1886** KIPLING *Departm. Ditties*, etc. (1899) 61 'Twas Fultah Fisher's boarding-house, Where sailor-men reside. **1948** *Sea Breezes* VI. 337/2 From Colchester sails Francis & Gilder's large fleet of 'sailor-men'. **1951** H. BENHAM *Down Tops'l* 187 *Sailorman*, the London River term for either a sailing-barge or a sailing-bargeman. **1961** G. FOULSER *Seaman's Voice* i. 20 The winter of 1936–7 was a rough one, with a lot of windbound intervals for the 'sailormen'. **1931** H. CRANE *Let.* 13 June (1965) 373 My usual household white *sailor pants and shirt. **1976** *National Observer* (U.S.) 2 Oct. 18/1 Today Stramler is in white sailor pants and a T-shirt. **1897** *Daily News* 24 Sept. 6/6 Some of the new felt hats are quite *sailor-shape. **1904** *Daily Chron.* 23 Aug. 8/2 The new French sailor shape of chapeau. **1902** *M.A.P.* 29 Mar. 327/1 There were many of the large, round, and *sailor-shaped collars now so much worn. **1880** *Harper's Mag.* Aug. 337/2 Excursionists in *sailor suits were playing croquet. **1885** C. M. YONGE *Nuttie's Father* II. xii. 145 We can't persuade ourselves to cut his hair, and it looks so lovely on his sailor suit. **1946** G. MILLAR *Horned Pigeon* iv. 53 He wore a sailor suit that was much too small for him—clothing that had been provided when a Messerschmitt had shot his Blenheim down into the sea. **1976** *Times* 27 Feb. 10/5 Susanna Agnelli was born in 1922... She and her brothers and sisters were dressed in sailor suits, blue in winter, white in summer. **1960** *Times* 3 Aug. 5/2 A juvenile delinquent cousin who appears *sailor-suited in the first act. **1977** *Times* 7 May 9/1 The sailor-suited members of the Vienna Boys' Choir. **1913** C. MACKENZIE *Sinister St.* I. I. v. 80 He..wished that he were not compelled to wear a *sailor-top that was slightly shabby. **1916** JOYCE *Portrait of Artist* (1969) i. 12 He had a blue sailor top on. **1962** G. AVERY *Greatest Gresham* i. 20 She had..a navy blue sailor top to her blue serge suit. **1971** *Vogue* Dec. 70 Gabardine trousers. Sailor top with big bow. **1851** M. REID *Scalp Hunters* xx. 69 *Calzoneros* of green velveteen. These are cut after the fashion of *sailor-trousers,—short-waist—tight round the hips, and wide at the bottoms.

c. Possessive combinations: **sailor's Bible** *U.S. slang*, Bowditch's *Navigator* (Cent. Dict. 1891); **sailor's blessing** *Naut. slang*, a curse; also **sailors' blessing**, such rigging or tackle as eases the sailors' work; **sailor's choice** *U.S.*, a name given locally to various American fishes; **sailor's farewell** *Naut. slang*, a parting curse; †**sailor's hat** *Obs.* = *sailor hat*; **sailors' home** (see quot. 1867); **sailor's knot**, any of the kinds of knot (KNOT *sb.*[1] 1) used by sailors; also, a kind of knot used in tying a neck-tie; **sailor's pleasure** *Naut. slang* (see quots.); **sailor's pocket, purse** *U.S.*, the egg case of a skate or oviparous shark ('in recent U.S. Dicts.', *N.E.D.*); †**sailor's suit** *Obs.* = *sailor suit* above; **sailor's waiter** *Naut. slang* (see quot.).

1876 F. W. H. SYMONDSON *Two Years abaft Mast* ii. 56 Poor 'doctor' not unfrequently comes in for a '*sailor's blessing' (a growl). **1944** J. MASEFIELD *New Chum* 166 Being almost new had all the latest sailors' blessings; nothing above her royals, double topgallant yards, a spike jib boom and no spanker gaff. *c* **1860** HOLBROOK in Goode, etc. *Nat. Hist. Aquatic Anim.* (1884) 399 The '*Sailor's Choice' makes its appearance in our waters about the month of April and continues with us until November. **1879** GOODE, etc. *Catal. Anim. Resources U.S.* 46 *Lagodon rhomboides*... Sailor's Choice. **1882** JORDAN & GILBERT *Synopsis Fishes N. Amer.* 551 *Pomadasys fulvomaculatus*... Sailor's Choice; Hog-fish. **1888** GOODE *Amer. Fishes* 80 *Diabasis chromis* the 'Sailor's Choice'. **1937** PARTRIDGE *Dict. Slang* 722/1 **Sailor's farewell*, a parting curse. **1974** *Listener* 10 Jan. 50/3 The sole baker there..found himself ruined, and in some anger he gave the village a sailor's farewell and announced that he was off. **1862** *Englishwoman's Domestic Mag.* V. 142/1 Two styles of *hat..seem to be equally in favour this season—one, the *sailor's hat with straight brim; the other, the turned-down or bell-shaped hat. **1885** *Outing* 7 Nov. 138/2 Their round straw hats, with flat-topped crowns, and shape usually termed by Americans 'sailor's hat'..were trimmed with a plain white ribbon around the crown. **1839** *New Orleans Commerc. Appeal* 18 Apr. 2/2 (*heading*) Public meeting to promote the establishment of a *Sailors' Home. **1840** R. H. DANA *Bef. Mast* 144 The establishment of Sailors' Homes. **1867** SMYTH *Sailor's Word-bk.*, *Sailors' home*, a house built by subscription, for the accommodation of seamen on moderate terms. **1843** POE *Mystery of Marie Rogêt* in *Ladies' Compan.* (N.Y.) Feb. 165/2 The '*sailor's knot' with which the bonnet-ribbon is tied. **1882** *Encycl. Brit.* XIV. 128/1 **Sailors' knots.* **1856** C. NORDHOFF *Merchant Vessel* 132 Others take what is called, *par excellence*, '*sailor's pleasure', in overhauling their chests, bringing their best clothing on deck to air, and counting over their stock of tobacco and pipes. **1932** J. W. HARRIS *Days of Endeavour* 57 They must have a sailor's pleasure on Sunday to see what can be raked up. *Ibid.* 232 *Sailor's pleasure*, overhauling contents of sea-chest and bag, and airing go-ashore clothes. **1933** P. A. EADDY *Hull Down* v. 122 Sunday at sea in a deep-water sailing-ship, especially if the weather is fine, and nearing port the sole topic of conversation, means 'sailor's pleasure'. **1869** G. MEREDITH *Let.* Dec. 19 (1970) I. 406 You should see Willie Godson in his *sailor's suit. **1840** R. H. DANA *Bef. Mast* iii, The crew call him [the second mate] the '*sailor's waiter', as he has to furnish them with spunyarn, marline, and all other stuffs that they need.

sailoress ('seɪlərɪs). [f. SAILOR + -ESS.] A female sailor.

1890 *Yacht Racing Cal.* 159/2 The introduction of sailoresses on board racing yachts. **1894** *Yachting* (Badm. Libr.) I. 236 Solent sailoresses.

sailoring ('seɪlərɪŋ), *vbl. sb.* [f. SAILOR + -ING[1].] The work of a sailor.

1864 C. GEIKIE *Life in Woods* i. (1874) 2 He had found the romance of sailoring [etc.]. **1886** STEVENSON *Kidnapped* xi, If ye miss that, ye must be as feckless at the sailoring as I have found ye at the fighting.

sailorizing ('seɪləraɪzɪŋ), *vbl. sb. colloq.* [f. SAILOR + -IZE + -ING[1].] The pursuits or work of sailors.

1876 DAVIS *Polaris Exp.* xi. 254 You will find them busy on various branches of work, such as shoemaking, patching, whittling out..miniature ships, and, in fact, sailorizing of all sorts. **1880** CLARK RUSSELL *Sailor's Sweeth.* (1881) I. iv. 118 With a high barometer and a harbour always under your lee, sailorizing can't fail to be enjoyable. **1898** F. T. BULLEN *Cruise 'Cachalot'* 209 Many of the crew were quite unable to do any sailorizing, as we term work in sails and rigging.
attrib. **1882** T. G. BOWLES *Flotsam & Jetsam* xi, Translated it into sailorizing language.

sailorless ('seɪləlɪs), *a.* [f. SAILOR + -LESS.] Without sailors.

1816 BYRON *Darkness* 75 Ships sailorless lay rotting on the sea. **1824** GALT *Rothelan* III. VI. i. 6 The seams of the sailorless ships yawned to the sun.

sailorly ('seɪləlɪ), *a.* [f. SAILOR + -LY[1].] Befitting a sailor; having the characteristics of a sailor.

1865 MRS. WHITNEY *Gayworthys* xxiv, Great asking of questions; brief sailorly answers. **1883** STEVENSON *Treas. Isl.* I. ii, He was not sailorly.

sailorship ('seɪləʃɪp). *rare.* [f. SAILOR + -SHIP.] Seamanship; the skill of a good seaman.

1820 J. SEVERN *Let.* 20 Sept. in H. E. Rollins *Lett. John Keats* (1958) II. 343 Keats this Morning brags of my sailorship. **1856** C. NORDHOFF *Merchant Vessel* 111 Fancy seizings and lashings bore witness to the sailorship of the mates and crew.

†**sailour.** *Obs. rare*[−1]. [a. OF. *sailleor*, f. *saillir* to dance: see SAIL *v.*[3]] A dancer.

?*a* **1366** CHAUCER *Rom. Rose* 770 Ther was many a timbestere, And saylours [*MS. Glasgow* saillouris], that I dar wel swere Couthe hir craft ful parfitly.

sailplane ('seɪlpleɪn). Also **sail-plane**. [f. SAIL *sb.*[1] + PLANE *sb.*[3]] A heavier-than-air aircraft without an engine (or having only a small engine which is not normally used except to take off); = GLIDER 2 a (but see quot. 1971).

1922 *Flight* XIV. 545/2 The gliding angle of a good 'sail-plane' might be in the neighbourhood of 1 in 16 or 1 in 18. **1933** *Sun* (Baltimore) 5 Aug. 15/5 During the day sport planes circled about his sailplane. *Ibid.* 23 Sept. 4/5 Federal officials..will gather..to witness a demonstration in sailplane flying. **1935** *Ibid.* 17 May 1/4 The cheapest flight from London to Paris was made this evening when Robert Kronfeld..landed..in his sailplane driven by a motor-cycle engine of five horsepower, having consumed $1.50 in fuel for the 210-mile flight. **1940** *Illustr. London News* CXCVII. 85/1 The type of sailplane (or, to use the popular, but less correct, term, 'glider') required for use in transporting troops must, of course, be very large. **1950** *Chambers's Jrnl.* 137/2 In tropical countries some birds utilise these thermals, as they are called by sailplane pilots, and indeed make no attempt to fly until the air has warmed up. **1961** *New Scientist* 18 May 362/2 The Olympia 460 is what is called a 'standard' class sailplane. That is to say, it has a span of only 15 metres instead of the 19 metres allowed in the open class for world championship flights. **1971** N. ELLISON *Brit. Gliders & Sailplanes* 9 The terms 'gliders' and 'sailplanes' nowadays are somewhat synonymous. When these terms were first introduced a sailplane was defined as 'a glider having a sinking speed of less than 0·8 metres (2·625 feet) per second'. Today, nearly all motorless aircraft are sailplanes and capable of soaring flight, i.e. flying without loss of height or gaining height.

Hence **'sailplaner**, in the same sense; **'sailplaning** *vbl. sb.*, the flying of sailplanes, gliding; also *transf.*

1923 *Flight* XV. 34/2 In order to encourage gliding and sailplaning in America, the National Aeronautic Association of U.S.A. have appointed a sub-committee to deal with this form of flying. **1930** *Daily Express* 8 Sept. 16 The first lesson in the art of sail-planing. **1962** *Punch* 15 Aug. 237/2 It [*sc.* the fulmar] makes distance at sea..by sailplaning and tacking. **1973** *Sci. Amer.* Dec. 134/2 The cockpit panel of a serious sailplaner shows 10 dials, plus radio, oxygen gear and cameras. **1977** *Maclean's Mag.* 2 May 58/2 For recreation they have turned to such exotic and often dangerous sports as..sailplaning.

†**'sailrife**, *a. Obs.* In 6 sailrif. [f. SAIL *sb.*[1] + RIFE *a.*] Abounding in sails.

1513 DOUGLAS *Æneis* I. v. 3 Quhen Iupiter, frome his hich spheir, adoun Blent on the sailrif seis [L. *velivolum mare*].

sails (seɪlz). *Naut. slang.* [pl. of SAIL *sb.*[1], used as sing.] A name for a ship's sailmaker.

1864 *Hotten's Slang Dict.*, *Sails*, the sail-maker on board ship. **1867** SMYTH *Sailor's Word-bk.*, *Sail-maker*, a qualified person who (with his mates) is employed on board ship in making, repairing or altering the sails; whence he usually derives the familiar sobriquet of *sails*.

sailsman ('seɪlsmən). [f. *sail's*, genitive of SAIL *sb.*[1] + MAN *sb.*[1]] A sailor; also one who manages a sailing-boat.

c **1601** KEYMOR *Observ. Dutch Fishing* (1664) 7 The Sailsmen and the Marriners..there cannot be less then 200. **1890** W. G. BLACK in *Pall Mall G.* 9 Sept. 1/3 They [the fisher-folk] live, in the main, by acting as ferrymen to steamers..and as pleasure sailsmen.

†**'sailworthy**, *a. Obs. rare.* [f. SAIL *sb.*[1] + WORTHY.] Of weather: Admitting of the use of sails.

c **1595** CAPT. WYATT *R. Dudley's Voy. W. Ind.* (Hakl. Soc.) 36 Yt blew soe much all the daie that it neither was saileworthy, nor coulde they possiblie use theire owers. **1633** T. JAMES *Voy.* 34 It began to blow a storme not sayle-worthy.

†**'saily**, *a. Obs.* [f. SAIL *sb.*[1] + -Y.] Having the appearance of a sail or sails.

1605 DRAYTON *Man in Moone* 193 His saily Wings. **1612** —— *Poly-olb.* x. 66 From Thrace when hee her tooke, And in his saylie plumes the trembling Virgin shooke.

sailyard ('seɪljɑːd). Forms: see SAIL and YARD. [f. SAIL *sb.*[1] + YARD *sb.*]

1. *Naut.* One of the yards or spars on which the sails are spread.

c **725** *Corpus Gloss.* 588 *Antemna*, segilgerd. *c* **1050** *Suppl. Ælfric's Gloss.* in Wr.-Wülcker 182/3 *Cornua*, þa twegen endas þære segilgyrde. **1295** in *9th Rep. Hist. MSS. Comm.* App. I. 258 Et in vno masto et vna seylyarde emptis pro eadem Galya. *c* **1400** MAUNDEV. (1839) xxvii. 271 Of the Mastes and the Seylle ȝerdes. *c* **1440** *Promp. Parv.* 65/1 Ceyl yerde, *antenna*. **1553** EDEN *Treat. Newe Ind.* (Arb.) 13 To be hanged on the sayle yarde of the shyp. **1625** K. LONG tr. *Barclay's Argenis* IV. xv. 289 They began to run whither the wind's violence drave them, leaving some sayles to the sayle-yard. **1725** POPE *Odyss.* v. 325 With crossing sail-yards dancing in the wind. **1834** WRANGHAM *Homerics* 11 Distant were sail and sail-yard thrown.

†**2.** One of the radiating beams bearing the sails of a windmill. *Obs.*

1351–2 *Durham Acc. Rolls* (Surtees) 553 In uno Saylyerde empt. pro molendino de Hesilden, iij s. viij d. *c* **1380** *Ibid.* 181 In uno Saleyerd empto pro eodem (molendino), iij s. *c* **1419** *Ibid.* 616 Canvace..pro vestura de lez Saylyerdez molendini ventritici de Fery. **1426** LYDG. *De Guil. Pilgr.* 5426 The seyl yerdys off the melle, Wych tournede abouten offte, Wer clad in cloth that was not soffte. **1523** FITZHERB. *Surv.* 39 b, The mylner shall neyle vp the bordes make his shafte and the sayle yardes vpholde.

†**3.** *Ent.* = ANTENNA. *Obs.*

1658 ROWLAND tr. *Moufet's Theat. Ins.* 1125 The sailyards and the nippers are of a watry red colour.

†**'sailyie, sailʒ(i)e**, *sb. Sc. Obs.* [Aphetic var. *assailʒe*, ASSAIL *sb.*] Hostile attack, assault.

c **1470** HENRY *Wallace* XI. 18 Still saxte dayis at sar sailʒe thai baid. Fortrace, and werk..Thai brak, and brynt, and put to confusioun. **1535** STEWART *Cron. Scot.* II. 13 The Romanes..maid ane sailʒe baith be se and land. *Ibid.*, Instrumentis..That neidful war to mak sailʒie or salt. **1550** LYNDSAY *Sq. Meldrum* 952 Now, vailʒe quod vailʒe, Upon the Ladie thow mak ane sailʒe. **1819** TENNANT *Papistry Storm'd* (1827) 169 Their hands wagg'd wapons a' kinkinds; And sic varietie o' graith, Gather't for sailzie and for skaith. *Ibid.* 204 Dissim'lar men, but sim'lar minds, In formidable sailyie, Cam whurrin' in.

†**'sailyie, 'sailʒ(i)e**, *v. Sc. Obs.* [Aphetic var. *assailʒe* ASSAIL *v.* See SAIL *v.*[2]] **a.** *trans.* To assault, make a hostile attack upon. **b.** *intr.* To make an attempt.

c **1470** HENRY *Wallace* v. 992, I wald sailʒe..Lowmaban hous. **1533** BELLENDEN *Livy* II. vi. (S.T.S.) I. 151 And þocht my aventure was first, euery ane of þame sall sailʒe as þai best may. **1819** W. TENNANT *Papistry Storm'd* (1827) 22 He and the clerk..shall no be laith To raise the mob,..and sailzie kirk wi' weir and wraith.

saim, dial. and obs. form of SEAM (lard).

‖**saimiri** (saɪ'mɪərɪ). Also 8 samiri (9 in Dicts. **saimari, saimir**). [Brazilian Pg. *saimirim*, a. Tupi *çahy miri* little monkey (*çahy* SAI[1] + *miri* little).] A small South American squirrel-monkey of the genus *Chrysothrix* (formerly *Saimiris*).

1774 GOLDSM. *Nat. Hist.* (1776) IV. 236 The fifth and last of the sapajou kind, or monkies that hold by the tail, is the Samiri, or Aurora; which is the smallest and the most beautiful of all. **1780** SMELLIE *Buffon's Nat. Hist.* (1791) VIII. 199 The saïmiri is commonly known by the name of the golden, orange, or yellow sapajou. **1863** HUXLEY *Man's Place Nat.* II. 97 The Saimiri (*Chrysothrix*).

sain (seɪn), *v.* Now *arch.* and *dial.* Forms: 1 **segnian, sénian, sægnian**, 2 **seinian**, 4–5 **seyne**, 4–6 **sayn(e**, 8–9 **sein**, 3–7 **saine**, 3–9 **sane**, 3– **sain**; *pa. t.* 4–5 **saynned**; *pa. ppl.* 8 **saint**. [OE. *segnian* = OS. *segnon* (MDu. *zechenen*, Du. *zegenen*), OHG. *seganôn* (MHG. *segenen*, mod.G. *segnen* to bless), ON. *signa* to sign with the cross, bless (Sw. *signa*, Da. *signe* to bless); ad. L. *signāre* to sign (in eccl. use to sign with the cross), f. *signum* SIGN *sb.*, whence OE. *segn* sign, banner, MLG. *segen*, MDu. *zeghen* sign of the cross, blessing (Du. *zegen* blessing), OHG. *segan* sign of the cross (MHG., mod.G. *segen* blessing).]

1. *trans.* To make the sign of the cross on (a thing or person) in token of consecration or blessing; or for the purpose of exorcizing a demon, warding off the evil influences of witches, poison, etc.

a **900** tr. *Bæda's Hist.* v. v. §2 (1890) 396 Þa sang he orationes ofer hiene & hiene gebletsade & gesegnade [L. *dixit orationem, ac benedixit eum*]. *c* **1000** ÆLFRIC *Saints' Lives* iii. 114 Þa sette he hælend..and mid his halgum handum husel senode. *c* **1175** *Lamb. Hom.* 127 We sculen ure forheafod..mid þere halie rode tacne seinian. *c* **1375** *Sc. Leg. Saints* xxvii. (*Machor*) 599 With þat þe cop in hand tuk he, & sanyt It dewotly. *a* **1400** *St. John Evang.* 228 in Horstmann *Altengl. Leg.* (1881) 471 Þou..saynede þe coppe [of poison] swetely and suppede it off syne: Thow hade no harme. **1508** KENNEDY *Flyting w. Dunbar* 457 Quhen that the schip was saynit, et vndir saile, Foul brow in holl thow preposit for to pas. **1575–6** *Durham Depos.* (Surtees) 272 Then the said Umphray saynd the said Thomas and corssed hym, and spyttyd, and said, 'Away, devill', many tymes. **1701** J. Brand *Descr. Orkney, Zetl.*, etc. (1703) 62 Especially on Hallow-Even, they use to sein or sign their Boats and put a Cross of Tar upon them... Their Houses also some use then to sein. **1802** Scott *Minstr. Scot. Bord.* II. 179 *note*, Many of the vulgar account it extremely dangerous to touch any thing which they may happen to find without *saining* (blessing) it, the snares of the enemy being notorious and well attested. **1887** W. Stokes tr. *Tripartite Life St. Patrick* 37 Patrick sained [Irish *senais*] the earth and it swallowed up the wizard. *Ibid.* 111 Patrick sained their hands, and their hands grew stiff.

b. *refl.* To cross (oneself).

*a*900 tr. *Bæda's Hist.* iv. xxv. §5 (1890) 348, & þa him ȝebæd & hine ȝesegnode mid Cristes rode tacne. *a*1300 *Cursor M.* 7986 He.. Bitaght him þan to godd at kepe, And sanid him and fel on-slepe. *c*1375 *Sc. Leg. Saints* i. (*Petrus*) 521 Sanct petir sowne come in hy, and sanyt hym with þe Rycht hand. **1377** Langl. *P. Pl.* B. v. 456 Þanne sat sleuthe vp and seyned hym swithe [*v.r.* to A. v. 229 seynide hyme faste], And made avowe to-fore god for his foule sleuthe. ?*a*1400 *Morte Arth.* 966 Thow saynned the vnsekyrly to seke to þese mountez. *c*1450 *Merlin* iv. 66 And she lifte vp hir hande, and hir sayned [*printed* fayned], and seide, 'A mercy god!' **1508** Dunbar *Tua Mariit Wemen* 444, I sane me as I war ane sanct. **1588** A. King tr. *Canisius' Catech.*, *Confession* 15 Needful alsua is it.. to saine ws aft, putting beffoir our eyes Christ Iesus crucifide. **1728** Ramsay *Monk & Miller's Wife* 159 Bess sain'd herself, cry'd 'Lord, be here!' **1768** Ross *Helenore* (1789) 65 She—frae the ill o't sain'd her o'er and o'er. **1788** Shirrefs *Poems* (1790) 332 She'd raise her hands, and sain hersel', And think you on the road to Hell. **1828** J. Ruddiman *Tales & Sk.* 62 I sained mysel' thrice this morning before I had seen the face o' man.

†**c.** *intr.* for *refl.* *Obs. rare.*

*c*1440 *Alphabet of Tales* 7 Þan þis monke saynyd for mervell & said, 'sur, whi say ye so?' **1571** *Satir. Poems Reform.* xxviii. 24 And with that word I went sum thing abak, And bad say on, and, with God saif me, sanit.

2. *trans.* To bless.

*a*1300 *E.E. Psalter* lxii. 5 Swa sal I saine þe in life mine. **13..** *E.E. Allit. P.* B. 746 Now sayned be þou sauiour. *a*1400 *Sir Perc.* 287 So Criste mote me sayne. *c*1400 *Laud Troy Bk.* 6080 And with his goddis he hem sayned, And bad hem gon In here name. *c*1460 *Towneley Myst.* vi. 106 And thou [Jacob] shal full well saynyd be. **1500–20** Dunbar *Poems* xiii. 41 Sum sanis the Sait, and sum thaim cursis. **1616** T. Scott *Philomythie* (ed. 2) B 1, Against wise vigilant Statists, who like Ianus, Looke both waies squint, and both waies guard and sane vs. **1721** Kelly *Sc. Prov.* 120 God sain your Eye, Man. Spoken when you commend a Thing without blessing it. **1780** *Archie O Cawfield* xxxvii. in Child *Ballads* (1889) III. 488/2 For the man had needs to be well saint That comes thro the hands o Dicky Ha. **1818** Scott *Hrt. Midl.* xxix, God sain us. **1824** Byron *Juan* xvi. *Beware! beware* vi, Heaven sain him! fair or foul. **1848** Kingsley *Saint's Trag.* ii. vi, Mary sain us! **1898** N. Munro *John Splendid* ii. 19 Blow, present, God sain Mackay's soul!

b. *esp.* in conjunction with *save*.

*c*1460 *Towneley Myst.* iv. 107 So now god the saif and sayne! **1710** Ruddiman *Gloss. to Douglas* s.v. *Sane*, Hence Scot. Bor. the expression, God safe you and sane you. *a*1839 Praed *Poems* (1864) I. 146 Mary, Mother, sain and save! **1842** Browning *In a Gondola* Poems 1863 I. 210 They trail me, these three godless knaves, Past every church that sains and saves. **1894** Crockett *Raiders* xl. 336 Guid save us an' sain us! I like not this day.

¶**c.** app. associated by some mod. writers with L. *sānāre* to heal (see SANE *v.*).

1832 J. H. Newman *Sonn.*, '*They do but grope*' in *Lyra Apost.* (1836) 47 As if such shapes and moods, which come and go, Had aught of Truth or Life in their poor show, To sway or judge, and skill to sain or wound. **1896** A. E. Housman *Shropshire Lad* xiv, There flowers no balm to sain him.

3. *trans.* To secure by prayer or enchantment *from* evil influence. Cf. BLESS *v.*[1] 3.

1670 Ray *Prov.* 293 Saine (bless) you weill fra the Devil and the Lairds bairns. **1721** Kelly *Sc. Prov.* 288 Sain your self from the Dee'l and the Laird's Bairns. **1768** Ross *Helenore* 6 The jizzen-bed wi' rantree leaves was sain'd. **1848** Kingsley *Saint's Trag.* ii. viii, While angels.. Will sain us from the roaming adversary With scent of Paradise.

Hence †**sained** *ppl. a.*; '**saining** *vbl. sb.*

1508 Dunbar *Tua Mariit Wemen* 102 Than ma na sanyne me save fra that auld Sathane. **1593** Napier *Plain Discov. Rev. St. John* 58 Beside their daylie crossings with their right hande on their fore-heads, which they cal saning. **1888** Edmonston & Saxby *Home Naturalist* 214 Jaimie instantly turned back, for he knew that they had power at such times, and the saining might be neglected.

sain, obs. f. SAINT, SAY *v.*, SEE *v.*, SEINE (net).

sainctify, sainctuary, obs. ff. SANCT-.

saind, Sc. var. SAND *sb.* (message, etc.).

saine, obs. f. SAY *v.*, SEE *v.*, SEINE (net).

sainfayle, obs. form of SANSFAIL.

sainfeldite ('seɪnfɛldaɪt). *Min.* [a. F. *sainfeldite* (R. Pierrot 1964, in *Bull. de la Soc. franç. de Min. et de Crist.* LXXXVII. 180/1), f. the name of P. *Sainfeld* who collected the material: see -ITE[1].] A hydrous arsenate of calcium, $Ca_5H_2(AsO_4)_4.4H_2O$, occurring as small rosettes of transparent monoclinic crystals.

1964 *Chem. Abstr.* LXI 14371 Three new naturally occurring minerals, which were already known as synthetic compounds, were weilite.., rauenthalite.., and sainfeldite. **1972** *Bull. de la Soc. franç. de Min. et de Crist.* XCV. 33/2 Sainfeldite is the least hydrated member of the group including vladimirite, $Ca_5H_2(AsO_4)_4.5H_2O$, and guérinite, $Ca_5H_2(AsO_4)_4.9H_2O$.

sainfoin ('seɪnfɔɪn). Forms: 7 S. Foyne, Saint-, St. Foine, sainct-foin, santfine, -foyne, 7–8 St. Foyne, 8 St. Foin, sainfoine, 6– saintfoin, 7– sanfoin, 8– sainfoin. [a. F. *sainfoin*, also †*saintfoin* (16th c.), app. f. *sain* health-giving, wholesome + *foin* hay.

The identification of the first syllable with *saint* holy, was common in Fr. in the 16th c., and in Eng. in the 17th c. Cf. *holy hay* (see HOLY 5 b), G. *heiligheu*, and Pg. *sanfeno*.]

A low-growing perennial herb, *Onobrychis sativa* (formerly *Hedysarum Onobrychis*), much grown as a forage plant. Also, locally, lucerne (*Medicago sativa*).

1626 A. Speed *Adam out of E.* xiv. (1659) 108 A Gentleman.. hath this yeer about thirty acres of S. Foyne. **1653** Blithe *Eng. Improv. Impr.* xxvii. 187 St. Foyne is a French Grass much sowed there, upon their barren, dry, hasky Lands, and sometimes in our Gardens hath a kind of it been much sowed, called the French Honysuckel. **1669** Worlidge *Syst. Agric.* 27 This St. Foyne, or Holy-hay, hath in several places of England, obtained the preferrence above Clover-grass, for that it.. is so great an improvement on our barren Lands. **1726** *Dict. Husb.* II. s.v., Saintfoin, or Holy-Hay, a sort of Grass otherwise call'd Medick-Fodder, Spanish Trefoil, and Snail or Horned Clover-grass. **1792** A. Young *Trav. France* I. 152 Large quantities of sainfoin, which he used for fattening oxen. **1844** H. Stephens *Bk. Farm* II. 554 It is possible to cultivate both lucern and saintfoin as a one or more years' crop of grass in rotation with corn crops instead of red clover. **1857** Kingsley *Two Y. Ago* III. 133 Pink saintfoin. **1886** C. Scott *Sheep-farming* 50 For early spring feed and summer fattening, .. sanfoin, mustard, and lucern, will be found invaluable.

attrib. **1676** *Lond. Gaz.* No. 1073/4 Pure Trefoile and Santfine Seed. **1733** Tull *Horse-hoeing Husb.* xiv. 195 Cut off the St. Foin Heads an Handful deep. **1764** *Museum Rust.* I. 465 Saintfoin hay is excellent food for horses. **1792** A. Young *Trav. France* I. 357 A considerable portion of these calcareous districts should be thrown into sainfoin courses. **1805** R. W. Dickson *Pract. Agric.* I. 350 Old saintfoin lays. **1902** Cornish *Nat. on Thames* 174 The crimson of stray sainfoin clusters.

saing fayle, variant of SANSFAIL.

†**sainse, saynsure**, obs. ff. CENSE *v.*[1] and CENSER.

1565 Calfhill *Answ. Treat. Cross* ii. 53 b, We haue sainsed thy saincts, we haue.. honored thy Crosse. *Ibid.*, The sweete perfume of prayer shuld haue arisen from the saynsure of your heart to me.

saint (seɪnt; unstressed sənt, snt), *a.* and *sb.* Forms: α. 2–6 seint, 3–6 seinte, seynt(e, sainte, 4–5 saynt, (2 zeinte, 3 sæinte, 5 seyntte, 6 seeynt, sayent), 4– saint. β. (prefixed to a name beginning with a cons.) 3–4 sein, 4 san, sen, 4–6 sayn, 5 sayne, sain, syn. γ. 3–5 sant, 4–6 sent, (3 sante, sente, 4 santt, sande, sont, 5 synt, scent, 6 sentt(e), 8–9 *Sc.* saunt. δ. (chiefly *Sc.*) 4–8 sanct (6 -e), 5 senct, 5–6 saynct, seynct, 6–7 sainct. [a. OF. *saint*, *seint*, fem. *sainte*, *seinte* (*sancte*, *saente*, *sente*), later *sainct*, as prefix occas. *saen*, *sain*, mod.F. *saint* = Pr. *sanct*, *sant*, It., Sp., Pg. *santo* (before a cons. Pr., It. Sp. *san*, Pg. *são*):—L. *sanctus*, properly pa. pple. of *sancīre* to enact, ratify, devote, consecrate (cf. SANCTION).

The Latin word was adopted in most of the Germanic langs.; the variants with vowel other than *a* are due, partly to loss of stress in the prefixed position, partly to Fr. influence: OE. *sanct*, OFris. *sankt*, *sunkt*, *sant*, *sent*, *sint*, (prefixed) *sancte*, *sente* etc., MDu. (chiefly as prefix) *sanct*, *sant(e*, *sent(e*, *sint(e*, *sunte*, *sonte*, Du. *sint*, dial. *seint*, *sunt*, *sünt*, Flemish *zant*, MHG. (prefixed) *sancte*, *sant(e*, *sent(e*, mod.G. (prefixed) *Sanct*, *sankt*, Da. *sankt*-, Sw. *sankt(e*-.

The forms *sauynt*, *sauyn* (printed *sanynt*, *sanyn*) in the *Ayenbite* are difficult to account for.]

A. *adj.* = HOLY, in various special applications.

1. Prefixed to the name of a canonized person (see B. 2), also to the names of the archangels: now felt to be the sb. used appositively. Commonly abbreviated S. or St. (see below).

[In OE. *sanctus* and *sancte* (orig. the L. vocative) were used for the masc. and *sancta* for the fem.]

The possessive of names preceded by 'Saint' is often used ellipt. in names of churches, as *St. Paul's*, *St. Peter's*. Hence various names of towns, villages, etc., as *St. Albans*, *St. Andrews*, *St. Bees*; also the anglicized forms of some foreign place-names, as †*St. Omer's* (= F. *St.-Omer*).

α. *c*1175 *Lamb. Hom.* 49 Seint gregori. *c*1200 *Trin. Coll. Hom.* 9 Ure louerd sainte powel. *c*1250 *Kent. Serm.* in *O.E. Misc.* 26 Ure lauedi seinte Marie. **1297** R. Glouc. (Rolls) 8423 Þis bataile ido was A seinte peteres eue. **1340** *Ayenb.* 233 Ase zayþ saint austin. *c*1386 Chaucer *Prol.* 173 The reule of seint Maure or of seint Beneit. **1452** *Cal. Anc. Rec. Dublin* (1889) 277 The feste of Seynte Michell the Archangle. *c*1510 More *Picus* Wks. 9/2 Which is as trew as the gospell of seint John. **1599** Thynne *Animadv.* (1875) 57 Seinte Hughe Bishoppe of Lincolne. **1828** Scott *F.M. Perth* v, The rites due to good Saint Valentine.

β. *c*1200 *Trin. Coll. Hom.* 71 Þe godspelle þe sein lucas makede. *a*1300 *Cursor M.* 16762 + 10 þe swerd of sorow was at hir hert, Als sayde san symeon. *a*1330 *Otuel* 1585 Bi sein geme. **1389** in *Eng. Gilds* (1870) 54 Ye sunday after ye Natiuite of sen Jon day, baptist. *c*1400 *Rule St. Benet* (Prose) 42 Sain Benet leris vs in þis sentence, how we sal chese vre abbesse. *a*1470 *Gregory's Chron.* in *Hist. Coll. Cit. Lond.* (Camden) 168 Syr Phylyppe Dymmoke, that rode in the halle i-armyde clene as Syn Jorge. **1538** Starkey *England* i. i. 20 Aftur the mynd of Sayn Poule.

γ. *c*1230 *Hali Meid.* 7 As sente pawel seið, Alle þinge turneð þe gode to god. *a*1300 *Cursor M.* 154 And hit sal be reddynn þanne O Ioachim and of sant tanne [*Fairf.* seynt anne]. *Ibid.* 469 Sent micheal.. Rais a-gain him for to fight. *c*1375 *Ibid.* 12863 (Fairf.) Sande Iohn nerehand him stode. **14..** in *Rep. Hist. MSS. Comm.* (1907) IV. 24 Synt Petyrys mynyster of Exeter. **1557** in *Shropsh. Parish Documents* (1903) 58 It' Re'd of thomas browne for sentmari day rent ii[s].

δ. **1375** Barbour *Bruce* v. 336 The folk.. Held to Sanct Brydis kirk thar way. *c*1470 Henry *Wallace* i. 282 Quha sperd, scho said to Sanct Margret thai socht. *c*1510 More *Picus* Wks. 12/2 And remember these wordes of Sainct Paule also. **1562** Winȝet *Cert. Tractates* iii. Wks. (S.T.S.) I. 27 Sanctis Hierome and Augustine. **1596** Dalrymple tr. *Leslie's Hist. Scot.* iv. 230 Sancte Columba.

¶ Abbreviations: S. and St., *pl.* SS. and Sts.

Since the 18th c. 'St.' is the form usually employed; but since about 1830 'S.' has been favoured by ecclesiologists. In place-names, and in family names derived from these, only 'St.' is used.

[*c*1122 *O.E. Chron.* (Laud MS.) an. 963 To Eliȝ, þær S. Æðeldrið lið. *c*1154 *Ibid.* an. 1132 On S' Petres messe dei.] *a*1400 *Wyclif's Bible* IV. 693 Fynding of S. Steuen martir. **1535** Coverdale *Bible*, The gospell of S. Mathew... The epistles of S. Paul. **1611** Bible *Transl. Pref.* ¶8 S. Chrysostome that liued in S. Hieromes time. **1638** Sir T. Herbert *Trav.* (ed. 2) 33 St. Francis Shyvier the Navarrean Jesuit. **1711** Shaftesb. *Charac.* (1737) I. 344 The storys of their giants, their dragons, and St. George's. **1850** J. H. Newman *Serm. Var. Occas.* xii. (1857) 263 Those early Religious, of which St. Benedict is the typical representative. **1852** (*title*) The Homilies of S. John Chrysostom.. on the Gospel of St. Matthew. **1877** J. D. Chambers *Div. Worship* 177 The Octave of S. Stephen.

2. *transf.* †**a.** of heathen deities, etc. *Obs.*

*c*1375 *Cursor M.* 7458 (Fairf.), I sulde him sla be seint Mahoun. *c*1400 *Rom. Rose* 5953 By my modir seint Venus. *Ibid.* 6781 My moder flemed him, Seynt Amour. **1588** Shaks. *L.L.L.* iv. iii. 366 Saint Cupid then, and Souldiers to the field.

b. allusively or ironically. *Obs.* in gen. use.

St. Monday: see MONDAY 2. *St. Lubbock's day*: a jocular name for any of the bank holidays instituted by Sir John Lubbock's Act, 1871: see BANK HOLIDAY.

1362 Langl. *P. Pl.* A. v. 40 Ȝe þat secheþ seynt Iame and seintes at Roome, Secheþ Seint Treuþe for he may sauen ow alle. **1540** Palsgr. *Acolastus* ii. i. I ij b, That holy saynte fylgutte or saynte panchart. **1592** Greene *Upst. Courtier* D 3 b, He sits down in the chaire wrapt in fine cloaths, as though the barber were aboute to make him a foot-cloth for the vicar of saint fooles. **1657** Titus *Killing no Murder* A 3 b, As Hugh Capet, in taking the Crown, pretended to be admonish't to it in a dreame by St. Valery, and St. Richard: so I beleeve will his Highnes [*sc.* Cromwell] doe the same, at the instigation of St. Henry and St. Richard his two Sonnes. **1665** Swan *Spec. M.* iv. §4 (ed. 3) 214, I think the best time to try this, is upon St. Jefferies day, which is neither before Christmass nor after it. **1690** C. Nesse *Hist. & Myst. O. & N. Test.* I. 39 Our late Anti-Sabbatarians.. call'd it Saint-Sabbath.

†**3.** Prefixed to various common nouns (in collocations taken over from Latin and French), esp. *Charity*, *Cross*, *Spirit*, *Trinity*. *Obs.*

Sometimes abbreviated as in 1.

In dedications of churches there occur *St. Cross*, *St. Faith*, *St. Saviour*, *St. Sepulchre*.

*a*1300 *Cursor M.* 21465 Bi sant drightin Mi thinc þe wers part es mine. **1377** Langl. *P. Pl.* B. xii. 104 Al-þough men made bokes, god was þe maistre, And seynt spirit þe saumplarye. *c*1386 Chaucer *Knt.'s T.* 863 But sle me first for seinte charitee. *c*1386 —— *Sompn. T.* 116 Chideth him weel, for seinte Trinitee. *c*1440 *Generydes* 4282 He.. askyd almes for seynt charite. **1470–85** Malory *Arthur* x. i. 413 By seynt crosse said syre Vwayne he is a stronge knyght. **1553** Becon *Reliques of Rome* (1563) 206 Cause a masse to be song or sayde in the honoure of Saint Spirite. **1602** Shaks. *Ham.* iv. v. 58 By gis, and by S. Charity, Alacke, and fie for shame. **1631** Weever *Anc. Funeral Mon.* 722 The Altar.. was that which was first built to Saint seruice. **1710** *Lond. Gaz.* No. 4688/1 The Annual Procession.. in Honour of the Saint Sudario [i.e. *il Santo Sudario*].

4. Attributive and possessive collocations of proper names with the prefix 'Saint' (St.) in sense 1.

a. Many plants, animals, and other objects have been named after saints of the calendar. For these appellations see the saints' names in their alphabetical places or the sbs. qualified by them.

b. Many diseases have been named after saints that are supposed to ward them off or relieve them.

A long list of these is given in Dunglison's *Dict. Med. Sci.* and *Syd. Soc. Lex.* For *St. Anthony's*, *St. Francis's fire*, see FIRE *sb.* 12. *St. Vitus' dance*: see DANCE *sb.* 6 d.

c. Many objects are called after a place-name or a surname beginning with 'Saint' ('St.'); the following are some of the more important.

St. Augustine grass, a coarse grass, *Stenotaphrum secundatum*, native to the southeastern United States and central America and named after a town in Florida; **St. Bees Sandstone**, a pebbly sandstone occurring in thick beds in northwest England, formerly regarded as Upper Permian but now as Lower Triassic; **St. Bernard (dog)**, in full ***Great St. Bernard dog***, a dog of a breed kept by the monks of the Hospice of the Great St. Bernard (a dangerous pass in the alps between Switzerland and Italy) for the rescue of travellers in distress; **St. Bernard('s) lily**, a perennial herb, *Anthericum liliago*, belonging to the family Liliaceæ and bearing racemes of white flowers; **St. Brigid('s) anemone**, a plant belonging to a garden race of *Anemone coronaria*, bearing single or double red or blue flowers; **St. Bruno's lily**, a rhizomatous perennial herb, *Paradisea liliastrum*, which resembles St. Bernard's lily but has larger flowers (cf. LILY

1 b); **St. Dabeoc's heath**, an Irish heath, *Dabœcia cantabrica* or one of its varieties, belonging to the family Ericaceæ and bearing white, pink, or purple flowers; **St. Domingo cuckoo**, etc., species of cuckoo, etc., found in San Domingo; **St. Domingo fever**, yellow fever; **St. George's mushroom**, a creamy-white, flattened mushroom, *Tricholoma gambosum*; **St. Germain pear**, a fine dessert pear; **St. Gobain glass**, a fine kind of plate glass manufactured at St. Gobain in France; **St. Helena tea** (see quots.); **St. Johnston's riband, tippet**, *&c.*, a halter or hangman's rope; (*St. Johnston* = Perth); **St. Kilda cold** (see quot.); **St. Kilda (field, house) mouse**, a variety of the long-tailed field mouse, *Apodemus sylvaticus hirtensis*, or the house mouse, *Mus musculus muralis*; **St. Kilda wren**, a local variety of the wren, *Troglodytes troglodytes hirtensis*, with paler plumage; **St. Leger**, the name of a horse-race for three-year-olds run at Doncaster: instituted by Colonel St. Leger in 1776; **St. Louis encephalitis** [*St. Louis*, city of Missouri, U.S.], a severe viral encephalitis transmitted by mosquitos; **St. Louis group**, a section of the mountain limestone of North America, well developed in states bordering on the upper Mississippi; **St. Lucia (Lucie) bark**, the bark of the West Indian shrub *Exostemma floribundum*, used in tanning; **St. Michael's**, the name of one of the Azores, which produced a fine quality of orange; †**St. Omer's** (corruptly *St. Thomas*) **worsted**, a kind of worsted manufactured at St. Omer's; **St. Patrick's cabbage** (see CABBAGE *sb.*[1] 2).

1905 W. J. SPILLMAN *Farm Grasses U.S.* xiii. 196 *St. Augustine grass occurs along the Atlantic coast from Charleston, S.C., southward. **1968** F. W. GOULD *Grass Systematics* v. 203 St. Augustine grass is relatively coarse. [**1836** *Trans. Geol. Soc.* IV. 398 The red sandstone of St. Bees Head is unquestionably the exact equivalent of the upper red sandstone of that series.] **1865** E. W. BINNEY in *Mem. Lit. & Philos. Soc. Manchester* II. 373 Fine-grained red sandstone, laminated and ripple-marked, same as that seen at Moat, .. Maryport, and other places, which may be conveniently called *St. Bees sandstone. **1946** L. D. STAMP *Britain's Struct. & Scenery* xxii. 224 The St. Bees Sandstone, .. of New Red Sandstone age, forms the red cliffs of St. Bees Head. **1969** BENNISON & WRIGHT *Geol. Hist. Brit. Isles* xi. 265 In this case the base of the St. Bees Sandstone, of Bunter age, may also be diachronous. **1839** SIR T. D. LAUDER in C. H. Smith *Dogs* (1840) II. 142 My *St. Bernard dog, Bass. **1877** *Encycl. Brit.* VII. 327/2 The Great St. Bernard Dog of the present day is a powerful animal, as large as a mastiff. **1884** *Harper's Mag.* Aug. 464/1 A big St. Bernard. **1883** W. ROBINSON *Eng. Flower Garden* 26/2 The *St. Bernard's Lily .. grows from 1 foot to 2 feet high, producing single, sometimes branched flower-spikes. **1900** W. D. DRURY *Bk. Gardening* x. 315 The St. Bruno and St. Bernard Lilies .. are fast becoming popular. **1964** H. RAMSBOTHAM tr. *Schauenberg's Bulb Bk.* III. 106 St. Bernard's Lily .. is a common plant in Alpine meadows. [**1894** *Jrnl. R. Hort. Soc.* XVII. p. liv, Award of Merit. To Anenome St. Brigid's strain .. from Earl Cowper, Panshanger, Hertford ([gardener] Mr. Fitt).] **1902** *Ibid.* XXVII. p. lxxxvi. Award of Merit. To the Alderborough strain of *St. Brigid Anemones. **1939** W. FORTESCUE *There's Rosemary* lxxix. 408 We had the joy .. of seeing his beautiful frail hands caress the petals of flaming St Brigid Anemones and slender tulips which bordered the drive of the Domaine. **1971** *Country Life* 2 Sept. 543/3 St. Brigid's anemones. Sown in April, they flower from August. **1795** *Curtis's Bot. Mag.* IX. 318 (*heading*) Savoy Anthericum, or *St. Bruno's Lily. **1883** W. ROBINSON *Eng. Flower Garden* II. 26/2 The major variety of the St. Bruno's Lily has much larger flowers than the type. **1964** H. RAMSBOTHAM tr. *Schauenberg's Bulb Bk.* III. 204 The English name of this lovely Alpine plant [*sc.* St. Bernard's Lily] is 'St. Bruno's Lily'. **1863** R. C. A. PRIOR *On Pop. Names Brit. Plants* 195 *St. Dabeoc's Heath, from an Irish saint of that name, a species found in Ireland. **1978** P. ROWE-DUTTON tr. *van de Laar's Heather Garden* 130 St. Dabeoc's Heath. A low, evergreen Irish native with broad fresh green leaves, silvery beneath. **1782** LATHAM *Gen. Synopsis Birds* I. II. 541 *St. Domingo Cuckow. *Ibid.* I. 111 St. Domingo Falcon. **1793** SMELLIE tr. *Buffon's Nat. Hist. Birds* VIII. 231 The St. Domingo Chesnut .. *Colymbus Dominicus*, Linn. **1822–34** *Good's Study Med.* (ed. 4) I. 644 From the depredations it has committed in the West Indies and on the American Coast, it has been called the *St. Domingo .. fever. **1891** M. C. COOKE *Brit. Edible Fungi* iv. 34 '*St. George's mushroom' .. makes its appearance about the time of St. George's Day. **1966** *Oxf. Bk. Flowerless Plants* 134/2 'St. George's Mushroom' .. grows in undergrowth on the edges of woods .. and in open grassland. **1693** EVELYN *De La Quint. Compl. Gard.* I. 93 This *St. Germain-pear, otherwise called the Unknown Pear of the Fare, has a very tender Pulp. **1858** O. W. HOLMES *Aut. Breakf.-t.* iv. (1859) 77 Milton was a Saint-Germain with a graft of the roseate Early-Catherine ... Russet-skinned old Chaucer was an Easter-Beurré. **1870** SAUZAY *Marvels of Glass-making* 91 *note*, According to M. Péligot the *St. Gobain glass is composed of, Silica 73·0, Lime 15·5, Soda 11·5. **1875** MELLISS *St. Helena* 239 *Frankenia portulacæfolia*, Spreng.... *Beatsonia portulacæfolia*, Roxb.; *St. Helena Tea. .. I find no record of the plant having been ever used as a substitute for tea. **1897** *Syd. Soc. Lex.*, *St. Helena tea*, a kind of tea made in the island of St. Helena by infusing the leaves of the plant *Beatsonia portulacifolia*. **1638** H. ADAMSON *Muse's Threnodie* (1774) 119 Hence of *St. Johnston's ribband came the word. **1816** SCOTT *Old Mort.* vii, To be sent to Heaven wi' a Saint Johnstone's tippit about my hause. **1897** *Syd. Soc. Lex.*, **St. Kilda cold* .. A variety of Influenza occurring in the Hebrides, believed to be brought by strangers from ships touching at the islands. **1899** G. E. H. BARRETT-HAMILTON in *Proc. Zool. Soc.* 78, I have now before me .. a fine adult pair .. of the *St. Kilda Mouse. **1913** —— *Hist. Brit. Mammals* II. 540 (*heading*) The St Kilda Field Mouse. *Ibid.* 661 (*heading*) The St Kilda House Mouse. **1960** M. BURTON *Wild Animals Brit. Isles* 78 St. Kilda field mouse .. with brown under parts. *Ibid.* 88 Since the human inhabitants left the island in 1930, the St. Kilda mouse has become extinct. **1976** *Islander* (Victoria, B.C.) 7 Mar. 3/3 The St. Kilda house mouse has become extinct. *Ibid.*, The St. Kilda field mouse is also larger. **1884** H. SEEBOHM in *Zoologist* VIII. 333 Those ornithologists who regard the climatic races of this bird as distinct species, will probably come to the conclusion that the *St. Kilda Wren is one of the most distinct. **1914** [see WREN 1 b]. **1944** J. S. HUXLEY *On Living in Revolution* ix. 96 The St. Kilda wren .. was for some time classified as a separate species. **1976** *Islander* (Victoria, B.C.) 7 Mar. 3/3 The St. Kilda wren is unique. **1778** in *Baily's Racing Reg.* (1845) I. 470/1 *St. Leger's Stakes of 25 gs. each. **1825** C. M. WESTMACOTT *Eng. Spy* (1907) I. 327 This is the settling day for all bets made upon the great Doncaster St. Leger. **1847** THACKERAY *Van. Fair* (1848) xxxiv. 302 He and his father fell to talking about odds on the *St. Leger. **1930** *Daily Express* 11 Sept. 9/5 The St. Leger was run in almost ideal conditions. **1977** *Times* 10 Sept. 22/1 Thirteen runners have finally stood their ground for this year's St Leger .. at Doncaster this afternoon. [**1933** *Jrnl. Amer. Med. Assoc.* 9 Sept. 860/2 (*heading*) The St. Louis encephalitis epidemic.] **1934** *Ibid.* 18 Aug. 462/2 The virus of *St. Louis encephalitis had an almost exclusively neurotropic activity. **1962** GORDON & LAVOIPIERRE *Entomol.* xix. 130 As regards western equine encephalomyelitis and St. Louis encephalitis .. the important vector appears to be *Culex tarsalis*. **1977** *Jrnl. Virol.* XXII. 608 The antigenic determinants of St. Louis encephalitis, Japanese encephalitis, and dengue virus envelope and nucleocapsid proteins were examined by solid-phase competition radioimmunoassay. **1863** DANA *Man. Geol.* 307 The *St. Louis limestone (250 feet thick), overlaid by ferruginous sandstone (200 feet). **1879** *Encyl. Brit.* X. 350/2 St. Louis group.—Limestones with shale, in places 250 feet. **1840** PEREIRA *Elem. Mat. Med.* II. 992 *St. Lucia Bark. **1852** MORFIT *Tanning & Currying* (1853) 94 St. Lucia Bark .. is said to be suitable for tanning. *c* **1830** *St. Michael's oranges [see ORANGE *sb.*[1] 1]. **1892** *Daily News* 22 Dec. 3/1 It may be that some day sweet St. Michaels may pour in upon us again. **1530** PALSGR. 269/1 *Seynt Homer's worstedde, *demy ostade*. **1552** *Inv. Church Goods* (Surtees) II. 61 A cope of read Saint Thomas worsted. **1851** C. A. JOHNS *Flowers of Field* I. 240 *S*[*axifraga*] *umbrosa* (London Pride or *St. Patrick's Cabbage). **1976** *Church Times* 14 May 14/5 Other flowers with religious or curious folk-names are 'Yellow Archangel' ..; 'St. Patrick's Cabbage' (one of the saxifrages); [etc.].

‖**d.** Similarly found in various place- or personal names of French origin, as **St. Cloud** (sẽklu), used *attrib.* to designate porcelain or faïence made at St. Cloud, Seine-et-Oise, in the late-seventeenth and eighteenth centuries; **St. Emilion** (sẽtemiljɔ̃), the name applied to various wines produced in the region of St. Emilion, Gironde, in south-west France; **St. Galmier** (galmje), an effervescent natural mineral water from St. Galmier, Loire, in central France; **St. Honoré** (ɔnɔre) (see quot. 1964); usu. *attrib.*, as ***gâteau St. Honoré***; **St. Paulin** (polẽ), a kind of cheese (see quots.); **St. Porchaire** (pɔrʃɛr), used *attrib.* to designate a kind of earthenware made at Saint-Porchaire, Deux-Sèvres, France, in the sixteenth century; **St. Raphael (wine)** (rafajɛl), an aperitif wine from St. Raphael, Var, in France.

[**1699** M. LISTER *Journey to Paris* 138, I saw the *Potterie of St. Clou* with which I was marvellously well pleased.] **1721** M. W. MONTAGU *Let.* June (1966) II. 6 If you have not allready laid out that small Summ in St. Cloud ware, I had rather have it in plain Lutestring. **1870** C. SCHREIBER *Jrnl.* 17 Feb. (1911) I. 71 We found an exquisite pâte tendre St. Cloud group. **1978** *Times* 4 Mar. 10/7 The Garrick Club have .. Thomas King's cane with a fine St Cloud porcelain handle. **1833** C. REDDING *Hist. Mod. Wines* v. 142 St. Emilion has plenty of body, and superior flavour. **1981** P. FOX *Satan's Messenger* II. xviii. 133 You don't serve a Château Lafite to two hundred people... The St. Emilion would be perfectly adequate. **1883** *Encycl. Brit.* XVI. 436/1 Classes I. and II. of alkaline waters .. are very abundant on the Continent, and .. some of the best-known ones enumerated below are .. French .. St. Galmier, Pougues, Chateldon. **1912** BEERBOHM *Seven Men* (1919) 114 'Apollinaris? St. Galmier? Or what?' I asked. He preferred plain water. **1907** *Yesterday's Shopping* (1969) 55/2 *Iced & Fancy Cakes*... Gâteaux St. Honore .. each 1/5. **1964** A. LAUNAY *Caviare & After* 143 *Saint Honoré*, a rich, round pastry filled with cream and topped with crystallized fruits. **1968** V. CANNING *Melting Man* v. 120 He .. came back with a concoction that made me feel I would never want to eat again... 'It is a *Saint-Honoré*. He was, you know, once Bishop of Amiens and is the patron saint of pastry-cooks. **1968** D. HOPKINSON *Incense-Tree* i. 6 Her dinner parties were graced with .. Gâteau St Honoré. **1956** A. SIMON *Cheeses of World* 73 *Saint-Paulin* is a semi-hard cheese made from cow's milk... The Trappists of .. Tamié .. used to sell their cheese as *St. Paulin*, but it is now sold as *Fromage de Tamié*. **1958** *Catal. County Stores, Taunton* June 9 *Cheese* .. St. Paulin—each 5/6. **1971** *Sunday Times* (Colour Suppl.) 28 Mar. 34/3 *Saint-Paulin*, resembles Port Salut in texture, taste and origins. First made in a Norman monastery, it is a rich yellow whole cow's milk cheese, at once soft and firm to the touch and very mildly ripe to taste. [**1899** P. GLAZIER *Man. Hist. Ornament* 81 Henri-deux, or St Porchards ware, now more properly described as Oiron ware, originated at St Porchard in 1524.] **1925** E. HANNOVER *Pott. & Porc.* III. i. 15 Specimens of the 'Henri II' (St. Porchaire) ware, which is also extremely rare, have repeatedly been offered for sale .. in our own days. **1960** [see HENRI DEUX]. **1975** *Times* 20 May 16/4 One of the greatest rareties in .. European ceramics, a St. Porchaire ewer, is to be offered for sale... St. Porchaire wares were made between about 1525 and 1565 and only 60 pieces have survived... St. Porchaire ware, also known as *faience de Henri II* .. was rediscovered by the public, like Palissy ware, as a result of the 1862 'Special Exhibition of Works of Art' at the South Kensington Museum. **1899** HARDY *Let.* 23 Aug. in *One Rare Fair Woman* (1972) 83, I have taken one bottle of St Raphael wine —and it has picked me up. **1951** [see LILLET]. **1971** *Guardian* 3 June 9/4 St. Raphael and Dubonnet are the sweetest [aperitifs]. **1980** E. LEATHER *Duveen Let.* xii. 138 Glasses of St Raphael and Vichy water were ordered.

B. *sb.* A holy person.

1. One of the blessed dead in Heaven. Usually *pl.*

[*a* **1000** *Cædmon's Satan* 355 þær habbað englas eadiȝne dream, sanctas singað.] **13..** *Cursor M.* 10402 (Gött) Felauschip .. Of saintes [*Cott.* halus] hye in heuen bliss. **138.** WYCLIF *Sel. Wks.* III. 467 A thowsand þowsandis bene moo seintis in heven þen we kanonysen in þo kalender. *c* **1420** *Prymer* (1895) 7 (*Te Deum*) Make hem to be rewardid wiþ seyntis in endeles blis. **1592** *Arden of Feversham* I. i. 329 To liue With God and his elected saints in heauen. **1657** JER. TAYLOR *Funeral Serm. Sir G. Dalstone*, The consummation and perfection of the saints' felicity shall be at the resurrection of the dead. **1781** COWPER *Truth* 150 She, half an angel in her own account, Doubts not hereafter with the saints to mount. **1851** G. RORISON *Hymn*, '*Three in One*', With the Saints here-after we Hope to bear the palm. **1864** BP. W. HOW *Hymn*, For all Thy Saints who from their labours rest. **1875** MANNING *Mission Holy Ghost* vii. 191 A multitude who have not been canonised on earth, though they are saints in heaven.

2. a. *Eccl.* One of those persons who are formally recognized by the Church as having by their exceptional holiness of life attained an exalted station in heaven, and as being entitled in an eminent degree to the veneration of the faithful; a canonized person. In Pre-Reformation use, the term implies that the persons so designated may be lawfully addressed in prayer for their intercession with God, and that miracles have been wrought through their aid after death. Also, a monk or anchorite, esp. in phr. *(is)land of saints*, Ireland. †***to seek, visit a saint***: to pay one's devotions at his shrine. (Cf. HALLOW *sb.*[1] 2.)

[*c* **1000** ÆLFRIC in Sweet *A.-S. Reader* (1894) 85 God ȝeswutelode þæt he haliȝ sanct wæs swa þæt heofonlic leoht of þæt ȝeteld astreht stod up to heofonum. *c* **1122** *O.E. Chron.* (Laud. MS.) an. 979, He wæs on life eorðlic cing, he is nu æfter deaðe heofonlic sanct.]

a **1300** *Cursor M.* 28604 To godd i merci cri .. And all seyntes of heuen sere. *a* **1310** in Wright *Lyric P.* xxxiv. 96 Preye we alle to oure levedy, Ant to the sontes that woneth hire by. *c* **1374** CHAUCER *Troylus* II. 69 (118) In a cave To bidde, and rede on holy seyntes lyves. *c* **1420** *Anturs of Arth.* xvii, I salle gerre seke sayntes for thi sake. **1426** LYDG. *De Guil. Pilgr.* 6287 For seyntys wych that suffrede so, I wot ryht wel that they be go To paradys. **1500–20** DUNBAR *Poems* xxv. 65 We pray to all the Sanctis of hevin, That ar aboif the sterris sevin. **1588** A. KING tr. *Canisius' Catech.* in *Cath. Tractates* (S.T.S.) 206 This præsent Kalendar quhairin is comprehendit the Sanctes and martyres vith the tyme of thair death or suffering. **1614** BP. HALL *No Peace with Rome* §21 Neither will we only glorifie God in his Saints .. but wee will magnifie the Saints .. for their excellent graces. **1726** BOYS *Expos. 39 Art.* 146 Pardons or Indulgences, which are promis'd to those that visit such a Saint or Chapel. **1756–7** tr. *Keysler's Trav.* (1760) III. 44 The castle of St. Elmo, or St. Eramo, so called from a church dedicated to that saint. **1847** YEOWELL *Anc. Brit. Ch.* xii. 134 A considerable number of churches are called after the names of the primitive saints of our island. **1862** BURTON *Bk. Hunter* IV. 323 Technically, to make a saint, there should be an act of pontifical jurisdiction. **1888** CHESTERTON *Ballad of White Horse* v. 102 His men were all as thin as saints. *Ibid.* 103 Though Ireland be but a land of saints, and Wales a land of thieves. **1904** C. WALSH in J. McCarthy *Irish Lit.* I. p. xvii, Her nationality and her national spirit have been recognized during the last twenty years as they never were since the days when Ireland was the 'island of saints and scholars', the land of intellectual light and leading in Europe. **1938** W. B. YEATS *New Poems* 13 My father upon the Abbey stage, before him a raging crowd. 'This Land of Saints' and then .. 'Of plaster Saints'. **1964** *Welsh Hist. Rev.* II. 122 The migrations of the 'saints' from Britain can be dated almost exclusively to the sixth century. *Ibid.* 123 We can picture these early British 'saints' (monks) seeking solitary places at home and abroad in which to serve God. **1979** *Guardian* 1 Oct. 2/8 It was the Pope's arrival at Dublin Airport .. which truly set the distinctive character of this personal pilgrimage to his 'island of saints'.

Proverb. **1550** BALE *Eng. Votaries* II. 105 b, These adages myght than haue bene founde true, suche saynt, suche shryn, suche bere, suche bottell.

b. A representation or image of a saint.

1563 *Homilies* II. *Agst. Images* III. Qqiij, Such a creple came and saluted this saint of Oke. **1679** *Roxb. Ball.* (1885) V. 594 And who, to furnish his own want, Can seize Gold Cross, or Silver Saint. **1817** LADY MORGAN *France* I. (1818) I. 92 Fruit in wax-work, and saints in *or moulu*. **1849** JAMES *Woodman* xv, Far readier to worship a gold angel than a painted saint. **1893** BATES *Eng. Relig. Drama* 27 As if the chiselled, painted saint himself .. stepped down .. from marble niche.

c. *transf.* Applied e.g. to persons who are the objects of posthumous reverence in non-Christian religions. †Also *rarely* to heathen deities, etc.

13.. *K. Alis.* 6763 Thou schalt fynde trowes two: Seyntes and holy they buth bo. *c* **1400** *Destr. Troy* 2000 All the buernes in the bote, .. Besoght vnto sainttes & to sere goddes. *Ibid.* 12071 þe sayntis of hell Were wode in hor werkis for wreke of Achilles. **1601** HOLLAND *Pliny* I. 4 Others .. are punished by the saints whom they adore, and the holy ceremonies which they obserue. **1626** METHOLD in Purchas *Pilgrimage* 999 One Saint they haue .. whom they expresse by a plaine round stone. **1876** A. J. EVANS *Through Bosnia* viii. 342 There are many gay kiosques rising over the graves of Moslem saints.

3. a. In biblical use, one of God's chosen people; in the New Testament, one of the elect under the New Covenant; a member of the Christian church; a Christian. Hence used by some religious bodies as their own designation, e.g. by some puritanical sects in the 16–17th c., the Mormons (see LATTER-DAY), and the Plymouth Brethren.

1382 WYCLIF *1 Cor.* i. 2 To the halowid in Crist Ihesu, clepid seyntis. **1526** TINDALE *Acts* ix. 32 As Peter walked throughoute all quarters, he cam to the saincts which dwelt at lydda. **1567** *Gude & Godlie B.* (S.T.S.) 103 God, for thy grace,.. Ceis not to send thy Sanctis sune support. **1597** Hooker *Eccl. Pol.* v. lvi. 123 The fellowship of his Saincts in this present world. **1610** B. Jonson *Alch.* II. v, A seruant of the exil'd Brethren, That deale with widdowes and with orphanes goods And make a iust account vnto the Saints: A Deacon. **1626** —— *Staple of N.* III. ii. 125 Ha' you in your prophane Shop, any Newes O'the Saints at Amsterdam? **1658** Cowley *Cutter Colman St.* III. i, What preaching, and houling, and fasting, and eating among the Saints! **1704** Nelson *Fest. & Fasts* xxxiv. (1739) 419 In the beginning of Christianity, the word Saint was applied to all Believers. **1710** [H. Bedford] *Vind. Ch. Eng.* 170 We seem to have forgot the *Saints Reign* from 41 to 60. **1782** C. Simeon in Carus *Life* (1847) 28 Now he scruples keeping a horse, that the money may help the saints of Christ. **1786** Burns *Sc. Drink* viii, Godly meetings o' the saunts, By thee inspir'd. **1838** G. V. Wigram *Let.* in T. S. Veitch *Story of Brethren Movement* (1933) iv. 59 The question I refer to is 'How are the meetings for communion of Saints in these parts to be regulated?' **1847** Yeowell *Anc. Brit. Ch.* iii. 31 It is not.. improbable.. that St. Paul should have become acquainted with some of these captives, by means of some of the Saints in Cæsar's household. **1863** Dickens *Uncomm. Trav.* xx, The Preface, dated Manchester, 1840, ran thus:—'The Saints in this country have been very desirous for a Hymn Book adapted to their faith and worship'. **1866** H. Groves *Darbyism* ii. 25 God so ordered it, that the anathemas which had divided the assemblies in Plymouth, should fall upon the saints assembling at Bethesda in Bristol. **1886** *Whitaker's Alm.* 204 Religious Sects... Saints. **1907** E. Gosse *Father & Son* iii. 72 She now had the care of a practised woman, one of the 'saints' from the Chapel. **1978** *Times Lit. Suppl.* 26 May 573/1 Critical intelligence and the world of the Plymouth Brethren proved.. incompatible: growing up meant leaving the Saints.

b. In biblical use applied to angels.

1382 Wyclif *Deut.* xxxiii. 2 The Lord.. aperide fro the hil of Pharan, and with hym thousandis of seyntis. **1611** Bible *Jude* 14 The Lord commeth with ten thousands of his Saints. **1667** Milton *P.L.* vi. 46 Gabriel.. lead forth my armied Saints.

4. a. A person of extraordinary holiness of life. Sometimes ironically, A person making an outward profession of piety. Also in colloq. use, an extremely good or long-suffering person.

1563 Foxe *A. & M.* 1258/2 *Boner.* Well mayster Controller, I am no sainct. *Ibid.* 1374/2 Surely you would moue a Saint with your impertinent reasons. **1596** Shaks. *Tam. Shr.* III. ii. 28 For such an iniurie would vexe a very saint. **1625** Bacon *Ess., Suspicion,* What would Men haue? Doe they thinke, those they employ and deale with, are Saints? **1677** W. Hughes *Man of Sin* II. v. 99 We have read of Cannibals that devour the flesh of Men. Tush! They are Saints to Papists. For, They devour their God! **1732** Pope *Ep. Cobham* 246 Odious! in woollen! 'twould a Saint provoke. **1749** Chesterf. *Lett.* ccix. (1792) II. 301, I have sometimes known Saints really religious. **1852** Thackeray *Esmond* III. iii. 92 'O how good she is, Harry,' Beatrix went on to say, 'O what a saint she is!' **1884** *Harper's Mag.* Jan. 296/1 Were you a saint at college? **1884** H. A. Jones *(title)* Saints and Sinners. *a* **1887** H. W. Beecher *Prov. Plymouth Pulpit* 178 It will not do to be saints at meeting and sinners everywhere else. **1978** R. Barnard *Unruly Son* xvii. 186 My mother.. always thought about me. She was a saint.

b. Proverb.

1500–20 Dunbar *Poems* xlvi. 35 Of 3ung sanctis growis auld feyndis but fable. **1552** Latimer *7th Serm. on Lord's Prayer* (1562) H 4 b, The old prouerb yong saints, old deuils. **1616** S. Price *Ephesus Warning* 73 That Prouerb inuented by the Diuell that young Saints proue old Diuels. **1655** Fuller *Serm.* iv. 4 David began to be good betimes, a young Saint, and yet crossed that pestilent Proverb, was no old devill. **1694** Motteux *Rabelais* IV. lxiv. 254.

5. A nickname for: **a.** A member of a religious association at Cambridge (see quots.). Now *Hist.*

1793 *Acc. Proc. agst. W. Frend* 107, I shewed them [*sc.* two letters] to some of my friends, as instances of the gratitude of the saints. **1803** *Gradus ad Cantabr.* 116 *Saints,* a set of men who have great pretensions to particular sanctity of manners and zeal for orthodoxy. **1882** Mrs. Oliphant *Lit. Hist. Eng.* III. 38 [Dean Milner] was at the head of the party vulgarly called the Saints, the preachers of world-renunciation and self-denial. Another leader of this party.. was Charles Simeon.

b. One of the party which promoted the agitation in England against slavery. Now *Hist.*

1830 N. S. Wheaton *Jrnl.* 281 The friends of negro emancipation.. are already (1823–4) honoured with the nickname of 'Saints'. **1832** Marryat *N. Forster* xv, 'But do you think that this is likely to occur?' 'I do, most certainly, if those who govern continue to listen to the insidious advice of the party denominated 'Saints'. **1880** S. Walpole *Hist. Eng.* III. xiii. 196 The West Indians were furious with Stanley for doing so much; the 'Saints' were annoyed with him for doing so little.

6. *attrib.* and *Comb.*, as ***saint-author, -martyr, -protectrice; saint-beseeming, -eyed, -faced, -holy, -pleasing, -seeming*** adjs.; ***saint-maker, -making, server, -worship, worshipper***; **saint's day**, (*a*) a day set apart by the Church for observing the memory of a saint; (*b*) = name-day 1; † **saint's head stone**, a name for a kind of limestone.

1711 Shaftesb. *Charac.* (1737) I. 165 A *saint-author of all men least values politeness. **1650** Baxter *Saints' R.* I. iv. §5. 29 That *Saint-beseeming work. **1778** *Epit. in Stretton Church Yard* in *Bye-Gones* 18 July (1894) 376 Go *saint-eyed patience from affliction's door. **1829** H. Hawthorn *Visit Babylon* 61 Some usurious and *saint-faced Quakers. *a* **1617** Bayne *On Eph.* (1658) 7 Such beleevers.. who will not be accounted *Saint-holy. **1604** Hieron *Answ. to Popish Ryme* B 2, Who made the Pope a *Saint-maker? **1760–72** H. Brooke *Fool of Qual.* (1809) III. 19 A man who was called the saint-maker.. married five shrews in succession, and made Grizels of every one of them. **1802** Ranken *Hist. France* II. ii. §2. 186 The church of Rome, desirous of engrossing this power of *saint-making. **1826** W. E. Andrews *Exam. Fox's Cal. Prot. Saints* 473 Fox being in want of a *saint-martyr, thought proper to canonize a self-destroyer. **1601** Weever *Mirr. Mart.* B 7 b, Thy sweete *saint-pleasing songs forgotten. **1711** Shaftesb. *Charac.* (1737) I. 273 The ladys.. were the *saint-protectrices to whom the champions chiefly paid their vows. *a* **1450** Myrc *Festial* 267 þogh we halowen but few *sayntes-dayes, 3et we ben full neclygent yn oure seruyce. **1726** Ayliffe *Parergon* 473, I cannot find.. that we can trace what we call the Saints'-Days higher than the eighth or ninth Century. **1847** C. Bronte *J. Eyre* xxi, Eliza was gone to attend a saint's-day service at the New Church. **1863** Hawthorne *Our Old Home* II. 100 On a Sunday or Saint's day. **1943** E. M. Almedingen *Frossia* iii. 149 It is my saint's day, we have guests coming. **1980** 'J. Le Carré' *Smiley's People* xxiii. 272 Felicity had called her in.. to have Russian company on her saint's day. *a* **1641** Bp. Mountagu *Acts & Mon.* (1642) 395 Their *saint-seeming sanctity. **1563** Man *Musculus' Commonpl.* 293 As the *Sainct seruers [L. *cultores diuorum*] doe in our dayes. **1763** *Museum Rust.* I. lxxxv. 379 There is frequently found in the clay very hard lyas, or *saints-head stones. **1601** Weever *Mirr. Mart.* E 7, Acton did march in *Saint-triumphing showes. **1677** Gale *Crt. Gentiles* III. 173 The imputation of *Saint-worship. **1775** Adair *Amer. Ind.* 207 The popish saint-worship. **1882–3** *Schaff's Encycl. Relig. Knowl.* III. 2098 The abuses of saint-worship. **1615** Byfield *Expos. Col.* i. 19 (1628) 127 Sancti-colists, Pharises and *Saint-worshippers. **1648** Gage *West Ind.* 174 All that were there present, as well Saint-worshippers, as indeed that Idols worshippers.

saint (seɪnt), *v.* Forms: see saint *sb.*; also 3 *pa. pple.* isonted. [f. saint *sb.*]

1. *pass.* To be or become a saint in Heaven. *Obs.* or *arch.*

a **1225** *Ancr. R.* 350 þeo pilegrimes þet goð touward heouene, heo goð forte beon isonted. **1603** Shaks. *Meas. for M.* I. iv. 34, I hold you as a thing en-skied, and sainted. **1854** Longf. *Birds of Passage, Prometheus* iv, Only those are crowned and sainted Who with grief have been acquainted.

2. a. *trans.* To call (a person) a saint, give the name of 'saint' to; to reckon among the saints; *spec.* to enroll among the number of saints formally recognized by the Church; to canonize.

1375 Barbour *Bruce* XVII. 875 This thomas, That on this vis maid martir was, Wes sanctit and myraclis did. **1553** Becon *Reliques of Rome* (1563) 180 He [*sc.* Pope John XXII] sainted also Thomas of Aquine the blackefrier. **1601** Weever *Mirr. Mart.* F 3, He praisd, adornd, and for a martyr sainted, Whilst I (Rome's scoffe) my rites of buriall wanted. **1622** Drayton *Poly-olb.* xxiv. 960 There other holy Kings were likewise, who confess'd, Which those most zealous times have sainted. **1628** Earle *Microcosm., Shee Hypocrite* (Arb.) 63 Shee doubts of the Virgin Marie's Saluation, and dare not Saint her. **1690** Norris *Beatitudes* (1692) 135 The most generous and brave Spirits, those whom Paganism has Deify'd, and Christianity has Sainted. **1705** Addison *Italy, Sienna* 391 A Shooe-Maker that has been Beatify'd, tho' never Sainted. **1830** Coleridge *Table-t.* 4 June, [Jeremy] Taylor.. saints every trumpery monk and friar, down to the very latest canonizations by modern popes. **1842** Tennyson *St. Simeon Stylites* 152 They shout, 'Behold a saint!' And lower voices saint me from above. **1906** *Westm. Gaz.* 19 June 5/1 The sandy shores of River Nid, where Holy Olaf's bones were laid to rest before he had been sainted.

†**b.** *fig.* (Also *absol.*) *Obs.*

1597 Bp. Hall *Sat.* I. vii, Sure will he saint her in his Calendere. *a* **1625** Fletcher *Hum. Lieut.* III. iii, If fortune dare play the Slut againe, I'll never more Saint her. **1632** Brome *Novella* IV. i, Lovers shall saint thee; and this day shall be For ever callenderd to Love and thee. **1727–46** Thomson *Summer* 1481 Alfred.. whose hallow'd name the virtues saint. **1728** Pope *Dunc.* II. 357 Prompt or to guard or stab, to saint or damn. *a* **1910** 'Mark Twain' in C. B. Taylor *Margins on Thackeray's 'Swift'* (1935) 47 It would have been enough merely to have forgiven Swift in this paragraph—not sainted him.

3. To cause to be regarded, or to appear, as a saint; to represent as a saint. *rare.*

1609 Daniel *Civ. Wars* I. liii, And in the vnconceiuing vulgar sort, Such an impression of his goodnes gaue As Sainted him. **1649** Milton *Eikon.* Pref. B 3, Though the Picture sett in Front would Martyr him and Saint him to befoole the people. **1701** *Baxter's Paraphr. N.T.* Postscr., However holy Salvian excuse them, and the Life of Bobeline saint them, the generality of Christian Writers disown them. **1853** J. Hamilton *Lives Bunyan,* etc. 176 He fell upon a time when the Church of England contained many men whose genius and piety would have immortalized and sainted them in an earlier age.

absol. **1887** Browning *Parleyings, Bernard de Mandeville* ii, Brave sins which saint when shriven.

†**4. a.** To ascribe holy virtues or a sacred character to. *Obs.*

1652 French *Yorksh. Spa* xvii. 119 Whether this Well was Sainted from its real vertues, or onely supposed vertues. **1655** Fuller *Ch. Hist.* II. iv. §22 After-Ages.. over-acted their part in shrining, sainting and adoring his Relicks. **1657** Reeve *God's Plea* 90 It is an easie matter.. to professe the Gospell, to Saint a fancied cause.

b. To name (something) after a saint. *Obs. rare*$^{-1}$.

1706 Baynard *Cold Baths* in Floyer *Hist. Cold Bathing* II. 319 A.. Well, Sainted with the Name of Anne.

5. *intr.* To act or live as a saint; to live a saintly life; to play the saint. In later use chiefly with *it.*

c **1460** *Towneley Myst.* xiii. 209 *Mak*... I must haue reuerence; why, who be ich?.. Bot, mak, lyst ye saynt? I trow that ye lang. **1530** Palsgr. 697/1, I praye God I saynte than. **1571** *Satir. Poems Reform.* xxviii. 204 Nane I accuse, I come not heir to Sant. *c* **1585** *Faire Em* III. 1280 Let Mistress nice go saint it where she list. **1599** Shaks., etc. *Pass. Pilgr.* 342 Thinke women still to striue with men, To sinne and neuer for to Saint. **1619** W. Sclater *Exp. 1 Thess.* (1630) 183 What need to Saint it in youth? time enough to repent in age. **1735** Pope *Ep. Lady* 15 Whether the Charmer sinner it, or saint it. **1737** Ramsay *Prov.* (1750) 76 Neither sae sinfu' as to sink, nor sae haly as to saunt. **1880** A. I. Ritchie *Ch. Baldred* 26 He sainted it and sinnered it in turns.

saint, variant of cent², seynt.

†**'saintage.** *Obs. nonce-wd.* [f. saint *sb.* after *homage*.] Honour (done) as to a saint.

1657 J. Watts *Vind. Ch. Eng.* 85 When he is before them they must do their Homage, and their saintage unto him.

saint-bell: see sanctus bell.

saintdom ('seɪntdəm). [f. saint *sb.* + -dom.] **a.** The condition or status of a saint. **b.** Saints collectively.

1842 Tennyson *St. Simeon Stylites* 6, I will not cease to grasp the hope I hold Of Saintdom. **1862** M. Napier *Life of Visct. Dundee* II. 82 Nor until that great man, Wodrow, arose, was the Saintdom of Scotland properly recorded. **1887** E. Johnson *Antiqua Mater* 202 Patience.. is a cardinal virtue of Jewish saintdom.

sainted ('seɪntɪd), *ppl. a.* Also 6 sancted. [f. saint *v.* + -ed¹.]

1. Enrolled among the saints; canonized; that is a saint in Heaven.

1631 Weever *Anc. Funeral Mon.* 301 These Sainted Arch-bishops. *a* **1633** Austin *Medit.* (1635) 224 Some others he [*sc.* the Pope] hath let in for Sainted Martyrs, of whom some.. beleeve, that they were rather executed Traitors. **1717** Pope *Eloisa* 312 Love's victim then, tho' now a sainted maid. **1845** Longf. *Norman Baron* x, The lightning showed the sainted Figures on the casement painted. **1855** Macaulay *Hist. Eng.* xx. IV. 397 Lewis [XIV].. instituted.. a new military order of knighthood, and placed it under the protection of his own sainted ancestor [St. Louis].

2. a. Of sanctified or holy life or character.

1605 Shaks. *Macb.* IV. iii. 109 Thy Royall Father Was a most Sainted-King. **1760–72** H. Brooke *Fool of Qual.* (1809) III. 15, I.. pray for a blissful issue to the union of the sainted pair. **1810** Scott *Lady of L.* II. viii, The eve thy sainted mother died. **1826** Disraeli *Viv. Grey* IV. iv, His virtuous and sainted wife. **1867** Freeman *Norm. Conq.* I. v. 302 The former home of sainted princesses.

b. Used trivially as an expletive in phr. ***my sainted aunt*** (also ***mother***)!

1869 'Mark Twain' *Innoc. Abr.* v. 52 'Twenty-five cigars, at 100 reis, 2500 reis!' Oh, my sainted mother! **1916** M. Diver *Desmond's Daughter* II. ii. 50 My sainted aunt! You did ought to have been in the anteroom just now. **1919** F. Hurst *Humoresque* 114 Your sainted mither!.. It's only because she was sainted I'm lettin' ye up in on her. **1921** [see aunt 5]. **1926** 'Sapper' *Final Count* v. 141 Oh! my sainted aunt! don't tell me that old gorse bush was Carl Peterson. **1939** Wodehouse *Uncle Fred in Springtime* xvii. 256 'Oh, my aunt! Don't tell me she's changed her mind and wants the stuff after all?'.. 'Exactly.' 'Oh, my sainted bally aunt!' **1971** R. Roberts *Classic Slum* viii. 127 Self-consciously we incorporated weird slang into our own oath-sprinkled banter—'Yarooh!' 'My sainted aunt!' 'Leggo!' and a dozen others.

3. Such as belongs to or befits a saint; sacred, holy.

1598 *Mucedorus* Epil. 21 Case vicious Diuels vnder sancted Rochets. **1601** Shaks. *All's Well* III. iv. 7 Bare-foot plod I the cold ground vpon With sainted vow my faults to haue amended. **1634** Milton *Comus* 11 Amongst the enthron'd gods on Sainted seats. **1652** French *Yorksh. Spa* xvii. 123 Let not any one judge me to be a Catholick by this my approbation of this Sainted Well. **1760** Smollett *Contn. Hist. Eng.* I. 10 Bolingbroke.. resided at Battersea, where he was visited like a sainted shrine by all the distinguished votaries of wit. **1817** Moore *Lalla R., Paradise & Peri* 351 And, like a glory, the broad sun Hangs over sainted Lebanon. **1848** Thackeray *Van. Fair* l, She rocked him in her arms, and wept silently over him in a sainted agony of tears.

Hence †**'saintedly** *adv.*, in a saintly manner.

c **1789** Terry in T. Campbell *Life of Mrs. Siddons* (1834) II. vi. 149 So saintedly beauteous is the sickness and the grief of Katharine.

St. Elmo (sənt 'ɛlməʊ). Also †**St. Elm, St. Helmo, San Telmo, sant-elmo.** [A corruption, via *Sant'Ermo*, of the name of *St. Erasmus* (martyred 303), Italian bishop and patron saint of Mediterranean sailors; cf. It. *fuoco di Sant'Elmo.*] Used in the possessive, *absol.*, and with *of* to denote the luminous appearance of a naturally occurring corona discharge about a ship's mast or the like, usually in bad weather. Now usu. as *St. Elmo's fire*; = corposant, Helena.

1561 Sant-elmo [see corposant a]. **1621** J. Chamberlain *Let.* 21 July (1939) II. 390 His comming was taken for a goode presage, like the appearing of St. Elmo after a tempest. **1774** Fires of St. Helmo [see fire *sb.* A. 10 b]. **1814** tr. *G. H. Von Langsdorff's Voy. & Trav.* II. iv. 102 In the winter months the air is often so charged with electricity, that for many hours together in the darkest nights a bluish green electrical light, called St. Helen's, or St. Elm's fire, may be seen. **1845** *Encycl. Metrop.* IV. 135/1 The fire of St. Elmo, so frequently seen upon the masts of vessels in the mediterranean, and from very early times connected with the names of Castor and Pollux, meets with a very simple explanation on the principle of a pointed conductor imbibing electricity. **1882** *Encycl. Brit.* XIV. 633/2 This glow is known to sailors as St Elmo's (San Telmo's) fire, in old days Castor and Pollux. **1942** *Tee Emm* (Air Ministry) II. 56 St. Elmo's Fire.. is caused by the aircraft passing through a charged area of cloud and thus charging up itself. .. A glow, and in more extreme cases long streaks of fire appear at the propellers, wing-tips or nose. **1956** G.

Durrell *My Family & other Animals* xvii. 235, I tell you, we'll find the chimney covered with Saint Elmo's fire one night, and before we know where we are we'll be drowned in our beds by a tidal wave. **1969** M. A. Uman *Lightning* 244 Ball lightning and St. Elmo's fire are sometimes confused. St. Elmo's fire is a corona discharge from a pointed conducting object in a strong electric field. Like ball lightning, St. Elmo's fire may assume a spherical shape. Unlike ball lightning, St. Elmo's fire must remain attached to a conductor, although it may exhibit some motion along the conductor. Further, St. Elmo's fire can have a lifetime much greater than the lifetime of the usual ball lightning. **1976** *Scotsman* 20 Nov. (Weekend Suppl.) 1/1 The top of the mast was surrounded with an eerie pale green phosphorescence. This was St. Elmo's Fire—known and feared by seamen of old—caused by static electricity.

saint-errant. *ironical.* ? *Obs.* [Modelled on KNIGHT-ERRANT.] A saint who travelled in quest of spiritual adventures.

1674 Josselyn *Voy. New Eng.* 156 Rhode-Island a Harbour for the Shunamitish Brethren, as the Saints Errant, the Quakers..&c. **1688** H. Wharton *Enthus. Ch. of Rome* 24 At last he [*sc.* Ignatius Loyola] resolved to become Saint-Errant. *Ibid.* 33 Don Quixot fancied that all Knight-Errants went to Heaven, or at least to Purgatory; and surely Saint-Errants deserved to be placed in a higher degree. **1839–40** W. Irving *Wolfert's R.* 316 The fate of these saints-errant had hitherto remained a mystery.

Hence **saint-errantry**, the character, practice, or spirit of a saint-errant.

1688 H. Wharton *Enthus Ch. of Rome* 24 Saint-Errantry was a much easier, and more certain way than Knight-Errantry. **1711** Shaftesb. *Charac.* I. 20 If something of this militant Religion, something of this Soul-rescuing Spirit, and Saint-Errantry prevails still. **1760** Sterne *Serm.* (1764) I. 30 If we can so order it, as not to be led out of the way, by the variety of prospects, edifices, and ruins which solicit us, it would be a nonsensical piece of saint-errantary to shut our eyes. **1826** Southey *Vind. Eccl. Angl.* 173 The system of Saint-Errantry..forms as conspicuous a part of history in this age, as Knight-Errantry in the succeeding centuries.

saintess (ˈseɪntɪs). [f. SAINT *sb.* + -ESS.] A female saint.

1449 in Nichols *Illustr. Manners Ant. Times* 132, Y beseche al the glorious seyntes and seyntesses in heaven [etc.]. **1509** Fisher *Funeral Serm. C'tess Richm.* Wks. (1876) 306 The moost blessyd company of payntes and sayntesses. **1625** Jackson *Creed* v. xxviii. §1 Saints are not our immediate intercessors, but some Saintesse may make immediate intercession. **1737** *Gentl. Mag.* VII. 287/2 This Maid of Orleans, whom divers French Historians picture out as a Saintess. **1865** Freeman in W. R. W. Stephens *Life & Lett.* (1895) I. 334, I made a speech likening her to all the crowned saintesses in ecclesiastical history.

sainthood (ˈseɪnthʊd). [f. SAINT *sb.* + -HOOD.] The condition, status, or dignity of a saint; also, saints collectively.

1550 Bale *Eng. Votaries* II. 85 b, Couplynge it with the degre of hys sayntwode. **1753** *World* No. 8. 45 The supreme honour of monkish sainthood. **1818** Scott *Hrt. Midl.* viii, He felt no call to any expedition which might endanger the reign of the military sainthood. **1879** Farrar *St. Paul* II. 554 The glorious prophecy of Christian sainthood.

†ˈ**sainting**, *vbl. sb. Obs.* [-ING¹.] Enrolment among the number of the saints; canonization.

1563–83 Foxe *A. & M.* 225/2 The saincting of Thomas Becket. **1630** W. T. *Justific. relig. now Prof.* ix. 62 Saints of the Popes Cannonizing and saynting. **1631** Weever *Anc. Funeral Mon.* 298 Theodore succeeded Deodat, as in seat, so in Sainting. *a* **1668** Davenant *Epit. to Mrs. K. Cross* 22 A Land, where many..themselves as Saints esteem; Yet Sainting after Death prophaness deem.

attrib. **1604** Hieron *Answ. to Popish Ryme* E 2, Thou ask'st who them canonized..? You say the Pope. I aske againe, Wilt thou that sainting power maintaine?

saintish (ˈseɪntɪʃ), *a.* [f. SAINT *sb.* + -ISH.] Saint-like. (Chiefly contemptuous.)

1529 More *Dyaloge* iv. Wks. 284/1 Seme he neuer so saintish with any new construccion of Christes holy gospell. **1576** Gascoigne *Steele Gl.* Epil., They be no diuels (I trow) which seme so saintish. **1612** T. Taylor *Comm. Titus* iii. 3 (1619) 618 The affectation of a Saintish puritie. **1814** *Sporting Mag.* XLIII. 375 He could not bear people to be so damned saintish. **1840** Hook in *New Monthly Mag.* LX. 285 Don't think I am getting saintish.

†ˈ**saintism.** *Obs. rare*⁻¹. [f. SAINT *sb.* + -ISM.] The principles or practice of a Puritan 'Saint' (see SAINT *sb.* 3).

1691 Wood *Ath. Oxon.* I. 829/1 The pains he took in converting him to Godliness, *i.e.* to canting Puritanism and Saintism.

saintite, -y, obs. forms of SANCTITY.

St. Kildan (sənt ˈkɪldən). Also †**St. Kildean, St. Kildian.** A native or inhabitant of the island of St. Kilda in the Outer Hebrides.

The island is now the property of the National Trust for Scotland. The last native inhabitants were formally evacuated on 29 Aug. 1930.

1764 K. Macaulay *Hist. St. Kilda* v. 77 The St. Kildians are too wise or too good protestants, to neglect their secular affairs on the festival days of Columba and Brendan. **1819** D. Webster *Topogr. Dict. Scotl.* 375/2 One of the St. Kildans coming to Harris, was attacked with the small-pox, and died. **1842** J. Wilson *Voyage round Coasts of Scotl.* II. i. 9 In another moment we stood on Terra-Kilda... The small group of St. Kildeans..seemed cheered by our arrival. **1861** R. Chambers *Domestic Ann. Scotl.* III. 181 Mr. Macaulay..mentions..that not only is a St. Kildian's person disagreeably odoriferous to a stranger, but 'a stranger's company is..as offensive to them.' **1939** *Geogr. Mag.* X. 73/2 Stac Lee..was much more easily and more often climbed by the St. Kildans than Stac an Armin. **1965** T. Steel *Life & Death of St. Kilda* 10 The St. Kildan can only be described as a St. Kildan, and his island home little else than a republic. **1980** *Times* 22 July 4/2 It is 50 years since the last St Kildans elected to leave the island.

ˈ**saintless,** *a. rare.* [f. SAINT *sb.* + -LESS.]

†**1.** That is no saint. *Obs.*

a **1603** T. Cartwright *Confut. Rhem. N.T.* (1618) 544 That Saintlesse Saint and sinfull Souldier of the Pope, Thomas Becket.

2. That has no patron saint.

1892 *Daily News* 1 Jan. 5/5 The saintless parish church.

ˈ**saintlike,** *a.* [See -LIKE.] Resembling a saint or that of a saint; of saintly life, character, etc.

c **1580** Jefferie *Bugbears* iv. v. in *Archiv Stud. neu. Spr.* XCIX. 40 Who so Saintelike as she? **1651** Howell *Venice* 70 This Prince, as he was one of the stoutest, so was he the Saint-likest man of all the Dukes. *a* **1711** Ken *Preparatives* Poet. Wks. 1721 IV. 113 That I, May Saint-like live, Saint-like to die! **1809** Miss Mitford in L'Estrange *Life* (1870) I. 75 The saintlike meekness and resignation of Lady Jane [Grey]. **1830** Tennyson *Poems* 32 And women smile with saintlike glances Like thine own mother's.

saintliness (ˈseɪntlɪnɪs). [f. SAINTLY + -NESS.] The condition or quality of being saintly.

1837 Howitt *Rur. Life* vi. ii. (1862) 418 The pageantry of processions and the merry saintliness of festivals. **1880** R. W. Dale *Evang. Revival* 268 The inner life of saintliness in all churches has a common root.

saintling (ˈseɪntlɪŋ). [f. SAINT *sb.* + -LING.] A little or petty saint. (Usually contemptuous.)

1622 Boys *Wks.* (1630) 780 For either they worship his saints as himselfe, or else their owne saintlings and not his saints. **1751** Lavington *Enthus. Meth. & Papists* iii. (1754) 180 All the Glory, which Popish and other Saintlings propose by afflicting the Body. **1829** Landor *Imag. Conv.*, *Mahomet & Sergius* Wks. 1853 I. 443/2 The blindest and tenderest young saintling that ever was whelped. **1854** Mrs. Oliphant *M. Hepburn* I. 118 In niches and smaller shrines apart, a host of little saintlings keep their place.

St. Lucian (sənt ˈluːʃən), *sb.* and *a.* **A.** *sb.* A native or inhabitant of St. Lucia in the West Indies. **B.** *adj.* Of or pertaining to St. Lucia.

1844 H. H. Breen *St. Lucia* v. 169 The early refugees, being unwilling to gratify the curiosity of the St. Lucians.. had rallied their numerous inquiries. **1952** S. Selvon *Brighter Sun* viii. 149 Ah sorry for all dem Grenadians and St. Lucians who come over here to make money. **1955** *Caribbean Q.* IV. ii. 99 St. Lucian life has had a consistency and continuity rare in the New World. **1971** *Advocate-News* (Barbados) 17 Sept. (Guyana Suppl.) p. i/1 Barbadians, St. Lucians, St. Vincentians, Grenadians, Dominicans..all of them Guyanese by definition though not by birth..these are the people one meets in almost every hinterland settlement in Guyana. **1973** *Caribbean Contact* Feb. 4/2 In a brief conversation with the St. Lucian born elevator attendant.. Salkey records valuable information. **1978** *Daily Tel.* 11 Mar. 13/1 Because of the to-ing and fro-ing of the two languages, it takes a St. Lucian to understand another St. Lucian when he breaks out into the local Creole patois.

saintly (ˈseɪntlɪ), *a.* [f. SAINT *sb.* + -LY¹.] Of, belonging to, or befitting a saint or saints; of great holiness or sanctity; sainted.

1660 R. Coke *Power & Subj.* 43 The Saintly King Edward Confessor. **1665–6** Pepys *Diary* 17 Jan., The same weake silly lady as ever, asking such saintly questions. **1781** Cowper *Truth* 105 Which is the saintlier worthy of the two? **1819** Keats *Eve of St. Agnes* v, Wing'd St. Agnes' saintly care. **1847** De Quincey *Sp. Mil. Nun* Wks. 1854 III. 53 Solitary Arab's tent, rising with saintly signals of peace, in the dreadful desert. **1868** Milman *St. Paul's* xi. 274 There might..be found Farrers and Bernard Gilpins, of most saintly lives.

†ˈ**saintly,** *adv. Obs.* [-LY².] Holily.

1532 More *Confut. Tindale* Wks. 720/2 Babble he neuer so sayntely. **1653** Ld. Vaux tr. *Godeau's St. Paul* 209 Doe not think your selves so saintly disposed, as is requisite.

sainˈtology. [f. SAINT *sb.* + -OLOGY.] Hagiology. So **sainˈtologist**, a hagiologist.

1848 *Blackw. Mag.* LXIII. 184 Do you know that we have historical painters for modern saintology. **1885** Beveridge *Culross & Tulliallan* I. ii. 65 The later saintologists had a rage for burying all their great saints together. **1892** *Public Opinion* (N.Y.) 5 Nov., The angelology and the saintology of orthodoxy.

saintpaulia (sənt'pɔːlɪə). [mod.L. (H. Wendland 1893, in *Gartenflora* XLII. 321), f. the name of Baron Walter von *Saint-Paul* (1860–1910), German explorer + -IA¹.] A stemless perennial herb of the genus so called, belonging to the family Gesneriaceæ, native to East Africa, and bearing ovate hairy leaves and clusters of violet, pink, or white flowers; esp. a pot plant of the species *Saintpaulia Ionantha*, the African violet.

1895 Hofmarschal Baron St. Paul in *Curtis's Bot. Mag.* CXXI. 7408 The *Saintpaulia* was discovered by my son, who lives in East Africa. **1946** M. Free *All about House Plants* xv. 127 If you carefully examine a Saintpaulia which has been growing in the house all winter you will see..that it has split up into several crowns. **1961** *Amateur Gardening* 14 Oct. 27/2 It would be best to divide the saintpaulia when it finishes flowering. **1974** *Times* 5 Oct. 12/2 Millions of African violets, saintpaulias, are sold every year, but vast numbers do not live for long in houses or flats.

†ˈ**saintrel.** *Obs.* [a. OF. *sainterel*, dim. of *saint.* Cf. SANTREL.] A saintling.

c **1440** *Promp. Parv.* 451/2 Seyntrelle, *sanctillus, sanctilla.*

saints-, saint's bell: see SANCTUS BELL.

saintship (ˈseɪnt-ʃɪp). [f. SAINT *sb.* + -SHIP.]

1. The condition or status of a canonized saint.

1631 Heylin *St. George* 206 From thence to prove St. George's Saintship. **1639** Fuller *Holy War* iii. xxii. 150 After his [*sc.* Dominic's] death, Pope Honorius for his good service bestowed a Saintship on him. **1700** Osborn *Let.* in Maundrell *Journ. Jerus.* (1707) T 4 b, His Body being found so entire would have entitled him to Saintship. **1818** Bentham *Ch. Eng.* 35 Saint Dunstan,..whose Saintship consisted in pulling the unclean spirit by the nose. **1866** Rogers *Agric. & Prices* I. vii. 138 The veneration for Becket's memory, acknowledged by his elevation to the honour of saintship.

2. The condition of being a saint or saintly person; saintliness of life or character.

1613 Purchas *Pilgrimage* 328 These must be beliued for this Saint-ship, although they lie neuer so shamefully. *a* **1675** Glanvill *Ess. Philos. & Relig.* vii. (1676) 31 Each Sect confin'd the Church, Saintship, and Godliness to it self. **1732** Pope *Ep. Bathurst* 349 The Dev'l was piqu'd such saintship to behold. **1812** Byron *Ch. Har.* i. xi, Whose.. eyes..Might shake the saintship of an anchorite. **1859** Geo. Eliot *A. Bede* ii, He had felt sure that her face would be mantled with the smile of conscious saintship. **1871** Lowell *Pope* Wks. 1890 IV. 11 From the compulsory saintship..of the Puritans men rushed..to the opposite cant of sensuality.

3. With possessive pron. prefixed, used as a kind of title. Often *ironical.*

1606 Warner *Alb. Eng.* xv. xcviii. 389 Their Saintships are as capable thereof as sinfull men. **1668** H. More *Div. Dial.* iv. xxvii. 151 Where he did his Devotions to his Saintship with prayer and fasting in most humble manner. **1717** De Foe *Mem. Ch. Scot.* 15 They pulled St. Giles out of his Throne,..threw his Saintship into the Dirt. **1850** P. Crook *War of Hats* 8 Beside his saintship stands the holy nun, who broke her vows. **1893** A. Walters *Lotos Eater in Capri* vii. 149, I feel bound to throw what light I can upon his saintship's rather obscure personality.

Saint-Simonian (ˌseɪnt-, səntsɪˈməʊnɪən), *a.* and *sb.* Also St.- [f. *Saint-Simon* (see below) + -IAN.] **a.** *adj.* Belonging to or characteristic of the socialistic system propounded by the Comte de Saint-Simon (1760–1825), who advocated state control of all property and a distribution of the produce according to individual vocation and capacity. **b.** *sb.* An advocate of this system. Also **Saint-Simonist, -Simonite** (ˈsaɪmənɪst, -aɪt) in the same sense (also *attrib.* or as *adj.*). Hence **Saint-Siˈmonianism, -ˈSimonism,** advocacy of or adherence to this system.

1829 J. S. Mill *Let.* 7 Nov. in *Wks.* (1963) XII. 40, I object altogether to the means which the St Simonists propose for organizing the *pouvoir spirituel.* **1830** —— *Ibid.* 9 Feb. 45 His objections to the Saint-Simonian philosophy. *Ibid.* 48 France must pass through several states before it arrives at St Simonism. **1831** *Monthly Repos.* Mar. 189 The exposition of the Saint Simonian faith or doctrine. *Ibid.* Apr. 279 The St. Simonite faith. *Ibid.* Feb. 82 The French sect of Saint Simonites and the 'New Christianity' of its Founder. **1831** J. S. Mill *Let.* 20–22 Oct. 76 A Christian would be positively less fit than a St Simonian (for example), to form part of a national church. **1832** *John Bull* 6 Feb. 46/3 Massacre of old men and women in the Midi—Abbé Chatel—and Saint Simonists. **1833** J. S. Mill *Let.* 25 Nov. 193 The great majority have retained of St Simonianism about as much as is good and true, dropping the rest. **1841** Mary Hennell in C. Bray *Philos. Necess.* II. 610 St. Simonianism and Fourierism. *Ibid.* 562 The completion of the St. Simonian doctrine is to be found in the future full development of the religious sentiment which it contemplates. *Ibid.* 555 *note*, The St. Simonians complain that Guizot in reviewing the course of history has borrowed the ideas of their master. **1848** Mill *Pol. Econ.* ii. i. §4 (1865) I. 264 The two elaborate forms of non-communistic Socialism known as St. Simonism and Fourierism. **1863** Fawcett *Pol. Econ.* ii. i. 122 St. Simonism, even if it alleviated poverty would introduce greater evils. **1952** F. A. von Hayek *Counter-Revolution of Sci.* iv. 144 The greatest of the Saint-Simonians..and the medium through whom many of them had received the doctrine of the master, was Auguste Comte. **1953** S. Spencer *Creative Element* ii. 54 At the end of *Une Saison en Enfer* Rimbaud seems, indeed, to wish to reconcile Christianity with Saint-Simonist socialism. **1974** *Times Lit. Suppl.* 25 Jan. 66/2 He suggests that Heine saw himself as a Saint Simonian prophet and that Saint Simonianism, not the 1830 revolution, drew him to Paris. **1976** A. W. Gouldner *Dialectic of Ideol.* xii. 274 The surprising continuities between the Saint-Simonian formulations and the Weberian.

St. Trinian's (sənt ˈtrɪnɪənz). The name of a girls' school invented by the cartoonist Ronald Searle (b. 1920) in 1941. Used *absol.* and *attrib.* to designate allusively the characteristic style of hoydenish behaviour, school uniform, etc., of the girls in the cartoons and the subsequent associated books and films.

Searle's daughters attended St. Trinnean's school in Edinburgh.

[**1941** R. Searle in *Lilliput* IX. iv. 313 (*caption*) Owing to the international situation the match with St. Trinian's has been postponed. **1948** D. B. Wyndham Lewis in R. Searle *Hurrah for St. Trinian's* 8 Those typical English Roses, the girls of St. Trinian's, a nightmare synthesis of Roedean, Heathfield and Wycombe Abbey.] **1958** *Times* 20 May 11/4 How the girls of to-day, finishing at St. Trinian's or taking their degrees at St. Jude's, will smile with affectionate tolerance at these meagre achievements in the scholastic line. **1961** *Guardian* 3 Mar. 10/4 A St Trinian's type of schoolgirl. **1964** C. DALE *Other People* iv. 88 She was big and fat and pasty... In her school uniform..she looked a complete St. Trinian's type. **1972** *Guardian* 25 Jan. 9/2 Louis Feraud..includes a group of dresses called schoolgirl frocks..Lolita lives again, and one longs for the innocence of St Trinian's. **1977** 'D. CORY' *Bennett* iii. 93 His high-pitched St Trinian's giggle. **1981** R. BARNARD *Sheer Torture* xi. 121 Aunt Kate..an overgrown product of St Trinian's.

†**saintuaire.** *Obs.* Also 4 **sa(y)ntuare, seyntwar(e,** *Sc.* **sanctwar,** 5 **sayntware.** [a. OF. *saintuaire, santuaire*, semi-pop. ad. late L. *sanctuārium* (see SANCTUARY).] Sanctuary.

a **1300** *Cursor M.* 688 And ilk waand þat þai þere bare He sperd wit-in þer santuare [*Gött., Trin.* seyntwar(e]. *Ibid.* 8274 þat hali arke þai bare A-bute, wit all þair santuare. *c* **1375** *Sc. Leg. Saints* vii. (*Jacobus Minor*) 65 He of þe apostolis all In-to þe sanctwar can ga. **1390** GOWER *Conf.* I. 14 In libraire Which longeth to the Saintuaire. *a* **1400–50** *Alexander* 1567 Of þe saynt-ware many sere thingis.

saintuary, obs. form of SANCTUARY.

†**sainty.** *Obs. rare*⁻¹. In 6 **seynty.** ? A mock-affectionate formation on SAINT *sb.*

a **1529** SKELTON *E. Rummyng* 583 There was a pryckemedenty, Sat lyke a seynty, And began to paynty, As thoughe she would faynty.

saip, Sc. var. SOAP.

saipheron, obs. f. SAFFRON.

sair, Sc. var. SAVOUR, SERVE *v.*, SORE.

saircenett, obs. form of SARSENET.

sais: see SAY and SEE *v.*; var. SYCE.

saise, saisen, etc., obs. ff. SEIZE *v.*, SEISIN.

saisin, variant of SASIN, Indian antelope.

†**saisne.** *Obs. rare.* Also **sasne.** [a. OF. *Saisne*:—L. *Saxonem* SAXON.] = SAXON.

c **1450** *Merlin* xii. 176 Thei were in grete affray, and withoute counseile of the saisnes, that all day rode thourgh the londe. *Ibid.* 172 We haue herde the trouthe that the sasnes of the kyn of Aungier, of Saxoyne, be entred in-to oure londes and in-to oure heritages.

sait, obs. Sc. f. SEAT *sb.*, SET *ppl. a.*; obs. pa. t. of SIT *v.*

Saite ('seɪaɪt), *sb.* and *a.* [ad. L. *Saītē-s* sb. and adj., a. Gr. *Σαΐτης*, f. *Σάϊς*, Sais: see -ITE.] **a.** *sb.* An inhabitant of Sais. **b.** *adj.* = SAITIC *a.*

1678 CUDWORTH *Intell. Syst.* 342 *marg.*, Theopompus affirmeth the Athenians to have been a Colony of the Saites. *Ibid.* 479. **1866** *Chamb. Encycl.* VIII. 432/1 Many fine statues of basalt of the 26th or Saite dynasty.

saithe (seɪθ). *Sc.* Forms: 7 **sheath,** 7–9 **seath,** 8 **seeth,** 8–9 **saith, seth,** 9 **se(e)the, seythe,** 9– **saithe.** [a. ON. *seið-r* (Edda Gl.), mod.Norw. *seid, sei,* Icel. *seið, seiði* fry of codfish. Cf. Gael. *saigh, saighean* (*saoidhean, saoithean*), the coal-fish; Irish *saoidhean* (Dinneen) the young of any fish, esp. of the codfish or coal-fish.] The mature coal-fish. Also *attrib.*

1632 LITHGOW *Trav.* x. 500 Ling, Turbet and Seaths. *c* **1680** in *Macfarlane's Geogr. Collect.* (S.H.S.) III. 248 It is called Shetland, because in old time, there were many Sheath-fish caught about its Coast. **1710** SIBBALD *Hist. Fife & Kinross* 52 *Asellus Niger*, the Cole-fish of the North of England; our Fishers call it a Colman's-Seeth. **1792** *Statist. Acc. Scotl.* IV. 79 The fish commonly taken on this coast, are cod,..whitings, saiths or cuddies. **1793** *Ibid.* VII. 397 The tenants have from their landlords..a halfpenny for a seth (colefish). **1836** YARRELL *Brit. Fishes* (1841) II. 251 Among the Scotch islands the Coalfish is called Sillock,..Sethe, Sey, and Grey Lord. **1863** JOHNS *Home Walks* 114 Shoals of small fish, principally Sethe and Lythe. **1873** BLACK *Pr. Thule* xxvii, He proposed he should go ashore and buy a few lines with which they might fish for young saithe or lythe over the side of the yacht. **1892** *Gentlew. Bk. Sport* I. 67 The process of making a saithe-fly is very simple. **1895** *Athenæum* 14 Sept. 349/2 The angler may easily make a large catch either of mackerel or of pollack, seythe or herrings.

Saitic (seɪ'ɪtɪk), *a.* [ad. L. *Saïtic-us*, a. Gr. *Σαϊτικός*, f. *Σαΐτης*: see SAITE and -IC.] Of or pertaining to Sais, the ancient capital of Lower Egypt. ***Saitic dynasties***: the 26th and four following dynasties of the kings of Egypt. Hence ***Saitic period, art,*** etc.

1678 CUDWORTH *Intell. Syst.* 506 That excellent Monument of Egyptian Antiquity, the Saitick Inscription often mentioned, I am all that Was, Is, and Shall be. **1826–7** G. C. RENOUARD in *Encycl. Metrop.* (1845) XVIII. 411/2 The third [mouth of the Nile], called the Saïtic. **1836** G. HIGGINS (*title*) Anacalypsis, an attempt to draw aside the veil of the Saitic Isis; or, an inquiry into the origin of languages, nations, and religions. **1884** AMELIA B. EDWARDS in *Encycl. Brit.* XVII. 21/2 The Saitic period (Dynasties XXVI. to XXX.) is distinguished by the minute finish and artistic beauty of its sculptured sarcophagi.

saitt, obs. Sc. f. SEAT *sb.*; obs. pa. t. of SIT *v.*

saiv, obs. Sc. form of SAFE.

Saiva ('ʃaɪvə), *sb.* and *a.* [a. Skr. *śaiva* relating, belonging, or sacred to Siva; a worshipper or follower of Siva.] **A.** *sb.* A member of one of the three great divisions of modern Hinduism, exclusively devoted to the worship of the god Siva as the Supreme Being. **B.** *adj.* Of or pertaining to this division of Hinduism.

1810 E. MOOR *Hindu Pantheon* 15 *Saivas* or worshippers of Siva. **1842** *Penny Cycl.* XXII. 65/2 The great Saiva reformer, Sankara Acharya. **1876** *Encycl. Brit.* IV. 210/1 The *Śaiva, Vaishnava,* and *Sākta* sects. **1974** *Encycl. Brit. Macropædia* VIII. 893/2 Most Śaiva worship is not systematic but a complex amalgam of pan-Indian Śaiva philosophy and local or folk worship.

Hence **'S(h)aivism** = SIVAISM; **'S(h)aivite** *sb.* and *a.* = SIVAITE.

1867 R. MILMAN *Jrnl.* 21 Nov. in F. M. Milman *Mem. R. Milman* (1879) iii. 48 This temple is reckoned..the holiest shrine in India..among Shaivites. **1877** MONIER WILLIAMS *Hinduism* viii. 97 Śaivism and Vaishṇavism are not opposite or incompatible creeds. **1882** *Encycl. Brit.* XIV. 228/1 Saivite gods or devils. **1924** E. M. FORSTER *Passage to India* xxxvii. 323 They cantered..past a Saivite temple, which invited to lust, but under the semblance of eternity. **1956** R. REDFIELD *Peasant Society & Culture* 88 The important Vaishnavaism and Shaivism are theistic and ethical. **1969** *Indo-Asian Culture* Oct. 70 Both Saivism and Vaishnavism were popular in Srihatta and the neighbouring region during the late Gupta and mediæval times. **1972** 'E. PETERS' *Death to Landlords!* x. 153 A Saivite sadhu seated in contemplation.

saixe, variant of SAX *sb.*¹ (a slater's tool).

saj (sɑːdʒ). [Hindi.] The Indian laurel, *Terminalia tomentosa*, a tropical tree of the family Combretaceæ, native to India and Burma and bearing terminal spikes of yellow flowers; also, the dark hardwood produced by this tree and others of the genus. Also *attrib.*

1839 E. W. LANE tr. *Arabian Nights* II. xiii. 384 Its door was of sáj, adorned with brilliant gold. **1931** J. W. BEST *Tiger Days* xii. 173 Nobler trees take their place; the stately saj and the dark-limbed ebony. **1952** J. MASTERS *Deceivers* viii. 88 The man..started back..and began to run toward a thin line of saj trees bordering the road.

sajene, variant of SAGENE.

‖**sajou** (saʒu). [Fr., shortened from *sajouassu* (Buffon), a. Tupi *saiuassu*, f. *sai* (*sahy, çahy*) monkey (see SAI) + *-uassu* augmentative suffix.] One of various small South American monkeys, varieties of Sapajous, and Capuchin monkeys.

1774 GOLDSM. *Nat. Hist.* III. 236 The third [of the sapajous] is the Sajou; distinguished from the rest of the sapajous by its yellowish, flesh-coloured face. **1855** W. S. DALLAS in *Orr's Circ. Sci., Zool.* II. 503 The White-throated Sajou (*Cebus hypoleucos*).

sak, obs. form of SAC¹, SACK *sb.*¹, *sb.*²

Saka ('ʃækə), *sb.* and *a.* Also **Çaka, Saca,** [Skr. *Saka*; cf. Gr. pl. *Σάκαι*, L. pl. *Sacæ*.]

A. *sb.* **a.** (A member of) an ancient Indo-Scythian people originating in central Asia. **b.** The language of this people, = KHOTANESE *sb.*

[**1601** P. HOLLAND tr. *Pliny's Nat. Hist.* VI. xvii. 123 Beyond the realme Sogdiana, inhabit the nations of the Scythians. The Persians were wont to call them in generall Sacas, of a people adjoining unto them, so named. **1795** J. NOTT tr. *Catullus' Poems* I. xi. 35 Whether he treads Hircanian ground; Or seeks the gentle Arab's home; The Parthians, for the dart renown'd; Or mid the Sacæ's doom'd to roam.] **1880** H. W. BELLEW *Races of Afghanistan* ii. 18 The province itself derived its name of Sákistán..from the Sáka, who were probably the same people as the Sáká Hámuvarga mentioned in the tables of Darius. **1934** AHMAD & AZIS *Afghanistan* vii. 45 Driven from their home in Central Asia the Sakas migrated into Kashmir. **1961** [see *Indo-Scyth* s.v. INDO-¹]. **1966** G. S. LANE in Birnbaum & Puhvel *Anc. Indo-European Dial.* 223 Of the fifty-one words submitted as possible borrowings from Iranian, twenty-one are attested in Saca (Khotanese), or on various grounds appear to be for the most part of Saca origin. **1972** W. B. LOCKWOOD *Panorama Indo-European Lang.* 237 The Persians are said by Herodotus to have called the various Scythian tribes Saka... Rich manuscript remains of Saka came to light in Turkestan... The language of Khotan is called Khotanese Saka or simply Khotanese... Saka appears to survive in the mountains to the west. **1974** *Encycl. Brit. Macropædia* I. 173/1 Iranian tribes of nomadic Śaka..seem, before 130 BC, to have made a pact with the Parthians and to have settled in Sīstān whence they spread eastward..into India.

B. *adj.* **a.** Of or pertaining to this people or their language. **b.** In Indian chronology, designating or pertaining to an era reckoned from A.D. 78

1883 [see MAHAYANA]. **1886** *Encycl. Brit.* XXI. 854/1 The ancient Aryan inscriptions usually employ the Saka (Salivahana) era, dating from 79 A.D. **1923** *Cambr. Hist. India* I. xxiii. 585 It was in consequence of its long use by the Çaka princes of western India that the era has become generally known in India as the Çaka era—a name which effectually disguises its origin, and one which has in no small degree perplexed modern scholars in their endeavours to unravel the secret of Kamishka! **1932** W. L. GRAFF *Lang.* 371 Other Middle Iranian documents, especially known through recent discoveries, represent the Sogdian and Saka dialects. **1956** R. PIERIS *Sinhalese Social Organization* II. 92 The Saka era was made use of in all legal instruments... It is said to date from a king Saka. **1958** O. CAROE *Pathans* iv. 63 Greek or Macedonian soldiers were needed to guard the frontier marches against the Saka nomads. **1974** *Encycl. Brit. Macropædia* IV. 574/2 The Śaka, or Salivāhana, era (AD 78), now used throughout India, is the most important of all. It has been used not only in many Indian inscriptions but also in ancient Sanskrit inscriptions in Indochina and Indonesia. The reformed calendar promulgated by the Indian government from 1957 is reckoned by this era. It is variously alleged to have been founded by King Kaniṣka or by the Hindu king Salivāhana or by the satrap Nahapāna.

Hence **'Sakian** = SAKA *sb.* b.

1933 L. BLOOMFIELD *Language* iv. 63 Other medieval Iranian languages, which have been identified as *Parthian, Sogdian,* and *Sakian.* **1939** [see KHOTANESE *sb.* and *a.*].

sakabula (sækə'bʊlə). *S. Afr.* Also **sac(c)aboola,** etc. [a. Zulu *iSakabuli* widow-bird.] The long-tailed widow-bird, *Euplectes progne*, of the family Ploceidæ, the male of which is black, with red patches on the wings and very long tail-feathers. Also *fig.*

1877 LADY BARKER *Year's Housekeeping S. Afr.* ix. 179 Lynx tails hung down like lappets on each side of her face which was over-shadowed and almost hidden by the profusion of sakabula feathers. **1885** RIDER HAGGARD *King Solomon's Mines* viii. 127 They wore upon their heads heavy black plumes of Sacaboola feathers, like those which adorned our guides. **1896** H. L. TANGYE *In New S. Afr.* iv. 105 One of the most strange inhabitants of the Transvaal is a small black bird, the Sakabula. **1912** *E. London Dispatch* 20 July 3 They bartered the highly prized tail feathers of the sakaboola bird. **1937** S. CLOETE *Turning Wheels* 362 A saccabula, gorgeous in his black spring feathers, his wings blotched with red, flew past them followed by his wives that were grey and dull. **1951** R. CAMPBELL *Light on Dark Horse* x. 144 The finest variety [of widow-bird], the 'Sakabula', is quite a common sight. **1973** *Weekend Post* (Port Elizabeth) 28 Apr. 3 The long-tailed black widow birds commonly known as sakabullas.

Sakai ('sɑːkaɪ), *sb.* (and *a.*) Also 9 **Sakkye.** [Malay, lit. subject, dependent.] **a.** An aboriginal people of the Malay peninsula (loosely used of Malayan aborigines collectively); a member of this people. **b.** The language of the Sakai. Also *attrib.* or as *adj.*

1839 T. J. NEWBOLD *Pol. & Statistical Acct. Straits of Malacca* I. vii. 421 The Semangs, Sakkye, or Orang Bukit, men of the hills. **1886** *Jrnl. Anthrop. Inst.* Feb. 285 In this state of Perak there is at present besides the Sakais one other race, the Sĕmang. *Ibid.*, The Sakai race inhabits the left bank of the Perak River. **1906** [see JAKUN]. **1920** R. J. WILKINSON *Hist. Peninsular Malays* (ed. 2) i. 3 The fair wavy-haired aborigines known as the Sakai inhabit both sides of the Malayan main range. *Ibid.* 8 The grammar..of Sakai is extraordinarily complex and inflected. **1932** L. GOLDING *Magnolia St.* III. vi. 538 The people seemed stranger to him than the pygmies of the African jungle or the Sakais of Malaya, who live up in the hills and make their clothes out of the bark of trees. **1952** P. D. R. WILLIAMS-HUNT *Introd. Malayan Aborigines* i. 1 *Sakai*, used generally for Aborigines is a derogatory term which is disliked by most jungle dwellers. **1966** *Telegraph* (Brisbane) 18 Nov. 2/3 Malaya's aborigines, the little brown jungle men called Sakai, tried out a little modern technology. **1977** P. THEROUX *Consul's File* 43 The local *sakais*—they might have been Laruts—had deported some wild monkeys there.

sakawinki (sækə'wɪŋkɪ). Also 8–9 **saccawinkee,** 9 **sakka winkee,** 20 **sak(k)iwinki(e.** [Corruptly a. Du. *sagwijntje*, dim. of *sagwijn*: see SAGOIN.] A South American monkey, the White-headed Saki, *Pithecia pithecia* or *capillamentosa*. Also, a South American squirrel monkey of the genus *Saimiri*.

1769 E. BANCROFT *Guiana* 135 The Saccawinkee is the smallest of the Ape tribe in Guiana. **1796** STEDMAN *Surinam* II. xvi. 13 So very delicate is the saccawinkee, and so sensible of the cold, that scarcely one of them is brought to Europe alive... The Dutch call them the *shagarintee*, from their being chagrined at the smallest trifle. **1845** *Encycl. Metrop.* XXIII. 396/1 *Pithecia Capillamentosus*, Spix;.. Native of French Guiana, where it is called the Sakka Winkee, and also of Brazil. **1903** DES VOEUX *Colonial Service* I. 90 One or two sakawinki or marmoset monkeys. **1954** G. DURRELL *Three Singles to Adventure* i. 38 'What are they?'.. 'Squirrel monkeys, but I don't know what they call them here.' 'Sakiwinkis, Chief.' **1958** J. CAREW *Black Midas* vi. 102 Behind us, sakki-winki monkeys chattered, and toucans screamed. *Ibid.* vii. 155 Red howlers roared..and tinamous and saki-winkies joined in.

sake (seɪk), *sb.*¹ Forms: 1 **sacu,** 2– **sake;** also 4–5 **sak(k,** (4 **saac, sack,** 5 **saacke,** 6 **sacke),** 4–6 *Sc.* **saik, sayk,** (5 **saike, salk,** 6 **saek, sayck).** [OE. *sacu* str. fem. = OFris. *sake, seke* affair, thing, sake, OS. *saka* lawsuit, enmity, guilt, thing (MLG., MDu. *sake* lawsuit, affair, cause, reason, guilt, Du. *zaak* lawsuit, cause, sake, thing), OHG. *sahha* cause, sake, thing (MHG. *sach(e,* mod.G. *sache* thing, affair), ON. *sǫk* crime, accusation, action at law, cause, sake (Sw. *sak*, Da. *sag* in the same senses; also, influenced by Ger., thing):—OTeut. **sakā*, related to the str. vb. **sak-*, represented by OE. *sacan* to quarrel, fight, claim at law, accuse, OS. *sakan* to accuse, OHG. *sahhan* to strive, quarrel, rebuke. From the same root are OE. *sæc(c* (:—**sakjā*), Goth. *sakjô* (:—**sakjōn*), strife. An ablaut-variant of OTeut. **sak-* is probably the **sōk-* represented by SEEK *v.*, q.v. for the cognates outside Teutonic.

The only use surviving in mod.Eng. ('for the sake of') has not been found in OE., and was prob. adopted from ON. It existed, however, in OHG. and OFris., and there is a possibility that it may have been in OE., though not evidenced in the literature. It seems to have arisen from the use of the sb. to denote a litigant's cause or case (see 1 b). Cf. L. *causā*.]

†**I.** As an independent substantive. *Obs.*

1. Contention, strife, dispute; in OE. also, a contention at law; a suit, cause, action.

Beowulf 154 Grendel wan hwile wið Hroðgar, heteniðas wæʒ..singale sæce. **a 1000** *Laws of Hlothhære & Eadric* 8 ðif man oþerne sace tihte. **c 1000** ÆLFRIC *Gen.* xiii. 7 Wearð ..sacu betwux Abrames hyrdemannum and Lothes. **c 1175** *Lamb. Hom.* 95 He ne remde ne of bitere speche nes, ne he sake ne asterde. **c 1205** LAY. 26290 And æðmodliche hine beden þat he wið Romleode summe sake arerde. **a 1250** *Owl & Night.* 1160 Oþer þu bodest cheste an sake. **c 1320** *Sir Beues* (A.) 3510 So þai atonede wiþ oute sake.

2. A charge or accusation (of guilt); a ground of accusation. ***without sake***, without good reason (= L. *sine causa*).

c 1200 ORMIN 10211 Her he forrbæd te cnihhtess ec..To sekenn sakess o þe follc, To rippenn hemm & ræfenn. **a 1300** *E.E. Psalter* iii. 7 Alle to me witherwendand With-outen sake or any skil [Vulg. *omnes adversantes mihi sine causa*]. **a 1300** *Cursor M.* 27483 If þou man gas þin offrand to mak, And þi broþer haf gain þi sak. **c 1300** *Harrow. Hell* 37 (Digby MS.) Hi nomen me wiþouten sake, Bounden min honden to mi bake. **c 1375** *Sc. Leg. Saints* ii. (*Paulus*) 167 Nero, mesure þi gret foly, and sla na man fore-owt sake. **a 1400** *Pistill of Susan* 204 We schul presenten þis pleint,..And sei sadliche þe soþ, riȝt as we haue sene, O Sake.

3. a. Guilt, sin; a fault, offence, crime. Often coupled with *sin*.

Beowulf 2472 Ða wæs synn and sacu Sweona and ʒeata,.. wroht ʒemæne. **a 1000** *Phœnix* 54 (Gr.) Nis ðær on ðam londe..synn ne sacu. **c 1200** ORMIN 1127 Þa lakess mihhtenn clennsenn hemm Off sakess & off sinness. **a 1300** *Cursor M.* 11553 For he moght find nan wit sak, On þe sakles he suld ta wrake. *Ibid.* 29022 Fasting flemes flexsli sakes. **13..** *E.E. Allit. P.* A. 800 þat gloryous gyltlez þat mon con quelle, With-outen any sake of felonye. **c 1400** A. DAVY *Dreams* 90 And so shilde fro synne & sake! **a 1400–50** *Alexander* 3213 þat sloȝe so þaire soueraine þat neuire sake hadd.

b. ***without sake***, without guilt, fault, or blame (both as adj. and as adv. phrase). Hence *transf.* = without physical blemish.

a 1250 *Owl & Night.* 1430 Heo mai hire guld at-wende arihte weie þurh chirche-bende, an mai efte habbe to make hire leof-mon wiþ-ute sake. **a 1272** *Luve Ron* 62 in *O.E. Misc.* 95 Him waxeþ þouhtes monye and fele hw he hit may witen wiþ-vten sake. **a 1300** *Cursor M.* 4043 He [Joseph] was fair, wit-outen sake. *Ibid.* 6067 And siþen sal ilk hus in-take A clene he lambe, wit-vten sake. **c 1375** *Sc. Leg. Saints* xxiv. (*Alexis*) 33 þat noble wyf anna,..treuly to god seruit ay in þe tempil, nycht & day, foure schore of ȝere, forout sak.

4. *nonce-use.* Regard or consideration for some one. [After *for the sake of* in sense 6.]

1590 SPENSER *F.Q.* I. v. 12 Tho mov'd with wrath, and shame, and Ladies sake.

5. (See quot. 1879[2]). *nonce-use.*

1876 G. M. HOPKINS *Wreck of Deutschland* xxii, in *Poems* (1967) 58 Five! the finding and sake And cipher of suffering Christ. **1879** —— *Henry Purcell* in *Ibid.* 80 Let him oh! with his air of angels then lift me, lay me! only I'll Have an eye to the sakes of him, quaint moonmarks, to his pelted plumage under Wings. **1879** —— *Lett. to R. Bridges* (1955) 83 *Sake* is a word I find it convenient to use:..it is common in German, in the form *sach.* It is the *sake* of 'for the sake of'. .. I mean by it the being a thing has outside itself, as a voice by its echo, a face by its reflection,..a man by his name, fame, or memory, *and also* that in the thing by virtue of which especially it has this being abroad,..as for a voice and echo clearness; for a reflected image light, brightness;..for a man genius, great achievements... In this case it is, as the sonnet says, distinctive quality in genius.

II. Phr. ***for the sake of*** (also †***for sake of***); ***for*** (one's, a thing's) ***sake***.

In the latter of these forms, the word which precedes *sake* is a possessive (noun or pronoun); but down to the middle of the 19th c. the *'s* of the possessive of common or abstract nouns was very commonly omitted (doubtless owing to the difficulty of pronouncing the two sibilants in succession), and from the 17th to the early 19th c. the two sbs. were often connected by a hyphen, as if forming an attributive compound. The omission of the *'s* is now obsolete, but it is still not uncommon to write *for conscience sake*, *for goodness sake*, *for righteousness sake*, etc., without the apostrophe which is ordinarily used to mark the possessive of words ending in a sibilant.

The paragraphs marked β contain illustrations of the omission of the *'s*; some of the early examples there placed must be explained by the fact that the sbs. occurring in them (e.g. *soul*) had originally no *s* in the genitive.

6. a. Out of consideration for; on account of one's interest in, or regard for (a person); on (a person's) account.

a 1225 *Leg. Kath.* 98 For hare sake ane dale ha etheold of hire ealdrene god. **a 1250** *Owl & Night.* 1589 þat gode wif ..al for hire louerdes sake haueþ daies kare & niȝtes wake. **a 1300** *K. Horn* 1454 þis tur he let make Al for þine sake. **1375** BARBOUR *Bruce* VII. 244 Scho said, 'all that traualand ere, For saik of ane, ar velcom here'. **c 1375** *Sc. Leg. Saints* ii. (*Paulus*) 596 Fore I hafe schawit hym quhat he mone thole for þe sayk of me. **1530** TINDALE *Gen.* xviii. 31, I will not distroy them for twenties sake. *Ibid.* 32, I will not destroy them for .x. sake. **1590** SHAKS. *Mids. N.* II. ii. 103 And run through fire I will for thy sweet sake. **1595** J. KING *Queens Day Serm.* in *On Jonas* (1618) 703 Hee spareth our countrie for his anointeds sake. **1784** COWPER *Task* VI. 637 Content to hear..Messiah's eulogy for Handel's sake! **1875** JOWETT *Plato* (ed. 2) I. 277 For my own sake as well as for yours, I will do my very best. **1884** J. PAYN *Some Lit. Recoll.* 6 When it became necessary for him to exert himself for the sake of his family.

β. **1338** R. BRUNNE *Chron.* (1810) 135, & þus quathe he his þing, for his soule sake. *Ibid.* 292 For þe comon sake. **1390** GOWER *Conf.* II. 229 For Thetis his moder sake. **a 1400–50** *Alexander* 1813 And for þaire souerayne sake þam send to þe galawis. **c 1420** *Avow. Arth.* xvii, This socur thou hase send me, For thi Sune sake! **c 1450** *Mirour Saluacioun* 4087 Crist descendid to helle fro the heven for mankynde sake.

†**b.** Occas. with unfavourable notion: On account of enmity to; because of the guilt of. *Obs.*

a 1300 *Cursor M.* 162 Herode kyng wit wogh For crist sak þe childer slogh. **c 1375** *St. Andreas* 96 in Horstm. *Altengl. Leg.* (1881) 5/1 Or els I sall for þi god sake Ger hang þe right on swilk a tre Als þou sais suld so honorde be. **1530** TINDALE *Gen.* iii. 17 Cursed be the erth for thy sake.

c. When the preceding genitive is pl., the pl. *sakes* is often used.

1530 TINDALE *Gen.* xviii. 26, I will spare all the place for their sakes. **1567** *Gude & Godlie Ball.* (S.T.S.) 181 All the exempillis of the Law Ar writtin..For our saikis. **1588** SHAKS. *L.L.L.* v. ii. 765 For your faire sakes haue we neglected time. **1596** —— *Tam. Shrew* v. ii. 15 For both our sakes I would that word were true. **1716** ADDISON *Freeholder* No. 9 ¶14 We desire you will put yourself to no farther Trouble for our sakes. **1864** TENNYSON *En. Ard.* 505 'Then for God's sake', he answer'd, 'both our sakes, So you will wed me, let it be at once'.

7. a. Out of regard or consideration for (a thing); on account of, because of (something regarded in the light of an end, aim, purpose, etc.); often = out of desire for, in order to attain, etc.

a 1225 *Ancr. R.* 4 Ye schullen..wel witen þe inre [riwle] & þe uttre vor hire sake. **1390** GOWER *Conf.* II. 217 For lucre and nought for loves sake. **1393** LANGL. *P. Pl.* C. v. 99 For consciences sake. **1593** Q. ELIZ. *Boeth.* v. pr. iv. 110 For argumentes sake, mark what wold follow. **1643** BURROUGHES *Exp. Hosea* vii. (1652) 281 Men in their prosperity are not regarded for any thing in themselves, but for their prosperities sake, for their moneys sake, for their cloaths sake. **1691** WOOD *Ath. Oxon.* II. 689 This year..one Fabian Philipps..was a Student and Sojournour in the University for the sake of the Bodleian Library. **1693** *Humours Town* 56 One that drinks for drink's sake. **1711** ADDISON *Spect.* No. 35 ¶10 He pursues no Point either of Morality or Instruction, but is Ludicrous only for the sake of being so. **a 1770** JORTIN *Serm.* (1771) I. i. 10 It is doing mischief for mischiefs sake. **1790** PALEY *Horæ Paul.* Wks. 1825 III. 132 The business for the sake of which the journey was undertaken. **1816** KIRBY & SP. *Entomol.* (1818) I. ix. 289 The icteric oriole is kept by the Americans in their houses for the sake of clearing them of insects. **1875** JOWETT *Plato* (ed. 2) III. 63 Flattering of rich men for the sake of a dinner. **1875** T. W. HIGGINSON *Hist. U.S.* ix. 66 There was no persecution for opinion's sake.

β. ? **a 1500** *Chester Pl.* ii. 274 Adam, husband, I red we take thes figg-leaves for shame sake. **1535** COVERDALE *Matt.* xiv. 9 Neuertheles for yᵉ ooth sake [*Mark* vi. 26 for the oothes sake]. **1571** DIGGES *Pantom.* III. xi. R iv, I shall for breuitie sake set foorth one onely rule generall. **1594** HOOKER *Eccl. Pol.* Pref. i. §1 To suffer all things, for that worke sake which we couet to performe. **1605** BACON *Adv. Learn.* I. vii. §16 It was mooued by some after supper, for entertainement sake. **1621** BP. MOUNTAGU *Diatribæ* 404 We are pitied, for fashion-sake of many, relieved of none. **1731** in *Swift's Lett.* (1766) II. 127 To flatter a man, from whom you can get nothing,..is doing mischief for mischief-sake. **1754** RICHARDSON *Grandison* (1810) IV. xiv. 111 For sex-sake, for example-sake, Lucy, let it not be known. **1784** COWPER *Let. to Unwin* Wks. 1836 V. 57, I am writing in the greenhouse for retirement sake. **1815** *Edin. Rev.* XXV. 398 Imagery or mere declamation, that is, speaking for speaking-sake. **1833** *Tracts for Times* No. 10. 3 It is our duty to reverence them for their office-sake. **1853** J. H. NEWMAN *Lect. Turks* i. (1854) 13, I shall call..the populations..Tartars, for convenience-sake. **1865** SWINBURNE *Chastelard* IV. i, For sweet marriage-sake.

†**b.** Because of, by reason of, through; in return or requital for. *Obs. rare.*

1340–70 *Alex. & Dind.* 283 But say þou nouht, sire king, for sake of enuie þat me were loþ of our lif ludus to teche. **a 1400–50** *Alexander* 2022 And for þe sake of þi sede þou sent wᵗ þi lettre, Loo, here a purse full of pepire my powere to ken. **c 1400** *Laud Troy Bk.* 8902 Some of hem her deth schal take, Er it be nyȝt, for that wounde sake. **1622** MABBE tr. *Aleman's Guzman d'Alf.* I. 158 Fearing lest for my sinnes-sake..I might be taken in some trap.

c. ***for one's name('s) sake***, out of regard for one's name; also ***for name sake***.

This has been suggested as the origin of NAMESAKE, q.v.

1526 TINDALE *Acts* ix. 16, I wyll shewe hym howe grett thynges he must suffer for my names sake. **1599** *Warn. Faire Wom.* II. 915, I love you for your name-sake. **1638** BRATHWAIT *Barnabees Jrnl.* III. (1818) 97 Thence to Harrington, be it spoken! For name-sake I gave a token To a beggar. **1685** BAXTER *Paraphr. N.T.* Matt. xix. 29 All.. that lose and forsake any thing here, for my Name-sake.

8. In exclamatory phrases of adjuration, as ***for God's sake***, ***for goodness' sake***.

For further illustration see GOODNESS 5, GOD *sb.* 11, MERCY *sb.* 4, PITY *sb.* 2 c.

a 1300 *Cursor M.* 4800 And i yow pray, for drightin sak [*Gött.* for goddes sake]. **c 1386** CHAUCER *Sompn. T.* 24 Now spede yow hastily for cristes sake. **a 1533** LD. BERNERS *Huon* lxxxviii. 279 For goddes sake aduyse you well that ye come not there. **1535** COVERDALE *Ps.* vi. 4 Oh saue me, for thy mercies sake. **1879** HOWELLS *L. Aroostook* xvi, Hold on, for Heaven's sake! **1885** 'F. ANSTEY' *Tinted Venus* 32 'For goodness' sake, say something', he cried wildly.

†**9.** With a pronominal adj. in place of the possessive. ***for that sake***, for the sake of that, on that account, for that reason. ***for any sake***, in any case, at all events. ***for many sakes***, out of consideration for many things. *Obs.*

Quot. 1879 appears to be an unauthorized extension of this use.

13.. *S. Eng. Leg.* (MS. Bodl. 779) in *Archiv Stud. neu. Spr.* LXXXII. 321/512 A frere hadde I-trespased & for þat ilke sake a disciplyne he cholde habbe. **c 1350** *Will. Palerne* 2019 þer-fore for soþe gret sorwe sche made, & swor for þat sake to suffur alle peynes. **a 1425** *Cursor M.* 3771 (Trin.) She sent him soone into aram To hir broþer þat het laban þere to soiourne for þat sake Til his broþþer wraþþe wolde slake. **1597** SHAKS. *Lover's Compl.* 322 Aye me I fell, and yet do question make, What I should doe againe for such a sake. **1754** RICHARDSON *Grandison* (1810) IV. xlii. 317 He shall, for many sakes, find it very difficult to provoke me. **1824** MISS FERRIER *Inher.* xv, For any sake let us have one night of peace and rest. **1879** L. S. BEVINGTON *Key-notes* 133 Men are aglow to live for some great sake, Or die, if need be.

10. Phr. †***for sake('s) sake***: (*a*) euphemistically = 'for God's sake', in adjurations; (*b*) for the sake of some person understood; (*c*) for its own sake. *Obs.* Also, ***for old sake's sake***: for the sake of old friendship.

1665 R. HOWARD *Four Plays, Committee* III. 101 Run after him, and save the poor Fellow for Sakes sake. **1690** DRYDEN *Amphitryon* II. i, Meaning some Body, that for sake-sake shall be nameless. **1728–9** MRS. DELANY *Life & Corr.* (1861) I. 191 Cupid knows he is only civil to me for sakes's sake. **1742** RICHARDSON *Pamela* III. 86 But alas, Madam, he was not so well pleased with my Virtue, for Sake's sake, as Lady Betty thinks he was. **1857** HUGHES *Tom Brown* I. iii, I've a been long minded to do't for old sake's sake. **1863** KINGSLEY *Water-Bab.* v. 216 Yet for old sake's sake she is still, dears, The prettiest doll in the world. **1886** STEVENSON *Dr. Jekyll* 17, I continue to take an interest in him for old sake's sake as they say.

11. ***sakes alive!*** and simply ***sakes!***: a vulgar exclamation expressing surprise. *dial.* and *U.S.*

1846 MRS. KIRKLAND *West. Clearings* 78 'Law sakes alive!' was the reply, 'I ain't no how'. **1860** BARTLETT *Dict. Amer.* (ed. 3) s.v., 'La sakes!' 'massy sakes!' 'sakes alive!' are very common exclamations among the venerable matrons of the interior parts of the country. The first two expressions are evidently corruptions of 'for the Lord's sake!' 'for mercy's sake!' **1883** *Harper's Mag.* Dec. 91/2 Good sakes alive!—what harm? **1896** J. DE BOYS in *Pall Mall Mag.* Apr. 548 Clever! Sakes! You call *him* clever!

‖**saké** ('sɑːkɪ, 'sækeɪ), *sb.*[2] Forms: 7 saque, 8 sakki, 9 saki, sake, saké. [Japanese *sake*.] A Japanese fermented liquor made from rice. (Hence used by the Japanese as a name for alcoholic liquors generally.)

1687 A. LOVELL tr. *Thevenot's Trav.* III. 112 Their ordinary drink is a kind of Beer (which they call Saque) made of Rice. **1797** *Encycl. Brit.* (ed. 3) IX. 71/1 Sakki, or rice-beer, is clear as wine, and of an agreeable taste: taken in quantity, it intoxicates for a few moments, and causes headach. **1878** MISS J. J. YOUNG *Ceramic Art* 170 Saki, or Sake, is the chief alcoholic drink of Japan, and is made from rice. **1901** HOLLAND *Mousmé* 315 Oblige me with a glass of whisky sake. **1916** [see *brown rice*]. **1917** E. POUND *Lustra* 189 We drink our parting in saki. **1931** G. B. SANSOM *Japan* I. iii. 52 The new season's rice and *sake* of the new brew. **1947** R. BENEDICT *Chrysanthemum & Sword* v. 101 Every sip of *sake* doled out to them before going into battle. **1947** J. BERTRAM *Shadow of War* 273 The guards looted the *saké* from their own stores. **1958** G. MIKES *East is East* 56 Drinking *sake*, watching dancing and listening to singing. **1978** M. PUZO *Fools Die* xxxv. 409 She kept filling my cup with some sort of wine, the famous sake, I guessed.

attrib. **1884** GORDON in *Mission. Herald* (Boston) 310/2 (Stanf.) A little beyond lives a young saké brewer. **1885** E. GREEY *Bakin's Captive Love* i. (1904) 12 Raising the saké-bottle from the hot-water vessel. *Ibid.* iii. 26 Acquaintances recently made in the saké-shops. **1957** A. THWAITE *Home Truths* 53 And fill my *saké* cup again. **1960** B. LEACH *Potter in Japan* v. 118 An immense sake bowl was filled with about 4 gallons of hot wine. **1979** 'J. MELVILLE' *Wages of Zen* ii. 17 Otani held out his *sake* cup and she refilled it.

sake, *v.* Aphetic form of FORSAKE.

a 1300 *Cursor M.* 17183 And sua ur sinnes for to sake [*Gött.* to forsake]. **c 1400** *Rule St. Benet* (Verse) 592 Trew charite so for to sake. **c 1420** *Metr. St. Kath.* (Halliw.) 11 For sche sakyth owre lay!

sake, obs. form of SAC[1], SACK *sb.*[1], SHAKE.

†**saked**, *a. Obs.* [f. SAKE *sb.* + -ED[2].] Guilty.

a 1300 *Cursor M.* 1223 Vnseli caym þat ai was saked [*Gött.* þat was forsakid]. *Ibid.* 27471 And if he wat and warnis noght O ded es he saked if it be wroght.

sakeen, variant of SKEEN (Himalayan Ibex).

Sakel: see SAKELLARIDIS.

sakelease, -lests: see SACKLESS.

Sakellaridis (sækə'lærɪdɪs), **Sakellarides** (-ɪdiːz). Also shortened to **Sakel** ('sækəl). [The name of Σακελλαρίδης, a Greek cotton-grower who originated the variety.] The name of a superior variety of Egyptian cotton, widely grown in the early 20th century.

1912 W. L. BALLS *Cotton Plant in Egypt* vi. 105 The main varieties at present cultivated on a commercially important scale are Yannovitch and Sakellaridis in the 'fine-spinning' group; [etc.]. *Ibid.* 106 One of the cherished fables of the practician teaches that heavy crops and fine staple cannot co-exist. The inaccuracy of this belief, though long suspected, has only recently been proved by the Sakel variety. **1915** J. A. TODD *World's Cotton Crops* xiv. 276 Sakellarides, or Sakel, as it is commonly called, is a comparatively new variety, dating from about 1907. **1931** *Times* 17 Nov. 13/1 With Sakellaridis at 7d. per lb. **1953** *New Biol.* XIV. 49 The famous Sakellarides variety, selected by a Greek of that name in the early years of this century, has become a parent of most or all of the better quality Egyptian varieties now being bred. **1955** CHRISTIDIS & HARRISON *Cotton Growing Probl.* iii. 119 After 1887, a number of varieties acquired prominence; among them.. Sakellaridis or Sakel (1909)..could be mentioned. All are now extinct, even Sakel. **1958** BROWN & WARE *Cotton* (ed. 3) iii. 71 In 1918 several crosses were made between Pima and Sakel (Sakellarides), the latter having become the most prominent variety in Egypt following Mit Afifi.

saker[1] ('seɪkə(r)). Forms: 5 sagre, 6 sagar, 5–9 sacre, 6– **saker**. [a. F. *sacre*, ad. Sp., Pg. *sacro*, It. *sagro*, prob. a. Arab. *çaqr*.

In form the Sp., Pg. and It. word coincides with the adj. repr. L. *sacer* SACRED; it has in consequence been supposed to mean 'sacred falcon' (cf. mod. scientific Latin *Falco sacer*), and Diez ingeniously conjectured that the designation was suggested by a confusion between Gr. ἱέραξ falcon and ἱερός sacred.]

A large lanner falcon (*Falco sacer*) used in falconry, esp. the female, which is larger than the male, the latter being distinguished as *sakeret*.

'A related falcon of western North America, *Falco polyagrus* or *F. mexicanus*, is known as the *American saker*' (Cent. Dict. 1891).

c **1400** MAUNDEV. (Roxb.) xxv. 117 Laneres, sagres [(1839) xxii. 338 *reads* Sacres], sperhawkes. **1486** *Bk. St. Albans* d iv, There is a Sacre and a Sacret. And theis be for a knyght. *c* **1530** LD. BERNERS *Arth. Lyt. Bryt.* (1814) 327 Some behelde the tournes and tournynges of the sakers and gerfawcons. **1580** HOLLYBAND *Treas. Fr. Tong, Vn Sacret*, the tiercelet of a Saker. **1606** BRETON *Sidney's Ourania* H 1 b, The princely Sagar and the Sagaret. **1623** MIDDLETON & ROWLEY *Span. Gipsy* II. i. 102 Let these proud sakers and gerfalcons fly. **1668** CHARLETON *Onomast.* 65 *Falco Sacer*..the Saker, or British Falcon. **1755** SMOLLETT *Quix.* (1803) IV. 87 As a saker or jerfaulcon darts down upon a heron. **1873** TRISTRAM *Moab* xii. 226 The Saker (*Falco sacer*) is much prized here, and is well known as distinct from the peregrine and the lanner. **1888** *Daily News* 25 Aug. 3/4 A fine Asiatic hawk (a Saker).

saker[2] ('seɪkə(r)). Now *Hist.* or *arch.* Also (6 sakir, *Sc.* saikyr), 6–7 sacre, (sakar, 7 sacar, 9 erron. sacker). [a. F. *sacre* (= It. *sagro*), a transferred use of *sacre* SAKER[1]. (Cf. *falconet*, *musket*.)] An old form of cannon smaller than a demi-culverin, formerly much employed in sieges and on ships.

1521 LD. DACRES in *Archæologia* XVII. 205 First of grete peces, a Saker, Two Faucons, viij small Serpentyns. **1546** *St. Papers Hen. VIII*, XI. 145 Mr. Seymour,..beyng chased furst by that knave cowerd Burley, and put in gret dawnger with the shot of a sacre. **1549** *Compl. Scot.* vi. 41 Mak reddy ȝour cannons,..saikyrs, half saikyrs, and half falcons. **1556** J. HEYWOOD *Spider & F.* lii. 23 Potgoons, sakirs, cannons, double and demie. **1624** CAPT. SMITH *Virginia* v. 197 He found small hope to recouer any thing, saue a Cable and an Anchor, and too good Sacars. **1652–62** HEYLIN *Cosmogr.* III. (1682) 226 Culverin, Sakar, Minion, and other the like Ordnance of Brass. **1713** DERHAM *Phys. Theol.* I. iv. 28 According to my own Observations made with one of Her Majesties [Qu. Anne] Sakers,..a Bullet.. flies [etc.]. **1881** PALGRAVE *Visions of Eng.* 135 Shooting from musket and saker a scornful death-tongue of flame. **1881** GREENER *Gun* 21 Four sizes of cannon..called respectively, cannons, culverins, sackers and falconets.

b. *attrib.* as ***saker shot***, etc.

1547 *Acts Privy Council* (1890) II. 133 Sacre-wheles shod and unshod, three payr. *c* **1556** TOWRSON in *Hakluyt's Voy.* (1599) II. II. 38 The 14 day we came within Saker-shot of the castle. *c* **1595** CAPT. WYATT *R. Dudley's Voy. W. Ind.* (Hakl. Soc.) 60 With a fayre saker shott they strake the verie blade of his leadinge staff into manie peeces. **1666** in *10th Rep. Hist. MSS. Comm.* App. v. 8 Captain John Bartlett.. returneing into his Majestie's store 40 saker shott, being six poundes weight. **1669** STURMY *Mariner's Mag.* v. xii. 65 A Saker-bore Piece of Iron. *a* **1690** RUSHW. *Hist. Coll.* III. II. 281 [1643] A Demi-Culverin, Four small Drakes in one Carriage, a Sacre-Cut [see CUT *sb.*[2] 31 a].

†**saker**[3]. *Obs. rare*⁻¹. [App. of Fr. origin: cf. '*sacquerelle*, a dock for a horses tayle' (Cotgr.); also *saquarelle* 1553 in Godefr.] = DOCK *sb.*[2] 2 a.

1607 MARKHAM *Caval.* v. (1617) 31 This done you shall buckle on his breast plate, and his crooper,..then you shall lace on his saker or docke.

sakeret ('seɪkərɪt). *Obs.* or *arch.* Forms: 5 sacrette, 5–7 sacret, 6 sagaret, 7 sakret, sacaret, sakaret, 8– **sakeret**. [a. F. *sacret*, dim. of *sacre* SAKER[1].] The male of the 'saker'.

c **1400** MAUNDEV. (1839) xxii. 238 Faukons gentyls, Lanyeres, Sacres, Sacrettes. **1486** Sacret, **1606** sagaret [see SAKER[1]]. **1610** W. FOLKINGHAM *Art of Survey* IV. iii. 83 Hawlkes: as the Falcon,..Saker, Sakret, Marline. **1655** WALTON *Angler* i. (1661) 13 Of the first kind [*sc.* long-winged hawks], there be chiefly in use amongst us..the Saker and Sacaret. **1688** R. HOLME *Armoury* II. 236/1 A Sacret or Sakaret is the male of a Saker or Sacre. **1721** BAILEY *Sakeret*, the Male of a Saker Hawk. And in later Dicts.

sakeret, obs. var. pa. t. and pa. pple. of SACRE *v.*

sakerfyse, obs. form of SACRIFICE.

sakering(**e**, **-yng**(**e**, obs. forms of SACRING.

sakett, obs. form of SACKET.

†'**sakful**, *a. Obs.* [OE. *sacfull*, f. *sacu* SAKE + *full* -FUL.] **a.** Contentious, quarrelsome. **b.** Guilty, criminal.

c **1000** ÆLFRIC *De octo vitiis* in *Lamb. Hom.* 301 Se seofoþa unþeaw is þæt se cristena mann beo sacfull [*c* **1175** *Ibid.* 113 sacful]. *a* **1300** *Cursor M.* 26678 Bot þai na be samen partenar Sekand til an sakful dede.

sakhaite ('sækheɪaɪt). *Min.* Also sahaite. [ad. Russ. *sakhaít* (I. V. Ostrovskaya et al. 1966, in *Zapiski vsesoyuznogo min Obshchestva* XCV. 193), f. *Sakha*, name of the locality in Siberia where it was discovered: see -ITE[1].] A hydrous borate and carbonate of calcium and magnesium, the crystals of which belong to the cubic system and occur as greyish white masses.

1966 *Chem. Abstr.* LXV. 3567 A new mineral, called sakhaite.., was found during study of magnesian skarns in Siberia. **1970** *Canad. Mineralogist* X. 694 The formula of sakhaite was recalculated in an attempt to determine whether a relationship existed between sakhaite and harkerite. **1975** *Soviet Physics Doklady* XIX. 559/1 We have studied the synthetic analog of sahaite..under hydrothermal conditions in the $CaO-MgO-B_2O_3-CO_2-H_2O$ system.

saki ('sɑːkɪ). [a. F. *saki* (Buffon), app. incorrectly a. Tupi *çahy*: see SAI.] A South American monkey of the family *Cebidæ*, of either of the two genera *Pithecia* or *Brachyurus*; also with various defining names.

1774 GOLDSM. *Nat. Hist.* (1776) IV. 236 Of the sagoins with feeble tails, there are six kinds. The first and the largest, is the Saki. **1780** SMELLIE *Buffon's Nat. Hist.* (1791) VIII. 201 The saki, which is commonly called the fox-tailed monkey,..is the largest of the sagoins. **1896** H. O. FORBES *Hand-bk. Primates* I. 183 The hairy Saki. *Pithecia monachus*. *Ibid.* 185 The white-headed saki. *Pithecia pithecia*. **1898** *Daily News* 22 Aug. 5/1 An interesting South American Saki monkey known as *Pithecia chiropotes*.

saki, variant of SAKÉ *sb.*[2]

‖**sakia** ('sɑːkɪə). Forms: 7 saki, 8 sakiah, 9 sakie, sackiyeh, sageer, sakhyia, sak(i)yeh, sakieh, sakia. [Arab. *sāqiyaʰ*, *fem. pr. pple. of saqā* to irrigate. In North Africa the *q* is pronounced (g), whence the form *sageer*.] A machine for drawing water for irrigation, consisting of a large vertical wheel to which a number of earthen pots are attached, and to which motion is imparted by a horizontal wheel turned by oxen or asses.

1687 A. LOVELL tr. *Thevenot's Trav.* I. 139 Eight Sakis turned all by Oxen, that discharge Water into a great Bason. **1796** MORSE *Amer. Geog.* II. 603 (Stanf.) One of the ways in which the water is generally raised is by the Sakiah, or Persian wheel. **1832** *Veg. Subst. Food* 21 The Nubian cultivators..employ sakies, or water-wheels, for the purpose of irrigating the fields during the summer. **1836** LANE *Mod. Egypt.* (1848) II. 163 Another machine..almost the only one used for the irrigation of gardens in Egypt, is the 'sákiyeh'. **1844** KITTO *Phys. Hist. Palestine* vii. 295 The *Sackiyeh*,..which is usually in all places called 'the Persian Wheel'. **1866** BAKER *Albert N'Yanza* II. 37 Saat..works away with his spoon like a Sageer (water wheel),..the soup disappearing like water in the desert. **1873** LELAND *Egypt. Sketch-Bk.* 50 A *sakhyia* or water-wheel, turned by oxen or donkeys. **1885** C. G. W. LOCK *Workshop Receipts* Ser. IV. 93/1 In Egypt, under the name of *sakia*, this machine is in common use.

attrib. **1873** W. CORY *Lett. & Jrnls.* (1897) 324 The two characteristic sounds are the sakyeh creak, and the chattering of villagers at sunset.

sakin, variant of SKEEN (Himalayan Ibex).

sakir, obs. form of SAKER[2] and SACRE *v.*

sakke, obs. form of SACK *sb.*[1], *sb.*[3]

sakket, **sakki**, obs. ff. SACKET, SAKÉ *sb.*[2]

saklace, **-las**, **-les**, obs. ff. SACKLESS.

Sakmarian (sæk'mærɪən), *a. Geol.* [ad. Russ. *Sakmarskiĭ* (first used as a stratigraphical term by A. Karpinsky 1874, in *Zap. Imperatorskago Min. Obshchestva* IX. 269), f. *Sakmara*, name of a river in the Southern Urals: see -IAN.] Name of a stage in the Lower Permian in the Soviet Union; of or pertaining to this stage and the rocks that characterize it, and the geological age during which they were deposited. Freq. *absol.*

1936 V. E. RUZHENTSEV in *Problemỹ Sovetskoĭ Geologii* VI. 506 The upper Carboniferous is overlain in complete conformity by the Permian system which begins with Schwagerina beds. The writer defines by the name Sakmarian the whole of the deposits with Schwagerina princeps Ehr. and with the Ammonoid fauna described for the first time from the Sakmara river... The Sakmarian consists of sandy-argillaceous beds among which there are many conglomerates. **1960** *Bull. Geol. Soc. Amer.* LXXI. 1766/2 It is now the official usage of the Geological Survey of the U.S.S.R. to draw the base of the Permian below the Sakmarian and equivalent beds in the Ufa Plateau. **1963** D. W. & E. E. HUMPHRIES tr. *Termier's Erosion & Sedimentation* i. 20 Lakes and marshes are known in the northern hemisphere which were contemporaneous with the Stephanian and Sakmarian glaciers of the Southern hemisphere. **1974** *Nature* 8 Feb. 396/1 McLachlan and Anderson have recorded orthocerid nautiloids, the brachiopod *Attenuatella*, [etc.]..from the base of the succession near Kimberley. They favoured a Sakmarian age for this marine incursion.

sakor, variant of SACRE *v.*

†'**sakre**. *Obs. rare.* Also sacre, sakar. [Of obscure origin.] Some kind of sea-going vessel.

1546 *St. Papers Hen. VIII*, XI. 255 He toke occation to aske me..whethur I wolde goo to Callayes or Boulloigne by land, orelles in the gallyes with hym, or in the sakre which was taken by the gallyes, the which the King his masters pleasour was should be delyveryd agayne. *Ibid.*, [The writer replied] neither seyeng that I wold receave the saied sacre, nor that I wold refuse her. **1590** NASH *Pasquil's Apol.* B 4, Penrie..was built but for a Flie-boate, to take and leaue, when the skyrmish is too hote for him to tarrie, he may sette vp his sayles and runne away... Tantara, tantara, is he fled indeede? let me sende a Sakar after him.

sakred, obs. var. pa. t. and pa. pple. of SACRE *v.*

sakret, variant of SAKERET.

sakring, **-ryng**, obs. forms of SACRING.

Sakta ('ʃɑːktə). Also 9 **Sacta**. [a. Skr. *śākta* relating to power or to the Sakti; a worshipper of the Sakti.] A member of one of the principal sects of modern Hinduism which worships the Sakti or divine energy, especially as indentified with Durgā, the wife of Siva. Also *attrib.* Cf. SAIVA *sb.* and *a.* Hence '**Saktism**, the worship of the Sakti.

1810 E. MOOR *Hindu Pantheon* 116 Those, of whatever sect, who worship exclusively the female power..are called Sactas. **1845** *Encycl. Metrop.* XXIV. 443/1 The Hindús are almost always either 1. Vaïshnavas..; 2. Saïvas..; or 3. Sáktas. **1877** MONIER WILLIAMS *Hinduism* ix. 123 Tāntrism, or Śāktism, is Hindūism arrived at its last and worst stage of medieval development. **1920** [see NADA[1]]. **1931** G. MACMUNN *Relig. India* 69 The Sakta groups have borrowed much from aboriginal practices and influence. *Ibid.* 160 The really secret cult of Saktism. **1974** *Encycl. Brit. Macropædia* VIII. 896/2 The Tantric movement is not rarely inextricably interwoven with Śāktism. *Ibid.* 897/2 Śākta adepts are trained to direct all their energies toward the conquest of the Eternal.

Sakti ('ʃæktiː). Also 9 **Sacti**; **Shakti** and with small initial. [a. Skr. *śakti* power, divine energy, f. *śak* to be able.] In Hindu religion, the female principle, esp. when personified as the wife of a god, as Durgā is the Sakti of Siva, etc.; supernatural energy embodied in the principle.

1810 E. MOOR *Hindu Pantheon* 10 All the principal, and several of the secondary deities..have wives assigned to them, who are called Sacti. **1842** *Penny Cycl.* XXII. 67/1 That thou, united with thy Sakti, dost in sport create the universe from thy own substance. **1862** MRS. J. B. SPEID *Our Last Yrs. in India* vii. 174 Seresvati, the goddess of letters, &c., Lackshmi, of prosperity, and Kali or Parvati, of destruction... These three goddesses, under the name of the Sactis, sometimes receive an exclusive worship. **1871** J. GARRETT *Classical Dict. India* 540 The Sakti is said to have originated in God, the Supreme Being... There are many special forms of Sakti-worship. **1918** J. WOODROFFE *Shakti & Shâkta* 49 According to Shâkta doctrine each man and woman contains within himself and herself a vast latent magazine of Power or Shakti. **1922** JOYCE *Ulysses* 499 It has been said by one: beware the left, the cult of Shakti. **1937** M. COVARRUBIAS *Island of Bali* x. 339 Every Balinese believes that his body, like an electric battery, accumulates a magic energy called *sakti* that enables him to withstand that attacks of evil powers... This *sakti* is not evenly divided; some people are born with a capacity to store a higher charge of magic than others; they become the priests, witch-doctors, and so forth, endowed with supernatural powers. **1962** A. HUXLEY *Island* xiii. 213 Paintings of tropical animals, Bodhisattvas and their bosomy Shaktis. **1968** A. WARHOL *A* 421 He doesn't have any bhakti it's all shakti. **1972** D. BLOODWORTH *Any Number can Play* xviii. 184 In thirty times thirty years will come one with the ears of the Buddha and with the *sakti*... Supernatural power. **1977** *N.Y. Times Mag.* 4 Dec. 144 Joya's famous *shakti*, or spiritual energy.

sakura (sə'kʊərə, ‖sa'kura). [Jap.] A flowering cherry tree belonging to one of the many varieties bred from various species of *Prunus*; also, the blossom or wood of a tree of this kind.

1884 tr. *J. J. Rein's Japan* II. iii. 471 *Yoshino*..once the residence of the anti-emperors, a famous old place with many Sakura (Prunus pseudocerasus). **1892** F. T. PIGGOTT *Garden of Japan* 19 *P*[*runus*] *pseudocerasus—sakura*, with enormous pink double flowers. **1911** *Encycl. Brit.* XV. 175/2 The wood used is generally that of the cherry-tree, *sakura*, which has a grain of peculiar evenness and hardness. **1948** C. INGRAM *Ornamental Cherries* 13 Will you please tell me why you are so very fond of our Sakura—our Cherries? **1963** *Times* 22 Apr. 11/7 Famous songs such as '*Sakura, Sakura*' (Cherry blossom, Cherry blossom) elicited no gleam of sentiment. **1970** J. KIRKUP *Japan behind Fan* 41 The season when the *sakura* or cherry blossom blooms.

sakyre, obs. variant of SACRE *v.*

‖**sal**[1] (sæl). *Chem.*, *Alch.*, and *Pharm.* [L. (masc. and neut.) = salt.]

† **1.** = SALT *sb.*[1] (in various senses). *Obs.*

c **1386** CHAUCER *Can. Yeom. Prol. & T.* 257 Sal tartre, Alkaly, and sal preparat. **1460–70** *Bk. Quintessence* 12 Sal comen preparate. *a* **1626** MEVERELL in *Baconiana Physiol.* (1670) 117, I can truly and boldly affirm, that there are no such principles as Sal, Sulphur, and Mercury, which can be separated from any perfect Metals. **1674** JEAKE *Arith.* (1696) 662 All Sublunary Bodies consist of the three principal Substances, Sal, Sulphur, and Mercury.

2. With qualifying word: †**sal anatron** = ANATRON; **sal attincar** = ALTINCAR; †**sal lambrot**, corrupt form of *sal* ALEMBROTH; †**sal marine** [med.L. *sal marinus*], common salt (see MARINE *a.* 1 b); **sal mirabile** (-is) [mod.L., 'wonderful salt', so named by Glauber], Glauber's salts, sulphate of soda; **sal soda**, †**sode** [med.L. *sal sodæ*], crystallized sodium carbonate; †**sal-tartre** [med.L. *sal tartari*], salt of tartar. See also *sal* ALEMBROTH, *sal* ALKALI, *sal* POLYCHREST; SAL-AMMONIAC, SAL ENIXUM,

SALERATUS, SAL-GEM, SAL-NITRE, SALPETRE, SAL-PRUNELLA, SAL VOLATILE.

1775 Ash, *Salanatron, Anatron, a kind of native salt. **1471** Ripley *Comp. Alch.* Adm. v. in Ashm. (1652) 190 *Sal Attinckarr. **1678** Phillips (ed. 4), **Sal Lambrot*, or *Salebrot*. **1670** W. Simpson *Hydrol. Ess.* 7 They..become determined into a saline Body; in one place into Allom, in another in *Sal-marine. **1875** *Ure's Dict. Arts* III. 739 Sal marine is common salt (chloride of sodium). **1719** Quincy *Compl. Disp.* 33 Glauber's *Sal Mirabilis, which is made of common Salt and Vitriol. **1879** *Encycl. Brit.* X. 675 Glauber's Salt,..formerly known as 'sal mirabile Glauberi'. **1471** Ripley *Comp. Alch.* Adm. v. in Ashm. (1652) 190 Sal Peter, *sal Sode, of these beware. **1884** A. Watt *Soap-making* 93 The dried sal-soda is produced by passing currents of hot air through the crystals until they fall into a powder. **1890** *Anthony's Photogr. Bull.* III. 129 Sal soda gives detail and bromide gives contrast. *c* **1386** *Sal tartre [see 1 above]. **1471** Ripley *Comp. Alch.* Adm. v. in Ashm. (1652) 190 Sal Tarter, sal Comyn, sal Geme most clere. **1610** B. Jonson *Alch.* i. iii, I, I know, you'haue arsnike, Vitriol, sal-tartre, argaile, alkaly, Cinoper. **1683** Pettus *Fleta Min.* ii. 121 Sal Tartar.

†**b.** Short for SAL VOLATILE. *Obs.*

1703 Rowe *Ulyss.* Epil., Your Sal, and Harts-horn Drops.

sal[2] (sɑːl). Also saul, zoll. [Hindī *sāl* = Skr. *sāla*.] A valuable timber tree of India, *Shorea robusta* yielding the resin dammar. Also *attrib.*

1789 Saunders in *Phil. Trans.* LXXIX. 80 Saul timber, bamboo, and plantains. **1800** *Suppl. Chron.* in *Asiat. Ann. Reg.* 131/2 The forest, thro' which we passed, consisted of saul trees, setsaul, bamboos. **1866** *Chamb. Encycl.* VIII. 435/2 Great sal forests exist along the southern base of the Himalaya Mountains. **1867** Smyth *Sailor's Word-bk.*, *Zoll*, or *Saul*, an Indian timber, much used in the construction of country vessels. **1873** Miss R. H. Busk *Sagas fr. Far East* 331 His death..took place under a Shala-grove, or grove of sal-trees. **1875** Bedford *Sailor's Pocket Bk.* ix. (ed. 2) 336 The Teak and Saul of India. **1901** *Harper's Mag.* CII. 775/2 The gate was of solid sal-wood.

†**sal**[3] (sæl). *Theatr. slang. Obs.* Abbrev. of SALARY *sb.* 1.

1844 E. R. Lancaster *Manager's Daughter* (ed. 2) in *Oxberry's Budget of Plays* I. 110/1 Who does he suppose was to cut comic mugs before noblemen, without being paid double sals.? **1870** O. Logan *Before Footlights* xxxii. 433 'You're earning your sal easy,' says Clown to him with some reproach. **1885** *Househ. Words* 29 Aug. 350/1, I say that part of this money shall be shared among us as 'sals', and some of the remainder shall be used for mounting the guv'nor's panto.

sal[4] (sæl). [f. S(ILICON + AL(UMINIUM).]

1. *Petrogr.* One of the two primary categories erected by Cross, Iddings, Pirsson, and Washington to classify igneous rocks and their characteristic minerals, and broadly including those rich in non-ferromagnesian aluminous and siliceous minerals such as quartz, feldspars, and feldspathoids. Hence **salic** ('sælɪk) *a.*[2], of or pertaining to this category of rocks. Cf. FEMIC *a.*

1902 W. Cross et al. in *Jrnl. Geol.* X. 573 To express concisely the two groups of standard minerals and their chemical characters in part, the words *sal* and *fem* have been adopted. The former is employed to designate group I, mnemonically recalling the *s*iliceous and *al*uminous character of its minerals. **1902**, etc. [see FEMIC *a.*]. **1931** A. Johannsen *Descr. Petrogr. Igneous Rocks* I. viii. 86 The classes are determined by the salic-femic ratio. The five classes are: I. Persalic. Ratio sal:fem greater than 7·00 [etc.]. **1974** I. S. E. Carmichael et al. *Igneous Petrol.* ii. 48 The most generally used index of magmatic evolution is the differentiation index (DI) proposed by Thornton and Tuttle (1960); this is simply the weight percentage of the.. salic components quartz.., albite.., orthoclase.., nepheline.., leucite.., and kalsilite.

†**2.** *Geol.* Also **Sal.** [a. G. *Sal* (E. Suess *Das Antlitz der Erde* (1909) III. ii. xxiv. 626), f. *S(i* + *al*, chem. symbols for silicon and aluminium.] = SIAL (now superseded by that term). *Obs.*

1909 [see NIFE]. **1922** *Geol. Mag.* LIX. 338 Wegener accepts the terminology of Suess, except that he follows Pfeffer in writing Sial instead of Sal. *Ibid.* 340 The boundary of the Sal should therefore be drawn at the foot of the continental slope, where the continental masses begin to rise from the ocean-floor. **1954** R. L. Parker tr. *P. Niggli's Rocks & Mineral Deposits* xi. 476 A granite-gneiss association takes the upper hand and is the reason for calling the entire outer crust the sial crust (sial or sal, containing Si and Al, besides alkalies, as the most important elements).

sal, obs. f. SAIL; obs. north. f. SHALL, SOUL.

‖**sala**[1] ('sala). [It., Sp., Pg. *sala*: see SALLE.] A hall or large apartment; *spec.* a dining-hall.

1611 Coryat *Crudities* 205 Hee had entred with his whole troupe of men into the Sala where the Duke sat. *a* **1668** Lassels *Voy. Italy* (1670) ii. 54 Passing from hence through the *Sala* again, I was led into the great room hard by. **1774** Wraxall *Tour North. Europe* iii. (1776) 26 The grand sala or dining-room [of the palace of Rosenbourg]. **1851** Mayne Reid *Scalp Hunt.* vii, [In Mexico] The ball room was a long oblong *sala*, with a 'banquette' running all round it.

‖**sala**[2] ('sɑːlə). [Hindī, Skr. *sālā* house.] An Indian rest-house or inn.

1871 Alabaster *Wheel of Law* 265 We find two Salas or travellers' rest-houses. **1890** H. S. Hallett *1000 Miles* 257 Passing through the village we put up at the *sala* or rest-house, which is situated on the banks of the Meh Wung.

salaam (səˈlɑːm), *sb.* Also 7 salame, sallam, salema, salom, selame, 7–8 selam, 7–9 salam, 8 schalam, 8–9 salem. [Arab. *salām* (hence in Pers. and Urdū) = Heb. *shālōm* peace.] The Oriental salutation (*as*)*salām* (*ɛalaikum*), Peace (be upon you). Hence applied to a ceremonious obeisance with which this salutation is accompanied, consisting (in India) of a low bowing of the head and body with the palm of the right hand placed on the forehead.

1613 Purchas *Pilgrimage* (1614) 546 He..presenteth himselfe to the people to receive their Salames or good morrow. **1634** Sir T. Herbert *Trav.* 113 Some of the bridemaids came out unto us, and after a Sallam or Congee began a Morisko. **1687** A. Lovell tr. *Thevenot's Trav.* i. 152 When they give one another the Selam, after the Prayer of Kouschlouk. **1779** Forrest *Voy. N. Guinea* 214 Tuan Hadjee got up, and, without making the ordinary selam, went abruptly out of the hall. **1800** *Suppl. Chron.* in *Asiat. Ann. Reg.* 152/2 On being informed that I was a Brahman, he made me some very respectful salems. **1835** Willis *Pencillings* II. xlvii. 65 We were received with a profusion of Salaams by the sultan's perfumer. **1837** *Lett. fr. Madras* (1843) 114 Good morning, sar: great chief, salam! **1849** E. E. Napier *Excurs. S. Africa* I. 287 After a long chat, I made my salaam, and went to inspect a most conspicuous object on a neighbouring height. **1867** 'Ouida' *Under Two Flags* II. viii. 213 The Moor rose instantly, with profound salaams, before her. **1892** Kipling & Balestier *Naulahka* 181 'Salaam, Tarvin Sahib', he murmured.

b. *transf.* Respectful compliments.

1786 Han. More *Let. to Lady Middleton* 14 June, Pray present my proper salams (is that spelt right?) to Mrs. Bouverie. **1899** Kipling *Stalky* 267 Rutton Singh sends his best salaams.

c. *attrib.* and *Comb.*, as ***salaam-like*** adj.; **salaam convulsion, -spasm**, a form of convulsion incident to children and characterized by nodding of the head.

1850 R. G. Cumming *Hunter's Life S. Afr.* xvii. II. 9 A 'salaam-like' movement of his trunk. **1850** *Lancet* I. 485 *Eclampsia nutans* of Mr. Newnham, or the 'salaam convulsion' of Sir Charles Clarke. **1886** *Buck's Handbk. Med. Sci.* II. 287 Wry-neck, writer's cramp, spinal trepidation, salaam spasm.

salaam (səˈlɑːm), *v.* [f. prec.]

1. *trans.* To make a salaam to; to salute with a salaam; to offer salutations to.

1693 T. Smith *Obs. Constantinople* in *Coll. Cur. Trav.* II. 71 They..take it ill to be salam'd or saluted by them. **1718** Ockley *Saracens* II. 182 Obeidollah appearing, Muslim did not Salàm or salute him. **1837** *Lett. fr. Madras* (1843) 111 Two rows of his own servants and ours, salaming him at every step. **1892** Kipling & Balestier *Naulahka* 199 He [*sc.* an ape] used to salaam me in the mornings like Luchman Rao, the prime minister.

2. *intr.* To make a salaam or obeisance.

1698 Fryer *Acc. E. India & P.* 18 It being their Custom only to Salam, giving a bow with their Hands across their Breasts. **1824** *Edin. Rev.* XLI. 41 They salaamed to me with an air that said [etc.]. **1827** D. Johnson *Ind. Field Sports* 139 He fell on the ground salaming (the most submissive obeisance). **1852** Miss Yonge *Cameos* I. xxix. 249 Putting their hands to their brow, and salaaming down to the ground. **1879** Mrs. A. E. James *Ind. Househ. Managem.* 49 When he comes into the room he salaams profoundly.

Hence **sa'laaming** *vbl. sb.* and *ppl. a.*

1816 'Quiz' *Grand Master* ii. 45 *note*, Salaming is the mode of salutation in India. **1879** Mrs. A. E. James *Ind. Househ. Managem.* 43 Hordes of respectfully salaaming natives from all parts of India.

salable, var. SALEABLE *a.*

salacious (səˈleɪʃəs), *a.* [f. L. *salāci-*, *salax*, f. root of *salīre* to leap: see -IOUS.]

1. Lustful, lecherous; sexually wanton.

1661 Feltham *Lett.* in *Resolves*, etc. x. 74 If you remember how you have seen the salacious and devouring Sparrow beat out the harmless Marten from his nest. **1675** Evelyn *Terra* (1729) 25 Pigeons, Poultry and other Salacious Corn-fed Birds. *a* **1704** T. Brown *Satire agst. Woman* Wks. 1730 I. 55 Let every man thou seest give new desires And not one quench the rank salacious fires. **1774** Goldsm. *Nat. Hist.* (1862) I. v. 427 Animals of the hare kind .. are remarkably salacious. **1822–34** *Good's Study Med.* (ed. 4) II. 484 A disorder of the spinal marrow incident to persons of a salacious disposition. **1865** *Sat. Rev.* 28 Jan. 101 The perusal of the amatory diaries and salacious confession of incipient guilt. **1897** *Allbutt's Syst. Med.* II. 992 Its [i.e. arsenic's] more immediate effect on the system is to make the people lively, combative and salacious.

2. Tending to provoke lust. *rare.*

c **1645** Howell *Lett.* II. xxvii, Which makes fish more salacious commonly than flesh. **1697** Dryden *Virg. Georg.* iii. 199 Feed him with Herbs..Of generous Warmth, and of salacious kind. **1775** *Sterne's Sent. Journ.* IV. 219 (*Consequence*) It is well known..that turtle is very salacious food.

Hence **sa'laciously** *adv.*, **sa'laciousness**.

1727 Bailey vol. II, *Salaciousness*, Salacity, Lechery, Lustfulness. **1755** Johnson, *Salaciously*, lecherously; lustfully. **1812** W. Taylor in *Monthly Rev.* LXVIII. 509 His frequent salaciousness is an aroma, disgusting to the pure and corruptive of the temperate taste. **1875** H. C. Wood *Therap.* (1879) 564 Small doses do cause evident salaciousness and irritation of the genital organs.

salacity (səˈlæsɪtɪ). [ad. L. *salācitāt-em*, f. *salāc-*, *salax* (see SALACIOUS). Cf. F. *salacité*.] The quality or condition of being salacious; lustfulness, lecherousness, sexual wantonness.

1605 Willet *Hexapla Gen.* 333 The salacitie and wantonnes of their nation. **1621** Burton *Anat. Mel.* ii. ii. i. ii. 317 Sparrows, which are..short liued because of their salacity. **1675** Evelyn *Terra* (1729) 6 Some Earths appear to be totally barren, and some though not altogether so unfruitful, yet wanting Salacity to conceive. **1769** E. Bancroft *Guiana* 385 Lepers are notorious for their salacity and longevity. **1822–34** *Good's Study Med.* (ed. 4) II. 485 Morbid salacity is no uncommon cause of madness. **1884** *World* 20 Aug. 9/2 The Oxford fellow whose conversation.. was traversed by a vein of salacity. **1903** *Sat. Rev.* 4 Apr. 428/1 A reading of this book inspires us with a fear lest French salacity is to be paraded in the English tongue.

salad ('sæləd). Forms: α. 5 selad, 5–7 salade, 6–7 sallade, 7–9 sallad, 7– salad; β. 6 sal(l)ett(e, -otte, -ite, 6–7 salat, 6–9 (now *dial.* or *arch.*) sallet, 7 sallat(e. [a. OF. *salade* (14th c.), a. Pr. *salada* = OIt. *salata*, Pg. *salada* (cf. It. *insalata*, Sp. *ensalada*):—popular L. **salāta*, f. **salāre* (It., med.L. *salare*, Pr., Sp., Pg. *salar*, F. *saler*) to salt, f. L. *sal* salt.

The Romanic word has been generally taken into the Germanic langs.: Du. *salade* (*salaet* in Kilian, also *sla* from **slade*), late MHG. *salât* (G. *salat*), Sw., Da. *salat*; also Russ. *salat*.]

1. a. A cold dish of herbs or vegetables (e.g. lettuce, endive), usually uncooked and chopped up or sliced, to which is often added sliced hard-boiled egg, cold meat, fish, etc., the whole being seasoned with salt, pepper, oil, and vinegar.

For an earlier wider use see quot. 1688 in β and cf. quot. 1687 s.v. SALADING.

α. **1481–90** *Howard Househ. Bks.* (Roxb.) 398 Item, for erbes for a selad j. d. **1533** Elyot *Cast. Helthe* (1539) 41 Yonge men..shell eate..salades of cold herbes. **1578** Lyte *Dodoens* 125 This herbe..is much vsed in meates and Salades with egges. **1601** Holland *Pliny* II. 37 If you would make a delicate sallad of Cucumbers, boile them first, then pill from them their rind, serue them vp with oile, vinegre, and honey. **1699** Dampier *Voy.* II. i. 72 Purslain..tis very sweet, and makes a good Salad for a hot Country. **1712** Arbuthnot *John Bull* i. xvi, She turned away one servant for putting too much oil in her sallad. **1726** Swift *Gulliver* iv. ii, Wholesome herbs, which I boiled, and eat as sallads with my bread. **1846** Ford *Gatherings from Spain* (1906) 147 The salad is the glory of every French dinner and the disgrace of most in England. **1855** Delamer *Kitch. Gard.* (1861) 107 The most approved autumnal salads are those mainly composed of endive.

β. *c* **1390** *Forme of Cury* (1780) 41 Salat. Take persel, sawge, garlec [etc.]..waische hem clene..and myng hem wel with rawe oile, lay on vyneger and salt, and serue it forth. **1550** J. Coke *Eng. & Fr. Heralds* §30 (1877) 64 Oyle olyve whiche was brought out of Espayne, very good for salettes. **1597** Hooker *Eccl. Pol.* v. lxxvi. §8 A Sallet of greene herbes. **1629** Parkinson *Paradis.* 468 Asparagus..whose young shootes..being boyled, are eaten with a little vinegar and butter, as a Sallet of great delight. **1660** Pepys *Diary* 14 May, A sallet and two or three bones of mutton were provided for a matter of ten of us. **1688** R. Holme *Armoury* iii. 84/2 Sallet, is either Sweet Herbs, or Pickled Fruits, or Cucumbers, Samphire, Elder-Buds, Broom-Buds, &c. eaten with Roasted Meats. **1707** *Curios. in Husb. & Gard.* 173 Samphire..is very good in Sallets. **1716** Addison *Freeholder* No. 30 ¶5 Pudding, which, it must be confess'd, is not so elegant a Dish as Frog and Sallet. **1908** A. Noyes *Drake* vi, Sallets mixed with sugar and cinnamon.

b. *fig.* and allusively, as a type of something mixed (†or savoury).

1601 Shaks. *All's Well* iv. v. 18 She was the sweete Margerom of the sallet, or rather the hearbe of grace. **1602** —— *Ham.* ii. ii. 462, I remember one said, there was no Sallets in the lines, to make the matter sauoury. *a* **1635** Corbet *Iter Bor.* (1647) 487 The Puritan, the Anabaptist, Brownist, Like a grand sallet. **1774** Goldsm. *Retal.* 11 Our Garrick's a salad, for in him we see Oil, vinegar, sugar, and saltness agree. **1831** Gen. P. Thompson *Exerc.* (1842) I. 373 How the united robbers, after a sallad of murder and *Te Deums*, of conflagrations and general fasts, succeeded in dividing Poland. **1856** F. Saunders (*title*) Salad for the Social. **1893** *Nation* (N.Y.) LVII. 133/1 Close at hand the building is an entertaining salad of styles.

2. a. Any vegetable or herb used in a raw state as an article of food, esp. in the kind of dish described in 1; = *salad-herb*. See also CORN-SALAD.

c **1460** J. Russell *Bk. Nurture* 97 Beware of saladis, grene metis, and of frutes rawe. *a* **1500** *Flower & Leaf* lix, They yede about gadring Plesaunt salades, which they made hem ete. **1577** B. Googe *Heresbach's Husb.* ii. (1586) 52 b, And your Potte hearbes and Sallets in another place. **1621** Burton *Anat. Mel.* i. ii. ii. i. 91 That all rawe hearbs and sallets breed Melancholy blood, except Buglosse and Lettice. **1643** Sir T. Browne *Relig. Med.* ii. §1, I could digest a Sallad gathered in a Church-yard, as well as in a Garden. **1673** Ray *Journ. Low C.* 395 They are very temperate in their diet, eating a great deal of sallet and but little flesh. **1784** Cowper *Task* vi. 304 To pick A cheap but wholesome sallad from the brook. **1870** Dickens *E. Drood* iii, The Cloisterham children grow small salad in the dust of abbots and abbesses, and make dirt-pies of nuns and friars. **1887** Moloney *Forestry W. Afr.* 273 Watercress (*Nasturtium officinale*..). The well-known salad.

b. *spec.* (*dial.* and *U.S.*) Lettuce.

1838 *Philadelphia Ledger* July (Bartlett), Salad goes to head by the middle of May, on Vancouver's Island. **1860** *Darlington's Amer. Weeds*, etc. 205 Those forms known as Curled and Head Salad. **1877** *Holderness Gloss.*, *Sallit*..the lettuce plant before preparation for the table.

†**c.** in proverbial or allusive use, *esp.* in ***to pick a salad***, (*a*) to be engaged in some trivial occupation, (*b*) to make a selection (*out of*). *Obs.*

1520 Whitinton *Vulg.* 2 He that laboreth nothyng holy, but catcheth a patche of euery thyng, is mete to pycke a salet. **1550** Bale *Eng. Votaries* ii. 5 b, Angisus..byshopp of Metis, vsurpynge the hygh stewardshypp of Fraunce, at layser made the kynge to go pyke a salett. **1568** in Strype *Ann. Ref.* (1709) I. lii. 525 As for your new Doctors, it is good to pick a Sallet out of them, now and then. **1590** Greene *Never too* *late* Wks. (Grosart) VIII. 102 If not, like an vnthankefull Hackney-man shee meant to tourne him into the bare leas, and set him as a tyrde iade to picke a sallet. **1601** SHAKS. *All's Well* IV. v. 15 'Twas a good Lady. Wee may picke a thousand sallets ere wee light on such another hearbe. **1603** DEKKER *Batchelors Banquet* Wks. (Grosart) I. 176, I would haue turnd the queane out of doors to picke a Sallet.

3. *attrib.*, as ***salad bowl, -cream, -dish, -dressing, -eater, fork, leaf, -plate, -root, -spoon***; **salad bar** chiefly *U.S.*, a servery from which a salad may be obtained; **salad basket**, (*a*) a wire basket in which superfluous moisture is shaken from the constituents of a salad after washing; (*b*) *slang* [tr. Fr. *panier à salade*], a police van, 'Black Maria'; **salad burnet**, the common burnet, *Poterium Sanguisorba*; † **salad clover**, *Melilotus cærulea*; **salad days**, days of youthful inexperience; also *attrib.* in *sing.*; **salad furniture** (see FURNITURE 6 b); **salad-herb** ? *Obs.*, = sense 2; **salad rocket**, *Eruca sativa* (Miller *Plant-n.* 1884); **salad servers**, a large spoon and fork for serving salads; † **salad sorrel**, ? *Oxalis Acetosella*. Also SALAD-OIL.

1976 *Amer. Speech 1974* XLIX. 116 **Salad bar*, counter in many restaurants, with ingredients from which the diner can make his own salad. **1978** *Times* 23 Apr. 12/6 The.. assistant manageress..led me to the salad bar with its two kinds of salad, four kinds of bread and four kinds of salad dressing. **1906** *Mrs. Beeton's Bk. Househ. Managem.* xxxv. 1092 Where a *salad basket is not available, the materials should be well drained and shaken in a colander. **1962** P. BRICKHILL *Deadline* vi. 83 A row of large 'Black Marias', or, as I learned, '*paniers à salade*' (salad baskets) as the French call them. **1966** J. DOS PASSOS *Best Times* (1968) ii. 54 The French cooks were already out..whirling the salad around in wire salad-baskets to dry it. **1975** H. MCCUTCHEON *Instrument of Vengeance* iii. 52 There will be a salad basket here soon... What you call, I think, a Black Maria. **1773** J. WEDGWOOD *Let.* 21 Nov. (1965) 156 *Sa[lad] Bowles, and boats. **1837** BARHAM *Ingol. Leg.* Ser. I. *Spectre of Tappington*, Curled like a head of celery in a salad-bowl. **1867** TROLLOPE *Last Chron. Barset* I. xxxii. 267 A bitter leaf will now and then make its way into your salad-bowl. **1921** *Daily Colonist* (Victoria, B.C.) 22 Oct. 7/7 (Advt.), China salad bowls—hand painted. **1980** *Berkeley Graduate* Oct. 5/2 Even in California, the salad bowl of the nation, thousands of people were hungry. **1854** S. THOMSON *Wild Fl.* III. (1861) 236 The *Poterium sanguisorba*,..derives its English name of *salad-burnet from its being used as a salad. **1562** TURNER *Herbal* II. 42, I know no Englishe name for it [sc. *Lotus urbana*]: howbeit, it may be named..gardin clauer or four clauer, or *sallat clauer. **1858** SIMMONDS *Dict. Trade*, **Salad-cream*, a prepared dressing for salads. **1976** D. CLARK *Dread & Water* ii. 26 A woman..was shaking salad cream from a bottle. **1606** SHAKS. *Ant. & Cl.* I. v. 73 My *Sallad dayes, When I was greene in iudgement, cold in blood. **1865** *Cornh. Mag.* May 554 Being in want of a horse at the time—it was in my salad days, reader—I looked through the advertisements in *The Times*, and noticed one which at any rate promised well. **1882** PEBODY *Eng. Journalism* xii. 83 All the newspapers that flourished in the green and sallet days of the Press have been replaced by more adventurous rivals. **1953** DYLAN THOMAS *Under Milk Wood* (1954) 60 She whispers to her salad-day deep self. **1963** *Times* 8 Mar. 15/4 This was a young concerto for a young pianist—it was, we have tried to suggest, not such a salad-day reading. **1688** R. HOLME *Armoury* (Roxb. Club) II. 4/1 A *sallett dish. **1710** SWIFT *Jrnl. to Stella* 26 Oct., And so you only want some salad-dishes, and plates. **1836–9** DICKENS *Sk. Boz, Scenes* xviii, An unrivalled compounder of *salad-dressing. **1947** AUDEN *Age of Anxiety* (1948) iii. 70 The parlour cars and Pullmans are packed also With scented assassins, *salad-eaters Who murder on milk. **1917** *Harrods Gen. Catal.* 892/2 Glass *salad forks... Prices on application. **1978** *Detroit Free Press* 5 Mar. A17/5 (Advt.), Stainless tableware..setting includes salad fork, dinner fork, [etc.]. **1538–48** ELYOT *Dict.*, *Acetarium*,..a gardeine, where *salet herbes do growe. **1588** KYD *Househ. Phil.* Wks. (1901) 243 An other garden full of all sorts of sallet hearbes. **1629** PARKINSON *Parad.* 468 Asparagus is a principall and delectable Sallet herbe..boyled. **1767** ABERCROMBIE *Ev. Man his own Gard.* (1803) 665/2 *Sallad Herbs*:..the principal..are lettuce, endive, cellery, and small herbs, such as cresses, mustard, radish, &c. **1796** Salad herb [see BURNET *sb.*[2] 1]. **1927** JOYCE *Pomes Penyeach*, The still garden where a child Gathers the simple *salad leaves. **1881** C. C. HARRISON *Woman's Handiwork* III. 219 The little *salad-plates were silver-gilt. **1976** G. MCDONALD *Confess, Fletch* (1977) xxxii. 150 Sylvia entered with salad plates. The salad consisted of..cold, canned peas. **1573** in Nichols *Progr. Q. Eliz.* (1823) I. 370 Item, for *salet roots o 2. **1907** *Yesterday's Shopping* (1969) 148/2 *Salad Servers, boxwood ..set 1/1. **1978** 'M. DELVING' *No Sign of Life* v. 94 Betsy is a carver... She carves the handles of salad servers and jugs for me. **1611** COTGR. s.v. *Salette, Petite salette*, Pettie Sorrell, *sallet Sorrell. **1858** SIMMONDS *Dict. Trade*, **Salad-spoon*, a wooden, ivory, or other spoon, for mixing and serving salad.

salade, var. form of SALLET, helmet.

‖**salade niçoise** (salad niswaz). [Fr., = salad of, or from, Nice in the south of France.] A variety of salad (see quots.).

1955 E. DAVID *Bk. of Mediterranean Food* 160 There may be anchovies, gherkins, artichoke hearts, lettuce... *Salade niçoise*..is made with the same variety of ingredients. **1960** —— *French Provincial Cooking* 145 (*heading*) *Salade niçoise* ..The ingredients depend upon the season and what is available. But hard-boiled eggs, anchovy fillets, black olives, and tomatoes, with garlic in the dressing, are pretty well constant elements in what should be a rough country salad, rather than a fussy chef's concoction. **1969** C. IRVING *Fake!* vii. 86 A gallery, as Elmyr put it, 'like a *salade niçoise*, a little bit of everything, mostly for the American tourists'. **1975** *Times* 22 July 14/3 Eight dinner guests fed on *salade niçoise* made with fresh French beans.

‖**saladero** (sala'dero). [Sp.] In Spain and Latin America, a slaughter-house where meat is also prepared by drying or salting.

1870 *Weekly Standard* (Buenos Aires) 19 Jan. 8/5 The sales of saladero ox and cowhides during the last fifteen days. **1885** *Encycl. Brit.* XIX. 762/2 The principal prison in the capital of the kingdom [*sc.* Spain] was nothing more than a converted slaughter house where pigs were killed and salted, as its name, the Saladero, implied. **1902** *Encycl. Brit.* XXXI. 461/2 The increase in the herds of recent years has caused the owners of *saladero* establishments in Argentina and Uruguay to try the working of factories in Paraguay for the preparation of *tasajo* (jerked beef). **1930** C. F. JONES *S. Amer.* xviii. 403 As a lean animal served the purposes of the saladero, or salting establishment, the native cattle proved quite satisfactory. **1960** H. S. FERNS *Brit. & Argentina in 19th Cent.* xiii. 416 The old-fashioned *saladeros* supplying the domestic market with fresh meat and foreign markets with dried and salted meat were faced with severe difficulties. **1973** M. KOCHAN tr. *F. Braudel's Capitalism & Material Life* iii. 135 *Charque*, boned and dried meat produced in the saladeros of Argentina (once again intended for slaves and the European poor), was to all practical purposes invented at the beginning of the nineteenth century.

saladine ('sælədɪn), *sb.*[1] *Obs.* and *dial.* Also 5 **salendyne**, 5–6 **-andyne**, 6 **saledyne**, **-endinne**, 9 **salladin**. Variant of CELANDINE.

c **1430**, **1486** [see CELANDINE 1 a]. **1530** PALSGR. 265/1 Salandyne..*celidoyne*. *c* **1550** LLOYD *Treas. Health* H 6 Let the rote of Saledyne stampte sethe in wyne. **1573** *Art of Limming* 2 The yellow milke of green salendine. **1626** BACON *Sylva* §639 Saladine hath a yellow Milk, which hath..much Acrimony. **1878** *Cumbld. Gloss.*, *Salladin*, the plant celandine, *Chelidonium majus*. **1886** *Cheshire Gloss.*, *Saladine*.

† **saladine**, *sb.*[2] *Obs.* ? = CELIDONY[2].

c **1430** LYDG. *Min. Poems* (Percy Soc.) 223 Wythe dyamandes fulle derely dyghte, Ryche saladynez sette on every syde.

'**Saladine**, *a.* (*sb.*[3]). *Hist.* [ad. med.L. *saladīnus* (in *decimæ saladinæ*), f. *Saladin*, the name of the Sultan of Egypt and Syria (1137–93).] ***Saladine tax*** (also absol.); a tax, consisting of the tenth of a man's income, first imposed in 1188 on England and France for the support of the crusade against Saladin (see above).

Modern writers substitute the proper name used attrib. or possessively.

1728 CHAMBERS *Cycl.* s.v., The Saladine-Tax was thus laid; That every Person who did not enter himself a Croise, was obliged to pay a Tenth of his yearly Revenue. **1752** *Ibid.*, The Carthusians, Bernardines, and some other religious, were exempted from the Saladine.

[**1832** *Encycl. Amer.* XI. 172/2 The Saladin Tenth. **1837** *Penny Cycl.* VIII. 185/2 Saladin's tithe. **1874** STUBBS *Const. Hist.* I. xiii. (1897) 597 The Saladin tithe.]

salading ('sælədɪŋ). Forms: see SALAD; also 7 **salletine**, 8 **salatine**. [f. SALAD + -ING[1].] Herbs and vegetables used for salad.

1664 EVELYN *Kal. Hort.* (1729) 190 Sow Chervil, Lettuce, Radish, and other..Salletings. *Ibid.* 216 Fill your vacant Beds with Sallading. **1670** NARBOROUGH in *Acc. Sev. Late Voy.* I. (1694) 69 Some Herbs..we boiled for Salleting. **1687** in Wood *Life* (O.H.S.) III. 236, 36 plates of sallating, piled high and copped, viz., oranges, lemmons, olives, samphire, &c. **1709** E. WARD tr. *Cervantes* p. v, Several Cart Loads of Endive, Celery, Celician, Lettice, and Tarragon, were sent into the Kitchen to accommodate the Table with raw Salatine. **1771** SIR J. BANKS *Jrnl.* (1896) 442 Garden stuff and salletting. **1851** *B'ham & Midl. Gardeners' Mag.* May 69 Continue to make sowings..of Peas, Beans, Turnips,..every fortnight, with small salading every week. **1884** *Public Opinion* 5 Sept. 301/1 The small saladings which make an intermittent appearance at the table.

b. *attrib.*: † **salading-burnet**, = *salad-burnet*.

1766 *Museum Rust.* VI. 27, I spoke of it as the garden pot-herb, and sallading burnet.

'**salad-oil.** Olive oil of superior quality, such as is used in dressing salads.

1558–9 *Will of T. Hynde* (Somerset Ho.), Layde out..for sallett oyle. **1582** HESTER *Secr. Phiorav.* III. xvii. 31 Take sweete Sallette Oile twentie pounde. **1620** VENNER *Via Recta* vi. 99 Oyle Oliue, which we commonly call Sallet Oyle. **1683** MOXON *Mech. Exerc.*, *Printing* II. 74 Paste, Sallad-Oyl, and such accidental Requisites as the Press-man in his work may want. **1867** BLOXAM *Chem.* 580 Salad oil, or sweet oil (olive oil), is obtained by crushing olives. **1874** GARROD & BAXTER *Mat. Med.* 302 The oil, *Oleum Olivæ*, called also Salad oil, is of a pale straw colour.

‖**Salagrama** (ʃaːla'graːma). Also **Salagram** and with small initial. [a. Skr. *śālagrāma* (see SHALGRAM).] = SHALGRAM. Freq. *attrib.*

1801 H. T. COLEBROOKE in *Asiatick Researches* VII. 240 A Sālagrāma stone ought to be placed near the dying man. **1833** R. EVEREST in *Ibid.* XVIII. II. 111, I have several times looked for such among the Salagrams in the Hindoo temples. **1913** J. N. FARQUHAR *Crown of Hinduism* 267 If he recognizes Vishnu, he may possess a discus, a *salagrama* stone, a conch shell or a *tulsi* plant. **1920** —— *Outl. Relig. Lit. India* vii. 293 The more usual symbols are: Vishnu, the Śālagrāma pebble.

salak (sə'læk). Also **salac**. [Malay.] A thorny palm tree belonging to the genus *Salacca*, native to tropical south-east Asia, esp. *S. edulis*, or its pear-shaped edible fruit.

1820 J. CRAWFURD *Hist. Indian Archipelago* I. iv. 445 The *Salak*, affords a fruit about the size of a pullet's egg, which consists of a hard stone, enveloped by a firm white pulp, which is covered by thin husks. **1856** B. SEEMANN *Pop. Hist. Palms* 345 Nothing is recorded of the other species of this genus,—for instance,..the Salak of Penang. **1937** M. COVARRUBIAS *Island of Bali* v. 105 *Salak*, a pear-shaped fruit that grows on a palm, tastes like pineapple, and is covered by the most perfect imitation snakeskin. **1952** W. MARCH *October Island* x. 125 He made up a poem from the names of the palm trees..and..would recite it... Salak, pigafettia, orania palindan,.. And the great royal palm. **1981** *Oxf. Encycl. Trees of World* 259/2 Many palms have edible fruits though rather few are widely cultivated for this product, amongst them Salac (*Salacca edulis*) of southeast Asia.

salal ('sæləl). Also **sallal**. [Chinook Jargon *sallal* (= Chinook *kl-kwu-shá-la*).] An evergreen shrub, *Gaultheria shallon*, belonging to the family Ericaceæ, native to western North America, and bearing racemes of pink or white flowers followed by edible purple berries. Also *attrib.*

1825 D. DOUGLAS *Jrnl. Trav. N. Amer.* (1914) 104 *Gaultheria shallon*; called by the natives 'Salal' not 'Shallon'. **1833** W. F. TOLMIE *Jrnl.* 29 Aug. (1963) 230 Have supped on Sallal & at dusk, shall turn in. **1838** PARKER *Expl. Tour* (1846) 221 The salalberry is a sweet and pleasant fruit of a dark purple color, oblong, and about the size of a grape. **1866** *Treas. Bot.* I. 522/2 The Shallon or Salal of the north-west coast of America. **1884** C. PHILLIPPS-WOLLEY *Trottings of Tenderfoot* 140 In front lay in the river-bed a grove of cottonwood, and the bush I think British Columbians call 'sal lal'. **1886** *Good Words* 73 Great woods of Douglas fir cover the whole region [of Vancouver Island], with a lovely undergrowth of arbutus, sallal, an evergreen shrub, and small maples. **1926** *Daily Colonist* (Victoria, B.C.) 11 July 16/3, I caught my foot in a trailing vine and ploughed head first into the salal bushes. **1946** [see BLACK-CAP 5]. **1952** *Beaver* Sept. 7/1 Fireweed blazes in the rear and salal sprouts out of the unpainted totem poles. **1977** J. GILLIS *Killers of Starfish* (1979) xii. 105 She started to lead the way through Mike's pile of salal cuttings.

salamander ('sælə,mændə(r), sælə'mæn-), *sb.* Also 4–5 **salamandre**; 5–7 in L. form. [a. F. *salamandre* (12th c.), ad. L. *salamandra*, a. Gr. σαλαμάνδρα. Cf. MHG., mod.G. *salamander*.]

1. a. A lizard-like animal supposed to live in, or to be able to endure, fire. Now only *allusive*.

1340 *Ayenb.* 167 þe salamandre þet leueþ ine þe uere. *c* **1430** LYDG. *Min. Poems* (Percy Soc.) 170 And salamandra most felly dothe manace. **1481** CAXTON *Myrr.* II. vi. 74 This Salemandre berith wulle, of whiche is made cloth and gyrdles that may not brenne in the fyre. [Cf. *salamander's wool* in 6.] **1590** GREENE *Roy. Exch.* Wks. (Grosart) VII. 230 The Poets..seeing Louers scorched with affection, likeneth them to Salamanders. *a* **1591** H. SMITH *Serm.* (1637) 9 Like the Salamander, that is ever in the fire and never consumed. **1616** R. C. *Cert. Poems* in *Times' Whistle*, etc. (1871) 119 Yet he can live noe more without desire, Then can the salamandra without fire. **1634** SIR T. HERBERT *Trav.* 20 The Aery Camelion and fiery Salamander are frequent there [*sc.* in Madagascar]. **1681** FLAVEL *Meth. Grace* xxvii. 464 Sin like a Salamander can live to eternity in the fire of God's wrath. **1688** R. HOLME *Armoury* II. 205/1, I have some of the hair, or down of the Salamander, which I have several times put in the Fire, and made it red hot, and after taken it out, which being cold, yet remained perfect wool. [Cf. 1481 above.] **1711** HEARNE *Collect.* (O.H.S.) III. 129 He had 2 Salamanders, which lived 2 hours in a great Fire. **1864** KINGSLEY *Rom. & Teut.* iv. 131 That he will henceforth [in the island of Volcano] follow the example of a salamander, which always lives in fire.

b. Any tailed amphibian of the urodelous family *Salamandridæ*, or some closely allied family.

The land salamanders form the typical genus *Salamandra*; the water salamanders are the newts or tritons.

1611 COTGR., *Salamandre d'eau*, the water Salamander; black-backed, red-bellied, and full of yellow spots. **1668** CHARLETON *Onomast.* 26 *Lacerta Salamandra aquatica*, the water Salamander. *c* **1711** PETIVER *Gazophyl.* VI. lviii, Small Cape Salamander... It squeaks like a Rat. **1753** CHAMBERS *Cycl. Supp.*, The *salamandra aquatica*, or water salamander. .. The *salamandra terrestris*, or land salamander. **1834** MCMURTRIE *Cuvier's Anim. Kingd.* 187 Aquatic Salamanders always retain the vertically compressed tail. **1835** KIRBY *Hab. & Inst. Anim.* II. xxii. 421 The other [sc. *Menopoma*]..has been called by American writers the giant salamander. **1870** GILLMORE tr. *Figuier's Reptiles & Birds* 30 The Black Salamander (*Triton alpestris*) has no spots. **1896** tr. *Boas' Text-bk. Zool.* 405 The Japanese Giant Salamander (*Cryptobranchus japonicus*).

c. A figure of the mythical salamander used as an emblem.

1688 R. HOLME *Armoury* II. 205/1 He beareth Argent, a Salamander in flames. **1780** EDMONDSON *Heraldry* II. Gloss. **1823** CRABB *Technol. Dict.*, *Salamander (Her.)*, an emblem of constancy, is represented in flames. **1834** L. RITCHIE *Wand. by Seine* 138 The last cavalier..belongs to the suite of the King of France, which is seen by the royal salamander on his back. **1841** G. A. POOLE *Struct. & Decor. Churches* 9/2 A salamander also appears on this font [in Winchester Cathedral],..in allusion to the words which St. John spake of our blessed Lord [Matt. iii. 11].

2. *transf.* and *fig.* applied to persons, etc. with reference to sense 1 a. **a.** *gen.*

1596 SHAKS. *1 Hen. IV*, III. iii. 53, I haue maintain'd that Salamander [= fiery-red face] of yours with fire, any time this two and thirtie yeeres. **1600** S. NICHOLSON *Acolastus* (1876) 45, I sate too hot, yet still I did desire, To liue a Salamander in the fire. **1666** SPURSTOWE *Spir. Chym.* 103 At a far cheaper rate they might have been Saints in Heaven than Salamanders in Hell. **1670** BROOKS *Wks.* (1867) VI. 441 God's people are true salamanders, that live best in the furnace of afflictions. **1854** *Househ. Words* VIII. 159/1 She is a salamander in temper..for all her innocent name. **1888** F. HUME *Mme. Midas* I. iv, Madame Midas was a perfect salamander for heat.

b. A spirit supposed to live in fire.

See Paracelsus *De Nymphis, Sylphis, Pygmæis, et Salamandris*, etc., Wks. 1658 II. 388 seqq.
1657 PINNELL *Philos. Ref.* 27 To the Fire or the Firmament doe belong the Vulcanals, Pennats, Salamanders. **1712** POPE *Rape Lock, To Mrs. Arabella Fermor*, According to these Gentlemen [*sc.* the Rosicrucians], the four Elements are inhabited by Spirits, which they call Sylphs, Gnomes, Nymphs, and Salamanders. **1712–14** *Ibid.* I. 60 The Sprites of fiery Termagants in Flame Mount up, and take a Salamander's name. **1821** SCOTT *Kenilw.* xxxiii, Like salamanders executing a frolic dance in the region of the Sylphs. **1871** B. TAYLOR *Faust* (1875) II. I. iv. 55 A prince I seemed o'er many a salamander.

†**c.** A woman who (ostensibly) lives chastely in the midst of temptations. *Obs.*
1711 ADDISON *Spect.* No. 198 ¶1 There is a Species of Women, whom I shall distinguish by the Name of Salamanders. Now a Salamander is a kind of Heroine in Chastity, that treads upon Fire [etc.]. **1771** *Generous Husb. or Hist. Lord Lelius* 37 The real beauty and avowed virtue of those lovely salamanders.

d. A soldier who exposes himself to fire in battle.
1705 SWIFT *Descr. of Salamander* 22 Wks. 1751 VII. 79 Call my Lord C[utts] a Salamander. [**1807** SIR R. WILSON *Jrnl.* 15 May in *Life* (1862) II. vii. 217 As I know that Buonaparte exposes himself as little as possible; not amongst his other vanities believing that he is a salamander. *c* **1849** in *Spectator* 21 May (1904) 810/2 Paddy Gough's a cross betwixt A bulldog and a salamander.] **1897** *Daily News* 20 Apr. 8/4 In battles a man who feared fire was of no use, and Mr. Gee was the soundest Salamander he had ever known.

e. *slang.* A fire-eating juggler.
(Cf. quot. s.v. SALAMANDERSHIP.)
1859 HOTTEN *Slang Dict.*, *Salamanders*, street acrobats and jugglers who eat fire. **1886** BESANT *Childr. Gibeon* I. vi, We ain't a show. Lotty ain't a clown; I ain't a jumping-horse; Liz ain't a salamander.

3. Applied to various articles used in fire or capable of withstanding great heat. †**a.** Asbestos. (Cf. *salamander-stone*; also F. *salamandre pierreuse*.)
1668 CHARLETON *Onomast.* 254 *Amianthus.. aliàs Asbestinus Lapis.. Salamandra..* the Salamandre, or incombustible stone, and Salamanders wool. *a* **1700** B. E. *Dict. Cant. Crew*, *Salamander*, a Stone (lately) found in Pensylvania full of Cotton, which will not consume in the Fire.

b. An iron or poker used red-hot for lighting a pipe, igniting gunpowder, etc.: see quots.
1698 W. KING tr. *Sorbière's Journ. Lond.* 27 Multitudes had little Tin Kettles in their Houses, with Small-coal kindled, to light their Pipes withal; though in some places they use Candles, in others Salamanders. *a* **1700** B. E. *Dict. Cant. Crew*, *Salamander*, .. a red-hot Iron to light Tobacco with. **1846** A. YOUNG *Naut. Dict.*, *Salamander*, a piece of metal with a handle attached, which is heated for the purpose of firing guns. **1847** HALLIWELL, *Salamander*, a large poker. **1868** G. MACDONALD *R. Falconer* I. xv. 196 Peggy appeared with a salamander—that is a huge poker, ending not in a point, but a red-hot ace of spades. **1898** *United Service Mag.* Mar. 621 The salamander—an iron kept red hot in the galley for firing the salutes.

c. *Metallurgy.* 'A mass of solidified material in a furnace hearth' (Raymond); called also *bear*, *horse*, and *sow*.
[**1866** *Jrnl. Franklin Inst.* 3rd Ser. LII. 128 The matte melting (rohschmelzen) of the Stefanshütte does.. not produce any secretions of metallic iron, (eisensauen, salamander).] **1871** [see HORSE *sb.* 12]. **1877** RAYMOND *Statist. Mines & Mining* 335 To throw away in mattes, slags, and salamanders the iron it [*sc.* hematite] contains.

d. *Cookery.* A circular iron plate which is heated and placed over a pudding or other dish to brown it.
1755 H. GLASSE *Art of Cookery* (ed. 5) 331 Put it in the Oven to brown, or do it with a Salamander. **1769** MRS. RAFFALD *Eng. Housekpr.* (1778) 253 Hold a hot salamander over it till it is very brown. **1804** FARLEY *Lond. Art Cookery* 192 Lay in the fritters, strew a little sugar over them, and glaze them over with a red-hot salamander. **1818** MOORE *Fudge Fam. Paris* viii. 84 Their chronometer spits—their intense Salamanders—their ovens—their pots, that can soften old ganders. **1845** ELIZA ACTON *Mod. Cookery* vii. 169 This is done with a salamander, as it is called... A kitchen shovel is sometimes substituted for it. **1943** F. TOMPSON *Candleford Green* iii. 54 The smith then heated red-hot one end of a large, flat iron utensil known as the 'salamander' and held it above the plate until the rashers were crisp and curled. **1958** *Observer* 18 May 10/5 Caramelise the sugar by passing a red hot salamander very close to the surface till the sugar melts.

e. (See quots. 1873–95.) Also (*N. Amer.*), a workman's brazier.
1873 *Chicago Tribune* 3 Feb. 1/7 It caught fire from the 'salamander' used in drying the plaster. **1875** *Ure's Dict. Arts* III. 1059 The milk of wax, thus prepared, may be spread with a smooth brush upon the surface of a painting, allowed to dry, and then fused by passing a hot iron (salamander) over its surface. **1875** KNIGHT *Dict. Mech.*, *Salamander*, a term sometimes applied to a fire-proof safe. **1895** *Funk's Standard Dict.*, *Salamander*, .. a metal drum or box for containing hot coals, etc., used in drying plaster. **1944** S. BELLOW *Dangling Man* 107, I warmed myself at a salamander flaming in an oil drum. **1971** R. LEWIS *Fenokee Project* viii. 151 They caught a glimpse of twinkling lights. .. 'Salamanders... The workers over there have set up fire pots made out of punctured oil drums.'

4. *local U.S.* A pouched rat or gopher, esp. *Geomys pinetis.*
1805 M. LEWIS *Jrnl.* 9 Apr. in *Orig. Jrnls. Lewis & Clark Exped.* (1904) I. 289 Their work resembles that of the salamander common to the sand hills of the States of South Carolina and Georgia. **1834** J. J. AUDUBON *Ornith. Biogr.* II. 264 Thousands of 'mole-hills', or the habitations of an animal called 'the salamander'.. presented themselves. **1859** S. F. BAIRD *Mammals N. Amer.* 371 The species [of *Geomys*] are termed 'gophers' in the west, but in Georgia and Florida they are almost universally called 'salamanders'. *Ibid.* 380 *Geomys pinetis*,.. Salamander. **1885** *S. Florida Sentinel* 8 Apr. 1/6 The gophers (Florida salamanders) proved its [*sc.* the garden's] destruction. **1943** A. G. POWELL *I can go Home Again* 225 The small burrowing rodent.. which others call the gopher, we called the salamander. **1964** W. H. BURT *Field Guide to Mammals* (ed. 2) 136 Southeastern pocket gopher.. (Salamander).

5. A form of drinking a toast common among German students.
The full expression is ***einem einen salamander reiben*** (cf. first quot. below).
1868 *Daily News* 12 Aug., [One of the ceremonies] is called 'rubbing a salamander'. Every student fills his glass.. to the brim, and at the command of the toastmaster rubs it on the table, while the latter counts three. **1891** *Times* 12 May 9/3 The German emperor when he responded to the 'thundering salamander' in which the Bonn students drank his health.

6. a. *attrib.* and *Comb.*, as ***salamander-gathering***, ***-like*** adj. and adv.; †**salamander('s) blood** (see quots.); **salamander-cloth**, an incombustible cloth made from asbestos; †**salamander-fly**, a kind of fire-fly; **salamander's hair** [cf. G. *salamanderhaar*], a kind of asbestos (see quot.); †**salamander safe** *U.S.*, a fire-proof safe; †**salamander stone** = AMIANTHUS 1; **salamander-stove** *U.S.*, a small portable stove for heating rooms; †**salamander('s) wool**, asbestos (cf. quots. 1481 and 1688 in 1).
1694 SALMON *Bate's Dispens.* 57/2 This Spirit, from its coming forth in red Vapours, is by some Authors called, The *Salamanders Blood. **1704** J. HARRIS *Lex. Techn.* I, *Salamanders Blood*, is a foolish Term that the Chymists give to the red Vapours, which in Distillation of Spirit of Nitre, towards the latter end, do fill the Receiver with red Clouds. **1841** *Penny Cycl.* XX. 337/1 The *salamander-cloth sent by the Tartar king to the Roman pontiff. **1668** CHARLETON *Onomast.* 46 *Pyrogonus*.. the Fire-fly, or *Salamandre Fly. **1821** LAMB *Elia* Ser. I. *All fools' Day*, Good master Empedocles, you are welcome. It is long since you went a *Salamander-gathering down Ætna. **1728** WOODWARD *Fossils* 14 English Talc, of which the coarser Sort is call'd Plaister, or Parget, the finer, Spaad, Earth-Flax, or *Salamander's Hair. **1593** NASHE *Christ's T.* Wks. (Grosart) IV. 68 On the *Salamander-like Ierusalem, haue I cast the coole water of my Teares. **1718** *Entertainer* No. 32. 219 A Person.. that Salamander like feeds in the Fire of Contention. **1798** C. DIBDIN *Song, 'The Anchorsmiths'*, While, Salamander-like, the pond'rous anchor lies. **1885** *Stand. Nat. Hist.* (1888) III. 308 Salamander-like animals with four well-developed but short limbs. **1840** *Merchant's Mag.* (U.S.) II. 280 The *Salamander Safe. **1845** in C. Cist *Cincinnati Misc.* I. 194/2 These Salamander safes are made of stout, wrought bar and plate iron, .. lined with a chemical preparation, which is a non-conductor of heat, and is indestructible by fire. **1852** *Hunt's Merchants' Mag.* XXVI. 256 In April, 1833 I [*sc.* C. J. Gayler] patented my 'Double Fire Proof Safe'. The same year the name 'Salamander' was applied to it, for the reason that one had been subjected to a very intense heat for a long time, and fully protected its valuable contents. **1858** SIMMONDS *Dict. Trade*, *Salamander-safes*, an American name for patent fire-proof iron safes. **1859** BARTLETT *Dict. Amer.* s.v. *Safe*, They are now generally made fireproof; and some of these are called 'salamander safes'. **1583** GREENE *Mamillia* Wks. (Grosart) II. 61 The *Salamander stone, once set on fire, can neuer be quenched. **1590** —— *Never too late* Ibid. VIII. 22 Their eyes are like Salamander stones, that fier at the sight of euery flame. **1852** HAWTHORNE *Blithedale Rom.* v. (1885) 42 She has been stifled with the heat of a *salamander-stove. **1892** *Daily News* 9 Aug. 5/4 Artificial heat was furnished by one hundred small salamander stoves. **1626** BACON *Sylva* §774 *Salamanders Wooll; Being a Kinde of Minerall, which whiteneth also in the Burning, and consumeth not. *a* **1633** AUSTIN *Medit.* (1635) 152 A Garment of Salamander-wooll. **1646** SIR T. BROWNE *Pseud. Ep.* III. xiv. 139 Incombustible napkins and textures which endure the fire, whose materialls are call'd by the name of Salamanders wooll. **1668** [see 3 a].

b. passing into *adj.* = SALAMANDRINE *a.* 1.
1711 ADDISON *Spect.* No. 198 ¶3 As for this part of the fair sex who are not of the salamander kind, I would.. advise them.. to avoid.. what religion calls Temptations. **1742** YOUNG *Nt. Th.* IX. 1356 And is Lorenzo's salamander-heart Cold and untouch'd, amid these sacred fires? **1814** SIR R. WILSON *Priv. Diary* II. 302, I would rather.. have gone through the same proportion of fire, as I have more salamander than dolphin properties.

Hence **sala'manderish** *a.* (*rare*$^{-1}$), **'salamandership** (cf. sense 2 e above).
1787 *Microcosm* No. 21 ¶11 This illustrious Phænomenon of *Salamandership* and Virtue [*sc.* Mr. Powel, the Fire-eater]. **1921** W. DE LA MARE *Mem. Midget* xxxii. 225 Even my salamanderish body sometimes gasped like a fish out of water.

'salamander, *v. rare.* [f. prec. sb.] **a.** *intr.* To live amidst fire, like the salamander.
1857 *Chamb. Jrnl.* VII. 25 In one apartment.. dwells a maker of lucifer-matches, salamandering in fire and brimstone.

b. *trans.* To submit to great heat.
1904 *Blackw. Mag.* Dec. 782/1 His [*sc.* the Arab peasant's] garments must be salamandered and his carcass must be baked.

c. *Cookery.* To brown by means of a salamander.
1878 *Amer. Home Cook Bk.* 65 When it is cooked, glaze the top and salamander it.

Hence **'salamandering** *vbl. sb.*
1943 F. THOMPSON *Candleford Green* iii. 54 Another cooking process.. which perhaps may have been peculiar to smithy families was known as 'salamandering'.

salamandrian (sælə'mændrɪən), *a.* and *sb.* [f. L. *salamandra* SALAMANDER + -IAN.] **A.** *adj.*
1. Resembling (that of) a salamander.
1600 W. WATSON *Decacordon* (1602) 2 The Iesuits were the first beginners thereof [of scandal], and haue continued on this Salamandrian smoake of vaporous heats. **1647** OWEN *Death of Death* Wks. 1852 X. 155 It is not.. any Salamandrian Complexion that was the motive to this undertaking.

2. Belonging to the genus *Salamandra*.
1850 *Fraser's Mag.* XLI. 656 A salamandrian larva. **1888** G. ALLEN in *Good Words* 232 A few other salamandrian creatures.

B. *sb.* A salamandrian batrachian.
1850 *Fraser's Mag.* XLI. 656 A great fossil salamandrian.

salamandrid (sælə'mændrɪd). [ad. mod.L. *Salamandridæ*, f. *salamandra* SALAMANDER: see -ID.] A salamander of the family *Salamandridæ*.
1863 DANA *Man. Geol.* 345 Salamandrids.—Species without gills or gill-openings in the adult state.

salamandriform (sælə'mændrɪfɔːm), *a.* [f. L. *salamandra* SALAMANDER: see -FORM.] Resembling or having the form of a salamander.
1869 HUXLEY *Introd. Classif. Anim.* v. 112 The Labyrinthodonta.—The body is salamandriform, with relatively weak limbs, and a long tail. **1877** LE CONTE *Elem. Geol.* III. (1879) 390.

salamandrine (sælə'mændrɪn), *a.* and *sb.* [f. L. *salamandra* SALAMANDER + -INE[1].] **A.** *adj.*
1. Resembling or characteristic of the salamander in being able to resist fire, or live in it.
1712 ADDISON *Spect.* No. 281 ¶13 A certain Salamandrine Quality, that made it capable of living in the midst of Fire and Flame. *a* **1849** POE *Hawthorne* Wks. 1865 III. 190 'It becometh not a divine', saith Lord Coke, 'to be of a fiery and salamandrine spirit'. **1870** *Illustr. Lond. News* 29 Oct. 446 They led their salamandrine dance over the glazed delft plaques vis-à-vis to the leaping flames. **1886** A. SIMSON *Trav. in Ecuador* xiv. 184 There was a hot fire and the necessity of carrying on culinary operations in its immediate vicinity, which tended to call our salamandrine qualities into requisition.

2. *Zool.* Of or pertaining to the *Salamandrinæ*.
1865 COPE in *Nat. Hist. Rev.* Jan. 104 The representatives of these [types] in the Palæotropical region do not exhibit such decided salamandrine tendencies. **1870** HUXLEY *Lay Serm.* xii. 287 Fashioning flank and limb into due salamandrine proportions. **1888** ROLLESTON & JACKSON *Anim. Life* 408 The Salamandrine *Amblystoma mexicanum*.

B. *sb.* **1.** = SALAMANDER 2 b.
1797 W. TAYLOR in *Monthly Rev.* XXII. 507 The charms of Amenoe, a salamandrine. **1846** *Blackw. Mag.* LX. 226 Every horrible legend of demon, ghost, goule, gnome, salamandrine, and fireking. **1885** BATTERSBY *Elf Islands* 15 Then perhaps the elves, and the fairies and the beautiful salamandrines will come back to us.

2. = SALAMANDER 1 b.
1891 in *Century Dict.*

salamandroid (sælə'mændrɔɪd), *a.* and *sb.* [ad. mod.L. *salamandroīdēs*, *-oīdeus*, f. *salamandra* SALAMANDER: see -OID.] **A.** *adj.* Resembling a salamander, salamandriform.
1854 OWEN in *Orr's Circ. Sci.*, *Org. Nat.* I. 194 Salamandroid fishes. **1877** LE CONTE *Elem. Geol.* (1879) 493 A Salamandroid Amphibian.. four feet long.

B. *sb.* A urodele of the genus *Salamandra* or allied genera.
1863 DANA *Man. Geol.* 344 Salamandroids, or *Batrachia Urodela*. **1872** NICHOLSON *Palæont.* 349 The skeleton of a Salamandroid of large size.

sala'mandrous, *a. rare*$^{-1}$. [f. L. *salamandra* SALAMANDER + -OUS.] Living as it were in fire; fiery, hot, passionate.
1711 G. CARY *Phys. Phyl.* 29 My Salamandrous Spirit.. my Ætnous burning Humours.

So **sala'mandry** *a.*
1610 BOYS *Expos. Dom. Epist. & Gosp.* Wks. (1629) 76 If a Salamandry spirit should traduce that godly labour, as the silenced Ministers haue wronged our Communion Booke.

salami (sə'lɑːmɪ). Also **salame**. [ad. It. *salame*, pl. *salami*, repr. pop. L. **salāmen*, f. *salāre* to salt.] **1.** An Italian variety of sausage, highly salted and flavoured.
1852 PFEIFFER *Journ. Iceland* 19 White bread and salami! **1858** MAYNE *Expos. Lex.*, *Salami*. **1907** *Westm. Gaz.* 19 Oct. 6/2 We must lunch on bread, cheese, and salame. **1937** *Time & Tide* 11 Sept. 1209/1 Everyone carried a basket with their food for the day—red wine, long rolls of bread, salami, cherries. **1956** A. WILSON *Anglo-Saxon Att.* II. iii. 363 Tea at Slough was a curious meal. There was *salami* and *mortadella* and caraway bread. **1973** C. BONINGTON *Next Horizon* x. 146 We had a mass of high protein food; nuts, cheese, salami [etc.].

2. *attrib.* and *Comb.*, as *salami sandwich*, *sausage*; **salami tactics**, the piecemeal attack on or elimination of (esp. political) opposition (see quot. 1952).
1925 N. COWARD *Fallen Angels* in *Three Plays* 258 At the last moment he said he wanted a Salami sandwich. **1977** C. MCFADDEN *Serial* (1978) xlviii. 102/2 I'm not going back to the same old lifestyle with.. me making salami sandwiches all the time. **1946** G. MILLAR *Horned Pigeon* iii. 50 The driver handed out a bit of Salami sausage and a small flask of wine. [**1947** *Time* (Latin Amer. ed.) 9 June 25/1 In

Budapest, the citizens considered that the Smallholders' Party had been wrecked. 'Rakosi has eaten the last of the salami', was the word.] **1952** *Times* 19 May 7/3 Mr. Rákosi describes one stage in it as 'salami tactics', by which slices of the Small-holders' Party were cut away and its strength worn down, even while the Small-holders' leader was Prime Minister and Mr. Rákosi his deputy. **1964** *Spectator* 29 May 731/2 Castro's skilful use of 'salami tactics' was helped by their prevailing reluctance to be considered 'witch-hunters'. **1978** *Times* 28 Apr. 17/7 If these salami tactics are continued it will not be long before they [*sc.* Kew Gardens] are closed on every public holiday.

sal-ammoniac (sælə'məʊnıæk). Forms: see AMMONIAC; also 5, 7 **sal almoniack**, 6 *Sc.* **sal aramoniakle, salmoniakill**, 7 **Sal Armeniac, salhormoniacke**. See also SALMIAC. [See AMMONIAC A. 1.] Ammonium chloride.

c **1325** *Chron. Eng.* 184 Salgemme and salpetre, Salarmoniac ther ys eke. **1390** GOWER *Conf.* II. 84 And the spirit which is secounde In Sal Armoniak is found. **1477** NORTON *Ord. Alch.* iii. in Ashm. (1652) 41 Or whether I shall sal Almoniack take? **1507–8** *Acc. Ld. High Treas. Scot.* IV. 104, ij pund sal aramomakle [*sic*; *read* aramoniakle]. **1540** *Ibid.* VII. 357 Quik silver, aqua vite, salmoniakill. **1601** HOLLAND *Pliny* II. 351 The white of an egg incorporat with salhormoniacke finely puluerized. **1670** EACHARD *Cont. Clergy* 55 To which Aqua-fortis if you put a fifth part of Sal-Almoniack, and set them in a gentle heat, it makes Aqua-Regia. **1686** PLOT *Staffordsh.* iv. 150 Equal quantities of spirit of Sal Armeniac and spirit of Wine mixt. **1718** QUINCY *Compl. Disp.* 33 Sal Armoniac very elegantly imitates the Branches of a Tree. **1786** tr. *Beckford's Vathek* 87 The camels, which had been left unmolested to make sal ammoniac. **1863** *Fownes' Chem.* (ed. 9) 294 Sal-ammoniac.. is now largely manufactured from the ammoniacal liquid of the gas-works.

Hence †**sal-ammo'niacal** *a.*, pertaining to sal-ammoniac.

1760 BROWN *Compl. Farmer* II. 63 Urine by Glauber is reckoned to be of a destructive..nature to vegetables, because of the sal-armoniacal quality that is in it.

Salampo(o)re, -pora, variant ff. of SALEMPORE.

salamstone (sə'læmstəʊn). *Min.* [ad. G. *salamstein* (Werner).] A blue variety of sapphire from Sri Lanka (Ceylon).

1816 JAMESON *Min.* (ed. 2) I. 32 Werner has formed a new subspecies of spinel, under the name Salamstone, which is the Indian name of that mineral. **1839** URE *Dict. Arts*, etc. 743 *Salamstone* is a variety which consists of small transparent crystals..of pale reddish and bluish colours.

salangane ('sæləŋgeın). *Zool.* Also 8 **saligan**, 9 **salagane**. [ad. F. *salangane* or mod.L. *salangāna*, sc. *avis*, f. *salamga*, name of the bird in Luzon.] One of the birds of the genus *Collocalia*, which make edible nests; an esculent swallow.

1793 SMELLIE tr. *Buffon's Nat. Hist. Birds* VI. 577 Nothing better shews that the Salangane has remained long unknown, than the different names bestowed on it. **1796** MORSE *Amer. Geog.* II. 589 The nest of the bird saligan affords that dissolving jelly. **1869–73** T. R. JONES *Cassell's Bk. Birds* II. 119 The Salangane usually builds in such deep and dark cavities that [etc.].

†**Sa'larian**, *a.*[1] *Obs.* [Incorrectly for **Saliarian*, f. L. *Saliāris*, f. *Saliī* (see SALIAN[1]).] = SALIAN[1].

1598 GRENEWEY *Tacitus, Ann.* II. xix. (1622) 60 A Salarian verse [orig. *Saliari carmine*], which Mars Priests were wont to sing. [Hence in **1656** BLOUNT *Glossogr.*]

sa'larian, *a.*[2] [f. L. *salāri-us* (f. *sal* salt) + -AN.]

†**a.** Pertaining to salt. *Obs.*

1656 BLOUNT *Glossogr.*

b. *Salarian Way*, the name of an ancient road, the *Via Salaria*, running from Rome north-east to Reate (now Rieti) and later extended to the Adriatic.

[*a* **900**: see WAY *sb.*[1] 1 c.] **1866** tr. *P. Guéranger's Life St. Cecilia* viii. 87 Two figures in the cemetery of Priscilla in the Salarian Way, have been reproduced by Agincourt. **1945** R. HARGREAVES *Enemy at Gate* 38 The Salarian Gate stood upon the Salarian Way, the road by which the Romans had been accustomed to carry sea-salt up to the country of the Sabines.

salariat (sə'lɛərıət). [a. F. *salariat*, f. L. *salārium* (see SALARY *sb.*) after *proletariat* PROLETARIATE, -AT.] The salaried class; salary-earners collectively.

1918 RECKITT & BECHHOFER *Meaning of Nat. Guilds* iv. 85 Hypnotized by the round 'O' in the figure of their pay, the salariat feel that they really are important members of the industry. **1922** *Q. Rev.* Apr. 288 The 'salariat' is almost as much enslaved as the proletariat. **1926** *Glasgow Herald* 2 Feb. 8/2 Departmental economies, involving..savings on the salariat. **1937** *Daily Herald* 8 Feb. 13/2 Sir Walter Citrine..stressed the fact that technological progress had enormously increased the importance of the 'salariat'. **1965** *Sunday Times* 17 Jan. 4/1 Mr. Iain Macleod..said..'The age of the Salariat is here, and the age of the wage earner is passing.' **1971** *Oxford Times* 26 Nov. 7/2 Most of its members came from the British salariat—he [*sc.* Clive Jenkins] preferred this to the usual term white collar workers. **1978** *Listener* 26 Jan. 106/1 The professions and the salariat.

†**sa'lariate**, *v.* *Obs.* [f. L. *salāri-um* SALARY + -ATE[3].] *trans.* To pay a salary to; to supply the salary of. Hence **sa'lariated** *ppl. a.*, salaried.

1656 J. HARRINGTON *Oceana* (1658) 202 The Senat of the Bean in Athens, because it was but annual, was moderately salariated. **1672** PETTY *Pol. Anat.* (1691) 37 Sallariated Masters of Chancery. *a* **1687** —— *Pol. Arith.* (1690) 49 About 72,000*l*, at the medium of 3*l* per Man, would Salariate the whole number of twenty four thousand.

salaried ('sælərıd), *ppl. a.* [f. SALARY *sb.* or *v.* + -ED.]

1. Having or receiving a salary.

1600 O. E. *Repl. Libel* I. i. 36 Most of them are his salaried schollers, or agents. **1818** SOUTHEY in *Q. Rev.* XIX. 96 A regular inspection of the school by the salaried overseer. **1858** MAX MÜLLER *Chips* (1880) III. i. 36 To become a salaried class of servants of the crown. **1894** J. KNIGHT *D. Garrick* iv. 59 He appeared as a salaried actor at Drury Lane.

2. Having a salary attached to it.

1836 LANDOR *Pericles & Aspasia* cxiv. Wks. 1853 II. 399/1 The other offices that are salaried are the lower. **1872** MINTO *Eng. Prose Lit.* II. x. 610 The poorly-salaried Chair of Civil History.

salary ('sælərı), *sb.* Forms: α. 4 **salerie**, 4–6 **-arye**, 4, 7 **sallery**, 4–8 **salarie**, 5 **saleri, selarie, -aré, celarie, -ye**, 5–7 **sallarie**, 5–8 **-ary**, 6 **sellary**, 7 **sallerey**, 8 **-erie**, 5– **salary**; β. 5 **sala(i)re**, 6 **-air**. [a. AF. *salarie* = OF. *salaire*, It. *salario*, Sp., Pg. *salario*, ad. L. *salārium*, orig. money allowed to Roman soldiers for the purchase of salt, hence, their pay; subst. use of neut. sing. of *salārius* pertaining to salt, f. *sal* salt.]

1. Fixed payment made periodically to a person as compensation for regular work: now usually restricted to payments made for non-manual or non-mechanical work (as opposed to *wages*).

From *c* 1390 to *c* 1520 commonly applied to the stipend of a priest, esp. a chantry priest.

α. **1377** LANGL. *P. Pl.* B. XIV. 142 Riȝt as a seruaunt taketh his salarye bifore & sitth wolde clayme more. *a* **1400** *Solomon's Bk. Wisdom* 40 in *Adam Davy*, etc. 83 Chese þe a witty hyne & loue hym with al þi miȝth; Of his Salerie wiþ holde þou nouȝth. **1428** in *E.E. Wills* (1882) 80 And to a prest for to singe for me and all cristin soulis, competent saleri for an hole here. **1483–5** *Rec. St. Mary at Hill* 121 Payde to the preste, Syr Iohn plommer, for hys celarie for ij yer, xiij li vj s viij d. **1516** *Test. Ebor.* (Surtees) VI. 2, I will that a descritt and an honest preste have sellary to syng for my soull. **1585** T. WASHINGTON tr. *Nicholay's Voy.* III. xii. 93 Phisitions..for their salarie haue euery one of them tenne aspres a day. **1602** WARNER *Alb. Eng.* Epit. (1612) 360 For competent viande and sallarie to vndergoe the defence of the Realme. **1651** HOBBES *Leviath.* II. xxviii. 166 Reward, is either of Gift, or by Contract. When by Contract, it is called Salary, and Wages. **1659** D. PELL *Impr. Sea* 69 Are not some so taken up with the..gilded Cabbins, Lanthorns, and great Salaries which they have, that they minde little else? **1677** *Seasonable Argt. Grand Juries* 3 Sir Humphry Winch, Baronet, hath from the Court 500*l.* per annum Sallery. **1718** LADY M. W. MONTAGU *Lett. to C'tess of Bristol* 10 Apr., The slaves..have no wages; but..clothes to a higher value than our salaries to any ordinary servant. **1776** ADAM SMITH *W.N.* v. i. II. 324 Fixed salaries were appointed to the judges. **1848** MILL *Pol. Econ.* I. iv. §2 (1876) 36 That large portion of the productive capital of a country which is employed in paying the wages and salaries of labourers. **1868** *Chamb. Encycl.* X. 37/1 A manager of a bank or railway—even an overseer or a clerk in a manufactory, is said to draw a salary. **1879** *Print. Trades Jrnl.* XXIX. 43 The salary of the Prime Minister is £5,000 per annum.

β. **1433** LYDG. *St. Edmund* I. 934 The laborer neded no stuff to borwe For his salaire abood nat til the morwe. **1456** SIR G. HAYE *Law Arms* (S.T.S.) 144 Suppos the ȝere be nocht all past, or bot begonnyn, his [*sic*] sall have his full feis and salare. **1563–7** BUCHANAN *Reform. St. Andros* Wks. (S.T.S.) 16 The salair of the rectour.

†**2. a.** Reward or remuneration for services rendered; fee, honorarium. *Obs.*

c **1440** *Gesta Rom.* xxiv. 88 (Harl. MS.), But if þou pay now, I shal holde thi wif to wed, tyll tyme that I be paied fully my salary. *c* **1477** CAXTON *Jason* 119 Shal I haue none other salaire ne none other gwerdon for all my merites? **1602** SHAKS. *Ham.* III. iii. 79 Oh this is hyre and Sallery, not Reuenge. **1622** MALYNES *Anc. Law-Merch.* 390 Their Exchanges are made vpon this imaginarie ducat of three hundreth seuentie and fiue Maluedies, to be payed in Banke, with fiue vpon the thousand, which is the sallarie of the Banker. **1641** *Termes de la Ley* 245 Salarie..signifies a recompence or consideration given unto any man for his paines bestowed upon another mans businesse. **1643** SIR T. BROWNE *Relig. Med.* II. §9 When I doe him [*sc.* my patient] no good, me thinkes it is scarce honest gaine, though I confesse 'tis but the worthy salary of our well-intended endeavours.

b. *gen.* Reward, recompense. *Obs.*

1484 CAXTON *Fables of Poge* vii, Alle the sallary or payment of them that mokken other is for to be mocqued at the last. *a* **1619** FOTHERBY *Atheom.* II. viii. §1 (1622) 279 Felicitie, which is the salarie and reward of Vertue, is giuen vs of God. **1684** *Contempl. St. Man* I. vi. (1699) 67 This is the Sallery which the Goods of the Earth bestow on those who serve them. **1686** tr. *Chardin's Trav. Persia* 406 You that have repented and are become good People, receive your Salary entring there for ever.

3. *attrib.*: ***salary bracket***, ***-earner***, ***man***, ***officer***, ***scale***; ***salary-fixing*** vbl. sb.; **salary grab**, an opprobrious term for the act of the U.S. Congress of 1873 by which the salaries of congressmen were increased.

1969 L. HELLMAN *Unfinished Woman* vi. 62 We were in what was called 'the same salary bracket'. **1926** *Socialist Rev.* Oct. 47 A minority of salary-earners receive also unearned incomes of varying sizes. **1961** *Guardian* 25 Oct. 1/7 The machinery for salary-fixing in the universities is complicated. **1879** A. JOHNSTON *Hist. Amer. Politics* (1884) 220 The Act..was commonly known as the Salary Grab. **1719** in A. McF. Davis *Tracts Currency Mass. Bay* (1902) 193 Salary Men, Ministers, School-Masters, [etc.]..are pincht and hurt more than any. **1962** *Spectator* 29 June 846/2 Expensive cameras are being crowded out as the ultimate dream of what the Japanese call 'salarymen'. They are being replaced by a little bubble of an automobile. **1816** *Deb. Congress U.S.* 4 Dec. (1854) 240 The only difference between a salary officer and a per diem, is simply in the mode of payment, and not in the amount. **1940** R. S. LAMBERT *Ariel & all his Quality* xi. 302 Grade and salary scales were defined, and every employee informed where he stood.

†**'salary**, *a.*[1] *Obs. rare.* [? f. SALE *sb.*[1] + -ARY.] Open to sale, venal, SALEABLE.

1593 NASHE *Christ's T.* (1613) 157 Can it be so many brothel-houses, of salary sensuality, and six-penny whoredome,..should be set vp and maintained? **1596** —— *Saffron Walden* To Rdr., Wks. (Grosart) III. 27 He [*sc.* Tetzel] that..first stird vp Luther, pronouncing from the Pope free salarie indulgence to anie man.

†**'salary**, *a.*[2] *Obs.* [ad. L. *salāri-us*, f. *sal* salt: see -ARY.] Saline.

1646 SIR T. BROWNE *Pseud. Ep.* VI. xii. 338 From such salary irradiations may those wondrous varieties arise, which are observable in..Peacocks feathers.

salary ('sælərı), *v.* [Chiefly f. SALARY *sb.* In early use a. F. *salarier* (15th c.).] *trans.* To recompense, reward; to pay for something done (*Obs.* or *arch.*); to pay a regular salary to.

c **1477** CAXTON *Jason* 128 How..shall I be salaryed of suche payement in the recompensacion of the saluacion of your lyf? **1637** J. WILLIAMS *Holy Table* 46, I am not salaried to defend the Writer of the Letter. **1659** HEYLIN *Exam. Hist.* I. 210 They..salared some Lectures in such Market Towns where the people had commonly lesse to do. **1814** D'ISRAELI *Quarrels Auth.* I. 218 He [*sc.* Cibber] knew he was no poet, yet he would string wretched rhimes, even when not salaried for them. **1837** HT. MARTINEAU *Soc. Amer.* II. 290 The seven Judges of the Supreme Court are salaried with the same moderation as other members of the federal government. **1865** LECKY *Ration.* II. 375 For the great majority of nations agriculture is the single source of wealth; all manufactures are ultimately salaried by it. **1872** LIDDON *Elem. Relig.* ii. 69 The good man..is often unhappy, while vice is not unfrequently salaried and crowned with rewards. **1893** G. TRAVERS *Mona Maclean* III. 198 The Chinese system—salary the doctor and stop his pay when you get ill.

‖**salaud** (salo). [Fr., f. *sale* dirty.] A French term of abuse: filthy beast, 'swine', 'bastard'.

1962 D. LESSING *Golden Notebk.* III. 374 Jules said he would only pay me three hundred dollars for it. Salaud! **1967** C. L. MARKMANN tr. *F. Fanon's Black Skin White Masks* 11 When in the words of a gang of *salauds* it is no longer possible to find the sense of non-sense. **1971** E. PAUL *Reluctant Cloak & Dagger Man* xv. 177 '*Salaud*,' Jean whispered... 'For that you are going to die.' **1977** FONTANA & VAN DE WATER in Douglas & Johnson *Existential Sociol.* iii. 109 In *Nausea* Sartre referred to the others as *salauds* ('swine'). They live a smug existence, feel no anguish, and easily find meaning and justification in their lives.

salband ('sɑːlbænd). *Geol.* Also 9 **salebande, sahlband**. [G. *salband* selvage, earlier *sahlband* (from 16th c.), alteration of *selb-ende* 'self-end' (cf. *selvage* = 'self-edge').] A thin crust or coating of mineral, etc.

1811 PINKERTON *Petral.* I. 594 *note*, The amber is found between two salbands of lignite. **1839** URE *Dict. Arts* 316 These are often found upon both sides of the vein, so as to form cheeks or salebandes. **1879** RUTLEY *Stud. Rocks* xi. 199 The tachylytes occur mostly as salbands or thin crusts at the sides or margins of basalt dykes.

salband: see SALE *sb.*[3]

salbe, freq. spelling in ME. and early mod.Eng. of *shall be*: see SHALL *v.*

salbutamol (sæl'bjuːtəmɒl). *Pharm.* [f. SAL(ICYL + BUT(YL + AM(INE + -OL.] A white crystalline sympathomimetic agent which is used esp. as a bronchodilator in the treatment of asthma and is given as tablets of the sulphate or as an aerosol; 1-(4-hydroxy-3-hydroxymethyl-phenyl)-2-t-butylaminoethanol, $C_{13}H_{21}NO_3$.

1969 *Brit. Jrnl. Dis. Chest* LXIII. 173 Salbutamol is a new, metabolically stable adrenergic stimulant apparently more specific than either isoprenaline or orciprenaline for adrenergic β_2-receptors. **1977** *Lancet* 23 Apr. 908/2 Aerosolised salbutamol 1500 μg had no significant effect on lung function. *Ibid.* 13 Aug. 354/2 In 208 women in premature labour oral salbutamol 8 mg 6-hourly prolonged pregnancy for more than 2 days in 90% of patients. **1980** *Brit. Med. Jrnl.* 29 Mar. Advt. between pp. x and xi, A metered-dose aerosol delivering 100 mcg salbutamol BP per actuation.

salcepareille, obs. form of SARSAPARILLA.

salcer, salcery, obs. ff. SAUCER *sb.*, SAUCERY.

salchow ('sælkɒv, 'sælkəʊ). *Skating.* Also **Salchow**. [f. the name of Ulrich *Salchow* (1877–1949), Swedish figure skater, who invented it.] In full, ***salchow jump***. A jump in which the skater takes off from the inside back

edge of one skate and lands, after a complete rotation, on the outside back edge of the other.
1921 B. MEYER *Skating* 113 *Salchow jump*, outside forward three with jump from the back inside edge to the outside back edge of the other foot. **1930**, **1959** [see AXEL]. **1968** *Daily Tel.* 6 Dec. 15/6 An inspired Haig Oundjian took the men's title. He never put a foot wrong and his brilliant triple salchow was the jumping highlight of this meeting. **1976** *Times* 19 Jan. 9/7 Beginning with a perfect triple salchow and a soaring double axel, Miss Pötzsch went through her programme with rare charm..marred only by a two-footed landing of a double salchow. **1980** *Times* 25 Jan. 9/3 The British champion did play for safety by eliminating the two triple jumps he is not totally sure of, the lutz and toe salchow.

†**sald**, *v.* *Obs.* [ad. It. *saldare*.] *trans.* To balance (an account, etc.).
1588 J. MELLIS *Briefe Instr.* E vij b, To salde them afterwardes in the Leager, ye shall make gaines and damages, of all these parcels, and the expences in their places Creditors. *Ibid.* F j b, In salding of the same accompt.

sald(e, obs. pa. t. of SELL *v.*

Saldanha (sælˈdɑːnə). The name of a bay in western Cape Province, South Africa, used *attrib.* in **Saldanha man, skull**, to designate a fossil hominid belonging to an archaic form of *Homo sapiens* or the fragments of it found at Hopefield by Singer and Jolly in 1953.
1953 M. R. DRENNAN in *S. Afr. Jrnl. Sci.* L. 8 (*caption*) Side view of the skull-cap of Saldanha Man. *Ibid.* 8/2 The Saldanha skull is thus somewhat shorter..than..the Rhodesian skull. **1954** *Amer. Jrnl. Physical Anthropol.* XII. 349 Fluorine tests also revealed that *Mesochoerus* and *Paleoloxodon* lived contemporaneously with Saldanha Man. *Ibid.* 352 The Saldanha skull..at present consists of a fairly complete 'cap' or vault. **1959** J. D. CLARK *Prehist. S. Afr.* iv. 83 Saldanha Man may..be considered to be representative of the kind of 'proto-Australoid' individual who was responsible for the final expression of the Earlier Stone Age cultures in southern Africa at the end of the Middle and beginning of the Upper Pleistocene. **1973** B. J. WILLIAMS *Evolution & Human Origins* xi. 184/2 The later find of the Saldanha skull provided another specimen almost identical to that of Rhodesian Man.

Saldanier (sældəˈnɪə(r)). *S. Afr. Hist.* Also **Saldanhar** (-ˈɑː(r)). [Afrikaans, f. the name of *Saldanha* Bay in Cape Province (cf. prec.).] A member of a Hottentot group that, in the seventeenth century, inhabited the region of Saldanha Bay; an African cattle-dealer.
[**1607** W. KEELING in R. Raven-Hart *Before Van Riebeck* (1967) 36 Saldanians alias Cafares.] **1838** D. MOODIE tr. *J. van Riebeck's Jrnl.* in *Record* I. 16 In the evening some of the Saldania Ottentoos came to the Fort... These two Saldaniers were much bolder and livelier men than the Strandlopers who daily live with us, but still having the same language and clothing. *Ibid.* 22 The Saldaniers..lay in thousands about Salt River with their cattle in countless numbers. **1900** A. H. KEANE *Boer States* p. xviii, *Saldaniers*, originally the Hottentots of the grassy Saldanha Bay district, who had always plenty of cattle to sell to the Dutch East India Company's people; later, any native livestock dealers. **1972** *Stand. Encycl. S. Afr.* V. 606/2 As soon as they arrived in South Africa the Portuguese..followed by the Dutch colonists in 1652, came into contact with a yellowish brown pastoral people at the Cape. The colonists at first called them Kaapmans and Saldanhars, but later on the name 'Hottentot'..became firmly established.

†**sale**, *sb.*[1] *Obs.* Forms: 1 sæl, sal-, 4–7 sale, 5 sall, saile, 5–6 saill, sayll. [OE. *sæl* (pl. *salu*) str. n., = OHG., MHG. *sal* (G. *saal*):—OTeut. **saloz-*, orig. an *-es*, *-os* stem (cf. OE. *salor*). Romanic adoptions of the Teut. word are F. *salle*, Pr., It., Sp. *sala*: see SALE *sb.*[4] and SALLE.
The form **saliz-* of the OTeut. stem is represented by OE. *sel*, *sele* hall (appearing as the second element in LEVESEL), OS. *seli*, OHG. *sali*, *seli*, ON. *salr*, which have become masculine *i* stems.]
A hall or spacious chamber; a king's or noble's lodging, palace, castle; occas. a tent.
In ME. alliterative poetry *in sale* is a frequent tag.
Beowulf 2075 (Gr.) Gæst yrre cwom, eatol æfengrom user neosan, ðær we ʒesunde sæl weardodon. *a* **1000** *Riddles* liii. 2 (Gr.) Ic seah ræpingas in ræced ferʒan under hrof sales hearde tweʒen. *a* **1300** *K. Horn* 1187 (Cambr. MS.), Wyn for to schenche, After mete in sale. *c* **1330** *Amis & Amil.* 444 And worthliest in ich a wede, And semliest in sale. *a* **1400–50** *Alexander* 502 Þe king was sett in his sale with septer in hand. *Ibid.* 4016 Þan sett he sales vp of silke & sacrifece makis. *c* **1420** *Liber Cocorum* (1862) 10 Kele hit with a litelle ale, And set hit downe to serve in sale. *c* **1470** *Gol. & Gaw.* 1150 The seymly souerane of the sall. **1470–85** MALORY *Arthur* XVII. xvi. 713 Ryghte soo as they sat at her dyner in the chyef sale. **1513** DOUGLAS *Æneis* VII. iv. 45 Thair stud ane gret tempill, or saill riall. **1522** *World & Child* A j b, My selfe semely in sale I sende with you to be.
b. *fig.*
14.. in *Tundale's Vis.* (1843) 158 A mey hym harbered yn hur hall, Scho socourd hym sotht[l]y yn hur sale.

sale (seɪl), *sb.*[2] Also 5 saale, sayll, 5–6 saill, 7 saile, 7–8 sail. [late OE. *sala*, prob. a. ON. *sala* wk. fem. (ON. had also *sal* neut.) = OHG. *sala*, MHG. *sale*, *sal* str. fem., f. root *sal-* of **saljan* to SELL.]
1. a. The action or an act of selling or making over to another for a price; the exchange of a commodity for money or other valuable consideration. Also, with qualification: (Ready, slow, etc.) disposal of goods for money; opportunity of selling.
bill of sale: see BILL *sb.*[3] 10. *bargain and sale* (Law): see BARGAIN *sb.* 6.
c **1050** *Suppl. Ælfric's Gloss.* in Wr.-Wülcker 180 *Distractio*, ceap. *Uenditio*, sala. *a* **1300** *Cursor M.* 19239 'Sai me', he said, 'Ananias, Qui has þou tempted sathanas, To mak sli lesing o þi sale?' *c* **1400** *Rule St. Benet* (Prose) 37 Better chepe sal ye selle þan þe men of þe werld dose, þat god may be payde of yure sale. **1411** *E.E. Wills* (1882) 19 Þ' forseyd sale of my londes and tenementes. *a* **1450** MYRC *Festial* 79 When he [*sc.* Iudas Skaryot] segh þat Crist was demed to þe deth by hys sale. *c* **1475** *Rauf Coilȝear* 245 Thow sall haue for thy Fewaill, For my sake, the better saill. **1553** EDEN *Treat. Newe Ind.* (Arb.) 26 In the cytie of Panchi there is great sale of silke. **1582** N. LICHEFIELD tr. *Castanheda's Conq. E. Ind.* I. xlii. 97 He was told what ill sales he shoulde finde there of such Merchaundize as he had brought. **1593** SHAKS. *2 Hen. VI*, I. iii. 138 Thy sale of Offices and Townes in France. **1611** BIBLE *Lev.* xxv. 50 The price of his sale shalbe according vnto the number of yeeres. **1706** E. WARD *Wooden World Diss.* To Rdr. (1708) A v b, Permit it..to hang in View at..some such eminent Place of Sale. **1727** GAY *Begg. Op.* I. vi, They are of sure sale from our warehouse at Redriff among the seamen. **1786** *Chamb. Cycl.* I. Pref. 4 The extensive sail of this edition. **1836** W. IRVING *Astoria* III. 231 The terms of sale were lowered by him to the standard fixed by Mr. Stuart. **1837** CHANNING *Addr. Temperance* 32 After these remarks, it will follow, that we should discourage the sale of ardent spirits.
b. *spec.* A putting up of goods to be sold publicly; a public auction. See also PORT-SALE.
1673 TEMPLE *Misc.* (1680) 136 Both those that won the Plate, and those which are thus sold, ought immediately to be marked so as they may never return a second time, either to the Race or to the Sale. **1700** [see CANDLE *sb.* 5 d]. **1718** *Free-thinker* No. 108 ¶1 On Thursday next..will begin another Publick Sale by Inch of Candle. **1753** *News, Boys, News!* (Oxf. Jrnl.) 11 Apr., On Saturday, the 14th Instant, ..will be held at the Town-Hall in this City, a Sale of great Part of the Goods..belonging to the..Old Interest of this County. **1867** TROLLOPE *Chron. Barset* II. lxiii. 205 He should pull down the bills advertising the sale of his effects. **1888** ANNIE S. SWAN *Doris Cheyne* viii. 128 An auction sale ..for behoof of the creditors of Robert Cheyne.
c. A special disposal of shop goods at rates lower than those usually charged in order to get rid of them rapidly, e.g. at the end of a 'season'
1866 *Chambers's Jrnl.* 30 June 402/2 (Advt.), Enormous and incredible sale.., for ten days only!!! **1875** L. TROUBRIDGE *Life amongst Troubridges* (1966) 124 We.. found a vague little shop where a sale was going on and everything was too ridiculously cheap. We bought some little silk scarves for a penny three farthings each. **1880** [see *clearance sale* s.v. CLEARANCE 10]. **1888** *Daily News* 10 Jan., The low prices at the stock-taking sales. **1894** *Westm. Gaz.* 11 Jan. 3/2 Wait till you see my pretty new sale-frock. **1900** *Ibid.* 4 Jan. 3/2 Sale-time, when everything at the shops, from a collar to a costume, is reduced to low prices.
d. *Bookselling.* The ordinary trade rate.
1900 *What will it Cost?* 48 [Trade phrases] *Sale*, 30% discount off published price.
2. Phrases. **a.** *to sale* = 'for sale' (see 2 e). Now only in *to put up to sale*, formerly † *to set to sale* (often *fig.*; in quot. 1576 app. to abandon), *expose*, etc. *to sale*.
c **1380** WYCLIF *Wks.* (1880) 393 Welle niȝ alle her blessyngis ben sett to sale and to prise. **1390** GOWER *Conf.* II. 297 The Ston he profreth to the sale. *a* **1400** *Octouian* 1909 And chepede me that chyld to sale, For syxty florencys all be tale. **1543–4** *Act 35 Hen. VIII*, c. 8 Such persons as brew for theyr owne prouision, and not to sale. **1576** GASCOIGNE *Philomene* (Arb.) 104 But Progne (now in priuie place) Set silence al to sale. **1592** TIMME *Ten Eng. Lepers* D 3 b, Whereby they have set to sale for money Christ himselfe. **1642** MILTON *Apol. Smect.* 7 A strong presumption that his modesty set there to sale in the frontispice, is not much addicted to blush. **1649** —— *Eikon.* viii. 66 She pawn'd and set to saile the Crown-Jewels. **1660** F. BROOKE tr. *Le Blanc's Trav.* 15 Fair piazza's,..where the Merchants..expose to sale their drugs. **1670** DRYDEN *Conq. Granada* V. ii, My price!—Why, king, you do not think you deal With one who sets his services to sale? **1760–72** H. BROOKE *Fool of Qual.* (1809) III. 58 Those who set themselves, their trusts, and their country, to sale. **1810** *Act 50 Geo. III*, c. 41 §6 Every Hawker, Pedlar, Petty Chapman, ..carrying to sell, or exposing to Sale, any Goods. **1838** PRESCOTT *Ferd. & Is.* II. xxv. III. 494 The most considerable offices in church and state were put up to sale.
†**b.** *to make sale (of)*: to sell. *Obs.*
c **1430** *Pilgr. Lyf Manhode* IV. ix. (1869) 180 Which if men made of you saale, mihte no man livinge overbigge yow. **1463** in *Bury Wills* (Camden) 26, I wille..the Sexteyn of Bury and the Priour of Dusgylde..make a sale of myn seid hefd place. **1552** HULOET, Make sale of vyle thynges and trifles, *agitor*. **1557** W. TOWRSON in Hakluyt *Voy.* (1589) 114 When God should sende vs to any place where we might make sale. **1616** R. C. *Times' Whistle* IV. 1441 Thou mayst make sale of it to whom thou list.
c. *to set on* (or †*a*) *sale* = 'to set to sale' (see 2 a); (*to be*) *on* or †*upon sale* = 'for sale' (see 2 e).
1546 J. HEYWOOD *Prov.* (1867) 63 Here is a tale, For honestie, meete to set the diuell on sale. **1556** OLDE *Antichrist* 72 They bestowe not only benefices..but also set a sale..the holy sacred gyftes of the holy Goost. **1634** *Documents agst. Prynne* (Camden) 59 How those bookes have been dispersed by them upon sale or otherwise. **1793** COWPER *Let. to Lady Hesketh* 30 June, If it is out of print, it is no longer upon sale. **1835** SOUTHEY *Cowper's Wks.* I. Pref. 6 A book which has been upon sale ever since it was published, twelve years ago. **1901** *Times* 16 Dec. 8/6 The Times is on Sale for 3d. per Copy at all railway bookstalls in England and Wales.
†**d.** *of sale*: that is to be sold; vendible, venal.
1588 SHAKS. *L.L.L.* IV. iii. 240 To things of sale, a sellers praise belongs. **1605** BACON *Adv. Learn.* II. x. §8 (1891) 141 As to the confections of sale which are in the shops. **1608** SHAKS. *Per.* IV. vi. 84 The house you dwell in proclaims you to be a creature of sale.
e. *for sale*: used adjectively, = intended to be sold; used advb., = with a view to selling.
1611 SHAKS. *Cymb.* I. iv. 92 The other is not a thing for sale. **1686** PLOT *Staffordsh.* iii. §28. 124 Then they draw them [*sc.* pots] for Sale, which is chiefly to the poor Cratemen. **1808** *Times* 24 Feb., Feathers and Quills for Sale. **1815** SCOTT *Guy M.* vii, They..sometimes had good pointers for sale. **1863** HAWTHORNE *Our Old Home* I. 257 We went into a bookseller's shop to inquire if he had any description of Boston for sale.
f. *sale and* (now usu. *or*) *return*: see quot. 1838. Freq. *attrib.*
1795 T. PEAKE *Cases Nisi Prius* 56 Two questions were made, first on the sale and return. *Ibid. marg.*, If goods are delivered on the terms of sale or return. **1838** BELL *Dict. Law Scot.*, *Sale and return* is a contract, by which goods are delivered by a wholesale dealer to a retailer, to be paid for at a certain rate, if sold again by the retailer; and if not sold, to be returned to the vendor. **1897** [see RETURN *sb.* 15]. **1952** E. COXHEAD *Play Toward* iv. 100 The tickets..were distributed on a sale-or-return basis to every child in the school. **1954** L. DURRELL *Let.* in *Spirit of Place* (1969) 122 The local bookseller..has been pestering me to help him re-arrange his shop... Is there any sale or return system? **1973** *Times* 17 Apr. 23/2 A clause forcing direct-sales firms to offer their goods on a 'sale or return' basis. **1978** S. HODGES *Gollancz* vii. 154 Reg Dignum, the London traveller, persuaded Victor to let him sell it [*sc. Guilty Men*] 'on sale or return', a practice which the firm normally never agreed to.
g. *sale of work*, a sale of articles that have been made by members of an association, congregation, or the like, held on behalf of some charitable, religious, or political object. Also, a commercial sale of handiwork.
1859 in F. K. Prochaska *Women & Philanthr. 19th-c. Eng.* (1980) 258 (*title*) Second annual report of the association for the sale of work by ladies of limited means. **1873** *Young Englishwoman* May 258/1 Can the Editor inform M.A.B. of any repository where needle or network by distressed gentlewomen is removed and sold for their benefit? (New Society for Sale of Work, North Audley Street W). **1890** *New Road Chapel Monthly Visitor* Feb. 18b/1 Sale of work and mothers' meetings. **1905** *Grand Mag.* June 810 Ladies ..are informed that..a shop or gallery for the sale of work is shortly to be opened. **1917** F. KLICKMANN *Between Larch-Woods & Weir* ii. 21 The vermilion satin cushion embroidered with yellow eschscholtzias, that had lain in a trunk in the attic since the last Sale of Work but two. **1969** JOYCE *Finnegans Wake* (1964) 446 'Tis post purification we will, sales of work and social service, completing our Abelite union by the adoption of fosterlings. **1973** A. BEHREND *Samarai Affair* iv. 54 A ride round the farm, a coffee morning or a Conservative sale of work. **1976** M. HINXMAN *End of Good Woman* vii. 99 The success of the last sale of work.
h. *sale and lease-back*: see LEASE-BACK.
3. a. *attrib.* and *Comb.*, as *sale catalogue*, *-factor*, *-goer*, *-market*, *-room*, †*-shop*; **sale-block**, a block on which slaves are exposed for sale; **sale-boat**, a boat that conveys fish from the fishing ground to market; **sale day**, (*a*) the day on which a sale is held; (*b*) *Austral.* and *N.Z.*, a market-day; **sale-leaseback** = *sale and lease-back* (LEASE-BACK); †**saleman** [cf. OHG. *salaman*, MHG. *sal(e)man*], = SALESMAN; **sale note** *U.S.* (see quot.); †**sale-piece**, ? the sample that attracts purchasers (in quots. *fig.*); **sale ring**, the ring of buyers formed round an auctioneer at a sale; †**sale-worth, -worthy** *adjs.*, saleable; **sale-yard** *Austral.* and *N.Z.*, an enclosure in which livestock is sold.
1887 J. C. HARRIS *Free Joe*, etc. (1888) 54 The prisoner was made to stand on the *sale-block so that all might have a fair view of him. **1840** R. BREMNER *Excurs. in Denmark*, etc. II. 389 They [fish] are recaptured at dawn to be again imprisoned on the *sale-boats. **1792** J. LACKINGTON *Mem. First 45 Yrs.* xxxi. 329, I soon after this proposed printing a *sale catalogue. **1852** *Fraser's Mag.* June 723/2 When he [*sc.* a wholesale bookseller] subscribes a book, or issues a sale catalogue. **1910** *Quaritch's Catal.* No. 286 (*title*) Sale-Catalogue of the library of David Garrick. **1840** *Spirit of Times* 25 Apr. 90/2 *Sale days. **1898** *Bulletin* (Sydney) 26 Mar. 31/1 Tuesday was sale-day. Monday afternoon was devoted to the yarding of cattle and the yarding and drafting of innumerable sheep. **1937** *Burlington Mag.* Nov. p. xix/1 Let us hope..that this game..will end on the sale-day. **1948** N. SCANLAN *Rusty Road* i. 12 Thursday was Sale Day.. market day, they would call it in England, but there was no market in these small New Zealand towns. **1770** LANGHORNE *Plutarch* (1879) II. 829/2 Nor would he trust to the common customs of *sale-factors, auctioneers [etc.]. **1927** *Daily Express* 4 July 3/3 *Sale-goers are advised to remember the date. **1973** *N.Y. Law Jrnl.* 1 Aug. 5/3 Private placement of mortgages, joint ventures, sale-leasebacks on income properties and land, [etc.]. **1978** *Detroit Free Press* 5 Mar. B1/2 The sale-leaseback arrangement, which enables the farmer to raise money for new equipment despite low farm prices. **1642** T. HILL *Trade of Truth* 34 Christians should be Chapmen to buy, rather than *Salemen to sell. **1883** MOLONEY *W. African Fisheries* 22 (Fish. Exhib. Publ.) The *sale-market is large and wide enough. **1856** BOUVIER *Law Dict.*, **Sale note*, a memorandum given by a broker to a seller or buyer of goods, stating the fact that certain goods have been sold by him on account of a person called the seller to another person called the buyer. **1621** BURTON *Anat. Mel.* III. ii. II. ii. (1651) 463 Sweet breath, white and even teeth, which some call the *sale-piece. **1650** BULWER *Anthropomet.* 135 White teeth being so justly accounted a precious and natural beauty, that they are hence called the Sale-piece. **1901** *Essex Herald* 9 Apr. 4/8 The whole of this choice herd came into the *sale ring. **1813** *Examiner* 10 May 297/1 Public *Sale-rooms. **1858** CARLYLE *Fredk. Gt.* IV. vi.

I. 446 The learned babble of the Sale-room. **1902** *Daily Chron.* 25 Oct. 3/7 These curious sale-room methods. **1757** *Connoisseur* (ed. 2) III. 151, I am sure we have cast-off cloaths sufficient to furnish a *sale-shop. **1789** WOLCOTT (P. Pindar) *Imit. Hor.* I. xii. 31 Who soon shalt keep a saleshop for good places. **1795** J. AIKIN *Manchester* 233 A sale shop for most articles. **1922** JOYCE *Ulysses* 285 In Lionel Marks's antique saleshop window..candlestick melodeon oozing maggoty blowbags. **1957** *Beaver* Autumn 38/1 The 'Saleshop' classification marked a modest type of urban transition, from fur trade to general store operation. **1976** *Derbyshire Times* (Peak ed.) 3 Sept. 18/5 (Advt.), Self service grocery stores with modern detached house... Spacious living accommodation..plus saleshop 31ft. × 19ft. 6 ins. fully fitted for the trade. **1481** in Foster *Par. Ch. Whaplode* (1889) 94 The said trees..when thei shall be felled..at such tyme as thei be *saleworth. *c* **1440** *Promp. Parv.* 441/1 *Sale worthy, *vendibilis*. **1547** *Bk. Marchauntes* c vj, I would wit.. if her marchantdyse were sale worthy. **1901** M. FRANKLIN *My Brilliant Career* iv. 18 He was a familiar figure at the Goulburn *sale yards every Wednesday. **1934** [see BACKING *ppl. a.*]. **1975** *N.Z. Jrnl. Agric.* Sept. 61/1 Normally stud stock are sold either from yards on the farm itself, or by auction at recognized centrally situated saleyards.

b. *Comb.* with **sales-**, modelled on SALESMAN, SALESWOMAN, e.g. ***sales appeal, area, campaign, chart, correspondent, curve, figures, force, -gentleman, girl, -goer, graph, -lady, -manager, -master, message, outlet, -people, -person, presentation, promoter, promoting, promotion, volume***; also with plural, **sales-book**, a book or record of sales; **sales clerk** *N. Amer.*, a shop asistant; **sales drive**, an energetic effort to sell goods extensively; hence **sales-drive** *v. trans.*; **sales engineer**, a salesman with technical knowledge of his goods and their market; hence **sales engineering; sales pitch** [PITCH *sb.*^{2} 5 b] = *sales talk*; hence **sales pitchery; sales rep**: colloq. abbrev. of next; **sales representative**, one who represents a commercial firm to prospective customers and solicits orders; a traveller (cf. REPRESENTATIVE *sb.* 4 a); **sales resistance**, the ability or disposition to resist buying something offered for sale; also *fig.*; hence **sales-resistant** *a.*; **sales room** = *sale-room* (see above); **sales slip**, a slip of paper recording the price of an article and other details of its sale; **sales talk**, persuasive rhetoric designed to promote the sale of goods or (*transf.*) the acceptance of an idea; **sales tax**, a tax levied on the retail sales of commodities; †**sales-work** = *sale-work* (see 4 a).

1931 C. BEDELL *Seven Keys to Retail Profits* iii. 36 Instead of using a $20 bill to give him *two* profit opportunities, a double sales appeal, many a retailer spends the entire twenty for a quantity of one item. **1936** *Jrnl. R. Aeronaut. Soc.* XL. 289 In the case of commercial aircraft, at any rate, by the gain in 'sales appeal' resulting from the general air of cleanness. **1966** *B.B.C. Handbk.* 39 Another sales area which has great potential—the distribution of programmes for non-theatric use in schools, universities, training colleges. **1771** *Encycl. Brit.* I. 619/1 *The Sales-book.* This book too is chiefly used by factors; and into it is posted, from the Waste-book, the particular sales of every consigned cargo. **1809** R. LANGFORD *Introd. Trade* 76 The manner that a Sales-book is ruled. **1969** D. C. HAGUE *Managerial Econ.* III. xiii. 288 We talk of price wars, sales campaigns, marketing strategies. **1959** 'F. NEWTON' *Jazz Scene* iv. 72 Rhythm and blues have not only swamped ordinary pop music in America and Britain, at least in terms of the sales-chart, [etc.]. **1934** WEBSTER, Sales clerk. **1968** *Globe & Mail* (Toronto) 17 Feb. 39 A 19-year-old Toronto sales clerk. **1979** *Honolulu Advertiser* 8 Jan. D-3/9 Sales Clerk..full time and part time. Apply at B.S. Co. Ward Warehouse. **1951** in M. McLuhan *Mech. Bride* (1967) 41/3 A book that ought to be read by all advertising writers, sales correspondents, editors and business-paper writers. **1961** *Evening Standard* 14 July 20/3 Sales Correspondent in an expanding Mail Order Organization. **1946** Sales curve [see ROOF *sb.* 2 a]. **1969** 'J. MORRIS' *Fever Grass* ix. 81 You know I'm worth it. Just watch your sales curves. **1951** M. MCLUHAN *Mech. Bride* (1967) 144/2 Every success drive and sales drive is committed to erasing this [*sc.* resistance] in all its varieties. **1962** *Punch* 21 Nov. 754/1 To..sales-drive their dish-washing machines. **1942** *Sun* (Baltimore) 16 July 2/6 Three self-styled 'sales engineers' stood to garner commission on millions of dollars of Government war work. **1969** *Sales Engineer* Mar. 29/1 (Advt.), A Sales Engineer is any person who is directly or indirectly selling technical products to industry. Sales Engineering is not a trade, it is a profession, and the readers of *Sales Engineer* are professionals. **1966** G. N. LEECH *Eng. in Advertising* x. 99 The only criterion of success known to the advertising profession—sales figures. **1934** WEBSTER, *Sales force*, the sales clerks or sales agents of an establishment. **1974** *Times* 9 Mar. 24/6 (Advt.), Opportunity for a girl..to join Sales Force in the exciting new ski development of Anzère. **1980** M. BABSON *Queue here for Murder* ii. 21 Soon the Bonnard's sales force would start clocking in, and..after that the customers. **1887** *Courier-Jrnl.* (Louisville, Kentucky) 2 Feb. 4/7 In order to cripple his old partner, he offered superior inducements to the sales girls to go with him. **1978** M. KENYON *Deep Pocket* xi. 136 The squeak of a salesgirl flattened against a wall. **1925** *Glasgow Herald* 6 Jan. 7/2 The large number of men among the sales-goers. **1967** R. JEFFRIES *Deadly Marriage* i. 8 I've returned with firm orders for three parlour-sheds... That'll put the old graph up... The sales graph. **1856** *Daily Alta California* (San Francisco) 29 Oct. 4/3 (Advt.), *Wanted*—By a young lady, a situation as *saleslady* in a dry goods, trimming, or millinery store. **1883** *Century Mag.* XXVI. 610/2 The..ranks of seamstresses and 'sales-ladies'. **1928** *Sunday Dispatch* 5 Aug. 5/6 An amatory porter and a sales-lady sitting on some dirty steps on the Underground. **1976** *Billings* (Montana) *Gaz.* 20 June 8-D/5 (Advt.), Mobile Lot-Imperial Park. All city utili. Call Real Estate saleslady Geri Erickson, 252-0264. **1913** *Writer's Mag.* Nov. 184/2 *The Accountant*, Detroit, Mich., is in the market for interesting business stories—material of interest to business managers, advertising and sales managers, [etc.]. **1933** H. NICOLSON *Diary* 5 Jan. (1966) 131 We are then met by..the sales-manager of Doubleday Doran. **1979** R. PERRY *Bishop's Pawn* i. 13 My cover as sales manager for a multinational electronics firm. **1890** *Farmer's Gaz.* 4 Jan. 1/3 The salesmasters and dealers. **1922** JOYCE *Ulysses* 392 A worthy salesmaster that drove his trade for live stock and meadow auctions hard by Mr Gavin Low's yard in Prussia street. **1966** G. N. LEECH *Eng. in Advertising* iii. 30 The kernel of the sales message..has to be in some way special and different for each product. **1957** C. SMITH *Case of Torches* iv. 46 We must..keep the Belgian company as healthy as possible otherwise we stand to lose their valuable sales outlets. **1977** *Times* 5 Nov. 12/7 For..the purchasers of holidays, there will be..a wider choice of sales outlets. **1876** *Scribner's Monthly* Feb. 599/2, I walked through the crowds of purchasers and salespeople. **1976** *Evening Standard* 14 June 24/8 (Advt.), 2 salespeople required to manage small gift shop. **1978** *Tucson Mag.* Dec. 33/1 If you find pleasure in being the only customer in the midst of a convention of used car salespeople, you'll love buying stereo equipment in Tucson. **1920** *Harper's Mag.* June 86 We have long been familiar with *salesman* and *saleswoman*—even, alas! with *saleslady*; and the latest member of the family to whom we have been introduced to, *salesperson*, a name intended to apply to employee of either sex. **1928** *Publishers' Weekly* 10 Nov. 1962/2 We shall be glad to send a complimentary copy of the novel on request to any retail salesperson to read. **1955** *Sun* (Baltimore) (B ed.) 12 Sept. 10/7 The 'pencil box' she bought for her grandson and which the salesperson called a 'companion', wasn't a box at all. **1976** *Evening Standard* 14 June 24/5 (Advt.), Salespersons required for expanding Northern based home improvement company. **1980** *Times* 18 Feb. 12/6 One of those cheap department stores where you may browse for several weeks without even locating a salesperson at all. **1962** *Listener* 18 Jan. 133/2 Ditchburn went through a masterly sales pitch. **1976** *National Observer* (U.S.) 19 June 1/5 In fact, as things turned out, it was an extraordinary sales pitch for Reagan himself. It drew $600,000 and made Reagan the new conservative star. **1980** *Jrnl. R. Soc. Arts* Feb. 145/2 Managers are impatient and practical people who, having accepted our sales pitch, will want to learn how to use what they have bought. **1968** *Punch* 7 Aug. 206/1 Close scrutiny reveals the fan of a camp follower beneath the canopy; or, perhaps, then as now, she was sketched in merely as a piece of crypto-sexual sales-pitchery. **1947** *Fortune* Nov. 175/1 (Advt.), They bring real 'theater' to a sales presentation. **1981** W. H. HALLAHAN *Trade* iv. 111 My firm is doing the sales presentation for the Essen Arms Company. **1935** *Punch* 4 Sept. 264/1 The great advantage of being a Sales Promoter is that the working hours are short. *Ibid.*, Sales Promoting is one of those lovely jobs in which it is impossible to judge by results. **1916** (*title*) Sales promotion by mail: how to sell and how to advertise. **1964** A. WYKES *Gambling* iii. 70 A young Indian businessman..went to Tokyo on a sales-promotion visit for his firm. **1979** *Jrnl. R. Soc. Arts* CXXVII. 346/2 Ingenuity, in..sales promotion..creates better value for the customer. **1969** *Observer* (Colour Suppl.) 23 Mar. 23/3 Sales reps in their company cars are my number-one headache. **1979** *Business Traveller* Nov.–Dec. 46/1 The sales rep has been sweating it out..in the hope of clinching a much bigger deal. **1949** *Daily Tel.* 21 Nov 2/5 Experienced Sales Representatives. **1981** 'E. FERRARS' *Experiment with Death* iv. 83 He's a sales representative for a firm of confectioners. **1925** *New Yorker* 4 July (verso front cover), 'Beggar on Horseback' presents no sales resistance problem... The buying public flocks. **1933** P. FLEMING *Brazilian Adventure* I. x. 88 Girls..sold flags for the Red Cross... Posters exhorted them to 'give our young men courage': an injunction which I suppose they thought it would be easier to obey if they first broke down the young men's sales resistance. **1972** M. BABSON *Murder on Show* xvi. 185 Heaven help you the day some woman gets her hooks into you—you've no sales resistance at all. **1979** E. H. GOMBRICH *Sense of Order* i. 19 In the history of Greek rhetorical theory such 'sales resistance' developed into an aesthetic prejudice on the part of purists against all forms of verbal fireworks. **1957** *Times Lit. Suppl.* 22 Mar. 174/3 His sympathies are so one-sidedly Jewish that he sometimes makes a reader sales-resistant. **1840** *Knickerbocker* XVI. 226 Ejecting a crowded audience from his sales-room, because an unlucky wight had the temerity to bid six-pence for a tattered copy of Paradise Lost. **1891** *Century Dict.*, *Salesroom*, same as sale-room. **1929** W. FAULKNER *Sanctuary* (1981) xvi. 186 The block.. was filled by a row of automobile sales-rooms. **1981** *Times* 20 July 18/5 Used vehicle outlets..in..'upmarket' salesrooms. **1962** *Lebende Sprachen* VII. 35/3 *Sales slip*, Barverkaufsschein, Kassenzettel. **1965** G. JACKSON *Let.* 25 Feb. in *Soledad Brother* (1971) 64, I asked Robert to send me some shoes... They have to be sent from Sears by the salesman, cost no more than $25, have the price or sales slip in the box. **1976** *New Yorker* 23 Feb. 35/1 Do you have a sales slip? **1926** *Amer. Speech* II. 97/2 Slang is regularly employed, especially in the 'sales-talk' letters [sent by business firms], but it must have a definite snap and appropriateness. **1933** *Punch* 1 Feb. 122/2 'No sales-talk?' 'No... These bolts sell themselves.' **1968** MRS. L. B. JOHNSON *White House Diary* 1 Aug. (1970) 697 Mayor Richard Daley..was giving Lyndon a sales talk about coming to Chicago. **1974** N. MARSH *Black as he's Painted* ii. 52 Motivated by sales-talk and embarrassment, he bought.. a cat bed-basket. **1921** *Daily Colonist* (Victoria, B.C.) 27 Oct. 2/6 An important decision affecting the Dominion sales tax was rendered by Judge Gunn here. **1940** *Economist* 31 Aug. 282/1 To secure additional tax revenue, the sales tax has been raised from 5 to 10 per cent [in New Zealand]. **1978** *N.Y. Times* 30 Mar. B1/2 His anti-government attitude and promise to veto any sales tax or income tax the Legislature may pass has won him many followers. **1959** *Listener* 26 Mar. 552/1 In order to increase the sales-volume of a new shade of lipstick. **1775** ASH, *Saleswork*, work done for sales, work slightly performed.

4. *attrib.* passing into *adj.* **a.** That is made to be sold; that may be purchased (not being needed for home use); hence, ready-made (as opposed to *home-made*); of inferior quality; e.g. ***sale bread, cloth, door, gimlet, ram, ware, work*** (also attrib.). Also, connected with or producing things sold or intended for sale, e.g. ***sale gardener, kiln, pond***. ? Now applied only to animals bred or fattened for sale.

1455 *Rolls of Parlt.* V. 304/1 The Subsidie and Awenage of sale Clothes, in the Counte of Wiltes. **1505** in *10th Rep. Hist. MSS. Comm.* App. v. 392 That there be no sale bread ..mad in towne, but by ffre men. **1600** J. PORY tr. *Leo's Africa* II. 69 In old time there were almost an hundreth shops of sale-bookes. **1600** SHAKS. *A.Y.L.* III. v. 43, I see no more in you then in the ordinary Of Natures sale-worke? **1601** DENT *Pathw. Heaven* (1603) 35 God hath not given such gifts unto men to the end they should make sale-ware of them. **1671** CLARENDON *Dial.* Tracts (1727) 314 They would find ample recompense in the first growth of their children, un-impaired by any ill qualities of sale-milk. **1679** SHADWELL *True Widow* Epil., Our Poet therefore Sale-work Habits makes. **1691** J. GIBSON in *Archæologia* XII. 191 Darby, at Hoxton,..is master of several curious greens that other sale-gardeners want. **1778** [W. MARSHALL] *Minutes Agric.* 20 Feb. an. 1777, A middling field-load of wheat will yield a sale-load of straw, of 1296 lb. **1805** R. W. DICKSON *Pract. Agric.* I. 396 Most of the farmers here burn lime for themselves..and think they have it much cheaper than it could be got from a sale kiln. **1815** S. PARKES *Chem. Ess.* I. 300 In the end they [*sc.* ash-pit doors] will be found to be more economical than any ready-make sale-doors. **1828** P. CUNNINGHAM *N.S. Wales* (ed. 3) II. 166 The common English sale gimlets are either soon broken at the point by our woods, or else the handle becomes loose. **1886** C. SCOTT *Sheep-farming* 151 The sale ewe lambs. *Ibid.* 157 These sale rams are injured, and in many cases rendered useless by overfeeding. **1895** *Funk's Standard Dict.*, *Sale-pond*,..a pond devoted to fishes kept for sale.

†**b.** That may be had for payment; venal, mercenary. (Cf. SALARY *a.*^{1}) *Obs.*

1591 SYLVESTER *Du Bartas* I. iii. 936 Sale-tongu'd Lawyers, wresting Eloquence, Excuse rich Wrong, and cast poore Innocence. **1602** DEKKER *Honest Wh.* I. vi, Belike then shee's some sale curtizan. **1609** HOLLAND *Amm. Marcell.* 293 A multitude thronged together of vendible or sale souldiors. **1650** MILTON *Eikon.* i. 12 Nothing troubl'd or offended at the working upward of thir Sale-venom thereupon.

†**sale**, *sb.*^{3} *Obs.* Also 6 **saile, sayle.** [Northern form of SOLE *sb.* (OE. *sál*). The form *saile* may represent directly the cognate ON. *seil*.] A rope for tying up cattle. Also *attrib.* †**saleband.**

c **1299** *Durham Acc. Rolls* (Surtees) 496 In tractubus, cordis, salband (etc.), 28*s.* 11*d.* **1434–5** *Ibid.* 232 Redyls, 6 hoxes bowes, 7 salys, ferrura boum et plowshon. **1599** *Mem. St. Giles's Durham* (Surtees) 27 Paid for a saile to the bull, *jd.* **1668** *Ibid.* 75 For a sayle and band to ty the Bull in.

†**sale**, *sb.*^{4} *Obs.* [a. or ad. OF. *sale* (see SALLE) or It. *sala*: cf. SALE *sb.*^{1}] A hall.

1632 LITHGOW *Trav.* IX. 401 This great Cell or Hall, is a yard deepe of blackish Water..: Hauing more than halfe way entered in this Sale [etc.]. *a* **1648** LD. HERBERT *Hen. VIII* (1683) 233 The next day, obtained Audience of the King; Who in a great Sale (or Hall) sate on his Throne.

sale, *v. rare.* [f. SALE *sb.*^{2}] **1.** *intr.* and *trans.* To sell.

1809 GIFFORD in *Mem. F. Hodgson* (1878) I. 115 Lord Byron's poem sales well I understand. **1922** JOYCE *Ulysses* 555 Lovely ladies saling gloves.

2. *intr.* To hold a sale; to shop at the sales. Hence **'saler**, a person who frequents sales; **'saleing** *vbl. sb.* All now *rare* or *Obs.*

1901 *Sketch* 3 July 443/1 To go 'saleing' in Bond Street. **1902** *To-Day* XXXV. 447/1 All London is 'saleing' at the present moment. **1928** *Daily Express* 19 June 3/2 Men went 'sale-ing' at lunch time. **1928** *Morning Post* 25 June 8 Many experienced 'salers' will tell you that it is an excellent plan to go to the sales with an open mind. **1928** *Daily Express* 31 Dec. 5/3 'Saleing' has become a specialised art. **1929** *Ibid.* 8 Jan. 3/4 The great furniture houses are 'saling'.

sale: see SAIL, SEAL, SOUL.

saleability (seɪlə'bɪlɪtɪ). Also **salability,** (irregularly) **salesability** [f. next: see -BILITY.] Saleableness.

1797 COLERIDGE in *Sotheby's Catal. Bks. & MSS.* 30 Nov. (1891) 58 So much for the priceableness of the volume —now for the saleability. **1818** MOORE *Mem.* (1856) VIII. 248 Saleability is the thing with the booksellers. **1881** JEVONS in *Contemp. Rev.* Mar., To throw taxation off land on to personalty..is to increase the value of English land; but to restrict its saleability or letting is to diminish its value. **1885** *Times* 9 Oct. 9/2 The saleability of Church property. **1940** E. GILL *Autobiogr.* vii. 195 The man who buys in order to sell can only judge of good by the saleability of what he has bought. **1940** M. LOWRY *Let.* 27 July (1967) 33 Whit.. has not..wanted to say anything..until some verdict has been reached..as to its salesability. **1972** *Nature* 28 Jan. 232/2 One is forced to the conclusion that the title was chosen with an eye to salability. **1975** *Language* LI. 447 It was a common practice..for grammatical works by well-known scholars to be more or less extensively emended and refashioned by later publishers, in order to enhance their usefulness and saleability. **1976** *Publishers' Weekly* 1 Nov. 70/1 Undoubtedly it enhances gift book salability. **1979** *SLR Camera* Jan. 14/2 Subjects of universal and eternal—as far as saleability was concerned—content.

saleable ('seɪləb(ə)l), *a.* Also (6 salehable), 6– salable. [f. SALE *sb.*^{2} + -ABLE.]

1. a. Capable of being sold; fit for sale; commanding an easy or ready sale. Also *absol.* or as quasi-*sb.*

1530 PALSGR. 323/1 Saleable, *vendible*. **1539** TAVERNER *Erasm. Prov.* (1552) 42 Wyne that is saleable and good nedeth no bushe. **1615** G. SANDYS *Trav.* 66 That which in England is not saleable, doth passe here amongst them for most excellent. *a* **1661** FULLER *Worthies, London* (1662) II. 219 His book.. had been more salable, if more conformed to our modern language. **1763** *Museum Rust.* I. 27 Being at a loss what to do with my crop, which was not saleable in my neighbourhood. **1845** STEPHEN *Comm. Laws Eng.* (1874) II. 621 *note*, Certain offices in the Queen's Bench and Common Pleas were saleable by the chief justices of those courts respectively till the year 1825. **1871** M. COLLINS *Mrq. & Merch.* I. vi. 189 A horse saleable at three hundred guineas. **1881** *Times* 29 Jan. 11 Grenada Cocoa is more readily salable than other qualities. **1886** C. SCOTT *Sheep-farming* 144 After .. the saleable lambs and draft ewes have been disposed of. **1945** *Sun* (Baltimore) 4 Aug. 8/7 Five hundred salables were offered and 2,500 went directly to packers. **1946** *Ibid.* 15 Jan. 10-O/2 Salables amounted to 2,500 head, compared with 5,000 head marketed a week ago.

Comb. **1868** *Rep. U.S. Commissioner Agric.* (1869) 233 To cut good, salable-sized potatoes for seed.

transf. **1565** JEWEL *Repl. Harding* Concl., As for your Eloquence,.. as it serueth wel, to make the mater more salehable in the sight of the simple, so [etc.].

†**b.** On sale, for sale. *Obs. rare*$^{-1}$.

1599 SANDYS *Europæ Spec.* (1632) 115 They were content to let it be translated.., as also some number of Copies to be saleable a while at the beginning.

c. Said of the price which an article will fetch.

1778 *Chron.* in *Ann. Reg.* 186 Divers goods to the saleable value of 17*2l.* **1881** H. GEORGE *Progr. & Pov.* VII. iii. 327 If the land belong to the people, why.. should the people pay its salable value for their own?

2. Venal, mercenary. Now *rare* or *Obs.*

1579 FENTON *Guicciard.* XIII. (1599) 624 The corruptions of men salable, would not be sufficient to transport the Empire from the Germaine nation to the house of France. **1598** SYLVESTER *Du Bartas* II. ii. III. *Colonies* 633 We finde the Alman in his fight courageous, But salable. **1650** FULLER *Pisgah* II. viii. 172 Saint Paul eloquently defended his innocence, against the salable tongue of Tertullus. **1798** MRS. INCHBALD *Lovers' Vows* V. i, Tell him, my honour has never been saleable.

'saleableness. [f. prec. + -NESS.] The condition of being saleable; fitness for sale.

1727 BAILEY vol. II. **1754** T. SECKER in Nichols *Illustr. Lit. Hist.* (1818) III. 492 You might probably give him a better notion of the value, that is, the saleableness of the work. **1807** SOUTHEY *Lett.* (1856) II. 6 My own judgement of the saleableness of books. **1894** *Times* 25 July 10/1 The intrinsic saleableness of his novel.

saleably ('seɪləblɪ), *adv.* [Formed as prec. + -LY[2].] In a saleable manner.

1755 JOHNSON, *Saleably*. **1898** *Times* 13 Apr., Every constituent.. is.. used up, and used up saleably.

‖**sale Boche, sale boche** (sal bɔʃ). [Fr., f. *sale* dirty + BOCHE.] A French term of abuse for a German.

1919 C. MACKENZIE *Sylvia & Michael* iii. 85, I get called *sale boche* if I open my mouth. **1934** D. L. SAYERS *Nine Tailors* 189 A man.. called him *sale Boche*—but Jean knocked him down. **1938** L. BEMELMANS *Life Class* I. iv. 67 'Go away!' he repeated. '*Sale Boche!*' I called him a French pig. **1979** D. ROBINSON *Eldorado Network* vi. 53 Marty.. blasted off the complete clip in the general direction of Mola's camp. '*Sales boches!*' he spat.

sa'lebrity. *rare*$^{-0}$. [ad. late L. *salebritās*, f. *salebra* roughness.] = SALEBROSITY.

1656 BLOUNT *Glossogr.* **1731** BAILEY vol. II.

salebrosity (sælɪ'brɒsɪtɪ). [ad. L. **salebrōsitās*, f. *salebrōs-us* SALEBROUS.] Ruggedness, unevenness. Also *fig.*

1638 R. BAILLIE *Lett. & Jrnls.* (1841) I. 140 His Grace here wiselie brought the Doctor off salebrosities, whence all his witts could not have delivered him with his credit. **1661** FELTHAM *Resolves, Upon Eccles.* 378 Yet is not this without its Thornes and salebrosity.

†**salebrot** = *sal* ALEMBROTH. *Obs.*

1678 PHILLIPS, *Sal Lambrot* or *Salebrot*.

salebrous ('sælɪbrəs), *a.* [ad. late L. *salebrōsus*, f. *salebra* roughness: see -OUS.] Rough, rugged. Also *fig.*

1633 *Battle of Lutzen* 30 The entrie of his Raigne.. was thorny and sallebrous. **1641** OUGHTRED in Rigaud *Corr. Sci. Men* (1841) I. 60 Others of my profession.. refuse to tread these salebrous and uneasy paths. **1681** COTTON *Wond. Peak* 54 We now again proceed Thorough a Vale that's salebrous indeed.

Hence †**'salebrousness.**

1727 BAILEY vol. II.

saléeite ('sæleɪaɪt). *Min.* orig. **saléite**; also without accent. [ad. F. *saléite* (Thoreau & Vaes 1932, in *Bull. de la Soc. géol. de Belgique* XLII. 96), f. the name of Achille *Salée* (d. 1932), Belgian palæontologist: see -ITE[1].] A hydrated phosphate of magnesium and uranium, $Mg(UO_2)_2(PO_4)_2 \cdot 10H_2O$, which occurs as yellow crystals in association with torbernite as an oxidation product of uranium minerals.

1934 *Chem. Abstr.* XXVIII. 5372 Saleite is the Mg analog of autunite. **1940** *Mineral. Mag.* XXV. 643 Saleeite. A. Schoep... The correct form of saleite. **1951** *Amer. Mineralogist* XXXVI. 681 Under the microscope, the saléeite from Portugal appears as rectangular plates with the corners sometimes truncated at 45°. **1959** in G. J. Williams *Econ. Geol. N.Z.* (1965) xiii. 206/2 The yellow coating of secondary uranium mineral.. forms small plates and is an unidentified member of the sabugalite-saleeite-novacekite group.

Salem ('seɪləm). [Name of a place in Gen. xiv. 18 (Heb. *Shālēm*), understood to be another name for Jerusalem and to mean 'peace' (Heb. *shālōm*).] Occasionally (chiefly in the nineteenth century) adopted by Methodists, Baptists, Independents, etc., as the name of a particular chapel or meeting-house. Hence used as a synonym for 'nonconformist chapel'. Cf. BETHEL 2, EBENEZER 2, ZION.

1857 GEO. ELIOT in *Blackw. Mag.* July 62/1 The Independent chapel, known as Salem, stood red and conspicuous in a broad street. **1880** TROLLOPE *Duke's Children* III. iii. 27 Every Salem and Zion and Ebenezer in his large parish would be closed. **1935** A. CRUSE *Victorians & their Bks.* iv. 66 Most Churchmen really did look down upon the Dissenters... The congregations that gathered in the Bethels and Ebenezers and Salems.. were, for the most part, made up of the less educated and less polished classes. **1963** W. H. BOORE *Valley & Shadow* ix. 43 Salem, Bryncoed, was square and dumpy... The place was private, too—just the Lord and His elect. **1970** *Guardian* 1 Aug. 9/8 The grey chapels called Salem and Zion.

Salempore ('sæləmpɔə(r)). Also 6 **Sarampura**, 7 **Salampora**, 7- **Salampore**, 8 **Sallampoore**, 8-9 **Salempore**. [= F. *salempouri* (18th c.), Du. *salamporij* (17th c.): of unascertained origin. Cf. *palampore*.] 'A blue cotton cloth formerly made at Nellore in India, and largely exported to the West Indies, where it was the usual slave cloth' (Knight *Dict. Mech.*).

1598 W. PHILLIP tr. *Linschoten* I. i. 28/1 This linnen.. is called Sarampuras, Cassas, Comsas, Beatillias, Satopassas, and a thousande such like names. **1614** in W. Foster *Lett. E. India Co.* (1897) II. 32 Salampora, being a broad white cloth. **1680** *Notes & Extr. Govt. Rec. Fort St. George* III. (1873) 16 (Y.) Salampores, Blew, at 14 Pagodas per corge. **1703** *Lond. Gaz.* No. 3933/4 The Cargo of the Star of the East, consisting of Long Cloth, Sallampoores, Betelles [etc.]. **1809** R. LANGFORD *Introd. Trade* 74, 8 Bales, each containing 60 Pieces Sallampores blue. **1834** M. SCOTT *Cruise Midge* iii. (1842) 40 Wide white petticoat trowsers.. made of some strong cotton stuff of the same fabric as the India salampore. **1863** W. C. BALDWIN *Afr. Hunting* i. 21 Paid them on arrival with brass wire and blue salempore, or calico. **1883** B. MITFORD *Through Zulu Country* xv. 189 On shelves against the walls are arranged blankets, Salampore cloth, [etc.]. **1928** E. SITWELL *Five Poems* 15 Gaze d' Ispahan and bulchauls, salampores.

†**salen.** *Obs.* [Cf. mod.L. *salēna* kind of fish found in Lake Como (Benedictus Jovius *a* 1544).]

1513 *Bk. Keruynge* in *Babees Bk.* (1868) 280 Grene fysshe, pyke, lampraye, salens, porpas rosted.

†**sal e'nixum.** *Chem. Obs.* Also -**on**. [mod.L. (Paracelsus): see SAL. The second word is the neut. of L. *ēnixus*, app. in the sense 'that has given birth' (*scil.* to the acid).] Crude potassium sulphate, produced in the manufacture of nitric acid.

[**1797** *Encycl. Brit.* (ed. 3) VI. 673 The sal enixum of Paracelsus is the caput mortuum of spirits of nitre with oil of vitriol, or what remains in the retort after the distillation of this spirit.] **1827** FARADAY *Chem. Manip.* xiii. 298 Sal-Enixum is an acid sulphate of potash. **1875** *Ure's Dict. Arts* III. 738 *Salenixon*.

salep ('sæləp). See also SALOOP. [= F. *salep*, Sp. *salép*, Pg. *salepo*, a. Turkish *sālep*, a. Arabic *thaʻleb* (pronounced in some parts *saʻleb*), taken to be a shortening of *khasyu 'th-thaʻlab* orchis (lit. 'fox's testicles'; cf. the Eng. name 'dogstones'.)] A nutritive meal, starch, or jelly made from the dried tubers of various orchidaceous plants, chiefly those of the genus *Orchis*; formerly also used as a drug.

1736 BAILEY *Househ. Dict.* 519 Put an ounce of salop or salep, into a quart of water. **1771** MRS. HAYWOOD *New Present* 43 To boil Salep. Take of the powder of salep a large teaspoonful [etc.]. **1837** M. DONOVAN *Dom. Econ.* II. 365 The root [of *Orchis mascula*] being washed, baked, and ground to powder, is salep. **1854** S. THOMSON *Wild Fl.* III. (1861) 295 Salep is used in the preparation of a mucilaginous jelly like arrow-root. **1858** CARPENTER *Veg. Phys.* §677 A nutritive substance termed Salep, somewhat resembling Arrow-root or Sago. **1861** [see SALOOP 1].

attrib. **1768** MOULT in *Phil. Trans.* LIX. 3 The jelly of Salep-powder is clear and transparent. **1841** *Penny Cycl.* XX. 345/2 One part of salep-powder with forty-eight parts of water boiled or heated forms a thick mucilage. **1868** WATTS *Dict. Chem.* V. 147 Salep-mucilage.

sale price. [SALE *sb.*[2]] **a.** Retail price. **b.** A price fetched at auction. **c.** A price reduced for a sale SALE *sb.*[2] 1 c).

1793 NEMNICH *Comptoir-Lex., Eng.* s.v., On the Sale price, *zum Verkaufspreise*. **1866** *London Society* Mar. 258/2 The sale price of the 'Marriage à la Mode' cannot therefore be again tested. **1897** (*title*) The sale prices of 1896. **1902** *To-Day* XXXV. 123/1 Some people, so long as they see 'Sale Price'.. written on a card pinned to some goods, are content to pay any price. **1940** C. MILBURN *Diary* 31 Aug. (1979) 55, I bought an evening frock in 1919 at sale price for £18 18s. od. **1970** R. JEFFRIES *Dead Man's Bluff* xix. 185 She'd been in and tried on some fur coats, including a mink at sale price. **1974** N. FREELING *Dressing of Diamond* 138 My wife gets her hairdressing free and her clothes at sale prices. **1980** M. BABSON *Queue here for Murder* i. 6 A diagonal red line through the original price and the sale price below it.

Hence **'sale-price** *v. trans.*, to set at a price for sale.

1959 *Time* 2 Nov. 6/2 In Seattle, the suburban Grinnell & McLean furniture store ballyhooed 'Mother-in-law-Mattresses', sale-priced at $9·95. **1978** *New York* 3 Apr. 74 (Advt.), And for just $50 more, we'll transform the Sofa into a queen-sized sleeper convertible! Of course, we've also sale-priced the pieces separately.

†**'saler.** *Obs.* Also 4 **salure**, 5 **salere**, **sallyer**, 5-6 **seler**. See also SALT-CELLAR. [a. OF. *sal(l)iere* fem., mod.F. *salière* (= Pr. *saliera*, *saleira*, It. *saliera*), also OF. *salier* masc.:—L. *salāriam*, *-um*, properly adj. 'pertaining to salt'; cf. SALARY *sb.*] A salt-cellar.

13.. *Coer de L.* 1099 The saler on the table stood. **13..** *Gaw. & Gr. Knt.* 886 Sanap, & salure, & syluer-in sponez. **1439** in *Archæol.* XXI. 36, ij Salers of gold, whereof yᵗ oon ys a man and yᵗ other a woman, holdyng yᵉ salers in her hondes. *c* **1475** *Babees Bk.* (1868) 7 The salte also touche nat in his salere Withe nokyns mete. *c* **1500** *For to serve a Lord* ibid. 368 The boteler or panter shall sette the seler in the myddys of the tabull accordyng to the place where the principall soverain shalle sette, and sette his brede iuste couched unto the salte-seler.

saleratus (sælə'reɪtəs). *U.S.* Also **salæratus**. [a. mod.L. *sal aerātus* 'aerated salt'.] An impure bicarbonate of potash containing more carbon dioxide than pearl-ash does, much used as an ingredient in baking-powders. Now also applied to sodium bicarbonate used for the same purpose.

1837 S. GRAHAM *Treat. Bread-Making* 46 Pearlash or saleratus is also used by them in considerable quantities. **1846** WORCESTER (citing ADAMS), *Saleratus*, a sort of refined pearl-ash. **1854** MRS. STOWE *Sunny Memories* xx. II. 19 Hot biscuits, hot corn-cakes, and other compounds got up with the acrid poison of saleratus. **1880** *New Virginians* II. I. 64 Bread made with carbonate of soda, saleratus, or any other kind of baking-powder. **1883** B. HARTE *Carquinez Woods* iv. 98 Without extra trouble kneaded flour, water and saleratus need not be essentially heavy.

attrib. **1846** *Knickerbocker* XXVII. 510 The white sal-æratus cake and the 'water bewitched' are quickly devoured. **1853** MRS. A. L. WEBSTER *Improved Housewife* 130 Salaeratus Biscuit. **1867** [MRS. WHITNEY] *Summer in L. Goldthwaite's Life* 71 They think it is only saleratus cakes and maple molasses. **1884** *Harper's Mag.* Jan. 297/1 Salæratus bread, heavy pastry, and fried meat do not form the best diet.

†**Salerne.** *Obs.* Anglicized f. L. *Salernum*, It. *Salerno*, the name of an Italian maritime town near Naples, used attrib. = SALERNITAN *a.*

1598 BP. HALL *Sat.* IV. iv, Tho neuer haue I Salerne rimes profest To be some Ladies trencher-critick guest. **1607** *Englishman's Docter* (1830) 125 The Salerne Schoole doth by these lines impart, All health to England's king. **1635** SWAN *Spec. M.* (1643) 240 The Salern school makes this demand, *Cur moriatur homo cui Salvia crescit in horto?*

Salernitan (sə'lɜːnɪtən), *a.* and *sb.* [ad. L. *Salernitān-us*, f. *Salernum* (see prec.).] **a.** *adj.* Of or pertaining to Salerno or the medical school which formerly flourished there. **b.** *sb.* A native or inhabitant of Salerno; a physician of the Salernitan school.

The reference in quots. 1621, 1826 is to the following lines of the poem *Regimen Sanitatis Salernitanum*, 'Si tibi deficiant medici, medici tibi fiant Hæc tria, mens læta, requies, moderata diæta.'

1608 TOPSELL *Serpents* II. 190 Some have called.. a toade the brother of the Salernitans, & the Lizard the brother of the Lombards. **1621** BURTON *Anat. Mel.* II. ii. VI. iv. 375 This is one of the three Salernitan Doctors, Doctor Merriman, D. Diet, and D. Quiet. **1826** C. M. WESTMACOTT *Eng. Spy* (1907) II. 57 Mirth is the principal of the three Salernitan doctors. **1878** VILLARI *Machiavelli* I. 254 A great admixture of the Neapolitan and Salernitan dialects.

Salesian (sə'liːʃən, sə'liːʒən), *a.* and *sb.* [ad. *Salésien*, f. the name of St. François de *Sales* + *-ien* -IAN.] **A.** *adj.* Of or pertaining to St. Francis of Sales (1567–1622), Roman Catholic mystic, or to communities founded by him or living according to his rule, as the nuns of the order of the Visitation founded in 1610 under his direction, and societies founded by St. John Bosco for the rescue of poor and neglected children. **B.** *sb.* A follower of St. Francis of Sales or a member of a Salesian order; a Brother or Sister of one of the orders founded by St. John Bosco.

1836 *Account Conversion of L.T.H. to Holy Catholic Church* 18 Till I had examined the Rules and visited a Convent of Salesian Nuns. **1884** *Month* Jan. 46 His [*sc.* Bosco's] institution henceforth went by the name of 'The Oratory of St. Francis of Sales', and his co-labourers were called 'Salesians'. **1884** H. B. MACKEY *St. Francis de Sales's Treat. Love of God* p. xxxiii, S. Francis also had his special characteristics, which, therefore, are not French but Salesian. **1890** LADY MARTIN tr. *Villefranche's Life Dom Bosco* xx. 232 His first missionary expedition.. included ten priests and coadjutor Salesian Brothers. **1912** *Catholic Encycl.* XIII. 399/1 The Salesians established themselves at Battersea in London. **1928** J. BRODRICK *Life & Work Cardinal Bellarmine* I. ix. 182 There is an added quality in his work, a characteristic Salesian grace which is the best part of it. **1930** *Tablet* 4 Oct. 425/1 This learned and zealous Salesian is already known as one of the ablest men in the

Church to-day. **1964** F. D. PARKER *Central Amer. Republics* vi. 179 Five Franciscans and one Salesian. **1974** *Oxf. Dict. Chr. Ch.* (ed. 2) 190/2 *St. John Bosco* (1815–88)... In 1859 he founded the 'Pious Society of St. Francis de Sales', commonly known as the 'Salesians'.

salesite ('seɪlzaɪt). *Min.* [f. the name of Reno H. *Sales* (1876–1969), U.S. geologist + -ITE[1].] A very rare basic iodate of copper, $CuIO_3(OH)$, found as bluish-green orthorhombic prisms at Chuquicamata, Chile, and also prepared synthetically.

1939 PALACHE & JARRELL in *Amer. Mineralogist* XXIV. 388 Salesite is an iodate of copper first found by the junior author in 1936 on the west side of Bench E-4 at the south end of the open pit at Chuquicamata, Chile. **1962** *Acta Crystallographica* XV. 1106/1 Rotation and Weissenberg photographs of the artificial $CuIO_3(OH)$.. indicate that it is identical with salesite in cell dimensions and the distribution of intensities.

salesman ('seɪlzmæn). Also 6 **salys-man**; and see *saleman*, SALE *sb.*[2] 3. [f. *sale's*, genit. of SALE *sb.*[2] + MAN *sb.*[1] Cf. *craftsman, tradesman.*] A man whose business it is to sell goods or conduct sales. Also *transf.*

The following are specific applications: **a.** One who sells goods or produce for another, e.g. one who acts as middleman between the grazier or the killer of cattle and the butcher. †**b.** One who sells ready-made clothing. (Cf. SALE *sb.*[2] 4 a.) **c.** orig. *U.S.* A commercial traveller (also *transf.*). **d.** † *salesman's dog*: a tout.

1523 FITZHERB. *Husb.* §134 It is not conuenient that the salesman, that selleth the wod, shuld be partener with the bier. **1548** W. FORREST *Pleas. Poesye* 441 in *Starkey's Life & Lett.* p. xcvi*, What the Salys-man is the ware ofte dothe teache. **1697** *Lond. Gaz.* No. 3341/8 Tho, Middleton late of West-Smithfield, London, Salesman, deceased. *a* **1700** B. E. *Dict. Cant. Crew, Salesman's-dog*, the same as *Barker*. *Ibid. Sales-men*, brokers who sell Cattel for the Graziers to the Butchers, before, and at the Beast-Market; also Sellers of ready-made Cloaths. **1717** PRIOR *Alma* I. 166 This looks, friend Dick, as Nature had But exercis'd the Salesman's Trade: As if She haply had sat down, And cut out Cloaths for all the Town. **1717** SWIFT *Prol. to Gay's Three Hours after Marriage* 25 Poets make Characters, as Salesmen Clothes. **1758** JOHNSON *Idler* No. 28 ¶3 Miss Mohair, the daughter of a salesman. **1777** HOWARD *Prisons Eng.* 183 A generous Benefactor (a salesman in Smithfield) often sends the Prisoners beef and bread. **1831** YOUATT *Horse* 47 He [*sc.* Eclipse] was.. sold at his death to Mr. Wildman, a sheep salesman for seventy-five guineas. **1851** MAYHEW *Lond. Labour* I. 378/2 Should the salesman [*i.e.* a pedlar] succeed with the mistress, he carries out his promise to the maid by presenting her with a cap ribbon, or a cheap neckerchief. **1851** Meat-salesman [see MEAT *sb.* 5]. **1851** Dead salesman [DEAD *sb.*[1] 6]. **1883** COTTON in *Law Times Rep.* XLIX. 723/1 The defendants have let all these stalls to salesmen. **1885** *Law Rep. 14 Q.B. Div.* 248 Salesmen had brought their carts with fruit or vegetables to Spitalfields Market on the market days. **1891** *Ibid.* Weekly Notes 80/1 A farmer in Northamptonshire sent certain meat to a salesman in the Central Meat market.. for sale. **1891** *Cent. Dict., Salesman*, ..a commercial traveler. [U.S.] **1912** J. SANDILANDS *Western Canad. Dict., Salesman*, a commercial traveller, a drummer, a store counter-man, or a man who canvasses real estate. **1930** *Amer. Speech* VI. 134 *Salesman*, confidence man. **1937** *Daily Herald* 15 Jan. 12/8 Increased employment means that people are replacing old-fashioned furniture for [*sic*] new, and the attractive designs made possible by veneering are good salesmen. **1942** BERREY & VAN DEN BARK *Amer. Thes. Slang* §507/3 *Pimp; procurer*..crack salesman, ..salesman. **1944** *Amer. N. & Q.* IV. 10/2 A transportation company in New Jersey now refers to its drivers and motormen as 'salesmen'. **1945** MENCKEN *Amer. Lang.* Suppl. I. 588 American milk-wagon drivers are called *milk-salesmen* and bakers' deliverymen *bread-salesmen*. **1968–70** *Current Slang* (Univ. S. Dakota) III–IV. 105 *Salesman*, n. Pimp; one who sells anything.

Hence **'salesmanship**, the condition or character of being a (good) salesman; also *fig.*

1880 BLACKMORE *Mary Anerley* II. ix. 162 He made a good stroke of salesmanship. **1887** *Old Man's Favour* I. II. i. 202 The art-pottery stall, under the attractive salesmanship of Canon Elwyn. **1930** *Economist* 20 Dec. 1164/2 The Prince of Wales, who is shortly leaving for Buenos Aires, where he will open the British Empire Trade Exhibition, delivered an outspoken address on salesmanship. **1936** *Discovery* Apr. 129/2 Consult any of the books on psychology and salesmanship so numerous on the market. **1937** WODEHOUSE *Ld. Emsworth & Others* v. 172 When a woman is to all intents and purposes waiting for a demon lover, it requires super-salesmanship to induce her to accept on the this-is-just-as-good principle an Ernest Plinlimmon. **1960** *Farmer & Stockbreeder* 12 Jan. 102/2 Salesmanship in food is liable to be overrated because nothing is more distasteful than.. food, when you have had enough.

saleswoman ('seɪlz,wʊmən). A woman who sells goods (e.g. in a shop).

1704 *Lond. Gaz.* No. 4025/4 Ann Scadding, of the Parish of St. Buttolp Aldgate, Saleswoman. **1880** *Libr. Univ. Knowl.* (U.S.) VIII. 800 In 1790 [she] went to Paris, where she was a saleswoman in a linen shop. **1887** *Old Man's Favour* I. II. i. 204 The stall was well-furnished, the saleswoman was pretty and animated. **1916** D. H. LAWRENCE *Amores* 97 She puts me away like a saleswoman whose mart is Endangered by the pilferer on his quest. **1932** L. GOLDING *Magnolia St.* III. vi. 548 She's one of the leading saleswomen in our firm.

Hence **'saleswomanship**, the position of a saleswoman; the character of being a (good) saleswoman.

1973 M. AMIS *Rachel Papers* 28 Gloria held the assistant pet-food saleswomanship in, handily, a Shepherds Bush emporium. **1977** *Church Times* 29 Apr. 11/2, I felt that a little saleswomanship might be a good thing.

salew, salewt: see SALUE, SALUTE.

salews, obs. pl. SALUTE *sb.*[2]

salf(e, salffe, obs. ff. SAFE, SALVE, SAVE.

†**salfay.** *Obs.* Also 5 **safye**, 6 *Sc.* **salfer** (?). [Origin unknown, but prob. ultimately connected with L. *salvus* SAFE.] The reward paid to the finder and restorer of lost goods.

c **1440** *Alphabet of Tales* 434 Bod þe riche man, when he had þe sakett agayn, wolde not pay þe salfay. *Ibid.*, Becauce he wold nott hafe gyffen þe pure man a hondreth talentis to safye, as he promysid he sulde do. **1551–2** *Reg. Privy Council Scot.* I. 123 All sik gudis stollin or reft, lauchfullie Convict, salbe restorit and redressit with the thre dowbillis and salfer.

salfe, obs. form of SAUGH, willow.

salfleme: see SAUCEFLEME.

salft, salfty, obs. forms of SALVE *sb.*[1], SAFETY.

salge, obs. form of SAGE.

sal-gem ('sæl,dʒɛm). Now *rare* or *Obs.* Also 4–9 **gemme**, 5–8 **-geme**, 7 **gemm**; and in L. form. [ad. med.L. *sal gemma* or *gemmæ*, lit. 'gem-like salt'. Cf. F. *sel gemme.*] Native chloride of sodium; rock-salt.

c **1325** [see SAL-AMMONIAC]. *c* **1450** *M.E. Med. Bk.* (Heinrich) 99 Poudres of sal gemme. **1471** RIPLEY *Comp. Alch.* Adm. v. in Ashm. (1652) 190 Sal Tarter, sal Comyn, sal Geme most clere. *c* **1550** LLOYD *Treas. Health* E iv, Make pouder of Roses suger and salgem. **1646** SIR T. BROWNE *Pseud. Ep.* VI. xii. 336 No other salt that I know will strike the colour with galles; neither Alom, Sal-gemme, Nitre, nor Armoniack. **1718** QUINCY *Compl. Disp.* 9 That which is termed fossile Salt, or Sal Gemma. **1836** T. THOMSON *Min. Geol.*, etc. I. 100 Rock salt, sal-gemme, muriate of soda. **1852** TH. ROSS tr. *Humboldt's Trav.* I. i. 8 The interior of Spain forms a vast plain,..covered with secondary formations, grit-stone, gypsum, salgem. **1867** BLOXAM *Chem.* 262 Perfectly pure specimens [of rock-salt]..are styled sal gem.

salgh(e, obs. forms of SALLOW, willow.

salgram, var. SHALGRAM.

Salian[1] ('seɪlɪən), *a.* and *sb.* [f. L. *Sali-us* (usually sb. pl. *Saliī*, lit. 'leapers, dancers', f. *salīre* to leap) + -AN.] **a.** *adj.* Of or pertaining to the Salii or priests of Mars in ancient Rome. **b.** *sb.* One of the Salii.

1653 R. SANDERS *Physiogn.* 22 Numa Pompilius also instituted 12 Salian Priests in the honour of Mars. **1781** GIBBON *Decl. & F.* xxviii. (1787) III. 71 The confraternities of the Salians, the Lupercals, &c. practised such rites, as might extort a smile of contempt from every reasonable man. **1857** H. SPENCER in *Westm. Rev.* Apr. 462 Among the Romans, too, there were sacred dances: the Salian and Lupercalian being named as of that kind. **1871** FARRAR *Witn. Hist.* iii. 107 The catacomb triumphed over the Grecian temple; the cross of shame over the wine-cup and the Salian banquet.

Salian[2] ('seɪlɪən), *a.* and *sb.* [f. late L. *Sali-ī*, the Salian Franks + -AN.] **a.** *adj.* Of or belonging to a tribe of Franks who inhabited a region near the Zuyder Zee, and to whom the ancestors of the Merovingian dynasty belonged. (Cf. SALIC *a.*[1]) **b.** *sb.* A Salian Frank.

1614 SELDEN *Titles Hon.* II. i. 175 The old Franks which were Teutonique, and calld also Salians. *a* **1727** NEWTON *Obs. Proph. Daniel* I. v. (1733) 43 By the access of these Gauls, and of the foreign Franks also,..the Salian kingdom soon grew very great. **1830** GRATTAN *Hist. Netherlands* 11 The Salians, and the other petty tribes of Franks, their allies, were essentially warlike. **1837** KEIGHTLEY *Hist. Eng.* I. 208 This regulation of the descent of the French crown, was said, though improperly, to depend on a law of the Salian Franks, hence called the Salic law. **1879** *Encycl. Brit.* IX. 529/2 There is in the Salian law no trace of a primitive nobility.

†**'saliaunce.** *Obs.* [f. *saliaunt*, SALIENT: see -ANCE. Cf. *salience.*] An assault, or sally.

1590 SPENSER *F.Q.* II. i. 29 Now mote I weet,..why with so fierce saliaunce,..ye did at earst me meet.

Salic ('sælɪk, 'seɪlɪk), *a.*[1] Also 6 **Salicque**, 6–7 **-like**, 7 **Sallick**, 7–8 **Salick**, 6–9 **Salique**. [ad. F. *salique* or med.L. *Salicus*, f. *Saliī* (see SALIAN[2]).]

1. *Salic law*: in early use, and still in popular language, the alleged fundamental law of the French monarchy, by which females were excluded from succession to the crown; hence *gen.* a law excluding females from dynastic succession. In this sense still often spelt *Salique* and pronounced (sə'li:k).

The ancient text which under the name of the 'Salic law' was adduced in favour of the succession of Philip V in 1316, and afterwards used to combat the claims of Edward III of England (and his successors) to the French crown, was really a quotation from the *Lex Salica* (see sense 2); the words however (cap. lix. §5 of modern editions) have no reference to succession to the crown, but merely state that a woman can have no portion of the inheritance of 'Salic land' (*terra Salica*); the precise meaning of this term is disputed, and in the earliest form of the code the word 'Salic' is omitted.

a **1548** HALL *Chron., Hen. V* (1550) 4 b, The lawe Salicque was only fayned and invented to put your noble progenitours and you [Hen. V.] from your lawfull right and true inheritaunce. For they say that Pharamond made the lawe for the land Salicque, which the glose calleth Fraunce. **1599** SHAKS. *Hen. V*, I. ii. 39. *Ibid.* 91 They would hold vp this Salique Law, To barre your Highnesse clayming from the Female. **1674** *Ch. & Crt. of Rome* 29 In despite of the Sallick Law, [they] endeavour that the Infanta..should succeed unto the Crown. **1837** [see SALIAN[2]]. **1842** W. IRVING *Life & Lett.* (1866) III. 233 By long usage, the Salique law of France..had become naturalized in Spain. **1847** TENNYSON *Princess* II. 117 She fulmined out her scorn of laws Salique.

transf. **1663** COWLEY *Verses & Ess.* (1669) 2 Orinda does in that too raign, Does Man behind her in proud Triumph draw, And Cancel great Apollo's Salick Law. **1773** HAN. MORE *Search Happ.* ii. 139, I scorn'd the salique law of pedant schools, Which chain our genius down by tasteless rules. **1870** HUXLEY *Lay Serm.* ii. 29 Nature's old salique law will not be repealed.

2. In the original sense of L. *Salicus*: Pertaining to the Salian Franks. Chiefly in ***Salic law*** or ***code*** (L. *Lex Salica*), a Frankish law-book, written in Latin, and extant in five successively enlarged recensions of Merovingian and Carolingian date.

1781 GIBBON *Decl. & F.* xxxviii. (1787) III. 583 Before the election of the Merovingian kings, the most powerful tribe, or nation, of the Franks, appointed four venerable chieftains to compose the Salic laws. *Ibid.* 594 Besides these royal and beneficiary estates, a large proportion had been assigned, in the division of Gaul, of allodial and Salic lands. **1879** *Encycl. Brit.* X. 476/1 The Salic code..shows us the Salian king as in all respects the centre of his state.

Hence **'salicly (saliquely)** *adv.*, with reference to the Salic law.

1784 H. WALPOLE *Lett. to C'tess Ossory* (1848) II. 207 Numerous as were the sons of Edward III., only Thomas, Duke of Gloucester, continued the masculine line, and I cannot (upon memory alone) affirm that. If he did, the Duke of Buckingham beheaded by Henry VIII., had *saliquely* speaking the best title to the Crown.

salic, *a.*[2]: see SAL[4] I.

salic ('seɪlɪk), *a.*[3] *Soil Sci.* [f. L. *sal* salt + -IC.] Applied to a soil horizon which is at least 15 cm. thick and is enriched with salts more soluble in water than gypsum (see quot. 1971).

1960 *Soil Classification* (U.S. Dept. Agric.) v. 60/1 A salic horizon is a horizon 6 inches or more thick with secondary enrichment of salts more soluble in cold water than gypsum. **1970** E. M. BRIDGES *World Soils* iii. 24/2 These soils develop a surface encrustation of salt... Such soils possess salic horizons. **1971** *Gloss. Soil Sci. Terms* (Soil Sci. Soc. Amer.) 26/2 A salic horizon is 15 cm or more in thickness, contains at least 2% salt, and the product of the thickness in centimeters and per cent salt by weight is 60% cm or more.

salicaceous (sælɪ'keɪʃəs), *a.* *Bot.* [f. mod.L. *salicāce-us*, f. L. *salic-*, *salix* willow: see -ACEOUS.] Belonging to the N.O. *Salicaceæ*, which consists of two genera, *Salix* (willow) and *Populus* (poplar). Also *transf.* (*joc.*), made of willow.

1846 in SMART Suppl. **1963** *Times* 13 June 13/3 This makes one wonder whether any of the aforetime Latinists ever called a bat a salicaceous implement.

salicet ('sælɪset). [a. G. *salicet* (1703 in Zedler), f. L. *salic-*, *salix* willow + -ET[1]. For the suffix cf. *dulcet* sb.] = SALICIONAL.

1852 SEIDEL *Organ* 104 Salicional, or 'salicet'..is one of the finest organ registers. **1876** HILES *Catech. Organ* ix. (1878) 66 Salicet in the Pedal is a soft 16 feet register.

salicetum (sælɪ'si:təm). Also **salictum**. Pl. **saleceta, -cetums.** [f. L. *salix*, *salic-* willow + -ETUM.] A plantation of willows, esp. a collection of different species and varieties of willow.

1776 A. HUNTER *Evelyn's Silva* xx. 252 In order to raise a Salictum, or a plantation of Willows for timber, the ground must be dug or plowed; and the cuttings for this purpose should be of the last year's shoot. **1838** J. C. LOUDON *Arboretum* I. I. 129 Woburn Abbey, where a salicetum, or salictum..was planted in 1825. *Ibid.* III. 1477 A Salictum is the only scene in which a complete collection of willows can be displayed to advantage. **1853** C. G. B. DAUBENY *Oxford Bot. Garden* (ed. 2) 16 Salicetum. On the opposite side of the garden outside of the walls, and bordering upon the river, there existed a few years ago a tolerably good collection of Willows. **1875** *Encycl. Brit.* III. 422/1 Mr. William Scaling..cultivates a salictum of about 100 acres. **1926** *Nat. Hist. Oxford District* 73 Many interesting Willows which were formerly grown in the Salicetum in the Botanic Gardens. **1952** G. TAYLOR *Victorian Flower Garden* x. 153 The Willow garden, or salicetum, as it was called, slightly antedates the pinetum. **1972** S. C. WARREN-WREN *Willows* ii. 32 A salictum should be a sizeable area of ground set aside for the express purpose of growing a fully representative group of willows. *Ibid.* 33 It may be considered wise to have two salicta. **1978** A. HUXLEY *Illustr. Hist. Gardening* ix. 307 The numerous species of *Salix* were gathered into salicetums or sally gardens.

salicify, erron. form of SILICIFY.

salicin ('sælɪsɪn). Also **-ine**. [ad. F. *salicine* (Leroux), f. L. *salic-*, *salix* willow: see -IN[1].] A bitter crystalline principle obtained from willow-bark, much used medicinally.

1830 *Philos. Mag.* VIII. 304 Salicine, burnt with oxide of copper in a proper apparatus, yielded a gas entirely absorbable by potash. **1840** *Ibid.* XVI. 210 Salicin is now.. employed in medicine as a substitute for quinine. **1879** *St.*

George's Hosp. Rep. IX. 230 The power of salicin and salicylic acid in counteracting the rheumatic poison.
attrib. **1887** *Athenæum* 26 Mar. 421/1 Salicine crystals.

salicional (sə'lɪʃənəl). Also erron. **salcional, salicinal.** [a. G. *saliz-*, *salicional* (18th c.), f. *salic-*, *salix* willow, with obscure suffix. Cf. SALICET.] An organ stop of a soft reedy tone resembling that of a willow pipe.

1843 *Mech. Mag.* XXXIX. 6 The plan has long been used in Germany for the Salcional. **1881** BROADHOUSE *Mus. Acoustics* 171 Pipes which are conically narrowed at the top, such as the salicional and the gems horn. **1884** BOSANQUET in *Encycl. Brit.* XVII. 833/1 The salicional, salcional, or salicet. **1897** F. E. ROBERTSON *Organ-building* 117 If there be any shade of difference between these stops, it is that the Salicional should be beautifully soft and stringy, yet not without fulness, the Dulciana quiet and a little less reedy, and the Vox Angelica the thinnest of all.

salicyl ('sælɪsɪl). *Chem.* Also **-yle, -ile, -ule.** [ad. F. *salicyle*, f. L. *salic-*, *-salix* willow: see -YL.] The diatomic radical of salicylic acid.

1840 *Turner's Elem. Chem.* (ed. 6) III. 852 Under the name of hydruret of salicule, a peculiar acid was made known by Piria, who discovered it as a product of the decomposition of salicine. **1857** MILLER *Elem. Chem.* (1862) III. 409 Hydride of salicyl. **1876** HARLEY *Royle's Mat. Med.* 415 Gently heated with sulphuric acid and bichromate of potash, it [*sc.* salicin]..is converted into fragrant oil of meadow sweet or hydride of salicyle.
attrib. **1842** T. GRAHAM *Elem. Chem.* 871 Salicyl Series of Compounds. **1857** MILLER *Elem. Chem.* (1862) III. 409 The salicyl group. **1888** FAGGE & PYE-SMITH *Princ. Med.* (ed. 2) I. 205 Salicyl compounds, invaluable as they are in rheumatic fever.

Hence ˌ**salicy'laldehyde**, *o*-hydroxybenzaldehyde, $C_7H_6O_2$, a colourless volatile liquid having an odour of bitter almonds, which is found in oil from meadowsweet and related species, and is used esp. in perfumery; **salicy'lamic** *a.*, derived from salicyl and ammonia; **sali'cylamide**, a compound formed when oil of gualtheria is dissolved in a solution of ammonia; **'salicylide**, the anhydride of salicylic acid; **sali'cylimide**, a yellow crystalline powder produced by the action of heat on salicylamic acid; **'salicylite**, a salt formed by the action of salicylol on oxides and hydrates of metals; **'salicylol**, a colourless or reddish oil intermediate in composition between salicylic acid and salicylic aldehyde; also, extended to include a class of bodies of this type in which part of the hydrogen is replaced by a metal; **salicyl'urate**, a salt of salicyluric acid; †**salicyl'uret**, a compound of salicyl with a metal; **salicy'luric acid**, an acid derived from the urine evacuated after the administration of salicylic acid.

1840 *Turner's Elem. Chem.* (ed. 6) III. 855 Saliculimide. *Ibid.*, Saliculite of Ammonia. **1842** T. GRAHAM *Elem. Chem.* 872 In the salicylites, the atom of hydrogen of the formula of salicylous acid is replaced by a metal. *Ibid.* 873 Solutions of alkalies and acids act upon salicylimide,..as they do upon amides. **1845** W. GREGORY *Outl. Chem.* II. 345 Salicyluret of ammonium..is formed when concentrated ammonia is poured upon hydruret of salicyle. **1857** MILLER *Elem. Chem.* (1862) III. 544 It [*sc.* benzamic acid] is isomeric with anthranilic acid and with salicylamide. *Ibid.* 567 Both salicylide and salicylic anhydride are rapidly converted into ordinary salicylic acid. *Ibid.*, The solutions of salicyluric acid give a violet colour with persalts of iron. **1863** *Fownes' Chem.* (ed. 9) 557 Salicylite of copper is a green insoluble powder. **1868** WATTS *Dict. Chem.* V. 150 *Salicylamic-acid*, ..this compound is produced by the action of ammonia on methylsalicylic or ethylsalicylic acid. *Ibid.* 167 *Salicylol*... Salicylous Hydride. Hydric Salicylite. Salicylous acid. *Ibid.* 172 Salicylurates.—The acid decomposes carbonates. Its salts crystallise easily. **1869** ROSCOE *Elem. Chem.* xxxix. 388 Salicyl Aldehyde, $C_7H_6O_2$. *Ibid.* 389 Sodium Salicilol. **1886** *Encycl. Brit.* XXI. 212/2 Salicin is eliminated from the system partly in the form of salicylic and salicyluric acids, and partly as saligenin. **1896** W. T. BRANNT *Animal & Vegetable Fats* (ed. 2) II. xix. 274 Salicylaldehyde..exists in the oils of meadow sweet and of other species of *spiraea*. **1973** *Nature* 4 May 37/2 Several compounds with specific odours, such as 2,4-pentanedione, morin, salicylaldehyde and acetic acid, are well known chelating agents for heavy metals.

salicylate (sə'lɪsɪlət), *sb. Chem.* [f. SALICYLIC + -ATE[1].] A salt or ester, or the anion (o-$C_6H_4(OH)COO^-$), of salicylic acid.

1842 T. GRAHAM *Elem. Chem.* 874 Salicylate of silver is an insoluble white precipitate, anhydrous. **1857** MILLER *Elem. Chem.* (1862) III. 180 The oil of winter green is a salicylate of methyl. **1878** BRISTOWE *Theory & Pract. Med.* (ed. 2) 900 By far the most..efficacious treatment of acute rheumatism is that by salicylic acid or salicylate of soda. **1964** W. G. SMITH *Allergy & Tissue Metabolism* iii. 40 Salicylate inhibits both the 'in vitro' activation of permeability globulin and its action on capillaries. **1972** *Sci. Amer.* Jan. 92/3 Physicians have found that most patients coming to the emergency room of a hospital with massive bleeding of the upper gastrointestinal tract have taken salicylates within the preceding 24 hours. **1977** *Addictive Dis.* III. 284 Researchers have called attention to the hazard to pregnant women of the easy accessibility of over-the-counter drugs such as salicylates.
attrib. **1897** *Allbutt's Syst. Med.* III. 13 The salicylate treatment pushed too freely.

salicylate (sə'lɪsɪleɪt), *v.* [f. next + -ATE[3].] *trans.* To mix or impregnate with salicylic acid.

1880 *Times* 28 Dec. 7/6 By salicylating the drinking-water of the beasts by the addition of two tablespoonfuls of the acid dissolved in hot water. **1883** MARTINDALE & WESTCOTT *Extra Pharmacop.* 71 Salicylated Camphor. **1886** *Lancet* 2 Oct. 638/1 The salicylated beer of Paris.

salicylic (sælɪ'sɪlɪk), *a. Chem.* Earlier **saliculic.** [f. SALICYL + -IC.]

1. *Chem.* Belonging to a group of benzene derivatives obtainable from salicin; esp. in ***salicylic acid***, a white crystalline substance, prepared commercially from sodium phenol, and much used as an antiseptic and in the treatment of rheumatism.

1840 *Turner's Elem. Chem.* (ed. 6) III. 857 Saliculic Acid. Discovered by Piria. **1842** T. GRAHAM *Elem. Chem.* 874 The salicylic acid is liberated by adding an excess of hydrochloric acid. **1857** MILLER *Elem. Chem.* (1862) III. 560 Salicylic Series. **1869** ROSCOE *Elem. Chem.* xxxix. 388 Salicylic group. The members of this group are closely connected with the benzyl and benzoyl series. **1881** *Athenæum* 4 June 754 The use of salicylic acid as a disinfectant.

2. *Therapeutics.* Made from, impregnated with, or involving the use of, salicylic acid.

1876 *Trans. Clinical Soc.* IX. 10 On the eleventh day the salicylic ointment was employed. **1880** MACCORMAC *Antisept. Surg.* 215 The inguinal regions..should be well padded with salicylic wool. **1897** *Allbutt's Syst. Med.* III. 57 As a rule such articular pains yield rapidly to salicylic treatment.

salicylism ('sælɪsɪlɪz(ə)m). [f. SALICYLIC + -ISM.] A toxic condition produced by the administration of salicylic acid or salicylates.

1889 *Lancet* 19 Jan. 114/2 If patients bleed at all as a result of salicylism, they should do so from their gums.

salicylize ('sælɪsɪlaɪz), *v.* [f. SALICYLIC + -IZE.] To treat with salicylic acid in order to prevent fermentation. Hence **'salicylized** *ppl. a.*

1881 *Nature* 12 May 48/1 It is estimated that 5,000,000 hectolitres of wine were salicylised in France in 1880. **1881** *Athenæum* 4 June 754/2 The daily use of salicylized food or drink does not..injure the health.

salicylous (sə'lɪsɪləs), *a. Chem.* Earlier **saliculous.** [f. SALICYL + -OUS. Cf. F. *salicyleux.*] ***salicylous acid***: an oily liquid obtained by distillation of salicin with sulphuric acid and bichromate of potash; salicyl aldehyde.

1840 *Turner's Elem. Chem.* (ed. 6) III. 854 Saliculous acid combines with metallic oxides to form the saliculites. **1842** T. GRAHAM *Elem. Chem.* 735 Oil of spiræa, or salicylous acid. **1876** HARLEY *Mat. Med.* (ed. 6) 415 Salicylous acid.. differing from salicylic acid by an atom less of oxygen.

salie ('sæliː). Also **saliehout, zalie.** [Afrikaans, a. Du. *salie* sage.] = *sage-wood* (*b*) s.v. SAGE *sb.*[1] 5 b.

1819 C. G. CURTIS *Acct. Colony Cape of Good Hope* 72 Saly hout..Hard and heavy. **1908** F. C. SLATER *Sunburnt South* 11 Wild-willows and feathery-flowered *zalie* trees grew in..profusion. **1932** [see *sage-wood* s.v. SAGE *sb.*[1] 5 b]. **1952** *Cape Times* 2 Aug. 9/3 Among indigenous trees, three are milkwood, salie and Kafir plum. **1973** *Stand. Encycl. S. Afr.* IX. 459/1 Saliehout... Tall, much-branched shrub.. with large, simple, opposite, grey-green leaves.

salie, variant of SAULIE *Sc.*

salience ('seɪlɪəns). [f. SALIENT: see -ENCE.]

1. The quality of leaping or springing up. *rare.*

1836 L. HUNT in *New Monthly Mag.* XLVII. 479 What fresh, clean, and youthful salience in the lynx! **1840** —— *Seer* I. 6 The suddenness and salience of all that is lively, sprouting, and new.

2. a. The fact, quality, or condition of being salient or projecting beyond the general outline or surface. Also of immaterial things.

1849 LYTTON *Caxtons* x. i, No wonder that thou seemest ..to have a great cavity where thy brain should have the bump of 'conscientiousness' in full salience! **1877** SYMONDS *Renaiss. It., Fine Arts* III. vi. 299 His character does not emerge with any salience from the meagre notices we have received concerning him. *a* **1878** SIR G. SCOTT *Lect. Archit.* (1879) I. 149 These subsidiary shafts may be..subordinated one to another, both in size and salience. **1884** *Contemp. Rev.* July 142 There is not the same unity of composition or salience of colour.

b. *Social Psychol.* The quality or fact of being more prominent in a person's awareness or in his memory of past experience.

1938 H. D. SPOERL tr. *Stern's Gen. Psychol. from Personalistic Standpoint* iv. 74 The different proportions of salience and embedding give the process and content of every experience its special character. **1938** G. W. ALLPORT *Personality* xx. 553 At other times..consciousness is embedded..more deeply; there is less clearness, less salience. Salience represents an act of pointing, a directedness of the person toward something that at the moment has special significance for him. **1953** C. I. HOVLAND et al. *Communication & Persuasion* v. 155 We shall refer to the degree to which..a specific group is present and prominent in a person's 'awareness' as the *salience* of that group. **1958** W. C. SCHUTZ *FIRO* vii. 147 If the reaction to the anxiety is withdrawal from interchange in that area, the area acquires a negative salience in that the actor tries to avoid it. **1965** T. M. NEWCOMB et al. *Social Psychol.* iii. 58 The difference between the centrality of an object to an individual and the closely related matter of its *salience*. **1972** *Jrnl. Social Psychol.* Aug. 256 Relatively low Salience problems..produced shifts predominantly towards greater risk.

3. A salient or projecting feature, part, or object.

1837 C. LOFFT *Self-formation* I. 144 To people who would merely lounge along, side by side, these saliences are sorely annoying, they are abominable things. **1890** C. H. MOORE *Gothic Archit.* ix. 299 Saliences are indicated conventionally [in illumination] by paling the colour. **1894** R. ELLIS *Phaedrus* 26 An imitator reproduces the saliences of his model. **1908** *Westm. Gaz.* 7 May 2/1 The Badakshan district ..forms a salience, running deeply into Russian territory.

saliency ('seɪlɪənsɪ). [f. SALIENT: see -ENCY.]

†**1.** Leaping or jumping. *Obs.*

1664 POWER *Exp. Philos.* I. 25 It [*sc.* the ant] trips so nimbly away without any saliency or leaping.

2. a. = SALIENCE 2 a.

1834 J. S. MACAULAY *Field Fortif.* vi. §1. 114 In order to give as great a saliency as possible to these lunettes. **1841** HOR. SMITH *Moneyed Man* III. viii. 208 The great attenuation of the face..gave a singular saliency to the features. **1863** LYTTON *Caxtoniana* II. 275 Its merits are not to be sought in the saliency of any predominating excellence. **1882** C. D. WARNER *Washington Irving* vi. 118 A man,.. whose..strong patriotism did not need the saliency of ignorant partisanship.

b. *Social Psychol.* = SALIENCE 2 b.

1965 T. M. NEWCOMB et al. *Social Psychol.* ii. 37 The notion of saliency has an interesting counterpart in the information storage of modern 'thinking machines' or large computers.

3. = SALIENCE 3.

1831 *Examiner* 68/2 They should be replete with saliencies, and..poke quaint peculiarities at the spectator. **1887** *Harper's Mag.* July 266 Their little chronology.. stepped briskly over the centuries solely on the names of kings and sanguinary saliencies.

salient ('seɪlɪənt), *a.* and *sb.* Also 6 **saliaunte,** 7 **salliant,** 7–9 **saliant,** 8 **saillant.** [ad. L. *salientem*, pres. pple. of *salīre* to leap. The form has been freq. assimilated wholly or partly to F. *saillant* (from the same source).] **A.** *adj.*

1. a. Leaping, jumping; *esp.* of animals, saltatorial.

Used by Sydney Smith app. for 'dancing': cf. SALTANT.
1646 SIR T. BROWNE *Pseud. Ep.* v. iii. 237 Salient animalls, and such as move by leaping. **1655** FULLER *Ch. Hist.* x. ii. §53 Behold a straw besprinkled with some drops of his blood..leaped up on this Wilkinson [etc.]..when this straw salient leaped first up into Wilkinson's lap [etc.]. **1803** SHAW *Zool.* IV. 167 Salient Blenny. *Ibid.* 585 Salient Mackrel. **1826** SYD. SMITH *Wks.* (1859) II. 89/1 With ten or a dozen stars and an Oonalaska chief, and followed by all vicious and salient London, Mrs. Clotworthy takes the field. **1848** MAUNDER *Treas. Nat. Hist.* 804 *Salient*, moving by leaps, as frogs.

b. Of water: Jetting forth; leaping upwards.

1669 BOYLE *Contn. New Exp.* iv. 17 We could take notice of the Lines describ'd by the Salient water, as the ejaculation of that Liquor grew still fainter and fainter. **1728** POPE *Dunc.* II. 162 Who best can send on high The salient spout, far-streaming to the sky. **1830** TENNYSON *Adeline* iii, Do beating hearts of salient springs Keep measure with thine own? **1892** LD. LYTTON *K. Poppy* II. 289 Nor any better could that Dragon sage Hinder the sources of the salient springs From listening.
fig. **1796** BURKE *Let. Noble Ld.* Wks. VIII. 46 He had in himself a salient, living spring, of generous and manly action.

c. Of the pulse: Beating strongly. *poet.*

a **1791** BLACKLOCK *Ode written when sick* 15 The salient pulse of health gives o'er.

d. Math. ***salient point*** (see quot.).

1845 *Encycl. Metrop.* II. 122 The points of curves which have been called shooting or saliant points, when the function $\frac{dy}{dx}$ becomes discontinuous by changing suddenly of value.

2. *Her.* Having the hind legs in the sinister base and the fore paws elevated near together in the dexter chief, as if in the act of leaping.

1562 LEGH *Armorie* 78 He beareth Argent, a Lion saliaunte,..this lifteth up hys right pawe to the right corner of the Escocheon, and the Rampande, lifteth up his left pawe to the same corner. **1605** CAMDEN *Rem.* (1637) 227 A demy Ramme salient Argent. **1718** A. NISBET *Ess. Armories* Index Terms, *Salient*, when any Beast is erected Bendways. **1864** BOUTELL *Her. Hist. & Pop.* xx. (ed. 3) 334 A Pegasus salient.
transf. **1740** *Gentl. Mag.* X. 460/1 [A little cur] salient on her nether feet, Extorts your very fav'rite bit.

3. a. ***salient point*** [= F. *point saillant*, mod.L. *punctum saliens*; the source of this use is Aristotle, *Hist. Anim.* VI. iii, Τοῦτο δὲ τὸ σημεῖον πηδᾷ καὶ κινεῖται ὥσπερ ἔμψυχον, 'this point [representing the heart in the egg] leaps and moves as alive']: in old medical use, the heart as it first appears in an embryo (cf. quot. 1706); hence, the first beginning of life or motion; the starting-point of anything. *Obs.* or *arch.*

1672 SIR T. BROWNE *Let. Friend* §5 His end was not unlike his beginning, when the salient point scarce affords a sensible motion. [**1706** PHILLIPS (ed. Kersey), *Punctum Saliens*, a little Speck or Cloud that appears in a Broodegg, and seems to leap before the Chicken begins to be hatch'd.] **1712** BLACKMORE *Creation* VI. 337 The Salient Point, so first is call'd the Heart. **1769** *Junius Lett.* (1820) 154 That was the salient point from which all the mischiefs..of the present reign took life. **1822** GOOD *Study Med.* II. 7 The heart is the salient point of the circulation. **1837** CARLYLE *Fr. Rev.* II. I. v, What a progress, since the first salient-point of the Breton Committee! **1869** GOULBURN *Purs. Holiness* iv. 39 What is the salient point, the spring, of a virtue?

b. Similarly, †***salient motion.***

1660 INGELO *Bentiv. & Ur.* II. (1682) 119 The earthly bud of young Life first appears in a salient Motion.

4. Of an angle: Pointing outward, as an ordinary angle of a polygon (opposed to *re-entrant*); chiefly in *Fortif.*, 'formed by two lines of works meeting and pointing towards the country' (Voyle), i.e. away from the centre of the fortification. So ***salient point***, etc.

1687 J. RICHARDS *Jrnl. Siege of Buda* 19 We pierc'd the Wall of the Lower Town looking into St. Paul's Valley, and carry'd on a 3d Angle Salliant. **1702** *Milit. Dict.* s.v. *Bonnet*, A Work consisting of two Faces, which make an Angle Saillant in the Nature of a small Ravelin. **1739** LABELYE *Short Acc. Piers Westm. Bridge* 79 Each Point, or Saliant Angle of each of the Piers. **1812** WELLINGTON in Gurw. *Desp.* (1837) IX. 12 When the attack upon the salient angle ..succeeded. **1816** R. JAMESON *Char. Min.* (ed. 2) 170 In ordinary crystals, the faces adjacent to each other always form salient, and never re-entering angles. **1838** *Penny Cycl.* X. 375/2 We obtain about 360 yards for the distance between the salient points F and E of the two bastions. **1876** VOYLE & STEVENSON *Milit. Dict., Salient Order of Battle*, an order of battle, the front of the army being formed on a salient or outward angle.

5. a. Of material things: Standing above or beyond the general surface or outline; jutting out; prominent among a number of objects.

1789 E. DARWIN *Bot. Gard.* I. 32 He..Crowns with high Calpè Europe's saliant strand. **1834** MCMURTRIE *Cuvier's Anim. Kingd.* 268 The hinge always furnished with salient and well-marked teeth. **1844** KINGLAKE *Eothen* vi. 93 The town is on a salient point. **1854** BADHAM *Halieut.* 451 Large salient eyes. **1859** GULLICK & TIMBS *Paint.* 201 The salient parts of the body and limbs should always be seen through the drapery. **1878** BOSW. SMITH *Carthage* 229 The salient physical features of the spot. **1881** MIVART *Cat* 480 The Mastoid is never salient.

b. Of immaterial things, qualities, etc.: Standing out from the rest; prominent, conspicuous; often in phr. ***salient point*** (cf. 3). Also *Psychol.*, standing out or prominent in consciousness.

1840 CARLYLE *Heroes* iii. 177 The great salient points are admirably seized. **1846** GROTE *Greece* I. xx. II. 87 His personal ascendancy..is the salient feature in the picture. **1862** STANLEY *Jew. Ch.* (1877) I. viii. 153 Some few salient points emerge full of eternal significance. **1873** SYMONDS *Grk. Poets* xii. 401 In the midst of our activity we have so little that is salient or characteristic in our life. **1874** GREEN *Short Hist.* vii. §7. 421 No salient peculiarity seems to have left its trace on the memory of his contemporaries. **1938** H. D. SPOERL tr. *Stern's Gen. Psychol. from Personalistic Standpoint* iv. 74 Dissonance is constant by being augmented or diminished. All experience consequently tends to become either *salient* against or *embedded* with the totality. **1938** G. W. ALLPORT *Personality* xx. 553 The most important of all facts about consciousness is that it is graded; sometimes it stands out, as it were, against the diffuse background of personal life. It is *salient*... The more salient an experience, the greater its objective meaning. **1953** C. I. HOVLAND et al. *Communication & Persuasion* v. 161 A communication will produce more immediate change when the opposing group norms are at a low level of salience than when they are highly salient. **1965** T. M. NEWCOMB et al. *Social Psychol.* ii. 37 We shall use the term 'salient' to describe stored information that has been prompted to the forefront of the individual's conscious thought.

6. Electr. ***salient pole***, a type of field pole used in electrical machinery in which the energizing coil is wound on a pole-piece projecting inside the yoke of a stator assembly or outside the cone of a rotor assembly.

1886 S. P. THOMPSON *Dynamo-Electric Machinery* (ed. 2) vii. 121 This pattern differs from that of the better known 'A' Gramme in using salient poles instead of having the 'consequent poles' at the middle points of the electro-magnets. **1920** *Whittaker's Electr. Engineer's Pocket-Bk.* (ed. 4) 169 The turbo-alternator is now the standard a.c. generator, and is almost invariably built with a cylindrical (or non-salient pole) rotor, the salient pole construction being confined to slow-speed alternators and water turbine-driven alternators. **1962** [see ALTERNATOR]. **1970** J. SHEPHERD et al. *Higher Electr. Engin.* (ed. 2) x. 331 An alternative arrangement to having uniform slotting on both sides of the air-gap is to have salient poles around which are wound concentrated coils to provide the field winding. The salient poles may be on either the stator or the rotor.

B. *sb. Fortif.* **1.** A salient angle or part of a work.

1828 J. M. SPEARMAN *Brit. Gunner.* (ed. 2) 209 If lunettes are constructed beyond the saliants of the bastions and ravelins. **1868** KINGLAKE *Crimea* (1877) III. i. 216 Two sides of a triangle whereof the salients pointed straight to the front. **1897** GEN. H. PORTER *Campaigning with Grant* in *Century Mag.* June 210 The fort was an enclosed work, and formed a salient upon the enemy's line.

2. a. A narrow projection or spur of land extending from a larger feature; a spur-like area of land, esp. one held by a line of offence or defence, as in trench-warfare; *spec.* (freq. with *the* and capital initial) that at Ypres in western Belgium, the scene of severe fighting in the war of 1914–18.

1864 W. G. MITCHELL in *War of Rebellion* (U.S. War Dept.) (1891) 1st Ser. XXXVI. I. 359 Conducted General Wright to a point near the Salient we had captured. **1903** A. F. MOCKLER-FERRYMAN *Milit. Sketching & Reconnaissance* ix. 88 Select..a line of level to be assumed as a crest-line, so situated that when drawn-in it will show the shape of all the principal salients and re-entrants. **1914** *War Illustr.* 5 Dec. 366/1 The British salient at Ypres fascinated the Kaiser. **1915** *N.Y. Tribune* 8 May 9/2 The salient at Ypres always has been dangerous. Formerly it made a semi-circular loop, with Ypres a little above the centre. After this successful movement of the Germans it took the shape of the eye in a hook and eye. **1927** R. H. MOTTRAM *Spanish Farm Trilogy* 238 Poperinghe was the railhead for that essentially English battle-field, the Ypres Salient. **1944** *Daily Progress* (Charlottesville, Va.) 2 Oct. 9/4 The British drove five miles north of the village of Oss at the north-western corner of their salient to the Maas. **1972** K. BONFIGLIOLI *Don't point that Thing at Me* xix. 172, I had almost succeeded in becoming..'Mad Jack' Mortdecai, V.D. and Scar, the ice-cool toast of the Ypres Salient. **1974** *News & Courier* (Charleston, S. Carolina) 28 Apr. A-1/6 An officer identified in a national radio interview as Yoav, commander of the southern salient.

b. *fig.*

1936 [see *industrial psychologist* s.v. INDUSTRIAL *a.* e]. **1969** *Daily Tel.* 31 Oct. 18 With this week's pamphlet on 'The Police and the Citizen'..he will be taking the council into a very hot salient indeed.

Hence **'saliently** *adv.*, in a salient manner.

1847–54 in WEBSTER. **1868** E. EDWARDS *Ralegh* I. Introd. 30 His name stands out saliently in several events which serve to mark epochs..in English history. **1870** *Contemp. Rev.* XVI. 159 They stand saliently in the van of civilization.

salientian (seɪlɪ'ɛntʃɪən, -'ɛntɪən), *a.* (and *sb.*) *Zool.* [f. mod.L. name of order *Salientia* (J. N. Laurenti *Synopsis Reptilium* (1768) 24), f. L. *salient-em* (see SALIENT *a.* and *sb.*) + -IA[1]: see -AN.] = ANURAN *a.* Also as *sb.*

1948 *Evolution* II. 29/2 The general trend of modified salientian ontogeny is towards withdrawal of development from water. **1951** [see CALCAR[2] 2]. **1956** *Nature* 18 Feb. 342/2 How, then, can the salientian trends so clearly shown in the hind limbs and girdle..be correlated with the absence of a functional sacrum? **1973** ESTES & REIG in J. L. Vial *Evolutionary Biol. Anurans* i. 43 This hypothesis does not afford an answer..to the question of placement of salientian origins.

saliewe, variant of SALUE.

saliferous (sə'lɪfərəs), *a.* [f. L. *sal*, *sali-* salt + -FEROUS, perh. after F. *salifère*. (Cf. Kirwan's *saliniferous*.)] Containing a large proportion of salt: said chiefly of strata.

Formerly used *Geol.* to define the Upper Trias.

1828–32 WEBSTER (citing EATON). **1833** LYELL *Princ. Geol.* III. 332 A saliferous red marl. **1833–4** J. PHILLIPS *Geol.* in *Encycl. Metrop.* (1845) VI. 612/2 Saliferous System of Europe. **1846** MCCULLOCH *Acc. Brit. Empire* I. 65 The name *saliferous* has sometimes been given to this group [*sc.* the new red sandstone series]. **1847** H. MILLER *First Impr.* x. 181 The saliferous district of Cordova. **1879** G. GLADSTONE in *Cassell's Techn. Educ.* IV. 315/1 The water in percolating through the saliferous strata will dissolve out the salt.

salifiable ('sælɪfaɪəb(ə)l), *a.* *Chem.* [a. F. *salifiable*, f. *salifier* to SALIFY.] Capable of combining with an acid to form a salt.

1790 KERR tr. *Lavoisier's Elem. Chem.* 150 Acids may..be considered as true salifying principles, and the substances with which they unite to form neutral salts may be called salifiable bases. **1836** BRANDE *Chem.* (ed. 4) 321 The salifiable oxides. **1882** *Nature* XXVI. 102 Under the proper conditions of temperature, moisture, supply of oxygen, and presence of salifiable base.

†**sa'lificate**, *a. Obs.* [ad. mod.L. *salificāt-us*, pa. pple. of *salificāre* to SALIFY.] Turned into a salt.

1657 G. STARKEY *Helmont's Vind.* 314 A very small portion of the Oyl will be turned into a resinous gumme, distinct from that which is salificate.

salification (ˌsælɪfɪ'keɪʃən). [ad. mod.L. *salificātiōn-em*, f. *salificāre* to SALIFY.] Conversion into a salt; the action or condition of being salified.

1684 tr. *Bonet's Merc. Compit.* XIX. 769/1 The liquor being filtrated and evapourated the salts run into crystals. Such kind of salification succeeds well [etc.]. **1828–32** in WEBSTER, and in recent Dicts.

salify ('sælɪfaɪ), *v.* *Chem.* Now *rare*. [ad. F. *salifier*, ad. mod.L. *salificāre*, f. L. *sal*, *sali-* salt: see -FY.] *intr.* To form a salt.

1790 [see SALIFIABLE].

saligenin (sæ'lɪdʒənɪn). *Chem.* Also 9 -ine. [a. F. *saligénine*, f. *sali(cine)* SALICIN: see -GEN and -IN[1].] A substance obtained in the decomposition of salicin by dilute acid.

1852 W. GREGORY *Org. Chem.* (ed. 3) 147 Salicine is composed of saligenine and sugar. **1863** *Fownes' Chem.* (ed. 9) 558 Saligenin forms colourless, nacreous scales, freely soluble in water, alcohol, and ether.

So **sa'ligenol, sa'ligenyl** (see quots.).

1886 *Encycl. Brit.* XXI. 212/2 It [*sc.* salicin] may be split up by digestion with emulsin or saliva into salicylic alcohol (saligenol, $C_7H_8O_2$) and glucose. **1897** *Syd. Soc. Lex.*, *Saligenyl*, the hypothetical radical of Saligenin.

saligot ('sælɪgɒt). Also 7–8 salligot. [a. OF. *saligot*.] The water-chestnut, *Trapa natans*.

Urquhart (quot. 1653) uses 'salligots' to render F. *tribars* (said to mean 'ragouts of tripe'), evidently because of Cotgrave's '*Tribule*, the water Caltrop, Saligot'.

1578 LYTE *Dodoens* IV. lxxii. 535 Theophrast and Dioscorides haue described two kindes of *Tribulus*, the one of the lande... The other of the water, called Saligot. **1597** GERARDE *Herbal* II. cclxxxiv. 677 The leaues of Saligot be giuen against all inflammations. **1653** URQUHART *Rabelais* II. xxxi, Gallant salligots with garlick [orig. *beaux tribars aux ails*]. **1666** J. DAVIES *Hist. Caribby Isles* 56 The Potatoe is a root much like the Saligots growing in Gardens, which are called Topinambous, or Jerusalem Artichokes. **1736** BAILEY *Househ. Dict.* 517 Salligot, or Water Caltrop. **1866** *Treas. Bot.*

saligram, var. SHALGRAM.

salimeter (sə'lɪmɪtə(r)). [f. L. *sal*, *sali-* salt + -METER.] An instrument for determining the amount of salt in a solution.

1866 ATKINSON tr. *Ganot's Physics* §109.

salina[1] (sə'laɪnə). [a. Sp. *salina*:—L. *salīna*, only in pl. *salīnæ* (sc. *fodīnæ*), fem. of **salīnus* SALINE.] A salt lake, pond, well, spring, or marsh; a salt-pan, salt-works. Also, a low, marshy area of land near the coast (orig. *Jamaican*).

1697 DAMPIER *Voy.* (1699) 265 A dry Salina or Salt-pond. **1748** BROWNRIGG *Art Making Salt* 16 Salinas of the same kind have been taken notice of by travellers, in many other parts of the world. **1756** P. BROWNE *Civil & Nat. Hist. Jamaica* 356 The Samphire of Jamaica... This plant is common in all the Salinas on the south side of Jamaica: it abounds with alkalious salts, but the manufacture of this commodity has not been yet attempted in that island. **1774** E. LONG *Hist. Jamaica* I. II. iv. 474 In making roads to traverse the salinas, or level grounds adjacent to the sea, and in swampy places, a *stratum* should first be laid. **1811** W. J. TITFORD *Sk. Hortus Bot. Amer.* 33 Herbaceous marsh samphire..grows in great plenty in Jamaica, on the Salinas and Marshes near the sea coast. **1829** W. IRVING *Conq. Granada* II. lxxxviii. 312 El Zagal relinquished his right to one half of the salinas, or saltpits, of Maleha. **1879** BEERBOHM *Patagonia* v. 76 We rode past a long chain of salinas, which glittered and sparkled whitely in the sun. **1889** *Nat. Geogr. Mag.* I. IV. 334 Beyond the narrow gateway in the hills, less than three miles of level swampy *salinas* reach to the surf of the Pacific.

Salina[2] (sə'laɪnə). *Geol.* The name of a town (now a part of Syracuse) in New York State, used *attrib.* and *absol.* to designate a group of sub-stages of the upper Silurian in New York State and adjacent areas, characterized by thick shale formations that contain beds of rock-salt; of or pertaining to this group or the time when it was deposited.

1863 J. D. DANA *Man. Geol.* III. ii. 246 With the opening of the Salina period there was a change by which shales or marls and marly sandstones, with some impure limestones, were formed over a portion of New York. **1905** H. RIES *Econ. Geol. U.S.* vi. 129 The vast beds of rock salt which occur in the Salina (Monroe) are exploited along the Detroit and St. Clair rivers. **1906** CHAMBERLIN & SALISBURY *Geol.* II. 388 Gypsum..is present in the Salina series. **1949** C. O. DUNBAR *Hist. Geol.* ix. 193 In central New York the salt-bearing shales of the Salina group..succeed the Niagaran limestone. **1960** R. L. BATES *Geol. Industr. Rocks & Minerals* vi. 216 An aggregate salt thickness of at least 1800 feet has been penetrated in oil test wells in the central part of the Michigan Basin, where the top of the Salina is some 8000 feet below the surface. **1974** *Encycl. Brit. Micropædia* VIII. 810/3 The Salina Group consists of two shale formations that attain a thickness of more than 300 metres (1,000 feet).

Hence **Sa'linan** *a.*

1909 *Jrnl. Geol.* XVII. 245 (*heading*) The Middle Siluric or Salinan. **1924** C. SCHUCHERT *Textbk. Geol.* (ed. 2) II. xxi. 264 Cayugan or Upper Silurian..Salinan.

salination (sælɪ'neɪʃən). *rare*[−1]. [ad. L. type **salīnātio*: see SALINE and -ATION.] Salting.

1705 GREENHILL *Embalming* 59 It is not improbable the Egyptians might have been accustom'd to wash the Body with the same Pickle they us'd in the Salination.

‖**sali'nator.** *rare.* [L. *salīnātor*, f. *salīna*: see SALINA[1] and -ATOR.] A salter.

1705 *Phil. Trans.* XXV. 2107 A Dissector or Anatomist; a Salinator or Salter. **1854** BADHAM *Halieut.* 67 *note*, The salt of Rome is at present monopolized by one or two *salinators*, who farm it from Government.

saline ('seɪlaɪn, sə'laɪn), *a.* and *sb.* [ad. L. **salīnus*, f. *sal* salt: see -INE[1]. Cf. F. *salin*, fem. *-ine* (17th c.), Sp., Pg., It. *salino*.] **A.** *adj.*

1. a. † Composed of salt (*obs.*); of the nature of salt; having salt as a preponderating constituent.

c **1450** *Mirour Saluacioun* 3377 Loths wif loking bakwards was turnyd til a stone Salyne. **1660** BOYLE *New Exp. Phys. Mech.* xxii. 167 Some saline Corpuscles dispers'd through the Air. **1693** J. EDWARDS *Author. O. & N. Test.* 136 Lot's wife turn'd into a saline pillar. **1733** P. SHAW *Chem. Lect.* iv. (1750) 67 Under the general Head of Saline Earths may be reckoned all those that are calcined or burnt in the Fire. **1802** PLAYFAIR *Illustr. Hutton. Theory* 364 The water would gain admission to the saline strata. **1832** DE LA BECHE *Geol. Man.* (ed. 2) 21 The saline contents of sea-water. **1878** HUXLEY *Physiogr.* 124 The river contains less saline matter.

b. Of natural waters, springs, lakes, etc.: Impregnated with salt or salts.

1789 in J. M. Brown *Polit. Beginnings Kentucky* (1889) 255 Kentucky in general appears to be a limestone soil.. abounding in..saline springs, which by simple evaporation plentifully supply the country with salt. **1805** W. SAUNDERS *Min. Waters* 230 A valuable property which this water possesses in common with the other bitter saline waters. **1826** KIRBY & SP. *Entomol* xlix. IV. 499 Brackish waters and saline marshes. **1840** in *Trans. Michigan State Agric. Soc.* (1855) VI. 289 Several saline springs and deer-licks were examined in the valley and vicinity of Maskego river. **1862** MERIVALE *Rom. Emp.* liii. VII. 240 *note* 2, Mehadia, long celebrated for its saline baths. **1872** JENKINSON *Guide Eng. Lakes* (1879) 265 Medicinal springs, saline and sulphurous.

¶**c.** *loosely* used for SALT *a.*[1] 2.

1812 CRABBE *Tales* vii. 21 With bacon, mass saline, where never lean Beneath the brown and bristly rind was seen.

2. Like that of salt; like salt; salty.

1651 BIGGS *New Disp.* ¶ 144 The acid saline vitriolated qualities of wine, vineger or juice of Limons. **1732** ARBUTHNOT *Rules of Diet* in *Aliments*, etc. 270 By this saline Quality, the Juices of Shell-Fish..are diuretick. **1774** J. BRYANT *Mythol.* I. 33 The fountain at Selinus in Sicily was of bitter saline taste. **1857** *G. Bird's Urin. Deposits* (ed. 5) 78 The..saline taste of nitre. **1875** DARWIN *Insectiv. Pl.* viii. 178 The solution was sufficiently strong to taste saline.

3. Of or pertaining to chemical salts; of the nature of a salt.

1771 *Encycl. Brit.* II. 70/1 The chemists have not yet been able to produce a saline substance by combining earth and water together. **1790** KERR tr. *Lavoisier's Elem. Chem.* 167 There is reason to believe that many of these supposable saline combinations [*viz.* neutral salts] are not capable of being formed. **1839** URE *Dict. Arts* 1085 A few have rashly offered to cut the knot, by excluding from the saline family, chloride of sodium, the patriarch of the whole. **1863** *Fownes' Chem.* (ed. 9) 269 The great resemblance in properties between the two classes of saline compounds, the haloid and oxy-salts. **1881** WILLIAMSON in *Nature* No. 618. 414 When a constitution, similar to that attributed to salts, was imagined for other compounds not saline in their character.

4. a. Of medicines: Consisting of or based upon salts of the alkaline metals or magnesium.

1789 W. BUCHAN *Dom. Med.* (1790) 681 Saline Mixture. Dissolve a drachm of the salt of tartar in four ounces of boiling water. **1802** *Med. Jrnl.* VIII. 32 The use of saline purgatives. **1876** BRISTOWE *Theory & Pract. Med.* 241 Saline effervescents may both relieve sickness and at the same time promote urine. **1887** *Brit. Med. Jrnl.* 26 Mar. 678/2 Saline aperients were..useful in children of full habit.

b. ***saline solution***, physiological saline (see PHYSIOLOGICAL *a.* 2 b.)

1833 J. FORBES et al. *Cycl. Pract. Med.* II. 213/2 In extreme cases, or when the practitioner is not called in till the very last stage of fever, Dr. Stevens thinks life may be occasionally saved by injecting a saline solution into the veins. We have lately adopted this saline treatment in some cases of typhous fever. **1890** F. TAYLOR *Man. Pract. Med.* 105 The intravenous injection of saline solutions has appeared to do good in some cases of profound collapse. **1932** L. N. KATZ in *Practitioners Libr. Med. & Surg.* I. xxv. 1170 Isotonic saline solution injected subcutaneously or intravenously is valuable. **1971** A. C. GUYTON *Basic Human Physiol.* xx. 223/2 The arterial pressure remained normal until the animals were required to drink 0·9 per cent saline solution.

5. Of plants, †animals: Growing in or inhabiting salt plains or marshes.

1802 SHAW *Zool.* III. 119 Saline Frog. *Rana Salsa*... It is an inhabitant of salt marshes in some parts of Germany. **1866** *Chamb. Encycl.* VIII. 441/1 Saline Plants are those which require for their healthy and vigorous growth a considerable supply of chloride of sodium..and other salts.

B. *sb.*

1. = SALINA[1].

c **1450** *Godstow Reg.* 669 One salyne that is called a salte pitte. **1533** BELLENDEN *Livy* I. xiv. (S.T.S.) I. 79 He biggit als In þe mouth of tyber þe ciete callit hostia, And mony Salynis war edifyt about þe samyn. **1589** M. PHILLIPS in Hakluyt *Voy.* 568 We came to the North side of the riuer of Panuco, where the Spanyards haue certaine Salines. **1748** BROWNRIGG *Art Making Salt* 15 The learned Doctor Shaw hath given us the most accurate description of several of these salines in the kingdom of Algiers. **1808** ASHE *Trav.* III. 3 It [*sc.* Salt River] received its name from the number of salines on its banks which impregnate its waters. **1888** *Harper's Mag.* Apr. 739 Its highest ridges do not rise more than the height of a man above the salines on either side.

2. (See quots.)

1662 MERRETT tr. *Neri's Art of Glass* cxvii. 173 Saline of the Levant. **1674** BLOUNT *Glossogr.* (ed. 4), Saline of the Levant, is a salt extracted from the froth of the Sea, coagulated through the extreme heat of the Countrey. **1850** OGILVIE, *Saline*,..potash before it is calcined. **1860** WORCESTER (citing LOUDON), *Saline*, a dry saline, reddish substance, obtained from the ashes of potato leaves, etc. **1895** *Funk's Standard Dict.*, *Salin*, the residue obtained from the evaporation or calcination of vinasse.

3. a. A saline purge (see A. 4 a).

1875 B. MEADOWS *Clin. Observ.* 71 Acids and alkalies, quinine and colchicum, rhubarb and salines, all kinds of remedies were useless. **1883** THOMSON & STEELE *Dict. Domestic Med. & Surg.* (ed. 17) 520/1 Pyretic saline. **1899** *Allbutt's Syst. Med.* VIII. 656 Free purgation with salines will often, as in eczema, alleviate the itching.

b. Physiological saline (see PHYSIOLOGICAL *a.* 2 b). Also *attrib.*

1926 S. WRIGHT *Appl. Physiol.* vi. 245 If saline is injected intravenously into a normal animal, a condition of hydræmic plethora results. **1951** [see HYPERTONIC *a.* 2]. **1952** E. F. DAVIES *Illyrian Venture* ix. 160 Saline injections followed, bottles hung above me, needles feeding into my arm. **1956** A. C. GUYTON *Textbk. Med. Physiol.* xxvi. 304/2 If the sodium chloride solution is isotonic with the body fluids (that is, the injected saline has exactly the same crystalloidal osmotic activity as do both the extracellular and intracellular fluids), it does not increase or decrease the crystalloidal osmotic pressure of the extracellular fluid. **1971** *Nature* 11 June 344/2 Cholera can be treated by killing the bacteria with antibiotics such as tetracycline and replacing the body fluid lost through diarrhoea with saline.

salinely ('seɪlaɪnlɪ), *adv. rare.* [f. SALINE *a.* + -LY[2].] In a saline or salty manner.

1929 W. FAULKNER *Sartoris* III. ix. 268 He still felt nausea, and he drank long of the tepid water from the tap. Immediately it welled salinely within him.

salineness. *rare.* [-NESS.] Salinity.

1674 R. GODFREY *Inj. & Ab. Physic* 59 It having..lost its salineness, and its vitality. **1757** tr. *Henckel's Pyritol.* 357 A vitriolic salineness.

†**saliner.** *Obs.* [a. OF. *salinier*, ad. late L. *salīnārius*, f. L. *salīna* SALINA.] A salt-maker.

1543 *St. Papers Hen. VIII* (1849) IX. 260 The saliners do gyve out of hande 15000 muys of salt to be delivred [etc.].

saliniferous (sælɪ'nɪfərəs), *a. rare.* [irreg. f. L. *salīn-us SALINE + -FEROUS.] Saliferous.

1799 KIRWAN *Geol. Ess.* 389 The saliniferous hill Konigshorn in Westphalia, consists of marly limestone.

salinification (sə,lɪnɪfɪ'keɪʃən). [f. SALINE *a.* + -IFICATION.] The action or process of becoming, or causing to become, saline.

1911 WEBSTER, *Salinification*, process of making salt. *Rare.* *a* **1961** in *Webster*, s.v., The..salinification of many agricultural soils. **1979** B. L. C. JOHNSON *Pakistan* v. 78/2 It may be necessary for Sind to restrict its irrigated area in order to ensure that whatever water is applied is given in sufficiently copious quantities to avoid salinification.

saliniform (sə'lɪnɪfɔːm), *a.* [irreg. f. L. *salīn-us SALINE + -FORM.] Having the form of salt.

1799 KIRWAN *Geol. Ess.* 399 Most metals..are found in four states, native, sulphurated, calciform, or saliniform.

salinitrous ('sælɪnaɪtrəs), *a.* [f. L. *sal*, *sali-* salt + NITRE + -OUS. Cf. SALITROSE, -OUS.] Pertaining to or containing nitre.

1731 BAILEY vol. II, *Salinitrous*, compounded with salt or salt-petre. **1901** *Westm. Gaz.* 5 Oct. 7/2 The salinitrous districts.

salinity (sə'lɪnɪtɪ). [f. SALINE + -ITY. Cf. F. *salinité*.] **1.** The quality of being saline; saltness.

1658 R. FRANCK *North. Mem.* (1694) 181 The Salinity of the Ocean. **1869** *Sci. Opinion* 14 Apr. 445/2 We want information..as to the degree of salinity..of the water at different levels. **1883** *Chamb. Jrnl.* 332 Deeper down [in the Dead Sea] the salinity amounts to saturation.

2. Special Comb.: **salinity crisis** *Geol.* and *Geogr.*, a period of increased evaporation and salinity in the Mediterranean at the end of the Miocene epoch which resulted in the local disappearance of marine life.

1967 C. RUGGIERI in Adams & Ager *Aspects Tethyan Biogeogr.* 286 The Gibraltar straits (probably the true asylum for the Indo-Pacific relicts during the salinity crisis of the Upper Miocene). **1977** A. HALLAM *Planet Earth* 231/1 This evaporative phase..is known as the 'salinity crisis' because of the extreme effect which it had upon the marine fauna and flora present in the late Miocene Mediterranean.

salinization (,sælɪnaɪ'zeɪʃən). [f. SALINE *a.* and *sb.* + -IZATION.] The accumulation of salts in the soil.

1928 A. A. J. DE 'SIGMOND in *Proc. & Papers 1st Internat. Congr. Soil Sci.* I. 334 Circumstances under which only the salinization took place, giving no chance for alkalization. **1951** W. P. KELLEY *Alkali Soils* iv. 77 Salinization is the initial step in the formation of an alkali soil. **1973** *Nature* 12 Jan. 105/2 With the available evidence strongly indicating salinity to be the primary cause of woodland mortality, it is necessary to offer some reason for the rapid and widespread salinization of Amboseli basin.

salino- (sə'laɪnəʊ), used as combining form of SALINE, in the sense 'consisting of salt (and...)', as ***salino-sulphureous***, ***-terrene***, ***terreous*** adjs.

1674 *Phil. Trans.* IX. 69 An Acid Salino-sulphureous steam. *a* **1691** BOYLE *Hist. Air* (1692) 49 Salino-sulphureous spirits. **1744** PARSONS in *Phil. Trans.* XLIII. 19 *note*, The salino-sulphureous Particles of the Blood. **1800** tr. *Lagrange's Chem.* I. 357 We are not acquainted with the action of salinoterreous matters on arsenic. **1828–32** WEBSTER, *Salino-terrene*, denoting a compound of salt and earth.

salinometer (sælɪ'nɒmɪtə(r)). [f. SALINE + -(O)METER.] An apparatus or instrument for ascertaining the salinity of water.

1844 *Mech. Mag.* XL. 34 Mr. J. Scott Russell's Salinometer. **1876** *Catal. Sci. App. S. Kens.* 97. **1884** KNIGHT *Dict. Mech.* Suppl., *Salinometer*, an instrument for testing the strength of a brine or salt pickle. **1963** G. L. PICKARD *Descriptive Physical Oceanogr.* vi. 86 One of the great advantages of the electrical salinometer is that it uses a null-balance method. **1977** M. G. GROSS *Oceanogr.* (ed. 2) v. 127 Salinometers are commonly used for salinity determinations on oceanographic ships and at shore-based laboratories.

Hence **sali'nometry**, the use of a salino-meter; measurement of the salinity of water.

1907 in WEBSTER. **1964** *Oceanogr. & Marine Biol.* II. 104 Magazine loading of samples and automatic print-out of results have been achieved for radioactive samples, and similar developments in salinometry would not be impossible.

†**sa'linous,** *a. Obs.* [f. L. *salīnus SALINE + -OUS.] Saline, salty.

1646 SIR T. BROWNE *Pseud. Ep.* II. i. 50 Salinous spirits, concretive juyces, and causes circumjacent. **1669** W. SIMPSON *Hydrol. Chym.* 327 Spaws of different sorts, as vitrioline, aluminous, nitrous, salinous. **1687** A. LOVELL tr. *Thevenot's Trav.* II. 119 Rain-water,..incorporating with that Salinous Earth, produces a Salt, that works out of the Surface of it.

salipyrin (sælɪ'paɪərɪn). [f. SALI(CYLIC) + (ANTI)PYRIN.] Salicylate of antipyrin.

1892 A. H. ALLEN *Comm. Org. Anal.* (ed. 2) III. II. 37 Salicylate of antipyrine has been employed with favourable results in medicine under the name of 'salipyrin'.

saliretin (sælɪ'riːtɪn). *Chem.* [ad. F. *salirétine* (Piria), f. SALI(CIN) + Gr. ῥητίνη RESIN.] A resinous substance obtained by the action of dilute acids on saligenin.

1840 *Turner's Elem. Chem.* (ed. 6) III. 861 The white precipitate obtained, when salicine is boiled in dilute muriatic or sulphuric acid is saliretine. **1853** *Pharmac. Jrnl.* XIII. 88 Saliretin is isomeric with hydruret of benzoyle.

Salisbury steak ('sɔːlzbərɪ steɪk). *U.S.* Also with small initial. [f. the name of J. H. *Salisbury* (1823–1905), American physician specializing in the chemistry of foods + STEAK.] A variety of hamburger steak initially promoted by Salisbury.

1897 A. K. ECCLES *Man. what to Eat* 9 To cook the Salisbury steak..place the Cakes on the broiler, turning frequently until done. **1914** D. C. C. L. ROPER *Scientific Feeding* ii. 61 *Salisbury steak.* Secure some fresh, thick, sliced round steak. Scrape or grind in a meat-cutting machine, and mould into flat, round cakes. Have an iron spider very hot and oiled... Lay the meatcake in, and turn from side to side till cooked sufficiently. **1945** MENCKEN *Amer. Lang.* Suppl. I. 429 During World War I an effort was made by super-patriots to drive all German loans from the American vocabulary. *Sauerkraut* became *liberty cabbage*, *hamburger steak* became *Salisbury steak*. **1953** R. CHANDLER *Long Goodbye* xix. 117 After a while I..ate one of Rudy's 'world-famous' salisbury steaks, which is hamburger on a slab of burnt wood, ringed with browned-over mashed potato, supported by fried onion rings and one of those mixed-up salads which men will eat with complete docility in restaurants. **1966** L. J. BRAUN *Cat who could read Backwards* vii. 80 'I'll eat with you' said Quilleran... Odd ordered Salisbury steak. **1970** T. COE *Wax Apple* xxiii. 162 Two plates of that kind of outsize hamburger usually called Salisbury steak and frequently served in places where large numbers of people are being fed without a choice of menu.

Salish ('seɪlɪʃ). Also †**Salisk, Selish.** [Southern Interior Salish *séˀliš* Flat-heads, Northern Okanagan *siylx* Salish: of uncertain ulterior etym.]

1. a. Formerly, an American Indian people of N.W. Montana, also called the Flat-heads (see FLAT-HEAD 1); now used to designate a group of American peoples, including the Flat-heads, inhabiting the N.W. United States and S.W. Canada.

The group is freq. subdivided geographically into ***Coast(al)*** and ***Interior Salish***.

1831 W. A. FERRIS *Life in Rocky Mts.* (1940) v. 88 They [*sc.* Flat-head Indians] call themselves in their beautiful tongue, 'Salish', and speak a language remarkable for its sweetness and simplicity. **1881** *Encycl. Brit.* XII. 826/2 Selish or Flat Heads. **1910** F. W. HODGE *Handbk. Amer. Indians* II. 415/2 Salish... Formerly a large and powerful division of the Salishan family, to which they gave their name, inhabiting much of w. Montana and centering around Flathead lake and valley. **1933** W. SCHMIDT *High Gods in N. Amer.* vii. 111 Of the three Amerindian groups whose religions include a High God, the Selish are the most recent. **1978** *Amer. Poetry Rev.* Sept./Oct. 15/3 The organization of the animal kingdom by a lunar divinity occupies a predominant place..in the myths of the Salish of North America.

b. The name of a group of languages spoken by the Salish. (In quot. 1848, the language of the Flat-heads.)

1848 R. G. LATHAM in *Jrnl. Ethnol. Soc. London* I. 158 *The Salish.*—This is an anonymous vocabulary from Duponceau's collection... It is evidently closely akin to the Okanagan. **1923** A. L. KROEBER *Anthropol.* v. 120 Chinook and Coast Salish, indeed, are in contiguity, and one may therefore have taken up the trait in imitation of the other. **1929** [see MOSAN *sb.*]. **1940** M. W. SMITH *Puyallup-Nisqually* 20 Although the language of the Puyallup-Nisqually is classified as Salish, the people themselves used no special language names. **1977** C. F. & F. M. VOEGELIN *Classification & Index of Worlds' Lang.* 302 The argument for leaving Salish unaffiliated with respect to phylum classification is given by Voegelin and Voegelin (1967).

2. *attrib.* or as *adj.*

1849 in *Ex. Doc. 31st U.S. Congress 1 Sess. Senate* (1850) No. 52. 170 The *Salish* or *Flat Head* Indians occupy from Bitter Root river, a fork of the Columbia, all the country that is drained by that stream down to what is called the Hell Gate. **1902** *Encycl. Brit.* XXV. 373/1 The Shoshone, Shahaptin, and Salish tribes are of middle stature. **1933** L. BLOOMFIELD *Language* 470 Quilleute, Kwakiutl, and Tsimshian..distinguish between visibility and invisibility in demonstrative pronouns; the latter peculiarity appears also in the neighboring Chinook and Salish dialects. **1965** *Canad. Jrnl. Linguistics* Spring 159 Several other Coast Salish languages distinguish by sex of referent in the older generation. **1977** *Islander* (Victoria, B.C.) 2 Oct. 14/1 She has in her studio..a Salish loom.

Salishan ('seɪlɪʃən), *sb.* and *a.* [f. prec. + -AN.] **A.** *sb.* = SALISH 1 b. **B.** *adj.* Of or pertaining to the Salish people or language group.

a **1886** J. W. POWELL in *7th Ann. Rep. U.S. Bureau Amer. Ethnol.* (1891) 104 Eastern Vancouver Island to about midway of its length was also held by Salishan tribes. **1897** [see KWAKIUTL]. **1902** G. W. JAMES *Indian Basketry* (ed. 2) v. 51 They are of the Salishan stock. **1937** H. H. TURNEY-HIGH *Flathead Indians of Montana* i. 11 That much of the North Pacific Coast is inhabited by Salishan people is a well-known ethnological fact. That a portion of western Montana is also inhabited by a Salishan group of tribes is also well-known. **1940** H. VOGT *Salishan Stud.* 1 During my stay with the Kalispel Indians..I had the opportunity of taking down some material on Spokan and Colville, Salishan languages related to Kalispel. **1959** E. TUNIS *Indians* viii. 112/2 Not far from the Kutenai, in southern Canada, lived the Salishan tribes, speaking a language that has no traceable connection with any other Indian speech. **1965** *Canad. Jrnl. Linguistics* Spring 88 In Salishan, Kutenai, Quileute and Nootka a *k-* or *q-* seems to be added in the numeral 'three'. **1973** *Amer. Speech 1969* XLIV. 232 Chinook jargon is a pidginized Chinukan-derived contact vernacular with Nootkan, Salishan, English, French, and Algonkian lexical elements. **1977** *Language* LIII. 502/2 In the Salishan languages, as elsewhere on the Northwest Coast, much of the burden which in other languages falls on the syntax is shouldered by the principles of word structure.

salit, variant pa. t. SALUE *v. Obs.*

‖**salita** (sa'lita). Pl. **salite, salitas.** [It.: see SALLY *sb.*[1]] In Italy, an upward slope or incline, a stretch of rising ground.

1910 H. G. WELLS *Hist. Mr. Polly* i. 35 Other countrysides have their pleasant aspects... Italy gives salitas and wayside chapels, and chestnuts and olive orchards. **1937** E. POUND *Fifth Decad Cantos* xliii. 16 The kalypygous Sienese females Get that way from the *salite* That is from continual plugging up hill. **1949** —— *Pisan Cantos* lxxx. 89 And Italy one eucalyptus pip From the salita that goes up from Rapallo. **1967** P. E. H. DURSTON *Mortissimo* xii. 100 A short, bulky Italian.. strolled casually toward the steep *salita* leading up to the Pincio.

salite, variant of SAHLITE.

salited, *ppl. a.* ? *Obs.* [f. L. *salīt-us*, pa. pple. of *salīre* to salt + -ED[1].] Impregnated with salt.

1784 CULLEN tr. *Bergman's Phys. & Chem. Ess.* I. 443 Salited magnesia dissolves in spirit of wine. **1796** KIRWAN *Elem. Min.* (ed. 2) II. 438 Salited Arsenic may also be precipitated in its Metallic form by Zinc.

†**sa'lition.** *Obs.* [ad. late L. *salitiōn-em*, n. of action f. *salīre* to leap.] Leaping.

a **1682** SIR T. BROWNE *Comm.-pl. Bks.* Wks. 1835 IV. 393 What kind of motion natation or swimming is,.. whether not compounded of a kind of salition, and volation.

salitre ('sælɪtə(r)). [a. Sp. *salitre* saltpetre: see SAL-NITRE.] Sodium nitrate.

1884 *Boston* (Mass.) *Jrnl.* 9 Nov. 4/2 The Committee of the Combination of Salitre Elaborators. **1895** *Funk's Standard Dict.*, *Saliter*, soda niter.

salitrose ('sælɪtrəʊs), *a.* [ad. Sp. *salitroso*, f. *salitre* (see prec.).] Containing saltpetre.

1845 FORD *Handbk. Spain* II. 559 Roads.. clouded in a salitrose dust. **1848** *Blackw. Mag.* LXIII. 726 The Bayou Salade especially, owing to the salitrose nature of the soil and springs, is the favourite resort.

So **salitrous** ('sælɪtrəs) *a.*

1897 GADOW *In North. Spain* 77 A spring of salitrous water.

†**'saliture.** *Obs. rare.* [ad. late L. *salītūra*, f. *salīre* to salt (see SALITED).] Salting, pickling.

1657 TOMLINSON *Renou's Disp.* 87 As Saliture and Farture rather seem to appertain to a Cooks [shop]. **1657** *Physical Dict.*, *Saliture*, the art of salting or seasoning any meats.

saliva (sə'laɪvə). Also 5 **salyve.** [a. L. *salīva.*]

1. Spittle; the mixed secretion of the salivary glands and of the mucous glands of the mouth, a colourless liquid, having normally an alkaline reaction, which mixes with the food in mastication. Also *fig.*

c **1400** *Pety Job* 40 in *26 Pol. Poems* 122 Thow woldest suffer neuer more Me to swolowe my salyue? **1676** WISEMAN *Chirurg. Treat.* IV. vii. 333 Not meeting with that disturbance from the *Saliva* as in the former work. **1748** tr. *Vegetius' Distemp. Horses* 172 He will.. pour out a great deal of Saliva, and his Gums will swell. **1847–9** *Todd's Cycl. Anat.* IV. I. 415/2 The presence of food in the mouth caused a rapid flow of saliva. **1877** FOSTER *Physiol.* II. i. 158 Saliva contains but few solids.

transf. and *fig.* **1818** KIRBY & SP. *Entomol.* xxi. (ed. 2) II. 247 The carrion-beetles.. defile us.. with brown fetid saliva. *a* **1957** R. CAMPBELL tr. *F. García Lorca's Romance de la Guardia Civil* in *Coll. Poems* (1960) III. 63 The Virgin cures the children With the saliva of the stars.

attrib. **1826** KIRBY & SP. *Entomol.* xl. IV. 110 The usual saliva-reservoirs. *Ibid.* xli. 125 The most usual number of the saliva-secretors is two. **1875** KNIGHT *Dict. Mech.*, *Saliva-pump* (*Dentistry*), a device to remove the saliva from the mouth during dental operations.

2. (See quot.)

1969 P. HOLLISTER *Encycl. Glass Paperweights* 303 *Saliva*, unwanted string or conglomerate of small bubbles that may be the result of insufficient expulsion of internal air or cooling of the gather during assembly.

3. *attrib.*, as ***saliva gland***; **saliva ejector**, †**extractor** *Dentistry*, a device incorporating a suction pump, for removing saliva from the mouth during a dental operation; **saliva test**, any scientific test performed on a sample of saliva.

a **1884** KNIGHT *Dict. Mech.* Suppl. 778/1 *Saliva ejector*, an instrument for carrying off the accumulating saliva in dental operations. **1897** E. C. KIRK *Textbk. Operative Dentistry* vii. 157 An excessive flow of saliva is uncomfortable to the patient, by its accumulation it impedes the operation... During the preparation of accessible cavities.. the accumulation may be carried off by the use of a saliva ejector. **1931** N. BENNETT *Dental Surg.* (ed. 2) xix. 774 The saliva ejector when first introduced met with considerable opposition, but its use is now almost universal, and if simple aseptic precautions are taken no objection can possibly be found to its adoption. **1963** C. R. COWELL et al. *Inlays, Crowns, & Bridges* v. 53 This permits a saliva ejector to be used, which retracts the tongue and keeps the teeth dry. **1877** J. TAFT *Operative Dentistry* (ed. 3) vi. 176 Various pumps were devised for removing the saliva... All.. have been superseded by the introduction and use of the rubber dam and saliva extractor... The profession is indebted.. for the latter to Dr. J. E. Fisk. **1915** W. OWEN *Let.* 13 Mar. (1967) 327, I noticed that my saliva-glands were a trifle addled. **1939** *New Yorker* 8 July 77/1 You might like to know something about just what the New York Racing Commission does to prevent tampering with horses. Every winner gets a saliva test. **1973** J. THOMSON *Death Cap* i. 9 The saliva test will prove that the person who licked the stamp belongs to the 'O' blood group. **1975** *Times* 21 May 3/4 Detectives have taken their first saliva test in the hunt for the Cambridge rapist.

Hence **sa'liva** *v. intr.*, to salivate; **sa'livaed** *a.*, flecked or covered with saliva.

1939 G. GREENE *Confidential Agent* I. ii. 84 He felt her hand rest on his knee: she wasn't romantic, she had said: this was an automatic reaction, he supposed, to the deep seats and the dim lights and the torch songs; as when Pavlov's dogs saliva'd. **1975** J. GOULET *Oh's Profit* xxx. 187 Oh's salivaed middle finger had stumbled across a pocket of ants directly in front of the television.

salival (sə'laɪvəl), *a.* and *sb.* Now *rare.* [ad. mod.L. *salīvāl-is*, f. L. *salīva*: see prec. and -AL[1]. Cf. OF. *salival.*] **A.** *adj.* = SALIVARY.

1646 SIR T. BROWNE *Pseud. Ep.* III. xvi. (1686) 116 Salival conduits and passages. **1662** H. STUBBE *Ind. Nectar* iii. 34 That salival ferment in the mouth which inchoates digestion. **1713** DERHAM *Phys.-Theol.* IV. xi. 195 To afford that noble digestive salival Liquor to be mixed with the Food in Mastication. **1740** *Phil. Trans.* XLI. 441 The Vessels called salival Ducts by Coschivitzius. **1826** KIRBY & SP. *Entomol.* xli. IV. 124 He suspects that they may be salival vessels. **1881** CLARK RUSSELL *Ocean Free-Lance* I. iii. 81 The salival froth dropping from the jaws of a bloodhound.

†**B.** *sb. pl.* The salivary glands. *Obs.*

1676 WISEMAN *Chirurg. Treat.* IV. viii. 334 Ranula is a soft Swelling possessing those Salivalls under the Tongue.

salivan (sə'laɪvən), *a. rare*[−1]. [f. SALIVA + -AN.] = SALIVARY 2.

1882 *Proc. Zool. Soc.* 14 Nov. 632 The.. salivan secretion.

salivant ('sælɪvənt), *a.* and *sb.* [ad. L. *salīvant-em*, pres. pple. of *salīvāre*, f. *salīva* SALIVA. Cf. F. *salivant.*] **a.** *adj.* Promoting salivation; sialagogic. **b.** *sb.* A sialagogue.

1846 WORCESTER (citing Caldwell), *Salivant, a.*, a promoting salivation. **1857** DUNGLISON *Dict. Med.*

salivarian (sælɪ'vɛərɪən), *a. Biol.* [f. mod.L. *Salivaria*, name of a section of the genus *Trypanosoma* (C. A. Hoare 1964, in *Jrnl. Protozool.* XI. 203/1), fem. of L. *sālīvā-rius* (see SALIVARY *a.*): see -AN.] Used to designate those species of *Trypanosoma* which occur in the bloodstream of the secondary host, and are transmitted from its mouth when it bites a vertebrate. Cf. STERCORARIAN *a.*

1969 *Jrnl. Protozool.* XVI. 466 (*heading*) A new organelle of bloodstream salivarian trypanosomes. **1971** P. C. C. GARNHAM *Progr. Parasitol.* iii. 27 The earlier evolution of these mammalian trypanosomes... At first.. eliminated in the faeces on to the inhospitable ground..; next, in the 'stercorarian' trypanosomes.. passed in the faeces and.. transferred to the mucous membrane of the new host; finally and best, in the 'salivarian' trypanosomes.. the organisms.. reach.. salivary glands and when the insect next bites, the infection inevitably enters the new host. **1977** SOLTYS & WOO in J. P. KREIER *Parasitic Protozoa* I. vi. 241 *Trypanosoma* (*N.*) *congolense* is a small salivarian trypanosome and varies in length between 8 and 24 μm. **1977** J. M. MANSFIELD in *Ibid.* viii. 310 Unlike other stercorarian trypanosomes, *T. rangeli* infects the hemolymph and salivary glands as well as the alimentary canal of its intermediate host. **1980** *Nature* 24 Jan. 383/2 Infection rates of salivarian trypanosomes (subgenera *Nannomonas*, *Duttonella* and *Trypanozoon*) in the tsetse fly *Glossina.*

†**sali'various**, *a. Obs.*[−0] [f. L. *salīvāri-us* SALIVARY + -OUS.] (See quot.)

1656 BLOUNT *Glossogr.*, *Salivarious*, clammy and thick like spettle.

salivarium (sælɪ'vɛərɪəm). Pl. **salivaria.** [f. SALIVA + -ARIUM; cf. med.L. *salivarium* a linen cloth used to catch discharged spittle (DuCange).] A spittoon, esp. one genteelly disguised with a lid, ornamental casing, etc.

1883 *Graphic* 25 Aug. 194 (Advt.), Inlaid Walnut Salivarium, 6s. 9d. **1939** JOYCE *Finnegans Wake* (1964) ii. 286 With his primal handstoe in his sole salivarium. **1960** [see NON-U *a.* and *sb.*].

salivary ('sælɪvərɪ), *a.* [ad. L. *salīvāri-us*, f. *salīva*: see SALIVA and -ARY.]

1. Secreting or conveying saliva.

The salivary glands in man are the parotid, submaxillary, and sublingual.

1709 *Brit. Apollo* II. No. 37. 2/1 The Salivary Glands. **1793** BEDDOES *Consumption* 142 Some persons whose skin is no sooner touched with quicksilver ointment than it is felt in the salivary glands. **1851** WOODWARD *Mollusca* 30 The encephalous mollusks are always furnished with well-developed salivary glands. **1852** *Fraser's Mag.* XLVI. 162 That.. mutton.. moved my salivary apparatus. **1880** GÜNTHER *Fishes* 124 Salivary glands.. are absent in fishes.

2. Consisting of saliva.

1841 T. R. JONES *Anim. Kingd.* 562 The auxiliary secretions subservient to digestion.. are the Salivary, the Hepatic, and the Pancreatic. **1880** M. MACKENZIE *Dis. Throat & Nose* I. 116 The salivary secretion cannot be swallowed.

3. Pertaining to or existing in the saliva or salivary glands.

1807 S. COOPER *First Lines Surg.* II. v. 228 A salivary fistula is an opening on the cheek, from which saliva escapes. **1846** G. E. DAY tr. *Simon's Anim. Chem.* II. 473 In man salivary calculi are of rare occurrence, but the formation of tartar on the teeth is continually observed. **1872** T. BRYANT *Pract. Surg.* 457 In salivary fistula, the salivary duct must find a natural outlet before its unnatural orifice can be expected to close.

†**'salivate**, *a. Obs. rare*[−1]. [f. SALIVA + -ATE[2].] = SALIVARY 1.

1710 T. FULLER *Pharm. Extemp.* 181 It [*sc.* the gargle].. helps.. the laxity of the salivate Glands.

salivate ('sælɪveɪt), *v.* [f. L. *salīvāt-*, ppl. stem of L. *salīvāre*, f. *salīva* SALIVA.]

1. *trans.* To produce an unusual secretion of saliva in (a person), generally by the use of mercury; to produce ptyalism in.

1669 *Phil. Trans.* IV. 1050, I designe to salivate her, in hopes to correct that vitious ferment. **1720** BECKET *ibid.* XXXI. 109 Any Proof.. that Persons had been Salivated in their Leprosy. **1827** J. W. CROKER in *C. Papers* 7 Aug. (1884) I. 380 He gave Mr. C[anning] so much [mercury] that he actually salivated him. **1879** KHORY *Princ. Med.* 4 Quinine salivates a few.

absol. **1708** J. KEILL *Anim. Secretion* 63 Why does Mercury salivate, or Nitre force Urine? **1845** P. H. LATHAM *Lect. Clin. Med.* I. xiii. 266 Even within this time mercury must be made to salivate, if mercury is made to cure.

2. *intr.* **a.** To secrete or discharge saliva. **b.** To secrete saliva in excess under the influence of sialagogues.

1681 tr. *Willis' Rem. Med. Wks.* Vocab., *Salivate*, to spit. **1706** PHILLIPS (ed. Kersey), To *Salivate*, to gather or make Spittle. **1725** HUXHAM in *Phil. Trans.* XXXIII. 381 Two adult Persons,.. who neither salivated, nor purged, except when some lenient Cathartics were given them. **1737** BRACKEN *Farriery Impr.* (1749) 152 Horses easilier salivate than Men. **1829** SIR R. CHRISTISON *Treat. Poisons* xiii. (1832) 369 She immediately began to complain of soreness of the mouth, salivated profusely, and even put on the expression of countenance of a salivating person. **1832** *Blackw. Mag.* XXXI. 843 He [*sc.* an American] salivates for some threescore years,.. and is gathered to his fathers, to spit no more.

c. *fig.* To display one's relish *at* some prospect or anticipated event, to 'lick one's lips'.

1970 *Guardian* 11 May 10/3 On May 1, the American military were delighted to be unleashed into the Cambodian sanctuaries. One officer said of his colleagues: 'They've been salivating at the prospect of this for months.' **1977** *Times* 1 Nov. 14/6 The double LP set has sold two million copies in America. Pye, who are marketing the records in Britain, are salivating at the sales prospects.

Hence **'salivating** *vbl. sb.* and *ppl. a.*

1657 G. STARKEY *Helmont's Vind.* 101 As the Devil is fabled not able to hide his cloven foot, so Mercury will still be betraying its.. salivating quality. **1676** WISEMAN *Chirurg. Treat., Lues Ven.* 8 The methods of Salivating are divers, but all by Mercury. **1694** SALMON *Bate's Dispens.* 513/2 It is more gentle than *Turpethum Minerale*, or any other salivating Precipitate. **1728** CHAMBERS *Cycl.* s.v. *Salivation*, A.. French Physician, M. Chicoyneau,.. has lately done some Discredit to the Practice of Salivating. **1829** [see 2 above].

salivation (sælɪ'veɪʃən). [a. F. *salivation* or its source late L. *salīvātio*, n. of action f. *salīvāre* to SALIVATE.] Secretion or discharge of saliva: *esp.* the production of an excessive flow of saliva by administering mercury.

1598 T. BASTARD *Chrestoleros* (1880) 10 Phisition Mirus talkes of saliuation. **1686** WOOD *Life* (O.H.S.) III. 202 Whore houses increase, surgeons have work, and great salivation used. **1733** CHEYNE *Eng. Malady* II. ii. §4 (1734) 127 Salivation by the internal Exhibition of Mercurials only, seldom succeeds. **1764** REID *Inquiry* vi. §17 [He] having been blind for some years of a *gutta serena*, was restored to sight by salivation. **1801** *Med. Jrnl.* V. 570 Salivation, a symptom that is often remarked at the period of teething. **1843** R. J. GRAVES *Syst. Clin. Med.* xvi. 192 His mouth was still sore in consequence of severe mercurial salivation. **1877** ROBERTS *Handbk. Med.* (ed. 3) I. 157 Caution must be exercised in the administration of narcotics, should there be much bronchial catarrh or salivation.

b. with *a* and *pl.* Now *Obs.* or *rare.*

1700 T. BROWN *Amusem. Ser. & Com.* viii. Wks. 1709 III. 74 As if they were all clapt, and under a Salivation for the cure on't. **1746** H. WALPOLE *Let. to Mann* 25 Apr., Lord Elcho was in a salivation. **1760** C. JOHNSTON *Chrysal* (1822) III. 310 She had lost her hair and teeth in a salivation! **1831** J. DAVIES *Man. Mat. Med.* 23 An old woman.. was affected with a considerable salivation every time she made use of opium.

†**c.** *concr.* Saliva or an excretion resembling it.

1601 HOLLAND *Pliny* II. 413 The noysome saliuation or spittle of the Aspis called Ptyas. **1677** PLOT *Oxfordsh.* 107 Engendered from the salivation and slime of snakes.

†**salivative**, *a. Obs.* [f. L. *salīvāt-*, ppl. stem of *salīvāre* to SALIVATE + -IVE.] Causing a flow of saliva; salivant.

1657 G. STARKEY *Helmont's Vind.* To Rdr., I have.. rejected all Mercurial and Antimonial Medicaments, whether Vomitive, Purgative or Salivative.

'salivator. *rare*[−1]. [f. SALIVATE *v.*: see -ATOR.] One who uses sialagogues.

1834 *Good's Study Med.* (ed. 4) I. 661 The salivators.. have not been more successful than other practitioners.

sali'vatory, *a. rare.* [f. late L. *salīvāt-* (see SALIVATE *v.*) + -ORY.] = SALIVARY.

1699 *Phil. Trans.* XXI. 241 Salivatory glands.

†sa'livous, *a. Obs.* [ad. L. *salīvōsus* or F. *saliveux*, f. *salīva* SALIVA: see -OUS.]

1. Pertaining to saliva; of the nature of saliva.

1567 MAPLET *Gr. Forest* 62 This last being kept awhile in the mouth dryeth vp the tongue and saliuous humor. **1658** SIR T. BROWNE *Gard. Cyrus* iii. 150 After a fuller mastication, and salivous mixture. **1661** LOVELL *Hist. Anim. & Min.* 285 Their [*sc.* snails'] salivous mucus which they vomit out when pricked. **1676** WISEMAN *Chirurg. Treat.* IV. vii. 333 An Elongation of the *Vvula* through the abundance of salivous Humour flowing upon it.

2. Using spittle (in baptism).

1813 MOORE *Post-bag* iv. 67 Let no one tell us To free such sad salivous fellows—No—no—the man baptized with spittle Hath no truth in him.

salix ('seɪlɪks, 'sælɪks). [a. L. *salix* willow.] = WILLOW *sb.* 1.

1775 T. BLAIKIE *Diary Scotch Gardener* (1931) 61 I found ..several sorts of *salixes.* **1965** P. WAYRE *Wind in Reeds* viii. 96 A hazel hen feeding quietly among the salix and lichens.

Salk vaccine (sɒlk, -ɔː-). *Med.* [Named after Jonas Edward *Salk* (b. 1914), U.S. virologist, who developed the vaccine in 1954.] The first vaccine developed against poliomyelitis, made from viruses of the three immunological types inactivated with formalin.

[**1954** *Brit. Med. Jrnl.* 6 Mar. 593/2 This is..the first large-scale trial of Dr. Salk's vaccine.] **1954** *Jrnl. Amer. Med. Assoc.* 10 July 1021/1 There is no chance that injections of Salk vaccine will cause human Rh-negative subjects to produce Rh antibodies. **1958** *Oxford Mail* 22 Aug. 1/9 Chicago has been completely free from polio this year for the first time, states the Health Department, which credited this to the extensive use of Salk vaccine. **1964** [see KILLED *ppl. a.* 1 c]. **1976** M. GROSSMAN in W. L. Drew *Viral Infections* ix. 246 The Salk vaccine is no longer manufactured nor used in the United States.

sall, obs. form of SOUL, and SHALL *v.*

sallad(e, obs. forms of SALAD, SALLET.

‖**salle** (sal). See also SALE *sb.*[3] [Fr.; of Teut. origin: cf. SALE *sb.*[1]]

1. a. A hall, room. *rare.* (Only with reference to foreign countries.)

1765 H. WALPOLE *Let.* 5 Dec. (1904) VI. 375 You may go into the *petit cabinet*, and then into the great *salle*, and the gallery. **1819** BYRON *Let.* 31 Dec., in Moore *Life* (1839) 432/1 Music, dancing, and play, all in the same *salle.* **1853** C. BRONTE *Villette* xx, A knowledge not merely confined to its open streets, but penetrating to all its galleries, salles, and cabinets. **1913** H. JAMES *Small Boy & Others* xxv. 359, I.. enjoyed the commemorative show of Delaroche given..in one of the rather bleak *salles* of the École des Beaux-Arts.

b. = *salle de jeu* (see sense 2 below).

1886 C. M. YONGE *Chantry House* II. xv. 144 Martyn was doing his best for him..while Lady Peacock was at the *salle.* **1966** G. GREENE *Comedians* I. iii. 89, I watched him leave the *salle.* He had over three hundred dollars to change now. **1970** 'J. MORRIS' *Candywine Devel.* xxiii. 247 He stood at the big roulette table in the main *salle.*

c. = *salle d'armes* (see sense 2 below).

1961 F. C. AVIS *Sportman's Gloss.* 197/1 *Salle*, the fencing hall or studio, often open to the public. **1973** *Where* Mar. 73/3 Among the luxuries enjoyed by school C..a fencing salle. **1975** *Oxf. Compan. Sports & Games* 306/2 A few schools, such as that of the famous *Angelos* and the *London Fencing Club*, founded in 1848, kept the sport alive in a few London *salles*, some public schools, and the universities.

2. In Fr. combinations. **salle-à-manger** (salamɑ̃ʒe), a dining-hall, dining room. **salle d'armes** (sal darm), a fencing-room, school or club; **salle d'attente** (sal datɑ̃t), a waiting-room (at a station); **salle d'audience** (sal dodjɑ̃s), a court-room; **salle d'eau** (sal do), a wash-room, shower-room, **salle de jeu** (sal də ʒø), a gambling house or room; **salle des pas perdus** (sal de pɑ pɛrdy), a waiting-hall (at a law-court, station, etc.), lobby; **salle privée** (sal prive), a private gambling room in a casino.

1762 STERNE *Let.* 14 Aug., The house consists of a good *salle à manger* above stairs [etc.]. **1862** THACKERAY *Philip* II. ix. 201 At a pretty early hour the various occupants of the crib at the Rue Poussin used to appear in the dingy little salle-à-manger, and partake of the breakfast there provided. **1887** RUSKIN *Præterita* II. 172 James Forbes and his wife were with us in the otherwise untenanted *salle-a-manger.* **1885** E. CASTLE *Schools & Masters of Fence* x. 159 How different a 'salle d'armes' in Paris or London in those days from the old Italian schools of Queen Bess and Henri III. **1902** G. B. SHAW *Let.* 4 Mar. (1972) II. 269 There should be a salle d'armes where stage combats & wrestlings could be practised. **1952** *Fencing* ('Know the Game' Ser.) 19/1 In a friendly encounter in the Salle d'Armes (Fencing Room) or Club, the sporting tradition of acknowledging a hit has been jealously preserved. **1863** *Miss Jemima's Swiss Jrnl.* 26 June (1963) i. 9 Passengers..are locked in the *salle d'attente* until the arrival of the train. **1879** FROUDE in *Fraser's Mag.* Nov. XX. 624 It was a large barely furnished apartment like the *salle d'attente* at the Northern Railway Station at Paris. **1882** SALA *Amer. Revis.* (1883) I. vii. 111 Without any crowding..we passed from the *salle d'attente* to the platform. **1909** E. NESBIT *Daphne in Fitzroy St.* iv. 44 The rout of dark-skinned, browbent, hurrying, preoccupied French folk..in the *salle d'attente* at the station. *a* **1666** EVELYN *Diary* an. 1644 (1955) II. 98 Within are severall Chambers, Courts, Treasures &c above that most rich and glorious Sale de l'Audiens. **1957** L. DURRELL *Spirit of Place* (1969) 138 Of course no lavatories and *salle d'eau* a rarity. Even in this lovely villa we wash from a bucket. **1964** *Punch* 14 Oct. 573/3 Town-dwellers in France who have a *salle d'eaux* [*sic*]..of their own. **1968** D. TORR *Treason Line* 130 They were in the *salle des jeux* [*sic*], the hushed sanctuary of the temple of chance. **1901** V. BETHELL *Monte Carlo Anecdotes* 4 In the year 1858 a grand banquet was held to inaugurate the opening of his *Salle-de-Jeux.* **1839** *Indispensable Eng. Vade Mecum Paris* 135 The most remarkable hall is that named *la salle des Pas-Perdus*, being 222 feet long, by 84 wide. **1885** H. JAMES *Little Tour in France* xvii. 120 The curious *salle des pas perdus*, or central hall, out of which the different tribunals open..is a feature of every French court-house. **1977** *Listener* 10 Feb. 183/1 The image is growing on me of Limbo as a large railway terminus..where the dead hang about in a *salle des pas perdus.* **1930** E. WAUGH *Labels* ii. 35 The cinema producer's version of the *salles privées*, with jewelled courtesans and ribboned grand-dukes, is a thing of the past. **1976** H. MACINNES *Agent in Place* xiv. 153 There were two wings.. the left one consisted of the *Salle Privée.*

3. With varying pronunc. (sɑːl, sɔːl). Also †**saul.** The finishing department of a papermill, in which sheets of paper are examined, sorted and packed.

1819 *Ree's Cycl.* XXVI. s.v. Paper, The paper, being sufficiently dried for the last time, is carried to the building where it is examined, finished, and pressed: this is called the *Saul.* **1854** C. TOMLINSON *Cycl. Useful Arts* II. 364/1 The paper..is taken down, carried to a building called the Saul ..where it is examined, finished, and pressed. **1888** CROSS & BEVAN *Paper-Making* 175 The sheets of paper are now ready to be examined before being finally sent away from the mill. This is done in the 'Finishing-house', or 'Salle' as it is sometimes called. **1946** H. WHETTON *Pract. Printing & Binding* xxviii. 345/1 If the paper is being sold in sheets it goes to the 'salle' or finishing department, where each sheet is examined top and bottom..and sorted. **1976** *Oxford Times* (City ed.) 12 Mar. 1/7 Sogat members at Wolvercote Mill could not recommend acceptance of the management's latest proposals for the 70 men in the salle.

sallee, var. SALLY *sb.*[4]

Sallee-man ('sæliːmæn). Also **Sally-man.** [f. *Sallee*, the name of a Moroccan seaport formerly of piratical repute.]

1. A Moorish pirate-ship. *Obs.* exc. *Hist.* So also **Sallee rover.**

1637 J. DUNTON *Jrnl. Sally Fleet* Ep. Ded., Being sent out Master and Pilote in a Sallyman of warre, with twenty-one Moores and five Flemish rennagadoes, unto the coast of England to take Christians. **1686** J. DUNTON *Lett. fr. New-Eng.* (1867) 29 One of the Seamen having descry'd to the S.W. a ship which he took for a Sally-Man. *Ibid.* 30 This Supposed Sally-Rover prov'd nothing else but a Virginia Merchant-Man. **1698** T. FROGER *Voy.* 2 On the 9th we had a sight of another Vessel,..she seem'd to be a Sally-man, and might carry about 30 pieces of cannon. **1734** *Extracts Rec. Convent. Burghs Scotl.* (1885) V. 593 A ship-master in Boness and his crew who were taken by a Salee Rover and are now at Algeirs. **1754** *Jackson's Oxf. Jrnl.* 24 Aug., A Sallee man, which cruizes from Cape Bon to the Isle of Galeta. **1760** C. JOHNSTON *Chrysal* II. xii. 235 A Sallee rover gave chace to our ship.

2. A marine hydrozoan, *Velella vulgaris.*

It floats on the sea with its vertical crest acting as a sail. **1756** P. BROWNE *Jamaica* 387 The Sally Man. This insect is more firm and opake than either of the foregoing. **1860** G. BENNETT *Gatherings Naturalist Austral.* 54 *Vellela limbosa*, or Sallyman, is abundant. **1863** WOOD *Illustr. Nat. Hist.* III. 739 A remarkable creature called by the popular name of *Sallee Man*, sometimes corrupted in nautical fashion into *Sallyman.*

sallender ('sæləndə(r)). Now only *pl.* Forms: 6–7 selander, 7 sellander, sellender, sallander, 8 solander; 8 selenders, 8–9 sallenders. [Of obscure origin: in F. *solandre* (1664 in Hatz.-Darm.).] A dry scab affecting the hock of a horse.

1523 FITZHERB. *Husb.* §95 A selander is in the bendynge of the legge behynde. **1607** MARKHAM *Caval.* VII. (1617) 79 A Mallander is a drie scabbe vpon the bought of the fore leg: and the Sellanders vpon the hinder. **1639** T. DE GRAY *Compl. Horsem.* 6 No way subject to mainge, mallender, sellender. **1685** *Lond. Gaz.* No. 2092/4 Stolen.., a large strong grey Gelding,..hath a small Sallander. **1725** BRADLEY *Fam. Dict.* II. s.v. *Malenders*, Others alledge, that what cures the Scratches will cure both the Malenders and Selenders. **1831** YOUATT *Horse* 273 In the inside of the hock ..there is sometimes a scurfy eruption called mallenders in the fore leg, and sallenders in the hind leg. **1884** *Sat. Rev.* 5 July 27/2 It is a breach of a warranty of soundness if the warranted horse suffers from..sallenders.

sallendine, obs. form of CELANDINE.

saller, obs. f. SOLLAR *Min.*, platform.

sallery, obs. form of CELERY, SALARY.

sallet ('sælɪt), **salade** (sə'lɑːd). *Antiq.* Forms: 5–8 sallet, 5–6 salett(e, salet (also 8–9 *arch.*), *Sc.* sellat, -et, (5 salecte, salate), 6 salett(e, (-att), 6–7 sallat(e, 7 sallad(e, 5–7, 9 *arch.* salad(e. [a. F. *salade*, ad. Sp. *celada* or It. *celata*, believed to represent L. *cælāta* (sc. *cassis* or *galea*), (a helmet) ornamented with engraving. Cf. MDu. *salade, sallade, salla.*

The L. adj. has not been found in this elliptical use. Cf. 'loricæ galeæque aeneæ, cælatæ opere Corinthio' (Cicero).]

1. In mediæval armour, a light globular headpiece, either with or without a vizor, and without a crest, the lower part curving outwards behind.

c **1440** *Eng. Conq. Irel.* iv. 11 (MS. Rawl.), Ham-Selfe wel wepenyd with haubergeons, and bryght Salletis and sheldys. **1465** MARG. PASTON in *P. Lett.* II. 189 Imprimis, a peyr brygandyrs, a salet, a boresper [etc.]. **1480** CAXTON *Chron. Eng.* cclv. (1482) 331 He toke syr vmfreys salade and his brigantyns..and also his gylt spores and arayd hym lyke a lord. *c* **1537** *Thersytes* 55, I wolde have a sallet to were on my hed, Whiche under my chyn with a thonge red Buckeled shall be. **1585** T. WASHINGTON tr. *Nicholay's Voy.* IV. xxviii. 146 b, On their heads [they] hadde sallets of leather. **1593** SHAKS. *2 Hen. VI*, IV. x. 9 Many a time but for a Sallet, my braine-pan had bene cleft with a brown Bill. **1594** R. ASHLEY tr. *Loys le Roy* 113 b, The men that were heauily armed had a salade, which couered their head, and came downe as far as their shoulders. *a* **1600** *Floddan F.* ii. (1664) 12 Some of a share can shortly make A sallate for to save his pate. **1786** GROSE *Anc. Armour* 11 The Salade, Salet, or Celate. Father Daniel defines a Salet to be a sort of light casque, without a crest, sometimes having a visor, and being sometimes without one. **1824** MEYRICK *Ant. Armour* III. Gloss., *Salett*,..a light head piece sometimes worn by the cavalry, but generally by the infantry and archers. It..was generally a steel cap greatly resembling the morian. **1844** JAMES *Agincourt* II. v. 109 He caused his archers to put on the cuirasses and salades. **1888** STEVENSON *Black Arrow* 4 Armed with sword and spear, a steel salet on his head, a leather jack upon his body.

b. *jocularly* referred to as a measure for wine.

1600 HEYWOOD *1st Pt. Edw. IV* (1613) Cj, Make a proclamation..That..Sacke be sold by the Sallet.

†c. *transf.* Headpiece, head. *nonce-use.*

1652 C. B. STAPYLTON *Herodian* 56 When Wine was got into his drunken Sallat.

†2. Some kind of iron vessel. *Obs.*

1472–3 *Rolls of Parlt.* VI. 51/2 With fyere brought with theym in a Salette thider. **1507–8** *Acc. Ld. High Treas. Scot.* IV. 101 Item, for ane sellat to mak gwn powdir vij s. **1582** HESTER *Secr. Phiorav.* III. cxvi. 141 Sette the same potte in a Sallette of Iron, and lute them close together.

Hence **†'saletted** *a.*, wearing a sallet.

1455 *Coventry Leet Bk.* (E.E.T.S.) 282 An hundred of goode-men..with bowes & arowes, Jakked & saletted. **1461** J. PASTON in *P. Lett.* II. 36 The peple was jakkyd and saletted, and riottously disposed.

sallet, sallfe, obs. forms of SALAD, SALVE.

†'salliable, *a. Obs. rare*$^{-1}$. [f. SALLY *v.*[2] + -ABLE.] Suitable for making a sally.

1598 BARRET *Theor. Warres* IV. i. 98 It is alwayes important for him to know the wayes..most salliable for the souldiers..out of the campe.

sallibube, obs. variant of SILLABUB.

†'sallier[1]. *Obs.*$^{-0}$ In 5 salyare. [f. SALLY *v.*[1] + -ER[1].] A dancer.

c **1440** *Promp. Parv.* 441/1 Salyare, *saltator, saltatrix.*

sallier[2] ('sælɪə(r)). *rare.* [f. SALLY *v.*[2] + -ER[1].] One who takes part in a sally.

1685 TRAVESTIN *Siege Newheusel* 10 The Salliers were obliged, without any more effect, to retire. **1848** AIRD *Trag. Wold* II. x. Poet. Wks. 39 Dunley with a party of salliers is fighting outside one of the open gates.

sallow ('sæləʊ), *sb.* Forms: α. 1 sealh, (seal, salh, salch); β. 4–5 salwe, (4 salew, salugh), 5–6 salgh(e, salow(e, (5 salwhe, 6 sallowe, sallo, 7 salloo), 4– sallow; γ. [1 saliȝ-], 3 selihe, salyhe, 5–6 saly, 6 salye, 6, 9 salley, 7– sally. (See also E.D.D., and the forms placed under SAUGH.) [OE. *sealh* (Anglian *salh*):—prehistoric **salho-z* masc.; cogn. w. OHG. *salaha* wk. fem. (MHG. *salhe*, mod.G. in comb. *salweide*):—**salhōn-*; ON. *selja* wk. fem. (Sw. *sälj, sälg*, Da. *selje*):—**salhjōn-*; cognates outside Teut. are L. *salic-, salix*, Gr. ἑλίκη, Irish *saileach*, Welsh *helyg* (collect.). The Fr. *saule* is an adoption from Teut.

The OE. nom. sing. is directly represented by the dialectal SAUGH. The β and γ forms above descend from the late Anglian flexional form *salȝ-, saliȝ-*, where the ȝ is introduced on the analogy of those sbs. in which final *h* is a euphonic modification of ȝ. The form SEAL appears partly to represent the normal flexional form of the stem in OE., as in *seales* genit. sing., *sealas* pl., and partly to be adopted from ON. *selja.*]

1. A plant of the genus *Salix*, a willow; chiefly, in narrower sense, as distinguished from 'osier' and 'willow', applied to several species of *Salix* of a low-growing or shrubby habit: see quot. 1866. Also, one of the shoots of a willow.

α. *a* **700** *Epinal Gloss.* 892 *Salix*, salch. *a* **800** *Erfurt Gloss.* 1767 *Salix*, salh. *c* **1000** *Sax. Leechd.* II. 18 Wiþ heafod ece ȝenim sealh & ele.

β. **1377–8** *Durham Acc. Rolls* (Surtees) 131 In posicione de Sallowys juxta ripam de Wer, xxd. *c* **1386** CHAUCER *Wife's Prol.* 655 Who so that buyldeth his hous al of salwes..Is worthy to been hanged on the galwes! **1388** WYCLIF *Lev.* xxiii. 40 And ȝe schulen take to ȝou..salewis [1382 withies] of the rennynge streem. *c* **1450** LYDG. & BURGH *Secrees* 2014 Afftir, ovir a ryveer rennyng, To be set Arrayed to thyn estat, With salwys, wyllwys Envyronnd preperat. **1555** EDEN *Decades* 38 Elmes, wyllowes, and salowes. **1583** L. M[ASCALL] tr. *Bk. Dyeing* 76 Take cole of a willo or sallo. **1697** DRYDEN *Virg. Georg.* II. 573 Sallows and Reeds, on Banks of Rivers born. **1725** T. THOMAS in *Portland Pap.* (Hist. MSS. Comm.) VI. 131 There is a small shrub growing over the greatest part of it ['the Carr', near Carlisle] which they call soft sallows. **1782** J. SCOTT *Poet. Wks.* 96 And lofty sallows their sweet bloom display. **1818** SHELLEY *Pr. Wks.* (1880) III. 18 We sit with Plato by old Ilissus..

among the sweet scent of flowering sallow. **1859** TENNYSON *Merlin & V.* 223 A robe..In colour like the satin-shining palm On sallows in the windy gleams of March. **1866** *Treas. Bot.*, *Sallow*, a name for *Salix cinerea*, *S. Caprea*, and the allied species, which are not flexible like the osier, but furnish the best charcoal for gunpowder. **1907** *Gentl. Mag.* July 38 The yellow sallows, locally sallys, which the cottage children call palms, flame in gold.

γ. *c* **1000** *Ags. Ps.* (Th.) xxxvi. 2 On saliȝ[um] we sariȝe, swiðe ȝelome, ure organan up-ahengan. *a* **1300** *E.E. Psalter* cxxxvi. 2 In selihes [*v.r.* salyhes, wilthes] in mide ofe ite Our organes henge we yhite. **1483** *Cath. Angl.* 317/1 Salghe for Saly *A.*), *salix.* **1664** EVELYN *Sylva* xix. 39 Of the Withy, Sally, Ozier, and Willow. *Ibid.* 40 We have three sorts of Sallys amongst us: The vulgar..and the hopping Sallys..: And a third kind..having the twigs reddish. **1694** WESTMACOT *Script. Herb.* 222 Sallies grow the faster, if planted within the reach of the Water. **1750** W. ELLIS *Mod. Husbandm.* IV. II. 41 (E.D.S.). **1882** *W. Worc. Gloss.*, *Sallies*, willow-boughs.

2. The wood of the sallow tree.

β. *c* **1400** *Lanfranc's Cirurg.* 118 If þe heed be smyte wiþ a liȝt drie staf as of salow. **1646** SIR T. BROWNE *Pseud. Ep.* II. v. 88 Smal-coale..is made of Sallow, Willow, Alder, Hasell, and the like. **1658** —— *Hydriot.* iii. 44 Sallow..makes more Ashes then Oake. **1843** HOLTZAPFFEL *Turning*, etc. I. 104 Sallow (*Salix caprea*), is white, with a pale-red cast, like red deal, but without the veins. **1882** *Athenæum* 26 Aug. 271/2 A Sussex trug..is a flat basket..of flakes of sallow braced with ash.

γ. **1546** *Yorks. Chantry Surv.* (Surtees) I. 113 Ther is a wood..conteynyng..xx acres of okes, asshes, salyes and other woodes. **1582** in W. H. Turner *Select. Rec. Oxford* (1880) 424 Spoylinge of hasells, salleys, and other woods readie for sale. **1640** BP. REYNOLDS *Passions* xxxvii. 453 They doe not take Sally, or Willow, or Birch, and such other Materialls. **1810** W. H. MARSHALL *Rev. Board Agric.*, *W. Departm.* 275 The softer woods, such as ash, sallies, alder, are regularly cut from twelve to fourteen years' growth. **1835** J. WILSON *Biog. Blind* 212 The old harp..the front of which is white sally, the back of fir.

3. a. A collectors' name for certain moths the larvæ of which feed on the sallow or willow; esp. a moth of the genus *Xanthia*.

1829 J. F. STEPHENS *Syst. Catal. Brit. Ins.* II. 98. **1832** J. RENNIE *Conspect. Butterfl. & M.* 85. **1880** O. S. WILSON *Larvæ Brit. Lepidopt.* 270.

b. ? = *sally-fly* (see 4 b).

1902 *Webster's Dict.*, Suppl., *Sally*, a stone fly.

4. a. *attrib.* as **sallow** (or **sally**) **bush, charcoal, land, pole, stake, switch, tree, twig, willow, wood.**

1883 *Eng. Illustr. Mag.* Nov. 69/2 A few low *sallow bushes. **1615** MARKHAM *Eng. Housew.* 81 Take of *Sallow Charcole vj. ounces. **1907** *Gentl. Mag.* July 38 Down by the river we have the Sallens, or *Sally lands. **1898** *B'ham Daily Post* 26 Mar. (E.D.D.), 'White and black *Sally poles' for sale. *c* **1440** *Pallad. on Husb.* XII. 139 And put a *saly stake in hit. **1802** H. MARTIN *Helen of Glenross* I. 55 A *sally switch. **1502** ARNOLDE *Chron.* (1811) 188 Take..half soo myche of coles of *salow or of wylow tree. **1850** K. H. DIGBY *Compitum* III. 206 A brook that winds through bending sally trees. *c* **1440** *Pallad. on Husb.* IV. 18 And softe a *saly twigge aboute hym plie. **1776–96** WITHERING *Brit. Plants* (ed. 3) II. 54 *Sallow Willow. *Salix caprea*... This is perhaps the most common of all our willows. *c* **1790** IMISON *Sch. Art* II. 17 Charcoal is to be chosen of *sallow wood.

b. Special comb.: **sally-fly**, some kind of stone fly; **sallow kitten**, a moth (see quot.); **sallow moth**, a moth of the genus *Xanthia* (*Cassell's Dict.*); **sally picker** *Anglo-Irish*, a name for the Chiffchaff, Sedge Warbler and Willow Warbler; **sallow thorn**, a plant of the genus *Hippophae*; **sallow (wattle)**, one of several Australian acacias that resemble willows in habit or foliage. **sallow †withe, withy** [= G. *salweide*] = sense 1.

1787 BEST *Angling* (ed. 2) 114 The Yellow *Sally Fly. Comes on about the twentieth of May... It is a four winged fly; as it swims down the water its wings lie flat on its back. **1880** O. S. WILSON *Larvæ Brit. Lepidopt.* 189 *Dicranura furcula*, Linn. The *Sallow Kitten. **1885** SWAINSON *Provinc. Names Birds* 25, 26, 28 *Sally picker (Ireland). **1847** W. E. STEELE *Field Bot.* 157 *Hippophae.* L. *Sallow-thorn. **1884** A. NILSON *Timber Trees New South Wales* 21 *A[cadia] dealbata*.—Silver Wattle; Sallow. **1965** *Austral. Encycl.* VII. 539/2 *A[cacia] longifolia*, *A. mucronata* and several related species with long flower-spikes are known as sallow wattles in Victoria. **1657** THORNLEY tr. *Longus' Daphnis & Chloe* 68 The Goats gnaw'd the green *Sallow With in pieces. **1893** *Wiltsh. Gloss.*, **Sally-withy*, a willow.

sallow ('sæləʊ), *a.* Forms: 1 **salo**, 4–6 **salowe**, (5 **salloh, salwhe**, 6 **sallowe**, 7 **salow**), 6– **sallow**. [OE. *salo* = MDu. *salu*, *saluwe* discoloured, dirty (Du. †*zaluw*), OHG. *salo*, *salew-* dark-coloured (MHG. *sal*, *salw-*, mod.Ger. dial. *sal*), Icel. *söl-r* yellow:—OTeut. **salwo-*, whence F. *sale*, It. *salavo* dirty. Cf. Russian *solovoy* cream-coloured.] **a.** Of the skin or complexion: Having a sickly yellow or brownish yellow colour.

a **1000** *Riddles* lxxx. 11 (Gr.) Good is min wise & ic [*sc.* ? a horn] sylfa salo. ? *a* **1366** CHAUCER *Rom. Rose* 355 Ful salowe was waxen hir colour. *c* **1400** *Rom. Rose* 7392 That false traitouresse untrewe Was lyk that salowe hors of hewe, That in the Apocalips is shewed. *c* **1430** *Pilgr. Lyf Manhode* I. lxix. (1869) 41 Al blac thei bicomen and salwh,..and elded. *c* **1440** *Promp. Parv.* 441 Salwhe of colowre (*P.* salowe), *croceus.* **1530** PALSGR. 323/1 Salowe yolowe coloured as ones skynne is for sycknesse, *jaunastre.* **1533** ELYOT *Cast. Helthe* (1541) 13 Colour of inward causes... Of inequalytie of humoures, wherof doo procede, blacke, salowe, or white onely. Red, Blacke, Salowe, do betoken domynion of heate... Salowe, choler citrine. **1592** SHAKS. *Rom. & Jul.* II. iii. 70 What a deale of brine Hath washt thy sallow cheekes for Rosaline! **1613** R. CAWDREY *Table Alph.* (ed. 3), *Salow*, white. **1656** EARL. MONM. tr. *Boccalini, Pol. Touchstone* (1674) 256 [She] is of so sallow a complexion, that she shadows upon the Moor. **1744** ARMSTRONG *Preserv. Health* IV. 48 Hence..The Lover's paleness; and the sallow hue Of Envy. *a* **1745** SWIFT *Panegyric on Dean* Wks. 1751 X. 170 Pale Dropsy with a sallow Face. **1794** S. WILLIAMS *Vermont* 194 They were of a sallow or brownish complexion. **1813** BYRON *Corsair* I. viii, That man.. Whose name appals ..And tints each swarthy cheek with sallower hue. **1856** BRYANT *Death Schiller* iii, The sallow Tartar. **1877** BLACK *Green Past.* xxx, The eldest daughter was rather pretty but sallow and unhealthy.

b. *transf.* and of things personified.

1746 COLLINS *Ode Evening* 45 While sallow Autumn fills thy lap with leaves. **1784** COWPER *Task* I. 438 He..who, imprisoned long..and a prey To sallow sickness,..Escapes at last to liberty and light. **1827** CARLYLE *Misc.* (1857) I. 50 They are believers; but their faith is no sallow plant of darkness. **1844** MRS. BROWNING *Drama of Exile* Poems 1850 I. 72 Pining to a sallow idiocy.

c. *Comb.*

1551 T. WILSON *Logike* (1580) 52 b, A man maie be high coloured, or *sallowe coloured, and yet not blacke. **1633** FORD *Love's Sacr.* IV. i, The sallow-coloured brat Of some vnlanded banckrupt. **1598** SYLVESTER *Du Bartas* II. ii. IV. *Columnes* 148 That *sallow-fac't, sad, stooping Nymph. **1877** BLACK *Green Past.* v, A tall, thin, sallow-faced man. **1910** W. DE LA MARE *Three Mulla-Mulgars* 81 There came spindling along an old *sallow-hued Earth-mulgar. **1892** ZANGWILL *Childr. Ghetto* 100 A *sallow-looking, close-cropped Pole. **1606** MARSTON *Parasitaster* III. sig. E1, A blacke hayred, pall-fac'de, *sallowe thinking Mistresse. **1853** KANE *Grinnell Exp.* xxxiii. (1856) 292 The *sallow-visaged party.

sallow ('sæləʊ), *v.* [f. SALLOW *a.*] *trans.* To make sallow.

1831 T. L. PEACOCK *Crotchet Castle* i, Her quondam lover, whose physiognomy the intense anxieties..had left blighted, sallowed, and crow's-footed. **1861** DU CHAILLU *Equat. Afr.* xviii. 325 The whole complexion is sallowed. **1868** LOWELL *Under the Willows* 41 July..sallows the crispy fields.

†sallowie. *Obs. rare*[−1]. Perh. a dial. form of *sallow-withe*; see SALLOW *sb.* 4 b.

1610 G. FLETCHER *Christ's Tri.* I. ii, Bees, that flie About the laughing bloosms of sallowie.

sallowish ('sæləʊɪʃ), *a.* [f. SALLOW *a.* + -ISH.] Somewhat sallow in hue.

1754 RICHARDSON *Grandison* (1781) III. v. 32 Her complexion, sallowish, streaked with red. *Ibid.* VII. xxxiv. 158 He..has..a complexion a sallowish brown. **1865** DICKENS *Mut. Fr.* I. xi, A youngish sallowish gentleman in spectacles. **1889** *Macm. Mag.* Apr. 410/2 'Twas now of a cold, sallowish green.

sallowness ('sæləʊnɪs). [f. SALLOW *a.* + -NESS.] The state of being sallow.

1722 BP. DOWNES in Nicolson *Ep. Corr.* 546 It..has cast such a sallowness (if there is such a word) on his countenance, that [etc.]. **1797–1805** S. & HT. LEE *Canterb. T.* IV. 13 He was still pale, even to sallowness. **1899** *Allbutt's Syst. Med.* VI. 595 A little yellowness of the conjunctiva and sallowness of the skin.

sallowy ('sæləʊɪ), *a.* [f. SALLOW *sb.* + -Y.] Abounding in sallows or willows.

1840 LOUISA S. COSTELLO *Summer amongst Bocages* II. 96 We waded along till we reached..the sandy and sallowy Isle du Vieux Pont. **1864** TENNYSON *Aylmer's F.* 147 Where the brook..ran By sallowy rims. **1871** —— *Last Tourn.* 421 Many a glancing plash and sallowy isle.

sally ('sælɪ), *sb.*[1] Forms: 6 **sale, saley, (salew), sallie**, 7–8 **salley**, 8 **sailly**, 7– **sally**. [a. F. *saillie* issuing forth, outrush, outbreak (hence 'sally' of wit, etc.), projection, prominence (also in OF. leap), f. *saillir*: see SAIL *v.*[3], SALLY *v.*[1]

Parallel formations on the etymologically equivalent vb. in the other Rom. langs. are Sp. *salida*, Pg. *sahida*, *saida*, exit, sortie, It. *salita* ascent.]

I. An issuing forth.

1. A sudden rush (*out*) from a besieged place upon the enemy; a sortie; esp. in the phrase *to make a sally*.

1560 DAUS tr. *Sleidane's Comm.* 414 b, The French men that wer besieged make many sales oute. **1617** MORYSON *Itin.* II. 141 That night the Spaniards made a salley..to disturbe our Campe. **1648** *Hamilton Papers* (Camden) 170 Poyer making lately a salley out of Pembrooke Castle, and those from Tenby..assisting him, they haue utterly defeated the besiedgers. **1682** BUNYAN *Holy War* (1905) 380 The Captains..of the Town of Mansoul agreed, and resolved upon a time to make a salley out upon the camp of Diabolus. **1786** W. THOMSON *Watson's Philip III* (1839) 375 A garrison..which is able to resist assaults..and often to make successful sallies. **1803** WELLINGTON in Gurw. *Desp.* (1837) II. 396 He there remained..without throwing away his ammunition excepting when he could do it with effect in judicious sallies. **1850** GROTE *Greece* II. lvii. (1862) V. 119 A well-timed sally..dispersed the Leontine land force.

fig. **1630** *R. Johnson's Kingd. & Commw.* 26 Courage, is able..with a sudden assault to surprise..the enemie. Iudgement hath its scouts ever abroad, to prevent such like sallies and cavalcadoes, that he be not taken sleeper. **1642** FULLER *Holy & Prof. St.* II. vii. 73 As for the..Orientall languages he rather makes sallies and incursions into them, then any solemn sitting down before them. **1844** EMERSON *Lect. New Eng. Ref.* Wks. (Bohn) I. 263 It is handsomer to remain in the establishment,..and conduct that in the best manner, than to make a sally against evil by some single improvement.

†b. A place whence a sally may be made; a sally-port. *Obs.*

1542 *St. Papers Hen. VIII*, IX. 149 Of this Abbey they have made a bulwerk, and a platforme above, and a salew unto the same out of the cytadell. **1590** SIR R. WILLIAMS *Brief Disc. War* 50 Euerie Bulwarke ought to haue two sallies, one for horse and foote, the other a little secret sallie. **1598** BARRET *Theor. Warres* Gloss. 252 Sallie..is also a secret issue for the souldiers to passe out of a wall, bulwarke, or fort.

2. A going forth, setting out, excursion, expedition (of one or more persons).

1657 HOWELL *Londinop.* 49 We will now make a salley out of Algate. **1697** DRYDEN *Virg.* Ded., A Lark, melodious in her mounting, and continuing her Song till she alights: Still preparing for a higher flight at her next sally. **1743** FIELDING *Wedding-day* II. iv, Doth this early sally of yours proceed from having been in bed early..? **1851** CARLYLE *Sterling* II. iv, Here..is notice of his return from the first of these sallies into England.

b. *transf.* and *fig.*

1650 EARL MONM. tr. *Senault's Man bec. Guilty* 50 She [the soul] makes out salleys which cause men to believe that though she be fastened to the body, yet she is not a Prisoner. **1722** DE FOE *Moll Flanders* (1840) 208, I made my second sally into the world. **1753** JOHNSON *Adventurer* 107 ⁋3 At our first sally into the intellectual world, we all march together. **1836** EMERSON *Nature, Prospects* Wks. (Bohn) II. 172 Is not prayer also a study of truth—a sally of the soul into the unfound infinite? **1849** W. IRVING *Goldsmith* iii. 49 [He] made his second sally forth into the world. **1855** TENNYSON *Brook* 24, I make a sudden sally.

3. A sudden start into activity.

1605 DANIEL *Philotas* v. *Chorus*, How well were we within the narrow bounds Of..Macedon, Before our kings inlardgd them with our wounds And made these sallies of ambition. **1665** GLANVILL *Def. Van. Dogm.* To T. Albinus, For what ever heat attends the first sallies of young Inventions, Time..cools these delights. **1703** COLLIER *Dissuas. fr. Playhouse* 15 [They would] make us believe the Storm was nothing but an Eruption of Epicurus's Atoms, a Spring-Tide of Matter and Motion, and a blind Salley of Chance. **1737** WHISTON *Josephus, Hist. Jew. War* I. Pref. §7 What places the Jews assaulted..in the first sallies of the war. **1807** WORDSW. *Ode on Intimat. Immort.* 89 Behold the Child..See, where 'mid work of his own hand he lies, Fretted by sallies of his mother's kisses. **1860** EMERSON *Cond. Life, Wealth* Wks. (Bohn) II. 358 Nature goes by rule, not by sallies and saltations.

4. A breaking forth from restraint; an outburst or transport (*of* passion, delight, or other emotion); a flash (*of* wit); a flight (*of* fancy).

16.. STILLINGFL. (J.), These passages were intended for sallies of wit; but whence comes all this rage of wit? **1710** STEELE *Tatler* No. 172 ⁋4 She is apt to fall into little Sallies of Passion. **1727** SWIFT & POPE *Misc.* I. Pref. 10 We have written some Things which we may wish never to have thought on. Some Sallies of Levity ought to be imputed to Youth. **1752** HUME *Ess. & Treat.* (1777) II. 225 It is difficult to abstain from some sally of panegyric. **1775** T. SHERIDAN *Art Reading* 292 When she [fancy]..acknowledges no superior, her vigorous and wild sallies..are..vain and fruitless. **1794** MRS. PIOZZI *Synon.* II. 10 That sudden burst of confident self-sufficiency, by the vigorous sailly of which virtue herself may be sometimes confounded. **1838** THIRLWALL *Greece* xi. II. 40 Sufficient guards against the sallies of democratical extravagance. **1838** PRESCOTT *Ferd. & Is.* II. xviii. III. 313 He was..sometimes hurried..into a sally of passion. **1841–4** EMERSON *Ess.*, *Friendship* Wks. (Bohn) I. 87 It [friendship] keeps company with the sallies of wit and the trances of religion. **1875** MANNING *Mission Holy Ghost* viii. 216 Sudden sallies and impetuosities of temper.

†b. Outlet, 'vent'. *Obs. rare.*

1799 C. WINTER in Jay *Mem.* (1843) 19 While Mr. Whitefield was giving full sally to his soul, and..inviting sinners to the Saviour.

5. A sudden departure from the bounds of custom, prudence, or propriety; an audacious or adventurous proceeding, an escapade. Now *rare*.

a **1639** WOTTON *Parallel Essex & Buckhm.* (1641) 3 At his returne all was cleere, and this excursion was esteemed but a Sally of youth. *a* **1715** BURNET *Own Time* I. viii. (1897) I. 386, I made at this time a sally that may be mentioned, since it had some relation to public affairs. **1723** WATERLAND *Wks.* (1823) III. 261 It might be on account of some of these uncautious sallies of Origen, that he was forced to purge himself to Pope Fabian:..after which..he..kept closer to the language of the Church. **1768** TUCKER *Lt. Nat.* I. II. xxi. 56 We find people very brisk and active in seasons of joy, breaking out continually into wanton and extravagant sallies. **1871** MERIVALE *Rom. Emp.* V. xliii. 219 But the sally [ed. 1 1856 V. 110 *reads* enterprise] of an obscure slave was far less formidable than the intrigues of illustrious nobles.

6. A sprightly or audacious utterance or literary composition; now usually, a brilliant remark, a witticism.

1756–82 J. WARTON *Ess. Pope* (ed. 4) II. viii. 34 We must not try the charming sallies of Ariosto by the rigid rules of Aristotle. **1779–81** JOHNSON *L.P.*, *Shenstone* Wks. IV. 219 His poems consist of elegies, odes and ballads, humorous sallies and moral pieces. **1790** BURKE *Fr. Rev.* 98 After this sally of the preacher of the Old Jewry, which..agrees perfectly with the spirit and letter of the rapture of 1648. **1791** BOSWELL *Johnson* an. 1765, Voltaire, in revenge, made an attack upon Johnson, in one of his numerous literary sallies. **1879** G. MEREDITH *Egoist* xiii, The sprightly sallies of the two won attention like a fencing match.

II. 7. A leaping movement. *Obs.* exc. *Naut.* (see quot. 1867) and *dial.*

1589 PUTTENHAM *Eng. Poesie* II. x. (Arb.) 98 As the Dorien because his falls, sallyes, and compasse be diuers from those of the Phrigien. **1718** STEELE *Fish-pool* 178 On every sally of the boat, the water in the Well must shift its place. **1867** SMYTH *Sailor's Word-bk.*, *Sally*,..a sudden heave or set. **1887** DONALDSON *Jamieson's Dict.* Suppl. 210 *Sally*,..a rush or dash; a swing from side to side, rocking; a continuous rising and falling,..the swinging or bounding motion of a ship at sea.

III. 8. a. *Arch.* A deviation from the alinement of a surface; a projection, prominence. b. *Carpentry* (see quot. 1842).

1665–6 *Phil. Trans.* I. 73 This Authour did first conceive, that they were not shadows but some Sallies or Prominencies in that Belt. 1739 LABELYE *Short Acc. Piers Westm. Bridge* 69 The Sally, or Projection of a.. Cornish. 1757 ROBERTSON in *Phil. Trans.* L. 292 Add to this the sally of the head, the weight of the forecastle [etc.]. 1842 GWILT *Archit.* Gloss., *Sally*, a projecture. The end of a piece of timber cut with an interior angle formed by two planes across the fibres. 1879 *Cassell's Techn. Educ.* I. 396 The 'sally', or point given to the end of each part to resist lateral pressure. 1887 DONALDSON *Jamieson's Dict.* Suppl. 208 *Saillie, Sailye, Sally*, a projection; outjutting; applied to a room, gallery, or other building projecting beyond the face of a house or wall.

sally ('sælɪ), *sb.*² *Bell-ringing.* Also 9 **sallie.** [Perh. an application of SALLY *sb.*¹ 7.]

1. The first movement of a bell when 'set' for ringing; a 'handstroke', as distinguished from the reverse movement of 'backstroke'; also, the position of a bell when it is rung up to a 'set' position. ? Now *local.*

1668 F. STEDMAN *Tintinnalogia* (1671) 54 Whole-pulls, is to Ring two Rounds in one change.. so that every time you pull down the bells at Sally, you make a new change. *Ibid.* 134 But sometimes the fault of the stroke [*i.e.* when longer on one side than the other] is in the Sally. 1677 —— *Campanologia* 26 The falling of the bells from a Sett-pull must gradually be done, by checking them only at Sally, until the low compass renders the Sally useless. 1688 R. HOLME *Armoury* III. 462/2 The several wayes of Ringing Bells. 1. Is the Under Salley, that is when the Bells are raised but Frame high, so as the Clapper strikes on both sides of the Bell. 2. Is the Hand Salley, when they are rung almost up, and one hand is put to the Rope to raise it. 1702 J. D. & C. M. *Campanalogia Impr.* 11 The first Step.. is to learn perfectly to set a Bell,.. and to have it so much at his Command, as that he may be able to cut it down, either at hand (being the Sally) or back Stroke. *Ibid.* 13 He must likewise be careful, when they lie under Sally, (for so 'tis term'd) to keep his Bell at so constant a Pull, as not to pull harder one time than another. 1872 ELLACOMBE *Ch. Bells Devon* 13 *note*, The half-wheel action is distinguished by the name of the dead-rope pull, there being no sally. *Ibid.*, *Bells of Ch.* x. 551 It was at this time that the bells were altered from the dead-rope pull to the sally. 1897 F. T. JANE *Lordship* vi. 66 The tuftin being worn, she hurt a man's hands a good deal on the sally, and had mainly to be rung on the back-stroke.

2. The woolly 'grip' for the hands near the lower end of a bell-rope, composed of tufts of wool woven into the rope.

1809 T. BATCHELOR *Anal. Eng. Lang.* 142 *Sally*, the serving, or pluffy part of a bell rope. 1869 TROYTE *Change Ringing* i. 2 The 'hand stroke' blow will be the one on which he pulls the 'sallie', or tuffing on the rope. 1871 T. HARDY *Desperate Remedies* Epil., Bright red 'sallies' of woollen texture.. glowed on the ropes.

3. *Comb.*: **sally beam** (see quot. 1872); **sally hole**, a hole through which the bell-rope passes; **sally-pin, -pulley, -wheel** (see quots.).

1872 *N. & Q.* 4th Ser. IX. 186/2 The *sally-beam is a beam.. through which the bell-rope is passed to steady it. 1901 H. E. BULWER *Gloss. Techn. Terms Bells* 5 *Sally-beams*, light wooden cross beams.. with guide pieces attached through which the bell-ropes pass. 1851 C. ROGERS ['Tom Treddlehoyle'] *Bairnsla Foak's Ann.* (E.D.D.), He wor drawn up bit bell an knocked his head again t' *sally-hoil. 1879 TROYTE in Grove *Dict. Mus.* I. 219/2 When the rope has been pulled enough to bring the fillet or '*sallie-pin' down to the nearest point to the ground pulley that it can reach. 1901 H. E. BULWER *Gloss. Techn. Terms Bells* 4 *Sally-pin*, a reel inserted between the 'shrouds' over the rope to assist the purchase of the latter, when the 'fillet-hole' is placed near the top of the 'wheel'. *Ibid.*, *Pulley*, a sheave of hard wood on the lower part of the frame which guides the rope to the wheel. In some localities it is called.. '*sally-pulley',.. '*sally-wheel'.

†**Sally** ('sælɪ), *sb.*³ *Obs.* Corruption of SAL ENIXUM. Also **Sally Nixon.**

1879 G. LUNGE *Sulphuric Acid* II. ii. 19 Sulphate known as 'nitre-cake', 'salonix' (= sal enixum), or 'sally'. 1882 W. CROOKES *Dyeing & Tissue-Printing* 81 The crystallized sulphate of soda, known.. in many dye-houses as Sally Nixon.

sally ('sælɪ), *sb.*⁴ *Austral.* Also **sallee.** [Variant of SALLOW *sb.*] One of several eucalypts or acacias that resemble willows in habit or appearance; (see quot. 1965).

1884 A. NILSON *Timber Trees New South Wales* 22 *A*[*cacia*] *falcata.*—Hickory; Sally;.. Willow. 1889 J. H. MAIDEN *Useful Native Plants Austral.* 149 *Acacia falcata*, .. 'Hickory'. 'Lignum-Vitae'. 'Sally'. *Ibid.* 250 *Eucalyptus stellulata*,.. 'Sally' or 'Black Gum'. *Ibid.* 335 *Acacia falcata*. .. Called variously 'Hickory',.. and 'Sally' or 'Sallee'. 1932 R. H. ANDERSON *Trees New South Wales* 58 Snow Gum or White Sally. *Ibid.*, Black Sally.. Also known as Sally or Muzzlewood. 1941 BAKER *Dict. Austral. Slang.* 62 Sally: an acacia. 1949 J. WRIGHT *Woman to Man* 17 In the olive darkness of the sally-trees Silently moved the air. 1957 *Forest Trees Austral.* (Austral. Forestry & Timber Bureau) 96/2 Swamp gum or broad leaved sally.. occurs in cold and damp situations. *Ibid.* 144/1 White sallee is usually only 30–60 feet in height. 1965 *Austral. Encycl.* VII. 539/2 Sallee, or sally, a corruption of the English 'sallow' which is applicable to certain willow species.. and commonly used for Australian eucalypts and wattles that are supposed to resemble them in habit or foliage. Black sallee and white sallee are the names standardized in the timber trade for the cold-loving *Eucalyptus stellulata* and *E. pauciflora* respectively. *Acacia floribunda* and *A. prominens* are among the eastern wattles which have been called sally.

Sally ('sælɪ), *sb.*⁵ *colloq.* [Alteration of SALVATION (ARMY).] 1. a. The Salvation Army. Also with *the*, and *attrib.*

1915 *N.Y. World Mag.* 9 May 14/3 *Sally*, nickname for Salvation Army. 1931 'D. STIFF' *Milk & Honey Route* v. 52 The Salvation Army, more intimately known in Hobohemia as 'The Sally'. 1977 *Gay News* 7–20 Apr. 7/3 (*heading*) Sally soldier... A Salvation Army social worker who indecently assaulted young boys was sent to jail for three years at the Old Bailey recently.

b. A member of the Salvation Army; usu. *pl.*, the Salvation Army.

1936 I. L. IDRIESS *Cattle King* xx. 189 The surest place to find Sid Kidman, when in town on a Saturday night, was among the crowd around the 'Sallies'. 1942 BERREY & VAN DEN BARK *Amer. Thes. Slang* §327/4 *Sally*, a Salvation Army girl. 1957 D. NILAND *Call me when Cross turns Over* ii. 31 The woman that runs it, she used to be some sort of a high-up with the Sallies down in Sydney. 1966 A. LA BERN *Goodbye Piccadilly* iv. 43 The constable recommended the Salvation Army hostel... Why not? Better men than Dick Blamey have slept with the 'Sallies'. 1977 C. MCCULLOUGH *Thorn Birds* iii. 65 It's a hotel for the workingman run by the Sallies.

2. A Salvation Army hostel.

1931 'D. STIFF' *Milk & Honey Route* 213 *Sallies*, Salvation Army hotels and industrial workshops. 1966 *New Statesman* 1 Apr. 479/2 Julie Felix sang against the Salvation Army—and we were.. miles away from the sad Sally where the meth-drinkers are deloused. 1977 *Church Times* 18 Nov. 9/1 He knew that the only other places to find a bed—the 'Sally', the Cyrenian shelter, even the fairly distant 'Spike'—would not have him that night.

3. *Comb.*, as **Sally Ann(e)** [with colloq. alteration of *Army*], the Salvation Army; a Salvation Army hostel; **Sally Army**, the Salvation Army.

1927 *Amer. Speech* II. 387/1 *Sally Ann* is the sobriquet for Salvation Army. 1961 W. A. HAGELUND *Flying Chase Flag* iii. 48 Now you go see the Major at the Johnson Street Sally Anne about some meal tickets and beds. 1976 *New Society* 5 Aug. 290/3 The Salvation Army?.. You'd never get me sleeping there... Everyone knows you pick all sorts of things up from the Sally Ann. 1961 E. WILLIAMS *George* xxiii. 386 Your dear Brother Tom has celebrated his thirteenth birthday with buying a uniform for the Sally Army. *Ibid.* xxvi. 441 Tom sat uneasily polishing his Sally-Army trumpet. 1978 *Guardian* 9 Aug. 7/5 At Christmas, the Sally Army gave her a slap-up lunch.

†'**sally**, *v.*¹ *Obs. rare.* Forms: 5 salyyn, 6 saly, 7 **sally.** [irreg. ad. F. *saillir*: see SAIL *v.*³]

1. *intr.* To leap, bound, dance.

c 1440 *Promp. Parv.* 441/1 Salyyn, *salio* (P. *salto*). 1543 BECON *Invect. agst. Swearing* 54 Herode also made a promyse to the doughter of Herodias, whan she daunced & salyed so plesantly before hym.

2. *trans.* Of a horse: To leap (a mare).

a 1693 *Urquhart's Rabelais* III. xxxvi. 300 They use to ring Mares.., to keep them from being sallied by Stoned Horses.

Hence †'**sallying** *vbl. sb.*, dancing.

c 1440 *Promp. Parv.* 441/1 Salyynge, *saltacio.*

sally ('sælɪ), *v.*² Forms: 6 salee, salie, saly, 7– **sally**, 9 **saully.** [f. SALLY *sb.*¹, which first appears at the same time. The sense of the vb. may have been influenced by association with its ulterior source, F. *saillir*: see SAIL *v.*³]

1. *intr.* Of a warlike force: To issue suddenly from a place of defence or retreat in order to make an attack; *spec.* of a besieged force, to make a sortie. Also *to sally out.*

1560 DAUS tr. *Sleidane's Comm.* 430 Duke Henry.. hauinge lost.. many of his men what tyme the Marques saleed out, and fought. 1590 SIR R. WILLIAMS *Brief Disc. War* 51 Hauing an easie entrie into the ditch, the defendants dare not sally. *Ibid.* 52 Alledging.. that the defendants may the better saly out. 1615 CHAPMAN *Odyss.* XXIV. 375 And now, all girt in armes; the Ports, set wide, They sallied forth. 1617 MORYSON *Itin.* II. 200 The happy repulse of the Spaniards sallying upon our Cannon. 1769 ROBERTSON *Chas. V*, IV. Wks. 1813 V. 367 Leyva, with his garrison, sallied out and attacked the rear of the French. 1777 W. HEATH in Sparks *Corr. Amer. Rev.* (1853) I. 338 The enemy had sallied, early one morning, and surprised one of our out-guards. 1865 LIVINGSTONE *Zambesi* xix. 382 A nest of lake pirates who sallied out by night to kill and plunder. 1881 JOWETT *Thucyd.* I. 172 The Mitylenaeans with their whole force sallied out against the Athenian camp.

fig. 1651 N. BACON *Disc. Govt. Eng.* II. xxvi. (1739) 114 Like a good Soldier, whilst his strength is full, he sallies upon the people's liberties.

2. Of a person or party of persons: To set out boldly, to go forth (from a place of abode); to set out on a journey or expedition. Const. *forth, off, out.*

1590 SPENSER *F.Q.* II. vi. 38 Where gladsome Guyon salied forth to land. 1662 EVELYN *Chalcogr.* 41 To return now into Italy from whence we first sallied. 1710–11 SWIFT *Jrnl. to Stella* 19 Feb., Where Sir Andrew Fountain dined too, who has just began to sally out, and has shipt.. his nurses back to the country. 1762 FOOTE *Lyar* I. Wks. 1799 I. 282 But let us sally. 1766 COWPER *Let.* 20 Oct., Wks. (1876) 23 After tea we sally forth to walk in good earnest. 1786 JEFFERSON *Writ.* (1859) II. 9 Vessels may enter and sally with every wind. 1837 W. IRVING *Capt. Bonneville* I. 52 These frontier settlers form parties.. and prepare for a bee hunt. Having provided themselves with a waggon.. they sally off, armed with their rifles. 1840 DICKENS *Barn. Rudge* i, [He] had risen and was adjusting his riding-cloak preparatory to sallying abroad. 1845 DARWIN *Voy. Nat.* vi. (1879) 112 In the morning we all sallied forth to hunt. 1888 W. S. CAINE *Round the World* i. 2 We settled down in our comfortable cabins.. and then sallied forth for a tour of inspection round the ship.

transf. and *fig.* 1820 W. IRVING *Sketch Bk.* I. 178 He.. takes pen in hand.. and sallies forth into the fairy land of poetry. 1871 PALGRAVE *Lyr. Poems* 87 Where the tall trees crowd round and sally Down the slope sides.

†b. *to sally out*: to make a digression in speech. *Obs.*

1660 *Trial Regic.* 51 And we have, with a great deal of Patience, suffered you to sally out. *Ibid.* 55 My Lords, this ought not to come from the Bar to the Bench; if you sally out thus about your Conscience. 1661 BOYLE *Style of Script.* (1675) 58 Sometimes the Prophets, in the midst of the Mention of particular Mercies,.. Sally out into Pathetical Excursions relating to the Messias.

3. Of things: To issue forth; *esp.* to issue suddenly, break out, burst or leap forth.

1660 F. BROOKE tr. *Le Blanc's Trav.* 237 A little Mountain, whence there sallies a stream of water that turns three Mills. 1670 COTTON *Espernon* Ded., It may very well .. pass amongst good natur'd men, with other things, that every day sally from the Press. 1725 POPE *Odyss.* XI. 646 Fierce in his look his ardent valour glow'd, Flush'd in his cheek, or sally'd in his blood. 1785 REID *Intell. Powers* II. vii. 265 It is not at all likely that the soul sallies out of the body. 1791 COWPER *Iliad* XI. 326 While yet his warm blood sallied from the wound. 1847 EMERSON *Poems, Merlin* i, When the God's will sallies free.

4. a. To move, sway, or run from side to side (see quot. 1887 and cf. SALLY *sb.*¹ 7); to progress by making a rocking movement from side to side. *dial.* and *Naut.*

1825 J. T. BROCKETT *Gloss. North Country Words* 181 *Sally*, to move or run from side to side; as is customary with the persons on board of a ship after she is launched. 1887 D. DONALDSON Jamieson, Suppl. 210 To *Sally, Saully*,.. to move or run from side to side, as children do in certain games, and as workmen do on board a ship after it is launched; to rock or swing from side to side, like a small boat at anchor; also, to rise and fall, like a ship on a rough sea. 1972 *Daily Tel.* 15 July 3/8 He told the court that he was 'sallying' down Lowther Street when a policeman stopped him. Asked by the Judge what 'sallying' meant, he said: 'I was just sitting on the saddle pushing the bike along with my foot on the kerb.'

b. *trans.* To rock (a stationary or slow-moving ship) by running from side to side in order to assist its progress. *Naut.*

1919 E. SHACKLETON *South* i. 33 The engines running full speed astern produced no effect until all hands joined in 'sallying' ship.

Hence '**sallying** *vbl. sb.* (also attrib.) and *ppl. a.*

1560 DAUS tr. *Sleidane's Comm.* 401 b, To leave behynde my backe no fortified place, out of the whiche any force or saleinge out is to be feared. 1590 SIR R. WILLIAMS *Brief Disc. War* 53 The salying of the asseged. 1727–46 THOMSON *Summer* 473 Delicious.. As to the hunted hart the sallying spring. 1838 THIRLWALL *Greece* xxvi. III. 424 A sallying place for marauding inroads. 1839 THACKERAY *Major Gahagan* iii, I found our sallying party.

sally ('sælɪ), *v.*³ [f. SALLY *sb.*²] *trans.* To bring (a bell) to the position of 'sally'.

1735 SOMERVILLE *Chase* II. 250 Hark! now again the Chorus fills. As Bells Sally'd awhile at once their Peal renew.

sallyer, variant of SALER *Obs.*

Sally Lunn ('sælɪ 'lʌn). [See quot. 1827.]

1. a. A kind of tea-cake (see quot. 1892).

1780 P. THICKNESSE *Valetudinarian's Bath Guide* (ed. 2) iii. 12, I had the misfortune to lose a beloved brother in the prime of life, who dropt down dead as he was playing on the fiddle at Sir Robert Throgmorton's, after drinking a large quantity of Bath Waters, and eating a hearty breakfast of spungy hot rolls, or *Sally Luns.* 1798 *Gentl. Mag.* LXVIII. II. 931/2 A certain sort of hot rolls, now, or not long ago, in vogue at Bath, were gratefully and emphatically styled 'Sally Lunns'. 1824 CARLYLE *Early Lett.* (1886) II. 289 Robinson gives me coffee and Sally Lunns. 1827 HONE *Every-day Bk.* II. 1561 The bun.. called the Sally Lunn, originated with a young woman of that name in Bath, about thirty years ago. She first cried them... Dalmer, a respectable baker and musician, noticed her, bought her business, and made a song .. in behalf of Sally Lunn. 1845 DICKENS *Chimes* iv, It's a sort of night that's meant for muffins. Likewise crumpets. Also Sally Lunns. 1849 THACKERAY *Pendennis* xxiii, A meal of green tea, scandal, hot Sally-Lunn Cakes, and a little novel-reading. 1892 *Encycl. Cookery* (ed. Garrett) II. 361/1 *Sally Lunns.*—These are sweet light teacakes... Sally Lunns should be cut open, well buttered, and served very hot.

b. *Sally Lunn pudding*, a kind of pudding made with a Sally Lunn cake.

1892 *Encycl. Cookery* (ed. Garrett) 361/2.

2. Applied loosely to several varieties of yeast and soda bread, esp. in the southern United States. Also *attrib.*

1901 *Picayune's Creole Cook Bk.* (ed. 2) 407/2 Sally Lunn is nothing more than the old breakfast dish known to the Creoles for generations as 'Pain à la Vieille Tante Zoë'. 1933 F. M. FARMER *Boston Cooking-School Cook Bk.* (rev. ed.) 53 Sally Lunn Tea Cakes... Make like Raised muffins. 1976 M. G. EBERHART *Family Fortune* vii. 70 Alice was tucking food away.. Alice asked for more Sally Lunn.

Sally-man, Sally rover: see SALLEE-MAN.

Sally Nixon: see SALLY *sb.*³

'**sallyport.** [f. SALLY *sb.*¹ + PORT *sb.*³]

1. *Fortif.* An opening in a fortified place for the passage of troops when making a sally; sometimes used for 'postern'. Also *transf.* and *fig.*

1649 G. DANIEL *Trinarch., Hen. IV* cccxii, Soe lyes the Worme, safe in her treeble hedge And eats the Purple

Garden, ere wee find Her Sally-Ports. **1651** CLEVELAND *Poems* 3 My slippery soul had quit the fort, But that she stopt the Salley-port. **1688** J. S. *Fortification* 69 Little Ports are made in the middle of the Courtains .. called Sally-Ports. **1694** CONGREVE *Double-Dealer* IV. v, Were you provided for an Escape? Hold, Madam, you have no more holes to your Burrough, I'll stand between you and this Sally-Port. **1704** *Lond. Gaz* No. 4008/2 The rest made their Escape out of a Sally-Port. **1802** C. JAMES *Milit. Dict.*, *Sally-ports*, or postern-gates .. are those underground passages, which lead from the inner to the outward works. **1819** SCOTT *Ivanhoe* xxx, In the outwork was a sallyport corresponding to the postern of the castle. **1859** F. A. GRIFFITHS *Artil. Man.* (1862) 261 The Sallyports are openings cut in the glacis... They are used in making sallies from the covered way.
attrib. **1799** WELLINGTON in Gurw. *Desp.* (1837) I. 36 Tippoo Sultaun's body was discovered in the sallyport gateway.

2. (See quot. 1867.)

1753 CHAMBERS *Cycl. Supp.*, *Sally-port*, in a fire ship, is a great opening in her side .. for the men to escape by, when they have .. fired their train. **1769** FALCONER *Dict. Marine* (1780) s.v. *Fire-ship*. **1867** SMYTH *Sailor's Word-bk.*, *Sally-port*, .. a large port on each quarter of a fire-ship, out of which the officers and crew make their escape into the boats. .. Also, the entering port of a three-decker.

3. A landing-place at Portsmouth set apart for the use of men-of-war's boats (Adm. Smyth).

1814 JANE AUSTEN *Mansf. Park* III. vii. 161 The three boys .. determined to see their brother .. to the salley-port. **1833** MARRYAT *P. Simple* iv, The porter wheeled my chest down to the Sally Port. **1836** —— *Midsh. Easy* xi, After which hour the sally-port is only opened by special permission.

salm, obs. form of PSALM.

salmagundi (ˌsælmə'gʌndɪ). Forms: 7–8 salmagondi, 8 salamongundy, (sallad-magundy, Solomon Gundy, salmi-, salmogundy, salmagunda), 8–9 salmagundy, 7– salmagundi. [a. F. *salmigondis* (in the 16th c. *salmiguondin*, *salmingondin*), of obscure origin.]

1. *Cookery*. A dish composed of chopped meat, anchovies, eggs, onions with oil and condiments.

1674 BLOUNT *Glossogr.* (ed. 4), *Salmagundi* (Ital.), a dish of meat made of cold Turky and other ingredients. **1709** W. KING *Cookery* ix, Delighting in hodge-podge, gallimaufries, forced meats, jussels, and salmagundies. **1710** P. LAMB *Royal Cookery* 118 To make Sallad-Magundy. **1751** SMOLLETT *Per. Pic.* I. xxxviii. 287 A barrel of excellent herrings for salmagundy, which he knew to be his favourite dish. **1764** ELIZ. MOXON *Eng. Housew.* (ed. 9) 103 To make Solomon Gundy to eat in Lent. **1892** *Encycl. Pract. Cookery* (ed. Garrett), *Salmagundi*.
attrib. **1892** *Encycl. Pract. Cookery* (ed. Garrett), *Salmagundi Salad*.

2. *transf.* and *fig.*

1761 T. TWINING in *Recreat. & Stud.* (1882) 18 After all this salmagondis of quotation, can you bear another slice of Aristotle? **1764** FOOTE *Patron* II. Wks. 1799 I. 340 By your account, I must be an absolute olio, a perfect salamongundy of charms. **1777** COLMAN *Prose on Sev. Occas.* (1787) III. 218 Unbuttoned cits .. Throw down fish, flesh, fowl, pastry, custard, jelly, And make a Salmagundy of their belly. **1781** H. WALPOLE *Let. to C'tess Ossory* 2 Jan., A salmagundi of black and blue, and red and purple, and white. **1797** MRS. M. ROBINSON *Walsingham* III. 316 His mind was a sort of salmagundi. **1833** *Westm. Rev.* Jan. 34 A kind of Salmagundi of law, literature, joke, and blunder. **1887** SAINTSBURY *Hist. Elizab. Lit.* (1894) 274 *The Devil's Law Case* .. despite fine passages, [is] a mere 'salmagundi'. **1894** *Sat. Rev.* 26 May 539/1 The House of Commons .. was chiefly busy with the Estimates, on which the usual Salmagundi of subjects was served up.

Salmanazar (sælmə'neɪzə(r)). Also **Salmanasar**. [ad. *Salmanasar*, the form in the Vulgate of the name of *Shalmaneser*, King of Assyria (II Kings xvii, xviii).] A large size of wine-bottle. Cf. BALTHAZAR, JEROBOAM, REHOBOAM 2.

1935 A. L. SIMON *Dict. Wine* 225 *Salmanazar*, the fancy name given to a fancy bottle large enough to hold a dozen reputed quarts, or 9·60 litres, equal to 338·025 fluid ounces. **1959** *Gloss. Terms Packaging* (B.S.I.) 28 *Salmanazar*, a wine bottle—capacity 12 reputed quarts. **1962** [see BALTHAZAR]. **1978** *Daily Tel.* 13 June 16/2 Edward Heath is to be given a salmanazar of champagne... A salmanazar contains the equivalent of 14 ordinary bottles.

salme, -ede, obs. forms of PSALM, PSALMODY.

salmi ('sælmɪ). Also 8 **salmy**. [a. F. *salmi*, according to Hatz.-Darm. shortened from *salmigondis*: see SALMAGUNDI. Cf., however, SALOMENE.] 'A ragoût of partly roasted game, stewed with sauce, wine, bread, and condiments' (Garrett's *Encycl. Cookery* 1892).

1759 W. VERRAL *Cookery* 132 (Stanf.) Salmis des becasses. Salmy of woodcocks. **1823** MOORE *Fables* 7 Truffles, salmis, toasted cheese. **1824** BYRON *Juan* XV. lxxi, The salmi, the consommé, the purée. **1847** DISRAELI *Tancred* II. xv, Tancred was going to give them a fish dinner .. cutlets of salmon, salmis of carp. **1887** L. OLIPHANT *Episodes* (1888) 150 Salmi of wild duck [India].
attrib. **1892** *Encycl. Cookery* (ed. Garrett) s.v. *Sauces*, Salmi Sauce.

salmiac ('sælmɪæk). *Min.* Also 8 **sælmiak**. [a. G. *salmiak*, contraction of L. *sal ammoniacum*.] Native sal-ammoniac.

1799 W. TOOKE *View Russian Emp.* I. 198 Large lumps of sulphur and salmiak. **1888** *Encycl. Brit.* XVI. 384, art. *Mineralogy*, Salmiac... A sublimate on active volcanoes.

salmine ('sælmiːn). *Biochem.* Also -in (-ɪn). [ad. G. *salmin* (A. Kossel 1896, in *Zeitschr. f. physiol. Chem.* XXII. 180), f. L. *salm-o* salmon: see -INE[5].] A protein, one of the protamines, isolated from the sperm of the salmon and related species.

1896 *Jrnl. Chem. Soc.* LXX. I. 582 The sulphate [of the protamine] from salmon sperm has the formula $C_{16}H_{31}N_9O_3, H_2SO_4$. That from sturgeon sperm has rather different solubilities in sodium chloride solutions, and the names *salmine* and *sturine* are suggested by [*sic*] the two protamines. **1949** *Proc. Soc. Exper. Biol. & Med.* LXX. 494/1 Salmin, an acid hydrolysis, was shown to yield arginine, proline, serine, valine, alanine, and isoleucine. **1963** F. HAUROWITZ *Chem. & Function of Proteins* (ed. 2) ii. 18 Heterogeneities have also been discovered .. in the protamines clupein and salmine of fish sperm.

salmody, obs. form of PSALMODY.

salmon ('sæmən), *sb.*[1] and *a.* Forms: 4–5 samoun, -own(e, (5 samoon, samwn, sawmon, sawmun), 4–6 samon, 7 sammon, 8 *Sc.* sawmont, 9 *Sc.* saumon; 4 salmoun, 4–7 *Sc.* salmond(e, 5 salmone, (6 saulmon, salmont, 7 sallmon), 4– salmon. [a. AF. *samoun*, *saumoun*, *salmun* (OF. and mod.F. *saumon*):—L. *salmōn-em*, *salmo* (Pliny); the spelling with *l* is from the Latin form.

Cf. Pr. *salmo*, Sp. *salmon*, Pg. *salmão*, It. *salmone*, *sermone*. The Latin word is prob. a derivative of the root of *salire* to leap.]

A. *sb.* **1. a.** A large fish belonging to the genus *Salmo*, family *Salmonidæ*, esp. *Salmo salar*, comprising the largest fish of this family, which when mature are characterized by having red flesh, and a silvery skin marked with large black and red spots; highly prized as an article of food.

In mod. use the collective sing. takes the place of the pl.; *salmons* being used only in scientific language to denote different species, or, *rarely*, individual specimens.

13.. *K. Alis.* 5446 (Laud MS.) And of perches, & of salmouns, Token & eten grete foysouns. **13..** *Coer de L.* 3515 Fysch, flesch, salmoun, and cungyr. **1375** BARBOUR *Bruce* II. 576 He wrocht Gynnys, to tak geddis & salmonys. **1387** TREVISA *Higden* (Rolls) I. 407 They eteþ hote samoun alway. *Ibid.* II. 13 Þere is grete plente of small fische, of samon, and of elys. *a* **1400** in *Eng. Gilds* (1870) 354 Eueryche cart comynge in-to towne wiþ samown. **1426** LYDG. *De Guil. Pilgr.* 15365 Swettere than samoun. *c* **1460** J. RUSSELL *Bk. Nurture* 823 Sewes on fishe dayes .. The baly of þe fresche samon. **1515** *Test. Ebor.* (Surtees) V. 67 Of my ferme of my fyshynges in Yarom I give her ij salmons yerely. **1596** DALRYMPLE tr. *Leslie's Hist. Scot.* I. (S.T.S.) 100 Thay saw the Scottis eit rawe Salmonte, new drawen out of the flude. **1604** SHAKS. *Oth.* II. i. 156 She that in wisedome neuer was so fraile, To change the Cods-head for the Salmons taile. **1655** WALTON *Angler* I. vii. (1661) 134 The Salmon is accounted the King of fresh-water-Fish. **1787** BURNS *Tam Samson's Elegy* vi, Now safe the stately Sawmont sail. **1819** SCOTT *Let. to Dk. Buccleuch* 15 Apr. in *Lockhart*, Where I lie, as my old grieve Tom Purdie said last night, .. 'like a haulded saumon'. **1837** DICKENS *Pickw.* viii, 'It wasn't the wine,' murmured Mr. Snodgrass, in a broken voice. 'It was the salmon'. **1859** DARWIN *Orig. Spec.* iv. (1873) 69 Male salmons have been observed fighting all day long. **1882** DAY *Brit. Fishes* I. Introd. 71 The so-termed land-locked salmon .. might prove invaluable to upper riparian proprietors. *Ibid.* II. 87 The 'blue poll' and 'blue cock' of the Fowey in Cornwall, .. are sold in Billingsgate as 'Cornish salmon'. **1886** *Encycl. Brit.* XXI. 222/1 In North America there occurs one Salmonoid .. viz., *Salmo salar*, var. *sebago*, L... This form is called variously the Landlocked Salmon or the Schoodic Salmon. *Ibid.* 225/1 A salmon newly arrived in fresh water from the sea is called a clean salmon, on account of its bright, well-fed appearance.

b. Applied to fishes belonging to other genera of the same family; esp., a fish of any of the species of the genus *Oncorhynchus*, called the ***Pacific salmon***.

1884 GOODE, etc. *Nat. Hist. Aquatic Anim.* 468 According to the latest system .. the first [group] for which the name *Salmo* is retained includes the Atlantic Salmon, and the black-spotted species of the west [etc.]... In this same group are included the Quinnat, or California Salmon, and its allies... These have been placed in the genus *Oncorhynchus*. **1888** —— *Amer. Fishes* 480 The Pacific Salmon... The English-speaking people call it [*Oncorhynchus gorbuscha*] generally the 'Hump-back Salmon', and often the 'Dog Salmon'... This is one of the smallest Salmons. *Ibid.* 482 The Blue-back is the most graceful of the Salmons. **1888** W. S. CAINE *Round the World* viii. 122 The Pacific salmon takes no bait or fly in fresh water, but may be taken readily in salt water.

c. Applied to fishes resembling a salmon, but not belonging to the *Salmonidæ*. (*a*) In U.S., the SQUETEAGUE; also the *pike-perch* (see PIKE *sb.*[4] 3). (*b*) In Australia and New Zealand, *Arripis salar*.

1798 D. COLLINS *Acc. N.S. Wales* I. 136 A fish, named by us, from its shape only, the salmon. **1880** GÜNTHER *Fishes* 393 *Arripis salar*, South Australia. Three species are known, from the coasts of Southern Australia and New Zealand. They are named by the colonists Salmon or Trout. **1884** *Century Mag.* Apr. 908/1 The pike-perch becomes a 'salmon' in the Susquehanna, Ohio, and Mississippi rivers. **1884** GOODE, etc. *Nat. Hist. Aquatic Anim.* 365 [The Spotted Squeteague] is usually known on the Southern coast as the 'Salmon' or 'Spotted Trout'.

†**d.** Phrase. ***to seek for a salmon's nest.*** (Cf. MARE'S NEST.) *Obs.*

1589 *Hay any Work* 30 Where hast ti bene, why man, cha bin a seeking for a Samons nest.

2. The name of a kind of potato with red 'flesh'.

1845 *Morn. Chron.* 22 Nov. 5/2 The salmons are considered a good potato for the chalky soil; they are what in some parts are called red kidneys. *Ibid.* 5/3 Salmon potatoes.

3. Short for *salmon colour* (see 4 c).

1873 [see PAPER *sb.* 8 b]. **1892** *Gard. Chron.* 27 Aug. 245/1 Hollyhocks, ranging in colour from pure white through yellows to salmons, pinks [etc.]. **1892** EMILY LAWLESS *Grania* I. 87 The horizon was tinged with faint salmon.

4. *attrib.* and *Comb.* **a.** simple attrib., as ***salmon boat***, ***farm***, ***fishery***, ***hatchery***, ***heck*** (HECK *sb.*[1] 2), ***hutch*** (HUTCH *sb.* 3 a), ***kettle*** (KETTLE 2 a), ***leister***, †***lumber-pie***, ***mousse***, ***paste*** (PASTE *sb.* 1 d), †***pie***, ***rawn*** (Sc.), ***river***, ***roe***, ***spear***, ***stream***; in names applied (chiefly locally) to a young salmon indicating the different stages of its growth, as ***salmon-fry***, ***mort*** (*sb.* [3]), ***peal*** (*sb.* [2]), ***pink***, ***smelt***, ***sprint***; in the names of appliances used in angling for salmon, as ***salmon bait***, ***fly***, ***gaff***, ***line***, ***reel***, ***rod***, ***tackle***, ***winch***. Also ***salmon-like*** adj.

1883 *Fisheries Exhib. Catal.* 51 *Salmon baits. **1894** *Rudder* Mar. 77 White Class—*Salmon boat, Canthelpit, Captain Jacobsen. **1905** J. LONDON *Tales of Fish Patrol* 23 The salmon boat got out its oars. **1868** PEARD *Water-farm.* i. 10 The .. construction of a *Salmon-farm. **1732** *Calendar State Papers: Colonial Ser.* (Publ. Rec. Office) (1939) XXXIX. 226 The *salmon fishery is still carried on in the several rivers and to advantage. **1762** *Ann. Reg.* II. 53/1 A gentleman who resides at Berwick, near the great salmon-fishery. **1888** W. S. CAINE *Round the World* viii. 121 A fresh development of the salmon fishery has sprung up. **1704–6** *Dict. Rust.* s.v. *Fishing-fly*, *Salmon Flies. **1856** 'STONEHENGE' *Man. Brit. Rural Sports* V. ii. 246/1 Salmon-flies are made on the same principle as the trout-flies. **1927** M. ASQUITH *Lay Sermons* v. 106 The Durham Ranger and Black Dog are salmon-flies. **1741** *Compl. Fam.-Piece* II. ii. 341 *Salmon-fry are taken with a fine Hair-line. [**1907** *Yesterday's Shopping* (1969) 669/3 Gaffs .. Salmon and Pike.] **1922** JOYCE *Ulysses* 558 Follow the footpeople with knotty sticks, *salmongaffs. **1886** *Encycl. Brit.* XXI. 224/2 *note*, The first important series of experiments .. was made at the *salmon-hatchery of Stormontfield. **1868** *Law Rep.* Q.B. Div. III. 289 In this side-stream .. the said *salmon-hutch or hutches are situated. **1773** J. S. *Ep. to R. Fergusson* 48 I'se tak ye up Tweed's bonny side .. And shaw you there the fisher's pride, A *sa'mon kettle. *a* **1625** JAS. I in Spottiswood *Hist. Ch. Scot.* (1677) VII. 529 [A longing he had to see the place of his breeding,] a *Salmon-like instinct [so he was pleased to call it]. **1850** 'EPHEMERA' *Bk. Salmon* 16 *Salmon-lines. **1834** *Salmon lister [see LEISTER]. **1881** J. GRANT *Cameronians* I. iv. 52 In the hall hung .. salmon-listers, whips [etc.]. **1665** R. MAY *Accomplisht Cook* (ed. 2) Index, *Salmon lumber pie. **1893** J. WATSON *Confess. Poacher* 168 There were 90 trout, 37 *salmon-mort, and 2 salmon. **1936** LUCAS & HUME *Au Petit Cordon Bleu* 43 Put a little of the aspic into a pan... Run a thin coating of this jelly on the top of the *salmon *mousse*. **1972** K. STEWART *Times Cookery Bk.* vi. 84 Salmon mousse... Allow several hours for mousse to chill. [**1917** *Harrods Gen. Catal.* p. lxvii/6 Salmon .. and Shrimp Paste.] **1939** T. S. ELIOT *Old Possum's Bk. Pract. Cats* 45 You might now and then supply .. Some potted grouse, or *salmon paste. **1533–4** *Salmon peal [see PEAL *sb.*[2]]. **1661** RABISHA *Cookery Dissected* 127 To bake a *Salmon Pie to be eaten hot. **1747** in MRS. GLASSE *Cookery* 115. **1805** J. DUNCUMB *Agric. Heref.* 16 The spawn .. are in some parts termed salmon-fry or *salmon-pinks. **1841** T. SOUTH *Fly Fisher's Handbk.* II. 13 *Salmon Reel Lines. **1883** *Fisheries Exhib. Catal.* 51 Salmon Reels. **1753** CHAMBERS *Cycl. Supp.* s.v. *Salmon*, The richest *salmon river in France. **1771** G. CARTWRIGHT *Jrnl.* 29 May (1792) I. 127 At the head of this place we found a very fine salmon river. **1886** *Critic* 16 Oct. 183 A map and an annotated list of salmon-rivers locate them chiefly north of the St. Lawrence. **1968** R. M. PATTERSON *Finlay's River* 88 The Yukon, a salmon river with a name nobody had ever heard of and which was not to be found on any map. **1841** T. SOUTH *Fly Fisher's Handbk.* iii. 40 The *salmon-rod should consist of four parts. **1824** SCOTT *Redgauntlet* let. vi, The water being in such a rare trim for the *saumon raun, he couldna help taking a cast. **1832** *Ibid. note*, The bait made of *salmon row salted and preserved. **1867** F. FRANCIS *Angling* vii. (1880) 265 The only things I resolutely bar .. are salmon-roe and wasp-grub. **1700** J. CHETHAM *Angler's Vade Mecum* (ed. 3) 110 *Salmon Smelts. **1551** *Salmon spear [see LEISTER]. **1602** CAREW *Cornwall* 31 An instrument somewhat like the Sammon-speare. **1790** GROSE *Provinc. Gloss.* Suppl., **Salmon-sprint*, a young salmon. North. **1847** T. T. STODDART *Angler's Compan.* xv. 284 Let the angler take his place at the head of the cast or *salmon stream. **1883** *Fisheries Exhib. Catal.* 51 *Salmon Winches.

b. objective, as ***salmon-breeding***, ***-fisher***, ***-rearing***, ***spearer***, ***spearing***; instrumental, as ***salmon-haunted*** adj.

1866 *Chambers's Encycl.* VIII. 447/2 *Salmon-breeding ponds. *a* **1670** *Salmon-fisher [see COBLE[1] 1]. *a* **1678** MARVELL *Poems, Appleton Ho.*, And now the salmon-fishers moist Their leathern boats begin to hoist. **1771** T. PENNANT *Tour in Scotl.* 1769 148 Near is a cave, where the Salmon-fishers lie during the season. **1925** F. SCOTT FITZGERALD *Great Gatsby* vi. 118 He had been beating his way along the south shore of Lake Superior as a clam-digger and a salmon-fisher. **1870** F. R. WILSON *Ch. Lindisf.* 33 The silvery and *salmon-haunted Tweed. **1884** *Encycl. Brit.* (1886) XXI. 226/2 *Salmon-rearing establishments. **1899** *Daily News* 29 June 6/3 The fly-fishers and *salmon spearers. **1879** DOWDEN *Southey* vi. 144 The guests went *salmon-spearing on the Tweed.

c. Special combinations: **salmon bass** *S. Afr.* = KABELJOU; †**salmon bellows**, ? the sound or air bladder of a salmon; **salmon belly** (*U.S.*), the belly of a salmon prepared for food by pickling; **salmon berry** (*U.S.*), *N. Amer.*, any of several species of *Rubus*, esp. the white-flowered

R. chamæmorus and *R. parviflorus* or the pink-flowered western raspberry, *R. spectabilis*; also *attrib.*; **salmon cast** (see CAST *sb.* 5 b, c); **salmon coble**, a boat used in salmon fishing; **salmon-colour** (see quots.); **salmon disease**, (*a*) a fatal epidemic skin disease of salmon; (*b*) = *salmon poisoning* below; **salmon fishing**, (*a*) the catching of salmon; (*b*) a place where salmon may be caught; a salmon-fishery; **salmon flounder** (see quot.); **salmon gum** (see quot. 1883); **salmon killer** (*U.S.*), a stickleback, *Gasterosteus aculeatus*, destructive to salmon fry and spawn (*Cent. Dict.* 1891); **salmon ladder**, a fish ladder for salmon; also, *transf.* 'a contrivance used in the chemical treatment of sewage' (*Cent. Dict.*); **salmon leap**, see LEAP *sb.* 2 b; **salmon louse**, 'a parasitic crustacean, *Caligus piscinus*, which adheres to the gills of salmon' (*Cent. Dict.*); **salmon pass** = *salmon ladder*; **salmon pipe**, 'an engine to catch Salmon' (Cowel *Interpr.* 1607); **salmon pit, pool** (see quots.); **salmon poisoning**, a fatal disease of dogs on the Pacific Coast of North America which affects lymphoid tissue and the central nervous system and is caused by rickettsias present in flukes infesting ingested salmon; **salmon-scurf**, a dial. name for the salmon trout; **salmon stair** = *salmon ladder*; **salmon steak**, a fried slice of salmon; **salmon-tithe**, a tithe payable in salmon; **salmon twine**, linen or cotton twine used in the manufacture of salmon-nets (*Cent. Dict.*); **salmon weir**, a weir for the taking of salmon (*Ibid.*).

1929 *Hardy's Anglers' Guide* (ed. 51) 48 The Kabeljaauw, known in Natal as *Salmon Bass..runs to as much as 150 lbs. **1957** S. SCHOEMAN *Strike!* iii. 70 The very big ones are variously referred to as..salmon, salmon bass and often even Cape salmon if caught from East London to Durban. *c* **1460** J. RUSSELL *Bk. Nurture* 719 Musclade or menows, with þe *Samoun bellows. **1883** GOODE *Fish. Industr. U.S.* (Fish. Exhib. Lit. 1884 V.) 32 Pickled *salmon-belly is a favourite delicacy of the region. **1844** A. SYLVESTER *Jrnl.* in *Oregon Hist. Q.* (1933) XXXIV. 359 A *salmon berry.. being put into the mouth of a fish [*sc.* a salmon], destroys the charm. *a* **1861** Salmon-berry [see HIAQUA]. **1868** *Rep. U.S. Commissioner Agric.* (1869) 178 The salmon-berry..(*Rubus chamaemorus*). **1901** J. GRINNELL *Gold Hunting in Alaska* 16 The other day we picked three quarts of salmon berries. **1971** *Islander* (Victoria, B.C.) 14 Mar. 16/2 Directing their steps toward the beach..they hurried..through the salmonberry thicket. **1977** J. GILLIS *Killers of Starfish* (1979) xxii. 217 A precipitous tangle of salmonberry and alder. **1875** W. McILWRAITH *Guide Wigtownshire* 20 In the vicinity of Penninghame House are some excellent *salmon-casts. **1883** *Fisheries Exhib. Catal.* 51 Salmon Casts, plaited gut [etc.]. **1787** BURNS *Auld Farmer's Salut. Mare* vii, Tho' now ye dow but hoyte and hoble, An' wintle like a *saumont-coble. **1881** W. GREGOR *Notes Folk-lore N.-E. Scotl.* 146 In going past a salmon cobble in the harbour, a fisherman would not have allowed his boat to touch it. **1973** W. ELMER *Terminol. Fishing* iii. 78 The salmon coble.. differs in structure from the rest of the cobles. **1813** J. CONSTABLE *Let.* 30 June (1964) II. 109 The paper will be a sort of *salmon color and the sofa & chairs crimson. **1842** D. R. HAY *Nomencl. Colours* (1846) 42 Salmon colour is the name usually given to such tints as those produced by the attenuation of orange. **1860** WORCESTER, *Salmon-color*, a golden-orange tinge. **1880** *Proc. R. Soc. Edin.* X. 242, I am led to believe that the so-called *salmon disease does not depend upon a pre-diseased condition of the fish. **1950** *Amer. Jrnl. Path.* XXVI. 617 (*heading*) The pathology and etiology of salmon disease in the dog and fox. **1964** G. W. STAMM *Dog Owner's Vet. Guide* 79 Salmon disease has been successfully treated with certain sulfa drugs and with penicillin. **1971** D. MILLS *Salmon & Trout* iii. 91 The salmon is subject to a number of diseases... The diseases include furunculosis, Dee disease, kidney disease, salmon disease,..and columnaris. **1588** *Rot. Scacc. Reg. Scot.* XXI. 336 The fewmaill of the *salmound fisching upoun the water of Connan. **1607** NORDEN *Surv. Dial.* 67 The like of a Salmon fishing, wherin the Lord lost two parts in three. **1808** FORSYTH *Beauties Scotl.* V. 153 A salmon-fishing of some value. **1833** J. RENNIE *Alph. Angling* 45 The finest salmon-fishing is in mild weather. **1815** J. ARBUTHNOT *Hist. Acc. Peterhead* 18 (Jam.) *Pleuronectes Flessus*, Flounder, vulgarly called *Fresh-water Fleuk*, **Salmon Flounder*. [**1883** F. VON MUELLER *Eucalyptographia* ix, *Eucalyptus salmonophloia*... A tree, when aged, attaining to fully 100 feet in height, known vernacularly as the 'Salmon-colored Gumtree', in allusion to the smooth grey and somewhat purplish bark of an oily lustre.] **1934** *Bulletin* (Sydney) 24 Oct. 20/3 A Digger mate and myself saw three *salmon gums, trees of the Westralian wheatbelt and eastern goldfields. **1969** CHIPPENDALE & JOHNSTON *Eucalypts* 72/1 The salmon gum has been regarded as an indicator of good, loamy soil on which much of the West Australian wheatbelt is developed. **1867** *Lond. Rev.* 22 June 696/1 One great obstacle to the erection of *Salmon-ladders. **1387** TREVISA *Higden* (Rolls) I. 369 Also in Irlond beeþ þre *samoun lepes. *c* **1730** BURT *Lett. N. Scotl.* (1818) I. 236 The Salmon leap (which is a steep slope composed of large loose stones). **1867–99** *Salmon-pass [see PASS *sb.*[1] 3 h]. **1533** *Act 25 Hen. VIII*, c. 7 No maner of persone..shall..take..in fludgate, *salmon pipe or at the tayle of any mylle or were..the yonge frye..of..Salmon. **1787** *Surv. Kirton-in Lindsey* in *N.W. Linc. Gloss.* (1877), There are particular places in the river (Trent) to which the Salmon resort that are called *Salmon Pits. **1925** *Jrnl. Amer. Vet. Med. Assoc.* LXVI. 638 A microscopic cyst has been found in the muscle of 'sore-back' salmon. When these fish were fed to dogs typical symptoms of so-called *salmon poisoning were produced. **1974** T. McGINNIS *Well Dog Bk.* 74 This fluke is host to an organism (a rickettsia) which causes a severe disease called salmon poisoning. **1866** *Mass. Rep.* 32 (Cent. Dict. s.v. *Pool*[1]) **Salmon-pools*, eddies where the salmon collect. **1874** W. LENNOX *My Recoll.* II. 72 My guide then informing me that within three miles there were several salmon pools, I lost no time in proceeding there. **1892** Salmon pool [see EASY B. 4 b]. **1846** BROCKETT *N.C. Wds.* (ed. 3), *Scurf*, or **Salmon-scurf*, salmon trout. Tees, Wear, &c. **1875** KNIGHT *Dict. Mech.*, **Salmon-stair*. **1902** BUCHAN *Watcher by Threshold* 6, I had breakfasted..on eggs and *salmon-steaks. **1828** SCOTT *F.M. Perth* xxx, He hath had frequent disputes with them about the *salmon-tithe.

B. *adj.* [The sb. used *attrib.*: cf. A. 3.] Of the colour of the flesh of salmon; a kind of orange-pink. Also *Comb.*, as ***salmon-pink, -red, -rose.***

1786 ABERCROMBIE *Gard. Assist.* 234 Radishes..both of the common short top and salmon kinds. [Cf. quot. 1824 s.v. SALMON-COLOURED.] **1876** MISS BRADDON *J. Haggard's Dau.* xi, A..room painted white and salmon. **1882** *Garden* 1 Apr. 223/2 Large blossoms..of a beautiful, deep, salmon-pink colour. *Ibid.* 29 Apr. 299/3 Carnations..Conqueror, salmon-rose. **1884** Salmon-pink [see CREVETTE]. **1885** BLACK *White Heather* iii, Just over them was a line of gleaming salmon-red. **1899** *Allbutt's Syst. Med.* VIII. 558 The patches in such parts may then assume a salmon tinge. *Ibid.* 573 The colour of the base has more of a salmon hue when fresh. **1901** *J. Black's Illustr. Carp. & Build., Home Handicr.* 38 A good salmon tint is produced by adding to the dissolved whiting a little of the same [venetian] red. **1979** *Country Life* 24 May 1618/3 The salmon-pink of dawn.

†**'salmon**, *sb.*[2] *Cant. Obs.* Also 6–8 **salomon**, 7 **saloman**, 8–9 **salamon**, 8 **solomon**. [Of obscure origin: cf. SAM *sb.*[1]] In oaths or asseverations, as ***by (the) salmon, so help me salmon.***

Harman's interpretation (quot. 1567) may be correct; it is doubtful whether any of the subsequent writers quoted really knew the word in actual use.

a **1550** COPLAND *Hye Way to Spyttel Hous* 1050 in Hazl. *E.P.P.* IV. 69 Cyarum by salmon and thou shalt pek my jere. **1567** HARMAN *Caveat* 83 Salomon, a alter or masse. **1611** MIDDLETON & DEKKER *Roaring Girle* v. i. K 4 My doxy I haue, by the *Salomon* a doxy, that carries a kitchin mort in her slat at her backe. **1641** BROME *Jov. Crew* II. (1659) F 4 b, By Salmon, I think my Mort is in drink. *a* **1700** B. E. *Dict. Cant. Crew, Salmon*, c. the Beggers Sacrament or Oath. *Solomon*, c. the Mass. **1815** SCOTT *Guy M.* xxxiv, She swore by the salmon. **1834** H. AINSWORTH *Rookwood* III. v, You must repeat the 'Salamon', or oath of our creed. *Ibid.*, So may help me, Salamon!

salmon, variant of SAMMEN *dial.*

'salmon-,coloured, *a.* = SALMON *a.*

1776–96 WITHERING *Brit. Plants* (ed. 3) IV. 170 Gills salmon-coloured. **1807–8** W. IRVING *Salmag.* (1824) 361, I have..sported a pair of salmon-coloured small-clothes. **1824** LOUDON *Encycl. Gard.* §3756 Radishes... Long sorts. Scarlet, or salmon-colored, and its subvarieties. **1848** DICKENS *Dombey* xviii, Salmon-colored worsted drawers.

Salmonella (sælmə'nɛlə). *Bacteriol.* Also **salmonella**. Pl. **-ellæ, -ellas,** (*erron.*) **-ella.** [mod.L. (coined in Fr. by J. Lignières 1900, in *Bull. de la Soc. centrale de Méd. Vét.* XVIII. 389), f. the name of Daniel Elmer *Salmon* (1850–1914), U.S. pathologist + L. *-ella* (see -EL[2]).]

1. A member of the genus of pathogenic, Gram-negative, rod-shaped bacteria so called, which includes some causing food poisoning, typhoid, and paratyphoid in man and various diseases in domestic animals.

1913 H. J. HUTCHENS tr. *Besson's Pract. Bacteriol.* 442 Lignières proposed to designate all those organisms which had the morphological and cultural attributes of the bacillus of hog-cholera..by the name Salmonella after Salmon. **1920** *Lancet* 10 Jan. 96/2 So long as there appeared to be but two types in this group of the Salmonellas,..there was little need to find a name in common for them. **1932** J. H. DIBLE *Rec. Adv. Bacteriol.* (ed. 2) iv. 79 White..adduces evidence of the presence of common antigenic complexes, relating these to the enteric and food-poisoning salmonellas. **1944** L. R. THOMPSON *Introd. Microorganisms* xix. 269 Salmonella have been ingested with meats, fish,..dairy products,..and drinking water. **1951** *Chambers's Jrnl.* Oct. 588/1 Dr. Williams Smith and Professor J. C. Cruickshank have been inquiring into the danger cats and dogs may convey by acting as reservoirs of the salmonellæ, noxious bacteria which cause food-poisoning in man. **1979** *Daily Tel.* 19 Sept. 12/8 Twenty-seven of 64 samples of poultry manure yielded salmonella. **1980** *Brit. Med. Jrnl.* 29 Mar. 928/2 Zoonotic pathogens, such as salmonellas.., may be present in any type of slurry.

2. = SALMONELLOSIS.

1962 *Telegraph* (Brisbane) 27 Aug. 32/2 He believed there was a risk in the sale of kangaroo meat. It..carried Q fever and salmonella. **1977** *Shooting Times & Country Mag.* 13–19 Jan. 27/3 There is still the possibility of such diseases as forms of Salmonella (now a notifiable disease) being spread over a wide area.

3. *attrib.*

1916 A. I. KENDALL *Bacteriol.* xv. 344 These organisms are variously known as the hog cholera, Salmonella, Gärtner, enteritidis, intermediate, paracolon or paratyphoid group. **1920** *Lancet* 10 Jan. 95/1 The whole Salmonella group is considered a particularly variable one. **1925** J. W. BIGGER *Handbk. Bacteriol.* xxviii. 259 There are two chief types of bacilli which are responsible for isolated cases or epidemics of food poisoning... Both these are exceedingly closely rated to B[acillus] paratyphosus B, and together with it form what is called the 'Salmonella' group. **1963** *Lancet* 19 Jan. 161/1 Most outbreaks of salmonella infection result from the contamination of a single article of food which is then eaten by a number of individuals. **1979** *Daily Tel.* 9 Aug. 7/3 A woman..died in hospital after an outbreak of salmonella food poisoning.

salmonellosis (,sælmənɛ'ləʊsɪs). *Path.* Also **Salmonellosis.** [ad. F. *salmonellose* (J. Lignières 1901, in *Recueil de Méd. Vét.* VIII. 416), f. prec.: see -OSIS.] Infection with or a disease caused by salmonellæ.

1913 in DORLAND *Med. Dict.* (ed. 7). **1931** *Nomencl. Diseases* (Min. of Health) (ed. 6) 104 *Bacterium* (*Salmonella*) *enteritidis..suipestifer.* Causes of epidemic food-poisoning in man (Salmonellosis) and occasionally of paratyphoid fever. **1947** *Ann. Rev. Microbiol.* I. 324 The classical case of the salmonellosis..is that of a generalized infection, namely that of typhoid fever. This human clinical picture has its close parallel in animal salmonellosis. **1965** *N.Z. News* 13 Apr. 3/1 Several thousand sheep have died since Christmas in salmonellosis outbreaks among stock in the Rotorua and Waikato districts. **1970** W. H. PARKER *Health & Dis. in Farm Animals* xiii. 178 Outbreaks of Salmonellosis in stock are a matter of concern for public health.

salmonet ('sæmənɪt). Also 6 **samonett.** [f. SALMON *sb.*[1] + -ET[1].] A samlet.

1576 in J. Noake *Worcestersh. Relics* (1877) 62 That noe maner of persons..use ne occupy anie manner of takynge of trowte or trowte samon or samonetts within the said streame. **1800** LADY HUNTER in *Jrnl. Sir M. H.* (1894) 154 A John Dory and some Salmonets. **1850** in OGILVIE.

salmonic (sæl'mɒnɪk), *a. Chem.* [f. SALMON *sb.*[1] + -IC.] ***salmonic acid*** (see quot.).

1868 WATTS *Dict. Chem.*, *Salmonic acid*, a reddish fatty acid, existing, according to Frémy and Valenciennes.., in the reddish muscles of various species of salmon.

salmonid ('sælmənɪd), *sb.* (and *a.*) Also **-ide.** [ad. mod.L. *Salmōnid-æ* pl., f. L. *salmōn-* SALMON *sb.*[1]: see -ID.] A fish of the family *Salmonidæ.* Also *attrib.* and as *adj.*

1868 *Rep. U.S. Commissioner Agric.* (1869) 329 The creature..looking..more like a spiritual polliwog than a real salmonide. **1882** A. NICOLS *Acclim. Salmonidæ at Antipodes* 83 The presence of migratory salmonids in their rivers. **1888** *Daily News* 19 May 7/3 Highly satisfactory results have attended salmonide culture this season. **1895** B. DEAN *Fishes, Living & Fossil* viii. 186 Eggs of Salmonids are deposited loosely in 'nests' on a clean, gravelly bottom. **1931** J. R. NORMAN *Hist. Fishes* xiii. 268 When the climate was considerably colder the range of migratory Salmonids extended much farther south. **1964** *Oceanogr. & Marine Biol.* II. 178 Further changes have been reported to occur after fertilization of the ova in another salmonid, the rainbow trout. **1970** *New Scientist* 19 Feb. 353/1 Ulcerative dermal necrosis..attacks salmon and other salmonid fish. **1975** *Nature* 14 Aug. 528/2 Fish farming in the UK has grown slowly in the freshwater and marine salmonid field under commercial patronage. **1978** *Ibid.* 2 Mar. 77/1 Evidence of large-scale gene loss following tetraploidy has been reported in both salmonid and catostomid fish.

salmoniform (sæl'mɒnɪfɔːm), *a.* [f. SALMON *sb.*[1] + -(I)FORM.] = SALMONOID.

1891 in *Century Dict.* (citing HUXLEY).

salmonize ('sæmənaɪz), *v.* [f. SALMON *sb.*[1] + -IZE.] *trans.* To make (a river) fit for salmon. Also, to (attempt to) introduce salmon into (a river, etc.) So **,salmoni'zation**; also **'salmonizing** *vbl. sb.*

1870 *Sat. Rev.* 30 Apr. 576/1 Why should I be 'chaffed' about the salmonization of the Thames? The Thames once produced plenty of salmon; why should not the Thames produce salmon again? **1886** *Longm. Mag.* VII. 293 Much is talked about 'salmonising' the Thames. **1901** *Chambers's Jrnl.* Sept. 585/2 It does not seem quite fair that a few gentlemen should be able to prevent the salmonising of such a large extent of water as is here indicated.

salmonoid ('sælmənɔɪd), *a.* and *sb.* [f. SALMON *sb.*[1] + -OID.] **A.** *adj.* Of or belonging to the family *Salmonidæ*; resembling a fish of this family.

1850 in OGILVIE. **1865** *Athenæum* No. 1948. 279/1 Salmonoid fishes. **1883** *Pall Mall G.* 12 May Suppl., An extensive collection of salmonidæ and salmonoid fishes.

B. *sb.* A fish of the family *Salmonidæ.*

1842 in BRANDE *Dict. Sci.*, etc. **1867** (*title*) Reports on the Natural History and Habits of Salmonoids in the Tweed. **1883** G. ALLEN in *Knowledge* 23 Mar. 175 There is one little peculiarity common to all the salmonoids—the graylings and gwyniads as well as the trout and charr.

†**'salmonsews.** *Obs.*$^{-0}$ [ad. AF. *salmonceux* pl. (1389–90 *Act 13 Ric. II.* st. 1 c. 19), dim. of *salmon*. Cf. HERONSEW.] Salmon-fry.

1607 COWEL *Interpr.*, *Salmon sewse* seemeth to be the young fry of Salmon. **1706** in PHILLIPS (ed. Kersey).

'salmon-'trout.

1. A fish of the species *Salmo trutta*, resembling the salmon, found in rivers of northern Europe.

1421 *Rolls of Parlt.* IV. 132/1 Frie de Samon-Trought. **1540** *Rutland MSS.* (1905) IV. 302 A great salmon trowtte. **1668** CHARLETON *Onomast.* 155 *Trutta Salmoneta*..a Salmon-Trout. **1756–7** tr. *Keysler's Trav.* (1760) I. 17 There is also a kind of salmon-trouts called Gangfische. **1884** *Sat. Rev.* 12 July 61/1 Jim, the black cook boy..caught a twenty-pound salmon-trout with bait.

2. In U.S. and N.S.W. applied to other fishes (see quots.).

1705 *Boston News-Let.* 15–22 Oct. 2/1 Our men were refresh'd with variety of Fish, especially Salmon Trouts, some whereof 2 foot long. **1806** W. CLARK *Jrnl.* 13 Mar. in *Orig. Jrnls. Lewis & Clark Exped.* (1905) IV. 166 The Salmon Trout are seldom more than two feet in length. **1848** E. BRYANT *What I saw in California* xi. 158 He had taken with his hook about a dozen salmon-trout. **1882** J. E. TENISON-WOODS *Fish N.S.W.* 35 *Arripis salar*,..is in the adult state the salmon of the Australian fishermen, and their salmon trout is the young. **1884** GOODE, etc. *Nat. Hist. Aquatic Anim.* 468 According to the latest system..the second group [of the old genus *Salmo*] includes the Chars, or Red-spotted Trout, and the gray-spotted species known as Salmon Trout, or Lake Trout. These are assigned to the genus *Salvelinus*. *Ibid.* 474 The Steel-head—*Salmo Gairdneri*. Large individuals are often called 'Salmon Trout'. **1939** *Nat. Geogr. Mag.* Feb. 212/2 Both of these species [*sc.* Dolly Varden and blackspotted trout] are known in some localities as 'salmon trout'.

salmony ('sæmənɪ), *a.* [f. SALMON *sb.*[1] and *a.* + -Y[1].] Somewhat salmon-coloured.

1935 E. FARJEON *Nursery in Nineties* 237 She has one evening dress..a salmony-pink brocaded with bunches of lemon-coloured flowers. **1948** V. S. PRITCHETT in E. Bowen et al. *Why do I Write?* 12 Lichfield..a nice, dull little place in glazed salmony Midland brick. *a* **1974** R. CROSSMAN *Diaries* (1977) III. 805 Anne looked fresh and exquisite, too, in her lovely salmony red suit.

† **sal-nitre.** *Obs.* [ad. med.L. *sal nitrī* 'salt of nitre': see SAL and NITRE. Cf. It. *salnitro*, Pr. *salnitre*; also Sp., Pg. *salitre* (whence SALITRE), G. *salniter*, *saliter*.] Saltpetre.

1416 in *Essex Rev.* (1907) XVI. 159 Sal niter. **1601** HOLLAND *Pliny* II. 420, I may not put off the treatise concerning the nature of Salnitre, approching so neer as it doth to the nature of salt. **1610** MARKHAM *Masterp.* II. cxlv. 447 Adde to it of Sal-niter an ounce. **1683** SALMON *Doron Med.* I. 320 Subliming it with Sal Niter.

Hence † **sal'nitral** *a.*, of the nature of saltpetre.

1683 TRYON *Way to Health* vi. (1697) 104 Until the Sun and Cœlestial Influences have endu'd it [*sc.* earth] with a Salnitral Vertue.

salod, var. pa. t. of SALUE *v.* *Obs.*

salol ('sælɒl). *Chem.* [f. SAL(ICYL) + -OL.] A white, crystalline, aromatic powder, prepared from salicylic and carbolic acids, used as an antipyretic and antiseptic. Also in *Comb.*

1887 *Athenæum* 19 Feb. 260/1 Salol is said to have a most powerful effect in cases of rheumatism. **1897** *Trans. Amer. Pediatric Soc.* IX. 129 Salol-coated permanganate pills.

† **salomene.** *Obs.* Also 5 salome, -mere. [Of obscure origin: cf. It. *salame* (see SALAMI); also F. *salmis* (see SALMI), which agrees closely in sense.] (See quot.)

c **1430** *Two Cookery-bks.* 21 Salomene. Take gode Wyne, an..pouder, & Brede y-ground, an sugre..; þan take Trowtys, Rochys, Perchys, oþer Carpys,..an..roste hem ..; þan hewe hem in gobettys:..fry hem in oyle a lytil, þen caste in þe brwet;..take Maces, Clowes [etc.]..an cast a-boue, & serue forth. *Ibid.* 33 Capoun in Salome. *Ibid.* 35 Soupes of Salomere.

salometer (sæ'lɒmɪtə(r)). [f. L. *sal* salt or *salum* brine + -(O)METER.] = SALINOMETER.

1860 MAURY *Phys. Geog. Sea* (Low) ii. §102 The salometer confirms it.

Salomonic (sæləʊ'mɒnɪk), *a.* [f. L. *Salomōn* Solomon. Cf. SOLOMONIC.] Of or pertaining to Solomon. So **Salo'monian** *a.*

1873 *Speaker's Comment. Bible* IV. 667/2 Those who have denied its Salomonic authorship. *Ibid.* 15/1 The description of the Divine Wisdom, Proverbs viii, in which the Salomonian theory culminated. **1881** W. R. SMITH *Old Test. Jewish Ch.* v. 122 The collection of Salomonic proverbs formed by the scholars in the service of King Hezekiah. *Ibid.* 403.

‖ **salon** (‖ salɔ̃, 'sælɔ̃, 'sælɒn). Also 8 sallon. [Fr.: see SALOON.]

1. a. A large and lofty apartment serving as one of the principal reception rooms in a palace or other great house. **b.** A room, more or less elegantly furnished, used for the reception of guests; a drawing-room.

Now only with reference to France or other continental countries. Cf. SALOON 1.

1699 M. LISTER *Journey to Paris* 196 The Castle is..most commodious. The Great Salon and the Gallery are extreamly well Painted. **1715** LEONI *Palladio's Archit.* (1742) I. 52 Great Halls or Sallons for Feasting. **1717** BERKELEY *Tour in Italy* Wks. 1871 IV. 523 It [the palace of the Barberini in Rome] hath many noble chambers and salons. *a* **1721** SHEFFIELD (Dk. Buckhm.) *Wks.* (1723) II. 276, I rise..about seven a-clock..to walk in the garden; or, if rainy, in a *Salon* filled with pictures. **1728** CHAMBERS *Cycl.*, *Salon*, or Saloon,..a very lofty, spacious Hall, vaulted at Top, and sometimes comprehending two Stories, or Ranges, of Windows... Embassadors, and other Great Visitors, are usually received in the Salon. **1758** H. WALPOLE *Let. to Chute* 22 Aug., I have seen the plan of their hall..and both their eating-room and salon are to be stucco, with pictures. **1834** H. GREVILLE *Diary* 23 Oct., Finding Barras had not come home he established himself with a book in the salon until he should return. **1881** *Q. Rev.* Oct. 505 The principal salon had a dome, which, turning day and night imitated the movements of the terrestrial bodies.

2. *spec.* The reception-room of a Parisian lady of fashion; hence, a reunion of notabilities at the house of such a lady; also, a similar gathering in other capitals.

1810 F. JEFFREY in *Edin. Rev.* XV. 485 When she [Mlle. de Lespinasse] is visibly within a few weeks of her end..she still has her *salon* filled twice a day with company. **1853** C. C. FELTON in *Longfellow's Life* (1891) II. 253 There is not a *salon* in Paris which is not proud to welcome him. **1888** BRYCE *Amer. Commw.* III. cv. 508 One hears of attempts made to establish political 'salons' in Washington. **1888** MRS. H. WARD *R. Elsmere* xvii. 225 Famous in London society for her relationship, her audacity, and the *salon* which..she managed to collect round her.

3. a. *the Salon*: the annual exhibition at Paris of painting, sculpture, etc. by living artists.

Originally held in one of the 'salons' of the Louvre.

1875 T. G. APPLETON in *Longfellow's Life* (1891) III. 252 The *Salon* is open. **1908** *Athenæum* 15 Aug. 191/2 He received a medal at the Salon of 1864..; two of his pictures were in this year's Salon.

b. ‖ **salon des refusés** (de rəfyze). [Fr., exhibition of rejected work], an exhibition ordered by Napoleon III in 1863 to display pictures rejected by the official Salon; also *fig.*

1896 J. C. BECKWITH in J. C. Van Dyke *Mod. French Masters* III. 220 His [*sc.* Manet's] works became known..at the exhibitions of the pictures refused at the Salon, which were for several years gathered together and shown in a building generously provided by the government, and called the Salon des Refusés. **1932** KONODY & LATHOM *Introd. Fr. Painting* xiii. 194 *Déjeuner sur l'herbe* [by Manet]..rejected by the Salon,..was exhibited in the *Salon des Refusés*, and frowned on by Louis Napoleon. **1981** *Listener* 1 Jan. 4/3 Roy Jenkins plus Shirley Williams..plus the non-reselected MPs in the *salon des refusés*.

4. An establishment in which the trade of a beauty specialist or hairdresser is conducted.

1913 *Vogue* 1 June 106/1 (Advt.), Firming the skin is the new process used exclusively by Elizabeth Arden... It is administered at the Salon by experts. **1917** *Harrods Gen. Catal.* 397 Enshrined in an atmosphere of refinement and artistic comfort, *Harrods Hairdressing Salons* are a favourite resort with ladies. **1932** *New Yorker* 9 Apr. 68/3 See the telephone book for nearest Salon. **1956** ASHLEY & STEVENSON *Hair Design & Colour* i. 12 The salon itself, as a background to modern hair-styling, must inevitably play a highly important part in creating the right atmosphere. **1973** A. MACVICAR *Painted Doll Affair* vii. 82 My wife swears it's much better than the expensive 'salon' she used to go to in Glasgow.

5. a. *attrib.*, as (sense 2) ***salon philosopher***, ***science***, ***volume***, ***-writer***; (sense 3) ***salon furniture***, ***norm***, ***-piece***, ***vocabulary***; (sense 4) ***salon facial***, ***service***, ***treatment***.

1974 *Times* 27 Aug. 9/2 All the products Marisa uses in the salon facials can be bought. **1973** R. HAYES *Hungarian Game* ii. 18 An incredibly tasteless collection of Regency and Salon furniture in the drawing room. **1942** WYNDHAM LEWIS *Lett.* (1963) 324 The artist is labelled 'decadent' who departs from the Salon norm..by the Hitlerite pundit of 'sanity'. **1947** A. EINSTEIN *Music in Romantic Era* iii. 26 The perfect type of the 'cultured musician' in the 19th century is represented by Franz Liszt, who was an essayist and salon philosopher. **1974** *Impressionism* (R. A. Catal.) 8 Daubigny ..moved to narrow the distinction between outdoor study and Salon-piece. **1977** P. JOHNSON *Enemies of Society* xv. 203 Not a true discipline at all, but..a salon science. **1974** *Harrods Christmas Catal.* p. ii, Make a Gift of Beauty with a Gift Token..to the value of whichever Salon Service or Treatment you require. **1963** *Times* 6 Mar. 13/2 The liveliest part is that of a tramp-artist with ragged costume and *salon* vocabulary. **1957** *Times Lit. Suppl.* 20 Dec. 778/2 The work has higher claims than that of being merely a salon volume designed for presentation. **1944** L. MACNEICE *Christopher Columbus* 13 Radio's contemporary triangle.. insists on a function of words which salon-writers are perhaps too apt to forget; this function is communication.

b. *attrib.* (passing into *adj.*) and *Comb.* with (occas. derogatory) reference to light music played as in a fashionable salon.

1914 *Étude* Oct. 708/1 Nearly all compositions for the piano by modern composers are Salon Music. **1935** *Vanity Fair* (N.Y.) Nov. 38/1 He's not making a salon man of me. **1946** R. BLESH *Shining Trumpets* xii. 266 So this music sings, not in the African tones of jazz, but in bathetic and sentimental accents. It is salon music. *Ibid.* 268 The reverse record side..is precisely like the mood-music prevalent today in the special salon-swing. **1947** A. EINSTEIN *Music in Romantic Era* xvii. 331 He was a somewhat eccentric salon-composer. **1948** MENCKEN *Amer. Lang.* Suppl. II. 706 A performer who..undertakes conventional music is a *commercial*, *salon-man*, *long-underwear* or *long-hair*. **1949** KOESTLER *Promise & Fulfilment* III. i. 301 Middle-class families in the Tel Aviv cafés applauded..the Russian marches played by salon orchestras in the Viennese style. **1950** BLESH & JANIS *They all played Ragtime* iv. 77 It is unsyncopated and in a light salon vein. **1955** *Times* 12 July 5/5 A Prelude and Fugue for string orchestra by Moszkowski..combined learned and *salon* styles with surprising success. **1979** *Guardian* 5 May 14/5 Jones..wrote the music for such skittish romances as Girl from Utah.. and San Toy. Excerpts from these propped up many a salon orchestra's repertoire.

‖ **salone** (sa'lone). [It.: see SALOON.]

1. a. = SALON 1 a. **b.** = SALON 1 b. (Only with reference to Italy.)

1902 H. JAMES *Wings of Dove* X. xxxiii. 515 She received me..in that glorious great *salone*. **1912** BEERBOHM *Christmas Garland* 134 A wintry Venetian sunshine poured in through the vast windows of his *salone*. **1960** E. BOWEN *Time in Rome* v. 140 The cavalier..charged through the *salone* and out again on to the balcony. **1969** 'I. DRUMMOND' *Man with Tiny Head* v. 74 He had despised her at their first meeting, in the huge Uccello *salone*.

‖ **salonfähig** (za'lɔ̃:ˌfɛ:ɪç), *a.* *rare.* [Ger.] Fit for (polite) society; socially respectable.

1905 W. JAMES in *McClure's Mag.* May 3/2 Neither in dress nor in manner did he ever grow quite 'gentlemanly' or *Salonfähig* in the conventional and obliterated sense of the terms. **1980** *Encounter* May 41/1 The Austrian initiative, whatever its underlying motivations, serves to lend an air of cultured respectability to a blood-stained struggle and to render Arafat *salonfähig* in Western Europe.

salonnière (sælɒnɪ'ɛə(r)). [Fr., f. SALON.] A woman who holds a salon; a society hostess.

a **1922** T. S. ELIOT *Waste Land Drafts* (1971) 27 Fresca's arrived (the Muses Nine declare) To be a sort of can-can salonnière. **1925** A. HUXLEY *Those Barren Leaves* II. i. 86 Mrs. Aldwinkle the salonnière, the hostess, the giver of literary parties and agapes of lions—is she not classical? a household word? a familiar quotation? **1964** *New Sattesman* 10 Apr. 572/2 For a time she [*sc.* Beatrice Elvery] worked in the Co-operative Stained Glass Studio run by Sarah Purser, a patriotic *salonnière*. **1976** S. J. DARROCH *Ottoline* iv. 60 Being a hostess gave many women a chance to use talents and abilities that would otherwise have had no outlet. They turned their houses into cultural or intellectual oases, or merely centres of gossip. And a few did so in such a style that they qualified for the exalted title of salonnière.

saloon (sə'lu:n). Also 8 salloon. [a. F. *salon* (= Sp. *salon*, Pg. *salão*), ad. It. *salone*, augm. of *sala* hall: see SALE[2].]

1. a. = SALON 1 a. **b.** = SALON 1 b. Now *U.S.*

1728 [see SALON]. **1748** RICHARDSON *Clarissa* (1811) III. 352 What Mr. Lovelace saw of the house (which was the saloon and two parlours) was perfectly elegant. **1753** HANWAY *Trav.* (1762) I. VII. xciii. 427 They were then lining the grand salloon with silesia marble. **1760** H. WALPOLE *Let. to Montagu* 19 July, Ditchley..is a good house, well furnished, has good portraits, a wretched saloon [etc.]. **1784** COWPER *Task* I. 414 Strange! there should be found, Who, self-imprison'd in their proud saloons, Renounce the odours of the open field. **1810** E. D. CLARKE *Trav. Russia* (1839) 21/1 The *coup d'œil* upon entering the grand saloon is inconceivable... The company consisted of nearly two thousand persons. **1823** P. NICHOLSON *Pract. Build.* 438 Saloons are frequently raised the whole height of the building. **1828** J. F. COOPER *Notions of Amer.* I. 261 A young American..is just as happy in the saloon, as she was a few years before in the nursery. **1841** *Penny Cycl.* XX. 365 *Saloon* signifies, in its stricter architectural meaning, a room .., not only the principal room as to spaciousness, but loftiness also... At present however..the name of saloon is indiscriminately or ostentatiously bestowed on any unusually large room. **1842** *Literary Gaz.* 3 Sept. 612/1 Neither was she received altogether in the saloon, as she was of too humble a grade to mix with gentry and nobility. **1860** MARSH *Eng. Lang.* xiii. 291 In all grades of society, from the wigwam to the saloon. *Ibid.* xx. 440 The aim of a numerous class of popular writers is..to make books..speak the dialect of the saloon. **1907** *Connoisseur* XIX. 139/2 [Eaton Hall] The saloon..forms part of the hall... Divided by pillars alone from the entrance hall, the two form one large room.

2. = SALON 2. Now *rare.*

1810 F. JEFFREY in *Edin. Rev.* XV. 461 It is to this..that the French are indebted for the superiority of their polite assemblies. Their saloons are better filled than ours. **1820** SHELLEY *Lett.* Pr. Wks. 1880 IV. 163, I find saloons and compliments too great bores. **1838** EMERSON *Addr., Lit. Ethics* Wks. (Bohn) II. 214 How mean to go blazing, a gaudy butterfly, in fashionable or political saloons. **1881** STANLEY *Chr. Institut.* (1882) 297 Materials of conversation at the dinner tables of London or the saloons of Paris.

3. A large apartment or hall, esp. in a hotel or other place of public resort, adapted for assemblies, entertainments, exhibitions, etc.; also, rarely, any unusually large apartment.

1747 *General Advertiser* 12 May, Mr. Rose and others will play in the Great Room, and in the Salloon in the Gardens. **1761** *Ann. Reg.* 126 In digging near the Latin-gate, two subterraneous saloons have also been discovered, in which were found four tombs. **1837** DICKENS *Pickw.* xxxvi, The great pump-room is a spacious saloon, ornamented with Corinthian pillars. **1858** HAWTHORNE *Fr. & It. Note-bks.* (1872) I. 11 The Restaurant des Echelles..has a handsomely furnished saloon. **1886** *Guide Exhib. Galleries Brit. Mus.* 40 In this saloon are two Table-cases containing tablets of baked and unbaked clay from Babylonia.

4. a. A large cabin in a passenger-boat for the common use of passengers in general or for those paying first-class fares; † the passenger cabin of an aeroplane. Also quasi-advb. in *to go* (etc.) ***saloon***.

c **1835** in M. Johnson *Amer. Advertising, 1800–1900* (1960), Fare to Bristol—In main Saloon, and cuddy state rooms, Thirty-Five Guineas; in fore and lower saloons, Thirty Guineas. **1842** DICKENS in Forster *Life* (1872) I. 271 One man lost fourteen pounds at vingt-un in the saloon yesterday. **1882** W. D. HAY *Brighter Britain!* I. ii. 57 If you can compass the means, go saloon—the extra comfort on a long voyage is well worth the extra price. **1884** *Whitaker's Almanack* (Advt. section) 20 These large, highest classed and full-powered Steamships..are fitted up in the latest and most approved fashion to ensure the comfort of Passengers, having the Saloon on Upper Deck. **1888** W. S. CAINE *Round the World* x. 147 The saloon accommodates just sixteen persons to table. **1892** [see STEERAGE 5]. **1900** H. LAWSON *Over Sliprails* 113, I should have gone over steerage with nothing..and come back saloon with a pile. **1921** *Daily Mail Year Bk.* 27/1 Eight passengers..in armchair seats in a draught-proof saloon. **1930** *Daily Express* 6 Oct. 2/3 R101 swept around in a wide circle, visible only by her red and green navigating lights and the glow of the illuminated saloons.

b. In full ***saloon car*** or ***carriage***: A railway carriage without compartments, furnished more or less luxuriously as a drawing-room or for a specific purpose, as ***dining***, ***sleeping saloon***. Also (U.S.) 'the main room of a compartment-car or a small subdivision of a sleeping-car' (*Funk's Standard Dict.*).

1842 *Illustr. London News* 18 June 89/1 Previous to the departure from Paddington, the Royal Saloon, the fittings of which are upon a most elegant..scale, were tastefully improved by bouquets. **1850** C. SCHREIBER *Jrnl.* 17 June (1950) 243 We had a saloon carriage. **1855** D. K. CLARK *Railway Machinery* 275/1 Saloon carriages may..be planned variously... The business public appear generally to prefer the ordinary partitioned carriage. **1859** *First Impressions New World* 214 There were four of these [state rooms], besides a general saloon in the middle; but the whole was greatly inferior to the elegance of Mr. Tyson's car on the Baltimore and Ohio Railway. **1886** *St. James Gaz.* 16 Oct. 6/2 He stepped lightly from the saloon-car. **1886** *Encycl. Brit.* XX. 247/1 Saloon carriages are occasionally used, so called because two or more of the ordinary compartments are merged in one. **1891** *Harper's Mag.* LXXXII. 581/1 The car at the head of the New York and Chicago Limited was divided..; the two small apartments 'amidships', so to speak, were arranged, one as a bath room, and the other as a barber-shop; and then came the more spacious saloon reserved for the smokers. **1899** *Westm. Gaz.* 19 Sept. 6/2 In the rear of the express was..the saloon in which the distinguished travellers were making their journey... They travelled..to Aberdeen in an ordinary sleeping saloon.

c. A type of motor car with a closed body for four or more passengers. Cf. SEDAN 1 c.

1908 *Motor Manual* (ed. 11) iii. 92 Other forms of bodies fitted to more expensive cars include the brougham, landaulet, saloon, double phaeton, [etc.]. **1927** B. K. SEYMOUR *Three Wives* I. x. 157 He..secured the services of a Buick saloon. **1935** AUDEN & ISHERWOOD *Dog beneath Skin* 12 Brought in charabanc and saloon along arterial roads. **1955** *Times* 6 June 7/7 A chauffeur-driven saloon draws up with a single passenger in the back—a prim little boy reading a school book. **1971** *Daily Tel.* 13 Apr. 2/4 A new saloon with front-wheel drive and transversely-mounted engine.. is announced today by Fiat. **1976** BOTHAM & DONNELLY *Valentino* vii. 48 The street, where a gleaming new four-door Ford saloon was parked.

5. a. An apartment to which the public may resort for a specified purpose, as ***billiard, boxing, dancing, shaving saloon***, etc.

1851 [see ICE-CREAM *attrib.*]. **1852** C. J. TALBOT *Meliora* Ser. I. 166 In London..we went to places of entertainment, and low dancing saloons. **1874** MAHAFFY *Soc. Life Greece* viii. 241 We hear of no hells, or low music halls, or low dancing saloons [at Athens].

b. = *saloon theatre* below.

1864 G. A. SALA *Robson* 14 The place was a 'saloon'—that is to say, drinking and smoking went on during the performance, but the pieces put upon the stage were all of a high class. **1902** *Encycl. Brit.* XXXI. 46/2 The principal 'saloons' were the 'Effingham' in the Whitechapel Road, the 'Bower' in the Lower Marsh, Lambeth, [etc.]. **1974** *Encycl. Brit. Micropædia* VII. 130/1 'Saloon' became the name for any place of popular entertainment; 'variety' was an evening of mixed plays; and 'music hall' meant a concert hall that featured a mixture of musical and comic entertainment.

6. In the U.S., a place where intoxicating liquors are sold and consumed; a drinking bar. Also, in British use, a refreshment bar in a theatre; a separate bar in a public house (as opposed to *public bar*), = *saloon bar* below.

1841 *Southern Lit. Messenger* VII. 764/1 After going into the saloon (grog-shop) to 'freshen the nip'—..they led me into the upper tier of boxes. **1841** DICKENS *Let.* 28 Dec. (1969) II. 454 This note is about the saloon... The refreshments are preposterously dear... There ought to be a boxkeeper to ring a bell or give some other notice of the commencement of the overture to the afterpiece. **1854** *Harper's Mag.* Apr. 586/2 As I re-entered the bar-room labeled 'saloon', of mine inn. **1884** *N.Y. Herald* 27 Oct. 6/3 [Two men] demanded drinks in the saloon of ——, Myrtle avenue, Brooklyn. **1888** W. S. CAINE *Round the World* vii. 106 Here [at Rogers Pass, Canada] is a collection of wooden shanties, used as liquor-saloons, music and dancing-houses. **1892** J. RALPH in *Harper's Mag.* LXXXIV. 716/2 The fee for a permit to maintain a saloon or hotel bar in cities of more than 100,000 population is $1000. **1893** LELAND *Mem.* I. 282 A rather first-class saloon, bar, and restaurant on Broadway. **1902** 'N. GUBBINS' *Dead Certainties* 106 Exactly thirty days from the day upon which I first entered the accursed swing-doors of the Bull and Beehive, late one night, a stranger entered the 'saloon'. **1946** *Amer. Speech* XXI. 277 The English saloon-keeper was the keeper of the 'saloon', or as it would now be termed 'refreshment bar', in a London theatre. **1949** *Columbus* (Ohio) *Sunday Dispatch* 16 Oct. c1/3 He returned to Westerville in 1887 and opened a saloon at a new location on State St. **1969** HOUSE & STOREY *Lett. Charles Dickens* II. 454 Macready had gone to great lengths to civilize the saloon. **1976** *National Observer* (U.S.) 28 Aug. 13/1 People have been tossed out of saloons in downtown Utica, N.Y., with more style.

7. *attrib.* and *Comb.*: **a.** simple attrib., as *saloon licence, passengers, steward*, etc.; **b.** special comb., as **saloon bar**, a separate bar in a public house offering more comfort, services, etc. than the public bar; **saloon car, carriage**, (*a*) see 4 b above; (*b*) = 4 c above; **saloon deck**, a deck for the use of saloon passengers; **saloon-keeper** *U.S.*, one who keeps a drinking saloon; also, in British use, the keeper of a refreshment bar in a theatre; **saloon man** *U.S.*, one who frequents drinking saloons; **saloon pistol, rifle**, light firearms for firing at short range; **saloon smasher** *U.S. slang*, one who practises or advocates the practice of the wrecking of drinking saloons as a protest against the liquor traffic; so also *saloon smashing*; **saloon theatre**: see THEATRE *sb.* 2.

1902 G. HILL in G. Sims *Living London* II. 292/3 The distinction between the 'private' bar and the '*saloon' bar is subtle... The saloon bar is the ante-chamber of the billiard room. **1932** L. GOLDING *Magnolia St.* I. iii. 45 The Public Bar, nothing like so grand as the Saloon Bar, nothing like so cosy as the Private Bar. **1977** 'J. GASH' *Judas Pair* ii. 17 The saloon bar was crowded. **1915** *Motor Manual* (ed. 18) xi. 135 Landaulets, cabriolets, and *saloon cars. **1931** D. L. SAYERS *Five Red Herrings* xv. 167, I observed Mr. Gowan's saloon car standing before the door. **1974** *Country Life* 17 Oct. 1112/1 In post-war years we have had some very exciting saloon-car racing. **1888** W. S. CAINE *Round the World* i. 3 The *saloon-deck presents the usual aspect. Ladies are grouped about in pleasant corners in easy deck-chairs. **1849** *Theatrical Mirror* 10 Sept. 21 The 'Mirror' is supplied at most moderate prices to the *Saloon Keepers, in order to enable them to sell it to advantage. **1873** 'MARK TWAIN' *Gilded Age* lix. 530 Leave the true source of our political power..in the hands of saloon-keepers. **1879** G. CAMPBELL *Black & White* 242 The publicans, or saloon-keepers, as they are called in America. **1944** B. A. BOTKIN *Treas. Amer. Folklore* I. 131 He followed the construction of a new line on the Southern Pacific Railroad as camp saloon-keeper. **1977** *Times* 9 July 9/1 His grandfather was a poor tenant farmer..who became a saloon keeper. **1892** J. RALPH in *Harper's Mag.* LXXXIV. 712/1 The *saloon licence system is another village development. **1870** J. W. MCCLUNG *Minnesota* 213 Spring Valley, with 400 population..and no saloon. '*Saloon men cannot live in Spring Valley.' **1915** J. LONDON *Star Rover* ii. 9 You can weave the political pull of San Francisco saloon-men and ward heelers into a position of graft. **1879** FROUDE in *Fraser's Mag.* Nov. 625 The *saloon passengers were taken next. **1899** KIPLING *Stalky* 65 Rabbit-shooting with *saloon-pistols. **1881** GREENER *Gun* 368 *Saloon rifles..are small, smooth-bore guns,..firing a bulleted breech-cap... Pistols..are also made on the same principle. In all saloon rifles and pistols the propellant is fulminating powder contained in a small copper case. **1901** *Westm. Gaz.* 10 Dec. 9/2 The notorious *saloon smasher. **1905** *Daily Chron.* 11 July 5/7 '*Saloon-smashing' methods of reform by wrecking with dynamite buildings in which liquor selling was carried on.

saloon, obs. variant of SHALLOON.

saloonist (səˈluːnɪst). *U.S.* [f. SALOON + -IST.]

a. A saloon-keeper. **b.** One who upholds the system of drinking saloons.

1870 *Territorial Enterprise* (Virginia, Nevada) 3 Mar. 3/2 (*heading*) New saloonists. **1882** *Chicago Advance* 3 Aug. 499 Just think of a saloonist coming into court expecting to justify..his 'business' by exhibiting his 'license' as a contract by the people to let him sell liquor. **188.** *Pop. Sci. Monthly* XXX. 16 (Cent. Dict.) Any persistent effort to enforce the Sunday laws against the saloon is met by the saloonist with the counter-effort to enforce the laws against legitimate business. **1946** *Chicago Daily News* 8 Nov. 18/2 Saloonists voted out of business in the Woodlawn local option election talk of going to court to upset the vote.

saloop (səˈluːp). Also 8 **salob, salup**, 8–9 **saloup, salop**. [Altered form of SALEP.]

1. = SALEP.

1712 MRS. CENTLIVRE *Perplexed Lovers* v. i, Salup, what is that Salup? I have often seen this Fellow sauntering about Streets, and cou'd not imagine what he sold. **1719** D'URFEY *Pills* (1872) VI. 125 Here's Salop brought from foreign Parts. **1727** A. HAMILTON *Acc. E. Indies* I. 125 They [in Sind] have a Fruit..called Salob... They dry it hard..and being beaten to a Powder, they dress it as Tea and Coffee are, and take it with powdered Sugar-candy. **1728** [see 2]. **1747** MRS. GLASSE *Cookery* 120 To boil Salup. It is a hard Stone ground to Powder, and generally sold for one Shilling an Ounce. **1753** CHAMBERS *Cycl. Supp.*, *Orchisroot*, in the materia medica, is otherwise named salep, vulgarly called saloop. **1756** P. BROWNE *Jamaica* 325 The Jamaica Salop... It may be used with great propriety as a stomachic. **1766** *Ann. Reg.* 112 This powder is no other than that of sago or China salop. **1804** CHARLOTTE SMITH *Conversations*, etc. I. 94 The roots..of the orchis of which saloop is made. **1826** HENRY *Elem. Chem.* II. x. 266 Salop or Saloop is the farina obtained from several species of *Orchis*, especially the *O. Mascula*. **1851** MAYHEW *Lond. Labour* I. 8 Saloop (spelt also 'salep' and 'salop') was prepared, as a powder, from the root of the *Orchis mascula*. **1861** BENTLEY *Man. Bot.* 667 *Eulophia vera* and *E. campestris*.—The tubercular roots of these species are used in India in the preparation of the nutritious substance known by the names of Salep, Salop, and Saloop.

2. A hot drink consisting of an infusion of powdered salep or (later) of sassafras, with milk and sugar, formerly sold in the streets of London in the night and early morning.

1728 E. SMITH *Compl. Housew.* 149 To make Salop. Take ..Water, and let it boil..; then put in a quarter of an ounce of Salop finely powdered, and let it boil..; drink it in China Cups as Chocolate. *c* **1759** *Roxb. Ball.* (1890) VII. 58 Here's fine saloop, both hot and good. **1803** *Censor* 1 Dec. 135, I was taking my pot of saloop, (for I am not so extravagant as to drink coffee). **1822** LAMB *Elia* Ser. I. *Praise Chimneysw.*, There is a composition, the groundwork of which I have understood to be..sassafras. This wood boiled down to a kind of tea, and tempered with an infusion of milk and sugar, ..is saloop. **1840** PEREIRA *Elem. Mat. Med.* 799 Sassafras tea, flavoured with milk and sugar, is sold..under the name of saloop. **1851** MAYHEW *Lond. Labour* I. 183 The vending of tea and coffee, in the streets, was little..known twenty years ago, saloop being then the beverage supplied from stalls. **1882** BESANT *All Sorts* xviii, Those now forgotten delicacies, saloop and tansy pudding.

b. *attrib.*, as ***saloop-house, -man, -stall***, etc.

1764 *Low Life* (ed. 3) 1 The Salop-man in Fleet-Street shuts up his Gossiping Coffee-House. **1791** 'G. GAMBADO' *Ann. Horsem.* xvii. (1809) 136 He knock'd down and went over Alice Turner, the Saloup Woman. **1851** MAYHEW *Lond. Labour* I. 8/2 The saloop-stalls were superseded by the modern coffee-stalls. **1873** THORNBURY *Old & New Lond.* I. 69 A 'saloop-house', where the poor purchased a beverage made out of sassafras chips. **1889** *N. & Q.* 7th Ser. VII. 35 Within the last twenty years saloop vendors might have been seen plying their trade in the streets of London.

3. ***saloop bush*** (see quot.).

1884 MILLER *Plant-n.*, Saloop-bush, of Australia, *Rhagodia hastata*.

Hence **saˈlopian** *a.*[2], *nonce-wd.*

1822 LAMB *Elia* Ser. I. *Praise Chimneysw.*, Mr. Read, who hath time out of mind kept open a shop..for the vending of this 'wholesome and pleasant beverage'..—the only Salopian house.

‖**salopette** (salopɛt). [Fr.] A pair of overalls or dungarees of a kind worn orig. in France by workmen and later introduced for general wear, esp. as a skiing garment. Also in *pl.*

1972 *Guardian* 31 Oct. 11/2 Basically, the salopette is a Frenchman's overalls with a high waist, a bib front and adjustable shoulder straps, modified for skiing only by a snow cuff fitting snugly round your ankles. **1973** *Country Life* 21 June 1847/2 A summer salopette suit in glazed cotton. **1974** N. FREELING *Dressing of Diamond* 130 The old man..in his sleeveless vest and bib-and-brace *salopette*. **1977** *Guardian* 16 Mar. 9/2 Peter Blacklay is a doctor and he made a pair of bright red and blue nylon salopettes in a weekend. **1978** *Daily Tel.* 2 Feb. 15/4 Salopettes are far warmer and more comfortable..than stretch ski pants. **1980** *Woman's Jrnl.* Jan. 35/1 He wears a navy blue salopette.

salophen (ˈsæləʊfɛn). *Chem.* [f. SAL(ICYLIC) + -O[1] + PHEN(OL).] A derivative of salicylic acid (*Syd. Soc. Lex.* 1897).

1899 *Allbutt's Syst. Med.* VIII. 474 Such drugs as salicylate of sodium, salicin, salol, salophen and salipyrin.

Salopian (səˈləʊpɪən), *a.*[1] and *sb.* [f. *Salop*, a name of Shropshire (evolved from *Sloppesberie*, an AF. corruption of OE. *Scrobbesbyriȝ*, Shrewsbury, the county town) + -IAN.]

A. *adj.* **a.** Of or belonging to Shropshire.

1706 FARQUHAR *Recruiting Officer* III. ii, Thou Peerless Princess of Salopian Plains. *c* **1814** SOUTHEY *Affair Arroyo Molinos* 38 Salopian vales. **1886** T. L. K. OLIPHANT *New English* I. i. 9 A Salopian bard.

b. Designating a variety of porcelain made at the former Caughley manufactory (closed 1814) near Broseley, Shropshire in the late eighteenth and early nineteenth centuries. Also *transf.* Cf. CAUGHLEY.

1850 J. MARRYAT *Coll. Hist. Pott. & Porc.* ix. 182 The Salopian ware is very similar to the Derby in pattern and colouring. **1857** —— *Hist. Pott. & Porc.* xii. 297 The early Salopian porcelain was originally made..at Caughley. **1910** J. F. BLACKER *ABC of Collecting Old Eng. China* (ed. 3) III. 49 Salopian blue is somewhat similar in tone to that of Worcester. **1933** W. B. HONEY *Eng. Pott. & Proc.* II. xii. 190 The Caughley porcelain was known as 'Salopian'. *Ibid.* 191 The Salopian blue-painting..was mostly cribbed from Worcester and Chantilly. **1957** *Encycl. Brit.* XVIII. 354/1 Some Liverpool factories and that at Caughley (the 'Salopian' factory)..may be regarded as offshoots of Worcester.

c. *Geol.* Of, pertaining to, or designating an alternative division of the Silurian comprising the Wenlockian and (lower) Ludlovian. Freq. *absol.*

1879 C. LAPWORTH in *Ann. & Mag. Nat. Hist.* III. Table facing p. 455 Silurian System: Middle Division (Salopian). **1880** —— in *Ibid.* V. 48 The second natural division of the Silurian system is undoubtedly Murchison's Great Mudstone series, which includes the so-called Wenlock and Lower Ludlow groups... In Shropshire this great mudstone or *Salopian* formation is by far the most important physical group in the Silurian. **1883** J. E. MARR *Classification of Cambrian & Silurian Rocks* 42 No higher Salopian beds, and no Downtonian beds occur in North Wales, partly perhaps owing to subsequent denudation. **1929** O. T. JONES in Evans & Stubblefield *Handbk. Geol. Gt. Brit.* III. iv. 92 In certain areas Lapworth's term Salopian is sometimes useful, since the line of separation between Wenlock and Ludlow, represented by that between Lower and Upper Salopian, is not easy to determine. **1940** *Q. Jrnl. Geol. Soc.* XCV. 335 (*heading*) The geology of the Colwyn Bay district: a study of submarine slumping during the Salopian period. *Ibid.* 374 The strike of these structures.. indicates that the floor of the Salopian area in the Colwyn Bay region sloped from north to south. **1971** *Jrnl. Geol. Soc.* CXXVII. 104 Lapworth's..term *Salopian* was eventually extended upwards by O. T. Jones..to include the whole of the Ludlow as well as the Wenlock. It is thus still employed from time to time... It finds no place in our classification.

B. *sb.*

a. A native or inhabitant of Shropshire.

1700 CONGREVE *Way of World* IV. ii, Ay, ay, come, will you March my Salopian? **1886** T. L. K. OLIPHANT *New English* I. i. 6 William de Shoreham..uses *e* like the Salopians.

b. A pupil of Shrewsbury School.

1866 *Blackw. Mag.* Apr. 432/2 He has left us specimens of Latin verses of which even modern Salopians might be proud. **1898** *Public School Mag.* Dec. 487/2 'Swilling', a substitute for baths, is still an institution, of which every Salopian is proud. **1932** PENDLEBURY & WEST *Shrewsbury School* xi. 82 Nearly 2,000 Salopians saw active service... A sum of money was set aside to assist in the education of the sons of Old Salopians who had been killed. **1964** P. COWBURN *Salopian Anthol.* p. vi, This book..is to enable Salopians..to know what has been written about this particular school.

salopian, *a.*[2]: see SALOOP.

‖**salotto** (saˈlɔtto). Also (erron.) **salotta**; pl. **salotti**. [It. dim. f. SALA[1].] In Italy, a drawing-room, reception room; a lounge.

1918 G. FRANKAU *One of Them* xii. 87 Can we repay those ..midnight cocktails of your flowered *salotti*. **1924** D. H. LAWRENCE in M. Magnus *Mem. Foreign Legion* 51 So we went into the salotta. 'Oh, what a beautiful room,' he cried. **1930** E. POUND *XXX Cantos* xxvii. 126 In the salotto of that drummer's hotel. **1932** *Times Lit. Suppl.* 21 Jan. 38/3 Her prototype..can always be found in the cheerless *salotto* of a certain kind of Florentine pension.

salow(e: see SALLOW *sb.* and *a.*, SALUE *v.*

salp (sælp). *Zool.* Also **salpe**. [a. F. *salpe*, ad. mod.L. *salpa*.] = SALPA².

1835 KIRBY *Hab. & Inst. Anim.* I. vii. 222 The Salpes or biphores, as the French call them—phosphoric animals so transparent that all their internal organs.. may be distinctly seen. **1850** OGILVIE, *Salpa* or *Salp*, a genus of soft-shelled or tunicated acephalous molluscs which float in the sea. **1896** tr. *Boas' Text-bk. Zool.* 540 The chains remain within the body-wall of the solitary salp.

‖**'salpa**¹. *Obs.* [L. *salpa*, ad. Gr. σάλπη. Cf. F. *saupe*.] Some kind of salt-water fish used by the ancients as stockfish.

c **1520** ANDREW *Noble Lyfe* lxxix. in *Babees Bk.*, Salpa is a fowle fisshe and lytell set by. **1555** EDEN *Decades* 269 Dryed fysshe as soles, maydens, playces, salpas, stocke-fysshes, and such other. **1624** MIDDLETON *Game at Chess* v. iii, The *Salpa* from Ebusus [in ed. 1 and MSS. Eleusis]; or the *Pelamis* (which some call Sommer Whiting). **1706** PHILLIPS (ed. Kersey), *Salpa*, the Goldlin; a sort of Fish.

‖**Salpa**² ('sælpə). *Zool.* Pl. **salpæ**; also **salpas**. [mod.L. *salpa* (Forskål *a* 1763); prob. an application of class. L. *salpa* (see prec.), but the reason for the selection of this word does not appear.] A genus of tunicates, the sole representative of the family *Salpidæ*; also, a tunicate of this genus.

1852 TH. ROSS tr. *Humboldt's Trav.* I. i. 27 The genus dagysa.. belongs to the salpas (biphores of Bruguière). **1854** A. ADAMS *Man. Nat. Hist.* 336 Those curious double gelatinous animals the *Salpæ*, which resemble two little glassy bells, one fixed to the inside of the other. **1860** H. SPENCER in *Westm. Rev.* Jan. 102 In the *Salpæ* the component individuals adhere so slightly that a blow on the vessel of water in which they are floating will separate them. **1883** C. F. HOLDER in *Harper's Mag.* Dec. 107/1 The fantastic glaucus and luminous salpa, hover about in close attendance.

Hence **sal'pacean**, a salpian or salp.

1841 *Penny Cycl.* XX. 366/1.

Salpausselkä ('sælpaʊsɛlkə). *Physical Geogr.* Also **-selka**. [Finnish.] Each of two long, wide end moraines in southern Finland that are regarded as marking the last readvance of the ice sheet at the end of the Pleistocene.

1923 *Bull. de la Commission Géologique de Finlande* No. 60. 8 The southern slope toward the Gulf of Finland and Lake Laatokka (Ladoga).. consists of two faces of different grade: (1) The larger inner part, the Lake District of Finland, extending to the belt of the recessional moraines of Salpausselkä ('the damming ridge') and (2) the narrower bow-shaped Coast zone between the Salpausselkä and the coasts of Lake Laatokka and the sea. **1937** WOOLDRIDGE & MORGAN *Physical Basis Geogr.* xxii. 390 The great sand and gravel ridge which extends from east to west through Finland and is known as the Salpausselka. **1957** J. K. CHARLESWORTH *Quaternary Era* II. xxxi. 675 The Salpausselkä readvance,..of 12,000 years ago, has been linked with a temporary increase of snowfall. *Ibid.* xlii. 1172 The First or Outer Salpausselkä has a maximum altitude of 70–80 m, an average width of 2·5 km. **1968** R. W. FAIRBRIDGE *Encycl. Geomorphol.* 919/1 The upper boundary of the Pleistocene.. must lie somewhere between 10,000 and 10,500 years B.P., and may be defined as.. the time equivalents of sediments overlying the terminal moraines of the Valders (in North America) or the Salpausselkä (in Europe).

†**salpege**. *Obs. rare*⁻¹. [ad. mod.L. *salpega*, corruption of L. *sol(i)puga*.] Some kind of serpent.

1569 J. SANFORD tr. *Agrippa's Van. Arts* lxxxi. 138 Serpents, Salpeges, Scolopenders.

†**sal'petre**. *Obs.* Also 4–6 **salpeter**, 5 **salpetyr**, 6 **-ir**, **sall-petter**, **saulpeter**. [a. OF. *salpetre* (mod.F. *salpêtre*), ad. med.L. *salpetra*, prob. for *sal petræ* 'salt of stone' (*sal*, see SAL¹; *petræ* gen. of late L. *petra*, whence F. *pierre* stone), so called because the salt occurs as an incrustation on stones. Cf. G. *salpeter*.] Saltpetre.

c **1325** [see SAL-AMMONIAC]. **1384–5** *Durh. Acc. Rolls.* (Surtees) 594 Item pro Salpetre emp. pro Gonnis, vij s. vj d. *c c* **1386** CHAUCER *Can. Yeom. Prol. & T.* 255 Sal peter, vitriole. **1483** *Cath. Angl.* 317/2 Salpetyr. **1500–20** DUNBAR *Poems* lix. 9 A refyng sone of rakyng Muris.. That fulle dismemberit hes my meter, And poysound it with strang salpeter. **1601** HOLLAND *Pliny* II. xxxi. x. 421 The true marke to know good sal-petre, Is to be verie light in hand [etc.]. **1667** BOYLE *Orig. Formes & Qual.* (ed. 2) 115 It [*sc.* vitriol] is wont to be reckon'd with Sal-petre, Sea-salt, and Sal Gem among true Salts.

Hence †**sal-petery**, **salpetrous** *adjs.*, impregnated with salpetre, nitrous.

1608 SYLVESTER *Du Bartas* II. iv. III. *Schisme* 674 Rich Jericho's (sometimes) sal-peetry soyl.. Brought forth no fruit. **1731** BAILEY (vol. II), *Salpetrous*. **1883** D. COOK *On Stage* I. 221 Sparks and smoke and fearful salpetrous fumes.

salpian ('sælpɪən). [f. SALPA² + -IAN.] An individual of the genus *Salpa*; a salp.

1851 WOODWARD *Mollusca* 49 The salpians produce long chains of embryos. **1854** A. ADAMS *Man. Nat. Hist.* 164 Others among them [*sc.* the Tunicaries] are free and pelagian, as the Salpians and Pyrosomes.

‖**salpicon** ('sælpɪkɒn). *Cookery.* [Fr., a. Sp. *salpicon*, f. *salpicar* to sprinkle, pickle, f. *sal* salt + *picar* to pick.] A kind of stuffing for veal, beef, or mutton, also used as a garnish for vol-au-vents and the like.

1723 J. NOTT *Cook's & Confectioner's Dict.* sig. Gg7, Make a Hole in your Piece of roast Meat.. and pour the Salpicon into the Hole. **1726** *Dict. Rust.* (ed. 3), *Salpicon*, a Ragoe usually made for large Joints of Beef, Veal, or Mutton, which are to be served up roasted for the side Dishes. **1824** BYRON *Juan* xv. lxvi, Then there was.. 'A l'Espagnole', 'timballe', and 'salpicon'. **1828–32** WEBSTER (citing Bacon, prob. in error). **1877** E. S. DALLAS *Kettner's Bk. of Table* 81 *Bouchées*—Morsels—These are small Vol-au-vents.. filled with a salpicon of chicken, game or fish. **1906** *Mrs. Beeton's Bk. Househ. Managem.* lxi. 1651 Salpicon.—This name is applied to the various mixtures used in filling timbales, bombs, patty-cases. **1936** LUCAS & HUME *Au Petit Cordon Bleu* 44 Mix the sauce into the salmon, mushrooms, and onions and pour this *salpicon* on to the bottom of the dish. **1965** E. DAVID *French Provincial Cooking* (ed. 2) 99 *Salpicon*. May be one of a score of mixtures comprising flavouring vegetables, herbs, ham, veal, fish or meat but always cut into very small dice and bound into a thick white or brown sauce. Used as a stuffing, or as a garnish for little tartlets or *vols-au-vent*. **1977** *Time* 25 Apr. 17/2 He makes.. a saddle of boned lamb stuffed with a mousse of chicken, accompanied by a salpicon of kidneys, brains and sweetbreads.

salpiglossid (sælpɪ'glɒsɪd). [f. SALPIGLOSSIS: see -ID.] A plant of the tribe *Salpiglossideæ* (typical genus *Salpiglossis*: see SALPIGLOSSIS), one of Bentham's divisions of the order *Scrophulariaceæ*.

1846 LINDLEY *Veg. Kingd.* 682 Mr. Bentham remarks that the nearest Order to Figworts is undoubtedly that of Nightshades, through the medium of Salpiglossids.

salpiglossis (sælpɪ'glɒsɪs). [mod.L. (H. Ruiz & J. Pavon *Floræ Peruvianæ et Chilensis Prodromus* (1794) 94), irreg. f. Gr. σάλπιγξ trumpet + γλῶσσα tongue, from the trumpet-shaped corolla.] An annual or perennial herb of the genus so called, native to Chile and bearing funnel-shaped flowers of various colours.

1827 W. J. HOOKER *Exotic Flora* III. 229 (*heading*) Straw-coloured Salpiglossis. **1846** LINDLEY *Veg. Kingd.* 682 Petunia and Salpiglossis, two genera closely allied in habit. **1882** *Garden* 11 Nov. 426/1 The garden varieties of Salpiglossis rank amongst the finest of all half-hardy annuals. **1915** H. H. THOMAS *Bk. Hardy Flowers* 392 The great improvement in the size and colour of the flowers.. renders the Salpiglossis very desirable for beds and groups in the border. **1931** A. N. SCOTT tr. *Carossa's Boyhood & Youth* v. 72 A whole host of the most beautiful salpiglosses. **1962** R. PAGE *Educ. of Gardener* xii. 328, I remember a fantastic planting of yard-high salpiglossis in warm reds. **1979** *Daily Tel.* 26 May 30/2 The handsome salpiglossis.. will do very well from a May sowing out of doors.

salpingian (sæl'pɪndʒɪən), *a.* [f. mod.L. *salping-*, SALPINX 2 + -IAN.] Of or pertaining to the Eustachian or the Fallopian tubes. So **sal'pingic** *a.*, in the same sense.

1891 *Century Dict.*, Salpingian. **1897** *Syd. Soc. Lex.*, Salpingian, Salpingic.

‖**salpingitis** (sælpɪn'dʒaɪtɪs). *Path.* [mod.L., f. Gr. σαλπιγγ- (see SALPINGO-) + -ITIS.] Inflammation of the Fallopian or the Eustachian tubes.

1861 *Lancet* 14 Dec. 571/1. **1899** *Allbutt's Syst. Med.* VII. 481 Tuberculous salpingitis.

Hence **salpingitic** *a.*, pertaining to salpingitis.

1891 in *Century Dict.*

salpingo- (sæl'pɪŋgəʊ), combining form of Gr. σαλπιγγ-, σάλπιγξ, lit. 'trumpet', but used in mod.L. form *salpinx* to denote either the Fallopian or the Eustachian tubes. In various compounds (*Anat.*, *Phys.* and *Obstet.*): **salpin'gectomy** [-ECTOMY], excision of a Fallopian tube; **sal'pingogram**, an image of the Fallopian tubes obtained with X-rays or ultrasound; ˌ**salpingo'graphic** *a.*, of or pertaining to salpingography; **salpin'gography** [ad. G. *salpingographie* (F. Schoker 1925, in *Zentralbl. f. Gynaekol.* XLIX. 290)], the process or technique of obtaining salpingograms; **salpin'golysis** [mod.L. (coined in Fr. by P. E. Goullioud 1914, in *Lyon Médicale* CXXII. 689): see -LYSIS], the removal of adhesions that constrain the Fallopian tubes in abnormal positions with respect to the ovaries and hence prevent conception; **salˌpingo'nasal** *a.*, of or pertaining to the Eustachian tube and the nose; **salˌpingo-oöpho'rectomy**, **-ovari'otomy**, excision of a Fallopian tube and ovary; **salpingo-oöpho'ritis**, salpingitis and oöphoritis occurring together; **salˌpingo-'palatal**, **-'palatine** *adjs.*, of or pertaining to the Eustachian tube and the palate; **salˌpingo-pharyn'geal** *a.*, belonging to the Eustachian tube and the pharynx; ‖**salˌpingo-pha'ryngeus**, an occasional muscle passing from the Eustachian tube to the pharynx; **salpingo-'pterygoid** *a.*, pertaining to the sphenoid and hamular processes; **salpin'gorrhaphy**, suturing of the Fallopian tube; **salpin'gostomy**, 'the operation of establishing an artificial fistula of the Fallopian tube' (*Syd. Soc. Lex.* 1897); **salpin'gotomy**, excision of or incision into the Fallopian tube (*ibid.*).

1888 W. H. & H. T. BYFORD *Pract. Med. & Surg.* (ed. 4) 816/2 (Index), *Salpingectomy. **1897** *Amer. Jrnl. Med. Sci.* CXIV. 497 (*heading*) The stump after salpingectomy. **1978** G. VIDAL *Kalki* i. 5 In perfect health and with maximum publicity at the Marie Stopes Clinic in Daly City, I underwent a bilateral partial salpingectomy, better known as 'Band-Aid Surgery'. **1927** *Surg., Gynecol. & Obstetr.* XLV. 140/2 By means of roentgenological study after the injection of iodized oil, an accurate uterogram and *salpingogram, visualizing the entire internal female generative tract, may be obtained in cases in which the Fallopian tubes are not occluded. **1964** BROWNE & MCCLURE BROWNE *Postgrad. Obstetr. & Gynaecol.* (ed. 3) xii. 158 If the salpingogram seems normal and tubercle is suspected, an endometrial biopsy should be done. **1927** *Surg., Gynecol. & Obstetr.* XLV. 132/2 Rosenblatt.. reported his *salpingographic observations on three women who had submitted to the Alexander-Adams operation for sterility. **1935** *Ibid.* LX. 228/1 *Salpingography is.. of value in determining the presence or absence of tubes in patients who have had a previous operation on the adnexa but are uncertain of its nature. **1976** G. BERCI *Endoscopy* xvii. 236/1 The use of combined laparoscopy and intra-operative salpingography employing television fluoroscopy with aimed spot films allows the most complete evaluation of uterine and tubal anatomy conducted during a single procedure. **1937** *Amer. Jrnl. Obstetr. & Gynecol.* XXXIII. 39 When the occlusion is at the fimbriated end [of the fallopian tubes], simple release of adhesions may suffice to restore the patency of the tube (*salpingolysis). **1980** *Fertility & Sterility* XXXIV. 223/1 In Table 1 are listed the pregnancy rates after bilateral salpingolysis, bilateral salpingostomy, [etc.]. **1890** *Johns Hopkins Hosp. Bull.* I. 57/1 Eight cases of *salpingo-oöphorectomy for fibroids are symptomatically relieved of their pressure symptoms. **1977** *Proc. R. Soc. Med.* LXX. 189/2 Fig 1 shows the ureter deliberately exposed in relation to a clamp placed across the infundibulopelvic ligament during the course of a hysterectomy and left salpingo-oophorectomy. **1904** *Brit. Med. Jrnl.* 3 Dec. *Epit.* 83 Acute appendicitis with concomitant *salpingo-oöphoritis. **1884** M. MACKENZIE *Dis. Throat & Nose* II. 253 The yellow orifice of the Eustachian tube can be seen, bounded by the *salpingo-palatine fold on its inner, and the *salpingo-pharyngeal fold on its outer side. **1891** E. SAJOUS in *Ann. Univ. Med. Sci.* II. Sect. G. 31 This operation he [Skutsch] calls *salpingostomy. **1899** *Allbutt's Syst. Med.* VIII. 491 A successful *salpingotomy for a hypertrophied left ovary.

‖**salpinx** ('sælpɪŋks). [Gr. σάλπιγξ; in sense 2 used as mod.L.]

1. *Antiq.* An ancient Greek trumpet.

1865 J. HULLAH *Transit. Period Mus.* 118 The pipe of Pan, the lyre of Mercury, the salpinx [etc.]. **1888** *Encycl. Brit.* XXIII. 592/2 The Roman tuba and the Greek salpinx are supposed to be one and the same instrument.

2. *Anat.* **a.** The Eustachian tube. **b.** The Fallopian tube.

1842 BRANDE *Dict. Sci.*, etc., *Salpinx*, the Eustachian tube, or channel of communication between the mouth and the ear. [In recent Dicts.]

‖**sal-prunella** (ˌsælpruː'nɛlə). Also 8 **sal prunellæ**, **prunel**, 9 **prunelle**. [mod.L. *sal prunella* or *prunellæ*: see SAL and PRUNELLA³.] Fused nitre cast into cakes or balls.

1681 tr. *Willis' Rem. Med. Wks.* Vocab., *Sal-prunella*, a salt made out of salt-peter. **1747** WESLEY *Prim. Physic* (1762) 30 Two teaspoonfuls of Sal Prunellæ an hour before the Fit. **1778** JOHNSON in *Boswell*, In Mrs. Glasse's Cookery.... salt-petre and sal-prunella are spoken of as different substances, whereas sal-prunella is only salt-petre burnt on charcoal. **1812** J. SMYTH *Pract. of Customs* (1821) 198 Sal Prunelle is a preparation of Saltpetre, useful in Medicine and in curing provisions. **1849** D. CAMPBELL *Inorg. Chem.* 108 Nitrate of potash.. when cast into moulds, solidifies, and is known in this form as sal-prunelle.

salrar, obs. form of CELLARER.

1473 *Rental Bk. Cupar-Angus* (1879) I. 201 Twynty suklar kyddis.. to be kepit and delyuerit at the ordinans of the salrar and wardane.

sals, obs. form of SAUCE.

salsa ('sælsə, ‖'salsa). [Sp.; cf. SAUCE *sb.*]

‖**1.** *Cookery.* A variety of sauce served with meat. Also *Comb.*

1846 R. FORD *Gatherings from Spain* xi. 132 What sort of a stew is it? Let me smell and taste the *salsa*. **1935** J. STEINBECK *Tortilla Flat* xvi. 289 Her two sons.. carried a wash-tub of salsa pura between them. **1973** *Listener* 18 Jan. 98/2 Serve the meat... Horse-radish, *salsa verde*, spicy tomato sauce.. all go very well. **1978** *Tucson Mag.* Dec. 84/3 Steak and salsa rate high.

2. [Amer. Sp.] A kind of dance music of Latin American origin which incorporates elements of jazz and rock music; a dance performed to this music.

1975 *New Yorker* 29 Sept. 41/3 The group I play with consists of some Latin kids who are not afraid to break out of pure salsa. **1975** *N.Y. Times* 11 Nov. 61/5 Take the sound and percussion rhythm of an eight-piece Latin band; add a mixture of mambo, cha cha and merengue dance steps;.. simmer gently for about 10 to 15 minutes on a crowded dance floor; add a pinch and a squeeze and you have it—salsa. **1976** *Monitor* (McAllen, Texas) 21 Oct. 5B/3 The Caribbean has given us gentle calypso and Trinidad's brash steel bands,.. the spicy latin 'salsa' of Puerto Rico and the whimsical chants and big beat of Jamaican reggae. **1978** *Detroit Free Press* 5 Mar. D16/5 San Juan's major hotels have lounge bands that specialize in salsa (Latin rhythm with a jazz beat). **1981** *Weekly Guardian* 12 July 17/1 Salsa music drifts out of the bar as a group of grease-spattered youths tinker with the engine of a new Toyota.

salsaf(a)y, salsage: see SALSIFY, SAUSAGE *sb.*

‖**salsamen'tarious,** *a.* *Obs.*$^{-0}$ [ad. L. *salsāmentāri-us* (f. *salsāmentum* pickling brine, pickled fish) + -OUS.] 'Of or belonging to salt, or to any salt thing' (Blount *Glossogr.* 1656).

salsaparilha, -illa, -illia, -perilla, -parillin: see SARSAPARILLA, -PARILLIN.

salsar, -ary: see SAUCER *sb.*, SAUCERY.

†**salsature.** *Alch. Obs.* [ad. med.L. *salsātūra* (Raymond Lull), f. L. *sals-us* salted, salt.]

1650 ASHMOLE *Chym. Collect.* 3–4 By another digestion it will be another thing, which we call Argent Vive, Earth, Water, and Ferment, Gumm and our second Salsature,.. In our Magisteriall there are three proper Earths, three Waters, and three proper Ferments; three proper Gumms, three Salsatures, three Argent Vives Congealing.

salse (sæls). *Geol.* [a. F. *salse* (Humboldt), ad. It. *salsa*, orig. proper name of a mud volcano at Sassuolo, near Modena.] A mud volcano.

1832 DE LA BECHE *Geol. Man.* 133 'Salses' or mud volcanoes. **1871** KINGSLEY *At Last* x, Now and then this 'Salse'.. is said to be seized with a violent paroxysm. **1878** HUXLEY *Physiogr.* 202 Conical hills, known as Salses, or mud volcanoes.

salser, -ery: see SAUCER *sb.*, SAUCERY.

salsify ('sælsɪfɪ). Also 7 **salsifax, (salsfy),** 8 **sassafy, salsafay,** 8–9 **salsafy.** [a. F. *salsifis* (in the 16–17th c. variously *sercifi, serquify, sassify, sassefy, sassefique, sassefrique*), believed to be corruptly ad. It. *sassefrica*, of unknown origin. Cf. Sp. *salsifí*, Pg. *sersifim*.]

1. A biennial composite plant, the Purple Goat's-beard, *Tragopogon porrifolius*, indigenous to Great Britain and the Continent of Europe, producing an esculent root.

meadow salsify (U.S.): the Yellow Goat's-beard, *Tragopogon pratensis* (Britton & Brown *Flora Northern U.S.* III. 269).

1706 PHILLIPS (ed. Kersey), *Salsifie, (Fr.)* Goats-bread [*sic*], an eatable root. **1707** MORTIMER *Husb.* 482 Salsifie or Goats-beard. **1731** MILLER *Gard. Dict., Tragopogon*.. commonly call'd Salssafy or Sassafy. **1747** MRS. GLASSE *Cookery* xiv. (1796) 229 So likewise you may dress root of salsify and scorzonera. **1767** ABERCROMBIE *Ev. Man his own Gard.* (1803) 85 Salsafay is estimable both for its roots.. and for the young shoots rising in the spring. **1830** LINDLEY *Nat. Syst. Bot.* 201 Many of the species are useful articles of food; ..for instance.. the roots of.. Tragopogon, or Salsafy. **1881** *Encycl. Brit.* XII. 287/2 The Salsafy (or Salsify).. is a hardy biennial, with long cylindrical fleshy esculent roots. **1882** *Garden* 11 Nov. 425/3 Salsafy.. when boiled in milk or fried in butter.. has a peculiar resemblance to oysters.

2. black, †**Spanish salsify,** *Scorzonera hispanica*, producing a dark esculent root, used in the same way as salsify (sense 1).

1699 EVELYN *Acetaria* 61 Salsifax, *Scorzonera.* **1707** MORTIMER *Husb.* 482 Spanish Salsifie or Scorzonera, is multiplied by Seed. **1891** *Century Dict.* s.v., *Black salsify*,.. a related plant... It is similarly used, and its flavor is preferred by some.

†**sal'sipotent,** *a.* *Obs. rare.* [ad. L. *salsipotentem* (as if f. *sals-um* neut. adj., salt), a false reading for *sali-potentem*, f. *sal-um* salt water + *potentem* POTENT *a.*] That rules the salt sea.

1575 LANEHAM *Let.* (1871) 33 The supreame salsipotent Monarch Neptune. **1656** in Blount *Glossogr.*

salsister, variant of SAUCISTER *Obs.*

†**'salsitude.** *Obs. rare.* [a. F. *salsitude*, ad. L. *salsitūdo*, f. *salsus* adj., salt: see -TUDE.] Saltness, brackishness.

1623 COCKERAM I, *Salcitude*, brine liquor that is salt. *Ibid.* II, *Brine*, salsitude. *a* **1693** *Urquhart's Rabelais* III. xxxii. 271 Their.. smarting Salsitude. **1696** J. EDWARDS *Demonstr. Exist. & Provid. God* I. 171 The heat of the sun is not the cause of the salsitude of the waters. **1721–** in BAILEY.

†**'salso-'acid,** *a.* and *sb.* *Obs.* [f. *salso-*, assumed comb. form of L. *salsus* adj., salt.] **a.** 'Having a taste compounded of saltness and sourness' (J.). **b.** *sb.* A substance partaking of the qualities of a 'salt' and an 'acid'.

1697 SIR J. FLOYER *Enq. Baths* 17 Salso-acid Baths. *Ibid.* 20 Salso-acid Medicines. **1707** —— *Physic. Pulse-Watch* 335 Salso Acids, volatile Salt, or fix'd Vitriolate, *Sal Catharticum* is a nauseous, bitterish, Salso Acid.

sal-soda: see SAL b.

‖**Salsola** ('sælsələ). [mod.L. (Cæsalpinus *De Plantis* 1583 IV. xxxix. 170), a. It. †*salsola*, dim. of *salso* salt *adj.*] A genus of herbaceous plants belonging to the N.O. *Chenopodiaceæ*, found on the sea-coasts and salt-impregnated soils of warm and temperate regions, chiefly in the Old World; esp. *S. soda*, a species yielding soda. Also, a plant of this genus.

1801 J. BARROW *Trav. S. Africa* ii. 91 The plant.. was a species of *salsola*, or salt-wort. **1890** E. F. KNIGHT *Cruise of 'Alerte'* iv. 57 [An island] green with salsola or saltwort and other alcalescent plants.

salsolaceous (sælsə'leɪʃəs), *a.* [See -ACEOUS.] Belonging to or resembling the genus SALSOLA.

1859 H. KINGSLEY *G. Hamlyn* xlii, The salsolaceous plants, so long the only vegetation we have seen, are gone. **1863** SPEKE *Source of Nile* i. 6 A small island.. covered with salsolacious shrubs. **1880** J. C. CRAWFORD *New Zealand & Austral.* 8 Dry plains thinly clad with a salsolaceous vegetation.

salss, obs. Sc. form of SAUCE.

†**'salster.** *Obs.* [Formed after SALTER: see -STER.] A female salter.

14.. *Nom.* in Wr.-Wülcker 692/37 *Hec salinaria*, a salster.

salsuginous (sæl'sjuːdʒɪnəs), *a.* Also 7 **-eous, -os.** [f. L. *salsūgin-em* saltness (f. *sals-us* adj., salt) + -OUS.] †**a.** Impregnated with salt; brackish. *Obs.* **b.** Of plants: Growing in salt-impregnated soil.

1657 TOMLINSON *Renou's Disp.* 677 A certain.. salsugineous liquor is educed. **1664** BOYLE *Experim. Colours* III. xl. Refl. 314 Salts.. are discriminated into Acid, Volatile, or Salsuginous (if I may for Distinction sake so call the Fugitive Salts of Animal Substances) and fix'd or Alcalizate. **1665** DUDLEY *Mettall. Martis* (1851) 38 His white Arcenical, Salsuginos and Sulphurious substance which is in that Cole. **1669** W. SIMPSON *Hydrol. Chym.* 54 If this acidulated water find a salsuginous glebe, it becomes coagulated. **1731** MEDLEY *Kolben's Cape G. Hope* II. 302 'Tis owing to the salsuginous nature of the valley grass, that the Cape graziers never give.. their.. cattle any salt to lick. **1897** *Syd. Soc. Lex., Salsuginous*, epithet applied to plants that grow in a soil that is impregnated with common salt.

†**'salsure.** *Obs.*$^{-0}$ [ad. L. *salsūra*, f. *sals-us* adj., salt.] 'A salting or seasoning brine' (Blount *Glossogr.* 1656).

1658 in PHILLIPS; **1721–** in BAILEY.

salt (sɒlt, -ɔː-), *sb.*[1] Forms: 1 **sealt,** (3 **salit,** *Ormin* **sallt),** 4–6 **salte,** (5 **sawte,** 6 **saulte),** 6–7 **sault,** 8–9 *Sc.* **saut, sawt,** 1– **salt.** [Com. Teut.: OE. *sealt* (*salt*) str. neut. = OFris. **salt* (mod.Fris. *salt, sâ(l)t, saut, solt*), OS. *salt* (MLG. *salt, solt*), MDu., Du. *zout*, OHG. (MHG., G.) *salz*, ON. (Sw., Da.), Goth. *salt*:—OTeut. *salto*^{m}, cogn. with Gr. ἅλ-ς masc., L. *sal* masc., neut. (whence F. *sel*, Sp., Pg., Pr. *sal*, It. *sale*), OIr. *salann*, W. *halen*, OSl. *solĭ*.]

1. a. A substance, known chemically as sodium chloride (NaCl), very abundant in nature both in solution and in crystalline form, and extensively prepared for use as a condiment, a preservative of animal food, and in various industrial processes. Salt for domestic use is manufactured from SEA-SALT (***marine-salt***, BAY-SALT), ROCK-SALT (***mineral salt***, † ***salt mineral***), and (now chiefly) from brine pumped up from rock-salt strata. Frequently called ***common salt***.

c **1000** *Sax. Leechd.* II. 76 Wiþ blæce, wyl eolonan on buteran, meng wiþ sote, sealt, teoro. *Ibid.* 344 Do haliʒes sealtes fela on. *c* **1200** ORMIN 1653 Forr witt & skill iss wel inoh þurrh sallt sallte smacc bitacnedd. *c* **1290** *S. Eng. Leg.* 187/95 So þat þe salt scholde is woundene frete with þe brenninde fuyre. **1398** TREVISA *Barth. De P.R.* XVI. xciv. (Bodl. MS.), Salte makeþ potage and oþer mete sauourye. **14..** *Pol. Rel. & L. Poems* (1903) 245 Nad I ben babtyzyd in water and salt. *c* **1460** J. RUSSELL *Bk. Nurture* 57 Loke þy salte be sutille, whyte, fayre and drye. **1557** SEAGER *Sch. Vertue* 440 in *Babees Bk.*, Saulte with thy knyfe then reache and take. **1620** VENNER *Via Recta* vi. 92 The best and most common of all Sauces is Salt. **1661** J. CHILDREY *Brit. Bacon.* 50 They boile Salt out of Salt-water. **1729** [see SALT-CELLAR]. **1774** GOLDSM. *Nat. Hist.* (1776) VII. 146 Salt seems to be much more efficacious in destroying these animals [*sc.* lizards], than the knife. **1833–4** J. PHILLIPS *Geol.* in *Encycl. Metrop.* (1845) VI. 614/2 Regular strata of gypsum below, and regular layers of salt above. **1839** URE *Dict. Arts* 1087 The rock is a mass of saccharoid and anhydrous gypsum, imbued with common salt. **1870** YEATS *Nat. Hist. Comm.* 380 Beds of salt occur.. in China, and many districts of North America.

b. With qualifying word.

white salt: salt prepared and refined mainly for household use (as contrasted with rock-salt, which is of a brownish red colour). † ***great salt***: salt in large crystals or lumps; rock-salt. † ***small salt***: salt powdered as for table use. † ***Pattow, Pateu salt*** [i.e. Poitou salt = F. '*sel de Poictou*, blacke salt, gray salt' Cotgr.]: ? a coarse kind of salt manufactured in Poitou. Also ***Newcastle, Spanish salt***.

c **1000** *Sax. Leechd.* I. 138 Cnuca mid greatan sealte. *Ibid.* III. 20 Ado.. hwites sealtes fela. **1377–8** *Durham Acc. Rolls* (Surtees) 586 In 2 quar. de Pattowsalt, 7*s.* 3*d.* **1390** GOWER *Conf.* II. 63 In stede of Oxes He let do yoken grete foxes, And with gret salt the lond he siew. **1486** *Bk. St. Albans* C vj, Put therto spanyshe salte. **1583–4** *Reg. Privy Council Scot.* Ser. I. III. 638 Na small salt sould be careit furth of this realme. **1614** T. GENTLEMAN *Eng. Way to Win Wealth* 24 Ships may come vnto them with Salt from Mayo, or Spanish salt. **1728** CHAMBERS *Cycl.* s.v., The Salt is brown when taken out of the Pits,.. in some Places they make it into White-Salt by refining. **1748** BROWNRIGG *Art of Making Salt* 50 Northumberland and Durham; from whence this salt is exported in large quantities, under the name of Newcastle salt. **1883** *Fisheries Exhib. Catal.* 74 Fishery Salt .. Common Salt, Middle Grain Salt, Table Salt,.. Kitchen Salt. **1886** *Encycl. Brit.* XXVI. 232/1 As usually made, white salt from rock-salt may be classified into two groups.

†**c.** ***salt upon salt***: see quot. 1748. *Obs.*

1580 HITCHCOCK *Politic Plat* A ij b, To.. barrill theim [*sc.* herrings] after the Flemishe maner, with salte vpon salte, whiche is the beste kinde of Salt. **1614** T. GENTLEMAN *Eng. Way to Win Wealth* 24 This place [*sc.* Ipswich] is also most conuenient for the erecting of Salt-pans, for the making of Salt vpon salt. **1682** J. COLLINS *Salt & Fishery* 13 Of Salt upon Salt, or Salt made by Refining of Forreign Salt. **1748** BROWNRIGG *Art of Making Salt* 49 Salt upon salt; which is bay salt dissolved in sea water, or any other salt water, and with it boiled into white salt.

fig. **1659** G. WITHER (*title*) Salt upon Salt: made out of certain ingenious verses upon the late Storm and the death of his Highness ensuing.

d. ***in salt***: sprinkled with salt or immersed in brine; in pickle.

1853 SOYER *Pantroph.* 187 Let it remain in salt during twenty-four hours.

2. Proverbial and allusive uses. **a.** *gen.*

1539 TAVERNER *Erasm. Prov.* (1552) 57 Passe not ouer salt and the table: as who shulde saye, neglecte not the Company of frendes, or breake not the lawe of amitie. *c* **1589** R. HARVEY *Pl. Perc.* (1860) 9 Seruice without salt, by the rite of England, is a Cuckholds fee, if he claime it. **1596** HARINGTON *Metam. Ajax* (1814) 3 The poor sheep would eat him without salt (as they say). *c* **1678** MARVELL *Growth Popery* 23 As much out of order, as if the Salt had been thrown down, or an Hare had crossed his way. **1681** FLAVEL *Meth. Grace* iii. 50 Some account the falling of salt upon the table ominous. **1865** S. EVANS *Bro. Fab. MS.*, etc. 49 If the salt thou chance to spill, Token sure of coming ill. **1884** *Harper's Mag.* Nov. 889/1 They threw the salt over their shoulders,.. in propitiation of evil powers, when they spilled it at table.

b. Taken as a type of a necessary adjunct to food, and hence as a symbol of hospitality. Phr. ***to eat salt with*** (a person), ***to eat*** (a person's) ***salt***: to enjoy his hospitality; also occas. to be dependent upon him. ***bread and salt***: see BREAD *sb.* 2 d.

1382 WYCLIF *Ezra* iv. 14 Wee thanne mynde hauende of the salt that in the paleis wee eeten. **1539** TAVERNER *Erasm. Prov.* 30 Trust no man onles thou hast fyrst eaten a bushel of salte with hym. [Cf. Gr. τῶν ἁλῶν συγκατεδηδοκέναι μέδιμνον.] **1581** PETTIE tr. *Guazzo's Civ. Conv.* I. (1586) 11 b, You who haue eaten much salt out of your owne house. **1608** BP. HALL *Epist.* I. viii, Abandon those from your table and salt, whom your own.. experience shall descry dangerous. **1809** WELLINGTON in Gleig *Life* App. (1862) 702 The real fact is .. I have eaten the King's salt. **1813** BYRON *Corsair* II. iv, Why dost thou shun the salt? that sacred pledge, Which, once partaken.. Makes ev'n contending tribes in peace unite. **1854** THACKERAY *Newcomes* I. v. 43 One does not eat a man's salt, as it were, at these dinners. There is nothing sacred in this kind of London hospitality. **1889** NORRIS *Miss Shafto* i, One has no business to eat a man's salt and then say nasty things about him.

c. In allusions to the jocular advice given to children to catch birds by putting salt on their tails.

1580 LYLY *Euphues* (Arb.) 327 It is.. a foolish bird that staieth the laying salt on hir taile. **1664** BUTLER *Hud.* II. i. 278 Such great Atchievements cannot fail, To cast Salt on a Woman's Tail. **1704** SWIFT *T. Tub* vii, Men catch Knowledge by throwing their Wit on the Posteriors of a Book, as Boys do Sparrows by flinging Salt upon their Tails. **1721** KELLY *Scot. Prov.* 380 You will ne'er cast Salt on his Tail. That is, he has clean escap'd. **1813** SOUTHEY *Nelson* viii, If they go on playing this game, some day we shall lay salt upon their tails. **1840** DICKENS *Barn. Rudge* xxvii, Having dropped a pinch of salt on the tails of all the cardinal virtues and caught them every one. **1893** STEVENSON *Catriona* I. viii, I will never be persuaded that you could not help us.. to put salt on Alan's tail.

d. ***with a grain of salt*** [= mod.L. *cum grano salis*]: (to accept a statement) with a certain amount of reserve. Also in similar phrases, now esp. ***with a pinch of salt***.

1647 TRAPP *Comm. Rev.* vi. 11 This is to be taken with a grain of salt. **1648** SPARKE *Pref. to Shute's Sarah & Hagar* b j b, Read them then but with such a grain of salt as intimated. **1883** *American* VI. 280 An Extremist,—and we may add more or less salt to his expressions. **1908** *Athenæum* 1 Aug. 118/1 Our reasons for not accepting the author's pictures of early Ireland without many grains of salt. **1948** F. R. COWELL *Cicero & Roman Republic* xvi. 243 A more critical spirit slowly developed, so that Cicero and his friends took more than the proverbial pinch of salt before swallowing everything written by these earlier authors. **1949** V. GROVE *Language Bar* ii. 29 Even if we accept such a statement with a pinch of salt, it is an undisputable fact that its writer did look upon Latin as a guiding mistress. **1965** M. SHADBOLT *Among Cinders* xxvi. 258, I take what he says with a half-pound of salt, after his review of that play. **1981** J. S. BRATTON *Impact of Victorian Children's Fiction* ii. 41 We must take William Jones's enthusiasm about the eagerness of [tract] readers with a pinch of salt.

e. With reference to the bitter saline taste of tears.

1595 SHAKS. *John* v. vii. 45 *Hen.* Oh that there were some vertue in my teares, That might releeue you. *John.* The salt in them is hot. **1602** —— *Ham.* I. ii. 154 The salt of most vnrighteous Teares. **1824** GALT *Rothelan* I. I. v. 43 There was salt as well as sorrow in her tears.

f. ***not to be made of sugar or salt***: not to be readily affected by moisture; hence, not to be disconcerted by wet weather.

1786 *Har'st Rig* lxxxi. (1794) 27 But Highlanders ne'er mind a douk, For they're na'e sawt. **1855** CARLYLE in *E. Fitz-Gerald's Lett.* (1889) I. 235, I persist in believing the weather will clear,.. at any rate I am not made of sugar or of salt. **1870** MISS BRIDGMAN *R. Lynne* I. xv. 254, I am made neither of sugar nor salt... Do you call this rain?

g. (*to be*) ***worth one's salt***: efficient or capable. Usually with expressed or implied negative.

1830 MARRYAT *King's Own* lii, The captain.. is not worth his salt. **1857** HUGHES *Tom Brown* II. v, Every one who is worth his salt has his enemies. **1883** STEVENSON *Treas. Isl.* xviii, It was plain from every line of his body that our new hand was worth his salt.

h. With reference to the saltness of the sea, in phrases denoting fondness for or adaptability to a seafaring life. (Cf. 11.)

1886 *Illustr. Lond. News* 10 July 42/3, 'I would be a sailor, if only before the mast'. 'Why there!' cried the admiral... 'What else could the boy be? He is salt all through'. **1901** *Daily Chron.* 24 May 3/3 The man.. with the salt in his blood, and a yearning for the blue water.

i. ***to rub salt in one's wounds***: to behave or speak to someone so as to aggravate a hurt already inflicted.

1944 [see CURL *v.*[1] 1 c]. **1967** WODEHOUSE *Company for Henry* x. 182 He could see that Henry was deeply stirred, and he had no wish to rub salt in his wounds. **1973** *Guardian* 16 Feb. 13/8 Mr. Nixon's treatment for war wounds is rubbing salt in them.

3. *fig.* **a.** ***the salt of the earth*** (after Matt. v. 13): the excellent of the earth; formerly, in trivial use, the powerful, aristocratic, or wealthy; now also applied to a person or persons of great worthiness, reliability, honesty, etc.

c **950** *Lindisf. Gosp.* Matt. v. 13 Ȝee sint salt eorðes. *c* **1386** CHAUCER *Sompn. T.* 488 Ye been the salt of the erthe and the savour. ?*c* **1420** 26 *Pol. Poems* xxi. 145 Of erþe ȝe ben cleped salt, For salt of wisdom soule saues. **1579** LYLY *Euphues* (Arb.) 141 The vniuersities of Christendome which should be.. the leauen, the salt, the seasoning of the world. **1790** H. VENN in Carus *Life C. Simeon* 84 They are the truly excellent of the earth—its salt, who.. reach the heart and conscience. **1842** *Literary Gaz.* 28 May 371/3 To dine like queens, kings, princes, potentates, and the other 'salt of the earth'. **1869** RAWLINSON *Anc. Hist.* 517 The army was, under the Imperial system, the 'salt' of the Roman world. **1871** MORLEY *Carlyle* in *Crit. Misc.* Ser. I. (1878) 195 A little band, the supposed salt of the earth. **1916** G. B. SHAW *Androcles & Lion* p. xv, They may not be the salt of the earth, these Philistines; but they are the substance of civilization. **1931** T. R. G. LYELL *Slang, Phrase & Idiom* 659 If he's a friend of yours, you're a lucky man, for if ever a fellow was one of the salt of the earth, he is. He's the best man I've ever met, in every way. **1948** E. S. GARDNER *D.A. takes Chance* x. 103 Eve was a mighty fine girl, and her mother is the salt of the earth. **1951** E. M. FORSTER *Two Cheers for Democracy* I. 56 If you don't like people, kill them, banish them, segregate them, and then strut up and down proclaiming that you are the salt of the earth. **1953** WODEHOUSE *Performing Flea* 78 You dine with the President on Monday, and he slaps you on the back and tells you you are the salt of the earth, and on Tuesday morning you get a letter from him saying you are fired. **1976** N. THORNBURG *Cutter & Bone* vi. 148 And such *good* friends they were too. Real salt of the earth.

b. That which gives liveliness, freshness, or piquancy to a person's character, life, etc. Often in phr. ***salt of youth***, from Shakspere.

1579 TOMSON *Calvin's Serm. Tim.* 688/1 They are such that haue neither salt nor sause in them. **1598** SHAKS. *Merry W.* II. iii. 56 Wee haue some salt of our youth in vs. **1698** NORRIS *Pract. Disc.* (1707) IV. 26 The Things of Religion, that Divine Salt, that will give a wholesome and relishing savour to our Conversation. *a* **1718** PENN *Tracts* in *Wks.* (1726) I. 732 A Man insipid, of no Sense or Salt. **1822** HAZLITT *Table-t.* II. ii. 24 His character has the salt of honesty about it. **1865** TROLLOPE *Belton Est.* xiv. 153 He was a man not yet forty years of age, with still much of the salt of youth about him. **1879** M. ARNOLD *Mixed Ess., Democracy* 19 A people without the salt of these qualities would arrive at the pettiness of China.

c. That which gives life or pungency to discourse or written composition; poignancy of expression; pungent wit; †point. ***Attic salt***: see ATTIC *a.* 2.

1573–80 BARET *Alv.* s.v., *Salte*, a pleasaunt and mery worde that maketh folke to laugh and sometimes pricketh. **1609** *Shaks.'s Tr. & Cr.* Ep. (Qo. 1), So much and such sauored salt of witte is in his Commedies, that [etc.]. **1639** MAYNE *City Match* II. iii, She speaks with salt, And has a pretty scornefulnesse. **1645** MILTON *Tetrach.* 63 Exceptions are not logically deduc't from a divers kind, as to say who so puts away for any naturall cause except fornication, the exception would want salt. **1682** SHADWELL *Medal of J. Bayes* 2 For Libel and true Satyr different be; This must have Truth, and Salt, with Modesty. *a* **1694** TILLOTSON *Serm.* clxiii. (1743) IX. 3884 He.. could with salt and sharpness enough upbraid those whom he sees guilty of them. **1734** tr. *Rollin's Anc. Hist.* V. 75 The prince comprehended all the salt and spirit of that ingenious pleasantry. **1766** FORDYCE *Serm. Yng. Women* II. viii. 20 That salt and poignancy.. derived from writers of taste. **1874** *Q. Rev.* CXXXVII. 106 Humour, the salt of well-bred conversation. **1894** K. GRAHAME *Pagan Papers* 120 We could not discover any salt in them [*sc.* the witticisms].

†**4.** *Alch.* and *Old Chem.* One of the supposed ultimate elements of all substances. *Obs.*

?*c* **1585** HESTER tr. *Paracelsus' 114 Exper.*, etc. C 8, These three mercurie, Salt and Sulphur can not bee one without another. **1605**, **1729** [see MERCURY *sb.* 8]. **1650** FRENCH tr. *Paracelsus' Nat. Things* 10 Mercury, Sulphur, Salt, of which all the seven Metalls are generated. For Mercury is the Spirit, Sulphur the Soule, and Salt the Body. **1651** —— *Distill.* vi. 181 Salt is that fixt permanent earth which is in the center of every thing that is incorruptible, and inalterable. **1670** D. CABLE tr. *Basil. Valent. Of Nat. & Supernat. Things* viii. 124 [Tin] hath no excess of Mercury, nor of Salt, and it hath the least of Sulphur in it. **1719** QUINCY *Lex. Physico-Med.* s.v. *Principle.*

5. *Old Chem.* †**a.** A solid soluble non-inflammable substance having a taste. *Obs.*

The name originally comprised such substances as resembled common salt (sense 1) in their appearance or properties, e.g. substances produced by the evaporation of watery liquids as salt is produced by the evaporation of sea-water. The quality of the taste was not originally considered to be a criterion of the class, but was added in the 18th c., when these substances were ultimately divided into 'acid salts' (*salia acida*), 'alkaline salts' (*salia alkalina*), and 'neutral salts' (*salia neutra, media*, or *salsa*), corresponding to the modern 'acids', 'alkalis', and 'salts'.

1426 LYDG. *De Guil. Pilgr.* 15632, I.. Yive hem vergows and vynegre.. And yive hem other sawtys mo. **1594** PLAT *Jewell-ho.* II. 10 Coppers.. Niter.. vitrial.. allom.. Borras, .. Suger.. Sublimate.. Saltpeter.. all these are diuers kindes of saltes. **1626** BACON *Sylva* §645 Out of the Ashes of all Plants, they extract a Salt which they use in Medecines. **1686** W. HARRIS tr. *Lemery's Course Chem.* I. xiv. 347 If there were any Salt in this petrified Plant, it would dissolve in hot water like other salts. **1707** *Curios. in Husb. & Gard.* 219 Sugar is a balsamick Salt. **1729** WOODWARD *Nat. Hist. Fossils* I. I. 98 The Vitriolic Salts, with which the Pyrites abounds. **1774** GOLDSM. *Nat. Hist.* I. 166 By divesting a quantity of earth of all its oils and salts. **1797** *Encycl. Brit.* (ed. 3) IV. 599 Salts.. are soluble in water, sapid, and not inflammable. They are either Acids or Alkalies.

b. Particular substances of this class are distinguished by defining words (q.v., and cf. SAL[1]); e.g. †***salt ammoniac*** (= SAL-AMMONIAC), †***essential s.***, †***fixed s.***, †***s. perlate***, †***s. sedative***, ***volatile s.***; †***salt of antimony***, †***of Mars***, †***of Saturn***, ***of soda***, †***of steel***, †***of wisdom***; †***salt anatron***, †***s. gem(me*** (= SAL-GEM), †***s. prunel(la*** (= SAL-PRUNELLA), †***s. nitre*** (= SAL-NITRE), †***salt sode*** (= sal-soda), †***s. tartar***; GLAUBER'S SALT, ***Rochelle s.***, etc. ***salt of lemon***, potassium hydrogen oxalate, used to remove ink-stains and iron-mould from linen; ***Carlsbad*** (or ***Karlsbad***), ***Vichy salts***, salts prepared from the mineral springs in these places, or imitations of them; ***Everitt's salt*** (see quot. 1939); †***Preston salts***, a variety of smelling-salts.

a **1400** *Stockholm Med. MS.* 4 A water þat is clepyd salt gemme. **14..** *Chaucer's Can. Yeom. Prol. & T.* 257 (Corpus & Petw. MSS.), Salt tartre. **1526** *Grete Herball* cccciii. (1529) Y j b, Salt armeniake is hote and drye in the fourth degre. *Ibid.* Y ij, Salt gemme.. hath the vertues of salt armonyake. **1565** COOPER *Thesaurus* s.v. *Ammoniacus*, Salte armonike. **1580** LYLE *Euphues* (Arb.) 439 Salt Sode for Glasse. **1601** HOLLAND *Pliny* II. 133 If some salt-nitre be put to them whiles they be a boiling ouer the fire. **1670** D. CABLE tr. *van Suchten's Secr. Antimony* 118 This Salt of Antimony.. performs almost all that the Salt of Gold doth. **1741** *Compl. Fam.-Piece* I. ii. 180 An Ounce of beaten Salt-prunel. **1756** WRIGHT in *Phil. Trans.* XLIX. 681 Fossil sea-salt or salt-gem. **1765** DELAVAL *ibid.* LV. 31 *note* f, A solution of salt-ammoniac. **1810** *New Family Receipt-bk.* 349 Essential Salt of Lemons. **1839** URE *Dict. Arts* 1084 Salt of amber is succinic acid. Salt of lemons is citric acid. **1858** P. L. SIMMONDS *Dict. Trade Products, Preston-salts*,.. smelling-salts.. containing carbonate of ammonia in small pieces, with a drachm of the following mixture added, viz. oils of bergamot, cloves, and lavender, and the strongest solution of ammonia. **1866** *Chambers's Encycl.* VIII. 453/2 The celebrated Preston smelling-salts are scented with oils of cloves and pimento. **1868** *Ibid.* X. 75/2 Ink-stains.. require to be taken out with.. the essential salts of lemon. **1890** BILLINGS *Med. Dict.* I. 482/1 *Everitt's salt*, a compound of cyanide of iron and potassium, formed when potassium ferrocyanide is decomposed by sulphuric acid. **1895** *Army & Navy Co-op Soc. Price List* 15 Sept. 696/1 Carlsbad Salts. *Ibid.* 710/2 Vichy Salts, Effervescing. **1901** *To-Day* 1 Aug. 38/1 'Eisklene Hat Wash', which I find far superior to oxalic acid, salts of lemon, or any of the usual articles used for the purpose. **1908** *Chem. Abstr.* II. 3126 Artificial crystallized 'Karlsbad salts' as sold on the market is really impure Na_2SO_4. **1939** *Thorpe's Dict. Appl. Chem.* (ed. 4) III. 471/2 Ferrous potassium ferrocyanide, $K_2Fe[Fe(CN)_6]$, (Everitt's salt) is produced by heating saturated potassium ferrocyanide solution for 40 hours at 90°C with an equal volume of 20% sulphuric acid. **1960** *Chem. Abstr.* LIV. 8120/2 Hexametaphosphate.. combined with 34% Vichy salts.. gives a detergent which restores the original whiteness of superpolyamide textiles. **1977** *Martindale's Extra Pharmacopoeia* (ed. 27) 1459/1 Artificial Carlsbad Salt... A crystallised preparation of sodium sulphate 55, potassium sulphate 1, sodium chloride 10, and sodium carbonate 35. *Ibid.*, Artificial Vichy Salt. Anhydrous sodium sulphate 40, anhydrous sodium phosphate 20, potassium bicarbonate 35, sodium chloride 75, sodium bicarbonate 830.

c. *colloq. pl.* (*a*) Smelling salts, consisting usually of ammonium carbonate.

1741 RICHARDSON *Pamela* II. 247 Mrs. Jewkes held her Salts to my Nose, and I did not faint. **1767** *Woman of Fashion* I. 73 [She] was several Times obliged to have recourse to her Salts. **1817** BYRON *Beppo* lxxxix, Much hartshorn, salts, and sprinkling faces. **1840** MARRYAT *Poor Jack* xiv, Virginia had run for the salts as soon as she perceived that her mother was unwell.

(*b*) Short for *Epsom salts* (see EPSOM). Also, ***like a dose of salts***: see DOSE *sb.* 2 c.

1772 *Chron.* in *Ann. Reg.* 98/1 A servant maid.. thinking to take some salts.. took arsenic instead thereof. **1877** *N.W. Linc. Gloss.* **1887** SERVICE *Life Dr. Duguid* xix, A neffow [= nieveful] of salts and a neffow of senna.

6. *Mod. Chem.* A compound formed by the union of an acid radical with a basic radical; an acid having the whole or part of its hydrogen replaced by a metal. (In wider theoretical use the term 'salt' includes acids as salts of hydrogen.) Also, †***ethereal salt***, an ester.

The first marked step towards the modern conception of a chemical salt was Rouelle's definition (*a* 1770) of a neutral salt as a compound formed by the union of an acid with any substance serving as a base for it and giving to it a concrete or solid form. Various modifications of this or earlier views were put forward until the publication of Lavoisier's definition of a salt as the union of an acid with an oxide; this definition, however, was found to be inadequate when the composition of the halogen compounds, sulphides, etc. came to be accurately known. A further revolution in the theory of salts was made by Berzelius, who divided them into two classes; viz. HALOID salts, formed of an electropositive element and a halogen, and AMPHID salts, resulting from the union of an acid and a base; the latter he subdivided into oxy-salts, sulpho-salts, selenio-salts, and telluri-salts. According to more recent conceptions (Arrhenius 1888) salts, including acids, are regarded as composed of positive ions or cations (hydrogen and metals) and negative ions or anions (halogens and acid radicals).

1790 KERR tr. *Lavoisier's Elem. Chem.* 150–1 Acids may therefore be considered as true salifying principles... This view of the acids prevents me from considering them as salts... I shall not arrange the alkalies or earths in the class of salts, to which I allot only such as are composed of an oxygenated substance united to a base. **1807** T. THOMSON *Chem.* (ed. 3) II. 151 [Acids] combine with all the alkalies, and most of the metallic oxides and earths, and form with them those compounds which are called salts. **1838** —— *Chem. Org. Bodies* 924 The tannin of areca gives a black colour to salts of iron. **1855** HARDWICH *Photogr. Chem.* 15 The principal Salts of Silver which are employed in the Photographic processes are four in number, viz. Nitrate of Silver, Chloride of Silver, Iodide of Silver, and Bromide of Silver. **1859** *Todd's Cycl. Anat.* V. 332/1 Most of the blood-salts are present in increased quantity in the gastric juice. **1876** *Encycl. Brit.* V. 553/2 The thio-acids also form ethereal salts. **1890** WALKER tr. *Ostwald's Outl. Gen. Chem.* 281 The conductivities of the neutral salts are additively composed of two values, one depending only on the metal or positive ion, the other only on the acid radical or negative ion. **1905** GOODCHILD & TWENEY *Technol. & Sci. Dict.* 633/2 Salts like ethyl acetate, derived from an organic acid and an alcohol, or from an alcohol and an inorganic acid, are called ethereal salts or esters.

7. a. = SALT-CELLAR.

1493 in *Somerset Med. Wills* (1901) 310 To John Wymer and Margarete his wif a cuppe and a salt of silver. **1495** *Trevisa's Barth. De P.R.* VI. xxii. 212 Knyues spones & saltes [*Bodl. MS.* salers] ben sett on yᵉ borde. **1531** *Rec. St. Mary at Hill* (1905) 47 Two Rownde saltes with a Couer. **1605** B. JONSON *Volpone* V. iii, One salt of agat. **1663** PEPYS *Diary* 29 Oct., Under every salt there was a bill of fare. **1775** in Picton *L'pool Munic. Rec.* (1886) II. 199 Eight silver salts for the Corporation. **1821** SCOTT *Kenilw.* xxxii, Another salt was fashioned of silver, in form of a swan in full sail. **1894** *Times* 7 Apr. 9/5 A pair of hexagonal salts, of Limoges enamel.

b. ***above*** (or ***below, beneath, under***) ***the salt***: at the upper (or lower) part of the table, *i.e.* among the more honoured (or less honoured) guests.

The reference is to the formerly prevailing custom of placing a large salt-cellar in the middle of a dining table.

1597 BP. HALL *Sat.* II. vi, That he do, on no default, Euer presume to sit aboue the salt. **1599** B. JONSON *Cynthia's Rev.* II. ii. (1616) 200 Hee neuer drinkes below the salt. **1602** DEKKER *Honest Wh.* D, Set him beneath the salt and let him not touch a bit, till euery one has had his full cut. **1658** *Wit Restor'd* 43 Hee.. humbly sate Below the Salt, and munch'd his Sprat. **1826** HONE *Every-day Bk.* I. 1333 The marshals were the lowest above the salt. **1870** LOWELL *Study Wind.* 347 At the banquet of fame they sit below the salt. **1885** J. PAYN *Luck of Darrells* xxxvii, Though of Tory sentiments, she by no means approved of those feudal times when the chaplain was placed below the salt.

8. A salt marsh or salting.

1621 in Boys *Hist. Sandwich* (1792) 705 Two acres of salts, overagainst the old crane.., granted to John Gason.. for the erecting of his waterworks. **1709** *Lond. Gaz.* No. 4525/4, 164 Acres of fresh Marsh, and 10 Acres of Salts, well water'd. **1796** MORSE *Amer. Geog.* I. 698 Immediately after you leave the salts, begin the valuable rice swamps. **1836** W. D. COOPER *Prov. Sussex, Salts*, marshes near the sea flooded by the tides. **1900** *Academy* 28 Apr. 364/2 There remains on her seaward front [*sc.* of Rye], that green space the Salts.

9. *pl.* Salt water entering a river from the sea.

1658 R. FRANCK *North. Mem.* (1694) 173 Here the Salmon relinquish the Salts because by the Porposses pursued up the Freshes. **1828–32** WEBSTER, *Salts*, the salt water of rivers entering from the ocean. *S. Carolina.* **1856** OLMSTED *Slave States* 469 'Freshes' and 'salts'. **1883** G. C. DAVIES *Norfolk Broads* xxxii. 225 The last incursion of the salts was seven years ago. **1897** *Westm. Gaz.* 14 Dec. 10/2 The stormy weather and high tides, which have caused 'salts', *i.e.* the forcing of the sea water up the rivers.

10. At Eton, money collected for the Captain at the Montem. Now *Hist.*

See *Brand's Pop. Antiq.* 1813 I. 337 seqq., and Maxwell Lyte *Hist. Eton Coll.* (1889) 507 seqq.

a **1769** in *Brand's Pop. Antiq.* (1813) I. 345 *note*, Every scholar gives a shilling for Salt; the noblemen more. **1806** D. & S. LYSONS *Magna Brit.* I. 558 Tickets inscribed with some motto.. are given to such persons as have already paid for *salt*, as a security from any further demands. **1825** C. M. WESTMACOTT *Eng. Spy* I. 75 As long as salt and sock abound. **1899** C. K. PAUL *Memories* 113 The sixth-form.. stopped coaches, post-chaises, and carriages,.. asking for 'Salt'.

11. *colloq.* A sailor, esp. one of much experience. (Cf. 2 h.)

1840 R. H. DANA *Bef. Mast* i, My complexion and hands were quite enough to distinguish me from the regular *salt*. **1877** SPURGEON *Serm.* XXIII. 416 If you want to hear about the sea, talk to an 'old salt'. **1884** 'H. COLLINGWOOD' *Under Meteor Flag* iii, The 'green' hands.. had been very judiciously intermingled with the experienced 'salts'.

12. *attrib.* and *Comb.* **a.** Simple attrib., as ***salt-backet*** (Sc.), ***barrow*** (BARROW *sb.*[3] 3), ***bed, boat, brig, coffer, crystal, district, gauge, girnel, incrustation, manufacture, market, monopoly, pannier, room, shop, shovel, -spoon*** (hence

-spoonful), *spring*, *trough*, *vase*, *-warehouse*; also (sense 5 c (*a*)), *salts-bottle*. **b.** objective, instrumental, similative, etc., as *salt-boiler*, *-burner*, *-cured*, *-curing*, *-heaver*, *holder*, *-incrusted*, *-laden*, *-loving*, *manufacturer*, *owner*, *-resembling*, *-seller*, *-spilling*, *-white* (also as *adj.*), *-worker*; *salt-blue*, *-bright*, *-caked*, *-eaten*, *-free*, *-licked*, *-strewn*, *-tanged*, *-wavy*, *-worn* adjs.

1756 Pennecuik *Coll.* 47, I spake nae mair than our *salt-backit. **1881** W. Gregor *Folk-lore Scot.* ix. 51 A wooden box in the shape of a house, with a round hole in the exposed end; it was the saat-backet. **1610** Holland *Camden's Brit.* (1637) 608 Certaine women .. put it [*sc.* salt] in baskets, they call them *Salt barowes, out of which the liquor runneth, and the pure salt remaineth. **1886** *Encycl. Brit.* XXI. 230/1 The Cheshire and Worcestershire *salt-beds are by some attributed to the Permian. **1922** *Salt-blue [see *sea-death* s.v. sea *sb.* 18 d]. **1791** R. Mylne *Rep. Thames & Isis* 51 The Droitwich *Salt boat stopt here. **1748** *Salt-boiler [see *salt-officer* in 12 c.]. **1897** Kipling *Capt. Cour.* viii, The Jersey *salt-brigs. **1930** E. Pound *XXX Cantos* xvii. 79 And in her hands sea-wrack *Salt-bright with the foam. **1910** G. T. Zoëga *Conc. Dict. Old Icelandic* 346/2 [*Salt*]*-karl*, .. *salt-burner. **1975** C. Fell tr. *Egil's Saga* iv. 5 Those who worked in the forests and the salt-burners and all those who hunt .. had to pay his taxes. **1903** J. Masefield *Ballads* 19 Dirty British coaster with a *salt-caked smoke stack. **1859** Geo. Eliot *A. Bede* vi, Where the only chance of collecting a few grains of dust would be to climb on the *salt-coffer. **1886** *Encycl. Brit.* XXI. 233/2 The mother-liquor .. becomes .. totally unfit for further service after yielding but two or three crops of *salt crystals. **1883** Moloney *W. African Fisheries* 40 (Fish. Exhib. Publ.) *Salt-cured fish during the 'scarce season'. *Ibid.*, *Salt-curing .. is somewhat resorted to, as is also 'smoking'. **1833–4** J. Phillips *Geol.* in *Encycl. Metrop.* (1845) VI. 615/2 The ancient hydrography of the *salt districts. **1916** Joyce *Portrait of Artist* (1969) iv. 170 Picking a pointed *salteaten stick out of the jetsam among the rocks, he clambered down the slope of the breakwater. **1909** *Practitioner* Dec. 867 When nephritis occurs, the child is given milk for some days, and then a *salt-free diet, or at least one poor in salt. **1977** J. Cheever *Falconer* 49 A salt-free diet .. no salt added. **1864** Webster, **Salt-gauge*, an instrument used to test the strength of brine or salt-water. *c* **1688** Dallas *Stiles* 584 Salt-Pans, and *Salt-Girnals .. lying in the said Parochin. **1892** *Labour Commission* Gloss., **Salt heavers*, men who discharge the salt from the barges by heaving or throwing it up, either upon the deck .. or into a tub. **1834** Lytton *Pompeii* I. iii, In the centre of the table, at the corners of which stood the Lares and the *saltholders. **1840** *Penny Cycl.* XVII. 471/1 Great tracts of the plain are covered with *salt incrustations. **1856** *Times* 5 May 5/2 The margin of the *salt-incrusted shallows of the Dead Sea. **1878** Smiles *Robt. Dick* iii. 25 He enjoyed the *salt-laden breath. **1962** A. Sampson *Anat. of Britain* xvi. 264 In the past the air force has been led by aviators, as the navy has been led by *saltlicked admirals. **1849** Johnston *Exp. Agric.* 142 *Salt-loving plants. **1836** *Rep. Comm. Salt Brit. India* 24 The Bullooah molunghees found that the *salt manufacture .. was no longer so profitable as of old. *Ibid.* App. 143 *a*, Two Petitions of *Salt Manufacturers in the Agency of Tumlook. **1477** in *Charters*, etc. *Edin.* (1871) 140 The *salt market to be haldin in Nudreis Wynde. **1790** Burke *Fr. Rev.* 332 The provinces which had been always exempted from this *salt-monopoly. **1673** in *Lauderdale Papers* (Camden Soc.) II. 244 The good of the kingdome, the King's profite, and the interest of the *salt-owners. **1530** in *Ancestor* Oct. (1904) 182 A staffe or in his hande and a *salt panyer v[ert] at his backe. **1611** Cotgr., *Nitre*, Niter; a (*Salt-resembling) substance of colour light-ruddie, or white. **1809** Kendall *Trav.* II. xlvi. 133 The water is now drawn into the last range of vats or rooms, called *salt-rooms. **1847** Mrs. Gore *Castles in Air* II. iv. 89 My mother sat .. with her *salts' bottle in her hand. **1848** Thackeray *Van. Fair* xiv, Madly inhaling her salts-bottle. **1611** Cotgr., *Saulnier*, a Salter, *Salt-seller, Marchant of salt. *Ibid.*, *Saulnerie*, a *Salt-shop, or Garner for salt. **1709** *Female Tatler* No. 3/2 Tea-Cups, Sugar-Tongs, *Salt-Shovels, and Gloves made up in Wall-nut-shells. **1833** L. Ritchie *Wand. by Loire* 153 The sin of *salt-spilling. **1820** M. Edgeworth *Let.* 4 June (1979) 144 *Salt spoons never to be seen. **1858** Ramsay *Scot. Life & Char.* iii. 33 Last time Mrs. Murray dined here, we *lost* a salt-spoon. **1872** Calverley *Fly Leaves* 15 O'er hard-boil'd eggs the saltspoon shook. **1837** Dickens *Pickw.* xlviii. 518 Tom Smart beat him in the drinking by about half a *salt-spoon-full. **1844** H. Stephens *Bk. Farm* II. 356 A salt-spoonful of salt. **1904** *Queen* 30 Jan. 211/3 A salt-spoonful of powdered cloves. **1892** W. B. Yeats *Countess Kathleen* i. 24 My curse upon the *salt-strewn road of monks. **1933** W. de la Mare *Fleeting* 119 This wide *salt-tanged vast of air. **1832** *Scoreby Farm Rep.* 18 in *Libr. Usef. Knowl.*, *Husb.* III, A *salt-trough, and a sheep-rack for hay, should be found with every flock. **1829** Landor *Imag. Conv.*, *Pitt & Canning*, From every *salt-vase a spoonful. **1883** 'Mark Twain' *Life on Mississippi* xli. 423 The old brick *salt-warehouses clustered at the upper end of the city. **1912** E. Pound *Ripostes* 27 That I on high streams The *salt-wavy tumult traverse alone. **1855** Bailey *Mystic*, etc. 78 Kerman's sands *salt-white. **1922** Joyce *Ulysses* 50 A corpse rising saltwhite from the undertow, bobbing landward, a pace a pace a porpoise. **1961** A. Sillitoe *Key to Door* xxvii. 426 Water foamed into salt-white patches below the stern. **1680** J. Collins *Salt & Fishery* To Rdr., Mr. William Martin .. who .. gave me an account of the sad Condition of those *Saltworkers. **1861** Neale *Notes Dalmatia* 72 A little white chapel for the salt-workers. **1921** W. de la Mare *Veil* 78 And the ocean water stirs In *salt-worn casemate and porch.

c. Special combs.: † **salt-ark**, a salt-box; **salt bag** (see quot.); **salt bath**, a bath of a molten salt or salts, as used in annealing; **salt-bearer** (at the Eton montem: see quots.); **salt block** *U.S.* (see quot.); **salt bottom** *U.S.* (see quot.); **salt bridge** *Chem.*, (*a*) a tube containing an electrolyte (freq. in the form of a gel) which provides electrical contact between two solutions; (*b*) a structure linking parts of a large molecule by means of a polar bond; *spec.* one formed between an acidic and a basic group; **salt-burn** = *salt-sore*; **salt bush**, any of the plants of the genus *Atriplex* (and of some allied genera) which grow extensively on the interior plains of Australia and in arid regions elsewhere; **salt-cake**, (*a*) salt in the form of a cake; (*b*) see quot. 1858; **salt cedar**, a tamarisk, *Tamarix gallica*, growing as a shrub or small tree in warm parts of the United States; † **salt-corn**, a grain of salt (in quot. *fig.*); **salt dome**, a dome-shaped geological structure formed around and over a salt plug, often the source of oil or other minerals; also, a salt plug; **salt-dropping** = BITTERN *sb.*[2]; **salt-duty** = GRANAGE; **saltgardens** [= G. *salzgärten*], shallow ponds laid out upon a sea-coast for the collection and evaporation of sea-water for the manufacture of salt; **salt glaze** (see quot.); also *transf.*, ceramic objects to which salt glaze has been applied; hence as *v. trans.*; **salt-glazed** *a.*, prepared with salt glaze; **salt-glazing**, (*a*) the use of salt glaze; (*b*) = *salt-glaze*; **salt-like** *a.*, *spec.* in *Chem.*, ionic; applied esp. to those hydrides which contain the anion H^-; **salt-looking** *a.*, of sailor-like appearance; **salt-master**, a collector of salt-duty; **salt mine**, a mine yielding rock salt; also *joc.* (esp. in *pl.*) with allusion to the practice of sentencing offenders to labour in a salt mine; *spec.* one's work or place of employment; **salt money**, † (*a*) salary; (*b*) salt used as a medium of exchange; (*c*) = sense 10; † **salt-office**, the office concerned with the collection of salt-duty; so **salt-officer**; **salt-pie** *dial.* a salt-box (see E.D.D.); **salt plug**, an approximately cylindrical mass of salt, typically a mile in diameter and several miles deep, which has been forced upwards by subterranean pressure, distorting the overlying strata and forming a salt dome; **salt-radical** *Chem.*, in the binary theory of salts, any body which forms a salt with a metal or its equivalent; **salt-raker** (see quot.); **salt-rock**, † (*a*) rock-salt; (*b*) rock impregnated with salt; † **salt-rover**, one who sails the seas; **salt-shaker** *U.S.* = *salt-sprinkler*; † **salt-silver** (see quots.); **salt sore**, a sore caused by exposure to salt water; **salt-spreader**, a vehicle that spreads salt on roads in order to melt snow and ice; hence **salt-spreading** *vbl. sb.* and *ppl. a.*; **salt-sprinkler**, a closed vessel for salt having holes through which it is sprinkled; † **salt stack**, a mound of earth from which salt was manufactured; **salt-stand**, a salt-cellar; **salt tablet**, a tablet of salt that is swallowed, usu. to replace salt lost in perspiration; **salt-tax** = GABELLE; **salt-tree**, a tree of the genus *Halimodendron*, esp. *H. argenteum*; **salt-weed**, (*a*) the Toad-rush, *Juncus bufonius*; (*b*) *U.S.* a plant of the genus *Hedeoma*; † **salt-wich**, a salt-pit; **salt-wife** [cf. G. *salzfrau*], a woman who sells salt. See also SALT-BOX, SALT-CAT, SALT-CELLAR, SALT LAKE, etc.

1348 *Durham Acc. Rolls* (Surtees) 43 In 1 *Saltark, 13d. **1481** *Ibid.* 97, j Saltarke. **1847** S. R. Maitland in *Brit. Mag.* XXXI. 367 *note*, He told me that when, as a freshman [at Cambridge], he was getting his gown from the maker, he made some remark on the long strips of sleeve by which such gowns are distinguished, and was told they were called **salt-bags*. **1913** *Lockwood's Dict. Mech. Engin.* (ed. 4), **Salt bath furnace*, a type of hardening furnace in which the temperature is regulated by the employment of fused salts. **1925** *Jrnl. Iron & Steel Inst.* CXI. 536 The purification of fused salt baths composed of equal parts of sodium and potassium chlorides by the additon of boric acid and charcoal is also dealt with. **1980** *Railway Gaz. Internat.* Jan. 59/2 Molten salt bath nitriding and induction hardening caused bore distortion. *a* **1769** in *Brand's Pop. Antiq.* (1813) I. 344 *note*, Two of the scholars called *Salt-bearers, dressed in white, with a handkerchief of Salt in their hands. **1864** R. Chambers *Bk. Days* II. 665/2 The salt-bearers were accustomed to carry .. a handkerchief filled with salt, of which they bestowed a small quantity on every individual who contributed his quota to the subsidy. **1875** Knight *Dict. Mech.* 2023/1 **Salt-block*, an apparatus for evaporating the water from a saline solution. The technical name for a salt-factory. **1859** Bartlett *Dict. Amer.*, **Salt-bottom*, a plain or flat piece of land covered with saline efflorescence. These places abound in Western Texas, New Mexico, and Arizona. **1915** *Jrnl. Amer. Chem. Soc.* XXXVII. 2781 Bjerrum's method of extrapolation .. is to add, to the voltage obtained by using 3·5 *M* KCl as a *salt bridge, the difference between this voltage and that obtained by using 1·75 *M* KCl as the salt bridge. **1929** H. T. S. Britton *Hydrogen Ions* viii. 109 These two solutions are connected through the 'salt bridge', a narrow inverted U-tube, containing saturated KCl solution. **1965** *Jrnl. Molecular Biol.* XIII. 656 This arrangement would allow the α-amino group of one β-chain to form a salt-bridge with the α-carboxyl group of its symmetrically related partner, resulting in the formation of two salt bridges on either side of the dyod axis. **1978** P. W. Atkins *Physical Chem.* xii. 347 Another way of eliminating the junction potential is to connect the two half-cells with a salt bridge formed by dissolving potassium chloride in a water-soluble jelly. **1978** *Nature* 23 Nov. 362/1 Protein subunits in the two layers of the disk of tobacco mosaic virus have very similar conformations. Much of the bonding between subunits is polar, including salt-bridge systems. **1917** D. H. Lawrence *Look! We have come Through!* 37 Nevertheless, once, the frogs, the globe-flowers of Bavaria, the glow-worms Gave me sweet lymph against the *salt-burns. **1863** Westgarth in J. Davis *Tracks of McKinlay* 14 As cattle can live upon the *salt-bush, this country is thus suitable for pastoral pursuits. **1870** Braim *New Homes* ii. 89 This inland salt-bush country suits the settler's purpose well. **1890** 'R. Boldrewood' *Col. Reformer* (1891) 100 Garrandilla consisted wholly of saltbush plains. **1901** M. Franklin *My Brilliant Career* xxii. 185, I listened with interest to stories of weeks and weeks spent .. crossing widths of saltbush country. **1909** Coulter & Nelson *New Man. Bot. Rocky Mts.* (ed. 2) 165 Atriplex L. Saltbush. Orache. **1911** C. E. W. Bean *'Dreadnought' of Darling* xv. 144 The grass might die off and the salt bush wither up. **1936** I. L. Idriess *Cattle King* ii. 10 He had never seen saltbush before. He felt strangely attracted by this little grey bush; its sombre colouring typical of the area. **1940** E. C. Jaeger *Desert Wild Flowers* 53 It [*sc.* the hoary saltbush] is one of the most widely distributed of American salt-bushes. **1944** *Living off Land* ii. 42 Lucerne leaves, nettles, saltbush and milk thistles can all be used as substitutes for spinach. **1973** *Stand. Encycl. S. Afr.* IX. 480/1 Several species of *Atriplex* .. are known as saltbush. *c* **1702** C. Fiennes *Journeys* (1947) I. 49 The thinner part [of the salt] runns through on Moulds they set to catch it which they call *Salt Cakes. **1818** Marsden tr. *Trav. Marco Polo* II. xxxviii. 421 They obtain a *saggio* of gold for sixty, fifty, or even forty of the salt-cakes. **1858** Simmonds *Dict. Trade*, *Salt-cake*, a name for sulphate of soda made at alkali works, for the use of crown-glass manufacturers and soap makers. **1883** H. J. Powell, etc. *Princ. Glass-making* 146 The 'salt-cake' .. or sulphate of soda, is likewise pulverized and afterwards sifted. **1881** *Harper's Mag.* Apr. 731/1 *Salt cedars and stunted live-oaks .. were the only trees growing from the thin soil. **1973** *Tucson* (Arizona) *Daily Citizen* 22 Aug. 58/3 We wound up tramping .. through the mud and salt cedars. **1445** tr. *Claudian* in *Anglia* XXVIII. 273 Thou strowist such *saltcornys [orig. *aspersis salibus*] amonge þi spechis as amphion is founde vnlike To the in talkyng. **1908** *Science* 28 Feb. 348/1 The expansive force of the salt from the crystallizing source will be very circumscribed and the *salt domes local in character. **1928** E. R. Lilley *Geol. Petroleum & Nat. Gas* xvi. 376 The salt dome .. is known in areas where it does not appear to be associated with oil. **1945** M. F. Glaessner *Princ. Micropalaeont.* ix. 232 Lower Tertiary, Cretaceous, and Upper Jurassic microfossils (foraminifera and ostracodes) have been described from the salt-dome area .. between the northern shore of the Caspian sea and the southern foothills of the Ural Mountains. **1964** W. C. Putnam *Geol.* vi. 134/1 Many of the Gulf Coast salt domes are crowned with an irregular covering of limestone, anhydrite, gypsum, and occasionally sulphur, termed the cap rock. **1976** *Billings* (Montana) *Gaz.* 5 July 4-A/2 It not only will transmit needed crude oil to the Midwest, it also will make usable the vast salt domes of the Williston basin for strategic storage of crude. **1805** Forsyth *Beauties Scot.* II. 278 A liquid, something of the appearance of oil, .. which .. the people here call *salt-droppings. **1710** J. Chamberlayne *St. Gt. Brit.* II. III. vi. (ed. 23) 509 The Commissioners and other Officers for the *Salt-Duty. **1848** *F. Knapp's Chem. Technol.* I. 257 These *salt-gardens are nothing more than a series of very shallow ponds, intended to spread the water over a very large surface. **1855** J. Scoffern in *Orr's Circ. Sci.*, *Elem. Chem.* 432 The Lambeth stone ware, and some other kinds are glazed by a thin .. varnish of silicate of soda... This is known by the appellation of '*salt glaze', from the method of imparting it, which is as follows:—Whilst the stoneware is yet glowing in the furnace, a door is opened, and common salt is thrown in. **1968** J. Arnold *Shell Bk. Country Crafts* 236 The studio potters produce various kinds of terracotta .. and saltglaze. **1977** *Ashmolean Mus. Rep. Visitors 1975–76* 23 A selection of white salt-glaze from the Church bequest. **1862** *Catal. Internat. Exhib.* II. x. 12 The patent *salt-glazed socketed drain pipes. **1884** *Health Exhib. Catal.* 59/1 Patent Salt-Glazed Earthenware Latrine. **1967** M. Chandler *Ceramics in Mod. World* ii. 52 Porous drainpipes are still often salt-glazed, a process that is unique among glazing processes. **1875** Knight *Dict. Mech.* 2023/1 **Salt-glazing*, a glaze for earthenware, prepared from common salt. **1885** *Cassell's Techn. Educ.* III. 37/1 Salt-glazing is .. almost invariably confined to down-draught kilns. **1928** *Chem. Abstr.* XXII. 3343 (*heading*) *Salt-like hydrides. **1952** D. T. Hurd *Introd. Chem. Hydrides* iii. 23 The salt-like hydrides are very susceptible to hydrolysis in aqueous solution. **1965** Phillips & Williams *Inorg. Chem.* I. xvii. 619 The non-interstitial carbides are, in some senses, intermediate in character between the metallic interstitial carbides and the reactive salt-like carbides. **1848** Dickens *Dombey* iv, He .. had been a pilot, or a skipper, or a privateersman, .. and was a very *salt-looking man indeed. **1656** in *Misc. Scott. Burgh Rec. Soc.* (1881) 11 The Comissioners .. had some treaty with the *salt-masters touching the farme of theyr salt. **1847** *Crabbe's Poet. Wks.* Life 2 He rose to be collector of the salt-duties, or Salt-master. **1685** E. Brown *Trav.* 70 Half an hours going from the City of Eperies in upper Hungary, there is a *Salt-Mine of great note. **1811** Holland in *Trans. Geol. Soc.* I. 56 In countries where salt-mines occur, fragments of primitive rocks appear in great abundance over these beds. **1963** *Times* 13 May 3/1 Rhodes is back in favour after a year or two in the saltmines for throwing. **1966** L. Deighton *Billion-Dollar Brain* xvii. 186 We finished our milk. 'Back to the salt mines,' said Harvey. **1975** B. Garfield *Hopscotch* xxvii. 281 I'd better get back to the salt mines. I've got a lot of unfinished jobs. **1977** *Listener* 10 Nov. 616/2 Harding was summoned by Sir John Reith and .. sent off to the salt-mines of Manchester. **1535** Cromwell in Merriman *Life & Lett.* cxxvii. (1902) I. 436 There is due unto his grace the hole pencion and *salt moneye for the last yere. **1625** Purchas *Pilgrims* II. VII. v. §7. 1055 *marg.*, Through all Æthiopia, Salt runneth as a principal merchandize. Salt-money. *a* **1769** Huggett in *Brand's Pop. Antiq.* (1813) I. 345 *note*, The price of the dinner to each is 10*s.* 6*d.* and 2*s.* 6*d.* for Salt-money. **1708** *Brit. Apollo* No. 24. 4/2 James Cardonnell Esq; is made a Commissioner of the *Salt-Office. **1748** Brownrigg *Art of Making Salt* 56 An office for his majesty's *salt officers, and a dwelling house for the salt boilers. **1483** *Cath. Angl.* 317/2 A *Salte pye, *salinum.* **1918, 1944** *Salt plug [see PLUG *sb.* 21 (ii)]. **1967** M. T. HALBOUTY *Salt Domes* vi. 87/2 Oil and formation waters migrated from sediments surrounding the salt plug and were trapped in porous sections of the cap rock. **1842** GRAHAM *Elem. Chem.* 163 The acid and oxygen are thus always together in the exact proportion to form the *salt-radical. **1863** *Fownes' Chem.* (ed. 9) 253 It has been found necessary to create two classes of salts: in the first division will stand those constituted after the type of common salt, which contain a metal and a salt-radical. **1837** A. MALLORY *Let.* 20 Apr. in J. J. Audubon *Ornith. Biogr.* (1839) V. 257 Several of the fishermen, and *salt-rakers,..frequent the keys to the windward of this place. **1858** SIMMONDS *Dict. Trade, Salt-raker,* a collector of salt in natural salt-ponds, or enclosures from the sea. **1693** *Act 5 Will. & Mary* c. 7 §24 Whereas *Salt-Rock or Rock-Salt taken out of pittes is in such great Lumps that it cannot be measured without breaking the same to powder. **1796** MORSE *Amer. Geog.* II. 242 This mine of salt-rock has been worked these 600 years past. **1834–6** P. BARLOW in *Encycl. Metrop.* (1845) VIII. 429/2 Salt rocks, in which the salt is combined more or less with earthy matter. **1620** MIDDLETON & ROWLEY *World Tost* 633 [*Land-captain to Sea-captain*] Proud *salt-rover, Thou hast the salutation of a thief. **1895** *Salt shaker [see *pepper shaker* s.v. PEPPER *sb.* 7]. **1931** W. CATHER *Shadows on Rock* II. i. 50 His ragged jacket was as much too tight as the trousers were too loose, and this gave him the figure of a salt-shaker. **1977** B. ROUECHÉ *Fago* (1978) I. iv. 72, I..picked up the kitchen salt shaker and rubbed it clean. **1363** in Kennett *Par. Antiq.* (1695) 496 Quilibet virgatarius dabit Domino unum denarium pro *Salt-Sylver per annum..vel cariabunt salem Domini de foro ubi emptus fuerit ad lardarium Domini. [*Ibid.* Gloss., *Salt-Sylver,* one penny paid at the Feast of St. Martin, by the servile Tenants to their Lord, as a commutation for the service of carrying their Lord's Salt from Market to his Lardar.] **1908** N. DUNCAN *Every Man for Himself* v. 140 [*Armenian loq.*] An' thee *salt-sores from thee feeshin' is on thee han's. **1979** F. FORSYTH *Devil's Alternative* 7 Those parts submerged in sea water soft and white between the salt-sores. **1951** *Sun* (Baltimore) 21 Dec. B32/6 The Board of Estimates is expected to approve today the purchase of 25 latest-type *salt spreaders. **1962** *B.S.I. News* Feb. 8/1 One London council whose salt-spreading was hindered because supplies had become 'rock-hard'. **1962** *Times* 27 Nov. 13/2 For the motorways, a fleet of snow ploughs and heavy salt-spreading vehicles is at constant readiness, day and night. The salt-spreaders can cover the whole of the M.1 at 40 to 50 m.p.h., within an hour. **1864** BOUTELL *Her. Hist. & Pop.* xxi. (ed. 3) 369 *Salt-sprinklers. **16..** ARCHBALD in W. Macfarlane *Geogr. Coll.* (1908) III. 189 Then they carry a sufficient quantity of the *Saltstack & spread it over the whole Coach. **1869** BLACKMORE *Lorna D.* I. xxi. 238, I know..their hospitality is more of the knife than the *salt-stand. **1944** *Living off Land* v. 102 The cure is a pinch of salt, or one of the *salt tablets now provided for the purpose, on the back of the tongue before each drink. **1976** A. PRICE *War Game* II. iv. 230 A heavy leather buff-coat..trapped the sweat and delayed the dehydration... So even though the salt tablets..were necessary, the discomfort was endurable. **1792** A. YOUNG *Trav. France* I. 555 The *gabelle,* or *salt-tax. **1834** MCCULLOCH *Dict. Comm.* (ed. 2) 1004 It was not the nature of the salt tax, but the absurd extent to which it had been carried, that rendered it justly odious. **1883** F. DAY *Indian Fish* 11 (Fish. Exhib. Publ.) The fisherman's and fish-curer's occupations are injured by the incidence of a heavy salt-tax. **1824** LOUDON *Encycl. Gard.* (ed. 2) Index, *Salt-tree, *robinia halodendron.* **1836** W. IRVING *Astoria* III. 42 A plant called *saltweed, resembling pennyroyal. **1847** HALLIWELL, *Salt-weed,* toad-rush. *Suffolk.* **1881** GEIKIE in *Macm. Mag.* XLIV. 237/1 Here and there [in the Bad Lands of Wyoming] a bunch of salt-weed. **1610** HOLLAND *Camden's Brit.* (1637) 607 These are very famous *Salt-wiches,..where brine or salt water is drawne out of Pittes. **1818** SCOTT *Hrt. Midl.* xl, Ye wad hae kend nae odds on her frae ony other *saut-wife.

†**salt,** *sb.*[2] *Obs.* Also 6 saute. [a. F. *saut* (lit. 'leap'):—L. *saltus* (*u*-stem), f. *salire* to leap. Cf. ASSAUT *adv.*, and, for the spelling, SALT *a.*[2]] Sexual desire or excitement (usually, of a bitch).

1519 HORMAN *Vulg.* 110 My dogge proferth to the saute or bytchewatch. *Canis meus catulit.* **1519** *Eng. Misc.* (Surtees) 33 That no man lett no bitchis un [? *read* in] salte go aboght in the town. **1528** TINDALE *Obed. Chr. Man* D ij b, The weddinges of oure virgyns..ar moare like vnto the saute of a bitche then the marienge of a reasonable creature. **1648** HERRICK *Hesp., Parting Verse* 25 The expressions of that itch And salt, which frets thy Suters.

SALT (sɒlt, -ɔː-), *sb.*[3] Also S.A.L.T., Salt. [Acronym f. the initials of *S*trategic *A*rms *L*imitation *T*alks.] Negotiations, involving esp. the U.S.A. and the Soviet Union, aimed at the limitation or reduction of nuclear armaments. Freq. *attrib.*

The last element, which is freq. redundant in *attrib.* uses, is also understood as *Treaty.*

1968 MRS. L. B. JOHNSON *White House Diary* 1 July (1970) 693 When and where the talks would start, we do not know. They are being referred to as Strategic Arms Limitation Talks. (SALT). **1969** *New Scientist* 14 Aug. 314/2 The progress of SALT is likely also to be slow. **1972** *Guardian* 6 June 4/4 The Secretary for Defence..told Congress today that the United States could not afford to relax its defence effort in spite of the SALT agreement. **1973** E. OSERS tr. *Waldheim's Austrian Example* xv. 196 The first ceilings set by the Salt Talks may prove to be an important landmark in limiting the arms race. **1975** *Daily Tel.* 23 Sept. 14/3 Whether the SALT discussions were a success or not is a matter of embittered controversy. **1976** *Survey* Summer–Autumn 24 The need for a further agreement in SALT remains paramount, given the threat to human survival posed by the nuclear arms race. **1979** *Sci. Amer.* Feb. 30/1 As the Senate prepares to debate the ratification of the new treaty emerging from the second round of strategic-arms-limitation talks (S.A.L.T. II) between the two superpowers.

salt (sɒlt, -ɔː-), *a.*[1] Forms: see SALT *sb.*[1] [OE. *sealt* = OFris. *salt,* MLG., LG. *solt,* Du. *zout,* ON. *salt-r*:—OTeut. **salto-z*:—pre-Teut. **sald-*; cf. L. *salsus,* f. **sald-* + *-tos.*

In certain collocations it is doubtful whether *salt* is to be regarded as an adj. or as the sb. used attrib. Cf. the Ger. compounds *salzfleisch* salt flesh, *salzfisch* salt fish, etc.]

1. Impregnated with or containing salt; hence, having a taste like that of salt; saline. **a.** Of water, brine-springs, etc. ***salt finger***, one of a number of alternating columns of rising and descending water produced when a layer of water is overlain by a denser, more salty layer; so ***salt fingering***, the occurrence of salt fingers; ***salt spray***, used *attrib.* to denote a test in which an article is subjected to a spray of salt water, and the associated apparatus. See also SALT SPRING, SALT WATER.

In ME. poetry *salt sea, salt flood* (now occas. *arch.*), *salt foam, salt stream* are frequent phrases for the sea.

a **900** CYNEWULF *Christ* 677 Sum mæȝ fromlice ofer sealtne sæ sundwudu drifan. *c* **1205** LAY. 6116 He..fram þan londe hælde ofer þane saltne strem. **13..** *Sir Beues* (A.) 3272 He was maroner wel gode, A stertte in to þe salte flode. *c* **1385** CHAUCER *L.G.W.* 1462 So longe he seylith in the salte se Til in the yle of lenoun aryuede he. **1398** TREVISA *Barth. De P.R.* XI. i. (1495) 383 The North see is but lytyll salte and the see that hyght Ponticum is as it were fressh. *c* **1407** LYDG. *Reson & Sens.* 1458 She roos of the foom most salt. *c* **1470** *Gol. & Gaw.* 302 The roy rial..socht to the cietie of Criste, our the salt flude. **1565** COOPER *Thesaurus, Salsilago*..a salt licour; bryne. **1590** SHAKS. *Mids. N.* III. ii. 393 His [*sc.* Neptune's] salt greene streames. **1625** N. CARPENTER *Geog. Del.* II. v. 76 We see water being wrung through ashes, to grow salt. **1799** KIRWAN *Geol. Ess.* 356 It appears that, the Baltic is much less salt than the ocean, and that it is salter under a westerly than under an easterly wind. **1856** STANLEY *Sinai & Pal.* vii. 286 *note,* It is sometimes supposed that the Dead Sea is the saltest water in the world. **1877** BRYANT *Odyss.* v. 553 He loosed The veil..And to the salt flood cast it. **1883** G. C. DAVIES *Norfolk Broads* xxxiv. 236 What are known as the salt-tides are chiefly the bane of the angler. **1885** R. BUCHANAN *Annan Water* iii, Day and night the salt spray of the ocean was blown upon it. **1967** *Deep-Sea Res.* XIV. 599 The opposite situation of a stable temperature gradient made unstable with a little salt leads to the formation of 'salt fingers'. **1977** *Sci. Amer.* Oct. 147/1 The warm salty water of the Mediterranean sets up the conditions for salt fingering as it flows through the Straits of Gibraltar and over the fresher, cooler waters of the Atlantic. **1978** J. A. KNAUSS *Introd. Physical Oceanogr.* ix. 187 It would appear that..at least some of the microstructure in the ocean is caused by salt fingers.

in phrases used attrib. **1599** ? GREENE *Alphonsus* v. Wks. (Grosart) XIII. 405 If that the salt-brine teares,..Can mollifie the hardnes of your heart. **1605** SHAKS. *Macb.* IV. i. 24 The rauin'd salt Sea sharke. **1798** WORDSW. *Peter Bell* I. 232 Bespattered with the salt-sea foam. *a* **1837** R. NICOLL *Poems* (1842) 20 The Sabbath's wander in the woods, An' by the saut-sea faem. **1918** *Proc. Amer. Soc. Testing Materials* XVIII. 237 (*heading*) Method of making the salt-spray corrosion test. **1945** *Electroplated Coatings of Nickel & Chromium on Steel & Brass (B.S.I.)* 18 Salt spray cabinet. **1962** *B.S.I. News* Feb. 18/2 A frequently-used test for determining resistance to corrosion is the salt spray test. *Ibid.* 606 Because of salt fingering, salt will escape across the bottom of this layer faster than heat. **1970** *Materials & Technol.* III. ix. 704 Exposure to a continuous mist of salt water, the so-called salt-spray test,..does not truly simulate atmospheric exposure.

b. Applied to tears; †also, to humours, etc.

See also SALT-RHEUM.

c **1200** ORMIN 13849 þurrh beȝȝske & salte tæress. *c* **1386** CHAUCER *Clerk's T.* 1028 With hire salte teeres She bathed bothe hire visage and hire heeres. *a* **1400–1500** *Alexander* 154 Sekand þar souerayn with many salt terys. **1483** CAXTON *Gold. Leg.* 196 b/1, In requyryng our lord with salte teris that..he wolde delyuer them of this pestylence. **1544** PHAER *Regim. Lyfe* (1560) B iv, An excessive rednesse..commynge of brente humours or of salte fleume. **1589** NASHE *Martins Months Minde* Wks. (Grosart) I. 193 His Stomacke, full of grosse and salt humors. **1591** SPENSER *Tears of Muses* 112 Her Sisters..their faire faces with salt humour steep. **1607** SHAKS. *Timon* IV. iii. 443 The Seas a Theefe, whose liquid Surge, resolues The Moone into Salt teares. **1717** RAMSAY *Elegy on Lucky Wood* xi, Could our saut tears like Clyde down rin. **1840** LONGF. *Wreck of Hesperus* xxi, The salt tears in her eyes. **1870** 'H. SMART' *Race for Wife* ii, She wept salt tears in the solitude of her own chamber.

c. Of tracts of land, marshes: Flooded by the sea. (See also SALT-MARSH.) Of rocks, ground: Having salt mixed with the earth; (in biblical use) barren. ***salt flat***, a flat expanse of land covered with a layer of salt; ***salt meadow*** (chiefly *N. Amer.*), a meadow liable to be flooded by salt water.

1279 *Feod. Prior. Dunelm.* (Surtees) 110 *note,* Cum toto prato quod vocatur Saltmedus. **1535** COVERDALE *Jer.* xvii. 5 In a salt and vnoccupied londe. **1611** BIBLE *Job* xxxix. 6 Whose house I haue made the wildernesse, and the barren lande [*marg.* Hebr. salt places] his dwellings. **1656** *New Haven* (Connecticut) *Town Rec.* (1917) I. 288 It was don.. by the cattell hurrying downe in to ye salt meddows. **1716** B. CHURCH *Hist. Philip's War* (1865) I. 157 They March'd.. until they came unto the Salt Meadow. **1789** J. MORSE *Amer. Geogr.* 287 There are large bodies of salt meadow along the Delaware. **1813** SIR H. DAVY *Agric. Chem.* (1814) 338 Virgil reprobates a salt soil. **1815** ELPHINSTONE *Acc. Caubul* Introd. 80 The range of salt hills. **1838** HALIBURTON *Clockm.* Ser. II. xix, Sea-mud, salt-sand,..and river-sludge. **1873** J. L. CRAWFORD in D. Eagan *6th Ann. Rep. Commissioner of Lands, Florida* (1874) 97 Hundreds of salt-works were erected upon the 'salt-flats' along the sea-shore within the limits of Wakulla. **1881** *Harper's Mag.* Jan. 254/2 The sluggish river winds through tracts of salt-meadow. **1886** *Encycl. Brit.* XXI. 231/2 The great salt range of the Punjab. **1931** *Amer. Speech* VII. 5 Sometimes the hunter found that he could make his best 'killings' at the 'salt licks' or 'salt flats' frequented by the buffalos. **1952** E. F. DAVIES *Illyrian Venture* i. 20 Why was the plain white? Was it snow? No, it looked more like salt flats. **1966** T. H. RADDALL *Hangman's Beach* III. xix. 286 A fringe of farms and salt meadows along the shore. **1972** *Guinness Bk. Records* (ed. 19) 128/2 The highest speed attained by any wheeled land vehicle is 631·368 m.p.h...on the Bonneville Salt Flats, Utah, on 23 Oct. 1970... The highest speed attained by a wheel-driven car is 429·311 m.p.h...on the salt flats at Lake Eyre, South Australia, on 17 July 1964.

d. Of other things, chiefly with regard to taste.

1398 TREVISA *Barth. De P.R.* XVI. lxix. (1495) 575 Nitrum is bytter soure and somdeale salt in sauour. **1477** NORTON *Ord. Alch.* v. in Ashm. (1652) 74 Five of these Nyne [Sapors] be ingendred by Heat, Unctuous, Sharpe, Salt, Bitter.., Doulcet. **1484** CAXTON *Fables of Æsop* v. x, I dayne not to ete of this mete..for it is to salte. **1600** J. PORY tr. *Leo's Africa* VIII. 297 They use a kinde of newe and extreme salt cheeses. **1639** T. DE GRAY *Compl. Horseman* 348 The leanest and saltest martlemas-beefe. **1849** HAWTHORNE *Twice-told T., Foot-pr. on Sea-shore* 2 That far-resounding roar is Ocean's voice of welcome. His salt breath brings a blessing along with it. **1873** BLACK *Pr. Thule* vi. 92 They drove on through the keen salt air.

2. Treated with salt as a preservative; cured, preserved, or seasoned with salt; salted. ***salt rising***: see RISING *vbl. sb.* 15; ***salt side*** (U.S.), salt pork (cf. SIDE *sb.*[1] 3).

909 in Birch *Cart. Sax.* II. 290, & tu hrieðeru oþer sealt oþer fersc. *c* **1000** in *Techmer's Zeitschr.* (1885) II. 125 Ðonne þu for hwylcere neode sealtflæsc wille. *a* **1300** *Cursor M.* 4688 Ma þan a thusand selers Fild he wit wins..And warnistore o salt fless. *c* **1390** in *Forme of Cury* (1780) 177 Great Salt Eels. *c* **1460** J. RUSSELL *Bk. Nurture* 554 Of alle maner salt fische, looke ye pare awey the felle. **1590** in *Black Bk. Taymouth* (Bann. Cl.) 306 Of..martis fresch and salt.. iii[xx] xiii martis iii quarteris ii m. **1617** MORYSON *Itin.* I. 259 We..omitted to provide any dried or salt meates at Candia. **1745** P. THOMAS *Jrnl. Anson's Voy.* 64 Two horses, which being..probably better feeding than their salt Beef and Pork, they killed and eat them. **1816** T. L. PEACOCK *Headlong Hall* ii, Packages of salt salmon. **1821** *John Bull* 19 Mar. 111/3 Salt butter sold as high as twenty shillings a stone. **1861** M. PATTISON *Ess.* (1889) I. 46 Many a cargo of salt cod for Lent. **1892** O. WISTER *Jrnl.* 25 Nov. in *Out West* (1958) 143 We fried some bread..and I cooked some salt side. **1961** *Amer. Speech* XXXVI. 266 The term *salt side* is probably a similar blend of Northern *salt pork* and Midland *side meat,* terms for bacon.

in phr. used attrib. or Comb. **1598** SHAKS. *Merry W.* II. ii. 290 Mechanicall-salt-butter rogue. **1611** COTGR. s.v. *Boeuf,* The salt beefe-eater needs no candle to find his liquor withall. **1710** P. LAMB *Roy. Cookery* 71 A Salt-Fish Pie. **1747** H. GLASSTONE *Art of Cookery* ix. 114 A Salt-Fish Pye. Get a Side of Salt-Fish, lay it in Water all Night [etc.]. **1966** M. WOODHOUSE *Tree Frog* x. 76 We fought our way through thick salt-beef sandwiches.

b. *Naut.* (*jocular*). **salt eel**: a rope's end; compared to the tail of an eel. **salt horse**: salted beef; also *transf.*, a naval officer with general duties. **salt junk**: see JUNK *sb.*[2] 3.

1622 MABBE tr. *Aleman's Guzman d'Alf.* II. 342 A good Ropes end, (which your Sea-faring men call a *salt Eele). **1663** PEPYS *Diary* 24 Apr. (1876) II. 188 Up betimes, and with my salt eele went down in the parler and there got my boy and did beat him. **1695** CONGREVE *Love for L.* III. vii, An he comes near me mayhap I may giv'n a salt eel for's supper. **1761** COLMAN *Jealous Wife* v. i, If you wou'd let me alone, I wou'd give him a Salt Eel, I warrant you. **1867** SMYTH *Sailor's Word-bk., Salt-eel,* a rope's end cut from the piece for starting the *homo delinquens.* **1836** MARRYAT *Mr. Midshipman Easy* III. i. 11 Why you stay in Midshipman berth—eat hard biscuit, salt pig, *salt horse? **1840** F. D. BENNETT *Whaling Voy.* I. 189 *note,* A return..to the 'salt horse', which no one is more ready to abuse than an old sailor. **1872** *Routledge's Ev. Boy's Ann.* 42/1 The..hard fare of 'weevily' biscuit and 'salt-horse'. **1914** F. T. JANE *Navy as Fighting Machine* viii. 69 A non-specialist officer (known colloquially as 'salt horse') serves as a watch-keeper. **1917** 'TAFFRAIL' *Sub.* v. 115 Next came Lieutenant Hinckson, the senior 'salt horse', two and a half striped Lieutenant. **1946** J. IRVING *Royal Navalese* 149 *Salt horse, A,* an officer who has not specialised in gunnery, torpedo, etc. and does not intend to. **1957** D. MACINTYRE *Jutland* ii. 33 Here was a simple 'salt-horse', indeed, and such were not often selected, in time of peace, for the higher ranks of the Service. **1960** J. BISSET *Commodore* 17 Officers in big ships called destroyer-officers 'salt horses'—meaning nonspecialists, a term of disdain. **1792** *Salt junk [see JUNK *sb.*[2] 3]. **1837** MARRYAT *Snarleyyow* I. xii. 152 So while they cut their raw salt junks, With dainties you'll be crammed. **1853** KANE *Grinnell Exp.* xxxiv. (1856) 309 The same sergeant-major, Canot, is now cooking salt junk in Baffin's Bay.

3. †**a.** Of fishes: Living in the sea: opposed to *freshwater.* **b.** Of plants: Growing in the sea or on salt marshes. ***salt grass*** (U.S.), one of a number of grasses growing in salt meadows or dry plains, esp. *Distichlis spicata* and several species of *Spartina*; ***salt hay*** (U.S.) hay made from salt grass.

1297 R. GLOUC. (Rolls) 14 Engelonde is vol ino3..Of foweles & of bestes..Of salt fichz & eke verss. **1598** SHAKS. *Merry W.* I. i. 22 The Luse is the fresh-fish, the salt-fish, is an old Coate. **1648** in *Mass. Hist. Soc. Coll.* (1852) 4th Ser. I. 204 Salt hay and fresh there thousands are of acres I do deeme. **1697** DRYDEN *Virg. Georg.* III. 606 From the marshy Land Salt Herbage for the fodd'ring Rack provide. **1704** *Early Rec. Providence, Rhode Island* (1894) V. 224 The which sd Cove is a place of Salt Grass called Thatch. **1732** J. HEMPSTEAD *Diary* 23 Sept. (1901) 252, I went to Mamacock & fetcht a L[oa]d of Salt hay alias Rushes. **1763** MILLS *Pract. Husb.* III. 413 This..answers for any sort of hay, except salt-hay and red clover. *a* **1816** B. HAWKINS *Sk. Creek Country* (1848) 43 Such is the attachment of horses to this moss, or as the traders call it, salt grass. **1843** *Knickerbocker* XXII. 34 Range your eye along the summits of the salt hay-stacks. **1857** FABER *Sir Lancelot* II. 478 The drowsy plains, Where brittle salt-herbs struggle with wild thyme. **1849** M. ARNOLD *Forsaken Merman* 38 Where the salt weed sways in the stream. **1859** BARTLETT *Dict. Amer.*, *Salt grass* and *Salt hay*, the grass and hay growing in salt marshes. **186.** WHITMAN *Elem. Drifts* Poems (1868) 269 Leaves of salt-lettuce, left by the tide. **1910** J. HART *Vigilante Girl* xxv. 350 The little stream..ran from the spring through bunches of salt grass. **1952** L. & J. BUSH-BROWN *America's Garden Bk.* (ed. 2) xii. 446 Salt hay is one of the most satisfactory materials mentioned [for winter mulching]. **1972** R. G. KAZMANN *Mod. Hydrol.* (ed. 2) v. 175 Salt grass will survive when the water table is as much as 12 ft. below the land surface.

†**4.** *fig.* Of experience, etc.: Bitter; vexatious.

c **1500** *Priests of Peblis* 1206 And he to me wit thow maid ony falt, To the that wil be ful sowre and salt. **1513** DOUGLAS *Æneis* XIII. Prol. 98 Wald thou..mak amendis, I sal remyt this falt; Bot, other wais, that sete sal be full salt. **1592** GREENE *Quip Upst. Courtier* Wks. (Grosart) XI. 241 The yoong vpstart that needes it, feels it salt in his stomack a month after.

5. Of speech, wit, etc.: Pungent, stinging. Now *rare*.

a **1600** HOOKER *Eccl. Pol.* VI. (1648) 92 Of which opinion Tertullian making (as his usuall manner was) a salt Apologie. **1605** CAMDEN *Rem.* (1637) 248 He salted, powdred, and made them stir with his salt and sharpe quipping speeches. **1609** ARMIN *Ital. Taylor* ad fin., Thy wit, not worthie's any Schoole, T'is salt, and too precise. **1656** TRAPP *Comm. Eph.* v. 4 Salt jests,..to the just grief or offence of another. **1890** *Spectator* 11 Jan., The far-reaching issues of human emotion, which by a sentence he bites into our memory, give exceptional if a rather salt truthfulness to his creations.

transf. **1606** SHAKS. *Tr. & Cr.* I. iii. 371 The pride and salt scorne of his eyes.

6. *slang.* and *dial.* Of expense, cost: Excessive in amount; costly, dear.

1710 RUDDIMAN *Gloss. to Douglas* s.v. *Salt*, I shall make it salt to you *i.e.* I shall make you pay dear for it. **1808** JAMIESON, *Salt*... 2. Costly, expensive; applied to any article of sale. **1860** HOTTEN *Slang Dict.* s.v. 'Its rather too salt', said of an extravagant hotel bill. **1887** *Fun* 21 Sept. 126 A magistrate who was lately fined 20*s.* for striking a man in the street, seemed somewhat astonished on hearing the decision, and remarked, 'It's rather salt'.

7. *slang.* Of high rank or great wealth. (Cf. SALT *sb.*[1] 3 a.)

1868 *Daily Tel.* 27 May, The salt ones of the earth in their private boxes.

8. *Comb.*, as ***salt-tasting***, ***-waved*** adjs.

1593 SHAKS. *Lucr.* 1231 Those fair suns..Who in a salt-waved ocean quench their light. **1904** 'ANTHONY HOPE' *Double Harness* ii. 17 The exhilaration of the salt-tasting air.

†**salt**, *a.*[2] *Obs.* Also 6 saut(e, sawt(e, 7 sault. [Aphetic f. ASSAUT *adv.* in phr. *to go* or *be assaut*. Cf. SALT *sb.*[2]] Of bitches: In heat.

1541 *Court Roll Pershore Portsmouth Manor, Worc.* 22 July (Westm. Chapter Munim.), Nullus permittet licescas catulantes vocatas 'Sawtebytches' adire ad largum. **1575** TURBERV. *Venerie* lxxiii. 200 They [*sc.* Otters] goe sault at suche times as firrets goe sault. **1577** B. GOOGE *Heresbach's Husb.* III. (1586) 154 b, The Dogge is thought better than the Bitche, because of the trouble shee bringeth when shee is sawte. **1616** SURFL. & MARKH. *Country Farme* 701 If you take a bitch Fox when she is salt. **1697** DRYDEN *Virg. Georg.* II. 518 Salt Goats, and hungry Cows. **1737** OZELL *Rabelais* II. 250 *note*[8], Smelling.., as Dogs do to a salt Bitch.

b. *transf.* of persons: Lecherous, salacious; hence (of desire), inordinate.

1598 BP. HALL *Sat.* IV. 1, Hee lies wallowing..on his Brothel-bed, Till his salt bowels boyle with poysonous fire. **1599** B. JONSON *Ev. Man out of Hum.* IV. iii. (1616) 142 Let mee perish, but thou art a salt one! **1603** SHAKS. *Meas. for M.* V. i. 406 Whose salt imagination yet hath wrong'd Your well defended honor. **1604** —— *Oth.* II. i. 244 His salt, and most hidden loose Affection. **1605** B. JONSON *Volpone* II. i. (1616) 464 It is no salt desire Of seeing countries..hath brought me out. *a* **1683** OLDHAM *Wks.* (1686) 3 Bawds shall turn Nuns, Salt D——s grow chast.

Comb. *a* **1616** BEAUM. & FL. *Bonduca* III. v. (1647) 59/2 Ye villains, Ambitious salt-itcht slaves:..The mountain Rams topt your hot mothers.

salt (sɒlt, -ɔː-), *v.*[1] Forms: α. 1 sealtan, (*Mercian pa. pple.* salten), 4-6 salte, 6 (8-9) *Sc.* saut, 7 sault, 4- salt; 4 *pa. t.* selt, salt. β. 1 seltan, syltan, (*pa. pple.* ȝeselt, ȝesylt); 4 *pa. t.* silt; *pa. pple.* 3 iselt, 4 isult(e, selt. [(1) OE. *sealtan*, ? redupl. str. vb., pa. pple. **sealten*, *salten*, = mod.Fris. (pa. pple.) *sâlten*, MLG. *solten* wk., Du. *zouten* wk., OHG. *salzan*, pa. t. *sialz* (MHG., G. *salzen*, wk.), ON. *salta* wk. (Sw. *salta*, Da. *salte*), Goth. *saltan*, pa. pple. (*un-*)*saltans*; f. OTeut. **salto-*:—preTeut. **saldo-* SALT *sb.*[1] Cf. the synonymous L. *sallĕre* (:—**sald-*). (2) OE. **sieltan* (Northumb. *sælta*), *seltan*, *syltan* (pa. pple. *ȝeselt*, *ȝesylt*):—prehistoric **saltjan*, f. OTeut. **salto-* SALT *sb.*[1] The form *salte* as it appears in the 13–14th c. prob. partly represents OE. *sealtan*, and partly is a new formation on SALT *sb.*[1]

OE. *syltan* may be either the late WS. form of **sieltan* or may represent an umlaut-formation on the stem *sult-*, from which are derived OE. *unsylt* unsalted, OS. *sultia*, MLG. *sülte*, OHG. *sulzia* (MHG., G. *sulze*, *sülze*), Du. *zult* salt water, salted flesh, etc.]

1. *trans.* To treat with salt as a preservative; to cure or preserve with salt, either in solid form or in the form of brine. Also with *down*, †*up*.

α. *a* **1300** *Cursor M.* 13230 In a wall his heued sco hid, Sco has it salted in a wall. **1375** BARBOUR *Bruce* XVIII. 168 Thai strak his hed of, and syne it Thai haf gert saltit in-till a kyt. **1398** TREVISA *Barth. De P.R.* XIX. lxxiii. (1495) 904 Butter is somdeele salted that it may the better be kepte. *c* **1460** FORTESCUE *Abs. & Lim. Mon.* x. (1885) 132 In Ffraunce the peple salten but lytill mete, except thair bacon. **1530** PALSGR. 697/2, I never salte my befe but in the potte. **1562** *Act 5 Eliz.* c. 5 §6 Any Herring, not being sufficiently salted, packed and casked. **1634** W. WOOD *New Eng. Prosp.* (1865) 38 They [*sc.* fish] are left on the dry ground, sometimes two or three thousand at a set, which are salted up against winter. **1661** BOYLE *Style of Script.* (1675) 183 As swine after their death are salted. **1764** E. MOXON *Eng. Housew.* (ed. 9) 75 Then salt it [*sc.* beef] with common salt and two ounces of saltpetre. **1836** *Penny Cycl.* V. 139/1 The French..were obliged to live chiefly on the flesh of their horses, which was salted down. **1851** *F. Knapp's Chem. Technol.* III. 55 The one [method] consists in salting the butter, which preserves it for immediate use by hindering the decomposition of the casein. **1869** TOZER *Highl. Turkey* I. 308 The custom of salting and keeping the heads of enemies killed in battle. **1875** *Chamb. Jrnl.* 46 [She] had fed herself..through the winter upon snails she had salted down in a barrel.

absol. *c* **1400** MAUNDEV. (1839) xiii. 149 Beside that Cytee, is a Hille of Salt; and of that Salt, every man takethe what he will, for to salte with.

β. *a* **1000** *Ags. Gloss.* in Wr.-Wülcker 212/40 *Condit*,.. selt. *c* **1000** ÆLFRIC *Gram.* xxx. (Z.) 192 Ic..sylte, *condio*. *c* **1000** *Sax. Leechd.* II. 234 Selte mon hiora mettas. **1297** R. GLOUC. (Rolls) 9164, & suþþe þe bones hii bere Wel iselt [*v.r.* isulte] & isode to þe abbeye of redinge. **1300–1400** *R. Gloucester's Chron.* (Rolls) App. xx. 35 Hit was wel isult & in mani leþer ido. **1398** TREVISA *Barth. De P.R.* XVII. xxxii. (1495) 623 The floures of Capparis ben selt and so kepte to gode vse.

b. slang. ***to salt down***, ***away***: to put by, store away (money, stock).

1849 N. P. WILLIS *Rural Lett.* viii. 355 'Calm as the shadow of a rock across the foam of a cataract', would be a neat thing to 'salt down' for Calhoun or Van Buren. **1873** LELAND *Egypt. Sketch-Bk.* 57 Give an Egyptian the same [*sc.* a sixpence], and instead of thanking or drinking, he will salt it down, and promptly beg for more. **1885** *Daily News* 3 Nov. 5/2 He was 'salting down' money for the joint benefit of Ward and himself. **1897** BARRÈRE & LELAND *Slang Dict.* s.v., To salt down stock, to buy stock and keep it for a considerable period. **1902** R. W. CHAMBERS *Maids of Paradise* vii. 126 No one to hinder you from salting away as many millions as you can carry off! **1931** *Kansas City* (Missouri) *Star* 19 Sept. 12/5 It is a well known fact that all gamblers salt away their ill-gotten gains and die inordinately rich. **1952** *New Statesman* 17 May 578/2 Many palms itched for the millions that the Nationalists had salted away. **1959** *Times* 22 Apr. 8/4 Undisclosed profits were 'salted away' in banks in Eire and Rhodesia. **1966** *Economist* 9 Apr. 172/3 Members of previous governments, some of them now restricted to their homes, have salted away enormous sums of hard currency in foreign banks during their period of office. **1974** *Socialist Worker* 26 Oct. 3/1 The press, the experts and the pontificators see nothing wrong or hypocritical in the fact that the Banks can salt away these millions and make still more in this time of crisis.

†**c.** *Students' slang.* To admit (a freshman in a university) with certain burlesque ceremonies, one of which was making him drink salt-and-water or putting salt in his mouth. *Obs.*

1570, etc. [see SALTING *vbl. sb.* 2]. **1611** CHAPMAN *May Day* II. i. 32, I warrant you Sir, I haue not beene matriculated at the Vniuersity, to be meretriculated by him: salted there to be colted here. *c* **1618** MORYSON *Itin.* IV. (1903) 317 At Witteburg they still retayne the old custome of Salting freshmen, or admitting them with ridiculous Ceremonyes,..and the Ceremony is by them called the deposition of hornes.

d. *trans.* To render (an animal) immune by inoculation; *intr.* of an animal: to become immune by suffering a disease. Cf. SALTED *ppl. a.* 4.

1898 *Cape of Good Hope Agric. Jrnl.* 9 Jan. 6 The expression *to salt a beast* means to render the animal immune to the disease, to immunize him. **1906** *Rep. Brit. Assoc. Adv. Sci. 1905* 545 Dr. Edington..reports that..by inoculating mules with Heart-water blood he has been able to salt them against Horse-sickness. **1912** *S. Afr. Agric. Jrnl.* July 54 All farmers agree that cattle which recover [from Lamziekte] do not *salt* from the disease, in other words, there is no immunity.

2. *trans.* **a.** In biblical use: To sprinkle salt upon (a sacrifice); to rub (a new-born child) with salt. **b.** To rub salt into (a wound). **c.** To sprinkle (snow) with salt in order to melt it; to sprinkle (a roadway) with salt in order to melt snow or ice.

a **1300** *Leg. Rood* (1871) 58 (Ashm. MS.) And of is flesc þat was vorbarnd þe wounden hi selte also [*Vernon MS.* salt, *Harl. MS.* silte]. **1382** WYCLIF *Ezek.* xvi. 4 And in water thou art not wasshen in to helth, neither bi salt saltid, neither wlappid in clothis. **1643** MILTON *Divorce* Introd. A 2 b, Till Time the Midwife..have washt and salted the Infant. *a* **1682** SIR T. BROWNE (J.), If the offering was of flesh, it was salted thrice. **1890** *Daily News* 31 Dec. 3/1 Many of the vestries..won't clear the snow away themselves, and they won't let us salt the roads. **1977** *Oxford Jrnl.* 2 Dec. 12/4 Roads will only be salted when it is absolutely certain a cold snap is on the way.

3. To season with salt.

α. *c* **975** *Rushw. Gosp.* Matt. v. 13 Ðif þæt salt awerdað in þæm þe hit bið salten? *c* **1000** in *Techmer's Zeitschrift* (1885) II. 125 Do mid þin þrim fingrum, swillce þu sealte. **1382** WYCLIF *Matt.* v. 13 That ȝif the salt shal vanyshe awey, wherynne shal it be saltid? *c* **1420** *Liber Cocorum* (1865) 19 Salt hit, serve hit, as I þe say. *Ibid.* 31 Salt and messe forthe. *c* **1430** *Two Cookery-bks.* 32 Þen kytte þin Brewes & skalde hem with þe same broþe; Salt it wyl. *Ibid.* 41 Salt it þan, & þanne serue forth. **1747** H. GLASSTONE *Art of Cookery* i. 3 Never salt your roast Meat before you lay it to the Fire, for that draws out all the Gravy. **1882** MME. BOUCHARD *How to live on Nothing* 17 All roasts should be peppered as well as salted, very little flour dredged over, and they should be served with a thick gravy. **1931** E. WEIR *When Madame Cooks* v. 55 After cleaning the fish..Salt and pepper the inside of each half and then grill them like a steak. **1965** *New Statesman* 5 Nov. 692/3 He..took up his knife and fork. He carefully salted his egg.

β. *c* **950** *Lindisf. Gosp.* Matt. v. 13 Ðif salt forworðes, in ðon ȝesælted bið? [*Ags. & Hatton* ȝesylt.] *c* **1000** *Ags. Gosp.* Mark ix. 50 Ðif þæt sealt unsealt biþ, on þam þe ȝe hit syltað? [*c* **1160** *Hatton* selteð, *v.r.* sealtað.]

4. To render salt or salty. Also *fig.*, to embitter.

1786 BURNS *Dream* xv, But ere the course o'life be thro', It may be bitter sautet. **1826** J. JEKYLL *Corr.* (1894) 164 Clever plan..to supply the new palace with fish, by salting the Serpentine river to breed tame turbot. **1906** *Westm. Gaz.* 11 Dec. 2/2 A sea which salts all the rivers that flow into it.

5. *fig.* To season; to render poignant or piquant.

[*c* **1000** ÆLFRIC *Hom.* (Th.) II. 536 Lareowum ȝedafenað þæt hi mid wisdomes sealte geleaffulra manna mod sylton.] **1576** FLEMING *Panopl. Epist.* A ij, Coriolanus..whose.. continuall course of life being leauened and salted with the best things that nature could deuise. **1758** *Misc.* in *Ann. Reg.* 381/1 Hardly any thing..was received there with applause, that was not salted with some obscene raillery. **1882** SPURGEON *Treas. Dav.* cxix. 116 It is not wrong to make resolutions, but it will be useless..unless we salt them well with believing cries to God. **1887** SAINTSBURY *Hist. Elizab. Lit.* vi. 230 Lodge began to write pamphlets vigorously.. salted with charming poems. **1889** SKRINE *Mem. Thring* 217 There was piety salted with practical good sense. **1895** MEREDITH *Amazing Marr.* I. ii. 22 He salted his language in a manner I cannot repeat; no epithet ever stood by itself.

b. *U.S. colloq.* To reprimand or dress *down*.

1904 *Springfield* (Mass.) *Weekly Republ.* 9 Sept. 6 Senator Depew salts down William Allen White, who has stated that the senator tried to bully the president. **1913** J. LONDON *Valley of Moon* viii. 61 You're too fresh to keep... You need saltin' down.

6. †**a.** To make (soil) barren by impregnating it with salt. *Obs.*

a **1586** SIDNEY *Ps.* CVII. xii, How many where doth he convert Well watred grounds to thirsty sand? And saltes the soile for with hart The dwellers beare that till the land! *a* **1682** SIR T. BROWNE *Tracts* x. (1683) 166 Salting and making barren the whole Soil.

b. To treat (land) with salt; to strew salt in (hay) to prevent mould. Also 'To fill with salt between the timbers and planks, as a ship, for the preservation of the timber' (Webster 1828–32).

1824 *Trans. Highl. Soc.* VI. 173 Of these, 40 falls were.. salted on the surface. **1825** LOUDON *Encycl. Agric.* §5233 Hay that had been flooded, was preferred by cattle to the best hay that had not been salted.

c. Orig. in *Soap-making*, to separate *out* (the soap) by adding salt to the lye after saponification. More generally in *Chem.*, to reduce the solubility of, or precipitate (an organic substance) by adding an electrolyte to the solution; similarly ***to salt in***, to increase the solubility of (an organic compound) by adding an electrolyte to the solvent.

1857 MILLER *Elem. Chem., Org.* (1862) III. 331 The coagulated soap is then to be re-dissolved in water, and salted out once or twice more. **1887** *Encycl. Brit.* XXII. 203/1 In curd soaps..the uncombined alkali and glycerin are separated by 'salting out'. **1928** [see CORTIN]. **1933** *Chem. Rev.* XIII. 91 There are numbers of cases in which the addition of certain salts increases the solubility of particular non-electrolytes causing them to be 'salted in'. **1939** *Thorpe's Dict. Appl. Chem.* (ed. 4) III. 286/2 The power of these electrolytes in 'salting out' organic compounds from their solutions. **1966** MAHLER & CORDES *Biol. Chem.* ii. 58 From the data in this figure, it is clear that at low ionic strengths the protein is salted in and at high ionic strengths the protein is salted out.

d. To provide (livestock) with salt. *N. Amer.*

1783 'J. H. ST. JOHN DE CRÈVECŒUR' *Sk. 18th-Cent. Amer.* (1925) 111 We..salt our cattle regularly once a week.. From the horses to the sheep everyone must have a handful given them. **1819** E. DANA *Geogr. Sk. Western Country* 234 It is rare in this country that cattle are either fed, salted, or sheltered. **1852** [see *lick-log* s.v. LICK *v.* 8]. **1878** *Scribner's Mag.* XVII. 51/2 They [*sc.* sheep] make many lively expeditions for the farm-boy—driving them out of mischief, ..or salting them on the breezy hills. **1931** *Amer. Speech* VI. 359 The absence of a salt sage diet on the summer range necessitates 'salting mutton'... Every second or third day one or two fifty-pound sacks of salt for every fifteen hundred sheep will be emptied into 'salt troughs' on the 'bed grounds'. **1968** R. M. PATTERSON *Finlay's River* 240 The packer..decided to leave those two [horses] here on the meadows to fill up and recuperate. He would salt them here.

7. a. *Photogr.* To impregnate (paper, etc.) with a solution of a salt or a mixture of salts.

1879 *Cassell's Techn. Educ.* III. 230 Excellent prints may, however, be produced upon paper which has been simply salted. **1878** ABNEY *Photogr.* (1881) 145 When a paper is weakly salted, say, having half the amount of chloride given in the formula for albumenising paper.

b. To treat with chemical salts.

1904 *Brit. Med. Jrnl.* 10 Sept. 558 Only from old cultures or from younger cultures which have been salted with ammonium sulphate can any poisons be obtained by filtration through porcelain.

8. *Comm. slang.* (See quots.) Cf. F. *saler*.

1882 OGILVIE s.v., *To salt an invoice, account*, &c., to put on the extreme value on each article, in some cases in order to be able to make what seems a liberal discount at payment. **1897** BARRÈRE & LELAND *Slang Dict.* s.v., Making fictitious entries in the books to simulate that the receipts are greater than they really are, when about to sell a business connection, is called salting the books. **1977** *New Yorker* 29 Aug. 54/3 That made it easy for me to salt their accounts, and that's what I did. I began putting checks from company accounts into their personal accounts, and from there into oblivion via dummy companies.

9. *Mining slang.* To make (a mine) appear to be a paying one by fraudulently introducing rich ore, etc., into it, sprinkling gold dust in it, etc. Also *transf.* and *fig.*

1852 in *Pioneer* (San Francisco) (1855) Mar. 146 The quicksilver which was procured at the Ranch, for the testing of the quartz, the victims declared was 'salted'; and they accused the *Rancheros* of conniving at the fraud. **1863** W. H. GOODE *Outposts of Zion* III. 415 The grounds have been 'salted'—gold dust scattered to deceive. **1864** HOTTEN *Slang Dict.* s.v., At the gold diggings of Australia, miners sometimes salt an unproductive hole by sprinkling a few grains of gold dust over it. **1880** *Harper's Mag.* Dec. 88/1 The deacon had stuck in a bit of Scriptur so's to salt it like. **1884** *World* 20 Aug. 6/1 The mine had possibly been 'salted', for no gold was forthcoming. **1892** MUDDOCK *Grip of Law* 285 He purchased some valuable specimens of gold quartz, with which he salted the estate. **1901** *Westm. Gaz.* 29 June 9/3 The supposed great oilfields in Florida have been fraudulently 'salted' with refined petroleum. **1924** G. B. STERN *Tents of Israel* vii. 114 The Nong-Khan mine had been cleverly 'salted'... Only spinel sapphires, of practically no value, were to be found in it. **1951** *Times* 13 Dec. 4/6 (*heading*) Gold samples 'salted'. **1966** W. S. RAMSON *Austral. Eng.* vii. 148 One interesting and now probably obsolete expression is *to salt a claim*, meaning 'to sprinkle salt over the dirt', the salt having the appearance of gold-dust and giving the impression that the miner concerned has 'struck it rich'. **1968** A. S. ROMER *Procession of Life* xviii. 296 The gravel pit it would seem, was 'salted' by someone (? Dawson) with specimens to be later excavated as seeming authentic fossils. **1977** J. B. HILTON *Dead-Nettle* ii. 20, I shall want to see some evidence that there really is a seam. No salting it, no faking.. your first job is to collect your showing.

10. *intr.* 'To deposit salt from a saline substance; as, the brine begins to salt' (Webster 1828–32).

salt, *v.*^{2} [f. SALT *a.*^{2}] In pa. pple. = SALT *a.*^{2}

1582 STANYHURST *Æneis* IV. (Arb.) 101 Thee winter season too wast in leacherye wanton, Retchles of her kingdom, with rutting bitcherye sauted [orig. *turpique cupidine captos*].

salt, saltable, var. ff. SAULT, SAULTABLE.

salta ('sæltə). [f. L. *saltāre* to leap, perh. imitating HALMA.] A game played on a checkerboard of 100 squares by two persons with fifteen pieces each, with the object of occupying the opponent's side of the board.

1901 *Daily Express* 23 Mar. 8/7 Salta is played on a board of 100 squares, each player having fifteen pieces. *Ibid.*, Like in the first international salta tournament.., a chess master has again held his own against the draughts and salta experts who competed. **1904** E. B. TWEEDIE *Behind Footlights* viii. 153 She [*sc.* Sarah Bernhardt].. plays Salta with her son. This game is a kind of draughts. **1969** R. C. BELL *Board & Table Games* II. iii. 59 Salta was invented about 1900, and is played on the black squares of a continental draughtsboard of 10 × 10 squares.

salta-di-banco: see SALTIMBANCO.

†'**saltage.** *Obs. rare*$^{-0}$. [f. SALT *sb.*^{1} + -AGE, after F. *salage.*] Salt-duty.

1611 COTGR., *Salage*, saltage.

‖**saltamar'tino.** *Obs.* [It.] A kind of ordnance: see quot. 1688.

1684 R. WALLER *Nat. Exper.* 145 We fitted upon a Carriage with Six Horses, a Saltamartino. **1688** R. HOLME *Armoury* III. xviii. (Roxb.) 138/1 The Saltamartino, a smal peece of the Venetians 15 diameters long and carrieth 4 pound ball.

'**salt-and-'pepper**, *a.* Applied to things and materials (esp. hair) which are of two or more colours, one being light. Cf. PEPPER-AND-SALT. Also (orig. and chiefly *U.S.*) applied *transf.* to places, schemes, etc., in which black and white persons are mixed.

1915 *St. Even. Post* 2 Jan. 8/3 Hattie Krakow ran her hand over her smooth salt-and-pepper hair. **1959** *Wall St. Jrnl.* 12 Aug. 19/2 Houston is considering the 'salt and pepper' plan which has been widely suggested but not yet used. It calls for initial integration in schools where there is least objection from parents and expansion into other areas later. **1966** J. S. COX *Illustr. Dict. Hairdressing* 130/2 *Salt and pepper hair*, a head of hair in which the hairs are of at least two different colours, one of which is white. **1971** *New Yorker* 21 Aug. 3 (Advt.), Braid-bound suit of salt and pepper tweed. **1972** *Ibid.* 23 Dec. 38/3 Detroit is a salt-and-pepper situation. A great mix of black and white. **1973** M. AMIS *Rachel Papers* 52 In common with every American over eight and under twenty-five, he looked like a middle-aged American sports-writer: freckled pinhead, cropped salt-and-pepper hair. **1978** R. LUDLUM *Holcroft Covenant* vi. 79 Thick eyebrows, the coiled, matted hair an odd mixture of black and white. Salt-and-pepper eyebrows.

saltant ('sæltənt), *a.* [ad. L. *saltant-em*, pres. pple. of *saltāre* (see SALTATE).]

1. Leaping, jumping, dancing. Now *rare* or *Obs.*

1601 HOLLAND *Pliny* VIII. xvi. I. 202 When he chaseth and followeth after other beasts, hee goeth alwaies saltant or rampant. **1711** SHAFTESB. *Charac.* (1737) III. 117 This prophesying spirit-errant, processional, and saltant. **1755** JOHNSON, *Saltant*, jumping; dancing. **1819** H. BUSK *Vestriad* I. 676 Thou, whose turn'd legs, main pillars of the stage, Support its glory in this saltant age. **1827** J. F. COOPER *Prairie* II. x. 28 No professor of the saltant art ever applied himself with greater industry than [etc.].

b. *Zool.* = SALTATORIAL.

In mod. Dicts.

c. *Her.* Applied to small animals when salient.

1850 OGILVIE, *Saltant*,.. a term applied to the squirrel, weasel, rat, and all vermin, and also to the cat, greyhound, ape, and monkey, when in a position springing forward.

‖**saltarello** (sæltə'rɛləʊ). Also **salterello, -ella, -arella.** Pl. **saltarelli, -ellos.** [It. *salterello* cracker, squib, jack of a spinet, animated dance, Sp. *saltarelo*; related to It. *saltare*, Sp. *saltar* to leap, dance.]

1. A very animated Italian and Spanish dance for one couple in which there are numerous sudden skips or jumps. Also, the music for this, or a movement resembling it in a musical composition.

[**1597** MORLEY *Introd. Mus.* III. 181 The Italians make their galliardes (which they tearme *saltarelli*) plaine, and frame ditties to them.] **1724** *Short Explic. For. Wds. in Mus. Bks.*, *Saltarella*, a particular kind of Jig so called. **1833** B'NESS BUNSEN in Hare *Life* (1879) I. ix. 378 A merry party of the inhabitants, who.. danced the saltarello in every variety. **1873** 'OUIDA' *Pascarel* II. 175 The salterello and the stornello were all the gayer and the sweeter on his mandoline. **1876** STAINER & BARRETT *Dict. Mus. Terms* 383/2 Saltarelli are frequently found as movements or separate pieces in harpsichord and pianoforte music. **1890** *Daily News* 17 Feb. 3/2 The finale.. including a saltarello, is more or less Mendelssohnian. **1928** E. CANZIANI *Through Apennines & Lands of Abruzzi* iv. 55 At Mascione, when the *saltarella* is danced, if lovers quarrel, the man or the woman kneels and asks, '*Cosa hai fatto?*' **1968** *Listener* 22 Aug. 249/3 The orchestra takes over from the voices and provides what might be regarded as a cue for dancing—as in the *saltarello* episode (in 'Sloth'). **1976** *Early Music* Oct. 457/1 Two of them are included on the Telefunken record already mentioned: the third of the manuscript's four saltarellos and 'Chominciamento di gioia'. **1980** *Ibid.* July 406/3 Apart from some isolated examples which have appeared in various anthologies, including some of the saltarelli and the popular *Lamento di tristano*, transcriptions have been restricted to scholarly editions.

2. The jack of a spinet or harpischord.

1598 [see JACK *sb.*^{1} 14]. **1882** OGILVIE, *Saltarello*,.. a harpsichord jack, so called because it jumps on the key being struck.

saltarter, -tartre: see SAL^1 2.

†'**saltary.** *Obs.* Also **-ery.** [ad. med.L. *saltārium*, f. L. *saltāre* to leap. Cf. SALTATORY *sb.*^{2}, SALTORY.] (See quots.)

1598 MANWOOD *Lawes Forest* xx. 160 Neither may any man make any salteries [*ed.* 1615 saltaries] or leaping places out of the Forrest into the Pouralles, where any Deere may easily leape in, but cannot returne backe againe. **1615** *Ibid.* xxii. 227 Any Saltaries or great gaps, called Deere leapes. *Ibid.* xxiv. 242 You shall enquire.. what saltaries and leapes they haue in hurt of the said Forest.

Saltash ('sɔːltæʃ). The name of a fishing-port in Cornwall used *attrib.* in **Saltash luck** (occas. **catch**), a thankless or fruitless task that involves getting wet through. *Naut. slang.*

1914 'BARTIMEUS' *Naval Occasions* xxiii. 225 One of the securing chains wants tautening... 'Saltash Luck' for some one! **1946** J. IRVING *Royal Navalese* 149 *Saltash luck*, a wet and thankless task such as securing up a bower anchor's slips in a seaway with the forecastle streaming with spray. **1962** GRANVILLE *Dict. Sailors' Slang* 99/2 *Saltash catch or Saltash luck*, 'a wet arse and no fish'. This West Country phrase has long been in use at sea, both in the Royal and Merchant Navies... It is believed to have originated in the lucklessness of fisherman at Saltash near Plymouth who sit on the bridge and catch nothing but the tide.

saltate ('sælteɪt), *v.* [f. L. *saltāt-*, ppl. stem of *saltāre* to dance, frequent. of *salīre* to leap.]

1. *intr.* To leap; to jump; to skip. Hence '**saltating** *vbl. sb. rare.*

1623 COCKERAM I I, To Dance. *Saltate, Tripudiate.* **1846** in WORCESTER (citing *Month. Rev.*). **1865** *Cornh. Mag.* Mar. 299, I must here confess that they saltated to a mandolin touched by this hand. **1852** DANA *Crust.* II. 1180 The species of Cyclops swim.. with a saltating motion.

2. *Physical Geogr.* To move by saltation (see SALTATION 1 d); also *trans.* (causatively). Chiefly as **saltating** *ppl. a.*

1941 R. A. BAGNOLD *Physics Blown Sand & Desert Dunes* viii. 104 The energy supplied to the saltating grains by the wind. **1961** N. D. OPDYKE in A. E. M. Nairn *Descript. Palaeoclimatol.* iii. 47 Millet seed sand grains.. show very high sphericity and roundness values due to their mode of transport which tends to round off the individual grains while they are being saltated. **1969** *Nature* 23 Aug. 792/2 Larger particles may be moved, not by the wind itself, but by momentum exchange with saltating grains. **1976** R. C. SELLEY *Introd. Sedimentol.* vi. 172 In a situation such as a river channel,.. gravel will be rolling along the bottom, sand will sedately saltate, and silt and clay will be carried in suspension.

saltation (sæl'teɪʃən). [ad. L. *saltātiōn-em*, n. of action f. *saltāre* to SALTATE.]

1. a. Leaping, bounding, or jumping; a leap.

1646 SIR T. BROWNE *Pseud. Ep.* v. iii. 236 Locusts.. being ordained for saltation, their hinder legs doe far exceed the other. **1710** T. FULLER *Pharm. Extemp.* 129 Those odd Epileptic Saltations called St. Vitus's Dance. **1834** MCMURTRIE *Cuvier's Anim. Kingd.* 396 The posterior legs of.. the Orthoptera, are remarkable for the largeness of their thighs, and for their spinous tibiæ, which are adapted for saltation. **1852** DANA *Crust.* II. 1062 The animal swims by saltations, with great agility. **1881** *Trans. Obstetr. Soc.* XXII. 152 The conclusion one might arrive at from the violent saltation of the fœtus. **1883** *Pall Mall G.* 11 Sept. 11/1 It is not every flea.. that is gifted with the power of saltation. **1897** *Syd. Soc. Lex.*, *Saltation*... Especially applied to the leaping sometimes noticed in cases of chorea.

b. *spec.* Dancing; a dance.

1623 COCKERAM I, *Saltation*, dancing. **1656** BLOUNT *Glossogr.*, *Saltation*, a dancing. **1685** E. BROWN *Trav.* 10 The old Pyrrhical Saltation, or Warlike way of Dancing. **1814** SCOTT *Wav.* xxviii, Still keeping time to the music.., he.. continued his saltation without.. intermission. **1879** MISS BRADDON *Clov. Foot* iv. 34 Her dancing was distinguished for its audacity rather than for high art. She was no follower of the Taglioni school of saltation. **1890** *Harper's Mag.* Oct. 797/2 These spangled saltations.

c. *fig.* An abrupt movement, change, or transition.

1844 GLADSTONE *Glean.* V. xviii. 94 He must substitute for the saltations by which he reaches his conclusions.. the patient and measured march of thought. **1854** EMERSON *Lett. & Soc. Aims* i. (1875) 61 The number of successive saltations the nimble thought can make.

d. *Physical Geogr.* A mode of transport of hard particles over an uneven surface in a fluid stream (as a wind or river), in which they progress in leaps, and on falling to the surface either bounce up for another leap or impart their momentum to other particles which on rising are accelerated forward by the stream. Cf. SALTATE *v.* 2.

1908 W. J. MCGEE in *Bull. Geol. Soc. Amer.* XIX. 199 Transportation may be regarded as the general movement of earth matter seaward by streams; it comprises carriage of material (*a*) in solution, (*b*) in suspension, and (*c*) in what may be denoted saltation. **1941** R. A. BAGNOLD *Physics of Blown Sand & Desert Dunes* ii. 20, I shall use the name 'saltation' for the motion of sand in air, but without prejudice to the question of whether or not the mechanism which causes the grain to jump from the surface is the same in the two fluids. In air it is certainly the impact of a grain with the surface; but this is rarely so in water. **1962** READ & WATSON *Introd. Geol.* I. iv. 206 The mechanisms of transport in the sea are similar to those already described in connection with rivers, namely, suspension, rolling and saltation. **1977** A. HALLAM *Planet Earth* 50 The sand grains suspended in the air are the smaller ones, movement of larger particles being along the ground by saltation—by a series of jumps.

†**2.** *spec.* Pulsation or spurting forth (of blood).

1672 WISEMAN *Treat. Wounds* II. ix. 64 If it [*sc.* the blood] flow.. from the left side, we suppose it the Artery, you will discover it by its saltation and florid colour. **1752** C. SMART *Hop-Garden* I. 146 His verdant blood In brisk saltation circulates and flows. **1767** GOOCH *Treat. Wounds* I. 87 When veins are wounded, the blood does not flow with that impetuosity and saltation, as when proceeding from an artery.

3. *Biol.* **a.** A mutation, esp. one with marked effects on several characters.

The 'saltations' studied by de Vries (see quot. 1906) are now known to have been translocations, which in *Œnothera* with its unusual system of chromosomes lead to large phenotypic changes.

1870 HUXLEY *Lay Serm.* xiii. 343 We greatly suspect.. that she [*sc.* Nature] does make considerable jumps in the way of variation now and then, and that these saltations give rise to some of the gaps which appear to exist in the series of known forms. **1906** *Pop. Sci. Monthly* June 485 The name 'saltation', or in recent years 'mutation', has been applied to extreme fluctuation, the immediate cause of which is unknown. *Ibid.*, Experiments of Dr. Hugo de Vries on the saltations of the descendants of an American form of evening primrose. **1919** *Jrnl. Exper. Zool.* XXVIII. 381 In our opinion, the attempted distinctions between 'saltations', 'mutations', and 'variations of slight degree' have led rather to confusion of thought than to clearer thinking. To us these are all a single class, 'mutations'. **1930** R. A. FISHER *Genetical Theory Nat. Selection* vii. 163 Unless such a resemblance formerly existed a gradual mimetic evolution is precluded, and we should be forced to admit that the mimetic females arose as sports or saltations totally unlike their mothers. *Ibid.* 164 A single saltation from a male of the same species. **1963** E. MAYR *Animal Species & Evolution* xv. 435 The sudden origin of new species, new higher categories, or quite generally of new types by some sort of saltation has been termed macrogenesis.

b. Change of phenotype occurring within a fungal colony.

1922 F. L. STEVENS in *Bull. Illinois Nat. Hist. Surv.* XIV. v. 157 The existing differences in definition and usage of the term mutation, as also our very limited knowledge of cytological conditions in the genus Helminthosporium and our ignorance as to whether it has sexual stages, have led me to select the term saltation for the variations here discussed. **1926** *Ann. Bot.* XL. 223 Changes of a more lasting nature may be conceived as arising gradually as a response or adaptation to certain growth conditions, or by sudden jumps. The latter type of phenomenon, which is known to occur in a considerable number of fungal genera,.. is usually described as a 'mutation', or more conservatively as a saltation. **1940** J. RAMSBOTTOM in J. S. Huxley *New Systematics* 414 The morphological range is often so great that a single saltation will give what would be considered as a new species. **1978** *Nature* 29 June 755/1 The common and poorly understood phenomenon of frequent somatic variation in certain supposedly haploid fungi (saltation) may perhaps be due to the loss of extra chromosomes that had been acquired previously.

Hence **sal'tational** *a.*, of, pertaining to, or occurring by means of saltation.

1963 E. MAYR *Animal Species & Evolution* xv. 435 The reorganization of the gene pool, required for successful speciation, is (except in the case of polyploidy) never saltational. *Ibid.* 437 Some saltational postulates are based on the assumption of essentially invariant evolutionary rates. **1978** *Sci. Amer.* Sept. 41/1 Even T. H. Huxley.. could not accept the gradual origin of higher types and new species; he proposed a saltational origin instead.

saltationist (sælˈteɪʃənɪst), *a.* and *sb. Biol.* [f. SALTATION + -IST.] **A.** *adj.* Of or pertaining to saltationism. **B.** *sb.* One who supports or advocates saltationism.

1954 R. A. FISHER in J. S. Huxley et al. *Evolution as Process* 93 Darwin's criticism of the saltationist theory of M. Mivart. **1978** *Sci. Amer.* Sept. 44/1 They were essentialists and saltationists, and they looked on mutation as the probable driving force in evolution. **1980** *Nature* 4 Dec. 430/1 T. H. Huxley himself was unable fully to accept Darwin's gradualism, and preferred the saltationist camp.

So **salˈtationism**, the theory that new species arise suddenly as a result of major mutations.

1975 KELLY & MCGRATH *Biology* vii. 213/2 DeVries.. insisted that a new species could arise by the introduction of a single mutation in an organism. His theory, called saltationism.., has been disproved, with one exception. **1978** *Sci. Amer.* Sept. 41/1 Saltationism was also popular with such biologists as Hugo De Vries, one of the rediscoverers of Gregor Mendel's laws of inheritance. **1979** M. RUSE *Darwinian Revolution* ix. 249 There were scientific reasons why many favored saltationism.

saltative (ˈsæltətɪv), *a. rare.* [f. SALTATE *v.* + -IVE.] = SALTATORY *a.* 2 a.

1829 [implied in SALTATIVENESS]. **1911** *Law Rep., King's Bench* I. 654 These Scotch sheep are of a peculiarly wandering and saltative disposition.

ˈsaltativeness. *nonce-wd.* [f. L. *saltāt-* (see SALTATE), after *acquisitiveness*.] The faculty of leaping or jumping.

1829 T. HOOK *Bank to Barnes* 105 He discovered the Organ of Saltativeness [in a flea's skull] magnificently developed.

‖**saltator** (sælˈteɪtə(r)). *Ornith.* [mod.L. use of L. *saltātor*, agent-n. f. *saltāre* (see SALTATE).] A tanagrine bird of the genus *Saltator*.

1882 *Proc. Zool. Soc.* App. 795 Allied Saltator (*Saltator similis*). **1886** SCLATER *Brit. Mus. Catal. Birds* XI. 282 The Saltators keep to the bushes and smaller trees outside the dense forests.

saltatorial (sæltəˈtɔərɪəl), *a.* [f. L. *saltātōri-us* SALTATORY + -AL[1].]

1. Of, pertaining to, or characterized by leaping (or *spec.* dancing).

1789 TWINING tr. *Arist. Poet.* I. vii. 72 [In tragedy] the Trochaic tetrameter was made use of, as better suited to the satyric and saltatorial genius of the Poem at that time. **1843** *Blackw. Mag.* LIV. 84 Yarrell..confines their saltatorial powers only within ten or twelve perpendicular feet. **1877** COUES & ALLEN *N. Amer. Rod.* 532 The saltatorial nature of the animal. **1893** W. A. SHEE *My Contemp.* ii. 39 Whirled away into every species of saltatorial excess.

2. Fitted or adapted for leaping; *spec.* belonging to the group *Saltatoria* of insects.

1842 *Chamb. Jrnl.* 30 July 220 A pair of thickened saltatorial legs. **1855** *Orr's Circ. Sci., Org. Nat.* II. 354 The *Orthoptera* fall readily into two great sections—namely, the saltatorial and cursorial Orthoptera. **1871** DARWIN *Desc. Man* (1890) II. x. 282 The males in the three saltatorial families in this Order are remarkable for their musical powers.

So **saltaˈtorian** *a.*, involving dancing.

1823 *New Monthly Mag.* IX. 297/2 The progress of the saltatorian drama. **1825** *Ibid.* XV. 390 Pantomimic and saltatorian representations.

saltatoric (sæltəˈtɒrɪk), *a. Path.* [Formed as prec. after G. *saltatorisch* (Bamberger): see -IC.] *saltatoric spasm*: a kind of nervous disease in which the patient when set on his feet begins to leap.

1877 GOWERS in *Lancet* 14 July 45/2 The saltatoric spasm persisted for nine months, and then gradually ceased. **1899** *Allbutt's Syst. Med.* VII. 902 They are wanting in the regularity and precision of those of saltatoric spasm.

saltatorious (sæltəˈtɔərɪəs), *a.* [Formed as prec. + -OUS.] = SALTATORIAL.

1816 KIRBY & SP. *Entomol.* xxii. (1818) II. 283 These maggots have long been celebrated for their saltatorious powers. **1826** *Ibid.* xlvi. IV. 345 *Saltatorious*... When the hind legs have strong incrassated thighs formed for leaping.

saltatory (ˈsæltətərɪ), *a.* and *sb.*[1] [ad. L. *saltātōri-us*, f. *saltātor*: see SALTATOR.] **A.** *adj.*

1. Of, pertaining to, characterized by, or adapted for dancing.

1656 BLOUNT *Glossogr., Saltatory*,..of or belonging to dancing, vaulting, &c. **1821** EDGEWORTH *Mem.* I. 93, I soon began to avoid exhibiting my saltatory talents, and I seldom danced. **1851** HAWTHORNE *Snow Image*, etc., *Old News* I. 155 There is an incidental notice of the 'dancing-school near the Orange-Tree', whence we may infer that the saltatory art was occasionally practised. **1869** J. MARTINEAU *Ess.* II. 183 He could make a saltatory automaton.

2. a. Pertaining to, characterized by, or adapted for leaping; *spec.* = SALTATORIAL 2.

1847 L. HUNT *Men, Women, & B.* I. iii. 43 The way in which sheep carry themselves on abrupt and saltatory occasions. **1874** MIVART *Common Frog* I What is a Frog?.. 'The Frog is a small saltatory Reptile', will probably be the reply of the majority. **1877** HUXLEY *Anat. Inv. Anim.* vi. 262 The Amphipoda..are characterized by..their ordinarily saltatory habits. **1891** *Punch* Christmas No. 8 The position of the Moon..is also favourable to saltatory exercise on the part of the cow. **1908** *Bull. Geol. Soc. Amer.* XIX. 199 The coarser particles due to corrosion..and to washing move forward at ever varying rates in saltatory fashion, the variable or leaping movements arising largely in combinations of friction with inertia.

b. *Path.* = SALTATORIC.

1881 J. ROSS *Dis. Nervous Syst.* II. 341 Saltatory Spasm. **1899** *Allbutt's Syst. Med.* VIII. 106 Or when placed on her feet [a patient] may be forced to progress by a series of springing movements (saltatory spasm).

c. *fig.* Proceeding by abrupt movement.

1844 EMERSON *Ess., Experience* Wks. (Bohn) I. 183 Nature hates calculators; her methods are saltatory and impulsive. **1894** H. F. OSBORN *From Greeks to Darwin* 200 Another highly characteristic feature of his theory was, that he [St. Hilaire] included in it what has recently been termed 'saltatory evolution', and strongly opposed Lamarck's fundamental principle that all transformation is extremely slow.

d. *Physiol.* Used to designate the mode of transmission in a myelinated nerve in which the nerve impulse 'jumps' from node to node.

1934 *Amer. Jrnl. Physiol.* CX. 308 The pictures could be accounted for if progression were saltatory and by a process such as Lillie (1925) has described as occurring in the iron wire model... Here, due to reactivation by eddy currents flowing around the segments, activity progresses in jumps from node to node and consequently is more rapid than in the simple model. **1949** *Jrnl. Physiol.* CVIII. 339 The finding..that a large decrease in node spacing can occur without a drop in conduction velocity is shown not to conflict with the theory of saltatory conduction. **1977** *Proc. Nat. Acad. Sci.* LXXIV. 211/1 Myelinated nerve conducts by transmission of electrical excitation from node to node through local electrical circuits. This 'saltatory' mode of conduction results from a discontinuity in the excitability properties of the axon: excitable regions (nodes) alternate with nonexcitable passive core conductors (myelinated internodes).

e. *Biol.* Of the movement of small particles within cells: proceeding in directed jerks.

1964 L. I. REBHUN in Allen & Kamiya *Primitive Motile Syst. in Cell Biol.* 503 Particles may at one time undergo Brownian movement and suddenly undergo a process converting this to sudden, discontinuous motion, i.e., saltatory motion. **1970** *Nature* 7 Feb. 559/1 It may well be ..that microtubules in brain function in the saltatory transport of material and vesicles from their site of formation in the cell body to their site of utilization at the synaptic endings. *Ibid.* 5 Sept. 1006/2 Translocation has been pictured as a saltatory interaction between enzyme-containing vesicles and fibrous proteins, chiefly microtubules.

3. Biol. ***saltatory replication***, a hypothetical evolutionary event in which very many identical copies of a short section of DNA are added to a genome.

1968 R. J. BRITTEN in *Carnegie Inst. Year Bk. 1966–7* 72/2 *Saltatory replications*, the hypothetical events by which families of hundreds of thousands of similar nucleotide sequences are produced in the DNA of an organism... Families are produced in a time short compared to the time required for their loss by divergence (a few hundred million years). **1968** —— & KOHNE in *Ibid.* 84/1 Events in which very many copies [of a DNA segment] are made in a short time interval (saltatory replication). Evidence is now available which clearly indicates saltatory replication. *Ibid.* 88/1 A saltatory replication producing 100,000 copies of the right sort of gene is a candidate for a genetic event with immense potentiality. **1970** *Nature* 12 Dec. 1043/2 Such gene expansion has been designated saltatory replication and is illustrated in Fig. 1 *C*.

†**B.** *sb.* A dancer. *Obs. rare*[−1].

a **1625** FLETCHER, etc. *Fair Maid Inn* III. i, A second, a lavolteteere, a saltatory, a dancer with a Kit at his bum.

ˈsaltatory, *sb.*[2] *Antiq.* [ad. med.L. *saltātōri-um*, neut. sing. of *saltātōrius* (see prec.) used subst. Cf. SALTORY.] = SALTARY.

1903 *Edin. Rev.* July 179 The saltatory was a contrivance by which deer could make their way into the park, but could not jump back again.

†**salˈtatress.** *Obs. rare*[−1]. [f. SALTATOR: see -TRESS. Cf. It. *saltatrice*.] A female dancer.

1784 R. BAGE *Barham Downs* I. 120 Her le volts were the highest of any Saltatress in Italy.

ˈsalt-box. [f. SALT *sb.*[1] + BOX *sb.*[2]]

1. a. A box for keeping salt for domestic use.

'Billy in the Salt-box' was the title of a caricature referring to Pitt's budget of 1805, in which the salt-tax was greatly increased.

1611 COTGR., *Saulnier*,..a Salt-box. **1812** *Examiner* 12 Oct. 651/2 A few grains from the salt-box. **1862** W. BARNES *Homely Rhymes Dorset Dial.* I. 5 The zalt-box an' the corner-cupb'ard.

b. (See quot. 1847–54.)

1763 B. THORNTON *Ode on St. Cecilia's Day* ad. fin., The saltbox..With clattering and clapping shall sound. **1774** J. T. SMITH *Bk. Rainy Day* (1861) 39 A famous player on the salt-box. **1813** *Sporting Mag.* XLII. 19 The divine harmony of the Gong, the French-horn, and the Salt-box. **1847–54** WEBSTER s.v., In burlesque music, the salt-box has been used like the marrow-bones and cleaver, tongs and poker, etc.

c. *U.S.* Used *attrib.* or *absol.* to designate a kind of frame-house which resembles a salt-box in shape, having two storeys at the front and one at the back.

1876 J. S. INGRAM *Centennial Exposition* 717 One of the chief oddities of the Exhibition—the Hunter's Cabin. It was built of logs in the 'salt-box' style and entirely open in front. **1900** J. DE F. SHELTON *Salt-Box House* I. 17 Colloquially, it was called a 'salt-box house', its lines repeating those of the wooden salt-box that hung in the kitchen chimney. The ridge-pole was set far to the front, from which a short roof sloped..down to the outer line of the ceiling of the ground floor. **1934** *Sun* (Baltimore) 14 Aug. 10/6 The first of the salt boxes were almost always made by adding the lean-to to the two-room house. **1944** *Sat. Rev.* (U.S.) 2 Sept. 30/1 (Advt.), New England saltbox in scenic New York setting. **1952** F. ALLEN *Big Change* II. viii. 126 New England salt-box-type houses with attached garages. **1967** V. SILTER *Biltmore Call* 57 Some were remodelled farm houses..and some were old saltboxes..and some were just plain old country houses. **1976** *New Yorker* 22 Mar. 125/1 Cunningly combining painted backcloths, a two-story saltbox frame, and picturesque detail in the way of furniture and properties, Ming Cho Lee's decor for the six different settings was at once varied, realistic, and romantic.

2. *slang.* (See quots.)

1812 J. H. VAUX *Flash Dict.*, *Salt-boxes*, the condemned cells in Newgate are so called. *Ibid.*, *Salt-box-cly*, the outside coat-pocket, with a flap. **1820** *Lond. Mag.* Jan. 29 Their..leaving the stone-jug, after a miserable residence in the salt-boxes, to be top'd in front of the debtor's door.

3. *Naut.* (See quot.)

1867 SMYTH *Sailor's Word-bk.*, *Salt-box*, a case for keeping a temporary supply of cartridges for the immediate use of the great guns.

ˈsalt-cat. [Originally northern. The original meaning of the second element is unknown; *cat* is used dialectally as a name for several mixtures of which clay is a constituent: see E.D.D.

Cf. '*Cat*, a chump of clay stone'; '*Clay-cat*, a kind of large roundish stone found in clay' (Barnes *Dorset Gloss.*).]

A mass of salt, or salt mixed with earthy or other matter; *esp.* a mixture of salt, gravel, old mortar or lime, cummin seed, and stale urine, used to attract pigeons and to keep them at home.

c **1400** MAUNDEV. (Roxb.) xii. 51 At þe riȝt side of þis see was Loth wyf turned intil a salt catte. **1453–4** *Durham Acc. Rolls* (Surtees) 149, j Saltcatt. **1483** *Cath. Angl.* 317/1 A Salte catte. **1629** *Howard Househ. Bks.* (Surtees) 264 To Mr. Chambers his manne bringing 3 salte catts. **1669** WORLIDGE *Syst. Agric.* 154 A Lump of Salt, which they usually call a Salt-cat, made for that purpose at the Salterns. **1765** *Treat Dom. Pigeons* 33 The best way is to put your salt cat in jars, with holes in the sides for them to peck it out. **1864** KNIGHT *Passages Work. Life* II. i. 17 The business-house of a young publisher had..the sort of attraction for flights of authors as a saltcat has for pigeons.

ˈsalt-ˌcellar. Forms: 5–6 saler, (5 sellere, seler, 6 celler), 5–8 seller, 6–7 sellar, 7– cellar. [f. SALT *sb.*[1] + SALER (which has been assimilated in spelling to CELLAR).] **a.** A small vessel used on the table for holding salt.

1434 *E.E. Wills* (1882) 102 A feir salt saler of peautre with a feyre knoppe. **1445** *Will* in Madox *Formul. Anglic.* (1702) 434 Duas Saltsellers Argenteas. **1483** *Cath. Angl.* 317/2 A Salte seler. **1513** *Bk. Keruynge* in *Babees Bk.* (1868) 269 Take thy salte seller in thy lefte hande. **1566** in Peacock *Eng. Ch. Furniture* (1866) 53 A salt celler for salt. **1633** WOTTON in *Reliq.* (1672) 464, I send you..a triangular Salt celler. **1669** WOODHEAD *St. Teresa* II. 269 A Sister..found at last a little Salt-celler in a Chest. **1729** SWIFT *Direct. Serv.* i. Wks. 1751 XIV. 23 Fold up the Table-cloth with the Salt in it, then shake the Salt out into the Salt-cellar to serve next Day. **1865** DICKENS *Mut. Fr.* III. iv, Putting down the glasses and salt-cellars as if she were knocking at the door.

attrib. *c* **1460** J. RUSSELL *Bk. Nurture* 60 Loke..þy salte sellere lydde towche not thy salt bye.

b. In phrases as in SALT *sb.*[1] 7 b.

1609 DEKKER *Gull's Horn-bk.* Wks. (Grosart) II. 244 You may giue any Iustice of peace, or yong Knight (if he sit but one degree towards the Equinoctiall of the Salt-seller) leaue to pay for the wine. **1645** MILTON *Colast.* 19 That which never yet afforded corn of savour to his noddle, the Salt-seller was not rubb'd. **1648** HERRICK *Hesp.*, *His Age* vii, If we can meet, and so conferre, Both by a shining Salt-seller. **1843** JAMES *Forest Days* ix, We have no salt-cellar here, to make a distinction between highest and lowest. **1847** LYTTON *Lucretia* 32 This green banquet of nature, in which at least no man sits below the salt-cellar.

c. *colloq.* Each of the pronounced hollows at the base of a thin neck. (Usu. with reference to young women.)

1870 O. LOGAN *Before Footlights* 26, I was a child of the most uninteresting age..a tall scraggy girl, with red elbows, and salt cellars at my collar-bones, which were always exposed, for fashion at that time made girls of this age uncover neck and arms. **1880** F. BELTON *Random Recoll. Old Actor* vi. 87 The bones of her elbows were painfully prominent, with enormous salt-cellar hollows in her neck. **1913** 'O. ONIONS' *Story of Louie* I. i. 25 The copper-haired girl with the long thin neck and the 'salt-cellars' showing through her white flannel blouse. **1913** *Queen* 17 May 35 (Advt.), 'Saltcellars' and thinness of the neck and shoulders. **1964** P. WHITE *Burnt Ones* 162 She was so thin, but he loved her even for her salt-cellars.

salt chuck. *N. Amer. colloq.* [Chinook jargon, f. SALT *a.*[1] + CHUCK *sb.*[6]] In western Canada and north-western U.S.: the sea, the ocean.

1868 F. WHYMPER *Trav. Alaska* iv. 45 An Indian, paddling in his 'frail kanim' on the great 'salt chuck' or sea, was swallowed—canoe and all—by a great fish. **1874** C. HORETZKY *Canada on Pacific* 132 A thick heavy mist hung over the valley, completely hiding the Cascade range which we had now to enter and pass through before reaching the 'salt-chuck'. **1909** E. I. DENNY *Blazing the Way* I. vii. 120 The fish, of many excellent kinds, from the 'salt chuck', brought fresh and flapping to our doors, in native baskets by Indian fishermen. **1938** G. CASH *I like Brit. Columbia* 61 Unless you are camped near a log dump—which means where a logging company is dumping logs into the salt chuck —you have quite a time gathering enough. **1958** R. G. LARGE *Skeena* (ed. 3) x. 65 Sailing the salt-chuck easily, o'er an oft familiar route. **1964** L. LINTON *Of Days & Driftwood* iv. 24 Even the gulls, screeching over the gray saltchuck.. were giving their last accolade to summer. **1975** *Islander*

(Victoria, B.C.) 27 July 14/2 In 1905, most people lived close to the saltchuck and along Rainey Creek.

Hence 'salt-chucker, a sea-water angler.

1958 in R. E. Watters *Brit. Columbia* 216 It is the spirit that counts, and that spirit extends to trying to make life happier for thousands of scattered salt-chuckers. **1963** *Sun* (Vancouver) 20 July 15/1 Now, however, with an average of almost two fish per short outing of a few hours each trip, I'm wearing the saltchucker's smug smirk.

†**'salt-cote, -coat.** *Obs.* [f. SALT *sb.*[1] + COTE *sb.*[1]] A salt-house.

c **1425** *Voc.* in Wr.-Wülcker 670 *Hec salina*, saltecote. **1473** *Rolls of Parlt.* VI. 78/2 A Saltcote, and 111 acres of pasture with their appurtenaunces. **1483** *Cath. Angl.* 317/2 A Salte cote, *salina, est locus vbi fit sal.* *a* **1552** LELAND *Itin.* (1769) IV. 111 There be a great number of Sault Coates or Furnaces about this Well. **1612** CAPT. SMITH *Map Virginia* 18 The Bay and rivers haue much marchandable fish and places fit for Salt coats. **1630** *Maldon, Essex, Doc.* Bundle 208. No. 7 Went downe to the saltcoate of Mr. John Hastler at the heith [= hythe].

salted ('sɒltɪd, -ɔː-), *ppl. a.* [f. SALT *sb.*[1] or *v.* + -ED.]

1. Cured, preserved, or pickled with salt.

13.. *Cursor M.* 4688 (Gött.) Ma þan a thousand celers Fild he wid wines neu and fress, And lardineris wid saltid fless [*Cott., etc.* salt]. **1555** EDEN *Decades* 55 They..gaue them great plentie of salted fysshe. **1686** tr. *Chardin's Trav. Persia* 74 It preserves the Moisture of Salted Meats. **1732** ARBUTHNOT *Rules of Diet in Aliments*, etc. 269 A Diet of salted Flesh throws Ships Crews sometimes into Diarrhœas. **1842** BROWNING *Pied Piper* ii, They..Split open the kegs of salted sprats. **1851** *F. Knapp's Chem. Technol.* III. 162 The preparation of sauerkraut and salted cucumbers. **1901** *Scribner's Mag.* XXIX. 474/2 The salted goose is a famous dish.

2. a. Having salt as an ingredient; containing or impregnated with salt. Now used esp. of prepared foods, as ***salted almond, peanut***, etc.

1526 *Grete Herball* xcix. (1529) F v b, Sethe these herbes ..in salted water or in kyndly salt water. **1700** DRYDEN *Iliad* I. 628 Their salted Cakes on crackling Flames they cast. **1755** *Man* No. 28. 4 Innumerable species of the finny tribe, taking their solace in the bosom of the salted ocean. **1765** A. DICKSON *Treat. Agric.* (ed. 2) 38 In one of the pots with the salted earth, and in one of those with the washed earth, he planted fennel. **1892** *Encycl. Pract. Cookery* I. 15/1 Salted and 'Devilled' Almonds. **1897** *Westm. Gaz.* 18 Feb. 6/3 The contact with the salted earth had caused considerable corrosion to the stone. **1921** A. HUXLEY *Crome Yellow* xix. 202 Georgiana ate only an olive, two or three salted almonds, and half a peach. **1935** M. MORPHY *Recipes of All Nations* 775 Salted Green Peas, first cooked in cinders and then salted like almonds, are among Persian delicacies. **1954** 'R. CROMPTON' *William & Moon Rocket* iv. 85 Salted nuts.. potato crisps..celery. **1970** E. DAVID *Spices, Salt & Aromatics in Eng. Kitchen* 231 Salted almonds, whatever the promises held out by the words vacuum-sealed or oven-fresh on tins and jars are not to be bought. **1972** A. MACVICAR *Golden Venus Affair* v. 49, I ordered a Pym's No. 1... We munched salted peanuts.

b. Treated with salt.

1824 *Trans. Highl. Soc.* VI. 174 The grass-crop on the salted land will not exceed two-thirds of the weight of what is promised on the parts not salted. **1831** BREWSTER *Optics* xii. 108 A spirit lamp with a salted wick. **1884** A. WATT *Soap-making* 42 Salted soda, is composed of soft soda and common salt.

c. *Photogr.* Impregnated with a salt or a mixture of salts in solution.

1855 HARDWICH *Photogr. Chem.* II. v. 279 This albumenized and salted paper will keep any length of time in a dry place. **1890** *Anthony's Photogr. Bull.* III. 9 The prints ..on plain salted paper.

3. *fig.* 'Seasoned' with wit or good sense; sensible.

(? Orig. with reference to Mark ix. 50.)

1647 WARD *Simp. Cobler* 40 It was a well salted speech. **1869** MRS. WHITNEY *We Girls* iv. (1874) 91 There's a pretty good piece of the world salted, after all. **1900** PHILLPOTTS *Sons of Morning* II. iv, I'd warn 'e to fill her mind with gude, salted sense.

4. *slang.* or *colloq.* Of horses, etc.: Seasoned (from having survived attacks of disease, etc.); hence of persons: Experienced in some business or occupation.

1864 T. BAINES *Explorations in S.W. Afr.* xv. 418 He asked carefully 'whether the horse was salted' (i.e. acclimatised by having recovered from the horse sickness). **1879** ATCHERLEY *Boërland* 209 A 'salted' horse will always command a good price. **1889** F. OATES *Matabele-Land* 236 The old man tells me that a man gets a pain in his head and lies down, and next morning, if he is alive, he is 'salted'. **1892** STEVENSON & L. OSBOURNE *Wrecker* i. 9 Mr. London Dodd, though he was new to the group of the Marquesas, was already an old salted trader. **1899** G. H. RUSSELL *Under the Sjambok* xiv. 137 My friend has a very good 'salted' horse, just the sort of thing you will require in the Low Country. **1905** *Westm. Gaz.* 1 July 9/2 An expert and thoroughly 'salted' journalist. **1977** BUXTON & FRASER *Animal Microbiol.* II. xlviii. 634/1 Horses and mules that have recovered from a natural attack of horse sickness are generally more resistant to disease than other equines and are known as 'salted', as are animals that have survived for a number of years in badly infected areas without ever showing obvious signs of the disease.

5. *slang.* (See SALT *v.*[1] 9.)

1862 *California Mag.* Jan. 355/1, I lost my $2,000 by buying a 'salted' claim. **1886** P. CLARKE *'New Chum' in Australia* vii. 71 Taken in with a 'salted claim', a 'pit' sold for a £10 note in which a nugget worth a few shillings had before been 'planted'. **1889** MRS. C. PRAED *Rom. Station* 200 Their bogus companies and their salted gold-mines. **1949** *This Week Mag.* 15 Oct. 27/4 They are occasionally called upon by unscrupulous characters whose main object is to sell them a 'salted' mine.

saltee ('sɔːltiː). *slang.* [Said to be ad. It. *soldi*, pl. of *soldo* = SOU.] A penny.

1859 HOTTEN *Slang. Dict.* **1861** READE *Cloister & H.* III. iv. 77 It had rained kicks all day in lieu of 'saltees', and that is pennies. **1875** FROST *Circus Life* xvi. 277.

salten ('sɒlt(ə)n, -ɔː-), *a. rare.* [f. SALT *sb.*[1] + -EN[4].] **a.** Salted. **b.** Made of salt.

1654 GAYTON *Pleas. Notes* IV. ix. 233 Bread, Broder, Bacon, Boutter salten. **1875** READE *Wand. Heir* iii. 67 Lot's wife, in salten pillar, still looks on.

salter[1] ('sɒltə(r), -ɔː-). [OE. *sealtere*, f. *sealtan* SALT *v.*[1]: see -ER[1].]

1. A manufacturer of or dealer in salt; also *spec.* = DRYSALTER, as in the title of one of the London livery companies (incorporated in 1558).

a **1000** *Colloq. Ælfric* in Wr.-Wülcker 97 Sealtera [*sic*], hwæt us fremaþ cræft þin? *c* **1000** ÆLFRIC *Gram.* ix. (Z.) 47 *Hic salinator*, þes sealtere. **1392** *Durham Acc. Rolls* (Surtees) 342 Rob's Scott salter. **1402** *Rolls of Parlt.* III. 519 Robt Brendewod, William Estace, Salters. **1418** *Jrnl. Archives City of London* I. 51 Sal emptum per Bemond et Edwardum, Salters, infra civitatem Londoniarum vend'. **1507** *Rec. St. Mary at Hill* (1905) 22 Andrewe Evyngar, Cytezen and Salter of london. **1573** *Reg. Privy Council Scot.* Ser. I. II. 293 The saidis salteris sall sell salt to the subjectis and carearis of this realme of sufficient mett and stuff. **1611** COTGR., *Maligne*, a Spring-tyde; called so by the Salters of Xaintonge. **1682** J. COLLINS *Salt & Fishery* 125 It is commonly sold in Salters-shops at Billingsgate. **1745** *De Foe's Eng. Tradesman* (1841) I. iv. 25 As a salter, A. B. has had experience enough in the materials for dyeing. **1846** LD. CAMPBELL *Chancellors* cxxiii. IV. 567 The subject of this memoir was the son of a grocer and salter at Exeter.

2. A workman at a salt-works.

1606 *Sc. Acts Jas. VI*, c. 10 That na persone..sall fie hyre or conduce ony saltaris Coilȝearis or coilberaris without ane sufficient testimoniall of thair Maister quhome they last seruit. **1824** SCOTT *Redgauntlet* ch. vii, If sae mickle as a collier or a salter make a moonlight flitting. **1869** ROGERS *Hist. Glean.* I. 103 The colliers and salters..were only finally emancipated in 1799.

3. One who salts meat or fish.

1611 J. SPICER (*title*) The sale of Salt, or, The seasoning of Soules, Namely such, as..whom the Author, which taketh the name of a Salter, is willing..to season with the Salt of the Word. **1714** R. SMITH *Poems* (1869) 12 Thy Colledge has been at Buckhaven, Where thou hast past thy time years seven among the Salters and the Fishers. **1757** W. THOMPSON *R.N. Advoc.* 41 They were salted by the King's Salters. **1778** *Projects* in *Ann. Reg.* 125/1 The salter..crams as much salt as he can into the belly of the fish. **1883** *Chamb. Jrnl.* 310 His wife and daughters are 'gutters' or packers or salters.

b. One who salts bodies, in embalming.

1705 GREENHILL *Embalming* 283 The Surgeon or Embalmer, and..all other inferior Officers under him, such as the Dissector, Emboweller, Pollinctor, Salter.

4. A large vessel in which flesh is salted. *dial.*

1884 JEFFERIES *Red Deer* 85 A farmer who had shot a deer put the animal as soon as possible into the salter out of sight. **1891** *Hartland Gloss.*, *Salter* (zălter), a large stone or earthenware trough used in salting bacon, etc.

†**'salter**[2]. *Building Obs.* (See quot.)

1688 HOLME *Armoury* III. viii. 343/1 The Salter or Brick Axe..is to cut the rough and knotty places of Bricks, to make them lye flat and even in the Bed of Mortar.

salter, obs. f. SALTIRE.

salter(e, obs. ff. PSALTER.

salterello, see SALTARELLO.

salteriun, obs. f. PSALTERION.

saltern ('sɒltən, -ɔː-). [OE. *sealtærn*: see SALT *sb.*[1] and EARN *sb.*] A building in which salt is made by boiling or evaporation; a salt-works; also, a plot of land, laid out in pools and walks, into which the sea-water is admitted and allowed to evaporate naturally.

858 in Birch *Cartul. Sax.* II. 101 Butan ðem sealtern et fefresham & butan ðem þioda ðe to ðem sealtern limpð. **1681** WORLIDGE *Syst. Agric.* 262 The refuse salt Earth that at the Salternes is cast out and of no value. **1682** J. COLLINS *Salt & Fishery* 32 A Boyling-House is called a Saltern. *c* **1710** CELIA FIENNES *Diary* (1888) 38 Ye greatest trade is by their Salterns. Ye sea water they draw into Trenches. **1748** BROWNRIGG *Art of Making Salt* 50 At some convenient place near the sea shore is erected the saltern. This is a long, low building, consisting of two parts; one of which is called the fore-house, and the other the pan-house or boiling-house. **1791** W. GILPIN *Forest Scenery* II. 88 The coast becoming flat between the place and Lymington, is commodiously formed into salterns. **1830** LYELL *Princ. Geol.* I. 234 A considerable precipitate of muriate of soda has taken place in these natural salterns. **1879** *Cassell's Techn. Educ.* IV. 338/2 When salt was much dearer than it is now, the sea-water used to be concentrated in salterns.

saltery ('sɒltərɪ, -ɔː-). [f. SALTER: see -ERY.]

†**1.** Only *attrib.* in ***saltery ware***: the goods dealt in by salt-merchants. *Obs.*

1628 *Order in Council* in Abram *Mem. Preston Guilds* (1882) 41/2 To sett on saile..any manner of..grocery wares, or saltery wares. **1643** *Ord. Parlt. for Levying Moneys by Way of Excise* 7 All sorts of Saltery-wares Imported.

2. A salt-works.

1899 H. G. GRAHAM *Social Life Scot. 18th C.* vii. I. 228 The salteries of Prestonpans, where the salters were bondsmen for life.

3. *N. Amer.* A factory where fish is prepared for storage by salting. Now chiefly *Hist.*

1903 *Sci. Amer. Suppl.* 21 Mar. 22751/3 During 1900 there was but one saltery operated solely as such in this district. It is situated on the Nushagak and had an output of 7,186 barrels of red-fish and 536 barrels of king salmon for the season. **1960** M. SHARCOTT *Place of Many Winds* viii. 132 A few bricks and a couple of rotted and barnacled pilings tell of a long-forgotten cannery or saltery. **1972** L. HANCOCK *There's a Seal in my Sleeping Bag* ix. 218 Alert Bay was once a small saltery to preserve salmon prior to shipment to Victoria.

'saltfat. Chiefly *Sc.* Also *β. Sc.* corruptly **saltfoot.** [OE. *sealtfæt*: see SALT *sb.*[1] and FAT *sb.*[1] Cf. LG. *saltfat*, Du. *zoutvat*, MHG. *salzfaz* (G. *-fass*), ON. *saltfat.*]

1. A salt-cellar.

a. *c* **1000** ÆLFRIC *Gloss.* in Wr.-Wülcker 126/32 *Salinare, uel salinum*, sealtfæt. *a* **1100** *Gerefa* in *Anglia* IX. 264 Sealtfæt, sticfodder, piperhorn. **1488** *Acc. Ld. High Treas. Scot.* I. 81 A litill coffre of siluer ouregilt, with a litil saltfat and a couir. **1589** *Reg. Privy Council Scot.* Ser. I. IV. 445 Ane coverit saltfatt. **1599** ALEX. HUME *Poems* (S.T.S.) vii. 44 Saltfats outshorne, and glasses chrystalline. **1640–1** *Kirkcudbr. War-Comm. Min. Bk.* (1855) 43 Ane gilt silver salt-fat.

β. **1679** LD. SOMERVILLE *Mem. Somervills* (1815) II. 394 Sir Walter Stewart of Allontoune..whose predecessors untill this man never came to sitt above the saltfoot when at the Laird of Cambusnethen's table. [Cf. SALT-CELLAR b, SALT *sb.*[1] 7 b]. **1798** *Monthly Mag.* VI. II. 437/2 A salt, or a salt-foot; a salt-cellar. **1863** R. CHAMBERS *Bk. Days* I. 647/2 One of the customs of great houses, in former times, was to place a large ornamental *salt-vat* (commonly but erroneously called salt-foot) upon the table.

†**2.** A salt 'boilery'. *Obs.*

a **1647** HABINGTON *Surv. Worcs.* in *Proc. Worcs. Hist. Soc.* II. 298 The owners of these saltphates have byn aunciently called Burgeses.

3. ***in saltfat***: in the pickling tub; hence, disposed of, out of the way.

1820 SCOTT *Monast.* ix, The sooner the skin is off, and he is in saultfat, the less like you are to have trouble.

†**'salt-house.** *Obs.* [OE. *sealthús*: see SALT *sb.*[1] and HOUSE *sb.*[1] Cf. OHG. *salzhûs*, G. *salzhaus.*] A building in which salt is made or stored.

c **1000** ÆLFRIC *Colloq.* in Wr.-Wülcker 185/36 *Salinarium*, sealthus. **1340** *Durham Acc. Rolls* (Surtees) 540 In sarracione plancorum pro le Saltehous. **1465–6** *Ibid.* 90 Pro le puyntyng super le caponhous et salthous. **1580** HOLLYBAND *Treas. Fr. Tong*, *La Saline*, a salte house, where salte is made. **1601** HOLLAND *Pliny* II. XXXI. x. 420 Into the salt-houses they let in sea water. **1670** [see BOILERY]. **1730** S. DALE *Taylor's Hist. Harwich* 13 *note*, Here is a Salt-house at which they refine Salt.

saltier: see SALTIRE.

saltigrade ('sæltɪgreɪd), *a.* and *sb.* *Zool.* [f. mod.L. *Saltigradæ* pl., f. *salt-us* leap + *gradī* to step, advance.] **a.** Belonging to the *Saltigradæ*, a group of vagabond spiders having legs adapted for leaping. **b.** *sb.* A spider of this group.

1840 *Cuvier's Anim. Kingd.* 464 The second section of the Wandering Spiders, that of Saltigrades. **1885** H. C. MCCOOK *Tenants Old Farm* 196, I was standing by a fence-post watching a small saltigrade spider mount into the air.

‖**saltimbanco** (sæltɪm'bæŋkəʊ). Also 7 saltinbancho, (erron. salta-di-banco), salt'in-, 8 saltinbanco, 9 **saltimbank** (pseudo-*arch.*), -banque. [It. (= Sp. *saltinbanco*, *-banque*), f. *saltare* to leap + *in* on + *banco* bench; whence also F. *saltimbanque.*] A mountebank; a quack.

1646 SIR T. BROWNE *Pseud. Ep.* I. iii. 11 Saltimbancoes, Quacksalvers, and Charlatans. **1664** BUTLER *Hud.* II. iii. 1007 He play'd the saltinbancho's part, Transform'd t'a Frenchman by my art. **1675** COTTON *Scoffer Scoft* 114 An Archer, Fidler, Poetaster, A kind of Salt'in-banco too. **1675** A. HUYBERTS *Corner-stone* 15 No more than what may serve the Salta-di-Banco's upon a Stage. **1850** JAMES *Old Oak Chest* I. 125 To make the contortions of their 'Saltimbanks', and 'tomblesteres' act as a sort of argument or introduction to what was to follow. **1865** SALA *Diary in Amer.* I. 368 Those..marchands forains, saltimbanques and buffoons, who in Europe are afoot on every holiday.

attrib. *a* **1734** [see NON-JURABLE].

Hence **saltim'banquism.**

1861 *Temple Bar* II. 508 That gorgeous temple of saltimbanquism in Leicester Square [*sc.* the Alhambra].

‖**saltimbocca** (sæltɪm'bɒkə). [It., f. *saltare* to leap + *in* IN *prep.* + *bocca* mouth.] A dish consisting of rolled pieces of veal and ham cooked with herbs. Also in *Comb.*, as ***saltimbocca (alla) Romana.***

1937 M. MORPHY *Good Food from Italy* 89 (*heading*) Veal and Ham à la Romana [Saltimbocca alla Romana]. **1959** *Good Food Guide* 224 Escalope Cordon Bleu, 'rather like a Roman Saltimbocca only deep fried in batter'. **1960** *Harper's Bazaar* Oct. 154/2 *Saltimbocca* combines paper-thin slices of veal with *prosciutto* and a sage leaf. **1969** G. GREENE *Travels with my Aunt* I. xiii. 126 He put a lot of *saltimbocca Romana* into his mouth. **1977** C. MCCULLOUGH *Thorn Birds* xvii. 447 I'll have pâté, some scampi and a huge plate of saltimbocca. **1978** *Chicago* June 237/1 [There are] half a dozen veal dishes (Saltimbocca alla Romana—with prosciutto, butter, herbs, and marsala—is a specialty), [etc.].

saltine ('sɒltiːn, -ɔː-). orig. and chiefly *U.S.* [f. SALT *sb.*[1] + -INE[4].] A salted cracker or thin crisp biscuit.

1907 *Grocery World* 4 Nov. 40/2 Crackers and cakes... Orange Cookies... Quaker City Mixed... Salted Strips... Saltines [etc.]. **1914** H. C. SHERMAN *Food Products* viii. 287 Crackers,..Pretzels... Saltines... Soda crackers (etc.). **1933** E. O'NEILL *Ah, Wilderness!* II. 63 Mrs. Miller. (as Norah comes back with a dish of saltines—begins ladling soup into the stack of plates before her). *c* **1938** *Fortnum & Mason Price List* 19/1 Southern American Biscuits.. Saltines..2/3. **1958** E. S. WARNER *Silk-Cotton Tree* xvii. 177 The Head was passing around a box of soggy-looking saltines. **1969** 'E. LATHEN' *Murder to Go* xiv. 134 'Would anybody..like some crackers?'.. He delayed his own departure until the appearance of a dish of saltines. **1975** *New Yorker* 14 Apr. 104/3, I sought him out in his office at Hi Corbett Field (where he was lunching on two Cokes and some saltines crumbled into a cup of soup). **1980** R. L. DUNCAN *Brimstone* v. 89 Have my lunch brought in. Milk and saltines.

saltiness ('sɒltɪnɪs, -ɔː-). [f. SALTY *a.* + -NESS.] The quality or condition of being salty. Also *fig.*

1670 W. SIMPSON *Hydrol. Ess.* 69 The last are indued with a saltiness. *c* **1885** LAFCADIO HEARN in Gould *Life* (1908) 89 Have you forgotten the divine saltiness of that unfettered wind? **1934** A. WOOLLCOTT *While Rome Burns* 26 Hansoms have the advantage of semi-privacy, and what their drivers lack in chic they make up in saltiness.

salting ('sɒltɪŋ, -ɔː-), *vbl. sb.* [f. SALT *v.*[1] + -ING[1].]

1. The curing of fish, meat, etc., with salt.

a **1300** *Cursor M.* 26751 Þai sal sal yow vp on balkes lift Als suine þat ar to salting tift. **1494** *Act 11 Hen. VII*, c. 23 The same Herring..should be of one Time taking and salting. **1565** COOPER *Thesaurus, Salsura*... The salting of porke or baken. *a* **1568** ASCHAM *Scholem.* I. (Arb.) 45 New fresh flesh, for good and durable salting. **1620** VENNER *Via Recta* iv. 82 Fish of long salting..is vnwholsome. **1879** *Cassell's Techn. Educ.* IV. 354/2 Fish can be the more readily cured dry after having been exposed to this preliminary salting.

fig. *a* **1536** TINDALE *Expos. Matt.* v. Wks. (1573) 196/2 True preachyng is a salting that stirreth vp persecution, and an office that no man is mete for, saue he that is seasoned hymselfe.

2. a. In various technical, colloquial, and slang uses (see the vb.).

1570 *Lamb. MS.* 807 in *Brit. Mag.* (1847) XXXII. 366 My lord edward zou[ch]..hys matriculation ij[s]...hys saltyng iiij[s]. [In a later account spelt also 'psalting'.] **1588** FRAUNCE *Lawiers Log.* Ded. ¶ iv b, Having once knowen the price of an admission, Salting, and Matriculation, with the intertayning of Freshmenne in the Rhetorike schooles. *a* **1644** TWYNE in *MS. Twyne* xxi. 753 (Bodl.), The saltinge of fresh men which hath beene antiently and is yet at Oxford vsed at their first comminge, was perhaps borrowed or continued from this custome at Athens [see Gregory Naz. *Orat. Fun. Basilii Magni* xvi]. **1693** J. BYROM *Let. to Aubrey* in *Lett. from Bodl.* (1813) II. I. 167 'Twas..said, that the college [at Eton] held some lands by the custome of salting. **1748** BROWNRIGG *Art of Making Salt* 69 When violent fires are used towards the end of the process, whilst the salt is forming, which they call the time of salting. **1856** *Santa Barbara* (Calif.) *Gaz.* 21 Feb. 2/5 The best yield I have seen is eighteen cents to the pan, and this was without any 'salting'. **1869** 'MARK TWAIN' *Lett.* (1917) I. 164 When it was discovered that those lumps were melted half dollars and hardly melted at that, a painful case of 'salting' was apparent. **1887** *Athenæum* 31 Dec. 886/2 The traffic in stolen and spurious diamonds, and the nefarious practice known as 'salting'. **1889** *Anthony's Photogr. Bull.* II. 376 Any..change in the number of grains to the ounce of salting in an emulsion or in a developer. **1949** *Sun* (Baltimore) 31 Oct. 3/4 Farrell and others pointed out that 'salting'..along nine miles of river shore would be pointless and profitless. **1951** *Times* 13 Dec. 4/6, ——, works manager, of Malvern, Johannesburg, was found Guilty at the Rand criminal sessions to-day on two counts of *falsitas* in the 'salting' (fraudulent enrichment) of the basal and leader reef third deflection core samples of the Erdeel 5 mine. **1972** *Courier-Mail* (Brisbane) 20 June 5/3 (*heading*) Cutler denies nickel salting.

b. Chem. *salting in, out* (cf. SALT *v.*[1] 6 c).

1857 MILLER *Elem. Chem.* (1862) III. 332 Chloride of potassium cannot be substituted for chloride of sodium in salting out. **1905** *Jrnl. Physiol.* XXXII. 329 The only method which, according to our present knowledge, leaves proteids absolutely unaltered is that of 'salting out'. **1926** R. WRIGHT in *Jrnl. Chem. Soc.* 1203 The mutual lowering of solubility which takes place when an electrolyte and an organic substance are dissolved together in water..is the basis of the process of 'salting out' when an organic compound is driven out of aqueous solution by the addition of a salt. What may be termed 'salting in' is the reverse phenomenon, that is, a mutual increase in solubility of electrolyte and organic compound when added to the same solvent, which in this case is not pure water but aqueous alcohol. **1939** *Thorpe's Dict. Appl. Chem.* (ed. 4) III. 286/2 The 'salting out' effect of electrolytes on hydrophilic colloids is due to their dehydrating action as well as to their power of neutralising the charge. **1957** G. E. HUTCHINSON *Treat. Limnol.* I. ii. 183 Salting out of charged silt particles by water of compensation currents. **1970** A. L. LEHNINGER *Biochem.* vii. 133 Salts containing divalent ions..are far more effective at salting-in than salts such as NaCl, NH_4Cl, and KCl.

3. Chiefly *pl.* Salt lands; in some parts *spec.*, lands regularly covered by the tide, as distinguished from salt-marshes. *local.*

1712 DERHAM in *Phil. Trans.* XXVII. 483 These Lands they call Saltings, when covered with Grass. **1788** *Trans. Soc. Arts* VI. 59 The land in front of my sea-wall to the southward (called saltings, from the sea overflowing it except at low water). **1825** *Sporting Mag.* XV. 309 Two extraordinary large eels were taken..upon the saltings at Steeple, in Dengie Hundred, Essex. **1855** *Fraser's Mag.* LI. 267 Here ran a broad bulwark bank, keeping the saltings and marshes distinct. **1901** *Spectator* 17 Aug. 215/2 The marsh ..is dotted with white-fleeced sheep and white-faced bullocks grazing on the saltings. **1903** KIPLING 5 *Nations* 25 At the bridge of the lower saltings the cattle gather and blare.

4. *attrib.*, as (sense 1) *salting beef, -house, kit* (KIT *sb.*[1]), *-pan, -press, -room, -shed, -trough, -tub*; (*Photogr.*: see SALT *v.* 7 a) *salting bath, solution*; (sense 3) *salting-mound*; **salting-box, point** (see quots.); **salting-place**, (*a*) a place where cattle resort to lick salt; (*b*) ? *nonce-use*, the place where a stream joins the sea.

1856 HARDWICH *Photogr. Chem.* (ed. 3) 122 The Strength of the *Salting Bath. **1778** *Learning at a Loss* I. 135 What Piece of *salting Beef should be ordered from the Butcher. **1802** C. JAMES *Milit. Dict.*, **Salting-boxes*,..are boxes..for holding mealed powder, to sprinkle the fuzes of shells, that they may take fire from the blast of the powder in the chamber;..these boxes are now laid aside. **1682** WARBURTON *Hist. Guernsey* (1822) 110 The fisher men.. were obliged to bring in all the congress they took..to the kings *salting house. **1805** R. W. DICKSON *Pract. Agric.* II. 1021 After the cheeses have been properly salted..they are carried from the salting-house to the cheese-room. **1855** J. R. LEIFCHILD *Cornwall Mines* 19 Inside the salting-house, companies of chattering and screaming females are building up pilchards to heights of four and five feet. **1719** *Will of John Hirst*, A *salting kitt. **1908** *Essex Rev.* XVII. 33 The mysterious *salting-mounds known as 'Redhills' on the marshes of the Essex coasts. **1816** JANE AUSTEN *Emma* II. iii. 43 My mother was so afraid that we had not any *salting-pan large enough. **1849** NOAD *Electricity* (ed. 3) 214 A large, common, glazed salting-pan. **1842** MRS. KIRKLAND *Forest Life* I. 180 In vain..do we employ every ingenious artifice of temptation—supplying our '*salting-place' with the great delicacy of the grazing people. **1865** W. CORY *Lett. & Jrnls.* (1897) 163, I could hear not only the waves, but the millstream tripping down to its salting-place. **1884** A. WATT *Soap-Making* xxvi. 219 After settling, he adds a solution of alum, chloride of lime, or crude pyroligneous acid, stirring thoroughly. If preferred, he evaporates to nearly '*salting point' before adding any of the substances mentioned above. *c* **1830** *Glouc. Farm Rep.* 24 in *Libr. Usef. Knowl., Husb.* III, When the cheeses are taken from the *salting-presses, they are put on the shelf in the dairy for a day or two. **1805** R. W. DICKSON *Pract. Agric.* I. 59 The *salting-room should be laid with flags. **1889** W. B. YEATS *Wanderings of Oisin* 82 Times from the *saltin' shed..I scarce could drag my feet. **1961** N. FROUD et al. tr. *Montagné's Larousse Gastronomique* 493/2 The fish is transported from the boat to the salting sheds. **1892** *Photogr. Ann.* II. 205 Certain modifications of the *salting solution. **1842** J. AITON *Domest. Econ.* (1857) 239 A *salting trough which has a gutter round its edges, to drain away the brine. **1556** *Richmond. Wills* (Surtees) 92 In the larder housse iij *sowlting tobbes. **1805** R. W. DICKSON *Pract. Agric.* I. 254 A cellar where salted meat had been kept for a great length of time in a salting-tub. **1818** SCOTT *Rob Roy* xxviii, A turf back and a salting tub, which stood on either side of the narrow exterior passage.

†**saltion.** *Obs. rare*[−1]. Also 6 salcion. [ad. L. type **saltiōn-em*, f. *salt-*, ppl. stem of *salīre* to leap. Cf. SALITION.] Leaping.

1533 ELYOT *Cast. Helthe* (1541) III. i. 52 b, Stertynge or saltion [*other edd.* salcion] of the members.

saltire ('sæltaɪə(r)). *Her.* Forms: 4-5 **sawturoure**, 5 **sawtire**, 7 **saltoyre, -tyr**, 8 **salteer, salter-**, 6-9 **saltier**, 6- **saltire**. [a. OF. *saut(e)oir, sauteur, -our, -ouer, salteur, saultoir* (from 13th c.), mod.F. *sautoir*, †(1) silken or hempen stirrup-cord (? forming a deltoid figure when in use), (2) stile to keep cattle from straying, (3) saltire:—L. *saltātōrium* (see SALTATORY).] An ordinary in the form of a St. Andrew's cross, formed by a bend and a bend sinister, crossing each other; also, a cross having this shape. Hence, *in saltire*: crossed like the limbs of a St. Andrew's cross. *per saltire* (see quot. 1828-40).

? *a* **1400** *Morte Arth.* 4182 He had sothely for-sakene the sawturoure engrelede, And laughte vpe thre lyons alle of whitte siluyre. *c* **1420** *Anturs of Arth.* xxiv, A sawtire engrelede of siluer fulle schene. *a* **1550** in Baring-Gould & Twigge *W. Armory* (1898) 5 Sa: a saltier engr: arg. **1562** LEIGH *Armory* 45 b, The seuenth particion is this. Partye per Saltier, Argent, and Sable. **1603** DRAYTON *Bar. Wars* II. xxiii, Upon his Surcote, valiant Nevil bore A Silver Saltoyre, upon Martiall Red. **1605** CAMDEN *Rem.* (1637) 346 King Henry the sixt had two feathers in saltire. *a* **1695** WOOD *Oxford* (O.H.S.) III. 169 Two keyes in saltire. *a* **1711** KEN *Hymns Evang.* Poet. Wks. 1721 I. 6 A saltire, which the martyr'd Andrew bore. **1801** SCOTT *Fire-King* xxxiv, The Saracens, Curdmans, and Ishamaelites yield To the scallop, the saltier, and crossleted shield. **1828-40** BERRY *Encycl. Her.* s.v., When the field of a coat, or any charge upon it, is divided by two diagonal lines, crossing each other,..it is termed *per saltier*. **1864** BOUTELL *Her. Hist. & Pop.* xxi. (ed. 3) 359 Two pastoral staves, in saltire. **1970** H. BRAUN *Parish Churches* viii. 104 The 'saltire' or diagonal cross formed of two struts crossing, was nearly always formed of two serpentine timbers. **1974** *Northern Times* (Golspie, Sutherland) 2 Aug. 3/4 The gift was a saltire—a St. Andrew's Cross in blue and white with the arms of the cross outlined in gold thread.

attrib. **1621** LADY M. WROTH *Urania* 98 So farre asunder, as they made from corner to corner the fashion of a Saltier crosse. **1727** BOYER *Dict., Eng.-Fr.* s.v., A Saltire Cross, *Croix de S. André*. **1851** R. HILL in Gosse *Nat. in Jamaica* 466 Zig-zag lacings of a thickened tissue corresponding to the Saltier position of the Spider's legs.

'**saltireways**, *adv.* [See -WAYS.] = next.

c **1550** in Baring-Gould & Twigge *W. Armory* (1898) 5 Arg: 5 martlets saltireways sa. **1816** SCOTT *Antiq.* vi, Two long and bony arms..folded saltire-ways in front of her person. **1872** ELLACOMBE *Bells of Ch.* in *Ch. Bells Devon* ix. 513 A shield in the centre cross keys, saltier ways.

'**saltirewise**, *adv.* [See -WISE.] With or in the form of a saltire; (disposed) like the arms of a St. Andrew's cross; in saltire.

1725 *Lond. Gaz.* No. 6382/2 Two Pens placed Salterwise. **1748** RICHARDSON *Clarissa* (1811) V. xxix. 295 Gules, two swords, saltire-wise. **1821** SCOTT *Kenilw.* xiii, The background was crossed saltierwise..by the masts of two lighters that lay waiting for the tide. **1848** J. GRANT *Adv. of Aide-de-camp* ii, Leathern gaiters, laced saltire-wise up the legs with red straps. **1864** BOUTELL *Her. Hist. & Pop.* x. (ed. 3) 63 Two Foxes are leaping, saltire-wise, on the ancient shield of Sir Watkin Williams Wynne.

saltish ('sɒltɪʃ, -ɔː-), *a.* [f. SALT *sb.*[1] or *a.*[1] + -ISH.] †**a.** [f. the sb.] Of the nature of, characteristic of, or like that of, salt; impregnated with salt; salt, salty. *Obs.* **b.** [f. the adj.] Chiefly in mod. use: Somewhat salt.

1477 NORTON *Ord. Alch.* v. in Ashm. (1652) 74 The Tast thereof must needs Saltish be. **1545** RAYNOLD *Byrth Mankynde* 112 Loke vpon her mylke, that it be not blackysshe, blueysshe, grey or reddysshe, neyther sowre, sharpe, saltysshe, or brackysshe. **1582** STANYHURST *Æneis* III. (Arb.) 75 A cold sweat saltish through my ioyntes fiercely dyd enter. **1590** SPENSER *F.Q.* I. iii. 31 Ofte soust in swelling Tethys saltish teare. **1620** VENNER *Via Recta* iv. 77 The..pickled Herring..giueth a saltish and vnprofitable nourishment. **1625** N. CARPENTER *Geog. Del.* II. v. (1635) 75 That the Sea is of a saltish Quality, no man hath euer doubted. *a* **1647** T. HABINGTON *Surv. Worcs.* in *Proc. Worcs. Hist. Soc.* II. 295 The channell or bottom, scorched with the heate of the sun, appearethe whyte and saltysh. **1686** PLOT *Staffordsh.* 104 A saltish soil most commonly is fat and unctuous. **1775** ADAIR *Amer. Ind.* 228 Deer, which come in the warm season, to eat the saltish moss and grass. **1805** SAUNDERS *Min. Waters* 299 The water..tastes saltish, like weak sea water. **1875** CROLL *Climate & T.* vi. 108 Thus we have a surface current of saltish water from the poles towards the equator.

Hence '**saltishly** *adv.* (1828-32 Webster).

saltishness ('sɒltɪʃnɪs, -ɔː-). [f. as prec. + -NESS.] The quality or state of being saltish.

1562 TURNER *Bathes* 9 The water..semeth to shewe a littel saltishnes. **1625** N. CARPENTER *Geog. Del.* II. v. (1635) 75 Those which defend the saltishnesse to bee accidentall. **1686** W. HARRIS tr. *Lemery's Course Chem.* (ed. 2) 12 The waters of the Sea may be said to receive their saltishness from nothing else but this Salt dissolved in them. **1747** tr. *Astruc's Fevers* 184 The saltishness is owing to the evaporation of the serosity of the mouth.

†'**saltitant**, *a.* *Obs. rare*[−1]. [ad. late L. *saltitant-em*, pres. pple. of *saltitāre*, frequent. of *saltāre* (see SALTATE).] Leaping or springing.

1654 GAYTON *Pleas. Notes* II. iii. 41 Which Goat-provisions were most agreeable with their Errant bodies, which were alwaies saltitant, passant or currant.

salt lake. [SALT *a.*[1]] A saline lake, usu. one with no outlet to the sea so that salts brought in by rivers accumulate in it; *esp.* one which is not particularly alkaline (cf. *bitter lake* s.v. BITTER *a.* 1 c).

1763 J. BELL *Trav. from St. Petersburg* I. 289 We set up our tents near a lake of brackish water, called Solonoy-Osera, or the salt lake. *Ibid.* 326 The 22d, we quitted the salt lake. **1836** *Penny Cycl.* VI. 343/2 A great number of smaller and larger salt lakes. **1882** [see BITTER *a.* 1 c]. **1923** J. S. HUXLEY *Ess. Biologist* i. 34 A salt-lake shrimp could tolerate an even higher concentrate of brine. **1970** [see EXOGENETIC *a.* 2 b].

saltless ('sɒltlɪs, -ɔː-), *a.* [f. SALT *sb.*[1] + -LESS. Cf. Du. *zouteloos*, G. *salzlos*, with sense 2.]

1. Without salt; unsalted.

1398 TREVISA *Barth. De P.R.* XIX. lxxiv. (1495) 905 Saltlesse chese is moost nouryysshynge and moysteth the body. **1658** SIR T. BROWNE *Pseud. Ep.* II. v. 96 He that hath beheld what quantity of lead the test of saltless ashes will imbibe. **1666** BOYLE *Orig. Formes & Qual.* 414 [He] took the Earth to be quite Saltlesse. **1823** BYRON *Island* III. iii, Its bounding crystal..gush'd from cliff to crag with saltless spray. **1863** *W. Smith's Dict. Bible* III. 1096/2 (*Salt*), It was the belief of the Jews that salt would, by exposure to the air .., become saltless. **1905** *Punch* 25 Oct. 290/1 It is the landsman's lusty throat That rends to-day a saltless air.

2. *fig.* Lacking piquancy, poignancy, interest, or liveliness; insipid, 'flat'.

1633 T. ADAMS *Exp. 2 Peter* ii. 8 A heavy and saltless oration is insufferable to a quick hearer. *a* **1658** CLEVELAND *Agst. Ale* iv. Poems (1687) 305 Saltless and galless be thy Curse. **1874** LISLE CARR *Jud. Gwynne* I. iii. 73 It promises to afford a slight pungency of flavour to my tasteless life in this saltless wilderness. **1885** D. C. MURRAY *Rainbow Gold* III. 219 The days went by, saltless, lifeless.

Hence '**saltlessness**.

1682 BOYLE in R. Fitzgerald *Salt-Water Sweetened* 16 The main thing of all that convinced me of the Saltlessness of the Water I speak of. **1867** QUEEN VICTORIA *Let.* 13 Feb. in R. Fulford *Your Dear Letter* (1971) 121 There is great bitterness in the constant depression..and total saltlessness of my life.

'**salt-lick.** [LICK *sb.* 2.] A place where cattle collect to lick the earth impregnated with salt. Also *fig.* Now chiefly *N. Amer.*

1751 [see LICK *sb.* 2]. **1764** *Museum Rust.* II. lxiv. 209 We give this name of salt licks to the salt springs, which, in various places, issue naturally out of the ground, and form each a little rill. **1767** HUNTER in *Phil. Trans.* LVIII. 39 The marsh, called the Salt-Lick, near the River Ohio. **1847** W. C. L. MARTIN *Ox* 10/2 They visit the salt-licks, and are there to be found at all seasons of the year; some leaving the saline morass, others travelling towards it. **1859** J. PALLISER *Jrnl.* 16 Feb. (1863) 129 A splendid ram..had been caught by setting a snare in a path leading to a 'salt-lick'. **1922** *Beaver* May 7/2 They [*sc.* bighorn sheep] being in the habit of seeking the salt-licks early in the morning and again late in the evening. **1948** C. DAY LEWIS *Poems 1943–47* 75 The sea rolled up like a blind, oh pitiless light Revealing, shrivelling all! Lacklustre weeds My hours, my truth a salt-lick. **1965** R. MCKIE *Company of Animals* vii. 113 Jim went at first light to check which animals were visiting a small salt-lick in the jungle. **1976** N. THORNBURG *Cutter & Bone* viii. 202 Immediately she was weeping in his arms, her face a lovely saltlick to his mouth.

saltly ('sɒltlɪ, -ɔː-), *adv.* [f. SALT *a.*[1] + -LY[2].] With the taste or smell of salt.

1736 AINSWORTH *Eng.-Lat. Dict.*, Saltly, *salse.* **1827** J. MITCHELL *First Lines Sci.* 63 Saltly bitter, saltly cooling. **1865** *Cornh. Mag.* XI. 354 The winds That whistle saltly south from Polar seas. **1903** *Blackw. Mag.* Aug. 237/1 A sickly yellow spume that saltly stank.

'salt-ˌmaker. [Cf. Du. *zoutmaker*, G. *salzmacher*.] A manufacturer of salt.

1483 *Cath. Angl.* 317/2 A Salte makere, *salinator.* **1591** PERCIVALL *Sp. Dict.*, *Salinero*, a salt maker. **1614** PURCHAS *Pilgrimage* v. x. 493 The *Betua* are Salt-makers. **1707** *Lond. Gaz.* No. 4373/4 Thomas Elmes, late of Milford in the County of Southampton, Salt-maker. **1807** P. GASS *Jrnl.* 179 About noon Captain Clarke with 14 men came to the salt-makers camp. **1886** *Encycl. Brit.* XXI. 233/1 The warping or buckling, the scaling, and the formation of 'cats', ..arising from leaks in the pan, are perhaps among the worst annoyances of the saltmakers. **1892** *Labour Commission* Gloss., *Salt Makers*, term embracing all the men directly engaged in the manufacture of white salt from brine.

So **'salt-ˌmaking**, the manufacture of salt; †also *pl.*, salt-works.

1534 *Lett. Suppress. Monast.* (Camden) 281 The chargys that belongythe to the salte makyng. **1611** COTGR., *Salaison*, Salt-making. *a* **1647** HABINGTON *Surv. Worcs.* in *Proc. Worcs. Hist. Soc.* II. 297 Some of meaner ranck had and have salt-makings heere. **1886** *Encycl. Brit.* XXI. 234/1 Saltmaking is by no means an unhealthy trade.

attrib. **1823** in Cobbett *Rur. Rides* (1885) I. 319 There are no excisemen in these salt-making places in France.

'salt-marsh. [SALT *a.*[1]: cf. G. *salzmarsch*.]

a. Marsh overflowed or flooded by the sea; *spec.* one in which the sea water is collected for the manufacture of salt. (Cf. SALTING 3.)

c **1000** *Ags. Ps.* (Th.) cvi. 33 He þa weaxendan wende eorðan on sealtne mersc [Vulg. *in salsuginem*]. [So: *a* **1300** *E.E. Psalter* cvi. 34 Stremes in wildernes sete he.. In salt-mersche land fruitberande. *a* **1325** *Prose Psalter* cvi[i]. 33 Saltmerche.] **14..** *Tretyce* in *W. of Henley's Husb.* (1890) 53 Good kyne go in good pasture off salt maries. **1583** in *Collect.* (O.H.S.) I. 234 If any lands or salt marsh are reclaimed from the sea. **1686** *Plymouth Col. Rec.* (1836) VI. 183 It is ordered, that Patience..shall haue..the vse of about two acres of salt marish att the island. **1725** *Fam. Dict.*, *Salt-marsh*, a sort of Grazing Ground near the Sea, which is commonly very rich land. **1728** CHAMBERS *Cycl.* s.v. *Salt*, Low Marshy Grounds, disposed by Nature for the Reception of the Sea-waters when the Tide swells, and provided with Banks and Sluices to retain the same, are called a Salt-marsh. **1828** J. E. SMITH *Eng. Flora* II. 95 In muddy salt-marshes. **1832** TENNYSON *Mariana in the South* 9 Down in the dry salt-marshes stood That house darklatticed.

b. *attrib.*, in specific names of plants and animals found on salt marshes.

1855 T. R. JONES *Anim. Kingd.* (ed. 2) 462 The salt-marsh shrimp, *Artemia salinus.* **1861** MISS PRATT *Flower Pl.* I. 198 The Salt-marsh Club rush (*Scirpus maritimus*). **1862** *Harper's Mag.* Nov. 737/2 'Salt-marsh fly'—is a nuisance found everywhere..near salt marshes. **1872** *Proc. Amer. Philos. Soc.* XII. 475 The salt-marsh terrapin. **1932** *Sun* (Baltimore) 23 Aug. 4/7 The salt marsh mosquito causes intense discomfort. **1972** SWAN & PAPP *Common Insects N. Amer.* xxii. 592 Salt-marsh Mosquito: *Aedes sollicitans. Ibid.*, The California Salt-marsh Mosquito..breeds in salt marshes and tide pools along the Pacific coast.

c. *attrib.* in general use.

1937 *Discovery* Apr. 98/2 The occupation was brought to an end with the onset of salt-marsh conditions. **1960** J. J. ROWLANDS *Spindrift* 91 The salt-marsh hayfields are favorite stopping-places for geese and ducks on their northward flight. **1975** J. G. EVANS *Environment Early Man Brit. Isles* vii. 180 Later stages in the saltmarsh succession form good sheep pasture.

saltness[1] ('sɒltnɪs, -ɔː-). [f. SALT *a.*[1] + -NESS.]

1. The property or state of being salt; the condition of being impregnated with salt.

In OE. only quasi-concr. transl. L. *salsilago, salsugo.*

c **825** *Vesp. Psalter* cvi. 34 Sette..eorðan westembere in saltnisse. [So Wycl. (1388) saltnesse; Vulg. *posuit..terram fructiferam in salsilaginem* or *salsuginem.*] **1387** TREVISA *Higden* (Rolls) I. 265 Þe rootes mowe not take depnesse and fatnesse for saltnesse of þe erþe. **1388** WYCLIF *Jer.* xvii. 6 He schal dwelle in drynesse in desert, in the lond of saltnesse. **1422** tr. *Secreta Secret., Priv. Priv.* 208 By the tonge we felen the dyuersite of Sauores, Swetnes and bittyrnesse, Saltenesse and egyrnesse. **1551** ROBINSON tr. *More's Utop.* II. vi. (1895) 187 The ebbinge, flowinge, and saltenes of the sea. *a* **1625** FLETCHER, etc. *Fair Maid Inn* II. i, If I had buried him in a wave at sea,..I would not to the saltnesse of his grave Have added the last teare. **1676** COLLINS in Rigaud *Corr. Sci. Men* (1841) II. 454 Being troubled with a scorbutic humour, or saltness of blood. **1764** E. MOXON *Eng. Housew.* 103 Boil them [some herrings] as soft as you would do for eating, and shift them in the boiling to take out the saltness. **1832** DE LA BECHE *Geol. Man.* (ed. 2) 5 The superior saltness of the Mediterranean..is attributed to the evaporation of its surface. **1883** F. M. CRAWFORD *Dr. Claudius* viii, The delicious sense of saltness and freedom one feels on the deck of a good ship.

2. Piquancy, poignancy.

1612 BACON *Ess.*, *Discourse* (Arb.) 17 Men ought to finde the difference betweene saltnesse and bitternesse. **1896** *Westm. Gaz.* 27 Apr. 3/1 By reliance on beauty shows, variety turns, or saltness of dialogue.

'saltness[2]. *rare*$^{-0}$. [f. SALT *a.*[2]] Lecherousness, salacity.

1611 COTGR., *Chaude-colle*, saltnesse, leacherousnesse.

‖**salto** ('salto). [It., leap; cf. SALTUS.]

1. salto mortale (mor'tale) [It., = fatal jump, somersault], a daring or flying leap (as of a trapeze artist, etc.); also *fig.*, a step that involves risk; an unjustified inference, a 'leap of faith'.

1896 W. CALDWELL *Schopenhauer's Syst.* vii. 361 He really solved it [*sc.* the question of altruism] only by a *salto mortale.* *a* **1910** W. JAMES *Ess. Radical Empiricism* (1912) ii. 67 The transcendentalist..holds knowing to consist in a *salto mortale* across an 'epistemological chasm'. **1937** J. M. MURRY *Necessity of Pacifism* vii. 115 England will take this glorious *salto mortale* into a more human future. **1952** R. MANNING-SANDERS *Eng. Circus* IV. xvii. 237 Let us look..at the act of the two Codonas,..after Alfredo, in 1922, had mastered that wonderful feat, the *salto mortale*, or triple somersault. **1968** M. GUYBON tr. *Solzhenitsyn's First Circle* (1971) xxviii. 164 He was escorted up another flight of steps—where, as in a circus during the *salto mortale*, there were nets to catch him if he jumped off. **1977** *Language* LIII. 44 While the enclitic nature of the copula is beyond question in itself, inferring 'aphaeresis' as a phenomenon consequential upon it has involved an epistemological 'salto mortale' which has not been very successful.

2. *Gymnastics.* A somersault.

1972 B. TAYLOR et al. *Olympic Gymnastics* iii. 35 With more advanced movements (such as a double back salto or double twisting back layout), a spotting belt is sometimes used. **1974** *Rules of Game* 36 *Compulsory exercises*... Arms backward, two or three running steps into forward piked salto, land on one leg. **1980** *Sunday Times* 20 July 28/2, I will show you a new dismount off the beam... It is double Salto off one leg with half a turn.

saltorel ('sæltərəl). *Her.* [app. ad. OF. **saltorel*, dim. of *saltoir* SALTIRE.] (See quots.)

1780 EDMONDSON *Heraldry* II. Gloss., *Saltorels*, the same as Saltiers. **1894** *Parker's Gloss. Her.* 518 The term *saltorel* is sometimes used when three or more saltires occur, but it is hardly required.

'saltory. Alteration of SALTARY after L. *saltātōrium* SALTATORY *sb.*[2]

1867 E. P. SHIRLEY *Eng. Deer Parks* viii. 179 This right of saltory or deer-leap was once not uncommon.

saltou, obs. f. *shalt thou*: see SHALL.

Saltoun ('sɔːltən). [Proper name: see quot. 1886.] A variety of artificial trout fly (see quots.).

1886 F. M. HALFORD *Floating Flies* v. 90 Saltoun. *Wings.* Palest starling. *Body.* Black silk, ribbed with silver wire. *Hackle and Whisk.* Pale ginger cock. *Hook.* oo or ooo. A very useful summer fly, invented by and named after the late Lord Saltoun [prob. Alexander Fraser, 17th Lord Saltoun, d. Feb. 1886], a prominent member of the old Stockbridge Club. **1892** M. O. MARBURY *Favorite Flies* (ed. 2) 379 (*heading*) Frederic M. Halford's floating flies for dry-fly fishing... No. 223 Saltoun. **1926** *Chambers's Jrnl.* 13 Feb. 164/1 There's a two-pounder at the stream-mouth that has risen twice to the saltoun. **1931** *Hardy's Anglers' Guide* (ed. 53) 66 Lake and Sea Trout Flies... No. 44. Saltoun. **1961** A. C. WILLIAMS *Dict. Trout Flies* (ed. 3) 302 *Saltoun*, an old pattern and a one-time favourite on the chalk streams. After falling into disuse, it has been revived in recent years as a lake fly.

saltoyre, obs. form of SALTIRE.

'salt-pan. [Cf. Du. *zoutpan*, G. *salzpfanne.*]

a. (Usually *pl.*) A shallow depression near the sea into which sea-water is allowed to flow, where it evaporates, leaving a deposit of salt; in Africa, applied (after Du. *zoutpan*) to dried-up salt lakes or marshes. **b.** A shallow vessel in which brine is evaporated in salt-making; *pl.*, a salt-works.

1493 *Newminster Cartul.* (Surtees) 195, iiij salt pannes standynge vp on the north syde of yᵉ water of Blyth. **1533** BELLENDEN *Livy* App. (S.T.S.) II. 265 *note*, Salynis ar callit certane places besyd þe se quhair þe salt Is made. We call þame salt pannys. **1573** *Reg. Privy Council Scot.* II. 265 Havand commissioun of the rest of awnars of the salt pannis of Dysert. **1708** J. C. *Compl. Collier* (1845) 11 The best Coals are best for the Salt Pans and Salt too, and make most and best Salt. **1748** BROWNRIGG *Art of Making Salt* 52 The salt pans are made of an oblong form, flat at the bottom, with the sides erected at right angles. **1785** G. FORSTER tr. *Sparrman's Voy. Cape G. Hope* II. 14 A good mile and a half from the river, we met with the capital *Zout-pan*, or Salt-pan. **1857** LIVINGSTONE *Trav.* iv. 78 In every salt-pan in the country there is a spring of water on one side. **1883** F. DAY *Indian Fish* 9 (Fish. Exhib. Publ.) The salt used there costing about threepence per 82⅔ lb. weight, whereas in the contiguous British territory it stood at the salt-pans at about four shillings.

saltpetre (sɒlt'piːtər, -ɔː-). Also 6–9 (now *U.S.*) **-peter**, 6 **petir, -ur**, 7 **-ar**, 6–7 **peeter**. [Alteration of SALPETRE after SALT *sb.*[1] (see sense 5 b).]

1. Potassium nitrate; = NITRE *sb.* 1 b. ***Chili*** or ***cubic saltpetre***: sodium nitrate.

Saltpetre is a white crystalline substance having a saline taste; it is the chief constituent of gunpowder, and is used medicinally.

1501–2 *Acc. Ld. High Treas. Scot.* II. 139 For ij pund salt petir to the leich. **1528–9** *Rec. St. Mary at Hill* 347 The tyme that the kyng caused Salte peter to be made in the said house. **1590** GREENE *Never too late* (1600) 21 Like Saltpeeter, that fiereth at the first, and yet proueth but a flash. **1612** WOODALL *Surg. Mate* Wks. (1653) 209 Salt-Peeter..is of excellent use for medicine. **1669** STURMY *Mariner's Mag.* v. xii. 80 The Shot is driven forth..by the Air's exaltation, or Wind, caused through the Salt-Peter. **1722** *Phil. Trans.* (abr. ed.) III. 371 The pendent Rocks were glazed with Salt Peter. **1768** BOSWELL *Corsica* i. (ed. 2) 52 There are also mines of allum, and of salt-petre, in several parts of Corsica. **1837** M. DONOVAN *Dom. Econ.* II. 241 On account of the property which saltpetre possesses of giving a pleasing redness to beef, it is always an ingredient in the brine with which meat is preserved. **1846** GREENER *Sci. Gunnery* 21 Gunpowder is an explosive propellant compound, consisting of saltpetre or nitre, charcoal, and sulphur. **1877** [see CUBIC *a.* 1 b]. **1886** *Encycl. Brit.* XXI. 235/2 A large quantity of saltpetre is now prepared from Chili saltpetre, the nitrate of soda.

†**b.** ***oil of saltpetre*** [? error for *oil of* PETRE]: petroleum. ***spirits of saltpetre***: nitric acid. *Obs.*

1685 BOYLE *Salubr. Air* 95 The Spirits of Salt-peter will readily corrode silver. **1692** in *Capt. Smith's Seaman's Gram.* II. xxxi. 144 Fill these with good Powder dust, moistned with Oyle of Salt-Peter.

2. *attrib.* and *Comb.*, as ***saltpetre-boiler, -boiling, cave, crystal, earth, -maker, work(s), -worker***; **saltpetre flour** (see quot.); **saltpetre house**, (*a*) a building in which saltpetre is made or stored; (*b*) = F. *la Salpêtrière*, a hospital for aged and infirm women at Paris; formerly a prison for women; **saltpetre-lye**, 'a liquid obtained by the treatment of saltpetre with water' (*Syd. Soc. Lex.* 1897); †**saltpetre man**, a man appointed to find saltpetre for the manufacture of gunpowder; **saltpetre paper** = TOUCH-PAPER; **saltpetre rot**, white efflorescence which forms on new or damp walls, caused by saltpetre working through to the surface; †**saltpetre salt** (see quot. 1683).

1580 *Faversham Par. Reg.* (MS.), Edward Hale, a *saltpeeter boyller. **1683** PETTUS *Fleta Min.* I. 333 Some Salt-Petre Boylers (who sell the raw unpurified Earth-Petre). *Ibid.* 338 A true large Instruction of the *Salt-Peter boyling. **1868** *Rep. U.S. Commissioner Agric.* (1869) 397 *Saltpeter Caves in the South. **1878** GURNEY *Crystallogr.* 7 These beautiful rods which we call *saltpetre crystals. **1601** HOLLAND *Pliny* I. Index, *Saltpetre earth good for plants. **1699** DAMPIER *Voy.* II. II. i. 8 Probably there may be Salt-Petre-Earth in other Places. **1848** *Knapp's Chem. Technol.* I. 373 The saltpetre is obtained as a snow-white powder, consisting of fine crystalline needles—'*saltpetre-flour'. **1683** PETTUS *Fleta Min.* I. 340 The fore-part of the *Salt-Petre House, wherein the Lee Tubs do stand. **1767** *Ann. Reg.* 77 A woman..condemned..to be branded and confined to the saltpetre-house for nine years. **1683** PETTUS *Fleta Min.* I. 321 How the weak *Salt-Petre Lee is to be made richer and boil'd to greater profit. **1799** G. SMITH *Laboratory* I. 49 Saw-dust, boiled in saltpetre-lye. **1611** COTGR., *Salpestrier*, a Salt-peter-man, or *Salt-peter-maker. **1843** *Civ. Eng. & Arch. Jrnl.* VI. 424/1 In 1627 the saltpetre-makers were authorized to take away the ground of all dove-houses, stables, lairs, or other places where cattle were kept. **1578** *Acts Privy Council Eng.* XXVIII. 382 For chardges fo William Shill and John Tyrret, *saltpeter-men. **1589** NASHE *Martins Months Minde* Ep. Ded., Wks. (Grosart) I. 147 That haue chosen a Saltpeter man for their foreman, and a gunne powder house..for their printing shop. **1617** MIDDLETON & ROWLEY *Fair Quarrel* I. i, They are saltpetre-men... And they bring commission, the king's power indeed. *a* **1691** BOYLE *Hist. Air* (1692) 43 We seldom find Salt-peter in the earth, but that there is sea-salt mixed with it, which puts the salt-peter-men to a great deal of trouble to separate it. **1832** BREWSTER *Nat. Magic* xiii. 320 The heat of the wire is always sufficient to kindle a piece of German fungus or *saltpetre paper. **1848** *Knapp's Chem. Technol.* I. 351 A floccular, white, crystalline efflorescence.. which is called *salt-petre rot. **1682** J. COLLINS *Salt & Fishery* 126 *Salt-Petre Salt as to goodness hath no great Repute. **1683** PETTUS *Fleta Min.* I. 337 The black or grey Salt-Petre Salt, which is found (in boyling Salt-petre) below in the Kettle and slender Tub. **1753** CHAMBERS *Cycl. Supp.* s.v. *Mortar*, The finest of all kinds of Mortar for *salt-petre work, is such as is had from the ruins of old buildings in a low situation. *Ibid.*, The common managers of the saltpetre-works. *Ibid.*, The *salt-petre workers in France using the Mortar of old buildings.

b. quasi-*adj.* Explosive.

1598 E. GUILPIN *Skial.* C 3, Tearms of quick Camphire & Salt-peeter phrases.

Hence **salt'petreing**, the formation of saltpetre rot; †**salt'petrish**, †**-'petrous** *adjs.*, pertaining to, of the nature of, or impregnated with, saltpetre.

1662 J. DAVIES tr. *Mandelslo's Trav.* 84 Their Salt-petrous Earth. **1683** PETTUS *Fleta Min.* I. 322 The..Clay of very old Walls..where the Earth it self is Salt-Petrish. **1885** *Spons' Mech. Own Bk.* 602 The surfaces of walls are often covered with an efflorescence of an unsightly character, formed by a process known as 'saltpetreing'.

'salt-pit. A pit where salt is obtained.

1398 TREVISA *Barth. De P.R.* XVI. xciv. (Bodl. MS.), [It] is somtyme idrawe oute of salte pittes and isode. **1535** COVERDALE *Zeph.* ii. 9 Moab shalbe as Sodome, and Ammon as Gomorra: euen drie thorne hedges, salt pittes and a perpetuall wyldernes. **1560** DAUS tr. *Sleidane's Comm.* 338 b, The daye before he died, he released the customes which he had imposed upon Salt pits. **1625** PURCHAS *Pilgrims* III. i. 3 Out of those Salt-pits Baatu and Sartach haue great Reuenues. **1769** FALCONER *Dict. Marine* (1789), *Salt-pits*, reservoirs on a coast, to contain sea-water for the purposes of making salt. **1889** *Helps Study Bible* xlii. 125 A ridge of salt-rock runs into that sea [*i.e.* the Dead Sea], and there are salt-pits, and a plain of salt.

'salt-pond. A natural or artificial pond into which sea-water is run in order to be evaporated: cf. SALT-PAN a.

1697 DAMPIER *Voy.* I. 49 On the South side..is a good Salt-pond, where Dutch Sloops come for Salt. **1748** *Anson's Voy.* I. vi. 69 We..sent an Officer on shore to the salt-pond ..to procure a quantity of salt. **1836** EARL CARNARVON *Portugal & Gallicia* II. 38 The salt-ponds, which are situated in the immediate neighbourhood of the sea. **1883** MOLONEY *W. African Fisheries* 48 (Fish. Exhib. Publ.) The many 'salt ponds' [*Note*, Brackish inlets or salt-water lakes] adjacent to the African coast line.

salt rheum. [See SALT *a.*[1] 1 b.]

†**1.** An irritating discharge of mucus from the nose; a running cold. *Obs.*

1590 SHAKS. *Com. Err.* III. ii. 131. **1604** —— *Oth.* III. iv. 51, I haue a salt and sorry Rhewme offends me.

2. *N. Amer.* **a.** A popular name for 'almost all the non-febrile cutaneous eruptions which are common among adults, except perhaps ring-worm and itch' (Webster 1854).

1809 E. KENDALL *Trav. Northern Parts U.S.* I. 325 In the neighbourhood, the greater number of patients that it attracts appear to be such as labour under scrofulous diseases. That, of which I heard the name in everyone's mouth, is the *salt rheum.* **1855** DUNGLISON *Dict. Med.*, *Rheum, Salt*, a popular name..for various cutaneous affections of the eczematous and herpetic forms more especially. **1877** R. J. BURDETTE *Rise & Fall of Mustache* 291 'Centennial Cordial and American Indian Aboriginal Invigorator'..has absolutely no equal for the cure of..salt rheum. **1901** *Daily Colonist* (Victoria, B.C.) 26 Oct. 8/1 This preparation seems to have magnetic powers in stopping the dreadful itching, burning sensations of salt rheum and eczema.

b. *attrib.* **salt-rheum weed**, *Chelone glabra*, which is supposed to be a remedy for herpes.

1846-50 A. WOOD *Class-bk. Bot.* 400.

salt river. *U.S.* [SALT *a.*[1]] †**1.** A river which is tidal a considerable distance from its mouth. *Obs.*

1659 *Early Rec. Providence, Rhode Island* (1892) I. 97 A percell of land..lieth upon the salt River at the further-most side of the towne boundes. **1704** *Ibid.* (1894) V. 224 Sd Cove ..lieth adjoyneing to the North side of the salt River called Pautuckett. **1791** W. BARTRAM *Trav. N. & S. Carolina* I. iv. 29 Numerous small rivers and their branches: these they call salt rivers, because the tides flow near to their sources.

2. a. The name of a river (perh. one in Kentucky) used as *attrib. phr.* to designate the inhabitants of the American backwoods region, esp. with reference to their uncultivated manner of speech. Also applied to the speech, etc., of these people. Now only *Hist.*

1828 *Western Intelligencer* (Hamilton, Ohio) 26 Dec. 1/4 A 'Salt River Roarer'. One of these two fisted backwoodsmen, 'half horse, half alligator, and a little touched with the snapping turtle'. **1835** *Knickerbocker* V. 403 They [*sc.* speeches in Congress] are chiefly made up of extracts from the common school collection of lessons for reading and speaking, sprinkled with scraps of dog-Latin, and a sort of patois, called Salt-river roaring. **1835** T. FLINT in *Athenæum* July 511/2 There is, in fact, a well-known rivalry between the collectors of the Downing dialect of New England, and the Crocket or Salt River dialect of the South and West. **1947** J. CONROY *Midland Humor* p. x, The ring-tailed roarers and Salt River screamers of the half-horse and half-alligator breed, both male and female, were ordinarily combinations of physical might and mother wit which enabled them to outsmart invaders from other regions.

b. *fig.* In slang phr. ***to row*** (someone) ***up Salt River*** and varr., to defeat (a political opponent); to overcome, send to oblivion. Also with intransitive vb., to be defeated or overcome, to go to oblivion; to get drunk. Freq. in allusive and proverbial uses. Now *rare.*

The simplest of the numerous explanations offered for this usage is that which connects it with sense 2a; see H. Sperber and J. N. Tidwell in *Amer. Speech* (1951) XXVI. 241-7.

1828 *Reg. Deb. Congress U.S.* 2 Feb. 1341 But, sir, I will venture to say this, that, in playing this game, if the Secretary of State is not influenced by the same courtesy which governed the courtiers of the great Frederick, never to beat the monarch at chess, that he could give the President twenty-nine, and as they say in Kentucky, 'row him up salt river'. **1830** *Cincinnati Chron.* 2 Jan. 1/2 He replied he didn't 'smoak me', and unless I cut cable in short order, he'd roar me up salt river. **1832** J. K. PAULDING *Westward Ho!* I. ix. 77 See if I don't row you up Salt River before you are many days older. **1832** *Spirit of Times* 28 Apr. 3/1 He 'rowed' Stanberry 'up a salt creek', and is now *being* tried by the House of Representatives for his unlucky propensity. **1832** *Washington* (Ohio) *Herald* 17 Nov. 3/4 The Jackson boys of Ohio have been enabled to give them another ride 'up Salt River'. **1835** D. CROCKETT *Tour down East* 46 [Judge Clayton] made a speech that fairly made the tumblers hop. He rowed the Tories up and over Salt river. **1838** *Bentley's Misc.* IV. 588, I can drink till the world gets too old to move. While another man rows up Salt River, I'm only putting the fire out in the forest. *Ibid.*, Rowing up Salt River is a slang term for getting intoxicated. **1848** BARTLETT *Dict. Amer.* 279 *To Row up Salt River*, is a common phrase, used generally to signify political defeat. The distance to which a party is *rowed up Salt river* depends entirely upon the magnitude of the majority against its candidates. **1852** *Chicago Democrat* 11 Nov., One Thomas Holt, lately a clerk in The Chicago Post Office, when last seen,..was on his way up 'Salt River' with Gen. Scott. **1855** HALIBURTON *Nat. & H. Nature* I. 27 We rowed him to the very head waters of Salt River in no time. **1880** in J. C. Andrews *Pittsburgh Post Gaz.* (1936) xvi. 218 For Salt River—The River Boat Democracy left its Wharf Tuesday, Nov. 2, 1880 bound up Salt River in search of the late lamented Samuel J. Tilden. **1941** L. D. BALDWIN *Keelboat Age on Western Waters* 97 It'd shore be harder'n rowin' up Salt River to find a cleverer parcel o' fellers 'n them keelers.

saltry, obs. form of PSALTERY.

saltsage, obs. form of SAUSAGE *sb.*

salt spring. [SALT *a.*[1]] A flow of salt water or brine out of the earth; a brine-spring, brine-well. Also as *attrib. phr.*

1601 HOLLAND tr. *Pliny's Nat. Hist.* II. xxxi. vii. 416 In some parts of Spaine there be salt springs. *a* **1647** HABINGTON *Surv. Worcs.* in *Proc. Worcs. Hist. Soc.* II. 301 After the deathe of Richard the Saltspringes of Wich fell to decaye. **1683** J. PETTUS *Fleta Minor* I. 321 Of Salt-Petre, Vitriol, Allum and Salt Springs. **1748** J. HILL *Hist. Fossils* 382 The Sea-water and Salt-springs sustain it [*sc.* alimentary salt]..in a liquid form. **1782** T. PENNANT *Journey Chester to London* 27 The Britons, who had, in several places, plenty of salt-springs. **1834** *Phil. Mag.* IV. 31 The comparative strength of the salt springs of that country at different depths. **1839** G. ROBERTS *Dict. Geol.*, *Salt Springs*, which contain a large quantity of common salt, obtained from them by mere evaporation. **1852** J. REYNOLDS *Hist. Illinois* 86 They discovered in the present county of Galatin, salt springs. **1853** *Trans. Mich. Agric. Soc.* IV. 9 The twenty-two sections of salt spring lands now unappropriated.

†**'salt-stone.** *Obs.* [OE. *sealtstán*: see SALT *sb.*[1] and STONE *sb.* Cf. Du. *zoutsteen*, MHG. *salzsteyn* (G. *-stein*), ON. *saltsteinn.*]

1. Rock-salt; a mass of rock-salt.

In early use chiefly in allusions to the fate of Lot's wife.

a **1000** *Cædmon's Gen.* 2564 (Gr.) Heo on sealtstanes sona wurde anlicnesse æfre siððan. *a* **1000** *Sax. Leechd.* I. 374 ðenim ȝeoluwne stan & salt stan & pipor. *a* **1300** *Cursor M.* 2855 In a salt stan men seis hir stand. *c* **1475** *Pict. Voc.* in Wr.-Wülcker 768/2 *Hic cautes*, a salt-stone. **1535** FISHER *Wayes to perfect Religion* Wks. (1876) 370. **1585** HIGINS *Junius' Nomencl.* 409 *Sal natiuus vel fossilis*,..Salt naturall, or that is digged out of the earth: saltstone. **1677** PLOT *Oxfordsh.* 37 Besides its saltness it [*sc.* the water] has such a stink, that it equals the salt stone. **1680** MORDEN *Geog. Rect.*, *Hungary* (1685) 94 The colour of the Saltstone is somewhat gray.

attrib. **1638** JUNIUS *Paint. Ancients* 91 The woman.. keeping still her old posture in the same salt-stone image.

2. A salt-cat for pigeons.

1425 in Kennett *Par. Antiq.* (1818) II. 255, i saltstone empt. pro columbario. **1584** in Rogers *Agric. & Prices* VI. 575/1, 4 saltstones for the dovecot @ 1/9. **1646** SIR T. BROWNE *Pseud. Ep.* III. xxii. 165 Pigeons delight in salt stones.

†**'saltuary.** *Obs.* [ad. med.L. *saltuāri-us*, f. *saltus* woodland, forest-pasture.] (See quot.)

1674 BLOUNT *Glossogr.* (ed. 4), *Saltuary*, a Forrester, Woodward, or Ranger.

†**'salture.** *Obs.* [ad. mod.L. *saltūra*, f. *salt-*, *salīre* to leap.] (See quot.)

1656 BLOUNT *Glossogr.*, *Salture*, a leaping or dancing.

‖**saltus** ('sæltəs). [L. = leap.] A 'leap' or sudden transition; a breach of continuity. Also in *Comb.* Cf. *salto mortale* s.v. SALTO 1.

1665 HOOKE *Microgr.* 228 No Experiment yet known to prove a Saltus, or skipping from one degree of rarity to another. **1875** WHITNEY *Life Lang.* xiv. 291 These would be the real analogues of speech, and would bridge the saltus of which some are so afraid. **1894** A. C. FRASER *Locke's Essay Annotated* II. IV. xii. 348 The inductive *saltus*, which transcends this datum. **1913** E. W. HOBSON *Squaring the Circle* ii. 18 There is no jumping to the limit as the supposed end of an essentially endless process, to be reached by some inscrutable *saltus*. **1923** G. B. SHAW in *Nation & Athenæum* 10 Feb. 714/2 He [*sc.* Wright] was hampered not only by the mistakes of Pasteur, but by a remarkable *saltus empiricus* made by a famous bacteriological acrobat..named Metchnikoff. **1934** A. C. EWING *Idealism* viii. 407 One can ..pass from one to the other without a *saltus in aliud genus*. **1951** J. HOLLOWAY *Lang. & Intelligence* iii. 55 There must be a *saltus naturae*, an innate idea of symbolization must come to fruition.

salt water, *sb.* and *a.* [SALT *a.*[1] Cf. LG. *salt-wat(t)er*, MDu. *sout-water*, G. *salz-wasser*.]

A. *sb.* **a.** (stressed *salt 'water*). Water impregnated with salt; sea-water.

a **1000** *Ags. Ps.* (Th.) lxxvi. 13 Sweȝ micel sealtera wætera. *c* **1200** *Trin. Coll. Hom.* 151 Ðe wop þe man wepeð for his aȝene sinne is swiðe biter alse saltwater. *c* **1440** *Promp. Parv.* 441/1 Salt water, or see water, *Nereis.* **1497** *Naval Acc. Hen. VII* (1896) 129 Gonnepoudre wett in saltwater. **1530** PALSGR. 265/1 Saltewater, *saulmevre.* **1580** LYLY *Euphues* (Arb.) 296, I laboured no otherwise, then..he that hauing sore eyes rubbeth them with salt water. **1610** HOLLAND *Camden's Brit.* (1637) 268 Salt-waters, out of which they boile salt. **1669** WORLIDGE *Syst. Agric.* 5 By watering the place with brine or Salt water. **1706** E. WARD *Wooden World Diss.* (1708) 8 Seeng his Spot of Territory incircl'd with Salt-water. **1841** *Penny Cycl.* XX. 368/2 Hot parts of the world where the soil is saline or there is salt water in the vicinity.

fig. *a* **1450** MYRC *Festial* xxvii. 120 When he passyth þrogh þe salt-watyr of payne of deþe.

b. Applied humorously to tears. (See SALT *sb.*[1] 2 e.)

c **1400** *Laud Troy Bk.* 15694 He wepis..Many a tere of salt watir. **1592** SHAKS. *Rom. & Jul.* II. iii. 71 How much salt water throwne away in wast, To season Loue that of it doth not tast. **1612** WEBSTER *White Devil* K, 'Faith, for some few howers salt water will runne most plentifully in euery Office o' th Court. **1833** L. RITCHIE *Wand. by Loire* 128 Let us hear what all this salt water is about.

c. Applied to the sea. Hence, a jocular form of address to a sailor.

1839 H. AINSWORTH *Jack Sheppard* I. vi. 111 'Hark'ee, Ben', said the old sailor,..'you may try, but dash my timbers if you'll ever cross the Thames to-night'. 'And why not, old saltwater?' inquired Ben. **1843** MARRYAT *M. Violet* xv, When this sun will have disappeared behind the salt-water.

B. *attrib.* as *adj.* (stressed *'salt-water*). **a.** Of, pertaining to, consisting of, or living in salt water.

1528 *Lett. & Pap. Hen. VIII*, IV. II. 2232 The warffs gittes and saltwater bancks, beginning at Calais and continuing to Graveling. **1601** SHAKS. *Twel. N.* v. i. 72 Notable Pyrate, thou salt-water Theefe. **1796** WITHERING *Brit. Plants* (ed. 3) IV. 129 Salt water ditches between Greenwich and Woolwich. **1810** SCOTT *Let. to Miss J. Baillie* 19 July in *Lockhart*, The salt-water loch called Loch an Gaoil. **1858** O. W. HOLMES *Aut. Breakf.-t.* i, It does not follow that I wish to be pickled in brine because I like a salt-water plunge at Nahant. **1859** DARWIN *Orig. Spec.* xii. 384 Salt-water fish can with care be slowly accustomed to live in fresh water. **1892** GUNTER *Miss Dividends* I. iv, The train.. crossing the Harlem, skirts that pretty little salt water river.

b. In specific names of sea animals.

1828 SIR H. DAVY *Salmonia* (1840) 72 The salt-water louse adheres to his sides. **1888** GOODE *Amer. Fishes* 405 The bluefish, which is called the 'Salt water Tailor'. **1892** *Chamb. Encycl.* s.v. *Terrapin*, The terrapin *par excellence* is the *Malacoclemmys palustris*, the diamond-back salt-water terrapin.

c. *U.S.* and *W. Indies.* Used to designate a recent, usu. black, immigrant (see quots.).

1774 E. LONG *Hist. Jamaica* II. III. iii. 410 The Creole Blacks differ much from the Africans, not only in manners, but in beauty of shape, feature, and complexion. They hold the Africans in the utmost contempt, stiling them, 'salt-water Negroes', and 'Guiney birds'; but value themselves on their own pedigree. **1818** H. B. FEARON *Sk. Amer.* 93 If I had my will there should never be a salt-water man employed in the States. *a* **1820** B. H. LATROBE *Jrnl.* (1905) iii. 63 The ferryman..is one of several who are children of a man and woman, negroes, brought from Africa—called here salt-water negroes. **1855** F. DOUGLASS *My Bondage* 323 The salt water slave who hung in the guards of a steamer.. has, by the publicity given to the circumstance, set a spy on the guards of every steamer departing from southern ports. **1961** F. G. CASSIDY *Jamaica Talk* viii. 156 A sort of half-way condition between the creole Negro and the salt-water Negro was the *salt-water Creole*—one born during the voyage to Jamaica. **1966** *Publ. Amer. Dial. Soc.* *1964* XLII. 39 Irish informants use *turkey* and *saltwater turkey* to designate a recent immigrant.

d. ***salt-water taffy*** (TAFFY[1], var. form of TOFFEE *sb.*) *U.S.*, a type of confectionery made chiefly from corn syrup and sugar, freq. sold at North-eastern (chiefly New Jersey) seaside resorts.

1894 *Official Gaz.* (U.S. Patent Office) 17 July 410/1 (*caption*) The representation of a four masted schooner with the words '*The Original Atlantic City Salt Water Taffy*'. **1910** H. T. PECK *New Baedeker* II. vi. 309 And there are also itinerant venders of every sort of edible..from 'salt-water taffy'..down to peanuts and 'hot dogs'. **1933** *Nat. Geogr. Mag.* May 520/2 Next to the visitor, Atlantic City's biggest 'Industry' is the making and shipping of 'salt-water taffy'. Legend says that in the early eighties a man had a candy stand on the beach. One day an unusually high tide splashed over a batch of old-fashioned, pulled taffy on a slab. Being an enterprising person, he told his customers that he had something new—'salt-water taffy'. **1954** W. RICHMOND *Choice Confections* xxi. 385 This formula produces a salt water taffy or kiss of very fine quality... The formula can be used for regular kiss-shaped pieces or long sticks of salt water taffy. **1960** J. J. ROWLANDS *Spindrift* 65 Through the grimy windows of the salt-water taffy counter you see the cold steel arms of the taffy puller motionless and empty-handed. **1979** *United States 1980/81* (Penguin Travel Guides) 48 Vermont cheese and maple syrup, salt-water taffy along the New Jersey shore..are all specialties of their respective regions.

Hence **salt-watery** *a.*

1812 *Sporting Mag.* XL. 167 All very greasy, blowsy, dabby, dusty, salt-watery, and so on.

'salt-well. [OE. **sealtwielle*, *-wylle* (Northumb. *-wælle*).] A salt spring, well, or pit; now, a bored well from which brine is obtained for salt-making.

c **950** *Lindisf. Gosp.* Prol. 1 Of saltwælla ðone æne in-dranc. [**1042** in Kemble *Cod. Dipl.* IV. 70 Ðer ofer ða stræt æfter ðam ȝemære in saltwyllan; of saltwyllan in seȝchæma ȝemær.] **1398** TREVISA *Barth. De P.R.* XIX. liii. (1495) 894 Some lycoure comyth of veynes of the erth: as water of salt welles. *a* **1647** HABINGTON *Surv. Worcs.* in *Proc. Worcs. Hist. Soc.* II. 296 The freashe water with exceedynge fluddes overflowethe the banckes and for a season drownethe the salt-wells. **1656** SMITH & WEBB *Vale-Royal Engl.* I. 19 The Salt-wells, which they call Brine-pits; out of the which, they make yearly a great quantity of fine white Salt. **1756** C. LUCAS *Ess. Waters* II. 30 Salt was..made in Cappadocia from salt wells. **1848** *Knapp's Chem. Technol.* I. 260 Salt wells..are..frequently found ready formed in nature, wherever a spring, during its course, has come in contact with a bed of rock-salt. **1892** JACKSON in Lee *Hist. Columbus* (Ohio) I. 791 While working in the saltwells of Virginia.

Hence †**saltweller**, one who works at salt-wells.

1624 *Maldon, Essex, Borough Deeds* Bundle 108 lf. 2 Samwell Smyth, saltweller.

'salt-works. Formerly also -**work**. [Cf. G. *salzwerk.*] A salt manufactory.

1565 ABP. PARKER *Corr.* (Parker Soc.) 258 Your letters requesting timber and firewood for your salt-works. **1674**

BOYLE *Saltness of Sea* 29 A friend of mine that is Master of a Salt-work. **1697** *Lond. Gaz.* No. 3307/4 At the Salt-Works of Samuel Acton in Namptwich. **1712–13** SWIFT *Jrnl. to Stella* 21 Feb., Griffin..says he knows nothing of a salt-work at Recton. **1796** MORSE *Amer. Geog.* II. 242 Gallicia.. is famous for its immense salt-works at Wielitzka. **1848** *Knapp's Chem. Technol.* I. 261 The salt-works at Salzhausen.

'saltwort. *Bot.* [prob. after Du. *zoutkruid*; cf. G. *salzkraut*.] A name for several maritime and salt-marsh plants. Cf. GLASSWORT.

1. Any plant of the genus *Salsola*, spec. *S. Kali* (Common or Prickly Saltwort); = KALI[1] 1.

1568 TURNER *Herbal* III. 37 Kali..hath no name in English... But lest this herbe shoulde be without a name, it maye be called Saltwurt, because it is salt in taste. **1671** SKINNER *Etymol. Ling. Angl., Bot., Salt-wort*, Kali. **1712** tr. *Pomet's Hist. Drugs* I. 101 A Plant..which the Botanists call Kali, and we Salt-wort. **1810** CRABBE *Borough* i. 41 Here sampire-banks and salt-wort bound the flood. **1828** J. E. SMITH *Eng. Flora* II. 18 *Salsola fruticosa.* Shrubby Saltwort. **1862** ANSTED *Channel Isl.* II. viii. 177 The salt-wort or glass-wort (*Salsola kali*), grows freely on most of the shores. **1884** [see KALI[1] 1].

2. Black Saltwort, *Glaux maritima.* = MILKWORT 2.

1597 GERARDE *Herbal* II. clix. 447 Of blacke Salt woort. **1760** J. LEE *Introd. Bot.* App. 326. **1861** MISS PRATT *Flower. Pl.* IV. 234 Sea Milkwort, or Black Saltwort. **1867** SOWERBY *Eng. Bot.* (ed. 3) VII. 154.

3. A plant of the genus *Salicornia*, esp. *S. herbacea*; = GLASSWORT a.

1597 [see GLASSWORT]. **1760** J. LEE *Introd. Bot.* 326. **1785** MARTYN *Rousseau's Bot.* xvii. (1794) 233 *note*, Marsh Sampire, called also jointed Glasswort or Saltwort. **1845** LINDLEY *Sch. Bot.* (ed. 14) 110b, *Salicornia annua* (Saltwort). **1864** GRISEBACH *Flora W. Ind. Islands* 787.

salty ('sɒltɪ, -ɔː-), *a.*[1] and *sb.* [f. SALT *sb.*[1] + -Y.]

A. *adj.* **1.** Containing or impregnated with salt; tasting of salt; = SALT *a.*[1] 1.

c **1440** *Promp. Parv.* 441/1 Salt, or salti..*salsus.* **1563** HYLL *Art Garden.* II. liv. (1608) 133 Infused in warm and salty water for a season. **1634** SIR T. HERBERT *Trav.* 65 Sand and salty Desarts. **1657** TOMLINSON *Renou's Disp.* 161 Any convenient humour, whether bitter, acerb, salty, or oyly. **1670** W. SIMPSON *Hydrol. Ess.* 59 This yellow green salty liquor. **1860** R. C. A. PRIOR *Danish Ball.* I. 5 Launching over the salty sea. **1872** J. HATTON *Valley Poppies* II. i. 27, I smell the salty breath of the wind. **1875** LANIER *Symphony* 222 Her eyes with salty tears are wet. **1889** A. T. PASK *Eyes Thames* 49 From this sandy salty loam is made the best Portland cement.

†**2.** Consisting of salt. *Obs. rare.*

1605 WILLET *Hexapla Gen.* 219 God could turne a womans bodie into a saltie piller. **1633** T. ADAMS *Exp. 2 Peter* ii. 7 [Lot's wife] was turned into a material salty pillar. **1665** NEEDHAM *Med. Medicinæ* 393 If the Salty part becomes extravagant for want of the Spirit and Sulphur to restrain..it.

3. Piquant; racy.

1866 *Athenæum* 10 Mar. 332/2 This..only makes the books more salty; and we must add, that the piquancy is not diminished by [etc.]. **1978** J. A. MICHENER *Chesapeake* 359 When Captain Turlock learned that his mate had studied with the rector, there was salty discussion of that churchman's habits.

4. *U.S. Naut. slang.* Of a sailor: tough; hard-bitten; aggressive. Cf. SALT *sb.*[1] 11.

1920 H. R. CHAMBERS *U.S. Submarine Chasers in Mediterranean* ii. 12 We were all very 'salty' and 'rolled' fore and aft along the deck instead of walking. **1926** ANDERSON & STALLINGS *Three Amer. Plays* III. 73, I lived with a Spanish girl at Cavite back in '99... In those days I was salty as hell, a sea-going buckaroo. **1926** J. W. CROSLEY *Bk. Navy Songs* II. 24 A salty bunch of Ensigns we, from the great Atlantic Fleet, And we're here to learn the reason why a valve must have a seat. **1939** *Sat. Even. Post* 23 Dec. 6/1 He was a salty old regular, with one of those wedge-shaped figures and an ugly underslung face of the texture and color of seamed leather. **1941** M. GOODRICH *Delilah* iii. 210 The consensus was that Delilah's men now, for some reason, thought they were 'salty' and were looking for trouble.

5. *U.S. slang.* Angry, irritated; hostile. *to jump salty*: to undergo a sudden change of mood or outlook; to become annoyed or angry (with someone).

1938 *Amer. Speech* XIII. 314/1 *Jump salty*, implies an unexpected change in a person's attitude or knowledge. The person may become suddenly angry, or an unhipped person may become hipped. **1938** *N.Y. Amsterdam News* 26 Feb. 17/2 Let's sound a high C on the postoffice man whose Girl Friday is 'jumpin' salty' 'cause he won't Reno the wife who thinks but isn't sure. **1944** C. CALLOWAY *Hepsters Dict., Salty*, angry, ill-tempered. **1952** C. BROSSARD *Who walk in Darkness* xi. 67 Why do you have to get so salty when people want to have fun? **1958** *Partisan Rev.* XXV. 292 That man jumped salty on me. **1967** J. A. WILLIAMS *Man who cried I Am* xvi. 187 Oops! The dozens, is it? I made you salty eh? **1975** P. G. WINSLOW *Death of Angel* vi. 137 He was furious when I said I didn't have any [money] and got very salty.

B. *sb.* Also **saltie.** A sea-going ship (as opposed to LAKER[1] 4). *N. Amer.*

1959 *Ottawa Citizen* 29 Apr. 53/1 Sixty or more ocean ships—called 'salties' by lake seamen—and inland ships were expected to be in transit today. **1961** *Times* 24 Apr. 16/6 Hundreds of miles eastward again the 'salties' are converging from all over the world, soon to thread the canals and locks linking our vast ocean-like lakes, and bringing a nostalgic Atlantic tang into the very heart of the Dominion. **1966** *Kingston* (Ontario) *Whig-Standard* 5 Jan. 19/7 The only saltie to visit Kingston that year, the 17,170 ton Malmanger of Norway, sailed with her holds only half full of grain. **1971** *Cleveland* (Ohio) *Plain Dealer* 14 Dec. c7 (*heading*) British salty will be last in Cleveland this season.

Hence **'saltily** *adv.*

1926 R. MACAULAY *Crewe Train* II. ix 172 Arnold's old flannel trousers were rolled above his knees; his white, slim, long legs glistened saltily beside Denham's firm, brown ones. **1945** C. MANN in B. James *Austral. Short Stories* (1963) 77 After a time he did not so much hear and saltily smell those myriad fish. **1955** *Times* 7 July 5/1 Parents should teach a straightforward, 'saltily realistic' approach to sexual questions. **1958** *Times* 24 Dec. 3/6 The drawings pay marked attention to the arts. Constable..is accompanied by ..the young Brangwyn, saltily caught by Phil May.

†**'salty,** *a.*[2] *Obs.* [f. SALT *sb.*[2] or *a.*[2] + -Y.] Of a bitch: In heat.

1603 SIR C. HEYDON *Jud. Astrol.* xx. 416 A bitch..is 9. daies saltie, goeth 9. moneths with whelps, and hath her whelps 9. daies blind. **1796** PEGGE *Derbicisms* Ser. I. 59 (E.D.S.) *Salty*, of a bitch, when she is proud, or in her heat.

saltyr, salu: see SALTIRE, SALUE *v.*

†**saluberrime,** *a. Obs. rare*[−1]. [ad. L. *salūberrim-us*, superl. of *salūbris*: see SALUBRIOUS.] Highly salubrious.

1509 WATSON *Ship of Fools* lx. (1517) Ovb, All vacabondes.., the which gothe beggynge from dore to dore ..come vnto me and I shall gyue you an almesse saluberryme.

salubrify (sə'l(j)uːbrɪfaɪ), *v. rare.* [f. L. *salūbri-s* (see next) + -FY.] *trans.* To render salubrious.

1842 *Jrnl. R. Agric. Soc.* III. II. 407 The rain..washes out from the subsoil those noxious ingredients.., sweetens and salubrifies it to the depth of the drains.

salubrious (sə'l(j)uːbrɪəs), *a.* [f. L. *salūbri-s* (f. *salū-s* health) + -OUS.] Favourable or conducive to health.

a. Of food, medicine, etc. Now *rare.*

1547 BOORDE *Brev. Health* 121 b, I myghte here shewe of many salubriouse medecines. **1667** FLAVEL *Saint Indeed* (1754) 121 The Unicorn's horn..in the Apothecaries shop, where it is made salubrious or medicinal. **1709** W. KING *Art of Love* VIII. 1065 Give the salubrious draughts with your own hand; Persuasion has the force of a command. **1748** *Anson's Voy.* II. viii. 220 A species of food so very palatable and salubrious as turtle. **1842** A. COMBE *Physiol. Digestion* (ed. 4) 341 The more slowly they [ices] are eaten, the more refreshing and salubrious will they become. **1871** NAPHEYS *Prev. & Cure Dis.* I. ii. 68 Fish. In the hot months all kinds are less salubrious than in cold weather.

b. Of air, climate, places, etc.

1615 G. SANDYS *Trav.* 8 The forraine merchants here [Zacynthus] resident..by their frequent deaths do disprove the aire to be so salubrious as is reported. **1774** PENNANT *Tour Scotl. in 1772*, 175 In summer the air is remarkably salubrious. **1807** G. CHALMERS *Caledonia* I. I. iv. 164 The Roman officers seem to have had many villas along its salubrious shore. **1833** HT. MARTINEAU *Berkeley the Banker* I. i. 3 Foreseeing the possibility of his having four or five Masters Cavendish as boarders in his salubrious.. establishment. **1875** BROWNING *Inn Album* 2 Hail calm acclivity, salubrious spot!

c. Of an occupation. *rare.*

1675 WORLIDGE *Syst. Agric.* xii. (ed. 2) 253 Angling; a moderate, innocent, salubrious, and delightful exercise.

d. Of physiological processes: = SALUTARY.

1855 RAMSBOTHAM *Obstetr. Med.* 70 The salubrious change which the fœtal blood undergoes, is accomplished in the placental mass.

e. *transf.* and *fig.*

1659 HAMMOND *On Ps.* xcvii. 485 Dispensed by the divine providence for many salubrious and beneficial ends. **1737** THOMSON *To Mem. Ld. Talbot* 147 In Senates, He to Freedom firm, Enlighten'd Freedom, plann'd salubrious Laws. *a* **1780** H. BLAIR *Serm.* II. 31 If that fountain [the heart] be once poisoned, you can never expect that salubrious streams will flow from it. **1809** CAMPBELL *Gertr. Wyom.* I. ix, And dwells in day-light truth's salubrious skies No form with which the soul may sympathise? **1855** LANDOR *Imag. Conv., A. Pollio & L. Calvus* ii. Wks. 1876 II. 443 Religions, like the sun, take their course from east to west: traversing the globe, they are not all equally temperate, equally salubrious: they dry up some lands, and inundate others.

Hence **sa'lubriously** *adv.*; **sa'lubriousness.**

1677 W. HUBBARD *Narrative* 1 In the..salubriousness of the Air..most resembling the Country from whence it borrowed its appellation. **1790** BURKE *Fr. Rev.* 238 Does not the sweat of the mason and carpenter..flow as pleasantly and as salubriously, in the construction and repair of the majestic edifices of religion, as in the painted booths and sordid sties of vice and luxury. **1888** *Schaff's Encycl. Relig. Knowl.* 1391 The salubriousness of their climate.

salubrity (sə'l(j)uːbrɪtɪ). [ad. L. *salūbritās*, f. *salūbri-s* SALUBRIOUS.]

1. The quality of being salubrious or healthful.

a. Of the air, a country, etc.

1432–50 tr. *Higden* (Rolls) I. 75 Paradise..hath salubrite [orig. *Habet enim salubritatem*] and wholsomnesse. **1604** R. CAWDREY *Table Alph., Salubritie*, wholesomeness. **1685** BOYLE (*title*) An Experimental Discourse of some unheeded Causes of the Insalubrity and Salubrity of the Air. **1767** *Byron's Voy. rd. World* 57 The salubrity of the air had a surprizing effect in strengthening both the appetite and digestion. **1799** *Monthly Rev.* XXX. 400 In many instances, salubrity will be promoted by inclosures. **1870** YEATS *Nat. Hist. Comm.* I. ii. 12 Penzance and Torquay, in mildness and salubrity, resemble Madeira. **1876** A. J. EVANS *Through Bosnia* ii. 73 This decrease of salubrity is attributed..to the great destruction of forests.

†**b.** Of food, etc.: Wholesomeness. *Obs. rare.*

1620 VENNER *Via Recta* iii. 69 The heart of a fat Calfe is for pleasantnes of taste,..and salubrity of iuyce, the best. **1733** TULL *Horse-hoeing Husb.* v. (Dublin) 41 What can we say then to the Salubrity of those Roots themselves, bred up and fatten'd amongst these Toads and Corruption?

†**c.** *fig. Obs.*

c **1643** *Observ. his Maj. late Answ. & Expresses* 8 A.. proofe of the integrity, and salubrity of that publick advice.

¶ **2.** Healthy condition, health. (Also *fig.*) *rare.*

1654 [see SALVIFICAL *a.*]. **1786** *Pogonologia* 58 This bushy hair on man's face must have an influence on the salubrity of the neighbouring parts. **1822–34** *Good's Study Med.* (ed. 4) II. 63 The feet..ulcerated and healed, with a speedy return of general salubrity.

‖**salud** (sa'luð), *int.* [Sp., = (good) health: see SALUTE *sb.*[1]] A toast before drinking: 'cheers!', 'good health!'

1938 E. HEMINGWAY *Fifth Column* I. ii. 7 Salud, Comrade Stamp Collector. **1940** G. GREENE *Power & Glory* II. ii. 139 'I will have a little brandy.' 'Salud!' **1961** J. WELCOME *Beware of Midnight* xi. 140 '*Salud*,' she said, lifting her glass. **1973** G. GREENE *Honorary Consul* III. iii. 148 'That is a very large whisky.'.. 'Large? Why, it is only half as big as mine. *Salud!*'

salud, var. pa. t. of SALUE *v. Obs.*

‖**saludador.** Spanish form of SALUTATOR.

1685 EVELYN *Diary* 16 Sept.

†**sa'lue,** *sb. Obs. rare.* Also **salew.** [a. OF. *salu* (in mod.Fr. written *salut*: see SALUTE *sb.*[1]) = Sp. *saludo*, It. *saluto*, a Com. Rom. vbl. sb. f. *salūtāre* SALUTE *v.*] A salutation.

c **1430** LYDG. *Min. Poems* (Percy Soc.) 8 They..Goyng owtward gave the kyng salue [*rime* dewe]. *c* **1450** *Merlin* xxvii. 506 The quene..seide thei were welcome, and thei dide yelde hir a-gein hir salew debonerly. **1485** CAXTON *Paris & V.* (1868) 32 Parys rendred hys salewes ayeyn moche humbly.

†**sa'lue,** *v. Obs.* Forms: 4–5 **saluwe, saliewe, salwe,** 4–6 **salew,** 5 **salowe,** 6 **salu,** 4–7 **salue;** *pa. t.* 4 **salewede, saluet,** 4–5 **salu(e)de, salewed, salwed, saluwed, saluyd,** 5 **salut(e, ? salit, salod, -ud, saylut, salowed, -id, saluid, saluyed,** 6 **salewd,** 4–7 **salued.** [a. F. *saluer* = Pr., Sp. *saludar*, Pg. *saudar*, It. *salutare*:—L. *salūtāre* to SALUTE.]

1. *trans.* = SALUTE *v.*

c **1300** *Harrow. Hell* 868 (MS. Sion) To Ierusalem come on a day Thre prestes of þe Iewery, Tille þe temple held þai streke þe way And saluede þe clergy. *c* **1320** R. BRUNNE *Medit.* 1076 Anone come petyr, with wepyng chere, And salude Mary and Ion yn fere. *c* **1374** CHAUCER *Troylus* II. 1619 (1668) Eleyn in al hire goodly soft wyse Gan hym salue and wommanly to pleye. *c* **1386** —— *Frankl. T.* 781 And he saleweth hire with glad entente. **1387** TREVISA *Higden* (Rolls) V. 101 Þey emperoures þat were to fore hym were i-salwed as iuges. *c* **1400** *Destr. Troy.* 4981 Þai salut not þat souerain with no sad wordes. *c* **1420** *Sir Amadace* (Camden) xi, Ho sayd, 'Sir, welcum most ȝe be!' A[nd] salit him anon ryȝte [Weber's ed. l. 112 And salod hym anon ryght]. *Ibid.* xxxvii, He saylut him anon ryȝte [Weber 409 Bot salud hym full ryght]. *c* **1430** LYDG. *Min. Poems* (Percy Soc.) 242 The amerous fowlys with motetys and carollys, Salwe that sesoun every morwenyng. *c* **1440** *Gesta Rom.* xxiii. 83 (Harl. MS.) Thei fille doun on kne..and salowid him, as thei aught to do to themperour. **1481** CAXTON *Godeffroy* xiii. 40 He.. salewed hym in the name of the Patriarke..of Surye. **1502** ARNOLDE *Chron.* (1811) 159 Salu me highly with honorable salutacions to the honorable Lordis. **1542** UDALL *Erasm. Apoph.* 122 Diogenes..salued or hailed hym wᵗ this verse of homere. **1596** SPENSER *F.Q.* IV. vi. 25 Glaucè..her salewd with seemely bel-accoyle, Joyous to see her safe after long toyle. **1601** HOLLAND *Pliny* II. 297 Euen Tiberius Cæsar.. required in that manner to be salued and wished well vnto, whensoeuer he sneezed.

fig. **1606** WARNER *Alb. Eng.* XIV. xci. 369 Great'st Ladies with their women, on their Palfries mounted faire,.. Which now in Coches scorne to be salued of the aire.

b. *absol.*

13.. *Gaw. & Gr. Knt.* 1473 Þe lady noȝt forȝate, Com to hym to salue. *c* **1386** CHAUCER *Pers. T.* ⁋ 333 Yet is ther a priuee spece of pride, that waiteth first to be salewed er he wole salewe [*Harl. MS.* to be saluet er he saliewe]. **1596** DRAYTON *Leg. Cromw.* 827 Peace, the good Porter,.. prayes him God to saue, And after saluing, kindly doth demand What was his will.

2. By confusion = *salve*, SAVE *v.*

1484 CAXTON *Fables of Æsop* v. ix, The lyon ansuerd to hym God salewe the swete frend come nyghe me and kysse me.

salue, written for *salve*, obs. form of SAVE.

salufer ('sæljʊfə(r)). [irreg. f. L. *salū-s* health (see SALUTARY) + *-fer* producing.] Silicofluoride of sodium, used as an antiseptic. Hence **sa'luferize** *v.*, to cleanse or purify with 'salufer'.

1894 *Times* 5 May 6/1 Mr. Thomson, the successor of Playfair..at the Manchester Royal Institution Laboratory. He has a plan of attacking the mud in the bottom of the canal with a powerful antiseptic compounded of sodium, silicon, and fluorine. Salufer the mixture is named. *Ibid.*, It may be requisite to saluferize not only the canal water, but that of the river for some distance higher up. **1905** *Brit. Med. Jrnl.* 27 May 1147 The ear was syringed once or twice daily with a solution of salufer in boiled water.

salugh, obs. form of SALLOW *sb.*

saluid, var. pa. t. of SALUE *v. Obs.*

†**sa'luing,** *vbl. sb. Obs.* [f. SALUE *v.* + -ING[1].] The action of the verb SALUE; a salutation.

c **1374** CHAUCER *Troylus* II. 1519 (1568) Lat vs of hire saluynges pace. *c* **1386** —— *Knt.'s T.* 791 Ther nas no good day ne no saluyng. *c* **1430** *Syr Gener.* (Roxb.) 916 Make him noo privey salewing, But openlie afore hem all Profre youre seruice in the hall. *c* **1489** CAXTON *Blanchardyn* v. 23 The knyght, right humbly and wyth a right lowe voyce,.. rendryd hym ayen his salewyng.

saluki (sə'lu:kɪ). Also **selugi, sleughi; slogie, slokee, sloug(h)i, slughi.** [ad. Arab. *selūķī*, f. *Saluķ* the name of a town in the Yemen.] A large, lightly built hound belonging to the breed so called, with feathered tail and feet and large pendant ears; formerly called the Persian greyhound. Also *attrib.*

1809 J. G. JACKSON *Acct. Empire of Marocco* v. 31 They often hunt the gazel with the (slogie) African greyhound. **1844** J. H. D. HAY *Western Barbary* xiii. 89/2 The beaters kept good and steady line, and woe to the wild ones that showed themselves to.. the swift-footed slokees on the plain. **1891** 'OUIDA' in *N. Amer. Rev.* Sept. 316 The Siberian and the Persian greyhounds are one and the same breed; called *sleughi* in Persia and Arabia. **1913** *Dress & Vanity Fair* (N.Y.) Oct. 110/2 Among them is a Saluki or gazelle hound. **1924** *Blackw. Mag.* Jan. 24/2 Among them.. a few Selugis, Persian greyhounds of as ancient and pure a strain as our own. **1924** G. BELL *Let.* 13 Feb. (1927) II. xxiii. 684 When I came in at 4 from the office I found Marie sitting in the garden looking like a female St. Jerome, with a needle for a book, a slughi dog for a lion and a tame red-legged partridge standing solemnly beside her instead of a quail. **1926** *Public Opinion* 30 July 102/2 A tall great sloughi came out of the house, beating his tail against the posts of the verandah. **1928** *Evening News* 5 May 9 He was requested by the Bey to bring him back a really fine English slougi. **1931** C. S. JARVIS *Yesterday & To-day in Sinai* xi. 212 A Saluki hunt on camel-back. **1938** J. W. DAY *Dog in Sport* i. 18 The fleet gazelle-hound of the desert, ancestor of the graceful, tassel-eared Saluki of to-day. **1945** C. L. B. HUBBARD *Observer's Bk. Dogs* 134 Being a member of the Greyhound family, the Saluki is extremely old and of the purest descent. It traces back to about 5,000 years B.C., when it was little different to the modern dog of the Arabs of to-day. **1953** A. SMITH *Blind White Fish in Persia* ii. 41, 100 miles along it there was a tea house, just a hut with a man outside smoking a hookah and a boy with two Salukis. **1973** *Country Life* 8 Feb. (Suppl.) 33/3 (Advt.), Afghans and Salukis, also Ibizans and Pharoahs (with whom we will be at Crufts). **1978** *Times* 7 Jan. 12/2 Bahrain's pure-bred saluki hound, which recently came close to extinction as a pedigree strain, is making a comeback.

‖**salumeria** (salume'ria). [It., grocer's or pork-butcher's shop, f. *salume* salted meat f. *sale* salt (L. *sal* salt).] A delicatessen.

1926 R. HALL *Adam's Breed* I. v. 42 There was Fabio's salumeria.. his ware's—the sausages, the paste, the rich yellow oil, the.. Chianti. **1967** P. JONES *Fifth Defector* ii. 10, I was just coming out of the Salumeria in Via Canzotti... Where we get that delicious smoked cheese?

salumin ('sæljʊmɪn). [f. SAL(ICYLATE) + (AL)UMIN(IUM).] Salicylate of aluminium used in nose and throat diseases.

1897 in *Syd. Soc. Lex.*

salure, variant of SALER, salt-cellar.

saluresis (sæljʊ'ri:sɪs). *Med.* [f. as next + DI)URESIS.] The renal excretion of a greater quantity of salts than is usual. Cf. next.

1959 *Lancet* 25 Apr. 866/1 The urinary output of salt is raised... The saluresis soon abates. **1975** *Aviation, Space & Environmental Med.* XLVI. 1358/1 Exogenous mineral-corticoid prevents the diuresis, saluresis, and kaluresis.

saluretic (sæljʊ'rɛtɪk), *a.* and *sb. Med.* [f. L. *sal* salt + DI)URETIC *a.* and *sb.*] **A.** *adj.* Promoting the renal excretion of salts. **B.** *sb.* A saluretic drug. Cf. prec.

1959 *Lancet* 25 Apr. 866/1 Recently a more potent saluretic agent, hydrochlorothiazide, has become available. .. The saluretic and antidiuretic actions were interdependent. **1964** L. MARTIN *Clin. Endocrinol.* (ed. 4) i. 53 Restriction of protein and salt in the diet has been advised, and hydrochlorthiazide may be used for its saluretic effect. **1975** *Jrnl. Pediatrics* LXXXVI. 831/2 In newborn infants the saluretics are the diuretics of choice. *Ibid.* 832/1 Mannitol has.. been used successfully, either alone or with one of the saluretic agents.

†**salus**, *sb. Obs.* Also **saluz.** [Perh. a. early OF. *saluz, salus*, subj.-case sing. or obj.-case pl. of *salu*: see SALUE *sb.*] A salutation.

a **1225** *Ancr. R.* 388 And wrot mid his owune blode saluz to his leofmon, of luue gretunge. *a* **1400–50** *Alexander* 4647 To Alexander.. salus & ioye. *c* **1400** *Destr. Troy* 3640 Let vs send to hom salus solemli by letre, Praiand hom.. To helpe vs in hast our harmys to venge. *c* **1450** *St. Cuthbert* (Surtees) 5923 þe schipmen wendys to þe priour, And haylsid him with honour, he said saluz agayne. *c* **1475** *Partenay* 896 The Erle ther saluz yilding ryght goodly Vnto euery man.

†**salus**, *v. Sc.* and *north. Obs.* Also 5 **salose**, 6 **saluse, saluis.** [f. prec. sb.] *trans.* = SALUTE *v.* Hence **salusing** *vbl. sb.*, greeting.

1375 BARBOUR *Bruce* IV. 509 Than went thai to the kyng in hy, And hym salusit full curtasly. *c* **1440** *Gesta Rom.* lxix. 318 (Harl. MS.) And so she come to him, and worshipfully she salusid him. *c* **1450** *St. Cuthbert* (Surtees) 3419 The abbot salust him on hyght. *c* **1470** HENRY *Wallace* x. 593 Thar salusyng was bot boustous and thrawin. *c* **1500** *Lancelot* 1309 Nothir of thi salosing, nor the, Ne rak I nocht. **1500–20** DUNBAR *Poems* xlvi. 18 With notis glaid.. This joyfull merle so salust scho the day. **1528** LYNDESAY *Dreme* 149 Me thocht ane lady.. Did salus me, with benyng contynance. **1533** BELLENDEN *Livy* I. vii. (S.T.S.) I. 41 And Incontinent all þe remanent pepil salust him as king and fader of þe romane ciete. *Ibid.* xviii. 105 Scho.. was þe first þat salust him king. **1560** ROLLAND *Crt. Venus* I. 290 Greit salusingis, with gretingis full of gloir. *Ibid.* II. 37 [He] saluist thame on his best wayis anone.

absol. *c* **1470** HENRY *Wallace* v. 576 Quhen Wallace saw that thai war ma than he, Than did he nocht but salust curtasle.

salus, salut: see SALUTE *sb.*[2] *Obs.*

‖**salus populi suprema lex (esto).** Latin phr. (occurring in Cicero *De Leg.* III. iii. 8): the safety of the people must be the supreme law. Also *ellipt.* as ***salus populi***. Similarly ***salus rei publicae***.

1612 BACON *Essaies* xxvii, Judges ought above all, to remember the Conclusion of the Romaine twelve Tables; *Salus populi suprema lex*, and to know that Lawes, except they bee in order to that end, are but things captious, and Oracles not well inspired. **1617** J. CHAMBERLAIN *Let.* 10 May (1939) II. 74 Necessitie hath no law, and yf *salus populi* be *suprema lex*, in this case *salus regis* was included too. **1788** GIBBON *Let.* 29 Nov. in *Wks.* (1796) I. 193 In so new a case the *salus populi* must be the first law. **1794** [see *political science* s.v. POLITICAL *a.* 6]. **1836** J. F. DAVIS *Chinese* I. vi. 251 These are contained in their sacred books, whose principle is literally, *salus populi suprema lex.* **1845** H. BROOM *Legal Maxims* i. 1 *Salus Populi Suprema Lex...* Hence there are many cases in which individuals sustain an injury for which the law gives no action. **1910** CHESTERTON *G.B. Shaw* 89 The real and ancient emotion of the *salus populi*, almost extinct in our oligarchical chaos. **1963** *Times* 8 Mar. 13/5 In matters concerning the safety of the state, the definition of which can be safely left to our Courts of Law, *salus rei publicae* must surely still be *suprema lex*? **1978** *Times* 10 May 17/5, I do not wish to pursue the arguments for and against birching.. except to express doubts as to whether the vague and potentially dangerous maxim 'salus populi suprema lex'.. is really the best possible guideline to be recommended to a court of law for the determination of a legal issue.

‖**salut** (saly), *sb.* Also with capital initial. [Fr., ellipt. for *salut du Saint Sacrement*, salutation (or benediction) of the Blessed Sacrament.] In French Roman Catholic churches: an evening service of Benediction (at which the Host is exposed and the hymn 'O Salutaris Hostia' is sung).

1694 J. DRUMMOND *Let.* 30 Mar. (1845) 17 One may be either offering the Holy Sacrifice in conjunction with the priests of God, or singing the praise of the Almighty God at the Saluts, or hearing exhortations. **1815** E. WYNNE *Diary* 15 Sept. (1952) xxxi. 536 We went into church while the *Salut* was going on. **1843** C. BRONTË *Let.* 2 Sept. in W. Gérin *C. Brontë* (1967) xiv. 241, I found myself opposite to Ste Gadule, and the bell.. began to toll for evening 'salut'. **1853** —— *Villette* xii. 43/2 At sunset or the hour of *salut*, when the externes were gone home. **1901** *Month* Sept. 268 The word *salut*, which is still in French-speaking countries the name most commonly employed to designate the service of Benediction, preserves the memory of an institution which most probably must be regarded as the primitive stock, upon which the Exposition of the Sacred Host and the blessing imparted with It are only an excrescence. **1967** W. GÉRIN *C. Brontë* xiii. 188 The great bell.. ringing to Matins, Vespers, and to 'Salut' throughout the catholic year.

‖**salut** (saly), *int.* [Fr., lit. 'health'; cf. SALUD *int.*, SALUTE *sb.*[1]] A toast: 'cheers!', 'good health!'

1933 E. HEMINGWAY *Homage to Switzerland* in *Scribner's Mag.* Apr. 206/2 'Prosit,' said Johnson... The other two porters said 'Salut'. **1938** L. DURRELL *Spirit of Place* (1969) 53 All the Best. I hope to look you two up soon.. Salut—Larry. **1966** L. COHEN *Beautiful Losers* I. 4 Salut F., old and loud friend! **1976** 'TREVANIAN' *Main* (1977) xiii. 253 She lifts her glass. 'Salut?' 'Salut.'

salut, variant pa. t. of SALUE *v. Obs.*

†**salutaire**, *a. Obs. rare.* Forms: 5 **saluter**, 6 **salutaire.** [a. F. *salutaire*, ad. L. *salūtāris* SALUTARY.] Salutary.

c **1450** *Mirour Saluacioun* 1234 And marie wombe flovred & broght forth ffruyt saluter to mankynde. **1593** A. HUME *Treat. Conscience* v. in *Poems*, etc. (S.T.S.) App. A. 108 Sicknes may be healed, by the application of salutaire medicaments. **1600** J. HAMILTON *Facile Traictise* Ep. Ded. 3 For the reduction of dissauit people in maters of religion, to the salutaire vnion.. of Christs halie Catholick kirk.

salutarily ('sæljʊtərɪlɪ), *adv.* [f. SALUTARY *a.* + -LY[2].] In a salutary manner.

1532 R. COPLAND in *Prymer of Salysbury vse* 27 b, The maner to lyue well, deuoutly and salutarily. **1846** in WORCESTER (citing *Ed. Rev.*). **1861** SALA *Dutch Pict.* xii. 175 Very many vagrants.. were salutarily scourged by the parish constable. **1882–3** *Schaff's Encycl. Relig. Knowl.* 1275 [Lanfranc] says that those who unworthily partake.. receive the essence of the body and blood of Christ, without, however, being salutarily affected thereby.

salutariness ('sæljʊtərɪnɪs). [f. SALUTARY *a.* + -NESS.] The property of being salutary.

1727 BAILEY vol. II. **1755** JOHNSON, *Salutariness*, wholsomeness; quality of contributing to health or safety. **1873** M. ARNOLD *Lit. & Dogma* (1876) 98 The desire felt by the pious Israelites for some new aspect of religion such as Jesus Christ presented, is.. the best proof of its.. salutariness. **1879** H. SPENCER *Data of Ethics* iii. 41 Insistence on the salutariness of a state in which the wills of slaves and citizens are humbly subject to the wills of masters and rulers.

salutary ('sæljʊtərɪ), *a.* (and *sb.*) [ad. F. *salutaire* (see SALUTAIRE) or its source L. *salūtāris*, f. *salūt-em*, *salūs* health, well-being: see -ARY[2].]

1. Conducive to health; *chiefly*, serving to promote recovery from disease, or to counteract a deleterious influence.

1649 JER. TAYLOR *Gt. Exemp.* I. Ad. §1. 15 Abana and Pharpar.. were not so salutary as the waters of Jordan to cure Naamans leprosie. **1685** BOYLE *Enq. Notion Nat.* 225 Experience hath oblig'd Physicians to divide Crises's.. into Salutary, that quite deliver the Patient, and Mortal, that destroy him. **1751** JOHNSON *Rambler* No. 83 ¶5 The man that first.. climbed the mountains for salutary plants. **1771** SMOLLETT *Humph. Cl.* 8 June, At Brambleton Hall, I.. breathe a clear, elastic, salutary air. **1810** E. D. CLARKE *Trav. Russia* xv. (1839) 69/1 When a current sets in from the sea, it [the water of the Sea of Azof] is more salutary. **1872** T. BRYANT *Pract. Surg.* 119 When due to plethora of the vessels from any cause, it [*sc.* epistaxis] is often salutary.

2. Conducive to well-being; calculated to bring about a more satisfactory condition, or to remedy some evil; beneficial, 'wholesome'. Often with figurative notion of sense 1.

In early instances often = 'bringing salvation'.

1490 CAXTON *Eneydos* xii. 43 Consideringe the waye salutary to reuerte sone her sorow in to gladnesse. **1541** R. COPLAND *Guydon's Quest. Chirurg.* Q ij, The sayd dissease is penaunce salutary for the saluacion of theyr soules. **1729** STACKHOUSE *Body Divin.* IV. i. §2 (1776) II. 422 The blessings of Christ's salutary passion. **1741** MIDDLETON *Cicero* II. xii. 569 Cicero's [virtue] will be found.. always beneficial, often salutary to the Republic. **1760–72** H. BROOKE *Fool of Qual.* (1809) III. 154 The French.. I look upon to be our natural and salutary enemies. They.. hold us in exercise, and keep quarrelsome people from falling out among themselves. **1855** MACAULAY *Hist. Eng.* xix. IV. 360 The plot which ruined Bohun.. produced important and salutary effects. **1865** LIVINGSTONE *Zambesi* ii. 45 The natives having a salutary dread of the guns.

†**3.** *absol.* as *sb. pl.* (See quot.) *Obs.*

1823 CRABB *Technol. Dict.*, *Salutaries* (*Med.*), such diseases as admit of an easy cure, and are supposed to have a salutary effect on the constitution.

salutation (sælju:'teɪʃən). Forms: 4–5 **salutacioun**, 4–6 **-acion, -acyon**, 5 **-acioune**, 6 **-atioun, -atyon, -asyon**, 6– **salutation.** [a. OF. *salutacion* (mod.F. *salutation*), ad. L. *salūtātiōn-em*, n. of action f. *salūtāre* to SALUTE. Cf. Sp. *salutacion*, It. *salutazione*.]

1. a. The action, or an act, of saluting; a manner of saluting; an utterance, form of words, gesture, or movement, by which one person salutes another.

1382 WYCLIF *Luke* i. 41 As Elizabeth herde the salutacioun of Marie, the ȝonge child in hir wombe gladide. *c* **1386** CHAUCER *Shipman's T.* 8 Swiche salutacions and contenaunces Passen as dooth a shadwe vp on the wal. **1387** TREVISA *Higden* (Rolls) IV. 307 þanne a poore sowtere fondede to teche a chouȝhe to speke and seie þe same salutacioun. **1471** CAXTON *Recuyell* (Sommer) II. 352 Whan hercules sawe the salutacion.. of this man, he toke hym by the hande [etc.]. *a* **1533** LD. BERNERS *Huon* lviii. 201 Whan all the company had made there salutasyons one to an nother. **1610** SHAKS. *Temp.* III. iii. *Stage Direction*, Enter seuerall strange shapes, bringing in a Banket; and dance about it with gentle actions of salutations. **1620** *Westward for Smelts* (Percy Soc.) 23 He.. kissed her.., after this salutation, he said [etc.]. **1650** JER. TAYLOR *Holy Living* ii. §5 (1686) 101 In all publick meetings, or private addresses.. use those forms of salutation.. which.. [are] usual amongst the most sober persons. **1706** J. POTTER *Antiq. Greece* IV. xix. (ed. 2) II. 374 The most common Salutation was by the conjunction of their right Hands. **1756–7** tr. *Keysler's Trav.* (1760) I. 88 The commonalty of late are, by their salutation, come to be immediately known, whether they are protestants or papists. Sixtus V.. granted an indulgence of one hundred days to the salutation, 'Praised be Jesus Christ', and the answer, 'For ever or amen'. **1821** SCOTT *Kenilw.* xix, Out into the yard sallied mine host himself also, to do fitting salutation to his new guests. **1851** HAWTHORNE *Ho. Sev. Gables* vii. (1852) 76 He made a salutation, or, to speak nearer the truth, an ill-defined, abortive attempt at courtesy. **1851** DIXON *W. Penn* iv. (1872) 32 He had bowed his head and taken off his hat in salutation. **1867** LADY HERBERT *Cradle L.* vii. 202 Their usual salutation was—'welcome'.

transf. **1594** SHAKS. *Rich. III*, v. iii. 210 The early Village Cock Hath twice done salutation to the Morne.

b. ***the Angelic(al salutation***, †***the salutation of our Lady***, etc.: the AVE MARY (see Luke i. 29). Also a representation of the Annunciation.

1459 in *Archæologia* XXI. 37 A Tablet of gold of yᵉ Salutacion of our Lady. **1534** in Peacock *Eng. Ch. Furniture* (1866) 197 A masar.. with a prynt in the bothom of siluer & gilte of the salutacion of ovr lady. ? *c* **1600** *Soc. Rosary* xiii. 192 Next after our Lords praier the Angells Salutation is vsually saide. *Ibid.* xi. 170 The Angelicall Salutation. **1852** MRS. JAMESON *Leg. Madonna* Introd. (1857) 25 Towards the end of the tenth century the custom of adding the angelic salutation, the 'Ave Maria', to the Lord's prayer, was first introduced.

c. Applied to certain liturgical formulas of greeting between the minister and the people. *esp.* in the Church of England: 'The Lord be with you'.

1450–1530 *Myrr. our Ladye* 294 The preste.. sayeth *Dominus vobiscum...* The quier answereth, *Et cum spiritu tuo*, And with thy spirite. In this salutacion of the preste, and answere of the people, or of the quier, the preste prayeth that oure lorde be with them, & they pray that oure lorde be with hym. **1832** W. PALMER *Orig. Liturg.* I. 161 Then followed the salutation and kiss of peace; after which the priest read the collect, 'ad pacem'. **1929** E. C. THOMAS *Lay Folk's Hist. Liturgy* II. v. 182 In 1552 the Salutation and Kyrie [in Morning Prayer] were postponed to the Creed.

1978 D. M. HOPE in C. Jones et al. *Study of Liturgy* II. III. ix. 231 The people said 'Amen' at its [*sc.* the Epistle's] conclusion and the Gospel continued.. after the salutation by the celebrant.

d. *Naut.* The action of saluting by firing of guns, lowering of flags, etc.; an instance of this, a salute. Now *rare.*

1585 T. WASHINGTON tr. *Nicholay's Voy.* I. xv. 15b, The chains of the hauen being opened with salutation accustomed of the one side & other. **1652** NEEDHAM tr. *Selden's Mare Cl.* Ep. Ded. 13 That egregious attempt upon your Shipping, under pretence of a friendly salutation. **1727–41** CHAMBERS *Cycl.* s.v. *Salutation,* Saluting with the flag, is performed two ways; either by holding it close to the staff, so as it cannot flutter, or by striking it so as it cannot be seen at all, which is the most respectful salutation. **1808** SCOTT *Marm.* VI. xxiii, And distant salutation past From the loud cannon's mouth.

2. Elliptically for 'I offer salutation'. *arch.*

1535 COVERDALE *Ezra* vii. 12 Vnto Eszdras.. peace and salutacion. **1588** SHAKS. *L.L.L.* v. i. 38 Most millitarie sir salutation. **1600** —— *A.Y.L.* v. iv. 39 Salutation and greeting to you all. **1871** ALABASTER *Wheel of Law* 224 The donor says: 'Salutation to this land with its produce, salutation to the priest to whom I give it'.

3. *Antiq.* A visit of ceremony paid to a Roman in his house.

a **1700** DRYDEN tr. *Horace, Epode* ii. 17 And court and state, he wisely shuns, Nor brib'd with hopes, nor dar'd with awe, To servile salutations runs. **1741** JOHNSON *Life Morin* Wks. IV. 478 It is easy to conceive that a man of this temper was not crouded with salutations; there was only now and then an Antony that would pay Paul a visit.

¶**4.** *nonce-use.* (Cf. SALUTE *v.* 5.)

c **1600** SHAKS. *Sonn.* cxxi, For why should others false adulterat eyes Giue salutation to my sportiue blood?

5. *attrib.* or passing into *adj.*

1713 ADDISON *Guardian* No. 137 ¶5, I have seen him in every inclination of the body, from a familiar nod, to the low stoop in the salutation sign. **1899** *Allbutt's Syst. Med.* VIII. 106 Thus a patient may be constantly making bowing movements (salutation spasm). **1903** SIR H. C. MAXWELL-LYTE in *Cal. Charter Rolls* (1903) I. Pref. 5 In form, a Charter is distinguished from Letters Patent by the salutation clause addressed to Archbishops, Bishops, Abbots, Earls, Barons and so forth.. by the *quare volumus* clause.

Hence **salu'tational, salu'tationless** *adjs.*

1855 *Household Words* XII. 388, I would not advise the shooting of squires for breaches of salutational reciprocity; only, if his worship did not take off his hat to me in return, I would never again take off mine to his worship. **1885** HOWELLS *Silas Lapham* II. 116 The two came out together, and parted in their salutationless fashion.

‖**salutator** (sæljʊ'teɪtə(r)). *Hist.* [eccl. L., use of L. *salūtātor* one who salutes, agent-n. f. *salūtāre* to SALUTE.] The designation given to a class of persons in Spain who professed to work miraculous cures in the name of St. Catherine. See also SALUDADOR, SALUTER.

1668–72 M. CASAUBON *On Credulity & Incred.* 147 The Salutators of Spain.

salutatorian (səˌljuːtə'tɔərɪən). *U.S.* [f. next + -AN.] In American schools and colleges the student who delivers the 'salutatory' oration at the annual commencement day exercises.

1847 in WEBSTER. **1887** *Harper's Mag.* Sept. 636 The graduating class were the heroes of the hour. The valedictorian, the salutatorian, the philosophical orator, walked on air. **1943** *Lafayette Alumnus* (Lafayette Coll., Easton, Pa.) Nov. 1/1 Lloyd Felmly.. was salutatorian of his class. **1977** *Transatlantic Rev.* LX. 130 Elwood was valedictorian; I was salutatorian.

salutatory (sə'ljuːtətərɪ), *a.* and *sb.* [ad. L. *salūtātōrius*, f. *salūtāre* to SALUTE.]

A. *adj.* **a.** Pertaining to, or of the nature of, a salutation.

1895 *Critic* 19 Jan. 57/2 Henry Ward Beecher's salutatory editorial. **1898** J. R. HARRIS in *Expositor* Sept. 175 Jowett's argument for the authenticity of the Epistle is based on the salutatory formulae.

b. *U.S.* The distinctive epithet of the address of welcome (usually in Latin), which introduces the exercises of commencement in American colleges and high schools.

It is delivered by the senior of second highest position in his class for four years, or sometimes by a junior who has the highest position in his class. Cf. *valedictory*.

1702 C. MATHER *Magn. Chr.* IV. Introd. (1852) 13 These exercises were, besides an oration usually made by the President, orations both salutatory and valedictory. **1846** WORCESTER (citing Kirkland), *Salutatory*, containing salutations; greeting, as 'a salutatory oration' (U.S.). **1940** W. L. FINK *Evaluation Commencement Pract. Amer. Public Secondary Schools* ii. 25 Time would not permit all of the members of the class to speak. Accordingly, certain pupils chosen on the basis of scholarship alone were given the honor of delivering the salutatory and valedictory addresses. **1947** E. A. KAUMP *High School Commencement Bk.* (rev. ed.) 93 (*heading*) The Salutatory. *Ibid.*, The Salutatory address is another honor speech.. given by the student who makes the second highest average during the high school years.

c. *Gram.* [tr. L. *salutatorius casus.*] ***salutatory case***: the vocative case.

1818 STODDART *Gram.* in *Encycl. Metrop.* (1845) I. 32/2 The fifth case is the vocative or salutatory.

B. *sb.*

†**1.** [= med.L. *salūtātōrium.*] An audience-chamber; *spec.* in a church or monastery, a chamber where visitors were received to give their salutations.

1641 MILTON *Reform.* II. Wks. 1851 III. 63 Coming to the Bishop with Supplication into the Salutatory, some out Porch of the Church, he was charg'd by him of tyrannicall madnes against God, for comming into holy ground. **1656** BLOUNT *Glossogr.*, *Salutatory* (*salutatorium*), a place where men stand to salute a Prince.

2. *U.S.* **a.** An address or greeting to the reader of the first number of a newspaper or magazine.

1869 'MARK TWAIN' in *Buffalo* (N.Y.) *Morning Express* 21 Aug. 2/3 Your new editor feels called upon to write a 'salutatory' at once. **1880** *Scribner's Mag.* July 455 Its salutatory is worth quoting as a piece of brave crowing. **1887** *Lit. World* (U.S.) 25 June 206/2 In his salutatory the editor declares his paper to be 'a very modest effort to assist in a practical way the "Literary Movement in Chicago"'.

b. The 'salutatory oration' (see A. b) delivered at 'commencement' in American colleges and high schools.

1779 *Pennsylvania Packet* 7 Oct. 1/1 John Woodword [gave] the salutatory in Latin. *a* **1851** *Amherst Indicator* II. 96 (Hall *College Words*) We ask our friends.. not to ask if he had the Valedictory or Salutatory. **1864** *Harper's Mag.* Sept. 501/1 Still another is the burlesque philosphical oration and the half Latin, half Saxon Salutatory. **1905** *N.Y. Even. Post* 12 June 12 The annual class day exercises of the University of Pennsylvania were held to-day. H. B. Taylor delivered the salutatory. **1932** *School Life* May 165/1 On 85 occasions fond.. parents had listened to the same old story: Salutatory, oratory, valedictory. **1947** [see A. b above].

Hence **sa'lutatorily** *adv.* (*rare*), by way of greeting or salutation.

1847 in WEBSTER. **1863** MRS. WHITNEY *Faith Gartney's Girlh.* vi, 'Well, Melindy', said Mrs. Griggs, salutatorily.

salute (sə'l(j)uːt), *sb.*¹ Also 5–6 salut, (6 saluyte). [a. F. *salut* masc., of twofold origin: (1) = Sp. *saludo*, It. *saluto*, vbl. sb. f. Common Rom. (L.) *salūtāre* to SALUTE; (2) originally fem., = Sp. *salud*, Pg. *saude*, It. *salute*:—L. *salūt-em* (nom. *salūs*) health, safety, salvation.]

I. An act of saluting.

1. An utterance, gesture, or action of any kind by which one person salutes another; a salutation. Now chiefly used with reference to other than verbal modes of saluting: cf. the following senses.

a **1400–50** *Alexander* 1490 'I bringe þe bodword of blis ser bischop' he said, 'With salutis of solas I am sent fra þe trone'. **1483** CAXTON *Gold. Leg.* 436/1 The preest.. tourneth hym toward the peple & saleweth them sayeng Dominus vobiscum and that sygnefyeth salut whyche our lorde gafe to his appostles after his blessyd resurrexyon. *c* **1511** *1st Eng. Bk. Amer.* (Arb.) Introd. 32/1, I Pope Iohn.. gyue saluyte the Emperour of Rome.. & also the kinge of France. **1597** DRAYTON *Heroic Ep., Mortimer to Q. Isabel* 1 As thy salutes my sorrowes doe adiourne, So backe to thee their interest I returne. **1633** FORD *Broken H.* v. i. I 3b, The doublers of a Hare, or, in a morning, Salutes from a splay-footed witch, .. Are not so boading mischiefe as thy crossing My priuate meditations. **1671** MILTON *P.R.* II. 67 O what avails me now that honour high To have conceiv'd of God, or that salute Hale highly favour'd, among women blest. **1702** ADDISON *Dial. Medals* II. Wks. 1766 III. 35, I shall not trouble myself nor my Reader with the first salutes of our three friends. **1790** J. BRUCE *Source Nile* I. 18 We passed near enough, however, to give them the usual salute, *Salam Alicum.* **1794** MRS. RADCLIFFE *Myst. Udolpho* iv, He waved his hand, and Valancourt.. returned the salute and started away. **1859** TENNYSON *Geraint & Enid* 723 Last, coming up quite close, and in his mood Crying, '.. Take my salute', unknightly with flat hand, However lightly, smote her on the cheek. **1878** BROWNING *La Saisiaz* 16 From no far mound Waved salute a tall white figure. **1879** —— *Pheidippides* 111 So, to this day, when friend meets friend, the word of salute Is still 'Rejoice!'

2. A kiss, by way of salutation. (Cf. SALUTE *v.* 2 e.)

1590 GREENE *Never too late* (1600) 93 To her hee goes, and after his wonted salute sat downe by her. **1684** EARL ROSCOMMON *Ess. Transl. Verse* 314 There, cold salutes, But here, a Lovers kiss. **1688** R. HOLME *Armoury* III. 169/2 In Dances,.. a Salute, a Kiss, or Kiss of the hand with a bow of the Body. **1719** D'URFEY *Pills* (1872) V. 80 With a kind Salute, and without Dispute, He thought to gain her for his own. **1782** MME. D'ARBLAY *Diary* 26 Oct., Dr. Johnson.. received me.. with a salute so loud, that the two young beaux.. have never done laughing about it. **1828** SCOTT *Fair M. Perth* xix, He folded the fair maiden in his arms, and was permitted to take the salute which she had refused to bestow. **1906** H. WALES *Mr. & Mrs. Villiers* vii, She extricated his right arm also, and was rewarded by the complimentary salute on the left cheek.

3. *Mil.* and *Naut.* **a.** A discharge of cannon or small arms, display of flags, a dipping of sails, a cheering of men, manning the yards, etc., as a mark of respect, or as military, naval, or official honour, for a person, nation, event, etc.

A salute is said to be of as many guns as there are volleys fired.

1698 FRYER *Acc. E. India & P.* 107 Their way of Salutes are with Even, as ours with Odd Guns. **1727–41** CHAMBERS *Cycl.* s.v. *Salutation*, Father Fournier has an express treatise of sea-salutes and signals. **1744** J. PHILIPS *Jrnl. Exped. Anson* 181 He saluted us with eleven Guns, and we returned the salute with three. **1832** R. & J. LANDER *Exped. Niger* III. xx. 232 As we passed Forday's town, a salute of seven guns was fired off. **1838** J. L. STEPHENS *Trav. Russia* 88/1 A frigate.. was firing a salute. **1876** VOYLE & STEVENSON *Milit. Dict.* (ed. 3) s.v., In firing salutes 10 seconds is to be allowed between each round. **1883** 'OUIDA' *Wanda* I. 307 The culverins on the keep fired their salutes.

transf. **1719** DE FOE *Crusoe* II. (Globe ed.) 569 As we found them [the enemy] within Gun-shot, our Leader ordered the two Wings to advance swiftly, and give them a Salvo on each Wing with their Shot... And indeed that Salute clogg'd their Stomach, for they immediately halted.

b. (See quot. 1876.)

1832 LYTTON *Eugene A.* I. v, 'Beg pardon, Squire,' said he, with a military salute. **1876** VOYLE & STEVENSON *Milit. Dict.* (ed. 3) s.v., A salute is made by an inferior meeting or passing his superior, when in uniform and even out of uniform, by raising his hand to his cap or chaco.

c. The position of the sword, rifle, hand, etc., or the attitude assumed in saluting. Phrase, ***to stand at (the) salute.***

1833 *Regul. & Instr. Cavalry* I. 36 Officers recover their swords.., and drop them to the 'Salute'.

d. With defining term prefixed, denoting the attitude adopted by the saluter, or his affiliation, as **raised-arm salute**, a salute made with the arm out-stretched at an angle of about 45° from the vertical; **clenched fist salute**, a raised-arm salute with fist clenched (chiefly in communist use); **Hitler** or **Nazi salute**, a raised-arm salute with hand outstretched.

1935 [see HITLER]. **1937** V. BARTLETT *This is my Life* x. 165 Hundreds of arms went out in the Hitler salute, hundreds of voices yelled the *Horst Wessel Lied.* **1943** D. GASCOYNE *Poems 1937–1942* 5 The centurions.. Greet one another with raised-arm salutes. **1959** *Chambers's Encycl.* XII. 173/2 Special forms of salute, the clenched fist salute of the Communists, the 'Roman salute' of the Fascists and the Hitler salute, have been a feature of modern political life. **1969, 1974** [see NAZI *adj.*]. **1976** *Times* 13 Nov. 4 (*caption*) Clenched fist communist salutes from a group of Madrid car workers who had earlier voted to join the strike. **1977** *Times* 27 Jan. 6/8 Riot police looked on impassively here [*sc.* Madrid] today as a massive crowd of mourners.. gave the clenched fist Marxist salute at the funeral of five lawyers gunned down on Monday night by right-wing terrorists.

4. *Fencing.* A formal greeting of swordsmen when about to engage, consisting of a conventional series of guards, appels, thrusts, parries, parades, etc.

1809 J. ROLAND *Fencing* 139 The salute of *carte* and *tierce* is practised on the same principle. **1889** POLLOCK, etc. *Fencing* (Badm. Libr.) 98 The Salute, or prelude to the Assault.

†**II. 5. a.** Safety, well-being, salvation. *Obs.*

1471 CAXTON *Recuyell* (Sommer) I. 275 She shall dye for the salute and helthe of troye. **1483** —— *Gold. Leg.* 430/2 As the auncyente thobye gaue to them admonestyng of salut techyng them ouer alle thynges to drede god. **1509** WATSON *Ship of Fools* Argt. A j, This booke compyled for the felycyte & salute of all the humayne gendre.

†**b.** Used *ellipt.* (= L. *salutem*) in epistolary salutations. *Obs.*

a **1533** LD. BERNERS *Gold. Bk. M. Aurel.* Let. iv. (1535) 107b, Marke oratour Romayn.. to the Domitian of Capue, salute and consolacion of the goddis. **1549** *Compl. Scot.* xiv. 116 Pausanias duc of spart, to the kyng xerxes salut.

sa'lute, *sb.*² *Obs.* exc. *Hist.* Forms: 5–8 **salut**, 6, 9 **salute**; *pl.* 5 **saluz, salutz, salews,** (**salux**), 5–6 *Sc.* **salutis**, (5, 8 **salus**). [a. OF. *salut*, *saluyt*, pl. *saluts*, *saluz*, *salus*, a special use of *salut* salutation, SALUTE *sb.*¹] A gold coin bearing a representation of the salutation of Gabriel to the Virgin Mary; struck by Charles VI of France, and also by Henry V and Henry VI of England for circulation in their French dominions.

1488 *Acc. Ld. High Treas. Scot.* I. 79 Item, in Hari nobilis and salutis fourti and ane. **1455** *Paston Lett.* I. 360 For the value and denobbrement of iiij. m¹. saluz of yerly rent. **145.** *Rolls. of Parlt.* V. 181/1 Oon obligation of the Duchesse of Burgoyne of XV m. salutz. **1475** *Bk. Noblesse* (Roxb.) 19 Johan.. paied to the said regent duc of Bedforde for his raunson and finaunce allone clx. M. salux. *c* **1483** CAXTON *Dialogues* 17 Ryallis nobles of englond, Salews of gold lyons, Olde sterlingis pens. *a* **1548** HALL *Chron., Hen. V* 75 The kyng of England.. caused a new coyne to be made called the Salute, where in wer the Armes of Fraunce, and the Armes of England and Fraunce quarterly. **1577** HARRISON *England* II. xxv. (1877) I. 363 We haue yet remaining, the riall.. the salut, the angell [etc.]. **1580** STOW *Chron.* 618 King Henry [VI] caused a peece to be stamped called a Salus, worth two and twentie Shillings and Blans of eyghtpence a peece. **1653** URQUHART *Rabelais* I. xlvi, The summe of three score and two thousand saluts (in English money fifteen thousand and five hundred pounds). **1688** R. HOLME *Armoury* III. 29/1 The Salute of England, worth six shillings ten pence. **1716** M. DAVIES *Athen. Brit.* III. 79 Hen. 5's Golden Coyns were Rose-Nobles, Half-Nobles and Farthings, and Salus. *Ibid.*, Hen. 6. brought in the Rials, or Royals, Angels, Angellets and Salut. **1837** *Penny Cycl.* VII. 331/1 To these [coins].. Henry V. [added] salutes, and half-salutes. Henry VI. coined salutes, angelots, and francs in gold.

salute (sə'l(j)uːt), *v.* Also 5 salewt. [ad. L. *salūtāre*, f. *salūt-em*, *salūs* health. (Cf. SALUE *v.*) It is possible that this may have coalesced with an independent formation on SALUTE *v.*]

1. *trans.* To accost or address with words expressive of good wishes, respect, or homage, esp. with some customary formula of that import; to greet in words.

c **1380** WYCLIF *Sel. Wks.* II. 9 Marie.. went mekeli in hast to salute her cosyn. **1387** TREVISA *Higden* (Rolls) II. 193 He saluted and grette þe senatoures, and spak to eueriche of þe peple þat come aboute hym by his owne name. **14..** *Sir Beues* 1283 + 291 (Camb.) [He] saluted þe kyng on þys manere, As ye may aftur here. *c* **1430** LYDG. *Min. Poems* (Percy Soc.) 78 With ave or kirye salute a kyng. **1483** CAXTON *Cato* A v, Thou sholdest salewt and grete the peple gladly. **1526** *Pilgr. Perf.* (W. de W. 1531) 180 Forgete not to salute her with this swete word Aue. *a* **1533** LD. BERNERS *Huon* xxi. 60 He drew thedyr & salutyd ye olde man in ye name of god. **1592** SHAKS. *Rom. & Jul.* II. iii. 32 *Rom.* Good morrow Father. *Fri.* Benedicite. What early tongue so sweet saluteth me? **1711–12** SWIFT *Jrnl. to Stella* 22 Jan., T'other day at the Court of Requests Dr. Yalden saluted me by name. **1845** M. PATTISON *Ess.* (1889) I. 22 Being admitted to his presence they saluted him in the queen's name. **1875** JOWETT *Plato* (ed. 2) IV. 160 He saluted me as an acquaintance whom he remembered from my former visit.

b. ***I salute you***: used as itself a formula of salutation. Similarly in the 3rd person, of one who 'sends greeting'. [So L. *salutare*.] *arch.*

1599 SHAKS. *Hen. V*, v. ii. 22 You English Princes all, I doe salute you. **1834** LYTTON *Pompeii* I. ii, 'Fair Julia, we salute thee', said Clodius. *c* **1850** *Arab. Nts.* (Rtldg.) 252 'My mistress', said she, 'salutes you, and I come from her to beg you to deliver this letter to the prince of Persia'. **1881** TENNYSON *To Virgil* x, I salute thee, Mantovano, I that loved thee since my day began.

†**c.** ***salute me*** used for: Give my greeting (*to*). Cf. *remember me to*... REMEMBER *v.* 8 c. *Obs.*

1700 PENN in *Pa. Hist. Soc. Mem.* IX. 5 Salute me to the commissioners.

d. To hail or greet (as king, etc.).

1560 DAUS tr. *Sleidane's Comm.* 101 b, All people saluted hym with the tytle of the Emperour Auguste. *Ibid.* 423 He is saluted Prynce Electour. **1593** SHAKS. *2 Hen. VI*, II. ii. 61 Be we the first, That shall salute our rightfull Soueraigne With honor of his Birth-right to the Crowne. **1595** —— *John* II. i. 30 Till that vtmost corner of the West Salute thee for her King. **1617** MORYSON *Itin.* II. 2 King Henrie.. for the time was saluted Lord of Ireland. **1642** MILTON *Apol. Smect.* 40 Now they heare it as their ord'nary surname, to be saluted the Fathers of their countrey. **1755** W. DUNCAN *Cicero's Sel. Orat.* xi. (1841) 217 It was but lately that L. Torquatus.. was, at my instance, saluted emperour from this province.

e. In extended sense: To accost or address (whether courteously or otherwise).

c **1420** ? LYDG. *Assembly of Gods* 438 On a rewde maner he salutyd all the rout, With a bold voyse, carpyng wordys stout. **1639** S. DU VERGER tr. *Camus' Admir. Events* 303 Adiute.. beeing returned to towne, saw himselfe saluted by a letter of defiance.

f. *poet.* Of birds, etc.: To hail or greet (the sun, the dawn) with song.

1682 CREECH tr. *Lucretius* II. 39 The Morning climbs the Eastern Skies, And tuneful birds salute her early rise. **1700** DRYDEN *Pal. & Arc.* II. 38 The Morning-Lark, the Messenger of Day, Saluted in her Song the Morning gray. **1821** SHELLEY *Hellas* 941 Victorious Wrong, with vulture scream, Salutes the rising sun, pursues the flying day!

2. To greet with some gesture or visible action conventionally expressive of respect or courteous recognition.

c **1440** *Gesta Rom.* xxiii. 83 (Add. MS.), All his [the emperor's] knyghtes and other men, whan thei sawe hym, worshipfully thei saluted hym. *a* **1533** LD. BERNERS *Huon* lxii. 216 Huon approchyd & salutyd hym humbly. *a* **1586** SIDNEY *Arcadia* I. Ecl. i. (1598) 82 When that noble toppe doth nodd, I beleeue she salutes me. **1590** SPENSER *F.Q.* I. i. 30 He faire the knight saluted, louting low. **1593** SHAKS. *Rich. II*, III. ii. 6 Deere Earth, I doe salute thee with my hand. **1655** STANLEY *Hist. Philos.* III. (1687) 80/1 As soon as the Sun arose, [he] saluted it, and retir'd. **1727–41** CHAMBERS *Cycl.* s.v. *Salutation*, In England, we salute one another by uncovering the head, inclining the body, &c. The orientals salute by uncovering their feet, laying their hands on the breast, &c. **1760–2** GOLDSM. *Cit. W.* lxxix, One curtsies to the ground, the other salutes the audience with a smile. **1762** KAMES *Elem. Crit.* (1763) III. xx. 67 Among the ancients, it was customary after a long voyage to salute the natal soil. *a* **1859** MACAULAY *Hist. Eng.* xxiii. V. 93 Were they to stand erect and covered while everybody else saluted him?

b. *absol.* and *intr.* To perform a salutation.

1589 PUTTENHAM *Eng. Poesie* III. xxiv. (Arb.) 292 With them [the men of the East] to congratulat and salute by giuing a becke with the head, or a bende of the bodie, with vs here in England, and in Germany.. to shake hands. **1600** SHAKS. *A.Y.L.* III. ii. 50 You told me, you salute not at the Court, but you kisse your hands. **1617** MORYSON *Itin.* III. 174 They.. salute by bending the body and laying their left hand on their right side.

c. *spec.* in *Mil.* and *Naval* use. (*a*) *trans.* To pay respect to (a superior) by a prescribed bodily movement, the presenting of arms, or the like. (*b*) Of a ship, a body of troops, a commander: To honour or ceremoniously recognize in the customary manner, by a discharge of artillery or small arms, by lowering of flags, or the like. (*c*) *absol.*, and *intr.* To perform a salute.

1582 N. LICHEFIELD tr. *Castanheda's Conq. E. Ind.* I. ii. 5 b, They came to sight of their Captaine Generall,.. and saluting him with many shot of ordinaunce, and with sound of Trumpets, they spake unto him. **1706** PHILLIPS (ed. Kersey) s.v., The Colours also salute Princes and Generals, which is done by Bowing them down to the Ground. **1725** DE FOE *Voy. round World* (1840) 94 We saluted the Spanish flag. **1727–41** CHAMBERS *Cycl.* s.v. *Salutation*, In the army, the officers salute by certain orderly, studied motions of the half-pike, &c. *Ibid.*, *Saluting with the Sails*, is performed by hovering the topsails half way of the masts.—Only those vessels which carry no guns, salute with the sails. **1744** J. PHILIPS *Jrnl. Exped. Anson* 148 We saluted the Governor of Macao with 11 Guns. **1769** *Regul. Sea-Service* in Falconer *Dict. Marine* (1780) K k 4, When a captain salutes an admiral .. he is to give him fifteen guns. **1802** C. JAMES *Milit. Dict.* s.v., When a regiment is to be reviewed by.. the king, or his general,.. the officers salute one after another, pointing their swords downwards. The ensigns salute together, by lowering their colours, when his Majesty, or any of the royal family, are present. **1803** NELSON in Nicolas *Disp.* (1845) V. 139 You are not to salute the Fort of his Catholic Majesty, unless you receive a positive assurance that an equal number of guns will be returned. **1844** *Regul. & Ord. Army* 32 Officers wearing Hats, are not on any occasion to take them off in saluting; but when their Swords are not drawn, they are to salute, by bringing up the right hand to the forehead horizontally, on a line with the eyebrow. **1877–81** VOYLE & STEVENSON *Milit. Dict.* Suppl. (ed. 3) s.v., Her Majesty the Queen as Empress of India is saluted in India with 100 guns; the viceroy and governor-general of India with 31 guns. **1878** D. KEMP *Man. Yacht Sailing* 341 The ensign is lowered or dipped as a means of saluting a commodore, &c. or member of a club. **1889** *Infantry Drill* I. 24 When a soldier is about to pass an officer, he will salute with the further hand on the third pace before reaching him, and will lower the hand on the third pace after passing him.

d. *Fencing. intr.* To perform the salute used in fencing. See SALUTE *sb.*[1] 4.

1809 J. ROLAND *Fencing* 135 As it is understood when you salute, that it is a compliment you pay to the company, you should, while forming the parade of carte, turn your face to the spectators. *Ibid.* 136 Although I have directed that in saluting you should, in general, do it in *carte first*, and tierce *afterwards*.

e. *trans.* To kiss, or greet with a kiss. *arch.*

1716 ADDISON *Drummer* III. (1722) 31 You have the prettiest Tip of a Finger—I must take the Freedom to salute it. *Ibid.* IV. 37 *Ab.* Ay! but you han't saluted me. *Fan.* That's right; Faith I forgot that Circumstance. [*Kisses her.*] **1766** GOLDSM. *Vic. W.* v, He.. was going to salute my daughters as one certain of a kind reception. **1773** JOHNSON *Let. to Mrs. Thrale* 30 Sept., I had the honour of saluting the far famed Miss Flora Macdonald. **1849** THACKERAY *Pendennis* viii, He once more saluted the tips of Mrs. Pendennis's glove.

intr. **1629** DAVENANT *Albovine* III. i, It is a piece of courtship to salute at parting.

†**f.** To honour (a person) *with* a present, gift, etc. Cf. GREET *v.* 3 d. *Obs.*

a **1592** GREENE *George a Greene* (1599) C 1 b, And first I saluted her with a greene gowne. **1601** ? MARSTON *Pasquil & Kath.* II. 249 Wouldst haue a Ballet to salute her with? **1632** LITHGOW *Trav.* VIII. 346, I saluted the Princesse Palatine, with certayne rare Relickes of the Holy Land.

g. *ironically* used for: To assail.

1607 ROWLANDS *Famous Hist.* 60 Here is a weapon that must do me right. So draws his sword, salutes him with the same About the head, the shoulders, and the side.

†**h.** ***to salute Tyburn***: jocularly, to be hanged. *Obs.*

1640 SOMNER *Antiq. Canterb.* 205 Conspired with the Holy Maide of Kent.. and saluted Tiburne for his paines.

†**3.** To pay one's respects to; to pay a complimentary visit to. *Obs.*

1585 T. WASHINGTON tr. *Nicholay's Voy.* I. xi. 13 The Ambassadour sent to salute the Caddy. **1591** SHAKS. *Two Gent.* I. iii. 41 To-morrow.. Don Alphonso, With other Gentlemen of good esteeme Are iournying, to salute the Emperor, And to commend their seruice to his will. **1638** *Hamilton Papers* (Camden) 26 Eayrlie in the morning they sent ther commissioners doune to salut me. **1698** FRYER *Acc. E. India & P.* 367 Having not saluted the Temple Twelve times since he began to Reign.

†**4.** *fig.* To begin acquaintance with. *Obs.*

1648 BP. HALL *Breathings Devout Soul* (1851) 190 Methusalah.. did not more truly live; than the child, that did but salute and leave the world. **1722** WOLLASTON *Relig. Nat.* iii. (1738) 60 Every one, who has but just saluted the mathematics and philosophy, must be convinced, that [etc.].

5. *transf.* and *fig.* Of inanimate things, in various applications: †To bow or incline towards (*obs.*); to appear or come forth as if in welcome of; to approach, come into contact with; †(in Shaks.) to affect or act upon in any way (*obs.*).

c **1440** *Pallad. on Husb.* XII. 62 And there let bowis multiplie, And afterlong on euery side hem plie, Salutyng eest & west, & north & south. **1588** SHAKS. *Tit. A.* II. i. 5 As when the golden Sunne salutes the morne. **1595** —— *John* II. i. 590 Not that I haue the power to clutch my hand, When his faire Angels would salute my palme. **1613** —— *Hen. VIII*, II. iii. 103 Would I had to being If this salute my blood a iot. **1660** WALLER *To King on Return* 88 Like Ears of Corn when wind salutes the field. **1830** J. G. STRUTT *Sylva Brit.* 59 It [the elm] is the first tree that salutes the early spring with its light and cheerful green. **1880** SHORTHOUSE *J. Inglesant* (1882) II. 119 A land bathed in sunset light, overarched by rainbows, saluted by cool zephyrs.

b. Of a sound or sight: To strike (the eye or ear).

a **1586** SIDNEY *Arcadia* II. (Sommer) 117 Her eyes were saluted with a tuft of trees. *c* **1586** C'TESS PEMBROKE *Ps.* LXXXVIII. x, And ere the light Salute my sight. **1665** BOYLE *Occas. Refl.* IV. ii. (1848) 173 Our Ears were saluted with the melodious Musick of a good number of Larks. *a* **1668** LASSELS *Voy. Italy* (1698) I. 100 You may look.. a huge way into their gardens, which even from thence will salute your eye with a fair prospect. **1771** SMOLLETT *Humph. Cl.*, *To Dr. Lewis* 28 Apr., The first object that saluted my eye was a child, full of scrofulous ulcers. **1791** COWPER *Retired Cat* 89 A long and melancholy mew, Saluting his poetic ears. **1805** T. J. DIBDIN *All's Well* 14 Some well-known voice salutes his ear.

Hence **sa'luted** *ppl. a.* In quots. used *absol.*

1658 MANTON *Exp. Jude* I. Wks. 1871 V. 9 This first verse presenteth us with the two first circumstances, the saluter and the saluted. **1804** W. HANNA *Earlier Years Lord's Life* 293 The Ruler.. who.. might have counted on being the saluted rather than the saluter, does not hesitate to address him thus: 'Rabbi, we know' [etc.].

salute, var. pa. t. of SALUE *v.* *Obs.*

saluter (sə'l(j)uːtə(r)). [f. SALUTE *v.* + -ER[1].]

1. One who salutes or greets.

1542 UDALL *Erasm. Apoph.* 250 b, We have enough of suche saluters as this at home alreadie. **1611** COTGR., *Bailleur de bons iours*, an ordinarie saluter of euery one he sees, or meets. **1730** WALL *Crit. Notes N.T.* 295 Both he [*sc.* Aristarchus] and Epaphras are mentioned as saluters. **1753** CHAMBERS *Cycl. Supp.* s.v. *Salutation*, The women too had their crowds of saluters attending them every morning. **1834** L. RITCHIE *Wand. by Seine* 69 With a great lady, the saluter fell upon his knees and kissed the hem of her gown.

2. = SALUTATOR.

1586 ROWLAND *Lazarillo* C vj *marg.*, A Saluter is a kinde of drunken prophets in Spaine which take vpon them the healing of mad dogges. **1591** PERCIVALL *Sp. Dict.*, *Saludador*, a saluter, a charmer, *Salutator, incantator.* **1738** [G. SMITH] *Curious Relat.* II. v. 152 The Saluters (a certain Order in Spain) make the People believe, that by uttering the Name of St. Catharine, they have Power to heal Wounds.

†**salutifere**, *a.* *Obs.* *rare*$^{-1}$. In 6 salutiffere. [a. OF. *salutifere* (*salutiffere*), ad. L. *salūtifer*: see next.] Salutiferous.

1549 *Compl. Scot.* Epist. 1 It bringis furtht salutiffere & hoilsum frute of honour.

salutiferous (sæljuː'tɪfərəs), *a.* Also 6 salutiferus. [f. L. *salūtifer* (f. *salūt-* health, safety, salvation + *-fer* bringing) + -OUS: see -FEROUS.]

1. Promoting or conducive to health.

1604 F. HERING *Mod. Defence* 35 Safe, wholesome and salutiferous Medecins. **1696** TRYON *Misc.* Pref. 4 The pleasant influences and salutiferous Breezes of Wind in a hot season. **1747** *Gentl. Mag.* 77 Such exercise is not much less salutiferous than riding. **1752** C. SMART *Hop-Gard.* I. 41 Tunbridgia's salutiferous hills. **1824** SCOTT *St. Ronan's* xxviii, As soon as the ancient priestess had handed him his glass of the salutiferous water. **1865** CARLYLE *Fredk. Gt.* XXI. iv. (1872) X. 41 Forcing-on his salutiferous drains and fruitful canals through the morasses of the Weichsel.

2. Conducive to well-being, safety, or salvation. (Very common in the 17th c.)

c **1540** tr. *Pol. Verg. Eng. Hist.* (Camden) I. 209 The fowntaine beetokened the salutiferus water of baptisme. **1629** H. BURTON *Truth's Triumph* 253 The sweet and salutiferous streames of the waters of life. **1636** BRATHWAIT *Rom. Emp.* 139 France: Which he furnished with things necessary, salutiferous, good Lawes and customes. **1756** C. LUCAS *Ess. Waters* II. 63 He means to instruct us in following his salutiferous steps. **1760** SARAH FIELDING *Ophelia* I. xxx. 266 Her Ladyship thought Fasting and Mortification most salutiferous for my Soul.

Hence **salu'tiferously** *adv.*

1678 CUDWORTH *Intell. Syst.* 509 The Chief Prince of this great City.. who governeth all things salutiferously. **1696** TRYON *Misc.* v. 142 [The] Preparations [of Corn Foods].. are very wholsom and salutiferously used in many Countries.

†**salu'tigerous**, *a.* *rare*$^{-0}$. [f. L. *salūtiger* (f. *salūt-em* health + *-ger* carrying) + -OUS.] 'That brings commendation from another, or that is sent with *How-d'yees*' (Blount *Glossogr.* 1656).

saluting (sə'l(j)uːtɪŋ), *vbl. sb.* [f. SALUTE *v.* + -ING[1].] **a.** The action of the verb SALUTE.

1533 *Mystik Rosary* A j b, The saluting of the wounde of the right fote of our Lorde. *a* **1617** CORYAT in Purchas *Pilgrims* II. 1824 The Turke doth neuer at the saluting of his friend.. put off his Turbant (as wee Christians doe our Hats one to another). **1811** W. R. SPENCER *Poems* 139 One day, Good-bye met How-d'y-do, Too close to shun saluting.

b. *attrib.* as ***saluting-base***, ***-colour***, ***-ground***, ***-point***.

1894 *Times* 19 May 10/1 The Queen then quitted the saluting-point. **1895** *Funk's Stand. Dict.*, *Saluting-color*, *Mil.*, a camp-flag, distinguished by a transverse cross. **1902** *Westm. Gaz.* 11 Aug. 7/2 The saluting-ground. **1905** *Ibid.* 13 Sept. 3/2 The grim guns are disclosed as the artillery rattle past the saluting-point. **1961** *John o' London's* 19 Oct. 447/2 All the Queen's horses.. gallop right past the saluting-base. **1976** C. EGLETON *State Visit* ix. 88 The Queen had climbed on to the saluting base... The Queen left the dais to inspect the Guard of Honour.

saluting (sə'l(j)uːtɪŋ), *ppl. a.* [f. SALUTE *v.* + -ING[2].] That salutes.

1800 *Chron.* in *Asiat. Ann. Reg.* 46/2 His suite arrived at this Presidency, under a salute of thirteen guns from the saluting battery. **1885** *Athenæum* 11 July 44/3 The English pilgrim passed to the palace between bewildered boys and saluting soldiers.

salutz, obs. pl. form of SALUTE *sb.*[2]

saluwe, variant of SALUE *v.* *Obs.*

saluy(e)d, var. ff. of pa. t. of SALUE *v.* *Obs.*

saluyte, obs. form of SALUTE *sb.*[1]

saluz, obs. var. SALUS; obs. pl. f. SALUTE *sb.*[2]

salvability (sælvə'bɪlɪtɪ). *Theol.* [Formed as next + -ITY.] Capability of being saved.

1654 WARREN *Unbelievers* 52 We have only a salvability by Christ, but no certainty of salvation. *a* **1663** SANDERSON *Five Cases Consc.* (1666) 4 Holding that there is no Salvability but in the Church. **1700** J. H. *Salvab. Heathen* 3 You and I do believe a Salvability for some Heathen. **1868** *Contemp. Rev.* VII. 355 Chillingworth makes good use of the concessions of his opponent as to the salvability of Protestants.

salvable ('sælvəb(ə)l), *a.*[1] [ad. L. **salvābilis*, f. *salvāre* to SAVE: see -ABLE.]

1. *Theol.* Capable of being saved, admitting of salvation.

1667 *Decay Chr. Piety* viii. ¶6. 167 Our wild Phancies about Gods Decrees have in event reprobated more than those Decrees,..and have bid fair to the damning of many, whom those left salvable. **1734** WESLEY *Wks.* (1872) XII. 50 He is not in a salvable state. **1839** BAILEY *Festus* xxiii. (1848) 294 If God be Love, Or man a being salvable. **1888** G. MACDONALD *Elect Lady* 253 It was enough to be a Christian like other good and salvable Christians.

2. Of a ship, cargo, etc.: That can be salved or salvaged.

1797 S. JAMES *Narr. Voy.* 130 The adventurers could not find anything that was salvable. **1892** *Standard* 30 Mar. 5/1 The vessel was in a salvable condition. **1905** *Westm. Gaz.* 21 Jan. 7/1 A number of the ships were possibly salvable.

Hence **'salvableness; 'salvably** *adv. rare*$^{-0}$.

1727 BAILEY vol. II, *Salvableness*, capableness of being saved. **1847–54** WEBSTER, *Salvably*, in a salvable manner.

†**'salvable,** *a.*[2] *Obs.* [f. SALVE *v.*[2] + -ABLE.]

1. Of a difficulty, doubt, etc.: That can be met, explained or cleared up (see SALVE *v.*[2] 2).

1661 BOYLE *Style of Script.* (1675) 88 We sometimes read him to have Answer'd, without being ask'd the Question (though that be otherwise salvable by a Critick). **1675** EVELYN *Terra* (1676) 112 Admitting this [doubt] to be salvable.

2. Of 'phenomena': see SALVE *v.*[2] 1.

1678 CUDWORTH *Intell. Syst.* 691 The Phænomena of Nature being no way Salvable, nor the Causes of things Assigneable, without a Deity.

Salvadorean (sælvə'dɔːrɪən), *a.* and *sb.* Also **Salvadoran, -ian.** [f. El *Salvador* (see below + -AN.] **A.** *adj.* Of or pertaining to El Salvador, a republic in Central America. **B.** *sb.* A native or inhabitant of El Salvador.

1886 *Encycl. Brit.* XXI. 268/2 The tree from which it [*sc.* Balsam of Peru] is obtained grows naturally nowhere else in the world except in a limited part of the Salvadorian seaboard known as the Balsam coast. **1887** *U.S. Consular Rep.* XXIII. No. 82. 292 However great the advantage given to the Salvadorean debtor by English commercial codes,..American is worth 3 per cent. more than English gold. **1895** *Handbk. Salvador (Bull. Bureau Amer. Republics No. 58)* 79 Salvadorians are such either by birth or naturalization. **1909** 'O. HENRY' in *McClure's Mag.* July 330/1 For a Salvadorian he was not such a calamitous little man. **1941** C. M. WILSON *Central Amer.* (1942) iii. 52 The distinctly Salvadoran Feast of the Holy Savior. **1947** M. LOWRY *Let.* Nov. (1967) 159 Mlle. Zaza, wife of Salvadorean new passenger. **1969** *Guardian* 19 July 8/2 The quarter of a million Salvadoreans in Honduras. **1979** *Daily Tel.* 20 Apr. 4/4 Another hostage, a Salvadorean who was the Israeli honorary consul. **1980** *Ibid.* 11 July 19/7 A Mexican and a Salvadoran have been charged..with illegally smuggling a group of aliens..into the United States. **1981** *Times* 24 Feb. 13/4 The victory of the Salvadorians is certain.

salvage ('sælvɪdʒ), *sb.* Also 7 silvage. [ad. med.L. *salvāgium* or a. OF. *salvage, -aige* (in sense 1), f. L. *salvāre* to SAVE: see -AGE.]

1. A payment or compensation to which those persons are entitled who have by their voluntary efforts saved a ship or its cargo from impending peril or rescued it from actual loss; e.g. from shipwreck or from capture by the enemy (called respectively *civil* and *military* or *hostile* salvage).

1645 in Rushw. *Hist. Coll.* IV. I. 186 Whether the Ambassadors had not cause to have acknowledged a kind and good respect in taking of Custom, or Silvage only, of that Ship. **1648–9** *Act Encouragem. Officers & Mariners* §4 The Proprietor shall pay for salvage one moyety of the true value of such ship so retaken; which salvage..shall be divided and distributed proportionably to the Captain..and other Officers and Marriners. *a* **1715** SALKELD *K.B. Rep.* (1775) I. 393 And therefore they are ready to deliver the goods, if the plaintiff will pay them 4*l.* for salvage, &c. **1799** NELSON in Nicolas *Disp.* (1845) IV. 112 What..would satisfy the Captains, Officers and Men, for their renouncing all claim to the French property and all salvages. **1815** DODSON *Adm. Rep.* I. 317 Whether civil salvage is to be given to the king's ship, in addition to the military salvage, to which she is entitled under the statute. **1901** *Scotsman* 1 Mar. 9/2 The Admiralty court yesterday awarded..the Southampton tugs..a total salvage of £10,372 for services rendered to the Antwerp steamship.

transf. **1879** G. MEREDITH *Egoist* xxx. (1889) 296 Mrs. Mountstuart told him he ought to pay salvage for saving the wreck of her party.

2. a. The action of saving a ship or its cargo from wreck, capture, etc. Phr. *to make salvage of.*

1713 *Act 13 Anne* c. 21 §2 Three of the neighbouring Justices of the Peace..shall thereupon adjust the Quantum of the Monies or Gratuities to be paid to the several Persons acting or being imployed in the Salvage of the said Ship Vessel or Goods. **1851** DICKENS *Our Eng. Watering-Place*, Repr. Pieces (1868) 168 These men [boatmen] live chiefly on the salvage of valuable cargoes. **1857** T. F. KNOWLES in *Merc. Marine Mag.* (1858) V. 57 In the salvage of the crew .., I have but done my duty. **1861** HUGHES *Tom Brown at Oxf.* ii, The stranger..succeeded in making salvage of Tom's coat. **1886** *Encycl. Brit.* XXI. 238/1 Salvage of life is rewarded at a higher rate than salvage of property.

b. *gen.* The saving of property from fire or other danger. (Cf. *salvage corps* in 4.) Also *fig.*

1878 HALE *Mrs. Merriam's Scholars* xxiii. 236 (Funk) They had no thought of using these minutes for any salvage of their little personal effects in the school-room. **1902** *Daily Chron.* 1 July 4/3 The happy turn taken by the King's illness ..is enabling some salvage to be made from the Coronation arrangements.

c. In wartime, esp. the war of 1939–45: the saving and collection of waste material, esp. paper, for recycling; also *transf.*, those who organized and carried out this collection.

1918 *Times* 2 Mar. 3/5 A National Salvage Council has been set up with the approval of the War Cabinet to deal with the problems of civil salvage and the recovery of waste products generally. **1942** *Oxford Mag.* 29 Jan. 147/1 Next week sees the end of the great drive for salvage of waste paper. **1943** *Punch* 20 Jan. 51/3 Careless of salvage we tore wildly at the wrapper and turned eagerly to the last page. **1944** M. LASKI *Love on Supertax* i. 13 A large pile of empty bottles bore witness to the family's constant failure to remember which day the salvage called. **1946** R. LEHMANN *Gipsy's Baby* 118 Found last week in turning out old papers for salvage. **1961** E. S. TURNER *Phoney War* xx. 291 Some notable gestures were made that summer [in 1943] by persons whose idea of sacrifice was not fulfilled by lending money to the State at interest or putting out old love-letters for salvage.

3. a. Property salved or saved.

1755 MAGENS *Insurances* I. 356 The trouble of Hinsch and Labée, who had been aboard the Ship, having chartered the same and took great Care of the Salvage. **1787** PARK *Mar. Insurances* 130 The question upon this case was, whether as the freight exceeded the salvage, this was not to be considered as a total loss. **1883** SIR W. B. BRETT in *Law Times Rep.* XLIX. 226/2 Whatever is recovered or preserved by the solicitor's exertions is to be treated as a salvage. **1893** *Scotsman* 28 June 7 Directly after the vessel disappeared beneath the water the boilers exploded with a loud report, throwing up a quantity of salvage.

b. *transf.* and *fig.*

1857 J. HAMILTON *Less. Gt. Biog.* (1859) 106 The Sabbath ..still survives, a small but precious salvage from the world's great shipwreck. **1858** HAWTHORNE *Fr. & It. Note-bks.* (1871) II. 38 The broad eaves of the houses, too, make a salvage of shade, almost always. **1881** MALLOCK *Rom. 19th Cent.* I. ii, I still retain a certain salvage of wisdom.

c. Waste material, esp. paper, suitable for recycling. (Cf. sense 2 c above.)

1939 *Times* 11 Nov. 8/4 The salvage department will collect and organize the use of salvage. **1942** *Times Lit. Suppl.* 9 May 229/2 Recently,..a perfect copy of Von Gerning's 'Tour Along the Rhine', with colour plates by Ackermann, was sent to his firm as salvage, together with other fine volumes. **1943** G. WINN in S. Briggs *Keep smiling Through* (1975) 187 Queen Mary.., whenever she sees salvage lying around unclaimed—bones, bottles, scrap iron —Her Majesty stops the car, has it picked up, and taken home in triumph to the village dump. **1945** 'R. CROMPTON' *William & Brains Trust* xi. 204 We'll say we're collectin' salvage if anyone comes. **1951** *Good Housek. Home Encycl.* 237/2 The local Councils in many districts still undertake the collection of salvage. **1959** *Chambers's Encycl.* XII. 176/1 Industrial salvage arises in some form at nearly all factories. Apart from waste paper and canteen scraps, there are textile and chemical wastes, used oils, metal scrap, sawdust [etc.]. **1978** CADOGAN & CRAIG *Women & Children First* x. 213 Older children could help the war effort; they.. collected salvage, joined fire-watching rotas.

4. *Comb.* **salvage** ***brigade, campaign, collector, -drive, -dump, man, operation, sack***; ***salvage-minded*** adj.; **salvage archæology, excavation** = *rescue archæology, excavation* s.v. RESCUE *sb.* 3 c; **salvage charge, loss** (see quots.); **salvage corps**, a body of men kept in some towns to save property from fire; a fire brigade; **salvage money** = sense 1 above.

1967 G. H. GROSSO *Cave Life on Palouse* in *Encycl. Sci. Suppl.* (Grolier) 30 '*Salvage archaeology' became a way of life for anthropologists in Washington after Grand Coulee Dam created Roosevelt Lake more than 20 years ago. **1977** *Jrnl. R. Soc. Arts* CXXV. 199/1 If the Canada Council spent 90 per cent of its funds on salvage archaeology in California, for example, defenders would be very hard to find. **1890** W. BOOTH *In Darkest England* II. ii. 115, I propose to establish in every large town..'A Household *Salvage Brigade',.. entrusted with the task of collecting the waste of the houses in their circuit. **1942** P. JEPHCOTT *Girls growing Up* iii. 47 Ordinary time-table lessons are suplemented by..*salvage campaigns. **1813** *Salvage charge [see *salvage loss* below]. **1941** 'R. CROMPTON' *William does his Bit* vii. 165 (*heading*) William—the *Salvage Collector. **1975** S. BRIGGS *Keep smiling Through* 187 The salvage collector assured her that the letters would not be read, but suggested that she could tear them into small pieces. **1866** C. F. T. YOUNG *Fires* 417 The following is a scheme for the formation of a *salvage corps. **1942** *Ann. Reg. 1941* 335 Such special occasions as a War Weapons Week or a *Salvage Drive. **1952** R. A. KNOX *Hidden Stream* p. vii, My store of back-numbers is full to bursting again, and calls for a fresh salvage-drive. **1943** *Punch* 14 Apr. 321/1 Since picking out of the *salvage-dump a book entitled Half-Hours with the Stars, my father, a municipal dustman, has become keen on astronomy. **1972** *Even. Telegram* (St. John's, Newfoundland) 29 June 14/3 Provision for the preservation or *salvage-excavation of archaeological and historical sites. **1813** R. STEVENS *Ess. Average* I. ii. (1835) 79 The charges incurred are called 'salvage charges'—the property saved is 'the salvage',—and the difference between the amount of the salvage (after deducting the charges) and the original cost, or value of the property, is called 'the *salvage loss'. **1866** *Arnould's Marine Insur.* (ed. 3) II. III. v. 838 The claim must be adjusted as a salvage loss—that is, the underwriter pays the difference between the prime cost, or insured value of the goods, and the net proceeds of the damaged sales. *a* **1945** in S. Briggs *Keep smiling Through* (1975) 187 The war is driving Hitler back But here's one way to win it: Just give your *salvage men the sack And see there's plenty in it. **1942** *R.A.F. Jrnl.* 13 June 23 (*caption*), I want all you hut orderlies to *get* *salvage-minded and *stay* salvage-minded. **1661** BLOUNT *Glossogr.* (ed. 2), **Salvage Money*, is a recompence, allowed by the Civil Law, in lieu of all damages sustained by that ship that rescues another ship, which was set upon by Pirates or Enemies. **1689** in Magens *Insurances* (1755) II. 473 The Recompence which shall be made to the Captain and Mariners of a Man of War, who retake a Ship or Vessel, ..shall be paid out of the Salvage-Money. **1919** 'SAKI' *Fate* in *Toys of Peace* 200 The billiard table..was not the best place to have chosen for the scene of *salvage operations. **1975** *Globe & Mail* (Toronto) 4 June 2/2 Even filet mignon and Spencer steaks from Mr. Dumais' meat salvage operation went into hamburger. **1942** *Times Lit. Suppl.* 9 May 229/2 Before dropping books into the *salvage sack, owners have been urged..to consult the nearest public or university librarian or literary friend.

salvage ('sælvɪdʒ), *v.* [f. prec. sb.] **1.** *trans.* To make salvage of; to save or salve from shipwreck, fire, etc. Also *fig.*

1889 *Times* 25 Nov. 6/5 A gang of men were at once set to work to salvage and remove the remainder of the grain. **1895** *Pall Mall G.* 3 July 2/2 Mr. Balfour, nevertheless, will endeavour to salvage enough Bills to reclaim the Session from absolute barrenness. **1903** *Blackw. Mag.* June 842 The records were salvaged with little loss.

2. *U.S.* and *Austral.* To take (esp. *euphem.* by misappropriation) and make use of (unemployed or unattended property).

1918 *Stars & Stripes* 8 Feb. 2 *Salvage*, to rescue unused property and make use of it. **1919** S. PRENTICE *Padre* xv. 266 When he came out five minutes later it was gone; someone had 'salvaged' it again. **1919** K. D. MORSE *Let.* 1 Jan. (1920) vi. 206 The boys were setting off pyrotechnics of all sorts 'salvaged' from the dump. **1920** RIGGS & PLATT *Hist. Battery F* 15 We manœuvred around and got a loaf of bread and anything else we could 'salvage' before the M.P.'s were put guarding it. **1928** J. B. WHARTON *Squad* i. 40 If you two'll collect up all the canteens, we'll go off an' see what we can salvage. **1941** BAKER *Dict. Austral. Slang* 63 *Salvage, to*: to steal, purloin.

3. To save and collect (waste material, esp. paper) for recycling.

1943 *Ann. Reg. 1942* 313 The great national campaign to salvage paper for re-pulping resulted in..the destruction of many..irreplaceable volumes.

Hence **'salvaged** *ppl. a.*, **'salvaging** *vbl. sb.*

c **1920** J. F. MCGRATH *War Diary* 171 Salvaged rabbits, chicken, beer, and wine to add to the rations. **1951** *Manch. Guardian* 20 Apr. 6/7 His salvaging rather from the morgue of the Rules Committee of the Marshall Plan. **1969** R. EMERSON *Judging Delinquents* x. 275 Hard-core, discredited delinquents most in need of salvaging.

salvage, obs. form of SAVAGE.

salvage, salvagee: see SELVAGE, -EE.

salvageable ('sælvɪdʒəb(ə)l), *a.* [f. SALVAGE *v.* + -ABLE.] Capable of being salvaged. Also *fig.*

1976 *New Yorker* 24 May 115/1 Some urban experts suggest that the blacks who were salvageable were swept up and out into the suburbs—into decent jobs, and all that. **1977** *Custom Car* Nov. 20/1 Result: one completely junked digger with only the engine salvageable. **1981** *Times* 2 Mar. 10/4 The party is still salvageable..but it will not be saved if its best members leave it.

salvager ('sælvədʒə(r)). *rare.* [f. SALVAGE *sb.* or *v.* + -ER[1].] One who salves or salvages; = SALVOR 1; see also quot. 1867.

1829 *18th Rep. Comm. Crts. Justice Irel.* 10 A petition having been presented to the [High] Court [of Admiralty] by Mr. Henry Pyne Masters, one of the salvagers. **1867** SMYTH *Sailor's Word-bk.*, *Salvager*, one employed on the sea-coast to look to the rights of salvage, wreck, or waif.

salvar, var. SHALWAR.

Salvarsan ('sælvəsæn). *Pharm.* Also **salvarsan**. [a. G. *salvarsan*, f. L. *salv-āre* to save + G. *arsenik* ARSENIC *sb.*[1] + *-an* -AN.] A former proprietary name for ARSPHENAMINE. Now chiefly *Hist.*

1910 *Official Gaz.* (U.S. Patent Office) 23 Aug. 987/2 Farbwerke vorm. Meister Lucius & Brüning, Höchst-on-the-Main, Germany. Filed Feb. 23, 1909. *Salvarsan.* **1910** *N.Y. Med. Jrnl.* 3 Dec. 1137/1 Ehrlich followed up the arsenic compounds, and after many, many trials, changes, and improvements, placed, carefully and well prepared, dioxydiamidoarsenobenzol or 'salvarsan', to give it its trade name, before the profession. **1911** *Brit. Med. Jrnl.* 14 Jan. 100/1 The remedy has rapidly undergone improvements and successively become '606 ideal', '606 hyperideal', and now 'Salvarsan'. **1913** A. B. REEVE *Poisoned Pen* iii. 91 In these tubes I have the now famous salvarsan. **1913** *Times* 9 Aug. 3/1 The spirillum of relapsing fever, cultures of which after treatment with salvarsan were no longer capable of infecting mice. **1927** *Glasgow Herald* 29 Dec. 4/1 Setting right a joint by manipulation is different from killing a spirochaete with salvarsan. **1937** M. COVARRUBIAS *Island of Bali* (1972) x. 352 But the reluctance of the Balinese to undertake foreign treatment, the forbidding cost of Salvarsan, and the natural promiscuity do not help the situation. **1956** B. HOLIDAY *Lady sings Blues* (1973) ii. 24 At the hospital they were giving everbody shots of salvarsan for syphilis—only it was called 'bad blood' then. **1973** *Sci. Amer.* Sept. 106/3 In 1907 Paul Ehrlich of Germany, after long travail, succeeded in synthesizing Salvarsan, an arsenic compound that would kill *Treponema pallidum*, the microorganism that causes syphilis.

‖**salvatella** (sælvə'tɛlə). In 7 anglicized **salvatel.** [med.L. *salvatella* (It., Pg. *salvetella*, F. *salvatelle*), f. *salvāre* to save + dim. suffix (see -EL[2]); framed to render Arab. *al-usailim*, a derivative with dim. form from the root *s-l-m* implying safety, salvation, etc.] Old name for a vein on the back of the hand near its ulnar edge; blood-letting from this vein was held to be of great efficacy in the cure of diseases (*Syd. Soc. Lex.* 1891).

c **1400** *Lanfranc's Cirurg.* 158 Sche is clepid saluatella or ellis epatica in þe ri3thond, & in þe lifthand splenatica. **1548** VICARY *Anat.* vii. 53 And there it is called *Saluatella.* **1656** BLOUNT *Glossogr.* s.v. *Vein, Salvatel vein.* [From Cotgr. 1611, *Veine salvatelle.*] **1849–52** *Todd's Cycl. Anat.* IV. II. 1407 The '*vena salvatella*'.

salvation (sælˈveɪʃən). Forms: α. 3 **sauvaciun,** 4–5 **sauvacion, -acioun, savacion, -acyon, -acioun,** 5 **savation, (savacyowne, -asyon, -aysione, sawacyon);** β. 4 **salvaciun,** 4–5 **-acioun(e, -acyoun,** 4–6 **-acion, -acyon, -atioun,** (5 **-acyone, -atioune,** 6 **-acione, -aciounn, -atiounn, -atyon,** *Sc.* **sallwatioun),** 4– **salvation.** [a. OF. *sauvacion, -un, salvatiun,* etc., mod.F. *salvation* (Pr., Sp. *salvacion,* Pg. *salvação,* It. *salvazione*), ad. late L. *salvātiōn-em,* n. of action f. *salvāre* to SAVE.] The action of saving or delivering; the state or fact of being saved.

1. a. The saving of the soul; the deliverance from sin and its consequences, and admission to eternal bliss, wrought for man by the atonement of Christ. [eccl. L. *salvatio,* rendering Gr. *σωτηρία.*]

a **1225** *Ancr. R.* 242 Hwat te were leouest efter þi sauuaciun. *a* **1300** *Cursor M.* 17958 (Arundel MS.) His owne sone shal he sende doun In erþe to monnes saluatioun. **1377** LANGL. *P. Pl.* B. v. 126 Sorwe of synnes is sauacioun of soules. **14..** HOCCLEVE *Ad beatam Virginem* 53 O spryng and welle of our sauuacioun. **1602** SHAKS. *Ham.* III. iii. 92 Some acte That ha's no rellish of Saluation in't. **1651** HOBBES *Leviath.* III. xxxviii. 245 The joyes of Life Eternall, are in Scripture comprehended all under the name of *Salvation,* or *being saved.* ?**1709** LADY M. W. MONTAGU *Lett., To Mrs. Hewet* (1887) I. 23 His first wife..ventured her own salvation to secure his. **1738–9** BP. BUTLER *Serm. S.P.G.* 9 It is indeed true, God willeth that all men should be saved: yet..the Salvation of every man cannot but depend upon his Behaviour. **1816** SCOTT *Old Mort.* xxx, Men who believed that the pale of salvation was open for them exclusively. **1841** TRENCH *Parables* ix. (1877) 181 The whole economy of salvation has been put into Christ's hands.

b. in formulas of asseveration.

c **1374** CHAUCER *Troylus* II. 332 (381) God so wys be my sauacioun. *c* **1386** —— *Manciple's Prol.* 58 By my sauacion I trowe lewedly he wolde telle his tale. **1598** B. JONSON *Ev. Man in Hum.* (Qo. 1601) II. iii. E 4, *Bob.* I assure you (vpon my saluation) 'tis true. **1617** MORYSON *Itin.* II. 154 Foure thousand Spaniards (for so the prisoner that we tooke delivered them to be upon his salvation).

†**c.** ***year of (man's) salvation,*** a year reckoned from the birth of Christ: after med.L. *anno salutis.*

1560 DAUS tr. *Sleidane's Comm.* 160 b, In the yeare of mans salvation .M.C.LXXI. **1610** HOLLAND *Camden's Brit.* (1637) 624 About the yeere of Salvation 1328.

d. *transf.* and *fig.*

1886 *Times* 14 May 9/5 Mr. Campbell-Bannerman 'found salvation' in the shape of a conviction of the necessity of Home Rule, some time after the general election.

e. Phr. ***to work out (one's own) salvation;*** freq. *fig.,* to be independent or self-reliant in striving towards one's goal.

1535 COVERDALE *Phil.* ii. 12 Euen so worke out youre awne saluacion with feare and tremblynge. **1678** S. BUTLER *Hudibras* III. i. 86 With Crosses, Relicks, Crucifixes, Beads, Pictures, Rosaries and Pixes: The Tools of working out Salvation, By meer Mechanick Operation. **1818** KEATS *Let.* 9 Oct. (1931) I. 243 The Genius of Poetry must work out its own salvation in a man: It cannot be matured by law and precept, but by sensation and watchfulness in itself. **1881** T. R. DAVIDS tr. *Buddhist Suttas* I. vi. 114 Decay is inherent in all component things! Work out your salvation with diligence! **1891** *Anthony's Photogr. Bull.* IV. 88 Only those who have worked out their own photographic salvation can realize the difficulties to be overcome. **1911** L. T. HOBHOUSE *Liberalism* iv. 80 Let every people be free to work out its own salvation. **1948** A. J. TOYNBEE *Civilization on Trial* x. 210 It is for other Muslims to work out their salvation for themselves as may seem good to them. **1957** A. THWAITE *Ess. Contemp. Eng. Poetry* ix. 142 His [*sc.* Robert Graves'] self-imposed isolation from English literary life has left him free to work out his own poetic salvation and to take an idiosyncratic view of what everyone else is writing. **1981** *Daily Tel.* 12 Jan. 14/3 There are those..who resist the radicals' attempts to force their 'rights' upon them, and prefer to work out their own salvation.

f. (With initial capital.) *ellipt.* for (a member of) the Salvation Army.

1889 *Longman's Mag.* Feb. 407 My father says he is shamed to be called an Inglishman when he sees how the Salvation is knocked about and prossecuted. He says people will hold a drunken man up, but will knock a Salvation down.

2. *gen.* Preservation from destruction, ruin, loss, or calamity. In mod. use chiefly with more or less allusion to sense 1.

†*for* or *in salvation of*: in order to save or preserve.

c **1374** CHAUCER *Boeth.* I. pr. iv. 10 (Camb. MS.) Shal I clepe it..a synne þat I haue desired the sauacion of the ordre of the senat. *c* **1384** —— *H. Fame* I. 208 That he shulde drenche Lorde and lady, grome and wenche, Of all the Troian nacion Withoute any savacion. **1411** *Rolls of Parlt.* III. 650/2, I havyng doute of harme of my body, in myn entent for salvation of myself dyd assemble thise persones. *c* **1430** *Brut* 438 To gouerne and kepe the londe..in sauacion of his pepull and good kepynge of his Rewme. *c* **1440** *Gesta Rom.* lxix. 317 (Harl. MS.) The lady drowe to a bord, the which bare hire to þe londe; And þe maister tooke an othir bord, and so passid to þe londe, But neither of hem knewe of otheris saluacion. **1465** MARG. PASTON in *P. Lett.* II. 202 In any thyng that he canne doo tochyng the savacyon of the dedys gode, other in lyflode, other in other godys, he sayth that he wyll doo. **1472–3** *Rolls of Parlt.* VI. 52/1 [Your Petitioner] in salvation of his lyffe..came forth and submitted hym to the said Riottours. **1544** tr. *Littleton's Tenures* (1574) 11 The wife may doe this for salvacion of the state of the wardeine in chivalry. **1611** BIBLE *1 Sam.* xiv. 45 Shall Ionathan die, who hath wrought this great saluation in Israel? **1806** *Med. Jrnl.* XV. 18 The remedy..to which I owe the salvation of numbers, is cold bathing. **1849–50** ALISON *Hist. Europe* X. lxvi. §35. 147 Many a Burgoyne has capitulated because the means of salvation were not..put into his hands. **1850** CARLYLE *Latter-d. Pamph.* ii. (1872) 65 When men have a purse and a skin, they seek salvation at least for these. **1861** BRIGHT *Sp. Amer.* 4 Dec. (1868) I. 184 What then do you think would have been the regard of the Government..for personal liberty, if it interfered with..the salvation of the State? **1898** *Daily News* 30 Sept. 2/3 He thought the salvation of the District Company,..depended to a certain extent on the substitution of electricity for steam.

3. A source, cause or means of salvation; a person or thing that saves. Now chiefly in phr. ***to be the salvation of.***

c **1374** CHAUCER *Compl. Mars* 213 My right lady, my sauacyon. *c* **1440** LYDG. *Horse, Shepe & G.* 42 (Lansdowne MS.) Hors in cronyclis, wo-so looke a-riht, Hav be savacion to many a worthi knyht. **1539** BIBLE (Great) *Ps.* xxvii. 1 The Lorde is my lyght, and my saluacion. **1849** MACAULAY *Hist. Eng.* i. I. 15 The talents and even the virtues of her first six French Kings were a curse to her. The follies and vices of the seventh were her salvation. **1878** HOLBROOK *Hyg. Brain* 62 Sleep is the salvation of the nervous system.

4. *Comb.,* as ***salvation banner, -monger, -work; salvation-contemning*** adj.; **salvation history** = HEILSGESCHICHTE; **Salvation Jane** = *Paterson's curse* s.v. PATERSON; **Salvation lassie** = LASS 1 d.

1931 R. CAMPBELL *Georgiad* II. 33 One or two whose love is not unfurled Like a *salvation banner to the world. **1919** KIPLING *Years Between* 63. Drunk with enormous, *salvation-contemning Love for a tinker. **1959** *Times Lit. Suppl.* 20 Mar. (Relig. Bks. Section) p. vi/4 Such people are also rejecting the Incarnation, Crucifixion and Resurrection as events in '*salvation-history'. **1962** [see KERYGMA]. **1977** E. QUINN tr. *Küng & Lapide's Brother or Lord* 20 We ought to ask..how far the Jew..can help us to reach a more authentic understanding of Jesus: an understanding which brings home to us afresh the continuity of salvation history. **1911** *Jrnl. Dept. Agric. S. Austral.* XV. 305 (*heading*) *Salvation Jane. **1912** *Ibid.* XV. 679, I went to considerable trouble..in cutting down every plant of 'Salvation Jane' on a portion of my farm. **1937** LADY ROCKLEY *Some Canadian Wild Flowers* 5 There are tracts in New South Wales and South Australia covered with a Viper's Bugloss..but there it is a noxious weed reprobated by the names of 'Paterson's Curse' and 'Salvation Jane'. **1970** P. W. MICHAEL in R. M. Moore *Austral. Grasslands* xxiii. 356/2 *Phalaris tuberosa* has been shown to give excellent control of Salvation Jane or Patersons's curse in south-eastern South Australia. **1891** A. JAMES *Diary* 7 Apr. (1965) 188 Lifting up her voice in prayer as she knelt among the *Salvation lassies. **1972** P. M. HUBBARD *Whisper in Glen* iv. 34 These slight, intense men had to have their pound of flesh, whether it was a blowsy trollop..or a Salvation lassie. **1874** MOTLEY *Barneveld* I. viii. 345 The arch-heretic Arminius, the *salvation-monger. **1656** T. WATSON *One Thing necessary* 9 *Salvation-work is difficult in regard of the deceits about the work.

salˈvational, *a. rare.* [-AL[1].] Relating to or concerned with salvation.

1858 J. EADIE *Comm. Philippians* 44 His present Christ-like frame of spirit was salvational, if the expression may be coined—it was an index of present attainment, and the sure instrument of subsequent glory. **1894** *Thinker* Aug. 107 This purpose was of vital importance, if Israel was really to become Jehovah's salvational people in behalf of the Gentile world.

Salvation Army. **1.** An organization, on a quasi-military model, founded by the Rev. William Booth for the revival of religion among the masses in Great Britain and other countries.

The name was adopted in 1878 (the body until then was styled 'the Christian Mission'). The officers bear military titles ('general', 'captain', etc.). In its early years, open-air evangelistic services were the most prominent feature of the Salvation Army's work; it has since become notable for its charitable service among the poor and homeless.

c **1880** BOOTH *Salvation Soldier's Song-bk.* No. 123 The Salvation Army is marching along. **1881** —— *Doctr. & Discipl. Salvation Army* §29 When the organization had been in existence some eleven years, we found that it was fashioned, substantially, on the model of an army, and as its object was the salvation of men, we named it..'The Salvation Army'.

2. *attrib.*

1881 W. CORBRIDGE *Salvation Mine* (recto front cover), Salvation Army Stores, 101 Queen Victoria Street. **1910** 'SAKI' *Lost Sarijak* in *Reginald in Russia* 16 The corpse was that of a Salvation Army captain. **1920** H. BEGBIE *Life W. Booth* II. ii. 17 Blasphemous handbills, supposed to be circulated by Salvation Army Officers. **1921** M. L. CARPENTER *Angel Adjutant* v. 49 The wives of Salvation Army Bandsmen make their sacrifices. **1921** J. LAW *Curate's Promise* xv. 133 He saw..two officers..go into a large Salvation Army Hostel for women. **1928** H. CRANE *Let.* 27 Mar. (1965) 320, I finally had to finish the night in a ward of the Salvation Army Hotel. **1956** [see ROWTON]. **1966** [see SALLY *sb.*[5] 1 b]. **1972** P. M. HUBBARD *Whisper in Glen* iv. 34 A Salvation Army lass with the body of a Rubens Venus. **1978** *Lancashire Life* Sept. 90/2 In her latest picture..she shows a Salvation Army band playing hymns in a northern town some time between 1920 and 1930.

Salˈvationer. *rare*[−1]. [-ER[1].]

= SALVATIONIST 1.

1889 'M. GRAY' *Reproach of Annesley* III. VI. v. 209 The frantic Salvationers..make night and day hideous with profane bawlings.

salˈvationism. [-ISM.] **a.** Religious teaching which lays prime stress on 'salvation', or the saving of the soul. **b.** The principles or methods of the Salvation Army.

1883 *American* VI. 233 The emotional variety of religion which is called 'salvationism'. **1889** *Academy* 11 May 319/3 The gentler aspects of Salvationism find their exponent here in the labours of a beautiful self-denying girl, who voluntarily gives herself to the service. **1902** W. JAMES *Varieties Relig. Exper.* viii. 167 In their extreme forms, of pure naturalism and pure salvationism, the two types are violently contrasted.

salˈvationist, *sb.* (and *a.*) [-IST.]

1. With capital initial. A member of the Salvation Army.

1882 *Standard* 17 Jan., As the 'Salvationists' started on their 'triumphant march',..they were pelted with mud and brickbats. **1892** *Guardian* 13 Jan. 33/2 The Eastbourne Salvationists seem to believe that they serve their cause by making Sunday hideous.

2. One who rescues from peril; a saviour.

1971 *Daily Tel.* 4 May 14 Our great wartime leader, and I think salvationist, Sir Winston Churchill.

3. *attrib.* or as *adj.*

1934 WEBSTER, *Salvationist,* n. & adj. **1943** J. S. HUXLEY *Evolutionary Ethics* vii. 56 What I may call salvationist ethics, aimed at achieving salvation in a supernatural other life. **1959** A. F. WRIGHT *Buddhism in Chinese Hist.* iv. 81 Salvationist Buddhism..is neither an anomaly nor a temporary aberration of an otherwise 'rational' people.

salˈvationize, *v.* [-IZE.] *trans.* To convert, save, preach salvation to.

1927 *Scribner's Mag.* Feb. 118/2 Molly never could get over bein' salvationized. Some persons, when they get salvationized, get more joyous and happy. *a* **1930** D. H. LAWRENCE *Phoenix II* (1968) 439 Power..isn't bossing, or bullying, hiring a manservant or Salvationizing your social inferior.

†**salvative,** *a. Obs. rare*[−1]. [ad. L. type **salvātīv-us,* f. *salvāre* to save: see -IVE.]

? Healing; or ? preservative (*for* = against).

1653 R. SANDERS *Physiogn.* b j b, Archangel, physiognomising the fingers, is salvative for the fellon breeding on those parts.

†**salˈvator**[1]. *Obs.* Also 5 **-owr,** 5–6 **-our.** [ME. ˌ*salvaˈtour,* ad. late L. *salvātōr-em* (accus.), agent-n. f. *salvāre* to SAVE. In quot. 1707 a. *salvātor* (nom.).] One who saves or delivers; esp. the Saviour, Christ.

a **1400** *Stacions of Rome* 298 (Vernon MS.) In þe Rof ouer þe popes se A saluatour þer may þou se Neuer I-peynted with hond of Mon. *c* **1450** HOLLAND *Howlat* 473 Our Saluatouris sepultur. **1493** *Festivall* (W. de W. 1515) 123 b, Though eche of these were..helpers: and in maner salvatours of the people..but there was never none that was unyversall savyoure..but our lorde. **1500–20** DUNBAR *Poems* xxix. 1 Sanct Saluatour! send siluer sorrow. **1560** ROLLAND *Crt. Venus* III. 860 Our Saluator to fell the feyndis feid Was he not borne of the bour virginall? **1707** E. WARD *Hud. Rediv.* II. VII. 18 His holy Nose b'ing something greater Than that which grac'd our late Salvator [*i.e.* William III].

†**salvator**[2]: see SALVATORY *sb.*

Salvatorian (sælvəˈtɔərɪən), *sb.* (and *a.*) [f. L. *salvātor* (It. *salvatore*), saviour + -IAN.] A member of a Roman Catholic congregation, the Society of the Divine Saviour, founded in Rome in the late nineteenth century. Also *attrib.* or as *adj.*

1903 F. M. STEELE *Monasteries & Relig. Houses Gt. Brit. & Ireland* 188 (*heading*) The Fathers of the Society of the Divine Saviour, or the Salvatorians. **1909** *Catholic Encycl.* V. 53/2 The Salvatorians have establishments in Italy, Sicily, Austria, Poland. **1931** *Tablet* 22 Aug. 252/2 Father Melchior Geses, a German Salvatorian of the mission of Shaowu in the Vicariate of Foochow. **1962** L. SMITH *Salvatorians* 7 The chief ways in which the Salvatorians play their part in the work of the Church for the salvation of souls, is by contributing their particular spirit to the ministry of external work, in preaching and teaching, in assisting the parochial clergy, in the Mass and administration of the sacraments, as well as in the specialized tasks of educational and youth work. **1979** *Tucson* (Arizona) *Citizen* 20 Sept. 5A/1 In 1970, the Salvatorian Fathers filed for bankruptcy, the first instance of legal insolvency in the history of the Church in this country. .. The Salvatorians, LaSalettes and Paulines—essentially unregulated by virtue of their religious status—were able to float bonds in violation of normal Securities and Exchange Commission requirements that money raised be spent on the advertised purpose.

salvatory (ˈsælvətərɪ), *sb.* Also 7–8 **salvator(e.** [ad. med.L. *salvātōri-um* place of preservation (only *spec.* a fishpond), f. *salvāre* to SAVE. Sense 1 is due to association with SALVE *sb.*[1]]

†**1.** A box for holding ointment. *Obs.*

1549 *Will of T. Laund* (Somerset Ho.), A salvatory of syluer. **1561** VICARY *Will* in *Anat.* 189 My best plaister box, garnisshed with siluer, my salvitory of siluer. **1612** WOODALL *Surg. Mate* Wks. (1653) 16 The Salvatorie if it contain six severall Unguents, it is sufficient for any present use. **1623** WEBSTER *Duchess of Malfi* IV. ii, Thou art a box of worme-seede, at best, but a saluatory of greene mummey. **1688** R. Holme *Armoury* III. 438/1 The Surgeons Salvator or Salvatory, or his Box of Unguents..is a Box with a Lid made generally of Latin or Tin. **1706** Phillips (ed. Kersey), *Salvatory*, a Surgeon's Box, with Partitions, to hold several sorts of Salves, Ointments, and Balsams. **1715** *Lond. Gaz.* No. 5370/4 A Salvatore furnished with Balsam.

2. *gen.* A repository for safe storage. *rare.*

a **1677** Hale *Prim. Orig. Man.* II. iv. 156 When I consider ..the admirable powers of Sensation, of Phantasie, of Memory, in what Salvatories or Repositories the Species of things past are conserved. **1863** Jean Ingelow *Poems* 98 (*A Dead Year*) 'All the kings of the nations lie in glory' [see Isa. xiv. 18]; Cased in cedar, and shut in a sacred gloom;..Silent they rest, in solemn salvatory.

salvatory ('sælvətərɪ), *a.* *rare.* [ad. L. **salvātōri-us*: see prec.] Saving, imparting safety or salvation (*to*).

1830 *Fraser's Mag.* I. 525 Such and such redeeming points..these salvatory accidents. **1852** Jerdan *Autobiog.* I. xvii. 131 To aid us in our salvatory endeavours [viz. to save a convict from execution]. **1865** Carlyle *Fredk. Gt.* xv. xi. (1872) VI. 74 Fine feat, salvatory to the Cause of Liberty, and destructive of French influence. **1898** M. Muriel Dowie *Crook of Bough* 124 The raw young thinker who believes in the salvatory power of education. **1921** *Challenge* 18 Feb. 241/2 Salvatory and reconstructive work. **1922** J. Y. Simpson *Man & Attainment of Immortality* xiv. 334 The fact of Christ remains, solitary and salvatory. **1958** J. Lodwick *Bid Soldiers Shoot* III. vii. 222 The murderer has but a single advantage: the patient police, who, in extended order, beat the bush in search of him, or of the macabre *trouvaille* of his hastily buried victim, do not..believe that they will encounter either, personally. Therefore, when they do..a salvatory hiatus follows.

†**salvatrice.** *Obs. rare.* [ad. med.L. *salvātrīc-em* (nom. *-trix*), f. *salvāre* to save.]

1. A female saviour.

1500-20 Dunbar *Poems* lxxxv. 67 [To our Lady] Oratrice, mediatrice, salvatrice.

2. Old name for one of the coats (*tunicæ*) of the eye; in full ***tunicle salvatrice*** (= L. *tunica salvatrix*).

1590 Barrough *Meth. Physic* I. xxx. (1596) 50 Some.. imagin but only two coates, the one whereof they tearme Saluatrix, because it saueth and keepeth the humors. *Ibid.* xxxiv. 54 The tunicle saluatrice. *Ibid.* 55 It is not safe to aduenture to cure it [the 'second pannicle'], when by continuance of time, it hath vnited it selfe with the saluatrice.

‖**salva veritate** ('sælvɑː ˌvɛrɪ'tɑːteɪ), *advb. phr.* [L.] Saving the truth, without infringement of truth.

1930 P. P. Wiener tr. *Nicod's Found. Geom.* III. v. 141 It will be found in all cases necessary and sufficient that the two relations be *equivalent*, that is to say,..that one can be replaced by the other and the field of one by the field of the other, *salva veritate*, in every proposition containing nothing besides logical or mathematical expressions. **1957** [see *inter-substitutability* s.v. Inter- 2 a]. **1963** J. Lyons *Structural Semantics* iv. 56 Attempts to handle synonymy in terms of substitutability throughout the language *salva veritate* are generally regarded as unsatisfactory.

salve (sælv, sɑːv), *sb.*¹ Forms: 1 salb, salf, sealf, sealfe, 2 sealfe, 3 (Orm.) sallfe, 4 sealve, (salft), 4–5 salf, save, *Sc.* sawve, 4–9 *Sc.* saw, 5 salffe, 6 saulve, *Sc.* saufe, 7 sawf, 3– salve. [OE. *sealf* fem. = OS. *salba*, MLG. *salve* (whence MSw. *salva*, Sw. *salfva*, Da. *salve*), MDu. *salve*, *salf* (Du. *zalf*), OHG. *salpa*, *salba* fem., *salb*, *salp* neut. (MHG., G. *salbe* fem.):—OTeut. **salbā* str. fem.:—pre-Teut. **solpā́*, cogn. w. Skr. *sarpís* clarified butter, *sṛpra* greasy, and Albanian *ǵalpe* butter; perh. also with Gr. ὄλπη, ὄλπις oil-flask.]

1. a. A healing ointment for application to wounds or sores. See also eyesalve, lipsalve.

a **700** *Epinal Gloss.* 635 *Malagma*, salb. *c* **1000** *Sax. Leechd.* I. 110 Ᵹenim þas yclan wyrte, wyrc to salfe [*v.rr.* sealfe, sealue]. *c* **1000** *Ags. Gosp.* Mark xiv. 5 þeos sealf mihte beon ȝesealde to þrim hund peneȝum. *c* **1200** Ormin 6477 Þe þridde þatt teȝȝ gæfenn himm Wass an full deore sallfe,..Myrra bi name nemmnedd. *a* **1225** *Ancr. R.* 370 Ure Louerdes sonde þet brouhte hire salue uorto helen hire tittes. *c* **1315** Shoreham i. 18 And for þe goute sealue Me makeþe. *c* **1375** *Sc. Leg. Saints* xlvi. (*Anastace*) 102 Bot mekly vald scho wesch þar fet, & with softe sawis þare saris bet. *c* **1386** Chaucer *Sqr.'s T.* 631 Now kan nat Canacee but herbes delue Out of the ground and make saues [*v.r.* salues] newe. **14..** *Sir Beues* 605 (MS. M.) With drinke and salffe she helid hym softe. **1530** Palsgr. 729/1, I splette a saulve abrode upon a clothe, *je placque*. **1612** Woodall *Surg. Mate* Wks. (1653) 21 If an old wife had openly applied her one salve for all sores. **1704** W. King *Orpheus & Eurydice* 152 She..bade him 'noint himself with salve; Such as those hardy people use, Who walk on fire without their shoes. **1804** Abernethy *Surg. Obs.* 242 Linen spread over with spermaceti salve. **1896** A. E. Housman *Shropshire Lad* xlv, 'Twill hurt, but here are salves to friend you, And many a balsam grows on ground.

b. Formerly often (now *arch.*) in proverbial collocation with *sore*.

a **1300** *Cursor M.* 27397 Til all sares sere es sett, salues sere to be wit bett. **1399** Gower *Praise of Peace* 122 Ley to this olde sor a newe salve. **1575-85** Abp. Sandys *Serm.* xxi. 363 Where there is no sore, there needes no salue. **1671** Milton *Samson* 184 Or if better, Counsel or Consolation we may bring, Salve to thy Sores. **1825** Jamieson s.v. *Saw*, Ye hae a saw for ilka sair.

c. A mixture, usually of tar and grease, for smearing sheep.

1523 Fitzherb. *Husb.* §44 To make brome salue [for sheep]. **1837** Youatt *Mountain Sheph. Man.* 31 The scab —a disease which the common salve, made of tar and grease, seems effectually to resist. **1844** Stephens *Bk. Farm* III. 1117 This compound..forms a salve for 100 sheep.

fig. **1528** Tindale *Obed. Chr. Man* 129 b, As when we saye of a wanton childe, this shepe hath magottes in his tayle, he must be anoynted with byrchin salve, which speach I borow of the shephardes.

2. *fig.* **a.** A remedy (esp. for spiritual disease, sorrow, and the like). Now *rare.* See also 1 b.

c **1200** Ormin 13489 Jesumm Mannkinne sawle sallfe,.. Himm hafe we nu fundenn. *c* **1225** *Ancr. R.* 276 Prudes salue is edmodnesse. *a* **1250** *Owl & Night.* 888 Ich helpe monne on eiþer halue, Mi muþ haueþ tweire kunne salue. *c* **1320** R. Brunne *Medit.* 1133 Þank we now oure sa[u]youre, þat salue vs haþ broȝt, Oure syke soules to saue, whan synne haþ hem soȝt. **1377** Langl. *P. Pl.* B. xx. 370 Contricioun..þat is the souereynest salue for alkyn synnes. *c* **1412** Hoccleve *De Reg. Princ.* 1245, I am so drad of monyes scantnesse..Wisseth me how to gete a golden salue. *c* **1430** in *Pol. Rel. & L. Poems* (1903) 203 And to my soule goosteli salue þou sende! **1563** *Homilies* II. *Repentance* II. (1859) 541 That they may receive at their hand the comfortable salve of God's word. **1574** *Satir. Poems Reform.* xlii. 766 Schir, ȝe knaw, This raritie will be ane saw, To mak the word estemit moir Nor euir it was heirtofoir. **1577** Hanmer *Anc. Eccl. Hist.* (1619) 457 Wherefore we have devised these letters as a salve for this mischiefe. *c* **1610** Rowlands *Terrible Batt.* 8 Sinne hath no salue but mercy.

b. *esp.* Something which serves to soothe wounded feelings or honour, a tender conscience, etc.

This use has prob. developed from a misinterpretation or punning acceptation of phrases containing salve *sb.*[4]

1736 *Gentl. Mag.* VI. 669/1 This however was no Salve for the tender Consciences of the Quakers. **1856** Merivale *Rom. Emp.* xli. (1865) V. 115 For them Horace had a salve in his specious disparagement of illustrious parentage. **1865** Kingsley *Herew.* iv, Ranald had this salve for his conscience. **1874** L. Stephen *Hours in Library* (1892) I. ii. 54 Let us hope that this little salve to self-esteem never lost its efficacy.

c. *slang.* See quot., and cf. lipsalve.

1864 Hotten *Slang Dict.*, *Salve*, praise, flattery, chaff. **1896** *Leeds Mercury Weekly Suppl.* 21 Nov., Put plenty o' sauve on him an' tha'll get owght aht on him 'at iver tha wants to. **1908** J. M. Sullivan *Criminal Slang* 21 *Salve*, getting on the right side of the arresting officer. **1926** Maines & Grant *Wise-Crack Dict.* 14/1 *Spread the salve*, soft, conciliatory talk.

3. *Comb.*, as ***salve-box***.

1663 Cowley *Cutter Colman St.* III. i, A Sawf-box for a Wounded Conscience.

†**salve**, *sb.*² *Obs.* [a. F. *salve* (16th c.), ad. It. *salva*: see salvo. Cf. G. *salve*.] A salvo or discharge of fire-arms.

1577-87 Holinshed *Chron.* III. 1151/1 At whose arriuall there..they sounded their trumpets, & with a thundering peale of great ordinance gaue a lowd salue vnto the Britains. **1587** Sir R. Williams *Let. to Leicester* 29 June (MS. Cotton Galba D I. 146-7), I and other English gentilmen will approch theire Boates in such sorte that we will force them to giue theire salue of Artillerie vppon vs. **1604** E. Grimstone *Hist. Siege Ostend* 182 They made a Salue, euery one of the Musketiers three shot. **1635** Barriffe *Mil. Discipl.* cxx. (1643) 420 A salve is when 2, 3, or more rankes powre out all their shot together in one volly. **1637** R. Monro *Exped.* II. 66 They were prepared with a firme resolution to receive us with a salve of Cannon and Muskets. **1666** *Lond. Gaz.* No. 47/2 In which state they entred the City of Naples, where the..Spanish Garrison, welcomed them with the continued thunder of the Cannons and salves of small shot. *a* **1693** *Urquhart's Rabelais* III. xxxiv. 288 The Thundring of Nineteen hundred Canons at a Salve.

†**salve**, *sb.*³ *Obs.* [Origin and meaning obscure: perh. some error.] Some kind of boat.

1588 Archdeacon tr. *True Disc. Army K. Spain* 36 There are 20. Carauels for the seruice of the aboue named Armie, and likewise 10 Salues with sixe Oares a peece. [Reproduced by Strype, Tindal and Hume.]

†**salve**, *sb.*⁴ *Obs.* [f. salve *v.*² Cf. salvo *sb.*¹]

a. A solution of a difficulty; also, a sophistical excuse or evasion. **b.** A 'salvo' or means of 'salving' a person's honour, etc.

a **1628** F. Grevil *Sidney* (1652) 11 In their losse.. there be buried many delicate images, and differences between the reall and large complexions of those active times, and the narrow salves of this effeminate age. **1646** Sir T. Browne *Pseud. Ep.* VII. xiii. 366 While we referre it unto the Moone, we give some satisfaction for the Ocean, but no generall salve for Creeks, and Seas which know no floud. **1651** N. Bacon *Disc. Govt. Eng.* II. xliv. 114 The worst point in the case was that the Duke was a Bastard,..nor was there other salve thereto but the Norman custom, that made no difference. **1651** Hobbes *Leviath.* I. xi. 49 They will rather hazard their honour, which may be salved with an excuse; than their lives, for which no salve is sufficient. **1657** *Treat. Conf. Sin* vi. 109 A discourse not capable of a Roman salve, but needing the spunge throughout, with a *deleatur*. **1665** Glanvill *Def. Van. Dogm.* 24 Whether what is said be a clear salve or a shuffle.

‖**salve** ('sælviː), *sb.*⁵ Also 6 salvy. [L. *salvē* 'hail!', 'good morning', 2nd sing. imper. of *salvēre* to be well or in good health. Cf. F. *salvé* in sense 2 (14th c. in Godefroy).]

1. The utterance of the word *salvē* (see above) or its equivalent; a greeting or salutation on meeting.

1583 Greene *Mamillia* Wks. (Grosart) II. 22 After he had curteously giuen her the *Salue*. *Ibid.* 196 To salute thee with a *Salue*. **1588** —— *Metam.* ibid. IX. 20 An interchange of salues passed, between her and me. **1641** J. Jackson *True Evang. T.* III. 176 His Salve, or Present, when he came to his Disciples, [was] Peace be with you. **1701** C. Wolley *Jrnl. New York* (1860) 56 But the amaze soon went off with a *salve tu quoque*, and a Bottle of Wine.

2. (With capital initial. More fully ***Salve Regina.***) In the R.C. Ch., an antiphon, beginning 'Salve, Regina', now recited after the Divine Office from Trinity Sunday to Advent; also sung as a separate office or 'devotion'. Also, a musical setting for this.

1428 *E.E. Wills* (1882) 81 Also to-fore oure ladi in Senct Marie Chapell..I Tapre of a pounde, to brenne euery euen of oure lady, and þe day as atte salue. **1486** *Rec. St. Mary at Hill* (1904) 5 That he be euery Day in the same Chirch after evensong, at the tyme of syngyng of Salue Regina. **1502** Arnolde *Chron.* (1811) 277 Item we fynde that for defaute of good prouision bothe of the chirche wardeyns and also of the mastirs of the salue, neither the priestis nor clarkis that ben retayned for the chirche wil nat com to our lady masse nor salue. **1557-8** in Swayne *Sarum Churchw. Acc.* (1896) 103 For the Syngyn men that song' at Salvy. *c* **1570** *Durham Depos.* (Surtees) 149 He dyd dyvers tymes help to singe salvaes at mattynes and even songe. **1789** Burney *Hist. Mus.* III. 529 The *salmi, stabat maters, misereres*, and *salve reginas*, with solo airs. **1888** *Century Mag.* Aug. 495/2 It is the hour of the Compline, the Salve, and the Angelus.

b. *attrib.*, as †***Salve time***; †**Salve-light**, a candle lighted during the singing of the *Salve*.

1439 *E.E. Wills* (1882) 114, ij Tapers to stonde on the Auter of our lady..þer to be lighte and brenne at Salue tyme. **1486** *Will of W. Cromwell* in *Misc. Gen. & Her.* Ser. III. I. 95 To the lighting of the Blessed Virgin Mary in the same chapel, called Salvelight.

salve (sælv, sɑːv), *v.*¹ Forms: 1 sealfian, 3 *Ormin* sallfenn, 5 salf(e, sauf, save, 6 sawve, (9 *dial.* sauve, soave, sove), 3– salve. [OE. *sealfian* = OFris. *salvia*, OS. *salbon*, MLG. *salven* (mod.LG. *salven*, *salfen*; Da. *salve* from LG.), MDu. *salven* (Du. *zalven*), OHG. *salbôn* (MHG. and mod.G. *salben*), Goth. *salbôn* :—OTeut. **salbōjan*, f. **salbā* salve *sb.*¹]

1. a. *trans.* To anoint (a wound, wounded part) with salve or healing unguent. *Obs.* or *arch.*

a **800** *Erfurt Gloss.* 325 *Delibutus*, ȝisalbot. *c* **1050** *Voc.* in Wr.-Wülcker 406/13 *Fotam*, sealfode. *a* **1400-50** *Alexander* 3132 (Dubl.) He gart seke þair sarys & þaim salue with suurgers noble. **1530** Palsgr. 697/2, I salve, or playster a sore bodye with salves, *je emplastre*. **1590** Spenser *F.Q.* I. v. 17 Where many skilfull leaches him abide To salve his hurts, that yet still freshly bled. **1650** S. Clarke *Eccl. Hist.* I. (1654) 38 Where is he that salved and cured him which was wounded by the Theives? **1658** A. Fox *Würtz' Surg.* II. xxvi. 176 There are some, who by all means would have Fractures salved and annointed. **1822** Scott *Nigel* viii, Marry, her husband that made the weapon might have salved the wound. **1865** Kingsley *Herew.* xxiii, Is there a wound on your limbs, which my hands have not salved?

†**b.** To anoint to an office. *Obs.*

c **1200** Ormin 13243, & Crist bitacneþþ uss þatt mann þatt smeredd iss & sallfedd, Nohht þurrh nan eorþliȝ smere, acc all þurrh Haliȝ Gastess sallfe.

c. In figurative contexts, where the language is literal; esp. in phr. ***to salve a sore.*** †Also with *up.*

c **1200** Ormin 9427 Alls iff he brohhte læchedom & herrtess eȝhesallfe, To sallfenn & to clennsenn firrst þe folkess herrtess eȝhe. *a* **1225** *Ancr. R.* 194 Þe gostliche hurtes ne þuncheð nout sore, ne ne salueð ham mid schrifte. *a* **1340** Hampole *Psalter* xxvi. 15 Þou ert god my hele þat salues þe wounde of my syn. *c* **1400** *Destr. Troy* 9193 There is no medcyn on mold, saue the maiden one, þat my sors might salue, ne me sound make. *c* **1430** Lydg. *Testament* Min. Poems (Percy Soc.) 248 Sauf al my soorys that they nat cankryd be With noon old rust of disesperaunce. **1576** Fleming *Panopl. Epist.* 52 Al which sores I haue salued vp with apt plasters. **1604** Churchyard (*title*) A blessed Balme to search and salve Sedition. **1623** T. Scot *Tongue-Combat* 54 Matters..did..salve vp this sore from further festring. **1873** Browning *Red Cott. Nt.-cap* 249 Since plain speech salves the wound it seems to make.

†**d.** *intr.* To smear salve *upon* a sore; in quot. *fig.* *Obs. rare.*

1579 Lodge *Def. Poetry* 42 But after your discrediting of playmaking, you salue vppon the sore somewhat.

e. *trans.* To smear (sheep) with a mixture of tar and butter, or the like. Cf. grease *v.* 2.

1523 Fitzherb. *Husb.* §44 A medicyne to salue poore mennes shepe, that thynke terre to costely. **1544** *Supplic. Hen. VIII* (E.E.T.S.) 39 A shepherde..which nother wolde nor coulde feade, handle, salue, nor ones see his shepe commytted to his charge. **1788** W. Marshall *Yorksh.* II. 349 To *salve sheep*, to dress them with tar and grease. **1860** Kay-Shuttleworth *Scarsdale* II. 79 He would linger three or four days to help to 'salve' the sheep.

†**2. a.** In extended sense: To heal or remedy (a disease). Chiefly *fig.*, to heal (sin, sorrow, etc.).

1411 *26 Pol. Poems* x. 164 Þe holy gost salueþ soule syknesse. **1426** Lydg. *De Guil. Pilgr.* 7719 No tryacle may the venym saue. *c* **1450** *Cov. Myst.* xxvi. (Shaks. Soc.) 253 Alle your langoris salvyn xal he. **1579** Tomson *Calvin's Serm. Tim.* 320/1 We are not worthie that God should salve our sinnes gently and with a fatherly affection. **1581** Marbeck *Bk. of Notes* 187 But Christ salueth this disease, for he fulfilled the lawe for vs. **1594** Greene & Lodge *Looking Glasse* (1598) D 3, Content thee sweet, ile salue thy sorrow straight. **1621** Burton *Anat. Mel.* II. i. i. (1651) 220 They can..salve gouts, epilepsies [etc.]. **1624** Quarles *Job* Div. Poems (1717) 180 Why, rather, didst not thou remove my sin, And salve the sorrows that I raved in?

†**b.** To heal (a person) *of* (sickness, sin, etc.).

Occas. found coupled with *save* (see quots. 1377, *c* 1470).

a **1225** *St. Marher.* 22 Of þis sunne lauerd loke me nu salue. *a* **1240** *Ureisun* in *Cott. Hom.* 202 For to saluen [*Lamb.*

Hom. 187 sauuin] seke ine sunnen. **1377** LANGL. *P. Pl.* B. XI. 212 Cryst to a comune woman seyde.. þat *fides sua* shulde sauen hir and saluen hir of alle synnes. *Ibid.* xx. 303 Go salue þo þat syke ben and þorw synne ywounded. *c* **1440** *York Myst.* xx. 266 þe sight of þe Hath salued vs of all oure sore. *Ibid.* xxix. 263 He salued þame of sikenesse. *c* **1470** *Gol. & Gaw.* 793 The king.. prayt to the grete God to grant him his grace, Him to saue and to salf. *a* **1591** H. SMITH *Serm.* (1637) 599 His stripes are plasters to salve me. **1596** SPENSER *F.Q.* v. v. 43 For, seeking thus to salve the Amazon, She wounded was with her deceipts owne dart.

†**c.** To soothe, mitigate, assuage (an 'appetite').

1577 NORTHBROOKE *Dicing* (1843) 11 Neuer endeauoring to tame and salue their wilde appetites.

†**3. a.** *fig.* To heal, remedy, mend, make good, make up, smooth over (something amiss, a troubled state of affairs, a defect, offence, disgrace, dispute, etc.).

In many examples not distinguishable from SALVE *v.*[2]

1575 FENTON *Gold. Epist.* (1582) 246 They seeke not to salue what is amisse. **1579** E. K. *Spenser's Sheph. Cal.* Ep. to Harvey ¶ 1, Which default whenas some endevoured to salve and recure. **1587** GREENE *Penelopes Web* D j, The lady Barmenissa,.. still salued her want with labour and her pouertie with patience. **1590** SPENSER *F.Q.* II. x. 21 But Ebranck salved both their infamies With noble deedes. **1610** HOLLAND *Camden's Brit.* I. 509 If my conjecture missed the truth, the confession of my errour may salue it. *c* **1622** FORD, etc. *Witch Edmonton* I. i, To salve the infamy Of my disgraced house. **1692** LUTTRELL *Brief Rel.* (1857) II. 341 Which, 'tis thought, will salve the difference betwixt the two houses about the treason bill. **1706** PHILLIPS (ed. Kersey), To *Salve the Matter*, to make up a Business, so as to come off well. **1712** PRIDEAUX *Direct. Ch.-wardens* (ed. 4) 63 His Confirmation salved all defects.

†**b.** with intensive *up*. *Obs.*

1594 CAREW *Huarte's Exam. Wits* xiii. (1596) 217 That steward, whom his master called to accompt, reseruing a good portion of the goods to his owne behoofe, salued vp all his reckonings, and got his quietus est. **1612** T. TAYLOR *Comm. Titus* iii. 2 (1619) 571 These speaches are farre off from saluing vp the matter. **1656** FINETT *For. Ambass.* 222 In observation of which direction I repaired to them, salved up all as dextrously as I could. **1668** H. MORE *Div. Dial.* I. II. 230 There will be a Θεὸς ἀπὸ μηχανῆς, Christ coming in the Clouds, that shall salve up all.

4. a. *fig.* (From sense 1, after phrases containing SALVE *v.*[2]) To soothe, 'lay flattering unction to' (irritated feeling, 'wounded pride', an uneasy conscience, etc.). Also ***to salve over***.

1825 LAMB *Unitarian Protests*, So long as you Unitarians could salve your consciences with the *équivoque*. **1831** CAMPBELL *Power of Russia* 70 Rome could impart what Russia never can—Proud civic right to salve submission's shame. **1850** KINGSLEY *Alt. Locke* xiv, I salved over that feeling, being desirous to see everything in the brightest light. **1852** R. S. SURTEES *Sponge's Sp. Tour* xii, At first Chousam would hear of nothing but 'l-a-w'. Bullfrog's wounded honour could only be salved that way. *Ibid.* xxv, Jack salved his conscience over with the old plea of duty. **1864** TREVELYAN *Compet. Wallah* (1866) 144 Or any of the other benefits by which we seek to compensate the natives.. and salve our own consciences. **1874** SYMONDS *Sk. Italy & Greece* (1898) I. xv. 343 A supreme satisfaction—salving over many wounds of vanity. **1878** BOSW. SMITH *Carthage* 373 In the endeavour to salve their wounded pride.

b. *to salve over*: to talk over or persuade by smooth speech. *colloq.*

1862 MRS. H. WOOD *Channings* I. xi. 157 'Lady Augusta and Dr. Burrows are great friends, you know'; and we hear that they have been salving over Pye—' 'Gently, Tom!' put in Mr. Channing. 'Talking over Pye, then,' corrected Tom.

†**salve,** *v.*[2] *Obs.* [app. ad. L. *salvāre* to SAVE.

In the astronomical sense 1, the L. form was prob. adopted because the vernacular *save* did not sufficiently indicate the technical import of the word. In this use the word became virtually equivalent to 'solve', 'explain', and it seems probable that sense 2 (though in our quots. appearing earlier) arose as a generalized application of this notion. The remaining uses were no doubt suggested by mod. Latin phrases like *salvo jure*, *salvo honore*, etc.; see SALVO *sb.*[1]]

1. *Astr.* To SAVE (*the appearances*, *the phenomena*), i.e. to frame a hypothesis which will account for all the observed facts of the apparent motions of the heavenly bodies. Hence *gen.*, to account for, explain by hypothesis. (Cf. SOLVE *v.*, used in the same phrases.)

1625 N. CARPENTER *Geog. Del.* I. vi. (1635) 140 To salue this Apparence, Ptolomy inuented a slow motion of the Starry Heauen. **1627** HAKEWILL *Apol.* II. iv. §4. 95 Who to salue these different observations invented a new Hypothesis, which yet was not received by Astronomers of after times. **1635** SWAN *Spec. M.* vi. §2 (1643) 207 Serving to no other purpose but to salve the annuall motion of the earth. **1646** [see PHENOMENON 1 c]. **1656** tr. *Hobbes' Elem. Philos.* IV. xxvi. 320 That circular motion (which is commonly attributed to them) about a fixed Axis,.. is insufficient to salve their Appearances. **1662** BOYLE *Def. Doctr. Spring of Air* II. v. 57 To salve the Phænomena of the Torricellian Experiment. **1662** STILLINGFL. *Orig. Sacr.* III. i. §18 Such perplexities must needs arise, when men will undertake to salve the inward operations of the soul by meer motion. **1672** SIR T. BROWNE *Let. Friend* §8 A remarkable coincidence, which tho Astrology hath taken witty pains to salve, yet hath it been very wary in making predictions of it. **1691** T. H[ALE] *Acc. New Invent.* p. xxix, Inventers, whose discoveries have only salved the Phænomena.

2. To clear up, explain, account for (a difficulty, point in dispute, etc.); to overcome (a doubt, objection); to harmonize or reconcile (a discrepancy).

1571 CAMPION *Hist. Irel.* xv. (1633) 48 Here Cambrensis to salve the contradiction, thinketh [etc.]. **1594** PLAT *Jewell-ho.* III. 80 If the first doubt may be salued. **1614** RALEIGH *Hist. World* II. (1634) 475 So, by making the seventeenth yeare of Jeroboam to be newly begun, all may be salved. **1620** SANDERSON *Serm. ad Pop.* ii. (1689) 172 As for those phrases then of *Repenting*, *Grieving*, &c., which are spoken of God in the Scriptures; that συγκατάβασις, whereof St. Chrysostom so often speaketh, salveth them. **1643** MILTON *Divorce* II. viii. Wks. 1851 IV. 80 What may we do then to salve this seeming inconsistence? **1655** FULLER *Ch. Hist.* I. v. §20 To salve all, some have found out another Patrick, called Seniour, or Sen Patrick. **1676** W. HUBBARD *Happiness of People* 3 The reason given by some Interpreters seems not sufficient to salve the Knot. *a* **1677** HALE *Prim. Orig. Man.* I. iii. 82 And this does salve two Objections at once. **1686** R. DUNNING *Overseer of Poor* 11 This Exception may be thus salved. **1722** WOLLASTON *Relig. Nat.* ix. (1724) 199 The objection before us, tho we could not salve the difficulties in it,.. yet to be no prejudice against the belief of the immortality of the soul. **1744** WESLEY *Wks.* (1872) VIII. I conceive, this will not salve the matter at all.

b. To explain away, excuse by a 'salvo'.

1628 PRYNNE *Cens. Cozens* 73 What answer can you make to mitigate or salue this bloody and soule-slaying sinne? **1640** BP. HALL *Episc.* II. §20. 202 He flew out into some expressions indeed, but yet such as in other places he doth either salve or contradict.

3. To render tenable, obviate the objections to (an opinion); to vindicate from incredibility (an alleged fact).

1596 BELL *Surv. Popery* III. ix. 397 To salue their beggerly doctrine. **1635** JACKSON *Creed* VIII. xviii. §2 Such.. labour to salve the truth of the Propheticall prediction. **1658** SIR T. BROWNE *Hydriot.* iii. 19 But the soul subsisting, other matter clothed with due accidents, may salve the individuality. **1659** PEARSON *Creed* (1839) 88 There was no way to salve the eternity or antiquity of the World.. but by supposing innumerable deluges and deflagrations. **1701** NORRIS *Ideal World* I. v. 298 As the *esse reale* salves the infinity, so the *esse formale* does equally secure the ideality. **1720** WATERLAND *Eight Serm.* 116 To salve their Hypothesis, They make bold with the.. Construction of the Words.

4. To preserve or maintain unhurt (one's honour, credit, reputation, etc.). Hence, to preserve the credit of, make good (one's oath, etc.).

In the later examples prob. apprehended by the writers as a figurative use of SALVE *v.*[1]: see SALVE *v.*[1] 4.

1596 SPENSER *F.Q.* IV. iv. 27 To salve his name And purchase honour to his friends behalve. **1605** B. JONSON *Volpone* IV. ii, I devised a formal tale That salv'd your reputation. **1628** HOBBES tr. *Thucyd.* I. (1629) 65 *marg.*, The Oracles were alwayes obscure, that evasion might be found to salue their credit. **1636** MASSINGER *Bashful Lover* V. i, My onely Child Being provided for, her honor salv'd too. **1657** W. MORICE *Cœna quasi Κοινή* Pref. 9 The gentleman hath in one respect salved the honor of his judgement. **1689** EVELYN *Diary* 15 Jan., They were all for a Regency, thereby to salve their oathes. **1697** T. SMITH *Voy. Constantinople* in *Misc. Cur.* (1708) III. 7 The Seamen, to salve their Credit, and to excuse their Error,.. pretended that we were set in by a strong Current. **1698** FRYER *Acc. E. India & P.* 262 He was forced to make use of an Equivocation to salve his Oath. *a* **1711** KEN *Christophil* Poet. Wks. 1721 I. 433 His Truth in Threats to punish Guilt, Was salv'd in Blood of Jesus spilt. **1803** MALTHUS *Popul.* IV. vii. (1806) II. 402 Those who believe that the character of a woman is salved by such a forced engagement. **1814** SOUTHEY *Roderick* XXII. 133 An afterthought to salve decorum.

b. *refl.* To save one's credit.

1657 W. MORICE *Cœna quasi Κοινή* xii. 156 Unless perhaps they can think to salve themselves by saying [etc.].

c. With *from*: To clear from a charge or imputation of.

1685 DRYDEN *Thren. August.* 243 Charles left behind no harsh decree For schoolmen with laborious art To salve from cruelty.

d. To save the credit of (an author).

1646 SIR T. BROWNE *Pseud. Ep.* IV. ii. 182 In these considerations must Aristotle be salved, when hee affirmeth the heart of man is placed in the left side.

salve (sælv), *v.*[3] [Back-formation from SALVAGE.] *trans.* To save (a ship, its cargo) from loss at sea; to save (property) from destruction by fire; to make salvage of.

1706 PHILLIPS (ed. Kersey), To *Salve*, to save or preserve: as *To Salve a Ship or the Goods of it.* **1715** *Lond. Gaz.* No. 5330/3 Clarets and White Wines salved.. out of two Dutch Ships lost in January. **1796** J. TROUTBECK *Scilly Isl.* 229 Part of her cargo was driven on shore, and.. consisted of wine and oil. After it was salved, some of the inhabitants insisted on one half in kind. **1888** in *Pall Mall G.* 1 June 10/2 In 1886 this gun was salved, having lain nearly 100 years below the sea. **1901** *Scotsman* 11 Mar. 8/7 The Steamer.. has stranded at the entrance to the harbour: means are being taken to lighten and salve her.

absol. **1885** *Daily Tel.* 21 Dec. (Cassell), Crews of twenty boats scattered all over the islands are salving as quickly as they can.

Hence **salved** *ppl. a.*, **'salving** *vbl. sb.* and *ppl. a.*

1869 *Pall Mall G.* 4 Oct. 7/2 The wreck lying in a favourable position for salving operations. **1884** SIR N. LINDLEY in *Law Rep.* 9 *Probate Div.* 203 The salving vessel is often herself exposed to imminent peril. **1893** *Westm. Gaz.* 8 Feb. 8/3 The value of the salved vessel was £225,000. **1899** F. T. BULLEN *Log Sea-waif* 113 The small craft which clung to our side receiving the salved cargo.

salve, obs. form of SAFE, SAVE.

†**salve'diction.** *Obs.*[—0] [f. L. *salvē* hail, imp. of *salvēre* to be well, after VALEDICTION.] Salutation on meeting.

1668 WILKINS *Real Char.* 237 *Salvediction*, accost, greet, hail. **1674** BLOUNT *Glossogr.* (ed. 4), *Salvediction*, a greeting or bidding God save.

†**salvee.** *Obs.* [Precise formation uncertain: cf. SALVE *sb.*[3]] A SALVO (of fire-arms).

1632 *Swed. Intelligencer* II. 169 Teaching them especially how to give a Charge or Salvee; some upon their knees, others behind them stooping forward; and the hindmost ranke standing upright, and all to give fire at once. *c* **1651** G. GORDON *Contin. Hist. Earls Sutherld.* (1813) 526 At the first incounter they gave the Lord Gordon a salvee of shot from the folds, where he was slayn, with dyvers others.

salvelin, -ine ('sælvɪlɪn), *a. Ichth.* [ad. mod.L. *salvelīnus* sb. (Linnæus), specific name of the char, prob. ad. Ger. *salbling* (in 17th c. *salvelin*, Willughby *Hist. Pisc.* 195): see SAIBLING.] Belonging to the species (now usually regarded as a sub-genus or genus) *Salmo salvelinus*, the char.

1804 SHAW *Gen. Zool.* V. I. 59 [heading of page] Salvelin Trout. **1891** *Century Dict.*, *Salveline.*

salvenap, variant form of SANAP.

†**'salver**[1]. *Obs. rare.* Also salvour. [f. SALVE *v.* + -ER[1].] One who salves or heals; applied to Christ or the Virgin Mary.

14.. *Tundale's Vis.* (1843) 146 Heyle tho saluer of our solace. *c* **1430** *Hymns Virg.* (1867) 4 Heil comeli queene,.. Heil þe saluour of al sore! *c* **1440** *York Myst.* xxv. 507 Hayll! saluer of our sores sere. *a* **1500–34** *Coventry Corpus Chr. Plays, Weavers* 956 But I troo amonst vs he [Christ] be sent To be the saluer of owre sore.

salver[2] ('sælvə(r)). Also 7 salvor. [Formed (with suffix *-er* after *platter* or some other word of like meaning) on F. *salve* (1666 in Hatz.-Darm.), a tray used for presenting certain objects to the king, ad. Sp. *salva* (= Pg. *salva*), primarily 'a foretasting, as to a prince' (Minsheu 1617), the 'assaying' of food or drink (= CREDENCE *sb.* 6), and hence a tray or salver on which the cup was placed when the tasting had shown that its contents were free from danger (cf. CREDENCE *sb.* 7), f. *salvo* SAFE *a.* or *salvar* to save, render safe, to 'assay' food or drink. Cf. the synon. SERVER (late 17th c.).

Minsheu 1617 explains Sp. *salva* as 'the lid of the cup, in which it is customary to taste the drink before presenting it to a prince', but this is perh. a misunderstanding.]

A tray, used for handing refreshments or for presenting letters, visiting-cards, etc.

For the earlier sense, see quot. 1661.

1661 BLOUNT *Glossogr.* (ed. 2), *Salver* (from *salvo*, to save) is a new fashioned peece of wrought plate, broad and flat, with a foot underneath, and is used in giving Beer, or other liquid thing, to save the Carpit or Cloathes from drops. **1685** in Swayne *Sarum Churchw. Acc.* (1896) 242 Presented for the use of this Ch. one Silver Salver. **1685** *Lond. Gaz.* No. 2068/4, 3 Silver Porringers, 3 Salvors one of them deep, two flat. **1687** A. LOVELL tr. *Thevenot's Trav.* I. 160 These Dishes have feet like our Salvers, but almost half a Foot high. **1701** FARQUHAR *Sir H. Wildair* II. i, Where are my new japan salvers? **1729** SWIFT *Direct. Serv.* i. Wks. 1751 XIV. 19 Gather the Droppings and Leavings, out of the several Cups and Glasses and Salvers, into one. **1731** POPE *Ep. Burlington* 159 Between each Act the trembling salvers ring, From soup to sweetwine, and God bless the King. **1745** *De Foe's Eng. Tradesman* xxii. (1841) I. 207 Six fine large silver salvers to serve sweetmeats. **1759** *Compl. Lett.-writer* (ed. 6) 229 The company treated.. with morning salvers of champaigne. **1818** SCOTT *Hrt. Midl.* xl, Nor would he permit her to break off a fragment, and lay the rest on the salver. **1842** MRS. KIRKLAND *Forest Life* I. 238 Great trays of tea and coffee and bounteous salvers of cake, biscuits [etc.]. **1866** MRS. GASKELL *Wives & Dau.* xv, Always brings in a letter on a salver. **1874** WHYTE MELVILLE *Uncle John* xiv. II. 96 A ubiquitous mess-waiter.. presently appeared with the visitor's card on a salver. **1888** M. ROBERTSON *Lombard St. Myst.* iv, On the silver salver enriching the hall-table.

†**b.** ? A dish on which a jelly or the like is served up for the table.

1747–96 MRS. GLASSE *Cookery* xxi. 332 If you want it for the middle, turn it out upon a salver. **1769** MRS. RAFFALD *Eng. Housekpr.* (1778) 187 When you turn them [the jellies] out, dip your bason in warm water,.. then turn your dish or salver upon the top of your bason, and turn your bason upside down.

c. *Comb.* **salver-shaped** *a.* (*Bot.*) = HYPOCRATERIFORM.

1760 J. LEE *Introd. Bot.* I. iii. (1776) 7 Hypocrateriform, Salver-shaped. **1776–96** WITHERING *Brit. Plants* (ed. 3) II. 218 Vinca.. Bloss. salver-shaped. **1849** BALFOUR *Man. Bot.* §380 Hypocrateriform or salver-shaped [corolla], when there is a straight tube surmounted by a flat spreading limb, as in Primula. **1877–84** F. E. HULME *Wild Fl.* p. x, Larger Periwinkle.—Corolla salver-shaped.

salver, obs. form of SALVOR.

salverform ('sælvəfɔːm), *a. Bot.* [f. SALVER[2] + -FORM.] = HYPOCRATERIFORM. (Cf. SALVER[2] c.)

1821 W. P. C. BARTON *Flora N. Amer.* I. 37 Corolla salverform. **1880** [see HYPOCRATERIMORPHOUS].

salvetee, -ie, obs. forms of SAFETY.

salvia ('sælvɪə). *Bot.* and *Gardening.* [L. *salvia* SAGE *sb.*[1]] A large genus (J.P. de Tournefort *Institutiones Rei Herbariæ* (1700) I. 180), of *Labiatæ*, including the common sage; a plant of this genus (in popular use, chiefly applied to the ornamental varieties). Also *attrib.* and *fig.*

1844 LADY G. FULLERTON *Ellen Middleton* (1854) II. xiv. 149 Some sprigs of the deep red salvia were fastened in her hair. **1873** 'OUIDA' *Pascarel* III. 43 There were great bands of scarlet salvia blossoming. **1884** ROE *Nat. Ser. Story* ix, The flower beds flamed with geraniums and salvias. **1900** MRS. DEVEREUX in *Academy* 3 Feb. 104/1 Terraces radiant with red salvia, and golden with orange trees. **1923** D. H. LAWRENCE *Birds, Beasts & Flowers* 66 If there were salvia-savage Bolshevists To burn the world back to manure-good ash, Wouldn't I stick the salvia in my coat! **1941** E. P. O'DONNELL *Great Big Doorstep* ii. 28 There were humming-birds working around a wild salvia bush in the grove. **1963** W. BLUNT *Of Flowers & a Village* 222 Mrs. Stringer insisted upon my going round to see her salvias.

sal'vific, *a.* [ad. late L. *salvific-us* saving, f. *salv-us*: see SAFE *a.* and -FIC.] Tending to save, causing salvation.

1591 R. BRUCE *Serm.* v. M 2 b, The mair that this Countrie is watered by that saluifik and heauenlie dewe. *a* **1660** HAMMOND *On Hebr.* xiii. 15 The sacrifice of salvifick praise. **1667** WATERHOUSE *Fire Lond.* 65 There is most use for them, when their presence is salvifique and repulsive. *a* **1711** KEN *Christophil* Poet. Wks. 1721 I. 511 To Souls born blind, their cheerful Sight, The Radiance of Salvifick Light. **1946** R. A. KNOX *Epistles & Gospels* 223 A salvific law, promising life to Israel only, might have seemed to contravene them [*sc.* the promises of God]; not a purely damnific Law like that of Sinai. **1958** *Times Lit. Suppl.* 17 Oct. 599/3 Stephen would have seen in the Crucifixion nothing 'salvific', but only the latest in a series of crimes committed against the prophets of the pure religion of Moses. **1967** E. R. FAIRWEATHER in Clark & Davey *Anglican/R.C. Dialogue* (1974) iv. 49 Anglican theology has revealed no sympathy with .. any other doctrine which would minimize the reality and the salvific role of Christ's human will. **1979** J. HICK in M. Goulder *Incarnation & Myth* vi. 199 It is no longer acceptable .. to assume the salvific uniqueness of one's own religion.

†**sal'vifical**, *a.* *Obs.* [See -AL[1].] = prec.

1581 STUBBES *Two Wunderf. Examp.* in *Shaks. Soc. Papers* (1849) IV. 85 Or els we neuer can be saued by Jesus Christ his death, A sacrifice saluificall to them that liue by faithe. **1637** BP. REYNOLDS *Serm. July 12th* (1638) 39 The Foundation of Salvation, whatsoever things are simply and absolutely necessary to the spirituall, vitall, and salvificall state of Christian. **1642** J. JACKSON *Bk. Conscience* 58 That faith is .. no true, justifying, salvificall faith. **1654** VILVAIN *Theol. Treat.* Ep. Ded. 1 Such [things] as concern our Souls salubrity or salvifical felicity. **1678** T. JONES *Heart & Right Sov.* 586 He is of this salvifical church.

Hence †**sal'vifically** *adv.*

1682 SIR T. BROWNE *Chr. Mor.* II. §11 There is but One Who died salvifically for us.

salving ('sɑːvɪŋ, 'sælv-), *vbl. sb.*[1] [f. SALVE *v.*[1] + -ING[1].] The action of anointing with salve (*lit.* and *fig.*); healing as if with salve, soothing. †Also semi-*concr.*, a healing application.

a **1300** *Cursor M.* 29020 Saluing þat es for þe fot es noght for mans heued bote. *c* **1440** *York Myst.* x. 334 Harke sone! sum saluyng of our sare. **1584** *Mirr. Mag.* 24 For the saluynge of which, and all other Infirmyties, of the commonwealth, her Godly wisdome .. established many Medicinable Lawes. **1587** GOLDING *De Mornay* xii. (1592) 177 Hauing recourse .. to searing, cutting, launcing, and sawuing of euery sore. **1669** W. SIMPSON *Hydrol. Chym.* 330 Some waters are better .. for .. washing, brewing, salving, boyling of meat. **1805** R. W. DICKSON *Pract. Agric.* II. 1154 On the approach of winter, they are .. brought home in order to undergo the operation of smearing or salving. **1867** LADY HERBERT *Cradle L.* vii. 183 Though a Moslem he drinks wine, but says aloud for the salving of his conscience, 'It is only sugar and water'. **1887** *Athenæum* 3 Dec. 745/1 There is no commonplace salving of her wounds by the provision of an earl or a viscount in the third volume.

†**'salving**, *vbl. sb.*[2] *Obs.* [f. SALVE *v.*[2] + -ING[1].] In senses of the vb.

1575 in W. H. Turner *Select. Rec. Oxford* (1880) 369 Therw[th] a salving allwaies of y[e] libertie of y[e] Cittie. **1590** SPENSER *F.Q.* II. i. 20 Now therefore, Lady, rise out of your paine, And see the salving of your blotted name. **1656** tr. *Hobbes' Elem. Philos.* (1839) 447 But how little soever some bodies may be, yet I will not suppose their quantity to be less than is requisite for the salving of the phenomena. **1678** CUDWORTH *Intell. Syst.* Pref. 6 Epicurus .. did by violence introduce Liberty of Will, into his Hypothesis; for the Salving whereof, he ridiculously devized, That his Third Motion of Atoms.

salving ('sɑːvɪŋ, 'sælv-), *ppl. a.* [f. SALVE *v.*[1] + -ING[2].] Healing as with salve, soothing.

1748 RICHARDSON *Clarissa* (1811) III. xli. 242 This was what I returned, with warmth, and with a salving art, too.

‖**Salvinia** (sæl'vɪnɪə). [mod.L., named by Micheli in 1729 after Antonio Maria *Salvini* (1653–1729), a Greek scholar of Florence.] The typical genus of the N.O. *Salviniaceæ* of small cryptogamous plants; a plant of this genus.

1887 *Athenæum* 7 May 610/3 The ferns with the salvinias and marsilias are united into one group.

Hence **salvini'aceous** *a.*, pertaining to the N.O. *Salviniaceæ*.

1858 MAYNE *Expos. Lex.*, *Salviniaceus*, applied by Bartling to a Family (*Salviniaceæ* ..), having the *Salvinia* for their type: salviniaceous. **1895** in *Funk's Stand. Dict.*

salviol ('sælvɪɒl). *Chem.* [f. L. *salvi-a* SAGE *sb.*[1] + -OL.] A liquid body present in oil of sage.

1877 MUIR & SUGIURA in *Lond.*, etc. *Philos. Mag.* 5th Ser. IV. 345 For this liquid, which represents the oxidized liquid constituent of sage-oil, we propose the name of salviol.

salvo ('sælvəʊ), *sb.*[1] [a. L. *salvō*, abl. neut. sing. of *salvus* uninjured, intact, SAFE *a.*, as occurring in med.L. law phrases like *salvo servicio forinseco*, 'foreign service excepted', *salvo jure* (*jūre* abl. sing. of *jūs* right) 'without prejudice to the right of' (some specified person).]

1. A saving clause; a provision that a certain engagement or ordinance shall not be binding where it would interfere with a specified right or obligation; a reservation. Const. *of*, †*to* (a right, etc.).

1642 tr. *Perkins' Prof. Bk.* x. §650 (1657) 241 In this case, this *Salvo* shall make the Donee to hold of the Donor by Knights service. **1647** N. BACON *Disc. Govt. Eng.* I. xli. (1739) 68 In case any one died intestate, the Children should equally divide the Goods; which I take to be understood with a salvo of the Wife's Dower or Portion. **1648** *Eikon Bas.* xiv. 114 They admit anie man's senses of it, though divers, or contrarie; with anie salvo's, cautions and reservations. **1655** *Clarke Papers* (Camden) III. 22 If they could propose any expedient with a salvo to the security of that Nation, hee was willinge to answer their desires therein. **1667** WATERHOUSE *Fire Lond.* 172 Neither let the condition of Books .. and Records burnt or lost, be unprovided for by some Good and Grave Salvo, pleadable for the Loosers Indempnitie. **1716** ADDISON *Freeholder* No. 53 ¶7 However any one may concur, .. it is still .. with a Salvo to his own private Judgment. **1754** HUME *Hist. Eng.* (1761) I. viii. 176 In these words was virtually implied a salvo for the rights of their order. **1819** J. MILNER *End Relig. Controv.* (ed. 2) 100 Judges have even refused to admit the following Salvo in addition to the Subscription. **1826** C. BUTLER *Life Grotius* vi. 105 With an express salvo of their right to liberty of conscience. **1849** MACAULAY *Hist. Eng.* ix. II. 532 He .. wished to find out some salvo which might sooth his conscience. **1865** BUSHNELL *Vicar. Sacr.* (1868) 109 A qualification, or salvo, that very nearly unchristianizes Christianity itself. **1875** STUBBS *Const. Hist.* II. xiv. 155 It contained a salvo of the rights of the nation.

†**b.** Reservation of a point in dispute. *Obs.*

a **1644** LAUD *Troub. & Trial* (1695) 274 Here I desired a Salvo, till I might bring Arch-Bishop Parker's Book, to shew his Judgment in this Point.

2. In unfavourable sense: A dishonest mental reservation; a quibbling evasion; a consciously bad excuse.

1665 SIR T. HERBERT *Trav.* (1677) 166 Within Spahawn I found that Column or Pillar of Heads of Men and Beasts which was erected as a Salvo and expiation of the King's Oath. **1677** GILPIN *Demonol.* (1867) 78 Some pitiful salvo or silly evasion to blind the eyes. **1699** BENTLEY *Phal.* xiv. 479 This looks now like a Salvo to come off with Mr. B. and to reconcile the New Piece and the Old together; but it's perfectly a Banter upon him. **1709** STEELE *Tatler* No. 73 ¶12 The new Salvo to satisfy a Man's Conscience in sacrificing his Friend. *a* **1711** KEN *Hymnotheo* Poet. Wks. 1721 III. 80 He flatt'ry hated, Counsel well could time, And never studied Salvos for a crime. **1718** HICKES & NELSON *J. Kettlewell* III. xliv. 299 Most also did seem bent to take up with any Shift or Salvo, which might ease them of such Duties. **1747** RICHARDSON *Clarissa* (1811) I. xxxv. 261 There never was a rogue who had not a salvo to himself for being so. **1757** J. EDWARDS *Orig. Sin* (1837) II. II. i. 135 This evasion of Salvo is so far from helping the matter, or salving the inconsistence, that it increases and multiplies it. **1809** MALKIN *Gil Blas* x. x. (Rtldg.) 369 My tongue gave consent; but with a salvo in my heart .. to give him the slip just at the moment of embarkation. **1828** J. W. CROKER *Diary* 26 Aug., Some new attempt on his part to find a salvo for staying in office. **1858** MERIVALE *Rom. Emp.* liv. (1865) VI. 400 For all the iniquities he himself practised, he had no doubt a salvo in his own breast.

†**b.** ***under the salvo of***: on pretext of. *Obs.*

1705 tr. *Bosman's Guinea* 471 After having taken our Leaves under the Salvoe of a chearful Glass, we weighed Anchor.

†**3.** A solution, explanation (of a difficulty), an answer (to an objection). *Obs.*

1659 *Gentl. Calling* viii. §25 Let not men therefore pretend the fear of reproach, as an excuse, since here is so ready a salvo for that objection. **1678** CUDWORTH *Intell. Syst.* 305 Some of the ancient and learned Fathers .. apprehended this to be a convenient Salvo for this Difficulty, to suppose that Orpheus had by Fits and Turns, been of different Humours and Perswasions. **1691** T. H[ALE] *Acc. New Invent.* p. cii, Great men are like the heavenly bodies that find much veneration but no rest, unless we find a Salvo for their having the latter, by saying what the Philosophers do of the Heavens, that *Movendo quiescunt*. **1770** FOOTE *Lame Lover* II. Wks. 1799 II. 71 *Jack*. But then how comes the note to remain in plaintiff's possession? *Serj*. Well put, Jack; but we have a salvo for that.

4. An expedient for saving (a person's reputation) or soothing (offended pride, conscience).

Cf. obs. F. *salve-d'honneur*, and the med.L. phrase *salvo honore*.

1754 RICHARDSON *Grandison* (1781) III. xvii. 138 Lady L. .. cannot help throwing in a salvo for the pride of her Sex. **1771** *Junius Lett.* xlii. (1820) 221 As a salvo for his own reputation, he has been advised to traduce the character of a brave officer. **1778** *Ann. Reg., Hist. Europe* 64 The minister was humorously advised, as the only means of extricating himself from that dilemma, and as affording the only salvo in his power for the indignity offered to that House, to impeach those ministers. **1784** J. BARRY in *Lect. Paint.* v. (1848) 180 This account of the matter affords the most favourable salvo for their reputation. **1792** *Anecd. W. Pitt* xxxix. (1810) II. 184 The only object of the present negotiation is to find a salvo for the punctilious honour of the Spaniards. **1855** MOTLEY *Dutch Rep.* v. ii. (1866) 678 This would be a salvo for the disgrace of removing them. **1874** H. R. REYNOLDS *John Bapt.* viii. 513 The law .. is transformed into a salvo to conscience, by which others are condemned rather than self rectified.

salvo ('sælvəʊ), *sb.*[2] In 6 salva. [Originally *salva*, a. It. *salva* (whence F. *salve*) = Sp., Pg. *salva* salutation, salvo, perh. a Common Rom. formation on L. *salvē* hail! (see SAFE *a.*).

The change from *-a* to *-o* in the ending of words from It., Sp., and Pg. is common: cf. -ADO.]

1. A salute consisting in the simultaneous discharge of artillery or other firearms.

1719 D'URFEY *Pills* (1872) III. 347 Display the Standard, let the News be shown, With Salvos raise the Genius of the Town. **1815** J. SCOTT *Vis. Paris* App. (ed. 2) 319 Salvoes of artillery were fired on the evening of the 24th to announce the commencement of the fête. **1834** E. EVERETT *Orations & Sp.* (1850) I. 522 When your cannons proclaimed his advent with joyous salvos. **1852** THACKERAY *Esmond* II. ix, Salvos of cannon saluting him. **1860** MOTLEY *Netherl.* (1868) II. xix. 485 Those ships of Spain, which lay there, .. discharging salvoes of anticipated triumph.

attrib. **1808** SCOTT *Marm.* I. iv, And, from the platform, spare ye not To fire a noble salvo-shot.

2. a. A simultaneous discharge of artillery or other firearms, whether with hostile intent or otherwise.

The earliest sense in Eng.; it was developed already in Italian.

1591 *Garrard's Art Warre* 11 If .. his company be commanded to discharge certain volies of shot, or a salua, he must either hold his Peece side-long the ranckes, or [etc.]. **1719** DE FOE *Crusoe* II. (Globe) 569 As we found them [the enemy] within Gun-shot, our Leader ordered the two Wings to advance swiftly and give them a Salvo on each Wing with their Shot. **1826** SCOTT *Woodst.* xvii, After bursting their gates with a salvo of our cannon. **1828** J. M. SPEARMAN *Brit. Gunner* (ed. 2) 83 Occasionally firing salvoes at the part to be brought down. **1879** FIFE-COOKSON *Armies of Balkans* viii. 124 The Russians .. were firing salvoes by batteries of eight guns. **1902** 'LINESMAN' *Words Eyewitness* 93 When a movement of men was discernible on the ridge, a salvo was discharged, and the blow .. would alter the shape of the rocks before our very eyes.

b. *transf.*

[Cf. F. *salve d'applaudissements*, etc.]

a **1734** NORTH *Exam.* III. vii. §95 (1740) 578 All which was performed with fitting Salvos of the Rabble echoed from the Club. **1845** E. HOLMES *Mozart* 277 Amidst deafening salvos of applause. **1860** HAWTHORNE *Marb. Faun* xlix, The fair occupants of the balcony favored Kenyon with a salvo of confetti. **1875** G. JACQUE *Hope*, etc. ii. 16 Peals of laughter break out here and there The dread sardonic salvos of despair. **1895** ZANGWILL *Master* II. viii. 221 A great round of applause from their ranks set everybody peering towards the door, only to encounter the stern gaze of the magnificent beadle, whose entry had prompted the salvoes. **1924** 'W. FRANK' (*title*) Salvos, an informal book about books and plays. **1955** *Times* 26 May 4/3 It [*sc.* a broadsheet] was intended to be the 'hush-hush' weapon, which by triumphant revelation at the last moment and, by its powerful propaganda salvo, would bring to submission any wavering voters still about. **1971** *Daily Tel.* (Colour Suppl.) 21 May 18/3 They can stay on deck, .. watch salvoes of gannets plummet in white streaks to the sea. **1977** W. M. SPACKMAN *Armful of Warm Girl* 43 He bought her the Hindu nose-jewel .. and gently slipped it on (which with little salvoes of apologetic kisses she had at once slipped off, and never worn again).

c. Of rockets, etc.

1799 [G. SMITH] *Laboratory* I. 38 Of Salvo's. These, in fire-works, are a great number of strong iron reports, fixed either in a post or plank, and, with a fire, discharged at once. **1895** *Funk's Standard Dict.* s.v., A salvo of rockets.

d. Of bombs dropped from aircraft.

1942 *R.A.F. Jrnl.* 27 June 36 A .. change of course saved the ship from a direct hit from the salvo dropped by the leading aircraft. **1949** *Sun* (Baltimore) 17 Oct. 1/5 These loads are dropped either in 'chain' (a trail of bombs, blasting out a path between two and three miles long) or in 'salvo', where the scores of 500-pounders tumble out of the bays together in an 'area' bombing operation.

†**3.** A salutation or salute. *Obs. rare.*

1653 H. COGAN tr. *Pinto's Trav.* xxiv. 89 Whereupon with great devotion and zeal we sung a Salvo, before an image of Our Lady. **1755** *Mem. Capt. P. Drake* II. viii. 218 Whenever an Opportunity offered, to .. meet her in the Street, I would give her a Hat Salvo, with a low Bow.

Salvo ('sælvəʊ), *sb.*[3] *Austral. colloq.* [f. SALV(ATIONIST + -O[2].] A member of the Salvation Army; *pl.*, the Salvation Army.

1896 *Bulletin* (Sydney) 31 Oct. 27 (*title*) The Salvo's Error. **1908** C. H. S. MATTHEWS *Parson in Austral. Bush* xxvii. 256 Well, I was rared a Carthlick, but I haven't followed it up much. To tell ye the truth, I class 'em all alike —priests, parsons, 'salvos', and all the lot of 'em. **1942** J. SWEENEY in Murdoch & Drake-Brockman *Austral. Short Stories* (1951) 382 We come to the Salvo hut where there is a big joker sitting on a form drinking coffee and eating biscuits. **1952** J. CLEARY *Sundowners* iii. 144 I've only met one other Rupert.. . That was when I was in the Salvos. **1962** A. UPFIELD *Will of Tribe* ix. 87 Can't help bringing out old clichés. The Salvo padre at Derby was down on them but we learned them quick. **1968** *Telegraph* (Brisbane) 29 June 16/6 Hundreds of former Diggers have similar stories of the morale-boosting work done by the 'Salvos'. **1978** R. MCKIE *Bitter Bread* 77 When workers everywhere got their notices and the slump showed every sign of lasting, the Salvos decided to open a doss house.

'salvo, *v.* [f. SALVO *sb.*[2]] *trans.* To salute (a vessel, etc.) by firing of a salvo or volley of guns; to drop a salvo of (bombs). Also *transf.*

1839 MARRYAT *Phant. Ship* viii, See the gunners ready with their linstocks to salvo the supercargo. **1895** H. G. HUTCHINSON *Peter Steele, Cricketer* vii. 155 He had just made his century, and been salvoed with applause. **1943** *Yank* 17 Dec. 5 The pilot feathered the props and kept on; the Fort limped in over the target and salvoed its bombs.

‖**'salvo**, *prep. rare*[−1]. [L. *salvō*: see SALVO *sb.*[1]] Excepting, saving.
1601 A. C[OPLEY] *Answ. Let. Jesuited Gentl.* 19 Let them either yet make amends.. or else be sure that they sit fast; for that (*saluo* the Appeale) they are like to carrie as good as they bring.

‖**salvoconducto** (ˌsalvokon'dukto). [Sp.: see SAFE-CONDUCT *sb.*] A pass, safe-conduct.
1955 W. GADDIS *Recognitions* II. vi. 545 What happened! What happened to Huss? John Huss, enticed by a salvoconducto up to Constance, where three bishops sat on his case, and he was burned. **1957** P. KEMP *Mine were of Trouble* i. 13 Just beyond the Spanish barrier we halted; Vicuña went into the control hut to report and to collect my *salvoconducto*.

sal volatile (ˌsæl vəˈlætɪlɪ). [a. mod.L. *sal volătile* 'volatile salt': see SAL and VOLATILE *a.*] Ammonium carbonate, *esp.* an aromatic solution of this used as a restorative in fainting fits.
1654 GAYTON *Pleas. Notes* IV. v. 197 'Tis that fire, that *sal volatile* which makes them of so strange agility. **1709** *Female Tatler* No. 16/3 Betty ran for a Glass of Water, her Sister, for the Sal-Volatile. **1727** SWIFT, etc. *Further Acc. E. Curll* Wks. 1755 III. I. 160 A sufficient quantity of the vivifying drops, or Byfield's *sal volatile*. **1833** *Penny Cycl.* I. 458/1 A preparation called in the *Pharmacopœia*, *Spiritus Ammoniæ Aromaticus*, and commonly *Spirit of Sal Volatile*. **1880** MRS. FORRESTER *Roy & V.* I. 124 Let me send for a glass of wine or some *sal-volatile*.
attrib. **1731** FIELDING *Lottery* iii, Here are some hartshorn and sal-volatile drops.

salvor ('sælvə(r), 'sælvɔː(r)). Forms: 7–8 **salver**, 9– **salvor**. [f. SALVE *v.* + -OR.]
1. One who saves or helps to save vessels or cargo from loss at sea; one who effects or attempts salvage.
1678 *Lond. Gaz.* No. 1277/4 A.. Ketch,.. being forsaken by all her men, was.. taken up by John Duncke.. and by him brought into that Port, and there secured by the Saluer until the right Proprietor shall appear and make out his Propriety. **1706** PHILLIPS (ed. Kersey), *Salver*, one that has sav'd a Ship or its Merchandizes. **1802** ABBOTT *Law Merch. Ships* III. x. 322 The labor and peril incurred by the salvors. **1839** STORY *Bailments* §622. 391 Wherever a ship and cargo, or any part thereof, are saved at sea by the exertions of any persons from impending perils, or are recovered after an actual abandonment or loss, such persons are denominated salvors; and they are entitled to a compensation for their services, which is known by the name of salvage. **1883** *Times* 28 Nov. 9 The salvors, at great personal risk, put off in a small skiff. **1885** RUNCIMAN *Skippers & Sh.* 61 The captain is beset by a gang of salvors.
b. One who saves or attempts to save some one from drowning.
1890 *Daily News* 16 Oct. 7/1 Among the.. cases of saving, or attempting to save life from drowning.. there are 13 in which the salvors' ages ranged from eight years to 16. **1891** *Ibid.* 24 Oct. 2/6 Watching the peril in which the salvor and his burden were placed.
2. A vessel used in salvage.
1815 DODSON *Adm. Rep.* I. 415 The question was, whether the post-office packet the *Eliza* was to be considered the sole salvor, or jointly with H.M. brig the *Challenger*. **1880** *Libr. Univ. Knowl.* (N.Y.) XIII. 83 Those who navigate the saved ship into port.. [have] double the share of those who remain on the salvor vessel.

salvor, obs. f. SALVER[2].

salvour, var. SALVER[1].

salvy ('sælvɪ, 'sɑːvɪ), *a. dial.* and *U.S.* [f. SALVE *sb.*[1] + -Y[1].] (See quots.)
1861 *Trans. Ill. Agric. Soc.* IV. 103 Care should be taken not to work it too much, as it will hurt the grain of the butter and make it salvy. **1884** SHELDON in *West. Daily Press* 24 May 3/6 It is this oxydation of the curd.. which.. develops the flavour of the cheese, and mellows down the casein into a salvy and textureless mass. **1887** *S. Chesh. Gloss.*, *Sauvy*, (1) of curd, greasy, buttery; (2) *metaph.* unctuous of speech and manner. **1887** *Kentish Gloss.*, *Salvey*, close, soapy; spoken of potatoes that are not floury. **1891** *Century Dict.*, *Salvy*, like salve or ointment. **1895** *Funk's Stand. Dict.*, *Salvy*, unctuous. **1907** *Daily Chron.* 16 July 4/4 British cheese should be mild, nutty, and salvy.

salwar, var. SHALWAR.

salweour, obs. form of SAVIOUR.

salw(h)e, saly(e, obs. forms of SALLOW.

Salyrgan ('sælәgәn). *Pharm.* Also **salyrgan**. A proprietary name (orig. used in Germany) for MERSALYL.
1924 *Official Gaz.* (U.S. Patent Office) 10 June 270/1 H.A. Metz Laboratories, Inc., New York,.. *Salyrgan*... Preparations for the treatment of spirochetal and other infectious diseases and as a diuretic. Claims use since about Apr. 11, 1924. **1924** *Trade Marks Jrnl.* 15 Oct. 2285 *Salyrgan*... Farbwerke vorm. Meister Lucius & Brüning... Hoechst am Main, Germany; Manufacturers.—16th August 1924. **1928** *Canad. Med. Assoc. Jrnl.* XVIII. 45/1 Salyrgan was first introduced as an antiluetic mercurial agent. **1956** *Internat. Rev. Cytol.* V. 223 Experiments.. indicate that salyrgan strongly inhibits the hydrolytic splitting of the high-energy phosphate bonds of ATP. **1976** *Amer. Jrnl. Clin. Path.* LXV. 685/1 High concentrations of salyrgan.. shortened the lag period.

salys-man, obs. form of SALESMAN.

Sam (sæm), *sb.*[1] *slang.* Also **Sammy**. [Of obscure origin.
Commonly identified with *Sam* shortened form of the Christian name *Samuel*, and hence written with capital S. The two uses may belong to different words.]
1. ***to stand Sam***: to pay expenses, esp. for refreshment or drink.
1823 MONCRIEFF *Tom & Jerry* III. v, Landlady, serve them with a glass of tape, all round; and I'll stand Sammy. **1840** H. COCKTON *Val. Vox* xli, They make John Bull stand Sam. **1887** FARRELL *How He Died* 61 I'll stand Sam this time for Jemima's sake.
2. ***upon my Sam***: a jocular mode of asseveration. Also without const.: an oath, a promise. [Cf. SALMON[2], SANG.]
1879 'FRANK' (F. J. SQUIRES) *Nine Days in Devon* 12 Or 'pon my zam! oi really think as Zal'd a zot on moine. **1899** KIPLING *Stalky* 17 'Pon my sacred Sam, though, it's enough to drive a man to drink. **1939** J. MASEFIELD *Live & Kicking Ned* 115 On that I swop my solemn sam. **1940** M. ALLINGHAM *Black Plumes* xii. 138 Upon my Sam I think you're both mad. **1966** 'J. HACKSTON' *Father clears Out* 71 He'd see that things were righted, upon his Sam he would.

Sam, *sb.*[2] Abbrev. of SAMBO (sense 2).
1867 W. H. DIXON *New Amer.* II. ii. 13 Sam—all negroes there are Sams—may be a Methodist. **1877** L. HEARN *Genius Loci* in *Cincinnati Commercial* 12 Aug. 6/4 I'm Rag-a-back Sam, And I don't care a d——m, Fur I sooner-be a nigger dan a poor white man. **1938** *Amer. Speech* XIII. 152/1 *Sam*, a negro who demeans himself to secure favor with white people. **1964** L. NKOSI *Rhythm of Violence* 4 Black Sams! Why don't they do somethin' so we can handle this once and for all! **1973** K. JOHNSON in T. Kochman *Rappin' & Stylin' Out* 148 *Sam*, a common name of black males, it is used to refer to any black male. In addition, the story character, Sambo, was black; perhaps the label derives from 'Little Black Sambo'.

sam (sæm), *v.*[1] *Obs.* exc. *dial.* Forms: *α.* 1 **samnian**, 3–4 **samen**, **samne** (3 Ormin **sammne-nn**), 4 **samin**, **sammyn**, **samyn**, 4–5 **sammen**, 5 **sampne**; *β.* 4–5 **same**, 4–7 **samme**, 9– *dial.* **sam**. [OE. *samnian*, *sǫmnian*, corresp. to OFris. *somnia*, OS. *samnon* (MLG. *samenen*, *samnen*, *sammen*), MDu. *samenen*, *samnen*, *samen*, OHG. *samanôn* (MHG. *samenen*), ON. *samna*, *safna* :—OTeut. **samanōjan*, f. **samanō* together: see SAMEN *adv.* Synonymous forms, with substitution of *l* for *n*, are MDu. and MLG. *samelen* (Du. *zamelen*), MHG. *samelen* (mod.G. *sammeln*); the Sw. *samla*, Da. *samle*, are from German.
For the ME. forms descending from OE. *sǫmnian*, see †SOMNE *v.*[1] The *β* forms exhibit the same simplification of final *mn* to *m* that appears in the pronunciation of *damn*, *limn*, *contemn*.]
†1. a. *trans.* To assemble (persons). *Obs.*
a **1000** *Daniel* 228 Þa he þyder folc samnode. *a* **1300** *Cursor M.* 2515 Quen he herd þan o þis typand; He did to-geder samen his men. **1338** R. BRUNNE *Chron.* (1810) 100 Whan he had samned his oste of folk fer & nere. *a* **1400–50** *Alexander* 1732 For þou has samed [*Dubl.* sampned], as men sais a selly nounbre Of wrichis & wirlingis out of þe west endis. *c* **1400** *Laud Troy Bk.* 3232 To alle the lordes that there were Were redy dyght and samed there With ther meyne. *c* **1440** *York Myst.* xxxiv. 43 Oure gere behoues to be grayde, And felawes sammed sone.
†b. To bring together, join (in marriage, friendship, love, etc.). *Obs.*
c **1200** ORMIN 322 Þatt Daviþ kingess kinness menn Off weress oþþr off wifess Wiþþ Aaroness kinness menn Off siþre wærenn sammnedd. *a* **1340** HAMPOLE *Psalter* cxxi. 7 Þat neghburs & breþere be samynd in charite.
refl. *a* **1300** *Cursor M.* 2239 Þis fol folk þam sammen þan Brathli þai þis werk bigan. *a* **1300** *E.E. Psalter* xlvi. 10 Princes of folke þai samened þam With þe God of Abraham.
†c. *intr.* for *refl.* To assemble, come together.
[*a* **1000** *Ags. Ps.* (Spelman) xxx. 17 Hi ȝederedon *vel* somnodon samod toȝeanes me.] *c* **1200** ORMIN 2412 Ȝa mihhte ȝho sket affterr þatt Wiþþ hire macche sammnenn. *c* **1250** *Gen. & Ex.* 434 He ches a stede toward eden, And to him sameden ðer men. *c* **1330** R. BRUNNE *Chron. Wace* (Rolls) 1932 Þe names of contres Ben chaunged.. Als straunge folk han hider y-samed.
2. *trans.* To bring together, collect (things); now only *dial.* (Yorks., Lancs., etc.), chiefly with *together*, *up*. †Also in occasional senses: To bring together the edges of (a wound), *OE.*; to join or fasten together; to amass, hoard up; to fill full *of*.
Modern dialectal uses (for which see E.D.D.) are ***to sam up***, to pick up eagerly; ***to sam hold of***, to clutch, grasp.
c **1000** *Sax. Leechd.* II. 22 Þonne samnað hio þa wunde & hælð. *c* **1200** ORMIN 1552 Þu sammnesst all þin mele inn an & cnedesst itt togeddre. **13..** *Gaw. & Gr. Knt.* 659 Vchone.. Ne samned neuer in no syde, ne sundred nouþ[er]. *a* **1400–50** *Alexander* 1520 He plyes ouire þe pauement with pallen webis, Mas on hiȝt ouire his hede for hete of þe sone, Sylours of sendale to sele ouire þe gatis, And sammes [*Dubl.* sampnez] þaim on aithire side with silken rapis. *Ibid.* 5290 Þan scho laches him be-lyfe & ledis him forthire, In-to a clochere with a key þe clennest of þe werde, Was sammed all of sipris & seder-tables. *c* **1400** *Cursor M.* 27762 (Cott. Galba) Slewth oft samnes sorow strang, and þat vnmekely lastand lang. **1824** W. CARR *Horæ Momenta Cravenæ* 11 If shoe nobbud cud git a bit a naturable rist, shoe wod sam up strength fast. **1893** SNOWDEN *Tales Yorksh. Wolds* 168 We sammed together all we could find. **1934** J. B. PRIESTLEY *Eden End* I. 10 I've been up in the back garret, samming up these old clothes for the doctor.
3. To coagulate (†const. *together*). Now only *dial.*, to curdle (milk) for cheese; also *absol.*
1615 CROOKE *Body of Man* 263 There is nothing to be seene but the seede coagulated or sammed together. *Ibid.* 429 Whereby those things which otherwise could hardly be sammed together might receiue their conglutination. **1691** RAY *N.C. Words* (ed. 2), *To samme Milk*, to put the running to it, to curdle it. **1788** W. MARSHALL *Yorksh.* II. 349 'When do you sam?' When do you set your milk? or, When do you make cheese?

sam (sæm), *v.*[2] *Leather Manuf.* Also **samm**. [Of doubtful origin: the explanation in quot. 1870 may point to derivation from some word with SAM- *prefix*.] See quots. Cf. SAMMY *v.* Hence **sammed** *ppl. a.*; **'samming** *vbl. sb.*
1870 *Eng. Mech.* 11 Feb. 534/2 Hang until about half dry, or, technically speaking, 'Sammed'. **1883** R. HALDANE *Workshop Receipts* Ser. II. 367/1 The skins are allowed to drain,.. and after 'samming', or damping with cold water, are staked. **1885** A. WATT *Art of Leather Manuf.* xii. 151 The butts are next piled in a heap to *sam*, or *samm*, as it is termed, for several days, by which the leather becomes tempered or in an uniformly moist and softened condition. **1909** H. G. BENNETT *Manuf. of Leather* xx. 256 *Samming* is an exceedingly important operation by which leather is brought into a uniformly half-dry condition, this state being quite necessary for many of the finishing operations... The 'sammed' condition may be obtained in three ways—by drying out completely and then wetting back by dipping through water (often tepid) and leaving 'in pile' for some hours; by drying the wet goods in suspension to the required consistency and no further, wetting back any parts that have become drier than the bulk and leaving in pile for a time to become uniform; and by machine samming, in which case the superfluous moisture is removed by the pressure of machine rollers.

†sam, *adv. Obs.* Forms: 3–5 **same**, 4–6 **samme**, **sam**. [Shortened form of SAMEN *adv.*] Together; mutually.
For *in sam(e*, see INSAME, I-SAME. For *to sam*, see TO SAME.
13.. *Sir Beues* (A.) 4561 Þe maide & Miles wer spused same In þe toun of Notinghame. **13..** *Cursor M.* 9750 (Gött.), I sal crie pes in lande i-wiss, And dome and pes do sam [*Cott.* samen] þen kis. **13..** *Gaw. & Gr. Knt.* 363 Syþen þay redden alle same, To ryd þe kyng wyth croun. **1390** GOWER *Conf.* II. 240 Doun thei seten bothe same. *c* **1430** *Syr Tryam.* 1127 They seyde, 'God be at yowre game!' He seyde, 'Welcome, alle same!' *c* **1450** *St. Cuthbert* (Surtees) 4895 Þe scottys were gadird sam. *c* **1460** *Towneley Myst.* xii. 179 Now god gyf you care foles all sam. **1513** DOUGLAS *Æneis* VII. iv. 59 And heyr full oft at buyrdis by and by The heris wer wont togiddir syt all sam. *c* **1525** *Tale of Basyn* 8 in Hazl. *E.P.P.* III. 44 Off a parson ȝe mowe here,.. And of his brother that was hym dere, And louyd well samme. **1579** SPENSER *Sheph. Cal.* May 168 For what concord han light and darke sam? *a* **1600** *Flodden F.* ii. (1664) 18 When they were all assembled Sam The town of Edenbrough before, Fifty great Lords there were of Fame. *Ibid.* vii. 68 All Sam the souldiers then replied.

sam- (sæm), *prefix. Obs.* exc. *dial.* [OE. *sam-*, repr. (with vowel-shortening usual in compounds) prehistoric **sǣm-*:—W.Ger. **sâmi-* (e.g. in OS. *sâmquik*, OHG. *sâmiqueck* = OE. *samcucu* 'half-quick', *semianimis*):—OTeut. **sǣmi-*:—Indogermanic **sēmi-*: see SEMI-.] = HALF-, in various adjs. as ***sam-crisp***, ***-dead***, ***-red***, ***-ripe***; **sam-hale**, 'half-whole', in poor health; **sam-sodden**, half cooked, half done; also *fig.* 'half baked', stupid.
c **1425** *Eng. Conq. Irel.* xxxix. 98 Yolowe her & *sam-crysp. **1297** R. GLOUC. (Rolls) 3416 Ȝut ichabbe leuere *samded hom ouercome þan hol & sound be ouercome. *a* **1023** WULFSTAN *Hom.* l. (Napier) 273 Nu ne beoþ naht fela manna ætsamne, ðæt heora sum ne si seoc and *samhal. *a* **1300** *Cursor M.* 5153, I mai noght rise, i am sam-hale. *Ibid.* 13262 Þe sam-hale fast til him þai soght. **1393** LANGL. *P. Pl.* C. IX. 311 Chiboles and chiruylles and chiries *sam-rede [MS. M. *sam-ripe]. *c* **1425** *Eng. Conq. Irel.* xxi. 54 (Dubl. MS.) He was samroed, with grey eghen. *c* **1440** *Ibid.* xxxvi. 89 (Rawl. MS.) The kynge henry the othyr, was a man same rede [*Dubl. MS.* saunrede]. *a* **1000** *Ecgberti Confessionale* §40 Ȝif man awiht blodiȝes þicȝe on healf-sodenum [MSS. X.Y. *sam-sodenum] mete. **1825** JENNINGS *Obs. Dial. W. Eng.* 85 Any thing heated for a long time in a low heat so as to be in part spoiled, is said to be zamzodden. **1891** 'Q.' (Quiller-Couch) *Noughts & Cr.* 97, I'm afeard you'm o' no account,.. but sam-sodden if I may say so.

samaca, samakade: see SAMBOCADE.

‖**samadh** (sə'mɑːd). [See next.] The tomb of a holy man or yogi who is assumed to have achieved samadhi rather than to have died. Cf. SAMADHI 1 b.
1828 *Asiatick Researches* XVI. 39 A temple, sacred to the deity whom they worship, or the *Samádh*, or shrine of the founder of the sect, or some eminent teacher. **1888** KIPLING *Departmental Ditties* (1890) (ed. 4) 80 They made a *samádh* in his honour, A mark for his resting-place. *Ibid.* 82 Thus the *samádh* was perfect, thus was the lesson plain. **1891** MONIER WILLIAMS *Brahmanism & Hinduism* 179 A native of Oudh, whose samadh or tomb is at Katwa. **1964** A. SWINSON *Six Minutes to Sunset* i. 16 A dilapidated domed *samadh* (or tomb).

‖**samadhi** (sə'mɑːdɪ). *Indian Philos.* [Skr. *samādhi* a placing together, f. *sam* together + *ā* prefix + *dhā* to place (see DO *v.*).] **1. a.** The state of union with creation into which a perfected yogi or holy man is said to pass at his apparent death. **b.** The voluntary burial of such a person before death in anticipation of this state; the site of the burial of a holy man (cf. prec.).

1795 *Asiatick Researches* IV. 218 Dhritara'shtra, in the state of *Samadhi*, quitted his terrestrial form to proceed to the..beatitude, which awaited him. **1891** Monier Williams *Brahmanism & Hinduism* 261 When such a man dies in India, his body is not burnt but buried, because in fact he is not supposed to die at all. He is believed to lie in a kind of trance, called Samadhi. **1925** *Glasgow Herald* 24 Sept. 7 The Sadhu did not commit suicide, but performed the religious rite of Samadhi. **1968** *Jrnl. Mus. Acad. Madras* XXXIX. 13 Something more beautiful and commodious must be built at his Samadhi to commemorate his work. **1979** *Times of India* 17 Aug. 34 The Janata party had betrayed the oath taken at Gandhi's samadhi that they would fulfil his dreams of a nationalist, socialist India by forming connections with the RSS, he said.

2. The highest state of meditation, in which the distinctions between subject and object disappear and unity with creation is attained; the last stage of yoga.

1827 *Trans. R. Asiatic Soc.* I. 25 The collection of *Yóga-sútras*..is distributed into four chapters or quarters..: the first on contemplation (*samád'hi*)..[etc.]. **1850** [see dhyana]. **1913** [see raja yoga]. **1939** A. Huxley *After Many a Summer* II. i. 189 Baby..is now walking about in a state of perpetual *samadhi*. **1958** J. Sykes *Quakers* I. i. 31 A moment almost of group samadhi, of the displacement of all by God's Being, and Becoming. **1960** J. Hewitt *Yoga* I. 7 By a programme of bodily and mental self-discipline we who move on lower levels of consciousness can achieve Samadhi (union with divine consciousness). **1965** *New Statesman* 16 Apr. 616/2 Ramakrishna's ability to pass into a trance-like state of 'higher spiritual awareness' known as samadhi. **1971** *Shankar's Weekly* (Delhi) 11 Apr. 22/2 From time to time, the Swamiji would come out of his samadhi to frown at the opening and closing of the compartment door. **1977** L. A. Govinda *Creative Meditation* III. vi. 135 Though samadhi may be the culmination in the meditative experience, we cannot remain in that state..but have to return to the world.

Samain, var. Samhain.

Samaj (sə'mɑːdʒ). Also **Somaj**. [a. Hindi and Bengali *samāj* society, f. Skr. *samāja* a meeting with, f. *sam* together + *aj* to drive.] An assembly or congregation in India; a church or religious body, as in ***Brahmo Samaj*** (see Brahmoism).

1875 C. M. Davies *Unorthodox London* 2nd Ser. (ed. 2) 193 The present representative of the Bramo Somaj in London, was to preach at Mr. Conway's chapel. **1876** *Encycl. Brit.* IV. 201/1 He gave a printing-press to the Samáj. *Ibid.* 201/2 They encourage the establishment of branch Samájes in different parts of the country. **1884** [see progressive *a.* 4]. **1913** J. N. Farquhar *Crown of Hinduism* 76 The truths of religion which they find there are the doctrines taught by the Samāj. **1948** [see sarvodaya]. **1958** W. de Bary et al. *Sources of Indian Tradition* xxii. 629 The Ārya Samāj (the Society of the Āryas, or 'noble men') which he [*sc.* Dayānanda] established at Bombay in 1875 has since reflected the militant character of its founder, and from its stronghold in the Punjab has contributed to the rise of Hindu nationalism.

Saman[1] ('sɑːmən). [a. Skr. *sāman* chant.] A sacred text or verse forming the third of the four kinds of Vedas; the name of the Veda thus formed. Also *attrib.* So **Samaveda** ('sɑːməˌveɪdə), the name of the third Veda.

1798 *Asiatick Researches* V. 364 Prayer..on beginning a lecture of the Samaveda. **1843** *Penny Cycl.* XXVI. 171/1 These are the Rĭch, Yajush, Sâman, and Atharvan'a. *Ibid.*, The Sâmaveda contains songs of lyrical character to be recited with melancholy. **1886** *Encycl. Brit.* XXI. 277/1 The sâman-hymnal consists of two parts, viz., the *Sâmaveda-samhitâ*, or collection of texts (rich) used for making up sâman-hymns, and the *Gâna*, or tune-books. *Ibid.* 278/1 The *Vamśa-brâhmaṇa*, a mere list of the Sâmaveda teachers. **1900** J. G. Frazer *Golden Bough* (ed. 2) I. i. 92 A particular hymn of the ancient Indian collection known as the Samaveda. **1913** J. N. Farquhar *Crown of Hinduism* 77 The *Sāman, Yajus*, and *Atharvan* exhibit the same polytheism. **1954** *Grove's Dict. Mus.* (ed. 5) IV. 456/1 The Sāmans (sacrificial chants) may, though rarely, be heard nowadays. **1968** *Jrnl. Mus. Acad. Madras* XXXIX. 105 *Samkirtana* is in itself *Brahman* and is greater than *Sama-veda*.

saman[2] (sæ'mɑːn). Also **samaan**, **samang**. [a. Amer. Sp. *samán*, f. Carib *zamang*.] = guango, zamang. Also *attrib.*

1888, etc. [see *monkey-pod (tree)* s.v. monkey *sb.* 18b]. **1951** J. C. Fennessy *Sonnet in Bottle* II. iii. 46 The huge tents of the saman trees were islands of blackness in the cooling streams of night air. **1958** G. Lamming *Of Age & Innocence* II. vii. 117 The tall black samaan tree at the curve of the hill-top. **1960** *Times* 10 Mar. 18/3 The saman trees..were full of holders of tree tickets. **1963** [see guango]. **1968** E. Lovelace *Schoolmaster* viii. 120 Christiana was sitting on the trunk of a fallen samaan tree in the shade near the cocoa house. **1974** *Times* 5 Feb. 12/4 Queen's Park Oval is unlike its namesake at Kennington. Where the gasholders should be there are some fine samaan trees, with a range of low, wooded hills right behind them.

Samang, var. Semang.

samango (sæ'mæŋgəʊ). [Native name.] In full, ***samango guenon*** or ***monkey***. An African monkey, *Cercopithecus mitis*, which has blue-grey fur with black markings.

1888 *Proc. Zool. Soc.* 564 The most notable additions during the month were:—..the Small-clawed Otter..the Samango Monkey. **1894** H. O. Forbes *Hand-bk. Primates* II. 71 (*heading*) The Samango Guenon. **1912** J. Stevenson-Hamilton *Animal Life in Afr.* xvi. 260 The Samango monkey..extends from the eastern part of Cape Colony, through Portuguese East Africa, and the whole of Rhodesia. **1932** S. Zuckerman *Social Life Monkeys & Apes* xi. 185 The Samango monkey is encountered in the forests of eastern South Africa. *Ibid.*, Very near where the Samangos were seen, I came across a party of seven Vervet monkeys. **1967** J. R. & P. H. Napier *Handbk. Living Primates* 104 (*caption*) Samango monkey..grooming.

‖**samara** ('sæmərə, sə'mɑːrə). *Bot.* [mod.L. use of L. *samara* or *samera* seed of the elm.] The indehiscent winged fruit of the elm, ash, sycamore (etc.).

1577 B. Googe *Heresbach's Husb.* II. (1586) 103 He that will plante a Groue of Elmes, must gather the seede called Samara. **1731** *Gentl. Mag.* I. 40 Sow the Sameria [*sic*] of the Elm, and Bay-berries, all which come up the first Year. **1830** Lindley *Nat. Syst. Bot.* 131 Its ovarium..finally changes into a samara which is 1-celled and 1-seeded by abortion. **1960** [see achene]. **1976** *New Yorker* 12 Jan. 66/2 The best-known samara is the maple key, which is much larger than the fruit of the birch.

samaria: see samarium.

samariform (sə'mærɪfɔːm), *a. Bot.* [f. samara + -(i)form.] Having the form of a samara.

1891 in *Century Dict.*

samarin: see zamorin.

Samaritan (sə'mærɪtən), *sb.* and *a.* Also 6 **Samerytane**, 6–8 **Samaritane**. [ad. late L. *Samarītānus*, f. Gr. Σαμαρείτης Samaritan, f. Σαμαρεία Samaria.] **A.** *sb.* **a.** A native or inhabitant of Samaria, a district of Palestine named from its chief city, anciently the capital of the kingdom of Israel; *esp.* one who adheres to the religious system which had its origin in Samaria.

c **1000** *Ags. Gosp.* Matt. x. 5 Ne ga ȝe innan samaritana ceastre. **1377** Langl. *P. Pl.* B. xvii. 48 Þanne seye we a samaritan sittende on a mule. *c* **1511** *1st Eng. Bk. Amer.* (Arb.) Introd. 31/2 There be some crystened that in the holy land is namyd samerytanes. **1577** Hanmer tr. *Eusebius' Eccl. Hist.* iv. xxi. 70 Sundry sectes among the children of Israell ..the Samaritans: the Sadduces: the Pharises. **1799** *Med. Jrnl.* I. 439 The Samaritans who, in a life of solitude and retirement, incessantly contemplating the deity, abstained from the use of flesh. **1841** *Penny Cycl.* XX. 376/1 Samaritans are still found in their old country, especially at Nablous, near Sichem, and also in Egypt. **1957** *Oxf. Dict. Chr. Ch.* 1211/1 *The Samaritan Pentateuch*, a slightly divergent form of the Pentateuch in Hebrew, current since pre-Christian times among the Samaritans. It is the only part of the OT accepted by the Samaritans. **1965** M. Spark *Mandelbaum Gate* iv. 91 Those Israelites, Samaritans, those boys. **1977** *Sci. Amer.* Jan. 100/1 Although the kingdom of Samaria vanished long ago, the Samaritans still survive today as perhaps the smallest ethnic minority in the world.

b. *fig.* (freq. in full, ***good Samaritan***) with reference to the 'good Samaritan' in Luke x. 33; also *transf.*, a kind and helpful person; hence (nonce-wds.) ***good Samaritanism, good Samaritanship.***

Samaritan's balsam, 'a mixture of wine and oil, formerly used in treating wounds' (*Cent. Dict.* 1891); **Samaritan hospital**, a hospital specially devoted to the sick poor; **Samaritan schools**, 'common name in the Unites States for ambulance classes' (*Syd. Soc. Lex.* 1897).

1640 N. Rogers (*title*) The good Samaritan, or an exposition on that parable, Luke x. ver. xxx–xxxviii. **1644** (*title*) The compassionate Samaritane: Vnbinding the Conscience, and powring oyle into the wounds which have beene made upon the Separation. **1649** P. Chamberlen (*title*) The Poore Mans Advocate, or, Englands Samaritan. **1823** Scott *Quentin D.* ii, The bonny Scot had already accosted the younger Samaritan. **1840** J. Ruskin *Let.* 4 July in *Let. to College Friend* (1894) 11 You have sacrificed half a Good Samaritanship to insult your friends with letters of brown paper. **1846** Ld. Ashburton in *Croker Papers* III. xxiv. 77, I wish some good Samaritan of a Conservative with sufficient authority could heal the feuds among our friends. **1887** Hall Caine *Deemster* xxxix, The Samaritans laughed and bade them not to think of price or money until their captain should return. **1898** 'A. Hope' *Rupert of Hentzau* iii. 42 Good Samaritans but not men of war, they returned to where I lay senseless on the ground. **1919** M. Beer *Hist. Brit. Socialism* I. i. v. 74 The new order would act as a good Samaritan and pour oil and wine into the wounds of the nation. **1923** *Virginia Law Rev.* Apr. 423 It is unreasonable that the priest and the Levite should go free while the good Samaritan should be forced to undergo the ordeal and expense of a trial. **1925** A. Huxley *Those Barren Leaves* II. vi. 156 On the faces of all my good Samaritans I noticed an expression of childlike earnestness. **1930** H. Redwood *God in Slums* 14 A co-opted partner in every kind of Good Samaritanism. **1950** T. S. Eliot *Cocktail Party* I. ii. 49 Don't you realise how lucky you are To have *two* Good Samaritans? *a* **1953** E. O'Neill *Touch of Poet* (1957) I. 9 Sure, the good Samaritan was a crool haythen beside you. **1963** *Reader's Digest* May 89/1 The best known and most effective curb of the malpractice-suit racket is California's so-called Good Samaritan law. **1977** *Times of Zambia* 7 Sept. 1/6 Shawa started as a Good Samaritan, trying to separate a fight in which Mr Sichinga was involved.

c. ***the Samaritans***, an organization founded in London in 1953 that offers counselling by telephone to those in distress or contemplating suicide; hence as *sing.*, a member of this organization. Also (in sing.) *attrib.*

[**1953** *Church Times* 27 Nov. 854/5 The Rev. Chad Varah ..intends to open a 'Good Samaritan' centre—on the telephone.] **1960** *Times* 29 Nov. 6/6 The vast majority of those who came to the Samaritans were not mentally ill... The Samaritans had helped people of all types, from a duke to a dustman. **1967** *Guardian* 8 June 3/5 The most common reasons for people calling the Telephone Samaritans for help in the Greater Manchester area..were depression, anxiety, and mental illness. **1969** *Listener* 10 Apr. 508/1 The girl..works for Oxfam and wants to be a Samaritan. **1973** J. Seabrook *Loneliness* 115 I'd break down, I'd be all trembling. I used to ring the Samaritans. I don't know what I'd have done without the man who was my counsellor. **1977** *Hongkong Standard* 14 Apr. 13/3 (Advt.), Discouraged/Depressed? Dial the Samaritans, day or night. **1978** M. Dickens *Open Bk.* xxi. 186 The Samaritans is a world-wide fellowship of men and women of all ages, creeds and races, dedicated to befriending people who are desperate enough to want to kill themselves. *Ibid.*, I went to the Samaritan centre in London to talk about the isolated and lonely people who I knew must be among their callers.

B. *adj.* **a.** Of or pertaining to Samaria or the Samaritans; used by the Samaritans. Also *Comb.*, as (sense b of the sb.) ***Samaritan-like*** adj.

Samaritan Pentateuch: a recension of the Hebrew Pentateuch used by the Samaritans; the MSS. are written in 'Samaritan' (i.e. archaic Hebrew) characters.

1382 Wyclif *Luke* x. 33 Forsoth sum man Samaritan, makynge iourney, cam bisydis the weye. **1624** in *Abp. Ussher's Lett.* (1686) 311 The five Books of Moses in the Samaritan Character. *Ibid.* 321, I also told him of your Samaritan Pentateuch. **1641** Milton *Animadv.* 21 As little doe wee esteem your Samaritan trumpery, of which people Christ himselfe testifies, Yee worship you know not what. **1858** G. F. Nicholls (*title*) A grammar of the Samaritan language. **1889** *Harper's Mag.* Sept. 582/1 The greatest of the Samaritan festivals, the Passover, is still celebrated on the top of Gerizim. **1973** E.-J. Bahr *Nice Neighbourhood* vi. 64 We callously discussed how Samaritan-like we'd been, having John over for dinner.

b. *absol.* (quasi-*sb.*) in various contextual uses, e.g. the Aramaic dialect formerly spoken in Samaria; the character in which this is written; the Samaritan text of the Hebrew Pentateuch.

1627 Abp. Ussher *Let. to Selden* 30 Nov. *Lett.* (1686) 385 In the numbering of the Years of these Fathers..there is not the like consent betwixt the LXX, and the Samaritan, as was before. **1653** *Ibid.* 588 The Persian Pentateuch..being translated not out of the Original, but out of the Chalde and the Hebrew Samaritan. **1770** [Luckombe] *Hist. Printing* 159 Pica Samaritan. **1787** *Printer's Gram.* 300 Long Primer Samaritan. **1797** J. Pratt *Prospectus New Polyglot Bible* 8 Printing the Samaritan and Syriac in a character familiar to the Hebrew scholar. **1886** *Encycl. Brit.* XXI. 648/2 The false notion that Samaritan is a mixture of Hebrew and Aramaic.

†**Sa'maritanish**, *a. Obs.* [f. Samaritan + -ish.] Belonging to Samaria; Samaritan.

[*c* **1000** *Ags. Gosp.* Luke x. 33 Sum samaritanisc man.] **1532** More *Confut. Tindale* Wks. 693/2 Of thys ye haue an ensample John .iiij. of ye Samaritanish wyfe.

Samaritanism (sə'mærɪtənɪz(ə)m). [f. Samaritan + -ism.]

1. The religious system of the Samaritans. In the 17th c. often *transf.*

a **1641** Bp. Mountagu *Acts & Mon.* (1642) 474 All these consented to the generall Samaritanisme, of receiving Moses his Law. **1683** L. Milbourne (*title*) Samaritanism Reviv'd. **1693** *Consid. Explic. Trinity by Dr. Wallis*, etc. 32 What the Mystical Divines teach, cannot be called an Explication; they deny all Explications: we must say therefore 'tis Samaritanism; for what our Saviour says of the Samaritans, by way of Reproof and Blame, that these Gentlemen profess concerning themselves, that they worship they know not what. **1886** *Encycl. Brit.* XXI. 244/1 Before that time Samaritanism cannot have existed in a form at all similar to that which we know. **1973** *Sci. Amer.* Jan. 80/1 Of all the multifarious forms of Jewish religious expression that arose, only two have survived and flourish today... A marginal survivor is Samaritanism, maintained by a tiny group of Samaritans..who continue to worship on their holy Mount Gerizim.

2. An idiom or form of expression belonging to the Samaritan dialect of Aramaic.

1889 *Harper's Mag.* Sept. 582/1 Insertions of foreign passages, alterations, Samaritanisms, and changes in support of Samaritan doctrine.

3. Imitation of the 'good Samaritan'.

1843 Syd. Smith in Lady Holland *Mem.* (1855) II. 522 Mankind are getting mad with humanity and Samaritanism. **1863** 'Ouida' *Held in Bondage* (1870) 348 A shrew's vituperations rewarded him for his Samaritanism.

samarium (sə'mɛərɪəm). *Chem.* [mod.L., coined in Fr. (P.-É. Lecoq de Boisbaudran 1879, in *Compt. Rend.* LXXXIX. 214): see samarskite and -ium.] A hard grey metallic element of the lanthanide series, found in small quantities in monazite sand, samarskite, and other rare earth minerals. Symbol Sm; atomic number 62.

1879 *Jrnl. Chem. Soc.* XXXVI. 890 A new metal to which the author gives the name Samarium. **1907** *Athenæum* 31 Aug. 244/3 A sulphide of calcium containing a trace of the rare element samarium. **1923** U. R. Evans *Metals & Metallic Compounds* II. 233 If an attempt is to be made to obtain pure compounds of samarium, europium, or gadolinium, the double magnesium salts are more satisfactory. **1955** *Sci. News Let.* 12 Mar. 164/1 Rare earth metals, such as samarium and europium, have long remained a mystery, simply because there was not enough of them available to find out what they could be used for. **1969** *New Scientist* 28 Aug. 430/2 Storage densities of 100 000 bits of information per square inch may be achieved with an orthoferrite containing samarium and terbium. **1974** *Encycl. Brit. Micropædia* VIII. 829/2 In addition to its more stable trivalent state, samarium..has a +2 oxidation state... Trivalent samarium..forms a series of yellow salts and solutions. **1977** *Gramophone* Oct. 590/1 (Advt.), It has an unusually tiny, samarium cobalt (rare earth) magnet of remarkably high power. **1980** *Sunday Times* 24 Aug. 14/8 The magnet within which the coil fits is now made of samarium cobalt.

Hence **sa'maria**, the oxide Sm_2O_3, a cream-coloured solid.

1885 *Jrnl. Chem. Soc.* XLVIII. II. 1025 The spectrum of a phosphorescent mixture of samaria 90 parts, and yttria 10 parts, in high vacua, shows none of the lines of yttrium, but is almost a facsimile of the spectrum of pure samarium. **1898** SIR W. CROOKES *Addr. Brit. Assoc.* 23 The persistence of the samarium spectrum in presence of overwhelming quantities of other metals, is almost unexampled in spectroscopy: thus one part of samaria can easily be seen when mixed with three million parts of lime. **1974** *Encycl. Brit. Macropædia* XV. 516/1 Mosander's didymia was resolved into several oxides—samaria (samarium; 1879), praseodymia.., neodymia.., and europia.

samaroid ('sæmərɔɪd), *a.* [f. SAMARA + -OID.] Resembling a samara.

1830 LINDLEY *Nat. Syst. Bot.* 111 Fruit either consisting of a 3 samaroid carpella, or berried with from 1 to 3 cells.

samarr, variant of SIMAR.

‖**samarra**[1] (sə'mærə). *Hist.* Also 8 **samarre.** [med.L.: see SIMAR.] A kind of cassock, painted with flames, etc., worn on the way to execution by persons condemned by the Inquisition to be burnt.

1731 CHANDLER tr. *Limborch's Hist. Inquis.* II. IV. xli. 295 They [prisoners designed for the fire] are..cloathed with the Sackcloth, or kind of Mantle, which some call the Sambenito, others the Samarra or Samaretta. **1736** —— *Hist. Persec.* 265 The infamous Samarre. **1841** BARHAM *Ingold. Leg.* Ser. II. *Auto-da-fé*, Each clothed in a garment more frightful by far, a Smock-frock sort of gaberdine, call'd a Samarra.

Samarra[2] (sə'mɑːrə). The name of a city in northern Iraq, used in phr. ***an appointment in Samarra*** to indicate the inevitability of death. Also *transf.*

In Maugham's play (see quot. 1933), the servant to a merchant meets Death in the market-place at Baghdad, and flees to Samarra to escape his clutches. When questioned by the merchant, Death explains his surprise at seeing the servant, replying as in quot. 1933.

1933 W. S. MAUGHAM *Sheppey* III. 112, I was astonished to see him in Bagdad, for I had an appointment with him tonight in Samarra. **1934** J. O'HARA (*title*) Appointment in Samarra. **1971** A. PRICE *Alamut Ambush* xi. 133 He had ridden out innocently..and had set up his own appointment in Samarra. **1973** *Times* 28 June 16/8 All Mr Heath's justified complacency as he watches the Labour Party destroying itself will avail him little if, come the next General Election, his own rendezvous with destiny turns out to be an appointment in Samarra.

samarskite ('sæmɑːskaɪt). *Min.* [ad. G. *samarskit* (H. Rose 1847, in *Ann. d. Physik* LXXI. 166), f. the name of Col. M. von *Samarski*, 19th-cent. Russian mining official: see -ITE[1].] A complex niobate and tantalate of yttrium, uranium, and iron, with small quantities of other metals including lanthanides, which is found as velvet-black or dark brown monoclinic prisms in granite pegmatites.

1849 J. NICOL *Man. Mineral.* 285 Samarskite... Rhombic; isomorphous with columbite..mostly imbedded in flat, somewhat polygonal grains. **1947** *Proc. Indian Acad. Sci.* A. XXV. 405 The samples of samarskite were secured from the Kodanda Rama mine in Nellore District. **1973** T. MOELLER in J. C. Bailar et al. *Comprehensive Inorg. Chem.* IV. xliv. 49 Minerals of lesser importance include.. samarskite, an yttrium earth-iron-calcium-uranyl niobate-tantalate, found in North Carolina, the Ural Mountains, and Madagascar.

Samaveda: see SAMAN[1].

samba ('sæmbə), *sb.*[1] [Pg., of Afr. origin.] A Brazilian dance of African origin; a ballroom dance imitative of this; also, a piece of music such as accompanies this dance. Also *attrib.*

1885 W. MOBERLY *Rocks & Rivers Brit. Columbia* 17 It was here I first saw the graceful South American dance—the Zemba Queca (I am not certain how it is spelt). **1911** B. MIALL tr. *P. Denis's Brazil* xiii. 324 It is during these festivals that the negro dances are performed; the *Coco* and the *Samba.* **1929** H. MILES tr. *P. Morand's Black Magic* p. i, 1919—Darius Milhaud arrives from Brazil. He..plays me those Negro *Sambas* which are shortly to serve for the music of his *Bœuf sur le Toit.* **1939** *Britannica Bk. of Year* (U.S.) 201/1 The samba is the national dance of Brazil, much as the fox trot is in the United States... In 1938, the samba was just beginning to make its way in the New York night clubs. **1942** D. PIERSON *Negroes in Brazil* ix. 248 It was of these *Bahianas* that Carmen Miranda sang when she recently captivated Broadway with the staccato notes of the rollicking *samba* by Dorival Caymmi, 'Que é a Bahiana tem?' *Ibid.* 249 The *samba*, or *samba batida*, a regional form of the old *batuque*, although it has now been taken over by the upper classes and in a modified form become not only one of the most characteristic musical forms but also one of the favorite dances of Brazil, is still enjoyed in its primitive simplicity by the Bahian lower classes. **1949** M. DICKENS *Flowers on Grass* ix. 240 Mervyn and Wanda were doing a Samba. **1950** J. VEDEY *Band Leaders* 132 He [*sc.* Edmundo Ros] states that many of the numbers published as Sambas are not really Sambas at all... In 1940..the Rumba was the only known dance of its kind, played in either slow or fast tempo. The Samba, which Ros himself actually introduced, followed. *Ibid.* 144 Who are these thousands of people packing the Palais de Danse and jiving wildly to the sambas and Bop arrangements of the popular bands? **1954** J. STEINBECK *Sweet Thursday* xxviii. 199 The crazy trumpet put a samba beat to the 'Wedding March'. **1965** W. SOYINKA *Road* 21, I have not seen any other tout who would stand on the lorry's roof and play the samba at sixty miles an hour. **1974** *Down Beat* 18 July 26/3 Zoot, Jaki and Al all get their say in a medley of sambas. **1977** *Gramophone* Aug. 353/3 Barlow specializes in the more traditional sequined ballroom fare of quicksteps, waltzes, foxtrots, a tango, cha cha chas, a samba, slow rumbas, a pasodoble and jive. **1979** P. FOX *Mantis* iv. 62 Great driving-music: hard rock Samba, plenty of guitar.

samba ('sæmbə), *sb.*[2] Variant of SAMBO (sense 1).

1958 J. CAREW *Wild Coast* ix. 126 It please me eyes to see you growing up into a proper samba man. **1959** J. MORRIS *Adversary* i. 9 A couple of upcountry *corregidors*..had three girls between them... One of them looked like a *samba.* **1974** *Black World* Aug. 55 The Dirty Tricks store window featured a grotesque, black-purple mask of a 'samba' sister with a bone through its nose.

samba ('sæmbə), *v.* [f. SAMBA *sb.*[1]] *intr.* To dance the samba. Also *fig.*

1950 in WEBSTER Add. **1959** 'J. DRUMMOND' *Black Unicorn* xviii. 128 He put his arm round my waist, and started trying to make me samba. **1972** *Time* 22 May 9/3 Brazil had sambaed away with the talks. **1975** *Times* 14 Apr. 12/4, 37 couples..were required to cha-cha, samba, rumba and paso doble. **1979** C. WOOD *James Bond & Moonraker* xi. 111 How do you kill five hours in Rio if you don't samba?

samba, var. SAMBUR

sambal ('sæmbəl, ‖sambal). Also **sambaal, sambel.** [Malay.] A highly seasoned condiment, of Malayan and Indonesian origin, consisting of raw vegetables or fruit prepared with spices and vinegar and used as a relish; found also in other (esp. *S. Afr.*) cookery. Cf. POL SAMBOL.

1815 A. PLUMPTRE tr. *Lichtenstein's Trav. S. Afr.* II. IV. xxxiii. 84 *Sambal* is a mixture of gherkins cut small, onions, anchovies, Cayenne pepper, and vinegar. **1817** S. RAFFLES *Hist. Java* I. 98 The most common seasoning..is the lombok; triturated with salt, it is called *sámbel.* **1839** T. J. NEWBOLD *Brit. Settlements in Straits of Malacca* II. xii. 178 The ordinary food of Malays..is rice, and in times of scarcity, sago seasoned with a little salt fish, Blachang, the caviar of the East, made with acid fruits, &c., into a variety of condiments termed Sambals. **1871** *Cape Monthly Mag.* June 334 They make a sort of chutnee out of quinces, which they call 'sambal'. **1933** L. AINSWORTH *Confessions Planter in Malaya* 145 The usual small side-dishes containing what are known as 'sambals', which consist of such things as fried ground nuts, shredded cucumber, burnt grated coconut, Bombay duck and red and green chillies. **1942** S. CLOETE *Hill of Doves* xxiii. 328 He thought of food once more—bobotee; breede, made of mutton ribs; cucumber sambal. **1950** *Cape Times* 7 June 16/1 Her letter has reference to *melktert*, brandied peaches, *kreef frikkadels*, quince *sambaal*—all things which are becoming a lost art to us. **1953** DU PLESSIS & LÜCKHOFF *Malay Quarter* i. 15 The spicy stew is enhanced by means of various *sambals* or condiments. **1971** L. CHARTERIS *Saint & People Importers* iii. 24 Order me some samosas, lamb curry, pilau rice, dhal, and all the sambals you can crowd on the table. **1978** *Courier-Mail* (Brisbane) 26 Oct. 25/3 We ordered..a made-on-the-premises sambal mixing pineapple, capsicum and mild chillies in soy sauce, sugar and vinegar.

‖**sambaquí** (samba'ki). [Tupi.] A form of shell heap, found on the S. Brazilian coast, resulting mainly from the action of the wind and the sea, in which remains of prehistoric and historic cultures have been found; also *attrib.* (See quot. 1946.)

1944 S. PUTNAM tr. *E. da Cunha's Rebellion in Backlands* ii. 50 The pre-Columbian of the 'Sambaquis'. **1946** A. SERRANO in J. H. Steward *Handbk. S. Amer. Indians* I. III. 401 The word 'sambaquí' is of *Tupi-Guaraní* origin and means 'hill of shells'. *Ibid.* 403 The sambaquis are littoral cordons or concentrations of shells, broken and reshaped by natural forces. *Ibid.* 404 Artifacts in the most ancient sambaquis, which are farthest from the sea, correspond to the primitive culture of Lagoa Santa. *Ibid.*, The prevailing idea..has been that of a cultural unity—a single sambaqui culture—that is distinctive and characteristic of these deposits. It is no longer possible to maintain this. **1953** *Jrnl. R. Anthrop. Inst.* LXXXIII. 60 On the coast, the classic *sambaquí* culture, called the 'Southern Phase', may succeed the chipped-axe phase. **1977** G. CLARK *World Prehist.* (ed. 3) x. 447 There is evidence from the shell mounds or sambaqui sites that intensive exploitation of coastal resources had begun.

‖**sambar** ('sambər). Also **sambhar.** [Tamil.] In South Indian cookery, a highly seasoned lentil gravy. Also *attrib.*

1957 S. RANGARAO *Good Food from India* vii. 68 Sambar powders go well into meat curries. **1967** M. WALDO *Internat. Encycl. Cooking* II. 541/2 *Sambar*, (Indian), a highly seasoned vegetable and lentil dish. **1972** *Indian Express* 28 Dec. 10/1 South Indian dishes—idli, dosa and sambhar—have become popular. **1973** *Times* 19 June (Bombay Suppl.) p. xv/3 The food of South India, especially the idli (spongy rice cakes) with sambar (liquid lentil juice) should not be missed. **1976** *Sunday Standard* (India) 11 Jan. 10/4, I distribute bread to these children everyday. I've also brought sambar to go with it. **1977** *Sunday Times* (Colour Suppl.) 27 Nov. 35/4 The food is as authentic as it is in Madras—..*sambar* (the thick lentil gravy cooked with vegetables and tamarind juice).

sambenit, -benita, -i, -o: see SANBENITO.

samber, sambhar, sambhur, var. ff. SAMBUR.

samble, var. SEMBLE *sb. Obs.*, assembly.

sambleblie, obs. form of SEMBLABLY.

sambo ('sæmbəʊ). Pl. **-bos, -boes.** Forms: 8 **samboe,** 9 **zambo,** 8– **sambo.** [a. Sp. *zambo*, applied in America and Asia to persons of various degrees of mixed Negro and Indian or European blood; also, a name for a kind of yellow monkey; perh. identical with *zambo* bandy-legged (according to Diez repr. L. *scambus*).]

1. (See quot. 1884.)

1748 *Earthquake Peru* iii. 240 Sambo de Mulatto, sprung from Negroes and Mulattos. *Ibid.*, Sambo de Indian, sprung from Negroes and Indians. **1796** STEDMAN *Surinam* (1813) I. xiii. 340 A Samboe is between a mulatto and a black. **1833** MARRYAT *P. Simple* xxxi, A quadroon looks down upon a mulatto, while a mulatto looks down upon a sambo, that is, half mulatto half negro. **1884** *Encycl. Brit.* XVII. 319/2 *Zambo*: any half-breed, but mostly the issue of Negro and Indian parents; in the United States, Peru, and West Indies of Negro and Mulatto.

attrib. **1748** *Earthquake Peru* iii. 240 Giveros, the Offspring of Sambo Mulattos and Sambo Indians.

2. (With capital S.) A nickname for a Negro. Now used only as a term of abuse. Also *attrib.*, esp. with reference to the appearance or subservient mentality held to be typical of the black American slave. [Perh. a different word; it has been suggested that it may be the Foulah *sambo* uncle.]

1704 *Boston News-Let.* 2 Oct. 2/2 There is a Negro man taken up supposed to be Runaway from his Master,..calls himself Sambo. **1735** J. ATKINS *Voy. to Guinea, Brazil & W. Indies* 170 If you look strange and are niggardly of your Drams, you frighten him; *Sambo* is gone, he never cares to treat with dry lips. **1781** I. JACKSON *Divorce* II. 34 So then, Sambo, you want to be in the fashionable world, I see?.. Timothy, show the black Gentleman down-stairs. **1818** 'A. BURTON' *Adventures J. Newcome* IV. 222 His Steward was a scoundrel Sambo, And in his own conceit a d——d beau; A true Barbadian being born, He others held in utter scorn. **1866** W. REED *Hist. Sugar* 32 Sambo tells him the skip is ready; but it would never do for the sugar master to seem to be taught by Sambo. **1922** JOYCE *Ulysses* 322 *Black Beast Burned in Omaha, Ga.* A lot of Deadwood Dicks in slouch hats and they firing at a sambo strung up on a tree with his tongue out and a bonfire under him. *Ibid.* 436 Tom and Sam Bohee, coloured coons in white duck suits, scarlet socks, upstarched Sambo chokers and large scarlet asters in their buttonholes leap out. **1927** G. B. SHAW *Doctors' Delusions* (1932) 137 When a vivisector says, in effect, 'I have a dread secret to wrest from Nature: so you must license me to sacrifice a guinea pig', the Sambo in us assents. **1957** [see BOOT *sb.*[3] 1 e]. **1959** S. ELKINS *Slavery* 227 What, then, of the 'reality' of Sambo? Did the Sambo role really become part of the slave's 'true' personality? **1962** L. DEIGHTON *Ipcress File* xix. 123 'I'd just better be right about you pale-face,' he said. 'You'd just better had, Sambo.' **1969** *N.Y. Rev. Bks.* 13 Mar. 3/1 The reasons for the development of the 'Sambo' response of the Negro slave to his environment which help to explain the paucity of slave revolts in America. **1969** *Guardian* 1 Apr. 7/4 The brothers wore Afro costume... Their loose jigging and gestures, open-mouthed, Sambo style, reverberated with their long solid jammed numbers. **1973** *Times Lit. Suppl.* 2 Mar. 230/2 The 'Sambo' stereotype of the loyal, lazy, affectionate and child-like slave. **1977** *Times* 10 June 8/5 A white Zambian..had called him a black sambo during the struggle for independence.

†**sambocade.** *Cookery. Obs.* Also in corrupt forms: 5 **samakade, samaca, samaka, semaka, samata, samartard,** 6 **semeca.** [f. L. *sambūcus* elder; cf. It. *sambucato* flavoured with elder flowers.] A kind of fritter flavoured with elder flowers.

?**1390** *Forme of Cury* (1780) 77 Sambocade. Take and make a Crust..& take a cruddes..do þerto sugar..& somdel whyte of Ayrene, & shake þerin blomes of elren. *c* **1420** in *Q. Eliz. Acad.* 90 Semaka fryez. *c* **1430** *Two Cookery-bks.* 59 Samaca. *Ibid.* 62 Frutoure Samata. *c* **1440** *Anc. Cookery* in *Househ. Ord.* (1790) 450 At the seconde course..a leche and samakade, and bake mete. *c* **1467** *Noble Bk. Cookry* (ed. Mrs. Napier 1882) 45 To mak samartard tak wetted cruddes [etc.]. **1502** *Arnolde's Chron.* Qiiij b/2 Freature semeca.

sambo(c)k, obs. forms of SJAMBOK *sb.*

samboo, var. SAMBUR.

sambook, var. SAMBUK.

‖**sambouse.** *Obs.* Also 7 **samboyse.** [Persian *sanbūsah* (phonetically *samb-*), whence Arab. *sanbūsah*, *-saj, -sak, -saq* (Dozy).] A pasty of hashed meats.

1609 W. BIDDULPH in T. Lavender *Trav.* (1612) 36 Wee dined [near Aleppo] with Musmelons, Sambouses, and a Muclebite. **1630** CAPT. SMITH *Trav. & Adv.* xiii. 25 Samboyses and Muselbits are great dainties.

sambre, variant of SAMBUR.

Sam Browne (sæm braʊn). [The name of Sir *Sam*uel James *Browne* (1824–1901), British general, who invented it.] In full, ***Sam Browne belt***: a belt with a supporting strap that passes over the right shoulder, worn by commissioned officers of the British Army and also by members of various police forces, etc. Also *transf.*, a commissioned officer.

1915 *Punch* 6 Oct. 288/3 Military Wedding Equipment. Sam Browne belt, single brace and frog, best bridal leather. **1916** E. C. MIDDLETON *Aircraft* xvi. 114 Should he be posted to the Army wing he will probably present himself to an astonished and apoplectic adjutant wearing two cross straps to his 'Sam Browne'. **1919** *Amer. Legion Weekly* 5 Sept. 27 It wasn't the privates or the acting corporals or the full-fledged Sam Brownes who had a monopoly on this particular quality. **1933** J. CARY *Amer. Visitor* xvii. 278 Stoker in a Sam Browne and Gore with a huge Webley strapped to his waist were interrogating Sam and Henry. **1942** E. WAUGH *Put out More Flags* i. 55 Taking in every detail of his uniform, the riding boots, Sam Browne belt, the enamelled stars of rank. *Ibid.*, I heard they had stopped wearing cross straps on the Sam Browne. **1972** J. WAMBAUGH *Blue Knight* (1973) i. 16, I loosened by Sam Browne for the joy of eating. **1977** 'A. YORK' *Tallant for Trouble* i. 13 He wore the khaki shorts and bush jacket, and the Sam Browne belt, of a police officer.

sambu, variant of SAUMBUE *Obs.*

‖**sambuca**[1] (sæm'bjuːkə). Also in anglicized forms: 4, 6 **sambuke**, 5 **-buce**, 6 **-buque**, 9 **sambuc**. [L. *sambūca*, ad. Gr. σαμβύκη, prob. of Eastern origin, cogn. with Aramaic *sabbᵉkā* which it renders in the Book of Daniel. See SACKBUT.]

1. *Ancient Music.* 'A triangular stringed-instrument of a very sharp shrill tone' (Lewis & Short).

1382 WYCLIF *Dan.* iii. 5 Harpe, sambuke, sautrie, symfonie. **1545** ASHAM *Toxoph.* I. (Arb.) 39 This I am sure, yat lutes, harpes, all maner of pypes, barbitons, sambukes, ..be condemned of Aristotle. **1845** *Encycl. Metrop.* IX. 451 The sambuc was, it is believed, similar to the psaltery. **1902** W. L. NEWMAN *Politics of Aristotle* III. 550 The *sambuca* was high-pitched and piercing in tone.

2. *Roman Antiq.* A military engine for storming walls.

1489 CAXTON *Faytes of A.* II. xxxv. 154 Sambuce is an engyn whiche is made in manere of a harpe able to perce a walle. **1594** R. ASHLEY tr. *Loys le Roy* 117 The rest followed them by the Sambuque.

‖**sambuca**[2] (sam'buka). Also **sambucca**, and with capital initial. [It., ad. L. *sambūc-us* elder tree: see SAMBUCENE.] An Italian liqueur resembling anisette.

1971 P. PURSER *Holy Father's Navy* xv. 121 They stared at me, coffee cups and brandies and *sambuccas* half-raised to lips. **1975** *Times* 11 Jan. 11/5 Sambuca, from Italy.. contains liquorice. **1977** *New Yorker* 20 June 26/1 It got so cold that..when they tried to pour anisette or Sambuca into their coffee in the early mornings to warm up, they sometimes found it frozen in the bottle.

sambucco, var. SAMBUK.

sambucene ('sæmbjuːsiːn). *Chem.* [f. L. *sambūc-us* elder tree + -ENE.] (See quot. 1875.)

1872 J. H. GLADSTONE in *Jrnl. Chem. Soc.* Ser. II. X. 3, I would suggest the following:—..Hydrocarbon from Elder. Sambucene. **1875** WATTS *Dict. Chem.* 2nd Suppl. 1073 *Sambucene*, $C^{10}H^{16}$, the terpene from elder oil.

sambuco, var. SAMBUK.

‖**sambuk** ('sæmbuːk). Also 6 **sambuco, zanbuco**, 9 **sambucco, sambook, zambuck, zanbuc**, 20 **-buq**. [Origin uncertain: in Arab. written *sanbūq*. Cf. Pg. *zambuco*, It. *sambuco*.] 'A kind of small vessel formerly used in Western India, and still on the Arabian coast' (Yule). Also *attrib.*

1582 N. LICHEFIELD tr. *Castanheda's Conq. E. Ind.* I. x. 26b, They discouered two Sambucos (which are little Pinnacies). **1582** N. LICHEFIELD tr. *Castanheda's Conq. E. Ind.* I. lxiii. 129b, Hee went to Mousanbique in a Zanbuco. **1855** BURTON *Pilgr. El-Medinah & Meccah* I. 263 The Sambuk [is a vessel] from 15 to 50 [tons burden]. **1872** BEETON & R. SMITH *Livingstone & Stanley* 15 Small vessels, called zambucks. **1887** L. OLIPHANT *Episodes* (1888) 15 A sambook or craft such as are now used in those seas [about India]. **1891** *Nat. Rev.* Feb. 729 Small barques, which they called zanbucs. **1906** H. W. SMYTH *Mast & Sail* 307 The Red Sea *sambuk* is generally from 18 to 20 tons only. **1938** F. STARK *Jrnl.* 1 Mar. in *Winter in Arabia* (1940) 201 A king ..sent for one thousand virgins from Somaliland across the sea; they were all shipped in a sambuq. **1942** [see MASHWA]. **1963** *Times* 1 Feb. 14/6 They want a sambuq to meet them at Bir Sukaiya at noon next Wednesday—it's three hours' sail by sambuq from there to Perim. **1974** *Nat. Geographic* Sept. 333 (caption) *Sambuk*, once the most common of Arab dhows, has ferried generations of Moslem pilgrims from Africa towards Mecca. **1975** *Financial Times* 31 Oct. 5/4 The monsoon was pushing the seas too high, even for the sturdy *sambuq* fishing boats.

sambuke, sambuque, obs. ff. SAMBUCA[1].

sambunigrin (sæmbjuː'naigrɪn). *Chem.* [ad. F. *sambunigrine* (Bourquelot & Danjou 1905, in *Compt. Rend.* CXLI. 598), f. mod.L. *Sambucus nigra*, taxonomic name of the common elder (f. L. *sambūcus* elder + *niger* black): see -IN[1].] A colourless crystalline glycoside of the nitrile of *d*-mandelic acid, found in the leaves of the elder and having the formula $C_6H_5{\cdot}CH(CN){\cdot}O{\cdot}C_6H_{11}O_5$.

1905 *Jrnl. Chem. Soc.* LXXXVIII. I. 912 The leaves of *Sambucus nigra* contain only traces of emulsin; it is therefore possible to extract from the air-dried or the fresh leaves the glucoside sambunigrin $C_{14}H_{17}O_6N$, which crystallises from ethyl acetate in long, colourless needles. **1965** ANSELL & GIGG in S. Coffey *Rodd's Chem. Carbon Compounds* (ed. 2) Ic. ix. 104 It [*sc.* hydrogen cyanide] is widely distributed in plants in the form of..glycosides of the cyanohydrins of various aldehydes and ketones (amygdalin, prunasin, sambunigrin,..etc.).

sambuq, var. SAMBUK.

sambur ('sæmbə(r)). Forms: 7 **sabre**, 9 **sabir, samboo, sambar, samber, sambhur, sambhar, sambre, sambur, saumer**. Also **samba**. [a. Hindī *sābar, sāmbar*.] Either of two large deer, *Cervus unicolor* or *C. equinus*, native to southern Asia.

1698 FRYER *Acc. E. India & P.* 175 Our usual Diet was.. spotted Deer, Sabre, Wild Hogs, and sometimes Wild Cows. **1813** in J. Forbes *Oriental Mem.* (ed. 2) II. 400 (Y.) Four large sabirs or samboos, one considerably bigger than an ox. **1862** BEVERIDGE *Hist. India* I. Introd. 11 The saumer, or black rusa of Bengal. **1864** TREVELYAN *Compet. Wallah* (1866) 161 Sambhur, a gigantic deer of the elk species. **1883** MRS. BISHOP in *Leisure Ho.* 85/1 The palandok..and the sambre may not be far off. **1913** L. WOOLF *Village in Jungle* ii. 25 He showed them the sambur lying during the day in the other great caves. **1964** LD. MEDWAY in Wang Gungwu *Malaysia* I. iii. 57 This large group includes several animals widespread in South-east Asia such as the..Sambar and Barking Deer.

attrib. **1829** E. T. BENNETT *Tower Menag.* 187 The Samboo Deer..belongs to the Rusa group. **1874** H. H. COLE *Catal. Objects Indian Art S. Kensington Mus.* ii. 107 Strips of sappan wood.., ebony and samber horn dyed green. **1883** LD. SALTOUN *Scraps* II. 175 Long yellow sambur-skin boots. **1898** R. G. BURTON *Tropics & Snows* 261 He may find a sambhur stag. **1950** J. H. WILLIAMS *Elephant Bill* xi. 166, I once jumped into a creek, ten yards from a tiger, that was..eating a freshly killed samba deer. **1969** J. LEASOR *Week of Love* v. 92 A dapper man..with sambur skin shoes.

Samburu (sæm'bʊruː), *sb.* and *a.* [Native name.] **A.** *sb.* **a.** A pastoral people of mixed Hamitic stock inhabiting northern Kenya; a member of this people. **b.** The Nilotic language of this people. **B.** *adj.* Of or pertaining to this people or their language.

1896 W. A. CHANLER *Through Jungle & Desert* vii. 281 They said they had originally belonged to the Berkenedji or Samburu tribe. *Ibid.* 306 On our way to the new zeriba we were approached by a band of 100 Samburu. **1927** W. M. ROSS *Kenya from Within* xxiv. 436 Heavy pressure was brought to bear on the local Government to grant land in actual use by the Samburu tribe to one or more of the European sheep-ranchers. **1947** [see MASAI]. **1959** A. MOOREHEAD *No Room in Ark* iv. 100 The Samburu..are a tall fine slender people with something of the ancient Egyptians about them. **1964** J. HILLABY *Journey to Jade Sea* 81 Lelean said something uncomplimentary in Samburu. **1965** P. SPENCER *Samburu* p. xxii, Pardopa clan was typical of less than a half of the Samburu clans. **1976** D. TOPOLSKI *Muzungu* xiv. 222 He answered, just as chattily in Samburu. *Ibid.* 223 An uncircumcised man is still considered to be a boy amongst the Samburu.

†'**sam-cloth.** *Obs.* [app. repr. OE. **séamclāð* (see SEAM *sb.*[1] and CLOTH *sb.*). Huloet's explanation might suggest derivation from SAM-, though that prefix is not found with sbs.] (See quots.)

a **1450** *Glossary* (*MS. Harl. 1002*), *Hoc perzoma*, a samcloth. **1552** HULOET, Samcloth or vesture from the bealye downward, *limus*. **1688** R. HOLME *Armoury* III. 98/2 A Samcloth, a cloth to sow on, a Canvice cloth. *Ibid.*, A Samcloth, vulgarly a Sampler.

samdel, variant of SOMEDEAL.

same (seɪm), *a.* (*pron.*, *adv.*) Forms: 4–7 **sam**, 5 **ssame**, 6 **some**, 3– **same**. [ME. *same*, a. ON. *same* masc., *sama* fem., neut., rarely in str. form *sam-r* (Sw. *samma, samme*, Da. *samme*); a Com. Teut. word, but lost in OE. and OS. (which have only the derived adv., in OE. *swá same*, OS. *so sama, -o*, likewise) and in the mod.Teut. langs. retained only in Eng. and Scandinavian. Cf. OHG. *sama* same (rare, though the derived adv. *sama, -o*, likewise, similarly, is common), Goth. *sama* same:—Indogermanic **somo-*, whence Skr. *samá* level, equal, same, Gr. ὁμό-ς same (cf. ὁμαλός level), OIrish *som* same.

Ablaut-variants of this root are (1) **sem-* in Gr. εἷς (:—**sems*) one; (2) **s'm-* in OTeut. **sumo-* SOME, Skr. *sama* any, every, Gr. ἅμα together, L. *similis* like, OIrish *samail* likeness, image, Welsh *hafal* like; also as prefix in Skr. *sakṛt* acting at once, Gr. ἁπλόος, L. *simplex* simple; (3) *sōm-* in Skr. *sāma* similarity, OSl. *samŭ* same, OE. *sóm* agreement (see SEEM *v.*).]

The ordinary adjectival and pronominal designation of identity, equivalent to the older ILK *a.*[1], to L. *idem*, Gr. ὁ αὐτός, Ger. *derselbe*. Normally preceded by *the*, exc. after a demonstrative; the omission of the article occurs only in dialectal or vulgar speech and in certain specially elliptical varieties of diction (e.g. in commercial correspondence). As the prefixed article is functionally a part of the word, it is often difficult to distinguish the simple predicative use (= 'identical') from the absolute and elliptical uses.

A. *adj.*

I. Not numerically different from an object indicated or implied; identical.

1. With forward reference: Identical with what is indicated in the following context.

It is remarkable that this use is all but entirely absent from the writings of Shakspere; the only clear instance appears to be quot. 1598 in 4 below.

a. Followed by a clause with relative pronoun (*that, who, which*) or relative adverb (*when, where*). Cf. VERY *a.*

In this construction *that* sometimes has not the strict pronominal syntax, but is equivalent in meaning to 'in (on, by, etc.) which', 'where', 'when'. Cf. the similar use of F. *que*.

c **1200** ORMIN 9914 He mihhte makenn cwike menn þær off þa same staness, þat stodenn þær bi Sannt Johan. **1340** HAMPOLE *Pr. Consc.* 4511 Þan sal Iewes þe sam lawe halde, þat þai haf. *Ibid.* 5288 þis taken..sal noght be þe sam cros, ne þe sam tre, On whilk God was nayled fot and hande. **1537** STARKEY *Let. to Pole* in *England* (1878) p. xlvij, Euen the same thyng wych you percas thynke hathe byn the chefe roote of thys motyon. **1633** EARL MANCH. *Al Mondo* (1636) 141 The old saying is a good one, Doe that every day, which thou wouldest doe the same day that thou dyest. **1702** ADDISON *Dial. Medals* I. Wks. 1766 III. 22 He would often show us the same face on an old Coin that we saw in the Statue. **1707** —— *Pres. State War* ⁋7 ibid. 246 The same causes which straiten the British commerce, will naturally enlarge the French. **1711** BUDGELL *Spect.* No. 77 ⁋5 At the same time that I am endeavouring to expose this Weakness in others. **1809** J. ROLAND *Fencing* 89, I return to the same situation where I found your blade at the time I began my first motion. **1810** SOUTHEY *Let.* 5 Aug. in *Life* (1850) III. 290 As for my contempt of the received rules of poetry, I hold the same rules which Shakspeare, Spencer, and Milton held before me, and desire to be judged by those rules. **1849** MACAULAY *Hist. Eng.* v. I. 561 Care was taken that the prisoner should pass through the same gate and the same streets through which Montrose had been led to the same doom. **1876** J. DENNIS *Stud. Eng. Lit.* 422 He defends it on the same ground that he would defend the 'Lycidas' of Milton. **1904** *Blackw. Mag.* Oct. 578/2 They may recite his [Shakspere's] works with the same restraint of gesture.. which interpreted his works in his own day.

b. With ellipsis of the relative pron. or adv. Also (in careless use) followed by a pa. pple with ellipsis of relative and copula.

1514 *Rec. St. Mary at Hill* 21 Vppon condicion that they shall kepe solemply, my seid Obett or Annuersary yerely for euermore þe same day of the Moneth my sowle shall depart from þe body, in þe parisshe church of Seint Mary at hill within london. **1647** CLARENDON *Hist. Reb.* v. §449 The standard itself was blown down the same night it had been set up. **1710** SWIFT *Jrnl. to Stella* 29 Sept., Why do you trouble yourself, Mistress Stella, about my instrument? I have the same the Archbishop gave me; and it is as good now the Bishops are away. **1831** SCOTT *Ct. Rob.* v, So many princes..aim, it is pretended, at nothing else than the same extravagant purpose announced by the brute multitude who first appeared in these regions. **1855** *Orr's Circ. Sci., Org. Nat.* III. 307 It is regarded with the same interest accorded in Europe to its red-breasted relative.

†**c.** In the 16–17th c. often followed by *that* with ellipsis of the verb, so that *the same that* becomes equivalent to 'the same as' or 'the same with'. *Obs.*

1577 FULKE *Answ. True Christian* 64 The Pope chosen by the councell of Constance, was of the same iudgement that the councell. **1582** G. MARTIN *Manif. Corrupt. Script.* iii. 44 Here he citeth many authors and dictionaries idly, to prooue that *idolum* may signifie the same that Image. **1601** HOLLAND *Pliny* I. 88 The next marches of this higher prouince is the same that the tract of Tarracon. *Ibid.* 105 The Pisidians..whose chiefe colony is Cæsaria, the same that Antiochia. **1643** TRAPP *Comm. Gen.* xi. 30 Some say, that Iscah in Chaldee signifieth the same that Sarai in Hebrew. **1652** LOVEDAY tr. *Calprenede's Cassandra* II. 132 And having applyed unto them the same things that to my Master's, they laboured to recover him from the sound he was in. **1664** H. MORE *Exp. 7 Epist.* viii. (1669) 124 So that I understand by φιλαδελφία the same that ἀγάπη, universal Love. **1671** MILTON *P.R.* III. 413 Such was thy zeal To Israel then, the same that now to me.

d. Followed by *as*. Now the commonest construction.

Four varieties of use may be noted. (*a*) *As* may serve as a relative adv. or pron. introducing a clause (cf. 1 a); (*b*) it may precede the subject or object of a verb omitted by ellipsis; (*c*) by ellipsis of the copula, it may be followed by sb. or pronoun denoting that with which identity is stated; (*d*) it may elliptically precede an adv. or phrase.

(*a*) **1340** HAMPOLE *Pr. Consc.* 835 Þan sal he on þe same wys hethen wende..right als he cam þe first day fra his moder wam. *c* **1400** *Rule St. Benet* (Verse) 2371 On þe sam wise sall ilk souerayn Do os þai wil take o-gayn. *a* **1548** HALL *Chron., Edw. IV* 196 He was the same person and of the same good mynde towarde the kynge, as he was before the tyme of hys legacion. **1705** ADDISON *Italy, Rome* 350 The Horse and Man on the Medal are in the same Posture as they are on the Statue. **1827** HALLAM *Const. Hist.* (1842) II. 257 *note*, She was exactly in the same predicament as Philip had been during his marriage with Mary I. **1861** M. PATTISON *Ess.* (1889) I. 40 A patent of Henry II.., in which he.. licenses the sale of Rhenish wine at the same price as French is sold at. **1894** SWINBURNE *Stud. in Prose & P.* 56 Entering college at the same age as Fletcher had entered six years earlier.

(*b*) **1691** *Emilianne's Frauds Romish Monks* 148 We follow'd this Troop of Pilgrims at a small distance, being Mounted in the same manner as they, tho' we could not joyn our selves in company with them. **1839** URE *Dict. Arts* 1086–7 Salt springs occur nearly in the same circumstances ..as the salt rock. **1881** JOWETT *Thucyd.* I. 179 The sailors in the fleet all received the same pay as the soldiers. **1895** CHITTY in *Law Times Rep.* LXXII. 866/1 Other rules in Order XLV. point in the same direction as the first rule of the order.

(*c*) **1715** tr. *Gregory's Astron.* (1726) I. II. 351 The Ratio of *GH* to *IK*, which is the same as the given Ratio of the Sines of the Arcs *AB, CD*. **1807** ROBINSON *Archæol. Græca* III. xxi. 325 Olympia, a city of the Pisæans, or, as some say, the same as Pisa.

(*d*) **1662** BP. HOPKINS *Funeral Serm.* (1683) 39 They return again to the same glut of lusts and pleasures as before. **1702** ADDISON *Dial. Medals* II. Wks. 1766 III. 69 You see the metaphor is the same in the Verses as in the Medal. **1716** —— *Freeholder* No. 42 ⁋6 We receive the same profit from them, as if they were the Produce of our own Island. **1845** M. PATTISON *Ess.* (1889) I. 24, 'I again consulted your magnificence, and you gave the same answer as before.'

e. Const. *with*. The regimen of *with* may denote either (*a*) a participant in the possession, attribute, etc. qualified by *the same*, or (*b*) that with which the object mentioned is said to be identical.

(*a*) **1387** TREVISA *Higden* (Rolls) II. 259 Þerfore of þre þe firste kyngdoms, as it were of þe same age wiþ þe kyngdom of Assiries, firste we schal write. **1601** DOLMAN tr. *La Primaud. Fr. Acad.* (1618) III. 803 The blossomes have the same nature with the fruite. *Ibid.* 804 The seede and roote of this plant have the same operation with the leafe. **1609** HOLLAND *Amm. Marcell.* 42 The bishop, being of the same mind and opinion with the rest, was [etc.]. **1660** BARROW *Euclid* VI. xxvi, Then is that Parallelogram about the same diagonal with the whole. **1699** BENTLEY *Phal.* Pref. 69 He is of the same size for Learning with the late Editor. **1740** *Johnson's Debates* 2 Dec. (1787) I. 23 Debate relating to a seditious paper of the same kind with the considerations on the Embargo on provisions. **1753** CHAMBERS *Cycl. Supp.* s.v. *Bridge*, Rochester bridge is built in the same style with that of London. **1763** GOLDSM. *Misc. Wks.* (1837) II. 502 They are incapable of the same docility with terrestrial animals, and are less imitative of human perfections. **1803** SOUTHEY *Let.* 9 June in *Life* (1850) II. 212 Scott, it seems, adopts the same system of metre with me. **1837** LOCKHART *Scott* I. x. 325 [He] died..at the same age with Burns and Byron, in 1811. **1842** R. I. WILBERFORCE *Rutilius & Lucius* 111 Words of the same nature with those he had heard were chanted at intervals. **1858** H. SPENCER *Ess.* I. 254 This..will be found to come under the same generalization with the others.

(*b*) *c* **1380** WYCLIF *Serm.* Sel. Wks. I. 319 As þe spirit þat is mannis soule is þe same persone wiþ him, so the secounde persone of God is þe same persone wiþ þis man. **1607** TOPSELL *Four-f. Beasts* (1658) 225 The Chaonian Horses are the same with the Apirrolan Horses. **1618** HALES *Gold. Rem.* II. (1673) 62 He could not be ignorant that his quality was the same with theirs. *a* **1641** BP. MOUNTAGU *Acts & Mon.* (1642) 179 She was native..of Phrygia and so peradventure was the same with Trojana. **1681** T. FLATMAN *Heraclitus Ridens* No. 30 (1713) I. 197 The third was a Paper of Directions, what, and how to plead, which was also denied him, being the same thing with allowing him Council. **1764** GOLDSM. *Introd. Gen. Hist. World* Misc. Wks. 1837 I. 531 The materials to which we have had recourse are the same with those which other historians for several ages have employed before us. **1829** JAS. MILL *Hum. Mind* (1869) II. 194 It rested with him to prove that the expectation of a pleasure, or of a pain, is the same thing with the desire, or aversion. **1873** FREEMAN *Hist. Ess.* Ser. II. 188 This was no difficulty to the Greeks and Macedonians, who looked on the Egyptian Ammon as the same god with their own Zeus.

†**f.** In certain rare constructions: (*a*) const. *of* (perh. a Gallicism); (*b*) const. *to*. *Obs.*

1692 DRYDEN *St. Euremont's Ess.* 5 'Tis an extraordinary thing to find a Successor endowed with the same Qualities of his Predecessor. **1721** BRADLEY *Philos. Acc. Wks. Nat.* 13 And the Nourishment and Difference of Colours given these Bodies..I suppose to be produced by a cause nearly the same of that which gives us the different Colours in the Leaves and Flowers of Vegetables. **1756** TOLDERVY *Hist. 2 Orphans* III. 33, I am of the same opinion to the gentleman, who spoke last. **1771–2** *Ess. fr. Batchelor* (1773) I. 96 They fancy themselves in the same situation of the Jews, when their being victors, or vanquish'd, solely depended on the raising or depressing of Moses's hands.

2. a. With backward reference: Identical with what has been indicated.

1340 HAMPOLE *Pr. Consc.* 25 Þe sam God sythyn was þe bygynnyng And þe first maker of alle thyng. **1340–70** *Alex. & Dind.* 896 Also ȝe sente vs to saie in þe same time Of oþur manerus mo miche for to lakke. **1362** LANGL. *P. Pl.* A. Prol. 106 Tauerners to hem tolde þe same tale Wiþ good wyn of Gaskoyne And wyn of Oseye. *c* **1400** *Pety Job* 76 in *26 Pol. Poems* 123 Into poudre must I crepe, ffor of that same kynde I am. *c* **1400** *Rule St. Benet* (Verse) 1234 And sche ken þe perils of cursing, Sche salbe cursid for þat same þing. *a* **1578** LINDESAY (Pitscottie) *Chron. Scot.* (S.T.S.) I. 147 About the same tyme rang money cuning men be quhose labouris & trawell goode letteris flurischit. **1685** BOYLE *Eng. Notion Nat.* 384 How great a Difference there may be between a Body consider'd absolutely, or by itself, and the same Body consider'd in such Circumstances, as it may be found in. **1886** LINDLEY in *Law Rep.* 32 *Chanc. Div.* 28 The same observations are true of all other contracts similarly circumstanced.

†**b.** = The aforesaid. *Obs.*

1338 R. BRUNNE *Chron.* (1810) 126 To Normundie ageyn suld turne þe duke Henry, & Ingland alle holy after Steuen þe kyng Suld turne to þe same Henry, withouten geynsaiyng. **1455** *Cal. Anc. Rec. Dublin* (1889) I. 286 And in case that the sam man or person in hys takyng, make recistens not to be take. **1480** *Coventry Leet Bk.* 429 We send yewe same bill herin enclosed. **1517** TORKINGTON *Pilgr.* (1884) 9 Thursday, the vij Day of May, we retornyed by the same watir of Brent to Venese ageyne. **1535** COVERDALE *Eccl.* xii. 9 The same preacher was not wyse alone, but taught the people knowlege also: he gaue good hede, sought out the grounde and set forth many parables.

†**c.** *the same day*: to-day. *Obs.*

c **1475** *Rauf Coilȝear* 848 On loud said the Sarazine: 'I heir the now lie! Befoir the same day I saw the neuer with sicht.'

3. a. Expressing the identity of an object designated by different names, standing in different relations, or related to different subjects or objects. In this use the sb. qualified by *same* often denotes an indeterminate or hypothetical object, so that *the* becomes (with a sing.) functionally equivalent to the indefinite article, or (with a plural) redundant; hence result occasional ambiguities.

Cf. the Fr. 'Deux mots qui signifient *une* même chose', '*De* mêmes causes doivent produire *de* mêmes effets' with the ambiguous English 'Two words which signify *the* same thing', '*The* same causes must produce the same effects'.

1621 BP. MOUNTAGU *Diatribæ* 553 Bacchus and Sabasius is the same god. **1662** STILLINGFL. *Orig. Sacræ* II. vi. §14 Both these Prophets considered the same people under the same circumstances, and with the same conditions. **1670** *Moral State Eng.* 160 At this time a Germain and a Fleming were in the same Pension in the Town. **1690** LOCKE *Hum. Und.* II. i. §9 Having Ideas, and Perception, being the same thing. **1713** STEELE *Englishman* No. 8. 55 The same Person is to be paid twice for the same thing. **1738** tr. *Guazzo's Art Conversation* 221 They cannot live peaceable together in the same House. **1765** A. DICKSON *Treat. Agric.* I. (ed. 2) 33 Some kinds of animals,..such as horses, cows, and sheep, are nourished by the same food. **1797** *Encycl. Brit.* (ed. 3) III. 457/2 The flowers are male and female upon the same or different roots. **1809–10** COLERIDGE *Friend* (1865) 142 Sooner or later the same causes, or their equivalents, will call forth the same opposition of opinion, and bring the same passions into play. **1828** SCOTT *F.M. Perth* xix, With whom I have so often sat at the same board, and drunken of the same cup. **1835** *Penny Cycl.* III. 437/2 The old barcarolle was sung in parts, at stem and stern of the same boat, by its own gondoliers. **1868** LOCKYER *Elem. Astron.* iii. §10 (1879) 55 All the planets travel round the Sun in the same direction. **1879** HARLAN *Eyesight* ii. 16 Even in the same eye, half of the iris is sometimes brown, and the other half blue. **1884** BRETT in *Law Times Rep.* 10 May 315/2, I have come to the conclusion..that the Legislature intended in this case to be verbose and tautologous, and to say the same thing twice over.

b. More explicitly, ***one and the same***.

[After L. *unus et idem*, Gr. (ὁ) εἷς καὶ ὁ αὐτός.]

1551 T. WILSON *Logike* S iv b, Out of one and the same floure the Bee sucketh hony, and the spider draweth poison. **1584** ?SIDNEY *Disc. Def. Earl of Leicester* Misc. Wks. (1829) 272 In sum, in one the same man, all the faults that in all the most contrary-humoured men in the world can remain. *c* **1650** LEIGHTON *Serm.* xviii. Wks. 1869 II. 227 Never think that one and the same soul can have much pride and much of Christ. **1659** H. MORE *Immort. Soul* II. i. 113 Perception being really one and the same thing with Reaction of Matter one part against another. *a* **1806** HORSLEY *Serm.* (1816) II. xxvi. 304 A sameness of the terms..would be an argument for assigning one and the same meaning to the promises. **1862** LATHAM *Channel Isl.* III. xviii. (ed. 2) 411 They belong to one and the same class.

4. Coupled for emphasis with a synonymous adj.: † ***that ilk*** (***thilk***) ***same***, † ***the same self***, † ***the same very, the very same***. See also SELFSAME.

The same self was exceedingly common in the 16th c.

13.. *Cursor M.* 1919 (Gött.) Þat ilk same day [*Cott.* þat ilk dai, *Fairf.* þat same day]. **1390** GOWER *Conf.* I. 95 Thilke same speche Which, as thou seist, thou schalt me teche. *a* **1450** MYRC *Par. Priests* 668 Þenne schale he wyth hys owne hondes Brenne þat ylke same bondes. **1503** *Rolls of Parlt.* VI. 522/2 They..shall have..lyke auctorite..as the same selfe Bisshoppes shulde, ought or myght do. **1526** *Pilgr. Perf.* (W. de W. 1531) 24 And the same selfe mysteryes he afterwarde declared to his discyples. **1589–90** *Reg. Privy Council Scot.* IV. 465 Baith haveing the same selff freindis and commoun enemeyis. **1590** L. LLOYD *Diall of Daies* 169 Q. Metellus triumphed over Creet at the same verie day that Pompei the great triumphed over the Pyrats on sea. **1594** SHAKS. *Rich. III*, III. ii. 49 This same very day. **1598** —— *Merry W.* IV. v. 37 Shee sayes, that the very same man that beguil'd Master Slender of his Chaine, cozon'd him of it. **1692** R. L'ESTRANGE *Fables* ix. 9 The Snake, after his Recovery, is the very same Snake still, that he was at first. *Ibid.* xviii. 19 Several of the very same Birds that she had forewarn'd.

5. Appended redundantly to a demonstrative (*this, these, that, those, yon*). Common in 16–17th c.; usually expressing some degree of irritation or contempt, sometimes playful familiarity. (Cf. the vulgar *this here, that there.*) Now *arch.*

Out of the 95 instances of the word *same* in Shakespeare, 55 occur in collocation with a demonstrative.

For examples in which *same* has its normal force when preceded by a demonstrative, see senses 1–3.

1340–70 *Alex. & Dind.* 197 In þis same wise. **1598** SHAKS. *Merry W.* V. i. 18 That same knaue (Ford hir husband). **1603** —— *Meas. for M.* V. i. 270 Call that same Isabell here once againe. **1625** BACON *Ess., Truth* (Arb.) 499 This same Truth, is a Naked, and Open day light. **1628** MILTON *Vac. Exerc.* 16, I pray thee then deny me not thy aide For this same small neglect that I have made. **1634** —— *Comus* 738 Be not cosen'd With that same vaunted name Virginity. **1726** SWIFT *On reading Young's Univ. Passion* Wks. 1751 X. 246 If that same *Universal Passion* With ev'ry Vice hath fill'd the Nation. **1808** SCOTT *Marm.* I. xxv, If this same Palmer will me lead From hence. **1816** J. WILSON *City of Plague* II. iii, What is the use of these same lamps? **1871** R. ELLIS *Catullus* x. 26 Just for courtesy lend me, dear Catullus, Those same nobodies.

6. Phrases. ***at the same time***: see TIME *sb.* ***by the same token***: see TOKEN *sb.* ***same difference***, the same thing, no difference (*colloq.*).

1945 E. WILSON *I am gazing into my 8-ball* xx. 106 'That fluff from my office.' 'Fluff?' laughed Miss Lawrence. 'Fluff, doll, same difference.' **1951** J. CORNISH *Provincials* II. i. 130 'I found you.' '*I* found *you*.' 'Same difference.' **1976** A. HILL *Summer's End* viii. 115 'In the first place,' he said, 'these'm *boats*, not barges.' 'Same difference,' Noggie insisted.

II. In modified senses.

7. a. Applied to an object as having the same attributes with another or with itself at another time; exactly agreeing *in* (amount, quality, operation, etc.). Of a person: Unchanged in character, condition of health, etc. Chiefly *predicative* (cf. B. 1, 2). Constructions as in 1–3.

Phrases. ***much the same***: approximately the same (cf. MUCH *adv.* 3). (***the***) ***same but*** (or ***only***) ***different*** (*colloq.*): almost the same; subtly different.

1667 MILTON *P.L.* I. 256 The mind is its own place, and in it self Can make a Heav'n of Hell, a Hell of Heav'n. What matter where, if I be still the same. **1669** STURMY *Mariner's Mag.* IV. 138 If the Course and Distance had been first agreed upon from the Place they were bound to, to be just the same, unto the..Land they first descried. **1718** *Free-thinker* No. 91 ⁋5 Human Nature is perpetually the same, ever subject to the same Passions and Corruptions. **1758** R. PRICE *Rev. Quest. Morals* viii. (1769) 293 *note*, A distinction much the same with this may be found in the letters between Dr. Sharp and Mrs. Cockburn. **1836** J. GILBERT *Chr. Atonem.* ix. (1852) 284 God himself remains the same before and after the interposition of Christ. **1838** PRESCOTT *Ferd. & Is.* II. vi. II. 518 Bigotry is the same in every faith and every age. **1855** MACAULAY *Hist. Eng.* xv. III. 585 His salary was the same with that of the Lord Lieutenant. **1860** LD. LYTTON *Lucile* II. II. iii, Do not think that years leave us and find us the same! **1861** M. PATTISON *Ess.* (1889) I. 48 The Steelyard passed with the rest of the parish by the same easy gradations from the old to the new faith. **1893** *Bookman* June 86/1 Her ambitions superficially so different at different times, and yet substantially the same. **1942** BERREY & VAN DEN BARK *Amer. Thes. Slang* §16/9 *Same but different*, nearly the same. **1977** *Lancashire Life* Nov. 60/1 More seasoned observers may remark that the scene's the same, only different.

b. *predicatively*. Of a person: Unchanged in behaviour *to* another.

1850 DICKENS *Dav. Copp.* ix, But she was always the same to me. She never changed to her foolish Peggotty.

c. Corresponding in relative position.

1672 PETTY *Pol. Anat.* (1691) 18 About 504 M. of the Irish perished..between the 23 of October 1641 and the same day 1652. **1848** THACKERAY *Van. Fair* xxviii, He and I were both shot in the same leg at Talavera. **1856** SIR G. C. LEWIS *Lett.* (1870) 317 The Foreign Office..now holds the same place in our social economy as the Colonial Office used to hold. **1891** 'J. S. WINTER' *Lumley* xii, The doctors..have decidedly better hopes than they had yesterday at the same time.

8. Predicatively: Equally acceptable or the contrary; indifferent. Also ***all the same***, ***just the same***.

1803 MARY CHARLTON *Wife & Mistress* I. 245 He don't vally what he says to young or old, man or woman—it's all the same to old gruffy! **1838** DICKENS *Nich. Nick.* vii, It's all the same to me. **1847** UPHAM *Mme. Guyon & Fénélon* II. iii. 31 (Funk) To Daniel the lion's den and the monarch's palace are the same. **1914** G. B. SHAW *Pygmalion* (1916) III. 157 *Pickering.* We have taken her to classical concerts and to music..halls; and its all the same to her: she plays everything..she hears right off when she comes home. **1962** L. DEIGHTON *Ipcress File* 8 If it's all the same to you, Minister, I'd prefer you to make a note of the questions, and ask me afterwards.

9. Predicatively, without article: Characterized by sameness, monotonous. *rare.*

1891 *Pall Mall G.* 3 Feb. 6/2 The choruses in 'Judith' are numerous, and to the lay mind perhaps a little same.

III. 10. *Comb.*, as ***same-aged***, ***-kidneyed***, ***-named***, ***-natured***, ***-seemingness***, ***-sexed***, ***-sidedness***, ***-sized***, ***-soundingness***; also ***same-day***, ***-sex***, ***-size*** attrib.; **same-level** *Social Science*, analogous; that uses an established principle in one field of research for the explanation or analysis of phenomena in another field; **same-ways** *adv.*, in the same direction.

1949 M. MEAD *Male & Female* xiv. 285 He will frown upon the *same-aged youth who has a reputation for active premarital sex relations. **1967** *Punch* 22 Feb. 258/3 And such cleaning and pressing, a *same-day service like you never seen. **1674** N. FAIRFAX *Bulk & Selv.* Ep. Ded., The *same-kidneyed men, who have..a sharp flowt at the end of their tongue. **1934** J. T. WISDOM in *Aristotelian Soc. Suppl. Vol.* XIII. 66 When the psychologist says 'I am in awe of you' means 'I fear and admire you' he is giving a more ostensive but still *same-level translation of the first sentence. **1936** *Mind* XLV. 442 All material analysis is 'same-level analysis'. **1958** M. ARGYLE *Relig. Behaviour* xii. 141 A third kind of theory explains an empirical result by showing that it is an example of a law in another field of research—this will be called a 'same-level' theory. *Ibid.* 143 This is clearly a 'same-level' explanation, postulating that religion is learnt by the same processes of socialization as are other attitudes and beliefs. **1954** S. DUKE-ELDER *Parsons' Dis. Eye* (ed. 12) xxviii. 473 In vertical palsies the paresis is due to failure of the '*same-named' rectus muscle (in the left superior area, the left superior rectus) or the most 'crossed-named' oblique muscle (right inferior oblique). **1696** J. SERGEANT *Method to Sci.* I. ii. 20 The same Causes upon the *same-natur'd Subjects, must work the same Effects. **1839–48** BAILEY *Festus* xx. 231 Lest long *same-seemingness should send me mad. **1949** M. MEAD *Male & Female* xiv. 284 Their sex, lightly anchored to the model of the *same-sex parent. **1917** *Same-sexed [see FRATERNAL *a.* c]. **1977** *Lancet* 24 Sept. 657/2 There is sometimes *same-sidedness in familial breast cancer. **1967** KARCH & BUBER *Offset Processes* v. 151 Set the camera for *same-size reproduction. **1764** *Museum Rust.* III. lii. 229 Let this be done deep, and still in the *same-sized ridges. **1951** W. DE LA MARE *Winged Chariot* 32 On every nut there swelled the same-sized husk. **1839–48** BAILEY *Festus* iv. 33 The sea..In its sublime *samesoundingness laughed out. **1887** SIR W. THOMSON in *Nature* 3 Oct. 546/2 Every A is at the centre of an equal and similar, and *same-ways oriented, tetrahedron of O's.

B. *absol.* and as *pron.* (Constructions as in A.)

1. a. The same person or persons.

1340–70 *Alex. & Dind.* 780 ȝe ben soþli þe same of wham þei so tolde. *c* 1366 CHAUCER *A.B.C.* 77 Now queen of comfort sithe þou art þat same To whom ȝ seeche for my medicyne [etc.]. 1616 B. JONSON *Epigr.* xxxiii, On Sir Iohn Roe.. To the same. 1817 JAS. MILL *Brit. India* II. v. ix. 707 An appeal from the King's Council, to the King in Council, was ridiculed, even by the opponents of the bill, as an appeal from the same to the same.

†**b.** Conjoined with a personal pronoun or with a designation of a person, to indicate identity with one who has been mentioned. *Obs.* [A latinism.]

1377 LANGL. *P. Pl.* B. III. 26 Thanne lauȝte þei leue, þis lordes, at Mede. With that comen clerkis to conforte hir þe same. 1548 UDALL, etc. *Erasm. Par. Acts* 1 With the aduise and consente of the moste prudent and the same his moste dere vncle. 1598 GRENEWEY *Tacitus, Ann.* II. xvii. (1622) 57 Shew the people of Rome Augustus neece, and the same my wife [L. *Augusti neptem eandemque conjugem meam*].

2. a. The same thing. (See A. 1, 2, 3.) †Formerly also ***that same, this same.***

1340–70 *Alex. & Dind.* 1009 But þe same þat ȝe so by vs silf trowe Longeþ, ludus, to ȝou þat liuen so in ese. 1390 GOWER *Conf.* I. 19 Who that here wordes understode, It thenkth thei wolden do the same. *c* 1400 *Destr. Troy* 9772 þe sam to my-self, sothli, may happyn. *c* 1400 *Rule St. Benet* (verse) 488 And also crist in his godspell Of þis same makes minde o-mell. *a* 1450 MYRC *Festial* 8 Anon he made to take hym, and constrayne hym forto haue done þe same. *a* 1536 TINDALE *Pathw. Script.* Wks. (1573) 383/2 What soeuer is done to the lest of vs.. it is done to Christ, and what soeuer is done to my brother (if I be a Christen man) that same is done to me. 1576 FLEMING *Panopl. Epist.* 142, I have commended S—unto you oftentimes: and do the same againe at this instant. 1677 GALE *Crt. Gentiles* II. IV. 489 Here that common Proverbe holds true, 'When two do the same it is not the same'. 1687 A. LOVELL tr. *Thevenot's Trav.* I. 112, I failed not to speak to our Vice-Consul of the Light I had seen in the Isle of Samos, and he told me all the same that the rest did. 1711 J. GREENWOOD *Eng. Gram.* Wallis's Pref. 2 So the French Words *guerre* [etc.].. signify the same with these English Words. 1812 SOUTHEY *Let. to Jas. White* 16 Feb. in *Life* (1850) III. 328 It is the same in our age that it was in our youth. 1848 KINGSLEY '*Bad Squire*' xiv, If your misses had slept, squire, where they slept, Your misses would do the same. 1864 NEWMAN *Apologia* v. (1904) 168/1 When I became a Catholic, nothing struck me more.. than the English out-spoken manner of the Priests. It was the same at Oscott, at Old Hall Green, at Ushaw. 1896 A. E. HOUSMAN *Shropshire Lad* xliii, Bring the eternal seed to light, And morn is all the same as night.

†**b.** Phrases. ***of the same***: in the same way. ***to the (this) same***: to the same effect. ***with the same***: at the same moment. *Obs.*

1399 LANGL. *Rich. Redeles* Prol. 14 All þe londe.. ros with him rapely to riȝtyn his wronge, For he shullde hem serue of þe same after. *c* 1400 *Rule St. Benet* (verse) 373 Also we se ȝit to þe same. *Ibid.* 461 For hali writ sais on þis wise: 'þe fole with word may non chastese.'.. And to þis sam, als clerks may kun, þe wise man sais: 'Chastise þi sun [etc.].' 1603 HOLLAND *Plutarch's Mor.* 1027 He spake the word, and with the same, Immediatly out came the name.

¶**c.** With omission of article. *rare*⁻¹.

1638 BRATHWAIT *Barnabees Jrnl.* II. (1818) 45 What I was once, same I am now.

d. ***(the) same again***: another drink of the same kind as the last; ***same here***: the same (thing) applies to me; my case is similar; I agree; ***(the) same to you***; I say the same thing to you (as you have just said); freq. used as a retort.

1896 W. C. GORE in *Inlander* Jan. 150 *Same here!* I agree. 1907 A. P. MCKISHNIE *Gaff Linkum* xi. 59 'I've enj'yed th' ride in th' moonlight jest as much as I enj'yed th' singin' school.' 'Same here,' said Mr. Goosecall. 1911 G. B. SHAW *Blanco Posnet* 404 *Blanco.* Dearly beloved brethren—*A Boy.* Same to you, Blanco. 1913 KIPLING *Diversity of Creatures* (1917) 288 'Do you know I've broken this man's neck?' 'Same here,' I says. 1925 *New Yorker* 17 Oct. 12/2 The same to you. 1929 D. H. LAWRENCE in *Star Rev.* Nov. 624 It is as if the young girl said to the young man today: I rather like you, you know. You are so thrillingly repulsive to me.—And as if the young man replied: Same here! 1938 L. MACNEICE *Earth Compels* 22 What will you have now? The same again? 1949 G. B. SHAW *Buoyant Billions* II. 21 A chain shopkeeper, not a country squire. *She.* Same here: my father is a famous lucky financier. 1959, etc. [see KNOB *sb.* 1 e]. 1962 *Sunday Times* 19 Aug. 18 'I'm a rugged individualist: I think for myself.' 'Me too.' 'Same here.' 1972 H. KEMELMAN *Monday Rabbi took Off* xxi. 136 'To tell the truth, I think it was the *rebbitzin* that wrote it and he signed it.' 'Same here.' 1975 D. O'SULLIVAN in D. Marcus *Best Irish Short Stories* (1977) II. 90 A thump on the counter brought the barmaid. .. 'Same again, ladies?'

†**3.** Pleonastically emphasizing a demonstrative, used absol. or with ellipsis of sb. *Obs.*

1588 SHAKS. *L.L.L.* II. i. 194 Sir, I pray you a word: What Lady is that same? 1591 —— *Two Gent.* III. i. 138 What Letter is this same? 1592 —— *Rom. & Jul.* IV. v. 147 What a pestilent knaue is this same. 1611 BIBLE *Acts* xxiv. 20 Let these same here [1881 *R.V.* these men themselves] say, if they haue found any evill doing in mee.

4. a. ***the same***, †***that*** (or ***this***) ***same***: the aforesaid person or thing. Often merely the equivalent of a personal pronoun; he, she, it, they. Now *rare* in literary use; still common in legal documents; also (with reference to things) in commercial language (where *the* is sometimes omitted). Cf. G. *der-, die-, dasselbe.*

1362 LANGL. *P. Pl.* A. III. 27 þenne [lauȝten] þei leue þis lordynges, at Meede. Wiþ þat þer come Clerkes to Cumforte þe same. *c* 1400 *Lansdowne Ritual* in *Rule St. Benet*, etc. 143 þe nouyce sal.. singe þare thrise: 'Suscipe me, domine' &c. þe couent.. sall reherce þe same again thrise, and 'Gloria patri'. *c* 1400 MAUNDEV. (1839) viii. 97 Upon that same schalle he sytte,.. righte as himself seyde. *c* 1450 *Cov. Myst.* ii. (Shaks. Soc.) 25 Take this appyl and ete this ssame, This ffrute is best as I the telle. 1474 CAXTON *Chesse* Ded., That ye sawe gladly the Inhabitants of ye same enformed in good, vertuous, prouffitable and honeste maners. 1484 —— *Fables of Æsop* III. vii, [Men] ought to preyse and loue the chirche and the commaundements of the same. 1500–20 DUNBAR *Poems* lii. 11 ȝour Hienes can nocht gett ane meter, To keip your wardrope, nor discreter, To rule ȝour robbis, and dress the sam. 1503 in Kerry *Hist. St. Lawrence, Reading* (1883) 111 Also ij staynyd clothis w^t ryddels to þe same. 1509 FISHER *Funeral Serm. C'tess Richmond* Wks. (1876) 290 Above all these same there is a foure maner of noblenes. 1535 COVERDALE *Lev.* xiii. 40 Whan the hayres fall out of the heade of a man or a woman, so that he is balde, the same is cleane. 1548–9 (Mar.) *Bk. Com. Prayer, Collect 1st Sunday after Epiphany*, Graunt that they maie both perceaue and knowe what thinges they ought to do, and also haue grace and power faithfully to fulfill the same. 1583 STUBBES *Anat. Abus.* II. (1882) 65 Watermen haunt the waters, and fishes swim in the same. 1590 SHAKS. *Com. Err.* IV. i. 11 In the instant that I met with you, He had of me a Chaine, at fiue a clocke I shall receiue the money for the same. 1596 SPENSER *F.Q.* IV. x. 5 That was a temple.. farre renowmed .. Much more then that which was in Paphos built, Or that in Cyprus, both long since this same. 1611 BIBLE *Matt.* xxiv. 13 But he that shall endure vnto the end, the same shall be saued. 1621 in Owen & Blakeway *Hist. Shrewsb.* (1825) I. 574 Laid out in stocking up of the gorst in Kingsland, making the same into faggottes. 1667 PRIMATT *City & C. Build.* 8 An over-shot-mill, which is the water brought to the top of the wheel, in landers or troughs which cast the same into Buckets made in the wheel for the receipt of the same, the force and weight of which water drives the same. 1772–84 *Cook's Voy.* (1790) V. 1755 The natives thinking we were determined to pay not the least consideration, at length ceased to apply for the same. 1818 CRUISE *Digest* (ed. 2) III. 324 If such tenant for life die on the day on which the same was made payable, the whole [rent must be paid]. 1819 KEATS *Isabella* ii, Her lute-string gave an echo of his name, She spoiled her half-done broidery with the same. 1901 M. FRANKLIN *My Brilliant Career* viii. 56 A big red-bearded man.. had received a letter from Mrs. Bossier instructing him to take care of me. He informed me also that he was glad to do what he termed 'that same'. 1926 in H. W. Fowler *Mod. Eng. Usage* 512/1 Sir,—Having in mind the approaching General Election, it appears to me that the result of same is likely to be as much a farce as the last. 1966 G. W. TURNER *Eng. Lang. in Austral. & N.Z.* vi. 135 A different influence of written language is seen in the use of *same* as a pronoun equivalent to *it*, as in 'put the tailboard up and secure same with a length of wire' from New Zealand (Wally Crump, 1964), a facetious borrowing of lawyer's English which is quite common. 1973 *N.Y. Law Jrnl.* 24 July 4/4 The following sentence in a brief is typical of its misuse as a noun: 'Waldbaum purchased the soda.. then stacked it on the shelves in order to sell the same.'

b. †As an answer when addressed by name; = 'I am he'. *Obs.* Also *colloq.* in confirming a conjecture as to the identity of a person mentioned by the speaker.

1599 SHAKS. *Much Ado* II. i. 191 *Ben.* Count Claudio. *Clau.* Yea, the same. 1889 *Chatterbox* 24 Aug. 323/1 'Have you ever heard of Red Jim?' 'The bushranger, do you mean?' asked Allan. 'The same. Well, this man [etc.]'.

†**c.** ***(the) same***; = DITTO *sb. Obs.*

1486 *Bk. St. Albans* b iij, Take the Juce of percelly Moris otherwise calde percelly Rootis, and thossame of Isop. 1615 R. COCKS *Diary* 18 June (Hakl. Soc.) I. 11 He gave me a present of 3 nestes gocas, with their trenchers and ladells of mother of perle, with 10 spoons same, and a peece of white Liquea cloth. 1663 GERBIER *Counsel* 72 Rafters ten and seven inches, Purloyns the same, Plates the same.

†**d.** Chiefly Her. ***of the same***: of the kind or description last mentioned. *Obs.*

a 1548 HALL *Chron., Hen. VIII* 25 The Kyng was appareilled in almayne ryuet crested & his vambrace of the same. ?*a* 1588 *Glover's Ordinary* 38 in *Edmondson's Her.* I, Ar. in fesse three pellets betw. two bars sa. in chief two goats heads erased gu. attired or.; in base one of the same. *Gethinge.* 1625 BACON *Ess., Building* (Arb.) 553 A Greene Court Plain, with a Wall about it: A Second Court of the same, but more Garnished.

5. a. quasi-*sb.* An identical thing. *nonce-uses.*

1690 DRYDEN *Amphitryon* v. i, *Tran.* Two drops of water cannot be more like. *Pol.* They are two very sames. 1700 —— *Ovid's Met.* xv. Fables 515 Ev'n our own Bodies daily change receive,.. Nor are to Day what Yesterday they were; Nor the whole same to Morrow will appear.

b. pl. *Linguistics.* Features or utterances that are identical.

[1926 BLOOMFIELD in *Language* II. 155 Within certain communities successive utterances are alike or partly alike. .. That which is alike will be called *same.* That which is not same is *different.* This enables us to use these words without reference to non-linguistic shades of sound and meaning. 1948 B. BLOCH in *Ibid.* XXIV. 10 Successive phonotations composed wholly of the same articulations are *the same.* Other aspects are different.] 1961 R. B. LONG *Sentence & its Parts* xvii. 378 The evidence of history warrants our regarding the italicized words in the following pairs as 'sames' in spite of the differences in meanings. We rode in the day *coach.* We went with the football *coach* [etc.]. 1962 [see FORM *sb.* 5 c]. 1964 CRYSTAL & QUIRK *Syst. Prosodic & Paralinguistic Features in Eng.* iv. 49 We should.. only subsequently look for the correlations between postulated 'sames' of tension and formal items in the linguistic and situational context which will enable us to make statements of meaning. 1977 *Trans. Philol. Soc. 1975* 9 Certain configurations in languages typically result from the principled ('lawful') divergence over time of original sames.

C. *adv.* and in adverbial phrases.

1. ***the same***: **a.** in the same manner; (in weakened sense) just *as.* Const. *as.* ***to think the same of***: to have the same (good) opinion of (a person). Similarly, ***to feel the same to.***

Now rare in literary use; common *dial.*, often with omission of *the.*

1766 *Museum Rust.* III. 240 Sow the seed broad-cast,.. then harrow it in, the same as turnep seed. 1827 D. JOHNSON *Ind. Field Sports* 154 There is a physical cause for this, which operates the same in India as in the holy land. 1857 'S. SONDNOKKUR' *Ryde fro Ratchda to Manchistur* (ed. 2) IV. 9 Aw kuddunt elp wundurin.. wether it wur to put iz grund coffi in, saym uz wi dun o whoam. *Ibid.* VI. 14 Thir wur o rattlin saym uz uv o lot a peawur looms. 1861 GEO. ELIOT *Silas M.* xviii. 325 You'll never think the same of me again. 1884 'MARK TWAIN' *Huck. Finn* ii. 10 Strange niggers would.. look him all over, same as if he was a wonder. 1930 W. FAULKNER *As I lay Dying* 4 She ought to taken those cakes when she same as gave you her word. 1933 M. LOWRY *Ultramarine* i. 16 He knows bloody well same as myself it doesn't pay to shout and be unkind to youngsters. 1957 L. P. HARTLEY *Hireling* viii. 65 But I shouldn't be able to serve them personally, same as I do now. 1975 *Listener* 6 Feb. 174/1 There was no work.. We were all bad years, because, same as I say, there was nothing.

b. = 'all the same': see 2. *Obs.* exc. *poet.*

1782 MISS BURNEY *Cecilia* v. viii, Suppose I am a cabinet-maker? When I send in my chairs, do I ask who is to sit upon them? No; it's all one to me..; I must be paid for the chairs the same, use them who may. 1884 BROWNING *Ferishtah* (1885) 39 For as our liege the Shah's sublime estate Merely enhaloes, leaves him man the same, So [etc.].

c. ***same like***: just like, the same as, in the same manner as. *dial.*, *illiterate*, or *joc.*

1898 W. P. RIDGE *Mord Em'ly* x. 142 Beef Pudding same like Mother makes! 1922 E. O'NEILL *Anna Christie* II. 134 Two my bro'der dey gat lost on fishing boat same like your bro'ders vas drowned. 1928 J. PETERKIN *Scarlet Sister Mary* iv. 47 E weddin-dress fits em same like a green shuck fits a young ear o corn. *Ibid.* xix. 207 I'll lay down on de ground an' holler same like a dog. *Ibid.* xxi. 227 'How you do today?' 'Fine. Same like a lamb a-jumpin.' 1959 A. CHRISTIE *Cat among Pigeons* ix. 107 'See no evil, hear no evil, think no evil. Same like the monkeys,' observed Sergeant Percy Bond. 1968 'L. EGAN' *Serious Investigation* vi. 78 But same like the gent in Holy Writ, Beware the anger of a patient man. 1973 G. MITCHELL *Murder of Busy Lizzie* xv. 185 Ain't going to be no share-out. Same like the boy with the apple-core, if you happen to know that story. 1980 I. MURDOCH *Nuns & Soldiers* vii. 382, I have rich friends, same like you.

2. ***all the same***: in spite of what has been mentioned; even if circumstances had been otherwise; nevertheless, notwithstanding.

1803 MARY CHARLTON *Wife & Mistress* I. 121 But who would have thought of my Lady Countess having a maid sent with young Miss, whilst my Dolly have nothing to do, but to milk a cow or two, and dust and scrub a bit, and cook a bit; and could all the same wait upon she too! 1845 DISRAELI *Sybil* VI. iv, What you say is well worth attention; but all the same I feel we are on the eve of a regular crisis. 1852 CLOUGH *Poems*, etc. (1869) I. 187 This winter is extraordinarily mild: to day a little hoar frost, but bright sunshine all the same. 1856 F. E. PAGET *Owlet of Owlst.* 164 No, thank you. Obliged to you, Henry, all the same. 1861 J. PYCROFT *Agony Point* (1862) 340 Audrey remarked that the said allowance made little difference; the money would have gone all the same. 1868 SWINBURNE *Blake* 176 A man is locked up, with keys of gold indeed, yet is he a prisoner all the same. 1878 RUSKIN *Let. to Dr. J. Brown* 21 Oct., I was very sorry to come away. All the same, I'm glad to be at home again.

3. ***just the same***: **a.** Exactly in the same manner. Const. *as.* **b.** None the less.

1874 ALDRICH *Prudence Palfrey* xiv. 281 And in the meantime Dillingham will continue his visits here just the same? 1901 H. MCHUGH *John Henry* 59 'My mother was a lady', so She said, but just the same She ate boiled cabbage with a knife Except when company came.

same, variant of SAM *adv.* and *v. Obs.*; obs. f. PSALM; var. SEAM, lard; obs. f. SHAME *sb.* and *v.*

†'**samed,** *adv. Obs.* Forms: 1 samod, somed, somod, 3 somed, someð, somet. [OE. *samod* = OS. *samod, samad*, Du. (17th c.) *samet*, OHG. *samet, samit, samant* (MHG., mod.G. *samt*), Goth. *samaþ*, f. OTeut. **samo-* SAME *a.*] Together.

Beowulf 1063 þær wæs sang and sweȝ samod ætgædere for Healfdenes hildewisan. *a* 900 CYNEWULF *Crist* 1236 þær bið on eadȝum eðȝesyne þreo tacen somod. *a* 1000 *Cædmon's Gen.* 789 (Gr.) þa hie fela spræcon sorhworda somed, sinhiwan twa. *c* 1205 LAY. 20132 Ford we biliue þeies ohte alle someð [? somed] heom to. *Ibid.* 25747 þat heo sculden somed faren. *a* 1225 *Leg. Kath.* 532 Ha somet seiden, þæt [etc.].

same(i)kle, etc.: Sc. ff. *so mickle*; see SO *adv.*

samel ('sæməl). Also 7 sammell, 7–8 sammel; *erron.* 8 sandal, -el. See also SAMMEN. [Of obscure origin; possibly repr. an OE. **samǣled* half-burnt, f. SAM- + pa. pple of *ǣlan* to burn.] Of a brick or tile: Imperfectly burnt.

1663 GERBIER *Counsel* 26 To suffer no Sammell Bricks to be made use of. *Ibid.* 28 See the Brick-layers take good sollid Bricks to hue, since if any thing Sammel the work will molder away. 1703 T. N. *City & C. Purchaser* 48 He had burnt several Kilns of Tiles and.. not had above 50 waste, broken, and Sandal Tiles in all. 1716 *Lond. Gaz.* No. 5446/8 All that are samel, or under burnt, to be excluded. 1727–51 CHAMBERS *Cycl.* s.v. *Brick, Samel,* or *sandal bricks*, are such as lie outmost in a kiln or clamp, and consequently are soft and useless; as not being thoroughly burnt. 1745 *De Foe's Eng. Tradesman* iii. (1841) I. 23 The brick-maker's men.. turned their hands from the grey, hard, well-burnt bricks, to the soft, sammel, half-burnt bricks. 1845 *Encycl. Metrop.* VIII. 443/2 The outside bricks are necessarily under-burned. These are called samel bricks.

'**sameliness.** [f. SAMELY *a.* + -NESS.]

†**1.** Identity. *Obs.*

1662 J. Chandler *Van Helmont's Oriat.* 22 An unexcusable disagreement of every Similitude, remote from identity or sameliness. *Ibid* 338.

2. Want of variety, monotony.

1897 Webster (citing Bayne). 1901 *Westm. Gaz.* 10 Oct. 4/2 The sameliness of Longfellow's trochaic metre in 'Hiawatha'.

samely ('seɪmlɪ), *a.* [f. SAME *a.* + -LY[1].] Without variety; monotonous.

1799 *Trans. Soc. Arts* XVII. 122 To..separate parts [of the forest] that were in some places too heavy and samely. 1821 Clare *Vill. Minstr.* I. 58 O samely naked leas, so bleak, so strange! 1844 Kinglake *Eöthen* xvii. (1864) 198 The earth is so samely, that your eyes turn towards heaven. 1902 *Monthly Mus. Record* 1 Jan. 16 Mr. Thomas F. Dunhill's Sixteen Variations on an original theme are too long and samely.

†**'samen**, *a. Sc. Obs.* Forms: 4 **saymne**, 4–6 **sammyn(e**, 4–7 **samyn**, 4–9 **samine**, 5–6 **samin**, **samyne**, 6 **sammin**, **samyng**, 7–8 **samen**. [A derivative of SAME *a.*; the formation is obscure; possibly due to the influence of next.] = SAME.

1375 Barbour *Bruce* I. 252 And in the samyn tym come him to His wyff. *c*1375 *Sc. Leg. Saints* v. (*Johannes*) 348 Sancte Iohne ȝet but abaysitnes þe saymne drink tuk neuir-þe-les. 1456 Sir G. Haye *Law Arms* (S.T.S.) 25 Alssua in the samyn wys, did the Emperour Frederike. *c*1480 Henryson *Test Cres.* 58 For worthie Chauceir, in the samin buik, In gudelie termis, and in Ioly veirs, Compylit hes his cairis. 1513 Douglas *Æneis* vii. v. 184 Geif that my mynd can ocht ymagine rycht, I wene that he suld be the samyn knycht. *a*1555 Lyndesay *Tragedy* 331 Brether,..quhen ȝe were consecrat, ȝe oblyste ȝow all on the sammyn wyse. 1577–95 *Descr. Isles Scotl.* in Skene *Celtic Scotl.* III. App. 428 Yit thai keip the lawis and uses of the samine for the maist part. *c*1600 Montgomerie *Cherrie & Slae* 1503 Lyk as befoir we did submit, Sae we repeit the samyn ȝit. 1638 Chas. I in Spalding *Troub.* (Bannatyne Cl.) I. 62 Wee have taken notice therof and doe give you heartiely thanks for the samen. 1671 R. MacWard *True Nonconf.* vii. 398 The samine is there truely and more fully to be found. 1678 Sir G. Mackenzie *Crim. Laws Scot.* ii. xv. §4 (1699) 214 He writes upon the Bill, soverty is found; & subscribes the samine. 1725 Ramsay *Gentle Sheph.* iii. iii, And had I fifty times as meikle mair Nane but my Jenny should the samen skair. 1815 Finlayson *Rhymes* 95 (E.D.D.) Thousands are o' the samen mind.

†**'samen**, *adv. Obs.* Forms: 1–3 **somen**, 3 *Orm.* **samenn**, 3–5 **samen**, 4 **saman**, **samine**, **sammin**, **sammyne**, **samun**, 4–5 **samin**, **sammyn**, 4–6 **samyn**, 4–7 **sammen**, 5 **samene**, **samne**, **sampnen**, **samyne**, **samynge**, **somun**, **somyn**. [OE. **samen*, *sǫmen* (with prep. *æt sǫmne*) = OFris. *samin*, *semin*, *to-semine*, *to saminen*, OS. *saman*, *at-samna*, *to samne* (MLG. *sam(m)ene*, *to samene*), MDu. *samen*, *te-samen* (Du. *tezamen*), OHG. *saman*, *zi samane* (MLG. *zesamene*, mod.G. *zusammen*), ON. *saman*, *til samans* (Sw. *samman*, *tilsamman(s*, Da. *sammen*, *tilsammen*), Goth. *samana*, f. root of SAME *a.* Cf. Skr. *samanā* together.] = SAM *adv.*, together, mutually. For *in samen* see INSAME.

*c*975 *Rushw. Gosp.* John xxi. 2 Werun somen simon petrus & ðe ðeʒn seðe wæs cweden didimus. *c*1200 Ormin 377 Þeȝȝ baþe samenn cwemmdenn Godd þurrh heore rihht-wisnesse. *c*1230 *Hali Meid.* (MS. Titus) 59 Ha ne muhen nawt somen [*MS. Bodl.* somet] earden in heuene. *c*1250 *Gen. & Ex.* 40 In firme beginning, of noght Was heuene and erðe samen wroght. *a*1300 *Cursor M.* 7151 Thre hundreth fox he samun knitt, (I wat noght hu he on þam hitte). *Ibid.* 11998 And iesus samen his handes smat, and said. 1340 Hampole *Pr. Consc.* 1849 Bot þe body and þe saul..Lufes mare samen þan man and hys wyfe. *c*1375 *Sc. Leg. Saints* i. (*Petrus*) 111 þan kissit þai [ilk] oþer sammyne, gretand faste with gastly gammyne. *c*1400 *Destr. Troy* 10118 Seyuyn dayes somyn sesit þai noght. *c*1400 Maundev. (Roxb.) xxviii. 128 þai ware all gadred sammen. *c*1420 *Sir Amadace* (Camden) lv, A fayre knaue child hade thay somun. 1435 Misyn *Fire of Love* 78 We suld schewe lufly songis, to we be ..broght in-to þe inward dwellynge-place, samne takand a seet emongis heuenly citesenes. *c*1450 *Mirour Saluacioun* 3217 In this ffasscicle of mirre ware bonden samen paynes alle. 1513 Douglas *Æneis* v. vi. 16 On athir half, than gaderis hym about Of Troianis samyn and Sicilianis a rowt.

†**'samen**, *v. Obs.* ? Aphetic for EXAMINE *v.*

?1613 Rowlands *Paire Spy-knaves* (1872) 6 They samen him according to their skils.

samen, obs. form of SAM *v.*

samene, variant of SAMEN *adv.*, together.

sameness ('seɪmnɪs). [f. SAME + -NESS.]

1. The quality of being the same; = IDENTITY 1, 2.

1581 Mulcaster *Positions* xxxii. (1887) 118 They were ill sundred, whom the samenes of time so vniteth together. 1607 *Schol. Disc. agst. Antichr.* i. i. 28 They meane a samenesse for some proportion that is betweene them. 1678 Cudworth *Intell. Syst.* i. iv. 559 We worship, the Father of Truth, and the Son the Truth it self, being Two Things as to Hypostasis; but one in Agreement, Consent, and Sameness of Will. 1690 C. Nesse *O. & N. Test.* I. 119 If there be the sameness in sinning, the same shall be in suffering. 1690 Locke *Hum. Und.* i. iv. §4 Our Idea of sameness, is not so setled and clear, as to deserve to be thought innate in us. 1736 Butler *Anal.* i. i. 17 Personal identity or the sameness of living agents. 1753 *Scots Mag.* XV. 17/2 The sameness of the electrical fire with that of lightning. 1759 Capell *Prolusions* Pref. (1760) 7 Sameness of rythmus, sameness of orthography, and a very near affinity of words and phrases. 1827 Whately *Logic* App. (ed. 2) 305 Sameness, in the primary sense, does not even necessarily imply Similarity. 1875 Jowett *Plato* (ed. 2) IV. 139 Likeness is sameness of affections.

2. Absence of variety, uniformity, monotony; an instance of this.

1743 H. Walpole *Let. to Mann* 27 Jan., We are in such a state of sameness that I shall begin to wonder at the change of seasons and talk of the Spring as a strange accident. 1766 Fordyce *Serm. Yng. Wm.* (1767) II. viii. 20 There will arise ..a sameness and a flatness. 1820 J. W. Croker in Smiles *Mem. J. Murray* (1891) II. xxiii. 86, I shall endeavour to enliven a little the sameness of my author. 1842 Vigne *Trav. Kashmir* II. 404 The scenery is sameness itself. 1886 Ruskin *Præterita* I. 238 The steady occupations, the beloved samenesses, and the sacred customs of home.

3. ? *nonce-use.* Agreement in character or style.

1790 in W. Wrighte *Grotesque Archit.* Frontisp., Each will require a sameness to the Spot, For this a Cell, a Cascade or a Grot.

†**'samenfere.** *Obs.* [f. SAMEN *adv.* + FERE *sb.*[1]] A fellow-traveller, an associate.

13.. *E.E. Allit. P.* B. 985 Þay slipped bi & syȝe hir not þat wern hir samen feres.

†**'samening.** *Obs.* Forms: 1 **somnung**, 1–2 **samnung**, 3 **samening**, **somnunge**, **sompnunge**, 4 **samenyng**, **samnyng**, **sampninge**. [OE. *samnung*, vbl. sb. f. *samn-ian* SAM *v.*: see -ING[1].] **a.** A gathering, an assembly. **b.** Intercourse, communion.

*c*950 *Lindisf. Gosp.* Mark i. 23, & wæs in somnung [*c*1160 *Hatton* samnunge] hiora monn in gast unclæne. *c*1200 *Trin. Coll. Hom.* 215 Me is andsete þe samninge of þe hinderfulle. *c*1230 *Hali Meid.* 12 (Bodley MS.) þet bestelich gederunge, þet scheomelese sompnunge [*Titus MS.* somnunge], þet ful of fulðe stinkinde & untohe dede. *c*1250 in *Rel. Ant.* I. 23 Hy troue hy þeli gast, and hely kirke, þe samninge of halghes. *c*1250 *Gen. & Ex.* 1442 He fatȝnede hire wið milde mod, Here sameni[n]g was clene and god. *c*1330 R. Brunne *Chron. Wace* (Rolls) 2719 Gret noise at her samny[n]g was. *Ibid.* 6718 At Londone þey sette a Parlement;..And þus þey seyde at þer sampninge.

†**'samenly**, *adv. Obs.* Also 4 **sammenly**. [f. SAMEN *adv.* together + -LY[2].] Together.

*a*1300 *Cursor M.* 28391 Munk, nunne, or spused wijf, þat sammenly aght to lede þair liue. 1357 *Lay Folks Catech.* 91 The hali gast, That samenly comes of bothe the fadir and the son.

†**'samentale**, *sb.* and *a. Obs.* Forms: α. 3 **somentale**, 4 **samentale**, **sammentale**. β. (as *adj.* only) 4 **samer-tale**, **samirtale**, **sammertale**. [App. f. SAMEN *a.* + TALE *sb.* Cf. SAMTALE *a.*

The β forms seem to represent a genitive phrase = 'of the same tale' (ON. **samrar*, unrecorded str. genit. sing. fem. of *sam-r* SAME *a.*; *tǫlu* genit. of *tala* TALE); the sb. may have arisen from the substitution of a phrase with prep. for the genitive phrase.]

A. *sb.* Concord, agreement.

*a*1225 *Ancr. R.* 426 Seihnesse & some [*MS. T.* sachtnesse & somentale]. *a*1375 *Cursor M.* 683 (Fairf.) þe bestes weren in samen tale [cf. B].

B. *adj.* Concordant, agreeing.

*a*1300 *Cursor M.* 683 þe bestes self war samer-tale. *Ibid.* 10169 Was suilk a cuple neuer nan, Sua sammertale [*Gött.* samirtale], wit-vten strijf. *Ibid.* 23521 þai er sa selcut samen tale.

†**'samenward**, *adv. Obs.* [f. SAMEN *adv.* + -WARD.] Together.

*a*1375 *Cursor M.* 15117 (Fairf.) þai geddered ham samneward & mened ham of þaire care.

sameria, variant of SAMARA.

†**'sameron.** *dial.* (Yorks.) *Obs.* Also 6 **samoron**, 6–7 **samron**, 7 **sameran**, 7 **sammaron**. See quot. 1684.

1556 *Knaresb. Wills* (Surtees) I. 73 Thre yerdes of sameron. 1564 *Ibid.* 96, xj pai of samoron and hardin sheetes, xiij s. iiij d. 1583 in *Ripon Charter Acts* (Surtees) 380, xl yeredes of sameron, 20s. 1598 *Knaresb. Wills* (Surtees) I. 211 My best blankett, samron and a harden shete. 1617–18 *Ibid.* II. 50 One pairre of sameran sheetes. 1638 *Ibid.* 162 One little paire of samron shetes. 1684 G. Meriton *Yorksh. Dial.* 45 Thy Sammaron web..Is stown. *Ibid.* 107 (Alphabetical Clavis), *Sammaron*, is a Cloath between Linnen and Hempen, not altogether so course as the one, nor fine as the other.

samer-tale: see SAMENTALE.

Samerytane, obs. form of SAMARITAN.

samey ('seɪmɪ), *adv.* and *a. dial.* and *slang.* [f. SAME *a.* (*pron.*, *adv.*) + -Y[6].]

A. *adv.* ***all the samey*** = SAME *adv.* 2.

1897 Kipling *Captains Courageous* x. 221 All the samey, something's got to be done about it.

B. *adj.* Identical, characterized by sameness; lacking in variety, monotonous. Hence **'sameyness.**

1929 E. Raymond *Family that Was* iii. 49 The days that followed, becoming 'samey'.., sank out of memory's sight. 1959 *Sunday Times* 19 July 10/6 Many of his pictures of expensive men and women on expensive horses seem samey. 1962 *Listener* 11 Jan. 90/3 All that 'samey' food and the lack of service. 1969 M. Tripp *Malice & Maternal Instinct* iv. 25 Arthur never varied his approach or technique. Arthur was samey. 1977 *Oxf. Times* 9 Dec. 17/3 Their thick sound tends towards sameyness, but the songs have enough character to retain one's interest. 1978 *Illustr. London News* Nov. 142/2 She moves beautifully and does all that a dancer could do to differentiate steps that are samey.

sameyel, samfast, obs. ff. SAMIEL, SHAMEFAST.

samfayl(e, -ffayl: see SANS FAIL.

Samfrau ('sæmfraʊ). *Geol.* [See quot. 1937.] The name of a geosyncline postulated to have extended across GONDWANALAND.

1937 A. L. Du Toit *Our Wandering Continents* iv. 62 A major geosyncline..traversing Bolivia, north and central Argentina, Cape, Weddell Sea, passing east of King Edward VII Land and through Edsel Ford land, crossing Tasmania and the eastern part of Australia to New Guinea... This feature, which seems to have played so vital a rôle during the evolution of Gondwana,..can conveniently be called the 'Samfrau' Geosyncline—a contraction of the words 'South America—South Africa—Australia'. 1959 *New Biol.* XXIX. 14 A further example of this type is the Samfrau geosyncline, of which Du Toit has suggested the remnants now occur in South America, South Africa, and Australia. 1971 M. H. P. Bott *Interior of Earth* vii. 202 Examples [of good fits of tectonic features on the assumption of continental drift] include..the fitting together of the Samfrau orogenic belt of Gondwanaland.

samfu ('sæmfu:). Also **samfoo**. [Cantonese *sāam·fu.*] A suit consisting of jacket and trousers worn by Chinese women, particularly in Malaysia and Hong Kong; also worn by men. Freq. *attrib.*, as ***samfu jacket, trousers***.

1955 D. Moore *We live in Singapore* 41 Her thin, pendulous breasts hung down inside her *samfoo* jacket like malignant deformities. 1963 J. Kirkup *Tropic Temper* ii. 23 Chinese girls in samfu, a kind of flowered pyjama suit with short flaring jacket. 1966 D. Forbes *Heart of Malaya* iv. 47 A Chinese woman dressed in a white peasant smock and blue *samfu* trousers. 1967 A. Cordell *Bright Cantonese* iv. 51 The people..came..to the bath, pulling their samfoo jackets over their heads. *Ibid.* vi. 69 He brought white samfoo trousers and a jacket heavily stained with crimson flowers. 1969 J. Bennett *Dragon* ii. 19 She was wearing a *samfu*, the blue or black suit which looks like the Viet Cong pyjama uniform. 1975 O. Sela *Bengali Inheritance* ii. 20 The witness was a frail, elderly Chinese... He wore a tattered black *samfoo*.

samgha, var. SANGHA.

‖**Samhain** (saʊn; 'saʊɪn, 'sawɪn). Also **Samain**, **Samhainn**. [a. Ir. *samhain* (Sc. Gaelic *samhuinn*), OIr. *samain*.] The first day of November, celebrated by the ancient Celts as a festival marking the beginning of winter and of the new year according to their calendar; All Saints' Day or Hallowmass. Also *attrib.* Cf. BELTANE.

The OIr. form *samain* is used only with reference to the ancient Celts. 'Samhain Eve' (quot. 1904) and 'the night of Samhain' (quot. 1910) are different renderings of Ir. *oidhche Shamhna* 'Hallowe'en'.

1888 J. Rhys *Lect. Orig. & Growth Relig. as illustr. by Celtic Heathendom* v. 518 The Samhain feast..was, like the Greek Apaturia, partly devoted to business..otherwise the feast, which occupied, not only Samain or the first of November, but also the three days before and the three days after it, was given up to the usual games. 1904 W. B. Yeats *Stories of Red Hanrahan* 1 The barn where some of the men were sitting on Samhain Eve. 1910 J. M. Synge *Deirdre of Sorrows* i. 5 And it raining since the night of Samhain. 1917 J. M. Clark *Vocab. Anglo-Irish* vii. 27 Irish folk-lore has kept alive words of such classic associations as..Samhain and shanahus..which mean..'All-Hallowtide' (Nov. 1) and 'a friendly chat' respectively. 1949 J. A. MacCulloch *Celtic & Scandinavian Religions* i. viii. 58 Samhain, which means 'summer end', naturally pointed to the fact that the powers of blight, typified by winter, were beginning their reign. But it may have been partly a harvest festival. 1957 W. R. Kermack *Scottish Highlands* 153 At Samhain (Hallowe'en, 31st October, the beginning of Winter) the Lewismen made libation to the sea-god Shony, who could send them plenty of seaweed to manure their fields. 1958 T. G. E. Powell *Celts* iii. 117 At *Samain*, sacrifices were certainly offered although no material descriptions have survived. 1968 *New Larousse Encycl. Mythol.* 236/1 The [Celtic] year began on what is now the first of November with the feast of *Samain*... The ordinary people felt less sanguine about the possibility that on the eve of *Samain* the people of the *side* left their domain and wandered in the world of man. 1970 *Q. Rev. Guernsey Soc.* XXVI. 60 These four were the feast of Beltainn the great Sungod in May; mid-summer, mid-August..and Samhainn or Hallowmass (November 1).

sam-hal: see SAM-.

Sam Hill (sæm hɪl). *N. Amer. slang.* Also **sam hill**, **samhill**. [Orig. unknown.] A euphemism for hell; used especially in expressions of impatience or irritation preceded by *in* or *the* with an interrogative word.

1839 *Havana* (N.Y.) *Republican* 21 Aug. 1/4 What in sam hill is that feller ballin' about? 1868 J. T. Trowbridge *Three Scouts* vi. 26 When you might a'married!—why in Sam Hill didn't ye, then? 1894 'Mark Twain' in *St. Nicholas* Jan. 257/2 Hateful people..giving me Sam Hill because I shirked. 1909 *N.Y. Even. Post.* 10 Apr. (Sat. Suppl.) 3/5 How in Sam Hill can she do it? She's just as hot when she gets to bilin' p'int as she'll ever be. 1918 M. E. Freeman *Edgewater People* 314 What in Sam Hill made you treat him so durned mean fur? 1927 W. James *Cow Country* 77 What the Sam Hill do you think we are out here, servants? 1948 *Salt Lake Tribune* 18 Dec. 10/7 He wondered who the Sam Hill the 'senator' was. 1962 H. Green *Time to pass Over* xii. 147 Why in the samhill didn't you step in and stop them, Mike. 1973 B. Broadfoot *Ten Lost Years* xxiii. 262 He probably never could have figured what the Sam Hill was going on.

Samhita ('sʌmhɪtɑː). Also **sanhita.** [Skr. *saṃhitā* union, connection, f. *sam* together + *dhā* to place.] A text treated according to sandhi; a version of the vedas which is the continuous text formed from the pada or separate words by the appropriate phonetic sound changes. Also *attrib.*

1805 H. T. COLEBROOKE in *Asiatick Researches* VIII. 476 Tradition.. reckons sixteen Sanhitas of the Rigveda. **1843** *Penny Cycl.* XXVI. 171/1 The Rigveda is the first in order and its Sanhitâ contains mantras.. to the elemental deities. **1887, 1917** [see PADA b]. **1920** J. N. FARQUHAR *Outl. Relig. Lit. India* i. 26 The Veda as handed down in the various schools.. soon showed considerable differences. It has come down to us in four distinct forms called *Saṁhitās.* **1953** in K. W. Morgan *Relig. of Hindus* vii. 265 The Upanishads are the philosophic and mystical elaboration of the truths first revealed to the Seers and recorded in the Saṁhitās. **1974** *Encycl. Brit. Micropædia* X. 375/3 The foremost collection, or Samhitā, of such hymns.. is the Ṛgveda.

Sami ('sɑːmɪ, sɑːm). Also †**Salme-Same; Saam(e, Sabme,** etc. [Lappish *Sami* (in earlier orthography, *Sabme, Samek*) of uncertain ultimate etym.; cf. also Sw. and Norw. *Same.*] The native name of the Lapps; occas. *sing.*, a Lapp.

This word is preferred to *Lapp* by scholars.

1797 *Encycl. Brit.* IX. 572/1 The Laplanders call themselves *Salme-Same,* and *Salmen-Almatjeh.* **1842** *Penny Cycl.* XXIII. 390/1 They [*sc.* the Laplanders] call themselves Sami. **1864** *Chambers's Encycl.* VI. 38/1 The Lapps, who call themselves the *Sami* or *Sahmelads,* are a physically ill-developed, diminutive race. **1935** S. J. BECKETT *Wayfarer in Norway* xx. 145 The Lapps call themselves Sami or Sahmelads, whilst they call the Finns Suomi (which, like the name Finn, means 'Fen', or marsh-dwellers). **1957** R. PAINE *Coast Lapp Society* I. i. 3 The people whom we know as Lapps have their own name for themselves—*sabme,* plural *sāmek.* In academic circles inside Scandinavia, the Lappish term is now replacing any other. .. Outside Scandinavia, however,.. *sabme* is not widely understood. **1964** S. DUNN et al. tr. E. D. Prokof'yeva in Levin & Potapov *Peoples of Siberia* 547 Some scholars have compared the name 'Samoyed' with the Lappish (Saam) words 'same-yedne' ('land of the Saams'). This is based on the fact that the territory settled by the Nentsy.. was in earlier times inhabited by the Lapps (Saams). **1968** [see POT *sb.*[1] 13 f]. **1977** *Daily Colonist* (Victoria, B.C.) 19 June 22/3 The.. reindeer herder is one of the Saame, better known as Lapps. **1980** *Times* 8 Feb. 14/7 The 2,000 or so Lapps, or more accurately Sami, who live in this area.

Samian ('seɪmɪən), *a.* and *sb.* [f. L. *Sami-us,* Gr. Σάμιος (f. *Sam-us, -os,* Gr. Σάμος) + -AN.]

A. *adj.* Of or pertaining to Samos, an island in the Ægean Sea, the birthplace of Pythagoras. **Samian earth** (see quot. 1728). **Samian letter,** the letter *Y*, used by Pythagoras as an emblem of the different roads of Virtue and Vice. **Samian stone** (see quot. 1728). **Samian ware,** originally, pottery made of Samian earth; hence (also with lower case initial), the designation of a fine kind of pottery found extensively on Roman sites.

1580 NORTH *Plutarch, Pericles* (1595) 182 The Samian prisoners. **1601** HOLLAND *Pliny* II. Table, Samian earth of two kinds. *Ibid.*, Samian stone. **1616** [see Y 1 b]. **1693** DRYDEN *Persius* iii. 109 Where the Samian *Y* directs thy Steps to run To Virtue's narrow Steep, and Broad-way Vice to shun. **1728** CHAMBERS *Cycl.*, *Samian Earth,* Earth brought from the Isle of Samos.. esteemed very astringent, proper to dry, and draw Wounds... There is also a *Samian Stone,* taken out of the Mines in the same Island... 'Tis astringent and cooling, and is also used by the Goldsmiths to burnish their Gold, and give it a greater Lustre. **1742** POPE *Dunc.* IV. 151 When Reason doubtful, like the Samian letter, Points him two ways, the narrower is the better. **1779** T. POWNALL in *Archæologia* V. 287 The one [*sc.* vessel] is a red sort, the Ionian, or particularly the Samian, which is most commonly found. **1821** BYRON *Juan* III. *Isles of Greece* xiii, Fill high the bowl with Samian wine! *c* **1841** W. T. P. SHORTT *Sylva Antiqua Iscana* 110 The great quantity of fragments of Roman Red Ware, especially of that beautiful description, known to the ancients by the generic term of Samian, is not by any means the least interesting of the curiosities dug up in the city of Exeter, of late years. **1844** *Gentl. Mag.* July 35/2 Whether that singularly beautiful red glazed earthenware.. of which such vast quantities have been since exhumed in every part of England and France where their respective records have assigned a Roman station, be really the identical Samian pottery of Pliny, is, I think, a question yet to be decided. **1848** *Jrnl. Brit. Archaeol. Assoc.* Apr. 2 The Samian ware is found throughout this country almost wherever Roman remains are met with. **1859** LUARD in *Archæol. Cantiana* II. 7 The articles found consisted of Samian ware of various shapes. *Ibid.*, The vases, urns, and Samian vessels, were filled with bones.

B. *sb.* **a.** A native or inhabitant of Samos.

1580 NORTH *Plutarch, Pericles* (1595) 181 He.. kept the Samians besieged within their owne citie. **1759** W. WILKIE *Epigon.* v. 138 Ulysses then, with thirst of glory fir'd, The Samian left, and to the prize aspir'd. **1886** *Encycl. Brit.* XXI. 249/2 The great battle of Mycale (480), which.. freed the Samians from the Persian yoke.

b. (freq. **samian.**) *ellipt.* for *Samian ware.*

1958 STANFIELD & SIMPSON *Central Gaulish Potters* I. 52 Black slip samian has a pinkish-red or buff-coloured core. **1967** *Antiquaries Jrnl.* XLVII. 192 It seems most likely that the later samian has come from pits dug into the rampart. **1981** P. SALWAY *Roman Britain* 202 Mr B R Hartley's study of the dies for the makers' stamps on samian pottery reveals that the amount of samian bearing the same stamps which comes from the two Walls is negligible.

samie, obs. form of SHAME *v.*

samiel ('sɑːmɪəl). Also 8 **sameyel.** [a. Turkish *samyel,* f. *sam* a. Arab. *samm* (see SIMOOM) + *yel* wind.] The Simoom.

(Sometimes confused with SHAMAL, north wind.)

1687 A. LOVELL tr. *Thevenot's Trav.* II. 54 Having spoken so much of the Samiel, it is but reasonable I should relate what I have been told of it. **1774** GOLDSM. *Nat. Hist.* (1824) I. 153 A very dangerous wind prevails, which the natives [of Persia] call the *sameyel.* **1815** J. SMITH *Panorama Sci. & Art* II. 49 The samiel or mortifying wind of the deserts near Bagdad. **1817** MOORE *Lalla R., Veiled Prophet* (ed. 2) 90 Burning and headlong as the Samiel wind. **1832** J. BELL *Syst. Geogr.* IV. 231 The most dreadful of all winds is the famous semoum or samiel,.. which prevails in the desert bounded by Bassora, Bagdad, Aleppo, and Mekka, and the effects of which are suffocation and immediate putrefaction of the body. **1962** [see LEVECHE].

samin, obs. form of SAM *v.*[1]

samin(e, var. ff. SAMEN *a.* and *adv. Obs.*

†'**saming.** *Obs.* [f. SAM *v.* + -ING. Cf. SAMENING.] A meeting, assembly.

c **1400** *Laud Troy Bk.* 3823 Suche a peple was neuere y-sene.. To-geder broght at o samyng.

samiri, variant of SAIMIRI.

samirtale: see SAMENTALE.

‖**samisen** ('sæmɪsɛn). Also 7 **shamshin,** 9 **samsi, samishen, samsien,** 9– **shamisen; shamisan.** [Japanese form of Chinese *san-hsien* (*san* three, *hsien* string).] A Japanese guitar of three strings, played with a plectrum.

1616 R. COCKS *Diary* 9 Oct. (1883) I. 188 The *tuerto* that plaid on the *shamshin.* **1822** F. SHOBERL tr. *Titsingh's Illustr. Japan* 94 Several young females came to bear them company, playing on the *samsi,* and dancing. **1840** *Chinese Repository* Dec. 630 The *samishen* is a three-stringed guitar, and is usually played with a plectrum. **1864** ENGEL *Mus. Anc. Nat.* 55 The *san heen* of China, and the *samsien* of Japan. The two instruments are almost identical. **1871** A. B. MITFORD *Tales of Old Japan* I. 243 The *shamisen,* a sort of banjo. **1880** I. BIRD *Unbeaten Tracks in Japan* I. 134 Yuki plays the *samisen,* which may be regarded as the national female instrument. **1895** CLIVE HOLLAND *Jap. Wife* (ed. 11) 4 The music of guitars or *samisens* being played in the tea-houses. **1936** K. SUNAGA *Japanese Music* i. 19 The instrument employed as the accompaniment for the songs of geisha girls.. was the *samisen....* It might be described as a three-stringed, rectangular banjo. **1955** E. POUND *Classic Anthol.* II. 115 And words soft as the shamisan Distinguish the thick-faced man. **1964** I. FLEMING *You only live Twice* i. 18 [Bond was] far from being.. bewitched by the inscrutable discords issuing from the catskin-covered box of the three-stringed *samisen.* **1970** J. W. HALL *Japan* x. 227 The music of the *shamisen.* **1972** *Times* 18 Sept. 5/4 Guests knelt on tatami and used chopsticks to eat while geisha girls played the samisen.

samite ('sæmaɪt). *Obs.* exc. *Hist.* Forms: 4 **samit, samet,** 4–5 **samyt,** 4–6 **samyte,** 5–6 **samite,** 6 *arch.* **samitte,** 9 *arch.* **samit(e, sammit.** [a. OF. *samit* = Pr. *samit,* Sp. *jamete* (older *xamete*), It. *sciamito,* med.L. *examitum, exametum, samitum, samittum,* ad. med. Gr. ἑξάμιτον (whence OSl. *oksamitŭ,* Russian *aksamit* velvet), f. Gr. ἑξα- combining form of ἕξ six + μίτος thread; cf. Gr. δίμιτος double-threaded, as sb. DIMITY. From Fr. the word passed into MHG. as *samit* (mod.G. *sammet, sammt, samt,* velvet). Cf. MSw. *examit.*

The med. Gr. name, lit. 'six-threaded', has been variously explained. Usually it has been supposed that the original 'samite' was woven of thread composed of six strands of silk; but according to Middleton in *Encycl. Brit.* XXIII. 210/1 it 'was so called because the weft threads were only caught and looped at every sixth thread of the warp, lying loosely on the intermediate part'.]

A rich silk fabric worn in the Middle Ages, sometimes interwoven with gold. Also, †a garment or a cushion of this material. Also *fig.*, *attrib.*, and *Comb.*

13.. *K. Alis.* 2094 (Bodl. MS.) Alisaunder sytt on a samyt And plaieþ atte ches in his delyȝt. ? *a* **1366** CHAUCER *Rom. Rose* 873 In an over-gilt samyt Clad she was. *c* **1450** *Merlin* xxx. 608 Ther-on hinge a gipser of purpill samyte bete with golde. **1470–85** MALORY *Arthur* I. xxv. 73 In the myddes of the lake Arthur was ware of an arme clothed in whyte samyte. *Ibid.* XVIII. xix. 760 That my barget be couerd with blak samyte ouer and ouer. *c* **1530** LD. BERNERS *Arth. Lyt. Bryt.* (1814) 156 She was vestured wyth a samyte of grene. **1599** THYNNE *Animadv.* (1875) 35 'Dalmaticam de eodem samitto..', which is to saye, 'the kinges dalmaticall garmente of the same samitte'. **1834** PLANCHÉ *Brit. Costume* viii. 93 [A robe for Hen. III] to be made of the best purple-coloured samite (a rich silk). **1842** [see MYSTIC A. 5 b]. **1847** THACKERAY *Barbazure* i, A surcoat of peach-coloured samite.. bespoke him noble. **1938** R. GRAVES *Coll. Poems* 63 Into their many-shielded, samite-curtained, Jewel-bright hall where twelve Kings sit at chess. **1971** 'A. BURGESS' *MF* xvii. 191 There were fireworks out tonight, thudding and searing the samite air.

¶*jocularly.* (Scarlet) plush.

1854 THACKERAY *Newcomes* I. vii. 69 Springing down from his station behind his mistress, the youth clad in the nether garments of red sammit discharged thunderclaps on the door of Mrs. Newcome's house.

samiti ('sæmɪtɪ). Also **samity.** [Hind. *samiti* meeting, committee.] In India and Bangladesh, an assembly or committee.

1930 M. L. DARLING *Rusticus Loquitur* v. 124 The 250 Mahila Samitis or Women's Institutes founded in Bengal by Mrs G S Dutt. **1950** M. MASANI *Our Growing Human Family* 41 The village assembly, known in Europe as the Folk-moot and in India as the Samiti. **1962** *Times* 26 Jan. (Survey of India) p. vi/6 Presidents of the various block *samitis* in a district form the *zila parishad.* **1975** *Bangladesh Times* 19 July 8/8 All the members of the Board of Directors of Bangladesh National Bidi Sramik Samabaya Samity.. have also applied for membership of the national party. **1976** D. HIRO *Inside India Today* 50 What then emerged was a three-tiered system whereby the old district boards.. were replaced by Zilla parishads (i.e. district councils) with responsibility for co-ordinating development plans to be channelled through panchayat samitis (i.e. council committees) consisting of a number of popularly elected panchayats encompassing one or more villages—all interlinked through indirect elections. This system, popularly known as the panchayat raj, was first introduced .. in 1959.

‖**samizdat** ('sæmɪzdæt, səmɪz'dat). Also with capital initial. [Russ., abbrev. of *samoizdátel'stvo* self-publishing house, f. *samo-* self + *izdátel'stvo* publishing house.] The clandestine or illegal copying and distribution of literature (orig. and chiefly in the U.S.S.R.); an 'underground press'; a text or texts produced by this. Also *transf.* and *attrib.* or as *adj. Phr. in samizdat,* in this form of publication.

1967 *Times* 6 Nov. (Russia Suppl.) p. xxii/4 A vast and newly educated [Soviet] population.. do not pass around the precious *samizdat* (unpublished) manuscripts. **1968** tr. I. A. Yakhimovich *Let.* in *Probl. of Communism* July–Aug. 48/1 One must not speculate with the honor of the state, even if a certain leader wants to end *samizdat.* **1968** *Time* 27 Sept. 22/2 Those lines [of Solzhenitsyn] have not been published in the Soviet Union. But they are nonetheless read and passed from hand to hand in *samizdat,* the readers' answer to Soviet censorship. **1970** *New Statesman* 20 Feb. 241/1 The underground distribution of manuscripts and their publication abroad means that the *samizdat* writers have—at least in the eyes of the authorities—opted out of the Soviet scheme of things. **1971** *Guardian* 15 July 13/8 Nicolae Ceausescu's latest puritanical damper on 'Bourgeois Influences' in Rumania coincides with the first case of underground 'Samizdat' literature to come from there. **1973** R. ROSENBLUM *Mushroom Cave* 55 I've told you how effective the samizdat network has been in circumventing the repression of criticism. **1977** M. WALKER *National Front* vii. 182 The NF *samizdats* which did so much to pollute the atmosphere of NF life during the year [*sc.* 1975]. **1977** *Time* 28 Nov. 30/2 An exhibit of clandestine *samizdat* in the Correr Museum. **1978** *Manch. Guardian Weekly* 27 Aug. 7 Jiri Hrusa's novel 'The Questionnaire', which was printed by the Prague Samizdat. **1980** *Times Lit. Suppl.* 3 Oct. 1094/4 The strongest works to have come out since 1962 —Solzhenitsyn's *The First Circle* [etc.].. —have appeared, and could only appear, in *samizdat.*

Hence **samiz'datchik** [Russ. *-chik,* agent suffix], one who takes part in the writing, copying, and distribution of *samizdat* material (pl. *samizdatchiki*).

1972 *N.Y. Times Mag.* 10 Sept. 92 To fill their reserves.. the *samizdatchiki* seek ties with other cities... They arrive with copies of the originals, which have been given abroad. **1979** *N.Y. Times Bk. Rev.* 20 May 3/2 He assiduously collects information for the samizdat journals.. writes pseudonymous articles for samizdat and spends weeks on end retyping the Chronicle and other materials from Moscow in multiple copies. He is the quintessential *samizdatchik.*

Samkhya, var. SANKHYA.

samlet ('sæmlɪt). [Contracted f. SALMON[1] + -LET. Cf. the earlier SALMONET.] A young salmon.

1655 WALTON *Angler* vii. (1661) 135 [There they leave the spawn] to become Samlets early in the spring next following. *a* **1672** WILLUGHBY *Hist. Pisc.* IV. iv. §11. 192 Salmulus, Herefordiæ *Samlet* dictus. **1742** R. CORNES in *Phil. Trans.* XLII. 129 What goes here by the Name of Samlet, a small Fish spotted with Red, not much unlike the Trout. **1769** PENNANT *Zool.* III. 253 The samlet is the lest of the trout kind. **1787** BEST *Angling* (ed. 2) 34 They commonly spawn in October, and the young become samlets the following year. **1834** MEDWIN *Angler in Wales* I. 62 They are called indifferently, samlets, par, last spring, or fingerlings. **1884** BRAITHWAITE *Salmonidæ Westmld.* v. 18 The samlets have in the fresh water been content with small worms [etc.].

‖**samlor** ('sæmlɔː(r)). Also **samlo.** [Thai.] Chiefly in Thailand, a three-wheeled vehicle, freq. motorized, used as a taxi.

1955 *Times* 6 May 11/6 Let him be insidiously towed in a motor *samlor* round this town of Bangkok. **1960** R. KIRKBRIDE *Innocent Abroad* xi. 82 We crossed a humped bridge.. in the city, dodging about amongst cycle-rickshaws and samlors. **1963** 'HAN SUYIN' *Four Faces* 54 Peter would photograph her in front of the temples of Angkor, stepping down from a *samlo,* the three-wheeled vehicle, man-propelled, in use in Cambodia. **1974** *Time* 7 Jan. 50/2 The Assembly even includes a *samlor* driver, who intends to park his three-wheel smoke-belching minitaxi at the National Assembly building.

†'**samly,** *adv. Obs.* [f. SAM *adv.* + -LY[2]. Cf. SAMENLY *adv.*] Agreeingly.

c **1350** *Will. Palerne* 1835 Kindeli eche oþer clipt and kessed ful oft,.. Slepten wel swetly samli to-gadere.

samme, obs. f. SAM *v.*; var. SAM *adv.*, together.

sammen (ˈsæmən). Also **salmon.** [Etymologizing alteration of SAMEL.] = SAMEL.
*a*1825 FORBY *Voc. E. Anglia, Sammen-bricks*, bricks insufficiently burned; soft and friable. They are commonly understood to be salmon bricks, and to be so called, because ..they..assume a reddish hue, supposed to be something like that of the flesh of the salmon. **1876** ADAMS in *Jrnl. Franklin Inst.* Mar. 162 The arches, from necessity, are overburned in consequence of prolonging the firing sufficiently to burn the top and sides of the kiln into respectable salmon. **1889** C. T. DAVIES *Bricks* (ed. 2) 47 This test applies only to hard-burned bricks, not to salmon stock.

sammen, obs. f. SAM *v.*; var. SAMEN, together.

sammenly, variant of SAMENLY *adv. Obs.*

sammentale, sammertale: see SAMENTALE.

sammier (ˈsæmɪə(r)). [f. SAMMY *v.* + -ER[1].] (See quot.)
1884 KNIGHT *Dict. Mech.* Suppl., *Sammier*, a machine for pressing water from skins in the process of tanning.

sammin, sammit: see SAMEN, SAMITE.

Sammy (ˈsæmɪ), *sb.* Also **Sammie.** [Familiar dim. of the name *Samuel*: see -Y[6].] †**1.** *slang.* A ninny, simpleton. Also in *Comb. Obs.*
1837 E. HOWARD *Old Commodore* II. iii. 54 You have been sammy-foozled by a rascally swindler. **1838** R. B. PEAKE *Quarter to Nine* I. ii. 10 What a Sammy, give me a shilling more than I axed him! **1897** F. T. JANE *Lordship Passen and We* xv. 165 Simple Sammy, as we called Mr. Pote, the new pastor.

2. *slang.* In British use: an American soldier in the war of 1914–18, so called from the name *Uncle Sam* (see UNCLE *sb.* 2 c). Now *rare* or *Obs.*
1917 *Punch* 13 June 384/2 As a term of distinction and endearment [for the American 'Tommies'] Mr. Punch suggests 'Sammies'—after their uncle. **1917** *Nation* (N.Y.) 16 Aug. 164/1 The 'Sammies' whom the headlines are featuring. **1918** *Stars & Stripes* 29 Mar. 4/1 A Sammie may be defined as an American soldier as he appears in an English newspaper or a French cinema. It is a name he did not invent, does not like, never uses and will not recognize. **1921** *Glasgow Herald* 8 July 7/2 While a French soldier costs on average 13 francs 37 per day, ..a 'Tommy' costs 31 francs 69, and a 'Sammy' 59 francs 30.

sammy (ˈsæmɪ), *v. Leather-dressing.* [Extended form of SAM *v.*[2]] *trans.* To dry partially (leather); also, to dampen (leather that has been allowed to dry out) slightly. See SAM *v.*[2]
1885 C. T. DAVIS *Manuf. Leather* xxix. 502 The eleventh step, which consists in 'sammying' the hides, is then carried into effect. **1891** J. W. STEVENS *Leather Manuf.* iii. 20 After being sammied, take one side at a time and..dampen it. *Ibid.* 24 Sammieing. This term..I have failed to learn the origin of... It appears to have originated in the Western and Southern states, for in the East, 'hardening' is generally used when the leather is hung on poles or in the lofts to dry out a certain percentage of moisture, in order to prepare it for splitting and stuffing. **1897** C. T. DAVIS *Manuf. Leather* (ed. 2) 416 If the light color is desired, the leather is hung up and allowed to harden, as it is termed in the East, or to sammy, as it is termed in the West, for setting. **1922** A. ROGERS *Pract. Tanning* xv. 449 After the leather has been dried out, in order to set the fiber it must again be dampened back or sammied before carrying out the finishing process. **1974** P. W. BLANDFORD *Country Craft Tools* xv. 199 The currier used a 'sleaker' to force out dirt, then the hide was 'sammied' by rolling either between a pair of rollers or under a heavy brass roller.

sammyn, samne(n: see SAM *v.*[1], SAMEN *adv.*

Samnite (ˈsæmnaɪt), *sb.* and *a.* Also 4 **sampnite,** 7 **samnit.** [ad. L. *Samnītēs* pl. (sing. *Samnis*); perh. etymologically cognate with SABINE.]
A. *sb.* **a.** One of a people of ancient Italy, believed to be an offshoot of the Sabines; their territory, called Samnium, was adjacent to Latium.
1390 GOWER *Conf.* III. 179 Whan the Sampnites to him broghte A somme of gold [etc.]. **1553** GRIMALDE *Cicero's Offices* II. (1556) M vj b, Caius Pontius the Samnite. **1618** BOLTON *Florus* (1636) 45 Then, moved upon the petition of the countrey of Campania, they invaded the Samnits. **1718** ROWE tr. *Lucan* II. 224 When the proud Samnites Troops the State defy'd. **1841** W. SPALDING *Italy & It. Isl.* I. 298 The Etruscans and Samnites by turns possessed both.
b. A type of gladiator.
1600 HOLLAND tr. *Livy's Romane Hist.* IX. 344 The Campaines upon a pride, and inveterate hatred that they bare against the Samnites, used to arme their swordplayers and fensers at the sharpe (which was a solemne sight and pastime they had at their great feasts) with this same attire, and termed them in mockerie, by the name of Samnites. **1957** *Encycl. Brit.* X. 383/2 The Samnites fought [in gladiatorial contests] with the national weapons—a large oblong shield, a vizor, a plumed helmet and a short sword. **1971** M. GRANT *Cities of Vesuvius* iii. 74/1 Down to the first century BC, 'gladiator' and 'Samnite' were synonymous terms; and then the latter became the name of a particular type of gladiator.
c. The language of the Samnites.
1859 B. W. DWIGHT *Mod. Philol.* I. 187 The Umbro-Samnite Dialects: Umbrian; Samnite or Oscan; Volscian; Marsian. **1882** [see MARSIAN *sb.* and *a.*].
B. *adj.* Of or pertaining to the Samnites; in use among the Samnites.
1753 CHAMBERS *Cycl. Supp.* s.v. *Shield*, The Germans, beside the samnite-shield, have two others pretty much in use. **1841** *Penny Cycl.* XX. 380/1 The Samnite war.

Hence **Samˈnitic** *a.* [ad. L. *Samniticus.*]
1753 CHAMBERS *Cycl. Supp.* s.v. *Shield*, The samnitic-shield used by the Romans. **1864** *Athenæum* 12 Mar. 375/3 Built..on the conclusion of the Samnitic war.

†**Samˈnitis.** *Obs.* [Of obscure origin: perh. some error.] Some poisonous plant.
1590 SPENSER *F.Q.* II. vii. 52 Mortall Samnitis, and Cicuta bad.

Samoan (səˈməʊən), *a.* and *sb.* [f. *Samoa*, an island kingdom of the Pacific, + -AN.]
A. *adj.* Pertaining to Samoa, or the Samoans.
Samoan dove or *pigeon*, the tooth-billed pigeon. (In Dicts.: cf. quot. 1864.)
1846 LUNDIE *Mission. Life in Samoa* xxii. 140 The Samoan language. **1864** *Reader* 28 May 687/1 A species of ground-pigeon from the Samoan Islands.
B. *sb.* **a.** A native of Samoa. **b.** The Samoan language.
1846 LUNDIE *Mission. Life in Samoa* xxi. 135 Mrs. Murray prayed in Samoan. **1856** J. C. PATTESON *Let.* in C. M. Yonge *Life J. C. Patteson* (1874) I. vii. 262 Another crew arrived with a Samoan teacher... I rode out pick-a-back on the Samoan, Leonard following on a half-naked Anaitean. **1871** C. M. YONGE *Pioneers & Founders* ix. 250 These Samoans, though they deified many animals, had no temples, idols, priests, nor sacrifices. **1875** JEVONS *Money* iv. 28 The fine woven mats so much valued by the Samoans. **1894** *Outing* (U.S.) XXIV. 355/1 Roast pig is a joy for ever to a Samoan.

Samoed, Samoid, etc.: see SAMOYED.

samoleon, var. SIMOLEON.

‖**samolus** (səˈməʊləs). [L. *samōlus* (Pliny); said to be a Celtic word.] **a.** *Antiq.* A plant said to have been used in ancient Druidical ceremonies. **b.** *Bot.* Adopted (by Linnæus) as the name of a genus of plants belonging to the order *Primulaceæ*. Also, a plant of this genus.
1753 CHAMBERS *Cycl. Supp.*, *Samolus*, in botany, the name of a genus of plants. **1866** *Treas. Bot.*, *Samolus*, small marsh plants with white flowers..belonging to the *Primulaceæ*. **1878** MISS BRADDON *Open Verd.* II. 14, I wonder whether he was going to gather the samolus, left-handed and fasting. **1884** C. ROGERS *Soc. Life Scot.* I. i. 16 The leaves of the Samolus were gathered by the priest fasting. **1905** *Longm. Mag.* Jan. 254 The selago flourished on the heath and the samolus by the running stream.

samon, obs. form of SALMON.

samony(e, obs. Sc. ff. *so many*: see SO *adv.*

samoom, variant of SIMOOM.

‖**samoreus.** [Du.] A kind of boat used on the Rhine.
1622 T. SCOTT *Belg. Pismire* 71 An infinite number of people are imployd in Shippes, Samoreuses, Hoyes [etc.].

samori, samorine, samorit: see ZAMORIN.

samoron, variant of SAMERON *Obs.*

samosa (səˈməʊsə). Also **samoosa, samusa.** [Hind.] A triangular pastry fried in ghee or oil, containing spiced vegetables or meat.
1955 R. P. JHABVALA *To whom she Will* ix. 67 Another plate was filled with..samusas. **1960** —— *Householder* i. 54 'They have made vegetable samusas with our tea,' Romesh told his father. **1971** *Weekend* (Colombo) 12 Sept. 6/3 (Advt.), Rizwana for cool cool Faluda and fresh hot Samosa. **1974** N. GORDIMER *Conservationist* 131 What'd you find to buy?—.. Samoosas.—.. He puts the neat, crisp, greasy triangle whole into his mouth. **1978** [see PAKORA].

Samosatenian (ˌsæməʊsəˈtiːnɪən), *sb.* and *a.* Also 7 **Samosatonian,** 9 **-anian.** [f. L. *Samosatēnus*, Gr. Σαμοσατηνός (f. *Samosata*) + -AN.]
a. *sb.* A follower of Paul of Samosata. = PAULIAN *sb.* I. **b.** *adj.* = PAULIAN *a.*
1597 HOOKER *Eccl. Pol.* v. lxii. §6 For the baptisme which Nouatianists gaue stoode firme, whereas they whome Samosatenians had baptised were rebaptised. **1645** PAGITT *Heresiogr.* (ed. 2) 123 With which are joyned the Samosatonians and Sabellians. **1697** STILLINGFL. *Disc. Trinity* 42 Directly contrary to the Samosatenian Doctrine. **1727–41** CHAMBERS *Cycl.* s.v., St. Epiphanius will have the Samosatenians to be real Jews, without any thing more than the name of Christians. *a*1861 CUNNINGHAM *Hist. Theol.* (1863) II. xxiii. 160 The Samosatanian heresy.

Samothracian (sæməʊˈθreɪʃ(ɪ)ən), *sb.* and *a.* [f. L. *Samothrācē*, Gr. Σαμοθράκη, an island in the Ægean Sea + -IAN.] **a.** *sb.* An inhabitant of Samothrace. **b.** *adj.* Of or pertaining to Samothrace; *esp.* with reference to the Cabiric mysteries which originated in Samothrace.
1653 COGAN tr. *Diodorus Sic. Hist.* VI. x. 249 The Samothracians do report, that among them there was another great deluge before that of Deucalion. **1753** CHAMBERS *Cycl. Supp.*, *Cabiri*, in antiquity, certain deities worshipped more especially by the Samothracians... 'Tis disputed..whether they be of Phœnician, Samothracian, or Egyptian origin. **1803** G. S. FABER *Cabiri* I. 351 The Samothracian mysteries. **1886** *Encycl. Brit.* XXI. 250/2 When the Samothracians sent a contingent to the Persian fleet.

samovar (ˈsæməʊvɑː(r), sæməʊˈvɑː(r)). [Russian *samovar*, 'self-boiler', f. *samo-* self + *varit'* to boil.] A Russian tea urn.
1830 tr. *Kotzebue's New Voy.* II. 22 *note*, A Samowar, or self-boiler..generally stands in the middle of the tea-table. **1882** *Pall Mall G.* 14 June 2/1 The samovar is a tea-kettle which has its fire in a tube running through it, and which, with a few pieces of lighted charcoal dropped into the tube, maintains the water at boiling point with a minimum of evaporation.

Samoyed (ˈsæməʊjɛd), *sb.* and *a.* Forms: 7 **Samoit, Samoed,** 7–8 **Samoid, Samoied,** 8–9 **Samojede,** 9 **Samoiede, Samoyede,** 7– **Samoyed.** [Russian *samoyed*. The rendering 'self-eater' (cf. *myasoyed* flesh-eater), interpreted as 'cannibal', is already mentioned by Purchas 1613.] **A.** *sb.* **1.** One of Mongolian race inhabiting Siberia.
1589 A. JENKINSON in Morgan & Coote *Early Voy. Russia & Persia* (1886) I. 36 The Tartars and Gentiles, called Samoydes. **1613** PURCHAS *Pilgrimage* (1614) 432 The Samoits or Samoyeds are clad from head to foot in Deeres-skinnes. **1688** BOYLE *Final Causes Nat. Things* iv. 129 The countries inhabited by the Samoids. **1726** BOLINGBROKE *Study of Hist.* (1777) II. 34 The Samojedes wondered much at the Czar of Muscovy for not living among them. **1756** DYER *Fleece* IV. 145 The hardy Samoid. **1812** SHELLEY in Dowden *Life* (1887) I. 319 The poor are as abject as Samoyeds. **1841** [see OSTYAK]. **1876** A. J. EVANS *Through Bosnia* i. 31 Among Lapps and Samoyeds. **1911** *Encycl. Brit.* XXIV. 118/1 The language now spoken by the Samoyedes belongs to the Finno-Ugrian group, and is allied to Finnish but has a more copious system of suffixes. **1944** [see NENETS]. **1972** *Language* XLVIII. 206 The Samoyeds make up only one small group of scattered tribes among the many non-Russian peoples who have inhabited Siberia.
2. Also with small initial. A white or buff dog belonging to the breed so called, once used as working dogs in the Arctic, and distinguished by a thick, shaggy coat, stocky build, pricked ears, and a tail curled over the back. Also *attrib.*
1889 *Pall Mall Gaz.* 30 Apr. 6/2 A beautiful brown silky-haired sharp-eared Samoyed dog. **1905** [see LAIKA]. **1914** N. NEWNHAM-DAVIS *Gourmet's Guide to London* liii. 340 [He] brought me in..to look at a delightful little Samoyede puppy. **1922** R. LEIGHTON *Compl. Bk. Dog* vii. 98 The white Samoyed is one of the most beautiful of all dogs. **1934** [see MALAMUTE]. **1954** M. K. WILSON tr. *Lorenz's Man meets Dog* ix. 90 Pointed muzzles, obliquely set Mongolian eyes and pricked ears pointing sharply upwards..that fascinating expression which distinguishes Greenland sledge-dogs, Samoyeds and Huskies. **1977** G. MARTON *Alarum* 61 The well-fed passengers..probably expected to be carried across immense ice fields by rough Samoyed dogs.
B. *adj.* Of or pertaining to the Samoyeds. Also quasi-*sb.*, their language.
1667 MILTON *P.L.* x. 695 From the North Of Norumbega, and the Samoed shoar. **1797** *Encycl. Brit.* (ed. 3) XVI. 639/1 It is said that all the Samoied women have black nipples. **1822** tr. *Malte-Brun's Universal Geogr.* I. XXIII. 571 The Tunguse is a dialect of the Mantchou; the Samoyede differs from it. **1875** WHITNEY *Life Lang.* xii. 230 The second branch [of the Turanian family of languages] is the Samoyed. **1956** J. WHATMOUGH *Language* 28 In the north, Samoyede, a member of the same family as the Finnish dialects.

Samoyedic (sæməʊˈjɛdɪk), *a.* Also **Samojedic, -iedic.** [f. SAMOYED + -IC.] Of or pertaining to the Samoyeds. Also quasi-*sb.*, their language.
1813 *Q. Rev.* Oct. 288 The Samojedic nations are situated north of the Tartars. **1834** *Penny Cycl.* II. 474/1 The nations of Samoiedic origin occupy two different countries distant from one another. **1858** CARLYLE *Fredk. Gt.* VI. vi. II. 78 Peter, the Russian (say rather Samoeidic [*sic*]) Czar. **1888** *Encycl. Brit.* XXIV. 2/2 Certainly Turkic lies much closer to Mongolic than it does to Samoyedic and Tungusic.

samp (sæmp). *U.S.* Also 7 **sampe.** [a. Algonkin *nasamp* (Wood *Vocab.* 1634), Narragansett *nasaump* (R. Williams), lit. 'softened by water', applied subst. to 'every kind of spoon meat, bouillon, or porridge' (Trumbull in *Archiv Stud. neu. Spr.* LV. 454). Cf. SUPAWN.] Coarsely-ground Indian corn; also a kind of porridge made from it.
1643 R. WILLIAMS *Key* 11 *Nasàump*, a kind of meale pottage, unpartch'd. From this the English call their Samp, which is the Indian corne, beaten and boild, and eaten hot or cold with milke or butter. **1672** JOSSELYN *New Eng. Rarities* 101 The corn is light of digestion, and the English make a kind of Loblolly of it, which they call Sampe. **1833** WHITTIER *Passaconaway* Prose Wks. 1889 I. 276 My squaws have fine mat, big wigwam, soft samp. **1899** *Jrnl. R. Agric. Soc.* Mar. 133 Samp, a beautiful form of hominy.

sampan[1] (ˈsæmpæn). Also 7–8 **champana,** 8 **champan, -e, sampane, siampan,** 9 **sampaan, sampang, sanpan.** [a. Chinese *san-pan* (*san* three, *pan* board); cf. Annamite *tam-ban* (*tam* three). Cf. the Sp. spelling *cempan* (Oviedo 1535); also Pg. *champana.*]
1. A Chinese word meaning 'boat', applied by Europeans in the China seas to any small boat of Chinese pattern.
1620 R. COCKS *Diary* (Hakl. Soc.) II. 122 Yt was thought fytt and brought in question by the Hollanders to trym up a China sampan to goe with the fleete. **1653** H. COGAN tr. *Pinto's Trav.* xx. 72 Quiay Panian pursued them in a Champana. **1730** CAPT. W. WRIGLESWORTH *MS. Log-bk. of the 'Lyell'* 9 Sept., Took in 2 Sampan Loads of Wood. **1745** T. PASCOE *Jrnl. Voy. S. Seas* 296 Several Chinese

Champans, or small Fishing-Boats. **1867** SMYTH *Sailor's Word-bk.*, *Sampaan*, or *Sampan*, a neatly-adjusted kind of hatch-boat, used by the Chinese for passengers, and also as a dwelling for Tartar families, with a comfortable cabin.

2. *U.S.* (See quot.)

1897 *Outing* (U.S.) July 362/2 But the bay has a boat whose style is peculiar to the place. It is called a 'sanpan', and is an eight-foot punt, made of a few pine boards, which in light winds simply skims along the surface of the water.

3. *Comb.*, as **sampan-wallah** [WALLAH], a boatman in charge of a sampan.

1932 *Times Lit. Suppl.* 29 Sept. 693/3 In time he became a sampan-wallah. **1934** 'G. ORWELL' *Burmese Days* vii. 123 The successful sampan-wallah turned and discharged at his rival a mouthful of spittle.

sampan[2] ('sæmpən). [Khoi-khoin *samban.*] = TAMPAN.

1898 W. C. SCULLY *Between Sun & Sand* i. 8 The ground beneath is full of the dreaded 'sampans', which bury themselves in the flesh and cause serious injury. **1920** *Glasgow Herald* 2 Sept. 4 The minor plagues of scorpions and 'sampans'.

sampel, obs. form of SAMPLE.

samphire ('sæmfaɪə(r)). Forms: 6 **sampere, sampiere, samphier,** 6–8 **sampier,** 6–9 **sampire,** 7 **sampeir, samper, samphyre,** 7– **samphire.** [In 16th c. *sampere, -pire* (the altered form may have been assimilated to *camphire*), a. F. (*herbe de*) *Saint Pierre* (Cotgr. 1611), lit. 'St. Peter's herb'. Cf. mod.L. *sampetra* (in Dodoens ed. 1616).

Diefenbach cites mod.L. *herba divi Petri* from a work of 1694. Cf. G. *meerpeterlein.* Possibly the attribution to St. Peter may have been suggested by late L. *petra* (F. *pierre*) rock.]

1. a. The plant *Crithmum maritimum* (growing on rocks by the sea), the aromatic saline fleshy leaves of which are used in pickles. Also called *rock samphire.*

1545 ELYOT *Dict.*, *Crethmos* uel *Cretamus*, an herbe growing on the sea rockes, whiche we call Sampere. **1578** LYTE *Dodoens* v. xxi. 577 Sampiere hath fat, thicke, long smal leaves. **1590** R. PAYNE *Descr. Irel.* (1841) 7 The Phisitians there [in Ireland] holde, that Samphier is a present remedie against the stone. **1605** SHAKS. *Lear* IV. vi. 15 Halfe way downe Hangs one that gathers Sampire: dreadfull Trade. **1610** HOLLAND *Camden's Brit.* (1637) 344 Stately cliffes bringing forth Samphyre in great quantity. **1661** J. CHILDREY *Brit. Baconica* 10 In this shire grows greater store of samphire and Sea-holly. *a* **1691** BOYLE *Hist. Air* (1692) 178 Sampier clothes the rock in abundance. **1702** FLOYER in *Phil. Trans.* XXIII. 1167 Sampire is of an Acrid Aromatic Taste. **1731** MILLER *Gard. Dict.*, Crithmum;.. Smaller Samphire, or Sea-Fennel. **1832** *Veg. Subst. Food* 194 Samphire.. almost the only wild plant.. gathered for.. luxury. **1863** BARING-GOULD *Iceland* 176 The water has to be given a flavor by the squeezed berries of the Samphire.

b. As a name for various other maritime plants, esp. the glasswort (*Salicornia*). For GOLDEN, MARSH[1], PRICKLY *samphire*, see those words.

1703 DAMPIER *Voy.* III. I. 121 The Mould is Sand by the Sea-side, producing a large sort of Sampier, which bears a white Flower. *c* **1710** PETIVER *Catal. Ray's Eng. Herbal* Tab. xvii, Golden Samphire. *Ibid.* xxviii, Prickley Sampire. *a* **1794** BARHAM *Hortus Amer.* 165 Sampier... There is another sort, which resembles the English *kali, kelp,* or glass-wort; another sort hath a thick juicy saltish leaf, in shape of purslane..; another sort hath a turnsole leaf. **1807** J. E. SMITH *Phys. Bot.* 122 *Articulatus*, jointed, as in Samphire, *Salicornia annua.* **1847–54** WEBSTER, *Samphire.* .. In the United States, this name is applied to *Salicornia herbacea*, which is called glass-wort in England. **1864** GRISEBACH *Flora W. Ind. Isl.* 787 Samphire: *Borrichia arborescens.* Jamaica Samphire: *Batis maritima.* **1907** *Westm. Gaz.* 7 Feb. 12/1 The glasswort is still called 'samphire' in Suffolk, and is gathered for purposes of pickling.

2. *Cookery.* The leaves of samphire, used chiefly as a pickle.

1624 BOYLE in *Lismore Papers* (1886) II. 138 A smale Barricke of Sampier. **1641** MURREL *Cookerie* (ed. 5) 68 To boyle Pigeons with Capers or Sampyre. **1661** RABISHA *Cookery* 3 To pickle Sampier green. **1732** ARBUTHNOT *Rules of Diet* in *Aliments*, etc. 244 All Pickles, especially Samphire, which is stimulating. **1741** *Compl. Fam.-Piece* I. ii. 147 Then put in the Meat, and a few Capers and Samphire shred. **1747–96** MRS. GLASSE *Cookery* xix. 306 Take the samphire that is green, lay it in a clean pan.

3. *attrib.* and *Comb.*

1810 CRABBE *Borough* i. 41 Here sampire-banks and salt-wort bound the flood. **1822** *Hortus Anglicus* II. 380 *Inula Crithmifolia.* Samphire-leaved Inula. **1849** C. H. STURT *Narr. Exped. Centr. Austral.* I. 367 A shallow salt lagoon also fringed round with samphire bushes. **1928** V. WOOLF *Orlando* iv. 148 Closer and closer they drew, till the samphire gatherers, hanging half-way down the cliff, were plain to the naked eye. **1941** I. L. IDRIESS *Great Boomerang* ii. 10 Out among the samphire bushes lay huddled the little cloud of sheep. **1970** S. TRUEMAN *Intimate Hist. New Brunswick* iii. 57 Come home with thoughts of periwinkles, dulse, maple cream, samphire greens. **1971** *Country Life* 28 Oct. 1132/3 The reference to samphire, which for most of us means *King Lear*, the blinded Gloster and the wretched samphire-gatherer on Dover cliff.

sampi ('sæmpaɪ). Also **sanpi.** [Late Gr. *σαμπῖ*, prob. f. *ὡς ἂν πῖ* like pi.] The modern name for an ancient Greek numeral (ϡ) = 900, which has been hypothetically identified with one of several sibilants in early Greek alphabets.

1833 *Penny Cycl.* I. 385/2 The letter *tsadi* has no representative in the Greek alphabet, unless, indeed, it bear any relation to the Greek figure called *sanpi*, which, however, was never used, as far as it is known, for an alphabetic character. **1875** *Encycl. Brit.* I. 609/2 Herodotus .. speaks of the 'same letter which the Dorians call *σάν*, the Ionians *σίγμα*'; and though *san* was no letter of the Ionic alphabet, the compound *sampi* (= *σαν* + *πι*) denoted 900. **1912** E. M. THOMPSON *Introd. Greek & Lat. Palaeogr.* vii. 91 A symbol derived from the old letter *san*,.. which, from its partial resemblance to *pi*, was called *sampi* (= *san* + *pi*), for 900. **1968** W. S. ALLEN *Vox Graeca* i. 58 This stage [*sc.* affricate stage of [ts]] is probably represented by some early Asiatic Ionic inscriptions which show in such cases a special letter T.., which may be derived from the Semitic '*tsade*' (and perhaps survives in the numeral symbol ϡ = 900, now known by the late Byzantine name of *σαμπῖ* < *ὡς ἂν πῖ*).

samplar, obs. form of SAMPLER.

sample ('sɑːmp(ə)l, 'sæm-), *sb.* Forms: 4 **sampel, saumpel, -pul, -ple, saunpil,** 4–5 **saumpil,** 4–6 **sampill, saumple,** 5 **sampill(e, sampull, saumpyl,** 4– **sample.** [ME. *sample*, aphetic f. *essample*: see EXAMPLE *sb.*]

†**1.** A fact, incident, story, or suppositious case, which serves to illustrate, confirm, or render credible some proposition or statement. (Cf. EXAMPLE *sb.* 1.) *Obs.*

a **1300** *Cursor M.* 10351 Yitt samuel.. And sampson als,.. Bath þam bar tua wimmen geld... þou trou þir samples witerli, For þou sal haf a child in hi. **13..** *E.E. Allit P.* A. 499 As mathew melez in your messe, In sothful gospel of god al-myȝt In sample he can full grayþely gesse. *c* **1380** WYCLIF *Serm.* xlix. Sel. Wks. I. 142 And efte Crist tellip a kyndely saumple. *a* **1400–50** *Alexander* 5306 þar in perchement depayntid his persons scho schedwid. Said 'se þi-selfe a sampill þat I þe sothe neuyn!' **14..** *Tundale's Vis.* (Wagner) 6 Of suche a sampull y wyll ȝou telle, That he, þat wyll hit well unþerstande, In herte he may be full dredande. *c* **1430** LYDG. *Min. Poems* (Percy Soc.) 230 A sample we mow se al day, That God sent amonges us alle. **1513** MORE *Rich. III*, Wks. 48/1 And as simple as that saumple is, yet is there lesse reason in our case, then in that. **1529** —— *Dyaloge* II. ibid. 202/2 Thys wer not like yᵉ sufferance of an vnconsecrate host, wherof ye putte the saumple.

2. a. A relatively small quantity of material, or an individual object, from which the quality of the mass, group, species, etc. which it represents may be inferred; a specimen. Now chiefly *Comm.*, a small quantity of some commodity, presented or shown to customers as a specimen of the goods offered for sale. (An individual article offered as a specimen of goods sold by number and not by weight or measure is now more commonly called a *pattern.*)

The commercial use is now apprehended as the primary one, the wider application being felt as transferred.

1428 *Surtees Misc.* (1888) 6 Of ye whilk plaster and lyme a sample ys redy in ye chambre to shew. **1561** *Aberdeen Reg.* (1844) I. 335 Nor na skaiffry, sic as sampill and scheit schakin, to be tane thairof [*sc.* of malt and meal]. **1573–4** in Cunningham *Revels Acc.* (Shaks. Soc.) 60 For making of vj patternes, and for cutting therof for samples for the gownes of Cloth of golde, iij s. *a* **1626** BACON *New Atl.* 45 In one of these [galleries] wee place Patternes and Samples of all manner of the more Rare and Excellent Inuentions. **1699** *Poor Man's Plea* 20 Ye might let People buy by Samples, or at Barn-doors. **1703** *Lond. Gaz.* No. 3963/3 The Cargo of the Ship No. 7,.. consisting of.. White Wines, Sweets and Brandy; Samples of which may be seen at the said Hall. **1706** PHILLIPS (ed. Kersey), *Sample*, some part of a Commodity, given as a Pattern, to shew the Quality or Condition of it. **1713** ADDISON *Guardian* No. 100 ¶3 The hands and face were the only samples they gave of their beautiful persons. **1745** *De Foe's Eng. Tradesman* xlvi. (1841) II. 181 The farmer.. rubs out only a few handfuls of it [wheat] with his hand, and puts it into a little money-bag; and with this sample, as it is called, in his pocket, away he goes to market. **1775** J. BRYANT *Mythol.* II. p. vi, From those curious samples of Egyptian Sculpture at the British Museum. **1831** SIR J. SINCLAIR *Corr.* II. 394, I was induced to apply to his Sicilian Majesty.. for samples of the seed. **1838** W. BELL *Dict. Law Scotl.* s.v., When goods are sold by sample, there is an implied warrandice that the bulk is of equal quality with the sample. **1896** *Daily News* 9 Nov. 3/5 The Bench were of opinion that samples were goods.

b. of immaterial things.

1706 E. WARD *Wooden World Diss.* (1708) 89 He.. is often-times shewing you a sample of his Ingenuity. **1788** FRANKLIN *Autobiog.* Wks. 1840 I. 169 It was by a private person giving a sample of the utility of lamps. **1821** LAMB *Elia* Ser. I. *Quakers' Meeting*, Once only.. I witnessed a sample of the old Foxian orgasm. **1849** MACAULAY *Hist. Eng.* v. I. 526 Of the general character of those outlaws an estimate may be formed from a few samples. **1888** BRYCE *Amer. Commw.* xlviii. II. 235 Illinois furnishes so good a sample of that [township] system in its newer form, that I cannot do better than extract from a.. trustworthy writer, the following account.

c. A specimen taken for scientific testing or analysis.

1878 HUXLEY *Physiogr.* xvi. 261 During these surveys, numerous samples of the sea bottom were secured. **1882** *Nature* XXVI. 297 The collection of samples of air for analysis. **1895** J. C. GUERNSEY *Urinalysis including Blanks* 11 If a sample of urine cannot be analyzed immediately upon its receipt, add ten to fifteen grains of salicylic acid. **1938** LUNDELL & HOFFMAN *Outl. Methods Chem. Analysis* iii. 21 In a chemical analysis, the first consideration is the use of a sample that truly represents the material under test. **1950** RACE & SANGER *Blood Groups in Man* i. 3 The reactions when different cell samples are tested against parallel titrations of the same antisera. **1973** J. G. DICK *Analytic Chem.* ii. 32 Samples of impure acidic substances were analyzed by a neutralization method.

d. *Statistics.* A portion drawn from a population, the study of which is intended to lead to statistical estimates of the attributes of the whole population.

1903, 1922 [see POPULATION[2] 2 d]. **1944** H. G. WELLS *'42 to '44* 42 He would get answers to his questions from Samples of his Consumers. **1951** [see MID-RANGE 1]. **1961** *Listener* 9 Nov. 780/2 There is the social survey of, say, the Young and Wilmott kind, with its planned interviews of samples. **1979** *Church Times* 9 Mar. 2/2 A nationally representative sample of 956 people was interviewed for the survey.

†**3.** A person's action or conduct viewed as an object of imitation; also, a person whose conduct deserves imitation; = EXAMPLE *sb.* 6. *Obs.*

a **1300** *Cursor M.* 409 Hymself þan gaf us sample þare. *c* **1400** *Rule St. Benet* (Prose) 22 O þis maner sal þabbesse foliȝe þe saumpyl of Iesu. **1548** PATTEN *Exped.* Pref. b iij b, Since what he could doo, they could not resiste, and what he should do, they had set hym a sample. **1579** SPENSER *Sheph. Cal.* July 119 And nowe they bene to heauen forewent, Theyr good is with them goe: Theyr sample onely to vs lent, That als we mought doe soe. **1594** CAREW *Tasso* (1881) 106 For if his errour such pardon accrew, More by his sample will be couraged. **1611** SHAKS. *Cymb.* I. i. 48 [He] Liu'd in Court (Which rare it is to do) most prais'd, most lou'd, A sample to the yongest.

†**4.** Precedent; = EXAMPLE *sb.* 5. *Obs.*

1534 MORE *Comf. agst. Trib.* II. Wks. 1193/1 Therefore is his case both playn against Goddes open precept, and the dispensacion straunge and withoute saumple.

†**5.** A warning; = EXAMPLE *sb.* 3. Phrases, ***in sample***, by way of warning. ***to take sample.*** *Obs.*

a **1300** *Cursor M.* 20889 Bath ananias and his wife For suike he dampnid tam o life, þat all suld tak þaim sample bi For to naman do tricheri. *c* **1375** *Sc. Leg. Saints* i. (*Petrus*) 595 þar-for, in sampill of ewill dede to wekit dede I sall ȝow lede. *c* **1420** *Brut* 196 In sample þat þe Scottes shulde haue in mynde forto bere ham amys aȝeynz her lorde eftesones. *c* **1470** HENRY *Wallace* VI. 403 On the sall fall the fyrst part off thir harmys, Sampill to geyff till all thi fals natioune. *Ibid.* XI. 834 Nane sampill takis, how ane othir has beyn For cowatice put in gret paynys fell.

6. *attrib.* and *Comb.* **a.** appositive, quasi-*adj.*, serving as a sample.

1820 SCORESBY *Acc. Arctic Reg.* I. 458 If the 'sample blade', that is, the largest lamina in the series, weigh 7 pounds, the whole produce may be estimated at a ton. **1849** THACKERAY *Pendennis* xliv, Why did you leave that.. sample-bottle of Hollands out of the cupboard? **1855** J. R. LEIFCHILD *Cornwall Mines* 263 It is just possible that the sample ores you see in London, or some other city, have come from any mine except the one projected, or offered to your consideration. **1863** *Reader* 12 Dec. 688 By culling a few sample-extracts. **1865** DICKENS *Mut. Fr.* III. ii, Miss Abbey filed her receipts, and kept her sample phials. **1895** W. SCHLICH *Man. Forestry* III. I. iv. 66 Having ascertained the volume of the sample plot, that of the whole wood can be calculated. **1970** G. A. & A. G. THEODORSON *Mod. Dict. Sociol.* 361 The extent to which generalizations based on sample data may be considered applicable to the total population from which the sample was drawn depends on the method used to select the cases included in the sample and the size of the sample. **1978** C. H. STODDARD *Essent. Forestry Pract.* (ed. 3) vi. 119 Timber estimators also measure and tally the trees in the strips or sample plots. **1978** R. V. JONES *Most Secret War* xix. 156 Maita had stayed in Salisbury because she was nervous about London, but she wanted to come for a sample weekend, and when would I recommend?

b. General *attrib.*, as ***sample investigation, method, study, survey*** (hence ***sample-survey*** vb. trans.).

1930 *Economist* 1 Nov. 801/2 Even so, his impressions are inevitably based on 'sample' investigations and must be read with these limitations in mind. **1944** H. G. WELLS *'42 to '44* 43 The sample method of dealing with human affairs is exemplified by various uses to which we can put a jury. **1965** J. MEUVRET in Glass & Eversley *Population in Hist.* xxi. 516 Other sample-studies in parish registers.. have revealed analogous results. **1966** *Economist* 12 Nov. 682/3 The development of economic knowledge sample-surveyed in these articles has been matched by a growing use of economists in business and government. **1975** *Listener* 6 Feb. 187/3 The study of human behaviour by.. sample surveys.

c. Used *attrib.* to denote various statistical attributes of a sample, as ***sample average, mean, range***, etc.

1939 A. E. TRELOAR *Elements Statistical Reasoning* x. 137 The standard error of the sample mean. **1941** *Ann. Math. Statistics* XII. 91 (*heading*) Determination of sample sizes for setting tolerance limits. **1947** O. L. DAVIES *Statistical Methods Res. & Production* ix. 217 One [chart] on which the sample averages $\bar{x}$ are recorded and the other on which sample ranges *w* are recorded. **1971** HICKMAN & HILTON *Probability & Statistical Analysis* ix. 153 The sample variance.. is said to be a point estimator of the population variance in the same sense that the sample mean.. is a point estimator of the population mean.

d. Special Comb.: **sample-bag**, a bag containing the samples carried by a commercial traveller; also, a small holland bag tied up with an attached tape, used by merchants and farmers to carry samples of corn, etc.; **sample book**, a book containing samples of fabrics for prospective buyers; **sample bottle**, a bottle in which samples of fluid from the body may be collected; **sample card**, a piece of cardboard to which is fastened a sample of cloth, etc.; = *pattern card*; **sample case**, a case containing samples carried by a travelling salesman; **sample cutter** (see quot.); **sample hand**, an operative employed in producing 'sample' goods; **sample passer**, one whose business it is to select the articles that are to serve as samples; **sample room**, (*a*) a room in which samples are kept for inspection; and (*b*) *U.S. slang*, a place where liquor is sold by the glass; **sample-trier** = *sample passer*.

1884 *Manch. Guard.* 26 Sept. 5/1 He..deposited his *sample-bag in the dining-room. **1938** *Burlington Mag.* Apr. 200/2 The distinguished firm of weavers, whose *sample-books of 100 years and more ago are still in existence. **1976** P. Clabburn *Needleworker's Dict.* 232/1 Old sample books still in existence are of the greatest value in telling later generations what was in fashion at a particular date. **1977** *Belfast Tel.* 22 Feb. 8/6 Doctors' hands.., little *sample bottles, having your arm draped in black as your blood pressure is taken. **1875** *North Alabamian* (Tuscumbia, Alabama) 30 Sept. 3/3 We were not glad to see him, as he had left his *sample case at home. **1935** [see keister 1 a]. **1971** D. E. Westlake *I gave at the Office* 123 A salesman rapping his knuckles on his sample case in a waiting room. **1884** Knight *Dict. Mech.* Suppl., **Sample cutter*, a species of rotary shears. A sharp edged disk on a table rolling against an edge and cutting narrow strips of cloth from the roll, to form tailor's or traveler's samples. **1902** *Daily Chron.* 29 Apr. 10/3 Experienced *sample hands for children's costumes, pelisses, &c. **1892** *Labour Commission Gloss.*, **Sample Passer*, a proficient smelter who chemically tests a sample of metal drawn from the furnace when to the eye it seems about the desired quality. **1865** G. A. Sala *My Diary in Amer.* II. 46 Sometimes the bar is at the side, screened off, and genteelly disguised under the name of '*sample room'. You enter ostensibly to purchase cherries, and immediately 'put yourself outside' a 'tot' of Bourbon. **1869** W. H. Brewer *Rocky Mountain Lett.* (1930) 10 'Saloons', 'bar-rooms', 'sample-rooms', 'liquor stores', 'lager beer', etc., furnish most of the signs on the places of business. **1874** Aldrich *Prudence Palfrey* xv. 297 Colonel Todhunter..had been refreshing himself at the sample-room attached to Odiorne's grocery. **1887** *Grip* (Toronto) 21 May 10/2 One of the drug travellers insisted..that the clerk..had, in the north sample room, first nicknamed Albendis 'Chippy'. **1892** *Hist. Rev. York County* (Pa.) 62/1 To the side is the reading and sample-rooms for the commercial traveler. **1895** *Daily News* 5 Dec. 5/1 Commercial institutions, of which inquiry offices, museums, and sample rooms..should form a leading feature. **1776** Pryce *Min. Cornub.* 217 In the knowledge of which the *sample-triers or Tin-dressers are very expert. **1814** W. Phillips in *Trans. Geol. Soc.* II. 143 When a pound or two of the ore is given to the sample-trier, as a fair sample of 50 or 100 tons.

sample ('sɑːmp(ə)l, 'sæm-), *v.* [f. sample *sb.*]

†**1.** *trans.* To be or find a match or parallel to; to parallel; to intend as a match *for*. Also, to put in comparison *with*. *Obs.*

1592 Ld. Vaux in Ellis *Orig. Lett.* Ser. iv. IV. 109 Throwgh uneath to be sampled infortunacy I may neither dispose of my owne to my requisite reliefe [etc.]. **1597** J. King *On Jonas* (1618) 702 Whensoeuer afterwards there was taken vppe any great lamentation, it was sampled and matched with that of Hadadrimmon. **1602** Dekker *Honest Wh.* Wks. 1873 II. 141 If Cambricke you wud deale in, there's the best, all Millan cannot sample it. **1616** B. Jonson *Devil an Ass* v. i, She would ha' had you, to ha' sampled you With one within, that they are now a teaching; And do's pretend to your ranck. **1619** W. Sclater *Exp. 1 Thess.* 173 Who can sample, amongst Heretiques, that [patience] of Laurence on the Gridyron? **1630** Lord *Banians* 9 Modest were her Aspect, and her eyes Indices of so melancholly sobernesse, and composed lookes, as if she seemed to be sampled for him that met her. *a* **1638** Mede *Wks.* (1672) iii. 635 This notion [is] nowhere else sampled in any Greek Author. **1640** Bastwick *Lord Bps.* ii. Biij, Which Prelacie he samples and parallells with the..Lordship, which Heathen Princes exercise over their people. **1689** Hickeringill *Ceremony Monger* v. Wks. 1716 II. 435 A Lean and Cadaverous Clergy, the whole Protestant World cannot sample such a jejune Crew.

†**2. a.** To set an example to. **b.** To set an example of. *Obs.*

1600 S. Nicholson *Acolastus* (1876) 5 The morne, who sampling men their sinnes to rue, Hath washt earths motley face in weeping dewe. **1606** Warner *Alb. Eng.* xvi. ciii. 406 We Church-men should to Lay-men sample good.

†**3.** To illustrate, to explain by examples or analogies; to symbolize. *Obs.*

1613 Purchas *Pilgrimage* (1614) 599 Ortelius..supposeth ..that Vmbilicus was accounted the Deitie it selfe..which shapelesse shape hee sampleth by many like in other Nations. **1633** Earl Manch. *Al Mondo* (1636) 191 Therefore this wee may doe, some way sample that, which no way we can expresse. **1664** H. More *Exp. 7 Epist.* Pref. (1669) (a 3), Mr. Mede..seems to insinuate that they should Prophetically sample unto us a sevenfold successive Temper and Condition of the whole visible Church.

†**4.** To imitate, to copy. *Obs.*

1613–16 W. Browne *Brit. Past.* ii. iii, Walla by chance was in a meadow by Learning to 'sample earth's embrodery. **1626** Bp. Hall *Contempl.*, *O.T.* xx. vii, A modell of this more exquisite frame is sent to Urijah, the priest; and must be sampled in Jerusalem. **1675** V. Alsop *Anti-Sozzo* 530 Is it not a strange Copy that differs in kind from its Idea?.. As if you should propound a House for your patern, and draw a Horse to sample it.

5. a. To take a sample or samples of; to judge of the quality of (a thing) by a sample or specimen; to obtain a representative experience of.

1767 Sterne *Tr. Shandy* IX. xxi, She..looks at it,—considers it,—samples it,—measures it. **1858** Hughes *Scour. White Horse* 196, I won't turn my back..on any man in the country at sampling wheat. **1883** V. D. Majendie in *Fortn. Rev.* May 647 Every cargo is sampled by the Customs on its arrival and chemically examined. **1890** N. Hibbs in *Big Game N. Amer.* 22 The Moose has a hump on his nose,..it excels any other meat dish I have ever had the pleasure of sampling. **1897** Mary Kingsley *W. Africa* 354 Some one who has personally sampled Africa. **1974** Harvey & Bohlman *Stereo F.M. Radio Handbk.* v. 119 The composite audio signal voltage is sampled at the midpoints by a train of short pulses and the sampled voltage level is held between pulses. **1978** *Nature* 13 July 135/2 A synchronous gating circuit..samples the V_2 signal at a selectable phase ('phase lock'), converting it to a proportional d.c. voltage.

b. To present samples or specimens of. Also, to serve as a sample of.

1870 Lowell *Study Wind.* (1871) 208 Chaucer never shows any signs of effort, and it is a main proof of his excellence that he can be so inadequately sampled by detached passages. **1873** J. Geikie *Gt. Ice Age* (1894) 607 The literature of the subject has grown to such an extent,.. that it is hopeless..to do more than sample it. **1880** *Daily Tel.* 8 July, The fifty thousand men who would have sampled the drill, discipline, and patriotism of a hundred and fifty thousand more. **1889** *Pall Mall G.* 16 Nov. 3/2 English editors of Irish chronicles and histories often make grave blunders, some of which he samples.

6. To provide with samples.

1935 A. P. Herbert *What a Word!* iii. 83 From a firm of 'Publishers and Educational Contractors for Handicraft Materials':..'We shall welcome the opportunity of *sampling* you with anything you would like to see.' 'We are *sampling* Norway with the new articles.' **1946** K. T. Keller in *Chrysler Corp. Ann. Rep.* XXI, The limited production to date of our new models has been inadequate to properly sample our dealers.

7. *Comb.*: **sample-and-hold** *adj. phr. Electronics*, applied to a circuit or technique in which a varying voltage is sampled periodically and the sampled voltage is retained in the interval until the next sampling.

1966 M. Schwartz et al. *Communication Syst. & Techniques* vi. 244 One difficulty in PAM systems used for time-division switching is that the short samples do not deliver very much average signal power to the individual receiving channels. The difficulty can be remedied by the use of a sample-and-hold circuit. **1974** Harvey & Bohlman *Stereo F.M. Radio Handbk.* v. 119 Using this sample-and-hold technique, good channel separation, low distortion and low subcarrier breakthrough may be realized. **1979** C.-T. Chen *One-Dimensional Digital Signal Processing* 435 The conversions between analog and digital signals are performed by sample-and-hold (S/H) circuits, analog-to-digital (A/D) converters, and digital-to-analog (D/A) converters.

sampled ('sɑːmp(ə)ld, 'sæm-), *ppl. a.* [f. sample *v.* + -ed.] **1.** Tested to ascertain the quality.

1877 Raymond *Statist. Mines & Mining* 241 An assay of sampled ore gives 40 ounces silver and 60 per cent. lead.

2. sampled data, data supplied at regular intervals, rather than continuously; freq. *attrib.*, designating a system whose behaviour is modified by such data.

1951 *Trans. Amer. Inst. Electr. Engin.* LXX. 1779/1 The design of a sampled-data servo system is as direct as the design of a conventional system. *Ibid.* 1779/3 A control system makes use of sampled data when it is impossible to supply continuous data to all its parts. **1955** J. G. Truxal *Automatic Feedback Control System Synthesis* ix. 500 Servo-mechanisms which operate on sampled data: *i.e.*, systems for which the input (or the activating signal) is represented by samples at regular intervals of time, with the information ordinarily carried in the amplitudes of the samples. **1968** *Brit. Med. Bull.* XXIV. 252/1 The breathing mechanisms must include a form of 'memory' and a so-called 'sampled data' system.

sampler ('sɑːmplə(r), 'sæm-), *sb.*[1] Forms: 4 **saumplarie, -ye, sawmplere,** 4–5 **samplere, saumpler,** 4–8 **samplar,** 6 **sawmplar,** 9 *dial.* **sampleth,** 6– **sampler.** [Aphetic f. OF. *essamplaire*: see exemplar.]

†**1.** An example to be imitated; a model, pattern; an archetype; the original from which a copy is or may be taken. *Obs.*

a **1300** *Cursor M.* 28073 Bot nu sal i tell þe her nest Hu þu sal sceu þi scrift to preist,..þat laud men mai sumquat lere To scape þair scrift wit þis samplere. *c* **1375** *Sc. Leg. Saints* xxvii. (*Machor*) 1439 For þai till hyme war as samplar to lewe his kyne þat mychty war, & þis gret pilgrimag to tak. **1377** Langl. *P. Pl.* B. xii. 104 Al-þough men made bokes god was þe maistre, And seynt spirit þe saumplarye and seide what men sholde write. **1382** Wyclif *Exod.* xxv. 40 Bihold and do after the sawmplere, that to thee is shewid in the hil. *c* **1475** *Partenay* 2947 Off ther beyng here will I leue and cease, To declare and say make me will redy, As of my samplere to procede plainly. **1565** Jewel *Repl. Harding* (1611) 382 There are not two sorts of Adoration..but one onely Adoration, both of the Image, and also of the Samplar, whereof the Image is. **1581** J. Bell *Haddon's Answ. Osor.* 445 But the Type is past, and the veritye supplyeth the place. Latt us make a comparison betwixt the sampler and ye trueth [Melchisedech and Christ]. **1597** Beard *Theatre God's Judgem.* (1612) 490 The verie whores..paid him a yearely reuenue for their bauderies: which act..is made a sampler to some of our holie Popes to imitate. **1608** Topsell *Serpents* (1658) 778 Arachne first invented..working with the needle, which this mayd of Lydia first learned from the Spiders, taking her first Samplers and patterns from them for imitation. **1636** Featly *Clavis Myst.* xvi. 208 Christ's baptism was the perfect sampler and patterne of ours. **1656** Jeanes *Fuln. Christ* 296 The holinesse of Christ, which God hath propounded unto us for a samplar to imitate. **1658** Manton *Exp. Jude* Wks. 1871 V. 85 God is the original fountain and sampler of holiness. *a* **1680** Charnock *Attrib. God* (1834) II. 259 True holiness consists in a likeness to the most exact sampler.

attrib. **1645** Rutherford *Tryal & Tri. Faith* (1845) 48 A stone,..some way conform to..Christ the Sampler-stone.

†**2.** An illustrative or typical instance; a specimen. Also, a representation, symbol, type. *Obs.*

a **1300** *Cursor M.* 10892 þat þou be noght o þis in weir, Ald elizabeth be þi samplere. **1623** Lisle *Ælfric on O. & N. Test.* (1638) 24 So thou maist yet at least be furthered somewhat by this little sampler [A.S. *bysne*]. **1644** Quarles *Barnabas & B.* 253 What is man but a sampler of weakness? **1683** *Pennsylv. Archives* I. 73 And God is giving some Specimens hereof, some Samplars. **1697** Burghope *Disc. Relig. Assemb.* 25 The Temple..a Type and Samplar..of the Heavenly Temple that is above.

3. †**a.** A piece of embroidery serving as a pattern to be copied. *Obs.*

1574 R. Scot *Hop Gard.* (1578) 54 The Hoppesackes that are brought out of Flaunders, may be good samplers for you to worke by. *a* **1586** Sidney *Arcadia* ii. (Sommer) 119 Alas then, O Loue, why doost thou in thy beautifull sampler sette such a worke for my Desire to take out, which is as much impossible? [**1608**: see 1.] **1675** Brooks *Gold. Key* Wks. 1867 V. 284 Such as begin to work with the needle, look much on their sampler and pattern.

b. A beginner's exercise in embroidery; a piece of canvas embroidered by a girl or woman as a specimen of skill, usually containing the alphabet and some mottos worked in ornamental characters, with various decorative devices.

1523 Skelton *Garl. Laurel* 789 The saumpler to sow on, the lacis to enbraid. **1546** Marg. Thomson *Will* in *Essex Rev.* (1908) XVII. 147, I gyve to Alys Pynchebeck my sawmpler with semes. **1592** Kyd *Sol. & Pers.* i. ii, When didst thou, with thy sampler..sit sowing? **1639** Mayne *City Match* ii. ii, Your schoole-mistresse..teaches To knit in Chaldee, and worke Hebrew samplers. **1758** Johnson *Idler* No. 2 ⁋ 3 Our girls forsake their samplers to teach kingdoms wisdom. **1789** Burns *Let. to Mrs. M'Murdo* 2 May, Never did little Miss with more sparkling pleasure show her applauded sampler to partial Mamma, than I now send my poem to you. **1803** R. Anderson *Cumbld. Ball.* 61 Sin I furst work'd a sampleth at Biddy Forsyth's. **1862** Calverley *Verses & Tr.* (1894) 80 Now not all they seek to do Is create upon a sampler Beasts which Buffon never knew. **1886** J. K. Jerome *Idle Thoughts* (1889) 136 There is a 'sampler' worked by some idiot related to the family.

attrib. **1859** Miss Cary *Country Life* i. (1876) 19, I see that it was marked with sampler letters in one corner. **1881** Besant & Rice *Chapl. of Fleet* I. 170 Esther, for her part, taught her embroidery and sampler work.

transf. and *fig.* **1627** W. Hawkins *Apollo Shroving* Prol. 5 Take out thy fescue, and spell here, in this one-leau'd booke. Tell the stitches in this sampler of blacke and white. **1717** Prior *Alma* ii. 448 Distinguished Slashes deck the Great; As each excells in Birth, or State His Oylet-holes are more, and ampler, The King's own body was a Samplar. **1819** Keats *Wks.* (1889) III. p. cxxv, The more he may love the sad embroidery of the *Excursion*, the more will he hate the coarse samplers of Betty Foy and Alice Fell.

4. *Forestry.* A young tree left standing when the rest are cut down.

1653 Blithe *Eng. Improv. Impr.* 161 Take a good straight Pole or sampler growing of Ash or Willow. **1785** J. Phillips *Treat. Inland Navig.* 19 Cutting down samplers and young trees even for faggot and stack wood..has been..a common practice. **1813** Vancouver *Agric. Devon* 246 Standards or samplers are always left, but seldom raised to timber.

5. = sample *sb.* 2 a, b.

1823 J. Badcock *Dom. Amusem.* 136 Test for proving Steel. Take weak aqua-fortis, and drop a little on the sampler in question. **1972** T. Kochman *Rappin' & Stylin' Out* p. xv, Minimally necessary would be a comparative sampler of the diverse preaching styles that exist in the black community. **1975** *Booksellers Weekly* 15 Sept. 55/3 The authors also include a sampler of foreign menus: continental, Italian, Greek, Mexican, oriental, Indonesian. **1976** *National Observer* (U.S.) 17 Jan. 14/1 (Advt.), Try this Vermont Sampler... We'll send you, on approval, our Vermont cob-smoked ham..and 1 lb. of our delicious cob-smoked bacon.

6. That which contains a sample or representative selection; *spec.* a gramophone record of examples of a performer, type of music, etc.

1969 *Nature* 10 May 599/1 This paperback is a sampler of letters, perodicals, and reports in the United States relating to the publication late in 1859 of Charles Darwin's 'Origin'. **1970** *Melody Maker* 20 June 27/4 We are promised jazz releases from A. & M. Records commencing shortly with a jazz sampler. **1977** *Linlithgowshire Jrnl. & Gaz.* 15 Apr. 6/6 And one of the best ways to start is with Atlantic Record's sampler containing numbers from the albums 'War Babies', 'Abandoned Luncheonette' and 'Whole Oates'.

7. *attrib.* and *Comb.*, as (sense 3 b) ***sampler rhyme***; (sense 6) ***sampler album*** (album[1] 6), ***collection, record.***

1977 *Zigzag* Mar. 28/3 He's also doing a *sampler album, with sleeve notes too, I think. **1973** A. Dundes *Mother Wit* p. xii, There are already *sampler collections of raw folklore data available. **1975** *Gramophone* May 2024/1 Gustav Leonhardt Portrait. *Sampler Record. **1951** W. de la Mare *Winged Chariot* 51 My cross-stitch *sampler-rhyme.

sampler ('sɑːmplə(r), 'sæm-), *sb.*[2] [f. sample *v.* + -er[1].] **1.** One whose business it is to sample goods; also, one employed in any other form of sampling.

1778 Pryce *Min. Cornub.* 216 To make a rough guess or coarse essay, the sampler takes a handful of it, and washes it on a shovel [etc.]. **1877** Raymond *Statist. Mines & Mining* 382 The sampler takes charge of the piles. **1906** *Act 6 Edw. VII*, c. 27 § 3 (2) An official sampler shall at the request of the purchaser..take a sample for analysis by the agricultural analyst of any such article. *c* **1950** G. van Delden *I have Plan* i. 15 He..came to the mine.., so they put him on the staff as a sampler. **1971** J. B. Carroll et al. *Word Frequency Bk.* p. xviii, The responsibility for judging whether or not a textual segment was an essentially English sentence was left to the sampler.

2. A device for obtaining samples for scientific study.

1902 *Bull. U.S. Fish Comm. 1901* XXI. 58 (*caption*) Soil sampler, after Delbecque. **1927** *Bull. Nat. Res. Council* (U.S.) No. 61. 237 A modification of the Davis peat-sampler. *Ibid.* 238 In deeper water the other sampler had to be used. **1946** *Geogr. Jrnl.* CVII. 164 The core-sampler gave relatively short cores or none at all... The piston-sampler constructed by Dr. Kullenberg—a modification of the original vacuum core-sampler—secured practically undisturbed cores down to a maximum depth of over 3600 metres. **1959** *Jrnl. Sci. Instruments* XXXIV. 3 (*heading*) Impaction sampler for size grading air-borne bacteria-carrying particles. **1974** *Nature* 25 Oct. 678/2 The air samplers do not register this excess presumably because the size of the spray particles is beyond the upper limit of collection of the sampling duct.

†**'sampler,** *v. Obs.* [f. SAMPLER *sb.*¹] = SAMPLE *v.*

1628 PRYNNE *Brief Survay* 54, I will therefore now confine my selfe to the Matter, and Substance of these Deuotions, which I will now Paralell, and Sampler with those Popish Authors.

samplery ('sɑːmplərɪ, 'sæm-). [f. SAMPLER *sb.*¹ + -Y.] The making of samplers; sampler work.

1613 T. MILLES tr. *Mexia's*, etc. *Treas. Anc. & Mod. T.* I. 762/2 Feare God, and learne womens huswiuery; not idle Samplery, or Silken follies. **1840** DICKENS *Old. C. Shop* viii, The art of needle-work, marking, and samplery.

sampling ('sɑːmplɪŋ, 'sæm-), *vbl. sb.* [f. SAMPLE *v.* + -ING¹.] The action of the vb. SAMPLE.

†**1.** Following an example, imitation. *Obs.*

a **1638** MEDE *Wks.* (1672) 158 And this conformity and sampling (as I may say) of Christ, extends not only to those Acts of his which he did as man, where the imitation is plain and direct.

2. The action of testing the quality of anything by means of samples; an instance of this.

1778 PRYCE *Min. Cornub.* 326 The persons employed are called Samplers; and the business itself Sampling. **1809** R. LANGFORD *Introd. Trade* 64 Sample Box, Sampling and Duty..5s. 6d. **1867** *Jrnl. R. Agric. Soc.* Ser. II. III. II. 476 Numerous gaugings and samplings of the sewage..have been undertaken. **1889** *Athenæum* 15 June 753/2 It is..not one to be estimated on..a chance sampling. **1924** J. STAMP *Stud. Current Probl. Finance & Govt.* 12 A second development of statistics, along the lines of the theory of probability, is in the important principle of 'sampling'... Under certain conditions 20 per cent., or even 5 per cent., samples may yield satisfactory and reliable results. **1935** *Brit. Birds* XXVIII. 332 Sampling is an attractive labour-saving device, but it presents a number of obstacles and pitfalls, and needs to be used with considerable caution. **1973** *Jrnl. Genetic Psychol.* CXXII. 249 This wide sampling yields a measure of a generalized expectancy of reinforcement.

3. *attrib.*, as ***sampling method, rate, survey***; **sampling distribution**, the theoretical frequency distribution of a statistic, as calculated from a sample, over all samples of the same size and kind; **sampling error**, error due to the use of a sample which does not perfectly characterize the population from which it is drawn.

1928 *Proc. R. Soc.* A. CXXI. 654 (*heading*) The general *sampling distribution of the multiple correlation coefficient. **1967** R. C. CAMPBELL *Statistics for Biologists* ii. 32 A sample statistic..has a sampling distribution. This last term is slightly misleading, because all the distributions we have considered arise from sampling; the name is however usually reserved for the distribution from sample to sample of a statistic calculated from each sample. **1914** *Psychol. Rev.* XXI. 109 The correlation (compensated for *sampling errors) between any two columns. **1955** *Times* 8 July 7/3 It is anticipated that..the estimated total population of the Sudan will have a sampling error of substantially less than 1 per cent. **1974** *Times* 11 Feb. 15/3 Polls are subject to considerable sampling error. **1943** *Ann. Math. Statistics* XIV. 289 The accuracy of a *sampling method may be measured by the variance of the estimate of the quantity which is of interest. **1975** *Listener* 6 Feb. 187/3 We accept sampling methods in our everyday life. **1947** *Bell Syst. Techn. Jrnl.* XXVI. 396 Any input wave can be represented by a series of regularly occurring instantaneous samples, provided that the *sampling rate is at least twice the highest frequency in the input wave. **1978** *Gramophone* Apr. 1789/2 The Sound Stream recorder, which sells for $70,000, is a full 6-bit binary conversion and recording system, with a sampling rate of 48K, frequency response to 17kHz,..and a tape speed of 30ips. **1960** *Amer. Speech* XXXV. 176 The picture is probably as true as a *sampling survey can give. **1972** H. KURATH *Stud. Area Linguistics* 76 A sampling survey carried out on a modest scale can reveal important aspects of the dialectal structure.

‖**sampot** (sɑ̃po). [Fr., ad. Cambodian *sampuet.*] A kind of Cambodian sarong.

1931 *N. & Q.* 22 Aug. 127/1 The women of Cambodia make *sampots.* These are the long and wide sashes of silk of many colours which they bind around their waists. **1957** *Encycl. Brit.* IV. 641/2 Both sexes wear the *sampot* (a copious sort of loincloth) which the men supplement with a short jacket, the women with a long scarf draped around the figure or a long clinging robe. **1963** 'HAN SUYIN' *Four Faces* 100 The woman in a Cambodian *sampot* and blouse.

samprasarana (sæmprə'sɑːrənə). *Philol.* [Skr. *samprasāraṇa*, lit. 'a stretching out, extending', f. *sam-* together + *pra-* forth + *-sāraṇa* extension.] In Sanskrit, the interchange between the vowels i, u, ṛi, lṛi and their corresponding semi-vowels y, v, r, l; hence, a similar process in other Indo-European languages.

1861 T. GOLDSTÜCKER *Pâṇini: his Place in Sanskrit Lit.* 169 It is probable, therefore, that Pâṇini did not invent these terms, but referred to them as of current use. On the other hand, he distinctly defines..*upadhá, lopa, samprasárana*, and *abhyá sa.* **1888** J. WRIGHT tr. *K. Brugmann's Elements Compar. Gram. Indo-Gmc. Lang.* I. 473 Vowel absorption often happens in languages with predominantly expiratory accentuation... If the absorption happens in such a manner that the syllable retains its value as a syllable, which is only possible, if another sound is able to undertake the part as bearer of the syllabic accent, we call the process samprasāraṇa (after the Indian grammarians). **1916** A. A. MACDONELL *Vedic Gram. for Students* 5 The Samprasāraṇa series. Here the accented high grade syllables *ya, va, ra*.. interchange with the unaccented low grade vowels *i, u, ṛ*. **1933** L. BLOOMFIELD *Language* xxi. 384 When a relatively sonorous phoneme is non-syllabic, it often acquires syllabic function; this change is known by the Sanskrit name of *samprasarana.* **1968** *Language* XLIV. 278 The forms **xʷarta-* and **ųarta-* are correct: they are doubtless full grade replacements for the zero grade in samprasarana roots.

Sampsæan (sæmp'siːən). *Eccl. Hist.* [f. Gr. Σαμψαῖ-οι pl. + -AN.

Epiphanius renders the name by Ἡλιακοί 'solar', regarding it as f. Heb. *shemesh*, Syriac *shemshâ* the sun. He does not, however, accuse the Sampsæans of sun-worship, though he says they venerated water almost as a deity. Perhaps the word is from the Heb.-Aram. root *sh-m-sh* to minister.]

An adherent of a heretical sect that existed in Persia, identified by Epiphanius with the Elcesaites.

1613 PURCHAS *Pilgr.* (1614) 148 And in worshipping of the Sunne, whereof they were called the Sampsæans, or Sunner, Sunmen, as Epiphanius interpreteth that name. **1875** LIGHTFOOT *Comm. Col.* 88 *note*, The historical connexion of the Sampsæans with the Essenes is evident.

Sampson: see SAMSON.

†**sampsuchine.** *Obs.* [ad. mod.L. (*oleum*) *sampsūchinum*, Gr. σαμψύχινον (oil) of marjoram, f. σάμψυχον, -ος marjoram.] Oil of marjoram.

1599 B. JONSON *Cynthia's Rev.* v. iv, I savour no sampsuchine in it.

samptsoo, sampull, obs. ff. SAMSHOO, SAMPLE.

‖**Samsam** ('sæmsæm). Now chiefly *Hist.* [Malay.] A person of mixed Malayo-Thai origin from the west coast of the Malay peninsula (see quot. 1961).

1836 J. LOW *Diss. Soil & Agric. Penang* viii. 293, I believe there are some converts also amongst the Samsams, or mixed descendants of Siamese and Malays. **1839** T. J. NEWBOLD *Pol. & Statistical Acct. Straits of Malacca* I. 420 The Samsams are a race of Malays who have adopted the religion and language of the Siamese. **1883** *Encycl. Brit.* XV. 322/2 A mixed Malayo-Siamese people, commonly known as Samsams, form the bulk of the population in the lower parts of Ligor and Sengora, and in the north of Kedah. **1961** L. D. STAMP *Gloss. Geogr. Terms* 403/1 *Samsam*.., a person of mixed Siamese-Malay origin, especially characteristic of the State of Kedah under Siamese suzerainty from 1821 to 1909.

‖**samsara** (sam'sɑːra). *Indian Philos.* Also **sangsara.** [Skr. *saṃsāra*, a wandering through, f. *sam* prefix expressing completeness + *sṛ* to run, glide, move.] The endless cycle of death and rebirth to which life in the material world is bound; also *attrib.* Hence **sam'saric** *a.*

1886 *Encycl. Brit.* XXI. 289/1 The notion of saṃsâra has become an axiom, a universally conceded principle of Indian philosophy. **1913** J. N. FARQUHAR *Crown of Hinduism* v. 213 All souls, whether living as gods, demons, men, animals, or plants, are afloat on the stream of transmigration (*samsāra*). **1928** W. Y. EVANS-WENTZ *Tibet's Great Yogi* p. xvi, The golden fish..symbolizes sentient beings immersed in the Ocean of Sangsaric (or Worldly) Existence. **1930** S. N. DASGUPTA *Yoga Philos.* 67 The metaphysics of the saṃsāra cycle in connection with sorrow, origination, disease, rebirth. **1935** W. Y. EVANS-WENTZ *Tibetan Yoga* 16 The Sangsāra, or external universe, is a psycho-physical compound of mind; matter, as we see it, being crystallized mental energy. **1963** 'MAYANANDA' *Tarot for Today* xi. 140 It [*sc.* Stellar Power] can be distributed and assimilated by the Earth and Solar System, generally, thus producing all the minutiæ of Samsaric detail. **1966** R. F. C. HULL tr. *Jung's Ulysses* in *Coll. Wks.* XV. 127 Ulysses..is for Joyce..the higher self who returns to his divine home after blind entanglement in *samsara.* **1977** L. A. GOVINDA *Creative Meditation* I x. 43 The basic qualities of human individuality binding us to our worldly existence (*samsāra*) are at the same time the means of liberation and enlightenment.

Samscred, obs. form of SANSKRIT.

†**Samscre'damic,** *a. Obs.* [f. *samscredam* (early transliteration of Skr. *saṇskṛtam*: see SANSKRIT) + -IC.] = SANSKRIT.

1800 *Acc. Bks.* in *Asiat. Ann. Reg.* 44/1 The Ethiopic alphabet, which has a certain resemblance to the Samscredamic.

Samscretan: see SANSKRIT.

‖**samshoo** ('sæmʃuː). Also 7 **sam shu,** 8 **samptsoo, samshew, samshue, samso,** 8–9 **samsu, samtchoo,** 9 **sams-choo, sam-shee, samshoe, samshoo, samshu, san-tchoo.** [Pidgin-English: said by S. W. Williams to be a. *sam shiu*, Cantonese pronunciation of Chinese *san shao* 'thrice distilled'; but Chinese scholars consider this doubtful.] The general name for Chinese spirits distilled from rice or sorghum.

1697 DAMPIER *Voy.* I. 419 The Officer brought aboard.. 2 great Jars of Arack..called by the Chinese, Sam Shu. **1727** A. HAMILTON *New Acc. E. Ind.* II. l. 222 He loaded me with fair Promises, and sent after me..a small Jar of Sam-shew, or Rice Arrack. **1744** J. PHILIPS *Jrnl. Exped. Anson* 155 We also received on board..a But of Samshue. **1795** ANDERSON *Brit. Embassy China* 52, 6 Large jars of sampt-soo..a liquor made in China. *Ibid.* 163 A small quantity of samtchoo, a spirituous liquor. **1836** J. F. DAVIS *Chinese* I. iii. 86 Ardent spirits, called samshoo, generally adulterated with ingredients of a stimulating and maddening quality. **1845** *Encycl. Metrop.* XXV. 1291/1 The Chinese make rice wine perfumed, and distil the lees, whence they obtain a spirit like brandy, which they call sam-tchoo, or san-tchoo. **1852** F. A. NEALE *Narr. Resid. Siam* 75 That most baneful and least desirably-flavoured spirit in the world, samshoe. **1876** *Encycl. Brit.* IV. 264 The Chinese beverage, sam-shee, is made from rice. **1888** A. J. LITTLE *Through Yang-tse Gorges* 218 The business of the day commenced with swallowing endless thimblefuls of hot 'samshu'.

samsi, var. SAMISEN

samsien: see SAMISEN.

‖**samskara** (san'skɑːra). *Indian Philos.* Also 9 **sanscara, sanskara.** [Skr. *saṃskāra* a making perfect, preparation, f. *sam* together + *kṛ* to make, perform.] **1.** A purificatory ceremony or rite marking a stage or an event in life; one of twelve rites enjoined on the first three classes of the Brahman caste.

1807 *Asiatick Researches* IX. 288 The *Jainas*..admit the same division into four tribes, and perform like religious ceremonies, termed *sanscaras*, from the birth of a male to his marriage. **1832** *Ibid.* XVII. 309 Some of the original rites are still preserved..in such of the Sanskaras, or purificatory ceremonies as are observed at the periods of birth, tonsure, investiture, marriage, [etc.]. **1891** MONIER WILLIAMS *Brāhmanism & Hindūism* (ed. 4) 353 Twelve purificatory rites, called Sanskāras were prescribed in the ancient collections of domestic rules..for the purification of the three higher castes. **1913** J. N. FARQUHAR *Crown of Hinduism* ii. 104 Debendranath Tagore..rebelled against the polytheistic and idolatrous character of the sacraments (*saṁskāras*) of the Hindu family. **1962** R. ZAEHNER *Hinduism* vii. 201 Saṁskaras or sacraments play an important part throughout the life of a Hindu. **1977** B. SARASWATI *Brahmanic Ritual Trad.* p. xii, Of all the social institutions, the institution of the *samskaras* serves as the corner-stone of the total cultural complex of the brahmanic society.

2. A mental impression, instinct, or memory.

1827 *Trans. R. Asiatic Soc.* I. 562 Thence comes passion (sanscára), comprising desire, aversion, delusion, &c. **1875** MONIER WILLIAMS *Indian Wisdom* iii. 79 *Saṇskāra*, implying—*a.* impetus as the cause of activity; *b.* elasticity; *c.* the faculty of memory. **1896** 'SWĀMI VIVEKĀNANDA' *Yoga Philos.* 233 *Samskâra*, impressions in the mind-stuff that produce habits. **1930** N. DUTT *Aspects Mahayana Buddhism* iii. 94 They have been blinded by avidyā (ignorance of the Truth), from which have followed the saṃskaras (impressions). **1952** H. ZIMMER *Philos. of India* III. ii. 324 The noun saṁskāra, signifying 'impression, influence, operation, form, and mold', is one of the basic terms of Indian philosophy. **1977** J. HEWITT *Yoga & Meditation* v. 42 The other is that which consists only of *Samskaras*, being brought on by the practice of the cause of complete suspension.

Sam Slick (sæm slɪk). *U.S.* The name of a peddling clock-seller, hero of a series of stories by T. C. Haliburton (1796–1865), Nova Scotian judge and political propagandist, used *transf.* of a type of smooth-spoken and sharp-practising New Englander, and hence *gen.* of any resourceful trickster or 'spiv'. Also *attrib.*

1897 R. G. HALIBURTON in *Haliburton: a Centenary Chaplet* 26 Sixty years ago the Southern States were familiar with the sight of Sam Slicks. **1916** M. AIKEN *Canada in Flanders* I. 118 A 'hyphenated' voice..cried out peevishly next evening: 'Say, Sam Slick, no dirty tricks tonight.' **1944** B. A. BOTKIN *Treas. Amer. Folklore* III. 358 For Yankee trickiness or slickness the name Sam Slick has become proverbial. **1962** *Amer. Speech* XXXVII. 84 Other items of the standard vocabulary of this 'Sam Slick' American were suggested rather than directly quoted.

Samsoe ('sæmsəʊ). Also **Samso, Samsø.** In full, ***Samsoe cheese***: a firm, buttery cheese from the Danish island of Samsoe.

1953 G. P. SANDERS *Cheese Varieties & Descriptions* 124 Swiss Cheese is made in many other countries besides Switzerland... Danish Swiss is called Samso. **1955** *Times* 10 May 12/4 Samsoe cheese..takes its name from the island of Samsoe. **1968** *Vogue* 15 Apr. 42/2 You need 8 oz. Danish Blue cheese, 4 oz. Samsoe cheese. **1968** L. DEIGHTON *Continental Dossier* 8 Local dishes are rare—specialities are found country-wide, like..'Samsø'—the Cheddar of Denmark. **1976** M. PATTEN *Barbecue & Outdoor Eating* 27/2 Grate 12 oz (350 g) Danish Samsoe cheese and slice 2–3 tomatoes.

Samson ('sæmsən). Also, except in senses 1 and 6, with small initial. Also 6–8 **Sampson.** [a. L. (Vulgate) *Sam(p)sōn*, Gr. (LXX) Σαμψών, a. Heb. *Shimshōn* (in Masoretic vocalization).]

1. The name of the Hebrew hero whose exploits are recorded in Judges xiii–xvi. Applied allusively to persons, with reference to

Samson's enormous strength, to his having been blinded, or to some incident in his story. Also ***Samson-like*** adj. and adv.; ***Samson-passion***.

1565 HARDING *Confut. Jewel* III. v. 147 Such mighty Samsons, such constant Laurences, your ioyly gospell breedeth. **1591** SHAKS. *1 Hen. VI*, I. ii. 33 None but Sampsons and Goliasses It sendeth forth to skirmish. **1620** SANDERSON *Serm.* I. 146 Then it [conscience] riseth, and Sampson-like rouseth up it self, and bestirreth it self lustily, as a giant refreshed with wine. **1649** *Alcoran* 417 To bring out to the open view of all, the blinde Sampsons of their Alcoran. **1651** R. WILD *Poems* (1670) 21 He stands, And snaps asunder, Samson-like, these bands. **1678** *Yng. Man's Call.* 52 Foolishness..is a Sampson, whose eyes are out, the scorn and derision of all. **1689** in W. W. Wilkins *Pol. Ballads* (1860) II. 4 They had on their heads such a Sampson-like power. **1701** NORRIS *Ideal World* I. vi. 399 Such as no Sampson could overthrow. **1796** SOUTHEY *Joan of Arc* IX. 359 By experience rous'd shall man at length Dash down his Moloch-gods, Samson-like And burst his fetters. *a* **1821** BYRON *Don Juan* (1956) III. variant line 8 And make him Samsonlike—more fierce with blindness. **1887** *Times* (weekly ed.) 1 July 14/3 Intellectual Samsons toiling with closed eyes in the mills and forges of Manchester and Birmingham. **1929** BLUNDEN *Near & Far* 49 Joy's masque and fashion of Time's Samson-passion Deceived no lark that springs from weed and clod.

2. †**a.** *dial.* = SAMLET. *Obs.*

1769 PENNANT *Zool.* III. 254 Near Shrewsbury (where they [the samlet] are called Samsons).

b. *Austral.* ***Samson-fish***: see quots.

1874 in Tenison-Woods *Fishes N.S. Wales* (1882) 60 The Samson-fish (*Seriola hippos*, Günth.) is occasionally caught. .. The great strength of these fishes is remarkable. **1882** TENISON-WOODS *ibid.* 190 Samson-fish. In Sydney *Seriola hippos*. In Melbourne, young of *Arripis salar*.

3. *Mech.* = CRAMP *sb.*[2] 3. Now *Hist.*

1852 in BURN *Naval & Mil. Tech. Dict.* I., s. vv. *Cric, Davier, Sergent.* **1965** E. TUNIS *Colonial Craftsmen* iv. 95 The wheelwright..pulled the joint hard together with a large threaded clamp called a samson. **1968** J. ARNOLD *Shell Bk. Country Crafts* 163 There was a samson, for drawing felloes together when the strakes were being nailed on.

4. Samson bar: = SAMSON'S POST 2 a.

1889 *East. Morn. News* 10 Apr. 3/8 The prisoner lashed him to the sampson bar and mizenmast.

5. *Logging* (see quots.). Hence **'samson** *v.*

1905 *Terms Forestry & Logging* (U.S. Dept. Agric. Bureau Forestry) 45 *Sampson*, an appliance for loosening or starting logs by horsepower. It usually consists of a strong, heavy timber and a chain terminating in a heavy swamp hook. *Ibid.*, *Sampson a tree, to*, to direct the fall of a tree by means of a lever and pole. **1913** [see KILHIG]. **1971** F. C. FORD-ROBERTSON *Terminol. of Forest Sci., Technol. Pract. & Products* 148/2 *Killig.., Pushpole..* = *Sampson* (USA). A stout pole, sometimes notched into the tree stem at one end and braced against the base of a peavey handle at the other, used to push a small tree manually in the desired direction.

6. Samson fox [in allusion to Judges xv. 4], a fox belonging to a variety of the North American red fox, *Vulpes fulva*, in which the fur lacks guard hairs and so has a scorched appearance. Also *absol.*

1910 E. T. SETON *Life-Hist. Northern Animals* II. xxxii. 709 Another freak is the 'scorched' or 'Samson Fox'. **1921** N. M. W. J. MCKENZIE *Men of Hudson's Bay Company* xvii. 160 Foxes that were burned like these were [what] we called 'Samsons', and were useless. **1933** E. MERRICK *True North* 305 He said he weren't goin' to..go clear into Canada to trap a few weasels and samson foxes. **1948** A. L. RAND *Mammals Eastern Rockies* 105 The Samson fox is a freak, in which the guard hairs are lacking.

Hence **'Samsoness** [-ESS], a female Samson.

1707 J. STEVENS tr. *Quevedo's Com. Wks.* (1709) 395, I am a Female Sampsoness, for all my strength lies in my Hair.

Samsonian (sæmˈsəʊnɪən), *sb.* and *a.* [f. SAMSON + -IAN.] **a.** *sb.* A strong man. **b.** *adj.* Of or pertaining to Samson; resembling Samson or his attributes.

1654 GAYTON *Pleas. Notes* 56 All Foyters, men o' th' sword, Hectors, Herculeneans, Samsonians. **1861** FITZPATRICK *Bp. Doyle* (1880) I. 208 The Samsonian determination with which he grasped the leading pillar of the Irish Church Establishment. **1865** W. H. L. TESTER *Poems* (1867) 69 A beard, 'maist Samsonian, sae knottit an' thready. **1884** A. A. PUTNAM *10 Yrs. Police Judge* iii. 20 Riddles of the Samsonian type are not easily expounded.

Samsonistic (sæmsəˈnɪstɪk), *a.* [f. SAMSON + -ISTIC.] Strong, powerful.

1849 E. B. EASTWICK *Dry Leaves* 212 He commenced dealing..the most ferocious and Samsonistic blows.

Samsonite[1] (ˈsæmsənaɪt). Also **samsonite.** [f. SAMSON + -ITE[1].] **1.** A variety of dynamite having an inert base of borax and salt.

1909 *Jrnl. Soc. Chem. Industry* 31 Aug. 915/2 The Secretary of State has made an Order adding the following explosives to the schedule..Nobel Ammonia Powder.. Samsonite..Titanite No. 1. **1915** A. MARSHALL *Explosives* 213 A charge of undoubtedly hard frozen Samsonite exploded whilst being rammed home with a wooden rammer. **1921** *Glasgow Herald* 28 Feb. 11 Illegal possession ..of 2980 gelignite cartridges, 10 samsonite cartridges. **1936** E. HART *Shotfirer's Man.* viii. 95 He then charged the shothole with 8 ozs of Samsonite No. 3 and fired it.

2. A proprietary term in the U.S. for a make of suitcases, briefcases, and other items of luggage, etc. Chiefly *attrib.*

1939 *Official Gaz.* (U.S. Patent Office) 21 Feb. 538/2 Shwayder Bros., Inc., Denver, Colo. Filed Oct. 17, 1938. *Samsonite Streamlite.* For trunks, suitcases, and traveling bags. Claims use since Apr. 18, 1938. **1963** *Times* 24 Apr. 16/4 After this generous present, it is a bit of a come-down for the eight regional winners to receive 'Samsonite bridge tables and chairs'. **1969** J. GARDNER *Compl. State of Death* iv. 40 The file was dropped into a slim brown Samsonite brief-case. **1971** D. MACKENZIE *Sleep is for Rich* vi. 196 The samsonite case would carry a hundredweight without collapsing. **1977** *Time* 28 Feb. 47/1 Just now, Linda is cooling out in Los Angeles after months of bashing about in planes and buses like a piece of lost Samsonite. **1977** C. MCFADDEN *Serial* (1978) xliv. 94/2 She dragged the Samsonite over the threshold.

samsonite[2] (ˈsæmsənaɪt). *Min.* [ad. G. *samsonit* (Werner & Fraatz 1910, in *Centbl. f. Mineral.* 331), f. the name *Samson* (see quot. 1910) + *-it* -ITE[1].] A sulphide of silver, antimony, and manganese which occurs as black prisms with a metallic lustre.

1910 *Mineral. Mag.* XV. 430 Samsonite... Found with pyrargyrite and pyrolusite in the Samson mine, St. Andreasberg, Harz. **1968** I. KOSTOV *Mineral.* 173 Samsonite ($Ag_4MnSb_2S_6$) is a mineral of peculiar composition, containing up to 5·96% Mn and crystallizing in the monoclinic system. **1969** *Acta Crystallographica* B. XXV. 1004/2 The presence of two atomic polyhedra—the squat pyramids, SbS_3, and slightly deformed octahedra, MnS_6,—is the most characteristic feature of the crystal structure of samsonite.

Samson's post. Also 9 Samson-, Sampson-post. [Prob. named in allusion to Judges xvi. 29.]

†**1.** A kind of mousetrap (see quot. 1609). *Obs.*

1577 HARRISON *England* III. vi. 107 b/2 [Halifax gibbet.] Which being drawne vp to the top of the frame is there fastned with a wooden pinne, (the one ende set on a peece of woode,..& the other ende being let into the blocke, holding the Axe, with a notche made into the same after the maner of a Sampsons post). **1609** C. BUTLER *Fem. Mon.* vii. (1634) 120 *note*, There is none [*i.e.* no mousetrap] better than a Samsons Post, which is a flat Coouer or Roofe supported by a triangular Pillar or Prop, whose three sides doe so hold one by another, through the Weight of the Roofe, that the loosing of one is the loosing of all, and so the Prop failing, the Roofe falleth. **1828** *Craven Gloss.*, *Sampson's-posts*, a mouse-trap. [Described.]

fig. **1593** G. HARVEY *New Let. Notable Contents* Wks. (Grosart) I. 262 Croatia may learne to be prouident in Triumph; which hath often fealt the ioyfulnesse of a Sampsons post.

2. a. *Naut.* A strong pillar or stanchion passing through the hold of a merchant-ship, or between the decks of a man-of-war; also, in a whaling vessel, a strong post, firmly fixed in the deck, to which the fluke-rope may be fastened. **b.** *Oil-mining.* (See quot. 1881.)

1769 FALCONER *Dict. Marine* (1780), *Samsons-post*, a sort of pillar erected in a ship's hold, between the lower deck and the kelson, under the edge of a hatchway, and furnished with ..notches that serve as steps. **1860** *Illustr. Lond. News* 29 Sept. 285/3 The schooner was showing a white light on the sampson-post. **1865** *Harper's Mag.* Apr. 573/2 The walking-beam is a heavy horizontal piece of timber, supported in the centre by a Samson-post. **1875** KNIGHT *Dict. Mech.*, *Samson-post.* **1881** RAYMOND *Mining Gloss.*, *Sampson-post*, an upright post which supports the walking-beam, communicating motion from the engine to a deep-boring apparatus. **1960** C. GATLIN *Petrol. Engin.* iv. 45/1 The walking beam is supported by the sampson post, and imparts the reciprocating motion to the drilling line.

samsu, -tchoo, variant forms of SAMSHOO.

†**samtale,** *a. Obs.* [f. SAME *a.* + TALE *sb.* Cf. SAMENTALE.] Accordant, agreed.

c **1200** ORMIN 5731 Swa þatt hiss bodiȝ wiþþ hiss gost Sammtale & sahhte wurrþe. *Ibid.* 1535, 6037.

Samuelite (ˈsæmjuːəlaɪt). [f. the name of Sir Herbert Louis *Samuel*, first Viscount Samuel (1871–1963), Liberal politician + -ITE[1].] A supporter of Sir Herbert Samuel; used *spec.* to designate a member of the official Liberal Party, which was led by Samuel, subsequent to the secession in 1931 of the Liberal National Party under Sir John Simon (see SIMONITE[2]). Freq. *attrib.*

1931 *Times* 13 Oct. 14/4 The Liberal Party was split into at least three well-marked divisions. There were the Simonites, who had thrown in their lot boldly with the national cause; the Samuelites, about whom he [*sc.* Churchill] was unable to give any correct information; and the Lloyd Georgeites. **1931** A. SINCLAIR *Let.* 3 Nov. in J. Bowle *Visct. Samuel* (1957) xvii. 286 If you will forgive me saying so..we don't want to be called..Samuelite Liberals as opposed to Simonite Liberals. **1936** *Ann. Reg. 1935* 87 Against it [*sc.* the Government] were..the Liberals without prefix, led by Sir Herbert Samuel, and commonly known as 'Samuelites'. **1952** VISCT. SIMON *Retrospect* x. 180 The Samuelite Liberals supported the vote of censure. **1976** C. COOK *Short Hist. Liberal Party 1900–1976* x. 118 In March 1932, the National Government's decision to introduce the Import Duties Bill provoked a rebellion by the Samuelite Liberals.

Samuel-Smilesian: see SMILESIAN.

samum, samun, var. ff. SIMOOM, SAMEN *adv.*

samurai (ˈsæmʊraɪ). Pl. **samurai,** occas. **samurais.** [Japanese.] **1. a.** In Japan during the continuance of the feudal system, one of the class of military retainers of the daimios; sometimes in wider sense, a member of the military caste, whether a samurai proper or a daimio. Also applied to any Japanese army officer. Also *attrib.*

1727 J. SCHEUCHZER tr. *Kaempfer's Hist. Japan* II. i. 396 'Tis from thence they are call'd *Samurai*, which signifies persons who wear two swords. **1795** tr. *C. P. Thunberg's Trav. Europe, Afr., & Asia* (ed. 2) III. 123 The people in office at this place, who wore two sabres, were called *Samrai.* **1841** *Chinese Repository* X. 17 Class 4 is that of the *samorai*, or military, and consists of the vassals of the nobility. **1874** LADY HERBERT tr. *Hübner's Ramble* II. i. (1878) 222 He has ..his vassals, his Samurais, or knights with two swords (the others having only one). **1885** E. GREEY *Bakin's Capt. Love* ii. (1904) 14 Amada, who had been a samurai, taught the lad to read and write. *Ibid.* iv. 30 For a samurai woman, even when mortally wounded, always endeavours to conceal her pain. **1896** L. HEARN *Kokoro* x. 172 The fear of the dead was held not less contemptible in a samurai than the fear of man. **1898**, etc. [see BUSHIDO]. **1904**, etc. [see HEIMIN]. **1906** SLADEN *Lovers in Japan* vi, Mr. Jevons told us that we ought to have Samurai servants. **1972** *Mainichi Daily News* (Japan) 6 Nov. 7/7 The Samurai were distinguished in dress most easily by the swords they wore.

b. *transf.* and *fig.*

1905 H. G. WELLS *Mod. Utopia* ix. 259 These people constitute an order, the *samurai*, the 'voluntary nobility', which is essential in the scheme of the Utopian State. **1918** G. FRANKAU *One of Them* xx. 151 Stern mitred prelates; Law-lords; back-woods Samurais Who flung to consequence a scornful 'Damn your eyes'. **1934** H. G. WELLS *Exper. Autobiogr.* II. ix. 735, I have told already.. how I tried to make the Fabian Society into an order of the Samurai. **1977** *Time* 24 Jan. 17/2 Yukio Mishima, the right-wing literary samurai who committed spectacular hara-kiri in 1970.

2. *attrib.* and *Comb.*, as ***samurai code, ethic, order, spirit, sword, warrior***; ***samurai-minded*** adj.

1971 *Times Lit. Suppl.* 20 Aug. 984/1 The *samurai code embraced more than the practice of Zen and the ethics of Japanese forms of Confucianism. **1970** *Newsweek* 7 Dec. 32/2 The Japanese militarists of the 1930s twisted the ancient *samurai ethic into the ideology of Fascism. **1938** *Times* 17 Feb. 16/1 In private conversation business men will unequivocally express disapproval of the course of events, a minority of **samurai*-minded ultra-patriots being the only exceptions. **1906** G. B. SHAW *Let.* 24 Mar. (1972) II. 614 A proposal for a set of observances of the *Samurai order. **1923** *Samurai spirit [see BUSHIDO]. **1961** I. MURDOCH *Severed Head* xix. 155 Was it..when I saw her cut the napkins in two with the *Samurai sword? **1977** *National Observer* (U.S.) 15 Jan. 5 Hayakawa..went on to even more fame as the '*samurai warrior' president of San Francisco State University.

samusa, var. SAMOSA.

‖**samyama** (samˈjama). *Indian Philos.* Also **sanyama.** [Skr. *saṃyama* restraint, control of the senses, f. *sam* together + *yam* sustain, hold up (*yāma* rein, bridle, self-control).] The name given to the three final stages of meditation in yoga, which lead on to *samadhi*, or the state of union.

1828 *Trans. R. Asiatic Soc.* III. 164 That which removes sin is Brahmanhood. It consists of..*Neyama*, and *Ripavas*, and *Dan*,..and *Sànyama*. **1884** R. C. BOSE *Hindu Philos.* 160 Three internal subservients, attention, contemplation, and meditation, collectively called by the name of 'subjugation' (sanyana). **1899** MAX MÜLLER *Six Syst. Indian Philos.* vii. 459 It is difficult to find a word for Saṃyama, firm grasp being no more than an approximate rendering. It is this Saṃyama, however, which leads on to the Siddhis, or perfections. **1959** E. WOOD *Yoga* xiii. 237 *Sanyama* is then a definite tool of mind, which can be used for gaining knowledge of various kinds. **1978** D. N. BRADSHAW tr. *Oki's Meditation Yoga* iii. 84 People usually assume that there are many preparations to be made before entering samyama, but the method of Yoga is simple and clear.

samyn(e, obs. ff. SAM *v.*, SAMEN.

san[1] (sæn). [Gr. σάν.] The name (first recorded by writers of the sixth century B.C.) for a sibilant (M) found in early Doric scripts (later displaced by sigma), which has been compared with various Semitic sibilants and SAMPI.

1584 B. RICH tr. *Herodotus' Famous Hystory* I. f.44[v], All the wordes in theyr language which consist of 4 or more sillables do commonly end in one letter: which letter the Dores cal San the Iones Sigma. **1709** I. LITTLEBURY tr. *Herodotus' Hist.* I. I. 89 All Names representing the Person or Dignity of a Man, terminate in that letter which the Dorians call San, and the Ionians Sigma. **1860** *Chambers's Encycl.* I. 169/2 In accommodating itself [*sc.* the Phoenician alphabet] to the necessities of the Greek tongue..the name *Sigma* was transferred to *San.* **1912** [see SAMPI]. **1915** J. SANDYS tr. *Pindar's Odes* 559 In olden days, the lay of the dithyramb was wont to wind its straggling length along, and the sibilant *san* was discarded. **1933** [see KOPPA]. **1961** L. H. JEFFERY *Local Scripts Arch. Greece* I. ii. 33 By the second half of the fifth century, the sign of *san* was no longer in use, except in conservative Crete, and as an emblem on the coins of Sikyon.

San[2] (sɑːn). Also **Saan.** [Bushman, app. of Khoikhoi (Hottentot) origin: cf. Nama *sā-* to inhabit.] **a.** The name used for themselves by the Bushmen of southern Africa (see BUSHMAN 1); also *attrib.* **b.** The principal language of the Bushmen.

1876 *Encycl. Brit.* IV. 575/1 Bushmen..so named by the British and Dutch colonists of the Cape, but calling themselves *Saab* or *Saan*, are an aboriginal race of South Africa. **1878** K. JOHNSTON *Africa* xxiv. 440 The Bushmen or Saan are the nomads of the Kalahari. **1881** [see NAMA *a.*]. **1907** *Rep. Brit. Assoc. Adv. Sci. 1906* 689 They are called

Baroa by the Basuto, Abatwa by the Kafirs, San by themselves. **1930** [see KHOIKHOI]. **1944** M. OLDEVIG *Sunny Land* v. 50, I had the rare good fortune to come upon a Saan Bushman, one of the few who still inhabit parts of the Namib desert. **1967** D. S. PARLETT *Short Dict. Lang.* 73 The Khoin or 'Click' languages..comprising to the south Bushman (San), to the north Hottentot (Nama) [etc.]. **1974** J. FLINT *Cecil Rhodes* i. 9 South Africa was the home of the San (the so-called Bushmen). **1977** C. F. & F. M. VOEGELIN *Classification & Index World's Lang.* 201 South African Khoisan. Central... 36. San = Saan.

san[3] (san). [Jap.: a contraction of the more formal *sama*.] A Japanese honorific title, equivalent to Mr., Mrs., etc., suffixed to personal or family names as a mark of politeness; also *colloq.* or in imitation of the Japanese form, suffixed to other names or titles (cf. MAMA-SAN).

When suffixed to a female personal name, and in more polite endearment, *san* is often coupled with the prefix *O-* (see quot. 1922).

1878 C. DRESSER in *Jrnl. Soc. Arts* XXVI. 175/1 Mr. Sakata, or, as they would say Sakata San, who was appointed ..as one of my escort through Japan. **1891** A. M. BACON *Japanese Girls & Women* xi. 304 He is a person to be treated with respect,—to be bowed to profoundly, addressed by the title San, and spoken to in the politest of languages. **1922** JOYCE *Ulysses* 321 The fashionable international world attended *en masse* this afternoon at the wedding... Miss Grace Poplar, Miss O Mimosa San. **1952** T. J. MULVEY *These are your Sons* vii. 146 'You go away, O'Reilly-san?' the little girl asked. **1964** I. FLEMING *You only live Twice* i. 16 'Bondo-san,' said Tiger Tanaka, Head of the Japanese Secret Service, 'I will now challenge you to this ridiculous game.' **1968** *Guardian* 23 Feb. 11/4 Corpsman Kenneth Corner..told her [*sc.* a Vietnamese girl]: 'It's going to be all right baby-san, it's going to be all right.' **1972** J. BALL *Five Pieces of Jade* xiv. 188 It would make me the greatest pleasure, Nakamura san.

San[4] (sæn). Also **san**. Colloq. abbreviation of SANATORIUM (esp. in sense 3).

1906 R. BROOKE *Let.* 1 Apr. (1968) 47, I started this disease..rather badly, and as the San. was full, we were put into a room in the house. **1914** 'I. HAY' *Lighter Side School Life* iii. 71 Broken neck, inflammation of the lungs, ringworm, and leprosy, old son... You are going to the San. **1936** M. KENNEDY *Together & Apart* III. 174, I was in quarantine for mumps, so I stayed in our school San. all the holidays. **1945** [see KNOW *v.* 1 b]. **1976** 'D. FLETCHER' *Don't whistle 'Macbeth'* 45, I sounded like some old-fashioned matron, soothing the felled captain of the First Eleven in the san.

san: see SANS.

†'**sanable**, *a. Obs.* [ad. L. *sānābilis*, f. *sānāre* to heal, f. *sān-us* healthy: see SANE *a.*]

1. That heals or is concerned with healing; curative. *rare*[−1].

1597 A. M. tr. *Guillemeau's Fr. Chirurg.* 1 b/1 *Therapeutica* is the curinge or sanable parte of Physicke.

2. That may be healed; curable. *lit.* and *fig.*

1623 COCKERAM I, *Sanable*, which may be healed. **1656** in BLOUNT *Glossogr.* **1664** H. MORE *Antid. Idolatry* To Rdr. §1 That those that are sanable or preservable from this dreadful sin of Idolatry may find the efficacy of our Antidote. **1694** WESTMACOTT *Script. Herb.* 10 No Plant..doth sooner.. cure all Sanable Burnings and Scaldings. **1718** HICKES & NELSON *J. Kettlewell* III. §69. 361 Whilst the corruptions seem Sanable and admit hopes of Cure.

Hence **sana'bility**, †'**sanableness**, the state of being curable.

1727 BAILEY vol. II, Sanableness. **1860** WORCESTER (citing *Med. Jour.*), Sanability.

sanachy, obs. variant of SENNACHIE.

sanad: see SUNNUD.

sanakatowzer (ˌsænəkə'taʊzə(r)). *Naut. slang. rare.* Also with capital initial. [Of uncertain origin: cf. TOWSER *sb.* and *bandowzer* in *D.A.E.*] An extremely forceful blow; something particularly large or powerful, such as a heavy wave.

1903 KIPLING in *Collier's Weekly* 15 Aug. 9/3 Mr. Ducane catches 'im a sanakatowzer of a smite over the 'ead with the flat of 'is sword. **1920** *Blackw. Mag.* Apr. 501/2 She shipped one Sanakatowzer that nearly swamped her.

†'**sanap**. *Obs.* Forms: 4 **sauvenap**, (**saufenap**, **sayfenap**, **salvenap**), 4–5 **savenap(e**, 4 **saunap(e**, **sawnap(e**, **sannap**, 4–5 **sanap**, (4 **sanop**), 5 **sanapp**, (**sanope**). See also SURNAPE. [Orig. *sauvenape*, *savenape*, a. OF. **sauvenape*, f. *sauve-r* to SAVE + *nape* table-cloth, NAPE *sb.*[2]

Latinized *salva mappa* in *Durh. Acc. Rolls* (Surtees) an. 1338 and 1343.]

A strip of cloth placed over the outer part of the table-cloth to preserve it from being soiled.

1312 *Finchale Priory Acc.* (Surtees) p. v, Duo mappæ, ij sauvenapys. **1313** *Bolton Compotus* 279 Pro mappis & Sauuenapys emptis apud London. xxx.s. vij.d. *c* **1330** *Durham Acc. Rolls* (Surtees) 518 In salvenap' conficiend., 7*d.* **1337** in Riley *Mem. Lond.* (1868) 200, j savenape iiij*d.* **13..** *Gaw. & Gr. Knt.* 886 A tapit..Clad wyth a clene cloþe, ..Sanap, & salure, & sylure-in sponez. **1391** *Will J. Marischall* in *Ingleby MS.* 62 Vnum tuallium cum vno sausenap [? *read* saufenap] de optimis. *c* **1400** MAUNDEV. (Roxb.) xxvi. 123 þai vse nowþer burde clath ne sawnape. **14..** *Nom.* in Wr.-Wülcker 721 *Hoc manutergium*, a sanope. **1430** *Will of Cheymy* (Somerset Ho.), j towells j sauenap. *a* **1440** *Sir. Degrev.* 1387 Towellus..Why3th as the seeys fame, Sanappus of the same, Thus servyd thei ware.

sanaphant ('sænəfænt). *Electronics.* [f. SANA(TRON + PHANT(ASTRON.] (See quots.)

1949 B. CHANCE et al. *Waveforms* v. 200 Although somewhat more complex than the screen-coupled phantastron, the sanatron and sanaphant can generate waveforms..as short as 1 μsec. **1955** *Electronic Engin.* XXVII. 397/2 This undesirable loading may be avoided by the use of the sanaphant circuit, in which the gating waveform is obtained by amplification of the voltage developed across a small resistor inserted in the cathode circuit of the charging valve. **1960** COOKE & MARCUS *Electronics & Nucleonics Dict.* 413/2 *Sanaphant*, a linear time-delay circuit similar to the sanatron, differing chiefly in the connections between the two pentodes.

Sanashy, sanasse: see SUNYASEE.

†**sanate**, *v. Obs.*[−0] [f. L. *sānāt-*, ppl. stem of *sānāre* to heal, f. *sān-us* SANE *a.*] (See quot.)

1623 COCKERAM, *Sanate*, to heale.

†**sa'nation**. *Obs.* [ad. L. *sānātiōn-em*, n. of action f. *sānāre*: see prec.] The action of healing or the process of becoming healed; an instance of this. Also *fig.*

c **1440** *Pallad. on Husb.* Tab. 301 Pechis, ablaqueacioun, putacioun, & sanacioun. **1491** CAXTON *Vitas Patr.* (W. de W. 1495) I. xlvii. 87 b/2 He that hathe made the, yeue the sanacyon and helthe atte thys presente tyme. **1541** R. COPLAND *Galyen's Terap.* 2 Ej b, That curacyon or sanacyon is none other thynge but a retourne to the fyrste symmetrye or commoderacyon of the sayd conduytes. **1634** BP. HALL *Contempl., N.T.* IV. v. 122 It is no marvell if the report of so miraculous, and universall sanations drew customers. **1677** PLOT *Oxfordsh.* 351 Which holy King Edward was the first to whom was granted the gift of Sanation. **1697** J. SERGEANT *Solid Philos.* 297 Reflecting on all Motions whatever, v.g. Generation,..Augmentation, Sanation, etc.

sanative ('sænətɪv), *a.* and *sb.* Also 5 **sanatyf**, (**sanetyf**). [a. OF. *sanatif* or med.L. *sānātīvus*, f. L. *sānāre*: see SANATE *v.* and -IVE.]

A. *adj.* **1.** Having the power to heal; conducive to or promoting health; curative, healing.

14.. *Stockh. Med. MS.* II. 912 in *Anglia* XVIII. 329 To woundys it is confortyf With oþer erbys sanatyf. **1497** BP. ALCOCK *Mons Perfect.* A ij, Herbes and floures sanatyf to remedy all syknesses. **1508** DUNBAR *Tua Mariit Wemen* 8 The sauar sanatiue of the sueit flouris. **1562** BULLEYN *Bulwark, Bk. Simples* (1579) 59 b, Gum Sarcocoll..is a sanatyue gum to incarnat woundes and sores. **1626** BACON *Sylva* §787 Brass hath, in it selfe, a Sanative vertue;..But Iron is Corrosive, and not Sanative. **1655** FULLER *Ch. Hist.* II. vi. §33 That..Kings should receive that peculiar Priviledge, and sanative Power, whereof daily Instances are presented unto us. **1704** NORRIS *Ideal World* II. ii. 91, I speak not of their medicinal operations, those alterative or sanative effects which they have upon our bodies. **1742** FIELDING *Jos. Andrews* I. xv, A sanative soporiferous draught. **1826** SOUTHEY *Vind. Eccl. Angl.* 166 Handkerchiefs used to be inserted..to touch the place whereon the body had first been laid, and derive a sanative influence. **1885** *Manch. Exam.* 18 Feb. 3/2 The special treatment which has been proved serviceable and sanative by practical hydropathists. **1892** STEVENSON *Across the Plains* iii. 108 The place was sanative; the air, the light, the perfumes..concord in happy harmony.

b. *fig.*, esp. Promoting moral or spiritual health.

a **1548** HALL *Chron., Hen. VII* 4 Vsing the same for a remedy & medicine of their peine, addyng euer somwhat therto that was sanatyue & wholsome. **1674** BOYLE *Excell. Theol.* I. iii. 91 The mysteries themselves, being duly considered, have had a very sanative influence on many that contemplated them. **1816** COLERIDGE *Statesm. Man.* App. D. (1852) 109 A sort of sanative counter-excitement, that holds in check the more dangerous disease of Methodism. **1831** CARLYLE *Sart. Res.* II. iii, Imposture is of sanative, anodyne nature. **1859** MASSON *Brit. Novelists* iv. 289 The sanative virtue of action..to dispel doubt and despair.

2. Of, pertaining to or concerned with healing.

1695 J. EDWARDS *Perfect. Script.* III. 180 How congruously do the Musical and Sanative Art meet together? **1822–34** *Good's Study Med.* (ed. 4) II. 146 The absorption of the fluid being the first step in the sanative process. **1883** *Brit. Q. Rev.* Oct. 397 The sanative process by which despair is transformed..into triumphant faith.

†**B.** *sb.* A remedy. *Obs.*

c **1440** *Pol. Rel. & L. Poems* 248 Other [healing] Erbys ther ben alsoo..'Operys satisfaccio' [ys] the souereyne sauetyff [? *read* sanetyff]. **1678** *Lively Orac.* viii. §3 As if he that had an ulcer in his bowels, should apply all his balsoms and sanatives only to his head.

Hence †'**sanativeness**, healing quality.

a **1661** FULLER *Worthies, Huntingdon.* (1662) II. 48 An obscure Village..called Haile weston whose very name Soundeth something of sanativeness therein.

Sanatogen (sə'nætədʒən). A proprietary name for a tonic wine.

[**1898** *Official Gaz.* (U.S. Patent Off.) 14 June 1657/2 Dietetic albuminous preparations. Bauer, Cie Berlin... Sanatogen... Used since October 25, 1897.] **1924** G. B. STERN *Tents of Israel* xii. 173 She dispensed a share in her jellies and Sanatogen and grapes. **1936** H. NICOLSON *Let.* 28 Apr. (1966) 259 Tell Gwen I do not need Sanatogen at present. **1939** *Trade Marks Jrnl.* 1 Mar. 290/1 *Sanatogen Tonic Wine*... Genatosan Limited, 43, Regent Street, Loughborough, Leicestershire; manufacturers.

sanatorium (sænə'tɔərɪəm). Pl. **sanatoria**, **sanatoriums**. Also *erron.* **sanatarium**. [a. mod.L. *sānātōrium*, f. *sānāre* to cure, heal: see SANATE *v.* and -ORY.

Cf. G. *sanatorium*. The erroneous form *sanatarium* is due to confusion with SANITARIUM.]

1. An establishment for the reception and medical treatment of invalids; in recent use chiefly either of convalescent patients, or of consumptives undergoing the open-air treatment. Also *fig.*

1839 *London Med. Gaz.* XXV. 406/2 Dr. Southwood Smith, Dr. Arnott, and some other gentlemen, have it in contemplation to establish, under the name of 'Sanatorium', an institution..where patients are provided with board and medical treatment on the payment of a certain sum per week. *Ibid.* 407/2 We anticipate..that the parties who have set about the Sanatorium will abandon the scheme before it has been brought into actual operation. **1840** *Mech. Mag.* 152 [A prospectus of 'The Sanatorium'—a self-supporting establishment for the lodging, nursing and cure of sick persons]. **1899** *Westm. Gaz.* 21 Aug. 6/1 Quite a little shoal of companies for the establishment of sanatoria has recently made its appearance. The latest company is the Harrogate Sanatorium for Consumptives. **1934** DYLAN THOMAS *Let.* 15 Apr. (1966) 104, I don't want to see my books; a library is a sanatorium of sick minds. **1973** *Sci. Amer.* Sept. 130/2 The care of the mentally ill in distant upland sanatoriums.

2. A place to which, on account of favourable climatic and other conditions, invalids resort for the improvement of their health; *spec.* a hill-station in a hot country, esp. in India, to which residents periodically resort to recuperate.

1842 VIGNE *Trav. Kashmir* I. 38 These ladies are known by the well-selected epithet of 'Grass Widows'; and there are sometimes more than fifty of them at each sanatorium. **1845** STOCQUELER *Handbk. Brit. India* (1854) 248 On a ridge of the outer Himalaya, stands the cantonment, or depôt, of Landour. It was established in 1827, as a sanatarium for European troops. **1859** TENNENT *Ceylon* (ed. 2) II. 263 Neuera-ellia, as a sanatarium, is little to be relied on for the relief of active ailments. **1865** *Pall Mall G.* 29 Sept. 11/1 An English physician, who, as the custom is, has taken one of the rising sanatoria on the shores of the Mediterranean under his especial patronage. **1880** *Athenæum* 24 Apr. 533/2 There was a time when Minnesota was regarded as a sanatorium for the victims of consumption.

3. A room or building in a boarding school for the accommodation of the sick. Cf. SAN[4].

1860 *Eton Gloss.* 30 Sanatorium. The Hospital—a modern improvement—where a boy seized with any infectious and dangerous illness is at once sent. **1901** *Eton Boy's Lett.* 98 They dont take measels to the Sanatorium as they arent dangerous. **1914** 'I. HAY' *Lighter Side School Life* iii. 71 When dragged from the scrummage he was in a half-fainting condition. He revived as he was being carried to the Sanatorium. **1981** E. NORTH *Dames* iv. 75 Should Sister move the general's daughter to the sanatorium?.. Polio was about at Eton..where many girls had brothers.

sanatory ('sænətərɪ), *a.* [As if ad. mod.L. *sānātōrius*, f. L. *sānāre*: see SANATE *v.* and -ORY.]

1. Conducive to healing; curative.

a **1832** BENTHAM *Deontol.* x. (1834) I. 151 There are, he [our moralist] tells you, three doses of the moral medicine. .. In the proper dose there is health and safety... Has he not noted down the sanatory quantity? Not he! **1833** I. TAYLOR *Fanat.* vi. 174 The righteous retribution of Heaven which..is altogether of a sanatory influence. **1843** BETHUNE *Sc. Fireside Stor.* 127 Sanatory excursions.

2. Of or pertaining to healing.

1870 JEVONS *Elem. Logic* vi. (1880) 48 It [the name *surgeon*] has long been specialized..to those who perform the mechanical parts of the sanatory art. **1879** McCARTHY *Own Times* II. xxvii. 318 Miss Florence Nightingale..had from a very early period turned her attention to sanatory questions.

¶**3.** Pertaining to health. (Misused for SANITARY.)

1846 *Punch* XI. 87 The Sanatory Condition of the City. **1847** *Illustr. Lond. News* 20 Nov. 347 A..meeting in favour of an effective and comprehensive sanatory bill took place.

sanatron ('sænətrɒn). *Electronics.* [Perh. irreg. f. SANITARY *a.* (cf. quot. 1951): see -TRON.] A circuit which generates a saw-tooth output waveform on receipt of a short trigger pulse, used in time-bases and similar applications.

1946 *Jrnl. Inst. Electr. Engineers* XCIII. IIIA. 1191/1 The circuit, known as the Sanatron, is illustrated in Fig. 5. **1951** O. S. PUCKLE *Time Bases* (ed. 2) ix. 181 The Royal Air Force used many slang terms. The name 'Sanatron' has been derived from the term 'sanitary', meaning satisfactory. **1955** *Electronic Engin.* XXVII. 397/2 Examination of the sanatron circuit also shows that the gating waveform is obtained by partial differentiation..and amplification of the sweep waveform. **1966** *McGraw-Hill Encycl. Sci. & Technol.* XIII. 645/1 The basic sanatron delay circuit, of which there are a number of variations, combines in two pentode tubes the function of a gate waveform generator, clamp and linear saw-tooth generator.

sanbenito (sænbeɪ'niːtəʊ). Forms: 6 (9 *arch.*) **San Benito**, 6 **S. Benito**, 6–7 **Sambenit(e**, 7 **Sambenita**, **San-benit**, 7–9 **san-**, **sambenito**. [a. Sp. *San Benito* St. Benedict (as common noun written *sambenito*). Cf. Pg. *sambenito*, It., F. *sanbenito* (16th c. F. *santbeni*).

So called from its resemblance in shape to the scapular introduced by St. Benedict.]

Under the Spanish Inquisition, a penitential garment of yellow cloth, resembling a scapular in shape, ornamented with a red St. Andrew's cross before and behind, worn by a confessed and penitent heretic; also, a similar garment of a black colour ornamented with flames, devils and other devices (sometimes called a SAMARRA) worn by an impenitent confessed heretic at an auto-da-fé.

c **1560** TOMSON in *Hakluyt's Voy.* (1589) 584 We were brought into the Church, euery one with a S. Benito vpon his backe, which is halfe a yard of yellow cloth, with a hole to put in a mans head in the midst. **1568** SKINNER tr. *Gonsalvius' Discov. Sp. Inquis.* Pref., A newe kinde of Consistory..set vp..to compell them..by Rackes.. Chaines, Halters, Barnacles, Sambenites. *Ibid.* 21 b, The marks [of having been 'within the Inquisitours pawes'] are commonly these:..A white linen garment with a red crosse called a Sambenit, and..a perpetuall slaunder and ignominy to all his stocke. *Ibid.* 45 b, Such as..defended their profession against their detestable falshoodes, weare the Sambenit vnto the very stake, which is a linen garment of the coulour of earth,..and all to be painted with black deuils. *c* **1582** M. PHILLIPS in *Hakluyt's Voy.* (1600) III. 480 The Inquisitors..bringing with them certaine fooles coats ..called in their language, *S. Benitos*, which coats were made of yellow cotten & red crosses vpon them, both before & behind. **1624** *Gag for Pope* 12 In the inquisition to be clothed with the Sambenito, a punishment as vituperious as the carting of Bawdes in England. **1672** MARVELL *Reh. Transp.* I. 276 Sambenitas, painted with all the flames and devils in hell. **1678** BUTLER *Hud.* III. ii. 1574 By laying Trains to..blow us up in th' open Streets; Disguis'd in Rumps, like Sambenites. **1731** CHANDLER tr. *Limborch's Hist. Inquis.* II. IV. xli. 294 Penitent Hereticks..received the blessed Sackcloth, commonly called the Sambenito... As to those who are designed for the Fire, viz. Such as have confessed their Heresy, and are impenitent... They are.. cloathed with the Sackcloth..which some call the Sambenito, others the Samarra or Samaretta. And tho' it be of the same make as the Sambenito is, yet it hath different Marks, is of a black Colour [etc.]. **1816** SCOTT *Old Mort.* xxxv, Who seemed as effectually doomed to death as if they wore the *sanbenitos* of the condemned heretics in an *auto-da-fe*. **1829** CARLYLE *Misc.* (1840) II. 107 Dreadful death-scenes painted like Spanish *Sanbenitos*. **1842** BARHAM *Ingol. Leg.* Ser. II. *Auto-da-fé*, All the flames and the devils were turn'd upside down On this habit, facetiously term'd *San Benito*.

sanbornite ('sænbɔːnaɪt). *Min.* [f. the name of Frank *Sanborn* (d. 1945), U.S. mineralogist + -ITE[1].] A triclinic silicate of barium, $BaSi_2O_5$, which occurs as white or colourless plates at a locality in California, and has been artificially prepared.

1932 A. F. ROGERS in *Amer. Mineralogist* XVII. 161, I am indebted to Mr. Frank Sanborn of the Division of Mines, Department of Natural Resources, State of California..for the specimen which contains the new mineral, sanbornite, herein described. **1950** *Jrnl. Amer. Ceramic Soc.* XXXIII. 43/1 Point *M*, the quintuple point for the fields of sanbornite, tridymite, and mullite..is therefore a eutectic. **1968** I. KOSTOV *Mineral.* 381 The structures of apophyllite, sanbornite, and gillespite are similar and correspond to a layered type with basic silicon sheets of condensed wollastonite chains.

sance, obs. form of SANS.

sance bell: see SANCTUS BELL.

Sancerre (sɑ̃sɛr). The name of a city in the Cher department of central France, used *attrib.* and *absol.* to designate a light white (occas. red) wine produced in its neighbourhood.

1787 A. YOUNG *Jrnl.* 1 June in *Trav. France* (1792) I. 13 We are now in Berri... We drank there excellent Sancere wine, of a deep colour, rich flavour, and good body. **1946** A. L. SIMON *Conc. Encycl. Gastron.* VIII. 148/2 *Sancerre*, a noted white wine..sold..under the name of *Château de Sancerre*. **1962** P. BRICKHILL *Deadline* iv. 61, I ordered a bottle of Sancerre and it came well chilled. **1977** C. MCCARRY *Secret Lovers* vii. 86 Cathy would take a half-bottle of Sancerre.

†‖**sanchet.** *Obs.* [F. *sanchet* 'an old coyne of gold worth about 2*s.* sterl.' (Cotgr.).]

1643 PRYNNE *Sov. Power Parlt.* App. 72 That the Estates should pay unto them for their expences an hundred thousand Sanchets, or other French money equivalent.

‖**sancho**[1] ('sæŋkəʊ). Also **sanko.** [Ashanti *osanku*.] A kind of simple guitar used by West African Negroes.

1817 BOWDICH, etc. *Mission to Ashantee* I. ii. (1819) 38 Small drums, sankos, stools [etc.]. **1854** MRS. LEE *Afr. Wand.* xvii, Sankos, which were wooden boxes, covered with deer skin. **1864** ENGEL *Mus. Anc. Nat.* 211 The sancho a small stringed instrument of the negroes of Guinea. **1876** STAINER & BARRETT *Dict. Mus. Terms, Sancho.*

Sancho[2] ('sænʃəʊ). The forename of *Sancho* Panza, the squire of Don Quixote (see DON *sb.*[1] 1 c, QUIXOTE *sb.*) used allusively of one who is a companion or foil to a quixotic person.

1870 D. G. ROSSETTI *Let.* 15 Mar. (1965) II. 817 He [*sc.* Stillman] is a complete Don Quixote in every way, and with such a Sancho as myself to back him, we ought not to lack for adventures. **1934** R. CAMPBELL *Broken Record* 10 Humanity can be divided roughly into two classes, the Quixotes and the Sanchos.

†**san'cite,** *v. Obs. rare*[−1]. [Irreg. f. L. *sancīre*: see SANCTION *sb.*] *trans.* To sanction.

1597 MIDDLETON *Wisd. Solomon* xviii. 9 Now righteousnesse beares sway, and vice put downe,..The lawe of God sancited with renowne.

‖**sancocho** (san'kotʃo). [Amer. Sp., a. Sp. *sancocho* half-cooked meal, f. *sancochar* to parboil.] In South America and the Caribbean: a rich soup containing meat, plantain, yucca, etc. (see quot. 1969).

1939 C. BROWN *S. Amer. CookBk.* 78 *Sancocho*, a truly native dish with its tropical ingredients, takes the place in the Dominican Republic of the pucheros encochidos in cooler Latin-American countries. **1954** M. WALDO *Compl. Round-the-World Cookbk.* 361 The wonderful soup-stew of Latin countries, *sancocho*, is undoubtedly the [Dominican Republic] people's choice for a national dish. **1969** R. & D. DE SOLA *Dict. Cooking* 199/2 *Sancocho*,..Latin-American souplike stew containing fish, fowl, meat, seafood, vegetables, and spices. **1977** *Time* 22 Aug. 23/1 Following a meal of *sancocho* (Panama's national soup) and hot chili sauce, Torrijos offered the following comments.

sanct (sæŋkt), *a. rare.* [a. L. *sanct-us* holy: see SAINT *a.*] Holy, sacred, consecrated.

1890 E. JOHNSON *Rise Christendom* 58 [tr. from Roman law] Sanct things..are such as the walls and gates of a city. **1895** PURCELL *Manning* I. xxix. 692 When the sanct and stately edifice is with the blessing of God completed.

sanct, obs. f. SAINT.

sancta, pl. SANCTUM.

sanctanimity (sæŋktə'nɪmɪtɪ). *rare.* [f. L. *sanct-us* holy + *anim-us* mind + -ITY. Cf. LONGANIMITY, MAGNANIMITY, etc.] Holiness of mind.

1801 W. TAYLOR in *Monthly Mag.* XI. 43 Would not these words be..fairly expressed by the single word sanctanimity or religion? **1873** F. HALL *Mod. English* i. 17 A *hath*, or a *thou*, delivered with conventional unction, now well nigh inspires a sensation of solemnity in its hearer, and a persuasion of sanctanimity of its utterer.

‖**sancta simplicitas** ('sæŋktə sɪm'plɪsɪtæs, 'sæŋktə sɪm'plɪkɪtɑːs), *Latin phrase.* [L. 'holy simplicity'.] An expression of astonishment at another's naïvety. Also used *substantively*.

These are said to have been the dying words of John Huss (1373–1415), Bohemian religious reformer and martyr, provoked by the sight of a simple peasant adding wood to the fire about his stake.

1847 F. A. KEMBLE *Let.* Dec. in *Rec. Later Life* (1882) III. 278 Miss L—ingenuously replied, 'Oh dear! that she'd never thought of that...' *Sancta Simplicitas!* **1889** G. B. SHAW in *Star* 13 July 4/4 She..thinks it would be too much to ask the public to listen to two sonatas. *Sancta simplicitas!* too much! **1894** M. BEERBOHM in *Yellow Bk.* Apr. 65 The day of sancta simplicitas is quite ended. **1936** *Times Lit. Suppl.* 31 Oct. 870/1 Setting and character perfectly fused..the *sancta simplicitas* of the Reverend Micah Balwhidder. **1963** L. MEYNELL *Virgin Luck* iv. 84 'Me? I've never had a bet in my life. I don't even know how to.' '*O Sancta simplicitas.* I wish I didn't.' **1980** —— *Hooky & Prancing Horse* xi. 187 'How on earth did you get in?' '*Sancta simplicitas*..which means you are still wet behind the ears.'

sancte, -ed, obs. forms of SAINT, SAINTED.

sanctefie, obs. form of SANCTIFY *v.*

†'**sancteous,** *a. Obs. rare*[−1]. [f. L. *sanct-us* holy, SAINT + -EOUS.] Pertaining to saints.

1631 J. DONE *Polydoron* 185 Pictures of sancteous histories are but notes of divine actions in humane characters.

sanc'ticolist. ? *nonce-wd.* [f. L. *sanctícol-a (f. *sancti-*, *sanctus* SAINT + *col-ĕre* to worship) + -IST.] A worshipper of saints.

1615 BYFIELD *Expos. Coloss.* i. 19 This also reproves the justiciaries and sancticolists, pharisees and saint-worshippers.

sanctifiable ('sæŋktɪfaɪəb(ə)l), *a. rare.* [f. SANCTIFY *v.* + -ABLE.] Capable of being sanctified. Hence **'sanctifiableness**.

1894 A. B. BRUCE *St. Paul's Concept. Chr.* xiv. 272 The body is sanctifiable. The flesh unsanctifiable. *Ibid.* 271 It teaches plainly the sanctifiableness of the flesh.

†**sanc'tificate,** *ppl. a. Obs. rare.* [ad. eccl. L. *sanctificāt-us*, pa. pple. of *sanctificāre* to SANCTIFY: see -ATE[2].] Sanctified, holy.

c **1485** *Digby Myst.* (1882) III. 1555 To þi blyssyd name sanctificatt. *c* **1502** *Joseph Arim.* 401, O Ioseph, sanctificate is thy fyrst foundation, Thy parentycle may be praysed of vs all. **15..** *Gold. Litany* in Maskell *Mon. Rit.* (1882) III. 264 By the concepcion of thy blyssid modir and virgine whyche was sanctificate in her mothers wombe: haue mercy on vs. **1538** BALE *God's Promises* VII. (Dodsley) 33 In thy mother's wombe wert thou sanctyfycate By my godlye gyft.

sanc'tificate, *v. rare.* [f. eccl. L. *sanctificāt-*, pple. stem of *sanctificāre*: see prec. and -ATE[3].] *trans.* To sanctify.

a **1677** BARROW *Serm.* (1686) II. xxxiv. 493 Wherefore like-wise doth Saint Peter ascribe our election to the Father predestinating, to the Son propitiating, to the Holy Ghost sanctificating? **1883** R. W. DIXON *Mano* I. iv. 8 Pope Gregory our arms sanctificates.

sanctification (ˌsæŋktɪfɪ'keɪʃən). [ad. eccl. L. *sanctificātiōn-em*, n. of action f. *sanctificāre* to SANCTIFY; cf. F. *sanctification* (16th c.; OF. had the semi-popular *saintification* from the 12th c.).]

1. a. *Theol.* The action of the Holy Spirit in sanctifying or making holy the believer, by the implanting within him of the Christian graces and the destruction of sinful affections. Also, the condition or process of being so sanctified.

By the majority of theologians sanctification is regarded as a gradual process, not (at least normally) completed in this life. The doctrine of *entire* or *perfect sanctification* (or of *Christian perfection*: see PERFECTION) is the view, held by some Protestants, that the condition of freedom from sin (though not from ignorance or infirmities) is attainable in the present life.

1526 *Pilgr. Perf.* (W. de W. 1531) 215 Whiche be the werkes of our sanctificacyon and glorificacyon. **1582** N.T. (Rhem.) *2 Thess.* ii. 13 That he hath chosen you..in sanctification of spirit [**1611** through sanctification of the spirit; *Tindale, etc.* sanctifying]. **1597** HOOKER *Eccl. Pol.* v. lvi. §10 That the grace of sanctification and life..might passe from him to his whole race as malediction came from Adam vnto all mankinde. **1616** W. FORDE *Serm.* 19 The Prophets were indued with a great measure of sanctification. **1645** USSHER *Body Div.* (1647) 202 The renewing of our nature according to the Image of God, in righteousnesse and true holinesse: which is but begun in this life, and is called Sanctification. **1681–6** J. SCOTT *Chr. Life* II. vii. Wks. 1718 I. 370 Another of these ordinary Operations of the Spirit, is Sanctification; which consists in the purifying our Wills and Affections from those wicked Inclinations and inordinate Lusts, which [etc.]. **1754** SHERLOCK *Disc.* viii. (1755) I. 247 The only sign of Sanctification is Holiness. **1788** WESLEY *Wks.* (1872) VI. 509 By sanctification we are saved from the power and root of sin, and restored to the image of God. **1876** J. P. NORRIS *Rudim. Theol.* I. iii. 65 Sanctification is that growth in holiness through the influence of the Holy Spirit, which must..follow justification.

¶ **b.** *nonce-use.* 'Sanctified' or pious demeanour.

1760–72 H. BROOKE *Fool of Qual.* (1809) II. 94 [She] was the holiest of all saints, without any parade of sanctification.

2. The action of consecrating or setting apart as holy or for a sacred use or purpose; hallowing.

15.. in Burnet *Hist. Ref.* III. Rec. xxi. §12 It appeareth also that in the Old Testament, in the ordering of Priests, there was both Visible and Invisible Sanctification. **1550** VERON *Godly Sayings* H vj b, All impletye and vngodlynes, which myght in any wise obscure the saintycation [sic] of his name, beyng banisshed away [from us]. **1597** HOOKER *Eccl. Pol.* v. lxx. §1 The sanctification of dayes and times is a token of that thankfulnesse..which we owe to God. **1637** GILLESPIE *Eng. Pop. Cerem.* III. i. 6 Sanctification is the setting apart of a thinge for a holy or religious vse, in such sort, that thereafter it may be put to no other vse. **1725** tr. *Dupin's Eccl. Hist. 17th C.* I. v. 125 This Prayer [Giving of thanks before Meat] was call'd Sanctification, because if it had not preceded, the eating and drinking were reputed Prophane, but became Holy by this Prayer. **1832** W. PALMER *Orig. Liturg.* I. 165 The liturgy of the Gallican church originally contained always some invocation or prayer to God for the sanctification of the elements.

3. *Eccl.* The action of making a person a saint; canonization.

1855 MILMAN *Lat. Chr.* VI. 418 Those honours of Beatification and Sanctification.

4. *slang.* Blackmail, esp. the extortion of political favours from a diplomat. Cf. SANCTIFY *v.* 9.

1975 *Observer* (Colour Suppl.) 23 Nov. 25/3 *Sanctification*, blackmail for the purposes of extracting political favours from a victim, not money. **1977** J. GARDNER *Werewolf Trace* x. 87 He told himself to be careful. They were not above trying a bit of sanctification.

sanctifi'cationist. *rare.* [f. SANCTIFICATION + -IST.] One who has attained 'entire sanctification' (see prec. 1).

1868 DIXON *Spir. Wives* II. 130 With the Methodists she took rank among the Sanctificationists, having many times lost her strength by a sudden illumination from some invisible sphere.

†**sanctificative,** *a. Obs. rare*[−1]. [f. eccl. L. *sanctificāt-*, ppl. stem of *sanctificāre* to SANCTIFY + -IVE.] Serving to sanctify or make holy.

1607 *Schol. Disc. agst. Antichr.* I. iii. 160 The hypocrisie of the Crosse in prayer is proued in respect it is thought to be operatiue, sanctificatiue, and helpfull thereto.

†**sanctificator.** *Obs. rare*[−1]. [ad. eccl. L. *sanctificātor*, agent-n. f. *sanctificāre* to SANCTIFY. Cf. OF. *sanctificateur*, 'a sanctifier, hallower' (Cotgr.).] = SANCTIFIER.

1556 OLDE *Antichrist* 113 b, So is ther none other sanctificatour mencioned..but he alone.

sanctified ('sæŋktɪfaɪd), *ppl. a.* [f. SANCTIFY *v.* + -ED[1].]

1. Of a person: Made holy, endowed with saintly character; *spec.* made holy by the divine grace of the Holy Spirit.

c **1485** *Digby Myst.* (1882) IV. 1001 Whom seke ye, women sanctifiede? **1548** R. HUTTEN *Sum of Div.* F ij b, That much infirmity and vice doeth remayne as yet, euen in them whyche be santifyed. **1579** W. WILKINSON *Confut. Familye of Loue* B iv, Monkes..seperated from the world,..for to live euen so as sanctified ones of God. **1597** SHAKS. *Lover's Compl.* 233 Lo this deuice was sent me from a Nun, Or Sister sanctified of holiest note. **1611** BIBLE *Isa.* xiii. 3, I haue commanded my sanctified ones. **1647** CUDWORTH *Serm. Ho. Comm.* Ded. 6 All Philosophy..to a truly sanctified Mind..is but..Matter for Divinity to work upon. **1762** GOLDSM. *Cit. W.* lxvii, He finds no character so sanctified that has not its failings, none so infamous but has somewhat to attract our esteem. **1848** R. I. WILBERFORCE *Doctr. Incarnation* x. (1852) 234 That sanctified humanity of the Son of God.

2. Affecting holiness; sanctimonious.

1600 SHAKS. *A.Y.L.* II. iii. 13 Your vertues gentle Master Are sanctified and holy traitors to you. **1602** —— *Ham.* I. iii. 130 Breathing like sanctified and pious bonds [*Theobald conj.* bawds], The better to beguile. **1662** *Rump Songs* II. 89 A sanctify'd Colonel in beaten Buff. **1694** tr. *Milton's Lett.*

State, To King of France May an. 1658, Those sanctifi'd Cut-throats, who professing themselves to be the.. Disciples of..Christ,..abuse his meek and peaceful Name ..to the most cruel slaughter of the Innocent. **1743** FIELDING *J. Wild* IV. iv, No mind was ever yet formed entirely free from blemish, unless peradventure that of a sanctified hypocrite. **1778** FOOTE *Trip Calais* III. Wks. 1799 II. 373 For all her sanctified looks. **1844** LD. BROUGHAM *Brit. Const.* xv. (1862) 237 About 120 men of puritanical and sanctified habits. **1860** EMERSON *Cond. Life* vi. (1861) 118, I see not why we should give ourselves such sanctified airs.

†**b.** *absol.*

1620 E. BLOUNT *Horæ Subs.* 59 The Separatists or Sanctified, as they terme themselues.

3. Of things: Holy or consecrated; rendered spiritually profitable.

1632 SANDERSON *Serm.* 555 A sober and sanctifyed vse of the Creatures. **1660** T. GOUGE *Chr. Directions* xvii. (1831) 93 When an evil report is raised of you, be not so much inquisitive who raised it, as to make a good use and sanctified improvement thereof. **1814** SCOTT *Wav.* xiv, He could not help testifying some displeasure against the Blessed Bear, which had given rise to the quarrel, nor refrain from hinting, that the sanctified epithet was hardly appropriate. **1864** PUSEY *Lect. Daniel* v. 251 Levi's fierceness had become a sanctified zeal. **1895** *Westm. Gaz.* 16 Apr. 7/2 Here are a body of men who will mix the anodyne in a spirit of 'sanctified commonsense' (Mr. Welldon's famous expression).

ironically. **1605** B. JONSON *Volpone* I. ii. (1607) B3 And will drop you forth a libell, or a sanctified lie, Betwixt euery spooneful of a Natiuity Pie. **1682** *Enq. Elect. Sheriffs* 9 Or suppose that they [Papists] are again provided of one or two bigotted Fellows..that have promised to do the sanctified job [the assassination of Charles II] for them.

b. Of ground, buildings, etc.: Consecrated, hallowed. *rare.*

1525 *Test. Ebor.* (Surtees) V. 201 To be beried within sanctified grownde whereso it please Almyghtie God that I shall departe. **1601** SHAKS. *All's Well* I. i. 152 Virginitie murthers it selfe, and should be buried in highwayes out of all sanctified limit, as a desperate Offendresse against Nature. **1797** MRS. RADCLIFFE *Italian* xvi, Remember this place is sanctified. **1828** SCOTT *F.M. Perth* xi, Out of respect to the sanctified ground, they lowered their weapons.

c. *transf.* = CONSECRATED 3.

1888 F. HUME *Mme. Midas* I. iv, Where everything is old-fashioned, cheery, and sanctified by long usage.

Hence '**sanctifiedly** *adv.* Now *rare.*

1633 T. ADAMS *Exp. 2 Peter* i. 2 There be many causes in nature to make men die quietly, not sanctifiedly. **1641** BROME *Jov. Crew* II. (1652) D2b, He never looks upon us, but with a sigh,..tho' we simper never so sanctifiedly.

sanctifier ('sæŋktɪfaɪə(r)). [f. next + -ER[1].]

1. *Theol.* One who sanctifies or makes holy; *spec.* the Holy Spirit.

1548 CRANMER *Catech.* 140 God the holy gost, is the commen sanctifier or halower, of all theim that haue a true faithe in God. **1612** R. SHELDON *Serm. St. Martin's* 50 God the Dignifier, the Sanctifier, and Beautifier of the sacrifice. *a* **1768** SECKER *Serm.* iii. (1770) I. 53 The Duties..which we owe to God, as the Father of our Lord Jesus Christ; to his Son, as our Redeemer; to his blessed Spirit, as our Sanctifier. **1875** MANNING *Mission Holy Ghost* i. 2 God the Holy Ghost is the Sanctifier.

2. *occas.* Something that sanctifies.

1753 RICHARDSON *Grandison* (1754) III. i. 1 Self..is a very wicked thing; a sanctifier..of actions, which, in others, we should have no doubt to condemn. **1829** E. BATHER *Serm.* II. 147 A great sweetener and a great sanctifier of your toil it shall be to you.

sanctify ('sæŋktɪfaɪ), *v.* Forms: 4 **seintefie**, 5 **seintifie, sayntifie, -efy,** (6 **santifye, -yfy**); 5 **saynctyfy**, 6 **saincti̇fy**; 5–7 **sanctifie**, 5–6 **sanctyfy**, 6– **sanctify.** [ME. *seintefie*, etc., later (after Latin) *sanctifie*, a. OF. *saintifier* (12th c.), *sant-, sanctifier*, etc., ad. eccl. L. *sanctificāre* to make holy or treat as holy, to sanctify, consecrate, dedicate, f. L. *sanctus* holy: see -FY.]

†**1.** *trans.* To set apart religiously for an office or function; to consecrate (a king, etc.). *Obs.*

1390 GOWER *Conf.* III. 234 Bot yit a kinges hihe astat, Which of his ordre as a prelat Schal ben enoignt and seintefied. **1413** *Pilgr. Sowle* (Caxton 1483) v. vi. 99 He hath blessyd and saynctyfyed a newe precious plante that is comen of theyr lyne and descendyd fro the stock of dauyd. **1526** TINDALE *John* x. 36 Saye ye then to hym, whom the father hath sanctified [ἡγίασε], and sent into the worlde: Thou blasphemest..? **1597** SHAKS. *2 Hen. IV*, IV. v. 115 Let all the Teares, that should bedew my Hearse Be drops of Balme, to sanctifie thy head. **1660** JER. TAYLOR *Worthy Commun.* i. §3. 59 Thus God sanctified Aaron.

†**2.** To canonize, make a saint of. *Obs.*

1390 GOWER *Conf.* III. 317 The feste and the profession ..Was mad with gret solempnete, Where as Diane is seintefied. **1483** CAXTON *Gold. Leg.* 427/1 Saint yues was borne in litel britayn..and was reuelyd to his moder in hyr slepe that he sholde be sayntefyed. **1529** [implied in SANCTIFYING *vbl. sb.*]. **1631** WEEVER *Anc. Funeral Mon.* 271 Sanctifying such as did..build them houses.

†**3. a.** To honour as holy; to ascribe holiness to; = HALLOW *v.*[1] 3. *Obs.*

c **1450** LOVELICH *Grail* xvi. 292 And Alle the tothere gonnen forth to gon, Cristes Name to sanctefien Anon. **1477** EARL RIVERS (Caxton) *Dictes* 35 Pitagoras saide that it is..a noble thing to serue god, & to sayntifie his sainctes to dispreyse the world [etc.]. **1526** *Pilgr. Perf.* (W. de W. 1531) 171 Sanctificetur nomen tuum: that is, Sanctifyed be thy name. **1526** TINDALE *1 Pet.* iii. 15 Sanctifie the lorde god in youre hertes. **1582** N.T. (Rhem.) *Matt.* vi. 9 Ovr father which art in heauen, sanctified be thy name [*other versions* hallowed]. **1601** SHAKS. *All's Well* III. iv. 11 Whilst I from farre, His name with zealous feruour sanctifie.

b. To manifest (God, his might, etc.) as holy.

1535 COVERDALE *Num.* xx. 13 This is ye water of strife, where the children of Israel stroue with the Lorde and he was sanctified vpon them [**1611** he was sanctified in them]. **1567** *Gude & Godlie Ball.* (S.T.S.) 116 In all his wayis the Lord is just and rycht, In all his warkis is sanctifyit his mycht. **1611** BIBLE *Ezek.* xxxvi. 23 And I will sanctifie my great Name which was prophaned among the heathen,.. and the heathen shall know, that I am the Lord,..when I shall be sanctified in you before their eyes.

4. a. To consecrate (a thing); to set apart as holy or sacred.

1483 CAXTON *Gold. Leg.* 260b/2 The ayer and the heuen were puryfyed by thassumpcion of the sowle..and the water was sayntyfyed by the wasshyng of the body. **1530** TINDALE *Prol. Exod.*, Sanctefie, to clense and purifie, to apointe a thinge vnto holie vses and to seperate from vnclene and unholye vses. **1535** COVERDALE *Gen.* ii. 3 And [God] blessed the seuenth daye, & sanctified it. *a* **1548** HALL *Chron., Edw. V* 8b, Which ground was sanctified by Sainct Peter him selfe. **1832** W. PALMER *Orig. Liturg.* I. 162 A verbal oblation of the bread and wine, and an invocation of God to send his holy Spirit to sanctify them into the sacraments of Christ's body and blood. **1899** W. M. RAMSAY in *Expositor* Nov. 437 The new moon was then declared and sanctified, even though it had not actually been seen and reported by any witnesses.

b. To keep (a day, etc.) holy; to keep or observe as holy. = HALLOW *v.*[1] 4.

1604 R. CAWDREY *Table Alph.*, *Sanctifie*, to make holie, hallowe, or keepe holy. **1709** ABP. SHARP *Serm.* (1754) I. ix. 241 Those men have little or no sense of religion, that make no conscience of sanctifying that day, or that put no difference between it and other days. **1727–41** CHAMBERS *Cycl.* s.v. *Sanctification*, By sanctifying the sabbath, is meant, the spending it in prayer, praise, &c. not in worldly concerns.

5. a. To make (a person) holy, to purify or free from sin; to cause to undergo sanctification.

1526 TINDALE *1 Cor.* vi. 11 Ye are wesshed: ye are sanctified: ye are iustified [etc.]. **1530** PALSGR. 697/2, I santifye, I halowe, or make holye, *je sanctifie*... We rede in Scripture that some have ben sanctyfyed in their mothers wombes. **1548–9** (Mar.) *Bk. Com. Prayer, Catechism*, God the holy goste, who sanctifyeth me. **1651** HOBBES *Leviath.* III. xxxv. 220 The Elect in the New Testament were said to bee sanctified. **1711** ADDISON *Spect.* No. 257 ¶8 What Actions can express the entire Purity of Thought which refines and sanctifies a virtuous Man? **1865** R. W. DALE *Jew. Temple* iii. (1877) 38 It is still true that we need the power of the Holy Ghost to sanctify our hearts.

absol. **1531** FRITH *Judgem. Tracy* Wks. (1573) 78/2 S. Paule committeth the power of sanctifying to Christ only. Heb. 2. **1841** MYERS *Cath. Th.* IV. §2. 185 All truth ennobles, and some sanctifies.

b. Chiefly in the Old Testament: To free from ceremonial impurity.

a **1500** in *Tundale's Visions* (1843) 128 Sche of prest halowed and sanctyfyed Retowrned hom all fully puryfyed. **1535** COVERDALE *Exod.* xix. 10 Go vnto the people, and sanctifie them today and tomorrow, yt they maye wash their clothes, and be ready agaynst the thirde daye. **1535** —— *Num.* xi. 18 Vnto ye people thou shalt saye: Sanctifye youre selues agaynst tomorow, yt ye maye eate flesh. **1611** BIBLE *Josh.* iii. 5.

6. To render holy, impart sanctity to (a thing, quality, action or condition); to render legitimate or binding by a religious sanction.

? **1402** QUIXLEY *Ball.* xi. in *Yorksh. Arch. Jrnl.* (1908) XX. 45 A wedloke suche was neuer gracieuse, Where god lyst not it to senitifie [sic]. **1526** TINDALE *1 Tim.* iv. 5 For all the creatures of God are good: and nothynge to be refused, yff it be receaved with thankes gevynge: For it is sanctified by the worde of god and prayer. **1597** SHAKS. *2 Hen. IV*, IV. iv. 4 Wee will our Youth lead on to higher Fields, And draw no Swords, but what are sanctify'd. **1700** DRYDEN *Sigism. & Guisc.* 164 That holy Man, amaz'd at what he saw, Made haste to sanctifie the Bliss by Law. **1718** POPE *Iliad* IX. 223 Yet, more to sanctify the word you send, Let Hodius and Eurybates attend. **1812** J. WILSON *Isle of Palms* III. 103 The Island Queen becomes thy bride And God and Nature sanctify the vow. **1863** KINGLAKE *Crimea* (1876) I. iv. 60 Ambition was sanctified by Religion. **1868** M. PATTISON *Academ. Org.* v. 320 The Puritans of a former age imagined, that by the employment of Scripture phraseology they sanctified common conversation. **1872** E. W. ROBERTSON *Hist. Ess.* 207 The Church could neither make nor unmake a king, she could only sanctify his election by her benediction.

7. *transf.* To impart real or apparent sacredness to; to entitle to reverence or respect; to give a colour of morality or innocence to; to justify, sanction. Now *rare* or *Obs.*

1606 SHAKS. *Tr. & Cr.* III. ii. 190 As true as Troylus, shall crowne vp the Verse, And sanctifie the numbers. **1701** ROWE *Amb. Step-Moth.* I. i. 179 Thy function too will varnish o're our Arts And sanctifie dissembling. **1738** POPE *Epil. Sat.* II. 246 Truth guards the Poet, sanctifies the line. **1749** JOHNSON *Irene* III. viii, Be virtuous Ends pursued by virtuous Means, Nor think th' Intention sanctifies the Deed. **1774** BURKE *Amer. Tax.* Sel. Wks. I. 109 Does not this Letter adopt and sanctify the American distinction of taxing for a revenue? **18..** BENTHAM *Draught of Code* Wks. 1843 IV. 380 Custom, which sanctifies all absurdities. **1817** JAS. MILL *Brit. Ind.* II. v. vii. 607 If under such circumstances as these a zeal for the Government which he served could sanctify his actions, then may Jefferies be regarded as a virtuous judge. **1818** SCOTT *Let. to Joanna Baillie* Dec. in *Lockhart*, So let the intention sanctify the error, if there should be one. **1865** KINGSLEY *Herew.* xxx, And he argued stoutly with St. Peter and with his own conscience, that the means sanctify the end, and that he had done it all for the best.

8. 'To make a means of holiness' (J.); to render productive of or conducive to holiness or spiritual blessing.

1597 HOOKER *Eccl. Pol.* v. lx. §5 The vertues which sanctified those sufferings and made them pretious in Gods sight. **1648** *Eikon Bas.* ii. 8 Those Judgments God hath pleased to send upon Mee, are..a means (I hope) which his mercie hath sanctified so to Mee, as to make Mee repent of that unjust Act. **1662** *Bk. Com. Prayer, Visit. Sick*, Sanctifie, we beseech thee, this thy fatherly correction to him. **1758** S. HAYWARD *Serm.* i. 8 Sufferings..are sanctified and made a means of preparing for heaven. **1802** GOUV. MORRIS in Sparks *Life & Writ.* (1832) III. 160 They have made peace, and may the Lord sanctify it to them.

9. *slang.* To blackmail (a person), esp. for the purposes of extracting political favours. Cf. SANCTIFICATION 4.

1977 J. GARDNER *Werewolf Trace* vii. 71 Can't you sanctify him, or give him a dose of measles? Isn't that how you people talk about blackmail and murder? *Ibid.* xiv. 127 They've sanctified Maubert... It's what they call it. They've made him holy, separated him. Blackmailed him.

sanctifying ('sæŋktɪfaɪɪŋ), *vbl. sb.* [f. SANCTIFY *v.* + -ING[1].] The action of the verb SANCTIFY.

1526 TINDALE *1 Thess.* iv. 3 Every one of you shulde knowe howe to kepe his vessel in sanctifyinge and honoure. **1529** MORE *Dyaloge* II. Wks. 199/2 Though those [saints] bee none whose writing ye wold authorise by their sanctifyeng. **1727–41** CHAMBERS *Cycl.* s.v. *Sanctification*, The sanctifying of the sabbath..is of divine..institution.

'**sanctifying,** *ppl. a.* [f. SANCTIFY *v.* + -ING[2].] That sanctifies.

1586 HOOKER *Serm. on Justif.*, etc. §3 (1612) 3 There is a glorifying righteousnes of men in the world to come; as there is a iustifying and a sanctifying righteousnes here. **1706** STANHOPE *Paraphr.* III. 525 Do not..provoke him to withdraw those sanctifying Graces from you, which are given you as an Earnest of your Salvation at the last Day. **1738** WESLEY *Ps.* LI. x, But perfectly my Soul renew By sanctifying Love. **1858** HOLLAND *Titcomb's Lett.* iv. 206 Both have been chastened..by a relation as sanctifying as it is sacred. **1886** WELLDON *Serm. Harrow* x. (1887) 151 It is to be in the world, yet not of it; to live above it; to let your presence be a sanctifying influence among men.

Hence '**sanctifyingly** *adv.*

1847 BUSHNELL *Chr. Nurt.* viii. (1861) 202 Sanctifyingly touched by his Spirit.

†'**sanctiloge.** *Obs. rare.* [After MARTILOGE: see next.] = next.

1526 R. WHYTFORD *Martiloge* Pref., And the addicyons for theyr more edificacyon, we gadered out of the sanctiloge, legendaurea, catalogo sanctorum. **1608** I. W. *Eng. Martyrol.* Advt. to Rdr., This little worke or Sanctiloge of myne.

sanctilogy (sæŋk'tɪlədʒɪ). *rare.* [f. L. *sancti-, sanctus* SAINT, after *martilogium* MARTILOGE.] A catalogue of saints, or a collection of saints' lives. Cf. SANCTOLOGY.

1867 [see FESTILOGY].

sanctiloquent (sæŋk'tɪləkwənt), *a. rare.* [f. L. *sancti-, sanctus* holy + *loquent-em*: see LOQUENT *a.* Cf. eccl. L. *sanctiloquus* speaking holily.] Speaking of or discoursing on holy or sacred things.

1656 BLOUNT *Glossogr.*, *Sanctiloquent*, that speaks holily. **1845** S. JUDD *Margaret* II. i, Grown sanctiloquent of late, he always knew how to say the right thing.

sanctimonial (sæŋktɪ'məʊnɪəl), *sb.* ?*Obs. rare.* [ad. OF. *sanctimoniale*, or directly ad. eccl. L. *sanctimōniāl-is* (Augustine) a nun, subst. use of late L. *sanctimōniālis* holy, pious: see next. Cf. MONIAL *sb.*] A nun.

1513 BRADSHAW *St. Werburge* I. 2594 The hye perfeccyon and proued holynesse Of this pure vyrgyn and sanctymonyall. **1659** H. L'ESTRANGE *Alliance Div. Off.* 265 Women were by women (meaning Diaconisses and Sanctimonials) to be taught. **1694** MOTTEUX *Rabelais* IV. xliii. 169 That is..what our Sanctimonials alias Nuns in their Dialect call ringing backwards. **1838** G. S. FABER *Inquiry* 421 All Religious Orders of Monks and Sanctimonials they reprobated: saying, that They are vain and superfluous.

†**sancti'monial,** *a. rare.* [ad. late L. *sanctimōniāl-is* holy, pious, f. L. *sanctimōnia*: see SANCTIMONY.] = SANCTIMONIOUS 1.

1721 BAILEY, *Sanctimonial*, pertaining to Holiness. **1773** J. ROSS *Fratricide* III. 12 (MS.) Not such was Abel's sanctimonial pledge, So favour'd at the Altar.

sanctimonious (sæŋktɪ'məʊnɪəs), *a.* [f. L. *sanctimōnia* SANCTIMONY + -OUS.]

†**1.** Possessing sanctity, holy in character; sacred, holy, consecrated. *Obs.*

1604 DEKKER *Honest Wh.* Wks. 1873 II. 58 Thou dost make me violate, The chastest and most sanctimonious vow. **1610** SHAKS. *Temp.* IV. i. 16. **1627** LEVER *Crucifix* lxxxvi, They gaze upon that sanctimonious tree The Holy Crosse, (O sacred worthinesse!). **1631** WEEVER *Anc. Funeral Mon.* 281 The sanctimonious puritie of one Odo. *Ibid.* 309 Inuested in the sanctimonious robes of a Bishop. **1759** MASON *Caractacus* 35 All that by sage and sanctimonious rites Might of the gods be ask'd, we have essay'd. **1796** MORSE *Amer. Geog.* II. 170 [Iona] is still famous for its reliques of sanctimonious antiquity. **1801** J. JONES tr. *Bÿgge's Trav. Fr. Rep.* iii. 43 There were two cloisters. One of those sanctimonious erections was converted into a barrack.

2. Of pretended or assumed sanctity or piety, making a show of sanctity, affecting the appearance of sanctity.

1603 SHAKS. *Meas. for M.* I. ii. 7 Thou conclud'st like the Sanctimonious Pirat, that went to sea with the ten Commandements, but scrap'd one out of the Table. *a* **1652** J. SMITH *Sel. Disc.* ii. 30 Easy to be appeased again by some flattering devotions, especially if performed with sanctimonious shows, and a solemn sadness of mind. **1692** R. L'ESTRANGE *Fables* ccclvi. 327 'Tis not a Sanctimonious Pretence..that will serve the Turn. **1744** AKENSIDE *Pleas. Imag.* III. 111 And, bending oft their sanctimonious eyes, Take homage of the simple-minded throng—Ambassadors of Heaven! **1837** LOCKHART *Scott* 12 Dec. an. 1796, The sanctimonious air which the murderer maintained during his trial. **1849** MACAULAY *Hist. Eng.* iii. I. 400 To that sanctimonious jargon which was his Shibboleth, was opposed another jargon not less absurd and much more odious. **1871** L. STEPHEN *Playgr. Eur.* (1894) iv. III. 237 He informed us that they were a set of sanctimonious humbugs and thieves.

Hence **sancti'moniously** *adv.*, **sancti'moniousness**.

1622 FLETCHER *Sea Voy.* I. i, Ye know deer Lady..How truly I have lov'd ye, how sanctimoniously Observ'd your honour. **1679** J. GOODMAN *Penit. Pard.* I. ii. (1713) 21 Upon all occasions he exposed the sanctimoniousness of their admired Pharisees. **1771** MRS. GRIFFITH *Hist. Lady Barton* I. 3, I will most sanctimoniously perform my part of the covenant. **1876** MISS BRADDON *J. Haggard's Dau.* II. 94 'Henceforward there is laid up for me a crown of glory'. There was no touch of sanctimoniousness or cant in her utterance of these words, only a childlike and implicit faith.

sanctimony ('sæŋktɪmənɪ). [a. OF. *sainct-*, *sant-*, *sanctimonie*, ad. L. *sanctimōnia* sacredness, sanctity, virtuousness, f. *sanct-us* holy: see -MONY.]

†**1.** Holiness of life and character; the profession of holiness; religiousness, sanctity. *Obs.*

1540-1 ELYOT *Image Gov.* 102 The chaste liuing, sanctimonie and prudence of our reuerend mother. **1546** COVERDALE *Calvin's Treat. Sacrament* C j, That we be therby more vehementlie stered vp to sanctimonie and puritie of lyfe. **1601** SHAKS. *All's Well* IV. iii. 59 Which holy vnder-taking [a pilgrimage], with most austere sanctimonie she accomplisht. **1623** R. CARPENTER *Conscionable Christian* To Rdr. B ij b, The sauing power of inward sanctimony. **1658** W. BURTON *Itin. Anton.* 252 In old times it florished for nothing more then the Sanctimony and learning of the Bishops. **1691** WOOD *Ath. Oxon.* I. 9 For conspicuous Vertue, sanctimony of Life, and acuteness..he was in great renown. **1725** BAILEY *Erasm. Colloq.* (1733) 238 It came into my Mind that, to arrive at universal Holiness all at once, I would take a Journey to the holy Land, and so would return Home with a Back-Load of Sanctimony.

b. Of a writer: Chastity or decorum of expression. *rare*⁻¹. Cf. SANCTITUDE 2.

1829 LANDOR *Imag. Conv., Lucian & Tim.* Wks. 1853 II. 27/1 While I admired, with a species of awe,..the majesty and sanctimony of Livy.

†**2.** Sacredness. *Obs.*

1583 STUBBES *Anat. Abus.* II. (1882) 111 If they should repose any religion, holinesse or sanctimonie in them [*sc.* surplice, tippet, etc.] as the doting Papists doe. **1613** PURCHAS *Pilgrimage* (1614) 321 The Rites are solemnized with greatest Sanctimonie, and Oathes taken of greatest consequence. **1629** WHITELOCKE in Rushw. *Hist. Coll.* (1659) I. 688 Is there such Sanctimony in the place [Parliament], that they may not be questioned for it elsewhere? **1683** *Brit. Spec.* 232 The whole Nation being bound to the Observance of this Law by the Sanctimony of an Oath, the Refusal whereof was made High Treason.

†**b.** *pl.* Things sacred. *Obs.*

a **1547** *Doctour Doubble Ale* 40 in Hazl. *E.P.P.* III. 304 And so this folish nation Esteme..all dum ceremonies, Before the sanctimonies, Or Christes holy writ.

3. Pretended, affected or hypocritical holiness or saintliness; assumed or outward sanctity.

a **1618** RALEIGH *War* E vij, Questionlesse there was great reason, why all discreet Princes should beware of yeilding hasty beliefe to the Robes of Sanctimonie. **1749-51** LAVINGTON *Enthus. Meth. & Papists* (1829) 319 Various appearances and arts of sanctimony. **1823** H. BELFRAGE *Monitor to Fam.* 241 With the frown of sanctimony on the countenance. **1830** DE QUINCEY *Bentley* Wks. 1863 VI. 69 *note*, This epithet, bestowed playfully upon Whiston by Swift, in ridicule of his sanctimony. **1831** THIRLWALL *Lett.* (1881) I. 102 The *Edinburgh* [Review] which has no great reputation for sanctimony. **1871** R. H. HUTTON *Ess.* I. 290 The hard and false sanctimony of Pharisaism.

¶**4.** App. misused for SANCTIMONIAL *sb.*

1630 RANDOLPH *Aristippus* 26, I haue done as great wonders as these, when I extracted as much chastity from a Sanctimony in the English Nunnery, as cur'd the Pope of his lechery.

sanction ('sæŋkʃən), *sb.* [a. F. *sanction* (16th c.) or ad. L. *sanctiōn-em* action of ordaining as inviolable under a penalty, also a decree or ordinance, n. of action f. *sancīre* to render sacred or inviolable, ordain, decree, ratify.]

1. A law or decree; esp. an ecclesiastical decree. [So L. *sanctio*; cf. F. 'sanctions ou ordonnances ecclesiastiques', 1516 in Godefroy.] *Obs.* exc. *Hist.*

pragmatic sanction: see PRAGMATIC A. 1.

1563-87 FOXE *A. & M.* (1596) 5/1 Whereas now both the rule of Scripture, and sanctions of the old councels set aside, all things..are decided by certeine new decretal or rather extra decretal and extravagant constitutions. **1577** HARRISON *England* II. xix. (1877) I. 311 Canutus..did at the last make sundrie sanctions and decrees. **1583** STUBBES *Anat. Abus.* II. (1882) 15 The breach or violation of any humane lawe, ordinance, constitution, statute, or sanction. **1660** JER. TAYLOR *Duct. Dubit.* II. i. rule ix. §9 But even in this original rule and great sanction God did dispense with the Israelites. **1668** DENHAM *Of Justice* 1 'Tis the first Sanction, Nature gave to Man, Each other to assist in what they can. **1670** *Moral State Eng.* 105 The sanctions and constitutions of his own Nation. **1700** DRYDEN *Cinyras & Myrrha* 97 Secure the sacred Quiet of thy Mind, And keep the Sanctions Nature has design'd. **1706** PHILLIPS (ed. Kersey), *Sanction*, Decree, Ordinance, especially such as relate to Ecclesiastical Affairs; as the Constitution made at the Council of Basil, for the Reformation of the Church. **1725** POPE *Odyss.* I. 107 Bid him..The Sanction of th' assembled pow'rs report: That wise Ulysses to his native land Must speed, obedient to their high command. **1844** S. R. MAITLAND *Dark Ages* 19 The bishop is to appoint priests and other prudent men, skilled in the divine law, and conversant with the ecclesiastical sanctions.

2. a. *Law.* The specific penalty enacted in order to enforce obedience to a law.

a **1633** AUSTIN *Medit.* (1635) 267 The feare, or Sanction, of the Commandements preserves the Memory of the Law in our hearts. **1671** [R. MACWARD] *True Nonconf.* 316 The sanction and pain of this divine Law being by sin incurred. **1696** STILLINGFL. *Doctr. Christ's Satisfaction* I. Pref. (1697) 15 If there were such a Sanction of the Law, whereby an Obligation to Punishment did follow the Offences forbidden by it. **1736** BUTLER *Anal.* I. ii. 35 If..civil Magistrates could make the Sanctions of their Laws take place, without interposing at all, after they had passed them. *c* **1750** SHENSTONE *Elegies* xxii. 59 When savage robbers every sanction brave. *c* **1765** BURKE *On Popery Laws* Wks. IX. 338 The mode of conviction is as extraordinary as the penal sanctions of this Act. **1781** COWPER *Truth* 553 He gives a perfect rule..And guards it with a sanction as severe As vengeance can inflict, or sinners fear. **1821** J. Q. ADAMS in C. Davies *Metr. Syst.* III. (1871) 278 To require, under suitable sanctions that all the weights and measures..should be conformable to the national standards. **1829** MACAULAY *Mill on Govt.* in *Edin. Rev.* Mar. 187 The fear of death..is the most formidable sanction which legislators have been able to devise. **1832** AUSTIN *Jurispr.* (1873) I. 92 The evil which will probably be incurred in case a command be disobeyed..is frequently called a *sanction*, or an *enforcement of obedience*. **1844** GLADSTONE *Glean.* V. liii. 122 [In the Bible] it is declared under the most awful Sanctions, that God will not endure that his honour shall be given to another. **1845** POLSON in *Encycl. Metrop.* II. 733/2 Sanctions of the Law of Nations... These sanctions..may ..be reduced to two classes:—(1) Reprisals... (2) War. **1875** MAINE *Hist. Inst.* ii. 39 Another example..of the want or weakness of the sanction in the Brehon law.

b. *Law.* Extended to include the provision of rewards for obedience, along with punishments for disobedience, to a law (***remuneratory***, as distinguished from ***vindicatory*** or ***punitive, sanction***).

1692 TYRRELL tr. *Cumberland's Law Nat.* iii. §13. 126 The strictest Sanction which any Soveraign Power can give unto its Laws, is, when it..hath..declared, That it will conferr a sufficient share of good Things, or Rewards, for so doing; and of Evils, or Punishments, upon any breach, or neglect of its Commands. **1727** J. MAXWELL tr. *Cumberland's Laws Nat.* v. §35. 247 A Law is a practical Proposition concerning the Prosecution of the Common Good, guarded by the Sanction of Rewards and Punishments. **1765** BLACKSTONE *Comm.* I. 56 Human legislators have for the most part chosen to make the sanction of their laws rather *vindicatory* than *remuneratory*. **1825** WHATELY *Ess. Pecul. Chr. Relig.* i. 44 The temporal sanctions of the [Mosaic] law, the plenty and famine, the victory and defeat. **1845** R. JEBB in *Encycl. Metrop.* II. 686/1 We feel fully warranted in classing rewards amongst legal sanctions.

c. The part or clause of a law which declares the penalty attached to infringement. Similarly in a charter (see quot. 1844). [So L. *sanctio*.] *Obs.* exc. *Hist.*

1651 BAXTER *Inf. Bapt.* 175 The Law hath two parts, the mandate and the sanction. **1765** BLACKSTONE *Comm.* I. 54 The sanction, or vindicatory branch of the law; whereby it is signified what evil or penalty shall be incurred by such as commit any public wrongs, and transgress or neglect their duty. **1844** LINGARD *Anglo-Sax. Ch.* (1858) II. App. H. 369 The sanction or close of the charter in these instruments is almost always the same, at least in substance—a sort of blessing promised to those who observe the grant, and of imprecation against those who break it.

d. *Pol.* Esp. in *pl.*, economic or military action taken by a state or alliance of states against another as a coercive measure, usu. to enforce a violated law or treaty.

1919 G. B. SHAW *Peace Conference Hints* vi. 84 Such widely advocated and little thought-out 'sanctions' as the outlawry and economic boycott of a recalcitrant nation. **1935** *Punch* 25 Dec. 728 'And you,' we replied in great excitement, 'are the very man to give it to him. Come, now, put on your beard, fly over to Italy, and—sanctions or no sanctions—put into his stocking your One Hundred and Eighty-Ninth Volume.' **1937** A. HUXLEY *Ends & Means* ix. 109 Military sanctions *are* war. Economic sanctions, if applied with vigour, must inevitably lead to war-like reactions on the part of the nation to which they are applied, and these war-like reactions can only be countered by military sanctions. **1943** H. A. WALLACE in *N.Y. Times* 26 July 10/6 He witnessed the collapse of sanctions under the League of Nations. **1948** P. D. WHITTING in M. Beloff *Hist.* 356/1 Abyssinia was annexed by Italy in May, 1936. Sanctions were dropped two months later. **1965** *New Statesman* 9 Apr. 562/2 Given sufficient pressures to ensure the cooperation of British firms and banks operating in Rhodesia..sanctions could work if they were maintained for an extended period. **1981** *Guardian* 20 July 12/2 If Israel is to be stopped from riding roughshod over Western interests in the Middle East.., American sanctions may have to be a lot more convincing.

3. *Ethics.* A consideration which operates to enforce obedience to any law or rule of conduct; a recognized motive for conformity to moral or religious law, operating either through the agent's desire for some resultant good or through his fear of some resultant evil.

As a technical term of Ethics, the word is favoured by the Utilitarians. For the classification of the different 'sanctions' see quots. 1780 and 1887. The sanction of law in the strict sense (see 2 above) is distinguished as 'legal' or 'political'. Bentham's 'moral sanction' corresponds to the 'social sanction' of other writers.

1681 S. PARKER *Demonstr. Law Nat.* 72 The most powerfull and effectual Sanction in the World, *viz.* the Pleasures or Torments of Conscience. **1754** RICHARDSON *Grandison* VI. xix. 90 Religious zeal is a strengthener, a confirmer, of all the social sanctions. **1758** R. PRICE (*title*) A Review of the principal Questions and Difficulties in Morals. Particularly Those relating to the Original of our Ideas of Virtue, its Nature, Foundation, Reference to the Deity, Obligation, Subject-matter and Sanctions. **1780** BENTHAM *Princ. Legisl.* iii. §2 There are four distinguishable sources from which pleasure and pain are in use to flow: considered separately, they may be termed the *physical*, the *political*, the *moral*, and the *religious*: and inasmuch as the pleasures and pains belonging to each of them are capable of giving a binding force to any law or rule of conduct, they may all of them be termed *sanctions*. **1794** PALEY *Evid.* II. ii. (1817) 55 To supply what was much more wanting than lessons of morality, stronger moral sanctions, and clearer assurances of a future judgement. **1817** JAS. MILL *Brit. India* II. v. ix. 709 The undivided reputation of good measures, the undivided ignominy of bad, redounded to the Court of Directors. The great sanction of public opinion therefore acted upon them with concentrated energy. **1861** MILL *Utilit.* iii. 39 With regard to any supposed moral standard—what is its sanction? what are the motives to obey it? **1874** SIDGWICK *Meth. Ethics* II. v. (1890) 164 These 'sanctions' we may classify as External and Internal. The former class will include both 'Legal Sanctions'..and 'Social Sanctions'. **1887** FOWLER *Princ. Morals* II. iii. 144 Physical sanctions are the pleasures and pains which follow naturally on the observance or violation of physical laws, the sanctions employed by society are praise and blame, the moral sanctions..are..the approval and disapproval of conscience; lastly, the religious sanctions are either the fear of future punishment, and the hope of future reward, or, to the higher religious sense, simply the love of God, and the dread of displeasing Him. **1896** 'M. FIELD' *Attila* IV. 102 For he rejects our sanctions, he is bound By nothing we are bound by.

4. Binding force given to an oath; something which makes an oath or engagement binding; †a solemn oath or engagement.

1611 B. JONSON *Catiline* I. C 4 There cannot be A fitter drinke, to make this Sanction in. Here I beginne the Sacrament to all. *a* **1745** SWIFT *Serm., Testimony Consc.*, This Word [honour] is often made the Sanction of an Oath; it is reckoned a great Commendation to be a Man of strict Honour. **17..** tr. *Rollin's Anc. Hist.* III. ii. (ed. 5, 1768) II. 28 [Sennacherib] The Assyrian, regarding neither the sanction of oaths nor treaties, still continued the war. **1817** SHELLEY *Rev. Islam* X. xxix, We swear by thee! and to our oath do thou Give sanction, from thine hell of fiends and flame. **1869** FREEMAN *Norm. Conq.* III. xii. 242 When he knew by how awful a sanction he had unwittingly bound his soul.

5. The action of rendering legally authoritative or binding; solemn confirmation or ratification given to a law, enactment, etc. by a supreme authority.

1658 PHILLIPS, *Sanction*, a decreeing, enacting, or establishing, any Law or Ordinance. **1660** JER. TAYLOR *Duct. Dubit.* II. i. rule i. §41 It became a law only by the authority and proper sanction of God. *c* **1680** BEVERIDGE *Serm.* (1729) I. 85 All which laws have their..sanction from the supreme lawgiver. **1699** T. BAKER *Refl. Learn.* xiv. 167 As to Lancelottus's Book of Institutes, which Dr. Duck seems to make a part of the Corpus, he is therein mistaken, for wanting Sanction and Authority, it is only yet a private work. **1784** COWPER *Epist. Jos. Hill* 57 Could a law like that which I relate Once have the sanction of our triple state? **1838** THIRLWALL *Greece* IV. xxxii. 221 It even appears that a decree might be first moved in the Assembly, and then be sent up to receive the formal sanction of the Council, which could not be withheld. **1849** MACAULAY *Hist. Eng.* i. I. 85 The day on which the royal sanction was, after many delays, solemnly given to this great Act, was a day of joy and hope. **1875** MAINE *Hist. Inst.* ii. 27 Thus when a body of Brehon judgments was promulgated by an Irish chief to a tribal assembly it is probable that convenience was the object sought rather than a new sanction.

6. a. An express authoritative permission or recognition (e.g. of an action, procedure, custom, institution, etc.).

1720 POPE *Iliad* XVII. 246 Then with his sable Brow he gave the Nod, That seals his Word; the Sanction of the God. **1749** SMOLLETT *Regicide* I. i. (1777) 7 And implore A parent's sanction to support my claim. **1769** *Junius Lett.* viii. (1788) 63 You pardon the offence, and are not ashamed to give the sanction of government to the riots you complain of. **1774** BURKE *Sp. Amer. Tax.* Sel. Wks. I. 95 He will permit me to apply myself to the House under the sanction of his authority. **1798** S. & HT. LEE *Canterb. T., Yng. Lady's T.* II. 103 [He] told her, this experiment had not only his sanction, but warmest approbation. **1813** SHELLEY *Q. Mab* II. 157 But what was he who taught them that the God Of nature and benevolence hath given A special sanction to the trade of blood? **1845** STEPHEN *Comm. Laws Eng.* (1874) I. 108 The mother country..had never hesitated to lend her sanction to that iniquitous method of cultivation. **1849** MACAULAY *Hist. Eng.* vi. II. 77 He had caused it to be announced that, at every church in the kingdom, a collection would be made under his sanction for their benefit. *Ibid.* ix. 441 He could not make a descent on England without the sanction of the United Provinces. **1883** SIR W. B. BRETT in *Law Rep. 11 Q. B. Div.* 561 The trustee may, with the sanction of a special resolution of the creditors, accept any composition offered by the bankrupt.

b. *fig.* Now also in looser sense, countenance or encouragement given (intentionally or otherwise) to an opinion or practice by a person of influence, by custom, public sentiment, etc.

1738 SWIFT *Pol. Conversat.* Introd. 34 Authentick Expressions, I mean, such as must receive a Sanction from the polite World, before their Authority can be allowed. **1756** C. LUCAS *Ess. Waters* III. 112 The multitude gave fiction the sanction of authority. **1774** PENNANT *Tour Scot. in 1772*, 298 Such length of time does it require to root out follies that have the sanction of antiquity. **1841** MYERS *Cath. Th.* III. §24. 87 This testimony, as popularly interpreted, does present great appearance of sanction to some of the views which are discountenanced in these Pages. **1849** MACAULAY *Hist. Eng.* vii. II. 183 Religion gave her sanction to that intense and unquenchable animosity. **1852** CONYBEARE & HOWSON *St. Paul* (1862) I. vii. 213 His behaviour was giving a strong sanction to the very heresy which was threatening the existence of the Church.

7. a. Something which serves to support, authorize, or confirm an action, procedure, etc.

1728 YOUNG *Love Fame* v. 154 We grant that beauty is no bar to sense, Nor is't a sanction for impertinence. **1856** PATMORE *Angel in Ho.* II. II. iv, The wedded yoke that each had donned, Seeming a sanction, not a bond. **1863** KINGLAKE *Crimea* (1876) I. iv. 60 To a cause having all these sanctions the voice of prophecy could not be wanting.

†**b.** A recommendation or testimonial. *Obs.*

1791 BOSWELL *Johnson* Advt., What reason I had to hope for the countenance of that venerable Gentleman to this Work, will appear from what he wrote to me upon a former occasion... Such a sanction to my faculty of giving a just representation of Dr. Johnson I could not conceal. **1813** C. MARSHALL *Garden.* (ed. 5) Pref., The author..thinks it [? *read* he] is but doing himself justice by republishing the following sanctions, as they occurred on the first Edition.

¶**8.** Assurance of protection under the laws of hospitality. (Confused with *sanctuary*?) *rare*$^{-1}$.

1754 RICHARDSON *Grandison* II. xlv. (III. xiii), I cannot forgive myself—To suffer myself to be provoked by two such men, to violate the sanction of my own house!

9. a. *attrib.* and *Comb.*, as (sense 2 d) ***sanction-breaker***, ***-buster***, ***-busting***; ***sanction-induced*** adj.

1968 *Guardian* 25 Apr. 1/8 British citizens would be able to come to Britain from Rhodesia 'unless they are known *sanction breakers or supporters of the illegal regime'. **1973** *Times* 8 June 27/1 (*heading*) Dutch move to stop the *sanction busters. **1973** *Guardian* 16 Apr. 1/6 The Smith regime in Rhodesia has carried out its most spectacular coup in *sanction-busting..with the triumphant announcement that three Boeing-707 jet airliners have been delivered. **1974** A. WILLIAMS *Gentleman Traitor* xii. 186 He studied the.. South African and Rhodesian economies, and how these interlocked with the complex methods of Sanction-Busting. **1970** D. GOLDRICH et al. in I. L. Horowitz *Masses in Lat. Amer.* v. 192 We can project the possibility..of *sanction-induced parochialism on the part of formerly more highly politicalized actors.

b. *attrib.* and *Comb.* in *pl.* (sense 2 d), as ***sanctions-breaker***, ***-breaking***, ***-buster***, ***-busting***; ***sanctions-busting*** adj.

1973 R. LEWIS *Blood Money* viii. 110 *Scathe* would not be publishing an exposé on the German businessman, *sanctions-breaker or not. **1935** *Times* 7 Nov. 14/6 It may be taken for granted..that the German conception of neutrality does not permit of what might be described as '*sanctions-breaking'. **1976** P. DRISCOLL *Barboza Credentials* I. ii. 29 Countries whose laissez-faire attitudes had encouraged sanctions-breaking. *Ibid.* III. i. 92, I had one immediate concern: the British consulate. *Sanctions-buster or not, I was in desperate need of their help. **1970** *Observer* 1 Mar. 4/4 It is disappointed that so little is being done to..promote the campaign against the *sanctions-busting ships. **1975** M. HARTMANN *Game for Vultures* ii. 22 He had started seriously in the sanctions busting game.

sanction (ˈsæŋkʃən), *v.* [f. prec. sb. Cf. F. *sanctionner* (18th c.).] *trans.* To give sanction to.

1. To ratify or confirm by sanction or solemn enactment; to invest with legal or sovereign authority; to make valid or binding.

1778 JEFFERSON *Autobiog.* App., Wks. 1859 I. 146 Preserving..the very words of the established law, wherever their meaning had been sanctioned by judicial decisions. **1784** COWPER *Task* v. 548 That charter sanction'd sure By th' unimpeachable and awful oath And promise of a God! **1791** BURKE *App. Whigs* 12 Tests against old principles, sanctioned by the laws. **1823** J. MARSHALL *Const. Opin.* (1839) 284 The titles held under the Indians were sanctioned by length of possession. **1838** PRESCOTT *Ferd. & Is.* I. iii. I. 182 They entered into a covenant sanctioned by all the solemnities of religion usual on these occasions, not to re-enter [etc.].

2. a. To permit authoritatively; to authorize; in looser use, to countenance, encourage by express or implied approval.

1797 MRS. RADCLIFFE *Italian* viii, My own voice never shall sanction the evils to which I may be subjected. **1798** FERRIAR *Of Genius* in *Illustr. Sterne*, etc. 286 Such a preference ought not to be sanctioned by philosophers. **1807–26** S. COOPER *First Lines Surg.* (ed. 5) 416 The employment of bandages in these cases is sanctioned by high authorities. **1812** H. & J. SMITH *Rej. Addr.* v, Nor..will I ever sanction a theatre with my presence. **1836** J. GILBERT *Chr. Atonem.* Notes (1852) 366 These statements are sanctioned by common sense. **1840** MACAULAY *Ess., Clive* ¶121 (1897) 536 The Directors..were not disposed to sanction any increase of the salaries out of their own treasury. **1844** H. H. WILSON *Brit. India* I. viii. I. 499 The system of commerce and administration which had been sanctioned by the existing charter. **1857** GLADSTONE *Glean.* VI. xli. 73 Etymologically it is not tied to the one rather than the other sense; and usage will sanction either. **1865** GROTE *Plato* I. v. 190 Positions..which the dialogues themselves do not even sanction, much less suggest. **1908** *Q. Rev.* Oct. 329 He renounced on principle..large profits sanctioned by usage.

b. To allege sanction for; to justify as permissible.

1876 L. STEPHEN *Eng. Th. in 18th C.* i. §21 I. 21 If Spinoza and Hobbes were accused of Atheism, each of them sanctioned his speculations by the sacred name of theology.

3. To enforce (a law, legal obligation, etc.) by attaching a penalty to transgression. Cf. SANCTION *sb.* 2 a, b.

1825 WHATELY *Ess. Pecul. Chr. Relig.* i. 45 The temporal rewards and punishments..which sanctioned that Law. **1832** AUSTIN *Jurispr.* (1873) I. 92 The command or the duty is said to be sanctioned or enforced by the chance of incurring the evil. *Ibid.* 522 Laws are sometimes sanctioned by nullities.

4. To impose sanctions upon (a person), to penalize.

A use of doubtful acceptability at present.—R.W.B.

1956 *Universe* 27 July 1/1 (*heading*) Let Church sanction road killers. **1978** *Daily Mail* 29 Nov. 9/1 Sir Geoffrey Howe..referred to Ford's being 'sanctioned'... Nobody.. made a protest about this violence being done to the English language (or about normal meanings being stood on their head).

sanctionable (ˈsæŋkʃənəb(ə)l), *a.* [f. SANCTION *v.* + -ABLE.] That may be sanctioned.

1891 in *Cent. Dict.* **1927** A. KOCOUREK *Jural Relations* 441 *Sanctionable acts*, unlawful acts which are visited by a sanction. **1944** *Scrutiny* XII. 155 The only sanctionable activities unconnected with religion are parlour games. **1976** *Interdisciplinary Sci. Rev.* I. 182/1 It was our visit to the Flower Children..that suggested to me the need for an alternative to the polar position—the need for a totally new and socially sanctionable drug.

sanctional (ˈsæŋkʃənəl), *a. rare.* [f. SANCTION *sb.* + -AL[1].] 'Of or pertaining to sanction or sanctioning' (*Funk's Standard Dict.* 1895).

sanctionary (ˈsæŋkʃənərɪ), *a. rare.* [f. SANCTION *sb.* + -ARY[1].] Relating to sanctions (see SANCTION *sb.* 1).

1845 R. BALMER *Lect. & Disc.* I. x. 403 The Son of God has so satisfied the preceptive and sanctionary demands of the violated law of God. **1850** J. BROWN *Disc. & Sayings of our Lord* (1852) I. 30 Such suffering..signally honoured the sanctionary part of the divine law.

sanctionative (ˈsæŋkʃənətɪv), *a. Law.* [f. SANCTION *sb.* + -ATIVE.] Pertaining to sanctioning.

c **1832** AUSTIN *Jurispr.* (1873) I. 389 Rights of Action are classed with Obligations; whilst obligations to suffer punishment (which are not more sanctionative than the former), are referred..to Public Law. *Ibid.* II. 947 If this be so, quasi-delicts should be classed with 'Sanctionative Rights and Obligations'. **1875** POSTE *Gaius* I. Comm. (ed. 2) 140 As women were capable of administration, the functions of the guardian, which in the case of infants were either administrative or sanctionative, in the case of women were confined to sanctioning.

sanctioned (ˈsæŋkʃənd), *ppl. a.* [f. SANCTION *v.* + -ED[1].]

1. Allowed by authority; that has received sanction or solemn recognition.

1799 GEO. [IV] *Let.* 7 Jan. in *Paget Papers* (1896) I. 149 So long as you are to be one of the sanctioned Spies, & hidden lamps of Lord Grenville. **1832** tr. *Sismondi's Ital. Rep.* v. 109 Their lives, too, sometimes endangered by sanctioned robbers, under the pretext of repressing usury. **1833** J. H. NEWMAN *Arians* I. iii. (1876) 41 On these academical bodies, as subsidiary to the divinely-sanctioned system, devolved the defence and propagation of the faith. **1888** *Pall Mall G.* 25 Sept. 11/2 The total sanctioned mileage open and under construction was 16,870 miles.

2. *Law.* Of a right: Defined or created by a sanction antecedently to any wrong. Cf. SANCTIONING *ppl. a.* 2.

c **1832** AUSTIN *Jurispr.* (1873) II. 797 Primary (or sanctioned) Rights and Obligations distinguished from sanctioning. **1875** POSTE *Gaius* I. Introd. (ed. 2) 4 Sanctioned, or primary, or final rights, are such rights as exist antecedently to any Wrong, rights whose Title or origin from which they spring,..is some circumstance other than a Wrong.

3. *Roman Law.* Used to translate L. *sanctus* 'inviolable'.

1875 POSTE *Gaius* II. §8 Sanctioned places are to a certain extent under divine dominion, such as city gates [etc.].

sanctioneer (ˌsæŋkʃəˈnɪə(r)). [f. SANCTION *sb.* + -EER.] = SANCTIONIST 1.

1937 G. FRANKAU *More of Us* v. 53 Ask not of him—my noble sanctioneers Whose peaceful intents of such warlike mood are. **1965** *Observer* 21 Nov. 3/2 The 'sanctioneers', as they are coming to be called, are highly satisfied with Mr. Heath. **1967** *Economist* 7 Jan. 19/1 South West Africa would offer the sanctioneers a far more permanent bridgehead, the chance of applying sanctions, in effect, against apartheid itself.

sanctioner (ˈsæŋkʃənə(r)). [f. SANCTION *v.* + -ER[1].] One who sanctions.

1846 GROTE *Greece* I. i. 9 Horkos, the ever-watchful sanctioner of oaths. *a* **1890** CHURCH *Oxford Movement* xvii. (1891) 305 He [W. G. Ward] admitted that he *did* evade the spirit, but accepted the 'statements of the Articles', maintaining that this was the intention of their original sanctioners.

ˈsanctioning, *ppl. a.* [f. SANCTION *v.* + -ING[2].]

1. a. That sanctions or authorizes.

1829 CARLYLE *Misc.* (1857) II. 51 What they call 'Honour', the sanctioning deity of which is that wonderful 'Force of Public Opinion'. **1868** GEO. ELIOT *Sp. Gypsy* IV. 305 Their keen love of family and tribe Shall no more thrive on cunning, hide and lurk In petty arts of abject hunted life, But grow heroic in the sanctioning light. **1880** G. MEREDITH *Tragic Com.* (1881) 87 They meet beneath the sanctioning roof of the amiable professor.

b. That imposes or maintains sanctions. Cf. SANCTION *sb.* 2 d. *rare.*

1976 *Individualist* Dec. 66/2 South Africa will surely fall, and another great satellite state will have been created in a powerful strategic position. Have the 'santioning' countries considered this?

2. *Law.* Of a right: Creating or providing a sanction; arising as a consequence of a delict or wrong. Cf. SANCTIONED *ppl. a.* 2.

1832 AUSTIN *Jurispr.* (1873) I. 45 Rights and duties which are consequences of delicts, are *sanctioning* (or preventive) and *remedial* (or reparative). *Ibid.* II. 790 Those [rights and duties] which I call secondary or sanctioning (I style them sanctioning because their proper purpose is to prevent delicts or offences) arise from violations of other rights and duties, or from injuries, delicts, or offences.

sanctionism (ˈsæŋkʃənɪz(ə)m). *rare.* [f. SANCTION *sb.* + -ISM.] The theory of economic or military sanctions; advocacy of such sanctions.

1938 *Nation* (N.Y.) 29 Jan. 115/2 The struggle against the 'highly civilised hordes of sanctionism'.

sanctionist (ˈsæŋkʃənɪst), *sb.* (and *a.*) [f. SANCTION *sb.* + -IST.] **1.** One who advocates or supports the employment of sanctions. Cf. SANCTION *sb.* 2 d.

1935 *Observer* 6 Oct. 18/3 The 'News Chronicle', a sanguinary sanctionist, had a displayed article last week called 'Christmas is coming'. **1937** A. HUXLEY *Ends & Means* ix. 111 Sanctionists reply by asserting that the mere display of great military force by League members will be enough to deter would-be aggressors.

2. *attrib.* passing into *adj.*

1935 *Observer* 6 Oct. 18/3 British policy and the sanctionist mania were originally based on the delusion that Signor Mussolini was bluffing. **1936** *Empire Rev.* LXIII. 145 Sanctionist policy. **1937** A. HUXLEY *Ends & Means* ix. 112 According to sanctionist theory, the League is to take military action in order to bring about a just settlement of disputes.

ˈsanctionless, *a.* [f. SANCTION *sb.* + -LESS.] Having no sanction or legal penalty attached.

1875 POSTE *Gaius* I. (ed. 2) 126 Consuetudinary law.. inflicted positive sanctions on acts that originally had only been prohibited by the sanctionless law of honour.

ˈsanctionment. *rare.* [f. SANCTION *v.* + -MENT.] The action of sanctioning.

1802–12 BENTHAM *Ration. Judic. Evid.* (1827) III. 403 Securities for trustworthiness [of evidence], viz. sanctionment, or interrogation, one or both of them. **1818** —— *Ch. Eng.* 112 Appropriate sanctionment given to each of these sorts of acts respectively.

sanctitude (ˈsæŋktɪtjuːd). [ad. L. *sanctitūdo*, f. *sancti-*, *sanctus* holy: see -TUDE.]

1. The quality of being holy or saint-like; holiness, sanctity. Now *rare.*

c **1450** HOLLAND *Howlat* 96 Be the rud I am richt rad For to behald ȝour halyness, or my tale tell; I may nocht suffyss to se ȝour sanctitud sad. **1535** STEWART *Cron. Scot.* (Rolls) II. 682 Insufficient I am for to discrywe Hir sanctitude, and eik hir halie lyfe. **1616** *Marlowe's Faust.* (1631) E 1, *Pope*... Finde the man that doth this villany, Or by our sanctitude ye all shall dye! **1667** MILTON *P.L.* IV. 293 In thir looks Divine The image of thir glorious Maker shon, Truth, Wisdom, Sanctitude severe and pure. **1738** H. BROOKE *Tasso* II. 26 For ill the Wizard's pedant Arts retain That Sanctitude which Macon's Laws ordain, Whose Tenets, all replete with Lore divine, Prohibit Idols from his hallow'd Shrine. **1824** LANDOR *Imag. Conv.*, *Johnson & Horne Tooke* Wks. 1846 I. 153 The sanctitude of Milton's genius gave it [*sc.* our language] support until the worst of French invasions overthrew it. **1825** SCOTT *Betrothed* xviii, Whether he goes to the Crusade or abides at home, the character of Hugh Lacy will remain as unimpeached in point of courage as that of the Archbishop Baldwin in point of sanctitude. **1870–4** J. THOMSON *City Dreadf. Nt.*, etc. (1880) 65 Through rhythmic years evolving like a psalm Of infinite love and faith and sanctitude.

†**b.** *pl.* (as attribute of more than one.) *Obs.*

1552 LYNDESAY *Monarche* 5862 That day, ȝour faynit Sanctytudis Sall nocht be knawin be ȝour Hudis.

2. = SANCTIMONY 1 b. *rare.*

1855 LANDOR *Imag. Conv.*, *Pollio & Calvus* ii. Wks. 1891 II. 122 [Sallust.] His manners ill corresponded with the austerity and sanctitude of his style.

sanctity (ˈsæŋktɪtɪ). Forms: 4–5 saunctite, sauntite, saintite, 6 saincite, santytie, 6–7 sanctitie, 7– sanctity. [a. OF. *saint-*, *sainctété*, *-ité*, mod.F. *sainteté* (= Prov. *sanctitat*, *sanctetat*, Catal. *santetad*, Sp. *santidad*, Pg. *santidade*, It. *santità*, *-ade*, *-ate*), ad. L. *sanctitās*, *-tātem*, f. *sancti-*, *sanctus* holy: see -ITY.]

1. Holiness of life, saintliness. ***odour of sanctity***: see ODOUR 5.

The phr. ***sanctity of manners*** was common in the 18th c.

c **1394** *P. Pl. Crede* 105 Of all men opon mold we Menures most scheweþ þe pure Apostells life wiþ penance on erþe, And suen hem in saunctite & suffren well harde. *a* **1400** *Minor Poems fr. Vernon MS.* 54/98 Heil temple of grace most, Temple of Sauntite [*templum sanctitatis*]. **1526** *Pilgr. Perf.* (W. de W. 1531) 201 b, For otherwyse myght God neuer be conceyued than in purite & sanctite. **1532** MORE *Confut. Tindale* Wks. 357/2 But woulde God they would ones rather folow him truely in faith & good workes, then in simulacion of like santytie with their holy salutacions. **1600** SHAKS. *A.Y.L.* III. iv. 14 His kissing is as ful of sanctitie, As the touch of holy bread. **1616** R. C. *Times' Whistle*, etc. (1871) 141 Puritanes..by whose apparant shew Of sanctity doe greatest evils grow. **1651** HOBBES *Leviath.* II. xxvi. 148

From seeing the Extraordinary sanctity of his life. **1686** tr. *Bouhours' St. Ignatius* VI. 402 Illustrious for his Saintity, his Miracles, and for his Zeal. **1712** Addison *Spect.* No. 349 ⁋8 One who does not resemble him [Sir T. More] as well in the Chearfulness of his Temper, as in the Sanctity of Life and Manners. **1780** Cowper *Progr. Err.* 116 The master of the pack Cries —— Well done, saint! and claps him on the back. Is this the path of sanctity? Is this To stand a way-mark in the road to bliss? **1784** —— *Task* III. 260 Fam'd For sanctity of manners undefil'd. **1790** Burke *Fr. Rev.* 216 A few of them [bishops] were men of eminent sanctity. **1855** Macaulay *Hist. Eng.* xvi. III. 697 He committed this base action with all the forms of sanctity. **1877** Froude *Short Stud.* (1883) IV. I. iii. 34 Alexander had no liking for Becket ..and had no belief in the lately assumed airs of sanctity. *personified.* **1611** Shaks. *Wint. T.* III. iii. 23 In pure white Robes Like very sanctity she did approach My Cabine.

b. *pl.*

1597 Shaks. *2 Hen. IV*, IV. ii. 21 The very Opener, and Intelligencer, Betweene the Grace, the Sanctities of Heauen, And our dull workings. **1820** Lamb *Elia* Ser. I. *Oxford in Vac.*, The coalition of the better Jude with Simon —— clubbing (as it were) their sanctities together, to make up one poor gaudy-day between them. **1856** Emerson *Eng. Traits, Relig.* Wks. (Bohn) II. 96 The priest translated the.. sanctities of the old hagiology into English virtues.

c. The rank of a (canonized) saint. *rare.*

1855 Milman *Lat. Chr.* XIV. ii. VI. 418 Saints at length multiplying thus beyond measure, the Pope assumed the prerogative of advancing to the successive ranks of Beatitude and Sanctity.

2. The quality of being sacred or hallowed; sacredness, claim to (religious) reverence; inviolability.

1601 Shaks. *Twel. N.* III. iv. 395 This youth that you see heere, I snatch'd one halfe out of the iawes of death, Releeu'd him with such sanctitie of loue. **1611** Bible *2 Macc.* iii. 12 The maiestie and inuiolable sanctitie of the Temple, honoured ouer all the world. **1665** Dryden & Howard *Ind. Queen* III. i, Princes are sacred. *Zemp.* True, whilst they are free; But Power once lost, farewel their Sanctity. **1667** Milton *P.L.* VIII. 487 On she came, Led by her Heav'nly Maker, though unseen, And guided by his voice, nor uninformd Of nuptial Sanctitie and marriage Rites. **1757** Burke *Abridgm. Eng. Hist.* Wks. X. 216 The idea of sanctity, which the Britains, by a long course of hereditary reverence, had annexed to that island. **1774** Goldsm. *Nat. Hist.* (1776) I. 211 It [the Ganges] is not only esteemed by the Indians for the depth, and pureness of its stream, but for a supposed sanctity which they believe to be in its waters. **1821** Lamb *Elia* Ser. I. *Imperf. Sympathies*, His affirmations have the sanctity of an oath. **1856** Stanley *Sinai & Pal.* v. (1858) 240 Gerizim, the oldest sanctuary in Palestine, retained its sanctity to the end. **1865** Lubbock *Preh. Times* 52 Stonehenge was at one time a spot of great sanctity. **1888** D. C. Murray *Weaker Vessel* I. xiii. 208 We have grown quite accustomed nowadays to the invasion of what used to be called the sanctity of private life.

b. *pl.* Sacred obligations, feelings, etc.; also quasi-*concr.*, objects possessing sanctity.

1808 Wordsw. *White Doe* v. 1295 Bear it to Bolton Priory, And lay it on Saint Mary's shrine; To wither in the sun and breeze 'Mid those decaying sanctities. **1849** Robertson *Serm.* Ser. IV. xvi. (1876) 210 Christian love which dreads to tamper with the sanctities of a brother's conscience. *a* **1890** Church *Oxf. Movemt.* iii. (1891) 41 He saw in it [Milton's poetry] only an intrusion into the most sacred of sanctities. **1894** H. Drummond *Ascent Man* 330 Woman completes her destiny by occupying herself with the industries and sanctities of the home.

3. = holiness 2. *rare.*

1633 T. Stafford *Pac. Hib.* II. vii. (1821) 314 The petition to the Popes sanctitie. **1897** *Daily Record* 21 Sept. 5/1 An encyclical from the Armenian Patriarch was read, in which his Sanctity exhorts the faithful to continue faithful to the Sultan.

†**'sanctize**, *v. Obs. rare*⁻¹. [f. L. *sanct-us* holy + -ize.] *trans.* To make holy, sanctify.

1691 Sir P. King *Worship Prim. Ch.* (1712) 119 But not attributing unto them any such Holiness as to Sanctise those Services that were performed in them.

sanc'tology. *rare.* [f. L. *sanct-us* saint + -(o)logy.] = sanctilogy. Hence **sanc'tologist**, the compiler of a 'sanctology'.

1824 G. Chalmers *Caledonia* III. 167 The sanctologies do not recognize such a saint; and we must look for some other Osbern, though of less sanctity. *Ibid.* 192 St. Marjorie is not mentioned by the Sanctologists.

sanctoral. Anglicized form of next.

1641 R. B. K. *Parall. Liturgy w. Mass-Bk.*, etc. 86 This abhominable Masse hath three parts; The Ordinary..: The Temporall..: The Sanctorall. **1955** A. A. King *Liturgies of Relig. Orders* iii. 195 The mediaeval sanctoral was similar to that in many of the calendars of the time. **1975** *Church Times* 7 Mar. 8/4 Priests of the Society of Retreat-Conductors gave him a desk and something described as a coffee-table calendar of the Church's year and sanctoral.

‖**sanctorale** (sæŋktɒ'reɪlɪ, -'rɑːlɪ). *Eccl.* [med.L. *sanctorāle*, f. *sanct-us* saint, after temporale. Cf. Sp. *santoral.*] That part of the breviary and missal which contains the offices proper for saints' days.

1872 Shipley *Gloss. Eccl. Terms* s.v. *Temporale*, The temporale..as opposed to the sanctorale..which treats of the Saints' days. **1905** M. Rule in *Athenæum* 7 Jan. 20/1 The Sanctorale of the Canterbury Missal.

Sanctorian (sæŋk'tɔərɪən), *a.* [f. mod.L. *Sanctōri-us* (It. *Santorio*), a Venetian physician (1561–1636): see -an.] Of or pertaining to Sanctorius, who made experiments and calculations on insensible perspiration by means of a 'statical chair'. **Sanctorian perspiration**, insensible perspiration, first discovered by Sanctorius. **Sanctorian table**, a register of the quantities of perspiration, etc.

For earlier references to the experiments of Sanctorius (not containing this adj.) see **1663** Boyle *Usef. Exp. Nat. Philos.* II. iv. 116 and **1711** Addison *Spect.* No. 25 ⁋2.

1740 Cheyne *Regimen* p. liii, To try, by a Sanctorian Chair, the Quantity and Quality of those Foods that perspire the most and soonest. **1743** Lining in *Phil. Trans.* XLIII. 318 Two Columns in my Sanctorian Tables, where I have daily supposed the Ingesta to be 100 Ounces. **1744** tr. *Boerhaave's Inst.* III. 306 Through these [vessels] is perpetually transpired a very subtle Humour from every Point of the Body, called from its Inventor the Sanctorian Perspiration. **1774** Goldsm. *Nat. Hist.* (1824) I. 219 *note*, From this experiment also, the learned may gather upon what a weak foundation the whole doctrine of the Sanctorian perspiration is built. **1849–52** *Todd's Cycl. Anat.* IV. 842/1 Sanctorius..made lengthened experiments on perspiration. The insensible perspiration has..been termed 'Sanctorian' in honour of him.

sanc'torium. *rare*⁻¹. [quasi-Latin, irreg. f. L. *sanctus* saint *sb.*¹ + -orium.] A shrine.

1816 Keatinge *Trav.* I. 326 Edriss,..the great saint of the Moors,..fled hither, and a sanctorium to his memory is now extant..near Fez, which..was founded by this sect.

†**sanc'torum.** ? *jocular. Obs.* [a. L. *sanctōrum*, gen. pl. of *sanctus* holy, saint.] **a.** ? Persons of superior rank. **b.** quasi-*adj.* Irreproachable.

1675 A. Huyberts *Corner-Stone* 19 The Sanctorum must not be made too common, nor the Commons be over-stock't. **1824** in *Spirit Publ. Jrnls.* (1825) 395 An age like this,..So bright its magisterial quorum, Its kings so holy in alliance, Its navy, every man sanctorum.

sanctuaried ('sæŋktjuːərɪd), *a. rare.* [f. sanctuary *sb.*¹ + -ed².] That is made, or that contains, a sanctuary.

1852 *Meanderings of Mem.* I. 175 If a thought Should cream the blood in sanctuaried court. **1897** F. Thompson *New Poems* 26 In the sanctuaried East.

‖**sanctu'arium.** *rare.* [L.] = sanctuary *sb.*¹ 2.

1796 *Mod. Gulliver's Trav.* 67 He knew me, so without ringing or inquiry, opened the portal of the sanctuarium.

sanctuarize ('sæŋktjʊəraɪz), *v. rare.* [f. sanctuar(y *sb.*¹ + -ize.] *trans.* To afford sanctuary to; to shelter by means of a sanctuary or sacred privileges.

1602 Shaks. *Ham.* IV. vii. 128 *Laer.* To cut his throat i' th' Church. *Kin.* No place indeed should murder Sanctuarize; Reuenge should haue no bounds. **1609** Sir E. Hoby *Let. to T. H[iggons]* 15 The Jesuites, you knew, were no ordinary guls, and therfore, if you ment to be Sanctuarised by them, it lay you in hand first, *Audere aliquid carcere dignum*, to ascertaine them by some audacious proiect, of your future fidelitie. **1829** James *Richelieu* xxxv, 'Were he charged with all the crimes which disgrace humanity,' replied the bishop, 'here he is sanctuarized.'

sanctuary ('sæŋktjuːərɪ), *sb.*¹ Forms: 4–6 **saint-, saynt-, seint-, seyntuary(e, -uarie, -(e)warie, -wary(e,** (4 **seyntiwarie,** 5 **sceyntewarye, seyntery);** 4–6 **sentuary(e, -uarie, -wary,** (6 **senttuary, centuary, sentory, centory, cent(e)ry);** 6 **santuary;** 5–7 **sainctuarie, -uary;** 4–7 **sanctuarye,** 4– **sanctuary.** [a. OF. *sain(c)tuarie, sain(c)tuaire* (whence the form saintuaire), mod.F. *sanctuaire* (= Pr. *sanctuari*, Cat. *santuari*, Sp., Pg., It. *santuario*), semi-pop. ad. L. *sanctuārium*, app. irreg. f. *sanct-us* holy (? on the analogy of sacrarium). The present form of the word, which is due to recourse to the original Latin, occurs almost as early as the forms taken from OF.

The Latin word is post-Augustan; in classical Latin (Pliny) it occurs only in the sense of 'the private cabinet of a prince' (L. & Sh.); the sense of 'holy place' is common in the Vulgate and in Christian Latin generally.]

I. A holy place.

1. a. *gen.* A building or place set apart for the worship of God or of one or more divinities: applied, e.g., to a Christian church, the Jewish temple and the Mosaic tabernacle, a heathen temple or site of local worship, and the like; also *fig.* to the church or body of believers.

a **1340** Hampole *Cant. Moysi* 21 in *Psalter* (1884) 507 Þi sanctuary lord þe whilk þi hend festynd; lord sall regne wiþouten end and ouyre. In þat sanctuary oure lord sall be kynge, þat is in all sauyd men, wiþouten end. **1382** Wyclif *Exod.* xxv. 8 And thei shulen make to me a seyntuarye, and Y shal dwelle in the myddil of hem. **1508** Fisher *Penit. Ps.* cii. Wks. (1876) 198 *Filij seruorum tuorum habitabunt.* The children of thy seruauntes shall be permanent in thy sentuary. **1530** Tindale *Prol. Exod.*, Sanctuarie, a place halowed and dedicate vnto god. **1535** Coverdale *Tobit* xiii. 11 The people shal come vnto the from farre, they shal bringe giftes, and worshipe yᵉ Lorde in the, and thy londe shal they haue for a Sanctuary, for they shal call vpon the greate name in the. **1603** Shaks. *Meas. for M.* II. ii. 171 Hauing waste ground enough, Shall we desire to raze the Sanctuary And pitch our euils there? **1671** Milton *Samson* 1674 Chaunting thir Idol, and preferring Before our living Dread who dwells In Silo his bright Sanctuary. *a* **1729** J. Rogers *Serm.* xvii. (1735) 371 Let it not be imagined, that they contribute nothing to the Happiness of the Countrey, who only serve God in the Duties of a holy Life; who attend his Sanctuary, and daily address his Goodness to pardon the Sins of the Land. **1830** Leake *Trav. Morea* II. 426 Strabo ..describes the Epidaurian sanctuary as 'a place renowned for the cure of all sorts of diseases'. **1863** H. B. Hackett in *Smith's Dict. Bible* III. 1278/1 Shiloh was one of the earliest and most sacred of the Hebrew sanctuaries. **1871** R. Ellis tr. *Catullus* lxiii. 3 When he near'd the leafy forest, dark sanctuary divine [L. *loca Deæ*]. **1888** W. R. Smith in *Encycl. Brit.* XXIII. 165/2 A temple implies a sanctuary; but a sanctuary or holy spot does not necessarily contain a temple.

b. *fig.* Used for: The priestly office or order.

c **1380** Wyclif *Serm.* Sel. Wks. I. 25 In þis dede þat Crist dide, he techiþ his Chirche to bygynne for to purge his seintuarie, þat ben preests and clerks þerof. **1781** Gibbon *Decl. & F.* xx. (1787) II. 217 But the Christian sanctuary was open to every ambitious candidate, who aspired to its heavenly promises, or temporal possessions.

c. Applied to Heaven.

1382 Wyclif *Deut.* xxvi. 15 Bihold fro thi sanctuary, fro the hiȝe dwellynge place of heuens [Vulg. *de sanctuario tuo*]. **1535** Coverdale *Ps.* ci[i]. 19 For He loketh downe from his Sanctuary, out of the heauen doth the Lorde beholde the earth. *a* **1586** Sidney *Ps.* xx. ii, From santuary hy Let him come downe. **1667** Milton *P.L.* VI. 672 Had not th' Almightie Father where he sits Shrin'd in his Sanctuarie of Heav'n secure, Consulting [etc.].

d. *transf.*

1445 in *Anglia* XXVIII. 261 Fides thyn herte enbracyth As hir propir sanctuary, and medelith with al thi deedys. **1584** Whetstone *Mirrour for Mag.* 23 The Dicing-houses and other lyke Sanctuaries of iniquitie. **1796** Morse *Amer. Geog.* II. 170 The famous isle of Iona was once the seat and sanctuary of western learning. **1821** Byron *Two Fosc.* IV. i, *Sen[ator].* I sought not A place within a sanctuary; but being Chosen..I shall fulfill my office. **1831** Brewster *Newton* x. 120 Admiring disciples crowded to this sanctuary of the sciences [*sc.* Tycho Brahe's observatory of Uranibourg] to acquire the knowledge of the heavens. **1870** Max Müller *Sci. Relig.* (1873) 142 Entirely expelled from the sanctuary of the human mind.

e. ***to weigh*** (or ***examine***) ***with the weights*** (or ***scales***) ***of the sanctuary***: to test by the standard of divine revelation. Also, to examine by an equal and just scale (see quot. 1728), after F. *peser une chose au poids du sanctuaire, dans la balance du sanctuaire* (Littré).

Suggested by Vulg. *ad* (or *juxta*) *pondus sanctuarii, pondere sanctuarii* Lev. v. 15, Num. vii. 13, 19, 25, 31, 37, xviii. 16. The force of the orig. Heb. expression would be more accurately rendered by 'according to the sacred shekel'.

1617 Moryson *Itin.* III. 43 Setting humane experience aside, we will waigh this by the holy scales of the Sanctuarie. **1728** Chambers *Cycl.* s.v., To..examine a Thing by the Weight of the *Sanctuary*, is to examine it by a just and equal Scale.

2. A specially holy place within a temple or church. **a.** In the Mosaic tabernacle and the Jewish temple: the holy place, including the 'Holy of holies' (see holy *sb.* 5); sometimes applied to the latter only.

† ***sanctuary*** (or ***sanctuaries***) ***of the sanctuary***: a literal rendering of the Vulg. *sanctuarium (-aria) sanctuarii*, which inaccurately represents the Heb. for 'Holy of holies'.

1382 Wyclif *Exod.* xxvi. 33 The veyle forsothe be it sett yn bi cercles, with ynne the whiche thou shalt put the arke of testymonye, and with the which the seyntuarye, and the seyntuarye [*v.r.* sayntuarise] of the seyntuarie [Vulg. *sanctuarii sanctuaria*] shulen be dyuydid. *a* **1656** Ussher *Power Princes* I. (1683) 66 To be put in Tables of Brass, and to be set up within the compass of the Sanctuary in a conspicuous place. **1737** Whiston *Josephus, Antiq.* III. vi. §4 It [the veil] was to be drawn this way or that way by cords, the rings of which..were subservient to the drawing and undrawing of the veil, and to the fastening it at the corner, that then it might be no hinderance to the view of the sanctuary, especially on solemn days.

b. *Eccl.* That part of a church round the altar, the sacrarium; also used by some for the chancel.

a **1400–50** *Alexander* 1567 (Dublin MS.), And of þe sanctuary [Ashm. MS. saynt-ware] mony seere þinges, With tabels & tapers & tretes of þe law. **1577** Hanmer tr. *Eusebius' Eccl. Hist.* x. iv. 189 *margin*, A space betwene the Sanctuary & the porche. **1585** Higins *Junius' Nomencl.* 307 *Sacrarium* ..the sanctuarie or chauncell. **1708–22** J. Bingham *Orig. Eccles.* VIII. vi. §11 Wks. 1726 I. 300 In the middle of the Bema, or Sanctuary. **1788** Gibbon *Decl. & F.* xlix. V. 97 That all the images should be removed from the sanctuary and altar to a proper height in the churches. **1870** F. R. Wilson *Ch. Lindisf.* 35 The sanctuary is raised one step. *a* **1878** Sir G. G. Scott *Lect. Archit.* (1879) II. 40 The chancel, or rather the sanctuary, was apsidal, with a surrounding aisle. **1885** *Cath. Dict.* (ed. 3), *Sanctuary*, the part of the church round the high altar reserved for clergy.

c. The most sacred part of any temple; the 'cella', 'adytum'.

1412–20 Lydg. *Chron. Troy* II. 3810 For þei cast no longer for to tarie, But prowdely entre in þe seintuarie, In-to þe chapel callid Cytheroun. *Ibid.* IV. xxx. (1513) Svb, With many flawme and many hydous lyght That brent enuyrowne in the seyntuarye [1555 sentuarye]. **1857** Wilkinson *Egypt. Pharaohs* 141 Within this sanctuary was the statue of the god, and the altar for sacrifice or for libation; and to it the priests alone had access. **1875** *Encycl. Brit.* II. 388/2 The sanctuary, *adytum* or σηκός (fig. 4), still contained the idol and its altar.

d. *fig.*

1642 D. Rogers *Naaman* Ep. Ded. 2 We are come now beyond the Porch and Sanctuary, even to the Holy of Holies. **1686** [Hickes] *Spec. B. Virg.* 38 They pray to her..to admit them within the Sanctuary of her Audience. **1795** Burke *Let. to W. Elliot* Wks. 1842 II. 244 But now the veil was torn, and, to keep off sacrilegious intrusion, it was necessary that in the sanctuary of government some-thing should be disclosed not only venerable, but dreadful. **1815** Shelley *Alastor* 38 And, though ne'er yet Thou hast unveiled thy inmost sanctuary. **1841** W. Spalding *Italy & It. Isl.* I. 129 His writings..form only the portico to the temple of wisdom; but the singular beauty of the approach invites the student, and its ease of access secures his progress to the sanctuary beyond.

†3. A shrine or box containing relics. *Obs.*

c **1386** CHAUCER *Pard. T.* 625 But by the croys which that seint Eleyne fond, I wolde I hadde thy coillons in myn hond In stede of relikes or of seintuarie. **1393** LANG. *P. Pl.* C. VI. 79 Popes and patrones poure gentil blod refuseþ, And taken symondes sone seyntewarie [*v.r.* sanctuarye] to kepe. *c* **1400** *Laud Troy Bk.* 18043 Thei did the relikes brynge,.. Here saynteuarius with al her gere... Diomedes was ffurst that swore, And made his othe vpon the flore, He swor by al here saynteuaries. *c* **1450** *Merlin* iv. 75 Than the kynge made be brought the hiest seintewaries that he hadde, and the beste relikes, and ther-on they dide swere as Merlin dide hem devyse. **1471** CAXTON *Recuyell* (Sommer) II. 664 Than cam the day that the grekes shold swere the peas faynedly vpon the playn felde vpon the sayntuaryes. **1481** —— *Godeffroy* xxxvii. 205 They helde the crosse and the saínctuaryes with whiche they blessyd the peple.

4. A piece of consecrated ground; the precincts of a church; a churchyard, cemetery. Now *dial.* (See also *sanctuary garth* in 8 below.)

There seems to have been some confusion between *seintuary*, *centry*, etc. (ME. forms of *sanctuary*) and CEMETERY.

1432-50 tr. *Higden* (Rolls) V. 65 [He] made a seyntuary [*Trevisa* chirchehawe, L. *cœmeterium*] in the cite of Rome, in the way callede Via Appia, to bery the bodies of martires. *a* **1450** MYRC *Par. Pr.* 330 Also wyth-ynne chyrche and seyntwary Do ryȝt thus as I the say. **1872** *J. Glyde's Norfolk Garland* i. 28 'If I were on any occasion to urge a parishioner to inter a deceased relative on the north side of the church, he would answer me with some expression of surprise, ..."No, sir, it is not in the sanctuary."'

II. 5. a. A church or other sacred place in which, by the law of the mediæval church, a fugitive from justice, or a debtor, was entitled to immunity from arrest. Hence, in wider sense, applied to any place in which by law or established custom a similar immunity is secured to fugitives.

By English common law, a fugitive charged with any offence but sacrilege and treason might escape punishment by taking refuge in a sanctuary, and within forty days confessing his crime and taking an oath which subjected him to perpetual banishment. By the act 21 Jac. I. c. 28 §7 (1625) the right of sanctuary in criminal cases was abolished. Certain places, chiefly actual or reputed precincts of former royal palaces, as Whitefriars, the Savoy, and the Mint, continued to be sanctuaries in civil cases until their privilege was abolished by the acts 8 & 9 Will. III. c. 27 §15 (1696-7) and 9 Geo. I. c. 28 (1722). The abbey of Holyrood is still by law a sanctuary for debtors, but the abolition of imprisonment for debt has rendered the privilege useless.

c **1374** CHAUCER *Boeth.* I. pr. iv. 10 (Camb. MS.) To whiche Iugement they nolden nat obeye but defendedyn hem by the sikernesse of holy howses, þat is to seyn fledden in to sentuarye. **1463-4** *Rolls of Parlt.* V. 507/2 Eny persone ..that shall dwelle or inhabit within the Saynțwarie and Procyncte of the same Chapell. **1474** *Ibid.* VI. 110/1 Such persones as were endetted..and by fraude went to seyntuaries. **1477** *Ibid.* 183/2 Eny persone or persones havyng eny places of Tuitionez comonly called Seintwaries, as to eny Privilege, Libertee, Tuition or Fraunches. **1480** CAXTON *Chron. Eng.* ccli. x2b, Also this same yere the shereuis of london fette oute of Seint Martins the graunt the sayntwarie fiue persones, whiche afterward were restored agayne to the Sayntwarie by the kynges Iustices. *c* **1500** in *Arnolde's Chron.* (1811) p. xxxix, Perkin Warbek..fled to Bewdeley sentwary [cf. **1556** *Chron. Gr. Friars* (Camden) 25 He flede to Bewdley sentuary]. **1534** in *Lett. Suppress. Monasteries* (Camden) 39 Men sayd that the sayntuary shall, aftre this settyng of the parliament, hold no man for dett, morder, nor felenye. **1537** *Orig. & Sprynge of Sectes* H vij, The churches are a centuary for mysdoers. **1596** SPENSER *F.Q.* IV. ix. 19 That all the while he by his side her bore, She was as safe as in a Sanctuary. **1610** HOLLAND *Camden's Brit.* (1637) 811 Who..withdrew himselfe into a monastery hard by, which was counted a Sanctuary, and therefore not to be forced or broken. *c* **1710** CELIA FIENNES *Diary* (1888) 68 Just by the Communion table is the Sanctuary or place of refuge where Criminalls flee for safety. **1819** SCOTT *Ivanhoe* xli, If thou breathest aught that can attaint the honour of my house, by Saint George! not the altar itself shall be a sanctuary. **1839** H. AINSWORTH *Jack Sheppard* I. ii. 42 In order to guard against accidents or surprises, watchmen or scouts..were stationed at the three main outlets of the sanctuary [*sc.* the mint at Southwark] ready to give the signal in the manner just described. **1863** GEO. ELIOT *Romola* xxiv, The church was a sanctuary which he had a right to claim.

b. Applied to a similar place of refuge in a non-Christian country; an asylum.

c **1400** MAUNDEV. (1839) vi. 66 That Cytee [Ebron] was also Sacerdotalle, that is to seyne, seyntuarie, of the Tribe of Juda: And it was so fre, that Men receyved there alle manere of Fugityfes of other places, for here evyl Dedis. **1662** J. DAVIES tr. *Olearius' Voy. Ambass.* 353 He caus'd the Place where he was kill'd to be encompass'd with a high Wall, made a Sanctuary of it. *c* **1700** *Tarquin & Tullia* 10 in *Poems Aff. St.* (1704) III. 319 To form his Party, Histories report, A Sanctuary was open'd in his Court, Where glad Offenders safely might resort. **1878** P. GARDNER in *Encycl. Brit.* VIII. 468/1 Besides being a place of worship, a museum, and a sanctuary, the Ephesian temple was a great bank. **1897** MARY KINGSLEY *W. Africa* xx. 466 From the penalty and inconveniences of these accusations of witch-craft there is but one escape, namely flight to a sanctuary. There are several sanctuaries in Congo Français.

c. *transf.* and *fig.*

1568 ASCHAM *Scholem.* I. (Arb.) 49 Vsing alwaise soch discrete moderation, as the scholehouse should be counted a sanctuarie against feare. **1685** CROWNE *Sir C. Nice* v. 49 My house is your Sanctuary, and here to offer you violence, wou'd prejudice myself. **1776** PAINE *Com. Sense* (1791) 34 The reformation was preceded by the discovery of America, as if the Almighty graciously meant to open a sanctuary to the persecuted in future years, when home should afford neither friendship nor safety. **1856** EMERSON *Eng. Traits, Ability* Wks. (Bohn) II. 41 They have made..London..a sanctuary to refugees of every political and religious opinion. **1861** TULLOCH *Eng. Purit.* I. 38 His [Abbot's] house was a sanctuary to the most eminent of the factious party.

d. An area of land within which (wild) animals or plants are protected and encouraged to breed or grow.

1879 A. P. VIVIAN *Wanderings in Western Land* xiii. 299 The suggestion..of setting apart certain districts as 'sanctuaries', within which the buffalo should never be molested, is one well worthy of consideration. **1887** [see *bird sanctuary* s.v. BIRD *sb.* 9]. **1897** *Cornh. Mag.* Jan. 37 The national forests will become, as the New Forest is now in some measure, sanctuaries for all the animals *feræ naturæ* of England. **1909** *Bull. N.Y. Zool. Soc.* June 511/2 Around the coast there is gradually being extended a chain of insular bird sanctuaries that means much to the avifauna of North America. **1943** J. S. HUXLEY *TVA* 54 Game management areas and game refuges or sanctuaries have been set up. **1975** M. RUSSELL *Murder by Mile* iii. 26 The glen's by way of being something of a bird and animal sanctuary. **1978** *Country Life* 16 Nov. 1632/1 Rare and vulnerable plants and animals will be protected by setting aside 'sanctuaries'.

6. a. Immunity from punishment and the ordinary operations of the law secured by taking refuge in a sanctuary (sense 5); the right or privilege of affording such shelter; shelter, refuge, protection as afforded by a church, etc. Also ***privilege of sanctuary***. †***to keep sanctuary***: to resort to a sanctuary for protection. ***to violate*** or ***break sanctuary***: to violate the privilege or right of a sanctuary or place of refuge.

c **1380** WYCLIF *Sel. Wks.* III. 294 þei chalengen fraunchise and privylegie in many grete chirchis, þat wikid men..þere schullen dwelle in seyntewarie, and no man empeche hem bi processe of lawe. *c* **1380** —— *Wks.* (1880) 280 þat þefte & raueynen & mansleyng & robberie be not meyntened in seyntiwarye vnder colour of priuylegie. *c* **1430** LYDG. *Min. Poems* (Percy Soc.) 167 He is like a fugitif that rennythe to seyntwarye For drede of hangyng. **1464** *Coventry Leet Bk.* 322 The parker & oþer Officers of Cheylesmore pretendyng..that eny persones owed not to be arrested there, seying that Cheylesmore was seyntwary. **1471** SIR J. PASTON in *P. Lett.* III. 15 The Erle of Oxenffordys bretheryn be goon owt off Sceyntewarye. **1509** in I. S. Leadam *Sel. Cas. Crt. Requests* (Selden Soc.) 12 Your pore orator..neuyr dare come oute off seyntory. **1513** MORE *Rich. III* in Hall *Chron., Edw. V* (1548) 8 That ye kynges brother should be fayne to kepe sanctuary. **1577-87** HOLINSHED *Chron.* III. 1079/1 This woman..fled in the night to Westminster for sanctuarie. **1594** SHAKS. *Rich. III*, III. i. 42 God forbid We should infringe the holy Priuiledge Of blessed Sanctuarie. *Ibid.* 47 You breake not Sanctuarie, in seizing him [the Dk. of York]. **1623-4** *Act 21 Jas. I*, c. 28 §7 And be it alsoe enacted..That no Sanctuarie or Priviledge of Sanctuary shalbe hereafter admitted or allowed in any case. **1624** HEYWOOD *Captives* III. ii. in Bullen *O. Pl.* IV. 155 Theft, rapine, contempt of religion, and breach of sanctury. **1708-22** J. BINGHAM *Orig. Eccles.* VIII. x. §12 Wks. 1726 I. 334 Both by general Custom and Law under the Christian Emperors, every Church was invested with the Privilege of an Asylum, or Place of Sanctuary and Refuge in certain Cases. **1781** GIBBON *Decl. & F.* xx. (1787) II. 223 The ancient privilege of sanctuary was transferred to the Christian temples. **1822** SCOTT *Nigel* xvi, Get into Whitefriars or somewhere for sanctuary and concealment, till you can make friends or quit the city. **1831** *Ibid.* Introd., Alsatia..possessing certain privileges of sanctuary, became for that reason a nest of..mischievous characters. **1859** TENNYSON *Guinevere* 140 Mine enemies Pursue me, but, O peaceful Sisterhood, Receive, and yield me sanctuary. **1871** R. W. DALE *Commandm.* vi. 148 The altar of God itself was to be no sanctuary for..an actual murderer. **1898** J. T. FOWLER *Durham Cath.* 63 Those who sought sanctuary fled to the church and knocked.

b. in non-Christian countries (see 5 b); also *transf.* and *fig.*

1601 HOLLAND *Pliny* I. 138 The Priuiledged place whereinto the Persians vse to retyre for sanctuarie. **1641** EVELYN *Diary* 7 Aug., The Chapell and Refectory [of the Convent] full of the goods of such poor people as at the approach of the Army had fled with them thither for sanctuary. **1654** in *T. Burton's Diary* (1828) I. Introd. 23 Which, if in truth any would offer to impeach, by violence from without, it could receive no sanctuary nor advantage at all from such a declaration. **1655** GURNALL *Chr. in Arm.* I. 32 A Heathen could say when a bird (scared by a Hawke) flew into his bosome, I will not betray thee unto thy enemy, seeing thou comest for Sanctuary unto me. How much lesse will God yield up a soule unto its enemy, when it takes Sanctuary in his Name. **1659** HAMMOND *On Ps.* lxii. 7 On him only I rely ..for sanctuary when any distresse surrounds me. **1692** R. L'ESTRANGE *Fables* liii. 53 A Stag that was hard set by the Huntsmen, betook himself to a Stall for Sanctuary, and prevail'd with the Oxen to Conceal him the best they could. *a* **1711** KEN *Past. Let.* Wks. (1838) 476 Many poor Protestant strangers are now fled hither for sanctuary, whom as brethren, as members of Christ, we should take in and cherish. **1741** *Compl. Fam.-Piece* II. i. 294 When a Bitch Fox is bragged, and with Cub, she is hardly to be taken; for then she lieth near the Earth, and upon hearing the least Noise, she betakes herself to her Place of Sanctuary. **1788** GIBBON *Decl. & F.* l. (1846) V. 18 The precincts of Mecca enjoyed the rights of sanctuary. **1828-40** TYTLER *Hist. Scot.* (1864) I. 43 The churches, to which the miserable inhabitants had fled for sanctuary, were violated and defiled with blood. **1849** GROTE *Greece* II. xlv. V. 469 Pleistoanax.. lived for a long time in sanctuary near the temple of Athênê, at Tegea. **1855** HAWTHORNE *Eng. Note-bks.* (1870) I. 397 It now rained heavily and..we..betook ourselves to sanctuary, taking refuge in St. Paul's Cathedral.

c. ***to take sanctuary***: to take refuge in a sanctuary. Also *transf.* and *fig.*

1429 *Rolls of Parlt.* IV. 360/2 Merchantz straungiers, yat ..have stollen away, and daily taken seyntuaries. **1472-3** *Ibid.* VI. 20/1 That he never toke eny seyntwary, ne withdrewe hym from your good grace. **1504** in I. S. Leadam *Sel. Cas. Crt. Requests* (Selden Soc.) 8 Your saide besechar whan he was at large toke saynteweary and lost his goodes. **1513** MORE *Rich. III* (1883) 31 What if a mannes wyfe will take saintuary because she lyste to runne from her husbande. **1556** J. HEYWOOD *Spider & F.* lii. 14 The spiders ..In the copweb took sentuarie for defence. **1592** *Arden of Feversham* v. ii. 12, I haue the gould; what care I though it be knowne! Ile crosse the water and take sanctuary. **1613** PURCHAS *Pilgrimage* (1614) 75 The fishes which are many, haue taken Sanctuary in these waters, and none dare take them, but holde them holy. **1625** J. ROBINSON *Ess.* xxiv. (1851) I. 110 What intention could be better or action worse? We must not therefore take the sanctuary of fools by good meanings without knowledge. **1640** YORKE *Union Hon.* 40 In the beginning of King Edward's raigne, she was forced to take sanctuary at Westminster. **1705** STANHOPE *Paraphr.* II. 627 The Evasions of this Nature being only such miserable Shifts, as the Jews of later Ages have taken Sanctuary in. **1708-22** J. BINGHAM *Orig. Eccles.* VIII. xi. §3 Wks. 1726 I. 335 Next..we are to consider..in what Cases they were allowed to take Sanctuary in their Churches. **1725** DE FOE *Voy. round World* (1840) 72 The gunner who had taken sanctuary in the woods. **1745** P. THOMAS *Jrnl. Anson's Voy.* 41 The Sea-Lions..will..if you pursue them, be glad to take Sanctuary in the Water. **1785** WILKINS tr. *Bhagvat* xiv. 97 They take sanctuary under this wisdom. **1878** STEVENSON *Inland Voy., Oise in Flood* 104 Terrified creatures taking sanctuary in every nook along the shore.

7. *Hunting*, etc.: The 'privilege of forest'; also 'close time'.

1603 OWEN *Pembrokeshire* (1892) 265 As for hartes and hindes..yett some there are, and those lyve without sanctuarye or priviledge of fforest, free for every man to chase and hunte, at theire pleasure. **1892** *Daily News* 19 Apr. 3/5 Application was made to the Chief Ranger..for her [the hind's] recapture; but he promptly refused, on the grounds that the Forest was a 'sanctuary', and any wild animal escaping into the same was 'of right free of the forest'. The impossibility of uncarting a deer and preventing its getting into the forest,..has by the enforcement of this 'right of sanctuary', aided the authorities in putting a stop to 'Easter deer-baiting'. **1898** *Westm. Gaz.* 3 May 3/1 He would..extend the weekly close time, and he believes that if the present period of sanctuary was doubled, in a year or two at most the nets would be catching far more fish [salmon] than they now do in the longer period.

III. 8. *attrib.* and *Comb.* **a.** Of senses 1-4, as ***sanctuary lamp***, †***observance***, ***stair***, ***temple***; †***sanctuary garth*** = sense 4.

c **1400** *Apol. Loll.* 35 Ȝe..han put kepars of my sanctuari obseruaunce to ȝor silf. **1412-13** *Durham Acc. Rolls* (Surtees) 610 Subtus cameram d'ni Prioris versus Seyntery-garth, 14*d.* *c* **1600** *Rites of Durham* (Surtees) 52 The sentuarie garth. *Ibid.* 53 The Sentory garthe. *c* **1624** *Ibid.* 205 *note*, Sanctuary garth. **1850** WILKINSON *Archit. Anc. Egypt* 82 Sanctuary Temples, consisting of a single chamber. **1862** H. E. M. tr. *Monnin's Curé d'Ars* Pref. 7 When I saw, by the light of the sanctuary-lamp, that wasted and withered form. **1866** *Direct. Anglic.* (ed. 3) 259 Sanctuary Lamp, that which burns before the Blessed Sacrament when it is reserved. **1893** F. THOMPSON *Poems* 45 The cowlèd night Kneels on the Eastern sanctuary-stair.

b. Of senses 5 and 6, as ***sanctuary-breaking***, ***knocker***, ***place***, ***-seat***, ***town***.

a **1529** SKELTON *Sp. Parrot* 496 So myche *sayntuary brekyng, and preuylegidde barrydd. **1886** *Encycl. Brit.* XXI. 255/2 The sanctuary seats at Hexham and Beverley and the *sanctuary knocker at Durham are still in existence. **1529** RASTELL *Pastyme* (1811) 297 Wherefore suche gentylmen as had appoynted to eyde the duke fled, some to *sentwary places, and some beyonde the sea. **1886** *Sanctuary seat [see *sanctuary knocker* supra]. *a* **1548** HALL *Chron., Hen. VIII* 54 Richard Horsnayle Bailyfe of the *sanctuary towne called Good Esture in Essex.

†c. sanctuary man (so also ***sanctuary woman***, etc.), a man who has taken refuge in a sanctuary or privileged place of protection. *Obs.*

1494 FABYAN *Chron.* VII. 530 They went to Westmynster, and toke wt them all maner of seyntwary men. **1513** MORE *Rich. III* (1883) 31 Verely I haue often heard of saintuarye menne. But I neuer heard erste of saintuarye chyldren. **1529** RASTELL *Pastyme* (1811) 282 She went into Westmyster, and there regystarde her selfe as a sentwary woman. **1622** BACON *Hen. VII* 39 If any Sanctuarie-man did by night or otherwise, get out of Sanctuarie priuily, and commit mischiefe and trespasse, and then come in againe, hee should loose the benefit of Sanctuarie for euer after.

'sanctuary, *sb.*[2] *dial.* [Corruption of CENTAURY.]

[**1530** PALSGR. 268/2 Seyntuary an herbe.] **1877** E. LEIGH *Chesh. Gloss.* 175. **1886** BRITTEN & HOLLAND *Eng. Plant-n.*

†'sanctuary, *v. Obs. rare.* [f. SANCTUARY *sb.*[1]] *trans.* To place in safety as in a sanctuary. Of a place: to afford protection or shelter (*from*).

1615 HEYWOOD *Foure Prentises* D 3, Thy purse is sanctuary'd. **1631** —— *Fair Maid West* I. 9 Feare not sweet Spencer, we are now alone, And thou art sanctuar'd in these mine armes. **1655** FULLER *Ch. Hist.* IV. iv. §19 The Kings enemies once Sanctuaried, daring him no less then the Iebusites in their strong fort of Sion defied David. *c* **1676** LADY CHAWORTH in *12th Rep. Hist. MSS. Comm.* App. v. 32 St. James's where she had lodgings to sanctuary her from debt.

‖**sanctum** ('sæŋktəm), *sb.* Also 9 *pl. rare* **sancta**. [L. *sanctum*, neut. of *sanctus* holy.]

1. The 'holy place' of the Jewish tabernacle and temple. Also applied to a sacred place or shrine in other temples and churches. Cf. SANCTUARY *sb.*[1] 2.

1577 tr. *Bullinger's Decades* III. v. 340 The tabernacle, that is diuided..into the *Sanctum* and the *Sanctum sanctorum*.

1847–8 H. Miller *First Impr.* ii. (1857) 24 Who, in exploring a magnificent temple, passed through superb porticoes and noble halls, to find a monkey enthroned in a little dark sanctum as the god of the whole. **1855** *Englishwoman in Russia* 72 We ladies are not allowed to enter the 'sanctum' [of the Kazan church].

fig. **1858** Trollope *Three Clerks* xvii, Flower shows..are open to ladies who cannot quite penetrate the inner sancta of fashionable life.

2. = sanctum sanctorum 2.

1819 T. Hope *Anastasius* (1820) III. xiv. 362 He..then dragged us by main force into what he called his sanctum. **1838** Lytton *Alice* iii. iii, He found the banker in his private sanctum. **1850** Kingsley *Alt. Locke* vi, His sanctum behind the shop. **1870** H. Smart *Race for Wife* ii, Maude flits away to her own little sanctum. **1883** Ld. R. Gower *My Remin.* I. ii. 26 This room was..the sanctum of a scholar and a man of refinement.

‖**sanctum sanctorum** (ˈsæŋktəm sæŋkˈtɔərəm). Pl. **sancta sanctorum**. [L. *sanctum* neut. nom. sing. and *sanctōrum* neut. gen. pl. of *sanctus* holy; a Hebraism, transl. (= LXX. τὸ ἅγιον τῶν ἁγίων) of *qōdesh haqqōdāshīm*, 'Holy of holies' (see holy *sb.* 1). The Vulgate (following the LXX) several times uses the pl. *sancta sanctorum* in the same sense as the sing., without any warrant from the original Hebrew.]

1. The Holy of holies of the Jewish temple and tabernacle. †In early use also pl. in the same sense.

c **1400** *Apol. Loll.* 35 Þei..schal not nye to al My sanctuari, bi þe sancta sanctorum [*Ezek.* xliv. 13]. ? **1493** *St. Katherine* (W. de W.) b iij a/1 (Stanf.) That holy place that is called Sancta sanctorum. **1558** Morwyng tr. *Joseph Ben Gorion's Hist. Jews* (1561) 36 b, Thei entred also into the Sanctuary, and attempted to enter into the *sanctum sanctōrum*. **1577** [see sanctum 1]. **1714** Addison *Spect.* No. 580 ¶3 In Solomon's Temple there was the *Sanctum Sanctorum*. **1787** *Minor* 181 Mysteries, which, like the sanctum sanctorum of the Jewish Tabernacle, should never be exhibited to the profane world. **1841** Catlin *N. Amer. Ind.* lviii. (1844) II. 232 The Jews had their sanctum sanctorums.

fig. **1622** Mabbe tr. *Aleman's Guzman D'Alf.* i. ii. iv. 123 [He] that buyes an Office, whose money only (without any other merit) hath inthroned him in the *Sancta Sanctorum* of the world. **1643** Sir T. Browne *Relig. Med.* i. §13 There is no danger to profound these mysteries, no *sanctum sanctorum* in Phylosophy. **1771** Smollett *Humph. Cl.* 5 June, The inner apartment, or 'Sanctum Sanctorum' of this political temple.

b. *transf.*

1598 W. Phillip *Linschoten* i. xliv. 82 The doore of their *Sancta Sanctorum*, or rather *Diabolorum*, being opened, it shewed within like a Lime-kill,..neither was ther any light in al the Church, but that which came in at the doore we entered by. **1738** *Gentl. Mag.* VIII. 146/2 The Door of the Inner Temple, or *Sanctum sanctorum* opened, and discovered the most frightful Idol that ever the wit..of men contrived. **1806** *Edin. Rev.* VIII. 95 Sometimes there is a smaller circle [of stones], which is a sort of *sanctum sanctorum*, in the centre. **1878** J. Payn *By Proxy* I. iii. 35 Oh, that is the *sanctum sanctorum*, in which the..blessed relic of Buddha is kept.

2. A person's private retreat, where he is free from intrusion.

1706 E. Ward *Wooden World Diss.* (1708) 7 The great Cabin is the *Sanctum Sanctorum* he inhabits. **1834** Beckford *Italy* II. 169 We went by appointment to the archbishop confessor's and were immediately admitted into his *sanctum sanctorum*, a snug apartment [etc.]. **1874** Aldrich *Prud. Palfrey* xvii. 368 And now, if you please, we will inspect the sanctum sanctorum of the late incumbent.

transf. **1832** W. Irving *Alhambra* (1875) 122 Here was the sanctum sanctorum of female privacy.

‖**sanctus** (ˈsæŋktəs). Also (senses 2 and 3) 6 **saunts, saunce, saunt(us, 6–7 sant, 7 santus, santo, santez,** 6 (9 *arch.*) **santis.** [L. *sanctus* 'Holy', the first word of the hymn: see saint *a.*]

1. The 'angelic hymn' (from Isa. vi. 3) beginning with the words '*Sanctus, sanctus, sanctus*' ('Holy, holy, holy, Lord God of hosts') which forms the conclusion of the Eucharistic preface; also called tersanctus (thrice holy). Also, the music to which the words are sung.

c **1380** Wyclif *Wks.* (1880) 169 Ioly chauntynge þat.. lettiþ men fro þe sentence of holy writt, as Magnyficat, sanctus & agnus dei. **1450–1530** *Myrr. our Ladye* 119 Therfore accordynge to the aungels, ye synge quyer to quyer, one Sanctus on the tone syde, and another on the tother syde. **1528** Roy *Rede Me* (Arb.) 36 Fare wele O holy consecration With blyssed sanctus and agnus dei. **1567** *Gude & Godlie B.* (S.T.S.) 129 Quhair day and nycht we sall not ceas Ay singand Sanctus sweit. **1895** Benham in W. Andrews *Cur. Ch. Cust.* 265 We always sang the Canticles, and the metrical Psalms..and a few Sanctuses.

†**2.** *transf.* An outcry. Also, something repeated with wearisome iteration. *Obs.*

1594 *2nd Rep. Dr. Faustus* xxii. I 2, The people on both sides exceedingly amazed and affrighted, especiallye the Turkes who sent out such a dolefull Sauntus that it would haue moued the stones to ruth. *a* **1670** Hacket *Cent. Serm.* (1675) 626 For all this they are at their old santez, *What do we?*

†**3. black sanctus,** a kind of burlesque hymn; a discord of harsh sounds expressive of contempt or dislike (formerly used as a kind of serenade to a faithless wife); 'rough music'. Also, *to sing the black sanctus*: to lament. *Obs.*

1578 Lupton *All for Money* B iij, I will make him sing the blacke sanctus, I holde him a grote. **1578** *Bk. Chr. Prayers* 37 But euery man singes his own song, as in a black sanctus. **1582** N. T. (Rhem.) *1 Cor.* xiv. 23 *note*, Singing Psalmes.., one in this language, and another in that, all at once like a blacke saunts, and one often not vnderstood of another. **1591** Lyly *Endym.* iv. ii. 33 It [the sonnet] is sette to the tune of the blacke Saunce, *ratio est*, because *Dipsas* is a black Saint. **1593** Nashe *Christ's T.* (1613) 128 A great number had rather heare a iarring blacke-sant, then one of their balde Sermons. **1598** Marston *Sco. Villanie* ii. vii. 85 The language that they speake Is the pure barbarous blacksaunt of the Geate. **1600** Holland *Livy* v. xxxvii. 204 An hideous and dissonant kind of singing (like a blacke Santus). *a* **1619** Fletcher *Mad Lover* iv. i, Lets sing him a blacke Santis. **1632** Heywood *2nd Part Iron Age* ii. i. D 2 b, Many a blacke-saint..Haue I sung at his window. **1635** Quarles *Embl.* i. x. 41 Sometimes their Stigian cries Send their Black-Santos to the blushing Skies. **1861** *All Year Round* V. 14 The surly sinners sing A horrible black santis, so to cheer The work in hand.

ˈ**sanctus bell.** Forms: *α.* 5– **sanctus bell.** *β.* 5–6 **sanctes, sauntes, (-ys),** 6 **santes, saunctes,** 7 **sants-.** *γ.* 5 **sawnse,** 6–7 **sans, savns, sawnce,** 6–7 (9 *arch.*) **saunce-, sance-.** *δ.* 6–7 **saints,** 7 **saynts-,** 7–8 **saint's.** *ε.* 7 **saint-, St. bell.** *ζ.* 6 **sauncte,** 9 **sancte bell.** [f. sanctus + bell *sb.*[1]] A bell, commonly placed in a 'cote' or turret at the junction of the nave and the chancel (but often a handbell), rung at the Sanctus at Mass; in post-Reformation times often used to summon the people to church, being rung immediately before the service, when the pealing had ceased. (In 16–17th c. freq. used jocularly or allusively.)

α. **1479–81** *Rec. St. Mary at Hill* 101 Item, for nayle to amende the whele of the Sanctus bell. **1661** Blount *Glossogr.* (ed. 2), *Sance Bell* (*campana sancta*), the sanctus Bell. **1875** *Encycl. Brit.* II. 472/2 Sanctus bells have also been placed over the gables of porches.

attrib. **1867** Walker *Ritual Reason Why* 113 Sanctus-bell-cotes remain in many of our churches. **1875** *Encycl. Brit.* II. 472/2 Sanctus Bell-Cot or Turret.

β. **1492–3** *Rec. St. Mary at Hill* 185 Item, to the smyth for mendyng of the sauntys bell, xxijd. *Ibid.* 186 For mendyng of the sanctes bell. **1553** *Ludlow Churchw. Acc.* (Camden) 56 For hangynge of the sauntes bell, and for the corde, ijd. *c* **1618** Moryson *Itin.* iv. v. i. (1903) 457 They ring a knell with one great Bell..or with the Santsbell where they haue none greater.

γ. **1499–1500** *Rec. St. Mary at Hill* 238 Item, ffor a Rope ffor the lytyll Sawnse bell. **1501–2** *Ibid.* 244 The Sans bell. **1538** in *Lett. Suppress. Monasteries* (Camden) 270 Item, ij belles, one a sauncebelle. **1592** G. Harvey *Four Lett.* iii. 47, I am neither so profanely vncharitable as to send him to the Sancebell, to trusse-vp his life with a trice. **1623–33** Fletcher & Shirley *Nt.-Walker* iii. iii, Alas, this is but the Sauncebell, here's a Gentlewoman Will ring you another peale. **1655** J. Phillips *Satyr agst. Hypocrites* 5 Like a crackt Sans-bell jarring in the Steeple. **1885** W. Rye *Hist. Norfolk* 233 A saunce bell or 'ting-tang' *in situ*.

attrib. **1848** B. Webb *Cont. Ecclesiol.* 111 Two sance-bell ropes still hang down in the middle of the Chancel.

δ. **1599** Bp. Hall *Sat.* v. i. 119 Whose shril saints-bell hangs on his louerie While the rest are damned to the plumberie. **1678** *Poor Robin's True Char. of Scold* 4 Her Tongue is the Clapper of the Devil's Saints-bell, that rings all-in to Confusion. **1716** Hearne *Collect.* (O.H.S.) V. 313 It hath 3 Bells and a Saints Bell. **1839** *Hints Study Eccl. Antiq.* (Cambr. Camden Soc. 1842) 24 A Saint's bell, long disused, still hangs in the tower of Great St. Mary's, Cambridge.

ε. **1688** R. Holme *Armoury* iii. 461/2 A Saint Bell, or Hand Bell. *Ibid.* 466/1 St. Bell, a little Bell rung in the Mass [etc.].

ζ. *a* **1553** in *Surrey Archæol. Coll.* IV. 18 Item a sauncte bell. **1854** *N. & Q.* 1st Ser. X. 434/1 The inscription 'Signis cessandis', &c...is..on the 'sancte' bell of the adjoining parish of Clapton. **1855** Rock *Ibid.* XI. 151/1 The first ringing was on the *signa*, or large bells; the last quarter of the hour's ringing was on the smaller bell, the sancte bell.

attrib. **1839** *Hints Study Eccl. Antiq.* (Cambr. Camden Soc. 1842) 25 Sancte-bell cot. A small but frequently elegant erection at the east end of the nave. **1845** *Ecclesiologist* IV. 282 A beautiful sancte-bell cot remains. [**1876** *Whitby Gloss.*, *Sancte cot*, a turret upon a Church roof for the 'Sacring bell'.]

sanctwar, Sc. form of saintuaire *Obs.*

†**sand,** *sb.*[1] *Obs.* Forms: 1–2 **sand, sond,** 3–6 **sand(e, sond(e,** 3 **saand, sund,** 5 **saande, sonnd, sound(e, soonde, sownde,** 4–5 *Sc.* **saynd(e.** [OE. *sand, sǫnd* str. fem., f. OTeut. **sand-* in **sandjan* to send.]

1. The action of sending; that which is sent, a message, present; (God's) dispensation or ordinance.

c **1000** Ælfric *Hom.*, *Judith* (Assmann) ix. 114, & him dæghwamlice com þurh heora drihtnes sande mete of heofenum. *a* **1300** *Cursor M.* 5099 Noght wit your rede, bot godds saand, Was i þus sent in-to þis land. *c* **1320** *Sir Tristr.* 2351 Bot vp he stirt bidene And heried godes sand Almiȝt. **1338** R. Brunne *Chron.* (1810) 114 At Rokesburghe his parlement he helde, þe folk did somon þorgh..& gaf þam sonde at wille in Inglond forto fare, Man & beste to spille. **1377** Langl. *P. Pl.* B. iii. 349 Þe soule þat þe sonde [of the text] taketh bi so moche is bounde. *c* **1380** Wyclif *Wks.* (1880) 292 Wheþer prelatis now ben more confermed in grace þanne was seynt petir þanne aftir sonde of þe holy goost? *c* **1386** Chaucer *Man of Law's T.* 728 She taketh in good entente The wille of Crist, and, kneling on the stronde, She seyde, 'lord! ay wel-com be thy sonde!' **1387** Trevisa *Higden* (Rolls) I. 415 Men hadde craft by Goddes sonde. *c* **1400** *Destr. Troy* 10506 A sonnd will I send by a sad frynd. *a* **1440** *Sir Degrev.* 1079 (Cambr. MS.) Thay thanked God of his sant [*rime* ferrant; *Linc. MS. corruptly* here shaunce, *with rime* ferrauns]. *c* **1440** *York Myst.* x. 244 It is goddis will, it sall be myne, Agaynste his saande sall I neuer schone. *c* **1440** *Promp. Parv.* 464/2 Sond, or sendynge, *missio*. Sond, or ȝyfte sent, *eccennium*. *c* **1450** *Ratis Raving*, *Craft Deyng* 4 To thank hyme [God] of al his sayndes and gyftes. *c* **1500** Kennedy *Passion of Christ* 914 This crabbit theif,..Betakinnis men, quhilk euer mair is murnand, The saynd of God ay reput myschance. *c* **1520** Skelton *Magnyf.* 2360 To thanke God of his sonde. ? *c* **1525** *Tale of Basyn* in Hazlitt *E.P.P.* III. 44 A riche man wer he..And knowen for a gode clerke thoro goddis sande.

b. The action of sending for; invitation.

1494 Fabyan *Chron.* vi. ccx. 225 This Robert was a monke of an howse in Normandy, & came ouer by the sonde of the kynge.

2. A person or body of persons sent on an errand; an embassy; an envoy, messenger.

1038 in Kemble *Cod. Dipl.* (1846) IV. 57 Þa com cristes cyrce sand to þam biscop. *a* **1122** *O.E. Chron.* (Laud MS.) an. 1095, Eac on þis ylcan ȝeare toȝeanes Eastron com þæs Papan sande hider to lande þæt wæs Waltear bisceop. **1154** *Ibid.* an. 1135, Here sandes feorden betwyx heom. *c* **1205** Lay. 3125 He sende hiis sande into þisse lande to Leir þan kinge. *a* **1225** *Ancr. R.* 190 Euerich worlich wo is Godes sonde. Heie monnes messager me schal heiliche underuongen. *a* **1300** *Cursor M.* 14158 Þe sandes soght ouer all Iude, Faand þai him noght in þat contre. *c* **1440** *York Myst.* xliv. 29 But firste he saide he schulde doune sende His sande. **1456** Sir G. Haye *Law Arms* (S.T.S.) 189 The saynde of God, the quhilk was to be send fra the fader of hevyn, war cummyn. *c* **1470** *Gol. & Gaw.* 47 [Arthur said:] 'I rede we send furth ane saynd to yone ciete'. **1470–85** Malory *Arthur* xxi. i. 840 Than Syr Mordred sought on quene Gueneuer by letters & sondes..for to haue hir to come oute of the toure of london.

b. *a*, *on sand*: on an embassy or message.

a **1300** *Cursor M.* 710 Bot adam son was sent a saand. *c* **1440** *Ipomydon* 2283 Syr Camppanus forthe ys gon on sond, To the kyng of Sesanay-lond.

3. A serving of food; a course, mess.

a **700** *Epinal Gloss.* 188 *Commeatos, commeatus* sandæ [*a* 800 *Erfurt Gloss.* sondæ]. *a* **1175** *Cott. Hom.* 233 And þer hi hadden brad and win and vii. sandon. *c* **1205** Lay. 24601 Þas beorn þa sunde from kuchene to þan kinge. *c* **1250** *Death* 106 in *O.E. Misc.* 174 Hwer beoð þine dihsches midd þine swete sonde. *c* **1250** *Gen. & Ex.* 2295 Of euerilc sonde, of euerilc win, most and best he gaf beniamin. **13..** *Sir Beues* 1927 And of eueriche sonde, þat him com to honde, A dede hire ete al þer ferst. *c* **1440** *Floriz & Bl.* 1072 (Trentham MS.) Þere was fest swythe breeme; I can not telle al þe sonde, But rycher fest was neuer in londe.

4. *Comb.*, **sand-man,** messenger, ambassador. (Cf. sandesman, sendman.)

c **1205** Lay. 12747 And heo us habbeoð worð isend bi vre sond-monnen.

sand (sænd), *sb.*[2] Forms: 1 **sand, sond,** 3–5 **sond,** 3–6 **sonde,** 4–7 **sande,** (4 **sonnd,** 5 **scand),** 3– **sand.** [Com. Teut. (but not recorded in Goth.): OE. *sand, sǫnd* neut. = OFris. *sond-*, OS., MLG. *sand*, MDu. *sant, sand-* (Du. *zand* neut.), OHG. *sant* (MHG. *sant, sand-*, mod.G. *sand* masc., dial. also neut.), ON. *sand-r* masc. (Sw., Da. *sand*):—OTeut. **sando-*, prob.:—earlier **samdo-*, **samado-* (? whence OHG. **samat*, MHG. *sampt*) corresp. to Gr. ἄμαθος.]

1. a. A material consisting of comminuted fragments and water-worn particles of rocks (mainly silicious) finer than those of which gravel is composed; often *spec.* as the material of a beach, desert, or the bed of a river or sea.

c **825** [see 2]. *c* **1000** Ælfric *Exod.* ii. 12 Þa ofsloh he þone Egiptiscan and behidde hyne on þam sande. *c* **1200** Ormin 14802, & Drihhtin þær toclæf þe sæ..& sett itt upp onn eȝȝþerr hallf All allse tweȝȝenn walless, & tær bitwenenn wass þe sand All harrd to ganngenn onne. *a* **1300** *Cursor M.* 12527 A nedder stert vte of þe sand, And stanged Iam in þe hand. *c* **1384** Chaucer *H. Fame* i. 486 Al the feld nas but of sond As small as man may see yet lye In the desert of Libye. **1480** Caxton *Chron. Eng.* cci. 182 A drope of drye blode and smale sond cleued on his hond. **1526** *Pilgr. Perf.* (W. de W. 1531) 64 Rose vp and wente forthe and fylled a greate sacke with sande. **1591** Shaks. *Two Gent.* ii. iv. 170 And I as rich ..As twenty Seas, if all their sand were pearle. **1695** Woodward *Nat. Hist. Earth* iv. (1723) 207 That finer Matter,..vulgarly called Sand, being really no other than very small Pebles. **1733** Pope *Ess. Man* iii. 102 Who taught the nations..to..Build on the wave or arch beneath the sand? **1799** *Med. Jrnl.* I. 254 Siliceous sand, flint, clay and loam, constitute the principal part of the soil. **1820** Shelley *Witch Atl.* iv, Ten times the Mother of the Months had.. bidden..the billows to indent The sea deserted sand. **1870** Morris *Earthly Par.* II. iii. 305 A shore of hard white sand Met the green herbage. **1878** Huxley *Physiogr.* 132 As a rule both the gravel and the sand consist chiefly of the substance called silica. **1897** Gladstone *Eastern Crisis* 1 Every grain of sand is a part of the sea-shore.

†**b.** *poet.* and *rhet.* used for: The shore (of a sea); also 'land' as opposed to 'sea', esp. in (*by*) *sea and sand*. *Obs.*

c **1205** Lay. 123, I þere Tyure he eode alond þer þa sea wasceð þat sond. *a* **1300** *Cursor M.* 10910 Þat all wroght.. Sun and mone, and se and sand. *c* **1330** R. Brunne *Chron. Wace* (Rolls) 14476 So longe he ferde & þe se sailand, & kynges slow by se & sand. **13..** *E.E. Allit. P.* C. 341 Þenne he [*sc.* Jonah] swepe to þe sonde in sluchched cloþes. *a* **1400–50** *Alexander* 4299 And we sitt all-way so sure be sand & be wattir, þat na supowell vndire sonne seke we vs neuire. *c* **1420** ? Lydg. *Assembly of Gods* 128 Er they myght be ware he [*sc.* Eolus] drofe hym on the sande. *c* **1460** *Towneley Myst.* ix. 141 Mahowne the menske, my lord kyng, And save by see and sand. *Ibid.* xiv. 399 Borne is newly, in this land, A kyng that shall weld se and sand. **1535** Stewart *Cron. Scot.* (Rolls) II. 589 He tuke the se,..In Ingland syne arryuit at ane sand, With all his power thair passit to the land.

c. With *a* and *pl.* A sand-bank, shoal.

1495 *Acts Crt. Requests* (1592) 11 De..spoliatione dictae nauis..existentis in periculo infra le Goodwine sandes in mari. **1546** J. Heywood *Prov.* (1867) 76 But you leaue all anker holde, on seas or lands. And so set vp shop vpon Goodwins sands. **1555** Latimer in Strype *Eccl. Mem.* (1721) II. App. 99 They that have buylded upon a Sande wilbe affraied, thoughe they se but a Clowde aryse. **1588** N. Gorges in *Defeat Sp. Armada* (Navy Rec. Soc.) I. 357 On the 30th of July, passing through the sands, we were becalmed. **1599** Shaks. *Hen. V*, iv. i. 100 *Williams*... What thinkes he of our estate? *King*. Euen as men wrackt vpon a Sand, that looke to be washt off the next Tyde. **1613** Purchas *Pilgrimage* (1614) 504 A ship (called Saint Peter) fell vpon sands..and split. **1738** Weddell *Voy. up Thames* 42 On a sudden our Ship struck on a Sand. **1815** *Chron.* in *Ann. Reg.* 95 She struck on a sand about three or four miles from Yarmouth. **1877** Huxley *Physiogr.* 181 The position of the principal sands in the estuary of the Thames.

d. A sandy soil. Chiefly *pl.*

1610 Holland *Camden's Brit.* (1637) 547 The West part is taken up with the Forrest of Shirewood..This part because it is sandy, the Inhabitants tearme The Sand, the other..the Clay. **1675** Evelyn *Terra* (1676) 19 As of Sands, so are there as different sorts of Clays. **1794** A. Young *Agric. Suffolk* 22 On bad sands trefoile and ray grass are chosen. **1846** J. Baxter *Libr. Pract. Agric.* (ed. 4) II. 241 Sands.—Some of the best description of these soils nearly approach to hazel moulds. *Ibid.*, Light Sands.

e. A grain of sand. (See also 2 a and 5.)

1596 *Edw. III*, iv. iv. 42–3 As many sands as these my hands can hold Are but my handful of so many sands. **1611** Shaks. *Cymb.* v. v. 120 One Sand another Not more resembles that sweet Rosie Lad [etc.]. **1675** Evelyn *Terra* (1676) 34 Clay consisted of most exceeding smooth and round Sands of several opacous colours.

f. *Geol.* and *Mining*. A stratum of sand or soft sandstone. ***oil sand***: see oil *sb.*[1] 6 e.

1851 Greenwell *Coal-trade Terms Northumb. & Durh.* s.v., 'The sand' is a stratum of soft sandstone, frequently met with in sinking through the lower new red sandstone. **1894** *Geol. Mag.* Oct. 464 Fawn-coloured Sands and Marls.

g. *Golf*. Sand-holes or bunkers on a course. ***to be in sand***, to be 'bunkered'.

1842 G. F. Carnegie in *Golfiana Misc.* (1887) 82 'Give me the iron!' either party cries, As in the quarry, track, or sand he lies. **1897** *Encycl. Sport* I. 466/1 Balls in Sand—When a ball lies in a sand bunker [etc.].

h. *Soil Sci.* Applied *spec.* to particles whose sizes fall within a specified range, and to soils having a specified proportion of such particles (see quots.). Hence ***sand-size*** sb. (adj.).

1873 E. W. Hilgard in *Amer. Jrnl. Sci. & Arts* CVI. 337 (*table*) Coarse Sand, 80–90 (1/180) mm... Finest Sand 20–22 (1/180) mm. **1900** R. Warington *Lect. Physical Properties Soil* i. 8 Coarse sand 0·5–1·00 mm... Fine sand 0·1–0·25 mm. **1925** P. Emerson *Soil Characteristics* i. 6 The different soil particles are designated according to size as follows... Very coarse sand 2·0 to 1·0 millimeters... Very fine sand 0·1 to 0·05 millimeter. *Ibid.* 7 The United States Bureau of Soils recognizes the following classes [of soil]: ..*Sand*: more than 25 per cent very coarse, coarse and medium sand, less than 50 per cent fine sand, more than 20 per cent silt and clay. **1952** L. M. Thompson *Soils & Soil Fertility* ii. 8 Based on size of soil particles there are three fractions, sand, silt and clay. **1957** Sand-size [see sedimentological *a.*]. **1964** K. W. Butzer *Environment & Archeol.* x. 158 The modified Wentworth grade scale..is most widely used in North America. It has the following logarithmic subdivisions:..sand 0·064–2 mm., silt 0.004–0·064 mm... The non-logarithmic, modified Atterberg scale widely used in Europe has slightly different nomenclature... coarse sand 0·2–2·0 mm... fine sand 0·02–0·06 mm., silt 0·002–0·02 mm. **1971** *Gloss. Soil Sci. Terms* (Soil Sci. Soc. Amer.) 14/2 *Sand*, a soil particle between 0·05 and 2·0 mm in diameter. *Ibid.* 18/1 *Sand*, soil material that contains 85% or more of sand; percentage of silt, plus 1·5 times the percentage of clay, shall not exceed 15. **1972** J. G. Cruickshank *Soil Geogr.* ii. 55 The products of physical weathering are usually large on the particle size scale; that is, they are stone, gravel, or sand size and less commonly as small as silt size.

i. A fashion shade resembling the colour of sand.

1923 *Daily Mail* 13 Feb. 13/2 (Advt.), Artificial silk hose ..in black, white, beaver, nude, cinnamon, sand, suede. **1930** *Daily Express* 6 Oct. 5/6 (Advt.), Imitation nutria fur sets... In dark grey, fawn, beaver, sand, and nutria. **1971** *Guardian* 28 Sept. 11/2 (*caption*) Quilted raincoat... In sand, orchid, or damson. **1979** *Country Life* 24 May (Suppl.) 55 (Advt.), The new Renault 5..comes in black, silver, blue or sand.

2. In various metaphorical and similative uses. **a.** With reference to the innumerability of the grains composing sand.

c **825** *Vesp. Psalter* lxxvii. 27, & rinde ofer hie swe swe dust flæsc & swe swe sond sæs ðа fleȝendan ȝefiðrede. *a* **1300** *Cursor M.* 2571 Þe barns þat o þe sal bred Namar sal þou þam cun rede, þan sterns on light and sand in see. **1591** Shaks. *Two Gent.* iv. iii. 33 A heart As full of sorrowes, as the Sea of sands. **1667** Milton *P.L.* ii. 903 They..Swarm populous, unnumber'd as the Sands Of Barca or Cyrene's torrid soil. **1817** Shelley *Rev. Islam* xi. xxiii, Great People! as the sands shalt thou become.

b. With reference to its instability as a foundation or a constructive material. ***rope of sand***: see rope *sb.*

c **975** *Rushw. Gosp.* Matt. vii. 26 Ӡelic..were..se ðe ȝetimberde hus his on sonde. **1542–5** Brinklow *Lament.* (1874) 91 It is a token that your foundacion was buylded vpon the sande. **1596** Shaks. *Merch. V.* iii. ii. 84 Cowards, whose hearts are all as false As stayers of sand. **1790** Burke *Fr. Rev.* Wks. V. 427 They cannot bear to hear the sands of his Mississippi compared with the rock of the church. **1817** Shelley *To Ld. Chancellor* xi, Their error—That sand on which thy crumbling power is built. **1835** Lytton *Rienzi* ix. ii, Schemes of sand. **1873** Trollope *Phineas Redux* I. vi. 53, I complain of no injustice. Our castle was built upon the sand. **1905** G. L. Dickinson *Mod. Symposium* 77, I have been watching..one building after another laboriously raised by each speaker in turn, only to collapse ignominiously at the first touch administered by his successor. And why? For the ancient reason, that the structures were built upon the sand. **1920** Galsworthy *In Chancery* ii. iii. 151 She put out her hand to him. 'I feel you're a rock.' 'Built on sand,' answered Jolyon. **1963** *Times* 9 Jan. 4/2 On slower courts the story with Hughes would be different, but here, where even the best stroke is not an outright winner until it has died, his game is indeed built on sand.

c. In phrases implying the exercise or employment of fruitless labour. ***to plough the sands***: see plough *v.* 10 b.

1576 Fleming *Panopl. Epist.* 194, I am in beliefe (I may peradueunture sowe my seede in the sande) that you will doe nothing vnto me. **1581** J. Bell *Haddon's Answ. Osor.* 218 b, Surely I shall seeme to measure the sandes, when I enter uppon the gulfe of thys Romish Ierarchy. **1842** Tennyson *Audley Court* 49, I might as well have traced it in the sands.

d. ***to bury*** (or ***hide***) ***one's head in the sand*** (and allusive varr.): to ignore unpleasant realities.

In some quots. with direct reference to the legendary belief that an ostrich buries its head in sand when threatened.

1844 [see ostrich[1] 2 a]. **1899** W. H. D. Rouse in North tr. *Plutarch's Lives* VI. 345 Like the ostrich that hides his head in the sand. **1916** W. Wilson in *N.Y. Times* 2 Feb. 1/1 America cannot be an ostrich with its head in the sand. **1929** L. MacNeice in *Oxford Poetry* 24 Asking..Whether it would not be better To hide one's head in the warm sand of sleep. **1937** F. P. Crozier *Men I Killed* vii. 137 Our new system of rearmament is at least..encouraging our Colonel Blimps to hide their heads, stupidly like the ostrich, in the sand! **1946** E. O'Neill *Iceman Cometh* iii. 201 He thrusts his head down on his arms like an ostrich hiding its head in the sand. **1976** *Star* (Sheffield) 29 Oct. 10/4 The people of England should not bury their heads in the sand and say it can't happen here.

3. *pl.* Tracts of sand: **a.** along a shore, estuary, etc. or composing the bed of a river or sea.

1450 W. Lomner in *Paston Lett.* (1897) I. 125 [He] leyde his body on the sonds of Dover. *a* **1548** Hall *Chron., Hen. VIII*, 94 b, The Cardinall received hym on the Sandes. **1610** Shaks. *Temp.* i. ii. 376 Come vnto these yellow sands. **1704** Pope *Spring* 61 O'er golden sands let rich Pactolus flow. **1774** Goldsm. *Nat. Hist.* (1776) I. 224 The great Rhine..a part of which is no doubt lost in the sands, a little above Leyden. **1817** Shelley *Rev. Islam* xii. xvii, A melody, like waves on wrinkled sands that leap. *a* **1858** Kingsley *Poems* (title) The Sands of Dee. **1859** Tennyson *Guinevere* 291 They found a naked child upon the sands Of dark Tintagil by the Cornish sea.

b. Sandy or desert wastes.

a **1547** Surrey *Æneid* iv. 832 May he..fall before his time vngraued amid the sandes. **1585** T. Washington tr. *Nicholay's Voy.* iii. xxi. 110 The long desarts and sandes, whereby they must passe. **1604** E. G[rimstone] *D'Acosta's Hist. Indies* ii. xiii. 112 Why is all the coast of Peru, being ful of sands, very temperate? **1667** Milton *P.L.* i. 355 Her barbarous Sons..spread Beneath Gibraltar to the Lybian sands. **1738** Gray *Tasso* 32 Oceans unknown, in-hospitable sands! **1781** Cowper *Friendship* 184 So barren sands imbibe the show'r, But render neither fruit nor flow'r. **1822** Shelley *Calderon* ii. 143 A pirate ambushed in its pathless sands. **1843** Borrow *Bible in Spain* vii, We were in the midst of sands, brushwood, and huge pieces of rock.

fig. **1816** Byron *Ch. Har.* iii. iii, A sterile track..O'er which all heavily the journeying years Plod the last sands of life, where not a flower appears.

†**c.** Phrase. (Sc.) ***to leave*** or ***put*** (a person) ***to the long sands***: app., to leave in the lurch, to place in a difficulty. *Obs.*

1671 Fountainhall in M. P. Brown *Suppl. Decis.* (1826) II. 539 It would appear Udney transacts for the haill [*sc.* bond for the payment of himself and Pitreichy], pays himself, and leaves Pitreichy to the lang sands. **1678** J. Brown *Life Faith* i. ii. (1824) 33 How quickly were they put again to the long sands (as we say).

4. a. As used for various economic purposes; also, as an adulterant. ***fire of sand*** = ***sand fire***: see 10.

1511–12 *Act 3 Hen. VIII*, c. 6 §1 Without eny more oyle brene moistur dust sonde or other thyng deceyvably puttyng to..the same Webbe. **1530** Palsgr. 265/1 Sande to skoure vessell with, *sablon*. **1666** Boyle *Orig. Formes* ii. vi. 345 The saline Corpuscles are distill'd over in a moderate Fire of Sand. **1848** Dickens *Dombey* xxiii, The walls had been cleaned..and everything..was..shining with soft soap and sand. **1850** Holtzapffel *Turning*, etc. III. 1090 Sand, which is nearly pure silex, is used in sawing and smoothing building stones and marbles. **1857** Hassall *Adulterations Detected* 188 There is..but little foundation for the tales we hear about the presence of sand in sugar.

b. as an ingredient of mortar.

1427–8 *Rec. St. Mary at Hill* 69 Also payd for a lode sonde .. vd. **1455–6** *Cal. Anc. Rec. Dublin* (1889) I. 290 The sayd Jhon shall repeyre sayd towyr and slype..with lym and scand. **1703** T. S. *Art's Improv.* 6 This Mortar is made of Lime..and Brook-Sand. **1862** Merivale *Rom. Emp.* liv. (1865) VI. 459 His system, as Caius said of his style, was sand without lime.

c. as used to dry wet ink-marks.

1753 Chambers *Cycl. Supp.*, White Sands... 1. A fine shining kind, commonly used for strewing over writing. **1806** J. Beresford *Miseries Hum. Life* (ed. 3) 175 In writing:—neither sand, blotting paper, nor a fire, to dry your paper. **1860** *All Year Round* No. 52. 33 He was continually shaking sand from a pepper-box over scrawling entries in marble-covered copy-books.

d. as used in making founders' moulds; *spec.* a mixture of common sand with a binding material.

dry, green sand: see green *a.* 9 d. ***facing, parting sand***: see facing, parting *vbl. sbs.*

1839 Ure *Dict. Arts* 518 The experienced moulder knows how to mix the different sands placed at his disposal.

5. The sand of a sand-glass or hour-glass; also, with *a* and *pl.*, a grain of this. Chiefly *fig.*

1557 *Tottel's Misc.* (Arb.) 138, I saw, my tyme how it did runne, as sand out of the glasse. **1593** Shaks. *3 Hen. VI*, i. iv. 25 The Sands are numbred, that makes vp my Life. **1608** — *Per.* v. ii. 1 Now our sands are almost run. *a* **1644** Quarles *Sol. Recant.* Solil. ix. 14 Deaths impartiall hand Wounds all alike, and death will give no sand. **1732** Pope *Ep. Cobham* 225 Time, that on all things lays his lenient hand, Yet tames not this; it sticks to our last sand. **1837** Disraeli *Venetia* v. x, The remaining sands of my life are few. **1899** J. Chamberlain *Sp.* in *Times* 28 Aug. 6/4 Will he [*sc.* President Kruger] speak the necessary words. The sands are running down in the glass.

†**6.** = arena. *lit.* and *fig. Obs.*

1587 Thynne *Contin. Ann. Scot.* Pref., in *Holinshed*, Thus hauing laid before thee, that he writeth best that trulie writeth publike affaires, that I was commanded by my deere freends to enter into this sand [etc.]. **1615** Crooke *Body of Man* 25 Andreas Laurentius hath taken worthy paines, and sweate much in this sande. **1618** Bolton *Florus* iii. xxi. (1636) 241 That citizens should encounter citizens, as if they were fencers..in the heart and forum of the city, as in a fighting ground or theatral sand.

7. *slang*. **a.** (See quots.)

1812 J. H. Vaux *Flash Dict.*, *Sand*, moist sugar. **1823** P. Egan *Grose's Dict. Vulg. Tongue*. **1918** L. E. Ruggles *Navy Explained* 20 Bread is called 'punk'; sugar, 'sand'. **1935** A. J. Pollock *Underworld Speaks* 86/1 *Pass the sand*, pass the sugar. **1945** *California Folklore Q.* 19 Oct. 46 Joe with cow and sand. **1971** M. Tak *Truck Talk* 100 *Load of sand*, a cargo of sugar.

b. Chiefly *U.S.* Firmness of purpose; pluck, stamina. Phr. ***sand in one's craw***. Cf. grit *sb.*[1] 5.

1867 G. W. Harris *Sut Lovingood* 102, I tell yu he hes lots ove san' in his gizzard; he is the best pluck I ever seed. **1872** *Newton Kansan* 5 Dec. 3/3 We hope to see Mr. Pettibone with sufficient 'sand in his craw' for this new position [*sc.* police judge]. **1875** B. Harte *Tales of Argonauts* 71 Blank me if I didn't think he was losing his sand, till he walked to position. **1883** E. Ingersoll in *Harper's Mag.* Jan. 202 Good, solid man he was, too, with heaps of sand in him. **1884** 'Mark Twain' *Huck. Finn* viii. 62 When I got to camp I warn't feeling very brash, there warn't much sand in my craw. **1924** Galsworthy *Forest* iv. ii. 120 By Jove, Mr. Farrell, there's sand in you. Tell me, isn't he ever ashamed of himself? **1933** J. Buchan *Prince of Captivity* iii. i. 264 A plain face with nothing showy about it, but all the horse-sense and sand in the world. **1954** 'W. Henry' *Death of Legend* 4 You losing your sand, Buck?

c. ***to raise sand*** (U.S.): to create a disturbance; to make a fuss.

1892 *Dialect Notes* I. 231 'To raise sand' is slang [in Kentucky] for to get furiously angry, the same as 'to raise Cain'. **1893** H. A. Shands *Some Peculiarities of Speech in Mississippi* 74 *Raise sand*,..to create a disturbance, to raise a row. **1948** *Sun* (Baltimore) 1 Dec. 17/4 Boudreau raised sand but the decision stuck. **1970** C. Major *Dict. Afro-Amer. Slang* 96 *Raise sand*,..to make an outcry; to brawl; to fight.

8. *Anat.* and *Path.* Applied to various substances resembling sand, present either normally or as pathological products in certain animal organs or secretions. ***brain sand***: see quot. 1856; also called ***pineal sand*** (Syd. Soc. Lex.). ***urinary sand***: a substance of finer particles than those of gravel (gravel *sb.* 4).

1577 Frampton *Joyf. News* i. 19 The chief vertue that it hath, is in the paine of the stone in the Kidneis and Raines, and in expellyng of Sande and stone. **1707** Sloane *Jamaica* I. 60 A Seaman much troubled with Sand and gross Humors, eating of it..found so much benefit [etc.]. **1822–9** *Good's Study Med.* (ed. 3) V. 522 Urinary sand..is of two kinds, white and red. **1856** Griffith & Henfrey *Microgr. Dict.* 559/2 Brain-sand, or the acervulus cerebri, is found in the pineal gland and the choroid plexus, sometimes also in the pia mater [etc.]. **1899** Cagney tr. *Jaksch's Clin. Diagn.* vii. (ed. 4) 290 Concretions of considerable size are occasionally to be seen with the naked eye in the urine (urinary sand).

9. General Combinations. **a.** simple attrib., as ***sand-barge, -bay, -beach, -canyon, -cart, down, -dune, -flat, -grain, heap, -island, -knoll, -land, -line, -mound, -pile, -reef, -rip*** (rip *sb.*[5]), ***-sack, -sea, -shore, -spit, -stretch, -vein, -waste***; 'made of sand', as ***sand core, walk***; employed in the storing, carrying, working, etc. of sand, as ***sand bin, creel*** (creel *sb.* 1), ***-scoop, -wheel***.

1840 R. H. Dana *Two Yrs. before Mast* 225 We were as deep as a *sand-barge. **1887** S. Samuels *From Forecastle to Cabin* 197 My ship was loaded as deep as a sand barge. **1645–52** Boate *Irel. Nat. Hist.* (1860) 22 A *sand-bay where it is good anchoring. **1709** J. Lawson *New Voy. Carolina* 151 The Sand-Birds..frequent our *Sand-Beaches. **1728** J. Comer *Diary* 7 Apr. (1893) 50 A schooner..was cast on shore on a sand beach at Westport. **1806** *Deb. Congress U.S.* (1852) 9th Congress 2 Sess. App. 1117 They passed a number of sand-beaches, and some rapids. **1878** Lanier *Poems, Marshes of Glynn* 54 Softly the sand-beach wavers away. **1888** *Lockwood's Dict. Mech. Engin.*, **Sand Bin*, a trough..in..foundries, used as a convenient receptacle for sand..for..the moulder. **1939** Auden & Isherwood *Journey to War* 120 *Sand-canyons, guarded by fantastic sandy spires and pinnacles. **1788** Cowper *Let.* 1 Feb. in R. Southey *Life & Wks. W. Cowper* (1836) VI. 117 Thinking myself an ass, and my translation a *sand-cart. **1825** J. Constable *Let.* 1 Aug. (1966) IV. 97 A scene on Hampstead Heath, with broken foreground and sand carts. **1834** *Chambers's Edin. Jrnl.* III. 233/3 It was like subjecting a pampered palfrey all of a sudden, to the sorrows of the sand-cart. **1923** *Glasgow Herald* 30 Jan. 9 There is generally a so-called sandcart, a sort of squat fly with an awning for two. **1875** *Ure's Dict. Arts* II. 474 The *sand cores for filling up that part of the shell which is to be hollow. **1402–3** *Durham Acc. Rolls* (Surtees) 217, 2 panyhers, et 1 par de *sande crelys. **1604** E. Grimstone *Hist. Siege Ostend* 14 The Souldiers were forced to recouer the..*sande downes. **1856** C. J. Anderson *Lake Ngami* 157 Soil as yielding as that of an English sand-down. **1830–3** *Sand-dune [see dune]. **1899** C. Reid *Orig. Brit. Flora* 13 Many of the sand-dune.. species are more properly desert plants. **1773** in E. W. McMullen *Eng. Topogr. Terms in Florida* (1953) 190 From this point runs a *sand flat 1½ mile from the shore of Anastasia Island. **1794** *Trans. Soc. Promotion Agric., Arts, & Manuf.* (U.S.) I. 143 He..kept him in a very poor pasture adjoining a creek where creek-thatch grew on sand-flats. **1826** J. J. Audubon *Ornithol. Biogr.* II. 41 The dead fish that frequently are found about the sand-flats of rivers. **1839** *Penny Cycl.* XV. 516/2 Locality... The sand-flats of the Cape of Good Hope. **1858** Froude *Hist. Eng.* III. 349 Two thousand men were in arms upon the sandflats towards Deal. **1922** Joyce *Ulysses* 41 Unwholesome sandflats waited to suck his treading soles. **1895** *Outing* (U.S.) XXVI. 27/1 Dusty with little *sand-grains. **1602** Carew *Cornwall* 19 b, A little before plowing time, they scatter abroad those.. small *Sand heapes vpon the ground. **1854** C. M. Yonge *Heartsease* II. iii. xv. 327, I hope she will take her down to the *sand-heap, where the children have been luxuriating all morning. **1974** *Times* 5 Oct. 12/2 That sand-heap played a large part in his method of teaching. **1840** Poe *Jrnl. of Julius Rodman* in *Compl. Wks.* (1902) IV. 43 *Sand-island. **1975** *Offshore Engineer* Dec. 16/3 A sand island could engulf a conventional steel or concrete platform. **1916** Joyce *Portrait of Artist* (1969) iv. 172 A ring of tufted *sandknolls. **1766** *Compl. Farmer* s.v., The grey, black, and ash-coloured *sand-land are the worst of all. **1963** *Times* 10 June 7/1 This is 73 percent above the average of 16 other *sandland farms carrying cattle and sheep as well as growing corn. **1972** *Plant Dis. Reporter* LVI. 695 This pathogen spread rapidly into all the tomato sand-land areas of Florida. **1891** W. B. Yeats *John Sherman & Dhoya* ii. 185 By the..edge of the lake.. there suddenly stood before him a slight figure, at the edge of the narrow *sand-line, dark against the glowing water. **1872** 'Mark Twain' *Roughing It* v. 51 He..climbs the nearest *sand-mound, and gazes into the distance. **1921** *Daily Colonist* (Victoria, B.C.) 8 Apr. 4/2 Organized playgrounds were a valuable asset to any city—a playground in which there were *sandpiles and wading pools for the little ones. **1976** *National Observer* (U.S.) 30 Oct. 16/5 She recalls playing 'kick the can' and burying each other in sand piles. **1883** 'Mark Twain' *Life on Mississippi* xxiv. 267 You can tell a *sand-reef—that's all easy. **1973** *Publ. Amer. Dial. Soc.* LX. 8 The mainland is..cut off from the Atlantic by the long lines of sand reefs called the Outer Banks. **1884** Goode, etc. *Nat. Hist. Aquatic Anim.* 195 They lie in wait for them on the *sand-rips and catch them as they swim over. **1889** W. B. Yeats *Wanderings of Oisin* iii. 49 But prone on the pathway, prone struggling, They lay 'neath the *sand-sack at length. **1875** Knight *Dict. Mech.*, **Sand-scoop*, a shovel for obtaining sand from the bottom of the river. **1936** M. H. Mason *Paradise of Fools* xix. 218 When we finally get stuck in the middle of the *Sand Sea..you'll have to carry everything. **1976** L. Deighton *Twinkle, twinkle, Little Spy* ii. 13 This road skirted the edges of the Sahara's largest sand-seas. **1859** Tennyson *Elaine* 301 The waste *sand-shores. **1854** V. Lush *Jrnl.* 5 Feb. (1971) 151 The boat beat about all the afternoon and towards evening ran fast upon the *sandspit off the mouth of the Mungamungaroa Creek. **1910** S. P. Hyatt *Diary of Soldier of Fortune* xv. 161 The town..stands on a little sandspit which juts out from a mangrove-circled bay. **1934** *Discovery* May 130/1 One result of the storm was that a sand spit was built out across a bay. **1974** *Nat. Geographic* Dec. 785/1 Its reef supported two islets, one a mere sandspit and the other some 350 yards long. **1930** E. Pound *XXX Cantos* ii. 9 Glare azure of water, cold-welter, close cover. Quiet sun-tawny *sand-stretch. **1922** Blunden *Shepherd* 28 Where the *sand-vein still bubbles its clear spring. **1766** *Compl. Farmer* s.v. *Walk*, *Sand walks are also frequently made in gardens. **1817** Coleridge *Lay Serm.* 26 The unprofitable *sand-waste. **1883** *Min. Proc. Inst. Civ. Engin.* LXXIV. 338 *Sand-wheel Motor... A large overshot wheel operated by sand instead of water. **1892** P. Benjamin *Mod. Mechanism* 589 Sand Wheels [in ore-dressing machinery] are..elevators..for raising the..tailings.

b. objective and obj. genitive, as ***sand-castor, crusher, -elevator, mixer, -rammer, -shaker, sifter, -strewer; sand-loving, -teasing*** adjs.

1897 'H. S. Merriman' *In Kedar's Tents* xxv. 281 Vincente was writing at the table... He smiled as he shook the small *sand-castor over the paper. **1924** [see Battersea]. **1940** R. Graves *Sergeant Lamb of Ninth* 206 The chest was filled with pens, ink, paper, sand-castors. **1875** Knight *Dict. Mech.*, *Sand Crusher and Washer. **1875** *Ure's Dict. Arts* III. 750 The sand..is again lifted by the *sand-elevator. **1915** R. Lankester *Diversions of Naturalist* 17 The rare *sand-loving plants of the dunes. **1967** *Oceanogr. & Marine Biol.* V. 505 Sand-loving species such as the tectibranch gastropod *Philine aperta*. **1888** *Lockwood's Dict. Mech. Engin.*, **Sand Mixer*, a machine used in mixing sand for foundry use. **1902** *Encycl. Brit.* XXXI. 802/2 The *sand-rammers employed in making foundry moulds. **1958** *Washington Post* 26 June A1/8 They [*sc.* microphones] would be located where the old and now empty '*sand shakers', once used as blotters, are placed on each desk. **1972** *Country Life* 3 Feb. 272/3 It [*sc.* a 1652 inkstand] opens to reveal.. on the right a sand-shaker. **1975** *New Yorker* 26 May 105/3 (Advt.), Sterling Silver Salt and Pepper Reproductions of the original sand shakers used by George Washington at Mt. Vernon. **1888** *Lockwood's Dict. Mech. Engin.*, **Sand Sifter*, a machine made for sifting foundry sand. **1922** Joyce *Ulysses* 428 Through rising fog a dragon *sandstrewer, travelling at caution, slews heavily down upon him, its huge red headlight winking. **1865** G. M. Hopkins *Poems* (1948) 33 Eye greeting doves bright-counter to the rook, Fresh brooks to salt *sand-teasing waters shoaly.

c. instrumental, as ***sand-blanched, -blown, -built, -buried, -cleaned, -faced, -hemmed, -invested, -laden, -obliterated, -rubbed, -silted, -smothered, -stained, -strewn*** adjs.

1932 W. Faulkner *Light in August* v. 105 A smooth, *sandblanched floor. **1907** C. C. Brown *China* 139 Low dunes and *sand-blown farmsteads. **1788** T. Dwight *Triumph of Infidelity* 6 As *sand-built domes dissolve before the stream,..The structure fled. **1830** Tennyson *Ode Mem.* 97 A sand-built ridge. **1916** Joyce *Portrait of Artist* (1969) iv. 160 The music passed..over the fantastic fabrics of his mind, dissolving them painlessly and noiselessly as a sudden wave dissolves the sandbuilt turrets of children. **1888** *Daily News* 3 July 6/1 The *sand-buried cities of Western Mongolia. **1960** Auden *Homage to Clio* 58 A sand-buried site. **1891** W. B. Yeats *John Sherman & Dhoya* 17 Our *sand-cleaned doorsteps. **1931** *Times Lit. Suppl.* 3 Sept. 668/2 Hand-made and *sand-faced [tiles]. **1976** *Liverpool Echo* 7 Dec. 11/2 They were hand-made, sand-faced Flemish bricks, mellowed by time and totally irreplaceable. **1852** M. Arnold *Consolation* 27 In a lone, *sand hemm'd City of Africa. **1870** Longf. *Div. Trag.* 1st Pass. ii. iii, The vast desert, silent, *sand-invested. **1902** D. G. Hogarth *Nearer East* 72 The chief ranges run north and south, weathered to fantastic outlines by the *sand-laden winds and keen frosts of winter nights. **1955** P. Larkin *Less Deceived* 41 Those few forbidding signs Of the continuous coarse Sand-laden wind, time. **1938** D. Gascoyne *Hölderlin's Madness* 47 The *sand-obliterated face. **1922** V. Woolf *Jacob's Room* i. 13 Wind-swept, *sand-rubbed, a more unpolluted piece of bone existed nowhere. **1945** C. Mann in Murdoch & Drake-Brockman *Austral. Short Stories* (1951) 259 It broke through the *sand-silted block. **1924** Lawrence & Skinner *Boy in Bush* 11 Clogged, ..*sand-smothered, that's what we are. **1916** A. Huxley *Burning Wheel* 50 Who marked the land-weeds and the *sand-stained foam. **1849** M. Arnold *Forsaken Merman* 35 *Sand-strewn caverns, cool and deep.

d. parasynthetic, as ***sand-beached, -bottomed, -rimmed, -roofed, -wharfed*** adjs.

1895 Kipling *2nd Jungle Bk.* 166 Some granite-tipped, *sand-beached islet. **1894** H. Nisbet *Bush Girl's Rom.* 12 *Sand-bottomed, clear but not shallow streams. **1857** J. G. Whittier *Poetical Wks.* II. 231 Mine the *sand-rimmed pickerel pond. **1845** Longfellow *Belfry of Bruges* 50 Whole villages of *sand-roofed tents. **1930** Blunden *Poems* 318 So unexpected and so beautiful That they live on in the *sand-wharfed pool.

e. adverbial, chiefly similative, as ***sand-blond, -coloured, -like -sized, -toned*** adjs.; locative, as ***sand-bogged, -burrowing, dwelling, -marooned, -mounded, -wading*** adjs.; ***sand-groping*** vbl. sb.

1953 C. Day Lewis *Italian Visit* ii. 32 The hills are *sand-blond. **1959** A. Upfield *Bony & Black Virgin* xi. 88 Lots of drift sand now. We'd find it rougher in the ute. Be *sand-bogged a lot. **1963** R. P. Dales *Annelids* i. 29 Such protonephridia..are found in phyllodocids and in the *sandburrowing nephthyids. **1627** May *Lucan* ix. 822 *Sand-colour'd Ammodytes. **1897** *Daily News* 9 Sept. 6/5 Sand-coloured cloth. **1911** F. O. Bowen *Plant-Life on Land* 128 Certain *sand-dwelling plants. **1963** R. P. Dales *Annelids* ii. 43 In lugworms, in the fusiform sand-dwelling opheliids. **1924** Lawrence & Skinner *Boy in Bush* 21 They walked off the timber platform into the sand, and Jack had his first experience of '*sand-groping'. **1630** J. Taylor (Water P.) *Sieges Jerus.* Wks. i. 10/1 [Adam] from whose Star-like, *Sand-like Generation, Sprung euery Kindred, Kingdome, Tribe, and Nation. **1946** W. de la Mare *Traveller* 19 Meagre his saddlebag as camel's hump When, *sand-marooned, she staggers to her doom. **1921** —— *Veil* 24 Rent hull, and broken mast, She sprawls *sand-mounded. **1965** G. J. Williams *Econ. Geol. N.Z.* xx. 365/2 In them [*sc.* sandstones] the clay mineral occurs as large *sand-sized aggregates. **1977** A. Hallam *Planet Earth* 24/2 Somewhat larger particles, sand-sized grains, offer sufficient air resistance to be briefly heated to incandescence by friction before being entirely destroyed in the upper atmosphere. **1916** *Chambers's Jrnl.* Sept. 635/2 In the midst of the mass of *sand-toned uniforms. **1884** *Cornh. Mag.* May 459 We had an hour's *sand-wading after leaving O-Bak.

10. a. Special combinations: **sand-ball**, a kind of toilet soap (see quot. 1884); **sand-bar**, a bank of sand formed at the mouth of a river or harbour by the action of the water; also, a sandbank in the course of a river or close to a beach; **sand-bar willow**, a North American shrub or small tree, *Salix longifolia*; **sand-bat, -battery** (see quots.); †**sand-bearded** *a.*, having a sandy-coloured beard; **sand belt**, an arid ridge of sand frequently extending many miles; **sand-belt machine**, a variety of sand-papering machine; **sand-binder**, a plant which tends to hold loose or shifting sand; **sand-blight** = *sandy-blight* (see sandy *a.* 5 b); **sand blow**, the removal or deposition of large quantities of sand by the wind; a place where this has occurred; **sand-blower** (see quot.); **sand board**, (*a*) a board or tray sprinkled with sand in which letters may be traced and obliterated in teaching the alphabet; (*b*) see quots. 1875–95; **sand-body** *Geol.*, a permeable underground mass of sand or sandstone (which may contain oil); **sand boil** *U.S.*, an eruption of water through the surface of the ground; **sand bowls**, bowls for playing upon sand; **sand brake**, an appliance for stopping a train by the automatic packing of the axles with sand; **sandbreak**, a patch of sandy ground in a landscape; **sand-brush**, the brush or underwood of a sandy district; **sand-bunker**, a small well-fenced sand-pit (Jam.); **sand-burned, burnt** *adjs.*, of a casting, injured by the partial fusion of the sand in the mould; **sand-burr** = *sand-bat* (see also sand-bur); **sand cake** [tr. G. *sandkuchen, sandtorte*], a kind of cake which crumbles in the mouth; **sand-canal** *Zool.* (see quot.); **sand-castle**, a structure of sand resembling the form of a castle, of the kind made by a child on the beach; also *fig.*; **sand cay** [cay], a small sandy island, usu. elongated parallel to the shore, freq. found on a coral reef and there composed of fine coral debris; = *sand key*; **sand-clock** = sand-glass 1; **sand-cloud**, a cloud-like mass of sand accompanying a simoom; **sand-club**, (*a*) = sandbag *sb.* 2 c (*Cent. Dict.*); (*b*) orig. *U.S.*, = *sand-iron* (b); **sand-coal, cone** (see quots.); **sand core**, a compact mass of sand that is dipped into molten glass and withdrawn, so as to serve as a core in the making of a hollow vessel; freq. *attrib.*; **sand-crack**, (*a*) a fissure in a horse's hoof; (without *a* and *pl.*) a condition so characterized; (*b*) a crack in the human foot caused by walking on hot sandy soil; (*c*) a crack in a moulded brick, prior to burning, due to imperfect mixing (*Cent. Dict.*); **sand crater** (see quot.); **sand culture** *Bot.*, a hydroponic method of plant cultivation in which the plants are rooted in beds of purified sand supplied with nutrient solutions, used esp. to determine their mineral requirements; a culture of this kind; usu. *attrib.*; **sand-dance**, a step-dance performed on a sanded surface; hence **sand-dancing, sand-dance** *vb.*; **sand-dashing** (see quot.); **sand-devil**, in Africa, a small whirlwind; **sand-drift**, drifting sand or an accumulation of this; **sand drown**, chlorosis of plants caused by magnesium deficiency in the soil; †**sand dust** *nonce-wd.* = dust *sb.*[1] 3 b; **sand filter**, a filter used in water purification consisting of layers of sand arranged with coarseness of texture increasing downwards; †**sand-fire** = sand-bath 1; **sand-flag**, ? = flag-sandstone (flag *sb.*[2] 5); **sand-flask**, a frame for a sand-mould; **sand-flaw**, a flaw in the surface of a brick due to the uneven coating of sand given to the clay in moulding; **sand flood**, an inundation of moving or drifting sand; **sand-furnace** = sand-bath 1; **sand-gall**, †**-gavel** (see quots.); **sand garden**, in Japanese landscape gardening, an open space covered with sand, the surface of which is raked into a pattern; so **sand gardening**, the practice of this style of landscape design; †**sand-gelt**, in Flanders, ? an impost levied on shipping to pay the cost of clearing the harbour from sand; **sand glacier** *Geomorphol.* (see quot. 1972); **sand gold**, gold dust; **sand grain** *Printing* (see quot. 1906); also *attrib.*; **sand-groper** *Austral.*, a jocular appellation for a native West Australian; **sand-grown** *a.*, designating a native of Blackpool; **sand-happy** *a.* (see -happy); **sand-hog** *U.S.*, a man who works underground, as in a caisson or in foundation-work; also *fig.*; **sand-hole**, (*a*) a small hole or flaw in a casting, also in glass or stone; (*b*) a water-hole in sand; (*c*) a hole in sand; **sand-iron**, (*a*) see quot. 1789; (*b*) *Golf*, an 'iron' adapted for lifting the ball out of sand; **sand-jet**, (*a*) = sand-blast *sb.* 1; (*b*) a jet of sand from the sand-box of a locomotive; **sand-joint** (see quot.); **sand key** *U.S.* [key *sb.*[3]] = *sand cay*; **sand-letter** (see quot.); **sand-lime**, used *attrib.* to denote a type of brick made by baking sand with a proportion of slaked lime under pressure; **sand-lug** *U.S.*, a low grade of tobacco, manufactured from leaves that grow near the ground (*Funk's Stand. Dict.* 1895); †**sand-mail**, ? = *sand-gavel*; **sand-man**, one who digs sand; also, in nursery language, a personification of sleep or sleepiness (cf. G. *sandmann, -männchen*, and dustman 2); **sand mortar** (see quot.); **sand-mould**, a mould for a casting, composed of sand; hence **sand-moulder**; **sand-moulding**, a process of moulding bricks in which the moulds are sprinkled with sand; **sand-painting**, the technique used esp. by the Navajo Indians of painting with coloured sands; an instance of this; **sand-picture**, a picture formed by laying coloured sands on an adhesive ground (Ogilvie 1882); also more *gen.*, a design made in sand; **sand pie**, wet sand formed by a child into the shape of a pie; **sand-pillar** = *sand-spout*; **sand-pipe**, (*a*) *Geol.* (see quot. 1839); (*b*) a pipe conducting sand to the rails from the sand-box of a locomotive; **sand-plain**, a sandy plain; *spec.* in *Geol.*, a flat-topped hill of peculiar structure formed as a delta at the margin of a Pleistocene ice sheet; **sand plant** = *sand-binder*; **sand-plate**, (*a*) = *sanding-plate* (Funk's Stand. Dict.); (*b*) a contrivance for facilitating the transporting of a life-boat over sand; †**sand-plot**, (*a*) = arena; (*b*) a patch of sand; **sand plug** (see quot.); †**sand-poke**, a sand-bag; **sand-pot**, †(*a*) an iron pot used with the sand-furnace; (*b*) *dial.* a quicksand; **sand-pump**, a pump for raising wet sand, detritus, etc., from a drill-hole, oil-well, caisson, etc.; also *attrib.*; **sand-red** *a.*, of a sandy red colour; **sand-reel** (see quot.); **sand ripple**, one of a series of small parallel ridges or undulations in the surface of sand; **sand-rock**, a sandstone rock; **sand-scratch** (see quot.); **sand shadow**, an accumulation of sand to the lee of an obstruction; **sand-shoes**, shoes adapted for wearing on the sands or at the sea-side, *spec.* canvas shoes with gutta-percha or hemp soles; **sand-shot** (see quot.); **sand-slinger** *Founding* (see quot. 1948); **sand-smoke**, a whirlwind or sandstorm; **sand-soap** = *sand-ball*; **sand-spout**, a pillar of sand raised by a whirlwind in a desert; **sand-stock (brick)** (see quot.); **sandstorm**, a desert storm of wind accompanied with clouds of sand; also *fig.*; **sand-strake** = GARBOARD (see quot.); **sand-table**, (*a*) a sand-covered surface on which letters or designs can be drawn and erased or models placed and removed; (*b*) = SAND-TRAP 1; **sand-tray**, (*a*) = *sand-table* (a); (*b*) = SAND-BOX 2 e; **sand-tube**, (*a*) *Geol.* (see quot. 1841); (*b*) *Zool.* = *sand-canal*; also, a protective tube of agglutinated sand formed by some annelids; (*c*) *Mech.*, a conductor for sand; **sand valve, vent** (see quots.); †**sand-walker** *dial.*, ? one employed in shrimping or other similar work on the sands; **sand warped**, swept by the tide on to a sand-bank; also, 'silted up, or choked with sand' (*Whitby Gloss.*, 1876); **sand-wash** *U.S.*, a sloping surface of sand spread out by an intermittent stream; **sand wave**, a wave-like formation in sand; *spec.* in *Physical Geogr.*, an undulation similar to a maripple but on a larger scale; **sand-wedge** = *sand-iron* (b); **sandweld** *v. trans.*, to weld (iron) with sand, which forms a fluid slag on the welding-surface (*Cent. Dict.*); **sand-whirl**, a whirlwind whose vortex is filled with dust and sand (*ibid.*).

1846 *Jewish Manual, or Pract. Information Jewish & Mod. Cookery* iv. 212 *Sand-balls are excellent for removing hardness of the hands. **1858** Simmonds *Dict. Trade*, *Sand-balls*. **1884** A. Watt *Soap-making* xix. 164 Sand-Balls are made by incorporating with melted and perfumed soap certain proportions of fine river sand. **1766** J. Bartram *Jrnl.* 29 Jan. in W. Stork *Descr. E. Florida* 55 Towards the opposite shore there is a *sand-bar. **1782** T. Jefferson *Notes State of Virginia* ii. 9 The Missisipi, below the mouth of the Missouri, is always muddy, and abounding with sand bars, which frequently change their places. **1796** A. Ellicott *Jrnl.* (1803) 14 The fog was so thick that we could neither discover sand-bars nor logs. **1807** P. Gass *Jrnl.* 77 A great many sand-bars [in the Missouri River]. **1897** *Outing* (U.S.) XXX. 50/2 This one sheet of water formed a small harbor to the lee of a sand-bar. **1935** M. M. Atwater *Crime in Corn-Weather* i. 2 The little river—at this season no more than a network of shallow runnels between thirsty sand bars. **1968** W. Warwick *Surfriding in N.Z.* 10/3 At a beach break ..the takeoff area is always changing due to drifting sand-bars. **1884** C. S. Sargent *Rep. Forests N. Amer.* 168 *Sand-Bar Willow... Very common throughout the Mississippi River basin. **1975** M. C. Davis *Near Woods* v. 64 A natural hedge of sandbar willows accompanied us for twenty yards or so into the lake. **1876** H. B. Woodward *Geol. Eng. & Wales* vii. 169 Beds of concretionary sandstone or sandy limestone called '*sand bats' or 'sand burrs'. **1873** F. Jenkin *Electr. & Magn.* xv. §1 This [galvanic] battery is made more portable by filling the cells with sand... In this form it is called the common *sand battery. **1624** Heywood *Captives* i. iii. in Bullen *O. Pl.* IV, A short fellowe..*sand-bearded and squint eyde. **1862** D. Wilson *Preh. Man* ii. (1865) 19 Superior Bay and its tributary rivers with their spits and *sand-belts. **1881** F. Oates *Matabele-Land* (1889) 238, I went on with the waggons.., finally stopping on a sandbelt near a pan of water. **1892** P. Benjamin *Mod. Mechanism* 763 The *sand-belt machine. **1887** Moloney *Forestry W. Afr.* 390 Creeping and twining plant, found on the sea-shore; it is a good *sand-binder. **1852** Mundy *Our Antipodes* (1857) 16 In New South Wales these storms sometimes cause the eye-blight, or *sand-blight, as the malady is indifferently called. **1922** *Chambers's Jrnl.* XII. 428/2 The drifting sand held sway... Towns and villages were devastated by it... *Sand-blow alone did not complete the desolation. For months great areas were covered with water. **1934** *Antiquity* VIII. 182 Vast sand-blows begun by cattle breaking down the dunes. **1980** *National Trust* Spring 15/1 They were isolated from the sea by the extraordinary thirteenth- and fourteenth-century sand-blows. **1875** Knight *Dict. Mech.*, **Sand-blower*, a device for powdering with sand a freshly painted surface, in order to make it resemble stone. **1817** A. Bell *Instr. Conduct. Schools* (ed. 6) 8 The scholars copy.. the capital printed letters on sand at the *sand board. **1875** Knight *Dict. Mech.*, *Sand-board*, a bar over the hind axle [of a vehicle] and parallel therewith. **1895** *Funk's Stand. Dict.*, *Sand-board*, in car-building, a spring-plank. **1910** R. H. Johnson in *Oil Investors' Jrnl.* 20 Feb. 70/3 The necessity of conceiving the shape of the *sand body as something different from the shape of the actual oil-containing reservoir is of great importance. *Ibid.*, I have found this of considerable value in predicting the shape of a 'sand-body'. **1911** —— in *Econ. Geol.* VI. 809 In order to emphasize the importance of shape I have suggested that the term sand-body be adopted, from the analogy of the word ore-body, to describe the reservoir, i.e., continuous mass of sand or sandstones sufficiently porous to be capable of containing oil and gas in commercial quantities. **1927** *Petroleum Devel. & Technol. 1926* (Amer. Inst. Mining Engin. Petroleum Div.) 202 He is also enabled to determine such vital subsurface conditions as (1) porosity, (2) density, (3) saturation, and (4) thickness of sandbodies. **1937** *Daily Progress* (Charlottesville, Va.) 2 Feb. 1/8 Dread '*sand boils' bursting up in the heart of.. Cairo [Illinois] forewarned of deeply undermined barriers guarding the..city today... The eruptions sprang from the terrific pressure of the flooded Ohio River waters slowly eating their way beneath the..levels. **1939** W. Faulkner *Wild Palms* 24 Even those who..had probably never before seen more water than a horse pond..could (and did) talk glibly of sandboils. **1954** *Encounter* Oct. 9/1 The owners of the..plantations along the Big River confederated..to hold the sandboils and the cracks. **1976** C. S. Brown *Gloss. Faulkner's South* 167 A sandboil must be neutralized promptly. This is done by building a wall of sandbags around it so that a column of water will be built up above it to equalize the pressure. *a* **1683** Shaftesb. in *Gentl. Mag.* (1754) XXIV. 160/1 A bowling green..long but narrow, full of high ridges..; they used round *sand bowls. **1884** Knight *Dict. Mech.* Suppl., **Sand Brake*. **1883** Stevenson *Treas. Isl.* xiii, This even tint was indeed broken up by streaks of yellow *sandbreak in the lower lands. **1871** Kingsley *At Last* i, A little swamp of foul brown water, backed up by the *sand-brush. **1824** Scott *Redgauntlet* Let. xi, A' the gangrel bodies that ye..find cowering in a *sand-bunker upon the links. **1875** Knight *Dict. Mech.*, **Sand-burned*. **1876** *Sand burr [see *sand-bat*]. **1892** *Encycl. Cookery* (ed. Garrett) I. 253 *Sand Cakes. Sand Cake with Marmalade (German). **1870** H. A. Nicholson *Man. Zool.* I. Gloss., **Sand-canal*, the tube by which water is conveyed from the exterior to the ambulacral system of the *Echinodermata*. **1854** C. M. Yonge *Castle Builders* v. 63 The children are..dabbling after sea-weed and shells, and building *sand castles. **1925** H. G. Wells *Christina Alberta's Father* i. iv. 95 They had..camped on the beach while Mr. Preemby and Christina Alberta had made sand-castles. **1975** C. A. Haddad *Moroccan* i. 5 We tried to build a sandcastle romance out of our few short months in the [desert] sand. **1980** D. Newsome *On Edge of Paradise* vii. 228 Playing like children on the beach.. making sand-castles. **1934** T. Wood *Cobbers* xvii. 219 You do not see it [*sc.* the Barrier Reef]... You see instead islands. .. Islands which are sand-cays covered with birds. **1937** *Geogr. Jrnl.* LXXXIX. 138 *Sand-cays may occur on almost any reef, but they are most typical of the inner reefs of the outer barrier. **1968** R. W. Fairbridge *Encycl. Geomorphol.* 972/2 During hurricanes, sand cays are liable to be swept clear of vegetation and may disappear completely in a single storm. **1865** *Student & Schoolmate* June 177 One evening, fifty years ago, the noiseless '*sand-clock' in Squire Allen's bar-room was fast running down. **1964** *Listener* 24 Dec. 1011/3 The watch makers of Nuremberg were still turning out sand clocks on the egg-timer principle. **1839** Bailey *Festus* xxxi. (1854) 517 The desert *sand-cloud or simoom. **1873** *Winfield* (Kansas) *Courier* 11 Sept. 1/7 A weapon of a peculiarly dangerous and for a time mysterious nature..is a *sand club, formed by filling an eel skin with sand. **1912** *Punch* 15 May 380/2 Incidentally I am pleased to know that Americans call a niblick a sand-club. **1977** P. Alliss *Play Golf with P. Alliss* 57 If you play on a heavy course with hard muddy bunkers then you will need a sand club with a sharpish leading edge. **1848** Ronalds & Richardson *Chem. Technol.* I. 33 Other kinds of coal..leave a coke of the same form without caking. When pulverized, they leave a powdery coke. This variety is called *sand-coal. **1902** Webster Suppl., **Sand cone*, a low pinnacle of ice on a glacier, protected from melting by a layer of sand. **1894** W. M. F. Petrie *Tell El Amarna* iv. 27 A tapering rod of metal was taken..; on the end of this was formed a core of fine sand... The rod and core were dipped in the melted glass. .. When the whole was finished, the metal rod in cooling would contract loose from the glass; it could then be withdrawn, the *sand core rubbed out, and the vase would be finished. **1933** *Antiquity* VII. 421 In the technique of glass-manufacture..the process of pressing into a mould as distinct from modelling on a sand-core came into vogue. **1934** *Greece & Rome* May 140 Vessels of glass made by the sand-core technique, a process well known in Egypt during the eighteenth dynasty. **1962** D. Harden *Phoenicians* xi. 154 From the seventh to the third century sand-core fabrics made up the bulk of existing glass vessels. **1754** J. Bartlet *Gentleman's Farriery* (ed. 2) 312 What is called a *sand-crack is a little cleft on the outside of the hoof. **1895** J. G. Millais *Breath fr. Veldt* (1899) 102 His feet were so sore with sand-cracks he could not walk. **1903** Somerville & 'Ross' *All on Irish Shore* 82 The glow from the fire illumined the smith's sardonic grin of remembrance. 'She had a sandcrack in the near fore that time, and there's the sign of it yet.' **1934** A. Russell *Tramp-Royal in Wild Austral.* xix. 120 This in a country where the hooves of horses develop sandcrack. **1976** *Horse & Hound* 3 Dec. 53 (Advt.), Daily use after sand-crack, seedy-toe, brittle or contracted feet, encourages the natural growth of healthy horn. **1856** Thoreau *Jrnl.* 9 Apr. (1949) VIII. 268, I..sit on the edge of that *sand-crater near the spring by the railroad. **1883** *Science* I. 67/2 'Sand-craters'..are shown to result from the wet quicksand being forced up through a vent..in the overlying clays. **1916** *Soil Sci.* II. 208 The *sand culture solutions giving low yields of tops are characterized by a wide range in the Mg/Ca ratio. **1936** *Phytopathology* XXVI. 279 Soil cultures were similarly prepared and kept with the sand cultures under the same conditions. **1940** [see *gravel culture* s.v. GRAVEL *sb.* 9]. **1978** *Fluoride* XI. 76 In *Helianthus annus* seedlings grown in sand culture for five weeks the concentration of fluoride in the root and shoot was generally proportional to the concentration in the substrate. **1879** Stevenson *Ess. Trav., Amateur Emigrants* (1905) 23 That's a bonny hornpipe now,..they dance the *sand dance to it. **1905** *Daily Chron.* 24 Feb. 6/3 Only an expert in *sand-dancing could have found a hair's-breadth of difference in their ability to sand-dance. **1833** Loudon *Encycl. Archit.* §1435. 683 The external walls to be of stone.., walled rough for stucco or *sand-dashing (rough-casting). **1901** *Lancet* 16 Mar. 771/1 A number of small whirlwinds, called '*sand-devils', which would pass slowly along sucking up quantities of sand and any light articles such as pieces of paper. **1977** H. Innes *Big Footprints* iii. ii. 282 There was nothing visible ..except here and there the dancing whirl of a sand devil. **1839** De la Beche *Rep. Geol. Cornwall*, etc. xiv. 445 Running streams of water arrest the progress of the *sand-drift. **1922** *Science* 22 Sept. 341/2 The popular name of this chlorosis is '*Sand Drown', a term referring to the fact that the disease is likely to occur in aggravated form in the more sandy portions of the field after heavy rainfall. **1968** B. C. Akehurst *Tobacco* v. 96 Magnesium deficiency (called sand drown) is shown by a characteristic chlorosis that starts with the tips of the bottom leaves, spreads across them and moves up the plant in a similar manner. **1604** Middleton & Dekker *Honest Wh.* i. i, What but faire *sand-dust are earths purest formes. **1677** W. Harris tr. *Lemery's Course Chem.* 57 Place the Matrass in a small *Sand-fire digesting for a day. **1747** tr. *Astruc's Fevers* 150 [The water] must be renewed as often as it is evaporated by the sand-fire. **1894** Rafter & Baker *Sewage Disposal in U.S.* xiv. 267 *Sand filters have considerable capacity for storing the nitrogenous matter at one period and later on converting it into nitrates. **1977** F. M. Middleton in H. I. Shuval *Water Renovation & Reuse* i. 13 Sand filters have been used for many years. **1814** Scott *Diary* 9 Aug. in Lockhart *Life*, These lofty cliffs are all of *Sand-flag, a very loose and perishable kind of rock. **1822** —— *Pirate* vii. **1884** C. G. W. Lock *Workshop Receipts* Ser. iii. 10/2 A *sand-flask is then placed upon the board over the model. **1884** C. T. Davis *Bricks & Tiles* 124 (Cent.) The brick shall contain no cracks or *sand-flaws. **1668** *Phil. Trans.* II. 722 A *Sand-floud, which hath lately over-whelmed a great tract of Land in..Suffolk. **1830** Lyell *Princ. Geol.* I. 301 The commencement of the sand-flood might have been long posterior to the formation of the greater portion of that continent. **1666** Boyle *Orig. Formes & Qual.* ii. vii. 370 We very gently in a *Sand-Furnace distill off the Menstruum. **1787** Grose *Provinc. Gloss.*, *Galls*, *sand-galls, spots of sand through which the water oozes. Norf. and Suf. ? **1811** *Agric. Surv. Dumbart.* 330 (Jam. s.v. *Gaw*) A few narrow sand gaws. **1876** H. B. Woodward *Geol. Eng. & Wales* xiii. 409 The Chalk is worn away into pipes and hollows. *Note.* Called 'Earth pots' in Norfolk, and sometimes 'Sand-galls'. **1936** T. Tamura *Art of Landscape Garden in Japan* 225 (*caption*) A *sand garden carefully raked to print lines and waves. **1965** 'S. Harvester' *Assassins Road* iii. 32 The lighted windows showed patches as desolate as a Japanese sand-garden. **1975** R. L. Duncan *Dragons at Gate* (1976) iii. 89 Calder only half heard what she was saying,..fixing his attention on the sand garden. **1960** *Spectator* 16 Feb. 261/1 It's an uneasy, foreign respect—the sort one feels for minor, inscrutable Japanese arts such as Noh or sand-gardening. **1663** S. Taylor *Gavelkind* ix. 113 In the same Lordship [of Rodely, Glos.] is also another called *Sand-gavel, which is..a Payment due to the Lord, for the liberty granted to the Tenents to Digg up Sand. **1527** *Chron. Calais* (Camden) 103 Without paying ..*sandgelt, wharfgelt [etc.]. **1875** *Encycl. Brit.* III. 599/1 Among the less ordinary geological phenomena [of the Bermudas] may be mentioned the '*sand glacier' at Elbow Bay. **1897** *Geogr. Jrnl.* IX. 286 Wind blowing outwards from a deep sand tract forms a horizontal plateau terminated by a talus as steep as the sand can rest. Under these conditions the encroachment of sand recalls the manner of advance of a glacier, and to this formation I restrict the term 'sand glacier'. **1919** *Proc. R. Soc. Victoria* XXXI. 416 The typical forms of sand accumulation known as 'sand glaciers', which have been described in various parts of the world are due to sand being blown up the sides of hills or mountains, thence finding a passage through any passes or saddles, and spreading out on the opposite sides to form wide fan-shaped plains. **1972** *Gloss. Geol.* (Amer. Geol. Inst.) 627/2 *Sand glacier*. (*a*) An accumulation of sand that is blown up the side of a hill or mountain and through a pass or saddle, and then spread out on the opposite side to form a wide fan-shaped plain. (*b*) A horizontal plateau of sand terminated by a steep talus slope. **1766** Amory *Buncle* (1770) IV. 110 It is found..sometimes in a powdery form, and then called gold-dust, or *sand-gold. **1906** Goodchild & Tweney *Technol. & Sci. Dict.* 203/1 *Sand Grain... A ground is laid as for etching; a sheet of sandpaper is then laid face downwards on the plate, which is passed through the printer's press with sufficient pressure for the grains of sand to pierce the ground. **1960** H. Hayward *Antique Coll.* 248/1 A sand-grain aquatint is obtained from a plate which has been pulled through the press with a piece of sand paper to roughen its surface. **1896** H. Lawson *Let.* 3 Sept. (1970) 62 W[estern] A[ustralia] is a fraud... The old *Sand-gropers are the best to work for or have dealings with. **1902** J. H. M. Abbott *T. Cornstalk* i, In delicate reference to the nature of their country the West Australians are [called] 'Sand-gropers'. **1934** [see BANANALAND]. **1946** K. S. Prichard *Roaring Nineties* 214 'I'm a sand-groper,' she snapped... 'Don't know anything about London or Paris.' **1974** *Sunday Tel.* (Austral.) 30 June, Mining millionaire Lang Hancock has a sizeable number of sandgropers prepared to support his view that Western Australia should be detached from the rest of the nation. **1969** *Listener* 6 Mar. 300/1 Natives of Blackpool are called *sand-grown men. **1972** *New Society* 16 Nov. 394/2 The 'sand-grown-'uns' (the Blackpool-born). **1943** *Fortune* Dec. 268 A British Tommy on the North African desert..may have gone..'*sand happy'. **1944** J. Gunther *D Day* 129 Many are what the officers call 'sand-happy'; this is a phrase almost equivalent to punch-drunk, except that it does not mean lack of fighting instinct. **1961** *Times* 14 Sept. 15/2 Captain Scott, weathered, expatriate, sand-happy. **1903** *Century Mag.* Nov. 43/1 The tunnel workers, or '*Sand Hogs', enter the lower chambers of the shield. **1904** *N.Y. Even. Post* 11 Jan. 3 The men who are employed as 'sandhogs' or excavators in the caisson for the new Manhattan Bridge. **1940** R. Chandler *Farewell, My Lovely* xiii. 98 He just got through working as a sandhog on the San Jack tunnel. **1965** *National Observer* (U.S.) 13 Dec. 12/1 Those who view Mr. Sweeney and his Appalachian Commission associates as 'sandhogs' are the other poverty operations. **1977** N. Hynd *Sandler Inquiry* xvii. 130 George McAdam was a 'sandhog'. *Ibid.* 131 The sandhogs were the British agents in oil intelligence. **1691** T. H[ale] *Acc. New Invent.* 96 Certain defects in Cast-lead..called by the Plumber Blow-holes and *Sand-holes. **1867** G. F. Chambers *Astron.* 615 Air bubbles, striae, sand-holes,..of course,..are bad [in an object glass]. **1887** [see *sand vent*]. **1896** R. S. S. Baden-Powell *Matabele Campaign* xiii, While they scoop the muddy water from the sand-hole for their tea. **1897** *Encycl. Sport* I. 457/1 Golf may be played.. where the..whins, *sand-holes and banks, supply the conditions which are essential to the proper pursuit of the game. **1910** W. de la Mare *Three Mulla-Mulgars* xx. 267 Home he goes to his leaf-thatched huddle or sand-hole. **1935** W. Empson *Poems* 22 By jackal sandhole to your air flung wide. **1796** Morse *Amer. Geog.* I. 464 Jared Eliot.. invented *sand-iron, or the making of iron from black sand, in 1761. **1862** *Sandiron [see NIBLICK]. **1881** FORGAN *Golfer's Handbk.* 28 He should..firmly grasp his weapon (Niblick or Sand-Iron). **1871** *Jrnl. Franklin Inst.* Sept. 155 The blocks [for engraving] are protected with an open design..and the steam *sand jet directed upon them. **1900** *Daily Express* 19 June 5/7 The switching-on of the sandjets [of a train]. **1888** *Lockwood's Dict. Mech. Engin.*, **Sand Joint*, the parting or joint between the different portions of the sand of a foundry mould. **1775** B. ROMANS *Conc. Nat. Hist. E. & W. Florida* App. p. xli, We found ourselves surrounded by three very small low *sand keys (full of prickly pears). **1829** in *Amer. State Papers: Naval Affairs* (U.S. Congress) (1861) IV. 968 An effort is now making to form a naval establishment on the insulated cluster of sand keys called the Dry Tortugas. **1837** J. W. WILLIAMS *Territory of Florida* 23 Anclote Sound is sheltered on the west, by Anclote, Jacs and Sand Keys. **1880** G. W. CABLE *Grandissimes* v. 34 A beautiful land of low, evergreen hills ..[looked] out across the pine-covered sand-keys of Mississippi Sound. **1930** J. F. DOBIE *Coronado's Children* xviii. 308 They landed the Laffites on a barren sand key with just enough provisions to keep them alive a few days. **1937** *Geogr. Jrnl.* LXXXIX. 143 The reefs which bear a sand-key, and on which there is no sub-aerial accumulation of coral-shingle, have a least depth of water of 3 feet. **1843** *Penny Cycl.* XXV. 456/1 Large letters..were formerly cast in sand-moulds, and hence called *sand-letters. **1910** *Encycl. Brit.* IV. 521/1 The so-called *sand-lime bricks are now made on a very extensive scale in many countries. **1933** *Archit. Rev.* LXXIV. 225/2 (*caption*) The whole of the internal walls are faced with cream sand-lime bricks. **1966** W. G. NASH *Brickwork* I. i. 30 There are four classes of sand-lime bricks. **1287** *Yorksh. Inquisitions* (Yks. Rec. Soc.) II. 61 *Sondemale, 10*d.* at Easter and Michaelmas. **1821** CLARE *Vill. Minstr.* I. 116 The *sand-man's delving spade. **1861** WEHNERT tr. *Andersen's Tales* (1869) 237 Of an evening, as soon as it begins to grow dark,..the Sandman comes. **1775** ASH, **Sandmortar*, mortar in which sand is a principal ingredient. **1843** HOLTZAPFFEL *Turning*, etc. I. 325 Plaster of Paris and *sand moulds. **1831** J. HOLLAND *Manuf. Metal* I. 55 There is hardly a single article..in wrought-iron the like of which the ingenuity of the *sand-moulder cannot produce in cast metal. **1843** *Min. Proc. Inst. Civ. Engin.* II. ii. 147 The process was a kind of intermediate one between slop and *sand-moulding. **1902** W. HOUGH in *Rep. U.S. Nat. Museum 1900* 467 The ceremonial *sand painting of the Hopi and Navajo, where the most beautiful effects are secured by allowing sand in slender streams of different colors to fall from the hand guiding it over the surface to form designs. **1908** *Encycl. Relig. & Ethics* I. 826/2 The sand-paintings..may be regarded as actual pictorial prayers. **1963** G. S. MAXWELL *Navajo Rugs* (1973) iii. 47 Sandpainting rugs are woven copies of actual sandpaintings. **1978** T. HILLERMAN *Listening Woman* i. 3 Tell me more about how these sand paintings got messed up. **1957** J. KIRKUP *Only Child* xiv. 188 There was a man who made wonderful sculptures in the damp sand... Once,..he made a low-relief *sand-picture of the Shields Town Hall. **1970** G. SAVAGE *Dict. Antiques* 369/2 Apart from the work of Zobel, sand-pictures are rarely signed, and must be identified from their characteristics. **1975** *Times* 6 Dec. 11/5 A collection of sand pictures, mostly made in the Isle of Wight. **1835** C. F. HOFFMAN *Winter in West* I. 148 A bevy of rosy little girls..were making '*sand pies' on the bank of the river. **1980** M. DRABBLE *Middle Ground* 181 Girls in a concrete playground, making sand pies. **1879** WEBSTER Suppl., **Sand-pillar*, a sand-storm in desert tracts, like those of the Sahara and Mongolia. **1839** LYELL in *Lond. & Edin. Philos. Mag.* XV. 257 On the tubular Cavities filled with Gravel and Sand called '*Sand-pipes', in the Chalk near Norwich. **1905** *Daily Chron.* 15 Dec. 5/5 The sand-pipes which are fixed in front of the wheels of the engine. **1818** A. EATON *Man. Bot.* (ed. 2) 291 On the *sand plains, at the foot of Pine-rock, in New-Haven, a [juniper] root.. often sends off shoots. **1903** *Westm. Gaz.* 18 Sept. 4/2 The sand-plains of Berlin. **1849** BALFOUR *Man. Bot.* §1139 *Sand plants; as *Carex arenaria*, *Ammophila arenaria* [etc.] which tend to fix the loose sand. **1902** *Encycl. Brit.* XXX. 232/2 (art. *Life-boat*) *Sand-plates. **1618** BOLTON *Florus* (1636) 267 The first field and *Sand-plot of civill Warre was Italy. **1745** P. THOMAS *Jrnl. Anson's Voy.* 163 The Bottom very foul, being Riffs of Coral Rocks, interspersed with small Sand-plots. **1888** *Lockwood's Dict. Mech. Engin.* s.v. *Plug*, A *sand plug..is..the ball of sand..with which the riser of a mould is covered while the metal is being poured at the ingate. **1415–16** *Durham Acc. Rolls* (Surtees) 612 Item in 2 uln. di. de canvas empt. pro 1 *Sand-poke, 10*d.* **1421–2** *Ibid.* 228 Pro sandepokes. **1758** *Elaboratory* 15 Procure a proper *sand-pot, and large plate for forming the sand-bath. **1877** E. LEIGH *Chesh. Gloss.*, *Sand Pot*, a quicksand. Often met with in draining. **1865** *Harper's Mag.* Apr. 573/2 A *sand-pump is a metal case from five to ten feet in length, constructed with a valve at the bottom. **1881** RAYMOND *Mining Gloss.*, *Sand-pump*. **1902** *Encycl. Brit.* XXVII. 530/2 Sand-pump dredgers. *a* **1639** WOTTON in *Reliq.* (1651) 524 She trips to milk the *Sand-red Cow. **1883** *Century Mag.* July 329/2 The *sand-reel..serves to lower or raise the sand-pump. **1879** T. D. FORSYTH in E. D. Morgan tr. *Prejevalsky's From Kulja to Lob-Nor* 27 The upheaval of the Gobi..causes an entirely independent direction of profile.. to that of the *sand-ripples which cover it. **1897** *Geogr. Jrnl.* IX. 279 The uniformity of the wind-ripple pattern is at all times remarkable. In water-formed sand-ripples no such uniformity has been recorded. **1941** R. A. BAGNOLD *Physics of Blown Sand & Desert Dunes* xi. 144 A sand ripple is merely a crumpling or heaping up of the surface, brought about by wind action, and cannot be regarded as a true wave in a strict dynamical sense. **1960** B. W. SPARKS *Geomorphol.* xi. 248 The formation of sand ripples is closely connected with the process of saltation. **1798** CHARLOTTE SMITH *Yng. Philos.* IV. 276 They took the way above the excavation of *sand-rock where I sat. **1872** DANA *Corals* ii. 155 These sand-banks..become cemented into a sand-rock. **1871** STORMONTH *Dict.*, **Sand-scratches*, in *geol.*, rocks or rock-surfaces worn smooth, or marked with scratches and furrows, by sand carried by the wind passing over them. **1941** R. A. BAGNOLD *Physics of Blown Sand & Desert Dunes* xiii. 188 Deposits caused directly by fixed obstructions in the path of the sand-driving wind... These *sand shadows and sand drifts are dependent for their continued existence on the presence of the obstacle. **1971** I. G. GASS et al. *Understanding Earth* xiii. 184/2 Left behind protecting shells or pebbles are elongate mounds of sand ('sand-shadows') which give the beach a distinctive appearance. **1855** PATMORE *Angel in Ho.* II. xii. 1 While the shop-girl fitted on The *sand-shoes. **1916** J. B. COOPER *Coo-oo-ee* xvi. 235 In the circumscribed space of the vessel, the men, clad in their blue dungarees, wearing white sand-shoes, prepared themselves for their future battles. **1931** V. WOOLF *Waves* 16 Those are Louis' neat sand-shoes firmly printing the gravel. **1948** J. BETJEMAN *Sel. Poems* 79 Don't empty children's sand-shoes in the hall. **1965** S. T. OLLIVIER *Petticoat Farm* vii. 96 Rather than walk the dusty road in their freshly cleaned sparkling white sandshoes the girls took a short cut across the paddocks. **1979** *Guardian* 23 May 31/4 The sand shoe and school sandal look which was justifiably popular last summer. **1867** BRANDE & COX *Dict. Sci.*, etc., **Sand Shot*. In Artillery, small cast-iron balls; so called because they have always been cast in sand. **1928** *Jrnl. Iron & Steel Inst.* CXVII. 805 Stripping machines are mounted on turntables, which bring the flasks within range of a *sand-slinger, and then delivers them to the mould conveyor. **1948** J. E. GARSIDE in H. W. Baker *Mod. Workshop Technol.* I. iii. 65 For the ramming of sand moulds, a machine known as the 'sand slinger' is often used. It ejects a stream of sand vertically downwards at a high speed, so that the sand is rammed by impact with the pattern. **1930** T. S. ELIOT tr. *St.-J. Perse's Anabasis* 49 These *sandsmokes that rise over dead river courses. **1855** PIESSE *Perfumery* viii. 166 *Sand Soap. **1899** *Allbutt's Syst. Med.* VIII. 931 Salicylic acid..followed by friction with pumice-stone or sand-soap, will [etc.]. *a* **1849** J. C. MANGAN *Poems* (1859) 264 A *sandspout out of that sandy ocean, upcurls. **1884** J. COLBORNE *Hicks Pasha* 176 The sand-spouts, so frequent in these regions. **1843** *Min. Proc. Inst. Civ. Engin.* II. ii. 145 The mould is dipped into water previous to its receiving the clay, instead of its being sanded as is the case in making *sandstock bricks. *Ibid.* 146 Sand-stock and slop-moulding. **1956** *Archit. Rev.* CXIX. 257/2 Leicestershire *sandstock bricks are used in the panel on the west elevation. **1973** *Parade* (Austral.) Oct. 28/3 'Sandstock' (handmade) bricks were made from clay in the valley. **1774** GOLDSM. *Nat. Hist.* (1824) I. 155 The *sand storm of Africa exhibits a very different appearance. **1928** H. CRANE *Let.* 27 Apr. (1965) 325 Efforts for a foothold in this sand-storm [*sc.* Hollywood] are still avid. **1966** 'J. HACKSTON' *Father clears Out* 139 We missed the old..weather... Missed our blinding sandstorms even. **1978** A. & G. RITCHIE *Anc. Monuments Orkney* 43 The people who were forced to abandon their homes in the final sandstorm had been using essentially the same sort of pottery vessels as their ancestors who founded the settlement. **1820** SCORESBY *Acc. Arctic Reg.* II. 448 *note*, Garboard-strake, or *sand-strake, is the first range of strakes or planks laid..next the keel. **1867** SMYTH *Sailor's Word-bk.* **1812** N. J. HOLLINGSWORTH *Address Madras Syst. Educ.* p. ix, To the finger and *sand-table may succeed the pencil and slate. **1911** *Encycl. Brit.* XX. 728/2 To get rid of them [*sc.* impurities] the esparto pulp when washed and bleached is run from the potcher into storage chests, from which it is pumped over a long, narrow serpentine settling table or 'sand-table'. **1928** *Daily Tel.* 7 Aug. 4/4 A thorough groundwork of tactical knowledge has been formed by sand-table and week-end schemes during the winter. **1955** F. G. PATTON *Good Morning, Miss Dove* 13 One group..modelled clay caribou for the sand table. **1963** R. R. A. HIGHAM *Handbk. Papermaking* ii. 67 With rifflers and sand tables the stock is passed at approximately 0·5% consistency along narrow channels. **1969** E. H. PINTO *Treen* 423 The sand table is a very ancient device and may be referred to by Isaiah 'Now go write it before them in a table'. **1971** J. WAINWRIGHT *Last Buccaneer* II. 243 'What..is a sand-table?'..'It's usually a tray, filled with sand. The army uses them. It's possible to mould the sand into the contours of geographic locations for demonstrating military tactics.' [**1817** A. BELL *Instructions for Conducting Schools through Agency of Scholars Themselves* II. i. 68 For writing on sand, smooth and level (trays or) boards, ten inches wide, with ledges on every side of an inch deep..are prepared.] **1893** *N. & Q.* 25 Mar. 233/1 Economy being a great feature in the plan, the *sand trays..were adopted. A full account of the system was published by the S.P.C.K. in 1840. **1968** *Guardian* 23 Aug. 7/6 A livid deputation approached me, waving the kitten's sand-tray. **1972** *Country Life* 6 Jan. 31/2, I was also interested in the 19th-century sand tray or abacus in the north aisle. This was used for teaching children to write with a wooden stick on the sand. **1814** *Trans. Geol. Soc.* II 532 *Sand Tubes. **1841** BRANDE *Chem.* (ed. 5) 276 *note*, What are termed sand-tubes appear to be formed by the passage of lightning through a sandy soil which it fuses in its passage. **1857** GOSSE *Omphalos* 202 Implements by which the sand-tube [of a Terebella] is thus built up. **1871** *Jrnl. Franklin Inst.* 195 An annular passage surrounding the sand tube. **1875** *Encycl. Brit.* II. 67/2 Large coherent masses of coarse gravel and sand-tubes are formed..by *Sabellaria*. **1888** *Lockwood's Dict. Mech. Engin.*, **Sand Valve*, the valve by which the escape of sand from the sand box of a locomotive is regulated. **1887** *Archit. Publ. Soc. Dict.*, *Sandhole* in stone; also called a *sand vent. A deposit of sand in a block of stone. **1637–8** *Maldon* (Essex) *Borough Deeds* (Bundle 149 No. 3), Warne all..ferrymen, marshmen, and *sandwalkers within your townshippe..to be and appeare before our..vice-admirall. *a* **1661** FULLER *Worthies, Cambs.* (1662) I. 159 Crossing Humber in a Barrow-boat, the same was *sand-warpt, and he drowned therein. **1867** SMYTH *Sailor's Word-bk.*, *Sand-warpt*, left by the tide on a shoal. Also, striking on a shoal at half-flood. **1901** *Science* 4 Jan. 38/1 From this point the party worked down the *sandwash of Rio San Ignacio (or Rio Altar) to the coast of the Gulf of California, where the Tepoka Indians lived until recently. **1937** *Discovery* Jan. 24/1 The sand-washes surrounding the wells in the Gobi. **1948** *Sierra Club, S. Calif. Chapter, Schedule* No. 129. 69 The campsite will be in the sand wash at the mouth of the Fan Hill Canyon. **1819** KEATS *Ode Melancholy*, Then glut thy sorrow on..the rainbow of the salt *sand-wave. **1899** *Geogr. Jrnl.* XIII. 624 The sand-waves which corrugate the beds of streams and rivers. **1902** 'MARK TWAIN' in *Harper's Mag.* Jan. 269/2 He started on a run, racing in and out among the sage-bushes a matter of three hundred yards, and disappeared over a sand-wave. **1917** *Bull. Geol. Soc. Amer.* XXVIII. 915 Cross-bedding..probably represents in many instances one phase of a phenomenon called sand waves, which are nothing more than current-made ripple-mark[s] of mammoth proportions... The crests are often 15 to 35 feet apart and rise from 2 to 3 feet above the troughs. **1939** W. H. TWENHOFEL *Princ. Sedimentation* vi. 190 The sand waves or antidunes move up-current as the individual sands move down-current. **1978** *Nature* 14 Sept. 101/2 Sandwaves are the largest scale of bedform.., with average heights and wavelengths markedly larger than those of megaripples. **1937** H. LONGHURST *Golf* I. xxii. 196 No chapter on bunker play would be complete without a description of..the ..*sand wedge. **1952** *Chambers's Jrnl.* May 298/1, I couldn't use a sand-wedge in a bunker because I hadn't the strength to swing it. **1971** 'D. HALLIDAY' *Dolly & Doctor Bird* xv. 215 Wallace Brady..landed in the long, pale trap in front of the green and stayed there doing explosive shots with a sand-wedge.

b. In the names of animals, etc., as **sand asp**, ? = *sand-lizard*; **sand-badger**, (*a*) a Javanese badger, *Meles ankuma*; (*b*) the Indian badger, *Arctonyx collaris*, also called **sand bear**; **sand-beetle** (see quot.); **sand bird**, a bird whose habitat is the seashore, esp. the SANDPIPER; **sand boa**, a snake of the genus *Eryx*, found in north and east Africa and south and east Asia; **sand-bug**, (*a*) a member of the family *Galgulidæ*; (*b*) *N. Amer.*, a sand-wasp, *Ammophila arenaria* (Ogilvie 1855); (*c*) a burrowing crab, *Hippa talpoida*; **sand-clam**, *N. Amer.*, the common Long Clam, *Mya arenaria*; **sand cock**, the redshank; **sand-collar** = *sand-saucer* (Cent. Dict.); **sand crab**, (*a*) a crab of the family *Ocypodidæ*; (*b*) the Lady Crab, *Platyonichus ocellatus*; also *fig.*; **sand-creeper** [? a. Du. **zandkruiper*], a South African fish; **sand-cricket**, *U.S.*, a cricket belonging to the genus *Stenopelmatus*, esp. *S. fasciatus*; **sand dab**, (*a*) either of two eastern North American flat-fishes, the American plaice, *Hippoglossoides platessoides*, or the windowpane, *Scophthalmus aquosus*; (*b*) *dial.* = DAB *sb.*[2]; **sand dart**, a moth, *Agrotis ripæ*; **sand-darter**, an etheostomine fish of the genus *Ammocrypta*, esp. *A. pellucida* (Cent. Dict.); **sand-diver**, a West Indian lizard fish, *Synodus intermedius* (Webster *Suppl.* 1902); **sand dollar**, a flattened, irregular sea urchin belonging to the order Clypeastroida; **sand fiddler** *U.S.*, a small burrowing fiddler crab of the genus *Uca*; **sand-fish**, (*a*) a fish of the family *Trichodontidæ*, esp. one of the genus *Trichodon* (Cent. Dict.); (*b*) a book-name for *Diplectrum formosum*; (*c*) *S. Afr.* = MOGGEL; (*d*) *S. Afr.*, the beaked salmon, *Gonorhynchus gonorhynchus*; **sand flea**, (*a*) = CHIGOE; (*b*) *U.S.*, a crustacean belonging to the genus *Orchestia*; (*c*) a brine-shrimp, *Artemia salina*; **sand fluke** *dial.*, a flat-fish, *Pleuronectes microcephalus*; **sand-gaper** = *sand-clam*; **sand goanna**, an Australian monitor lizard, *Varanus gouldii*; **sand goby**, the common goby, *Pomatoschistus minutus*; **sand-hopper**, a crustacean, *Talitrus locusta*; also, a sand flea of the genus *Orchestia*; **sand-hornet**, a sand-wasp; esp. one of the family *Crabronidæ* (Cent. Dict.); **sand-jumper** = *sand-hopper*; **sand-lance** = *sand-launce*; **sand-launce** = SAND-EEL 1; **sand lizard**, (*a*) a common European lizard, *Lacerta agilis*; (*b*) *U.S.*, a fringe-toed lizard of the genus *Uma* or the striped race-runner, *Cnemidophorus sexlineatus*; **sand lob** = *sand-worm* (Cent. Dict.); **sandlurker** = PRIDE *sb.*[2]; **sand martin**, a variety of the MARTIN, *Riparia riparia*, which nests in the side of a sand-pit; **sand-mason**, a burrowing polychæte tube-worm belonging to the genus *Lanice*; also *attrib.*; **sand-mole** [Du. *zandmoll*], a mole of the S. African species *Bathyergus maritimus*; **sand monitor**, (*a*) the land-crocodile, *Monitor* or *Psammosaurus arenarius* (Cassell's Encycl. Dict. 1887); (*b*) = *sand goanna*; †**sand-mussel** (see quot.); **sandnecker**, a flat-fish, *Platessa limandoides*; **sand-partridge**, a partridge of the genus *Ammoperdix* (Cent. Dict.); **sand-peep**, a familiar name in the U.S. for various small sandpipers; **sand perch** *U.S.*, a small bass, *Roccus americanus*, found in marine and fresh water in eastern North America; **sand pigeon**, (*a*) see quot.; (*b*) the stock-dove, *Columba œnas* (E.D.D.); **sand-pike** (see PIKE *sb.*); **sand plover**, a local name for plovers of the genera *Ægialitis* and *Squatarola*; **sand-prey, -pride** = PRIDE *sb.*[2]; **sand rat**, a N. American rat of the genus *Thomomys*, esp. *T. talpoides*; **sand roller**, the trout perch (Webster *Suppl.* 1902); **sand-runner**, a sand-plover or sandpiper (Newton); **sand-saucer** (see quot.); **sandscrew**, an amphipod, *Lepidactylis arenaria*; **sand-shark**, (*a*) *U.S.*, a kind of shark (see quot. 1884); one belonging to the family Carchariidæ, esp. *Carcharias taurus*; (*b*) *Australia*, a variety of ray-fish (see quot. 1882); = *guitar-fish* s.v. GUITAR *sb.* b; **sand shell**, a yellow river mussel, or naiad

(*Lampsilus anodontoides*) of the Mississippi River; also, applied to *L. rectus* (Webster *Suppl.* 1902); **sand shrimp**, a shrimp, esp. *Crangon vulgaris* (Cent. Dict.); **sand-skink**, a skink found in sandy places; esp. *Seps ocellatus* (ibid.); **sand-skipper** = *sand-hopper*; **sand-smelt**, the smelt *Atherina presbyter*; **sand-snake**, (*a*) a snake of the genus *Eryx* = AMMODYTE 1; (*b*) = *desert-snake* (Cent. Dict.); **sand-snipe** (see quot.); **sand-sole**, the sole *Solea lascaris*; **sand-star**, a starfish of the genus *Ophiura*, esp. *O. texturata*; **sand-sucker**, (*a*) the flat-fish *Platessa limandoides*; (*b*) *U.S.*, a popular name for soft-bodied animals which hide in the sand, as ascidians, holothurians, or nereids (*Cent. Dict.*); **sand-swallow** (see quot.); **sand-viper**, (*a*) = *sand-snake* (a); (*b*) *local U.S.*, a snake of the genus *Heterodon* (Cent. Dict.); **sand-wasp**, a digger-wasp (see DIGGER 4, quot. 1847); **sand whiting**, (*a*) see quot. 1883; (*b*) the Carolina whiting *Menticirrhus Americanus* (Webster *Suppl.* 1902); **sand-worm**, the lug-worm *Arenicola marina* or *piscatorum*. Also SAND-EEL, -FLY, -GROUSE, -LARK, SANDPIPER, etc.

1833 COLERIDGE *Love's Apparition*, A ruined well, Where the shy *sand-asps bask and swell. **1873** *Proc. Zool. Soc.* 761 Two *Sand-badgers (*Meles ankuma*..), presented. **1894** LYDEKKER *Roy. Nat. Hist.* II. 89 The sand-badger ..(*Arctonyx collaris*). **1883** *Encycl. Brit.* XV. 440/1 The best-known species is *Arctonyx collaris*, the *Sand-Bear. **1854** A. ADAMS, etc. *Man. Nat. Hist.* 188 *Sand-Beetles (*Trogidæ*). **1709** J. LAWSON *New Voy. Carolina* 151 The *Sand-Birds are about the Bigness of a Lark, and frequent our Sand-Beaches. **1796** MORSE *Amer. Geog.* I. 213 Sand birds, *Tringa parva*. **1878** *Masque Poets* 51 Far off some sand-bird pipes its evening song. **1917** T. G. PEARSON *Birds Amer.* I. 234 White-rumped Sandpiper.. Sand-bird. **1910** R. L. DITMARS *Reptiles of World* IV. 233 The *Sand Boas, *Eryx*, are degenerate burrowing species,.. with a flat body, very stumpy tail, a small head,.. and tiny eyes. **1970** *E. Afr. Standard* 23 Jan. 6/4 These [snakes] include.. a sand boa and two boa constrictors. **1854** A. ADAMS, etc. *Man. Nat. Hist.* 242 *Sand-Bugs (*Galgulidæ*). **1884** GOODE, etc. *Nat. Hist. Aquatic Anim.* 779 The Sand Bug—*Hippa talpoida*, Say. This is.. related to the Hermit Crabs. **1809** KENDALL *Trav.* II. xlvii. 144 Rich in fish and in *sand-clams (*sabella granulata*). **1804** BEWICK *Birds* II. 91 Redshank. Red-legged Horseman, Pool Snipe, or *Sand Cock (*Scolopax calidris* Lin.). **1844** J. E. DEKAY *Zool. N.Y.* VI. 6 This [sc. *Platycarcinus irroratus*] and the succeeding species [sc. *P. sayi*] are both designated by our fishermen as the Spotted Crab and *Sand Crab. *a* **1851** J. G. DALYELL *Powers of Creator* I. 183 *Cancer* (*portunus*) *pusillus*.—The Sand Crab. **1877** *Encycl. Brit.* VI. 642/1 The swift-footed sand-crabs (Ocypoda) are exclusively terrestrial. **1883** SWEET & KNOX *On Mexican Mustang through Texas* 24 The calling of each other names, such as 'sand-crabs' and 'mud-turtles', is one of the harmless ways in which they ventilate their spleen. **1884** GOODE, etc. *Nat. Hist. Aquatic Anim.* 774 The 'Lady Crab', or 'Sand Crab' [*Platyonichus ocellatus*], is abundant ..from Cape Cod to Florida. **1946** K. TENNANT *Lost Haven* (1947) xii. 199 The little cream sand-crabs swift as impatient foam. **1952** W. J. DAKIN *Austral. Seashores* xv. 190 The sand bubbler-crab... This little crab may be found.. resting at the bottom of a vertical chimney-like burrow. **1955** V. PALMER *Let Birds Fly* 108 No, you ol' sandcrab, you don't know Charlie. *a* **1672** WILLUGHBY *Hist. Pisc.* (1686) App. 24 [*Pisces Indici*] *Sand Creeper *Belgis*. **1731** MEDLEY *Kolben's Cape G. Hope* II. 203 There is a fish at the Cape call'd a Sand-Creeper, from its keeping near sandy shores. **1885** *Standard Nat. Hist.* (1888) II. 185 Throughout the Rocky Mountain region.. are found several species of large, fierce looking insects... They are popularly known as *sand-crickets. **1839** D. H. STORER *Rep. Ichthyol. Mass.* 143 *Platessa dentata*..known by the fishermen as the '*Sand-dab' in the Boston market. **1880–4** DAY *Fishes Gt. Brit.* II. 33 Of Yorkshire it [*Pleuronectes limanda*] is.. abundant, and known as the 'sand-dab' at Redcar. **1884** GOODE, etc. *Nat. Hist. Aquatic Anim.* 197 The Sand Dab, or Rough Dab, *Hippoglossoides platessoides*.. is taken in winter by the line fishermen of New England. **1903** T. H. BEAN *Fishes N.Y.* 726 Sand Dab.. is also known as the rusty dab. **1924** J. A. LA GORCE et al. *Bk. Fishes* 15/1 The Sand Dab, lying on the sand, has harmonizing blotches imprinted all over the upper part of its body. **1954** J. STEINBECK *Sweet Thursday* xxiv. 155 Joe Elegant ordered sand dabs for supper. **1880** O. S. WILSON *Larvæ Brit. Lepid.* 243 *Agrotis ripæ*, Hub. The *Sand Dart. **1884** GOODE, etc. *Nat. Hist. Aquatic Anim.* 839 The '*Sand Dollar', or 'Flat Sea Urchin' (*Echinarachnius parma*), of the New England coast. **1884** *Bull. U.S. Nat. Museum* No. 27. 123 The so-called 'sand dollar'.. inhabits the east coast. **1923** *N. & Q.* 18 Aug. 133/1 The stone pies appear to be the fossilized remains of certain echinoderms kindred to the North American sand-dollar. **1962** [see KEYHOLE *sb.* 4]. **1969** R. LOWELL *Notebk. 1967–68* 70 His face an azure sand-dollar on the pail of a child. **1976** *National Observer* (U.S.) 6 Nov. 17-A/4, I stare down at the water-stained sand, hoping to find a sand dollar. **1852** C. H. WILEY *Life in South* 30/1 *Sand-fiddler,.. the local name for a small animal of the shell-fish kind. **1973** *Publ. Amer. Dial. Soc.* LX. 1 The long beaches are left to the sun and the surf, the sand fiddlers, the gulls and the pelicans. **1896** JORDAN & EVERMANN *Fishes N. & Mid. Amer.* I. 1207 *Sand-fish. **1925** *Ann. S. Afr. Mus.* XXI. 125 Beaked Salmon or *Sand Fish. .. Greyish brown above, silvery below. **1946** L. G. GREEN *So Few are Free* x. 135 The sandfish.. migrates at spawning time. **1947** [see MOGGEL]. **1949** VESEY-FITZGERALD & LAMONTE *Game Fish of World* v. 375 The sandfish, a species of *Labeo* characterised by the inferior position of the mouth, is another common inhabitant of this river system [*sc.* the Olifants river]. **1953** J. L. B. SMITH *Sea-fishes S. Afr.* 87 Sandfish or Beaked Salmon (Austral.). **1796** STEDMAN *Surinam* xiv. 352 The chigoe.. is a kind of small *sand-flea, that gets in between the skin and the flesh. **1848** BARTLETT *Dict. Amer.*, *Sand-Flea*, or *Beach-Flea* (Genus, *Orchestia*. Leach). **1884** E. INGERSOLL in *Harper's Mag.* Aug. 391/2 You are surrounded by clouds of little sand-fleas (*Artemia salina*). *c* **1640** J. SMYTH *Hund. Berkeley* (1885) III. 319 The *sand flooke, resemblinge the sole. **1880–4** DAY *Fishes Gt. Brit.* II. 29 *Pleuronectes microcephalus*... Sand-fleuk, Edinburgh. **1887** G. B. GOODE, etc. *Fisheries U.S.* v. II. 580 English books and people call it [*Mya arenaria*] the '*sand-gaper', the 'old maid', &c. **1968** K. WEATHERLY *Roo Shooter* 119 A *sand goanna.. has no respect for snakes at all; he would give most of them a very rough time of it. **1911** F. WARD *Marvels of Fish Life* ii. 13 The *sand goby.. merely scoops out a hollow. **1935** D. B. WILSON *Life of Shore & Shallow Sea* viii. 88 Sand gobies.. could not possibly see the bait. **1971** *Nature* 21 May 150/2 Other workers have found that the scarcity of the sand goby in inshore waters is matched by an increase offshore. **1790** HASSELL *Tour Isle of Wight* II. xxv. 131 Another particular species of fish.. to which they give the name of *Sandhopper, from its motion, which consists of a hop or bound, like that of a grasshopper; in all other respects it resembles a shrimp, as well in make as in colour. **1818** *Sporting Mag.* II. 158 Such insects as 'sea-lice' and 'sand-hoppers'. **1871** DARWIN *Desc. Man* II. ix. 337 The male sand-hopper (Orchestia) does not acquire his large claspers.. until nearly full-grown. **1900** CROCKETT *Little Anna Mark* xviii, Pools to dabble your feet in.. out among the dulse and the *sand-jumpers. **1776** PENNANT *Brit. Zool.* III. 137 *Sand Launce. **1864** P. H. GOSSE in *Gd. Words* 358 What is this writhing, wriggling thing, that looks like a narrow tape of burnished silver? It is a Sand-launce. **1905** D. S. JORDAN *Guide to Study of Fishes* II. xxix. 521 The small family of sand-lances.. comprises small, slender, silvery fishes, of both Arctic and tropical seas. **1975** *New Yorker* 12 May 80/3 The sand lances had both the length and the diameter of standard pencils. **1855** OGILVIE Suppl., **Sand-lizard*. **1882** *Encycl. Brit.* XIV. 734/1 The Sand-Lizard (*Lacerta agilis*), which is confined to some localities in the south of England. **1910** R. L. DITMARS *Reptiles of World* III. 173 The Sand Lizard or Striped Race-Runner.. is the only species of its genus ranging into the southeastern portion of the United States. **1915** E. G. BOULENGER *Reptiles & Batrachians* I. iv. 81 The Sand Lizard.. is a very local creature with us, confined to sandy heaths. **1928** *Bunker's Mag.* Jan. 73 The little sand lizards so common in West Texas possess the same ability to snap off their tails when they get into a tight corner. **1954** R. C. STEBBINS *Amphibians & Reptiles Western N. Amer.* 224/1 Buried sand lizards can sometimes be frightened from the sand. **1979** *Jrnl. R. Soc. Arts* CXXVII. 405/2 The heathland.. is the habitat of reptiles such as the smooth snake and sand lizard. **1859–62** RICHARDSON, etc. *Mus. Nat. Hist.* II. 111/1 The various names of Prid, Pride, Sandpride, *Sand-lurker [etc.]. **1668** CHARLETON *Onomast.* 90 *Hirundo riparia*.. the *Sand, or Bank Marten. **1678**, **1774** [see MARTIN[1]]. **1884** *Cassell's Fam. Mag.* Mar. 220/1 Steep banks of sandstone, riddled with the holes of the sand-martin. *a* **1851** J. G. DALYELL *Powers of Creator* (1853) II. 183 *Terebella littoralis, seu arenaria*. The *Sand Mason. **1935** E. G. BOULANGER *Nat. Hist. Seas* v. 77 Another common worm is the Sand Mason.., the tubes of which few can have overlooked. **1977** *Radio Times* 12–18 Nov. 19/1 Now he has photographed the denizens of mudflats: sea urchins, sand-mason worms, and the dog-whelk. **1850** A. WHITE *Pop. Hist. Mammalia* 232 Another member of this family.. is also a native of South Africa: this is the Coast Rat or *Sand-Mole (*Bathyergus maritimus*). **1975** H. G. COGGAR *Reptiles & Amphibians Austral.* 236/1 Gould's Goanna or *Sand Monitor... A widespread species subject to considerable geographic variation in colour, pattern and size. **1681** GREW *Musæum* I. VI. ii. 147 The *Sand-Muscle. *Tellina*. They live much in the Sand. **1835** L. JENYNS *Man. Vertebr. Anim.* 459 *Platessa Limandoides*, Nob. (*Sandnecker). **1872** COUES *Key N. Amer. Birds* 254 This species and the last are usually confounded under the common name of '*sandpeeps'. **1878** C. HALLOCK *Sportsman's Gazetteer* 378 *Sand Perch, or Bachelor Perch;.. Apparently a cross between the yellow belly and silver perch. **1946** *Richmond* (Va.) *Times-Dispatch* 4 Aug. IV. 4-D/2 There is always the likelihood of catching.. sand perch and blue-nosed perch. **1965** A. J. MCCLANE *Stand. Fishing Encycl.* 737/1 The sand perch.. is one of the small sea basses distributed from North Carolina to Texas. **1884** COUES *Key N. Amer. Birds* (ed. 2) 562 The Sand-grouse (better *Sand-pigeons) or *Pterocletes*. **1842** MACGILLIVRAY *Brit. Ornith.* II. 52 *Charadrius Hiaticula*. Ringed *Sand-Plover. *Ibid.* 53 *Charadrius Cantianus*. Kentish Sand-Plover. **1889** PARKER *Catal. N. Zealand Exhib.* 116 (Morris) But two genera of the group [Wading Birds] are found only in New Zealand, the Sand-plover and the Wry-billed Plover. **1836** YARRELL *Brit. Fishes* II. 459 The Pride, and *Sandpride. *Sandprey, and Mud lamprey. **1781** PENNANT *Quadrupeds* II. 466 *Sand Rat. *Mus Arenarius*. **1894–5** LYDEKKER *Roy. Nat. Hist.* III. 149 In size the naked sand-rats (*Heterocephalus*) may be compared to a common mouse. **1894** A. NEWTON *Dict. Birds* III. 813 *Sand-runner, like the foregoing [*sc.* sand-plover], but perhaps sometimes used more for Sandpiper. **1913** H. K. SWANN *Dict. Eng. & Folk-Names Brit. Birds* 205 Sand Runner: The Dunlin. Also the Ringed Plover and the Sanderling on the Humber. **1979** *Bull. Yorks. Dial. Soc.* Summer 7 We would find eggs on the sand at the sea side of the Point laid by a bird we called a sand runner. **1885** *Standard Nat. Hist.* (1888) I. 346 The egg masses of the *Nauticas* bear the common name *sand-saucers. **1863** WOOD *Illustr. Nat. Hist.* III. 623 *Sand-screw, *Sutcator arenarius*. .. So called from the odd movements which it makes when laid upon dry sand, wriggling along [etc.]. **1882** TENISON-WOODS *Fishes N.S. Wales* 93 *Rhinobatus granulatus*, blind or *sand shark. **1884** GOODE, etc. *Nat. Hist. Aquatic Anim.* 671 The Sand Shark—*Odontaspis littoralis*. This species.. is found.. from New England southward to Charleston. **1938** A. H. VERRILL *Strange Fish* ix. 92 Certain species of sharks.. may be considered harmless to man. Such are the sand-sharks and dogfish. **1949** W. W. SMALL in Vesey-Fitzgerald & Lamonte *Game Fish of World* v. 381 A sandshark (really a shovelnose skate) ..can give an angler hell. **1961** E. S. HERALD *Living Fishes of World* 17/2 Sand sharks—Family Carchariidæ. **1968** D. O'GRADY *Bottle of Sandwiches* 51 He said it was only a sand-shark, or shovel-nose. **1871** DARWIN *Desc. Man* II. ix. 334 This same naturalist separated a male *sand-skipper (so common on our sea-shores), *Gammarus marinus*, from its female. **1836** YARRELL *Brit. Fishes* I. 214 The Atherine, or *Sandsmelt. **1753** CHAMBERS *Cycl. Supp.*, Ammodytes.. or *sand-snake, from its sand-like colour. **1896** LYDEKKER *Roy. Nat. Hist.* V. 193 From their allies, the sand-snakes are distinguished by the small scales being either smooth or singly keeled [etc.]. **1848** *Zoologist* VI. 2137 All the sand-pipers.. are indiscriminately known as '*sand-snipes' [Leicestershire]. **1880–4** DAY *Fishes Gt. Brit.* II. 42 *Solea lascaris*... The.. '*sand-sole' from the localities it frequents. **1841** E. FORBES *Brit. Starfishes* 23 Common *Sand-star. *Ophiura texturata*. Lam. *Ibid.* 27 Lesser Sand-star. *Ophiura albida*. Forbes. **1862** GÜNTHER *Cat. Fishes Brit. Mus.* IV. 405 *Hippoglossoides limandoides*. The rough Dab or *Sandsucker. **1876** SMILES *Sc. Natur.* xiv. (ed. 4) 287 Amongst the rare fishes caught by them were the Sandsucker, *Platessa limandoides* [etc.]. **1797** BEWICK *Birds* I. 258 Sand Martin. (*Cotile riparia*.).. *Sand Swallow. (*Hirundo riparia*.) **1668** CHARLETON *Onomast.* 30 *Ammodites*,.. the *sand Viper. **1896** LYDEKKER *Roy. Nat. Hist.* V. 233 Another well-known poisonous European snake is the long-nosed, or sand-viper (*Vipera ammodytes*). **1802** BINGLEY *Anim. Biog.* (1813) III. 257 The Blue *Sand-wasp. **1896** tr. *Boas' Text-bk. Zool.* 270 Sand-wasps (*Crabronidæ*, *Pompilidæ*). These.. have a simple trochanter, a stalked abdomen, and a sting. **1776** PENNANT *Brit. Zool.* III. 207 The next baits in esteem are.. *sand worms, muscles, and limpets. **1896** LYDEKKER *Roy. Nat. Hist.* VI. 435 We may take as our first example [of the group Tubicola] the sand-worm (*Arenicola piscatorum*).

c. In the names of plants: **sand blackberry** (see quot.); **sand cherry** *N. Amer.*, a shrub or small tree, *Prunus pumila*, of central North America, or a related species, *P. besseyi*, of the western states; also, the fruit of these plants; **sand elm**, a variety of elm, *Ulmus suberosa*; **sand flower** = SANDWORT; **sand grass**, (*a*) any species of grass which grows in sand and serves the purpose of a sand-binder (see quots.); (*b*) *N.Z.* = PINGAO; †**sand-hooker tree** = *sand-box tree* (see SAND-BOX 3); **sand-jack** (see quot.); **sand-leek**, the rocambole, *Allium Scorodoprasum* (Cassell's Encycl. Dict. 1887); **sand lily**, (*a*) *U.S.*, a stemless rhizomatous herb, *Leucocrinum montanum*, belonging to the family Liliaceæ and bearing clusters of fragrant white flowers; (*b*) a bulbous plant, *Pancratium maritimum*, belonging to the family Amaryllidaceæ, native to the Mediterranean region, and bearing fragrant white flowers; = *sea-daffodil* s.v. SEA *sb.* 23 f; **sand myrtle**, a small evergreen shrub, *Leiophyllum buxifolium*, of the family Ericaceæ, native to eastern North America and bearing pink or white flowers; **sand-oat** = *sand-reed*; **sand pear**, an oriental species of pear, *Pyrus pyrifolia*; **sand pine, pink** (see quots.); **sand-reed**, the marram grass, *Ammophila arenaria*; cf. MARRAM 1; **sand rocket**, the wall mustard; †**sand-rush** *U.S.*, perh. *Equisetum arvense*; **sand-sedge** = *sand-reed*; **sand spurry**, a plant of the genus *Spergularia* (Cent. Dict.); **sandstay** (see quot.); **sand verbena** *N. Amer.*, a trailing herb of the genus *Abronia*, belonging to the family Nyctaginaceæ, found in western North America, and bearing clusters of fragrant red, yellow, or white flowers; **sand-weed** = SANDWORT; **sand-willow**, *Salix fusca*; **sand wood** (see quot.).

1847 W. DARLINGTON *Amer. Weeds* (1860) 128 *Rubus cuneifolius*,.. *Sand Blackberry. **1778** J. CARVER *Trav. N. Amer.* 30 Near the borders of the Lake [Michigan] grow a great number of *sand cherries. **1796** MORSE *Amer. Geog.* I. 168 On its banks are found amazing quantities of sand cherries. **1800** A. HENRY *Jrnl.* 17 Aug. in E. Coues *New Light Early Hist. Greater Northwest* (1897) I. ii. 40 We found an abundance of sand-cherries, which were of an excellent flavor. **1970** J. H. GRAY *Boy from Winnipeg* 55 When we tired of that [*sc.* swimming] we would go picking sand-cherries. **1878** *Encycl. Brit.* VIII. 152/1 The Dutch or *Sand Elm is a tree very similar to the wych elm. **1916** W. DE LA MARE *Songs of Childhood* (rev. ed.) 80 Alliolyle where the *sand-flower blows Taught three old apes to sing. **1937** DYLAN THOMAS in *Life & Letters* Spring 70 He stumbled on over sand and sandflowers like a blind boy in the sun. **1856** GRAY *Man. Bot.* (1860) 556 *Triplasis purpurea* (*Sand-Grass)... In sand, Massachusetts to Virginia along the coast, and southward. **1857** HENFREY *Bot.* §594. 426 The sand-grasses, *Elymus arenarius*, *Arundo arenaria*,.. are valuable binding weeds on shifting sandy shores. **1905** *Sand grass [see PINGAO]. **1959** A. H. MCLINTOCK *Descr. Atlas N.Z.* 31 Planting of sand grass, lupins, and, in places, pines.. is needed to protect farm land. **1796** STEDMAN *Surinam* II. xxiii. 164 The *sand-hooker tree.. receives its name from the fruit, which being divested of its seed, is used as a sand-box by writers. **1884** SARGENT *Forests N. Amer.* 153 *Quercus cinerea* Michaux... Upland Willow Oak. Blue Jack. *Sand Jack. **1909** WEBSTER, **Sand lily*, a white-flowered scapose liliaceous plant.. of the western United States. **1929** *Encycl. Brit.* XIX. 939/1 Sand Lily.. native to plains and mountain valleys from South Dacota and Nebraska west to California. **1951** T. H. KEARNEY et al. *Arizona Flora* 177 The star-lily or sand-lily.. is to be looked for in northern Arizona. **1956** G. DURRELL *My Family & Other Animals* xvi. 215 The smooth curve of the dune.. was the only place on the island [*sc.* Corfu] where these sand lilies grew, strange, misshapen bulbs buried in the sand, that once a year sent up thick green leaves and white flowers above the surface. **1973** HITCHCOCK & CRONQUIST *Flora Pacific Northwest* 691 Fl[ower]s white, rather showy, borne in clusters... Sand lily, star lily. **1814** F. PURSH *Flora Americana* I. 301 *Ammyrsine buxifolia*.. known by the name of *Sand-myrtle among the inhabitants of New Jersey. **1845–50** Sand myrtle [see MYRTLE *sb.* 2b]. **1882** *Harper's Mag.* June 71 Of the smaller shrubs now in bloom we find the sand-myrtle, with its terminal umbel-like clusters of small pinkish flowers. **1943** R. PEATTIE *Great Smokies &*

Blue Ridge 266 Tangled growths of rhododendrons..with some amounts of mountain laurel, blueberry, smilax, and occasionally sand myrtle. **1881** *Encycl. Brit.* XII. 60/1 The dunes show a tendency, except where the Dutch prevent it by planting wood or *sand-oats, to wear away on the side towards the sea. [**1629** J. PARKINSON *Parad.* III. xxi. 593 The *Sand peare is a reasonable good peare, but Small.] **1880** [see KIEFFER]. **1951** *Dict. Gardening* (R. Hort. Soc.) IV. 1722/2 Sand Pear... Edible var[ietie]s are grown in China and Japan. **1884** SARGENT *Forests N. Amer.* 199 *Pinus clausus* Vasey... *Sand Pine. **1852** *Cottage Gard. Dict.* (ed. G. W. Johnson) 325 *Dianthus arenarius* (*sand pink). **1805** *Edin. Rev.* Oct. 109 In Iceland, the grain of *sand-reed approaches so nearly to maturity, that [etc.]. **1849** W. H. HARVEY *Sea-Side Bk.* i. 12 The sand-reed..naturally grows on the sandy shores of Europe. **1879** *Scribner's Monthly* Sept. 651/1 After laboriously cleaning their fish, they laid them among the sand-reeds. **1910** *Encycl. Brit.* XIII. 590/2 The most common plant here is the stiff sand-reed. **1975** M. C. DAVIS *Near Woods* i. 3 On a wave-lashed slope, this sand reed measures land's end. **1857** MISS PRATT *Flower. Pl.* I. 153 *Sinapis muralis* (*Sand-rocket). **1805** LEWIS & CLARK *Trav. Missouri*, etc. (1815) II. xii. 2 The..*sandrush, and narrow dock, are also common. **1842** J. B. FRASER *Mesopot. & Assyria* xv. 361 There is no combat here, such as when the sand-reed or *sand-sedge..endeavours to climb above the perpetually accumulating sands. **1866** *Sand spurry [see SPURREY 2]. **1960** *Oxf. Bk. Wild Flowers* 112/2 The Cliff Sand Spurrey (*S. rupicola*), found on rocky coasts in the south and west, has glandular hairy stems... Sand Spurrey (*S. rubra*), common in sandy and gravelly places, is a rather hairy plant. **1889** J. H. MAIDEN *Usef. Pl. Australia* 642 *Leptospermum lævigatum*..'*Sandstay'... This shrub is the most effectual of all for arresting the progress of drift sand. **1898** A. M. DAVIDSON *Calif. Plants* 174 The wild four o'clock and the *sand verbena are classed in this group [of beautiful weeds]. **1929** *Encycl. Brit.* XIX. 940/1 The white sand-verbena,..with very numerous fragrant flowers, occurs from Iowa to Idaho. **1946** D. C. PEATTIE *Road of Naturalist* i. 16 Pervading the sunny waste with fragrance, rose sprawling sand-verbenas. **1849** D. G. ROSSETTI *Let.* 18 Oct. (1965) I. 78 Curse the big mounds of *sand-weed! **1786** J. ABERCROMBIE *Arrangem.* in *Gard. Assist.* 35/2 *Sand willow, downy leaved. **1840** PAXTON *Bot. Dict.* s.v., *Sand-wood. *Bremontiera Ammoxylon.*

sand (sænd), *v.* [f. SAND *sb.*²]

1. *trans.* To run (a ship) on a sandbank; also *pass.* of a person, to be run aground.

1560 JEWEL *Answ. to Cole's 3rd Let.* 98 b, Although ye be sanded, & set aground, yet ye kepe vp the sail stil, as if ye had water at your will. **1592** WYRLEY *Armorie* 129 This skyphier haue I seen through dotage To sand his ship in calme and quiet floud. **1621** BURTON *Anat. Mel.* I. ii. IV. iii. (1651) 148 Seamen..when they have been sanded or dashed on a rock, for ever after fear that mischance.

2. To sprinkle with or as with sand.

c **1374** CHAUCER *Troylus* II. 773 (822) This gardeyn was large and rayled all þe aleyes..and sonded alle þe weyes. **1453** in S. Bentley *Excerpta Hist.* (1831) 391 þat the place where þat the said bataille shalbe be..wel graveled and sanded. **1607** HIERON *Wks.* I. 154 If now, when the way is thus sanded forth vnto you, you will say, as they did of old, 'We will not walke therein'. *Ibid.* 414 If we desire fame, we see here the way sanded out vnto vs; Doe worthily, and be famous. **1712** J. JAMES tr. *Le Blond's Gardening* 34 All these Paths should be sanded. **1742** YOUNG *Nt. Th.* IX. 2308 This wide waste of worlds; this visto vast, All sanded o'er with suns. **1818** MOORE *Fudge Fam. Paris* xii. 62 He wrote,—Upon paper gilt-edged,..Then sanded it over with silver and azure. **1870** F. R. WILSON *Ch. Lindisf.* 102 The floors are sanded in the most primitive country-inn fashion. **1883** *Harper's Mag.* Oct. 716/1 Tawdry modern cast-iron work, 'sanded' to represent stone. **1897** *Allbutt's Syst. Med.* IV. 472 The skin [in myxœdema] becomes rough and scaly, almost as if it were sanded.

3. a. To overlay with sand, to bury under a sand drift; also *to sand up, over*.

1624 SANDERSON *Serm.* I. 224 This weather, that flood, such a storm, hath blasted our fruits, sanded our grounds [etc.]. **1789** *Trans. Soc. Arts* I. 222 That vessel perished..in Dunbar Bay, and..was thought to be sanded up. **1860** *Merc. Marine Mag.* VII. 39 Should the broken tree be sanded over,..it will be difficult..to find the..channel. **1881** M. A. LEWIS *Two Pretty G.* I. 239 The hay crop in the Lower Croft had been hopelessly sanded. **1918** GALSWORTHY *Five Tales* ix. 61 They would..sand up his only well in the desert. **1956** PETERSON & FISHER *Wild Amer.* xxxiv. 369 Novashtoshnah, which means 'the new growth' (newly sanded up from island to peninsula), is the northeast point of St. Paul.

b. To put sand upon (land) as a dressing.

1721 J. EDMONDS in Mortimer *Husb.* I. 101 'Tis now..twenty four Years since he sanded it first. **1867** *Jrnl. R. Agric. Soc.* Ser. II. III. II. 662 The heaviest clay lands are being sanded to a depth of 3 or 4 inches.

4. To intermix sand with (sugar, wool, etc.) for purposes of fraud.

1848 KINGSLEY *Yeast* xv, To sand the sugar, and sloe-leave the tea. **1880** in Goode, etc. *Hist. & Meth. Fish.* (Fish. Industr. U.S. v.) 1887 II. 840 To affirm..that the packers in question were sanding their sponges would not perhaps be justifiable. **1892** WALSH *Tea* (Philad.) 133 Sanding or adulterating with a variety of mineral matter, chiefly iron or steel filings, to add to the weight.

5. a. To grind or polish with sand. Also in phr. *to sand and canvas* (orig. *Naut. slang.*), to clean thoroughly; also *fig.*

1858 *Skyring's Builders' Prices* (ed. 48) 90 Old Sienna,..or other similar marbles,..sanded, polished, and re-set. **1912** J. MASEFIELD in *Eng. Rev.* Oct. 345 Unless you're clean we'll sand-and-canvas you. **1914** *Dialect Notes* IV. 151 *Sand and canvas*,..to clean. **1933** P. A. EADDY *Hull Down* 187 The Mate was anxious to get on with the 'sand and canvasing' of the bright work.

b. = SANDPAPER *v.*

1928 E. W. HOBBS *Mod. Furnit. Veneering* vii. 84 The wood finish..is sprayed on, allowed about three hours to dry, and sanded lightly with No. 400 waterproof paper and water. **1939** PATTOU & VAUGHN *Furnit.* II. vi. 197 Sand all first coaters with the grain and do not lap the sanding more than necessary. **1958** *Listener* 11 Sept. 399/1 After sanding the piece of furniture, you will be using oil paint to give a hard, durable surface. **1976** F. E. SHERLOCK *Enjoying Home Carpentry & Woodwork* xi. 116 When the project has been glued and cleaned-up.., it must be sanded.

6. *intr.* To become clogged or bunged *up* with sand.

1926 *Summary of Operations, California Oil Fields* (Calif. State Mining Bureau) Oct. 9 The well..stopped of its own accord, probably sanding up.

sandal ('sænd(ə)l), *sb.*¹ Also 4 **sandalie**, 5 **sendell**, 6 **sandale, -dell**, 7 **sandall**, 7– **sandal**. [ad. L. *sandalium* (pl. *sandalia*, whence as fem. sing. Sp., Pg. *sandalia*, F. *sandale*), ad. Gr. σανδάλιον, dim. of σάνδαλον (whence It. *sandalo*) = Æolic σάμβαγον; the remoter etymology is unknown.]

1. a. A kind of shoe with an open-work top, originally and still frequently consisting of a sole fastened by straps or thongs passed over the instep and round the ankle.

'The common foot-gear of the ancient Greeks and Romans, and still in use among some Oriental peoples. Of late years sandals have been used somewhat extensively in England instead of shoes for children, and sometimes for adults.' (*N.E.D.*)

1382 WYCLIF *Mark* vi. 9 And he clepide twelue,..and comaundide hem, that thei schulde not take ony thing in the weye.., but schoon with sandalies [**1388** schod with sandalies; *c* **1520** NISBET schod with sandalis]. **1493** *Dives & Paup.* (Pynson) b v, Do on thy galoches or sandalynes [? *read* sandalyes; ed. 1534 has sandalines]. **1526** TINDALE *Acts* xii. 8 And the angell sayd vnto him: gyrde thy silfe and bynde on thy sandalles. **1567** *Gude & Godlie Ball.* (S.T.S.) 195 Preistis..preiche the Euangell on zour feit, And set on Sandellis full meit, Bot cast zour pantonis of. **1590** SPENSER *F.Q.* I. vi. 35 His sandales were with toilsome travell torne. **1637** MILTON *Lycidas* 187 While the still morn went out with Sandals gray. **1666-7** PEPYS *Diary* 23 Jan., The Priest was in his cell, with his hair clothes to his skin, bare-legged, with a sandall only on. **1698** FRYER *Acc. E. India & P.* 30 The Moors and Persians shod with Sandals. **1725** DE FOE *Voy. round World* (1840) 267 Shoes..tied on like sandals. **1813** WELLINGTON in Gurw. *Desp.* (1838) XI. 34 The Basques and Navarrois..wear sandals. **1871** R. ELLIS *Catullus* lxviii. 72 Lightly the polish'd floor creak'd to the sandal again.

b. *Her.* used as a bearing.

1688 R. HOLME *Armoury* III. 13/2 He beareth Or, two Sandals, Sable. **1828-40** BERRY *Encycl. Her.* I.

2. a. A kind of half-shoe of red leather, silk, etc., richly embroidered and fastened with straps and bands, forming part of the regalia of a sovereign or of the official dress of a bishop or abbot.

c **1485** in *Rutland Papers* (Camden) 17 His hosen, sendellis, and spurres. *Ibid.* 19 With regall sandelles and spurres. **1579** FULKE *Refut. Rastel* 754 As for shauen crownes, and purple sandales,..they were neuer taken for..mysteries. **1687** F. SANDFORD *Coronat. Jas. II* 38 The [King's] Sandals were made with a dark-colour'd Leather Sole, and a Wooden Heel covered with Red Leather, the Straps or Bands..were of Cloth of Tissue. **1849** ROCK *Ch. of Fathers* II. vi. 238 The richest silks, elaborately embroidered, were used in England for making episcopal sandals.

b. Applied to various kinds of low shoes, slippers, etc.

1794 MRS. RADCLIFFE *Myst. Udolpho* xxvi, Barnardine was wrapt in a long dark cloak, which scarcely allowed the kind of half-boots, or sandals, that were laced upon his legs, to appear. **1900** T. W. GREIG *Ladies' Dress Shoes* Finis, Dancing sandals worn in the ballet by Madame Cerri, made of pink satin.

c. *U.S.* 'An india-rubber overshoe, having very low sides and consisting chiefly of a sole with a strap across the instep' (*Cent. Dict.* 1891).

3. A strap for fastening a low shoe or slipper, passed over the instep or round the ankle.

1829 *R. Ackerman's Repos. Fashions* 4 Cherry-colour shoes and sandals. **1833** HT. MARTINEAU *Cinnamon & Pearls* v. 86 Alice, love, come and tie my sandal. **1836-9** DICKENS *Sk. Boz, Scenes* xx, Her white satin shoes..being firmly attached to her legs with strong tape sandals. *Ibid.*, *Char.* ix, A young lady, with her shoes tied in sandals all over her ankles.

4. *attrib.*, *sandal-footed* adj.; *sandal-mark*, *-shoe*; **sandal-foot**, used *attrib.* and *absol.* to designate a kind of stocking with a non-reinforced heel, suitable for wearing with sandals.

1959 *Vogue* June 71 Coming in..are the *sandal-foot stockings... Aristoc have fully-fashioned sandal-foots. **1970** *Focus* June 10/2 Sandalfoot is used to indicate a vision or non-reinforced heel. **1978** *Detroit Free Press* 2 Apr. 2B (Advt.), Sheer, sandalfoot pantyhose with bone or self-colour panty knit right in. **1927** D. H. LAWRENCE *Mornings in Mexico* 83 A white, *sandal-footed man following with the silent Indian haste. **1949** R. CAMPBELL tr. St. John of the Cross in *Coll. Poems* I. 167 Tracking your *sandal-mark The maidens search the roadway for your sign. **1603** SHAKS. *Ham.* IV. v. 26 By his Cockle hat and staffe, and his *Sandal shoone. **1882** W. D. HAY *Brighter Britain!* II. 127 Sandal-shoes upon their feet.

sandal ('sænd(ə)l), *sb.*² Forms: 5 **sandell**, 6 **sandall, sandol(e**, 5– **sandal**; β. 6 (in Lat. form) **sandalum**, (in It. forms) **sandolo, sandalo**. [a. med.L. *sandalum* = Sp. *sándalo*, Pg., It. *sandalo*, F. †*sandal*, also OF. *sandle* (whence G. *sandel*), *sandre* (whence the older Eng. SANDERS); a med.L. variant *santalum* survives in mod.L. as generic name (hence mod.F. *santal*). The ultimate source appears to be Skr. *čandana* (Hindī *čandan*); cf. Arab. *çandal*, late Gr. σάνδανον, σάνταλον.] = SANDALWOOD, in its various applications. †Also, an ointment made of powdered sandalwood.

c **1400** tr. *Secreta Secret., Gov. Lordsh.* 81 With sandell confyt ennoynt his body. *c* **1450** LYDG. & BURGH *Secrees* 2016 Anoynted..With the Onyment callyd Sandal. **1526** *Grete Herball* ccccxvii. (1529) Y v, Sandales is a wood called Sandres. **1588** T. HICKOCK tr. *Frederick's Voy.* 5 These barkes be lade in with all sorts of spices, with..Sandole [etc.]. **159.** FITCH in *Hakluyt's Voy.* (1599) II. I. 265 The white sandol is wood very sweet &..the Indians..grinde it with a litle water and anoynt their bodies therewith. **1698** FRYER *Acc. E. India & P.* 93 Senting themselves with Essence of Sandal. **1715** J. STEVENS *Hist. Persia* 110 The King..loaded his Ship with Sandal and dismiss'd him. **1813** W. MILBURN *Oriental Comm.* (1825) 158 The merchants sometimes divide sandal into red, yellow, and white; but these are all different shades of the same colour. **1847** TENNYSON *Princess* Prol. 19 Fans Of sandal. **1864** *Intell. Observer* IV. 74 Sandal..being a most excellent wood for carving.

β. **1553** EDEN *Treat. Newe Ind.* (Arb.) 21 *Sandalum*, called saunders. **1588** T. HICKOCK tr. *Frederick's Voy.* 19 b, Euery yeare hee sendeth a small Ship to Timor to lande white Sandolo. **1588** PARKE tr. *Mendoza's Hist. China* Comm. xxiv. 400 When the king..doth die, they do..burne his bodie with wood of Sandalo. **1594** BLUNDEVIL *Exerc.* v. xii. (1636) 557 From the Ile Timor doth come..the white and pale medicinable simple called Sandalum.

b. *attrib.*, as ***sandal-dust***, ***oil***; **sandal-tree**, (*a*) the white sandalwood tree; (*b*) a tree of the meliaceous genus *Sandoricum*; **sandalwort**, Lindley's name for a plant belonging to the order *Santalaceæ*.

1873 W. CORY *Lett. & Jrnls.* (1897) 343 We bought *sandal-dust in the drug bazaar. **1823** BYRON *Island* IV. viii, And *sandal oil to fence against the dew. **1864** *Intell. Observer* IV. 75 The..almug trees..are supposed to have been *sandal-trees. **1866** *Treas. Bot.* 1014/2 Sandal-tree. *Sandoricum.* **1846** LINDLEY *Veg. Kingd.* 787 *Santalaceæ.*—*Sandalworts.

sandal ('sænd(ə)l), *sb.*³ [a. Turkish and Persian *sandal*, Arab. *çandal* (Dozy). Cf. late Gr. σάνδαλον, σανδάλιον, F. *sandale*.] A long, narrow two-masted boat used in the Levant and on the northern coast of Africa.

1742 WOODROOFE in Hanway *Trav.* (1753) I. I. xxiii. 149 There are some larger vessels..of 30 or 40 tuns, which are called sandalls. **1877** A. B. EDWARDS *Up Nile* xi. 295 He..bounded into his own ricketty sandal, and rowed away.

sandal ('sænd(ə)l), *v.* [f. SANDAL *sb.*¹]

1. *trans.* To furnish with or as with sandals.

1713 C'TESS WINCHILSEA *Misc. Poems* 301 These feet shall bear me sandal'd to the battle. **1821** SHELLEY *Epipsych.* 218 Then, from the caverns of my dreamy youth I sprang, as one sandalled with plumes of fire. *a* **1822** —— *Ess. & Lett.* (1840) I. 157 Socrates..walked barefoot upon the ice; more easily..than those who had sandalled themselves so delicately. **1884** J. COLBORNE *Hicks Pasha* 47 The bare foot being sandalled.

2. To fasten with sandals (SANDAL *sb.*¹ 3).

1897 GUNTER *Susan Turnbull* xxi, Little white dancing slippers are sandaled on her delicate ankles with satin bows.

Hence **'sandalled** *ppl. a.*

1802 H. K. WHITE *Elegy Mr. Gill* vi, As early I..Hail the grey-sandal'd morn. **1803** HEBER *Palestine* 311 There barbarous kings their sandal'd nations led. **1833** TENNYSON *Poems* 75 She from the ripple cold Updrew her sandalled foot. **1885** J. B. LENO *Boot & Shoemaking* i. 11 Sandalled slippers..remained in fashion till the early portion of the reign of Victoria.

sandal: see SAMEL, SENDAL.

sandal(i)e, obs. forms of SANDAL *sb.*¹

sandaliform ('sændəlɪfɔːm), *a.* *rare*⁻⁰. [f. SANDAL *sb.*¹ + -(I)FORM.] Shaped like a sandal.

1848 in CRAIG. **1889** WAGSTAFFE *Mayne's Med. Vocab.* (ed. 6), *Sandaliform*, Bot., having the appearance of a sandal or slipper.

[**sandaline**: see SANDAL *sb.*¹ 1, quot. 1493.]

sandaling ('sændəlɪŋ). Also **sandling**. [f. SANDAL *sb.*¹ + -ING¹.] Elastic web woven in narrow strips for 'sandals' (SANDAL *sb.*¹ 3).

1881 *Daily News* 22 Aug. 3/6 In elastic webs there is a better inquiry for gussets... There is also an improved trade in sandalings. **1894** *Times* 19 Mar. 13/2 The elastic web trade is quiet... Cords, braids, dress-boltings, and sandlings, however, sell freely. **1909** *Price List Elastic Webs*, Black Silk Sandling, White Silk Sandling, Bronze Silk Sandling.

sandalo: see SANDAL *sb.*²

sandalwood, *sb.* (and *a.*) Also sandal-wood. Also 6 **sandelen-**, 7 **sandall-**, 8 **sandle-wood**. [SANDAL *sb.*²]

1. A scented wood obtained from several species of *Santalum*; also, an inodorous dye-wood, *Pterocarpus santalinus*, RED SANDERS.

white sandalwood is obtained from *S. album*, a tree resembling the myrtle, found on the Malabar coast. ***citron*** or ***yellow sandalwood*** is from *S. Freycinetianum*, found in the South Sea Islands. ***red sandalwood*** = RED SANDERS (see also 2 below).

c **1511** *1st Eng. Bk. Amer.* (Arb.) Introd. 29/1 Whyte & red sandelen wodde. **1600** J. Pory tr. *Leo's Africa* VII. 295 There is great plentie of ciuet and Sandall-wood. **1796** Morse *Amer. Geog.* I. 112 Sandle wood, which is of a yellowish colour, and has a most agreeable smell. **1820** Shelley *Witch Atl.* xxvii, While on her hearth lay blazing many a piece Of sandal wood, rare gums, and cinnamon. **1846** Lindley *Veg. Kingd.* 787 The Sandal-wood of the Sandwich Islands is the wood of Santalum Freycinetianum and paniculatum.

2. Applied, usually with distinguishing epithet, to trees of other genera, which produce a wood often used as a substitute for the true sandalwood.

1846 Lindley *Veg. Kingd.* 553 A deep red is yielded by the chips of *Adenanthera pavonina*, called in India *Ruktachundun*, or Red Sandal-wood. **1866** *Treas. Bot.* 1014/2 Queensland Sandalwood. *Eremophila Mitchelli.* **1874** *Ibid.* Suppl. 1339/2 False sandal-wood of Crete. *Quercus abelicea.* **1886** *Encycl. Brit.* XXI. 256/1 *Bucida capitata*.. is known in the West Indies as sandalwood. **1898** Morris *Austral Eng.* 401 *Eremophila mitchelli*.. Bastard Sandalwood... *E. sturtii*.. Scentless Sandalwood... *Alyxia buxifolia*,.. called Native Sandalwood in Tasmania.

3. A perfume derived from sandalwood oil.

1865 E. Rimmel *Bk. Perfumes* viii. 143 Indra.. appears very partial to scent, for he is always represented with his breast tinged with sandal-wood. **1973** G. Butler *Coffin for Pandora* viii. 161 Her heavy scent of heliotrope and sandalwood.

4. A fashion shade resembling the colour of sandalwood, a light yellowish brown. Also as *adj.*

1926 *Daily Express* 1 Sept. 10 (Advt.), Shades of mulberry, sandalwood, purple, [etc.]. **1927** *Ibid.* 26 Feb. 5 This attractive model is designed in sandalwood face-cloth. **1937** [see mist *sb.*[1] 1 e]. **1976** *Country Life* 26 Feb. 502/3 Stockings.. in.. a browny colour called Sandalwood.

5. *Comb.*, as **Sandalwood English** = Beach-la-mar; **sandalwood oil**; a strongly aromatic oil obtained by distillation of sandalwood (*Santalum*), used in perfumes and cosmetics and formerly as a genito-urinary antiseptic.

1922 Jespersen *Language* 216 The so-called *Beach-la-mar* (or Beche-le-mar, or Beche de mer English); it is also sometimes called *Sandalwood English. **1936** S. Robertson *Devel. Mod. Eng.* iv. 89 Beach-la-Mar or Sandalwood-English, spoken.. all over the Western Pacific. **1950** J. C. Furnas *Anat. Paradise* v. 355 *Beach-la-mar* (sometimes Sandalwood English) is the specific name of this pidgin. **1971** I. F. Hancock in D. Hymes *Pidginization & Creolization of Lang.* VII. 523 Melanesian Pidgin English, also known as Neo-Melanesian, Sandalwood English, Bêche-de-mer, Beach-la-mar, etc. **1851** *Illustr. Catal. Gt. Exhib.* IV. 878/2 *Sandal-wood oil.. from Mangalore and Canara. **1901** W. H. White *Text-bk. Pharmacol. & Therapeutics* 586 Sandal-wood oil is very similar in its action to the oils of copaiba and cubebs. **1952** Kirk & Othmer *Encycl. Chem. Technol.* IX. 589 The Australian sandalwood oils and the West Indian sandalwood oils are distilled from different species. **1965** F. Sargeson *Memoirs of Peon* v. 109 He was so knowledgeable about the virtues of copaiba and sandalwood oil,.. not to mention a chemist who would be of great assistance to me.

† **sandapile.** *Obs.*$^{-0}$ [a. L. *sandapila.*] 'A Coffin or Beere' (Cockeram 1623).

sandar, pl. of sandr, sandur.

sandarac (ˈsændəræk). Forms: 6 **sandarache**, 7–8 **-arack**, 7–9 **-arach**, 8 **-arick**, 9 **-aric**, 7 **sanderick**, 8 **sandrick**, 9 **sandrake**, 8–9 **sandrac**, 7– **sandarac**. [ad. L. *sandarac-a*, a. Gr. σανδαράκη, -άχη (senses 1 and 3), prob. a foreign word. Cf. F. *sandaraque* (Cotgr. 1611 *sandarac, -ache*), Sp., Pg. *sandaraca* (senses 1 and 2), It. *sandaraca, sandracca* (sense 1).

It is difficult to see any connexion between the three senses; possibly two distinct words were already confused in Gr. Sense 2, in mod.L. *sandaracha Arabum*, represents Arab. *sandarūs* (Dozy, from P. de Alcalá 1505), also *sandalus* (Freytag, from Golius); but the word cannot be native Arabic. According to the Persian and Urdū dictionaries, Pers. *sandaros, sandara* and Urdū *sandaros* are used both in sense 1 and in sense 2. Connexion with Skr. *sindūra* (Hindī *sindūr*), red lead, vermilion, seems unlikely on the ground of form.]

1. Red arsenic sulphide. = realgar.

[**1398** Trevisa *Barth. De P.R.* XIX. xxix. (1495) 878 Sandaracha growyth in Topasion.. is of red coloure.. and is founde amonge metall of golde and of syluer.] *c* **1550** Lloyd *Treas. Health* Y ij, Take.. of Sandarache, whyte and red [etc.]. **1646** Sir T. Browne *Pseud. Ep.* II. v. 90 Arsenick red and yellow, that is, Orpement and Sandarach may perhaps doe something, as being inflamable. **1756** P. Browne *Jamaica* 41 The Sandarack is an inflammable fossil substance. **1890** E. Johnson *Rise of Christendom* 264 A hollow bull of bronze was filled with naphtha, sandarac, sulphur and lead.

2. In full ***gum sandarac***. A resin which exudes from the tree *Callitris quadrivalvis*, native of N.W. Africa; it is used in the preparation of spirit varnish and pounce.

1655 Culpepper, etc. *Riverius* I. i. 4 Take.. Frankinsence and Sandarach, of each two Scruples. **1666** Boyle *Orig. Formes & Qual.* II. iv. 321 Spirit of Wine will dissolve some Bodies, as Sanderick, Mastick, Gum-Lac, &c. **1687** A. Lovell tr. *Thevenot's Trav.* II. 87 A most excellent Varnish .. is made of Sandarack and lintseed Oyl. **1727** W. Mather *Yng. Man's Comp.* 73 To make the Paper bear Ink well,.. rub the Paper with the fine Powder of Gum sandrick, tied in a Rag. **1812** J. Smyth *Pract. of Customs* (1821) 99 Gum Juniper or Sandrake. **1849** Balfour *Man. Bot.* §1046 *Callitris quadrivalvis* (*Thuya articulata*), the Arar-tree, supplies a solid resin called Sandarach or Pounce.

attrib. **1825** J. Nicholson *Operat. Mechanic* 744 Sandarac Varnish. **1878** Hooker & Ball *Marocco* 389 The Arar, Thuja or Gum Sandrac Tree.

†**3.** = bee-bread 2. *Obs.*

1609 C. Butler *Fem. Mon.* x. (1623) V ij, Breake the Combes.. into three parts; the first sheere Honie and Wax, the second Honie and Wax with Sandarach, the third dry Wax. **1657** S. Purchas *Pol. Flying-Ins.* 179 This Bee.. gathers as the Hive-Bee sandaracha. **1747** R. Maxwell *Bee-master* §419 (1756) 113 The Sandrach or Bee-bread.

Sandawe (sænˈdɑːweɪ), *sb.* (and *a.*) Also **Sandawi.** [Native name.] The name of a tribe in central Tanzania having racial, cultural, and linguistic affinities with the Hottentots; a member of this tribe; their language; also *attrib.* or as *adj.*

1924 *Jrnl. Afr. Soc.* XXIV. 26 Farther to the south-east, another 'click' language is met with, the Sandawi. **1925** *Ibid.* XXIV. 219 A section of Wanyaturu some 5,000 strong, who for generations have lived with them, accepting the rule of the Sandawi headmen. *Ibid.* 226 The Sandawi is a bowman. *Ibid.* 334 For a description of the Sandawi language I must refer to some notes by Father Lemble... Its most interesting feature is its clicks. **1947** *Jrnl. R. Anthrop. Inst.* LXXVII. 61/1 The Sandawe are a tribe, some 21,000 strong, inhabiting part of the Kondoa Irangi District.. in the Central Province of Tanganyika. **1958** J. P. Moffett *Handbk. Tanganyika* v. 158 The members of the Sandawi tribe occupy the south-western part of the Kondoa District. **1963** in Oliver & Mathew *Hist E. Afr.* iii. 62 It should be added that the pastoralism of the Hottentots *seems* to be older and more deep-seated than that of the Sandawe. **1974** *Encycl. Brit. Macropædia* XVII. 1029/2 During the Stone Age, bands of hunter-gatherers of the Bushmen type inhabited parts of the country [*sc.* Tanzania]. The Sandawe are vestiges of this early group.

ˈ**sandbag**, *sb.* Also **sand-bag.** [sand *sb.*[2] Cf. G. *sandsack.*] A bag filled with sand.

1. *gen.* (Used in proverbial simile.)

1599 B. Jonson *Cynthia's Rev.* II. v, All the Ladies and Gallants lie languishing... And (without we returne quickly) they are all (as a youth would say) no better then a few Trowts cast a shore, or a dish of Eeles in a Sand-bag. **1611** Middleton & Dekker *Roaring Girl* H 3 b.

2. *spec.* **a.** *Fortif.* (see quots.)

1590 Sir R. Williams *Brief Disc. War* 50 Wooll sackes, gabions, sand bagges, faggots and such deuices. **1710** J. Harris *Lex. Techn.* II, *Sand-bags*, in Fortification, are Bags holding about a Cubick Foot of Sand or Earth: they are used for raising Parapets in haste, or to repair what is beaten down. **1799** Wellington in Gurw. *Desp.* (1837) I. 29 We did all our work last night except filling the sand bags. **1885** *Standard* 7 Apr. 5/4 [They] marched out.. to build.. a block-house with timber and sand bags.

attrib. **1884** *Milit. Engineering* (ed. 3) I. II. 72 The tools.. required are.. a clean sandbag, and a sandbag fork.

b. used as ballast; esp. for a boat or balloon.

1831 Carlyle *Sart. Res.* II. v, A hapless Air-navigator, plunging, amid torn parachutes, sand-bags, and confused wreck, fast enough, into the jaws of the Devil! **1855** Lardner *Hand-bk. Nat. Phil., Hydrost.*, etc. 184 The aeronaut.. is provided with ballast composed of sand-bags, by casting out which he diminishes the weight of the balloon. **1867** Smyth *Sailor's Word-bk., Sand-bags*, small square cushions made of canvas and painted, for boats' ballast.

c. as a weapon. In early use, a bag of sand attached by a string to the end of a staff; also, one similarly attached to the arm of a quintain. In recent use (chiefly *U.S.*), a weapon used by ruffians, consisting of a long cylindrical bag (sometimes an eelskin) filled with sand, by which a heavy blow may be struck without leaving a mark.

1594 *1st Pt. Contention* D 1 b, Enter at one doore the Armourer.. with a drum before him, and his staffe with a sand-bag fastened to it, and at the other doore, his man with a drum and sand-bagge. **1656** Earl Monm. tr. *Boccalini's Advts. fr. Parnass.* II. iii. (1674) 136 [He] was set upon by some.. who beat him so cruelly with Sand-bags, as they left him for dead. **1678** Butler *Hud.* III. ii. 80 They now begun With law and conscience to fall on.. Engag'd with money-bags, as bold As men with sand-bags did of old. **1728** Chambers *Cycl.* s.v. *Quintain*, A slender Beam.. at one of whose Ends was a sloap or flat Board, and at the other a Bag of Sand or Dirt.—The Sport was.. to ride a-tilt at the Board, and.. to escape the Blow of the Sand-Bag. **1871** Rossetti *Poems, Last Confess.* 512 And there I handed him [the mountebank] his cups and balls And swung the sand-bags round to clear the ring. **1894** Stead *If Christ came* 354 The predatory rich do not shrink even from using the sandbag and the revolver—of course by deputies.

d. A bag or cushion filled with fine sand, used (*a*) in *Engraving*, as a support for the plate; (*b*) in *Surg.* as a support for a set limb.

1658 Phillips, A *Sand-bag*, in Etching or Graving, is that on which they use to turn their plate. *c* **1790** Imison *Sch. Art* II. 46 Let the table.. be firm.. upon which place your sand-bag with the plate upon it. **1837** Whittock, etc. *Bk. Trades* (1842) 214 (*Engraver*) The sand-bag, or cushion,.. is for laying the plate upon, for the conveniency of turning it in any direction, but is seldom used by artists. **1873** E. Spon *Workshop Receipts* Ser. I. 149/1 A sand-bag, on which to rest the block whilst engraving it.

1875 W. R. Smith *Lect. Nursing* viii. 144 The rest of the limb must now be bandaged, and sand bags placed along either side of it.

e. A long narrow cylindrical bag, usually of flannel, containing fine sand, and used to cover a crevice and exclude draught or light.

1808 E. Weeton *Let.* 8 Nov. in *Jrnl. of Governess* (1969) I. 123 Scarce a window or a door was permitted to be opened. My room window was fastened down, and stuffed with sand-bags. **1858** Simmonds *Dict. Trade.* **1908** A. C. Benson *Altar Fire* 225 The poky, comfortable arrangements,.. the sand-bags for the doors, all spoke of a timid invalid life.

3. The stomach of a crab.

1895 in *Funk's Standard Dict.* (marked 'Eng.').

ˈ**sandbag**, *v.* [f. prec.]

1. a. *trans.* To furnish with sandbags.

1860 *Cornh. Mag.* Oct. 440 The Bank [was] sandbagged and barricaded. **1906** *Daily Chron.* 11 Dec. 10/5 He not only fastens all his windows, he sandbags them.

b. *intr.* To attend to sandbags.

1928 *Sat. Even. Post* 4 Feb. 100/2 One of the chauffeurs had just finished fueling the plane. 'You fly her,' said Andy. 'I'll sandbag.'

2. To fell with a blow from a sandbag. Also *fig.*, to bully or coerce; to criticize or lambaste.

1887 *Courier-Jrnl.* (Louisville, Kentucky) 2 Feb. 6/2 The next day Claytor turned up at Central Station with a fairy story that he had been sand-bagged on his way home. **1889** *Columbus* (Ohio) *Dispatch* 16 Sept., John Lehner and Henry Koontz were sandbagged Saturday night. **1897** Howells *Landl. Lion's Head* 421 He had not been sand-bagged, or buncoed. **1901** *Congress. Rec.* 23 Jan. 1345/1 [This district] is lying in wait, as it were, from one year's end to the other, awaiting an opportunity to sandbag the public. **1903** 'O. Henry' in *Ainslee's Mag.* Feb. 59/2 About what figure had you and the kalsominer agreed to sandbag the state for? **1919** *Daily News* 12 Mar. 8/1 While the [German] revolution was being side-tracked in Parliament it was being sand-bagged in the proletariat. **1973** *Globe & Mail* (Toronto) 4 May 6/1 Each will attempt to sandbag the Liberals into adopting its policies. **1974** *Listener* 27 June 818/1 Mr Heath and Mr Wilson sandbagging each other at televised press conferences.

3. *Poker.* To refrain from raising at the first opportunity in the hope of raising by a greater amount later.

1940 O. Jacoby *On Poker* v. 36 The time to sandbag is when you have three of a kind or better. **1950** G. S. Coffin *Poker Game Compl.* vi. 71 Jacks back sometimes offers a fine chance to sandbag. **1977** D. Anthony *Stud Game* i. 7 He fondled his stack of blue chips. He was sandbagging me. I gave him the same dose of silence. **1978** *Sci. Amer.* July 112/3 By under-representing a strong hand (sand-bagging) and thus keeping his opponents from folding a player may increase the pot he expects to win.

ˈ**sandbagged**, *ppl. a.* [f. sandbag *v.* + -ed[1].] Having or equipped with sandbags. Also *fig.*

1916 *Blackw. Mag.* May 615/2 He had betaken himself.. to a blockhouse which guarded a section of the.. railway... The outlook from this sand-bagged sanctuary was extensive and curious. **1930** Wodehouse *Very Good, Jeeves!* viii. 223 The Snettisham.. was standing there with a sand-bagged look watching her nominee pass right out of the betting. **1940** *Economist* 20 July 91/2 Claims under personal accident ..were higher, for the black-out and sand-bagged pavements produced many minor injuries. **1952** Dylan Thomas *Coll. Poems* 43 Man-in-seed, in seed-at-zero, From the star-flanked fields of space, Thunders on the foreign town With a sand-bagged garrison. **1959** I. Jefferies *Thirteen Days* ii. 26 The Yehudi convoys used to form up.. with iron-clad buses and sand-bagged lorries. **1977** *Time* 21 Feb. 14/1 The demilitarized zone in Nicosia.. separates sandbagged Turkish- and Greek-Cypriot gun emplacements.

sandbagger (ˈsændˌbægə(r)). *U.S.* [f. sandbag *sb.* and *v.* + -er[1].]

1. One who uses a sandbag as a weapon. Also *fig.*

1882 G. W. Peck *Peck's Sunshine* 203 Suppose all the men that have been robbed in the past year by cowardly sand-baggers, could have 'put up their hands'. **1884** *Chicago Advance* 10 Apr., Not a prize fighter, or street loafer,.. or sand-bagger appears among them. **1893** *Chicago Tribune* 26 Apr. 6/4 One of the Chicago papers recently complained that Illinois had no first-class highwaymen. It must have overlooked the legislative 'sand-baggers'. **1894** Stead *If Christ came* 340 The sand-bagger and blackmailer. **1929** C. E. Merriam *Chicago* 343 A matter to be carefully watched here [in subcommittees of the city council] is room for blackmail, even in the case of worthy measures unless the sandbaggers are offset by those of an opposite persuasion. **1981** P. McCutchan *Shard calls Tune* xiii. 148 Senglea.. had had its quota of sandbaggers once, evil men who lurked upon roofs and swung heavy sandbags to strike sailors on the head so that their pockets could be rifled.

2. A sailing-boat that uses sandbags as ballast.

1894 *Outing* (U.S.) XXIV. 477/2 He.. enjoys the sea in every form, whether racing in a sandbagger [etc.].

3. *Poker.* One who sandbags. Cf. sandbag *v.* 3.

1940 O. Jacoby *On Poker* v. 36 In this event the sand-bagger intends to raise. **1950** G. S. Coffin *Poker Game Compl.* v. 56 We have bet aces up so many times in last position when all checked after the draw, and butted into triplets and sandbaggers.

ˈ**sand-bank.** [f. sand *sb.*[2] + bank *sb.* 1.]

1. A bank of sand formed in a river or sea by the action of tides and currents.

1589 Rider *Bibl. Scholast.* 1268/60 A sand banke in the Sea,..*pulvinus*. **1659** D. Pell *Impr. Sea* 510 Frothy breaches of the Seas over the Sand-banks. **1725** De Foe *Voy. round World* (1840) 147 She tailed aground upon a sand-bank. **1877** A. B. Edwards *Up Nile* xix. 524 The Nile flows wide among sandbanks, like a tidal river near the sea.

fig. **1855** Motley *Dutch Rep.* VI. i. (1866) 781 Its foundation was the shifting sandbank of female and royal coquetry.

2. *Founding.* (See quot.)

1888 *Lockwood's Dict. Mech. Engin., Sand Bank.* In foundries where small pipes are cast in quantities the moulding boxes are placed, and the metal run on a bank of sand.

'sand-bath. [f. SAND *sb.*² + BATH *sb.*¹]

1. A vessel of heated sand used as an equable heater for retorts, etc. in various chemical proceses.

1677 W. HARRIS tr. *Lemery's Course Chem.* 11 These Furnaces may also serve for Distilling by the Refrigeratory, in..the Sand-Bath. **1758** REID tr. *Macquer's Chem.* I. 214 Set the retort in a sand-bath fixed over a reverberating furnace. **1880** C. & F. DARWIN *Movem. Pl.* 178 Six of the radicles in a jar..which stood on a sand-bath, raised to a temperature varying from 76° to 82° F., became hooked.

attrib. **1839** URE *Dict. Arts* 454 This process must be preceded by the sand-bath operation.

2. A medicinal bath of heated sand or sea-sand.

1869 TOZER *Highl. Turkey* I. 75 We saw a patient undergoing the sand-bath..for rheumatism.

3. A bath taken by fowls in sand; a dust-bath.

1891 in *Century Dict.*

'sand-bed. [f. SAND *sb.*² + BED *sb.*]

1. A bed, layer or stratum of sand.

c **1475** *Pict. Voc.* in Wr.-Wülcker 798/13 *Hec sertis*, a sandbedde. **1611** COTGR., *Sablonniere*, a sand bed. **1684** T. BURNET *Th. Earth* I. 137 Factitious islands..have been made..by..the aggestion of sands and sand-beds. **1839** URE *Dict. Arts* 969 Where the strata are connected with rivers, sand-beds filled with water, or marsh lands. **1889** C. T. DAVIS *Treat. Manuf. Bricks* x. 303 Micaceous sand-bed. *Ibid.* 304 It reposes on a sand-bed.

b. *transf.* One who 'absorbs' much liquor; a toper. *Sc.* (see E.D.D.).

1824 SCOTT *St. Ronan's* xxiii, That sandbed old MacTurk, upon whom whole hogsheads make no impression.

2. *Founding.* A bed of sand into which the iron from a blast-furnace is run; also, any bed of sand in which castings are made.

1873 R. HUNT *Weale's Dict. Terms* s.v., The side troughs in the sand-bed are called pigs.

'sand-blast, *sb.* [f. SAND *sb.*² + BLAST *sb.*¹]

1. A contrivance for depolishing or grinding glass, stone, wood or hard metal by means of a jet of sand impelled by compressed air or steam. Also *attrib.*, esp. ***sand-blast process.***

1871 *Jrnl. Franklin Inst.* 155 An engraving produced by the use of the sand-blast... This is then passed beneath the sand-blast, and the cutting obtained. **1884** *Health Exhib. Catal.* 136/1 Permanent Tablets, being texts and mottoes..engraved by the Sand-blast process. **1888** *Lockwood's Dict. Mech. Engin.*, *Sand Blast Sharpening*, the sharpening of files by the direction of a current of sand and water across the teeth.

2. A blast of sandy or sand-laden wind or liquid. Also *attrib.*

1898 T. WATTS-DUNTON *Aylwin* XII. iv, Hot and stifling as sand-blasts of the desert. **1913** V. B. LEWES *Oil Fuel* iii. 69 A big gusher would, by sand-blast action, cut through the chilled steel shields in a few days.

'sand-blast, *v.* [f. SAND *sb.*² + BLAST *v.*; cf. SAND-BLAST *sb.*] To subject to a blast of sand or the like, esp. so as to clean or polish. Also *fig.*

1888 *Texas Siftings* 6 Oct. 6/3 'Sleigh-bells! Well, I'll be sand blasted!' said the business man. 'What do you mean by trying to sell sleigh-bells in this section of the country? Don't you know it never snows here?' **1924** *Jrnl. Inst. Metals* XXXII. 294 The present-day practice is to sand-blast almost every article which is to be metal sprayed. **1939** A. K. LOBECK *Geomorphol.* xi. 376 (*caption*) The sand grains have been sand-blasted away but the more durable binding silica ..has resisted the attack. **1972** *Timber Trades Jrnl.* 3 June 47/1 The metal surfaces to be coated are first sand-blasted to remove grease and impurities. **1979** H. MCCLOY *Smoking Mirror* 176 The old buildings..had been sand-blasted to preserve their fabric.

Hence **'sand-blasted** *ppl. a.*, scored by wind-driven sand; **'sand-blaster,** (*a*) a workman who uses sand-blast; (*b*) = SAND-BLAST 1; **'sand-blasting** *vbl. sb.*

1881 *Instr. Census Clerks* (1885) 89 Glass Sand Blaster. **1904** GOODCHILD & TWENEY *Technol. & Sci. Dict.* 257/1 Sand blasting is another method of producing an etched effect upon glass. **1908** *Edin. Rev.* July 82 In Triassic times England itself was a desert, as the sand-blasted granite boulders of Charnwood Forest attest. **1920** *Public Health Rep.* (U.S. Public Health Service) XXXV. 518 (*heading*) The efficiency of certain devices used for the protection of sand blasters against the dust hazard. **1935** H. R. SIMONDS *Finishing Metal Products* xii. 105 The term 'sand blasting' is commonly used to describe the application of an abrasive material under pressure to surfaces to be cleaned or otherwise treated. Even when steel grit is used as the abrasive, the term 'sand blasting' is frequently retained. **1937** U. R. EVANS *Metallic Corrosion Passivity & Protection* xiii. 545 A roughened (sand-blasted) surface appears necessary for good adhesion. **1974** *Nature* 5 Apr. 502/1 Abraiding freshly made implements in a tumbling mill, or sandblaster. **1975** M. BRADBURY *Hist. Man* iii. 44 Another [student] brought a sand-blaster and cleaned off the walls of the basement. **1975** *New Yorker* 19 May 11/3 (Advt.), Polished and sandblasted stainless-steel sculptures. **1976** 'TREVANIAN' *Main* (1977) iv. 76 The sandblasters have cleaned..a façade that used to bear the comfortable patina of soot... For months now, they have been sand-blasting the building. **1977** *New Yorker* 24 Oct. 42/1 Dissolution, leaching, sandblasting, cracking and melting of fireproof doors.

'sand-blind, *a.* Now *arch.*, *poet.*, and *dial.* [Prob. a perversion of OE. **samblind* (see SAM- and BLIND *a.*), after SAND *sb.*²

Cf. Johnson's explanation: 'Having a defect in the eyes, by which small particles appear to fly before them'.]

Half-blind, dim-sighted, purblind. Also *fig.*

14.. *Nom.* in Wr.-Wülcker 709/34 *Luscus*, he that is sand-blynde. **1538** ELYOT *Dict.*, *Lippio*, to be poreblynde, or sande blynde. **1549** CHALONER *Erasm. on Folly* Hj, If one that is sandblynde woulde take an asse for a moyle. *a* **1578** LINDESAY (Pitscottie) *Chron. Scot.* (S.T.S.) I. 347 Drumlanrick being sum thing sand blind and saw nocht weill. **1596** SHAKS. *Merch. V.* II. ii. 37 This is my true begotten Father, who being more then sand-blinde, high grauel blinde, knows me not. *a* **1623** FLETCHER *Love's Cure* II. i, I have been Sand-blinde from my infancie. **1627** W. SCLATER *Exp. 2 Thess.* (1629) 50 His minde, no more than sand-blind in the things of God. **1790** A. WILSON *Rabby's Mistake* Poet. Wks. (1846) 102 Sic was the day, whan san'-blin' Rab,..Set out in eager search for game. **1831** CARLYLE *Sart. Res.* I. x, Thou hitherto art a Dilettante and sandblind Pedant. **1849** C. BRONTE *Shirley* xxxv. He is bald, sand blind, grey-haired. **1864** G. M. HOPKINS *Poems* (1967) 15 Are you sand-blind? Slabs of water many a mile Blaze for him all this while. **1938** W. DE LA MARE *Memory* 46 Hope.. Led sand-blind Despair To a clear babbling wellspring And laved his eyes there.

Hence **'sand-blindness.**

1552 HULOET, Sandblindnes, *luscio.* **1905** *Outlook* 16 Dec. 852/2 But there is a sort of sand-blindness endemic in the Liberal party just now.

'sand-box. [f. SAND *sb.*² + BOX *sb.*²]

1. A box with a perforated top for sprinkling sand as a blotter upon the wet ink of a manuscript. *Obs.* exc. *Hist.*

1572 HULOET (ed. Higins), Sandboxe, or a duste boxe, to spreade dust on writing. **1626** MIDDLETON *Women Beware Women* IV. ii, He would prick my skull as full of holes as a scrivener's sand-box. **1681** *Lond. Gaz.* No. 1637/8 Stolen,.. a Silver Inkhorn, the Sand box to it left behind. **1740** SWIFT *Will* Wks. 1751 XIV. 272, I bequeath to Deane Swift, Esq.; ..an Ink Pot, a Sand Box and Bell. **1858** CARLYLE *Fredk. Gt.* VI. vi. (1872) II. 187 '*Erz-Sandstreuer*', who solemnly brings up the Sandbox (no blotting-paper yet in use) when the Holy Roman Empire is pleased to write.

2. A box holding sand for various purposes; esp. **a.** A sand-mould. **b.** A box of sand on a locomotive (see quot. 1849) for use when the wheels slip. **c.** A receptacle for the sand used to 'tee' the ball on a golf course.

1688 R. HOLME *Armoury* III. 382/2 He beareth Gules, a Lapidaries Sand Box, or Dust Box, covered, Or... In such kind of Boxes with covers, Lapidaries keep their fine Dust of Diamond..made into a kind of Sand. **1833** J. HOLLAND *Manuf. Metal* II. 39 So largely has the sand-box superseded the anvil in this manufacture [of scissors]. **1849** WEALE *Dict. Terms*, *Sand-boxes*, in locomotive engines, boxes filled with sand, usually placed near the driving wheels, with a pipe to guide the sand to the rails. **1859** BARTLETT *Dict. Amer.*, *Sand-Box*, a primitive sort of spittoon, consisting of a wooden box filled with sand. **1875** *Ure's Dict. Arts* III. 750 The sand-box [of a sand-blast apparatus]. **1901** *Scotsman* 5 Nov. 8/4 Proceeding to the sand-box at the first tee.

d. A small low-sided sand-pit (cf. SAND-PIT 3). Chiefly *U.S.*

1937 [see HUH *int.*]. **1968** *Globe & Mail* (Toronto) 17 Feb. 39 Divided they stand not unlike urchins defying each other in the sandbox. **1969** [see MICKEY MOUSE 1]. **1976** *National Observer* (U.S.) 8 May 20/4 All the men in her life, from sandbox playmate to lip-smacking savage.

e. A box kept indoors and filled with sand or other material for a cat to defecate in.

1967 L. J. BRAUN *Cat who ate Danish Modern* viii. 73 Qwilleran showed Koko the new location of his sandbox and gave him his old toy mouse. **1971** J. MCCLURE *Steam Pig* viii. 98 The *Daily Post*..an evening rag not worth putting in the cat's sand-box. **1974** M. G. EBERHART *Danger Money* (1975) iv. 40 I've fixed up a sandbox for the cat.

3. The fruit of the West Indian forest tree, *Hura crepitans*. Also, the tree itself.

1750 G. HUGHES *Barbadoes* 114 The Sand-box Tree. *Ibid.* 115 These Trees are called Sand-boxes from the Use that is made of their Fruit to that Purpose. **1757** PARSONS in *Phil. Trans.* L. 405 This is undoubtedly the young Sand-box, or fruit of the Hura. **1885** LADY BRASSEY *The Trades* 178 We made our first halt, under a large sand-box-tree.

'sand-boy. [f. SAND *sb.*² + BOY *sb.*¹]

1. ? A boy who hawks sand for sale. In proverbial phr. ***as happy*** (or ***jolly,*** etc.) ***as a sandboy.***

1821 P. EGAN *Life in London* II. v. 289 Logic..appeared to be as happy as a sand-boy, who had unexpectedly met with good luck in disposing of his hampers full of the above-household commodity. **1823** 'JON BEE' *Dict. Turf, Sand-boy*, all rags and all happiness; the urchins who drive the sand-laden neddies through our streets, are envied by the capon-eating turtle-loving epicures of these cities. 'As jolly as a sand-boy', designates a merry fellow who has tasted a drop. **1840** DICKENS *Old C. Shop* xviii, The Jolly Sandboys was a small road-side inn.., with a sign, representing three Sandboys increasing their jollity. **1841** E. FITZGERALD *Lett.* (1889) I. 70 We will smoke together and be as merry as sandboys. **1892** ZANGWILL *Childr. Ghetto* I. xxiv, Everything combined to make him as jolly as a sand-boy. **1928** *Daily Express* 17 Mar. 3/1 The King was in his element here... He was happy as a sandboy. **1958** *Daily Sketch* 2 June 11/3 Brimming with health, polished like a Derby cup, happy as a sandboy. **1973** *Perthshire Advertiser* 17 Feb. 18/3 It isn't hot, but they're as happy as sandboys.

2. = *sand-man*: see SAND *sb.*² 10.

1873 *St. Paul's Mag.* Feb. 139 But you are sleepy—the sand-boys are in your eyes.

sand-bur ('sændbɜː(r)). *U.S.* Also **sand-burr.** [f. SAND *sb.*² + BUR *sb.*] The small prickly fruit of any of several plants, esp. a bur-grass of the genus *Cenchrus* or an annual herb, *Franseria acanthicarpa*; also, any of several plants bearing such a fruit. Also *attrib.*

1830 W. A. FERRIS *Life in Rocky Mts.* (1940) vi. 28 These grass-knots, are called 'Sand-burrs'. **1834** A. PIKE *Prose Sk. & Poems* 48 To add to our comforts, the ground here was covered with sand-burs. **1867** E. EGGLESTON in *Little Corporal* Sept. 37/1 A bad name..sticks to you like a sand-burr. **1896** *Voice* (N.Y.) 12 Mar. 4/4 The Prohibitionists of the state [Kansas] are soon to meet at Topeka again and feed sand-burs to Governor Morrill. **1904** *Topeka* (Kansas) *Daily Capital* 11 June 4 A sandbur will grapple on to a man's coat tail and stay there all day just to get a chance to fall into his bed at night. **1948** F. BLAKE *Johnny Christmas* I. 39 Weatherby stalked back to his bed, knocked the sandburs from his socks, and..pulled his blankets over his ears. **1957** L. EISELEY *Immense Journey* 69 There passed before my eyes the million airy troopers of the milkweed pod and the clutching hooks of the sandburs. **1971** *Country Life* 4 Nov. 1193/1 These [impurities] include the long spiky seeds of shepherd's needle..and the viciously armed burs of the sand-bur grasses..from South America.

'sand-cast, *v. Founding.* [f. SAND *sb.*² + CAST *v.*] *trans.* To make (a casting) by pouring molten metal into a sand mould.

1949 C. J. SMITHELLS *Metals Ref. Bk.* 596 Nearly all alloys can be sand cast, including relatively hot short materials. **1952** WOOD & VON LUDWIG *Investment Castings for Engineers* xvii. 371 The preference for location of bosses in parts which are to be sand cast is on internal surfaces rather than external ones.

So **'sand-cast** *ppl. a.*; **'sand casting** *vbl. sb.*, (*a*) an object cast in a sand mould; (*b*) the process of casting in a sand mould.

1934 *Jrnl. Inst. Metals* LIV. 103 A sand-cast ingot. **1939** *Light Metals* II. 361 (*heading*) The production of aluminium-alloy sand castings. **1949** C. J. SMITHELLS *Metals Ref. Bk.* 596 Sand casting offers the widest scope of all the casting processes. *Ibid.*, In weight, sand castings range from less than an ounce up to more than 100 tons. **1960**, **1964** [see *gravity die-casting* s.v. GRAVITY 8 b]. **1967** A. H. COTTRELL *Introd. Metall.* xiii. 184 In sand casting a wooden pattern of the required shape, slightly enlarged to allow for shrinkage of the casting, is firmly packed in sand in a moulding box... A green sand casting is made in sand bonded with clay. **1981** *Pop. Hot Rodding* Feb. 22/1 The only engine components that should be changed are the pistons, and only if they are of sand-cast manufacture.

sande ('sændeɪ). Also **sandee**, and with capital initial. [W. Afr.] The name of a cult for women based on secret rites of initiation, etc., widespread amongst tribes in Sierra Leone and Liberia. See also PORO.

1803 T. WINTERBOTTOM *Acct. Native Africans Sierra Leone* II. 235 In the river Sherbró,..which is inhabited by Bulloms, there is a society of girls called Sandee girls, who, besides being initiated into various mysteries, are instructed to dance in public. **1930** *Harvard Afr. Exped. 1926–27* I. v. 83 Most of the tribes in Liberia still practice certain ceremonies connected with the initiation of both boys and girls in the bush schools... The..girls' school is known as *sande.* **1954** R. LEWIS *Sierra Leone* i. 9 Quite a number of the mauve- and green-uniformed but nubile-looking schoolgirls who walk in crocodile through the streets will be rushed through Sande in the holidays. **1968** HARRIS & SAWYER *Springs of Mende Belief* i. 2 *Sande*..plays a more restricted role in the community. Its main concern is to cultivate in adult women the qualities of wifehood and motherhood. *Ibid.* vi. 104 This accusation..includes..any attempts to watch the masked *sande* dancers remove their head-piece.

sande, obs. form of SAINT, SANDY *sb.*

sanded ('sændɪd), *ppl. a.* [f. (in senses 1–4) SAND *sb.*² and (senses 5–7) SAND *v.*]

†**1.** Of a sandy colour = SANDY *a.* 3, 4. *Obs.*

1590 SHAKS. *Mids. N.* IV. i. 125 My hounds are bred out of the Spartan kinde, So flew'd, so sanded. **1607** TOPSELL *Four-f. Beasts* (1658) 515 The colour of Swine is uncertain, ..some are white, some branded, some sanded, some red. **1667** COTTON *Scarron.* IV. 10 The Sun..that spruce light-headed fellow With frizled locks of sanded yellow. **1686** *Lond. Gaz.* No. 2136/4 A white Sanded gray Mare, eight years old.

†**2.** Sand-blind. *Obs.*

1629 GAULE *Pract. Theories* Rules to Rdrs., My Poring, Prying, Pious Reader; With sanded, searching or with simple Eye. **1787** GROSE *Provinc. Gloss.*, *Sanded*, short-sighted. N[orth].

†**3.** Composed of or covered with sand; sandy.

1702 ROWE *Tamerl.* II. ii. 26 With Nations like the sanded Shore. **1726–46** THOMSON *Winter* 100 Dreadful down it [the river] comes..Then o'er the sanded valley floating spreads.

†**4.** Cast in sand, as opposed to 'minted'. *Obs.*

1732 in J. Tait *Two Cent. Border Ch. Life* iii. (1889) 64 Uncurrent money..consisting of doits, Irish halfpennies and sanded bodles. **1759** in *Scott. N. & Q.* 2nd Ser. (1902) IV. 5/2 Bad sanded halfpennies.

5. Sprinkled with sand.

1760–2 GOLDSM. *Cit. W.* xxx, The sanded floor that grits beneath the tread. **1860** TYNDALL *Glac.* II. xxvii. 377 Fine lines resembling those produced by the passage of a rake over a sanded walk. **1869** TROLLOPE *He Knew*, etc. xxxii. (1878) 181 [He] was up-stairs in the sanded parlour of the Full Moon public-house.

b. Of wood, etc.: Covered with a layer of sand to represent stone.

1883 *Harper's Mag.* Oct. 716/1 Tawdry modern cast-iron work, 'sanded' to represent stone. **1889** C. T. DAVIES *Bricks* ii. (ed. 2) 56 It is not considered an honest treatment of material to make painted and sanded wood take upon itself the appearance of stone.

c. Of land: Dressed with sand.

1707 MORTIMER *Husb.* (1721) I. 106 In well sanded Lands little or no Snow lies.

6. Adulterated with sand.

1883 *Daily News* 21 Nov. 6/7 They never would get free from this sanded wool so long as they paid such big prices for it, since it really paid better at the price obtainable than the clean wool. **1895** *Min. 9th Nat. Council Congr. Ch. U.S.* 151 To refrain from short yardsticks and sanded sugar.

7. Reduced to sand-like grains.

1897 *Syd. Soc. Lex., Sanded gum*, powdered gum arabic.

'sand-eel. Also 4–5 **sandel**, 4 **sandhell**, 5 **sawndel**, 6 **sand el**. [f. SAND *sb.*[2] + EEL *sb.*]

1. A fish of the genus *Ammodytes*, having a slender, cylindrical, silvery body resembling that of an eel.

1307 *Durh. Acc. Rolls* (Surtees) 3 In c de makerell, .. cccc di. merling. et sandelis. **1338** *Ibid.* 35 In Sandhells empt. pro familia die Veneris, 14*d.* **1425–6** *Ibid.* 620 Et de 3*s.* 4*d.* rec. pro tractatu de Sandeelez. *c* **1440–60** [see SANDLING[1] 1]. [**1558** RONDELET *Gesn. Hist. Anim.* IV. 1260 De Ammodyte pisce, vt nos vocauimus, pro Anglico Sandilz.] **1671** RAY in *Phil. Trans.* VI. 2276 Those little long fishes, which our Fishermen dig out of the Sands at low water, and therefore call in some places Sand-Eeles. *c* **1711** PETIVER *Gazophyl.* VI. lix, Brasil Sand Eel... About 9 Inches long; very good Meat. **1880** GÜNTHER *Fishes* 550 The 'Sand-eels' or 'Launces' (*Ammodytes*) are extremely common on sandy shores of Europe and North America.

2. *New Zealand.* The fish *Gonorhynchus greyi.*

1891 in *Century Dict.*

Hence **'sand-eeling**, fishing for sand-eels.

1862 ANSTED *Channel Isl.* II. ix. (ed. 2) 212 Sand-eeling at midnight .. is one of the amusements of all classes.

sandel: see SAMEL, SENDAL.

sandelen wood: see SANDALWOOD.

sandeling, obs. form of SANDLING[1].

sandell, obs. form of SANDAL *sb.*[1] and *sb.*[2]

Sandemanian (sændɪ'meɪnɪən), *sb.* and *a.* Also erron. **Sandimanian, Sandymanian**. [f. the name *Sandeman* + -(I)AN.] *sb.* A member of a religious sect developed by Robert Sandeman (1718–71) from the Glassites. *adj.* Of or belonging to the Sandemanians.

1766 B. STEVENS *Let.* 21 Jan. in E. Stiles *Extracts from Itineraries & Other Misc.* (1916) 566 In the late times of oclocracy some small damages have been done to the Sandimanian meeting house. **1773** *Massachusetts Gaz.* 8 Apr. 3/1 The Fire likewise communicated to the Sandemanian Meeting House. **1792** BELKNAP *Hist. New Hampsh.* III. 324 In the town of Portsmouth there is a society of Sandemanians. **1810** W. WILSON *Dissent. Ch. Lond.* III. 326 The discipline in this church is conducted pretty much in the same manner as in other Sandemanian societies. **1876** *N. Amer. Rev.* CXXIII. 224 The Sandemanian heresy. **1882–3** *Schaff's Encycl. Relig. Knowl.* III. 2109 The sect .. called 'Glassites' in Scotland, and 'Sandemanians' in England and America. **1926** A. HUXLEY *Let.* 10 Aug. (1969) 272 Faraday .. was at once a Sandemanian and a Fellow of the Royal Society. **1935** B. RUSSELL *Relig. & Sci.* vii. 171 Faraday was a Sandymanian, but the errors of that sect did not seem, even to him, to be demonstrable by scientific arguments.

Hence **Sande'manianism**.

1766 *Causes Pres. Declension Congr. Churches* title-p., Interspersed with Reflections on Methodism and Sandimanianism [*sic*]. **1822** J. BROWN *Mem. J. Hervey* 453 Fuller of Kettering .. opposes Sandemanianism.

sander ('sændə(r)), *sb.* [f. SAND *v.* + -ER[1].]

1. One who or something which sands or sprinkles with sand; one who collects sand.

1627 HAKEWILL *Apol.* IV. viii. §3 (1630) 396 The *Arena*, .. so called, for that it was strowed ouer with sand .., and officers they had purposely for this businesse, .. termed *Arenarii*, Sanders. **1854** E. GIFFARD *Deeds Nav. Daring* 262 Mr. Edward Henry A'Court, with a marine and seven seamen, was despatched from the Blanche in the red cutter to collect sand... The midshipman and his party of sanders [etc.]. **1889** *Blackw. Mag.* Sept. 321/2 A sudden whirl of the driving-wheels, .. followed by the application of the steam sanders [of a locomotive]. **1908** *Daily Chron.* 21 Feb. 10/6 Drum (Single), 28in. automatic feed sander .. to be Sold.

2. A workman employed to sandpaper the soles of boots and shoes.

1881 *Instr. Census Clerks* (1885) 76 Boot and Shoe Making: .. Levanter. Sander.

3. A sand-papering machine.

1895 in *Funk's Stand. Dict.* **1930** *Engineering* 23 May 688/1 The combination consists of a saw-table, .. a disc sander. **1975** M. BRADBURY *Hist. Man* iii. 43 Students .. with a rented sander exposed, and then waxed yellow with a rented waxer, the good old wood of the floors.

†**'sander**, *adv. Obs.* Also 5 **sannyr, sonder**. [Comparative of ME. *sōne*, SOON *a.*, with vowel-shortening and euphonic *d*; the phonology is somewhat obscure.] Sooner.

a **1450** MYRC *Festial* 43 Moche more and sannyr he heruth hom þat callyth to hym wyth all hor hertys. *Ibid.* 166 Þat he may þe sondyr come to beleue. *Ibid.* 267 Þis day your prayers schull be sandyr herd of God þen anoþer day. **1482** *Monk of Evesham* (Arb.) 29 How y might the sandyr and lyghter scape. *Ibid.* 37 Mony of them that sodenly scapyd .. and sander hastid hem selfe thanne other to go the weye that was before hem. **1532** *St. Papers Hen. VIII*, VII. 373 A litle brieff information .. emprinted .. to make theym the sander to understande the same. *Ibid.* 403 That suche thinges as are promissed .. suld the sander comme to passe.

sanderbode: see under SANDESMAN.

sanderick, obs. form of SANDARAC.

sanderling ('sændəlɪŋ). Also 7 **sanderlin**, 7, 9, **sandling**. [Possibly repr. OE. **sand-yrðling*, f. *sand* SAND *sb.*[1] + *yrðling* ploughman (see EARTHLING[1]), also the name of some bird (? the plover).] A small wading bird, *Calidris arenaria.*

1602 CAREW *Cornwall* 35 Coots, Sanderlings, Sea-larkes. **1623** N. H. in Whitbourne *Newfoundland* 114 The Fowles and Birds .. of the Sea are .. Teale, Snipes, .. Sanderlins. **1684** E. CHAMBERLAYNE *Pres. St. Eng.* (ed. 15) 6 Sandlings, knot, curlew. **1785** LATHAM *Gen. Synopsis Birds* III. 197 Sanderling, *Charadrius calidris*, Lin. **1804** CHARLOTTE SMITH *Conversations*, etc. II. 34, I rather think, Sanderling, .. is the name .. tho' the fishermen call them Sandlings. **1856** KANE *Arct. Expl.* I. xx. 259 A sanderling, the second migratory land-bird we have seen, came to our brig today. **1873** LONGF. *Wayside Inn* III. Prel. 77 The plover, peep, and sanderling, That .. pipe along the barren sands.

sander(r)man(n, var. ff. SANDESMAN *Obs.*

sanders[1] ('sɑːndəz, 'sæn-). Forms: 4 **saundres, (zaunders)**, 5 **sawndres, -dyrs, saun-, sawnderys**, 4–8 **saunders**, 6– **sanders**; with sing. form 4 **zawndre, sandery**, 5 **sander, sandrey**, 5–7 **saunder**. [a. OF. *sandre* (Hatz.-Darm. s.v. *santal*), var. of *sandle*: see SANDAL[2]. The word has in Eng. been most commonly plural in form, and occas. in construction.]

1. = SANDALWOOD, in its various applications. (Cf. RED SANDERS.)

1329–30 *Durham Acc. Rolls* (Surtees) 16 In .. 2 unceis de Saundres, 3*s.* **1340** *Ibid.* 35 Saundres pro colore. **1388** *Ibid.* 48 In una li. de zawndre. **1390** *Ibid.* 49 Di. li. de zaunders, 2*s.* 6*d.* **1331** *Acc. Chamberl. Scotl.* (1771) 25 Et de 484 lib. diversarum confectionum .. 2 lib. de sandery [etc.]. ? *c* **1390** *Form of Cury* xx. in Warner *Antiq. Culin.* (1780) 19 Color it with saundres a lytel. **1390** GOWER *Conf.* I. 225 That I mai stonde in thilke rowe Amonges hem that Saundres use. *c* **1430** *Two Cookery-bks.* 12 Þen take Sawnderys, an Vynegre, an cast þer-to. **14..** *Noble Bk. Cookry* (1882) 30 To mak longe de bef, tak ox tunges .. then tak .. parsly, ysope, tyme sandrey [etc.]. **1526** *Pilgr. Perf.* (W. de W. 1531) 22 b, A precyous tree: wherof the stock is saundres, the barke synamom, the fruyt nutmygges or maces. **1598** W. PHILLIP *Linschoten* I. lxxiv. 120/2 There are 3. sorts of Sanders, that is, white, yellow and red. **1623** MARKHAM *Eng. Housew.* (ed. 2) 108 Take .. good store of suger, cinamon, a few saunders and rosewater. **1791** HAMILTON *Berthollet's Dyeing* I. I. II. iv. 205 With the addition of sanders [F. *santal*] .. they stand much better. **1864** GRISEBACH *Flora W. Ind. Isl.* 787 Sanders, yellow: *Bucida capitata.*

†**2.** The sandalwood tree; sandalwood trees.

1613 PURCHAS *Pilgrimage* (1614) 507 In Tymor, an Iland by Iaua, are whole woods of Sanders. **1783** JUSTAMOND tr. *Raynal's Hist. Indies* II. 94 The santalum or sanders grows to the size of a walnut-tree.

3. *attrib.*, as ***sanders-beater, cup, powder, tree***; **sanders-wood** = sense 1.

1544 *Will of R. Osborne* (Somerset Ho.), I will that the *saunder beaters at Grocer's Hall beare my boddy to the churche. **1617** in Heath *Grocers' Comp.* (1869) 434 Payde the saunder beaters .. 1 l. 3 s. 4 d. **1491** *Will of Vaughan* (Somerset Ho.), My *saunder cupp. **1481–9** *Howard Househ. Bk.* (Roxb.) 42 Item, *sander poder di. lb. ij. s. vj. d. **1640** PARKINSON *Theat. Bot.* 1605 The *Saunders tree .. groweth to be as bigge as the Wallnut tree. **1615** *Cal. St. Papers, E. Ind.* (1862) 380 *Sanders wood. **1812** J. SMYTH *Pract. of Customs* (1821) 52 Brandy .. having its red colour from burnt sugar, Saunders wood, &c. **1846** *Penny Cycl. Suppl.* II. 190/1 Dyed red with the aromatic saunders-wood. **1866** *Treas. Bot., Sanders-wood.*

sanders[2] ('sɑːndəz, 'sæn-). Also **saunders**. (See quot. 1892.)

1827 *New Syst. Cookery* 51 To dress the same [*sc.* cold beef], called Sanders. **1864** *Englishw. in India* 128 Saunders. Put a layer of mashed potatoes [etc.]. **1892** *Encycl. Cookery* (ed. Garrett) II. 377 Sanders. This name is given to a preparation of minced beef or other meat.

sandery, obs. form of SANDERS[1].

sandesh ('sændɛʃ). [a. Bengali *sandesh* a sweetmeat.] An Indian sweetmeat resembling cheese fudge.

1944 in D. K. Gupta *Best Stories Mod. Bengal* I. 72 She .. pushed a plate full of Sandesh towards me. **1953** R. GODDEN *Kingfishers catch Fire* xi. 122 *Sandesh*, which is like toffee, and *jilibis* that are rings of clear sugar. **1966** J. & R. GODDEN *Two under Indian Sun* iv. 103 Indian sweets, jillipis or sāndesh. **1973** *Times* 19 June (Bombay Suppl.) p. xv/3 West Bengal's rosogollas and sandesh.

†**'sandesman.** *Obs.* Forms: α. 2 **sander man**, *Ormin* **sanderrmann**, 3 **sonder(e man**, 3–4 **sandirman**. β. 3 **sondes-**, 4 **sondezmon**, 4–5 **sondes-, sandes-, sandis-, soundis-**, 5 **sayndis-man**. [f. ME. *sandes*, genit. of SAND *sb.*[1] + MAN *sb.*[1] The α forms come from Scandinavian districts, and the *-er* seems to represent the ON. genitive ending *-ar*, although SAND *sb.*[1] does not appear to have existed in ON. Cf. *sand-man* s.v. SAND *sb.*[1]; also SENDMAN.] A messenger, envoy, ambassador.

α. **1123** *O.E. Chron.* (MS. Laud), & þær comen þes eorles sander men of Angeow to him. *c* **1200** ORMIN 19383 He [S. John Bapt.] nass nohht Crist .. Acc sanderrmann biforenn Crist To kiþenn Cristess come. *c* **1250** *Gen. & Ex.* 1410 Laban and his moder wið-ðan faȝneden wel ðis sondere man. *a* **1300–1400** *Cursor M.* 21408 (Gött.) Þan sent þe king costantine, sandirmen [*Cott.* send men] till his moder eline. β. *c* **1205** LAY. 13595 Heo .. nomen ænne sondes-mon and senden toward Lunden. **13..** *E.E. Allit. P.* B. 469 He sechez an oþer sondez-mon & settez on þe douue. *a* **1400–50** *Alexander* 2399 Now ere þe sandismen sett on þaire horsis. *c* **1400** *Destr. Troy* XXI. 8866 Then sent were þere sone soundismen two, To Priam, the prise kyng, purpos to hold. *c* **1470** *Gol. & Gaw.* 326, I rede ane sayndis-man ye send to yone senyeour.

So †**'sanderbode.** [BODE *sb.*[1] Cf. ON. *sendiboðe.*]

c **1200** *Trin. Coll. Hom.* 89 And þo tweien sander-bodes ferden and cudden in þe bureh, þat þe helende was þiderward.

sandever, -devoire: see SANDIVER.

†**'sand-eyed**, *a. Obs. rare*[−1]. [f. SAND *sb.*[2], supposed to be the first element in SAND-BLIND *a.*] Sand-blind.

1592 GREENE *Disput.* Wks. (Grosart) X. 223 A sawcie Signor there is, whose purblind eyes can scarcely discerne a Lowse from a Flea... I doubt the sandeyde Asse, will kicke .. if I rubbe him on the gaule.

'sand-fly. [f. SAND *sb.*[2] + FLY *sb.*[1]]

1. a. A small blood-sucking fly belonging to the family Simuliidæ or Psychodidæ or a biting midge of the family Ceratopogonidæ.

1748 *Anson's Voy.* I. v. 46 The muscatos .. were succeeded by an infinity of sand-flies. **1816** KIRBY & SP. *Entomol.* iv. (1818) I. 111 The burning-fly (*brulot*) or sand-fly of America and the West Indies. **1867** A. L. ADAMS *Wand. Naturalist India* 59 That prince of gallynippers, the sand-fly, whose bite produces a painful and irritable swelling. **1896** tr. *Boas' Text-bk. Zool.* 276 The Sand-fly (*Simulia*), a small fly-like Midge, the females of which .. are blood suckers. **1907** FOUNTAIN & WARD *Rambles Austral. Naturalist* xi. 121 The sand flies .. irritated us greatly. **1932** [see *owl fly* s.v. OWL *sb.* 7 b]. **1947** I. L. IDRIESS *Isles of Despair* xxxii. 214 Barbara was fortunate that it was beautiful weather; .. no hellish mosquitoes or burning sandflies to torture her naked hide. **1962** GORDON & LAVOIPIERRE *Entomol. for Students of Med.* xxi. 141 Members of the family Simuliidæ are widely known as 'buffalo-flies' and 'black flies', but in some parts of the world, as in Australia, they are .. designated by other names such as 'sandflies' or 'midges'. **1972** SWAN & PAPP *Common Insects N. Amer.* xxii. 595 The biting midges .. include some very annoying pests, variously called no-see-ums, punkies, sand flies, moose flies, and gnats.

b. An artificial fly used in angling.

1681 CHETHAM *Angler's Vade-m.* (1700) 229 Sand Fly... Made of the Wooll gotten off the Flank of a black Sheep. **1892** LOWNDES *Camping Sk.* 202 The dace were rising furiously, and we got to work at once with a sandfly and a blue dun.

2. ***sand-fly bush***: see quot.

1889 J. H. MAIDEN *Usef. Nat. Pl. Australia* 282 *Zieria Smithii*, Andr... Colonial names are 'Sandfly Bush' and 'Turmeric'.

3. sand-fly fever, an acute viral fever transmitted by flies of the genus *Phlebotomus.*

1911 DORLAND *Med. Dict.* (ed. 6) 629/2 *Phlebotomus papatasii* [printed *papatassii*] .. is thought to convey by its bite an infection known as sandfly fever. **1936** *Indian Jrnl. Med. Res.* XXIII. 870 The lesion in dengue fever .. differs to some extent from that in sandfly fever. **1962** GORDON & LAVOIPIERRE *Entomol. for Students of Med.* v. 26 There remain certain virus infections, such as sandfly fever and dengue, which cause disease in man, but for which no animal reservoir has, as yet, been demonstrated.

sandfracing, sand fracing ('sændfrækɪŋ), *vbl. sb. Oil Industry.* Also **-fraccing, -fracking**. [f. SAND *sb.*[2] + FRAC(TUR)ING *vbl. sb.*] A method of stimulating production from an oil field by forcing fluid containing sand grains into the reservoir rock. So **'sandfrac** *sb.*, a name for this process; **sand frac(k** *v. trans.* and *absol.*, to apply this treatment to (an oil field).

1953 *Petrol. Engineer* XXV. B108/2 This well had two sandfrac treatments, using .. round grained sand. **1957** *Times* 11 Dec. 16/4 It is believed that sandfraccing and drilling in proven areas will maintain the present rate of production. **1960** *Oil & Gas Reporter* XII. 1034 After the well was completed, Phillips contracted with *D* to sand frack. *Ibid.* 1035 Phillips arranged .. to sand frack the producing formation to increase productivity. **1961** *Ibid.* XIV. 111 On December 9, 1959, Gregg et al. requested the Commission to enter field rules including one which would authorize any operator to 'sand frac' by using a maximum of 20,000 gallons of fluid and 40,000 pounds of sand per well. **1961** *Texas Law Rev.* XXXIX. 359 It is suggested that compulsory pooling is a workable and effective method of solving the small tract problem and, more specifically, the issues arising from an alleged trespass caused by sand-fracing.

sandgiac, variant of SANJAK.

'sand-glass. [f. SAND *sb.*[2] + GLASS *sb.*[1]]

1. A contrivance for measuring time, consisting of two glass vessels of approximately conical shape, connected at the apex by a narrow neck, and containing so much sand as will take a given time to flow from the receptacle placed uppermost into that placed below; an hour-glass, a minute-glass, an egg-boiler, or the like. Also *fig.*

1556 WITHALS *Dict.* (1562) 65 b/2 A sande glasse, or houre-glasse, *vitreum horologium.* **1570** DEE *Math. Pref.* d iv, Houre, halfe houre, and three houre Sandglasses. **1687** A. LOVELL tr. *Thevenot's Trav.* I. 268 They turn a half minute Sand-Glass, .. and then drop the Log from the Stern. **1779** BOSWELL *Let.* 22 Oct. in *Life Johnson*, But my sand-glass was now beginning to run low, as I could not trespass too long on the colonel's kindness. **1824** SCOTT *St. Ronan's* xxiii, My span must be a brief one, but let not your hand shake the sand-glass! **1902** *Westm. Gaz.* 30 Oct. 1/1 The two-minute sandglass on the table of the House of Commons . . has to be turned, and whilst the sand is running down the division bells are set in motion.

†**2.** = SAND-BOX 1. *Obs.*

1806–7 J. BERESFORD *Miseries Hum. Life* VIII. xxiv, Emptying the ink-glass, (by mistake for the sand-glass) on a paper which you have just written out fairly.

'sand-grouse. [SAND *sb.*[2]] Any bird of the group *Pteroclomorphæ*, inhabiting sandy tracts of the old world, consisting of two genera *Pterocles* (esp. *P. arenarius*, the Sand-grouse proper, and *P. alchata*, the Pin-tailed Sand-grouse) and *Syrrhaptes*.

1783 LATHAM *Gen. Synopsis Birds* IV. 751 Sand Grouse. *Tetrao arenaria*. This is bigger than the Partridge. **1864** *Intell. Observer* IV. 197 The new British Sand-Grouse. (Pallas's Three-toed Sand-Grouse—*Syrrhaptes paradoxus*.) **1867** A. L. ADAMS *Wand. Naturalist India* 119 The painted or lesser sand-grouse (*Pterocles fasciatus*). **1895** J. G. MILLAIS *Breath fr. Veldt* (1899) 29 In the early morning the Namaqua sandgrouse come to their margins . . to drink.

'sand-heat. [SAND *sb.*[2]] Heat applied by means of heated sand; also = SAND-BATH 1.

1610 B. JONSON *Alch.* II. iii, I meane to tinct C. in sand-heat, to morrow, And giue him imbibition. **1677** W. HARRIS tr. *Lemery's Course Chem.* 317 You may distil the Spirit on a Sand-heat. **1746** R. JAMES *Moufet's Health's Impr.* Introd. 42 By a Sand-heat, gradually increased, it yields first a . . Liquor, . . then a white volatile Salt. **1857** MILLER *Elem. Chem.* (1862) III. 13 By evaporating the solution . . to dryness by a strong sand heat.

sandhi ('sandɪ). *Philol.* Also †**sundhi**, and with capital initial. [a. Skr. *saṃdhí* junction, combination, f. *sam* together + *dhā* to place (see DO *v.*).] The term applied orig. by Sanskrit grammarians to assimilative changes occurring in Sanskrit in the final and initial sounds of words in a sentence (*external sandhi*), and in the final sounds of stems in word-formation (*internal sandhi*); extended by modern philologists to analogous phenomena in other languages.

1806 W. CAREY *Gram. Sungskrit Lang.* I. iii. 15 (*heading*) Of Sundhi, or the permutation of letters occasioned by the junction of syllables. **1841** H. H. WILSON *Introd. Gram. Sanskrit Lang.* ii. 8 The changes to which letters are subject for the sake of euphony are numerous, and carefully defined, forming that part of Sanskrit grammar which is termed . . Sandhi, 'a holding together', 'a function'. **1888** H. SWEET *Hist. Eng. Sounds* 15 An equally primitive stage is preserved in the Sanskrit sandhi, only here it is generally the end of a word that is modified. **1888** J. WRIGHT tr. *Brugmann's Elem. Compar. Gram. Indo-Europ. Lang.* I. 501 Owing to the scantiness of the Umbrian-Samnitic materials, handed down to us, it remains doubtful at what period certain processes of sandhi took place in Latin. **1901** A. A. MACDONELL *Sanskrit Gram.* p. ii, The rules of Sandhi are based chiefly on the avoidance of hiatus and on assimilation. **1933** *Eng. Stud.* XV. 41 O[ld] E[nglish] *æt þam ende*, which became *atten ende*, and then, through sandhi, *at an ende*. **1939** [see MORPHOPHONEMICS *sb. pl.*]. **1952** [see NUCLEAR *a.* (and *sb.*) 1 c]. **1976** *Language* LII. 212 There is ample evidence that much of Sanskrit external sandhi is the result of sweeping generalizations.

2. *attrib.* and *Comb.*

1888 J. WRIGHT tr. *Brugmann's Elem. Compar. Gram. Into-Europ. Lang.* I. 488 The fettered language of the Vedas already furnishes the proof that the sandhi-system of the classical Sanskrit is not a thing of natural growth. **1933** L. BLOOMFIELD *Language* xxiii. 418 There resulted sandhi-alternants of words like *water*: . . ['wɔtə] . . ['wɔtər iz] . . . This . . resulted in the sandhi-form *the idea-r is*. . . English sandhi-alternation is limited largely to cases like the above. **1935** *Amer. Speech* X. 86/1 The sandhi customs are different in English from what they are in Dutch. *Ibid.*, A preliminary statement of the sandhi rules of the dialect or language studied. **1945** *Mod. Lang. Notes* Dec. 539 The sandhi-affricate formed in the sequence *right here*. **1961** R. E. KELLER *German Dialects* 264 This sandhi-lenition is not indicated in the orthography of the *Lux[emburger] W[ör]t[er]b[uch]*. **1969** *Eng. Stud.* Suppl. p. lxxxi, At a conservative estimate twenty-two of the above twenty-eight instances support a spoken *sandhi*-distribution of voiced and voiceless final consonants. **1975** *Language* LI. 551 Words may have more than one form, due to sandhi processes such as French liaison and elision.

'sand-hill. [SAND *sb.*[2]] **a.** A hill or bank of sand; esp. a dune on the sea-shore.

c **725** *Corpus Gloss.* (Hessels) A 440 *Alga*, scaldhyflas *uel* sondhyllas. *c* **1440** *Promp. Parv.* 464/2 Sond hylle, or pytte, *sorica*. *a* **1603** SIR F. VERE *Comm.* 88 The space betwixt the sea and the sand-hills or Downs. **1709** PRIOR *Lady's Looking-Gl.* 2 Celia and I . . Walk'd o'er the Sand-hills to the Sea. **1830** LYELL *Princ. Geol.* I. 300 Chains of sand-hills have also accumulated on the shores of the delta of the Nile. **1855** KINGSLEY *Westw. Ho!* xxviii, Easily, on the flowing tide, . . she has slipped up the channel between the two lines of sand-hill. **1890** *Murray's Handbk. for Lincolns.* Introd. 26 The sand-hills or 'dunes' have little beauty beyond their wildness.

b. sand-hill crane, a North American crane, *Grus canadensis*; also *absol.*

1805 W. CLARK *Jrnl.* 31 Oct. in *Orig. Jrnls. Lewis & Clark Exped.* (1905) III. 176 Jo killed a Sand hill Crane. **1834** J. K. TOWNSEND *Narr. Journey Rocky Mts.* (1839) i. 12 We observed great numbers of the brown, or sandhill crane, . . flying over us. **1894** *Outing* (U.S.) XXIV. 305/1 The great sand-hill cranes . . looking as big as the horses we rode. **1907** W. O. LILLIBRIDGE *Where Trail Divides* 115 He can . . stalk a sandhill crane where there isn't cover to hide your hat. **1938** C. H. MATSCHAT *Suwanee River* 186 He seen the sandhills a-dancin' their matin' dance. **1949** *Natural Hist.* Oct. 378/1 Once heard, the far-reaching call of the sand-hill crane is a sound that can never be forgotten. **1960** R. T. PETERSON *Field Guide Birds of Texas* 79 Sandhill Crane . . A long-legged, long-necked gray bird with a bald red forehead. **1977** *New Yorker* 9 May 113/1 He had later seen a pair of sandhill cranes.

c. sand-hill rosemary, a small heath-like evergreen shrub, *Ceratiola ericoides*.

1895 T. W. SANDERS *Encycl. Gard.*

d. *Canad. pl.* A region of southeastern Alberta; in the mythology of Plains Indians, the abode of departed spirits.

1949 J. G. MACGREGOR *Blankets & Beads* 113 Nothing marks the spot where some mighty chief or minor brave sleeps, while his spirit travels the trails of the Great Sand Hills. **1957** *Camsell Arrow* (Edmonton, Alberta) Christmas 77/1 The sun dance site is in the heart of the 50-mile-square Blood reserve about 40 miles south of Lethbridge. There are situated the sacred sand hills and the happy hunting grounds for departed spirits. **1959** N. SLUMAN *Blackfoot Crossing* 13 Little Tree would have to go unadorned to the Sand Hills, for her daughter could not part with the red glass beads. **1963** R. D. SYMONS *Many Trials* xiii. 138 He [*sc.* a missionary] had been saying that it would not be long now before he [*sc.* an Indian] would be called to the Sand-hills. **1975** *Alberta Hist.* Spring 16/2 Indians tell that a blizzard came up and blue and yellow lightning coloured the sky when Wolf Collar's ghost departed for the Sand Hills, the home of the dead.

Hence **'sand-hiller**, one of a class of 'poor whites' living in the pine-woods that cover the sandy hills of Georgia and South Carolina.

1848 *Congress. Globe* 30th Congress 1st Sess. App. 137/1 The thing is whispered even among the sandhillers of South Carolina. **1850** E. P. BURKE *Reminisc. Georgia* 205 These people are known at the South by such names as crackers, clay-eaters, and sand-hillers. **1856** OLMSTED *Slave States* 506 The sand-hillers . . are small, gaunt, and cadaverous, and their skin is just the color of the sand-hills they live on. **1872** [see *piney-woods cracker* s.v. PINEY WOOD b]. **1944** [see *piney-woods tacky* s.v. PINEY WOOD b]. **1958** H. BABCOCK *I don't want to shoot an Elephant* 155 Barefooted and shirtless, the sandhiller was sprawled listlessly on the porch when I arrived.

‖**sandhya** ('sandja:). [a. Skr. *saṃdhyā* a holding together, junction: cf. SANDHI.] **a.** Twilight. **b.** The period which precedes a yuga or age of the world. **c.** Morning or evening prayers.

1868 *Chambers's Encycl.* X. 327/1 A long mundane period of years, which is preceded by a period called *Sandhya*, 'twilight'. **1876** MONIER WILLIAMS *Indian Wisdom* (ed. 3) 248 The two Sandhyas of sunrise and sunset. **1891** —— *Brahmanism & Hinduism* 401 The first act of the Morning Sandhyā Service . . is sipping water. **1913** J. N. FARQUHAR *Crown of Hinduism* 164 The daily devotions (sandhya) are restricted to the three castes. **1971** *Leader* (Durban) 7 May 9/4 They were all saying the 'sandhya', the evening prayers. In perfect Hindi! **1974** *Encycl. Brit. Micropædia* VIII. 850/1 *Sandhyā* . . , Hindu religious acts performed by the twice-born (the three higher castes) at the three divisions of the day (morning, noon, and night).

‖**sandia** (san'dia). [Sp.] A water-melon.

1648 GAGE *West Ind.* 87 Excellent fruits, especially Pines and Sandia's. **1902** in WEBSTER Suppl.

sandifer, obs. form of SANDIVER.

†**san'diferous**, *a. Obs. rare*[−1]. [f. SAND *sb.*[2] + -(I)FEROUS.] Producing sand.

1578 SIDNEY *Wanstead Play* in *Arcadia* (1629) 619 What said that Troian Æneas, when he soiourned in the surging sulkes of the sandiferous seas.

sandiness ('sændɪnɪs). [f. SANDY *a.* + -NESS.]

1. The quality or condition of being sandy.

c **1642** *Observator Def.* 6 The sandinesse and incoherence of the Animadversors consequence. **1783** W. F. MARTYN *Geog. Mag.* II. 132 The sandiness of their walks. **1873** ROBERTS *Handbk. Med.* 173 The eyes are injected and watery, with a feeling of soreness and sandiness.

2. *U.S. slang.* The quality of having 'sand' or pluck. (Cf. SAND *sb.*[2] 7 b.)

1897 FLANDRAU *Harvard Episodes* 31 Their persistent 'sandiness' compelled his admiration.

sanding ('sændɪŋ), *vbl. sb.* [f. SAND *v.* + -ING[1].] The action of the vb. SAND in various senses.

1670 J. SMITH *Eng. Improv. Reviv'd* 10 Lands . . Improved by . . Marling, Liming, Sanding, . . and such like helpes. **1725** BRADLEY *Fam. Dict.*, *Sanding*, a Term in Gardening, signifying the placing of Sand in an Alley. **1842** GWILT *Archit.* §2277 The process of sanding . . is performed with fine sand thrown on the last coat of paint while wet. **1860** DICKENS *Uncomm. Trav.* xxviii, It was the subject of more stamping and sanding than I had ever seen before. **1887** R. RATHBUN *Hist. & Meth. Fisheries* (Fish. Industr. U.S. v.) II. 821 The New York dealers advocate their [*sc.* sponges'] sale by count, in order to circumvent certain fraudulent practices . . such as sanding and liming. *Ibid.* 840 The sanding process consists in mixing with the sponges . . fine sand.

b. *attrib.* and *Comb.*, as ***sanding-box***, ***-gear***, ***-machine***; **sanding plate**, a lap (LAP *sb.*[4]) used, with sand and water, in grinding marble.

1897 *Outing* (U.S.) XXX. 367/2, I knew his *sanding-box would be empty before he shook it over his writing. **1905** *Westm. Gaz.* 15 Aug. 9/3 An engine with . . valve motion, break-gear, and *sanding-gear complete. **1882** *Builder* 18 Nov. 668/1 Watering and *sanding machines. **1850** HOLTZAPFFEL *Turning*, etc. III. 1210 The [horizontal revolving] lap, or as it is called the *sanding plate. **1866** *Cycl. Useful Arts* (ed. Tomlinson) II. 127/2 In the grinding of works of small or moderate size . . sanding-plates are used.

Sandinista (ˌsændɪ'ni:stə, -'nɪstə), *sb.* (*a.*) [Sp., f. the name of Augusto César *Sandino* (1893–1934), Nicaraguan nationalist leader + *-ista* -IST.] A supporter of Sandino; a member of the revolutionary Nicaraguan guerrilla organization founded by him or of a similar organization founded in his name in 1963. Also *attrib.* or as *adj.*

1928 *Nation* (N.Y.) 29 Feb. 232/2 Everybody from here on was a Sandinista; the trail was full of Sandinistas. **1931** *Foreign Affairs* (N.Y.) IX. 499 A purely objective view of the facts hardly warrants calling the Sandinistas 'bandits'. **1954** *Southwestern Social Sci. Q.* (U.S.) Sept. 140 The Guardia's inability to destroy the *Sandinista* movement did not permit the early withdrawal of the marines. **1967** N. MACAULAY *Sandino Affair* iii. 55 On November 2 [1926] he led this force in an attack on the two-hundred-man government garrison at Jícaro, near San Albino. The Sandinistas killed some of the defenders. **1974** *N.Y. Times* 29 Dec. 1/4 The guerrillas, members of the so-called Sandinista Front, were said to have demanded the release of some 40 political prisoners. **1977** *Time* 31 Oct. 16/1 Others, like the Sandinista guerrillas of Nicaragua or the Islamic Marxists of Iran, have specific targets. **1980** *Ann. Reg. 1979* 66 A new Government, formed by the Sandinistas, was quickly recognized by the US.

sandirman, variant of SANDESMAN *Obs.*

†**'sandish**, *a. Obs. rare.* [f. SAND *sb.*[2] + -ISH.] Somewhat sandy.

1664 EVELYN *Kal. Hort.* Oct. 77 You may plant some Anemonies . . in fresh sandish earth. **1675** —— *Terra* (1676) 22 Some of them [*sc.* Chalks] have a Sandish, others a blacker and light surface.

sandisman, variant of SANDESMAN *Obs.*

sandiver ('sændɪvə(r)). Forms: 4 **saundyuer**, 5 **sandifer**, 7 **sandivoir(e**, **sandevoire**, **sandover**, 7, 9 **sandever**, 6– **sandiver**. [App. a. F. *suin de verre* (*suin*, now *suint*, exudation from wool, app. f. *suer* to sweat; *de* of; *verre* glass).] A liquid saline matter found floating over the glass after vitrification; glass-gall.

13 . . *E.E. Allit. P.* B. 1036 [Dead Sea.] Þe clay þat clenges þer-by arn corsyes strong, As alum & alkaran, . . Soufre sour, & saundyuer, & oþer such mony. **1477** NORTON *Ord. Alch.* iii. in Ashm. (1652) 39 Calx vive, Sandifer, and Vitriall. **1587** MASCALL *Govt. Cattle* (1627) 145 Then put of the powder of Sandiuer finely made, into his eye. **1607** TOPSELL *Four-f. Beasts* 357 Martin saith, that hee alwaies vsed to blow a little sandiuoire [**1658** Sandivoir] into the [horse's] eie once a day. **1662** MERRETT tr. *Neri's Art of Glass* ix, The water may take from it a sort of salt called *Sandever*. **1683** PETTUS *Fleta Min.* I. v. 118 One may melt the clean and rich Gold slicks . . in a Crucible with a little of *Caput Mort.* and Sandover. **1778** PRYCE *Min. Cornub.* 39 Sandiver, Scoria Vitri, is the fæces and dregs of glass. **1832** G. R. PORTER *Porcelain & Gl.* 166 Sandiver is purchased by refiners of metals, who use it as a powerful flux.

sandjak, -djakate: see SANJAK, SANJAKATE.

sand lark, sand laverock. [f. SAND *sb.*[2] + LARK *sb.*[1], LAVEROCK.]

1. A name applied, chiefly locally, to some of the smaller limicoline birds.

1658 R. FRANCK *North. Mem.* (1694) 181 Besides here [*sc.* Ross] are Eagles, . . Seapyes, Sandelevericks [etc.]. **1800** WORDSW. *Idle Sheph. Boys* 24 Along the river's stony marge The sand-lark chants a joyous song. **1831** J. RENNIE *Montagu's Ornith. Dict.*, *Dulwilly* (*Charadrius Hiaticula*). Provincial. . . Sand Laverock. *Ibid.*, *Sand Lark*, a name for the Ringed Plover, and the Sandpiper. *Ibid.*, *Sandpiper* (*Totanus hypoleucus*). . . Provincial. . . Sand Lavrock. Sand Lark. **1880** J. E. HARTING *Rodd's Birds Cornw.* 103 Under a variety of names, as Dunlin, . . Sandlark, the bird [*Tringa alpina*] is well known to shore-shooters. **1905** A. R. WALLACE *Life* I. 335 Sand-grouse and sand-larks were occasionally seen.

2. A lark of the genus *Ammomanes*.

1869–73 *Cassell's Bk. Birds* I. 199 The Sand Larks (*Ammomanes*) easily recognisable by their strong beaks . . and sand-coloured plumage.

3. *Austral.* The Red-capped Dottrel, *Charadrius ruficapilla*. (Morris *Austral Eng.*)

1867 W. RICHARDSON *Tasmanian Poems* Pref. 11 The nimble sand-lark learns his pretty note.

sandle wood: see SANDALWOOD.

sandling[1] ('sændlɪŋ). Also 5 **sandel-**, **sawndelynge**. [f. SAND *sb.*[2] + -LING[1].]

†**1.** = SAND-EEL 1. *Obs.*

c **1440** *Promp. Parv.* 441/1 Sandel, or sandelynge, fische, *auguilla arenalis*. *c* **1460** *Ibid.* (Winchester MS.), Sawndel, or sawndelynge. **1526** *Househ. Exp. Sir T. Le Strange* (B.M. Add. MS. 27448, lf. 30 b), Item, in whytyngs and sandlyngs, xid.

2. A small flat-fish; a dab.

1611 COTGR. *Barbue*, . . a kind of lesse Turbot, or Turbot-like fish, called by some, a Dab, or Sandling. **1694** MOTTEUX *Rabelais* IV. lx. 236 Dabs and Sand[l]ings. **1834** A. SMART *Rhymes* 90 (E.D.D.) Down by the Watermou' to wade An' howk for sandlings side by side Wi' nimble hand. **1907** *Nation* (N.Y.) 5 Oct. 13/1 Dabs or sandlings with the white side semi-transparent.

sandling[2] ('sændlɪŋ). *local.* [f. SAND *sb.*[2] + -LING[1].] (See quots.)

1794 A. YOUNG *Agric. Suffolk* 12 The title of sandling being given peculiarly to the country south of the line of Woodbridge and Orford, where a large extent of poor, and even blowing sands is found. *Ibid.* 42. **1847** *Jrnl. R. Agric.*

Soc. VIII. II. 265 The eastern maritime sandy districts or sandlings, and the north-west sandy districts or fieldings.

sandling, var. SANDALING, SANDERLING.

sand lot. *U.S.* Also with hyphen and as one word. **1.** A plot of empty or undeveloped land, esp. in a town or suburb. Also used (usu. *attrib.*) to designate the followers of Dennis Kearney, the leader of a socialistic or communistic party which existed 1877–80 (see quot. 1888).

1878 *N.Y. Tribune* 14 Aug. 4/3 Mr. Kearney, the 'sandlot orator' of California..came East with the prestige of a victorious leader. **1880** *San Francisco News Let.* 3 July 10/1 The Sand-lot barely escaped a Kilkenny fight on Sunday last. **1885** *Mag. Amer. Hist.* Feb. 201/2 One Dennis Kearney [*sic*]..made his headquarters in what were known as the 'Sand lots', near San Francisco. **1886** *Atlantic Monthly* Sept. 416/2 We can or could appoint a Fenian [as ambassador] to London,..a sand-lot politician to China [etc.]. **1888** BRYCE *Amer. Commw.* III. v. xc. 232 On the west side of San Francisco..there..was a large open space, laid out for building,..covered with sand, and hence called the Sand Lot. Here the mob had been wont to gather for meetings. *Ibid.* 245 After the session of 1880..what remained of the Sand Lot group was reabsorbed into the Democratic party. **1898** G. F. ATHERTON *Californians* 37 She drew Helena into a sand lot opposite. **1913** J. LONDON *Valley of Moon* 78 I've known [about his bad thumb] since he first got it as a kid fightin' in the sandlot at Watts Tract. **1930** J. DOS PASSOS *42nd Parallel* 192 The scorched sandlots and pinebarrens laid out into streets. **1949** *Sun* (Baltimore) 8 Jan. 9/5 The survey revealed that of the 18 direct fatalities [in football games] occurring in 1948, 6 were in 'sandlots'. **1978** *Verbatim* May 13/1 The sandlot in Washington Square has a sign 'Sandlot reserved for children and their guardians'.

2. Used *attrib.* (now usu. as one word) with reference to sports and games of the kind played by amateurs in a sand lot.

1890 *Breeder & Sportsman* (San Francisco) (Base Ball Suppl.) 7 June 3/3 Why..'skates' and 'wafters' are kept in the team simply because at one time they were alleged good players by some sand lot critic. **1921** *Daily Colonist* (Victoria, B.C.) 10 Apr. 10/1 The National Baseball Federation, the governing body of the sandlot baseball, today went on record as opposing the 'Black Sox'. **1932** *Sun* (Baltimore) 6 Sept. 14/4 The Bugle nine will be composed of the pick of sand lot teams. **1942** *Short Guide Gt. Brit.* (U.S. War Dept.) 12 'Village cricket' which corresponds to sandlot baseball. **1954** *Encounter* Oct. 8/2 Interpret what this goddamn cotton market is going to do tomorrow, and we can both quit chasing this blank blank sandlot ball team. **1964** R. MURPHY *Pond* iv. 64 He played sandlot football in the afternoons. **1979** *Amer. Poetry Rev.* Mar./Apr. 24/1 Just once the kid with bad eyes hit a home run in an obscure sandlot game.

Hence **sand lotter** (also with hyphen and as one word), (*a*) a follower of Kearney; (*b*) one who plays in a sandlot team.

1887 *Chicago Advance* 17 Feb. 107 [The California Chinese Mission] raised the last year in California $3,756, hoodlums, sandlotters and politicians to the contrary notwithstanding. **1889** *Breeder & Sportsman* (San Francisco) 14 Dec. 485/1 The local sports kicked like old sand-lotters; they visited the judges stand..and told the poolseller that their money would never be paid. **1979** *N.Y. Times* 6 Aug. C2/1 These White Sox..are stocked with college players, sandlotters and, as Lonborg says, 'guys who love the game but, well, have some deficiencies'.

sandol(e, -dolo: see SANDAL *sb.*[2]

‖**sandolo** ('sandolo). Also sandalo (pl. -i), *erron.* sandola. [It.] A flat-bottomed rowing-boat of the kind used in the waterways of Venice.

1928 D. H. LAWRENCE *Lady Chatterley* xvii. 314 He was a sandola man, a sandola being a big boat that brings in fruit and produce from the islands. **1940** V. WOOLF *Roger Fry* iv. 100 Row out across the lagoons in a sandolo. **1962** N. MITFORD *Water Beetle* 123 Young men..ferry tourists from the steamer to the village in sandolos. **1966** J. G. LINKS *Venice for Pleasure* 223/2 Take a gondola or the smaller *sandolo* from Burano. **1969** B. MALAMUD *Pictures of Fidelman* vi. 154 Sandali sailed under bridges, heaped high with eggplants. **1974** *Encycl. Brit. Macropædia* XIX. 72/2 There are almost as many different kinds of watercraft in Venice as there are surface vehicles in a mainland city, from the dainty little *sandolo*, rowed standing with crossed oars, to giant ocean liners.

sandover, obs. form or SANDIVER.

Sandow ('sændəʊ). The name of Eugen *Sandow* (1867–1925), Russo-German exponent of physical culture, used as the type of a strong man; also applied *attrib.* and in the possessive to exercises, an exercise machine, and societies endorsed by him. Also *fig.*

1898 *Physical Culture* I. 112/2 If 'Cantab' had proposed the theory that Sandow's system would have produced as good a ten-stone oar as Oxford training made of Mr. Kent, he would have stated a definitely arguable proposition; for if Sandow's system is to be applied to rowing at all, this is one of the results we shall immediately ask it to produce. **1905** W. B. YEATS *Let.* July (1954) III. 454, I have got into my routine here... To this I have added Sandow exercises twice daily. **1911** L. STONE *Jonah* I. ix. 100 He threw down the hammer with the air of a Sandow. **1914** C. MACKENZIE *Sinister St.* II. III. ii. 531 They talked instead of Sandow exercises and mountain-climbing. **1932** A. HUXLEY in *Lett. D.H. Lawrence* p. xiii, How bitterly he [*sc.* Lawrence] loathed the Wilhelm-Meisterish view of love as an education, as a means to culture, a Sandow-exerciser for the soul. **1947** N. COWARD *Peace in our Time* I. iv. 51 Nora: You're thinner than you were when—when you went away. Stevie: I'm Sandow to what I was when I left the prison camp. **1947** C. GRAY *Contingencies* i. 21 A complete fallacy ..that it is possible for aesthetic sensibility to be imparted.. by any such methods of spiritual jerks or intellectual Sandow exercisers. **1952** D. DAVIE *Purity of Diction in Eng. Verse* 175 He [*sc.* G. M. Hopkins] has no respect for the language, but gives it Sandow-exercises. **1962** *Listener* 2 Aug. 166/2 The founding of hundreds of Sandow physical-culture clubs throughout England and Wales. **1965** F. SARGESON *Mem. Peon.* v. 116 Anyone who engaged in Sandow exercises.

Hence **'Sandowism**, the principles of physical culture advocated by Sandow.

a **1930** D. H. LAWRENCE *Phoenix* (1936) 656 Physical training and Sandowism altogether is a ridiculous and puerile business.

'sandpaper, *sb.* (and *a.*) Also with hyphen and as two words. [f. SAND *sb.*[2]]

1. a. Paper upon which a layer of sand has been fixed by means of an adhesive, used chiefly for smoothing or polishing woodwork by abrasion.

1825 J. NICHOLSON *Operat. Mechanic* 641 The surface of the work [must] be carefully rubbed down with sand-paper. **1850** HOLTZAPFFEL *Turning*, etc. III. 1091 Sand Paper is made with the common house sand, and only of one degree of coarseness, but in other respects exactly like glass paper. **1877** HUXLEY *Physiogr.* ix. 134 The sand and finer particles ..scour the walls..as effectually as though they were well rubbed with fine sand-paper.

b. *fig.* Chiefly *attrib.* or as *adj.*, rough, abrasive, aggressive.

1953 'N. BLAKE' *Dreadful Hollow* II. xi. 145 The voice which had that sandpaper timbre of the overdriven. **1976** *Time* 20 Dec. 22/1 With his sandpaper style and naked drive for power, Burton had quite a few enemies.

2. *attrib.* and *Comb.*, as ***sandpaper maker***; **sandpaper stick**, a shoemaker's tool for finishing the soles of boots; **sandpaper tree**, a name for several tropical trees, the rough leaves of which are used by the natives for polishing (see quots.).

1899 *Allbutt's Syst. Med.* VIII. 917 Examples of which [*sc.* dermatitis] are seen in the case of stone-cutters, *sand-paper makers [etc.]. **1882** *Worc. Exhib. Catal.* (ed. 2) 240 The Shoemaker's 'buff knife and *sandpaper stick'. **1863** SPEKE *Discov. Nile* 567 The *sand-paper tree [*Kigelia pinnata*], whose leaves resemble a cat's tongue in roughness. **1866** *Treas. Bot.*, Sandpaper-tree, *Curatella americana*. **1882** J. SMITH *Dict. Pop. Names Plants* 367 Sandpaper Trees—*Dillenia scabrella* and *D. sarmentosa*,..natives of India.

Hence **'sandpapery** *a.*, resembling sandpaper, rough.

1957 V. NABOKOV *Pnin* 22 The sandpapery side of his head. **1970** E. MCGIRR *Death pays Wages* iii. 53 He.. massaged a sand-papery jaw. **1975** T. ALLBEURY *Special Collection* xi. 77 His hand was dry and sandpapery.

'sandpaper, *v.* [f. prec.] *trans.* To smooth with or as with sandpaper; also with *down*.

1846 MRS. GORE *Eng. Char.* (1852) 122 The body-coachman..caused himself to be..sandpapered and scrubbed into presentability. **1869** 'MARK TWAIN' *Innoc. Abr.* xii, Surely the..smooth..turnpikes are jack-planed and sand-papered every day. **1879** *Cassell's Techn. Educ.* IV. 221 The whole is then sand-papered down thoroughly.

Hence **'sandpaperer**; **'sandpapering** *vbl. sb.*

1881 *Instr. Census Clerks* (1885) 60 Tobacco Pipe Making: ..Sand Paperer or Scourer. **1885** J. B. LENO *Boot & Shoemaking* xxiv. 199 Sand-papering Machine.

sandpiper ('sændpaɪpə(r)). [f. SAND *sb.*[2] + PIPER[1].]

1. A common name for any limicoline bird which is not a plover or a snipe; esp. *Tringoides* or *Actitis hypoleucus*, the Common Sandpiper, and *A. macularia*, the common N. American Sandpiper.

1674 RAY *Collect. Words* 90 Sand-piper: *Tringa minor*. **1768** G. WHITE *Selborne, To Pennant* 8 Oct., The sandpiper, *tringa hypoleucus*. **1785** LATHAM *Gen. Synopsis Birds* III. 170 Green Sandpiper. *Tringa ochropus*, Lin. **1824** J. F. STEPHENS *Shaw's Zool.* XII. 130 Wood Sandpiper. (*Totanus glareola.*) *Ibid.* 144 Spotted Sandpiper. (*Totanus macularia.*) *Ibid.* 146 Purple Sandpiper. (*Totanus maritimus.*) **1835** AUDUBON *Ornithol. Biogr.* III. 444 The Curlew Sandpiper. *Tringa subarquata*, Temm. **1886** NEWTON in *Encycl. Brit.* XXI. 260/1 The birds commonly called Sandpipers seem to form three sections,..*Totaninæ*, *Tringinæ*, and *Phalaropodinæ*. **1892** STEVENSON *Across the Plains* ii. 78 Sandpipers trot in and out by troops after the retiring waves.

2. A kind of lamprey (see quot.).

1880 GÜNTHER *Fishes* 693 The 'Pride' or 'Sand-Piper' or Small Lampern (*Petromyzon branchialis*).

'sand-pit. Also as one word. [f. SAND *sb.*[1] + PIT *sb.*[1]]

1. A pit from which sand is excavated.

c **1440** *Promp. Parv.* 464/2 Sond hylle, or pytte, *sorica*. **1530** PALSGR. 265/1 Sandepytt, *sabloniere*. **1565** COOPER *Thesaurus*, *Arenarius*.., one that kepeth sande pittes. **1726** LEONI *Alberti's Archit.* I. 35/2 There is no want of Sand-pits. **1862** *Chamb. Encycl.* IV. 823/1 (*Golf*), The ground is diversified by knolls, sand-pits, and other *hazards*. **1876** BUCKLEY *Short Hist. Nat. Sci.* xxxix. 418 Tools were found in..the sandpits of Abbeville.

2. *Founding.* (See quot.)

1888 *Lockwood's Dict. Mech. Engin.* s.v. *Foundry Pit*, Foundry pits are either sand pits or open pits... Sand pits are so termed because the mould is of so weak a character as to require the support of sand rammed around in the space between it and the walls of the pit.

3. A space in a garden or park enclosed by low walls and filled with sand in which children may play.

1898 G. B. SHAW *Candida* I. 80 A park..containing..a sandpit..imported from the seaside for the delight of children. **1908** G. JEKYLL *Children & Gardens* xi. 90 You will find out endless ways of playing with the sand-pit. **1937** T. ADAMS *Playparks* 49 Sandpits are not desirable in crowded playgrounds of large towns. **1959** *Oxf. Mail* 11 Mar. 6/4 Nurseries featuring merry-go-rounds, sand-pits, and attendants dressed as clowns are supplied free of charge. **1960** F. G. LENNHOFF *Exceptional Children* vii. 138 He found some release through child-like games..including sandpits and mud. **1976** 'D. HALLIDAY' *Dolly & Nanny Bird* ix. 118 Grover..was given half an Italian Easter egg and was sick in the sandpit.

‖**sandr, sandur** ('sændør, 'sændə(r)). *Physical Geogr.* Pl. sandar; also sandr, sandrs, sandurs. [a. older Icel. *sandr* (pl. *sandar*) SAND *sb.*[2] In mod. Icel. the sing. is spelt *sandur*.] A broad, flat or gently sloping, sheet of glacial outwash.

1893 *Proc. Boston Soc. Nat. Hist.* XXVI. 172 This would lend much support to the theory that the sand and gravel plains of the Cape, of Long Island, and of the outlying islands, are to be regarded as confluent fan-deltas built up by streams issuing from the ice sheet, at times when its edge lay along the northern margin of the plains. They are therefore homologous with the sandr of Greenland,..and the gravel fans of Alaska. **1899** *Geogr. Jrnl.* XIII. 299 Here they [*sc.* glacial streams] cover vast areas with gravelly or sandy deposits, the equivalent of the 'sandr' of Iceland. **1937** W. B. WRIGHT *Quaternary Ice Age* x. 138 The outer moraine is distinguished from the inner by its great development of *sandr* or outwash sand plains. The inner moraine here lacks the *sandr* altogether. **1946** F. E. ZEUNER *Dating Past* v. 113 Analysis of the zones of moraines and sandrs of the Scandinavian Glaciation confirmed that there were at least three major glaciations. **1969** J. L. DAVIES *Landforms Cold Climates* xi. 180 The Icelandic sandurs have an overall gradient of about 1 : 200 to 1 : 250. **1976** H. M. FRENCH *Periglacial Environment* viii. 177 Periglacial sandar are particularly well developed in the broad valleys which drain towards the Beaufort Sea in the western Arctic.

sandrac, variant of SANDARAC.

†**sandragon.** *Obs.* Also 5 **sank dragoun**, 7 **sangdragon**. [a. F. *sang* (*de*) *dragon*.] = DRAGON'S BLOOD.

1334–5 *Durham Acc. Rolls* (Surtees) 525 In Sandragon, Coppros, et vertegrece empt. pro pede j equi. *c* **1400** *Lanfranc's Cirurg.* 35 Leie aboue þe wounde a poundir maad oon partie of frankencense, & of two parties of sandragoun. *Ibid.* 151 þe poudre of lym ffrankensence and sank dragoun. **1601** HOLLAND *Pliny* II. 476 The true Cinnabaris or Sangdragon is worth fiftie sesterces by the pound. **1615** MARKHAM *Eng. Housew.* (1660) 17 Take..of Sandragon one dram.

sandrake, obs. form of SANDARAC.

†**sandre.** *Obs. rare.* Shortened form of ALEXANDER *sb.*, a species of striped silk.

1511 *Acc. Ld. High Treas. Scot.* IV. 192 Item,..vij elnis and half ane quartar gray sandre; price elne xiiij *s.*

sandrey, -drick, obs. ff. SANDERS[1], SANDARAC.

'sand-ridge. [f. SAND *sb.*[2] + RIDGE *sb.*] A ridge of sand; a sandbank. Hence **'sand-ridged** *a.*

c **1000** ÆLFRIC *Gram.* ix. (Z) 75 *Haec syrtis* þes sandhricg. **1610** HOLLAND *Camden's Brit.* (1637) 210 This Banke or Sand-ridge, Portland. **1823** in Cobbett *Rur. Rides* (1885) I. 330 Westerham..lies between the sand-ridge and the chalk-ridge. **1897** MARY KINGSLEY *W. Africa* 417 The lagoons behind the sand-ridged beach.

sandstone ('sændstəʊn). [f. SAND *sb.*[2] + STONE *sb.*] A rock composed of consolidated sand. ***Old*** and ***New Red Sandstone***: two series of British rocks lying respectively below and above the carboniferous.

1668 CHARLETON *Onomast.* 241 *Saxum Arenarium*, Sandstone. **1761** CATCOTT *Deluge* III. (1768) 249 A red Sandstone. **1820** FOSBROOKE in *Q. Jrnl. Sci., Lit. & Arts* IX. XVII. 45 Old red sandstone. **1830** LYELL *Princ. Geol.* I. 263 Fair Island, said to be composed of sandstone with high perpendicular cliffs. **1842** H. MILLER *O.R. Sandst.* xi. (ed. 2) 235 We enter on a district of New Red Sandstone. **1855** LONGF. *Hiaw.* IV. 261 There the ancient Arrow-maker Made his arrow-heads of sandstone. **1855** J. PHILLIPS *Man. Geol.* 65 Sandstones are essentially littoral and shallow sea formations. **1879** HARE *B'ness Bunsen* II. viii. 437 Low round-headed arches of red sandstone.

attrib. **1796** KIRWAN *Elem. Min.* (ed. 2) I. 358 Sandstone Porphyry. **1823** P. NICHOLSON *Pract. Build.* 287 A sandstone quarry. **1877** RAYMOND *Statist. Mines & Mining* 127 Sandstone-schist.

'sand-trap. [f. SAND *sb.*[2] + TRAP *sb.*[1]]

1. A device for separating sand and other impurities from a stream of water or pulp passing through it, esp. in the manufacture of paper.

a **1877** KNIGHT *Dict. Mech.* III. 2027/2 *Sand-trap*, a device for separating sand, etc., from water flowing through a pipe. **1885** *Encycl. Brit.* XVIII. 221/2 From them the pulp is pumped into the supply-box, which communicates with the sand-traps by means of a regulating cock. **1927** T. WOODHOUSE *Artificial Silk* 22 These sand traps are long, shallow, wooden troughs, the bottoms of which are covered by suitable rough-haired felt and baffle plates. **1963** R. R. A. HIGHAM *Handbk. Papermaking* ii. 68 Sand traps..are the small recesses in the trough of a beater or breaker which are covered with a perforated metal plate.

2. *Golf.* A bunker. Also *fig.*

1922 Wodehouse *Clicking of Cuthbert* iv. 99 As for the deep sand-trap in front of the seventh green, he spent so much of his time in it that there was some informal talk.. of charging him a small weekly rent. **1927** *Daily Express* 29 Oct. 3/3 We cannot eliminate from the game that part of it which is played within the confines of the sandtraps. **1971** 'D. Halliday' *Dolly & Doctor Bird* xv. 212 He doesn't like soft sculpted sand-traps, which he likes to call bunkers. **1980** *Amer. Speech* LV. 127 Sixteen pages of notes and documentation attest to the authors' concern for accuracy and good scholarship, even though the inevitable sandtraps occur where nonspecialists attempt specialized courses.

sandveld ('sændvɛlt, ‖ 'sæntfɛlt). Also **sand veld, sand-veld, zandveld.** [a. Afrikaans, f. *sand* SAND *sb.*[2] + *veld* VELDT, VELD.] In southern Africa, (the name of) a region of light sandy soil.

1824 W. J. Burchell *Trav. S. Afr.* II. ix. 242 The plains on the other side [of the Langberg], are called by the name of *Zandveld.* **1873** *Cape of Good Hope Blue Bk.* App. p. JJ3, Several hundred trees have been planted along the main road to Cape Town.. on 'Zandveld'. **1919** *S. Afr. Geogr. Jrnl.* III. 73 The Free State farmer in the early spring-time treks to the 'sand veld' with his stock. **1937** Marais & Sim in D. J. Seymore *Handbk. Farmers in S. Afr.* (Dept. of Agric. & Forestry, S. Afr.) 704 In the sandveld the production of a grain crop is not easy—the soil is a light sand, not particularly fertile. **1939** 'D. Rame' *Wine of Good Hope* I. xiii. 158 They left the last of the wheat and came to a queer sand-veld. **1944** M. Oldevig *Sunny Land* vi. 51 The Kalahari, the waterless sandveld of Bechuanaland and South West Africa. **1953** D. Lessing *Five* iii. 121 This.. was farming country,.. a pocket of good, dark, rich soil in the wastes of the light sandveld. **1959** [see Africander, Afrikander 3]. **1964** *Listener* 6 Aug. 192/1 He plants the first rose on the burnt sandveld.

'**sandwich**, *sb.*[1] [The name of the town of *Sandwich*, Kent.] †**1.** Used *attrib.* to designate some kind of cord used in the 15–16th c. *Obs.*

1494 in Rogers *Agric. & Prices* (1882) III. 560/3 Sion.. 6 pieces sandwich line @/4. **1498** *Churchw. Acc. St. Dunstan's Canterb.*, Sandwyche corde for the clothe afore ye Roode. **1526–7** *Rec. St. Mary at Hill* 339 Item, paid for a pece of Sandwych lyne for the church, iiij d. **1572** in Feuillerat *Revels Q. Eliz.* (1908) 164 Sandwiche corde, packthreade, twyne.

2. Sandwich tern, a black, grey, and white tern, *Sterna sandvicensis*, found in Europe and Africa.

1785, 1888 [see tern *sb.*[1]]. **1914** *Chambers's Jrnl.* May 308/1 These birds are the ring-ouzel.. and the sandwich tern. **1934** *Discovery* Oct. 293/1 Many species like the.. Sandwich tern, and puffin are growing scarcer. **1968** [see machine *sb.* 3]. **1971** *Country Life* 18 Feb. 356/2 Two birds, at least, which breed nowhere else in Spain, have important colonies here: the black-headed gull and the Sandwich tern.

sandwich ('sændwɪtʃ), *sb.*[2] [Said to be named after John Montagu, 4th Earl of *Sandwich* (1718–1792), who once spent twenty-four hours at the gaming-table without other refreshment than some slices of cold beef placed between slices of toast.

This account of the origin of the word is given by Grosley *Londres* (1770) I. 262. Grosley's residence in London was in 1765, and he speaks of the word as having then lately come into use.]

1. An article of food for a light meal or snack, composed of two thin slices of bread, usu. buttered, with a savoury (orig. *spec.* meat, esp. beef or ham) or other filling. Freq. with specifying word prefixed indicating contents, as ***ham, egg, watercress, peanut butter*** (see peanut 3 a) ***sandwich***, or form, as ***club*** (see club *sb.* 20), ***Dagwood, Denver, hero*** (see hero *sb.* 5), ***poor boy*** (see poor *a.* (*sb.*) 8), ***submarine sandwich*** (see submarine *sb.*). Occas. with only one slice of bread, as in ***open*** or ***open-faced sandwich*** (see open *a.* (*adv.*) 22 c), or with biscuits, sliced buns, or cake.

1762 Gibbon *Jrnl.* 24 Nov., Misc. Wks. 1796 I. 110 *note*, I dined at the Cocoa Tree... That respectable body.. affords every evening a sight truly English. Twenty or thirty.. of the first men in the kingdom,.. supping at little tables.. upon a bit of cold meat, or a Sandwich. **1771** Foote *Maid of B.* I. Wks. 1799 II. 208 *Sir Chr.* Not a morsel, Tom, if you would give me the universe! *Rack.* Pho, man! only a Sandwich or so. **1800–1** Jane Austen *Lett.* (1884) I. 231 At Oakley Hall.. we did a great deal—eat some sandwiches all over mustard [etc.]. **1803** Beddoes *Hygëia* XI. 21 Our Nimrods.. have felt.. the propriety of carrying a sandwich into the field. **1836–9** Dickens *Sk. Boz*, *Tales* iii, The supper consisted of small triangular sandwiches in trays. **1866** *Chamb. Encycl.* VIII. 468 A.. Glasgow confectioner.. has the credit of making one hundred different kinds of sandwiches. **1872** *Cassell's Househ. Guide* III. 224 Egg Sandwiches. **1885** Mabel Collins *Prettiest Woman* xxvi, He ordered a hasty lunch of claret and sandwiches. **1925** S. Lewis *Arrowsmith* xxiv. 280 You might bring me a Denver sandwich from the Sunset Trail Lunch. **1932** G. Greene *Stamboul Train* I. i. 11 Get me a sandwich... I'm so empty I can hear my stomach. **1954** *Good Housek. Cookery Bk.* (rev. ed.) 443/1 Buns and cakes, provided they are not too sweet may be cut in thin slices and used for sweet sandwiches. **1977** *Rolling Stone* 16 June 12/1 Our past albums were like Dagwood sandwiches because you had to listen to them 30 or 40 times on very sophisticated equipment to hear everything we'd dub in. **1978** G. Mitchell *Mingled with Venom* iv. 37 Take Diana the smaller of my two sponge sandwiches.

transf. and *fig.* **1790** T. Wilkinson *Mem.* III. 154, I will, by way of a sandwich, halt for a few minutes refreshment, and present the reader [etc.]. **1848** Thackeray *Van. Fair* lviii, A pale young man.. came walking down the lane *en sandwich*— having a lady, that is, on each arm. **1866** *Cornh. Mag.* Oct. 468 A naval potentate.. whose talk was a perfect sandwich of oaths and orders. **1884** Edna Lyall *We Two* iv, The very oddest day, a sort of sandwich of good and bad.

b. A form of training involving alternate periods of practical and theoretical instruction. Freq. *attrib.* or as *adj.* (cf. sense 3 below).

1913 Fleming & Bailey *Engineering as Profession* ii. 113 A sandwich arrangement comprising short alternating periods of technical and practical training until the full course in each is completed. **1955** *Times* 14 July 2/6 This professional training scheme is organized over four or five years on a 'sandwich' basis. **1961** *Technology* Aug. 197 For its support of the sandwich principle *Technology* has often been taken to task by teachers in the colleges of advanced technology. **1965** *Listener* 2 Dec. 887/2 An undergraduate comes up in October, spends two terms in the college. In April he begins his first six-month spell in industry... This is the Brunel sandwich evolved over the past eight years. **1972** *Guardian* 20 June 18/6 The polytechnics.. have a special interest in sandwich degree courses.., either the thick sandwich, with one year out of a total of four spent in an industrial job, or the thin sandwich, during which the student spends alternating periods.. in college and in industry. **1980** *Jrnl. R. Soc. Arts* Feb. 157/1 We have a lot to learn and the sandwich graduates may possibly help to bridge that gap.

c. A laminated board or panel consisting of a layer of light-weight material situated between and bonded to two thin sheets of a strong material, used in light constructions, esp. in aircraft.

1944 *Use of Wood for Aircraft in U.K.* (U.S. Forest Products Lab. Publ. No. 1540) 21 The fuselage.. is composed of a plywood and balsa wood sandwich about 1/2 inch thick. **1946** *Rep. & Mem. Aeronaut. Res. Comm.* No. 1987. 2 The various kinds of sandwich considered are those in which the faces are of steel or duralumin, and the fillings of onazote, balsa wood or plywood. **1954** D. M. Desoutter *All about Aircraft* viii. 134/2 Corrugated metal.. makes a good filling for sandwiches. In this kind of sandwich two thin sheets are held apart by the corrugated metal between, and they are attached to it by welding or any other means. **1976–7** *Sea Spray* (N.Z.) Dec./Jan. 86/3 The Adelaide boat, built of foam/glass sandwich in a highly sophisticated layup technique was designed as a good all-rounder.

d. Used *attrib.* in *Chem.* to denote (complexes having) a structure in which a metal atom is bonded between two parallel cyclic ligands in different planes, as in ferrocene.

1952 *Jrnl. Amer. Chem. Soc.* LXXIV. 4971/2 A projection on the (*x*, *y*) plane concomitant with the 'sandwich' structures proposed by Wilkinson [et al.].. immediately appeared. **1966** Phillips & Williams *Inorg. Chem.* II. xxvii. 336 It does not appear that the benzene ring can act as a bridging sandwich-ligand, but two metal atoms can be 'sandwiched' between two benzenes. **1973** *Nature* 2 Nov. 3/1 Wilkinson used the name 'sandwich compounds' for the metallocenes. **1974** *Ibid.* 11 Jan. 85/1 In the so-called 'sandwich' molecules $(C_6H_6)_2Cr$ and $(C_5H_5)_2Fe$, the metal atoms are symmetrically placed between the rings.

2. Applied to a man carrying two advertisement boards suspended from the shoulders, one in front and the other behind; = *sandwich-man*.

[**1836–9** Dickens *Sk. Boz*, *Char.* ix, So, he stopped the unstamped advertisement—an animated sandwich, composed of a boy between two boards.] **1864** *Spectator* 24 Dec. 1460 The poor 'sandwiches' might justifiably have been kept moving, but to prohibit them altogether is a bit of unreasonable tyranny. **1885** *Pall Mall G.* 2 Feb. 12/2 We have, and not so very long ago, seen girls employed as 'sandwiches'.

3. *attrib.*, as (sense 1 a) ***sandwich-bag, bar, bell, bread, counter, grill, loaf*** (also *ellipt.*), ***lunch, paper, shop, spread, supper tray***; (sense 1 b) ***sandwich course, student, system, training***; (sense 2) ***sandwich advertisement***; **sandwich beam** (see quot.); **sandwich-board**, a board carried by a sandwich-man; **sandwich-board man** = sense 2; also *fig.*; **sandwich-boat**, the boat which rows in two divisions of the bumping races at Oxford and Cambridge, occupying the last position in a higher division and the first position in a lower division; **sandwich box**, a box or case in which to carry sandwiches; **sandwich boy**, (*a*) = sense 2; (*b*) a student on a sandwich course; **sandwich cake** = *layer cake* s.v. layer *sb.* 5; **sandwich case** = *sandwich box* above; **sandwich construction**, the structure or method of fabrication of sandwich panels; **sandwich flag**, a miniature flag that identifies the filling of a sandwich; **sandwich-man** = sense 2.; **sandwich panel**, a panel constructed as a sandwich.

1884 *Times* 27 Oct. 4/2 Yesterday.. I met.. a procession of.. girls,.. bearing *sandwich advertisements. **1837** Dickens *Pickw.* xvi, A closet in which the day boarders hung their bonnets and *sandwich-bags. **1955** H. Smith *Making Money in Catering Business* vi. 51 (*heading*) Analysis of operating costs of a small provincial snack and *sandwich bar. **1971** E. Paul *Reluctant Cloak & Dagger Man* x. 122, I found a sandwich bar, settled on a stool and ordered sandwiches and beer. **1977** *Lancashire Life* Mar. 101/1, I once met a chap who worked behind the counter of a sandwich bar at a railway station. **1887** *Archit. Publ. Soc. Dict.*, **Sandwich beam*, a name sometimes given to the flitch girder. **1922** Joyce *Ulysses* 284 Under the sandwichbell lay on a bier of bread one last, one lonely, last sardine. **1897** Mary Kingsley *W. Africa* 572 Some of my other men are only fit to carry *sandwich-boards for Day and Martin's blacking. **1890** W. Booth *In Darkest England* p. xv, The expense of providing boards for 'sandwich' board-men. **1936** W. B. Yeats *Lett. on Poetry* (1940) 124 When I excluded Wilfred Owen.. I did not know I was excluding a revered sandwich-board Man of the revolution. **1961** K. Reisz *Technique Film Editing* (ed. 9) ii. 199 Sandwich-board man carrying airline advertisement placard. **1884** *Oxf. & Camb. Undergrad. Jrnl.* 28 Feb. 273/1 Wadham was the *sandwich-boat. **1848** Dickens *Dombey* xv, *Sandwich-boxes. **1835** *Bell's Life in London* 11 Oct. 1/1 The *Sandwich boy took the hats and bonnets at the street-door. **1958** *Daily Mail* 19 Sept. 11/3 The first of the 'sandwich boys'.. have won diplomas in technology. **1971** B. Malamud *Tenants* 103 A loaf of *sandwich bread on the table. **1911** C. E. W. Bean '*Dreadnought' of Darling* xxv. 221 The thin layer of jam or chocolate in a *sandwich cake. **1929** J. B. Priestley *Good Companions* I. ii. 54 Mrs. Chillingford said this with immense gusto, then went slap into a piece of sandwich cake. **1968** 'P. Hobson' *Titty's Dead* vi. 70 At her elbow stood a pot of strong Indian tea and half a sandwich cake. **1817** J. Mayer *Sportsman's Direct.* (ed. 2) 203 Do not forget the *sandwich-case and flask of brandy. **1908** Sandwich-case [see *patch pocket* s.v. patch *sb.*[1] 8]. **1948** F. Thompson *Still glides Stream* ii. 40 'That fool of a groom'.. had carried off with him his mistress's sandwich case. **1944** *Use of Wood for Aircraft in U.K.* (U.S. Forest Products Lab. Publ. No. 1540) 3 *The sandwich construction so effectively used in the Mosquito fuselage consists of birch plywood faces and a balsa core, affording a relatively thick section of high strength and rigidity, and good sound and thermal insulating qualities. **1946** *Rep. & Mem. Aeronaut. Res. Committee* No. 1987. 2 Considerable interest has recently been shown in the possibilities of the so-called 'sandwich' construction in the design of stressed-skin wings and fuselages. **1963** H. R. Clauser et al. *Encycl. Engin. Materials & Processes* 587/1 The largest single reason for the use of sandwich construction and its rapid growth to one of the standard structural approaches during the past 10 years is its high strength or stiffness-to-weight ratio. **1913** S. Story *Spirit of Paris* I Cafés.. have been elbowed away by vulgar bars and automatic sandwich counters. **1960** R. E. Wolf tr. *T. Henrot's Belgium* 189 Department stores with low-price sandwich counters. **1978** 'A. Stuart' *Vicious Circles* 3 The sandwich counter of the Bar Roma.. Russian salad, prosciutto, baby pizzas. **1955** *Times* 15 July 9/7 This can be arranged in the '*sandwich' course, which alternates periods of study in college with periods of training in industry. **1957** *Technology* Apr. 44/4 Up to fifteen of these students will be Vickers undergraduate apprentices using the 'thick' sandwich course. **1966** *New Scientist* 13 Oct. 8/2 Most of the 2000 first-degree students are on sandwich courses which generally last 4½ years. **1972** *Accountant* 5 Oct. 436/1 The first paper was on sandwich courses. **1980** *Jrnl. R. Soc. Arts* Feb. 155/1 The apathy of senior management to design was felt in our BA (Hons) 4-year Sandwich course. **1907** *Yesterday's Shopping* (1969) 352 B/3 (*heading*) *Sandwich flags... Stamped in Gold and Colours, with different names such as—Anchovy.. Tongue.. Foie Gras. **1950** *Vogue* Aug. 100/3 Intellectuals.. spend very little on.. sandwich flags. **1962** F. T. Day *Introd. to Paper* viii. 87 Sandwich flags are designed to distinguish party dishes. **1955** *Sandwich grill [see master *sb.*[1] 31]. **1937** D. L. Sayers *Busman's Honeymoon* iv. 83 How many loaves would you be wanting?.. A cottage and a *sandwich. And a small brown? **1943** C. Milburn *Diary* 30 Jan. (1979) 166, I got two sandwich loaves. **1978** F. Weldon *Praxis* xxii. 194 On the estate bread was a sandwich loaf and the cheese cheddar or processed. **1932** D. L. Sayers *Have his Carcase* i. 9 She carried.. little.. beyond a pocket edition of *Tristram Shandy*, a vest-pocket camera, a small first-aid outfit and a *sandwich lunch. **1959** *Economist* 3 Jan. 26/2 About 15 per cent of men eat a sandwich lunch. **1973** K. Benton *Craig & Jaguar* vi. 67 There will be a sandwich lunch for us on the way. **1864** *Morn. Star* 26 May 4 He encounters a *sandwich man bearing placards. **1946** *Rep. & Mem. Aeronaut. Res. Comm.* No. 1987. 2 A *sandwich panel is one in which a thick sheet of a relatively weak 'filling' is interposed between two thin sheets of a more orthodox structural material, such as steel, duralumin or plywood. **1953** *Archit. Rev.* CXIV. 132/3 Walls are sandwich panels made up of two asbestos cement sheets with a cellular core. **1963** H. R. Clauser et al. *Encycl. Engin. Materials & Processes* 586/2 When a sandwich panel is loaded as a beam, the honeycomb and the bond resist the shear loads while the facings resist the moments due to bending forces, and hence carry the beam bending as tensile and compressive loads. **1923** T. S. Eliot *Waste Land* iii. 14 The river bears no empty bottles, *sandwich papers. **1924** [see carton[2] b]. **1970** 'D. Halliday' *Dolly & Cookie Bird* vii. 108 The empty packets of cigarettes, the greasy sandwich paper. **1948** Mencken *Amer. Lang.* Suppl. II. 580 Eat shop, *sandwich shop. **1967** A. Bailey in L. Deighton *London Dossier* 55 Sandwich shops abound to feed the mid-day lunch-hungries. **1978** *Detroit Free Press* 2 Apr. 11A/2 Business at the sandwich shops and stores on the edge of the campus was brisk. *c* **1938** *Fortnum & Mason Price List* 37/2 *Sandwich Spread—per glass 10½d. **1950** A. Wilson *Such Darling Dodos* 134 Dainty bridge rolls filled with sandwich spread. **1972** R. P. Jhabvala *New Dominion* I. 69 Your ketchup—and this is something new—sandwich spread—I thought you'd like to try it for your tea. **1963** *Times* 24 May (London Underground Suppl.) p. xv/4 The quaintly described dip. tech. *sandwich student has his place. **1975** *Times* 1 Sept. 10/8 The difficulty of finding places for sandwich students. **1802** Lemaistre *Rough Sk. Mod. Paris* xxxii. 297 With only a standing or *sandwich supper. **1954** J. Betjeman *Few Late Chrysanthemums* 26 Settles down to sandwich supper and the television screen. **1919** *Proc. Inst. Automobile Engineers* XII. 450 This training should be taken along with their apprenticeship... The *sandwich system has been in existence in Glasgow for over 70 years. **1940** *Nature* 21 Dec. 812/2 Some large firms testify highly to the value of the product of such a 'sandwich' system. **1956** *Ibid.* 3 Mar. 412/1 All its departments have increased their facilities to students,.. and in particular the 'sandwich system' has been established. **1971** *New Scientist* 1 Apr. 36/2 Industry is not yet prepared to cooperate sufficiently with educational establishments to make the sandwich system work as it should. **1957** *Technology* Mar. 10/3 Student apprentices, on completing their first two years *sandwich training, are also transferred to the main works. **1978** *Jrnl. R. Soc. Arts* CXXVI. 347/1 The Tech's part-time study, which was a form of sandwich training. **1799** *Hull Advertiser* 28 Dec. 3/1 Desert sets of dishes, plates, &c., and *Sandwich Trays.

Sandwich ('sændwɪtʃ), *sb.*[3] The name of a town on Cape Cod, Massachusetts, U.S.A., applied to a factory and to glass produced there from 1825 to 1888.

1881 C. C. HARRISON *Woman's Handiwork* III. 227 American finger-bowls..are made at the sandwich factory in Massachusetts. **1922** *Antiques* Feb. 57/2 Until recently no one had taken the trouble to look into the sources of sandwich glass. **1935** J. C. LINCOLN *Cape Cod Yesterdays* 164 The buttery shelves of every house in our town were filled with Sandwich glass at that period. **1947** R. P. COFFIN *Yankee Coast* 276 Long shelves across the north windows, every inch of them covered with sandwich glass drinking the pure north light. **1964** J. CLEARY *Flight of Chariots* vi. 251 She bought four-poster beds, Windsor chairs, Sandwich glass, hooked rugs.

sandwich ('sændwɪtʃ), *v.* [f. SANDWICH *sb.*[2]]

1. *intr.* ? To make a light repast.

1815 J. WILSON in *Mem.* vi. (1879) 133, I called..at Glencorse where I sandwiched for an hour.

2. *trans.* To put in or as in a sandwich; chiefly *fig.*, to insert (something) between two other things of a widely different character; to place (different elements) alternately; rarely, to enclose like a sandwich. Freq. const. *in.*

1861 WYNTER *Soc. Bees* 204 If capital would only turn its attention to the supplies of animal food..every man might have a slice of good beef sandwiched between his free-trade bread. **1864** *Daily Tel.* 28 Nov. 4/4 Mr. Disraeli sandwiches between sensible suggestions some of his very worst thoughts. **1881** *Times* 24 Feb. 8/3 The target was formed of two steel plates, 'sandwiching' an inch of deal. **1888** F. HUME *Mme. Midas* I. v, The wash..being sandwiched in between a bed of white pipe-clay and a top layer of brownish earth. **1896** KIPLING *Seven Seas* 78 (The Song of the Banjo) ..I'm sandwiched 'tween the coffee and the pork. **1900** *Times* 7 July 10/1 To offend the ear still further these calls of screeching boys are sandwiched by 'Any seat, Sir, but the first four rows'. **1924** H. DE SÉLINCOURT *Cricket Match* iv. 104 He liked to sandwich the weak and the strong, the swift and the slow. **1937** 'G. ORWELL' *Road to Wigan Pier* ii. 29 The miner does that journey to and fro, and sandwiched in between..are seven and a half hours of savage work. **1942** *R.A.F. Jrnl.* 27 June 30 Since the D.H. was sandwiched between them..he was almost pulverised. **1957** *Technology* Mar. 16/2 Mechanical engineering students at Hendon Technical College sandwich eight weeks of study with eight weeks of factory work. **1977** *Time* 30 May 40/3 He sits in a rocker sandwiched between speakers blaring the hard rock music of the Grateful Dead.

intr. for *refl.* **1898** *Engineering Mag.* XVI. 103 The way in which the different functions 'sandwich' in with each other. **1931** *Times Lit. Suppl.* 18 June 484/2 Tobogganing and their other misdemeanours agreeably sandwich with the humours of the always optimistic Waterall.

3. *intr.* To be employed as a sandwich-man.

1886 [implied in SANDWICHING *vbl. sb.*].

Hence **'sandwiching** *vbl. sb.*

1877 E. S. DALLAS *Kettner's Bk. of Table* 334 In puff paste the butter and the paste are separate and there is no mixing or kneading—only what may be called fine sandwiching. **1886** *Gd. Words* 247 Election sandwiching is paid for at higher rates than ordinary advertisement sandwiching. **1886** *Times* 1 Apr. 9/1 The sandwiching of the Budget between the two declarations of policy.

†**'Sandwicher.** *Obs.* [-ER[1].] A native of the Sandwich Islands in the Pacific Ocean (named by Cook in 1778 after the fourth Earl of Sandwich); a Sandwich Islander.

1817 SOUTHEY in *Q. Rev.* XVII. 9 One of the Sandwichers was ordered a few days after to commit the murder. **1824** W. E. ANDREWS *Rev. Fox's Bk. Martyrs* I. 402 Where are the persecutions to try the faith of the Sandwichers?

sandwort ('sændwɜːt). [f. SAND *sb.*[2] + WORT, plant.] A name given to the genus *Arenaria* and other plants growing in sandy localities.

1597 GERARDE *Herbal* II. xcvi. 347 Buckeshorne..is called also by certaine bastarde names, as *Harenaria*, or Sandwort. **1796** WITHERING *Brit. Plants* (ed. 3) II. 421-4. **1856** GRAY *Man. Bot.* (1860) 57 *Alsine*..Grove Sandwort. **1866** *Treas. Bot.* 1015/1 Spurrey sandwort, *Spergularia*. **1882** *Garden* 21 Jan. 34/3, I have not yet tried these Sandworts in shade.

Sandy ('sændɪ), *sb.* Also 5 **Sande**, 6 **Sandie**. A shortened form of the name Alexander, chiefly used in Scotland. Hence used as a nickname for a Scotchman. Cf. SAWNEY.

1473 *Acc. Ld. High Treas. Scot.* I. 17 Item fra Sandy Wardrowpar, iij elne of blac. *Ibid.* 89 Item, to Sande Boyd ..iiij li. x s. **1508** DUNBAR *Poems* iv. 69 He has Blind Hary, et Sandy Traill Slaine with his schour of mortall haill. **1585** *Sc. Acts Jas. VI* (1814) III. 390/2 Sandie clark. **1785** GROSE *Dict. Vulg. Tongue*, *Sawny* or *Sandy*, a general nick name for a Scotchman. **1888** *Harper's Mag.* Sept. 493 A party of Lowland Sandies who filled the other seats.

sandy ('sændɪ), *a.* Forms: 1 **sandiȝ**, 4 **sondi**, 4-5 **sondy(e**, 4- **sandy**. [OE. *sandiȝ*: see SAND *sb.*[2] and -Y. Cf. Du. *zandig*, MHG. *sandic* (G. *sandig*), ON. *sǫndug-r* (Sw., Da. *sandig*).]

1. Of the nature of sand; composed of or containing a large proportion of sand.

c **1000** *Sax. Leechd.* I. 94 Ðeos wyrt..wihst..on sandiȝum landum. **1382** WYCLIF *Acts* xxvii. 17 Thei vseden girdyng to gidere of schipp, dredynge lest thei schulden falle into sandy placis. *c* **1440** *Pallad. on Husb.* III. 447 Lond myxt with cley, or sondy cley, faat sonde. *c* **1586** C'TESS PEMBROKE *Ps.* LXXVIII. vi, Where the deepe did show his sandy flore. **1663** GERBIER *Counsel* 28 The Mason must work no Stone with Sandy veines. **1697** DRYDEN *Virg. Georg.* IV. 285 With sandy Ballast Sailors trim the Boat. **1709** POPE *Ess. Crit.* 55 In other parts it [the ocean] leaves wide sandy plains. **1787** *Trans. Soc. Arts* V. 216 Rubbed in with a brickbat or sandy stone. **1813** SIR H. DAVY *Agric. Chem.* (1814) 200 The term sandy..should never be applied to any soil that does not contain at least seven eighths of sand. **1868** *Rep. U.S. Commissioner Agric.* (1869) 169 A subsoil, the deeper the sandier. **1878** BROWNING *Poets Croisic* xi, The spit of sandy rock which juts Spitefully northward.

b. Of or containing sand as used for measuring time. (Cf. SAND-GLASS.) *poet.*

1591 SHAKS. *1 Hen. VI*, IV. ii. 36 Ere the Glasse that now begins to runne, Finish the processe of his sandy houre. **1607** HEYWOOD *Wom. Killed w. Kindn.* Wks. 1874 II. 138 O God, that it were possible..That time could turne vp his swift sandy glasse..to redeeme these houres! **1893** F. THOMPSON *Poems* 31 The sandy glass hence bear—Antique remembrancer.

2. *fig.* Resembling sand as lacking the quality of cohesion or stability.

1590 NASHE *Pasquil's Apol.* I. A iij b, You may easily perceiue what successe they are like to haue, that deale with so leaden and sandie braines. **1592** —— *Four Lett. Confut.* Wks. (Grosart) II. 265 The short shredder out of sandy sentences without lime. *a* **1609** DONNE *Lett.* (1654) 162 It were no service to you, to send you my notes upon the Book, because they are sandy, and incoherent ragges. **1628** PRYNNE *Cens. Cozens* 29 Who build the Antiquitie of their Canonicall Howers vpon such a sandy foundation. **1687** DRYDEN *Hind & P.* II. 105 But mark how sandy is your own pretence. *a* **1720** SEWEL *Hist. Quakers* III. (1722) 107 He said they [*sc.* the Quakers] were built upon a sandy Foundation, and so call'd them Shakers. **1822** B. CORNWALL *Dram. Scenes, Amelia Wentworth* i, Oh, what a picture have I raised upon My sandy wishes. **1861** BUCKLE *Civiliz.* II. i. 41 Now it was that men might clearly see on how sandy a foundation the grandeur of Spain was built.

3. Having hair of a yellowish-red colour; of hair, yellowish-red.

1523 FITZHERB. *Husb.* §68 A sandy colte, lyke an yren grey. **1575** *Gamm. Gurton* IV. i, Hath your browne cow cast hir calfe, or your sandy sowe her pigs? **1613** PURCHAS *Pilgrimage* (1614) 841 The Tocomans..are sandie, small, but not so little as they say of the Pigmees. **1731** SWIFT *Cassinus & Peter* Wks. 1755 IV. I. 163 Why, plague confound her sandy locks. **1833** MARRYAT *P. Simple* viii, He was a florid young man..with sandy hair. **1845** DISRAELI *Sybil* II. xi, The ladies Fitz-Warene were sandy girls.

4. Qualifying the names of colours.

1819 WARDEN *United States* II. 409 Oak, sandy red. **1851** BORROW *Lavengro* xcix, My mother's sandy-red cat. **1885** J. BEDDOE *Races Brit.* 266 Red [hair], and a sort of sandy-flaxen hue. **1894** R. B. SHARPE *Handbk. Birds Gt. Brit.* I. 67 Wing-coverts edged with sandy-buff. *Ibid.* 78 The.. plumage is obscured by sandy-rufous edges to the feathers.

5. Comb., parasynthetic, as ***sandy-bottomed, -coloured, -haired, -pated.***

1596 SHAKS. *1 Hen. IV*, III. i. 66 From the Banks of Wye, And *sandy-bottom'd Seuerne. **1661** LOVELL *Hist. Anim. & Min.* 86 The red or *sandy coloured are the best. **1871** HOWELLS *Wedd. Journ.* (1892) 272 Her hair was cut..so as to cover her forehead with a straggling sandy-coloured fringe. *a* **1817** JANE AUSTEN *Persuasion* (1818) IV. iii. 49 Colonel Wallis's companion..certainly was not *sandy-haired. **1848** THACKERAY *Van. Fair* ii, She was..pale, sandy-haired. **1687** T. BROWN *Saints in Uproar* Wks. 1730 I. 77 Your *sandy-pated companions.

b. Special Comb., as **sandy blight** *Austral.*, a kind of ophthalmia in which the eye feels as if full of sand (Morris); **sandy carpet**, a moth (see quot.); **sandy hill crane** = *sand-hill crane* s.v. SAND-HILL b; **sandy laverock** = SAND LARK; **sandy mocking-bird** *U.S.*, the brown thrush, *Harporynchus rufus*; **sandy pate**, a sandy-haired person; **sandy pear** = *sand pear* s.v. SAND *sb.*[2] 10 c; **sandy ray**, *Raia circularis*, also *R. maculata*.

1869 J. F. BLANCHE *Prince's Visit* 20 The Prince was suffering from the *sandy blight. **1829** J. F. STEPHENS *Syst. Catal. Brit. Ins.* II. 148 [*Emmelesia decolorata*] *Sandy Carpet. **1819** D. THOMAS *Trav. Western Country* 210 A bird inhabits this country called the *sandy hill Crane. **1825** Sandy hill crane [see LYED *ppl. a.* var. LYE *v.*[2]]. **1710** FOUNTAINHALL in M. P. Brown *Suppl. Decis.* (1826) IV. 793 To restrict him to the fifth part of the rent, was to send him to lift the rest of his stipend from windle-straws and *sandy laverocks. **1816** SCOTT *Old Mort.* vii, I had rather that the rigs..bare naething but windle-straes and sandy lavrocks. *a* **1700** B. E. *Dict. Cant. Crew*, **Sandy-pate*, one red-hair'd. **1785** GROSE *Dict. Vulg. Tongue*. **1884** tr. *A. de Candolle's Orig. Cultivated Plants* 233 *Sandy Pear, Chinese Pear. **1870** GÜNTHER *Cat. Fishes Brit. Mus.* VIII, *Raja circularis*. *Sandy Ray. **1880-4** DAY *Brit. Fishes* II. 346 *Raia maculata*. .. Sandy ray. *Ibid.* 348 *Raia circularis*... Sandy-ray.

'sand-yacht. Also **sand yacht, sandyacht.** [f. SAND *sb.*[2] + YACHT *sb.*] A sail-driven craft mounted on a three- or four-wheeled chassis, used for sailing on sand.

1912 *Car* 6 Nov. 458/2 Some of the sand-yachts have three wheels; others have four wheels. **1924** F. M. FORD *Joseph Conrad* IV. 227 Knocke was just within the Belgian border. You could run in a sand-yacht in front of the dunes, right to Sluys. **1960** L. LAMPLUGH *Sixpenny Runner* ii. 21 By sailing he meant sand-yacht sailing..along the four-mile stretch of sands. **1967** *Daily Tel.* 21 Feb. 15/1 Sand yachts in the first race across the Sahara..are 70 miles from Tindouf. **1970** R. MARR in *Sports Stories for Boys* 309 The *Sandsprite* was a sand yacht, a sleek, streamlined vessel of gleaming aluminium and scarlet enamel, mounted on three motor-cycle wheels. **1980** *West Lancs. Even. Gaz.* 23 June 5 Action from the sandyacht racing at Fylde International Sand Yacht Club.

Hence **'sand-yachter**, one who uses a sand-yacht; **'sand-yachting** *vbl. sb.* and *ppl. a.*; **'sand-yachtsman** = *sand-yachter* above.

1922 *Car* 6 Nov. 458/2 (*heading*) Sand-yachting on the Belgian coast. **1937** *Illustr. London News* 21 Aug. 315 Sailing the desert at 45 m.p.h.: the thrilling sport of sand-yachting at an R.A.F. station in Egypt. **1960** L. LAMPLUGH *Sixpenny Runner* vii. 76 Keith had spent most of the week with the sand-yachters..on Brenstowe beach. *Ibid.* xv. 157 His sand-yachting pals. **1967** *Sunday Times* 28 May 19 Forty sand yachtsmen from six countries had a disappointing day at St. Annes, Lancashire, yesterday when races for the international..sand yacht championships were unable to be started. **1970** *Daily Tel.* 23 May 9 Sensible sand-yachters wear a crash helmet. **1973** *Country Life* 25 Jan. 218/1 Ideal wind speeds for sand yachting are between 12 and 20 m.p.h. **1980** *West Lancs. Even. Gaz.* 23 June, The following Fylde sandyachters were chosen for the British team.

sandyish ('sændɪɪʃ), *a.* [f. SANDY *a.* + -ISH.] Somewhat sandy.

1793 *Trans. Soc. Arts* XI. 130 A light sandyish soil. **1862** MISS BRADDON *Aur. Floyd* vii, A tuft of sandyish hair.. ornamented his low forehead. **1871** C. GIBBON *Lack of Gold* ii, He had fair hair, sandyish beard.

‖**sandyx** ('sændɪks). *Hist.* Also **sandix** (Dicts.). [L. *sandyx, -dix*, a. Gr. σάνδυξ, -διξ.] A red pigment, mentioned by ancient writers.

[**1398** TREVISA *Barth. De P.R.* XIX. xxix. (1495) 878 Cerusa ..yf it is euen tostyd and medlyd wyth Rubrita thenne it torneth in to Sandix.] **1601** HOLLAND *Pliny* II. 533 Calcine this [Sandarach] and Ruddle together, and..you shall haue the color called Sandyx. **1728** CHAMBERS *Cycl.*, *Sandix*, a kind of Minium, made of Ceruss or rather of red Masticot, calcined and rubified, called also a *Factitious Sandaract*. **1891** O. WILDE *Intentions* 106 On a wall of fresh plaster, stained with bright sandyx.

sane (seɪn), *a.* [ad. L. *sānus* healthy; cf. F. *sain*, Sp., It. *sano*, Pg. *são*.

The almost entire restriction in Eng. to the sense 'mentally sound' is due to the use in antithesis with *insane*, which (like the L. *insānus*, its source) always referred to mental condition.]

1. Of the body, its organs or functions: Healthy, sound, not diseased. *rare.*

[**1694** MOTTEUX *Rabelais* v. Ep. by Lymosin 251 For in veracity these Times denote Morbs to the Sane, and Obits to th' Ægrote.]

1755 JOHNSON, *Sane*,..sound; healthy. Baynard wrote a poem on preserving the body in a sane and sound state. **1777** MASON *Ep. to Dr. Shebbeare* 135 As Pringle, to procure a sane secretion, Purges the *primæ viæ* of repletion. **1826** MRS. SHELLEY *Last Man* II. 231 Pestilence had become a part of our future..it became our part to..raise high the barrier between contagion and the sane. **1844** KINGLAKE *Eothen* xviii, He touches the gland, and finds the skin sane and sound. **1872** BROWNING *Fifine* lxxxviii, Mind, sound in body sane, Keeps thoughts apart from facts.

2. Sound in mind; in one's senses; not mad. Also, of the mind: Not diseased.

1721 BAILEY, *Sane*, sound, whole, in his Sences. **1809-10** COLERIDGE *Friend* (1818) I. 2 The activity of sane minds in healthful bodies. **1842** DICKENS *Amer. Notes* iii. (1850) 32/1 Every patient is as freely trusted with the tools of his trade as if he were a sane man. **1884** TENNYSON *Falcon* I. i. 46 To call a madman mad Will hardly help to make him sane again.

b. *of sane memory*: see MEMORY 2 b.

1628 COKE *On Litt.* I. 166 If Coparceners make partitions at ful age and vnmarried, and of sane memorie of Lands in Fee simple, it is good & firme for euer.

3. Sensible, rational; free from delusive prejudices or fancies.

1843 BETHUNE *Sc. Fireside Stor.* 44 A drunken physician, is an anomaly from which every sane man must turn with feelings of dislike. **1859** TENNYSON *Enid* 917 One of our noblest, our most valorous, Sanest and most obedient. **1899** [see IMPERIALISM 2]. **1908** *Athenæum* 29 Aug. 232/1 This is a sane and lucid study of twelve poets.

†**sane**, *v. Obs.* [ad. L. *sānāre*, f. *sān-us* healthy: see SANE *a.*] *trans.* To cure, to heal.

c **1386** CHAUCER *Pars. T.* ¶973 For, as seith Ierom, by fasting be saned [Skeat prints *saved*; Pseudo-Jerome (Migne xxx. 616) has *sanandæ*] the vices of flesh, and by prayere the vices of the soule. *c* **1400** *Hymn to Jesus Christ* 40 in *Relig. Pieces fr. Thornton MS.* (1867) 84 He will..with his mercy sane my sore. *c* **1420** *Anturs of Arth.* 693 (Thornton MS.) Surgeones sanede [*Douce MS.* saued] thayme, sothely to saye.

sanedrim, -drist, obs. ff. SANHEDRIM, -DRIST.

sanely ('seɪnlɪ), *adv.* [f. SANE *a.* + -LY[2].] In a sane manner.

1803 M. EDGEWORTH *Let.* 19 Mar. (1979) 101, I am not famous for judging sanely of strangers. **1876** GEO. ELIOT *Dan. Der.* ii, Her mind was still sanely capable of picturing balanced probabilities. **1884** TENNYSON *Freedom* viii, Of saner worship sanely proud.

saneness ('seɪnnɪs). *rare*$^{-0}$. [f. SANE *a.* + -NESS.] The condition of being sane, sanity.

1727 BAILEY vol. II, *Saneness*, Soundness of Health.

sanetyf, obs. form of SANATIVE.

sanfaile, sanfoin: see SANS FAILE, SAINFOIN.

san fairy ann (sæn 'fɛərɪ æn). *slang.* Also **san ferry ann**, etc. [Jocular form repr. F. *ça ne fait rien* 'it does not matter', said to have originated in army use in the war of 1914-18.] An expression of indifference to, or resigned acceptance of, a state of affairs. Also *ellipt.* as **Fairy Ann.**

1919 W. H. DOWNING *Digger Dial.* 43 *San ferry ann*,..it doesn't matter. **1921** *Amer. Legion Weekly* 8 Apr. 14 Son fairy Ann. **1922** B. A. COLONNA *Hist. Company B, 311th*

Infantry 78 If he did not sign he did not get paid and often when he does sign he don't get paid. So 'sanferriens'. **1924** *Radio Times* 19 Dec. 589/1 My mottoe's still san fairy Han. **1927** H. Kimber *San Fairy Ann* ix. 312 'There is a magic charter,' he whispered. 'It runs, "San Fairy Ann".' **1930** Kipling *Thy Servant Dog* III. 88 We said we were wonderful brave dog... He said 'Fairy Ann! Fairy Ann!' **1941** W. P. Crozier *Diary* Mar. in D. Ayerst *Guardian* (1971) xxxiv. 544 Gradualness, san faery ann. **1956** F. B. Vickers in *Coast to Coast 1955–6* 72 'Ya. Good night.' 'San ferry ann, Joe.' 'Which means black you, Jack, I'm all right,' Tom shouted. **1965** L. Brain *It's Free Country* xx. 181 'I wish you'd thought of my ulcer before you—' he began, and then broke off. 'Oh, san fairy anne!' **1973** *Times* 22 June 20/1 (Advt.), San fairy Ann... It doesn't matter to us whether it is fixed wing or helicopter because we sell the best of both.

‖**Sanfan** ('sanfan). Also **San-fan, San Fan** and with small initial. [Chinese *sānfǎn*, f. *sān* three + *fǎn* anti-, against.] Used *attrib.* to designate an official campaign conducted in China in 1951–2 against corruption, waste, and bureaucratism in State affairs. Cf. Wufan.

1956 *Contemp. China 1955* I. 63 The *san-fan* movement directed against the 'three evils' of corruption, waste and bureaucracy in state institutions and enterprises. **1966** F. Schurmann *Ideol. & Organization in Communist China* v. 318 The regime resorted to terror to enforce controls. This took the form of the Three-Anti (*Sanfan*) and Five-Anti (*Wufan*) movements. The *Sanfan* campaign which started in the winter of 1951 was directed against corruption, waste, and bureaucratism. **1971** H. Trevelyan *Worlds Apart* viii. 98 The early campaigns were followed by the 'San-fan' and 'Wu-fan' movements, the so-called Three Antis and Five Antis, directed against corrupt Government officials and businessmen, but doubtless also against the politically unreliable. **1974** tr. *Wertheim's Evolution & Revolution* 333 In the early fifties, the *San Fan* (three-anti) campaign was directed at all kinds of malpractices in the newly built state apparatus.

Sanfedist ('sænfɛdɪst), *sb.* (and *a.*) [ad. It. *sanfediste* (also used), f. *santa fede* holy faith, used in the title of the society known as the Bande della Santa Fede + -ist.] A member of an Italian political and military organization of the late 18th and early 19th centuries loyal to the Papacy and hostile to republicanism. Also *attrib.* or as *adj.*

1842 F. W. Faber *Foreign Churches* II. 268 It has been asserted..that among the higher orders of society in the Papal States another party has been formed, which includes within itself a few of the princes of the Church and affords some disquiet to the Austrian embassy at Rome. The members of this society call themselves Sanfedists. It is indeed but a revival of old Guelphic principles... The Sanfedists are said to have arisen in 1780 as an anti-Austrian party at Turin, Gregory VII, and Sixtus V, being the great objects of their admiration. **1881** *Encycl. Brit.* XIII. 486/1 In a short while, the Carbonari societies, with Sanfedisti and many other revolutionary associations, had extended their organization through the length and breadth of the peninsula. **1920** J. P. Trevelyan *Short Hist. Ital. People* xxvii. 475 During the reign of..Leo XII..Romagna was ravaged by the blood feuds of Carbonari and Sanfedisti. **1960** E. E. Y. Hales *Revolution & Papacy* vii. 123 The most interesting..Sanfedist leader was Cardinal Ruffo. *Ibid.* xvi. 264 During Leo's..reign—he died on February 10, 1829—the discontent in the Papal States..grew more serious. The policy of using the Sanfedists..was now encouraged from Rome, with a view to suppressing..the secret societies. **1965** C. Hibbert *Garibaldi & his Enemies* I. iv. 48 At Ancona twenty-eight *Sanfedisti*, murderous anti-liberals who acted in the name of the faith, were assassinated.

Sanforized ('sænfəraɪzd), *a.* Also **sanforized.** [f. the name of *Sanford* L. Cluett (1874–1968), U.S. inventor of the process + -ize + -ed[1].]

a. A proprietary name for cotton and other fabrics which have been preshrunk by a special process. Also *transf.*

1930 *Official Gaz.* (U.S. Patent Office) 30 Sept. 737/1 Cluett, Peabody & Co., Inc., Troy, N.Y... *Sanforized* for piece goods of cotton, linen, woolen, silk, rayon, and combinations thereof. **1938** *Times* 21 Feb. 11/1 A water-repellant finish is demonstrated at the stand of the Bleachers' Association, where Sanforized cotton and linen cloths are shown. **1939** *Trade Marks Jrnl.* 24 May 706/2 *Sanforized*... Piece goods of textile material but not including cotton piece goods. Cluett, Peabody & Co., Inc., ..Troy, New York..; manufacturers. **1944** T. D. Clark *Pills, Petticoats & Plows* 221 A frugal backwoods customer adequately sized up the complications of the 'sanforized' era in men's clothing when he sauntered into the Harbour Pitts store. **1952** M. Steen *Phoenix Rising* i. 21 If this were the States..you'd be in a tuxedo and a sanforized shirt. **1963** *New Yorker* 15 June 78 Made in the Orient of fine Sanforized cotton. **1970** *Which?* Nov. 340/1 Some jeans carried a Sanforised label. **1975** G. Howell *In Vogue* 104/2 In shops people were asking for uncrushable fabrics like zingale, and for cottons, linens and spun rayons which were Sanforized—preshrunk. **1978** *Church Times* 25 Aug. 8 Soap-operas featuring sanforised nurses or grubby Lancastrians—everyday stories of boring folk.

b. *fig.*

1968 *Observer* (Colour Suppl.) 11 Feb. 24 (Advt.), The Sanforized Big Car. £567. The Imp is the big car shrunk small before it reaches you. **1970** S. J. Perelman *Baby, it's Cold Inside* 130 The next time I go shopping for naïve art, I'll make bloody well sure it's Sanforized.

Hence '**Sanforizing**, this process.

1948 *Time* 11 Oct. 91/3 The company was also lucky in its Vice President Sanford Cluett, the original families' only remaining executive. Cluett was an experiment-minded man. His tinkering had turned up Sanforizing. **1963** A. J. Hall *Textile Sci.* v. 241 Recently the inventors of the Sanforizing machine have been able to use a 2-inch thick rubber belt in a modified machine and so enable fabrics to be shrunk up to 20% in length.

San Franciscan (ˌsæn frænˈsɪskən), *sb.* and *a.* [f. *San Francisc(o* (see below) + -an.] **A.** *sb.* A native or inhabitant of San Francisco in California, U.S.A. **B.** *adj.* Of or pertaining to San Francisco.

1875 *Scribner's Monthly* July 277/2 San Franciscans are remorseless critics. **1886** F. C. Baylor *On Both Sides* iv. 227 The glasses rattled as if in a San Franciscan earthquake. **1899** Kipling *From Sea to Sea* II. xxv. 8 It may be this sense of possible disaster..that makes San Franciscan society go with..a whirl. **1949** *Los Angeles Times* 6 June 2/5 San Franciscans wear overcoats and furs even in the summer. **1960** Partridge *Charm of Words* 55 *Beatniks*, as the San Franciscan press christened members of the Beat community. **1973** S. Cohen *Diane Game* (1974) iv. 43 I'm afraid I've become a San Franciscan. **1977** W. Marshall *Thin Air* ii. 16 His soft San Franciscan accent.

sang (sæŋ), *sb.*[1] *Sc.* and *north.* [Of obscure origin: cf. Sam *sb.*[1] 2.] Used in the asseverative phrase (*by*) *my sang*; also shortened to *sang*.

1787 Grose *Provinc. Gloss.*, *Sang is't*, indeed it is. N. **1790** A. Wilson *Poems* 87 But by my sang! now gin we meet, We'll hae a tramp right clever. **1894** A. Robertson *Nuggets*, etc. 70 'Ma sang!' said McKeel, 'ye've come to the richt shop.'

sang (sæŋ), *sb.*[2] *U.S.* colloq. abbrev. of ginseng.

1843 'R. Carlton' *New Purchase* I. xxvii. 256 The store-keeper was obliged to book the nine and a quarter cents, to be paid in 'sang'. **1886** *Harper's Mag.* June 58/2 Formerly, digging 'sang', as they call ginseng, was a general occupation. **1897** W. E. Barton *Sim Galloway's Daughter-in-Law* 20 The sang was short this year. **1948** E. N. Dick *Dixie Frontier* 32 He spent some time digging ginseng, or 'sang' as they called it. **1978** *Nat. Parks & Conservation Mag.* Feb. 18/1 Hunters of 'sang', as ginseng is known in Virginia and West Virginia, can tell..exciting stories about finding the 'big root' or 'patch'.

attrib. **1859** Bartlett *Dict. Amer.* (ed. 2) 379 *Sang-hoe*, the implement used in gathering ginseng. **1878** C. B. Coale *Life & Adventures Wilburn Waters* xxi. 124 These hill-sides are a godsend to 'sang-diggers'. **1899** M. G. Kains *Ginseng* 31 The average 'sang' digger has very little conscience. **1927** K. Eubank *Horse & Buggy Days* 53 The trail of death which lasted for twenty years started over the ownership of a 'sang-digger' hog. **1949** J. Nelson *Backwoods Teacher* xxii. 233 Thar I was in them deep woods huntin' sang roots. **1975** C. Bogue in E. Wigginton *Foxfire 3* 247 A man could go 'sang' hunting and return with a fortune.

Hence as *v. intr.*, to gather ginseng; '**sanging** *vbl. sb.*

1848 Bartlett *Dict. Amer.* 282 *Sang*,..is or was also used in Virginia as a verb; *to go a sanging*, is to be engaged in gathering ginseng. **1859** *Ibid.* (ed. 2) 379 In Alleghany Co., Maryland, is Sang Run near which is a well-known 'sanging ground'. **1877** *Field & Forest* III. 40 Why, I have sanged all over it [*sc.* the mountain]. **1892** J. L. Allen *Blue-Grass Region of Kentucky* 249 In the wildest parts of the country..entire families may still be seen 'out sangin'. **1975** C. Bogue in E. Wigginton *Foxfire 3* 247 With some domestic sale, as well as a continuing foreign market, 'sanging' became a business.

‖**sang** (sʌŋ), *sb.*[3] Also **srang**; pl. **sang**, (anglicized) **-s**. [Tibetan *s(r)ang* ounce.] A former Tibetan unit of currency, consisting of 100 *sho*; a coin or note of this value.

1902 S. C. Das *Journey to Lhasa & Central Tibet* vii. 182 The Government revenue for each *kang* is, on an average, fifty *srang* (125 rupees), or about one hundred and fifty *khal* of grain. **1947** *Whitaker's Almanack* 886/2 The present currency [of Tibet] is reckoned in *sangs*... The 1939 value was about 8 sangs = 1 rupee. **1962** R. A. G. Carson *Coins* 545 Since 1935 on various srang values in silver..has been the lion with a background of mountains. **1962** L. Davidson *Rose of Tibet* ix. 174 The current yuan went 330 to the Tibetan sang: the sang six and a half to the rupee. **1970** R. D. Taring *Daughter of Tibet* xviii. 242 Thubtenla lent me six hundred *sangs* (about £6). **1974** D. Norbu *Red Star over Tibet* ii. 36 His profits and premium from Chang Thang amounted to 600 *sang*.

sang, var. Sheng[1].

Sanga ('sæŋgə). [Amharic.] A bull or cow belonging to the East African breed so called, distinguished by large, lyre-shaped horns. Also *attrib.*

1814 H. Salt *Voy. Abyssinia* 258, I was gratified by the sight of the Galla oxen, or Sanga. **1862** *Chambers's Encycl.* IV. 583/1 Galla Ox, or Sanga, a remarkable species or variety of ox inhabiting Abyssinia. **1912** R. Lydekker *Ox & Its Kindred* vii. 160 These Galla or Sanga cattle are generally white and have small or no humps, their muzzles being black... In stature these oxen are very large. **1959** J. D. Clark *Prehist. S. Afr.* xi. 283 The indigenous long-horned African breed—the Sanga cattle. **1970** W. J. A. Payne *Cattle Production in Tropics* I. ii. 46 East Africa is the most likely centre of origin of the earliest Sanga cattle.

sanga, var. f. sunga.

sangar ('sæŋə(r)), *sb.* Now chiefly *Mil.* Also **sanga, sanger, sung(h)a, sungar.** [Pashtō *sangar* = Panjābī *saṅghar.*] A breastwork of stone. Also, a strong point or fortified look-out post.

1841 in Sir T. Seaton *Cadet to Colonel* (1866) I. viii. 215 [Havelock, who was turning one of the spurs of the hill, called out] 'Here's the sunga; come on, it's nothing.' **1857** Bellew *Jrnl. Mission Afghanistan* II. i. (1862) 127 They had thrown up barricades and breastworks of wood and stone ('murcha' and 'sanga' respectively). **1879** C. R. Low *Afghan War* iii. 210 A stone breast-work, or *sungha*,..obstructed the flankers. **1892** Kipling *Barrack-R. Ball.*, *Ball. King's Mercy* 51 When the red-coats crawl to the sungar wall. **1893** *Edin. Rev.* July 214 Fire was opened on us from numerous sangas opposite. **1897** Ld. Roberts *41 Yrs. in India* xxxv. II. 15 The summit [of the hill] was strengthened by *sangars*. **1938** D. Forbes *My Life in S. Afr.* v. 68 Small sangers were put up at other commanding positions to hold the enemy back until the fort was finished. **1944** *N.Y. Times* 25 Apr. 5/5 It was about noon..when he climbed out of his own 'sanger',—a type of rocky foxhole characteristic of this section [of Italy]. **1951** G. Wilson *Brave Company* vii. 135 Our sangars are much more elaborate. We have erected roofs reinforced by sandbags and screw pickets. **1962** *Times* 2 May 14/7 The pickets settled down in their *sangars* [in a wadi, W. Aden]. **1974** *Sunday Times* 17 Feb. (Colour Suppl.) 27/3 High look-out platforms called *sangars* [in Northern Ireland]. **1979** *Observer* 4 Mar. 11/1 The man on sangar duty must look out through a narrow slit and observe movements for up to four hours at a time. **1982** *Times* 12 June 5/4 To the commando crouching in his damp 'sanger', a slit trench built up with rocks, there has seemed little reason for the wait.

Hence '**sangar** *v. trans.*, to fortify with a sangar.

1900 W. S. Churchill in *Morning Post* 25 July 5/7 Both infantry and guns are strongly sangared among the rocks and stones of the kopjes. **1901** 'Linesman' in *Blackw. Mag.* June 758/1 The night was spent in 'sangaring' the position. **1905** E. Candler *Unveiling of Lhasa* viii. 147 At other times they [*sc.* the Tibetans] will forsake a strongly sangared position at the first shot.

sangarede, variant of sangrede *Obs.*

sangaree (sæŋgəˈriː), *sb.* Also **sangarie, sangre(e.** [a. Sp. *sangría* (lit. 'bleeding'), 'a drink composed of lemon water and red wine' (*Novísimo Dicc.*, 1868).] A cold drink composed of wine diluted and spiced, used chiefly in tropical countries.

1736 *Gentl. Mag.* Sept. 551 Mr. Gordon, a Punch-seller in the Strand, had devised a new Punch made of strong Madeira wine and called Sangre. **1785** Grose *Dict. Vulgar Tongue*, *Sangaree*, rack punch was formerly so called in bagnio's. **1795** Potter *Dict. Cant* (ed. 2), *Sangree*, rack punch. **1796** Stedman *Surinam* I. 293 Sherbet, sangaree, and wine and water. *Ibid. note*, Water, Madeira wine, nutmeg, and sugar. **1801** Charlotte Smith *Lett. Solit. Wand.* I. 302 The worthy manager then retired to his sangarie. **1843** Marryat *M. Violet* xxvii, Which..enabled the fortunate owner to take his last tumbler of port-wine sangaree. **1865** *Indian Dom. Econ.* (ed. 6) 329 Sangarie. Mix three bottles of red wine with three half pints of water [etc.]. **1891** Kipling *Light that Failed* vii, Come, and I'll show you how to brew sangaree.

attrib. **1872** E. Braddon *Life in India* i. 4 The Anglo-Indian is generally believed to be a luxurious idler, whose life is spent in hookah-smoking,..sangaree-drinking.

Hence **sangaree** *v. trans.*, to make (wine) into sangaree.

1835 J. H. Ingraham *South-West* I. 115 [Devotees of domino are] clustered around the tables, with a tonic, often renewed and properly sangareed, at their elbows. **1860** R. Fowler *Med. Vocab.*, *Sangareed*, reduced in strength and sweetened.

‖**sang-de-bœuf** (sɑ̃dəbœf). [Fr.: lit. 'bullock's blood'.] 'A deep red colour found on old Chinese porcelain' (Stanf.). Also *transf.*, a ceramic glaze of this colour; porcelain bearing such a glaze. Also *attrib.*

1881 C. C. Harrison *Woman's Handiwork* II. 104 A number of antique Chinese vases in high glaze, sang de bœuf, céladon, gray, rose, mandarin, yellow. **1886** *Athenæum* 13 May 650/3 His claret-jug with a body of *sang de bœuf*. **1897** *Daily News* 29 July 2/7 A slender vase of splashed sang-de-bœuf crackle. **1900** F. Litchfield *Pott. & Porc.* iv. 45 The pottery made in self-colour, such as *sang de boeuf*. **1957** Mankowitz & Haggar *Conc. Encycl. Eng. Pott. & Porc.* 88/2 The monochrome copper-red glazes of the Chinese were successfully imitated in the closing decades of the nineteenth century by Bernard Moore and the Burtons. These glazes were designated *Sang de Boeuf* and 'Flambé'. **1960** O. Manning *Great Fortune* II. 121 She had seen an Italian tea-set of fine *sang-de-bœuf* china. **1965** D. Torr *Diplomatic Cover* vi. 102 A scholarly, balding man..was examining a plain deep red vase. Janine was saying, ..'It's a genuine Lang Yao sang de boeuf, seventeenth century.' **1972** *Trans. Oriental Ceramics Soc.* XXXVIII. 47 All these transmutations can be seen..in the *sang de boeuf* bowl No 231 where the almost colourless rim shows faintly green. **1974** Savage & Newman *Illustr. Dict. Ceramics* 254 *Sang-de-bœuf*,..a brilliant red glaze which exhibits patches resembling the coagulation of ox-blood... The colouring agent was copper oxide fired in a reducing atmosphere, and it was developed in China during the Ch'ing dynasty.

sangdragon, variant of sandragon.

sange, sangeak: see song, sanjak.

sanger, var. sangar.

Sängerfest ('sɛŋəfɛst). *U.S.* Also **Saengerfest**, *erron.* **Sangfest.** [a. Ger. *sängerfest*, f. *sänger* singer + *fest* fest.] A choral festival.

1865 *Harper's Weekly* 5 Aug. 490/2 Arrangements were made for the Saengerfest, which will be celebrated at Philadelphia in 1867. **1903** *Forest & Stream* 24 Jan. 78 It is thought that the event will attract several hundred shooters from all over the United States, as the Saengerfest will be in progress here the week of the shoot. **1950** 'D. Divine' *King of Fassarai* xxvii. 241 They've got a *Sangfest* on down at the *falu*.. Teresa's leading the choir. **1966** *Amer. Speech* XLI. 13 In 1853 the first *Sängerfest* took place in New Braunfels

[Texas], at which singing societies from neighboring towns participated. Several *Sängerfests* still take place annually.

sangester, obs. form of SONGSTER.

sangewyn, obs. form of SANGUINE *a.*

‖**sang-froid** (sɑ̃frwa). [F. *sang-froid*, lit. 'cold blood' (*sang* blood, *froid* cold).

In the 17th c. the expression was in France often written erroneously *sens froid*, as if it contained *sens* 'sense' instead of the homophonous *sang* 'blood'.]

Coolness, indifference, absence of excitement or agitation.

1750 CHESTERF. *Lett.* (1792) III. 27 Don Louis, with the same *sang froid* as constantly persisted, till he at last prevailed. **1790** J. P. ANDREWS *Anecd., Add.* Index 5 Sang-froid of a chess-player. **1823** BYRON *Juan* VIII. cxxi, With great sang-froid.., he sat smoking Tobacco. **1888** 'ANNA K. GREEN' *Behind Closed Doors* v, Cameron accepted the situation with his usual *sang froid.*

‖**sangha** ('saŋa). *Buddhism.* Also 9 **Thanga**; **samgha** and with capital initial. [Hind. *saṅgha*, Skr. *saṃgha*, f. *sam* together + *han* to come in contact.] The community or order of monks. Also *transf.*

1858 P. BIGANDET *Life or Legend of Gaudama* 234 The Budhist Religious constitute the Thanga, or assembly of the Perfect. They are the strict followers of Budha. **1876** *Encycl. Brit.* IV. 429/2 The Sangha, or Society, as Buddha's order of mendicants was called. **1921** C. ELIOT *Hinduism & Buddhism* III. xxxvi. 71 The Sangha has always shown a laudable reserve in interfering directly with politics... In 1886, when the British annexed Burma, the Head of the Sangha forbade monks to take part in the political strife. **1951** E. CONZE *Buddhism* ii. 53 The core of the Buddhist movement consisted of monks... The entire 'brotherhood' of monks and hermits is called the *Samgha.* The Samgha naturally always formed only a small minority of the Buddhist community. **1968** T. WOLFE *Electric Kool-Aid Acid Test* xxi. 292 Boise in that moment is in the tiny knot of Perfect Pranksters, the inner circle, ascending into the *sangha* for good! **1978** C. HUMPHREYS *Both Sides of Circle* xii. 135 The adoption of Twelve Principles became my major Buddhist activity in Japan, and their later presentation to the Sanghas and leading Buddhists of Thailand, Burma and Ceylon was..my major interest in those countries.

sangiac(c)o, -iac(h, -ia(c)que: see SANJAK.

sangister, obs. form of SONGSTER.

sangle, obs. form of CINGLE.

†'**sanglier.** *Obs.* Forms: α. 5 **synglere**, 5, 7 **singuler**, 7, 9 **singler**; β. 6 **sangleir, sangweler**, 6–7, 9 **sanglier**, 6, 8 **sangler**. [a. OF. *sengler*, *sangler*, *sanglier* (mod.F. *sanglier*) = Pr. *singlar-s*, *senglar-s*, It. *cinghiale*, *cignare*:—L. *singulārem* solitary (see SINGULAR *a.*), used subst. in late L. (Vulg. Ps. lxxix. 14 after Gr. μονιός in the LXX) for a boar separated from the herd.

The forms *synglere*, *singler* show normal phonetic development from early ME. **sengler*, a. OF. *sengler*; the form *singuler* is due to assimilation to the Latin.]

A full-grown wild boar (see quots.).

?*a* **1400** *Morte Arth.* 3124 Boyes in þe subarbis bourdene ffulle heghe, At a bare synglere that to þe bente rynnys. **1513** DOUGLAS *Æneis* x. xii. 47 Lyke to the strengthy sangler, or the bore. **1541** *Acc. Ld. High Treas. Scot.* VII. 472 Ane pale of tymmer within the park of Falkland to the sangweleris. **1575** TURBERV. *Venerie* 100 The next yere he shall be called a Sanglier of three yeres old. **1598** MANWOOD *Lawes Forest* iv. §5 (1615) 43 After the fourth yeere, if not before, hee departeth from the Sounder, and then you shall call him, a Singler, or rather, Sanglier. **1688** R. HOLME *Armoury* II. 132/1 A Boar [of 5 years is] a Singuler, or more properly a Sanglier. **1725** BRADLEY *Fam. Dict.* s.v. *Wild Boar*, He is also call'd Singlet or Sangler. **1805** J. SIBLEY *Let.* 10 Apr. in *Deb. Congress U.S.* (1852) 9th Congress 2 Sess. App. 1104 There were innumerable quantities of..deer, foxes, sangliers, or wild hogs [etc.]. **1842** W. TOLMIE *Jrnl.* 7 May in *Physician & Fur Trader* (1963) 356 The Sanglier or wild boar is still found there. **1896** C. M. YONGE *Release* II. xiii. 198 It is like having to do with a set of tame pigs..turned loose among the wild sangliers.

Sango ('sæŋgəʊ). [Native name.] An African language of the Adamawa-Eastern group of the Niger-Congo family, *spec.* that pidginized version of Sango spoken as a lingua franca in the Central African Republic and elsewhere in central Africa.

1948 M. GUTHRIE *Classification Bantu Lang.* 74 Full classified list of the Bantu languages... Zone B... Group 10... B. 14 Cira, i-(Saŋgo). **1955**, etc. [see NGBANDI]. **1967** W. J. SAMARIN *Gram. of Sango* 17 Sango is a creolized language because it stands in somewhat the same relationship to vernacular Sango as Haitian Creole to French. **1971** B. MAFENI in J. Spencer *Eng. Lang. W. Afr.* 112 Pidgin languages have been known to develop in circumstances where no master-servant relationship existed between the groups in contact. Pidgin Sango, spoken in the Central African Republic, is a good example. **1977** C. F. & F. M. VOEGELIN *Classification & Index World's Lang.* 128 *Sango*,..a lingua franca..with many French and Bantu words.

Sangoan (sæŋ'gəʊən), *a. Archæol.* [f. the place-name *Sango* Bay in Uganda + -AN.] Of, pertaining to, or designating a palæolithic culture in central Africa, roughly contemporary with the Mousterian culture in Europe, and the people and tools associated with it. Also *absol.*, this culture.

[**1924** *Man* XXIV. 169 The large tools of the Sango types ..are now known to occur practically wherever extensive beds of quartzite crop out.] **1931** L. S. B. LEAKEY *Stone Age Cultures of Kenya Colony* x. 232 Kamasian pluvial. Sub-divisions unknown but may include Mr Wayland's Kafuan and Sangoan. **1952** *Geol. Survey Uganda Memoir* VI. II. 64 The typical Sangoan pick is an elongated steep-sided, double-ended implement with small flat dorsal and large ventral faces... The most finely finished product is somewhat canoe-like in shape. **1959** J. D. CLARK *Prehist. S. Afr.* ii. 40 The cultures of the First Intermediate period.. can be subdivided into two contemporary cultures—the Fauresmith and the Sangoan. **1969** *Geol. Survey Uganda Memoir* X. 87 The occurrence of tranchets and pressure flaked lances, together with mint-fresh, steeply flaked duck-head and other small hand axes..invites correlation with the latest Sangoan or upper Lupemban. **1977** G. CLARK *World Prehist.* (ed. 3) i. 34 The leading artefacts of the Sangoan continued to be bifacial, including core-axes, picks and narrow lanceolate forms.

Sangrado (sæŋ'grɑːdəʊ). [The name of a character in Le Sage's *Gil Blas*, a physician whose sole remedies were bleeding and the drinking of hot water; suggested by Sp. *sangrador* bleeder.] A medical practitioner resembling Dr. Sangrado; a doctor given to bleeding, or an ignorant pretender to medical knowledge.

1812 BYRON *Works* (1898) II. 429 After feeling the pulse and shaking the head over the patient, prescribing the usual course of warm water and bleeding—the warm water of your mawkish police, and the lancets of your military—these convulsions must terminate in death, the sure consummation..of all political Sangrados. **1820** SCOTT *Lett.* (1894) II. 90 One is sadly off in France and Italy, where the Sangrados are of such low reputation, that it were a shame even to be killed by them. **1873** E. H. CLARKE *Sex in Educ.* 63 Our fathers' physicians were too often Sangrados.

‖**sangrador** (sangra'dor). [Sp. = 'bleeder'.] = SANGRADO.

1832 SIR W. HAMILTON *Discuss.* (1852) 248 In Spain, every village has even now its *Sangrador*, whose only cast of surgery is blood-letting; and he is rarely idle.

sangrail (sæŋ'greɪl). In 5 **sangrayle, -grayll(e, seynt graal**, 7–9 **sangreal**, 9 **sangreall**. [a. OF. *Saint Graal* 'Holy Grail': see SAINT *a.* and GRAIL².

The pseudo-etymological form *sang roial* (confusing the word with SANG-ROYAL 2) appears in AF. of the 15th c.: see Godefr. *Compl.* s.v. SANC. Another spurious etymology formerly common appears in the following quot.:—

1685 STILLINGFL. *Orig. Brit.* i. 13 Others think that the word was *Sangreal*, being some of Christ's real blood..said to be somewhere found by King Arthur.]

1. = GRAIL².

a **1450** *Le Morte Arth.* 10 The knights of the table Round, The sangrayle when they had sought. *c* **1450** *Merlin* ii. 32 Thi boke shalbe cleped the boke of the seynt Graal. **1470–85** MALORY *Arthur* II. xi. 88 Soone after the aduentures of the Sangrayll shalle come among yow and be encheued. **1808** SCOTT *Marm.* I. *Introd. Epist.* 268 He took the Sangreal's holy quest. **1871** G. MEREDITH *H. Richmond* II. 145 They bear the veiled sun like a sangreal aloft to the wavy marble flooring of stainless cloud.

†**2.** The book of the Grail. *Obs.*

1470–85 MALORY *Arthur* II. xiii. 91 As it telleth after in the sangraylle.

‖**sangre azul** ('sangre a'θul). [Sp.] The 'blue blood' of the old and aristocratic Spanish families (see note s.v. BLOOD *sb.* 8).

1834 [see BLOOD *sb.* 8]. **1846** F. FORD *Gatherings from Spain* xix. 259 *Sangre azul* is the ichor of demigods which flows in the arteries of the grandees. **1876** *Gentl. Mag.* Nov. 601 The sephardim..once contained the *sangre azul* of the nation. **1975** H. MCCLOY *Minotaur Country* vii. 74 Carlos.. was the embodiment of *sangré azul.*

†'**sangrede.** *dial.* (Suffolk). *Obs.* Also 6 **sangarede, sangered, sangred.** [Of obscure origin: perh. f. OE. *sang* SONG + *rǣde* reading.] A service chanted for the souls of the departed.

1463 in *Bury Wills* (Camden) 30, I wil the seid Willm Baret..paye yeerly..iiij s. iiij d. for a sangrede, that my soule, my fadrys and modrys sowlys, and my frendys, may be preyd fore in the pulpet on the Sunday. **1492** *Ibid.* 80 That aftyr myn decesse be song and kepte yerely..a sangrede for the sowlys of the seyd John Odeham, Margarete hys wyff [etc.]. **1504** in Wright *Dict. Obs. & Prov. Eng.* II. 821 To the sepulkyr lyght vi. hyves of beene to pray ffor me and my wyffe in the common sangered. **1539** *Will of Bryan* (Somerset Ho.), That myn Executours kepe.. by the space of xx^ti yeres a Sangrede for my sowle.

Sangria (sæŋ'griːə). Also **sangria.** [a. Sp. *sangría* (see SANGAREE).] A cold drink of Spanish origin composed of red wine variously diluted and sweetened.

1961 'J. WELCOME' *Beware of Midnight* x. 119 Hugo ordered a dry Martini for himself and a jug of *Sangria* for the others..'It's a sort of Spanish Pimms.' **1966** *House & Garden* Dec. 79/3 Visitors to Spain soon become familiar with sangria—the national iced wine cup. The simplest form consists of slices of fruit..soaked in a rough Spanish red wine and with a little water..and ice added. **1972** D. LEES *Zodiac* 107, I ordered a pitcher of sangria to go with the couscous. **1978** *Times* 23 Apr. 12/8 There was time for a glass of the house Sangria (a sweet wine tasting of Cherry-ade).

†'**sangris.** *Obs. rare*⁻¹. [Of obscure history, but repr. mod.L. *synagris* (Rondelet 1554), a. Gr. συναγρίς.] A fish of the genus *Synodus.*

1598 *Epulario* F iiij, To dresse a Sangris or tooth fish [It. *dentale*].

†**sang 'royal.** *Obs.* Also 5 **sanke royall, saunke realle**, 6 **sangue, sank royall.** [Fr.; *sang* (OF. *sanc*) blood, *royal* ROYAL.]

1. Royal blood.

?*a* **1400** *Morte Arth.* 179 Taghte mene and towne..Of saunke realle in suyte, sexty at ones. **1430–40** LYDG. *Bochas* VIII. xxv. (1558) 16 As Sanke royall doth playnly determyne. *a* **1548** HALL *Chron., Hen. VII* 6 One that descended from the high progeny of the Sangue royall.

derisively. **1522** SKELTON *Why not to Court* 490 He came of the sank royall, That was cast out of a bochers stall.

2. The blood of Christ.

1523 SKELTON *Garl. Laurel* 1463 That goodly place.. Where the sank royall is, Crystes blode so rede.

sangsara, var. SAMSARA.

sangstar(e, obs. forms of SONGSTER.

sangsue ('sæŋsjuː). ? *nonce-wd.* [a. F. *sangsue*: see SANGUISUGE.] A leech.

a **1849** POE *Tale Ragged Mount.* Wks. 1865 II. 320 The poisonous sangsue of Charlottesville may always be distinguished from the medicinal leech by its blackness.

sanguane, -guen(e, obs. ff. SANGUINE *a.*

sangue royall, variant of SANG ROYAL *Obs.*

sangueyn(e, obs. forms of SANGUINE *a.*

sanguicolous (sæn'gwɪkələs), *a.* [f. mod.L. **sanguicol-a*, f. L. *sangui-s* blood + *col-ĕre* to inhabit: see -OUS.] Inhabiting the blood, as a parasite.

1891 in *Century Dict.*

'**sanguiduct.** [f. L. *sangui-s* blood + *ductus* DUCT *sb.*] †**a.** A blood-vessel (*obs.*). **b.** *nonce-wd.* (after *aqueduct*). A drain for carrying off blood.

1681 tr. *Willis' Rem. Med. Wks.* Vocab., *Sanguiducts*, the vessels that carry the blood through the body, as the veins and arteries. **1853** J. W. CROKER *Hist. Guillotine* 81 It became necessary to build a kind of sanguiduct, to carry off the streams of blood from the Guillotine.

sanguiferous (sæŋ'gwɪfərəs), *a.* [f. mod.L. **sanguifer*, f. L. *sangui-s* blood: see -FEROUS.] Bearing or conveying blood.

1682 T. GIBSON *Anat.* (1697) p. v, A vein is a sanguiferous vessel. **1793** ABERNETHY in *Phil. Trans.* LXXXIII. 60, I shall first relate those varieties of the sanguiferous system which were found on the thoracic side of the diaphragm. **1857** BULLOCK *Cazeaux' Midwif.* 191 The sanguiferous apparatus of the yolk of fowls.

san'guific, *a. rare.* [ad. mod.L. **sanguificus*, f. L. *sangui-s* blood: see -FIC.] Blood-producing.

1684 tr. *Bonet's Merc. Compit.* VIII. 294 Upon the failing of the fermentation and sanguifick virtue of the Bloud. **1822–29** *Good's Study Med.* (ed. 3) IV. 543 It [swooning] more commonly originates in the sanguificor digestive organs.

sanguification (ˌsæŋgwɪfɪ'keɪʃən). [ad. mod.L. *sanguificātiōn-em*, n. of action f. *sanguificāre*: see SANGUIFY *v.* Cf. F. *sanguification.*] The formation of blood, conversion into blood.

1578 BANISTER *Hist. Man* v. 80 The liuer the shoppe of sanguification. **1665** NEEDHAM *Med. Medicinæ* 381 The work of Sanguification or bloud-making is performed by the Bloud. **1702** FLOYER *Hot & Cold Bath.* I. iv. (1709) 101 The Sanguification of the Chyle. **1761** STERNE *Tr. Shandy* III. iv, The lungs the only organ of sanguification. **1835** BROWNING *Paracelsus* Note 215 It appears..that he had discovered the circulation of the blood, and the sanguification of the heart. **1856** in *Orr's Circ. Sci., Pract. Chem.* 305 The aggregate of the changes which..foods undergo up to sanguification is called digestion. **1876** MCKENDRICK *Outl. Physiol.* 206 Sanguification, or the preparation of a nutritive fluid called the Blood, which [etc.].

b. *transf.* and *fig.*

1651 HOBBES *Leviath.* II. xxiv. 130 This Concoction, is as it were the Sanguification of the Common-wealth. **1731** MILLER *Gard. Dict.* s.v. *Sap*, Botanists are now generally agreed, that all Plants are furnish'd with Organs and Parts necessary both for Chylification and Sanguification.

†**san'guificative**, *a. Obs.* [ad. mod.L. *sanguificātīvus*, f. *sanguificāre*: see -ATIVE.] Blood-producing.

1662 J. CHANDLER *Van Helmont's Oriat.* 209 Because the Liver was not a Kitchin, but a family Governour by its own Sanguificative ferment.

†'**sanguifier.** *Obs.* [f. SANGUIFY *v.* + -ER¹.] Something that produces blood.

1615 CROOKE *Body of Man* 40 It is the first Sanguifier or the workhouse wherein the bloud is made. **1696** FLOYER *On Humours* (J.), Bitters, like choler, are the best sanguifiers, and also the best febrifuges.

†**san'guifluous**, *a. Obs.* [f. mod.L. **sanguiflu-us* (f. L. *sangui-s* blood + *flu-ĕre* to flow) + -OUS.] Flowing with blood.

1684 tr. *Bonet's Merc. Compit.* IX. 340 When Bile and Phlegm falls by a sanguifluous Vein. **1727** in BAILEY vol. II.

1860 R. FOWLER *Med. Vocab.* 1897 *Syd. Soc. Lex.*, *Sanguifluous*, flowing or running into blood.

† **'sanguify**, *v. Obs.* [ad. mod.L. *sanguificāre*, f. L. *sangui-s* blood: see -FY.]

1. *intr.* To produce blood.

1624 BP. HALL *True Peacemaker* in *Var. Treat.* (1627) 540 The head to deuise and command, the eies to see, .. the liuer to sanguifie. **1652** CULPEPPER *Eng. Physic.* (1656) 375 If the Liver be weak and cannot make Blood enough, (I would have said sanguifie if I had written only to Schollers). *a* **1677** HALE *Prim. Orig. Man.* I. i. 29, I do not digest, sanguifie, nor my Heart move, nor my Blood circulate .. by any immediate command of my Will.

fig. **1644** MILTON *Divorce* II. xvii. (ed. 2) 66, I doubt his will like a hard spleen draws faster than his understanding can well sanguifie.

2. *trans.* To convert into blood.

1650 BAXTER *Saints' R.* (1655) III. xi. § 11. 218 As the chyle is sanguified in the Liver, Spleen, and Veins. **1707** FLOYER *Physic. Pulse-Watch* 265 When the Relicks of the Chyle which are not sanguify'd are not excreted.

Hence † **'sanguifying** *ppl. a.*

1620 VENNER *Via Recta* ii. 40 Which .. it doth .. enfeeble, and dispoliate of its sanguifying facultie. **1665** NEEDHAM *Med. Medicinæ* 400 The liquor hath less of a Vital Sanguifying power than it had before.

sanguigenous (sæŋ'gwɪdʒɪnəs), *a.* [f. L. *sangui-s* blood + -GEN + -OUS.] Producing blood.

1852 W. GREGORY *Org. Chem.* (ed. 3) 496 The food of animals should contain a due admixture of sanguigenous and respiratory food.

† **sangui'naceous**, *a. Obs.* [f. L. *sanguinem*, *sanguis* blood + -ACEOUS.] (See quot.)

1816 T. BROWN *Elem. Conchol.* 163 *Sanguinaceous*, of a blood colour, or resembling blood.

‖ **sanguinaria** (sæŋgwɪ'nɛərɪə). *Bot.* and *Pharm.* [mod.L. (J. J. Dillenius in Linnæus *Systema Naturæ* (1735)) application of L. *sanguināria* (sc. *herba*), fem. of *sanguinārius* pertaining to blood: see SANGUINARY *a.*

The plant so called in classical Latin (identified by Pliny with Gr. πολύγονον POLYGONUM) had the name from its real or supposed property of stanching blood; the modern application refers to the blood-red colour of the root.]

The blood-root, *Sanguinaria canadensis*; also the rhizome of this, used in medicine.

1808 [see *Jersey tea* s.v. JERSEY[2]]. **1842** BRYANT *Fountain* iv, The flower Of sanguinaria, from whose brittle stem The red drops fell like blood. **1875** H. C. WOOD *Therap.* (1879) 435 As an emetic, sanguinaria has fallen into well-deserved disuse. **1887** *Homeopathic World* 1 Nov. 506 In reference to Sanguinaria, he said that its most brilliant triumphs were in edematous laryngitis.

† **sangui'narian**, *a. Obs.* [f. L. *sanguināri-us* (see SANGUINARY *a.*) + -AN.] = SANGUINARY *a.* 2.

1637 HEYLIN *Answ. Burton* 89 Such a rayling Rabsakeh, so sanguinarian a spirit.

sanguinarily ('sæŋgwɪnərɪlɪ), *adv.* [f. SANGUINARY *a.* + -LY[2].] In a sanguinary manner.

1850 in OGILVIE. **1893** *Cornh. Mag.* Sept. 243 A mosquito .. adhered sanguinarily to the side of his aristocratic nose.

sanguinarine ('sæŋgwɪnərɪn). *Chem.* Also -in; earlier **sanguinarina**. [f. SANGUINARIA + -INE[5]. Cf. F. *sanguinarine*.] (See quots.)

1838 T. THOMSON *Chem. Org. Bodies* 292 Of Sanguinarina. This substance was discovered by M. Dana in the root of the *sanguinaria canadensis*. **1852** GREGORY *Handbk. Org. Chem.* (ed. 3) 366 Sanguinarine .. forms a grey powder, which is alkaline and yields red salts. **1874** GARROD & BAXTER *Mat. Med.* (1880) 194 Meconidine is Homologous with Sanguinarin, an alkaloid contained in *Chelidonium majus*, a papaveraceous plant. **1897** *Syd. Soc. Lex.*, *Sanguinarin*, $C_{17}H_{15}NO_4$. The alkaloid of blood-root, the rhizome of *Sanguinaria canadensis*... Also, $C_{34}H_{15}NO_8$, a brown, resinoid substance obtained by precipitation from a tincture of the root of *Sanguinaria canadensis*.

'sanguinariness. [f. SANGUINARY *a.* + -NESS.] The quality of being sanguinary.

1689 *Myst. Iniq. working* 30 The Treachery, Sanguinariness, Violence and Cruelty which the Papal Principles mould, influence, and oblige Men unto. **1881** A. C. GRANT *Bush Life Queensland* II. xxxi. 150 Blucher accompanies them, and greatly amuses his master by the excessive sanguinariness of his disposition.

† **sangui'narious**, *a. Obs. rare.* [f. L. *sanguinări-us* SANGUINARY + -OUS.] Sanguinary.

1654 GAYTON *Pleas. Notes* III. iv. 89 To express his Sanguinarious Nature, he [etc.].

† **'sanguinary**, *sb. Obs.* [ad. L. *sanguināria*, fem. of *sanguinārius* pertaining to blood (see SANGUINARY *a.*), used *ellipt.* as a name for various plants (see 1 below and SANGUINARIA), also, in med.Latin as the name of a jewel (see 2 below).]

1. A name applied to certain plants having styptic properties, esp. milfoil, *Achillea Millefolium*, and shepherd's purse, *Capsella Bursa-pastoris*; also to *Polygonum Hydropiper* (see 2nd quot. 1526). In some recent Dicts. said to be used in the sense of SANGUINARIA.

c **1440** *Promp. Parv.* 441/1 Sanguinarye, herbe, or myllefolye .., *sanguinaria, millefolium*. **1526** *Grete Herball* lxxii. (1529) E ij b, Bursa pastoris is shepeherdes purs, some call it sanguynary, bycause it stauncheth bledynge of the nose. *Ibid.* cccliii. T v b, Persicaria... Some call it sanguynary or blodeworte bycause it draweth blode in places that it is rubbed on.

2. A kind of BLOOD-STONE.

1465 *Will of Blyton* (Somerset Ho.), Anulum .. cum lapide infix. vocat. Sanguinarye. **1504** in Wadley *Bristol Wills* (1886) 178 A cheyne of gold with a Sanguinarye. **1567** MAPLET *Gr. Forest* A vij b, The Sanguinarie which in Greek is called Amatites, which being well chafed and rubbed, bleedeth. **1600** in Nichols *Progr. Q. Eliz.* (1823) III. 511 Item one sworde, with a pomell of sanguimarie [*sic*].

sanguinary ('sæŋgwɪnərɪ), *a.* (and *sb.*) [ad. L. *sanguinārius*, f. *sanguin-em*, *sanguis* blood: see -ARY. Cf. F. *sanguinaire*, Sp., Pg., It. *sanguinario*.]

1. Attended by bloodshed; characterized by slaughter; bloody. Of laws: Imposing the death-penalty freely.

1625 BACON *Ess., Unity in Relig.* (Arb.) 431 We may not .. propagate Religion, by Warrs, or by Sanguinary Persecutions, to force Consciences. *c* **1645** HOWELL *Lett.* (1655) IV. xxix. 70 The eagerst, and most sanguinary Warrs are about Religion. **1647** CLARENDON *Hist. Reb.* I. § 107 For the Penal Laws (those only excepted which were Sanguinary, ..) were never more rigidly executed. *a* **1720** SEWEL *Hist. Quakers* (1795) I. IV. 368 Here endeth this sanguinary act. **1788** GIBBON *Decl. & F.* xlix. V. 137 His [Charlemagne's] laws were not less sanguinary than his arms. **1841** ELPHINSTONE *Hist. Ind.* VI. i. II. 21 A sanguinary conflict took place, and the prince gained a complete victory. **1877** BROCKETT *Cross & Cr.* 27 Twenty-one years out of ninety were spent in war, often of the most sanguinary character.

2. a. Bloodthirsty; delighting in carnage.

1623 COCKERAM II, *Blood thirsty*, sanguinary. **1656** BLOUNT *Glossogr.*, *Sanguinary*, cruel, thirsty, bloody, desirous of, or delighted in shedding blood. **1732** LEDIARD *Sethos* II. x. 357 They aggravated the treacherous and sanguinary ambition of Daluca. **1751** HARRIS *Hermes* Wks. (1841) 170 The facetious Fuller, speaking of one Morgan, a sanguinary bishop in the reign of Queen Mary, says of him, that [etc.]. **1841** JAMES *Brigand* xvi, Brissac is somewhat of a sanguinary person to deal with.

† **b.** *absol.* as *sb.* A sanguinary person. *Obs.*

a **1550** *Image Ipocr.* I. in *Skelton's Wks.* (1843) II. 415 He that thus dothe cary Is a mercenary, Yea, a sangunary. **1632** B. JONSON *Magn. Lady* I. v, A Souldier .. Who being by custome growne a Sanguinarie .. Is more delighted i' the chase of an enemy .. Then all the .. happinesse of Issue could bring to him.

3. Of or pertaining to blood. *rare.*

1684 tr. *Blancard's Phys. Dict.*, *Mater tenuis*, a Membran which .. clothes the Brain and Cerebellum, extreamly full of sanguinary Vessels. **1908** P. T. FORSYTH in *Expositor* Sept. 215 Sacrifice, in the ritual sense, in the sanguinary sense, has long had no real place in our religion.

¶ **4.** *slang.* Used as a jocular euphemism for BLOODY, in reports of vulgar speech.

1890 KIPLING in *Macm. Mag.* LXI. 155/1 This is sanguinary. This is unusual sanguinary. Sort o' mad country. **1891** —— *Lett. of Marque* xv. 110 'Eres this sanguinary down mail a stickin' in the eye of the Khundwa down! **1910** G. B. SHAW *Lett. to Granville Barker* (1956) 168 The inhabitants raise up their voices and call one another sanguinary liars. **1942** *Tee Emm* (Air Ministry) II. 131 Lovely crate, but lousy on the approach with that sanguinary great nose sticking up in front of you.

† **sangui'nation.** *Obs.* [n. of action f. L. *sanguināre* to bleed, f. *sanguin-em*, *sanguis* blood: see -ATION.] A flow of blood.

1597 A. M. tr. *Guillemeau's Fr. Chirurg.* 51 b/1 There followeth such a superfluous sanguination, that by noe meanes it can be restraygned. **1599** —— *Gabelhouer's Bk. Physicke* 67/2 Vse this every moneth in the increasing of the Moon, till the sanguination be stenched.

sanguine ('sæŋgwɪn), *a.* and *sb.* Forms: 4–5 **sangueyn(e, -gweyn(e,** 4–6 **sanguyn(e, -gwyn(e,** 4–8 **sanguin,** 5 **sangewyn, -gwayn, -gwen, -gwynne,** 6 **sangwane, sanguane, -uene,** 7 **sanguen,** 4– **sanguine.** [a. F. *sanguin* (fem. *sanguine*), ad. L. *sanguineus*: see SANGUINEOUS. Cf. Sp. *sanguino*.] **A.** *adj.*

1. a. Blood-red. Also ***sanguine red*** (sometimes hyphened), † ***red sanguine***, † ***brown sanguine***. Now only *literary*.

1382 WYCLIF *Ecclus.* xlv. 12 With .. blyu vyolet silc, and sanguyn silc [Vulg. *hyacintho et purpura*]. *c* **1386** CHAUCER *Knt.'s T.* 1310 His colour was sangwyn. **1398** TREVISA *Barth. De P.R.* XIX. xxiv. (1495) 877 Sinopis is a red colour and is callyd Rubrica for it is nexte to redde sangweyne. **1399** in *Hampole's Wks.* (1896) II. 449 A longe sangwyn gowne furryd with Calabir. **1444** *Test. Ebor.* (Surtees) II. 106, ij girdils ye tone redde and tother sangvyn. *c* **1470** HENRY *Wallace* IX. 1932 His colour was sangweyn. **1494** *Somerset Med. Wills* (1901) 323 A sangewyn kyrtyll and a smoke. **1513** DOUGLAS *Æneis* VII. ii. 4 Within hir rosy cartis cleirlie schane Aurora vestit into broun sanguane. **1526** *Grete Herball* xxviii. (1529) B v b, It is an vnpure thynge and hath a sanguyne coloure. **1601** HOLLAND *Pliny* II. 625 Interlaced .. with certain knots, both white and also of a sanguine red. **1637** MILTON *Lycidas* 106 Like to that sanguine flower inscrib'd with woe. **1650** BULWER *Anthropomet.* 153 In Persia the womens pale colour is made sanguine by adulterate complexion. **1666** DRYDEN *Ann. Mirab.* clii, Her flag aloft, spread ruffling to the wind, And sanguine streamers seem the flood to fire. *a* **1668** LASSELS *Voy. Italy* (1698) I. 112 The vault is painted with a deep sanguin red. **1757** GRAY *Bard* 185 Yon sanguine cloud, Rais'd by thy breath. **1784** COWPER *Task* VI. 158 The lilac, various in array, now white, Now sanguine. **1820** SHELLEY *Cloud* 31 The sanguine sunrise, with his meteor eyes, And his burning plumes outspread. **1864** LOWELL *Fireside Trav.* 26 In an obscure corner grew the sanguine beet. **1885** G. MEREDITH *Diana* iii, The beautiful virgin devoted to the sanguine coat.

b. *Nat. Hist.* Chiefly in names of animals and plants, usually as transl. of mod.L. *sanguineus* in specific names.

1783 LATHAM *Gen. Synopsis Birds* IV. 657 Sanguine Turtle. **1809** SHAW *Gen. Zool.* VII. II. 487 Sanguine Paradise-bird, *Paradisea sanguinea*. **1816** KIRBY & SP. *Entomol.* xvii. (1818) II. 82 The sanguine ants at length rush upon the negroes. **1839** LINDLEY *Introd. Bot.* III. (ed. 3) 480 Sanguine; dull red, passing into brownish black. **1865** GOSSE *Land & Sea* 261, I may compare the Sanguine Sponge to an uneven, rather than a hilly country.

2. a. Of or pertaining to blood; consisting of or containing blood. Now *rare*.

1447 BOKENHAM *Seyntys* (Roxb.) 259 Dyssentyrye .. Wych .. Sendyth owte sangweyn agestyoun. **1584** COGAN *Haven Health* cxl. 125 The tongue is of a spungie and sanguine substance. **1656** BLOUNT *Glossogr.*, *Sanguin flesh* .. is that which is engendred of blood; of which sort is the flesh compounded in the Muscles, the Heart [etc.]. **1706** E. WARD *Wooden World Diss.* (1708) 60 The Barber, that has stept from the demolishing of Beards, to the Practice of more sanguine Operations. **1716** M. DAVIES *Athen. Brit.* III. *Diss. Physick* 4 Without any Pretensions to that Sanguine Discovery [of circulation of blood], or knowing any thing considerable of it, much less of his Teaching it to Dr. Harvey. **1769** E. BANCROFT *Guiana* 300 That this Poison may duely operate, it is necessary that it should be externally admitted into the sanguine vessels. **1800** tr. *Lagrange's Chem.* II. 368 The colouring part seems to be richer in the sanguine principle. **1812** [see FRUSTUM 2]. **1860** RUSKIN *Mod. Paint.* V. VII. iv. § 17. 146 It was .. to serpents, that the Greeks likened the dissolving of the Medusa cloud in blood. Of that sanguine rain .. I cannot yet speak. **1873** MRS. H. KING *Disciples, Giov. Nicotera* (1877) 307 One sanguine sacramental cup.

b. Causing or delighting in bloodshed; bloody, sanguinary. Now *poet.* or *rhetorical*.

1705 HICKERINGILL *Priest-cr.* I. (1721) 19 The *Inquisition*, the *Hangman*, the *Dragoons*, and the *Jaylors*, are the Holy Pillars of their Sanguine Priest-craft. **1727** A. HAMILTON *New Acc. E. Ind.* II. xlii. 115 Ordered both their Heads to be struck off, which ended their Disputes effectually .. but Governor Sowdon was sent for to Fort St. George, and another sent in his Place less sanguin. **1736** LD. J. HERVEY *Mem. Geo. II* (1847) I. 346 The long and sanguine war that soon followed. **1817** SHELLEY *Rev. Islam* I. xxxi, And Fear, the demon pale, his sanguine shrine forsook. **1872** BLACKIE *Lays Highl.* 85 The fiends in hell delight to view The sanguine slaughter done. **1884** SYMONDS *Shaks. Predec.* ix. 331 The craziest career which ever closed a brilliant dynasty in sanguine gloom.

3. a. In mediæval and later physiology: Belonging to that one of the four 'complexions' (see COMPLEXION *sb.* 1) which was supposed to be characterized by the predominance of the blood over the other three humours, and indicated by a ruddy countenance and a courageous, hopeful, and amorous disposition.

In the strict use as connected with the doctrine of the four 'complexions', the word is now only *Hist.*; but the modern writers (chiefly phrenologists) who have attempted a classification of 'temperaments' usually retain it as one of their descriptive terms.

c **1386** CHAUCER *Prol.* 333 Of his complexioun he was sangwyn. **1398** TREVISA *Barth. De P.R.* XVII. cxxxi. (1495) 689 The vse of pepyr is not prouffitable to Sangueyne men. *c* **1430** LYDG. *Min. Poems* (Percy Soc.) 196 The sangueyn man of blood hath hardynesse, Wrouhte to be lovyng, large of his dispence. **1538** STARKEY *England* I. ii. 58 The iiij [*sc.* complexions] .. sanguyn, melancolyk, phlegmatyk, and coleryke. *a* **1548** HALL *Chron. Edw. IV* 192 b, A prince of haut corage, young lusty and sanguyne of complexion. **1587** GREENE *2nd Pt. Tritameron* Wks. (Grosart) III. 144 The Saturnine temperature is necessarie to dry vp the superfluities of the sanguine constitution. **1707** FLOYER *Physic. Pulse-Watch* 309 A fat sanguine Woman. **1727–41** CHAMBERS *Cycl.* s.v., Sanguine constitutions require a frequent use of phlebotomy. Sanguine people are usually observed to be brisk, bold, daring, and even presumptuous. **1781** J. MOORE *View Soc. It.* (1790) II. lxii. 228 [A disease] more apt to seize people of a sanguine constitution than others. **1843** R. J. GRAVES *Syst. Clin. Med.* xxvii. 346 Persons of a sanguine temperament are in general the most susceptible. **1855** BROWNING *An Epist.* 109 The man—it is one Lazarus a Jew, Sanguine, proportioned. **1874** CARPENTER *Ment. Phys.* I. ii. § 88 (1879) 98 Small brains and great activity, betoken what are known as the sanguine and nervous temperaments.

b. *Astrol.* Of signs, etc.: Favourable to the sanguine complexion.

1647 LILLY *Chr. Astr.* vi. 48 [The First Quadrant is] called the Orientall, Vernall, Masculine, Sanguine, Infant quarter.

c. With reference to 'complexion' in the modern sense (see COMPLEXION *sb.* 4): Red in the face. Cf. sense 1.

1684 *Lond. Gaz.* No. 1982/4 He is very tall, having curled brown Hair, or sanguine Complexion. **1839** DE QUINCEY *Recoll. Lakes* Wks. 1862 II. 138 A sanguine complexion had, of late years, usurped upon the original bronze-tint.

4. a. Of persons or their dispositions: Having the mental attributes characteristic of the sanguine complexion (see sense 3 above); chiefly, disposed to hopefulness or confidence of success.

1509 HAWES *Past. Pleas.* xvi. (Percy Soc.) 73 For sanguyne youth it is al contrary. **1599** B. JONSON *Cynthia's*

Rev. II. iii, He is neither too fantastickally Melancholy; too slowly Phlegmatick, too lightly Sanguine. **1700** DRYDEN *Fables* Pref. *B, Our two Great Poets, being so different in their Tempers, one Cholerick and Sanguin, the other Phlegmatick and Melancholick. **1841** BREWSTER *Mart. Sci.* II. iv. (1856) 147 He was of sanguine temperament. **1855** PRESCOTT *Philip II*, I. I. vii. 97 Philip was not of that sanguine temper which overlooks .. the obstacles in its way. **1882** PEBODY *Eng. Journalism* xix. 144 It was published .. under difficulties which would .. have killed any man of less sanguine temperament.

b. Of persons and expectations, etc.: Hopeful or confident with reference to some particular issue.

1673 *Lady's Call.* Pref. (1684) 4 When the most sanguine of his Disciples had denied, yea forswore, and all had forsaken him. **1712** LADY M. W. MONTAGU *Let. to Mr. W. Montagu* 9 Dec., Sanguine groundless hopes, and .. lively vanity .. make all the happiness of life. **1735–6** T. SHERIDAN in *Swift's Lett.* (1768) IV. 151 Do not think me sanguine in this; for more unlikely and less reasonable favours have been granted. **1785** BURKE *Sp. Nabob of Arcot's Debts* Wks. IV. 242 In the fond imaginations of a sanguine avarice. **1836** W. IRVING *Astoria* III. ix. 139 He now looked forward with sanguine hope to the accomplishment of all his plans. **1863** MISS BRADDON *J. Marchmont* iii, It's kind of you to look at it in this sanguine way, Arundel. **1876** A. J. EVANS *Through Bosnia* ix. 417 And yet how fascinating is Ragusa still! It far surpassed our most sanguine expectations.

5. *Comb.*, parasynthetic and adverbial, as ***sanguine-coloured***, ***-complexioned***, ***-flowered***, ***-streaming***, ***-valiant*** adjs.; **sanguine-bilious** *a.*, partly sanguine and partly bilious; **sanguine-heart** *a.*, *nonce-wd.*, crimson at the heart; **sanguine-nervous** *a.*, partly sanguine and partly nervous; †**sanguine-rod**, the wild cornel or dogwood; **sanguine root** = BLOOD-ROOT; †**sanguine stone** (see quot. 1727–41); also *ellipt.* as *sb.*

1843 R. J. GRAVES *Syst. Clin. Med.* xxxi. 424 Jane McKernan, aged 28—*sanguine bilious. **1552** *Inv. Ch. of Surrey* (1869) 31 A *sangwyne coloured coope of Sattyn. **1888** STEVENSON *Black Arrow* 24 Wrapped warmly in a sanguine-coloured cloak. **1692** *Lond. Gaz.* No. 2773/4 Round Shoulder'd and *sanguine Complexion'd. **1922** JOYCE *Ulysses* 44 His fustian shirt, *sanguine-flowered, trembles its Spanish tassels at his secrets. **1840** BROWNING *Sordello* III. 356 Where in maple-chamber glooms, Crowned with what *sanguine-heart pomegranate blooms, Advanced it ever? **1842** A. COMBE *Physiol. Digestion* (ed. 4) 277 A mixture of the sanguine and nervous, the ****sanguine-nervous***. **1601** HOLLAND *Pliny* II. 189 The plant called the *Sanguin-Rod. **1578** LYTE *Dodoens* I. xxxiii. 48 The sixth [kind of Geranium] is called .. *Sanguine roote, or Bloud roote. **1486** *Bk. St. Albans, Her.* a iii, The .v. stone is calde a Loys, a *sanquine stone or sinamer hit is calde in armys. *Ibid.*, Aloys is calde sinamer or sanquine in armys. **1727–41** CHAMBERS *Cycl.*, *Sanguine stone*, lapis Sanguinalis, a kind of Jasper, brought from New-Spain. **1799** H. GURNEY *Cupid & Psyche* xiii. (1800) 35 And *sanguine-streaming fires arise Meteorous from the trembling ground. **1837** CARLYLE *Fr. Rev.* I. III. iii. 101 Audacity and hope alternate in him with misgivings; though the *sanguine-valiant side carries it.

B. *sb.*

†**1.** A cloth of blood-red colour, also a piece of this.

1319 in Riley *Mem. Lond.* (1868) 131 [Also two] sanguynes [in grain, value 15 pounds]. *c* **1386** CHAUCER *Prol.* 439 In sangwyn and in pers he clad was al. **1411** in *Somerset Med. Wills* (1901) 51 [To the aforesaid Alice two] Kirtells, [one of] Sangwyn.

2. †**a.** A blood-red colour. *Obs.*

a **1500** *E.E. Misc.* (Warton Club) 90 Thanne ȝour flote is made fore ȝour sangweyns, and also for ȝour viollettes saddere thanne ȝour morreys. **1543** GRAFTON *Contn. Harding* (1812) 592 Grained clothe of sondrie coloures, as scarlettes, crimosins, sanguines. *a* **1568** ASCHAM *Scholem.* II. (Arb.) 114 This face [in a picture] had bene more cumlie, if that hie redde in the cheeke, were somwhat more pure sanguin than it is. **1590** SPENSER *F.Q.* II. i. 39 From which forth gusht a stream of gore blood thick, .. And into a deep sanguine dide the grassy grownd. **1594** NASHE *Unfort. Trav.* Wks. (Grosart) V. 68 They .. had all the coate coulours of sanguin, purple, crimson, copper, carnation that were to be had in their countenaunces. **1612** PEACHAM *Gentl. Exerc.* I. xxiii. (1634) 80 With which water you may Diaper and Dammaske upon all other blewes, and sanguines to make them shew more faire and beautifull.

b. *Her.* (See quots.)

1562 LEIGH *Armorie* 21 The last of all collours, of Armory, which is called Murrey. This is blazed Sanguine, and is a princely colour. **1610** GUILLIM *Heraldry* I. iii. 11 The last of the seuen mixed colors we doe commonly call Murrey, but in Blazon, Sanguine. **1704** J. HARRIS *Lex. Techn.* I, *Sanguine*, the Heralds term for the Colour usually called *Murry*, being made of Lake with a little Spanish Brown. **1868** CUSSANS *Her.* iii. 51 Sanguine [is represented] by diagonal lines intersecting each other.

†**3.** The sanguine 'complexion' or temperament.

1530 PALSGR. 265/1 Sanguyn a complexion, *sanguin.* **1594** LADY RUSSELL in Ellis *Orig. Lett.* Ser. I. III. 40 Your Lordships so honorable most kynde .. visitacion, as turned melancoly into a sanguin. **1656** H. MORE *Enthus. Tri.* (1712) 25 That it is the Reign of Sanguine, not the rule of the Spirit, is discoverable both from the Complexion of the Head of this Sect, as also from the general disposition of his followers. **1718** HICKES & NELSON *J. Kettlewell* I. ii. 15 His temper was a Mixture of Sanguine and Choler.

4. *Art.* A crayon coloured red with iron oxide; a drawing executed with red chalks.

1854 FAIRHOLT *Dict. Terms Art*, *Sanguine*, a deep blood colour, prepared from oxide of iron. **1882** HAMERTON *Graphic Arts* 115 When an artist uses red chalk or sanguine he does not intend to produce a very powerful effect. *Ibid.*, Examples of fine sanguines are .. extremely frequent in every large collection of drawings by the old masters. **1886** *Academy* 21 Aug. 127/2 An interesting Greuze sketch in sanguine.

†**'sanguine**, *v. Obs.* [f. SANGUINE *a.*]

1. *trans.* To stain or paint a sanguine colour.

1591 PERCIVALL *Sp. Dict.*, *Pavonado*, sanguined as a sword hilt. *Politus.* **1601** HOLLAND *Pliny* II. 558 Iron-smiths also haue much vse of bitumen, and namely, in sanguining or colouring their ironworke. **1611** COTGR., *Sanguine*, the bloud-stone wherewith Cutlers doe sanguine their hilts. **1665** SIR T. HERBERT *Trav.* (1677) 140 His face was also sanguined with Vermilion. **1688** R. HOLME *Armoury* III. 91/2 Sanguining, is to make it [the Hilt and Pommell] of a pure Purple colour.

2. To stain with blood.

1610 GUILLIM *Heraldry* II. vi. (1611) 54 It is the honour of a generous minde, to put off his belt, and not to sanguine his blade with cold blood. **1689** J. BENT *Bloody Assizes* 16 He breathed Death like a destroying Angel, and sanguined his very Ermins in Blood.

Hence **'sanguined** *ppl. a.*, stained with blood; of eyes: bloodshot.

1700 PARNELL *Battle Frogs & Mice* I. 111 He rolls his sanguin'd Eyes. *a* **1814** *Gonzanga* III. i. in *New Brit. Theatre* III. 126 That life .. Which .. Heav'n did preserve In battle on Bulgaria's sanguin'd plains.

sanguinean(e, var. ff. SANGUINIAN *Obs.*

†**'sanguineless**, *a. Obs. rare*⁻¹. [f. SANGUINE *sb.* + -LESS.] Bloodless.

1675 J. SMITH *Chr. Relig. App.* II. 45 But they shall see her, in her native dress, Such as she is 'mongst shades, pale, sanguinless.

sanguinely ('sæŋgwɪnlɪ), *adv.* [f. SANGUINE *a.* + -LY².] In a sanguine manner.

1. Hopefully; confidently.

1653 in *Nicholas Papers* (Camden) II. 29 My Lord of Rochester hath written very sanguinely hither about his negotiations at the Dyett. **1790** BURKE *Fr. Rev.* Wks. V. 334, I cannot speculate quite so sanguinely as he does. **1857** BUCKLE in A. H. Huth *Life* (1880) I. ii. 140 My mother is a little better, and writes very sanguinely about herself.

†**2.** In a manner characterized by bloodshed. *Obs.*

1765 *Hist. Europe* in *Ann. Reg.* 2/2 Intermarriages, by which the heretofore so sanguinely rival houses of Austria and Bourbon have been drawn nearer to each other.

sanguineness ('sæŋgwɪnnɪs). [f. SANGUINE *a.* + -NESS.] The quality of being sanguine. †**a.** Of 'complexion' (see SANGUINE *a.*). *Obs.* **b.** Hopefulness, confidence of success.

1530 PALSGR. 265/1 Sanguynesse, *sanguinevr.* **1659** *Gentl. Calling* (1696) 94 Whether the Sanguineness of their Temper make them lustful, or the melancholy revengeful. **1727** EARBERY tr. *Burnet's St. Dead* (1728) I. 3 To give a wicked Man a little View of that World he must enter into, divested of Flesh and Blood, may make him drop some of his Arguments supported only by the Sanguineness of his Constitution. **1832** L. HUNT *Sir R. Esher* (1850) 417 The sanguineness of my temper kept me in a constant expectation of my friends return. **1891** E. KINGLAKE *Australian at H.* 13 A boy of eighteen or twenty has, as a general rule, a healthy fund of sanguineness with which to start on life's journey.

sanguineo- (sæŋ'gwɪnɪəʊ), used as combining form of L. *sanguineus* SANGUINEOUS, SANGUINE *a.*, prefixed (with hyphen) to adjs., forming physiological terms with the sense 'partly sanguineous (or sanguine) and partly something else'; also in **sanguineo-'vascular** *a.*, pertaining to blood-vessels. Cf. SANGUINO-.

1803 *Med. Jrnl.* IX. 417 Of a sanguineo phlegmatic temperament. **1845** *Encycl. Metrop.* VII. 257/1 Sanguineo-vascular Ganglia. **1846** G. E. DAY tr. *Simon's Anim. Chem.* II. 144 The sanguineo-bilious temperament. **1879** LEIGHTON *Lichen-Flora* (ed. 3) 521 *Sanguineo-black*, blood-red black.

sanguineous (sæŋ'gwɪnɪəs), *a.* [f. L. *sanguine-us* (f. *sanguin-*, *sanguis* blood) + -OUS.]

1. Of or pertaining to blood; of the nature of or containing blood.

1646 SIR T. BROWNE *Pseud. Ep.* III. ix. 127 This part, or animall of Plato, containeth not only sanguineous and reparable particles, but is made up of veynes, nerves, arteries. **1673–4** GREW *Anat. Trunks* I. ii. §34 As the Sanguineous Vessels in an Animal are composed of a number of Fibres. **1704** RAY *Creation* II. 332 To supply the sanguineous Mass with Nitro-Ærial Particles. **1808** BARCLAY *Muscular Motions* 225 Different organs secrete and assimilate different substances from the sanguineous fluid. **1897** *Syd. Soc. Lex.*, *Sanguineous cyst*, a cyst containing blood, whether it be primarily a blood-cyst, or one into which hæmorrhage has secondarily occurred. **1899** *Allbutt's Syst. Med.* VIII. 466 In exceptional cases vesications are produced .. whose contents may become sanguineous or puriform.

†**b.** Of animals: Having blood. *Obs.*

1646 SIR T. BROWNE *Pseud. Ep.* III. xvi. 144 Sanguineous corticated animals, as Serpents, Toads, and Lizards. **1664** POWER *Exp. Philos.* I. 59 It is plain that a Louse is a Sanguineous Animal. **1667** BOYLE *Orig. Formes & Qual.* (ed. 2) 323 Perfect and sanguineous animals.

2. Of the colour of blood.

sanguineous creeper, honey-eater, book-names for *Certhia sanguinolenta* (1811–1826 Shaw and Stephens *Gen. Zool.* VIII. 232, XIV. 263).

c **1520** *Interl. Beauty & Gd. Prop. Women* A j, I know that nature hath gyuyn me bewte with sanguynyous compleccyon fauour & fayrenes. **1686** GOAD *Celest. Bodies* I. xviii. 120 He may give an account also of a Red-angry Sun, *Sol Rutilus*, in Kepler, which others call Sanguineous. **1819** KEATS *Lamia* II. 76 His passion, cruel grown, took on a hue Fierce and sanguineous. **1826** KIRBY & SP. *Entomol.* IV. xlvi. 280 Sanguinous (*Sanguineus*), red with a tint of black. **1837** CARLYLE *Fr. Rev.* II. III. i, For swinging of incense-pans and Eighty-three Departmental Banners, we have waving of the one sanguineous *Drapeau-Rouge.* **1861** HAGEN *Synopsis Neuroptera N. Amer.* 59 Wings sanguineous at base. **1882** *Garden* 20 May 356/3 Large flowers .. [of] a very deep sanguineous crimson.

3. Of or pertaining to bloodshed; giving rise to bloodshed; bloodthirsty, sanguinary. Now *rare.*

1612 R. SHELDON *Serm. St. Martin's* Ep. Ded. 2 A detestation against all Popish, Ignatian, bloody, and sanguineous attempts. **1642** HALES *Schism* 11 No occasion hath produced more frequent, more continuous, more sanguineous Schismes, than this hath done. **1663** J. H. *Hist. Cromwell* v. in *Harl. Misc.* (1744) I. 275 His other Victories .. were very sanguineous, and fatally cruel. **1843** *Blackw. Mag.* LIV. 244 When a chancellor, more experienced than Rhadamanthus, more sanguineous than Draco, shall have the care of the innocent flock! **1854** THACKERAY *Newcomes* I. 305 Sanguineous histories of queens who sewed their lovers into sacks.

4. Of persons, their constitution or temperament: = SANGUINE *a.* Also, in later use, Full-blooded, plethoric. ***sanguineous fever*** (see quot. 1753).

1732 ARBUTHNOT *Rules of Diet* in *Aliments*, etc. 287 All things which accelerate the Motion of the Blood are hurtful to sanguineous Constitutions. **1753** CHAMBERS *Cycl. Supp.*, *Sanguineous fevers*, a term used by the medical writers to express a kind of fever, in which there is always a plethora, or fullness of blood. **1806** SIR C. BELL *Anat. Expression* vi. (1844) 144 Courage .. is witnessed in the pale and fragile, more than in the strong and sanguineous. **1843** R. J. GRAVES *Syst. Clin. Med.* xxxi. 421 Edward Fitzgerald, labourer .. temperament sanguineous. **1877** F. T. ROBERTS *Handbk. Med.* (ed. 3) I. 6 Four principal temperaments are described, the sanguineous, lymphatic, bilious, and nervous.

b. Of mental temperament: = SANGUINE *a.* 4.

1847 DISRAELI *Tancred* v. v, Therèse, who was of a less sanguineous temperament than her sister, affected despair.

Hence **san'guineousness**, in quot., the condition of having a blood-red colour.

1865 SALA in *Daily Tel.* 7 June, The women .. are ruddy to sanguineousness.

†**san'guinian**, *a.* and *sb. Obs.* Also 4 **sanguinien**, 6–7 **sanguinean(e**. [a. OF. *sanguinien*, f. *sanguin*: see SANGUINE *a.*] **a.** *adj.* Having the sanguine temperament. **b.** *sb.* A person of sanguine temperament.

1340 *Ayenb.* 157 þane colrik mid ire and mid discord. þane sanguinien mid ioliueté and mid luxurie. **1560** ROLLAND *Crt. Venus* Prol. 11 The secund is Sanguineane sicklike. **1607** EARL STIRLING *Cæsar* IV. ii, No corpulent Sanguinians make me feare. **1655** MOUFET & BENNET *Health's Improv.* (1746) 347 Sanguineans must take no more of it than lightly to relish their unsavoury Meat. **1681** COLVIL *Whigs Supplic.* (1751) 119 Sanguinians did only laff, Choleric Melancholians chaff.

†**san'guinical**, *a. Obs.* [f. SANGUINE *a.* + -IC + -AL¹.] = SANGUINE *a.* 3.

1632 LITHGOW *Trav.* (1906) 130 He was .. of a sanguinicall complexion, and a couragious stomacke.

sangui'nicolous, *a. rare*⁻⁰. = SANGUICOLOUS.

1897 *Syd. Soc. Lex.* s.v.

sangui'niferous, *a.* = SANGUIFEROUS.

1891 in *Century Dict.*

sanguinification (sæŋ,gwɪnɪfɪ'keɪʃən). [f. L. *sanguin(i)-*, *sanguis* blood: see -FICATION.] = SANGUIFICATION.

1875 H. WALTON *Dis. Eye* 536 The functions most at fault, whether of digestion, assimilation, or sanguinification, must be carefully attended to.

sanguinism ('sæŋgwɪnɪz(ə)m). *rare.* [f. SANGUINE *a.* + -ISM.] Sanguineness of temperament.

1897 *Times* (weekly ed.) 5 Oct. 656/2 The mingled *insouciance* and sanguinism of that fair-haired adventuress.

†**'sanguinist.** *Obs.* [f. SANGUINE *a.* + -IST.] A person (or animal) of a sanguine temperament.

1628 JACKSON *Worthy Churchman* 36 To sanguinists we must pipe; to melancholists mourne. **1725** *Bradley's Fam. Dict.* II. 5 Y 4, The Black [Horses] with white Marks, are Sanguinists.

sanguinity (sæŋ'gwɪnɪtɪ). [f. SANGUINE *a.* + -ITY.]

1. †**a.** = Consanguinity. [So OF. *sanguinité*, med.L. *sanguinitas.*] *Obs.* **b.** (see quot. 1897.)

c **1470** HARDING *Chron.* LXIII. xi, Alle menne hym loued for his sanguynite [*v.r.* consanguynyte (he was the uncle of the empress Helena)]. **1741** H. WALPOLE *Let. to Mann* 22 Oct., Some say that the duel would have been no breach of sanguinity. **1897** *Syd. Soc. Lex.*, *Sanguinity* .. the quality of likeness or unlikeness between parents.

2. The quality of being sanguine. *rare.*

1737 SWIFT *Let. to Sheridan* Wks. 1761 VIII. 278 But I distrust your sanguinity so much (by my own desponding temper) that [etc.]. **1822** J. MACDONALD *Mem. J. Benson* 291 Whatever severity might appear from time to time in Mr. Benson's manner .. may be attributed to the sanguinity of his temper. **1979** *Time* 8 Jan. 72/2 Nevertheless, Lasch, a history professor .., legitimately finds cracks of doom in our sanguinity.

sanguinivorous (sæŋgwɪˈnɪvərəs), *a.* [f. L. *sanguin(i)-*, *sanguis* blood: see -VOROUS.] = SANGUIVOROUS.
1828–32 in WEBSTER. **1895** A. H. MILES *Nat. Hist. in Anecd.* 38 The Vampire Bat of South America has long been credited with sanguinivorous habits.

sanguino- (ˈsæŋgwɪnəʊ), used as combining form of SANGUINE *a.*, prefixed with hyphen to adjs. to form physiological terms with the sense 'partly sanguine and partly something else'. Also in **sanguino-ˈpurulent** *a.*, consisting of pus mixed with blood. Cf. SANGUINEO-.
a **1697** AUBREY *Lives* (1898) I. 138 He was..sanguino-cholerique, middle sized, strong. **1876** *Trans. Clinical Soc.* IX. 160 Oosing of sanguino-purulent fluid.

‖**ˈsanguinole.** *Obs.* [Fr., f. *sanguin* SANGUINE *a.*] A kind of pear.
1693 EVELYN *De La Quint. Compl. Gard.* I. 123 The Sanguinole or Bloody-Pear, August. **1786** ABERCROMBIE *Arr.* in *Gard. Assist.* p. xii, Pears principally for Baking... Sanguinole or blood pear.

sanˈguinolence. *rare*$^{-0}$. [See -ENCE.] = next.
1891 in *Century Dict.*

†**sanˈguinolency.** *Obs.* [f. next: see -ENCY.] The quality of being sanguinolent; in quot., addiction to bloodshed.
1664 H. MORE *Myst. Iniq.* 247 That great red Dragon with seven Heads is so called from his Sanguinolency.

sanguinolent (sæŋˈgwɪnəʊlənt), *a.* [ad. L. *sanguinolentus*, f. *sanguin-*, *sanguis* blood: see -OLENT.]
1. Of or pertaining to blood; tinged or stained with or containing blood. Now chiefly *Path.* †Also of a patient: Suffering from hæmorrhage.
1597 A. M. tr. *Guillemeau's Fr. Chirurg.* 47 b/2 The Dysenteria or bloodye flixe is a sangvinolent excrement of the Bellye. **1599** —— tr. *Gabelhouer's Bk. Physicke* 67/1 Agaynst bleedinge of the Nose... Take the Mosse of a dead mans Cranium,..and applye that to the sanguinolent Patient his nose, and it helpeth. **1613** MARSTON *Insatiate Countess* v. Wks. 1856 III. 181 Yet the sanguinolent staine would extant be! **1697** HEADRICH *Arcana Philos.* 39 Preparation in Sanguinolent Vlcers. **1850** BLACKIE *Æschylus* I. 194 Find a home In some grim lion's den sanguinolent. **1898** *Allbutt's Syst. Med.* V. 598 Pericarditis with abundance of sanguinolent effusion.
†**2.** Having the colour of blood, blood-red. *Obs.*
c **1450** *Mirour Saluacioun* 4109 Fore rede sangvinolent was alle cristis clothing. **1513** DOUGLAS *Æneis* x. v. 141 The comete stern sanguynolent, Wyth hys red cullour trist and violent.
3. Bloodthirsty; cruel; merciless. *rare.*
1577–87 HOLINSHED *Chron.* III. 1115/2 Others of good behaviour, have beene most cruellie cast awaie by these former sanguinolent thirstie lawes. **1716** M. DAVIES *Athen. Brit.* III. 30 He makes Sanguinolent outcrys against those of the Clergy who [etc.]. **1853** *Blackw. Mag.* LXXIV. 569 From the days of sanguinolent Sulla until now.

sanguinous (ˈsæŋgwɪnəs), *a.* [ad. OF. *sanguineux*, ad. late L. *sanguinōsus*, f. *sanguin-*, *sanguis* blood: see -OUS.]
†**1.** Of eyes: Bloodshot. *Obs.*
1490 CAXTON *Eneydos* xxvii. 103 Her fayre eyen..were incontynent tourned in-to a right hidouse lokynge mobyle, & sangwynouse to see.
†**2.** Bloodthirsty; attended by bloodshed; cruel, merciless. *Obs.*
1755 T. H. CROKER *Orl. Fur.* XXXVI. xxx, The skirmish terrible and sanguinous.
3. Of or pertaining to blood.
1833 J. EBERLE in *Trans. Amer. Pediatric Soc.* (1897) IX. 18 [It] depends mainly, if not wholly, on great sanguinous engorgement of the pulmonary blood-vessels.

sanguisorb (ˈsæŋgwɪsɔːb). [ad. mod.L. *Sanguisorba*, f. L. *sangui-s* blood + *sorbēre* to absorb; so called from the use of burnet as a styptic.]
1. A plant of the N.O. *Sanguisorbaceæ*, typified by the genus *Sanguisorba* (now a sub-genus of *Poterium*), which includes the common burnet.
1846 LINDLEY *Veg. Kingd.* 561 Its habit, indeed, is by no means that of Sanguisorbs.
¶ **2.** quasi-etymologically: A 'blood-sucker'.
1884 G. ALLEN *Philistia* I. 73 A pluralist and a sanguisorb of the deepest dye.

†**ˈsanguisuge.** *Obs.* Also 7 sanguisug. [ad. L. *sanguisūga*, f. *sangui-s* blood + *sūg-ĕre* to suck.] **a.** A blood-sucker (*fig.*). **b.** A leech.
a **1550** *Image Ipocr.* II. in *Skelton's Wks.* (1843) II. 431 That blody judge And Mighty sanguisuge, The Pope that is so huge, Is ever ther refuge. **1575** BANISTER *Chyrurg.* I. (1585) 23 Sanguisuges also serue to this purpose. *a* **1609** A. HUME *Ep. to G. Mont-Creif* 175 As sanguisugs quhilk finds the feeding gud, Cleaues to the skin.

sanguiˈsugent, *a. rare*$^{-0}$. [f. L. *sangui-s* blood + *sūgent-em*, pr. pple. of *sūgĕre* to suck.] Blood-sucking.
In recent Dicts.

sanguisugous (sæŋgwɪˈsjuːgəs), *a.* [f. L. *sanguisūga* (see SANGUISUGE) + -OUS.] Blood-sucking; †also *fig.* bloodthirsty, cruel.
1615 T. ADAMS *Lycanthropy* Ep. Ded., To expose his foming malice and sanguisugous cruelty to mens censure and detestation. *Ibid.* 29 These were the sanguisugous wolues, Papists. **1897** in *Syd. Soc. Lex.*

[**sanguivolent** (in Dicts.), misprint for *sanguinolent* in (? Beaum. & Fl.) *Faithful Friends* III. iii.]

sanguivorous (sæŋˈgwɪvərəs), *a.* [f. L. *sanguis* blood: see -VOROUS.] Feeding on blood.
1842 BLYTH in *Jrnl. Asiatic Soc. Bengal* XI. I. 255 Notice of the predatory and sanguivorous habits of the Bats of the genus Megaderma. **1883** G. E. DOBSON in *Nature* XXVII. 412 The vampire..believed by the older naturalists to be thoroughly sanguivorous in its habits.

sangweler, var. form of SANGLIER *Obs.*

sanhedrim, sanhedrin (ˈsænɪdrɪm, -ɪn). *Jewish Antiq.* Also 6–7 **sanedrim,** 7 **-in.** [a. late Heb. *sanhedrīn*, a. Gr. συνέδριον council, lit. 'sitting together', f. σύν together + ἕδρα seat. The incorrect form *sanhedrim*, which has always been in England (from the 17th c.) the only form in popular use, seems to have arisen from a notion that the ending of the word was the Aramaic plural suffix *-īn*, the Heb. equivalent of which was *-īm*. Cf. G. *sanhedrin*, F. *sanhédrin*, It., Sp. *sanedrin*, Pg. *sanedrim*.] 'The name applied to the highest court of justice and supreme council at Jerusalem, and in a wider sense also to lower courts of justice' (W. Bacher in *Hastings' Dict. of the Bible*, s.v.); the 'Great Sanhedrim' is said to have consisted of 71 members. Also, the title given to the assembly of representative Jewish rabbis and laymen convened by Napoleon I in 1807 to report on certain points of Jewish law.
1588 J. UDALL *Demonstr. Discipl.* i. (Arb.) 15 For priests, pastours;..for rulers of the Synagogue, Elders;..for the Sanedrim, the Eldershipp. **1625** T. GODWIN *Moses & Aaron* v. (1641) 190 The greater court by way of excellency, was called the Sanhedrim, which word came from the Greek συνέδριον, a place of judgement. *a* **1656** USSHER *Ann.* VI. (1658) 146 Ezra the President..of this Sanedrin, or great Synagogue. **1656** BLOUNT *Glossogr.*, *Sanhedrim* or *Sanhedrin*. **1662** STILLINGFL. *Orig. Sacræ* II. v. §3. 169 The cognizance and tryal of false Prophets did peculiarly belong to the great Sanhedrim. *c* **1800** MOORE *Devil among Schol.* 56 Priest and holy Sanhedrim Were one-and-seventy fools to him! **1877** C. GEIKIE *Christ* lii. (1879) 618 The great ecclesiastical court of the nation, known in the Talmud as the Sanhedrim.
b. *transf.*
1653 *Clarke Papers* (Camden) III. 4 The management of the Governement is now resolved to bee by a Sanedrim or 70 of the best men that can bee thought of through England. **1797** BURKE *Affairs Ireland* Wks. IX. 464 This Protestant Apostle is as much above all suspicion of Popery as the greatest and most zealous of your Sanhedrim in Ireland can possibly be. **1837** CARLYLE *Fr. Rev.* VI. i, Occupied in that way, an august National Assembly becomes for us little other than a Sanhedrim of Pedants. **1865** LOWELL *Reconstruction* Prose Wks. (1890) V. 222 Here [is]..an acknowledgment of the human nature of the negro by the very Sanhedrim of the South. **1875** E. WHITE *Life in Christ* I. vii. (1878) 68 It is quite possible for whole sanhedrims of the most respectable divines..to misunderstand important doctrines of revelation.

sanhedrinist (ˈsænɪdrɪnɪst). [f. SANHEDRIN + -IST.] = SANHEDRIST.
1880 A. J. MASON in *Academy* 10 Jan. 20/3 What their authors deemed good for an ideal Sanhedrinist.

sanhedrist (ˈsænɪdrɪst). Also 6 **sanedrist.** [f. SANHEDR(IM) + -IST.] A member of the Sanhedrim; also *fig.*
1593 G. HARVEY *Pierce's Super.* Wks. (Grosart) II. 179 Me thinkes the wisest Sanedrist of a thousand, should hardly persuad me, that he is a frend of Princes, and no enemie of Monarchies. **1879** FARRAR *St. Paul* (1883) 4 The inquisitorial agent of Priests and Sanhedrists.

sanhita, var. SAMHITA.

Sanhiwal, var. SAHIWAL.

‖**san hsien** (san ʃɛn). *Mus.* Also 9 **san heen, hien; san-hsien.** [Chinese *sānxián*, f. *sān* three + *xián* string of musical instrument.] A Chinese three-stringed plucked instrument with a long neck and oval-shaped body. Cf. SAMISEN.
1839 *Chinese Repository* May 43 The *san heĕn.* Three-stringed guitar... The *san heĕn* is played as an accompaniment to the *pepa*, as its sounds are low and dull. **1848** S. W. WILLIAMS *Middle Kingdom* II. xvi. 169 The *san hien*, or three stringed guitar, resembles a rebeck in its contour. **1874** *Jrnl. North-China Branch R. Asiatic Soc.* VIII. 115 The *San-hsien* is usually played as an accompaniment to the *P'i-p'a*, its sound being low, and dull, and deficient in character. **1917** *Encycl. Sinica* 388/2 Hsien tzŭ or San hsien is a three-stringed instrument with a small oval body covered above and below with snake-skin, and a neck about thirty inches long. There are no frets. It is played with a plectrum of jade. **1933** N. WALN *House of Exile* 204 An orchestra..played serpent-bellied *san hsien.* **1954** *Folk Arts of New China* 34 Before he came to Peking, the blind minstrel Han Chi-hsiang, as he frankly admitted, was some-what complacent about his technique on the *san hsien* (a Chinese three-stringed musical instrument). **1975** C. P. MACKERRAS *Chinese Theatre in Mod. Times* 22 The other principal plucked instruments are the *yüeh-ch'in* and the *san-hsien*, both of which function as secondary accompanying instruments in many dramatic styles... The name *san-hsien* means 'three strings'... It produces a characteristic twanging sound.

saniacco, -iacho, -iack(e, etc.: see SANJAK.

Sanibin (ˈsænɪbɪn). Also **Sani-bin** and with small initial. [f. SANI(TARY *a.* + BIN *sb.*] The proprietary name of a receptacle for refuse.
1921 *Trade Marks Jrnl.* 16 Mar. 550 Sanibin. 411,006. Bins and the like Receptacles... Robert Bailey and Son Limited,..Stockport, Cheshire; Manufacturers of Surgical Dressings. **1963** *Spectator* 1 Mar. 273/2 Cosi-jade sanibins. **1966** A. E. LINDOP *I start Counting* xviii. 219 Under the sink where he kept the Sani-bin. **1975** *Listener* 25 Dec. 879/1 A blaze in one of the downstairs sani-bins.

sanicle (ˈsænɪk(ə)l). Also 5 **sanycle,** 6 **sanickle,** 6–7 **sanikell,** (7 **sanikl,** 8 **sanicula**). [a. OF. *sanicle* (12th c. in Hatz.-Darm.; AF. *c* 1265 in Wr.-Wülck. 553/9), ad. med.L. *sanicula*, *saniculum*, prob. f. L. *sān-us* healthy, with reference to the healing powers formerly attributed to the plant. Cf. Sp., Pg. *sanícula*, It. *sanicola*, G. *sanikel* (late OHG. *sanikela*).]
1. The umbelliferous plant *Sanicula europæa* (more fully **wood sanicle**). Also, in extended sense, any plant of the genus *Sanicula*, as *S. marilandica*, the black snakeroot.
14.. *Stockholm Med. MS.* I. 263 in *Anglia* XVIII. 302 Take sanycle and grynde it smal. **1548** TURNER *Names Herbes* (E.D.S.) 86 Sanicula is named in englishe Sanicle. **1643** J. STEER tr. *Exp. Chyrurg.* xvi. 66 With a sufficient quantity of the juice of Sanicle..make thereof Trochisqus. **1852** TH. ROSS *Humboldt's Trav.* I. vii. 254 A sanicle not unlike the S. Marilandica. **1872** OLIVER *Elem. Bot.* II. 183 Compare, also, fruits of Sanicle, covered with stout hooked prickles. **1889** *Daily News* 20 May 5/2 Patches of wood-sanicle.
2. Applied to various plants of other genera. †**a.** = SATYRION (*obs.*). †**b.** = SAXIFRAGE (*obs.*). **c.** With defining words, as **alpine, bear's ear sanicle,** the primulaceous plant *Cortusa matthioli*; **American sanicle,** *Heuchera villosa* (Miller *Plant-n.*, 1884); **(American) bastard sanicle,** the genus *Mitella*; †**great sanicle,** Lady's mantle, *Alchemilla vulgaris*; **Indian, white sanicle** *U.S.*, the white snakeroot, *Eupatorium ageratoïdes* (Cent. Dict.); †**Yorkshire sanicle,** butterwort, *Pinguicula vulgaris.*
14.. *Voc.* in Wr.-Wülcker 613/33 *Stinctum*, i. *Satirion*, sanycle. **1578** LYTE *Dodoens* I. xcviii. 140 Great Sanicle or Ladies Mantell, groweth in some places of this countrey. **1597** GERARDE *Herbal* II. cclxiii. 643 *Pinguicula*..Butter-wort, or Yorkshire Sanicle. *Ibid.* 645 The first is called..in English spotted Sanicle; of our London dames pratling Parnell. **1657** W. COLES *Adam in Eden* xi. 24 The Bears eares according to their name Sanicle are no lesse powerful for healing then the former. **1705** tr. *Cowley's Plants* Wks. 1711 III. 345 Next Spotted Sanicle and Navel-wort. **1760** J. LEE *Introd. Bot.* 326 Sanicle, *Saxifraga. Ibid.*, Sanicle, American Bastard, *Mitella.*

sanidine (ˈsænɪdiːn). *Min.* [a. G. *sanidin* (K. W. Nose 1808), f. Gr. σανιδ-, σανίς board: see -INE[5].] A glassy variety of orthoclase, found in flat crystals (Chester).
1815 AIKIN *Man. Min.* (ed. 2) 197 Glassy Felspar. Sanidin. **1849** J. NICOL *Man. Min.* 121 The glassy felspar or sanadine is by some considered a distinct species. **1867** BRANDE & COX *Dict. Sci.*, etc., *Sanidine*,..a name given to Glassy Felspar, on account of the tabular form of its crystals.
Hence **saniˈdinic** *a.*, containing sanidine. **ˈsanidinite,** a rock consisting largely of sanidine.
1885 *Encycl. Brit.* XVIII. 748/2 Modern volcanic rocks (quartzose trachyte, amphiboliferous and sanidinic trachyte). **1887** *Mineral. Mag.* VII. 227 The blocks of sanidinite and laacher-trachyte occur of all sizes up to masses measuring two feet in diameter... The sanidinite consists principally of sanidine, or of sanidine and nosean. **1916** J. A. THOMSON in David & Priestley *Brit. Antarctic Exped. 1907–9: Geol.* II. 139 Trachytes appear to have the power of converting inclusions of such rocks as older trachytes, gneisses and granulites into sanidinites. **1962** *N.Z. Jrnl. Geol. & Geophysics* V. 395 The finest examples of sanidinites..were obtained from a zone of yellowish-green glass, in some places as much as half an inch in thickness, formed at the contact between porcellanite and overlying basalt.

‖**sanies** (ˈseɪnɪiːz). [L. *saniēs.* Cf. F. *sanie.*]
1. *Path.* A thin fetid pus mixed with serum or blood, secreted by a wound or ulcer.
1562 BULLEYN *Bulwark, Soarnes & Chir.* 27 Now sanies is nothyng els, but corrupted foode or nourishemente which natur was not able to digest. **1608** TOPSELL *Serpents* (1658) 789 For the stanching of bloud, the curation of ulcers, the hindering of sanies. **1650** TRAPP *Comm. Lev.* xv. 4 Paul found it as noisom to his soul..as the sanies of a plague-sore to a rich robe. **1707** P. BLAIR *Misc. Observ.* (1718) 43 There flowed out a great deal of Sanies and Ichor, scarce any purulent Matter. **1804** ABERNETHY *Surg. Obs.* 220 A bloody sanies was discharged. **1897** MARY KINGSLEY *W. Africa* 283 The whole hand was a mass of yellow pus, streaked with sanies.
†**b.** *fig. Obs.*

1651 JER. TAYLOR *Serm. for Year* ii. II. (1653) 19 Gods heavie hand shall press the *sanies*..out from all our sins.

†**2.** Any watery fluid of animal origin. *Obs.*

1661 LOVELL *Hist. Anim. & Min.* 54 The Sanies, or matter of a Goats liver rosted, helps the dimnesse of sight. **1792** BELKNAP *Hist. New Hampsh.* III. 184 Mr. Peck..has assured me, that 'the sanies of many testaceous marine animals will give the same tint'. **1826** KIRBY & SP. *Entomol.* III. xxviii. 5 Those having..cold white sanies in the place of blood. **1834** MACGILLIVRAY *Lives Zoologists* 59 Every living creature has a humour, blood, or sanies the loss of which produces death.

†**sa'niferous**, *a. Obs.* [f. late L. *sānifer*, f. *sān-us* healthy: see -FEROUS.] Health-bringing.

a **1706** EVELYN *Sylva* II. iii. (1776) 342 Not that there are no nociferous trees, as well as saniferous.

sanification (sænɪfɪ'keɪʃən). *rare.* [f. SANIFY *v.*: see -FICATION.] The action or process of making healthy.

1895 W. JAMES *Let.* 16 June (1920) II. 21 Just about to get a little health into me, a little simplification and solidification and purification and sanification.

sanify ('sænɪfaɪ), *v.* [f. L. *sān-us* healthy (see SANE *a.*) + -(I)FY.]

1. *intr.* To become sane or reasonable.

1836 HOR. SMITH *Tin Trump., Anger*, This seasonable arrest of our functions gives us time to sanify.

2. *trans.* To make healthy; improve the sanitary conditions of (a city, etc.).

1872 [see below]. **1891** *Nation* (N.Y.) 3 Dec. 423/2 Palermo is transformed—cleansed, sanified, and.. beautified. **1895** *Chamb. Jrnl.* XII. 691/2 To sanify Jeddah and its vicinity.

Hence '**sanified** *ppl. a.*

1872 W. R. GREG *Enigmas Life* 30 *note*, The premature deaths of the bread-winners [will] disappear before sanified cities and vanishing intemperance.

sanikell, sanikl, obs. forms of SANICLE.

Sanio ('sænɪəʊ). *Bot.* The name of Gustav *Sanio* (1832–91), German botanist. †**a.** [First designated, as *Sanio'sche balken*, by C. Müller 1890, in *Ber. d. Deutsch. Bot. Ges.* VIII. 23.] Used in the possessive and with *of* to designate a thickening of the primary wall or medial lamella separating or inclosing pits in wood, esp. of the radial walls of tracheides in gymnosperms. *Obs.*

1891 *Jrnl. R. Microsc. Soc.* 488 'Sanio's Bands' in the Coniferæ.—By this term (*Sanioische Balken*) Herr C. Müller proposes to designate the beams or thickenings commonly found in the xylem-elements, chiefly in the tracheids of Coniferæ. **1915** *Jrnl. Linn. Soc.: Bot.* XLI. 462 All the Indian species of *Pinus* show Sanio's rims. **1916** *Ann. Bot.* XXX. 425 Sanio's bars are small rods crossing the tracheides, cambium, and phloem elements in many conifers. **1920** *Bot. Gaz.* LXX. 431 Considerable importance was attached for some years to the presence or absence of 'bars' or 'rims' of Sanio. **1935** C. J. CHAMBERLAIN *Gymnosperms* xi. 245 A cytological study of the origin and development of the bordered pit and the bars and rims of Sanio would be interesting.

b. *Sanio's law*: any of a set of empirical results that describe the growth of tracheides in conifers.

1903 MUDGE & MASLEN *Class-bk. Bot.* ii. 51 It follows from Sanio's law that the elements of the phloem and xylem, unless subjected to subsequent disturbances, should be arranged in radial rows. **1915** BAILEY & SHEPARD in *Bot. Gaz.* LX. 66 (*heading*) Sanio's laws for the variation in size of coniferous tracheids. *Ibid.* 70 It is evident from Table V that Sanio's second law is applicable to *Picea rubens* as well as to *Pinus sylvestris*. **1961** *Forestry* XXXIV. 125 The foundation of the study of tracheid and fibre-length variation was laid by Sanio (1872) who presented his results of studies on Scots pine (*Pinus sylvestris*) in a set of five conclusions which, for some time now, have been regarded as 'Sanio's Laws'. **1975** S. CARLQUIST *Ecol. Strategies of Xylem Evol.* 5 The variations noted in Sanio's laws have been confirmed for a number of conifers and dicotyledons.

sanious ('seɪnɪəs), *a.* [ad. F. *sanieux*, ad. L. *saniōsus*, f. *saniēs*: see SANIES and -OUS.] Of the nature of sanies; consisting of, or containing sanies; yielding a discharge of sanies.

1562 BULLEYN *Bulwark, Soarnes & Chir.* 22b, Take heede..that passage be left in the loweste parte, for sanious matter. **1676** WISEMAN *Chirurg. Treat.* II. iv. 177, I was sent for, and observing the Ulcer sanious, proposed Digestion. ? **1780** COWPER *Recipr. Kindness* 15 The cure was wrought; he wip'd the sanious blood. **1797** M. BAILLIE *Morb. Anat.* (1807) 351 Cells..containing a sanious fluid. **1884** M. MACKENZIE *Dis. Throat & Nose* II. 394 The ulcer presenting the well-known raised, hard, ragged edges, and sanious base.

‖**sanitar** (sænɪ'tɑː(r)). [Russ.] In Russia, a hospital attendant; *spec.* a medical orderly in the army.

1916 H. WALPOLE *Dark Forest* I. i. 33 Then I came to Petrograd and through the English Embassy found a place in one of the hospitals, where I worked as a sanitar for three months. **1927** —— in *Daily Express* 21 Dec. 8/6 He was my servant during part of 1915, when I was a sanitar in the Russian army. **1933** —— *Vanessa* IV. 674 The sanitars began to dig a grave. **1974** F. FARMBOROUGH *Nurse at Russian Front* II. 30 The 1st *Letuchka*, (Flying Column)..was staffed with four surgical sisters,..two doctors,..about 30 *sanitars* (ambulance orderlies) and an officer.

sanitarian (sænɪ'tɛərɪən), *sb.* and *a.* [f. SANITARY *a.* + -AN.]

A. *sb.* **a.** One who studies sanitation; one who is in favour of sanitary reform.

1859 HELPS *Friends in C.* Ser. II. Introd. 11, I will go with you and see the chief sewers..and if that is not an inducement to offer to a sanitarian [etc.]. **1865** *Cornh. Mag.* May 602 Energetic and practical 'sanitarians' had made successful war upon dirt, overcrowding, and foul air. **1883** *Harper's Mag.* May 924 A crusade in favor of 'fresh air' was fought by the sanitarians.

b. *U.S.* A public health officer.

1946 *Richmond* (Va.) *News* 20 Mar. 4/2 A field trip to observe high-temperature, short-time pasteurization was one of the high-lights today of the closing session of the Virginia Association of Milk Sanitarians. **1974** *Index-Jrnl.* (Greenwood, S. Carolina) 23 Apr. 12/1 J. D. Kirby, chief sanitarian with the health department, said the vaccine is 'the safest, most reliable yet perfected and is specified by the Public Health Services'. **1976** *National Observer* (U.S.) 23 Oct. 10/2 The boss is Dale Reeves, senior public-health sanitarian and head of the consumer-protection program.

B. *adj.* Pertaining to sanitary matters; advocating sanitary reforms.

1884 *Athenæum* 5 Apr. 446/2 Its serious interest is rather antiquarian than sanitarian. **1886** FROUDE *Oceana* 275 In some sanitarian salon Macaulay's New Zealander..will exhibit his sketch.

Hence **sani'tarianism**.

1881 R. N. BOYD *Chili* 3 The monotonous regularity prescribed by modern sanitarianism is observed. **1891** EBSWORTH *Roxb. Ball.* VII. 425 At which some of our modern puritanic hypocrites affect to be shocked, resenting it as an outrage on their fastidious Sanitarianism.

sanitarily ('sænɪtərɪlɪ), *adv.* [f. SANITARY + -LY[2].] With regard to sanitary condition.

1881 A. ELWES tr. *Pinto's How I crossed Africa* I. ii. 36 A small amount of goodwill would make it, sanitarily, far better than it is. **1884** *Pall Mall G.* 17 Apr. 14/1 A miniature mansion, tastefully and sanitarily fitted. **1889** *Twentieth Cent.* (N.Y.) 6 Apr., You can make a prison..as sanitarily perfect and as administratively humane as you like.

sanitariness ('sænɪtərɪnɪs). [f. SANITARY *a.* + -NESS.] The condition of being sanitary.

1889 *Pall Mall G.* 3 Dec. 2/2 To secure the sanitariness of all premises within its area.

sanitarist ('sænɪtərɪst). [f. SANITARY *a.* + -IST.] = SANITARIAN *sb.*

1859 KINGSLEY *Misc.* I. 130 This new 'National Association' seems the most hopeful and practical move yet made by the sanitarists.

sanitarium (sænɪ'tɛərɪəm). [quasi-Lat., f. *sānitās* health: see next and -ARIUM.] = SANATORIUM 1 and 2.

1851 LADY BENTHAM in *Mech. Mag.* LV. 304 Sanitariums, wherein the diseased of all ranks might, at moderate cost obtain superior medical advice. **1861** J. H. BENNET *Winter Medit.* I. vii. (1875) 192 Mentone has made a great step in advance..as a winter sanitarium. **1865** *Pall Mall G.* 27 Sept. 5/1 The Mansion House committee for the provision of sanitaria for diseased cattle have thrown up their work.

sanitary ('sænɪtərɪ), *a.* Also *erron.* sanitory. [ad. f. *sanitaire* (1812 in Hatz.-Darm.), as if ad. mod.L. **sānitārius*, f. L. *sānitās* health: see SANITY and -ARY[2].]

1. a. Of or pertaining to the conditions affecting health, esp. with reference to cleanliness and precautions against infection and other deleterious influences; pertaining to or concerned with sanitation. Also *occas.* of conditions or surroundings: Free from deleterious influences. Also ***sanitary reform, reformer.***

sanitary cordon: see CORDON 4.

1842 (*title*) Report on the Sanitary Condition of the Labouring Population of Great Britain. **1849** *Act 11 & 12 Vict.* c. 63 §1 Provision..for improving the Sanitary condition of Towns and populous places. **1849** MACAULAY *Hist. Eng.* iii. I. 427 It may well be..that sanitary police and medical discoveries may have added several more years to the average length of human life. **1850** C. KINGSLEY *Alton Locke* I. i. 4 A sanitary reformer would not be long in guessing the cause of my unhealthiness. **1857** —— *Two Years Ago* II. iv. 68 Sanitary reform is thrust out of sight, simply because its necessity is too humiliating to the pride of all. **1875** HELPS *Soc. Press.* iii. 38 A committee of persons was formed, who were supposed to have some skill in sanitary science. **1875** *Act 38 & 39 Vict.* c. 55 §5 Urban sanitary authorities and rural sanitary authorities..invested with the powers in this Act mentioned. **1883** *Encycl. Brit.* XV. 798/1 The want of constant supervision of the slaughter-houses is thought..to be a serious defect in the sanitary law of the country. **1884** *Times* 4 Oct. 4/5 Dr Jaeger's sanitary woollen system has been adopted by some of our most eminent sanitary reformers. **1966** N. LONGMATE *King Cholera* xi. 112 The sanitary reformer triumphed over the cleric: the churches were shut for one whole Sunday. **1974** H. R. F. KEATING *Underside* iv. 41 There's an immense amount to be done in sanitary reform.

b. Used as the distinctive epithet of appliances specially contrived with a view to sanitary requirements; e.g. of certain makes of wall-paper, of glazed tiles for flooring and walls, of non-absorbent pipes for drainage; and the like.

1862 *Catal. Internat. Exhib.* II. x. 27 Flanged and unflanged sanitary tubes, from four to twelve inches in diameter. **1872** CROOKES *Wagner's Handbk. Chem. Technol.* 321 Sanitary ware is one of the largest branches of stoneware manufacture. **1877** T. L. NICHOLS *Herald of Health Almanack* 21 (Advt.), O for the muse of Dryden, or of Pope To hymn thy praises, *Sanitary Soap!* **1884** A. WATT *Soap-making* xii. 112 Chloridised Sanitary Soap. **1934** A. HUXLEY *Beyond Mexique Bay* 2 The last word in cocktail bars and peach-pink sanitary fittings. **1940** *Chambers's Techn. Dict.* 740/1 *Sanitary ware*,..glazed earthenware used for some sanitary fittings. **1977** *Times* 30 July 10/4 Plain colours..in bath and sanitary ware.

2. Intended or tending to promote health.

1853 KANE *Grinnell Exp.* xxxiv. (1856) 298 All hands went out for a sanitary game of romps in the cold light. **1861** TROLLOPE *Orley F.* (1862) I. xxxi. 229 The judge, though he rode everyday on sanitary considerations, had not a sportsman's celerity in leaving and recovering his saddle. **1870** LOWELL *Study Wind.* (1871) 154 Solitary communion with Nature does not seem to have been sanitary or sweetening in its influence on Thoreau's character. **1872** FISKE *Myths & Myth-Makers* ii. 61 (Funk) In Sweden sanitary amulets are made of mistletoe twigs, and the plant is supposed to be a specific against epilepsy and an antidote for poisons.

3. Special collocations: **sanitary belt**, a belt to which a sanitary towel is attached; **Sanitary Commission** *U.S. Hist.*, one of various commissions established to supervise matters of health and sanitation, *spec.* that set up by the U.S. government in 1861 to care for soldiers and their dependants during the Civil War; **sanitary engineer**, one whose profession is the design, construction, or maintenance of sanitary appliances or sewerage; a plumber; hence **sanitary engineering**; **sanitary inspector**, an officer appointed to inspect sanitary conditions, a public health inspector; **sanitary napkin** (*U.S.*), **pad, towel**, a pad worn by women to absorb menstrual flow.

1908 *Sears, Roebuck Catal.* 998/2 The EZ *Sanitary Belt ..fits the body so smoothly that it is not felt when either worn over or under garments. **1969** B. MALAMUD *Pictures of Fidelman* ii. 55 He trotted to get her anything she had run out of—drawing pencil, sanitary belt, safety pins. **1861** *N.Y. Times* 25 June 4/4 A week ago we noticed the formation in Washington of the *Sanitary Commission for the volunteers, and its approval by the Army Medical Bureau and by the Government. **1898** *Kansas City* (Missouri) *Star* 19 Dec. 2/5 The sanitary commission's work can all be done by a state veterinarian. **1949** J. B. HERRICK *Mem. 80 Yrs.* 1 A clearer war memory is that of the fair of the Sanitary Commission, held in Chicago in the summer of 1865. **1873** B. LATHAM *Sanitary Engin.* Pref., The whole range of works in which the *Sanitary Engineer is engaged. **1901** *Daily Colonist* (Victoria, B.C.) 5 Oct. 6/2 The septic tank system of sewerage..is highly recommended by some of the most eminent sanitary engineers in Europe and America. **1974** 'M. YORKE' *Mortal Remains* v. iv. 156 Her grandfather had been a sanitary engineer, making lavatory basins. **1868** B. LATHAM (*title*) Inaugural address..before the Society [of Engineers]..upon..the results of *sanitary engineering. **1957** *Encycl. Brit.* XVIII. 740/2 A barrister by profession, he [*sc.* Edwin Chadwick] mastered the elements of sanitary engineering, then a little-understood science. **1863** *Times* 24 June 7/5 We shall leave it to the report of the *sanitary inspector... He was astonished..to find the rooms so nice and clean. **1897** *Act 60 & 61 Vict.* c. 38 The expression 'sanitary inspector' means a sanitary inspector appointed by the local authority. **1907** *Nature* 21 Feb. 400/1 Among the recommendations are..the provision of an expert staff of inspectors under the medical officer, whose title shall be altered from that of 'Inspector of Nuisances' to 'Sanitary Inspector'. **1943** *Our Towns* (Women's Group on Public Welfare) iii. 88 A Sanitary Inspector gave evidence that the majority of houses have outside W.C.'s only. **1956** *Act 4 & 5 Eliz. II* c. 66 §1 Sanitary inspectors appointed under the local Government Act, 1933, or the London Government Act, 1939, shall henceforth be designated public health inspectors. **1977** *Lancashire Life* Dec. 92/3 Not only did Christopher become Burnley's first fire brigade chief and first sanitary inspector. **1917** W. J. ROBINSON *Sex Knowledge for Women & Girls* vi. 45 Menstrual blood..is discharged from the uterus.. to the outside, where it is caught on cotton, *sanitary napkins or some other pad. **1975** D. RAMSAY *Descent into Dark* 74 She had experienced no traumas over the change from sanitary napkins to tampons. **1926** *Daily Colonist* (Victoria, B.C.) 2 Jan. 7/7 (Advt.), The hazards of the old-time *sanitary pad have been supplanted with a protection both absolute and exquisite. **1974** *Times* 27 Apr. 1/6 One [line]..will always have to be sold cheaply.. denture powder, sanitary pads and tampons, nappies. **1881** *Trans. Obstetr. Soc.* XXII. 188 Dr. Galabin showed the new ladies' *sanitary towels manufactured by Messrs. Southall, Barclay, & Co., of Birmingham. They were extremely light and soft, and contained a pad of absorbent cotton wool. **1896** *Eng. Illustr. Mag.* Aug. 8/2 (Advt.), Ladies will find the use of Southalls' Sanitary Towels in assorted sizes to be a great convenience and a great saving. **1917** *Lancet* 28 July 145/2 (*heading*) The destruction of sanitary towels and surgical dressings. *a* **1935** T. E. LAWRENCE *Lett.* (1938) 503 You'd think they'd have had some other place for their sanitary towels. **1977** B. FREEMANTLE *Charlie Muffin* iii. 33 On the wall..there was still a white outline where the sanitary-towel dispenser had been.

Sanitas ('sænɪtæs). [a. L. *sānitās* health.] (See quot. 1897.)

1878 *Med. Times & Gaz.* 12 Jan. 51/1 'Sanitas'. This fluid has been brought out as 'the only true antiseptic and disinfectant combined'. **1897** *Syd. Soc. Lex.*, *Sanitas*,.. name for a commercial preparation consisting of an aqueous solution of oxidised oil of turpentine, the active principle of which is peroxide of hydrogen. Used as an antiseptic.

sanitate ('sænɪteɪt), *v.* [Back-formation from SANITATION.] *trans.* To put in a sanitary condition; to provide with sanitary appliances. Also *absol.*

1882 SALA *Amer. Revis.* II. viii. 106 An epidemic which.. will..scourge her again..unless the town be 'sanitated'. **1886** KIPLING *Departm. Ditties* (1899) 15 Rustem Beg of Kolazai.. Lusted for a C.S.I.—so began to sanitate. **1892** B. W. RICHARDSON in *Longm. Mag.* Dec. 201 We in rural England are better sanitated than are the rural populations of France.

†**'sanitating,** *ppl. a. Obs.* [f. L. *sānitās* + -ATE[3] + -ING[1].] Health-giving; healing.

1656 S. HOLLAND *Zara* I. vi. (1719) 39 Searching about the Grove for some sanitating Simple; he at last lighted upon that..weed called *Morsus Diaboli.*

sanitation (sænɪ'teɪʃən). [irreg. f. SANIT(ARY) + -ATION.] **1.** The devising and application of means for the improvement of sanitary conditions. Also *spec.* (the provision of) toilet facilities.

1848 CLEVE (*title*) Hints on Domestic Sanitation. **1880** JEFFERIES *Hodge & M.* II. 242 Rural sanitation, again, comes to the front day by day. **1881** P. S. ROBINSON *Under the Punkah* 84 The Government sent down its chiefs of sanitation. **1901** V. BETHELL *Monte Carlo Anecdotes* p. xii (Advt.), *Hotel Metropole*... Sumptuous private suites, excellent cuisine, perfect sanitation. **1934** M. V. HUGHES *London Child* x. 117 Sanitation was not known at Reskadinnick, neither earth nor water nor any such thing.

2. In *Comb.*, designating a person or vehicle employed in the removal and disposal of domestic refuse, as ***sanitation man, truck, van*** (*U.S.*).

1939 *N.Y. Times* 16 Sept. 19/2 Sweepers and drivers.. will be known as '*sanitation men'. **1975** *New Yorker* 8 Sept. 111/1 The city paid the sanitationmen $713,500 at time-and-a-half rates to clean up the debris that had accumulated because the strikers had refused to collect it. **1958** *N.Y. Times* 18 Nov. 26/6 'Some kind of job action' by the crews of *sanitation trucks can be expected. **1974** *Anderson* (S. Carolina) *Independent* 23 Apr. 3B/4 Among the critically hurt was a crewman on a sanitation truck that happened to be picking up refuse at the..building. **1973** *Times* 27 Aug. 5/7 My wife explained that this caper was weightier than that by defining dust cart as Garbage truck, or, in Current American, *sanitation van.

Hence **sani'tationist**, one who is skilled in or who advocates sanitation.

1888 *Pall Mall G.* 27 Aug. 4/1 'Sanitationists' (will that be the terrible word?) will contract to supply so much public health per 1,000 for so much a year. **1894** *Liberal* 24 Nov. 42/2 Such farseeing sanitationists.

sanite, obs. form of SANITY.

†**sani'tiferous,** *a. Obs.* [irreg. f. L. *sānitās* health: see -(I)FEROUS.] Health-bringing.

1657 TOMLINSON *Renou's Disp.* 214 Those whose spirits want refection..require sanitiferous Perfumes.

'sanitist. *rare.* [f. SANIT(ARY) + -IST.] = SANITARIAN.

1882 in OGILVIE (citing *Examiner*).

sanitize ('sænɪtaɪz), *v.* [Formed as prec. + -IZE.] **1.** *trans.* To make sanitary; to disinfect.

1836 *New Monthly Mag.* XLVII. 14 Human industry is God's vicegerent in sanitizing, if I may dare to coin a word, the earth we tread, and the air we breathe. **1899** *N.B. Daily Mail* 28 Feb. 4 He, too, was closured, and every precaution taken to sanitise his surroundings. **1950** C. A. LAWRENCE *Surface-Active Quaternary Ammonium Germicides* VI. 90 It can be said that dishes are sanitized by adequate cleaning. **1968** *National Observer* (U.S.) 22 Apr., His demand: an injunction directing the companies to sanitize their smoke or close down. **1971** *Listener* 11 Nov. 659 Air-conditioning sanitises the air. **1978** *Detroit Free Press* 5 Mar. 20/2 (Advt.), This formula permanently and completely removes urine and sanitizes your carpet.

2. *transf.* and *fig.*, esp. (*U.S. slang*) to render more acceptable, clean up, as by the removal of undesirable, improper, or confidential material.

1934 *N.Y. Times* 7 July 2/4 New words are being manufactured at NRA's code factory... Leon Henderson, economic adviser, has just turned out two which may some day find their way to dictionaries. 'Sanitize' is one. Mr. Henderson says it means putting 'sanity and sanitation in business'. **1966** *Amer. Speech* XLI. 300 After it [*sc.* a document] has been *sanitized*, or redrafted to remove the secret information. **1974** *News & Courier* (Charleston, S. Carolina) 28 Apr. A-10/4 Aides claim the transcripts are accurate, but they have been 'sanitized' to delete Nixon's profanity and character slurs spoken in confidence. **1977** *Rolling Stone* 13 Jan. 38/1 The Congressional Joint Committee on Atomic Energy reacted to the criticism by trying to sanitize the report. **1978** *Listener* 30 Mar. 394/3 The language of the Pentagon is designed (if I may use an Americanism) to sanitise disagreeable realities and disreputable motives. **1978** *Guardian Weekly* 27 Aug. 15/4 NBC also has said that the rape scene was essential to the film's artistic integrity, although the network sanitized the scene after the furor created by the initial showing. **1980** *Times Lit. Suppl.* 7 Nov. 1258/4 A writer has no duty to sanitize his imagination; if defilement is what Potter most wants to write about, write about it he should. But..we do not have to like the taste of greasy hamburger.

Hence **'sanitized** *ppl. a.*

1950 C. A. LAWRENCE *Surface-Active Quaternary Ammonium Germicides* VI. 93 In those tests in which the number of bacteria did not exceed 100 per swab, the glasses were considered adequately sanitized regardless of the chemical agent used. **1970** *Nature* 17 Oct. 203/2 The commission found no consensus..that explicit sexual materials (the commission's sanitized word for 'pornography') should be banned. **1973** *Ibid.* 5 Oct. 231/1 The 'sanitised' transcripts of the proceedings have contained virtually no discussion of the possible implications of the programme. **1973** *Philadelphia Inquirer* (Today Suppl.) 7 Oct. 44/2 The towels are in place, the bed's made, even the 'sanitized' slip is still over the toilet. **1977** N. FREELING *Gadget* IV. 173 A hotel with..sanitized lavatory seats. **1979** G. ROBERTSON *Obscenity* 274 The press published the original text, juxtaposed with the sanitised version prepared by the Corporation, after the director and dramatist had publicly protested against 'this new and Orwellian form of political censorship'.

sanitizer ('sænɪtaɪzə(r)). [f. SANITIZE *v.* + -ER[1].] A substance which sanitizes: a disinfectant, or a preservative of food.

1950 *Jrnl. Milk & Food Technol.* XIII. 63/2 The most recent trend has been toward the use of the quaternary ammonium detergent sanitizer. **1968** SHAFFER & STUART in Lawrence & Block *Disinfection, Sterilization & Preservation* x. 160/1 Acceptances of chemicals as sanitizers have been based in the past on tests conducted under conditions of actual use. **1979** *Nature* 19 Apr. p. xvii/1 The Brentchem range of 14 specifically developed detergents, sanitisers and ancillary products for use in laboratories has been recently improved.

sanitory, erron. form of SANITARY.

†**'sanitude.** *Obs. rare*[−1]. [As if ad. L. *sānitūdo, f. *sān-us* healthy: see SANE *a.* and -TUDE.] Healthy condition.

1652 FRENCH *Yorksh. Spa* ix. 81 Nature..will..the sooner recover its natural vigour, and sanitude.

sanity ('sænɪtɪ). Also 5 **sanite**, 6–7 **sanitie.** [a. F. *sanité*, ad. L. *sānitās*, f. *sān-us* healthy: see SANE *a.* and -ITY.]

1. Healthy condition, health. *arch.*

1432–50 tr. *Higden* (Rolls) I. 333 The flesche of that cuntre inducethe sanite to men of that londe. **1586** B. YOUNG *Guazzo's Civ. Conv.* IV. 192 For safetie and sanitie of his stomacke. **1646** SIR T. BROWNE *Pseud. Ep.* IV. xiii. 230 Therapeuticke or curative Physicke, we tearme that which restoreth the Patient unto sanity. **1744** ARMSTRONG *Art Preserv. Health* II. 94 Each extreme From the blest mean of sanity departs. **1778** [W. MARSHALL] *Minutes Agric.* 16 Jan. an. 1776, His heart, liver, entrails, and nutriment in each state, bear every mark of perfect sanity. **1837** CARLYLE *Fr. Rev.* VII. i, Slow regular growth, though this also ends in death, is what we name health and sanity. **1885** PATER *Marius* I. 33 *Salus*—salvation—for the Romans, had come to mean bodily sanity.

fig. **1682** SIR T. BROWNE *Chr. Mor.* I. §1 Whether thou hast yet entred the narrow Gate, got up the Hill and asperous way, which leadeth unto the House of Sanity. **1829** SOUTHEY *Sir T. More* (1831) II. 156 A restoration of national sanity and strength.

†**b.** Wholesomeness. *Obs.*

1613 PURCHAS *Pilgrimage* (1614) 907 They had Tabacco in religious estimation, not onely for sanity but for sanctity also. **1731** MEDLEY *Kolben's Cape G. Hope* II. 176 A raging wind clears the country of all the Flies and Fleas it meets with, and restores sanity to the air.

2. The condition of being sane; soundness of mind; mental health.

1602 SHAKS. *Ham.* II. ii. 214 A happinesse, That often Madnesse hits on, Which Reason and Sanitie could not So prosperously be deliuer'd of. **1746** FRANCIS *Horace, Sat.* I. v. 59 Is there a Blessing, in the Power of Fate, To be compar'd, in Sanity of Mind, To Friends of such companionable Kind? **1809–10** COLERIDGE *Friend* (1865) 193 The same sanity of mind will the true patriot display. **1854** EMERSON *Lett. & Soc. Aims, Comic* Wks. (Bohn) III. 206 The perception of the comic is..a pledge of sanity. **1873** HAMERTON *Intell. Life* XII. ii. (1875) 442 Much of the sanity of his [Goethe's] genius may have been due to his residence in so tranquil a place as Weimar. **1902** *Edin. Rev.* Apr. 512 The sense of limit belongs to sanity, and is natural to normally constituted minds.

†**3.** Soundness (of material). *Obs. rare.*

1760–72 H. BROOKE *Fool of Qual.* (1809) III. 58 Want of sanity in the materials can never be supplied by any art in the building.

†**4.** *Comb.*, **sanity-institution**, a hospital. *Obs.*

1799 W. TOOKE *View Russian Emp.* II. 177 From this brief account of the medical college..we will proceed to describe the sanity-institutions connected with it.

‖**sanjak** ('sændʒæk). Forms: 6 **saniac, saniacho, sania(c)ke, saniaque, sanjake, senjaque, zanziac,** 6–7 **sangiac(c)o, sangia(c)que,** 6, 8–9 **sangiac,** 7 **sangiach, saniacco, saniack, sanjack, sansack, sansiak, sanzack(e, -ake, -iack, zaniacci, -o, zanzack,** 7–8 **sangiak,** 9 **sandgiac, -jak, sangiack, sangeak,** 8– **sanjak.** [Turkish *sanjāq*; lit. 'banner'.]

1. In the former Turkish Empire, one of the administrative districts into which an eyalet or vilayet was divided.

1537 *St. Papers Hen. VIII*, VII. 706 *note*, The Begeler Bey of Grece..hath seven sanjakes. **1640** E. DACRES tr. *Machiavelli's Prince* 25 Deviding his whole Kingdome into divers Sangiacques or Governments, he sends severall thither. **1802** *Edin. Rev.* I. 52 A pachalic is divided for military purposes, into certain districts, called sangiacs, or standards. **1888** *Encycl. Brit.* XXIII. 654/2 The immediate possessions of the sultan are divided into vilayets (provinces), which are again subdivided into sanjaks or mutessariks. **1895** *Times* 25 Nov. 5/1 Perfect tranquillity reigns..in the sandjaks of Ismid, Zor, and Tchataleja.

†**2.** Misused for SANJAKBEG. *Obs.*

1546 P. ASHTON tr. *Jovius' Turk. Chron.* 126b, The Saniackes..be the lyeutenauntes and Capitaynes of the prouinces. **1546** HARVEL in *St. Papers Hen. VIII*, XI. 160 The Saniacho of Bossena, a man of grete estimacion. **1590** SIR J. SMYTH *Disc. Weapons* 41b, The Bashas, Bellarbies and Senjaques of the Turkes. **1632** LITHGOW *Trav.* II. 73 Sanzacks, or Iudges deputies of Iurisdictions. **1788** GIBBON *Decl. & F.* xl. IV. 99 The residence of a Turkish sanjak. **1832** *Encycl. Amer.* XI. 196 *Sangiac* (Turkish *horsetail*) signifies, in the Turkish army, an officer who is allowed to bear only one horsetail, the pachas having two or three.

Hence †**'sanjakry,** †**'sanjakship,** = sense 1.

1615 G. SANDYS *Trav.* 211 Tendring to the Testadar or Treasurer the reuenew of that Sanziackry. **1630** *R. Johnson's Kingd. & Commw.* 539 Servia..was taken by the Turke in 1438, and reduced into a Sangiak-ship under the Beglerbeg of Buda. **1762** tr. *Busching's Syst. Geog.* II. 121 It ..consists of three Sangiakships. **1814** tr. *Klaproth's Trav.* 9 These three names..are yet borne by a city and sangiackship in the Turkish pachalik of Servia.

sanjakate ('sændʒəkət). Also 7 **sangiacat,** 9 **sandjakate, sangiacat(e.** [f. SANJAK + -ATE[1].] = SANJAK 1.

1687 A. LOVELL tr. *Thevenot's Trav.* II. 11 The Sangiacat of Sefet hath been annexed to Saide and its dependances. **1876** A. J. EVANS *Through Bosnia* Map, The Vilayet of Bosnia, including the Herzegovina or Sandjakate of Mostar.

‖**'sanjakbeg, -bey.** [Turkish: see SANJAK and BEG *sb.*[1], BEY.] The governor of a sanjak.

1524 in *Hakluyt's Voy.* (1599) II. I. 83 It was reported to vs from the campe, there were three saniacbeis, that is to say, great seneshalles or stuards. **1589** HAKLUYT *Voy.* 170 Last of all the Beglerbegs, and Zanziacbegs. **1599** *Ibid.* II. I. 181 Whereas sundry exactions..be offered ours by such Byes, Sanjacbies iustices and Cadies. **1687** A. LOVELL tr. *Thevenot's Trav.* I. 71 Sangiac Bey is like a Lord of a Manor. **1802** *Edin. Rev.* I. 53 The janizaries..and timariots of the district, are obliged in case of war, to unite under the colours of a commander, called Sangiac-bey.

San Joaquin (sæn wɑː'kiːn). [The name of a river in southern California.] ***San Joaquin Valley fever***: = COCCIDIOIDOMYCOSIS.

1958 *New Biol.* XXVII. 65 [Coccidioidomycosis] was originally known as the San Joaquin Valley fever from the part of California with which fatalities from the disease were associated. **1974** M. C. GERALD *Pharmacol.* xxvi. 450 (*table*) *Coccidioides*—San Joaquin Valley fever.

†**sank,** *v. Obs.* Also 4 **sanck.** [a. ON. *samka*, rarely *sanka* (Sw. *samka*, Da. *sanke*), frequentative f. *samna, safna* to collect (see SAM *v.*).] **a.** *trans.* To assemble; bring together. **b.** *intr.* To come together. Hence †**'sanking** *vbl. sb.*, an assembly.

a **1300** *Cursor M.* 13843 He dos vs mani geddering mak, And mani sancking for his sak. *Ibid.* 27663 O nith cums.. conspiraciun, als quen þam sankes samen þe nithful men. *c* **1375** *Ibid.* 16042 (Fairf.) Alle þai geddered atte his court & þer þai sammyn sanke.

sank(e royall, variant ff. SANG-ROYAL *Obs.*

Sanka ('sæŋkə). Chiefly *U.S.* [Repr. abbrev. form of F. *sans caffeine* without caffeine.] The proprietary name of a make of decaffeinated coffee.

1923 *Official Gaz.* (U.S. Patent Office) 14 Aug. 251/1 Société Anonyme Fabriques de Produits de Chimie Organique de Laire, Issy, France... *Sanka*... Teas and coffees; tea and coffee extracts, both dry and liquid, and tea and coffee substitutes. Claims use since Mar. 19, 1910. **1933** *Ibid.* 18 Oct. 642/1 Sanka Coffee Corporation, New York... *Sanka.* For coffees. **1952** *Trade Marks Jrnl.* 17 Dec. 1176/1 *Sanka*... Coffee. General Foods Corporation.., New York. **1964** H. CAMPBELL *Why did They name It...?* 10 Dr. Roselius named the new product *Sanka*—a contraction of the French phrase *sans caffeine.* **1975** *New Yorker* 26 May 28/1 For breakfast, he ordered orange juice, a boiled egg (five minutes), toast and Sanka. **1978** G. VIDAL *Kalki* viii. 192 Giles served Jason Scotch. Prager asked for Sanka. 'I have an ulcer,' he said.

‖**Sankaracharya** (ʃaŋkaraː'tʃaːria). Also **sankaracharya.** [Skr.] The name and title of Sankara Acharya, a famous teacher of Vedānta philosophy (prob. of the eighth century A.D.), used as the title of one of various Indian religious teachers and leaders.

1947 K. M. PANNIKAR *Survey of Indian Hist.* xii. 133 Soon, however, especially after the disappearance of Buddhism, the Mutts became centres of luxury like the great abbeys and the Sankaracharyas who presided over them assumed pontifical dignities. **1960** KOESTLER *Lotus & Robot* i. 54 The nearest to an authoritative position..was attributed to the five Sankaracharyas, leaders of an important Traditionalist sect. **1969** *Cultural News from India* Nov. 43 The annual *Agama Silpa Vidwat Sadas* inaugurated a few years ago by the Sankaracharya of Kanchi Kamakoti Peetam bids fair to be an event of increasing importance and to establish a wholesome tradition. **1977** *Times* 20 Jan. 6/8 India's mass spectacle of faith during the Kumbh Mela Fair started before dawn... Many sages—sankaracharayas, nahatmas [*sic*] and guru—rode on elephants or in chariots.

sank dragonn, variant of SANGDRAGON.

sanke, obs. form of SHANK.

†**'sanker.** *Obs.*

a **1548** HALL *Chron., Hen. VIII* 83b, The kynge of England gaue to the Frenche kynge a colloure of Iewels.. the Sanker furnished with great Diamantes and Perles.

‖**Sankhya** ('sɑːŋkɪa). Forms: 8–9 **Sanchya;** 9– **Sankhya, Samkhya.** [Skr. *sāṃkhya*, lit. = relating to number, prob. referring to the 'enumeration' of the twenty-five principles of the philosophy.] One of the six orthodox systems of Hindu philosophy, based on a dualism of matter and soul.

1788 G. CAUL in *Asiatick Researches* I. 344 Both these works contain a studied and accurate enumeration of natural bodies and their principles; whence this philosophy is named Sánc'hya. **1808** H. T. COLEBROOKE *Amarasimha's Cósha*; *or*, *Dict. Sanskrit Lang.* III. iv. §xxvi, The third quality, according to the Sán'chya system of philosophy: darkness or illusion, contrasted to truth and passion. **1838** *Penny Cycl.* XII. 234/1 The *Sânkhya* system of philosophy ..maintains that true knowledge can alone secure perfect deliverance from evil. **1877** MONIER WILLIAMS *Hinduism* 193 The Sānkhya philosophy, founded by a sage named Kapila, though probably prior in date, is generally studied next to the Nyāya, and is more categorically dualistic. **1934** J. BAILLIE *And Life Everlasting* v. 117 In opposition to such monism, arose the dualistic Sankhya system. According to this teaching human souls are not all united in one impersonal *atman*, but exist separately, each in its own right. **1957** *Encycl. Brit.* XII. 251/1 The *Sāmkhya* is a reaction against the idealistic monism of the Upanishads. It believes in a real matter and an infinite plurality of individual souls which are not emanations of a single world-soul. **1959** *Listener* 17 Sept. 431/2 This [religion] again has resemblances to Brāhmanism and to Sānkhya. **1977** J. HEWITT *Yoga & Meditation* iii. 19 Yoga borrows extensively from the Samkhya (or Sankhya) system.

‖**sanko**, variant of SANCHO[1].

San Luiseño: see LUISEÑO.

sanmartinite (sæn'mɑːtɪnaɪt). *Min.* [f. *San Martín*, name of a town in San Luis Province, Argentina + -ITE[1].] Monoclinic zinc tungstate, $ZnWO_4$, usu. also containing some iron, calcium, and manganese, found as dark brown microcrystalline aggregates in quartz, in association with scheelite.

1948 ANGELELLI & GORDON in *Notulae Naturae* (Acad. Nat. Sci. Philadelphia) 9 Apr. 1 (*heading*) Sanmartinite, a new zinc tungstate from Argentina. *Ibid.* 2 While usually compact, the sanmartinite may be quite porous, and in color varying from dark brown to dark gray depending upon the amount of admixed scheelite. **1968** I. KOSTOV *Mineral.* 483 Sanmartinite is a zincian member $(Zn,Fe)WO_4$, containing about 18% ZnO.

†**sann**, *v.* *Obs.* [a. ON. *sanna* to maintain as true, affirm (Sw. *sanna*, Da. *sande*) = OE. *sóðian*:—OTeut. **sanþōjan*, f. **sanþo-* true (see SOOTH *a.*).] *intr.* To argue.

c **1200** ORMIN 11289, & ȝiff þatt aniȝ læredd mann Shall sannenn her onnȝæness [etc.]. *Ibid.* 17930 þatt hise Lerninng-cnihhtess Tokenn to sannenn fasste onnȝæn þe Judewisshe lede Off Johaness fulluhht.

‖**sannah** ('sænə). ? *Obs.* Also 7 **sannow**, 8 **sano, sanno, sana.** [Of obscure origin; presumably East Indian.] Some kind of cotton fabric formerly exported from India.

1696 J. F. *Merchant's Ware-ho.* 36, I could mention many other sorts, as Sannows a sort of Callico. **1708** SEWEL *Eng. Du. Dict.* (ed. 2), *Sanoes*, sanen. **1720** *Lond. Gaz.* No. 5815/3 A Parcel of Sannoes. **1757** *New Hist. E. Ind.* II. 144, 6900 pieces sanas. **1850** OGILVIE, *Sannah*, the name of certain kinds of India muslin.

sannap, variant of SANAP *Obs.*

sannup ('sænəp). *Amer. Ind.* In 7 **sannop, sanapp.** [a. Narragansett *sannop* = Penobscot *senombi*, Abnaki *seenanbé*.] A married male member of the community; the husband of a squaw (*Cent. Dict.*).

1630 WINTHROP *Hist. New Eng.* (1853) I. 58 Chickatabot came with his sannops and squaws. **1632** *Ibid.* I. 103 Where he had lodged two nights with his squaw, and about twelve sanapps. **1725** S. WILLARD *Jrnl.* in *Appalachia* (1881) II. 342 Our Indian said there was Squaws as well as Sannups. **1847** EMERSON *Poems*, *Musketaquid* Wks. (Bohn) I. 484 Through which at will our Indian rivulet Winds mindful still of sannup and of squaw.

‖**sannyasi** (sæn'jɑːsiː). *Anglo-Ind.* Forms: 7 **sanasse**, 8 **saniasi, sanashy, sannyasin, sinnasse, sinassie, senassie, sunniassy, -asse**, 9 **sanyasi, sanyassi, senassea, sunyasee, -as(s)i, sunnyas(s)ee, -asi**; 9– **sannyasi**; 20 **sanyas(s)in.** [a. Urdū, Hindī *sannyāsī*, = Skr. *saṃnyāsin* laying aside, abandoning, ascetic, f. *saṃ* together + *ni* down + *as* to throw.] A Brahman in the fourth stage of his life; a wandering fakir or religious mendicant. Also *attrib.*

1613 PURCHAS *Pilgrimage* v. ix. 417 Some [Bramenes] wander from place to place begging: Some (an vnlearned kinde) are called Sanasses. **1766** J. RENNELL *MS. Let.* 30 Aug. (Y.) The Sanashy Faquirs (part of the same Tribe which plundered Dacca in Cossim Ally's Time). **1773** W. HASTINGS *Let.* 2 Feb. in Gleig *Life* (1841) I. 282 You will hear of great disturbances committed by the Sinassies, or wandering Fackeers. **1777** STEWART in *Phil. Trans.* LXVII. 483 This Indian..must have travelled as a Faquier or Sunniassy through Bengal into Thibet. **1812** J. MALCOLM in *Asiatick Researches* XI. 267 That crowd of holy mendicants, Sanyásis and Fakírs, with whom India swarms. **1839** *Lett. fr. Madras* xxiii. (1843) 244 A Sunnyassee, or Hindoo devotee, came to pray in the middle of the river. **1854** GEO. ELIOT tr. *Feuerbach's Essence Christianity* xvii. 167 No regenerate man could assume the rank of a Sanyassi,..if he had not previously paid three debts. **1876** Sannyasin [see BHIKSHU]. **1885** G. S. FORBES *Wild Life in Canara* 88 A Hindoo sunyási, or hermit, lived in a cave under the overhanging rock. **1891** MONIER WILLIAMS *Brahmanism & Hinduism* 55 He was a Sannyāsī and an unmarried Smārta Brāhman. **1938** W. S. MAUGHAM *Writer's Notebk.* (1949) 280 At his birth his horoscope was taken, and the astrologer said that he would either become a very rich, successful man, a king among men, or a sanyasin. **1957** *Contributions to Indian Sociol.* I. 17 Now, what one is in the habit of calling Indian Thought is for the very great part the thought of the sanyasi. **1960** E. R. LEACH *Aspects of Caste in S. India, Ceylon & N.W. Pakistan* 6 It is open to every man to become a *sannyasi* and receive the adulations of his society. **1978** *Times* 5 Aug. 7/8 Dom Bede Griffiths, a Benedictine monk who has spent the past 16 years of his life as a *sannyasi* —a kind of hermit—at a Hindu ashram at Kerala in India. **1980** *Daily Tel.* 13 Feb. 15/4 She joined a group of sanyassins, and became fascinated with the guru's writings.

Sanocrysin (seɪnəʊ'kraɪsɪn). *Pharm.* Also **sano-, -chrysin.** [a. Da. *sanocrysin*, irreg. f. L. *sān-us* healthy, SANE + -O + Gr. *χρυσ-ός* gold + *-in* -IN[1].] A colourless crystalline complex salt of gold, sodium (dithiosulphato)aurate(1), $Na_3[Au(S_2O_3)_2].2H_2O$, formerly used in the treatment of tuberculosis.

A proprietary term in the U.S.

1924 H. MØLLGAARD *Chemotherapy of Tuberculosis* ii. 24 The compound built by this synthesis is registered under the name: Sanocrysin. **1924** *Brit. Med. Jrnl.* 8 Nov. 870/2 Arrangements have been made for producing it in bulk in Denmark under the name 'sanocrysin'. **1925** *Official Gaz.* (U.S. Patent Office) 10 Mar. 255/1 *Sanocrysin*... Medicine for phthisis. Claims use since Mar. 16, 1924. **1926** D. MASTERS *How to conquer Consumption* 103 Möllgaard's treatment is generally referred to..as the 'gold treatment', because it consists of a metallic compound of gold, which the discoverer has named 'sanocrysin'. **1929** *Daily Express* 7 Jan. 4 In the treatment of consumption..by sanochrysin. **1943** *Thorpe's Dict. Appl. Chem.* (ed. 4) VI. 117/2 Sodium aurothiosulphate..has been of considerable interest since 1924 when it was introduced..under the name 'Sanocrysin' for the treatment of tuberculosis. **1965** *Biochem. Pharmacol.* XIV. 1174 Gold sodium thiosulphate ('Sanochrysin'), Platinum Chemicals Ltd., Asbury Park, N.J., U.S.A.

sanope, sanpan: see SANAP, SAMPAN[1].

‖**sanpaku** (san'paku). [Jap., lit. 'three white', f. *san* three + *haku* white.] Visibility of the white of the eye below the iris, as well as on either side. Also *attrib.* or as *adj.*

1963 *N.Y. Herald Tribune* 18 Aug. 23/1 George Ohsawa, the Japanese philosopher and prophet of the Unique Principle walked through the streets of New York yesterday. .. There were many beautiful girls... But so many *sanpaku*. **1964** T. WOLFE in *N.Y. Herald Sunday Mag.* 12 Jan. 15/2 Abdul Karim Kassem, President Ngo Dinh Diem and President Kennedy; all *sanpaku* and, now, all shot to death, all destroyed by the fate of the *sanpaku*. **1965** W. DUFTY tr. *Sakurazawa Nyoiti's Macrobiotics* (1972) 60 Any sign of sanpaku meant that a man's entire system—physical, physiological and spiritual—was out of balance. **1970** W. BURROUGHS JR. *Speed* 162 Had I had a rose, I'd have held it in my teeth all morning with sanpaku eyeballs.

San Pellegrino (ˌsæn pɛlɛ'griːnəʊ). The name of a village in Lombardy, used *attrib.* and *absol.* to designate a mineral water obtained from springs there; a bottle or glassful of this water.

1924 W. STORMONT *Summer in Italy* (ed. 2) 174 The following is an abridged classification of the principal waters:..Affections of the Stomach and Intestines: Agnano, ..San Pellegrino, Telese. **1953** G. COOPER *Your Holiday in Italy* (ed. 2) II. 49 Mineral waters *aranciata* (made from oranges—ask for 'San Pellegrino'). **1964** H. ROSE *Your Guide to N. Italy* II. 94 San Pellegrino mineral water is mentioned in historical literature as early as the twelfth century. **1965** 'W. HAGGARD' *Hard Sell* xi. 116 To drink?.. A bottle of Recoardo. No Recoardo? Then San Pellegrino. **1971** M. MCCARTHY *Birds of Amer.* 283 He had had noodles, a salad, and a small San Pellegrino. **1981** R. THOMAS *Mordida Man* xxviii. 242 In front of Abedsaid was a small bottle of San Pellegrino mineral water.

sanpi, var. SAMPI.

sans (sænz), *sb.* *Typog.* Also **Sans** (esp. as the proper name of particular type-faces). A shortened form of SANSERIF.

1927 A. J. WATKINS *Advertisement Lay-Out & Copy-Writing* 116/2 *Serifs*,..not present on block letters or sans type. **1932** H. A. MADDOX *Printing* (ed. 2) iii. 40 (*caption*) Sans-serif (Gill Sans in light, medium, and bold). **1959** O. MILLS *Stairway to Murder* ii. 16 Brash cardboard notices in harsh Sans letters. **1966** BERRY & POOLE *Annals Printing* 208/1 Modern sans include Futura (1927), Cable (1927), [etc.]. **1969** J. WAINWRIGHT *Big Tickle* 124 The double-column headline was in Sans Heavy Italic. **1978** *Antiques & Art Monitor* 28 Oct. 19/2 The result was a series of type-faces, 'Perpetua' and 'Sans', which remain some of the noblest and least fussy in the world.

sans (sænz, sɑ̃(z)), *prep.* Forms: α. 4 **san, saune, (saunt)**, 4–5 **saun.** β. 4–5 **sanz, saunz**, 5–6 **sauns**, 5–7 **saunce**, 6–7 **sance**, 4– **sans.** See also SANS FAIL. [a. OF. *sen* and *sens*, later *san* and *sans*, *sanz*, mod.F. *sans* = Pr. *senes*, *sens*, *ses*, OCat. *senes* (mod. *sens*), OSp. *sen* and *senes*, mod.Sp. *sin*, Pg. *sem*, formerly *sen*, OIt. *sen*:—pop.L. **sene* (for class. L. *sine*) and **senes* (with analogical *s*).

The It. *senza* is now believed to represent L. *absentia* absence, prob. with some influence from the popular L. prep.]

1. a. Without. Now *arch.* (chiefly with reminiscence of Shakspere), *joc.*, and *Her.*

Before the time of Shaks. used almost exclusively with sbs. adopted from OF., in collocations already formed in that language, as ***sans delay, sans doubt, sans fable, sans pity, sans return***. Even in some of our earliest examples, however, a native Eng. synonym has been substituted for the Romanic sb. in the phrase, as in ***sans biding*** = *sans delay*.

α. *c* **1320** *Sir Tristr.* 2253 þat mani man miȝt y se San schewe. **13..** *K. Alis.* 600 He schal beo poisond, saun return Of his owne traitour. *Ibid* [see FABLE *sb.* 1 d]. **1375** *Canticum de Creatione* 62 in *Anglia* I. 304 Bote mete founde þeȝ non saun doute such as hy hadden byfore. *a* **1400** *Pistill of Susan* 181 (MS. A) þe prestes saun pite, And ful of falshede. *c* **1425** *Cast. Persev.* 74 in *Macro Pays* 79 þe vycys arn ful lyckely þe vertues to opresse saun dowte.

β. *c* **1320** *Gosp. Nicod.* 127 (Sion MS.), Saunz doute swa dide þai alle bydene. **13..** *Coer de L.* 681 Go in, sans bydyng. **1377** LANGL. *P. Pl.* B. XIII. 286 Religioun sanz reule and resonable obedience. *c* **1400** *Beryn* 2150 Tell on, saunce delay. **1470–85** MALORY *Arthur* IX. xli. 407 Here came a knyght called sir Breuse saunce pyte. **1471** CAXTON *Recuyell* (Sommer) II. 478 Thou art sauns faulte the tyrant that I seke. **1587** HARRISON *England* II. vi. 168/1 It is a greefe vnto them though now sans remedie sith the thing is doone and past. **1588** SHAKS. *L.L.L.* v. ii. 415 My loue to thee is sound *sans* cracke or flaw. **1600** —— *A.Y.L.* II. vii. 166 Second childishnesse, and meere obliuion, Sans teeth, sans eyes, sans taste, sans euery thing. **1610** *Muses Gard. for Delights* II. ii. 3 My life thou may'st command saunce doubt. **1631** WEEVER *Anc. Funeral Mon.* 765 A man is compleat Armour in brasse, sans Helme. **1686** PLOT *Staffordsh.* 210 If we step higher to trees *sans* date. *a* **1687** COTTON *Poems* (1689) 94 The Bears and Foxes, who *sans* question Than we by odds have warmer Vests on. **1688** HOLME *Armoury* III. xiii. 470 Some term this tower, Sans Port, or Gate. **1797** BRYDGES *Hom. Trav.* II. 239 There-fore, sans favour and affection, Take thou, my boy, thy own election. **1828–40** BERRY *Encycl. Her.* s.v., A dragon or griffin, sans wings. **1841** CATLIN *N. Amer. Ind.* II. 208 Sans accident we arrived,..and sans steamer..we were obliged to trust to our little tremulous craft. **1883** BURTON & CAMERON *Gold Coast* I. i. 13 A sailer-made-steamer, sans boats, sans gunwales. **1901** G. B. SHAW *Admirable Bashville* III. 324 And my blows unpaid, Sans stakes, sans victory, sans everything I had hoped to win. **1922** L. STRACHEY *Let.* 6 Feb. in *Let.*: *V. Woolf & L. Strachey* (1956) 97, I am sans eyes, sans teeth, sans prick, sans..but after that there can be no more sanses. **1929** *Oxford Poetry* 45 Here, foundling and cheat, my Lord Parvenu suns His armorial lie, sans remorse and sans pother. **1942** *Tee Emm* (Air Ministry) II. 78 *Sans* rank, *sans* aircraft, *sans* everything to show off about, he'll be just a foolish little figure. **1970** *Nature* 28 Feb. 781/2 The specimen, though sans its right hind paddle, is a fine example of *Ichthyosaurus platyodon* (Conybeare). **1975** *Publishers Weekly* 18 Aug. 58/2, 75 relevant illustrations sans razzle-dazzle. **1977** *Rolling Stone* 30 June 68/1 It offers anxiety enough for the Rhodesians themselves,..to face the prospect of starting life afresh in some harsher, colder country, sans servants, sans swimming pool, sans sunshine, sans supremacy. **1979** A. HAILEY *Overlord* III. i. 196 The result was a high-quality recording, sans commercials, which the adults and other families watched later at their leisure.

†**b.** With the exception of. [So in Fr.]

1659 EVELYN *Let. to Boyle* 3 Sept., All play interdicted, sans bowls, chess, &c.

2. ‖**a.** Used in various Fr. phrases and combinations (not naturalized) either in their original Fr. use or in derived applications: **sans appel**, used *subst.*, a person from whom there is no appeal; **sans blague**, you don't say! I don't believe it!; **sans cérémonie**, unceremoniously, without the usual ceremony or polite form; also *attrib.* suitable for unceremonious occasions; †**sans dener** [see DENIER[3]], a penniless person; **sans dire**, without saying anything, without mentioning (something specified); **sans doute**, doubtless, no doubt; **sans façon** = *sans cérémonie*; **sans-gêne** [*gêne* constraint], disregard of the ordinary forms of civility or politeness; **sans-pareil**, lit. not having its like, †(*a*) used subst. for a kind of perfume or smelling salts; (*b*) (as two words) unique, unequalled; hence **sans-pareilly** *a. nonce-wd.*, unexampled; **sans peur**, without fear, fearless, often in (or with allusion to) the phr. ***sans peur et sans reproche***, which was applied to the Chevalier de Bayard; **sans phrase** [after *la mort sans phrase*, the alleged words of Sieyes in giving his vote for the death of Louis XVI], without more words, without circumlocution, without exceptions or qualifications; **sans prendre** (see VOLE); †**sans-punie**, with impunity; **sans recours** (*Law*) [cf. RECOURSE *sb.*[1] 4 b], 'without recourse (to me)', an endorsement on a bill of exchange absolving the endorser or any other party from liability as such party; **sans reproche**, without reproach, blameless (see *sans peur* above); **sans souci**, lit. without care or concern; as *sb.*, unconcern; also, †a free-and-easy social gathering; hence **sans-souciant** *a. rare*, carefree, unworried; **sans-souci-ism**, unconcern.

1855 KINGSLEY *Westw. Ho!* II. xi. 299 He had followed in full faith such a *sans-appel as he held Frank to be. **1922** JOYCE *Ulysses* 398 A drenching of that violence, he tells me, **sans blague*, has sent more than one luckless fellow in good earnest posthaste to another world. **1967** *New Yorker* 25 Feb. 39/1 *Aristide*..I happen to be only forty-four. *Auto-coiffeur. Sans blague?* I would have put you at twice that age. **1645** EVELYN *Diary* 23 Feb., The burying-place for the common prostitutes, where they are put into the ground, *sans ceremonie. **1773** H. WALPOLE *Let. to Mann* 27 Apr., The Sheriffs of Middlesex, *sans cérémonie*, summoned Wilkes, instead of Luttrell. **1807** W. IRVING *Salmag.* (1811) I. 158 The honest old comfortable *sans-ceremonie* furniture is discarded. **1857** 'C. BEDE' *Verdant Green* III. ii, This evil ..obliged neighbours to be hospitable to each other, sans cérémonie. **1469** *Paston Lett.* II. 349 We pore *sanz deners of Castr have brook iij. or iiij. stelle bowys. **1881** TROLLOPE *Ayala's Angel* II. xxviii. 68 I ain't. You might as well let that accident pass, *sans dire. **1890** E. DOWSON *Let.* 17 June (1967) 154 **Sans doute* you know your way by this time. **1918** 'K. MANSFIELD' *Let.* 11 Jan. (1977) 90 A pimp getting *in* [a train] to hold a seat for some super-pimp gave me such a blow in the chest that it is blue today. I thought: 'This is Marseilles, *sans doute*.' **1672** W. PERWICH *Desp.* (Roy. Hist. Soc.) 224 His Maty replyed hee might doe it at that time **sans façon*. **1838** GRANVILLE *Spas Germ.* 257 The simple, quiet, and *sans façon* manner in which this daily intercourse ..took place. **1865** 'OUIDA' *Strathmore* II. xxiii. 305 His usual sans façon, good-humoured style. **1893** SALTUS *Sapphira* 87 With the **sans-gêne* of a married man, Nevius dropped in a chair. **1749** LADY LUXBOROUGH *Lett. to Shenstone* (1775) 167 Methinks I smell the **sans pareille* hither. **1753** J. COLLIER *Art of Tormenting* 55 Hastily take snuff, or smell to your sans-pareil. **1766** [ANSTEY] *Bath Guide* iii. 26 Eau de Chipre, Eau de Luce, Sans Pareil, and Citron Juice. **1962** *John o' London's* 20 Sept. 287/1 This conducted tour..must be quite *sans pareil* for..candour. **1818** KEATS *Wks.* (1889) III. p. cxxxi, An unpardonable offence, so **sans pareilly*. **1812** *Amer. St. Papers* For. Relat. (1832) III. 556 He told them that he had nothing to fear, that he was '**sans peur et sans reproche*'. **1827** DISRAELI *Viv. Grey* VII. xiii[x], The Knight, sans peur et sans reproche. **1847** BARHAM *Ingol. Leg.* Ser. III. *Blasphemer's Warning*, He had been *sans reproche*, as he still was *sans peur*. **1808** SCOTT *Let.* in *Lockhart* (1837) II. iv. 139, I hope you will remember how impatient I shall be to hear your opinion **sans phrase*. **1885** *Encycl. Brit.* XVIII. 793/2 This study gives us the science of empirical psychology, or, as it is now termed, psychology *sans phrase*. **1919** D. RUSSELL *Let.* Nov. in *Tamarisk Tree* (1975) v. 78, I got him to accept sans phrase for the moment. **1956** *Ann. Reg. 1955* 8 If they chose to expel him, he would become Independent *sans phrase*. **1961** J. WILSON *Reason & Morals* iii. 161 Thus we might say (almost *sans phrase*, as some early Christian authorities did) 'sex is bad'. **1976** *Times Lit. Suppl.* 26 Mar. 337/1 A. J. P. Taylor is the representative historian of our century... He is a historian *sans phrase*, not a man using history as the vehicle for other gifts. **1728** VANBR. & CIB. *Prov. Husb.* v. iii. 110 Laying down a *Vote*, **sans prendre*. **1731** FIELDING *Mod. Husb.* I. iv, If it had not been for a cursed Sans-prendrevole, that swept the whole table. **1609** [BP. W. BARLOW] *Answ. Nameless Cath.* 138 His Proclamations..must bee either calumniated, or *sans-punie transgressed. **1874** J. B. BYLES *Treat. Law Bills of Exchange* (ed. 11) v. 38 A safe and proper mode in which an agent may indorse, so as to avoid personal responsibility, is by adding the words, **sans recours* or *without recourse to me*. **1974** D. W. FIDDES *Business Terms, Phr. & Abbrev.* (ed. 14) 184 Sans recours is a phrase used in the endorsement of bills and notes. When an endorser wishes to free himself of responsibility, he adds the words *Sans Recours*, or *Without recourse to me*. **1847** **Sans reproche* [see *sans peur*]. **1858** TROLLOPE *Three Clerks* III. i. 23 His conduct had been *sans reproche*. **1781** H. WALPOLE *Lett.* (1858) VIII. 65 Mrs. Hobart did not invite me to her **sans souci* last week, though she had all my other juvenile contemporaries. **1797** *Encycl. Brit.* (ed. 3) VIII. 685/1 Their *tout ensemble* indicates health and delight, or at least an air of *sans souci*. **1826** W. SCOTT *Jrnl.* 10 Mar. (1972) 109, I have in my odd *sans souciant character a good handful of meal from the grist of the Jolly Miller who—once Dwelld on the river dee. **1837** *Tait's Mag.* IV. 390 Buoyant with youth, wine, *sans-souci-ism, and a holiday.

b. In jocular nonce-wds.: **sans-breech** = SANS-CULOTTID; **sans-potato**, an indigent Irishman.

1837 CARLYLE *Fr. Rev.* XVIII. iv, Our intercalary Days Sans-breeches. **1839** —— *Chartism* iv. (1840) 25 The Sanspotatoe is of the selfsame stuff as the superfinest Lord Lieutenant.

‖**sansa** ('sænsə). Also **sanse, zanza, zanze.** [Marungu (Bantu), ad. Arab. *ṣanj*, Pers. *sinj* cymbals.] An African musical instrument consisting of a wooden box having at the top tongues of bamboo or iron which the performer vibrates with his thumb and forefingers. Cf. *Kaffir piano*, MARIMBA.

1864 C. ENGEL *Music Most Anc. Nations* 14 Nos. 4, 5, and 6 show the notes of three *zanzes*. **1874** —— *Descr. Catal. Musical Instruments S. Kensington Museum* (ed. 2) 297 The *zanze*, or sansa, is to be found principally among the Negro tribes of upper and lower Guinea. **1876** STAINER & BARRETT *Dict. Mus. Terms., Zanze*... Known also by the names of mambira, ambira, marimba, ibeka, vissandschi, in different parts of Africa. **1909** *Cent. Dict.* Suppl., Sanse. **1929** *N. & Q. Anthropol.* (ed. 5) II. 299 The 'musical-box' is an elaborated mechanical analogue of the *sansa*. **1970** *Guardian* 24 Apr. 9/1 They improvise together on the xylophone, sansas (thumb pianos), guitar, or piano. **1975** S. MARCUSE *Mus. Instruments* (rev. ed.) 455/1 *Sansa*, linguaphone consisting of tuned metal or split-cane tongues fitted to a wooden board or resonator, so that one end of the lamellae can vibrate freely. *Sansa* is the name of the linguaphone among the Marungu people of the Congo; by extension it has come to be used in a generic sense for all similar instr[ument]s.

sansack, obs. form of SANJAK.

sans bell, obs. form of SANCTUS BELL.

sanscara, var. SAMSKARA.

Sanschrite, -screet, -scrita, obs. ff. SANSKRIT.

‖**sansculotte** (sænzkju:'lɒt, as Fr. sɑ̃kylɔt). [Fr., f. *sans* without (see SANS) + *culotte* knee-breeches: usually explained as one wearing trousers instead of knee-breeches; but the origin is disputed (see Littré Suppl.).]

1. In the French Revolution, a republican of the poorer classes in Paris. Hence *gen.* an extreme republican or revolutionary.

1790 *Hist. Eur.* in *Ann. Reg.* 13/2 The numerous army of ragged *Sans Culottes*. **1793** BURKE *On policy of Allies* Wks. 1802 IV. 104 A desperate set of obscure adventurers, who led to every mischief, a blind and bloody band of Sans-Culottes. **1794** *Gentl. Mag.* LXIV. 863 A *Sans-Culotte* approaching him [i.e. Robespierre] very coolly pronounced these words in his ears, *there exists a Supreme being*. **1794** LD. TORRINGTON *Diary* 5 May (1938) IV. 10 Nor do I hope to live to see the Sans Culottes of this land laying all distinction waste. **1902** R. W. CHAMBERS *Maids of Parad.* vii. 120 He was no crude Belleville orator; ..no *sans-culotte* with brains ablaze. **1927** G. B. SHAW *Gt. Composers* (1978) I. 18 Mozart was still to him the master of masters..but he was a court flunkey in breeches while Beethoven was a Sansculotte. **1940** [see DEFLATE *v.* 2 b]. **1955** *Times* 18 July 6/1 So it is the crowd of *sans autos*—the modern *sans-culottes?*—who are left to swarm over the streets, empty of all but the buses (each with its little crest of Tricolor flags for the occasion) and taxis, to celebrate with a certain fervour their annual rites. **1969** *N.Y. Rev. Bks.* 30 Jan. 8/1 The term plebs is convenient for the *sans-culottes* and similar movements made up mainly of small shopkeepers, artisans, journeymen; proletariat for factory workers.

attrib. **1796** BURKE *Let. to Noble Ld.* 65 The true sans-culotte criticks. **1812** J. BRADY *Clavis Calend.* I. 35 The *Sans Culotte* adherents of Robespierre. **1837** CARLYLE *Fr. Rev.* II. III. v, Sansculotte Scylla hardly weathered, here is Aristocrat Charybdis gurgling under his lee! **1906** B'NESS ORCZY *I Will Repay* xviii, The sansculotte mob of Paris.

2. *transf.* 'A man shabbily dressed; a tatterdemalion; a ragamuffin' (Worcester).

1812 *Sporting Mag.* XXXIX. 4 The Hampshire barber being no *sans culotte*, but in buff. **1815** SCOTT *Guy M.* xliv, Bertram..was dragged..across the threshold, amid the continued shouts of the little *sans culottes*.

sansculotted, *a. nonce-wd.* [f. prec. + -ED.] Unbreeched.

1801 W. FELTON *Carriages* 131 The head of the horse imitates much the head-dress of a French lady, while the posteriors are left sansculotted.

‖**sansculotterie** (sænzkju:'lɒtərɪ, as Fr. sɑ̃kylɔtri). Also anglicized **-ery**. [Fr., f. *sansculotte* (see above) + *-erie* -ERY.]

1. The principles, spirit or behaviour characteristic of sansculottes.

1794 tr. *Brissot to his Constituents* 99 Certain hypocritical chiefs who talk continually of *Sans Culotterie* whilst they are affecting an insolent luxury. **1814** COLERIDGE *Princ. Genial Crit.* iii, The Sans-culotterie of a contemptuous ignorance. **1831** *Blackw. Mag.* XXX. 817 The hoof of modern Sansculotterie..will trample on the bowers of Chatsworth. *a* **1834** COLERIDGE in *Lit. Rem.* (1839) IV. 231 Modern Unitarianism is..the *sans-culotterie* of religion.

2. Sansculottes collectively.

1796 BURKE *Let. to Noble Ld.* 72 The rabble rout of this Sans Culotterie of France. **1837** CARLYLE *Fr. Rev.* III. III. ii, What profit were it for the Paris Sansculottery to insult us?

sansculottic (sænzkju:'lɒtɪk), *a.* [f. SANSCULOTTE + -IC. Cf. *culottic*.]

1. Pertaining to the sansculottes or to sansculottism; revolutionary.

1822 C. BUTLER *Remin.* xv. 211 The reader probably remembers the *sans-culottic* exhibitions, equally ridiculous and disgusting, of the Goddess of Reason. **1837** CARLYLE *Fr. Rev.* II. v. i, Those Sansculottic violent Gardes Françaises, or Centre Grenadiers. **1903** *Q. Rev.* July 133 The rising storm of sansculottic frenzy.

2. *allusively.* Without breeches, unbreeched; hence, inadequately or improperly clothed.

1833 CARLYLE *Misc. Ess., Diderot* (1888) V. 54 He is utterly unclean, scandalous, shameless, sansculottic-samoeidic. **1871** KINGSLEY *At Last* iii, He would not have gone on ordinary days in a sansculottic state. He would have worn that most comfortable of loose nether garments.. slops. **1883** *Times* 13 Feb. 9 These poor wretches were denied clothes altogether, and..there is a sort of fitness in the accompaniment of bad language which they provided for their sansculottic Sunday.

sansculottid (sænzkju:'lɒtɪd). Also **-ide**. [a. F. *sansculottide*, f. *sansculotte* (see above).] One of the five (in leap-years six) complementary days added at the end of the month Fructidor of the Republican Calendar; *pl.*, the festivities held during these days. Also attrib. in *sansculottid days*.

1813 SOUTHEY in *Q. Rev.* X. 96 The festivals in their new Calendar were called Sans Culottides. **1877** MORLEY *Robespierre* in *Crit. Misc.* Ser. II. 93 If Greece..had its Olympian games, France too shall solemnize her sans-culottid days. **1904** *Daily Chron.* 19 July 4/7 Its five or six Sans-culottide days thrown in at the end of the year.

sansculottish (sænzkju:'lɒtɪʃ), *a.* [f. SANSCULOTTE + -ISH.] = SANSCULOTTIC.

1798 *Spirit Public Jrnls.* (1805) II. 286 Because the *sans-culottish* example of a crop administration would ruin all the hair-dressers in the three kingdoms. **1885** MORLEY in *Macm. Mag.* Feb. 254/2 You are just as *sans-culottish* and rash as I would have you.

sansculottism (sænzkju:'lɒtɪz(ə)m). [ad. F. *sansculottisme*, f. *sansculotte*: see above and -ISM.] The principles or practice of sansculottes.

1794 J. B. S. MORRITT *Let.* 22 May (1914) ii. 32 His enemies charge him with sansculottism. **1799** *Spirit Public Jrnls.* III. 148 Liberty, Equality, and Sansculottism. **1833** *Q. Rev.* XLIX. 42 The abolition of all distinctions of dress, language, condition, and refinement; in a word, the establishment of general *sans-culottism*. **1886** A. WEIR *Hist. Basis Mod. Europe* 572 The *sansculottism* of the early revolution.

So **sanscu'lottist**, one who favours sansculottism; also *attrib.* **sanscu'lottize** *v. trans.*, to make republican in character; *intr.*, to favour sansculottic or republican principles.

1798 *Anti-Jacobin* No. 32. 254/2 The *Citizen Imitator* seems to have Sans-culottized the Original. **1831** SIR C. WETHERELL in *Hansard's Parl. Deb.* Ser. III. IV. 862 The sans-culottizing principles of the French Revolution. **1831** A. W. FONBLANQUE *Eng. under 7 Administr.* II. 103 [Sir C. Wetherell] is..full of fears lest the Bill should loosen the braces of the Constitution, and..'*sansculottise*' it... He should be the last person in the world to talk of *sansculottising* with such horror. **1831** CARLYLE *Sart. Res.* I. ix, Teufelsdröckh, though a Sansculottist, is no Adamite. **1878** SEELEY *Stein* III. 404 The vain sansculottist scribblers.

sansei ('sænseɪ). [Jap., f. *san* three, third + *sei* generation.] An American born of nisei parents (see NISEI); a third-generation Japanese American.

1945 in WEBSTER Add. **1950** *Amer. Speech* XXV. 242 Further distinctions lie in other colloquialisms such as *sansei* ('third generation'), the few descendants of *nisei*. **1971** *Newsweek* 19 Apr. 108/1 Aoki says bluntly that nisei and sansei (second and third generation) are too educated and don't work hard enough. **1975** *Time* (Canad. ed.) 20 Oct. 39/1 Carl Takamura, a young sansei (third generation) state legislator.

sanserif (sæn'serɪf). *Typog.* Also **sans serif, sansserif(f, -surryph, -ceriph.** [Prob. f. SANS *prep.* + SERIF (q.v.).

The word *serif*, however, has not hitherto been found till much later than the first appearance of *sanserif*, and it has been suggested that it may have been evolved from the supposed compound.]

A form of type without serifs: called also *grotesque*. Also *attrib.* Cf. CERIPH.

1830 *Figgins's Spec. Printing Types*, 8 Lines Pica San-Serif. **1832** *Blake & Stephenson's Spec. Printing Types*, Ten Lines Sans-Surryphs. **1879** *Print. Trades Jrnl.* XXVI. 23 Calendars, occupying half the space set in sans-serif figures looking twice as bold. **1888** *Encycl. Brit.* XXIII. 699/1 Sanserifs or grotesques, which have no serifs, as **M.** **1903** *N. & Q.* 23 May 418 His initials G. M., written in sanserif characters. **1961** *Guardian* 17 June 14/6, I saw a..truck bearing in white sans serif capitals the name Fay Improvement Company. **1970** *Brit. Printer* July 77/2 Bold sans serifs have remained popular on posters up to the present day. **1976** *Visible Language* X. 88 Sans serif, to him, was the best, if not the only kind of type suitable for the modern world.

sansevieria (sænsɪ'vɪərɪə). Also **sanseveria, sanseviera.** [mod.L. (C. P. Thunberg *Prodromus Plantarum Capensium* (1794) I. 65), f. the title of Raimond de Sansgrio, Prince of Sanseviero (1710–71) + -IA[1].] A herbaceous perennial of the genus so called, belonging to the family Liliaceæ, native to tropical Africa or south-eastern Asia, and bearing racemes of white or greenish flowers and rosettes of stiff, erect, variegated leaves yielding a strong white fibre; also called bowstring hemp. Also *attrib.*

1804 *Curtis's Bot. Mag.* XIX. 739 (*heading*) Chinese Sanseviera. **1851** *Illustr. Catal. Gt. Exhib.* IV. 882/2 Liliaceous plants, such as..the Sanseviera, the pine-apple, and even the plantain. **1899** F. V. KIRBY *Sport E. Central Afr.* xxiv. 268 Quantities of the sansevieria plants..yield a valuable fibre. **1955** *Sci. News Let.* 2 Apr. 213/2 Kenaf is seen as a substitute for jute, sanseveria for manila hemp. **1959** J. D. CLARK *Prehist. S. Afr.* ix. 248 The knife or scraper used by the Hukwe Bushmen in Northern Rhodesia for shredding *sansevieria* leaves to obtain fibre for rope and string is also made of wood. **1961** [see MOTHER-IN-LAW 4]. **1976** *Hortus Third* (L. H. Bailey Hortorium) 1002/2 Sansevierias are commonly grown as durable porch and house plants.

†**sans fail.** *Obs.* Forms: α. 3–5 **saun**, 4–5 **san**, 5 **sain, saing, sawm, sawn**, 5–6 **sam**; β. 4 **sauntz**, 4–5 **sauns, sans**, 4–6 **saunz, sans**, 5 **saunce**; 3–6 **faile**, 4 **feil**, 4–5 **fayle, faille**, 4–6 **fayl, fail**, 5 **fayll, faill**, 6 **fale**. [a. OF. *sansfail(l) e*: see SANS and FAIL *sb.*[2]] Without fail; without doubt, doubtless; in ME., a common riming tag.

α. **1297** R. GLOUC. (Rolls) 8360 Go & seie hom þis þat hii turne aȝen to me & icholle to hom saun faile [*v.rr.* samfayle, san fail(l)e, sawmfaile]. **13..** *K. Alis.* 217 Of hire faired, saun faile, He hadde in hert gret mervaile. ? *a* **1400** *Arthur* 439 þe Muchelnesse of Men sainfayle Ys nat victorie in Batayle. **14..** *Sir Beues* 4021 (MS. M.) All oure londis Hathe the kynge arested, samffayll, Thorouȝe Brians counsell of Cornwayll. *c* **1475** *Partenay* 1592 [He] both his penon And baner sanfaill Put within the town, so making conqueste.

β. *c* **1325** *Chron. Eng.* 285 in Ritson *Metr. Rom.* II. 282 Ant Luces the emperour, sauntz fayle, He overcom in bataille. *c* **1380** *Sir Ferumb.* 2350 'It is now', quaþ he, 'sanzfaile to late þer-to to gon'. *c* **1384** CHAUCER *H. Fame* I. 188 (Fairf.) And seyde he most vnto Itayle As was hys destanye sauns faille. **1421–2** HOCCLEVE *Dial.* 461, I feele now, sanz faille, That in this cas yee can nat wel consaill. *c* **1450** *Merlin* 91 Antor ansuerde, 'This is the childe that the kynge me praide to norisshe of my wif'... And he seide, 'It is the same saunz-faile'. **1513** DOUGLAS *Æneis* I. vi. 61 ȝe bene in the marchis of Libie, sans fail, Inhabeit with peple vndowtable in battail. *c* **1530** *Crt. of Love* 117 Under the cloth of their estate, saunz faile [*rime* availe], The king and quene ther sat.

¶ Misused as if = 'sans avail'.

1597 *Guistard & Sismond* II. C 4 b, But all his excuse was euin samfayll.

Sansi ('sɑːnsɪ). Also **Sansiya, Sansya**. [Origin uncertain (see quot. 1896).] A low-status caste group of the Punjab, India; a member of this group. Also *attrib.*

1882 E. J. GUNTHORPE *Notes on Criminal Tribes* xiii. 78 Kunjurs are..a branch of the great family of Sansya robbers, who claim their descent from Sainsmull. **1883** D. C. J. IBBETSON *Outl. Panjáb Ethnogr.* vi. 311 The thieving Sánsis are said to admit any caste to their fraternity except the Dhedhs and Mhangs; and the man so admitted becomes ..a Sánsi. **1896** W. CROOKE *Tribes & Castes North-Western Provinces & Oudh* IV. 277 Sânsiya. A vagrant thieving tribe... Of their name no satisfactory account has been given. Some derive it from the Sanskrit *svâsa*, 'breathing', or *srasta*, 'separated', others with *svagâ nika*, 'one who has to do with dogs', or *svapâka*, 'dog-cooking', a person of a degraded and outcaste tribe, who, by the older law, was required to live outside towns, to eat his food in broken vessels, to wear the clothes of the dead, and to be excluded from all intercourse with other people... The Sânsiya is no doubt the near kinsman of the other degraded wandering races who occupy the same part of the country, such as the Kanjar. **1901** KIPLING *Kim* iv. 86 They meet a troop of long-haired, strong-scented Sansis, with baskets of lizards and other unclean food... The Sansi is deep pollution. **1931** E. A. H. BLUNT *Caste System N. India* ix. 149 The Beriya, Bhantu, Habura, Karwal, and Sansiya..may be regarded as offshoots of a single nomadic race. **1972** S. R. SHARMA in F. Singh *Hist. Punjab* III. xvi. 366 Prostitution had come to be associated with certain castes—Kanjai, Bangali, Sansi and Pema.

sansiak, obs. form of SANJAK.

sansing bell: see SAUNCING BELL.

sanskara, var. SAMSKARA.

Sanskrit, Sanscrit ('sænskrɪt), *sb.* and *a.* Forms: 7 (Samescretan), Sanscreet, 8 Shanscrit(t)a, -krit, -chrite, -creet, -kreet, Sansskirrit, Samscred, Hanscrit, 8–9 Shan-, Sham-, Sanscrit, 9 Sung-, Sangskrit, 8– Sanskrit. [ad. Skr. *saṃskṛta* (neut. *saṃskṛtam*) put together, well-formed, highly wrought, perfected, f. *sam-* together (related to *sama*: see SAME *a.*) + *kṛ* to make, do, perform. Cf. F. *Sanscrit*.

The 18th c. form *Hanscrit*, which occurs also in Fr. at the same period, has not been satisfactorily explained.]

A. *sb.* The ancient and sacred language of India, the oldest known member of the Indo-European family, in which the extensive Hindu literature from the Vedas downward is composed. In a narrower sense, the 'classical Sanskrit' (opposed to the 'Epic' and 'Vedic'), the grammar of which was fixed by Pāṇini (? 4th c. B.C.).

1617 PURCHAS *Pilgrimage* v. xi. 636 The Iesuites conceiue that these Bramenes are of the dispersion of the Israelites, and their bookes (called *Samescretan*) doe somewhat agree with the Scriptures. **1696** OVINGTON *Voy. Surat* 248 It is the Learned Language among them [*sc.* the Bramins], called the *Sanscreet*. **1760** J. H. GROSE *Voy. E. Indies* I. 202 (Y.) They have a learned language peculiar to themselves, called the Hanscrit. **1770** *Phil. Trans.* LX. 448 Their language is the Nagri..more ancient than even the Shanscritta. **1785** C. WILKINS (*title*) The Bhăgvăt-Gēētā,..translated from the original, in the Sănskrēēt, or ancient language of the Brāhmăns. **1797** *Encycl. Brit.* (ed. 3) VIII. 518/2 The language called *Shanscrit* or *Sanscrit*. **1801** H. LEBEDEFF *Gramm. E. Ind. Dial.* Pref. p. ix, The alphabetical characters of the Shamscrit. **1841** ELPHINSTONE *Hist. Ind.* I. III. v. 277 There are, in Shanscrit, treatises on rhetoric and composition. **1876** WHITNEY *Lang. & Study* vi. 225 We possess it in two some-what varying forms, the classical Sanskrit, and the older idiom of the so-called Vedas.

¶ In corrupt form **Sanscript** used for 'Sanskrit writings'.

1698 FRYER *Acc. E. India & P.* 161 Who founded these, their Annals nor their *Sanscript* deliver not.

b. *attrib.* and *Comb.*

1794 [MATHIAS] *Purs. Lit.* (ed. 6) 286 With Jones, a linguist, Sanskrit, Greek, or Manks. **1831** B. E. P[OTE] *Assassins of Parad.* 98 Explained by a Shanscrit Authority. **1841** *Penny Cycl.* XX. 404/1 A. W. von Schlegel and Lassen have founded in Bonn a Sanscrit school. **1844** H. H. WILSON *Brit. India* II. 578 The institution of a Sanscrit college in Calcutta for the tuition of Brahmans. **1874** L. J. TROTTER *Hist. India* I. iii. 25 Sanskrit-speaking Hindus.

B. *adj.* Of, belonging to, or written in Sanskrit.

1773 *Gentl. Mag.* XLIII. 498 The loss of the Sans-skirrit language, and the confinement of it to the priesthood. **1798** *Phil. Trans.* LXXXVIII. 582 The Sanscrita words are spelt according to the method practised by Sir William Jones. **1800** *Asiat. Ann. Reg.* V. 44/1 The Samscred language. **1804** W. CAREY *Gram. Skr. Lang.* 35 There are six Declensions of Sungskrit Nouns. **1842** PRICHARD *Nat. Hist. Man* 164 They retain very few vestiges of their Indian original, except their Sanskrit speech. **1876** WHITNEY *Lang. & Study* vi. 225 The Prakrit dialects are chiefly preserved in the Sanskrit dramas.

Sanskritic (sæn'skrɪtɪk), *a.* Also **-critic**. [f. SANSKRIT + -IC. Cf. F. *sanscritique*, mod.L. *Samscriticus*.] Relating to, derived from, based on, or resembling Sanskrit; using the Sanskrit language.

1848 MAX MÜLLER in *Rep. Brit. Assoc. Adv. Sci. 1847* XVII. 336 There is still another more Sanscritic termination in *e*, for the locative of words ending in a consonant or the vowel *a*. **1853** —— *Chips* (1880) I. iii. 79 A form [of word] peculiarly Sanskritic. **1883** *Athenæum* 21 July 85 The Sanskritic vernaculars of Northern India. **1889** I. TAYLOR *Orig. Aryans* vi. 305 The very foundations of the Sanskritic school of interpretation.

Sanskritist ('sænskrɪtɪst). Also **Sanscritist**. [f. SANSKRIT + -IST. Cf. F. *sanscritiste*.] A person versed in the Sanskrit language or writings. Also, one who bases a mythological theory upon Sanskrit myths. Also *attrib.*

1853 W. D. WHITNEY in *Jrnl. Amer. Oriental Soc.* III. 292 This little work..gave perhaps the most powerful impulse to that movement which has since carried all Sanskritists irresistibly to the study of the Vedas. **1864** T. H. KEY in *Reader* 4 June 717/1, I have thus endeavoured to show, in defiance of the Sanskritists, that the first person of this pronoun derives its nominative from the same base as its other cases. **1884** MAX MÜLLER in *Athenæum* 11 Oct. 462/3 The first place among Sanscritists, both dead and living. **1889** I. TAYLOR *Orig. Aryans* vi. 316 Mannhardt, after having been a disciple of the Sanskritist school, has been obliged to confess that comparative mythology has not borne the fruit that was at one time expected. *Ibid.* 317 The case of the Sanskritists rests on these four Indian names, Bhaga, Parjanya, Varuna, and Dyaus.

Sanskritize ('sænskrɪtaɪz), *v.* [f. SANSKRIT + -IZE.] **a.** *trans.* To translate into Sanskrit; to reduce to a Sanskrit form; to introduce Sanskrit elements into.

1881 *Academy* 1 Oct. 251/2 That prince's foreign name would never have been Sanskritised in such a form in the seventeenth century. **1887** MAX MÜLLER *Sci. Thought* vii. 344 *note*, Mistakes in sanskritising vulgar, apabhramsa, and Paisâki words.

b. *trans.* To adapt to the beliefs or practices of a high Hindu caste.

1952 M. N. SRINIVAS *Relig. & Society among Coorgs of S. India* ii. 38 Some Coorg families are more Sanskritized than their neighbours.

Hence **Sanskriti'zation**.

1884 KERN tr. *Saddharma-Pundarîka* Introd. p. xi *note*[2], An erroneous Sanskritisation of the present tense dakkhanti. **1952** M. N. SRINIVAS *Relig. & Society among Coorgs of S. India* ii. 30 A low caste was able..to rise to a higher position in the hierarchy by adopting vegetarianism and teetotalism, and by Sanskritizing its ritual and pantheon. In short, it took over, as far as possible, the customs, rites, and beliefs of the Brahmins... This process has been called 'Sanskritization' in this book, in preference to 'Brahminization', as certain Vēdic rites are confined to Brahmins and the two other 'twice-born' castes. **1964** *Diogenes* XLV. 99 (*heading*) Sanskritization and cultural mobility. **1974** tr. *Wertheim's Evolution & Revolution* iii. 240 Even if a sub-group within a caste..achieved a certain measure of prosperity and aiming at a higher status through 'sanskritization', has constituted itself as a separate sub-caste, [etc.].

sans nombre, † sans number. Now only *Her.* Also 6 **saunce**, 7 **sance**. [a. F. *sans nombre*: see SANS and NUMBER *sb.*] Innumerable. Also occas. as adv.: innumerably, infinitely.

1550 J. COKE *Eng. & Fr. Heralds* (1877) 85, vi. thousande lordes, knyghtes, and esquiers, and of the commons, sans nombre. *c* **1557** ABP. PARKER *Ps.* 104 Theare liuing things saunce number creepe. **1627** W. SCLATER *Exp. 2 Thess.* (1629) 146 Locusts sans number and monstrous. **1655** FULLER *Ch. Hist.* IV. 155 Any Author of a Book may multiply them [*sc.* Patrons] Sance-number. **1688** SHADWELL *Sqr. Alsatia* v. i. 60 We'll swinge these Rogues with Indictments for a Riot, and with Actions *Sans Nombre*. **1868** CUSSANS *Her.* viii. 119 *Semé, Aspersed, Gerated, Sans Nombre*, and *Powdered*: These terms are used to signify that a Shield or Charge is covered with an indefinite number of minor Charges promiscuously scattered over the surface. *Powdered, Gerated, Sans Nombre*, and *Aspersed*, however, commonly imply that the Charges are to be smaller, and more thickly distributed than *Semé*.

† sans-peer, saunce-pere. *Obs.* Forms: see SANS and PEER *sb.* As *adj. phr.*: Without equal, peerless. Also occas. *advb.*: As one that has no equal. Often used as a proper name or surname; hence *sb.*, a person who has no equal.

a **1400** *Pistill of Susan* 33 (MS. I) Prestes hye of priuylage were praysed saune pere. **1426** LYDG. *De Guil. Pilgr.* 14087, I wolde be holden ay sanz per, And by my syluen synguler. *c* **1460** *Pol. Rel. & L. Poems* 291/19 Lady saunzpere. *a* **1529** SKELTON *Bouge of Court* 51 The owner therof is lady of estate, Whoos name to tell is dame Saunce-pere. **1576** N. R. in Gascoigne *Steele Gl.* To Author (Arb.) 46 In Elegies, and wanton loue writ laies Sance peere were Naso, and Tibullus deemde. **1600** W. WATSON *Decacordon* (1602) 8 The Iesuits being men holden of all,..to be sance peres of the Christian globe. *Ibid.* 16 All..right Alchumists, that is, sance peeres in all things.

sans-seriff, variant of SANSERIF.

Sansya, var. SANSI.

sant, variant of CENT[2].

1591 GREENE *Notable Disc. Coosenage* (1592) B 2 b. **1596** LODGE *Wits Miserie* 41.

sant, obs. var. SAINT and SANCTUS (senses 2, 3).

‖**'santa**. *Obs. rare*$^{-1}$. A female saint.

App. ad. L. *sancta*, with assimilation to SAINT.

a **1450** *Knt. de la Tour* (1906) 5 For-yete not..to recomaunde you to the seintes and santas.

Santa Ana ('sæntə 'ænə). *U.S.* Also **Santa Anna, Santana** (sæn'tænə). [Sp., = Saint Anne.] A hot, dry, föhn-type wind of desert origin, freq. strong and dust-laden, which blows on the coastal plain of southern California after being channelled and heated adiabatically during its descent of the Santa Ana Mountains. Also ***Santa Ana wind***.

The suggestion made in some dicts. that this is named after Antonio Lopez de *Santa Anna* (?1795–1876), Mexican revolutionary leader and president, seems without foundation.

1887 *Ann. Meteorol. Rev. Calif. 1886* (Calif. State Agric. Soc.) 128 Another health-giving, but extremely disagreeable wind, is the 'Santa Ana', or 'norther'. *Ibid.*, The 'Santa And' wind receives its name, because it frequently issues from the Santa Ana Pass. **1889** G. DAVIDSON *Pacific Coast: Coast Pilot of Calif.* (U.S. Coast & Geodetic Survey) (ed. 4) 40 In November, 1888, when the Santa Ana wind had passed its greatest strength, a reverse current of wind was drawing along the shore from Anaheim Landing towards Newport Bay. **1915** *Nature & Sci. Pacific Coast* (Amer. Assoc. Adv. Sci.: Pacific Coast Comm.) 22 Known locally as Santa Anas, these wind storms constitute the most disagreeable feature of the weather in the great valley of the south. **1931** A. A. MILLER *Climatol.* viii. 150 The Santa Annas of southern California and the Northers of the Sacramento Valley are hot, dry winds. **1941** B. SCHULBERG *What makes Sammy Run?* iv. 56 The music came at us like a Santa Ana wind. **1970** KOENIG & DIXON *Children are Watching* xxi. 181 Out in the sunset the Santana scoured the beach and hurled fine sand with enough force that hands cupped protectively over eyes. **1972** C. WESTON *Poor, Poor Ophelia* xi. 58 Santa Ana wind, he thought. No fog tomorrow, desert heat instead. **1973** R. HAYES *Hungarian Game* xlii. 248 A Santa Ana, that dry desert wind, blew away the smog.

Santa Claus ('sæntə 'klɔːz). Orig. *U.S.* Also 9 **Santiclaus**; *dial.* and *colloq.* **Santy**. [a. Du. dial. *Sante Klaas* (Du. *Sint Klaas*), Saint Nicholas: see NICHOLAS.] **a.** In nursery language, the name of an imaginary personage, who is supposed, in the night before Christmas day, to bring presents for children, a stocking being hung up to receive his gifts. Also, a person wearing a red cloak or suit and a white beard, to simulate the supposed Santa Claus to children, esp. in shops or on shopping streets. Also *transf.*, *fig.*, *attrib.*, and *ellipt.* as ***Santa***.

Now virtually synonymous with *Father Christmas*.

1773 *N.Y. Gaz.* 26 Dec. 3/1 Last Monday the Anniversary of St. Nicholas, otherwise called St. A Claus, was celebrated at Protestant-Hall. **1808** *Salmagundi* 25 Jan. 407 The noted St. Nicholas, vulgarly called Santaclaus—of all the saints in the kalendar the most venerated by true hollanders, and their unsophisticated descendants. **1821** *Weekly Visitor* IV. 262/1 For time immemorial the Dutch had a tradition, that there existed a being of no *earthly birth*, who was called *Santa Claus*. **1828** LONGF. in *Life* (1891) I. 152 Gew-gaws for the *Bifana*, who acts here the same comedy for children that Santiclaus does in America. **1850** SUSAN WARNER *Wide Wide World* xxviii, I used to think that Santa Claus came down the chimney. **1863** MISS YONGE *Chr. Names* I. 213 The Dutch element in New England has introduced Santa Klaus to many a young American who knows nothing of St. Nicholas or of any saint's day. **1872** BRET HARTE (*title*) How Santa Claus came to Simpson's Bar. **1886** P. STAPLETON *Major's Christmas* 201 Papas and mammas..planned the Santa Claus performance which was to come when the inquisitive eyes were closed in slumber. **1909** *Chicago Daily News* 10 Aug. 8/3 Uncle Sam is by no means an impartial Santa Claus. **1913** *Sat. Even. Post* 6 Dec. 50/1 If you want to act the part of Santa this Christmas. **1925** T. DREISER *Amer. Trag.* (1926) I. II. xxix. 356, I know something Santy has brought my Dad that he'll like. **1932** J. BEAMES *Gateway* vi. 108 You're just as kiddish as what you was when you'd be up at three in the mornin' to see what Santy had brung you. **1934** *Amer. Mercury* May 5/2 The Santa Claus theory of relief may be appropriate to a genuine emergency like an earthquake or a big fire. **1943** K. TENNANT *Ride on Stranger* iii. 24 Come on down, Ma. Come and see what Santa's brought you. **1956** H. GOLD *Man who was not with It* (1965) xxxii. 310 It was practically Christmas, too, with all the Santy Clauses peddling in the streets. **1957** [see GOOD-TIME *a.*]. **1973** 'D. HALLIDAY' *Dolly & Starry Bird* i. 2 The Zodiac Trust is the Santa Claus of worldwide astronomy. A private foundation richly funded .., it makes grants to struggling centres. **1975** *Times* 10 Dec. 4/4 Being a man was a genuine occupational qualification for a Santa Claus. **1976** M. MACHLIN *Pipeline* ix. 103 A huge, heavy-set man,..with a bushy unkempt Santa Claus beard, walked unsteadily toward their table. **1976** *Scotsman* 24 Dec. (Weekend Suppl.) 1/1 Stop rakin', Rikki. Santy says ye've had enough. **1976** *Scottish Daily Express* 27 Dec. 2/8 She was one of nine women charged with prostitution in Dallas, Texas, for propositioning Vice Squad officers disguised as Santas. **1977** *Times* 24 Dec. 16/5 Santa must have been updated over the years. Presumably girls hang out their tights now, instead of a solitary stocking.

b. (*collect. sing.*) Christmas presents; Christmas delicacies. *U.S. dial.*

1929 W. FAULKNER *Sound & Fury* 107 Buy yourself some Santy Claus. **1939** *These are our Lives* (Federal Writers' Project, U.S.) 22 One Christmas we ask him for fifty dollars for some clothes and a little Santy Claus for the chil'en.

Santa Gertrudis ('sæntə gə'truːdɪs). The name of the Santa Gertrudis division of the King Ranch, Kingsville, Texas, used to designate a breed of large red-coated beef cattle suitable for hot climates, developed there between 1910 and 1940 by crossing Brahmans and Shorthorns; an animal of this breed. Also *attrib.*

c **1946** R. J. KLEBERG *Santa Gertrudis Breed of Beef Cattle* 8 The bull on the ranch known as 'Monkey'.. marks the real beginning of the improved breed of Santa Gertrudis cattle. *Ibid.* 11 Santa Gertrudis calves at eight months of age will average over 500 pounds. **1949** *Jrnl. Heredity* XL. 115/1 One of the most noteworthy contributions to livestock breeding has been the creation and development of the Santa Gertrudis breed of beef cattle. **1955** *Times* 16 July 11/5 The Zebu and Santa Gertrudis breeds are suitable in country where grasses lack nutriment for a great part of the year. **1960** *Times* 1 Oct. 7/7 A remarkable artificial insemination programme [in Queensland].. aims to transform a herd of 30,000 Shorthorn cattle into one of 70,000 high grade Santa Gertrudis. **1962** *Listener* 6 Dec. 956/1 Mr Joyce had introduced Santa Gertrudis cattle from Texas. **1978** J. B. FRIEND *Cattle of World* 148/2 The Santa Gertrudis today carry approximately ⅝ Shorthorn blood and ⅜ Brahman blood.

santal[1] ('sæntəl). [a. F. *santal* (16th c.), ad. med.L. *santal-um*, a. Gr. σάνταλον: see SANDAL *sb.*[2]]

1. Sandalwood. Also ***santal-wood.***

1727-41 CHAMBERS *Cycl.* s.v. *Santalum*, There are santals of three different colours; citrine, white, and red. **1797** *Encycl. Brit.* (ed. 3) VI. 214/2 The santal or saunders is a hard wood imported from the Indies. **1883** MARTINDALE & BENNETT *Extra Pharmacopœia* 194 Capsules of Santal Oil are prepared. **1899** *Allbutt's Syst. Med.* VIII. 932 Oil of santal wood very rarely causes even a slight erythema.

2. *Chem.* A substance ($C_8H_6O_3$) obtained from sandalwood.

1894 in MUIR & MORLEY *Watts' Dict. Chem.* IV. 427.

Santal[2] ('sæntæl). Also **Santhal**, **Sonthal**. [Native name.] A Kolarian people of north-eastern India; a member of this people. Also, the language of this people (see SANTALI *sb.* and *a.*). Also *attrib.*

1852 J. PHILLIPS *Introd. Sántál Lang.* i. 1 *The Sántál*, having been hitherto an unwritten language, has.. no characters of its own. *Ibid.* 3 Pronouns in Sántál, are.. completely interwoven with the declension of nouns. **1866** [see MUNDA *sb.* and *a.*]. **1873** L. O. SKREFSUD *Gram. Santhal Lang.* p. iii, Santhali is the language spoken by a people called by foreigners the Santhals or Santals, inhabiting the western frontier of Lower Bengal. *Ibid.* i. 8 *Semi-consonants.* k', ch', t', p'. The sounds, which these letters represent, are peculiar to the Santal language... The 'Schnalz-laute' (click-sounds) mentioned by Dr. Lepsius, as existing in some of the African languages, appear to have some similarity to these Santal jerks. **1891** MONIER WILLIAMS *Brahmanism & Hinduism* (ed. 4) xxii. 578 We came to what appeared to be a good typical example of a Santal village-community. **1891** KIPLING *City of Dreadful Night* 85 We have any amount of Sonthals besides Mahomedans and Hindus of every possible caste. **1936** *Times Lit. Suppl.* 3 Oct. 788/4 The pictures of Sonthal life are evidently based on personal and intimate knowledge. **1941** J. H. HUTTON in L. O'Malley *Mod. India & West* xii. 422 The ignorance and honesty of the Santal enabled the first adventurous traders from the plains to make rapid fortunes out of the hill-men. **1969** *Illustr. Weekly of India* 27 July 29/1 Santal women do not wear much jewellery. **1971** *Ibid.* 25 Apr. 42/2 (*caption*) Resettled Santhals in the Malkanagiri zone of Dandakaranya Project. The Santhals are also found in the border districts of West Bengal. **1974** W. G. ARCHER *Hill of Flutes* i. 19 Flanked by rows of tall palmyra palms, Santal villages have an air of genial comfort. *Ibid.* 24 Within this neat and ordered setting most Santals lead calm and happy lives.

santalaceous (sæntə'leɪʃəs), *a.* [-ACEOUS.] Belonging to the N.O. *Santalaceæ*, typified by the genus *Santalum* or sandalwood.

1845 G. DON in *Encycl. Metrop.* VI. 179*/1.

santalate ('sæntələt). *Chem.* [Formed as SANTALIN + -ATE.] A salt of santalic acid.

1849 *Chem. Gaz.* VII. 132 Santalate of baryta and lime.

Santali (sæn'tɑːlɪ), *sb.* and *a.* Also 9 **Santalee**; Santhali, Sonthali. [f. SANTAL[2] + adj. suff. *-i.*] **A.** *sb.* The Munda language of the Santals. **B.** *adj.* Of or pertaining to the Santals or their language.

1873 [see SANTAL[2]]. *c* **1875-9** E. L. BRANDRETH *On Non-Aryan Lang. India* 7 The Santali verb.. has twenty-three tenses. **1891** KIPLING *City of Dreadful Night* 96 Sonthali.. is more elaborate than Greek. **1927** *Other Lands* July 138/2 At one house I was presented with a burnt arm to examine, and having no Santali with which to explain that I was not a doctor, the only thing to do was to look at it carefully and express, by nods and smiles, great satisfaction at the state of its progress. **1961** WEBSTER, Santhali. **1969** [see MADAL]. **1974** *Times* 18 Apr. 16/6 Elmhirst took his first group of students into the Moslem, Hindu and Santali villages of the district early in 1922. **1974** W. G. ARCHER *Hill of Flutes* 343 The Santali Language. According to Grierson's Linguistic Survey, Santali is an Austro-Asiatic Language.

santalic (sæn'tælɪk), *a. Chem.* [Formed as next + -IC.] ***santalic acid***: †**a.** An acid said to have been found in 1849 by Leo Meier in white sandalwood (*obs.*); **b.** = SANTALIN.

1849 *Chem. Gaz.* VII. 131 Santalic acid. **1876** HARLEY *Mat. Med.* (ed. 6) 646 A resinous ruby-coloured crystalline substance called santalin or santalic acid.

santalin ('sæntəlɪn). *Chem.* Also -ine. [a. F. *santaline*, f. mod.L. *santal-um* (see SANDAL *sb.*[2] and -IN).] The colouring principle of red sanders.

1833 *Lond. & Edin. Philos. Mag.* III. 312 Santaline. **1838** T. THOMSON *Chem. Org. Bodies* 410 Santalin. *Ibid.*, The colouring matter which it [*sc.* red sanders] contains was examined by Pelletier in 1814, who distinguished it by the name of *santalin.* **1839** URE *Dict. Arts* 1092 Santaline.

santalol ('sæntəlɒl). *Chem.* [f. SANTAL + -OL.] Either of two isomeric terpenoid alcohols, $C_{15}H_{24}O$ (known respectively as α- and *β-santalol*), which are fragrant liquids found in sandalwood oil.

1895 *Pharm. Jrnl.* I. 118/1 Chapoteaut, after a very careful study of the oil, announced some time ago that it consisted almost entirely of two bodies, $C_{15}H_{26}O$ [*sic*], an alcohol termed santalol, and $C_{15}H_{24}O$, probably the corresponding aldehyde. **1935** *Jrnl. Chem. Soc.* 312 Tautomerism is observed also in the two santalols themselves, since they yield on ozonolysis both formaldehyde and acetylcarbinol. **1966** *McGraw-Hill Encycl. Sci. & Technol.* XIII. 497/2 Santalol occurs in sandalwood oil and is used in perfumery. **1976** *Nature* 5 Aug. 487/2 The essential oils D-bornyl acetate, α- and β-santalol and several plant sesquiterpene hydrocarbons have been shown to induce sexual excitement in male American cockroaches.

Santa Lucia ('sæntə luː'tʃiːə). The name of a range of mountains in south-western California, used *attrib.* in **Santa Lucia fir** to designate the bristlecone fir, *Abies bracteata*, which is native to the region.

1905 *Occasional Papers Calif. Acad. Sci.* IX. 7 Santa Lucia Fir is found in only a few cañons of the Santa Lucia Mountains in Monterey County. **1948** *Sierra Club Bull.* (San Francisco) Mar. 137 Among these were the Santa Lucia fir.. and hosts of others. **1965** *Listener* 20 May 742/3 You mentioned a Santa Lucia fir just now, and you were saying that in its original habitat it is sadly depleted. **1977** *Daily Colonist* (Victoria, B.C.) 7 Aug. 1/1 The Marble Cone fire has destroyed two-thirds of the Ventana Wilderness Area, home of the Santa Lucia fir which grows nowhere else.

‖**Santa Maria** ('santa ma'ria). [Sp. = Saint Mary.] The calaba-tree, *Calophyllum Calaba*, of tropical America, and its timber.

1696 SLOANE *Catal. Plant. Jamaica* 180 Bastard Mammee Tree or Santa Maria. **1756** P. BROWNE *Jamaica* 372 The Santa Maria.. is reckoned pretty good timber-wood. **1827** O. W. ROBERTS *Voy. Centr. Amer.* 178 Very stout timbers of the wild calabash, bally or Santamaria Wood. **1894** *Outing* (U.S.) XXIII. 353/2 Strong posts of indestructible santa maria.

†**santar.** *Thieves' slang. Obs.* (See quot.)

1591 GREENE *2nd Pt. Conny-catching* (1592) Table, In lifting Law. He that first stealeth, the lift. He that receiues it, the Markar. He that standeth without and caries it away, the Santar.

san-tchoo, variant of SAMSHOO.

sante, santer, obs. forms of SAINT, SAUNTER.

‖**santé** (sɑ̃te), *int.* Also in anglicized form **santy** ('sæntɪ). [Fr., lit. 'health'.] An exclamation used as a salutation before drinking. Cf. HEALTH *sb.* 6.

1903 KIPLING *Traffics & Discoveries* (1904) 43 Here's santy to us all! **1952** P. FRANKAU *Wreath for Enemy* I. 18 She cried, '*Santé, santé*' raising her glass to each of us. **1966** J. FOWLES *Magus* iv. 21 She had poured herself a whisky. '*Santé.*' **1975** D. GRAY *Ride on Tiger* iv. 30 He raised his own glass of champagne and said, '*Santé*!' **1980** P. HARCOURT *Tomorrow's Treason* II. ii. 141, I watched him.. pour us each a generous tot. '*Santé*!' He grinned.

‖**santeria** (sante'ria). Also **Santeria**. [Sp., lit. 'holiness, sanctity'.] An Afro-Cuban religious cult with many Yoruba elements.

1950 *Southwestern Jrnl. Anthropol.* VI. 64 The worship of African deities, as it is practised in Cuba today, is known as *santeria.* The deities and the men and women who work with them are known by the Spanish words *santos, santeros*, and *santeras*, or by the Yoruba words *orisha, babalorisha*, and *iyalorisha.* **1953** [see SANTERO 2]. **1956** *Publ. Amer. Dial. Soc.* XXVI. 34 In Cuba the practitioners of a religion known as Santeria use a variety of African language called Lucumí in their religious services. **1972** W. R. BASCOM *Shango in New World* 20 A second major center of santeria in the United States, perhaps even more important than Miami, is New York City, where a Shango temple has been established. Apparently this has attracted not only Cuban refugees but also Puerto Ricans and New York Negroes.

‖**santero** (san'tero). Fem. santera. [Sp.]

1. In Mexico and Spanish-speaking areas of south-western U.S.: a maker of religious images.

1931 R. L. BARKER *Caballeros* xiii. 333 As the colonists became more securely rooted on the prados and mesas of Nuevo México certain men developed greater proficiency as carvers and painters. They were called santeros, the saint-makers, who signed and dated their work on the backs of the santos de retablos. **1944** *Horizon* Jan. 23 At about the same period [*sc.* 18th and 19th centuries] the *santero* of New Mexico produced for religious needs starkly primitive paintings and sculpture (*retablos* and *bultos*). **1951** *Western Folklore* Apr. 153 The following material about *santeros* was collected in the San Luis Valley, where there still remains a definite *santero* tradition... Southern Colorado is.. the one remaining place where something may still be learned of the *santero* and his art.

2. A priest (or priestess) of a religious cult, esp. *santeria.*

1950 [see SANTERIA]. **1953** *Language* XXIX. 157 Lucumí is a term here used to refer to a language spoken in Cuba by practitioners of the religion known as *Santería.* In Cuba both the *santeros* and the language are often called Lucumí. **1972** W. R. BASCOM *Shango in New World* 20 Refugee santeros and santeras have.. spread to many other parts of the New World. **1977** *N.Y. Rev. Bks.* 4 Aug. 27/3 He did many odd jobs for his neighbors,.. served as a *santero*, or priest, in two religious cults.

santes bell, obs. form of SANCTUS BELL.

santez, obs. var. SANCTUS (senses 2 and 3).

santfine, -foyne, obs. forms of SAINFOIN.

santifye, obs. form of SANCTIFY *v.*

‖**santir, santour** (sæn'tɪə(r), sæn'tʊə(r)). Also **santur**. [Arab. *santīr* (Pers., Turkish *sāntūr*), corruption of Gr. ψαλτήριον PSALTERY; cf. Biblical Aramaic *p'santerin.*] The dulcimer of the Arabs and Persians.

1853 LAYARD *Discov. Nineveh & Babylon* xx. 454 An instrument not unlike the modern santour of the East, consisting of a number of strings stretched over a hollow case or sounding-board. **1864** ENGEL *Mus. Anc. Nat.* 43 The Persians possess.. a dulcimer called *Santir*, which in construction and in the mode of its treatment is almost identical with the German Hackbret.

santis, obs. var. SANCTUS (senses 2 and 3).

‖**santo** ('santo). [Sp. or Ital. *santo.*]

1. = SANTON.

1638 SIR T. HERBERT *Trav.* (ed. 2) 235 The Church-men, Clerks, and Santos. **1687** A. LOVELL tr. *Thevenot's Trav.* I. 150 The Santo's, or Mad-men. **1901** *Scribner's Mag.* XXIX. 451/1 Like the new bits of cloth sewn on the tattered cloak of a 'Santo'.

2. A wooden representation of a saint or other religious symbol from Mexico or south-western U.S.

1834 A. PIKE *Prose Sk. & Poems* 146 The santos and other images had been brought from Mexico. **1948** F. BLAKE *Johnny Christmas* I. 19 The lines of prayer benches, the altar with its tapestry and candlesticks, the religious santos set in niches. **1976** *National Observer* (U.S.) 1 May 18/1 *Folk sculpture USA*... Santos from the Southwest, trade signs, voodoo cult objects.

santo, obs. var. SANCTUS (senses 2 and 3).

Santobrite ('sæntəbraɪt). [f. the name of the Mon*santo* Chemical Company.] A proprietary name for preparations of sodium pentachlorophenate (s.v. PENTA-), used as a fungicide, wood preservative, insecticide, etc.

1936 *Official Gaz.* (U.S. Patent Office) 2 June 14/2 Monsanto Chemical Company, St. Louis, Mo... *Santobrite.* For preservatives for wood, lumber, and other cellulosic materials. Claims use since Apr. 2, 1936. **1938** [see *pentachlorophenate* s.v. PENTA-]. **1944** *Trade Marks Jrnl.* 29 Nov. 567/1 *Santobrite...* Insecticides, germicides, algicides, [etc.]. **1959** [see *pentachlorophenate* s.v. PENTA-]. **1971** N. E. HICKIN *Wood Preservation* 89 The technical materials are also known as 'Santobrite' (the Monsanto Chemical Co.) and 'Dowicide G' (the Dow Chemical Co.).

Santo Domingan ('sæntəʊ dəʊ'mɪŋgən), *a.* [f. *Santo Domingo* (see below) + -AN.] Of or pertaining to Santo Domingo, former name of the Dominican Republic, and also the name of a district, and of the capital city of the Dominican Republic.

1934 in WEBSTER. **1947** J. C. RICH *Materials & Methods Sculpture* x. 291 The West Indian *Swietenia mahogani* is marketed as Cuban, Santo Domingan, or Spanish mahogany... Santo Domingan mahogany is one of the hardest and heaviest varieties. **1976** B. LECOMBER *Dead Weight* x. 118 A little Santo Domingan whore.

‖**Santolina** (sæntə'laɪnə). [mod.L., ? alteration of *santonica, santonicum*: see SANTONICA. (Cf. LAVENDER COTTON, quot. 1577 'some call it.. Santonia'.) Cf. It. *santolina* (Florio), F. *santoline.*] A genus of fragrant undershrubs, allied to the camomile, native of the Mediterranean region; Lavender Cotton. Also, a plant of this genus.

1578 LYTE *Dodoens* I. xix. 29 Some of the later writers do call it *Santolina* and *Camphorata*:.. some call it in English Lauender Cotton, and som Garden Cypres. **1731** MILLER *Gard. Dict.* **1865** *Athenæum* No. 1990. 848/2 The flowers of *santolina.*

santon ('sæntɒn). Also 6–7 **santone**, 7 **zanton**, sancton, santoon. [a. F. *santon* (in the 16th c. also *sainton, santoron, sanctoron* santon, hypocrite), or its source Sp. *santon* santon, also hypocrite, f. *santo* SAINT. Cf. Pg. *santão.*]

1. A European designation for a kind of monk or hermit among the Muslims, a marabout; also, incorrectly † a yogi, Hindu ascetic.

1599 HAKLUYT *Voy.* II. I. 204 There go in this foreward 6 Santones with red turbants vpon their heads. **1617** MORYSON *Itin.* I. 220 The Santons or Turkish Priests. *Ibid.* 224 This Chappell is kept by a Turkish Zanton, that is a kind of their Priests. **1660** F. BROOKE tr. *Le Blanc's Trav.* 125 These Santons, Joguies, or Indian Anchorites, lodge in the field, in hollow trees. **1786** tr. *Beckford's Vathek* (1834) 49 Calenders, santons, and derwiches. **1825** SCOTT *Talism.* xx, A little old Turk, poorly dressed like a marabout or santon of the desert.

Comb. **1873** LELAND *Egypt. Sketch-Bk.* 43 The wretchedest mosques and most beggarly Santon-tombs.

2. The chapel or shrine of a santon. [So. F. *santon*. Cf. MARABOUT 2.]

1835 tr. *Lamartine's Pilgr. Holy Land* II. 241 For the purpose of supporting..the roof of a santon.

3. Chiefly in Provence: a figurine adorning a representation of the manger in which Christ was laid.

1926 E. I. ROBSON *Wayfarer in Provence* xviii. 226 The little home-made crèches, the simple figures known as the Santons,..the pastoral ceremonies..at the famous midnight mass of Les Baux, are all witnesses to the way in which the Nativity story went home to the hearts of the Provençals. **1952** *Spectator* 10 Oct. 478/1 The pretty *santons*, the traditional clay figures of the Holy Family and the ancient trades of Provence. **1963** G. K. WILKINSON *Guinea-Pigs* xii. 189 Christmas will soon be on us and I hope that you will arrange the Holy Crêche and the Santons in the church. **1976** N. ROBERTS *Face of France* iii. 40 These days *santons*, the little pottery crib figures introducing characters from daily life..into the Nativity scene, are known far beyond their native Provence.

santonate (ˈsæntənət). *Chem.* [f. SANTON-IC + -ATE[1].] A salt of santonic acid.

1841 *Penny Cycl.* XX. 409/1 Santonate of soda and santonate of lime. **1874** GARROD & BAXTER *Mat. Med.* (1880) 293 Santonin..dissolves in solutions of the caustic fixed alkalies, forming definite compounds called santonates.

Santonian (sænˈtəʊnɪən), *a. Geol.* [ad. F. *Santonien* (H. Coquand 1857, in *Bull. de la Soc. géol. de France* XIV. 749) f. *Santon*, native or characteristic of Saintes, a town in Charente-Maritime Dept. (f. L. *Santoni* or *Santones*, ancient name of a people of Aquitania), + *-ien* -IAN.] Name of a stage in the Upper Cretaceous in France and adjacent areas, corresponding to the middle Senonian and to part of the Upper Chalk in Britain; of or pertaining to this stage and to the strata which characterize it, or the geological age during which it was deposited. Freq. *absol.*

1869 H. COQUAND in *Q. Jrnl. Geol. Soc.* XXV. 239, I have divided the Cretaceous formation of the south-west [of France] in the following manner..Santonian stage (of Saintes). **1885** A. GEIKIE *Text-bk. Geol.* (ed. 2) 833 This stage [*sc.* the Senonian]..consists mainly of white chalk separable into the two divisions of: 1st, Micraster (Santonian) sub-stage composed of chalk beds [etc.]. **1924** C. SCHUCHERT *Text-bk. Geol.* (ed. 2) II. xxxviii. 537 Upper Cretaceous [of Europe]... Senonian... Santonian. **1971** *Nature* 18 June 439/2 Misfit motion in the African plate closed this rift in Santonian time. **1974** *Encycl. Brit. Micropædia* VIII. 886/2 In northern Europe the Santonian is represented by the Granulaten Chalk, the equivalent of portions of the Upper Chalk in Great Britain.

santonic (sænˈtɒnɪk), *a. Chem.* [ad. L. *Santonic-us*: see next.] **santonic acid**: an acid derived from santonin.

1836–41 BRANDE *Chem.* (ed. 5) 1252 *Artemisia santonica.* The seeds contain a substance which has been called *santonin* or *santonic acid.* **1876** HARLEY *Mat. Med.* (ed. 6) 539 Heated with an alkali, santonin is converted into santonic acid, which is isomeric with santoninic acid.

santonica (sænˈtɒnɪkə). [a. L. *Santonica* (sc. *herba*), a kind of wormwood, fem. sing. of *Santonicus* pertaining to the Santones or Santoni, a people of Aquitania. The plant was also called *absinthium Santonicum* (Pliny), Gr. (ἀψίνθιον) σαντονικόν, σαντόνιον. Cf. 16th c. F. *santonique*.] The dried unexpanded flower-heads of species of *Artemisia*, produced in Turkestan, used as an anthelmintic; Levant or Alexandrian wormseed.

1658 J. ROWLAND *Moufet's Theat. Ins.* 1119 Such things as we said to be good against Worms..such as are Wormwood, Southernwood, Santonicum. **1871** RANSOM in *J. R. Reynolds' Syst. Med.* III. 198 A very general concurrence of opinion..in favour of the use of santonica or worm-seed.

santonin (ˈsæntənɪn). *Chem.* Also **-ine**. [f. SANTON-ICA + -IN. Cf. F. *santonine*.] A bitter principle obtained from santonica and used as a powerful anthelmintic.

1838 T. THOMSON *Chem. Org. Bodies* 133 Santonin. **1879** ROOD *Chromatics* viii. 95 Persons under the influence of santonin cannot see the violet end of the spectrum.

santoˈninic, *a. Chem.* [f. SANTONIN + -IC.] **santoninic acid**: an acid obtained from santonin, isomeric with santonic acid.

1875 WATTS *Dict. Chem.* 2nd Suppl. 1076

santoon, obs. form of SANTON.

Santorin (sæntəˈriːn, ˈsæntərɪn). Also **santorin, Santoˈrini**. [ad. Gr. Σαντορίνη Santorini, former name for Thira, ad. It. *Sant' Irene* St. Irene, Italian name for the island.] In full **Santorin earth**. A natural volcanic ash, similar to pozzolana, found on the island of Thira in the Cyclades.

1868 WATTS *Dict. Chem.* V. 191 *Santorin*, an argillaceous mineral, occurring on the island of Santorin, which yields an excellent cement. **1876** *Min. Proc. Inst. Civil Engineers* XLV. 291 For hydraulic works on the Mediterranean coast Santorin earth recommends itself through facility of excavation and lading and economical transport at sea. **1951** LADOO & MYERS *Non-Metallic Minerals* (ed. 2) 407 Santorini or Santorin earth is a variety of pumice mined on Santorin Island (Greece), used in making pozzuolana cement. **1971** *Materials & Technol.* II. ii. 106 Cements ground together with siliceous materials other than pozzolan—such as santorin earth (Greece), trass..and diatomaceous earth (USA)—are also named pozzolan cement.

Santorinian (sæntəˈrɪnɪən), *a.* [f. the name *Santorini* + -AN.] Named after the Venetian anatomist Santorini (1681–1737), as, the Santorinian plexus.

In recent Dicts.

Santos (ˈsæntɒs). The name of a port in Brazil, used *ellipt.* and *attrib.* of coffee exported from there.

[**1885** C. F. VAN D. LAËRNE *Brazil & Java: Rep. Coffee-Culture* x. 267 The second or Santos zone lies..between 21 and 24 degrees S.L. but a little further landwards, as it does not begin till about 150 kilometers from Santos. *Ibid.* 289 The coffee-shrub in the Santos zone is much larger than the coffee-shrub in the Rio zone, besides being almost twice as productive.] **1888** C. G. W. LOCK *Coffee* vi. 112 As to impurities:—San Domingo is usually very dirty; Ceylon, East India, Rio, Santos, Martinique, and Java, generally well prepared and clean. **1899** [see JAMAICA b]. **1956** A. E. HAARER *Mod. Coffee Production* xvii. 398 Though an ever-increasing number are beginning to pick ripe coffee and prepare it by the wet method,..most planters still follow the old dry method. Of the latter there are two kinds, those who process only ripe cherry and take more care in its preparation,..and those who strip the crop from the trees at the stage when most of it is ripe... The first of these two methods produces a softer and milder product such as Santos coffee. **1975** *Times* 6 Mar. 7/7 Blue Sumatra, 82 p per pound..very strong aroma. Santos, 72 p, the best Brazilian, rich flavour.

santour, variant of SANTIR.

santre, obs. form of SAUNTER.

†**ˈsantrel**. *Obs. rare*[−1]. [ad. OF. *sainterel* or It. *santarello* (Florio), diminutives of *saint, santo* SAINT: see -REL and SAINTREL.] A little saint.

1653 URQUHART *Rabelais* I. xxvii. 129 With a thousand other jolly little Sancts and Santrels [orig. *et mille autres bons petis saincts*].

‖**san ts'ai** (san tsaɪ). Also **san-ts'ai**. [Chinese *sāncǎi*, f. *sān* three + *cǎi* colour.] Chinese pottery, esp. of the Tang dynasty, decorated in three colours; decoration in three enamel colours applied to pottery and porcelain. Also *attrib.*

1901 C. MONKHOUSE *Hist. & Descr. Chinese Porc.* I. caption facing p. 35 Squirrel and grapes: *San-ts'ai* water pourer. **1906** S. W. BUSHELL *Chinese Art* II. II. viii. 37 For a typical example of the *san ts'ai*, or 'three-coloured', decoration *sur biscuit*, see the pictures..of a fish-shaped water pourer, which is painted with the brownish-purple, green, and yellow enamels of this *genre*. **1915** R. L. HOBSON *Chinese Pott. & Porc.* II. x. 151 The Dresden collection is peculiarly rich in this kind of *san ts'ai*. **1959** H. CHEVALIER tr. *Grousset's Chinese Art & Culture* vi. 292 The main categories of Ming ceramics are..: 1. *San-ts'ai* or 'three-colours', namely green.., yellow.., and aubergine-violet. **1972** *Trans. Oriental Ceramics Soc.* XXXVIII. 29 The combination of green, blue and yellow-brown glaze which constitutes the famous T'ang polychromes ('three-colour ware', *san-ts'ai*) appear to belong..to the first half of the 8th century. **1978** P. VAN GREENAWAY *Man called Scavener* xi. 159 A priceless san ts'ai bowl.

santsbell: see SANCTUS BELL.

santuare, variant of SAINTUAIRE.

santuary, obs. form of SANCTUARY.

santur, variant of SANTIR.

santus, obs. var. SANCTUS (senses 2 and 3).

†**ˈsanty**. *Obs.* Also **santie, sancti**, *pl.* **sonties**. [Of obscure origin: perh. corruption of *saintitie* SANCTITY.] Used in a form of oath, (**God's**) **santy, by God's sonties**.

c **1570** W. WAGER *The longer thou livest* 459 (Brandl), Gods santie, this is a goodlie Booke in deede. *Ibid.* 763 Santy amen, here are saintes a great sort. *Ibid.* 1828 *Sancti*, Amen, where is my goodly geare? **1596** SHAKS. *Merch. V.* II. ii. 47 Be Gods sonties 'twill be a hard waie to hit. **1604** DEKKER *Honest Wh.* xiii. K 2, Gods santy yonder come Friers.

santy: see SANTÉ.

Santy (Claus): see SANTA CLAUS.

Sanusi, Sanusiya(h: see SENUSSI.

sanyama: see SAMYAMA.

sanyas(s)i, sanyas(s)in, varr. SANNYASI.

sanz, obs. form of SANS.

sanzack(e, -zake, -ziac, obs. ff. SANJAK.

sanze (sanȝe), obs. Sc. form of SENE.

s-aorist: see S I. 1 b.

Saorstát Éireann (ˈsiːrstaːt ˈeːrjən, ˈseːr-). [Ir., = The Free State of Ireland.] = *Irish Free State* s.v. IRISH *adj.* 2 c. Also *ellipt.* as **Saorstát**.

1922 *Bille um Bun-reacht Shaorstáit Eireann* (*Constitution of Saorstát Eireann Bill*) 2 Article 1. The Irish Free State/Saorstát Eireann is a co-equal member of the community of nations. **1923** *Glasgow Herald* 18 June 9/8 One was Article 12 where the Northern Government was entitled to pass a resolution against entrance into the Saorstat. **1924** W. B. YEATS *Senate Speeches* (1961) 69 Your Committee is gravely impressed by the responsibility now laid upon the Saorstat towards the Irish people. **1938** S. BECKETT *Murphy* 197 Turf is compulsory in the Saorstat, but one need not bring a private supply to Newcastle.

saouari, souari (saʊˈɑːrɪ). Also **souarri, s(o)u(w)arrow, sawarrow, sawarra, sawari, sawarri, saouwarri, sewarri**; *corruptly* **savory**. [a. Galibi (Cayenne) *sawarra*; in the Gal.-Fr. dict. of 1763 written *saouari*.] **saouari nut**, the 'butter-nut' of *Caryocar nuciferum* and *C. tomentosum*, lofty trees of Guyana. **saouari wood**, the hard durable timber of these trees, used for shipbuilding.

1806 PINCKARD *W. Indies* III. 287 The Souwarrow nut. **1829** *Encycl. Metrop.* (1845) XX. 7 The Savory tree is famed for its immense fruit. **1836** *Penny Cycl.* VI. 333/2 The Suwarrow or more properly Saouari nuts of commerce. **1842** *Penny Cycl.* XXIII. 184/2 Suarrow-nut (*Caryocar*). **1849** BALFOUR *Man. Bot.* §808 *Rhizobolaceæ*, the Souari-nut Family. **1855** H. G. DALTON *Hist. Brit. Guiana* II. 213 Saouwarri, saouari, or sewarri nut. **1858** BAIRD *Cycl. Nat. Sci.* 410/2 *Pekea tuberculosa* yields a nut known in the shops by the name of the Saouari or Sawarra nuts. **1866** *Treas. Bot.*, *Saouari* or *Souari-wood*. *Ibid.*, Souari-nuts. **1884** *Encycl. Brit.* XVII. 664/2 The Souari or Surahwa nut, called also the 'Butter nut of Demerara', and by fruiterers the 'Suwarrow nut'. **1885** LADY BRASSEY *The Trades* 112 The souari or butter-nuts..contain even more oleaginous matter.

sap (sæp), *sb.*[1] Forms: 1 sæp, sep, 4 *Kentish* zep, 5 saap(pe, 5–7 sappe, 6 sape, sapp, 4– sap. [Com. WGer.: OE. *sæp*, genit. *sæpes* (prob. neut.) = MLG., LG., MDu., Du. *sap*, neut. (Flemish *zap*), OHG. *saf*, genit. *saffes*, neut. (MHG. *saf, saft*, neut., mod.G. *saft*, masc., whence Sw. *saft*, fem., Da. *saft*), prob. repr. OTeut. types **sapo*[m], **sappo*[m]:—pre-Teut. **sapnó-*, cogn. w. ON. *safi*, masc., sap (Sw. *safve, saf*, masc.):—OTeut. **safon-* or **sabon-*:—pre-Teut. **sapon-*.

On this assumption the Teut. words may be cognate with L. *sapĕre* to taste, *sapor* taste, savour; also with *sapa* must boiled thick, whence (with change of meaning prob. due to association with the WGer. word) Pr., Sp. *saba*, Fr. *sève* sap. The hypothesis that the WGer. word was adopted from L. *sapa* is improbable in view of its relation to the Scandinavian synonym; besides, the assumed development of meaning in popular Latin (of which the Rom. words afford the only evidence) appears unlikely unless as a result of extraneous influence.]

1. a. The vital juice or fluid which circulates in plants.

a **900** CYNEWULF *Crist* 1177 (Gr.) Ða wearð beam moniȝ blodiȝum tearum birunnen..sæp wearð to swate. *a* **1000** *Gloss.* in *Germania* N.S. XI. 391 *Sucum*, sep. *c* **1000** ÆLFRIC *Gloss.* in Wr.-Wülcker 139/16 *Cedrus*, cederbeam. *Cedria*, his sæp. **1340** *Ayenb.* 96 þet zep of þo traue and þe tyeres weren uour wel preciouses þinges. ?*c* **1377** *Pol. Poems* (Rolls) I. 218 Weor that impe ffully growe, That he had sarri, sap, and pith [etc.]. **1523** FITZHERB. *Husb.* §127 Alwaye se that the toppe lye hyer than the rote a good quantyte for els the sappe wyll nat renne into the toppe kyndely. **1596** SPENSER *F.Q.* IV. ii. 43 Like three faire branches budding farre and wide, That from one roote deriv'd their vitall sap. **1615** W. LAWSON *Country Housew. Gard.* (1626) 7 The sap is the life of the tree, as the bloud is to mans body. **1667** MILTON *P.L.* IX. 837 Whose presence had infus'd Into the plant sciential sap. **1787** M. CUTLER in *Life*, etc. (1888) II. 398 The sugar maple is a most valuable tree... The sap is extracted in the months of February and March. **1820** SHELLEY *Sensit. Pl.* III. 84 The sap shrank to the root through every pore. **1864** C. GEIKIE *Life in Woods* xi. (1874) 183 We kept some sap for vinegar. **1875** BENNETT & DYER tr. *Sachs' Bot.* 650 All functions are brought into play only when the temperature of the plant..rises to a certain height above the freezing-point of the sap.

b. *transf.* and *fig.*

1526 *Pilgr. Perf.* (W. de W. 1531) 43 The barke þat defendeth the tree from stormes and tempestes, is hope. And the sap that gyueth lyfe to bothe, is charite. **1594** SHAKS. *Rich. III*, IV. iv. 277 A hand-kercheefe, which..did dreyne The purple sappe from her sweet Brothers body. **1692** BENTLEY *Boyle Lect.* ix. 335 The Moral part of the Law of Moses, which is the Sap and Marrow of the whole. **1791** A. WILSON *Eppie & Deil* Poet. Wks. (1846) 86 Ye maybe think that spinning's naething! And that it wastes na sap nor breathing? **1832** LYTTON *Eugene A.* I. vi, The sap of youth shrinks from our veins. **1865** G. M. HOPKINS *Poems* (1967) 169 My sap is sealed, My root is dry. **1942** T. S. ELIOT *Little Gidding* i. 7 Between melting and freezing The soul's sap quivers. **1961** B. J. CHUTE *Moon & Thorn* iv. 37 An old man ..gave her a more than reflective look as she passed, the sap still plainly rising in his branches.

c. Moisture in stone.

1881 *Dict. Arch. Publ. Soc.*, *Quarry Damp*, or *Sap*, the natural dampness of the stone when in the quarry. **1892** MIDDLETON *Anc. Rome.* I. 5 *note*, What stone-masons call the 'sap' should always be allowed to dry out of stone before it is used.

d. *Cytology.* **cell sap** [tr. G. *zellsaft*] (see quot. 1875); ***nuclear sap***, the fluid within the nuclear membrane.

1875 BENNETT & DYER tr. *J. Sachs's Text-bk. Bot.* I. i. 62 The term Cell-sap may be understood in a wider or in a narrower sense. In the former it would express the collective mass of all fluids by which the cell-wall, the protoplasm-body, and all other organised structures of the cell are saturated, and would also embrace the fluids contained in the vacuoli of the protoplasm; in a narrower sense the latter only is ordinarily designated as cell-sap. **1884** *Jrnl. Bot.* XXII. 124 The rich, violet-coloured cell-sap in the flower of *Justicia speciosa*.. crystallizes very easily into minute slender prisms. **1887** *Jrnl. R. Microsc. Soc.* 979 Linin and paralinin, the substance respectively of the nuclear threads.. and of the intermediate matrix or 'nuclear sap'. **1955** *Internat. Rev. Cytol.* IV. 293 Another suggestion for the origin of nucleolar material is that it is formed from nuclear sap. **1971** VILLEE & DETHIER *Biol. Princ. & Processes* vi. 152 The activation of amino acids for protein synthesis, the process of glycolysis and many other reactions occur in the soluble cell sap. *Ibid.* xvi. 499 The plant cell, inside its cellulose wall, has one or more large vacuoles filled with cell sap. **1975** *Nature* 4 Sept. 21/1 Similar preparations were..made from rat liver chromatin but after previous removal of 'nuclear sap' which contains soluble nuclear proteins. **1978** B. S. BECKETT *Illustr. Biol.* xxxi. 62/1 As root hairs take up water their cell sap is diluted and soon becomes a weaker solution than the sap of cells deeper inside the root.

†**2.** Ear-wax. *Obs.*

c **1440** *Promp. Parv.* 441/1 Saap [*Winchester MS.* sap] of the ere, *pedora*.

†**3.** Juice or fluid of any kind. *Obs.*

Cf. *Sc.* and *north.* '*Sap*, anything used for drinking, esp. milk or beer'; *sap-money*, money allowed to servants for liquor. (See E. D. D.)

1527 ANDREW *Brunswyke's Distyll. Waters* bij, Other lyquor or sape which ye wyl puryfye from all troublous and unclere substaunces. **1535** COVERDALE *Song Sol.* viii. 1 The swete sappe of my pomgranates. **1589** *Pappe w. Hatchet* To Indiff. Rdr., It is said that camels neuer drinke, til they have troubled the water with their feete, and it seemes these Martins cannot carouse the sapp of the Church, til by faction they make tumults in religion. **1601** HOLLAND *Pliny* I. 449 That the three principall Elements whereof the world is made, namely, Water, Aire, and Fire, should haue no tast, no sauor, nor participation of any sap and liquor at all.

fig. **1613** SHAKS. *Hen. VIII*, I. i. 148 If with the sap of reason you would quench, Or but allay the fire of passion.

4. a. = SAP-WOOD.

c **1374** CHAUCER *Boeth.* III. pr. xi. (1868) 97 þat thilke thing þat is ryht softe as the marye (i. sapp) is. **1483** *Cath. Angl.* 318/1 þe Sappe of a tre, *suber*. **1592** GREENE *Upst. Courtier* Wks. (Grosart) XI. 270 The ioyner though an honest man, yet hee maketh his ioynts weake, and putteth in sap in the mortesels, which should be the hart of the tree. **1627** CAPT. SMITH *Seaman's Gram.* ii. 14 Deale of thirty foot long, the sap cut off. **1699** DAMPIER *Voy.* II. II. 57 The old black-rinded Trees..have less sap, and require but little pains to chip and cut it. The sap is white and the heart red. **1737** HOPPUS *Salmon's Country Build. Estim.* (ed. 2) 22 To lay a Barn Floor with double Deals,.. and to List off the Sap. **1864** *Intell. Observ.* IV. 74 The sandal cutters carefully remove the outer..portion of the wood, which they term the 'sap'. **1898** RIDER HAGGARD *Farmer's Yr.* (1899) 121, I noticed that the wood was as hard as iron, and that there was ..practically no 'sap', that is, soft outer wood, which is useless for most purposes.

b. *U.S. slang.* A club; a short staff. So *saps* (see quot. 1899).

1899 'J. FLYNT' *Tramping with Tramps* 396 *Saps*, a clubbing with weapons made from saplings. **1915** *N.Y. World Mag.* 9 May 14/3 *Sap* or *sapstick*, a crutch, cane or club. **1926** J. BLACK *You can't Win* vii. 83 The town marshal would then appear with a posse armed with 'saps', which is short for saplings, young trees. **1932** J. DOS PASSOS *1919* 436 He could hear the crack of saps on men's skulls. **1940** R. CHANDLER *Farewell, my Lovely* xvi. 116 He had the sap out this time, a nice little tool about five inches long, covered with woven brown leather. **1955** W. FOSTER-HARRIS *Look of Old West* vii. 218 Its [*sc.* a quirt's] handle, or butt, would probably be loaded with an iron spike or with buckshot, thus giving you a handy sap when you needed one. **1974** D. SEARS *Lark in Clear Air* iv. 49 His main staff of office was a lead sap that must have weighed two pounds.

5. The core (of unaltered iron) in the middle of a bar of blister steel.

1884 W. H. GREENWOOD *Steel & Iron* 411.

†**6.** = SAP-GREEN. *Obs.*

1572 in Feuillerat *Revels Q. Eliz.* (1908) 178 Sapp.. Crymsen..white. **1573** *Ibid.* 210 Sape .j. quarterne xx[d].

7. *attrib.* and *Comb.*: as *sap-boiling, -flow, -monger, -pressure, -trough, -vessel*; *sap-clear, -consuming, -filled, -rife, -sucking* adjs.; **sap-ball**, a local name for certain fungi of the genus *Polyporus*, 'the stems of which, after the juice has been squeezed out, are sometimes used by boys as their foundation for tennis-balls' (*Treas. Bot.* 1866); **sap-beetle** *U.S.*, any beetle of the family *Nitidulidæ* (Cent. Dict.); **sap-colour** (see quot.); †**sap-pate**, = SAP-HEAD, SAPSKULL; **sap pine** *U.S.* [perversion of F. *sapin*], the pitch-pine, *Pinus rigida*; **sap-rot**, a disease of timber, dry-rot; **sap-stain**, discoloration of sap-wood, esp. a bluish discoloration by fungi; so **sap-stained** *a.*, **sap-staining** *sb.* and *a.*; **sap-sucker**, a name in N. America for many of the smaller woodpeckers, esp. those of the genus *Sphyropicus*; †**sap-time**, the time of year when the sap circulates; **sap-tree**, the mountain ash, *Pyrus aucuparia*; also the sycamore, *Acer pseudo-platanus* (E.D.D.); **sap-tube**, a vessel that conveys sap (Ogilvie, 1850); **sap-whistle** *dial.*, 'a whistle made from the green twig of a tree, esp. mountain ash or sycamore' (E.D.D.); in quot. 1737 referred to proverbially; †**sap-wiser**, an instrument for indicating the motion of the sap in plants; **sap-wort** (see quot.). Also SAP-GREEN, -LATH, -WOOD.

1953 E. SITWELL *Gardeners & Astronomers* 31 The gardener plays upon his *sap-clear flute. **1816** S. PARKES *Chem. Catech.* (ed. 7) 532 **Sap-colours*, a name given to various expressed vegetable juices of a viscid nature, which are inspissated by slow evaporation for the use of painters, &c. Sap-green, gamboge, &c. are of this class. **1590** SHAKS. *Com. Err.* v. i. 312 Though now this grained face of mine be hid In *sap-consuming Winters drizled snow. **1915** D. H. LAWRENCE *Rainbow* xiii. 383 Her own world of warm sun and growing, *sap-filled life was turned into nothing. **1935** C. DAY LEWIS *Time to Dance* 64 We remember them as the glowing fruit remembers *Sap-flow and sunshine. **1652** CULPEPER *Eng. Physic.* (1656) 383 Let such *Sap-mongers answer me to this Argument, If the Sap fal into the Root in the fal of the Leaf, and lye there al the winter, then must the Root grow only in the winter. *a* **1700** B. E. *Dict. Cant. Crew*, **Sap-pate*, a Fool. **1808** PIKE *Sources Mississ.* (1810) 56 A new species of pine, called the French *Sap pine. **1866** *Treas. Bot.* s.v. *Pine*, Sap Pine, *Pinus rigida*. **1976** *Sci. Amer.* May 104/3 Hales measured the springtime *sap pressure by placing open mercury manometers on a cut vine. **1942** W. FAULKNER *Go down, Moses* 326 Wet and *saprife spring in their ordered immortal sequence. **1838** *Civil Eng. & Arch. Jrnl.* I. 191/1 The sap-wood is the part in which the decomposing operations commence, and hence the propriety of the term *sap-rot. **1918** J. W. HARSHBERGER *Mycol. & Plant Path.* xxxv. 545 Sap-rot (*Polystictus versicolor* (L.), Fr.).—*Polystictus versicolor* is one of the most cosmopolitan species of fungi known... It grows on the sapwood of every species of deciduous tree known. It is the most serious of all the wood-rotting fungi, destroying probably 75 per cent. of the timber used for railroad ties. *Ibid.* 558 Sap-rot (*Daedalea quercina* (L.) Pers).—One of the most important enemies of structural oak, produces a soft, mushy decay of the wood. **1971** *Country Life* 4 Nov. 1224/2 The chestnut for the frames is cleft..soon after cutting to prevent sap rot. **1910** *Bot. Gaz.* L. 147 *Sap stain is in general produced in two ways, by the attacks of fungi and by chemical discoloration. **1953** F. T. BROOKS *Plant Dis.* (ed. 2) xii. 199 Several species of Ceratostomella and allied genera, together with many Fungi Imperfecti, cause sap-stain or blueing of the sap-wood of soft and hard timber felled for lumber, and of pulp-wood... Affected wood is reduced in marketability as the stain is unsightly in timber used for certain purposes. **1976** B. M. BAKSHI *Forest Path.* III. 281 The fungi causing soft rot, like those causing sap stain, belong to the Ascomycetes and Fungi Imperfecti. **1910** *Bot. Gaz.* L. 142 The examination of microscopic sections of this *sap-stained lumber reveals the fact that the colored substance, produced by the chemical reaction, is most conspicuously developed in the wood rays and wood parenchyma cells. *Ibid.*, Favorable conditions for *sap-staining are found during warm weather. **1921** *Phytopathology* XI. 214 As a sap-staining organism *Lasiosphaeria pezizula* has been previously reported by Humphrey. **1976** B. M. BAKSHI *Forest Path.* III. 280 Sap staining fungi..do not cause any wood decay. **1805** LEWIS & CLARK *Jrnl.* 8 Apr. in *Orig. Jrnls. Lewis & Clark Exped.* (1905) VI. 187 [I saw] the small woodpecker or *sapsucker as they are sometimes called. **1808** A. WILSON *Amer. Ornith.* (1831) I. 167 This, and the two former species [i.e. *Picus varius*, *P. villosus*, and *P. pubescens*] are generally denominated sap-suckers. **1834** J. J. AUDUBON *Ornith. Biogr.* II. 81 The Downy Woodpecker..is best known in all parts of the United States by the name of Sap-sucker. **1872** 194 Genus *Sphyrapicus* Baird... Of the several small species commonly called 'sapsuckers' they alone deserve the name. **1941** *Sun* (Baltimore) 25 Jan. 6/1 The cardinals have been flashing to and fro, and the flickers and sapsuckers and the tiny snowbirds. **1962** T. A. IMHOF *Alabama Birds* 329 These far-ranging woodland birds are called Peckerwoods and Sapsuckers in the South. **1971** *Islander* (Victoria, B.C.) 13 June 13/2 A sapsucker tapped out an accompaniment on his favorite tree. **1884** COUES *Key N. Amer. Birds* (ed. 2) 485 *Sphyropicus*... *Sap-sucking Woodpeckers. **1523** FITZHERB. *Husb.* §133 Beware, that thou croppe hym not, nor heed hym (specially) in *sappe-tyme. **1701** GREW *Cosm. Sacra* I. v. §22. 20 The Liquor of the adjacent *Sap-Vessels. **1737** BRACKEN *Farriery Impr.* (1757) II. 123 If he would not be a *Sap-whistle, he might be a Sling at any time. **1979** *Bull. Yorks. Dial. Soc.* Summer 7 Here's a sap whistle, lads er aw alike, Here's en aad knife, en a nut off a bike [in a boy's pocket]. **1670** TONGE in *Phil. Trans.* V. 2071 *Sap-wiser. **1844** H. STEPHENS *Bk. Farm* III. 948 In damp situations, *Œnanthe crocata*, water *sap-wort, grows.

b. *N. Amer.* With *spec.* reference to the sap of the sugar maple, as *sap beer, -boiling, bucket, -cider, -gatherer, -house, -kettle, pail, pan, season, sled, syrup, trough, tub, weather, works, yield*; **sap-boiler**, a furnace with pans for evaporating the sap of the maple (Knight *Dict. Mech.*); **sap-bush**, a grove of sugar-maples; **sap neckyoke** = *sap yoke*; **sap orchard** = *sap bush*; **sap porridge** (see quots.); **sap run**, an increased flow of sap in a sugar-maple tree; **sap spout**, a spout through which sap is drawn from a sugar-maple tree; **sap sugar** = *maple sugar* s.v. MAPLE 3; **sap tree**, the sugar maple, *Acer saccharum*; **sap weather**, the kind of weather that encourages the flow of sap in a sugar-maple tree; **sap yoke**, a yoke used for carrying sap pails.

1950 H. & S. NEARING *Maple Sugar Bk.* ix. 202 The other maple product is *sap beer. **1876** W. BOYD in Bartlett *Dict. Amer.*, The great event of the spring is the *sap-boiling in the maple-woods. **1845** S. JUDD *Margaret* I. iii. 12 [Here were] frows, *sap-buckets, a leach-tub. **1969** E. H. PINTO *Treen* 94 A maple sap bucket of coopered pine,..is shown. .. The wire loop, for suspending it on a nail below the sap incision in the tree, can be seen in the photograph. **1980** *Blair & Ketchum's Country Jrnl.* (Brattleboro, Vermont) Oct. 102/1 I've used mine [*sc.* a wooden packboard] to carry 200 sap buckets up the washed-out road to the sugar-house and to carry finished gallons of syrup back down. *a* **1882** T. WEED *Autobiogr.* (1883) I. ii. 12, I now look with great pleasure upon the days and nights passed in the *sap-bush. **1845** J. F. COOPER *Chainbearer* II. v. 60, I don't think anything of bringing you..a little water,..nor should I had we any beer or *sap-cider. **1874** *Rep. Vermont Board Agric.* II. 719 The '*sap-gatherer' or 'draw-tub', as it is called, is a hogshead containing from one hundred to one hundred and fifty gallons. **1917** D. CANFIELD *Understood Betsy* vii. 110 The *sap-house, where Cousin Ann and Uncle Henry were making syrup. **1939** I. B. WOLCOTT *Yankee Cook Bk.* 338 Any one who..returns to the sap house. **1904** M. E. WALLER *Wood-Carver of 'Lympus* ii. 51 [I] drew trees and sheep and loggers' camps on the flat stones beneath the crotch set for the *sap-kettles. **1968** E. R. BUCKLER *Ox Bells & Fireflies* iv. 77 You thought..about the sap kettle in the cool green shadow, waiting to be emptied at noon. **1905** W. M. WEBB in A. E. Cowles *Past & Present City of Lansing & Ingham County, Michigan* 441 One neighbor whittled out brooms... Another gauged the *sap neckyokes and another made ox yokes. **1861** *Boston Herald* 12 Apr. 2/6 Owners of *sap orchards can afford to work day and night. **1947** K. M. WELLS *Owl Pen Reader* (1969) I. 44 Jim..followed him, hanging *sap pails to the already dripping spouts. **1874** *Rep. Vermont Board Agric.* II. 729 Russia iron is the best material for home made *sap pans as the niter can be removed from it more easily. **1842** *Amer. Pioneer* I. 346 '*Sap porridge',.. when made of sweet corn meal, and the fresh sacarine juice of the maple, afforded both a nourishing and a savory dish. **1948** E. N. DICK *Dixie Frontier* 290 Corn-meal mush was a regular supper dish. In the spring it was made with maple sap and was known as sap porridge. **1876** J. BURROUGHS *Winter Sunshine* 119 A '*sap-run' seldom lasts more than two or three days. **1950** H. & S. NEARING *Maple Sugar Bk.* ix. 202 Maple vinegar..is made of sap run at the end of the season. *Ibid.* iii. 48 Much of the boiling was done far from home, and the sugar makers camped out in the deep woods until the *sap season was over. *Ibid.* v. 98 The loaded *sap sled..moves down rather easily. **1878** *Rep. Vermont Board Agric.* V. 105 We now have the Eureka *sap spout, the tin bucket, [etc.]. **1949** *Highway Traveler* Feb. 16/2 A sap spout, or 'spile' as your boss may call it, is driven into the opening with a few taps of a hammer. **1800** C. D. R. D'ERES *Mem.* 63 The squaws in particular, would make me many and valuable [presents]..consisting of *sap sugar. **1895** S. O. JEWETT *Life of Nancy* 105 [She] handed us sap sugar on one of her best plates. **1951** T. CAPOTE *Grass Harp* I. 11, I could hear the tantalizing tremor of their voices flowing like *sapsyrup through the old wood. **1843** *Knickerbocker* XXII. 161 One felled the proper trees, taking care to leave the '*sap-trees, the sugar-maple, untouched. **1804** T. G. FESSENDEN *Orig. Poems* (1806) 41 Your love I well repaid By..a *sap-trough neatly made. **1840** GOSSE *Canadian Nat.* 11 The timber..is..made into sap-troughs for the sugary. **1897** R. E. ROBINSON *Uncle Lisha's Outing* x. 84 These 'ere boots... They're stiffer'n sap troughs. **1872** *Rep. Vermont Board Agric.* I. 215 When I was a boy I purchased one hundred *sap tubs, and commenced sugaring on my own hook. **1950** H. & S. NEARING *Maple Sugar Bk.* vi. 137 The 20-degree-night and the 45-degree-day, sunny-days and cold-night formula for *sap weather is very far from telling the whole story. **1832** J. J. STRANG *Diary* 19 Feb. in M. M. Quaife *Kingdom of St. James* (1930) 202, I expect to dismiss my school soon and leave the place..for the people want their boys to work in the *sap works. **1849** *Knickerbocker* XXXIII. 279 '*The Sugar Bush*' has vividly recalled to memory..the pale blue smoke curling up from the 'sap-works'. **1950** H. & S. NEARING *Maple Sugar Bk.* iv. 82 There is some evidence that length of trunk plays a part in *sap yield. **1878** *Rep. Vermont Board Agric.* V. 105 The sap was lugged with *sap yoke and pails on their shoulders.

†**sap**, *sb.*[2] *Obs.* [a. F. *sappe* (now *sape*): see SAP *sb.*[3]] Some kind of spade or mattock.

1566 *Wills & Inv. N.C.* (Surtees) I. 254, I giu to Richard walton my..stele sappe. **1598** FLORIO, *Zappa*, a mattocke to dig and delue with, a sappe.

sap (sæp), *sb.*[3] *Mil.* Forms: 6–7 **zappe**, 6–8 **sappe**, 7–8 **sapp**, 8– **sap**. [Late 16th c. *zappe*, *sappe*, ad. It. *zappa* and a. F. *sappe* (16th c. also *zappe* after It.; now *sape*) spade, spadework, sap. Cf. Sp. *zapa*, late L. *sappa* (6th c.). The ulterior origin is uncertain: see Diez and Körting.]

1. †The process of undermining a wall or defensive work (*obs.*); the process of constructing covered trenches in order to approach a besieged place without danger from the enemy's fire.

1591 UNTON *Corr.* (Roxb.) 247 The King now resolveth to gaigne the fort by the zappe. *Ibid.* 248 Now we labor by sappe to win the fort. **1633** T. STAFFORD *Pac. Hib.* III. xii. 334 Untill such time as they might gaine it by Sapp or Myne. **1683** SIR J. TURNER *Pallas Armata* 316 This Sappe or Zappe is nothing else but a digging. **1704** J. HARRIS *Lex. Techn.* I, *Sappe*, in Fortification, formerly signified the undermining, or deep digging, with Pick-axe and Shovel at the Foot of a Work to overthrow it without Gunpowder. **1710** *Ibid.* II, *Sap*, in Fortification, is digging deep under the Earth,..to open a way to come under cover to the Passage of the Moat. **1742** YOUNG *Nt. Th.* VI. 22 Like pow'rful armies trenching at a town, By slow, and silent, but resistless sap. **1747** *Gentl. Mag.* XVII. 328/1 The French advanced, by sap, quite up to the foot of our entrenchment. **1812** WELLINGTON in Gurw. *Desp.* (1838) VIII. 549 We had made some progress by sap towards the crest of the glacis. **1828** J. M. SPEARMAN *Brit. Gunner* (ed. 2) 368 The sap is a mode of carrying on the approaches at a siege, under cover. **1867** SMYTH *Sailor's Word-bk.*, *Sap*, that peculiar method by which a besieger's zig-zag approaches are continuously advanced in spite of the musketry of the defenders. **1875** CLERY *Min. Tactics* xvii. 253 A solid redout..made it necessary to advance from house to house by sap.

b. *fig.* Applied to stealthy or insidious methods of attacking or destroying something.

1748 RICHARDSON *Clarissa* (1811) III. iii. 35 Be my end what it may, I am obliged, by thy penetration, fair one, to proceed by the sap. **1791** COWPER *Odyss.* VII. 317 Exempt forever from the sap of age. **1828** P. CUNNINGHAM *N.S. Wales* (ed. 3) II. 52 A hock of pickled pork and a pound of sixpenny sugar, conveyed by way of sap to undermine the virtue of one of our Newgate nuns. **1862** ELLICOTT in *Aids* *to Faith* ix. 396 It is simply an endeavour by slow sap to weaken the authority of some of the writers of the New Testament.

†**c.** ? *transf.*

1794 Sullivan *View Nat.* I. 327 Water may rise..either by running channels or by sap or percolation.

2. A covered trench made for the purpose of approaching a besieged place under the fire of the garrison. ***flying sap***: see flying *ppl. a.* 4 d.

1642 Hexham *Princ. Art Milit.* II. (ed. 2) 38 In the Interim a Sapp is begun, that runneth towards the Bulwark. **1672** J. Lacey tr. *Tacquet's Milit. Archit.* 48 You cut a strait Channel LH, commonly called a Sappe, thorough the outbrestwork, to the very ditch of the Fortification. **1674** Clarendon *Hist. Reb.* VIII. §151 His soldiers..began their approaches by saps. **1687** J. Richards *Jrnl. Siege of Buda* 34 The Duke of Lorrain order'd a large Sap to be made into the Ditch. **1702** *Milit. Dict.* s.v. *Attack*, The Works the Besiegers carry on, either Trenches, Galeries, Sappes, or Breaches to reduce a place. **1782** *Encycl. Brit.* (ed. 2) IX. 6952/1 There are several sorts of saps; the single, which has only a single parapet; the double, having one on each side; and the flying, made with gabions, &c. **1812** Wellington in Gurw. *Desp.* (1838) IX. 35, 200 men likewise of the covering party will rush from the right of the sap into the salient angle of the covered-way of the ravelin. **1893** Forbes-Mitchell *Remin. Gt. Mutiny* 104 To protect this part of their route a flying sap was constructed.

3. *Comb.*: **sap battery**, a battery at the head of a sap; **sap-faggot**, a fascine used in sapping, to fill up the spaces between gabions; **sap-fork** (see quot. 1842); **sap-head**, the foremost end of a sap; **sap-roller**, a large gabion covering the sap-head; **sap-shield** (see quot. 1876).

1810 *Naval Chron.* XXIV. 368 The Namur and Valiant took it day and day about to fight a *sap battery. **1834** J. S. Macaulay *Field Fortif.* 222 The *sap-faggot has a strong stake in the middle. **1842** Brande *Dict. Sci.*, etc., **Sap fork*, an instrument like a boat hook, used to push on a sap roller in sapping. **1884** *Mil. Engineering* (ed. 3) I. II. 75 According as the gabion has to be pulled towards the trench or pushed away from it, which must be done entirely with the sap-fork. **1878** *Text Bk. Fortif.* §332 The rate of progress of the *sapheads, therefore, regulates the rate of progress of the siege. **1834** J. S. Macaulay *Field Fortif.* 222 The head of the sap is covered by a *sap-roller, viz. a large stuffed gabion. **1876** Voyle & Stevenson *Milit. Dict.*, **Sap-shield*, a steel plate mounted on wheels for the purpose of giving cover to the sapper in a single sap.

sap (sæp), *sb.*[4] *School slang.* [prob. f. sap *v.*[3], though appearing earlier in our quots.]

1. One who studies hard or is absorbed in books.

1798 Charlotte Smith *Yng. Philos.* I. 48 He obtained the character of a sullen, cold-blooded fellow, and a sap. **1827** Lytton *Pelham* ii, When I once attempted to read Pope's poems out of school hours, I was laughed at, and called 'a sap'. *a* **1833** W. Wilberforce in *Life* (1838) I. 11 The tutors [at Cambridge, *c* 1776] would often say..that 'they were mere saps, but that I did all by talent'. **1862** *Rep. Publ. Schools Comm.* (1864) III. 284 (Eton), You do not consider a boy who is considered what is called a sap, is looked down upon by the rest?—No.

2. Study, book-work. *Eton College slang.*

a **1862** Q. Hogg *Let.* in E. M. Hogg *Quintin Hogg* (1904) ii. 32 The night before last I..worked the whole night... I hope I shall take well after all my sap. **1901** *Quiet Evening* in *Eton Echoes* 13 Soon a drowsiness steals o'er you, and all thought of 'sap' is banished.

sap (sæp), *sb.*[5] [Short for sapskull.] A simpleton, a fool.

1815 Scott *Guy M.* xlviii, They're sporting the door of the Custom-house, and the auld sap at Hazlewood-House has ordered off the guard. **1818** —— *Rob Roy* xiv, He maun be a saft sap, wi' a head nae better than a fozy frosted turnip. **1836** Mrs. Sherwood *H. Milner* III. xi, Do you think that we are such saps that we cannot say No? **1852** *Meanderings of Mem.* I. 164 He crowned his head but with another cap Than Cardinal's—for that he wants no Sap. **1930** *Sat. Even. Post* 26 July 145/1 In some ways Angelo's a sap, but I never thought he'd get himself in a spot like that. **1940** Wodehouse *Quick Service* xix. 240 You were a sap to come away. **1945** 'N. Shute' *Most Secret* vii. 154 But when you come to think of it, I'd have been a sap. **1959** I. & P. Opie *Lore & Lang. Schoolch.* x. 181 The word 'sap'..the children define as meaning a sissy or a softy ('soft in that he does not do anything wrong'), and suggest other moist alternatives, as 'milksop', 'soppy date', a 'wet', or a 'drip'. **1968** *Globe & Mail* (Toronto) 3 Feb. 35/1 Bobby Mull.., is a sap if he accepts less than $100,000 from the tight-fisted.. management. **1973** 'H. Howard' *Highway to Murder* vi. 72 My brother was a prize sap... Guess he knows better now.

sap (sæp), *v.*[1] [a. F. *saper* (earlier *sapper*) = It. *zappare*, f. *zappa*: see sap *sb.*[3] Cf. Sp. *zapar*.]

1. a. *intr.* To dig a sap or covered trench; to approach a besieged place by means of a sap. Also *to sap up, on.*

1598 Florio, *Zappare*, to digge, or delue, or grubbe the ground, to sap. **1642** Hexham *Princ. Art Milit.* II. (ed. 2) 38 Then one begins to Sapp from H to I. *Ibid.* 45 After you have sapt through the Counterscharfe. **1647** Sprigge *Anglia Rediv.* IV. vii. (1854) 259 They sapt up towards the castle. **1882** Sir R. Temple *Men & Events India* xx. 483 Where the Muhammadan besiegers erected batteries, sapped, undermined, stormed.

b. *fig.* To make way in a stealthy or insidious manner. Also *trans.* in *to sap one's way.*

1732 Pope *Ep. Bathurst* 34 In vain may Heroes fight, and Patriots rave; If secret Gold sap on from knave to knave. **1839** Landor *Andrea & Giov.* Wks. 1846 II. 540 Lies, while they sap their way and hold their tongues, Are safe enough.

2. a. *trans.* To dig under the foundations of (a wall, etc.). Also *transf.* of natural agencies, etc.: To undermine; to render insecure by removing the foundations.

1652 C. B. Stapylton *Herodian* x. 79 But see the chance, from off the Mountaines rapt A sudden flood, which strong Foundation sapt. **1689** *Lond. Gaz.* No. 2482/1 We have begun to sappe the Glacis. **1695** Blackmore *Pr. Arth.* III. 57 Sinking Isles, Sap'd by the Flame,.. Fall down with mighty Cracks. **1696** Phillips (ed. 5), To *sap*, a Term in War, to dig under the Foundations of a Wall to throw it down and destroy it. To dig under the Glacis, in order to pass the Moat securely. **1700** Dryden *Ovid's Met.* I. 397 Sap'd by floods, Their houses fell. **1718** Pope *Iliad* XII. 25 The Weight of Waters saps the yielding Wall. **1726** Leoni *Alberti's Archit.* I. 18/1 Drains..shou'd..not do any harm to the House, either by sapping of dirtying it. **1816** Byron *Siege Cor.* xxiv, Huge fragments, sapp'd by the ceaseless flow. **1838** Prescott *Ferd. & Is.* I. xiii. II. 108 Galleries were also wrought,..to sap the foundations of the walls. **1840** Dickens *Old C. Shop* xxi, A crazy building, sapped and undermined by the rats. **1867** Parkman *Jesuits N. Amer.* xviii. (1875) 263 The flood still rose,..and threatened to sap the magazine.

b. *fig.* with reference to a metaphorical wall, foundation, etc.

1711 Addison *Spect.* No. 163 ¶5 A Heart in Love has its Foundations sapped. **1751** Johnson *Rambler* No. 111 ¶2 To sap the difficulties which it expected to subdue by storm. **1761** Churchill *Night* Poems 1767 I. 80 How damps and vapours..sap the walls of health. **1835** I. Taylor *Spir. Despot.* i. 13 He takes his stand..upon advanced ground which is already sapped. **1857** Buckle *Civiliz.* I. viii. 544 There was..not one who did not..sap the foundation of some old opinion.

c. To approach (a fortress) or to pierce (ground) with saps.

In some recent Dicts.

d. To erode by glacial sapping (sapping *vbl. sb.*[1] 2 b).

1910 *Geogr. Jrnl.* XXXV. 269 Lack of glacial scratches or polish in uplands sapped by this process should not be allowed to weigh too heavily in reconstructing the glacial history of the district. **1940** *Geogr. Rev.* XXX. 81 Whether these glaciers, when at their maximum thickness, were able to sap vigorously the very bottom of the head walls..is a little doubtful.

3. *fig.* **a.** To weaken or destroy insidiously (esp. health, strength, courage, or the like).

Probably often coloured by association with sap *sb.*[1], as if the primary notion were 'to drain the vital sap from'.

1755 *Connoisseur* No. 82 (1774) III. 83 A Drunkard; one that takes an unaccountable pleasure in sapping his constitution. **1770** Goldsm. *Des. Vill.* 393 Till sapped their strength, and every part unsound, Down, down they sink. **1836** J. H. Newman in *Lyra Apost.* (1849) 96 But sloth had sapped the prophet's strength. **1850** Tennyson *In Mem.* cvi, Ring out the grief that saps the mind, For those that here we see no more. **1858** Merivale *Rom. Emp.* (1865) VI. liv. 412 The spirit of inquiry..was sapping the positive beliefs of the day. **1877** Dowden *Shaks. Primer* vi. 117 His moral energy is sapped by a kind of scepticism.

¶ **b.** ? To drain *of* something.

1893 Kate D. Wiggin *Cathedr. Courtship* 68 He sapped me of all my ideas, and gave me none in exchange.

sap (sæp), *v.*[2] *Obs.* [f. sap *sb.*[1]]

1. *trans.* To remove the sap from (wood).

1725 *Bradley's Fam. Dict.* s.v. *Poplar*, The Wood is useful for the Engraver, and being saw'd into Boards and sapt dry, continues a long while.

2. To remove the sap-wood from (a log).

1875 [implied in sapping *vbl. sb.*[3]].

sap (sæp), *v.*[3] *School slang.* [Prob. a fig. use of sap *v.*[1] I. Cf. sap *sb.*[4], which is recorded earlier.] *intr.* To pore over books; to be studious.

1830 H. Angelo *Remin.* II. 371 Preferring a continental visit to sap-ing..three years at college for a fellowship. **1853** Lytton *My Novel* I. I. xii. 80 They say he is the cleverest boy in the school. But then he saps. *a* **1884** M. Pattison *Mem.* (1885) 21 It was unworthy of a man of his position to 'sap'.

sap (sæp), *v.*[4] *U.S. slang.* [f. sap *sb.*[1]] *trans.* To hit or club (someone) with a sap (see sap *sb.*[1] 4 b). Also with *up* and *intr.* in *to sap up on* (someone).

1926 J. Black *You can't Win* vii. 83 The posse fell upon the convention and 'sapped up' on those therein assembled and ran them..out of town. **1926** *Clues* Nov. 162/1 *Sapped*, beaten up. **1931** 'D. Stiff' *Milk & Honey Route* 213 *To get sapped* means to be clubbed by the bulls. **1935** A. J. Pollock *Underworld Speaks* 101/1 *Sapped*, struck with a club or billy by a police officer. **1940** R. Chandler *Farewell, my Lovely* xxxviii. 178 He slumped sideways and clawed at a corner of the desk, then rolled on his back. It was nice to see someone else get sapped for a change. **1971** *Black World* Apr. 65 My eye was swole... I remember how you sapped me up somethin awful.

‖**sapa** ('seɪpə). [L.] **a.** *Antiq.* New wine boiled to a syrup. †**b.** *Pharm.* = rob *sb.*

1624 Middleton *Game at Chess* V. iii, With *Far* and *Sapa*; Flower and cockted Wine. **1688** R. Holme *Armoury* III. xx. (Roxb.) 249/2 Sapa, Boiled wine. **1725** Sloane *Jamaica* II. 3 A Sapa is made of it for sore throats. **1858** Simmonds *Dict. Trade*, *Sapa*, a thickened confection of grapes. **1897** *Syd. Soc. Lex.*, *Sapa*, Syn. for *Rob.*

sapadillies, -dillo: see sapodilla.

sapajou ('sæpədʒuː). Also 7 sapaiou, 9 sapago. [a. F. *sapajou*, in 1614 *sapaiou*, given by D'Abbeville as a Cayenne word.] A South American monkey of the genus *Cebus.*

1698 T. Froger *Voy.* 130 The sapaiou is a kind of a little monkey. **1774** Goldsm. *Nat. Hist.* (1776) IV. 235 Those with muscular holding tails, are called Sapajous. **1875** *Encycl. Brit.* II. 153/2 The genus *Cebus*, the typical genus of American apes, is composed of the sapajous, so commonly seen in captivity.

sapan, sappan ('sæpən). Also 6–7 sapon, 7 sappon. [a. Malay *sapaŋ*, of South Indian origin: cf. Tamil *shappangam*, Malayālam *chappaṅnam*. The proximate source in the 17th c. was prob. Du. *sapan(hout)*; cf. Pg. *sapão*, Fr. *sapan*.] A dye-wood yielding a red dye, obtained from trees belonging to the genus *Cæsalpinia*, indigenous to tropical Asia and the Indian Archipelago, esp. *C. Sappan.* Now only ***sapan wood.***

1598 W. Phillip tr. *Linschoten* I. xxii. 36 The wood Sapon, whereof also much is brought from Sian, it is like Brasill to die withall. **1616** R. Cocks *Diary* (Hakl. Soc.) I. 209 Ofring to deliver me money for all our sappon which was com in this junk. **1626** Methold in Purchas *Pilgrimage* (ed. 4) 1004 A wood to die withall called Sapan wood, the same we heere call Brasill. **1662** J. Davies tr. *Mandelslo's Trav.* II. 197 A sort of wood called Sappan. **1687** *Lond. Gaz.* No. 2269/2, 210 100 l. [*i.e.* 210 quintals] of Siams Sapan Wood. **1780** *Phil. Trans.* LXX. App. 7 For which they give in return sugar, ripe cloves, sappan wood, ivory. **1861** Bentley *Man. Bot.* 529 The roots of the same tree [*Cæsalpinia Sappan*], under the names of Yellow-wood and Sappan-root, are..employed for dyeing yellow. **1881** *Daily News* 22 Jan. 5/8 Great store of Sapanwood from the Indies is also aboard.

†**sape,** *sb. Obs.* Anglicized form of sapa.

c **1440** *Pallad. on Husb.* III. 1142 In water first this opium relent Of sape until it have similitude. **1642** A. Ross *Mel Heliconium* (1643) 56 Let me taste of that sweet sape Which dropp'd from this squeezed grape. **1657** Tomlinson *Renou's Disp.* 102 Make them into conserves, sapes, and syrups. **1657** *Physical Dict.*, *Sapes*, are medicinated juyces which having been pressed out of fruits and herbs, have been brought to a consistency by standing in the sun.

†**sape,** *v.*[1] *Obs.* Also 7 *pa. t.* **sapped.** [Of obscure origin: cf. dial. *sap*, 'to drench, soak' (E.D.D.); also sop *v.*] *intr.* ? To be steeped (*in* sin, etc.). Hence †**saped** *ppl. a.*

1571 Golding *Calvin on Ps.* xvii. 14 The men..whom thou hast suffered too sit saping too long in the dregges of their prosperitie [orig. *quos nimis diu in prosperitatis suæ fæcibus residere passus es*]. **1583** —— *Calvin on Deut.* v. xxxii. 191 Such as..are caryed away with their owne lewdnesse, and as it were saped in their sinnes [Fr. *qui se sont transportez en leurs iniquitez, et y sont comme confits*]. **1587** —— *De Mornay* i. 11 Saped in wickednesse [Fr. *confites en meschancetez*]. **1633** D. R[ogers] *Treat. Sacram.* ii. 30 Say not, there is no hope for so saped a wretch as thou. **1642** —— *Naaman* 175 When she is sapped and soked in Selfe. **1693** Evelyn *De La Quint. Compl. Gard.*, Dict., *Saped*,..is any thing that is too much soaked in water.

†**sape,** *v.*[2] *Burlesque nonce-wd.* [ad. L. *sapĕre.*] *intr.* To be wise.

1694 Motteux *Rabelais* V. 252 If then you sape, as we are cogitating [Fr. *Et si tu es (comme cogitons) sage*].

sape, obs. form of sap *sb.*[1], shape, soap.

sapego, variant of serpigo.

Sapei, var. Sebei.

sapele (sə'piːliː). The name of a port on the Benin River, southern Nigeria, used to designate the reddish-brown hardwood timber of *Entandophragma cylindricum*, a large West African forest tree belonging to the family Meliaceæ. Also *attrib.*

1904 *Timber Trades Jrnl.* 2 Apr. 740/2 A fair amount of the African wood [*sc.* mahogany]..was sold. There were submitted 346 lots of Lagos..69 logs of Sapeli, Benin, padouk, birch and Gaboon logs. **1914** E. W. Foster *Notes Nigerian Trees & Plants* 20 The wood..has been exported to Europe under the name of 'Unscented Mahogany' presumably to distinguish it from the 'Sapele Scented Wood'. **1928** *Sunday Express* 29 July 15/4 We take the most handsome pieces of burr walnut, of rosewood and sapele mahogany... We place these on the surface of our furniture in such a way that they provide all the beauty and decoration that is needed. **1936** *Nature* 9 May 790/1 The following woods amongst others have been used: laurel wood,.. Sapele. **1954** *Archit. Rev.* CXV. 189/3 Display shelves are of sapele wood supported by light steel rods, cellulosed black and orange. **1958** [see mansonia]. **1960** *News Chron.* 21 Apr. 6/2, 11 steps, with treads of sapele (an African hardwood), lead to a landing above the hall. **1964** R. W. J. Keay et al. *Nigerian Trees* 265 This [*sc. Entandophragma cylindricum*] is one of Nigeria's largest and finest trees, producing the well known Sapele Wood. **1972** 'K. Royce' *Miniatures Frame* ix. 117 A board room..with steel tubular chairs running the length of a sapele mahogany table. **1981** *Times* 24 Apr. 12/2 Great sapele logs are stacked along the banks of the Oubangy river.

sapful ('sæpfʊl), *a.* [f. sap *sb.*[1] + -ful.] Abounding in sap or moisture.

1674 N. Fairfax *Bulk & Selv.* 185 Those layers, that are made of sapful and growthsom earths. **1847** Chr. G. Rossetti *Dead City* Poems (1904) 101/1 Strong and sapful were the root, The top boughs, and all between. **1881** Fairbairn *Stud. Life Christ* iv. 65 The roots of the glorious flower are bedded deep in the sapful soil.

sap-green, *sb.* (and *a.*). [f. sap *sb.*[1] + green, prob. after Du. *sapgroen.*]

1. A green pigment prepared from the juice of buckthorn berries; also, the colour of this pigment.

1578 in Feuillerat *Revels Q. Eliz.* (1908) 294 Sape greene quarter li. ii[s]. **1612** PEACHAM *Gentl. Exerc.* 83 Take Sappe greene, and lay it in sharpe vinegar. **1686** BLOME *Gentl. Recr.* I. 219 Sap-green is a dirty dark Green, and of little use, except to Shadow in the dark places. **1797** *Encycl. Brit.* (ed. 3) III. 366/2 The next operation is the sprinkling the leaves of the book; which is done by dipping a brush into vermilion and sap-green. **1861** BENTLEY *Man. Bot.* 520 The colour called Sap-green is prepared by evaporating to dryness the juice of the Buckthorn berries previously mixed with lime. **1881** E. J. WORBOISE *Sissie* xxxviii, St. Peter in royal purple and sap-green.

2. *attrib.* and *adj.*

1658 W. SANDERSON *Graphice* 42 Her Knots and choyce Riband sap-green and silver. **1824** SCOTT *St. Ronan's* xi, Landscapes with sap-green trees and mazareen-blue rivers. **1848** *Zoologist* VI. 1979 Those specimens I saw myself were of a yellowish sap-green colour.

'sap-head. [f. SAP *sb.*[1] (sense 4). Cf. the earlier SAPSKULL.] A fool, a simpleton.

1798 T. G. FESSENDEN in *Farmer's Weekly Museum* 2 Jan. 4/1 The poet nimbly trips it back—Over the Union courses rapid, And squibs each Jacobinick saphead. **1828** *Craven Gloss.*, *Sap-head*, a blockhead. **1884** 'MARK TWAIN' *Huck. Finn* iii. 23 You don't seem to know anything, somehow—perfect sap-head.

So **sap-headed** *a.*, foolish, stupid.

1665 HEAD *Eng. Rogue* (1666) I. iv. 31 *Culle*, a Sap-headed Fellow. **1821** in Cobbett *Rur. Rides* (1885) I. 31 Sap-headed fools! They will [etc.]. **1902** *Harper's Mag.* Jan. 266/2 Of all the sap-headed milksops I ——.

sapheir, obs. form of SAPPHIRE.

‖**saphena** (sə'fiːnə). *Anat.* Also α. 7 **saphen**, 7, 9 **saphena**; β. 5 **sophena**, 6 **sopheyne**. [med.L. *saphena*, *sophona*, ad. Arab. *çāfin* saphena; also 'a vein lying deep in the arm' (Lane). Cf. F. *saphène* (1314 in Hatz.-Darm.), Pg., It. *safena*.

The usual statement that the word is from Gr. σαφηνής 'manifest, clear', is baseless. The Gr. word does not mean 'conspicuously visible', but is used only in intellectual senses.]

The distinctive name of two veins in the leg: (1) the ***long*** or ***internal saphena***, which extends from near the ankle-joint along the inner surface of the leg, and ends in the femoral vein; (2) the ***short***, ***posterior***, or ***external saphena***, which extends from the foot along the calf of the leg, and finally joins the popliteal vein. Also ***saphena vein***.

1398 TREVISA *Barth. De P.R.* VII. lvii. (1495) 271 The veyne whyche hight Saphena is vnder the ancle boon of the fote. *c* **1400** *Lanfranc's Cirurg.* 177 þer ben ij. oþer veynes in þe holow of þe foot withinne, & þat oon is clepid sophena, & þat oþer is clepid vena ventris. **1541** COPLAND *Guydon's Quest. Chirurg.* K iij b, The sopheynes that are vpon the ancle. **1597** A. M. tr. *Guillemeau's Fr. Chirurg.* 30/1 The second, Saphena, or mother vayne, we open on the insyde of the legge. **1656** BLOUNT *Glossogr.* s.v. *Vein*, *Saphen vein* (*saphena*), the mother Vein; the first branch of the thigh vein. **1693** tr. *Blancard's Phys. Dict.* (ed. 2), *Saphæna*, the Vein of the Leg, or Crural Vein. **1813** J. THOMSON *Lect. Inflam.* 151 This..has of late years been often done by tying the saphena veins. **1846** BRITTAN tr. *Malgaigne's Man. Oper. Surg.* 53 Bleeding in the Foot. The internal saphena vein may be opened in front of the internal maleolus, or the external saphena in front of the external maleolus. **1876** tr. *Wagner's Gen. Path.* 198 The saphena can usually be distinctly felt.

b. *attrib.* in ***saphena nerve***: see quot.

1849–52 *Todd's Cycl. Anat.* IV. 1411 The internal saphena vein is accompanied, from the ankle to the knee, by the internal saphena nerve.

saphenal (sə'fiːnəl), *a.* [f. SAPHENA + -AL[1].] = SAPHENOUS *a.*

1831 R. KNOX *Cloquet's Anat.* 517 Of the internal popliteal nerve. External Saphenal branch.

saphenous (sə'fiːnəs), *a.* Also *erron.* (quasi-Latin) **saphenus**. [f. SAPHENA + -OUS.] Pertaining to or connected with the saphena. ***saphenous vein***: the saphena. ***saphenous nerve*** = 'saphena nerve' (see SAPHENA b.).

1840 G. V. ELLIS *Anat.* 626 The oval aperture in the fascia lata, now exposed, is the saphenous opening. **1840** E. WILSON *Anat. Vade M.* (1842) 345 It receives several muscular and articular veins, and the external saphenous vein. **1881** *Trans. Obstetric Soc. Lond.* XXII. 22 The course of the long saphenous nerve.

sapher(e, -eron(e, -ian, -ic(k(e: see SAPPHIRE, SAFFRON, SAFFIAN, SAPPHIC.

‖**saphie** ('sæfiː). *North Africa.* Also 9 **saffi**, **safie**. [Mandingo *safaye*.] A charm.

1799 M. PARK *Trav.* xvi. (ed. 2) 206 He..desired me to write him a saphie. **1817** BOWDICH, etc. *Mission Ashantee* II. iv. (1819) 271 The most surprising superstition of the Ashantees, is their confidence in the fetishes or saphies they purchase so extravagantly from the Moors. **1847** MRS. R. LEE *Afr. Wand.* xvii. (1854) 290 Scraps of the Koran, esteemed as charms, and called safies. **1904** MARY GAUNT *Arm of Leopard* 256 The more or less Arabic charms known as Saphis. **1905** R. A. FREEMAN *Golden Pool* 108, I..hung round my neck a saffi or amulet.

saphier, Saphik: see SAPPHIRE, SAPPHIC.

saphion, -ique: see SAFFIAN, SAPPHIC.

saphir(e, -irine: see SAPPHIRE, -IRINE.

‖**saphir d'eau** (safir do). Also **sapphir(e) d'eau**. [Fr., lit. 'sapphire of water'.] A translucent blue variety of cordierite occurring in Sri Lanka; = WATER-SAPPHIRE.

In Fr. the term was orig. used by mineralogists to refer to blue quartz.

1820 R. JAMESON *Syst. Mineral.* (ed. 3) I. 174 The sapphire d'eau of collectors. **1897** L. FLETCHER *Introd. Study Mineral.* 106 Cordierite is a silicate of magnesium, iron and aluminium; its transparent variety is the *Saphir d'eau* of jewellery. **1925** KRAUS & HOLDEN *Gems & Gem Materials* II. 165 Ceylon is the most important locality, and the gems from that country have sometimes been called *saphir d'eau*, or 'water sapphire'. **1936** H. P. WHITLOCK *Story of Gems* 175 Iolite. This silicate of magnesium, aluminium and iron is better known as *water-sapphire* (saphir d'eau).

saphron, obs. form of SAFFRON.

sapid ('sæpɪd), *a.* Also 7 **sapide**. [ad. L. *sapid-us* savoury, f. *sapĕre* (see SAPIENT *a.*). Cf. F. *sapide*; the direct descendant is *sade* (*obs.*).]

1. Of food, etc.: Readily perceptible by the organs of taste, having a decided taste or flavour; *esp.* having a pleasant taste, savoury, palatable.

1646 SIR T. BROWNE *Pseud. Ep.* III. xxii. 165 Thus Camels to make the water sapide do raise the mud with their feet. **1656** BLOUNT *Glossogr.*, *Sapid*, well seasoned, savory, that hath a smack. **1761** ARMSTRONG *Day* 140 In salt itself the sapid savour fails. **1837** M. DONOVAN *Dom. Econ.* II. 103 It [venison] is certainly more sapid than any butchers' meat, and is even strong. **1898** P. MANSON *Trop. Diseases* xxi. 325 If the patient attempts to take any sapid food..the pain and burning in the mouth are intolerable.

2. In neutral sense: Having the power of affecting the organs of taste; having taste or flavour.

1634 T. JOHNSON *Parey's Chirurg.* XXVI. vii. 1034 Therefore Nature observes this order in the concoction of sapide bodies, that at the first the acerbe taste should take place, then the austere, and lastly, the acide. **1686** GOAD *Celest. Bodies* I. ix. 32 They are genericall Natures, common to all Sapid and Odorate Bodies. **1756** C. LUCAS *Ess. Waters* II. 95 Epsom water..scentless, and hardly sapid. **1831** J. DAVIES *Manual Mat. Med.* 10 Those [salts] which are insoluble in water are insipid; such..as are soluble in it, are more or less sapid. **1862** G. WILSON *Relig. Chem.* 5 Neither plants nor animals can exist..in any of the odorous or sapid gases.

3. *fig.* Grateful to the mind or mental taste.

1640 HOWELL *Dodona's Gr.* 217, I must confesse there may some few criticismes or graines of browne salt, and small dashes of vineger be found here and there, to make the discourse more sapid, but this tartnesse is farre from any gall or venome. **1649** JER. TAYLOR *Great Exemp.* I. Dis. iv. 125 The life of the spirit, is lessened and impaired according as the gusts of the flesh grow high and sapid. *a* **1677** HALE *Prim. Orig. Man.* IV. viii. 373 These are things..more grateful, sapid, and delightful to the Mind, than the best Apparatus or Provisions of a sensible Good. **1690** NORRIS *Refl. Cond. Hum. Life* (1691) 179 Such Books..as are Sapid, Pathetic, and Divinely-relishing. **1864** CARLYLE *Fredk. Gt.* IV. 356 Pamphlets..sapid, exhilarative. **1868** *Sat. Rev.* 19 Dec. 794/2 Quite as important as the possession..of all these faculties, is the temper, spirit, tone, or manner of their use, the something which makes them sapid.

4. *absol.* **a.** ***the sapid***, that which is sapid, sapidity. **b.** quasi-*sb.* A sapid substance.

1715 *Pancirollus' Rerum Mem.* II. v. 299 Sugar..seems to tame and to triumph over all Sapids. **1831** T. L. PEACOCK *Crotchet Castle* iv, I speak of the cruet sauces, where the quintessence of the sapid is condensed in a phial.

sapidity (sə'pɪdɪtɪ). [ad. L. **sapiditātem*, f. *sapid-us* SAPID: see -ITY.] The quality of being sapid or having taste and flavour.

1646 SIR T. BROWNE *Pseud. Ep.* III. xxi. 158 The body of that element [air] is ingustible, void of all sapidity. **1837** M. DONOVAN *Dom. Econ.* II. 3 The epicure with whom the single quality of sapidity outweighs every other consideration. **1878** M'KENDRICK *Outl. Physiol.* 224 There must always be a certain amount of sapidity or flavour in the food.

b. *fig.* (Cf. 'relish'.)

1656 BLOUNT *Glossogr.*, *Sapidity*, pleasantness of taste or savor; also pleasantness of talk. **1784** J. BARRY in *Lect. Paint.* vi. (1848) 230 [Rembrandt's] tints..have the same truth, high relish, and sapidity, as those of Titian. **1907** *Sat. Rev.* 29 June 815/1 It is the clash of personalities which gives the sapidity to the life of a politician.

'sapidless, *a.* *nonce-wd.* [Badly f. SAPID + -LESS.] Flavourless.

1821 LAMB *Elia* Ser. I. *Grace bef. Meat*, To come home..expecting some savoury mess, and to find one quite tasteless and sapidless.

†**'sapidness.** *Obs.* [f. SAPID + -NESS.] Sapidity (*lit.* and *fig.*).

1649 JER. TAYLOR *Gt. Exemp.* Pref. ¶2 God gave man reason and abilities..to perceive the sapidnesse and rellish of those objects. **1680** BOYLE *Scept. Chem.* IV. 246 We see that sapidness and volatility are wont to denominate the Chymists Mercury or Spirit.

sapience ('seɪpɪəns). Also 4–6 **sapyence**, 4–5, *Sc.* 6, 8 **sapiens**. [a. OF. *sapience*, ad. L. *sapientia*, f. *sapient-em* SAPIENT: see -ENCE.]

1. Wisdom, understanding. (A learned synonym. Now *rare* in serious use: see sense 2.)

13.. *E.E. Allit. P.* B. 1626 þat þou has in þy hert holy connyng, Of sapience þi sawle ful soþes to schawe. **1377** LANGL. *P. Pl.* B. XII. 42 For what made Lucyfer to lese þe heigh heuene, Or salamon his sapience or sampson his strengthe? **1412–20** LYDG. *Chron. Troy* I. 3854 But whan monhod is meynt with sapience, Who considereth, it may double avayle. **1509** WATSON *Ship of Fools* ii. (1517) A iv, All the scyence and all the sapyence of men shall not excuse them. **1549** *Compl. Scotl.* vi. 43 Appollo, that the poietis callis the god of sapiens. **1603** HARSNET *Pop. Impost.* 99 It is a point of high Sapience in the Church of Rome to choose [etc.]. **1659** *Queries on Proposalls of Officers of Armie to Parlt.* 4 As that Supreme Master of Politicall Sapience doth assert. **1724** RAMSAY *Vision* xv, A king..Quhase pusiens, and sapiens, Sall richt restore and saiv. **1730** SWIFT *Traulus* I, Yet many a Wretch in Bedlam..still has Gratitude and Sap'ence, To spare the Folks that give him Ha'pence. **1836** HOR. SMITH *Tin Trump.* s.v. *Praise*, Silence is sapience. **1874** BLACKIE *Self-Cult.* 71 'Honour all men' is one of the many texts of combined sanctity and sapience with which the New Testament abounds. **1901** CORVO *Ho. Borgia* 20 That letter..written..with the unerring sapience of a saint.

†**b.** as an attribute of God. Hence applied to the Word or second person of the Trinity. *Obs.*

c **1386** CHAUCER *Prioress' Prol.* 20 Of whos vertu, whan he thyn herte lighte, Conceyued was the fadres sapience. *c* **1400** *Sowdone Bab.* 2 God..That all thinge made in sapience. **1489** CAXTON *Faytes of A.* IV. vii. 247 The diuyne puissaunce and the sapience of almyghty god. **1536** *Primer Eng. & Lat.* 55 b, He that is the greate profounde sapience And dyuyne trueth of the father on hye. **1605** BACON *Adv. Learn.* I. vi. § I. 27 b, All learning is knowledge acquired, and all knowledge in God is originall. And therefore we must looke for it by another name, that of wisdome or sapience, as the scriptures call it. **1698** [R. FERGUSON] *View Eccles.* 100 Herein is the Immense Sapience and the Superlative Goodness of God to be admired.

†**c.** Spiritual wisdom, knowledge of divine things.

[*c* **1430** LYDG. *Min. Poems* (Percy Soc.) 9 God the ffulfylle withe intelligence, And withe a spyrut of goostly sapience. *c* **1570** W. WAGER *The longer thou livest* 1654 (Brandl), As scripture calleth this the hiest sapience, God to know, to feare, to loue, and obey.] **1598** BARCKLEY *Felic. Man* VI. (1603) 589 Let us now examine Sapience..or that part of wisedome which is conversant in the contemplation of God and divine matters. **1614** RALEIGH *Hist. World* I. (1634) 21 The eie of the soule, or receptacle of Sapience and divine knowledge.

†**d.** sometimes contradistinguished from *prudence* (see quots.). *Obs.*

1606 BRYSKETT *Civ. Life* 252 This light of reason (as much as concerneth mens actions) is nothing else but Prudence,..euen as sapience or wisedome is the guide and gouernesse of speculation. **1651** HOBBES *Leviath.* I. v. 22 As, much Experience, is Prudence; so, is much Science, Sapience. For though wee usually have one name of Wisedome for them both; yet the Latines did alwayes distinguish between *Prudentia* and *Sapientia*; ascribing the former to Experience, the later to Science. *a* **1677** BARROW *Serm.* (1686) III. xiv. 156 Wisedom..may denote either sapience, a habit of knowing what is true; or prudence, a disposition of chusing what is good.

†**e.** Correct taste and judgement. *Obs.*

1667 MILTON *P.L.* IX. 1018 Eve, now I see thou art exact of taste, And elegant, of Sapience no small part, Since to each meaning savour we apply, And Palate call judicious. **1692** WOOD *Athen. Oxon.* II. 540 (Heneage Finch) A person of so eloquent and fluent speech, and of so great sapience, that he was usually stiled the English Roscius and the English Cicero. **1796** BURNEY *Mem. Metastasio* III. 174 The sapience of Horace, that is, the correct judgment which reigns in all you think and write.

2. Used depreciatingly or ironically: Would-be wisdom.

c **1374** CHAUCER *Troylus* I. 515 Loo þer goþe he þat is man of so grete sapience and held vs louers leest in reuerence. **1642** MILTON *Apol. Smect.* Wks. 1851 III. 287 This is a piece of sapience not worth the brain of a fruit-trencher. **1664** BUTLER *Hud.* II. iii. 794 Staring round with Owl-like Eies, He put his face into a posture Of Sapience, and began to bluster. **1781** COWPER *Charity* 519 Just as the sapience of an author's brain Suggests it safe or dang'rous to be plain. **1893** MORLEY *Sp. at Manchester* 8 Nov., Wisdom is the real article and sapience is the sham article.

†**3.** The apocryphal book of 'Wisdom'. *Obs.*

In *Piers Plowman* perh. used as a general name for the 'sapiental books' of the Bible.

1362 LANGL. *P. Pl.* A. VIII. 47 So seiþ þe sauter and sapience boþe. **1377** *Ibid.* B. III. 330 Se what Salamon seith in Sapience bokes. **14..** *Wyclif's Bible*, *Wisd.* ad. fin., Here endith the book of Sapiens. **1534** MORE *Comf. agst. Trib.* II. Wks. 1199/1 Of this arowe speaketh the wise man in the .v. Chapter of Sapience. **1563** *Homilies* II. *Rogation Wk.* III. 245 b, Wherein is expressed further in Sapience howe God geueth his elect an vnderstandyng of the motions of the heauens.

sapient ('seɪpɪənt), *a.* and *sb.* [a. OF. *sapient* or ad. L. *sapient-em* wise, sb. wise man, pres. pple. of *sapĕre* to have a taste or savour, to be sensible or wise.]

A. *adj.*

1. a. Wise. (A learned synonym, in serious use now only *poet.*)

1471 RIPLEY *Comp. Alch.* V. viii. in Ashm. (1652) 150 Of thys Pryncyple spekyth Sapyent Guydo. **1515** BARCLAY *Egloges* ii. (1570) B v b, Thou haste me saued by councell sapient Out of hell mouth. **1549** *Compl. Scot.* Epist. 5 That maist sapient prince..ihone of loran. **1622** CALLIS *Stat. Sewers* (1824) 334 In Scripture he is not counted sapient that before he build a house will not first count the charge of it. **1667** MILTON *P.L.* IX. 442 Where the Sapient King Held dalliance with his faire Egyptian Spouse. **1809** WORDSW. *Sonn.*, '*Alas! what boots the long laborious quest*', If sapient Germany must lie deprest Beneath the brutal sword. **1868** LONGF. *Dante's Inferno* iv. 149 Another way my sapient Guide conducts me.

b. now usually *ironical*.

a **1763** SHENSTONE *Economy* I. 3 Nor think some Miser vents his sapient saw. **1784** COWPER *Task* II. 531 Now tell me, dignified and sapient Sir. **1790** BURKE *Fr. Rev.* 337 The œconomy which has been introduced by the virtuous and sapient assembly. **1822** Lamb *Elia, Bks. & Reading*, I think I see them at their work—these sapient trouble-tombs. **1886** Hall Caine *Son of Hagar* II. xvi, Then the group of women at the gate separated with many a sapient comment.

c. Having knowledge *of*, aware *of*. *rare*$^{-1}$.
1764 Grainger *Sugar Cane* II. 306 The herds, as sapient of the coming storm.. In troops associate.

†**2.** Used in the orig. sense of L. *sapĕre*: Having a taste or savour, sapid. *Obs.*
1599 A. Hume *Hymns* ii. 75 Of euerie substance sapient, the sapor and the taist..the mouth will try in haist.

3. *Anthrop.* Of, pertaining to, or characteristic of modern man, *Homo sapiens*.
1971 *Nature* 28 May 213/1 At sites in East Africa can be seen evidence of the various stages of human evolution—the older levels have the remains of the australopithecines and the younger levels have, in succession, early hominines and, finally, fully sapient types. **1976** *Ibid.* 5 Aug. 487/1 It [*sc.* the Ndutu cranium] differs from Swanscombe and Steinheim in its occipital curvature and in that the mastoid of Steinheim is sapient in form.

B. *sb.* **1.** [= L. *sapiens*.] A wise man, sage. In later use only *jocularly*.
1549 *Compl. Scot.* xvi. 142 Conformand til ane addagia of ane of the seuyn sapientis callit mimus publianus. **1592** Chettle *Kind-harts Dr.* (1841) 38 Mirth, in seasonable time taken, is not forbidden by the austerest sapients. **1600** W. Watson *Decacordon* (1602) 110 He must be an Antiquary with Nestor: an Historian with Plutarch, and a Sapient with Cato. **1827** Scott *Two Drovers* i, 'She canna do that', said another sapient of the same profession.

†**2.** = sapience. [? A confusion or mis-writing.]
a **1400–50** *Alexander* 622 þan was he lede furthe be-lyfe to lere at þe scole, As sone as to þat sapient him-self was of elde. *Ibid.* 2526 þare had I siȝt of þe segg, his sapient [*Dubl. MS.* sapiens] I herde.

sapiential (seɪpɪˈɛnʃəl), *a.* Also 5 sapyencyall, 7 sapientiall. [a. F. *sapiential*, or ad. eccl. L. *sapientiāl-is*, f. *sapientia* sapience.]
1. Belonging to or characterized by wisdom; esp. belonging to the wisdom of God (cf. sapience 1 b).
c **1485** *Digby Myst.* (1882) II. 80 For your sapyencyall wyttes I gyf commendacion. **1656** Hobbes *Quest. Liberty, Necess. & Chance* 212 Some distinctions are Scholastical onely, and some are Scholastical and sapiential also. **1663** Baxter *Div. Life* 11 Man being made at first the Natural and Sapiential image of God. **1675** —— *Cath. Theol.* II. i. 20 Under Gods sapiential Government of the World. *a* **1680** J. Corbet *Free Actions* II. iii. (1683) 16 God..can do with it as he pleaseth, by a sapiential Government.
2. Epithet of the 'wisdom' books of the Bible (Proverbs, Ecclesiates, Canticles, Wisdom, Ecclesiasticus); also applied occas. to kindred writings outside the canon. [So in eccl.L. and Fr.] Also applied to similar writings in Old English.
1568 Bible (Bishops') Introd. 8 b, The Bible..is of diuers natures, some legall, some historicall, some sapientiall, and some propheticall. **1673** O. Walker *Educ.* I. vi. 50 Let him also frequently..read some part of the Scripture, and the Historical and Sapiental Books rather then the other. **1880** W. Sanday in *Expositor* XI. 358 The Sapiential books in the Apocrypha. **1882** Farrar *Early Chr.* I. 278 This Sapiential literature of Alexandria,..represented by the books of Ecclesiasticus and Wisdom and in the writings of Philo. **1970** *N. & Q.* Dec. 445/1 Old English sapiential poetry has received a good deal of scholarly attention.
Hence **sapiˈentially** *adv.*
1846 Worcester (cites Baxter).

sapientious (seɪpɪˈɛnʃəs), *a. rare.* [f. L. *sapienti-a* + -ous.] Characterized by sapience.
1852 Jerdan *Autobiog.* I. xii. 90 Many a..sapientious declination of his head had the perplexed and bemused editor. **1860** Worcester (cites Chambers).

†**sapientipotent**, *a. Obs. rare.* [ad. L. *sapientipotent-em*, f. *sapient-* sapient (or *sapientia* sapience) + *potentem* powerful.] Mighty in wisdom. Also *absol.* as *sb.*
1656 Blount *Glossogr.*, *Sapientipotent*, mighty in wisdom. **1675** J. Smith *Chr. Relig. App.* I. 25 Æacus his Progeny were a stolid Generation, that acted by main strength, not by policy, being belli-potents not sapienti-potents.

ˈ**sapientize**, *v. nonce-wd.* [-ize.] *trans.* To make sapient or wise.
c **1810** Coleridge in *Lit. Rem.* (1838) III. 219 Truly evangelical way of..sapientizing Calvin's *tolerabiles ineptias* by making them *ineptias usque ad carcerem et verbera intolerantes*!

sapiently (ˈseɪpɪəntlɪ), *adv.* [-ly².] In a sapient manner, wisely, Now usually ironically = with apparent or would-be wisdom.
1477 Norton *Ord. Alch.* v. in Ashm. (1652) 77 Plato wrote full sapiently. **1816** Kirby & Sp. *Entomol.* (1818) II. xxiv. 382 From whence he very sapiently concludes, that not the tail but the mouth must be their organ of sound. **1872** W. R. Greg *Enigmas Life* 112 No government and no statesman has ever yet dared thus to supplement the inadequacy of personal patriotism by laws so sapiently despotic. **1882** Mrs. J. H. Riddell *Pr. Wales' Garden-Party* 189 'Still property is property,' remarked Mrs. Briart, sapiently.

sapin. Also 5–6 -yn, 7 -ine. [a. OF. (and mod.F.) *sapin*, ad. L. *sapīnus*.] A kind of fir or pine. Usually ***sapin tree***.
1323–4 *Ely Sacr. Rolls* (1907) II. 47 In xxiv arboribus de sapin empt. pro stagyngg, 2^{li} 8^{s} 0^{d}. *c* **1489** Caxton *Sonnes of Aymon* ix. 242, I lefte hym here by this sapyn tre. **1526** *Grete Herball* xv. (1529) B j, Agaryke is an excrescens that groweth nyghe to the rote of a sapyn tre. **1585** T. Washington tr. *Nicholay's Voy.* I. iv, They pul from the said Sapins great abundance of rosin. **1604** E. G[rimstone] *D'Acosta's Hist. Indies* v. xxvi. 403 Which they died blacke with the fume of sapine, or firre trees, or rosine. **1793** E. Wynne *Diary* 14 Sept. (1935) I. xii. 216 Not such Sapin and Pine woods as in the Country of St. Gall but Oak's. **1813** A. Henry *Jrnl.* 14 Dec. in E. Coues *New Light Early Hist. Greater Northwest* (1897) II. xxiv. 772 The place is deeply shaded with spruce, pine, sapin, etc. **1927** *Brit. Weekly* 1 Sept. 470/3 Across the valley..are the mountain slopes, with the valient *sapins* sending their spear points, in massed formation, to the highest level at which a tree can grow.

sapindaceous (sæpɪnˈdeɪʃəs), *a. Bot.* [f. mod.L. *Sapindus*, the typical genus of the order: see -aceous.] Belonging to the N.O. *Sapindaceæ*.
1845 G. Don in *Encycl. Metrop.* VI. 174*/2 Sapindaceous trees.

Sapiny (ˈsæpɪnɪ). Also Sabiny, Sapin, Saviny. [Native name.] = Sebei.
1909 A. C. Hollis *Nandi* I. 2 It seems probable that the tribes allied to the Nandi who live on or near Mount Elgon (the Lako, Kony, Mbai, Sabaut, Sapin, Pôk, and Kâpkara) are only a section of the migrants. **1964** Sabiny [see Kipsigis]. **1977** C. F. & F. M. Voegelin *Classification & Index World's Lang.* 323 *Nandi*... Sapiny = Sabei = Savei = Sebei = Saviny = Kamecak (572,000; Uganda).

Sapir-Whorf hypothesis (səˈpɪə(r) hwɔəf). [f. the names of Edward *Sapir* (1884–1939) and Benjamin Lee *Whorf* (1897–1941), American linguists.] A hypothesis, first advanced by Sapir in 1929 and subsequently developed by Whorf, that the structure of a language partly determines a native speaker's categorization of experience. Cf. Whorfian *a.*
1954 H. Hoijer *Language in Culture* I. 93 The central idea of the Sapir-Whorf hypothesis is that language functions, not simply as a device for reporting experience, but also..as a way of defining experience for its speakers. **1954** —— in *Mem. Amer. Anthropol. Assoc.* LXXIX. 95 Differences..which reflect a people's habitual and favorite modes of reporting, analyzing, and categorizing experience, form the essential data of the Sapir-Whorf hypothesis. **1956** J. B. Carroll in B. L. Whorf *Lang., Thought, & Reality* 27 Whorf's principle of linguistic relativity, or, more strictly, the Sapir-Whorf hypothesis (since Sapir most certainly shared in the development of the idea) has..attracted a great deal of attention. **1976** *Word 1971* XXVII. 242 This is 180 degrees different from what has been known about the Sapir-Whorf hypothesis, which advocates that it is language that has the power to dictate man's world view in a tyrannical way.

sapi-utan (sapiˈutan). Also -outan, -utang, -utung. [Malay *sāpi ūtan* 'wild ox' (*sāpi* ox, *ūtan* wild: cf. orang-outang.] A small wild ox of Celebes, *Anoa* (or *Bos*) *depressicornis*.
1868 Bickmore *Trav. E. Ind. Archip.* 325 There dwells the *sapi-utung* or 'wild ox'. *Ibid.* 334 The wild ox, *sapi-utung*. **1869** A. R. Wallace *Malay Archip.* I. 414 On their way they caught a young Sapi-utan and five pigs.

sap lath. Also 7 sapt lath. [sap *sb.*¹ 4.] A lath made of sap-wood.
1350 in Riley *Mem. Lond.* (1868) 261 [Also 30000] saplathes, [value 2s. per thousand]. **1415** in *York Minster Fabric Rolls* (Surtees) 35 In m.ccc. saplates emptis de Johanne Bateman de Topclyff, 5s. 10d. **1421** *Ibid.* 44 In m.m. saplattes emptis ab eodem, 8s. **1514** *MS. Acc. St. John's Hosp., Canterb.*, Payd for ij C off sep lath. **1577** Harrison *England* II. xii. (1877) I. 235 Made fast here and there with saplaths. **1630–1** in Swayne *Sarum Churchw. Acc.* (1896) 192 Three hundred of sapt lathes, 2s. 3d. **1766** *Compl. Farmer* s.v. *Lath*, Heart of oak, sap laths, and deal laths. **1825** J. Nicholson *Operat. Mechanic* 611 Laths are also distinguished into heart and sap laths.

†ˈ**saple.** *Obs. rare*$^{-1}$. Altered form of sapling.
1589 T. Lodge *Scillaes Metam.* B 2, Her breast..From whence..her armes doo sweetly spred Like two rare branchie saples in the Spring.

sapless (ˈsæplɪs), *a.* [f. sap *sb.*¹ + -less.]
1. Of plants, wood, etc.: Destitute of sap; dry, withered.
1591 Shaks. *1 Hen. VI*, II. v. 12 Pyth-lesse Armes, like to a withered Vine, That droupes his sappe-lesse Branches to the ground. **1678** H. Vaughan *Thalia Rediv., Affliction* (1858) 224 Flowers that in sunshine riot still, Dye, scorched and sapless. **1762** *Poetry in Ann. Reg.* 225 Sapless wood but makes a blaze. **1786** tr. *Beckford's Vathek* (1868) 46 Their summits..till then had never been covered but with sapless thistles and fern. **1818** Shelley *Euganean Hills* 43 Like sapless leaflets..Frozen upon December's bough. **1892** Walsh *Tea* (Philad.) 161 But if old and 'sapless' they [the tea leaves] will be found rough and 'chaffy' to the touch.
fig. **1594** J. Dickenson *Arisbas* (1878) 29 The saplesse frutes of greene youth, and pithlesse blossomes of a simple Authors vnripe wit.
b. Of soil: Dry, without moisture; also barren, unproductive.
1655 Moufet & Bennet *Health's Impr.* (1746) 78 A dry, crumbling, sapless and unmingled Earth. **1665** Sir T. Herbert *Trav.* (1677) 37 These Troglodites well knowing how little advantage that great Monarch would get by entring their sapless Country, scornfully refused it. **1827** Lytton *Pelham* liv, I live, as it were, on a rock, barren, and herbless, and sapless. **1895** Salmond *Chr. Doctr. Immort.* II. v. 262 His creative might will bring life out of the sapless dust of Sheol.
2. *transf.* and *fig.* **a.** Of persons: Lacking vital moisture, energy, or vigour. Also with reference to mental qualities: Lacking in character, insipid.
1598 Marston *Sco. Villanie* III. viii. 214, I am not saplesse old or reumatick. ? *c* **1600** *Distracted Emp.* I. i. in Bullen *O. Pl.* III 168 Theres not enough to cherrish a desyer Left in his saplesse nerves. **1647** Trapp *Comm. 1 Cor.* ii. (1656) 663 Such was that Sapless fellow Psal. 14. 1. that may have a disciplinary knowledge..but not an intuitive *per speciem propriam*. **1680** Baxter *Answ. Stillingfl.* vi. 16 An unexperienced sapless Teacher. **1700** Dryden *Ovid's Met.* xv. 349 Now sapless on the verge of Death he stands. **1821** Shelley *Hellas* 706 Hear ye the blast,..Whose spirit shakes the sapless bones Of Slavery? **1875** Jowett *Plato* (ed. 2) III. 33 Ghosts and sapless shades, and the rest of their Tartarian nomenclature. **1903** *Daily Chron.* 31 Oct. 3/2 In ten years he was friendless, his children sapless and sensitive, his wife lonely.
b. Of age, etc.
1591 Shaks. *1 Hen. VI*, IV. v. 4 When saplesse Age, and weake vnable limbes Should bring thy Father to his drooping Chaire. **1618** G. Strode *Anat. Mortal.* 161 The euill dayes of sickly and saplesse old age. **1842** Tennyson *Love & Duty* 16 The staring eye glazed o'er with sapless days. **1864** Lowell *Fireside Trav.* 318 A somewhat sapless womanhood.
c. Of immaterial things, ideas, sayings, etc.: Destitute of inner worth, insipid, trivial, pointless.
1602 Marston *Antonio's Rev.* I. iii, Blowe hence these saplesse jestes. **1642** Milton *Apol. Smect* x. Wks. 1851 III. 310 Pestring their heads with the saplesse dotage of old Paris and Salamanca. **1664** H. More *Myst. Iniq.* 292 It is to make the Prophecy guilty of a sapless and useless Tautologie. **1732** Waterland *Script. Vind.* III. 38 Those heartless, sapless Services, which had no Godliness in them, were not the Services which God required. **1850** Marsden *Early Purit.* (1853) 408 The evangelical principles of the Reformation had begun to decline..into a dry and sapless orthodoxy. **1891** *Academy* 20 Aug. 171/2 Old stories and sapless anecdotes. **1897** W. P. Ker *Epic & Rom.* 358 The growth of a kind of dull, parasitic, sapless language over the old stocks.
Hence ˈ**saplessness**.
1851 Ruskin *Stones Ven.* I. xxvii. §23 The good in it, the life of it.., are Protestantism in its heart; the rigidity and saplessness are the Romanism of it. **1866** Neale *Sequences & Hymns* 26 Now this saplessness shall flush to green.

sapling (ˈsæplɪŋ). Forms: 5 sapp(e)lynge, 6 sapplyne, 7 saplyn, 7–9 saplin, 8 sappling, 6– sapling. [f. sap *sb.*¹ + -ling¹. Cf. sipling.]
1. A young tree; *esp.* a young forest-tree with a trunk a few inches in diameter.
1415 in *York Minister Fabric Rolls* (Surtees) 35 In ij sappelynges emptis de Gilberto Walker pro gauntrees, 3s. 8d. **1513** Douglas *Æneis* xi. xi. 43 And scars this sentens prent into hys mynd, Hys douchtir for to clos wythin the rynd And stalwart sapplyne or bark of cork tre. **1543** *Mem. Fountains Abb.* (Surtees) I. 412 Yonge saplings. *Ibid.* 413 Smale saplings. **1594** Shaks. *Rich. III*, III. iv. 71 Behold, mine Arme Is like a blasted Sapling, wither'd vp. **1607** Norden *Surv. Dial.* v. 212 To preserue the timber trees, and saplins likely to become timber trees, Oke, Elme, and Ashe. **1681** Dineley *Jrnl. Tour Irel.* in *Trans. Kilkenny Archæol. Soc.* Ser. II. IV. 332 The Roof of this Church is admirable, of whole Saplyns. **1775** Adair *Amer. Ind.* 310 If the hunter chance to miss his aim, he speedily makes off to a sappling, which the bear..cannot climb. **1810** Scott *Lady of L.* I. xiv, The broom's tough roots his ladder made, The hazel saplings lent their aid. **1818** Cruise *Digest* (ed. 2) I. 149 Saplins not proper to be cut as timber. **1896** A. E. Housman *Shropshire Lad* xxxi, The gale, it plies the saplings double.
b. used as a switch.
a **1712** W. King *Old Cheese* 69 Slouch..saw his wife's vigorous hand Wielding her oaken sapling of command.
2. *transf.* A young or inexperienced person.
1588 Shaks. *Tit. A.* III. ii. 50 Peace tender Sapling, thou art made of teares, And teares will quickly melt thy life away. **1738** Lillo *Marina* I. ii, *Bawd.* You're a sapling to talk so to one of my experience. **1828** P. Cunningham *N.S. Wales* (ed. 3) II. 255 The saplings from Carter's Barracks, Sidney, are three times greater nuisances than the 'full growths' in the Penitentiary there. **1847** Marryat *Childr. N. Forest* xi, Right, my sapling; right and well said. **1905** *Academy* 7 Oct. 1031/2 What god or mortal reared up so fair a sapling?
3. A young greyhound (see quots.).
1832 [cf. *sapling stake* below]. **1853** 'Stonehenge' *Greyhound* xiv. 274 The young greyhound is called a sapling till he is a year old, after which he becomes a puppy till two years old. **1892** *Coursing & Falconry* (Badm. Libr.) 56 A sapling is a greyhound whelped on or after January 1 of the same year in which the season of running began.
4. a. *appositively* or as *adj.* That is a sapling.
1700 Dryden *Theod. & Hon.* 129 A Saplin Pine he wrench'd from out the Ground. **1807** Wordsw. *White Doe* I. 121 Mourns she for lordly chamber's hearth That to the sapling ash gives birth. **1869** Tozer *Highl. Turkey* II. 280 The branch of a sapling tree.
b. simple *attrib.*, as ***sapling pole***, ***stick***, (sense 3) ***sapling stake***. Also **sapling-cup, -tankard**, an open cup or tankard formed of wood, with staves hooped like a diminutive barrel.
1851 *Archæol. Jrnl.* VIII. 427 A *Sapling cup—an oaken tankard for drinking new ale. **1762** Mills *Syst. Pract. Husb.* I. 437 They [the corn-bins] are made of *sapling poles, three or four inches diameter. **1832** in *Altcar Coursing Cal.* (1839) 47 *Sapling Stakes. **1885** *Field* 21 Feb. 228/3 Having conspired to run in a sapling stake..a greyhound which was not a sapling. **1828** Scott *F.M. Perth* xiv, He bore no

weapon in his hand, excepting a small *sapling stick, with a hooked head. **1900** H. LAWSON *Over Sliprails* 59 The wheel was boxed in, mostly with round sapling-sticks.

Hence ˈ**saplinghood**, the condition or state of being a sapling.

1868 NETTLESHIP *Browning* vi. 218 Just as one having a rare tree..would not, in its saplinghood, set it..in a forest of full-grown giant trees. **1903** EDNA K. WALLACE in *Critic* XLIII. 315 Then..I grew From sapling-hood to a Tree.

sapo, var. form of SARPO, toadfish.

sapodilla (sæpəʊˈdɪlə). Forms: 7 sapadilloe, (*pl.*) sapadillies, 7–8 sapadillo, 8 sappadilla, -o, sapodylle, sabatille, 9 sapotilla, sapadilla, sappodilla, zapotilla (in Dicts.), 8– sapodilla. [a. Sp. *zapotilla* (whence F. *sapotille*), dim. of *zapote* SAPOTA; for the change of *t* to *d* cf. Du. *sapodille*, G. *sappadill*.]

1. A large evergreen tree, *Achras Sapota*, native of tropical America, having a durable wood and an edible fruit. Also called NASEBERRY.

1697 DAMPIER *Voy.* I. 39 Where there grow great Groves of Sapadillies, which is a sort of Fruit much like a Pear, but more juicy. **1699** L. WAFER *Voy.* 58 The Sambaloe's are.. cover'd with variety of Trees; especially with Mammees, Sapadilloes, and Manchineel, &c. **1753** CHAMBERS *Cycl. Supp.* App., *Sappadilla*, a name used by some for the *cainito*, or *chrysophyllum*, of botanists. **1794** G. ADAMS *Nat. & Exp. Philos.* III. xxix. 193 Deal wood makes very good pendulum-rods; the wood called sapadillo is said to be still better. **1871** KINGSLEY *At Last* xi, The glossy foliage of the mangos and sapodillas. **1892** [see NASEBERRY].

2. The fruit of this tree.

1750 G. HUGHES *Barbadoes* 148 The inside pulp of the fruit is milky, and of a soft sweet taste, not unlike a Sappadillo. **1764** GRAINGER *Sugar Cane* II. 441 The sweetest sappadillas oft he brought. **1782** P. H. BRUCE *Mem.* XII. 423 They [the people of the Bahamas and adjacent islands] have tamarinds,..sapodylles, bananas, sowersops [etc.]. **1796** STEDMAN *Surinam* II. xxvi. 242 We had also the fruit called sabatille, which grows on a large tree. **1804** tr. *Piguenard's Zoflora* I. 33 Negroes, who came..with oranges, lemons, pine apples, sapotillas, and all the different fruits of the country to sell. **1885** LADY BRASSEY *The Trades* 323 Among the fruits of the Bahamas the sapodilla is abundant and cheap.

3. *attrib.*, as *sapodilla wood*; **sapodilla-plum** = sense 2; **sapodilla-tree** = sense 1.

1830 LINDLEY *Nat. Syst. Bot.* 181 The *Sappodilla Plum, the Star Apple [etc.]. **1697** DAMPIER *Voy.* I. 202 The *Sapadillo-Tree is as big as a large Pear-tree. **1908** R. W. CHAMBERS *Firing Line* xxxvii, Under the sapodilla-trees on the lawn. **1866** *Treas. Bot.* s.v., The West Indian *Sapodilla-wood..is a fancy wood used for furniture.

sapogenin (səˈpɒdʒɪnɪn). *Chem.* [f. SAPO(NIN) + -GEN + -IN. Coined in G. by P. A. Bolley 1854, in *Ann. d. Chem. u. Pharm.* XC. 216.] A crystalline compound obtained 'by treating saponin with dilute mineral acids'. In mod. use, a generic term for any of the steroid aglycones of the saponins.

1862 WATTS tr. *Gmelin's Handbk. Chem.* XV. 53. **1916** *Jrnl. Biol. Chem.* XXVIII. 443 Hydrolysis [of a new saponin] yielded a sapogenin. **1955** *Sci. Amer.* Jan. 57/1 The steroid part of a saponin is called a sapogenin. **1977** LEWIS & ELVIN-LEWIS *Med. Bot.* ii. 19/2 Some of the plants having useful steroidal sapogenins include *Dioscorea* spp. (yams, Dioscoraceae), *Agave* spp., and *Smilax* spp. (Liliaceae).

sapon, obs. form of SAPAN.

saponaceous (sæpəˈneɪʃəs), *a.* [f. mod.L. *sāpōnāce-us* (F. *saponacé*), f. L. *sāpōn-em* SOAP *sb.*: see -ACEOUS.]

1. Of the nature of, or resembling, soap; consisting of, or containing, soap; soapy.

1710 T. FULLER *Pharm. Extemp.* 109 A Saponaceous Draught. **1731** ARBUTHNOT *Aliments* i. (1735) 13 The Gall ..is a saponaceous Substance, being compos'd of an Alkaline Salt, Oil, and Water, all which can be extracted from it. **1748** *Phil. Trans.* XLV. 553 These..made a kind of Soap, or sulphureous saponaceous Salt, resembling Soap of Tartar. **1757** DYER *Fleece* I. 70 Rich saponaceous loam, that slowly drinks The blackening show'r. **1770** *Cook's 1st Voy.* III. viii. in *Hawkesworth's Voy.* (1773) III. 634 It was.. saponaceous to the touch, and almost as heavy as white lead. **1812** BRACKENRIDGE *Views Louisiana* (1814) 105 A kind of clay, of a dirty yellow, and of a saponaceous appearance. **1826** HENRY *Elem. Chem.* II. 293 Caustic fixed alkalis convert wax into a saponaceous compound. **1839** MURCHISON *Silur..Syst.* I. vi. 81 Some portions of which [*sc.* shale] have a saponaceous feel. **1878** T. BRYANT *Pract. Surg.* I. 575 A saponaceous tooth powder should be used.

2. *jocularly.* 'Soapy', *lit.* and *fig.*; unctuous in manner; 'slippery', evasive.

1837 SYD. SMITH *Let. to Archd. Singleton* Wks. 1859 II. 294/1 Among all his pecuniary, saponaceous, oleaginous parishioners. **1860** SALA *Baddington Peerage* I. xi. 192 Then did the uncertain chase after the pig with the saponaceous tail take place. **1864** LD. WESTBURY in *Daily Tel.* 16 July, This so-called synodical judgment was, no doubt, a well-lubricated form of words, but it was so oily, so saponaceous, that no one could grasp it.

sapoˈnacity. *rare* (*jocular*). [irreg. f. SAPONACEOUS + -ITY.] Soapiness.

1845 THACKERAY *Cornhill to Cairo* vii, You little knew what saponacity was till you entered a Turkish bath. **1860** WORCESTER (citing *Dublin Rev.*).

saponaria (sæpəˈnɛərɪə). [med.L. *sāpōnāria* (see SAPONARY *a.* and *sb.*), adopted as a generic name by Linnæus (*Systema Naturæ*, 1735).] = SOAPWORT 1. Cf. SAPONARY *sb.* 1, SAPONER.

1865 M. EYRE *Lady's Walks S. of France* vii. 87, I gathered..eye-bright, saponaria, and ling. **1900** J. M. ABBOTT in W. D. Drury *Bk. Gardening* vii. 237 Saponarias ..are dwarf hardy annuals..of the Pink family. **1951** *Dict. Gardening* (R. Hort. Soc.) IV. 1865/2 Saponarias mostly grow readily in well-drained soils.

saponarin (sæpəˈnɛərɪn). *Chem.* Formerly also -ine. [a. G. *saponarin* (G. Barger 1902, in *Ber. d. Deut. Chem. Ges.* XXXV. 1296), f. med.L. *sāpōnār-ia* (see below and SAPONARY *a.* and *sb.*) + *-in* -IN[1].] A white or pale yellow crystalline flavonoid diglycoside, ${}_2C_7H_{30}O_{15}$, first found in soapwort, *Saponaria officinalis*. Hence **saponaˈretin** [-ETIN], a monoglycoside derived from this by hydrolysis.

1902 *Jrn. Chem. Soc.* LXXXII. I. 387 Saponarin dissolves in about 1000 parts of hot water and crystallises on cooling in minute, birefringent needles. **1905** G. BARGER in *Rep. Brit. Assoc. Adv. Sci. 1904* 531 Unless the solution be dilute, a second product of hydrolysis separates as a thick yellow oil, which has not yet been obtained crystalline. The name saponaretin is suggested for it. **1923** *Nature* 25 Aug. 304/2 The formation of a glucoside (saponarine) in the mitochondria. **1950** *Thorpe's Dict. Appl. Chem.* (ed. 4) X. 687/1 Saponarin..dried in air is a white powder, but after drying *in vacuo* becomes pale yellow. **1967** *Chem. Abstr.* LXVI. 10485/2 Saponaretin..was obtained by chromatog[raphy] of flavonoids on a polyamide column. **1969** *Acta Chemica Scandinavica* XXIII. 2910/2 At the time of Molisch's investigation the constitution of saponarin was not known. It is now identified as isovitexin-7-glucoside (apigenin-6-*C*-7-*O*-diglucoside).

†**saponariness.** *Obs. rare*$^{-1}$. [f. SAPONARY + -NESS.] Saponaceous quality.

1669 W. SIMPSON *Hydrol. Chym.* 189 Whence proceeds the saponaryness of all fix'd salts.

†**saponary**, *a.* and *sb.* *Obs. rare.* [ad. med.L. *sāpōnārius*, f. L. *sāpōn-em* (*sāpo*) soap (see -ARY).]

A. *adj.* Saponaceous, soapy.

1661 BOYLE *Cert. Physiol. Ess.* (1669) 199 By digesting a good while a solution of Salt of Tartar with Oyl of Almonds, I could reduce them to a soft Saponary substance. **1699** *Phil. Trans.* XXI. 247 The Bile is generally allow'd to have much of a saponary nature.

B. *sb.*

1. The plant soapwort, *Saponaria officinalis*. Cf. SAPONER.

1526 *Grete Herball* ccclxxxiv. (1529) X iij, Saponaria..is called saponary fullers grass..and crowsoppe.

2. *sb. pl.* Substances convertible into soap (see quot.).

1684 tr. *Bonet's Merc. Compit.* XIX. 831 Alkalines and Enixa, which on this account are called Saponaries.

†**saponer.** *Obs. rare*$^{-1}$. [ad. med.L. *sāpōnāria*.] The plant soapwort; = SAPONARY *sb.* 1.

a **1400–50** *Stockh. Med. MS.* 156 Saponer or lesse crow[so]pe: *Saponaria minor.*

saponifiable (səˈpɒnɪfaɪəb(ə)l), *a.* [f. SAPONIFY *v.* + -ABLE.] Capable of being saponified or converted into soap.

1835–6 *Todd's Cycl. Anat.* I. 411/1 Seroline..is a white slightly opalescent substance,..not saponifiable. **1873** RALFE *Phys. Chem.* 19 Which causes the saponifiable fats to dissolve out, leaving the non-saponifiable in solution.

saponification (səˌpɒnɪfɪˈkeɪʃən). [a. F. *saponification*, f. *saponifier* SAPONIFY *v.*: see -FICATION.] **a.** The process of saponifying; the decomposition of a fat by the addition of an alkali which combines with its fatty acids to form a soap, the remaining constituent, glycerine, being consequently liberated.

1821 URE *Dict. Chem.* s.v. *Fat*, Saponification by potash. **1836–41** BRANDE *Chem.* (ed. 5) 1137 The general results of saponification. **1884** J. PATON in *Encycl. Brit.* XVII. 740/2 The saponification of stearin with sodic hydrate.

b. *saponification equivalent*, a 'term signifying the number of grammes of any oil saponified by one gramme of an alkali' (*Syd. Soc. Lex.* 1897); now usu. defined in terms of the amount of alkali required to saponify a particular quantity of oil, *spec.* the number of milligrammes of potassium hydroxide required by one gramme of oil; also *saponification number*, *value*.

1877 in Moloney *Forestry W. Afr.* (1887) 49 Saponification equivalent [of palm oil from] Brass 280·2. **1895** PEARMAIN & MOOR *Aids to Analysis of Food & Drugs* 89 The saponification value of an oil may be stated in terms of alkali absorbed per cent., or the number of grammes of the oil which would be saponified by one litre of normal solution of alkali, which is usually known as the 'saponification equivalent'. **1896** *Analyst* XXI. 192 The ether value thus obtained, added to the acid value, gave the saponification number. **1944** *Industrial & Engin. Chem. (Analytical Ed.)* XVI. 53 The indicator..is therefore recommended for use in the determination of acid numbers and saponification equivalents. **1946** F. SCHNEIDER *Qualitative Organic Microanalysis* vi. 163 For the identification of the acid portion of the ester use the titrated solution from the determination of the saponification equivalent. **1964** C. J. BONER *Gear & Transmission Lubricants* iii. 68 The saponification number divided by two will give a close approximation of the percentage of fat in a compounded oil. **1975** *Materials & Technol.* VIII. i. 17 The saponification value..expressed as the number of milligrams of potassium hydroxide required to saponify one gram of fat.

c. (See quot. 1877.)

1877 LITTLEJOHN in *Encycl. Brit.* VII. 475/1 On the other hand, in cool weather the progress of liquefaction [of a corpse] is arrested, and the soft parts become solidified, owing to their conversion into adipocire, a peculiar kind of animal soap. To this stage..Devergie gives the name of saponification. **1882** TIDY *Legal Med.* I. 115 Partial saponification may be expected..after three months' submersion in water, and after twelve months' burial in earth.

saponifier (səˈpɒnɪfaɪə(r)). [f. next + -ER[1].]

1. An apparatus for isolating glycerine and the fatty acids by saponification.

188. *Sci. Amer. Sup.* 2562 (Knight).

2. An alkali used in saponification.

1872 CROOKES *Wagner's Handbk. Chem. Technol.* 242 Natrona refined saponifier.

saponify (səˈpɒnɪfaɪ), *v.* [ad. F. *saponifier*, ad. mod.L. *sāpōnificāre*, f. *sāpōn-* SOAP: see -IFY.]

1. *trans.* To convert (a fat or an oil) into soap by combination with an alkali.

1821 URE *Dict. Chem.* s.v. *Fat*, Each of the constituents of natural fat were then saponified by the addition of potash. **1854** R. D. THOMSON *Cycl. Chem.* 441/1 Ricinoleic Acid.. Sherry-coloured syrupy acid.., obtained by saponifying castor oil. **1879** *Cassell's Techn. Educ.* IV. 192/2 They [articles to be gilded] are, therefore, first boiled in caustic alkali in order to saponify and render soluble all traces of grease. **1897** *Allbutt's Syst. Med.* III. 132 The fat must be emulsified or saponified before it can be absorbed.

2. *intr.* To become converted into soap.

1823 URE *Dict. Chem.* (ed. 2) s.v. *Soap*, Those [oils or fats] which saponify best,..are, 1. Oil of olives..2. Animal oils [etc.]. **1884** W. S. B. MCLAREN *Spinning* (ed. 2) 46 The best oils are those which..saponify with the greatest facility with carbonate of soda. **1900** *Lancet* 29 Sept. 950/1 Kelpion..is a greasy, dark-olive-coloured substance which refuses to saponify with strong soda solution.

Hence **saˈponified, saˈponifying** *ppl. adjs.*

1821 URE *Dict. Chem.* s.v. *Fat*, The saponified fat of the sheep. **1856** *Orr's Circ. Sci., Pract. Chem.* 311 Finely divided and saponified fats. **1880** W. C. ROBERTS *Introd. Metallurgy* 9 The saponifying powers of litharge. **1899** *Allbutt's Syst. Med.* VI. 259 The saponifying ferment—lipase—which Hanriot has discovered in blood-serum is probably one of the agents concerned in disposing of the fat.

saponin, -ine (ˈsæpənɪn, -aɪn). *Chem.* [a. F. *saponine*, f. L. *sāpōn-* soap: see -IN.] A glucoside obtained from *Saponaria officinalis*, *Quillaia saponaria*, and many other plants. In mod. use, any of a large class of steroid glycosides obtained from plants, which are usu. toxic (esp. to fish), causing hæmolysis, and are characterized by the property of foaming in aqueous solution.

1831 J. DAVIES *Manual Mat. Med.* 127 Saponine.. presents the physical properties of a solution of soap. **1836–41** BRANDE *Chem.* (ed. 5) 1230/2 Saponin [obtained] from the *Saponaria officinalis.* **1884** A. DANIELL *Princ. Physics* xi. 247 If a magnetic needle be so adjusted as to have its lower surface in contact with the surface of a solution of saponine, it will remain in any position in defiance of the directive force of the earth's magnetism. **1891** *Jrnl. Chem. Soc.* LX. II. 1531 The author [*sc.* R. Kobert] considers that there are a series of saponins of the general formula $C_nH_{2n-8}O_{10}$, several of which are known. **1916** *Jrnl. Biol. Chem.* XXVIII. 443 A new saponin, $C_{24}H_{40}O_{14}$, was isolated from the rootstock of *Yucca filamentosa*. **1953** C. W. & E. SHOPPEE in E. H. Rodd *Chem. Carbon Compounds* II. B. xix. 1035 Saponins..are haemolytic when injected into the bloodstream of animals and therefore highly toxic intravenously but comparatively harmless when ingested. **1977** LEWIS & ELVIN-LEWIS *Med. Bot.* ii. 19/2 The recent importance of plant steroidal compounds, especially the steroid saponins, is their suitability as cortisone and hormone precursors.

saponite (ˈsæpənaɪt). *Min.* [f. L. *sāpōn-em* soap + -ITE; formed by Svanberg 1841 as a rendering of the Ger. name *seifenstein* (= soap-stone).] A hydrous silicate of aluminium and magnesium, occurring in soft, soapy, amorphous masses, filling veins in serpentine and cavities in trap-rock.

1849 J. NICOL *Man. Min.* Index. **1862** DANA *Man. Min.* 145. **1866** LAWRENCE tr. *Cotta's Rocks Class.* (1878) 22 Saponite occurs in fissures of serpentine rock. **1883** M. F. HEDDLE in *Encycl. Brit.* XVI. 414/2 Saponite,..Massive; sectile, and very soft... White, orange-yellow, pale green, and reddish brown... Occurs in all the above colours in the later igneous rocks of Scotland, commonly.

saponule, -ul (ˈsæpənjuːl, -ʌl). *Chem.* [f. L. *sāpōn-* soap: see -ULE.] (See quot. 1897.)

1794 G. PEARSON *Table Chem. Nomencl.* Pl. 4 end, Saponules of Turpentine, &c. **1802** T. THOMSON *Chem.* II. 182 The French chemists have proposed to give the combinations which these bodies form with the volatile oils the name of *savonules*, which Dr. Pearson has translated by the term *saponules.* **1897** *Syd. Soc. Lex.*, *Saponule*, term for an imperfect and partial soap formed by incomplete saponification of volatile..oils by means of various bases.

sapor, sapour (ˈseɪpɔː(r), -pə(r)). Also 6 sapowr. [a. L. *sapor*, *sapōr-em* taste (whence F. *saveur* SAVOUR), f. *sapĕre* to taste, to be sapid.] A quality such as is perceived by the sense of taste, as sweetness, bitterness, sourness, etc.; a taste, savour; the taste or savour of a substance, esp. of an article of food or drink. Now chiefly in scientific use.

†*sapor Pontic*, *sapor styptic*: particular 'sapors' frequently mentioned by the alchemists as indicative of the nature or condition of substances under examination (see also PONTIC, STYPTIC).

1477 NORTON *Ord. Alch.* v. in *Ashm.* (1652) 63 Which I teach you to knowne by signes fowre, By Colour, Odour, Sapor and Liquore. *Ibid.* v. 69 As Sapor of Meates chaungeth your Tastinge. *c* **1480** HENRYSON *Orpheus & Eurydice* 23 Lyke as a strand of water or a spring Haldis the sapour of his fontall well. **1513** DOUGLAS *Æneis* v. Prol. 54 Not jawyn fra tun to tun, In fresche sapour new fro the berrie run. **1552** LYNDESAY *Monarche* 6158 In thare mouth, ane taist, as I heir tell, Off sweit and Supernaturall Sapowris. **1615** CROOKE *Body of Man* 628 The other Nerue is sprinckled into the flesh of the Tongue..and by that meanes the Tongue is made apprehensiue of *Sapors*. **1638** FEATLY *Transubst.* 76 You tast nothing but bread in the one, and the sapour of wine in the other. **1682** CREECH tr. *Lucretius* IV. 117 Whil'st Colours strike the Eyes, Odours the Smell, Sapours the Tast. **1699** EVELYN *Acetaria* 91 Without being over-power'd by some Herb of a stronger Taste, so as to endanger the native Sapor and Vertue of the rest. **1725** WATTS *Logic* II. iii. §1 To discover the shape of those little particles of matter which distinguish the various sapors, odors, and colors of bodies. **1826** HOR. SMITH *Tor Hill* (1838) III. 314 The exquisite sapor of their French dishes. **1849–52** *Todd's Cycl. Anat.* IV. 857/1 There remains a large class of pure sapors, of which we take cognizance without the assistance of smell, and which are altogether dissimilar to any tactile impressions: such as the bitter of quinine. **1861** LANKESTER *On Food* 256 We will call these substances which are tasted, *sapours*, in opposition to those which are called *odours*.

fig. *c* **1568** LAUDER *Min. P.*, *Ane Godlie Tractate* 110 Tha want the Sapour of the spreit Of Christ Jesus. **1677** GALE *Crt. Gentiles* II. IV. 62 This deservedly rules al offices which flow from its empire, are tinctured with its color and sapor, and ought to be referred to it.

b. In generalized sense: Quality in relation to the sense of taste.

1650 BULWER *Anthropomet.* i. 10 The gullet and conveying parts are [not] appertaining unto sapor. **1680** BOYLE *Scept. Chem.* VI. 394 Sapour being an Accident or an Affection of matter that relates to our..Organs of Tast. **1704** J. HARRIS *Lex. Techn.* I, *Saporifick Particles*, are such as by their Action on the Tongue occasion that Sensation which we call Taste or Sapor.

†**'saporal**, *a. Obs. rare*$^{-1}$. [f. SAPOR + -AL[1].] Of or pertaining to taste or 'sapor'.

1651 BIGGS *New Disp.* ¶80 How many sowre things are there which by their saporall rules should be most cold, which notwithstanding are most hot.

saporific (sæpə'rɪfɪk), *a. rare.* [ad. mod.L. *sapōrificus*, f. *sapōr-em*: see SAPOR and -(I)FIC. Cf. F. *saporifique.*] 'Having the power to produce tastes' (J.); imparting flavour or taste.

1704 [see SAPOR b]. **1721** BAILEY, *Saporifick*, causing Taste. **1768** [W. DONALDSON] *Life Sir B. Sapskull* II. xxv. 212 He..always insisted upon a saporific crust to stimulate the flavour of the punicious fluid.

saporine, *a. rare*$^{-1}$. [f. SAPOR + -INE.] Pertaining to the sense of taste.

1813 T. BUSBY tr. *Lucretius* II. IV. *Comm.* p. xxxiv, They more readily receive the impressions, which, by the saporine nerves, are transmitted to the sensorium.

saporosity (sæpə'rɒsɪtɪ). *rare.* [f. mod.L. *sapōrōs-us*: see next and -ITY.] That property of a body by which it imparts the sensation of taste.

1794 E. DARWIN *Zoon.* I. 115 Unless we may use the words Saporosity and Odorosity for these common properties, which are possessed by our organs of taste and smell, and by the particles of sapid and odorous bodies.

saporous ('seɪpərəs), *a. rare.* [ad. mod.L. *sapōrōsus*, f. *sapōr-em*: see SAPOR and -OUS.] Of or pertaining to taste; having flavour or taste; yielding some kind of taste. †Also, agreeable to the taste, savoury.

a **1670** HACKET *Cent. Serm.* (1675) 283 We read of Manna that it was saporous to all palates. **1704** J. HARRIS *Lex. Techn.* I, *Saporous*, are such Bodies as are capable of yielding some kind of Taste when touch'd with our tongue; but those that afford no Taste, are called *Insipid*. **1813** T. BUSBY tr. *Lucretius* II. IV. 748 The sharp and jagged in their progress tear The suffering nerves, and wage saporous war. **1828** *Blackw. Mag.* XXIII. 590 We omit no solitary supplement ..which can contribute to such cunning combinations as result in saporous felicity.

‖**sapota** (sə'pəʊtə). Forms: 6–9 **sapote**, 7 **sapotte**; 7 **supota, supporter, sappota**, 9 **zapota**, 8– **sapota**. [repr. Sp. and Pg. *zapote* (whence F. *sapote*), a. Mexican *zapotl*, *çapotl*. The form now in use is from mod. Latin.] **a.** The tree *Achras Sapota* and its fruit; = SAPODILLA 1, 2; (see also quot. 1887). As mod.L., a genus, the type of the *Sapotaceæ*, now referred to *Achras*.

white sapota, the greenish yellow fruit of the Mexican tree *Casimiroa edulis* (*Funk's Stand. Dict.* 1895). **mammee-sapota**, see MAMMEE 3.

?*c* **1560** TOMSON in *Hakluyt's Voy.* (1600) III. 454 There are many goodly fruits in that Countrey, whereof we haue none such, as Plantanos, Guyaues, Sapotes, Tunas. **1648** GAGE *West. Ind.* 42 There we had..the Plantin, Sapotte, Chicosapotte, Pine-fruit, and all other fruits that were to be found in Mexico. **1760** J. LEE *Introd. Bot.* App. 326 Sapota, *Achras*. **1760–72** tr. *Juan & Ulloa's Voy.* (ed. 3) I. 75 The sapotes are round, about two inches in circumference. **1811** PINKERTON *Mod. Geog.*, *West Indies* (abr., ed. 3) 666 The sapota or sapadilla. **1866** MARY B. CLARKE *Mosses fr. Rolling Stone* 120 Zapotas, rough and brown. **1887** BRIGHAM *Guatemala* 131 There is no little confusion in the nomenclature of the sapotes or sapodillas. What is usually called a sapote in Guatemala does not belong to the genus Sapota, but to an allied genus, Lucuma, and is known in the W. Indies as the mammee-apple... The sapoton or big sapote does not even belong to the Sapota family, but is a Pachira.

b. *attrib.*, as ***sapota plum***, ***wood***.

1797 *Encycl. Brit.* (ed. 3) I. 68/2 Achras or Sapota Plum. **1844** *Civil Eng. & Arch. Jrnl.* VII. 94/1 The material of the beams of the doors was sapote wood. *a* **1881** L. H. MORGAN *Contrib. Amer. Ethnol.* 273 They used sapote wood usually for lintels.

sapotaceous (sæpəʊ'teɪʃəs), *a. Bot.* [f. mod.L. *Sapotāce-æ* (f. SAPOTA): see -ACEOUS.] Of or pertaining to, or characteristic of the *Sapotaceæ*, a N.O. of gamopetalous plants typified by the *Achras* (formerly *Sapota*).

1845 G. DON in *Encycl. Metrop.* VI. 178*/1.

sapotad ('sæpəʊtæd). [f. SAPOT-A + -AD 1 d.] Lindley's term for: A plant of the N.O. *Sapotaceæ*.

1846 LINDLEY *Veg. Kingd.* 590.

sapote, variant of SAPOTA.

sapotilla, sapotte, obs. ff. SAPODILLA, SAPOTA.

sapotoxin ('sæpəʊtɒksɪn). *Chem.* Also **-ine**. [a. G. *sapotoxin* (R. Kobert 1887, in *Arch. f. exper. Path. u. Pharm.* XXIII. 241), f. med.L. *sāpōnāria* (see below and SAPONARY *a.* and *sb.*): see TOXIN.] A saponin found in the bark of the Chilean soap-bark tree, *Quillaja saponaria*; also, any markedly toxic saponin.

1891 *Jrnl. Chem. Soc.* LX. 1532 The sapotoxin of *Agrostemma githago* (corn cockle)..is absorbed both by the subcutaneous tissues and by the intestinal canal, and thus acts as a dangerous poison. **1892** *Ibid.* LXII. 350 The sapotoxin of *Agrostemma* has the same composition as those of *radix saponariæ albæ* and of quillaja bark, but differs from them in its physiological properties. **1924** C. T. KINGZETT *Chem. Encycl.* 486 Saponins from quillaya bark..are stated to consist of one-third quillajic acid and two-thirds of a body named sapotoxin. **1927** *Glasgow Herald* 11 June 4 The saponine and sapotoxine in effluents from beet-sugar factories. **1941** *Martindale's Extra Pharmacopœia* (ed. 22) I. 910 Quillaia... Contains quillaic acid..and sapotoxin, $C_{17}H_{28}O_{10}$..closely allied to saponin.

sapour, variant of SAPOR.

sappadilla, -o, obs. forms of SAPODILLA.

†**'sappar(e.** *Min. Obs.* [a. F. *sappare* (De Saussure 1789 in *Jrnl. de Physique* XXXIV. 213).

De Saussure copies from the label of his specimen (received from the Duke of Gordon) a statement indicating that the name came from the records of the abortive attempt to find gold in Scotland in the reign of James VI. In Atkinson's book of 1619, *Discovery and History of Gold Mynes in Scotland* (ed. Bannatyne Club, pp. 15, 67), 'the sapparr, saxere, and salineere stones' are mentioned as minerals in conjunction with which gold may be expected to be found. It is very doubtful whether these terms had any real meaning; the description of 'sappar-stone' on p. 15 would seem to suit quartz; it certainly does not refer to cyanite.]

An obsolete synonym of CYANITE.

1796 KIRWAN *Elem. Min.* (ed. 2) I. 209 Sappare. Cyanite of Werner. **1862** DANA *Min.* 173 Kyanite..is also called *sappar*, a corruption of sapphire.

sapped (sæpt), *ppl. a.* [f. SAP *v.*[1] + -ED[1].] Undermined. Also, eroded or broken off by glacial sapping.

1716 GAY *Trivia* III. 389 Her sap'd Foundations. **1840** DICKENS *Old C. Shop* liii, Here were the rotten beam, the sinking arch, the sapped and mouldering wall. **1972** J. G. McCALL in C. Embleton *Glaciers & Glacial Erosion* xi. 220 The general lack of any further frost action on the 'sapped' blocks of rocks which formed the moraine and screes in the area.

sappelynge, obs. form of SAPLING.

sapper[1] ('sæpə(r)). [f. SAP *v.*[1] + -ER[1], after F. *sapeur.*]

1. One who saps; *spec.* a soldier employed in working at saps, the building and repairing of fortifications, the execution of field-works, and the like.

The non-commissioned officers and privates of the Engineers were formerly called the (*Royal*) *Sappers and Miners*, but in 1859 they became the Royal Engineers. (The privates are still unofficially called *sappers*.)

1626 tr. *Boccalini's New-found Politicke* 92 These are.. tooles belonging to Pioners, Sappers, Diggers [etc.]. **1642** HEXHAM *Princ. Art Milit.* II. (ed. 2) 37 He..continues the Sap,..and then followes another Sapper presently, who [etc.]. **1782** *Encycl. Brit.* (ed. 2) IX. 6952/1 A brigade of sappers generally consists of eight men, divided equally into two parties; and whilst one of these parties is advancing the sap, the other is furnishing the gabions, fascines, and other necessary implements, who relieve each other alternately. **1811** WELLINGTON in Gurw. *Desp.* (1837) VIII. 601, I would beg to suggest..the expediency of adding to the Engineers' establishment a corps of sappers and miners. **1851** *Ord. & Regul. Roy. Engineers* §2. 7 Officers of Engineers, are restrained from employing Soldiers of the Corps of Royal Sappers and Miners, as Servants. **1868** *Regul. & Ord. Army* ¶762 A Gunner, Sapper or private, as the case may be. **1872** *Pall Mall G.* 6 Apr. 8 For use by the officers and sappers of the Royal Engineers for torpedo operations. **1896** KIPLING *Seven Seas* 175 The Lord He created the Engineer, Her Majesty's Royal Engineer, With the rank and pay of a Sapper!

2. *attrib.* and *Comb*, as ***sapper officer***, etc.; **sapper-pumper**, *nonce-wd.*, used for F. *sapeur-pompier* a member of a (French) fire-brigade.

1876 VOYLE & STEVENSON *Milit. Dict.* (ed. 3) s.v. *Engineers*, On active service, an engineer officer is sometimes a *sapper officer. **1841** THACKERAY *Sec. Funeral Napoleon* iii, The *Sapper-pumpers, with ditto. **1894** DU MAURIER *Trilby* VI. (1895) 288 All the sapper-pumpers..with their beautiful brass helmets! **1900** *Daily News* 21 May 7/6 A telegraph cart manned by *sapper telegraphists.

sapper[2] ('sæpə(r)). *Mech.* [f. SAP *sb.*[1] + -ER[1].] A tool for cutting away sap-wood (see quots.).

1822 *Amer. Jrnl. Sci.* V. 147 On this shaft [of a rotary saw machine] are the saw and sappers... The sappers which are crooked pieces of iron, steel edged,..cut the sap off the log. **1891** *Century Dict.*, *Sapper*, a chisel used in some sawing-machines to cut away waste or sap-wood and reduce a log to a cylindrical shape.

sapper[3] ('sæpə(r)). *Eton slang.* [f. SAP *v.*[3] + -ER[1].] One who 'saps' or studies hard.

1825 C. M. WESTMACOTT *Eng. Spy* (1907) I. 52 Pleasant clever Hawtrey, and careful Okes, and that shrewd sapper, Green..: these form his classic escort to the cloisters.

‖**sapperment** (sapər'mɛnt), *int.* [G. *sapperment*, corruption of *sakrament* SACRAMENT.] An oath put in the mouth of a German speaker.

1815 SCOTT *Guy M.* xxxiii, 'That won't pass, Mr. Captain'. 'That *must* pass, Mr. Justice—sapperment!' **1823** —— *Quentin D.* xxii, Sapperment—what a shy fairy it is! **1894** DU MAURIER *Trilby* II. (1895) 106 But you are not listening, sapperment!

sappharine, obs. form of SAPPHIRINE *a.*

Sapphic ('sæfɪk), *a.* and *sb.* Also 6 **Saphik, Saphic(ke**, 6–8 **Sap(p)hick**, 7 **Sap(p)hique**. [a. F. *saphique*, †*sapphique* (16th c. in Godefroy), ad. L. *Sapphic-us*, a. Gr. *Σαπφικός*.] **A.** *adj.* Of or pertaining to Sappho (*Σαπφώ*), the famous poetess of Lesbos (*c* 600 B.C.); *spec.* epithet of the metres used by her (see B).

1501 DOUGLAS *Pal. Hon.* II. iv, Metir saphik, and also elygie. **1585** T. WASHINGTON tr. *Nicholay's Voy.* II. ix. 43 She inuented the verses which after her name are called Saphic. **1656** BLOUNT *Glossogr.*, *Sapphique Verse*. **1706** A. BEDFORD *Temple Mus.* v. 100 Iambick, and Sapphick Verses. **1871** *Public Sch. Lat. Gram.* 472 Catullus has two Sapphic Odes. **1872** CALVERLEY *Fly Leaves* (1884) 97 She'd throw off odes, again, whose flow And fire were more than Sapphic.

B. *sb.* A metre used by Sappho or named after her. Chiefly *pl.*, verses written in the Sapphic stanza.

greater Sapphic: a logaœdic distich of which the first line is -∪∪-∪-∪ and the second (the Greater Sapphic verse) is ∪̲∪̲-∪̄-∪∪-‖-∪∪-∪-∪̄. ***lesser Sapphic***: a logaœdic hendecasyllable with a dactyl in the third place (-∪-∪̄-∪∪-∪-∪̄). The 'Sapphic stanza' consists of three Lesser Sapphics followed by an Adonic (-∪∪-∪̄).

a **1586** SIDNEY *Arcadia* I. (1598) 78 Zelmane..tooke out of his hand the Lute, and..sung these Saphikes. **1586** W. WEBBE *Eng. Poetrie* (Arb.) 81 For tryall of which I haue turned the new Poets sweete song of Eliza into such homely Sapphick as I coulde. *c* **1645** HOWELL *Lett.* (1650) II. 50 Give me leave to salute you first in these Sapphics. **1730** SWIFT *Dan Jackson's Picture*, To give us a Description graphick Of Dan's large Nose, in modern Saphick. **1892** LOUNSBURY *Stud. Chaucer* II. vii. 49 Lumbering hexameters and dolorous sapphics consequently made their appearance in English literature.

sapphire ('sæfaɪə(r)). Forms: 3–6 **saphyr**, 3–7 **saphir**, 4–5 **safir(e**, (**zaphire**), **safer(e**, 4–6 **saffer(e**, **safyr(e**, **sapher**, 4– 7 **saphyre**, 4–8 **saphire**, 5 **saffyr**, **saffre**, **safewr**, (**safour**, **safur**), 5–6 *Sc.* **sapheir**, 6 **saphere**, **saphier**, (**safure**, **saffure**, **-oure**, *Sc.* **saufir**), 7 **sappheir**, *Sc.* **saiffer**, 8–9 **sapphyr**, 8– **sapphire**. [a. OF. *safir* (12th c. in Littré), mod.F. *saphir* (Pr. *saphir*, *safir*, Sp. *zafir*, *zafiro*, Pg. *safira*, *zafira*, It. *zaffiro*), ad. L. *sapphīr-us*, also *sapp(h)ir* (both fem.), a. Gr. *σάπφειρος*, fem., said to mean lapis lazuli (our sapphire being perh. the *ὑάκινθος*, L. *hyacinthus*); prob. a. some Semitic form, cf. Hebr. *sappīr*, rendered *σάπφειρος*, *sapphirus* in the LXX and Vulg.

The word, however, does not appear to be ultimately of Semitic origin. As Heb. *sappīr* may represent an earlier **sampīr* (cf. Jewish Aramaic *sampīrīnā*), some scholars have conjectured that the source may be Skr. *çanipriya* (lit. 'dear to the planet Saturn'), the name of some dark gem, perh. sapphire or emerald. The Pers. *saffīr* and mod.Arab. *çafīr* may be from Greek.]

1. a. A precious stone of a beautiful transparent blue. It is a variety of native alumina akin to the ruby.

a **1272** *Luue Ron* 173 in *O.E. Misc.* 98 Hwat spekstu of eny stone..Of iaspe, of saphir, of sardone. **13..** *K. Alis.* 5667 (Bodl. MS.), Safyres Smaragdes & Margarites. **1340** *Ayenb.* 82 Hy wenеþ of a gles þet hit by a safir. *c* **1386** CHAUCER *Monk's T.* 478 Of Rubies, saphires [*v.rr.* safferys, safers], and of peerles white Were alle hise clothes brouded vp and doun. c1430 Lydg. *Min. Poems* (Percy Soc.) 159 A poore man proud is nat comendable, Nor a fayr saphir set in a copir ryng. c1450 *Guy Warw.* (C.) 11403 Some were of safewrs and some of saradyn. c1475 *Rauf Coilȝear* 464 With stanis of Beriall deir, Dyamountis and Sapheir. 1554 *Bury Wills* (Camden) 145 Oon gold ringe wt a saffer. 1583 Greene *Mamillia* Wks. (Grosart) II. 61 Though the Polipe chaungeth colour euery houre: yet the Saphyre will cracke before it consent to disloyaltie. 1597 Shaks. *Lover's Compl.* 215 The heauen hewd Saphir. 1624 Quarles *Sion's Sonn.* Div. Poems (1630) 299 With veines, like Saphyres, winding in and out. 1676 Evelyn *Diary* 26 Aug., He reported prodigious depth of ice, blew as a sapphire, and as transparent. 1711 Pope *Temp. Fame* 252 Bright azure rays from lively sapphyrs stream. 1873 Black *Pr. Thule* (1874) 13 The sky..was as blue and clear as the heart of a sapphire.

b. *Min.* Used as a general name for all the precious transparent varieties of native crystalline alumina, including the ruby. A colourless variety is called ***white*** or WATER SAPPHIRE.

1668 Wilkins *Real Char.* 68 Saphire White. 1698 Fryer *Acc. E. India & P.* 215 There are three sorts, one perfect Blue, and very hard... The second is perfect White, and very hard... The third, called Water-Saphires, are of small Esteem, being not so hard as the other, and commonly of a dead Waterish Colour. 1829 Crawfurd *Jrnl. Emb. to Crt. of Ava* (1834) II. 201 All the varieties of the sapphire, as well as the spinelle, are found together. 1834 McCulloch *Dict. Comm.* (ed. 2) s.v., The red sapphire, or Oriental ruby.

c. *transf.* and *fig.*

14.. Hoccleve *Min. Poems* (1892) 70 Lady, þat clept art 'modir of mercy', Noble saphir. 1614 Drumm. of Hawth. *Poems* II. Sonn. ii, Those Eyes, those sparkling Saphires of Delight! 1667 Milton *P.L.* IV. 605 Now glow'd the Firmament With living Saphirs.

d. The pure bright blue of the sapphire.

1686 Goad *Celest. Bodies* I. v. 14 He [the Sun] brighteth the Air into a chearful Saphir. 1813 Byron *Corsair* III. i, Again his waves in milder tints unfold Their long array of sapphire and of gold. 1855 Tennyson *Maud* I. XVIII. vi, It seems that I am happy, that to me A livelier emerald twinkles in the grass, A purer sapphire melts into the sea.

e. *Her.* The tincture blue or azure, in blazoning by the names of precious stones.

1562 Leigh *Armorie* 12 Azure..whose preciouse stone is the Saphier. 1572 Bossewell *Armourie* II. 90 Hys fielde is of the Saphire, the Sunne propre; or thus. He beareth Azure, a Sunne d'Or. 1777 Porny *Elem. Her.* (ed. 3) 109 Party per Saltier Sapphire and Pearl.

f. A sapphire used as a stylus for gramophone records.

1943 *Electronic Engin.* XVI. 121/2 The portion of the wire between the ribbon and the sapphire provides sufficient vertical compliance to minimise mechanical noise. 1957 [see *playing-life* s.v. PLAYING *vbl. sb.* 2]. 1964 P. J. Guy *Disc Recording & Reproduction* vii. 99 In the author's experience some sapphires have a very much shorter life.

2. a. A name for certain humming-birds.

1843 *Penny Cycl.* XXV. 272/2 [Humming-Birds.] The Sapphires. 1861 Gould *Trochilidæ* V. Pl. 330 *Eucephala Grayi*, Blue-headed Sapphire. *Ibid.* 342 *Hylocharis sapphirinus*. Red-throated Sapphire.

b. A sapphire mink (see sense 3 c).

1951 *Genetics* XXXVI. 575 Several color phases result from the combination of two or more of these mutant genes, the sapphire..and the 'red-eyed' pastel..being of most commercial importance at the present time.

3. *attrib.* and *Comb.*, as ***sapphire-blaze***, ***-blue*** (adj. and sb.), ***colour***, ***crown***, ***hue***, ***jewel***, ***ring***, ***throne***; ***sapphire needle***, ***point***, ***stylus*** (sense 1 f); ***sapphire-coloured***, ***-hued***, ***-shot***, ***visaged*** adjs.; † **sapphire loop** (see LOOP *sb.*[4] 2); **sapphire quartz**, a rare indigo-blue variety of quartz; = SIDERITE[1] 5; **sapphire stone** = sense 1.

1754 Gray *Poesy* 99 The living Throne, the *sapphire-blaze, Where angels tremble while they gaze. 1782 Latham *Gen. Synopsis Birds* II. 775 The fore part of the neck and breast are of a rich *sapphire blue. 1798 Greville in *Phil. Trans.* LXXXVIII. 420, I have some specimens of a sapphire-blue stone. 1885 Lady Brassey *The Trades* 390 Another sea, of the deepest and clearest sapphire-blue. 1477 Norton *Ord. Alch.* v. in Ashm. (1652) 65 The *Saphire Colour, that Orient Blewe. a1586 Sidney *Arcadia* II. (Sommer) 152 b, There fall those *Saphir-coloured brookes. c1630 Milton *Ode Sol. Music* 7 That undisturbed Song of pure content, Ay sung before the saphire-colour'd throne. 1634 —— *Comus* 26 And gives them leave to wear their *Saphire crowns. c1430 Lydg. *Min. Poems* (Percy Soc.) 8 They had on bawderykys alle of *saffer hewe. 1446 —— *Nightingale Poems* ii. 2 Towardes Even the *Saphyre-huwed sky Was westward meynt with many Rowes Rede. 1613 Purchas *Pilgrimage* (1614) 578 He wore about his necke a *saphire jewel. c1400–1548 *Sapphire loop [see LOOP *sb.*[4] 2]. 1940 *Chambers's Techn. Dict.* 740/1 *Sapphire needle. 1943 *Gramophone* Dec. 107/2 In the last two years of manufacture of radiograms in this country practically all of them came thru with sapphire needles as standard equipment. 1899 *T. Eaton & Co. Catal.* Spring & Summer 191 Graphophone Supplies... Recorder, with *sapphire point, $5.00. Reproducer, with sapphire point, $5.00. 1972 *Country Life* 28 Dec. 1777 We..listened avidly to Mr Alfred Heather's rendering of *I'll sing thee songs of Araby* on our sapphire-point Pathé gramophone. 1868 J. D. Dana *Syst. Min.* (ed. 5) 193 Siderite, or *Sapphire-quartz. Of indigo or Berlin-blue color. 1904 L. J. Spencer tr. *M. Bauer's Precious Stones* 488 Sapphire-quartz (azure-quartz or siderite) is a blue, crystalline quartz... It is used to a very small extent and is correspondingly low in price. 1971 *Country Life* 3 June 1382/3 Quartz, however, may be variously tinted:.. sapphire quartz—blue; [etc.]. 1634–5 in *Anc. Invent.* (Halliw.) 6 One *Sapphire ringe. 1883 G. M. Hopkins *Poems* (1967) 95 Yet such a *sapphire-shot, Charged, steepèd sky will not Stain light. 1382 Wyclif *Exod.* xxiv. 10 As a werk of a *saphire stoon. c1820 S. Rogers *Italy* (1839) 6 The lake Blue as a sapphire-stone. 1947 *Gramophone* Oct. 74/1 This..has the..replaceable *sapphire stylus, for which the makers claim 1,000 playings before replacement is necessary. 1974 *Encycl. Brit. Macropædia* XVII. 54/1 When, between 1933 and 1935, attempts were made to use sapphire styli with electrical pickups weighing 50 to 150 grams.., record wear was found to be excessive. 1667 Milton *P.L.* VI. 758 A *Saphir Throne, inlaid with pure Amber. 1745–6 Collins *Ode Poet. Char.* 32 Himself.. plac'd her on his Saphire Throne. a1593 Marlowe *Hero & L.* 11, The *sapphire-visag'd god.

b. quasi-*adj.* Resembling the sapphire, sapphire-coloured.

1433 Lydg. *St. Edmund* App. 173 A saphir skye ladde Israel be day-light Toward the lond of promyssyoun. 1508 Dunbar *Gold. Targe* 37 The cristall air, the sapher firmament. a1600 Montgomerie *Misc. P.* xxxv. 55 Hir saphir veins, lyk threids of silk. 1630 Drumm. of Hawth. *Flowers of Sion* 10 The Sunne..faintly iourneyes vp Heauens saphire Path. 1667 Milton *P.L.* IV. 237 How from that Saphire Fount the crisped Brooks..Ran Nectar. 1726 Pope *Odyss.* xx. 128 Loud from a saphire sky his thunder sounds. 1819 Keats *Eve St. Agnes* xxxvi, Like a throbbing star Seen mid the sapphire heaven's deep repose. 1837 Carlyle *Fr. Rev.* VIII. iii, Beyond that sapphire promontory, which men name St. Bees, which is not sapphire either, but dull sandstone, when one gets close to it. 1862 Calverley *Verses & Tr.* (1894) 60 In the sapphire West the eve yet lingered.

c. used in denominating some animals (see quots.). **sapphire mink**, a variety of mink with blue fur (see also sense 2 b); also, the fur of this animal.

1664 R. Hubert *Catal. Rarities* (1665) 40 A Saphir flie so called for his bright shining blew colour. 1729 *Dampier's Voy.* III. 425 The Saphire-beetle has green Wings, with a Gold Gloss. 1782 Latham *Gen. Synopsis Birds* II. 775 Sapphire Humming Bird. 1861 Gould *Trochilidæ* III. Pl. 178 *Pterophanes Temmincki*. Temminck's Sapphire-wing. 1960 *Guardian* 26 Aug. 6/4 A generously wide sapphire mink stole. 1974 *Genetika* XII. II. 109 The interactions between genes are demonstrated to result in a significant rearrangement of cells and the development of a new pigmentation type in sapphire minks. 1976 *S. Wales Echo* 25 Nov. 22/7 (Advt.), Full-length Sapphire Mink, £850.

sapphired ('sæfaɪəd), *ppl. a. rare*[−1]. [f. SAPPHIRE + -ED[2].] Painted with sapphire blue.

1820 Keats *Cap & Bells* v, As in old pictures tender cherubim A child's soul thro' the sapphir'd canvas bear.

sapphir(e) d'eau, var. SAPHIR D'EAU.

sapphiric (sə'fɪrɪk), *a. rare.* [f. SAPPHIRE + -IC.] Resembling or of the nature of a sapphire.

1605 Timme *Quersit.* II. v. 130 Wine..partaketh very much of the vitriolated nature; which may be gathered..by the saphiric and reddy colour of those that are ripe. 1882 Jas. Walker *Jaunt to Auld Reekie* 175 Badged garters twinkling with sapphiric stones.

sapphirine ('sæfɪraɪn), *sb. Min.* Also **saphirine**. [f. SAPPHIRE + -INE[5].] **a.** A silicate of aluminium and magnesium found in pale blue grains. **b.** A blue variety of spinel. †**c.** An early name for blue chalcedony (*obs.*).

The term (in Ger. form *saphirin*) was applied in its now usual meaning by Giesecke 1819; it had been used in 1808 by K. W. Nose for haüynite.

1823 H. J. Brooke *Crystallogr.* 489. 1836 T. Thomson *Min., Geol.*, etc. I. 218 *Sapphirine*. This mineral was discovered by Sir Charles Giesecke, in Greenland... It has a pale sapphire blue colour. 1866 Brande & Cox *Dict. Sci.*, etc. s.v. *Mineralogy* 533/1 Chalcedonic Quartz... Saphirine. 1883 M. F. Heddle in *Encycl. Brit.* XVI. 386/2 Spinel.. Sapphirine is pale sapphire-blue to greenish or reddish blue.

sapphirine ('sæfɪraɪn), *a.*[1] Forms: 5 **saphyryn**, 7 **saphyrin**, 7–8 **saphirine**, 8–9 **sappharine**, 7– **sapphirine**. [ad. L. *sapphirinus*, a. Gr. σαπφείρινος, f. σάπφειρος SAPPHIRE.] Consisting of or like sapphire, having the qualities of sapphire, esp. the colour.

sapphirine gurnard: see GURNARD.

1413 *Pilgr. Sowle* (Caxton) v. v. (1859) 76 This Cercle in his bordure was of mesurable brede of coloure, saphyryn, and was redyly lyned by ordre, and set full of sterres. a1631 Donne *Elegy* [xi.] Poems (1633) 296 She was too Saphirine and cleare to thee; Clay, flint, and jeat now thy fit dwellings be. 1672 *Phil. Trans.* VII. 5044 The same water..appears of a Saphyrin blew. 1672 Boyle *Ess. Orig. & Virt. Gems* I. 38 Jewellers reckon among Saphires..another sort of Stones, because of their Saphirine degree of hardness. 1769 Pennant *Zool.* III. 176 The irides sappharine; the head flat. *Ibid.* (1776) III. 245 Sapphirine Gurnard. 1833 *Fraser's Mag.* VIII. 63 The sapphirine pavement of heaven. 1835 Browning *Paracelsus* II. 46 No nymph..Or sapphirine spirit of a twilight star. 1878 T. Hardy *Ret. Native* IV. v, The sapphirine hue of the zenith in spring.

b. *absol.*

1822 W. Tennant *Thane of Fife* I. xxxi, He..with his feet ..Smote soundingly the pavement's sapphirine. 1887 Browning *Parleyings, Gerard de Lairesse* xi, Thunder from the safe sky's sapphirine.

'sapphirine, *a.*[2] [f. mod.L. *Sapphirina*, subst. use of the fem. of L. *sapphirin-us*: see prec.] Of or pertaining to, or characteristic of the *Sapphirina*, a genus of copepods of the N.O. *Sapphirinidæ*.

1897 *Jrnl. Mar. Zool.* Dec. 111 Sapphirine copepods.

sapphirinid (sæfɪ'rɪnɪd). *Zool.* [ad. mod.L. *Sapphirinidæ*, f. *Sapphirina*: see prec.] A member of the N.O. *Sapphirinidæ* of parasitic copepods. So also **sapphi'rinoid** *a.*, of or pertaining to the *Sapphirinidæ*.

1895 *Funk's Stand. Dict.* Sapphirinid. Sapphirinoid. 1897 *Jrnl. Mar. Zool.* Dec. 111 When seen swimming the Sapphirinids present a magnificent play of metallic colours.

sapphirite ('sæfɪraɪt). *Min.* [f. SAPPHIRE *sb.* + -ITE[1].] = SAPPHIRINE *sb.* a.

1883 M. F. Heddle in *Encycl. Brit.* XVI. 409/1.

Sapphism ('sæfɪz(ə)m). [f. name of *Sappho* (see SAPPHIC), who was accused of this vice: see -ISM.] Homosexual relations between women.

1890 Billings *Nat. Med. Dict.* 1901 *Lancet* 1 June 1548/1 As yet in this country the novelist..has not arrived at the treatment in romance of excessive morphiomania, or Sapphism, or vaginismus, all of which diseases will be found in French novels.

So **'Sapphist**, 'one addicted to sapphism' (*Webster's Suppl.* 1902); **sa'pphistically** *adv.*, in the manner of a Sapphist.

1913 R. Brooke *Let.* 13 Dec. (1968) 547 A woman..who loved Lulu sapphistically. 1923 V. Woolf *Diary* 19 Feb. (1978) II. 235 She is a pronounced Sapphist, & may..have an eye on me. 1925 [see PÆDERAST]. 1975 'M. Orr' *Rich Girl, Poor Girl* (1977) xviii. 247 Winifred knew herself to be ..a Sapphist on the prowl for a desirable *jeune fille*.

Sappho ('sæfəʊ). [Applications of the name of the poetess (see SAPPHIC).]

1. *Ornith.* In mod.L. the name of a genus of humming-birds. Hence, a bird of this genus; = COMET *sb.* 3; usually ***Sappho comet***.

1843 *Penny Cycl.* XXV. 272/1 [Humming-Birds] 11th Race. The Sapphos. 1861 Gould *Trochilidæ* III. Pl. 174 *Cometes sparganurus*. The Sappho Comet. 1862 [see COMET 3].

2. *Astr.* The name of the eightieth asteroid.

1875 Proctor in *Encycl. Brit.* II. 807/2 Sappho [discovered] 1864, May 3.

†**'sappily**, *adv. Obs.* [f. SAPPY *a.* + -LY[2].]

1. By means of sap; through the operation of sap.

1684 *Phil. Trans.* XIV. 774 The Glastenbury Thorne, whose arising time being between Michaelmas and Christmas being sappily prepared by the beginning of the hard Frost [was almost destroyed].

2. Mustily.

1724 Ramsay *Wyfe of Auchtermuchty* xiv, The first it smellt sae sappylie, To touch the lave he did not grein.

sappiness ('sæpɪnɪs). [f. SAPPY *a.* + -NESS.]

1. The condition of being full of sap.

1552 Huloet, Sapines or naturall humour or moysture, *vligo*. 1594 Plat *Jewell-ho.* III. 33 For want of moysture and sappinesse. 1610 W. Folkingham *Art of Survey* I. iii. 6 They prosper and thriue in burgening, sappines, flowers, fruit. 1727 Bailey vol. II, *Sappiness*, the having Sap. 1731 *Ibid.* (ed. 5), *Sappiness*, the being sappy. 1812 J. Smyth *Pract. of Customs* (1821) 282 According to the size or sappiness of the tree. 1891 T. Hardy *Tess* xxvii, That green trough of sappiness and humidity, the valley of the River Var.

2. *colloq.* The quality of being sappy or foolish.

a1909 In recent Dicts. 1943 *New Yorker* 20 Feb. 22/1 She was..convinced..that a floppy feminine hat was a symbol of celluloid sappiness.

sapping ('sæpɪŋ), *vbl. sb.*[1] [f. SAP *v.*[1] + -ING[1]]

1. The action of the verb SAP in various senses; an instance of this.

1672 J. Lacey tr. *Tacquet's Milit. Archit.* 51 The sapping of the out-breastwork must be intercepted by a counter and transverse Sappe. 1726 Cavallier *Mem.* IV. 341 They were obliged to.. make their approach by Sapping. 1822–29 *Good's Study Med.* (ed. 3) III. 480 The general health had borne up under all these chronic sappings, undisturbed. 1880 G. Meredith *Tragic Com.* (1881) 238 A rather petulant objection to her use of analogies, which he called the sapping of language.

attrib. 1904 *Daily News* 16 Dec. 7/1 The sapping trenches will have to be run through frozen ground.

2. *Physical Geogr.* **a.** Undercutting by water, esp. backward erosion by a waterfall of softer layers of rock at its base; headward erosion of hillsides by springs.

1863 J. R. Green *Lett.* (1901) II. 126, I have noticed..the wonderful sapping of the chalk cliffs going on here [Margate]. 1902 W. M. Davis in *Bull. Mus. Compar. Zoöl.* XXXVIII. 328 Whatever flood plains may have been produced during the excavation of the present basin floor, the streams have now so well taken advantage of their opportunity for lateral corrosion or 'sapping' that terraces at high and intermediate levels are everywhere obliterated. 1932 W. H. Emmons et al. *Geol.* vi. 133 As the swirling water back of the falls loosens the soft, shaley formation it removes it piecemeal and undermines the capping limestone, until finally it remains as an inadequately supported overhanging ledge from which large masses of rock plunge into the pool at the bottom of the falls. This process of undercutting is termed sapping. 1936 *Proc. Geologists' Assoc.* XLVII. 40 A coombe formed in jointed chalk by the sapping back of springs. 1957 *Ibid.* LXVIII. 31 There remains the curious series of right-angled bends in the Ravensburgh Valley system, which has been attributed to sapping along major joints. 1970 R. J. Small *Study of Landforms* ii. 53 On rocks such as chalk and limestone the actual sources of streams are extended into escarpments and steep slopes by the process known as 'spring sapping'. This involves underground chemical erosion, surface stream erosion, and slumping of moistened debris around the springhead.

b. Undermining by glacial erosion; (*loosely*) plucking; *spec.* erosion of rock slopes by frost action under the margins of a glacier.

1899 W. D. Johnson in *Science* 20 Jan. 106/1 An unrecognized process was set forth, that of sapping, whose action is horizontal and backward... The tendency of the sapping process is to produce benches and cliffs. **1938** *Geol. Mag.* LXXV. 261 As the wall at the head of the cirque retreats under the action of sapping and plucking, immediately downstream the ice abrades and smoothes. **1954** *Jrnl. Glaciol.* II. 421 In accounting for these features [*sc.* roches moutonnées] the assumption ordinarily made is that rock has been removed by plucking or sapping from the downstream side, leaving that face steep and irregular. **1968** R. W. Fairbridge *Encycl. Geomorphol.* 741/1 The walls have been kept steep and caused to retreat by the collapse of unsupported rock faces as they have been undercut by the process of glacial 'sapping'... The explanation of sapping appears to be found in rending and disintegration of rock by the freeze-and-thaw process. **1972** J. G. McCall in C. Embleton *Glaciers & Glacial Erosion* xi. 217 The term sapping, as used here, implies frost-riving on the rock slopes under the margins of a glacier. It is produced by the freezing of any water which flows in under the 'cold' glacier and, in the case of cirques, it results in a horizontal retreat of the headwall.

sapping (ˈsæpɪŋ), *vbl. sb.*[2] *School slang.* [f. sap *v.*[3] + -ing[1].] The action of studying hard.

1821 *Salt-Bearer* No. 26. 303 When at Eton, boxing, rowing, cricket, and even *sapping*, had by turns the honour of possessing a stall in his hobby stable. **1825** C. M. Westmacott *Eng. Spy* (1907) I. 91 Have you patronized learning, or sapping commended? **1861** Hughes *Tom Brown at Oxf.* i, I never was much of a hand at sapping, and..the light work suits me well enough. **1922** S. Leslie *Oppidan* iv. 48 That..was why *sapping* was unnecessary.

sapping (ˈsæpɪŋ), *vbl. sb.*[3] [f. sap *v.*[2] + -ing[1].] The action of the verb sap[2] 2. In quot. *attrib.*

1875 Knight *Dict. Mech.*, *Sapping-machine*, a circular saw for slabbing balks and sawing bolts for shingle stuff.

sapping (ˈsæpɪŋ), *ppl. a.* [f. sap *v.*[1] + -ing[2].] That saps or undermines.

1819 Byron *Venice* i, Thus they creep..through their sapping streets. **1831** E. Irving *Expos. Rev.* I. 90 The stormy winds and sapping streams of infidelity which are overthrowing the house of those who [etc.]. **1908** Sir I. Hamilton in *Manch. Courier* 27 Oct. 10/5 The slow and sapping struggle against starvation.

sappodilla, obs. form of sapodilla.

sappota, obs. form of sapota.

sappy (ˈsæpɪ), *a.* (*sb.*) [f. sap *sb.*[1] + -y. Cf. MLG. *sapich*, MHG. *saffec*, *saffic*.]

1. Of a plant or tree or its parts, of wood: Abounding in sap.

1100 *Aldhelm Gloss.* i. 546 in Napier *O.E. Glosses* 16/1 *Suculentus*, sæpiᵹ stela. *c* **1440** *Promp. Parv.* 441/1 Sapy, or fulle of sap, *cariosus*. *a* **1555** Samuel *Let.* in Foxe *A. & M.* (1583) 1705/1 Began they not first with the greene and sappie tree? **1579** W. Wilkinson *Confut. Familye of Love* Ep. Ded. *ij, The Vine..stretcheth abroad his sappy braunches. **1592** Shaks. *Ven. & Ad.* 165. **1600** Surflet *Country Farm* ii. liv. 383 The citron tree is a great deale more sappie and full of iuice for to make nourishment of then the limon tree. **1693** Evelyn *De la Quint. Compl. Gard.* II. 58 Branches, of which the Wood is..extreamly Pithy, or Sappy. **1708** J. Philips *Cyder* ii. 75 When the sappy Boughs Attire themselves with Blooms. **1842** Tennyson *Amphion* xii, But these [*sc.* exotic plants], tho' fed with careful dirt Are neither green nor sappy. **1884** Bower & Scott *De Bary's Phaner.* 425 Sappy masses of parenchyma.

Comb. *a* **1722** Lisle *Husb.* (1757) 393 The fat sappy-leaved clover has been agreeable.

2. *fig.* in various applications. **a.** Full of vitality.

1558 Phaer *Æneid* vi. Qj b, Well agyd now, but sappy strength he kepes of grener yeres. **1879** J. Burroughs *Locusts & Wild Honey* (1884) 114 A rank, sappy race like the English or German.

b. Full or 'goodness' or substance.

1563 L. Blundeston *Pref.* to B. Googe *Eglogs* (Arb.) 30 The sappye Sence of this his passyng Ryme. **1567** Drant *Horace, Ep.* To Rdr. *vj, He that is least acquainted with suche trashe, and pelfe wyll better perceaue suche thinges whych be sauerye and sappye. **1587** Greene *Card of Fancy* Wks. (Grosart) IV. 90 The sugered eloquence, which so sweetlie flowed from the sappie wit of Gwydonius. **1601** ? Marston *Pasquil & Kath.* iv. 43 What thinke you of the lines of Decius? Writes he not a good cordiall sappie stile? **1948** F. R. Leavis *Great Tradition* ii. 111 *The Portrait of a Lady* belongs to the sappiest phase of James's art, when the hypertrophy of technique hadn't yet set in.

†**c.** Immature, unseasoned. *Obs.*

a **1627** Hayward *Edw. VI* (1630) 3 When he had passed this weake and sappie age he was committed to Dr. Coxe. **1654** Whitlock *Zootomia* 365 A Creature of that Sappy Sapience (for it selfe) as too green to burn for Religion.

†**3.** Juicy; succulent. **a.** Of fruit. Also as epithet of the juice.

1562 Bulleyn *Bulwark*, *Compounds* 33 Make your balles with the sappie iuce of the beries. **1590** Spenser *F.Q.* ii. xii. 56 The riper fruit..Whose sappy liquor, that with fulnesse sweld, Into her cup she scruzd. **1604** E. G[rimstone] *D'Acosta's Hist. Indies* vii. ix. 519 *Tomates* which is a great sappy and savourie graine. **1652** Culpepper *Eng. Physic.* (1656) 33 After which succeed round, reddish, sappy Berries. **1671** Grew *Anat. Plants* vii. §11 In its first and juvenile Constitution, it is a very Spongy and Sappy body.

b. Of meat, fish, etc.

1536 Bellenden *Cron. Scot.* (1821) I. *Cosmogr.* vi. 29 In this region ar mony fair ky and oxin,..the talloun of thair wambis is sa sappy, that it fresis nevir. *a* **1758** Ramsay *To Hamilton* (*Herrings*) i, Braw sappy fish As ane could wish. **1825** J. Wilson *Noct. Ambr.* Wks. 1855 I. 25 Their flesh will be the sappier.

4. Fat; plump. *Obs.* exc. *dial.*

1694 *Lond. Gaz.* No. 2998/4 She [a mare] is spay'd, and has a heavy Eye, somewhat sappy. *a* **1813** A. Wilson *Epit. Auld Janet* Poet. Wks. (1840) 288 A sonsier dame, or sappier wame, Ne'er hotcht alangst the cawsey. **1819** *Blackw. Mag.* V. 637 Your frame so sappy, and your face so smug.

5. a. Full of moisture; moist; wet; sodden; rainy. *Obs.* exc. *dial.* Cf. soppy *a.*

c **1470** Henryson *Mor. Fab.* viii. (*Preach. Swallow*) xiv, To se the soill..Sappie, and to resaue all seidis able. **1806** J. Beresford *Miseries Hum. Life* (ed. 3) iii. ix, At cricket..on very sloppy ground, so that your hard ball presently becomes, muddy, sappy, and rotten. **1885** Hall Caine *Shadow Crime* xxiv, It's cold and sappy, Mrs. Garth.

b. Of meat: Putrescent, tainted. *dial.* (See E.D.D.)

1573 Baret *Alv.* s.v. *Restie*, Sapie or vnsauerie flesh. **1783** Lemon *Etymol. Dict.*, *Sapy*, a moisture contracted on the outward surface of meats, which is the first stage of dissolution.

6. Consisting of or containing sap-wood.

1466 in Willis & Clark *Cambridge* (1886) III. 93 This tymbir shalbe white oke, not doted, nor storvyn, nor sappy. **1711** *Milit. & Sea Dict.* (ed. 4) s.v. *Trenel*, These T[r]enels must be well season'd, and not sappy. **1776** G. Semple *Building in Water* 84 Be exceeding careful how you make use of any sort of sappy Timber.

7. Foolish. (Cf. sap *sb.*[5]) Also as *sb.* Hence ˈ**sappyhead**, a foolish person. Cf. sap-head.

1670 *2nd Pt. Peoples Liberties Asserted* 6 When unlimited Prerogatives have sprung up, like Mushromes out of the sappy Apprehensions..of inferior Officers. **1797** Mrs. A. M. Bennett *Beggar Girl* (1813) I. 242 'Where', said she fretfully, 'can he have taken his sappy head?' **1894** G. W. Appleton *Co-Respondent* I. 150, I am a fat-headed, sappy, bally ass. **1922** Joyce *Ulysses* 114 Martin could wind a sappyhead like that round his little finger without his seeing it. **1930** D. H. Lawrence *Nettles* 23 You know that they've got to think that they're happy... Oh so happy, you sappy.

punningly. **1848** Lowell *Fable for Critics* Poet. Wks. 1890 III. 61 The women he draws from one model don't vary, All sappy as maples and flat as a prairie.

‖**sapræmia** (sæˈpriːmɪə). [mod.L., f. Gr. σαπρό-ς putrid + -αἱμα blood.] 'Septic intoxication, or poisoning by means of septic or putrefactive organisms' (*Syd. Soc. Lex.* 1897).

1886 *Encycl. Brit.* XXI. 666/2 When the wound is due to a saprophyte the absorption of the ptomaine has been termed 'Sapræmia'. **1889** J. M. Duncan *Clin. Lect. Dis. Wom.* v. (ed. 4) 16 It not very rarely leads to death from putrid intoxication or sapræmia.

sapræmic (sæˈpriːmɪk), *a.* [f. prec. + -ic.] Of or pertaining to sapræmia; affected with sapræmia.

1889 J. M. Duncan *Clin. Lect. Dis. Wom.* xiv. (ed. 4) 106 Inflammation of the cyst is set up, with fever and sapræmic symptoms. **1902** G. S. Woodhead in *Encycl. Brit.* XXXI. 521/2 A distinction must be drawn between sapræmia and septicæmia... So long as no micro-organisms follow the toxins, the condition is purely sapræmic.

sapric (ˈsæprɪk), *a.* *Soil Sci.* [f. Gr. σαπρ-ός rotten, putrid + -ic.] Of a soil or soil horizon: characterized by the presence of highly decomposed organic material.

1965 Farnham & Finney in *Adv. Agronomy* XVII. 138 In the classification of organic soils presented here, only three types of horizons are considered diagnostic... These are the fibric, mesic, and sapric horizons, listed in order of increasing decomposition. **1972** J. G. Cruickshank *Soil Geogr.* vi. 187 At the other extreme, sapric..soils or horizons are well decomposed and contain a high proportion by weight of mineral material.

†**saprine.** *Chem. Obs.* Also -in. [ad. G. *saprin* (L. Brieger *Untersuchungen über Ptomaine* (1885) II. 46), f. as prec.: see -ine[5].] A ptomaine of doubtful identity isolated from putrefying flesh.

1887 [see cadaverine]. **1894** *Watts's Dict. Chem.* IV. 346/2 Saprine is isolated by means of its platinochloride. **1910** *Practitioner* June 830 Ptomaines obtained from putrid meat and other albuminous bodies:..Saprin $C_5H_{16}N_2$.

‖**sapristi** (sapristi), *int.* [Fr., corruption of *sacristi* in same sense.] An exclamation of astonishment, exasperation, etc.; a mild oath.

1839 Thackeray *Cox's Diary* in *Comic Almanack 1840* 33 Shouting out, 'Aha!' and '*Sapprrrristie*!' **1867** 'Ouida' *Under Two Flags* II. i. 3 Sapristi! And what did he say? **1932** A. Christie *Peril at End House* xxii. 244 And the card—*my* card! *Ah! Sapristi*—she has a nerve! **1957** O. Nash *You can't get there from Here* 97 So when I sight my island home I'll salvage but a single tome, Which is—what should it be, *sapristi*, But any book by Agatha Christie? **1966** A. Christie *Third Girl* ii. 10 Ah *Sapristi*! That must be a woman—undoubtedly a woman. **1972** A. MacVicar *Golden Venus Affair* i. 9 Sapristi, what a condition he's in!

saprobe (ˈsæprəʊb). *Biol.* [f. Gr. σαπρό-ς putrid + β-ίος life; cf. G. *saprobie* (Kolkwitz & Marsson 1902, in *Mitteilungen aus der K. Prüfungsanstalt f. Wasserversorgung und Abwässerbeseitigung* I. 46).] Any organism that derives its nourishment from decaying organic matter.

1932 G. W. Martin in *Bot. Gaz.* XCIII. 427 The word *saprophyte* and its derivatives, implying that a fungus is a plant, can be replaced by saprobe (σαπρός + βίος), which is without such implication. **1952** C. J. Alexopoulos *Introd. Mycol.* i. 30 Fungi obtain their food either as parasites or saprobes. Some are obligately parasitic or saprobic. **1971** G. C. Ainsworth *Ainsworth & Bisby's Dict. Fungi* (ed. 6) 518 Saprobe is the preferred usage for fungi.

saprobial (səˈprəʊbɪəl), *a.* *Ecol.* [f. saprob(ic *a.* + -ial.] Serving as a measure of saprobity.

1965 *Hydrobiologia* XXV. 523 The secondarily introduced methods of statistical calculation and expression of saprobial indices may only pretend an exact mathematical basis. **1970** J. Schwoerbel *Methods Hydrobiol.* vii. 155 The saprobial valency is better characterized than the allotment to a single zone of the saprobic system.

saprobic (səˈprəʊbɪk), *a.* *Ecol.* [f. G. *saprob-ie* saprobe + -ic.] **a.** Characterized by the prevalence of decaying organic material; *spec.* = *polysaprobic* adj. s.v. poly- 1; ***saprobic system***, a system by which a body of polluted water is divided into zones characterized by the presence of certain organisms that are treated as indicators of the degree of pollution.

1913 *Bull. Illinois State Lab. Nat. Hist.* IX. x. 498 We will distinguish..three stages of impurity, by use of the following terms applicable both to the waters themselves and to the characteristic organisms, given here in the order of a diminishing impurity, namely: (1) septic or saprobic [etc.]. **1925** [see *polysaprobic* adj.]. **1967** A. F. Bartsch in Olson & Burgess *Pollution & Marine Ecol.* vi. 294 Various North American biologists have expressed doubt as to the applicability of the saprobic system to coastal and estuarine environments. **1971** R. J. Benoit in L. L. Ciaccio *Water & Water Pollution Handbk.* I. iv. 255 The general relationship between the saprobic zones and the zones shown by oxygen sag curves has been illustrated. **1975** D. F. Westlake in B. A. Whitton *River Ecol.* iv. 126 In general macrophytes are not good indicators for use in the saprobic system of classifying rivers.

b. Pertaining to or characteristic of a saprobe; deriving nourishment from decaying organic matter.

1932 *Bot. Gaz.* XCIII. 429 The nutrition of the Phycomycetes is saprobic or parasitic. **1960** H. B. N. Hynes *Biol. Polluted Waters* xiii. 161 Complex organic..molecules encourage the growth of saprophytic plants and saprobic animals. **1976** *Nature* 27 May 336/2 The free-living saprobic form found in soil is mycelial.

Hence **saˈprobical** *a.* = saprobial *a.*; **sapro'bicity** = saprobity.

1961 *Arch. Hydrobiol.* LVII. 405 Tables of the saprobical valency of species studied by the authors as well as examples of the saprobiological evaluation are appended. **1971** *Ann. Rev. Microbiol.* XXV. 565 The rate of multiplication of the test organism, i.e., optimum biomass produced, is considered to be an integrated biological measure of the content of biologically active organic nitrogen in the water and thus a measure of the saprobicity. **1975** G. A. Cole *Textbk. Limnol.* iv. 61/2 Saprobicity, the total of all the processes that are antithetical to primary production, is another classification of heterotrophy.

saprobiology (ˌsæprəʊbaɪˈɒlədʒɪ). [f. as next + biology.] The study of saprobic environments.

1958 *Ecology* XXXIX. 547/2 It can be stated in terms used in saprobiology that the polysaproby was changed into alpha-mesosaproby. **1965** *Hydrobiologia* XXV. 524 The applicability in practice is..the main criterion of an applied scientific branch, as saprobiology is.

Hence ˌ**saprobioˈlogical** *a.*; **saprobiˈologist**.

1960 *Biol. Abstr.* XXXV. 3801/2 The saprobiological analysis is based on the determination of approximately 8,500 organisms. **1965** *Hydrobiologia* XXV. 526 Such problems as the influence of different amino acids..on the stimulation of the growth of *Sphaerotilus* and *Leptomitus* cannot be solved by the saprobiologists alone. **1971** *Ann. Rev. Microbiol.* XXV. 574 Caspers & Karbe..have proposed a saprobiological classification of waters.

saprobiotic (ˌsæprəʊbaɪˈɒtɪk), *a.* *Biol.* [f. Gr. σαπρός putrid + βιωτικ -ός pertaining to life.] = saprobic *a.*

1940 *Chambers's Techn. Dict.* 740/2 *Saprobiotic*, feeding on dead or decaying animals or plants. **1950** P. D. F. Murray *Biology* xlvii. 52 A saprobiotic organism (the term covers 'saprozoic' and 'saprophytic') is one which lives on the dead bodies of other organisms or their inanimate products. **1960** E. N. Willmer *Cytol. & Evolution* ix. 151 Many flagellates..depend for their energy supplies on the extraction of materials dissolved in the fluid in which they are swimming, i.e. they lead a saprobiotic existence.

Hence **saprobiˈotically** *adv.*

1957 G. E. Hutchinson *Treat. Limnol.* I. ix. 623 Living plankton metabolizing its reserves or living saprobiotically.

saprobity (səˈprəʊbɪtɪ). *Ecol.* [f. saprob(ic *a.* + -ity.] The degree to which the decomposition of organic material is occurring in an aquatic environment.

1956 *Archiv für Hydrobiol.* LI. 389 Utilization of the running water Macroorganism as Indicators of the water saprobity degrees (sensu Kolkwitz-Marsson). **1965** *Hydrobiologia* XXV. 523 The saprobity system is applicable only to organic pollution undergoing bacterial decomposition and it is useless for the assessment of the effects of poisons or other pollutional matters. **1973** Bayly & Williams *Inland Waters & their Ecol.* xii. 254 The 'saprobity indices' of several European workers..are indirect measures of pollution based upon a combination of chemical, bacteriological, and biological features.

saprogenic (sæprəʊˈdʒenɪk), *a.* [f. Gr. σαπρό-ς putrid + -gen + -ic.] Causing decay or putrefaction; also, produced by putrefaction.

1876 tr. *Wagner's Gen. Pathol.* 599 Saprogenic or putrid infection. **1882** Huxley in *Nature* 9 Mar. 439 The results of recent researches, which tend to show that pathogenic bacteria are mere modifications of saprogenic forms. **1900** A. C. JONES tr. *A. Fischer's Struct. Bacteria* 49 Zymogenic, saprogenic and saprophile bacteria.

saprogenous (sæ'prɒdʒɪnəs), *a.* [f. Gr. σαπρό-ς putrid + -GEN + -OUS.] = prec.

1876 tr. *Wagner's Gen. Pathol.* 92 *Bact. termo* is the ferment of putrefaction, the saprogenous ferment. **1890** BILLINGS *Nat. Med. Dict.*, *Saprogenic* or *Saprogenous*, producing putrefaction or decay. **1900** B. D. JACKSON *Gloss. Bot. Terms*, *Saprogenous*, growing on decaying substances.

saprol ('sæprɒl). *Chem.* [f. Gr. σαπρό-ς putrid + -OL.] (See quot. 1897.)

1892 *Brit. Med. Jrnl.* 17 Sept. 47/3 Laser (..August 18th, 1892) gives an account of an inquiry made by him into the properties of saprol. **1897** *Syd. Soc. Lex.*, *Saprol*, name for a crude mixture of creosols with carbohydrates and pyridine, used for rough disinfection.

‖**Saprolegnia** (sæprəʊ'lɛgnɪə). *Bot.* [mod.L., f. Gr. σαπρό-ς putrid + λέγν-ον border.] A genus of fungi (the type of the N.O. *Saprolegnieæ* or *Saprolegniaceæ*), which chiefly infests the bodies of fish.

1866 BERKELEY in *Treas. Bot.* s.v. *Saprolegnieæ*, The same animal has been observed, when immersed, to produce a *Saprolegnia*, and when surrounded merely by air to produce a *Mucor*. **1882** HUXLEY in *Nature* 9 Mar. 438/2, I tried some experiments on the transplantation of the *Saprolegnia* of the living salmon to dead animal bodies. **1885** KLEIN *Micro-Organisms* 146 Saprolegnia: colourless tubular threads, forming gelatinous masses on living and dead animal and vegetable matter in fresh water.

Hence **sapro'legnious** *a.* (see quot. 1900); **sapro'legnized** *ppl. a.*, diseased with saprolegnia.

1882 HUXLEY in *Nature* 9 Mar. 439/1 The conditions under which my saprolegnised flies were placed. **1900** B. D. JACKSON *Gloss. Bot. Terms*, *Saprolegnious*, allied to the genus *Saprolegnia*.

saprolite ('sæprəʊlaɪt). *Geol.* [f. Gr. σαπρός putrid + -LITE.] Soft, clay-rich, thoroughly decomposed rock formed *in situ* by chemical weathering of igneous and metamorphic rocks.

1895 G. F. BECKER in *16th Ann. Rep. U.S. Geol. Survey* III. 289, I propose the term *saprolite*. *Ibid.* 290 The deposits referred to..are gold-bearing saprolites. **1935** *Jrnl. Geol.* XLIII. 745 In the Appalachian Piedmont of the southern states, weathering has reduced the granitic rocks to an extensive mantle of incoherent clay, or saprolite, that in places extends to a depth of over 100 feet. **1948** *Prof. Papers U.S. Geol. Survey* No. 213. 125/2 The upper parts of the lodes were in the saprolite zone and were worked as residual placer deposits, but at the base of the saprolite these deposits graded into solid lodes. **1977** A. HALLAM *Planet Earth* 48/1 Chemical weathering can produce a rotted rock-form known as a saprolite, which is the product of chemical changes which have taken place *in situ*.

Hence **sapro'litic** *a.*; ˌ**saproliti'zation**, the process of formation of saprolite.

1904 L. J. SPENCER tr. *Bauer's Precious Stones* 361 Several crystals of rhodolite were found..embedded in a decomposed saprolitic rock. **1970** D. CARROLL *Rock Weathering* iii. 20 Extensive areas in arid Western Australia are underlain by saprolitic rocks on which lateritic profiles have developed (probably in the Pliocene). *Ibid.*, Saprolitization also occurs in rocks that are covered by later deposits that protect them from erosion. An example is saprolitization under a cover of river gravel or sand through which water percolates.

sapropel ('sæprəʊpɛl). *Geol.* [a. G. *sapropel* (H. Potonié 1904, in *Sitzungsber. Ges. naturforsch. Freunde Berlin* 13 Dec. 243), f. as next.] An unconsolidated nitrogen-rich slime or sludge, formed of incompletely decomposed aquatic micro-organisms, esp. algæ, found in anaerobic environments on the bottoms of lakes and seas.

1907 *Rep. Brit. Assoc. Adv. Sci. 1906* 748 The sapropel is formed from the excrements and bodies of completely aquatic animals and plants which have lived in stagnant water, and therefore, because the water is stagnant, do not decay completely. *Ibid.*, Cannel coal..is a fossil sapropel. **1929** H. B. MILNER *Sedimentary Petrogr.* (ed. 2) 335 The coal-substance has been regarded by Potonié as 'sapropel', a solidified jelly-like carbonaceous slime. **1970** *Nature* 17 Oct. 200/1 Cores from the Mediterranean's three deep basins also yielded dolomites,..diatomites and organic sapropels. **1978** *Ibid.* 16 Nov. 259/2 The preservation of non-siliceous algae is uncommon, although found in the sapropel deposits of the USSR.

sapropelic (sæprəʊ'pɛlɪk), *a. Geol.* and *Zool.* [ad. G. *sapropelisch* (R. Lauterborn 1901, in *Zool. Anzeiger* XXIV. 50), f. Gr. σαπρός putrid + πηλός mud, earth, clay: see -IC.] Found in, characterized by, or derived from sapropel.

1901 *Jrnl. R. Microsc. Soc.* 144 'Sapropelic' Fauna... Dr. R. Lauterborn uses the term '*sapropelische*' to denote the organisms found in the muddy debris covering the bottom of stagnant fresh-water pools. **1918** [see HUMIC *a.*]. **1963** D. W. & E. E. HUMPHRIES tr. *Termier's Erosion & Sedimentation* xi. 239 The presence of a sapropelic bottom inhibits aerobic life over the whole of the lower part of the basin. **1966** [see HUMIC *a.*]. **1971** *Nature* 31 Dec. 508/1 They [*sc.* labyrinthodonts] are never found in humic coals, but usually in sapropelic coals, laid down in the deep anaerobic mud which formed in stagnant conditions.

saprophagan (sæ'prɒfəgən). *Ent.* [f. mod.L. *saprophag-us* (see next) + -AN.] (See quot.)

1842 BRANDE *Dict. Sci.*, etc., *Saprophagans*, the name of a tribe of Coleopterous insects, comprising those which feed on..substances in a state of decomposition.

saprophagous (sæ'prɒfəgəs), *a.* [f. mod.L. *saprophag-us* (f. Gr. σαπρός putrid + -φάγος eating) + -OUS.] Living on decomposing matter.

1819 MACLEAY *Horæ Entomol.* I. 27 Saprophagous insects or such as feed on putrid or decomposed vegetable matter. **1849** HARDY in *Proc. Berw. Nat. Club* II. No. 7. 361 Species whose larvæ are..either fungivorous or saprophagous.

saprophile ('sæprəʊfaɪl), *sb.* and *a.* [f. Gr. σαπρός putrid + -φίλος loving: see -PHILE.]

a. A bacterium inhabiting putrid matter. **b.** *adj.* Of bacteria: Found in putrid matter. So **sa'prophilous** *a.*

1882 A. W. BLYTH *Foods* 544 There are, however, certain animalcules..that specially point to sewage contamination. This class have been called 'saprophiles'. **1890** BILLINGS *Nat. Med. Dict.*, Saprophilous. **1900** A. C. JONES tr. *A. Fischer's Struct. Bacteria* 49 Such bacteria may be termed *saprophile*.

fig. **1934** S. BECKETT *More Pricks than Kicks* 67 A little saprophile of an anonymous politico-ploughboy setting him off.

saprophyte ('sæprəʊfaɪt). [f. Gr. σαπρό-ς putrid + φυτόν plant: see -PHYTE.] Any vegetable organism that lives on decayed organic matter.

1875 *Encycl. Brit.* III. 691/1 There are other degraded allies of green plants, which are content to work up again the imperfectly broken down products of decay. Such plants are termed *Saprophytes*. **1882** S. WALPOLE & HUXLEY in *Q. Jrnl. Microsc. Sci.* XXII. 332 The common moulds,..which are habitually saprophytes (that is to say, live on decaying organic matter).

Hence **sa'prophytal** (B. D. Jackson *Gloss. Bot. Terms* 1900), **saprophytic** (-'fɪtɪk) *adjs.*, of or pertaining to saprophytes; **sapro'phytically** *adv.*, after the manner of saprophytes; **sa'prophytism**, the state of living as a saprophyte.

1882 H. M. WARD in *Q. Jrnl. Microsc. Sci.* Jan. 2 The appearance of various saprophytic fungi on the old shrivelled spot indicates the completion of the destruction. **1887** GARNSEY & BALFOUR tr. *De Bary's Fungi* 356 Species of purely and strictly saprophytic..mode of life. **1890** A. WHITELEGGE *Hygiene & Public Health* x. 227 Cultivation in non-living media, in other words, a form of saprophytism, is [etc.]. **1898** *Allbutt's Syst. Med.* V. 257 The fungus being merely saprophytic. **1904** *Brit. Med. Jrnl.* 3 Dec. 1509 All the known parasitic bacterial species (with the exception of the leprosy bacilli)..can thrive also saprophytically.

sapsago (sæp'seɪgəʊ). *U.S.* [Corrupt form of SCHABZIEGER.] A kind of hard cheese made in Switzerland, flavoured with melilot.

1846 in WORCESTER. **1858** SIMMONDS *Dict. Trade.*

sapskull ('sæpskʌl). Now *dial.* (see E.D.D.). [f. SAP *sb.*[1] (sense 4) + SKULL.] = SAP-HEAD.

1735 H. CAREY *Honest Yorkshire-man* 9 Welcome to London, dear 'Squire Sapscull. **1785** GROSE *Dict. Vulgar Tongue*, *Sapscull*, a simple fellow. **1796** *Sporting Mag.* VII. 55 Poor sapskull, thus craftily put to the blush. **1974** J. AIKEN *Midnight is Place* i. 11 Idiot! Sapskull! How dared you write?

‖**sapucaia** (sæpuː'kaːjə). Also 7 iacapucaya, 9 sapucaya. [Brazilian; according to Von Martius f. *sopia* egg + *acaia* a kind of forest tree; the fruit with its seeds resembling a nest containing eggs. Gandavo 1576 (Pg.) writes *zabucaes* pl.]

1. a. A South American tree of the genus *Lecythis.*

b. The fruit of the tree, a sapucaia-nut.

1613 PURCHAS *Pilgrimage* (1614) 843 Of Fruits, he reckons the Iacapucaya, like a pot..with a couer on it. **1869** R. F. BURTON *Highl. Brazil* I. 120 Hereabouts also are two noble lofty Sapucaias, vestiges of the forest primeval.

2. *attrib.*, as *sapucaia tree*; **sapucaia-brown** *Chem.* (see quot.); **sapucaia-nut**, the edible fruit of *Lecythis Zabucajo* and *L. Ollaria*; **sapucaia-oil, -wine** (see quots.)

1868 WATTS *Dict. Chem.* V. 195 The shell of the fruit contains a tannin..which..in the older fruits is converted into a brown substance (*sapucaia-brown). **1820** tr. *von Wied's Trav. Brazil* I. 126 Some baskets..full of bananas, oranges, *sapucaya-nuts [etc.]. **1866** *Treas. Bot.* s.v. *Lecythis*, Under the name of Sapucaia nuts, the seeds of *L. Zabucajo* are commonly sold in our fruit shops. **1884** *Encycl. Brit.* XVII. 746/1 **Sapucaia oil*, yielded by *Lecythis ollaria*. **1820** tr. *von Weid's Trav. Brazil* I. 105 The young foliage of the *sapucaya tree. **1868** WATTS *Dict. Chem.* V. 195 The juice (*sapucaia-wine) which flows from incisions in old trees.

'sap-wood. [SAP *sb.*[1]] = ALBURNUM.

1791 E. DARWIN *Bot. Gard.* I. Add. Notes 96 The placental vessels..are transformed from sap-wood..into inert wood. **1815** J. SMITH *Panorama Sci. & Art* I. 258 Boards..free from..sap-wood. **1887** MOLONEY *Forestry W. Afr.* 353 A deep reddish-brown heartwood and light sap-wood.

saque, saquem, obs. ff. SAKÉ *sb.*[2], SACHEM.

sar (sɑː(r)). [a. F. *sar*, variant of *sargue*, *sargo*, etc., ad. L. *sargus*: see SARGON, SARGUS.] A fish of the sparoid genus *Sargus*.

1838 *Encycl. Metrop.* (1845) XXIV. 320/2 The Sars are shore fish, are common on the Southern coasts of France. **1880** GÜNTHER *Fishes* 406 Several of them occur in the Mediterranean and the neighbouring parts of the Atlantic, and are popularly called 'Sargo', 'Sar', 'Saragu'.

sar: see SAVOUR, SERVE, SHEAR, SORE.

Sarabaite (særə'beɪaɪt). *Eccl. Hist.* Also 4 Serabite, 6 Sarrabaite, 6- Sarabite. [ad. eccl. L. *Sarabaīta* (Cassianus, 4–5th c., who says that the word is Egyptian; but no light has been thrown on it from that language).

Sarabite is the form commonly found in English translations of the Rule of St. Benedict.]

One of a class of monks in the early Church who lived together in small bands without rule or superior. †Also as *adj.*, applied to certain followers of the Franciscan rule (see quot. *c* 1380), prob. the *Fratricelli*.

138. WYCLIF *Wks.* (1880) 12 ȝif þei pursuen to þe deþ pore freris serabitis, þat kepen fraunseis reule and testament to þe riȝte vndyrstondynge and wille of fraunceis wiþ outen glose of antecristis clerkis. **1516** BP. FOX *Rule of Seynt Benet* i, The .iii. kynde, maner, or secte, is of Sarabites, a secte detestable: whiche lyue not vnder obedience of any superior. **1537** *Orig. & Sprynge of Sectes* A vij b, These Sarrabaites be sayd..to come of Ananias & Saphira..by lynage & kynred. **1693** D'EMILIANNE *Mon. Ord.* viii. 59 Sarabaites, who were a sort of People following only their own Wills. **1728** CHAMBERS *Cycl.* s.v., St. Benedict gives a frightful Idea of these Sarabaites in the First Chapter of his Rule. **1765** MACLAINE tr. *Mosheim's Eccl. Hist.* Cent. IV. II. iii. §15 Those wandering fanatics, or rather impostors, whom the Egyptians called Sarabaites. **1801** RANKEN *Hist. France* I. 224 The Sarabaites, who associated two or three together, lived sometimes in solitude, but always without rule or order. **1904** GASQUET *Eng. Mon. Life* 8 The Gyrovagi and Sarabites.

saraband[1] ('særəbænd). Also 7-8 sarabrand, 8-9 sarabande. [ad. F. *sarabande*, ad. Sp. *zarabanda* (= Pg. *sarabando*), prob. of Oriental origin.]

1. A slow and stately Spanish dance in triple time.

1616 B. JONSON *Devil an Ass* IV. iv, Coach it to Pimlico; daunce the Saraband. **1675** CROWNE *Country Wit* IV. 51, I can dance Corantoes and Jiggs and Sarabands. **1726** *Adv. Capt. R. Boyle* (1768) 186 He went away to his own Chamber, leaving room in all our Pockets for the Devil to dance a Saraband. **1741** RICHARDSON *Pamela* III. 324 Oh! that I could but dance as well as thou sing'st! I'd give you a Saraband, as old as I am. **1776** HAWKINS *Hist. Mus.* IV. 388 *note*, Within the memory of persons now living, a Saraband danced by a Moor was constantly a part of the entertainment at a puppet-shew. **1809** CAMPBELL *Gert. Wyom.* I. v, Nor far some Andalusian saraband Would sound to many a native rondelay.

attrib. **1696** tr. *Du Mont's Voy. Levant* 284 They begin.. with a Saraband-Step, two steps forward and three backwards.

b. *transf.* and *fig.*

a **1658** LOVELACE *Posth. Poems* (1659) 10 So you but with a touch from your fair Hand Turn all to Saraband. **1703** *Rules of Civility* 22 'Tis pleasant, in troth, to see a lame Person find fault with a Step in such a Sarabrand. **1860** R. A. VAUGHAN *Mystics* (ed. 2) II. 75 In that unswept brain of his..the super-subtile fancies of theosophy, have danced a whirlwind saraband. **1863** I. WILLIAMS *Baptistery* II. xxxi. (1874) 181 When the loose villager Weaves 'neath the moon his rustic saraband.

2. A piece of music composed for this dance or in its rhythm, in which the second note of the measure is commonly lengthened.

1625 B. JONSON *Staple of N.* IV. ii, How they are tickl'd with a light ayre! the bawdy Saraband! **1657** R. LIGON *Barbadoes* 96 As Musitians, that first play a Preludium, next a Lesson, and then a Saraband. **1760–72** H. BROOKE *Fool of Qual.* (1809) III. 152 The lady called to the orchestre for a saraband. **1776** BURNEY *Hist. Mus.* (1789) IV. i. 114 Corelli in the saraband of his eleventh concerto. **1820** SCOTT *Monast.* xxviii, He hummed a saraband. **1860** O. W. HOLMES *Elsie V.* xxv, Elsie rattled out a triple measure of a saraband. **1884** HAWEIS *My Mus. Life* I. 8 Those simple and severe gigues and sarabands.

Saraband[2] ('særəbænd). Also Sarabend, Serabend, etc. [ad. *Saravand*, name of a district in western Iran.] A kind of Persian rug characterized by a pattern of leaf or pear forms. Also *attrib.*

1901 J. K. MUMFORD *Oriental Rugs* vi. 68 The 'pear' [*sc.* a motif] seems to have..original association with Persia... In the Sarabands..it covers the whole field. *Ibid.* xi. 197 The Saraband rugs are made in the district of Sarawan. **1913** W. A. HAWLEY *Oriental Rugs* ix. 130 In Mir-Sarabends one of two threads encircled by a knot is doubled under the other at back. In Royal Sarabends each is equally prominent. **1931** [see *palm-leaf pattern* s.v. PALM-LEAF c]. **1943** *Burlington Mag.* May 130/2 A Saraband carpet, the property of Mrs. Gilbert Russell. **1962** C. W. JACOBSEN *Oriental Rugs* 278 Choicest antique Sarabends will have as many as 350 knots to the square inch. **1975** 'E. LATHEN' *By Hook or by Crook* viii. 78 An old and valued customer was.. closing a deal for an old and valued Saraband. **1975** *Oxf. Compan. Decorative Arts* 612/1 Serabend rugs with all-over cone designs.

sarabatane, obs. form of SARBACANE.

sarabrase, variant of SABRAS *Obs.*, an infusion.
14.. *Nom.* in Wr.-Wülcker 740/35 *Hoc sarabracium*, sarabrase.

Saracen ('særəsən), *sb.* and *a.* Forms: α. 1 *pl.* Sarracene, Sarocine, 3 Sarezin, 3–4 Sarrezin, 3–7 Sarazin(e, 4 -sene, Sarisine, -zene, -ezyne, 4–6 Sarasyn(e, -in(e, 4–7 -cene, (5 Saresoun, -ezen, -esyn, -aseyn, Sarracene, -ysyne), 5–6 Sarazyn(e, Sarrasyn, 5–7 -zen(e, Sarrasin(e, (6 Sarason, -asen, -ezon, 7 -icin, -acin), 3– Saracen. β. 1 *pl.* Sarcine, 3–5 Sarzin(e, 4–5 -zyn, 4–6 -syn, 5 -sin(e, -s(e)yne, -cyne, -zene, -soun, 6 -son, 9 -zan. [In OE., ad. late L. *Saracēnī* pl; in ME., a. OF. *Sar(r)azin, -cin*, mod.F. *Sarrasin* (= It. *Saracino*, Sp. *Saraceno*, Pg. *Sarraceno*), ad. late L. *Saracēnus*, a. late Gr. *Σαρακηνός*.
The ultimate etymology is uncertain. The derivations from Arabic commonly given (of which the most usual is Arab. *sharqī* eastern, oriental, f. *sharq* sunrise) are not well founded. In mediæval times the name was often associated with Sarah, the wife of Abraham; St. Jerome (*Ezek.* VIII. xxv) identifies the Saracens with the *Agareni* (Hagarens, descendants of Hagar) 'who are now called Saracens, taking to themselves the name of Sara'.]

A. *sb.* **1. a.** Among the later Greeks and Romans, a name for the nomadic peoples of the Syro-Arabian desert which harassed the Syrian confines of the Empire; hence, an Arab; by extension, a Muslim, *esp.* with reference to the Crusades.
α. **c893** K. ÆLFRED *Oros.* I. i. 12 Moneʒe þeoda.. þæt is, Comagena & Fenitia.. Iudea, & Palestina, & Sarracene [orig. *absque Saracenis*]. **a950** *Durham Ritual* (Surtees) 196 On india saracena [L. *in India Saracenorum*]. **a1300** *Cursor M.* 16 How charles kyng and rauland faght, Wit sarazins wald þai na saght. **1387** TREVISA *Higden* (Rolls) II. 293 Peple þat cleped hem self Saracenys, as þogh þey were i-come of Sarra. **1390** GOWER *Conf.* I. 363 To passe over the grete See To werre and sle the Sarazin. **c1449** PECOCK *Repr.* I. xvii. 99 The lawe of Macomet and of Sarezenis. **c1475** *Partenay* 309 Lesse worth am I then any sarysyne, Whiche is in beleue of sory mahound! **1555** EDEN *Decades* (Arb.) 51 He hath quite dryuen out of Spayne the Moores or Sarasens. **1590** SIR J. SMYTH *Disc. Weapons* 33 That braue Saladin, Souldan of Egipt, with his notable milicia of Mamelucks (by many called Sarasins). **1602** BRETON *Wonders worth Hearing* (Grosart) 7/2 Standing.. with a Sarazins face, his nose too long for his lips, his cheekes like the iawes of a horse [etc.]. **1632** LITHGOW *Trav.* IV. 161 The Sarazens are descended of Esau. **1788** GIBBON *Decl. & F.* l. V. 181 From Mecca to the Euphrates, the Arabian tribes were confounded by the Greeks and Latins, under the general appellation of Saracens. **1848** LYTTON *Harold* I. iv, Here.. might be seen the swarthy Saracen, with wares from Spain and Afric. **1905** *19th Cent.* Aug. 268 The African hordes, generically termed Saracens, who were established near Villefranche as late as the early part of the tenth century.
β. ?**a900** *Malchus* in Cockayne *Shrine* (1864) 42 Wit urnon.. for sarcina herʒunge. **a1300** *Cursor M.* 11072 His [*i.e.* St. John Baptist's] fest it es in somers time, it halus bath Iu and sarzine. **a1375** *Joseph Arim.* 55 þei ferden to A Cite faste bi-syde, þat was called sarras þer sarsyns sprongen, Erest þorw Abrahames wyf þat wonede þer-inne. **1387** TREVISA *Higden* (Rolls) VI. 153 þat ȝere Sarzyns com out of Egipt into Affrica. **a1529** SKELTON *Agst. Garnesche* I. 36, I sey, ye solem Sarson, alle blake ys your ble. **1530** PALSGR. 265/1 Sarsyn a man.

†**b.** A Turk's head for tilting at. *Obs.*
1637 EARL MONM. tr. *Malvezzi's Rom. & T.* 231 Who passionately run their lances against a Saracin of wood. **1652** URQUHART *Jewel* Wks. (1834) 228 He carryed away the ring fifteen times on end, and broke as many lances on the Saracen. **1656** FLECKNOE *Relat. 10 Yrs. Trav.* x. 26 A solemn Justing or Running at Ring and Sarazen.

†**2. a.** A non-Christian, heathen, or pagan; an unbeliever, infidel. *Obs.*
c1250 *Meid. Maregrete* ix. 35 Sone wolde þe sarezin habben hire to wiue. **1297** R. GLOUC. (Rolls) 4522 Eiȝte hundred ssipes in to þis londe he broȝte Vol of saracens [*MS.* δ of Saxons fulle]. **a1300** *K. Horn* 42 (Cambr. MS.), He fond bi þe stronde,.. Schipes fiftene, Wiþ sarazins kene. **c1330** *Arth. & Merl.* 2067 Danmark Sarrazins þat were of Angys lins. **1377** LANGL. *P. Pl.* B. XI. 151 Nouȝt þorw preyere of a pope.. Was þat sarasene [*sc.* Emperor Trajan] saued. **1433** LYDG. *Edmund & Fremund* II. 381 in Horstm. *Altengl. Leg.* (1881) 403 Edmond that day was Cristis champioun,.. Among sarseynes he pleied the lioun. **c1450** *Merlin* 193 That day Gawein slowgh many a sarazin of the saxouns more than eny of his felowes. **1526** *Pilgr. Perf.* (W. de W. 1531) 289 That they shall loue, as the chylde his parentes, and the pagane or Sarasyn his false goddes. **1552** ABP. HAMILTON *Catech.* (1884) 50 Thou art made as ane Pagan, Saracen or Enfidele.

†**b.** *fig.* An ignorant and tasteless person, a 'barbarian', 'Goth', 'Vandal'. *Obs.*
1714 MANDEVILLE *Fab. Bees* (1733) I. 331 Methinks I hear them.. ask what brute of a Saracen it is that draws his ugly weapon for the destruction of learning.

†**3.** The Saracen people or territory. *Obs.* [So OF. *sarrazin*.] Cf. SARACENÉ below.
a1300 *Cursor M.* 6984 þai.. lefte þe lagh of hei drightin, And ledd þe law of sarazin. *Ibid.* 22286 Ouer Iubiter and apoline, þat godds war o sarazine. **1303** R. BRUNNE *Handl. Synne* 185 Here fadyr was prest of sarysyne [Fr. orig. *paenete*].

4. *Comb.*, as *Saracen-like* adj.; **Saracen corn**, buckwheat (see SARRASIN); † **Saracen's all-heal**, † **comfrey**, † **consound**, *Senecio saracenicus*, said to have been used by the Saracens in healing wounds; † **Saracen's birth-wort** = SARAZINE; **Saracen's corn**, *Sorghum vulgare*; also = *Saracen corn* or buckwheat, *Fagopyrum esculentum*; † **Saracen's earth**, ? Lemnian earth; **Saracen's head**, the head of a Saracen, Arab, or Turk used (*a*) as a charge in heraldry, (*b*) as an inn sign, etc.; **Saracen's herb** = SARAZINE; † **Saracen's mint** = SARAZINE; † **Saracen's soap**, a mixture of soap-lye and olive-oil; **Saracen's stone** = SARSEN; † **Saracen's woundwort** = *Saracen's consound*.
1687 A. LOVELL tr. *Thevenot's Trav.* II. 46 We saw a Field sowed with Maez or *Sarazin Corn. **1887** BENTLEY *Man. Bot.* 653 The fruits of *Fagopyrum esculentum*,.. Common Buckwheat or Saracen Corn. **a1704** T. BROWN *Lett. to Gent. & Ladies* Wks. 1709 III. II. 122 His Eye-brows are.. somewhat *Saracen-like. **1786** *Saracen's all-heal [see SARACENICAN]. **1597** GERARDE *Herbal* II. ccxcvii. 696 The later writers haue ioined vnto them a fift named *Saracens Birthwoort. **1578** *Saracen's comfrey, *Saracen's consound [see CONSOUDE]. **1585** HIGINS *Junius' Nomenclator* 109/2 *Milium Indicum*.., Indian millet: Turkishe wheate, or *Saracens corne. **1600** R. SURFLET tr. *Stevens & Liebault's Maison Rustique* I. xi. 53 Let her cause to be ground amongst her corne beanes, pease, fetches or sarrasins corne in some small quantitie. **1804** M. WILMOT *Russ. Jrnls.* (1934) I. 123 So many different sorts of Corn.. the Sarazens' Corn so white, the flax with its blue flowers, the peas so green. **1526** *Grete Herball* ccccxliv. (1529) Z v, Terra sigillata is otherwyse called *sarazyns erthe or siluered clay. **1510** *Nottingham Rec.* III. 108 Unius mesuagii nuncupati 'le *Sarezon' Hed'. **1726** S. KENT *Banner Display'd* 532 He beareth Gules, a Saracen's Head eras'd at the Neck Argent. **1838** DICKENS *Nich. Nick.* iv, The coach-yard of the Saracen's-Head Inn. **1838** *Penny Cycl.* XII. 142/2 Many of these [charges], such as crosses,.. Saracens' heads, &c., were assumed during the Crusades. **1585** HIGINS *Junius' Nomenclator* 116/2 *Aristolochia sarmentitia*.. *nonnullis herba Saracenica*.., *Saracens herb. **1525** *Grete Herball* cclxxiv. (1529) P v, It is called mynte romayne, or *sarazyns mynt. **1526** *Ibid.* cccxcviii. X vj, *Sarazyns sope is made of a lye called capitellium and oyle olyue syden together tyll it be thycke. **1644** SYMONDS *Diary* (Camden) 151 A place so full of a grey pibble stone of great bignes as is not usually seene.., the inhabaitants calling them *Saracens' stones. **1597** GERARDE *Herbal* II. xcvii. 347 Saracenes Consounde is called in Latine *Solidago Saracenica*, or Saracens Comfrey,.. English Saracens Consound, and *Saracenes Woundwoort. **1760** J. LEE *Introd. Bot.* App. 326 The true Saracen's Wound-wort *Senecio*.

B. *adj.* **a.** = SARACENIC. (By Sir C. Wren erroneously applied to Pointed or 'Gothic' architecture.)
a1300 *Cursor M.* 4247 For men war þar o sarzin lede. **c1450** LOVELICH *Grail* xlv. 721 Whiche were to holden the better lay, whethir the Cristene lawe, Oþer Sarazine. **c1477** CAXTON *Jason* 29 Jason dide do sowne trompettis, tabours, and cornes sarasins. **1519** HORMAN *Vulg.* 279 Let vs daunce the haye, shypmens, sarson, and maurys daunce. *Saltemus geranion*. **1613** PURCHAS *Pilgrimage* (1614) 86 Syria.. was with the first subdued to Saracene servitude. **1713** WREN in *Parentalia* (1750) 297 This we now call the Gothick Manner of Architecture... I think it should with more Reason be called the Saracen Style. **1818** MILMAN *Samor* 207 When mad Orlando met On that frail bridge the giant Sarzan king. **1842** *Catal. Classic Contents Strawberry Hill* 162 A magnificent table of Saracen mosaic. **1862** W. H. JERVIS *Hist. France* v. (1872) 67 The Saracen governor of Saragossa.

†**b.** *Cookery*. In ***browet, sauce Saracen***. *Obs.*
?**c1390** *Form of Cury* (1780) 44 Sawse Sarzyne. Take heppes and make hem clene, take Almaundes blaunched. **c1430** *Two Cookery-bks.* 19 Bruette Sareson. *Ibid.* 30 Sauke Sarsoun. Take Almoundys, & blaunche hem. *Ibid.* 113 Saug saraser [*so printed*]. Tak Almandes, frye hem in oille.

Hence † **Saracené**, the land of the Saracens.
c1450 LOVELICH *Grail* xlv. 724 A gret Semble Of Alle the Maistres Of Sarrasene.

Saracenian (særə'siːnɪən), *a.* [f. late L. *Saracēnus* + -IAN.] Saracenic.
1818 MILLS *Hist. Crusades* (1822) I. i. 17 Some direful effects of Saracenian zeal.

Saracenic (særə'sɛnɪk), *a.* [ad. med.L. *Saracēnic-us*, f. late L. *Saracēn-us* SARACEN: see -IC. Cf. F. *sarracénique*.] Of, pertaining to, or characteristic of the Saracens.
1638 SIR T. HERBERT *Trav.* (ed. 2) 38 The Mammoody and Roopee are good silver.. and (after the Saracenic sort who hate Images in Coyne) cover'd with Arabick letters. *Ibid.* 280 The iron yoak of Saracenic bondage. **1816** *Sporting Mag.* XLVIII. 9 Those nations.. have to acknowledge their obligations to Saracenic or Arabian instructors. **1819** SCOTT *Ivanhoe* ix, The Saracenic music of the challengers. **1832** G. DOWNES *Lett. Cont. Countries* I. 231 Specimens of Saracenic Armour. **1897** DOWDEN *Fr. Lit.* III. vii. 226 The strife between French chivalry and Saracenic hordes.

b. Applied to Islamic architecture in its various forms, or to any features of it.
In the 18th and early 19th c. often erroneously applied (after Wren: see SARACEN *a.*) to 'Gothic' architecture.
1768 RIOU *Grec. Orders Archit.* 10 The heavy Gothic by Sir C. Wren, is distinguished as Anglo-Saxonic, the lighter as Saracenic. **1829** SCOTT *Anne of G.* xxi, A considerable part of the edifice was less in the strict Gothic than in what has been termed the Saracenic style. **1842** W. F. AINSWORTH *Trav. Asia Minor*, etc. I. 197 Its numerous remains of Mohammedan buildings, chiefly in a rich style of Saracenic architecture. **1846** THACKERAY *Cornhill to Cairo* Wks. 1898 V. 726 A great, large Saracenic oriel window. **1877** A. B. EDWARDS *Up Nile* i. 11 Saracenic doorways.

c. *transf.* Barbaric, heathenish.
1837 DICKENS *Pickw.* xvii, Swearing at him in a most Saracenic and ferocious manner.

Saracenical (særə'sɛnɪkəl), *a.* [Formed as prec.: see -ICAL.] = SARACENIC.
1613 PURCHAS *Pilgrimage* (1614) title-p., The Ancient Religions before the Flood, the Heathnish, Jewish, and Saracenicall in all Ages since. **1632** LITHGOW *Trav.* IV. 144 A Saracenicall Sultan of Persia. **1672** *Rosemary & Bayes* 6 It is not manifest unto me by the Sarracenical histories.. that Mahomet had not two companions. **1768** TUCKER *Lt. Nat.* (1834) II. 297 The Saracenical caliphs.

† **Saracenican** (særə'sɛnɪkən), *a. Obs.* [Formed as prec. + -AN.] = SARACENIC. **Saracenican groundsel**, *Senecio saracenicus*.
1607 TOPSELL *Four-f. Beasts* 734 Dib (otherwise *Dijb*) is an Arabian or Saracenican word. **1786** J. ABERCROMBIE *Arrangem.* in *Gard. Assist.* 67/1 Saracenican helvetian groundsel, called Saracen's all-heal.

Saracenism ('særəsənɪz(ə)m). *rare.* [ad. med.L. *Saracēnism-us* race or country of the Saracens, f. *Saracēnus* SARACEN. Cf. OF. *Sarasinesme* country of the Saracens.] The political or religious organization of the Saracens.
1659 GAUDEN *Tears Ch.* 356 Saracenism, Barbarism, and Atheisme. **1855** MILMAN *Lat. Chr.* XIV. vi. VI. 524 The Saxondom of his [*sc.* Arthur] foes recedes, the Paganism, even the Saracenism takes its place. **1907** *Edin. Rev.* Apr. 445 It was Saracenism that beat back the Cross on the plains of Syria.

† **'Saracenly**, *adv. Obs.* [f. SARACEN + -LY².] Like a Saracen; ? with heathenish violence.
1596 NASHE *Saffron Walden* O 2 b, Whiles he was thus saracenly sentencing it against mee.

saracennet, obs. form of SARSENET.

‖ **saraf** (sa'rɑːf). Also 6 xaraffe, -affo, 7 charaff, xeraffo, 9 sarraf, saraff, serof, -aff. See also SHROFF. [Pers., etc., a. Arab. *ṣarrāf*, f. *ṣarafa* to exchange, corresp. to Heb. *ṣāraph* to refine, assay (gold or silver), whence *ṣōrēph* refiner, worker in gold. Cf. F. *cherafe* (17th c.), Pg. *xarrafo*, *ṣarafo* (16th c.).] A banker or money-changer in the East; = SHROFF.
1598 W. PHILLIP tr. *Linschoten* I. xxxiii. 66/1 There is in euery place of the street exchangers of mony, by them [*sc.* Heathens] called Xaraffos, which are all christian Jewes. *Ibid.* 244 Xaraffes. **1662** J. DAVIES tr. *Olearius' Voy. Ambass.* VI. 330 The money-changers, whom they call Xeraffi [in Persia]. **1678** J. P. tr. *Tavernier's Trav.* I. II. 4 There is no considerable payment made, which is not received by the Cheraff or Banker. **1811** *Niebuhr's Trav. Arab.* liii. in *Pinkerton's Voy.* X. 71 He sent us to receive the money from his Saraf, or banker. **1877** MᶜCOAN *Egypt as it is* 115 The mâmour.. till the recent reform appointing a Controller-General of Receipts, received the taxes from the saraffs. **1883** C. J. WILLS *In Land of Lion & Sun* xvii. 192 The business of the serof is despised as being a usurer on the sly. **1897** *Blackw. Mag.* July 24/2 They [*sc.* Armenians] prospered as our 'Sarrafs'.

‖ **sarafan** ('særəfæn). Also 8–9 **-phan(e**. [Russian *sarafan*.] A long mantle, veil, or sleeveless cloak, forming part of the national dress of Russian peasant women.
1799 W. TOOKE *View Russian Emp.* I. 366 The quality of the saraphan is various according to circumstances. **1833** R. PINKERTON *Russia* 301 A ribbon, which reaches to the hem of their sarafan. **1855** *Englishw. in Russia* 28 The national dress, the sarafane, which was generally of.. blue or red cotton, having no bodice. **1896** *Daily Tel.* 27 May 7/1 The Grand Duchesses.. wore.. the.. national veil or scarf, called sarafan.

saragoy, var. SARIGUE.

Sarah ('sɛərə). [f. *s*earch *a*nd *r*escue *a*nd *h*oming.] Name given to a portable radio transmitter used by wrecked airmen to signal their position to rescue ships or aircraft. Also *attrib.*
1955 *Times* 31 Aug. 8/3 'Sarah', the device demonstrated yesterday, weighs only about 3lb. and can be carried in a Mae West. It contains a beacon battery of 24 hours operating capacity which can send signals to a Shackleton aircraft 75 miles away. A wrecked airman can start 'Sarah' working quite easily and can speak on it to those who are searching for him. **1956** *Times* 18 July 10/7 Tryout for 'Sarah'.. 'Sarah', the R.A.F.'s new air-sea rescue system, had its first real test yesterday. **1962** S. CARPENTER in *Into Orbit* 59 One of these beacons, a British invention called 'Sarah'—for 'Search and Rescue and Homing'—put out the signal that helped tell the search planes exactly where I was. *Ibid.* 60 There was one Sarah beacon aboard the capsule.

sarai, var. SERAI.

saralasin (sə'ræləsɪn). *Pharm.* [Contraction of 1-*sar*-8-*ala*- angiotens*in*, f. SAR(COSINE + ALA(NINE + *angioten*)*sin* (f. ANGIO- + HYPER)TENSIN).] A synthetic octapeptide which blocks the pressor action of hypertensin II, thereby reducing high blood pressures.
1974 *Lancet* 28 Dec. 1535/1 Angiotensin-II blockade by the competitive antagonist sar¹-ala⁸-angiotensin II ('Saralasin').. Blockade of angiotensin II with saralasin has been advocated. **1977** *Ibid.* 24/31 Dec. 1317/1 Two types of renin-angiotensin inhibitor have been tested in renal hypertension—competitive antagonists of angiotensin II, such as saralasin, and inhibitors of the converting enzyme.

Saramaccan (særə'mækən), *sb.* and *a.* Also **Saramak(k)an.** [f. the name of the river *Saramacca* in Surinam.] **A.** *sb.* **a.** A native or inhabitant of the upper reaches of the river Saramacca. *rare.* **b.** A creole language of this region; = *Jew Tongo* s.v. JEW *sb.* 3c. **B.** *adj.* Of or pertaining to the people or language of this region.

1959 J. VOORHOEVE in *Word* XV. 436 (*title*) An orthography for Saramaccan. *Ibid.* 437 The phoneme analysis was based on a Saramaccan story and a series of test-words. *Ibid.*, The Rev. Schmidt is a Saramaccan by birth. **1961** *Compar. Stud. Society & Hist.* III. 278 Saramakkan is spoken only by the Bush Negroes on the upper reaches of the Surinam or 'Saramakka' river. **1968** [see *Jew Tongo* s.v. JEW *sb.* 3c]. **1970** *Language* XLVI. 408 (*title*) A Saramaccan narrative pattern. **1976** *Amer. Speech 1974* XLIX. 141 Saramakkan and other creoles of the Americas with a higher proportion of African linguistic content are recognized tone languages.

sarampura, obs. var. SALEMPORE.

Saran (sə'ræn). orig. *U.S.* Also **saran.** A proprietary name for PVC, esp. as a film. Also ***Saran Wrap*** (hence ***Saran-Wrapped*** adj.).

1940 *Official Gaz.* (U.S. Patent Office) 26 Nov. 809/2 The Dow Chemical Company, Midland, Mich. Filed Sept. 27, 1940. *Saran* for thermoplastic synthetic resins comprising polymers and co-polymers derived from vinylidene chloride. Claims use since Aug. 21, 1940. **1942** [see POLY-VINYLIDENE]. **1948** *Textile Colorist* Feb. 46/3 Plastic Sales Division—of the Dow Chemical Company has formally released its trademark rights to the name 'saran' permitting it to become the descriptive name of the product. **1958** *Trade Marks Jrnl.* 26 Nov. 1214/2 *Saran*..Wrapping (packaging) materials included in Class 16 in the form of films. The Dow Chemical Company..Manufacturers. **1966** N. SIMON *Odd Couple* II. i. 64 After the..leftovers have been Saran-Wrapped—what do we do? **1968** T. WOLFE *Electric Kool-Aid Acid Test* xxvii. 391 Dresses made out of ..supermarket Saran Wrap. **1969** W. R. R. PARK *Plastics Film Technol.* vi. 161 The three plies, 'Saran' 18 (outer), PVC 88 (center), and 'Saran' 22 (inner) each serve a specific function. **1974** D. E. WESTLAKE *Help* ii. 15, I was stretching Saran Wrap over the toilets. **1979** *Maclean's Mag.* 21 May 9/1 Clark began by granting interviews in a separate compartment aboard his plane but by the fifth week of the campaign, Tory campaign manager Lowell Murray sensed that the party was taking the heat for a Saran-Wrapped strategy. **1980** *Yachts & Yachting* 29 Feb. 656/2 Blown saran to produce an easily worked filler.

sarang, rare var. SERANG.

‖**sarangi** ('sɑːrəŋgɪ). Also 9 **sarungee.** [Skr.] An Indian musical instrument resembling a violin. Cf. SARINDA.

1851 *Illustr. Catal. Gt. Exhib.* IV. 913/2 Sarungee and bow, or Hindoostanee fiddle. **1886** GONDAL *Jrnl. of Visit to Eng. in 1883* 155 Those niceties of sweet sounds which a *sitar* or a *sârangi* can alone give. **1891** C. R. DAY *Mus. & Mus. Instruments S. India* vi. 93 The use of Sârangi in Southern India..is rapidly being discontinued. **1921** [see ESRAJ]. **1929** *Radio Times* 4 Jan. 38/3 The *sarangi* has a sweeter, slightly deeper tone than the violin. **1969** [see DILRUBA]. **1980** *Early Music* July 351/2 This, as can be heard when listening to recordings of the sarangi, does not chop a note from the string but leaves a small *bruyard* to escape.

sarape, var. SERAPE.

sararre, obs. f. compar. of SORE.

Sarasen, -son, etc., obs. forms of SARACEN.

Saratoga (særə'təʊgə). [f. *Saratoga Springs*, the name of a summer resort in New York State.]

1. In full ***Saratoga trunk***: a large kind of trunk much used by ladies.

1858 *N.Y. Tribune* 26 July 3/1 The Saratoga Trunk is an article that has been a theme of story for some time. **1874** B. F. TAYLOR *World on Wheels* I. ix. 72 It is not a carpet-bag, nor a valise nor a Saratoga. **1893** F. F. MOORE *Forbid Banns* xix, 'Oh, Eric, do help Miriam with that Saratoga,' cried Mrs. Hardy,..pointing to where Miriam was struggling with a large trunk that had just been hoisted from the hold. *Ibid.* xxx, Three Saratoga trunks. **1894** HOWELLS *Trav. from Altruria* 95, I found the porter..with his wrist bound up. He said he had strained it in handling a lady's Saratoga.

2. In Combinations: **Saratoga chips, (fried) potatoes** *U.S.*, thinly-sliced fried potato served cold, potato crisps; **Saratoga water** *U.S.*, a mineral water obtained from the springs at Saratoga.

1880 F. M. A. ROE *Army Lett.* (1909) 262 The *Saratoga chips were delicate and crisp. **1947** *Reader's Digest* Feb. 95/2 She compromised on..a broiled lobster drenched with butter, Saratoga chips, and a fancy ice cream. **1973** *Daily Colonist* (Victoria, B.C.) 4 Feb. 24/2 An Indian—an American Indian—was a chef in Saratoga, N.Y., in 1853 when he had an order for French fries—sliced thin. He sliced them too thin and they came out crunchy, and for the next 40 or 50 years, they were known as Saratoga chips. **1876** M. N. HENDERSON *Cooking* 194 Nothing deteriorates more by getting cold or keeping than fried potatoes (with the exception of *Saratoga fried potatoes, which are served cold). **1877** *Golden Hours* Apr. 187/2 (*heading*) *Saratoga Potatoes. **1911** *Oysterman & Fisherman* Mar. 25/2 Serve with oysters.. French-fried or Saratoga potatoes. **1829** *Amer. Advertiser* (Philadelphia) 29 July 3/6 (Advt.), Fresh *Saratoga or Congress Spring Water. **1893** *Harper's Mag.* Jan. 323/1 In front of me was the sign: 'Saratoga water. All you wish for five cents.' **1969** R. & D. DE SOLA *Dict. Cooking* 200/1 *Saratoga water*, any of several mineral waters bottled at their source in Saratoga Springs, New York.

sarau, -aw, variant of SEROW.

sarawakite (sə'rɑːwəkaɪt). *Min.* [a. G. *Sarawakit* (Frenzel 1877), f. *Sarawak* (in Borneo): see -ITE.] A compound of antimony found in minute colourless crystals.

1882 G. J. BRUSH *3rd App. Dana's Min.* 106 Sarawakite... Found in cavities in the native antimony of Borneo.

saray, variant of SERAI.

†**Sara'zantic**, *a.* *Obs.*$^{-0}$ [app. alteration of *Saracenic* after *Byzantine*.] Saracenic.

1726 BAILEY, *Sarazantick*, like a Sarazen.

sarazin, variant of SARRASIN.

Sarazin(e, etc., obs. forms of SARACEN.

†**'sarazine.** *Obs.* [a. OF. *sarazine, sar(r)asine* aristolochia:—pop. L. *sarracīna* for late L. *sarracēna* (sc. *herba*), fem. of *sarracēnus* SARACEN.] Birthwort.

1525 *Grete Herball* cclxxiv. (1529) P v b, Mynte romayne or sarazyne is hote & drye in yᵉ seconde degre. **1866** *Treas. Bot.*, Sarazine, *Aristolochia Clematitis.*

sarbacane ('sɑːbəkeɪn). *Obs.* exc. *Antiq.* Also 7 **sarabatane,** 8 **sarbacan,** 9 **sabarcane** (?), **sarbacand** (?). [a. F. *sarbacane* (16th c.; earlier *sarbatenne*) 'a long trunke to shoot in' (Cotgr.), also, a speaking-trumpet (Littré), ad. Sp. *cebratana*: see CEBRATANE.]

1. A blow-tube or pipe for shooting with. *Hist.*

1765 H. TIMBERLAKE *Mem.* 45 Children, who..are very expert at killing with a sarbacan. **1825** SCOTT *Talism.* xxi, These cowardly caitiffs come against us with sarbacanes and poisoned shafts. **1869** BOUTELL *Arms & Armour* vi. 87 Substituting for the bow..the Sabarcane [*sic*], Sumpitan, or blow-tube, the Malays strike objects at great distances. **1878** *Pop. Sci. Monthly* XIII. 258 Thus originated..slings, *sarbacands*, lassos.

†**2.** An ear-trumpet. *Obs.*

1644 DIGBY *Nat. Bodies* xxviii. 251 To this art belongeth the making of sarabatanes, or trunkes, to helpe the hearing.

sarbet, obs. form of SHERBET.

sarbut ('sɑːbət). *local slang.* Also **sarbot, sarbutt.** [App. a proper name.] In Birmingham: a police informer. Also as *v. intr.* = INFORM *v.* 7b.

[**1896** *Birmingham Daily Mail* 17 Apr. 2/5 'Old Sarbot' says that..the Corporation have no legal powers to superannuate them from the rates.] **1897** *Ibid.* 5 Aug. 3/1, I knew him as one of those men who were engaged by the police for the purpose of putting up robberies and then giving information about them... They are called touts, 'sarbuts' or something else. **1928** F. C. TAYLOR *Language of Lags* in *Word-Lore* Oct. 122 Should one of the fraternity turn informer, he is for ever afterwards known as a *nark*, a *sarbot*, a *copper*. *Ibid.* 124 May be she'll sarbot to the D. who clobbered the kids. **1969** R. BUSBY *Robbery Blue* iii. 24 Your sarbut's story wasn't good enough... We were fooled. **1976** —— *New Face in Hell* viii. 110 The hand-picked city crime squad..recruited their 'sarbuts', the city slang for informants. **1978** *Daily Mail* 25 Jan. 12/2 In Birmingham an informer..is a 'sarbutt'.

sarc (sɑːk). *rare.* Abbrev. of SARCASM. Cf. SARKY *a.*

1926 E. WALLACE *Square Emerald* xv. 236 She always knew when her young lady was indulging in what Lucretia described as 'sarc'.

sarcasm ('sɑːkæz(ə)m). Also 6-7 in L. form **sarcasmus.** [ad. late L. *sarcasm-us*, a. late Gr. σαρκασμός, f. σαρκάζειν to tear flesh, gnash the teeth, speak bitterly, f. σαρκ-, σάρξ flesh.] A sharp, bitter, or cutting expression or remark; a bitter gibe or taunt. Now usually in generalized sense: Sarcastic language; sarcastic meaning or purpose.

α. **1579** E. K. in *Spenser's Sheph. Cal.* Oct., Glosse, Tom piper, an ironicall Sarcasmus, spoken in derision of these rude wits, whych [etc.]. **1581** J. BELL *Haddon's Answ. Osor.* 324 With this skoffe doth he note them..by a certayne figure called Sarcasmus. **1605** J. DOVE *Confut. Atheism* 38 He called the other Gods so, by a figure called *Ironia*, or *Sarcasmus*. **1621** BURTON *Anat. Mel.* I. ii. IV. iv, Many are of so petulant a spleene, and haue that figure Sarcasmus so often in their mouths,..that [etc.]. **1661** FELTHAM *Resolves* II. l. 284 Either a Sarcasmus against the voluptuous; or else, 'tis a milder counsel.

β. **1619** H. HUTTON *Follie's Anat.* (Percy Soc.) 10 Muse, shew the rigour of a satyres art, In harsh sarcasmes, dissonant and smart. **1690** C. NESSE *Hist. & Myst. O. & N. Test.* I. 234 No lye, but an irony..a witty way of speaking.. such sarcasms Elijah used. **1725** BLACKWALL *Introd. Class.* (ed. 3) 179 When a dying or dead Person is insulted with Scoffs and ironical Tartness 'tis usually call'd a Sarcasm. **1814** SCOTT *Ld. of Isles* IV. xxviii, With many a sarcasm varied still On woman's wish, and woman's will! **1862** MRS. H. WOOD *Channings* I. ix. 133 He looked upon the remark as a bit of sarcasm. **1866** GEO. ELIOT *F. Holt* II. xxx. 227 Blows are sarcasms turned stupid. **1871** FREEMAN *Norm. Conq.* (1876) IV. 127 William's return was accompanied by a confiscation and distribution of laws on so wide a scale that it could be said with indignant sarcasm that he gave away the land of every man.

†**sarcas'matical**, *a.* *Obs. rare.* [f. SARCASM + -ATICAL.] Sarcastic. Hence †**sarcas'matically** *adv.*, sarcastically. So †**sar'casmatize** *v.*, to speak sarcastically of.

1716 M. DAVIES *Athen. Brit.* III. 94 A haughty Jesuit.. publish'd an Anonymous, sarcasmatical Pamphlet. *Ibid.* II. 71 Mr. Wood calls the first a Calvinistical Bishop (who was then, as it seems, marry'd, says he, very Sarcasmatically). *Ibid.* III. 33 So easy it is from Scorning and Sarcasmatizing a deceas'd Protestant Bishop..to proceed to quarrel with a living Brother Bishop.

†**sar'casmical**, *a.* *Obs. rare.* [f. SARCASM + -ICAL. Cf. med.L. *sarcasmicus.*] Sarcastic. Hence †**sar'casmically** *adv.*, sarcastically.

1602 FULBECKE *2nd Pt. Parallel* 26 The Graecians did allow such taunts and biting sarcasmicall speeches. **1658** J. JONES *Ovid's Ibis* 42 It is inhumane sarcasmically to insult over a captive as a Cat over a Mouse.

So †**sar'casmous** *a.*, sarcastic.

1663 BUTLER *Hud.* I. ii. 578 So say the Wicked—and will you Make that Sarcasmous Scandal true? *a* **1734** NORTH *Exam.* I. ii. § 124 (1740) 98 When he gets a sarcasmous Paper against the Crown, well backed with Authority. *Ibid.* iii. § 36. 144 A sarcasmous Reflection on the House of Commons itself.

sarcast ('sɑːkæst). [ad. Gr. type *σαρκαστής, f. σαρκάζειν (see SARCASM).] A sarcastic writer or speaker.

1654 GAYTON *Pleas. Notes* III. vi. 108 The slave Sancho doth supra-parasite it, turnes mime, Satyr, Sarcast, Hyperaspist. **1859** *Knickerb. Mag.* Nov. 478 Jerrold has been called a cynic and a sarcast. **1886** *Sat. Rev.* 19 June 845 Dr. Parker; or, the Sarcast. **1898** *Daily News* 8 June 2/2 'Mr. Disraeli', he [*sc.* Gladstone] said..'was a great sarcast'.

sarcastic (sɑː'kæstɪk), *a.* Also 7-8 **-ick.** [ad. Gr. type *σαρκαστικός, f. σαρκάζειν: see SARCASM and -IC. Cf. F. *sarcastique.*] Characterized by or involving sarcasm; given to the use of sarcasm; bitterly cutting or caustic.

1695 J. EDWARDS *Author. O. & N. Test.* III. 380 Sarcastick speeches, gibes, taunts. **1751** JOHNSON *Rambler* No. 177 ⁋11 Their merriment bluntly sarcastick. **1848** THACKERAY *Van. Fair* xi, Mrs. Firkin..flung up her head and said, 'I think Miss *is* very clever,' with the most killing sarcastic air. **1862** CALVERLEY *Verses & Transl.* (1894) 43 Poising evermore the eye-glass In the light sarcastic eye. **1879** FROUDE *Cæsar* xxii. 385 He had spoken his thoughts with sarcastic freedom.

Hence **sar'casticness.**

1903 *Times* 30 Sept. 10/5 His habitual sarcasticness.

sarcastical (sɑː'kæstɪkəl), *a.* [Formed as prec.: see -ICAL.] = prec.

1641 'SMECTYMNUUS' *Vind. Answ.* § 2 Such a sarcasticall Declaration. **1697** S. PATRICK *Comm. Exod.* v. 17 Nothing could be more Sarcastical, than to tell them they were idle, when they sunk under their Burdens. **1756** P. POTT *Treat. Ruptures* vi. Wks. II. 123 He will be inclined to believe the sarcastical distinction between cures, and escapes, not ill-founded. **1834** *Gentl. Mag.* CIV. I. 185 The active and sarcastical mockery of the ruthless tyrant upon its victims. **1877** MRS. FORRESTER *Mignon* I. i. 14 'You mean that to be sarcastical', she laughs.

Hence **sar'casticalness.**

1709 MRS. MANLEY *Secret Mem.* (1720) III. 244, I could never give my self a Reason why the Ephesian Matron of Petronius should please so much, unless it were for the Sarcasticalness.

sarcastically (sɑː'kæstɪkəlɪ), *adv.* [f. prec. + -LY².] In a sarcastic manner; with sarcasm.

1647 J. TRAPP *Matt.* xiii. 55 As a Christian Schoolmaster fitly answered Libanus, sarcastically demanding: what the Carpenters son was now a doing? **1664** H. MORE *Myst. Iniq.* xii. 39 Or whether pursuing, or in a journey, or asleep somewhere, as Elias sarcastically argues concerning Baal. **1785** BURKE *Sp. Nabob of Arcot's Debts* 25 It is not necessary that the right honourable gentleman should sarcastically call that time to our recollection. **1847** C. BRONTË *J. Eyre* xviii, 'I suppose, now', said Miss Ingram, curling her lip sarcastically [etc.]. **1855** MACAULAY *Hist. Eng.* xvii. IV. 49 If, it was sarcastically said, all our notions of right and wrong ..are to be suddenly altered by a few lines of manuscript found in a corner of the library at Lambeth. **1887** *Courier* 16 June 16/4, 'I am as hungry as a wolf. I work like a horse, but I can't sleep.' 'You had better see a veterinary surgeon,' said the doctor, sarcastically.

sarce, obs. form of SEARCE *sb.* and *v.*

Sarcee ('sɑːsiː), *a.* and *sb.* Also † **Sursee, Sussee, Sarsee, Sarsi.** [ad. Blackfoot *saaxsííwa*; 18th-c. forms ad. Cree *sasiw*, pl. *sasiwak*.] **A.** *adj.* Of or pertaining to the Sarcee or their language (see below). **B.** *sb.* **a.** An Athapaskan people of Alberta in Canada; a member of this people. **b.** Their language.

[**1772** M. COCKING *Jrnl.* 1 Dec. in *Trans. R. Soc. Canada* (1909) II. II. 111 There are 4 Tribes, or Nations, more, which are all Equestrians Indians, Viz... Pegonow or Muddy-water Indians & Sassewuck or Woody Country Indians.] **1790** E. UMFREVILLE *Present State of Hudson's Bay* i. 78 Those Indians from whom the Peltries are obtained are known to us by the following names, *viz.* The Ne-heth-aw-a Indians. The Assinne-poetuc Indians. The Fall Indians. The Sussee Indians [etc.]. **1801** A. MACKENZIE *Voy. from Montreal* p. lxxi, The Sarsees, who are but few in number, appear from their language, to come..from the North-Westward, and are of the same people as the Rocky-Mountain Indians. **1820** D. W. HARMON *Jrnl. Voy. & Trav. Interior N. Amer.* 313, I have been acquainted with fifteen different tribes of Indians, which are the..Black feet Indians, Blood Indians, Sursees [etc.]. **1904** *Jrnl. Amer.*

Folklore July–Sept. 180 (*heading*) Traditions of the Sarcee Indians. *Ibid.*, The Sarcee Indians of Alberta, N.W.T., Canada, claim to have belonged at one time to the Beaver Indians. **1915** *Univ. Calif. Publ. Amer. Archaeol. & Ethnol.* XI. III. 190 The Sarsi are an Athapascan-speaking group of Indians who have been closely associated with the Northern Blackfoot of Alberta. **1919** *Anthropol. Papers Amer. Mus. Nat. Hist.* XVI. IV. 273 The text itself was dictated by Eagle-ribs..a younger son of the head chief of the Natsilt'inna, one of the four Sarsi bands. *Ibid.*, A..running account of the sun dance was recorded as a text in Sarsi. **1921** E. SAPIR *Language* 213 The buffalo culture of the Plains (Sarcee). **1933** L. BLOOMFIELD *Language* iv. 72 The Athabascan family covers all but the coastal fringe of northwestern Canada (Chipewyan, Beaver, Dogrib, Sarsi, etc.). **1936** D. MCCOWAN *Animals Canad. Rockies* ix. 81 Amongst the Stony and Sarcee Indians there was formerly a vague superstition imposing a sort of taboo on the cougar. **1965** *Language* XLI. 171 Harry Hoijer and Janet Joël, 'Sarsi nouns'. **1965** [see ATHAPASCAN, -PASKAN *sb.* 2]. **1973** A. H. WHITEFORD *N. Amer. Indian Arts* 92 Checks, diamonds, and terraced triangles were old patterns among the..Sarcee. **1977** T. A. SEBEOK *Native Lang. Americas* II. 316 The term Mountain..has been applied also to groups speaking Beaver, Chipewyan, Kaska, Sarsi, Slave, Tsetsaut and Yellowknife.

†**'sarcel.** *Obs.* Also 5, 7 sercell, sercil, 6–7 sarcell, 7 sarcill. [a. OF. *cercel* (mod.F. *cerceau*):—late L. *circellus*, dim. of *circus* circle (see CIRCUS).] A pinion feather of a hawk's wing. Also ***sarcel feather.***

1496 *Bk. St. Albans, Hawking* a v b, The feders that some calle the pynyon feder of a nother foule: of an hawke it is callyd the Sercell. **1575** TURBERV. *Faulconrie* 272 Within Sixe or Seven dayes she will caste..hir Sarcels or flagges. **1591** SYLVESTER *Du Bartas* I. v. (1641) 45 The Marlin, Lanar, and the gentle Tercell, Th' Ospray, and Saker, with a nimble sarcell, Follow the Phœnix. **1611** COTGR., *Cerceau*, ..the Sercell, or Sarcell (feather) of a hawkes wing. **1678** PHILLIPS (ed. 4), *Sercil*. **1688** HOLME *Armoury* II. xi. 237/1 The Sarcell Feathers, are the extream pinion Feathers in the Hawks Wing.

b. *fig.* or in fig. context.

1610 W. FOLKINGHAM *Art of Survey* Ep. Ded. p. ii, Skie-towring Faulcons, whose Quills imped with strong Sarcells of the Grace of Greatnes. **1630** DRUMM. OF HAWTH. *Flowres of Sion* 33 My Knowledge sharpen, Sarcells lend my thought. **1649** G. DANIEL *Trinarch., Hen. V*, xxxvii, Vnfledg'd Witt Imp't from the ragged Sarcill Chaucer drop't.

sarcelle (sɑː'sɛl). Also 4 cercelle, 5 sorcell (?), 6 sarcell. [a. OF. *cercelle* (13th c.), mod.F. *sarcelle* = Pr. *sercela* (cf. med.L. *cercella*, Higden):—pop. L. **cercedula-*, for class. L. *querquedula*.] A name for the teals and closely allied ducks (*e.g.* the garganey, the long-tailed duck).

1387 TREVISA *Higden* (Rolls) I. 371 In Lagenia is a ponde; þere is Seynt Colman his briddes; þe briddes beeþ i-cleped cercelles. *c* **1450** *Two Cookery-bks.* 79 Take a Sorcell or a tele, and breke his necke. **1513** *Bk. Kernynge* (W. de W.) B j b, Take a sarcell or a teele, and reyse his wynges.

1793 tr. *Buffon's Nat. Hist. Birds* IX. 217 The Sarcelles, which we cannot better paint in general terms than by saying, that they are ducks much smaller than the others. *Ibid.* 240 The White and Black Sarcelle; or, the Nun. *Ibid.* 243 The Brown and White Sarcelle. **1802** MONTAGU *Ornith. Dict.* **1818–22** *Encycl. Metrop.* (1845) XIV. 266/2.

sarcelled ('sɑːsəld), *a.* *Her.* [Anglicized f. *sarcelle*, SARCELLY.]

1. = SARCELLY 2.

1688 R. HOLME *Armoury* I. v. 49–50 A Cross double parted Voided Flory... It is like the Cross Moline Sawed, or cut into 4. quarters, and disposed at a convenient distance; And therefore may be fitly termed a Cross Moline Sarcelled. **1722** NISBET *Syst. Her.* I. xv. 113 If the Voiding be of another Colour..than the Field, the Cross is then said to be charged with another Cross; for which our English Heraulds have some needless Terms, as *Sarcelled* and *Resarcelled*. **1828–40** BERRY *Encycl. Her.* I, *Cross pattée sarcelled* at bottom in the form of a ʌ reversed. *Ibid.*, *Cross double voided*, by some called *a cross voided sarcelled*, or *sarcelled resarcelled*, that is double or twice sawed asunder. **1847** *Parker's Gloss. Her.* 101 Cross moline sarcelled, or voided throughout, cross recercelée or recersile, or recercelée voided or disjoined, which has also been called a cross fleury biparted.

2. = SARCELLY 3.

1828–40 BERRY *Encycl. Her.* I, *Sarcelled*, cut through the middle. Beasts and birds, thus cloven throughout, and the halves..endorsed..is no uncommon bearing in.. Germany.

sarcelly ('sɑːsəlɪ), *a.* *Her.* Forms: 6 sarsile, 6–7 (9) sarcele, 7 sarcelie, 8 cercilé, cercelly, 9 sarcel(l)é, 8– sarcelly, cercelée. Also *erron.* 9 sarcell. [a. AF. *sercelé, cerselé* = OF. *cercelé* hooped, ringleted, curled, pa. pple. of *cerceler*, f. *cercel* (see SARCEL).

F. *cercelé* and *recercelé* (see RECERCELÉ(E) were used synonymously in sense 1 (below). Beside these there was a F. *resarcelé* (see RESARCELÉE, of obscure origin) applied to a cross on which another is placed of a different colour. *Recercelé*, and consequently *cercelé, sarcelly*, were confused with *resarcelé* and used for it (sense 2). The cross resarcelée was later sometimes blazoned as a cross voided (*i.e.* having the central part cut out), and recent English heraldic writers have further extended the use of *sarcelly* (and *sarcelled*) by applying them to birds and beasts cut through the middle (sense 3).]

1. Used to designate a variety of the cross moline in which the points are recurved or curled back.

The Book of St. Albans blazons this cross as *retornyt* and *reuersit*, F. *recercilee*, L. *inversa*.

c **1500** *Sc. Poem Heraldry* 141 in *Q. Eliz. Acad.*, etc. 99, xj crois fichye; xij sarsile fere. **1562** LEGH *Armory* 59 The fielde Or, a crosse Sarcele Geules. **1572** BOSSEWELL *Armorie* II. 25 b, Gules, on a Crosse Sarcele D'or, fiue mollettes of the firste. **1780** EDMONDSON *Her.* Gloss., *Cross-Cercelée.* This Cross is like the Cross Moline, but with this difference, that the points are turned round. *Ibid.*, *Sarcelly*, the same as *Cercelly*. **1864** BOUTELL *Heraldry* 79 *Cercelée* or *Recercelée*, curling at the extremities. **1897** W. K. R. BEDFORD *Blazon Episc.* (ed. 2) 217 Gules, a cross sarcelly ermine.

2. Applied to a cross (esp. a cross moline) voided and open at the ends. (Cf. RESARCELÉE.)

1661 MORGAN *Sph. Gentry* II. 9 Sarcele Cross [= *infra* 14 Recercile]. **1722** NISBET *Syst. Her.* I. xv. 118 A Cross moline, altogether voided, which some of them call a Cross Cercilé. **1828–40** BERRY *Encycl. Her.* I, *Cross sarcele, sarcell*, or *sarcelle*, is a *cross voided*, or, as it were, sawed apart. **1889** ELVIN *Dict. Her.* p. xiii, Cross voided, also term sarcelle.

3. Cut through the middle. (Cf. SARCELLED 2.)

1864 BOUTELL *Heraldry* 87 *Sarcellée*.

sarcen, variant of SARSEN.

sarcenchyme (sɑː'sɛŋkaɪm). [f. Gr. σαρκ-, σάρξ flesh, after PARENCHYME.] Sollas's name for a connective tissue in certain sponges (see quot.).

1887 SOLLAS in *Encycl. Brit.* XXII. 419/2 In the higher sponges (*Geodia, Stelletta*) it [*sc.* the mesoderm] consists of small polygonal granular cells either closely contiguous or separated by a very small quantity of structureless jelly, and in this form may be termed sarcenchyme. **1898** SEDGWICK *Text-bk. Zool.* I. 79.

Hence **sarcen'chymatous** *a.*

1888, 1900 [see CHONDRENCHYMA].

sarcenet(t, obs. forms or variants of SARSENET.

sarch(e, var. or obs. ff. SEARCE; obs. ff. SEARCH.

sarcic ('sɑːrsɪk). [ad. Gr. σαρκικός, f. σαρκ-, σάρξ flesh.] (See quot.)

1876 tr. *Hergenröther's Cath. Ch. & Chr. State* II. 293 Neither is it true that the clergy were only regarded as men of the spirit, and the laity only as men of the flesh; the Church had long rejected the Gnostic distinction between pneumatics and sarcics.

‖**Sarcina** ('sɑːsɪnə). *Bot.* Pl. -inæ (ɪniː). [L. = bundle, f. *sarcīre* to patch, mend.] A genus of schizomycetous fungi or bacteria, forming masses of cells united in fixed numbers, which are found in various animal fluids. Also *attrib.*

1842 GOODSIR in *Edin. Med. & Surg. Jrnl.* 434 These circumstances gave the whole organism the appearance of a wool-pack, or of a soft bundle bound with cord... From these very striking peculiarities of form, I propose for it the generic name of Sarcina. *Ibid.* 435 The Sarcinæ were found grouped as it were in colonies, in certain portions of the ropy fluid. **1866** *Chamb. Encycl.* VIII. 486/1 The sarcinæ occurring in urine are about half the size of those occurring in the stomach, and the aggregations of sarcina cells are also smaller. **1884** KLEIN *Micro-org.* 39 A group of four (tetrade or sarcinaform) is thereby produced. *Ibid.* 43 Small sarcinæ occur on boiled potatoes. **1888** *Jrnl. Chem. Ind.* 30 June 449/1 Cultivations of sarcina in sterilised beer-wort.

†**sarci'narious,** *a.* *Obs.* [f. L. *sarcinārius*, f. *sarcina* bundle, pack.]

1656 BLOUNT *Glossogr.*, *Sarcinarious*, of or belonging to Packs, Fardels, &c., serving to carry burthens or loads.

†**'sarcinate,** *v.* *Obs.* [f. L. *sarcināt-*, ppl. stem of *sarcināre* to load a beast, f. *sarcina* load, pack.] *trans.* To load (a beast of burden); *fig.* to overload (but cf. FARCINATE).

1623 COCKERAM II, To Lade a beast, *Sarcinate*. **1645** *Martin's Echo* in Prynne *Discov. Blazing-Stars* 23 Extend your panches, cram your bellies, sarcinate your ventricles. [*But* 'MARTIN MAR-PRIEST' *Martin's Eccho* (? 1645) 2 *has* farcinate.] **1656** BLOUNT *Glossogr.*

Hence †**sarci'nation.**

1658 PHILLIPS, *Sarcination*, a loading with packs or fardells.

†**'sarcinator.** *Obs.* [L. agent-n. of **sarcināre* = *sarcīre* to botch.] A mender, patcher.

1646 MAYNE *Serm. on Unity &c.* 31 There wants only a Sarcinator, or Botcher, to assume to himselfe the Crowne.

sarcine ('sɑːsɪn). *Chem.* Also -kin(e. [ad. G. *sarkin* (Strecker), f. Gr. σαρκ-, σάρξ flesh: see -INE.] A base existing in the juice of flesh. Also *attrib.*

1858 *Q. Jrnl. Chem. Soc.* X. 121 A well characterised organic base, which I [i.e. Strecker] will provisionally distinguish by the name *Sarcine*. *Ibid.* 123 Its [*sc.* sarcine] solution in baryta-water, deposits, on addition of a larger quantity of the baryta-solution,..crystals of sarcine-baryta. **1887** A. M. BROWN *Anim. Alkaloids* 70 Sarkine or hypoxanthine, so widely distributed in the organic world, both animal and vegetable.

sarcinet, obs. form of SARSENET.

sarcinoid ('sɑːsɪnɔɪd), *a.* [ad. mod.L. *Sarcinoīdēs* (used by Blainville, 1834, in neut. pl. *-oidea*), f. Gr. σάρκινο-ς fleshy (f. σαρκ-, σάρξ flesh): see -OID.] Belonging to the group *Sarcinoidea* of polyps.

1841 *Penny Cycl.* XX. 432/1 The Sarcoid (or sarcinoid, or carnose) Polypiaria.

sarcinous ('sɑːsɪnəs), *a.* [f. SARCINA + -OUS.] Pertaining to or involving sarcinæ.

1874 GARROD *Mat. Med.* (ed. 6) 143 Sarcinous vomiting.

sarcle ('sɑːk(ə)l), *sb.* (Only in renderings of the L. word.) [ad. L. *sarculum*. *-us*, instrumental noun f. *sar(r)īre* to weed.] A hoe.

1745 tr. *Columella's Husb.* II. xii, The roots of the corn are laid open and uncovered with the sarcle. **1875** *Encycl. Brit.* I. 311/2 A history of this implement [*sc.* the plough], tracing its gradual progress from the ancient *Sarcle* to its most improved form at the present day.

sarcle ('sɑːk(ə)l), *v.* ? *Obs.* Also 7 **sarkle.** [a. OF. *sarcler*:—L. *sarculāre*, f. *sarculum* (see prec.).] *trans.* To weed with a hoe. Chiefly in *vbl. sb.*

1543 tr. *Act 25 Edw. III*, c. 1 (*Stat. labourers*) And that none pay in the time of sarcling or heymaking but .i.d. the day. **1601** HOLLAND *Pliny* II. 20 After the ground is sowne, it requireth weeding, sarcling, or raking. *Ibid.* 28 That they must not be sarcled, nor have the earth opened & laid hollow about them. **1611** FLORIO, *Risarchiàre*, to sarkle, to harrow or rake ouer againe. **1617** MINSHEU *Ductor*, *Sarceling time*, or *time of Sarceling*, seemeth to bee the time when the Countryman weedeth his corne. **1745** tr. *Columella's Husb.* II. xii, There are many who are of opinion that they should be sarcled. *Ibid.*, After we have finished our sowing, our next care is of sarcling.

Hence **'sarcler,** a weeder.

1707 FLEETWOOD *Chron. Prec.* 158 In 1351..Sarclers (that is Weeders) and Hay-makers, by the Day, oo*l.* oo*s.* o1*d.* [**1885** *Q. Rev.* Apr. 327 On 220 acres in Suffolk, 60 sarclers or weeders were employed on one day at 2*d.* a piece.]

sarcnet, obs. form of SARSENET.

sarco- ('sɑːkəʊ, sɑː'kɒ), combining form of Gr. σαρκ-, σάρξ flesh, occurring as prefix in many scientific terms (the more important are given as Main words): **sarco-acid,** short for SARCOLACTIC *acid.* ‖**'sarcobasis** *Bot.*, a very fleshy gynobase; = CARCERULE. **'sarcoblast,** (*a*) one of the minute yellow bodies present in rhizopods; (*b*) a germinal particle of protoplasm. **'sarcocyte:** see quot. **sar'cognomy** *Psych. rare* [after *physiognomy*], the study of the sympathy and correspondence between the body and the brain. ‖**'sarcomatrix,** in protozoa (see quot.). **'sarcoplasm,** ‖**sarco'plasma,** the interfibrillar hyaline substance of muscle. ‖**sarco'soma** [Gr. σῶμα body], the 'bark' of corals. **'sarcosperm** *Bot.* = SARCODERM. ‖**sarco'stosis** *Path.* [Gr. -οστωσις as in ἐξόστωσις EXOSTOSIS], ossification of flesh (Craig 1849). **'sarcostyle,** ‖**sarco'theca** [Gr. θήκη case]: see quots. **'sarcotome** *Surg.* [Gr. -τόμος that cuts]: see quot.

1882 *Encycl. Brit.* XIV. 197/1 The *sarco-acid has precisely the same structure as ordinary lactic acid. **1866** *Treas. Bot.*, **Sarcobasis*, the same kind of fruit as the Carcerulus. **1895** J. C. WARREN *Surg. Path.* ix. 235 Some authorities believe that the new growth proceeds from the muscular cells or *sarcoblasts. **1898** SEDGWICK *Textbk. Zool.* I. 57 In many forms [of Gregarines] there are longitudinal fibrillar thickenings of the cuticle, and occasionally a special superficial layer of the ectoplasm immediately beneath the cuticle is distinguished as the *sarcocyte. **1878** J. R. BUCHANAN *Psychophysiol. Sci.* 74 *Sarcognomy. **1882** *Banner of Light* (Boston, U.S.) 19 Aug., The entire symptomatology of diseases must be deficient in regard to mental symptoms,..without the guidance of sarcognomy. **1884** J. R. BUCHANAN (*title*) Therapeutic Sarcognomy, a scientific exposition of the mysterious union of soul and body, and a new system of therapeutic practice without medicine. **1895** *Jrnl. Mar. Zool.* Mar. 13 The extra-capsular substance consists of two well defined layers, the inner (*sarcomatrix) which invests closely the capsule, is protoplasmic. **1900** BOURNE *Comp. Anat.* I. 96 They [*sc.* sarcostyles] are prismatic in section, and are separated from one another by a more fluid substance known as *sarcoplasm. **1890** C. F. MARSHALL in *Q. Jrnl. Microsc. Sci.* CXI. 67 According to Rollett, the 'muscle-columns' are the essential parts of the fibre, and the '*sarcoplasma' is simply interfibrillar material. **1865** *Nat. Hist. Rev.* 363 The *sarcosoma or bark of the coral is next described [by Lacaze-Duthiers]. **1849** BALFOUR *Man. Bot.* § 578 The secundine.. when it assumes a fleshy character,..has received the name of *sarcosperm or sarcoderm. **1888** ALLMAN in *Challenger Rep., Zool.* XXIII. *Hydroida* p. xix, I shall..adopt here the terminology proposed by Hincks, and use the term **sarcostyle* for the fleshy offset from the cœnosarc, and that of **sarcotheca* for the chitinous receptacle by which this is protected. *Ibid.*, The Sarcothecæ occur in the Plumularinæ under two principal forms. **1874** *Trans. Clinical Soc.* VII. 138 Description of the *Sarcotome, an Instrument for painlessly cutting through the soft Tissues of the Body. By W. Ainslie Hollis.

sarcocarp ('sɑːkəʊkɑːp). *Bot.* [ad. F. *sarcocarpe* (Richard), f. Gr. σορκο-, σάρξ flesh + καρπός fruit.] The fleshy part of a drupaceous fruit lying between the epicarp and the endocarp, being the part usually eaten.

1819 LINDLEY tr. *Richard's Obs. Fruits & Seeds* 2, I propose naming the epidermis of fruit Epicarp, the parenchyma Sarcocarp. **1849** BALFOUR *Man. Bot.* § 525 In the Date,..the pulpy matter is the mesocarp or sarcocarp. **1870** HOOKER *Stud. Flora* 237 Olea europæa yields oil in its fleshy sarcocarp.

sarcocele ('sɑːkəʊsiːl). *Path.* [ad. mod.L. *sarcocēlē* (G. Valla, 1501), a. Gr. σαρκοκήλη, f.

σαρκο-, σαρξ flesh + κήλη tumour.] Hard fleshy enlargement of the testicle.

1742 tr. *Heister's Surg.* II. (1768) II. 115 A recent Sarcocele may frequently be suppurated by digestive Medicines. **1783** JOHNSON *Let. to Mrs. Thrale* 22 Sept., The complaint about which you enquire is a sarcocele: I thought it a hydrocele and heeded it but little. **1861** BUMSTEAD *Ven. Dis.* (1879) 634 Syphilitic sarcocele, orchitis, or albuginitis, as it is variously termed.

sarcococca (sɑːkəʊ'kɒksə). [mod.L. (J. Lindley 1826, in *Bot. Reg.* XII. 1012), f. SARCO- + Gr. κόκκος seed.] A small evergreen shrub of the genus so called, belonging to the family Buxaceæ, native to India, China, and Malaysia, and bearing clusters of white, often fragrant, flowers followed by black or red berries.

1914 W. J. BEAN *Trees & Shrubs Hardy in Brit. Isles* II. 500 The hardy Sarcococcas, all Chinese, are neat and pleasing shrubs,.. the flowers white, fragrant. **1972** *Country Life* 16 Mar. 624/2 Equally valuable for winter flowering are the evergreen sarcococcas.

sarcocol(l ('sɑːkəkɒl). Now *rare*. [ad. late L. *sarcocolla*: see next.] = next.

c **1400** *Lanfranc's Cirurg.* 153 Take oile of rosis..mirre, sarcocol [etc.]. **1526** *Grete Herball* ccclxxxviii. (1529) X iv, Sarcocolle is hote and drye in the thyrde degre. *c* **1550** H. LLOYD *Treas. Health* M ij, A fumigacion made of Sarcocoll upon hote Coles. **1612** tr. *Valentinus' Enchir. Med.* 98 Mastich and sarcocol mixt together. **1712** tr. *Pomet's Hist. Drugs* I. 198 Sarcocol is a Gum that flows from a little prickly Shrub, whereof the Leaves are like the *Palta Sena*. **1819** J. G. CHILDREN *Chem. Anal.* 286 Sarcocoll; colour yellow, resembles gum arabic in appearance. **1846** LINDLEY *Veget. Kingd.* 577 A sub-viscid, sweetish..gum-resin called Sarcocol..is said to be produced by various species [of *Penæa*].

‖**sarcocolla** (sɑːkə'kɒlə). [late L., a. Gr. σαρκόκολλα, f. σαρκο-, σάρξ flesh + κόλλα glue: so called because of its reputed property of agglutinating wounds.] A sub-viscid gum-resin brought from Arabia and Persia in light yellow or red grains.

Its source is not certainly known: see quots. 1830, 1887.

1599 HAKLUYT *Voy.* II. 278 Sarcacolla, from Persia. **1601** HOLLAND *Pliny* II. 197 As touching Sarcocolla, some bee of opinion that it is the gum or liquor issuing from a certain thornie plant or bush. **1658** A. FOX tr. *Würtz' Surg.* II. v. 59 Congealed blood..is a right flesh-glue, exceeding a Sarcocolla. **1763** W. LEWIS *Phil. Comm. Arts* 367 Sprinkle in the same quantity of sarcocolla. **1830** LINDLEY *Nat. Syst. Bot.* 72 A subviscid, sweetish, somewhat nauseous gum-resin, called Sarcocolla, is produced by Penæa mucronata (and others). **1887** BENTLEY *Man. Bot.* 531 The gum known as *Sarcocolla*, which is imported into Bombay from.. Bushire, is..considered by Dymock to be derived from a species of *Astragalus*, or from one nearly allied to that genus.

sarcocollin (sɑːkə'kɒlɪn). *Chem.* [ad. F. *sarcocolline* (Pelletier): see prec. and -IN.] A principle contained in sarcocolla.

1830 LINDLEY *Nat. Syst. Bot.* 72. **1838** THOMSON *Chem. Org. Bodies* 645.

sarcocyst ('sɑːkəʊsɪst). *Microbiology* and *Vet. Sci.* [f. SARCO- + CYST.] **a.** A cyst in muscle tissue containing spores or sporoblasts of sarcosporidia. **b.** An individual of the genus *Sarcocystis* of sarcosporidia.

1892 G. FLEMING tr. *Neumann's Treat. Parasites & Parasitic Dis.* VI. i. 662 The Sarcocysts of Miescher are very frequent—at least, in certain countries and at certain periods. **1932** GAIGER & DAVIES *Vet. Path. & Bacteriol.* xxii. 333 The sarcocyst in the muscles is the only stage of the parasite which is known. *Ibid.* 334 Sarcocysts may die *in situ*. **1938** SOUTHWELL & KIRSHNER *Guide Vet. Parasitol. & Entomol.* (ed. 2) ii. 19 Sarcocysts are included in the Sporozoa, though it is doubtful if they really belong to this class. **1970** [see SARCOSPORIDIUM].

Hence **sarco'cystic** *a.*

1927 [see SARCOSPORIDIAL *a.*]. **1979** *Acta Leidensia: Scholae Medicinae Tropicae* XLVII. 46 Schizogonic and sarcocystic stages.

sarcodal (sɑː'kəʊdəl), *a.* [f. SARCODE + -AL[1].] = SARCODIC.

1869 H. J. CARTER in *Ann. Nat. Hist.* Sept. 191 Their walls formed of sarcodal rugæ more or less curled.

sarcode ('sɑːkəʊd), *sb.* and *a. Biol.* [a. F. *sarcode* (Dujardin 1835), f. σαρκ-, σάρξ flesh: see -ODE[1].]

A. *sb.* The PROTOPLASM of animals.

1853 *Bot. & Physiol. Mem.* (Ray Soc.) 535 The protoplasm of Botanists and the..sarcode of Zoologists, if not identical, are at all events..analogous formations. **1871** T. R. JONES *Anim. Kingd.* (ed. 4) 4 The body of the Protozoon consists chiefly of the elementary substance known as *sarcode* or animal protoplasm. **1883** W. SAVILLE KENT in Adderley *Fish. Bahamas* 35 The *Euplectella*, as sold in the market, being then divested of the buff-coloured gelatinous flesh or sarcode.

B. *adj.* Sarcodic; protoplasmic.

1855 *Orr's Circ. Sci., Org. Nat.* II. 209 This gelatinous coating is found to consist entirely of an immense number of aggregated sarcode-cells. **1859** J. R. GREENE *Protozoa* 19 Gemmule, embedded in sarcode substance. **1898** P. MANSON *Trop. Dis.* xxxii. 501 The bulk of the embryo is occupied by a number of sarcode globules.

sarcoderm ('sɑːkədɜːm). *Bot.* Also in L. form **sarcoderma** (-'dɜːmə) [ad. mod.L. *sarcodermis* (De Candolle), f. Gr. σαρκο- SARCO- and δέρμα DERMA.] The fleshy layer in some seeds lying between the internal and external integuments.

1848 LINDLEY *Introd. Bot.* II. 26 The testa..consists..of three portions;..3. of an intervening substance..called sarcoderm by De Candolle. **1861** BENTLEY *Bot.* 337 Some botanists..describe a third integument under the name of sarcoderm; this layer, however, is commonly and more accurately considered as but a portion of the outer integument.

sarcodic (sɑː'kɒdɪk), *a. Biol.* [f. SARCODE + -IC.] Of, pertaining to, of the nature of sarcode; protoplasmic.

1864 *Reader* 2 Apr. 434/1 A spherical sarcodic mass. **1866** DARWIN *Orig. Spec.* vi. (ed. 4) 216 Sarcodic tissue not furnished with any nerve. **1870** ROLLESTON *Anim. Life* 257 The 'sarcodic expansions', as the pseudopodia have been called.

sarcoid ('sɑːkɔɪd), *a.* and *sb.* [f. Gr. σαρκ-, σάρξ flesh + -OID. Cf. Gr. σαρκώδης.]

A. *adj.* **1.** Resembling flesh; flesh-like: applied to sponges, plants, etc.

1841 *Penny Cycl.* XX. 423/1 In the Sarcoid..Polypiaria we may imagine the distinct collected axis of Corallium or Pennatula to be ramified and reticulated. **1858** MAYNE *Expos. Lex.*, *Sarcoides*,..sarcoid. **1864** WEBSTER (citing DANA).

2. *Path.* Pertaining to or resembling sarcoidosis.

1935 *Proc. Soc. Exper. Biol. & Med.* XXXIII. 403 A sarcoid lesion of the skin..was removed. **1962** *Lancet* 26 May 1107/2 Sarcoid tissue obtained from a skin lesion was suspended in saline solution. **1976** EDINGTON & GILLES *Path. in Tropics* (ed. 2) xi. 522 The presence [in Crohn's disease] of a sarcoid reaction in the tissues of the bowel wall, and regional lymph nodes.

B. *sb.* **1.** A sponge particle.

1875 H. A. NICHOLSON *Man. Zool.* v. 70 The 'sponge-flesh'..is found upon a microscopical examination to be composed of an aggregation of rounded amœbiform bodies—the so-called 'sponge-particles' or 'sarcoids'.

2. a. *Path.* Sarcoidosis; also, a tumour resembling a sarcoma.

1899 C. BOECK in *Jrnl. Cutaneous & Genito-Urin. Dis.* XVII. 543 (*heading*) Multiple benign sarkoid of skin. **1941** *Arch. Ophthalm.* XXVI. 358 The term sarcoid was adopted by Boeck in 1899 for lesions simulating sarcomas and leukemic conditions of the skin. He believed the condition to be one only of the skin. Later he recognized his mistake in the term and changed it to multiple miliary lupoid. **1963** JUBB & KENNEDY *Path. Domestic Animals* II. x. 565/1 Sarcoids are usually multiple and occur most frequently about the base of the ear, on the neck, and on the lower limbs. **1977** *Proc. R. Soc. Med.* LXX. 484/2 Greenberg *et al.* (1964) found parotitis in 23 (6%) of 388 patients suffering from sarcoid. **1978** *Price's Textbk. Pract. Med.* (ed. 12) III. 275/2 Subcutaneous telangiectases or haemangiomata become visible in some patients. The latter may develop into small tumours or 'sarcoids' up to a centimetre across.

b. *Comb.*, as ***sarcoid-like*** adj.

1943 *Arch. Dermatol. & Syphilol.* XLVII. 62 Sarcoid-like lesions have..been produced by the injection of bovine tubercle bacilli of low virulence into rabbits. **1968** A. ROOK et al. *Textbk. Dermatol.* xxvi. 937/1 Beryllium causes either a local or a systemic sarcoid-like reaction.

sarcoidal (sɑː'kɔɪdəl), *a. Path.* [f. prec. + -AL.] = SARCOID *a.* 2.

1961 *Jrnl. Amer. Med. Assoc.* 4 Nov. 476/1 Employing a suspension of human sarcoidal tissue as test material. **1962** *Lancet* 26 May 1108/1 If sarcoidosis were produced by many agents..then a series of sarcoidal test-tissues would presumably be necessary.

sarcoidosis (sɑːkɔɪ'dəʊsɪs). *Path.* [f. as prec. + -OSIS.] A chronic disease characterized by the widespread appearance of sarcoid granulomata derived from the reticuloendothelial system.

1936 *New England Jrnl. Med.* CCXIV. 346 (*heading*) Hutchinson-Boeck's disease (generalized 'sarcoidosis'). **1955** *Lancet* 26 Mar. 640/2 There is no general agreement on whether any form of treatment is effective for pulmonary sarcoidosis. **1975** *Guardian* 25 Feb. 6/1 He recorded a verdict of death from natural causes after hearing that Mrs Rogers died of acute adrenal insufficiency due to sarcoidosis, a chronic illness which can affect all the organs of the body.

sarcolactic (sɑːkəʊ'læktɪk), *a. Chem.* [f. SARCO- + LACTIC.] ***sarcolactic acid***: an acid, isomeric with lactic acid, obtained from muscular tissue.

1862 MILLER *Elem. Chem., Org.* (ed. 2) III. 376 The sarkolactic acid from muscular tissue may be distinguished as the variety α [of lactic acid]. **1887** *Brit. Med. Jrnl.* 221/2 A new product appears in the urine after liver-extirpation. This is sarcolactic acid.

Hence **sarcolactate**, a salt of sarcolactic acid.

1882 *Encycl. Brit.* XIV. 197/1 The sarcolactates in general are more readily soluble than ordinary lactates.

sarcolemma (sɑːkə'lɛmə). *Anat.* Also **-lema**. [mod.L., f. SARCO- + Gr. λέμμα (see LEMMA[2]).] The fine transparent tubular sheath investing muscular fibre.

1840 BOWMAN in *Phil. Trans.* CXXX. 474 Of the Sarcolemma, or Tunic of the Primitive Fasciculus. **1849** NOAD *Electricity* 449 The tendinous fibres are continued among the muscular fibres, whilst the sarcolema merely envelopes the said muscular fibres. **1872** HUXLEY *Physiol.* ii. 36 The muscular fibres of the heart..have no sheath or sarcolemma.

attrib. **1899** *Allbutt's Syst. Med.* VI. 276 Proliferation of the sarcolemma nuclei.

Hence **sarco'lemmal** *a.*, of or pertaining to the sarcolemma.

1912 *Brain* XXXIV. 370 In some places the saracolemmal nuclei were much increased in numbers. **1974** *Nature* 1 Mar. 69/2 Our data favour the hypothesis that sarcolemmal sensitivity to ACh is regulated by a mechanism located in or near the muscle membrane.

sarcolite ('sɑːkəlaɪt). *Min.* [f. SARCO- + -LITE.] A silicate of aluminium, sodium, and calcium found in flesh-coloured crystals. Also = GMELINITE.

1814 AIKIN *Dict. Chem. & Min.* App. 56 Sarcolite. Colour flesh red. **1836** T. THOMSON *Min., Geol.*, etc. I. 337 Analcime. Cubizite, sarcolite. *Ibid.* 340 Hydrolite. Gmelenite, sarcolite of Vauquelin. **1858** NICOL *Elem. Min.* 130 Sarkolite, from Vesuvius. **1869** PHILLIPS *Vesuv.* x. 291 Sarcolite [occurs] in ejected blocks with Wollastonite [etc.].

sarcology (sɑː'kɒlədʒɪ). [f. SARCO- + -LOGY. Cf. F. *sarcologie*.]

1. That branch of anatomy which treats of the fleshy parts of the body.

1728 CHAMBERS *Cycl.* s.v., Anatomy is divided into Two principal Parts; Osteology and Sarcology. **1796** SOUTHEY *Lett. fr. Spain* (1799) 470 The Professor shall begin his instructions with Osteology upon the skeleton,..proceed with Sarcology, and conclude with the organs of the senses.

2. The therapeutic method or theory which involves or advocates the internal administration of the extractives of the organs of animals for the purpose of affecting the corresponding organs of the human body.

1893 *Science* (N.Y.) 22 Sept. 162 The science of sarcology and the new way opened up by Brown-Séquard and Dr. Hammond suggest higher possibilities.

Hence **sarco'logic, -ical** *adjs.*, belonging to sarcology; **sar'cologist**, a professor of sarcology.

1828–32 WEBSTER, *Sarcological*. **1855** OGILVIE Suppl., *Sarcologist*. **1882** OGILVIE, *Sarcologic*.

sarcoma (sɑː'kəʊmə). Pl. **sarcomata**, **sarcomas**. [mod.L., a. Gr. σάρκωμα (Galen), f. σαρκοῦν to become fleshy, f. σάρξ, σαρκ- flesh.]

1. *Path.* †**a.** A fleshy excrescence. *Obs.*

1657 *Physical Dict.*, *Sarcoma*, flesh growing in the nostrils like the proud flesh in a sore. **1742** tr. *Heister's Surg.* (1768) II. 249 Some call them [*sc.* polypuses] *Sarcoma's*, others *Hypersarcoma's*. *Ibid.*, We sometimes meet with Excrescences of various Sizes and Figures... These are usually called Sarcomata of the Uterus. **1752** CHAMBERS *Cycl.* s.v., Every polypus is a sarcoma; but not *vice versa*. The sarcoma frequently degenerates into a polypus.

b. A tumour composed of embryonic connective tissue. Now applied to almost any malignant tumour not derived from epithelial tissue.

1804 ABERNETHY *Surg. Obs. Tumours* 19 The first genus may be denominated from its most obvious character (that of having a firm and fleshy feel) Sarcoma or Sarcomatous Tumours. *Ibid.* 26 Adipose Sarcoma. This is a very common species of Sarcomatous Tumours. **1872** PEASLEE *Ovarian Tumors* 19 A cystic sarcoma is merely a development of cysts in a fibroid tumor. **1880** M. MACKENZIE *Dis. Throat & Nose* I. 350 As a rule Sarcomata rapidly attain a considerable size. **1894** *Dublin Rev.* Oct. 350 A poor woman with an extensive sarcoma of the face. **1971** *Nature* 21 May 147/2 In human populations only about 10 per cent of cancers are sarcomas; the other 90 per cent are carcinomas—cancers of tissues of epithelial, not mesodermal, origin. **1975** *Sci. Amer.* Nov. 64/2 The cancers are divided into three broad groups. The carcinomas arise in the epithelia... The much rarer sarcomas arise in supporting structures such as fibrous tissues and blood vessels. The leukemias and lymphomas arise in the blood-forming cells.

fig. **1850** J. BROWN *Lett.* (1907) 82, I often look upon myself as one sarcoma of selfishness and indolence.

2. *Bot.* Link's term for the fleshy disc surrounding the ovary.

1832 LINDLEY *Introd. Bot.* I. ii. 137. **1856** HENSLOW *Dict. Bot. Terms*.

‖**sarcomatosis** (sɑːkəʊmə'təʊsɪs). *Path.* [mod.L., f. Gr. σαρκωματ-, SARCOMA + -ωσις, -OSIS.] Sarcomatous degeneration.

1890 BILLINGS *Nat. Med. Dict.* **1897** *Allbutt's Syst. Med.* III. 726 In generalised sarcomatosis the mucous membrane may contain numerous small secondary growths.

sarcomatous (sɑː'kəʊmətəs), *a.* [Formed as prec. + -OUS. In mod.L. *sarcomatosus*.] Pertaining or relating to, of the nature of, sarcoma.

1754 SMELLIE *Midwifery* II. 113 Bonetus..gives several instances of sarcomatous and glandular tumours, which were mistaken for the uterus. **1804** [see SARCOMA]. **1897** *Allbutt's Syst. Med.* IV. 446 These infantile tumours are almost invariably sarcomatous.

†**sarcome.** *Obs.* = SARCOMA 1.

1626 MINSHEU *Ductor*, A *Sarcome*, a bunch of flesh in ones nose.

sarcomere ('sɑːkəʊmɪə(r)). *Anat.* [f. SARCO- + -MERE.] A unit of a myofibril in striated muscle, consisting of a dark band and the nearer half of each adjacent pale band.

1891 E. A. SCHAFER in *Proc. R. Soc.* XLIX. 281 The segment of a saracostyle comprised between two transverse membranes may be termed 'muscle-segment' or 'sarcomere'. **1897** *Jrnl. Anat. & Physiol.* XXXI. 336 [Schäfer] regards the sarcostyle as divided at regular intervals by Krause's transverse membranes into 'muscle segments' or 'sarcomeres', which are only new names for Krause's 'muscle caskets'. **1900** BOURNE *Comp. Anat.* I. 96

The sarcostyle itself is made up of a number of segments, called sarcomeres, separated from one another by fine membranes. **1930** W. BLOOM *Maximow's Text-bk. Histol.* viii. 205 In the invertebrates (arthropods)..sarcomeres as long as 17μ have been found. The length of the sarcomere and the physiologic peculiarities of the muscle have not.. been correlated. **1970** T. S. & C. R. LEESON *Histol.* (ed. 2) ix. 162/2 It is customary to consider the muscle fibril as composed of structural units. Each unit extends between adjacent z lines and is termed a sarcomere. **1980** CRAWFORD & JAMES in R. Owen et al. *Sci. Foundations Orthopaedics & Traumatol.* x. 68/1 Changes in sarcomere length occur by movement of the thick myosin filaments along the thin actin filaments, their own length remaining unchanged.

sarcomic (sɑːˈkəʊmɪk), *a. nonce-wd.* [f. SARCOMA + -IC.] = CANCEROUS *a. fig.*

1958 J. STEINBECK *Once there was War* p. xx, We are poisoned in our souls by fear, faceless, stupid sarcomic terror.

sarcophagal (sɑːˈkɒfəgəl), *a. rare.* [f. L. SARCOPHAG-US + -AL[1].]

1. Flesh-devouring, flesh-consuming.

1614 T. ADAMS *Phys. Heaven* in *Diuells Banket* vi. 307 This naturall Balme..can (at vtmost)..giue a short and insensible preseruation to it [*sc.* the body], in the sarcophagall graue. **1905** *Daily News* 23 June 6 [A vegetarian] denounces my meat-eating habits as 'cannibal' and 'sarcophagal'.

2. Represented on sarcophagi.

1874 W. H. WITHROW *Catacombs of Rome* (1877) 292 The sarcophagal and other representations of this event.

sarcophagan (sɑːˈkɒfəgən). *Zool.* [f. mod.L. *Sarcophaga*, n. pl. or fem. sing. of *sarcophagus* (see SARCOPHAGUS) + -AN.] **a.** An animal of the group *Sarcophaga* (flesh-eating animals). **b.** A fly of the genus *Sarcophaga*; a flesh-fly.

In recent Dicts.

†**ˈsarcophage.** *Obs.* [ad. L. SARCOPHAGUS.]

1. = SARCOPHAGUS 1, 2.

1623 COCKERAM, *Sarcophage*, a graue, a sepulchre. **1656** BLOUNT *Glossogr.*, *Sarcophage*,..a stone called Eat-flesh. **1811** PINKERTON *Petral.* I. 229 [Green universal bricia.] The celebrated sarcophage, in the British Museum, is of this stone.

2. A flesh-eater; = SARCOPHAGUS 3.

1852 *Meanderings of Mem.* I. 210 Yon vermined Sarcophage.

So †**sarˈcophagist** in sense 2.

1699 EVELYN *Acetaria* 86 Whilst Men Sarcophagists (Flesh-Eaters) in all this time were yet to seek.

sarcophagize (sɑːˈkɒfədʒaɪz), *v.* [f. SARCOPHAG-US + -IZE.] *trans.* To enclose in a sarcophagus. Also *intr.* for *pass.* (*nonce-use*).

a **1876** M. COLLINS *Pen Sk.* (1879) I. 146 [He] lies sarcophagised in red granite. **1953** E. SITWELL *Gardeners & Astronomers* 9 The hue of honey sarcophagising or of sard.

sarcophagous (sɑːˈkɒfəgəs), *a. rare.* [f. L. *sarcophag-us* (see SARCOPHAGUS) + -OUS.]

1. **a.** 'Flesh-eating, feeding on flesh' (J.). **b.** Belonging to the group *Sarcophaga* (flesh-eaters) of mammals.

In recent Dicts.

2. Resembling a sarcophagus.

1885 *Edin. Rev.* Jan. 38 The faded palazzo with their sarcophagous courtyards and precincts.

‖**sarcophagus** (sɑːˈkɒfəgəs). Pl. -phagi (fədʒaɪ). Also 8 -fagus. [L., a. Gr. σαρκοφάγος, orig. adj., f. σαρκο-, σάρξ flesh + -φάγος eating.]

1. A kind of stone reputed among the Greeks to have the property of consuming the flesh of dead bodies deposited in it, and consequently used for coffins. *Obs.* exc. *Antiq.*

1601 HOLLAND *Pliny* XXXVI. xvii. II. 587 Near vnto Assos, a city in Troas, there is found in the quarries a certaine stone called Sarcophagus. *a* **1680** BUTLER *Rem.* (1759) II. 461 His Entrails are like the Sarcophagus, that devours dead Bodies in a small Space. **1750** tr. *Leonardus' Mirr. Stones* 232 Sarcofagus, is a Stone of which the Antients built their Monuments, and took its Name from its Effect.

2. A stone coffin, esp. one embellished with sculptures or bearing inscriptions, etc.

1705 ADDISON *Italy* (1733) 198 Several Sarcophagi that have inclosed the Ashes of Men or Boys, Maids or Matrons. **1762–71** H. WALPOLE *Vertue's Anecd. Paint.* (1786) I. 285 A sarcophagus with ribbed work and mouldings. **1838** MURRAY *Handbk. N. Germ.* 103 Their effigies, formed of Italian alabaster, repose upon a sarcophagus. **1838** ARNOLD *Hist. Rome* (1846) I. 325 The sarcophagus which contained the bones of L. Cornelius Scipio was discovered in 1780. **1869** RAWLINSON *Anc. Hist.* 63 Suphis I, the builder of the 'Third Pyramid' which contained his sarcophagus.

fig. **1619** PURCHAS *Microcosmus* xxxv. 329 This (*venter impiorum insaturabilis*)..consumes..generally twice a day all the flesh therein interred; so true a Sarcophagus is the belly. **1855** MOTLEY *Dutch Rep.* Introd. xiv. 85 The monastic spirit..which now kept it [*sc.* learning]..stiffening in the stony sarcophagus of a bygone age. **1870** tr. *Pouchet's Universe* (1871) 98 The Emperor Moth..emerges from its horny sarcophagus without catching a hair of its velvet wings against it.

3. A flesh-eating person or animal. ? *Obs.*

1617 COLLINS *Def. Bp. Ely* II. x. 420 No Transformators, no such sauage *Sarcophagi*, as S. Cyrill bends his penne against. **1864** PUSEY *Lect. Daniel* vii. 429 Dr. Browne informs me; 'There are met with in asylums *sarcophagi*, individuals who have desired to eat..human flesh.'

4. A wine-cooler.

In recent Dicts.

1833 LOUDON *Encycl. Archit.* 1045 Fig. 1871 is a pedestal sideboard... There is an open sarcophagus-shaped wine cooler beneath... Castors are sunk into the plinth of the sarcophagus.

Hence **sarˈcophagus** *v. trans.*, to deposit or enclose in a sarcophagus.

1862 MISS MULOCK in *Macm. Mag.* V. 464 The handful of mere dust that lies Sarcophagused in stone and lead. **1888** W. H. H. ROGERS *Mem. of West* App. 391 She rests in a wedge-shaped coffin, which is sarcophagused within the tomb in the presbytery.

sarcophagy (sɑːˈkɒfədʒɪ). *rare.* [ad. Gr. σαρκοφαγία, f. σαρκοφάγος: see prec. and -PHAGY.] The practice of eating flesh.

1650 SIR T. BROWNE *Pseud. Ep.* III. xxv. (1658) 209 There was no Sarcophagie before the flood. **1901** H. G. WELLS in *Eng. Illustr. Mag.* Nov. 112 The movements against vivisection, opium, alcohol, tobacco, sarcophagy, and the male sex.

sarcoplasmic (sɑːkəʊˈplæzmɪk), *a. Anat.* [f. *sarcoplasm* s.v. SARCO- + -IC.] Of, pertaining to, or containing sarcoplasm; ***sarcoplasmic reticulum***, the characteristic endoplasmic reticulum of striated muscle.

1891 *Internat. Monatsschrift für Anat. u. Physiol.* VIII. 229 The optical effect produced by the enlarging sarcoplasmic accumulations will involve more and more of the segment. **1902** *Encycl. Brit.* XXXI. 733/1 The muscle-cells of the ventricles are thicker, less sarcoplasmic, and more clearly striated than the auricular muscle. **1948** *Jrnl. Neurol., Neurosurg. & Psychol.* XI. 78/1 The dense areas showed an accumulation of pale oval sarcoplasmic nuclei. **1953** BENNETT & PORTER in *Amer. Jrnl. Anat.* XCIII. 69 The disposition of the larger masses of this sarcoplasmic reticulum is interpreted as evidencing an arrangement entirely analogous to the cross-fiber reticulum of Thin (1876), Melland (1885)..and others. **1970** T. S. & C. R. LEESON *Histol.* (ed. 2) ix. 164/2 Sarcoplasmic reticulum corresponds to the endoplasmic reticulum of other cell types, but its membranes are not associated with ribosomes. The sarcoplasmic reticulum comprises an extensive, continuous system of membrane-limited sarcotubules enclosing each myofibril as in a net. **1970** *Nature* 31 Oct. 417/2 The group of muscle fibres in the centre of the section show sarcoplasmic basophilia.

sarcopside (sɑːˈkɒpsɪd). *Min.* [ad. G. *sarkopsid* (Websky 1868), irreg. f. Gr. σαρκ-, σάρξ flesh + ὄψις sight.] Phosphate of iron and manganese exhibiting a flesh-red colour or fracture.

1877 DANA *Text-bk. Min.* 347 Sarcopside.—Near triplite. Valley of the Mühlbach, Silesia.

sarcopterygian (ˌsɑːkɒptəˈrɪdʒɪən). [f. mod.L. name of subclass *Sarcopterygii* (A. S. Romer 1955, in *Nature* 16 July 126/2) + -AN: see SARCO- and PTERYGO-.] A fossil or living fish belonging to the subclass Sarcopterygii, distinguished by fleshy fins.

1966 A. S. ROMER *Vertebr. Paleontol.* (ed. 3) v. 71/2 Many later sarcopterygians have simple bony scales. **1974** D. & M. WEBSTER *Compar. Vertebr. Morphol.* v. 96 Among the sarcopterygians there are striking differences between the pectoral girdles of the living lungfish, Dipnoi, and the living coelacanth, *Latimeria*.

‖**Sarcoptes** (sɑːˈkɒptiːz). *Zool.* [mod.L. (Latreille 1804), irreg. f. Gr. σαρκ-, σάρξ flesh + κόπτειν to cut.] A genus of parasites comprising the itch-mite; a mite of this genus.

1874 *Ann. Nat. Hist.* Jan. 75 The two genera in question differ from the true *Sarcoptes* in not piercing canals in the epidermis of their host. **1876** *Van Beneden's Anim. Parasites* 133 No other species but those of Sarcoptes can be transferred from animals to man. *Ibid.* 135 A sarcoptes (*S. mutans*) which produces a disease among fowls.

Hence **sarˈcoptic** *a.*, caused by itch-mites.

1886 *Order of Council* in *Field* 24 July 160/3 A horse, ass, or mule affected with sarcoptic mange.

sarcoptid (sɑːˈkɒptɪd). [f. mod.L. family name *Sarcoptidæ*, f. generic name *Sarcoptes* (P. A. Latreille *Hist. Nat. Crustacées & Insectes* (1802) III. 67): see SARCOPTES and -ID[3].] An itch or mange mite of the family Sarcoptidæ. Also *attrib.* or as *adj.* Also **ˈsarcopt** in the same sense.

1870 A. S. PACKARD *Guide Study of Insects* 666 Various Sarcoptids occur on birds. **1892** G. FLEMING tr. *Neumann's Treat. Parasites Domestic Animals* I. v. 121 The sarcopt of scabies..has the body slightly oval. **1932** L. VAN ES *Princ. Animal Hygiene* xliii. 736 Sarcopts are the most common cause of mange in dogs. **1962** GORDON & LAVOIPIERRE *Entomol. for Students of Med.* xliv. 264 (*caption*) The life-cycle of a sarcoptid mite.

sarcosine (ˈsɑːkəsɪn). *Chem.* Also **sarkosin(e, sarcosin.** [a. G. *sarkosin* (Liebig 1847), irreg. f. Gr. σαρκ-, -σάρξ flesh + -INE.] A nitrogenous substance, one of the constituents of creatine; methyl glycocoll.

1848 *Chem. Gaz.* VI. 4 Sarcosine. This substance is obtained by boiling a saturated solution of kreatine with crystallized hydrate of baryta. **1857** MILLER *Elem. Chem.*, *Org.* III. 323 Lactamide..is isomeric with sarcosine. **1869** ROSCOE *Elem. Chem.* 383 Sarcosine can be artificially prepared by acting upon monochloracetic acid with methylamine.

Hence **sarcoˈsinic** *a.* (see quot.).

1877 *Pharmac. Jrnl.* 28 Apr. 872/2 J. Hertz has extracted from a Mexican species of shell-lac, termed 'Soma de Sonora', which exuded from the *Mimosa Coccifera*, a body which he has designated 'sarcosinic acid'.

sarcosome (ˈsɑːkəʊsəʊm). *Biol.* [ad. G. *sarcosom* (G. Retzius 1890, in *Biol. Untersuchungen* Neue Folge I. 76): see SARCO- and -SOME[4].] A large mitochondrion found in striated muscle.

1899 tr. *Verworn's Gen. Physiol.* v. 464 The granules, or sarcosomes, lying in the sarcoplasm between the individual fibrillæ were enormously enlarged in the fatigued..muscle. **1912** *Amer. Jrnl. Anat.* XIV. 5 The 'exoplasmic granules' (J granules and Q granules) and the 'endoplasmic granules' of Holmgren correspond to the 'Sarcosomes' of Retzius which in turn correspond to Kölliker's true interstitial granules. It is possible that Retzius and Holmgren may have occasionally confused fat droplets with sarcosomes. **1919** *Anat. Rec.* XVI. 217 The wing muscle of the mantis furnishes an exceptionally favorable material for the investigation of the interfibrillar sarcoplasmic granules, or 'sarcosomes', characteristic of insect wing muscle. **1956** *Physiol. Rev.* XXXVI. 3 It is proposed in this article..to use the term sarcosome in its original sense as a general term to describe the lipoprotein granules which lie between the myofibrils and which can be seen with the light microscope. **1970** *Sci. Amer.* Feb. 101 The specialized mitochondria of the myocardial cell are unusually large; they are called sarcosomes.

sarcosporidiosis (ˌsɑːkəʊspɒrɪdɪˈəʊsɪs). *Vet. Sci.* [f. next + -OSIS.] Infection with, or a disease caused by, sarcosporidia.

1893 *Bull. Bureau Animal Industry, U.S. Dept. Agric.* No. 3. 80 Barrows' description renders it almost certain that this was a case of sarcosporidiosis. **1953** R. P. HALL *Protozool.* vi. 326 Sarcosporidiosis of man is apparently rare, although cases are reported occasionally. **1978** AYERS & JONES in K. Benirschke et al. *Path. Laboratory Animals* I. i. 14/1 Sarcosporidiosis is probably the most common parasitic disease of the heart seen in laboratory animals.

sarcosporidium (ˌsɑːkəʊspɒˈrɪdɪəm). *Microbiology* and *Vet. Sci.* Also **Sarco-**. Pl. **-sporidia.** [mod.L., ad. F. *sarcosporidie* (G. Balbiani, in *Jrnl. de Micrographie* (1882) VI. 262, (1883) VII. 87): see SARCO- and SPORIDIUM.] A spore-forming protozoan of the genus *Sarcocystis* that is a common parasite in the muscle tissue of many vertebrates, esp. domestic and laboratory mammals. Usu. *pl.*

1891 *Jrnl. Compar. Med. & Vet. Arch.* XII. 693 The small cysts found in the muscular fibres of various animals and known as Sarcosporidia. *Ibid.*, The negative results obtained..from feeding meat infected with sarcosporidia to various animals. **1927** *Indian Jrnl. Med. Res.* XV. 142 It is suggested that this parasite is an undescribed species of sarco-sporidium infecting the human host. **1930** *Jrnl. Parasitol.* XVI. 111 From the economic standpoint Sarco-sporidia are of chief interest to the veterinarian rather than the physician. **1970** JUBB & KENNEDY *Path. Domestic Animals* (ed. 2) I. ii. 121/2 Of those parasites with an affinity for muscle, the ubiquitous Sarcosporidia are the most common. The sarcocysts may be found in the Purkinje cells as well as in the myocardial fibres and normally appear to be of little detriment.

Hence **ˌsarcospoˈridial** *a.*, **-spoˈridian** *a.* and *sb.*

1903 E. A. MINCHIN in E. R. Lankester *Treat. Zool.* I. II. 301 The dangerous effects of the Sarcosporidian parasites. **1913** *Proc. Cambr. Philos. Soc.* XVII. 221 (*heading*) *Sarcocystis colii*, n. sp., a Sarcosporidian occurring in the red-faced African mouse bird. **1924** HEGNER & TALIAFERRO *Human Protozool.* xi. 372 (*caption*) Sarcosporidian spores. **1927** *Indian Jrnl. Med. Res.* XV. 142 Sarcocystic (Sarcosporidial) infection is common in cattle. **1949** C. A. HOARE *Handbk. Med. Protozool.* xiv. 271 Sarcosporidial infection has been reported in the muscles of the heart, larynx, tongue and the extremities. **1957** SMITH & JONES *Vet. Path.* xx. 704 Myocarditis... Sarcosporidial..cysts are common in the heart muscle.

†**sarˈcotic,** *a.* and *sb. Obs.* [ad. mod.L. *sarcōtic-us*, a. Gr. σαρκωτικός, f. σαρκοῦν (see SARCOMA).]

A. *adj.* Producing flesh; inducing the growth of flesh; = INCARNATIVE *a.*

1656 RIDGLEY *Pract. Physick* 127 Sarcotick remedies. **1684** tr. *Bonet's Merc. Compit.* III. 81 Ointment of Woodbine is a most excellent Sarcotick Medicine.

B. *sb.* = INCARNATIVE *sb.*

1657 TOMLINSON *Renou's Disp.* IV. i. 129 The best Sarcotick, confected of *Ceratum*, and a twelfth part of Verdigrease. **1676** WISEMAN *Chirurg. Treat.* 340 Where there is loss of Substance, there he must assist Nature with his Sarcoticks. **1676** JAS. COOKE *Marrow Chirurg.* (1685) IV. ix. 216 Use first exceedents and then Sarcoticks.

†**sarˈcotical,** *a.* and *sb. Obs.* [Formed as prec.: see -ICAL.] = prec.

1638 A. READ *Chirurg.* ix. 63 All Sarcoticall medicaments ..ought to be voyd of a sharp and biting quality. **1656** RIDGLEY *Pract. Physick* 285 [A boil] is cured by suppurating medicaments; after that by Sarcoticals. **1657** TOMLINSON *Renou's Disp.* III. iv. 124 If it [*sc.* a plaster] a sarcotical, herein it helps Nature, that it generates flesh more easily.

sarcous (ˈsɑːkəs), *a.* [f. Gr. σαρκ-, σάρξ flesh + -OUS.] Consisting of flesh or muscular tissue.

sarcous elements: see quot. 1840.

1840 W. BOWMAN in *Phil. Trans.* CXXX. 493 The primitive fasciculi of voluntary muscle consist of elongated polygonal masses of primitive component particles, or sarcous elements... It is the assemblage of these particles, which may most properly be styled 'Sarcous tissue'. **1875** DARWIN *Insectiv. Pl.* vi. 100 Parallelograms of sarcous matter. **1898** *Allbutt's Syst. Med.* V. 890 The process of fatty degeneration of the cardiac muscle consists..in the gradual replacement of the sarcous elements by fatty granules.

†'**sarculate**, *v. rare*$^{-0}$. [f. ppl. stem of late L. *sarculāre*, f. *sarculum* (see SARCLE).] *trans.* To hoe. So †**sarcu'lation** *rare*$^{-1}$, hoeing.

1623 COCKERAM, *Sarculate*, to weed. *Sarculation*, a weeding. **1733** TULL *Horse-Hoeing Husb.* vii. 62 Their Sarculation was used but amongst small Quantities of sown Corn.

sarcynet, obs. form of SARSENET.

sard (sɑːd), *sb.*[1] Also 4 saarde. [In mod. use prob. a. F. *sarde*, ad. L. *sarda*, a synonym of *sardius*: see SARDIUS.

In quot. 1382 ad. L. *sardius*; in quot. 1601 ad. L. *sarda*.]

A variety of CORNELIAN[1], varying in colour from pale golden yellow to reddish orange.

1382 WYCLIF *Exod.* xxxix. 10 And he putte in it foure ordres of gemmes; in the first veers was saarde, topazi, smaragd. **1601** HOLLAND *Pliny* II. 618 The Indian Sardes or Cornallines are transparent. **1809** KIDD *Outl. Min.* I. 227 This variety [of Carnelian] seems to be the sard of the present day. **1815** AIKIN *Man. Min.* (ed. 2) 180 Sarde. **1839** URE *Dict. Arts* 570 The sard of the English jewellers..is a stone of the nature of agate. **1863** GEO. ELIOT *Romola* xxxix, A fine sard, engraved with a subject from Homer. **1901** *Q. Rev.* Oct. 430 The gem is a golden sard.

attrib. **1881** PALGRAVE *Vis. Eng.* 70 Sardstones ruddy as wine.

Sard (sɑːd), *a.* and *sb.*[2] Also ‖Sarde. [ad. It. *Sardo*, L. *Sardus*.]

A. *adj.* = SARDINIAN *a.* and *sb.*

1823 W. ROBINSON in J.A. Heraud *Voy. & Mem. Midshipm.* viii. 142 The Sard costume. **1861** J. H. BENNET *Winter Medit.* II. xiii. (1875) 464 Little wiry Sard horses.

B. *sb.* **1.** = SARDINIAN *sb.* 1

1822 W. ROBINSON in J.A. Heraud *Voy. & Mem. Midshipm.* v. (1837) 81 Boats manned by Genoese, French, Sards, and Neapolitans. **1845** *Encycl. Metrop.* XXIV. 318/2 The Sards are greatly attached to the pleasures of the table. **1889** C. EDWARDES *Sardinia & Sardes* vi. 147 The foreman was a Sarde of an advanced type. **1932** [see SARDINIAN *sb.* 2]. **1968** *Listener* 29 Feb. 267/1 No Sard will betray another. .. There's the unwritten law of *omerta*, of silence.

2. = SARDINIAN *sb.* 2.

1885 [see LOGUDORO]. **1889** C. EDWARDES *Sardinia & Sardes* iii. 59 Modern Sarde is what Sardinia's conquerors made it—a language much more nearly kin to Latin than Italian. **1957** *Whitaker's Almanack 1958* 899/1 Sard, the dialect of Sardinia, is accorded by some authorities the status of a distinct Romance language. **1975** *Times Lit. Suppl.* 25 Apr. 452/4 Gramsci was a humane and intelligent man, but in no sense an 'authority' on anything except Mussolini's prisons and Sard.

†**sard**, *v. Obs.* Also 5 serd. [In OE. only once (Northumb.) in imp. *serð*, app. a. ON. *serða* (str. vb.) = MLG. *serden*, MHG., early mod.G. *serten*. OE. may have had the normal **seordan*.] *trans.* = JAPE *v.* 2. Hence †'**sarding** *vbl. sb.*

c **950** *Lindisf. Gosp., Matt.* v. 27 Ne serð þu oðres mones wif. *c* **1425** *Cast. Persev.* 1163 in *Macro Plays* 112 þanne mayst þou bultyn in þi boure, & serdyn gay gerlys. **1530** PALSGR. 697/2, I sarde a queene, *je fous*. **1535** LYNDESAY *Satyre* (ed. Laing) 3028 Freirs, Quhilk will, for purging of their neirs: Sard up the ta raw, and doun the uther. **1598** FLORIO, *Fottere*, to iape, to sard. *Fottarie*, iapings, sardings. **1659** HOWELL *Eng. Prov.* 17 Go teach your Grandam to sard; a Nottingham Proverb.

†'**sardachate**. *Obs.*$^{-0}$ [ad. L. *sardachātēs*; see SARD *sb.*[1] and ACHATE *sb.*[1]] (See quots.)

1706 PHILLIPS (ed. Kersey), *Sardachates*, a kind of Agate, of a Cornelian Colour. **1828–32** WEBSTER, *Sardachate*, the clouded and spotted agate, of a pale flesh color. In some recent Dicts.

†'**sardan**, *a. Obs. rare*$^{-1}$. [ad. L. *Sardonius* (? with supposed correction of form after Gr. Σαρδάνιος).] = SARDOIN *a.*

1649 OGILBY *Virg. Eccl.* VII. 43, I bitterer to thee then Sardan grass..shall seeme.

‖**sardana** (sar'dana). [Sp.] A popular Catalan dance performed to pipes and drum.

1922 *Glasgow Herald* 28 Apr. 8 The music played by amateur orchestras, even in small villages, to the Sardanas or national Catalonian dances is delightful. **1934** C. LAMBERT *Music Ho!* III. 172 The Catalan sardanas..have added to their primitive basis sophisticated and foreign elements. **1953** *Observer* 13 Sept. 9/2 To describe the new local dance, the Sardana from Spanish Catalonia, Mr. O'Brian has essayed a poetic prose. **1965** *Listener* 10 June 877/3 Spain retains small keyless shawms..and also has modern keyed forms in the sardana bands of Catalonia. **1976** D. MUNROW *Instruments Middle Ages & Renaissance* 40/3 The Catalonian *coblas* of north-eastern Spain which play for the *sardana*, the 'national' dance of the region.

Sardanapalian (sɑːdənə'peɪlɪən), *a.* [f. L. *Sardanapālus*, Gr. Σαρδανάπαλος, the name given by Gr. historians to the last king of Nineveh, proverbial as the type of luxurious effeminacy.] Resembling Sardanapalus and his attributes; luxuriously effeminate. So †**Sardana'palical** *a.* (in quot. erron. *-panicall*). †**Sarda'napalize** *v.*, *trans.* to represent or describe as a Sardanapalus.

1555 EDEN *Decades* 101 Tumanama..with all his Sardanapanicall famelye. **1673** MARVELL *Reh. Transp.* II. 179 You muster up all Christian Princes to Neronize and Caligulize them, unless they..will chuse..to be Uilenspiegled and Sardanapalized by you. **1863** R. H. GRONOW *Recoll. & Anecd.* 117 He [Eugène Sue] was supposed..to lead a very Sardanapalian life. **1876** A. J. EVANS *Through Bosnia* vi. 267 [He] lived in Sardanapalian luxury.

sardane, obs. form of SARDINE *sb.*[2]

sardanique: see SARDONIC.

sardar: see SIRDAR.

[**sardel**, A precious stone. Error for *sardine* or *sardius*.

[**1721** BAILEY, *Sardel, Sardine*, a sort of Fish.] **1755** JOHNSON, *Sardel, Sardine Stone, Sardius*, a sort of precious stone. [Johnson omits Bailey's meaning 'a sort of Fish', but combines his *Sardel, Sardine* with *Sardius*.] Hence in **1828–32** WEBSTER, **1850–82** OGILVIE, and some later Dicts.]

sardelle (sɑː'dɛl). Also 6–7 sardell, 8–9 sardel. [ad. It. *sardella*, dim. of *sarda*:—L. *sarda*, a. Gr. σάρδη sardine. Cf. F. †*sardelle* (16th c.), G. *sardelle*, Du. *sardel*.] A fish, *Clupea* or *Sardinella aurita*, resembling the sardine and prepared like it in certain Mediterranean ports.

1598 FLORIO, *Sardella*, a little pickled or salt fish like an anchoua, a sprat or a pilcher, called a sardell or sardine. **1657** C. BECK *Univ. Charac.* K vj b, Sardell fish. **1745** tr. *Columella's Husb.* VIII. xvii, It is proper that rotten.. pilchards should be given them; and sardels consumed with salt, and rotten sardines. **1799** W. TOOKE *View Russian Emp.* III. 169 Anchovies and sardelles. **1889** *Boston* (Mass.) *Jrnl.* 19 Dec. 2/8 Certain fish put up in brine in wooden packages, ..and known as 'sardelles'. **1896** BRANNT *Anim. & Veg. Fats* (ed. 2) II. 66 Anchovy oil or sardel oil..from *Engraulis enerasicholus* Cuv. the anchovy.

sardenian, -denyk: see SARDONIAN, -DONYX.

sardeos, sardeyn: see SARDIUS, SARDINE *sb.*[2]

Sardian ('sɑːdɪən), *a.* and *sb.* [ad. L. *Sardiānus*, a. Gr. Σαρδιανός, Ionic -ηνός, f. Σάρδεις pl., L. *Sardīs, Sardēs*, the name of the ancient capital of Lydia.] **A.** *adj.* Of or pertaining to Sardis.

Sardian acorn, nut, a chestnut, *Castanea vesca*. ***Sardian stone*** = SARD *sb.*[1]

1551 TURNER *Herbal* I. (1568) H vj, Castanea..is named in englyshe a chesnut tree... The frute of it is called of som glans sardiana, that is a sardiane acorne. **1714** EUSDEN *On Addison's Cato* A.'s Wks. 1830 II. 57 Here the Sardian stone is seen, The topaz yellow, and the jasper green. **1830** tr. *Aristoph., Acharnians* 9 Tell me clearly,..lest I dip you in a Sardian dye. **1847** GROTE *Greece* II. xvii. III. 343 His monument..erected near Sardis by the joint efforts of the whole Sardian population.

B. *sb.*

1. An inhabitant of Sardis.

1598 GRENEWEY *Tacitus, Ann.* III. xiii. (1622) 83 The Sardians brought in matters of latter memory. **1601** SHAKS. *Jul. C.* IV. iii. 3 You haue condemn'd, and noted Lucius Pella For taking Bribes heere of the Sardians. **1846** P. FAIRBAIRN tr. *Hengstenberg's Comm. Ps.* xliv. 14 People would figuratively call a miserable man a Jew, just as liars were called Cretans, wretched slaves, Sardians.

2. = *Sardian stone* (see A), SARD *sb.*[1]

1741 CHAMBERS *Cycl.* s.v., The Sardian [*ed.* **1728** *has* Sardoin] is most used for seals, as graving easily, yet taking a fine polish. **1860** C. W. KING *Ant. Gems* 398 [tr. Marbodus] The blood-red Sardian to its birthplace owes Its name, to Sardis, whence it first arose.

sardiane, obs. Sc. form of SARDINE *sb.*[1]

†'**Sardic**, *a. Obs. rare*[1]. In 6 **Sardique**. [f. L. *Sard-īs* (see SARDIAN) + -IC.] = SARDIAN *a.* *Sardic stone* = SARD *sb.*[1]

1586 FERNE *Blaz. Gentrie* I. 142 The first, is called a Sardique stone, and sheweth in cullor lyke vnto red claie.

sardine ('sɑːdaɪn), *sb.*[1] Forms: 4 sardiner, sardyn, *Sc.* sardiane, 6– **sardine**. [ad. late L. *sardinus*, occurring in the Vulgate of Rev. iv. 3 (if the genitive *sardinis* of the usual text be a mistake for **sardini*; but the word may be the genit. of **sardo*, a. Gr. σαρδώ, genit. -δοῦς, some gem), where it renders Gr. σάρδινος, a variant reading for σάρδιος (or σάρδιον) SARDIUS, which mod. editors adopt.

The Gr. σάρδινος occurs in one other passage (see L. & Sc.): late L. *sardinus* is quoted by Du Cange from the Old Latin version of Prov. xxv. 12. OF. *sardine* 12th c. may perh. represent this word, or it may be a variant of *sardoine* (see SARDOIN).]

A precious stone mentioned in Rev. iv. 3. In the non-Biblical examples perh. used for SARDOIN.

13.. *E.E. Allit. P.* B. 1469 And safyres, & sardiners [? *read* sardines], & semely topace. *c* **1375** *Sc. Leg. Saints* vi. (*Thomas*) 279 Preciuse stanys, as sardiane, topias fyne, Iaspis. **1382** WYCLIF *Rev.* iv. 3 Lijk to the siȝt of a stoone iaspis, and to sardyn. *c* **1400** MAUNDEV. (1839) xxvii. 276 Degrees..of Sardyne [Roxb. xxx. 136 sardone]. **1526** TINDALE *Rev.* iv. 3 Lyke vnto a iaspar stone, and a sardyne stone [so **1611**; **1881** (*Revised*) a sardius]. **1574** tr. *Marlorat's Apocalips* (1578) 300 The sixt a Sardine. This stone is all of one colour lyke bloud.

sardine (sɑː'diːn), *sb.*[2] Forms: 5–6 sardyn, 5 sardeyn, 6, 8 sardin (6 surdone), 7 sardane, 7 sardino, sirdena (surdiny, *pl.* sirdena's, -dinasses), 7–8 **sardina** (7 *pl.* -aes), 9 **Sardinia**, 6– **sardine**. [a. F. *sardine*, ad. It. *sardina*:—L. *sardīna* (Columella; cf. late Gr. σαρδήνη and σαρδῖνος), f. *sarda*, = Gr. σάρδη, the sardine or some similar fish. In the 17th and 18th c. the Italian form was often used.

The Latin and Greek word may be related to the name of the island, L. *Sardinia*, Gr. Σαρδώ: cf. SARD *a.*]

1. a. A small fish of the Herring family, *Clupea pilchardus*, abundant off the shores of Sardinia and Brittany, or a young pilchard of the Cornish coast, when cured, preserved in oil and packed in tins or other cases for sale as a table delicacy.

c **1430** *Two Cookery Bks.* 24 Sardeynez. **1547** BOORDE *Introd. Knowl.* xxviii. 195, I was borne in Aragon,..Masyl baken, and sardyns, I do eate and sel. **1580** HOLLYBAND *Treas. Fr. Tong, Sardelle, ou Sardine*,..a kinde of fishe called a Sardine. **1583** FOXE *A. & M.* (ed. 4) 2154/1 [At Rochelle] there was sent to them euery day in the Riuer (by the hand of the Lord no doubt) a great multitude of fishe (called surdones). **1585** T. WASHINGTON tr. *Nicholay's Voy.* I. xii. 14 There flew a fish into our Gallie of the length, colour and bignesse of a great sardin. **1601** HOLLAND *Pliny* I. 244 The Pike and Sardane [L. *trichias*] breed twice a yere. *a* **1623** FLETCHER *Loves Cure* II. i, A Pilcher, Signior, a Surdiny, an Olive. *a* **1625** —— *Loves Pilgr.* I. i, *Inc.* He looks as he would eat partridge, this guest... *Hostesse.* With a Sardina, and Zant oil? **1658** SIR T. BROWNE *Pseud. Ep.* III. xxvi. (ed. 3) 143 The Reliques are like the skales of Sardinos pressed into a mass. **1690** STRUTTON *Relat. Cruelties French* 9 Our Breakfast, viz. a six Denire Loaf, and one Sirdena per Man. *Ibid.* 40 Our Supper here was a piece of Bread and two Sirdinasses. **1740** R. BROOKES *Art of Angling* II. xxxix. 157 There is another Sort of Fish sold instead of Anchovies call'd a Sardin, which is very probably a young Pilchard. **1777** *Ann. Reg.* 179 Figure to yourself these feeding on scanty portions of rotten sardines. **1850** L. HUNT *Autobiog.* II. xvii. 303 The anchovies, or Sardinias, that we eat. **1864** MATHIAS *Sport in Himalayas* (1865) 33 Unless I shoot something or other, I shall have to fall back on biscuits and sardines. **1879** *Encycl. Brit.* IX. 253/2 Curing establishments were..set up.., and 'Cornish sardines', or 'pilchards in oil', were prepared..with.. success. **1883** *Fisheries Exhib. Catal.* 215 Spiced Sardines..Mustard Sardines..Oil Sardines. **1886** *Encycl. Brit.* XXI. 307/2 Another of the *Clupeidæ* (*C. scombrina*) is the 'oil-sardine' of the eastern coast of the Indian Peninsula.

b. *U.S.* (See quots.)

1870 L. M. ALCOTT *Old-Fashioned Girl* xiii. 266 We've got sardines, crackers, and cheese. **1876** GOODE *Anim. Resources U.S.* (1879) 186 (Smithsonian Coll. XXIII) Canned menhaden, in oil, 'American sardines'. Canned herring, in oil, 'Russian sardines'. **1884** GOODE, etc. *Nat. Hist. Aquatic Anim.* 576 The Gulf Menhaden [*Brevoortia patronus*] has several vernacular names. At Key West it is called 'Sardine'. *Ibid.* 611 A species of Anchovy, *Stolephorus Browni*, is extremely common about Fort Macon, where it is known as the 'Sardine'.

c. *Austral.* (See quot.)

1898 MORRIS *Austral Eng.*, *Sardine*,..a fresh-water fish, *Chatöessus erebi*, Richards., of the herring tribe.

d. In colloq. phr. ***to be packed (in) like sardines***: to be crowded or confined tightly together, as sardines in a tin.

1911 W. OWEN *Let.* 12 Sept. (1967) 80 The entrance hall ..where for half an hour the boys stand waiting packed like sardines. **1922** *Dialect Notes* V. 172 We were packed in there like sardines in a box. **1974** *Daily Mirror* 11 Nov. 4/3 Lodgers at a lorry drivers' digs hit by a horror blaze were 'packed in like sardines', it was claimed yesterday.

e. *pl.* (const. as *sing.*) A party game of hide-and-seek, in which each seeker joins the hider upon discovery until one seeker remains. Also ***sardines-in-the*** (also ***a)-box*** (U.S.).

1924 in Mendel & Meynell *Weekend Bk.* 241 *Sardines* is gaudier still. Only one player hides, all the others seek; the first to find him hides with him, the next..squashes in alongside,..till everybody's hiding in the same spot but one Seeker. **1925** F. SCOTT FITZGERALD *Great Gatsby* v. 82 'Hide-and-go-seek' or 'sardines-in-the-box' with all the house thrown open to the game. **1935** N. MARSH *Enter Murderer* xx. 242 Give us all the light in the house. I refuse to play sardines with Mr. Hickson. **1959** J. BYROM *Take only as Directed* xiii. 147, I remembered the big linen-chest... I had once hidden there playing Sardines. **1960** N. HALE *New England Girlhood* 113 We used to play hide-and-go-seek, and a game called sardines-in-a-box. **1962** B. COBB *Murder: Men Only* iv. 37 That game—'Sardines,' isn't it?—in which men hide with girls in cupboards. **1974** N. FREELING *Dressing in Diamond* 116 Tomorrow is a holiday... So we weekend... And play sardines. **1980** G. M. FRASER *Mr. American* xiii. 259 The festivities were strictly of the nursery variety..musical chairs, 'sardines', and hide-and-seek.

2. *attrib.* and *Comb.*, as ***sardine boat, can, factory, -fishery, fishing, fleet, sandwich, tin***; ***sardine-packed*** adj.; **sardine box**, a box in which sardines are packed; also, an ornamental box to hold sardines for the table; **sardine shears** (see quot.); **sardine tongs**, tongs used in serving sardines; **sardine-wise** *adv.*, like sardines in a box.

1927 L. RICHARDSON *Brittany & Loire* 128 The early type of *sardine boat had no overhang—a long, straight keel, straight stem. **1976** F. GREENLAND *Misericordia Drop* II. xiii. 161 A converted sardine-boat. **1855** *Harvard Mag.* I. 266 O ghosts of innumerous *sardine-boxes, and emptied cracker-kegs. **1873** LELAND *Egypt. Sketch-bk.* 24 The brass *etiquette* or advertisement-label cut from a sardine-box. **1892** *Encycl. Pract. Cookery* (ed. Garrett) II. 379/2 Ornamental Sardine-box. **1977** *Modern Railways* Dec. 484/1 The first run was with an eight-car formation of this stock forming the 18.00 down Clacton packed to *sardine-can condition. **1979** P. DRISCOLL *Pangolin* ii. 22 The tram..was more crowded than usual..a clanking sardine can. **1891** *Chamb. Jrnl.* 7 Mar. 155/2 The *sardine factories of Kent. **1859** JEPHSON *Brittany* xii. 193 It sends several goats to the *Sardine-fishery. **1775** J. SCHAW *Jrnl. Lady of Quality* (1921) iv. 220

Above a hundred boats engaged in the *sardine fishing. **1939** H. M. Miner *St. Denis* ii. 23 There is still some commercial eel- and sardine-fishing, but this has declined. **1942** 'A. Bridge' *Frontier Passage* iv. 65 The many-coloured dancing shapes of the *sardine-fleet. **1917** Wyndham Lewis *Let.* Sept. (1963) 92, I am now absolutely *sardine-packed with the quintessence of the prosperous slums of a Protestant country. **1954** B. Malamud in *Partisan Rev.* Nov.–Dec. 587 Leo fixed tea and a *sardine sandwich. **1978** F. Weldon *Praxis* vii. 42 She had lit the fire and made sardine sandwiches. **1884** Knight *Dict. Mech.* Suppl., **Sardine Shears*,.. scissors.. for cutting open the tin boxes containing sardines. **1890** W. Booth *In Darkest Eng.* II. ii. 121 Most of the toys which are sold in France on New Year's Day are almost entirely made of *sardine tins. **1933** M. Allingham *Sweet Danger* xv. 187 'Leave that smelly little sardine tin [*sc.* a motor car] alone.'... 'The exhaust smells a little, but that's nothing.' **1973** 'A. Hall' *Tango Briefing* x. 124 A rip-string and I pulled it, opening the polyester like a sardine-tin. **1895** *Army & Navy Co-op. Soc. Price List*, *Sardine Tongs. **1894** Du Maurier *Trilby* II. v. 120 The guests were not packed together *sardine-wise, as they are at most concerts.

sardine (sɑːˈdiːn), *v. colloq.* (orig. *U.S.*). [f. SARDINE[2].] *trans.* To pack closely, as sardines in a tin; to crowd, cram, press tightly.

1895 W. C. Gore in *Inlander* Dec. 114 *Sardine*,.. to pack closely, side by side. 'We sardined ourselves in front of the Law Building and howled.' **1896** *Advance* 24 Dec. 916/2 There are 350 people outside.., and in some way we are going to sardine them in. **1940** H. Walpole *Roman Fountain* vii. 124 We were pressed back and sardined together. **1953** Dylan Thomas *Under Milk Wood* (1954) 69 Mrs Probert.. is the one love of his sea-life that was sardined with women. **1968** *N.Y. Times* 22 Apr. 36 Hundreds of thousands of people.. will be sardined into the famous amusement park. **1977** *New Yorker* 11 July 79/1 Once sardined in place, they are subject to terrifying hazards in case of fire.

sardinia, obs. form of SARDINE *sb.*[2]

Sardinian (sɑːˈdɪnɪən), *a.* and *sb.* [f. *Sardinia* (see below) + -AN.] **A.** *adj.*

1. a. Of or pertaining to Sardinia, i.e. either the large island adjacent to Corsica, or the kingdom of Sardinia (1720–1859), which had its capital at Turin, and included the island of Sardinia as well as Piedmont and adjacent territories.

1748 H. Walpole *Let. to Mann* 29 Apr., The Sardinian Minister has refused to sign too. **1841** W. Spalding *Italy & It. Isl.* III. 342 The Sardinian States. The dominions of the King of Sardinia consist of 51 provinces in all. **1851** *Life A. Gentili* 228 At the Sardinian chapel in London, he twice preached.. for two consecutive Sundays. **1876** Voyle & Stevenson *Milit. Dict.* (ed. 3), *Sardinian Huts*, wooden huts made by many English officers in the Crimea and by the Sardinians for their men.

b. Designating a Romance language (or group of dialects) spoken by the Sardinians.

1835 G. C. Lewis *Origin & Formation Romance Lang.* i. 48 Niebuhr.. says that 'specimens of the Sardinian language from the civilized districts exhibit peculiarities which are more than varieties of dialect'. **1960** W. D. Elcock *Romance Lang.* v. 474 In.. perceiving that the 'outlandish' character of Sardinian speech lay in its approximation to Latin the poet-philologist [Dante] had almost divined the truth concerning the origin of the Romance languages. **1974** *Encycl. Brit. Macropædia* XV. 1029/1 It is sometimes said that these last two [*sc.* Sassarian and Gallurian] are not Sardinian dialects but rather Corsican.

c. ***Sardinian warbler***, a black, brown, and white warbler, *Sylvia melanocephala*, found in the Mediterranean region.

1909 C. Whymper *Egyptian Birds* 209 Sardinian Warbler.. Rare. **1954** D. A. Bannerman *Birds Brit. Isles* III. 150 In Sicily.. the Sardinian warbler is the commonest warbler. **1971** *Country Life* 1 July 27/3 Our most familiar sounds by day were.. the chatter of Sardinian warblers among the mastic bushes.

†**2. a.** Used for SARDONIAN, SARDONIC. **b.** transl. of L. *sardonius*, as the epithet of the plant producing 'sardonic' laughter. *Obs.*

1615 Chapman *Odyss.* xx. 457 A laughter.. most Sardinian, With scorn and wrath mix'd. **1697** Dryden *Virg. Past.* vii. 61 May I become.. Rough as a Bur, deform'd like him who chaws Sardinian Herbage to contract his Jaws. **1752** Johnson *Rambler* No. 188 ⁋4 What the Latins call Sardinian Laughter, a distortion of the face without gladness of heart.

¶**3.** ***Sardinian acorn, nut*** = SARDIAN acorn, nut.

1895 in T. W. Sanders *Encycl. Gard.* **1897** in *Syd. Soc. Lex.*

B. *sb.* **1.** An inhabitant of the island or of the kingdom of Sardinia.

1598 Grenewey *Tacitus, Ann.* iv. xii. (1622) 109 All the contention rested betwixt the Sardinians & Smyrnæans. **1748** H. Walpole *Let. to Mann* 29 Apr., The Sardinian to have the cessions made to him by the Queen. **1793** Burke *Policy of Allies* Wks. VII. 142 Bands of English, Spaniards, Neapolitans, Sardinians [etc.]. **1908** *Daily News* 29 Sept. 4 The Siberians and Sardinians [*sc.* foxes] that are introduced from time to time.

2. A Romance language (or group of dialects) spoken in Sardinia.

1813 *Q. Rev.* Oct. 259 Bolognese.., Sicilian.., Sardinian. **1841** *Penny Cycl.* XX. 427/1 A book was published at Cagliari, in both Sardinian and Italian, called 'Moriografia Sarda'. **1894** W. M. Lindsay *Latin Lang.* ii. 34 Short *ŭ* and *ō* of Latin are distinguished not only in Sardinian.., but also in Roumanian and in the Latin element of the Albanian language. **1932** G. F.-H. Berkeley *Italy in Making* I. iv. 52 French was permitted for the Savoyards and Valdostani, Genoese for the Ligurians, and Sardinian for the Sards. **1965** W. S. Allen *Vox Latina* i. 25 At what period such a [phonetic] change took place it is impossible to say, but Sardinian suggests that it was very late. **1974** *Encycl. Brit. Macropædia* XV. 1026/1 On linguistic grounds Sardinian (not the language of an independent nation since the 14th century) and Occitan (the medieval Provençal) are usually regarded as languages rather than dialects. *Ibid.* 1029/1 The first documents in Sardinian are legal contracts dating from about 1080.

‖**sardius** (ˈsɑːdɪəs). Also 4, 6 **sardis**, 6 **sardeos**, **-ios**, **-ious**; also in the anglicized forms 6 **sardye**, 7 **sardie**. [L. *sardius* (Vulg.), ad. Gr. *σάρδιος*, *σάρδιον*, f. *Σάρδεις* Sardis: see SARDIAN.] A precious stone mentioned by ancient writers; see SARD *sb.*[1] (Chiefly in translations of or allusions to the Bible or classical writers.)

1382 Wyclif *Ezek.* xxviii. 13 Eche precious stoon thi keuerynge, sardius, topacius, and iaspis. **1390** Gower *Conf.* III. 132 The Ston which that this sterre alloweth, Is Sardis. **1526** Tindale *Rev.* xxi. 20 The sixt sardeos [**1560** (Genev.) Sardious]. **1530** —— *Exod.* xxxix. 10 Sardios [**1535** Coverdale a Sardis], a Topas and smaragdus. **1567** Maplet *Gr. Forest* 19 The Sardye is a kind of Gemme red coloured. **1596** Lodge *Wits Miserie* 76 The stone Sardius hindreth the properties thereof [wrath]. **1608** Willet *Hexapla Exod.* 640 The sardie is red and somewhat of a fierie colour. **1611** Bible *Exod.* xxxix. 10. **1681** Grew *Musæum* III. i. iv. 290 The Sardius or Cornelian. **1865** J. H. Ingraham *Pillar of Fire* (1872) 219 There were present merchants from Ind with boxes of precious stones, including the diamond and the sardius.

†**sardoin**, *sb. Obs.* Forms: 3–5 **sardone**, 3 **sardoine**, 5 **-oyne**, 7 **sardoin**. [a. OF. *sardoine*, ad. L. *sardonyx* SARDONYX.] = SARDONYX.

a **1272** *Luue Ron* 173 in *O.E. Misc.* 98 Hwat spekstu of eny stone þat beoþ in vertu.. Of iaspe of saphir of sardone [etc.]. *a* **1300** *Floriz & Bl.* 285 þe smale stones.. beoþ þer funden.. Boþe saphirs and sardoines. *c* **1400** Maundev. (1839) xxvii. 275 The principalle ȝates of his Palays ben of precious Ston, that men clepen Sardoyne [*Roxb.* xxx. 136 sardones]. **1601** Holland *Pliny* II. 615 The ground of these Sardoins is found in the Indian stones to resemble wax or horne.

†**sardoin**, *a. Obs. rare*$^{-1}$. [ad. L. *sardonius* (? influenced in form by prec.).] Epithet of the herb fabled to produce 'sardonic' laughter.

1633 P. Fletcher *Purple Isl.* viii. 48 The Sardoin herb with many branches filling His [Flattery's] shield, was his device: the word, *I please in killing*.

sardone, var. SARDOIN *sb. Obs.*, sardonyx.

†**sarˈdonian**, *a.* and *sb. Obs.* Also 6 **sardenian**. See also SARDINIAN *a.* 2. [f. L. *sardoni-us* + -AN.

The Latin adj. is ad. Gr. *Σαρδόνιος* Sardinian, which in late Gr. was substituted for *σαρδάνιος* (Homer, etc.; of obscure origin), as the descriptive epithet of bitter or scornful laughter; the motive of the substitution was the notion that the word had primary reference to the effects of eating a 'Sardinian plant' (L. *herba Sardonia* or *Sardōa*), which was said to produce facial convulsions resembling horrible laughter, usually followed by death.]

A. *adj.* = SARDONIC *a.*

1586 Bright *Melanch.* xvii. 99 The perturbations of melancholie are.. sometimes merry in apparaunce, through a kinde of Sardonian, and false laughter. **1589** Greene *Menaphon* (Arb.) 62 Haue you fatted me so long with Sardenian smiles, that.. I might perish in your wiles? **1596** Spenser *F.Q.* v. ix. 12 And with Sardonian smyle Laughing on her, his false intent to shade. **1620** Bp. Hall *Hon. Mar. Clergy* iii. vi. 282 It is then but a Sardonian laughter that my Refuter takes vp at our complete Antichrist. **1742** Hume *Ess.* xiv. (1825) 123 This unprovoked piece of rusticity.. caused no farther resentment in Philip than to excite a Sardonian smile. **1794** [T. Taylor] *Pausanias' Descr. Greece* III. 149 Homer first, and others after him, call laughter, which conceals some noxious design, Sardonian.

†**B.** *sb.* One who flatters with deadly intent.

App. alluding to the 'Sardinian plant' (see the etymological note above) which was said to kill by exciting laughter. Cf. quot. s.v. SARDOIN *a.*

1609 Bp. Barlow *Answ. Nameless Cath.* 254 His nature is too.. noble, to be a Sardonian: Fawning and Crouching hee leaues to such base bone-gnawers as Fa. Parsons.

sardonic (sɑːˈdɒnɪk), *a.* Also 7 **sardonick**, **sardanique**. [a. F. *sardonique* (16th c.) = Sp. *sardónico*, Pg., It. *sardonico*, as if ad. L. **sardonicus*, an alteration (by substitution of suffix: see -IC) of *sardonius*: see SARDONIAN.

Hobbes's form *sardanique* is assimilated to Gr. *σαρδάνιος*: see prec.]

a. Of laughter, a smile: Bitter, scornful, mocking. Hence of a person, personal attribute, etc.: Characterized by or exhibiting bitterness, scorn or mockery.

1638 Sir T. Herbert *Trav.* (ed. 2) 190 He.. gives a Sardonick smile to think how blest hee was in this attonement. **1675** Hobbes *Odyssey* xx. 276 Then smil'd Ulysses a Sardanique smile. **1713** Steele *Guard.* No. 29 ⁋10 The Horse-Laugh, or the Sardonic, is made use of with great Success in all kinds of Disputation. **1766** Goldsm. *Vic. W.* xx, Our cousin received the proposal with a true sardonic grin. **1826** Scott *Woodst.* iv, The knight meanwhile darted a sardonic look.. on his nephew. **1830** Carlyle *Misc.* (1857) II. 140 His countenance, strangely twisted into Sardonic wrinkles. **1833** I. Taylor *Fanat.* v. 119 The sardonic historian, whose rule it is to exhibit human nature always as an object of mockery. **1866** Howells *Venet. Life* v. 68 The favourite drama of the Burattini appears to be a sardonic farce, in which the chief character.. deludes other.. puppets into trusting him, and then beats them. **1872** Darwin *Emotions* x. 251 We see a trace of this same expression [the sneer] in what is called a derisive or sardonic smile. **1878** Bayne *Purit. Rev.* ii. 27 He would have found exercise for dramatic sympathy and sardonic humour.

b. *Path.* (See quot. 1897.)

1822–29 *Good's Study Med.* (ed. 3) IV. 374 The nostrils are drawn upward, and the cheeks backward toward the ears; so that the whole countenance assumes the air of a cynic spasm or sardonic grin. **1897** *Syd. Soc. Lex.*, *Risus sardonicus*, sardonic grin. The involuntary, convulsive drawing down of the angles of the month in *Tetanus*. *Ibid.*, *Sardonic laugh*. See *Risus sardonicus*.

c. *Comb.*, as ***sardonic-looking*** adj.

1921 D. H. Lawrence *Tortoises* 29 She is.. A little sardonic-looking, as if domesticity had driven her to it.

Hence **sarˈdonicism**, the quality or state of being sardonic; an instance of this; a sardonic remark.

1928 *Daily Express* 6 Jan. 8/3 The old Spartan régime has gone, but there is a relentlessness about the public school system that engenders secret terrors at every turn. It may be the fear of ridicule, or the sardonicisms of a satiric master, or one of a dozen things. **1930** W. de la Mare *On Edge* 197 A corrosive sardonicism had come into her voice. **1940** W. Faulkner *Hamlet* ii. i. 100 He would speculate now and then with cold sardonicism. **1964** *Listener* 29 Oct. 667/2 Because familiarity with the role has made Sean Connery feel able to play Bond more relaxedly, an agreeable sardonicism has been added to the earlier deliberately overdone Superman masculinity.

sardonical (sɑːˈdɒnɪkəl), *a.* [f. SARDONIC + -AL[1].] = SARDONIC *a.*

1859 Thackeray *Virgin.* lxxii, He would.. begin a very pleasant sardonical discourse upon the fall of man.

sardonically (sɑːˈdɒnɪkəlɪ), *adv.* [-LY[2].] In a sardonic manner.

1842–51 Tennyson *E. Morris* 59 'What should one give to light on such a dream?' I ask'd him half-sardonically. **1865** Carlyle *Fredk. Gt.* xii. xi. IV. 247 An enlightened public grinned sardonically, and was not taken in. **1872** Liddon *Elem. Relig.* i. 33 The dreary criticism which makes a solitude in the human spirit and then sardonically calls it peace. **1898** *Westm. Gaz.* 13 Sept. 10/1 Maximilian Harden is making himself sardonically merry over the most appropriate inscription for the sarcophagus of Bismarck.

[**sardonican**, *a.* Error for SARDONIAN *a.*

[**1794** [T. Taylor] *Pausanias' Descr. Greece* III. 149 Homer first, and others after him, call laughter, which conceals some noxious design, Sardonian.] **1837** Richardson, Sardonican [quoting this as 'Sardonican']. Hence in *Cassell's Encycl. Dict.*, *Century Dict.*, Webster (1911).]

sardonyx (ˈsɑːdənɪks). Forms: *α.* **sardonyse**, (**sardony**), 4–7 **sardonix**, (6 *Sc.* **sardonice**), 7– **sardonyx**, (7 *pl.* **sardonyches**); *β.* 4 **sardenyk**, 6 **sardonique**, 7 **sardonic(k**. [a. L. *sardonyx* (pl. *sardonyches*), a. Gr. *σαρδόνυξ* (pl. *σαρδόνυχες*), app. f. *σάρδ-ιος* SARDIUS, SARD *sb.*[1] + *ὄνυξ* ONYX. The *β* forms are ad. the late L. *sardonychus* (late Gr. *σαρδόνυχος*); as this occurs only in apposition with *lapis* stone, it may perh. be an adj.] A variety of onyx or stratified chalcedony having white layers alternating with one or more strata of sard.

13.. *E.E. Allit. P.* A. 1006 þe sardonyse þe fyfþe ston. **1382** Wyclif *Job* xxviii. 16 It shal not be comparisound.. to the most precious sardenyk ston or safyr. **1382** —— *Rev.* xxi. 20 The fyuethe [foundement], sardonix [1388 sardony]. *c* **1520** Nisbet *N.T. in Scots* Rev. xxi. 20 The fijft, sardonice. **1562** Legh *Armorie* 21 b, The precious stone to this colour [Sanguine] annexed, is the Sardonix. **1585** T. Washington tr. *Nicholay's Voy.* iv. xi. 123 b, In this place are also found the Sardonique stones. **1586** Ferne *Blaz. Gentrie* i. 144 The Sardonix, consisting as it were of two rich gemmes, the Sardix, and the Onix: it is blacke in the bottome, red in the middest, and white aboue. **1601** Holland *Pliny* II. 615 The Sardonyx.. was taken for the pretious stone which seemed to be a Cornalline vpon white,.. and both together transparent.. they verily doe name all.. that are not cleare and shew not through them, Blind Sardonyches. **1652** Evelyn *Diary* 1 Aug., Lennier.. shew'd me her [Q. Elizabeth's] head, an intaglia in a rare sardonyx, cut by a famous Italian. *a* **1668** Lassels *Voy. Italy* ii. (1670) 388 A little Vase of the rootes of Emmeraud. An other of Sardonick. A great cup of Agate. **1762–71** H. Walpole *Vertue's Anecd. Paint.* (1786) I. 173 Hillyard.. cut the images of Henry VIII. and his children on a sardonyx. **1860** C. W. King *Ant. Gems* 8 The Sardonyx is defined by Pliny as 'candor in sarda', that is to say, a white opaque layer superimposed upon a red transparent stratum of.. Sard; and no better description can be given of a perfect gem of this species. **1867** A. Billing *Sci. Gems* 11 Should one of the layers [of onyx] be sard, which is of various shades of orange, brown, or brownish red, it is called sardonyx. **1875** Jowett *Plato* (ed. 2) I. 491 Our highly-valued emeralds and sardonyxes.

b. *attrib.*

a **1691** Boyle in T. Birch *Life* B.'s Wks. 1772 I. p. clix, I give and bequeath to my eldest brother, Richard.. a sardonyx seal ring. **1867** A. Billing *Sci. Gems* 68 Variegated brown sardonyx-agates which look somewhat like tortoise-shell. **1901** *Q. Rev.* Oct. 432 The large sardonyx cameos of the Augustan age.

Sardoodledom (sɑːˈduːd(ə)ldəm). [f. blend of the name of Victorien *Sardou* (1831–1908), French dramatist + DOODLE *sb.* + -DOM.] A fanciful word used to describe well-wrought, but trivial or morally objectionable, plays considered collectively; the characteristic milieu in which such work is admired.

1895 G. B. SHAW in *Sat. Rev.* 1 June 725/2 (*heading*) Sardoodledom. **1897** —— in *Ibid.* 17 Apr. 410/2 It is rather a nice point whether Miss Ellen Terry should be forgiven for sailing the Lyceum ship into the shallows of Sardoodledom for the sake of Madame Sans-Gêne. **1931** *Times Lit. Suppl.* 1 Jan. 2/1 The 'cup-and-saucer' comedy of Robertson and what Mr. Shaw christened 'Sardoodledom'..opened a new phase of theatrical history. **1959** *Listener* 30 July 186/3 Sardoodledom is not forgotten. **1960** *Times* 15 Jan. 16/1 We do not want to try to rebut Shaw's criticism of 'Sardoodledom'.

sardye, anglicized form of SARDIUS.

sare, obs. form of SERE *a.*, SORE.

saree: see SARI.

sarell, anglicized form of SERAIL.

saresnet, obs. form of SARSENET.

Saresoun, -syn, obs. forms of SARACEN.

saretree, variant of SARTRY *Obs.*

Sarezin, -zon, obs. forms of SARACEN.

sargasso (sɑːˈgæsəʊ). Forms: 7 sargossa, -o, saragossa, 7–9 sargaso, (8 sargazo), 6– sargasso. [a. Pg. *sargaço*, whence Sp. *sargazo*, F. *sargasse* (mod.L. *Sargassum* as generic name).]

a. = GULF-WEED; also a mass or a species of this. Also *fig.*, esp. in sense 'a confused or stagnant mass'.

1598 W. PHILLIP *Linschoten* I. xcv. 176/1 Then wee entred into the sea, called Sergasso, which is all couered with hearbes... The hearbe is like Samper, but yellow of colour... The Portingalles call it Sargasso, because it is like the herbes that groweth in their welles in Portingall, called Sargasso. **1634** SIR T. HERBERT *Trav.* 19 About the Cape Sargassoes and Trumbaes floate fifty leagues into the Seas. **1687** *New Atlantis* I. 169 The watry Field, Spread with Sargossa. **1688–9** SLOANE *Voy. Eng.* 26 Mar. in *Jamaica* (1725) II. 342 We saw much Saragossa a floating here, called by the Seamen Gulf-weed. **1760–72** tr. *Juan & Ulloa's Voy.* (1772) II. 337 The sea was covered with a kind of weed called Sargasso, which pickled, is by many thought equal to Samphire. **1835–6** [see GULF-WEED]. **1855** MAURY *Phys. Geog.* ii. §132 There is in each ocean a Sargasso into which all drift matter..finds its way. **1871** KINGSLEY *At Last* i, The Sargassos..are a genus of themselves and by themselves.

fig. **1934** DYLAN THOMAS *18 Poems* 12 The dry Sargasso of the tomb Gives up its dead to such a working sea. **1968** A. C. CLARKE *2001: Space Odyssey* xlii. 206 It had swept him across the Galaxy, and dumped him..in this celestial Sargasso. **1976** *Listener* 12 Feb. 182/3, I started the week with a careful schedule and ended in bed with 'flu, lost in a Sargasso of phone-ins, pop, news, avant-garde operas and the reminiscences of David Niven. **1977** *Mystery Writers' Choice* 62, I waited..adrift in a sargasso of conflicting feelings.

b. *attrib.*, as *sargasso bed, weed*; **Sargasso Sea** (see quot. 1855; also *fig.*).

1830 *Philos. Mag.* VIII. 459 In the North Atlantic Ocean, coming from the south, you fall in about the tropic with the Sargasso weeds. **1855** MAURY *Phys. Geogr. Sea* (1859) §13 Midway the Atlantic, in the triangular space between the Azores, Canaries, and the Cape de Verd Islands, is the Sargasso Sea. **1855** KINGSLEY *Westw. Ho!* iii, All around floated the sargasso beds, clogging her bows. **1885** LADY BRASSEY *The Trades* 168 The patches of sargasso weed that floated past. **1961** P. SOLOMON in B. E. Flaherty *Psychophysiol. Aspects Space Flight* III. 275 Deprived of sensory input, the mind is cut adrift and regresses inexorably into that Sargasso Sea of the primary process, where time disappears,..where vivid, multicolored hallucinations swirl and befuddle the senses. **1966** C. H. HAPGOOD *Maps of Anc. Sea Kings* ii. 25 We found ourselves in a veritable Sargasso Sea of uncertainties. **1966** J. RHYS (*title*) The wide Sargasso Sea. **1979** P. O'CONNOR *Into Strong City* I. xix. 68, I was experiencing a severe London pea-soup fog... I swam through an impenetrable ochre sargasso sea.

sargassum (sɑːˈgæsəm). [mod.L. (G. E. Rumpf *Herbarium Amboinense* (1755) VI. tab. 76): see SARGASSO.] **a.** A large floating seaweed of the genus so called, found in masses in warm or temperate seas. Cf. GULF-WEED, SARGASSO.

1905, etc. [see sense b below]. **1951** G. M. PAPENFUSS in G. M. Smith *Man. Phycol.* vii. 119 *Sargassum*..forms immense floating masses in the Sargasso Sea, between the West Indies and the coast of North Africa. **1969** J. M. KINGSBURY *Seaweeds of Cape Cod* 116 The berry-like bladders..serve to identify *Sargassum* or 'gulfweed' as it is sometimes called.

b. sargassum angler, fish, a small toadfish, *Pterophryne histrio*, which lives in clusters of sargassum; **sargassum weed** = sense a above.

1961 *Sargassum angler [see *sargassum weed* below]. **1905** D. S. JORDAN *Guide to Study of Fishes* II. xxxi. 549 (*caption*) *Sargassum-fish. **1928** W. BEEBE *Beneath Tropic Seas* iii. 26 An unexpected performance was suddenly staged in the jar of sargassum fish. **1962** K. F. LAGLER et al. *Ichthyol.* iv. 119 The sargassum fish (*Pterophryne*) and the alga-resembling seadragon..are the most frequently cited examples of the extension of the skin into flaps. **1928** W. BEEBE *Beneath Tropic Seas* iii. 24 On several days great masses of *sargassum weed drifted into the bay. **1961** E. S. HERALD *Living Fishes of World* 283/1 The sargassum angler can make slight changes in its colour pattern to match its background, but seems to be limited to those shades found in the sargassum weed.

sarge (sɑːdʒ). orig. *U.S.* Also **Sarg(e), serg.** Colloq. abbrev. of SERGEANT *sb.* (Freq. used as a term of address.) **a.** *Mil.* = SERGEANT *sb.* 9a. Also *Comb.*

1867 W. L. GOSS *Soldier's Story* 98 You look hungry too, Sarg. *Ibid.* 258 Sarge, the Colonel has got his mad up, and you'll be sent into the stockade. **1913** *Sat. Even. Post* 5 Feb. 6 'Sergeant Tanner?' asked the bartender incredulously. 'The sarge,' replied Kennedy with some satisfaction. **1919** W. H. DOWNING *Digger Dial.* 43 *Sarge* (n.), sergeant. **1929** F. A. POTTLE *Stretchers* (1930) 238 But sarge, I've been out since five without a bite. **1940** PARTRIDGE *S.P.E. Tract* LV. 191 The Regular Army's pre-1914 slang..consisted mainly of words from Hindustani and Arabic..and abbreviations (..*sarge* 'sergeant'). **1958** M. K. JOSEPH *I'll soldier no More* ix. 166 Hey, sarge, there's another bugger out in the middle of the field. **1973** *Jewish Chron.* 19 Jan. 14/2 We are never allowed to forget the grim and earnest purpose behind the farcical square-bashing and sarge-baiting.

b. = SERGEANT *sb.* 10.

1926 *Scribner's Mag.* Aug. 193/2 'Quiet, serg.,' volunteered the desk man. 'Too quiet,' corrected the sergeant. **1934** J. M. CAIN *Postman always rings Twice* x. 115 Just a few minutes, sarge. **1938** G. GREENE *Brighton Rock* III. i. 106 'You aren't pulling my leg, are you?' the sergeant said. 'Not this time, sarge.' **1959** M. GILBERT *Blood & Judgement* i. 15 Garn, Sarge, *this* isn't Guy Fawkes, it's Father Christmas. **1977** 'J. BELL' *Such a Nice Client* xi. 106 'I want you over here,' said Sergeant Thomas... 'Right, sarge,' answered the constable.

sarge, variant of CIERGE.

1544 *Aberdeen Reg.* (1884) I. 206 Ane sarge of new walx.

sargeancie, -ge(au)nt: see SERGEANCY, -ANT.

sargo (ˈsɑːgəʊ). [a. Sp. *sargo*:—L. *sargus*: see SARGUS. Cf. SAR.] **a.** (See quot. 1880.) **b.** *U.S.* (See quot. 1884.)

1880 GÜNTHER *Fishes* 406 Sargus..comprises twenty species; several of them occur in the Mediterranean and the neighbouring parts of the Atlantic, and are popularly called 'Sargo', 'Sar', 'Saragu'. **1884** GOODE, etc. *Nat. Hist. Aquatic Anim.* 400 On the California coast occur two species of this family [Grunts]; one known to the fishermen by the name 'Sargo', *Pristipoma Davidsoni*, is found from San Pedro southward to Cerros Island.

†ˈsargon, ˈsargot. *Obs.* [a. F. †*sargon*, †*sargot*, derivatives of L. *sargus*.] = SARGUS.

1598 SYLVESTER *Du Bartas* II. i. III. *Furies* 70 Th' hidden love that..unites so well Sargons and Goats. **1601** HOLLAND *Pliny* I. 269 The Sargots [F. *les sargots*] haue another trick ..: for he that finds himselfe taken fretteth the line in twaine, whereto the hooke hangeth, against a hard rocke. **1635** SWAN *Spec. M.* (1670) 339 The Sargon..is an adulterous fish, daily changing mates.

Sargonid (ˈsɑːgənɪd), *sb.* and *a.* Also -ide. [f. the Akkadian royal name *Sargon* + *-id*, after SELEUCID, etc.: cf. -ID³.] **A.** *sb.* A member of the Assyrian dynasty founded by Sargon II (ruled 722–705 B.C.), which remained in power until the fall of Assyria in 607 B.C.

1887 Z. A. RAGOZIN *Assyria* ix. 295 (*heading*) The Sargonides. **1913** H. R. HALL *Anc. Hist. Near East* x. 516 Sennacherib was the first Sargonid who no longer went forth to war himself.

B. *adj.* Of, pertaining to, or designating this dynasty.

1913 H. R. HALL *Anc. Hist. Near East* x. 517 (*heading*) Sargonide dynasty. **1925** *Cambr. Anc. Hist.* III. ii. 43 The days of the 'Sargonid' dynasty. *Ibid.* 45 A fanciful genealogy of the Sargonid house.

‖**sargus** (ˈsɑːgəs). [L. = Gr. σάργος.] A fish of the genus *Sargus*, the type of the family *Sparidæ*, the sea-breams.

1591 SYLVESTER *Du Bartas* I. v. 206 Th' adulterous Sargus ..Courting the Shee-Goats on the grassie shore. **1607** TOPSELL *Four-f. Beasts* 260 There is a prettie comparison of a Harlottes loue to a fisherman which putteth vpon him a goats skin with the hornes, to deceiue the Sargus-fish. **1752** J. HILL *Hist. Anim.* 255 Spari... The Sargus. **1844** KITTO *Phys. Hist. Palestine* viii. 416 Three species of Sargus—namely, the Hoarse Sargus, the Common Sargus, and the Ringed Sargus.

sari, saree (ˈsɑːriː). Forms: 8 saurry, 9 sar(r)ie, sahree, sarhi, 9– saree, sari. [Hindī *sāṛhī, sāṛī*.]

1. a. A long wrapping garment of cloth or silk, usually of a bright colour, worn by Hindu women; also, the material of which this is composed.

In use one end is passed several times round the waist to form a kind of petticoat and the remaining end passing across the bosom and left shoulder is thrown over the head.

[**1598** W. PHILLIP *Linschoten* I. xvi. 28/2 They make whole pieces or webbes of this hearbe [of Bengalen]... These webs are named Sarrijn, and it is much vsed and worne in India.] **1785** in Seton-Karr & Sandeman *Sel. fr. Calcutta Gaz.* (1864) I. 90 Her clothes were then taken off, and a red silk covering (a saurry) put upon her. **1800** *Misc. Tracts* in *Asiat. Ann. Reg.* 301/1 From Burhampoor they receive turbans, saries, and other stained goods. **1879** E. ARNOLD *Lt. Asia* VI. (1881) 147 One arm clasping her crimson sari close To wrap the babe. **1895** MRS. B. M. CROKER *Village Tales* (1896) 128 In spite of their fine silk sarees and gold ornaments. **1907** *Blackw. Mag.* Feb. 241/1 Held in a fold of the *sarhi*, they sport with their mother's ear-rings. **1908** [see CHOLI]. **1930** *Aberdeen Press & Jrnl.* 6 May 6, I was struck today by the international character of London. Indians in gay saris, a group of Japanese,..all passed me. **1960** [see CHOLI]. **1969** *Hindu* 3 Aug. 12/4 A petition on behalf of over 4,000 handloom weavers of Salem and other parts of Tamil Nadu was presented to the Rajya Sabha on Tuesday urging the immediate implementation of the order reserving manufacture of coloured sarees for the handloom sector. **1969** *Femina* (Bombay) 26 Dec. 8/4 The piece-de-resistance of the show, a smart zip-up sari, found great favour with the foreigners in the audience. **1971** [see MANIPURI *a.* and *sb.*]. **1971** R. RUSSELL tr. *A. Ahmad's Shore & Wave* i. 14 Love for the dark-skinned maidservants in their grubby sarees. **1976** *Leicester Trader* 24 Nov. 22/1 (Advt.), Also we clean.. dresses, bedspreads, sarees, etc.

‖**b.** 'An embroidered long scarf of gauze or silk.' [Perhaps a misunderstanding of prec. sense.]

1858 in SIMMONDS *Dict. Trade.* **1882** in CAULFEILD & SAWARD *Dict. Needlework.* And in recent Dicts.

2. *attrib.* and *Comb.*

1936 J. FLANNER in *New Yorker* 22 Aug. 65/1 The Hindu hockey team, and its handsome, sari-clad womenfolk. **1955** R. P. JHABVALA *To whom she Will* xiv. 96 Radha..would walk into a sari-shop, because she was so fond of looking at nice silks. **1968** *Guardian* 19 Sept. 7/3 Embroidered sari silks for evening dresses. **1978** 'M. M. KAYE' *Far Pavilions* xxvi. 392 There was little chance of seeing her..save as a sari-shrouded figure on the occasion of her marriage.

Hence **ˈsareed** *a.*, wearing a saree.

1958 E. A. ROBERTSON *Justice of Heart* xv. 212 The sari'd head wagged slower. **1975** O. SELA *Bengali Inheritance* vii. 53 Oval-eyed, smiling sareed girl with skin like brown silk.

sarie: see SERRY *v.*

sarif, obs. form of SERVE.

‖**sarigue** (sarig). Also 7–8 sarigoy, 9 (Dict.) saragoy, 8 CERIGO, -GON. [Fr. (Buffon), a. Pg. *sarigué*, in 16th c. *çarigué, cerigoé, serigoé* (whence the earlier forms); used erron. for Brazilian *sarigueya*, a derivative of *Sarigué*, which is the name of an Indian people.

Several other forms of the word are quoted by Ray *Syn. Quad.*, 1693, Pennant *Hist. Quad.*, 1781, and Smellie tr. *Buffon's Nat. Hist.* 1780–5.]

A South American opossum, *Didelphys opossum*.

1683 TYSON in *Phil. Trans.* XIII. 379, I am apt to think 'twas by removing these Scent-bags rather then taking out the Kidneys; that they made the Sarigoy edible. **1828–32** WEBSTER, *Saragoy*, the opossum of the Molucca Isles. **1847** *Ibid.*, *Sarigue*. [And in later Dicts.]

Sarik, var. SARYK.

sariliche, Sarisine, obs. ff. SORRILY, SARACEN.

Sarin (ˈsɑːrɪn). Also **sarin.** [Ger., of unknown origin.] The name of an odourless organo-phosphorus nerve gas.

1951 *Acta Physiol. Scandinavica* Suppl. No. 90. 106 (*table*) Isopropoxy-methyl-phosphoryl-flouride (sarin). **1967** *New Scientist* 26 Jan. 196/3 At Newport, Indiana, there is a plant making Sarin,..and loading it into rockets, land mines and artillery shells. **1968** *Observer* 16 June 9/1 By the end of the war, three of these gases—compounds of phosphorus—were known in Germany: tabun, sarin and soman. **1978** A. MELVILLE-ROSS *Blindfold* ii. 18 Bad stuff 'Sarin'. Nerve gas containing fluorine and phosphorus... Absorption through the skin..means paralysis and death.

‖**sarinda** (ˈsaːrindaː). Also 9 sarindah. [Hind., dial. var. of *sārangi* SARANGI.] An Indian stringed musical instrument played with a bow (see quots.)

1851 *Illustr. Catal. Gt. Exhib.* IV. 913/2 Musical Instruments... Sarindah or fiddle..from Moorshedabad. **1872** *Catal. Special Exhib. Anc. Musical Instruments* (S. Kensington Mus.) 35 *Sarinda.* A kind of Violin. **1921** H. A. POPLEY *Music of India* vii. 109 The Sārindā is another variety of the sārangī, peculiar to Bengal. **1944** W. APEL *Harvard Dict. Music* 801/1 In India fiddles called *sarinda* have truly fantastic shapes such as only the Indian fancy could have produced. **1964** S. MARCUSE *Musical Instruments* 456/2 *Sārindā*, folk sārangī of India, with thin wooden body of irregular shape, and skin belly covering only the lower part of the body, short neck, 3 gut or hair strings that are bowed. **1969** [see DILRUBA]. **1977** G. WELLS in *Early Music* Apr. 250/2 A sarinda from Northern India.

‖**sarissa** (səˈrɪsə). *Antiq.* Pl. -æ. [Gr. σάρισσα, better σάρῑσα.] A long lance used in the Macedonian phalanx.

1734 tr. *Rollin's Anc. Hist.* (1827) VIII. 69 The sarissæ or long spears. **1856** GROTE *Greece* II. xcii. XII. 77 The sarissa of this cavalry may have been fourteen feet in length.

sark (sɑːk), *sb. Sc.* and *north.* (and occas. *arch.*). Forms: 1 serc, serce, syrce, 2 syric, suric, 3 serc, 3–6 (9 *Sc. local*) serk, (4 scherk), 4–5 serke, 4–7 sarke, 4– sark. [OE. *sęrc*, masc. (also in extended form *serce*, wk. fem.) = ON. *serk-r* (Sw. *särk*, Da. *særk*):—OTeut. type **sarki-z*. Affinities outside Teut. are doubtful: OSl. *sraka* tunic does not correspond phonetically, but some scholars believe it to be adopted from Teut.

The final *k* instead of *ch* is due to the fact that the word has come down only in the northern dialect. The anomalous form *scherk* (quot. 13..) app. proceeds from a southern scribe to whom the word was unknown.]

1. A garment worn next the skin; a shirt or chemise; occas. a nightshirt; also *transf.* a surplice.

In Sc. still the ordinary word for 'shirt'.

Beowulf 1111 Æt þæm ade wæs eþgesyne swat-fah syrce. *a* **1100** *Ags. Voc.* in Wr.-Wülcker 328/12 *Colobium, uel* *interula*, syric. *a* **1200** *Ibid.* 547/25 *Colobi(um)*,.. suric. *a* **1300** *Cursor M.* 17243 For-sak þi serc o silk and line. *Ibid.* 21527 Of he kest al to his serk. **13..** *Coer de L.* 3630 Tyl he have maad al playn werk Off thy clothes of gold, into thy scherk. *c* **1338** R. BRUNNE *Chron.* (1810) 161 Bare in serke & breke Isaac away fled. **1377** LANGL. *P. Pl.* B. v. 66 She shulde vnsowen hir serke and sette þere an heyre To affaiten hire flesshe. *c* **1440** *Gesta Rom.* ix. 24 (Harl. MS.) If it happe me to dye.. for þe in batill.., þat þu sette out my blody serke on a perch afore. **1503** DUNBAR *Thistle & Rose* 46 In serk and mantill [eftir hir] I went In to this garth. **1571** *Satir. Poems Reform.* xxviii. 69 My Steming Sark & Rokket was laid doun, Fra tyme that I hard tell the King was deid. **1572** *Ibid.* xxxiii. 369 Buft brawlit hois, Coit, Dowblet, sark, and scho. **1578** *Inv. R. Wardr.* (1815) 215 Ane hieland syd serk of yallow lyning pasmentit with purpour silk and silver. Foure Inglis sarkes with blak werk. *a* **1634** W. ROW *Contin. J. Row's Hist. Kirk* (Maitl. Cl.) 204 Shee, being in hard labour in chyld-birth, posted away her servant.. to St. Allarit's Chapell.. with her sarke. **1725** RAMSAY *Gent. Sheph.* III. ii, Aneath his oxter is the mark, Scarce ever seen since he first wore a sark. **1790** BURNS *Tam o' Shanter* 153 Had.. Their sarks, instead o' creeshie flannen, Been snaw-white seventeen hunder linnen! *Ibid.* 171 Her cutty sark, o' Paisley harn, That while a lassie she had worn. *a* **1802** in Scott *Minstr. Scott. Bord.* III. 152 Jenny shall wear the hood, Jocky the sark of God. **1809** T. DONALDSON *Poems* 158 The Clerk, Wha croons his notes like morning lark Before the man i' Holy Sark. **1816** SCOTT *Old Mort.* xxiv, And Cuddie at the heels o' him, in ane o' Sergeant Bothwell's laced waistcoats.. and a ruffled sark, like ony lord o' the land. **1849** LONGF. *Building of Ship* 219 Speeding along.. Like a ghost in its snow-white sark. **1870** MORRIS *Earthly Par.* III. IV. 70 A silken sark wrought wondrously In some far land across the sea.

fig. c **1410** *26 Pol. Poems* 40 þey wil.. resceyue þe charge.. To wasche synful soules serkis. **14..** HENRYSON *Garmont Gude Ladeis* iii, Hir sark suld be hir body nixt Of chestetie so quhyt.

Proverbs. ? *a* **1598** D. FERGUSON *Prov.* (1785) 26 Near is the kirtle, but nearer is the sark.

b. Phrase. ***sark alane***, with a sark as the only covering of the body.

1538 *Aberdeen Reg.* (1844) I. 155 Thai ordane the said Besse.. to gang, sark alane, afore the procession. **1786** *Har'st Rig* (1794) 35 Auld *Seonet* comes in sark-a-lane.

†**c.** ***sark of mail***: a shirt of mail. *Obs.*

1515 *Test. Ebor.* (Surtees) V. 62 My sark of mayll and a battell axe.

2. *attrib.*, as ***sark-neck***, ***-skirt***, ***-tail***.

1786 BURNS *Author's Cry* x, There's some *sark-necks I wad draw tight, And tie some hose well. *c* **1440** *Alphabet of Tales* 302 And þis man.. with his *sark skirte, wypid it [*sc.* the leper's nose] als softlye as he cuthe. **1715** RAMSAY *Christ's Kirk Gr.* II. v, Some did their *sark-tails wring. **1721** KELLY *Sc. Prov.* 139 He was wrap'd in his Mother's Sark Tail.. The Scots.. believing that this Usage will make him well-beloved among Women. **1896** CROCKETT *Grey Man* xv, Some fought like Highlandmen in their sark-tails.

sark (sɑːk), *v.* orig. *Sc.* and *north.* [f. SARK *sb.*]

1. *trans.* To furnish with or clothe in a sark.

1483 *Cath. Angl.* 330/2 Serked, *camisiatus, jnterulatus.* **1789** D. DAVIDSON *Th. on Seasons* 15 On's back a coat.. And, underneath well sarket Wi' harn, that day. *a* **1869** C. SPENCE *Fr. Braes of Carse* 166 They told me.. How drink had brought me to sic fash; How I was neither clad nor sarkit.

2. *Building.* To cover (a roof) with wooden boards or sarking felt (see quot. 1771 and SARKING *vbl. sb.*).

1464-5 [see SARKING *vbl. sb.* 1]. **1568-9** *Durham Acc. Rolls* (Surtees) 717 For sarking of the inner howse in the dorture, 7*s.* 9*d.* **1642** in J. Watson *Jedburgh Abbey* (1894) 86 Item for making of the roofe and sarking of it,.. 300 mks. **1771** PENNANT *Tour Scot. in 1769*, 121 The roofs are sarked, *i.e.* covered with inch-and-half deal, sawed into three planks, and then nailed to the joists, on which the slates are pinned. **1961** *Guardian* 21 Feb. 2/7 (Advt.), Other kinds of Sisalkraft will insulate buildings, cure concrete, sark roofs. **1977** *Belfast Tel.* 19 Jan. 24/2 (Advt.), Roofspace partly floored, sarked and felted.

Sarkese (sɑːˈkiːz), *sb.* and *a.* [f. the place-name *Sark* (see below) + -ESE.] **A.** *sb.* **a.** *collect.* Also **Sarkees.** The inhabitants of the Channel Island of Sark. **b.** The language of Sark, a variety of Norman French. **B.** *adj.* Of or pertaining to Sark.

1845 G. W. JAMES *Sark Guide* vii. 78 Most of the Sarkese now manufacture their own lobster pots... The Sarkese certainly love money even to a fault. **1882** D. F. S. *Channel Islands* 77 The kind-hearted Sarkese thought the sentence too severe... The good Sarkese women kept her company. **1928** L. E. HALE tr. *J. L. V. Cachemaille's Island of Sark* 105 This.. harbour.. has a history of its own, interesting to the Sarkese, and also to the tourist. **1935** E. PLATT *Sark as I found It* iv. 29 The Sarkees adore litigation. **1957** *Sunday Times* 10 Feb. 3/8 The debates in the *Parlement* are conducted in Sarkese which is apparently a slightly modernised version of Ancient Norman. **1958** J. W. DAY *Lady Houston* ix. 127 No other race of people but the Sarkese speak it [*sc.* 'Norman-French'] today. **1965** 'J. CHRISTOPHER' *Wrinkle in Skin* vi. 71 He had been one of the Sarkees engaged in the carriage business. **1978** *Times Lit. Suppl.* 26 May 572/5 Some of the Sarkese still reproach her with fraternization with the Germans.

sarkful (ˈsɑːkfʊl). *Sc.* [f. SARK *sb.* + -FUL.] In phrase ***a sarkful of sore bones***, a sore body.

1721 KELLY *Sc. Prov.* 396 I'll give you a Sarkful of sore Bones. **1815** SCOTT *Guy M.* xlv.

sarking (ˈsɑːkɪŋ), *vbl. sb.* orig. *Sc.* and *north.* [f. SARK *v.* and *sb.* + -ING¹.]

1. *Building.* The action of SARK *v.* 2; also *attrib.*, as ***sarking-board***, ***felt***, ***-nail***.

1464-5 *Durham Acc. Rolls* (Surtees) 154 Pro M¹ sarkyngnale, 5*s.* **1597** *Ibid.* 740 For sawinge Sarkyn boordes.. for the churche. **1571** *Burgh Rec. Lanark* (1893) 64 The laith to be all sarking like Sanct Nicolus kirk, and to be rignit with hewin stane. **1610** *Churchw. Acc. Pittington*, etc. (Surtees) 157 For xx yeardes of sarkin bordes. **1636** *Ibid.* 189 Item.. for.. laying the sarking bordes for the leades. **1821** GALT *Ann. Parish* xxvii, I told them of the sarking of the roof, which was as frush as a paddock-stool. **1833** LOUDON *Encycl. Archit.* §983 A course of five-eighths inch deal sarking (boarding), 9 inches broad, to be laid along the eaves. **1844** H. STEPHENS *Bk. Farm* I. 170 All the gables of the external walls.. should.. be entirely filled up to the sarking or tiles, as the case may be. **1882** CHRISTY *Joints used by Builders* 76 As a rule, slates are most likely to keep out the weather when laid on close or open jointed sarking or rough boarding.. with felt between it and the slates. **1885** C. G. W. LOCK *Workshop Receipts* Ser. IV. 40/1 Line the inside of the structure with rough sarking boards. **1894** *Northumbld. Gloss.*, *Sarkin*, the cleading of wood laid on the rafters of a house when a strong and tight roof is required. The slates are laid over the sarkin. **1908** *Laxton's Price Bk.* (ed. 91) 151 Roof linings... Asphalte Sarking Felt. **1926-7** *Army & Navy Stores Catal.* 308/2 Ruberoid Sarking Felt. Rolls contain 24 sq. yds. **1957** *Archit. Rev.* CXXI. 354/4 In addition to these they will show their extensive range of general purpose papers for sarking and damp-proofing. **1958** *N.Z. Timber Jrnl.* July 73/1 *Sarking boards*, close boarding to carry roof tiles, shingles, or slates. Thin boards used as a lining. *Ibid.*, *Sarking felt*, a bituminous underlining placed beneath slates or tiles.

2. A material for the making of 'sarks'. More fully ***sarking-cloth***, ***linen***.

a **1670** SPALDING *Troub. Chas. I* (Bannatyne Cl.) I. 287 Order was given to search the countrie for gray hydes, and gray cloath, and sarking cloath. **1804** STAGG *Misc. Poems* (1808) 142 Wi' monny mair see Meggy Houpe, Wi' her bit sarkin' linen. **1810** *R. H. Cromek's Rem. Nithsd. & Gall. Song* 95 My kimmer and I gade to the fair, Wi' twal' pun' Scots in sarking to ware. **1821** GALT *Ann. Parish* iv, It [the lint] was intended for sarking to ourselves, and sheets and napery.

sarkinite (ˈsɑːkɪnaɪt). *Min.* [Named (Sarkinit) in 1885 by A. Sjögren, f. Gr. σάρκιν-ος fleshy, in allusion to its flesh-red colour and greasy lustre + -ITE.] Arsenate of manganese, of flesh-red or rose-red colour.

1887 *Jrnl. Chem. Soc.* LII. I. 346 Sarkinite, a New Manganese Arsenate. **1890** *Ibid.* LXVIII. II. 715 Crystals of Sarkinite.

sarkless (ˈsɑːklɪs), *a. Sc.* and *north.* [f. SARK *sb.* + -LESS.] Without a sark. Also *transf.*

a **1774** FERGUSSON *Drink Ecl.* Poems (1845) 51 You hae been blythe to hack Your a' upon a sarkless sodger's back. **1882** *Lanc. Gloss.*, *Sarkless*, shirtless.

sarky (ˈsɑːkɪ), *a. colloq.* [f. abbrev. of SARCASTIC *a.* + -Y¹: cf. SARC.] Sarcastic. (Widely used amongst schoolchildren.) Also in *Comb.* Hence **ˈsarkily** *adv.*; **ˈsarkiness.**

1912 D. H. LAWRENCE *Let.* 1 Feb. (1962) I. 97 Why are you so sarky? **1924** H. DE SÉLINCOURT *Cricket Match* iii. 46 He says it sarky-like and sneering. **1930** *Diary of Public School Girl* 76 Made some currant buns. Bob very sarky about them. **1949** E. TAYLOR *Wreath of Roses* vii. 107 She's funny with Ernie, very sarky sometimes the way she answers him back. **1958** C. WATSON *Coffin, scarcely Used* iii. 25 The bland and (he had heard) 'sarky' inspector. **1965** *New Statesman* 30 July 163/1 John's saturnine profile, George's sarkiness, Paul's ageing chorister naughtiness and Ringo's deadpan outsider appeal are well brought out by David Watkin's restless camera. **1967** M. WADDELL *Otley Pursued* xv. 139 'Eating it would have been bad for your digestion, I suppose,' she said sarkily. **1977** 'J. BELL' *Such Nice Client* xvi. 161 You needn't be sarky, I've never refused you.

sarlac (ˈsɑːlæk). Also **sarlik, sarlyk.** [Calmuck *sarluk*, cited by Gmelin in *Novi Comm. Acad. Sci. Petrop.* (1760) V. 341.] = YAK.

1781 PENNANT *Hist. Quad.* I. 23 Sarlyk. **1828-32** WEBSTER, *Sarlac.* **1852** J. E. GRAY *Catal. Mammalia Brit. Mus.* III. 40 *Poephagus grunniens.* The Yac or Sarlyk. **1864** WEBSTER (citing *Baird*). In recent Dicts.

Sar-Major (sɑːˈmeɪdʒə(r)). Also **Sarmajor**, etc. and with small initial. Mil. colloq. abbrev. of SERGEANT-MAJOR 2. (Freq. used as a term of address.) Cf. SARGE; SARN'T.

1919 W. H. DOWNING *Digger Dial.* 43 *Sarmajor*, Sergeant-major. **1958** P. SCOTT *Mark of Warrior* I. 26 Thank you, Sar-Major. I congratulate you on your staff. **1969** D. CLARK *Nobody's Perfect* iii. 109 There's some.. think because a man's been a sar' major he'll want to turn the place into a training depot. **1974** P. MCCUTCHAN *Call for Simon Shard* i. 6 What's up, Sar-Major?

‖**sarmale** (sarˈmale), *sb. pl.* Also **sarmalas** and in sing. **sarmala.** [Romanian.] A Romanian dish of forcemeat and other ingredients wrapped in leaves, esp. cabbage or vine leaves.

1945 A. L. SIMON *Conc. Encycl. Gastron.* VII. 107/2 *Sarmalas.* Rub a little garlic on some raw beef and mince the beef with a little ham, a scrap of onion, parsley and other seasonings. Dip some spinach or young vine leaves in hot water and roll up the mince in them... Braise very slowly. **1958** W. BICKEL tr. *Hering's Dict. Classical & Mod. Cookery* 509 *Sarmale*, Saurkraut Rolls: ground beef and pork mixed with boiled rice, seasoned with garlic, salt, pepper and finely chopped onions, wrapped in leaves of cabbage pickled in whole heads and rolled together. **1969** *Listener* 2 Jan. 31/1 Local dishes include sarmale (meat and rice in pickled cabbage leaves). **1970** 'M. UNDERWOOD' *Silent Liars* II. xii. 131 First we have mamaliguta... Then Sarmale which are meat balls in cabbage leaves.

Sarmatian (sɑːˈmeɪʃən), *a.* and *sb.* [f. L. *Sarmatia* the land of the *Sarmatæ* (Gr. Σαρμάται, also Σαυρομάται, whence the form SAUROMATIAN).

In mod. Latin *Sarmatia* has been extensively used for Poland: hence occas. in English poetry, e.g.

1799 CAMPBELL *Pleas. Hope* I. 376 Sarmatia fell, unwept, without a crime.]

A. *adj.* **a.** Of or belonging to the region north of the Black Sea, anciently known as Sarmatia, now included in the U.S.S.R.

1613 PURCHAS *Pilgrimage* (1614) 394 Ptolemey.. confineth Sarmatia Europæa with the Sarmatian Ocean. **1800** SHAW *Gen. Zool.* I. II. 430 Sarmatian Weesel, *Viverra Sarmatica.* **1841** ALISON *Hist. Europe* (1847) IX. 187 [Vienna was] anciently the frontier station of the Roman empire upon the Sarmatian wilds.

b. *Geol.* = SARMATIC b.

1882 GEIKIE *Text-Bk. Geol.* 867 Sarmatian or Cerithium Stage. *Ibid.*, The Sarmatian stage is characterized by the prodigious number of individuals of a comparatively small number of species of shells.

B. *sb.* **a.** One of a nomadic people formerly inhabiting Sarmatia.

1613 PURCHAS *Pilgrimage* (1614) 393 Of the Scythians, Sarmatians, and Seres. **1671** MILTON *P.R.* IV. 78. **1771** ROBERTSON *Hist. Amer.* I. (1851) I. 22 The wandering tribes, which they called by the general name of Sarmatians or Scythians. **1886** *Encycl. Brit.* XXI. 311/1 Scythians and Sarmatians spoke almost the same language.

b. The language of the Sarmatians, known only from Greek inscriptions in the southern U.S.S.R., and now regarded as a member of the Iranian group.

1922 O. JESPERSEN tr. R. Rask in *Language* ii. 39, I divide our family of languages in this way: the Indian.. Iranic.. Thracian.. Sarmatian (Lettic.. and Slavonic),.. Gothic.. and Keltic. **1939** L. H. GRAY *Foundations of Lang.* 320 Old Sakian.. and Old Sarmatian are preserved only in a few proper names and glosses. **1972** W. B. LOCKWOOD *Panorama of Indo-Europ. Lang.* 235 The exiguous records of the Median language are of the same character as those of Scythian and Sarmatian.

Sarmatic (sɑːˈmætɪk), *a.* [Formed as prec. + -IC.] = SARMATIAN *a.*; in quot. 1723 = Polish.

Sarmatic polecat, the Mottled Polecat, *Putorius sarmaticus.* (In recent Dicts.: cf. *Sarmatian weasel.*)

1723 MATHER *Vind. Bible* 402 In Poland.. when the priest was about to pronounce the words of the Gospel at the altar, the noblemen drew their swords in part out of the scabbards..: a Sarmatick sacrament.

b. *Geol.* (See quot.)

1874 *Geol. Mag.* July 325 Newer Tertiary beds—the three stages of the Vienna Tertiaries occur, the Marine, the Sarmatic, and the Congeria beds, but they are not always separately mapped.

sarment (ˈsɑːmənt). Now *rare* (*Bot.*). [ad. L. *sarmentum*, chiefly in pl., twigs lopped off, brushwood, f. *sarpĕre* to prune, trim (trees, branches). Cf. F. *sarment* shoot of vine, woody climbing stem.] A twig, †a cutting of a tree.

1398 TREVISA *Barth. De P.R.* XIX. xxxvi. (1495) 879 Cerusa.. comyth of vapour of stronge vyneygre effusyd and shedde on thynne plates of leed and layed vpon whyte Sarmentes. *c* **1440** *Pallad. on Husb.* IV. 33 He.. nygh the roote ingraffeth his sarment. *Ibid.* XII. 356. **1657** *Physical Dict.*, *Sarments*, twigs of trees. **1766** SMOLLETT *Trav.* 176 [For lighting fires] the people of these countries use the sarments or cuttings of the vines. **1837** GRAY *First Less. Bot.* Gloss., *Sarmentaceous*, bearing long and flexible twigs (*sarments*), either spreading or procumbent.

sarmentaceous (sɑːmənˈteɪʃəs), *a.* [f. L. *sarment-um*: see SARMENT and -ACEOUS.] = SARMENTOSE.

1830 LINDLEY *Nat. Syst. Bot.* 32 [The Cocculus tribe.] Shrubs, with a.. sarmentaceous habit. **1831** MACGILLIVRAY tr. *Richard's Elem. Bot.* 470 This family is composed of sarmentaceous and climbing shrubs.

sarmentiferous (ˌsɑːmənˈtɪfərəs), *a.* [f. mod.L. *sarmentifer-us*, f. *sarmentum*: see SARMENT and -FEROUS.] = SARMENTOSE.

1858 in Mayne *Expos. Lex.* **1900** B. D. JACKSON *Gloss. Bot. Terms.*

†**sarmenˈtitious**, *a. Obs.*⁻⁰ [a. L. *sarmentītius*, *-tīcius*, f. *sarmentum*: see SARMENT and -ITIOUS.] (See quot.)

1656 BLOUNT *Glossogr.*, *Sarmentitious*, of or belonging to twigs or branches.

sarmentose (sɑːmənˈtəʊs), *a. Bot.* [ad. L. *sarmentōs-us*, f. *sarmentum*: see SARMENT and -OSE. Cf. OF. *sarmenteux.*] (See quot. 1863.)

1760 J. LEE *Introd. Bot.* III. iv. (1776) 181 Sarmentose; when they [*sc.* stems] are Repent and Subnude. **1783** JUSTAMOND tr. *Raynal's Hist. Indies* III. 341 It's stem.. is.. knotty at intervals, and sarmentose, as that of the vine. **1863** BENTHAM *Flora Austral.* I. Introd. 5 Stems are.. sarmentose, when the branches of a woody stem are long and weak, although scarcely climbing. **1870** HOOKER *Stud. Flora* 108 Creeping herbs or sarmentose shrubs.

sarmentous (sɑːˈmɛntəs), *a.* [ad. L. *sarmentōs-us*: see prec. and -OUS.] = prec.

1721 BAILEY, *Sarmentous*, twiggy or branching. **1753** CHAMBERS *Cycl. Supp.* s.v. *Stalk*, Creeping, or sarmentous stalk, that which emits roots as it runs along. **1756** P. BROWNE *Jamaica* 327 The large sarmentous Satyrium with mottled flowers. **1883** *Century Mag.* XXVI. 354 It is of sarmentous growth.

sarmientite (sɑːmiːˈɛntaɪt). *Min.* [f. the name of Domingo Faustino *Sarmiento* (1811–88), Argentinian educator and statesman + -ITE[1].] A monoclinic hydrated basic arsenate and sulphate of ferric iron, $Fe_2(AsO_4)(SO_4)(OH).5H_2O$, found as pale yellow-orange microcrystalline nodules.

1941 ANGELELLI & GORDON in *Notulae Naturae* (Acad. Nat. Sci. Philadelphia) 16 Sept. 1 (*heading*) Sarmientite, a new mineral from Argentina. **1941** *Science* 26 Sept. (Suppl.) 9/1 Called sarmientite.., the new mineral is found in fair-sized nodules of great purity, of a pale yellow-orange color, in iron sulfate deposits of the Santa Elena mine. **1968** *Amer. Mineralogist* LIII. 2081 When heated at 300° C for one hour sarmientite yields a buff colored product, amorphous to X-rays.

sarmon(d, -one, -oun, etc.: see SERMON.

sarnes, obs. form of SORENESS.

sarnie (ˈsɑːniː). *slang.* Also **sarney.** [Prob. f. *sarn-*, repr. colloq. or (north.) dial. pronunc. of initial element of SANDWICH *sb.*[2] + -Y[6], -IE.] = SANDWICH *sb.*[2] 1. Freq. in *pl.*

1961 PARTRIDGE *Dict. Slang* Suppl. 1259/1 *Sarnies*, sandwiches. **1966** F. SHAW et al. *Lern Yerself Scouse* 39 *Sarneys, abnabs*, sandwiches. **1973** *Observer* 22 Apr. 27/5 Most people clamour for tea and sarnies within an hour, but I'm funny where dope's concerned. **1980** *Times* 11 Sept. 8/1 Questions like the protein content of bacon butties.. and the vitamin rating of corned beef sarnies.

Sarn't (sɑːnt). Also **Sarnt, Sar'nt,** etc. and with small initial. Mil. colloq. abbrev. of SERGEANT *sb.* 9 a. (Freq. used as a term of address.) Also **Sarn't-major** = SERGEANT-MAJOR 2. Cf. SAR-MAJOR.

1930 BROPHY & PARTRIDGE *Songs & Slang* 159 *Sarnt*, a smart and soldierly pronunciation of sergeant. Only used before the N.C.O.'s surname, e.g. 'Sarnt Smith', but 'Here's the Sergeant'. Also in *Sarnt-Major*, but here it could be used without the surname. **1945** *Gen* 30 June 50/1 An erb would turn up from no-where, come up to the sarnt and 'Flight Sarnt So-and-So's compliments, Sarnt, and can A. C. Actor be released from polo practice'. **1946** [see PEE *v.*[2] 2 b]. **1959** I. JEFFERIES *Thirteen Days* i. 21 'Ah, Sar'nt,' he said, nodding to my salute. **1972** G. BELL *Villains Galore* vii. 85 'Get out of there. Sarn't major...' They got out and were searched. The sergeant-major was thorough. **1972** F. DURBRIDGE *Bat out of Hell* v. 157 Let me put you in the picture, Sar'nt. **1978** R. MARK *Office of Constable* iii. 39 A bugler whose lip split whilst blowing the single-note half-hour call provoked the falsetto scream, 'Sarn't major... Take his name for idle blowing of the 'orn.'

‖**sarod** (sæˈrəʊd). Also **saroda, sarode,** etc. [Hindi.] An Indian stringed musical instrument of Persian origin, variously bowed or plucked. Also *attrib.* and *Comb.*

1865 *Proc. R. Irish Acad.* IX. I. 115 *Sarrooda*, may be called the tenor or second fiddle... The *sarrooda* is.. powerful but.. difficult of execution; and it combines the effect of a guitar.. and the violin. **1898** B. A. PINGLE *Indian Music* (ed. 2) ii. 58 On the.. Saroda.. the limit of a Ghasita is not fixed. **1921** H. A. POPLEY *Music of India* vii. 109 The *Sāroda* or *Sarrawat* is a sārangi played with the plectrum instead of the bow. **1957** *New Oxf. Hist. Music* I. iv. 224 The *sarod*, played with a plectrum held between the fingers, has no frets. **1961** *Observer* 26 Nov. 28/1 Two sarod recitals. Srimati Sharan Rani. Foremost woman sarod player, acc. by Chatur Lal (tabla). **1961** *Guardian* 8 Dec. 10/6 Sharan Rani, the famous Indian sarode player, was.. in London today. **1975** R. P. JHABVALA *Heat & Dust* 96 They had a tape playing of sarod music.

†**sarole-man.** *Obs.* (See quot. Cf. SAROSEL.)

1662 MERRETT *Neri's Art of Glass* 244 These Glasses are put into Iron pans.. call'd Fraches, which by degrees are drawn by the Sarole man all along the Leer,.. that the Glasses may cool *Gradatim*.

‖**saron** (ˈsɑːrɒn). [Javanese.] An Indonesian musical instrument, normally having seven bronze bars which are struck with a stick.

1817 T. S. RAFFLES *Hist. Java* I. viii. 470 The *sáron*.., the *démong*.., and *selántam*.., are *staccátos* of metallic bars, and a sort of bells placed on a frame. They contain a regular diatonic scale, and nearly two octaves. **1940** C. SACHS *Hist. Mus. Instruments* (1942) xii. 239 The Javanese *saron* cannot have been constructed much earlier than 900 A.D. The modern saron has a wooden resonance box which frequently is carved in the shape of a crouching dragon... Sarons are constructed in four main sizes an octave apart. **1961** [see *metallophone* s.v. METALLO-]. **1964** S. MARCUSE *Mus. Instruments* 457/1 *Saron*, metallophone of Bali and Java, first depicted at Borobudur (*ca.* 800). In modern sarons the bars are set above a wooden trough resonator.

sarong (səˈrɒŋ). [Malay *sārung*, prob. from some mod. form of Skr. *sāranga* variegated.]

1. a. The Malay national garment, resembling a skirt, which consists of a long strip of (often striped or brightly-coloured) cloth worn round the waist and sometimes the chest by both sexes. (Its use is not restricted to Malaysia.)

1834 G. BENNETT *Wand. N.S.W.*, etc. II. 217 He was attired in a dirty sarong around his waist, and a loose baju or jacket. **1895** SWETTENHAM *Malay Sk.* 172 The Sārong is the Malay national garment, a sort of skirt, usually in tartan, worn by men and women alike. **1911** *Encycl. Brit.* XVII. 483/1 The silk is imported raw and is re-exported in the form of Malay clothing (*sarongs*) of patterns and quality which are widely celebrated. **1923** D. H. LAWRENCE *Kangaroo* i. 6 Somers had.. opened the bags, so she fished out an Indian sarong of purplish shot colour, to try how it would look across the table. **1953** G. M. DURRELL *Overloaded Ark* ix. 166 Here he removed his sarong and proceeded to bathe. **1965** R. MCKIE *Company of Animals* iv. 77 They.. pulled up their checked sarongs to spit between their crossed legs. **1971** *Sun* (Colombo) 20 Sept. 5/2 When it comes to crossing a stream groin deep the man in sarong has an advantage over the one in long trousers.

b. *attrib.* and *Comb.*

1913 L. WOOLF *Village in Jungle* vii. 193 In the roof between the thatch he found the two sarong cloths. **1944** *Film Star Parade*, Dorothy Lamour... Paramount tested her for the leading part in 'Jungle Princess' and it was thus that she first became the 'sarong girl'. **1972** M. SHEPPARD *Taman Indera* 40 Thin cut out panels with another sarong design were fitted into the end wall at the same level. **1979** W. H. CANAWAY *Solid Gold Buddha* xiii. 95 Both men wore sarong-like lower garments.

‖**2.** (See quot.)

1858 SIMMONDS *Dict. Trade, Sarong*,.. a woven or printed fabric imported into the Dutch ports of the Eastern archipelago.

Hence **saˈronged** *a.*, wearing or attired in a sarong.

1934 R. V. C. BODLEY *Jap. Omelette* iii. 19 The good-natured smile of the saronged Malays and their cousins the Sudanese and Madoerese concealed no sinister thoughts. **1962** *Punch* 18 July 106/1 We barely have time to settle down from the last lot of celluloid raptures enacted beneath our palms when some other super-colossal unit arrives to shoot further bouts of saronged amour.

Saronic (səˈrɒnɪk), *a.* [ad.L. *Saronicus*, Gr. Σαρωνικὸς.] Of, pertaining to or designating the *Saronic Gulf*, a part of the Aegean Sea between Attica and the Peloponnese. Also † **Saˈronian** *a.*

1601 HOLLAND tr. *Pliny's Nat. Hist.* I. IV. iv. 73 The one side thereof is called the Corinthian gulfe, the other, the Saronian. **1845** *Encycl. Metrop.* XIX. 725/1 To the Myrtoan Sea belonged the deep Saronic Gulf, (Σαρωνικὸς). **1890** J. G. FRAZER *Golden Bough* I. i. 6 Hippolytus.. had been killed by his horses on the sea-shore of the Saronic Gulf. **1956** A. TOYNBEE *Historian's Approach to Relig.* I. 44 The pinnacle of Acrocorinthus a stone's throw away, just across the Saronic gulf. **1977** *Times* 11 June 11/3 Spetses.. one of the Saronic islands.

‖**saros** (ˈsɛərɒs). [Gr. σάρος or σαρός (Berossos), a. Assyro-Babylonian *šār(u).*]

1. *Antiq.* The Babylonian name for the number 3600, and hence for a period of 3600 years.

The notion expressed in quot. 1662, that the saros consisted of 3600 *days*, is due to the desire to rationalize the incredible statements of Berossos with regard to the lengths of the reigns of the antediluvian kings of Babylon. Other expedients for the same purpose were adopted by early writers on chronology.

1613 PURCHAS *Pilgrimage* (1614) 54 Sarus with them is three thousand sixe hundred yeares. **1662** STILLINGFL. *Orig. Sacræ* I. v. §4. 80 The learned Monks, Panodorus and Anianus,.. make a Saros to contain 120. months of 30. dayes a piece.

2. *Astr.* Adopted by modern astronomers as the name of the cycle of 18 years and 10⅔ days, in which solar and lunar eclipses repeat themselves.

This use is founded on the statement of Suidas (app. due to some mistake) that the length of the saros was 18½ years.

1812 WOODHOUSE *Astron.* xxxv. 353 The period of 223 lunations, called by the Chaldean Astronomers, the Saros. **1868** LOCKYER *Elem. Astron.* iii. §18 (1879) 102 This period of 18 years 10 days is a cycle of the Moon, known to the ancient Chaldeans and Greeks under the name of Saros.

†**sarosel.** *Glass-making. Obs.* (See quot.)

1662 MERRETT *Neri's Art of Glass* 244 The mouth thereof [the leer] enters into a room, where the Glasses are taken out and set. This room they call the Sarosel, and the Sarole-men those who draw the Fraches along the Leer.

Sarouk (sæˈruːk). Also **Saruk.** The name of a village near Arak in Iran, used *attrib.* or *absol.* to designate various types of rug made there.

1900 J. K. MUMFORD *Oriental Rugs* xi. 204 Persian magnates.. never demur at the loose colours which are the only drawback to the Saruks. **1913** W. A. HAWLEY *Oriental Rugs* ix. 126 Probably not one in a score.. of the Sarouks now offered for sale in this country was woven there. **1920** [see KASHAN]. **1931** A. U. DILLEY *Oriental Rugs & Carpets* iv. 121 The best Saruks are now all woven in Sultanabad. **1962** C. W. JACOBSEN *Oriental Rugs* iii. 32 In the City of Arak.. and in the surrounding villages, a good many thousand Sarouks have been woven each year, especially for the American market. *Ibid.* II. 281 The early Sarouks were very fine and short pile rugs... No large Sarouks were made until about the turn of the century. **1975** 'E. LATHEN' *By Hook or by Crook* x. 97 A Sarouk, gleaming on the wall like a Rembrandt. **1977** *Times* 10 Sept 14/6 A Saruk carpet of about 1930 fetched £2,100 in Sotheby's sale.. yesterday.

sarp, obs. form of SHARP.

‖**sarpanch** (ˈsarpantʃ). [Hindi-Urdu, = head arbitrator, foreman of a jury or council.] In India: the head of a panchayat or village council.

1963 F. G. BAILEY *Politics & Social Change* I. i. 55 In order to run the panchayat one of the.. members is selected as head and another as his assistant. The head is called the 'Sarpanch' and his assistant is the 'Naib Sarpanch'. **1971** *Hindustan Times* (New Delhi) 7 Apr. 12/4 They went around with Girdhari Lal, the village sarpanch. **1976** D. HIRO *Inside India Today* 50 Forty to fifty panchayats are banded together to form a panchayat samiti (covering a population of 30,000 to 100,000). Its membership consists of the sarpanches of the constituent panchayats and ten co-opted members.

†**sarp-cloth.** *Obs.* Also 6 **serpe-cloth.** [Shortened f. SARPLIER + CLOTH. Cf. the Sc. forms *sarplaith, sarpleth*, under SARPLIER.] = SARPLIER.

1580 HOLLYBAND *Treas. Fr. Tong, Serpeilliére, ou serpillére*, a serpe-cloth. **1611** COTGR., *Serpillere*, a Sarpler, or Sarp-cloth, a piece of course Canuas to packe vp things in. **1726** *Dict. Rust.* (ed. 3), Sarpliar or Sarp-cloth.

†**sarpe**[1]. *Obs.* [a. OF. *sarpe* (mod.F. *serpe*), app. f. L. *sarpĕre* to prune.] A pruning hook.

1388 WYCLIF *1 Sam.* xiii. 20 That ech man schulde scharpe his schar, and picoise, and ax, and sarpe [1382 purgyng hook]. *Ibid., Isa.* vii. 25 And alle hillis that schulen be purgid with a sarpe [1382 wode bil]. **1474** CAXTON *Chesse* III. v. eij, He ought to haue on his gyrdel a sarpe or crokyd hachet for to cutte of the superfluytees of the vignes.

†**sarpe**[2]. *Obs.* Also **sarp, serpe.** [Of obscure origin.] A collar, neck-ring of gold or silver.

1429 *Sc. Acts Jas. I* (1814) II. 18/1 Ande at nane vthir weir broudry.. bot aray þaim.. in all vthir honest aray as serpis beltis vches & chenzeis. **1438** *E.E. Wills* (1882) 110 Item to Robert Greyndoor,.. my Serpe of siluer and my cheyne of goold. **1456** SIR G. HAYE *Law Arms* (S.T.S.) 46 He.. tuke .. a grete wreth of golde, callit a sarp be sum men, and put it about his hals. *c* **1460** FORTESCUE *Abs. & Lim. Mon.* vii. (1885) 125 Rich stones, serpes, bauderikes, and oþer juels. **1470–85** MALORY *Arthur* XX. xiv. 822 Alle they were arayed in grene veluet with sarpys of gold about their quarters. *c* **1485** in *Rutland Papers* (Camden) 4 The King.. arraied in a doblet of gren.., a long goune of purpur velwet,.. with a riche sarpe and garter. **1488** *Acc. Ld. High Treas. Scotl.* (1877) I. 86 Memorandum:—fund in a blac coffre.. It. the first, the grete sarpe of gold contenand xxv schaiffis with the fedder betuix.

sarpego, sarpent: see SERPIGO, SERPENT.

sarplier (ˈsɑːplɪə(r)). Forms: 4–7 **sarpler,** (4 **sarpuler**), 5 **sarpeler(e,** (**sarplar, -pelar, -pliar**), 6– **sarplier;** *Sc.* 5 **sarplare, -air, sarpleth,** 7 **serplaith.** [a. AF. *sarpler* (*Rolls of Parlt.* I. 413, 1321–2), OF. *sarpillere* (mod.F. *serpillière* packing cloth) = Pr. *sarpelheira*, Cat. *sarpallera, xarpallera*, Sp. *arpillera*, Pg. *sarapilheira*.

Littré suggests that the word is a derivative (with suffix *-ˈaria*: see -ER[2] 2) of late L. *xērampelinus* (med.L. corruptly *xeropellinus, serampelinus, serapellinus*) a. Gr. ξηραμπέλινος, of the colour of withered vine-leaves, f. ξηρός dry, withered + ἄμπελος vine. But this derivation has been contested by later philologists. Cf. Fr. dial. (16th c.) *serpol* bride's trousseau. MDu. had *sarpelier, serplier*, pack of wool (also *sarpeel*).]

†**1.** A large sack of coarse canvas for wool; a sack or bale of wool containing eighty tods; also used as a measure of quantity for wool.

[**1353–4** *Durham Acc. Rolls* (Surtees) 554 Et in 4 sarplers novis pro lanis cariandis.] *c* **1374** CHAUCER *Boeth.* I. pr. iii. 6 (Camb. MS.) They ben ententyf abowte sarpuleris or sachels vnprofitable for to taken [orig. *circa diripiendas inutiles sarcinulas occupantur*]. *c* **1380** *Sir Ferumb.* 4371 Hyre sarplers dud he with hay be fild, & bonde hem to hure sadels gyld. **1425** *Rolls of Parlt.* IV. 290/1 The which Cokett contenes the hool nombre of sarplers. *c* **1430** LYDG. *Min. Poems* (Percy Soc.) 204 Though many a robe hath be shente On hire sarpelere and on hire sak. **1436** *Sc. Acts Jas. I* (1814) II. 23/2 Gudis þat aw na custum or þat aw custum eftir þe fraucht of þe serplaith þat is to say it at payis as a serplaith in fraucht. *c* **1440** LYDG. *Hors, Shepe & G.* 415 The.. Duke of Burgon Cam befor Caleis with Flemynges nat a fewe, Which yaff the sakkis & sarpleres of the toun To Gaunt & Brugis his fredam for to shewe. *a* **1513** FABYAN *Chron.* VII. (1811) 395 The Kyng.. commaunded a new subsydie to be leuyed vpon all yᵉ sarplers of wolle goynge out of Englande. **1581** J. BELL *Haddon's Answ. Osor.* 51 b, You besturre yourselfe: & packe and stuffe together a whole sarpler full of Tullies owne sentences. **1609** SKENE *Reg. Maj., Treat.* 141 In Merchandice na Merchant sall passe over the sea, except he haue thrie Serplaiths of wooll, of hiw awin proper gudes.

†**2.** A wrapper of sackcloth (or other coarse material) for packing merchandise. *Obs.*

1565 COOPER *Thesaurus, Segestre*, a sarplier: a thyng to packe vp merchandice in. **1601** HOLLAND *Pliny* I. 392 It serued as wast Paper for sarplers to wrap and packe vp wares in. **1653** URQUHART *Rabelais* Prol. (Rtldg.) 18 His Orations did smell like the sarpler, or wrapper of a foul.. oil vessel. **1686** tr. *Chardin's Trav. Persia* I. 74 The other [tent] is cover'd with a great Sarpler of Wooll, for their Cattel and Horses. **1725** BRADLEY *Fam. Dict.* s.v. *Ointment*, If.. the Fire should catch, you must have a Covering or Sarplier ready, which you have dipt in Water and well wrung. **1847** HALLIWELL, *Sarpelere*, a coarse packcloth made of hemp. *Glouc.*

3. A large sack into which hops are gathered and carried to the kiln. *local.*

1893 C. WHITEHEAD *Hop Cultiv.* 36 When picked, the hops are measured.. into 'pokes', 'greenbags', or sacks, holding 10 bushels. *Note.* In Hampshire and Surrey these sacks are called 'sarpliers', and hold fourteen bushels.

sarplys, obs. pl. of SURPLICE.

sarpo (ˈsɑːpəʊ). Also 8 **sarpoe,** 9 **sapo.** [a. Sp. *sapo*, lit. 'large toad'.] (See quots.)

1753 CHAMBERS *Cycl. Supp., Sarpoe*, a name given to the fish called by authors *salpa*. **1884** GOODE, etc. *Nat. Hist. Aquatic Anim.* 251 A form [of the Toad-fish] found only in the Gulf, *Batrachus pardus*.. is known to the fishermen as the 'Sarpo' and the 'Sea-robin'. **1891** *Century Dict., Sapo*, the toad-fish, *Batrachus tau*.

sarpuler, Sarra, obs. ff. SARPLIER, SAHARA.

‖**Sarracenia** (særəˈsiːnɪə). *Bot.* Also 8 **sarracena, -sena.** [mod.L.; orig. *Sarracēna* (Tournefort 1700, after Dr. D. Sarrazin of

Quebec who sent him the plant).] A genus of insectivorous plants, the type of the N.O. *Sarraceniaceæ*, to which belong many of the plants popularly known as *pitcher-plants*. Hence **sarra'ceniad**, Lindley's name for a plant of this Order (*Veg. Kingd.* 1846, p. 429).

1786 ABERCROMBIE *Arrangem.* 66 in *Gard. Assist.*, *Sarracenia*, or side-saddle flower. **1796** C. MARSHALL *Gardening* xix. (1813) 370 *Sarrasena* is a native of the bogs of North America. *Ibid.* 360 *Sarracena*, or side-saddle flower. **1879** LUBBOCK *Sci. Lect.* i. 5 Sarracenia. In this genus some of the leaves are in the form of a pitcher. **1884** *Pall Mall G.* 14 July 5/1 Great tropical carnivores like the beautiful Sarracenias.

sarrail: see SERAIL.

sarralia: see SERAGLIO.

†**'sarraly**, *adv. Obs.* Forms: 4 **sarreliche, sarrely, sarrilich, sarraly**. [f. **sarree* (a. F. *serré* in close order, pa. pple. of *serrer* to shut tightly, lock:—popular L. **serrāre*, L. *serāre*, f. *sera* bolt, lock) + -LY. Cf. SERRY *v.*] In close order or array, closely.

c **1330** *Arth. & Merl.* 6047 (Kölbing) Cleodalis Stode on fot, & mani of his Aboute him stode sarreliche. *Ibid.* 5279, 7846, 8044. *c* **1330** R. BRUNNE *Chron. Wace* (Rolls) 13536 Doun wyþ þe hil þey toke þe weye Al sarrely in to þe valeye. **13..** *K. Alis.* 2127 (Bodl. MS.), þise brouȝtten fourty þousynde And comen sarrilich byhynde. **1375** BARBOUR *Bruce* VIII. 222 The kyng..Saw first cumand thair first eschele Arrait sarraly and weill.

‖**sarrasin** ('særəzın). In quots. **sar(r)azin, sarassin.** [a. F. *sarrasin* (16th c.), for *blé sarrasin* 'Saracen wheat'.] Buckwheat.

1621 LODGE *Summary Du Bartas* I. 135 That graine, which we call Sarazin Wheate, or Turky Wheate. [**1687** Sarazin corn: see SARACEN 3.] **1840** T. A. TROLLOPE *Summer in Britt.* I. 308 A small quantity of black bread, made of sarazin. **1865** *Pall Mall G.* 30 Aug. 3/2 The fields of sainfoin and sarassin. **1888** *19th Cent.* June 836 The Russian peasant will not always sell his wheat and live on sarrazin and rye.

Sarrasin, sarrature: see SARACEN, SERRATURE.

†**sarray**, *adv. Sc. Obs. rare*$^{-1}$. [a. F. *serré*: see SARRALY *adv.*] = SARRALY *adv.*

1375 BARBOUR *Bruce* VIII. 296 And the formast of his menȝe Enbraist vith that thar scheldis braid And richt sarray togidder raid.

Sarrazin, sarre, obs. ff. SARACEN, SORE.

sarreliche, -ly, var. ff. SARRALY *adv. Obs.*

sarreverence: see SIR-REVERENCE.

sarrie, sarrilich: see SERRY *v.*, SARRALY *adv.*

†**sa'rrition.** *Obs. rare.* [ad. L. *sarrītiōn-em*, n. of action f. *sarrīre* to hoe, weed.] The action of hoeing or stirring the soil.

a **1722** LISLE *Husb.* (1752) 79 This sarrition was performed in dry burning lands. **1733** TULL *Horse-Hoeing Husb.* xv. (Dublin) 202 They scratch'd it again and again with the same wooden Instruments, this was call'd Sarrition.

sarrusophone (sə'rʌsəfəʊn). [f. *Sarrus* (see quot. 1884) + Gr. φωνή voice, sound.] A brass instrument of the oboe class, played with a double reed. Hence **sa'rruso,phonist**, a performer on the sarrusophone.

1875 KNIGHT *Dict. Mech.*, *Sarrusophone.* **1884** *Encycl. Brit.* XVII. 707/1 In 1856..M. Sarrus, thought out the construction of a family of brass instruments... Gautrot of Paris realized the inventor's idea, and, under the name of 'sarrusophones', has created a complete family, from the sopranino in E♭ to the contrabass in B♭. **1894** G. B. SHAW in *World* 7 Mar. 23/1, I want a craftsman to take the matter up, with the object, not of inventing some new instrument like the saxophone or sarrusophone which nobody wants, but of giving us back the old instruments. **1906** *Daily News* 21 Feb. 12 M. Leruste, the only sarrusophonist in the Garde Republicaine Band. **1926** WHITEMAN & MCBRIDE *Jazz* ix. 196 The sarrusophone, which is made in seven or more sizes, is named with the wood winds although it is metal. For this reason, it is sometimes mistakenly called a metal oboe. **1975** *Gramophone* Oct. 611/3 Since the nine encyclopaedic columns..nowhere spell out the forces required by Schmitt's score, I feel justified in giving them here:..two bassoons, sarrusophone, two E flat clarinets [etc.].

sarry, obs. variant of SAVOURY *a.*

sarsa ('sɑːsə). Also **sarza**. [Short for next.] = SARSAPARILLA 1. Also *attrib.*

1625 BACON *Ess., Friendship* (Arb.) 167 You may take Sarza to open the Liuer. **1698** FRYER *Acc. E. India & P.* 182 These [Mangoes] and Sarsa being their usual Diet. **1849** BALFOUR *Man. Bot.* §1054 The root of various species of Smilax constitutes the Sarsaparilla or Sarza of the pharmacopœias. **1889** *Syd. Soc. Lex.*, *Sarsa.*

sarsaparilla (sɑːs(ə)pə'rılə). Forms: α. 6–8 **zarza parilla**, (6 **parille**), 7–8 **sarzaparilla**, 6–7 **sarcaparilla**, 6 **-parillia, -perilla, sarsaparilia**, 7 **-perilla**, 8 **-parill**, 7– **sarsaparilla**; β. 6–7 **salsaperilla**, 6–8 **-parilla**, 6 **-pariglia, -perillia**, 7 **-parillia, salcepereille**, 9 **salsaparilha**; γ. 7 **sassaparilla**. [a. Sp. *zarzaparrilla*, f. *zarza* (? a. Basque *sartzia*) bramble; the latter part is said in A. Matthioli *Comm. in Dioscoridem* (1565) 184 to be **parilla*, dim. of *parra* vine, the sarsaparilla being a climbing plant, and its berries having some resemblance to grapes. The word appears, with etymologizing corruption after It. *salso* adj. salt, in It. *salsapariglia* (whence the β forms), F. *salsepareille* (whence the γ form).

The above etymology is given in Gerarde's *Herbal* 1597; and (as an original conjecture) in Monlau's *Diccionario etimol. de la lengua castellana* 1856. The statement of many writers, that the word comes from the name of a Dr. Parillo, has not been traced to any authoritative source.]

1. A plant belonging to any of the species of the order *Smilaceæ*, indigenous to tropical America from Mexico to Peru; esp. *Smilax officinalis* the Jamaica sarsaparilla.

1577 FRAMPTON *Joyfull Newes* II. 79 Of the Sarcaparillia [Sp. orig. (Monardes) *çarçaparrilla*] of Guaiquill. *Ibid.* 79 b, This Sarcaparilla, dooeth growe at the side of a Riuer, which commeth from the Mountaines of the Peru. *Ibid.* 80 Sarcaperilla. **1597** GERARDE *Herbal* II. cccii. 710 We haue great plentie of the rootes of this Bind-weed of Peru, which we vsuallie call Zarza, or Sarsa Parilla. **1620** J. MASON *Newfound-land* (Bannatyne Cl.) A 4, The common wild herbes of the Countrie are Angelica, Violets,..Sarsaparilla [etc.]. **1712** E. COOKE *Voy. S. Sea* 150 All along the Banks grow abundance of Mangroves and Sarzaparilla. **1731** MILLER *Gard. Dict.*, *Smilax*... Rough Virginian Bindweed, with a smooth Ivy Leaf, commonly call'd Zarzaparilla. **1851–9** HOOKER in *Man. Sci. Enq.* 427 The so-called Jamaica Sarasaparilla grows near the Chiriqui Lagoon in the state of Costa Rica. **1873** SYMONDS *Grk. Poets* x. 313 Clematis and polished garlands of tough sarsaparilla wed the shrubs with clinging, climbing arms.

b. The dried roots of plants of the various species of *Smilaceæ*; esp. Jamaica sarsaparilla, *Smilax officinalis*; also, a medicinal preparation of the root used as an alterative and tonic. (The early mentions often relate to the supposed efficacy of the drug in the treatment of syphilis.)

1577 FRAMPTON *Joyfull Newes* II. 80 b, For these euilles they haue an other maner of Water, that is, takyng of foure ounces of Sarcaparilla. **1582** HESTER *Secr. Phiorav.* I. xxviii. 32 Let hym take Sarsaparilia, or Lignum Vitæ. *Ibid.* III. xlvi. 65 The Salsa pariglia is a Roote that commeth from the Indes, the which is hot and dryng. **1621** BURTON *Anat. Mel.* II. iv. I. iii, And to such as are cold, the Decoction of Guacum, Salsaperilla [etc.]. **1671** SHADWELL *Humorists* I, Hast thou not rais'd the price of Sarsaperilla, and Guiacum all over the Town. **1712** tr. *Pomet's Hist. Drugs* I. 49 *Sarsaparilla*, or *Salsaparilla*, is a very long Root, like a small Cord. **1840** PEREIRA *Mat. Med.* II. 661 Jamaica Sarsaparilla, offic. *Ibid.* 662 Brazilian Sarsaparilla: Lisbon, Portugal, or Rio Negro Sarsaparilla... Lima Sarsaparilla. *Ibid.* 663 Honduras Sarsaparilla; Mealy Sarsaparilla; Vera Cruz Sarsaparilla; Mexican Sarsaparilla. **1843** R. J. GRAVES *Syst. Clin. Med.* xxix. 369 We will..give him mild aperients, light nutritious diet, and sarsaparilla. **1846** LINDLEY *Veg. Kingd.* 216 Nees and Ebermaier say that it [root of *Smilax aspera* and *S. excelsa*] sometimes comes into the market under the name of Italian Sarsaparilla. **1853** A. R. WALLACE *Amazon & Rio Negro* 140 The trade here is principally in Brazil-nuts, salsaparilha,..farinha, and salt-fish. **1857** BALFOUR *Cycl. India*, etc. 1659/1 A large quantity is shipped at the Brazils and is called Lisbon sarsaparilla. **1875** H. C. WOOD *Therap.* (1879) 422 If, therefore, sarsaparilla have any value whatever in disease, it must be simply as an alterative. **1886** *Encycl. Brit.* XXI. 313/1 Sarsaparilla... *Smilax officinalis*.. and *S. Medica*..yield respectively the so-called 'Jamaica' and the Mexican varieties. *Ibid.* 313/2 The varieties of sarsaparilla met with in commerce at present are the following:—Jamaica, Lima, Honduras, Guatemala, Guayaquil, and Mexican... 'Jamaica' sarsaparilla..derives its name from the fact that Jamaica was at one time the emporium for sarsaparilla.

2. Applied to plants of other genera, resembling the true sarsaparilla or furnishing a root used as a substitute for it (see quots.).

German sarsaparilla: see GERMAN *a.*[2] 4.

1840 PEREIRA *Mat. Med.* II. 904 The root of *Hemidesmus indicus*..is used in India under the name of 'country sarsaparilla'... It has been called 'Indian' or 'scented sarsaparilla, nannari'. **1847** W. DARLINGTON *Amer. Weeds* (1860) 155 *Aralia*, L. Wild Sarsaparilla. Ginseng. *Ibid.* 156 *Aralia nudicaulis*, L... Sarsaparilla. False Sarsaparilla. **1858** BAIRD *Cycl. Nat. Sci.* 107/2 *Carex arenaria*..has also a certain reputation on the continent as a diaphoretic and diuretic, and is used as such under the name of German sarsaparilla. **1866** *Treas. Bot.* s.v., New Zealand Sarsaparilla, *Ripogonum parviflorum.* **1883** F. M. BAILEY *Synops. Queensl. Flora* 114 Native Sarsaparilla. The roots of this beautiful purple-flowered twiner (*Hardenbergia monophylla*) are used by bushmen as a substitute for the true sarsaparilla. **1891** *Coo-ëe* (ed. Mrs. P. Martin) 258 On the hills..cyclamen, sundew, purple sarsaparilla, and the scarlet pea.

3. *attrib.*

1634 S. R. *Noble Soldier* IV. ii. in Bullen *O. Pl.* (1882) I. 317 Sirra, you Salsa-Perilla Rascall,..doe you heare, Monsire? **1657** B. W. tr. *Bauderon's Expert. Phys.* 110 Let the drink bee decoction of Sarsa Parilla roote. **1849** BALFOUR *Man. Bot.* §1053 Smilaceæ, the Sarsaparilla Family. **1868** M. H. SMITH *Sunsh. & Sh. N.Y.* 61 A famous house..built by a successful sarsaparilla man.

‖**sarsar** ('sɑːsɑː(r)). [Arab. *çarçar* a cold wind.] (See quots.)

1786 tr. *Beckford's Vathek* 207 She..thus penetrated the very entrails of the earth, where breathes the Sansar [*sic*], or icy wind of death. **1801** SOUTHEY *Thalaba* I. xxxvi, The Sarsar can pierce through The Icy Wind of Death.

sarsartie, var. SOSATIE.

sarse: see SAUCE, SEARCE.

sarsen ('sɑːs(ə)n). Also **sarsden, -don, sarcen.** [App. identical with *Sarsen*, var. of SARACEN.] (In full ***sarsen-stone, boulder***.) One of the numerous large boulders or blocks of sandstone found scattered on the surface of the chalk downs, esp. in Wiltshire.

[**1644**: see SARACEN *sb.* 4.] *a* **1691** AUBREY *Nat. Hist. Wilts* (1847) 44 They are also (far from the rode) commonly called Sarsdens or Sarsdon stones. **1743** STUKELEY *Abury* 16 The people call these great stones, sarsens; and 'tis a proverb here, *as hard as a sarsen.* **1834** *Gentl. Mag.* CIV. I. 174 The stones outside of the work,..as well as the five large trilithons, are all of that species of stone called *Sarsen*, which is found in the neighbourhood. **1879** JEFFERIES *Wild Life in S. Co.* 217 Yonder lies a great grey sarsen boulder. **1888** J. PRESTWICH *Geol.* II. 342 The isolated blocks called Greywethers or Sarsen stones, scattered on the surface of the chalk downs.

Sarsen, obs. form of SARACEN.

sarsenet, sarcenet ('sɑːsnıt). Forms: 5 **sarsinett, -ynett, sarssinette**, 6 **sarssynet, sarsenett(e, (saresnet, sesynet, saircenett, sercenett, sarsnett**, 7 **sarcnet, sarcenett)**, 6–9 **sarsnet**, 5– **sarcenet**, 6– **sarsenet**. [a. AF. *sarzinett* (1373 in *Exch. Accts.* 397/16, Publ. Rec. Office: see *N. & Q.* 8th Ser. I. 129), prob. a dim. of *sarzin* SARACEN (see -ET[1]), suggested by OF. *drap sarrasinois*, med.L. *pannus saracenicus*, lit. 'Saracen cloth'.

Godefroy's sole example of the alleged OF. *sarcenet*, taken from Du Cange, is a mistake; it comes from a York Cathedral inventory of 1530, and the word is English. Palsgrave 1530 renders the Eng. *sarcenet* by F. *taffetas*. The only trace of the existence of the word in continental Fr. appears to be the Swiss dial. *sarcenet* 'lustrine de coton' cited by Godefr.]

1. A very fine and soft silk material made both plain and twilled, in various colours, now used chiefly for linings; a dress made of this.

1463 *Bury Wills* (Camden) 41 My tepet of blak sarsenet. **1477** *Rolls of Parlt.* VI. 189/1 It shal be leefull..to use and were in their Colers, Ventes, and Slefes of their Gownes and Hukes, Sateyn, Chamelet, Sarcenet, or Tarteron. **1496–7** *Rec. St. Mary at Hill* 30 Item, ij Curtens of Russet sarsynet frengid with sylke. **1542** *Nottingham Rec.* III. 220 Dublet lyned wyth sarcenet. **1581** in Feuillerat *Revels Q. Eliz.* (1908) 346 Tincells, taffeta, sarcenetes, & single sarcenetes. **1662** PEPYS *Diary* 15 Apr., We saw some new-fashon petticoats of sarcenett. **1687** *Lond. Gaz.* No. 2302/4 A Scarlet Coat lined with green Sarcenet. **1712** ADDISON *Spect.* No. 265 ¶9 The palest Features look the most agreeable in white Sarsenet. **1798** JANE AUSTEN *Northang. Abb.* xv, I remember, too, Miss Andrews drank tea with us that evening, and wore her puce-coloured sarsenet. **1881** BESANT & RICE *Chapl. of Fleet* I. 182 The citizen's daughters making a gallant show in hoops, patches, lace, sarsnet and muslin.

†**b.** With following adj. (after Fr. use).

1483 *Coronat. Rich. III* in *Antiq. Repert.* II. 250 The other [shert] made of ij yerds di' of sarsynet crymysyn. **1507** *Justes May & June* 28 in Hazl. *E.P.P.* II. 122 Of horse and man fyrst day was theyr araye Sarcenet blue.

2. *attrib.* passing into *adj.* Composed of sarsenet.

1521 *Test. Ebor.* (Surtees) V. 133 My best sayrsnett tippit. **1547** BOORDE *Brev. Health* xxxiii. 18 b, Hange over the eye or eyes a greene sarsenet cloth. **1672** in Willis & Clark *Cambridge* (1886) II. 295 For making up ye Sarcenet Curtain. **1728** POPE *Dunc.* III. 248 Yonder cloud..Whose sarcenet skirts are edg'd with flamy gold. **1836–7** DICKENS *Sk. Boz, Sentiment*, The linendrapers of Hammersmith were astounded at the sudden demand for blue sarsenet ribbon, and long white gloves.

†**b.** *adj., fig.* Resembling sarsenet in softness. (Said of speech, manners, etc.) *Obs.*

1596 SHAKS. *1 Hen. IV*, III. i. 56 You sweare like a Comfit-makers Wife:..And guiest such Sarcenet suretie for thy Oathes, As if thou neuer walk'st further then Finsbury. Sweare me, Kate,..A good mouth-filling Oath. **1646** CHAS. I in Carte *Ormonde* (1736) II. App. 14, I have received your sarsenet dispatches by this bearer. **1820** SCOTT *Monast.* ii, With many a *fye* and *nay pshaw*, and such sarsenet chidings as tender mothers give to spoiled children.

†**'Sarsenish**, *a. Obs.* In 4–5 **Sarsaneis, Sarcynesse, Sarsinesshe, -ynneis.** [a. OF. *Sar(r)asinois*, fem. *sar(r)asinesche*, adj. of nationality f. *sarrasin* SARACEN. OE. had *Saracenisc*.] Saracenic; in OE. *sb.*, a Saracen.

In 'bruet of Sarcynesse' (quot. 1381) the word is erron. made into a sb.; cf. *bruette sareson* (*c* 1430 s.v. SARACEN *a.* b).

a **1366** CHAUCER *Rom. Rose* 1188 Largesse hadde on a Robe fresh Of Riche purpur Sarsynysh [*MS.* Sarlynysh, Fr. orig. *sarazinesche*]. **1381** in *Form of Cury* (1780) 110 For to mak a Bruet of Sarcynesse. Tak the lyre of fresch Buf [etc.]. *c* **1400** *Laud Troy Bk.* 9429 He was leyd In that paleis, That was of riche werk Sarsaneis. *c* **1400** *Siege of Troy* 1076 in *Archiv. Stud. neu. Spr.* LXXII. 38 Diuerse melodye..Of trumpis, tabouris and nakeres, Pypers sarsynneis and symbaleris. [Cf. OF. *cors sarrazinois*.]

†**'Sarsenry.** *Obs. rare*$^{-1}$. Also 5 **sarsynrye.** [f. *Sarsen*, SARACEN + -RY.] The Saracen people.

c **1440** CAPGRAVE *Life St. Kath.* I. 877 It was neuyr seyn ȝet þat þe sarsynrye [*v.r.* sarsenrye] Was left a-lone vn-to a wommanes hande.

sarshan, variant of SAGENE[1].

1783 W. F. MARTYN *Geog. Mag.* II. 41 A sarshan, or fathom, which contains three arshines.

Sarsi, var. SARCEE.

Sarson, -oun, obs. forms of SARACEN.

†**sart**, *sb.*[1] *Obs.* [a. OF. *sart*:—med.L. *sartum*, neut. pa. pple. (for *sarrītum*) of *sarrīre* to hoe, weed.] = ASSART *sb.* Also in *Comb.* **sart-silver**, a payment made by tenants for the right of taking brushwood from land.

c **1290** *S. Eng. Leg.* I. 463/46 Lazarus hadde þat haluendel: of al Ierusalem, Of wodes and fieldes and of sart: almest to bedleem. **1408** *Nottingham Rec.* II. 56 Dicta villata ei debet pro sartsilver spectante Domino Regi annuatim solvendo de praedicta Oxton v s. **1451** *Rolls of Parlt.* V. 223/1 Consideryng that oure seide Collage hath noo Woode liyng yerto within xxiiii myle; whereof xx acres they have by wey of a sart..; and other xx acres..by wey of almes. *c* **1518** *Rental Bk. Earl Kildare* in *Jrnl. Kilkenny Archæol. Soc.* Ser. II. (1862) IV. 133 Item ij pullis in Kyltecrenyn in pledge of iiij^{xx} kyene for the Sart of William Naco is doughter sett yerelye for iiij merkis. [**1706** PHILLIPS (ed. Kersey), *Sart*, a piece of Woodland turned into Arable. See *Assart*.]

Sart (sɑːt), *sb.*[2] and *a.* [Turki.] **A.** *sb.* **a.** A member of a settled people of mixed Turkoman and Iranian descent, living as town-dwellers and traders in Turkestan and parts of Afghanistan. Cf. TAJIK. **b.** The Eastern Turkic dialect of Uzbek spoken by the Sarts. **B.** *adj.* Of or pertaining to this people or their language.

The name is widely used, with varying degrees of exactness, to designate the sedentary people of this region. They are thus contrasted with the Kurds and others, by whom the term is considered derogatory. Other commentators view the Sarts as an ethnologically distinct people.

1871 R. B. SHAW *Visits to High Tartary* ii. 26 All the Khokandees whom I met with in Eastern Toorkistân agreed in affirming that Sart is merely a word used by the Kirghiz to denote all who do not lead a nomad existence like themselves, whether they be Tajiks or Oosbeks. **1879** *Encycl. Brit.* IX 85/2 Tajiks..in the chief towns and central districts, who are known as Sarts, show a large infusion of Uzbeg and other Turki blood. **1898** BEALBY & HEARN tr. *Hedin's Through Asia* v. 61 Guided by some Sart boys, I threaded my way through a labyrinth of narrow lanes. **1900** 'ODYSSEUS' *Turkey in Europe* iii. 101 Sart, though now commonly used as a name for the Jagatai Turkish spoken in those provinces [sc. Fergana, Turkestan, etc.] is, strictly speaking, not a linguistic designation, but denotes a dweller in cities and a merchant, as distinguished from a countryman and agriculturist, called Tajik. **1920** *Glasgow Herald* 31 Aug. 8 It is among the highly intelligent Sarts and Tadjiks, speaking Persian and Arabic fluently and many of them conversant with Hindustani, that the Bolshevists find their cleverest agents. **1946** F. M. BAILEY *Mission to Tashkent* iii. 36 Sart writers sometimes refer to themselves as Turks but this word is..misleading. **1953** O. CAROE *Soviet Empire* iii. 34 It was to sedentary dwellers of this kind, whether bilingual or speaking only Tajik, that the true Turks formerly applied the pejorative appellation of 'Sart'. **1954** PEI & GAYNOR *Dict. Linguistics* 190 *Sart*, an Asiatic language; member of the Central Turkic group of the Altaic sub-family of the Ural-Altaic family of languages. **1964** R. A. PIERCE in N. J. Couriss tr. *Pahlen's Mission to Turkestan* 10 Pahlen..regarded the Sarts as a distinct ethnic group with their own language. Originally..the word was applied to the sedentary, and..urban, population of Turkestan without any reference to race or language. A Sart might.. be of Tadzhik.., Uzbek.., or of mixed Iranian and Turkic stock; and..speak..Tadzhik or Uzbek... There is no such thing as a Sart language. During the Soviet régime the word acquired a derogatory significance and is now no longer used.

sartage ('sɑːtɪdʒ). *U.S.* [a. OF. *sartage*, f. *sarter* to clear ground, f. *sart* SART *sb.*[1]] (See quots.)

1887 *Detroit Free Press* (Lond.) 2 July 6/4 'Sartage' is the practice of setting fire to trees in order to clear the ground. **1891** *Century Dict.*, *Sartage*, the clearing of woodland for agricultural purposes, as by setting fire to the trees.

sartan, -tayne, -teyn, obs. forms of CERTAIN.

sarten, sartente, obs. ff. CERTAIN, CERTAINTY.

c **1435** *Torr. Portugal* 717 The sarten to sey with-owt lese, A scheff-chambyr he hym ches. **1484** *Cely Papers* (Camden) 152 The man ys goode Inowythe [= enough] were we yn sartente of þes betwyxte Flaunders and us. **1572** in Feuillerat *Revels Q. Eliz.* (1908) 411 A note of sarten thinges.

sartin, repr. an illiterate pronunc. of CERTAIN *a.*

1762 G. COLMAN *Mus. Lady* I. 4 Indeed it was, sir!—I am sartin it was. **1890** W. A. WALLACE *Only a Sister* 86 Look here, that's proof for sartin.

sartor ('sɑːtɔː(r)). *Humorously pedantic.* [a. L. *sartor* patcher, mender, f. *sarcīre* (ppl. stem *sart-*) to botch, patch.] A tailor.

1656 BLOUNT *Glossogr.*, *Sartor*, a Tailor, a Botcher, a Mender of old Garments. **1843** O. W. HOLMES *Terpsichore* Poet. Wks. (1895) 55/1 And coats whose memory turns the sartor pale. **1870** (*title*) The Sartor, or British journal of cutting, clothing, and fashion.

sartorial (sɑː'tɔərɪəl), *a.* [f. L. *sartōri-us*, f. *sartor*: see SARTOR and -AL[1].] Of or belonging to a tailor or his art; characteristic of a tailor.

1823 SYD. SMITH *Wks.* (1859) II. 24/2 A little wicked tailor arrives... He is turned over to a settler, who leases this sartorial Borgia his liberty for five shillings per week. **1831** CARLYLE *Sart. Res.* I. v, The First Chapter..turns on Paradise and Fig-leaves, and leads us into interminable disquisitions of a mythological, metaphorical, cabalistico-sartorial..cast. **1832** —— *Misc.* (1840) IV. 108 His visitor.. we suppose, sat upon folios, or in the sartorial fashion. **1893** VIZETELLY *Glances Back* II. xxxvii. 337 The sartorial artist ..had been vainly trying to obtain payment.

sartorially (sɑː'tɔərɪəlɪ), *adv.* [f. SARTORIAL *a.* + -LY[2].] With regard to clothes.

1905 W. J. LOCKE *Morals of Marcus Ordeyne* xii. 146 When she puts her foot upon my sartorially immaculate knee. **1916** —— *Wonderful Year* xvii. 245 Like a woman clothes-starved for years.. Martin ran sartorially mad. **1928** *Daily Express* 16 Apr. 3/4 Sartorially magnificent in all-over woolly tights. **1970** *Daily Tel.* 30 Dec. 9/2 Sartorially speaking, men are at last catching up with the women. **1972** *Ibid.* 14 Mar. 13/7 Sartorially, the beginning of the Chinese 'thaw' is to be seen in the gaily-coloured clothes worn by girls and women. **1974** 'M. UNDERWOOD' *Pinch of Snuff* ii. 12 The club's most sartorially elegant member.

sartorian (sɑː'tɔərɪən), *a. rare.* [f. L. *sartōri-us* (see SARTORIAL *a.*) + -AN.] = SARTORIAL *a.*

1668 WILKINS *Real Char.* 243 Clothing, Sartorian Trades. **1813** L. HUNT in *Examiner* 5 Apr. 209/1 The reader will excuse this sartorian metaphor.

sartorite ('sɑːtəraɪt). *Min.* [Named by J. D. Dana in 1868 after Sartorius von Waltershausen, who first described it: see -ITE.] Sulpharsenide of lead, found in dark, lead-grey, orthorhombic crystals.

1868 DANA *Min.* (ed. 5) 87.

‖**sartorius** (sɑː'tɔərɪəs). [mod.L. *sartōrius* (*musculus*): see SARTORIAL *a.*

So called as being concerned in producing the cross-legged position in which a tailor traditionally sits at work.]

A long narrow muscle which crosses the thigh obliquely in front.

1704 J. HARRIS *Lex. Techn.* I, *Sartorius*, a Muscle of the Leg. **1802** PALEY *Nat. Theol.* ix, The Sartorius or tailor's muscle..enables us by its contraction to throw one leg and thigh over the other. **1840** E. WILSON *Anat. Vade M.* (1851) 256 The Sartorius (tailor's muscle).

Sartrean, Sartrian ('sɑːtrɪən), *a.* Also Sartreian. [f. the name of *Sartre* (see below) + -AN, -IAN.] Of, pertaining to, or characteristic of the French writer and philosopher Jean-Paul Sartre (1905–80), his writings, or his existentialist philosophy. Hence as *sb.*, an admirer of the ideas of Sartre.

1948 [see COMMITMENT 6 c]. **1949** E. L. MASCALL *Existence & Analogy* vi. 126 Given their atheist dogma, the Sartrians are quite right in asserting that existence is absurd, that the world does not make sense. **1951** N. ANNAN *Leslie Stephen* viii. 247 In the 'forties Sartrian Existentialism..was a bizarre attempt to justify the duties to society which are inescapably binding upon individuals, who, whether they like it or not, are forced to commit themselves. **1958** *Spectator* 25 July 141/2 That unique Sartrean blend of intellectual and moral disintegration. **1961** *Encounter* June 42/2, I cannot claim to be either a Sartrian or a Thomist. **1962** *Listener* 24 May 920/2 From the Sartrian standpoint, Rousseau went about this enterprise in the wrong way. **1970** J. D. CAUTE *Fanon* iii. 35 Fanon's prose reverberates with Sartreian concepts, phrases, dialectical juxtapositions, paradoxes and essentialist abstractions. **1975** J. SYMONS *Three Pipe Problem* xix. 218 Were they both dead, joined in a permanent squabble in some Sartrean hinterland? **1977** *New Yorker* 16 May 147/1 Soyinka discusses material.. with ample cross-references to Greek drama, Nietzschean aesthetics, Jungian philosophy and Sartrean opinionizing.

†'**sartry.** *Obs.* In 5 saretree, sartre. [a. OF. *sartrerie*, f. *sartre*:—L. *sartor*: see -ERY.] A tailor's workshop.

1447–8 *Durham Acc. Rolls* (Surtees) 186 In repar. cujusdam fontis ex opposito le Saretree. **1448–9** *Ibid.*, j crooke pro porta de le Sartre, 12*d.*

†**sartryn.** *Obs. rare*$^{-0}$. [a. OF. *sartrin (recorded as *sartrain*), ad. med.L. *sartrīnum* tailor's shop, related to SARTOR.] A tailor's shop.

1483 *Cath. Angl.* 318/2 A Sartryn, *sartorium*, *sutrinum*.

saru-, graphic var. of *sarv-*, obs. form of SERV-.

Saruk, var. SAROUK.

‖**Sarum** ('sɛərəm). [med.L. *Sarum* (indeclinable), app. evolved from a misunderstanding of the abbreviation *Sarȝ* for *Sarisburia* Salisbury.] The ecclesiastical name of Salisbury, used attrib. in **Sarum Use**, the order of divine service used in the diocese of Salisbury from the 11th century to the Reformation; so ***Sarum missal, office, rubric***. Also *absol.*

1570 FOXE *A. & M.* 237/1 Thus..Osmundus bishop of Salisbury, deuised that ordinary, which is called the vse of Sarum. *Ibid.* Table, Sarum vse when it was deuised. **1832** W. PALMER *Orig. Liturg.* I. 186 Their rubrics are sometimes less definite than those of the Sarum 'Use'. *Ibid.* 357 *note*, This epistle, according to the Sarum rubric, was taken from the 'commune unius Apostoli'. **1882** G. H. FORBES *Missale Drummond.* 7 *margin*, In the Sarum Office this is the Alleluia for Mondays. *Ibid.* 8 *margin*, This Communio does not occur in the Sarum. **1929** S. LESLIE *Anglo-Catholic* x. 117 His ritual was simple: two lights, Sarum Use and Sarum colours with simple vestments of linen. **1954** O. CHADWICK *Founding of Cuddesdon* v. 133 This was just the time when the old-fashioned cassock was giving way to the Sarum cassock, which was intruding from about 1887 onwards and conquering by 1897. **1957** *Oxf. Dict. Chr. Ch.* 1209/1 In the years preceding the Reformation the output of Sarum books was enormous. The much increased knowledge which has followed their discovery..has led to the revival of Sarum customs and ornaments in many English cathedral and parish churches. **1966** J. BETJEMAN *High & Low* 55 And there we'll sing the Sarum rite Tae English Hymnal airs. **1972** C. STEPHENSON *Merrily on High* iv. 64 SS. Philip & James, very Sarum, and St. Margaret's close by very western, were the centre of great turmoil at one stage when the vicar of Phil & Jim was making it western and the vicar of St. Margaret's was busy taking off the six candles from the altar and substituting two while introducing Sarum practices. **1974** *Encycl. Brit. Micropædia* VIII. 908/3 The Sarum chants resemble Gregorian ones in the use of free rhythm, modes.., psalm tones.., musical form, and the addition of tropes.

sarus ('sɛərəs). Also **sarrus**. [Hindi *sāras*.] The Indian crane *Grus antigone*.

1838 *Penny Cycl.* XII. 173/2 The gigantic Indian or Sarrus Crane, *Grus Antigone* of Linnæus. **1879** MRS. A. E. JAMES *Ind. Househ. Managem.* 65 The handsome *sarus*.

sarve, obs. form of SERVE.

sarves, sarvice, -is, obs. forms of SERVICE.

‖**sarvodaya** (sar'vodaja). [Skr., f. *sárva* 'all' + *udayá* 'uplift, prosperity'.] The welfare of all; the name given to the new social order advocated by the Indian leader M. K. Gandhi (1869–1948) and his followers. Also *attrib.*

[**1908** M. K. GANDHI (*title*) Sarvodaya.] **1919** *Bombay Chron.* 8 Apr. 713 The committee has selected the following prohibited books for dissemination:..*Sarvodaya* or *Universal Dawn* by M. K. Gandhi. **1941** K. G. MASHRUWALA *Practical Non-Violence* (1946) 45 This is the civilization of Sarvodaya (the wellbeing of all). **1948** *Harijan* 4 Apr. 54/2 *Samaj*, which corresponds more to brotherhood than to association... The Sarvodaya Samaj has been established to strive..towards a society based on Truth and Non-violence, in which there will be no distinction of caste or creed. **1954** B. KUMARAPPA *Sarvodaya* (1958) p. iii, Sarvodaya, as the welfare of all, represents the ideal social order according to Gandhiji. Its basis is all-embracing love. **1962** B. SMITH *Portrait of India* vi. 45 Vinoba..became at Gandhi's death, the leader of the *Sarvodaya* movement of selfless service. *Ibid.* 46 Gandhi's *sarvodaya* embodied the idea of regeneration in the individual and in society. **1965** E. LINTON *World in Grain of Sand* ix. 163, I thought of the Gandhians in their present dilemma as expressed later at the Sarvodaya Conference at Vedchi. **1971** *Peace News* 10 Sept. 8/2 The concept of the freedom march was born in the minds of Indian Sarvodaya workers. **1974** *Times* 7 Dec. 5/4 The village is conceived of in Gandhian or *sarvodaya* terms as a miniature, self-governing republic. **1978** *Times Lit. Suppl.* 3 Feb. 121/2 India's own home-spun village socialist movement known as *Sarvodaya* acquired its name, significantly, from the word used by Gandhi to translate the title of Ruskin's book, *Unto This Last*.

sarwan, var. SURWAN.

sarych, saryf, obs. forms of SEARCH, SERVE.

Saryk (sæ'riːk). Also **Sarik**. [Native name.] **a.** One of several Turkic tribes inhabiting the Turkmen Soviet Socialist Republic; a member of this tribe. **b.** *attrib.* Used to designate a carpet or rug made by this tribe, similar in design to a Bokhara carpet. Also *absol.*

1885 E. W. HAMILTON *Diary* 9 Apr. (1972) II. 831 The news reached me that the Russian Colonel—Alikhanoff—attacked the Afghans at Penjdeh on the 30th,..and that Alikhanoff had actually instigated the Sariks (a Turcoman tribe in that neighbourhood) to attack the English party... The Sariks fortunately declined the offer. **1889** G. CURZON *Russia in Central Asia* v. 96 Transcaspia...includes..the minor oases inhabited by the Sarik and Salor Turkomans. **1899** SKRINE & ROSS *Heart of Asia* II. iv. 268 The Merv oasis was inhabited by the Sāriks,..who were engaged in a struggle with the Khivans. **1922** H. CLARK *Bokhara, Turkoman & Afghan Rugs* p. xiv, In the course of years I acquired..specimens of Salor, Saryk..and Afghan Turkoman rugs... A Saryk Turkoman rug of the early 18th century, nearly square in shape and of wonderful colouring. **1957** C. W. HOSTLER *Turkism & Soviets* ii. 69 The Turkmens are divided into seven main tribes (the Chauders, ..Sariks, Salors and Ersaris). **1960** H. HAYWARD *Antique Coll.* 248/2 *Saryk rugs*, Turkestan rugs, generally not so fine in texture as Bokhara rugs.., but bearing a similar design. **1962** C. W. JACOBSEN *Oriental Rugs* II. 286 Even today nine out of ten dealers have never heard of the name 'Saryk'. **1964** *Sunday Times* (Colour Suppl.) 19 Jan. 25 Sarik. Carpet from a Turcoman tribe almost destroyed by the Tekkes in the last century. **1974** *Encycl. Brit. Macropædia* XVIII. 800/1 The number of people in other tribes (the Salyr, Saryk, Groklen, and Choudor) fluctuated between 20,000 and 40,000.

sarynes, obs. form of SORRINESS.

sarza, Sarzan: see SARSA, SARACEN.

sas, var. SASS *sb.*

‖**sa, sa** (sɑː sɑː), *int. Obs.* See also SESSA. The Fr. exclamation *çà, çà*, redupl. of *çà* (lit. here, hither), 'interjection familière pour exciter, encourager' (Littré). Formerly used by fencers when delivering a thrust. Also *attrib.* as in *sa-sa man* [cf. F. *faire le çà-çà galant homme* (16th c. in Littré)]; and quasi-*sb.* as a nickname for a fencing master.

Cf. Du. *sa sa*, 'come on, cheer up, quickly, an interjection much used to stir up fighting dogs' (Sewel).]

1607 TOURNEUR *Rev. Trag.* V. i, Sa, sa, sa! thumpe, there he lyes. **1608** SYLVESTER *Du Bartas* II. iv. III. *Schisme* 224 Sa, sa (my hearts) let's cheerly to the charge. **1697** VANBRUGH *Æsop* Pt. II. 9 He's none of your Fencers, none of your Sa Sa men. **1698** FARQUHAR *Love & Bottle* II. ii, And what are you good Monsieur, sa, sa? **1826** SCOTT *Woodst.* xxviii, 'Do you ever take bilboa in hand?—Sa—sa!' Here he made a fencing demonstration with his sheathed rapier.

sasafras, obs. form of SASSAFRAS.

sasaitie, var. SOSATIE.

Sasak ('sɑːsæk), *sb.* and *a.* Also 9 **Sassak**. [Native name.] **A.** *sb.* One of the Malay inhabitants of the island of Lombok. Also, the language of the Sasaks. **B.** *adj.* Of or pertaining to the Sasaks.

1817 T. S. RAFFLES *Hist. Java* II. p. cxcviii, Comparative vocabulary of the Bugis, Makasar, Mandhar, Búton, Sásak, Bíma, Sembáwa, Tembóra, and Endé Languages. **1869** A. R. WALLACE *Malay Archipel.* I. xi. 256 Beyond Mataram.. is Karangassam, the ancient residence of the native or Sassak Rajahs before the conquest..by the Balinese. *Ibid.* 270 The aborigines of Lombock are termed Sassaks. They are a Malay race... They are Mahometans. **1897** E. J. TAYLOR tr. *W. Cool's With Dutch in East* III. 121 The language of the Sassaks is totally different from that spoken by the Balinese; although the Sassaks have borrowed many words from their neighbours, still they are unable to understand each other's language. **1937** M. COVARRUBIAS *Island of Bali* ii. 30 In 1885 there was a rebellion of Sasaks, the vassals of the Balinese in Lombok... The Sasak chiefs complained to the Dutch, asking to be freed from the tyranny of the Balinese princes. **1954** E. D. LABORDE tr. *C. Robequain's Malaya, Indonesia, Borneo & Philippines* II. xii. 24 Balinese Hinduism is isolated between Java and Lombok, for Islam has..almost wholly won over Lombok... Sasak converts to Islam form the great majority..of the population. **1961** P. KEMP *Alms for Oblivion* xi. 163 Almost nine-tenths of this population are Sasaks, a simple agricultural people of Malay stock. *Ibid.* 166 We enlisted the Eurasian as an extra interpreter, for..he spoke Dutch, Malay, Balinese and Sasak. **1965** *Language* XLI. 294 Madurese, like some of its neighboring languages (Sundanese, Javanese, Balinese, and Sasak), has socially determined choices of words. **1974** *Encycl. Brit. Micropædia* VI. 308/3 The population of Lombok is composed largely of Sasaks of Malay origin.

Sasanian, var. SASSANIAN *a.* and *sb.*

Sasanid, var. SASSANID *sb.* and *a.*

sasanqua (sə'sænkwə, -kə). Also **sasank(w)a**. [Jap. *sasankwa* mountain tea-flower.] An evergreen shrub, *Camellia sasanqua*, belonging to the family Theaceæ, native to Japan, and bearing fragrant white or pink flowers and seeds yielding an edible oil also used in the production of silk and soap.

1866 LINDLEY & MOORE *Treas. Bot.* I. 207/2 *C. Sasanqua* (Sasanqua is the Japanese name of the plant) is found in many parts of China and Japan. **1878** *Trans. Asiatic Soc. Japan* VI. 216 A kind of evergreen with poplar-like leaves.. is called *Sasanka* by the Japanese. **1884** tr. *J. J. Rein's Japan* 441 In November and December Sasankwa and Cha.. blossom. **1962** J. L. THRELKELD *Camellia Bk.* i. 3 In the gardens of Japan the sasanqua predominates.

sasarara, variant of SISERARY.

sasatie, var. SOSATIE.

sase, obs. form of SAUCE, SEIZE.

saser, obs. form of SAUCER *sb.*

sash (sæʃ), *sb.*¹ Forms: 6–7 **shash**, 7 **shass(e**, **sasche**, 7– **sash**. [Originally *shash*, a. Arab. *shāsh* muslin, turban-'sash' (Dozy).]

†**1.** A band of a fine material worn twisted round the head as a turban in some Middle-Eastern countries. *Obs.*

159. R. FITCH in *Hakluyt's Voy.* (1599) II. I. 255 Great store of cloth is made there of cotton, and Shashes for the Moores. **1615** G. SANDYS *Trav.* 63 All of them weare on their heads white Shashes and Turbants, the badge of their religion. **1617** MORYSON *Itin.* III. 174 The Greekes and other Christians..weare Shasses, that is, striped linnen (commonly white and blew) wound about the skirts of a little cap. **1650** FULLER *Pisgah* II. xiv, The silk in Judea, called Shesh in Hebrew, whence haply that fine linen or silk is called shashes, worn at this day about the heads of Eastern people. **1685** G. MERITON *Nomencl. Cleric.* 63 A Shash or Turbant, *Tiara*. **1718** OZELL tr. *Tournefort's Voy. Levant* II. 287 [They] weare the white Sash round their Turbant as well as the Turks.

†**b.** Put for: One who wears a 'sash'. *Obs.*

1657 HOWELL in Rumsey *Org. Salutis* b 2 b, As they who have conversed with Shashes and Turbants doe well know.

2. A scarf, often with fringe at each end, worn by men, either over one shoulder or round the waist; spec. *Mil.* (see quot. 1876). Also, a similar article worn round the waist by women and children.

1681 R. KNOX *Hist. Ceylon* 89 A blew or red shash girt about their loyns. **1684** J. P. tr. *Tavernier's Relat. Seraglio* xi. 58 He..thrusts the Ponyard into his Sasche before his Breast. **1687** *Lond. Gaz.* No. 2295/4 Officers Sashes and Ribons. **1715** J. STEVENS *Hist. Persia* 25 Girdles, or Sashes ever were, and still are Badges of Honour, and Dignity in Persia. **1787** M. CUTLER in *Life*, etc. (1888) I. 233 Dr. Rogers with a large white sash... These sashes, I was informed, were given the last week at a funeral. **1829** *R. Ackermann's Repos. Fashions* 4 The skirt is plaited in full round the waist, and has a border of white *tulle*... Sash to correspond. **1864** KNIGHT *Passages Work. Life* I. i. 19 A white frock with a black sash—the indication that I had lost my mother. **1876** VOYLE & STEVENSON *Milit. Dict.* (ed. 3), *Sash*, part of the dress of an officer and non-commissioned officer. It is worn across the shoulder by officers and sergeants of the infantry; it is made of crimson silk for the former, and of a mixture of crimson and white cotton for the latter. **1884** *Pall Mall G.* 13 Feb. 8/2 The brides-maids.. wore dresses of cream soie épinglé and plush..and large tied sashes of satin merveilleux.

b. *attrib.* and *Comb.*, as *sash ribbon*; *sash-capped* adj.; *sashways*, *-wise* advs.

1827 G. DARLEY *Sylvia* 137 Hurrah! the *sash-capt cymbal swingers! **1861** *Ladies' Gaz. Fashion* Nov. 87/2 The waist is round, and worn with a *sash ribbon. **1731** *Gentl. Mag.* I. 427 An old piece of crimson Ribbon ty'd *Sashways about him. **1842** F. E. PAGET *Milford Malvoisin* 28 An embroidered baldric or sword-belt, worn *sash-wise over the right shoulder.

sash (sæʃ), *sb.*² Also 7 **shash**, **shas**. [A corruption of CHASSIS, app. mistaken for a plural.]

1. a. A frame, usually of wood, rebated and fitted with one or more panes of glass forming a window or part of a window; *esp.* a sliding frame or each of the two sliding frames of a SASH-WINDOW. Also (? now only *U.S.*) applied to a casement.

In early use denoting a glazed frame of wood as distinguished from a leaded window, but now usually applied to a sliding frame in contradistinction to a casement. *French sash*, a French window (see FRENCH A. 3).

1681 COTTON *Wond. Peak* 82 The primitive Casements modell'd were no doubt By that through which the Pigeon was thrust out, Where now whole Shashes are but one great eye. *a* **1704** T. BROWN *Lett. to Gent. & Ladies* Wks. 1709 III. II. 108 Why have I not seen you shine out of the Sash this Morning? **1712** STEELE *Spect.* No. 510 ¶ 1 My eye was ..catch'd with..the Face of a very fair Girl..fixed at the Chin to a painted Sash, and made part of the Landskip. **1716** GAY *Trivia* II. 141 Shops breathe Perfumes, thro' Sashes Ribbons glow. **1716** SWIFT *Progr. Beauty* Wks. 1755 III. II. 165 She ventures now to lift the sash. **1781** COWPER *Conversat.* 331 The southern sash admits too strong a light, You rise and drop the curtain—now it's night. **1784** —— *Task* IV. 763 The casements lin'd with creeping herbs, The prouder sashes fronted with a range Of orange. **1794** HOME in *Phil. Trans.* LXXXV. 14 Lines..rendered confused by reflections from the cross bars of the sash of the window. **1842** GWILT *Archit.* §2164 French sashes, which open like doors. **1870** E. PEACOCK *Ralf Skirl.* I. 32 Some of the Gothic windows had been divested of their tracery and fitted with sashes. **1876** PAPWORTH in *Encycl. Brit.* IV. 494/2 Sashes are either hung upon hinges or hung with lines, pulleys, and weights. Fixed sashes are put into frames... Sashes hung with hinges are usually called casements. **1881** YOUNG *Ev. Man his Own Mechanic* §824 In most cases the sash.. consists of a frame in which one large pane is set, or..the space is divided into two parts by one vertical bar, or into four parts by a vertical bar and a horizontal bar crossing each other at right angles. **1902** R. STURGIS *Dict. Archit.* III. 409 In the United States the term 'sash' is often applied to the movable woodwork of a casement or glazed door. **1908** *Times* 22 Apr. 5/5 A pane of glass was broken just above the meeting of the two sashes.

†**b.** A window-frame covered with paper or linen. Cf. CHASSIS. *Obs.*

1687 [see SASH-WINDOW]. **1822** IMISON *Sci. & Art* II. 422 The use of a sash, made of transparent or fan paper,..will preserve the sight.

c. A glazed light of a glass-house or garden frame; a sash-light.

1707 *Curios. in Husb. & Gard.* 279 Keep them..under Bell-Glasses and Sashes. **1725** BRADLEY *Fam. Dict.* s.v. *Green-house*, The Glass in the Front, whether it be in Sashes or Casements, must be so contrived, that it may..slide..to give Air to the Plants. **1856** DELAMER *Fl. Gard.* (1861) 28 They are..safest..in raised beds covered with shutters or sashes in winter.

2. *U.S.* **a.** *Hydraulic Engin.* A guide or string piece for sheet-piling.

1838 *Civ. Engin. & Arch. Jrnl.* I. 148/1 [Potomac Aqueduct.] Wales, or stringers, twelve by six inches, to guide sheet piling, called in America the lower and upper *sash*.

b. A rectangular frame in which a saw-blade is stretched to prevent its bending or buckling.

1875 KNIGHT *Dict. Mech.* **1877** *Lumberman's Gaz.* 8 Dec. 362 The old 'sash saw' was so thin that it had to be kept strained within a frame or 'sash' to prevent its 'buckling' or bending when crowded into the cut.

3. *attrib.* and *Comb.*, as *sash fastener*, *lifter*, *mortise chisel*, *moulding*; *sash-boring*, *-mortising*, *-planing*, *-tenoning*, vbl. sbs. (Knight *Dict. Mech.* 1875); **sash bar**, each of the bars dividing the glass in a sash; also, the shaped material of which such bars are made; **sash bead**, each of the beads or guides which keep the sashes in place; †**sash-casement**, a sash-window; **sash cord**, a cord used for hanging window sashes; **sash cramp** (see quot. 1964); **sash-door**, a door fitted with a glazed sash in the upper part; also, a French window; **sash fillister** (see quot.); **sash frame**, (*a*) a frame fixed in the opening of a wall to receive the sash or sashes of a window; also, a sash or sash-light; (*b*) *U.S.* = 2 b above (Knight); **sash gate** (see quot.); **sash light**, a sash or sash-window; **sash line** = *sash cord*; **sash-pane**, each of the panes of glass in a sash-window; **sash pocket**, 'the space formed in the sash frame in which the weight runs up and down' (*Archit. Publ. Soc. Dict.*, 1887); **sash pulley**, a pulley in a window frame over which the sash cord runs; **sash saw**, (*a*) a small sized tenon saw used in making sashes; (*b*) *U.S.* a frame saw; **sash sluice** (see quot.); **sash strip**, each of the vertical strips which support the glass of a glass-house; **sash tool**, a glaziers' brush (see quot. 1842); also, a small painters' brush suitable for painting sashes; **sash weight**, a weight attached to each of the two cords of a sash to counterbalance it and to facilitate the raising and lowering of it; **sashwork**, the glazing of sashes or sash-windows. Also SASH-WINDOW.

1837 *Civ. Engin. & Arch. Jrnl.* I. 24/2 The *sash-bars.. should be of copper. **1851** *Guide-bk. Industr. Exhib.* 10 The length of sash-bar used is 205 miles. **1844** *Regul. & Ord. Army* 237 Whenever Troops are directed to clean the windows of their Barrack-Rooms, they are in no instance to be allowed to remove the *sash-beads. **1757** BORLASE in *Phil. Trans.* L. 500 The *sash-casements jarred. **1776** G. SEMPLE *Building in Water* 18 A long Piece of *Sash-cord. **1964** J. S. SCOTT *Dict. Building* 275 **Sash cramps*, cramps between 2 and 5 ft long used for clamping sashes during gluing. **1969** E. H. PINTO *Treen* 381/2 Wooden cramps. The general run of both G cramps and sash cramps are too familiar to need any special description. **1726** D. EATON *Let.* 25 Sept. (1971) 60, I think the *sash door at Little Deen ought to be oak, and these planks we have will do very well. **1739–40** RICHARDSON *Pamela* (1740) I. 95 In this green Room was a Closet, with a Sash-door and a Curtain before it. **1747** RICHARDSON *Clarissa* II. viii. 46 My closet, whither I retired..and pulled the sash-door after me. **1876** *Encycl. Brit.* IV. 494/2 French casements, or sash doors, as they are called when they open down to the ground. **1790** *Trans. Soc. Arts* VIII. 237 His improved *sash-fastener. **1812** P. NICHOLSON *Mech. Exerc.* 112 The *sash fillister is a rebating plane..mostly used in rebating the bars of sashes for the glass. **1693–1700** MOXON *Mech. Exerc.* (1703) 266 *Shas Frames. **1793** SMEATON *Edystone L.* §279 The casting of sash frames of copper, each in one piece. **1855** DELAMER *Kitch. Gard.* (1861) 16 Sash-frames to cover hotbeds or cold-pits. **1875** KNIGHT *Dict. Mech.*, **Sash-gate* (Hydraulic Engineering), a stop valve sliding vertically to and from its seat. **1844** H. STEPHENS *Bk. Farm* I. 218 Brass *sash-lifters. **1693–1700** MOXON *Mech. Exerc.* (1703) 266 *Shas Lights. **1710** *Tatler* No. 178/4 Advt., The whole House being well wainscotted, and sash'd with 30 Sash Lights. **1767** *Jrnl. Byron's Voy. rd. World* 74 The sash lights [of Scilly light-house] are eleven feet six inches high. **1794** *Rigging & Seamanship* I. 65 *Sash-line of 4 strands. **1881** YOUNG *Ev. Man his own Mechanic* §259 One or two..*sash mortise chisels..will be necessary. *Ibid.* §824 Except in fancy work for greenhouses and conservatories, *sash mouldings are now but seldom used. *c* **1806** D. WORDSWORTH *Jrnl.* (1941) I. 311 The dwelling-house was distinguished from the outer buildings..by a chimney and one small window with *sash-panes. **1762** STERNE *Tr. Shandy* V. xix, The *sash pullies, when the lead was gone, were of no kind of use. **1812** P. NICHOLSON *Mech. Exerc.* 136 The *Sash Saw..is used by sash makers in forming the tenons of sashes. **1877** [see 2 b above]. **1875** KNIGHT *Dict. Mech.*, **Sash-sluice*, a sluice with vertically sliding valves. **1901** *J. Black's Carp. & Build., Home Handicr.* 69 In the matter of rafters and *sash-strips strength should be sought in depth. **1825** J. NICHOLSON *Operat. Mechanic* 636 A glazing-knife,..a duster, and *sash-tool. **1842** GWILT *Archit.* §2226 The sash tool is used wet, for taking the oil from the inside after the back putties are cleared off. **1737** HOPPUS *Salmon's Country Build. Estim.* (ed. 2) 93 *Sash Weights, &c. at 18*s. per* C. **1762** STERNE *Tr. Shandy* V. xxiii, I wish..instead of the sash weights I had cut off the church spout. **1825** J. NICHOLSON *Operat. Mechanic* 635 Glazier's work may be classed under three distinct heads, *sash-work, lead-work, and fret-work.

sash (sæʃ), *v.*¹ [f. SASH *sb.*¹] *trans.* To dress or adorn with a sash. Cf. SASHED *ppl. a.*²

1796 BURKE *Regic. Peace* Wks. IX. 46 Now they are powdered and perfumed,..and sashed and plumed. **1888** HENLEY *Bk. Verses* 117 As here you loiter, flowing-gowned And hugely sashed.

sash (sæʃ), *v.*² [f. SASH *sb.*²] *trans.* To furnish with sash-windows; to construct or glaze as a sash-window.

170. CELIA FIENNES *Diary* (1888) 300 It is sashed up to the top with low windows to sit in. **1750** MRS. DELANY in *Life & Corr.* (1861) II. 562, I am new sashing the room. **1781** COWPER *Retirement* 483 Suburban villas,..Tight boxes, neatly sash'd, and in a blaze With all a July sun's collected rays. **1886** WILLIS & CLARK *Cambridge* I. 227 The chamber windows were sashed.

sashay (sæ'ʃeɪ), *sb. N. Amer.* [f. next.]

1. A venture, a sally; an excursion, trip, or expedition.

1900 G. ADE *More Fables* 184 Lutie never got out of her Dream until she made a bold Sashay with a Concert Company. **1935** H. L. DAVIS *Honey in Horn* 15 If you yank him out for any all-night sashay on these roads, you ought to be ashamed of yourself. **1941** *Sat. Even. Post* 16 Aug. 68/3 On my first sashay into the flying field. **1952** E. B. WHITE *Let.* 6 Apr. (1976) 355 Spring is making little sashays about coming to town, but it has been a fairly unconvincing demonstration so far. **1961** R. M. PATTERSON *Buffalo Head* v. 183 He could make a long sashay north along the foot of the range. **1968** —— *Finlay's River* 147 Swannell, Copley and Alexander and the two dogs..set out for a three-day sashay up the strong creek that flowed into the Ingenika.

2. A step in square dancing (see quot. *c* 1940). Also *transf.* and *attrib.*

c **1940** *Square Dance* (Writers' Program, Illinois) 40 The Sashay is a series of short quick steps directly to the side, either to the right or to the left... The gent holds the lady's left hand in his right, and her right hand in his left. **1941** R. J. MCNAIR *Western Square Dances* XIX. 78 The Sashay step is a quick side step. **1956** R. HOLDEN *Contra Dance Bk.* iv. 45 Sashay, the American chassez. **1971** *Flying* (N.Y.) Apr. 49/1 It's got a marvelous sort of sashay movement because it's such a big airplane that when you roll you can feel those booms kind of rolling around behind you. **1974** 'J. MARKS'

Mick Jagger 32 The juvenile Jagger... Trying a few quick sashays and eating a banana.

sashay (sæ'ʃeɪ), *v. colloq.* (chiefly *U.S.*). Also **sasshay, sashy.** [Mispronunciation of CHASSÉ *v.*]
1. *intr.* **a.** To perform a chassé, esp. in square dancing; freq. *transf.*, to perform a movement similar to the chassé. **b.** To glide, walk, or travel, usu. in a casual manner. **c.** To move diagonally or sideways; to travel an irregular path; to wander or saunter. **d.** To move or walk ostentatiously, conspicuously, or provocatively; to strut or parade. Freq. with *adv.*

1836 *Franklin Repository* (Chambersburg, Pa.) 4 Oct. 1/3 If you don't sashay across, button your lip, and go home quietly, you and I will have to promenade all around, and swing corners into the watch house. **1860** O. W. HOLMES *Elsie V.* vii, The Doctor looked as if he should like to rigadoon and sashy across as well as the young one he was talkin' about. **1865** 'MARK TWAIN' in *Californian* 18 Mar. 8/1 For all they're so handy about keeping her sasshaying around from shanty to shanty..none of 'em's ever got a good word for her. **1878** F. H. HART *Sazerac Lying Club* 83 S'pose, gentlemen, that we sashay up to the bar. **1888** J. C. HARRIS *Free Joe*, etc. 49 What were you doing sasshaying around in his room last night? **1891** B. HARTE *First Fam. Tasajara* II. vii, Ye remember how he sashayed round newspaper offices in Frisco until he could write a flapdoodle story himself? **1905** *Dialect Notes* III. 64 They sashayed back and forth to beat the band. **1913** C. E. MULFORD *Coming of Cassidy* v. 80 Logan..is about thirty miles east. You must 'a sashayed some to get only this far in four days. **1917** H. GARLAND *Son of Middle Border* xv. 163 At dancing parties they balanced or 'sashayed' in *Honest John* or *Money Musk.* **1935** Z. N. HURSTON *Mules & Men* I. v. 113 John was callin' for de new set: 'Choose yo' partners.'.. 'Sashay all.' **1942** E. PAUL *Narrow St.* ix. 74 He staggered eastward toward the Panthéon and I sashayed westward to the rue Lafayette. **1944** C. HIMES *Black on Black* (1973) 201, I picked up my sack and sorta sashayed off. **1949** K. M. WELLS *Owl Pen Reader* (1969) III. 246 Fireflies danced by Moonstone Creek. They dipped and cavorted, they sashayed like a million wee stars gone mad. **1951** E. PAUL *Springtime in Paris* v. 114 Instead of continuing toward the rue de la Huchette, Christophe hopped and sashayed to the left. **1960** F. RAPHAEL *Limits of Love* I. iii. 41 A large Negro ..was sashaying through the crowd towards them. **1968** J. UPDIKE *Couples* iv. 311 Sashaying from the shower nude, her pussy of a ferny freshness. **1973** S. ALSOP *Stay of Execution* (1974) II. 201 Stewart brought a pretty..girl friend home. As she sashayed through the living room, Andrew remarked, 'I like the way she wiggles her things.' **1978** J. A. MICHENER *Chesapeake* 270 He hoped that Nelly Turlock would not sashay in, demanding dividends for her family. *Ibid.* 545, I see her sashayin' past in a dress I know she stole from Miss Susan.

2. *trans.* To cause (someone or something) to sashay; to walk or parade (a person); to carry or convey (an object); to manœuvre (a vehicle).

1928 L. H. NASON *Sergeant Eadie* 130 What the hell good a rifle does to me sashayin' these jugheads up an' down the road, I don't know. **1944** J. S. PENNELL *Hist. Rome Hanks* 189 Take them guns thar—tuck 'em from the Yanks at the fust battle of Manassas, an' been a-farin' 'em eveh since an' sashayin' 'em all oveh hell an Vuhginny. **1963** T. PYNCHON *V.* i. 22 Rachel would gee and haw this MG around Route 17's bloodthirsty curves and cutbacks, sashaying its arrogant butt past hay wagons. **1977** J. GARDNER *Werewolf Trace* i. 17 'James Bond rules. Okay?' chuckled Bud, sashaying the car neatly between a pair of taxis.

Hence **sa'shaying** *vbl. sb.* and *ppl. a.*

1935 R. STOUT *League of Frightened Men* xx. 272 It did mean his sashaying out of the house twice in two days, which was an all-time record. **1976** *New Yorker* 8 Mar. 109/1 He'd start with a fusillade of rim shots, sink into a sashaying figure that strode back and forth between his tomtoms.

sashed (sæʃt), *ppl. a.*[1] [f. SASH *v.*[2] or *sb.*[2] + -ED.] Furnished or constructed with a sash or with sash-windows. ***sashed door, window*** = SASH-*door*, SASH-WINDOW.

1710 STEELE *Tatler* No. 203 ¶8 A sashed Roof, which lets in the Sun at all Times. **1762** *Jackson's Oxf. Jrnl.* 6 Nov., A Freehold modern-built sashed house. **1814** SCOTT *Wav.* ix, A sashed-door opening from the house. **1816** JANE AUSTEN *Emma* II. vi. 98 He stopt for several minutes at the two superior sashed windows which were open. *Ibid.* III. xiv. 260 A brick house, sashed windows below, and casements above. **1862** SHIRLEY *Nugæ Crit.* i. 8 A..room, whose sashed windows open upon a terraced flower-garden.

sashed (sæʃt), *ppl. a.*[2] [f. SASH *v.*[1] or *sb.*[1] + -ED.] Dressed or adorned with a sash.

1869 'MARK TWAIN' *Innoc. Abr.* vii. 69 Turbaned, sashed and trowsered Moorish merchants. **1894** MRS. H. WARD *Marcella* ii, The frilled and sashed splendours of her companions. **1970** *Daily Tel.* 27 Apr. 14 A good sashed white midi coat for £25.

sashen, variant of SAGENE[1].

sashery ('sæʃərɪ). *rare*[−1]. [f. SASH *sb.*[1] + -ERY.] Sashes collectively.

1864 CARLYLE *Fredk. Gt.* XVII. vii. IV. 594, I have seen staff officers, distinguished only by their sasheries and insignia, who would not [etc.].

‖**sashimi** ('sæʃɪmɪ). [Jap., f. *sashi* pierce + *mi* flesh.] A Japanese dish consisting of thin slices of raw fish served with grated radish or ginger and soy sauce. Also *attrib.* or as *adj.*

1880 I. L. BIRD *Unbeaten Tracks in Japan* I. 239 The preparation of raw fish cut into oblong strips called *sashimi.* **1920** *Japan Advertiser* 22 Aug. 5 Sashimi or arai..is raw tai, tunny or kare, served with horseradish. **1933** P. PETO *Recipes Rare from Everywhere* 29 *Sashimi.* The fish is skinned, cleaned and cut into fillets about $\frac{1}{10}$ inch thick; it is arranged on a dish and garnished with fresh thinly sliced vegetables, and is eaten with Shoyu blended with Japanese shredded horseradish. **1936** K. TEZUKA *Jap. Food* 14 *Sashimi* (raw sea-bream, flounder, tunny, etc. cut into thin slices). **1959** R. KIRKBRIDE *Tamiko* vii. 54 They had hors d'oeuvres of raw wild vegetables, sashimi, thin slices of raw tuna [etc.]. **1967** *Guardian* 8 Dec. 8/2 Finding fish fresh enough to serve sashimi (raw) is very difficult. **1969** R. HOWE *Far Eastern Cookery* 189 *Sashimi*..is a truly Japanese speciality... I took myself to a small *sashimi* bar..and ordered *sake.* **1973** J. GORES *Final Notice* x. 60 Waiting for the Japanese waitress to arrive with the sukiyaki and sashimi. **1978** *Maclean's Mag.* 13 Nov. 47/1 Each spring the tiny fishing village 20 miles south of Halifax prepares to satisfy the yearnings of 100 million Japanese for sashimi.

sashine, variant of SAGENE[1].

sashing ('sæʃɪŋ), *vbl. sb.* [f. SASH *sb.*[1] or *v.*[1] + -ING[2].] = SASHERY.

1864 CARLYLE *Fredk. Gt.* XVI. vi. IV. 318 Silver helmets, sashings, housings.

sashless ('sæʃlɪs), *a.* [f. SASH *sb.*[2] + -LESS.] Without a sash or glazed frame.

1841 LADY F. HASTINGS *Poems* 159 Within those sashless walls. **1883** STEVENSON *Silverado Sq.* 41 The other gable was pierced by a sashless window.

†**sa'shoon.** *Obs.* exc. *U.S.* Also 7 **sashune, shashune, shasoon.** [Corruptly a. F. *chausson.*] A stuffed leather pad formerly worn inside the leg of a boot; also, see quot. 1875.

1687-8 in *Sussex Archæol. Coll.* (1849) II. 113 June 29th, paid Henry Sharpe of Cuckfield for a pair of bootes and sashoones, 13s. **1688** R. HOLME *Armoury* III. 13/2 A Sashune or Shashune, is stuffed or quilted Leather, to be bound about the small of the Leg. **1692** *Scarronides* II. 34 His gouty Hocks, with fleshy Sashoons, Like Horses lookt that has the Fashions. **1694** MOTTEUX tr. *Rabelais* IV. ix. 37 One nam'd his [wench], my Slipper, and she him, my Foot. Another my Boot, she him, my Shasoon. **1706** PHILLIPS (ed. Kersey), *Sashoons*, Leather put under a Boot about the Small of the Leg. **1875** KNIGHT *Dict. Mech.*, *Sashoon*, a soft leathern pad placed inside a shoe to ease the pressure on a tender spot.

'sash-'window. [f. SASH *sb.*[2]] A window consisting of a SASH or glazed wooden frame; esp. one having a sash or a pair of sashes made to slide up and down, as distinguished from a casement.

1686 *Lond. Gaz.* No. 2135/8 Any Person may be furnished with Glasses for Sashwindows..at Mr. Dukes Shop. **1687** J. SMITH *Painting in Oil* xx. (ed. 2) 97 The manner of Painting Cloth, or Sarsnet Shash-Windows. **1699** LISTER *Journ. Paris* 191 The House it self was but building; but it is one of the finest in Paris... He shewed us his great Sash Windows; how easily they might be lifted up and down, and stood at any height; which Contrivance he said he had out of England,.. There being nothing of this Poise in Windows in France before. **1709** ADDISON *Tatler* No. 162 ¶6 Having lately observed several..Shops, that stand upon Corinthian Pillars, and whole Rows of Tin Pots showing themselves, in order to their Sale, through a Sash-Window. **1820** SCOTT *Abbot* xviii, This maiden of Morton. 'Tis an axe, man—an axe which falls of itself like a sash window. **1862** LYTTON *Str. Story* I. xxiv. 164 It was the man servant's business to see that the sash-window was closed.

attrib. **1689** in Willis & Clark *Cambridge* (1886) I. 107 Materialls and worke of 5 sash window frames. **1718** *Free-thinker* No. 95 ¶5 All the Sash-Window Shop-keepers in London.

Hence **sash-windowed** *ppl. a.*, furnished with sash-windows; **sash-windowing** *vbl. sb.* (*nonce-wd.*), the action of furnishing with sash-windows.

1714 J. MACKY *Journ. Eng.* (1724) II. ix. 129 Handsome Houses, Sash-windowed. **1826** MISS MITFORD *Village* Ser. II. 14 By dint of..sash-windowing and fresh-dooring the.. farm-house has become a very genteel-looking residence.

sashy, see SASHAY *v.*

sasin ('sæsɪn). Also **saisin.** [Nepalese.] The common Indian antelope, *Antilope bezoartica* or *cervicapra.*

1834 *Penny Cycl.* II. 72 The Sasin or Common Antelope. **1842** *P. Parley's Ann.* III. 76 The common antelope or sasin is found over the vast continent of India. **1846** GRAY *Catal. Hodgson's Specim. Brit. Mus.* 26 The Black Antelope, or Sasin. **1850** R. G. CUMMING *Hunter's Life S. Afr.* (1902) 14/1 This exquisitely graceful and truly interesting antelope [springbok]..in its nature and habits reminded me of the saisin of India.

sasine ('seɪsɪn). *Sc. Law.* [Sc. var. of SEISIN (q.v. for obsolete forms), after Law Latin *sasina.*] The act of giving possession of feudal property. Also, 'colloquially, the instrument by which the fact of possession of feudal property is proved' (Bell).

Precept of Sasine; see PRECEPT *sb.* 4 b. *Register of Sasines*: the court at Edinburgh in which all sasines must be recorded within sixty days of execution.

1669 *Sc. Acts Chas. II* (1820) VII. 609/1 Together with the precept of sasine following vpon the said charter and instrument of sasine following vpon the said precept. **1693** *Sc. Acts Will. & Mary* (1822) IX. 271/2 All Infeftments whether of property or annual-rent, or other Reall Rights, wherupon Sasines for hereafter shall be taken. *Ibid.*, According to the date and priority of the Registrations of the Sasines. **1782** *Encycl. Brit.* (ed. 2) XVI. 661 *Sasine*, or *Seisin.* **1826** SCOTT *Woodst.* iii, Will you take sasine and livery? **1828-40** TYTLER *Hist. Scot.* (1864) I. 28 Sasine or legal possession of the land, was immediately to be given by a brief from Chancery. **1869** *Act 31 & 32 Vict.* c. 101 §3 Sched. B, A disposition..bearing date as in the precept of sasine herein-after inserted. **1884** *Law Rep.*, 9 *App. Cases* 305 The trustee's infeftment in the heritable estate was recorded in the register of sasines at Glasgow.

saskatoon (sæskə'tuːn). Also **saskootoom.** [Contracted a. Cree *misâskwatomin* (Lacombe, *Dict. de la langue des Cris*), f. *misâskwat* the Amelanchier + *min* fruit, berry.] Canadian name of the shrub or small tree *Amelanchier canadensis* (var. *alnifolia*), and its fruit, also called June-berry, shad-berry, and service-berry.

1875 EARL OF SOUTHESK *Saskatchewan & Rocky Mts.*, Table of Contents vii, Saskootoom Berries. [Not in the text, which gives the Indian name *Meesasskootoom-meena.*] **1894** C. L. JOHNSTONE *Wint. & Summer Excurs. Canada* 47 The wild saskatoon is a very luscious fruit, like a black currant and bilberry combined. **1904** *Blackw. Mag.* July 74 The uncleared bush is thick with ash, maple, cherry, and saskatoon.

sasne, variant of SAISNE *Obs.*, SAXON.

sasone, obs. Sc. spelling of *so soon.*

sasoun(e, obs. forms of SEASON.

sasquatch ('sæskwɒtʃ). *Canad.* Also **Sasquatch.** [Salish.] A name for a huge, hairy, man-like monster supposedly inhabiting the north-west of the U.S. and Canada. Also *collect.* and *attrib.*

1929 *Maclean's Mag.* 1 Apr. 61/1 The strange people, of whom there are but few now—rarely seen and seldom met —..are known by the name of Sasquatch, or, 'the hairy mountain men'. **1950** C. P. LYONS *Milestones on Mighty Fraser* 28 Indian lore has it that a mysterious race of giants, known as the Sasquatch, live in the high mountains around Harrison Lake. **1958** *Encycl. Canadiana* IX. 233/1 Known originally to the Indians..as Saskehavas (wild men), they are called by the..whites Sasquatch (hairy men). **1966** *Globe Mag.* (Toronto) 11 June 3/3 Most villagers relate every Sasquatch sighting to the amount of alcohol they insist must have been consumed immediately prior to the monster's appearance. **1971** W. HILLEN *Blackwater River* xi. 108 Stories of strange lights and huge, wild, hairy men, or 'sasquatch', circulate periodically, usually toward spring. **1972** L. HANCOCK *There's a Seal in my Sleeping Bag* vi. 123 We scanned the steep forested slopes of the pass for Sasquatch. **1974** *New Yorker* 25 Feb. 92/2 The Northwest's legendary Sasquatch, a huge, humanoid seven-or-so-foot creature akin to the Abominable Snowman of Tibet. **1976** *Toronto Star* 31 Jan. 7/1 A nine-man team, using computerized information and electronic detection gear, will go sasquatch hunting in British Columbia in April or May. **1977** *New Yorker* 20 June 72/2 It was lumpy, pitted, pocked, rough, ugly—an apparent filling from the tooth of a Sasquatch. **1979** T. GIFFORD *Hollywood Gothic* (1980) v. 53, I feel like a sasquatch has been using me for a soccer ball.

Sasquehanno, -sahannock, etc., obs. varr. SUSQUEHANNOCK.

sass (sæs), *sb. U.S. colloq.* Also **sas.** [var. SAUCE *sb.*] **1. a.** = SAUCE *sb.* 4 a.

1775 J. STEVENS *Jrnl.* 5 May in *Essex Inst. Hist. Coll.* (1912) XLVIII. 43 Steven Barker come down & brought us som sas. **1836** B. TUCKER *Partisan Leader* II. xxxv. 124 The fellow talked to me about living at home on codfish, and potatoes, and cider, and pies, and *all sorts of sass.* **1860** *Knickerbocker* July 102 White turnip, yellow turnip, or any sort of sass, long sass, or short sass. **1945** M. LYON *Fresh from Hills* iv. 46 A family could get along without garden sass.

b. = SAUCE *sb.* 4 b.

1913 H. KEPHART *Our Southern Highlanders* xiii. 293 Your hostess, proffering apple sauce, will ask, 'Do you love sass?'

2. = SAUCE *sb.* 6 b.

1835 [see CHUNK *v.*[1] 1]. **1853** G. C. HILL *Dovecote* 88 I've a precious good mind to duck you for your sass! **1876** 'MARK TWAIN' *Tom Sawyer* i. 23 If you give me much more of your sass I'll take and bounce a rock off'n your head. **1880** J. C. HARRIS *Uncle Remus* iv. 31 Brer Rabbit wuz bleedzed fer ter fling back some er his sass. **1897** 'O. THANET' *Missionary Sheriff* 21, I shall take more advantage of it if you give me any sass. **1935** J. T. FARRELL *Judgement Day* ii. 25 It must have been something of the old Studs Lonigan left in him that led to his not taking sass, risking a fight. **1967** P. WELLES *Babyhip* iii. 46 Is this what we get? Sass? No gratitude. **1977** *Time* 3 Jan. 21/1 If she's mostly given over now to laughter, pride and sass, she has earned her fun.

sass (sæs), *v. U.S. colloq.* [var. SAUCE v.]

1. *trans.* = SAUCE *v.* 4 d.

1856 'J. PHOENIX' *Phoenixiana* xvi. 125 While the squire.. sasses all respectable persons With his talk of pills he's invented. **1867** 'MARK TWAIN' *Celebr. Jumping Frog* 166 You ought never to 'sass' old people—unless they 'sass' you first. **1887** MARY E. WILKINS *Humble Romance* i. 9 An' she might sass you so you'd be ready to back out, too. **1896** *N. Y. Dramatic News* 18 July 2/3 When he was requested to desist he 'sassed' the officer. **1920** S. LEWIS *Main Street* ix. 118 There had to be one man in town independent enough to sass the banker! **1929** W. FAULKNER *Sound & Fury* 67 Dont you sass me, nigger boy. **1956** W. H. WHYTE *Organization Man* (1957) VII. xxvi. 358 If little Johnny sasses Mrs. Erdlick just once more. **1966** K. L. MORGAN in A. Dundes *Mother Wit* (1973) 602/1 She wanted to know if it was all right to 'sass' the woman the way she did since she was 'trash'. **1978** J. A. MICHENER *Chesapeake* 536 'But, Missy, I done clean it.' 'Don't you sass me!' she screamed.

2. *intr.* To speak impertinently; ***to sass back***, to reply impertinently, to 'answer back'.

1880 J. C. HARRIS *Uncle Remus* iv. 29 You been runnin' roun' here sassin' after me a mighty long time. **1884** 'MARK TWAIN' *Huck. Finn* (1885) xxvii. 237 The king sassed back, as much as was safe for him. **1891** O. W. Holmes *Over Teacups* 154, I suppose Me-Number-Two will 'sass back'. **1976** *National Observer* (U.S.) 24 July 10/3 No teacher chooses to teach students who are sleeping or throwing chalk or sassing.

Hence **'sassing** *vbl. sb.*

1962 W. H. Gass in Foley & Burnett *Best Amer. Short Stories* 112 Listen to me, Jorge, I've had enough to your sassing. **1967** P. Welles *Babyhip* iii. 48 'Don't you get hysterics,' Mrs Green warned, 'or I'll throw cold water on you. I'll have none of this sassing.' **1977** *New Yorker* 6 June 48/3 Far worse than any welts he ever got when his father or Abel beat him in the shed for misbehaving or sassing.

sassaby (sə'seɪbɪ). Also 9 **sas(s)ayby, sassaybe, sassaybi, sassabye, tsessebe, tsessabi.** [a. Sechwana *tsessébe, tsessábi.*] A large antelope (*Alcelaphus lunata*), a native of S. Africa, sometimes called the Bastard Hartebeest.

1820 S. Daniell *Sk. S. Africa* 18 The Sasayby is an Antelope, heretofore not described, found in the Booshwana country. **1833** *Penny Cycl.* II. 90/2 They consider it as a kindred species with the Hartebeest of the colonists... The Booshwanas call it Sassaby. **1850** R. G. Cumming *Hunter's Life S. Afr.* (1902) 156/1 Presently I came across two sassaybys, one of which I knocked over. **1857** Livingstone *Trav.* vii. 135 The tsessebe. *a* **1875** T. Baines *Gold Regions S.E. Afr.* (1877) 66 Gee shot a Sassaybe, or bastard hartebeest. **1897** H. H. Johnston *Brit. Centr. Afr.* 326 The tsessebe or sassaby of S. Africa. **1907** W. C. Scully *By Veldt & Kopje* 201 Opportunity to lay low koodoo, sable and tsessabi.

sassafras ('sæsəfræs). Also 7 **saxe-, sasafras, sassa-, saxa-, sarsafrax,** 7–8 **sassafrass,** 8–9 **saxafras.** [a. Sp. *sasafras* (whence Pg. *sassafraz, salsafraz,* F., G. and mod.L. *sassafras.*

It is doubtful whether the Sp. word is a transferred application (which, indeed, would be difficult to account for) of a Sp. representation of L. *saxifraga* SAXIFRAGE, or whether it was adopted from some American language; in the latter case the American word seems to have influenced the form of the Sp. name for saxifrage, which according to the native lexicographers has the forms *saxifraga, -fragia, -fragua, salsifragia, salsifrex, saxafrax.* The Spanish writer Monardes (1571) regards the Sp. name as adopted from Fr., which seems unlikely; he gives the native Indian name as *pauame.*]

1. a. A small tree, *Sassafras officinale* (N.O. *Laurineæ*), also called Sassafras Laurel and Ague-tree, with green apetalous flowers and dimorphous leaves, native in North America, where it is said to have been discovered by the Spaniards in 1528.

The name is frequently applied (chiefly with defining word) to trees of other genera which have similar medicinal properties; e.g. **Australian** or **Tasmanian sassafras** (*Atherosperma moschata*), see PLUME-NUTMEG; **Brazilian sassafras** (*Nectandra Puchury*), see PICHURIM; **Cayenne sassafras** (*Laurelia sempervirens*); **oriental sassafras** (*Sassafras Parthenoxylon*); **swamp sassafras** (*Magnolia glauca*).

1577 Frampton *Joyfull Newes* II. 46 Of the Tree that is brought from the Florida, whiche is called Sassafras. **1597** Gerarde *Herbal* III. cxxxvi. 1341 The roote of Sassafras hath power to comfort the liuer. **1622** Capt. Smith *New Eng. Trials* 260 About three hogsheads of Beuer skins and some Saxefras. **1641** R. Evelin in *Descr. New Albion* (1648) 21 There are Cedars, Cypresse, and Sassafras. **1666** J. Davies *Hist. Caribby Isles* 47 They afford Sandal-wood, Guiacum, and Sasafras, all of which are so well known. **1684** Penn *Let.* in *Academy* 11 Jan. (1896) 36/3 The trees that grow here are the Mulberry,..chesnut, Ash, Sarsafrax. **1726** Shelvocke *Voy. round World* (1757) 54 The sassafras, so much esteemed in Europe. **1745** P. Thomas *Jrnl. Anson's Voy.* 12 Sassafrass is here in great Plenty. **1817–18** Cobbett *Resid. U.S.* (1822) 5 The Sassafras in flower, or, whatever else it is called. It resembles the Elder flower a good deal. **1856** Bryant *Ind. Story* x, And there hangs on the sassafras, broken and bent, One tress of the well known hair. **1887** T. N. Page *Ole Virginia*, etc. (1893) 140 An old field all grown up in sassafras.

b. The wood or timber of this tree.

1728 *Rec. Early Hist. Boston* (1883) VIII. 222 No Popler, ..Sassifax, Black ash, Basswood, or Ceder Shall be Corded up. **1900** *19th Ann. Rep. U.S. Bureau Amer. Ethnol. 1897–98* I. 422 Sassafras is tabued as fuel among the Cherokee..perhaps for the practical reason that it is apt to pop out of the fire when heated. **1921** C. C. Deam *Trees of Indiana* 165 Floors were made of sassafras to keep out the rats and mice.

2. a. The dried bark of this tree, used medicinally as an alterative; also an infusion of this.

1577 Frampton *Joyfull Newes* II. 50 Many of them that had Tertians did take Water of the Sassafras. **1605** B. Jonson *Volpone* II. ii, No Indian drug had ere beene famed, Tabacco, Sassafras not named. **1714** *Fr. Bk. of Rates* 96 Sax-a-fras per 100 Weight, 05 00. **1822** Lamb *Elia* Ser. I. *Praise Chimney-Sweepers*, A composition, the groundwork of which I have understood to be the sweet wood yclept sassafras. **1837** R. Ellis *Laws & Regul. Customs* III. 405 Sassafras, is the bark of the *Lauris Sassafras*. **1863** *Rio Abajo Weekly Press* (Albuquerque, New Mexico) 14 Apr. 2/3 Sassafras.—Those who use this drink will find [etc.]. **1871** E. Eggleston *Hoosier Schoolmaster* 88 He drank his glass of water, having declined even her sassafras. **1912** M. Nicholson *Hoosier Chron.* 44 Sassafras in the spring, and a few doses of quinine in the fall,..were all the medicine that any good Hoosier needed.

b. *oil of sassafras* = *sassafras oil* (see 3).

1753 Chambers *Cycl. Supp.* s.v. *Oil*, The oil of sassafras is peculiarly liable to crystallization in certain circumstances. **1838** T. Thomson *Chem. Org. Bodies* 479 Oil of Sassafras is obtained from the root of the laurus sassafras.

3. *Comb.*, as ***sassafras-bark, -bush, -chips, -pith, -root, -tree, -wood***; **sassafras laurel** = sense 1; **sassafras nut** (see PICHURIM); **sassafras oil**, an oil distilled from the root of the common sassafras, from the bark of the Tasmanian sassafras, or from the sassafras nut; **sassafras soap** *U.S.*, a soap scented with sassafras; **sassafras tea**, an infusion of sassafras formerly used in making saloop.

1681 Grew *Musæum* II. I. i. 180 Being well chewed, it hath the self same Tast with that of *Sassafras-Barque. **1848** G. C. Furber *Twelve Months Volunteer* 54 The field, or the larger part of it, growing up with tall weeds and *sassafras bushes. **1944** T. D. Clark *Pills, Petticoats & Plows* 261 The graveyard is scraped bare of crab grass,..Johnson grass and sassafras bushes to give them a 'cared-for' appearance. **1875** *Ure's Dict. Arts* III. 543 [Recipe for 'Athenian Hair-wash'.] *Sassafras chips. **1878** Hoblyn *Dict. Med.* s.v., *S. officinale*, or *Sassafras Laurel, grows in North America. **1830** Lindley *Nat. Syst. Bot.* 30 The *Sassafras nuts of the London shops are the fruit of the Laurus Puceri. **1800** *Misc. Tracts* in *Asiat. Ann. Reg.* 74/1 The sassafras tree, the bark of which yields the costly coelilawang, and all its roots the *sassafras oil. **1861** Bentley *Man. Bot.* 631 *Sassafras pith is used in America as a demulcent like quince seeds. **1607** in *3rd Rep. Hist. MSS. Comm.* 53/2 Our easiest and richest commodity being *sassafras roots, were gathered up by the sailors. **1875** T. W. Higginson *Hist. U.S.* vii. 51 Gosnold went back to England with a cargo of sassafras-root. **1860** J. G. Holland *Miss Gilbert's Career* 108 Arthur took his accustomed seat at the head of the table, with Leonora at his right hand,..[in an] atmosphere of *sassafras-soap. **1863** B. Taylor *H. Thurston* I. 256 An old woman with two sentimental daughters, who..always smelt of sassafras-soap. **1783** M. Garthshore in *Med. Commun.* I. 245 She.. drank *sassafras tea. **1817** T. Dean in *Indiana Hist. Soc. Publ.* (1918) VI. 324 We took some bread and sassafras tea. **1960** I. Wallach *Absence of Cello* 41 Perry sipped a cup of sassafras tea. **1597** Gerarde *Herbal* III. cxxxvi. 1341 The *Sassafras tree. **1864–5** Wood *Homes without Hands* xiv. (1868) 3 The insect called *Saturnia promethea*, which lives on the Sassafras-tree. **1681** tr. *Belon's Myst. Physick* 16 One dram or two of *Sassafrax-wood. **1736** Bailey *Househ. Dict.* 13 Sassafras-wood and China-root, of each ½ oz.

sassafrid, -ide ('sæsəfrɪd, -fraɪd). [f. SASSAFR(AS) + -ID(E used irreg.] A substance extracted from the root-bark of sassafras.

1852 Morfit *Tanning & Currying* (1853) 87 Sassafride. **1876** Harley *Mat. Med.* (ed. 6) 460 A red colouring matter ..called sassafrid.

sassafy, sassage: see SALSIFY, SAUSAGE *sb.*

Sassanian (sæ'seɪnɪən), *a.* and *sb.* Also **Sasanian.** [f. *Sasan* (Pers. *Sāsān*) + -IAN.]

a. *adj.* Of or pertaining to the family of Sasan, whose grandson Ardashir I founded the dynasty which ruled the Persian Empire A.D. 211–651. Also, of, pertaining to, or characteristic of the period of this dynasty. **b.** *sb.* A member of this family, esp. one of the Sassanian kings.

1788 Gibbon *Decl. & F.* V. li. 285 The fall of the Sassanian dynasty. **1855** Fergusson *Handbk. Archit.* VIII. i. 371 The Sassanians took up the style where it was left by the builders of Al Hadhr. **1866** *Jrnl. Asiat. Soc. Bengal* XXXV. I. 133 The kingdom of the Sasanians. **1908** *Athenæum* 28 Mar. 380/1 The causes of the decay of the Byzantine and the Sasanian empires. **1928** C. Dawson *Age of Gods* iv. 84 In historical times we find the influence of the Sassanian culture of Persia following very much the same paths. **1929** E. C. Thomas *Lay Folks' Hist. Liturgy* I. v. 22 Persia..was conquered by the Mohammedans in 651, thus ending the native Sassanian dynasty, which was founded in 223 B.C. **1931** A. W. Seaby *Art in Life of Mankind* 80 The Sasanians were as bitter enemies of the Christian eastern or Byzantine empire as they had been of pagan Rome. **1940** *Burlington Mag.* July 31/1 An important feature in Sasanian and Muslim architecture. **1958** A. Toynbee *East to West* 167 On bas-reliefs of the Sasanian age one is shocked to find the goddess Anahita holding her ground beside Ormuzd. **1971** R. Russell tr. *Ahmad's Shore & Wave* viii. 93 Strange houses. One like a dreadnought..one in Japanese style, one displaying Sassanian arches. **1976** *Nature* 10 June 472/1 The Venus-Jupiter conjunction of 650 was one recorded by the Chinese; this conjunction was later regarded by Masha'allah as signifying the fall of the Sasanians and the rise of the Arabs. **1977** *Ashmolean Mus. Rep. Visitors 1975–76* 17 (*title*) Parthian and Sasanian metalwork in the Bomford collection. **1980** J. Lees-Milne *Harold Nicolson* xiv. 303 The Sassanian city of Istakh, destroyed during the Arab conquest in the seventh century A.D.

Sassanid ('sæsənɪd), *sb.* and *a.* Also 8–9 **-ide.** Also **Sasanid.** [ad. med.L. *Sassanidæ* pl., f. *Sassan, Sasan*: see prec. + -ID.] **a.** *sb.* A descendant of Sasan (see SASSANIAN), esp. a king of the Sassanian dynasty. **b.** *attrib.* and *adj.* = SASSANIAN *a.*

1776 Gibbon *Decl. & F.* (1782) I. viii. 256 *note*, The dynasty of the Sassanides. **1867** C. M. Yonge *Pupils of St. John* xvii. 270 The Sassanid princes had taken up all the traditions of their supposed ancestry. **1871** P. Smith *Anc. Hist. East* xviii. §7 (1881) 379 The Sassanids..adopted a sacred standard of leather emblazoned with gems. **1895** Salmond *Chr. Doctr. Immort.* I. vi. 101 [Zoroastrianism] held the Persian mind till the end of the Sassanid dynasty. **1904** F. C. Burkitt *Early Eastern Christianity* 25 The rise and decay of Christianity in the Sasanid Empire. **1910** [see AQUAMANILE]. **1929** E. C. Thomas *Lay Folks' Hist. Liturgy* I. v. 22 In A.D. 202 Abjar IX., Prince of Edessa, adopted Christianity, but this Church [in Persia] was barely tolerated by the Parthians and often persecuted by the Sassanids. **1958** A. Toynbee *East to West* 165 The capital of the Sasanid Persian Empire's Arab wardens of the Arabian marches. **1977** *Field* 31 Mar. 525/1 For the early Persian dynasties such as the Archamedians and Sassanids, the rug may have been used as a gift from one ruler to another.

sassaparilla, obs. form of SARSAPARILLA.

sassarara: see SISERARY.

†**sassa'rollo.** Also **sassorolla,** anglicized **sassorol.** [a. It. *sassaruolo*, now *sassajuolo*, f. *sasso* rock.] The Rock Pigeon (*Columba livia*).

1753 Chambers *Cycl. Supp.*, Sassarollo. **1850** Ogilvie, *Sassorol, Sassorolla.*

sassatje, var. SOSATIE.

†**sasse.** *Obs.* Also 7 **soss.** [a. Du. *sas*, of obscure origin. The Fr. *sas* of the same meaning is prob. from Du.] = LOCK *sb.*[2] 9.

1642 Sir C. Vermuyden *Disc. Drain. Fens* 22 A Sasse to be set to let water into old Welland to preserve Navigation. **1661–2** Pepys *Diary* 25 Jan. **1665** Dodson *Design Drain. Fens* 7 The Sosses at Stanground,..and others,..are of singular good use, yet I do affirm, there will be a necessity of having a Soss and Sleuce near Ditton. **1861** Smiles *Engineers* I. 57 A navigable Sasse or Sluice at Standground.

Sassella (sæ'sɛlə). Also **sassella.** [It.] The name of a red wine from the Valtellina district, Lombardy, in Italy.

1935 A. L. Simon *Dict. Wine* 227 *Sassella*, one of the best red wines of the Valtellina (Lombardy). **1967** A. Lichine *Encycl. Wines & Spirits* 330/1 In this district [*sc.* Valtellina], centred around the town of Sondrio, the three almost identical red wines are Sassella, Grumello, and Inferno, all from Nebbiolo grapes grown on the more manageable Alpine slopes. **1970** *House & Garden* May 140/2 Of all the Lombardy wines..I have most enjoyed..sassella—a red wine. **1975** 'S. Marlowe' *Cawthorn Jrnls.* xix. 166 A bottle of the dark, velvety Sassella stood on the table.

Sassenach ('sæsənæx). Also 8 **Sassenaugh, Sacsanagh,** 8–9 **Sassenagh, Sassanagh,** 9 **Sacsanach.** [repr. Gael. *Sasunnach* adj. English, sb. an Englishman = Irish *Sasanach, Sacsanach*, f. *Sasan-*, repr. the Teut. ethnic name SAXON. (Cf. Gael. *Sasunn*, Irish *Sasana, Sacsain*, England.)] The name given by the Gaelic inhabitants of Great Britain and Ireland to their 'Saxon' or English neighbours. (Sometimes attributed to Welsh speakers: the corresponding Welsh form is *Seisnig.*)

1771 Smollett *Humph. Cl.* 3 Sept., The Highlanders have no other name for the people of the low country, but Sassenaugh, or Saxons. **1814** Scott *Let. to Morritt* 11 Nov. in *Lockhart*, I believe the frolics one can cut in this loose garb are all set down by you Sassenachs to the real agility of the wearer. *a* **1820** Drennan in *Spirit of Nation* (1845) 24 Unarm'd must thy sons and thy daughters await The Sassenagh's lust or the Sassenagh's hate. *a* **1845** T. O. Davis *Fontenoy* v, Revenge! remember Limerick! dash down the Sacsanach. **1876** Grant *Burgh Sch. Scot.* II. xiii. 410 *note*, A brave and patriotic Sassenach may be said to have wiped out this stain.

attrib. **1869** W. S. Gilbert *Bab Ball.* 187 All loved their McClan, save a Sassenach brute, Who came to the Highlands to fish and to shoot.

sasser, obs. form of SAUCER *sb.*

sasshay: see SASHAY *sb.* and *v.*

sassinate, sassination, *rare*⁻⁰, aphetic forms of ASSASSINATE, ASSASSINATION.

1623 Cockeram, *Sassination*, murder. **1656** Blount *Glossogr.*, *Sassinate*: see *Assassinate*.

†**'sassinous,** *a. Obs.* (Only in Lithgow.) [App. f. It. *sasso*:—L. *saxum* rock.] Rocky, stony.

1632 Lithgow *Trav.* III. 88 This sassinous and marine passage. *Ibid.* VIII. 350 Coasting the sassinous shoare of Genoaes reuieroe.

sassoline ('sæsəʊli:n). *Min.* Also **-lin.** [a. G. *sassolin* (Karsten), f. the name of the Lago del *Sasso* in Tuscany + -IN, -INE[5], with euphonic *l.*] Native boracic acid, found as a crystalline deposit in the hot springs of Tuscany.

1807 Aikin *Dict. Chem. & Min.* II. 286 *Sassolin* is the native Boracic Acid of Sasso in Tuscany. **1818** Parkes *Chem. Catech.* (ed. 8) 219 *note*, Sassoline. **1888** *Encycl. Brit.* XVI. 387 Sassoline.

So **'sassolite** = prec.

1868 Dana *Syst. Min.* (ed. 5) 594 Sassolite.

sassorol(la: see SASSAROLLO.

‖**sassy** ('sæsɪ), *sb.* Also **sass, saucy.** [W. African; believed to represent the Eng. SAUCY *a.*] Used *attrib.* in ***sassy-tree***, the African tree *Erythrophlœum guineense* (*Cynometra Mannii*); also in ***sassy-bark, -wood***, the bark of this tree, a decoction of which is used in West Africa as an ordeal poison.

1856 *Pharmaceut. Jrnl.* XVI. 233 Several very perfect specimens of the inflorescence of the Sassy bark tree. *Ibid.*, The Sassy tree. **1874** *Treas. Bot.* Suppl. s.v. *Erythrophlœum*, The Sassy-tree has a powerfully poisonous bark. **1883** *Jrnl. Chem. Ind.* 29 Mar. 137/2 On Erythrophleïne, the Principle of the Sassy Bark. **1894** Amanda Smith *Autobiog.* xxvii. 219 She was accused of being a witch, and..the penalty was to drink the sassy wood. **1897** Mary Kingsley *W. Africa* 464 In both the sass-wood and Calabar bean drink the only chance for the accused lies in squaring the witch-doctor.

sassy ('sæsɪ), *a. colloq.* (orig. and chiefly *U.S.*). [Var. SAUCY *a.*[1]] Impudent, saucy, 'cheeky'; outspoken, provocative; conceited, pretentious; self-assured, spirited, bold; vigorous, lively; stylish, 'chic'. Also quasi-*adv.*

[**1815** D. HUMPHREYS *Yankey in Eng.* I. 22 'Ah, you sly boots. Don't be saucy.' 'Saisy!']. **1833** S. SMITH *Life & Writings J. Downing* 128 If I should give out now.., them are sassy chaps in Portland would laugh at me. **1862** C. F. BROWNE *A. Ward his Book* 200 A hansum yung gal, with.. a sassy little black hat tipt over her forrerd, sot in the seat with me. **1870** 'MARK TWAIN' *Lett. to Publishers* (1967) 38 And then I talked sassy to him for a page or two. **1880** J. C. HARRIS *Uncle Remus* ii. 24 Brer Rabbit pacin' down de road ..dez ez sassy ez a jaybird. **1908** J. H. SHINN *Pioneers & Makers Arkansas* xxxii. 258, I have seen sassy people, but of all sassy people in the world Arkansassy people are the worst. **1917** T. H. COMSTOCK *Man thou Gavest* 12, I kept the sassy little hen. **1936** WODEHOUSE *Laughing Gas* vii. 77 Have you ever had to look after a sassy, swollen-headed, wisecracking child star? **1945** L. SAXON et al. *Gumbo Ya-Ya* xii. 233 My ma was hard-headed and sassy, and she'd talk right back to anybody, Massa or nobody. **1958** J. KEROUAC *On Road* I. x. 75 You can fill your filthy belly and get fat and sassy right before my eyes. **1961** *New Statesman* 11 Aug. 193/2 The film..is big and sassy, full of generous visual effects. **1969** N. COHN *A Wop Bopa Loo Bop* (1970) xviii. 169 They looked at the things the Who did and analysed them and thought up sassy names for them. If the Who smashed up their instruments..was that violence? Certainly not: it was auto-destruction. **1974** K. MILLETT *Flying* (1975) III. 368 Celia's voice sweet brave sassy, 'Of course I'll be okay.' **1977** *Time* 7 Feb. 57/1 He has..a stand-up lush of an ex-wife..whose sassy words rain mockery on all. **1977** *Spare Rib* July 50/1, I learned a lot of things from the Beatles about sassiness. I always thought they were sassy, that was my label for them. **1979** *Arizona Daily Star* 5 Aug. I. 10/4 She plays a leading character, Persona Non Grata, a hip, wise, slightly sassy new friend of Alic. **1980** W. SAFIRE in *N.Y. Times Mag.* 21 Sept., The Oxford American Dictionary, a sassy and helpful addition to any library. *Ibid.* 9 Nov., He initials 'MFC', a sadly sassy signal that means 'measure for coffin'.

Hence **'sassily** *adv.*; **'sassiness**.

1976 C. WESTON *Rouse Demon* (1977) xii. 56 'Go ahead, ask me something,' he urged sassily. **1976** 'TREVANIAN' *Main* vi. 128 Now that his first panic is over, something of his haughty sassiness returns.

†**'sastange, 'sasting.** *Obs.* Forms: 4 **saa stange,** 5 **sastange,** 5–6 **saystang(e, sasteing,** 6 *Sc.* **say styng.** [f. *sa*, northern form of SOE, bucket + STANG, STING *sbs.* Cf. Sw. *såstång*, Da. *saastang.*] A pole passed through the two ears of a bucket, to form a handle by which two might carry it.

c **1375** *Cursor M.* 21144 (Fairf.) A wikkid iew wiþ mikil wrange, smate him wiþ a saa stange [*Gött.* a walker stange]. *c* **1470** HENRY *Wallace* II. 33 He bar a sasteing in a boustous poille. **1483** *Cath. Angl.* 319/1 A Sastange (*A.* Saystange), *falanga, tinarium.* **1538** *Aberdeen Reg.* XVI. (Jam. s.v. SAY *sb.*), Ane cumyeone, ane bukat, say & say styng. **1593** HOLLYBAND *Dict. Fr. & Eng.*, *Vne Courge*, a coulestaffe, a saystang [*misprinted* sayslang].

sa sterre, sa storre, obs. forms of SEA-STAR.

sastra, sastri: see SHASTRA, SHASTRI.

sastruga (sæ'struːgə). Also **zastruga**; chiefly as pl. **sastrugi** (-ɪ). [a. G. *sastruga*, f. dial. Russ. *zastrúga* small ridge, furrow, f. *zastrugát* to plane, smooth, f. *strug* plane.] One of a series of irregular ridges formed on a snow surface by wind erosion and deposition, aligned parallel to the direction of the prevailing wind.

1840 E. SABINE tr. *von Wrangell's Narr. Exped. Polar Sea* vii. 146 We were guided by the wave-like stripes of snow (sastrugi) which are formed, either on the plains on land or on the level ice of the sea, by any wind of long continuance. *Ibid.* 147 It often happens that the *true* permanent sastruga has been obliterated by another produced by temporary winds. **1878** E. L. MOSS *Shores of Polar Sea* vi. 42 The sloping shore hills are barred with 'sastrugi'—wind-made ridges of snow—but the abrupt scooped-out rifts between them are smothered over with deep snow in gentle undulations. **1911** R. F. SCOTT *Jrnl.* in *Last Exped.* (1913) I. 517 The hard surface gave place to regular sastrugi. **1937** *Geogr. Jrnl.* LXXXIX. 195 He remarks on sastrugi 6 inches high, then for three days very few. **1960** *Times* 17 Feb. 10/3 Much of the traverse was conducted over a difficult surface rippled with *sastrugi.* **1975** E. HILLARY *Nothing venture, Nothing Win* xiii. 243 The surface, which had appeared so smooth from above, was..liberally peppered with large sastrugi—some of them up to three feet in height. **1979** R. FIENNES *Hell on Ice* v. 70 The sastruga ripples we encountered along the summit ridges. **1982** B. ALDISS *Helliconia Spring* ii. 89 Only Yuli had experience of the tundras and zastrugi, which stretched away to the north of the Quzint.

satai, var. SATAY.

Satan ('seɪtən). Also 3–5 **saton,** 5 **satone;** 3–7 **sathan,** 4, 6 **sathane,** 5 **sathon(e.** [a. L. *Satān* (Vulg., only in the O.T.) = Gr. *Σατάν* or *Σατᾶν* (once in the LXX and once in the N.T.), a. Heb. *ṣāṭān* adversary, one who plots against another, f. *ṣāṭan* to oppose, plot against.

In the Old Testament the Heb. word ordinarily denotes a human adversary, but in some of the later portions (Job, Chron., Zech., Ps. cix) it occurs (chiefly with definite article) as the designation of an angelic being hostile to mankind, who tempts men to evil and accuses them to God. In both applications the ordinary rendering of the LXX is *διάβολος* slanderer (see DEVIL *sb.*); the more accurate *ἐπίβουλος* (plotter) occurs once; the one instance in which the Heb. word is retained (1 Kings xi. 14) relates clearly to a human enemy, but may have been misapprehended. In the Gr. N.T. the ordinary form is *Σατανᾶς* (once only *Σατᾶν*), which is followed by the Vulgate and hence by Wyclif (see SATANAS); but the English versions from Tindale onwards (including the Rheims N.T.) all substitute the Heb. form *Satan.* Cf. OF. *Sathan, Satan*, Fr., Sp., It., G. *Satan.*

The pronunciation ('sætən), which is mentioned disapprovingly by Walker (1828), and is ignored in later Dictionaries, was still not uncommon in British liturgical and pulpit use *c* 1900.]

1. The proper name of the supreme evil spirit, the Devil. See DEVIL *sb.* 1 and LUCIFER 2.

Now always with capital S.

a **900** CYNEWULF *Christ* 1522 (Gr.) Farað nu..on ece fir, þæt wæs Satane..ȝeȝearwad. *a* **1000** *Cædmon's Gen.* 347 (Gr.) Satan maðelode, sorȝiende spræc. ? *a* **1300** *XI Pains of Hell* 17 in *O.E. Misc.* 147 Wiltu ihere me sathan. *a* **1300** *Cursor M.* 12023 þou wreche sede o felunny! Werck o dred, sun o sathan [*Fairf.* saton, *Gött.* sathane, *Trin.* sathone]. *Ibid.* 19884 For-sakes þou sathan [*Gött.* sathane, *Trin.* satone]. **1377** LANGL. *P. Pl.* B. IX. 61 For þei seruen sathan her soule shal he haue. *c* **1425** *Cast. Persev.* 552 in *Macro Plays* 93 Be Satan, þou art a nobyl knawe to techyn men fyrst fro goode! **1550** J. COKE *Eng. & Fr. Heralds* §117 (1877) 93 Dyvers bysshopes of Rome, beynge annabaptystes, heretyques, scismatiques, and chyldren of Sathan. **1567** *Gude & Godlie B.* (S.T.S.) 10 To saue vs... Fra Sathanis subteltie and slycht. **1590** SHAKS. *Com. Err.* IV. iv. 57, I charge thee Sathan, hous'd within this man, To yeeld possession to my holie praiers. **1622** GATAKER *Spirituall Watch* (ed. 2) 54 No marvaile if Sin and Sathan finde free entrance at will. **1847** TENNYSON *Princess* v. 32 Satan take The old women and their shadows! (thus the king Roar'd). *fig.* **1843** CARLYLE *Past & Pr.* IV. i, Could he [the modern preacher] but find the point again... Will he discover our new real Satan, whom he has to fight; or go on droning through his old nose-spectacles about old extinct Satans?

¶ **b.** In the etymological sense of 'adversary', with allusion to Matt. xvi. 23, Mark viii. 33.

1685 BAXTER *Paraphr. N.T., Matt.* xvi. 23 To hinder us in God's work and mens Salvation, is to be Satans to us. O how many Satans then are called reverend Fathers, who silence and persecute men for God's work.

†**2.** In wider sense: A devil. *Obs.*

a **1668** DAVENANT *Man's the Master* v. 67 A thousand Sathans take all good luck. *a* **1688** BUNYAN *Jerus. Sinner Saved* (1886) 103 We in all likelihood are to possess the very places from which the Satans by transgression fell.

b. Applied to a person or animal as a term of abhorrence. Now *rare.*

1596 SHAKS. *1 Hen. IV*, II. iv. 509 That villanous abhominable mis-leader of Youth, Falstaffe, that old white-bearded Sathan. **1600** W. WATSON *Decacordon* (1602) 9 How many Sathans and begotten of the diuell did he tearme them? **1754** RICHARDSON *Grandison* III. i. 9, I called her a little Satan. **1867** AUGUSTA WILSON *Vashti* xi, My mistress will say it was my fault, and she will stand by the grey satans [*sc.* ponies] through thick and thin. **1900** G. SWIFT *Somerley* 148 Let me go! you fiends! you Satans! let me go!

3. *attrib.* and *Comb.*, as ***Satan-mad***; **Satan monkey,** the black saki, *Chiropotes satanas*, which is found in dense forest in parts of South America and has thick reddish-black fur; **Satan shrimp,** any 'shrimp' of the family *Luciferidæ.*

1918 W. DE LA MARE *Motley* 51 Not simple happy mad like me,.. But that foul Satan-mad. **1906** E. INGERSOLL *Life of Animals: Mammals* 44 (*caption*) Black Saki, Cuxio, or Satan Monkey. **1941** J. S. HUXLEY *Uniqueness of Man* ix. 205 Others, like..the Satan monkey with his fine beard, are curiously reminiscent of ourselves.

satan, obs. form of SATIN.

Satanas ('sætənæs). *Obs.* exc. *arch.* Also 1 **satanus,** (3 *gen.* **Sathanesses**), 4 **saternas,** 4–5 **satanase, satenas, satnace;** 5 **sathonas,** 1–6, 9 **sathanas.** [a. L. (Vulg.) *Satanās*, a. Gr. *Σατανᾶς*, ad. Jewish Aramaic *ṣāṭānā*, emphatic form of *ṣāṭān* (a. Heb.): see SATAN. Cf. F. *satanas* (OF. also *satenas, sathanas, satrenas*, etc., whence some ME. forms), Pr. *Sathanas, Sadanas*, Sp. *Satanas*, Pg. *Satanaz*, OIt. *Satanasse, Satanaso.*]

1. = SATAN 1.

a **1000** *Cædmon's Satan* 371 (Gr.) Satanus swearte. *c* **1000** *Ags. Gosp.* Mark iii. 23 Hu mæȝ satanas satanan [*c* **1160** *Hatton Gosp.* sathanas sathana] ut adrifan. *c* **1220** *Bestiary* 96 Forsaket ðore satanas, and ilk sinful dede. *c* **1275** *Sinners Beware* 221 in *O.E. Misc.* 79 From sathanasses wrenche. *a* **1300** *Cursor M.* 11903 He [Herod] es bileft wit satanas [*Trin.* sathonas], And wit þe traitur sir iudas. *c* **1315** SHOREHAM i. 2170 Ac he hyt hadde wel priue For saternases lyste. ? *a* **1400** *Morte Arth.* 3813 Bot Satanase his sawle mowe synke in-to helle! **1482** *Monk of Evesham* xxi. (Arb.) 50 The wekyd angelle of that deuyl Sathenas. **1526** *Pilgr. Perf.* (W. de W. 1531) 37 b, By the operacyon & werkynge of sathenas. **1590** SIR J. SMYTH *Disc. Weapons* Ded. 13 A very offering of sacrifice vnto Satanas, or rather to Belzebub himselfe the Prince of feendes. **1819** SCOTT *Ivanhoe* xxxiii, Speak, Jew—have I not ransomed thee from Sathanas?—have I not taught thee thy *credo*, thy *pater*, and thine *Ave Maria*? **1855** KINGSLEY *Westw. Ho!* xxvi, Satanas must need help those who serve him.

¶ **b.** With etymological sense: = SATAN 1 b. *Obs.*

15.. *Exam. Thorpe* in Foxe *A. & M.* (1583) 533/1 The Priest that preacheth not the word of God..he is Antichrist and Sathanas.

†**2.** Applied to a fierce animal. (Cf. SATAN 2 b.)

c **1420** *Avow. Arth.* v, We schalle that Satnace [*sc.* a boar] see, Giffe that he be thare. *Ibid.* viii, Were he neuyr so hardy, ȝone Satenas to say, To brittun him, and downe bringe, With-oute any helpinge.

Satanic (sə'tænɪk), *a.* [f. SATAN + -IC. Cf. eccl. Gr. *Σατανικός*, F. *satanique* (16th c.), Sp. *satánico*, Pg., It. *satanico.*]

1. Of or pertaining to Satan.

1667 MILTON *P.L.* VI. 392 The faint Satanic Host. **1839** LANE *Arab. Nts.* I. 66 Satanic magic, as its name implies, is a science depending on the agency of the Devil and the inferior evil Jinn. **1881** JAS. GRANT *Cameronians* I. ii. 23 Two large yellow rings..drawn by the sword of an evil Montgomerie, who had trafficked in Satanic influence. **1896** WAITE *Devil-Worship in France* 119 The Grand Master seized one of the fakirs and cut his throat upon the altar, chanting the satanic liturgy amidst imprecations, curses [etc.].

2. (Freq. with lower-case initial.) Characteristic of or befitting Satan; extremely wicked, diabolical, devilish, infernal.

1793 HOLCROFT tr. *Lavater's Physiog.* xxix. 142 A criminal ..who with satanic wickedness had murdered his benefactor. **1804** *Ann. Rev.* II. 196/2 The satanic art of destroying the fetus in the womb. **1817** COLERIDGE *Biog. Lit.* xxiii. (1907) II. 199 Count Bertram..avows with open atrocity, his Satanic hatred of Imogine's Lord. **1878** J. E. JENKINS *Haverholme* 79 With an ingenuity almost satanic.

3. ***Satanic school***: Southey's designation for Byron, Shelley, and their imitators; subsequently often applied to other writers similarly accused of defiant impiety and delight in the portraiture of lawless passion.

1821 SOUTHEY *Vis. Judgement* Pref. iii. 21 Men of diseased hearts and depraved imaginations..hating that revealed religion which..they are unable utterly to disbelieve... The school which they have set up may properly be called the Satanic school; for..their productions..are more especially characterized by a Satanic spirit of pride and audacious impiety. **1831** CARLYLE *Sart. Res.* II. vi, Teufelsdröckh.. had only one of three things which he can next do: Establish himself in Bedlam; begin writing Satanic Poetry; or blow-out his brains. **1843** —— *Past & Pr.* II. xvii, Satanic-school, Cockney-school, and other Literatures.

Satanical (sə'tænɪkəl), *a.* Now *rare.* Also 6–7 **sathanicall.** [Formed as prec.: see -ICAL.]

†**1.** Resembling Satan, devilish. *Obs.*

a **1548** HALL *Chron., Hen. VI* 109 b, Allured and intised by a deuilishe wytche, and a Sathanicall enchaunteresse. **1553** BECON *Reliques of Rome* (1563) 34 A Satanicall swarme of shamelesse shauelynges. **1657** FIENNES *Sp. Parl.* 20 Jan. 12 We doubt not, but that the Prince of those Satanical Spirits..will in God's good time split himself also upon this Rock. **1711** HICKES *Two Treat. Chr. Priesth.* (1847) I. 320 The Church of England, whose ruin this Satanical sect of men seek. **1759** LAW *Lett. Import. Subj.* 195 Adam's turning from God to hear the voice and instruction of his own reason and imagination, and the suggestions of a satanical serpent, was [etc.].

2. Of or pertaining to Satan: = SATANIC *a.* 1.

1590 H. HOLLAND *Treat. agst. Witchcraft* (title-p.), The most certen meanes ordained of God, to discouer, expell, and to confound all the Sathanicall inuentions of Witchcraft and sorcerie. **1608** WILLET *Hexapla Exod.* vii. 84 Seeing these Magicians by their Satanicall craft do so strongly deceiue. **1779** W. ALEXANDER *Hist. Women* (1782) II. 98 Those ideas of sorceries, witchcrafts, and satanical possessions with which the minds of the people were infected. **1887** B. O'REILLY *Life Leo XIII* 354 They felt these satanical festivities to be directed against Christ Himself.

3. Of things, actions, or qualities: = SATANIC *a.* 2.

1547–64 BAULDWIN *Mor. Philos.* (Palfr.) 138 b, All cursed crimes and sleights satanicall. **1632** LITHGOW *Trav.* I. 2 Such be the Satanicall opinions of this hell-borne age. **1748** HARTLEY *Observ. Man* II. iv. 410 Self-Righteousness and Satanical Pride. **1762** KAMES *Elem. Crit.* xxi. (1833) 411 Iago's character..is insufferably monstrous and satanical. **1907** A. C. BENSON *Altar Fire* 153 A Satanical sort of pride —the pride of correct information.

Hence **Sa'tanically** *adv.*, in a satanic manner; †**Sa'tanicalness,** the quality of being satanic.

1606 *Proceedings agst. Garnet* S 4 b, Hall the Iesuit..in stead of..a sence of the wickednesse of the Treason, fell.. Sathanically to argue for the iustification of the same. **1668** H. MORE *Div. Dial.* III. xix. (1713) 216, I was only a going to add something of the Madness of the Heathenish Priests, as the last Note of the Satanicalness of their Religion. **1824** *Examiner* 276/2 Satanically false. **1906** H. B. SWETE *Apocalypse* xvi. 13 *note*, *Ψευδοπροφήτης*..is used in the N.T. of..persons Satanically inspired.

satanisco, obs. form of SATINISCO.

Satanism ('seɪtənɪz(ə)m). [f. SATAN + -ISM. Cf. F. *satanisme* (= sense 3 below).]

1. A satanic or diabolical disposition, doctrine, spirit, or contrivance.

1565 HARDING *Confut. Jewel* II. ii. 42 b, Meaning the time when Luther first brinced to Germanie the poisoned cuppe of his heresies, blasphemies, and sathanismes. **1639** VISCT. FALKLAND *Elegy on Donne* Poems (Grosart) 36 So mild was Moses countenance, when he pray'd For them whose Satanisme his power gainsaid. **1855** BAGEHOT *Lit. Stud.*, *Cowper* (1879) I. 285 The whole burning soul breaks away into what is well called Satanism—into wildness, and bitterness, and contempt. **1893** GOLDW. SMITH *Ess.* 2 That sort of social revolution which may be called Satanism, as it seeks, not to reconstruct, but to destroy. **1900** A. LANG in *Daily News* 27 June 6/2 With such a mixture of..loyalty, mysterious Satanism, and reputation for conquests over her sex..Bothwell must have fascinated the Queen.

2. The characteristics of the 'Satanic school'.

1822 *Blackw. Mag.* XI. 445 His Lakeism or his Satanism will not save the piece from being damned, if it be stupid. **1833** *Fraser's Mag.* VIII. 524 This scene of Byron's is really sublime, in spite of its Satanism.

3. The worship of Satan, alleged to have been practised in France in the latter part of the 19th century; the principles and rites of the Satanists.

1896 A. LILLIE *Worship Satan in Mod. France* Pref. 18 There are five temples of Satanism in Paris itself.. Satanism has the *Bulletin au Diable* and other organs.

Satanist (ˈseɪtənɪst). Also 6–7 **sathanist(e**. [f. SATAN + -IST. Cf. F. *Sataniste*.]

1. One who is regarded as an adherent of Satan.

1559 AYLMER *Harborowe* H j b, The Anabaptistes, with infinite other swarmes of Satanistes. **1565** HARDING *Confut. Jewel* II. ix. 81 b, Be ye Zuinglians, Arians,.. Anabaptistes, Caluinistes, or Sathanistes? **1589** NASHE *Martins Months Minde* H 4 b, By nature an Athiest, By arte a Machiuelist, In summe a Sathanist, loe here his hire. **1662** HIBBERT *Body of Div.* I. 16 By profession a Christian, by conversation a Satanist. **1833** *Fraser's Mag.* VIII. 570 The aboriginal races of just men distinguished themselves by this very title, Alibenim, theogonists, or God's sons, from the atheistical Sathanists, or evil-seekers.

2. A Euchite.

1874 *Blunt's Dict. Sects*, etc. 518.

3. A Satan-worshipper; *spec.* one of a sect alleged to have existed in France in the latter part of the 19th century.

1896 MRS. LYNN LINTON in *Life* xxi. (1901) 323 There are two sects, the Satanists and the Luciferists—and they pray to these names as Gods. **1897** J. MCCABE *Twelve Yrs. in Monast.* v. 98 It is believed on the Continent that apostate priests frequently consecrate for the Satanists and Free-masons. **1926** C. CONNOLLY *Let.* 16 May in *Romantic Friendship* (1975) 126, I think he's a satanist. **1974** *Encycl. Brit. Macropædia* XIX. 899/2 Such modern satanists as Aleister Crowley and Gerald Gardner. **1976** *Eastern Even. News* (Norwich) 29 Nov., The sisters.. are on the trail of a group of Satanists, believed to have caused a young man's death.

4. A writer of the 'Satanic school'.

1921 *Glasgow Herald* 9 Apr. 6/3 Thus he [*sc.* Baudelaire] is a Satanist in the Miltonic sense of a rebel against stifling power.

Satanistic (seɪtəˈnɪstɪk), *a. rare.* [f. SATANIST + -IC.] Of or pertaining to the Satanists; adhering to Satanism (sense 3).

1895 *Westm. Gaz.* 17 Dec. 1/3 Huysmans declares that there existed a Satanistic Society in America some years ago. *Ibid.* 2/1 The case of a nun which caused such excitement in 1865 is a strange one. This nun, who had been corrupted by a Satanistic priest when fifteen years of age, was placed in a convent.

Satanity (səˈtænɪtɪ). *rare.* [f. SATAN + -ITY.] Satanic conduct or character.

1864 BLACKMORE *Clara Vaughan* liv. (1889) 202 The author of such Satanity. **1903** *Protestant Observer* Dec. 190/1 This charge of Satanity is illustrated by the following facts.

Satanize (ˈseɪtənaɪz), *v. rare.* [f. SATAN + -IZE.] *trans.* To render like Satan; to make into, or like a devil.

1598 TOFTE *Alba*, etc. (1880) 132 Oh let not Sinne my Soule still Satanise. **1646** TRAPP *Comm. John* vi. 71 How fearfully was he [*sc.* Judas] satanized and transformed into a breathing devil. **1832** *Blackw. Mag.* Apr. 592 [Satan] Look'd back upon France; for he sympathized With a nation so thoroughly Satanized.

Hence ˈ**Satanized** *ppl. a.*

1610 BARRET *Sacred Warre* in Southey *Roderick* (1814) Notes p. xiv, In all parts Violence had vogue, and on sathanized earth Fraud, Mischief, Murder martialled the camp. **1625** JACKSON *Creed* v. vi. §5 Nothing but Satanized affection deeply rooted in the heart could afford such store of malignant nutriment as this hellish slip must be fed with. **1891** *Dublin Rev.* Jan. 186 A thirst for blood is the characteristic of the brutalised, or rather satanised man.

Satanology (seɪtəˈnɒlədʒɪ). [f. SATAN + -(O)LOGY.] That part of knowledge which relates to Satan.

1862 W. K. TWEEDIE *Satan as revealed in Script.* 42 In a Satanology the portion of revelation which has now been considered is the foundation of all our knowledge. **1883** EDERSHEIM *Life Jesus* II. 752 The difference between the Satanology of the Rabbis and of the New Testament is, if possible, even more marked than that in their Angelology.

Satanophany (seɪtəˈnɒfənɪ). [f. SATAN, after *theophany*: see -PHANY.] The appearing, or visible manifestation, of Satan.

1864 WEBSTER (cites *O. A. Brownson*). **1892** *Nation* 4 Feb. 91/1 As to the ass,.. it is believed that he brays because he has a vision of Satan, a Satanophany. **1896** A. J. GORDON *Biog.* 325 No theory can explain this grotesque satanophany, this incredible perversion of early Christianity.

Satanophobia (ˌseɪtənəˈfəʊbɪə). [f. Gr. σατανᾶς SATAN + -φοβία: see -PHOBIA.] Morbid dread of Satan.

1860 READE *Cloister & H.* xcvi, Impregnated as he was with Satanophobia, he might perhaps have doubted still whether this distressed creature, all woman, and nature, was not all art, and fiend. **1897** *Syd. Soc. Lex.*, *Satanophobia*, a morbid or insane dread of the devil.

Satanry (ˈseɪtənrɪ). *rare*$^{-0}$. [f. SATAN + -RY, after DEVILRY.] 'Satanic conduct or wiles; a course or action appearing as if inspired by Satan' (*Funk's Stand. Dict.* 1895).

Satanship (ˈseɪtənʃɪp). *rare.* [f. SATAN + -SHIP.] The quality of being a Satan.

1647 HAMMOND *Power of Keys* iv. 93 One main act of his Satanship is exprest in accusing us before God. **1884** HELEN MATHERS *Eyre's Acquittal* I. vii, [They] felt their conviction of his Satanship rudely shaken.

satara (səˈtɑːrə). [Named from *Satara*, a town and district in the Bombay Presidency, India.] A woollen cloth (see quots.).

1878 BARLOW *Hist. & Princ. Weaving* 442 *Sataras*, ribbed cloths highly dressed, lustred and hot pressed. **1888** J. PATON in *Encycl. Brit.* XXIV. 662/1 Of cloths milled and cropped bare there are venetians, sataras, and diagonals. **1904** *Woollen Draper's Terms* in *Tailor & Cutt.* 4 Aug. 480/1 Satara: A peculiar make of broadcloth, rather heavy, and having a horizontal rib to it.

satay (ˈsæteɪ). Also **satai, saté**. [Mal. *satai, sate*, Indonesian *sate*.] An Indonesian and Malaysian dish, consisting of small pieces of meat grilled on a skewer and usually served with a spiced sauce.

1934 *Willis's Singapore Guide* 149 'Satai' I am given to understand was introduced into this Country by the Chinese, the word being spelt 'Satae', meaning three pieces of meat. **1937** M. COVARRUBIAS *Island of Bali* v. 108 The *saté* can be made of pork or chicken, but turtle remains the favourite of the Balinese of Den Pasar. **1955** P. ANDERSON *Snake Wine* II. vi. 163 The Malays crouch over their portable stoves, fanning the embers below sticks of spicy broiled goat known as *satay*. **1967** L. DEIGHTON *London Dossier* 56 You can eat Malay Satay in the Singapore restaurant in Allen Street, W8. **1971** *Carry Singapore in your Pocket* (Singapore Tourist Promotion Board) (ed. 3) 30 One of the most famous Malay dishes is satay which is tenderised and spiced mutton, chicken or beef barbecued over charcoal and dipped in a chilli-hot peanut sauce. They are served skewered. **1971** *National Geographic* Jan. 16/2 Saté consists of bits of meat skewered on bamboo slivers, grilled over charcoal, and served with a spicy peanut sauce. **1976** *Outdoor Living* (N.Z.) I. II. 64/1 The sate is Asia's answer to the shishkebab. The sate is usually all meat, beautifully spiced and traditionally served on small wooden skewers. **1980** *Times* 5 July 11/2 A menu that ranges from Indonesian satay.. to Persian khoresh faisinjan.

‖**sat-bhai** (ˈsɑːtbɑːi). Also **saht-bai, sathbhai**. [Hind. *sātbhāī*.] An Indian jungle babbler, *Turdoides striatus*, a large brown bird with a long tail and slightly curved bill; = SEVEN SISTERS 4.

1863 T. C. JERDON *Birds of India* II. 65 It [*sc.* the large grey babbler] leaves the jungles and wilds, and becomes the familiar and unscared.. *Sat bhai*. **1886** KIPLING *Departmental Ditties* (ed. 2) 62 The blue jay screams and flutters where the cheery *sát-bhai* dwell. **1928** H. WHISTLER *Pop. Handbk. Indian Birds* 32 The vernacular name [of the jungle babbler] is 'Sathbhai', the Seven Brethren. **1953** S. ALI *Birds of Travancore & Cochin* 28 A frowzled, untidy-looking earthy brown bird.. invariably in flocks of half a dozen or so, whence its popular Hindustani name Sātbhai (= seven brothers). **1978** 'M. M. KAYE' *Far Pavilions* ii. 27 The normal noises of an Indian morning:.. the harsh cry of a peacock.. and the chatter and chirrup of tree-rats *saht-bai* and weaver-birds.

satchel (ˈsætʃəl), *sb.* Forms: 4 (**cachel**), **sachil**, 4–7 **sachel**, 5 **cechelle, secchell**, 5–7 **sachell**, 6 **sechell, setchel(l**, 6–7 **satchell**, (7 **setchal**), 5– **satchel**. [a. OF. *sachel*:—L. *saccellus*, dim. of *saccus* SACK *sb.*[1]]

1. a. A small bag; *esp.* a bag for carrying schoolbooks, with or without a strap to hang over the shoulders.

13.. *S. Eng. Leg.* in *Archiv Stud. neu. Spr.* LXXXII. 316/233 Ne tit þe purs ne cachel þin mete þer-in to bere. *a* **1340** HAMPOLE *Psalter* xxxviii. 11 My substance.. is anence the & with the.. not in sachelis [*v.r.* sacles]. *c* **1380** WYCLIF *Serm.* Sel. Wks. I. 177 [*Luke* x. 4] Nyle ȝe, he seiþ, bere sachil ne scrippe, ne hosis, ne shoon. *c* **1440** *Alphabet of Tales* 191 He tuke a sachell full of sylver. *c* **1440** *Promp. Parv.* 64 Cechelle, *saccellus*. *c* **1440** *York Myst.* xxvii. 172 Satcheles I will ȝe haue. ? *a* **1500** *Chester Pl.* (Shaks. Soc.) 123 My secchell to shake oute To sheapardes am I not shamed. **1552** HULOET, Bagges for money, or sachelles. **1557** SEAGER *Sch. Virtue* 109 in *Babees Bk.* 338 This done, thy setchell and thy bokes take, And to the scole haste see thou make. **1585** T. WASHINGTON tr. *Nicholay's Voy.* III. ix. 84 b, Refreshing themselues with such victualles as they haue brought with them in their satchel. **1589** RIDER *Bibl. Schol.* s.v., A sachell, or great bag for money, *fiscus*. **1600** SHAKS. *A.Y.L.* II. vii. 145 Then, the whining Schoole-boy with his Satchell.. creeping.. Vnwillingly to schoole. **1675** HOBBES *Odyssey* (1677) 21 And fine flour twenty measures at the least In good thick leather satchels let me have. **1688** R. HOLME *Armoury* III. 336/1 A Setchal or Leather Bag.. is the Plow Mans Pantry, in which his Provision is put, and carried on his Shoulder. **1695** KENNETT *Par. Antiq.* vi. 22 At the other end [of a beam] they hang a leathern bag or satchel of gravel. **1709** SWIFT *Descript. Morn.* 18 And School-Boys lag with Satchels in their Hands. **1823** SCOTT *Quentin D.* ii, The young traveller.. had at his back a satchel, which seemed to contain a few necessaries. **1862** BORROW *Wales* (ed. 2) 200 A small leather satchel with a lock and key. **1888** ANNA K. GREEN *Behind Closed Doors* ii, She took nothing but a little hand satchel.

b. *transf.* and *fig.*

c **1450** *Mankind* 128 in *Macro Plays* 6 Now opyn yowur sachell with Laten wordis, Ande sey me þis in clerycall manere! **1593** G. HARVEY *Pierces Super.* Wks. (Grosart) II. 297 Lewes the French king, one of the busiest, ielousest, and craftiest Princes, that euer raigned in that kingdome, might haue borrowed the Foxes Satchell of him. **1646** SIR T. BROWNE *Pseud. Ep.* v. i. 234 The chowle or croppe adhering unto the lower side of the bill, and so descending by the throat; a bagge or sachell very observable, and of capacity almost beyond credit.

2. *attrib.*, as *satchel cutter*; **satchel charge** (see quot. 1973); †**satchel date**, the fruit of the †**satchel palm**, *Manicaria saccifera*.

1961 WEBSTER, *Satchel charge. **1969** *New Yorker* 20 Sept. 145/1 Setting off satchel charges and other explosives at police stations. **1973** J. QUICK *Dict. Weapons* 385/1 *Satchel charge*, a number of blocks of explosive taped to a board fitted with a rope or wire loop for carrying and attaching. **1977** *Time* 20 June 6/3 The troops used satchel charges to widen the gap made by the armored car, causing thunderous explosions that awoke sleeping villagers. **1900** *Daily Chron.* 23 Jan. 11/2 *Satchel Cutter wanted. **1659** LOVELL *Herbal* 516 The *Sachell date, *Palma saccifera*. **1658** SIR T. BROWNE *Gard. Cyrus* iii. 48 The codde of the *Sachell palm.

satchel (ˈsætʃəl), *v. rare.* [f. prec.] *trans.* **a.** To make a 'bag' of (game). **b.** To fasten (something) on one, as in a satchel. In quot. *fig.*

1828 COL. HAWKER *Diary* (1893) I. 342, I contrived to satchel 48 partridges (besides 3 brace lost). **1839** LANDOR *Andrea of Hungary* IV. ii. 70 Since thy services may soon Be call'd for, satchel on thee my experience, Then set about thy work.

satchelled (ˈsætʃəld), *a.* [f. SATCHEL *sb.* + -ED[2].] Having or carrying a satchel.

1749 *Whitehall Evening Post* No. 535 To Country School, the satchel'd Youths are sent. **1855** DOBELL *Sonn., Amer.*, Back, and see Thy satchelled ancestor! Behold, he runs To mine, and, clasped, they tread the equal lea To the same village-school.

sate (seɪt), *v.* Also 7 **satt**. [App. a pseudo-etymological alteration of SADE *v.*, after L. *sat*, *satis* enough: cf. SATIATE *v.*]

1. a. *trans.* To fill or satisfy to the full (with food); to indulge or gratify to the full by the satisfaction of any appetite or desire.

1613–16 W. BROWNE *Brit. Past.* II. i, A pious.. sonne, Who.. bringing.. home Dried figs, Dates, Almonds,.. sates the want Therewith of those, who, from a tender plant, Bred him a man for armes. **1634** MILTON *Comus* 714 Wherefore did Nature powre her bounties forth,.. But all to please, and sate the curious taste? *a* **1639** W. WHATELEY *Prototypes* II. xxvi. (1640) 84 So that no outward benefits may glut and satt our hearts. **1713** JOHNSON *Guard.* No. 8 ¶4 As his resentment was sated. **1719** YOUNG *Busiris* I. i, Artaxes' friends.. Were swept away by banishment or death, In throngs and sated the devouring grave. **1791** BURKE *Corr.* (1844) III. 303 When your curiosity is sated with the Rhine. **1840** THIRLWALL *Greece* lvi. VII. 199 He had sated his vengeance. **1876** MERIVALE *Rom. Triumvirates* vii. 144 He.. sated the populace with largesses.

b. To surfeit or cloy by gratification of appetite or desire; to glut, satiate.

1602 SHAKS. *Ham.* I. v. 56 So Lust, though to a radiant Angell link'd, Will sate it selfe in a Celestiall bed, & prey on Garbage. **1712** STEELE *Spect.* No. 522 ¶1 They are immediately sated with Possession, and must necessarily fly to new Acquisitions of Beauty. **1719** YOUNG *Revenge* III. i, 'Twas time to get another, When her first fool was sated with her beauties. **1828** CARLYLE *Misc.* (1857) I. 161 Sated to nausea, as we have been with the doctrines of Sentimentality. **1833** SIR R. PEEL in *Croker Papers* 29 Sept. (1884) II. 214, I saw some extracts from it in the newspapers, which sated my appetite for such reading. **1876** BLACK *Madcap V.* xv, Violet, who was not sated with the ordinary sights and occupations of London life, was enjoying herself thoroughly.

c. To wear *away* through satiety. *nonce-use.*

1817 BYRON *Lam. Tasso* ii, Successful love may sate itself away, The wretched are the faithful.

¶**d.** *intr.* To pall (*on*). *rare*$^{-1}$.

1794 MRS. A. M. BENNETT *Ellen* III. 75 A passion, which.. had no chance of sating on his imagination.

e. *intr.* (for *refl.*). To become sated. *rare.*

1869 BROWNING *Ring & Bk.* IV. XI. 179 Let me turn wolf, be whole, and sate, for once.

†**2.** *trans.* To saturate. (Cf. SATIATE *v.* 3.) *Obs.*

1673 RAY *Journ. Low C.* 60 These Waters seemed to me more brisk and sprightly, and better sated with Mineral Juices than any I have tasted in England. **1677** PLOT *Oxfordsh.* 26 The Banks of the Thame are so well sated with some kind of acid. **1759** B. MARTIN *Nat. Hist. Eng.* I. *Oxford* 397 A spring strongly sated with a kind of salt.

Hence ˈ**sating** *ppl. a.*

1818 BYRON *Ch. Har.* IV. clix, There is more In such a survey than the sating gaze Of wonder pleased.

sate (seɪt), *sb. Blacksmithing.* [Var. SET *sb.*[1]] A heavy chisel or punch used for cutting metal. Cf. SET *sb.*[1] 33

1906 T. MOORE *Handbk. Pract. Smithing & Forging* ii. 15 The cold sate.. is a very simple tool in itself, and easy to make. *Ibid.* 17 The hot sate.. is made in much the same way as the cold sate. **1942** W. H. ATHERTON *Workshop Pract.* (ed. 2) V. 198 Making two small holes.. by slitting with the hot sate and opening out slightly.. will widen the hole sufficiently to take a drift of the size required. **1962** [see SET *sb.*[1] 33].

sate: see SEAT, SET *v.*[1], SIT *v.*

saté, var. SATAY.

sated (ˈseɪtɪd), *ppl. a.* [f. SATE *v.* + -ED[1].] Glutted, satiated; cloyed or surfeited by indulgence of appetite.

1699 POMFRET *Love Triumphant* 262 Who, when the sated Appetite is tir'd, Even loath the Thoughts of what they once admir'd. **1745** COLLINS *Ode to Lady* 48 Till William seek the sad retreat, And bleeding at her sacred feet, Present the sated sword. **1762** GOLDSM. *Cit. W.* xcvii, The sated reader turns from it with a kind of literary nausea. **1855** LONGF. *Hiaw.* VIII. 217 Till Kayoshk, the sated sea-gulls, From their banquet rose with clamour. **1873** Symonds *Grk. Poets* v. 129 To prevent the palling of so much luxury on sated senses.

Hence '**satedness**.

1847 R. W. Hamilton *Rew. & Punishm.* i. 51 Do their sophisms quite convince them? Is all within at ease? Know they no satedness and disgust?

sateen (sə'tiːn). [Altered f. SATIN, after *velveteen.*] **1.** A cotton or woollen fabric with a glossy surface like that of satin.

1878 Barlow *Hist. & Princ. Weaving* 442 *Sateens*, light cloths for ladies' dresses. **1882** Miss Braddon *Mt. Royal* II. x. 206 Loose flowing tea-gowns of old gold sateen.

2. *Comb.*, as ***sateen-backed*** adj.

1939–40 *Army & Navy Stores Catal.* 629/2 Down quilts .. Figured Rayon Marocain, Sateen backed. **1960** *Farmer & Stockbreeder* 15 Mar. (Suppl.) 4/1 This wool-lined, sateen-backed quilted pad, with elastic waist belt, fits snugly.

satefy, variant of SATIFY *v. Obs.*

sateless ('seɪtlɪs), *a.* Chiefly *poet.* [f. SATE *v.* + -LESS.] Not to be sated, insatiable. Const. *of*, *in*.

1701 Cibber *Love Makes Man* II. ii, Happy he .. that unconfin'd may lave and wanton there in sateless Draughts of ever-springing Beauty. **1742** Young *Nt. Th.* VII. 512 His sateless thirst of pleasure, gold, and fame. **1838** *Fraser's Mag.* XVIII. 519 And Ate, his fell bride, sateless of blood. **1864** Neale *Seaton. Poems* 71 The thirst Of sateless Moloch. **1935** L. Luard *Conquering Seas* 6 The heedless voice of the land sateless in greed.

satell, obs. form of SETTLE *v.*

‖**satelles** (sə'tɛliːz). *Obs.* Pl. **satellites** (sə'tɛlɪtiːz). [L. *satelles*, *satellit-*.] Used by some writers of the 17th and early 18th c. for SATELLITE *sb.* 2.

1666 *Phil. Trans.* I. 246 The other three Satellites in the time of this Eclipse, made by the Satelles, were Westwards of the Body of Jupiter. *a* **1708** Beveridge *Priv. Th.* II. (1712) 337, I behold him there surrounded with an innumerable Company of holy Angels, as so many fixed Stars, and of glorified Saints as Planets enlightened by him; all his *Satellites* or Servants waiting upon him. **1708** *Brit. Apollo* No. 65. 2/2 The Moon is the Earth's Satelles. **1732** Pope *Ess. Man* I. 42 Or ask of yonder argent fields above, Why Jove's Satellites are less than Jove?

sa'tellitary, *a. rare*$^{-1}$. [f. SATELLITE *sb.* + -ARY, after *planetary*.] Belonging to satellites.

1867 Glennie in *Athenæum* 21 Dec. 855/1 New Laws of Planetary and Satellitary Motions.

satellite ('sætɪlaɪt), *sb.* Also 6 **-yte**, 7 **-it**. [a. F. *satellite* (14th c. in Littré), ad. L. *satellit-em* (nom. *satelles*) attendant or guard. Cf. SATELLES.]

1. An attendant upon a person of importance, forming part of his retinue and employed to execute his orders. Often with reproachful connotation, implying subserviency or unscrupulousness in the service. (Occas. with allusion to sense 2.)

This sense is not in J., and save for quot. *a* 1548 does not appear in our material until near the end of the 18th c. Quot. 1656 follows Cooper's explanation of L. *satelles*, supplemented from Cotgrave's definition of the Fr. word.

a **1548** Hall *Chron.*, *Rich. III* 52 b, Environed with his satellytes and yomen of the crowne. **1656** Blount *Glossogr.*, *Satellite*, one retained to guard a mans person; a Yeoman of the Guard; a Serjeant, Catch-pole, one that attacheth. **1797** S. James *Narr. Voy.* 147 Our most august visitant .. followed by his naked train of satellites. **1850** W. Irving *Goldsmith* xiii. 159 Boswell was .. made happy by an introduction to Johnson, of whom he became the obsequious satellite. **1852** Mrs. Stowe *Uncle Tom's C.* xxxii, Legree encouraged his two black satellites to a kind of coarse familiarity with him. **1860** Trollope *Framley P.* x, The satellites of the nursery. **1864** Kirk *Chas. Bold* II. IV. iii. 384 Tyrants, encompassed by their armed satellites.

2. a. A small or secondary planet which revolves round a larger one. (See also SATELLES.)

[The L. *satellites* was first applied in 1611 by Kepler to the secondary planets revolving round Jupiter, recently discovered by Galileo, who had named them *Sidera Medicæa*.]

1665 *Phil. Trans.* I. 71 A Satellite of Jupiter. *Ibid.*, The shadow of the Satellit between Jupiter and the Sun. **1692** Bentley *Boyle Lect.* viii. (1693) 14 Jupiter and Saturn .. have many Satellites about them. *a* **1721** Keill *Maupertius' Diss.* (1734) 33 The Moon is the Earth's Secondary or Satellite. **1784** Cowper *Task* I. 766 We can spare The splendour of your lamps; they but eclipse Our softer satellite. **1870** Proctor *Other Worlds* viii. (1872) 187 We have no satisfactory evidence that the satellites of Jupiter and Saturn turn always the same face towards their primary.

b. *transf.* and *fig.*

1771 Smollett *Humph. Cl.* 2 June, He, too, like a portentous comet, has risen again above the court horizon. .. Who are those two satellites that attend his motions? **1839** Darwin *Voy. Nat.* xvii. (1845) 377 The archipelago is a little world within itself, or rather a satellite attached to America. **1887** Olivia M. Stone (*title*) Tenerife and its six satellites. **1891** Freeman *Sk. fr. French Trav.* 126 At Poitiers the interest of the cathedral church is far smaller than that of its satellite the baptistery.

c. A man-made object placed (or designed to be placed) in orbit around an astronomical body (usu. the earth).

[**1880** W. H. G. Kingston tr. *Verne's Begum's Fortune* xiii. 180 A projectile, animated with an initial speed twenty times superior to the actual speed, being ten thousand yards to the second, can never fail! This movement, combined with terrestrial attraction, destines it to revolve perpetually round our globe... Two hundred thousand dollars is not too much to have paid for the pleasure of having endowed the planetary world with a new star, and the earth with a second satellite.] **1936** *Discovery* Sept. 299/2 The scheme for building a metal outpost satellite and propelling it in a fixed orbit 600 miles above the earth's surface. **1945** A. C. Clarke in *Wireless World* Oct. 305/2 This 'orbital' velocity is 8 km per sec. (5 miles per sec), and a rocket which attained it would become an artificial satellite, circling the world for ever with no expenditure of power. **1955** *Times* 30 July 6/1 The satellite is expected to be about the size of a basketball, and will be shot into the upper atmosphere by a rocket, where it will circle the earth at an altitude of between 200 and 300 miles at a speed of about 18,000 miles an hour. **1956** *Spaceflight* I. 6/2 After the Earth satellite stage, the next target will almost certainly be the Moon. **1957** *Ibid.* 49/1 Each satellite will be launched into its orbit by being ejected from the third stage of a multiple stage rocket. **1957** *Times* 7 Oct. 8/1 The Russian satellite soaring over the United States seven times a day has made an enormous impression on American minds. **1961**, etc. [see *communication(s) satellite* s.v. COMMUNICATION 12]. **1964** *Ann. Reg. 1963* 185 Among other notable American achievements in space during the year was the launching of a communications satellite. **1972** *Computers & Humanities* VII. 49 An experiment .. was conducted during the fall of 1971 at Stanford, where users were able to communicate with a computer by using NASA's ATS-1 experimental satellite. **1977** *Times* 16 Dec. 16/1 Killer satellites are small space-craft. They carry an explosive charge which destroys itself and any nearby satellite on detonation.

3. The name of **a.** a moth; **b.** a humming-bird.

1832 J. Rennie *Conspect. Butterfl. & M.* 62 The Satellite (*Glæa Satellitia*, Stephens) appears in September. **1861** Gould *Trochilidæ* III. Pl. 142 *Calothorax Calliope.* Mexican Satellite. **1882** *Cassell's Nat. Hist.* VI. 65 One of the largest species is the Satellite (*Scopelosoma satellitia*), which sometimes expands nearly two inches.

4. Geom. ***satellite line***, ***point***: see quot. 1857. Also used simply = *satellite line*.

1857 Cayley *Curves of 3rd Order* in *Coll. Papers* II. 383 It is a well-known theorem, that if at the points of intersection of a given line with a given cubic tangents are drawn to the cubic, these tangents again meet the cubic in three points which lie in a line; such line is in the present memoir termed the *satellite line* of the given line, and the point of intersection of the two lines is termed the *satellite point* of the given line; the given line in reference to its satellite line or point is termed the *primary line*. **1873** Salmon *Higher Plane Curves* (ed. 2) v. §207 A case where the satellite cuts the sides of the asymptotic triangle.

5. ***satellite vein***: a vein that accompanies an artery (mod.L. *vena satelles*, *vena comes*).

1846 Brittan tr. *Malgaigne's Man. Oper. Surg.* 126 On the upper third of the fore-arm, the artery .. has always two satellite veins. **1849–52** *Todd's Cycl. Anat.* IV. II. 816/2 The satellite vein of the right subclavian artery. **1897** in *Syd. Soc. Lex.*

6. a. A country or state politically or economically dependent upon and subservient to another.

[**1776** T. Paine *Wks.* (1796), II. 24 In no instance hath nature made the satellite larger than its primary planet; and as England and America .. reverse the common order of nature, it is evident that they belong to different systems: England to Europe, America to itself.] **1800** J. Adams *Wks.* (1854) IX. 49 A great deal is yet to be done to prevent our becoming a mere satellite to a mighty power. **1827** Macaulay *Ess.*, *Machiav.* (1897) 43 The governments of the Peninsula ceased to form an independent system. Drawn from their old orbit by the attraction of the larger bodies which now approached them, they became mere satellites of France and Spain. **1930** *Economist* 8 Nov. 844/2 Do they portend a military alliance against France between a Fascist Italy and a Fascist Germany, with a bevy of East European satellites—Bulgaria, Albania, Hungary, Austria—to balance Poland and the Little Entente? **1936** *Pacific Affairs* Sept. 404 Outer Mongolia may well be called a satellite of the Soviet Union. **1941** *Ann. Reg. 1940* 204 This [*sc.* the Tripartite Pact of the Axis Powers] made Hungary a mere satellite of Germany. **1948** *Sun* (Baltimore) 9 Jan. 1/2 Several of the Soviet Union's satellites. **1974** M. B. Brown *Econ. of Imperialism* xii. 286 Cuba is not a satellite of the USSR in the same sense that other Latin American States are satellites of the USA. **1977** *Time* 21 Feb. 8/1 In Czechoslovakia, East Germany, Poland and even some of the less volatile satellites, the Russians and their local rulers are being forced to put out brushfires of discontent.

b. A community or town that is economically or otherwise dependent on a nearby larger town or city.

1912 G. R. Taylor in *Survey* (N.Y.) 5 Oct. 14/2 In some sections of the South scarcely a city of any size lacks one or more satellites thrumming with spindle and shuttle. **1935** *Archit. Rev.* LXXVII. 188 (*caption*) 19th Century. Came the railways and with them the first general exodus, suburbs and satellites springing up round the railway stations. **1947** [see OVERSPILL *sb.* a]. **1958** *Manch. Guardian* 30 June 6/2 And if Manchester itself is some way from Tatton, Manchester's proposed satellite at Lymm is much nearer. **1977** *R.A.F. News* 27 Apr.–10 May 8/2 No. 50(B) Squadron was then based at Skellingthorpe, west of Lincoln (a satellite of Swinderby).

7. *Spectroscopy.* A spurious or subordinate spectral line; *spec.* one caused by an irregularity in the positions of lines in a diffraction grating. Also ***satellite line***.

1904 *Astrophysical Jrnl.* XIX. 118 The appearance and disappearance, according to circumstances, of the satellite lines still remains a most curious fact. **1924** *Phil. Mag.* XLVIII. 501 On moving the eyepiece back, the line broadened and a faint black 'satellite' split off from it, moving slowly across the grating. **1945** R. A. Sawyer *Exper. Spectrosc.* vii. 175 It often happens that satellites or diffuse edges will be observed for strong lines at the best obtainable focus. **1969** [see *Rowland ghost*]. **1971** *Physics Bull.* July 388/3 The centre line is due to Rayleigh scattering and the satellites arise from transverse (T) and longitudinal (L) phonons.

8. *Anat.* Chiefly as ***satellite cell***. Each of the cells that go to make up the membrane surrounding the nerve cell bodies in many ganglia, analogous to the Schwann cells that surround their axons; also, formerly, a Schwann cell.

[**1908** G. Marinesco in *Compt. Rend. Hebdom. des Séances et Mém. de la Soc. de Biol.* LXV. 99 De toutes ces recherches, il résulte qu'il existe à l'état normal un équilibre entre la nutrition des cellules satellites et celle des cellules des ganglions sensitifs.] **1928** W. Penfield in E. V. Cowdry *Special Cytol.* II. xxx. 1055 Specific stains showed the perivascular and perineuronal oligoglia satellites to be definitely increased. **1954** M. Singer in R. O. Greep *Histology* xi. 216 Each cell body of spinal, cranial, and autonomic ganglia is completely encapsulated by a thin membrane composed of so-called satellite cells which contains small, scattered, and flattened nuclei. **1958** *Exper. Cell Res. Suppl.* V. 33 The structural characteristic which is present in all fibers so far studied .. is the Schwann or satellite cell which .. appears everywhere to enclose the axon. **1960** G. Causey *Cell of Schwann* v. 69 The regeneration of nerve fibres and their satellite cells in the tail of the tadpole. **1971** W. M. Copenhaver et al. *Bailey's Textbk. Histol.* (ed. 16) x. 259/1 When these companion cells are in association with a nerve cell body .., they are called satellite cells; when they provide ensheathment for axons, they are called neurilemma cells, or cells of Schwann.

9. *Cytology.* A short section of a chromosome demarcated from the rest by a constriction (if terminal) or by two constrictions (if intercalary). [The sense is due to S. G. Navashin, who used Russ. *spútnik* satellite (*Izvestiya Imper. Akad. Nauk* (1912) VI. 378).]

1926 C. D. Darlington in *Jrnl. Genetics* XVI. 246 Chromosome 'G' is seen to be approaching the pole with the satellite foremost; this means that the satellite is endowed with special responsiveness to the attraction of the pole. **1960** *Lancet* 14 May 1063/2 In some chromosomes the additional criterion of the presence of a satellite is available (table 1), but in view of the apparent morphological variation of satellites, they and their connecting strands are excluded in computing the indices. **1975** A. & D. Löve *Plant Chromosomes* I. i. 26 A secondary constriction may demarcate a short part of the chromosome, either intercalary or, most frequently, terminally. Such a terminal piece is called a satellite.

10. *Bacteriol.* A bacterial colony growing in culture near a second colony which is the source of a diffusible substance which promotes the growth of the first but is not produced by it; it consequently shows accelerated growth, or resists a substance which would otherwise poison it. Usu. *attrib.*

1938 in Dorland & Miller *Med. Dict.* (ed. 18) 1243/1. **1940** M. Frobisher *Fund. Bacteriol.* (ed. 2) xxv. 355 (*caption*) 'Satellite' formation by *Hemophilus influenzae* on 'chocolate-agar' plate. **1943** *Jrnl. Bacteriol.* XLV. 522/1 The development of satellites depended upon the concentration of sulfonamide, the susceptibility of the satellite strain, the temperature of incubation, and the size of the inoculum of both satellite and inhibitor. **1975** *Jrnl. Clin. Microbiol.* I. 90/2 The satellite growth of *Haemophilus* species around a colony of *Staphylococcus* can be attributed not only to NAD but also to catalase, which is produced by staphylococci.

11. *Molecular Biol.* A portion of the DNA of a genome distinguished from the rest of the genome by its distinctive base composition and density. Freq. *attrib.*

1961 S. Kit in *Jrnl. Molecular Biol.* III. 711 The mean buoyant densities of the principal and the satellite mouse DNA bands were 1·701 and 1·690 g cm^{-3}, respectively. **1962** *Ibid.* IV. 439 Calf thymus satellite was found at the same position in each of three different DNA preparations isolated from thymus tissue obtained from different animals. **1970** *New Scientist* 27 Aug. 406/1 Discovered originally in the mouse, where it constitutes some 10 per cent of the total DNA in each cell of the animal, satellite DNA can be distinguished from the rest by its different density, and by the fact that it apparently consists of repeating base sequences—i.e., multiple copies of a given sequence repeated again and again. **1977** Rees & Jones *Chromosome Genetics* ii. 22 Exceptional DNA segments may have an unusually high or low G + C content. When plotted, these fractions appear as heavy or light satellites respectively at the tails of the 'main-band' DNA. Heavy satellites are found in the guinea pig and in human DNA. Light satellites .. are less common.

12. Used *attrib.* to designate a computer or computer terminal distant from, but connected to and serving, a main computer.

1966 C. J. Sippl *Computer Dict. & Handbk.* 278 As a satellite system the real-time system relieves the larger system of time consuming input and output functions as well as performing preprocessing and postprocessing functions. **1970** O. Dopping *Computers & Data Processing* vi. 95 Input data in cards or paper tape are converted to magnetic tape by the satellite computer. **1971** E. F. Schoeters in B. de Ferranti *Living with Computer* viii. 68 The way in which their huge networks of small satellite computers, or calculating terminals, connected to big machines in London behave .. will show just how much more work has to be done.

13. *attrib.* and *Comb.*, as (sense 2 c) ***satellite camera***, ***communication(s)***, ***killer***, ***launcher***, ***navigation***, ***observatory***, ***programme***, ***-tracking***; ***satellite-borne*** adj.; ***satellite-to-home*** adj. phr.; (sense 6) ***satellite city***, ***community***, ***country***, ***government***, ***nation***, ***state***, ***town***, ***township***; **satellite airfield**, an airfield auxiliary to and serving, if necessary, as a substitute for a larger airfield; **satellite broadcasting**,

broadcasting in which the signal is transmitted via an artificial satellite; *spec.* = *direct broadcasting by satellite* s.v. DIRECT *a.* 6i; **satellite photo(graph)**, a photograph taken from an artificial satellite; so **satellite photography; satellite picture**, a satellite photograph; **satellite station**, (*a*) an artificial satellite; *spec.* (see quot. 1950); (*b*) a secondary radio station which receives and retransmits programmes, so as to improve local reception; **satellite telescope**, a telescope in orbit beyond the range of atmospheric distortion; **satellite television**, television in which the signal is transmitted via an artificial satellite.

1941 F. H. JOSEPH *Lett. Home from Brit. at War* (1942) 38 Clear skies over West Raynham's *satellite airfield, Massingham. **1951** O. BERTHOND tr. *P. Clostermann's Big Show* I. 20 We spent the last three weeks of our training at Montford Bridge, a small satellite airfield lost in the hills. **1968** *Wall St. Jrnl.* 25 Sept. 36/1 Flight delays at World Chamberlain and the satellite airfields are almost non-existent. **1962** W. B. THOMPSON *Introd. Plasma Physics* i. 4 Recently, rocket- and *satellite-borne counters have detected belts of energetic radiation, electrons and ions, high above the earth's atmosphere. **1974** *Sci. Amer.* June 132/2 Within less than a decade the bulk of trans-oceanic telephony (and all transoceanic television) has become satellite-borne. **1964** M. MCLUHAN *Understanding Media* xxv. 252 [Man's] central nervous system..is now approaching an extension of consciousness with *satellite broadcasting. **1984** *Listener* 8 Mar. 2/1 Barry Fox tries to make sense of the current debate about satellite broadcasting. **1987** *Sunday Tel.* 22 Feb. 23/7 Cotton spent the next two years working on the BBC's plans, now effectively shelved, for satellite broadcasting. **1963** *Satellite camera [see *satellite picture* below]. **1966** P. O'DONNELL *Sabre-Tooth* xiv. 185 The end of the journey..was on neutral ground, in an area where spy-plane or satellite cameras would never seek. **1912** G. R. TAYLOR in *Survey* (N.Y.) XXIX. 5 Oct. 23/1 Like camp sutlers, the traffickers in demoralization are quick to follow the trail of *satellite cities. **1960** *Washington Post* 20 Dec. A14 They urge that the growth of this region from some 4 million to 9 million persons in the remainder of this century be organized in a pattern of some 50 new satellite cities, each of 75,000 to 150,000 population. A dozen of them would fill the corridor between Baltimore and Washington. **1977** *New Yorker* 13 June 94/2 The new Taichung port..is to include a separate satellite city. **1959** J. H. STRAUBEL et al. *Space Weapons* 243 (Index), *Satellite communication. **1960** *Signal* XIV. 32/1 A means of communication is needed that will immediately provide several hundred channels linking key cities throughout the world. This requirement will be filled by a satellite communication system. **1961** *Times Rev. Industry* Feb. 26/3 Last autumn a team of British experts visited the United States to discuss with their opposite numbers the feasibility of establishing a satellite communications system. **1964** *Economist* 1 Aug. 481/2 Complex legal controversies arising from satellite communications systems. **1946** *Nature* 13 July 39/2 The Manchester request for compulsory powers to buy land for the creation of *satellite communities. **1970** R. STAVENHAGEN in I. L. Horowitz *Masses in Lat. Amer.* vii. 254 Not only in the city but also in the 'satellite communities' is commerce usually in Ladino hands. **1956** *Times* 7 Feb. 8/5 Dropping leaflets over the *satellite countries..was begun by Radio Free Europe in April, 1954. **1969** A. G. FRANK *Latin Amer.* (1970) i. 4 Relations between the satellite underdeveloped and the now developed metropolitan countries. **1976** B. FREEMANTLE *November Man* iv. 43 The Americans actually believe we [*sc.* the Russians] are going to withdraw all our troops from the satellite countries. **1949** KOESTLER *Promise & Fulfilment* I. xii. 133 Experts of the Foreign Office..tried to set up a puppet Jewish Agency as a kind of *satellite Government. **1977** *Guardian Weekly* 2 Oct. 15/2 A new weapon that could destroy Soviet satellites in space... Vought is expected to have a battle version of the *satellite killer ready to test in space in about two years. **1977** *Time* 17 Oct. 32/1 The U.S. will now emphasize efforts to design an American satellite killer to defend against the Soviet version. **1959** *Daily Tel.* 2 July 5/5 This *satellite launcher is about 110 ft long and 15 in in diameter at the base. **1961** *New Scientist* 19 Jan. 133/1 Several of these countries will discuss the specific proposal for the development of a satellite-launcher based on *Blue Streak*. **1916** C. M. MEREDITH tr. *F. Naumann's Central Europe* vi. 180 What is meant by a *satellite nation..? We might also say a planet State. Such States have their own life. **1956** E. E. CUMMINGS *Let.* 26 Nov. (1969) 253 Urging (via night & day broadcasts) the socalled satellite nations to revolt from colossal Russia. **1967** *Oceanogr. & Marine Biol.* V. 145 In February 1965 *Atlantis* II returned to the area to carry out a hydrographic and coring survey of this area using a *satellite navigation system and ship-board computer for the location of this small area. **1975** *Offshore Progress—Technol. & Costs* (Shell Briefing Service) 7 With satellite navigation, however, the rig can fix its own position by computer, processing signals received from orbiting satellites. **1953** J. N. LEONARD *Flight into Space* 159 They suspect that the human intellect is approaching a boundary of mystery which its present tools cannot penetrate. Some of them feel that the *satellite observatory may be the necessary tool. **1976** H. KEMELMAN *Wednesday the Rabbi got Wet* xii. 61 The noon broadcast had been almost entirely devoted to..Hurricane Betsy. There were..*satellite photos of the eastern coast. **1963** VAN DIJK & RUTHERFORD in Wexler & Caskey *Rocket & Satellite Meteorol.* 305 *Satellite photographs were obtained of a cut-off low over southeast Australia. **1977** A. HALLAM *Planet Earth* 43 (*caption*) A satellite photograph of the Andes. **1971** P. O'DONNELL *Impossible Virgin* v. 107 I'll have it checked by our own Map Section... There's *something* there which is detectable by *satellite photography. **1963** VAN DIJK & RUTHERFORD in Wexler & Caskey *Rocket & Satellite Meteorol.* 305 Facility in interpretation of meteorological *satellite pictures can best be achieved by exercises in which clouds of known type and distribution are charted and compared with pictures of the same cloud taken by satellite camera. **1977** L. P. WHITE *Aerial Photogr. & Remote Sensing for Soil Survey* vii. 73 Early examination of coverage of this kind did, however, serve to indicate the possibility of using automatic satellite pictures for purposes other than meteorology and oceanology. **1959** *Daily Tel.* 13 May 1 Britain has decided to take the essential steps to enable scientists here to participate in a *satellite programme. **1916** C. M. MEREDITH tr. *F. Naumann's Central Europe* vi. 181 Round about the *satellite States there still exists a certain mass of unorganised national material. **1943** *Ann. Reg. 1942* 176 Their [*sc.* Pan-Germans'] plan was that Germany.. should carve out in the Danube basin several satellite states. **1950** *Sun* (Baltimore) 17 July 11/2 Fortifications toughening the ragged western borders of central Europe's satellite states. **1976** *Survey* Summer-Autumn 41 Here was the authentic voice of the unconscious Western desire to believe that the satellite states of the Soviet Union were free. **1945** *Wireless World* Oct. 306 (*caption*) Three *satellite stations would ensure complete [radio] coverage of the globe. **1950** W. PROELL *Handbk. Space Flight* 174 *Satellite station*, synonym for space station... *Space station*, a habitable vehicle placed in a satellite orbit around a planetary body, for use in refueling of space ships, communications relaying, or military use. **1954** E. PANGBORN *Mirror for Observers* (1955) I. i. 21, I understand men will have their first *satellite station in a very short time, four or five years. **1959** *Times Lit. Suppl.* 30 Oct. 631/4 The cost of building a moon rocket at a satellite station, including the fuel of the rockets carrying the materials, he estimates as £40m. **1959** *Proc. Inst. Electr. Engineers* V. 416/1 A number of low-power satellite stations are therefore planned... They will be designed to..pick up signals from an existing B.B.C. station and retransmit them on a different channel for local reception. *Ibid.*, The B.B.C.'s plan for extending and improving the coverage of the television service and of.. sound services on v.h.f. by building low-power satellite stations in various parts of the country. **1962** *Rep. Comm. Broadcasting 1960* 197 in *Parl. Papers 1961-2* (Cmnd. 1753) IX. 259 It is possible to provide low-powered relay stations ..to extend coverage still further... These satellite stations ..have been planned as a stage by stage project. **1951** J. P. MARBARGER *Space Med.* 26 If we turn such a *satellite telescope to the outer reaches of the universe, the planets and the stars, we shall find observation conditions which no terrestrial observatory could equal. **1960** *Aeroplane* XCIX. 358/1 It turns out that this is a design study into a stabilised platform for a small satellite telescope. **1966** *B.B.C. Handbk.* 53 The BBC's first *satellite television transmissions were shown in 1962. **1971** L. KOPPETT *N.Y. Times Guide Spectator Sports* xii. 194 Satellite television. **1967** *Economist* 1 July 32/2 What about lasers? What about direct *satellite-to-home broadcasting?.. Perhaps the only way in which the federal government could expect to keep abreast of the developments in communications technologies would be to set up a Department of Communication. **1973** *Computers & Humanities* VII. 226 The uses of such wonders as switched data networks, computer terminals, mobile radio transceivers, and satellite-to-home-receiver television transmission. **1925** C. B. PURDOM (*title*) The building of *satellite towns. **1929** *Times* 17 July 17/6 Since neither complete decentralization nor the proposal to 'departmentalize' the government of Greater Paris is found to give general satisfaction, the system of 'satellite towns' has been suggested as a way out. **1933** *Archit. Rev.* LXXIV. 166/2 The proposed formation of a ring of satellite towns around the immediate radius of London. **1946** F. J. OSBORN *Green Belt Cities* I. 182 *Satellite Town.* This term was first used in Great Britain in 1919 as an alternative description of Welwyn Garden City... Some planning writers have thoughtlessly renewed the old confusion by using the term Satellite Town to describe an Industrial Garden Suburb. It is better reserved for a Garden City or country town, at a moderate distance from a large city, but physically separated from that city by a Country Belt. **1955** *Sci. Amer.* Jan. 40/3 As population continues to move from cities out to ever more distant suburbs and satellite towns [etc.]. **1971** *Rand Daily Mail* 27 Mar. 3/7 A giant new *satellite township near Pretoria..will provide housing..for about 200 000 White people. **1958** A. BUDRYS in Aldiss & Harrison *Decade 1950s* (1976) 68 I'm assigned to the *satellite-tracking station. **1969** *Listener* 20 Feb. 233/2 Satellite tracking is not as easy as it appears.

14. *attrib.* passing into *adj.* That is a satellite to something else; subsidiary, subordinate; associated; ancillary.

1892 B. POTTER *Jrnl.* 8 Aug. (1966) 245 We..found the thirteen or fourteen vans drawn up in the town square, and covered with a tarpaulin, with several satellite peep shows. **1923** N. SHAW *Forecasting Weather* v. 115 Two detached secondary or satellite depressions. **1931** *Economist* 17 Oct. 699/1 The Indian currency and..the various 'satellite' currencies of the Crown Colonies and Possessions. **1939** *Oxoniensia* IV. 13 Post-holes 1..., 3 and 6 were also provided with from two to four satellite sockets and slots for supports. **1949** *Caribbean Q.* I. III. 43 A central model farm..would carry on intensive dairy farming... The satellite farms would be run by skilled farmers. **1957** *Observer* 8 Sept. 7/3 When fashion makes a decisive move innumerable satellite trades are affected. **1965** B. SWEET-ESCOTT *Baker St. Irregular* iii. 77 This was to be their home for the next four years and became in due course surrounded by a series of satellite premises. **1967** *Boston Sunday Globe* 23 Apr. (Mag.) 33/1 Satellite clinics for children and pregnant mothers.. run jointly by several Harvard affiliated hospitals and the City of Boston. **1969** *Wall St. Jrnl.* 1 Dec. 9/1 Pan Am..is trying to sell passengers on use of the 'satellite' terminal facilities around the New York metropolitan area. **1972** *Accountant* 26 Oct. 518/2 Satellite reports, or supplementary reports, would be prepared for the particular interests of particular users. **1976** *NBR Marketplace* (Wellington, N.Z.) III. 37/2 The satellite seminar was joined by dozens of doctors and nurses. **1976** *Offshore Engineer* July 20/3 A cluster of 10 wells with four satellite wells for water and gas injection.

satellite ('sætɪlaɪt), *v.* [f. prec.]

1. *intr.* To orbit like a satellite.

1959 *IRE Trans. Military Electronics* III. 62/2 Mission periods of the order of one year (including a brief period.. of satelliting about the target planet).

2. *trans.* To transmit by way of a communications satellite.

1974 *Listener* 14 Dec. 826 The telephone woke me. It was Peter Lynch, our contact in Tel Aviv (from where our film was being satellited). **1976** A. DAVIS *Television* iv. 50 During the war in Cyprus in 1974, film shot by British cameramen was flown to Tel Aviv where it was processed, then satellited to Rome, where it was fed into the Eurovision network. **1978** *Broadcast* 23 Oct. 5/1 BBC TV News reporter Bob Friend ..satellited the pictures to London from Tai Pei.

satellited ('sætɪlaɪtɪd), *a.* [f. SATELLITE + -ED².]

1. Attended *by* a satellite.

1895 K. GRAHAME *Golden Age* 92 A dingy tramp, satellited by a frowsy woman and a pariah dog.

2. *Cytology.* Having a satellite or satellites (SATELLITE *sb.* 9).

1934 L. W. SHARP *Introd. Cytol.* (ed. 3) xviii. 319 (*caption*) Synaptic configurations..after deletion of portion of shorter arm of satellited chromosome. **1938** *Jrnl. R. Microsc. Soc.* LVIII. 103 Every primary diploid plant or animal generally has one pair of satellited chromosomes which..produce by fusion a single nucleolus. **1971** *Nature* 21 May 195/1 In the Australasian superfamily Dasyuroidea, all species have seven pairs of chromosomes, the autosomes including..two small pairs of chromosomes of which one has a satellited short arm.

satellitic (sætɪ'lɪtɪk), *a.* [f. SATELLITE *sb.* + -IC.] Of, pertaining to, or of the nature of, a satellite or lesser planet.

1823 *Monthly Mag.* LV. 8 One..who..has seen the stony masses, the aërolites, fall from satellitic bodies. **1882** STALLO *Concepts Mod. Physics* 277 The stellar, solar, planetary, satellitic, and meteoric systems.

transf. **1851** RUSKIN *Stones Venice* II. App. ix. 384 Small satellitic shafts [*sc.* of a clustered column].

sate'llitious, *a.* ? *Obs.* [f. L. *satelliti-um* (see SATELLITIUM) + -OUS.] Consisting of, having the character of, satellites.

1715 CHEYNE *Philos. Princ. Relig.* I. 208 Their Satellitious Attendance, their Revolutions about the Sun [etc.]. **1807** W. TAYLOR in *Ann. Rev.* V. 499 A halo of their brilliance may overspread even the satellitious vapours that strive to ornament their course.

satellitism ('sætɪlaɪtɪz(ə)m). [f. SATELLIT(E + -ISM.] **1.** *Bacteriol.* The occurrence of satellites (SATELLITE *sb.* 10); the promotion of bacterial growth by the proximity of a colony of different bacteria.

1951 WHITBY & HYNES *Med. Bacteriol.* (ed. 5) xvi. 282 Staphylococci secrete enough of the factor to stimulate growth of *H[æmophilus] influenzæ*; colonies of the latter on a blood plate are always larger when they lie near a staphylococcal colony (satellitism). **1975** *Jrnl. Clin. Microbiol.* I. 89 (*heading*) New satellitism test for isolation and identification of *Haemophilus influenzae* and *Haemophilus parainfluenzae* in sputum.

2. *Pol.* The fact or condition of being a satellite (state); the role of a satellite.

1955 O. LATTIMORE *Nationalism & Revolution in Mongolia* 41 (*heading*) Anatomy of satellitism. **1962** —— *Nomads & Commissars* viii. 155 Stalin..and Mongolia's loyalty to the Soviet alliance bring up the question of satellitism. **1964** *Economist* 10 Oct. 101/1 Only by helping to create a state much closer in strength to the super-powers can we escape satellitism or neutralism. **1969** D. WIDGERY in Cockburn & Blackburn *Student Power* 137 Wilson's satellitism to Washington forces an attack on Government spending.

‖**sate'llitium.** *Astrol. Obs.* [L. = body-guard, retinue, f. *satelles* SATELLES.] ? A retinue or company (of planets).

1669-96 AUBREY *Brief Lives, Hobbes* (1898) I. 328 His horoscope is Taurus, having in it a *satellitium* of 5 of the 7 planets. It is a maxime in astrologie—vide Ptol. Centil.—that a native that hath a *satellitium* in his ascendent becomes more eminent in his life then ordinary.

satellitosis (sætɪlaɪ'təʊsɪs). *Path.* [f. SATELLIT(E + -OSIS.] A proliferation of neuroglial cells around nerve cells in the brain.

1928 W. PENFIELD in E. V. Cowdry *Special Cytol.* II. xxx. 1055 From this satellitosis a perivascular and even a perineuronal leucocytic infiltration must be carefully distinguished. **1969** BROWN & BERTKE *Textbk. Cytol.* xxiii. 549 Oligodendrocytes..may increase in number during aging to produce a satellitosis, which is often seen in aging organs. **1979** *Jrnl. Compar. Path.* LXXXIX. 490 Some of the ganglion cells showed satellitosis.

satellize ('sætəlaɪz), *v.* [f. SATELL(ITE + -IZE.]

1. *intr.* To cluster *about. rare.*

1916 E. V. LUCAS *Variety Lane* 60 A little band of important men hurried up, satellizing about a quiet, gentle-looking but distinguished man.

2. *trans.* To make into a political or economic satellite.

1951 *Melbourne Herald* 16 Apr., Dr. W. E. Stanner.. introduced..the verb *to satellise*. Dr. Stanner used it when referring to other countries which, in given conditions, Russia might *satellise*. **1965** *Observer* 19 Sept. 2/3 Pakistan ..will not become a satellite of India; but..she will not be satellised by China either.

Hence **satelli'zation**, the action of making into a satellite; the condition or process of being satellized; **'satellized** *ppl. a.*

1958 *Times* 13 May 8/5 Mr Rountree, Assistant Secretary of State..told the committee:..'Satellization of the Middle East now seems less a danger than it did a few months ago.' **1962** *Economist* 12 May 551/2 A small communist country which..wants to escape satellisation by China. **1968** 'HAN SUYIN' *Birdless Summer* I. iii. 56 Japan's terms were the permanent satellization of China. **1969** A. G. FRANK *Latin Amer.* (1970) i. 7 The satellized national, regional, and local metropoles in Latin America find that their economic development is at best a limited or underdeveloped development. **1976** *Globe & Mail* (Toronto) 18 June 7/3 In spite of the somewhat unsure character of its national identity and its excessive satellization by the American economic and cultural empire, Canada-without-Quebec has enough 'difference' left, [etc.].

satelloid ('sætəlɔɪd). [f. SATELL(ITE + -OID.] A craft designed to follow approximately a free-fall orbit, but to expend power to overcome air resistance or to change its course.

1955 *Times* 3 Aug. 8/5 He has constructed a special earth satellite, the 'Satelloid' which goes to an altitude of 100 miles and from there is moved forward by an engine. **1956** *Jrnl. Brit. Interplanetary Soc.* XV. 166 Dr. Krafft A. Ehricke, of the guided missile group of Convair, has suggested that a weakly-powered satellite might be placed in a lower orbit than that required for an unpowered satellite, and used the word 'satelloid' to describe such a vehicle when discussing it at the I.A.F. meeting in Copenhagen. He said that the satelloid might be placed in an orbit at 80 miles altitude. **1960** *Aeroplane* XCVIII. 496/1 The authors examine various statements which have been made by U.S. military leaders on the merits of arching ballistic missiles, jump-down bombs, variable orbit satelloids, and boost-glide devices.

satem ('sɑːtəm). *Philol.* Also **satəm**. [f. Avestan *satəm* hundred, from its pronunciation with (s), as opposed to CENTUM: first used by P. von Bradke 1890 in *Über Methode und Ergebnisse der avischen Alterthumswissenschaft* I. iv. 63.] A name given by philologists to one, chiefly eastern, group of Indo-European languages, distinguished by their use of sibilants where the corresponding sounds in cognate words in the western group (cf. CENTUM) are velar stops.

1901, etc. [see CENTUM]. **1933** L. BLOOMFIELD *Language* xviii. 316 Many scholars suppose that the earliest traceable division of the Primitive Indo-European unity was into a western group of so-called '*centum*-languages' and an eastern group of '*satem*-languages'. **1952** O. R. GURNEY *Hittites* vi. 119 The main characteristics of the Indo-Iranian (or so-called 'Satem') languages (change of original *k* to *s*, *qu* to *k*, and *e* and *o* to *a*). **1973** *Word 1970* XXVI. 3 The time when the back velar stops moved forward in satem languages.

saten, Satenas, obs. ff. SATIN, SATANAS.

sater, obs. form of PSALTER.

sater, var. SAETER, SETTER.

Saterday, Sateresday, etc., obs. ff. SATURDAY.

saterick(e, obs. forms of SATIRIC.

saterion, obs. variant of SATYRION.

Saternas, obs. form of SATANAS.

†**saternight.** *Obs.* [OE. *Sæterniht*, f. *Sætern*: see SATURDAY.] The night before Saturday, Friday night.

c **1000** ÆLFRIC *Hom.* I. 216 His lic læȝ on byrȝene þa sæter-niht and sunnan-niht. **1297** R. GLOUC. (Rolls) 11650 In a lammasse niȝt, saterniȝt þat was.

Satersday, obs. form of SATURDAY.

satesfet, -fit: see SATISFY *v.*

sateyn, obs. form of SATIN.

Sathan, etc.: see SATAN, etc.

sathbhai, var. SAT-BHAI.

sati: see SUTTEE.

satia: see SETTEE (ship).

satia'bility. *rare*⁻¹. In 6 sas-. [f. next + -ITY.] Capability of being satiated.

1528 LYNDESAY *Dreme* 586 Thare is plentie of all plesouris perfyte..; Withouttin hunger, Sasiabilitie.

satiable ('seɪʃɪəb(ə)l), *a.*[1] [ad. L. **satiābil-is*, f. *satiāre* to SATIATE: see -ABLE.]

1. That can be satiated.

1570 LEVINS *Manip.* 3 Satiable, *satiabilis*. **1813** SHELLEY *Q. Mab* VII. 217 War, Scarce satiable by fate's last death-draught. **1864** *Jrnl. R. Agric. Soc.* XXV. II. 346 There are some soils which swallow up manure, with, so to speak, no satiable appetite.

†**2.** ? Satisfactory, plausible. (Cf. SATISFIABLE a.)

1592 GREENE *Philomela* Wks. (Grosart) XI. 156 Though my wife returned a taunting letter to him openly, yet she might send him sweete lines secretlye: her satiable answere, was but a cloak for the rayne.

Hence '**satiableness** *rare*⁻⁰. †'**satiably** *adv.*, so as to satiate.

1627-8 FELTHAM *Resolves* II. xxi. Wks. (1677) 205 The daily Laboring Man sells both his strength, his time, and his ease, for that alone which will not satiably content his craving Belly. **1882** OGILVIE, *Satiableness*.

'satiable, *a.*[2] Colloq. reduced form of INSATIABLE *a.* Used in phr. '*satiable curiosity* in allusion to Kipling's *Just So Stories* (see quot. 1900).

1900 KIPLING *Just So Stories* (1902) 63 There was one Elephant..—an Elephant's Child—who was full of 'satiable curtiosity, and that means he asked ever so many questions. **1963** L. EGAN *Run to Evil* i. 6 Talk about the Elephant's Child... Nobody could really dislike the Brandon boy, even with his 'satiable curiosity. **1974** K. BENTON *Craig & Tunisian Tangle* v. 52 She's like the Elephant's Child, full of 'satiable curiosity.

satiate ('seɪʃɪət), *pple.* and *ppl. a.* Now *rare.* Forms: 5-6 **saciat(t, -ate, sacyat(t, -atte, -ate,** (6 **saceat, satyett**), 6-9 **satiate.** [ad. L. *satiāt-us*, pa. pple. of *satiāre* to satiate, f. *satis* enough.]

†**a.** *pple.* Equivalent to the later *satiated*, pa. pple. of SATIATE *v. Obs.* **b.** *ppl. a.* Satiated, filled to repletion, glutted, gratified to the full. Const. *with*, †*of*; also †with inf.

c **1440** *Alphabet of Tales* 403 þai war saciatt & fulfyllid þer-with as it had bene with meate or drynk. *c* **1450** *Man-kind* 304 in *Macro Plays* 12 My soull ys well sacyatt With þe mellyfluose doctryne of þis worshyppfull man. **1485** CAXTON *Paris & V.* (1868) 55 And whan messyre Iaques had redde the letter, he coude not be sacyat of redyng, he took so grete playsyr therin. **1526** in Ellis *Orig. Lett.* Ser. II. I. 338 He..made suche good relacyon of the Kings Highnes and of your Grace that they coulld not be sacyate to talke with hym. **1534** MORE *Comf. agst. Trib.* III. Wks. 1221/2 Neuer was he saciate of hearinge his owne prayse. **1583** STUBBES *Anat. Abus.* II. B 3, When the Sodomits, and Gomorreans had filled vp the measures of their iniquitie, and saciate themselues in sinne. **1593** DRAYTON *Idea* No. 31 Euery drudge doth dull our satiate eare. **1611** BIBLE *Jer.* xlvi. 10 The sword shal deuoure, and it shall be satiate, and made drunke with their blood. **1640** R. BAILLIE *Canterb. Self-convict.* Pref., Their furious desire of revenge must be satiate. **1667** MILTON *P.L.* I. 179 Let us not slip th' occasion, whether scorn Or satiate fury yield it from our Foe. **1737** POPE *Hor. Epist.* I. i. 9 Our Gen'rals now, retir'd to their Estates, Hang their old Trophies o'er the Garden gates, In Life's cool Ev'ning satiate of Applause. **1781** CRABBE *Library* 410 [491] Satiate with power, of fame and wealth possess'd. **1889** G. GISSING *Nether World* I. xii. 262 The gratuity expected from each guest as he rose satiate.

satiate ('seɪʃɪeɪt), *v.* Also 6-7 **saciat(e**, 7 **satiat.** [f. L. *satiāt-*, ppl. stem. of *satiāre*: see prec.]

1. *trans.* To fill, satisfy (with food). Hence *gen.*, to gratify to the full (a person or his desires). Const. *with*, rarely † *of*, †*in*. Now *rare* (the prevailing use being in sense 2).

c **1532** DU WES *Introd. Fr.* in *Palsgr.* 954 Saouler, to saciate. *a* **1548** HALL *Chron., Hen. VII* 30 To thentent that ..the boylynge heate of her malicious harte mighte be fully saciated with hys innocent bloude. **1571** BUCHANAN *Admonitioun* Vernac. Writ. (1892) 35 To that fyne yat.. Thay may saciat yair cruell hartis of blude, yair obstinat will of vengeance. **1611** BIBLE *Jer.* xxxi. 14, I will satiate the soule of the priests with fatnesse. **1634** SIR T. HERBERT *Trav.* 221 Able to satiate the most couetous. **1713** C'TESS WINCHELSEA *Misc. Poems* 254 A Lyon, satiated with Food. **1749** SMOLLETT *Regicide* II. x, My starv'd revenge Thy blood alone can satiate! **1817** JAS. MILL *Brit. Ind.* II. IV. vii. 247 The idea that satiating the servants of the public with wealth is a secret for rendering them honest. **1828** D'ISRAELI *Chas. I*, II. xi. 268 A terrible enmity which nothing could satiate short of life. *a* **1853** ROBERTSON *Serm.* Ser. III. xx. 258 The outcast son tried to satiate his appetite with husks.

absol. *c* **1645** HOWELL *Lett.* (1650) I. v. xxv. 162 Hee had so far transgressed the Fannian Law, which allows a chirping cup to satiat, not to surfet. **1657-83** EVELYN *Hist. Religion* (1850) I. 242 It is then that, cleared of all suffusion, we shall contemplate that fulness, which can only satiate without satiety.

2. To gratify beyond one's natural desire; to weary or disgust by repletion; to glut, cloy, surfeit.

1620 VENNER *Via Recta* 84 The Carpe..quickly satiateth the stomacke. **1651** N. BACON *Disc. Govt. Eng.* II. i. (1739) 4 The King being rather satiated than satisfied with Victory and Honour, returned home to enjoy what he had. **1667** MILTON *P.L.* IX. 248 But if much converse perhaps Thee satiate, to short absence I could yeild. **1693** LOCKE *Educ.* §167 (1699) 297 Whatever that [*sc.* novelty] presents, they are presently eager to have a Taste of, and are as soon satiated with it. **1780** BURKE *Œcon. Reform* Wks. III. 258 Quite fatigued and satiated with this dull variety. **1789** MRS. PIOZZI *Journ. France* II. 187 Here at Venice there are paintings to satisfy, nay satiate connoisseurship herself. **1849** RUSKIN *Sev. Lamps* iv. §19. 109 They only satiate the eye. **1855** BREWSTER *Newton* II. xvii. 134 But Newton was satiated with fame.

absol. **1667** MILTON *P.L.* VIII. 214 Sweeter thy discourse is to my eare Then Fruits of Palm-tree..; they satiate and soon fill. **1836** KINGSLEY *Lett.* (1877) I. 33 She longed for.. a love that should never satiate.

b. *intr.* (for *refl.*). To become satiated. *rare.*

1797 MRS. A. M. BENNETT *Beggar Girl* (1813) II. 162 The eye of taste would never tire, nor the soul of sensibility satiate.

†**3.** *trans.* To saturate. *Obs.* (Cf. SATE *v.* 2.)

1674 *Phil. Trans.* IX. 175 The colour argued it abounding with Sulphureous or Oily parts, and the weight, that it was highly satiated with the Saline. **1680** BOYLE *Produc. Chem. Princ.* II. 93 A quantity of Calcin'd Corall, sufficient to satiate the Acid Corpuscles. **1704** NEWTON *Optics* (1721) 352 Why does not Salt of Tartar draw more Water out of the Air than in a certain Proportion to its quantity, but for want of an attractive Force after it is satiated with Water? **1791** MACIE in *Phil. Trans.* LXXXI. 373 A piece of Tabasheer.. was first let satiate itself with distilled water.

Hence '**satiated** *ppl. a.*, '**satiating** *vbl. sb.* and *ppl. a.*

1611 COTGR., *Saoulement*, a glutting, filling, saciating, cloying with. **1657** *Divine Lover, Holy Exerc.* 304 Loue is all kind of Prayer by which our soule tends towards God as her only All, and satiatinge end. **1691** LOCKE *Lower. Interest* 85 Buying of Land is the result of a full and satiated Gain. **1769** E. BANCROFT *Guiana* 344 Enabling some to squander the bread of provinces in a profusion of satiating pleasures. **1824** MISS MITFORD *Village* Ser. I. 251 Her loveliness..is such a fulness of bloom, so luxuriant, so satiating. **1935** ADAMS & ZENER tr. *Lewin's Dynamic Theory of Personality* viii. 255 Both agreeable and disagreeable tasks are comparatively more rapidly satiated than neutral ones. **1969** J. D. DAVIS et al. in *Jrnl. Compar. & Physiol. Psychol.* LXVII. 407 Intake of milk by fasted rats was reduced 50% below normal after their blood had been transfused with that of satiated rats. **1975** SCHNEIDER & TARSHIS *Physiol. Psychol.* xvi. 283 These studies have shown that the size of the cells in the ventromedial hypothalamus are larger and thus presumably more active in satiated animals than in deprived animals.

satiation (seɪʃɪ'eɪʃən). [ad. L. **satiātiōn-em*, n. of action f. *satiāre* to SATIATE.] **a.** The action of satiating or fact of being satiated.

1638 T. WHITAKER *Blood of Grape* 4 As if Satiation were the Usher of diseases. **1656** S. HOLLAND *Zara* III. vi. (1719) 140 What do we get by these Gim-cracks? Satiation of our Lusts. **1811** SHELLEY *St. Irvyne* x, From my earliest youth, before it was quenched by complete satiation, curiosity.. was the passion by which all the other emotions of my mind were intellectually organized. **1839** DE QUINCEY *Recoll. Lakes* Wks. 1862 II. 54 The same satiation never can take place, which too frequently deadens the genial enjoyment of those who have a surfeit of books, and a monotony of leisure. **1856** GROTE *Greece* II. xciv. XII. 244 Clinging to the hope that Alexander, when possessed of the three southern capitals and the best part of the Persian empire, might have reached the point of satiation.

b. *Psychol.* The point at which satisfaction of a need or familiarity with a stimulus reduces or ends an organism's responsiveness or motivation. Also *attrib.*

1935 ADAMS & ZENER tr. *Lewin's Dynamic Theory of Personality* viii. 254 The progressive process of satiation is evidenced by such typical criteria as variation, dissolution of the whole.., inattention, forgetting. **1944** KÖHLER & WALLACH in *Proc. Amer. Philos. Soc.* LXXXVIII. 276/1 We propose to call only the alterations of *T*-objects 'figural after-effects' and to refer to the affection of the medium as 'satiation'. **1954** WOODWORTH & SCHLOSBERG *Exper. Psychol.* (rev. ed.) xiv. 426/1 Satiation.. is not offered as an explanation of the illusion itself, but as a cause of its reduction and final destruction. **1967** J. R. MILLENSON *Princ. Behavioral Analysis* (1969) xv. 367 There are drive operations that reduce or eliminate reinforcing value... The most universal of these is *satiation*—repeatedly presenting the reinforcer until it loses its power to reinforce. **1975** SCHNEIDER & TARSHIS *Physiol. Psychol.* xvi. 276 Studies have confirmed the notion that the ventro-medial hypothalamus comes into play during satiation to inhibit eating. *Ibid.* 283 The transfused rats no longer seemed to be hungry... Davis took this to mean that the blood does carry an off, or satiation, signal. **1978** F. LEUKEL *Essent. Physiol. Psychol.* xii. 197/2 Satiation stimuli are more readily aroused.

satiety (sə'taɪɪtɪ). Forms: 6-7 **sacietie, -ty,** (6 **-tee**), **satietie,** 6- **satiety.** [ad. F. *satiété* (12th c. *sazieted*, 16th c. *societé*), ad. L. *satietātem* abundance, satiety, f. *satis* enough.

The pronunciation (sə'saɪɪtɪ) is mentioned by Walker (1828) as all but universally current in his time, and as accepted by Sheridan and other orthoepists. His protest against it, as contrary to all analogy, was effectual: the condemned pronunciation is now quite obsolete.]

1. a. The state of being glutted or satiated with food; the feeling of disgust or surfeit caused by excess of food.

1533 ELYOT *Cast. Helthe* (1541) 40b, The dyner moderate, that is to say, lasse than sacietie or fulness of bealy. **1583** STUBBES *Anat. Abus.* (1877) 104 Dooth not the impletion and sacietie of meates and drinks prouoke lust? *c* **1610** *Women Saints* (E.E.T.S.) 215 They began to feele some sacietie of theire ordinarie simple sustenance. **1762** GOLDSM. *Cit. W.* xv, His cooks had a hundred different ways of dressing it, to solicit even satiety. **1791** COWPER *Iliad* IV. 407 And quaff your wine Delicious, 'till satiety ensue. **1865** LIVINGSTONE *Zambesi* xix. 388 It is always a case of famine or satiety.

b. *gen.* The condition of having any appetite or desire gratified to excess; hence, weariness or dislike *of* (an object of desire) caused by gratification or attainment.

1553 T. WILSON *Rhet.* 108b, It offendeth and werieth mens eares with saciety. *a* **1586** SIDNEY *Arcadia* III. (Sommer) 291 Where desire neuer wanted satisfaction, nor satisfaction neuer bred sacietie. **1604** SHAKS. *Oth.* II. i. 231 When the Blood is made dull with the Act of Sport, there should be a game to enflame it, and to giue Satiety a fresh appetite. **1605** BACON *Adv. Learn.* I. viii. §5 Of knowledge there is no sacietie, but satisfaction and appetite are perpetually interchangeable. **1647** CLARENDON *Hist. Reb.* II. §101 He never apprehended a greater censure than a sequestration from all public employments, in which it is probable he had abundant satiety. **1667** MILTON *P.L.* VIII. 216 Thy words with Grace Divine Imbu'd, bring to thir sweetness no satietie. **1669** CLARENDON *Ess.* in *Tracts* (1727) 127 Satiety of all things naturally produces a satiety of life itself. **1712** ADDISON *Spect.* No. 412 ¶3 That Satiety we are apt to complain of in our usual and ordinary Entertainments. **1820** SHELLEY *To Skylark* 80 Thou lovest —but ne'er knew love's sad satiety. **1832** R. & J. LANDER *Exped. Niger* I. iv. 192 The eager curiosity of the natives has been glutted by satiety. **1865** SEELEY *Ecce Homo* iv. (ed. 8) 36 Prosperous villany carried to an honoured grave in the fulness of years and in the satiety of enjoyment.

†**c.** In favourable sense: The condition of being filled or fully gratified; full attainment of an object of desire. *Obs.*

1548 UDALL, etc. *Erasm. Par. Matt.* v. 6 Where there is euer hungar and euer thurst, and blessed sacietie & fulnes. **1590** SPENSER *F.Q.* II. ii. 39 Thus fairely shee attempered her feast, and pleasd them all with meete satiety. *a* **1617** BAYNE *On Eph.* (1658) 45 In Gods presence is the saciety of everlasting delight. **1712** ADDISON *Spect.* No. 387 ¶12 Which..will produce a Satiety of Joy, and an uninterrupted Happiness. **1722** WOLLASTON *Relig. Nat.* ix. 208 *note*, There being no Satiety of Knowledge in this life, we may hope for future opportunities when [etc.].

d. ***to satiety***: to an amount or degree which satisfies or gluts desire. [= L. *ad satietatem*.]

1607 TOPSELL *Four-f. Beasts* (1658) 189 They must be suffered to eat of them to saciety. **1726** POPE *Odyss.* XXI. 59 To full satiety of grief she mourns. **1775** BURKE *Sp. Conc. Amer.* Sel. Wks. I. 215 The Colonies not only gave, but gave to satiety. **1837** J. H. NEWMAN *Par. Serm.* III. iii. 31 They had miracles even to satiety. **1878** C. STANFORD *Symb. Christ* xii. 325 Their earthly nature..is filled to satiety with earth's good things.

e. *Psychol.* Satisfaction of a need (esp. hunger) as it is registered physiologically; also *attrib.* and *Comb.*, as ***satiety hormone, mechanism, process***; **satiety centre**, an area of the brain concerned with the regulation of food intake.

1951 *Amer. Jrnl. Physiol.* CLXIV. 186 The physiological release of enterogastrone is apparently not involved in the production of satiety. **1962** *Science* CXXXV. 374/2 The so-called 'feeding center' of the lateral hypothalamus and the 'satiety center' of the medial hypothalamus are well known. **1969** J. D. DAVIS et al. in *Jrnl. Compar. & Physiol. Psychol.* LXVII. 407/1 Is food intake..regulated by a 'satiety hormone' which terminates feeding when it reaches a threshold level? **1971** K. H. PRIBRAM *Lang. of Brain* x. 192 Somehow the lesion had impaired the patient's *feelings* of hunger and satiety and this impairment was accompanied by excessive eating! *Ibid.* 195 The term 'motivation' can be restricted to the operations of appetitive 'go' processes..and the term 'emotion' to the operations of affective 'stop' or satiety processes of equilibrium. **1974** J. OLDS in W. R. Adey et al. *Brain Mechanisms* vii. 379 In one of these areas, known as the 'satiety center', destruction of tissues caused animals to overeat and become obese. **1975** F. P. VALLE *Motivation* xii. 227 There are several hypotheses regarding the variables that govern the activity of the 'satiety center' in the ventromedial nuclei. **1977** N. R. CARLSON *Physiol. of Behav.* xii. 324 The fact that we stop eating before a significant amount of food is digested makes it necessary to postulate a satiety mechanism. *Ibid.* 325 Satiety has many sources, from several kinds of detectors. **1978** F. LEUKEL *Essent. Physiol. Psychol.* xii. 203/1 The first center is the ventromedial nucleus of the hypothalamus. This nucleus appeared to function as a satiation, or satiety, centre.

2. A sufficiency or abundance. [So in L.] *rare.*

1635 HEYWOOD *Hierarch.* II. 68 This, of himselfe all Fulnesse, all Satietie, Is then the sole Incomprehensible Deitie. **1884** LUSHINGTON in Knight *Mem. J. Nichol* (1896) 222 Here is a satiety or (nimiety) for you, about a man, for whom I have a loving admiration.

'satify, *v.* Chiefly *Sc.* Also 5 satefy, 6 satyfy, satifie. [a. OF. *satifier*, *satefier*, var. of *satisfier*: see SATISFY.] *trans.* = SATISFY.

Still locally used in Scotland, in the form *settifee*.

c **1475** *Partenay* 1917 Hit is gret reson ye were satefied Off your ful good will don And applied. **1513** DOUGLAS *Æneis* v. xi. 11 Juno,..Not satyfyit of hir auld fury nor wroik. **1533** BELLENDEN *Livy* Prol. (S.T.S.) I. 4 Be sum meretis þare Ire war satifyit. *Ibid.* II. II. 285 For quhen thir pepill maye nocht be gottin to satify his crewelte, he behufit finallie to rage in him selff. *c* **1555** HARPSFIELD *Divorce Hen. VIII* (1878) 271 It is worse for a man to break good laws to..satify his sensual appetite. **1596** DALRYMPLE tr. *Leslie's Hist. Scot.* (S.T.S.) II. 454 To satifie his askeng.

satin ('sætɪn), *sb.* (and *a.*) Forms: 4-5 satyne, -ine, 4-6 satyn, sat(t)on, 5 sathan, 5-6 saten, sateyn, 5-7 sattyn, 5-8 satten, 6 satte(i)ne, sat(t)an, satyng, *Sc.* saiting, satteing, salting, 6-8 sattin(e, 6- satin. [a. F. *satin* (14th c. in Hatz.-Darm.; the supposed popular OF. form *saïn*, cited by Diez, is an error), app. ad. It. †*setino*, prob. repr. late L. **(pannus) sētinus* silken (cloth), f. *sēta* silk. Cf. Pg. *setim* (? from It.), late med.L. *satinius*, *satinus* (from Fr.), *setīnus* (1594, from Spain); also Du. *satijn*.

The word cannot be connected etymologically with the app. synonymous Arab. *zaitūnī*, f. *Zaitūn* name of a city in China (the locality of which is disputed). F. Hirth (*Arch. Stud. neu. Spr.* LXVII, 1882, p. 204) suggests that the Arabs may have confused the name of the town with the Cantonese *sze-tün* = Mandarin *ssŭ-tuan*, satin; but the conjecture that the Cantonese form is the source of It. *setino* is extremely improbable.]

I. 1. A silk fabric with a glossy surface on one side, produced by a method of weaving by which the threads of the warp are caught and looped by the weft only at certain intervals. † ***satin of Cypres***: see CYPRESS³ 1 b.

? *a* **1366** CHAUCER *Rom. Rose* 1104 The barres were of gold ful fyne, Upon a tissu of satyne. [The word is not in the original Fr.] *c* **1369** —— *Dethe Blaunche* 253 Ryght wel cledde In fyne blak satyn de owter mere. *c* **1400** *Brut* 458 And iij. other estates with hem, clothed in oon sute, in rede fyne saten crymsyn furred with Martrons. **1435** in Dugdale *Bar. Eng.* (1675) 246/1 Item, Three Penons of Satten, entertailed with Raggedstaffs, price the peece 2ˢ. *c* **1440** *Promp. Parv.* 441/2 Satyne, clothe of sylke, *satinum*. *c* **1460** *Towneley Myst.* xxx. 325 With youre bendys and youre bridyls of sathan, the whilke sir sathanas Idyls you for tha ilke This gill knaue. **1506** in *Bury Wills* (Camden) 107 A vestement of whyte sateyn and poudrid wᵗ Seynt Nicholas armes. **1530** PALSGR. 265/1 Sattyn of cypres—*ostadine*. *a* **1555** LYNDESAY *Trag.* Prol. 21 In Rayment reid..Off vellot and of Saityng Crammosie. **1580** *Aberdeen Reg.* (1848) II. 36 Ane [cloak] lynt witht salting, ane uther witht taffetie. **1603** in *38th Rep. Deputy Kpr. Records* App. 444 Sattins reverses, sattins of Cipres, Spanish sattins. **1628** FELTHAM *Resolves* I. xviii. 56 Poore men, though wise, are but like Sattens without a glosse. **1748** RICHARDSON *Clarissa* (1811) III. 29 Her coat white sattin, quilted. **1853** C. BRONTE *Villette* xxi, The middle distance was filled with matrons in velvets and satins, in plumes and gems. **1855** TENNYSON *Maud* I. xxii. 9 In gloss of satin and glimmer of pearls. **1880** MISS BRADDON *Just as I am* xi, The draperies and chair and sofa coverings were of amber satin.

transf. **1616** R. C. *Times' Whistle* vii. 2938 Her skin sleek sattin or the cygnettes brest.

b. Applied to certain fabrics resembling satin, but composed wholly or in part of other materials than silk. † ***satin of Bruges (Bridges)***, ***Bruges satin***: see quot. 1728. ***Denmark satin***: a smooth worsted material used for ladies' slippers.

1517-1599 [see BRUGES]. **1728** CHAMBERS *Cycl.* s.v., The Sattins of Bruges have their Warp of Silk, and their Woof of Thread. **1875** *Ure's Dict. Arts*, *Denmark satin*, a stout worsted stuff used for ladies' shoes.

c. A woman's satin dress.

1787 'T. WIGNELL' *Contrast* I. 2 She is to be married in a delicate white sattin. **1866** MRS. GASKELL *Wives & Daughters* I. xxvi. 287, I remember the time when Mrs Kirkpatrick wore old black silks..and now she is in a white satin. **1932** [see *low-cut* s.v. LOW *adv.*]. **1958** J. CANNAN *And be a Villain* iv. 100 A high-waisted pomegranate satin with gold lace sleeves.

†**2.** A kind of pear. *Obs.*

1693 EVELYN *De La Quint. Compl. Gard.* I. 109 b, A Summer Satin-pear. *Ibid.* 121 The Green-Satin-Pear, January. **1706** LONDON & WISE *Retir'd Gard.* I. vii. 33 The Satin is round; its Coat is yellow, and smooth like Satin; 'tis a melting sugar'd Pear, and in good Esteem.

3. The plant Honesty, *Lunaria biennis*. Also ***white satin***. Cf. *satin-flower* in 8 b.

1597 GERARDE *Herbal* II. cxvii. 378 We cal this herb in English Pennie flower..in Northfolk Sattin, and white Sattin. **1668** WILKINS *Real Char.* 103 Bulbonach, Honesty, Sattin. **1785** MARTYN *Rousseau's Bot.* xxiii. (1794) 320 The brilliant whiteness of these silicles has occasioned this plant [Honesty] to be called White Sattin.

4. *slang.* Gin. Also ***white satin***.

1845 J. R. PLANCHÉ *Golden Fleece* I. 13 An ardent spirit, known By several names..Some 'Cupid's eye water' the liquor call, 'White Satin' some. **1854** *Househ. Words* VIII. 75 For..gin, we have ten synonyms: max, juniper,..cream of the valley, white satin, old Tom. **1865** *Slang Dict.*, *Satin*, gin; 'a yard of satin,' a glass of gin. **1934** T. S. ELIOT *Rock* ii. 66, I brought you along a drop o' satin. Four glasses and all.

5. A collector's name for a glossy white moth. Also ***white satin***.

1766 M. HARRIS *Aurelian* (1778) 9 White Sattin. **1819** G. SAMOUELLE *Entomol. Compend.* 248 Satin moth. **1832** J. RENNIE *Conspect. Butterfl. & M.* 41 The Satin..appears in July. **1857** STAINTON *Brit. Butterfl. & Moths* I. 134 *Stilpnotia Salicis* (White Satin). **1869** E. NEWMAN *Brit. Moths* 36 The Satin Moth (*Liparis Salicis*).

6. A domestic rabbit belonging to the breed so called, developed in America during the early 1930s by Walter A. Huey and distinguished by smooth fur with a satin-like sheen. Also *attrib.*

1934 W. L. COTTA in *Fur Animals* Aug. 3/1, I take great pleasure in describing, for the first time publicly, the most amazing rabbit of all time, the Satin Havana. **1935** *Small Stock Mag.* Aug. 7/2 Anything in the nature of a boom will do the satin more harm than good. **1946** *Amer. Rabbit Jrnl.* XVI. 44/2 In 1936 the American Satin Rabbit Breeders Association was organized. *Ibid.* 45/1 With the exception of the Satin Havanas, none of the Satin breeds have an Approved Working Standard. **1947** *Fur & Feather* 9 May 191/3 The Satin..a beautiful animal..comes in various colours, white, an orange, blue, black... Its fur feels like satin. It is a breed about nine years old and was started from a freak litter of Havanas. **1957** J. C. SANDFORD *Domestic Rabbit* i. 2 A second mutation of a coat character is the Satin. *Ibid.* 3 The Satin coat has also been combined with a number of colours. **1979** G. R. SCOTT *Rabbit Keeping* i. 26 The Satin rabbit is another mutation. *Ibid.*, The early Satins were ivory in colour.

II. Attrib. and Comb.

7. *attrib.* passing into *adj.* **a.** Made of satin.

1521 *Test. Ebor.* (Surtees) VI. 6 My blake sattan jackett. **1580** *Aberdeen Reg.* (1848) II. 36 Item, ane pair of satteing breikis. **1599** MARSTON *Sco. Villanie* 166 Each sattin sute, Each quaint fashion-monger, whose sole repute Rests in his trim gay clothes. **1606** PRICKET in Farr *S.P. Jas. I* (1847) 101 A sattin sute, bedawb'd with silvered lace, Beyond desert doth vildest clownship grace. **1676** HALE *Contempl.* I. 497 When you are in the Publick Worship and Service of God, ..if the weather be too cold, wear a satten cap. **1750** GRAY *Long Story* 14 His high-crown'd hat and sattin-doublet. **1866** GEO. ELIOT *F. Holt* i, You shall have nothing to do now but to be grandmamma on satin cushions.

fig. **1635** QUARLES *Emblems* v. vii. 270 A land, where each embroydred Sattin word Is lin'd with Fraud.

b. Resembling satin in texture or surface.

1826 MISS MITFORD *Village* Ser. II. 60 The satin palms with their honeyed odours are out on the willow. **1838** T. THOMSON *Chem. Org. Bodies* 42 When sublimed, it [Benzoic Acid] assumes the form of long flat prismatic needles, having a beautiful satin lustre. **1851** MAYHEW *Lond. Labour* I. 369 The best satin note-paper. **1866** *Reader* 12 May 471 The papers..retain the gloss, the bright 'satin' surface of the albumenized material. **1913** C. MACKENZIE *Sinister St.* I. I. vii. 103 Boys emerged from the tuckshop, sucking gelatines and satin pralines and chocolate creams. **1930** E. POUND *XXX Cantos* vii. 27 Square even shoulders and the satin skin, Gone cheeks of the dancing woman. **1975** P. MOYES *Black Widower* v. 56 A single big tear ran down her black satin cheek. **1977** *Hot Car* Oct. 59/2 The finish will be a nice satin which is a sod to keep clean.

c. Clothed in satin. (In 17th cent. a mark of dandyism).

1603 DEKKER *Wonderfull Yeare* Aiij, The stinking Tobacco-breath of a Sattin-gull. *a* **1613** OVERBURY *A Wife, &c.* (1638) 35 Where if his Russet-friend would chance to dine, Whether his Satten-friend would fill him wine. **1624** HEYWOOD *Captives* IV. ii. in Bullen *O. Pl.* IV. 187 The pesent with his homespoon lasse As many merry howers may passe As coortiers with there sattin guerles. **1912** W. DE LA MARE *Listeners & Other Poems* 8 Her satin bosom heaving slow With sighs that softly ebb and flow.

8. General combinations: **a.** simple attrib., as ***satin-like*** adj.; **b.** instrumental, similative, and parasynthetic, as ***satin-clad***, ***-faced***, ***-frilled***, ***-leaved***, ***-lidded***, ***-lined***, ***-purfled***, ***-sandalled***, ***-shimmering***, ***-shining***, ***-smooth***, ***-striped***, ***-worked***, adjs.

1881 'MARK TWAIN' *Prince & Pauper* xxxii. 349 *Satin-clad officials are flitting and glinting everywhere. **1891** KIPLING *Light that Failed* iii, A portly middle-aged gentleman in a *satin-faced frockcoat. **1949** BLUNDEN *After Bombing* 25 Enchanting poppies *satin-frilled. **1897** MARY KINGSLEY *W. Africa* 570 Patches of *satin-leaved begonias. **1879** E. ARNOLD *Lt. Asia* 84 The *satin-lidded eyes, with lashes dropped Sweeping the delicate cheeks. **1699** M. LISTER *Journey to Paris* 59 A very smooth *Sattin-like Skin. **1719** LONDON & WISE *Compl. Gard.* IV. ii. 68 When mellow, the Skin is slick and Satin-like. **1919** E. POUND *Quia Pauper Amavi* 16 There is a satin-like bow on the harp. **1891** *Lock to Lock Times* 24 Oct. 12/1 A *satin-lined Inverness cape. **1862** G. M. HOPKINS *Poems* (1967) 10 And trample and tread The *satin-purfled smooth to foam. **1917** BLUNDEN *Poems* (1930) 44 *Satan-sandalled Chloes glimmering. **1952** R. CAMPBELL tr. *Baudelaire's Poems* 89 On *satin-shimmering, downy avalanches. **1859** TENNYSON *Vivien* 222 A robe..In colour like the *satin-shining palm On sallows. **1847** C. BRONTË *J. Eyre* xiv, This *satin-smooth hazel hair. **1882** CAULFEILD & SAWARD *Dict. Needlework*, **Satin-striped Canvas*..is a fancy variety of embroidery Canvas. **1799** *Hull Advertiser* 30 Nov. 1/1 *Satin worked..muslins.

9. Special combinations. **a.** Used to designate materials resembling, or woven in the same manner as, satin; as **satin cloth**, a woollen cloth woven like satin, chiefly produced at Roubaix in France; **satin-damask** (see quot.); **satin-finish**, a polish for silver produced by means of a metallic brush; also any effect resembling satin in texture or surface produced on materials in various ways; **satin foulards** (see quot.); **satin jean** (see quot. 1875); **satin leather**, **satin oil**, leather finished so as to resemble satin; **satin-paper**, a fine writing paper; **satin sheeting**, a composite material of waste silk and cotton; **satin stitch**, a kind of stitch in embroidery and wool-work, imitating the appearance of satin; **satin-straw**, soft flexible straw used for hats; **satin-tails**, streamers of satin attached to ladies' dresses; **satin weave** (see quot. 1897); **satin wire** (see quot. 1925).

1882 CAULFEILD & SAWARD *Dict. Needlework*, **Satin Cloth*, a French woollen material of Satin make. **1557-71** A. JENKINSON *Voy. & Trav.* (Hakl. Soc.) I. 90 *Satton damaske with diuers other things. **1882** CAULFEILD & SAWARD *Dict. Needlework*, *Satin Damask*, a very costly silk material. **1865** MRS. STOWE *House & Home Papers* 157 For *satin finish,..American papers equal any in the world. **1901** *Daily Chron.* 7 Dec. 8/3 [Ornaments] made in art silver, with what is called a satin finish. **1929** *Encycl. Brit.* XXIX. 7/2 Frequently the surface [of glass] had been dulled by acid so as to produce a 'satin' finish. **1959** *Gloss. Packaging Terms* (*B.S.I.*) 32 *Satin finish*, a decorative matt finish mechanically or chemically applied to aluminium and tinplate sheets. **1969** *New Yorker* 27 Sept. 92/3 (Advt.), It's Norway Pewter with the gleaming, never-tarnish satin finish. **1972** *Homes & Gardens* Mar. 106/2 They [*sc.* paints] are obtainable in gloss, semi-gloss, eggshell and satin finishes. **1974** *Harrods Christmas Catal.* 8 Housecoat in washable satin-finish flocked nylon. **1882** CAULFEILD & SAWARD *Dict. Needlework*, **Satin Foulards*..are silk stuffs printed in various designs and colours. **1875** KNIGHT *Dict. Mech.*, **Satin-jean*, a twilled cotton goods, having a smooth satiny surface. *c* **1885** *Weldon's Pract. Needlework* IV. 3/1 Executed..on a ground of white satin jean. **1802** *Monthly Mag.* XIV. 203/2 White and chamois leather..are evidently in danger of being beat out of the market by the English *satin-leather. **1903** L. A. FLEMMING *Pract. Tanning* xiv. 264 Wax calf and satin leather are finished upon the flesh or inner side. **1971** T. C. COLLOCOTT *Dict. Sci. & Technol.* 1033/1 *Satin leather*.., leather with a perfectly smooth finish and without grain marks. **1895** *Montgomery Ward Catal.* Spring & Summer 517/3 Men's *Satin Oil Congress Gaiters. **1897** C. T. DAVIS *Manuf. Leather* (ed. 2) xxviii. 424 This blacking is for satin oil, glove grain, plow grain, oil grain and dongola. **1834** M. EDGEWORTH *Tour in Connemara* (1950) 55 Mʳ Jones wrote me as elegant a note as ever you saw on *satin paper. **1840** THACKERAY in *Fraser's Mag.* XXI. 684/1 I'll keep everything: the red wax, because it's like your lips; the black wax, because it's like your hair; and the satin paper, because it's like your skin! **1866** W. COLLINS *Armadale* III. xiii, Supply me with a quire of extra double-wove satin paper, and a gross of picked quills. **1882** CAULFEILD & SAWARD *Dict. Needlework*, **Satin Sheeting*, one of the 'waste-silk' materials. **1684** HAN. WOOLLEY *Queen-like Closet* Suppl. 57 Work it in *Satten-stitch. **1840** MRS. F. TROLLOPE *Widow Married* ii, The profusion of elaborate satin-stitch bestowed upon its cuffs and collar. **1900** *Daily News* 3 Mar. 6/5 There are many varieties of *satin straws and grades of varying suppleness. **1841** THACKERAY *Chron. Drum*, Lovely Court ladies in powder, And lappets, and long *satin-tails. **1897** STEPHENSON & SUDDARDS *Text Bk. Ornamental Design Woven Fabrics* 104 What is known in textile manufacturing as a *satin weave, which is a construction of cloth where the weft comes to the surface in greater proportion than the warp, or *vice versa*, in a certain definite order. **1964** *McCall's Sewing* iv. 52/2 Satin weaves produce smooth, lustrous fabrics. **1969** *Sears Catal.* Spring/Summer 20 Blazer stripes in a satin weave on sand beige. **1899** in A. Adburgham *Shops & Shopping* (1964) xxii. 261 *Satin wire. **1925** G. E. MARTIN *Make your Own Hats* (rev. ed.) i. 4 *Satin wire*, the thickest wire used in millinery, covered with a padding of cotton and then wrapped with silk; sometimes used for head line and edge wires. **1966** Satin wire [see MILLINERY 3].

b. In names of birds, insects, plants, and minerals having a satin-like lustre or smoothness: **satin beauty**, a moth, *Boarmia abietaria* (Stainton *Brit. Butterflies & Moths.* 1859); **satin bell** = MARIPOSA LILY; **satin-bird** or **satin bower-bird**, *Ptilorhynchus violaceus*; **satin-carpet**, a moth, *Cerotopacha fluctuosa*; also = *satin beauty*; **satin-flower**, (*a*) Honesty, *Lunaria biennis*; †(*b*) French Honeysuckle, *Hedysarum coronarium*; (*c*) the Greater Stitchwort, *Stellaria Holostea*; (*d*) in Australia, the umbelliferous plant *Actinotus helianthi*; (*e*) a small herb of the genus *Sisyrinchium*, esp. *S. douglasii*, which is native to western North America and has grass-like leaves and small blue or purple flowers; †**satin-grakle**, an Australian bird, perh. *Calornis metallica*; **satin gypsum**, a fibrous variety of gypsum, with a pearly lustre; **satin-leaves** (see quot.); **satin moth** (see 5); **satin-pug**, a moth, *Eupithecia sericeata*; **satin-pygmy**, a moth, *Microsetia sericiella*; **satin-spar**, a fibrous variety of carbonate of lime; also = *satin-gypsum*; **satin-sparrow** (see quot.); **satin-stone** = *satin gypsum*; **satin-walnut** *U.S.*, a trade name for the Sweet Gum Tree, *Liquidambar styraciflua*; **satin wave**, a white moth, *Sterrha subsericeata*; **satin-white**, artificial sulphate of lime; **satin-wood**, the wood of the Indian tree *Chloroxylon Swietenia* and of several W. Indian trees esp. *Fagara flava*; also, the similar yellowish wood of any of several African or Australian trees, esp. *Daphnandra micrantha* or *Zanthoxylum brachyacanthum*; also, any of the trees producing this timber; the colour of this timber.

1898 A. M. DAVIDSON *Calif. Plants* 123 Mariposas are.. sometimes called globe tulips,..the *satin-bell or fairy's lantern. **1925** W. L. JEPSON *Man. Flowering Plants Calif.* 237 White Globe Lily..Also called Snow-drops, Indian Bells, and Satin Bells. **1825–6** VIGORS & HORSFIELD in *Trans. Linnean Soc.* (1827) XV. 264 The natives call it Cowry, the colonists *Satin Bird. **1860** G. BENNETT *Gatherings Nat. Austral.* 234 Satin-birds are now seen very frequently in captivity in Sydney. **1848** GOULD *Birds Austral.* IV. pl. 10 *Ptilonorhynchus holosericeus* Kuhl. *Satin Bower-bird. **1832** J. RENNIE *Conspect. Butterfl. & M.* 82 The *Satin Carpet appears the middle of June. **1869** E. NEWMAN *Brit. Moths* 64 The Satin Carpet (*Boarmia abietaria*). *Ibid.* 239 The Satin Carpet (*Cymatophora fluctuosa*). **1597** GERARDE *Herbal* II. cxvii. 377 Bolbonac or the *Sattin flower, hath hard and round stalkes. **1629** PARKINSON *Paradisus* 339 *Hedysarum clypeatum.* The red Sattin flower. **1854** MISS PRATT *Flower. Pl.* (1861) I. 245 Greater Stitchwort, Satin-flower, or Adder's Meat. **1860** G. BENNETT *Gatherings Nat. Austral.* 358 A profusion of the Sunflower Actinotus, also called Satin-flower by the colonists. **1882** G. P. LATHROP *Echo of Passion* iv. 76 Marigolds and satin-flowers..were growing in the midst of rank weeds. **1971** *Daily Colonist* (Victoria, B.C.) 18 Apr. 22/2 Numerous clumps of satin flower blend their purple hued petals with the rosy shooting star. **1822** LATHAM *Gen. Hist. Birds* III. 171 *Satin Grakle... Inhabits New-Holland. **1836–41** BRANDE *Chem.* (ed. 5) 682 A beautiful fibrous variety, called *satin gypsum, is found in Derbyshire, applicable to ornamental purposes, such as beads, broaches, &c. **1864** GRINDON *Brit. & Gard. Bot.* 152 The old-fashioned 'honesty', or *Lunaria*, the beauty of which lies in the great oval silvery shields that form the partitions of its seed-pods. .. They are often as large as florins, and in Cheshire are called '*satin-leaves'. **1832** J. RENNIE *Conspect. Butterfl. & M.* 132 The *Satin Pug. *Ibid.* 205 The *Satin Pygmy.. appears the end of May. **1802** AIKIN in *Tilloch's Philos. Mag.* XII. 364 The *satin spar..is a mineral as yet peculiar to the neighbourhood of Alston Moor, in Cumberland. **1804** JAMESON *Syst. Min.* I. 498 Common Fibrous Limestone... The sattin spar found in Derbyshire belongs to this kind. **1875** DAWSON *Dawn of Life* vii. 188 The prismatic structure of satin-spar may be said..to resemble that of a shell. **1894** NEWTON *Dict. Birds* 814 *Satin-sparrow, the name in Tasmania for *Myiagra nitida*, a Flycatcher. **1829** *Glover's Hist. Derby* I. 101 Fibrous or silky Gypsum..has a curious cat's-eye appearance, and is commonly called *Satin stone. **1897** G. B. SUDWORTH *Nomencl. Arborescent Flora U.S.* 205 Sweet Gum..*Satin Walnut. **1901** *Daily Chron.* 22 Aug. 7/5 'Sweet gum' is the name most generally used in the United States, and the wood was a drug until its name was changed by a smart trader to 'satin walnut'. **1949** COLLINGWOOD & BRUSH *Knowing your Trees* 247/1 Sweetgum..is frequently marketed as satin walnut. **1908** R. SOUTH *Moths Brit. Isles* 2nd Ser. 117 The *Satin Wave... The wings of this species are glossy whitish. **1958** W. J. STOKOE *Caterpillars Brit. Moths* II. 29 The Satin Wave..is widely distributed throughout England and Wales. **1839** *Civ. Engin. & Arch. Jrnl.* II. 141/1 The satin ground is laid with *satin white. **1792** G. IMLAY *Topogr. Descr. W. Territory N. Amer.* 214 *Satin-wood tree. Not classed. **1799** *Times* 1 June 4/1 (Advt.), Cabinet articles..in mahogany, satin, and other woods. *Ibid.*, Valuable, and seasoned stock of Mahogany and satin wood in lots, planks, boards, and veneers. **1823** P. NICHOLSON *Pract. Build.* App. 47 With respect to mahogany, satin and other choice woods. **1847** TENNYSON *Princess* II. 90 She herself Erect behind a desk of satin-wood. **1866** *Treas. Bot.* s.v., *Bahamas Satinwood*, a timber supposed to be the produce of *Maba guineensis*. **1871** KINGSLEY *At Last* x, Here..was a house of satin-wood and cedar not two years old. **1884** SARGENT *Rep. Forests N. Amer.* 31 *Xanthoxylum Caribæum*... Satin Wood. Semi-tropical Florida [etc.]. **1884** A. NILSON *Timber Trees New South Wales* 50 D[*aphnandra*] *micrantha.*—Satin-wood; Light yellow-wood... Timber fragrant, quite yellow when fresh. *Ibid.* 125 Z[*anthoxylum*] *brachyacanthum.* Satinwood; Thorny Yellowwood. **1902** G. S. BOULGER *Wood* v. 97 About 1750, Satinwood..became fashionable for coach-panels. **1907** *Yesterday's Shopping* (1969) 145/1 Stains..as used by the Working Ladies Guild, colours:—Rosewood, Satinwood, Oak, [etc.]. **1908** [see OBECHE]. **1920** [see AFRORMOSIA]. **1926–7** [see MAPLE 2 b]. **1936** R. H. ANDERSON *Trees New South Wales* 127 Socket Wood..is also known as Light Yellow-wood, Satin Wood, and occasionally as Sassafras. **1958** *N.Z. Timber Jrnl.* July 73/2 There is a great variety of satinwoods. **1962** S. WYNTER *Hills of Hebron* v. 73 The indent where the pulse beat was smooth, like satinwood.

c. In Fr. combinations (some of them anglicized in form) serving as trade names for certain textile fabrics, as **satin beauté**, a soft finely woven material with a dull crêpe back and brilliant satin finish; **satin de chine**, a silk fabric with a silk finish; **satin de laine** [= 'wool satin': see DELAINE]; **satin de Lyon(s)** (see quots.); **satin lisse** [F. *lisse* smooth]; **satin sultan**, **satin turk** [F. *turc* = Turkish] (see quots.).

1922 *Daily Mail* 18 Dec. 8 Her gown, in the Early Italian style, will be of cream *satin beauté. **1928** *Times* 9 May 10/6 A draped gown of lavender satin beauté, embroidered with silver. **1880** L. HIGGIN *Handbk. Embroidery* ii. 14 '*Satin de Chine*', and other silk-faced materials of the same class. **1895** *Army & Navy Co-op. Soc. Price List* 15 Sept. 1095/1 Satin de Lyon..Satin de Chine, for dress linings. **1969** R. T. WILCOX *Dict. Costume* 303/2 *Satin de chine*,..was known in medieval Europe... Because of its exquisite texture, it became a court favorite. **1851** *Satin de laine [see MOUSSELINE 1 b]. **1858** SIMMONDS *Dict. Trade*, *Satin-de-laine*, a black cassimere manufactured in Silesia, from wool. **1881** C. C. HARRISON *Woman's Handiwork* II. 115 *Satin de Lyons, of a fine close quality, may be used with water-colors. **1915** L. HARMUTH *Dict. Textiles* 137/2 *Satin de Lyon*, silk satin made with a twilled back, and finely striped face, used for lining. **1969** R. T. WILCOX *Dict. Costume* 303/2 *Satin de lyon*, satin with a ribbed back. Used for masculine evening wear trim such as top hat, waistcoat, lapel or trouser stripes. **1882** CAULFEILD & SAWARD *Dict. Needlework*, **Satin Lisse*, a French dress material made of cotton, but having a Satin-like lustre. *Ibid.*, **Satin Sultan*, a textile somewhat resembling Bengaline in the method of its manufacture, but having a satin face. **1858** SIMMONDS *Dict. Trade*, **Satin-Turk*, a trade term for a superior quality of satinette.

satin ('sætɪn), *v.* [f. SATIN *sb.* Cf. F. *satiner.*] *trans.* To give (to wall-paper) a glossy surface resembling that of satin. Hence '**satining** *vbl. sb.* (also *attrib.*).

1839 URE *Dict. Arts* 921 Pieces intended to be satined, are grounded with fine Paris plaster. *Ibid.* 922 A final satining, ..is communicated by the friction of a finely polished brass roller. **1875** KNIGHT *Dict. Mech.*, *Satining-machine*, a machine for imparting the 'satin' finish to paper.

Satin, obs. form of SATAN.

†**sati'nade.** *Obs. rare*⁻⁰. In quot. **sattinade.** [a. F. *satinade*, f. *satin*: see -ADE.] = SATINETTE.

1728 [see SATINETTE 1 a].

‖**satiné** (satine). [Fr. (*bois*) *satiné* (Aublet *Hist. Pl. Guiane*, 1775).] A kind of satin-wood.

1866 *Treas. Bot.*, *Satiné*, a cabinet-wood of French Guiana, the produce of *Ferolia guianensis*. **1875** LASLETT *Timber & Trees* 161 Satiné. This wood is red in colour, hard, heavy [etc.].

satined ('sætɪnd), *ppl. a.* [f. SATIN *sb.* or *v.* + -ED, after F. *satiné.*] **a.** Having a satin-like surface. Also, having a satin-finish.

1707 SLOANE *Jamaica* I. 154 A brown membranaceous capsula,..containing three sattin'd seeds. **1897** *Sears, Roebuck Catal.* 415 Solid Sterling Silver [bracelet], chased satined links.

b. Clothed in satin.

1817 JANE AUSTEN *Venta* in *Minor Wks.* (1954) VI. 457 The Lords & the Ladies were sattin'd & ermin'd.

sati'netta. *nonce-wd.* Pseudo-It. form of next. (Attributed to 'the Euphuist'.)

1820 SCOTT *Monast.* xxi, Standing on end with double piled velvets, satins, and satinettas!

satinette, satinet (sætɪ'nɛt, 'sætɪnɪt). Also 8 **sattinet.** [a. F. *satinet*: see SATIN *sb.* and -ET¹.]

1. a. An imitation of satin woven in silk, or silk and cotton.

1703 *Lond. Gaz.* No. 3915/4 Stolen.., a Cloth colour Silk Sattinet Gown and Petticoat. **1709** *Female Tatler* No. 9/1 Fine Mohairs, Silk Sattinets, Burdets, Persianets [etc.]. **1728** CHAMBERS *Cycl.*, *Sattinet*, or *Sattinade*, a very slight, thin Sattin, chiefly used by the Ladies for Summer Night-gowns, &c. and ordinarily striped. **1849** C. BRONTË *Shirley* xxv, You shall have a black satin dress for Sundays—a real satin—not a satinet or any of the shams. **1891** PINERO *The Times* I. 3 Beryl is cotton, you are silk; each material in itself is estimable, but cotton and silk beget satinet.

b. A material woven with a cotton warp and woollen weft, having a satin-like surface.

1837 HT. MARTINEAU *Soc. Amer.* II. 227 At Lowell, in Massachusetts, there was in 1818, a small satinet mill, employing about twenty hands. **1860** HOLLAND *Miss Gilbert* ii. 42 Old Ruggles looked down on his rusty satinet suit, perfectly conscious he was out of place. **1882** CAULFEILD & SAWARD *Dict. Needlework*, *Satinet*, an American cloth of mixed materials, both cheap and durable. **1904** *Woollen Draper's Terms* in *Tailor & Cutter* 4 Aug. 480/1 Satinette: A cheap fabric, composed of cotton and wool.

2. A fancier's name for a kind of pigeon.

1876 *Fulton's Bk. Pigeons* 312 The Satinette. **1881** LYELL *Fancy Pigeons* 232.

†**sati'nisco.** *Obs.* Also 7 **sattinisco, satanisco.** [pseudo-Sp., f. SATIN *sb.*, after words like MORISCO.] An inferior quality of satin.

1615 *Overbury's Char.*, *Fellow of House* (ed. 6) L 3, His meanes..afford him Mock-veluet or Satinisco. **1619** PURCHAS *Microcosmus* xxvii. 268 The new deuised names of Stuffes and Colours,..*Callimanco, Sattinisco* [etc.]. **1639** GLAPTHORNE *Wit in Constable* I. (1640) B 3, You meere Schollers Know no degree of garment above Serge, Or Satanisco. *a* **1661** FULLER *Worthies, Norwich* (1662) II. 274 Also [there were stuffs called] Perpetuano..Satinisco, Bombicino, Italiano, &c.

†'**satinist.** *Obs. rare*⁻¹. [f. SATIN *sb.* + -IST.] A wearer of satin, a dandy.

1632 SHIRLEY & CHAPMAN *Ball* IV. i, If it be so, Ile call you cosin still, my satinist.

sa'tinity. *nonce-wd.* [f. SATIN *sb.* + -ITY.] Smoothness, like that of satin.

1830 LAMB *Let. to Gilman* (1837) II. 267 Your friend B—— (for I knew him immediately by the smooth satinity of his style) must excuse me for [etc.].

satinize ('sætɪnaɪz), *v.* [f. SATIN *sb.* + -IZE.] *trans.* To impart a satin-like surface to. Hence '**satinized** *ppl. a.*

1869 TANNER *Pract. Med.* (ed. 6) II. 595 Baths..in repute for softening and whitening ('satinizing') the skin. **1883** J. MILLINGTON *Are we to read Backwards?* 77 The system of 'satinizing' the paper largely prevailing in France. **1972** *Guardian* 18 July 11/1 Satinised cotton trousers. **1975** *Harper's & Queen* June 96 Shocking pink shawl in satinised cotton.

satiny ('sætɪnɪ), *a.* [f. SATIN *sb.* + -Y.] Resembling satin in smoothness, gloss, or polish.

1786 ABERCROMBIE *Arrangem.* 82 in *Gard. Assist.*, Its moon shape, sattiny pellucid seed-pods. **1819** G. SAMOUELLE *Entomol. Compend.* 423 Geometra subsericeata. The satiny Wave [moth]. **1830** LINDLEY *Nat. Syst. Bot.* 45 They have the appearance of thin satiny paper. **1839** LADY LYTTON *Cheveley* (ed. 2) I. iii. 57 Her hair of that rich sattiny [*sic*], nameless brown, like a hazel-nut. **1862** MILLER *Elem. Chem.* (ed. 2) III. 264 Melissin..crystallizes..in satiny crystals. **1882** *Garden* 11 Feb. 91/1 This variety bears flowers of a satiny crimson-blush colour.

†'**sation.** *Obs.* Also 5 **-oun.** [ad. L. *satiōn-em*, f. ppl. stem *sat-* of *serĕre* to sow.] 'A sowing of seed, a planting' (Blount *Glossogr.* 1661).

c **1440** *Pallad. on Husb.* XII. 9 Ek summen seyn the benes satioun In placis coold is best to fructifie. **1651** BIGGS *New Disp.* §297 Some there are, which want sation and occatory operations. **1658** SIR T. BROWNE *Gard. Cyrus* iv. 63 It hath not succeeded by sation in any maner of ground.

Satirdai, -day, obs. forms of SATURDAY.

satire ('sætaɪə(r)), *sb.* Also 6–8 **satyre**, 7–8 **satyr**, 8 **satir.** [a. F. *satire* (= Sp. *sátira*, Pg., It. *satira*, G. *satire*), or directly ad. L. *satira*, later form of *satura*, in early use a discursive composition in verse treating of a variety of subjects, in classical use a poem in which prevalent follies or vices are assailed with ridicule or with serious denunciation. The word is a specific application of *satura* medley; this general sense appears in the phrase *per saturam* in the lump, indiscriminately; according to the grammarians this is elliptical for *lanx satura* (lit. 'full dish': *lanx* dish, *satura*, fem. of *satur* full, related to *satis* enough), which is alleged to have been used for a dish containing various kinds of fruit, and for food composed of many different ingredients.

Formerly often confused or associated with SATYR (see esp. sense 4), from the common notion (found already in some ancient grammarians) that L. *satira* was derived from the Gr. σάτυρος satyr, in allusion to the chorus of satyrs which gave its name to the Greek 'satyric' drama. The words *satire* and *satyr* were probably at one time pronounced alike, as the derivatives *satiric* and *satyric* are still; and the common use of *y* and *i* as interchangeable symbols in the 16th and 17th c. still further contributed to the confusion.]

I. 1. A poem, or in modern use sometimes a prose composition, in which prevailing vices or follies are held up to ridicule. Sometimes, less correctly, applied to a composition in verse or prose intended to ridicule a particular person or class of persons, a lampoon.

Also used *Hist.* as the rendering of L. *satura* in its preclassical sense of a poetic 'medley': see the etymological note above.

1509 BARCLAY *Shyp of Folys* (1874) I. 134 Therfore in this satyre suche wyll I repreue. **1566** DRANT (*title*) A Medicinable Morall, that is, the two Bookes of Horace his Satyres, Englyshed. **1595** LODGE (*title*) A Fig for Momus: Containing Pleasant varietie, included in Satyres, Eclogues, and Epistles. **1605** CAMDEN *Rem.*, *Rythmes* (1623) 309 The Exchequer officers were extortors in the time of King Henry the fourth, otherwise Henry Bell..would neuer haue written a riming long Satyr against them. **1672** SIR T. BROWNE *Let. Friend* §33 Impotent Satyrs write Satyrs against Lust [1682 —— *Chr. Mor.* I. §33 upon Lust]. **1711** STEELE *Spect.* No. 88 ¶2 This honest Gentleman, who is so desirous that I should write a Satyr upon Grooms, has a great deal of Reason for his Resentment. **1756** J. WARTON *Ess. Pope* (1782) I. iv. 254 The *Rape of the Lock*, is the best

Satire extant. **1841** Elphinstone *Hist. Ind.* II. 251 They had the merit of introducing satires on manners and domestic life into Asia. **1878** Dowden *Stud. Lit.* 278 A great proportion of the book [Middlemarch] is only not a satire because with the word satire we are accustomed to associate the idea of exaggeration and malicious purpose.

†**b.** *transf.* A satirical utterance; a speech or saying in ridicule of some person or thing. *Obs.*

1642 Fuller *Holy & Prof. St.* III. xxi. 210 Speaking constant satyrs to the disgrace of others. **1678** R. L'Estrange *Seneca's Mor., Epist.* ii. (1696) 467 The Poor Man wants many things, but the Covetous Man wants All. Can any Flesh forbear being delighted with This saying, though a Satyr against his own Vice?

c. *fig.* A thing, fact, or circumstance that has the effect of making some person or thing ridiculous.

1693 Norris *Pract. Disc.* (1698) IV. 11 Religion has no advantage from the Commendations of those whose Lives are a constant Satyr upon it. **1770** *Junius' Lett.* xxxviii. (1788) 207 Their very names are a satire upon all government. **1848** Thackeray *Van. Fair* lvii, You..whose rank may be an ancestor's accident, whose prosperity is very likely a satire. **1863** B. Taylor *H. Thurston* i. 15 Seth was an awkward, ungainly person, whose clothes were a continual satire on his professional skill.

2. a. The species of literature constituted by satires; satirical composition.

1589 Puttenham *Eng. Poesie* I. xiii. (Arb.) 46 The said auncient Poets vsed for that purpose [of reproving the people], three kinds of poems reprehensiue, to wit, the Satyre, the Comedie, and the Tragedie. **1659** *Gentl. Calling* IV. xiii. 404 If any shall think this character partakes of the satyr, I shall beseech him to compare it with the true state. *a* **1661** Holyday *Juvenal* Pref. (1673) 2 According to the ancient use and law of Satyre, it should be nearer the Comedy, then the Tragedy, not declaiming against Vice, but jeering at it. **1682** *Lenten Prol.* 36 in *Third Coll. Poems* (1689) 26/1 Baye's crown'd Muse, by Sovereign Right of Satyre, Without desert, can dub a man a Traitor. **1693** Dryden *Juvenal* Ded. (1697) 35 Thus..I..have prov'd, I hope, from the best Critiques, that the Roman Satire was not borrow'd from thence [Greece], but of their own Manufacture. **1728** Young *Love Fame* I. 1 My verse is satire; Dorset, lend your ear, And patronise a muse you cannot fear. **1841** Elphinstone *Hist. Ind.* I. 295, I have seen no specimen of Hindú satire. **1845** H. Thompson in *Encycl. Metrop.* X. 391/2 Lucilius is asserted by Horace to have been the founder of the New Satire. **1880** Goldw. Smith in *Atlantic Monthly* Feb. 199 There are different kinds of satire: the epicurean, which laughs at mankind,..the stoical, which indignantly lashes mankind,..the cynical, which hates and despises mankind.

b. The employment, in speaking or writing, of sarcasm, irony, ridicule, etc. in exposing, denouncing, deriding, or ridiculing vice, folly, indecorum, abuses, or evils of any kind.

c **1675** ? Villiers (Dk. Buckhm.) *Follies Men of Age* 6 Nothing helps more than Satyr to amend Ill manners, or is trulier Virtues Friend. **1699** Bentley *Phal.* ii. 31 His Animadversions have other faults besides Satyr and Abuse. **1705** Addison *Italy, Caprea* 265 This..is therefore interpreted by many as a hidden Piece of Satyr. **1724** R. Welton *Chr. Faith & Pract.* 359 Those Pharisees, whom our Blessed Saviour, with the utmost satyre, and indignation, call'd painted sepulchres. **1736** Butler *Anal.* II. vii, The Mythological [Writing], and the Satyrical where the Satyr is, to a certain Degree, concealed. **1816** 'Quiz' *Grand Master* IV. 75 Disgraceful too, to human nature,— Unworthy even, of his satire. **1828** Scott *F.M. Perth* xxxi, Rothsay thought he discovered a smile upon his countenance; and to be the subject of this man's satire, gave him no ordinary degree of pain. **1847** Tennyson *Princess* II. 445 And often came Melissa hitting all we saw with shafts Of gentle satire, kin to charity, That harm'd not. **1877** Mrs. Oliphant *Yng. Musgrave* I. 10 Even now there would be a tone of satire in her voice when she noted the late marriage of one or another of her old adorers.

c. *fig.* Effect in making ridiculous. (Cf. 1 c.)

1848 Thackeray *Van. Fair* xxiv, Some few score of years afterwards, when all the parties represented are grown old, what bitter satire there is in those flaunting childish family portraits.

d. *personified.*

1820 Shelley *Fragm. Satire on Sat.* 17 If Satire's scourge could wake the slumbering hounds Of Conscience, or erase the deeper wounds, The leprous scars of callous Infamy. **1855** Milman *Lat. Chr.* IX. viii. (1864) V. 380 Satire began to aim its contemptuous sarcasms at the pope and the papal power. **1870** Swinburne *Ess. & Stud.* (1875) 252 Satire in earlier times had changed her rags for robes. Juvenal had clothed with fire, and Dryden with majesty, that wandering and bastard Muse.

3. Satirical temper, disposition to use 'satire'.

1829 Lytton *Devereux* I. iv, The kindness of his temper so softened the satire of mine.

†**II. 4.** A satirical person, satirist. *Obs.*

[Perh. to be regarded as a misuse of Satyr.]

1596 Harington *Ulysses upon Ajax* E 1 b, Harke in thine eare, Misacmos is a Satire, a quipping fellow. **1628** Shirley *Witty Fair One* I. iii. (1633) B 3 b, Prethee Satyre chuse another walke, and leaue vs to inioy this. *a* **1629** T. Goffe *Courageous Turk* II. iii. (1632) D 2 b, Poore men may love, and none their wils correct: But all turne Satyres of a Kings affect. **1640** Shirley *Hum. Courtier* I. i. B j b, We may As well condemne our fathers, and declaime 'Gainst them for our begetting, come Orseollo, Desist to be a Satire. **1656** Earl Monm. tr. *Boccalini's Advts. fr. Parnass.* II. xxxii. (1674) 182 It being..forbidden to play the Satyre, gallant men who saw things..committed, which ought publickly to be declaimed against, were forc'd to see, and to say nothing. **1709** Pope *Ess. Crit.* 592 Leave dang'rous truths to unsuccessful Satires, And flattery to fulsome Dedicators.

fig. *c* **1600** Shaks. *Sonn.* c, Rise resty Muse, my loues sweet face suruay, If time haue any wrincle grauen there, If any, be a *Satire* to decay, And make times spoiles dispised euery where.

III. 5. *attrib.* and *Comb.*

1553 T. Wilson *Rhet.* 24 b, The whiche thyng appereth plaine by the Satyre Poete. **1687** Dryden *Hind & P.* III. 1187 Frontless and Satyr-proof he scow'rs the streets. **1691** *Satyr agst. French* 2 The Town, alas, is now grown Satyr-proof.

satire ('sætaɪə(r)), *v.* [f. the sb.] *trans.* = satirize *v.* 2 a.

1905 S. Joyce in *Lett. J. Joyce* (1966) II. 104 He doesn't think the critics will approve, or the people satired. **1961** in *Amer. Speech* XXXVI. 138 Hawthorne in his story 'Earth Holocaust' satires Emerson's idea of books.

satire, obs. form of satyr.

sati'rette. *nonce-wd.* [f. satire *sb.* + -ette.] A small satire.

1870 F. Harrison *Choice Bks.*, etc. (1886) 150 The characters even have merit... They are happy satirettes.

satiri: see satyr.

†**sa'tirial,** *a. Obs. rare.* In 6 satyrial(l. [f. satire *sb.* + -ial.] Satirical.

1579 Twyne *Phisicke agst. Fort.* I. lxxxi. 104 b, As the Satyrial Poet sayeth. **1580** G. Harvey *Two Other Lett.* Wks. (Grosart) I. 83 This bolde Satyriall Libell.

satiric (sə'tɪrɪk), *a.* and *sb.* Forms: 6 **satyryke, satyricque, satiricke, 6–8 satyrick, 7 (satericke), satyryck, -ique, 7–8 (9) satyric, 8 satirick, 8– satiric.** [ad. F. *satirique*, ad. late L. *satiricus* (*a.* and *sb.*), f. *satira* satire *sb.* Cf. Sp. *satírico*, Pg., It. *satirico*. (Formerly often confused with satyric.)] **A.** *adj.*

1. Of, pertaining to, or of the nature of satire; consisting of, or containing satire; that writes or composes satires.

[**1387** Trevisa *Higden* (Rolls) IV. 177 Oracius þe poete satiricus and liricus.] **1509** H. Watson *Ship of Fools* Prol. (1517) A v b, My boke satyryke I gyue vnto you for example. **1581** Sidney *Apol. Poetrie* (Arb.) 28 The most notable [kinds of poets] bee the Heroick, Lirick,..Satirick, Iambick,..and certaine others. **1611** Rich *Honest. Age* (Percy Soc.) 68 For Satyryck inueyghing at any mans pryuate person, it is farre from my thought. **1613** R. Cawdrey *Table Alph.* (ed. 3), *Satericke*, belonging to a scoffing verse. **1665** Sir T. Herbert *Trav.* (1677) 215 When so long a fare-well was least thought on, he and his are hewn down, making good that of the Satyric Poet, *Ad generum Cereris* [etc.]. **1732** Swift *Let. to Dr. Jenny* 8 June, He hath been often engaged in a kind of flirting war of satiric burlesque verse with certain wags both in town and country. **1738** Warburton *Div. Legat.* I. 112 A fabulous and satyric Writer. **1796** Morse *Amer. Geog.* II. 674 Horace, the Roman lyric and satiric poet. **1812** Crabbe *Tales* xix. *Convent* 163 Satiric novels, poets bold and free. **1852** Thackeray *Esmond* III. iii, All this comedy was full of bitter satiric strokes against a certain young lady. **1861** Wright *Ess. on Archæol.* II. xxiii. 240 The Latin literature of the thirteenth century..is extremely rich in comic and satiric verse.

†**2.** Addicted to satire, satirical. *Obs.*

1627 Drayton *To H. Reynolds* 113 And surely Nashe, though he a Proser were A branch of Lawrell yet deserues to beare, Sharply Satirick was he. **1638** Cowley *Love's Riddle* I. i, Why so Satyrick, Shepherd? I believe You did not learn these Flashes in the Woods. **1729** Swift *To Dr. Delany, on Libels* (end), On me when Dunces are satyrick, I take it for a Panegyrick. **1754** J. Shebbeare *Matrimony* (1766) II. 106 You are satyrick this Morning. **1763** J. Brown *Poetry & Mus.* vii. 139 The Spirit of Sarcasm being once awakened, it would of course proceed from occasional Strokes of Raillery, to the Recital of ridiculous Actions, for the..Entertainment of a lively and satyric People.

B. *sb.*

†**1.** A writer of satires; a satirist. *Obs. rare.*

1387 Trevisa *Higden* (Rolls) IV. 407 þere were more poetes þan satirices [orig. *Fuerent autem plures poetæ quam satirici*]. **1589** Puttenham *Eng. Poesie* I. xi. (Arb.) 41 Their inuectiues were called Satyres, and them selues Satyricques. **1598** Barckley *Felic. Man* 168 Which agreeeth aptly with the saying of the Satyricke. *Ille crucem sceleris pretium ferat, hic diadema.* **1603** R. Johnson *Kingd. & Commw.* (1611) 120 Hiperbolus, who,..for his boldnesse and saucy impudency, was the onely Subiect in his time, for all Satyricks & Commedians to worke vpon.

2. *pl.* Satiric writings. *rare.*

1600 W. Watson *Decacordon* (1602) 9 Together with sundrie Satyrickes [*printed* Satyricals: *corrected in errata*] of Maister Blackwels. *Ibid.* 194 Infamous libelling or Ouidian inuectiues, or Horatian Satyriques. **1825** (*title*) Facetiæ Cantabrigiensis, consisting of Anecdotes, Smart Sayings, Satirics, Retorts, &c.

satirical (sə'tɪrɪkəl), *a.* Forms: 6 **saturicall, 6–7 satyricall, 6–8 (9) -ical, (8 satyracal), 8– satirical.** [f. late L. *satiric-us* (see prec.) + -al[1].]

1. Of or pertaining to satire; of the nature of or containing satire; satiric.

a **1529** Skelton *Agst. Garnesche* iv. 139 If thow war aquentyd with alle The famous poettes saturicall. **1579** E. K. in Spenser *Sheph. Cal.* Gen. Argt. ¶3 For eyther they [these xij Æglogues] be Plaintive,..or Recreative,..or Moral, which for the most part be mixed with some Satyrical bitternesse. **1581** J. Bell *Haddon's Answ. Osor.* 262 b, In steade of a Rhetoricall acclamation, concluding with a Satyricall skoffe he doth advertize hym. **1617** Moryson *Itin.* I. 108 Attella, whence were the old satyricall Comedies, which were full of baudery, and were called Attellane. **1644** Milton *Areop.* (Arb.) 38 Nor was the Satyricall sharpnesse, or naked plainnes of Lucilius, or Catullus, or Flaccus, by any order prohibited. **1738** Chambers *Cycl.* (ed. 2) s.v., Satyrical prints, and medals. **1845** S. Austin *Ranke's Hist. Ref.* III. 427 Satirical songs were sung against Johann Rode. **1880** McCarthy *Own Times* lxvii. IV. 536 It has some of the brightest and bitterest satirical passages in the literature of our time.

2. Disposed to or given to satire; fond of indulging in satire; characterized by satire; sarcastic.

1590 Greene *Never too late* (1600) 51 Isabel..outwardly withstood such in satyrical tearmes as did inueigh against the honestie of Francesco. **1596** Nashe *Saffron Walden* Wks. (Grosart) III. 183 The satyricallest confuters. **1601** B. Jonson *Poetaster* IV. iii, A sharpe thornie-tooth'd satyricall rascall [*sc.* Horace]. **1612** Bacon *Ess., Discourse* (Arb.) 17 Certainly he that hath a Satyricall vaine, as he maketh others afraid of his wit, so he had need be afraid of others memory. **1657** T. M. (*title*) The Life of a Satyrical Pvppy, Called Nim, who worrieth all those Satyrists he knowes, and barkes at the rest. **1693** Southern *Maid's Last Prayer* III. i, O law! Mr. Granger, you're so strangely s'terical [sic], I belieue you laugh at us all behind our backs. *a* **1715** Burnet *Own Time* (1766) I. 516 Sometimes a satyrical temper broke out too much. **1717** Lady M. W. Montagu *Let. to Lady Rich* 1 Apr. (1790) 67 Disdainful smiles and satyrical whispers..never fail in our assemblies, when any body appears that is not dressed exactly in the fashion. **1727** Swift *Let. to Yng. Lady* Wks. 1751 V. 61 The satyrical part of Mankind will needs believe, that it is not impossible to be very fine [in dress] and very filthy. **1814** R. Bland *Proverbs* I. Pref. 8 In his humorous and satyrical declamation. **1829** Lytton *Devereux* I. ii, 'To educate them himself,' answered my mother, with a sort of satirical gravity. **1856** Emerson *Eng. Traits, First Visit* Wks. (Bohn) II. 7 He [Carlyle] took despairing or satirical views of literature at this moment. **1872** Geo. Eliot *Middlem.* xxi, She was not coldly clever and indirectly satirical, but adorably simple and full of feeling.

satirically (sə'tɪrɪkəlɪ), *adv.* [f. satirical *a.* + -ly[2].] In a satirical manner; by derisive censure, ridicule or sarcasm.

1594 Carew *Huarte's Exam. Wits* (1616) 109 For which cause, Iuuenall..did Satirically nip him, saying [etc.]. **1697** Dryden *Pref. to Virg. Past.* ***b, One of the Ancients has observ'd truly, but Satyrically enough, that Mankind is the Measure of every thing. **1794** Mrs. Radcliffe *Myst. Udolpho* xvi, Montoni smiled satirically at what Emily had written. **1884** Courthope *Addison* i. 9 The Tory fox-hunter of the *Freeholder*, though somewhat satirically painted, is a fair representative.

satiricalness (sə'tɪrɪkəlnɪs). [f. satirical *a.* + -ness.] The quality of being satirical.

a **1661** Fuller *Worthies, Essex* (1662) I. 334 Some Poets, if debarr'd profaness, wantoness, and Satyricalness, (that they may neither abuse God, themselves, nor their neighbours,) have their tongues cut out in effect. **1673** O. Walker *Educ.* xi. 125 Wit is the mother of facetiousness, conceits, jests, raillery, satyricalness. **1683** Kennet tr. *Erasm. on Folly* Pref. Ep. (1709) 8 To reply now to the objection of satyricalness, wits have been always allowed this priviledge. **1829** *Blackw. Mag.* XXVI. 591 [He] had a smeddum of satiricalness.

†**sa'tirien,** *a. Obs. rare*[−1]. In 6 satyrien. [a. OF. *satirien*: see satire *sb.* and -ian.] Satirical.

1509 Barclay *Shyp of Folys* Argt. (1874) I. 17 As olde Poetes Satyriens in dyuers Poesyes conioyned repreued the synnes and ylnes of the peple at that tyme lyuynge.

satirion(e, obs. forms of satyrion.

'satirism. *rare.* [f. satire *sb.* + -ism.] Indulgence in satire; satirical temper or utterance.

1593 Nashe *Christ's T.* To Rdr., I haue nothing to spend on you but passion. A hundred vnfortunate farewels to fantasticall Satirisme. **1602** Dekker *Satirom.* L 3 b, Bitter Satirisme. **1610** Healey *St. Aug. Citie of God* v. xxvii. 234 Their tongue-ripe Satyrisme may more easily disturbe the truth of this world then subuert it. **1683** Cave *Ecclesiastici* Introd. 47 He had a quick Wit, but too much inclin'd to Satyrism. **1716** M. Davies *Athen. Brit.* II. To Rdr. 39 Where others have trod before, with various Sarcasms and Satyrisms. **1950** *Scrutiny* XVII. II. 145 What strikes one in reading, however, is not so much the variety of these satirisms..but simply their ubiquity.

satirist ('sætɪrɪst). [f. satire *sb.* + -ist.

In the first quot. app. partly representing (with misapprehended sense) Gr. σατυριστής player of satyric drama.]

A writer of satires. Also (const. *of*) one who satirizes some person or thing.

1589 Puttenham *Eng. Poesie* I. xiii. (Arb.) 46 They made wise as if..Satyres or Siluanes should appeare and recite those verses of rebuke,..whereupon the Poets inuentours of the deuise were called Satyristes. **1592** Greene *Groat's W. Wit* (1617) 36 Young Iuuenall, that byting Satyrist. **1597** G. Harvey *Trim. Nashe* Wks. (Grosart) III. 63 We heare howe you threatned to spoile our stirring Satirist: alas, haue thy writings such efficacie? **1641** Brathwait *Nat. Emb.* Ded. A ij, It is high time for the Satyrist to pen somthing which may diuert them from their impietie. **1706** Pope *Epit. on Dorset* 7 Blest Satyrist! who touch'd the Mean so true, As show'd, Vice had his hate and pity too. **1762** Goldsm. *Cit. W.* xcix, Her very appearance was sufficient to silence the severest satirist of the sex. **1796** Burke *Reg. Peace* Wks. VIII. 354 It is for the satyrist to expose the ridiculous. **1837** Syd. Smith *Wks.* (1867) II. 261, I am not setting myself up as the satirist of Bishops. **1875** Helps *Soc. Press.* xiv. 194 A satirist, for instance, has generally some idea of improving mankind by his satire.

satirize ('sætɪraɪz), *v.* Also 7 **satyrise, 7–8 satyrize, 8–9 satirise.** [ad. F. *satiriser* (= Sp., Pg. *satirizar*), f. *satire*: see satire *sb.* and -ize.]

1. *intr.* To write satires; to assail some one or something with satire. Now only as absol. use of 2; formerly †const. *on, upon.*

1601 B. JONSON *Poetaster* III. v, What? when the man that first did satyrise, Durst pull the skin ouer the eares of vice; ..shall I forbeare? **1620** BRATHWAIT *Five Senses* 129 They shew the vnworthinesse of their Nature in Satyrizing vpon the weaker. **1703** DE FOE *Let. to Mr. How* in *Misc.* 337, I find you no more talking to me, till you come to Page 25, where you are pleased to Satyrize upon my Title and Preface. **1728** YOUNG *Love Fame* I. 34 Shall authors smile on such illustrious days, And satirise with nothing—but their praise? *a* **1734** NORTH *Exam.* III. x. Concl. (1740) 692 It is as bad a Fault in History to panegyrise, as to Satyrise without Reason. **1745** *De Foe's Eng. Tradesman* xxii. (1841) I. 211 Satirizing on the blindness and folly of mankind. **1821** BYRON *Juan* III. lxxviii, He being paid to satirise or flatter. **1879** FARRAR *St. Paul* I. 217 It was easy to satirise and misrepresent.

2. *trans.* To assail with satire; to make the object of, or to expose to, satire or censure; to describe or ridicule in a satirical manner.

1630 J. TAYLOR (Water P.) *Kicksey Winsey* Wks. II. 36, I will Satyrize, Cauterize, and Stigmatize all the whole kennell of curres that dare [etc.]. **1676** GLANVILL *Seasonable Reflect.* 153 Those Wits..that Satyrize humane nature. **1715** M. DAVIES *Athen. Brit.* I. Pref. 4 Pamphlets..pretend to..Satyrize the Frankness of Tories [etc.]. **1727** POPE *Th. Var. Subj.* in Swift's Wks. 1755 II. I. 226 It is as hard to satirize well a man of distinguished vices, as to praise well a man of distinguished virtues. **1782** J. WARTON *Ess. Pope* VII. II. 61 Chaucer takes every opportunity of satyrizing the follies of his age. **1803** SIR J. MACKINTOSH *Def. Peltier* Wks. 1846 III. 259 If you should believe that it is ascribed to Jacobinical writers for the sake of satirising a French Jacobinical faction. **1870** DISRAELI *Lothair* viii, The parasite ..had been on the point of satirising his hostess, but, observing the quarter of the wind, with rapidity went in for praise. **1873** SYMONDS *Grk. Poets* iv. 108 Alcaeus exercised his poetical talent in satirizing Pittacus.

b. *fig.* To be a 'satire' upon. (Cf. SATIRE *sb.* 1 c.)

1798 ROSCOE tr. *Tansillo's Nurse* 1. *Notes* i. (1800) 7 This detestable custom, which outrages nature, and satirizes humanity, is..more frequent in Italy than in this country.

Hence **'satirized** *ppl. a.*

1793 D'ISRAELI *Cur. Lit.* II. 276 Satirists, if they escape the scourges of the law, have reason to dread the cane of the satirised.

satirizer ('sætɪraɪzə(r)). [f. SATIRIZE *v.* + -ER[1].] One who satirizes.

1867 LEGGE *Confucius* 249 By the *fung* or phœnix, his satirizer or adviser intended Confucius. **1889** *Spectator* 5 Jan. 22 The sprightly satiriser of Lord Eldon and the Tories.

'satirizing, *ppl. a.* [f. SATIRIZE *v.* + -ING[2].] That satirizes.

1716 *Loyal Mourner* 39 My Satyrizing Muse. **1771** LUCKOMBE *Hist. Print.* 235 Expressions..by which they intend to convey to the reader either instructing, satyrizing, admiring, or other hints and remarks. **1804** CHARLOTTE SMITH *Conversations*, etc. II. 23 But we are getting into a grave and satyrizing vein. **1861** WRIGHT *Ess. Archæol.* II. xxiv. 278 The satirising and reforming spirit of the age appeared not unfrequently on the stage.

satirus, satiry: see SATYR.

satisdation (sætɪs'deɪʃən). *Civil Law. ? Obs.* [a. L. *satisdatiōn-em* a giving of bail or security, n. of action f. *satisdare* to give bail, f. *satis* enough + *dare* to give. Cf. OF. *satisdacion, -ccion, -tion*, 13th c. in Godefr.] (See quot. 1656.)

1656 BLOUNT *Glossogr.*, *Satisdation*, a putting in of Surety or Bail sufficient for performance of Covenants, or for payment of moneys. **1726** AYLIFFE *Parergon* 425 There is another Exception stiled an Exception of not giving Satisdation or Security. **1774** HALLIFAX *Rom. Civ. Law* III. iii. 88 Not unlike the Satisdations required from an Actor and *Reus* by the Roman laws.

satisdiction. *nonce-wd.* [f. L. *satis* enough + *dictiōn-em* saying (see DICTION), after *satisfaction*.] Saying enough.

1647 WARD *Simp. Cobler* 14 They desire not satisfaction, but satisdiction, whereof themselves must be judges.

satisfaction (sætɪs'fækʃən). Forms: 4–8 **satis-**, 4–6 **satys-**; 4 **-facciun**, 4–7 **-faccion**, 4–5 **-fac(c)ioun**, **-faccio(u)n**, 5 **-faccyo(u)n**, **-facion**, **-faccione**, (**-faccoun**), 5–7 **-factioun**, 6 **-faccyon**, **-factyon**; 5– **satisfaction**. [a. F. *satisfaction* (12th c. *satisfactiun*, 13th c. *satisfacion, -fecion*) = Pr. *satisfactio*, Sp. *satisfaccion*, Pg. *satisfacção*, It. *satisfazione, soddisfazione*, ad. L. *satisfactiōn-em*, n. of action f. *satisfacĕre* to SATISFY.] The action of satisfying; the state or fact of being satisfied.

I. With reference to obligations.

1. a. The payment in full of a debt, or the fulfilment of an obligation or claim; the atoning *for* (rarely †*of*) an injury, offence, or fault by reparation, compensation, or the endurance of punishment. Also quasi-*concr.*, the pecuniary or other gift or penalty, or the act, by which a debt or obligation is discharged or an offence atoned for. Phrases, ***to make*** (or †***do***) ***satisfaction***; ***in satisfaction*** (***of***). Now chiefly in *Law.*

[The sense is found earlier in legal AF.: e.g. **1306** *Rolls of Parlt.* I. 212/1 Quil ne purroient a nul temps de ce faire suffisauntz amendes ne due satisfaction.]

c **1400** *Destr. Troy* 5017 Angers me full euyll your angard desyre, When ye couet..Satisfaccioun to be sent fro my selfe euyn, Syn ye are cause of þis care. *c* **1420** ? LYDG. *Assembly of Gods* 221 Beholde how the teares from hys eyen go. Hit ys satysfaccion half for hys trespase. **1432–50** tr. *Higden* (Rolls) V. 5 'My successor schalle iugge and do to the satisfaccion.' The wedowe seide, 'What schalle that profite the and if thy successour do satisfaccion for me'. **1477** EARL RIVERS (Caxton) *Dictes* 1 In satisfaccoun & recompence of myne Inyquytees. **1480** *Coventry Leet-bk.* 431 That the seid Chamberleyns shuld in recompense & satisfaccion of their seid disobeysaunce..bryng [etc.]. **1531** *Test. Ebor.* (Surtees) VI. 24, xl s...in satisfaction of a distres that I toke of hyr. **1563** *Homilies* II. *Repentance* II. 287 b, Zacheus..was most wyllyng..to make satisfaction vnto all them, that he hadde doone iniurie and wrong vnto. **1602** SHAKS. *Ham.* IV. v. 209 If by direct or by Colaterall hand They finde vs touch'd, we will our Kingdome giue,..and all that we call Ours To you in satisfaction. **1602** MARSTON *Ant. & Mel.* III. Wks. 1856 I. 43, I would be glad to make you satisfaction, if I have wronged you. **1621** ELSING *Debates Ho. Lords* (Camden) 86 Fyne, 10,000 marks;..publique satisfaccion of his faulte by submission and acknowledgement thereof. *a* **1651** CALDERWOOD *Hist. Kirk* (Wodrow Soc.) II. 303 Mr. Patrik Creigh..was ordeaned to make satisfaction in the kirk of Edinburgh two severall Sabboth dayes,..for celebrating marriage..without proclamatioun of bannes. **1659** MILTON *Civil Power* 63 Who by subjecting us to his punishment in these things, brings back into religion that law of terror and satisfaction, belonging now only to civil crimes. **1660** MARVELL *Corr.* Wks. (Grosart) II. 25 The Excise of Forain Commodityes is to be continued apart untill satisfaction of publick debts and ingagements secured upon the Excise. **1667** in *10th Rep. Hist. MSS. Comm.* App. v. 52 Sir Robert..is indebted to your petitioner in £320 by bond, but..utterly refuseth to give your petitioner satisfaction. **1667** MILTON *P.L.* III. 212 Unless for him Som other able, and as willing, pay The rigid satisfaction, death for death. **1683** *Brit. Spec.* 46 He..himself escaped Shipwrack, and received Satisfaction for his Losses out of the publick Treasury. **1725** DE FOE *Voy. round World* (1840) 313 The Captain..promised to have the fellows punished, and satisfaction to be made. **1818** CRUISE *Digest* (ed. 2) I. 215 A devise of an annuity to the wife..has been held not to be in satisfaction of dower. **1845** POLSON in *Encycl. Metrop.* II. 796/1 The party injured may agree to accept a certain sum or other thing as a compensation—an arrangement technically styled *accord and satisfaction*. **1848** THACKERAY *Van. Fair* ix, He had a savage pleasure in making the poor wretches [his creditors] wait, and in shifting from court to court and from term to term the period of satisfaction. **1875** MAINE *Hist. Inst.* ix. 262 'Distress'—its primary object is to compel the person against whom it is properly employed to make satisfaction.

b. In particularized use: An act of compensation or amends; an amount paid in compensation; a penalty. Now *rare.*

c **1440** *Alphabet of Tales* 281 He..made hur to hafe a due satisfaccion for hur hurte. **1598** BACON *Sacr. Medit., Exalt. Charitie* Ess. (Arb.) 107 The seconde degree is to pardon our enemies, though they persist and without satisfactions and submissions. **1603** DEKKER & CHETTLE *Grissil* IV. iii. (Shaks. Soc.) 75 Grissil's two babes are dead, and kill'd by scorn, But that fair issue, that shall now be born, Shall make a satisfaction of all wrongs. **1609** B. JONSON *Sil. Wom.* IV. v, Thinke vpon some satisfaction, or termes to offer him. *c* **1622** FORD, etc. *Witch Edmonton* I. i, I cannot request a fuller satisfaction Then you have freely granted. **1649** MILTON *Eikon.* ii. 21 We may well perceave to what easie satisfactions and purgations he had inur'd his secret conscience. **1766** BLACKSTONE *Comm.* II. 406 The mere mechanical operation of writing, for which it directed the scribe to receive a satisfaction.

c. Law. ***to enter*** (***up***) ***satisfaction***: to place on the record of a court a statement that the payment ordered by it has been duly made. So ***entry of satisfaction***.

1782 J. IMPEY *Pract. King's Bench* 378 Entry of Satisfaction. If satisfaction is made of a judgment, a warrant of attorney should be given to the attorney by the plaintiff..to enter up satisfaction on record. **1828** ARCHBOLD *Forms & Entries* (ed. 2) 276 Whereas I, the said John Nokes, have received satisfaction for the same [damages and costs]: These are therefore to desire and authorize you..to acknowledge and enter satisfaction upon the record of the said judgment.

2. *Eccl.* (The earliest recorded use in Eng.) The performance by a penitent of the penal and meritorious acts enjoined by his confessor as payment of the temporal punishment due to his sin: the last of the constituent parts of the sacrament of penance. Cf. DEEDBOTE. (Phrases as in 1.)

a **1300** *Cursor M.* 28620 For it mai be na penance right Bot man him pain to bete his plight, þat satisfaccion es cald, And þis parti it es thrid-fald, In almus, fastyng, and orisun. *Ibid.* 29121 Generali nu haf i tald þe pointes þat ar for to hald Til ilk sinful þat es bun For to do satisfacciun. *a* **1340** HAMPOLE *Psalter* cxviii. 118 þai will syn and will noght make satisfaccioun til god. **1340** *Ayenb.* 32 Nele arere þet heued to gode be zorȝe ne grede harou be ssrifte ne arere þe honden be satisfaccioun [*gloss c* 1400 dedbote]. **1377** LANGL. *P. Pl.* B. XIV. 94 Satisfaccioun..as it neuere had ybe to nouȝt bryngeth dedly synne. *c* **1386** CHAUCER *Pars. T.* ⁋955. *c* **1400** *Jacob's Well* xxix. 189 Satysfaccyoun is, to fulfylle þi penaunce, enioyned of þe preest, & to pay þi dettys to qwyke & dede & to holy cherche, & to restore, þat þou hast falsely gett, to makyn amendys for þi wrongys & þe harmys, þat þou hast don, & no more to turne aȝen to þi synne. **1450–1530** *Myrr. our Ladye* 99 Thre partes of penaunce, that ys contrycyon, confessyon, and satysfaccion. **1509** HAWES *Past. Pleas.* xli. (Percy Soc.) 204 With dame Contricion, which gan to bewayle My synnes great with hole repentaunce, And Satisfaccion without any fayle. **1563** *Homilies* II. *Repentance* II. 286 Judas..did also make a certain kynde of satisfaction [as well as his confession], when he did cast their money vnto them agaime. **1579** TOMSON *Calvin's Serm. Tim.* 16/2 The Papistes holde, that we must get Paradise by our desartes, and what wanteth we must supplie by our satisfactions. *a* **1600** HOOKER *Eccl. Pol.* VI. v. §6 Amongst the works of satisfaction, the most respected have been alwayes these three, Prayers, Fasts, and Almes deeds. **1725** tr. *Dupin's Eccl. Hist. 17th. C.* I. VI. i. 217 He [Melancthon] does not believe that Confession and Satisfaction are necessary. **1885** *Cath. Dict.* (ed. 3) s.v. *Penance* (4) The penitential discipline of the early Church witnesses to the belief that satisfaction by penitential works is necessary in itself, and is required as a part of the sacrament of penance.

3. *Theol.* The atonement made by Christ for sin, according to the view that His sufferings and merits are accepted by the Divine justice as an equivalent for the penalty due for the sins of the world. So ***doctrine of satisfaction***. Occas. said of Christ himself as the victim by whose sacrifice the satisfaction was made.

c **1380** WYCLIF *Sel. Wks.* II. 282 And so, siþ Crist is God and man, satisfaccioun for þis synne þat he made þus freli is better þan oþer þat man or angel myȝt make. **1542** BECON *Potation for Lent* E vij, Christ alone is the omnisufficient satysfaccion for all oure synnes vnto God the father. **1549** LATIMER *Serm. Ploughers* (Arb.) 33 By hym selfe and by none other, Chryste made purgacion and satisfaction for the whole worlde. **1563** *Homilies* II. *Repentance* I. 276 b, For he alone dyd with the sacrifice of his body and blod make satisfaction vnto the Iustice of god for our sinnes. **1630** PRYNNE *Anti-Armin.* 158 Which cooperates and concurres with the aduocation and satisfaction of Iesus. **1643** MILTON *Divorce* II. vii. Wks. 1851 IV. 78 The prime end of the Gospel is not so much to exact our obedience, as to reveal grace and the satisfaction of our disobedience. **1657** *Treat. Conf. Sin* 314 There is a propitiatory satisfaction, which is Christ Jesus, for our sins and the sins of the whole world. **1696** STILLINGFL. (*title*) A Discourse concerning the Doctrine of Christ's Satisfaction. **1741** WATTS *Improv. Mind* I. v. §3 And some writers for the Trinity and Satisfaction of Christ have exposed themselves and the sacred doctrine by their feeble and foolish manner of handling it. **1872** J. G. MURPHY *Comm. Lev.* v. Introd., In satisfaction..the mediator renders a perfect obedience to the law, and the penitent sinner who relies on his good offices is justified or accepted and treated as righteous.

4. a. The opportunity of satisfying one's honour by a duel; the acceptance of a challenge to a duel from the person who deems himself insulted or injured. Chiefly in phrases, ***to give, demand satisfaction***.

1602 EARL NORTHUMBLD. in Collins *Peerage* (1779) II. 410 Seeke not by fryvelous shiftes to dyverte this course of satisfaction. **1611** SHAKS. *Cymb.* II. i. 16, I gaue him satisfaction? would he had bin one of my Ranke. **1630** *R. Johnson's Kingd. & Commw.* 190 The English Gentleman, with mature deliberation, disputeth how farre his honour is ingaged, by the injury offered, and judiciously determineth his manner of satisfaction, according to the quality of the offence. **1709** STEELE *Tatler* No. 25 ⁋5 It is called *Giving a Man Satisfaction*, to urge your Offence against him with your Sword. **1724** DE FOE *Mem. Cavalier* (1840) 180 He was ready to give him satisfaction. **1771** SMOLLETT *Humph. Cl.* 24 Apr. (1815) 36 If he thinks himself injured, he knows where to come for satisfaction. **1802** C. JAMES *Milit. Dict.* s.v., When an officer or other person goes out to fight with one whom he has offended, or by whom he has been offended, he is said to give or take satisfaction.—Hence to demand satisfaction is tantamount to challenge, &c.—To call to account. **1834** MEDWIN *Angler in Wales* II. xxvi. 152 If it prove so, and you will give me your card, I will see that you shall shortly have the satisfaction you require. **1843** MIALL in *Nonconf.* III. 489 The satisfaction consists in giving to the offender a chance of becoming either a murderer or murdered.

†**b.** ***to give oneself satisfaction***: to be avenged *on* an offender. *Obs.*

1684 DRYDEN tr. *Maimbourg's Hist. League* 163 Who dar'd not to arrest any of them singly, the two remaining being at liberty, and in condition to give themselves satisfaction on the Aggressours.

II. With reference to desires or feelings.

5. a. The action of gratifying (an appetite or desire) to the full, or of contenting (a person) by the complete fulfilment of a desire or supply of a want; the fact of having been gratified to the full or of having one's desire fulfilled. Phrases, ***to the satisfaction of***; ***to give satisfaction***.

The first quot. is a mere literalism from the Vulgate, and the translator prob. attached no definite meaning to the word. One MS. adds the gloss 'or a covenable ansuere'.

1382 WYCLIF *Lev.* x. 20 The which thing whanne Moyses hadde herde, he resseyuede satysfaccioun [Vulg. *recepit satisfactionem*; Heb. lit. 'and Moses heard, and it was good in his eyes']. **1538** STARKEY *England* II. i. 146 Though nature hath gyuen to man..natural inclynatyon to hys increse; yet, bycause man ys only borne to cyuylyte and polytyke rule, therfore he may not, wythout ordur or respecte, study to the satysfactyon of thys natural affecte. **1603** SHAKS. *Meas. for M.* III. i. 275 If for this night he intreat you to his bed, giue him promise of satisfaction. **1622** FLETCHER & MASSINGER *Prophetess* II. ii, Hate to vow'd enemies findes a full satisfaction in death. **1649** JER. TAYLOR *Gt. Exempt.* §1. 14 When the Blessed Virgin was so ascertained, that she should be a Mother and a Maid,..then all her hopes and all her desires received such satisfaction, as filled all the corners of her heart. **1662** STILLINGFL. *Orig. Sacræ* III. iv. §1 For the satisfaction of our curiosity as to the true Origine of Nations. **1690** NORRIS *Beatitudes* (1694) I. 90 The Desire of Happiness is not absolutely secure of Satisfaction, but only upon Condition. **1771** *Junius Lett.* xlix. (1788) 265 The profound respect I bear to the gracious Prince who governs this country with no less honour to himself than satisfaction to his subjects. **1860** TYNDALL *Glac.* I. xxiii. 168 My guide ..did his duty entirely to my satisfaction. **1880** McCARTHY *Own Times* xl. III. 219 The difficulty was settled to the satisfaction of everyone. **1894** BOTTONE *Electr. Instr. Making* (ed. 6) 191 This having been effected to the operator's satisfaction, he turns his attention once again..to the glass bulb.

b. Satisfied or contented state of mind; now usually, gratification or pleasure occasioned by some fact, event, or state of things. Const. *at*, *with*, †*of*; also followed by *that* with clause expressing the cause.

1477 EARL RIVERS (Caxton) *Dictes* 7 The grettest richesse is satisfacion of the herte. *a* **1627** SIR J. BEAUMONT *Miserable St. Man* 4 His whole felicity is endlesse strife, No peace, no satisfaction, crownes his life. **1612** SHELTON *Quix.* I. iv. (1620) 27 Who..did trauell towards his village, with very great satisfaction of himselfe. **1648** GAGE *West Ind.* 103, I had not very great satisfaction of the whole Family. **1711** LADY M. W. MONTAGU *Let. to Mr. W. M.* 24 Mar., Nothing touches me with satisfaction but what touches my heart. **1744** *Life & Adv. M. Bishop* 147, I was as happy in my Station, and enjoyed as much Peace and Satisfaction in my own Breast, as possibly the Duke of Marlborough could in his. **1749** FIELDING *Tom Jones* XVII. v, Mrs. Miller expressed great satisfaction in these declarations. *Ibid.* ix, Jones expressed the utmost satisfaction at the account. **1781** GIBBON *Decl. & F.* xix. II. 151 Sapor..expressed his satisfaction that his brother, Constantius Cæsar, had been taught wisdom by adversity. **1797–8** JANE AUSTEN *Sense & Sens.* xliii, All within Elinor's breast was satisfaction, silent and strong. **1834** J. H. NEWMAN *Par. Serm.* I. vi. 88 Is it not the way of men to dwell with satisfaction on their good deeds, particularly, when for some reason or other, their conscience smites them? **1848** W. H. BARTLETT *Egypt to Pal.* xxiv. (1879) 480 The satisfaction of the traveller at Nazareth comes from the presence of those natural objects and scenes which alone remain unchanged.

c. A particular instance of satisfaction; an experience, fact, or circumstance that occasions gratification.

1687 A. LOVELL tr. *Thevenot's Trav.* I. 88, I could earnestly have wished the Door had been open that I might have gone in..; but I had not that satisfaction. **1692** R. L'ESTRANGE *Fables* lxviii. 68 A Freedom,..not to be Parted with for All the Sensual Satisfactions under the Sun. **1712** STEELE *Spect.* No. 423 ¶2 Gloriana has very good Sense, a quick Relish of the Satisfactions of Life. **1716** ADDISON *Freeholder* No. 9 ¶3 You own it would be a great Satisfaction to you to be placed upon the Throne by our Endeavours. **1719** DE FOE *Crusoe* I. (Globe) 112, I cannot express what a Satisfaction it was to me, to come into my old Hutch. **1774** GOLDSM. *Nat. Hist.* (1824) I. 1 Human curiosity..gives higher satisfactions than what even the senses can afford. **1869** J. D. BALDWIN *Preh. Nations* ii. (1877) 26 It has undoubtedly furnished many satisfactions to those whose calling did not afford a more profitable occupation. **1883** H. SPENCER in *Contemp. Rev.* XLIII. 8 The savage thinks only of present satisfactions, and leaves future satisfactions uncared for.

†**d.** *bad satisfaction*: dissatisfaction, dissatisfying result. *Obs.*

1656 EARL MONM. tr. *Boccalini's Advts. fr. Parnass.* I. xxxix. 81 Amongst all these bad satisfactions, nothing distasted..the Nobility more, then the severe Magistracy of the Censors. *Ibid.*, *Polit. Touchstone* 414 Flanders..was there-fore begun to be governed by forreiners, with such jealousies,..which ingendered those ill humors, and gave that bad satisfaction, which was the rise of the civil war that insued.

e. *Psychol.* The satisfying of a need or desire as it affects or motivates behaviour.

1911 E. L. THORNDIKE *Animal Intelligence* vi. 244 The Law of Effect is that: Of several responses made to the same situation, those which are accompanied or closely followed by satisfaction to the animal will..be more firmly connected with the situation, so that when it recurs, they will be more likely to recur. **1922** R. S. WOODWORTH *Psychol.* xix. 488 Dancing also gives a chance for muscular activity which is obviously one source of satisfaction in the more active games. **1951** J. M. FRASER *Psychol.* xiv. 161 Another group of satisfactions can be drawn, not perhaps from the work itself, but from the surroundings in which it is carried out. **1966** KATZ & KAHN *Social Psychol. of Organizations* xii. 363 If there is one confirmed finding in all the studies of worker morale and satisfaction, it is the correlation between the variety and challenge of the job and the gratifications which accrue to workers. **1976** R. H. MOOS *Human Context* viii. 265 Once workers feel competent with the transition, they often report long term gains in satisfaction or morale.

6. a. 'Release from suspense, uncertainty, or uneasiness' (J.); information that answers a person's demands or needs; removal of doubt, conviction. Phrase, *to (a person's) satisfaction*.

†*in heavy satisfaction*: in sorrowful acceptance of the truth.

1586 MARLOWE *1st Pt. Tamburl.* II. iii. 5 What think'st thou, man, shall come of our attempts? For, even as from assured oracle, I take thy doom for satisfaction. **1601** SHAKS. *All's Well* v. iii. 100 But when I..inform'd her fully, I could not answer in that course of Honour As she had made the ouerture, she ceast In heauie satisfaction, and would neuer Receiue the Ring againe. **1601** —— *Jul. C.* II. ii. 73 *Cæ s.* The cause is in my Will, I will not come, That is enough to satisfie the Senate. But for your priuate satisfaction, Because I loue you, I will let you know. **1615** CROOKE *Body of Man* 270 Because these things are some-what obscure, we referre you for further satisfaction to the Controuersies next ensuing. **1662** STILLINGFL. *Orig. Sacræ* II. x. §10. 359 Thus abundantly to the satisfaction of the minds of all good men hath God given the highest rational evidence of the truth of the doctrine which he hath revealed to the world. **1725** DE FOE *Voy. round World* (1840) 43 Prove it to my satisfaction. **1833** HT. MARTINEAU *Brooke Farm* xi, I made my retreat, and was obliged to wait till the afternoon for further satisfaction. **1862** BAGEHOT *Lit. Stud.* (1878) II. 404 An offence not proved to the 'satisfaction of the Court' escapes the judgement of the Court.

†**b.** Satisfying proof. *Obs.*

1601 LD. MOUNTJOY *Let.* in Moryson *Itin.* (1617) II. 123 Hereafter I doubt not but to giue you satisfaction that I am not worthy of this wrong. **1646** SIR T. BROWNE *Pseud. Ep.* I. vii. 26 In naturall Philosophy..it carryeth but slender consideration, for that also proceeding from setled principles, therein is expected a satisfaction from scientificall progressions, and such as beget, a sure and rationall beleefe. **1722** DE FOE *Plague* (1754) 249, I have had very good Satisfaction, that it was utterly false.

†**c.** Solution (of a difficulty). *Obs.*

a **1547** COVERDALE *Fruitf. Less.* (1593) Mm 2, But this satisfaction concerning drunkennes,..is made with all meeknes, and yet with sinceritie and stedfastnes, not lordly, or braggingly, although he [*sc.* Peter] was highly endewed with the holy Ghost. **1650** FULLER *Pisgah* II. iv. 103 But seeing they [*sc.* commentators] professe their calling to be a satisfaction of difficulties, it is in them an unexcusable lazinesse.

III. 7. *attrib.*, **satisfaction-money**, money paid in satisfaction; **satisfaction note** *Insurance*, an acknowledgement of satisfaction with repairs made to a car signed by one claiming repair costs from an insurance company; **satisfaction piece** *Law*, a formal acknowledgement given by one who has received satisfaction of a mortgage or judgement, to authorize the entry of such satisfaction on the record; **satisfaction theory** *Theol.* = *doctrine of satisfaction* (see sense 3).

1868 BP. S. WILBERFORCE in R. G. Wilberforce *Life* (1882) III. x. 280 That the *satisfaction-money for vested rights should be in a common fund. **1971** *Reader's Digest Family Guide to Law* 533/1 When repairs [to a car] are finished, the policy-holder is usually asked to sign a *satisfaction note... Before signing, inspect the vehicle carefully and, if possible, take it for a test drive. **1973** *Times* 15 Dec. 19/7 Normally you will have to sign a 'satisfaction note' for the repairers before you can regain possession of your car after it has been repaired. **1782** J. IMPEY *Pract. King's Bench* 378 *Satisfaction piece. **1887** *48th Deputy Kpr. Rep.* 628 The Satisfaction Pieces of the Court of Common Pleas do not differ in any essential feature from those of the Court of Queen's Bench. **1932** *Satisfaction theory [see ANSELMIC *a.*]. **1969** *Dict. Christian Theol.* 23/1 Anselm..in his work *Cur Deus Homo?*,..interpreted the doctrine [of atonement] in terms of the 'satisfaction' or 'juridical' theory.

satisfactional (sætɪsˈfækʃənəl), *a.* [-AL^{1}.] Belonging to, or of the nature of, a satisfaction.

1874 BUSHNELL *Forgiven. & Law* Introd. 11 Its satisfactional substitute.

†**satisˈfactionar, -er.** *Obs. rare*$^{-1}$. = next.

1561 T. NORTON *Calvin's Inst.* III. iv. §38. 152 As for those thinges that are commonly founde in the bookes of olde wryters concerning satisfaction, they litle moue me... Many of them..haue..spoken to crabbedly and hardely: but I will not graunt that they were so rude and vnskilfull as to haue wrytten those thynges in that sense that the newe Satisfactionars [**1562** (ed. 2) satisfactionaries, **1578–1611** -ars, **1634** -ers] do reade them.

†**satisfactionary.** *Obs. rare*$^{-2}$. [ad. mod.L. *satisfactiōnārius* (Calvin): see SATISFACTION and -ARY.] A believer in 'satisfaction' by penance.

1562 [see prec.]. **1628** GAULE *Pract. Theorists Panegyr.* (1629) 33 There be a sort of Satisfactionaries, that boast their abilitie to quit them of their Aduersarie, they dare not say for their Talents, yet for their Farthings.

satisfactionist (sætɪsˈfækʃənɪst). *rare.* [f. SATISFACTION + -IST.] One who holds the doctrine that Christ suffered punishment as satisfaction for the sins of man: see SATISFACTION 3.

1668 PENN *Sandy Foundation* 28 Some..of the same spirit with the Satisfactionists and Imputarians of our time. **1669** OWEN *Declar. & Vind. Doctr. Trinity* 205 Is this your retribution, O injurious Satisfactionists? **1858** J. MARTINEAU *Stud. Chr.* 145 Yet where is there any trace in it of the satisfactionist's redemption?

satisˈfactionless, *a. rare*$^{-1}$. [f. SATISFACTION + -LESS.] Without satisfaction.

1839 BAILEY *Festus* xii. (1852) 143 Wait for what Is on the wing already, or else have The aimless satisfactionless result As of a lunge into the empty air.

satisfactive (sætɪsˈfæktɪv), *a.* and *sb. rare.* [as if ad. L. **satisfactīvus*, f. *satisfact-*, *satisfacĕre* to SATISFY: see -IVE.] **A.** *adj.* †**a.** ? Adequate to the requirements of the case. *Obs.* **b.** In Bentham's use: Consisting in or concerned with 'satisfaction' or reparation.

1646 SIR T. BROWNE *Pseud. Ep.* VI. xi. 334 By a finall and satisfactive discernment of faith, we lay the last and particular effects upon the first and generall cause of all things. **1829** BENTHAM *Justice & Cod. Petit.*, *Abr. Petit. Justice* 79 The two remedies which wrong in every shape calls for: namely, the satisfactive and the punitive. **1830** —— *Offic. Apt. Maximized* Pref. 25 *note*, Punishment, together with the several other remedies, which the nature of things admits of:—namely, satisfactive, suppressive, and preventive.

†**B.** *sb.* 'An act of satisfaction; compensation; requital; amends' (*Cent. Dict.* 1891).

†**satisfactor.** *Obs. rare*$^{-1}$. [quasi-Lat. agent-n. f. L. *satisfacĕre* to SATISFY.] One who makes satisfaction (for sin).

1540 COVERDALE *Confut. Standish* (1547) fvj, Yet call ye them happie that punishe them selues, and take vpon them to be satisfactours in that behalfe.

satisfactorily (sætɪsˈfæktərɪlɪ), *adv.* [f. SATISFACTORY *a.* + -LY^{2}.] In a satisfactory manner.

1587 in W. M. Williams *Ann. Founders' Co.* (1867) 68 He was bothe oulde and partly blind, and..lacked knowledge to do them satisfactorilye. **1646** SIR T. BROWNE *Pseud. Ep.* III. xxi. 157 Bellonius hath beene more satisfactorily experimentall. **1748** HARTLEY *Observ. Man* II. ii. 105 We cannot yet, perhaps never shall, interpret it satisfactorily. **1791** *Gentl. Mag.* 33/1 Dr. Farmer had most satisfactorily proved that Shakspeare was not versed in Greek or Latin. **1839** JAMES *Louis XIV*, III. 138 He was denied the opportunity..of explaining satisfactorily the facts which tended to criminate him. **1869** H. AINSWORTH *Hilary St. Ives* II. vii, All seemed going on as smoothly and satisfactorily as those interested..could desire.

satisfactoriness (sætɪsˈfæktərɪnɪs). [f. SATISFACTORY *a.* + -NESS.] The state or character of being satisfactory.

1648 BOYLE *Seraph. Love* vi. (1700) 40 'Tis a good sign.. when the Incompleatness of our Seraphick Lover's happiness in his Fruitions proceeds not from their want of Satisfactoriness. **1649** PRYNNE *Subst. Sp. Ho. Comm.* title-p., Wherein the Satisfactorinesse of the Kings Answers..is clearly demonstrated. **1671** BAXTER *Holiness Design Chr.* xliii. 12 The satisfactoriness and meritoriousness of the Death or Sacrifice of Christ. **1865** DICKENS *Mut. Fr.* I. viii, Where's the satisfactoriness of the money as yet? **1891** *Spectator* 14 Mar., Much of the satisfactoriness of the arrangement will depend upon their perfect trustworthiness.

†**satisfacˈtorious,** *a. Obs. rare*$^{-2}$. [f. med.L. *satisfactōri-us* (see SATISFACTORY *a.*) + -OUS.] Making satisfaction. Hence †**satisfacˈtoriously** *adv.*, satisfactorily.

1561 DAUS tr. *Bullinger on Apoc.* (1573) 97 Acknowledgyng their sinnes in the feare of God, but yet with a true fayth hopyng for remission of sinnes, knowyng that they are thorough Christ reconciled to God the father. The Monasticall, Heremiticall Satisfactorious, and Pharisaicall faction doth not fully acknowledge this doctrine. *a* **1623** W. PEMBLE *Justif.* (1629) 242 Christ hath deserued for them to make them [*sc.* our workes] satisfactorious. **1661** BOYLE *Style of Script.* Rdr.'s Pref., There is great hope that some Answering this Objection, another that, and a third another, they may at length be all of them Satisfactoriously reply'd to.

satisfactory (sætɪsˈfæktərɪ), *a.* and *sb.* [ad. F. *satisfactoire* (14th c. in Hatz.-Darm.), ad. med.L. *satisfactōri-us*, f. L. *satisfacĕre* to SATISFY. Cf. Sp., Pg. *satisfactorio*, It. *satisfattorio*.] **A.** *adj.*

1. *Eccl.* and *Theol.* Serving to make satisfaction or atonement for sin. (Cf. SATISFACTION 2, 3.)

1547 *Act 1 Edw. VI*, c. 14 §1 Vain Opinions of Purgatory and Masses satisfactory, to be done for them which be departed. **1631** GOUGE *God's Arrows* I. xxvii. 41 The satisfactory, expiatory, and propitiatory sacrifice of Christ Jesus. **1656** JEANES *Fuln. Christ* 324 Like pretended satisfactory punishments. **1664** H. MORE *Myst. Iniq.* 113 That is to say, as Satisfactory penances, and not by way of correction and emendation of life. **1786** A. GIB *Sacred Contempl.* 271 His meritorious service must be considered as running through all his satisfactory sufferings. **1897** *Cath. Dict.* (ed. 5) s.v. *Redemption*, Christ..atoned by His passion, He merited by His holy actions, yet so that His actions were also satisfactory and His passion meritorious.

2. Serving to satisfy a debt or obligation. *rare.*

1604 R. CAWDREY *Table Alph.*, *Satisfactorie*, that dischargeth, or answereth for. **1781** COWPER *Conversat.* 202 Then each might show, to his admiring friends, In honourable bumps his rich amends, And carry, in contusions of his skull, A satisfactory receipt in full.

†**b.** *to stand satisfactory to*: to consent to fulfil (a request). *Obs.*

1576 FLEMING *Panopl. Epist.* 59 If you will stand satisfactorie to my request.

†**3.** Of an explanation or argument: Serving merely to satisfy the inquirer, or objector; merely plausible. *Obs.* (Only in Bacon.)

1605 BACON *Adv. Learn.* II. vii. §7 The handling of finall causes..hath..giuen men the occasion, to stay vpon these satisfactorie and specious causes, to the great arrest..of furder discouerie. *Ibid.* xxv. §12 It is true, that knowledges reduced into exact Methodes haue a shew of strength... But this is more satisfactorie then substantiall. *Ibid.* II. xiii. §4.

4. a. Sufficient for the needs of the case, adequate. Of an argument: Convincing. †Of an author: Treating adequately of his subject. **b.** That justifies a feeling of satisfaction; such as one may be content or pleased with.

1640 BP. HALL *Episc.* III. iv. 240 How gladly should we heare him out, and returne him a satisfactory answer. **1641** J. JACKSON *True Evang. T.* III. 206, I will..referre onely him that is scrupulous herein, unto a most learned, and satisfactory Author, Grotius. **1663** COWLEY *Ess. & Verses, Greatness* Wks. 1710 II. 745 [The prince] could find out no Delight so satisfactory, as the keeping of little singing Birds, and hearing of them, and whistling to them. **1651** *Life Father Sarpi* 56 They first moved the Patriarch Priuli to deprive him of his faculty of confessing, thereby to shorten the father of his wonted, but poore, and yet satisfactory allowance. **1683** DR. ROBINSON in *Ray's Corr.* (1848) 135 It [the letter] was not so satisfactory as I wished. **1687** A. LOVELL tr. *Thevenot's Trav.* II. 89, I could not learn of any a satisfactory reason for that last signification. **1756** BURKE *Subl. & B.* Pref., Wks. I. 83, I have endeavoured to make this edition something more full and satisfactory than the first. **1822** LAMB *Elia* Ser. I. *Chimney-sweepers*, It is the time when..the kennels of our fair metropolis give forth their least satisfactory odours. **1849** MACAULAY *Hist. Eng.* vi. II. 45 But James supposed that the Primate was struck dumb by the irresistible force of reason, and eagerly challenged His Grace to produce..a satisfactory reply. **1860** TYNDALL *Glac.* II. xxiv. 361, I also made a few experiments at Rosenlaui,..but the result was not satisfactory. **1863** GEO. ELIOT *Romola* Introd., [He] went home with a triumphant light in his eyes after concluding a satisfactory marriage for his son. **1907** HODGES *Elem. Photogr.* 28 A cheaper but less satisfactory method.

†**B.** *sb.* **a.** A place or means of atonement or retribution. **b.** One who makes satisfaction (for the sins of another). *Obs.*

1530 TINDALE *Answ. More* Wks. (1573) 307/2 For to punishe a man that hath forsaken sinne of his owne accorde, is not to purge him, but to satisfie the lust of a tyrant. Neyther ought it to be called Purgatory, but a Iayle of tormenting and a satisfactory. **1587** GOLDING *De Mornay* xvii. (1592) 277 Among all people we see there were.. Sacrifices to appease Gods wrath, Mysticall washings, and Satisfactories or Notaries that were charged with the sinnes of some whole Realme, Citie, or State.

satisfiable (ˈsætɪsfaɪəb(ə)l), *a.* [f. SATISFY *v.* + -ABLE.] †**a.** In active sense: Satisfactory. *Obs. rare.* **b.** Capable of being satisfied, able to be or that may be satisfied.

1609 T. MORTON *Answ. Higgons* 6, I shall presently returne him.. a satisfiable answer. **1638** MAYNE *Lucian* (1664) 296 Having but one belly satisfyable with a little. **1641** 'SMECTYMNUUS' *Vind. Answ.* vii. 96 This may satisfie (if this man be satisfiable) that bold challenge of the former page. **1647** H. MORE *Song of Soul* To Rdr. 6 Nor is reason unback'd with better principles mathematically satisfiable in matters of this kind. **1681** T. FLATMAN *Heraclitus Ridens* No. 7 (1713) I. 42, I will give you Satisfaction if you be satisfiable. **1874** RUSKIN *Fors Clav.* xlvi. 241 Merely expressing anxiety for my welfare, not satisfiable but by letters, which do not promote it. **1942** W. S. CHURCHILL *End of Beginning* (1943) 228 All these conditions were satisfiable around 23rd October. **1944** *Annals Math. Stud.* XIII. 91 Formulas which are valid (or satisfiable) in every domain of individuals. **1952** R. L. WILDER *Introd. Foundations Math.* ii. 26 An axiom system Σ is satisfiable if there exists an interpretation of Σ. **1978** *Sci. Amer.* Jan. 106/3 When the machine is given a yes instance of a problem in *NP*, its operation is described by a satisfiable sentence, whereas the operation of a machine given a no instance is described by a sentence that cannot be satisfied.

Hence ˌ**satisfiaˈbility**.

1944 *Annals Math. Stud.* XIII. 90 We may study the decision problem from the point of view either of validity or of satisfiability, instead of that of provability. **1952** R. L. WILDER *Introd. Foundations Math.* ii. 26 Where a system [of axioms] is consistent, we are usually unable to tell the fact from 1.1. But.. we have a very simple test showing 'satisfiability' in the sense of 1.3. **1977** *Word 1972* XXVIII. 285 Something which, with Hockett, we may term the 'productivity' of the description, one of the fundamental conditions of its acceptability or 'satisfiability'.

ˈ**satisfice, -fise,** *v.* [Alteration of SATISFY (influenced by L. *satisfacĕre*).]

1. *trans.* = SATISFY *v. Obs.* exc. *north.* (see E.D.D.).

1561 DAUS tr. *Bullinger on Apoc.* (1573) 168 b, That their founders were nourished by suckyng of a wolfe: so haue all that people wolues mindes, neuer satisfised with bloud, euer greedy of dominion and hungryng after riches. **1597** in Feuillerat *Revels Q. Eliz.* (1908) 417 The other officers will nott be satisficed. **1721** KELLY *Scot. Prov.* 325 Satisfic'd, that is, satisfied.

2. *intr.* To decide on and pursue a course of action that will satisfy the minimum requirements necessary to achieve a particular goal. Hence ˈ**satisficer;** ˈ**satisficing** *ppl. a.* and *vbl. sb.*

1956 H. SIMON in *Psychol. Rev.* LXIII. 129/2 Evidently, organisms adapt well enough to 'satisfice'; they do not, in general, 'optimize'. *Ibid.* 136/1 A 'satisficing' path, a path that will permit satisfaction at some specified level of all its needs. **1957** —— *Models of Man* iv. 205 The key.. appeared to lie in substituting the goal of satisficing, of finding a good enough move, for the goal of minimaxing, of finding the best move. **1958** MARCH & SIMON *Organizations* vi. 141 To optimize requires processes several orders of magnitude more complex than those required to satisfice. **1963** G. P. E. CLARKSON in A. R. Oxenfeldt *Models of Markets* II. 340 Two important innovations.. have occurred... The first of these is the modified concept of rational behavior known as 'satisficing'... Important changes in the theory of the firm have been brought about by the introduction of the satisficing concept of behavior. **1967** H. SIMON in N. Rescher *Logic of Decision & Action* i. 19 It is easy to see how GPS can be made into a satisficer. **1973** *N.Y. Times* 11 Feb. III. 1/2 Big business executives don't really try to maximize profits but '*satisfice*'—that is, they try to make enough profit to keep stockholders and boards of directors happy without bringing the wrath of government regulators, consumer groups or business competitors down on them. **1977** P. N. KHANDWALLA *Design of Organizations* xi. 404 To the seat-of-the-pants 'satisficer', scientific analysis may be acceptable in dealing with relatively trivial problems. **1977** JANIS & MANN *Decision Making* ii. 32 A much more serious flaw of this complex form of satisficing lies in its failure to ensure that the alternatives retained are.. superior to those eliminated.

satisfied (ˈsætɪsfaɪd), *ppl. a.* [f. SATISFY *v.* + -ED¹.]

1. Contented, pleased, gratified.

1816 J. SCOTT *Vis. Paris* (ed. 5) 78 [He] might rest his satisfied looks on this trophy of his success. **1831** SCOTT *Ct. Robt.* xiii, She.. felt.. elated, perhaps, with a certain degree of satisfied pride while under his momentary protection. **1867** AUGUSTA WILSON *Vashti* xix, It was impossible to mistake the satisfied expression that flashed over her countenance. **1872** RUSKIN *Eagle's N.* §205 Bright fancies, satisfied memories.

2. Of a debt or obligation: Discharged, paid in full.

1817 W. SELWYN *Law Nisi Prius* (ed. 4) II. 659 A satisfied term set up by a mortgagor against a mortgagee. **1845** *Act 8 & 9 Vict.* c. 112 §1 Every satisfied Term of Years.. shall on that Day absolutely cease and determine as to the Land upon the Inheritance or Reversion whereof such Term shall be attendant.

Hence ˈ**satisfiedly** *adv.*; ˈ**satisfiedness**.

1571 GOLDING *Calvin on Ps.* xvii. 15 David dooth woorthely terme this peace or joy of the spirit, by the name of satisfyednesse. **1593** NASHE *Christ's T.* To Rdr., Buy who list, contemne who list, I leaue euery Reader his free libertie. If the best sort of men I content, I am satis-fiedly successfull. **1667** WATERHOUSE *Fire Lond.* 189 My satisfiedness in, and adhæsion to the piety and probity of my breeding and belief. **1867** MISS BROUGHTON *Not Wisely* II. xi. 230 His eyes sought her face and dwelt there satisfiedly.

satisfier (ˈsætɪsfaɪə(r)). [f. SATISFY *v.* + -ER¹.] One who or something which satisfies.

1547–64 BAULDWIN *Mor. Philos.* (Palfr.) 140 The conscience of man is.. also a satisfier or ioyfull quieter of the minde in all his doings. **1593** NASHE *Christ's T.* (1613) 190 Wee believe thee to be an absolute satisfier for sinne. **1624** F. WHITE *Repl. Fisher* 556 By the vertue thereof men are made satisfiers of Diuine Iustice, together with Christ. **1706** BP. W. SHERIDAN *Disc.* III. 97 It was fit that the satisfier should be God and man. **1892** H. RICE in *Home & For. Miss. Rec.* (Scot.) Mar., Christianity.. the satisfier of all human aspirations.

satisfy (ˈsætɪsfaɪ), *v.* Forms: 5–6 **satysfy(e,** 5–7 **satisfye,** (6 **satisfey,** *Sc.* **satisffi,** *pa. pple.* **satesfet, -fit),** 6–8 **satisfie,** (7 **sattisfy),** 6– **satisfy.** Also SATIFY. [a. OF. *satisfier* (also *satifier, satefier*), irregularly (see -FY) ad. L. *satisfacĕre*, orig. two words, *satis* enough, *facĕre* to do. Cf. OF., F. *satisfaire*, Pr. *satisfar*, Sp. *satisfacer*, Pg. *satisfazer*, It. *satis-*, *soddisfare*.]

I. With reference to debt or obligation.

1. *trans.* To pay off or discharge fully; to liquidate (a debt); to fulfil completely (an obligation), comply with (a demand). Now somewhat rare exc. in *Law*.

In the first quot. perh. *intr.* = to pay what is due.

c **1430** LYDG. *Min. Poems* (Percy Soc.) 43 To satisfye it is but impossible,—It may not be parformed as for me, What eyled me, lord, maryed for to be. **1578** *Knaresb. Wills* (Surtees) I. 128 After all my dettes are satisfied. **1596** BACON *Max. & Use Com. Law* I. viii. (1636) 33, I shall satisfie my contract with a sixpenny piece so raised. **1655** TERRY *Voy. E. India* xxiii. 384 When they cannot satisfie their Debts. **1677** YARRANTON *Eng. Improv.* 36 At this day many Gentlemen.. have sold Land since they entered into these Bonds, and the Bonds not satisfied. **1766** BLACKSTONE *Comm.* II. 485 Before his [a bankrupt's] debts are satisfied or agreed for. **1784** COWPER *Task* III. 783 'Tis finish'd, and yet, finish'd as it seems, Still wants a grace, the loveliest it could show, A mine to satisfy th'enormous cost. **1818** CRUISE *Digest* (ed. 2) VI. 276 The personal estate was not sufficient to satisfy legacies. **1847–9** HELPS *Friends in C.* (1851) I. 117 Claims which cannot be satisfied, ought not to be satisfied, and which, being unsatisfied, embitter people. **1886** *Law Rep., Weekly Notes* 196/1 The reserve fixed by the judge was not sufficient to satisfy the first and second mortgage debentures.

†**b.** *impers.* in passive, *it is satisfied*: full payment has been made (*to* a person *of* or *for* a debt).

c **1450** *Godstow Reg.* 198 To hold her distresse til þat hyt were satisfiede to þe foreseyde abbas & couent for all pynges. *Ibid.* 411 Yf hit were not I-satisfied fully in ony terme to the said mynchons.. of the said rent. *Ibid.* 486, 530.

†**c.** With the money paid as object. *Obs.*

1617 MORYSON *Itin.* I. 199 The one hundred pounds which my brother and I carried in our purses, would not satisfie the five hundred pound we had spent. **1818** SCOTT *Hrt. Midl.* xxvi, Though I ken my father will satisfy every penny of this siller, whatever there's o't, yet I wadna like to borrow it frae one that maybe thinks of something mair than the paying o't back again.

d. To pay (a creditor). Const. *of* (the debt, a sum of money); †formerly occas. with the debt, etc. as second object. Now *rare* exc. in legal use.

1433 *Rolls of Parlt.* IV. 425/1 Ye said Lords.. agreed.. to make hym to be satisfied and paide of the seid yerly sommes. **1455–6** *Cal. Anc. Rec. Dublin* (1889) 289 Tyll he satysfy the courte of the sayd sowme. **1558** CARD. POLE *Let.* in Strype *Ann. Ref.* ii. (1709) 50, I thought it my duty before I should depart,.. to leave all persons satisfied of me. **1611** TOURNEUR *Ath. Trag.* III. i, That shee [Earth] is satisfied what he did owe, Both principall and use. **1667** in J. Watson *Jedburgh Abbey* (1894) 89 [The council] ordains James Fall to be satisfied of the sum of £200 for timber bought by him. **1692** R. L'ESTRANGE *Fables* xxix. 28 The Defendant [a sheep] was cast into Costs and Damages, and forc'd to sell the Wool off his Back to satisfie the Creditor. *a* **1768** SECKER *Serm.* (1770) III. vii. 165 It is very true, that Motives, not at all akin to Pride, frequently induce those of high Rank to neglect or even refuse satisfying their Creditors. **1818** CRUISE *Digest* (ed. 2) II. 141 A tenant by the curtesy may also redeem a mortgage, and hold the lands till he is satisfied. **1825** T. LEE *Dict. Pract. Civ. Actions* (ed. 2) II. 1224 The said —— .. acknowledges himself to be satisfied by the said —— of the damages, costs, and charges aforesaid,.. therefore the said —— is acquitted of the said damages, costs, and charges.

fig. *c* **1510** MORE *Picus* Wks. 8/2 Compelled him within thre daies to satisfie nature, and repaie her the life which he receiued of her.

†**e.** To remunerate; to pay for services. *Obs.*

1623 BINGHAM *Xenophon* 141 We are ready to depart, as soone as they, by whose meanes you enjoy the land, are satisfied for their pay. **1624** CAPT. SMITH *Virginia* IV. 126 We thought our selues now fully satisfied for our long toile and labours. **1697** DAMPIER *Voy.* I. v. 128 These Indians did us good service,.. and for this their service we satisfied them to their hearts content. **1771** LUCKOMBE *Hist. Print.* 388 It is not a Compositor's duty; especially where he has no expectation of being satisfied for it.

†**2.** To make compensation or reparation for (a wrong, injury); to atone for (an offence). *Obs.*

c **1460** *Wisdom* 1084 in *Macro Plays* 71 Yet of my selff I may not satysfye my trespas. *a* **1586** SIDNEY *Arcadia* III. (Sommer) 319 b, Thy death shall satisfie thy iniurie, & my malice. **1590** GREENE *Mourn. Garm.* (1616) 66 Repentance satisfies the deepest offences. **1590** SPENSER *F.Q.* II. viii. 28 Why should not that dead carrion satisfye The guilt? **1611** BEAUM. & FL. *Knt. Burning Pest.* III. i, Come, by this hand you dye, I must have Life and blood to satisfie Your fathers wrongs. **1649** BP. HALL *Cases Consc.* (1654) 23 He is bound either to prevent the buyers wrong; or if heedlesly done, to satisfy it. *a* **1715** BURNET *Own Time* (1823) I. 343 A complaint of a ship taken was ready to have been satisfied, but Downing hindered it.

b. To make atonement or reparation to (a person, his honour, etc.).

1602 EARL NORTHUMBLD. in Collins *Peerage* (1779) II. 413 Sir Frauncis Verre was willing to satisfye his Lordshipp [in a duel]. **1674** BREVINT *Saul at Endor* 237 Now it seems he hath satisfied Divine Justice, in case I do satisfie it my self. *a* **1711** KEN *Christophil* Poet. Wks. 1721 I. 432 God's Holiness, by Sin defy'd, The Lamb unspotted satisfy'd. **1860** PUSEY *Min. Proph.* 556 In the way of justice He satisfied for men, delivering Himself for their faults to the pain of death, to satisfy the honour of the Divine Majesty, so that sin should not remain unpunished.

3. *intr.* To make satisfaction, full payment, reparation, or atonement. Const. *for*, *to* (a debt or offence). *Obs.* exc. *Theol.* (said of Christ).

c **1450** *Godstow Reg.* 45 Vndur the condicion that they satisfye & make good to hym thorow whose londys they make her cundyt for the harmys. **1491** CAXTON *Vitas Patr.* (W. de W. 1495) I. ix. 14 b/2 If thou wylt promyse tamende thy conscyence & satysfye for thy synnes we shal praye god for the. **1529** MORE *Suppl. Soulys* Wks. 326/2 Obiectyng that no men mai satisfy for another. **1556** *Aurelio & Isab.* (1608) N iij, Thinckinge be me selfe where in I mighte doo you service agreable for to satisfye to my fautes. **1562** COOPER *Answ. Priv. Masse* vii. 47 b, May.. an other mans penance satisfy for your sinnes? **1565** in Calderwood *Hist. Kirk* (1843) II. 303 Persons lying in fornication, under promise of mariage, which they differe to solemnize, sould satisfie publicklie in the place of repentance, upon the Lord's Day, before they be maried. **1570–6** LAMBARDE *Peramb. Kent* (1826) 205 Wanting otherwise to satisfie for his raunsome, and having good leysure to devise for his deliveraunce. **1590** MARLOWE *Edw. II*, III. iii. (1598) F 2, For which ere long, their heades shall satisfie: T'appeaze the wrath of their offended king. **1639** S. DU VERGER tr. *Camus' Admir. Events* 2 Having beene bound in a great summe of money for one of his friends, whom misfortune had made unable to satisfie. *c* **1660** SOUTH *Serm. John* vii. 17 (1715) I. 219 That he should die and satisfy for the Sins of the World. **1667** MILTON *P.L.* III. 295 So Man.. Shall satisfie for Man, be judg'd and die. **1684** *Contempl. St. Man* II. x. (1699) 237 If the malice of Sin be so exorbitant, that nothing can satisfie for it, less than God. **1701** J. LAW *Counc. Trade* (1751) 218 If he have not to satisfy for the theft, then to be condemned for any time, not exceeding six years more. **1732** *Wedding Serm.* i. Ded. 2 The Son of the Highest died to satisfy for it [*sc.* sin]. **1860** [see 2 b].

II. With reference to feelings or needs.

4. *trans.* To meet or fulfil the wish or desire or expectation of; to be accepted by (a person, his taste, judgement, etc.) as all that could be reasonably desired; to content.

to satisfy the examiners: in English Universities, the technical phrase indicating that a person has 'passed' an examination, but is not entitled to 'honours'.

c **1489** CAXTON *Sonnes of Aymon* xiv. 348 And yf this can not satysfye your mynde I shall doo yet more. Playseth it to you for to pardonne my bredern and I shall forswere Fraunce for evermore. **1494** FABYAN *Chron.* VI. cxc. 193 With whiche fayre speche, the duke.. was wele satysfyed & content. **1526** *Pilgr. Perf.* (W. de W. 1531) 2 b, My herte good lorde can not be satysfyed in this worlde. **1530** PALSGR. 698/1 It is harde to satisfye all men. *a* **1548** HALL *Chron., Edw. V* 7 b, Muche parte of the common people were therewith right well satisfied. *a* **1586** SIDNEY *Arcadia* II. (Sommer) 109 These two young Princes to satisfie the king [who had sent for them] tooke their way by sea, towards Thrace. *a* **1715** BURNET *Own Time* (1823) I. 351 He was cheerful and seemed fully satisfied with his death. **1764** GOLDSM. *Trav.* 154 The sports of children satisfy the child. **1784** COWPER *Task* I. 199 Nature inanimate employs sweet sounds,.. To sooth and satisfy the human ear. **1840** DICKENS *Barn. Rudge* x, 'It's well I am easily satisfied,' returned the other with a smile. **1842** W. C. TAYLOR *Anc. Hist.* viii. §7 (ed. 3) 219 The Dorian mountains were ill calculated to satisfy men whose ancestors had inherited the fertile plains of the Peloponnesus. **1849** MACAULAY *Hist. Eng.* v. I. 548 That every exertion would be made to satisfy him. **1861** J. E. T. ROGERS *Educ. Oxf.* 37 Certain persons who, attempting only to satisfy the examiners, do more than satisfy them, are by the practice of the schools, and under the sanction of the statute, distinguished by having an honorary class.. assigned to them. **1878** R. W. DALE *Lect. Preach.* iii. 68 The theological creed of the Church to which they belong satisfies them perfectly.

b. with obj. a desire, expectation, etc.

1570 DEE *Math. Pref.* 2 My sincere endeuour to satisfie your honest expectation. *c* **1595** CAPT. WYATT *R. Dudley's Voy. W. Ind.* (Hakl. Soc.) 40 Albeit the sayd Baltizar had not throughlie satisfied the expectacion of our Captaine, yet did hee wiselie dissemble his conceipte. **1603** SHAKS. *Meas. for M.* III. i. 170 Do not satisfie your resolution with hopes that are fallible, to morrow you must die, goe to your knees, and make ready. **1717** LADY M. W. MONTAGU *Let. to Pope* 1 Apr., I have it in my power to satisfy your curiosity. **1823** LAMB *Elia* Ser. II. *Old Margate Hoy*, The incapacity of actual objects for satisfying our preconceptions of them. **1871** FREEMAN *Norm. Conq.* (1876) IV. xviii. 215 A few names awaken curiosity without satisfying it.

†**c.** *refl.* To make oneself content (*with* something); to consider it sufficient *to do* something. Also, to bring or persuade oneself *to do* something distasteful. *Obs.*

1611 BIBLE *Transl. Pref.* ¶ 11 Ioash the king of Israel did not satisfie himselfe, till he had smitten the ground three times. **1660** F. BROOKE tr. *Le Blanc's Trav.* 2, I..shall satisfie my self for the present to tell you, that..we sailed happily for some few dayes. **1719** DE FOE *Crusoe* I. (Globe) 110 Nor could I satisfy myself to eat them, tho' I kill'd several. *Ibid.* II. 397 The two English Men were so encourag'd, that they could not satisfy themselves to stay any longer there..but away they went in Quest of the Savages. **1782** MISS BURNEY *Cecilia* VIII. iv, Mr. Delvile, should he find a daughter-in-law descended..from Egbert, ..won't be so well off as if he had satisfied himself with you.

d. In *passive*, To be content (*with*); with *inf.*, to find it sufficient, desire or demand no more than *to do* something (cf. the reflexive use c). Phrase, ***to rest satisfied***. Also in stronger sense, to be well pleased (*with*, †*at*).

a **1533** LD. BERNERS *Huon* lxii. 217 The melodye..was so swete..that euery man was satysfyed with the herynge therof. **1597** HOOKER *Eccl. Pol.* v. lxii. §21 God was satisfied with that she did. **1603** SHAKS. *Meas. for M.* II. ii. 104 Be satisfied; Your Brother dies to morrow; be content. **1654–66** EARL ORRERY *Parthen.* (1676) 643 The King seems to be much more satisfied at it, than any other concerned in it. **1686** tr. *Chardin's Trav. Persia* 41 M. de la Haye bid 'em rest satisfi'd. **1687** A. LOVELL tr. *Thevenot's Trav.* I. 170 We were fain to rest satisfied then, with what we saw of that Monastery from the top of the Mount. **1732** LEDIARD *Sethos* II. 2 The heroes of Greece..not satisfy'd with making the passage of the seas known. **1784** COWPER *Task* VI. 394 While he, Not satisfied to prey on all around,..first torments ere he devours. **1809** MALKIN *Gil Blas* IV. vii. ¶15 Not satisfied to humbug a silly old gentleman with a tale of love. **1831** SCOTT *Ct. Robt.* xx, She must be satisfied..to know that her husband is under the guidance of a friend. **1852** MRS. STOWE *Uncle Tom's C.* xix, Can you be satisfied with such a way of spending your probation? **1863** GEO. ELIOT *Romola* xxxix, He had the air of a man well satisfied with the world.

5. *absol.* and *intr.* To cause or give satisfaction or contentment.

1600 *Chester Pl.* Proëm 44 If the same be likeinge to the comons all, then our desier is to satisfie—for that is all our game. *a* **1649** WINTHROP *New Eng.* (1825) I. 210 This would not satisfy, but they called him to answer publickly. **1831** *Westm. Rev.* Jan. 243 What would have satisfied from the Duke will not satisfy from Lord Grey. **1836** EMERSON *Nature* iii. Wks. (Bohn) II. 145 But in other hours, Nature satisfies by its loveliness, and without any mixture of corporeal benefit. **1903** *Heart of Heretic* vi. 33 The first and last need of an aspect of religious truth is that it shall *satisfy*.

6. *trans.* To cause to have enough; to supply fully the needs of; to put an end to (an appetite, a want) by fully supplying it.

1500–20 DUNBAR *Poems* xvii. 37 Sum wald tak all this warldis breid, And ȝit not satisfeit of thair neid [*Maitl. MS.* not ȝit can be satisfeid]. *a* **1533** LD. BERNERS *Huon* xxii. 66 Yf he were in the gretest famyn.., he sholde be satysfied as well as though he had eten al that he wolde wysshe for. **1588** SHAKS. *Tit. A.* II. iii. 180 So should I rob my sweet Sonnes of their fee, No let them satisfie their lust on thee [Lavinia]. **1593** —— *Lucr.* 422 As the grim Lion fawneth ore his pray, Sharpe hunger by the conquest satisfied. **1611** BIBLE *Ecclus.* xii. 16 Hee will not be satisfied with blood. **1667** MILTON *P.L.* x. 991 So Death shall be deceav'd his glut, and with us two Be forc'd to satisfie his Rav'nous Maw. **1690** NORRIS *Pract. Disc.* (1694) I. 88 There are some Appetites of Man which are never satisfied. **1800** *Med. Jrnl.* IV. 209 He takes a great deal of food without being satisfied. **1857** H. H. WILSON tr. *Rig-veda* III. 158 Indra..has inundated the dry lands, and (satisfied) the thirsty travellers.

refl. **1585** T. WASHINGTON tr. *Nicholay's Voy.* IV. xv. 129b, They cannot satisfie them of the pleasure which is there.

7. To furnish with sufficient proof or information; to assure or set free from doubt or uncertainty; to convince.

1520 NISBET *N.T.*, *Summe Matt.* (S.T.S.) I. 6 The angell satisffijs Josephs mynd. **1538** STARKEY *England* I. i. 8 You haue ryght wel satysfyd me in my dowte. **1611** SHAKS. *Cymb.* III. v. 92 No farther halting: satisfie me home, What is become of her? **1611** BIBLE *Transl. Pref.* ¶8 If any doubt hereof, he may be satisfied by examples enough. **1628** EARLE *Microcosm.* xlvi. (Arb.) 67 He finds reason in all opinions, truth in none: indeed the least reason perplexes him, and the best will not satisfie him. **1643** SIR T. BROWNE *Relig. Med.* I. §10 Where I cannot satisfy my reason, I love to humour my fancy. **1771** BURKE *Corr.* (1844) I. 275 All I can do is, to satisfy you, and to leave you to satisfy those whom you think worthy of being informed. **1849** MACAULAY *Hist. Eng.* vi. II. 119 These expressions were far from satisfying the Chancellor. **1856** SIR B. BRODIE *Psychol. Inq.* I. iii. 104 He..cannot comprehend, the arguments which satisfy men of sober sense that his views are erroneous.

absol. **1605** BACON *Adv. Learn.* II. xvii. §7 Methodes are more fit to winne Consent; or beleefe; but lesse fit to point to Action; for they carrie a kinde of Demonstration in Orbe or Circle, one part illuminating another; and therefore satisfie.

refl. **1604** E. G[RIMSTONE] *D'Acosta'a Hist. Indies* III. xiv. 162 For to satisfy my selfe vpon this point and question, I demaunded particularly of the said Pilot, how he found the tides in the straight. **1709** BERKELEY *Th. Vision* §31 Which is the very matter of Fact, as any one that pleases may easily satisfie himself by Experiment. **1769** E. BANCROFT *Guiana* 332 They seem by no means sollicitous to satisfy themselves on this subject.

b. const. *of*, †*in*.

1596 SHAKS. *Merch. V.* v. i. 296, I am sure you are not satisfied Of these euents at full. **1600** HAKLUYT *Voy.* III. 304 That the kings Maiestie..shall in part be satisfied of the diligence which I haue vsed in his seruice. **1614** SIR R. DUDLEY in *Fortesc. Papers* (Camden) 11 This for the present is as much as I can saye to satisfye his Majestye in this point. **1690** LOCKE *Hum. Und.* II. i. §16 This I would willingly be satisfy'd in. **1736** BUTLER *Anal.* Advert., No one can..be satisfied of the contrary. **1749** FIELDING *Tom Jones* v. vi, When Sophia was well satisfied of the violent passion which tormented poor Jones, and no less certain that she herself was its object. *Ibid.* XVIII. vi, You need be under no Apprehension, Sir, I shall satisfy Mr. Allworthy very perfectly of that Matter.

refl. **1663** BP. PATRICK *Parab. Pilgr.* xxxvi. (1668) 461 The Young man..soon satisfied himself in the truth of what he said.

c. with *subordinate clause*. Also parenthetically, ***I am*** (***he is***, etc.) ***satisfied***.

1621 ELSING *Debates Ho. Lords* (Camden) 32 Desyres to be satisfyed whether sylke may be so dyed or noe. **1662** J. DAVIES tr. *Olearius' Voy. Ambass.* 205 Two good deep ditches built about with Free-stone, which satisfy'd us they were the ruins of an impregnable Fortress. **1758** S. HAYWARD *Serm.* iv. 125 We are satisfyed the foundation upon which we build is safe. **1766** *Compl. Farmer* s.v. *Surveying*, Being satisfied what shall be the distance between the center and every angle, with that distance describe a circle. **1851** MAYHEW *Lond. Lab.* I. 324/2 It's a great thing, I'm satisfied, in a street-trade,..to understand the goods you're talking about. **1884** *Manch. Exam.* 22 May 5/2 The success of the French at Sontay..had no doubt satisfied the Chinese that their troops were no match for those of France.

refl. *a* **1687** PETTY *Pol. Arith.* Pref. (1690) a3b, Having satisfied myself, that the..Affairs of England are in no deplorable Condition. **1860** TYNDALL *Glac.* II. xxvi. 370 We have at all events satisfied ourselves that [etc.]. **1892** T. W. ERLE in *Law Times* XCIII. 417/1 Information..to enable anybody to satisfy himself as to how things are done.

8. To answer sufficiently (an objection, a question); to fulfil or comply with (a request); to solve (a doubt, a difficulty).

1581 PETTIE tr. *Guazzo's Civ. Conv.* II. (1586) 108 If I should throughlie satisfie your request, this daie would not be inough to doe it. *a* **1626** BACON *New Atl.* (1626) 10 And I shall gladly, and briefly, satisfie your demaund. **1650** FULLER *Pisgah* 420 Many shrewd objections may be alleadged to the contrary, which we shall endevour to satisfie in order. **1765** H. WALPOLE *Otranto* v, Thou hast not satisfied my question. **1784** COWPER *Task* II. 527 'Tis revelation satisfies all doubts. **1834** J. H. NEWMAN *Par. Serm.* I. xviii. 264 Revelation was not given us to satisfy doubts, but to make us better men. **1862** H. SPENCER *First Princ.* I. i. §4 (1875) 16 They are liable to forget that information, however extensive it may become, can never satisfy inquiry.

9. To answer the requirements of (a state of things, a hypothesis, etc.); to accord with (conditions). †Also *rarely* of a person: To fulfil the requirements of.

1651 HOBBES *Leviath.* III. xxxiv. 208 Where none of these can satisfie the sense of that word in Scripture. **1665** GLANVILL *Def. Van. Dogm.* 47, I met an ingenious Account, among some excellent Geometricians of this Probleme, which perhaps may satisfie the difficulty. *a* **1754** SIR J. STRANGE *Reports* (1782) I. 58 Pratt J. This man has fully satisfied the words of the act of Parliament. **1855** BAIN *Senses & Int.* III. iv. 4 When there are four or five different conditions to satisfy, the range of choice must be so much the wider. **1883** CHRYSTAL in *Encycl. Brit.* XV. 244/1 The assumption of uniform magnetization will enable us to satisfy the law of induction. In point of fact, substituting.. and transposing, we get three linear equations to determine A_1, B_1, C_1 in terms of a_0, β_0, γ_0.

b. *Algebra.* Of a known quantity: To fulfil the conditions of, to be an admissible solution of (an equation).

c **1826** *Encycl. Metrop.* (1845) I. 544/1 A value of the unknown quantity, which thus converts the equation into an identity, is said to *satisfy* the equation. **1842** COLENSO *Elem. Algebra* vi. (ed. 3) 53. **1878** GURNEY *Crystallogr.* 25 Any three numbers which will satisfy this equation.

satisfying ('sætɪsfaɪɪŋ), *vbl. sb.* [-ING¹.] The action of the verb SATISFY in various senses.

1560 DAUS tr. *Sleidane's Comm.* 107 They oughte of necessitie to answere to this poinct, for the satisfynge as well of his father as his fellowes. **1647** SANDERSON *Serm.* II. 215 For the satisfying of their lusts. **1795** in Picton *L'pool Munic. Rec.* (1886) II. 270 The satisfying of their own minds as to the cause of such appearances. **1869** MRS. WHITNEY *Hitherto* xii, In the great, full world of powers, and knowledges, and possible joys and satisfyings.

satisfying ('sætɪsfaɪɪŋ), *ppl. a.* [f. SATISFY *v.* + -ING².] That satisfies, in the senses of the verb.

1604 SHAKS. *Oth.* v. i. 9 He hath giuen me satisfying Reasons. **1725** WODROW *Corr.* (1843) III. 232 It's satisfying to me to find him so warm and earnest for our Redeemer's Proper and Supreme Deity. **1759** ROBERTSON *Hist. Scot.* v. Wks. 1851 II. 46 A satisfying answer was given to the regent's demands. **1900** P. C. SIMPSON *Fact of Christ* v. 184 Any true or satisfying view of life must take account of death.

Hence **'satisfyingly** *adv.*, **'satisfyingness**.

1643 TORSHELL *Case Consc.* 13 Satisfyingly. *a* **1709** J. NIMMO *Narr.* (S.H.S. 1889) 30 That word came satisfienglie in ther minde, Isay 41 & 10. **1856** FABER *Creator & Creature* III. i. (1858) 332 There is also a satisfyingness about it [*sc.* the sense of pardon], which seldom accompanies other joys. **1885** *Manch. Exam.* 25 Mar. 3/3 An etching from a small Landseer..has been satisfyingly executed by Mr. C. O. Murray.

satispassion (sætɪs'pæʃən). *Theol.* [ad. med.L. **satispassiōnem*, f. phrase *satis patī* to suffer enough (*satis* enough, *patī* to suffer): cf. PASSION.] Atonement by an adequate degree of suffering.

1614 BP. ANDREWES *96 Serm.* (1629) 77 This, this is the great *With us*:..With us, in all the vertues and merits of His life; With us, in the satisfaction and satis-passion (both) of His death. **1678** J. S. *Unerrable Church* 311 This is don either by Satispassion suffering the pains of Purgatorie for a certain time; or [etc.]. **1890** W. J. B. RICHARDS *Catech. Indulg.* 8 This [reparation for sin] may be made..by satispassion, or sufferings simply endured. **1897** *Cath. Dict.* (ed. 5) s.v. *Redemption*, Like His satispassion, so His satisfaction embraces the whole earthly career of the Saviour.

†**'sative**, *a. Obs.* [ad. L. *satīv-us* that may be sown or planted, f. *sa-*, root of *serĕre* to sow: see -TIVE.] Sown or planted; cultivated, not wild.

1599 H. BUTTES *Dyets Drie Dinner* P4b, Tabacco... Translated out of India in the seed or roote; Natiue or satiue in our own fruitfullest soiles. **1664** EVELYN *Sylva* (1679) 2 These [trees] we shall divide into the greater and more ceduous..and such as are sative and hortensial. **1725** *Bradley's Fam. Dict.* s.v. *Pine*, The wild Pine differs no otherwise from the Sative.

†**'sativous**, *a. Obs.* [f. L. *satīvus*: see SATIVE *a.* and -OUS.] = SATIVE.

1786 ABERCROMBIE *Arrangem.* 72/1 in *Gard. Assist.*, Sativous, or cultivated common garlick.

satle, satling, obs. ff. SETTLE, SETTLING.

Satnace, Saton(e, obs. ff. SATANAS, SATAN.

saton, obs. form of SATIN *sb.*

Satorday, obs. form of SATURDAY.

‖**satori** (sa'toːri). *Zen Buddhism.* [Jap., = spiritual awakening.] A sudden indescribable and uncommunicable inner experience of enlightenment. Also *transf.* Hence **sa'toric** *a.*, pertaining to or inducing satori.

1727 J. G. SCHEUCHZER tr. *Kæmpfer's Hist. Japan* I. III. vi. 242 This profound Enthusiasm is by them call'd *Safen*, and the divine truths revealed to such persons *Satori*. **1921** A. WALEY *Nō Plays of Japan* 58 The only escape from this 'Wheel of Life and Death' lies in *satori*, 'Enlightenment', the realization that material phenomena are thoughts, not facts. **1921** D. T. SUZUKI in *Eastern Buddhist* May 33 The power to see into the nature of one's own being lies also hidden here [in the subconscious]. Zen awakens it. The awakening is known as *Satori*, or the opening of a third eye. **1933** —— *Ess. Zen Buddhism* 2nd Ser. I. 21 When you have satori you are able to reveal a palatial mansion made of precious stones on a single blade of grass; but when you have no satori, a palatial mansion itself is concealed behind a simple blade of grass. **1949** C. HUMPHREYS *Zen Buddhism* ii. 33 *Satori*, the immediate experience of truth as distinct from understanding about it. **1957** *New Yorker* 31 Aug. 35/1 It takes at least ten years of meditation and *koans* to attain even one flash of *satori*. **1968** T. WOLFE *Electric Kool-Aid Acid Test* viii. 102 It was as if Cassady..was in a state of satori, as totally into this very moment, Now, as a being can get. **1970** W. BURROUGHS JR. *Speed* vii. 154 His music was improvised to fit short declarations and imaginary rhyming words, prayers and questions to the audience that he fit together in a satoric sound that brought me back to and into the running water. **1974** *Sci. Amer.* Oct. 140/2 Thought, like the kingdom of life, grows and evolves slowly; the book focuses on 'the inner work of synthesis' and not on the claimed *satori* of one chance page.

†**sa'torious**, *a. Obs.* [f. L. *satōri-us* (f. *sator*, agent-n. f. *sa-*, *serĕre* to sow) + -OUS.] (See quot.)

1656 BLOUNT *Glossogr.*, *Satorious*,..belonging to a Sator, or to him that sows, sets, or plants.

satrangi, satranji, varr. SITRINGEE.

satrap ('seɪtræp, 'sætræp). Forms: 4–5 **satrape**, 4–5, 8– **satrap**; also in L. form 6–8 **satrapa**, (*pl.* **satrapæ, satrapaes**), 6 *erron.* **satrapas, satrapos**. [ad. L. *satrapa*, *satrapes*, a. Gr. σατράπης, also ἐξατράπης, *ἐξαιθράπης (implied in the derivative ἐξαιθραπεύειν to be a satrap), ad. OPers. *xšaθra-pāvan-*, lit. 'protector of the country', f. *xšaθra-* country (= Skr. *kshatra*) + *pā-* to protect. The OPers. word appears in Heb. as *ăḥashdarp'nīm* (*pl.*) in Masoretic vocalization.

Cf. F. *satrape*, Sp. *sátrapa*, It. *satrapo*.]

1. A governor of a province under the ancient Persian monarchy. (In the Book of Daniel anachronistically attributed to the Babylonian empire.)

1382 WYCLIF *Dan.* iii. 3 Than satrapes weren gedrid. **1532** HERVET *Xenophon's Househ.* (1768) 17 In somme countreys of Persia, a great lord, that they cal Satrapa, occupieth the rowme of bothe lyeutenauntes. **1594** LODGE & GREENE *Looking Glass* (1598) E4b, I am not chiefe, there is more great then I, What greater then Th'assirian Satrapos? **1601** HOLLAND *Pliny* I. 135 The royall pallace of their great dukes & potentates, named Satrapæ. *a* **1618** RALEIGH *Maxims of State* Rem. (1664) 17 To that end serves the Persian practise, in having a Band, or Train of the Satrapa's children, and other Nobles to attend the Court. **1738** GLOVER *Leonidas* IV. 297 Th'innumerable host Roll back by nations, and admit their lord With all his Satraps. **1815** BYRON *Vis. Belshazzar* i, The King was on his throne, The Satraps throng'd the hall. **1838** THIRLWALL *Greece* xiii. II. 185 The satraps were accountable for the imposts of their several provinces. **1885** BIBLE (R.V.) *Dan.* iii. 3 The satraps, the deputies, and the governors.

2. *transf.* A subordinate ruler; often suggesting an imputation of tyranny or ostentatious splendour.

[The sense 'domineering person' appears in med.Latin, and in all the Rom. langs.]

c **1380** WYCLIF *Wks.* (1880) 7 þat schal not be dispensid wiþ but reserued to a grettere satrap. *a* **1529** SKELTON *Agst. Garnesche* i. 6 But sey me now, Syr Satrapas, what autoryte ye haue In your chalenge, Syr Chystyn, to cale me knaue? **1549** LATIMER *2nd Serm. bef. Edw. VI* (Arb.) 63 The byshoppe would beare nothynge at all wyth hym, but played me the Satrapa. **1598** MARSTON *Pygmal.*, *Sat.* i. 137 For shame leaue running to some Satrapas, Leaue glauering on him in the peopled presse. **1827** HALLAM *Const. Hist.* iv. (1876) I. 210 Elizabeth..must have shuddered at the thought of seeing a republican assembly substituted for those faithful satraps her bishops. **1838** LYTTON *Alice* II. ii, A private secretary to one of our Indian satraps. **1861** GOLDW. SMITH *Irish Hist.* 121 Louis XIV..acted on England through his subsidized satraps.

satrapaire, variant of SATRAPER.

satrapal (ˈsætrəpəl), *a.* [f. SATRAP + -AL[1].] Of or pertaining to a satrap or satraps.

[*a* **1693** URQUHART *Rabelais* III. xxxviii. 316 Satrapal fool.] **1887** B. V. HEAD *Hist. Numorum* 512 Satrapal Coinage in Ionia. *Ibid.* 676 A series of uncertain Satrapal coins.

satrapate (ˈsætrəpeɪt). [f. SATRAP + -ATE.] A province governed by a satrap.

1888 *Times* 12 Sept. 5/3 Who have the ambition to see Servia become a Russian satrapate.

†**ˈsatraper.** *Obs.* Also 5 **satrapaire, satropar.** [f. SATRAP + -ER.] A satrap.

a **1400-50** *Alexander* 1913 Þe soueraynest of my seniourie my sa[t]roparis [*Dubl. MS.* satrapers] hatten. *Ibid.* 2694 Ȝour satrapaires [*Dubl. MS.* satrapers]. *Ibid.* 2758 Þus send I to my satraparis [*Dubl. MS.* satrapars].

satrapess (ˈseɪtrəpɪs, ˈsætrəpɪs). [f. SATRAP + -ESS.] A female satrap.

1832 C. T[HIRLWALL] in *Philol. Museum* I. 376 Alexander ..left Ada as queen or satrapess of Caria.

satrapial (səˈtreɪpɪəl), *a.* [f. SATRAP + -IAL.] = SATRAPAL.

1869 RAWLINSON *Anc. Hist.* 558 The satrapial system, which had been introduced by the Persians.

satrapian (səˈtreɪpɪən), *a.* [f. SATRAP + -IAN.] Of or pertaining to a satrap; tyrannical.

1822 *New Monthly Mag.* V. 270 After many similar satrapian invectives.

satrapic (səˈtræpɪk), *a.* [f. SATRAP + -IC.] Of, pertaining to, or characteristic of a satrap.

c **1535** J. AP RICE in Ellis *Orig. Lett.* Ser. III. II. 356 Also I require more modestie, gravitie, and affabilitie, which wolde purchase hym more reverence than his owne setting foorth and Satrapike countenance. **1852** GROTE *Greece* II. lxxiii. IX. 363 Near the satrapic residence.

satrapical (səˈtræpɪkəl), *a.* [f. SATRAPIC + -AL[1].] Of or pertaining to a satrap; also *fig.* cruel, tyrannical.

1823 SYD. SMITH *Botany Bay* Wks. 1859 II. 23 These Asiatic and satrapical proceedings. **1852** GROTE *Greece* II. lxx. IX. 140 They then found themselves amidst several villages, wherein were regal or satrapical residences.

†**ˈsatrapon.** *Obs.* [ad. It. *satrapone*, augm. of *satrapo* SATRAP.] An important personage.

1650 HOWELL *Giraffi's Rev. Naples* I. 34 The peeple shew'd it to their Satrapons [orig. It. *Satraponi*] and Councel.

satrapy (ˈseɪtrəpɪ, ˈsætrəpɪ). [a. F. *satrapie*, ad. L. *satrapīa, satrapēa*, a. Gr. σατραπεία, f. σατράπης SATRAP.]

1. A province ruled over by a satrap.

1603 KNOLLES *Hist. Turks* (1638) 127 At length they with their Kingdome, and all the rest of the Turkish Satrapies, were..swallowed vp and deuoured. *a* **1727** NEWTON *Chronol. Amended* iv. (1728) 325 When Cyrus took Babylon, he changed the Kingdom into a Satrapy or Province. **1821** BYRON *Sardan.* II. i. 408 Repair to your respective satrapies Of Babylon and Media. **1847** GROTE *Greece* II. xxxiii. IV. 315 Darius distributed the Persian empire into twenty satrapies.

b. *transf.*

a **1641** SIR H. SPELMAN *Anc. Govt. Eng.* Posth. Wks. (1698) 50 The Temporal Government was likewise divided into Satrapies or Dukedoms, which contained in them divers Counties. **1864** *Even. Stand.* 29 Sept., Major General Butler..was ill calculated to rule a Federal satrapy with profit to his government. **1882** FARRAR *Early Chr.* II. 110 They [the Galileans] detested..alike the Roman dominion and the Herodian satrapy which was its outward sign. **1887** GOLDW. SMITH in *Times* 3 Dec. 10/3 The abolition of what is now styled an Austrian satrapy.

2. The dignity of a satrap: in quots. *transf.*

1641 MILTON *Ch. Govt.* I. i. 4 Yea the Angels themselves ..are distinguisht and quaterniond into their celestiall Princedomes, and Satrapies. **1839** BAILEY *Festus* xxxi. (1852) 506 Jewels well worth the satrapies of Heaven.

†**3.** The body of satraps. *Obs.*

1693 RYMER *Short View Trag.* 11 Xerxes went also in person, with all the Maison de Roy, Satrapie and Gendarmery.

4. The period of rule of a satrap.

1846 GROTE *Greece* I. xv. I. 454 A century afterwards, during the satrapy of Pharnabazus.

satringee, satrungee, varr. SITRINGEE.

satropar, variant of SATRAPER.

satsang (sætˈsæŋ). *Indian Philos.* Also **Satsang.** [ad. Skr. *satsaṅga* association with good men, f. *sat* good man + *saṅga* association.] A spiritual discourse, a sacred gathering.

1929 J. N. FARQUHAR *Mod. Relig. Movements in India* iii. 171 As in Theosophy, you may be a Rādhā Soāmi and yet remain a Hindu, a Muḥammadan or a Christian... Yet it is definitely stated that the religion is for all, and that outside the Satsaṅg there is no salvation. **1971** *Shankar's Weekly* (Delhi) 4 Apr. 5/4 Local communists had been watching with uneasiness at this priest's continual attendance at kirtans and satsangs and were even of the mind that he should be denounced as a CIA spy. **1972** *Times* 23 Oct. 12/1 There [in Delhi] they will sit at the boy's feet, listen to his spiritual discourses (*satsangs*) or just enjoy his physical presence. **1977** *New Society* 30 June 672/3 The 'satsangs' (spiritual discourses) given at the recent Wembley festival.

Satsuma (ˈsætsjʊmə, now (esp. in sense 2) freq. sætˈsuːmə). Also **Satzuma.** [The name of a province in the island of Kiusiu, Japan.]

1. Used *attrib.* in ***Satsuma ware***, a kind of cream-coloured Japanese pottery. Also *absol.*

1872 CHAFFERS *Keramic Gallery* I. Pl. 99 Satsuma-Ware Bottle... Satsuma Bowl. **1875** AUDSLEY & BOWES *Keramic Art Japan* II. Pl. xi, Three vases of middle period Satsuma faïence..good representatives of a style of decoration but seldom met with in Satsuma ware. **1880** T. W. CUTLER *Grammar Jap. Ornament* 16 Modern Satsuma is largely decorated at Tokio and elsewhere. **1909** M. DIVER *Candles in Wind* ix. 86 Roses..filling every available bowl, even the sacred Satzuma. **1974** SAVAGE & NEWMAN *Illustr. Dict. Ceramics* 255 True Satsuma is comparatively rare outside Japan.

2. (Freq. with lower-case initial.) A small tangerine belonging to a variety of *Citrus reticulata* so called; also, the variety itself. Also *attrib.* as ***Satsuma orange***.

1882 E. S. HART in *Proc. 18th Session Amer. Pomological Soc. 1881* 67/1 One [variety of tangerine] from Japan called Satsuma, bore a temperature of 16°. **1905** *Flora & Sylva* III. 66/1 Satsuma, an early fruiting Mandarine. **1909** *Circular Bureau Plant Industry U.S. Dept. Agric.* XLVI (*title*) The limitation of the Satsuma orange to trifoliate-orange stock. **1922** [see MIKAN]. **1926** H. H. HUME *Cultivation of Citrus Fruits* xxix. 477 Satsuma oranges are susceptible to the disease. **1943** WEBBER & BATCHELOR *Citrus Industry* I. v. 551 The Satsuma was first introduced into the United States in 1876 by Dr. George R. Hall... It is characteristic of Satsuma fruits that although they mature and fill with juice ..the rind frequently remains green or shows only slightly colored. **1967** [see CLEMENTINE]. **1980** 'M. YORKE' *Scent of Fear* vii. 64 She bought..some tangerines—or satsumas, as they were called nowadays.

satt(e, obs. forms of pa. t. of SIT *v.*

sattan, sattee: see SATIN, SETTEE (ship).

satteine, -eing, -en(e: obs. ff. SATIN.

Satterdaie, -day, obs. ff. SATURDAY.

satti, sattie: see SUTTEE, SETTEE (ship).

sattil, obs. form of SETTLE *v.*

sattin(e, satton, obs. forms of SATIN.

sattle, satty(e, obs. ff. SETTLE, SETTEE (ship).

sattrangee, var. SITRINGEE

sat-upon (ˈsætəpɒn), *ppl. a. colloq.* [See SIT *v.* 26 d.] Downtrodden, humiliated, 'squashed'.

1892 *Times* 30 July 8/2 In his concession, where he is an apologetic and much sat-upon importation, the foreign resident does no harm. **1893** *Chambers's Jrnl.* 25 Feb. 128 With that sat-upon sort of man..you never know where he may break out.

satur, obs. form of SALTIRE.

a **1440** *Sir. Degrev.* 1030 He beres in cheef of azour, Engrelyd with a satur.

saturable (ˈsætjʊərəb(ə)l), *a.* [ad. L. *saturābilis*, f. *saturāre* to SATURATE: see -BLE.] **a.** Capable of saturation.

1570 LEVINS *Manip.* 4/14 Saturable, *saturabilis.* **1701** GREW *Cosm. Sacra* I. iii. 13 Consequently the Water would be Saturable with the same Quantity of any Salt. **1966** *Electronics* 31 Oct. 44 The transmittance of the saturable absorber increases with the light flux. **1979** *Nature* 19 Apr. 748/2 A stereospecific, saturable, high affinity binding site for ^{3}H-diazepam has recently been characterised in membrane fractions isolated from the brains of mammals.

b. Of magnetic systems: capable of retaining a saturating magnetic field (see SATURATE *v.* 4 b). ***saturable reactor***: an iron-cored coil whose impedance to alternating current can be varied by varying the direct current in an auxiliary winding so as to change the degree of magnetization of the core.

1944 W. D. COCKRELL *Industr. Electronic Control* x. 84 Another device by means of which we make deliberate use of the saturating effect for loads both large and small is the saturable reactor. **1956** [see *ferro-resonance* s.v. FERRO- 1 c]. **1962** F. I. ORDWAY et al. *Basic Astronautics* v. 187 The flux gate magnetometer..consists essentially of a flux gate of two, identical, high-permeability, saturable coils, oppositely wound with identical coils. **1966** *McGraw-Hill Encycl. Sci. & Technol.* XII. 37/1 Saturable-core reactors are used to control large alternating currents where rheostats are impractical. Theater light dimmers often employ saturable reactors. **1975** D. G. FINK *Electronics Engineers' Handbk.* XIII. 82 The response time of saturable reactors is the combination of the time constants of the control circuit and of the gate-winding circuit.

Hence **saturaˈbility.**

a **1909** In some recent Dicts. **1979** *Nature* 19 Apr. 747/2 If the direct linkage EGF-receptor complex is a complex of EGF and its physiological receptor, the saturability for reversible EGF binding and direct complex formation should be similar.

saturant (ˈsætjʊərənt), *a.* and *sb.* [ad. L. *saturantem*, pr. pple. of *saturāre* to SATURATE.]

A. *adj.* Saturating; impregnating to the full.

1755 in JOHNSON; and in later Dicts.

B. *sb.* = ABSORBENT *sb.* 1.

1775 in ASH; and in later Dicts.

saturate (ˈsætjʊrət), *a.* [ad. L. *saturātus*, pa. pple. of *saturāre*: see next.]

†**1.** Satisfied, satiated.

? *a* **1550** *Schole-ho. Women* 946 in Hazl. *E.P.P.* IV. 142 Salomon saith, three things here be Seldome or neuer saturate. **1557** PAYNELL *Barclay's Jugurth* 79 Whan they were full saturate and ingorged. **1604** R. CAWDREY *Table Alph.*, *Saturate*, filled or glutted.

†**2.** Complete, perfect. *Obs.*

1682 H. MORE *Annot. Glanvill's Lux O.* 112 All will be turned into a more full and saturate Brightness and Glory.

3. Soaked through, saturated with moisture. Chiefly *poet.*

1784 COWPER *Task* I. 494 The lark is gay, That dries his feathers, saturate with dew, Beneath the rosy cloud. **1798** SOUTHEY *Sonn.* xiii. '*I marvel not, O Sun!*' Earth asks thy presence, saturate with showers. **1842** TENNYSON *Will Waterpr.* 87 A season'd brain..Unsubject to confusion, Tho' soaked and saturate, out and out, Thro' every convolution.

b. *transf.*

1868 BROWNING *Ring & Bk.* VI. 1518 There she lay,.. Wax-white, seraphic, saturate with the sun O' the morning. **1894** *Athenæum* 3 Mar. 285/1 'Calais Pier', a silvery and limpid jewel, saturate with light, by D. Cox.

4. Of colours: Intense, deep. (Cf. SATURATED 5, SAD *a.* 8.)

1669 W. SIMPSON *Hydrol. Chym.* 121 It would yield a deep saturate green tincture. **1684** tr. *Bonet's Merc. Compit.* XIX. 807 The quickness of cooling makes the Blood of a more saturate colour. **1891** *Century Dict.*, *Saturate*, in *Entom.*, deep; very intense: applied to colors: as, saturate green, umber, black, etc.

†**5.** *Chem.* = SATURATED.

1782 KIRWAN in *Phil. Trans.* LXXIII. 70 If a piece of copper be put into a saturate solution of silver, the silver will be precipitated. **1805** R. CHENEVIX *ibid.* XCV. 126 A single drop of a saturate solution of neutralized nitrate or muriate of mercury.

saturate (ˈsætjʊəreɪt), *v.* [f. L. *saturāt-*, ppl. stem of *saturāre*, f. *satur* full, satiated, cogn. w. *satis* enough.]

I. †**1.** *trans.* To satisfy, satiate. *Obs.*

1538 ELYOT *Dict.*, *Saturo*, to saturate or fyl with any thing superfluousely, moste commonly in eating. **1570** LEVINS *Manip.* 41/12 To satiate, *saturare.* To saturate, *idem, placare.* **1596** BELL *Surv. Popery* II. I. iv. 153 So to saturate their insatiable hunger. **1683** *Lond. Gaz.* No. 1864/2 Cruel Persons whose Blood-thirsty minds nothing could Saturate, but the Sacrifice of two Princes at once. **1799** in *Spirit Publ. Jrnls.* III. 271 These subaltern modes of chicane..could by no means saturate his ambition. **1816** KIRBY & SP. *Entomol.* (1818) I. viii. 229 They [*sc.* ants] march in long files..to any place where sugar is kept; and when they are saturated, return in the same order.

2. To impregnate, soak thoroughly, imbue *with.*

1764 HARMER *Observ.* iii. 8 These lands of Ægypt..are.. so saturated with moisture, that [etc.]. **1873** BLACK *Pr. Thule* xiv, Thatch that had got saturated with the smoke. **1891** E. PEACOCK *N. Brendon* I. 151 The sleeve of the shirt was saturated with blood.

b. *fig.*

1756 BURKE *Tracts Popery Laws* Wks. IX. 369 To a mind not thoroughly saturated with the tolerating maxims of the Gospel. **1837** LYTTON *E. Maltravers* II. ii, He had saturated his intellect with the Pactolus of old. **1882** A. AUSTIN in *Comtemp. Rev.* Jan. 129 Reflective Poetry, which is indeed Poetry because saturated with imagination.

c. *Mil.* To overwhelm (enemy defences) by aerial attack, esp. by intensive bombing.

1942 *Times* 1 June 4/3 The plan for saturating the defences of Cologne was an undoubted success. **1943** *Times* 12 Mar. 8/4 Air Marshal Sir Arthur Harris and his commanders and staffs have displayed extraordinary fertility in tactical ideas. The monster raids saturating the enemy's active and passive systems of defence is one example. **1944** *Ann. Reg. 1943* I. 74 The ultimate possibility of saturating the enemy's defences both on the ground and in the air. **1956** A. H. COMPTON *Atomic Quest* 228 The areas attacked were saturated with bombs.

d. To supply (a market) to the point of over-satisfaction of demand for a product.

1958 *Engineering* 4 Apr. 435/1 The Swiss vehicle market, if not saturated, seems to be reaching a certain stabilisation of demand. **1976** 'G. BLACK' *Moon for Killers* i. 18 The market was saturated, and Robert bought two thousand of them at a throw-away price. **1978** *Times Lit. Suppl.* 27 Jan. 84/5 *Man watching* will saturate the market and maintain its well-deserved primacy.

3. a. *Chem.* To cause (a substance) to combine with or dissolve the utmost possible quantity of another substance. Const. *with.* Also, to cause to become saturated (see SATURATED *ppl. a.* 3 b).

1681 tr. *Belon's Myst. Physick* Introd. 49 Which clearly demonstrates, that the Menstruum is sufficiently saturated. **1782** KIRWAN in *Phil. Trans.* LXXIII. 39 A body is said to be saturated with another, when it is so intimately combined with that other as to lose some peculiar characteristic property which it possesses when free from that other. **1788** *Trans. Soc. Arts* VI. 143 The mineral Alkali saturates much more acid than an equal quantity of..vegetable Alkali. **1857** MILLER *Elem. Chem.* (1862) III. 9 This process consists in saturating a portion of the acid liquid with potash or with soda. **1866** *Notices Proc. R. Inst. Gt. Brit.* IV. 419 This new molecule—we call it hypochlorous acid—we open again: again two attraction units are liberated and saturated by a second atom of bivalent oxygen. **1878** Huxley *Physiogr.* 217 The waters covering this plain would be more or less completely saturated with the soluble materials. **1926** H. G. Rule tr. *J. Schmidt's Text-bk. Org. Chem.* 26 Thiele assumes that all such unsaturated compounds possess a double bond, but that the two affinities do not completely saturate one another, leaving a certain residual affinity or partial valency in excess on each carbon atom. **1972** *Materials & Technol.* V. x. 282 Such isomers may arise from the addition of hydrogen at a double bond which is normally not saturated by natural processes. **1977** *Lancet* 20 Aug. 401/1 Many dietitians tell patients not to re-use the oil more than once because reheating is thought to saturate the double bonds.

b. *Physiol.* To cause (tissues of the body) to retain the greatest amount of inert gas possible at the given pressure during a saturation dive.

1965 *Jrnl. Appl. Physiol.* XX 1269/2 The decompression schedule after and while breathing helium takes longer than with nitrogen because the helium saturates a greater proportion of the body tissues. **1971** J. Salzano et al. in C. J. Lambertsen *Underwater Physiol.* 347 (*heading*) Arterial blood gases, heart rate, and gas exchange during rest and exercise in men saturated at a simulated seawater depth of 1000 feet. **1974** *Encycl. Brit. Macropædia* X. 926/1 For any given depth,..there is a saturation point, at which body tissues are saturated with inert gas; after that, no matter how long a worker stays under pressure his decompression time does not increase.

4. *Physics.* **a.** To charge (air or vapour) with the utmost quantity of moisture that it can hold in suspension.

1812–16 Playfair *Nat. Phil.* (1819) I. 315 T and *t* are the temperatures of two equal portions of air, H and *h* the humidity contained in them when saturated. **1860** Tyndall *Glac.* I. xxv. 184 Atmospheric regions already saturated with moisture. **1871** —— *Fragm. Sci.* (1879) I. ii. 62 Saturated with the vapour of sulphuric aether. **1878** Huxley *Physiogr.* 68 If the air were thoroughly saturated with moisture, evaporation would be utterly impossible.

b. To magnetize (a piece of metal), that the intensity of its magnetization is the greatest which it can retain when not under the inductive action of a strong magnetic field. Also, to charge (a body) with the greatest charge of electricity that it can receive.

1832 *Nat. Philos.* II. *Magnetism* i. §42. 11 (Usef. Knowl. Soc.) A steel bar, which has as great a degree of magnetic power as it is capable of retaining, is said to be saturated with magnetism. *Ibid., Electric.* ii. §49. 13 In this state they may be considered as saturated with the electric fluid. **1891** S. P. Thompson *Electromagnet* iv. 151 The iron is..more saturated round the edge than at the middle... If the edge is already far saturated you cannot by applying higher magnetizing power increase its magnetization much. **1928** [see sense 6 below]. **1962** R. D. Pettit in G. A. T. Burdett *Automatic Control Handbk.* v. 18 The core flux is initially saturated negatively.

5. *Electronics. trans.* To cause or maintain a state of saturation in (a device or a current); *pass.*, to be in a state of saturation. Cf. saturation 3 d, f.

1919 J. A. Crowther *Ions, Electrons, & Ionizing Radiations* ii. 17 The effects when the current is not saturated are in general very complex. **1956** J. C. Logue in L. P. Hunter *Handbk. Semiconductor Electronics* xv. 30 It is possible to have a high degree of saturation or just barely to saturate the transistor. **1962** Simpson & Richards *Physical Princ. Junction Transistors* xvi. 388 The base current chosen must be sufficient to saturate the transistor. **1969** J. J. Sparkes *Transistor Switching* i. 18 This equation applies only when the transistor is saturated. **1976** Millman & Halkias *Electronic Fund. & Appl.* iv. 81 A knowledge of h_{FE} tells us the minimum base current..which will be needed to saturate the transistor.

II. 6. *intr.* To reach or exhibit a condition of saturation, in any sense; to reach a state in which no further change or increase is possible.

1928 *Observer* 17 June 26/3 The essential thing is the current that can be carried without any danger of saturating the core... If the core saturates there will at once be a falling-off in the quality of reception. **1947** F. G. Spreadbury *Electronics* iv. 184 The thermionic current does not truly saturate, but continues to increase slowly. **1953** *Physical Rev.* XCI. 632/2 As the rf level is increased, the peak amplitudes labeled M_1 and M_2 in Fig. 2 saturate quite readily. **1957** R. D. Middlebrook *Introd. Junction Transistor Theory* ii. 28 The hole flow very soon reaches a limit as the potential is increased. This occurs when all the available holes are being drawn out of the *p*-region. The electron current saturates in a similar way. **1962** R. D. Pettit in G. A. T. Burdett *Automatic Control Handbk.* v. 21 When the flux in element A saturates, that in element B is unsaturated. **1969** J. J. Sparkes *Transistor Switching* iii. 74 The circuit can be designed so that the output transistor saturates. **1975** *Nature* 6 Nov. 85/1 Figure 1 shows that the steady-state amplitude saturates at a relatively low stimulus level. **1976** [see saturation 3 a]. **1977** *Nature* 21 Apr. 709/1 This ratio tends to saturate for crystallite sizes less than 40 Å.

saturate (ˈsætjʊrət), *sb. Chem.* [f. the vb.] A saturated fat or fatty acid.

1959 R. H. Potts in E. S. Pattison *Industr. Fatty Acids* ii. 13 In selecting a raw material, one always considers that more saturates can be made if required, but the unsaturated requirements must be purchased with the raw material. **1977** *Nature* 3 Nov. 2/2 Pursuit of the lipid hypothesis does not mean just swapping polyunsaturates for saturates.

saturated (ˈsætjʊəreɪtɪd), *ppl. a.* [f. saturate *v.* + -ed[1].]

†**1.** Completely satisfied, filled to repletion. *Obs.*

1668 H. More *Div. Dial.* I. 213 Therefore it is fit that, as well-saturated Guests, we should at length willingly recede from the Table. **1820** C. R. Maturin *Melmoth* (1892) III. xxviii. 119 Sleep which is as often the refuge of intolerable misery, as of that of saturated enjoyment.

2. a. Penetrated with moisture, soaked through.

1728–46 Thomson *Spring* 217 And saturated earth Awaits the morning beam. **1784** Cowper *Task* III. 479 Shaking.. From the full fork, the saturated straw. **1840** Dickens *Barn. Rudge* xvii, His saturated clothes clinging with a damp embrace about his limbs. **1897** Mary Kingsley *W. Africa* 502, I arrived in the evening in a saturated condition.

b. *transf.* Filled to capacity; *spec.* in *Econ.*, of a market in which demand is completely satisfied.

1962 S. Strand *Marketing Dict.* 653 *Saturated market*, the ultimate point of absorption of a product or service within a territory. Now limited to parts replacement. **1965** *Monthly Economic Let.* (First National City Bank, N.Y.) Apr., Household durables with 'highly saturated markets'—those which the vast majority of families already have, such as refrigerators or black-and-white television sets—achieved sales gains through growing replacement demand.

3. *Chem.* **a.** That has combined with or taken up in solution the largest possible proportion of some other substance. In mod. use, applied to solutions containing as much solute as is possible in equilibrium conditions (in contrast to those that are supersaturated).

1788 Blagden in *Phil. Trans.* LXXVIII. 299, I took a saturated solution of nitre. **1799** *Med. Jrnl.* I. 290 The preparation of the digitalis best adapted to that purpose, appeared to be the saturated tincture, of which [etc.]. **1867** Bloxam *Chem.* 47 Such a solution would be called a *cold saturated solution* of saltpetre. **1939** *Thorpe's Dict. Appl. Chem.* (ed. 4) III. 452/2 Removal of solvent from a saturated solution at this point results in the solution becoming supersaturated. **1978** P. W. Atkins *Physical Chem.* viii. 220 If a lump of solid is left in contact with a solvent it will dissolve until the solvent has become saturated. The saturated solution corresponds to the case in which the chemical potential of the pure solid is equal to the chemical potential of the solute in the saturated solution.

b. Orig., applied to compounds which contained the greatest possible proportion of some element, and to (the chemical 'affinities' of) atoms, radicals, etc., which had entered into chemical combination to the maximum extent. Now applied to organic compounds, molecules, groups, etc., which have structures containing the greatest possible numbers of hydrogen atoms, and hence have no multiple bonds between carbon atoms; occas. applied also to carbon atoms in such structures.

1866 *Notices Proc. R. Inst. Gt. Brit.* IV. 429 We have thus been led..to a distinction of a novel kind, that of finished and unfinished molecules; or, to use the more frequently employed expression, that of saturated and non-saturated compounds. **1876** *Phil. Mag.* II. 167 The group OH is related in one case to a carbon atom a large number of whose affinities are already 'saturated' (to use a common term). **1888** Brannt *Anim. & Veg. Fats & Oils* 48 These hydrocarbons cannot absorb any further atoms of hydrogen, and are therefore termed 'saturated hydrocarbons'. **1935** A. K. Anderson *Essent. Physiol. Chem.* iv. 67 Chemically, fats differ from oils in that fats contain saturated fatty acids whereas oils contain rather large quantities of unsaturated fatty acids. **1949** *Thorpe's Dict. Appl. Chem.* (ed. 4) IX. 6/2 In the higher land-animals the most abundant component acids are always the monoethenoid oleic and the saturated palmitic acid. **1961** [see polyunsaturated *a.*]. **1968** Murthy & Nathan *Org. Chem. made Simple* vii. 122 A saturated carbon atom may be represented by a model showing only the tetrahedrally directed linkages. **1971** *Jrnl. Gen. Psychol.* LXXXV. 155 Increasing the amount of saturated fat..resulted in a similar increase in the excitatory process. **1976** *Sci. Amer.* Mar. 35/2 Such multiple-ring, or polycyclic, compounds are said to be saturated if all the bonds of the carbon atoms, beyond the minimum needed for carbon–carbon bonding, are linked to hydrogen atoms.

c. *Min.* and *Petrol.* Of a mineral (see quot. 1913). Of a rock: containing neither free quartz (or some other specified oxide) nor any undersaturated minerals.

1913 S. J. Shand in *Geol. Mag.* Decade V. X. 508 Of the various minerals which enter into the composition of igneous rocks, about one-half are capable of forming in presence of free silica... These may..be termed saturated minerals. *Ibid.* 510 A rock which contains only saturated minerals may be termed a saturated rock. **1947** [see oversaturated *ppl. a.*]. **1951** Turner & Verhoogen *Igneous & Metamorphic Petrol.* iii. 54 Saturated minerals are those which are compatible with excess silica under magmatic conditions, and are therefore commonly associated with quartz. **1968** B. Bayly *Introd. Petrol.* vi. 53 All saturated rocks fall within the shaded area in Fig. 6·1. The commonest such rocks are made of feldspar with pyroxene or amphibole.

4. a. *Physics.* Charged to the full extent of its capacity. (See saturate *v.* 4 a, b.) ***saturated steam***: see quot. 1881.

1848 tr. *Regnault* in *Chem. Rep. & Mem.* (Cavendish Soc.) 296 Temperature of the Saturated Steam. **1858** Lardner *Hand-bk. Nat. Phil.* 316 Quantity of vapour in saturated space depends on temperature. **1880** C. R. Markham *Peruv. Bark* II. ix. 388 Its rains are therefore heavy, and are accompanied by dense fogs and a saturated atmosphere. **1881** J. Hill in *Metal World* No. 22. 342 Saturated steam (that is, steam charged with such an amount of heat that any reduction thereof would produce condensation, and any increase thereof would produce super heat) is substantially a perfect gas. **1883** W. N. Shaw in *Trans. Cambr. Philos. Soc.* XIV. 39 The saturated air was then sent through all four tubes, and the gain in weight of each tube determined.

b. *Electronics.* Characterized by or exhibiting saturation (senses 3 d, f); of or pertaining to a device in such a state.

1896 *Phil. Mag.* XLII. 394 For a given intensity of radiation the current through the gas does not exceed a certain maximum value whatever the electromotive force may be, the current gets, as it were, 'saturated'. **1899** *Ibid.* XLVII. 160 The gas tends to become more readily saturated with diminution of pressure. **1933** *Proc. IRE* XXI. 1667 The practical limitation of this 'saw-tooth' generator lies in the fact that there is no such thing as a completely saturated thermionic tube. **1956** J. C. Logue in L. P. Hunter *Handbk. of Semiconductor Electronics* xv. 11 It is necessary to impose an upper limit on r_c in the saturated region. This is to ensure that the voltage drop between the emitter and collector terminals is small when the transistor is in a saturated state. **1967** *Electronics* 6 Mar. 122/2 They permit a whole spectrum of products with the highest speed possible with saturated logic. **1977** Taub & Schilling *Digital Integrated Electronics* i. 18 When a base current I_B is supplied, the transistor is able to furnish a current $I_C = h_{FE}I_B$. If the current I_C is actually less than $h_{FE}I_B$, the transistor is said to be in saturation. However, such is the case because of the constraint imposed by the circuit and not by the transistor. Hence, strictly, we should speak of a saturated circuit and not a saturated transistor.

c. ***saturated diving*** = *saturation diving* s.v. saturation 5.

1968 *New Scientist* 17 Oct. 125/2 The important element in saturated diving is that after six days or six months of exposure to a given depth or pressure, the diver requires a single, fixed decompression period. **1971** *Petroleum Rev.* July 248/1 Saturated diving requires a considerable increase in equipment sophistication and diver training.

5. Of colours: Free from admixture of white. (Cf. saturate *a.* 4, saturation 4.)

1853 Herschel *Pop. Lect. Sci.* vi. §41 (1873) 257 The green being by no means a saturated or full green. **1878** [see saturation 4]. **1901** *Athenæum* 31 Aug. 293/2 In the figures grouped round the table rich and saturated tones predominate.

saturating (ˈsætjʊəreɪtɪŋ), *vbl. sb.* [-ing[1].] The action of the vb. saturate. In quots. *attrib.*

1850 Daubeny *Atom. Theory* vii. (ed. 2) 193 Yet there is no fundamental difference between the two acids, and their saturating power is exactly the same. **1857** Miller *Elem. Chem.* (1862) III. 168 The sulphuric acid thus combined with the elements of alcohol, loses half its saturating power.

saturating (ˈsætjʊəreɪtɪŋ), *ppl. a.* [f. saturate *v.* + -ing[2].] In senses of the vb.

1760–72 H. Brooke *Fool of Qual.* (1792) I. 182 After a saturating meal, and an enlivening cup, they departed. **1860** Emerson *Cond. Life, Behaviour* Wks. (Bohn) II. 381 The persevering talker, who gives you his society in large saturating doses. **1862** Dana *Man. Geol.* §52. 50 Aluminium combines with a saturating quantity of oxygen to form alumina. **1897** Mary Kingsley *W. Africa* 44 An over supply of rain, and equally saturating mists.

saturation (sætjʊəˈreɪʃən). [ad. late L. *saturātiōn-em*, n. of action f. L. *saturāre* to saturate. Cf. F. *saturation.*] The action of saturating; the condition of being saturated.

†**1.** Complete satisfaction of appetite; satiation.

?**1554** Coverdale *Hope Faithful* xxxi. 212 For tediousnesse and grefe runneth customably wyth saturacion or fulnesse. **1816–30** Bentham *Offic. Apt. Maximized, Extract Const. Code* (1830) 16 For the perpetual saturation of appetites essentially unsaturable. **1831** Carlyle *Sart. Res.* II. ix, The Shoeblack..would require..for his permanent satisfaction and saturation, simply this allotment, no more, and no less. **1831** Syd. Smith *Wks.* (1850) 565 The advocates of Boroughmongers must be crammed to saturation, before there is a morsel of bread for the man who does not sell his votes. **1832** L. Hunt *Transl.* Poet. Wks. 243 When I have eat and drank—yea, ev'n to saturation.

2. The action of thoroughly soaking with fluid; the condition of being thoroughly soaked.

1846 J. Baxter *Libr. Pract. Agric.* (ed. 4) II. 358 That the saturation of any vegetable fibre or compost with liquid manure or urine is of great use to the crop. **1882** Vines tr. *Sach's Bot.* 814 In one case the amount of water present in the soil was 10 per cent...of the amount requisite for complete saturation. **1897** Mary Kingsley *W. Africa* 555, I am wet through, but it is not uncomfortable at this temperature,..if you can..forget the risk of fever which saturation entails.

3. a. The action of charging, or the state of being charged, up to the limit of capacity; *spec.* in *Chem.* the condition of a substance when combined with or holding in solution the largest proportion of another substance that it can take (cf. unsaturation.); in *Physics*, the condition of holding as much suspended matter, or of being as highly charged with electricity, heat, etc. as possible. (See saturate *v.*) ***point of saturation***: the degree of charge at which a substance becomes saturated. More widely in *Physics*, a condition or phenomenon in which a quantity (usu. the value of some property) no longer increases in response to an increase in the magnitude of some external influence, or ceases to alter in the usual way; *spec.* in *Spectroscopy* (see quot. 1976). See also senses 3 c, d, f following.

1659 H. More *Immort. Soul* I. ii. 13 To both these may be applied the termes of Reduplication and Saturation. **1673** *Phil. Trans.* VIII. 5190 And this injection of calcin'd Tartar must be continued, untill all Fermentation do cease, that is, to the very degree of Saturation. **1758** Reid tr. *Macquer's Chym.* I. 20 The instant when such proportions of the two saline substances are mixed together, that the one is incorporated with as much of the other as it can possibly take up, is called the *Point of Saturation.* **1799** Sir H. Davy in Beddoes *Contrib. Phys. & Med. Knowl.* 34 Since the word gas..is intended to express the chemical combination or rather the saturation of bodies with caloric. **1807** T. Thomson *Chem.* (ed. 3) II. 99 This augmentation varies with the quantity of salt dissolved. In general, it is the greater the nearer the solution approaches to saturation. **1848** tr. *Regnault* in *Chem. Rep. & Mem.* (Cavendish Soc.) 293 The law regulating the densities of aqueous vapour in a state of saturation or non-saturation, at different pressures and different temperatures. **1857** Miller *Elem. Chem.* (1862) III. 231 It then produces a base..which requires two atoms of a monobasic acid for its saturation. **1860** Tyndall *Glac.* I. xxiv. 174 An atmosphere charged to saturation with aqueous vapour. **1866** *Notices Proc. R. Inst. Gt. Brit.* IV. 422 The saturation of these two units [of attraction] by the trivalent nitrogen atom. **1882** Geikie *Text Bk. Geol.* III. II. ii. §1. 328 This vapour remains invisible until the air containing it is cooled down below its dew-point, or point of saturation. **1902** J. B. Cohen *Theoret. Org. Chem.* xvii. 240 The saturation of one unsaturated carbon atom necessitates that of the other. **1948** *Physical Rev.* LXXIII. 683/1 As H_1 is increased, the thermal contact between spin system and lattice eventually proves unable to cope with the energy absorbed by the spin system, the spin temperature rises, and the relative absorption..diminishes. It is the onset of this saturation effect which has been used to measure the spin-lattice relaxation time. **1953** *Ibid.* XCI. 206/2 From the saturation of the absorption and a measurement of the rf field, a spin-lattice relaxation time of approximately one millisecond is calculated. **1959** G. Troup *Masers* iii. 37 If the energy density of radiation falling on an assembly of molecules having an excess upper state population is increased, there comes a time when the energy of induced emission is no longer linearly dependent on the incident radiation energy density. This phenomenon is known as saturation. **1961** G. R. Choppin *Exper. Nuclear Chem.* v. 62 The higher the atomic number of the scattering material, the larger is f_b [back-scattering factor]. Also, f_b increases with thickness up to a saturation thickness beyond which it is a constant. **1964** N. G. Clark *Mod. Org. Chem.* vi. 89 By partial saturation of this triple bond with hydrogen, an olefin is produced. **1968** A. A. Baker *Unsaturation in Org. Chem.* vi. 71 His formulas..illustrate the progressive saturation of a diatomic carbon molecule to acetylene, to ethylene, and to completely saturated ethane. **1972** McFarlane & White *Techniques of High Resolution N.M.R. Spectroscopy* v. 55 The gross observable effects of saturation are a general broadening of the spectrum with associated loss of peak height and resolution. **1976** D. Shaw *Fourier Transform N.M.R. Spectroscopy* ii. 20 Saturation is the equalisation of the population in the ground and the excited state which occurs because relaxation from the excited state is slow and with a strong exciting field a dynamic equilibrium can be set up. In this equilibrium the number of nuclei in the upper and lower states become [*sic*] equal, and the signal saturates, or disappears.

b. *transf.* and *fig.*

1820 T. G. Wainewright *Ess. & Crit.* (1880) 55 Corregio's mind must have been full to saturation, of the honey-dew of Christianity, when he gave birth to this mysterious conception. **1848** H. Miller *First Impr.* viii. (1857) 128 A long series of historic events had served..to fill with it to saturation every recess of the popular mind. **1859** Smiles *Self-Help* x. (1860) 265 Abernethy was of opinion that there was a point of saturation in his own mind, and that if he took into it something more than it could hold, it only had the effect of pushing something else out.

c. *Magnetism.* The condition of being as strongly magnetized as possible, or so strongly magnetized that an increase in magnetizing force produces no appreciable increase in magnetization.

1837 Brewster *Magnet.* 134 It was magnetized to saturation. **1864** *Chamb. Encycl.* VI. 262/2 Magnets, when freshly magnetised, are sometimes more powerful than they afterwards become. In that case, they gradually fall off in strength, till they reach a point at which their strength remains constant. This is called the *point of saturation.* **1920** *Whittaker's Electr. Engineer's Pocket-bk.* (ed. 4) 144 In addition to the limitations imposed by saturation, the parts of the magnetic circuit where the flux is continually changing in value are further restricted by losses due to eddy-currents and hysteresis. **1962** *Newnes Conc. Encycl. Electr. Engin.* 463/2 The coercivity is the magnetizing force necessary to remove the magnetism completely from a specimen which has been magnetized to saturation. **1974** *Encycl. Brit. Macropædia* XI. 333/2 It was suggested in 1907 that a ferromagnetic material is composed of a large number of small volumes called domains, each of which is magnetized to saturation.

d. *Electronics.* The condition in which increase in the potential difference between two electrodes in a gas-filled or evacuated vessel leads to no increase in the current flowing between them, owing to the limitations of the gas as a current-carrier or the electrode as an electron-emitter.

1896 *Phil. Mag.* XLII. 394 It is evident that this saturation must occur if the current destroys the conducting power of the gas. **1899** *Ibid.* XLVII. 158 The great difficulty in producing complete saturation, i.e. to reach a stage when all the ions produced reach the electrodes, may be due to one or more of three causes. **1947** R. Lee *Electronic Transformers & Circuits* v. 116 In plate-modulated class C amplifiers, sufficient excitation must be applied so that grid saturation still obtains at 100 per cent modulation; otherwise output would not be proportional to plate voltage. **1962** D. F. Shaw *Introd. Electronics* x. 192 Other cathode materials, such as metallic oxides, do not exhibit full saturation.

e. *Psychol.* A term used in mental testing based on the theory of two-factor analysis put forward by C. S. Spearman (1863–1945) for the degree to which the general factor (*g*) saturates the specific factor or ability in question; also *attrib.*

1904 C. S. Spearman in *Amer. Jrnl. Psychol.* XV. 276 Intellective saturation, or extent to which the considered faculty is functionally identical with General Intelligence. *Ibid.* 277 Mathematics, for example, has a saturation of 74 and Common Sense has one of about 96. **1927** *Psychol. Bull.* XXIV. 392 Slocombe..applies the intellective saturation formula of Spearman to nine group tests. **1940** C. L. Burt *Factors of Mind* xii. 299 Let us suppose that both the variances for the different factors and the saturation coefficients for the different tests are everywhere equal. **1951** R. H. Thouless *Gen. & Social Psychol.* (ed. 3) xxiii. 367 This degree of dependence on the general factor was called by Spearman the saturation with *g* of the ability in question; the term more commonly used at the present time is the general factor loading.

f. *Electronics.* The state of operation of a transistor in which the collector current becomes independent of the base voltage, arising when the base-collector junction becomes forward-biased.

1956 J. C. Logue in L. P. Hunter *Handbk. of Semiconductor Electronics* xv. 48 In pulse-type computer systems, the length of time that the transistor is driven into saturation is controllable. **1962** Simpson & Richards *Physical Princ. Junction Transistors* xvi. 389 'External' control causes the 'on' position to be largely independent of transistor parameters..and makes heavy base overdrive possible without danger of saturation. **1975** D. G. Fink *Electronics Engineers' Handbk.* xvi. 13 When the collector current I_C reaches its maximum possible value.., saturation occurs and the collector junction becomes forward-biased.

g. The retention by the blood of the greatest amount of inert gas possible under the given pressure, as during a saturation dive (see sense 5 below); also *transf.*, a saturation dive.

1971 J. K. Summitt et al. in C. J. Lambertsen *Underwater Physiol.* 519 A study of five trained men during compression to a simulated depth of 1000 FSW, during subsequent saturation at this pressure for 77 hr and 30 min, and during decompression. **1974** *Encycl. Brit. Macropædia* X. 926/1 Reasonably safe and efficient decompression from saturation at depths up to 600 feet..can be accomplished by a decompression at the rate of 15 minutes per foot.., or about 100 feet..per day. **1975** *BP Shield Internat.* May 5/1 In excess of 14,000 diver man hours were spent in saturation without a single decompression problem or lost time accident. **1975** *Offshore Engineer* Dec. 7/2 A 17-day saturation involving six divers at depths of up to 260m carried out by Strongwork Diving (International) has given a British company a new record.

4. a. *Chromatics.* Degree of intensity (of a colour); relative freedom from admixture of white. Cf. hue *sb.*[1] 3 c.

1878 *Encycl. Brit.* VIII. 824/1 Saturation, which depends on the amount of white the colour contains; thus, it is saturated when there is no white, as in the pure colours of the spectrum, and there may be an infinite number of degrees of saturation from the pure colour to white. **1879** Rood *Mod. Chromatics* iii. 39 Purity and luminosity are the factors on which the intensity or saturation depends. **1966** [see hue *sb.*[1] 3 c]. **1967** E. Short *Embroidery & Fabric Collage* i. 12 The hues are all used at their full strength or saturation, i.e. they are not diluted in any way by black or white. **1970** *Nature* 19 Sept. 1183/1 Discrimination tests revealed that sorters identified stamps most easily if seven colours were used each at two distinct levels of saturation, for example, dark blue and light blue, dark green and light green. **1978** *Sci. Amer.* Mar. 87/3 The color pictures were generated by first determining the spectral irradiance of Mars in each of the regions and then computing the hue, brightness and saturation of color for the range of wavelengths to which the human eye is sensitive.

b. *transf.* The name of a control on a colour television set used to adjust the quality of colours in the picture.

1964 M. S. Kiver *Color Television Fundamentals* (ed. 2) v. 144 There is also a color saturation control to adjust the vividness or depth of color. **1967** *Punch* 12 Apr. 532/3 It is good to be able to report that the colour sets shown at the Ideal Home Exhibition in London..had one colour control only. For reasons impossible to conjecture it is labelled 'Saturation'. Twisting this knob does not release a jet of water, however; it simply changes the picture from black-and-white to any strength of colour desired. **1968** *Guardian* 5 July 8/5 There is a secondary colour knob marked either 'saturation' or 'colour' which enables you to control the shade you receive. **1974** A. G. Priestly *Receiving PAL Colour Television* v. 103 A good saturation control is not easy to design. The control itself is usually situated on the front of the receiver for use by the viewer.

5. *attrib.* and *Comb.*, as ***saturation charge***, ***experiment***, ***recording***, ***time***, ***weapon***; **saturation current**, the greatest current that can be carried by a gas or electronic device (cf. senses 3 d, f above); **saturation dive**, a dive made with the diver's blood-stream saturated with an inert gas, usu. helium or nitrogen, at the pressure of the surrounding water, so that the time required for decompression afterwards is independent of how long the dive lasts; so **saturation diver**, **diving** *vbl. sb.*; **saturation point**, the state or condition at which saturation begins; the limit of acceptance; freq. *fig.*; **saturation (vapour) pressure** *Physics* (see quot. 1969).

1969 *Saturation charge [see *saturation time* below]. **1896** *Phil. Mag.* XLII. 403 The *saturation current depends only on the number of conducting particles produced by the rays. **1929** *B.B.C. Year-bk. 1930* 450/2 As the anode voltage applied to a three-electrode valve is increased, the anode current also increases up to a point, when a further increase in anode voltage does not increase the anode current. This maximum value of the current is called the 'saturation current'. **1954** L. M. Krugman *Fund. Transistors* iii. 43 The saturation current is composed of two components. The first is formed by thermally generated carriers which diffuse into the junction region. The second component is an ohmic characteristic which is caused by surface leakage across the space charge region. **1976** Millman & Halkias *Electronic Fund. & Appl.* iv. 79 In addition to the variability of reverse saturation current with temperature, there is also a wide variability of reverse current among samples of a given transistor type. **1966** *Sci. Amer.* Mar. 27/1 It is clear..that the 'partial pressure' of oxygen should be kept between about 150 and 400 millimeters of mercury during the at-depth phase of a long *saturation dive. **1974** *Daily Tel.* 22 Feb. 7/6 The record saturation dive in the North Sea was 621ft. The diver took a day to get down, and after surfacing spent $3\frac{1}{2}$ days in a decompression chamber. **1970** *Sci. Jrnl.* Feb. 15 The *Argyronète*, a self-propelled submersible combining a house in which *saturation divers can live (under sea bottom pressure) and a conventional submarine with a crew at normal atmospheric pressure. **1974** *Encycl. Brit. Macropædia* X. 926/1 In practice, saturation divers are compressed slowly to working pressure, generally in the deck chamber, and are then transferred as needed to and from the work site sealed in the diving bell. **1975** *BP Shield Internat.* May 5/4 It is..not uncommon for saturation divers to spend from two to three weeks under saturation conditions. **1966** *Sci. Amer.* Mar. 27/1 Although this '*saturation diving' is efficient, it imposes an extra technical burden, because the schedules for the ultimate decompression must be calculated and controlled with particular care. **1970** *New Scientist* 26 Mar. 617/2 The experiment successfully demonstrated the feasibility in scientific research of saturation diving—a technique which relies on the fact that once the body tissues become saturated with gases breathed under pressure, the time to remove them during decompression remains the same no matter how much longer the person stays at that pressure. **1974** *Daily Tel.* 22 Feb. 7/6 Bone necrosis is a growing fear connected with saturation diving. **1976** *Offshore Platforms & Pipelining* 122/3 Any diving inspection beyond the 140-ft. depth, which requires any appreciable time on the bottom, is carried out by using saturation diving. **1904** *Brit. Med. Jrnl.* 10 Sept. 563 By *saturation experiments we can remove the one opsonine after the other. **1858** O. W. Holmes *Aut. Breakf.-t.* v. 52 The *saturation-point of each mind differs from that of every other. **1902** *Encycl. Brit.* XXXIII. 631/2 It is a fair inference that similar behaviour would be observed up to the saturation-point if surface condensation could be avoided. **1927** *Sunday Times* 13 Feb. 2 Those controlling the industry realize that the world production of motor-cars has by no means reached saturation point. **1932** Wodehouse *Louder & Funnier* 71, I rather fancy that sinister jewel-trackers have about reached saturation-point. **1977** *Times* 30 Apr. 3/3 The popularity of the forest may have reached saturation point. **1884** A. Daniell *Princ. Physics* xiii. 346 Each volatile liquid has its own *saturation pressure for each temperature. **1902** *Encycl. Brit.* XXXIII. 631/1 The values of the saturation-pressure have been very accurately determined for the majority of stable substances. **1975** D. G. Fink *Electronics Engineers' Handbk.* xxiii. 56 There are two methods of recording called saturation and nonsaturation. With *saturation recording, material under the head is fully saturated throughout the material thickness. **1969** J. J. Sparkes *Transistor Switching* i. 23 The turn-off time is divided into two parts. First the *saturation time,..during which the saturation charge..is used up and the collector current does not significantly change. Second, the fall time. **1955** *Sci. Amer.* Mar. 74/2 For every temperature there is a '*saturation vapor pressure' at which the rates of escape and of deposit at a step balance. Under these conditions the crystal does not grow. It can grow only when the vapor is supersaturated. **1969** *Gloss. Terms Vacuum Technol.* (*B.S.I.*) I. 9 *Saturation vapour pressure*, the pressure exerted by a vapour when in equilibrium with its solid or liquid phase. **1955** *Bull. Atomic Sci.* Jan. 14/3 The construction of '*saturation weapons' became possible when it was discovered that under certain circumstances a tiny amount of matter transforms into a tremendous amount of energy.

b. Designating an activity intended to achieve the complete saturation of its object; orig. *Mil.*, referring to intensive bombing operations, esp. in ***saturation bombing***; hence ***saturation bomb*** vb.; more widely, applied to an intensive operation in the fields of marketing, advertising, security, and the like.

1942 *Sun* (Baltimore) 15 Oct. 13/5 The fact that only nine bombers were lost..was taken to mean that the 'saturation technique' was used to crowd so many planes over the area in a short raid that the strong defenses..were swamped. **1943** *Time* 7 June 29/3 According to U.S. testimony, the precision bombing of the American forces is more effective, ton for ton, than the saturation bombing of the R.A.F. *Ibid.* 30 Aug. 33/2 The greatest air force the world has known: a combination of the daylight precision bombing planes of the U.S. Eighth Air Force and the heavy night-time saturation raiders of the R.A.F. *Ibid.* 6 Sept. 36/3 Of the 73 raids Berlin had experienced, this was the worst, the first of the kind of saturation raids that had wrecked Hamburg. **1944** *Times* 28 Mar. 4/5 A great weight of high-explosives and incendiaries pounded Essen in a 'saturation' attack which lasted just under half an hour. **1957** Clark & Gottfried *Dict. Business & Finance* 314/2 *Saturation* selling involves making a product available in every outlet in an area, and using every possible means of sales promotion. **1958** *Listener* 5 June 950/3 Mrs. Ancsa's father had been killed in a saturation air-raid. **1962** *Economist* 2 June 920/3 The large number of copies of each film necessary for this so-called 'saturation release'. **1966** *Times* 12 July 11/3 It is simply not true to say that America has engaged in saturation bombing. **1971** *Wall St. Jrnl.* 13 Aug. 14/1 He came to realize such journalism is possible through 'saturation reporting'. **1975** R. H. Rimmer *Premar Experiments* (1976) i. 19 The days when we believed we could change things—like the draft, or the saturation bombing of Vietnam, or the Pentagon running the universities. **1977** *Time* 28 Nov. 29/2 As the deadline arrived.., West Germany's national airline responded with a policy of saturation security for its 411 daily scheduled flights worldwide. **1979** P. NIESEWAND *Member of Club* xxi. 165 The Cubans were saturation bombing the camp. **1981** I. A. GORDON in *N.Z. Listener* 18–24 Apr., The big idea behind the saturation-bombing of consumers with a trade-name is to persuade you that X (and not Y or Z) is the brand to remember.

saturator (ˈsætjʊəreɪtə(r)). Also **saturater**. [f. SATURATE *v.* + -OR. Cf. late L. *saturātor*.] One who or something which saturates: *spec.* **a.** A device for supplying air saturated with water-vapour to a room or inclosed space.

1883 W. N. SHAW in *Cambr. Phil. Soc. Trans.* XIV. 37 A saturater (A) for supplying saturated air at the temperature of the room. *Ibid.* 39.

b. An apparatus for saturating oxygen with ether for the purposes of the ether-oxygen lime-light.

1894 *Brit. Jrnl. Photogr.* XLI. Suppl. 2 The more recent forms of saturators..give a very good light.

Saturday (ˈsætədeɪ, -dɪ). Forms: *α.* 1 Sæternes-, Seternes dæȝ, 3 Sæternes dæȝ, 5 Saturnesday, 7 *Sc.* Saturnsday; 1 Sæterndæȝ, 2 Sætern-daiȝ, 5 Saturneday, 7–8 *Sc.* Saturnday; *β.* 1 Sæteres dæȝ, 3 Saeteresdai, 3–4 Settresday, 4 Seters-dai, 5 Setrys-day, 7 Saters-day; *γ.* 1 Sæter-dæȝ, 2 Sæter-daiȝ, Saterdei, 3 Sætterdæi, *Orm.* Saterrdaȝȝ, 4 Satirdai, Saturdaie, Seterdai, Setre-, Setret-, Settir-, Set(t)urday, Zeterday, -dey, 4–5 Seter-, Setirday, 4–6 Saterdaye, Satir-, Setterday, 4–7 Saterday, 5 Scaturday, Setryday, Set(t)yrday, 5–6 Satyrday, 5–7 Satterday, 6 Satterdaie, Sat(t)orday, Saturdaye, 6–7 Saterdaie, 9 *dial.* Settherday, 3– Saturday. [OE. *Sætern(es)dæȝ*, corresp. to OFris. *saterdî, saterdei*, MDu. *saterdach* (Du. *zaterdag*, earlier *zaturdag*), MLG. *sater(s)dach* (LG. *saterdag*), whence northern HG. dial. *satertag*; a half-translated adoption of L. *Sāturnī diēs* day of (the planet) Saturn; cf. Irish, Gael. *dia Sathuirn*, Welsh *dydd Sadwrn*.]

1. The seventh day of the week.

The advb. use of the names of the days of the week (*Saturday* = 'on Saturday') is now chiefly *U.S.*, exc. in collocations like 'next Saturday', 'last Saturday'. Formerly ***the Saturday*** was often used advb. but is now rare or obs. exc. with some defining phrase.

a **900** tr. *Bæda's Hist.* II. iii. (Schipper) 125 Æȝhwilce sæternes dæȝe. **971** *Blickl. Hom.* 71 Ærest on þæm Sæteres dæȝe he awehte Ladzarum of deaþe. *c* **1000** *Ags. Gosp.* Luke xxiii. 54 Sæter-dæȝ on-lyhte. *Ibid.* 56 On sætern-dæȝ. *c* **1175** *Lamb. Hom.* 45 Ic ham ȝeuereste..from non on saterdei a þa cume monedeis lihting. *c* **1200** ORMIN 4350 Forr Saterr-daȝȝ wass haliȝ daȝȝ O þatt Judisskenn wise. *c* **1290** *S. Eng. Leg.* I. 66/451 On a satur-day at niȝht. *c* **1300** *St. Brandan* 543 For ich am her ech Soneday and fram Sater-dayes Eve. *a* **1300** *Cursor M.* 17673 Als i stod saiand mi bede, þe seterdai. **1340** *Ayenb.* 213 Yef god het zuo straytlic[h]e loki þane zeterday ine þe yealde laȝe þet he made ane man to stene..uor þet he hedde y-gadered a lite wode þane zeterdey. **1362** LANGL. *P. Pl.* A. v. 14 On a Seterday at euen. *c* **1375** *Sc. Leg. Saints* x. (*Mathou*) 336 þan yrtacus..þe next setret-day..a congregacion has gert ma. **1418** *E.E. Wills* (1882) 28 On Setrysday in þe vygyle of þe Holy Trynyte. **1421** *Coventry Leet-bk.* 30 Euery Saturneday in the yer. *c* **1447** in *Jarrow & Wearmouth* (Surtees) 242 Apon Saturnesday next be for Palmsonday. *c* **1475** *Partenay* 2724 So it cam and fill in a scaturday, That Raymounde loste the fair melusine. *c* **1500** *Melusine* 15 That he wil promytte to the that neuer on the Satirday he shall see the. *c* **1511** *1st Eng. Bk. Amer.* Introd. (Arb.) 34/2 Noman ther ouer can passe, excepte ye saterdaye. **1556** *Chron. Gr. Friars* (Camden) 36 The satterday after, that was Wytson evyn, [she] came from the tower thorow London. **1581** J. HAMILTON *Cath. Treat.* V viij, God commandit yat ve suld Keip halie ye Sabaoth day, quhilk is Setterday. *c* **1610–15** *Lives Women Saints* 93 From Thursday vntill Satersday. **1637–50** ROW *Hist. Kirk* (Wodrow Soc.) 515 On Saturnsday, Aprile 27, they disbanded their men. **1671** [R. MACWARD] *True Nonconf.* 119 That the Churches meeting recorded to have been on the first day of the week, sayeth not that they antiquated the Saturnday. **1703** *Extracts Burgh Rec. Stirling* (1889) 99 Against Saturnday next. **1775** T. PERCIVAL *Ess.* (1777) III. 194 Saturday, the mint continued to grow and to ascend, looking vigorous and fresh. **1793** BURKE *Obs. Cond. Minority* Wks. VII. 236 Although the House does not usually sit on Saturday. **1845** T. W. COIT *Puritanism* 495 The Puritan way of eating fish is, to eat it Saturday instead of Friday. **1870** M. D. CONWAY *Earthw. Pilgr.* xxviii. 344 On Saturday the English people are among the most sensible people in the world. **1885** *Cath. Dict.* (ed. 3) 561/1 The office of the Blessed Virgin is said on all Saturdays.

2. With specific epithet. **Black Saturday** *Sc.*, (*a*) the 10th Sept. 1547, the date of the Battle of Pinkie; (*b*) the 4th Aug. 1621, the date of the ratification of the articles of Perth. **Egg Saturday**: see EGG *sb.* 7. **Holy Saturday**, the Saturday of Holy Week; Easter eve. **Hospital Saturday**: see HOSPITAL *sb.* 6.

1657 MURE *Ho. Rowallane* Wks. (S.T.S.) II. 255 He died in battell at the Black Satterday in the year of our Lord 1547. **1717** DE FOE *Mem. Ch. Scot.* II. 45 The Day got the Name of black Saturday, upon this Account, as well as on the Occasion of the black Work they had been about.

1398 TREVISA *Barth. De P.R.* IX. xxxi. (1495) 368 Also to Ester perteynyth the euyn therof that for passynge holynesse is callyd Sabbatum Sanctum the holy Saterday. **1730** tr. *Fleury's Eccl. Hist.* IV. Index, Saturday, holy, even Children fasted on that Day. **1885** *Cath. Dict.* (ed. 3) 405/2 The Mass celebrated at midnight belonged rather to the morning of Easter Sunday than to Holy Saturday.

3. a. *attrib.* and *Comb.*, as ***Saturday-afternooner, concert, kirtle, morning, night, office, sabbath,*** † ***wit***; **Saturday penny**, a penny or small sum of money given to a child on Saturday as pocket-money; † **Saturday-sabbatharian** = SABBATARIAN *sb.* 3.

For *Saturday('s slop* or *slap* Sc. (in some Dicts. erron. *stop*), see SLOP *sb.*

1906 *Saturday-afternooner [see *early-closer* s.v. EARLY *a.* 7]. **1889** HUEFFER *Half Cent. Mus. Eng.* 14 The Crystal Palace *Saturday Concerts. **1557** *Will of T. Howgill* (Somerset Ho.), My *saturday kyrtyll. **1641** BEST *Farm. Bks.* (Surtees) 77 On *Satterday-morninge the 11th of December. **1785** BURNS (*title*) The Cotter's *Saturday Night. **1859** SIR J. PAGET in *Mem. & Lett.* (1901) 224 In bringing-up the book 'to Saturday night'. **1686** [HICKES] *Spec. B. Virginis* 13 One of the Lessons for the *Saturday-Office of the B. Virgin. **1972** *Homes & Gardens* Apr. 60, I am old enough to remember the small child's pocket money called the '*Saturday penny'. **1979** *Church Times* 27 Apr. (Mayflower Suppl.) p. iii/2 When I was in trouble with my Mum and Dad and they wouldn't give me my 'Saturday penny'..I had at least twelve other homes where there were relations where I could go and 'con' them for a penny. **1645** PAGITT *Heresiogr.* (1661) 192 Mr. Hebden a prisoner in the New-prison, that lay there for holding *Saturday-Sabbath. **1705** HICKERINGILL *Priest-cr.* IV. (1721) 204 Without an express Command (as ye have against the *Saturday-Sabbatharians) in the New Testament. **1593** G. HARVEY *Pierces Super.* 145 Phy, long Megg of Westminster would haue bene ashamed to disgrace her Sonday bonet with her *Satterday witt.

b. ***Saturday-to-Monday***: a period beginning on Saturday and ending on Monday; often *attrib.* with reference to railway and other excursion tickets.

1886 C. E. PASCOE *London of To-day* xviii. (ed. 3) 182 In one of the delightful Saturday to Monday trips on the Thames. **1892** MRS. H. WARD *D. Grieve* IV. ii, A..warm invitation..to spend an October Saturday-to-Monday at Benet's Park had been accepted.

Saturdaying (ˈsætədeɪɪŋ, -dɪɪŋ), *vbl. sb.* [f. SATURDAY + -ING[1], after Russ. *subbótnik*.] An English rendering of SUBBOTNIK. So **ˈSaturdayite**.

1920 *Manch. Guardian* 5 Feb. 9/7 In Moscow it has been found worth while to set up a special bureau for 'Saturdayings'. **1920** *Contemp. Rev.* Oct. 504 For members of the Bolshevik party, 'Saturdaying' had become compulsory. **1932** C. HOGARTH tr. *Kollontai's Free Love* 233 She will persuade you..that it is necessary..to deny oneself everything that gives joy, to live only for the 'Saturdayites'.

Saturday night. [SATURDAY 3.]

1. Used *attrib.* of activities taking place on or as on a Saturday night, esp. some form of revelry.

[**1847** H. MELVILLE *Omoo* xii. 49 The evening of the last day of the week was always celebrated by what is styled on board of English vessels, 'The Saturday-night bottles'. Two of these were sent down into the forecastle, just after dark.] **1896** 'M. RUTHERFORD' *Clara Hopgood* xii. 121 Saturday-night drunkenness and looseness in the relations between the young men and young women. [**1938** G. GREENE *Brighton Rock* III. 124 'Saturday,' he thought, 'today's Saturday,' remembering the room at home, the frightening weekly exercise of his parents which he watched from his single bed. *Ibid.* VII. 320 The Boy was shaken again with his nocturnal Saturday disgust. He couldn't blame his father now... You couldn't even blame the girl.] **1942** BERREY & VAN DEN BARK *Amer. Thes. Slang* §509/17 *Saturday-night habit, week-end habit*, indulgence in small amounts of narcotics at irregular intervals. **1951** *Evening Sun* (Baltimore) 27 Mar. 4/1 The graduate 'hype' was a 'student' or 'hoosier fiend' who 'dabbled' with drugs occasionally. He had what is known as 'chippy habit', a 'Saturday night habit', or an 'ice cream habit'. **1963** R. I. MCDAVID *Mencken's Amer. Lang.* xi. 742 Most cats consider it necessary to probe the mystic depths with the assistance of wine, a joint of pot.., peyote buttons and large infusions of invigorating jazz music—..in any event indulged in with friends as part of the Saturday night kicks. **1964** *New Statesman* 17 Apr. 606/2 Is the Saturday-night blind..any less characteristic of the modern urbanised proletariat than of the traditional rural peasantry? **1976** *N.Y. Times Mag.* 10 Oct. 111/2 [In the southern States of the U.S.] there were all those cross burnings, lynching bees and Sairday Nite Socials.

2. *spec. attrib.* uses: ***Saturday night palsy*** or ***paralysis***, temporary local paralysis of the arm, esp. wrist drop, after it has rested on a hard edge for a long time, as during sleep following a bout of drinking (*colloq.*); ***Saturday night pistol*** (*U.S. colloq.*) = *Saturday night special*; ***Saturday night soldier***, a member of a volunteer army, as opp. a regular soldier; ***Saturday night special*** (*U.S. colloq.*), a cheap, low-calibre pistol or revolver such as might be used by a petty criminal.

1927 I. S. WECHSLER *Textbk. Clin. Neurol.* III. 249 The frequent occurrence of wrist drop in alcoholics who fall asleep and lean heavily on the arm has given rise to the common designation of 'Saturday night palsy'. **1942** *Sun* (Baltimore) 23 Apr. 22/2 A similar ailment is called 'shelter paralysis'—formerly known as 'Saturday night paralysis' because its victims were generally payday tipplers. **1951** E. PAUL *Springtime in Paris* xii. 216 Berthe was suffering from what is known in the United States as Saturday-night paralysis,..when drunken men go to sleep in gutters, with one arm across a sharp kerbstone. **1974** PASSMORE & ROBSON *Compan. Med. Stud.* III. xxxiv. 35/1 Wrist drop thus produced is known as a 'Saturday night palsy'. **1929** M. A. GILL *Underworld Slang, Saturday night pistol*, 25 automatic. **1917** A. G. EMPEY *Over Top* 311 '*Terrier*', Tommy's nickname for a Territorial or 'Saturday-night soldier'. **1974** *Maclean's Mag.* Oct. 30/1 My husband was a Saturday Night soldier, the militia, and he couldn't wait for the war and when it started, zoom, he was called up and then he was happy. **1968** *N.Y. Times* 17 Aug. 1/1 Title IV of that law bans the importation of the cheap, small-caliber 'Saturday night specials' that are a favorite of holdup men. **1976** *Pioneer* (Big Timber, Montana) 30 June 4/2 A ban on 'Saturday Night Special' handguns. **1977** C. MCFADDEN *Serial* xlvi. 98/1 I'm not packing a Saturday-night special, *really*.

Hence **Saturday nighter**, a person who attends an entertainment on a Saturday night; **Saturday-night** *v. intr.*, to spend a Saturday night in enjoyment or revelling.

1962 D. LESSING *Golden Notebk.* IV. 462 The fellows were out Saturday-nighting true-hearted, the wild-hearted Saturday-night gang of true friends. **1966** *Listener* 24 Mar. 422/2 The Korean script announced that *Dr No* was showing inside. So he was..and half the population of Korea was inside, too..all of us lapping up James Bond like Surbiton Saturday nighters.

†**ˈsature.** *Obs.* [as if ad. L. **satūra*, f. *sa-*, *serĕre* to sow (pa. pple. *satus*).] Sowing.

1657 TOMLINSON *Renou's Disp.* 238 Its seed germinates.. about forty or fifty dayes after its sature.

†**satureie.** *Obs.* Forms: 1 satureȝe, 3–5 satureie, 5 saturege, satureye. [ad. L. *saturēia*.] = SAVORY.

c **1000** *Sax. Leechd.* (Rolls) III. 24 Satureȝe. *c* **1265** *Voc. Plants* in Wr.-Wülcker 557/12 *Satureia*, satureie, timbre. **1390** GOWER *Conf.* III. 132 His herbe is cleped Satureie, So as these olde bokes seie. *c* **1440** *Pallad. on Husb.* XI. 336 And forto make a wyn to drynke swete, Of saturege or fenel putte in meete.

saturgresse, obs. f. SETTER-GRASS *dial.*

saturicall, -rioun: see SATIRICAL, SATYRION.

†**saˈturity.** *Obs.* [ad. L. *saturitās*, f. *satur* full, satisfied.] Fulness, repletion, satisfaction.

1533 tr. *Erasmus' Commune Crede* 19 In which worlde..is there..neither perfyghte puryte and clennes, neither full saturyte and satisfyeng of mannes mynde. **1548** UDALL, etc. *Erasm. Par. Matt.* v. 6 Sumtime the saturitie doth more vexe them that be ful, than the hunger dyd trouble them before. **1643** TRAPP *Comm. Gen.* xlvii. 13 Saturity and security had so besotted them, that they feared nothing, till they felt it. **1752** HODGES *Chr. Plan* (1755) 53 The primary idea of it is saturity and fulness.

Saturn (ˈsætən). Forms: 1–6 **Saturnus** (1 *genit.* **Saturnes**); 5 **Satourn**, 5–7 **Saturne**, 7– **Saturn**. [ad. L. *Sāturnus*, perh. f. the root *sa-* to sow.]

1. *Mythol.* An Italic god, in the original native religion the god of agriculture, but in classical times identified with the Greek Cronos, who was deposed from the sovereignty of the gods by his son Zeus (Jupiter).

c **888** K. ÆLFRED *Boeth.* xxxv. §4 Iob Saturnes sunu. *Ibid.* xxxviii. §1 þa sceolde þæs Iobes fæder bion eac god; þæs nama wæs Saturnus. **1398** TREVISA *Barth. De P.R.* VIII. xii. (1495) 318 Saturnus hath that name of saturando, makynge fulnesse and plente. **1508** DUNBAR *Ballad Ld. B. Stewart* 75 Saturnus doune, withe fyry eyn, did blent. **1513** DOUGLAS *Æneis* VIII. vi. 39 By quham the land of Saturn, war and wys, Hes left and changit his auld name oft sys. *c* **1600** SHAKS. *Sonn.* xcviii. 4 When proud pide Aprill..Hath put a spirit of youth in euery thing: That heauie *Saturne* laught and leapt with him. **1667** MILTON *P.L.* I. 519 Or who with Saturn old Fled over Adria to th' Hesperian fields. **1819** SHELLEY *Prometh. Unb.* II. iv. 33 Then Saturn, from whose throne Time fell.

2. *Astr.* The most remote of the seven planets known to ancient astronomy. In OE. also † ***Saturnes steorra***.

Saturn is now known to be the sixth planet in distance from the sun. It is surrounded by several thousand rings, composed of small icy particles and occupying a wide band of orbits, and has at least fifteen moons.

In *Astrology*, on account of its remoteness and slowness of motion, Saturn was supposed to cause coldness, sluggishness, and gloominess of temperament in those born under its influence, and in general to have a baleful effect on human affairs.

c **888** K. ÆLFRED *Boeth.* xxxvi. §3 Siððan to þan cealdan stiorran þe we hatað Saturnes steorra. *Ibid.* xxxix. §3 Saturnus se steorra. **1398** TREVISA *Barth. De P.R.* VIII. xii. (1495) 319 Though Saturnus be kyndly leeddy by clerenesse of Iubiter whan he is coniunct with hym he is made white and bright. *c* **1400** *Treat. Astron.* 6 (MS. Bodl. Add. B. 17), A Saturne is a planete maliuole and wycked. *c* **1430** LYDG. *Min. Poems* (Percy Soc.) 197 Satourn disposith to malencolye. **1588** SHAKS. *Tit. A.* II. iii. 31 Though Venus gouerne your desires, Saturne is Dominator ouer mine. **1640** HOWELL *Dodona's Gr.* (1645) 107 Saturne that dull and malevolent planet. **1741** WATTS *Improv. Mind* I. xvi. §2 Inform them that Saturn has five moons of the same kind attending him. **1784** COWPER *Tiroc.* 634 The moons of Jove, and Saturn's belted ball. **1832** TENNYSON *Pal. of Art* iv, Still as, while Saturn whirls, his stedfast shade Sleeps on his luminous ring. **1875** *Encycl. Brit.* II. 811/1 Saturn is the largest planet but one of the solar system. **1964** R. H. BAKER *Astronomy* (ed. 8) viii. 225 Saturn is encircled by three concentric rings... There is no gap between the bright ring and the crape ring. **1974** *Encycl. Brit. Macropædia* XVI. 274/2 Saturn has ten satellites... Janus, the most elusive and closest to the planet, was found by A. Dollfus in 1966.

3. a. *Alch.* The technical name for lead.

† ***salt, extract of Saturn***: lead acetate, sugar of lead. † ***spirit of Saturn***: app. impure acetic acid distilled from sugar of lead.

c **1386** [see JUPITER 2 b]. **1471** RIPLEY *Comp. Alch.* III. vii. in *Ashm.* (1652) 140 For sum men can wyth Saturne it multeply. **1594** PLAT *Jewell-ho.* III. 89 To congeale Mercurie with the spirit of Saturne. **1651** FRENCH *Distill.* iii. 73 Take of the Calx of Saturn, or else Minium. **1694** SALMON *Bate's Dispens.* I. ii. (1713) 66/1 This Spirit of Saturn, drawn from its Salt, is an inflamable Liquor, and is thus made: ℞Salt of Saturn, so much as may fill your Glass or Earthen Retort two Thirds full; put it into a Furnace [etc.]. **1706** PHILLIPS (ed. Kersey), *Salt of Saturn*, otherwise call'd *Saccharum Saturni*, or Sugar of Lead, is the Body of that Metal, open'd and reduc'd to the form of a Salt, by Distilled Vinegar. **1727-51** [see BALSAM *sb.* 2 b]. **1758** [see JUPITER 2 b]. **1829** *Glover's Hist. Derby* I. 32 It.. is said to have this effect, as soon, and completely, as extract of Saturn.

allusively. **1797** W. JOHNSTON tr. *Beckmann's Invent.* I. 398 One may justly doubt whether, at present, Mars, Venus, or Saturn, is most destructive to the human race.

b. *Comb.* † **Saturn cinnabar** (*Syd. Soc. Lex.*), † **Saturn red** (in recent Dicts.), names for red lead; **Saturn's tree** [tr. med.L. *arbor Saturni*], a lead tree (in recent Dicts.).

4. *Her.* The tincture sable, in blazoning by the names of heavenly bodies.

1572 [see JUPITER 2 c, MARS 2 c].

saturnal (sə'tɜːnəl), *a.* and *sb.* [ad. L. *Sāturnālis*, f. *Sāturn-us* SATURN: see -AL[1].]

† **A.** *adj.* Pertaining to Saturn or his astrological influence. *Obs.*

1591 GREENE *Farew. Folly* Wks. (Grosart) IX. 324 Yet remaines there in the minde certain *Scyntillulæ voluptatis*, which confirmed by a saturnall impression, were harder to root out than were they newly sprong vp in youth. **1651** J. F[REAKE] *Agrippa's Occ. Philos.* 96 They that are to gather a Saturnall, Martiall, or Joviall Hearb must look towards the East, or South. **1666** J. SMITH *Old Age* 109 He that shall call the.. poor bloud returning home in the Veins, Earthly, Saturnal, Gross, shall make no Schisme.. in the.. doctrine of Circulation. **1683** TRYON *Way to Health* 649 Are not the Saturnal and Martial Strings and Notes as material and useful as the Jovial and Venerial?

B. *sb.*

† **1.** ? One born under the influence of Saturn. *Obs.*

1605 TIMME *Quersit.* I. 47 There are starres which haue their most colde and moyst spirites, as the Saturnalls and Lunaries.

2. *pl.* [a. F. *saturnales* fem. pl. (14th c. *saturneles* in Littré).] † **a.** = SATURNALIA 1. **b.** = SATURNALIA 2.

1487 CAXTON *Bk. Gd. Manners* I. xv. (W. de W. *c* 1515) E ij, As enseyg[n]eth Macrobe in his boke of Saturnelles. [**1513** DOUGLAS *Æneis* I. Prol. 68 Of the writis Macrobius.. In his grete volume clepit Saturnail.] **1619** B. JONSON *Masque, Pleas. Reconc. to Virt. (init.)*, I know it is now such a time as the Saturnalls for all the World. **1647** A. ROSS *Mystag. Poet.* xi. (1675) 286 At certain Feasts of Minerva in March, the Maids were wont to be served by their Mistresses, as in the Saturnals the Men-servants by their Masters. **1654** OGILBY *Virg. Georg.* I. (1684) 47 *note*, Macrobius in the first of his Saturnals, *c.* 21. **1705** TATE, etc., tr. *Cowley's Hist. Plants* (1795) 191 But yet these wild Saturnals shall not last. **1864** *Athenæum* 5 Mar. 345/3 To compose that swaggering song, 'They shall not have our Rhine,' for these saturnals.

‖ **Saturnalia** (sætə'neɪlɪə), *sb. pl.* [L. *Sāturnālia*, neut. pl. of *Saturnālis* SATURNAL *a.*]

1. *Roman Antiq.* The festival of Saturn, held in the middle of December, observed as a time of general unrestrained merrymaking, extending even to the slaves. (Also, the title of a work by Macrobius.)

Now always with capital S.

1591 L. LLOYD *Tripl. Triumphes* B 3, Imitating the orders and maners in the feast Saturnalia. *a* **1654** SELDEN *Table-T.* (Arb.) 33 Christmas succeeds the Saturnalia. **1788** GIBBON *Decl. & F.* xli. IV. 176 The first days, which coincided with the old Saturnalia, were [etc.]. **1886** *Encycl. Brit.* XXI. 321/2 Saturnalia. This, the great festival of Saturn, was celebrated.. after Cæsar's reform of the calendar on the 17th of December. Augustus decreed that the 17th should be sacred to Saturn and the 19th to Ops. Hence-forward it appears that the 17th and 18th were devoted to the Saturnalia.

2. *transf.* and *fig.* A period of unrestrained licence and revelry. Sometimes construed as *sing.*

In this sense not unfrequently with small initial.

1775 *Answer to Pamphlet, entitled Taxation no Tyranny* 61 Thus you would establish a Saturnalia of cruelty, and expose these devoted men to the brutality of their own slaves. **1782** H. WALPOLE *Let. to W. Mason* 8 July, Malignity at least will have its Saturnalia. **1818** BYRON *Ch. Har.* IV. xcvii, But France got drunk with blood to vomit crime, And fatal have her Saturnalia been, To Freedom's cause. **1856** OLMSTED *Slave States* 101 From Christmas to New-Year's Day, most of the slaves, except house servants, enjoy a freedom from labor; and Christmas is especially holiday, or Saturnalia, with them. **1899** RIDER HAGGARD *Farmer's Yr.* 147 This was the beginning of a perfect saturnalia of tail-cutting and other operations [among the lambs].

Saturnalian (sætə'neɪlɪən), *a.* and *sb.* [f. prec. + -AN.] **A.** *adj.* Pertaining to the Saturnalia; appropriate to Saturnalia.

Saturnalian coin: a medal struck in commemoration of the Saturnalia, and intended to be used in the present-giving common at that season.

1721-2 AMHERST *Terræ Fil.* No. 1 ¶4 The famous Saturnalian Feasts among the Romans, at which every Scullion and Skipkennel had Liberty to tell his Master his own. **1796** BURKE *Let. to Windham* Corr. (1844) IV. 404, I make use of the saturnalian liberty with which you have indulged your Davus at the close of this December. **1825** FOSBROKE *Encycl. Antiq.* II. 895 Saturnalian Coins. **1831** CARLYLE *Sart. Res.* III. v, Amid wailings from some, and saturnalian revelries from the most, the venerable Corpse is to be buried. **1853** HUMPHREYS *Coin-Coll. Man.* xxvii. II. 396 A coin of Gallienus, which has been described as a Saturnalian coin. **1855** MILMAN *Lat. Chr.* VI. iii. (1864) III. 450 That coarse saturnalian humour which pleases the Italian.. ear.

B. *sb.* One who celebrates Saturnalia.

1885 'G. FLEMING' *Andromeda* I. vi. 105 The sight.. brought much confusion upon these innocent saturnalians.

† **sa'turnally**, *adv. Obs.* [f. SATURNAL *a.* + -LY[2].] Under the influence of Saturn.

1603 FLORIO *Montaigne* II. xii. (1632) 305 So are they more or lesse merily and Giovially, or rudely and Saturnally incorporated.

Saturn(e)day, obs. forms of SATURDAY.

saturnelles: see SATURNAL *sb.*

† **sa'turnial**, *a. Obs.* [f. L. *Sāturni-us* pertaining to SATURN + -AL[1].] Pertaining to the planet Saturn; born under the influence of Saturn.

1591 SPARRY tr. *Cattan's Geomancie* 133 In things Saturnial it is ill. **1652** GAULE *Magastrom.* xxvi, So far forth as it pronounceth him Saturnial, or Jovial, &c.

† **Sa'turnian**, *sb.*[1] *Obs.* [ad. eccl. L. *Sāturniānus*, incorrectly f. *Sāturnīnus* or *Sāturnilus*, the name of the founder of the sect.] An adherent of a sect of Gnostic heretics of the second century.

1598 GOLBURNE tr. *De Voyon's Catal. Doctors* To Rdr. A 8, The Saturnians, Montanists, Origenians, Tertullianists, & Hyeraists. **1607** T. ROGERS 39 *Art.* i. (1625) 11 Those men which held.. that, Christ.. was man in appearance onely, as the Manichies.. and the Saturnians.

Saturnian (sə'tɜːnɪən), *a.* and *sb.*[2] [f. L. *Sāturni-us* (f. *Sāturn-us* SATURN) + -AN.]

A. *adj.* **1. a.** Pertaining to the god Saturn.

Chiefly with reference to the 'golden age' under the reign of Saturn (L. *Saturnia regna*). ***Saturnian land*** (L. *Saturnia tellus*), Italy.

1612 J. SELDEN in Drayton *Poly-olb.* sig. A4, This later age.. hath, in our greatest Latine Critiques.. so receiued that Saturnian Language, that, to Students in Philology, it is now grown familiar. **1640** HOWELL *Dodona's Gr.* 58 The Saturnian times of Gold let none henceforth admire. **1728** POPE *Dunc.* I. 28 Here pleas'd behold her mighty wings outspread To hatch a new Saturnian age of Lead. **1820** SHELLEY *Œdipus* I. i. 174 Through the fortunate Saturnian land, Into the darkness of the West. **1827** CARLYLE *Misc.* (1857) I. 51 A new social order was to bring back the Saturnian era to the world. **1862** LONGF. *Wayside Inn* I. *K. Robt. Sicily* 106 And now returned again To Sicily the old Saturnian reign.

b. *nonce-use.* Resembling Saturn (in conduct).

1891 F. THOMPSON *Sister-Songs* (1895) 55 Ere Saturnian earth her child consumes.

2. The distinctive epithet of the metre (*versus Saturnius*) used in early Roman poetry, before the introduction of Greek metres.

Although a considerable number of Saturnian lines have been preserved, the nature of the metre is still disputed, some scholars believing it to be quantitative, and others accentual.

1693 DRYDEN *Juvenal* Introd. (1697) 29 The Romans.. had certain Young Men, who at their Festivals Danc'd and Sung after their uncouth manner, to a certain kind of Verse, which they call'd Saturnian. **1783** T. WILSON *Archæol. Dict.*, Saturnian Verses. **1842** MACAULAY *Let.* 22 Aug., in Trevelyan *Life* (1880) II. 119 The Saturnian metre is catalectic dimeter Iambic, followed by three trochees. **1894** LINDSAY *Lat. Lang.* 159 The Saturnian verse recognizes this secondary accent, if we are right in regarding it as accentual and not quantitative verse, with three accents in the first hemistich and two in the second.

3. a. Of or pertaining to the planet Saturn; due to the baleful influence of Saturn.

1557 GRIMALDE in *Tottel's Misc.* (Arb.) 115 Mauortian moods, Saturnian furies fell. **1794** G. ADAMS *Nat. & Exp. Philos.* IV. xliii. App. 176 But, like the Jovian and Saturnian machines, they are only made from particular orders. **1806** HERSCHEL in *Phil. Trans.* XCVI. 466 We may infer the existence of a Saturnian atmosphere. **1865** PROCTOR *Saturn & Syst.* 115 The only possible interpretation of the stability of the Saturnian rings. **1922** W. B. YEATS *Seven Poems & Fragment* 6 Stretch out your limbs and sleep a long Saturnian sleep.

b. *nonce-use.* Resembling Saturn in slowness.

1796 BURKE *Regic. Peace* Wks. IX. 93 The slow-paced Saturnian movements of Spain.

c. *Physics.* Of or pertaining to a model of the nuclear atom in which electrons are assumed to orbit in rings around a central nucleus, thus resembling the appearance of Saturn. Now *hist.*

1904 H. NAGAOKA in *Phil. Mag.* VII. 445 The system differs from the Saturnian system considered by Maxwell in having repelling particles instead of attracting satellites. *Ibid.* 455 There are various problems which will possibly be capable of being attacked on the hypothesis of a Saturnian system, such as chemical affinity and valency. **1911** *Phil. Mag.* XXI. 688 Nagaoka has mathematically considered the properties of a 'Saturnian' atom which he supposed to consist of a central attracting mass surrounded by rings of rotating electrons. **1967** D. TER HAAR *Old Quantum Theory* iii. 31 Nagaoka (1904) had considered earlier the properties of a 'Saturnian' atom. **1974** G. REECE tr. *Hund's Hist. Quantum Theory* iv. 56 Nuclear types of atom included.. the 'Saturnian system' of H. Nagaoka (1904).

† **4.** = SATURNINE. *Obs.*

1656 BLOUNT *Glossogr.*, *Saturnian* or *Saturnine*, barren, dull, heavy, melancholly; also unlucky or unfortunate. **1738** CHAMBERS *Cycl.*, *Saturnine*, or *Saturnian*, a term applied to persons of dark, sullen, melancholic complections.

B. *sb.*

† **1.** One born under the influence of the planet Saturn; a person of saturnine temperament. *Obs.*

1591 SPARRY tr. *Cattan's Geomancie* 31 A man being a Saturnian, is much more apte and prompt vnto things of Magicke, then he that is borne vnder an other Planet. **1598** MARSTON *Pygmal.* iv. 150 What cold Saturnian Can hold, and heare such vile detraction?

2. An inhabitant of the planet Saturn.

1738 *Gentl. Mag.* VIII. 315/2 Some cold Saturnian, when the lifted tube Shows to his wond'ring eye our pensile globe, Pities our thirsty soil, and sultry air. **1870** PROCTOR *Other Worlds* vi. 153 The provision of satellites and of the rings.. is altogether inadequate to increase the supply of light received by the Saturnians to any such extent as has been imagined.

3. *pl.* Saturnian verses.

1899 MACKAIL *Life Morris* I. 284 English, like Latin, has changed too deeply in structure to revert to its Saturnians.

4. *nonce-use.* The son of Saturn, Jupiter (tr. Gr. Κρονίων).

1820 SHELLEY *Hymn Merc.* xxxviii, Where the ambrosial nymph with happy will Bore the Saturnian's love-child, Mercury. *Ibid.* lii, I appeal to the Saturnian's throne.

saturnian (sə'tɜːnɪən), *sb.*[3] [f. mod.L. generic name *Saturnia* + -AN.] = SATURNIID *sb.*

1842 T. W. HARRIS *Treat. Insects Injurious to Vegetation* 276 These insects.. belong to a family called Saturnians.

saturnic (sə'tɜːnɪk), *a.* [f. SATURN + -IC.] Affected with lead-poisoning.

1879 *St. George's Hosp. Rep.* IX. 206 One patient was a total abstainer. Two took 1½ pint of beer (both saturnic). Three took 2 pints of beer (one was gouty and saturnic).

† **Sa'turnical**, *a. Obs.* [f. SATURN + -ICAL.]

1. Belonging to the god Saturn.

1561 DAUS tr. *Bullinger on Apoc.* (1573) 101 A Saturnicall or golden age. **1582** STANYHURST *Æneis* IV. (Arb.) 97 Thus toe Venus turning spake thee Saturnical empresse [*sc.* Juno, daughter of Saturn].

2. Saturnine.

1605 VERSTEGAN *Dec. Intell.* iii. (1628) 80 Crodo was also mistaken for Saturnus, not in regard of any saturnicall qualitie. **1616** R. COCKS *Diary* (Hakl. Soc.) I. 134, I think it is the saturnecall humor of the ould king. **1652** PEYTON *Catastr. Ho. Stuarts* (1731) 62 Nor lean, nor too Saturnical, nor too Jovial, but in Golden Temper. **1701** WARWICK *Mem. Chas. I* 33 Where this malevolent saturnical man, named Felton,.. gave him that mortal wound.

saturnicentric (sə,tɜːnɪ'sɛntrɪk), *a.* [f. SATURN, after *geocentric.*] Calculated with reference to the centre of Saturn.

1790 HERSCHEL in *Phil. Trans.* LXXX. 432 In order to reduce the Saturnicentric situation of the satellites to the apparent one. **1868** LOCKYER *Guillemin's Heavens* (ed. 3) 253 In advancing as far as 63° of Saturnicentric latitude, we shall [etc.].

saturniid (sə'tɜːnɪɪd), *a.* and *sb. Ent.* Also **Saturniid.** [f. mod.L. family name *Saturniidæ*, f. generic name *Saturnia* (F. von P. Schrank *Fauna Boica* (1802) II. 149): see SATURNIAN *a.* and *sb.*[2]] **A.** *adj.* Of, pertaining to, or belonging to the family Saturniidæ, which includes large, mainly tropical moths with a few species of temperate regions. **B.** *sb.* A moth of the family Saturniidæ.

1892 W. L. DISTANT *Naturalist in Transvaal* 122 The fine Saturniid moth *Urota sinope.* **1928** G. H. CARPENTER *Biol. Insects* xii. 378 The large Chinese Saturniid silk-moth.. is represented in Japan and Java by readily distinguishable forms. **1952** *Bull. Amer. Mus. Nat. Hist.* XCVIII. 355/1 The saturniid moths appear to be most closely related to the small South American families Oxyteridae and Cercophoridae. *Ibid.* 365/2 The eyes of saturniids are large in relation to the head. **1964** [see LASIOCAMPID *sb.* and *a.*]. **1979** *Smithsonian* X. 68 (*caption*) Saturniid moth.. is one of the many colorful insects harbored in Costa Rica's forests.

saturnine ('sætənaɪn), *a.* and *sb.* [ad. med.L. **Sāturnīnus*, f. *Sāturnus* SATURN. Cf. F. *saturnin*, Sp., Pg., It. *saturnino.*] **A.** *adj.*

1. a. *Astrol.* Born under or affected by the influence of the planet. **b.** Hence (in later use without allusion to the primary sense), sluggish, cold, and gloomy in temperament.

Saturnine mount, in *Palmistry* = *Mons Saturni*: see MONS.

1433 LYDG. *St. Edmund* II. 275 This cursid Bern, enuyous and riht fals, And of complexioun verray saturnyne. **1587** GREENE *2nd Pt. Tritam.* I 4 b, The Saturnine temperature is necessarie to dry vp the superfluities of the sanguine constitution. **1599** NASHE *Lenten Stuffe* 64 Saturnine heauy headed blunderers. **1621** BURTON *Anat. Mel.* I. ii. I. ii. 62 Gregorius Tolosanus makes seauen kindes of ætheriall.. Divels, according to the number of the seauen Planets, Saturnine, Iouial, Martiall, &c. **1642** HOWELL *For. Trav.* v. (Arb.) 30 Go first to the Operations of the Soule, the one is Active and Mercuriall, the other is Speculative and Saturnine: the one Quick and Ayry, the other Slow and Heavy. **1668** DRYDEN *Def. Dram. Poesy* Ess. (ed. Ker) I. 116 My conversation is slow and dull; my humour saturnine and reserved. **1696** AUBREY *Misc.* (1721) 172 Toads (Saturnine

Animals) are killed by putting of Salt upon them. **1711** ADDISON *Spect.* No. 179 ¶1, I may cast my Readers unto two general Divisions, the *Mercurial* and the *Saturnine*. *a* **1779** WARBURTON *Div. Legat.* IX. Introd., Wks. 1788 III. 593 The Indolent, the Active, the Sanguine, the Flegmatic, and the Saturnine have all their correspondent Theories [of morality]. **1822** SCOTT *Nigel* xiii, The former..was grave and saturnine in every thing he did. **1848** DICKENS *Dombey* xxxv, Towlinson is saturnine and grim. **1855** MACAULAY *Hist. Eng.* xvi. III. 634 One of the most remarkable peculiarities of this man [William III], ordinarily so saturnine and reserved, was that danger acted on him like wine. **1865** LONGF. *Dante's Purgat.* Introd. Sonn., O poet saturnine! **1871** TYLOR *Prim. Cult.* I. 113 Chiromancy.. finds proof of melancholy in the intersections on the saturnine mount.

2. Pertaining to the planet Saturn. *rare*$^{-1}$.

1862 G. WILSON *Relig. Chem.* 59 The Mercurial day being, like our own, twenty-four hours long, the Saturnine only ten.

3. Of or pertaining to lead.

1669 W. SIMPSON *Hydrol. Chym.* 7 You shall find the water to have contracted no saturnine impression. **1753** CHAMBERS *Cycl. Supp.* s.v., Saturnine tincture, *tinctura saturnina*. **1782** E. FORD in *Med. Commun.* I. 96 A scabby eruption, which..yielded to a saturnine application. **1813** J. THOMSON *Lect. Inflam.* 445 An emollient or saturnine poultice forms..the best application to the ulcer. **1835** G. FIELD *Chromatogr.* 95 Red Lead, Minium, or Saturnine Red. **1874** GARROD & BAXTER *Mat. Med.* (1880) 120 Acetate of lead and other Saturnine preparations.

b. *Path.* Of disorders: Caused by absorption of lead. Of a patient: Suffering from lead-poisoning.

1823 J. BADCOCK *Dom. Amusem.* 105 Spasmodic cholic, or the satumine [*read* saturnine], as it is termed, from the causation thereof, generally follows a debauch of wine, of the pale kinds particularly. **1855** DUNGLISON *Med. Lex.*, *Saturnine breath*, the peculiar odour of the breath in one labouring under Saturnismus. **1885** T. STEVENSON in *Encycl. Brit.* XIX. 278/1 Potmen, who drink beer which has rested for some time in pewter vessels, are also the occasional victims of saturnine poisoning. **1897** *Allbutt's Syst. Med.* II. 982 The increase or diminution of the uric acid was in no way proportional to the severity of the colic, and old saturnine patients tended to pass it in excess.

†**B.** *sb.* A person born under the planet Saturn; a gloomy person.

1631 BRATHWAIT *Whimzies, Launderer* 56 A Launderer is a linnen barber, and a meere saturnine; for you shall ever finde her in the sudds. **1653** R. SANDERS *Physiogn.* 151 So much for the Physiognomy of the Saturnines; now for the Jovialists.

saturninely (ˈsætənaɪnlɪ), *adv.* [f. SATURNINE *a.* + -LY².] In a saturnine manner.

1895 *Daily News* 6 Feb. 5/6 Lord Salisbury was saturninely humorous in his criticism of the Ministerial programme.

saturninity (sætɜːˈnɪnɪtɪ). [f. SATURNINE *a.* + -ITY.] The quality of being saturnine.

1903 *Critic* XLIII. 353/2 The two dominating traits of the Englishman's character are a love of battle and a tendency to saturninity.

†**saˈturnious**, *a. Obs.* [f. L. *Sāturni-us* pertaining to Saturn + -IOUS.] Saturnine, gloomy.

1591 SPARRY tr. *Cattan's Geomancie* 229 It shall be by Saturnyous, melancholy and vitious men.

saturnism (ˈsætənɪz(ə)m). Also in mod.L. form. [a. mod.L. *Saturnism-us*, f. L. *Sāturn-us* SATURN: see -ISM.] Lead-poisoning.

1855 DUNGLISON *Med. Lex.*, *Saturnismus*, poisoning by lead; lead-poisoning; saturnine cachexy. **1879** *St. George's Hosp. Rep.* IX. 179 Four had suffered from fits, one from saturnism.

†**ˈsaturnist.** *Obs.* [f. SATURN + -IST.] One born under the influence of the planet Saturn; a saturnine person.

1569 J. SANFORD tr. *Agrippa's Van. Artes* 50 b, She pronounceth this man a Saturniste, or Jouialist. **1598** MARSTON *Sco. Villanie* I. ii. 175 What icye Saturnist, what Northerne pate, But such grosse lewdnesse would exasperate? **1654** WHITLOCK *Zootomia* 507 Grum-sirs hate Jovialists; they the sad, The active Soule a Saturnist.

†**saturnite.** *Min. Obs.* [f. SATURN + -ITE.] (See quot. 1896.)

1784 KIRWAN *Min.* 361 (Chester) Saturnite. **1795** W. NICHOLSON *Dict. Chem.* II. 801 *Saturnite*. By this name Kirwan distinguishes a substance said by Monnet to be found in the lead mines of Poullaouwen in Brittany, and separated from the lead ore during its torrefaction. **1896** CHESTER *Dict. Names Min.*, *Saturnite*, the name given to a furnace product from lead smelting, at first considered a simple mineral.

saturnize (ˈsætənaɪz), *v.* [f. SATURN + -IZE.]

†**1.** *trans.* To combine or impregnate with lead.

1694 SALMON *Bate's Dispens.* (1713) 477/1 *Nitrum Saturnisatum*, Nitre saturnised, or with Lead.

2. *nonce-use.* To castrate.

[In allusion to the mutilation of Saturn by Jupiter.]

1829 LANDOR *Imag. Conv.*, *Lucian & Timoth.* Wks. 1853 II. 18/2 My grandfather..likes no horses but what are Saturnized.

†**ˈSaturnlike,** *adv. Obs.* [f. SATURN + -LIKE.] Resembling Saturn.

1569 SPENSER *Vis. Bellay* (earlier version) vii. 4 A grisly forehed and Saturnelike face. *a* **1633** AUSTIN *Medit.* (1635) 147 But since the Sunne of righteousnesse hath rose from the Saturne-like and dull Earth on our Sunday; wee [etc.].

Saturnsday, obs. form of SATURDAY.

Saturnus: see SATURN.

satury: see SATYR.

‖**satya** (ˈsatja). [Skr.] In Indian philosophy: truth, truthfulness.

1943 C. S. LEWIS *Abolition of Man* i. 10 Righteousness, correctness, order, the *Rta*, is constantly identified with *satya* or truth, correspondence to reality. **1956** E. WOOD *Yoga Dict.* 139/2 *Satya*. (Truthfulness). The second of the abstinences. **1974** *Encycl. Brit. Macropædia* VIII. 900/1 The ancient ideals of *ahiṃsā*, chastity, observances, and *satya* (Truth, which he [*sc.* Gandhi] identified with God) were the main principles of his undogmatic doctrine and social and political practice. **1975** DASTUR & AIYAR in H. M. Patel et al. *Say not the Struggle Nought Availeth* 192 In Gandhi's view, truth (*satya*) and non-violence (*ahimsa*) were inter-related.

‖**satyagraha** (saˈtjaːgraha). [a. Skr. *satyāgraha* insistence on truth, f. *satya* truth + *āgraha* pertinacity.] The Indian form of passive resistance, as formulated by M. K. Gandhi. Also *transf.* and *attrib.*

1920 M. K. GANDHI *Non-Co-operation* (1921) 46 But all the painful experience that I then gained did not in any way shake my belief in Satyagraha or in the possibility of that matchless force being utilised in India. **1928** V. G. DESAI tr. *Gandhi's Satyagraha in S. Afr.* xii. 173 A small prize was therefore announced in *Indian Opinion* to be awarded to the reader who invented the best designation for our struggle... Sr. Maganlal Gandhi..suggested the word 'Sadagraha', meaning 'firmness in a good cause'. I..corrected it to 'Satyagraha'. Truth (Satya) implies love and firmness (Agraha) engenders and therefore serves as a synonym for force. I thus began to call the Indian movement 'Satyagraha', that is to say, the Force which is born of truth and love or non-violence, and gave up the use of the phrase 'passive resistance'. **1929** *Daily Express* 10 Jan. 1/5 The ex-soldiers expressed their intention of performing satyagraha until their leader was released. **1930** *Aberdeen Press & Jrnl.* 7 Apr. 7/1 The 'Untouchables', dissatisfied with his campaign, have threatened counter satyagraha. **1955** *Times* 5 July 10/5 But there were signs of official uneasiness; Sikh dignitaries were arrested before offering satyagraha, Press censorship was imposed in Amritsar, [etc.]. **1958** *Economist* 26 July 280 Delay in producing this Bill was one of the grievances advanced by the Tamil minority when they launched their satyagraha campaign in the spring. **1963** *Times* 3 May 12/2 Negro and white youngsters, organized by bodies such as the student non-violent coordinating committee and the south Christian leaders' conference, will be offering their own kind of satyagraha throughout the deep south. **1969** *Pioneer* (Lucknow) 13 Aug. 7/7 A batch of 12 girls were taken into custody..when they staged satyagraha in support of a separate Telengana. **1976** *Times* 23 Jan. 9/2 The opposition..is pursuing its campaign of *satyagraha* (non-violent demonstration) in traditional Indian style. **1980** *Times Lit. Suppl.* 21 Nov. 1339/1 For him [*sc.* Michael Scott], the world desperately needs a moral force which will work for justice. He finds this in *satyagraha*, the soul-force, more positive than non-violence or passive resistance, an active weapon of good in its perennial fight against evil.

So **satˈyagrahi** (with pl. **satyagrahi** or **satyagrahis**), **satˈyagrahist**, an exponent or practitioner of *satyagraha*.

1928 V. G. DESAI tr. *Gandhi's Satyagraha in S. Afr.* xx. 233 Rama Sundara was the first Satyagrahi prisoner. *Ibid.* xlv. 468 Only thus could the Satyagrahis..bring their struggle to a triumphant end. **1930** *Aberdeen Press & Jrnl.* 6 Mar. 8/6 He [*sc.* Gandhi] will be accompanied by a band of satyagrahists or home rule volunteers, who will march on foot. **1934** H. MILLER *Tropic of Cancer* 102 The little band of Satyagrahists imitated the devotion of their master. **1968** H. J. N. HORSBURGH *Non-Violence & Aggression* i. 22 Belligerents do, and satyagrahi do not, claim finality for their interpretation of a just settlement. **1976** *New Yorker* 24 May 43/1 According to Gandhi, a satyagrahi, or votary of satyagraha, is governed by the belief that the soul can be saved from evil in the world, and so helped along in its search for Brahma, by truth and truth alone.

satyr (ˈsætə(r)). Forms: α. (repr. L. *satyrus*, pl. *satyrī*) 4 satirus; *pl.* 4–6 satiri, satyri, (4–5 satiry, satury, satarye). β. 5–7 satyre, 6 satyer, 6–8 satire, 6– satyr. [ad. L. *satyrus*, a. Gr. σάτυρος. Cf. F. *satyre*, Sp. *sátiro*, Pg., It. *satiro*.]

1. a. *Myth.* One of a class of woodland gods or demons, in form partly human and partly bestial, supposed to be the companions of Bacchus.

In Greek art of the pre-Roman period the satyr was represented with the ears and tail of a horse. Roman sculptors assimilated it in some degree to the faun of their native mythology, giving to it the ears, tail, and legs of a goat, and budding horns.

In the English Bible the word is applied (without precedent either in the LXX or the Vulgate) to the hairy demons or monsters (Heb. *ṣᵉʿīrīm*) of Semitic superstition, supposed to inhabit deserts.

c **1374** CHAUCER *Tr. & Cr.* IV. 1516 (1544) And þis, on euery god celestial I swere it ȝow,..On euery Nymphe and deyte infernal On satury and fawny more and lesse, þat halue goddes ben of wildernesse. *c* **1387** TREVISA *Higden* (Rolls) I. 169 þere is ofte by nyȝte i-seie fire, fauni, and satyri. **1390** GOWER *Conf.* II. 171 The Greks..Sein ek that of the helles hihe The goddes ben in special, Bot of here name in general Thei hoten alle Satiri. **1484** CAXTON *Fables of Auian* xxii, The wodewose or Satyre ledde the pylgrym in to his pytte. **1569** J. SANFORD tr. *Agrippa's Van. Artes* 111 The woode Satires. **1581** PETTIE *Guazzo's Civ. Conv.* III. (1586) 157 A milkemaide of the countrie, who will haue as good a grace amongst other women, as a Satyre would haue amongst the Nymphes. **1584** R. SCOT *Discov. Witchcr.* VII. xv. (1886) 122 They have so fraied us with bull beggers, spirits, witches, urchens, elves, hags, fairies, saytrs, pans, fauns, sylens [etc.]. **1594** NASHE *Terrors Nt.* Wks. (Grosart) III. 222 Fawnes, Satyres, Dryades, & Hamadryades. **1595** *Locrine* V. iv. 203 You Driades and lightfoote Satiri. **1602** SHAKS. *Ham.* I. ii. 140 So excellent a King, that was to this Hiperion to a Satyre. **1611** BIBLE *Isa.* xiii. 21 Satyres [1885 (*Revised*) satyrs (*margin* or he-goats)] shall daunce there. **1700** CONGREVE *Way of World* III. xviii, Sure I was born with budding Antlers like a young Satyr. **1848** MRS. JAMESON *Sacr. & Leg. Art* (1850) 64 The head has the god-like ugliness and malignity of a satyr.

b. *fig.* as the type of lustfulness.

1781 COWPER *Conversat.* 38 The heathen law-givers of ancient days,..Would drive them forth from the resort of men, And shut up ev'ry satyr in his den. **1877** RUSKIN *Laws Fesole* I. 206 The essential character of Renaissance art, —the pride of Thieves, adorned by the industry of Fools, under the mastership of Satyrs.

¶**c.** The confusion between the words *satiric* and *satyric* gave rise to the notion that the satyrs who formed the chorus of the Greek satyric drama had to deliver 'satirical' speeches. Hence, in the 16–17th c., the frequent attribution to the satyrs of censoriousness as a characteristic quality. See also SATIRE *sb.* 4.

?**1580** LODGE *Repl. Gosson's Sch. Abuse* 36 They presented the liues of Satyers, So that they might wiselye vnder the abuse of that name, discouer the follies of many theyr folish fellow citesens. **1593** GREENE *Mamillia* II. To Rdrs., Let Momus mocke, and Zoilus enuie,..yea, let the sauage Satyre himselfe, whose cynicall censure is more seuere than need, frowne at his pleasure. **1650** B. *Discolliminium* 46 A..lumpe, compounded of..Satyres Splens, Polecatts Lites.

2. A kind of ape (so Gr. σάτυρος); in modern use, the orang-utan, *Simia satyrus*. *rare.*

1398 TREVISA *Barth. De P.R.* XVIII. xcvi. (1495) 842 Some ape is callyd Satirus, plesynge in face wyth mery meuynges and playenges. **1613** PURCHAS *Pilgrimage* (1614) 558 Other Apes there are store, and as Solinus reporteth, Satyres with feet like Goats, and Sphynges, with breasts like women. **1698** FRYER *Acc. E. India & P.* 188 For their Solitariness called Men of the Woods, or more truly Satyrs. **1776** BURNEY *Hist. Mus.* (1789) I. ii. 304 Satyr is a name given by some authors to the Orang-outang, or man of the woods. **1780** *Ann. Reg.* 196 Gough..unchained a large fierce animal ..it proved to be a man satyr... Gough is a dealer in wild beasts. **1842** BRANDE *Dict. Sci.*, etc., s.v., In Zoölogy, the ourang-outang..is sometimes called satyr.

3. Any butterfly of the group *Satyridæ*.

1871 NEWMAN *Brit. Butterflies* 77.

†**4.** *Cant.* (See quot.) *Obs.*

1714 A. SMITH *Lives Highwaym.* (ed. 2) II. 136 He left off picking Pockets, and got into a Gang of Satyrs who are Men living wild in the Fields, that keep their Holds and Dwellings in the Country and forsaken Places, stealing Horses, Kine, Sheep, and all other sort of Cattle.

†**5.** *Her.* = SATYRAL. *Obs.*

1889 [see SATYRAL].

6. *attrib.* and *Comb.*, as ***satyr-brood, -dance, forest, -shape, -spring, -talk, train; satyr-charming, -footed, -hairy, -haunted, -like, -shrewd*** adjs.; **satyr-drama** = SATYRIC *drama*; **satyr-pug**, a British geometer moth, *Eupithecia satyrata*.

1924 E. SITWELL *Sleeping Beauty* i. 11 Smiling dim as *satyr-broods. **1883** J. G. WHITTIER *Bay of Seven Islands* 31 Calm as the hour, methinks I feel A sense of worship o'er me steal; Not that of *satyr-charming Pan. *a* **1746** HOLDSWORTH *Rem. Virgil* (1768) 23 Virgil here speaks of a feast just like this; and of the Pan or *Satyr-dance. **1850** LEITCH tr. *C. O. Müller's Anc. Art* §386 (ed. 2) 499 The old *satyr-drama. **1598** E. GUILPIN *Skial.* (1878) 35 Thys leaden-heeled passion is to dull, To keepe pace with this *Satyre-footed gull. **1933** E. SITWELL *Five Variations* 2 Mowhair for *satyr forests. **1953** —— *Gardeners & Astronomers* 29 Like the first budding of the small red *satyr-hairy leaves upon the fruit-boughs. **1924** —— *Sleeping Beauty* xv. 53 From *satyr-haunted caverns drip These lovely airs on brow and lip. **1835** POE in *Southern Lit. Messenger* I. 637/2 *Satyr-like figure of Mentoni himself. **1882** 'OUIDA' *Maremma* I. viii. 187 The figure of a shepherd, satyr-like and clad in goatskin. **1869** NEWMAN *Moths* 126 The *Satyr Pug. **1850** TENNYSON *In Mem.* xxxv, In his coarsest *Satyr-shape. **1928** BLUNDEN *Retreat* 38 And almost catch the horned and rude Woodgod at gaze ere *satyr-shrewd He dodges by. **1922** E. SITWELL *Façade* 7 Like red Furred buds of *satyr-springs long dead. **1944** L. MACNEICE *Springboard* 49 Not smut but *satyr-talk, not clever but wise. *a* **1717** PARNELL *To Pope* 27 A *Satyr Train Peeps o'er their Heads, and laugh behind the Scene.

satyr, obs. form of SATIRE *sb.*

‖**satyra** (ˈsætɪrə). [L., a. Gr. σατύρα, fem. of σάτυρος SATYR.] A female satyr.

1850 LEITCH tr. *C. O. Müller's Anc. Art* §385 (ed. 2) 497 Double herma of a satyr and a satyra.

satyral (ˈsætɪrəl). *Her.* [a. OF. *satirel*, *-al*, dim. of *satire* SATYR.] (See quot.)

1780 EDMONDSON *Heraldry* II. Gloss., *Satyral*, a fictitious beast, said to have the body of a lion, the tail and horns of an antelope, and the face of an old man. **1889** ELVIN *Dict. Her.*, *Satyr* or *satyral*.

Satyrday, satyre: see SATURDAY, SATIRE *sb.*

satyresque (sætɪˈrɛsk), *a.* Also -esk. [ad. It. *satiresco*, f. *satiro* SATYR: see -ESQUE.]

Resembling a satyr; having the characteristics of a satyr.

1755 *Phil. Trans.* XLIX. 497 It..represents a Priapus, which is not satyresque. **1850** LEITCH tr. *C. O. Müller's Anc. Art* §329 (ed. 2) 388 The gelasinus in the cheeks also only becomes satyresk beauties.

satyress ('sætɪrɪs). [-ESS.] A female satyr.

1840 H. DRUMMOND *Let. to T. Phillips* 24 Satyresses suckling their little cubs. **1890** *Sat. Rev.* 11 Oct. 437/1 The fauness or satyress..grows a little monotonous. **1952** [see NIXIE[1]]. **1978** *Daily Tel.* 12 Apr. 14/4 A Tiepolo drawing, 'A Centaur with a Satyress', was bought for £4,000.

satyri, satyrial(l: see SATYR, SATIRIAL *a.*

satyrian, obs. form of SATYRION.

‖**satyriasis** (sætɪ'raɪəsɪs). *Path.* Also 7 saturyasis. [mod. L., a. Gr. σατυρίασις, f. σατυριᾶν to suffer from satyriasis, f. σάτυρ-ος SATYR: see -ASIS.]

1. 'Excessively great venereal desire in the male. Also, synonym for *Priapism*' (*Syd. Soc. Lex.* 1897).

1657 W. COLES *Adam in Eden* cclxxx, Being put into Plaisters and applyed to the Reines, it helpeth the Satyriasis or continuall standing of the Yard. **1696** FLOYER *On the Humours* (J.), If the chyle be very plentiful it breeds a satyriasis. **1874** BUCKNILL & TUKE *Man. Psych. Med., Insanity* 452 Satyriasis and Nymphomania, as examples of Monomania, are, therefore, liable to the objection that they are spinal or cerebro-spinal affections.

fig. **1629** QUARLES *Argalus & P.* I. 46 Now..euery eare Hath got the Saturyasis to heare This tragicke sceane. **1847** DE QUINCEY *Notes on Landor* Wks. 1858 IX. 285 Afflicted with the very satyriasis of curiosity.

2. 'Old term applied to a variety of *Elephantiasis græcorum*, or leprosy, on account of its hideous appearance' (*Syd. Soc. Lex.* 1897).

[**1684** *Blancard's Phys. Dict., Satyriasis...* 'Tis taken sometimes for the Leprosy, because in that Disease the Skin acquires the Roughness of a Satyr.] **1884** A. LAMBERT in *Contemp. Rev.* Aug. 211 Elephantiasis, Satyriasis, Leontiasis, serve only to render more vividly the real fact of uttermost misery..concealed now under the common name of Leprosy.

satyric (sə'tɪrɪk), *a.* and *sb.* Also 7 satir-, satyrique, 8 satir-, satyrick. [ad. L. *satyric-us*, Gr. σατυρικ-ός, f. σάτυρ-ος SATYR: see -IC.]

A. *adj.* Pertaining to satyrs; *esp.* as the epithet of that species of Greek drama in which the chorus was habited to represent satyrs.

1607 TOPSELL *Four-f. Beasts* 13 That..there are certaine little hilles full of the *Satyrique-Ægipanæ*, and that in the night time they vse great fires, piping and dansing. **1693** DRYDEN *Juvenal* Ded. (1697) 32 In the Olympique Games, where the Poets contended for four Prizes, the Satirique Tragedy was the last of them. **1776** J. BRYANT *Mythol.* III. 196 They had also..the satyric dance, which was common among the Thracians, and the people of Greece. **1783** T. WILSON *Archæol. Dict.* s.v. *Scene*, According to Vitruvius there were three sorts of scenes, *Tragic, Comic*, and *Satyric*. **1819** SHELLEY (*title*) The Cyclops. A Satyric Drama Translated from the Greek of Euripides. **1871** NESBITT *Catal. Slade Coll. Glass* 167 Five columns, surmounted by satyric masks. **1877** RUSKIN *Fors Clav.* lxxxiii. 360 Which satyric dance and sirenic song accomplished [etc.].

†**B.** *sb.* A satyric drama. *Obs.*

1693 DRYDEN *Juvenal* Ded. (1697) 32 Amongst the Plays of Euripides,..there is one of these Satyriques. *Ibid.* 33 The Satyrique, says he [Casaubon], is a Dramatique Poem, annex'd to a Tragedy; having a Chorus, which consists of Satyrs.

satyric, obs. form of SATIRIC.

satyrical (sə'tɪrɪkəl), *a.* [f. L. *satyric-us* (see prec.) + -AL[1].] = SATYRIC *a.*

1590 L. LLOYD *1st Pt. Diall of Daies* Oct. 43 Picus and Faunus two Satyricall Gods. **1601** HOLLAND *Pliny* I. 296 Those satyricall gesticulations of theirs like Antikes. **1699** BENTLEY *Phal.* 243 The true Thespis's Plays were all Satyrical, (that is, the Plot of them was the story of Bacchus, the Chorus consisted of Satyrs). **1763** J. BROWN *Poetry & Mus.* vii. 144 In this Union of comic Representation and a satyrical Choir, we see the genuine, though imperfect and rude Form of the old Greek Comedy. *a* **1846** MRS. BROWNING *Lett. R. H. Horne* (1877) II. liv. 98 There are certain objections..such as the difficulty of sustaining the right Satyrical tone.

satyrical, obs. form of SATIRICAL *a.*

sa'tyrically, *adv. rare.* [f. SATYR.] In the manner of a satyr.

1887 SWINBURNE *Let.* 14 Aug. (1962) V. 209, I have written a poem..called 'Pan and Thalassius'... Pan is figured in all his different shapes or phases..lord of the mystery of earth and immanent godhead of—or in—the terrene All: only not of the human soul, the stars, Urania, and the sea—on whose general behalf the intruder in his domain has the last word—while recognizing the folly and falsehood of the cry that 'Pan is dead'..over which premature cry the old wood-god chuckles satyrically.

Satyrid (sə'tɪrɪd), *sb.* and *a.* [a. mod.L. family name *Satyridæ*, f. generic name *Satyrus* (P. A. Latreille & J. B. Godart *Encyclopédie Méthodique* (*Insectes*) (1819) IX. 11): see SATYR and -ID[3].] **A.** *sb.* A small, usually brown, butterfly belonging to the subfamily Satyrinæ of the family Nymphalidæ. **B.** *adj.* Of or pertaining to a butterfly of this kind.

1901 D. SHARP in *Cambr. Nat. Hist.* VI. vi. 348 The species of the genus *Pierella* connect these transparent Satyrids with the more ordinary forms. **1912** H. ROWLAND-BROWN *Butterflies & Moths* viii. 79 The Continental Satyrids..and our 'Grayling',..well-nigh invisible on the tree trunks where they love to perch. **1936** *Discovery* Dec. 370/2 A shining silvery insect..quite different from the general run of Satyrid butterflies. **1963** V. NABOKOV *Gift* ii. 126 His father accompanied him up a trail through the pinewoods in order to show him, with a smile of condescension for this European trifle, the Satyrid recently described by Kuznetzov, which was flitting from stone to stone. **1975** *Zool. Jrnl.* CLXXVII. 333 *Zethera hestioides* Felder, a Philippine Satyrid..shows unimodal mimicry.

satyrion (sə'tɪrɪən). Forms: 5 saturioun, 6–7 satirion, 7 satyrian, saterion, 6– satyrion. Also 8 in L. form **satyrium.** [a. L. *satyrion, -um*, a. Gr. σατύριον, f. σάτυρ-ος SATYR, in allusion to the reputed aphrodisiac properties of the plant so named.] A name given to various kinds of Orchis.

The name *Satyrium* has been given in botanical Latin to a sub-tropical orchidaceous genus.

a **1400** *Stockholm Med. MS.* ii. 732 in *Anglia* XVIII. 325 Of dragans arn spycis iij..Bothe arn callyd saturioun. **1526** *Grete Herball* cccxci. (1529) Xv, Satirion..groweth on hylles & playne feldes. **1548** TURNER *Names Herbes* (E.D.S.) 70 The great Satyrion may be called in englishe whyte satyrion or great satyrion. **1597** GERARDE *Herbal* I. civ. 172 Red handed Satyrion is a smal lowe and base herbe. **1625** BACON *Ess., Gardens* ¶1 The Sweet Satyrian, with the White Flower. **1681** OTWAY *Soldier's Fort.* v. (1735) 108 'Tis the root Satyrion, a very precious plant. **1731** MILLER *Gard. Dict., Orchis*,..Satyrion, or Fool-Stones. **1752** J. HILL *Hist. Plants* 591 (Jod.) The undivided bulbed satyrium, with lanceolated leaves. **1844** KITTO *Phys. Hist. Palestine* vii. 241 Moon-trefoil; knapweed; satyrion.

attrib. **1637** HEYWOOD *Dial.* xvi. 237 There nothing is to boot Between a Bean and a Satyrion root. **1661** RABISHA *Cookery* 220 To preserve Saterion roots.

satyrique, obs. form of SATIRIC *a.*

satyrish ('sætɪrɪʃ), *a.* [f. SATYR + -ISH[1].] Characteristic of a satyr (sense 1); erotic, sensual.

1932 W. FAULKNER *Sartoris* III. vi. 233 Simon chuckled again, unctuously, a satyrish chuckle rich with complacent innuendo. **1937** J. C. POWYS *Maiden Castle* v. 198 His satyrish pleasure in the exposed curves of her limbs.

satyrisk ('sætɪrɪsk). *Antiq. rare.* [ad. Gr. σατυρίσκος, dim. of σάτυρος SATYR.] A little satyr.

1850 LEITCH tr. *C. O. Müller's Anc. Art* §386 (ed. 2) 500 Heron also..mentions Satyrisks with wine-skins.

satyromaniac (ˌsætɪrəʊ'meɪnɪæk), *a.* and *sb.* [f. SATYR + -O + -MANIAC.] **A.** *adj.* Of a man: exhibiting excessive sexual desire. **B.** *sb.* A man who exhibits excessive sexual desires; a sex maniac.

1889 *Cent. Dict., Satyromaniac, a.* and *n.* I. *a.* Affected with satyromania. II. *n.* A person affected with satyromania. **1892** G. B. SHAW *Let.* 12 Aug. (1965) I. 360, I hear from Oxford that de Mattos is ravishing every maiden in the country... York Powell writes to me privately urging the importance of dissociating ourselves from the satyromaniac W. S. de M. **1909** — *Let.* 22 June (1972) II. 847, I have read the play... It is made impossible by your nymphomania. There are two men in it.., one a satyromaniac, the other a mere imaginary male figment to focus the nymphomania of all the women. **1944** D. L. SAYERS *Let.* 18 Oct. in J. Brabazon *D. L. Sayers* (1981) x. 112 All Satyromaniacs, sadists, connoisseurs in rape.

Satzuma: see SATSUMA.

sau, obs. pa. t. of SEE *v.*; obs. f. SAW, SOW.

sauba ('sɔːbə, ‖sa'uba). In quots. saüba. [Tupi *sauba.*] The leaf-cutting ant (*Œcodoma cephalotes*) of tropical South America.

1863 BATES *Nat. Amazons* i. (1864) 11 Another far more interesting species was the Saüba... Large mounds of earth,..forty yards in circumference,..were the work of the Saübas. **1864–5** WOOD *Homes without Hands* vii. (1868) 122 The Saüba or Coushie Ant.

sauce (sɔːs), *sb.* Forms: 4–5 sawse, *Sc.* salss, 4–8 sawce, sause, 5 saus, sace, 5–6 *Sc.* sals(e, 6 saulce, sace, 9 *vulgar* sarse, saase, sass, 4– sauce. See also SOUSE. [a. F. *sauce* (in OF. also *sausse*) = Pr., Sp., Pg., It. *salsa*:—popular L. *salsa*, fem. of *salsus* salted: see SALT *a.*[1] The etymological sense is thus identical with that of SALAD.]

1. a. Any preparation, usually liquid or soft, and often consisting of several ingredients, intended to be eaten as an appetizing accompaniment to some article of food. †Formerly occas. applied to a condiment of any kind.

Often with qualifying word denoting the predominant ingredient, as ***bread, egg, mint, parsley sauce***, or with qualifying *adj.*, as ***black, brown, hard, white sauce***. †Also (15th c.) in many adopted Fr. terms, as ***sauce cameline, galantine, gansell***, etc.: see *Two Cookery-bks.* 77 (*c* 1450) and 108–110 (*c* 1430). Occas., in the names of sauces taken unchanged from French into English, found with the qualifying word following; in such cases the Fr. pronunc. (sos) may be heard. † ***Robert sauce*** [tr. F. *sauce Robert*], now usu. ***sauce Robert*** (sos rɔbɛr): a sauce consisting of chopped onions cooked with butter and seasoned. See also ALLEMANDE *sb.* 3, BÉARNAISE, MORNAY, SOUBISE 2.

1350 *Will. Palerne* 1882 þei ete at here ese as þei miȝt þanne, boute salt oþer sauce or any semli drynk. **13..** *E.E. Allit. P.* B. 823 [Lot's wife] sayde softely to hir self 'þis vn-sauere [*MS.* vn-fauere] hyne Louez no salt in her sauce'. *c* **1386** CHAUCER *Nuns Pr. T.* 14 Of poynaunt sauce [*v.rr.* sawce, sause] hir neded neuer a deel. *c* **1420** *Liber Cocorum* (1862) 52 For grete lordis þou schalt take wyne With safroune to þy sawce ful fyne. *c* **1450** HOLLAND *Howlat* 705 Many sawouris salss with sewaris he send. *c* **1480** HENRYSON *Test. Cress.* 421 The swete Meitis, seruit in plaittis clene, With Saipheron sals of ane gude sessoun. **1481–90** *Howard Househ. Bks.* (Roxb.) 109 Otmele j.d. Sasis j.d. Clos and mas j.d. **1558** WARDE tr. *Alexis' Secr.* (1568) 42 Use it at meales in the maner of a saulce. **1573** 'C. HOLLYBANDE' *French Schoole-maister* 114 Cut some of these loynes of the hare, drest with a blacke sauce. **1578** LYTE *Dodoens* II. lxxvi. 250 This herbe is also used..in Salades and sawces. **1633** P. FLETCHER *Purple Isl.* I. xxvii, While sugar hires the taste the brain to drown, And bribes of sauce corrupt false appetite. *a* **1656** BP. HALL *Rem. Wks.* (1660) 186 A sharp kind of sowrenesse in sawces is esteemed pleasing and tastfull. *a* **1682** SIR T. BROWNE *Misc. Tracts* (1684) 81 Sawce made of Raisins stamped with Vinegar. **1723** J. NOTT *Cook's & Confectioner's Dict.* sig. Bb6, *To dress Pikes* à la Sainte Robert [*sic*]..make your Sauce Robert in the following manner. *Ibid.* sig. D[v], *Artichokes with white Sauce...* Make a Sauce for them with the Yolks of Eggs, a Drop or two of Vinegar, and a little Gravy. **1725** *Bradley's Fam. Dict.* s.v. *Roast-Meats*, An old wild Boar must be dress'd..with Pepper and Vinegar, or Robert-Sauce. **1750** W. ELLIS *Country Housewife's Comp.* 246 For Sauce to such a Pudding, they strew a little Sugar over it when out of the oven, and then it becomes so palatable that [etc.]. **1764** ELIZA MOXON *Eng. Housew.* (ed. 9) 123 To make Sauce for tame Ducks. **1806** J. SIMPSON *Compl. Syst. Cookery* 293 Pigs feet au gratin, ears shredded, and sauce robert. **1845** E. ACTON *Mod. Cookery* iv. 116 *Bechamel.* This is a fine French white sauce, now very much served at good English tables. *Ibid.* 127 Parsley-green, for colouring Sauces. *Ibid.* 130 *Sauce Robert...* Large onions,..butter,..flour... Gravy... Mustard. **1884** *Girl's Own Paper* May 427/3 Boiled chicken ..covered with white sauce. **1909** *Cent. Dict.* Suppl., *Hard sauce*, a creamy sauce of butter and sugar, usually flavoured with vanilla or the like. **1911** WEBSTER, Brown sauce = Espagnole sauce. **1928** S. LEWIS *Man who knew Coolidge* I. 103 A..Plum Pudding..with both hard and soft sauce. **1935** 'R. HULL' *Keep it Quiet* xxix. 279 A brown substance ..called generally 'Sauce Robert', which disfigures cutlets and suchlike. **1939** A. L. SIMON *Conc. Encycl. Gastron.* I. 29/2 In U.S.A., a Hard Sauce is made with one measure of fresh butter to two of castor sugar... A squeeze of lemon is then added... It is usual, in some States,..to add some Brandy or Rum... In England, a similar sauce is called Brandy Butter or Rum Butter. **1960** *Good Housek. Cookery Bk.* (rev. ed) 196/1 The foundation of all brown and white sauces in which flour is the thickening agent is the roux, formed by cooking the butter and flour together. For white sauces the butter should be melted, the flour added and the two stirred and cooked together until well incorporated. The liquid should then be added by degrees. **1974** E. MCGIRR *Murderous Journey* 90 His man had a certain way with Sauce Robert which gave it an added piquancy. **1981** M. C. SMITH *Gorky Park* III. 304 She'd brought cartons of spaghetti with meat, clam and white sauces.

b. In proverbial expressions, as ***sweet meat will have sour sauce, what's sauce for the goose is sauce for the gander***, and the like.

1562 J. HEYWOOD *Prov. & Epigr.* (1867) 158 Sweete meate will haue soure sauce, to this reason feate, Ioyne this conuersion soure sauce will haue sweete meate. **1581** T. HOWELL *Deuises* (1879) 200 Aye me that such soure sauce, false fortune should procure. **1607** HIERON *Wks.* (1614) I. 20 The sweet meats of wickednes will haue the sowre sauce of wretchednes and misery. **1700** COLLIER *2nd Def. Short View* 37 That that's Sawce for a Goose is Sawce for a Gander. **1845** DISRAELI *Sybil* III. i, We were holding out for our rights, and that's sauce for any gander. **1900** UPWARD *Eben. Lobb* 295 It seemed to me as though what was sauce for the insured ought to have been sauce for the annuitant. **1905** *Athenæum* 5 Aug. 167/1 What is sauce for the verb is surely sauce for the verbal substantive.

c. *transf.*

1362 LANGL. *P. Pl.* A. VII. 249 Ete not, Ich hote þe, til hunger þe take, And sende þe sum of his sauce to sauer þe þe betere. **1375** BARBOUR *Bruce* III. 540 Thai soucht [nane othir] sals thar-till Bot appetyt. **1542** UDALL *Erasm. Apoph.* 13 b, Houngre & thirste is for all thynges the beste sauce in the worlde. **1555–1634** [see HUNGER *sb.* 1 c]. **1693** LOCKE *Educ.* §13. 13 Flesh once a Day,..without other Sawce than Hunger, is best.

d. *U.S. slang.* (See quot.)

1919 E. V. RICKENBACKER *Fighting Flying Circus* p. xi, *Sauce*, petrol or gasoline.

e. *slang* (orig. *U.S.*). Alcoholic liquor; occas., a narcotic drug.

1940 J. O'HARA *Pal Joey* 114 It made him sad and he almost began hitting the sauce. **1953** W. BURROUGHS *Junkie* (1972) xiii. 134 The first thing you have to do is cut down on the sauce and build up your health. You look terrible. **1960** WODEHOUSE *Jeeves in Offing* xvii. 176 Her first husband,.. was..a constant pain in the neck to her till one night he most fortunately walked into the River Thames while under the influence of the sauce and didn't come up for days. **1970** M. BRAITHWAITE *Never sleep Three in Bed* vi. 66 Which means any occasion when any group of the brothers and sisters.. have got into the sauce. **1975** N. FREELING *What are Bugles blowing For?* xii. 74 Castang found a narcotics squad cop... Patricia was known, but not well. 'She got off the sauce for nearly a year.' **1976** W. TREVOR *Children of Dynmouth* v. 114 'You often get loonies in joints like that,' he remarked on the street. 'They drink the sauce and it softens their brains for them.' **1978** H. C. RAE *Sullivan* I. ii. 25 You're not in debt, on the sauce, going gay... I can't blackmail you.

2. *fig.* Something which adds piquancy to a word, idea, thought or action. Also in Fr. phr. ***sauce piquante.***

a **1500–20** DUNBAR *Poems* lxvii. 19 Quha maist it servis sall sonast repent: Off quhais subchettis sour is the sals. **1533**

MORE *Debell. Salem* Wks. 969/2 But this good host of ours ..geueth vs thereto one litle messe of sace to it. **1552** [see SAUCY *a.*[1] 1 *fig.*]. **1642** FULLER *Holy & Prof. State* II. xiii. 183 Sleep it self is a recreation; adde not therefore sauce to sauce. **1692** R. L'ESTRANGE *Fables* lxxiv. 74 That which we call Raillery, in This Sense, is the very Sawce of Civil Entertainment. **1821** HAZLITT *Table-T.* Ser. I, *Character of Cobbett* 121 How fine were the graphical descriptions he sent us from America:..what a fine *sauce piquante* of contempt they were seasoned with! **1831** SCOTT *Ct. Robt.* xiii, What is enticing to other men, must, to interest them, have the piquant sauce of extreme danger. **1907** A. C. BENSON *Altar Fire* 16 Fame is only one of the sauces of life. **1934** C. LAMBERT *Music Ho!* III. 206 They are only thorns protecting a fleshy cactus—a sauce piquante poured over a nice juicy steak.

3. Phrases. **a.** ***to serve with the same sauce***: to subject to the same kind of usage (as one has suffered, or as has been inflicted on another). Similarly, ***a sop of the same sauce, to taste of the same sauce***.

1523 LD. BERNERS *Froiss.* I. ccccxv. 726 If the flemynges had achyued the prise ouer them, they had bene serued of the same sauce. **1555** EDEN *Decades* (Arb.) 70 They serue them with like sause, requitinge deathe for deathe. **1587** GREENE *Euphues his Censure* Wks. (Grosart) VI. 223 Hee [Cleophanes] thought to giue them a soppe of the same sauce, and to thrust out one wyle with another. **1593** *Telltroth's N. Y. Gift* (1876) 7, I wil not liue alone in sorrow, but will make thee taste of the same sauce. **1605** *Trag. End Sir J. Fites* (1860) 24 The other man who was close by him ..might wel haue beene served with the same sawce likewise. **1704** J. PITTS *Acc. Mohammetans* 152 They sent for the French Consul, intending to serve him the same Sause. **1889** 'R. BOLDREWOOD' *Robbery under Arms* xxxvi, You deserve the same sauce..for..letting that ruffian torment these helpless ladies.

†**b.** ***to have eaten sauce, to have drunk of sauce's cup***: to be abusive. *Obs.*

Cf. sense 6b, and SAUCE *v.* 4c, d.

1526 SKELTON *Magnyf.* 1404 Ye haue eten sauce, I trowe, at the Taylers Hall. *a* **1529** —— *Bouge of Court* 72 To be so perte..she sayde she trowed that I had eten sauce; She asked yf euer I dranke of saucys cuppe.

†**c.** ***to pay sauce***, to pay dearly; ***to cost*** (a person) ***sauce***, to cost him dearly. *Obs.*

1678 J. PHILLIPS tr. *Tavernier's Trav.* I. IV. viii. 168 This penitence costs the criminal Sawce. **1686** tr. *Chardin's Coronat. Solyman* 107 All the Court..believ'd 'twould cost his ambition sauce; as indeed it fell out. **1694** WESTMACOTT *Script. Herb.* 9 We pay Sauce for sophisticated stuff. **1718** MOTTEUX *Quix.* (1733) II. 116 The Innkeeper..swore.. that they should pay him Sauce for the Damage.

†**d.** ***in no sauce***: under no possible circumstances, by no persuasion or inducement. *Obs.*

[Cf. Fr. 'cela ne vaut rien à quelque sauce qu'on le mette'.]

1542 UDALL *Erasm. Apoph.* 265b, An haulte courage towarde, and that could in no sauce abyde to bee putte backe. **1550** LATIMER *Last Serm. bef. Edw. VI* (1562) 113b, And yet I remember I had preached vpon thys Epistle once afore Kyng Henry the .viii. but now I could not frame wyth it, nor it liked me not in no sauce. **1565** T. STAPLETON *Fortr. Faith* 10 The lerned therefore amonge the protestants will in no sauce make papistry so late a matter.

4. a. Chiefly *U.S.* Vegetables or fruits, fresh or preserved, taken as part of a meal, or as a relish. Often = SALAD. See also GREEN SAUCE.

In U.S. ***long sauce*** = beet, carrots, and parsnips; ***short sauce*** = potatoes, turnips, onions, pumpkins, etc.

1629 PARKINSON *Parad.* title-p., A Kitchen Garden of all manner of herbes,..and fruites, for meate or sause vsed with vs. **1705** BEVERLY *Hist. Virginia* IV. xvii. (1722) 253 Roots, herbs, vine-fruits, and Sallad-flowers..they dish up..and find them very delicious Sauce to their Meats. **1809** W. IRVING *Knickerb.* III. vii. (1820) 204 Some buxom country heiress,..deeply skilled in the mystery of making apple sweetmeats, long sauce, and pumpkin pie. **1813** BATCHELOR *Agric. Bedford.* 76 (E.D.D.) The potatoe..is also the principal vegetable used for sauce. **1893** ZINCKE *Wherstead* xxvii. 261 Vegetables are, with us [in East Anglia], 'sauce'.

b. *U.S.* A dish of fruit-pulp stewed with sweetening or flavouring.

In recent Dicts.; the examples cited are *apple-sauce* and *cranberry sauce*, which as used in England belong to sense 1.

1846 MRS. KIRKLAND *West. Clearings* 24 Among custards, cakes, and 'saase' or preserves, of different kinds, figured great dishes of lettuce [etc.].

5. A solution of salt and other ingredients used in some manufacturing processes. Cf. PICKLE *sb.*[1] 3.

So F. *sauce*: see Littré s.v.

1839 URE *Dict. Arts* 617 (Gold) This pickle or sauce, as it is called, takes up..a notable quantity of gold. *Ibid.* 1255 (Tobacco) Watering each layer [of tobacco]..with a solution of sea salt, of spec. grav. 1·107, called sauce. **1876** J. DUNNING *Tobacco* (Brit. Manuf. Industr.) 16 In other countries liquors or 'sauces' (as they are called) are generally employed.

6. [? Evolved from SAUCY *a.*] †**a.** *Vocatively.* An impudent person, a 'saucebox'. *Obs.* Cf. *Jack sauce* s.v. JACK *sb.*[1] 36 and SAUCEBOX.

a **1553** UDALL *Royster D.* III. iii. (Arb.) 48 Backe sir sauce, let gentlefolkes haue elbowe roome. **1591** *Troub. Raigne K. John* (1611) 27 Good words sir sauce, your betters are in place. *c* **1592** MARLOWE *Jew of Malta* III. (1633) F 2b, Go to, sirra sauce, is this your question? get ye gon. **1697** CIBBER *Woman's Wit* III. 40 Why what's that to you, Sawce!

b. Sauciness, impertinence. *colloq.* and *dial.*

1835 MARRYAT *Jac. Faithf.* ii, He's full of his sauce, sir, —you must forgive it. **1872** *Routledge's Every Boy's Ann.* 614/1 Dennis had been in his tantrums..; he'd..given sauce to the monitors. **1897** C. MORLEY *Stud. Board Sch.* 217 My husban' wouldn't take none of his sauce.

7. *attrib.* and *Comb.*, as ***sauce-bottle, -bowl, cook, -deviser, -dish, maker, -plate, -tureen; sauce-stained*** adj.; **sauce-garden** *U.S.*, a garden in which vegetables are grown for the table; **sauce-man** *U.S.*, one who deals in vegetables; **sauce oyster**, a large oyster used in making sauce.

1925 HODKIN & COUSEN *Textbk. Glass Technol.* v. 49 Glasses..of the type usually used for ordinary white flint glass, for medical, paste, and *sauce bottles, and for those used in machines with automatic feeding devices. **1973** *Country Life* 1 Nov. 1313/1 The autumn gathering [of mushrooms] went to make ketchup, put up in old sauce bottles. **1765** J. WEDGWOOD *Let.* 2 Mar. (1965) 29, I have sent the Green & Gold *Sauce bowles and stands..in a box. **1908** *Daily Chron.* 5 Aug. 6/2 A *sauce cook, at the Bath Club. **1884** TENNYSON *Becket* Prol. 52, I know thee..A *sauce-deviser for thy days of fish. **1837** HALIBURTON *Clockm.* Ser. I. xii. 103 They vegitate like a lettuce plant in *sarse garden. *a* **1410** in *1st Rep. Hist. MSS. Comm.* 109/1 All the folks of the *salsemakercrafte..did at their own costs and charges together maintain..the pageant. **1562** TURNER *Herbal* II. (1568) 22 The succot makers and saucemakers. **1837** HAWTHORNE *Twice-told T.* (1851) I. xvi. 249 Behind comes a '*sauceman', driving a wagon full of new potatoes, green ears of corn [etc.]. **1891** *Daily News* 10 Oct. 5/4 *Sauce oysters are unusually large and excellent. **1922** JOYCE *Ulysses* 44 His breath hangs over our *saucestained plates, the green fairy's fang thrusting between his lips. **1772** J. WEDGWOOD *Let.* 17 Feb. (1965) 119, I thank you..for the hint respecting the *sauce Terrine. **1776** [see TUREEN β]. **1835** DICKENS *Sk. Boz, Tales, Mr. W. Tottle* ii, On one side of the table two green sauce-tureens, with ladles of the same. **1971** *Country Life* 1 Apr. 765/2 At the dining table, the classical urn was, of course, readily applied..to the now popular sauce tureen.

sauce (sɔːs), *v.* Forms: 5–6 sause, sawse, 5–7 sawce, 6 saulce, 5– sauce. [f. SAUCE *sb.* Cf. F. *saucer.*]

1. a. *trans.* To season, dress, or prepare (food) with sauces or condiments.

c **1440** *Promp. Parv.* 441/2 Sawcyn, *salmento.* Sawcyn, wythe powder, *idem quod* Powderyn. *c* **1450** *Douce MS.* 55 in *Two Cookery Bks.* 50 Sauce him withe powdre of pepyr and gyngevere & mustarde vynegre & salt and serve him forth. **1556** J. HEYWOOD *Spider & F.* vi. 30 Of a goose with garlicke sauste: so late I eete. **1584** COGAN *Haven Health* cxxvi. (1636) 125 A..powder, to strow upon..Quinces, or Wardens, or to sauce a hen. **1594** R. ASHLEY tr. *Loys le Roy* 15 Eche countrey hauing his peculiar meates, and a seueral kinde of dressing, preparing, sauouring, saulcing, rosting, and boyling them. **1632** tr. *Bruel's Prax. Med.* 242 His meate may be sawced with iuyce of Pomegranates. **1667** L. STUCLEY *Gospel-Glass* xxxii. (1670) 305 Nothing has pleased your squeamish stomachs, but meat so sawced. **1699** EVELYN *Acetaria* 81 Garcius and others, assure us, that the Indians..universally sauce their Viands with it [Fœtid Assa]. **1741** *Compl. Fam.-Piece* I. ii. 152 Sauce them [the cutlets] with Mustard, Butter, Shallot, Vinegar and Gravy. **1883** *American* VII. 120 However poor the meat it is well sauced. **1973** *Jewish Chron.* 2 Feb. 19/1 If..I choose to sauce them, then I find the ordinary four-to-a-fish fillets quite suitable. **1975** *Times* 4 Oct. 12/4 A sole dish..said to be sauced with cream, wine and egg... The pale yellow sauce tasted sour.

b. In proverbial phrase. (See quots.)

1579 GOSSON *Sch. Abuse* (Arb.) 73 Hunger sauceth every meate. **1641** J. SHUTE *Sarah & Hagar* (1649) 136 Saith Saint Basil 'Fasting..sauceth best the use of meats'.

†**c.** *transf.* To make bitter. *Obs.*

1614 BP. HALL *Contempl., O.T.* v. i. 10 So to craue water, that it may not be sauced with bitternes.

2. *fig.* **a.** To furnish a pleasing accompaniment to; to make pleasant or agreeable, to reduce the asperity or severity of.

1514 BARCLAY *Eglog* ii. (1570) Bjb, Their disputation Is swetely saused with adulation. **1561** T. HOBY tr. *Castiglione's Courtyer* I. B4, Other..do..sauce their sorowes with sweetenesse. **1576** FLEMING *Panopl. Epist.* 281 Sawce the same with laughter. **1598** GRENEWEY *Tacitus, Ann.* IV. vii. (1622) 99 These continuall causes of sorrow, were sauced with some small contentment. **1621** in Birch *Crt. & Times Jas. I* (1848) II. 127 This sad news I shall sauce with a little that is more pleasant. **1661** R. L'ESTRANGE *State-Divinity* Pref. 2 Whoever Sauces not his Earnest with a Tang of Fooling misses his Marque. **1837** HAWTHORNE *Twice-told T.* (1851) I. xi. 182 A slice of the densest cloud within his reach, sauced with moonshine.

†**b.** To qualify with a mixture of bitterness. *Obs.*

c **1510** BARCLAY *Mirr. Gd. Manners* (1570) Dv, Joy sauced is with payne. **1565** T. STAPLETON *Fortr. Faith* I. v. 25 Caluin..sauceth the swete and true doctrine, with the cancred venim of heresy. **1617** MORYSON *Itin.* I. 75 Tyrone writ to the Earle of Ormond, whose Letter he sauced with general complaints against the Earle. **1647** FULLER *Wounded Consc.* xv. 112 It being just, that the sweetnesse of his corporall pleasure should be sauced with more spirituall sadnesse. **1655** TERRY *Voy. E. India* iii. 120 The Contents there found by such as have lived in those parts, are sour'd and sauc'd with many unpleasing things.

c. To 'season', make piquant.

1555 WATREMAN *Fardle Facions* II. xi. 238 When this countrefeicte prophet had saused his secte with these wicked opinions: he gaue them his lawe. **1633** BP. HALL *Hard Texts, O.T.* 208 He gave them abundance of food..but withall, hee sauced it with judgement. *a* **1661** HOLYDAY *Juvenal* v. Notes (1673) 80 He endeavour'd to sauce their dishes with his scurrility. **1908** *Westm. Gaz.* 23 Oct. 3/2 Now it [history] must be sauced and savoured,..lest our sickened appetites refuse to taste the dish.

¶**3.** An alleged technical term for: To prepare (a capon, a plaice, a tench) for the table. (Cf. quot. 1513.) Now pseudo-*arch.*

c **1486** *Bk. St. Albans* fvijb, A Capoon sawsede. *Ibid.*, A Tenche sawced. **1513** *Bk. Keruynge* in *Babees Bk.* (1868) 266 Sauce that capon. Take vp a capon, & lyfte vp the ryght legge and the ryght wynge,..& laye hym in the plater as he sholde flee, & serve your soueryne & knowe well that capons or chekyns ben arayed after one sauce; the chekyn shall be sauced with grene sauce or vergyus. **1688** R. HOLME *Armoury* III. iii. 78/1 Sauce that Plaice and Tench,..Sauce that Capon. **1840** H. AINSWORTH *Tower of London* II. xxxix, In the old terms of his art, he leached the brawn, reared the goose, sauced the capon [etc.].

4. In various jocular or colloquial uses. †**a.** To make (a person) 'pay sauce' (see SAUCE *sb.* 3c): to charge extortionate prices to. *Obs.*

1598 SHAKS. *Merry W.* IV. iii. 11 Ile make them pay: Ile sauce them.

†**b.** To belabour, flog. Also *fig. Obs.*

1598 B. JONSON *Ev. Man in Hum.* III. v. (1601) H3b, Oh he hath basted me rarely, sumptiously: but I haue it heare will sause him. *a* **1693** AUBREY *Lives, Dr. Triplet* (1898) I. 265 'And doe not sawce me openly.' 'Yes sir, I'll sawce you openly.' *a* **1726** VANBRUGH *Journey to London* I. (1728) 14 But heavy George and fat Tom are after 'em..; they'll sawce their Jackets for 'em, I'll warrant 'em.

c. To rebuke smartly. Now only *dial.*

[Cf. F. '*saucer quelqu'un*, le gronder, le réprimander fortement' (Littré).]

1600 SHAKS. *A. Y. L.* III. v. 69 As fast As she answeres thee with frowning lookes, ile sauce Her with bitter words. **1602** DEKKER *Satiro-mastix* E3, I wod alwaies haue thee sawce a foole thus. **1882** A. B. TAYLOR *Westmorld. Sk.* 5 (E.D.D.) Sheed tell em a lot a lees to git off being sased for spillin t'cofe an stuff.

d. To speak impertinently to. *vulgar.* Also *transf.* Cf. SASS *v.*

1862 H. ADAMS *Let.* 10 Jan. in N. Longmate *Hungry Mills* (1978) iv. 61, I found myself this morning sarsed through a whole column of *The Times* and am laughed at by all England. **1864** *Doncaster Chron.* 4 Mar., I have never been saucy to Mr. Sykes; I have 'sauced' the men who have been working for him. **1865** DICKENS *Mut. Fr.* I. vii, Dont sauce me in the wicious pride of your youth. **1868** 'HOLME LEE' *B. Godfrey* li. 289 If a chap sauces you.., let him sauce on. **1885** J. K. JEROME *On the Stage* 117 They bully the slavey (but then the slavey sauces them, so perhaps it is only tit for tat). **1892** B. POTTER *Jrnl.* 6 Oct. (1966) 274 He puts on wrong postage..and will sauce anybody who is unprovided with small change; he wants reporting. **1962** D. LESSING *Golden Notebk.* II. 274 He sauced her with his eyes; sitting up broad, solid, pink-cheeked; very sure of himself.

sauce-alone ('sɔːsəˌləʊn). [app. f. SAUCE *sb.* + ALONE, implying that the plant serves as a sufficient sauce by itself.] The plant *Sisymbrium Alliaria*, a tall hedge-weed formerly used as a flavouring for salads and sauces.

1530 PALSGR. 265/2 Sauce alone an herbe. **1548** TURNER *Names Herbes* (E.D.S.) 82 Alliaria is called in english Sauce alone or Iacke of the hedges. **1579** LANGHAM *Gard. Health* (1633) 592 Sausalone: It is vsed of some instead of Garlike. **1597** GERARDE *Herbal* II. cclxvii. 650 Sauce alone, or Jack by the hedge... Diuers eate the stamped leaues heerof with salt fish, for a sauce. **1699** EVELYN *Acetaria* 29 Sauce-alone has many Medicinal Properties. **1785** MARTYN *Rousseau's Bot.* xxiii. (1794) 323 The garlick-smelling [species of Erysimum], called thence Sauce-alone,..has heart-shaped leaves. **1896** J. DAVIDSON *Fleet St. Eclogues* Ser. II. 93 And white the lady-smocks a-row And sauce-alone in the hedge.

sauce-boat ('sɔːsbəʊt). [BOAT *sb.* 2a.]

1. A small vessel with a lip, used for serving sauce.

1747 MRS. GLASSE *Cookery* 6 You may do Half the Quantity and put it into your Sauce-Boat or Bason. **1750** H. WALPOLE *Let. to Mann* 1 Sept., For one article of the plate she ordered ten sauceboats. **1841** THACKERAY *Sam. Titmarsh* iv, I had..pretty nearly all the oysters out of the sauce-boat. **1892** *Encycl. Pract. Cookery* (ed. Garrett), *Sauceboats*, small vessels of various shapes and designs in which sauce is served at table. In the illustrations the Sauceboats are served in the dish.

2. *Archæol.* A vessel of the Early Helladic and Early Cycladic cultures resembling a sauce-boat and prob. used for drinking or pouring liquids.

1967 R. HIGGINS *Minoan & Mycenean Art* ii. 55 Sauceboats like the popular Mainland variety..were decorated with an all-over wash. *Ibid.* iii. 67 Favourite shapes are now the so-called 'sauceboats', a very common type whose function is unknown. *Ibid.* iii. 70 Only one form of gold or silver plate has been recorded from mainland Greece for this period. That form, known in two surviving examples, is a translation into gold of the common pottery 'sauceboat' shape. **1977** G. CLARK *World Prehist.* (ed. 3) IV. 157 Another unusual ceramic vessel common to the three areas is the sauce-boat which also occurs in Early Helladic Greece in gold.

saucebox ('sɔːsbɒks). *colloq.* [f. SAUCE *sb.* 5 + BOX *sb.*] A person addicted to making saucy or impertinent remarks. Also *attrib.*

1588 *Marprel. Epist.* (Arb.) 6 Why sawceboxes must you be pratling? **1675** COTTON *Scoffer Scoft* 34 For which, Sir Sawce-box, dost thou see, Since thou'lt make them, I'll unmake thee. **1741** RICHARDSON *Pamela* I. 29 And so I am to be expos'd, am I, said he.., to the whole World, by such a Saucebox as you? **1820** MISS MITFORD in L'Estrange *Life* (1870) II. 121 She's a goosecap, you know, and a romp, and a saucebox. **1825** in C. E. Pearce *Life & Times Madame Vestris* (1923) 116 We thought that the stamping sort of sauce-box air with which she marched away to the tune of the 'Dashing White Sergeant' was too much in keeping with her notorious male-attire exhibitions. **1875** R. G. WHITE in *Galaxy* XIX. 558 What delight it must have given this she sauce-box to make that answer to her own father. **1969** V. C. CLINTON-BADDELEY *Only a Matter of Time* 89 He hadn't used 'camp' for several weeks—not since his sauce-box notice of *Idomeneo.*

sauced (sɔːst), *ppl. a.* [f. SAUCE *v.* + -ED[1].] Seasoned, flavoured.

c **1592** MARLOWE *Jew of Malta* IV. (1633) H 4 b, He liues vpon Pickled Grashoppers, and sauc'd Mushrumbs. **1651** BIGGS *New Disp.* §160 Their sauc'd Julaps.

†**saucefleme**, *sb.* and *a.* *Obs.* Forms: 4 sawcefleem, 4, 6 sausfleme, 5 sawflom, salce-, salfleme, sawse-, sawceflewm(e, sauseflem(e, 6 sawce-, salsefle(a)gme, sawce-, sauce-, sausfleume, sawsfleam, -flame, 7 sauce-, sausfleame, saucefleme, 5–6 saucefleme. See also SAUCELINE. [a. OF. *sausefleme*, semi-popular ad. med.L. *salsum flegma* 'salt phlegm'; *salsum*, neut. of L. *salsus* salt, adj., *flegma* PHLEGM.] **A.** *sb.* A swelling of the face accompanied by inflammation, supposed to be due to salt humours.

Also in translated form *salt fleume*: cf. SALT *a.*[1] 1 b.

[**1398** TREVISA *Barth. De P.R.* VII. lix. (1495) 1 vij, Carbunculus..comeþ of salte flewme.] *a* **1400** in *Rel. Ant.* I. 189 And on is in the mydde for-hevede, For lepre saus-fleme mot blede. *c* **1450** *St. Cuthbert* (Surtees) 4116 His face was deformed and bolnyd And with' rede salfleme suolnyd. **1542** UDALL *Erasm. Apoph.* 71 Litle pymples or pushes, suche as of cholere and salsefleagme budden out in the noses and faces of many persones. **1586** LUPTON *Thousand Not. Things* (1675) 14 Scurviness, Sawsfleme, or Redness of the face. **1597** GERARDE *Herbal* II. cccxxvi. 765 Cucumber [thus prepared]..doth perfectly cure all manner of sawcefleagme and copper faces. **1601** HOLLAND *Pliny* II. 113 The red pimples or sauce-flegme in the face.

B. *adj.* Afflicted with this disease.

c **1386** CHAUCER *Prol.* 625 A Somonour was ther with vs in that place That hadde a fyr reed Cherubynnes face ffor sawcefleem he was with eyen narwe. **1542** BOORDE *Dyetary* x. (1870) 257 It [whey] doth purge redde colour, and is good for sausfleme faces. **1547** —— *Brev. Health* clxx, A sauce fleume face, which is a rednes about the nose and the chekes, with small pymples. **1639** O. WOOD *Alph. Bk. Phys. Secrets* 166 For a Red gum, or Sausfleame face old or new.

Hence †**saucefleméd** = SAUCEFLEME *a.* †**sauceflemıng** = SAUCEFLEME *sb.*

a **1450** *Knt. de la Tour* 116 Wyne..makithe the uisage salce fleumed rede, and full of white whelkes. **1592** in *Vicary's Anat.* (1888) App. IX. 229 Þe vayn..to opyn for Þe ..sauce-flemyng in the face. **1631** BRATHWAIT *Whimzies, Piper* 145 This sauce-fleamed porcupine..will bee many times monstrously malapert.

saucege, -eidge, obs. forms of SAUSAGE *sb.*

sauceless ('sɔːslıs), *a.* [f. SAUCE *sb.* + -LESS.] Having no sauce, or sauces; *fig.* lacking piquancy.

1882 MISS C. F. WOOLSON *Anne* iv. 67 Seeking a place [in New York] where his knowledge..would have been prized by exiled Frenchmen in a sauceless land. **1899** *Month* June 621 Even vice would be in many ways sauceless and insipid in the absence of faith.

†**sauceline**, *sb.* and *a.* *Obs.* In 5 sawcelyne, -lyme, sawslem, 6 saucelin, sauslyme. [Corrupt form of SAUCEFLEME.] = SAUCEFLEME.

14.. *Stockholm Med. MS.* p. 4 in *Archæologia* XXX. 412/2 Good for sawslem skabbe & mannys lymys. *c* **1440** *Promp. Parv.* 441/2 Sawcelyne [*Winch. MS.* sawcelyme]. **1537** *St. Papers Hen. VIII*, V. 96 The fellowe with the fowle sauslyme face. **1542–3** *Act 34–35 Hen. VIII*, c. 8 The stone ..saucelin and morfew, and suche other lyke diseases.

†'**sauceliness.** *Obs. rare*[−0]. [f. **saucely* (f. SAUCE *sb.* + -LY[1]) + -ness.] Sauciness.

1552 HULOET, Wantonnes or saucelines in askynge or crauynge, *procacitas*.

saucely, obs. form of SAUCILY.

†**sauce malapert.** *Obs.* [See under SAUCY *a.* 2.] Impertinence, insolence. Hence †**sauce malapertly** *adv.*, in a manner insolently abusive.

1529 MORE *Supplic. Soulys* Wks. 305/2 He vseth a figure of rethorike that men cal sawce malapert. **1556** J. HEYWOOD *Spider & F.* xcv. 74 Not blowing hensforth (so sausmalapertlie) My masters and maistres meate.

†**sauce-medley.** *Obs.* [app. a. AF. **sauce medlee*, lit. 'mixed sauce'.] A concoction, a mixture compounded by art.

1579 TOMSON *Calvin's Serm. Tim.* 678/1 The Papists haue made an hotchepoche and a sawse medley of lyes that they haue scraped together from all corners.

saucepan ('sɔːspən). [f. SAUCE *sb.* + PAN *sb.*[1]]

1. a. In early use, 'a small skillet with a long handle, in which sauce or small things are boiled' (J.). Now, in wider application, a vessel of metal, with a long handle projecting from the side, and usually with a lid; the utensil most commonly employed for culinary boiling, except for large joints of meat.

1686 *Lond. Gaz.* No. 2120/8 Two Silver Porringers, one Silver Sawce-pan. **1697** E. LHWYD in *Phil. Trans.* XXVII. 468 With these Plates he makes Furnaces, Pots,..Sauce-Pans, &c. **1729** SWIFT *Direct. Serv.* ii. (1751) 38 If you have a Silver Sauce-pan, and the Butter smells of Smoak, lay the Fault upon the Coals. **1817** LADY MORGAN *France* I. (1818) I. 65 He found his gold-headed cane, silver saucepan, baggage, every thing in short in *statu quo*. **1865** DICKENS *Mut. Fr.* III. iv, I would recommend examination of the bacon in the saucepan on the fire. **1892** *Photogr. Ann.* II. 174 As an oilbath a small cast-iron saucepan answers well.

b. *Phrase.* (Cf. SAUCE *sb.* 6.)

a **1700** B. E. *Dict. Cant. Crew*, *Your Sauce-Pan runs over*, you are exceeding bold.

2. *attrib.* and *Comb.*, as ***saucepan-brush***; **saucepan crab**, the crab *Limulus Polyphemus*, the shell of which is used, in tropical America, for a ladle; **saucepan lid**, rhyming slang for (*a*) a 'quid', a one-pound note; (*b*) a 'kid', a child.

1926–7 *Army & Navy Stores Catal.* 181/1 Steel *saucepan brush. Each— -/6. **1944** C. MILBURN *Diary* 30 Dec. (1979) 260 A few oddments at the ironmonger's..a dish mop, a baking tin, a colander, a saucepan brush. **1952** *Observer* 12 Oct. 5/3 Won't dish-mops, saucepan-brushes and swabs, rubbers, and all kitchen cloths one day be of nylon? **1884** *Leisure Hour* Nov. 687/2 King crabs..are sometimes called the horseshoe crab..as also *saucepan crab. **1861** E. D. COOK *Paul Foster's Daughter* viii, Do you call that *saucepan lid clean?—because I don't. **1951** P. HOSKINS *No Hiding Place!* xvii. 191/2 *Saucepan lid*, £1 note. **1960** J. FRANKLYN *Dict. Rhyming Slang* 119/1 *Saucepan lid*,..kid.

saucepanful ('sɔːspənfʊl). [f. SAUCEPAN + -FUL.] The contents of a saucepan; the amount a saucepan will hold.

1868 DICKENS *Holiday Romance* II, in *All Year Round* 8 Feb. 206/2 The other Princes and Princesses were squeezed into a..corner to look at the Princess Alicia turning out the saucepan-full of broth, for fear..they should get..scalded. **1976** *Horse & Hound* 3 Dec. 34/4 Two or three saucepansful may be needed simultaneously and it is a good idea to put a spoon in the glass when dispensing. **1980** J. O'FAOLAIN *No Country for Young Men* iv. 71 Judith boiled a saucepanful [of water].

saucer ('sɔːsə(r)), *sb.* Forms: 4–6 sawser(e, 4–8 sawcer(e, 5 sawsesere, sauscyre, sawssor, sowcer, 5–6 salser, *Sc.* salsar, 5, 7 sausser, 6 sawsser, sawecere, sasser, salcer, *Sc.* sasar, 6–7 saser, 4– saucer. [a. OF. *saussier* masc., *saussiere* fem. (mod.F. only *saucière*) vessel for holding sauce, f. *sauce* SAUCE *sb.* Cf. Sp. *salsera*, Pg. *salseira*, It. *salsiera*, med.L. *salsārium*.]

†**1.** A receptacle, usually of metal, for holding the condiments at a meal; a dish or deep plate in which salt or sauces were placed upon the table.

13.. *Coer de L.* 1489 Now, styward, I warne the, Bye us vessel gret plenté, Dysschys, cuppys, and sawsers. *c* **1340** *Nominale* (Skeat) 503 Dobler saucer of lynde. **14..** *Metr. Voc.* in Wr.-Wülcker 626/9 Sawsesere, *salsarium*. **1434** in *E.E. Wills* (1882) 101, ij sauseres of peautre. *c* **1481** CAXTON *Dialogues* 7/31 Now must ye haue Platers of tyn, Disshes, saussers, Sallyers, trenchours. **1488** *Acc. Ld. High Treas. Scot.* I. 82 Item, tuelf salsaris. **1504** in *Bury Wills* (Camden) 97 Item I wyll that myn executo^rs shall geve to xx^ti maydens ..xij pecys of pewtyr, that ys to sey, iiij platers, iiij dysshys, and iiij sawssers. **1538** in *Lett. Suppress. Monasteries* (Camden) 272 Item, iij. platters, a dysshe, and a sawecere xij^d. **1541** *Aberdeen Reg.* (1844) I. 176 Ane playt, a dische, a salsar, a chandlar of brace. **1588** ARCHDEACON tr. *True Discourse Army K. Spain* 69 Dishes, Cuppes, Sassers. **1600** HAKLUYT *Voy.* III. 338 The women, going to dance, did weare about their girdles plates of golde as broad as a sawcer. **1674** T. P. etc. *Eng. & Fr. Cook* 31 And send with the serving it up some Saucers of Green-sauce. **1728–42** BAILEY, *Saucer*, a little Dish to hold Sauce.

2. a. Any small shallow dish or deep plate of circular shape. Now commonly felt as an extended use of sense 3.

Somewhat specialized applications are: †a receptacle for the blood in blood-letting (*obs.*); a small earthenware plate on which cake water-colours are rubbed in water; a shallow vessel placed under a flower-pot, sometimes holding water to be drawn up through a hole in the bottom of the pot.

1607 B. BARNES *Divils Charter* Prol., Presently the Pronotary strippeth vp Alexanders sleeue and letteth his arme bloud in a saucer. **1615** CROOKE *Body of Man* 254 Blood.. caked as it is in a Saser after blood-letting. **1630** *Churchw. Acc. Pittington*, etc. (Surtees) 184 Two litle plates or sawcers for carying and setting the bread on itt, at the tyme of the Communion. **1665** in *Phil. Trans.* I. 118 The last Blood was received in a Sawcer. **1806–7** J. BERESFORD *Miseries Hum. Life* III. xxxvi, Rubbing Indian ink, or cake colours, in a very smooth saucer. **1822** LOUDON *Encycl. Gard.* 328 The Flower Pot-Saucer is a flat, circular vessel, with a rim from one to two inches high. **1848** THACKERAY *Van. Fair* xxvi, A quantity of orange marmalade spread out in a little cut-glass saucer. **1856** GLENNY *Gard. Every-d. Bk.* 259/1 The pot had feet to keep the drain hole above the water in a common saucer, and the saucers for common pots had a flat rim inside.

transf. **1615** G. SANDYS *Trav.* 173 The Armenians..in stead of musicall instruments, have Sawcers of brasse (which they strike against one another) set about with gingles.

b. ***pink saucer***: see PINK *a.*[1] C. c.

1855 PIESSE *Art of Perfumery* 222 Pink Saucers.

c. = *flying saucer* s.v. FLYING *vbl. sb.* 3. Also *attrib.*

[**1878** *Denison* (Texas) *Daily News* 25 Jan., in C. & J. Lorenzen *UFOs* (1969) i. 10 When directly over him it [*sc.* a flying object] was about the size of a large saucer and was evidently at a great height.] **1947** *Daily Progress* (Charlottesville, Va.) 5 July 1/4 Describing what they saw as flat, translucent plates 12 to 15 inches in diameter, several Port Huron, Mich., residents reported seeing the 'saucers'. **1958** *Times Lit. Suppl.* 16 May 274/3 The author declares he was arrested while camping out in a fertile saucer district and narrowly escaped a mental examination court. It all affords a good occasion to re-tell certain saucer stories the author inquired into. **1966** *McGraw-Hill Encycl. Sci. & Technol.* V. 363/2 Light reflections from material objects account for most reports of saucers. **1978** D. A. J. SEARGENT *UFO's* vi. 122 People frequently shy away from traditional religions and look for salvation from the 'saucers'.

3. A small round shallow vessel, usually with concave sides and flat at the bottom, used for supporting a cup (esp. a tea or coffee cup), and catching any liquid that may be spilled from it.

c **1702** C. FIENNES *Journeys* (1947) III. v. 177, I went to this Newcastle in Staffordshire to see the makeing the fine tea-potts cups and saucers of the fine red earth. **1753** RICHARDSON *Grandison* (1781) I. ix. 49 Down went his cup and sawcer. **1776** WILKES in Boswell *Johnson* (1791) II. 86 If a poet had to speak of Queen Caroline drinking tea, he must endeavour to avoid the vulgarity of cups and saucers. **1840** MARRYAT *Poor Jack* xvi, Don't pour your tea in your saucer —that's vulgar! **1861** J. R. GREENE *Man. Anim. Kingd., Cœlent.* 66 The constrictions deepen until the Strobila becomes not unlike a pile of cups or saucers.

4. In similative phrases. Cf. SAUCER EYE. So (*slang*), an eye. Also *attrib.*

This use orig. belonged to sense 1. Cf. AF. 'les oyls granz com deus saucers', *Boeve de Haumtone* 1760 (13th c.).

13.. *Seuyn Sag.* (W.) 2784 With eghen that war ful bright and clere, And brade, ilkone, als a sawsere. **1598** BP. HALL *Sat.* VI. i. G 8, Her eyes like siluer saucers fayre beset With shining Amber and with shady Iet. **1663** DRYDEN *Wild Gallant* v. i, We met three or four hugeous ugly Devils, with Eyes like Sawcers. **1679** *Hist. Jetzer* 3 The eyes of these Dogs as Jetzer thought,..were bigger than Saucers. **1789** WOLCOT (P. Pindar) *Ode to Devil* 93 Wks. 1816 II. 23, I thought That thou a pair of horns hadst got, With eyes like saucers staring! **1864** M. LEMON *Jest Bk.* 185, I always know when he has been in his cups by the state of his saucers. **1876** tr. *Andersen's Fairy Tales* 128 There sat the dog with eyes as big as saucers, glaring at him. **1958** *Spectator* 22 Aug. 246/2 Nor were they wasting any saucer stares on National Savings or 'Taking up a Career in the Midland Bank'.

5. †**a.** *Phys.* = COTYLEDON 1, ACETABULUM 2 d.

1683 SNAPE *Anat. Horse* I. xxviii. (1686) 62 Any of those Glandules that are..called *Cotyledons* or Sawcers. **1684** tr. *Bonet's Merc. Compit.* I. 2 Slimy humours which loosen the acetabula (or saucers) of the womb.

b. *Bot.* Any part of a plant resembling a saucer, as the involucre of *Euphorbiaceæ*, and the tubercle of lichens in which the seeds are imbedded.

1578 LYTE *Dodoens* III. xxix. 356 The flowers are yellow and grow out of litle dishes or sawsers. **1796** WITHERING *Brit. Plants* (ed. 3) I. 370 The rising particle, which is destined to form a concave saucer, becomes hollow and green at the top,..the saucer becomes larger and more and more open... At length it becomes a perfect saucer, either sitting, or supported on a short foot. **1862** DARWIN *Orchids* vi. 277 In Dendrobium chrysanthum the nectary consists of a shallow saucer.

6. *Mech.* In various uses: see quots.

1747 HOOSON *Miner's Dict.*, *Sawcers*, those round Pieces of Iron fixt on the Sawcer-hooks, on which the Leathern Suckers are put in Chain-Pumps. **1750** BLANCKLEY *Nav. Expositor*, *Saucers*, are round thick Pieces of Iron, on which the Spindle of the Capstons work. **1794** *Rigging & Seamanship* I. 8 *Saucer*, a bolt with a flat head. **1867** SMYTH *Sailor's Word-bk.*, *Saucer*,..a socket of iron let into a wooden stock or standard..to receive the spindle or foot on which the capstan rests and turns round.

7. *attrib.* and *Comb.* **a.** = belonging to a saucer, as ***saucer-hook*** (see sense 6); **b.** = of the shape of a saucer (sense 3), as ***saucer-barrow***, ***-brooch***, ***-cap***, ***-cloud***, ***-dome***, ***-eyeball***, ***-hat***, ***-head***; **saucer bath**, a wide shallow bath usu. kept in a bedroom and used for sponging oneself down; **saucer-buried** *a.*, formerly in the southern U.S., applied to a Black person whose burial was paid for by donations placed in a saucer laid on or near the corpse; hence **saucer-burial**; **saucerman**, a being imagined or believed to be the pilot or passenger of a flying saucer. **c.** parasynthetic, as ***saucer-blue***, ***-headed***, ***-shaped*** adjs.; also ***saucer-like*** adj. and adv.

1941 *Proc. Prehist. Soc.* VII. 88 The *saucer-barrow may be defined as a low mound, generally one or two feet high.. enclosed in a ditch and outer bank. **1899** SOMERVILLE & 'ROSS' *Some Experiences Irish R.M.* ii. 38 A conspicuous object outside the door was a *saucer bath full of something that looked like flour. **1927** G. MURRAY *Classical Trad. in Poetry* 4 He used a sponge and a tooth-brush and a saucer bath. **1951** C. V. WEDGWOOD *Last of Radicals* i. 19 The patriarchal old gentleman, who rose every morning to a cold saucer-bath. **1925** W. DE LA MARE *Miss Jemima* 12 She was staring about her..with her *saucer blue eyes. **1912** *Archaeologia* LXIII. 167 The find included no less than four *saucer brooches, one decorated with the star with incurved sides..and three with spirals. **1965** A. H. SMITH in Bessinger & Creed *Medieval & Linguistic Stud.* 61 The presence of artifacts in the Avon valley cemeteries, like applied, disc, and saucerbrooches..has been interpreted as a mixed culture. **1963** P. POLLACK *Photography* xxvii. 351/1 A picture of a *saucer burial taken in Alabama. **1925** DU B. HEYWARD *Porgy* I. 25 It had even become a grievous reproach to have a member of the family a '*saucer-buried nigger'. **1885** C. LOWE *Bismarck* I. 17 He got himself up in the traditional long-boots, velvet jacket, and *saucer cap. **1911** H. S. WALPOLE *Mr. Perrin & Mr. Traill* iv. 72 Faint blue skies, dim and shining like clear glass with a hard yellow sun stuck like a tethered balloon between *saucer-clouds. **1895** *Westm. Gaz.* 7 Oct. 8/2 Work has been begun upon the third *saucer-dome. *a* **1732** GAY *Story of Apparition* 19 Wks. 1737 II. 55 Night roaming ghosts, by *saucer eye-balls known. **1940** M. SADLEIR *Fanny by Gaslight* I. 30 My own tartan frock..and tiny *saucer hat. **1965** J. POTTS *Only Good Secretary* iv. 68 Her head, topped with its black saucer hat. **1815** *Falconer's Dict. Marine* (ed. Burney) s.v. *Bolt*, Those ..have commonly small round heads, somewhat flatted, called *saucer heads. *Ibid.*, **Saucer-headed Bolt*. **1815** SCOTT *Guy M.* xxxvi, A muckle great saucer-headed cutlugged stane, that they ca' Charlies Chuckie. **1650**

BULWER *Anthropomet.* 75 This affectation then of great *Sawcer-like eyes is a fancie against the rule of nature. **1861** READE *Cloister & H.* xxxviii, On reaching them the rustic rider's eyes opened saucer-like. **1967** *Time* 4 Aug. 40/2 Barney and Betty Hill..whose 'abduction' by *saucermen during an auto trip was described in the fast-selling book [etc.] **1971** *New Scientist* 30 Sept. 722/1 Visiting saucermen from Mars might well report back to base that all our Gods must be hard of hearing. **1847–9** *Todd's Cycl. Anat.* IV. 213/2 At the bottom of the sac is situated a *saucer-shaped body. **1901** *Athenæum* 27 July 132/1 The same church has a saucer-shaped paten, 1652.

'saucer, *v.* [f. the sb.] **1.** *intr.* To be saucerlike; to take the shape of a saucer, be as shallow as a saucer.

1925 W. DE LA MARE *Broomsticks* 112 The immense starry sky that saucered in the wide darkness of the Moor. **1977** *Times* 19 Nov. 1/6 They prophesy that the rate is now 'saucering' and that after a brief dip into single figures it will rise again.

2. *trans.* To make saucerlike; to shape (something) like a saucer.

1934 WEBSTER, *Saucer, v.t. & i.* To make or be saucerlike. **1977** *Whitaker's Almanack 1978* 1058/1 The site has been successfully 'saucered' to disguise the bulk and reduce the overall height.

3. *trans.* To pour (a liquid) into a saucer, esp. from a cup.

1938 *Atlantic Monthly* Oct. 552/2 'Want a sasser o' sorghum?... The visitor would 'sasser' some sorghum. **1944** A. CLARKE *Coll. Plays* (1963) 246 Mind you don't utter A word..Until you have eaten six slices of bread With plenty of butter—and saucered your tay! **1951** H. GILES *Harbin's Ridge* x. 100 Granny saucered her coffee and blew on it. **1978** *New Yorker* 9 Jan. 41/3 Have you ever heard the old Texas expression 'saucered and blowed'?.. If a cowboy's coffee is too hot, he puts some in a saucer and blows on it. A cowboy will say to a friend, 'Take mine, it's already saucered and blowed.' Jim needs to get the energy bill saucered and blowed.

saucer eye. Usually *pl.* **a.** An eye as large and round as a saucer, formerly freq. ascribed to spectres and ghosts. Cf. SAUCER *sb.* 4.

1664 BUTLER *Hud.* II. i. 131 Some have mistaken Blocks and Posts, For Spectres, Apparitions, Ghosts, With Sawcer-eyes, and Horns. **1718** PRIOR *Hans Carvel* 77 The devil.. without saucer-eye or claw Like a grave Barrister at Law. **1808** WOLCOT (P. Pindar) *One more Peep at Roy. Acad.* Wks. 1812 V. 371 With mealy face and saucer eyes. **1837** BARHAM *Ingol. Leg., Spectre of Tappington*, Don't suppose you can palm off your saucer eyes on me. **1846** C. BONER tr. *Andersen's Danish Story-bk.* K 6b, He struck the flint, and the well-known dog with saucer-eyes stood before him. **1970** 'D. HALLIDAY' *Dolly & Cookie Bird* vi. 78 She still had the huge saucer eyes I remembered, with false eyelashes and then spikes drawn in under the lashes. **1976** G. MOFFAT *Short Time to Live* v. 48 'This is the astonishing thing—' she turned to Miss Pink with saucer eyes.

b. *transf.*

1849 DE QUINCEY *Eng. Mail-Coach* Wks. 1862 IV. 326 The huge saucer eyes of the mail, blazing through the gloom.

So **saucer-eyed** *a.*, having saucer eyes; also *transf.*, of an expression, emotion, etc.

In quot. 1968 the sense is 'susceptible to seeing flying saucers'.

1622 MASSINGER & DEKKER *Virg. Mart.* III. iii, Clouen footed, Blacke, saucer-eyde, his nostrils breathing fire. **1843** *Ainsworth's Mag.* IV. 5 The frightful, open-mouthed, saucer-eyed expression of wonder. **1883** T. HARDY in *Longm. Mag.* July 268 A thin saucer-eyed woman of fifty-five. **1934** A. WOOLLCOTT *While Rome Burns* 57 He rushed at me in saucer-eyed excitement. **1968** *Listener* 27 June 823/1 As if people haven't tended in such matters to see the expected thing in the expected form, as if they were unlikely to go saucer-eyed to their vigils. **1978** J. IRVING *World According to Garp* xvii. 361 Garp looked for the strange saucer-eyed girl. **1979** N. FREELING *Widow* xvii. 108 I've been shot at... Don't look so saucer-eyed..don't let's dramatize.

saucerful ('sɔːsəfʊl). [f. SAUCER *sb.* + -FUL.] As much as fills a saucer. Also, the contents of a saucer, and *fig.*

1852 MRS. GASKELL *Cranford* (1853) viii. 156 She..mixed a saucer-full for him, and put it down for him to lap. **1860** O. W. HOLMES *Elsie V.* vii. 87 With a saucerful in each hand. **1917** D. CANFIELD *Understood Betsy* vi. 123 She herself ate three saucerfuls. **1927** [see *grape-nuts* s.v. GRAPE *sb.*[1] 9]. **1944** M. LASKI *Love on Supertax* viii. 77 A saucerful of margarine. **1973** K. GILES *File on Death* ii. 48 Here, sit at the table, and I'll give you a saucerful.

saucerian (sɔː'sɪərɪən), *a.* and *sb.* [f. SAUCER + -IAN.] **A.** *adj.* Of or pertaining to a flying saucer (see FLYING *vbl. sb.* 3). **B.** *sb.* **a.** A believer in the existence of flying saucers. **b.** An entity which travels by flying saucer.

1950 *Jrnl. Brit. Interplanetary Soc.* IX. 300 This passage ..surely deserves immortality. We..happen to believe it is true—but perhaps not in the saucerian sense that the author intended. **1965** *New Society* 9 Sept. 14/4 The definition of the situation in occult terms began in 1950 with the publication of..the first saucerian book complete with little green men..looked upon by saucerians as the beginning of the tradition. **1973** C. SAGAN *Cosmic Connection* (1975) vi. 43 Likewise, the category of contact story, now quite fashionable in some UFO enthusiast circles, of sexual contact between human and saucerian..must be relegated to the realm of improbable fantasy. Such crossings are about as reasonable as the mating of a man and a petunia.

saucerization (ˌsɔːsəraɪ'zeɪʃən). *Surg.* [f. SAUCER + -IZATION.] The surgical excision of bone or flesh so as to leave a shallow saucer-shaped cavity. So **'saucerize** *v. trans.*

1928 P. LEWIN *Orthopedic Surg. for Nurses* xv. 252 In chronic osteomyelitis the entire infected area must be removed, the so-called 'saucerization'. **1940** *Lancet* 13 July 32/1 No method of treating such a case can compare with closed plaster after saucerisation, which may include laying open all heavily infected areas. **1946** *Jrnl. Bone & Joint Surg.* XXVIII. 19 The wounds are saucerized and then packed. **1964** W. A. LARMON in L. Davis *Christopher's Textbk. Surg.* (ed. 8) xxv. 1105/1 This operation is termed saucerization because the bone cavity is made as shallow and broad as possible by the surgeon.

saucerless ('sɔːsəlɪs). [f. SAUCER *sb.* + -LESS.] Having no saucer.

1831 TRELAWNY *Adv. Younger Son* vii, Cups, saucerless and chipped. **1873** TRISTRAM *Moab* ii. 22 Three handleless, saucerless blue china cups.

†'saucery. *Obs.* Forms: 5 salserie, 5–6 sawcery(e, 6 salcerie, salcery, saulcery, 7 sausery, 8 salsary, 6–8 saucery(e. [a. OF. *sausserie*, med.L. *salsāria*, f. OF. *sausse*, med.L. *salsa* SAUCE *sb.*: see -ERY.]

1. The department of a household entrusted with the preparation of sauces.

c **1440** in *Househ. Ord.* (1790) 38 There is none that dyneth in their offyces, savinge onely the cookes, the scullery, the sawcerye [etc.]. **1502** in *Priv. Purse Exp. Eliz. York* (1830) 2 To the Saulcery xs. **1520** in *Rutland Papers* (Camden) 40 Item, the skullary and sawcery. **1541** *Act 33 Hen. VIII*, c. 12 §3 The Grome of the Salcerie..of the same housholde.. shalbe..redye withe vyneger and colde water. **1708** J. CHAMBERLAYNE *St. Gt. Brit.* I. II. xiv. (1710) 121 Vinegar and cold Water, brought by the Groom of the Saucery.

2. That part of a house in which sauces were prepared; the apartments of the servants engaged in the preparation of sauces.

1468 in *Priv. Purse Exp. Eliz. York* (1830) 223/2 In the squillery and salserie a yeoman a groom and a page. **1649** *Descr. Richmond Crt.* in Nichols *Progr. Eliz.* (1823) II. 412 One other little room called the Saucery. **1650** *Surv. Nonsuch* in *Archæologia* V. 435 One little timber building,.. commonly called the Saucery House, conteyning foure little roomes used by the yeomen of the sauces.

3. *attrib.* **salsary-man.** (See quot.)

1708 J. CHAMBERLAYNE *St. Gt. Brit.* II. III. 537 Salsary-man. [An officer of the Queen's Pastry.]

saucester, -cestour, -cestr, var. ff. SAUCISTER.

sauch, var. SAUGH; obs. Sc. pa. t. of SEE *v.*

sauchen, sauchie, var. ff. SAUGHEN, SAUGHY *a.*

saucht(e, -ine, var. ff. SAUGHT, SAUGHTEN.

†'sauciate, *v. Obs. rare.* [f. L. *sauciāt-*, ppl. stem of *sauciāre*, f. *sauci-us* wounded.] *trans.* To wound, hurt. Hence **'sauciated** *ppl. a.*; so **sauci'ation** [ad. L. *sauciātio*], wounding.

1644 HAMMOND *Of Conscience* 27 Any such act of willfull sinne..is a naturall meanes..of sauciating and wounding the soule. **1656** BLOUNT *Glossogr.*, *Sauciate (saucio)*, to hurt, to wound, to cut. **1657** TOMLINSON *Renou's Disp.* 283 Balm ..which distills out of a sauciated Tree. **1658** PHILLIPS, *Sauciation*, a wounding.

†'sauciate, *pa. pple. Obs.* [ad. L. *sauciāt-us*, pa. pple. of *sauciāre*: see prec.] Wounded, hurt.

1509 BARCLAY *Shyp of Folys* (1874) II. 17 Murdred is Mars, and with woundes sawciate The bondys of peas hath dryuen the tyrant hens.

saucidge, -ige, obs. forms of SAUSAGE *sb.*

‖saucier (sosje). [Fr.] A sauce cook.

1961 *Evening Standard* 14 Sept. 29/3 (Advt.), Saucier required for first class London Club. Interesting position with good wages. **1976** *National Observer* (U.S.) 10 Apr. 5/1 She..gained 10 pounds that could be attributed almost entirely to the magic of the finest sauciers in town. **1980** J. CARTWRIGHT *Horse of Darius* xvii. 269 Chef Leon..took three under-chefs, a *saucier*, a vegetable cook, and his dessert chef.

saucily ('sɔːsɪlɪ), *adv.* Also 6 saucely, 6–7 sawcely, 7 sawcily. [f. SAUCY + -LY[2].] In a saucy manner, in various senses of the adj.

1548 ELYOT *Dict.*, *Proterue*, proudely, immoderately, shamefully, saucily, knappishely. **1552** HULOET, Sawcely. **1592** WARNER *Alb. Eng.* VII. xxxvii. 166, I beare a mind lesse bace than that I can digest your Drudge with me so saucely should chat. **1599** *Broughton's Lett.* vi. 19 You began to stirre,..malepartly answering his Grace with scornfull letters, and subscribing them..most saucely. **1617** MORYSON *Itin.* II. 63 The Townes..stood so saucily upon their priviledges, as a sharpe rod and strong hand were requisite to amend them. **1651** DAVENANT *Gondibert* II. i. 31 Even from the Temples, Angels soon withdrew; So sawcely th' afflicted there complain'd. **1668** CLARENDON *Contempl. Ps.* Tracts (1727) 443 We have..saucily used and prophaned some of the expressions which by the dictate of God's own spirit they have thought fit to make use of. **1709** STEELE *Tatler* No. 44 ⁋5 [He] makes him speak sawcily of his Betters. **1712** ARBUTHNOT *John Bull* II. xi, The more young and unexperienc'd he us'd to teach to talk Saucily. **1768** *Priv. Lett. Ld. Malmesbury* (1870) I. 218 Some printers who saucily mentioned our debates were ordered to attend. **1853** READE *Chr. Johnstone* xv. 276 She then smiled saucily in his face. **1900** CROCKETT *Love Idylls* (1901) 27 Bell's saucily unconscious air of command piqued him.

sauciness ('sɔːsɪnɪs). Also 6–7 sawcines(se, 7 sawcyness, sawsinesse. [f. SAUCY *a.*[1] + -NESS.] The quality of being saucy, in various senses of the adj. In early use as a term of serious reprobation: Insolent presumption, haughtiness, arrogance. Now with milder sense: Impertinence, rudeness to superiors; often used playfully in mock dispraise (cf. SAUCY *a.*[1] 2 c).

1548 ELYOT *Dict.*, *Proteruitas*,..saucinesse. **1576** FLEMING *Panopl. Epist.* 383 To the intent you may take him in hand, suppresse his saucinesse, and make him leaue off his mallapertnesse. **1582** N.T. (Rhem.) *Luke* iii. 36 marg. note, Whereby we learne the intolerable saucines of the Caluinists, and their contempt of holy Scripture, that dare so deale with the very Gospel it self. **1590** SHAKS. *Com. Err.* II. ii. 28 Your sawcinesse will iest vpon my loue, And make a Common of my serious howres. **1600** HOLLAND *Livy* xxv. 547 The magistrates..gaue place to the furious rage and malapart saucinesse of a few. **1676** GLANVILL *Ess. Philos. & Relig.* vii. 6 All demean'd themselves with much sawciness and irreverence towards God. **1710** STEELE *Tatler* No. 225 ⁋3 Familiarity in Inferiors is Sauciness. **1713** ADDISON *Trial Count Tariff* 9 Speaking against his Superiours with Sauciness and Contempt. **1753** JOHNSON *Adventurer* No. 84 ⁋13 Thus we travelled on four days..without any endeavour but to outvie each other in superciliousness and neglect; and when any two of us could separate ourselves for a moment, we vented our indignation at the sauciness of the rest. **1835** MARRYAT *Jac. Faithf.* xxi, What might be called sauciness in a girl, may be thought something more of in a young woman. **1866** GEO. ELIOT *F. Holt* v, Her sauciness was always charming because it was without emphasis. **1879** FROUDE *Cæsar* viii. 81 He [Sylla] experienced, however, himself, in a milder form, an explosion of military sauciness.

saucing ('sɔːsɪŋ), *vbl. sb.* [f. SAUCE *v.* + -ING[1].] The action of the verb SAUCE.

1548 UDALL *Erasm. Par.* Pref. 5 b, The sawcing of pleasures with some kynd of misfortune. **1586** J. HOOKER *Hist. Irel.* in *Holinshed* V. 83/1 He..being in a chafe for the wrong sawcing of a partridge, arose suddenlie from the table.

‖'saucisse. *Obs.* Also 7 saulcisse. [a. F. *saucisse* SAUSAGE *sb.*, applied transf. with allusion to the shape.] = SAUCISSON 3.

1604 E. GRIMSTONE *Hist. Siege Ostend* 144 He causeth Saulcisses to be made (so they call certaine things made of wood, tyed together). **1702** *Milit. Dict.* (1711), *Saucisse*, a long Train of Powder roll'd up in a Pitch-Cloth, and sew'd together in Length, so that it reach from the *Fourneau*, or Chamber of the Mine, to the Place where the Engineer stands to spring the Mine... There are generally two Saucisses to every Mine, that if the one fail, the other may hit. **1738** CHAMBERS *Cycl.* (ed. 2) s.v. *Mine*, The saucisse [1728 (ed. 1) *reads* Saucidge] of the mine is the train; for which there is always a little aperture left. **1795** *Amer. State Papers, For. Relat.* (1832) I. 523 (Stanf.) All arms and implements serving for the purposes of war, by land or sea, such as..carcases, saucisses, &c.

‖saucisson (sosisɔ̃). [Fr., augmentative of *saucisse* SAUSAGE *sb.*]

1. A large thick sausage. Freq. with Fr. qualifying words designating spec. types of sausage. Also *attrib.*

Following Fr. usage the term usu. describes a sausage which does not need to be cooked, as opp. to a *saucisse*.

1760–72 tr. *Juan & Ulloa's Voy.* (ed. 3) I. 361 The better to preserve its strength, it [*sc.* tobacco] is dried, and tied up in the form of a saucisson. **1834** MARRYAT *P. Simple* xxiii, French saucissons seasoned with garlic. **1958** W. BICKEL tr. *Hering's Dict. Cookery* 31 *Marinated sausage*: saucissons à l'huile: sliced cervelat, marinated in French dressing with chopped onions. *Viennese sausage*: saucissons de Vienne: heat up in boiling water, serve with grated horseradish, mustard, saurkraut or goulash sauce. **1962** *Harper's Bazaar* Aug. 69/1 A few slices of *saucisson d'ail* and *saucisson sec*. **1965** *House & Garden* Jan. 60 *Saucisson à l'ail* (*garlic sausage*), a type that includes many of the large sausages such as saucisson de Lyon and cote-chino. *Saucisson d'Arles* (*Arles sausage*)..is dried and delicately seasoned. *Saucisson de Lyon*, a sausage from Lyon made of pork, with fat and lean mixed. **1972** *Guardian* 11 Mar. 15/3 [The] Brasserie du Nord..is noted..for its *saucisson* and *rognon* dishes. **1975** *Woman's Jrnl.* Sept. 73/3 We started off with a plate of beetroot and tomato and *saucisson*. **1980** J. DITTON *Copley's Hunch* I. ii. 60 A little *saucisson sec*, bread and apples.

2. A kind of firework, consisting of a tube of paper or canvas packed with gunpowder.

1634 J. B[ATE] *Myst. Nature* 86 Saucissons are of two sorts eyther to be placed upon a frame,..and so to be discharged .. or else to bee discharged out of the morter-peece. **1688** R. HOLME *Armoury* III. xvi. (Roxb.) 91 In this Balloone must be put Rockets serpents, stars, petards, and one or two saucissons to Break the Balloone.

3. *Mil.* [Cf. SAUCISSE, SAUSAGE *sb.* 3.] **a.** A large fascine.

1702 *Milit. Dict.* (1711), *Saucissons* or *Saucisses*, Faggots made of the Bodies of Underwood, or of the large Branches of great Trees. **1756** *Gentl. Mag.* XXVI. 508 The 11th and 12th were employed in making gabions, saucissons, and fascines. **1876** VOYLE & STEVENSON *Milit. Dict.* (ed. 3), *Saucisson*... This name is also given to an extra large fascine.

b. A long tube of waterproofed canvas or other material packed with gunpowder and used as a fuse for firing a mine.

1827 SOUTHEY *Hist. Penins. War* II. 300 The saucisson was fired, and the explosion, as Bouchard had expected, threw down the entrenchments. **1862** *Chamb. Encycl.* VIII. 496/2 The electric spark is now preferred to the saucisson. **1876** VOYLE & STEVENSON *Milit. Dict.* (ed. 3), *Saucisson* (French = sausage).—A long tube of linen, filled with gunpowder..used for exploding fougasses or mines.

†'saucister. *Obs.* In 4 sausither, 4–5 salsister, 5 sawster, -styre, -sestyr, sawcystre, -cistre, saucestr, -cestour, -cester. [? Altered adoption of

F. *saucisse* SAUSAGE *sb.*, by assimilation to some word in *-ister*.] A sausage.

1347 *Durham Acc. Rolls* (Surtees) 41 In Salsisters emp. vjd... Salsisters emp. in villa, 3s. 3d. *a* **1387** *Sinon. Barthol.* (Anecd. Oxon.) 29 *Mazakata*,..vulgaliter salsicia, i. sausither. **14..** *Nom.* in Wr.-Wülcker 741/24 *Hec salsucia*, a sawstyre. **1434** *Durh. Acc. Rolls* (Surtees) 62 In sawsestyrs empt. 4s. 11d. *c* **1440** *Promp. Parv.* 441/2 Sawcyster, lynke, *hirna*. **1483** *Cath. Angl.* 317/1 A Salsister, *hirna*.

sauconite ('sɔːkənaɪt). *Min.* [f. *Saucon*, name of a valley near Bethlehem, Pennsylvania + -ITE¹.] A clay mineral of the montmorillonite group containing a high proportion of zinc.

1875 F. A. GENTH *Prelim. Rep. Mineral. Pennsylvania* v. 120 The first [peculiar clay] occurs at the Ueberoth Zinc Mine near Friedensville, Lehigh county, where it has been discovered by Prof. W. Th. Roepper, who named it 'Sauconite'. **1946** *Amer. Mineralogist* XXXI. 414 Sauconite proves to be a member of the montmorillonite group of minerals in which three bivalent zinc ions proxy two trivalent alumina ions in octahedral positions in the lattice structure. **1968** I. KOSTOV *Mineral.* 373 Additional representatives of the sub-groups are the following corresponding varieties:..Zn-saponite (sauconite) with about 35% ZnO.

saucy ('sɔːsɪ), *a.*¹ Forms: 6 sausy, -ie, *Sc.* **sawsy**, 6–7 sawsie, 6–8 sawcy(e, -ie, 8 *vulgar* saasy, 6– saucy. [f. SAUCE *sb.* + -Y¹.]

†**1.** Flavoured with or pertaining to sauce; resembling sauce; savoury. *Obs.*

1508 DUNBAR *Flyting* 191 Quhair thow lyis sawsy in saphron, bak and syd. **1604** E. G[RIMSTONE] *D'Acosta's Hist. Indies* IV. xxv. 279 Delicate, and of a sawcie and delicious taste. **1630** J. TAYLOR (Water-P.) *Gt. Eater Kent* Wks. I. 146/1 Nor in all his life time the queasinesse of his stomacke needed any sawcy spurre or switch of sowre Veriuice or acute Vineger.

fig. allusively. **1552** LATIMER *Serm. Lincolnsh.* i. (1562) 65 But he that wilbe a christen man, that intendeth to come to heauen, must be a sausye felow: he must be well poudered with the sause of affliction and tribulation.

2. a. Of persons, their dispositions, actions, or language: Insolent towards superiors; presumptuous. Now chiefly *colloq.* with milder sense, applied to children and servants: Impertinent, rude, 'cheeky'.

In the 16th c. often *saucy (and) malapert*, whence More's SAUCE MALAPERT. † *saucy Jack*: an impertinent fellow.

1530 PALSGR. 323/1 Saucy to perte or homlye, *malapert*. **1548** UDALL *Erasm. Par. Luke* v. 17–20 What a more shamelesse or sawcie pranke coulde there bee, then to take downe the tyling of an other mannes house, and to toumble in such a lothely syght before such a presence to behold it? **1553** *Respublica* I. iii. 26 Whoo buzzeth in myne eare so? what? ye sawecye Iacke? **1556** OLDE *Antichrist* 24 Symon magus was so sawcye as to name him selfe the mightie power of God. **1599** B. JONSON *Ev. Man out of Hum.* v. v, That saucie stubborne generation, the Iewes. **1600** SHAKS. *A.Y.L.* III. ii. 313, I wil speake to him like a sawcie Lacky, and vnder that habit play the knaue with him. **1602** FULBECKE *1st Pt. Parall.* Introd. 7 Comparisons wer of al things most saucy and malepert. **1617** MORYSON *Itin.* II. 70 My Lady Rich her letter he termed an insolent saucy malapert action. **1620** BEAUM. & FL. *Philaster* II. i, My father would preferre the boyes he kept to greater men then he, but did it not till they were too sawcy for himselfe. **1646** H. MARKHAM *Let.* in *12th Rep. Hist. MSS. Comm.* App. v. 2, I shall not trouble your Ladyship with her scandelous and sawcy language of my Lord or yourselfe. **1663** DRYDEN *Wild Gallant* IV. i, Sawcy Rascal, to disturb my Meditations. **1693** CONGREVE *Old Bach.* IV. xii, Base Man! Was it not enough to affront me with your sawcy Passion? *a* **1721** SHEFFIELD (Dk. Buckhm.) *Jul. C.* I. ii. Wks. 1723 I. 217 Betters! thou sawcy Citizen, be silent. **1791** BOSWELL *Johnson* an. 1773, 29 Sept., A clergyman's widow..having acquired great influence over the father, was saucy to the son. **1821–2** SHELLEY *Chas. 1st* ii. 35 Mark you what spirit sits in St. John's eyes? Methinks it is too saucy for this presence. **1843** SYD. SMITH in *Mem.* (1855) II. 499, I was sorry to be forced to give —— such a beating, but he was very saucy and deserved it. **1879** DIXON *Windsor* II. xvi. 171 Alençon had a saucy tongue. **1888** BURGON *Lives 12 Good Men* II. v. 16 He forwarded a copy of his letter to Lord John, who sent him in reply a saucy comment on it.

b. occas. with the notion: Wanton, lascivious.

In Shaks. as a term of serious condemnation; in modern examples only playful and in coy use: 'daring', smutty, suggestive.

1603 SHAKS. *Meas. for M.* II. iv. 45 To remit Their sawcie sweetnes, that do coyne heauens Image In stamps that are forbid. **1611** —— *Cymb.* I. vi. 151 If he shall thinke it fit, A sawcy Stranger in his Court, to Mart As in a Romish Stew. **1871** R. ELLIS *Catullus* xvi. 3 You that lightly a saucy verse resenting, Misconceit me. **1962** *Times* 13 Apr. 18/4 The comedy is all reduced to relentlessly 'saucy' sniggering farce. **1975** *Radio Times* 3 Apr. 17 George Formby..died 15 years ago. His songs, especially the saucy ones, have passed into legend. **1977** *News of World* 17 Apr. 9/7 He [*sc.* Mozart] won a reputation as a bed-hopping gambler and earned a fortune... Experts unearthed the saucy truth when they studied the great man's personal accounts.

c. Now often used in mock dispraise, as an endearing or admiring epithet implying piquancy or sprightliness.

1710 SWIFT *Jrnl. to Stella* 21 Sept., Here must I begin another letter, on a whole sheet, for fear saucy little *MD* should be angry. **1742** RICHARDSON *Pamela* (1785) IV. xxxiii. 190 Never was a saucier dear Girl, than you, in your Maiden Days. **1838** MISS MITFORD in L'Estrange *Life* (1870) III. 93, I love to see my tame pigeons feed at the window, and the saucy hen tap the glass, if the casement be shut. **1851** RUSKIN *Stones Ven.* (1874) I. App. 362 Some saucy puppies on their hind legs. **1888** HENLEY *Bk. Verses* 155 She has..the sauciest nose. **1904** A. GRIFFITHS *50 Yrs. Publ. Serv.* 17 They were old brother officers in the Saucy Sixth.

d. Applied to a ship or boat: †(*a*) In early use (with figurative context): Presumptuous, rashly-venturing (*obs.*). (*b*) In modern use (cf. 2 d): Smart, stylish.

c **1600** SHAKS. *Sonn.* lxxx, My sawsie barke (inferior farre to his) On your broad maine doth wilfully appeare. **1606** —— *Tr. & Cr.* I. iii. 42 Where's then the sawcy Boate, Whose weake vntimber'd sides but euen now Co-riual'd Greatnesse? **1652** CRASHAW *Alexias* Wks. (1904) 287 Seas had not bin rebuk't by sawcy oares. **1828** *Sporting Mag.* XXI. 341 Several East India ships..with such saucy rigging that would have made the Yachters raving in envy. **1873** G. C. DAVIES *Mount. & Mere* xix. 173 Slow moving trawlers and saucy little crab boats. **1878** W. C. BENNETT *Sea Songs* 78 Tight and saucy—tight and saucy, Trim's the ship we hail from.

†**e.** quasi-*adv.* = SAUCILY.

1598 Q. ELIZ. tr. *Plutarch* x. 13 Suche vers as Archi-Lochus againe women Lewdely and ful sawsy made. **1713** SWIFT *Jrnl. to Stella* 21 Feb, Methinks I writ a little saucy last night.

†**3.** Dainty, fastidious, 'spoilt'. *Obs.* exc. *dial.*

1573 TUSSER *Husb.* (1878) 214 Where cocking Dads make sawsie lads. **1611** COTGR., *Friand*..saucie, lickorous, daintie-mouthed, sweet-toothed. **1676** HALE *Contempl.* II. 174 Thou hast a sawcy and a luxurious Palate. **1886** *Cheshire Gloss.*, *Saucy*, dainty as to food. **1904** A. BENNETT *Great Man* vi. 50 He ate a little of the lean, leaving a wasteful margin of lean round the fat..; then he unobtrusively laid down his knife and fork. 'Come, Henry,' said Aunt Annie, 'don't leave a saucy plate.'

4. Scornful, disdainful. Now *dial.*

1716 GAY *Trivia* I. 117 In sawcy State the griping Broker sits. *a* **1774** FERGUSSON *Poems* (1807) 300 Sin Merlin laid Auld Reikie's causey, And made her o' his wark right saucy. **1786** BURNS *Twa Dogs* 91 They gang as saucy by poor folk As I wad by a stinkan brock. **1867** ELLEN JOHNSTON *Poems* 180 Had ye drest like a clark, aye in a clean sark, I vow I wad ne'er been sae saucy.

5. *Comb.*, as ***saucy-looking*** adj.; †**saucy-box** = SAUCEBOX; **saucy-face**, an impertinent person.

1684 OTWAY *Atheist* III. i, Robb'd, Sir! No, Mr. Saucy-face. **1711** SWIFT *Jrnl. to Stella* 21 Nov., Well, but I won't answer your letter now, sirrah saucyboxes, no, no; not yet. **1740** RICHARDSON *Pamela* (1824) I. 92 Come, saucy-face, give me another glass of wine. **1748** —— *Clarissa* IV. xxi. 96 For why? The dear saucy-face knows not how to help herself. **1848** THACKERAY *Van. Fair* li, Becky laughed, gay, and saucy-looking.

†**'saucy**, *a.*² *Obs.* [f. *sauce-* in SAUCEFLEME + -Y.] Affected by SAUCEFLEME.

1600 SURFLET *Country Farm* III. lxxiii. 604 This virgins milke is good to heale..saucie and red faces [orig. *goutte roses & taches rouges du visage*]. **1623** MARKHAM *Eng. Housew.* (ed. 2) 20 For a pympled or a red-saucy face.

saucy: see SASSY *sb.*

‖**saudade** (sau'dadə). [Pg.] Longing, melancholy, nostalgia, as a supposed characteristic of the Portuguese or Brazilian temperament.

1912 A. F. G. BELL *In Portugal* i. 7 The famous *saudade* of the Portuguese is a vague and constant desire for something that does not and probably cannot exist, for something other than the present, a turning towards the past or towards the future; not an active discontent or poignant sadness but an indolent dreaming wistfulness. **1936** R. GALLOP *Portugal* xi. 262 In a word *saudade* is yearning: yearning for something so indefinite as to be indefinable: an unrestrained indulgence in yearning. **1957** R. CAMPBELL *Portugal* p. ix, It [*sc.* Portugal] is an intensely poetic country, and it is the country of *saudade*, that mysterious melancholy which sighs at the back of every joy. **1976** *Gramophone* Aug. 320/1 The vigour and the *saudade*, the two Brazilian qualities with which the Preludes are imbued, are here replaced by a *gaucho* nostalgia.

saudan(t, variant forms of SOLDAN, sultan.

saudeor, -der, -diour, obs. forms of SOLDIER.

sauder, -dre, obs. forms of SOLDER.

Saudi ('saʊdɪ, 'sɔːdɪ, sɑː'uːdɪ), *sb.* and *a.* [ad. Arab. *sa'ūdī*, f. the name *Sa'ūd* (see below) + -I.] **A.** *sb.* **a.** A member of the Arabian Sa'ūd dynasty, the rulers of Nejd since the eighteenth century and of the kingdom of Saudi Arabia since 1932. **b.** = SAUDI ARABIAN *sb.* **B.** *adj.* **a.** Of or pertaining to the Sa'ūd dynasty. **b.** = SAUDI ARABIAN *a.*

1933 K. WILLIAMS *Ibn Sa'ud* i. 18 Muhammad took Riyadh... The Sa'udis could neither forget nor forgive their humiliation. *Ibid.* 23 Was the star of the Sa'udi scion..not to appear? *Ibid.* ii. 28 Arabia knew that a Sa'udi was..again master of Riyadh. **1949** *Britannica Bk. of Year* 51/1 A fraternal declaration which it was hoped would be the beginning of friendlier relations between the Saudi and Hashimi dynasties. **1957** *Encyl. Brit.* II. 169/1 The name Arabia is quite often used, incorrectly, when reference is intended to the Saudi kingdom only. **1959** W. THESIGER *Arabian Sands* xii. 227 At that time I was dressed as a Saudi. *Ibid.* xiii. 245 They were dressed in Saudi fashion, in long white shirts, gold-embroidered cloaks, and white head-cloths. **1962** *Listener* 5 Apr. 587/1 The Saudis could not bear the thought of an expansion of Hashimite power into Syria. **1974** *Encycl. Brit. Macropædia* XVI. 275/2 The 10,000 Saudi Arabs employed by Aramco..are exposed to modern industrial skills, technology, [etc.]. **1976** *Daily Record* (Glasgow) 22 Nov. 15/2 While I was there, Lebanese and Saudis in exquisite white silk suits, sipped pink champagne and peeled off £20 tips to English waitresses. **1976** *Star* (Sheffield) 3 Dec. 14/7 Sheffield workers got a pat on the back..for helping to save a Saudi customer waiting.

Hence **'Saudian, 'Saudite** *adjs.*

1949 [see HASHIMITE *a.* and *sb.*]. **1950** W. THEIMER *Encycl. World Politics* 378/1 Some experts believe that the Saudian oilfields contain one-half of the world's oil reserves.

Saudi Arabian ('saʊdɪ ə'reɪbɪən, 'sɔːdɪ ə'reɪbɪən), *a.* and *sb.* Also **Sa'udi Arabian**, and with hyphen. [f. *Saudi Arabia* (see below): cf. SAUDI *sb.* and *a.*, ARABIAN *a.* and *sb.*] **A.** *adj.* Of or pertaining to Saudi Arabia, a kingdom founded in 1932 by Abdul Aziz ibn Sa'ūd (1882–1953), comprising the greater part of the Arabian peninsula. **B.** *sb.* A native or inhabitant of Saudi Arabia.

1934 *Times* 23 Nov. 13/7 Sheikh Hafiz Wahba, the Saudi Arabian Minister to the Court of St. James's, is about to return to Mecca. **1947** K. PHILBY *Let.* in F. Maclean *Take Nine Spies* (1978) vii. 251 Ignorance and arrogance make a bad combination, and the Saudi Arabians have both. **1951** *Britannica Bk. of Year* 48/1 Syria undertook to supply Syrian goods for Saudi-Arabian consumption. *Ibid.*, The Saudi Arabian province of Hasa on the Persian Gulf. **1959** *Chambers's Encycl.* I. 504/2 The financial strength of the Sa'udi Arabian government has been greatly increased by the granting of foreign concessions for oil and minerals. **1959** G. A. LIPSKY *Saudi Arabia* i. 2 Loyalty to the family ..and loyalty to the tribe are the strongest bonds felt by most Saudi Arabians. **1976** *Alyn & Deeside Observer* 10 Dec. 9/6 A group of Saudi Arabians in Chester, celebrated one of their own religious feasts last week.

saue, obs. form of SAW *sb.*²

sauerbraten ('saʊə,brɑːt(ə)n, ‖'zaʊər,braːtən). *U.S.* [Ger., f. *sauer* sour + *braten* roast meat.] A dish of German origin consisting of oven- or pot-roasted beef that has been marinaded in vinegar with peppercorns, onions, garlic, and bay-leaves before being cooked.

1889 B. K. KRAMER '*Aunt Babette's' Cook Bk.* 62 (*heading*) Sauerbraten. **1923** *Ladies' Home Jrnl.* Mar. 133/1 A demure little Mennonite maid..will invite you cordially to 'sit up' to a table arrayed with the wealth of cup cheese and pot cheese and sugar cakes and *sauerbraten* and noodles and all the rest of the savory dainties..on the menu of a Pennsylvania Dutch family. **1931** *Better Homes & Gardens* Mar. 44/3 The Sauerbraten mit Kartoffelklossen—that pot roast with the wonderful sauce. **1938** L. BEMELMANS *Life Class* I. i. 29 They lived on a diet of sauerbraten and cabbage. **1964** S. BELLOW *Herzog* 80 We eat in twenty minutes. Good chow. Sauerbraten. **1966** N. FREELING *King of Rainy Country* 84 There was a very good delicate sauerbraten, with almonds and raisins in it, not too vinegary. **1978** *Detroit Free Press* 16 Apr. (Detroit Suppl.) 28/2 Or the sauerbraten, the German version of roast beef, is always good, marinated with a vinegar mixture which later is used to make the rich brown gravy.

‖**sauerkraut** ('saʊə,kraʊt). Also 7 **sawer-kraut**; for the anglicized forms, see SOUR CROUT, SOUR-CROUT. [Ger.; *sauer* sour + *kraut* vegetable, cabbage, whence F. *choucroute*. Cf. obs. Du. *zuurkruid*; the mod.Du. word is *zuurkool* (*kool* cabbage).] **1.** A popular article of diet in Germany, consisting of cabbage which has undergone an acid fermentation.

1633 HART *Diet of Diseased* I. xiv. 52 They pickle it [cabbage] up in all high Germany, with salt and barberies, and so keepe it all the yeere, being commonly the first dish you have served in at table, which they call their *sawerkrant* [*sic*]. **1825** LAMB *Eliana, Mem. Mr. Liston*, A German empiric, who, in this extremity, prescribed a copious diet of *sauer-kraut*. **1845** COOLEY *Pract. Receipts* (ed. 2) 704 Saur kraut. *Prep.* Clean white cabbages [etc.]. **1863** P. S. DAVIS *Young Parson* 48 [You] eat the best of roast beef, while I have to put up with sauerkraut and spec. **1875** LOWELL *Spenser* Prose Wks. 1890 IV. 269 Mr. Sibbald..seems to find a sort of national savor therein, such as delights..the German in his *sauer-kraut*. **1892** S. BARING-GOULD *Strange Survivals* vi. 130 Such an umbrella..was sufferable as spread over an old woman vending *sauerkraut*. **1945** C. A. PRICE *German Settlers in S. Austral.* ii. 14 Various Silesian recipes such as..Sauerkraut (pickled cabbage), etc., made their appearance and even penetrated to the English colonists. **1973** *Times* 29 Dec. 10/2 The stereotypes of the German as a man born with a monkey wrench in his hand and eating vast quantities of sausage and sauerkraut.. should really be discarded. After all, the French eat more sauerkraut.

2. *U.S. slang.* (Often with capital initial.) A German. Cf. SOUR CROUT 2 and KRAUT 2.

1858 J. A. STONE *Put's Golden Songster* 41 Sauer-Kraut was looking for a Justice of the Peace. **1909** *Sat. Even. Post* 3 July 7 I'll expurgate you, you old Dutch Sauerkraut!

3. *attrib.* and *Comb.*, as ***sauerkraut barrel, cutter***; **sauerkraut-eater** *slang* = sense 2 above.

1888 *Century Mag.* Mar. 807/1 The representative Americans of the present day..[are] the Micks and the Pats, the Hanses and the Wilhelms, redolent still of the dudeen and sauerkraut barrel. **1969** *Canadian Antiques Collector* Aug. 21/1 Another..bargain is a primitive sauerkraut cutter, which she..purchased for twenty-five cents. **1918** R. BRAMBLETT *Let.* 9 June in K. Cowing *Dear Folks at Home* (1919) 217 We will scatter those 'sauerkrauter eaters' [*sic*] before the summer is over.

‖**sauf** (sof), *prep.* [Fr.: cf. SAVE *quasi-prep.* and *conj.*] Used for: except for, apart from.

c **1844** H. TAYLOR *Let.* in F. A. Hayek *John Stuart Mill & Harriet Taylor* (1951) 115 Your liability to take an over large *measure* of people—sauf having to draw in afterwards. **1847** J. S. MILL *Let.* 9 Mar. in *Wks.* (1963) XIII. 708, I have had a book to write..which I have now..completed, sauf the revising. **1864** G. MEREDITH *Let.* 1 June (1970) I. 259 Her Papa can't bear to lose her, though he always lets his daughters have their way in this matter, *sauf* the guarantee of moral character.

sauf, variant of SAUGH.

sauf(e, -fand: see SAFE, SALVE, SAVING.

†**saufey.** *Sc.* and *north. Obs.* Also 5 salfay, safye, 6 salfer, saufer, sawpheir, saufeir, 6–7 saiffer, 7 sau(l)ffer, saifare, 7, 9 saufey. [Of obscure origin; prob. connected with SAVE *v.*; the last syllable may possibly represent FEE *sb.* or FEER. Cf. the synonymous SAUGHE, SAW-SILVER.] The sum paid for recovering lost property.

Persons convicted of having stolen cattle were adjudged to pay *double and saufey*, i.e. app. double the value, together with a sum representing what would have been due to one who had restored the cattle when it had strayed.

c **1400** *Alphabet of Tales* 434 Bod þe riche man, when he had þe sakett agayn, wolde not pay þe salfay. *Ibid.*, Becauce he wold nott hafe gyffen þe pure man a hondreth talentis to safye, as he promysid he sulde do. **1551–2** *Reg. Privy Council Scot.* I. 123 It is..ordanit, that all sik gudis stollin or reft, lauchfullie convict, salbe restorit and redressit with the thre dowbillis and salfer. **1561–2** *Ibid.* I. 201 That he.. sall..relief him of ane bill fylit upoun him of thre horsis takin fra the Lord Gray, with the dowble and saufer thairof. **1578–9** *Ibid.* III. 82 And that he that is offendit unto ressave his redres with dowbill and sawfeir according to the buke and lawis [of Marchis] foirsaid. **1605** *Ibid.* VII. 712 In matteris of auld thiftis..*quo jure procedendum*? quhidder by dowble sauffer or be single? *Ibid.* 744 That it mayе be lawfull to any man to give saifare for speiring of his goodis or geir stollen, provyding it does not exceade the double of the availle of the goods stollen. **1649** W. G. *Surv. Newcastle* 33 These Highlanders..come down..into the low Countries, and carry away Horses and Cattell so cunningly, that it will be hard for any to get them..except they be acquainted with some Master Thiefe; who for some mony (which they call Saufey mony) may help they to their stoln goods.

Hence †**saufey** *v.*, *trans.*, to redeem by payment of 'saufey'.

1571 *Reg. Privy Council Scot.* II. 90 That na maner of persoun..furneis money to the saidis rebellis..under cullour of saulffiing thair geir.

sauff(e, -ffand, -ffing: see SALVE, SAVING.

sauffer, variant of SAUFEY *Obs.*

saufftye, saufte, -tie, obs. ff. SAFETY.

saugeour, obs. form of SOLDIER.

sauger ('sɔːgə(r)). The smaller American pike-perch (see quot. 1882).

1882 JORDAN & GILBERT *Synopsis Fishes N. Amer.* 526 *Stizostedium canadense*... Sauger; Sand-pike; Gray-pike; Horn-fish. **1893** *Outing* (U.S.) XXII. 88/1 She fished on, adding now a bass, then a pike or a sauger to her trophies.

saugh, sauch (sɑx). *Sc.* and *north.* Also 4 salfe, 7–9 sauf, etc.: see E.D.D. [repr. OE. *salh* (Anglian) = WS. *sealh* SALLOW *sb.*] = SALLOW.

1368 *Durham Halm. Rolls* (Surtees) 73 De Waltero Biscopp pro una salfe detent. prec. 18d. **1472** *Rental Bk. Cupar-Angus* (1879) I. 163 Plantatioun of treys that is to say eysses, osaris, and sauch. **1501** *Acc. Ld. High Treas. Scotl.* II. 83 Item, to George Cambel, gardiner of Strivelin, to by sauchis and to set thaim, iiij Franch crouns. **1641** BEST *Farm. Bks.* (Surtees) 120 Att Martymmasse..wee sette our foreman to cuttinge of white-wilfes, reade-wilfes, and saughs. **1786** BURNS *Auld Farmer's Salut. Mare* x, Nae whip nor spur, but just a wattle O' saugh or hazel. *a* **1834** R. SURTEES in G. Taylor *Mem.* (Surtees) 241 They made a bier of the birken boughs, Of the sauf and the espin gray. **1844** H. STEPHENS *Bk. Farm* III. 1178 Of the woods best adapted for the purpose, I may name the common saugh or willow. **1891** ATKINSON *Last of Giant Killers* 132 Lower about the slacks were alders and saughs or sallows.

†**b.** A rope made of twisted sallow-withes. *Obs.*

1508 DUNBAR *Flyting* 245 Filling of tauch, rak sauch, cry crauch, thow art our sett. **1570** *Satir. Poems Reform.* xii. 56 For this foule deid ȝour seid man rak ane sauch.

c. *attrib.*, as ***saugh slip, tree, woody*** (= withy).

1842 J. AITON *Domest. Econ.* (1857) 171 [For] screening the dunghill, *saugh slips may be planted,—or better, *saugh stobs, four feet long, may be driven into the ground. **1513** DOUGLAS *Æneis* VII. xi. 73 Thair targettis bow thai of the lycht *sauch tre. **1548** TURNER *Names Herbes* (E.D.S.) 70 Salix is called..in english a wylow tree, a salowe tree or a saugh tree. **1815** SCOTT *Guy M.* xxii, Did ye notice if there was an auld saugh tree that's maist blawn down. *a* **1802** in Scott *Minstrelsy* II. 142 O wae betide the frush *saugh wand! **1789** BURNS *To Dr. Blacklock* vi, I hae a wife and twa wee laddies,..But I'll sned besoms—thraw *saugh woodies, Before they want.

saugh, obs. form of SOUGH, channel.

†**saughe.** *Sc. Obs.* [If not a misreading, app. identical with the first element in SAUFEY, SAW-SILVER.] = SAUFEY.

1561 in R. Keith *Hist. Aff. Ch. & St. Scotl.* (1734) App. 95 For any Attemptat done since the said 20th Day of September last, Deliverance and Redress shall be made with Double and Saughe.

saughen, sauchen ('sɑx(ə)n), *a. Sc.* [f. SAUGH + -EN.] Pertaining to or made of sallow. Also *fig.*, 'soft, weak, wanting in energy' (E.D.D.).

1724 PEDEN in *Biogr. Presbyt.* (1838) I. 82 He caused dig a Cave, with a Saughen-bush covering the Mouth of it. **1875** J. VEITCH *Tweed* 172 They brought him slow From the hills on a sauchen bier.

†**saught**, *sb. Obs.* (since 14th c. only *Sc.* and *north.*). Forms: 1 seht, seaht, 3 sæht(e, saht(e, seaht(e, seht(e, saihte, seihte, (seþte), sauht, 3–5 saght, 4 saȝt(e, sahut, saughte, 5 sauȝt, 8 *north.* saft, 6–9 saught, 7 saucht. [Late OE. *seht*, *seaht* masc., prob. a. ON. **sæht*, **saht* fem. (OIcel. *sætt*, *sátt*):—earlier **sahti-z*, f. OTeut. **sah-* perh. identical with L. *sac-* in *sancīre* to hallow, make binding (a treaty, etc.), *sacer* sacred.

The forms with *a* and *au* directly represent the ON. word.]

1. An agreement, covenant.

1038–50 in Kemble *Codex Dipl.* (1846) IV. 118 Se seht ðe Godwine eorl worhte betweðnan ðam arcebisceop & ðam hirede æt sancte Augustine & Leofwine preoste. *a* **1122** *O.E. Chron.* (Laud MS.) an. 1091, On þisum sehte wearð eac Eadgar eþeling wið þone cyng ȝe sæhtlad.

2. Agreement, freedom from strife, peace. Frequent in the phrase (*to be*) *at saught.*

c **1100** in *Bæda's Hist.* IV. xxii. [xxi.] ad fin. (Camb. MS.), Sib wæs syððan seaht & sib [*earlier texts* Ðære sibbe wære] mycelre tide æft þon betwyh ða ylcan cyningas & heora rice awunode. **1154** *O.E. Chron.* (Laud MS.) an. 1140, & sib & sæhte sculde ben betwyx heom & on al Engle land. *c* **1205** LAY. 2139 þa luueden heom þeos leoden mid sibben & mid sahten. *a* **1225** *Ancr. R.* 250 God lihte to eorðe uorte makien þreouold seihte—bitweonen mon & mon [etc.]. *c* **1275** *Serving Christ* 1 in *O.E. Misc.* 90 Hwi ne serue we crist and secheþ his sauht. *a* **1300** *Cursor M.* 3964 Iacob þan sent him of his aght Giftes large, al for þe saght. **1460** *Lybeaus Disc.* 1030 They ryden forth all yn saght. **1603** *Philotus* cxliii, The feind wald faine man be your wyfe, Can neuer sit in saucht. **1768** ROSS *Helenore* 27 For as her mind began to be at saught. *Ibid.* 29 'Tis true, she had of warlds gear a fraught: But what was that to peace an' saught at hame. **1781** J. HUTTON *Tour to Caves* Gloss., *Saft*, heart's ease, as *to be at saft*, to be easy and contented, also reconciled. **1806** R. JAMIESON *Pop. Ball.* I. 207 O gin wi' thee, regretted maid! I in the mools at saught were laid.

†**saught**, *a. Obs.* Forms: 1 seht, sæht, 2–3 seht, saht, 3 *Ormin* sahhte, 3 sæht(e, sauchte, swahte, 3–4 sauht(e, 3–5 saght(e, 4 sawht, sawght, saught(e, (sayct), 4–5 sauȝt(e, saȝt, 5 sawcht, 4–6 *Sc.* saucht. [Late OE. *seht*, *sæht*, prob. a. ON. **saht-r* (OIcel. *sáttr*):—OTeut. type **sahto-*, a passive pple. f. **sah-*: see SAUGHT *sb.*] In agreement, free from strife, at peace, reconciled.

956 in Birch *Cartul. Sax.* III. 172 And sæ bisceop Stigandæ and sæ hiræd on ealdan mynstræ him þæs ȝætiþodon wið scwlcon ȝersumen swylce hi þa sehtte wæron. *c* **1175** *Lamb. Hom.* 15 And eour eyþer sunegað bi-foran drihtan and ec leter ȝe beoð sahte. *c* **1200** ORMIN 5731 þe seoffnde seollþess ædiȝleȝȝc Iss griþþ i manness herrte,.. Swa þatt hiss bodiȝ wiþþ hiss gast Sammtale & sahhte wurrþe. *a* **1272** *Luue Ron* 134 in *O.E. Misc.* 97 Alle heo schule wyþ engles pleye some and sauhte in heouene lyhte. *a* **1300** *Cursor M.* 3540 þou and i er selden saght, Abute our forbirth er we wrath. *c* **1320** *Cast. Love* 552 And Pees and Riht cussen and be sauȝt and some. **1375** BARBOUR *Bruce* x. 300 Qwhen the king ves thus vith him saucht. **1390** GOWER *Conf.* I. 371 Of this point ye have me tawht, Toward miself the betre sawht I thenke be, whil that I live. *Ibid.* III. 313 The wyndy Storm began to skarse,..The Schipman.. Whan that he sih the wyndes saghte, Towardes Tharse his cours he straghte. *c* **1450** MYRC *Festial* 26 Scho beþoght hur how þat chyldern don no vengeans, but lyghtly ben saȝt, þogh þay ben wrothe. **1513** DOUGLAS *Æneis* II. vii. 48 Now lat ws change scheildis, sene we bene saucht. **1570** *Satir. Poems Reform.* xiii. 179 We trowit from thence thay suld haif sittin saucht, And suld haif tyrit of all thair tyrannie.

†**saught**, *v. Obs.* Forms: 1 sehtan, ȝesehtian, 2–5 sauȝt(e, 3 sæhte, seyte, 4 saght, 3–4 sauhte, sahut, saȝt, 4–5 saucht, 5 saughte. [Late OE. *sehtan*, *ȝe-sehtian*, f. *seht* SAUGHT *sb.* Cf. ON. **sæhta* (OIcel. *sætta*).]

1. *trans.* To bring to peace, reconcile.

c **1000** in Thorpe *Ags. Laws* II. 304 Cristenum cyninge ȝebyreð..þæt he..eall cristen folc sibbie & sehte mid rihtre laȝe. *Ibid.* 312. **1154** *O.E. Chron.* an. 1101, Ac þa heafod men heom betwenan foran & þa broðra ȝesehtodan on þa ȝerad. *c* **1250** *Hymn Virg.* 40 in *Trin. Coll. Hom.* App. 256 Help me to mi liues ende & make me wið þin sone isauȝt. **1297** R. GLOUC. (Rolls) 11008 Hii broȝte him þer to To makie a poruеance..þut lond uor to seyte. *c* **1320** *Cast. Love* 933 Godes sone, þ^t fro heuene to eorþe wolde come To sauȝte his sustren. *a* **1400** *Hymns Virg.* 108 Loke þou assay, To sauȝten hem þenne at on assent.

2. *intr.* To become reconciled.

a **1375** *Cursor M.* 3964 (Fairf.) Iacob sende him of his aȝt giftes large wiþ him to saȝt [*Gött.* to sahut; *Cott.* al for þe saght]. *c* **1400** *Gamelyn* 150 Graunte me my bone Of thing I wil thee aske and we schul saughte sone. *c* **1450** HOLLAND *Howlat* 844 Thai forthocht that thai faucht, Kissit samyn and saucht.

Hence †'**saughting** *vbl. sb.*

a **1300** *Cursor M.* 17198 And blith o saghting þou me bedis. *c* **1375** *Sc. Leg. Saints* I. (*Katerine*) 921 Wald þu..ask forgiffnes of þi syne, yheit mycht þu sauchtyng with hym wine. *a* **1400** *Minor Poems fr. Vernon MS.* 573 Wraþþe gedereþ gret hate, Loue norisscheþ sauȝtynge.

saught, obs. pa. t. and pa. pple. of SEEK.

†**saughtel**, *v. Obs.* Forms: 2 sæhtle, 2–3 sahtle, 3 sawghtle, *Ormin* sahhtlenn, 4 saȝttel, sa(u)ghtle, -til, sauhtill, (saxtel), 4–5 saȝtle, sauȝt(e)le, saghtel, 5 saȝtill, saghtill, sahtil, saghetylle, sauȝthle, saughtel, -tille. [In 12th c. *sahtlian*, *sæhtlian*, f. *sæht*, **saht*: see SAUGHT *a.*]

1. *intr.* To come to agreement, become reconciled.

1154 *O.E. Chron.* (Laud MS.) an. 1140, Sithen þer efter sahtleden þe king & Randolf eorl at Stanford. **1340** HAMPOLE *Pr. Consc.* 1470 Now lofe we, now hate, now saghtel, now strife. *c* **1375** *Cursor M.* 3580 (Fairf.) [When a man is old] þen ys ethe to make him wraþ & for tille saxtel sumdel laþ. **1377** LANGL. *P. Pl.* B. x. 183 It is no science for sothe forto sotyle [*v.r.* sauȝtele] Inne. ? *a* **1400** *Morte Arth.* 330, I salle hym surelye ensure, þat saghetylle salle we never. *a* **1400–50** *Alexander* 865 Sire, latt þi wreth a-wai wende & with þi wyfe saȝtill. *a* **1440** *Sir Degrev.* 1757, I rede ye sauȝthle with the knyȝt.

b. To become calm or quiet.

13.. *E.E. Allit. P.* B. 445 As þat lyftande lome [*sc.* the ark] luged aboute,..Hit saȝtled on a softe day synkande to grounde. *Ibid. C.* 232 He [Jonah] was no tytter out-tulde þat tempest ne sessed, þe se saȝtled þer-with, as sone as ho moȝt. *Ibid.* C. 529 For-þy when pouerte me enprecez & paynez in-noȝe, Ful softly with suffraunce saȝttel me bihouez.

2. *trans.* To reconcile (persons). Also *refl.*

a **1122** *O.E. Chron.* (Laud MS.) an. 1066, þa eodon gode men heom betwenen & sahtloden heom. *Ibid.* an. 1070, þa tweȝen kyngas Willelm & Swæȝn wurðon sæhtlod. *c* **1200** ORMIN 6024 He riseþþ upp & sahhtleþþ himm Wiþþ Godd þurrh rihht dædbote. *a* **1300** *Cursor M.* 28565 Quen man think to traueil lath, to saghtil men þat er wrath. **13..** *E.E. Allit. P.* B. 1139 For when a sawele is saȝtled & sakred to dryȝtyn, He holly haldes hit his. *c* **1400** *Ywaine & Gaw.* 3917 Thou sal do thi power,..To saghtel the Knyght with the liown And his lady of grete renowne.

Hence †'**saughteling** *vbl. sb.*

a **1300** *Cursor M.* 964 Tell me..Howgat and wit quat-kinthing I sal couer þi saghteling. *c* **1330** R. BRUNNE *Chron. Wace* (Rolls) 3256 For þat saughtlyng [of the brothers] was mykel blisse. *c* **1400** *Ywaine & Gaw.* 3680 Than asked the king Wha had so sone made saghteling Bitwix tham thai had bene so wrath. *c* **1420** *Anturs of Arth.* 661 (Douce MS.) Withe outene more lettynge, Diȝte was here saȝtlynge.

†'**saughten**, *v. Obs.* Forms: 2 sahtnie, 2–3 sehtne, 3 sahtne, sæhtne, -nie, sehtnie, seihtni, sachtni, 4 sauhtne, sahutin, sauȝtne, -tene, (saxtend), *Sc.* sauchtine, 5 saughten. [f. SAUGHT *a.* + -EN[5].]

1. *trans.* To reconcile.

c **1175** *Lamb. Hom.* 39 þet seste is þat þu scalt sahtnien þa þe beoð unisahte mid alle þine mahte. *Ibid.* 83 He isehtnede god & man. *c* **1205** LAY. 8776 Nu þu must me ræden sæhtnien me wið þene kæisere. *Ibid.* 30036 Heo..spileden bitweonen þat heo wolden alle þa kinges sehtnie. *a* **1225** *Ancr. R.* 28 Vorte seihtni [*v.r.* sachtni] me wiþ þe deore-wurðe Louerd. *c* **1375** *Sc. Leg. Saints* xviii. (*Egipciane*) 1485 Dere lady, I þe pray, þat..þu succure me, & sauchtine me & þi sowne.

2. *intr.* To become reconciled or at peace.

c **1205** LAY. 8254 Wið þon þe þu hine ȝeue grið & late hine sæhtne þe wið. **1362** LANGL. *P. Pl.* A. IV. 2 Seseþ, seide þe kyng..ȝe schulle sauȝtene [MS. D. *c* **1480** saughten] forsothe and serue me bothe.

Hence †'**saughtening** *vbl. sb.* (*attrib.*).

a **1300–1400** *Cursor M.* 3954 (Gött.) Iacob sent þan for-to fonde, Esau wid sahutinyng sonde. *c* **1320** *Sir Tristr.* 1805 Made was þe sauȝtening And alle forȝeue bi dene. *c* **1375** *Sc. Leg. Saints* xxi. (*Clement*) 742, & sic mystreutht I here forsak, & with ȝoure god wil sauchtnyng mak. *c* **1425** WYNTOUN *Cron.* V. xi. 3165 Qwhil at þe last þe hail barne Off Brettane knyt þaim in sauchtenynge. **1513** DOUGLAS *Æneis* X. xiv. 176 Na frendschip in thy handis, Nane syk trety of sauchnyng nor cunnandis, My son Lawsus band vp with the.

sauȝter, obs. form of PSALTER.

†'**saughtliness.** *Obs. rare*[−1]. In 4 saghtlines. [f. SAUGHT *sb.* or *a.* + -LY[1] + -NESS.] Reconciliation. Cf. SAUGHTNESS.

a **1300** *Cursor M.* 29125 If he be funden in þam treu his saghtlines þat sal him neu.

†'**saughtness.** *Obs.* Forms: 1 sehtnyse, 2 sahtnys, 3 seht-, seih(t)-, saht-, seht-, sæht-, sachtnesse, 4 saght-, sawghtnes, sauht-, seiȝtnesse. [OE. *sehtnys*, *sahtnys*, f. *seht* SAUGHT *a.*: see -NESS.] The condition of being reconciled.

c **1000** ÆLFRIC *Hom.* II. 198 Ðam dom-bocum þe se Heofonlica Wealdend his folce ȝesette to some, and to sehtnysse. *a* **1122** *O.E. Chron.* (Laud MS.) an. 1066, Geaf þa þone cyng .xl. marc goldes to sahtnysse. *c* **1200** ORMIN 3515 He wass borenn her Sahhtnesse & griþþ to settenn Bitwenenn Drihhtin..& mannkinn. *c* **1200** *Trin. Coll. Hom.* 5 Cum louerd and biwind us on seihtnesse. *c* **1205** LAY. 2809 He sette þis lond he sahtnesse wrohte. *a* **1225** *Ancr. R.* 250 Pax uobis! Seihtnesse beo bitweonen ou. *Ibid.* 426 þis is o þing..þet is God leouest—seihnesse & some [*v.r.* sachtnesse & somentale]. *a* **1300** *Cursor M.* 4014 Sli strength es o þe holi gast, To saghtnes mak þar wrath es mast. *c* **1320** *Cast. Love* 474 Euer on þat ilke stryf þat a-mong my sustren is a-wake, þorw sauhtnesse mowe sum ende take. *a* **1330** *Otuel* 570 Sitte eche man oppon his kne, & biddeth to god..Sende seiȝtnesse bi-twene þo kniȝtes.

saughy ('sɑxɪ), *a. Sc.* Also sauchie. [f. SAUGH + -Y.] = SAUGHEN.

1818 *Edin. Mag.* Oct. 328/1 Deep down in the sauchie glen o' Trows, Aneth the cashie wud. **1897** 'L. KEITH' *Bonnie Lady* v. 47 She might have twisted him like a sauchie bough in her tender fingers.

‖**saugrenu** (sogrəny), *a.* Also fem. pl. saugrenues. [Fr.] Absurd, preposterous, ridiculous.

1876 W. JAMES *Let.* 5 July in R. B. Perry *Tht. & Char. W. James* (1935) I. 371 The *saugrenu*, comic Shakespeare scenes. **1889** E. DOWSON *Let.* 18 Oct. (1967) 110, I have many adventures to tell you of—some assez saugrenues. **1908** 'ODYSSEUS' *Turkey in Europe* (ed. 2) xiii. 440 The Great Powers of Europe are very like ordinary prejudiced individuals, not to say the lower animals. What they shy at one day, what they denounce with diminishing invective as impossible, revolutionary *sangrenu*, or crude, they accept a few years later as a matter of course. **1933** *N. & Q.* CLXV. 378/2 If we take 'chevalier' as addressed by Christ to the poet, do we not get merely a retort—frigid, and, by reason of the historical association a little *saugrenu*?

sauht, obs. form of SAULT *sb.*[1] *Obs.*

Sauk (sɔːk). Also Sac; 8 Sacky, Sax. [ad. Canad. F. *Saki*, f. Ojibwa *osākī*; cf. Sauk *asākīwa* person of the outlet.] An Algonquian Indian people inhabiting parts of the central United States, formerly in Wisconsin, Illinois, and Iowa, now in Oklahoma and Kansas; a member of this people. Also, the language of this people, a dialect of Fox. Also *attrib.* or as *adj.*

1722 D. COXE *Descr. Carolana* 48 The Nations who dwell on this River, are Outogamis,..Sacky, and the Poutouatamis. **1762** [see MENOMINEE]. **1789** *Deb. Congress U.S.* 25 May (1834) 41 The treaties..with the sachems and warriors of the Wyandot, Delaware,..and Sac nations,.. appear to have been negotiated [etc.]. **1810** Z. M. PIKE *Acct. Expeditions Sources Mississippi* App. I. 20 The Sauks and Reynards are planting corn. **1810** in *Deb. Congress U.S.* (1853) 12th Congress 1 Sess., App. 1858 A considerable number of Sacs went..to see the British superintendent. **1835** [see MENOMINEE]. **1836** J. HALL *Statistics of West* 53 On this prairie is a small village of the Sauk and Fox Indians. **1877** L. H. MORGAN *Anc. Society* II. vi. 169 The Shawnees had a practice, common also to the Miamis and Sauks and Foxes, of naming children into the gens of the father or of the mother or any other gens. **1881** *Encycl. Brit.* XII. 832/1 The *Sacs* and *Foxes*, now one tribe, located in Indian Territory, were originally separate, living near Green Bay, Wisconsin... A few still remain in Iowa, Nebraska, and Kansas. **1933** L. BLOOMFIELD *Language* iv. 72 The Algonquian family..includes the languages of..the Great Lakes region (..Menomini, Sauk, Fox, Kickapoo, [etc.]). **1946** G. FOREMAN *Last Trek of Indians* 187 Treaties were thus made with the following tribes: Delawares, Kansas, Sauk and Foxes of the Mississippi, Sauk and Foxes of the Missouri, [etc.]. **1972** J. MOSEDALE *Football* i. 3 The famous Sac and Fox warrior, Chief Blackhawk. **1974** *Encycl. Brit. Micropædia* VIII. 921/1 In the 1970s there were about 1,000 Sauk. **1978** *Handbk. N. Amer. Indians* XV. 654 Organized as the Sac and Fox tribe of Indians of Oklahoma under the Oklahoma Indian Welfare Act of 1936, the Sauk had an elected chief and business committee.

saul, variant of SAL[2], SOUL.

saulce, -ery: see SAUCE, SAUCERY.

sauldyer, obs. form of SOLDIER.

†**saule**, *v. Obs.* [a. OF. *saouler* (mod.F. *soûler*), f. *saoul* (mod.F. *soûl*) full of meat or drink = Pr. *sadol*, It. *satollo*:—L. *satullus*, dim. of *satur* full: see SATURITY.] *trans.* To satisfy, fill with food.

c **1430** *Pilgr. Lyf Manhode* I. lxix. (1869) 41 Thei wer namore sauled ther with than if [etc.].

saule, obs. form of SAIL, SOUL.

†**'saulee.** *Obs.* Also 4 saule, 5 sawle(e. [a. OF. *saoulee* (mod.F. *soûlée*), f. *saouler*: see SAULE *v.*] Satisfaction of appetite; a satisfying meal or quantity of food.

1377 LANGL. *P. Pl.* B. XVI. 11, I wolde..forto haue my fylle of þat frute forsake al other saulee [*Gloss* edulium]. *c* **1400** *Lanfranc's Cirurg.* 272 He schal drinke no newe wijn, & he schal ete no greet saule. *c* **1400** tr. *Secreta Secret., Gov. Lordsh.* xliv. 73 Wherfore it nedys þanne..to abstene to mekyll ete and drynke, and fro greet saule. **1426** LYDG. *De Guil. Pilgr.* 6178 My voyded herte to fulfylle Wych so longe ..hath voyde be, And neuere ne hadde hys ful sawlee. *c* **1430** *Pilgr. Lyf Manhode* I. v. (1869) 4 Good it were to faste a litel for to haue ful saulee at the sopere.

saulf(e, -ff, obs. forms of SAFE, SAVE.

saulffer, saulftie: see SAUFEY, SAFETY.

saulie ('sɑlɪ). *Sc. Obs.* exc. *Hist.* Also saullie, sawlie, sal(l)ie, saly, sauley. [Of obscure origin; perh. short for some comb. of *saul* SOUL.] A hired mourner at a funeral.

1621 *Sc. Acts Jas. VI* (1816) IV. 626/1 That no duillweidis be givin to herauldis, Trumpetoris or saullies Except by the Earlis and lordis and thair wyffes And the number of the saullies to be according to þe number of duilweiddis. **1654** in C. Rogers *Soc. Life Scotl.* (1884) I. v. 161 [(Funeral of Earl of Buccleuch.) In front marched forty-six] salies [or hired mourners with hoods and bearing black staves]. **1773** R. FERGUSSON *Poems* (1800) 169 How come mankind, whan lacking woe, In Saulie's face their hearts to show? **1815** SCOTT *Guy M.* xxxvii, And then the funeral pomp set forth; saulies with their batons, and gumphions of tarnished white crape. **1864** in R. Paul *Mem.* xix. (1872) 304, I see in imagination a tall unbendable fellow..grave as a sauley. **1898** W. DRYSDALE *Old Faces* 47 When hearses came into fashion, people of distinction were conveyed therein, and were preceded by 'saulies'.

saull(e, obs. forms of SOUL.

saullie, variant of SAULIE.

saulm, saulmon, obs. ff. PSALM, SALMON.

saulpeter, variant of SALPETRE *Obs.*

†**sault,** *sb.*[1] *Obs.* Forms: 3–6 saut, 4 saght, sauȝt, 4–5 sauht, sawt, 4–6 saute, sawte, 4–6 salt, 6 sault. [Early ME. *saut*, aphetic form of *assaut* ASSAULT *sb.*, with later insertion of *l* as in that word.] = ASSAULT *sb.*, in various senses.

1297 R. GLOUC. (Rolls) 11870 Wiþ a lance he broȝte a kniȝt atte verste saut þer doune. **1338** R. BRUNNE *Chron.* (1810) 125 þe Gyour of his oste at þat saut [*sc.* on Lincoln] was slayn. *a* **1340** HAMPOLE *Ps.* xii. 4 The deuel..makes his saute in vs, and bost bifor god, to gare vs be dampned if he may ouere com vs in any temptacioun. *c* **1350** *Will. Palerne* 2651 þe king bi-seget þe cite selcouþli harde, & mani a sad sauȝt his sone þer-to made. **1375** BARBOUR *Bruce* XVII. 356 [At the siege of Berwick] Thai trumpit till ane sawt [*v.r.* salt] in hy. *c* **1380** WYCLIF *Epist. Domin.* iv. Sel. Wks. II. 365 þat ȝe may stonde aȝens þe fendis sautis. **1452** J. PASTON in *P. Lett.* I. 232 Charlis Nowell with odir hath in this cuntre mad many riot and sautes. *c* **1477** CAXTON *Jason* 11 Tho fewe that yet lyue dare not now yssue out more for to make ony saulte or scarmusche ayenst their ennemyes. **1510** *Sel. Cases Crt. Star Chamber* (Selden) 206 Thomas Withiford..and dyuerse moo made a Sawte on Thomas powes and wold haue take hym With stroung hande owte of his schoppe. *c* **1520** SKELTON *Magnif.* 2329 Remedy pryncypall Agaynst all sautes [*v.r.* fautes] of your goostly foo. **1523** EARL OF SURREY *Let. to Wolsey* in Ellis *Orig. Lett.* Ser. I. I. 215, I being at the sault of th' abbay, whiche contynued unto twoo houres within nyght. **1556** J. HEYWOOD *Spider & F.* lxv. 74 Sir captaine our mind is, To giue saute to the copweb. *a* **1600** *Flodden F.* iii. (1664) 22 Though with hard saults they him assaild.

†**sault,** *sb.*[2] *Obs.* Forms: 4 saut, 5 sawte, 6 saute, 7–8 salt, sault. [a. F. *saut*:—L. *saltus* (*u* stem), f. *salīre* to leap; for the form cf. prec.]

1. A leap, jump; *spec.* of horses (see 1728–52).

a **1350** *John Bapt.* 105 in Horstm. *Altengl. Leg.* (1881) 125 Scho daunced and tumbild diuers saut Ful faire and wele, with-outen faut. *c* **1400** *Brut* iv. 11 þerfore þe place is called ȝit in-to þis day 'þe sawte of Gogmagog'. **1607** MARKHAM *Caval.* I. (1617) 14 They are many of them naturally giuen to bound, & to performe saults aboue ground. **1616** B. JONSON *Devil an Ass* II. vi, [Love] could make More wanton salts from this braue promontory. **1623** MARKHAM *Cheap Husb.* I. ii. (ed. 3) 15 The loftinesse of a horses salts and leapes. **1653** URQUHART *Rabelais* I. xxiii, He rode..a light fleet horse, unto whom he gave a hundred carieres, made him go the high saults, bounding in the aire. **1688** R. HOLME *Armoury* III. xix. (Roxb.) 183/2 Ground salts, is to take vp his fore leggs from the ground both togather, and bringing his hinder feet in their place. **1728–52** CHAMBERS *Cycl.*, *Salts*, or *Saults*, in the menage, denote the leaps, or high airs and vaults of an horse... A *step and a salt* is an high air, wherein the horse rising, makes a curvet between two salts, or caprioles... *Two steps and a salt* is a motion composed of two curvets; ending with a capriole.

2. *a sault out*: a sally.

1560 DAUS *Sleidane's Comm.* 323 b, To the ende the Townes men shoulde make no salt out [L. *eruptionem*].

3. *to go to sault* = 'to go assault': see ASSAUT *adv.* and SALT *sb.*[2]

1567 PAINTER *Pal. Pleas.* II. 185 And yet you see this great ..Duchesse..run after the male, like a female Wolfe or Lionesse (when they goe to sault).

‖**sault** (səʊ, commonly suː), *sb.*[3] *North Amer.* [Colonial Fr. *sault*, 17th c. spelling of *saut*: see SAULT *sb.*[2]] A waterfall or rapid.

1600 *Hakluyt's Voy.* III. 234 The Captaine prepared two boats to goe vp the great River to discouer the passage of the three Saults or falles of the River [Canada]. **1809** A. HENRY *Trav.* 16 Lachine..is at the head of the Sault de Saint-Louis, which is the highest of the saults, falls, or leaps, in this part of the Saint-Lawrence. **1860** BARTLETT *Dict. Amer.* (ed. 3), *Sault*, pronounced *soo*. (Old French.) The rapids of the St. Lawrence and those connecting the Upper Lakes retain the French name; as, the Sault St. Mary, etc.

†**sault,** *v.*[1] *Obs.* Forms: 4–5 saute, sawte, 5 sawlte, 6 saut, sawt, saulte, salt, 6, 9 sault. [ME. *saute*, aphetic form of *assaute* ASSAULT *v.*] *trans.* = ASSAULT *v.* in various senses.

1387 TREVISA *Higden* (Rolls) VIII. 552 And thenne the kynge sente therle marchal vnto Louers, whiche they sawted. **1448** METHAM *Wks.* (E.E.T.S.) 55/1474 Offte this serpent gan saute the bugyl blak The qwyche vpon hys helmet stod. *c* **1489** CAXTON *Sonnes of Aymon* xvi. 384 Yf ye sawte Reynawde, we four that ben here shall helpe hym agaynste you. **1556** J. HEYWOOD *Spider & F.* lxxiv. 11 To sawt this castell a fresh, they haue purueyde. **1560** PHAER *Æneid* IX. E e iij b, A towre..whom all the Italians totall strength incessaunt stil did saulte.

absol. c **1471** in *Pol. Poems* (Rolls) II. 278 At Algate thay sawtid in an ill seasoun. **1489** CAXTON *Faytes of Armes* I. ix. B iv, To teche hem bettre in all thynges to fighte & to sawte, they were oftymes put in arraye of batailles. *c* **1500** *Melusine* xxxvi. 291 And there they rested them by the space of viii dayes, without sawtyng ne scarmysshing.

Hence †**'saulting** *vbl. sb.*

c **1489** CAXTON *Sonnes of Aymon* vi. 149 Reynawde made ..all yᵉ castell to be closed rounde aboute wyth double walles, ..that it fered no sawtynge of no side of it. **1490** —— *Eneydos* lxii. 161 Anoone as Eneas herde turnus speke he.. lefte the sawtyng of the walles and of the toures.

†**sault,** *v.*[2] *Obs. rare.* Forms: 4 saute, 5 sawlte. [a. F. *sauter*:—L. *saltāre*, freq. of *salīre* to leap.] *intr.* To leap, dance.

1377 LANGL. *P. Pl.* B. XIII. 233, I can..noyther sailly ne saute ne synge with þe Gyterne. **1422** tr. *Secreta Secret., Priv. Priv.* 152 Thay hym yaue pryuely a lytill toode in a drynke, and by crafte thay makyd hit grow in his bely, and his bely sawlte hit wax grete.

sault, obs. f. SALT *sb.*[1] and *v.*[1]

†**'saultable,** *a. Obs.* Also 6 sawt-, sautable, 7 saltable. [f. SAULT *v.*[1] + -ABLE.]

1. = ASSAULTABLE *a.*

1556 J. HEYWOOD *Spider & F.* lxv, Ere they could anie peece of the walles batter To make it sawtable. **1568** GRAFTON *Chron.* II. 1357 Certayne..souldiers..mountyng the top of the breache brought report that the place was saultable. *a* **1652** BROME *Covent Gard.* v. iii, The Enemie made saltable six hundred paces there.

2. Capable of being used in assaults.

1563 FOXE *A. & M.* (1596) 246/2 He began to giue sharp assaults [on the city], with all maner of Saultable engins. *Ibid.* 306/2 With ensignes and other munition sautable.

saulte, obs. form of SALT *sb.*[1]

saulted, erron. spelling of SALTED *ppl. a.* 4.

a **1879** A. K. JOHNSTON *London Geogr.* (1880) 402 A 'saulted' horse, or one which has been bitten [by the tsetse fly] and has recovered. **1893** *Westm. Gaz.* 18 Sept. 3/1 'Saulted horses'..are only claimed to be proof against 'horse sickness'.

saulter, saulve: see PSALTER, SALVE *sb.*[1]

†**'saumbu.** *Obs.* Forms: 4 sambu, saumber, *Pl.* 5 sambu(e)s, sambutes, saumbues. [a. OE. *sambue*:—med.L. *sambūca*, app. ad. OHG. *sambuoh* saddle-cloth, litter.] A saddle-cloth.

13.. *K. Alis.* 176 (Bodl. MS.) Wiþ sadel of gold sambu of sylk. *c* **1330** *Arth. & Merl.* 2976 (Kölbing) Saumbers, quissers & aketoun. *a* **1400** *Launfal* 950 Her sadell was semyly sett, The sambus wer grene felvet, I paynted with ymagerye. *c* **1420** *Anturs of Arth.* 24 Here sadel sette of þat ilke, Saude withe sambutes of silke. *a* **1450** *Le Morte Arth.* 2360 Yuory sadyll and white stede, Saumbues of the same threde.

†**'saumbury.** *Obs. rare*$^{-1}$. Also sambury. [A derivative or corrupt form of prec.] A litter.

1393 LANGL. *P. Pl.* C. III. 178 And shope þat a shereyue sholde bere mede Softliche in saumbury [*MS. C.C.C. Cambr.* in his Sambury] fram syse to syse.

saume, saumon: see PSALM, SALMON.

saumpel, -ler, etc.: see SAMPLE, SAMPLER.

‖**Saumur** (somyr). [The name of a town in the department of Maine-et-Loire in France.] A French white wine resembling champagne.

1888 H. J. NEWMAN in *Encycl. Brit.* XXIV. 606/1 In 1874 sparkling Saumur was introduced into the United Kingdom in its own name. **1906** *Daily Chron.* 25 Sept. 7/6 Tasting the wine, the witness pronounced it to be Saumur.

saun, obs. f. SANS; obs. pa. pple. of SOW *v.*

sauna ('sɔːnə, ‖'sɑuna), *sb.* [Finn.] A bath-house or bathroom in which the Finnish steam bath is taken; the steam bath itself, taken in very hot steam produced by throwing water on to heated stones. Also *attrib.* and *Comb.*, as ***sauna bath***, ***heat***, ***stove***, ***suite***; **sauna-like** *a.*, oppressively hot and steamy.

1881 P. D. DU CHAILLU *Land of Midnight Sun* II. xvii. 206 One of the most characteristic institutions of the country is the *Sauna* (bath-house), called *Badstuga* in Swedish. **1897** E. B. TWEEDIE *Through Finland in Carts* iii. 42 Every house in the country, however humble that house may be, boasts its *bastu*, or bath-house, called in Finnish *Sauna*. **1936** *Discovery* Apr. 110/1 A speciality of Finland which everyone who visits the country ought to try is the *Sauna*—the special steam-baths which Finnish people from time immemorial have been in the habit of taking. **1939** *Daily Tel.* 18 Dec. 1/5 The Finnish soldiers..continue to take their celebrated 'sauna' steam baths wherever they are stationed. **1957** A. BUCHWALD *I chose Caviar* 31 But in Finland a sauna is not just a bath—it is a way of life. A sauna is to a Finn what a pub is to a Britisher, what a café is to a Frenchman, what a television set is to an American. **1959** *Times* 2 Dec. 5/4 A move to make British business men sauna bath conscious begins next week with the opening of a Finnish-style sauna in the City of London... City Wall sauna, as it is called, has the requisite little wooden rooms with a stove containing a pile of heated stones on to which water is sprinkled to produce the sauna heat, and showers and rest cubicles. Bunches of leafy birch twigs will also be available, price 2s. 6d., for bathers to whisk up their circulation; the sauna itself costs 15s. **1971** *Country Life* 26 Aug. 512/3 It stands in six acres, with frontage to the river, and has a..sauna bath, stables, [etc.]. **1975** *N.Y. Times* 13 Apr. x. 1/2 The sauna, otherwise known as the Finnish bath, is a wood-lined room with benches built up toward the ceiling. A special sauna stove (today, usually electric) heats small rocks piled atop it and the rocks in turn radiate a dry heat. **1976** *Times* 22 July 4/4 The sauna-like conditions of the Oxford court during the [last] five weeks. **1978** *Morecambe Guardian* 14 Mar. 15/3 Preparing for the play involved the cast in a trip to the sauna suite at Lancaster Baths.

'sauna, *v.* [f. the sb.] *intr.* To take a bath in a sauna, to visit a sauna.

1967 J. EASTWOOD *Little Dragon from Peking* iv. 28 Do you sauna? **1972** *Vogue* June 118/1 You could retire here to.. shower, sauna, ring your friends.

saunape, variant of SANAP *Obs.*

saunce, obs. form of SANCTUS, SANS.

sauncing bell. Alteration of *saunce-bell* SANCTUS BELL, after *sacring-bell*.
1600 *England's Helicon* L 2 b, It [*sc.* LOVE] is perhaps that sauncing bell, That toules all into heauen or hell. [Repeated by Heywood in *Lucrece* 3rd Song, with the form *sansing bell*.]

sauncte(s bell, obs. forms of SANCTUS BELL.

sauncite, obs. form of SANCTITY.

†**'saunder.** *Obs.* Shortened f. ALEXANDERS.
1561 HOLLYBUSH *Hom. Apoth.* 43 b, Put therto a litle butter, and a litle salte, and a litle Saunder.

saunders, etc.: see SANDERS.

saunders blue ('sɔːndəzbluː). [Phonetic corruption of F. *cendres bleues* (sɑ̃drbløe) 'blue ashes'.] A name for ultramarine ashes.
1850 *Weale's Dict. Terms*; and in later Dicts.

saune, sauns, obs. forms of SANS.

saunke realle, var. SANG-ROYAL *Obs.*

saunpil, obs. form of SAMPLE.

saunt: see CENT², SAINT, SANCTUS, SANS.

†**'saunter,** *sb.*¹ *Obs. rare*⁻¹. [Of obscure origin: possibly an alteration of *sauntes* or *sauntus* SANCTUS.] ? An incantation.
1562 TURNER *Herbal* II. 3, I went aboute this busynes all figures, coniuryngcs, saunters, charmes, wytchcrafte, and sorseryes sett a syde [tr. Tragus *de Stirpium Hist.*, 1552, I. clxxxvi. 544 *Nullis characteribus, nullis coniurationibus, nullis preculis, nulla denique superstitione usus sum, sed citra huiusmodi Magicas uanitates*, etc.].

saunter ('sɔːntə(r)), *sb.*² [f. SAUNTER *v.*]
1. The action or habit of sauntering; 'lounge; idle occupation' (Seager).
1728 YOUNG *Love of Fame* I. 231 The tavern! park! assembly! mask! and play! Those dear destroyers of the tedious day! That wheel of fops! that saunter of the town! Call it diversion, and the pill goes down.
2. A sauntering manner of walking; a leisurely, careless gait.
1712 HENLEY *Spect.* No. 518 (*ad fin.*), So likewise the *Belles Lettres* are typified by a Saunter in the Gate;..an Insertion of one Hand in the Fobb [etc.]. **1853** LYTTON *My Novel* XI. ii, Men who make money rarely saunter; men who save money rarely swagger. But saunter and swagger both united to stamp *prodigal* on the Bond Street Lounger. **1859** GEO. ELIOT *Adam Bede* xxvii, The other, turning round, walked slowly, with a sort of saunter, towards Adam.
3. A leisurely, careless, loitering walk or ramble; a stroll.
1828 W. IRVING in *Life & Lett.* (1864) II. 330 A quiet saunter about a cathedral..has the effect upon me of a walk in one of our great American forests. **1881** LADY D. HARDY *Through Cities & Prairie Lands* 105 In one of our saunters through the city we met two..girls.

saunter ('sɔːntə(r)), *v.* Also 5–8 **santer**, (7 **sawnter**, *dial.* **sonter**). [Of obscure origin.
It is doubtful whether the word represented by the quots. under sense 1 is identical with the modern word, the unequivocal history of which begins with the mention by Skinner (quot. *a* 1667 under sense 2); for the supposed 15th c. examples see SAUNTERING *vbl. sb.* 1.
The current suggestion that the word is a. AF. *sauntrer* (= *s'auntrer*), to venture oneself, is unlikely (apart from difficulties of meaning) on the ground that the AF. word, of which only one instance has been found (1338 in *Yearbks. Trinity* 12 Edw. III, p. 619) is app. an adoption of ME. *auntre* to ADVENTURE *sb.*, and possibly a mere nonce-word; the conjecture that it represents a med.L. type **exadventūrāre* is phonologically inadmissible.]
†**1.** *intr.* ? To muse, be in a reverie. *Obs.*
c **1475** *Partenay* 4653 But yut he knew noght uerray certainly, But santred and doubted uerryly Wher on was or no of this saide linage. **1548** FORREST *Pleas. Poesye* 29 in *N. & Q.* Ser. v. IV. 397 [To Edw. VI] When straungers greate yowre presence hathe none take of yowre nobles youe compenye too keepe: doo not your selfe sitt santeringe alone: as wone that weare in studye most deepe. **1589** R. HARVEY *Pl. Perc.* (1590) A ij b, I stood sauntring ouer it, like a whelp that had scalded his mouth.
2. †**a.** To wander or travel about aimlessly or unprofitably; to travel as a vagrant. *Obs.* **b.** To walk with a leisurely and careless gait; to stroll. Also, to travel by vehicle in a slow and leisurely manner.
a **1667** SKINNER *Etymol. Ling. Angl.* (1671), *To Saunter up and down*, à. Fr. G. *Sauter*, Sauteller, Saltare, Saltitare, q.d. huc illuc Saltitare seu Discurrere. **1677** MIEGE *Dict. Eng.-Fr.*, To Saunter about, *rouler en vagabond d'un côté & d'autre.* **1678** BUTLER *Hud.* III. i. 1343 What hast thou gotten by this Fetch?..By Santring still on some Adventure, And growing to thy Horse a Centaur. **1691** RAY *S. & E. Country Words* 111 To *Santer* about; or go *Santering* up and down. It is derived from *Saincte terre*, *i.e.* The Holy Land, because of old time..many idle persons went from place to place, upon pretence that they..intended to take the Cross upon them, and to go thither. **1692** R. L'ESTRANGE *Fables* cxliv. 131 The Cormorant is still Sauntering by the Sea-side, to see if he can find any of his Brass cast up. **1693** S. HARVEY in *Dryden's Juvenal* IX. 1 Tell me, why saunt'ring thus from Place to Place, I meet thee (Nevolus) with a Clouded Face? **1703** THORESBY *Let. to Ray* in *Philos. Lett.* (1718) 337 [List of Yorkshire words] To *Sonter*, to loiter, a *santring* or *sontring* Body, one that squanders the time in going idly about. **1713** *Guardian* No. 171 His customers can santer up and down from corner to corner. **1742** POPE *Dunc.* IV. 311 Led by my hand, he saunter'd Europe round, And gather'd ev'ry Vice on Christian ground. **1782** MISS BURNEY *Cecilia* III. viii, Mr. Harrel sauntered into the breakfast room. **1826** SCOTT *Woodst.* ii, The preacher..left the church and sauntered through the streets of Woodstock. **1873** 'OUIDA' *Pascarel* II. 54 He sauntered about Florence with me. **1883** STEVENSON *Silverado Sq.* 3 The people of hill and valley go sauntering about their business as in the days before the flood. **1932** R. FRY *Let.* 6 June (1972) II. 671 We sauntered through North Italy and saw a lot of lovely things.
3. To loiter over one's work, to dawdle. Also in *indirect passive*, *trans.*, and quasi-*trans.* with *away*.
1673, **1693** [implied in SAUNTERING *ppl. a.*]. **1693** LOCKE *Educ.* §118. 146 Aversion to his Book that makes him saunter away his time of Study. *c* **1731** BOLINGBROKE *Let. to Swift* in *Pope's Wks.* (1741) II. 107 But I know men..who to preserve their health, saunter away half their time. **1752** CHESTERF. *Let. to Son* 5 Mar., Business must not be sauntered and trifled with. **1776** ADAM SMITH *W.N.* I. i. I. 11 A man commonly saunters a little in turning his hand from one sort of employment to another. **1926** D. H. LAWRENCE *Plumed Serpent* ix. 153 Sauntering the day away. **1970** *Daily Tel.* 14 Nov. 9/3 If you're not fond of boats you soon will be..sauntering the sunny quay, watching the gulls.

saunterer ('sɔːntərə(r)). [f. SAUNTER *v.* + -ER¹.] One who saunters; a lounger; †a dawdler, trifler.
1688 PETT *Happy Future St. Eng.* 251 The fantastick Vtopias, Oceanas, and new Atlantis'es that our late Visionaries and idle Santerers to a pretended new Jerusalem troubled England with. **1735** BERKELEY *Querist* §413 (1750) 46 And quit the Life of an insignificant Saunterer about Town, for that of an useful Country-Gentleman. **1798** EDGEWORTH *Pract. Educ.* (1822) I. 149 Alcibiades might have been a saunterer at his book. **1832** SCOTT *St. Ronan's* Introd. ¶3 Thither, too, comes the saunterer, anxious to get rid of that wearisome attendant *himself*.

sauntering ('sɔːntərɪŋ), *vbl. sb.* [-ING¹.]
†**1.** (Sense uncertain; possibly not from the existing verb.) *Obs.*
The interpretation 'loitering, vagrancy' does not well suit the context, and the corresponding sense of the vb. has not been found before the middle of the 17th c. If SAUNTRELL means 'pretended saint', *sauntering* may be a back formation from it, with the sense 'a pretending to holiness'.
c **1440** *York Myst.* xxxv. 70 Thoo sawes schall rewe hym sore For all his saunteryng sone. *Ibid.* 150 Nowe all his gaudis no thyng hym gaynes, His saunteryng schall with bale be bought.
2. The action of the vb. SAUNTER; strolling about; †dawdling, trifling.
1678 DRYDEN *Kind Kpr.* v. i, When the Cuckold finds no Company, he will certainly go a santring again. *c* **1685** VILLIERS (Dk. Buckhm.) *Char. Chas. II* in *Coll. of Poems* 156 A bewitching kind of Pleasure, called Santring, and Talking, without any Constraint, was the true Sultana Queen he delighted in. **1693** LOCKE *Educ.* §120. 148 When his sauntring at his Book is cured. **1813** L. HUNT in *Examiner* 22 Mar. 178/1 His saunterings and his drinking parties with Tom, Dick, and Harry. **1849** MACAULAY *Hist. Eng.* ii. I. 168 Charles came forth from that school with social habits,..fond of sauntering and of frivolous amusements. **1885** MISS BRADDON *Wyllard's Weird* I. i. 42 Bothwell was fond of late saunterings in the grounds.
attrib. **1796** G. M. WOODWARD *Eccentric Excurs.* (1807) 20 This is a general sauntering place for men and cattle.

sauntering ('sɔːntərɪŋ), *ppl. a.* [-ING².]
1. a. Of a person, his habits or dispositions: That saunters; given to strolling about carelessly; †given to dawdling over one's work.
1673 O. WALKER *Educ.* (1677) 99 Others are to all purposes slow and sawntring. **1693** LOCKE *Educ.* §116. 141 This Sauntring Humour I look on as one of the worst Qualities can appear in a Child. *Ibid.*, Upon the first suspicion a Father has, that his Son is of a Sauntring Temper, he must [etc.]. **1703** ROWE *Fair Penit.* Epil., We'd teach the Saunt'ring Squire, who loves to roam, Forgetful of his own dear Spouse and Home. **1740** RICHARDSON *Pamela* (1824) I. xii. 250 Jackey..was the most thoughtless, whistling, sauntering fellow you ever knew. **1855** MACAULAY *Hist. Eng.* xiii. III. 307 The idle sauntering habits of an aristocracy.
b. *transf.* Of time: Occupied in leisurely pursuits, not strenuous.
1818 BYRON *Ch. Har.* IV. xxxiii, The brawling brook, where-by, Clear as its current, glide the sauntering hours With a calm languor. **1849** ROBERTSON *Serm.* Ser. I. ii. (1866) 24 In our inattentive, sauntering, wayside hours. **1854** S. DOBELL *Balder* iii. Poet. Wks. 1875 II. 20 Taskless thro' the round of sauntering day.
†**2.** Of a story: Trumpery, foolish. *Obs.*
Perh. a different word; cf. north. dial. *saunter* in *auld wife saunter* (= 'auld wife's aunter'), an old woman's tale.
1726 THRELKELD *Synopsis Stirp. Hib.* D 5 b, A great Sputter has been made about Fern-Seed, and several sauntring Stories feigned concerning its Collection on St. John's-eve.
Hence **'saunteringly** *adv.*
1842 *Blackw. Mag.* LI. 249 A gay good-looking young man rode saunteringly up the main street. **1881** D. C. MURRAY *Joseph's Coat* I. vii. 140 You come saunteringly to a little rise.

sauntes bell: see SANCTUS BELL.

sauntite, obs. form of SANCTITY.

†**'sauntrell.** *Obs. rare*⁻¹. In 5 **sawntrelle**. [Of obscure origin and meaning; perh. a var. of SAINTREL with the sense 'pretended saint'. Cf. SAUTERELL.] Used as a term of contempt.
c **1440** *York Myst.* xxviii. 190 To take Jesus, þat sawntrelle.

†**'sauntry,** *a. Obs. rare*⁻¹. [f. SAUNTER *sb.*² or *v.* + -Y.] Characterized by sauntering.
1732 LORD TYRAWLY in *Buccleuch MSS.* (Hist. MSS. Comm.) I. 381, I live a sort of a sauntry strolling life.

saunts, sauntus, obs. forms of SANCTUS.

sauntys bell: see SANCTUS BELL.

saun(t)z (fail): see SANS, SANS FAIL.

‖**saupiquet.** *rare*⁻¹. [Fr., f. *saupiquer* = Sp. *salpicar*: see SALPICON.] A piquant sauce.
1656–7 DAVENANT *Entert. Rutland Ho.* Wks. (1673) 357 Your Pottages, Carbonnades, Grillades, Ragouts, Haches, Saupiquets,..and Entre-mets.

saurel (sɒ'rɛl). [a. F. *saurel*, 'the Bastard Mackerel' (Cotgr.).] A fish of the genus *Trachurus*.
1882 JORDAN & GILBERT *Synopsis Fishes N. Amer.* 431 *Trachurus*, Rafinesque. Saurels. *Ibid.* 432 *T. saurus* Raf. —Horse Mackerel; Skip Jack; Saurel.

‖**Sauria** ('sɔːrɪə), *sb. pl. Zool.* [mod.L. (Brongniart 1799), f. Gr. σαύρ-α, σαῦρ-ος lizard. (Oppel used the masc. form *Saurii*.)] An order of Reptiles, originally including the Lizards and Crocodiles; subsequently restricted to the Lizards alone. The term is now little used, being commonly replaced by *Lacertilia*.
1834 MCMURTRIE *Cuvier's Anim. Kingd.* 169 The *Sauria*, or *Lizards*, whose heart has two auricles, and whose body, supported by four or two feet, is covered with scales. **1851** MANTELL *Petrifactions* iii. §5. 261 And equally differ from the vertebræ of the Iguanæ, Monitors, and all existing Sauria. **1878** BELL tr. *Gegenbauer's Comp. Anat.* 420 In the Saurii the so-called 'crural pores' lead into glands, which look like compound tubes, and which secrete cells which harden and fill up the lumen of the glands.

saurian ('sɔːrɪən), *a.* and *sb.* [f. prec. + -AN. Cf. F. *saurien*.] **A.** *adj.*
1. *Zool.* Belonging to the order *Sauria*.
1807–29 *Edinb. Encycl.* (1830) XI. 23/1 Saurian Reptiles. **1851** MANTELL *Petrifactions* iii. §5. 308 The *Amblyrhynchi*, the most exclusively vegetable feeders of the saurian order.
2. Pertaining to or characteristic of a saurian.
1826 *Ann. Rep. Yorksh. Philos. Soc.* 14 in Lyell *Princ. Geol.* (1830) I. 129 *note*, Having found a saurian vertebra. **1844** MRS. BROWNING *Drama of Exile* 738 Earth methinks, Will..class these present dogmas with the rest Of the old-world traditions, Eden fruits And Saurian fossils. **1864** DAY in *Geol. Mag.* I. 61 They were not mixed up with Saurian remains, or those of any other species of Hybodus.
3. Also *fig.*
1864 W. BAGEHOT in *National Rev.* XVIII. 525 Much of *Tristram Shandy* is a sort of antediluvian fun, in which uncouth Saurian jokes play idly in an unintelligible world. **1929** G. MITCHELL *Mystery of Butcher's Shop* i. 8 Mrs. Beatrice Lestrange Bradley..smiled the saurian smile of the sand lizard and basked in the sun. **1940** —— *Brazen Tongue* vi. 67 Lady Selina had never approved..the deep affection of her daughter Sally for this oddly saurian aunt. **1970** [see MORNING-GLORY 1].
B. *sb.* **1.** (*Zool.*) A reptile of the order *Sauria*. Now chiefly in popular use, applied esp. to crocodiles and to large extinct lizard-like animals such as the ichthyosaurus, plesiosaurus, etc.
1807–29 *Edinb. Encycl.* (1830) XI. 23/2 Flat-tailed Saurians. **1830** LYELL *Princ. Geol.* I. 148 The vertebra..of a saurian..has been met with in the mountain limestone of Northumberland. **1832** *Ibid.* II. 103 Of the great saurians, the gavials which inhabit the Ganges differ from the cayman of America, or the crocodile of the Nile. **1851** MANTELL *Petrifactions* iii. §5. 302 Bones and teeth of marine saurians. **1888** J. INGLIS *Tent Life in Tigerland* 3 The long ugly serrated back of the man-eating saurian. **1891** F. THOMPSON *Sister-Songs* (1895) 31 Like the back of a gold-mailèd saurian Heaving its slow length from Nilotic slime.
2. Also *fig.*
1923 H. G. WELLS *Men like Gods* I. i. 13 A car with the voice of a prehistoric saurian warned him. **1953** A. HUXLEY *Let.* 25 Sept. (1969) 684 The mesozoic reptiles of the Ford Foundation are being as mesozoic as ever... Hutchins has recently flown to New York and has promised to do what he can with the saurians. **1974** V. NABOKOV *Look at Harlequins* (1975) II. i. 130 He was one of the very few larger saurians in the *émigré* marshes.

'saurio-'coprolite. *Palæont.* [f. *saurio-* (used as combining form of SAURIAN) + COPROLITE.] The fossilized excrement of a saurian.
1877 *Encycl. Brit.* VI. 353/2 The true ichthyo-coprolites and saurio-coprolites.

‖**sauriosis** (sɔːrɪ'əʊsɪs). *Path.* [mod. medical L., f. Gr. σαύρ-α, σαῦρ-ος lizard + -OSIS.
Also, more correctly, *sau'riasis* (Gould *Illustr. Dict. Med.* 1894, *Syd. Soc. Lex.* 1897).]
A form of ichthyosis (also called in mod.L. *Ichthyosis sauroderma*) in which the skin resembles that of a lizard.
1890 in BILLINGS *Nat. Med. Dict.* **1897** in *Syd. Soc. Lex.*

saurischian (sɔː'rɪskɪən), *a.* and *sb.* [f. mod.L. *Saurischia* (H. G. Seeley 1887, in *Proc. R. Soc.* XLIII. 170), f. Gr. σαύρα, σαῦρος lizard + ἰσχίον ISCHIUM + -AN.] **a.** *adj.* Relating or pertaining to the *Saurischia*, a sub-order or order of dinosaurian reptiles with the inferior pelvic elements directed downwards. **b.** *sb.* A member of the *Saurischia.*

1887 SEELEY in *Q. Jrnl. Geol. Soc.* XLIV. 86 This .. is an intelligible modification of the Saurischian type. **1891** in *Century Dict.* **1933** A. S. ROMER *Vertebr. Paleontol.* ix. 181 We shall here use a conservative classification which divides the saurischians into two suborders. *Ibid.* 184 (*caption*) The manus in saurischian dinosaurs. **1970** *Nature* 11 Apr. 109/1 It was carnivorous and is thus classified in the Theropoda within the saurischian dinosaurs. **1973** J. UPDIKE *Museums & Women* 197 The two saurischians entered his party with the languid confidence of the specially cherished. **1977** *Radio Times* 17 Dec. 45 One of the liveliest of these disputes concerns the two great groups of dinosaurs, the saurischians (with hip-bones like those of lizards) and the ornithischians.

sauro- ('sɔːrəʊ), before a vowel saur-, combining form of Gr. σαῦρο-ς lizard, entering into many scientific terms. **saurodont** ('sɔːrəʊdɒnt), *Palæont.* [Gr. ὀδοντ- tooth] *a.*, of or pertaining to the *Saurodontidæ*, an extinct family of fishes; *sb.*, a fish of this family. **saurography** [-GRAPHY], 'term for a description of the saurian reptiles' (Mayne *Expos. Lex.* 1858). **saurophagous** (sɔː'rɒfəgəs), *a. Ornith.* [see -PHAGOUS], eating or feeding on lizards and other reptiles (*Ibid.* and in recent Dicts.). **saurophidian** (sɔːrəʊ'fɪdɪən) [see OPHIDIAN] *a.*, of or pertaining to the order *Saurophidia* of reptiles; *sb.*, a reptile of this order (used in quot. 1882 for a hypothetical reptile combining the characteristics of a lizard and a snake). **sauropterygian** (ˌsɔːrəʊptə'rɪdʒɪən), *Palæont.* [Gr. πτερύγιον wing, fin] *a.*, of or pertaining to the *Sauropterygia* (usually called *Plesiosauria*), an order of extinct marine reptiles in Owen's classification (*Palæont.* 1860, 209); *sb.*, a reptile of this order; a plesiosaur.

1896 *Roy. Nat. Hist.* V. 486 The Extinct *Saurodonts. *Ibid.*, All the members of the group are collectively spoken of as the saurodont fishes. **1882** MISS HOPLEY *Snakes* xv. 263 We might the rather wonder if there were not .. many unsuspected species of reptiles, compound ophiosaurians, or *saurophidians in those inaccessible depths. **1861** OWEN *Monogr. Fossil Reptilia Kimmeridge Clay* I. 15 The huge dimensions of the present species of short-necked *Sauropterygian. **1865** —— *Fossil Reptilia Liassic Format.* III. 17 There is no sufficient ground for encumbering the Sauropterygian group with one or two additional generic names.

saurognathous (sɔː'rɒgnəθəs), *a. Ornith.* [f. mod.L. *Saurognathæ* pl., f. Gr. σαῦρο-ς lizard + γνάθ-ος jaw: see -OUS.] Of, pertaining to, or characteristic of the *Saurognathæ*, W. K. Parker's superfamily of birds, the woodpeckers and their allies, characterized by an arrangement of the bones of the palate similar to that in lizards. So **sau'rognathism**, saurognathous formation of the palate.

1874 W. K. PARKER in *Trans. Linnean Soc.* Ser. II. *Zool.* (1879) I. 9, I am confident that the term 'saurognathous' for this kind of palate will not be thought inappropriate. **1884** COUES *Key N. Amer. Birds* (ed. 2) 173 Saurognathism. **1891** *Proc. Zool. Soc.* 3 Feb. 122 On the Question of Saurognathism of the Pici. By R. W. Shufeldt.

sauroid ('sɔːrɔɪd), *a.* and *sb.* [a. F. *sauroïde* (Agassiz), ad. Gr. σαυροειδής like a lizard, f. σαῦρο-ς lizard + -ειδής: see -OID.] **A.** *adj.*

1. Resembling a saurian or lizard; a distinctive epithet of an order of fishes (mod.L. *Sauroidei*).

1836 BUCKLAND *Geol. & Min.* xiv. §13 (1837) I. 274 M. Agassiz has already ascertained seventeen genera of Sauroid Fishes. **1849–52** OWEN in *Todd's Cycl. Anat.* IV. 881/1 It is in this .. that the Sphyrænoid fishes .. approach the Sauroid type. **1860** GOSSE *Rom. Nat. Hist.* 363 An Enaliosaur,—a marine reptile of large size, of sauroid figure. **1875** CROLL *Climate & T.* xviii. 304 The corals and huge sauroid reptiles which then inhabited our waters.

2. *Path.* Akin to sauriosis.

1879 *St. George's Hosp. Rep.* IX. 742 In parts the eruption may be called sauroid, said to have come after scarlatina.

B. *sb.*

1. A sauroid fish.

1836 BUCKLAND *Geol. & Min.* xiv. §13 (1837) I. 282 *note*, The Pycnodonts, as well as the fossil Sauroids, have enamelled scales. **1857** AGASSIZ *Contrib. Nat. Hist. U.S.* I. 187 Ganoids; with three orders, Cœlacanths, Acipenseroids, and Sauroids.

2. An animal belonging to the Sauroidea, the second of the three primary groups of *Vertebrata* in Huxley's earlier classification; afterwards named by him SAUROPSIDA.

1863 HUXLEY *Elem. Comp. Anat.* v. (1864) 74 The Vertebrata are capable of being grouped into three provinces: (I.) the Ichthyoids .. (II.) the Sauroids ..; and (III.) the Mammals. **1875** *Encycl. Brit.* I. 750/2. **1886** *Ibid.* XX. 437/2.

Hence **sau'roidal** *a.* (*rare*) = SAUROID *a.* 1.

1858 GEIKIE *Hist. Boulder* v. 63 The massive bone-covered sauroidal fish.

Sauromatian (sɔːrəʊ'meɪʃən). *Hist.* [f. Gr. Σαυρομάται: see SARMATIAN.] = SARMATIAN.

1611 BIBLE *Transl. Pref.* ¶8 The Hebrew tongue .. is turned .. into the Language of .. Armenians, and Scythians, and Sauromatians.

sauropod ('sɔːrəʊpɒd), *a.* and *sb.* [f. mod.L. *sauropoda* (O. C. Marsh 1884, in *Nature* 20 Nov. 68/2), f. Gr. σαῦρο-ς lizard + ποδ-, πούς foot.]

a. *adj.* = SAUROPODOUS *a.* **b.** *sb.* A member of the suborder *Sauropoda* of gigantic herbivorous dinosaurs.

1891 *Century Dict.*, *Sauropod* [adj. and sb.]. **1905** *Westm. Gaz.* 3 May 9/3 'Sauropod' is one of the many terrible names they call the poor thing [*Diplodocus Carnegii*]. **1933** A. S. ROMER *Vertebr. Paleontol.* ix. 189 A first step in sauropod development is perhaps illustrated by *Anchisaurus*. *Ibid.* 190 The sauropods were massively built. **1971** *Nature* 15 Jan. 153/1 The great herbivorous dinosaurs known as sauropods are inevitably the most impressive exhibit in any natural history museum. **1976** *Ibid.* 8 Apr. 559/2 The laminar bone of sauropod dinosaurs is indistinguishable from that of some of the larger artiodactyls and it is presumed that this indicated a similar metabolism.

sauropodous (sɔː'rɒpədəs), *a.* [Formed as prec. + -OUS.] Of, pertaining to, or connected with the *Sauropoda* (see prec.).

1887 LYDEKKER in *Q. Jrnl. Geol. Soc.* XLIV. 55 This huge bone .. is clearly Sauropodous. **1895** —— in *Knowledge* Mar. 70/1 Gigantic sauropodous dinosaurs.

‖**Sauropsida** (sɔː'rɒpsɪdə), *sb. pl. Zool.* [mod.L., f. Gr. σαῦρ-α, σαῦρ-ος lizard + ὄψις appearance: see -ID.] The second of the three primary groups of *Vertebrata* in Huxley's classification, comprising reptiles and birds, etc. Also in anglicized form **sau'ropsid**. Hence **sau'ropsidan** *a.*, of or pertaining to the *Sauropsida*; *sb.*, a member of the *Sauropsida*. **saurop'sidian** *a.* = *Sauropsidan*.

1864 HUXLEY *Elem. Comp. Anat.* 220 *note*, Mr. Parker agrees with my suggestion .. that the basi-temporals of the *Sauropsida* (or Birds and Reptiles) are the homologues of the *linguæ sphenoidales* of Man. **1864** W. K. PARKER in *Geol. Mag.* I. 56 This exaltation of the 'Sauropsidan' or oviparous type by the substitution of feathers for scales, wings for paws, warm blood for cold, .. —this sudden glorification of the vertebrate form is one of the great wonders of Nature. **1873** MIVART *Elem. Anat.* 47 In Sauropsidans the number [of cervical vertebræ] is greater. **1881** MARSH in *Amer. Jrnl. Sci.* Apr. 340 It is apparently a generalized Sauropsid. **1881** P. M. DUNCAN in *Academy* 23 Apr. 303 The head is less sauropsidian and more chelonian.

'**saurous**, *a.* ? *Obs.* [f. Gr. σαῦρ-ος lizard + -OUS.] Resembling a lizard; saurian.

a **1843** J. F. SOUTH *Zool.* in *Encycl. Metrop.* (1845) VII. 308/2 The Saurous or Lizard-like Reptiles are distinguished from the Serpents by the large gaps on the sides of the Skull. *Ibid.* 312/1 In the Saurous Order, the Ribs [etc.].

saurus ('sɔːrəs). *rare.* [quasi-L., ad. Gr. σαῦρος lizard: after *ichthyosaurus*, etc.] A saurian.

1834 T. HAWKINS *Mem. Ichthyosauri* 27 'One more trial, my boys, your own reward, if successful—ye-o'—the saurus is safe! **1841** TH. PARKER *Pharisees* Wks. 1864 IX. 142 The sauri of gigantic size, the mammoth, and the mastodon, are quite extinct.

saury ('sɔːrɪ). [app. irreg. ad. mod.L. *saurus*, a. Gr. σαῦρος lizard.] A name applied to various fishes (tr. mod.L. *saurus*), esp. the skipper or bill-fish, *Scomberesox saurus*; also *attrib.* as ***saury elops, pike, salmon.***

1771 PENNANT *Tour Scotl.* 1769, 284 Saury. *Saurus* Rondel. 232. **1776** —— *Brit. Zool.* III. 284 Saury Pike. **1804** SHAW *Gen. Zool.* V. I. 66 Saury salmon. *Salmo Saurus*... Shape much elongated: length about twelve inches. *Ibid.* 125 Saury elops. *Elops Saurus*. *Ibid.* 126 In general habit the Saury Elops bears some resemblance to a Pike, or rather to a Salmon. **1882** JORDAN & GILBERT *Synopsis Fishes N. America* 374 *Scomberesox*, Lacépède. Sauries. *Ibid.* 375 *S. saurus* .. Saury; Skipper; Bill-fish.

saury, saus, obs. forms of SAVORY, SAUCE.

sausage ('sɒsɪdʒ, -ɔː-), *sb.* Forms: α. 5 **sawsyge**, 6 **sawsege, -cedge, sausige, saucege, saussege**, 6–7 **sausedge**, 7 **sausidge, sausege, sauceidge, sawcege, -sidge, -sadge, -sedge, saussage, saucige, sossage**, 7–8 **sawsage, saucidge**, (7, 9 *vulgar* **sassage**, 9 *vulgar* **sossige**), 6– **sausage**; β. 7 **salsage, soulsage, saltsage**. [ME. *sausige*, a. ONF. *saussiche* (Central OF., mod.F. *saucisse*) = Sp., Pg. *salchicha*, It. *salsiccia*:—late L. *salsīcia*, fem. sing. or perh. neut. pl. of **salsīcius* (? prepared by salting), f. *sals-us* salted: see -ITIOUS.

For the representation of original (-tʃ) in unstressed syllables by (-dʒ), cf. *cabbage*, *knowledge*, and the usual pronunciation of *Greenwich*, *Woolwich*, *Norwich*, *spinach*.]

1. In the original use, a quantity of finely chopped pork, beef, or other meat, spiced and flavoured, enclosed in a short length of the intestine of some animal, so as to form a cylindrical roll (usually, one of the 'links' formed by tying the containing intestine at regular intervals); later also, in generalized sense, meat thus prepared. Since the 19th c. the application of the word has been greatly extended; in its widest use, it denotes a preparation of comminuted beef, veal, pork, mutton, or a mixture of these, either fresh, salted, pickled, smoked or cured, with salt, spices, flour (sometimes with the addition of fats, blood, sugar, vegetables, etc.), stuffed into a container made from an intestine, stomach, bladder, or other animal tissue.

There are more than 150 kinds of sausage, distinguished by names indicating the ingredients and the method of manufacture. They are divided into two classes, in the U.S. known as ***dry sausage***, which is a cured product, subjected to a process of drying lasting several weeks, and ***fresh*** or ***wet sausage***. ***Bologna sausage***: see BOLOGNA. ***polonian, polony sausage***: see POLONY². ***German sausage***: see GERMAN *a.*² 4.

α. **14..** *Voc.* in Wr.-Wülcker 609/5 *Salsicia* [*printed* salsicix], a sawsyge. **1553** EDEN *Treat. Newe Ind.* (Arb.) 29 Keping it in a certayne pickle as we do regottes or sausages. **1573** BARET *Alv.* s.v. *Pudding*, A pudding called a sawsege, *tomaculum*. **1585** T. WASHINGTON tr. *Nicholay's Voy.* II. xi. 46 Certain sauceges and other good .. refreshments. **1586** D. ROWLAND *Lazarillo* C j, The euil eaten sausedge came gushing out after. **1598** *Epulario* C iij, To make good Sausseges of Pork or other flesh. **1617** MORYSON *Itin.* I. 70 Sawsages the pound ten sols. **1641** *Conf. J. Browne, Jesuit* A 3, He .. brought them of his Holinesses bread, and wine, and other rarities, as Bolognean Sassages, and such dainties. *c* **1645** HOWELL *Lett.* (1650) I. v. xxxviii. 174 She must go adorn'd with chaines of Sausages. *c* **1700** W. BISHOP in *Ballard MSS.* XXXI. 122 Your best Oxford Sossages. **1755** JOHNSON, *Sausage*, a roll or ball made commonly of pork or veal, and sometimes of beef, minced very small, with salt and spice; sometimes it is stuffed into the guts of fowls, and sometimes only rolled in flower. *a* **1845** HOOD *Sausage Maker's Ghost* 34 To meet the call from streets, and lanes, and passages, For first-chop 'sassages'. **1848** THACKERAY *Van. Fair* xl, Her fingers were like so many sausages. **1850** DICKENS *Dav. Copp.* vii, Poor Traddles in a tight, sky-blue suit that made his arms and legs like German sausages. **1853** SOYER *Pantropheon* 390 Pheasant sausages, a delicious mixture of the fat of that bird, chopped very small, and mixed with pepper. **1863** W. C. BALDWIN *Afr. Hunting* ix. 367, I .. made a sheep into sausages. **1887** HENLEY *Culture in the Slums* i. 2 'Look sharp', ses she, 'with them there sossiges.'

β. **1634** SIR T. HERBERT *Trav.* 183 The fruit [Banana] is long in fashion of a soulsage. **1648** J. RAYMOND *Il Merc. Ital.* 182 In Bolonia .. I took a taste of those famous Saltsages, that are compos'd at Bolonia.

2. *transf.* and *fig.* **a.** Applied to a thing having the appearance of a sausage or string of sausages.

1650 W. D. tr. *Comenius' Gate Lat. Unl.* (1656) 63 Parted as it were into ropes, or sawsidges [Lat. *in funes aut farcimina*], which the anatomists call muscles. **1685** *Roxb. Ball.* (1885) V. 599 The iron Sawsages I wear [*i.e.* fetters]. **1879** STEVENSON *Trav. with Donkey* (1886) 79 The sack .. hung at full length across the saddle, a green sausage six feet long.

b. Applied to certain kinds of indiarubber.

1903 *Times* 14 Feb. 4/6 India Rubber.—Mozambique, good stickless sausage, 3*s.* 2½*d.* .. sausage softish, 2*s.* 10*d.*

c. = *sausage-balloon*.

1858 *Househ. Words* 30 Jan. 168/1 Down came the grand royal blue sausage. **1874** *Belgravia* Aug. 170 This sausage was incased in the ordinary net-work and dependent shrouds, encircled by the ordinary hoop, and sustaining the ordinary car—a big circular basket capable of containing four persons comfortably. **1916** J. BUCHAN *Battle of Somme* 20 Captive balloons, the so-called 'sausages', glittered in the sunlight. **1916** J. R. MCCONNELL in *World's Work* Nov. 53/2 Norman Prince became obsessed with the idea of bringing down a German 'sausage', as the observation balloons are called. **1928** C. F. S. GAMBLE *Story N. Sea Air Station* xx. 356 While the first pilot brings the boat down to 1,000 feet and flies over the air station to have a careful look at the 'sausage' to confirm the wind direction. **1929** HALL & NILES *One Man's War* 164 A balloon job is either a success or a failure the very first time you try, as the crew on the ground haul in their 'sausage' at the first note of warning from the observers. **1940** [see OBBO].

d. *slang.* A German. Also *attrib.* ? *Obs.*

1890 BARRÈRE & LELAND *Dict. Slang* II. 203/2 *Sausage game* (billiards), a German game. **1909** *Sat. Even. Post* 3 July 30 The durned old beer-swillin' sausage! **1919** *Athenæum* 8 Aug. 727/2 The German was known by several names, as 'Jerry', .. 'Sausage', [etc.]. **1923** J. MANCHON *Le Slang* 255 *Sausage* .. sobriquet de l'Allemand. **1929** E. A. DOLPH *Sound Off!* 186 In the World War .. our soldiers not only sang about the 'Huns', 'Krauts', and 'sausages', but they even took a fling at the .. French.

e. *slang.* A German trench-mortar bomb, so called because of its shape. ? *Obs.*

1915 [see *Bath Oliver* s.v. BATH *sb.*² 2 a]. **1918** H. W. MCBRIDE *Emma Gees* 164 At first we called them 'sausages', then 'rum-jars' .. then they became 'flying pigs'. **1926** F. M. FORD *Man could stand Up* II. v. 184 What the Germans called *Minenwerfer* might project what our people called sausages.

f. *colloq.* A person, esp. in phr. ***silly old sausage*** and varr.

[**1900** *Dialect Notes* II. 57 *Sausage*, 1. A person easily imposed upon. 2. An easy-going, inoffensive person.] **1934** W. GIBSON *Fuel* 72 His mother's stopped Waving, to wipe her eyes, the silly old sausage! **1955** 'A. GILBERT' *Is she Dead Too?* ii. 38 Dr Grieve .. was a silly old sausage. **1972** K. BONFIGLIOLI *Don't point that Thing at Me* v. 54 Very good customer of mine .. Very nice old sausage. **1977** *Harper's & Queen* Nov. 308/4 He's only had five letters, the dear old sausage.

g. colloq. phr. ***not a sausage*** (and varr.), nothing at all.

1938 M. ALLINGHAM *Fashion in Shrouds* xix. 349 I've been .. to Ben's and I dropped in at Conchy Lewis's. Not a sossidge [*sic*] anywhere. **1943** P. BRENNAN et al. *Spitfires over Malta* 29 Nothing happened, & we came back very brassed off, not having seen a sausage. **1955** J. BINGHAM *Paton Street Case* viii. 139 Don't go and quarrel with the old geezer, or he'll cut you off without a sausage. Hang on, and you'll get the lot. **1963** V. NABOKOV *Gift* iii. 179 Time flies, he gets older, she blossoms out—and not a sausage. Just walks by and scorches you with a look of contempt. **1970** P. LAURIE *Scotland Yard* iii. 69 We do this for three nights and don't get a sausage—we stop lots of people but they're all relatively straight. **1978** J. WAINWRIGHT *Ripple of Murders* 134 'Anything?' 'Not a sausage, Dick.' **1981** *Times* 29 June 12/6 Mr Healey said the press did not print Labour's actual policies. 'Not a sausage.'

h. A length of padded fabric that can be placed at the foot of a door to stop draughts.

1961 PARTRIDGE *Dict. Slang Suppl.* 1259/1 *Sausage*,..a draught-excluder placed at foot of a door. **1962** *Times* 10 Feb. 11/3 Red twill coated, sand filled sausages along window ledges. **1977** *Times* 30 Apr. 20/1 Keeping the maximum heat indoors by..using sandfilled sausages against gaps under doors.

3. *Mil.* = SAUCISSE, SAUCISSON 3.

1645 *Enchiridion of Fortif.* 34 The figure..Presents the form of a Saucidge, the use whereof is to secure the foundations of Workes in Moorish..grounds. **1688** R. HOLME *Armoury* III. xvi. (Roxb.) 102/2 Sauceidges are things made of fagotts and brush wood to fill vp ditches. **1704** J. HARRIS *Lex. Techn.* I. s.v., Two of these Saucidges are commonly applied to every Mine, to the end that if one should fail, the other may take effect. **1763** R. ORME *Milit. Trans. Hindostan* I. 276 A serjeant of artillery, carrying a barrel of gunpowder with a long sausage to it, went forward [etc.]. **1845** W. H. MAXWELL *Hints to Soldier* I. 65 A sergeant..leaped upon the covered way with intent to cut the sausage of the enemy's mines.

4. *attrib.* and *Comb.* **a.** simple attrib., as in ***sausage-factory***, ***-shop***; **b.** objective, as in ***sausage-maker***, ***-seller***, ***-stuffer***; also in names of appliances used in making sausages, as ***sausage-cutter***, ***-filler***, ***-grinder***, ***-stuffer***; ***sausage-eating*** adj.; **c.** similative, as in ***sausage-finger***; ***sausage-fingered***, ***-pink***, ***-shaped*** adjs.

1891 *Century Dict.*, **Sausage-cutter*, a machine for cutting sausage-meat. **1913** 'SAKI' *When William Came* xii. 206 A highly civilized race like ours..is not going to be held under for long by a lot of damned *sausage-eating Germans. **1922** JOYCE *Ulysses* 324 And as for the Prooshians and the Hanoverians,..haven't we had enough of those sausageeating bastards? **1837** DICKENS *Pickwick* xxxi, 'Celebrated *Sassage factory', said Sam. **1875** KNIGHT *Dict. Mech.*, **Sausage-filler*, a small machine for stuffing sausage-meat into intestines. **1884** *Health Exhib. Catal.* 110/2 Sausage Fillers. **1910** *Practitioner* Jan. 33 The fingers..as large at their tips as at their base—the so-called *sausage fingers. **1841** THACKERAY *Men & Coats* Wks. 1900 XIII. 602 The old *sausage-fingered Berlin gloves. **1875** KNIGHT *Dict. Mech.*, **Sausage-grinder*, a machine for mincing meat for sausages. **1797** *Encycl. Brit.* I. 212/1 Æschines..the son of Charinus a *sausage-maker. **1922** JOYCE *Ulysses* 59 The ferreteyed porkbutcher folded the sausages he had snipped off with blotchy fingers, *sausagepink. **1572** HULOET (ed. Higins), *Sawsage seller, one that selleth sawsages, *allantopola*. **1839** LINDLEY *Introd. Bot.* III. (ed. 3) 454 **Sausage-shaped* (*botuliformis*); long, cylindrical, hollow, curved inwards at each end; as the corolla of some Ericas. **1926** J. S. HUXLEY *Ess. Pop. Sci.* 251 It will become simpler ..and finally be converted into a sausage-shaped semi-opaque mass of tissue. **1956** *Nature* 18 Feb. 320/2 Dr. Dessens mentioned a small sausage-shaped (presumably organic) type of particle. **1767** STERNE *Tr. Shandy* IX. v. 12 A Jew who kept a *sausage shop in the same street. **1859** DICKENS *T. Two Cities* I. v, At the sausage-shop. **1873** Sausage-shop [see CORNER *sb.*[1] 2 b]. **1875** KNIGHT *Dict. Mech.*, **Sausage-stuffer*, a device for stuffing cleaned intestines with sausage-meat.

d. Special comb.: **sausage balloon**, (*a*) an elongated aeronautical balloon; †(*b*) *slang*, a kite balloon used for observation (*obs.*); **sausage board**, a surf-board rounded at both ends; **sausage-burger** [BURGER], a hamburger made with sausage meat; **sausage curl**, a curl resembling a sausage; also, *esp.* a horizontal curl (see quots.); **sausage dog** *colloq.*, a dachshund; †**sausage-eater** *slang*, a German (*obs.*); †**sausage-hose**, ? hose padded so as to resemble sausages; **sausage machine**, a machine for manufacturing sausages; also *fig.*, esp. with reference to an institution that is held to 'process' its members so that their views, outlook, etc., are routinely identical; also *attrib.*; **sausage-meat**, meat minced and spiced to be used in sausages or as a stuffing; also *transf.* and *attrib.*; **sausage poison**, a peculiar ptomaine sometimes developed in sausages; so **sausage-poisoning**; **sausage roll**, a sausage, or a roll of sausage-meat, enveloped in a cover of flour paste, and cooked; **sausage toad** *colloq.* (see quot. 1937); **sausage-tree**, an evergreen tree, *Kigelia pinnata*, belonging to the family Bignoniaceæ, native to tropical Africa, and bearing red, bell-shaped flowers followed by pendulous, hard-shelled fruits shaped like large sausages.

1874 *Belgravia* Aug. 170, I am not, at this length of time, quite certain as to whether the body of the '*sausage' balloon was provided with two valves—one at each end of the cylinder—or whether there was but a solitary trap for the emission of gas at the convexity of the summit. **1916** F. M. FORD *Let.* 28 July (1965) 67 The air is full of sausage balloons, swallows, larks & occasional aeroplanes. **1917** 'SAPPER' *No Man's Land* 97 A row of sausage balloons like a barber's rash adorned the sky. **1930** BLUNDEN *De Bello Germanico* 79 Daylight relieving still prevailed, despite the hovering sausage-balloons. **1965** J. POLLARD *Surfrider* ii. 18 Or it might be a '*sausage board'—straight for most of its length and rounded at both ends. **1970** *Studies in English* (Univ. of Cape Town) I. 28 Older designs [of surfboard] include the *sausage board*; rounded at both ends. **1942** *Better Homes & Gardens* Aug. 41/3 (Advt.), *Sausageburgers. Add 1 tsp. Heinz Horseradish (soaked 10 minutes in 1 tbs. water) to 1 lb. bulk pork sausage. Shape into four cakes. Pan-broil, turning often. **1979** *Good Housekeeping* Nov. 367/2 *Sausage burgers.* 450g..pork sausagemeat. 125g.. fresh white breadcrumbs [etc.]. **1828** *Lights & Shades* II. 298 Misses in their 'Boucles d'Angoulême' (Anglice, *sausage curls). **1899** KIPLING *Stalky* 40 Who, in a gray skirt and a wig of chestnut sausage-curls,..represented the Widow Twankey. **1966** J. S. COX *Illustr. Dict. Hairdressing* 131 *Sausage curl*, a wide, croquignole-wound curl. Not to be confused with a spirally-wound drop or hanging curl. **1968** J. IRONSIDE *Fashion Alphabet* 198 *Sausage curls*, similar to ringlets but laid horizontally. **1974** *Country Life* 28 Mar. 712/3 Pearls, ringlets and sausage curls. **1938** J. W. DAY *Dog in Sport* v. 77 From Royal circles the snaky '*sausage dog' permeated downward through the aristocracy to the ranks of the common or show-bench exhibitors. **1958** L. DURRELL *Mountolive* xv. 298 The door..opened and a dispirited-looking sausage-dog waddled into the room. **1972** *Country Life* 21 Dec. 1727/3 They poke fun at my toy German sausage dog. **1918** *Sat. Even. Post* 22 June 70 The *sausage eaters decided to drop a few samples on our escadrille. **1633** B. JONSON *Tale Tub* I. iv, His long *sawsedge-hose. *c* **1840** C. WEBB *Vagrant* I. i. 14 *Coco.* [*Furiously.*] Why you infernal old Tomahawk!—you Patent Mangler!—you *Sausage Machine to young men! **1850** *New England Farmer* II. 379 Sausage or Mincing Machine. This is a small, compact machine, remarkably strong and durable. **1860** BARTLETT *Dict. Amer.* (ed. 3), *Sausage-machine*, a machine for chopping or mincing meat for the purpose of making sausages. **1889** KIPLING in *Pioneer Mail* 20 Nov. 647/3 They will be sorry that they began tampering with the great sausage-machine of civilization. **1934** R. MACKENZIE *Maitlands* II. 64 When I became a schoolmaster I was full of hope... But I soon saw I was just part of a sausage-machine. **1960** *Encounter* Jan. 40/2 Producing a stock of plays and playwrights to feed the relentless sausage-machines of the drama departments. **1976** *Howard Jrnl.* XV. I. 55 Rise in the incidence and severity of juvenile delinquency may increase pressures towards an even more 'sausage-machine' and delinquency-orientated approach.., with no better results. **1723** J. NOTT *Cook's & Confectioner's Dict.* sig. Hh4v, Lay in..some *Sausage-meat fry'd. **1741** E. SMITH *Compl. Housewife* (ed. 10) 66 Slice a penny white loaf..and work it in well with your Sausage-meat. **1806** A. HUNTER *Culina* (ed. 3) 49 If required, the sausage meat may be put into skins. **1845** E. ACTON *Mod. Cookery* xi. 301 (*heading*) Sausage-meat cake; or, pain de porc frais. **1861** MRS. BEETON *Bk. Househ. Managem.* x. 249 (*heading*) Sausage-meat stuffing, for Turkey. **1876** BESANT & RICE *Gold. Butterfly* xvii, No wonder, I thought, that the men who wrote these things, were chopped up into sausage-meat. **1843** R. J. GRAVES *Syst. Clin. Med.* Introd. Lect. 34 In this class appear miasms, contagions, the similar *sausage poison of Würtemburg. **1876** A. W. BLYTH *Dict. Hygiene* 506/1 Four hundred cases of *sausage-poisoning are stated to have occurred in Wurtemburg alone during the last fifty years. **1881** *Syd. Soc. Lex.*, *Allantiasis*, sausage poisoning. **1852** *1st Rep. Commissioners Exhib. 1851* App. XXIX. 150 *Sausage Rolls [consumed] 28,046. **1875** V. LUSH *Jrnl.* 30 Jan. (1975) 157 Mrs O'Keefe and Mrs Spencer sent a large quantity of peaches and Mamma sent sausage rolls for the teachers. **1881** E. J. WORBOISE *Sissie* xx, Arnold..had nothing but a sausage-roll for his dinner. **1937** PARTRIDGE *Dict. Slang* 728/1 **Sausage toad*, sausage toad-in-the-hole: eating-houses' coll[oquialism]: late C. 19–20. **1958** B. PYM *Glass of Blessings* xiv. 159 Would you even have sausage toad if I ordered it? **1915** L. H. BAILEY *Stand. Cycl. Hort.* III. 1738/1 The 'fetish-tree' and '*sausage-tree', is offered in S[outhern] Calif[ornia], and specimens may be expected in botanical collections in the W. Indies. **1944** *Sun* (Baltimore) 6 Dec. 8-D/3 An 'Admirer Visiting in Florida' sends me a colored picture postal-card view of a sausage tree... There they hang, the sausage-like seed pods, amid a background of wonderful green foliage. **1956** E. E. EVANS-PRITCHARD *Nuer Relig.* xii. 298 The man who has committed incest..cuts in two the fruit of a sausage-tree. **1962** *Times* 9 Oct. (Uganda Suppl.) p. viii/4 The incredible sausage-tree with its dangling woody fruits. **1977** D. BEATY *Excellency* xii. 133 The sausage trees with heavy fruits shaped like giant loofahs.

sausage, *v. rare.* [f. prec.] *trans.* To subject (a person or thing) to treatment reminiscent of the manufacture or shape of a sausage.

1922 JOYCE *Ulysses* 500 He is sausaged into several overcoats. **1949** DYLAN THOMAS *Let.* 13 Oct. (1966) 329 So that I won't..have at once to set into motion again the.. little machines that sausage out crumbs and coppers for me. **1951** N. MITFORD *Blessing* II. ii. 168 'Sometimes they only sausage them.' 'They what?' 'Tie them up like sausages, brr round and round.' **1965** *Sunday Times* (Colour Suppl.) 11 July 9/2 Once or twice we had a bit of an indiscretion, might sausage a motor into an island, or over a muddy pasture.

sauscyre, **sause**, obs. ff. SAUCER *sb.*, SAUCE.

sausedge, obs. form of SAUSAGE *sb.*

sauseflem(e, variant ff. SAUCEFLEME *Obs.*

sausenap, rare variant form of SANAP *Obs.*

†**'sauserling.** *Obs. rare.* Also 5 **sawsyrlyng.** [? f. SAUCISTER (contracted) + -LING[1].] A sausage.

1475 *Pict. Voc.* in Wr.-Wülcker 789/29 *Hec ulla*, a sawsyrlyng. *c* **1570** W. WAGER *The longer thou livest* 254 (Brandl), There be good Poddings at the signe of the Plough, You neuer did eate better Sauserlinges.

sausfle(a)me, obs. variant ff. SAUCEFLEME.

sausi(d)ge, **sausie**, obs. ff. SAUSAGE *sb.*, SAUCY.

sausither, variant of SAUCISTER *Obs.*

sauslyme, variant of SAUCELINE *Obs.*

saussage, **-ege**, obs. forms of SAUSAGE *sb.*

sausser, obs. form of SAUCER *sb.*

Saussurean (səʊ's(j)ʊəri:ən), *a.* Also **Saussurian.** [f. the name *Saussure* (see below) + -AN.] Of, pertaining to, or characteristic of the Swiss scholar Ferdinand de *Saussure* (1857–1913) or his linguistic theories. Hence as *sb.*, an adherent of these theories; also **Sau'ssureanism.**

1937 J. ORR tr. *I. Iordan's Introd. Romance Linguistics* iii. 194 His [*sc.* Gilliéron's] linguistic is descriptive, or, in the Saussurian terminology, 'synchronic'. **1939** P. CHRISTOPHERSEN *Articles* 16 A word has thus two aspects: verbal image and meaning (in the well-known Saussurean terms: *signifiant* and *signifié*). **1943** *Language* XIX. 55 In its essence it is Saussurean, but differs in certain respects also from the practices of the major European groups that follow the teachings of Saussure. **1952** *Word* VIII. 264 Eleven papers are devoted to general problems and methodology, among them..the Saussurean opposition between synchrony and diachrony. **1954** *Ibid.* X. 391 Orthodox Saussureanism of the Geneva school. **1968** J. LYONS *Introd. Theoret. Linguistics* ix. 429 This fact is expressed in Saussurean terms by saying that each language imposes a specific *form* on the *a priori* undifferentiated *substance* of the content-plane. **1971** [see PAROLE *sb.* 3]. **1975** LASS & ANDERSON *Old Eng. Phonol.* IV. i. 117 Without adhering to the Saussurean dichotomy one can still realize that diachronic evidence does not crucially determine choices for synchronic ordering. **1977** *Language* LIII. 391 The history of Saussureanism—perhaps one of the most challenging topics that a historian of linguistics could undertake. *Ibid.* 398 As a Saussurean, K views with suspicion any suggestion 'that linguistics might not yet have reached the status of an autonomous science'.

saussurite ('sɔ:sjʊəraɪt). *Min.* [Named after Prof. H. B. de *Saussure* (1740–99) who first described it: see -ITE[1].] A very compact variety of zoisite. Also *Comb.* **saussurite-gabbro**, a variety of gabbro in which the component feldspar and diallage have been partly altered to saussurite.

1811 PINKERTON *Petral.* I. 362 Saussurite..from the western isles of Scotland. **1880** F. W. RUDLER in *Encycl. Brit.* XIII. 541/1 H. B. de Saussure..found a greenish mineral, of singular toughness, which he described as jade. .. Its chemical composition, however, is quite unlike that of jade, and Beudant separated it as a distinct mineral under the name of 'saussurite'. **1885** JUDD in *Q. Jrnl. Geol. Soc.* XLI. 398 The saussurite-gabbros.

Hence **saussu'ritic** *a.*, resembling, pertaining to, or characterized by the presence of saussurite; **saussuriti'zation** (also incorrectly **saussuri'zation**), conversion into saussurite, or the process by which saussurite is formed; '**saussuritized** *ppl. a.*, converted into saussurite, or having component minerals converted into saussurite.

1885 BONNEY *Addr. Geol. Soc.* 70 The felspar being changed into a saussuritic mineral. **1889** M'MAHON in *Q. Jrnl. Geol. Soc.* XLV. 532 The felspar in all these rocks affords more or less evidence of incipient saussurization. **1893** GEIKIE *Text-Bk. Geol.* (ed. 3) 618 Saussuritization, the alteration of plagioclase into an aggregate of needles, prisms, or grains..imbedded in a glass-like matrix.., by an exchange of silica and alkali for lime, iron and water. **1907** J. S. FLETT in W. A. E. Ussher *Geol. Plymouth & Liskeard* 101 There are..saussuritized residues of felspar. **1954** *Mineral. Mag.* XXX. 525 The high density..of the rock.. distinguishes it from saussuritized gabbros. **1974** *Nature* 25 Jan. 195/2 The plagioclase of the gabbros is often saussuritised.

sausy, obs. form of SAUCY.

†**saut**[1]. *Obs. rare. Irish.* Also **saulte**, **sawt(e**, **sould(e.** [Of obscure origin.] A ransom for murder or manslaughter.

1528 in *10th Rep. Hist. MSS. Comm.* App. v. 403 William Marten..dessired of the Courte and Comens Thomas Marten [his] saut, the which saut was jugid uppon the town by Pers Lynch..in recompenc of the slaght and saut of Thomas Marten. **1533** *St. Papers Hen. VIII*, II. 163 Alterages, biengis, saultes, and slauntiaghes. **1534** *Ibid.* 211 Sautes, otherwyse called raunsomes. **1537** *Ibid.* 496 Neyther canes, erykes, sawtes, ne byenges.

saut[2] (so). [Fr., = 'leap'.]

1. Saut Basque (also in pl. and with small initials), a dance of the French Basque provinces (see quots.).

1895 L. GROVE *Dancing* x. 313 The *Mutchico*, or *Saut Basque*, of the French Basque provinces, is held during winter nights in large kitchens or on threshing-floors. **1930** R. GALLOP *Bk. of Basques* iv. 56 A hundred years ago it was not unusual to see the village priest lead the *Saut Basque* on a Sunday evening. *Ibid.* vi. 104 The *jantziak* or *sauts basques* ..are neither wholly ritualistic nor yet purely recreational. **1948** 'LA MERI' *Spanish Dancing* iv. 39 The *Sauts Basques* is also danced by men and women and is now recreational, although its origin is ritualistic... The Sauts is better known in the French provinces of the Basque country than in the Spanish. **1964** W. G. RAFFE *Dict. Dance* 445/1 *Saut Basque*, a dance of French Basque provinces, especially Basse Navarre, where it has two forms—a recreational dance in a large kitchen or on a threshing-floor; and a more ceremonial form, out of doors.

2. *Ballet.* A leap in dancing; chiefly used in the names of special steps, as ***saut de Basque***, ***saut de l'ange*** (see quots. 1957).

1948 A. CHUJOY tr. *Vaganova's Basic Princ. Classical Ballet* vii. 91 Saut de basque... Both legs in this pas should be fully turned out. **1952** KERSLEY & SINCLAIR *Dict. Ballet Terms* 84 *Saut*, a jump in which the dancer springs off both feet and lands in the same position. **1957** G. B. L. WILSON

Penguin Dict. Ballet 240 *Saut de Basque*, lit. a Basque jump. Turning step performed in the air with one leg straight and the other in a retiré position. *Ibid.* 241 *Saut de l'ange*, lit. angel's jump. Similar to a temps de poisson..but the body is held obliquely to the ground in the direction of travel. **1972** H. J. SUMMERS *Guide to Ballet* 155 *Saut de l'ange*, an angel's jump, or a forward leap with the body obliquely to the ground and arms *en couronne* and legs slightly bent. **1976** *New Yorker* 24 May 146/1 From this one performance, I seem to recall Baryshnikov landing from a double saut de basque in a split on the floor.

saut, sautable, var. ff. SALT, SAULT, SAULTABLE.

‖**sauté** (sote), *a.* and *sb. Cookery.* [Fr., pa. pple. of *sauter* to leap (see SAULT *v.*[2]), used *trans.* in causative sense.] **A.** *adj.* (Sometimes as pa. pple.) Of meat, vegetables, etc.: Fried in a pan with a little butter over a high heat, while being tossed from time to time.

1869 GOUFFÉ *Roy. Cookery Bk.* I. vi. 90 Beef kidney can also be *sauté* in the following way.

B. *sb.* A dish cooked in the above manner.

1813 L. E. UDE *Fr. Cook* (1827) 194 Mind, you must never let the *sauté* be too much done. **1827** LYTTON *Pelham* lxvii, 'Long life to the Solomon of *sautés*', was my audible exclamation. **1869** GOUFFÉ *Roy. Cookery Bk.* I. vi. 93 For *sautés*, the fire should be brisk. **1870** DUBOIS *Artistic Cookery* 56 A *sauté* of chickens.

attrib. **1813** [see the vb. below]. **1845** ELIZA ACTON *Mod. Cookery* 163 The sauté-pan..is much used by French cooks instead of a frying-pan. **1846** A. SOYER *Gastron. Regenerator* 341 Melt two ounces of butter in a sauté-pan. **1960** E. DAVID *French Provincial Cooking* 68 Few English kitchens seem to possess sauté pans.

Hence **sauté** *v.* = SAUTER *v.*; **sautéing** *vbl. sb.*

[**1813** L. E. UDE *Fr. Cook* (1827) 192 Cut your scollops.., dip them into some clarified butter, in a *sauté*-pan, *sautez* them over a brisk fire.] **1859** *Eng. Cookery Bk.* 51 Frying or Sauteing, Broiling, Toasting and Braising of Animal Food. **1868** MARY JEWRY *Warne's Model Cookery* 51 To 'Sauté' anything means to dress it quickly, in a small pan, with a very little butter [etc.]. *Ibid.*, The art of sauté-ing well consists in doing it quickly, to keep the gravy..in the meat. **1907** [see JARDINIÈRE 2]. **1953** ROMBAUER & BECKER *Joy of Cooking* 73/1 Dice bread and sauté it in butter. **1968** *Globe Mag.* (Toronto) 13 Jan. 16/3 Halve frankfurters lengthwise. Melt butter in heavy skillet, add onion and saute over low heat until just tender but not brown.

saute, var. SALT *sb.*[2], SAULT *sbs.* and *vbs. Obs.*

sauteer, obs. form of PSALTER.

‖**sauter** (sote), *v.* [Fr. (inf.): see SAUTÉ *a.*] *trans.* (See quot.)

1869 GOUFFÉ *Roy. Cookery Bk.* I. 5 *To sauter* is to fry with little butter over a brisk fire. **1891** in *Century Dict.*

sauter(e, etc., obs. ff. PSALTER, etc.

†**sauterell.** *Obs. rare.* Also **sawterell**. Var., possibly erroneous, of SAUNTRELL.

c **1440** *York Myst.* xxxi. 310 Carpe on knave cautely and caste þe to corde here, And saie me nowe somwhat, þou sauterell with sorowe. *Ibid.* xxxii. 91 Yone sauterell he sais, He schall caste doune oure tempill..And dresse it vppe dewly with-in thre daies. *Ibid.* xxxii. 274 Ȝitt schalte þou noȝt, sawterell, þu sune for-sake it.

‖**Sauternes** (sotɛrn, səʊˈtɜːn). Also **Sauterne**. [Named from the district *Sauterne* near Bordeaux, where it is made.] A white French wine of the Bordeaux class.

1711 *Lond. Gaz.* No. 4817/6 For Sale.., 32 Hogsheads.. of..Sauternes White Wine. **1833** REDDING *Wines* 154 The first [wines] in quality are Carbonieux,..Sauterne, Bommes, Barsac, and Preignac. **1836** DICKENS *Sk. Boz, Boarding Ho.* i, Mr. Simpson, Mr. Calton, and Mr. Hicks produced respectively a bottle of sauterne, bucellas, and sherry. **1895** *Army & Navy Co-op. Soc. Price List* 165 Sauternes... 18/0. **1908** [see SAUVIGNON a]. **1959** W. JAMES *Word-bk. Wine* 168 The sauternes-types made in Australia, South Africa, and California are most frequently a well-sulphured mixture of white wine and fortified grape juice. **1967** A. LICHINE *Encycl. Wines* 486/2 The wines to be met with in many other places in the world which call themselves sauternes—or even sauterne, as if to justify bad practice by bad spelling—are not what they claim to be.

sautir, sautre, obs. forms of PSALTER.

‖**sautoir** (sotwar). [Fr.: cf. SALTIRE.] A long necklace consisting of a fine gold chain usu. set with jewels.

1936 *N.Y. Times Mag.* 6 Dec. 10/1 It was the era of sunbursts, sautoirs, immense brooches and flaming diamonds. **1957** M. B. PICKEN *Fashion Dict.* 284/1 *Sautoir* .., long jeweled chain of gold. **1960** *Times* 29 Mar. 22/7 A pearl and diamond sautoir. **1969** R. T. WILCOX *Dict. Costume* (1970) 304/1 *Sautoir*, a long, fine gold or silver chain upon which women carried a watch, or a small gold or silver chain purse, or, perhaps, a medallion. **1980** *Times* 18 Oct. 7/4 Sautoirs, or long neckchains..were very popular at the beginning of the century.

sautre, -trie, -triȝe, -try, obs. ff. PSALTERY *sb.*

sauvage, obs. form of SAVAGE.

sauve, obs. form of SAFE, SAVE.

‖**sauvegarde**, Fr. form of SAFEGUARD 11.

1840 *Cuvier's Anim. Kingd.* 274 Some [monitors], more particularly termed *Sauvegardes*, have the tail more or less compressed. **188.** *Cassell's Nat. Hist.* IV. 276 The Common Teguexin, or South American Sauvegarde.

sauvenap, rare variant of SANAP *Obs.*

sauveo(u)r, obs. f. SAVIOUR.

‖**sauve-qui-peut** (sovkipø). [Fr., subst. use of a phrase = 'Save (himself) who can'.] A general stampede or complete rout. Also as a phrase in the original Fr. sense. Hence as *vb.*, to stampede or scatter in flight.

[**1802** C. JAMES *Milit. Dict.*, *Sauve qui peut!* Fr. Let those escape that can. This expression is familiar to the French in moments of defeat, and great disorder.] **1815** SCOTT *Let.* in Lockhart *Life* (1837) III. xi. 361 The marshals followed his [Buonaparte's] example; and it was the most complete *sauve qui peut* that can well be imagined. **1855-6** THACKERAY *Four Georges* i. (1861) 41 What a fine satirical picture we might have had of that general *sauve qui peut* amongst the Tory party! **1875** *Encycl. Brit.* III. 321/2 *Sauve qui peut* was the universal cry; and..in less than six weeks above seventy banking establishments were swept off. **1907** ANTHONY HOPE *Tales of Two People* 133 The poor Stock fell two points more: there had been a *sauve qui peut* of the timid holders. **1939** tr. *E.N. Marais's My Friends the Baboons* iii. 35 All the baboons do in such a case is *sauve qui peut* with an alarm-call that makes the mountains echo. **1964** *Reading Teacher* Dec. 211/1 Working-class whites, themselves anthropologically unsophisticated, join the *sauve qui peut* in search of a suburban haven. **1973** *Times* 26 Nov. 15/4 It is difficult to understand the Government's present policy, or indeed that of any of the oil users. *Sauve qui peut* will serve no one well in the long run. **1980** *Guardian* 11 Nov. 10/8 It is in those hallowed halls of the UN..that I feel most keenly the theatre of anarchy; of sauve-qui-peut.

sauver, obs. f. SAVER.

sauvete, obs. form of SAFETY.

Sauveterrian (səʊvˈtɛrɪən), *a. Archæol.* [ad. F. *Sauveterrien* (E. Octobon 1930, in *Actes XV Congr. Internat. d'Anthrop. & Archéol.* (1931) 332), f. *Sauveterre* (see below) + -IAN.] Of, pertaining to, or designating the mesolithic culture of which remains were first discovered at Sauveterre-la-Lémance, in Lot-et-Garonne, France. Also *absol.*

1940 C. F. C. HAWKES *Prehist. Foundations Europe* iii. 50 We are..in the region of Azilian tradition, but the industry might almost equally well be a 'Middle Tardenoisian', with its crescentic and angular microliths and its moderate but not excessive development of micro-burin technique, and the French now propose to call such industries in general Sauveterrian, reserving the name Tardenoisian in a strict sense for the later stage. *Ibid.* 66 In Britain,..microlithic technique was never carried beyond the Middle Tardenoisian or Sauveterrian stage. **1952** *Proc. Prehist. Soc.* XVIII. 109 Since then, the discovery of mesolithic tools which preceded the Tardenoisian on the Causses west of the Massif Central has added 'Sauveterrian' to the terminology. **1963** E. S. WOOD *Collins Field Guide Archaeol.* iv. 50 The character of the mesolithic of all but the south-east and east of England shows affinities with the French mesolithic culture called *Sauveterrian*. *Ibid.* 103 The mesolithic people of the Sauveterrian were particularly fond of rock-shelters. **1975** *Nature* 3 July 33/2 This radiocarbon evidence from the Pennines indicates conclusively that simple 'broad blade' microlithic industries identical to those of Thatcham and Star Carr precede 'narrow blade' (sometimes termed 'Sauveterrian') industries with small scalene triangles and rod-like microliths. **1975** J. G. EVANS *Environment Early Man Brit. Isles* v. 92 On the high moors of north-east Yorkshire another group of industries, also Mesolithic.., occurs. These..contain..a profusion of microliths. The name Sauveterrian—after the type site in France of Sauveterre-la-Lémance—has been applied to them.

sauveur, obs. form of SAVIOUR.

‖**Sauvignon** (soviɲɔ̃). [Fr.] **a.** A white grape of France; the white wine made from this grape. Also *attrib.* or as *adj.*

1846 C. COCKS *Bordeaux* II. 142 The following are the names of the most esteemed white wines. 1. The *Sauvignon*, of a yellowish or greyish brown-spotted wood. **1875** H. VIZETELLY *Wines of World* 18 The fine white wines of the Gironde are produced from the Sauvignon and Semillon grapes, the former of which yields a limpid, perfumed, delicate-flavoured, amber-coloured, heady wine. **1888** *Encycl. Brit.* XXIV. 604/2 The principal vines used in the Médoc are..for white wines, the Semillon, the Sauvignon, and the Muscatelle. **1908** E. & A. VIZETELLY *Wines of France* 82 Sauternes and the better Graves..are chiefly the produce of the Sauvignon and Semillon grapes. **1935** SCHOONMAKER & MARVEL *Compl. Wine Bk.* v. 142 Corvo, a..dry white wine, made..out of two native Sicilian grapes blended with the famous Sauvignon grape of Sauternes. **1959** W. JAMES *Word-bk. Wine* 168 *Sauvignon*, one of the three white grape varieties used in Sauternes and grown to a limited extent in South Africa, Australia, and California for high-quality white wines. **1969** V. ROSE *Loire* 30 Pouilly-Fumé..is made from the Sauvignon grape. **1973** *Times* 30 June 11/4 Wines made solely from the Sauvignon Blanc grape..are now to be found in many of the French wine regions. *Ibid.* 11/5 Many merchants list Sauvignons. **1976** *Times* 6 Mar. 13/5 A classic Sauvignon..comes from Haut Poitou..with the steely flavour of this great great..wine of astonishing quality.

b. Short for Cabernet-Sauvignon, a black grape of France; also the red wine made from this grape.

1846 C. COCKS *Bordeaux* II. 140 The *Carmenère*, or grosse *Vidure*, called also *grand Carmenet, Carbonet*, or *Sauvignon*, has..grapes..of a bright colour. **1895** *Army & Navy Co-op. Soc. Price List* 166 'Imperial', from finest Sauvignon grapes. **1907** *Yesterday's Shopping* (1969) 97/3 Sauvignon ..(Burgoyne) 16/0. **1917** *Harrods Gen. Catal.* 1289/2 Sauvignon, full bodied..1/11. **1952** A. LICHINE *Wines of France* 46 The wine..comes from a vineyard planted two-thirds in Cabernet Franc and Sauvignon... No white wine is made.

sauvour, obs. form of SAVIOUR.

sav, abbrev. of SAVELOY.

1936 J. CURTIS *Gilt Kid* 75 Cup o' tea, sav and a slice. **1969** C. DRUMMOND *Odds on Death* vi. 130 Some home-made savs —not the shop kind.

savable, saveable (ˈseɪvəb(ə)l), *a.* Also 5 **sauvable**. [f. SAVE *v.* + -ABLE. Cf. OF. *sauvable, salvable.*] Capable of being saved; orig. chiefly in *Theol.* sense. Cf. SALVABLE *a.*[1]

c **1450** *Mirour Saluacioun* (Roxb.) 103 Nowe in it be cristis vertue growes the noumbre of the sauuable. **1530** PALSGR. 323/1 Savable, *saluable*. **1638** CHILLINGW. *Relig. Prot.* I. Pref. §39 Those who doe subscribe them are in a saveable condition. **1751** [J. YOUNG] *Affect. Narr. of Wager* 25 Our unfortunate Lot was cast, where our Lives were however saveable. **1832** *Examiner* 51/2 They [*sc.* small rotten boroughs] are not of a saveable size. **1882-3** SCHAFF *Encycl. Relig. Knowl.* II. 1211 Who has shown himself by his works savable?

¶? Conducive to salvation.

a **1706** EVELYN *Hist. Relig.* (1850) I. 374 And we find more admirable and saveable matter in one only Sermon of Jesus, upon the Mount, than in all the morals of the philosophers.

Hence †**ˈsavableness**.

1638 CHILLINGW. *Relig. Prot.* I. Concl. 411 Saveablenesse of Protestants.

savacu: see SABICU.

savage (ˈsævɪdʒ), *a.* and *sb.*[1] Also α. 3-6 **sauvage**, (*rare* 4 **saveage**, 5 **sawage, saffage**, 7 **savadg(e)**; β. 4, 6-9 (now *arch.*) **salvage**, (7 **salvadge**). [a. F. *sauvage* (in OF. also *salvage*) = Pr. *salvatge*, Sp. *salvage*, Pg. *salvagem*, It. *selvaggio* (in the sense wooded, woodland; also in learned forms *salvatico, selvatico* wild), Romanian *sălbatic* :—L. *silvāticus* (in popular L. also with vowel-assimilation *salvāticus*) woodland, wild, f. *silva* wood, forest: see SILVAN and -AGE, -ATIC.]

A. *adj.*

I. That is in a state of nature, wild.

1. Of animals: Wild, undomesticated, untamed. Often, and in later use exclusively, with the contextual implication of ferocity (cf. sense 9).

α. *a* **1300** *Dial. betw. Body & Soul* 30 (MS. Digby 86) To binden leounes sauuage. *a* **1330** *Roland & V.* 92 [Presents offered to the emperor] Sauage bestes... Gold & siluer, & riche stones. **1483** CAXTON *Knt. de la Tour* a j, But a lytel I rejoyced me in the sowne and songe of the fowles sauuage. **1572** BOSSEWELL *Armorie* II. 58 b, An Asse sauage passante. **1596** SHAKS. *Merch. V.* v. i. 78 Youthful and vnhandled colts ..Their sauage eyes turn'd to a modest gaze, By the sweet power of musicke. **1610** GUILLIM *Heraldry* III. xx. (1611) 163 Now of those [Fowles of Prey] which are Predable, whereof some are Sauage, some Domesticall: the Sauage I call those that are not subiect to mans gouernment, but doe naturally shun their societie. **1774** GOLDSM. *Nat. Hist.* (1776) III. 272 An angry and ferocious disposition, renders the dog, in its savage state, a formidable enemy to all other animals. **1820** SHELLEY *Hymn Merc.* xlvi, A story so absurd As that a new-born infant forth could fare Out of his home after a savage herd.

β. **1542** UDALL *Erasm. Apoph.* 148 b, Yᵉ partie had the mynde or stomake, not of a manne, but of a veraye brute & salvage beaste. **1550** J. COKE *Eng. & Fr. Herald.* §7 (1877) 59 We have almaner of bestes salvages that you have, and more plente of them to chase. **1628** WITHER *Brit. Rememb.* I. 815 Whom late the salvage Bore..Hath rooted up, with purpose to devoure. *a* **1701** MAUNDRELL *Journ. Jerus.* (1721) 39 Lyons and other Salvage Creatures.

2. Of country, land, scenery: †**a.** Uncultivated, wild. *Obs.* **b.** Hence (by association with branch II), Horribly wild and rugged.

α. *c* **1300** *Arth. & Merl.* 5433 (Kölbing) þe .xii. Drians of þe Forest sauage, A strong kniȝt of heiȝe parage. **1426** LYDG. *De Guil. Pilgr.* 17134, I fyl a-noon, in my passage Into a wood ful savage. **1523** LD. BERNERS *Froiss.* I. xvii. 18 Northumbrelande..was a sauage and a wylde countrey, full of desartis and mountaignes. **1585** T. WASHINGTON tr. *Nicholay's Voy.* II. ix. 43 The moste part of the yle is hilly and sauage. **1671** MILTON *P.R.* III. 23 Affecting private life, or more obscure In savage Wilderness. **1774** PENNANT *Tour Scotl. in 1772*, 22 The prospect on all sides quite savage, high barran hills or dreary wet sands. **1810** SCOTT *Let.* in *Lockhart* (1837) II. ix. 326 The scenery is quite different from that on the mainland, dark, savage, and horrid. **1860** TYNDALL *Glaciers* I. ii. 11 The view from this place had a savage magnificence. **1907** BP. ROBERTSON in *Trans. Devon Assoc.* 47 Savage and forbidding scenes have laid aside their grandeur.

β. **1553** EDEN *Treat. New Ind.* (Arb.) 27 It is throughout baren & saluage, so that it is not able to nourishe any beastes for lacke of pasture. *a* **1645** WALLER *To my Lord Admiral* 12 Eurydice, for whom his num'rous moan Makes listning trees and savage mountains groan. **1713** *Guardian* No. 101 ⁋5 Fountaine-bleau..is situated among Rocks and Woods, that give you a fine Variety of Salvage Prospects. **1853** G. JOHNSTON *Nat. Hist. E. Bord.* I. 96 The old salvage character of the hill has disappeared.

†**3.** Of a plant, tree, etc.: Wild, uncultivated.

α. **1422** tr. *Secreta Secret., Priv. Priv.* 244 Letus sauage, that is y-callid scariole. *c* **1580** R. WILLES in *Hakluyt's Voy.* (1599) II. II. 79 The greater part of the quadrangle [is] set with sauage trees, as Okes, Chestnuts, Cypresse. **1732** POPE *Ess. Man* II. 182 As fruits..On savage stocks inserted, learn to bear. **1733** TULL *Horse-Hoeing Husb.* xiv. (Dublin) 178 St. Foin..grows naturally savage without sowing or tillage, upon the Calabrian Hills near Croto. **1820** SHELLEY *Ode to*

Liberty iv, The vine, the corn, the olive mild, Grew savage yet, to human use unreconciled.

β. **1599** HAKLUYT *Voy.* II. I. 202 A place..which yeeldeth balme in great plenty, but saluage, wilde, and without vertue. **1697** DRYDEN *Virg. Georg.* II. 24 Thus the salvage Cherry grows.

4. a. Of movements, noise, demeanour, manners, etc.: Wild, ungoverned; rude, unpolished. *arch.*

c **1420-30** LYDG. *Dance Machabree* in *Bochas* (1554) 221, I haue nought learned here toforn to daunce, no daunce in sooth of footyng so sauage. **1599** SHAKS. *Much Ado* IV. i. 62 But you are more intemperate in your blood, Than Venus, or those pampred animalls, That rage in sauage sensualitie. **1606** —— *Tr. & Cr.* II. iii. 135 The sauage strangenesse he puts on. **1611** —— *Wint. T.* III. iii. 56 A sauage clamor. **1667** MILTON *P.L.* VII. 36 The Race Of that wilde Rout that tore the Thracian Bard In Rhodope,..till the savage clamor drownd Both Harp and Voice. **1781** COWPER *Convers.* 421 Oh to the club, the scene of savage joys, The school of coarse good fellowship and noise. **1784** —— *Task* III. 325 Delights which who would leave..For all the savage din of the swift pack, And clamours of the field? **1822** SHELLEY *Tri. Life* 142 The wild dance maddens in the van, and those Who lead it ..without repose Mix with each other in tempestuous measure To savage music, wilder as it grows.

†**b.** Of colouring: Crude, harsh, violent. *Obs.*

β. **1706** *Art of Painting* (1744) 163 He tam'd the fierceness of his colours, which were too salvage.

5. Of peoples or (now somewhat *rarely*) of individual persons: Uncivilized; existing in the lowest stage of culture.

α. **1588** SHAKS. *L.L.L.* IV. iii. 222 Like a rude and sauage man of Inde. **1589** PUTTENHAM *Eng. Poesie* I. iii. (Arb.) 22 He brought the rude and sauage people to a more ciuill and orderly life. **1600** E. BLOUNT tr. *Conestaggio* 27 Taking for their leader the Earle of Desmond and others, as Oneale, and some other of the sauage Irish. **1652** NEEDHAM tr. *Selden's Mare Cl.* 196 The Britains were for the most part an abject savage people. **1755** GRAY *Progr. Poesy* 60 She [the Muse] deigns to hear the savage youth repeat, In loose numbers, wildly sweet, Their feather-cinctur'd chiefs and dusky loves. **1772** *Ann. Reg.* 41/1 The highlanders, whom more savage nations called Savage. **1781** GIBBON *Decl. & F.* xxx. III. 170 The barriers, which had so long separated the savage and the civilised nations of the earth. **1842** TENNYSON *Locksley Hall* 168, I will take some savage woman, she shall rear my dusky race. **1871** FREEMAN *Norm. Conq.* (1876) IV. xvii. 73 The south..was, through its neighbourhood and intercourse with Gaul, somewhat less savage than the rest of the island. **1906** A. MACHEN *House of Souls* Note 7 We know..how the enemies of the cruel Star Chamber caused the savage Indian to disappear from the land.

β. **1614** RALEIGH *Hist. World* II. xiii. §7. 435 In these times Greece was very saluage, the inhabitants being often chaced from place to place, by the captaines of greater Tribes. **1690** LOCKE *Hum. Und.* I. iii. §12 The more than Brutality of some salvage and barbarous Nations. **1698** FRYER *Acc. E. Ind. & P.* 271 From a Salvage Prince rendred himself a tame Follower of the Patriarch St. Gregory.

b. *salvage man*: the conventional representation of a savage in heraldry and pageants; a human figure naked or enveloped in foliage. *arch.*

1575 GASCOIGNE *Princely Pleas. Kenelworth* (1587) A iv, There met her in the Forest as she came from hunting one clad like a Sauage man, all in Iuie. **1575** LANEHAM *Let.* (1871) 14 Oout of the woods, in her Maiestiez return roughly came thear foorth Hombre Saluagio [*marg.* The sauage man.] with an Oken plant pluct vp by the roots in hiz hande, himself forgrone all in moss and Iuy. **1815** SCOTT *Guy M.* xli, On either side stood as supporters..a salvage man proper, to use the language of heraldry, wreathed and cinctured. **1819** —— *Ivanhoe* viii, Beside it stood his squire, quaintly disguised as a salvage or silvan man. **1820** —— *Monast.* xvi, The flesh-coloured silken doublet..in which I danced the salvage man at the Gray's-Inn mummery. **1874** GREEN *Short Hist.* vii. §7. 415 The 'Faerie Queen'..in its alternation of the salvage-men from the New World with the satyrs of classic mythology.

c. Pertaining to or characteristic of savages.

α. **1614** RALEIGH *Hist. World* I. vii. §3. 102 The first people which after the generall floud inhabited Italie, were the Camesenes,..which people liued altogether a sauage life. **1788** GIBBON *Decl. & F.* liii. V. 494 The Grecian princess was torn from the palace of her fathers, and condemned to a savage reign and an hopeless exile on the banks of the Borysthenes. **1809-10** COLERIDGE *Friend* (1865) 161 The civilized man gives up those stimulants of hope and fear which constitute the chief charm of savage life. **1857** BUCKLE *Civiliz.* I. iv. 176 This is the purely savage state; and it is the state in which military glory is most esteemed, and military men most respected. **1899** R. C. TEMPLE *Univ. Gram.* 24 The 'savage' nature of the languages comes out even more clearly if we apply the theory in another way.

β. **1614** RALEIGH *Hist. World* I. viii. §5. 140 There is no man so impious, as to beleeue that Noah..could..set vp or deuise any Heathen saluage, or idolatrous adoration. **1697** DRYDEN *Æneid* VII. 925 Like Hercules himself, his Son appears, In Saluage Pomp a Lyon's Hide he wears.

†**d.** Remote from society, solitary. *Obs.*

1667 MILTON *P.L.* IX. 1085 O might I here In solitude live savage, in some glade Obscur'd. **1680** OTWAY *Orphan* II. vii, I, methinks, am Salvage and forlorn, Thy presence only 'tis can make me blest.

†**6.** Of decoration: Rustic, imitating natural vegetation. *Obs.*

a **1548** HALL *Chron., Hen. VIII* 156 b, The Jawe peces.. were karved with Vinettes and trailes of savage worke.

II. With reference to disposition or temper.

†**7.** Indomitable, intrepid, valiant. *Obs.*

α. **13..** *Coer de L.* 485 An hardy knyght, stout and savage, Hent a schafft with gret rage. *c* **1330** *Arth. & Merl.* 8270 (Kölbing) Þe .v. was Dedinet, þe saueage. *c* **1350** *Will. Palerne* 4022 But sone sauage men þat seten in þe halle henten hastili in honde what þei haue miȝt,..to wende him [the werwolf] after wiȝtli to quelle. **1470** HENRY *Wallace* VIII. 813 With v thowsand welle garnest and sawage. *Ibid.* v. 534 A worthy clerk, bath wys and rycht sawage.

†**b.** In bad sense: Reckless, ungovernable. *Obs.*

c **1400** *Laud Troy Bk.* 4759, I praye the, my broder dere, ..That thow be wyse and not sauage; ȝif the not to outrage. *a* **1500** *Bernard. de cura rei fam.* (E.E.T.S.) 300 A mane..of wyne þat has vsage Ande habundance, and syne is nocht saffage Th[r]ow mychtines and confort of þe wyne At temporance bydis and sobyr syne.

†**8.** Rude, harsh, ungentle (also *transf.* of the sea, a river). *Obs.* (merged in the stronger sense 9). In the 17th c. a Gallicism.

α. **13..** *K. Alis.* 4089 (Laud MS.) Darrie hete..Remuen his tentes..and setten hem bisides Estrage, A colde water and a sauage.

β. **1390** GOWER *Conf.* II. 77 Bot vertu set in the corage, Ther mai no world be so salvage, Which mihte it take and don aweie, Til whanne that the bodi deie. *Ibid.* III. 230 For as the wilde wode rage Of wyndes makth the See salvage, And that was calm bringth into wawe. *Ibid.* 332 And if ye wiste what I am, And out of what lignage I cam, Ye wolde noght be so salvage. **1655** F. G. tr. *Scudery's Artemenes* VII. III. 189 Her reputation is high, though her vertue be neither salvage nor austere.

9. Fierce, ferocious, cruel. **a.** of animals.

α. *c* **1407** LYDG. *Reson & Sens.* 3680 Lyouns proude in ther rage, And many beste ful Savage. **1420-2** —— *Thebes* III. in *Chaucer's Wks.* (1561) 374 b, Grekes wening that were yong of age That this Tygre hadde be sauage And cruely besetting al the place Rounde about. **1579-80** NORTH *Plutarch, Theseus* (1595) 5 The wild sauage Sowe of Crommyon, otherwise surnamed Phæa. **1611** BIBLE *Wisd.* xvii. 19 A roaring voice of most sauage wilde beasts. **1630** BP. HALL *Occas. Medit.* xxvii. (1633) 70 Even the Savagest Beasts are made quiet and docible, with want of food, and rest. **1706** ADDISON *Rosamond* I. iv, What savage tiger would not pity A damsel so distressed and pretty! **1820** SCOTT *Let.* in *Lockhart* (1837) IV. xi. 348 For all the kind [of dogs] are savage at night.

β. **1632** SANDERSON *Serm.* 148 Wherein Iob alludeth to ravenous and salvadge beasts. **1696** TATE & BRADY *Ps.* vii. 2 Lest, like a salvage Lion, he My helpless Soul devour.

b. of persons, their attributes or actions.

α. **1579-80** NORTH *Plutarch, Theseus* (1595) 5 Of a cruell, wicked, and sauage pleasure. **1588** SHAKS. *L.L.L.* IV. iii. 348 O then his lines would rauish sauage eares, And plant in Tyrants milde humilitie. **1594** —— *Rich. III*, I. iv. 265 [*Murderer.*] Relent? no: 'Tis cowardly and womanish. *Cla.* Not to relent, is beastly, sauage, diuellish. **1599** —— *Hen. V*, II. ii. 95 What shall I say to thee Lord Scroope, thou cruell, Ingratefull, sauage, and inhumane Creature? **1697** CONGREVE *Mourn. Bride* I. i. 1 Musick has Charms to sooth a savage Breast, To soften Rocks, or bend a knotted Oak. **1749** SMOLLETT *Regic.* I. i, A wretch Of soul more savage breathes not vital air. **1780** BURKE *Sp. at Bristol* Wks. 1842 I. 261 The operation of the old law is so savage, and so inconvenient to society, that [etc.]. **1800** MRS. HERVEY *Mourtray Fam.* IV. 190 It would be downright savage to leave Lady Miramont now. **1808** SCOTT in *Lockhart* (1837) I. i. 32 The magistrates of Edinburgh..encouraged a savage fellow,..one of the under-masters, in insulting his [Dr. Adam's] person and authority. **1845** DISRAELI *Sybil* III. vii, With a countenance..rather brutal than savage. **1848** THACKERAY *Van. Fair* ix, He had a savage pleasure in making the poor wretches [his creditors] wait. **1849** GROTE *Greece* II. lii. (1862) IV. 457 His queen the savage Parysatis. **1879** FROUDE *Cæsar* xxiv. 419 The troops were savage, and killed every man that they overtook.

β. **1637** SALTONSTALL *Eusebius' Constantine* 137 Hee hath changed all mansutude and graciousnesse with salvage fury and cruelty. *a* **1694** TILLOTSON *Serm.* xlii. (1742) III. 198 With what a salvage and murderous disposition they fly at one another's reputation and tear it in pieces.

c. *transf.*

1634 MILTON *Comus* 358 Within the direfull grasp Of Savage hunger, or of Savage heat. **1818** SHELLEY *Homer's Hymn to Castor* 9 When wintry tempests o'er the savage sea Are raging. **1821** —— *Epipsych.* 332 So that the savage winds hung mute around. **1857** EMERSON *Poems* 12 The bellowing of the savage sea.

10. (Chiefly *colloq.*) Enraged, furiously angry. Also, rough or unsparing in speech.

1825 T. HOOK *Sayings* Ser. II. *Sutherl.* (Colburn) 29 Don't let Emmy know that we have split, else she'll be savage with us. **1851** LYTTON *Not so bad* II. i. 32 You're so savage on Softhead, I suspect 'tis from envy. **1861** FLOR. NIGHTINGALE *Nursing* (ed. 2) 45 Almost any sick person..if he can speak without being savage..is exercising self control. **1870** EMERSON *Soc. & Solit., Old Age* Wks. (Bohn) III. 134 Michel Angelo's head is full of masculine and gigantic figures as gods walking, which make him savage until his furious chisel can render them into marble. **1875** W. S. HAYWARD *Love agst. World* 3 Come, Jasper, you need not look so savage. **1899** E. PHILLPOTTS *Human Boy* 110, I think the Doctor was pretty savage with old Briggs.

III. 11. *Comb.*, as †*savage-fierce*, *-hearted*, *-looking*, *-spoken*, †*-wild*.

1784 COWPER *Task* VI. 487 Vicious in act, in temper *savage-fierce. **1819** MRS. GRANT in *Mem. & Corr.* (1844) II. 223 His *savage-hearted prototype. **1795** SEWARD *Anecd.* II. 272 They were the most *savage-looking men that I had ever beheld. **1848** THACKERAY *Van. Fair* xliv, He..glared at him with savage-looking eyes. **1894** *Outing* (N.Y.) XXIV. 230/1 A *savage-spoken old Scotch woman. **1592** SHAKS. *Rom. & Jul.* V. iii. 37 The time, and my intents are *sauage wilde.

B. *sb.*

†**1.** A wild beast. *Obs.*

1682 SOUTHERNE *Loyal Brother* IV. i, What unfrequented coast am I thrown on, Naked, and helpless, to be made a prey To the next coming Salvage of the field? **1750** JOHNSON *Rambler* No. 11 ¶12 The suspicion and solicitude of a man that plays with a tame tiger, always under a necessity of watching the moment in which the capricious savage shall begin to growl. **1770** LANGHORNE *Plutarch* I. 9 Crommyon was infested by a wild sow named Phæa... This savage he [Theseus]..killed. **1831** MACAULAY *Ess., Hampden* ¶14 The man who, in a Spanish bull-fight, goads the torpid savage to fury, by shaking a red rag in the air.

b. A bad-tempered horse. Cf. SAVAGE *v.* 4.

1869 'WAT. BRADWOOD' *The O.V.H.* vi, His experience of similar animals led him to house a donkey in the same box with Warrener, with whom the savage soon fraternised, and displayed corresponding improvement in his temper. **1888** W. DAY *Horse* 419 We also have in Paradox a modern savage, like his grey prototype.

2. A person living in the lowest state of development or cultivation; an uncivilized, wild person.

α. **1588** SHAKS. *L.L.L.* V. ii. 202 Vouchsafe to shew the sunshine of your face, That we (like sauages) may worship it. **1605** CAMDEN *Rem., Impreses* 174 His conceit was obscure to mee which painted a savadge of America pointing toward the Sun, with *Tibi accessv, mihi decessv.* **1632** LITHGOW *Trav.* VI. 292 Some scattering Arabs, sold vs Water... Two of which Sauages our Captayne hyred, to guide vs. **1672** DRYDEN *1st Pt. Conq. Granada* I. i. 7, I am as free as Nature first made man, 'Ere the base Laws of Servitude began, When wild in woods the noble Savage ran. **1763** J. BROWN *Poetry & Mus.* iii. 29 The Iroquois, Hurons, and some less considerable Tribes, are free and independent Savages. **1907** G. TYRRELL *Oil & Wine* 24 To the savage every stranger is therefore an enemy.

β. **1610** SHAKS. *Temp.* II. ii. 60 Doe you put trickes vpon's with Saluages, and Men of Inde? **1612** CAPT. SMITH, etc. *Map of Virginia* II. i. 3 Wee traded with the Salvages at Dominica. **1719** DE FOE *Crusoe* I. (1883) 40 Among strangers and salvages.

fig. **1642** FULLER *Holy & Prof. St.* III. ii. 156 Seeing we are civilized English men, let us not be naked Salvages in our talk.

b. *transf.* A cruel or fierce person. Also, one who is destitute of culture, or who is ignorant or neglectful of the rules of good behaviour.

1606 SHAKS. *Tr. & Cr.* V. iii. 49 *Hect.* Fie sauage, fie. *Troy.* Hector, then 'tis warres. **1672-5** COMBER *Comp. to Temple* (1702) 130 But who would imagine that our Christned Albion should breed such Salvages? **1762** COLMAN *Mus. Lady* II. 20 *Sophy*... Oh—the people here are all downright Goths. *Mask.* Absolute savages—an English catch, a Scotch jigg, and an Irish howl are all their ideas of harmony. **1784** COWPER *Task* VI. 422 Witness the patient ox, ..Driv'n to the slaughter..while the savage at his heels Laughs at the frantic suff'rer's fury. **1826** DISRAELI *Viv. Grey* I. iii, However,..the young savages at Burnsley Vicarage had caught a Tartar. **1847** TENNYSON *Princess* III. 230 Peace, you young savage of the Northern wild! **1898** HAIG-BROWN in *Westm. Gaz.* 1 Feb. 8/1 Schoolboys..are not such savages as in the old days.

3. a. = *salvage man* (see A. 5 b). **b.** The 'Jack of the clock' (see JACK *sb.*[1] 6).

1575 LANEHAM *Let.* (1871) 15 This Sauage, for the more submission, brake hiz tree a sunder. **1708** [HATTON] *New View Lond.* I. 231 The Ornament of this Church [*sc.* St. Dunstans in the West] consists..of the Clock..here being two Figures of Savages or wild Men, well carved in Wood, ..with each a knotty Club in his Hand wherewith they alternately strike the Quarters. **1780** EDMONDSON *Heraldry* II. *Gloss., Savage, Wood-man,* or *Wild-man.* **1803** MALCOLM *Lond. Rediv.* III. 461 Their clock and savages, whose fascinating movements attract twenty pair of eyes every quarter of an hour. **1908** *Daily Chron.* 9 Oct. 4/7 [About 1762] it was customary for the Lord Mayor's procession to be headed by a body of men called 'whifflers'... These, with the assistance of some twenty 'savages' or 'greenmen', as they were termed, who let off..fireworks, effectively cleared the way for the City Fathers and the 'Show'.

Savage ('sævɪdʒ), *sb.*[2] The name of Arthur *Savage*, inventor, of Brooklyn, N.Y., used *attrib.* and *absol.* as a brand name (proprietary in the U.S.) of a repeating rifle produced by him in 1894, and of other firearms produced by the Savage Arms Company.

1892 *Ann. Rep. Chief of Ordnance to Secy. of War* (U.S.) App. IX. 224 *Savage*... This arm was brought before the board by Mr. Arthur Savage, of Brooklyn, N.Y. **1902** *Encycl. Brit.* XXXII. 657/2 The Savage magazine rifle, model 1899, is a 'hammerless', lever-action repeating arm. **1903** *Kynoch Jrnl.* Feb.–Mar. 62/1, I had my ·301 Savage. [**1914** *Official Gaz.* (U.S. Patent Office) 18 Aug. 989/2 Savage Arms Company, Frankfort, N.Y. Filed Apr. 25, 1913... Particular description of goods.—Rifles, Pistols, and Cartridges. Claims use since Jan. 1. 1906.] **1964** H. L. PETERSON *Encycl. Firearms* 30/2 This system was later used by the Mexican Obregon pistol and in a slightly modified form by Savage pistols. **1968** *Globe & Mail* (Toronto) 17 Feb. 1/1 Police seized a battered, old ·303-calibre Savage hunting rifle.

savage ('sævɪdʒ), *v.* Also 6 **salvage.** [f. SAVAGE *a.*]

†**1.** *intr.* To act the savage; to indulge in cruel or barbarous deeds. *Obs. rare.*

1563 SACKVILLE *Mirr. Mag., Compl. Dk. Buckingham* xlix, My hart agryesd that such a wretche should raygne, Whose bluddy brest so salvaged out of kynde, That Phalaris had never so bluddy a minde. **1646** SIR T. BROWNE *Pseud. Ep.* VII. xix. 384 Though the blindnesse of some ferities have savaged on the dead, and beene so injurious unto wormes, as to disenterre the bodies of the deceased; yet had they therein no designe upon the soule.

2. *trans.* To render savage, barbarous, or fierce.

1611 SPEED *Hist. Gt. Brit.* IX. viii. (1623) 563 Dispositions not despicable, if they had not been sauaged with a too carelesse rudenesse. **1727-46** THOMSON *Summer* 1081 Dependants, friends, relations, Love himself, Savag'd by woe, forget the tender tie, The sweet engagement of the feeling heart. **1748** SMOLLETT *Rod. Rand.* xxii, I was so savaged by my wrongs that I delighted in the recital of this adventure. **1828** SOUTHEY *Epist., Anniv.* 13 Its bloodhounds savaged by a cross of wolf. **1899** *Contemp. Rev.* Dec. 882

They are extremely good-natured and mild-tempered dogs, unless carefully 'savaged' by their masters.

†**3.** To behave savagely to. *Obs.*

1796 CHARLOTTE SMITH *Marchmont* III. 146 She used to savage me so..that I shall never go near them any more.

4. Of an animal, *esp.* a horse: To attack with the teeth, bite. Also *transf.* and *fig.*

1880 W. DAY *Racehorse in Train* v. 38 In the stalls the bars should be put up between them, so that..they may be hindered kicking and savaging each other. **1891** N. GOULD *Double Event* 12 A dangerous horse had thrown Thurton to the ground, and was 'savaging' him. **1894** *Pall Mall G.* 1 Nov. 7/3 Alexander III was daily caricatured as a bear with an Imperial crown, who wished to savage the best of his subjects. **1896** W. C. F. MOLYNEUX *Campaigning in S. Afr. & Egypt* 173 [The horse] galloped about with rolling eyes, savaging every horse or man it could reach. **1923** *Public Opinion* 2 Sept. 103/2 Human lust and hatred has first savaged them to death. **1926** *Bulletin* 9 June 13 He is much too severe on the form of novels—the Cogglesby comedy in 'Evan' is savaged, for example. **1929** CHESTERTON *Poet & Lunatics* 107, I can no more see him savaging somebody like poor young Saunders than I can see him kicking a crippled child. **1962** I. MURDOCH *Unofficial Rose* xxxiv. 319 Once he stroked it [*sc.* a picture] absently, as he had done when it was his, and was savaged by an attendant. **1963** [see CUT *ppl. a.* 6]. **1977** *Time* 26 Dec. 36/1 Minnelli is only the latest in a long line of actresses savaged by Simon.

†**'savaged,** *a. Obs. rare.* [f. SAVAGE *sb.*[1] and *v.* + -ED.] Savage, barbarous, uncivilized; also, rendered savage or cruel.

1611 SPEED *Hist. Gt. Brit.* v. vii. §10. 42 Icones and Patternes of their first and most sauaged times. **1642** H. MORE *Song of Soul* III. App. xxxviii, Madnesse and stupor seize His salvag'd heart.

savagedom ('sævɪdʒdəm). [f. SAVAGE *a.* or *sb.*[1] + -DOM.] The condition of being a savage; the realm of savages, savage people collectively.

1845 E. WARBURTON *Crescent & Cross* I. 311 We had been already five weeks in Savagedom, among sands, and deserts, ..and..had had enough of it. **1889** JESSOPP *Coming of Friars* ii. 87 The people..goaded to frequent outbursts of ferocious savagedom by hunger. **1908** O. CRAWFURD in *19th Cent.* Jan. 63 In the early ages of savagedom this region was eagerly colonised by Rome.

savageism, variant of SAVAGISM.

savagely ('sævɪdʒlɪ), *adv.* [f. SAVAGE *a.* + -LY[2].] In a savage manner; †recklessly (*obs.*), cruelly, barbarously, fiercely.

a **1400** *Launfal* 130 So savagelych hys good he besette, That he ward yn greet dette, Ryght yn the ferst yere. **1563** WINȜET *Vincentius Lirin.* To Q. Marie, Wks. (S.T.S.) II. 7 Raigeing I say, nocht only aganis our mother the haly, catholik kirk, bot maist sauagelie aganis thame selfis. **1605** SHAKS. *Macb.* IV. iii. 205 Your Castle is surpriz'd: your Wife and Babes Sauagely slaughter'd. **1749** SMOLLETT tr. *Gil Blas* II. vii. (1782) I. 174 Mergellina being..withal so savagely virtuous that she could not so much as endure the look of a man. **1848** THACKERAY *Van. Fair* xiv, Captain Crawley looked savagely at the Lieutenant. **1891** KIPLING *Light that Failed* xiii. (1900) 223 He was savagely angry against Torpenhow.

savageness ('sævɪdʒnɪs). Also 7–8 **salv-**. [f. SAVAGE *a.* + -NESS.] The state or condition of being savage, uncivilized, barbarous, cruel, fierce.

α. **13..** *Sir Beues* 2363 (MS. S.), I haue herde of [*MS. N.* in] sauagenes, Whenne ȝonge men were in wyldernes, þat þey toke hert and hinde..; þey slowen hem and soden hem in her hide; þus doon men, þat in wood abyde. **1600** SURFLET *Country Farm* II. liv. 371 He [the vnruly bull] will become gentle, forgetting his naturall sauedgenes. **1604** SHAKS. *Oth.* IV. i. 200 She will sing the Sauagenesse out of a Beare. **1748** RICHARDSON *Clarissa* (1811) IV. xxxiv. 261 He kissed my hand with such a savageness, that a redness remains upon it still. **1866** GEO. ELIOT *F. Holt* ii, When the latent savageness of his nature was thoroughly roused.

β. **1660** F. BROOKE tr. *Le Blanc's Trav.* 353 Leaving them by reason of their salvagenesse. **1701** W. NICHOLS *Consol. to Parents* 8 A Salvageness and Ferity which the cruelest of Brutes are not subject to.

†**savagerous** ('sævɪdʒərəs, sə'vædʒərəs), *a. U.S. dial. Obs.* Also **sawagerous, servagerous, sevagerous.** [f. SAVAGE *a.* + DANG)EROUS *a.*] Fierce, wild, violent, dangerous. Also as quasi-*adv.*

1832 F. TROLLOPE *Dom. Manners Amer.* I. xiii. 186 The visitor took it [*sc.* a dagger] up, and examining it with much emotion, exclaimed, 'What! do you really jab this into yourself sevagarous?' **1837** R. M. BIRD *Nick of Woods* I. iv. 71 The strongest men in Kentucky, and the most sevagarous at a tussle. **1845** W. T. PORTER *Big Bear of Arkansas* 121 They war mighty savagerous arter likher. **1850** *Wilmington* (N. Carolina) *Commercial* 7 Mar. 1/6 Of all the untiring, unaccountable, and unspeakable 'Savagerous' rumpuses ever kicked up Cape Horn takes the banner. **1859** 'DOW, JR.' *New Patent Sermons* 263 A very sawagerous creature called the Youknowcan. **1866** C. H. SMITH *Bill Arp* 54 It [*sc.* Habeas Corpus] is, perhaps, *when suspended*, the most savagerous beast that ever got after tories and traitors. **1927** *Amer. Speech* II. 363/2 *Servagerous* (adj.), very active. 'That is a servagerous coon dog.'

savagery ('sævɪdʒrɪ, 'sævɪdʒə rɪ). [f. SAVAGE *a.* + -RY, after F. *sauvagerie.*]

1. The quality of being fierce or cruel; savage disposition, conduct, or actions; also with *a* and *pl.* a cruel action or deed.

1595 SHAKS. *John* IV. iii. 48 This is the bloodiest shame, The wildest Sauagery, the vildest stroke That euer wall-ey'd wrath..Presented to the teares of soft remorse. **1794** COLERIDGE *Relig. Musings* 182 In savagery of holy zeal. **1840** CARLYLE *Heroes* iv. (1841) 227 They err greatly who imagine that this man's courage was ferocity, mere coarse disobedient obstinacy and savagery, as many do. **1877** TENNYSON *Harold* II. ii. 210 Hast thou never heard His savagery at Alençon? **1883** BURTON & CAMERON *Gold Coast* I. iii. 75 We shall seldom see these savageries on the eastern coast of the island.

2. The condition of being wild or uncivilized; the characteristics of savages; the savage state of human society.

1825 COLERIDGE in *Lit. Rem.* (1836) II. 327 The progress from savagery to civilization is evidently first from the hunting to a pastoral state. **1864** R. F. BURTON *Dahome* I. 19 At certain hours the bugle-call from Santa Cecilia intimates that all about me is not savagery. **1865** DICKENS *Mut. Fr.* I. iii, There was a curious mixture in the boy, of uncompleted savagery, and uncompleted civilisation. **1870** LUBBOCK *Orig. Civiliz.* i. (1875) 3 A tribe which had sunk from civilisation into barbarism would by no means exhibit the same features, as one which had risen into barbarism from savagery. **1904** SIR R. RODD *Sir W. Raleigh* ii. 23 Ireland.. remained abandoned to the savagery of the primeval Celt.

3. Wildness, as of nature or scenery, etc.

1872 B. HARTE *Mrs. Skaggs's Husbands* 1, Except for the rudest purposes of shelter from rain and cold, the cabin possessed but little advantage over the simple savagery of surrounding nature. **1884** SALA *Journ. due South* I. vii. (1887) 97 The appearance of the rock-bound coast is one of unrelieved savagery.

4. *collect.* in occasional uses: †Wild vegetation (*obs.*); savage beasts or savages collectively.

1599 SHAKS. *Hen. V*, V. ii. 47 Her fallow Leas, The Darnell, Hemlock, and ranke Femetary, Doth root vpon; while that the Culter rusts, That should deracinate such Sauagery. **1867** JEAN INGELOW *Story of Doom* VI. 10 And had made A fire, to scare away the savagery That roamed in that great forest. **1896** R. S. S. BADEN-POWELL *Matabele Campaign* xviii. (1897) 464 That the white settlers were not entirely overwhelmed in the first mad, blood-thirsting rush of relentless savagery is a matter for marvel.

savagess ('sævɪdʒɪs). *rare.* [f. SAVAGE *sb.*[1] + -ESS[1]. Cf. F. *sauvagesse.*] A female savage.

1640 tr. *Verdere's Rom. of Rom.* I. vii. 24 The Empresse would needs visit the fair Savagesse. *Ibid.* xxxii. 143 Silvan and the fair Savagess his wife. **1858** THACKERAY *Virgin.* xl, The savage and savagess retired together.

†**savagine,** *a.* and *sb. Obs. rare.* Also **-yne.** [a. F. *sauvagin*, f. *sauvage* SAVAGE *a.* Cf. Sp. *salvagina*, Pg. *selvagina*, *salvagina*, It. *selvaggina*, *salvaggina* venison, game.]

A. *adj.* Savage, wild.

c **1430** LYDG. *Min. Poems* (Percy Soc.) 246 Savagyne, voyd of al resoun. **1430–40** —— *Bochas* II. xvi. (1494) h ij, Of the forests the bestes sauagyne.

B. *sb.* A savage.

a **1400–50** *Alexander* 3914 Þai..Sloȝe of þa sauagyns [*printed* -yus] a sowme out of nombre.

†**savagious,** *a. Obs. rare.* [f. SAVAGE *a.* + -IOUS.] Savage. Hence †**savagiously** *adv.*

1650 HOWELL *Giraffi's Rev. Naples* I. 51 So they sent for Doctor Iulio Genovino a most savagious man. **1632** LITHGOW *Trav.* VI. 296 The people generally are..as sauagiously tame (I protest) as the foure footed Citizens of Lybia.

savagism ('sævɪdʒɪz(ə)m). Also **savageism.** [f. SAVAGE *a.* + -ISM.] = SAVAGERY 2.

1796 W. TAYLOR in *Monthly Mag.* II. 465 Virtues..could alone keep the world from that relapse into savagism to which mankind is ever tending. **1798** A. P. *Tour in Wales* 30 (MS.) We began to omit clambering among..ruins, merely for the assurance of Superstition and Savageism having existed when these terror striking fabrics were erected. **1841** MARY HENNELL in C. Bray *Philos. Necess.* II. 616 Fourier.. divides the history of humanity into four forms or periods, incoherently social—savagism, patriarchalism, barbarism and civilization. **1877** SPARROW *Serm.* xiii. 175 There are various kinds of life..there is that of youth and age, of ignorance and knowledge, of civilization and savageism, with numerous subdivisions under each.

savagize ('sævɪdʒaɪz), *v. rare.* [f. SAVAGE *a.* + -IZE.] *trans.* To render savage or cruel.

1848 *Tait's Mag.* XV. 140 Earnshaw has been allowed to grow up on the farm, a man savageized. **1864** GILFILLAN in *Mem.* (1892) 349 It was but natural that a man, who when he was close on middle-age had still his reputation and fortune to make [etc.],..should be soured and half savagised.

SAVAK ('sævæk, ‖'savak). [Acronym f. the initial letters of Persian *Sāzmān-i-Attalāt Va Amniyat-i-Keshvar* National Security and Intelligence Organization.] The secret intelligence organization of Iran, established in 1957 and disbanded in 1979.

1967 *Time* 6 Oct. 47/2 All candidates must be approved by SAVAK, his powerful security police. **1975** *New Yorker* 8 Dec. 128/2 They speak matter-of-factly of a conspiracy that includes the C.I.A. and SAVAK (the Iranian secret police) and the Sheriff of Cole County. **1976** *Maclean's Mag.* 17 May 41/3 This is a police state ruled over by one of the most ruthless secret police forces in the world, the dread SAVAK. **1977** *Time* 28 Nov. 36/2 Documented charges by both Amnesty International and the International Red Cross that Iran's secret police organization, SAVAK, had systematically persecuted dissidents. **1979** M. MCCARTHY *Cannibals & Missionaries* i. 18 SAVAK, the Shah's secret police, would scarcely have the same sociable attitude as the New York State wardens and guards. **1981** *Times* 13 Aug. 2/2 A former member of Savak, the Shah of Iran's secret police, killed himself..after being told he was to be deported back home.

‖**'savalo.** *Obs. rare*[−1]. [Sp., now written *sábalo*: see SABALO.] The shad. Only *attrib.*

1622 MABBE tr. *Aleman's Guzman d'Alf.* II. 115 Your Savalo-pyes for the holy weeke.

savan: see SAVANT.

savannah (sə'vænə). Forms: 6 **zavana,** 7 **savanar, savanah,** *pl.* **savanæ,** 7–8, 20 **savana,** 7– **savanna, savannah.** [In 16th c. *zavana*, a. Sp. *zavana*, *çavana*, given by Oviedo 1535 as a Carib word. The later form *savana* (mod. Sp. *sabana*) is an instance of the usual N. American Sp. substitution of *s* for *z*. Cf. F. *savane*, G. *savanne*.

The Sp. *sabána* savanna is not, as has been supposed, the same as *sábana* sheet. The difference in accent is shown by verse examples to have existed already in the 16th c.; and the words originally began with different consonants.]

1. a. A treeless plain; *properly*, one of those found in various parts of tropical America. In mod. use, an open plain of long grass, freq. with scattered drought-resistant trees, such as is characteristic of certain tropical and subtropical regions having distinct wet and dry seasons; grassland or vegetation of this kind.

1555 EDEN *Decades* III. iii. (Arb.) 148 Hauynge towarde the southe a playne of twelue leages in breadth and veary frutefull. This playne, they caule *Zauana*. **1604** E. G[RIMSTONE] *D'Acosta's Hist. Indies* IV. xxx. 291 The plaines, which they call *Savanas*. **1655** I. S. *Brief Jrnl. Proc. Army W. Indies* 18 Open ground and plaine Fields, or Savanars as they there call them. **1661** HICKERINGILL *Jamaica* 13 Nor are the Woods a more plentiful Nursery for the Hoggs then the *Savana's* are for the Beeves and wild Cattel. **1672** SIR W. TALBOT *Discov. John Lederer* 25 The Woods being full of Fallow, and Savanæ of Red-Deer. **1697** DAMPIER *Voy.* I. 87 In the Bay of Campeachy are very large Savanahs, which I have seen full of Cattle. **1699** *Ibid.* II. II. 53 The neighbouring Savannahs. **1719** DE FOE *Crusoe* I. 115 On the Bank of this Brook I found many pleasant Savana's, or Meadows, plain, smooth, and cover'd with Grass. **1753** WASHINGTON *Jrnl.* Writ. 1889 I. 17 He told me that the nearest and levellest Way was now impassable, by Reason of many large mirey Savannas. **1756** P. BROWNE *Jamaica* 11 The more extended plains are commonly called Savanas. **1819** BOWDICH, etc. *Mission to Ashantee* II. xiii. 448 The red and yellow ochres brought to me, were dug in the neighbourhood of a savannah three journies south-eastward of Empoöngwa. **1826** SCOTT *Woodst.* v, Glades..anon opening yet wider into little meadows, or savannahs. **1836** N. ISAACS *Trav. & Adventures E. Afr.* I. vi. 88 This we did for the purpose of calling at some hamlets and savannas, in our course, to obtain cattle and curiosities. **1865** PARKMAN *Huguenots* iv. (1875) 57 Next came the broad sunlight and the wide savanna. **1900** DOYLE *Gt. Boer War* xiv. 235 Between these hills there lie wide stretches of the green or russet savannah. **1903** W. R. FISHER tr. *Schimper's Plant-Geogr.* 261 Tropical grassland, wherever it has not been modified by human agency, occurs chiefly as savannah, more rarely as steppe. **1920** M. E. HARDY *Geogr. of Plants* iii. 142 The treeless savana is called 'campo vero';..if the savanas are strewn with clumps of low trees, they are 'serrados'. **1926** D. H. CAMPBELL *Outl. Plant Geogr.* viii. 292 The outstanding feature of this savanna was a noble fan-palm..which formed groves of considerable extent. **1955** *Times* 28 May 7/6 The Rupununi river flows almost due north through Southern British Guiana. On either side are the wide open savannahs, broken only here and there by small clumps of stunted sandpaper bushes and groups of anthills. **1957** P. DANSEREAU *Biogeogr.* ii. 73 The somewhat drier types [of climate]..show a very uneven distribution of rainfall and generally support woodland or savana. **1958** L. VAN DER POST *Lost World of Kalahari* vii. 123, I met a man ..walking out of the bush into a long savannah of buffalo grass. **1968** R. W. FAIRBRIDGE *Encycl. Geomorphol.* 979/2 Savanna passes in drier regions to steppe or desert, and in wetter areas into savanna woodland. **1969** S. M. SADEEK *Windswept & Other Stories* 29 The cart rolled on..into the savannah of sagebush and beezie-beezie reeds and razor-grass. **1974** H. F. GARNER *Origin of Landscapes* v. 267/2 The small forest areas on savannahs differ botanically in no great measure from more continuous rain forest elsewhere. **1976** WEST & AUGELLI *Middle Amer.* (ed. 2) ii. 47/1 One of the most puzzling features of the natural vegetation in the tropical rainy areas of Middle America is the presence of large expanses of grassland, called 'savannas', in areas that receive as much as 80 to 100 inches of rain annually, with no dry period or a quite short one... The largest of the humid savannas is found along the Caribbean margin of Nicaragua and northeastern Honduras.

fig. **1866** *N. & Q.* Ser. III. IX. 273/1 The allusions..so profusely scattered through the vast savannahs of literature. **1893** F. THOMPSON *Poems* 49 Whether they swept, smoothly fleet, The long savannahs of the blue.

b. *spec.* In the West Indies and Guyana, a particular tract of such land within definable limits; a meadow, a paddock.

1934 J. RHYS *Voyage in Dark* I. i. 4 When the black women sell fishcakes on the savannah they carry them in trays on their heads. **1952** S. SELVON *Brighter Sun* i. 13 Opposite the school was a large savannah on which cattle and donkeys grazed. **1960** *Tamarack Rev.* XIV. 48 Mittelholzer..took a walk every evening about five or six around the Port-of-Spain savannah. **1964** S. M. SADEEK *Windswept & Other Stories* (1969) 19 You don't have to go galavanting the settlements and savannahs like some coot.

2. (See quots.)

1827 O. W. ROBERTS *Voy. Centr. Amer.* 113 Close to an extensive and beautiful pine savannah. *Ibid.* 114, I had a long walk into the savannah, which is pretty closely covered with detached clumps of pine trees of all ages and sizes. **1865** *Reader* 23 Sept. 236/3 The army has been moving through magnificent pine-woods—the savannahs of the South, as they are termed.

3. *U.S.* A tract of low-lying damp or marshy ground.

1671 in *S. Carolina Hist. Soc. Coll.* (1897) V. 333 You will finde..great Creeks, mar[s]hes, or Savanoes on the other side. **1737** J. Wesley *Jrnl.* 2 Dec. (1910) I. 401 There is a little [soil] of a better kind, especially in the savannahs,..so they call the low, watery meadows, which are usually intermixed with pine-lands. **1895** *Dialect Notes* I. 380 *Savannah*, stretch of bog or moorland. **1905** *Bull. Bureau of Forestry* (U.S. Dept. Agric.) No. 64. 7 Loblolly is the first pine to take possession of the savannas, or marshy pairies. **1938** J. R. Carpenter *Ecol. Gloss.* 236 *Savannah*, a tract of damp level land with a growth of grass or reeds (S[outhern] U.S.).

4. *attrib.* **a.** simple attrib.

1697 Dampier *Voy.* I. 50 Plain even Savanah Land, without any Trees. **1719** De Foe *Crusoe* I. (Globe) 110, The open or Savana Fields. **1844** Mrs. Browning *Sonn.*, '*O Dreary Life*' 7 Savannah-swards Unweary sweep. **1867** Latham *Black & White* 118 'Savanna land', meaning wet land.

b. In the names of birds, plants, etc.: **savannah bird, blackbird**, the *Crotophaga ani* of the West Indies; †**savannah crane**, ? the Whooping Crane, *Grus americana*; †**savannah finch**, the grasshopper-sparrow of the U.S., *Coturniculus passerinus*; **savannah flower**, 'a West Indian name for various species of *Echites*' (Treas. Bot. 1866); **savannah fox** (see quot.); **savannah sparrow**, a sparrow of the genus *Passerculus*, esp. *P. savanna*, common throughout the greater part of North America; **savannah-wattle**, the West Indian trees *Citharexylum quadrangulare* and *C. cinereum*; †**savannah woodcock**, Latham's name for *Gallinago undulata*.

1694 Ray in *Lett. Lit. Men* (Camden) 200 In referring the *Savanna bird to the Lark-kind. **1725** Sloane *Jamaica* II. 306 The Savanna Bird..is four Inches long [etc.]. **1862** Wood *Illustr. Nat. Hist.* II. 569 The food of the *Savannah Blackbird is mostly of an animal nature. **1791** W. Bartram *Carolina* 220 Amongst other game, they brought with them a *savanna crane which they shot in the adjoining meadows. **1783** Latham *Synopsis Birds* III. 270 *Savanna Finch. **1696** Sloane *Catal. Plant. Jamaica* 89 *Savanna Flour. **1756** P. Browne *Jamaica* 182 The Savanna Flower. This plant is common in the Savannas about Kingston. **1852** G. W. Johnson *Cottage Gard. Dict.* 350 *Echites suberecta* (..Savannah flower). **1879** Wood *Waterton's Wanderings* 412 Fox (*Vulpes cancrivora*).—This animal is generally called *Savannah Fox by the colonists, and Mikang by the natives. **1808–13** A. Wilson *Amer. Ornith.* (1831) II. 249 *Fringilla savanna*, Wilson.—*Savannah sparrow. *Ibid.*, The female of the Savannah sparrow is five inches and a half long. **1864** Grisebach *Flora W. Ind. Islands* 787 *Savannah-wattle. **1785** Latham *Synopsis Birds* V. 132 *Savanna Woodcock.

c. Special Combs.: **savannah forest, woodland**, grassland similar to savannah but with a denser growth of trees, though not enough to provide continuous cover; **savannah grass**, a stoloniferous carpet grass, *Axonopus compressus*, native to tropical and subtropical America.

1903 W. R. Fisher tr. *Schimper's Plant-Geogr.* 260 The *Savannah-forest..is more or less leafless during the dry season, rarely evergreen, is xerophilous in character, usually, often much, less than twenty meters high, park-like, very poor in underwood, lianes, and epiphytes, rich in terrestrial herbs, especially in grasses. **1958** G. Lienhardt in Middleton & Tait *Tribes without Rulers* 99 Boundaries between different political communities are often not apparent to the eye in such savannah-forest areas. **1756** P. Browne *Civil & Nat. Hist. Jamaica* 137 The small *Savannah Grass with echinated valves..grows in the Savanna about Kingston. **1859** G. W. Perry *Turpentine Farming* 9 Every kind of turf should be turned over, such as ..wire grass, savanna grass, and broom-sage grass. **1954** *Farmer's Guide* (Jamaica Agric. Soc.) 232 Savannah Grass —Carpet Grass (*Axonopus compressus*)... In the West Indies it is an important pasture grass. **1970** A. T. Semple *Grassland Improvement* viii. 177 In Malaya, fertilizer trials with savanna grass..showed a marked response. **1976** P. D. Driscoll *Barboza Credentials* v. iv. 233 A parade-ground, now overgrown with savanna grass. **1903** W. R. Fisher tr. *Schimper's Plant-Geogr.* 836/2 (Index), *Savannah woodland. **1960** N. Polunin *Introd. Plant Geogr.* xiv. 442 Savanna-woodland..is found very widely in tropical and subtropical regions including much of Cuba and elsewhere in the Caribbean, Brazil and northern Argentina, East and central Africa.., and occupying much of India and China as well as of northern and eastern Australia. **1968** Savannah woodland [see sense 1].

‖**savant** (savɑ̃). Also †sçavant, savan. [Fr.; subst. use of *savant* adj., orig. pr. pple. (synon. with *sachant*, now the only form in this use) of *savoir* to know:—popular L. **sapēre* = class. L. *sapĕre* to be wise: cf. sapient.

The misapprehension of the obs. Fr. spelling *savans* of the plural has given rise in Eng. to the incorrect form *savan*.]

A man of learning or science; esp. one professionally engaged in learned or scientific research.

1719 F. Hauksbee *Phys. Mech. Exper.* v. 225 [He] made a Report thereof to the Royal Academy of Sciences of France; and, upon his return home, those Scavans thought it worth their while to re-examine the matter. **1750** Chesterf. *Let. to Son* 24 May, At Paris..you will find a cargo of letters, to very different sorts of people, as *beaux esprits, sçavants, et belles dames*. **1765** H. Walpole *Let. to G. Montagu* 22 Sept., I dined to-day with a dozen *savans*. **1805** *Edin. Rev.* VII. 232 On one of these occasions, the *savants* in waiting were Quintus Icilius and Thiebault. **1848** E. FitzGerald *Lett.* (1889) I. 189, I saw Alfred [Tennyson], and the rest of the sçavans. **1864** *Chamb. Encycl.* s.v. *Manzoni*, His mother [being] the gifted daughter of the great savan, the Marquis Beccaria. **1874** Sidgwick *Meth. Ethics* III. v. 263 How shall we compare..the service of the *savant* who discovers a new principle with that of the inventor who applies it?

‖**savante** (savɑ̃t). [Fr., fem. of *savant*: see savant.] A learned (French) woman.

1766 H. Walpole *Let. to Gray* 25 Jan., Madame de Rochfort is different... Her manner is soft and feminine, and though a *savante*, without any declared pretensions. **1813** Byron in Moore *Lett. & Jrnls.* (1830) I. 457 Annabella ..is..an only child, and a *savante*, who has always had her own way. **1844** Marg. Fuller *Woman in 19th Cent.* (1862) 57 There is on her no hue of the philosopher, the heroine, the *savante*, but she looks great and noble.

savar, obs. Sc. form of savour.

‖**savarin** (savarɛ̃). [f. the name of Anthelme Brillat-*Savarin* (1755–1826), French gastronome.] A light, ring-shaped cake made with yeast, soaked in syrup flavoured with liqueur, and served with fruit and cream. Also *attrib.*

1877 E. S. Dallas *Kettner's Bk. of Table* 402 Little has been said about the Bath bun, the Banbury cake, the Scotch shortbread, the Brioche, the Baba, the Savarin, the Gauffre. **1894** G. du Maurier *Trilby* I. ii. 127 The cakes were of three kinds—Babas, Madeleines, and Savarins... The Savarin..is shaped like a ring, very light, and flavoured with rum. **1928** J. Rhys *Postures* xviii. 180 A savarin, an éclair, two meringues—the ones you like, and I've ordered tea. **1943** A. L. Simon *Conc. Encycl. Gastron.* IV. 115/1 Savarin paste. **1958** [see baba[2]]. **1963** R. Carrier *Great Dishes of World* xv. 252 The *savarin* cake mixture..is the basis of rum baba as well as many other famous sweets. *Ibid.* 253 Butter a deep cake tin or savarin mould and half-fill it with dough. **1969** *Daily Tel.* 12 Nov. 15/6 A hinged cake-tin with two interchangeable bases, one for deep sponges, the other—fluted, with a funnel—for savarins.

‖**savate** (savat). [Fr.; lit. a kind of shoe: see sabaton.] A method of fighting (commonly employed instead of or in conjunction with boxing) in which the feet are used. Also *Comb.*, as ***savate kick***. Hence ‖**savateur** (savatœr), one who is skilled in the savate.

1862 Wraxall *Hugo's Miserables* cxxx. II. 79 The Parisian gamin..is clever at the savate, and all creeds are possible to him. **1889** E. B. Michell *Boxing* (Badm. Libr.) 132 While the practice of the *Savate*, in which the feet as well as the hands are used, was growing up in France, an exactly similar style of boxing was being separately developed in the remote countries between India and China. **1898** *Daily News* 25 Oct. 8/5 This mixture of savate with a sort of elementary boxing would appear to be only effective when both parties use it. **1899** *Ibid.* 30 Oct. 6/6 Charlemont, the French savateur. **1969** J. Fredman *Fourth Agency* xi. 104 He came at me in a crouching horizontal leap and dealt me a great big savate kick. **1975** P. Audemars *Nightmare in Rust* xi. 157 He..launched a tremendous *savate* kick at the base of the old man's spine.

savation (seɪˈveɪʃən). *dial.* (see E.D.D.). [f. save *v.* + -ation. Cf. *savacion*, obs. f. salvation.] A saving (of money).

1724 Macky *Journ. thr. Engl.* (ed. 2) II. xii. 181 Which (to use that Country People's Word) was a great Savation of Money to my Lord Duke.

†**save**, *sb.*[1] *Obs.* [ad. L. *salvia* sage *sb.*[1], whence OE. *saluie*; assimilated to save *v.*] Sage.

c **1386** Chaucer *Knt.'s T.* 1855 Fermacies of herbes, and eek saue They dronken, for they wolde hir limes haue. ? *a* **1450** *Pol. Rel. & Love Poems* 287 So þat he drynke save or anteoche.

save (seɪv), *sb.*[2] [f. save *v.*]

1. An act of saving; a piece of economy. *dial.* and *vulgar*. (See E.D.D.)

1906 *Daily Chron.* 9 Feb. 4/4 The fact is, apart from..the save in gas and firing,..when the year's finished I've calculated I shall make a profit on it.

2. *Football, Hockey*, etc. An act of preventing the opposite side from scoring. Now usu. such an action performed by the goal-keeper.

1890 *Field* 1 Nov. 670/1 Coventry [a half-back] came to the rescue with a plucky save. **1892** *Pall Mall G.* 1 Mar. 2/1 Gay, in goal, made no mistake and several excellent saves. **1942** *Sun* (Baltimore) 26 Jan. 4/1 Gil Schuerholz..made astounding saves all afternoon. **1954** *Encounter* Feb. 58/2 The highlights of a [football] game, a spectacular save, a beautiful evasive run..become evocative images. **1960** B. Liddell *My Soccer Story* x. 68 One save of Bert's..was of the truly miraculous type... The ball..sped like a bullet towards the left-hand corner..but with a marvellous leap.. Bert turned it over the bar. **1977** *News of World* 17 Apr. 23/4 Arsenal lost the match the precise second that Liverpool's England goalkeeper Ray Clemence made a world-class save from Frank Stapleton.

3. *Bridge.* = sacrifice *sb.* 5 d. Freq. in phr. ***cheap save***.

1927 *Observer* 31 July 14/5 Now consider the position if Z had doubled 'Six Hearts' instead of going on with Spades.. which would have saved the game and rubber. A cheap save and well worth while! **1928** A. E. M. Foster *Auction Bridge* IV. 200 (*heading*) A good save on majority bidding. **1974** *Country Life* 3 Oct. 975/3 A hand from a recent session... Trying for a cheap save.

save (seɪv), *v.* Forms: *α.* 3–5 (6 *Sc.*) salve; *Sc.* 5–6 sa(u)lf(f, 6 salfe, salffe. *β.* 3–5 sauve; also (chiefly *north.* and *Sc.*) 3–6 sauf(e, 4–5 sawf(e, sawff, 4–6 sauff. *γ.* 4 *Kent.* sove (sovi, sovy). *δ.* 3– save; also (chiefly *north.* and *Sc.*) 4–6 saw(e, 4–5 saf(e, 4–6 saff(e; *Sc.* 5–6 saif(f, (6 saaf). [a. OF. *salver, sauver* (= Pr., Sp., Pg. *salvar*, It. *salvare*):—late L. *salvāre* to save, f. L. *salv-us* safe.]

I. To rescue or protect.

1. *trans.* To deliver or rescue from peril or hurt; to make safe, put in safety. Const. *from*, †*out of*.

a. a living being.

c **1250** *Kent. Serm.* in *O.E. Misc.* 32 Lord saue us for we perisset. **13..** *Guy Warw.* 7226 God..þat..heldest Daniel fram þe lyoun, Saue me fram þis foule dragoun. *c* **1375** *Sc. Leg. Saints* xxxiii. (*George*) 116 To saf his douchtir fra þat wrak. *c* **1470** *Gol. & Gaw.* 1099 Thus may thow saif me fra syte. *a* **1533** Ld. Berners *Huon* xc. 284 He that alwayes hath saued me out of all perelles wyll not forsake me at this tyme. *a* **1578** Lindesay (Pitscottie) *Chron. Scot.* (S.T.S.) II. 55 Gif ȝe..salve his servandis ffre the daith so far as ȝe may. **1591** Shaks. *Two Gent.* IV. iv. 3 One that I sau'd from drowning. **1692** R. L'Estrange *Fables* ix. 9 Save a Thiefe from the Gallows, and he'll Cut your Throat. **1719** De Foe *Crusoe* I. (Globe) 63 Did not you come Eleven of you into the Boat, where are the Ten? Why were not they sav'd and you lost? **1848** Thackeray *Van. Fair* xxxii, She fell on her knees, and thanked the Power which had saved her husband. **1852** Mrs. Stowe *Uncle Tom's C.* vii, 'O Mr. Symmes!—save me —do save me—do hide me!' said Eliza.

b. one's life (similarly, one's body, carcass, head, neck, etc.). ***to save one's skin***, to escape unhurt. ***to save one's bacon***: see bacon *sb.* 5 a. Also used colloq. in *fig.* phr. ***to save*** (someone's) ***life***, to give timely assistance, esp. a stimulating drink.

1297 R. Glouc. (Rolls) 9231 So þat to saui is lif þe castel vp hii ȝolde. **13..** *K. Alis.* 3811 He lefte his pray, and fleygh to hors, For to save his owne cors. **1470** Henry *Wallace* II. 271 His fostyr modyr..Did mylk to warme, his liff giff scho mycht saiff. *a* **1533** Ld. Berners *Huon* lxvii. 230 He besought our lorde god to saue his body fro mysfortune. *c* **1570** W. Wager *The longer thou livest* 477 (Brandl), Neither mockes nor gaudes shall your skinne saue. **1611** Shaks. *Cymb.* v. iii. 67 To day, how many would haue giuen their Honours To haue sau'd their Carkasses? **1685** [see neck *sb.*[1] 3 d]. **1803** *Med. Jrnl.* IX. 458 A great many lives were saved by the salutary practice of inoculation. **1855** Macaulay *Hist. Eng.* xxi. IV. 544 To have done all in his power to save both the head of Stafford and the head of Russell. **1896** A. E. Housman *Shropshire Lad* xlvii, See my neck and save your own. **1914** [see gesundheit]. **1938** E. Waugh *Scoop* I. ii. 14 God bless you, Julia. You've saved my life. **1950** 'J. Tey' *To love & be Wise* xii. 153 Saved my life, you have! I missed the bus. **1955** M. Allingham *Beckoning Lady* iv. 62 Tea, darling? Bless you, you're saving my life. **1977** D. Bagley *Enemy* xxviii. 218 'A sherry,' she said. 'A sherry, to save my life.'

c. a people, state, city.

c **1375** *Sc. Leg. Saints* xxxiii. (*George*) 106 His douchtir.. to þe dragone suld be gyffine, to sauff þe ton. **1474** Caxton *Chesse* II. v. (1883) 59 He shold employe alle his entente to saue the comyn wele. **1533** Bellenden *Livy* I. v. (S.T.S.) I. 34 My citee was sauffit be þi helpe. **1607** Shaks. *Cor.* v. iii. 133 If it were so, that our request did tend To saue the Romanes, thereby to destroy The Volces whom you serue. **1728** Pope *Dunc.* I. 197 Could Troy be sav'd by any single hand. **1852** Tennyson *Ode on Wellington* 200 Yea, let all good things await Him who cares not to be great, But as he saves or serves the state. **1894** J. T. Fowler *Adamnan* Introd. p. xxi, The Bards were saved, but reformed.

d. To rescue (property) from shipwreck, fire, etc.

1582 N. Lichefield tr. *Castanheda's Conq. E. Ind.* I. xli. 95 There was kindled in the same [ship] a great fire, so that nothing was saued, but onely the men. **1591** Shaks. *Two Gent.* I. i. 156 Go, go, be gone, to saue your Ship from wrack. **1615** R. Cocks *Diary* (Hakl. Soc.) I. 73 The fyre was so vehement that littell or nothing was saved. **1787** Park *Mar. Insurances* 141 Whereas the circumstance of the lighters being saved, and the ship lost, was accidental. **1878** Mrs. Hungerford *Molly Bawn* xxxviii, I saved them [*sc.* diamonds] from the fire.., and have had them re-set.

e. *absol.*

1560 Bible (Geneva) *Isa.* lix. 1 The Lords hand is not shortened, that it can not saue. **1593** Shaks. *Rich. II*, II. ii. 80 Your husband he is gone to saue farre off, Whilst others come to make him loose at home. **1732** Pope *Ess. Man* II. 201 The same ambition can destroy or save. **1781** Cowper *Charity* 226 Oh, 'tis a godlike privilege to save! **1860** W. Whiting *Hymn*, Eternal Father, strong to save.

f. Hyperbolically in trivial use, as ***to save*** (one's) ***life*** (or occas. ***soul***): usu. following statement in negative, denoting lack of ability or intention to do something.

1848 Trollope *Kellys & O'Kellys* III. v. 106, I shan't remain long. If it was to save my life and theirs, I can't get up small talk for the rector and his curate. **1873** C. M. Yonge *Pillars of House* III. xxvii. 88 'Does she go to their church?' 'Oh no, she wouldn't to save her life—she thinks it quite shocking.' **1893** Yonge & Coleridge *Strolling Players* iii. 21, I couldn't act to save my life. **1916** A. Bennett *These Twain* III. xix. 436 'What will you have to eat?' said Maggie. 'Nothing. I couldn't eat to save my life.' **1920** E. O'Neill *Beyond Horizon* III. i. 128, I couldn't get to sleep to save my soul. **1941** J. Cary *Herself Surprised* xxxiv. 82 It took even Bill six months to get her into a motor, when motors came in, and she wouldn't telephone now to save her life. **1973** E. Berckman *Victorian Album* 192 She must have..dressed in record time, but to save my life I couldn't tell you how she looked or what she had on.

2. *Theol.* To deliver (a person, the soul) from sin and its consequences; to admit to eternal bliss. [Gr. σῴζειν, L. (Vulg.) *salvum facere, salvare, salvificare*.]

a **1225** *Leg. Kath.* 1025 Monnes unmihte; þet he neodeles nom upon him seoluen, us for to saluin. **1340** *Ayenb.* 98 Godes zone þet com to þe wordle to zeche an to souy þet þet wes uorlore. **1362** Langl. *P. Pl.* A. I. 82 Tech me..Hou I may saue my soule. 1382 Wyclif *Mark* xvi. 16 He that schal bileue, and schal be baptisid, schal be sauyd [*v.r.* saaf]; sothli he that schal bileue not, schal be dampned. [So 1535 Coverdale, 1611.] —— *James* i. 21 In myldenesse receyue ȝe the word insent, that mai saue ȝoure soules. [So in later versions.] *c* 1449 Pecock *Repr.* II. xviii. 261 If it be seid ..'The crosse of Crist saued the world..', the dewe vndirstonding ther of is this: 'Crist bi his crosse..saued the world'. *a* 1500–34 *Coventry Corpus Chr. Plays, Shearmen* 546 A seyd there schuld a babe be borne,..To sawe mankynd that wasse for-lorne. 1526 *Pilgr. Perf.* (W. de W. 1531) 20 b, I am passed my purgatory, and I am saued. 1549 Latimer *6th Serm. bef. Edw. VI* (Arb.) 166 We can not be saued wythout fayeth, and fayth commeth by heryng of the worde. 1601 Shaks. *Twel. N.* III. ii. 75 For there is no christian that meanes to be saued by beleeuing rightly, can euer beleeue such impossible passages of grossenesse. 1666 Bunyan *Grace Abound.* §202, I was again much under this Question, Whether the Blood of Christ was sufficient to save my Soul? 1786 Burns *For G. H. Esq.* 4 But with such as he, where'er he be, May I be sav'd or d——'d. *c* 1830 Moore *Epitaph on Tuft Hunter* 20 He'd rather be Genteelly damn'd beside a Duke Than sav'd in vulgar company. 1840 Carlyle *Heroes* iv, Luther learned now that a man was saved not by singing masses, but by the infinite grace of God. 1893 F. Thompson *Poems* 61 There is no expeditious road To pack and label men for God, And save them by the barrel-load.

absol. *a* 1340 Hampole *Psalter* xiii. 1 Þat is, þare is na god þat dampnnes or safes. 1858 Arnot *Laws fr. Heaven* Ser. II. xiii. 101 It is grace accepted that saves.

b. in asseverative phrases, ***as I hope to be saved***, † ***so God*** (or ***Christ***) ***save me***, etc.

c 1386 Chaucer *Can. Yeom. Prol.* & *T.* 808 Ye shul paye fourty pound, so god me saue. *c* 1450 Holland *Howlat* 120 So me Crist saif. *c* 1530 Ld. Berners *Arth. Lyt. Bryt.* 300 As I be saved, ye be ful gentil and noble. 1710 Swift *Jrnl. to Stella* 23 Dec., Remember poor Presto, that wants you sadly, as hope saved. 1711 *Ibid.* 30 June. 1749 Fielding *Tom Jones* VIII. xi, As I hope to be saved, I will never mention a word of it.

c. *transf.* To reclaim from moral laxity, or the like; to be the 'salvation' of.

1894 Sir E. Sullivan *Woman* 98 How often you hear it said that marriage has improved a man—that it has saved him!

3. Used in certain formulas of benediction, greeting, etc.; as ***God save you!*** †Also (in greetings) with omission of the subject.

(*God*) ***save the mark***: see MARK *sb.*[1] 18.

c 1330 *Arth. & Merl.* 7034 (Kölbing) Wele yfounden, child Wawayn, Crist saue þi miȝt & þi mayn. *c* 1386 Chaucer *Knt.'s T.* 2250 God saue al this faire compaignye. Amen. 1530 Palsgr. 698/1 God save you, whiche sayeng we use whan we come firste to ones presence. 1591 Shaks. *Two Gent.* I. i. 70 Sir Protheus: 'saue you: saw you my Master? 1632 Massinger *City Madam* IV. iv, *Luke.* Then, as I said ..you were tickl'd when the beggars cry'd, Heaven save your honour. 1706 Farquhar *Recruit. Officer* III. ii, Save ye, save ye, Gentlemen. 1888 Lowell *Heartsease & Rue* 178, I have seen him some poor ancient thrashing Into something (God save us!) more dry.

b. *esp.* in ***God save the king!*** and the like.

c 1290 *Beket* 755 in *S. Eng. Leg.* I. 128 Sire king, he seide, god þe loke, and saui þi dignite! 1340–70 *Alex. & Dind.* 811 Þus dindimus þe dere king enditeþ his sonde, & god bysecheþ to saue þe soueraine prinse. 1350–70 in *Eulogium Hist.* (Rolls) III. 87 *Regem* [*Henricum II*] *Theutonica lingua sic affatur*: Godde saue the kyng. [In *Giraldus* (Rolls) VIII. 180 God houlde dhe, cuning.] 1535 Coverdale *2 Sam.* xvi. 16 He sayde vnto Absalom: God saue the kynge. 1540 Palsgr. *Acolastus* II. iii. Mj b, *Aue rex*, or god saue your royall maiestie. 1558 *Procl.* in Strype *Ann. Ref.* (1709) I. II. App. i. 389 God save the quene. *a* 1627 Sir J. Beaumont *Bosw.-field* (1629) 9 Some with loud shouting, make the valleyes ring, But most with murmur sigh: God saue the King.

†4. To spare instead of killing, allow to live, give (one) his life. Often coupled with *slay*. *Obs.*

a 1300 *Cursor M.* 5549 Þis midwimmen..did noght als þe king þam badd, Bot sauued þai þar childer liues. *c* 1385 Chaucer *L.G.W.* 1917 So that the site was al at his wille, To sauyn hem hym leste or ellis spille. 1470 Henry *Wallace* IV. 256 Wallace commaundede thai suld na wermen saiff. 1474 Caxton *Chesse* II. iv. (1883) 52 Whan he sauyth the lyf of them that he may slee. 1549 *Compl. Scot.* xii. 100, I ordand ȝou to slay doune al the romans, and nocht to saif ane of them. 1588 Lambarde *Eiren.* IV. xvi. 586 To saue or slay the Sparow that he holdeth closed in his hand. 1593 Shaks. *2 Hen. VI*, IV. vii. 124 And therefore yet relent, and saue my life. 1642 *Laws of War Army Earl Essex* 20 None shall save a man that hath his offensive Armes in his hands, upon paine of losing his prisoner.

absol. *c* 1386 Chaucer *Prol.* 663 For curs wol slee, right as assoillyng sauith. 1390 Gower *Conf.* III. 207 Where him hapneth the victoire, His lust and al his moste gloire Was forto sle and noght to save.

5. To deliver *from* some evil which is likely to befall one; to protect from something which would be unwelcome or untoward; to ensure (one) immunity from some hurt or annoyance.

a 1300 *Cursor M.* 2985 Fra toche of hir i saued þe, þat þou suld not sin in me. 1362 Langl. *P. Pl.* A. I. 23 Þat on Clothing is from Chele ow to saue. *c* 1450 Myrc *Festial* 293 Þonkyng hym þat sauid hym wyth hys blessing from poysynnyng. 1530 Palsgr. 698/1, I save one from daunger, as harnesse doth ones persone, or as medecyne, or preservatyve dothe ones helth, *je contregarde.* *a* 1533 Ld. Berners *Huon* lv. 186 The good harneys saued Huon fro all hurtes. *a* 1586 Sidney *Arcadia* II. (Sommer) 103 But Zelmanes comming saued Dorus from further chiding. 1827 O. W. Roberts *Voy. Centr. Amer.* 226 He saved me from much interruption and many annoying questions. 1860 Tyndall *Glac.* I. xvi. 118 A sudden effort was necessary to save me from falling. 1886 C. E. Pascoe *Lond. of To-day* xviii. (ed. 3) 162 This route has the advantage, too, of saving one from the crowd.

b. used in invocation or aspiration: esp. with sarcastic emphasis.

1738 Pope *Univ. Prayer* 33 Save me alike from foolish Pride, Or impious Discontent. 1784 Cowper *Task* I. 499 But save me from the gaiety of those Whose head-aches nail them to a noon-day bed. 1798 Canning *New Morality* 210 in *Anti-Jacobin* 9 July, Save, save, oh! save me from the candid friend!

c. To be a protection, defence, or means of deliverance to.

1412–20 Lydg. *Troy Bk.* III. 90 And some wil haue also no viser To saue his face, but only a naser. 1470 Henry *Wallace* II. 71 Couert of treis sawit him full weille. 1543 Grafton *Contn. Harding* 489 A goodly glose, by the whiche that place that may defend a thefe, may not saue an innocent. 1771 *Junius Lett.* lxvii. 333 But it shall not save you. The very sunshine you live in is a prelude to your dissolution.

6. *refl.* (in senses 1 and 5). Often = to get away, escape (F. *se sauver*).

a 1225 *Ancr. R.* 98 O none wise ne muwe ȝe betere sauuen ou suluen. *c* 1320 *Sir Beues* 836 Him com strokes so gret plente þat fain he was to weren is hed And saue him self fro þe ded. *c* 1450 Myrc *Festial* 133 Wherfor, gentyll knyght, gos hens fast and saue þyselfe. 1593 Shaks. *3 Hen. VI*, V. ii. 48 Flye Lords, and saue your selues. *a* 1715 Burnet *Own Time* (1724) I. 585, I saved my self out of those difficulties by saying to all my friends, that I would not be involved in any such confidence. 1729 W. Funnell *Voy.* 144 He and his company got to his boat, and so saved themselves to the ship. 1817 *Ballad of Waterloo* 18 All panic struck, the legions fled, 'Twas *save himself who could.* 1819 Scott *Ivanhoe* xl, The only course by which he could save himself from degradation and disgrace.

†b. *refl.* and *intr.* To avoid loss. *Obs.*

a 1548 Hall *Chron., Hen. VI* 139 b, So both parties, rather myndyng to gain or save then to lose, departed for that tyme. *Ibid.* 141 b, Thenglishemen sometyme saved, and sometyme gained, but the moste losse lighted on the Frenchemen. 1696 Phillips (ed. 5) s.v., A Tradesman is said to save himself that neither gets nor loses.

7. †a. To heal, cure, restore to health. *Obs.* **b.** Later only as a specific use of sense 1: To rescue from a sickness which threatens to prove mortal; = to save the life of.

1362 Langl. *P. Pl.* A. VIII. 17 Hou heore schabbede schep schal heore wolle saue. 1387 Trevisa *Higden* (Rolls) VI. 387 He was hard i-holde with a strong siknesse, and myȝte nouȝt be i-heled noþer i-saved wiþ no manere medecyne. 1390 Gower *Conf.* III. 32 Bot as a man that wolde him save, Whan he is sek, be medicine. *a* 1400–50 *Alexander* 2558 Myself with a serop sall saue [*Dublin MS.* safe] ȝow belyue. 14.. *Officium Resurrect.* 7 in *Non-Cycle Myst. Plays* 3 Why suffred he so forto dy, Sithe he may all sekenes saue? 1615 R. Cocks *Diary* (Hakl. Soc.) I. 63 Soe our chirurgion was sent for to assist the Duch chirurgion to save the [wounded] man, yf it were possible. 1848 Thackeray *Van. Fair* xli, Her own little boy was saved, actually saved, by calomel, freely administered, when all the physicians in Paris had given the dear child up.

8. To keep, protect or guard (a thing) from damage, loss, or destruction.

1387 Trevisa *Higden* (Rolls) IV. 429 And so þe strokes were i-lette, and þe walles i-saved. 1387 *Charters*, etc. *Edinb.* (1871) 35 To cast the watir owte and to save the werc for the watir. *c* 1450 Myrc *Festial* 39 Hys hall was yche day of the ȝere new strawed..forto saue knyghtys cloþys þat setton on þe flore. 1553 Wilson *Rhet.* (1585) 117 Fond is his purpose, that being in the Raine, casteth his garment in a bush, and standeth naked himself, for sauing the glosse of his gay coate. 1669 Sturmy *Mariner's Mag.* v. xii. 63 A Ferril of Brass may be put thereon to save the Head from cleaving. 1672 Wiseman *Wounds* II. 90 If the Toes with part of the foot was shot off, cut off the lacerated parts smooth, but with care to save as much of the foot with the heel as you can. 1712–14 Pope *Rape Lock* II. 93 To save the powder from too rude a gale. 1735 —— *Donne Sat.* ii. 72 His Office keeps your Parchment fates entire, He starves with cold to save them from the fire. 1907 Hodges *Elem. Photogr.* 97 Over-exposed prints may possibly be saved by further diluting the developer.

†b. To guard (property) from loss or from passing into other hands; to keep in safe possession (for oneself or another). *Obs.*

1389 in *Eng. Gilds* (1870) 81 Also, ye skyueyns of ye gylde yat hauen ye catel in hande, scholene fynden borwes to ye alderman, for to sauen ye catel, and for to bringe it forht at ye general morspeche, wyht-outen ani lettyng. 1393 Langl. *P. Pl.* C. x. 272 When þy lord lokeþ to haue a-louaunce for hus bestes, And of þe monye þow haddist þer-myd hus meoble to saue. 1526 Tindale *1 Tim.* vi. 20 O Timothe save that which is geven the to kepe. 1533 Bellenden *Livy* I. ii. (S.T.S.) I. 15 The realme of latynis and troianis was sauffit to þis childe Ascanius be prudent tutorie of lavinia his moder.

†c. To have (a person) in safe keeping. *Obs.*

c 1386 Chaucer *Doctor's T.* 200, I deeme anon this cherl his seruant haue; Thou shalt no lenger in thyn hous hir saue.

†d. To make (a place) secure. *Obs.*

1338 R. Brunne *Chron.* (1810) 294 Þe toun he suld so saue, þat he suld not ascape.

e. ***to save one's pocket***: to avoid spending one's money.

1883 *Law Times Rep.* XLIX. 9/1 The tenant for life may have indirectly benefited himself or saved his own pocket.

f. ***to save one's face***: to avoid being disgraced or humiliated. Similarly, *to save* (another's) *face.* Hence ***save-face*** adj. = *face-saving* ppl. adj. s.v. FACE *sb.* 27, and *absol.* as *sb.*

[Originally used by the English community in China, with reference to the continual devices among the Chinese to avoid incurring or inflicting disgrace. The exact phrase appears not to occur in Chinese, but 'to lose face' (*tiu lien*), and 'for the sake of his face', are common.]

1898 *Westm. Gaz.* 5 Apr. 5/1 Unquestionably the process of saving one's face leads to curious results in other countries than China. 1900 *Daily News* 25 June 4/5 The communiqué in the Russian 'Official Messenger' provides the necessary formula by the adoption of which the Chinese Government can save its face. 1917 *Chambers's Jrnl.* Jan. 13/2 The civilian native staff had bolted at the first sign of trouble, 'going to report to the authorities' being their 'save face' for it! 1935 *Times* 7 Oct. 9/4 The closing phase of the War—namely, a save-face, patched up peace. 1966 R. Standish *Widow Hack* i. 8 A save-face formula to enable Janet to plead *force majeure.*

9. To keep intact or unhurt, preserve, maintain, safeguard (honour, credit, chastity, and the like).

a 1300 *Cursor M.* 11232 Right sua al plain,..he com and yede, Saufand his moder hir maidenhede. *c* 1350 *Will. Palerne* 527 My worschipe to saue. 1375 Barbour *Bruce* II. 338 Wyrk yhe then apon swylk wyss, That ȝour honour be sawyt ay. *c* 1386 Chaucer *Sqr.'s T.* 523 Til that myn harte ..Graunted hym loue, vpon this condicioun, That eueremore myn honour and renoun Were saued. 1390 Gower *Conf.* I. 19 Good is to save With penance and with abstinence Of chastite the continence. 1588 Shaks. *L.L.L.* IV. i. 26 Thus will I saue my credit in the shoote. 1617 Moryson *Itin.* I. 148 Who to save the reputation of the Virgin, confessed that he came to rob the house. 1665 Boyle *Occas. Refl.* II. xi. (1848) 130 'Twould be much easier for the mistaken Physitian to save his Credit, than for the unprepar'd Sinner to save his Soul. 1733 Pope *Ep. Cobham* 125 Must then at once (the character to save) The plain rough Hero turn a crafty Knave? 1851 Lytton *Not so Bad* II. i. 29 The loan saved my credit, and made my fortune.

b. To safeguard (a right, possession) *to* a person.

c 1460 Fortescue *Abs. & Lim. Mon.* xiv. (1885) 144 Whether the kynge mey gyve such rewarde..off his revenues, savynge to hym selff sufficiant ffor the sustenance off his estate. 1499 *Reg. Privy Seal Scotl.* I. 50/1 A precept of confirmation of the crownarschip of Carrik..Salffand to the kingis hienes service auch and wont. 1544 tr. *Littleton's Tenures* 41 b, Yf a man let lande to another for terme of lyfe sauynge the reuersyon to him. 1571 *Act 13 Eliz.* c. 29 §6 Savinge to all and every person or persons..all such Rightes ..w[ch] they..had, might or should have had, of, in or to any the Mannors Lordshippes [etc.]. 1642 tr. *Perkins' Prof. Bk.* x. §648. 279 The Lord doth grant the rent unto a stranger saving unto him his seignory. 1863 H. Cox *Instit.* I. v. 23 We find a clause..introduced saving the king's rights.

†c. ? To keep, observe (a duty, rule). *Obs.*

1390 Gower *Conf.* I. 85 Wherof I can noght bothe save My speche and this obedience. *c* 1400 *Rule St. Benet* (verse) 538 And all þai aw be day & night To saue þis rewle in all þer myght.

†d. To preserve the credit of (one's word, oath).

c 1425 *Eng. Conq. Irel.* xxix. 72 A man stode þer besyde & herd, & wold, hys thankes, saue [*v.r.* Sawe] þe prophetes sawe. 1595 *2nd Pt. Contention* (1843) 125 Ile shew your grace the waie to saue your oath.

e. ***to save the situation***, to avert disaster.

1907 W. Raleigh *Shakespeare* v. 135 If Cordelia had been perfectly tender and tactful, there would have been no play. The situation would have been saved. 1908 A. Bennett *Old Wives' Tale* IV. ii. 467 Those dogs saved the situation, because they needed constant attention. 1922 J. Williamson *Short Hist. Brit. Expansionism* v. iii. 514 Starvation more than once threatened annihilation, but on each occasion the timely arrival of food-ships saved the situation.

10. With adj. complement: To keep or preserve *whole, unhurt*, etc.

† ***to save harmless***: see HARMLESS *a.* 2.

a 1300 *Cursor M.* 5037 Lauerd..sauue mi childir hale to me. *c* 1440 *Alphabet of Tales* 223 Ane angell..opynd þe dure and savid þe seale hale at Saynt Remigius sett on itt. 1535 Coverdale *Ezek.* xviii. 27 When the wycked man turneth awaye from his wickednesse..he shal saue his soule alyue. 1595 Shaks. *John* II. i. 225 To saue vnscratch'd your Citties threatned cheekes. 1611 Bible *2 Kings* vii. 4 If they saue vs aliue, we shall liue. 1784 Cowper *Task* I. 566 Which, kindled with dry leaves, just saves unquench'd The spark of life. 1859 Tennyson *Enid* 894 To Save her dear lord whole from any wound.

†11. To store, preserve, keep in sound condition.

1398 Trevisa *Barth. De P.R.* v. xxxvi. (Bodl. MS.), He [the heart] is holowȝ to fong blood, and he is þikke to saue it. 1601 Holland *Pliny* II. 507 After that, it ought to be dried in the Sun, and saued in a brasen box. 1602 Carew *Cornwall* (1723) 33 They [the Fish] are saued three maner of wayes: by fuming, pressing, or pickelling. 1728 Pope *Dunc.* I. 151 There sav'd by spice, like mummies, many a year, Dry Bodies of Divinity appear.

b. *intr.* To remain in good condition, to last without spoiling, to 'keep'. ? *U.S.*

1891 *Century Dict., Save*..To be capable of preservation: said of fish: as, to *save* well.

12. *trans.* **a.** Astr. ***to save the appearances, the phenomena*** [tr. Gr. σώζειν τὰ φαινόμενα (e.g. in Proclus *Hypotyp.* v. §10); cf. It. *salvar le apparenze*, F. *sauver les apparences*]: said of a hypothesis which satisfactorily explains the observed facts. See also SALVE *v.*[2] 1. *Obs.* exc. *Hist.*

1625, 1643 [see PHENOMENON I c]. 1667 Milton *P.L.* VIII. 82 When they come to model Heav'n And calculate the Starrs, how they will weild The mightie frame, how build, unbuild, contrive To save appearances. 1946 A. Huxley *Let.* 3 Sept. (1969) 547 My primary preoccupation is the achievement of some kind of over-all understanding of the world, directly and, at one remove, through the building up of some hypothesis that accounts for the facts and 'saves the appearances'. 1957 O. Barfield (*title*) Saving the appearances. 1981 *Country Life* 26 Feb. 528/3 His single professional aim is to perceive order in the physical world, not merely to save the appearances but to discover an ordered reality.

Hence (? orig. allusively) **b.** ***to save appearances***: to contrive to keep up an appearance of propriety, solvency, or the like. (So in Fr. and It.) Cf. APPEARANCE 12 b.

1711, 1761 [see APPEARANCE 12 b]. 1844 THIRLWALL *Greece* VIII. lxiii. 222 Sparta sent only a handful of men to save appearances. 1876 'OUIDA' *Winter City* viii. 234, I suppose it 'saves society', at least it saves appearances.

13. To prevent the loss of (a game, match, wager, etc.). Also, in Racing slang, to 'hedge' so as to protect (oneself, one's 'book') from loss, or so as to recover (a certain sum) out of one's losses.

1611 SHAKS. *Cymb.* II. iv. 94 The description Of what is in her Chamber, nothing saues The wager you haue laid. 17.. in Lillywhite *Cricket Scores* (1863) I. Pref. 10 If a striker nips a Ball up just before him he may fall before his Wicket, or pop down his Batt before Shee comes to it to Save it. 1837 D. WALKER *Sports & Games* 217 The striker..must never follow a ball so far that, in case of no runs being obtained, he cannot return to save his wicket. 1862 PYCROFT in *London Soc.* II. 114/1 As to his bowling, it might have saved the game. 1869 'WAT. BRADWOOD' *The O.V.H.* xx, And even his lordship began to grudge that he had not just saved his book upon him [a horse] in consonance with the Major's advice. 1885 *New Bk. Sports* 58 But in the Eton field..even in the sorest straits, by the feet, and by the feet alone, must the goal be saved.

†**b.** To make (a dangerous voyage) safely. *Obs.*

1698 FRYER *Acc. E. India & P.* 77 This holds with little intermission till..the first Full Moon in August; when our Europe Ships, if they save their Passage about the Cape, venture to make in here.

14. 'To take or embrace opportunely, so as not to lose' (J.); to be in time for, manage to catch.

1732-3 SWIFT *Reas. Rep. Sacram. Test.* Wks. 1751 IX. 245 The same Persons..were..faithful Subjects to Cromwell, yet being wise enough to foresee a Restoration, they seized the Forts and Castles here [in Ireland]..; just saving the Tide, and putting in a Stock of Merit sufficient to preserve [etc.]. 1802 CANNING in G. Rose *Diaries* (1860) I. 456, I have but a moment to save the post. 1833 I. TAYLOR *Fanat.* vi. 203 That they may save the hour of..appointment. 1849 THACKERAY 12 June in *Scribner's Mag.* I. 409/2 The note must go this instant to save the post. 1865 TROLLOPE *Belton Est.* vii. 73 There arises a question whether under such circumstances the train can be saved.

†**b.** ***to save one's distance, time***: to manage to arrive at (a given point or time) after being delayed.

1790 R. CUMBERLAND *Observer* No. 142 §3 (1791) V. 184 Whether Nicolas saved his distance..we shall not just now enquire. 1806 J. BERESFORD *Miseries Hum. Life* VI. iv, Riding out to dinner, many miles off, on a beast that will not quit his walk, while you know that nothing short of a full gallop will save your time.

II. To reserve, lay aside.

15. To keep for a particular purpose or as likely to prove useful; to set apart, lay by, reserve.

*c*1400 *Rule of St. Benet* (verse) 1582 Þat euer-ilkon wil of hir laue þe third part til hir sopper saue. 1592 SHAKS. *Rom. & Jul.* I. v. 9 Good thou, saue mee a piece of Marchpane. 1719 DE FOE *Crusoe* I. (Globe) 136, I saved the Skins of all the Creatures that I kill'd. 1747 MRS. GLASSE *Cookery* (1796) xiv. 210 Take..a bunch of turnips, pare them, save three or four out, put the rest into the water. 1845 *Visit to Bury St. Edmunds* 90, I have one pair [of shoes]; they were almost worn out when father died, and as mother can't buy any more, I save them for Sundays.

16. *spec.* To collect and keep (seed) in stock for sowing.

1657 W. COLES *Adam in Eden* xxiii. 47 The Roots [of Clary]..perish after the Seed-time: it is most usuall to save it; for the Seed seldom riseth of its own shedding. 1763 MILLS *Syst. Pract. Husb.* IV. 128 The best way to save the seeds of this paint, is [etc.]. 1801 *Farmer's Mag.* Jan. 92 It is feared the bulk of the people will not be able to save seed for next crop.

b. To dry (corn, hay, peat) by exposure to the air; to harvest, stack. Cf. *win*.

1719 DE FOE *Crusoe* I. (Globe) 120 When it [the corn] was growing and grown, I have observ'd already, how many Things I wanted, to Fence it, Secure it, Mow or Reap it, Cure and Carry it Home, Thrash, Part it from the Chaff, and Save it. 1764 *Museum Rust.* I. lxxxiii. 361 The farmers pile them up in one of their offices, with an outside facing of bog turf well *saved*. 1824 MISS MITFORD in L'Estrange *Life* (1870) II. 183 The Northumberland people have an idiom of 'saving hay' for 'making hay'. 1892 JANE BARLOW *Irish Idylls* i. 8 A turf-stack..when newly 'saved'..looks like a solidified shadow of the little house.

c. To extract (gold) from quartz.

1877 RAYMOND *Statist. Mines & Mining* 69 The gold is easily saved, being clean, angular, and not very small; hence the proportion saved by the mill-process is notably greater than in any other locality in California.

d. ***to save clean*** in *Whaling* (see quot.).

1891 *Century Dict.* s.v., *To save clean*, to save all (the blubber) in cutting in: a whaling-term.

17. To store up or put by (money, goods, etc.) by dint of economy; to reserve instead of spending, consuming, or parting with.

1362 LANGL. *P. Pl.* A. VIII. 27 Treuþe..Bad hem Bugge Boldely what hem best lykede, And seþþen sullen hit a-ȝeyn And saue þe wynnynge. 14.. *How Good Wife taught Dau.* 170 in *Q. Eliz. Acad.* 49 Þei..þat wyll thryue, and þer gode saue. 1600 SHAKS. *A.Y.L.* II. iii. 39, I haue fiue hundred Crownes, The thriftie hire I saued vnder your Father. 1753 JOHNSON *Adventurer* No. 84 ¶14 A nobleman's butler, who has furnished a shop with the money he has saved. 1842 TENNYSON *Dora* 50 But Dora stored what little she could save, And sent it them by stealth. 1856 FROUDE *Hist. Eng.* (1858) II. vi. 95 He was able to save money for his son's education.

b. *absol.* Now used esp. with reference to or in exhortations concerning the purchase of savings certificates, etc., instead of consumer goods.

1595 LODGE *Fig for Momus* H 1 b, Counsell, how to spend, and saue. 1776 ADAM SMITH *W.N.* II. iii. I. 410 Whatever industry might acquire, if parsimony did not save and store up, the capital would never be the greater. 1859 SMILES *Self-help* ix. 234 Add guinea to guinea; scrape and save; and the pile of gold will gradually rise. 1878 JEVONS *Pol. Econ.* ix. 86 It is idle to say that the better-paid working men cannot save. 1916 *War Savings* Oct. 12/2 A large number of circulars headed 'Save for England' have been distributed by the school children. *Ibid.* 13/1 Men and women are saving in Gloucestershire who never saved before because they have been taught that their 6d. per week..will help to end the War. *Ibid.* 16/1 Men are encouraged to save and help their country by joining the Association. 1942 J. A. SCHUMPETER *Capitalism, Socialism & Democracy* xviii. 210 Nor am I going to ask the reader to rely on the individual comrades' propensity to save. 1948 G. CROWTHER *Outl. Money* (ed. 2) v. 169 By every imaginable device of publicity people are exhorted to save. 1961 E. S. TURNER *Phoney War* xx. 292 This was merely an ingenious way of getting people to save. 1969 *Whitaker's Almanac 1970* 353/1 The Chancellor..went on to introduce a contractual savings scheme—for which he said he was glad to appropriate (from the Conservatives) the title 'Save As You Earn'. 1978 *Times* 15 Mar. 21/8 The publication of Keynes' *General Theory* by its emphasis on the propensity to save (rather than the propensity to import) as the major cause of the insufficiency of demand, diverted attention from Harrod's approach.

c. with *up*. Also *absol.*

1834 [see SAVED *ppl. a.* 2]. 1850 SMEDLEY *Frank Fairlegh* iv, A parting gift from my little sister Fanny, who..had saved up her pocket-money during many previous months, in order to provide funds for this munificent present. 1884 BLACKLEY *Thrift & Indep.* 20 To try the system of saving up a little week by week. *Ibid.* 57 If, by an effort, he save up ..£30. *Ibid.* 91, I set myself to save up for my own old age.

18. To avoid spending, giving, or consuming (money, goods, etc.); to keep (a given amount) from being spent or consumed or lost and so retain it in one's possession. Also with indirect obj. (with or without *to*): To enable a person to avoid spending, giving, or losing.

*a*1400 *Minor Poems fr. Vernon MS.* 545/345 *Ki sauuer veut soun doner, Corteis seit de soun manger*;..He may saue moneye and gete þat wol be curteys of his mete. 1539 in W. A. J. Archbold *Somerset Rel. Houses* (1892) 73 Ther will be a great soome of money that shalbe salved to the kinges highnes therbye. 1590 SIR J. SMYTH *Disc. Weapons* 6 b, And so consequentlie in their whole Armies to saue the pay of a great sort of Captaines..and other Officers. 1596 SHAKS. *1 Hen. IV*, III. iii. 48 Thou hast saued me a thousand Markes in Linkes and Torches. *Ibid.* v. i. 99, I..will, to saue the blood on either side, Try fortune with him, in a Single Fight. 1617 MORYSON *Itin.* I. 207 The said Ianizare..will easily save a man more then his wages. 1661 PEPYS *Diary* 20 Aug., When we came to look for our coach we found it gone, so we were fain to walk home afoot and saved our money. 1693 in C. R. Wilson *Old Fort William* (1906) I. 12 That old Maxim..That a Penny saved is two Pence gott. 1712 SWIFT *Let. Eng. Tongue* Wks. 1755 II. I. 197 You have already saved several millions to the publick. 1801 *Farmer's Mag.* Nov. 406 By carrying this plan into execution, the public.. would save not less than four millions *per annum*. 1854 RONALDS & RICHARDSON *Chem. Technol.* (ed. 2) I. 257 With suitable flues, the saving of fuel is much greater when turf and wood are employed than is the case with coal;..⅓rd being saved in the case of wood, and ¼th only in that of coal. 1860 TROLLOPE *Framley P.* xxxii, Mr. Sowerby then got into another cab... Anyone else would have saved his shilling, as Mrs. Harold Smith's house was only just across Oxford Street.

†**b.** *absol.* Of a commodity: To effect a saving in use, 'to be cheap' (J.).

*a*1626 BACON *Compounding of Metals* Baconiana (1679) 94 Brass Ordnance..saveth both in the quantity of the Material, and in the charge and commodity of mounting & carriage.

c. With immaterial obj., e.g. labour, time, distance to be travelled, etc.

1579 W. WILKINSON *Confut. Fam. Love* B ij, Therefore saue labour for making any further reply hereunto, least you doe but lose your trauaile herein. 1600 SHAKS. *A.Y.L.* II. vii. 8 He saues my labor by his owne approach. 1601 —— *Twel. N.* II. ii. 6 You might haue saued mee my paines, to haue taken it away your selfe. 1612 BACON *Ess., Despatch* (Arb.) 248 To chuse time, is to saue time. 1687 A. LOVELL tr. *Thevenot's Trav.* II. 3 Fair weather beginning with the New Moon, made the Captain repent that he had not passed through the Phare of Messina, which would have saved him fifty miles in his course. 1847 MARRYAT *Childr. N. Forest* iv, Edith..baked all the oatmeal cakes, which saved Alice a good deal of time. 1889 J. K. JEROME *Three Men in Boat* 149 We had dispensed with tea, so as to save time.

d. ***to save one's breath*** or ***wind***, to refrain from wasting one's argument or energy on a lost cause. (Perh. an ellipt. use of the proverbial phr. *to keep* (*save*, etc.) *one's breath to cool one's porridge*: see PORRIDGE *sb.* 4.)

1926 F. W. CROFTS *Inspector French & Cheyne Mystery* xi. 146 If your story's going to be more lies about St John Price and the Hull succession you may save your breath. 1941 MENCKEN in *New Yorker* 24 May 22/1 He might very well have saved his wind, for Bill soon had him. 1952 E. CALDWELL *Lamp for Nightfall* iv. 36 Now stop making me mad, talking about a new dress that you haven't any need of. Save your breath for something dearer. *Ibid.* x. 101 You'd better be saving your wind for road work, and for doing chores.

19. To be careful or economical in the use of; to use or consume sparingly.

1600 SHAKS. *A.Y.L.* II. vii. 160 His youthfull hose well sau'd, a world too wide For his shrunke shanke. 1719 DE FOE *Crusoe* I. (Globe) 62 For I eat sparingly; and sav'd my Provisions (my Bread especially) as much as possibly I could. 1729 SWIFT *Direct. Serv., Butler* Wks. 1751 XIV. 21 To avoid burning Day-light, and to save your Master's Candles. 1816 SCOTT *Old Mort.* xl, Next she enlarged on the advantage of saving old clothes to be what she called 'beet-masters to the new'. 1847 C. BRONTE *Jane Eyre* xxix, Everything..including the carpet and curtains—looked at once well worn and well saved.

20. To treat carefully, so as to obviate or reduce fatigue, wear and tear, etc. ***to save oneself***, to reduce the amount of one's exertions.

[1756 CHESTERF. *Let. to Son* 14 Dec., Adieu! I am going to the ball, to save my eyes from reading, and my mind from thinking.] 1785 G. A. BELLAMY *Apology* (ed. 3) III. 82 To make use of the theatrical phrase, I never saved myself, but often suffered my feelings to possess me so entirely, as that they deprived me of the power of voice. 1847 MARRYAT *Childr. N. Forest* xviii, My eyes are getting weak, and I wish to save them as much as possible. 1856 WHYTE MELVILLE *Kate Cov.* v. 52 White-Stockings, whom I had ridden down [to the races], to save Brilliant. 1859 GEO. ELIOT *Lifted Veil* ii, Supposing that he wished merely to save her nerves. 1907 SYMONS-JEUNE *Art of Punting* 17 Beginners..in order to save themselves and ease the strain on their arms..shove crooked and turn the punt round.

III. To avoid or prevent (something undesirable).

A development from sense 18; sense 21 arises naturally from the sense 'to avoid paying or losing'. Cf. also sense 5.

21. To avoid for one's own part or enable another to avoid (some burden or inconvenience): *occas.* to avoid or obviate the necessity for. *Const.* indirect obj. of the person (oneself or another) who is relieved.

1606 G. W[OODCOCKE] tr. *Justin* Epit. Emp. Hh 3 b, By meanes whereof, a little tract of time would saue him a great deal of wrath. 1615 R. COCKS *Diary* (Hakl. Soc.) I. 75 And about midnight [he] departed towards Crates; which saved the geveing a present of 2 damaskt fowling peeces, yf he had staid till morninge. 1654 GAYTON *Pleas. Notes* IV. xvii. 259 How might'st thou by this *effugium* have sav'd all thy misfortunes? 1681 DRYDEN *Span. Friar* IV. ii. 58 Will you not speak to save a Lady's Blush? 1699 —— *Ep. J. Driden* 11 Without their cost you terminate the cause And save the expense of long litigious laws. 1780 *Mirror* No. 95 Take my advice, my dear Bell, and save yourself the trouble. 1790 SCOTT *Let.* in *Lockhart* (1837) I. vi. 168 My letters lie there for me, as it saves their being sent down to Rosebank. 1813 SOUTHEY *Nelson* II. 135 The hurt done by their splinters would have been saved also. 1815 SCOTT *Guy M.* xxiii, The best way's to let the blood barken upon the cut—that saves plasters. 1886 *Manch. Exam.* 13 Mar. 5/2 The only use of paper money is in saving the wear and tear of gold. 1899 *Allbutt's Syst. Med.* VIII. 77 A tendency to take quick steps, as if running forward to save a fall.

†**b.** ***to save*** (a woman's) ***longing***, to anticipate and so prevent it. Also *transf. Obs.*

1593 *King Leir* I. ii. 133 (Malone Soc.), Madam, to saue your longing, this it is. 1607 SHAKS. *Timon* I. i. 261 Sir, you haue sau'd my longing, and I feed Most hungerly on your sight. 1614 B. JONSON *Barth. Fair* III. i. (1631) 48 Looke, Win, doe, looke a Gods name, and saue your longing. 1656 OSBORN *Adv. Son* II. xvi. 54 Our Beldame Eve, to save her longing, sold us all for an Apple. 1665 HEAD *Eng. Rogue* (1874) I. 88 Come hither Sirrah, I know what you would have, I'le save your longing.

c. *Games.* To prevent the opposing side from gaining (a run, goal, etc.). ***to save two, three, four runs*** (Cricket): to prevent the scoring of a second, third, or fourth run for a hit. Also (in football, hockey, etc.) *absol.* = to save a goal.

1816 LAMBERT in Box *Eng. Game Cricket* (1877) 34 Long Stop.—This man should stand a proper distance behind the wicket, to save a run, if the ball should not be stopped by the striker, or wicket keeper. 1850 'BAT' *Cricket. Manual* (1851) 49 Long Leg.. usually stands to save four runs. 1867 SELKIRK *Guide to Cricket Ground* 35 *Saving the Run.*—Stopping and returning the ball so quickly that the batsmen dare not attempt a run for fear of being run out. 1889 *Field* 5 Jan. 29/3 For the losers, Jackson in goal saved well on several occasions [hockey]. *Ibid.* 12 Jan. 65/2 But his shot was saved by the goal-keeper [football].

d. ***well saved***: an applauding expression used when a rider has avoided a fall; also (in games) when a brilliant 'save' has been made.

1859 WHYTE MELVILLE *Digby Grand* I. i. 10 As he fell upon his head into the road, and recovered himself without unhorsing me,..'Well saved, my lad, and devilish well ridden too', said the jolly General.

†**22.** To afford protection from. *Obs.*

1583 *Leg. Bp. St. Androis* Pref. 46 in *Satir. Poems Reform.* I. 348 The plesant plane-trie will the leavs unfauld With fairest schaddow to save the sone in symmer.

†**23.** To meet or overcome (a doubt); = SALVE *v.*[2] 2. *Obs. rare.*

1591 SPENSER *M. Hubberd* 194 Right well, deere Gossip, ye advized have, (Said then the Foxe) but I this doubt will save.

IV. Idiomatic uses of certain parts of the verb. (For those of the pr. pple. see SAVING *prep.*)

24. The infinitive *to save* has been used to mean: †**a.** On condition of not injuring. Cf. sense 9.

1297 R. GLOUC. (Rolls) 1260 Ac ich wolde to sauui lif & lume bringe him to ech lawe. [Cf. ante 1242: þat he vor his neueu wolde..Do hey amendement, sauue lume & lif.]

†**b.** Saving, having regard to (one's honour, 'presence'). See SAVING *prep.* 2.

1375 BARBOUR *Bruce* III. 173 'Schyr', said he,..'To sauff ȝour presence, it [is] nocht swa'. *c*1470 *Gol. & Gaw.* 1008

And grant the frekis on fold farar to fall, Baith thair honouris to saif.

†**c.** Except, excepting; = SAVE *prep.*

c **1425** WYNTOUN *Orig. Cron.* IV. ix. 1170 Al þe cite þan fande þai Withe þar fais nere wptane, To sauff þe Capitalle allane. *Ibid.* IV. xvi. 1600 For nane þare gouernalle þar had, To sauff barnnys of ȝoutheide.

†**25.** The pa. pple. *saved* was used in absolute construction with a sb., with the sense: Preserving..safe or intact, without detriment to, making reservation of. Cf. SAFE *a.* 5.

Sometimes placed before the sb.: cf. *except, considered.*

c **1400** *Apol. Loll.* 52 And þus he may lefuly, sauid his ordre. **1432-50** tr. *Higden* (Rolls) VIII. 79 That he wolde submitte hym to his grace, his honoure and crowne of his realme salvede. **1487** *Rolls of Parlt.* VI. 390/2 Saved alwey to youre Grace..of the said Fee Ferme xviii li. v s. **1539** in W. A. J. Archbold *Somerset Rel. Houses* (1892) 71 We haue determyned (your lordeshippes pleasure savyd) to differ the same vnto our return. **1580** LYLY *Euphues* (Arb.) 335, I haue aunswered your custome, least you should argue me of coynes, no otherwise then I might mine honour saued, and your name vnknowen.

†**V. 26.** In combinations of verb-stem + object, used *attrib.* or *adj.*, as *save-soul, save-stake.*

1654 WHITLOCK *Zootomia* 178 Such A Spirit were of A Save stake, if not promoting Prudence, as they call it. **1799** E. DU BOIS *Piece Family Biog.* III. 129 Martha was gone on a save-soul pilgrimage to a neighbouring village.

save (seɪv), quasi-*prep.* and *conj.* Forms: *α.* 3-5 **sauf,** 5-6 **saufe,** 5 **sawf, sauff, saauf;** 3-5 **saf,** 4-5 **safe, saaf,** 4-6 **saff(e,** 5 **sef;** 5-6 **salf,** 6 **salfe, saulfe;** 5-6 *Sc.* **saif(f.** *β.* 3-4 **sauve,** 4 **sawve,** 5 **sawe,** 4-6 **salve,** 4- **save.** [Developed from SAFE *a.* 5, in imitation of the similar development in the use of the equivalent F. *sauf.*

Already in OF. the adj. *sauf*, fem. *sauve*, prefixed to a sb. in the absolute construction (= L. *salvō, salvā*: see SAFE *a.* 5) had often the sense 'being excepted', so that it became (like the analogous *except* ppl. adj. in Eng.) functionally equivalent to a prep., and was eventually treated as such, the masc. form *sauf* being used even before a fem. sb. Cf. Sp. *salvo*, Pr. *sal.*

The *β* forms may partly represent the OF. *sauve* in collocation with a fem. sb., and partly the ME. form of the plural adj. But the later exclusive use of the form *save* is probably due to the identification of the word with the imperative of the vb.: cf. *except*, which appears to have been similarly apprehended as an imperative.

The use of a nominative after *save* (see 1 b) may perhaps be a trace of the originally adjectival character of the word; it is, however, to be noted that the same thing occurs with all the quasi-prepositional words of the same meaning, including even *saving* and *excepting*, which are in origin pr. pples. of transitive verbs.]

1. quasi-*prep.* Except, with the exception of, but. Often strengthened by the addition of *only* (*alone,* †*alonely,* †*anerly,* †*one*); also tautologically ***save and except,*** Sc. †***bot saiff.***

α. a **1300** *Cursor M.* 17288 + 438 Alle to-geder þai whore sauf thomas of ynde allone. **13..** *E.E. Allit. P.* B. 1749 Heȝest of alle oþer, saf onelych tweyne. *c* **1470** HENRY *Wallace* XI. 134 Sexte and vi and xvi to ded has dycht, Bot saiff vii men at fled out of thair sycht. **1470-85** MALORY *Arthur* XX. vii. 808 Howe they were alle slayne sauf hym self al only. *a* **1533** LD. BERNERS *Gold. Bk. M. Aurel.* (1546) S v, Al thinges haue an ende at last by deth, saufe onely deathe. **1538** WRIOTHESLEY *Chron.* (1875) I. 86 All the lightes of waxe in every church to be taken downe, saffe onely the roode-loft light. **1579** in *10th Rep. Hist. MSS. Comm.* App. v. 430 No kynd of..tymber..salfe onely fuell of wood for fyre.

β. a **1300** *Cursor M.* 19485 Disciplis folud þai sa herd þat þai þam draf vte o þair ward, Sauue þe apostels þat þam ledd. **13..** *Gosp. Nicod.* 482 (Addit. MS.) Bedrede I lay ffourty ȝhere fully sawe two. **1362** LANGL. *P. Pl.* A. II. 210 Saue Meede þe Mayden no mon dorste abyde. *c* **1380** WYCLIF *Last Age of the Church* (1840) 28 Euery lettre in þe abece may be souned wiþ opyn mouþ saue .m. lettre one. *c* **1425** *Eng. Conq. Irel.* vi. 18 Trew frendes fonde he non, sawe Robert, steuenes son. **1451** *Rolls of Parlt.* V. 220/1 The last day save oon of august. **1548** HALL *Chron., Hen. IV* 21 No Chronicler save one, maketh mencion what was the very cause. **1617** MORYSON *Itin.* I. 77 The aforesaid boats are.. covered all save the ends with black cloth. **1749** FIELDING *Tom Jones* VIII. xi, We spent the next evening, save one, in London. **1808** G. ELLIS *Let.* in Lockhart *Scott* (1837) II. iv. 143 The most pleasing poem in our language—save and except one or two of Dryden's fables. **1850** TENNYSON *In Mem.* cv. 23 No dance, no motion, save alone What lightens in the lucid east. **1878** STUBBS *Const. Hist.* III. xviii. 140 All that remained to England in France, save Calais, was lost.

b. followed by the nominative of a pronoun. (App. the normal construction.)

α. c **1400** MAUNDEV. (1839) xxii. 245 Saf only thei that ben dwellynge with hym. *a* **1450** *Knt. de la Tour* 25 For ferde that ani other shulde haue the loue of her sauf he hym selff. *c* **1500** *Three Kings' Sons* 133 Then were they alle slayne, sauf y.

β. c **1386** CHAUCER *Can. Yeom. Prol. & T.* 802 Saue I and a frere, In Engelond ther kan no man it make. **1430-40** LYDG. *Bochas* IX. xxi[i]. (1494) F vj, There is a lyue left none of the blode Saue I alone of the royall lyne. **1528** TINDALE *Obed. Chr. Man* 79 b, Wilt thou so teach..that no man shall have knowlege..in Gods worde save thou only? **1601** SHAKS. *Jul. C.* III. ii. 66, I do intreat you, not a man depart, Saue I alone, till Antony haue spoke. *Ibid.* v. v. 69 All the Conspirators saue onely hee, Did that they did, in enuy of great Cæsar. **1667** MILTON *P.L.* II. 814 That mortal dint, Save he who reigns above, none can resist. **1821** BYRON *Juan* III. *Isles of Greece* xvi, Where nothing, save the waves and I, May hear our mutual murmurs sweep. **1866** DASENT *Gisli* 5 No one has ever challenged me before this day, save thou.

c. followed by the accusative of the pronoun.

1382 WYCLIF *Ecclus.* xxxvi. 5 For ther is noon other God, saue thee, Lord. **1607** SHAKS. *Timon* IV. iii. 507 But all saue thee I fell with Curses. **1893** F. THOMPSON *Hound of Heaven* 180 Whom wilt thou find to love ignoble thee, Save Me, save only Me?

†**d.** = but for. *Obs.*

1522 MORE *De quat. Noviss.* Wks. 83/1 Spiritual pride.. carieth with it a blindnes almost incurable saue gods gret mercye. **1820** KEATS *Eve of St. Agnes* xxv, She seem'd a splendid angel, newly drest, Save wings, for heaven.

2. *conj.* Introducing a sentence which states an exception; now only in the full form ***save that;*** = EXCEPT C. 1.

α. a **1300** *Fall & Passion* 23 in *E.E.P.* (1862) 13 God ȝaf him..foules bestis an þe frute saf o tre he him forbede. **1387** TREVISA *Higden* (Rolls) VII. 339 In his tyme þe monkes of Caunterbury..were nouȝt onliche to seculer men, sauf þat þey lefte nouȝt [liȝt]liche her chastite. **1463** *Bury Wills* (Camden) 36 Lych to the tothir, saf they be not garnysshed. **1501** DOUGLAS *Pal. Hon.* II. vii, My curage grew, for quhat cause I nocht wait, Saif that I hald me payit of thair estait. *a* **1533** LD. BERNERS *Golden Bk. M. Aurel.* (1546) M j, His face was lyke a man, saufe it hadde but one eye.

β. c **1350** *Will. Palerne* 436 Min hert hol i haue now..saue a fers feintise folwes me oft. *c* **1386** CHAUCER *Frankl. T.* 216 He was despeyred, no thyng dorste he seye, Saue in his songes somwhat wolde he wreye His wo. **1388** WYCLIF *Mark* vi. 5 And he myȝte not do there ony vertu, saue that he helide a fewe sijk men. **1547** *Test. Ebor* (Surtees) VI. 265 Salve onlie that the said Thomas shall [etc.]. **1617** MURE *Misc. Poems* xx. 6 My muse, q[ch] noght doth challenge worthy fame, Saue from Montgomery sche hir birth doth clayme. **1634** SIR T. HERBERT *Trav.* 187 Naked from the waste vpwards, saue that their heads are couered. **1750** GRAY *Elegy* 9 Save that from yonder ivy-mantled tow'r The moping owl does to the moon complain. **1842** R. I. WILBERFORCE *Rutilius & Lucius* 270 Then all was still, save that a vast gush of fire rose up for a moment. **1871** R. ELLIS *Catullus* xiv. 1 Calvus, save that as eyes thou art beloved, I could verily loathe thee for the morning's Gift.

¶ *confused use.*

1530 TINDALE *Answ. More* III. Wks. (1573) 305/2 M. More..proueth nothing saue sheweth his ignoraunce.

b. = 'But that', 'were it not that'. Cf. 1 d. ? *Obs.*

c **1600** SHAKS. *Sonn.* lxvi. 14 From these would I be gone, Saue that to dye, I leaue my loue alone.

c. Introducing a hypothetical case of exception, = 'unless', 'if..not'; cf. EXCEPT C. 2.

1390 GOWER *Conf.* II. 119 And thus I mai you sothli telle, Save only that I crie and bidde, I am in Tristesce al amidde And fulfild of Desesperance. **1870** TENNYSON *Holy Grail* 80 Who wept and said, That save they could be pluck'd asunder, all My quest were but in vain. *Ibid.* 86 Save that he were the swine thou spakest of. **1897** F. THOMPSON *New Poems* 186 'Tis said there were no thought of hell, Save hell were taught.

†**d.** As an adversative, = 'but on the contrary'.

1362 LANGL. *P. Pl.* A. Prol. 77 Saue hit nis not bi þe Bisschop þat þe Boye precheþ. *c* **1400** *Lanfranc's Cirurg.* II. v. 163 And if..þe herte be hurt, þere liiþ no cure þeron, saue he schal die anoon; for þe herte takiþ no lijf of no lyme of al þe bodi, saue þe herte ȝeueþ lyues to euery lyme of þe bodi. **1422** tr. *Secreta Secret., Priv. Priv.* 188 Kynde vs hath grantid two eighen and two eeris, Saue but one tonge.

3. Followed by an adv. or advb. phrase or clause, expressing the manner, time, etc., in regard to which an exception is to be made; = EXCEPT C. 3.

α. c **1420** HOCCLEVE *Min. Poems* 154/405 Womman, with my swerd, slee wolde I thee heere, Sauf for awe of god. *c* **1450** *Merlin* i. 12 Be-fill yowe neuer this merveyle saf ones? **1540-1** ELYOT *Image Gov.* (1549) 113 Beyng not instructed in any occupacion or science, saulfe onely in feates perteynyng to warre.

β. c **1320** *Sir Beues* 2270 Al is þes þar ichaue went, Saue in þe lond of Dabilent. **1390** GOWER *Conf.* II. 172 And yit withoute experience Salve only of illusion. **1577** KENDALL *Flowers of Epigr.* 7 Thy garments all and some Do smell of Mirrhe, and saue of Mirrhe no sent doth from thee come. **1598** H. B. *Rdr. to Chaucer* in *Speght* a v b, Unknowne to vs, saue only by thy bookes. **1611** BIBLE *1 Kings* xxii. 31 Fight neither with small nor great, saue only with the king of Israel. **1667** MILTON *P.L.* XII. 258 Over the Tent a Cloud Shall rest by Day, a fierie gleame by Night, Save when they journie. **1750** GRAY *Elegy* 7 Save where the beetle wheels his droning flight. **1864** M. J. HIGGINS *Ess.* (1875) 165 Save and except in a dead calm she is utterly unseaworthy. **1875** MANNING *Mission Holy Ghost* xiv. 397 For fifty years he never left Rome, save only when he went out of the walls to visit the Seven Churches. **1879** FROUDE *Cæsar* viii. 79 There was no longer, therefore, any excuse for its meeting, save on special occasions.

b. Followed by an inf. (with or without *to*).

c **1400** *Beryn* 660 He..had no thing to doon Saff shake a lite his eris, & trus, & be goon. *c* **1450** MYRC *Festial* 17 'What schall þat serues ben'. Þen sayde he: 'þe same, worde for worde, þat ys yn hor natyuyte, saue turne þe natyuyte ynto þe concepcyon'. **1534** TINDALE *John* xiii. 10 He that is wesshed, nedeth not save to wesshe his fete. **1819** SCOTT *Ivanhoe* xl, If thou hast aught to do, save to witness the misery thou hast caused.

c. ***save for:*** exception being made for, but for.

1594 SHAKS. *Rich. III*, IV. iv. 303 Of all one paine, saue for a night of groanes Endur'd of her, for whom you bid like sorrow. **1610** —— *Temp.* I. ii. 282 Then was this Island (Saue for the Son, that [s]he did littour heere..) not honour'd with A humane shape. **1879** ESCOTT *England* xxv. (1881) 403 The well-conducted soldier, save and except for a more or less constant *ennui*..may pass his days in comparative comfort. **1879** MCCARTHY *Own Times* II. 283 The Black Sea is, save for one little outlet.., a huge land-locked lake. **1894** HALL CAINE *Manxman* IV. xvi. 262 Saue for the slumbering fire, all was dark within the house.

¶**4.** Phrases like *save your grace, save your reverence* belong to SAFE *a.* 5. See also GRACE *sb.* 6 d, REVERENCE *sb.* 5; and cf. SAVING.

'Save your displeasure' (quot. *c* 1500) is perh. due to a confusion between this use and sense 1 above.

13.. *Seuyn Sag.* (W.) 687 Sauue your grace, wene ich hit nowt, Hit euere com in his thout. *c* **1500** *Three Kings' Sons* 139 It semeth, sauf your displeasir, that [etc.].

save, obs. form of SAFE, SALVE *sb.*[1]

saveable: see SAVABLE.

†**'saveage.** *Obs. rare*[−1]. [f. SAVE *v.* + -AGE. Cf. SALVAGE.] The action of saving.

1507 in Leadam *Sel. Cases Crt. Star Chamber* (Selden Soc.) 243 The seid ij gromes wer fyne for the sauege of their lyues to draw out their weppyns.

save-all ('seɪvɔːl). [f. SAVE *v.* + ALL.]

1. A means for preventing loss or waste.

a **1655** SIR T. MAYERNE *Archimag. Anglo-Gall.* Pref. (1658) 2 This Book is a Save-all; It suffers nothing to be lost. **1776** ADAM SMITH *W.N.* I. xi. III. I. 281 [The poultry] as they are fed with what would otherwise be lost, are a meer save-all. **1870** *Echo* 28 Nov., Wretched shifts and savealls of reserve and recruiting systems are enough to engage their attention, so far as their war administration is concerned.

2. A receptacle for collecting matter which would otherwise be lost and not utilized. Also *attrib.*

1797 *Monthly Mag.* III. 301 A refrigerator, from which proceeds an additional worm, to receive the spirit [in cooling and condensing], before it goes to the save-all. **1823** J. BADCOCK *Dom. Amusem.* 149 The fat of every kind collected in our kitchens, being rendered, or melted down from day to day, and cast into a 'save-all tub', will be found to produce very good soap. **1833** LOUDON *Encycl. Archit.* §1443 There is, immediately beneath the fountain [for spirits], a saveall, or pierced plate of pewter, through which the drippings from the glasses percolate, and are collected in a shallow basin below. **1884** *Health Exhib. Catal.* 71/2 Front Damper acting as a 'Tidy Betty' with Cinder-sifter or Save-all attached.

3. A contrivance to hold a candle-end in a candlestick while burning so that it may burn to the end; a common form is a pan with a projecting pin in the centre on which the candle-end is fixed.

c **1645** HOWELL *Lett.* (1655) IV. xxi. 58 In som this light goes out with an ill-favor'd stench; But others have a save-all to preserve it from making any snuff at all. **1682** HARTMAN *True Preserv. Health* 348 Heat the pin of a save-all, and then thrust it into the bigger end [of a small candle], and so set it upon a candlestick. **1747** *Gentl. Mag.* XVII. 444/2 Death's a dark-lanthorn, life a candle's-end Stuck on a save-all, soon to end in stink. **1895** *Army & Navy Price List* 15 Sept. 1316/2 [Candle] Saveall, White..each 0/4½.

4. A money-box to receive small savings or contributions. Also *dial.* (see quot. 1841).

1837 HOWITT *Rur. Life* (1842) 228 In this manner..enter your rooms..monks with their little savealls in their hands, collecting for hospitals. **1841** HARTSHORNE *Salopia Ant.* 555 *Save-all*,..an earthen bottle with slits at the sides, destin'd to receive all the savings of children.

5. A niggardly, stingy, miserly person. Now *dial.*

1785 GROSE *Dict. Vulgar Tongue, Saveall*,..also a miser. **1820** KEATS in *Life* II. 63 There is old Lord Burleigh, the high-priest of economy, the political save-all.

6. *Naut.* A sail set under another sail or between two other sails. Also *attrib.*

1794 *Rigging & Seamanship* I. 83 Vessels with one mast.. have..above the cross-jack, a small sail, called a save-all top-sail. **1846** in YOUNG *Naut. Dict.* **1878** D. KEMP *Man. Yacht Sailing* 366 *Save-all*, a water sail; a sail set underneath booms in light weather.

7. A pinafore; overall. *dial.*

1864 MRS. LLOYD *Ladies of Polcarrow* 103 Ever since I was a boy in a save-all. **1888** JESSIE FOTHERGILL *Lasses of Leverhouse* iv. 34 The black alpaca monstrosity which I.. denominated a save-all.

8. *attrib.* or *adj.* Parsimonious, stingy.

1812 SOUTHEY *Ess.* (1832) I. 141 The paltry proceedings of those save-all politicians, who boast of their economy in banishing newspapers from the public offices. **1856** R. W. PROCTER *Barber's Shop* xi. (1883) 65 Still pursuing his save-all theory of a pin a day is a groat a year.

saved (seɪvd), *ppl. a.* [f. SAVE *v.* + -ED[1].]

1. a. Delivered from damnation. Also *absol.*

a **1300** *Cursor M.* 10867 His folk al saued þan sal he mak. **14..** *Less. of Dirige* 409 in 26 *Pol. Poems* 120 Þe sauyd excusyd, þe dampnyd accusyd, As thay deseruyd echon haue. **1509** H. WATSON *Ship of Fools* Prol. (1517) A ij b, That thorugh theyr labour they may be of the nombre of ye saued. **1688** BUNYAN *Jerus. Sinner Saved* (1886) 123 If thy desires be firm..to become the saved of Christ, and His servant. **1868** H. LAW *Beacons of Bible* 78 Every saved soul shines for ever a monument of..sanctifying grace.

b. ***saved by the bell*** (*Boxing*) (see quot. 1971); hence *fig.* in general use, saved (as from an unpleasant occurrence) by timely interruption.

[**1932** *Ring* Nov. 3 Floored in the first session by a terrific right to the jaw, the bell saving the Jersey boy at the count of seven. **1954** F. C. AVIS *Boxing Dict.* 98 *Saved by bell*, a boxer saved from being counted out because the end of the round is signalled.] **1959** A. SILLITOE *Loneliness of Long-Distance Runner* 31 'Ain't it next door to a pub, then?' I wanted to know. He answered me sharp: 'No, it bloody well aint.'.. 'Then I don't know it,' I told him, saved by the bell. **1963** *Times* 18 May 8/5 If, in future, the bell interrupts a count, the count will continue until the boxer is counted out —unless he gets up in the meantime... The expression 'saved by the bell' will, therefore, become an anachronism. **1971** L. KOPPETT *N.Y. Times Guide Spectator Sports* v. 116 If a man is knocked down in the closing seconds of a round, so that the bell rings ending the round before the count of 10 has been reached, he can be 'saved by the bell'. **1976** G. SIMS

End of Web I. 13 Had he been saved by the bell... Was there still a chance of some lovers' games?

2. a. Hoarded, laid by; also with *up*. **b.** Economized; not spent or wasted.

1732 POPE *Ep. Bathurst* 194 Benighted wanderers, the forest o'er, Curse the sav'd candle and unop'ning door. **1834** S. BAGSTER *Managem. Bees* Pref. 6 Often.. have I spent the saved-up shilling to run into..the old menagerie in Exeter 'Change. **1875** SMILES *Thrift* vi. 93 Saved money, however little, will serve to dry up many a tear.

Savei, var. SEBEI.

saveine, obs. form of SAVIN.

saveloy ('sævəlɔɪ). [Corruption of F. *cervelas* (sɛrvəla): see CERVELAT.]

1. A highly seasoned cooked and dried sausage.

1837 DICKENS *Pickw.* lv, Mr. Solomon Pell..regaling himself..with a cold collation of an Abernethy biscuit and a saveloy. **1887** SMILES *Life & Labour* 333 Soyer, the gastronomist,..would stop at a stall in the Haymarket and luxuriate in eating a penny saveloy.

2. ***saveloy marble*** (see quot.).

1839 *Civil Engin. & Arch. Jrnl.* II. 452 *Cervellata.* Saveloy marble, red ground, white and green, with very fine interlaced white veins.

†**'savement.** *Obs.* Also **sauvement.** [a. OF. *sauvement*, f. *sauver* SAVE *v.*: see -MENT. Cf. Pr. *salvamen.*] Safety, salvation.

13.. *Guy Warw.* 3840 Iesu,..Saue him fram cumberment, & him oȝain bring in sauement. *c* **1315** SHOREHAM 7 *Sacram.* 406 Þorwe creymie anoynt strange he bi-compe His sauuement to winne. **13..** *E.E. Allit. P.* B. 940 Þer soȝt no mo to sauement of cities aþel fyue. *a* **1450** *Knt. de la Tour* cxi. (1906) 151 Symeon..saide with a high voys, 'Lo! here the clere light, and the sauement of the worlde'. **1485** CAXTON *Chas. Gt.* 236 By the is made the path of sauement.

saven, obs. form of SAVIN.

savenap(e, rare var. ff. SANAP *Obs.*

saveo(u)r(e, obs. forms of SAVIOUR, SAVOUR.

saver ('seɪvə(r)). Also 4 **sauver**, 4–5 **savere**, 6 ? **sawar.** [f. SAVE *v.* + -ER[1]. Cf. SAVIOUR.]

1. a. One who saves, preserves, or rescues from death, evil, or destruction; a saviour or preserver.

In early use said of Christ = SAVIOUR; now only used when *saviour* would seem inappropriate.

a **1300** *Cursor M.* 10541 Of hir sal cum þat man sauuer [*other MSS.* sauere]. *c* **1410** HOCCLEVE *Mother of God* 10 Modir of mercy..Saver of us by thy benevolence. **1538** BALE *Brefe Comedy Baptist* in *Harl. Misc.* (1744) I. 99 Your kynge, your sauer and redemer. *Ibid.*, For all men shall se their mercyfull sauer playne. **1608** B. JONSON *Masque at Ld. Haddington's*, Sauer of his King. **1700** C. NESS *Antid. Armin.* (1827) 58 Salvation is the work of the saved, not of the saver. **1833** M. SCOTT *Tom Cringle* xix, A statue erected to Lord Rodney the saver of the Island as he is always called from having crushed the fleet of Count de Grasse. **1872** TENNYSON *Gareth & Lynette* 858 For strong thou art and goodly therewithal, And saver of my life. **1891** *Longman's Mag.* Feb. 373 He hated his rescuer and saver.

†**b.** One who keeps or preserves a thing from destruction or waste. *Obs.*

1422 tr. *Secreta Secret., Priv. Priv.* 213 And therfor the nedyth to haue a constabil that shal not bene a destruere of thy trees, but a Kepere and a Sauere. **1573** TUSSER *Husb.* (1878) 168 Where all thing is common, what needeth a hutch? where wanteth a sauer, there hauocke is mutch.

c. One who saves (property) from wreck or destruction; a salvor.

1629 in Boys *Sandwich* (1792) 749 And do further ill entreat the savers and finders thereof [wrecks]. **1820** W. SCORESBY *Acc. Arctic Reg.* II. 329 The propriety of appropriating all wrecked stores to the use of the savers.

†**2.** 'One who escapes loss, though without gain' (J.). (Primarily a gaming term.) ***to make*** (oneself or another person) ***a saver***: to insure against or compensate for a loss. *Obs.*

1591 FLORIO *2nd Fruites* 71 *S.* What can I doe withall? I can not mend it. *A.* If I thought one hand would make me a sauer, I would play. *c* **1613** MIDDLETON *No Wit like a Womans* II. iii. (1657) 58 You'd need have a clear way, because y'are a bad pricker. *Mrs. Low.* Yet if my Bowl take bank, I shall go nigh To make my self a saver. **1668** HOWE *Bless. Righteous* xx. 388 Heaven were a poor Heaven, if it would not make us savers. **1676** LEE *Sophon.* IV. i. 45 Your Armies are the Cards which both must play; At least come off a saver if you may. **1687** DRYDEN *Hind & P.* III. 344 For laws of arms permit each injured man To make himself a saver where he can. **1691** —— *Arthur* II. 18 He puts the gain of Britain in a Scale, Which weighing with the loss of Emmeline, He thinks he's scarce a Saver. *a* **1700** SEDLEY *Poems* Wks. 1722 I. 46 We'll Game and give off Savers too.

3. One who saves, economizes, or hoards up.

1548 FORREST *Pleas. Poesye* 56 Some muste bee Sauers, Store is no sore. **1601** F. GODWIN *Bps. of Eng.* 460 A good sauer makes a well doer. **1727** SWIFT *St. Irel.* Wks. 1755 V. II. 167 Hence alone comes the dearness of land, since the savers have no other way to lay out their money. **1755** JOHNSON, *Saver*... 3. A good husband. **1830** CUNNINGHAM *Brit. Paint.* I. 319 A saver of bits of thread. **18..** COBDEN in Smiles *Self-help* (1859) 218 The accomplishment of all other great works..has been done by the savers, the thrifty. **1869** *Daily News* 14 Dec., The small farmers are great savers.

4. A means of saving or economizing.

1664 EVELYN *Sylva* xxii. (1679) 111 We find it [*sc.* the Fir] an extraordinary saver of Oak. **1901** *Munsey's Mag.* XXV. 393/2 The railroad,..when it can be used, is a wonderful saver. **1903** *Westm. Gaz.* 26 Oct. 15/1 The invention is a great labour-saver.

5. *Racing slang.* A hedging bet. Also *transf.*

1891 N. GOULD *Doub. Event* xvii. 123 Wells says Perfection will win,..but I've put a saver on Caloola. **1917** A. B. PATERSON *Three Elephant Power* 17 'I had a quid on,' he says. 'And..I had a saver on the second, too.' **1950** N. CARDUS *Second Innings* 163, I.. suggest a saver each way on Gunga Din. **1958** G. CASEY *Snowball* xvii. 168 A lot of people who had bet on Benny—and made sure of a saver on the Negro—put on a few shillings more at the ringside. **1974** RATHER & GATES *Palace Guard* II. v. 51 Nixon..decided to slap a deuce or two on a couple of long shots, as a 'saver'—just in case.

saver(e, saveray, obs. ff. SAVOUR, SAVORY.

save-reverence: see SIR-REVERENCE.

saverey, -ie, obs. forms of SAVORY, SAVOURY.

†**savernapron.** *rare.* [? corruption of AF. **save-naperon*, f. *saver* SAVE *v.* + *naperon*: see APRON. Cf. *savenappe* SANAP.] A table-napkin.

1422–3 *Abingdon Rolls* (Camden) 94 Item vij sauernaprons. Item x alie sauernaprons debiles.

saverous, obs. form of SAVOROUS.

savery(e, obs. forms of SAVORY, SAVOURY.

savete(e, saveure: see SAFETY, SAVOUR.

saveyne, savico: see SAVIN, SABICU.

Savile Row ('sævɪl rəʊ). The name of a street in London celebrated for fashionable and expensive tailoring establishments, used *attrib.* to designate such tailors, their styles, or wares, esp. men's suits.

1896 G. B. SHAW in *Sat. Rev.* 13 June 597/2 A suit turned out by a Savile Row tailor. **1934** *Cornh. Mag.* Sept. 366 Sinai, like a Savile Row tailor,..does not display its goods in the shop window for all to see. **1946** A. CHRISTIE *Hollow* xxiv. 206 She took in the Savile Row cut of Edward's clothes. **1948** 'J. TEY' *Franchise Affair* xii. 126 'I'll come along and help.' 'Not in that Savile Row suit, you won't.' **1955** T. H. PEAR *Eng. Social Differences* vii. 172 The tendency to conform with fashion, but not its extremes, marks the Savile Row tailor. **1972** M. FARHI *Pleasure of your Death* ii. 43 Van Loon..looked like a foetus—stillborn in a Savile Row suit.

savin, savine ('sævɪn). Forms: α. 1 **safene, -ine**, 1, 5– **savine**, 4–6 **savyne, saveine**, 5–6 **-eyne**, 7 **saven**; 4, 6– **savin**; β. 6–7, 9 **sabine**, 8 **sabin**. [a. OF. *savine* (in mod.F. replaced by the learned form *sabine*, whence the β forms above) = Sp., Pg. *sabina*, It. *savina*:—L. (*herba*) *Sabīna*, lit. 'Sabine herb' (*Sabīna* fem. of *Sabīnus* SABINE).

Cf. G. *saben-*, *sevenbaum* (for the many corrupt forms see Grimm), Du. *zevenboom.*]

1. A small bushy evergreen shrub, *Juniperus sabina*, a native of Europe and Western Asia, with spreading branches completely covered with short imbricating leaves, and bearing a small, round, bluish-purple berry.

The name is also applied to certain trees or shrubs resembling *Juniperus sabina*, as the Sea Wormwood, *Artemisia maritima*; the dwarf Juniper, *Juniperus nana*; *Cæsalpinia pulcherrima* (Indian savin); in the U.S. to the Red Cedar, *Juniperus virginiana*, and to *Torreya taxifolia*, one of the stinking cedars; and in the W. Indies to *Cæsalpinia bijuga*, *Fagara lentiscifolia* and *Xanthoxylum pterota*.

c **1000** *Sax. Leechd.* II. 312 Nim þas wyrte safenan & mersc mealwan. *Ibid.* III. 38 Wyll in buteran þas wyrta.. sauinan & curmeallan & feferfuȝean. *a* **1387** *Sinon. Barthol.* (Anecd. Oxon.) 18 *Ebel, i.* savin. **1390** GOWER *Conf.* III. 130 Ther is an herbe which men calleth Saveine. *a* **1400** *Pistill of Susan* 69 Þe sauyne [*MS. Phillipps* saveyne] and sypres, selcouþ to sene. **1567** MAPLET *Gr. Forest* 61 Sauin, is one of those kindes which..beareth leafe all seasons of the yeare. **1590** SPENSER *F.Q.* III. ii. 49 But th' aged Nourse..Had gathered Rew, and Savine. **1607** TOPSELL *Four-f. Beasts* 240 Agolethros and Sabine are poyson to Goates. **1707** MORTIMER *Husb.* (1721) II. 188 Sabin or Savin will make fine Hedges, and may be brought into any sort of Form by clipping. **1811** A. T. THOMSON *Lond. Disp.* (1818) 730 Ointment of Savine. Take of fresh leaves of savine, two parts; yellow wax, one part; lard, four parts. **1838** T. THOMSON *Chem. Org. Bodies* 464 Oil of sabine. It is obtained from the leaves of the *juniperus sabina*. Limpid. Has the odour and flavour of sabine. This plant furnishes a great deal of oil. **1861** MRS. STOWE *Pearl Orr's Isl.* I. 8 Only savins and mullens, with their dark pyramids or white spires of velvet leaves, diversified the sandy wayside. **1884** SARGENT *Rep. Forests N. Amer.* 183 *Juniperus Virginiana*... Red Cedar. Savin. *Ibid.* 186 *Torreya taxifolia*... Stinking Cedar. Savin.

2. The dried tops of this shrub, used as a drug.

Savin is strongly poisonous; it possesses emmenagogic properties, and hence was a common means of procuring abortion. It is also an anthelmintic, used chiefly in veterinary practice.

c **1000** *Sax. Leechd.* II. 100 Wiþ þon ilcan ȝenim safinan ȝnid to duste. **1573** TUSSER *Husb.* (1878) 97 Sauin, for the bots. **1590** BARROUGH *Meth. Physick* III. lvi. 193 Incessions made of the decoction of laurell berries, & leaues,.. motherwort, horehound, saueine, althæa, cammomill [etc.]. **1614** MARKHAM *Cheap Husb., Bull* xxix. 58 There is nothing killeth wormes in the bodies of cattell sooner than Sauen chopt small and beaten with sweet Butter. **1693** DRYDEN *Juvenal* vi. 775 Help her to make Manslaughter; let her bleed, And never want for Savin at her need. **1736** BAILEY *Househ. Dict.* 521 *Savin*, is of an incisive, penetrative and attenuating quality..; being powdered and mix'd with fresh butter, it is given to the quantity of a dram to persons troubled with the asthma. **1843** R. J. GRAVES *Syst. Clin. Med.* xxvi. 334 They were treated with lapis infernalis, Plenk's liniment, and powdered savine.

3. *attrib.* and *Comb.*, as ***savine-berry, -bush, -cerate, -oil, -tops, -tree; savin-leaved*** adj.

1681 GREW *Musæum* II. §ii. i. 219 *Savine-Berrys. About as big as those of the common Juniper, and of a blackish blew. **1672** JOSSELYN *New Eng. Rarities* 3 In these Gullies grow *Saven Bushes. **1826** S. COOPER *First Lines Surg.* (ed. 5) 448 A discharge should be kept up from the blistered surface by means of the *savine cerate. **1829** *Glover's Hist. Derby* I. 126 *Lycopodium alpinum*, mountain or *savin-leaved club-moss. **1858** SIMMONDS *Dict. Trade*, **Savine-oil*, an essential oil obtained by distilling the tops of the savine plant. **1695** BLACKMORE *Pr. Arth.* VII. 645 Henbane, Wormwood, Hemlock, *Savine Tops. **1611** TOURNEUR *Ath. Trag.* IV. i, There growes a *Sauin-tree next it forsooth. **1696** SLOANE *Catal. Plant. Jamaica* 128 Savine Trees. *Ibid.* 149 Indian Savin Tree. **1864** GRISEBACH *Flora W. Ind. Islands* 737 Savin tree: *Cæsalpinia bijuga* and *Fagara lentiscifolia.*

saving ('seɪvɪŋ), *vbl. sb.* [f. SAVE *v.* + -ING[1].]

1. The action of the verb SAVE; an instance of this. **a.** The action of rescuing or protecting; †a deliverance.

a **1300** *Cursor M.* 12775 Wijt we þan for quat resun For sauueing of vr dampnacioun, þat he now suilk baptiszing mass? *a* **1340** HAMPOLE *Psalter* xi. 6 Safynge of rightwis and dampnynge of wickid. *c* **1460** FORTESCUE *Abs. & Lim. Mon.* vi. (1885) 123 For the repressynge off rovers, sauynge off owre marchauntes, owre ffishers, and the dwellers vppon owre costes. **1523** LD. BERNERS *Froiss.* I. xxxix. 53 Syr Henry wolde nat let his wepon go for sauyng of his honour. **1571** GOLDING *Calvin on Ps.* xviii. 50 This election was myghtely ratifyed by continewall successe of savinges. **1611** BIBLE *Heb.* xi. 7 Noah..prepared an Arke to the sauing of his house. **1676** MOLLOY *De Jure Marit.* II. v. (1688) 240 If the Ship perishes only, and the Goods are safe, in that case the Goods ought to pay a proportion of a fifth or tenth penny, according to the easie or difficult winning or saving of the said Goods. **1848** CLOUGH *Amours de Voy.* I. 21 All the foolish destructions, and all the sillier savings.

b. The action of saving or economizing in expenditure (of money, time, labour, etc.); an instance of this, a reduction in expenditure.

1551 *Cal. Anc. Rec. Dublin* (1889) 426 For the..sawing of expenssis to the citizens. **1640** G. HERBERT *Jacula Prud.* 119 No Alchymy to saving. **1731–8** SWIFT *Pol. Conversat.* ii. Wks. 1751 XII. 259 *Lord Smart.* Come, hang Saving! bring us up a Halfp'orth of Cheese. **1772** C. HUTTON *Bridges* 5 Fewer arches..will produce great savings in the expence. **1832** HT. MARTINEAU *Life in Wilds* vi. 77 A great saving of time and labour. **1848** MILL *Pol. Econ.* I. v. §5 (1876) 45 Saving, in short, enriches, and spending impoverishes. **1854** RONALDS & RICHARDSON *Chem. Technol.* (ed. 2) I. 257 The saving of fuel is much greater when turf and wood are employed. **1883** *Law Rep. 11 Q.B. Div.* 569 The object of the society being the encouragement of saving.

c. In games: cf. SAVE *v.* 21 c.

1889 *Field* 26 Jan. 123/1 It was only the brilliant saving of Holmes, and the sound defence of the backs generally, that averted two or three scores.

2. *concr.* A sum of money saved; chiefly *pl.* sums of money saved from time to time (by the exercise of economy) and put by or hoarded up.

1737 *Gentl. Mag.* VII. 656/2 If he could save 500 or 1000*l.* a Year out of his Estate, he would certainly apply that Saving towards discharging his small Debts. **1786** MRS. A. M. BENNETT *Juvenile Indiscr.* I. 215 My hard savings and earnings. **1809** MALKIN *Gil Blas* V. i. ¶62 More than half my savings were laid out on repairs. **1824** MISS MITFORD *Village* Ser. I. 239 She had three or four hundred pounds to bequeath, partly her own savings, and partly a legacy from a distant relative. **1888** BRYCE *Amer. Commw.* II. xliii. II. 132 The working man who puts his savings into the house he lives in.

b. In the navy: (see quot. 1815).

1815 *Falconer's Dict. Marine* (ed. Burney), *Savings of Provisions*, implies the bread, wine, spirits, beef, pork, butter and cheese, which have been saved by the different persons or messes in any of his Majesty's ships, from the established allowance of those species; and for which the purser pays them, at the expiration of one, two, or three months at furthest, agreeable to the credit prices stated in his instructions. **1901** *Westm. Gaz.* 28 Aug. 8/2 The Committee dwells upon the difficulty of framing an ideal ration so long as canteens and the 'savings' system exist.

3. A salvo, reservation, saving clause. Now only in *Law*.

1477 *Rolls of Parlt.* VI. 171/1 All Offices, Fees, Rents and Annuitees..other than Rents services, be in no wise comprised or conteyned in this saving. **1542–3** *Act 34 & 35 Hen. VIII*, c. 5 §9 The sauinges reseruinges and prouisions ..of the saide former act. **1765** BLACKSTONE *Comm.* I. 367 Therein the tenant swore to bear faith to his sovereign lord, in opposition to all men, without any saving or exception. **1875** DIGBY *Real Prop.* viii. (1876) 343 The Statute of Uses contained a saving in favour of wills made before the first day of May, 1536. **1884** SELBORNE in *Law Times Rep.* L. 315/1 The savings from a repealing clause would not apply to any express antecedent provision of the Act inconsistent with them.

4. *attrib.* and *Comb.*: Now usu. with *pl.* **savings**: †**saving bank**: see SAVINGS BANK; †**saving-box**, a money-box for savings; **savings account**, a deposit account; **savings and loan** *U.S.*, used *attrib.* to designate a co-operative association which operates in the manner of a building society, though now offering additional services, as loans for purchases other than houses, and the issue of cheques to account-holders; also *absol.*; **savings book**, a book in which an official record is kept of sums deposited and withdrawn by the holder and of interest accrued; **savings-box** = *saving-box*; **saving(s institution** = SAVINGS BANK; †**(war) savings certificate**, introduced February 1916, renamed 1920, **(national) savings certificate**, a certificate declaring that the holder has invested a small sum in government funds, encashable at any time with accrued interest, and usually maturing after five or ten years. Cf. SAVINGS BANK.

1691 *D'Emilianne's Frauds Rom. Monks* 151, I have since understood, that all Tradesmen in Italy do each of them keep a *Saving-box, into which they put what Mony they can spare during the whole Year in order to their going in Pilgrimage. **1830** J. T. PRATT *Hist. Savings Banks* p. vij, The imperious necessity of *Saving Institutions for the industrious Poor. **1911** *Daily Colonist* (Victoria, B.C.) 29 Apr. 8/6 Encourage your boy to save by opening a *savings account for him. **1978** S. SHELDON *Bloodline* xxxix. 350 A London savings account with a balance of twenty-five thousand pounds. **1978** *Washington Post* 16 Feb. F5/4 (Advt.), You earn a high 6% on regular savings accounts. **1980** *Travel & the TSB* (Trustee Savings Bank Central Board), You'll need to show your Savings Account passbook and some identification. [**1877** *Acts & Resolves Gen. Court Mass.* ccxxiv. 613 The words 'coöperative saving fund and loan association' shall form a part of the name. **1882** *Chicago Business Directory* 86/1 Union Savings, Loan & Building Assn.] **1884** *Lakeside* (Chicago) *Ann. Directory of Business 1884-5* 1489/1 Sharpshooters' Building, *Savings and Loan Association. **1887** *Laws of State of N.Y.* dlvi. 720 All associations formed under the provisions hereof shall be known as co-operative savings and loan associations; and the name of every association, so formed, shall contain as a part thereof the words Co-operative Savings and Loan Association. **1921** *Proc. 34th Ann. Convention N.Y. State League of Savings & Loan Assoc.* 7 They believe in the State organization of savings and loan associations. **1962** J. H. EWALT *Business Reborn* i. 3 The typical predepression association [was] known more often as a building and loan than as a savings and loan. **1975** *New Yorker* 5 May 98/3 The Gibraltar Savings Association, of Houston, which is a subsidiary of the Imperial Corporation of America, a holding company that owns a number of savings-and-loan companies in four of the Western states. **1936** N. STREATFEILD *Ballet Shoes* xv. 232, I was quite ashamed of your *savings book... I care.. that you have a nice lot saved for when you are grown up. **1977** 'J. FRASER' *Hearts Ease in Death* ix. 103 The proprietor.. was standing beside the Post Office counter when Aveyard came in, pushing a savings book.. through the grille. *c* **1863** T. TAYLOR *Ticket-of-Leave Man* II. 32 I've put away a shilling every week out of my savings... It's all here. (Goes to table, and.. puts a *savings-box into his hand.) **1922** JOYCE *Ulysses* 30 Three, Mr Deasy said, turning his little savingsbox about in his hand. **1978** *Church Times* 27 Jan. 14/1 (*heading*) Savings box for Lent. **1916** *Times* 19 Feb. 5/1 The new War *Savings Certificates, which can be bought from today for 15s. 6d. each at any money-order office. **1919** *Saving* 3 Dec. 140/2 Leyton school children have bought Savings Certificates to the value of over £48,000. **1920** *Act 10 & 11 Geo. V* c. 12 (*title*) An Act.. to extend to National Savings Certificates the enactments relating to War Savings Certificates. **1927** W. DEEPING *Doomsday* xix. 209 Seventy-five pounds in Savings Certificates. **1932**, **1941** [see *National Savings Certificate* s.v. NATIONAL *a.* 5]. **1961** E. S. TURNER *Phoney War* x. 131 If I buy three Savings Certificates at 15s. each the State will have to pay me interest and eventually repay my capital. **1978** F. MACLEAN *Take Nine Spies* vii. 235 Into his Foreign Office black leather briefcase.. he crammed nearly £300 in notes and a bundle of Savings Certificates. **1832** *Encycl. Amer.* XI. 216/2 **Savings Institutions*, or, as they are often called *Savings Banks*.

saving ('seɪvɪŋ), *ppl. a.* [f. SAVE *v.* + -ING².]

1. a. That delivers, rescues or preserves from peril; that protects or guards from anything undesirable.

1535 COVERDALE *Ps.* xii[i.] 5 My hert is ioyfull in thy sauynge health. **1692** R. L'ESTRANGE *Fables* xxix. 29 There's No Living however without Law: and there's No Help for't in many Cases, if the Saving Equity be Over-rul'd by the Killing Letter of it. **1718** G. SEWELL *Proclam. Cupid* 15 Woman.. A Guardian Angel, and a saving Saint. **1804** WORDSW. *Vaudracour & Julia* 194 The silver shower, whose reckless burthen weighs Too heavily upon the lily's head, Oft leaves a saving moisture at its root. **1885-94** R. BRIDGES *Eros & Psyche* June xvi, And with that lie the wounded man they slew, Hiding the saving truth which well they knew.

b. *saving piece*: a piece of wood to prevent injury to the machine in the process of cutting.

1839 URE *Dict. Arts*, etc. 160 [Machine for cutting the edges of books, banknotes, &c.]. Upon this latter board is placed the 'material to be cut', with a saving piece between it.

2. *Theol.* That delivers from sin and eternal death by the power of God's grace.

a **1300** *Cursor M.* 8097 Sceu vs þe sauuand tre, sir king. **1597** HOOKER *Eccl. Pol.* v. lx. §2 That they.. might.. obteine as well that sauing grace of imputation which taketh away all former giltines. **1671** MILTON *P.R.* 474 But to guide Nations in the way of truth By saving Doctrine. *a* **1711** KEN *Hymns Festiv.* Poet. Wks. 1721 I. 309 May I from his own Writings learn His Love, and Saving-Truths discern. **1712** POPE *Messiah* 107 But fix'd his word, his saving pow'r remains. **1732** BERKELEY *Alciphr.* VII. §11 That notion of a saving faith which is required in a Christian. **1809-10** COLERIDGE *Friend* (1865) 207 Good works may exist without saving principles..; but saving principles.. never can exist without good works.

3. *gen.* That delivers from moral or intellectual error; also, of a quality, 'redeeming', exempting from unqualified condemnation or censure. Often as a direct transference from sense 2. Now freq. in phr. *saving grace*.

1599 SHAKS. *Hen. V*, v. ii. 217 If euer thou beest mine, Kate, as I haue a sauing Faith within me tells me thou shalt. **1735** POPE *Prol. Sat.* 40 And drop at last, but in unwilling ears, This saving counsel, 'Keep your piece nine years'. **1852** TENNYSON *Ode Dk. Wellington* iv, Foremost captain of his time, Rich in saving common-sense. **1865** M. ARNOLD *Ess. Crit.* ix. (1875) 373 The obedience demanded by theology and the knowledge demanded by philosophy are alike saving. **1902** ELIZ. BANKS *Newspaper Girl* 210, I am not, I believe, without a saving sense of humour. **1910** W. G. COLLINGWOOD *Dutch Agnes* 168 She plied me with questions until I was very nearly tormented into confession. But I had the saving grace, I trust, to remember John Bell's adage of *Vir sapit qui pauca loquitur*. **1932** J. B. PRIESTLEY *Self-Selected Ess.* 282 Here, in its plain lack of ideas, is the saving grace of this dull company. **1960** C. DAY LEWIS *Buried Day* viii. 170 Tchehov.. has indeed said, but with all the saving grace of his felicitous compassion, that we are not put on the earth to be happy. **1978** *Lancashire Life* Oct. 36/1 In all the shouting, the bitter recriminations, there was the saving grace of native good humour.

4. Accustomed to save, hoard up, or economize; avoiding unnecessary expenses; tending to reduce expenses; parsimonious, economical.

1581 PETTIE *Guazzo's Civ. Conv.* II. (1586) 88b, If you will haue riches to be a help to Gentrie, it shall behooue a man rather to bee sauing, that he may be able to keepe himselfe rich. **1606** CHAPMAN *Mons. D'Olive* I. i, Indeed that's the savingst way. **1625** BACON *Ess., Expense* (Arb.) 53 A Man had need, if he be Plentifull, in some kinde of Expence, to be as Sauing againe, in some other. As if he be Plentifull in Diet, to be Sauing in Apparell. **1712** ARBUTHNOT *John Bull* I. x, Not but that she lov'd Mony, for she was of a saving Temper. **1729** SWIFT *Direct. Serv., Butler* Wks. 1751 XIV. 26 Be saving of your Candles. **1771** LUCKOMBE *Hist. Print.* 225 A saving way, similar to this, was .. from three sets of Punches.. to cast six different Bodies of Letter. **1848** THACKERAY *Van. Fair* xi, Mrs. Crawley was a saving woman and knew the price of port wine.

†**5.** 'Not turning to loss, though not gainful' (J.); neither winning nor losing. *Obs.*

1614 ? BRETON *I would & would not* lxxiii, When weather-beaten Sailes, with winde, & raine, Scarce make a Sauing-Voyage home againe. **1632** in *10th Rep. Hist. MSS. Comm.* App. v. 478 The greate plentie of corne that remaines uppon their handes, and which they cannot utter at any saveing price. **1645** WITHER *Vox Pacif.* 94 A likely means, to get a saving-game. **1709** POPE *Let. Wycherley* 20 May *Lett.* (1735) I. 40, I can be content with a bare saving Game, without being thought an eminent Hand. **1713** ADDISON *Guard.* No. 97 ¶3 Silvio.. was resolved to make a saving bargain of it. **1765** *Museum Rust.* IV. 174, I have no great expectations from this plantation, though, I fancy, it will be a saving crop. **1826** SCOTT *Mal. Malagr.* iii, A country, where industry and skill can but play a saving game, at best, against national disadvantages. **1828-32** WEBSTER (with example: 'the ship has made a saving voyage').

6. Making a reservation; furnishing a proviso.

1700 TYRRELL *Hist. Eng.* II. 853 With a Saving Clause, that it should not be drawn into Example. **1838** DICKENS *Nich. Nick.* I, 'Will you prevent me?' asked Sir Mulberry, with a laugh. 'Ye-es, if I can;' returned the other, promptly. 'A very proper saving clause, that last', said Sir Mulberry; 'and one you stand in need of'. **1855** BROWNING *Before* 32 Now, enough of your chicane of prudent pauses, Sage provisos, sub-intents, and saving-clauses.

saving ('seɪvɪŋ), *prep.* and *conj.* [absol. use of the pr. pple. of SAVE *v.* Cf. *excepting*.] **A.** *prep.*

1. Excepting, except; = SAVE *prep.* 1.

c **1386** CHAUCER *Knt.'s T.* 1980 No man myghte gladen Theseus Sauynge his olde fader Egeus. *c* **1440** *Alphabet of Tales* 139 His guidis wer all tane fro hym safeyng a mantill. **1513** DOUGLAS *Æneis* I. Prol. 155 The thre first bukis he hes ourhippit quyte, Salfand ane little twiching Polidorus, And the tempest sent furth be Eolus. **1569** *Reg. Privy Council Scot.* Ser. I. II. 4 Sauffing suche as ar attaynted. **1650** TRAPP *Comm. Exod.* v. 4 Anie thing seem's due work to a carnal minde saving God's service. **1808** SOUTHEY *Lett.* (1856) II. 115 Saving Joanna Baillie, we had no very interesting people this season. **1887** SAINTSBURY *Hist. Elizab. Lit.* viii. (1890) 302 There is no complete collection even of the poems, saving a privately printed one.

†**b.** ***all saving but, ne saving but***: excepting only. *Obs.*

a **1400-50** *Alexander* 3707 A lande, as þe buke tellis, a large & a noble, All sauand bot serpentis & oþire sere bestis. *Ibid.* 4037 Sen at we Ioy nouthire gemmes, ne Iuwels in cofirs, Pelour, pirre, ne perle, ne na proude wedis, Ne sauand bot to sustene with oure awen sary craftis.

†**c.** With pers. pron. in the nominative. *Obs.*

1526 TINDALE *Rev.* ii. 17 And in the stone a newe name wrytten, which no man knoweth, savinge he that receaveth hit. [So **1611**.] **1588** PARKE tr. *Mendoza's Hist. China* 254 Al their people [were] cast away, sauing they, who escaped by vsing great diligence. **1594** SPENSER *Amoretti* xxxv. 14 All this worlds glory seemeth vayne to me, And all their showes but shadowes, saving she.

†**d.** = but for; cf. SAVE *prep.* 1 d. *Obs.*

1540 *Aberd. Reg.* (1844) I. 173 And to deliuer thair schip agane, with hir pertinentis, safand awentour of see, to the saidis Thomas and Robert.

2. Without prejudice or offence to. ***saving (one's) reverence***: see REVERENCE *sb.* 5 b.

c **1386** CHAUCER *Merch. T.* 522 And finally he dooth al his labour As he best myghte sauynge his honour To haste hem fro the mete in subtil wyse. **1387** TREVISA *Higden* (Rolls) VIII. 79 Savynge his owne worschippe [L. *salvo honore suo*]. *c* **1400** [see REVERENCE *sb.* 5 b]. *c* **1400** *Destr. Troy* 7587 Therfore, sothely me semeth, sauyng your wille, Hit is bettur þis bold kyng in the burgh hold. **1530** TINDALE *Answ. More's Dial.* Wks. (1573) 253/2 When we say.. I be-shrew him sauing my charitie, there we take it for patience. **1562** WINȜET *Cert. Tractates* I. (S.T.S.) I. 9 And zow (saifing zour dew honoris we speik). **1577** FULKE *Confut. Purg.* 382 But sauing his wisedome, he must geue vs leaue to aunswere for our selues. **1596** HARINGTON *Metam. Ajax* Answ. Let., Euen so I must write in this discourse, some time indeede as homely (sauing your worship) as you shall lightly see. **1596** SHAKS. *Tam. Shr.* II. i. 71 Sauing your tale Petruchio, I pray let vs that are poore petitioners speake too? **1607** NORDEN *Surv. Dial.* I. 15 Sauing your tale, Sir, we poore Country-men doe not thinke it good to haue our Lands plotted out. **1611** BEAUM. & FL. *Knt. Burn. Pestle* II. ii, You lookt so grim, and, as I may say it, saving your presence, more like a Giant than a mortal man. **1837** HALLAM *Lit. Eur.* I. iii. §96 His own opinions, saving the authority of the church, he was willing to defend. **1907** ELIZ. ROBINS *Convert* ii. 24 There's nothing I should quite so much hate talking about as politics —saving your presence.

b. ***saving correction*** [= F. *sauf correction*]: subject to correction; if I am not mistaken. *rare.*

1830 A. W. FONBLANQUE *Eng. under 7 Administr.* (1837) II. 65 It seems to me, saving correction, that this does not concern us.

†**3.** With the reservation of. *Obs.*

1477 *Exch. Rolls Scotl.* VIII. 403 *note*, To be haldin.. to the said Johne and Agnes.. saulfing alanerly to ws and oure successouris the cariage of samekl of the saidis landis as the said Johne and Agnes occupiis [etc.]. **1609** SKENE *Reg. Maj.* 43 Saifeand alwise the service to the other over-lord, for the lands haldin of him.

†**4.** In default of, for lack of. *Obs. rare.*

c **1400** *Destr. Troy* 1126, I will say for myself, sauyng a bettur, As me thinkes full throly with-outyn threp more.

B. *conj.*

1. = EXCEPT, SAVE *conjs.* **a.** With clause introduced by *that*. Also, †with ellipsis of *that*.

1535 COVERDALE *Eccl.* v. 12 And what pleasure more hath he that possesseth them, sauynge that he maye loke vpon them with his eyes? **1578** LYTE *Dodoens* I. iii. 8 The wilde kinde of Buglosse is like to the small Buglosses.. sauing the leaues be rougher, smaller, and narrower. **1600** J. PORY tr. *Leo's Africa* VI. 269 The flesh.. tasteth not much vnlike to the flesh of a dunghill-cocke, sauing that it is more tough. **1720** MRS. MANLEY *Power of Love* I. 40 The Count of Briançon's Affairs seemed to keep the same Situations, saving his Love more and more increased, as his Hopes abated.

b. With advb. phrase. Also (rarely) ***saving for*** = but for, except as regards.

1473 *Rental Bk. Cupar-Angus* (1879) I. 168 Wilzam beand alegyt and fre of al aucht and wunt seruys, savand gyfe in tyme of harueyst we gader our tendis that he supple and help efter as we neyd. **1523** LD. BERNERS *Froiss.* I. cclxviii. 397 The duke of Lancastre.. thought to haue gone and dyned in the frenchmens lodgynges (sauynge for the fyre and smoke that they had made wolde not suffre him). **1538** CRANMER in *St. Papers Hen. VIII*, I. 590 To graunte hensforth none other lycence to any other printer saving to theym, for the printyng of the said Bible. **1550** CROWLEY *Last Trump.* 1218 Delite in nothyng sauinge in doynge thy duty. **1611** BIBLE *Matt.* v. 32 Whosoeuer shall put away his wife, sauing for the cause of fornication, causeth her to commit adultery. *a* **1661** FULLER *Worthies, Suff.* (1662) III. 54 Though the general breadth be but twenty [miles], saving by the Sea-side. **1840** DICKENS *Old C. Shop* i, Saving in the country I seldom go out until after dark. **1877** SWINBURNE *Note C. Brontë* 54 Saving for her 'plentiful lack' of inborn baby-worship.

†**2.** Provided that. *Obs.*

1592-3 in Ellis *Orig. Lett.* Ser. III. IV. 111 The which Clergie government they would have to be exempted from the temporall government, saving they speake not agaynst the Prynces government towching the supremacye.

'**savingly**, *adv.* [f. SAVING *ppl. a.* + -LY².]

1. In saving, a sparing, or frugal manner.

1553 GRIMALDE *Cicero's Offices* I. (1558) 47 To leade our life sauinglie [L. *parce*], chastelie, sagelie, and soberlie. **1673** R. HEAD *Canting Acad.* 167 They begin to quaff at *Ut*, savingly. **1883** R. G. WHITE *Wash. Adams* 7 Having lived savingly in the past on fewer hundreds a year.

2. *Theol.* In a way that ensures salvation. Common in the 17th c.

1629 H. BURTON *Babel no Bethel* 31 If any.. come to beleeue otherwise then that Church teacheth them, to wit, sauingly, whence haue they that beleefe? **1648** JENKYN *Blind Guide* iv. 120 The naturall man hath no power to know savingly the things of the Spirit of God. **1719** DE FOE *Crusoe* I. 260, I seriously pray'd to God, that he would enable me to instruct savingly this poor Savage. **1877** W. BRUCE *Comm. Rev.* 5 Practical love is the last link in the chain which connects man savingly with his Maker.

savingness ('seɪvɪŋnɪs). *rare.* [-NESS.]

1. 'Tendency to promote eternal salvation' (J.).

a **1658** DURHAM *Comm. Rev.* II. iii. (1660) 123 One in the search and trial of the sincerity and savingnesse of his Grace, is not only [etc.]. *a* **1677** MANTON *Christ's Eternal Exist.* vii. (1685) 193 Now if the fulness of the Godhead dwelt in him who gave this Covenant, we cannot deny either the certainty or the perfection, or the savingness of it.

2. The quality of being saving, sparing, frugal or parsimonious.

1727 BAILEY, vol. II, *Savingness*, Frugality. **1755** in JOHNSON. **1876** A. J. EVANS *Through Bosnia* i. 32 The savingness of the race was noticeable in their clothing, which was the same they had brought with them from Bulgaria.

savings bank. Orig. saving bank, also savings' bank. [f. *savings* pl. (see SAVING *vbl. sb.* 2) + BANK *sb.*³] An institution for encouraging thrift, by receiving small deposits at interest.

In the United Kingdom the principal institution of this kind is now the ***National Savings Bank***, a government-owned organization whose services are available at post office counters, formerly known as the POST OFFICE *Savings Bank*. *Trustee Savings Banks* were originally designed for the small investor and were managed by unpaid trustees (under the control of the National Debt Commissioners) but have now become a public limited company offering the full range of banking services and retaining only the abbreviated title *TSB*.

1817 *Act 57 Geo. III*, c. 105 Sched. A, The sum above stated is the exclusive Property of the Saving Bank specified in this our Order. **1819** *Ann. Biography* III. 215 In him [*sc.* G. Rose] the..system of saving banks found an active friend and patron. **1844** *Regul. & Ord. Army* 150 The Regimental Savings' Bank. **1886** C. E. PASCOE *London of To-day* xxvi. (ed. 3) 242 Investments in Consols have been placed within the reach of the poor through the medium of the Savings Bank. *Ibid.* xliii. (ed. 3) 382 Communications from the Savings Bank Department.

Saviny, var. SAPINY.

saviour ('seɪvjə(r)). Forms: 3-4 **sauveur**, 3-5 **sauveour**, 3-5 **saveour(e**, 4 **sauveor**, **saveor**, **-iur**, **-our**, **safeoure**, *Sc.* **safare**, **saweoure**, 4, 6 **sauvour**, **savioure**, 4-6 **savyour(e**, 5 **savyowur**, 5-6 **savyor**, 6 **salveour**, **-iour**, *Sc.* **salvior**, **salweour**, 4, 6-8 (9 chiefly *U.S.*) **savior**, 4- **saviour**. [a. OF. *sauveour* (mod.F. *sauveur*) = Pr., Sp., Pg. *salvador*, It. *salvatore*:—late L. *salvātōr-em*, agent-n. f. *salvāre* to SAVE.]

1. a. One who delivers or rescues from peril.

a **1300** *Cursor M.* 4666 His nam þai chaunged, fra þat our, And cald him 'warld sauueour'. *c* **1375** *Sc. Leg. Saints* i. (*Petrus*) 674 And petir till hym [Paul] þis can say:..far wele ay..lledar of heile and saweoure!' **1535** COVERDALE *Ecclus.* xlvi. 1 A greate sauioure vnto the electe of God. **1560** DAUS tr. *Sleidane's Comm.* 120 Saynct Genevefa is the saviour of Paris. **1611** BIBLE *Neh.* ix. 27 Thou gauest them sauiours, who saued them out of the hand of their enemies. **1711** POPE *Temp. Fame* 163 Bold Scipio, saviour of the Roman state; Great in his triumphs, in retirement great. **1774** WILKES *Corr.* (1805) IV. 185 Those who..now dare to persecute the saviour of India. **1871** BROWNING (*title*) Prince Hohenstiel-Schwangau: Saviour of Society. **1887** A. E. HOUSMAN *Shropshire Lad* i, To fields that bred them brave, The saviours come not home to-night.

b. *transf.* in nonce-uses.

c **1399** CHAUCER *Purse* 16 (Fairf.) Now purse that ben to me my lyves lyght And saveour as doun in this worlde here. **1552** LATIMER *Serm. 1st Sund. Epiph.* (1584) 297 Likewise shippes and boates..vpon the Seas are Sauiours, for they saue vs from the fury, rage, and tempest of the Sea. **1804** *Something Odd* III. 126 Thus died the means I had looked to as the saviour of myself and children.

2. a. He who saves mankind from sin and its consequences: as a title of God, and esp. of Christ (in the latter application often ***Our Saviour***). Now always with capital S.

a **1300** *Cursor M.* 15015 Welcum sauuer! lang has þou ben, Al sal thoru þe be bett. **13..** *Coer de L.* 2087 He swore a ful grete othe, By Jesu Cryst our Saviour. **1362** LANGL. *P. Pl.* A. XI. 66 Whi wolde god vr saueour suffre such a worm In such a wrong wyse the wommon to bigyle? *a* **1450** MYRC *Instr. Par. Priests* 12 3ef þow plese thy sauyoure 3ef thow be not grete clerk Loke thow moste on thys werk. **1472** *Rec. St. Mary at Hill* 16 In the name of our lord Ihesu Criste our Savyour: Amen. *c* **1500** *Lancelot* 2096 This is the vyrgyne, this is the blessit flour That Ihesu bur that is our salweour. **1513** BRADSHAW *St. Werburge* II. 354 The yere of our saueour in his humanite viii hundreth complet .v. and seuentie. **1602** SHAKS. *Ham.* I. i. 159 That Season.. Wherein our Sauiours Birth is celebrated. **1643** SIR T. BROWNE *Relig. Med.* I. §3 At the sight of a Crosse or Crucifix I can dispense with my hat, but scarse with the thought or memory of my Saviour. **1667** MILTON *P.L.* III. 412 Hail Son of God, Saviour of Men. *a* **1738** SWIFT *Serm. Mutual Subj.* (1744) 11 Our Saviour tells us that every Man is our Neighbour. **1753** HANWAY *Trav.* (1762) I. III. xxviii. 121 Who is the king, the lawgiver, the redeemer, and the savior. **1813** SHELLEY *Q. Mab* VII. 144 Millions shall live and die, Who ne'er shall call upon their Saviour's name. **1864** TENNYSON *En. Arden* 783 O God Almighty, blessed Saviour,..Uphold me, Father.

†**b.** ***to receive one's Saviour, to give*** (a person) ***his Saviour***, etc.: common ME. phrases referring to the reception and administration of the Eucharist.

c **1400** *Rom. Rose* 6434 But thou yeve me my Saviour At Ester. *a* **1450** MYRC *Instr. Par. Priests* 1883 And 3ef he aske hys sauyour, Gyf hym hyt wyþ gret honour. **1470-85** MALORY *Arthur* XVII. xi. 706 Thenne asked she her saueour and as soone as she had receyued hit the soule departed from the body.

3. Saint Saviour. (See SAINT *a.* 3.) †**a.** Used in oaths. *Obs.* **b.** [= eccl. L. *ecclesia Sancti Salvatoris*], the title of the cathedral church of Rome, usually called St. John Lateran. **c.** The title of the monastic order founded by St. Bridget.

13.. *Guy Warw.* 5318 Þou wroche glotoun losaniour, Þou schalt þe 3eld, bi seyn Sauour. *c* **1330** *Arth. & Merl.* 2908 (Kölbing) Forth went anon sir Kay & ledde his fader, sir Antour, to þe chirche of seyn sauour. **1728** CHAMBERS *Cycl.* s.v., Order of St. Saviour, is a religious Order founded by St. Bridget. **1873** J. H. BLUNT *Myrr. our Ladye* p. xi, The Monastery of St Saviour and St Bridget of Syon of the Order of St Augustine.

4. *attrib.* (appositive), as in ***saviour-ark***, ***-arm***, ***-god***, ***-youth***; also ***saviour-like*** adj.

1836 GLADSTONE in *Good Words* (1871) 366 Is there..no *saviour ark That..bears the children, loved of God and blest, Unto the land of rest? **18..** SHELLEY *Assassins* ii. Prose Wks. 1888 II. 158 How many holy liars..would his *saviour arm drag from their luxurious couches. **1738** WESLEY *Ps.* XXIV. vi, This is the chosen Royal Race That seek their *Saviour-God to see. **1587** GOLDING *De Mornay* xxx. 568 There are two commings of Christ, the one in lowlynes.., Poore, Lowely, and *Sauiourlyke; and the other in maiestie. **1801** SOUTHEY *Thalaba* x. xxxv, Laila rush'd between To save the *saviour Youth.

b. Special combinations: **saviour's blanket**, **flannel**, in Sussex and Kent, a local name for several plants with greyish downy leaves, esp. lamb's ears, *Stachys lanata*, or mullein, *Verbascum thapsus*.

1882 H. FRIEND *Gloss. Devonshire Plant Names* 10 In Sussex the small plant (*Stachys lanata*) with a similar leaf is called 'Saviour's Blanket'. **1927** V. WOOLF *Jrnl.* 4 July (1980) III. 144 They [*sc.* slightly furred cheeks] are like saviours flannel, of which she picked me a great bunch, in texture.

Hence **'savioress**, a female saviour; **'saviourhood**, **'saviourship**, the quality or fact of being a saviour.

c **1553** LATIMER in Foxe *A. & M.* (1563) 1309/2 When men can not be content that she [*sc.* our Lady] was a creature saued, but as it were a sauioresse, not neding saluation. **1649** JER. TAYLOR *Gt. Exemp.* III. Disc. xix. 143 Polycrita Naxia [expired] being saluted the Saviouresse of her countrey. **1650** FULLER *Pisgah* IV. v. 91 Finding an Egyptian wronging an Israelite he kils him; shewing therein some signes of that Saviour-ship, which God intended him for. **1864** P. BROOKS *Myst. Iniq.*, etc. xviii. (1893) 317 What if there had been for ever a Saviourhood in the Deity. **1893** *Athenæum* 30 Dec. 919/2 The Indian Buddhist Cult of Avalokita and his Consort Tārā the Savioress. **1900** R. J. CAMPBELL in *Chr. World Pulpit* 31 Jan. 71 The Saviourhood of Christ. **1905** MARZIALS *Browning* 49 Unfolding the mysteries of his saviourship of society.

saviour, savir, obs. forms of SAVOUR.

†**'savite.** *Obs.* [f. the name of Professor P. *Savi* + -ITE[1].] = NATROLITE.

1852 *Amer. Jrnl. Sci. & Arts* Ser. II. XIV. 64 *Savite.*

savite, saviur, obs. ff. SAFETY, SAVIOUR.

‖**savoir** (savwar). [Fr., = to know.] Knowledge. Used *ellipt.* for SAVOIR FAIRE or SAVOIR VIVRE.

1823 LADY BLESSINGTON *Jrnl.* 12 Aug. in E. Clay *Lady Blessington in Naples* 64 Glad as I was to profit by the *savoir* of Sir William Gell.., yet I could have wished to ramble alone. **1911** A. BENNETT *Card* x. 236 He had latterly acquired a considerable amount of social *savoir.* **1952** W. STEVENS in *Nation* 6 Dec. 519 It is as if We had come to an end of the imagination, Inanimate in an inert savoir.

‖**savoir faire** (savwar fɛr). [Fr.; *savoir* (formerly often miswritten *sçavoir*) to know, know how (inf. used subst.) + *faire* to do.] Tact, address; the instinctive knowledge of the right course of action upon any given emergency.

1815 SCOTT *Guy M.* xxxv, He had great confidence in his own *savoir faire.* **1840** BARHAM *Ingol. Leg.* Ser. II. *Black Mousquetaire*, He..show'd so much of the true *sçavoir faire.* **1886** *Manch. Exam.* 15 Mar. 5/5 Sir Charles Warren has the versatility and *savoir-faire* which will enable him to do good work as Chief Commissioner of the London police. **1897** E. A. BARTLETT *Battlefields of Thessaly* iv. 74 He was a fine powerful man, with plenty of courage and *savoir faire.* **1924** *Granta* 25 Apr. 361/2 He had, it seems, spent previously some months at Deauville and Paris..and there acquired that polished French and developed that *savoir-faire*, both so typical of him. **1965** A. RENOIR in Bessinger & Creed *Medieval & Linguistic Stud.* 159 If he is indeed the speaker's husband and Wulf her lover, we could hardly expect him to stretch the limits of *savoir faire* to the point of offering the latter a cup of mead at the family table. **1974** J. BETJEMAN *Nip in Air* 28 A luncheon and a drink or two, a little *savoir faire*——.

‖**savoir vivre** (savwar vivr). [Fr.; *savoir* (see prec.) + *vivre* to live.] Ability in the conduct of life, knowledge of the world and of the usages customary in good society.

1755 MASON *Let. to Gray* (1853) 30 Though France is remarkable for its *savoir vivre* and Italy for its *virtù*, yet Germany is the reservoir of solid literature. **1806** J. PINKERTON *Recoll. Paris* II. 98 The use of red wine with oysters shews great want of sçavoir vivre. **1878** GEO. ELIOT *Dan. Der.* xlviii, People with any *savoir vivre* don't make a fuss about such things.

Savonarola (sævɒnə'rəʊlə). [The name of the Dominican monk, Girolamo *Savonarola* (1452–98), famed for his fierce opposition to ecclesiastical, moral, and political licence and corruption.] **1.** Used allusively to designate someone considered puritanical in attitude, esp. in regard to the arts.

1916 G. B. SHAW *Androcles & Lion* p. xv, They save society from ruin by criminals and conquerors as well as by Savonarolas and Knipperdollings. **1963** W. K. ROSE in *Lett. Wyndham Lewis* (1963) III. 122 This might change abruptly to an angry, mind-scourging Savonarola. **1980** R. LUDLUM *Bourne Identity* xvi. 252 He was a Savonarola, but without religious principles, only his own odd morality.

2. In full, ***Savonarola chair.*** A kind of folding chair typical of the Italian Renaissance (see quots.).

1918 G. L. HUNTER *Italian Furnit. & Interiors* (1920) I. p. iv, Of Italian chairs there are more types than were until recently known to exist:..folding 'X' chairs of the type sometimes called 'Savonarola', wonderful 'Dante' chairs. **1927** EBERLEIN & RAMSDELL *Pract. Bk. Ital., Span. & Port. Furnit.* 71 The really correct name for both the so-called 'sedia Dantesca' and the so-called 'sedia Savonarola' is *sedia del campo* or *field chair*... Being readily portable when folded up, they were carried on campaigns... These chairs were likewise commonly used by the Florentines for resting, dining, writing and reading... The finest of the 'Savonarola' chairs were made of walnut. **1969** *Observer* 11 May (Colour Suppl.) 17 Savonarola's folding chair..gave its name to this characteristic piece of Renaissance furniture —a savonarola. **1972** *Country Life* 23 Mar. 723/1 Knowledgeable inspection of the oak will reveal these shams which have been sold under such names as Dante and Savonarola chairs.

Hence **Savona'rolan** *a.*

1960 K. CLARK *Looking at Pictures* 184 Savonarolan puritanism has made Botticelli renounce the physical beauty which he still thought appropriate to the blessed spirits in his Dante drawings. **1976** *Jrnl. R. Soc. Arts* Mar. 167/2 Michelangelo himself, of course, had a strong strain of Savonarolan puritanism in his background.

‖**savonette** ('sævɔnɛt). Also 8 **savonet.** [Fr. (now written *savonnette*), dim. of *savon* soap: see -ET[1].] (See quots.)

1706 PHILLIPS (ed. Kersey), *Savonet*, (*Fr.*) a Wash-Ball or other sort of Compound, to wash the Face or Hands with. **1866** COOLEY *Toilet* 438 Savonettes; Soap balls; Wash Balls ..are made of any of the mild toilet-soaps, scented at will, generally with the addition of powdered starch or farina, and sometimes, sand.

b. ***savonette-tree*** [= F. *arbre à savonnettes*], a W. Indian tree, *Pithecolobium micradenium*, the bark of which is used as a substitute for soap.

1864 GRISEBACH *Flora W. Ind. Islands* 787.

Savonius (sə'vəʊnɪəs). The name of Sigurd J. *Savonius* (*fl.* 1930), Finnish engineer, used *attrib.* to designate a device developed by him consisting of two opposed semicylindrical blades (see quot. 1948), used in various forms to measure the speed of air and water currents and as a windmill rotor in the generation of electricity from wind power.

1925 *Mech. Engin.* Nov. 912 In slow winds the Savenius [*sic*] wing rotor might have to be provided with an auxiliary motor... In strong winds, however, its own turning moment would be sufficient. **1948** P. C. PUTNAM *Power from Wind* vi. 101 The Savonius rotor was a vertical cylinder sliced in half from top to bottom, the two halves being pulled apart by about 20 per cent of the diameter... In principle it resembled a cup anemometer... The Savonius design possessed fairly high efficiency. **1955** E. W. GOLDING *Generation of Electricity by Wind Power* xii. 197 The Savonius rotor has the two halves of the bent sheet displaced so that the wind can pass between them... A number of Savonius type machines were built some years ago but only in small sizes. **1963** G. L. PICKARD *Descriptive Physical Oceanogr.* vi. 79 An alternative..is the Savonius rotor which is not sensitive to vertical motion. **1974** *Undercurrents* Mar.–Apr. 3/3 A double Savonius rotor windmill directly driving a screw pump.

Savonnerie (savɔnri). [Fr., lit. 'soap factory', f. *savon* soap.] The name of a factory established in a former soap works in Paris in the 17th century, used *attrib.* and *absol.* to designate hand-knotted pile carpets made there. Also used of similar products from elsewhere in France.

1876 *Encycl. Brit.* V. 129/2 The most celebrated and artistic textures of this class are the Aubusson, Savonnerie, and Beauvais carpets of France. **1899** R. GLAZIER *Man. Hist. Ornament* 118 About 1590, some carpets called Savonnerie were made in the Louvre, the technique being somewhat similar to the Persian carpets. **1912** *Loan Exhib. Tapestries, Carpets & Silk Fabrics from Mobilier Nat. Paris* (Victoria & Albert Mus.) 4 The chief characteristic of the Savonnerie carpets was the application of the technical methods used in..Oriental specimens to designs prepared in the contemporary style of French decorative art. **1922** KENDRICK & TATTERSALL *Hand-Woven Carpets* I. I. vii. 73 The factory of the Savonnerie, which has provided a generic name for all French hand-knotted carpets, was founded in 1626. **1933** *Burlington Mag.* Dec. p. xxiv/2 Savonnerie panels in silk, brocades etc. **1949** N. MITFORD *Love in Cold Climate* II. iv. 225 My Savonnerie, my Sèvres, my sanguines, all my treasures gone and I confess I am very low about it. **1966** M. JARRY *Carpets of Manuf. de la Savonnerie* 18 Le Château de Fontainebleau..is fitted up with Savonnerie carpets. **1972** K. BONFIGLIOLI *Don't point that Thing at Me* i. 2 That..is a valuable Savonnerie rug. **1977** *Times* 11 Oct. 17/6 The sale will contain..16 antique Oriental carpets and one Savonnerie.

savor: see SAVOUR *sb.* and *v.*

savorous ('seɪvərəs), *a.* Also 4-7 **saverous**, 5 **savoruss**, *Sc.* **sawouris**, 5-7 **savourous.** [a. OF. *saverous*, *savorous* (mod.F. *savoureux*):—late L. *sapōrōsus*, f. *sapōr* SAPOR: see -OUS.]

1. Of good savour, pleasant to the taste.

c **1450** HOLLAND *Howlat* 705 Many sawouris salss with sewaris he send. **1520** NISBET *N.T.*, *Mark* ix. 49 Salt is gude; gif salt be vnsauorous, in quhat thing sal ye mak it sauorous? **1604** E. G[RIMSTONE] tr. *Acosta's Hist. Indies* III. xvi. 170 There are two kindes of fishes breed in this Lake.., the one they call Suches, which is great and savorous. **1891** F. TENNYSON *Daphne*, etc. 274 Garden sweets..And savorous herbs that lay together crush'd.

†**b.** *fig.* That is relished or enjoyed; delightful.

? *a* **1366** CHAUCER *Rom. Rose* 84 Than yonge folk entenden ay For to ben gay and amorous, The tyme is than so savorous. **1483** CAXTON *Gold. Leg.* 366/4 Though she were resplendysshaunt, wel sauerous and ryght ful of grete myracles. **1567** PAINTER *Pal. Pleas.* II. 157b, To gather that soote and sauorous frute which louers so egerly sue for at maydens handes. **1657** tr. *'Idiota's' Div. Lover, Holy Exerc.*, But if it proue..that some other worke, or Exercise, is, or would be more sauourous or rellishinge to thy Spirit.

†**2.** Full of relish, greedy. *Obs.*

1491 CAXTON *Vitas Patr.* (W. de W. 1495) I. cxv. 138 b, Many notable lordes..somwhat to content his sauourous appetyte..send oft tymes to hym grete sommes of money.

Hence 'savorously *adv.*

1480 CAXTON *Ovid's Met.* xv. iii, The tyme was somtyme that the peple lyvyd wᵗ out etyng of flesshe; & wer norysshyd saverously of the fruytes of the trees & of herbes.

savory ('seɪvərɪ), *sb.* Forms: [1 sæþerie], 4–6 **saverey**, 5 **savereye, saferay, savry**, 5–6 **saveray**, 6–7 **savery(e, saverie, savorie**, 7 **savourie**, 7–9 **savoury**, 7– **savory**. [Ultimately from L. *saturēia*; the form-history is uncertain.

On the one hand the ME. *saverey* might descend (with substitution of v for ð) from OE. *sæðerie*, a. early OF. *sa*ðereie* (later *sarrie*, whence the dim. *sarriette* surviving in mod.Fr.) = Pr. *sadreia* (whence 16th c. Fr. dial. *sadriege*, Sp. *ajedrea*, and perh. by metathesis the synon. *sagerida*):—L. *saturēiam*. On the other hand, Heresbach (*De Re Rustica*, 1570) cites an It. *savoreggia* and F. *savoreie*, and the latter appears in Cotgr. 1611 as *savorée*. The existence of these forms suggests that the ME. *saverey* may be an adoption of an unrecorded OF. form which had the *v* either as a phonetic development in hiatus (cf. F. *pouvoir* for early OF. *pooir*) or through the influence of *saveur* SAVOUR.

Independent adoption of the Latin word appears in OE. *saturege*, ME. SATUREIE, MHG. *saterje* (G. *saturei*), It. *satureja*, corruptly *santoreggia*, Pg. *saturagem*.]

1. Any plant of the genus *Satureia* (N.O. *Labiatæ*), esp. the annual herb *Satureia hortensis* (garden, summer savory), or the perennial *S. montana* (mountain or winter savory), natives of the south of Europe, cultivated for use as flavouring ingredients in cooking.

[*c* **1000** *Sax. Leechd.* II. 314 Feldmoran sæd, sæþerian sæd, petorsilian sæd.] *a* **1387** *Sinon. Barthol.* (Anecd. Oxon.) 37 *Satureia, tymbra idem*, saverey. *c* **1420** *Liber Cocorum* (1862) 32 Take sawge, persoly, ysope, saveray, Onyons gode. *c* **1430** *Two Cookery-bks.* 18 Take a Capoun ..& sethe hym in Water, percely, Sauereye & Salt. *c* **1440** *Pallad. on Husb.* Tabula 374 Coriaundir, popy, saury, senuy, oynet. **1483** *Cath. Angl.* 319/1 Saferay, *s[a]tureia, herba est.* **1502** ARNOLDE *Chron.* (1811) 171 And ete alle maner fishe wᵗ..vergews made with good erbis sawge & sauery. **1573** TUSSER *Husb.* (1878) 94 Summer sauerie. **1597** GERARDE *Herbal* II. clxv. 460 Winter Sauorie is a plant resembling Hyssope. **1697** DRYDEN *Virg. Georg.* IV. 43 Wild Thyme and Sav'ry set around their Cell. **1786** ABERCROMBIE *Gard. Assist.* 79 Savory—sow of the summer and winter kind. **1849** BALFOUR *Man. Bot.* §967 Many Labiates, such as Thyme..Savoury,..&c., are used..to flavour sauces and dishes. **1881** *Encycl. Brit.* XII. 289 The Winter Savory, *Satureja montana*, a hardy evergreen undershrub.

2. *dyer's savory*, the Saw-wort, *Serratula tinctoria*.

1874 *Treas. Bot.* Suppl.

3. *attrib.* and *Comb.*: *savory-seed*; *savory-leaved* adj.; **savory oil** (see quot.); **savory thyme**, *Thymus virginicus*, an American herb.

1822 *Hortus Anglicus* II. 394 *Aster Linariifolius.* *Savory-leaved Star Wort. **1896** BRANNT *Anim. & Veg. Fats* II. 577 *Savory oil... Both the summer savory, *Satureja hortensis*, L., and the winter savory, *S. montana*, yield by distillation.. a volatile oil. *c* **1440** *Pallad. on Husb.* III. 580 Now *saury seed in faat vndunged londe Doth wel. **1822** *Hortus Anglicus* II. 105 Virginian or *Savory Thyme.

savour, savor ('seɪvə(r)), *sb.* Forms: 3–5 **savur**, 4 **safour, safer, sauvur, savoyre**, *Sc.* **sawure, -oure, -or, -eoure**, 4–5 **savore**, 4–6 **savoure, saver**, 5 **saveure, saveoure, savowre, savyr**, *Sc.* **sawour**, 5–6 **savir**, 6 **savre, savour, savyour, savar, sawr-**, 7 **saviour**, 8 *Sc.* **sa'r**, 4– **savour, savor**. [a. OF. *savur, savour* (mod.F. *saveur*) = Pr., Sp., Pg. *sabor*, It. *savore*:—L. *sapōrem* taste, savour (see SAPOR), f. *sapĕre* to taste.]

1. Quality in relation to the sense of taste; a specific mode of this quality, as sweetness, bitterness, etc.; a taste. Also in fig. context.

Now *rare*, exc. as denoting a touch or admixture of some taste other than the proper or prevailing taste of a substance, a 'smack'.

a **1225** *Ancr. R.* 102 Þes cos, leoue sustren, is a swetnesse & a delit of heorte, so unimete swote & swete, þet euerich worldes sauur is bitter þer aȝeines. *a* **1300** *Cursor M.* 13404 He dranc and feild gode sauur. **1303** R. BRUNNE *Handl. Synne* 9988 Hit semeþ brede, as be syȝt, And as brede, sauer haþ ryȝt. *c* **1315** SHOREHAM *Poems* I. 686 Ne lef non oþer, crysteman, For safour ne coloure. For þat colour, ne þat sauour Ne beþ nauȝt þer inne cryste. **13..** *E.E. Allit. P.* B. 995 For his make was myst, þat on þe mount lenged In a stonen statue þat salt sauor habbes. **1393** LANGL. *P. Pl.* C. xv. 187 Þe larke..is loueloker of lydene, And swettur of sauour. **1422** tr. *Secreta Secret., Priv. Priv.* 208 By the tonge we felen the dyuersite of Sauores, Swetnes and bittyrnesse, Saltnesse and egyrnesse, and other Saueoure. *a* **1510** DOUGLAS *K. Hart* I. 420 Servit thai war of mony dyuerss meis, Full sawris sweit. **1587** GOLDING *De Mornay* i. (1617) 7 Sounds, Sents, Savors, and Feelings. **1600** SURFLET *Country Farm* III. xlix. 533 Cyders differ one from another, especially in colour and sauour or relish. **1671** MILTON *P.R.* II. 342 Meats of noblest sort And savour. **1725** POPE *Odyss.* xv. 155 Viands of various kinds allure the taste Of choicest sort and savour; rich repast! **1774** tr. *Chesterf. Let. to Son* (8 June 1741), [The waters] are very heating, and disagreeable to the taste, having the savour of rotten eggs. **1841** ELPHINSTONE *Hist. Ind.* I. 233 Qualities of body; namely,—colour, savour, odour, feel [etc.].

b. The power of affecting the sense of taste, esp. agreeably; sapidity, tastiness.

c **1440** *Alphabet of Tales* 65 Ther wyne had nowder colour nor savor. **1483** CAXTON *G. de la Tour* m iv b, They ete black brede and metes of lytyll sauoure. **1816** SCOTT *Old Mort.* xiii, I see auld fruit has little savour—our suffering and our services have been of an ancient date. **1882** 'OUIDA' *Maremma* I. 12 The lads felt that when no more tales could be told of the king of Maremma, savour would be gone out of the goatsflesh roasted in the charcoal in the woods.

†**c.** Flavouring, spice. *Obs.*

1422 tr. *Secreta Secret., Priv. Priv.* 187 Lette hungyre yeue the talent, and not Sause ne Saueure.

2. A smell, perfume, aroma. *poet.* and *arch.*

[So occas. L. *sapor* and the verb *sapĕre* (Pliny). Some traces of this use occur in OF., though it seems to have been rare; in mod.Fr. it is entirely unknown.]

a **1300** *Cursor M.* 1381 And cipres, be þe suete sauur, Bi-takens ur suete sauueur. **1303** R. BRUNNE *Handl. Synne* 11567 She broȝt a smel of grete sauour. **1382** WYCLIF *John* xii. 3 The hous is fillid of the sauour of oygnement. *c* **1400** *Laud Troy Bk.* 6027 The boydies that ther ded lay, That hadde be sclayn In fight that day; Ther come of hem a foul sauour. *c* **1450** MYRC *Festial* 142 Þus as þe flesche rostyd, þe sauer þerof went out into þe strete. **1481** CAXTON *Myrrour* II. vi. 75 [The panther] gyueth oute of his mouth so swete a savour and smell, that anon the bestes that fele it seche hym. **1508** DUNBAR *Tua Mariit Wemen* 8 Throw the sauar sanatiue of the sueit flouris. *a* **1593** MARLOWE *Edw. II*, V. v, I was almost stifeled with the sauour. **1631** GOUGE *God's Arrows* III. §88. 349 Plagues oft arise..from noisome savours. **1697** DRYDEN *Virg. Georg.* IV. 88 Then Melfoil beat, and Honey-suckles pound, With these alluring Savours strew the Ground. **1820** SHELLEY *Hymn Merc.* xxii, For the sweet savour of the roasted meat Tempted him though immortal. **1871** FARRAR *Days of my Youth* ii. (1876) 20 Like a sweet savour, like a precious heritage, it lingers here.

b. in figurative context.

a **1225** *St. Marher.* 4 He is leoflukest lif for to lokin uppon, and swotest to smeallen; ne his swote sauur, ne his almihte mihte..ne mei neauer littlin ne aliggen. *c* **1502** *Joseph Arim.* (E.E.T.S.) 51 Heyle, tresour of Glastenbury moost imperyall, In sauour smellynge swete as eglantyne.

c. In the translations of the Bible from Tindale (1526) onwards, *savour* occurs very freq. as rendering of Gr. ὀσμή, Heb. *rēᵃḥ* smell; in the Old Testament *lit.* of the smell of sacrifices and incense regarded as pleasing to God, in the N.T. *fig.* chiefly with reference to spiritual sacrifices.

See, e.g., *Gen.* viii. 21, *Num.* xxviii. 13, *Ezek.* vi. 13, *2 Cor.* ii. 15, *Eph.* v. 2.

d. Used *fig.* for: Repute, estimation; = ODOUR 4 b. Now only *poet.*

1535 COVERDALE *Exod.* v. 21 Ye have made the sauoure of us to stynke before Pharao. **1639** FULLER *Holy War* II. xv. (1640) 64 Since which time the bad sauour of his life came to the Popes nose, who sent a Legate to depose him. **1726** W. PENN in *Life* Wks. (1782) I. 53 These several Things agreed upon, being of good Savour and Report. **1872** TENNYSON *Gareth* 377 Then came in hall the messenger of Mark, A name of evil savour in the land, The Cornish king.

3. In various uses, originally *fig.* from sense 1.

†**a.** Attractive quality, merit, value. *Obs.*

a **1225** *Ancr. R.* 138 Salt bitocneð wisdom; vor salt ȝiueð mete wordnesse & wisdom ȝifð sauur. **13..** *K. Alis.* 2839 (Bodl. MS.) Tofore þe kyng com on harpoure And made a lay of gret sauoure. *c* **1320** *Cast. Love* 72 Þauh hit on Englisch be dim and derk, Ne nabbe no sauer bi-fore a clerk. **1483** CAXTON *Golden Leg.* 220 b, She had sothly the bame of good odour and sauoure in conuersacion.

†**b.** Character, style, sort. *Obs.*

1605 SHAKS. *Lear* I. iv. 258 This admiration Sir, is much o' th' savour Of other your new prankes. **1639** ROUSE *Heav. Univ.* x. (1702) 153 Let the excellent and unmatchable ointments of Christ Jesus give an excellent savour to your works.

c. Essential virtue or property: with allusion to Matt. v. 13 (and Luke xiv. 34). Also, power to excite relish, interest.

1650 I. WEEKES *Truth's Confl.* i. 11 This is to put a non-sense upon the place, and to destroy the savor that is in it. **1850** MARSDEN *Early Purit.* (1853) 334 Principles which are permitted to lie barren soon lose their savour. **1885** PATTISON *Mem.* 298 All the savour of life is departed.

d. A 'smack', tinge, or admixture.

1795 BURNS *'O ay my wife'* 5 Some sa'r o' comfort still at last, When a' my days are done, man. **1867** MACFARREN *Harmony* ii. 66 Practised by modern musicians when they wish to give an antique savour to any particular passage.

†**4.** Relish or taste for something; delight, satisfaction. *to catch (a) savour*: to acquire a taste or liking. *Obs.*

a **1225** *Ancr. R.* 232 We ne iuindeð swetnesse in none þinge þet we wel doð, ne sauur of heorte. **13..** *Coer de L.* 3047 To mete hadde he no savour To wyn, ne watyr, ne no lycour. ? *c* **1400** LYDG. *Æsop's Fab.* Prol. 2 Wysdom is more of pris than gold in cofres To theym, that have savour in lettrure. *Ibid.* i. 65 Losengeours..Whiche have savour in slewth and sluggardy. *Ibid.* ii. 101 When a iorrour haþe caught sauour ones To be forsworn, custom makeþ hym strong. *c* **1412** HOCCLEVE *De Reg. Princ.* 393 Hast þou in me ony gretter sauour þan þat þou haddest first whan þou me sy. *c* **1430–40** *Abbey of Holy Ghost* in Horstm. *Hampole* I. 333 Plente of oyle, þat es for to hafe delyte and sauoyre in god. **1483** CAXTON *G. de la Tour* m iv, Good wynes, whereto the good heremyte tooke soo good a sauoure that he had.. dranke soo moche, that he was dronke. **1555** WATREMAN *Fardle of Facions* II. iv. 140 When they had caughte a sauour in this holye daye loytering,..thei made a longe holy daye also of the whole seuenth yere.

†**5.** Perception, understanding. *Obs.*

1387–8 T. USK *Test. Love* III. iv. (Skeat) 79 Of this have I yet no savour, without better declaration. **1548** UDALL, etc. *Erasm. Par. Matt.* iii. 1–6 Christ..of whome they had a certayne sauour and vnderstandyng. **1633** G. HERBERT *Temple, Dialogue* iii, But as I can see no merit, Leading to this favour: So the way to fit me for it, Is beyond my savour.

savour, savor ('seɪvə(r)), *v.* Forms: 3 **savur(e**, 4 **savir, savyre, safer**, 4–5 **savere**, 4–6 **saver, savoure**, 5 **savre, savyr**, 4– **savor, savour**: *Sc.* 4 **sawer**, 5 **sawour**, 6 **sair-, sawr-**, 8 **sar, sa'r**. [a. OF. *savourer, savorer* (mod.F. *savourer*) = Pr. *saborar*, Sp., Pg. *saborear*, It. †*savorare* (now in learned form *saporare*):—late L. *sapōrāre*, f. *sapōr-* SAVOUR *sb.*]

I. To have a savour.

†**1.** *intr.* Of food or drink: To taste (well or ill); chiefly, to have an agreeable taste. Often with *dative*; hence *trans.* to be agreeable to the taste of. *Obs.*

a **1300** *Cursor M.* 3647, I sal þam dight til his be-houe, A mete als he was wonto loue; It sal him sauur al to will, Ete he sal þer-of his fill. **1362** LANGL. *P. Pl.* A. VII. 249 Ete not, Ich hote þe til hunger þe take, And sende þe sum of his sauce to sauer þe þe betere. *c* **1386** CHAUCER *Pars. T.* ¶48 For soothly, there is no thyng that sauoureth so wel to a child as the Milk of his Norice. **1432–50** tr. *Higden* (Rolls) VIII. 17 Þer was noo licoure that savoured his mowthe or that he myȝhte discerne in that hit made his chekes colde. **1530** PALSGR. 698/2 This potage savoureth, whiche we use whan the meate is sodden to the pottes bottome. **1563** HYLL *Art Garden.* (1593) 129 In the fourth day, to sprinckle your seedes with water,..for by that meanes (saith he) they will sauour much better. **1634** G. HERBERT tr. *Cornarus' Treat. Temperance* 8 That Proverb, wherewith Gluttons use to defend themselves, to wit, *That which savours, is good and nourisheth.* **1686** W. HARRIS tr. *Lemery's Course Chem.* 119 Water..that's heated or boil'd in a Copper vessel for a whole day together, savours not at all, or not so much, of the Copper.

†**b.** *fig.*

c **1450** tr. *De Imitatione* III. xxxix. 109 To whom þou sauorist, what shal not sauore him ariȝt? and to whom þou sauorist not, what þinge may turne him to mirþe? [L. *cui tu sapis.. Et cui tu non sapis.*] **1526** *Pilgr. Perf.* (W. de W. 1531) 8 Syth the mater is all spirituall, it shall but lytell sauour or please the taste of them that be carnall.

2. *intr.* To give forth a (specified) scent or odour; to smell *of* something. *arch.*

13.. *Cursor M.* 6368 (Gött.) Þa wandis..euer þai held lijf and flour, Sauirand wid a suete sauur. **1303** R. BRUNNE *Handl. Synne* 1396 As a medue hyt was grene,..And saueryd swete as spycerye. **13..** *E.E. Allit. P.* C. 275 Þer in saym & in sorȝe þat sauoured as helle, Þer was bylded his bour. *c* **1450** MYRC *Festial* 50 For þer nys no brent sence þat sauereth so swete yn mannys nase, as doþe a deuote oreson yn Goddys nase. **1500–20** DUNBAR *Poems* xxxiv. 34 'Fy', quod the Feynd, 'Thow sairis of blek, Go clenge the clene and cum to me'. **1526** *Pilgr. Perf.* (W. de W. 1531) 184 Was dulcet & swete to yᵉ mouth..& sauoured wele to the nose. **1549** LATIMER *Ploughers* (Arb.) 18 As the saffrone bagge.. doth euer after sauoure and smel of the swete saffron that it conteyned. **1601** HOLLAND *Pliny* II. 111 Parthenium.. bringeth forth a white floure, sauouring like an apple, and having a bitter tast. **1870** W. MORRIS *Earthly Parad.* III. IV. 218 The spilt blood savoured horribly.

†**b.** Without qualifying word: To smell offensively, stink. *Obs.*

1536 *Primer Eng. & Lat.* 121 b, Whan he [*sc.* Lazarus] in the same foure dayes had lyen So that hys body beganne to sauoure. *a* **1591** H. SMITH *Serm.* (1637) 348 Like the snuffe of a candle, which all men looked upon even now when it shined, and now it so savours, that they tread it under foot.

3. *fig.* †**a.** To be agreeable or pleasing. Const. *to* or *dative*. *Obs.* **b.** With qualification: To be *well* or *ill* pleasing. *arch.*

a **1300** *Cursor M.* 25885 'Man', he sais, 'quin cuth þow fele Hu pine o þis lijf sauure wele'. **1362** LANGL. *P. Pl.* A. IX. 102 But ȝit sauereþ me nat þi siggynge. **1450–1530** *Myrr. our Ladye* 4 That lyke it [the service] goyth dayle as throughe your mouthes so let yt synke & sauoure contynually in youre hartes. *a* **1609** SIR F. VERE *Comm.* (1657) 94 This advise could not savour to that young Nobleman. *a* **1660** *Contemp. Hist. Irel.* (Ir. Archæol. Soc.) I. 275 All the sermon of that daie..was of this and such other like stuffe, as not pleasinge or sauoringe unto Christian eares. **1668** HOWE *Bless. Righteous* (1825) 78 Nothing savours with me; I take comfort in nothing. **1842** TENNYSON *Vision of Sin* xxiv, What is loathsome to the young Savours well to thee and me.

4. a. *to savour of*: to show traces of the presence or influence of; to have some of the characteristics of; to have the appearance of proceeding from.

1548 CRANMER *Catech.* Ep. Ded., [We] sauer longest of that thynge that we fyrste receaue and taist of. **1577** HANMER *Anc. Eccles. Hist.* 110 The phrase of that epistle sauoreth very muche of the Greeke tongue. **1612** DRAYTON *Poly-olb.* To Rdr. A 1, The Idle Humerous world must heare of nothing that..sauors of Antiquity. **1647** N. BACON *Disc. Govt. Eng.* I. iii. 9 The matter of that Epistle savoureth of the purer times of the Church. **1700** DRYDEN *Fables* Pref. *A 2, I have written nothing which savours of Immorality or Profaneness. **1722** RAMSAY *Three Bonnets* I. 120 Your courtship sars sae rankly O' selfish interest. **1749** FIELDING *Tom Jones* I. x, Such solicitations from superiors too often savour strongly of commands. **1790** BURKE *Fr. Rev.* 234 But the institutions savour of superstition in their very principle. **1870** J. H. NEWMAN *Gram. Assent* II. viii. 332 Cromwell, whose actions savoured of the boldest logic, was a confused speaker. **1894** H. DRUMMOND *Ascent of Man* 47 A spectacular act..savours of the magician.

b. *trans.* in the same sense.

1574 WHITGIFT *Def. Answ.* ii. 109 For it neyther savoureth the spirite of God, neither yet any modest and good nature, but [etc.]. *a* **1634** RANDOLPH *Muses Looking-gl.* III. iii. (1638) 53 Would thou wert worth the killing. *Colax.* A good wish, Savouring as well discretion, as bold valour. **1667** MILTON *P.L.* x. 1043 Wilful barrenness, That.. savours onely Rancor and pride. **1906** *Athenæum* 23 June 758/2 'One ail for thee and me', instead of 'wail'; 'went by her like their flames', instead of 'thin flames'—these savour the printer.

II. To give a savour to.

†**5.** *trans.* To flavour with salt or spice. *Obs.*

13.. *E.E. Allit. P.* B. 825 þenne ho sauerez with salt her seuez vchone. **1387** TREVISA *Higden* (Rolls) IV. 243 Flesche i-savered i-not by what vertu of herbes. *c* **1400** *Lanfranc's Cirurg.* 75 Kyddes & lambres, & kalffes isaveryde with agresta. *c* **1440** *Pallad. on Husb.* XII. 494 Yf hit be not sauered worth a flie, Olyues grene ygrounde in hit let stie. **1508** DUNBAR *Flyting* 192 Powderit with prymross, sawrand all with clowiss. **1693** LYDE *Retaking 'Friend's Adventure'* 9 Beef without any Salt to savour it.

†**6.** To impart a taste or flavour to. *Obs. rare*$^{-1}$.

1303 R. BRUNNE *Handl. Synne* 9986 þarfore hys wysdom, hys owne rede, Sauerþ hyt [Christ's flesh] yn wyne and brede.

7. To season, flavour; to give tone or character to.

1579 LYLY *Euphues* (Arb.) 44 These old huddles, hauing ouercharged their gorges with fancie, accompt al honest recreation meere folly, and hauing taken a surfet of delight, seeme now to sauour it with despight. **1889** J. JACOBS *Æsop's Fables* I. 196 He..has left out..that pinch of humour that has savoured the fabulist.

8. To impart a savour or scent to.

1832 HT. MARTINEAU *Ireland* ii. 28 On many a petition, savoured with a scent of potheen, did he turn his back.

III. To perceive a savour.

9. *trans.* To taste, to perceive by the sense of taste. In mod. use, to taste with relish, to dwell on the taste of; also *fig.*, to give oneself to the enjoyment or appreciation of.

c **1430** *Pilgr. Lyf Manhode* II. cxxix. (1869) 125 And j shulde neuere be at ese if j sauowrede swete thing. *c* **1440** *Gesta Rom.* lvi. 373 (Add. MS.) When he sauours the soure barke with oute for bitternesse he leuyth the swete kyrnelle with in. **1865** *Pall Mall G.* 17 June 11/1 We savour at our leisure the delicate satire which we were too excited to appreciate duly. **1869** BROWNING *Ring & Bk.* XI. 1762 Deal each judge His dole of flattery and feigning,—why, He turns and tries and snuffs and savours it As an old fly the sugar-grain. **1883** 'HOLME LEE' *Loving & Serving* I. iii. 42 He moved hither and thither about his silent house,.. savouring his strange pain. **1889** MAX O'RELL *Jacques Bonhomme* 70 Savoring in advance the long list of dainties for the day.

†**b.** To relish, enjoy (flavours). Also *absol. Obs.*

1387 TREVISA *Higden* (Rolls) VIII. 17 He wolde seie þat he savered water, for hit kelede his mouþ and his jowes. **1426** LYDG. *De Guil. Pilgr.* 16990 For tyl I hadde gone to Scole with Trybulacion, I savoured fful lytil in the soote mylk of grace. **1566** *Pasquine in Traunce* 65 If a man giue them any deintier meate, they can not sauour it, and suche as they sauoure not, they vtterly dispise.

10. To be conscious, or sensible of (an odour). †Also *absol. Obs.* or *arch.*

1382 WYCLIF *Ecclus.* xxx. 19 What shal profiten sacrifice to the maumet? and forsothe he shal not eten, ne sauouren [Vulg. *nec odorabit*]. *c* **1450** MYRC *Festial* 191 And þerwyth he felde þe swetyst smell þat euer he saverde. *a* **1542** WYATT *That the Season of Enjoyment* 23 What vaileth the flower To stand still and wither; If no man it savour It serves only for sight. **1605** SHAKS. *Lear* IV. ii. 39 (1st Qo.) Filths sauor but themselues. **1864** *Daily Tel.* 8 Sept., You have the moor pretty much to yourself, can savour all its wild perfume, and listen to all its cries.

11. To relish, like, care for. *Obs.* or *arch.*

So *thou savourest* in all versions of Matt. xvi. 23 from Wyclif 1380 to 1611; Vulg. *sapis*, Gr. *φρονεῖς*, Revised Version 1881 *thou mindest*.

c **1340** HAMPOLE *Prose Tr.* 1, I sauyre noghte joye that with Jhesu es noghte mengede. *c* **1390** CHAUCER *Truth* 5 Savour no more than thee bihove shal. **1451** CAPGRAVE *Life St. Aug.* 1 To þese both þe holy apostell saide he was dettour, to paye ech of hem aftir þat he sauoured. **1526** *Pilgr. Perf.* (W. de W. 1331) 148 b, Some blynded with sensualite & carnall pleasure, sauouryng nothynge but y^{t} onely that is delectable to ye body. **1584** LODGE *Alarum* (Shaks. Soc.) 77 Those that are earthly minded savor not the things that are of God. **1599** B. JONSON *Cynthia's Rev.* III. iv, Sauours himselfe alone, is onely kind And louing to himselfe. **1633** FORD *Broken H.* I. i, Beauteous Penthea wedded to this torture By an insulting brother,.. he savours not humanity, Whose sorrow melts not into more than pity, In hearing but her name. **1678** BUNYAN *Pilgr.* I. (1900) 23 He [Worldly Wiseman] savoureth only the doctrine of this world. **1693** NORRIS *Pract. Disc.* (1698) IV. 223 Those false Relishes and depraved Tastes of the Soul which dispose it to Mind and Savour the Earth, and Earthly things. **1868** E. EDWARDS *Ralegh* I. xviii. 376 To give prominence to such rumours as they know will be savoured at their own Court.

†**12.** To perceive, apprehend; to discover traces of. Also, to experience. *Obs.*

a **1340** HAMPOLE *Psalter* xciii. 8 The vnwis, withouten kunynge, & fulis, withouten puruyaunce of the tother warld, that ere in noumbire of cristen men, vndirstandis and sauyrs this. *c* **1440** *Gesta Rom.* (Add. MS.) 110 But wolde god, that wrechid man.., sauered and vndirstode, and ordeyned for his laste Ende! **1509** BARCLAY *Shyp of Folys* (1874) I. 248 Such seldom savour fortune's happiness. **1567** *Gude & Godlie B.* (S.T.S.) 146 That we, in hartis, may sauour Thy mercy and thy fauour. **1602** WARNER *Alb. Eng.* XIII. lxxvii. (1612) 317 By now, perhaps, thow sauorests [*sic*] some Godhead. **1659** HEYLIN *Certamen Epist.* 8 In your writings I savour a spirit so very distant from my disposition, that I have small hopes that my words will escape your displeasure.

†**b.** *to savour out*: to scent out, get wind of. *Obs.*

1714 RAMSAY *Elegy John Cowper* i, There's none..Could sa'r sculdudry out like John.

†**c.** *intr.* To have a suspicion *of. Obs. rare*$^{-1}$.

1594 MARLOWE & NASHE *Dido* III. ii, Sister, I see you sauour of my wiles.

savour, obs. form of SAVIOUR.

†**'savourable**, *a. Obs. rare*$^{-1}$. [a. OF. *savourable*, f. *savourer* to SAVOUR.] Pleasing to the taste.

1502 ATKYNSON tr. *De Imitatione* III. vi. 200 Loue..that maketh..bitter thynges swete & sauorable.

savoured ('seɪvəd), *ppl. a.* [f. SAVOUR *sb.* + -ED.] Having savour, with defining adv.

1590 SPENSER *F.Q.* II. vii. 51 Hearbs and fruits..Not.. sweet and well savored, But direfull deadly black. **1609** *Shaks. Tr. & Cr.* Ep. ¶2 (1st Qo.), So much and such sauored salt of witte is in his Commedies, that they seeme.. to be borne in that sea that brought forth Venus.

savourer ('seɪvərə(r)). [f. SAVOUR *v.* + -ER^{1}.] One who savours (in various senses).

1655 FULLER *Ch. Hist.* IV. ii. §61. 172 She was..a great Savourer and Favourer of Wickliffe his Opinions. **1898** MONEY-COUTTS *Rev. St. Love* 3 Be all the blight of God's immediate ban on savourers of poison at the feast of Love.

savourie, obs. form of SAVORY and SAVOURY.

savourily ('seɪvərɪlɪ), *adv.* Also savorily. [f. SAVOURY *a.* + -LY^{2}.]

1. In a savoury manner, with a pleasing smell or taste, appetizingly. Also, †with relish or appetite.

1398 TREVISA *Barth. De P.R.* XVIII. ix. (Bodl. MS.), A serpent..eteþ more sauoryly [*ed.* 1495 sauvurly] þanne þaie dede bifore þe chaunginge of þe skynne. **1617** MORYSON *Itin.* III. II. iii. 81 Apples or peares first dried, then prepared with cinamon and butter very sauourily. **1670** NARBOROUGH *Jrnl.* in *Acc. Sev. Late Voy.* (1711) 49, I can eat Foxes and Kites as savourily as if it were Mutton. **1790** BLAKE in Gilchrist *Life* (1863) I. 86 Here and there I saw one savourily picking the flesh off his own tail. **1823** LAMB *Elia* Ser. II. *Old China*, We would eat our plain food savorily. **1841** *Fraser's Mag.* XXIII. 679 Two small pullets were brought in,..smelling most savouryly. **1886** R. F. BURTON *Arab. Nts.* (abr. ed.) III. 103 Roasted meat, With basting oil so savourily replete!

†**2.** *fig.* Heartily, pleasurably; appreciatively. Also, in religious use (cf. SAVOURY *a.* 2 b).

1643 MILTON *Divorce* II. iii. (1644) 38 Yet that he commanded the allowance of adulterous and injurious divorces for hardnes of heart,..they can very savourily perswade themselves. **1662** J. CHANDLER *Van Helmont's Oriat.* 12 Which being seen, and savourily known, I admired my former ignorances. **1676** O. HEYWOOD *Diaries*, etc. (1883) III. 147 A blind man prayed pertinently and savourily.

savouriness ('seɪvərɪnɪs). [f. SAVOURY *a.* + -NESS.] The quality of being savoury, in various senses of the adj.

1398 TREVISA *Barth. De P.R.* XIII. i. (1495) 438 The.. lyghtenesse and sauerynesse therof [*sc.* of reyne water] shewyth the subtylnesse of her substaunce. **1576** GASCOIGNE *Steel Gl.* (Arb.) 72 These be my priests, the seasning of the earth Which wil not leese their Savrinesse, I trowe. **1599** MINSHEU *Span. Gram.* 82 It is great sauorines to dine or eate, and not to paie any shot. **1681** H. MORE *Exp. Dan.* Pref. 53 This was the tenour of the Testimony..which they witnessed with great savouriness and assurance. **1792** A. YOUNG *Trav. France* I. 277 All sorts of vegetables have a savouriness and flavour, from rich sauces, that are absolutely wanted to our greens boiled in water. **1801** *Sketch of Paris* I. xxxviii. 455 The savouriness of their cooking. **1859** GEO. ELIOT *Adam Bede* I. v, His mental palate..found a savouriness in a quotation from Sophocles or Theocritus that was quite absent from your text in Isaiah or Amos.

savouring ('seɪvərɪŋ), *vbl. sb.* [f. SAVOUR *v.* + -ING^{1}.]

1. The action of the vb. SAVOUR in various senses.

c **1386** CHAUCER *Pars. T.* ¶885 Thy fiue wittes, that been sighte, heryng, smellyng, tastynge or sauouryng, and feelynge. *c* **1430** *Pilgr. Lyf Manhode* I. lxxii. (1869) 42 Ne that shulde not meeue thee that at the taast, and at the sighte, at the smellinge, and at the sauouringe, bred and wyn it may seeme thee. *a* **1450** *Knt. de la Tour* (1868) 59 Touchinge, and cussinge and saweringe made of fals delite that Eue dede to ete the apille. **1574** tr. *Life* 70 *Archb. Canterb.* C v b, If they had been closed in lead, and well spiced,..they might haue been kepte from sauoringe yet a while.

†**2.** *concr.* A perfume. *Obs.*

1382 WYCLIF *Rev.* v. 8. Golden fioles ful of saueringis, whiche ben the preyers of seyntis.

†**3.** Something that gives a faint notion. *Obs.*

1513 DOUGLAS *Æneis* i. Prol. 44 3it with your leif, Virgill ..I wald..Write sum savoring of thi Eneados.

'savouring, *ppl. a.* [f. SAVOUR *v.* + -ING^{2}.]

1. Having a (defined) smell or taste.

1578 LYTE *Dodoens* I. i. 2 The highe Almaignes do call it ..sweete smelling, or sauering Southrenwood. **1596** DALRYMPLE tr. *Leslie's Hist. Scot.* I. 44 Sueit sairing flouris. **1612** WOODALL *Surg. Mate* Wks. (1653) 39 Cynamon water ..helpeth a bad or evil savouring breath.

2. Pleasing, relishing.

1598 DANIEL *Civ. Wars* I. xciv, He who had no thought so hie to clime (With savouring comfort still allur'd along).

3. Imparting savour or relish.

1886 *Athenæum* 17 Apr. 517/2 The lotos there has its sweets sharpened with a savouring bitterness.

savouringly ('seɪvərɪŋlɪ), *adv.* [f. prec. + -LY^{2}.] In a relishing manner.

1647 TRAPP *Comm. Jas.* iv. 9 And mourn savouringly and soakingly, with a deep and down right sorrow. **1848** *Fraser's Mag.* XXXVIII. 311 You would..have done just what I did,—smilingly, gently, savouringly, peel, slice, and eat, three raw turnips.

savourless ('seɪvəlɪs), *a.* Also 6 saverles, *Sc.* sairles, 7, 9 savorless, 9 *Sc.* sareless, saurless. [f. SAVOUR *sb.* + -LESS.] Destitute of savour; tasteless or odourless; of immaterial things, void of interest or efficacy, insipid.

1398 TREVISA *Barth. De P.R.* III. xx. (1495) 67 The tongue is sauourles that he maye the better take all maner sauour of thynges. **1552** HULOET, Sauourles or wythoute sauoure, *inodorus.* **1627** DONNE *Serm.* xxii. (1640) I. 223 In my grave ..I..shall be all insipid, tastlesse, savourlesse dust. **1633** BP. HALL *Occas. Medit.* §128. 319 The rose-tree hath a sweet flowre, but a savour-lesse root. **1657** TRAPP *Comm. Ps.* xxxiv. 8 All flesh is savourles to him that hath tasted of the Spirit. **1886** BRUCE *Mirac. Elem. Gosp.* ii. 74 Cast out as savourless salt. **1907** *Outlook* 12 Oct. 451/2 Most of his jests when repeated seem almost savourless.

Hence **'savourlessness.**

1841 H. F. CHORLEY *Music & Manners* III. 179 The intrinsic savourlessness of the Mass which it [the orchestra] was performing, a *fade* composition by Morlacchi.

†**'savourly**, *a. Obs.* Also 4 saverly. [f. SAVOUR *sb.* + -LY^{1}.] = SAVOURY *a.*

13.. *E.E. Allit. P.* A. 226, I hope no tong mo3t endure No sauerly saghe say of þat sy3t. **1583** GOLDING *Calvin on Deut.* lxiii. 383/2 Manna..was a good & sauorly nourishment. **1608** WILLET *Hexapla Exod.* 669 The burning of flesh of it selfe is not so pleasant and sauourly.

†**'savourly**, *adv. Obs.* Forms: 4–6 saverly, 5 saverely, 6 savor-, saverlie, 6–7 savourely, savorly, 5–7 savourly. [f. SAVOUR *sb.* + -LY^{2}.]

1. With enjoyment; with relish; pleasantly; agreeably; keenly.

13.. *Gaw. & Gr. Knt.* 1937 þen acoles he (þe) kny3t, & kysses hym þryes, As sauerly & sadly as he hem sette couþe. *c* **1440** *York Myst.* xxix. 80 Wherfore we counsaile you This cuppe sauerly for to kisse. **1495** [see SAVOURILY 1, quot. 1398]. **1560** PILKINGTON *Expos. Aggeus* H ij, The labouryng man..feedes sauerly on brown bread, thin drynke, and a poore supper. **1637** *Brief Relat. Passages Star Chamber* 25 A Bee came and pitched on the Nosegay, and began to suck the flowers very savourly. **1683** TRYON *Way to Health* 350 The Cannibals feed on Humane Flesh, and will most savourly gnaw a Shoulder of Man. **1690** DRYDEN *Amphitryon* I. i, He ..snuffs up Incense so savourly, when 'tis offer'd him by a fair Hand.

b. Of weeping: Passionately, bitterly.

1662 H. MORE *Antid. Ath.* III. iv. §4 Other sometimes bearing the Image of Christ in her arms, weeping savourly. **1722** DE FOE *Col. Jack* ii, Then I fell a-crying as savourly as I did before, when I thought I had lost it.

2. With understanding; with appreciation; wisely; effectively.

c **1450** tr. *De Imitatione* I. i. 2 For who euere wol understonde þe wordes of crist pleinly and sauerely, he must studie to conforme all his lif to his lyf. **1529** MORE *Supplic. Soulys* Wks. 301/1 But than he speaketh so sauorlie hereof, that it well appereth of hys wyse wordes he neyther canneth anye skill therof, nor neuer came in the house. **1619** FOTHERBY *Atheom.* II. vi. §1 (1622) 246 Which folly that wise King derided very sauorly. **1663** BUNYAN *Chr. Behav.* Wks. 1692 I. 595/2 For Christians to commune savourly of God's Matters one with another, it is as if they opened to each other Nostrils Boxes of Perfume. **1664** H. MORE *Myst. Iniq.* vi. 119 Which life I conceive S. Paul describes very savourly, when he saith, That the Kingdom of Heaven is.. righteousness, and peace, and joy in the Holy Ghost.

savoursome ('seɪvəsəm), *a.* Also 6 savorsome. [f. SAVOUR *sb.* + -SOME^{1}.] Full of savour (in various senses).

1595 CHAPMAN *Ovid's Banquet of Sence* xxxii, Come soueraigne Odors, come..Wax hotter ayre, make them more sauorsome. **1922** *19th Cent.* Sept. 513 Hot savoursome shellfish the inn people gave us. **1958** *Times* 9 Oct. 7/1 Mr. Derek Francis is a savoursome Casca.

savoury ('seɪvərɪ), *a.* and *sb.* Forms: α. 3 savure, *compar.* savurure; β. 4–5 savery, savori, 4–6 saverey, 5 saveray, sauvury, 6 savrie, savourye, *Sc.* sau'rie, 6–7 savourie, savorie, 7 saverie, 4–9 savory, 6– savoury; γ. *contracted* 5 sarry. [Early ME. *savure*, app. a. OF. *savouré* sapid, fragrant, pa. pple. of *savourer*: see SAVOUR *v.* In the 14th c. the ending was associated with the native *-y*, so that the adj. was apprehended as f. SAVOUR *sb.* + -Y.]

A. *adj.* **1.** Pleasing to the taste; appetizing; agreeable.

1382 WYCLIF *Mark* ix. 48 Forsoth euery man schal be saltid, or maad sauori, with fier. **1387** TREVISA *Higden* (Rolls) I. 365 At Glyndalkan aboute þe oratorie of Seint Keynewyn wilewys bereþ apples as it were appel treen, and beeþ more holsom þan sauory. **1393** LANGL. *P. Pl.* C. XIX. 65 Tho þat sitten in þe sonne-syde sonner aren rype, Swettour and saueriour. *c* **1400** MAUNDEV. (Roxb.) xxx. 136 þai er ri3t sauoury in þe mouth. **1584** COGAN *Haven Health* cxcii. (1636) 172 Cookery..may make that savoury, which of it selfe is unsavoury. **1611** BIBLE *Gen.* xxvii. 31 And hee also had made sauoury meate, and brought it vnto his father. **1725** POPE *Odyss.* IV. 300 All..with keen gust the sav'ry viands share. **1837** M. DONOVAN *Dom. Econ.* II. 35 The natives of some part of Australia eat a kind of caterpillar.. of which they compose a dish to them highly savoury. **1865** KINGSLEY *Herew.* v, Savoury was the smell of fried pilchard and hake; more savoury that of roast porpoise.

b. Gratifying to the sense of smell; fragrant.

Now rare exc. in negative context: cf. *unsavoury.*

1560 DAUS tr. *Sleidane's Comm.* 209 b, They..perfume the house with the graines of Juniper, and other savoury thinges [L. *aliisque rebus odoratis*]. **1859** DICKENS *T. Two Cities* II. i, Cruncher's apartments were not in a savoury neighbourhood. **1871** R. ELLIS *Catullus* xiii. 11 Perfume savoury.

2. *fig.* **a.** Pleasant; acceptable.

a **1225** *Leg. Kath.* 1527 Mi swete lif, se swoteliche he smecheð me & smelleð þat al me þuncheð sauure & softe þat he sent me. *c* **1230** *Hali Meid.* 39 Ah schal ifinden him ai swettere & sauurure. *c* **1374** CHAUCER *Troylus* I. 405 If it be wikke, a wonder thinketh me, Whenne every torment and adversitee That cometh of him, may to me savory thinke. **1545** *King's Primer, Graces* **iv, O Lord Jesu Christ without whom nothing is swete nor sauery,.. blesse vs & our supper. **1602** SHAKS. *Ham.* II. ii. 463 One said there was no Sallets in the lines, to make the matter sauoury. *a* **1677** BARROW *Serm.* Wks. (1716) III. 57 The sense of having lived well.. is a far more solid and savoury pleasure than the most ample revenue can afford. **1875** RUSKIN *Fors Clav.* xlix. 11 The delicious parable, savouriest of all Scripture to rogues. **1885** R. L. & F. STEVENSON *Dynamiter* 100 Something taking in the way of colour, a good, savoury choice of words.

†**b.** In religious phraseology. (*a*) Full of spiritual 'savour'; spiritually delightful or edifying. (*b*) Having the savour of holiness; of saintly repute or memory. *Obs.*

(*a*) *c* **1449** PECOCK *Repr.* I. xvi. 89 The maner of outring which is sauory in a sermonyng. **1450–1530** *Myrr. our Ladye* 49 An other [wyse] is to take hede to the letter only, after the lytterall understondynge. And thys ys sometyme sauory, sometyme bareyne, after that the letter ys. **1563** FOXE *A. & M.* 1354/2 Many such like answers and reasons, mery, but sauery.. proceaded from that man. **1626** BP. HALL *Contempl. O.T.* XXI. i. 336 A forced discontinuance, makes deuotion more sauoury, more sweet to religious hearts. *a* **1720** SEWEL *Hist. Quakers* (1795) I. III. 230 Practised by the savouriest of people called Quakers. **1726** PENN in *Life* Wks. (1782) I. 98 Leaving the Man in a sensible and savoury Frame. **1855** MACAULAY *Hist. Eng.* xiii. III. 295 His letters and speeches are, to use his own phraseology, exceeding savoury... He had a text of the Old Testament ready for every occasion.

(*b*) **1642** D. ROGERS *Naaman* Ep. Ded. 4 Hath made your name sweet and savoury in the Church of God. **1731** WODROW *Corr.* (1843) III. 487 You need not be told what a great loss this Church will be at by this good and worthy gentleman's death, whose name will be for ever savoury in this Church.

3. Used, in contradistinction to *sweet*, as the epithet of articles of food having a stimulating taste or flavour.

1661 RABISHA *Cookery Dissected* 157 If you would have it baked savoury, season it with Pepper, Salt, Cloves [etc.]. **1769** MRS. RAFFALD *Eng. Housekpr.* (1778) 283 Pigeons in Savory Jelly. **1806** A. HUNTER *Culina* (ed. 3) 278 Omelette, a Savoury one.

B. *sb.* A savoury dish (see A. 3); *spec.* a cooked dish, flavoured with appetizing ingredients, served at the beginning or end of a dinner as a stimulant to appetite and digestion.

1661 RABISHA *Cookery Dissected* 138 Another way for a savory. **1844** TUPPER *Heart* xvii. 168 The board was overloaded with solid sweets and savouries. **1896** ANTHONY HOPE *Phroso* i, 'Why, how early you two have dined!' cried Beatrice. 'You're at the savoury, aren't you? We've only just come.'

savoury, savowr(e: see SAVORY, SAVOUR.

Savoy (sə'vɔɪ). Also 6 Savoie, Savoye. [a. F. *Savoie*, the name of a region of S.E. France, south of the Lake of Geneva.]

1. In full, *Savoy cabbage* (†*cole*, †*colewort*, †*kail*, *sprouts*). A rough-leaved hardy variety of the common cabbage, much grown for winter use.

1578 LYTE *Dodoens* IV. vi. 552 Sauoye Colewurtes. **1597** GERARDE *Herball* II. xxxvi. 247 Sauoie Cole is also numbred among the headed Coleworts or Cabbages. **1657** W. COLES *Adam in Eden* lxxxvi, The Savoy Cole and the Cole-flory.. must be sowed in April. **1689** in *Thanes of Cawdor* (Spald. Club) 353, 1 unce Savoy kaell. **1699** EVELYN *Acetaria* §11 The Broccoli from Naples.. are very delicate, as are the Savoys. **1707** MORTIMER *Husb.* (1721) II. 132 The Savoy Cabbage, which is one of the best sort and very hardy. **1747** MRS. GLASSE *Cookery* 58 Savoys Forced and Stewed. **1764** ELIZA MOXON *Eng. Housew.* (ed. 9) 132 To boil Savoy Sprouts. **1855** DELAMER *Kitch. Gard.* (1861) 57 There is a vulgar idea.. that Savoy cabbages are improved by exposure to frost. **1856** GLENNY *Gard. Every-d. Bk.* 17/1 Frosts, that will kill all other greens, will leave Savoy Sprouts.. untouched. **1881** *Encycl. Brit.* XII. 287/2 The savoys come into use in autumn, and continue until the spring.

2. In full, *Savoy biscuit*. A kind of sponge-biscuit, made of finger-shaped pieces of paste covered with sifted sugar which when baked are joined together in pairs; so also *Savoy drop*, *ring*. Similarly *Savoy cake*, a large sponge cake baked in a mould; also called a *Savoy mould*. **Savoy bag**, a bag with a narrow orifice through which the paste for making the biscuits is laid out.

1723 J. NOTT *Cook's & Confectioner's Dict.* sig. Fv, *Savoy Biskets*... Eggs.. Rose-water.. Sugar.. beaten as thick.. as Cream... The finest flour... Bake. **1764** ELIZA MOXON *Eng. Housw.* (ed. 9) Suppl. 10 Slips of bread cut long like Savoy biskets. **1822** *Cook's Oracle* (ed. 4) 494 Savoy Cake, or Sponge Cake in a Mould. **1854** G. READ *Compl. Biscuit & Gingerbr. Baker's Assist.* (ed. 2) 76 Savoy Cakes... Almond Savoy Cakes. *Ibid.* 77 Savoy Biscuits and Drops. **1862** FRANCATELLI *Eng. & Foreign Confectioner* 96 These Savoy biscuits should present a smooth surface, and be of a light fawn colour. **1866** *Massey's Biscuit Bk.* 3 Savoy Drops... Savoy Rings. **1889** R. WELLS *Bread & Biscuit Baker* 47 The Savoy Biscuits must be laid out from a savoy bag on 'cap' paper one half round and one half long. The French Savoys must be laid out oval, and when baked two are to be put together. **1892** *Encycl. Pract. Cookery* (ed. Garrett) I. 138/2 A Biscuit-bag, sometimes called a 'savvy-bag' being used very much to prepare Savoy Biscuits.

3. The name of the *Savoy* Theatre in London, used *attrib.* to designate the Gilbert and Sullivan operas originally presented there by the D'Oyly Carte company.

1889 G. B. SHAW in *Star* 13 Dec. 2/4 A new Savoy opera is an event of no greater artistic significance than.. a new oratorio by Gounod. **1893** —— in *World* 11 Oct. 23/2 The announcement of a new Savoy opera always throws the middle-aged playgoer into the attitude of expecting a surprise. **1902** *Encycl. Brit.* XXXIII. 56/2 The Savoy operas did not aim at intellectual or emotional grandeur, but at providing innocent and wholesome pleasure. **1907** W. S. GILBERT in *Daily Mail Year Bk.* 90/1 Savoy opera.. was snuffed out by the deplorable death of my distinguished collaborator, Sir Arthur Sullivan. **1930** *Times* 22 Mar. 13/4 Savoy Opera is a tree deeply rooted in our national fantasy. **1961** *Sunday Times* 30 Apr. 12/3 Today only the Savoy operettas and the Bab Ballads remain alive to judge him [*sc.* W. S. Gilbert] by.

†**Sa'voyan**, *a.* and *sb.* *Obs.* = SAVOYARD.

1601 E. A. *True Disc. Queen's Voy.* title p., Herevnto is annexed, the first Sauoyan; wherein is set forth the right of the conquest of Sauoy by the French, and the importance of holding it. **1607** TOPSELL *Four-f. Beasts* 46 They are vsed by the Lotharingians and Sauoyens for meat. **1611** COTGR., *Rave de Savoye*, the Sauoyan Rape, the greatest kind of Turnep. **1653** A. WILSON *Jas. I* 94, The Savoyan Agents bringing more Gold in their hands than on their backs.

Savoyard (sə'vɔɪɑːd), *sb.* and *a.* [a. F. *savoyard* (fem. *-arde*), f. *Savoie*: see SAVOY and -ARD.]

A. *sb.* **1.** A native or inhabitant of Savoy.

Well known in other countries as musicians itinerating with hurdy-gurdy and monkey.

1756–7 tr. *Keysler's Trav.* (1760) I. 271 The steward of the houshold is the marquis de Coudray,.. a Savoyard. **1770** [see HURDY-GURDY 1]. **1839** *Penny Cycl.* XV. 517/1 They [*sc.* marmots] are taken by the Savoyards and others principally that they may be exhibited by those itinerants. **1906** W. WALKER *Calvin* vii. 166 The Savoyards pressed Geneva and made travel unsafe on the roads.

2. An inhabitant of the precinct of the Savoy Palace in London, which formerly possessed the right of sanctuary.

a **1700** B. E. *Dict. Cant. Crew*, *Rum-dukes*, the boldest Fellows amongst the Alsatians, Minters, Savoyards, &c. **1855** MACAULAY *Hist. Eng.* xxii. IV. 775 At length, in 1697, a bill for abolishing the franchises of these places.. received the royal assent. The Alsatians and Savoyards were furious.

3. a. A member of the D'Oyly Carte company which originally played at the Savoy theatre in productions of the Gilbert and Sullivan operas. **b.** A devotee of the Savoy operas. Cf. SAVOY 3.

1890 W. S. GILBERT (*title*) Songs of a Savoyard. **1893** G. B. SHAW in *World* 11 Oct. 24/2, I enjoyed it [*sc.* Utopia Limited] and.. the majority of Savoyards will share my appreciation of it. **1908** R. BARRINGTON *Rec. 35 Years' Exper. Eng. Stage* xxi. 265 To have been an 'old Savoyard', that is to say, one of the original company, seems to confer not only a great measure of dignity but.. a greater natural activity in old age. **1922** *Glasgow Herald* 26 July 9/1 The death is announced of Mr George Thorne, the famous Savoyard.. well known to the older generation of Glasgow admirers of Gilbert and Sullivan. He.. appeared regularly with the [D'Oyly Carte] company at the Royalty Theatre, Glasgow. **1930** *Times* 24 Mar. 15/5 As an old Savoyard and senior vice-president of the Gilbert and Sullivan Society, I .. heard with dismay Mr. Henry Lytton's tentative announcement of his possible retirement. **1961** *Times* 12 Dec. 5/3 In *Trial by Jury*.. we remarked with horror.. an anachronism as horrible to the designers of Printing House Square as is the fear of a rock 'n roll *Mikado* to good Savoyards. **1977** *Times* 14 July 12/7 While.. the words and music of Gilbert and Sullivan are the main attraction, Savoyards have a powerful respect for the spirit of the original productions. **1978** *Lancashire Life* Feb. 62/1 My music teacher was the mother of Martyn Green the world-famous Savoyard, who was a Boltonian.

B. *adj.* Belonging to Savoy.

1741 M. W. MONTAGU *Let.* 15 Nov. (1966) II. 259 This Town [*sc.* Chambéry].. is wholly inhabited by the poor Savoyard Nobillity. **1820** RANKEN *Hist. France* VII. i. VII. 238 The Savoyard army. **1841** JAMES *Brigand* ii, Why baron, who would have thought to meet you thus in a Savoyard inn? **1905** LD. COLERIDGE *Story of Devonshire House* xvi. 239 You will find the girl in the garden with a coarse Savoyard straw hat. **1975** P. TOPPING in Setton & Hazard *Hist. Crusades* III. v. 154 The Savoyard prince secretly intrigued with Theodore despite his agreements with Venice.

savoyre, savre, obs. forms of SAVOUR.

savrie, savry, savte, savur, obs. ff. SAVOURY, SAVORY, SAFETY, SAVOUR.

savvy ('sævɪ), *sb.* and *a.* *slang.* Also 8 **scavey**, 9 **savey** (*Sc.* **savie**), **savvey**. [The Sc. *savie* is perh. a. F. *savez(-vous)* do you know? The later slang use is f. SAVVY *v.*: see also SABE *sb.*]

A. *sb.* Practical sense, intelligence; 'nous', gumption.

1785 [see SAVVY *v.*]. **1825–82** JAMIESON, *Savie*, knowledge, experience, sagacity, Loth. ?**185.** B. HARTE *Chiquita* 9 Hedn't no savey—hed Briggs. **1884** E. INGERSOLL in *Harper's Mag.* Sept. 508/2 They don't need much savvey for that. **1890** 'R. BOLDREWOOD' *Col. Reformer* (1891) 47 He could ride the best, but the black boy had twice as much savey. **1923** R. CUMMINS *Sky-High Corral* 31, I don't just get the savvy of this. **1936** W. R. TITTERTON *Chesterton* II. iii. 138 Which idea.. Armstrong actively disliked because, having more savvy than I had, he saw it meant death to his doctrine. **1951** K. CRICHTON *Marx Brothers* x. 134 He had bounce, stage savvy, and the optimism of a Rotarian. **1964** E. B. WHITE *Let.* 1 Feb. (1976) 515, I felt deeply envious of their skills, their savvy, their self reliance, and their general deportment. **1974** *Publishers Weekly* 11 Feb. 58/1 Full of baseball savvy, the book is also at times very funny. **1978** J. CARROLL *Mortal Friends* v. i. 496 Kennedy's reputation was for more savvy than that. He knew his history, didn't he, and its humbling lesson?

B. *adj.* Of persons, etc.: having practical sense, quick-witted; knowledgeable, wily, experienced. Also wise *to* (something).

1905 K. INGLEWOOD *Patmos* I. ix. 124 'How very savvy of you to think of that,' he said. **1946** *Calif. Folklore Q.* Oct. 377 From the safe landing of an airplane which has followed the homing radio beam (beacon), a person who is thinking clearly, performing an act correctly, that is, who is *savvy*, is *in the groove* or *on the beam*. **1964** H. WAUGH *Missing Man* xiii. 65 The kid might give himself away and Lambert's savvy enough to pick it up. **1974** *Publishers Weekly* 27 May 65/1 Norman Two Bull is a modern and savvy 15-year-old Sioux. **1975** BYFIELD & TEDESCHI *Solemn High Murder* iv. 77 She's older and been around and savvy to a lot of things the rest of them aren't. **1978** *Guardian Weekly* 5 Feb. 15/5 They are savvy hands, and if they do not speak persuasively they do speak precisely. **1980** *Economist* 16 Aug. 51/3 A savvy tenant putting a deposit on his house gains a 12-month option to buy at the price ruling when he made the deposit.

savvy ('sævɪ), *v.* *slang.* Also 8 **scavey, savey, savvey,** 20 **savee.** [Orig. Negro-Eng. and Pigeon-Eng., after Sp. *sabe usted* you know: see also SABE *v.*] *trans.* To know; to understand, comprehend. Freq. used in the interrogative (= 'do you understand?') following an explanation to a foreigner or to one considered slow-witted. Also *absol.*

1785 GROSE *Dict. Vulgar Tongue*, *Scavey*, sense, knowledge; 'massa me no scavey', master I don't know, (*negroe language*) perhaps from the French scavoir. **1828** *Life Planter Jamaica* 137 Dey hab not savey dat de store-keeper hab be deir broder Joseph. **1833** MRS. CARMICHAEL *West Indies* II. 131 As I went on, I paused and asked them if they 'savey' what I said, (comprehended me). *Ibid.* 135 Misses, you no peak lie, me savey dat well. **1850** L. H. GARRARD *Wah-to-Yah* 105 You've got so much 'fofarraw' stuck 'bout you, this child didn't savvy at fust! **1890** 'R. BOLDREWOOD' *Col. Reformer* (1891) 51 Now do you savey? **1897** A. H. LEWIS *Wolfville* 45 You've got to quit; savey? **1908** E. J. BANFIELD *Confessions of Beachcomber* II. iii. 315 'You savee?' The 'savee' touched Harry's dignity. 'What for you say savee? You take me for a blurry Chinaman?' **1914** S. LEWIS *Our Mr. Wrenn* iv. 59 Gotta do what I say, savvy? **1917** [see CHAIR *sb.*[1] 1 d]. **1920** D. H. LAWRENCE *Touch & Go* II. 49 *Gerald.* Yes, I want to be told. *Anabel.* That's rather mean of you. You should savvy, and let it go without saying. *Gerald.* Yes, but I don't savvy. **1933** M. LOWRY *Ultramarine* iii. 128 Let's have two starboard lights. Savee starboard lights? **1949** *True* Jan. 61/3 When there are ladies present, we say it in Mexican. The hounds savvy either. **1955** *Times* 27 July 10/6 The secretary was a literate man who 'savvied book'. **1964** E. PALMER tr. *Martinet's Elem. Gen. Linguistics* v. 155 Everywhere we find the word *savvy* 'know', which.. is automatically used by a monoglot English speaker who tries to make himself understood by a foreigner.

savyour, savyr(e, obs. forms of SAVOUR.

savyte, obs. form of SAFETY.

saw (sɔː), *sb.*[1] Forms: 1 **sagu, saga,** 4 **sagh,** 4–7 **sawe,** 5 **sae, saghe, saȝe,** 5– **saw.** [OE. **sagu* str. fem., in oblique cases *sage* (also *saga* wk. masc.) = OHG. *saga*, MLG., MDu. *sage* (Du. *zaag*), ON. *sǫg* (Sw. *såg*, Da. *sav*, †*saug*):—OTeut. **sagā* str. fem.; the ablaut-var. **segā* appears in OHG. *sega* (MHG. *sege*, mod.G. *säge*); cogn. w. OE. *seax* (:—**sahso-*) knife, SAX *sb.*[1], f. pre-Teut. root **sok-*: **sek-* to cut; cf. L. *secāre* to cut.]

1. a. A cutting tool consisting of a plate (or, in some forms, a band or a tube) of metal (usually steel), one edge of which is formed into a continuous series of teeth. (Some saws for cutting stone are without teeth.) In the original form of the tool, represented by the HAND-SAW, and in some varieties of more modern invention, e.g. the pit-saw (see PIT *sb.*[1] 15), the saw is moved backwards and forwards, each movement in one direction deepening the groove or 'kerf' made in the wood or other material to be cut. In other varieties, as the circular saw and the band-saw, a continuous movement in one direction is substituted for the reciprocating movement.

Ordinarily *saw* means the complete instrument including the handle, frame, or the like, necessary to fit it for use; but sometimes the word is applied to the 'saw-plate' or 'saw-blade' alone.

Also with defining words, indicating special varieties of form, structure, mode of operation, or purpose, as in *band saw, circular saw, compass saw, drag saw, endless saw, frame saw, fret saw, gate saw, hand saw, ice saw, joint saw, keyhole saw, lock saw, meat saw, mill saw, panel saw, pit saw, rabbet saw, rip saw, sash saw, tenon saw, web saw*. These terms, so far as they have been thought to require notice in this Dictionary, are treated either under their first element or as main words. A considerable number of kinds of saws used for surgical purposes are distinguished by the names of their inventors, as *Butcher's, Ferguson's, Gowan's, Hey's, Liston's saw*.

c **1000** ÆLFRIC *Gloss.* in Wr.-Wülcker 106/22 *Serrula*, saga, *uel* snide. *a* **1100** *Gerefa* in *Anglia* IX. 263/1 He sceal ..habban..æcse, adsan, sage. *a* **1300** *Cursor M.* 27376 Away to sagh þam ilk crote, wit þe sagh o penance treu þat þe frut spring efter neu. *c* **1340** *Nominale* (Skeat) 525 File sawe and spindelle. **1387** TREVISA *Higden* (Rolls) II. 383 þis Perdix.. took a plate of iren, and fyled it, and made it i-toþed as a rugge boon of a fische, and þanne it was a sawe. *a* **1400–50** *Alexander* 4096 A burly best with a bake as bedell as a saȝe. **1432–50** tr. *Higden* (Rolls) II. 75 After that Ysay was kytte with a sae of tree. **1533** *Ld. Treas. Acc. Scotl.* VI. 155 Ane saw send to the werkmen in Lochaber to cut the tymmer for the artailzerie. **1681** Grew *Musæum* iv. §i. 360 A Box of Anatomick Instruments; sc. Saws, Steel and Ivory Knives [etc.]. **1784** Cowper *Task* v. 145 No sound of hammer or of saw was there. **1816** J. Smith *Panorama Sci. & Art* I. 16 Saws for cutting metals, are made very narrow, ..and stretched by a screw at one end. **1886** *Encycl. Brit.* XXI. 343/2 The principal modern use of the saw is to divide wood.

transf. and *fig.* **1593** Shaks. *Lucr.* 1672 Euen so his sighes, his sorrowes make a saw, To push griefe on, and back the same grief draw. **1621** Burton *Anat. Mel.* I. ii. III. viii. 138 Faction, hatred, livor, emulation, which..are, *serræ animæ*, the sawes of the soule. **1871** Kingsley *At Last* iv, You..see aloft the saw of the mountain ridges against the black-blue sky.

†**b.** In obsolete phrases. ***to draw the saw*** (***of contention*** or ***controversy***): to keep up a fruitless dispute. ***to be under the saw of contention***: (of a question) to be the subject of profitless dispute. ***to hand the saw***: to take turns, change parts, *with* another in some work or function. ***to hold*** (a person) ***at the long saw***: to keep in suspense.

1654 Jer. Taylor *Real Pres.* A 1, The Question of Transubstantiation, which hath already so many times passed by the Fire and under the Saw of Contention. **1659** Bp. Walton *Consid. Considered* 305 Yet if he think fit to draw this saw of contention further,..I [etc.]. **1674** N. Fairfax *Bulk & Selv.* 101 Now because ghost cannot hand the saw thus with body..Thence 'tis [etc.]. **1688** *Lond. Gaz.* No. 2329/3 It would be of little avail to draw the Saw any longer of Answers and Retorts. **1710** Prideaux *Orig. Tithes* Pref. 12 Neither will I draw the saw of contention with any one in answering any of the Cavils. *a* **1733** North *Life Ld. Kpr.* (1742) 79 So, between the one and the other, he was held at the Long Saw above a Month. **1768** Wesley *Wks.* (1872) XIV. 343 Having neither leisure nor inclination to draw the saw of controversy.

c. A flexible saw used as a musical instrument, played with a bow.

1931 *Daily Mail* 6 Oct. 16/3 Saw solos. **1938** *Oxf. Compan. Mus.* 872/1 *Singing saw.* This is an ordinary hand saw which is held between the player's knees and played on by a violin bow; its blade is meanwhile bent, under a lesser or greater tension, by the player's left hand, so producing the different pitches. **1961** *Times* 18 Jan. 15/5 An instrument believed to be wholly new in the orchestra pit, the musical saw. **1977** *Times* 14 Dec. 14/8 The Anal Zephyr Trio *does* exist..(apart from the pianist) it includes a saw and bottles.

2. *Zool.* A part or organ with teeth like those of a saw. Also Comb. *saw-bearing* adj.

1664 Hubert *Catal. Rarities* (1665) 32 A very great Saw, or weapon of a Saw-fish, with the which he torments the Whale. **1747** Gould *Eng. Ants* 4 The double Saw is a hard bony Substance. *Ibid.*, They [*sc.* Ants] have four or five Teeth in a Saw. **1754** Fielding *Voy. Lisbon* Wks. 1882 VII. 64 The sting or saw of a wasp. **1854** A. Adams, etc. *Man. Nat. Hist.* 222 Saw-bearing Hymenoptera (*Securifera*). **1866** *Chamb. Encycl.* VIII. 508/2 Whales are said to be sometimes killed by sawfishes, and the saw has been sometimes driven into the hull of a ship. **1871** T. R. Jones *Anim. Kingd.* (ed. 4) 360 The saws of the various species of Tenthredo are as diversified as the habits of the insects to which they belong. **1885** G. S. Forbes *Wild Life Canara* 51 A great saw-fish, which measured about twenty-one feet from the end of the saw to the tail.

3. [Properly a distinct word, f. saw *v.*] **a.** A sawing movement. (In Dicts.). **b.** *Whist.* = see-saw *sb.* 1 c.

1746 Hoyle *Whist* (ed. 6) 36 You gain the Advantage of establishing of a Saw. **1755** *Connoisseur* No. 60 ¶ 4 (1761) II. 195, A forces B, who, by leading Spades, plays into A's Hand, who returns a Club, and so they get a Saw between them. *c* **1890** *Up to Date Games of Cards* 37 Saw, is when each partner trumps a different suit, and they play those suits to each other for that purpose.

4. Short for sawfish. *rare.*

1888 G. H. Kingsley *Sport & Travel* vi. (1900) 180 Across the mouth of the bay cruised a pair of saws, some ten or twelve feet long.

5. *attrib.* and *Comb.* **a.** simple attrib., as ***saw-blade***, ***-carriage***, ***machine***, ***-mandrel***, ***-mark***; **b.** objective, as ***saw-filer***, ***-filing***, ***-grinder***, ***-maker***, ***-piercer***, ***-setter***, ***-setting***; **c.** similative, as ***saw-backed***, ***-beaked***, ***-leaved***, ***-like***, ***-shaped***, ***-toothed***, ***-topped*** adjs.

1903 Kipling *Five Nations* 176 The same old *saw-backed fever-chart. **1924** R. Campbell *Flaming Terrapin* v. 77 The angel cowboys..Vaulting on the saw-backed ridges Where they tear the sky to strips. **1961** C. H. D. Todd *Popular Whippet* 33 One is often asked about a 'saw-backed' dog and what can be done about it. **1869–73** T. R. Jones *Cassell's Bk. Birds* III. 95 The *Saw-beaked Alcyons (*Syma*). **1831** J. Holland *Manuf. Metal* I. 275 Of the elastic steel, a *saw-blade may be considered an example. **1886** *Encycl. Brit.* XXI. 345/1 Here they are rolled upon skids leading to the *saw-carriage. **1890** W. J. Gordon *Foundry* 200 Where the *saw-edged knife in one of the cylinders perforates the web. **1881** Young *Every Man his own Mech.* §347 This *saw-filer's vice may be obtained [etc.]. **1875** Knight *Dict. Mech.*, **Saw-filing machine*, one for sharpening the teeth of saws. **1861** *Sat. Rev.* 21 Dec. 635 The *Sawgrinders' Union in Sheffield. **1822** *Hortus Anglicus* II. 252 *Saw-leaved Vetch. **1611** Cotgr. s.v. *Scie*, *Scie de mer*, a kind of Whall which hath a *Saw-like snowt. **1881** Newton in *Encycl. Brit.* XII. 358/1 Fine, horny, saw-like teeth. **1822** T. Gill *Techn. Repos.* II. 217 An improved *Saw Machine. **1662** *Comenius' Janua Ling. Triling.* 103 The *saw-maker [maketh] saws. **1816** J. Smith *Panorama Sci. & Art* I. 9 Saw makers first harden their plates in the usual way. **1858** Simmonds *Dict. Trade*, **Saw-mandrel*, a holdfast for a saw in a lathe. **1873** J. Richards *Operator's Handbk.* 117 Saw mandrils..should be as strong as possible, to stand the speed. **1875** *Ure's Dict. Arts* I. 420 The cross cords become embedded in the *saw-marks by the pressure of the sewing thread. **1858** Simmonds *Dict. Trade*, **Saw piercer*, a workman who cuts the teeth of saws. **1881** Young *Every Man his own Mech.* §342 Any itinerant *saw-setter, who goes his regular round..with his bench and files. *Ibid.* §346 Useful contrivance for *saw setting [etc.]. **1842** Brande *Dict. Sci.* etc., s.v. *Securifers*, The females have a *saw-shaped or hatchet-shaped terebra. **1868** *Rep. Munitions of War* 102 The rifling is what is termed in England the Scott or saw-shaped system. **1588** Fraunce *Lawiers Log.* I. vi. 36 b, Shee is splayfooted, crookbacked, tunnebellied, *sawtoothed, &c. **1857** A. Gray *First Less. Bot.* (1866) 229 *Saw-toothed*: see *serrate*. **1866** Owen *Anat. Vertebr.* II. 495 The saw-toothed Sterrink (*Stenorhynchus serridens*). **1874** Eassie *Wood & Uses* 165 Figs. 217 and 218 are each of the kind known as the saw-toothed roof,..used in weaving and other sheds.

d. Special combinations: **saw-bar**, either of the two bars which hold the saw in a fretwork machine; † **saw battle**, a disposition of troops in which the battalions form a serrated front; **saw-bearing** *a.* (see sense 2); **saw-belly** *U.S.*, a name for the glut herring (*Clupea æstivalis*), and the alewife (*C. serrata*); **saw-bench**, a circular saw with a bench to support the material and advance it to the saw; † **sawboard**, timber sawn into boards; † **saw-carf** = *saw-kerf*; **saw-cut** *sb.*, an incision made with a saw; **saw-cut** *v. Bookbinding*, to make saw-cuts in (the back of a book); **saw-doctor**, (*a*) 'an instrument having an angular punch for cutting pieces out of the edge of a saw-blade, to increase the depth of the interdental spaces; a saw-gummer' (Knight); (*b*) a craftsman who maintains saws in an efficient condition; **saw-edge**, a serrated edge (in quot. of a ridge of rock); **saw-edged** *a.*, having a serrated edge; **saw-file**, a file specially adapted for sharpening the teeth of saws; **saw-frame**, (*a*) the frame in which a saw-blade is stretched; (*b*) the sash or gate of a mill saw; **saw-gin**, a form of cotton-gin in which the fibres are torn from the seed by revolving toothed discs or circular saws; **saw-ginned** *a.*, prepared by means of the saw-gin; **saw-grass**, (*a*) = *saw-wort*; (*b*) *U.S.*, a sedge of the genus *Cladium*; **saw-gummer** = gummer[1] b; **saw-handle**, (*a*) the handle of a saw; (*b*) *slang*, the handle of a 'saw-handled' pistol; **saw-handled** *a.*, having a handle shaped like that of a saw; **saw-horned** *a.*, having serrate antennæ; **saw-horse**, a frame or trestle for supporting wood that is being sawn, a saw-buck; **saw-kerf** *sb.* = kerf *sb.* 2; *v. trans.*, to make a saw-kerf in; hence **saw-kerfing** *vbl. sb.*; **saw-log** (see quot.); † **saw-muscle** = serratus; **saw-pad** (see pad *sb.* 8); **saw palmetto**, a palmetto, *Serenoa serratula*, with prickly leaf-stalks; also, a small cluster palm, *Acoelorrhaphe wrightii*, of southern Florida and central America; **saw-pierced** *a.*, cut out with a frame-saw or piercing-saw; so **saw-piercing**; **saw-plate**, (*a*) the blade of a saw; (*b*) iron in plates of the thickness of the blade of a saw; **saw-sash** *U.S.* (see sash *sb.*[2] 3 b); **saw-scale** = *saw-scaled viper*; **saw-scaled viper**, a small venomous rough-scaled snake, *Echis carinatus*, of the family Viperidæ, found in Africa and southern Asia; **saw-set**, an instrument for setting the teeth of a saw: also *attrib.*; **saw-shark**, a small shark of the family Pristiophoridæ, found in southern seas from Africa to Australia and distinguished by a saw-like flattened snout; **saw-sharpener**, (*a*) one who sharpens saws; (*b*) a name for the Great Titmouse, *Parus major* (cf. *saw-whetter*); **saw-spindle**, the shaft of a circular saw; † **saw-stage**, ? = saw-pit; **saw-tail**, a bird (*Temnurus truncatus*) inhabiting Cochin China (T. R. Jones *Cassell's Bk. Birds*, 1869–73); **saw-timber**, timber suitable for sawing into boards or planks; **saw-way** = *saw-kerf*; **saw-whet** *N. Amer.*, a small dark brown owl, *Ægolius acadica*, found in eastern North America; **saw-whetter**, (*a*) = *saw-whet*; (*b*) the marsh titmouse, *Parus palustris*; **saw-work** *Fortif.* (see quot.); **saw-wrack** *Bot.*, the seaweed *Fucus serratus*; **saw-wrest** = *saw-set*. Also sawbill, sawbuck, etc.

1875 Seaton *Fret Cutting* 18 An iron eye, screwed in exactly under the lower *saw bar. **1598** Barret *Theor. Warres* 80 The *Saw battell containeth 3 sharpe angles framed of 6 battalions. **1884** Goode, etc. *Nat. Hist. Aquatic Anim.* 582 Around the Gulf of Maine this species is also known by the names 'Kyack' or 'Kyauk', '*Saw-belly', and 'Cat-thrasher'. **1846** Holtzapffel *Turning*, etc. II. 793 The flooring boards..were grooved on each edge upon an ordinary *saw bench. **1869** Rankine *Cycl. Machine & Hand Tools* Pl. Q 16 Improved self-acting saw bench. **1495** *Naval Accts. Hen. VII* (1896) 226, vij[ml] fote of *Sawborde price the c—ij[s]. **1778** [W. Marshall] *Minutes Agric.* 9 Dec. 1775 The *saw-carf, instead of binding, is always kept gaping. **1846** Holtzapffel *Turning*, etc. II. 706 The chalk line..marks the edges of the intended *saw-cuts with sufficient certainty. **1874** Knight *Dict. Mech.* s.v. *Bookbinding*, Sewing [comes] after *saw-cutting the backs for the cords. **1936** A. M. Rust *Whangarei Early Reminisc.* 163 Timber was being got..along its..foreshore. Hundreds of bushmen..were employed besides stackers, *saw doctors, benchmen and mill-hands in the different sawmills. **1949** J. L. Carvel *One Hundred Years in Timber* ix. 140 No sawmill can function long without efficient tool-rooms, and at the City Saw Mills the saw-shop and grinding-shop supply these essentials. These are supervised by the saw-doctor. **1977** *Belfast Tel.* 22 Feb. 22 (Advt.), C.D. Monninger Ltd. require Saw Doctor to take charge of the day-to-day running of their new Belfast Service Centre. **1857** Kingsley *Two Y. Ago* xxi, From the highest *saw-edges, where Moel Meirch cuts the golden sky, down to the very depth of the abyss. **1846** Louisa S. Costello *Tour Venice* 446 A wall of *saw-edged perpendicular rocks. **1846** Holtzapffel *Turning*, etc. II. 689 The files used in sharpening saws are triangular, round, half-round, and mill *saw-files. **1825** J. Nicholson *Operat. Mechanic* 442 Let a transverse groove..be cut in the *saw-frame to receive that pin. **1801** Miller & Whitney in *Amer. Jrnl. Sci. & Arts* (1832) XXI. 222 The machine for separating cotton from its seeds, commonly called the *Saw Gin. **1873** *Beeton's Dict. Comm.* s.v. *Cotton*, Good fair to good *saw-ginned Surat cotton. **1822** W. H. Simmons *Notices E. Florida* ii. 24 They were obliged to defend their horses' feet with wrappings of cow-hide, in order to prevent their being injured by the sharp *saw grass. **1847** Whittier *Drovers* 56 Cows..Disputing feebly with the frogs The crop of saw-grass meadows! **1855** Ogilvie *Suppl.*, *Saw-grass*, a kind of coarse grass, bog-rush. **1882** 'Ouida' *Maremma* I. 187 Thrusting their snouts amidst the saw-grass. **1891** Villiers-Stuart *Equat. Forests* 110 It turned out to be really a vast expanse of water hidden beneath saw-grass, which in some places attains a height of twenty feet. **1860** Bartlett *Dict. Amer.* (ed. 3), **Saw-gummer*, see Gummer. **1837** Lever *Harry Lorrequer* v, My friend there..is a very neat shot when he has the *saw-handle. **1892** *Daily News* 4 Aug. 7/1 The plaintiff..was a saw-handle maker. **1899** Ld. Rosebery *Peel* 26 But scarcely..is there any memory of so peppery a politician with so constant an inclination to the 'sawhandles'. **1837** Lever *Harry Lorrequer* v, Didn't I tell ye, that pistol always threw high... Oh, Fin, if you had only given me the *saw-handled one. **1862** T. W. Harris *Insects Injur. Veget.* (ed. 3) 45 Serricorn or *saw-horned beetles. **1778** [W. Marshall] *Minutes Agric.* 9 Dec. 1775 The common *saw-horse makes the cutting of it [*sc.* firewood] a tedious labour-consuming piece of business. **1883** *Harper's Mag.* Mar. 601/2 A hen..came in and settled herself in a corner behind a saw-horse. **1688** R. Holme *Armoury* III. 101/1 Kerf, or *Saw Kerf. **1886** *Encycl. Brit.* XXI. 344/2 Gang-saws are seldom thicker than 14-gauge, and are successfully worked at 18-gauge, making a saw-kerf or waste of but ⅛ inch. **1887** *Archit. Publ. Soc. Dict.* s.v. *Saw Curf*, Soufflot in 1779 employed workmen to *saw-kerf the joints of the piers..of S. Geneviève... Wood-bending is often facilitated by *saw-kerfing. **1799** D. W. Smyth *Short Topogr. Descr. Upper Canada* 32 The *saw logs are conveyed to this mill in a very remarkable manner. **1842** Mrs. Kirkland *Forest Life* II. 194 We had made perhaps half the distance when we met a prodigious 'saw-log'—that is, the huge trunk of a tree, drawn by oxen, on its way to the mill. **1916** *Daily Colonist* (Victoria, B.C.) 1 July 6/6 The timber returns for the month of May..show that the total scale of sawlogs for the Province amounted to 94,771,871 ft. [etc.]. **1971** *Timber Trades Jrnl.* 14 Aug. 38/1 It is estimated that quantities from British forests should increase significantly in the next decade and with the improving quality of sawlogs home producers can look forward to obtaining an increasing share of consumption of sawnwood. **1615** Crooke *Body of Man* 795 The second muscle is called *Serratus maior* or the greater *saw-muscle. **1846** Holtzapffel *Turning*, etc. II. 712 The key-hole or fret saw-blade..is held in a *saw-pad. **1797** B. Hawkins *Let.* 18 Feb. in *Georgia Hist. Soc. Coll.* (1916) IX. 85 The whole country was a pine barron, with wiregrass and *saw palmetto. **1861** *Amer. Cycl.* XII. 704/1 The saw palmetto..occurs on the southern islands of South Carolina, and in sandy soils southward to Florida. **1894** B. Torrey *Florida Sketch-Bk.* 3 The ground [was] covered thickly with saw palmetto. **1938** M. K. Rawlings *Yearling* xxv. 317 The bears were..eating the berries of the saw palmetto. **1942** S. Kennedy *Palmetto Country* 4 Shrub-like saw palmetto underlies the pine flat-woods. **1879** *Navy List* Sept. 490/1 On the star to be mounted a dead gilt laurel wreath and *saw pierced garter with regimental motto. **1892** *Daily News* 10 May 2/4 A saw-pierced picture frame. **1902** *Daily Chron.* 15 Oct. 10/7 Art Metal, leaf-beating and *saw-piercing. **1837** Lt.-Col. Reid in *Civ. Engin. & Arch. Jrnl.* I. 6/1 Long iron needles pass through holes in the strips of *saw-plate, and pin them to the ground. *Ibid.*, To retain the front ones in their places, ties are used made of saw-plate iron. **1865** I. T. F. Turner *Slate Quarries* 16 A continuous dropping of water washes particles of flint sand beneath the saw-plate. **1964** J. Hillaby *Journey to Jade Sea* 121 *Saw-scales sound like kettles of boiling water. **1935** N. L. Corkill in *Sudan Notes & Records* XVIII. 245 The Carpet or *Saw-scaled Viper is usually considered to be a form restricted to a sandy habitat. **1966** C. Sweeney *Scurrying Bush* xii. 168 A very violent saw-scaled viper crawled out into the open, hissing and rustling its scales against each other. **1846** Holtzapffel *Turning*, etc. II. 697 The *saw-set ..consists of a narrow blade of steel, with notches of various widths for different saws... In some few cases saw-set pliers are used. **1881** Young *Every Man his own Mech.* §345 The teeth can be bent to the right or left, as may be requisite, with the saw-set. **1882** Tenison-Woods *Fishes N.S. Wales* 98 The *saw-shark must not be confounded with saw-fish. **1906** D. G. Stead *Fishes Austral.* xii. 236 The Little Saw-Shark..is a small species, having a somewhat flattened body, and attaining a length of about 4 feet. **1931** J. R. Norman *Hist. Fishes* iii. 35 In..one of the Saw Sharks..there may be as many as six or seven [gill-clefts]. **1961** E. S. Herald *Living Fishes of World* 49/1 The four known species of saw sharks have small pectoral fins with the gill openings just ahead of these fins. **1885** Swainson *Prov. Names Birds* 33 Great Titmouse (*Parus major*)..*Saw sharpener. **1895** P. H. Emerson *Birds*, etc. *Norfolk Broadland* 63 They [*sc.* great titmice] are sometimes called 'saw-sharpeners' in the building season, from the well-known and peculiar grating noise made by the cock. **1905** *Daily Chron.* 22 Mar. 8/7 Wood Turner, Fret Cutter and Saw Sharpener. **1819** *Rees' Cycl.* XXI. 5 D/1 Circular *saw-spindles are frequently burnt..their motion being very quick. **1846** HOLTZAPFFEL *Turning*, etc. II. 754 The saw spindle is frequently squared at one end. **1522** *MS. Acc. St. John's Hosp., Canterb.*, For drawyng out of ij battis to yᵉ *sawstage. **1932** *Sun* (Baltimore) 17 Sept. 4/6 The cutting is always done selectively, large trees being taken for *saw timber for new buildings and repairs, and weed trees and defective trees for fuel. **1979** *Sci. Amer.* Feb. 65/3 In the Western national forests, which constitute..50 percent of the nation's entire supply of standing saw-timber. **1823** P. NICHOLSON *Pract. Build.* 220 If planks are sawed longitudinally, through their thickness, the *saw-way is called a ripping-cut. **1834** J. J. AUDUBON *Ornith. Biogr.* II. 567 The Little Owl is known in Massachusetts by the name of the '*Saw-whet', the sound of its love-notes bearing a great resemblance to the noise produced by filing the teeth of a large saw. **1839** AUDUBON *Synopsis Birds Amer.* 24 *Ulula Acadica*,..Acadian Night-Owl... Saw-whet. **1872** COUES *Key N. Amer. Birds* 206 *Nyctale acadica*... Acadian Owl. Saw-whet Owl. **1894** *Outing* XXIII. 406/1 The little 'saw whet' under his tiny glass globe. **1949** *Amer. Forests* Oct. 23/1 The saw-whet owl has a peculiar voice. **1959** W. R. BIRD *These are Maritimes* vi. 183 Now I rather like the little fellows [*sc.* owls], especially the saw-whets. **1977** *New Yorker* 5 Sept. 24/1 Saw-whet owls and long-eared owls roost in evergreens in winter. **1784** BELKNAP *Tour to White Mts.* (1876) 10 The Dr. saw a blue bird, with a white head, which is said to be a *saw-whetter. **1840** GOSSE *Canadian Nat.* 92 The sound..is usually thought to resemble the whetting of a saw, and hence the bird from which it proceeds is called the Saw-whetter. **1885** SWAINSON *Prov. Names Birds* 33 Marsh Titmouse (*Parus palustris*)..Saw whetter. **1728** CHAMBERS *Cycl.*, *Redens*,..or *Redan*, in Fortification, a Kind of Work indented in Form of the Teeth of a Saw... It is also call'd *Saw-work. **1868** PAXTON *Bot. Dict.*, **Saw-wrack*. **1678** MOXON *Mech. Exerc.* v. 94 Then with the *Saw wrest..they set the Teeth of the Saw. **1728–52** CHAMBERS *Cycl.* s.v. *Saw*, This is done by putting an Instrument, called a *Saw-wrist*, between every other two Teeth, and giving it a little Wrench. **1841** *Penny Cycl.* XX. 477/1 A *saw-wrest* is used for setting the teeth.

saw (sɔː), *sb.*² Forms: 1 **saȝu** (**saȝe**), ? **saȝa**, 2–5 **saȝe**, 3 **sæȝe**, **sahe**, 3–7 **sawe**, 4 **sa**, **sach(e**, **sau(e**, **sauue**, **sawȝe**, 4–5 **sagh(e**, 4– **saw**. *Pl.* 3 **sæȝen**, **sahen**, **sawen**, 4 **saȝez**, **sauez**, **sawus**, 5 *Sc.* **sawiss**. [OE. *saȝu* str. fem. = MLG., MDu. *sage*, *zage*, OHG. *saga* str. and wk. fem. (MHG., mod.G. *sage*), ON. *saga* wk. fem. (see SAGA):—OTeut. **sagā*, **sagōn-*, f. root of **sagǣjan* SAY *v.*¹ Cf. Lith. *pa-saka* (:—*sokā*) story.]

†**1.** A saying; discourse; speech. *Obs.*

9.. *Voc.* in Wr.-Wülcker 221/28 *Dictu i. dicione*, saȝu, *uel oratione*. *c* **1000** ÆLFRIC *Gloss.* ibid. 165/27 *Elogium*, *uel dictio*, saȝa. *c* **1000** *Ags. Gosp.*, *Luke* xi. 45 Lareow teonan þu wyrhcst us mid þisse saȝe. *c* **1175** *Lamb. Hom.* 133 Ðeo apostles hine beden þet he scalde suggen hwet þeo saȝe bicweðe and he seide *Semen est uerbum dei*. *c* **1205** LAY. 749 Heo wenden þat his sawen [*c* **1275** sawes] soðe weren. *Ibid.* 29658 Þa he isaid hauede þa sæȝen of ure drihten. *c* **1220** *Bestiary* 600 He sweren bi ðe rode..and he ðe leȝen sone, mid here saȝe and mid here song. *a* **1225** *Ancr. R.* 360 Þis is Seinte Poules sawe. *a* **1225** *Leg. Kath.* 358 Alle ich iseo þine sahen sotliche isette. *a* **1300** *Cursor M.* 4167 And þan wil naman mak on sau þat we him suld haue broght on dau. *Ibid.* 24112 Luue wald i spak, might me wit-stode, Mi reut was all apon þat rode, Na sagh [*Edin. MS.* sache] þar moght i sai. **1303** R. BRUNNE *Handl. Synne* 3557 He was wunt to seye wykked sawes. *c* **1350** *Will. Palerne* 1112 Alle seide at o sawe 'sire, we ȝou rede'. **13..** *E.E. Allit. P.* B. 109 Thenne þe sergauntez, at þat sawe, swengen þer-oute. *c* **1375** *Sc. Leg. Saints* xv. (*Barnabas*) 84 Quhen þe paianis hard þis sa, þai sad [etc.]. *c* **1386** CHAUCER *Knt.'s T.* 668 Ful litel woot Arcite of his felawe That was so ny to herknen al his sawe. **1387** TREVISA *Higden* (Rolls) I. 383 Hit is comoun sawe þat [þe] contray þat now hatte Scotlond is an out strecching, and is þe norþ partie of þe more Bretayne. *c* **1450** *St. Cuthbert* (Surtees) 1501 Bot ay boisil dedis and sawes he folowed. **1456** SIR G. HAYE *Law Arms* (S.T.S.) 106, I will nocht that men understand be my sawis na the King of Jerusalem has gude rycht. **1553** T. WILSON *Rhet.* 78 Thus we se howe and in what maner pleasaunt sawes are gathered and used, upon the occasion of divers wordes spoken. *a* **1586** *Satir. Poems Reform.* xxxvii. 12 Thair sawis to be suythe sum will suspect. **1621** T. WILLIAMSON tr. *Goulart's Wise Vieillard* 100 The counsell and sawe of old men hath in it somewhat..that is pleasing to heare, gracefull, and of venerable regard.

†**2.** A story, tale, recital. *Obs.*

c **1320** *Cast. Love* 619 Such wonder nas neuer I-herd in sawe. **1338** R. BRUNNE *Chron.* (1810) 205 Þis þat I haf said it is Pers sawe, Als he in romance laid, þer after gan I drawe. *c* **1375** *Sc. Leg. Saints* ii. (*Paulus*) 53 Aymo recordis In his saw, þat [etc.]. *c* **1400** *St. Alexius* 393 (Laud MS.) His moder ne miȝth lete sorouȝ, Neiþer at euene ne at morowe, In sawȝe as it is seide. *c* **1460** *Emare* 319 As y haue herd menstrelles syng yn sawe.

†**3.** A decree, command. *Obs.*

a **1300** *Cursor M.* 8333 Of his sauues þis was an, þat of his barnage sa bald was nan,..in his chamber..A fote to set, bot þai war cald. **1338** R. BRUNNE *Chron.* (1810) 250 What for þe kynges sawe, & skille þei vnderstode, & þorgh þe londes lawe, & descent of blod, þe triours alle þat caste, & put þer saw tille on. **14..** 26 *Pol. Poems* 23 That leueþ trouþe, and falshed vse, And lyue not after goddis sawe. *c* **1440** *York Myst.* xlviii. 211 A! myghtfull god, here is it sene, Þou will fulfille þi forward right, And all þi sawes þou will maynteyne. **1566** STERNHOLD & H. *Ps.* cxix. 97 What great desire and feruent loue, do I beare to thy saw: All the day long my whole deuise, is onely on thy law. **1595** SPENSER *Col. Clout* 884 So love is Lord of all the world by right, And rules the creatures by his powrfull saw.

4. A sententious saying; a traditional maxim, a proverb. For *(old) said saw* see SAID *ppl. a.*

a **1275** *Prov. Ælfred* 35 (Trin. Coll. MS.) Þis werin þe sawen of kinc Alfred. *Ibid.* 361 Þurch saȝe mon is wis. *c* **1320** R. BRUNNE *Medit.* 853 Of salamons sawys ȝe are nat auysed. **1362** LANGL. *P. Pl.* A. VIII. 124 'Lewede lorel!' quod he 'luite lokestou on þe Bible, On Salamones sawes seldom þou bi-holdest'. **13..** *E.E. Allit. P.* B. 1599 His sawle is ful of syence, saȝes to schawe. *c* **1375** *Sc. Leg. Saints* vii. (*Jacobus Minor*) 653 Fore It is sad in elderys saw: 'ful harde is hungyre in hale maw.' *c* **1440** *Promp. Parv.* 441/2 Sawe, or proverbe, *proverbium*, *problema*. **1470–85** MALORY *Arthur* x. lxi. 519 Euer hit is an old sawe gyue a chorle rule and there by he wylle not be suffysed. **1530** PALSGR. 265/1 Sawe a proverbe, *prouerbe*. **1563** B. GOOGE *Eglogs* i. (Arb.) 31 And many a saged sawe lies hyd within thine aged brest. **1600** SHAKS. *A.Y.L.* II. vii. 156 Full of wise sawes, and moderne instances. **1632** E. ROBERTSON in *Lithgow's Trav.* To Author B 4, How ruld with Lawes The South world is: their Rites, Religious sawes. *c* **1705** POPE *Jan. & May* 219 We, Sirs, are fools; and must resign the cause To heath'nish authors, proverbs, and old saws. **1764** *Oxf. Sausage* 172 Alone from Jargon born to rescue Law, From Precedent, grave Hum, and formal Saw! **1849** MACAULAY *Hist. Eng.* x. II. 635 The great question now depending was not to be decided by the saws of pedantic Templars. **1861** FLOR. NIGHTINGALE *Nursing* (ed. 2) 50 It is an ever ready saw that an egg is equivalent to a lb. of meat; whereas it is not at all so. **1884** TENNYSON *Becket* v. ii, For I was musing on an ancient saw, *Suaviter in modo, fortiter in re*.

saw (sɔː), *v.*¹ Pa. t. **sawed**; pa. pple. **sawed**, **sawn**. Forms: 4 **sagh**, **sau**, 5 **saghe**, **saȝe**, 5–6 **sawe**. *Pa. t.* α. *weak* 3 **sahede**, 5 **sawede**, 5– **sawed**; β. *strong* 5 **suwe**, **sew**. *Pa. pple.* α. *weak* 3 **isahet**, 4 **i-sawed**, **saede**, **sawid**, 6 **saw'de**, **sawyde**, 7– **sawed**; β. *strong* 5–7 **sawen**, 5 **sowen**, 6 **sawin**, 9 **sawn**. [f. SAW *sb.*¹; cf. the equivalent MLG., MDu. *sagen* (Du. *zagen*), OHG. *sagôn*, *segôn* (MHG. *sagen*, *segen*, mod.G. *sägen*), ON. *saga* (Sw. *såga*, Da. *save*).

The pa. t. was sometimes conjugated strong in the 15th c. The str. pa. pple., which came into use at the same time, is now perh. equally current with the wk. form in the compound tenses of the vb., and as ppl. adj. is much more common.]

1. a. *trans.* To cut with a saw. Also with advs., *asunder*, *away*, *off*, *through*; and const. *into*.

a **1225** *Life St. Juliana* 38 Ich makede þen wittie ysaye beon isahet þurh and þurh to deaðe. *a* **1300** *Cursor M.* 27375 Þe preist bi-gin..Away to sagh þam ilk crote. *c* **1400** *Wyclifite Bible* Prol. to Prophets (1850) III. 225 Manasses ordeynede and demyde Isaye to be sawid with ynne a cedre tree. *c* **1400** *Melayne* 60 His wyffe & his childire three Byfore his eghne þat he myghte see Be in sondre sawenn. *c* **1430** *Pilgr. Lyf Manhode* II. cxlviii. (1869) 135 In Iacob and Esau þou hast seyn þe figure; I sawede hem and vnioyned hem. *c* **1450** *Mirour Saluacioun* (1888) 10 Some with sawes he suwe. **1483** *Cath. Angl.* 319/2 To saghe a tre, *serrare*. **1483** CAXTON *Golden Leg.* 248/2 She..was taken of the deuyls and departed and sowen a sondre. **1496** *Ld. Treas. Acc. Scotl.* I. 281 Item, to othir tua sawaris, at sew with thaim, xvij s. viij d. **1538** ELYOT *Dict.*, *Runcino*, to sawe tymber. **1573** TUSSER *Husb.* (1878) 42 Now sawe out thy timber, for boord and for pale. **1577** HANMER *Anc. Eccl. Hist.* To Rdr. *vb, Their legges sawed of, their tongues cutte. **1597** SHAKS. *2 Hen. IV*, v. i. 70 If I were saw'de into Quantities, I should make foure dozen of such bearded Hermites staues, as Master Shallow. **1611** BIBLE *1 Kings* vii. 9 Hewed stones, sawed with sawes. —— *Heb.* xi. 37 They were stoned, they were sawen asunder. **1646** SIR T. BROWNE *Pseud. Ep.* III. i. 107 By sawing away of trees. **1664** J. WILSON *A. Commenius* v. i, 'Twere better dye at once, Than be thus saw'd in pieces. **1678** MOXON *Mech. Exerc.* v. 95 When they direct any of their Underlins to saw such a piece of Stuff..seldom say Saw that piece of Stuff. **1719** J. CONDUIT in *Phil. Trans.* XXX. 917 The Letters probably were either sawed off, or turned inwards. **1795** J. HOLT *Agric. Surv. Lancaster* 48 He takes a hand-saw..and saws the top level. **1847** *Act 10 & 11 Vict.* c. 89 §28 Every Person who..hews, saws, bores, or cuts any Timber or Stone. **1876** *Encycl. Brit.* IV. 43/1 (*Bookbinding*) The volumes are then adjusted and clamped up..for the operation of sawing the back. Two or three grooves are..sawn straight across the back of the volume, according to the number of bands on which the book is to be sewed. **1879** FROUDE *Cæsar* xxii. 368 Trees were cut down and sawn into planks. **1886** *Encycl. Brit.* XXI. 344/1 With a cutting edge of so light a gauge as to waste but little of the valuable timber to be sawed.

fig. **1579** G. HARVEY in *Three Proper Lett.* (1580) 63 The sixte..is also in the same Predicament, vnlesse happly one of the feete be sawed off wyth a payre of Syncopes. *a* **1680** BUTLER *Rem.* (1759) I. 316 Until between these different Usurpations, that pull several ways, the whole Nation will in the end be sawed in Pieces. **1879** FARRAR *St. Paul* (1883) 119 The agony of hatred which was sawing their hearts asunder.

b. To cut as a saw does. Also *absol.* or *intr.*

a **1225** *St. Marher.* (1862) 22 Ant let scharpe sweord ant eke smart scher hire bi the schuldren ant sahede hire thurhut. *a* **1325** *Prose Psalter* (E.E.T.S.) li[i]. 2 Þou dost treccherie as a rasour sharp sauaand. **1664** HUBERT *Catal. Rarities* (1665) 31 A tayl of a Stingray, it will saw like an Iron saw.

transf. **1865** DICKENS *Mut. Fr.* I. xii, The grating wind sawed rather than blew.

c. To form by cutting with a saw.

1530 PALSGR. 698/2 Have you sawed nothyng but these two plankes to daye. **1678** MOXON *Mech. Exerc.* v. 87 When you Saw the Bevelling angles upon the square ends of Pieces. **1856** EMERSON *Eng. Traits, Character* Wks. (Bohn) II. 59 They saw a hole into the head of the 'winking Virgin' to know why she winks. **1875** SEATON *Fret Cutting* 15 To most people, this method of sawing out a pattern is inconvenient.

transf. **1871** TYNDALL *Fragm. Sci.* (1879) I. ix. 289 This wonderful fissure has been sawn through the mountain by the waters of the Tamina. **1906** BELLOC *Hills & Sea* 17 All the way down the gorge for miles, sawing its cut in sheer surfaces through the rock, crashes a violent stream.

d. *absol.* To use a saw; to cut with a saw.

c **1340** *Nominale* (Skeat) 116 M. cleuyth the borde and sawith. **1465** *Maun. & Househ. Exp.* (Roxb.) 309 My mastyr made comenaunt wyth ij. sawers of Donwyche: and thei schalle haue euery werke day that thei saw, vj. d. **1678** MOXON *Mech. Exerc.* v. 83 You must not Saw just upon the struck line,..Saw therefore right down with the Tennant Saw. **1692** R. L'ESTRANGE *Fables* cxiii. 106 Then, 'tis Call the Doctor, Pothecary, Surgeon; Purge, Flux, Launce, Burn, Saw. **1852** MRS. CARLYLE *Lett.* II. 184 Carpenters, into whose head the devil put it to saw the whole day.

e. *intr.* with passive force. To admit of being sawn.

1726 LEONI *Alberti's Archit.* I. 27/1 Beech..will saw into extreme thin Planks. *Ibid.* 57/1 A white sort of Stone..which Saws easier than Wood itself.

2. *transf.* With reference to the movement used in sawing. **a.** *trans.* *Phr. to saw the air*: to gesticulate with the hands as if sawing something invisible. Also *to saw one's hand*.

1602 SHAKS. *Ham.* III. ii. 5 Do not saw the Ayre too much your hand thus, but vse all gently. **1819** CRABBE *Tales of Hall* XIX. 158 'And what is proud', said Frances, 'but to stand Singing at church, and sawing thus your hand?' **1824** MISS FERRIER *Inher.* lxix, He was puffing, and blowing, and sawing the air with his arms, without ever gaining a single step upon them. **1884** *Sat. Rev.* 14 June 778/1 With her right hand she ceaselessly saws the air.

b. To work (the bit) from side to side in a horse's mouth. Also with the mouth as obj.

1850 SMEDLEY *Frank Fairlegh* v, I..got her head up by sawing her mouth with the snaffle, and pulled her [the mare] fairly at it. **1856** 'STONEHENGE' *Rural Sports* 536 If a horse obstinately refuses to stir, the bit may be gently 'sawed' from side to side.

c. *intr.* Said of one playing a stringed instrument with a bow.

1736 *Gentl. Mag.* VI. 615/1 Then saw'd and thrumm'd on ev'ry string! **1977** J. CROSBY *Company of Friends* v. 36 Czernowski sawed away at Mozart.

d. *trans.* Phr. *to saw wood*, to attend to one's own affairs; to continue working steadily. *U.S. colloq.*

1894 *Congress. Rec.* 24 Jan. 1347/2 Is it possible that the framers of the bill hold a grudge against the voters who 'sawed wood' last November? **1909** 'O. HENRY' *Options* 75 During all these wintry apostrophes, Barbara, cold at heart, sawed wood—the only appropriate thing she could think of to do. **1913** F. H. BURNETT *T. Tembarom* xxix. 359 Say nothing and saw wood... It means 'shut your mouth and keep on working'. **1933** J. BUCHAN *Prince of Captivity* III. i. 264 He sees the next job and sits down to it—stays still and saws wood, as Lincoln said.

e. Phr. *to saw a chunk* (*length, piece*) *off*, to copulate. *slang.*

1961 PARTRIDGE *Dict. Slang* Suppl. 1259/2 *Saw off a chunk* or *a piece*, to coït: Canadian: since ca. 1920. **1977** J. WAINWRIGHT *Do Nothin'* v. 86 The act is..known, in polite circles, as 'copulation'. Known, in less polite circles, as ..'sawing a length off'.

3. *transf.* With reference to the sound made by sawing; *to saw gourds*, etc., to snore loudly. *slang* (orig. *U.S.*).

1870 F. H. LUDLOW *Heart of Continent* ii. 91 In five minutes..we were all 'sawing gourds' together in the land of Nod. *a* **1897** 'R. SANDERS' *Sk. Country Life* (1898) xxx. 188 When the day's work is done..he can draw his bobtail night shirt about him..knowin that while he sleeps and dreams and saws gourds his worldly possessions are growin. **1939** J. WORBY *Spiv's Progress* ii. 12 I've been in the town and got the grub while you've been sawing them off. **1946** *Penguin New Writing* XXVIII. 184 The deaf-mute was asleep and sawing them off horribly. **1961** PARTRIDGE *Dict. Slang* Suppl. 1259/2 *Saw them off*, to snore; to sleep soundly... Ex the noise made with a saw clumsily handled. **1980** A. FOX *Kingfisher Scream* iii. 49 Rosemary would be asleep too now, with Don sawing wood beside her.

4. *intr.* (See quot.) ? *Obs.*

1630 in Binnell *Descr. Thames* (1758) 68 No Fisherman..shall..saw or search for Barbel within the Limits of London Bridge.

5. *trans.* To give a serrated outline to. *rare*⁻¹.

1780 A. YOUNG *Tour Irel.* I. 242 The coast is perfectly sawed by bays.

†**saw**, *v.*² *Obs.* (? *nonce-wd.*) [f. SAW *sb.*²] *intr.* To speak in saws.

1648 JENKYN *Blind Guide* i. 13 He saith, or rather *saweth* thus,..The time will come that youthfull Turnus shall Wish dearly Pallas ne'er has been encountred.

saw, obs. form of SAVE *v.*, SHOW *v.*, SOW *v.*

sawagerous, var. SAVAGEROUS *a.*

‖**sawah** (ˈsɑːwa). Also 8 **sawoor**; **sawa**. [Malay.] In Malaysia and Indonesia: an irrigated rice-field.

1783, **1839** [see LADANG]. **1937** M. COVARRUBIAS *Island of Bali* iv. 71 The most striking element of the Balinese landscape is the ever present ricefield, the *sawa*, a patch of land filled with water held by dikes cut out of the red earth. **1961** P. KEMP *Alms for Oblivion* vii. 105 The slopes are terraced with superb skill in tier after tier of *sawas*, or small paddy-fields, that produce each year two crops of the finest rice in South-East Asia. **1978** *Times* 25 Mar. 13/1 All around us were the..rice-fields. We had watched the ploughing of the water-logged *sawahs*.

sawar, obs. form of SOWER.

sawbill (ˈsɔːbɪl). [f. SAW *sb.*¹ + BILL *sb.*²] A name applied to various birds with serrated bills. **a.** The mergansers (also *sawbill diver* or *duck*). **b.** A humming-bird of the genus *Rhamphodon* (also *sawbill humming-bird*). **c.** *U.S.* A motmot (also *sawbill roller*).

1763 tr. *A.S. Le Page du Pratz's Hist. Louisiana* II. II. ii. 235 We are disturbed in the night, by the hideous noise of the numberless water-fowls,..such as cranes, flamingo's, wild geese, herons, saw-bills, ducks, &c. **1833** W. F. TOLMIE

Jrnl. 1 Sept. (1963) 232 Saw the Sawbill Duck once or twice riding down on a log. **1835** *Ibid.* 12 June 311 Shot a sawbill with rifle at the upper end of lake. **1843** YARRELL *Brit. Birds* III. 293 This bird [*Mergus merganser*] like the Red-breasted Merganser, is also called Saw-bill and Jacksaw. **1849** *Zoologist* VII. 2393 The red-breasted merganser [is] a saw-bill duck. **1856** F. O. MORRIS *Hist. Brit. Birds* V. 284 Goosander... Sawbill. Jack-saw. **1861** GOULD *Trochilidæ* I. pl. 1 *Grypus nævius*. Saw-bill. **1864-5** WOOD *Homes without Hands* xiii. (1868) 235 The Sawbill Humming Bird (*Grypus nævius*). **1869-73** T. R. JONES *Cassell's Bk. Birds* III. 83 The Saw-bill Rollers (*Prionites*)..occupy the..forests of South America. **1872** COUES *N. Amer. Birds* 178 *Momotidæ* (motmots or saw-bills). **1894** A. NEWTON *Dict. Birds* III. 814 Sawbill, a name commonly given to the Goosander and Merganser. **1973** *Nature West Coast* (Vancouver Nat. Hist. Soc.) 167 The 'toothed' bill, a necessity for holding slippery fish, has earned this bird [*sc.* the red-breasted merganser] the name 'sawbill'.

So **'saw-billed** *a.*, having a serrated bill.

1785 LATHAM *Gen. Synopsis Birds* VI. 579 Saw-billed Pelican. **1797** —— in *Trans. Linnean Soc.* IV. 121 Saw-billed Ducks or Divers.

sawbones ('sɔːbəʊnz). *slang.* [f. SAW *v.*[1] + BONE *sb.*] A surgeon.

1837 DICKENS *Pickw.* xxx, 'What, don't you know what a Sawbones is, Sir', enquired Mr. Weller; 'I thought every body know'd as a Sawbones was a Surgeon.' **1874** R. TYRWHITT *Sketch. Club* 166 The vivisectors and sawboneses. **1898** RIDER HAGGARD *Doctor Therne* 196, I found her the affianced bride of a parish sawbones.

Hence **'sawbonesing** *vbl. sb.* (*nonce-wd.*).

1870 MISS BROUGHTON *Red as Rose* I. 196 If I had..had to earn my bread quill-driving..or sawbones-ing.

sawbuck ('sɔːbʌk). *U.S.* [ad. Du. *zaagbok* trestle, saw-horse: cf. SAW *sb.*[1] and BUCK *sb.*[7]]

1. a. = BUCK *sb.*[7]

1862 *Rep. Comm. Patents: Agric. 1861* (U.S.) 141 The sheep is then laid upon his back in a kind of saw-buck. **1869** 'MARK TWAIN' *Innoc. Abr.* vi. (1872) 39 The saddles were peculiar... They consisted of a sort of saw-buck, with a small mattress on it. **1877** R. J. BURDETTE *Rise & Fall of Mustache* 308 You might as well tell a joke to a sawbuck as to his wife. **1906** W. CHURCHILL *Coniston* 390 He was standing with his foot upon the sawbuck and the saw across his knee. **1920** S. LEWIS *Main Street* 83 In back yards their sawbucks stood in depressions scattered with..flakes of sawdust. **1948** *Sat. Even. Post* 10 July 83/2 I'd roped everything around the ranch—calves, hounds, horses, fence posts, sawbucks.

b. In full, *sawbuck* (*pack*)*saddle*. A pack-saddle shaped like a sawbuck.

1881 E. W. NYE *Bill Nye & Boomerang* 67 This summer, however, I will get me a little blue jackass and put a sawbuck on his back. **1907** S. E. WHITE *Arizona Nights* ii. 12 We skirmished around and found..a sawbuck saddle with kyacks. **1913** *Outing* Jan. 425/1 The most practical equipment for pack animals is the ordinary crosstree or sawbuck pack saddle for all-round use. **1933** F. H. CHELEY *Camping Out* 461 While the Government has adopted the aparejo as its pack saddle, the cross-tree or sawbuck is the best one for ordinary use. **1938** M. THOMPSON *High Trails of Glacier National Park* 138 If you are going on a camping trip you utter an instinctive protest as your packer cinches up the 'sawbuck' packsaddle and loads his animal.

2. *slang.* **a.** Ten dollars; a ten-dollar note. Also *double sawbuck* (*a*) s.v. DOUBLE *a.* A. 6.

In allusion to the x-shaped (Roman x = 10) ends of the sawyer's buck: cf. also BUCK *sb.*[8] dollar.

1850, etc. [see *double sawbuck* (*a*) s.v. DOUBLE *a.* A. 6]. **1852** *Oregon Statesman* 13 Nov. 1/1 Dod rabbit it, there goes another 'saw-buck', on the plag'uey jack. **1870** J. H. B. NOWLAND *Early Reminisc. Indianapolis* 315 In former years he was ever ready to..risk what he called a 'sawbuck' (a ten dollar note), on his success. **1933** [see BITE *sb.* 1 i]. **1973** J. WAMBAUGH *Blue Knight* ii. 41, I gave him a ten, which was just like folding up a sawbuck and sticking it in his arm. He'd be in the same shape twelve hours from now.

b. A ten-year prison sentence. Also *double sawbuck* (*b*) s.v. DOUBLE *a.* A. 6.

1925 *Flynn's* 25 Mar. 511/1 *Sawbuck*,..a ten-year sentence. **1929** *Sat. Even. Post* 13 Apr. 50/4 A prisoner with ten years brings in a saw-buck. **1938** D. CASTLE *Do Your Own Time* iii. 28 'I'm doing two saw-bucks.' 'Oh, yeah? Whatever that is.' 'Two ten spots. Twenty years.' **1945**, **1950** [see *double sawbuck* (*b*) s.v. DOUBLE *a.* A. 6].

‖**Sawbwa** ('sɔːbwə). Also **Chobwa, Tsaubwa,** etc. [Burmese.] The hereditary ruler of a Shan state in Eastern Burma.

1800 M. SYMES *Acct. Embassy to Kingdom of Ava* xvi. 375 We were told that there were fifty-six Chobwas dependent on the Birman state; if it be true, their territories must be very inconsiderable. **1829** J. CRAWFURD *Jrnl. Embassy to Court of Ava* xv. 395 The only class of public officers which can be called hereditary under the Burmese Government, are the Thaubwas, or Saubwas, the tributary princes of the subjugated countries. **1858** H. YULE *Narr. Mission sent to Court of Ava* xiii. 303 The Tsaubwas..retain all the forms and appurtenances of royalty. **1875** H. A. BROWNE *Jrnl.* 18 Jan. in *Reminisc. Court of Mandalay* (1907) 67 Kut-Loon.. is in the jurisdiction of the Maing-maw Tsawbwa, or Chinese Shan chieftain. **1911** *Encycl. Brit.* XXIII. 802/1 Politically, where not under the direct control of Chinese magistrates, the tribes are organized under their own chiefs, who are recognized by the Chinese government and endowed with official rank and title. In Burmese such native chiefs are termed *Sawbwa*. **1929** F. T. JESSE *Lacquer Lady* III. 276 The Shan Sawbwas were in open revolt. **1962** *Listener* 25 Oct. 646/2 Some of the Shans, led by some of the Sawbwas, agitated for separation from Burma. **1973** *Dict. World Hist.* 1378/2 The Shans have retained their racial identity and a high degree of separatism, with numbers of small states each until recently having its own ruling chief. The chiefs were known as Sawbwas, Myosas, or Ngwegunhmus, according to rank.

sawce, sawcer, etc.: see SAUCE, SAUCER *sb.*, etc.

sawd(e, variant forms of SOLD *Obs.*

sawdan, sawdant, var. ff. SOLDAN, sultan.

†**'sawdee.** *Obs.* [a. OF. *soudée* (corresp. to Pr. *soudada, soldada*, med.L. *solidāta*), f. *souder*: see SOLD *v.*] Soldier's pay.

c **1500** *Melusine* 148 'By my feyth', said Uryan, 'we are not come hither for to take sawdees ne for no syluer.'

sawden, var. form of SOLDAN *Obs.*, sultan.

sawder ('sɔːdə(r)), *sb. colloq.* [App. a use of *sawder* SOLDER *sb.*] In full *soft sawder*: flattery, blarney.

1836 HALIBURTON *Clockm.* Ser. I. x. 78 If she goes to act ugly, I'll give her a dose of 'soft sawder'. **1846** SHAFTESB. in *Life* xiv. (1887) 342 Soft sawder to the mill-owners (unless it is skilfully applied) is a damper to the men. **1854** E. FITZGERALD *Lett.* (1889) I. 232 He..by dint of good dinners and soft sawder finally draws the country gentry to him. **1854** D. G. ROSSETTI *Let.* 11 May (1965) I. 193 MacCrac.. offers £50 for the water-colour, with all manner of soap and sawder into the bargain. **1880** 'C. E. CRADDOCK' in *Atlantic Monthly* Jan. 103/2 That ain't the right sort o' sawder fur a candidate. **1886** 'SARAH TYTLER' *Buried Diamonds* v, Till he had done listening to the 'soft sawder' of Crabtree the banker's..wife.

sawder ('sɔːdə(r)), *v. colloq.* [f. SAWDER *sb.*] *trans.* To flatter, to 'butter'. Also *absol.* and as *soft-sawder v.*

1834 LOVER *Leg. & Stories of Irel.* Ser. II. 297 His vagabone mother sawdhered him up afther a manner. **1843** HALIBURTON *Attaché* ii. 46, I don't like to be left alone with a gall, it's plaguy apt to set me a soft sawderin' and a courtin'. **1853** HICKIE tr. *Aristoph.* (1887) I. 26 As often as any one soft-sawdered you. **1863** R. F. BURTON *Wand. W. Africa* II. 287 Now 'ryling up' the agent, then sawdering him down. **1883** *Manch. Exam.* 26 Nov. 5 When the Irish electors were to be soft-sawdered.

Hence **'sawderer,** in quot. *soft-sawderer*.

1851 *Blackw. Mag.* Dec. 714 The highest law officer of the State..condescending to enact the part of a 'soft-sawderer'.

sawder, -dre, obs. forms of SOLDER.

sawdour, -oyer, obs. forms of SOLDIER.

sawdust ('sɔːdʌst), *sb.* [f. SAW *sb.*[1] + DUST *sb.*]

1. a. Wood in the state of small particles, detached from a tree, plank, etc. in the process of sawing.

1530 PALSGR. 265/1 Sawedust, *sievre dais.* **1563** *Respublica* I. iv. 344 What is your brain-pan stufte with-all? wull or sawduste? **1573** TUSSER *Husb.* (1878) 42 Saue sawe dust, and brick dust, and ashes so fine, for alley to walke in, with neighbour of thine. *a* **1680** BUTLER *Elephant in Moon* (long verse) 218 Make Chips of Elms produce the largest Trees, Or sowing Saw-dust furnish Nurseries. **1712** J. JAMES tr. *Le Blond's Gardening* 175 Ants..are driven away by strewing very fine Saw-dust. **1854** RONALDS & RICHARDSON *Chem. Technol.* (ed. 2) I. 60 Winkler enclosed his specimens in crucibles surrounded with saw-dust. **1884** MRS. C. PRAED *Zero* xi, My doll is stuffed with sawdust.

b. *transf.* and *fig.* (Sometimes with reference to the use of sawdust for stuffing dolls or puppets.)

a **1873** MRS. SPOFFORD in *Casq. Literature* IV. 9/2 The deviled turkey sizzled..away to saw-dust. **1890** L. C. D'OYLE *Notches* 16 I'll knock the saw-dust out of any two men in this hole of a place. **1908** *Nation* 12 Sept. 833/2 The other characters are all sawdust and wires.

2. In wider sense: Dust of any material produced in the process of sawing. *rare.*

1672 WISEMAN *Wounds* II. 138 That done we cleansed the wound from the Saw-dust. **1835-6** P. BARLOW in *Encycl. Metrop.* (1845) VIII. 650/1 [Ivory] rubbed over with a little of its own sawdust.

3. a. *attrib.* and *Comb.*, as *sawdust-pad*; *sawdust-like* adj.; **sawdust game** *U.S. slang*, a type of confidence trick; **sawdust-powder**, a substitute for gunpowder, prepared by treating sawdust with acids.

1872 G. P. BURNHAM *Mem. U.S. Secret Service* 404 A new device for skilful robbery of the uninitiated has been introduced..known as the '*Sawdust' or 'Circular' Game. **1939** *Times Lit. Suppl.* 9 Sept. 530/2 We hear all about..the 'sawdust game', (selling bad notes). **1899** RODWAY *Guiana Wilds* 145 The *sawdust-like cassava bread. **1879** *St. George's Hosp. Rep.* IX. 308 Great comfort was derived from the use of the *sawdust-pads. **1883** F. A. ABEL in *Encycl. Brit.* XI. 278/2 Preparations allied to gun-cotton, in the production of which wood fibre is used as the starting-point, are manufactured..under the name of Schultze's powder, *sawdust powder, and patent gunpowder.

b. With reference to the use of sawdust for strewing the floor of a place of public entertainment (as a circus, etc.) or (*U.S.*) the arena used by a travelling evangelist.

1864 P. PATERSON *Glimpses of Real Life* xii. 120 As good as the general run of sawdust plays. **1883** *Century Mag.* XXV. 746/1, I was not flattered at being taken for a sawdust artist. **1883** Sawdust ring [see RING *sb.*[1] 13 a]. **1902** R. W. CHAMBERS *Maids of Paradise* xvii. 296 Once only they [the circus procession] circled the saw-dust ring. **1913** *Collier's* 26 July 7/3 And down the aisle, 'hitting the sawdust trail', they come in ones and twos and dozens, until 476 have stood before that multitude to shake the evangelist's hand and signify their intention of starting another life. **1915** T. S. ELIOT in *Catholic Anthol.* 2 One-night cheap hotels And sawdust restaurants with oyster-shells. **1946** S. H. HOLBROOK *Lost Men of Amer. Hist.* 312 Many of these suddenly patriotic pleaders..like repentant sinners at a revival, hurried down the sawdust path. **1964** A. WYKES *Gambling* vii. 170 The terms 'carpet joint' and 'sawdust joint' meant broadly the degree of luxury or squalor to be expected in American gambling saloons. **1977** *Time* 11 July 41/2 Sawdust Evangelist Rex Humbard, likes to exhort: 'You'd better straighten out and fly right with God.' **1978** M. PUZO *Fools Die* xiv. 152, I spent the day going through all the casinos in town on the Strip and the sawdust joints in the center of town.

Hence **'sawdusty** *a.*, abounding in, savouring of, or resembling sawdust; of the nature of sawdust.

1861 DICKENS *Gt. Expect.* iv, I remember Mr. Hubble as a tough high-shouldered stooping old man, of a sawdusty fragrance. **1863** —— *Uncomm. Trav.* xxi, A bagatelle-board shadily visible in a sawdusty parlour. **1880** *Confess. Frivolous Girl* 172 In his society I sometimes felt that life was stupid, but never that it was hollow and sawdusty. **1893** J. T. HOSKINS *Mr. P.'s Diary* 356 Dry, tasteless, sawdusty white bread. **1896** MRS. CAFFYN *Quaker Grandmother* 55, I never liked dressing dolls, it brought one into too close contact with their sawdusty insides.

sawdust ('sɔːdʌst), *v.* [f. SAWDUST *sb.*] *trans.* To cover, sprinkle, or strew with sawdust. Hence **'sawdusted** *ppl. a.*, **'sawdusting** *vbl. sb.*

1844 ALB. SMITH *Adv. Mr. Ledbury* xiii, A..sawdusted tavern. **1855** DICKENS *Dorrit* I. ix, The sweeping and saw-dusting of the common room. **1882** P. FITZGERALD *Recreat. Lit. Man* I. 249 All is duly sawdusted. **1895** J. DAVIDSON *Earl Lavender* 177 In the midst of the sawdusted floor.

sawdyer, sawdyn: see SOLDIER, SOLDAN.

sawdyo(u)r, sawecere: see SOLDIER, SAUCER *sb.*

sawed (sɔːd), *ppl. a.* [f. SAW *v.*[1] and *sb.*[1] + -ED.]

1. a. That has undergone the operation of sawing; = SAWN *ppl. a.* Also in comb. *sawed-off* (see also senses 1 b, c).

1553 EDEN *Treat. Newe Ind.* (Arb.) 15 Certayne sawed bordes of the thickenes of halfe a hande breath. **1597** A. M. tr. *Guillemeau's Fr. Chirurg.* 38/1 The skinn and muscles sinck agayne downwardes, and cover the sawed bone. **1677** YARRANTON *Eng. Improv.* 114 The Great Duke of Saxony hath three great Manufactures; one of Iron,..another of Linnen,..the third of Sawed Timbers of all sorts. **1796** C. MARSHALL *Garden.* iii. (1813) 37 Espalier trees should rather be trained to sawed materials properly framed together. **1841** ORDERSON *Creoleana* iii. 30 Cedar posts, sawed stones. **1895** KIPLING *2nd Jungle Bk.* 149 A couple of sawed-off antlers. **1899** *Daily News* 13 June 4/4 In 1894 Congress passed an Act taking the duty off sawed boards, shingles [etc.].

b. *sawed-off fig.*, short, undersized. Freq. of persons, etc.: below average height. Also *ellipt.* Cf. SAWN *ppl. a.* 2 b. *U.S. colloq.*

1887 C. B. GEORGE *40 Yrs. on Rail* 22, I remember..the little sawed-off cars jolting along the uneven track. **1901** S. E. WHITE *Westerners* 220 Most marvellous was a clean-limbed, deep-chested, slender running horse, accompanied by a sawed-off English groom. **1902** G. H. LORIMER *Lett. from Self-Made Merchant* 160, I didn't understand football, but understood that little sawed-off. **1919** *Dialect Notes* V. 65 A tall girl never looks well dancing with a sawed-off. **1930** J. DOS PASSOS *42nd Parallel* 100 Two soldiers on guard, toughlooking sawedoff men. **1947** *Richmond* (Va.) *Times-Dispatch* 9 Nov. B7/7 Grover Jones, the sawed-off fullback who played one war year for Penn. **1973** *Black World* Jan. 63/1, I..heard her say to that little sawed-off runt she calls a man.., 'I think she tried to communicate with me.'

c. *sawed-off*: *spec.* (*U.S.*) used to designate a (shot)gun of which the barrel has been specially shortened to make it easier to handle and give a wider field of fire. Also *ellipt.* Cf. SAWN *ppl. a.* 2 a.

1898 *Scribner's Mag.* Jan. 86/2 There was another roar from the messenger's sawed-off shotgun. **1912** W. M. RAINE *Brand Blotters* 80 The 'shotgun messenger' was indolently rolling a cigarette, his sawed-off gun between his knees. **1930** *Sat. Even. Post* 26 July 145/1 The other laughed harshly. 'Did they knock him off?' he grunted. 'Nothin' but a sawed-off full in the chest an' half a dozen shots from an automatic as a chaser!' **1935** 'L. FORD' *Burn Forever* 255 He'd have used a revolver, a sawed-off shotgun or a sub-machine gun. **1962** A. LURIE *Love & Friendship* xiv. 280, I suppose a sawed-off shot-gun would be more his speed. **1977** *Time* 16 May 18/1 He pulled out a sawed-off sub-machine gun.

2. Serrated.

1607 TOPSELL *Four-f. Beasts* 506 Vulgar Mice..drinke by licking or lapping, although their teeth be not sawed. **1757** A. COOPER *Distiller* III. lii. (1760) 236 This tree hath sawed Leaves, and large open Flowers. **1839** LINDLEY *Introd. Bot.* III. (ed. 3) 461 Sawed (*serratus*), having sharp straight-edged teeth pointing to the apex. **1900** B. D. JACKSON *Gloss. Bot. Terms*, *Saw-toothed* or *Sawed*, serrate.

Comb. **1786** ABERCROMBIE *Gard. Assist.* 127 Cutting them with a long, narrow, sawed-edged knife.

sawen, obs. pa. pple. of SOW *v.*

sawen(t, obs. forms of SEVEN.

saweoure, obs. form of SAVIOUR, SAVOUR.

sawer ('sɔːə(r)). Also 6 **saer, sawar.** [f. SAW *v.*[1] + -ER[1].] One who saws. Now *rare*; as a designation of employment superseded by SAWYER.

1379 *Poll-tax West Riding* in *Yorks. Archæol. Jrnl.* VI. 324 Willelmus Sagher, Sagher vjd. **1457** *Nottingham Rec.* II. 365 Rodger Saxton, sawer. **1536** *MS. Acc. St. John's Hosp., Canterb.*, Payd to the saers vij s. vij d. **1589** [? LYLY] *Pappe w. Hatchet* C b, Martin & his mainteiner are both sawers of timber. **1664** in Holmes *Pontefract Bk. Entries* (1882) 372

Ordinances made for the good governance..of the.. cowpers, patenners, turners, sawers. **1865** Mrs. Carlyle *Lett.* (1883) III. 271, I send you a..letter of Madame Venturi's, with vignette of Venturi sawing... I advise you to read it [another letter] now, with a key: 'The Gorilla' means George Cooke,..the sawer Venturi.

sawer(e, obs. forms of savour, sewer.

sawerkraut, obs. form of sauerkraut.

sawete, sawf, obs. forms of safety, salve.

sawfish ('sɔːfɪʃ). [saw *sb.*[1] Cf. L. *serra* sawfish (*lit.* 'saw').] A fish of the genus *Pristis*, the snout of which ends in a long flat projection with teeth on each edge; a saw-shark of the family Pristiophoridæ (cf. *saw-shark* s.v. saw *sb.*[1] 5 d). Also applied to fishes of certain allied genera.

1664 Hubert *Catal. Rarities* (1665) 17 A Saw-fish, vulgarly called the Sword-fish. **1668** Charleton *Onomast.* 123 *Monoceros Clusii*, the little Vnicorn, or Saw-fish. **1681** Grew *Musæum* 1. §v. i. 84 The Saw-Fish. *Pristis.* **1796** Stedman *Surinam* I. i. *11 Another animal, which is called the saw-fish, carries also an offensive weapon. **1860** G. Bennett *Gatherings Naturalist Austral.* 35 There is a species of Saw-fish peculiar to the Australian seas. **1863** Wood *Illustr. Nat. Hist.* III. 216 The Tentaculated Saw-fish (*Pristiophorus cirratus*). **1880** A. C. L. G. Gunther *Introd. Study of Fishes* 335 These Sharks [*sc.* Pristiophoridæ] resemble so much the common Saw-fishes as to be easily confounded with them. **1934** *Sun* (Baltimore) 6 July 1/7 A saw fish measuring ten feet nine inches..was landed. **1978** O. White *Silent Reach* xii. 124 Sometimes you catch sawfish and barramundi there.

sawflom, sawfte: see saucefleme, safety.

'saw-fly. [saw *sb.*[1]] An insect of the family *Tenthredinidæ*, distinguished by the saw-like construction of the ovipositor.

The saw-flies are very destructive to vegetation, and several species are designated from the plants attacked by them, as ***pine saw-fly, rose saw-fly, turnip saw-fly***.

1773 T. P. Yeats *Inst. Entom.* 177 The Tenthredo is called, by some English Authors, the Saw-fly, from the formation of its sting, which differs from that of all other insects..in being dentated..like the instrument from which its name is taken. **1802** Bingley *Anim. Biog.* (1813) III. 249 The saw-fly of the gooseberry-tree. **1840** [see rose *sb.* 23 c]. **1851** H. Stephens *Bk. Farm* (1855) II. 74 The turnip saw-fly, *Athalia spinarum.* **1886** *Encycl. Brit.* XXI. 343/1 The Pine Saw-Fly (*Lophyrus pini*) causes great damage to plantations of young Scotch firs.

attrib. **1816** Kirby & Sp. *Entomol.* xxiii. (1818) II. 331 The saw-fly tribes (*Tenthredinidæ*).

'saw-gate[1]. [f. saw *sb.*[1] + gate *sb.*[2]]

† **1. a.** ? The passage of a saw through the wood that is being sawn. **b.** The channel made by a saw; a saw-kerf. *Obs.*

1601 Holland *Pliny* I. 493 You must except the Oke and the Box wood, which although they be greene, do stiffely withstand the saw-gate. **1793** Smeaton *Edystone L.* §74 By supporting the Saw-gate with wedges, the whole of the superstructure..might have been expeditiously severed from the solid.

2. In fret-sawing, a hole bored to make way for the entrance of the saw.

1873 *Routledge's Ev. Boy's Ann.* 535 Study your [fret-work] pattern and see where to bore the holes, or saw-gates, as they are called. **1875** Seaton *Fret Cutting* 15 Now put the ..saw-gate over the V, with the bow of the saw frame turned to the right.

'saw-gate[2]. [gate *sb.*[1]] = gate *sb.*[1] 8 b.

1857 *Proc. Inst. Civ. Engin.* XVII. 25 The saw-gate of this machine [for sawing ship-timber] is formed of hollow wrought-iron bars. **1875** Knight *Dict. Mech.*, *Saw-gate*, the rectangular frame in which a mill-saw or gang of mill-saws is stretched.

†**'sawgeat.** *Obs.* [a. AF. **saugeat*, f. *sauge* sage *sb.*[1]] (See quot.)

c **1390** *Forme of Cury* (1780) 72 Sawgeat. Take Pork..&.. take and close litull Balles in foiles of sawge.

†**sawger.** *Obs. rare*—[0]. [a. OF. *sauger, -ier,* f. *sauge* sage *sb.*[1]] A bed or garden of sage.

c **1440** *Promp. Parv.* 441/2 Sawger, *salgetum.* **14..** *Voc.* in Wr.-Wülcker 609/1 *Salgearium*, a sawger.

sawier, sawin, obs. ff. sawyer, seven.

sawin, obs. pa. pple. of sow *v.*

sawing ('sɔːɪŋ), *vbl. sb.* [f. saw *v.*[1] + -ing[1].]

1. The action of the verb saw; an instance of this.

c **1440** *Jacob's Well* xxxvi. 233 Þat ȝe be sauyd fro sawyng & brennyng of feendys to ioye & blysse euere-lastynge! **1477–9** *Rec. St. Mary at Hill* 82 Paid to Stere for sawyng of iij kervis of the same, iij d. **1515** *Ld. Treas. Acc. Scotl.* V. 11 Item for the sawing of theme ij s. vj d. **1678** Moxon *Mech. Exerc.* v. 95 The Excellency of Sawing is, to keep the kerf exactly in the line marked out to be Sawn. **1839** Ure *Dict. Arts* 160 (*Bookbinding*) We thus see that Mr. Hancock dispenses entirely with the operations of stitching, sewing, sawing-in. **1873** J. Richards *Operator's Handbk.* 130 After sawing comes planing.

2. *pl.* Sawdust. Now only *Sc.*

1512–13 in Willis & Clark *Cambridge* (1886) I. 611 Certeyn refuse ston and sawyngs of both Weldon..and Clypsham and molded stones. **1598** Florio, *Segatura*,.. sawings, saw-dust. **1857** Livingstone *Trav.* xix. 367 It closely resembles wood sawings and on that account is named 'wood-meal'.

3. *attrib.* and *Comb.*, as ***sawing action, -machine, stage, table, -windmill***; **sawing-bench** = *saw-bench* (see saw *sb.*[1] 4 d); **sawing-block** (see quot.); **sawing horse, stool, trestle** = *saw-horse* (see saw *sb.*[1] 4 d); **sawing-mill, pit** = sawmill, saw-pit; **sawing-stop,** a contrivance to assist in holding wood on the bench while being sawn.

1898 *Cycling* 64 It has the further advantage of eliminating the friction and '*sawing' action that takes place between the threads of ordinary canvas. **1845** *Encycl. Metrop.* VIII. 386/1 Circular *sawing benches. **1846** Holtzapffel *Turning*, etc. II. 714 The back-saws..are often assisted or guided by *sawing-blocks, in which one or more saw-kerfs..serve to guide the blades. *Ibid.* 711 The log is..laid on the common X-form *sawing-horse. **1841** *Penny Cycl.* XX. 479/1 Attempts have been made to introduce *sawing-machines with two sets of saws. **1722** *Lond. Gaz.* No. 6070/7 The Stone-Yard and *Sawing-Mill. **1905** A. R. Wallace *My Life* I. 79 Large builders and contractors, who had planing and sawing-mills of their own. **1560** *Acc. Fratern. Holy Ghost, Basingstoke* (1882) 12 For a pece of tymber lyenge at yᵉ *Sawinge pitt. **1612** *MS. Acc. St. John's Hosp., Canterb.*, For making of a *saing stagge [= *saw-stage*] viij d. **1846** Holtzapffel *Turning*, etc. II. 709 The board..is rested upon a *sawing stool or trestle. **1875** *Carpentry & Join.* 37 The *sawing stop..will be found a very convenient adjunct to the fittings of the work bench. **1873** *Routledge's Ev. Boy's Ann.* 534, I am supposing you to be using a *sawing table (fret-cutting machine), such as I have described. **1611** Cotgr., *Chevalet*,..a Nagge, or little horse..also, a *sawing Tressle. **1679** Locke in P. King *Life* (1830) I. 248 See..the *sawing-windmill.

sawing ('sɔːɪŋ), *ppl. a.* [f. saw *v.*[1] + -ing[2].]

† **1.** Of teeth: Like the teeth of a saw; serrate.

1398 Trevisa *Barth. De P.R.* xvii. xxviii. (1495) 788 Houndes whelpes ben whelpyd wyth sawyng teeth.

2. Of sounds: Rasping, harsh.

1851 D. Jerrold *St. Giles* v. 41 This reproof and interrogation were put in a hoarse, sawing voice by a man. **1879** *St. George's Hosp. Rep.* IX. 85 A sawing diastolic (subsequently double) murmur was heard along the sternum.

sawkeye, sawl: see sockeye, soul.

sawld, obs. Sc. pa. t. of sell *v.*

sawlter, obs. form of psalter.

sawmfaill: see sans fail.

sawmill ('sɔːˌmɪl). [f. saw *sb.*[1] + mill *sb.* Cf. Du. *zaagmolen*, G. *sägemühle*.] A factory in which wood is sawn into planks or boards by machinery (formerly propelled by water, wind, or animal power, or steam; now usually by electricity).

1553 Eden *Treat. Newe Ind.* (Arb.) 40 Goodly ryuers vpon the which are bylded manye sawe mylles. **1677** Yarranton *Eng. Improv.* 114 At the descent of the Hills, are infinite of Saw-Mills that go by Water. **1786** Jefferson *Writ.* (1859) II. 12 There are abundance of saw-mills in all the States. **1825** J. Nicholson *Operat. Mechanic* 441 Saw-mills, constructed for the purpose of sawing either timber or stone, are moved by animals, by water, by wind, or by steam. **1886** *Encycl. Brit.* XXI. 345/1 The modern saw-mill stands upon the banks of a river or pond.

attrib. **1654** *Suffolk County* (Mass.) *Deeds* (1883) II. 26, I Edward Colcott..doe hereby giue..vnto Thomas Rucke.. one third pte of a saw mill worke. **1716** *Duxbury* (Mass.) *Rec.* (1893) 113 We began at the waste gate belonging to the saw mill..and run from said gate Easterly as the old saw mill dam stood. **1818** T. G. Fessenden *Ladies' Monitor* 35 His elbows, hoofs and paws That rip and rend and rive like saw mill-saws. **1875** Knight *Dict. Mech.*, *Sawmill dog, Sawmill gate.* **1888** Barrie *When a Man's Single* ii, The men and women in the saw-mill kitchen. **1897** Mary Kingsley *W. Africa* 197 He was up in the sawmill shed.

Hence **'sawmiller** [cf. Du. *zaagmolenaar*, G. *sägemüller*], the proprietor or manager of a sawmill; **'sawmilling,** the business of sawing wood in a sawmill.

1845 Thoreau *Jrnl.* 5 July (1949) I. 361, I lodged at the house of a saw-miller last summer. **1878** *N. Amer. Rev.* CXXVI. 501 All..printers, gunsmiths, sawmillers,..shall pay twenty-five cents on every hundred dollar's worth of gross receipts. **1881** *Times* 1 July 4/1 The respondent..is a farmer and saw-miller. **1901** *J. Black's Carp. & Build., Scaffolding* 73 The man who is interested in sawmilling.

sawmont, obs. Sc. form of salmon.

sawmplar, sawmplere, obs. ff. sampler *sb.*[1]

sawn (sɔːn), *ppl. a.* Also 6–8 **sawen,** 7 **sawne.** [pa. pple. of saw *v.*[1]] **1.** That has undergone the operation of sawing; = sawed *ppl. a.*

1536 *Fabric Rolls York Minster* (Surtees) 108 Pro j.c. sawen burdes. **1634** W. Wood *New Eng. Prosp.* i. v. 16 One kind [of trees] being more fit for clappboard, others for sawne board. **1678** Moxon *Mech. Exerc.* vi. 110 The Sawn-away slit between two pieces of stuff is called a kerf. **1679** *Ibid.* ix. 171 Single Quarters are Sawen stuff. **1707** Mortimer *Husb.* (1721) II. 202 As for sawn Pales they are as dear, considering their lasting, as Brick or Stone. **1870** J. Power *Handy-bk.* 41, 1751. About this date bookbinders began to use sawn-backs, whereby the bands on which the book is sewn were let into the backs of the sheets. **1891** *Daily News* 5 Feb. 5/4 Sawn timber in brief is rapidly gaining the ascendency.

2. ***sawn-off*** (now more usu. than *sawed-off* exc. in *N.Amer.*). **a.** Of a (shot)gun: = sawed *ppl. a.* 1 c.

1915 A. Conan Doyle *Valley of Fear* vi. 113 In the latter was a sawn-off shot-gun, so he came with the deliberate purpose of crime. **1937** N. Marsh *Vintage Murder* ii. 14 A salute of two sawn-off shotguns. **1959** *Encounter* July 59/1 A fifteen-year-old highschool boy who had taken a sawn-off shotgun into the classroom and blown off the head of a classmate. **1978** R. Westall *Devil on Road* xx. 186 A sawn-off shotgun..sprays lead like a hose.

b. = sawed *ppl. a.* 1 b. *colloq.*

1936 R. Campbell *Mithraic Emblems* 162 Yet could I trudge in sawn-off trousers, And redden up like logs at Yule. **1944** *Coast to Coast 1943* 56 He was a sawn-off little bloke, and they reckoned there couldn't have been much grass about when he was born. **1954** 'J. Christopher' *22nd Cent.* 104 It's a little sawn-off town up in Scotland. **1960** J. Mortimer *Call me Liar* 431 Found him, have you?.. That sawn-off, bald, damp-eyed old hundred per cent British duodenal with..no convictions known.

sawn (sɔːn), *sb.* Austral. slang abbrev. of sawney *sb.* 2.

1953 K. Tennant *Joyful Condemned* xvii. 145 I'm always getting into trouble through sawns. **1961** Partridge *Dict. Slang* Suppl. 1259/2 *Sawn*, a softy, a 'dope': low Australian.

sawn, obs. pa. pple of sow *v.*

sawnap(e, variant forms of sanap *Obs.*

sawnce bell: see sanctus bell.

sawndelynge, obs. form of sandling[1].

sawndres, -dyrs, obs. forms of sanders[1].

sawney ('sɔːnɪ), *sb.* [In sense 1, repr. a Sc. local variant of Sandy, short for Alexander; the connexion of the other senses is doubtful.]

1. *colloq.* A derisive nickname for a Scotchman.

a **1704** T. Brown *Highlander* Wks. 1730 I. 117 And learn from him against a time of need To husband wealth, as *sawny* does his weed. **1710** Addison *Whig Exam.* No. 4 ⁋12 Sawney [i.e. a Scotchman just mentioned] turned about in a great passion. **1764** Wilkes *Corr.* (1805) III. 125 The list of the company (of the *Macs* and *Sawneys* not in the French service) would divert you. **1785** [see Sandy *sb.*]. **1883** R. Cleland *Inchbracken* viii. 55 To..amuse his superior mind with Sawney at his devotions.

2. *colloq.* A simpleton, fool. [? Cf. zany.]

a **1700** B. E. *Dict. Cant. Crew*, *Sawny*, a Fool. *He's a meer Sawney*, he is very soft. **1807** [Ireland] *Mod. Ship of Fools* 226 Quite a sawney. **1882** 'Edna Lyall' *Donovan* xxiv, A regular sawney—..weak as water.

3. *slang.* Bacon.

1812 J. H. Vaux *Flash Dict.*, *Sawney*, bacon. **1856** Mayhew *Gt. World Lond.* 46 'Sawney-hunters', who purloin cheese or bacon from cheesemongers' doors.

4. *techn.* (See quots.)

1892 *Labour Commission Gloss.*, *Sawney*, term used to denote the accident when all the threads in a mule are broken at the same time by some faulty action of the mule. **1901** *N. & Q.* Ser. ix. VIII. 170/1 If a minder in a cotton mill have four or five hundred 'ends' or threads broken through the chance intervention of an obstacle when the carriage is on the outward run, or through the sudden breaking of a band, he is said to 'have a sawney'.

sawney ('sɔːnɪ), *a.* [app. f. sawney *sb.*]

1. Foolish; foolishly sentimental; ? canting, wheedling.

1805 Foster *Ess.* ii. vi. 201 A sawney clown on the road. **1843** J. Abbott *Journ. Heraut to Khiva* I. 21 A tall, sawney, miserly looking fellow. **1847** Disraeli *Tancred* i. v, She spoke in her sawney voice of factitious enthusiasm. **1873** Miss Broughton *Nancy* vii, The bronze of his face is a little paled by emotion, but there is no sawny sentiment in his tone, none of the lover's whine. **1900** H. Lawson *Over Sliprails* 163 A good-hearted, sawny kind of chap.

2. ? *transf.*

1847 Disraeli *Tancred* i. i, Curzon Street, after a long straggling sawney course, ceasing to be a thoroughfare.

sawney ('sɔːnɪ), *v.* [f. sawney *sb.* (in sense 2).] *intr.* **a.** To wheedle, cant. **b.** To act the sawney, to fool. Hence **'sawneying** *ppl. a.*

1808 Southey *Lett.* (1856) II. 63 It looks like a sneaking sawneying Methodist parson. **1871** Besant & Rice *Ready-money Mort.* viii, What's he coming sawneying over here about, I wonder?

sawnse bell: see sanctus bell.

sawoor, var. sawah.

sawor, -our(e, obs. form of savour.

'saw-pit. [f. saw *sb.*[1] + pit *sb.*]

a. An excavation in the ground, over the mouth of which a framework is erected on which timber is placed to be sawn with a long two-handled saw by two men, the one standing in the pit and the other on a raised platform.

1408 *Nottingham Rec.* II. 62 Rogerus Parker fecit unum sawpytt in alta via. **1486** *Ibid.* III. 256 For drawyng of þe seid tymber fro þe wrightes to þe sawe pitt. **1598** Shaks. *Merry W.* iv. iv. 53 Let them from forth a saw-pit rush at once. **1627** Capt. Smith *Seaman's Gram.* i. 1 To those Docks..belongs their wood-yards, with Saw-pits. **1719** De Foe *Crusoe* i. (Globe) 116 Two Sawyers, with their Tools, and a Saw-Pit would have cut six of them..in half a Day. **1811** Moore *Mr. Orator Puff* iii, He tripped near a sawpit, and tumbled right in. **1876** *Encycl. Brit.* IV. 476/1 The facility with which sawing whole timber is now done by the aid of the upright saw-frame [etc.], has in large factories and workshops caused the saw-pits to be out of date.

transf. and *fig.* **1648** JENKYN *Blind Guide* i. 5 In Satans saw-pit school'd he was. **1865** DICKENS *Mut. Fr.* I. xii, Every street was a sawpit.

b. *N.Amer.* A wooden framework serving the function of a saw-pit.

1876 H. W. RAVENELL in *Yale Rev.* (1936) XXV. 763 The saw-pit was a rude structure about seven feet high, made of strong posts set in the ground wide enough apart to hold one or two pieces of heavy pine timber, and the sawyers, one above and one beneath, sawed out one hundred feet per day. **1961** J. W. ANDERSON *Fur Trader's Story* x. 87 Next they would erect, from smaller trees in the vicinity, what we used to call a saw-pit, which was not really a pit at all but a frame set entirely above the ground.

sawqui: see SOCKEYE.

sawr-: see SAVOUR.

†**sawsykylle.** [a. AF. *solsecle*, ad. L. *solsequium*.] The heliotrope.

c **1425** *Voc.* in Wr.-Wülcker 644/18 *Hoc solsequium*, sawsykylle.

sawsyrlyng, variant of SAUSERLING *Obs.*

sawt(e: see SALT, SAULT, SAUT.

sawter(e, -tery: see PSALTER, PSALTERY.

sawterell, sawtire: see SAUTERELL, SALTIRE.

saw tooth. [SAW *sb.*[1]]

1. a. A tooth of a saw. **b.** A tooth (of an animal, also, of a machine) shaped like a saw, or forming one of a serrated series.

1601 HOLLAND *Pliny* I. 337 The saw teeth run one betweene another,.. as we see in serpents, fishes, and dogs. **1835** URE *Philos. Manuf.* 113 The saw-teeth of the gin, in tearing the fibres from the seeds, broke several of them. **1880** BALE *Woodworking Machinery* 332 A circular holder.. fitted to a circular notch at the root of the saw tooth. **1886** *Encycl. Brit.* XXI. 344/1 Inserted teeth [in circular saws] are of various forms and shapes, from that of the ordinary saw tooth.. to a 'chisel point'.

c. *Electronics.* A wave-form showing a slow linear rise and rapid linear fall, or the reverse; a voltage or current varying in this way. Usu. *attrib.*, as ***saw-tooth generator, wave-form.***

1933 *Proc. IRE* XXI. 1666 The variation of intensity of both horizontal and vertical deflecting fields plotted against time is of a 'saw-tooth' shape. **1935** M. G. SCROGGIE *Television* iv. 37 The sudden charge of the condenser, followed by a slower discharge, yields a saw-tooth wave-form. **1940** [see KEYSTONE *v.*]. **1942** *Electronic Engin.* XIV. 666/2 The time-base circuit is.. adapted for single sweep operation and the saw-tooth generated can be expanded symmetrically with respect to the centre of the tube. **1947** R. LEE *Electronic Transformers & Circuits* ix. 251 Probably the most common application of sawtooth amplifier transformers is to provide a linear sweep to horizontal plates of a cathode ray oscilloscope. **1969** J. J. SPARKES *Transistor Switching* iii. 63 All sawtooth-wave generators integrate a constant voltage or current with respect to time.

2. *attrib.* = saw-toothed. **saw-tooth roof**, a roof with a serrated profile incorporating windows in the steeper sides, which face in the direction of the equator; **saw-tooth sterrinck**, the Crab-eating Seal, *Lobodon carcinophaga*.

187. *Cassell's Nat. Hist.* II. 243 The Crab-eating Seal or Saw-tooth Sterrinck of Owen [cf. *saw-toothed* 1866 in SAW *sb.*[1] 5]. **1884** W. S. B. MCLAREN *Spinning* (ed. 2) 228 All of which are covered with garnet saw-tooth licker-in wire. **1900** *Engineering* 9 Feb. 173/2 The factory consists of four bays, each covered with a saw-tooth roof running east and west, and glazed on the north side only. **1942** ASHER & HEAL *Send no Money* 58 It had plenty of windows, a sawtooth roof to provide light, and it was airy and spacious. **1966** L. COHEN *Beautiful Losers* I. 10 The sun was just coming up over the sawtooth roof of the factory next door.

sawtre(e, -trie, -try, obs. forms of PSALTERY.

sawtrer, obs. form of PSALTERER *Obs.*

sawturoure, sawtyr: see SALTIRE, PSALTER.

sawure, sawve: see SAVOUR, SALVE.

sawwort ('sɔːwɜːt). Also 6 **sawewoort**, 9 **sawort**. [f. SAW *sb.*[1] + WORT.] A name given to various species of the genera *Serratula* (esp. *S. tinctoria*) and *Saussurea*, and to *Carduus arvensis*.

1597 GERARDE *Herbal* III. ccxxxi. 577 Sawewoort groweth in woods and shadowie places. *c* **1710** PETIVER *Cat. Ray's Eng. Herbal* Tab. xxii, Broad Saw-wort. **1777** LIGHTFOOT *Flora Scot.* I. 448 *Serratula alpina*... Alpine Saw-wort. **1796** WITHERING *Brit. Plants* (ed. 3) III. 697 *Carduus arvensis*... Corn Saw-wort. **1800** tr. *Lagrange's Chem.* II. 287 There are a great many other ingredients proper for dyeing yellow; such as saw-wort. **1838** T. THOMSON *Chem. Org. Bodies* 424 *Serratula tinctoria*, sawort. **1866** *Treas. Bot.* s.v. *Serratula*, The genus is represented in England by *S. tinctoria*, the Common Sawwort.

sawyer ('sɔːjə(r)). Also 4–5 **sawier**, 6–7 **sawyere**, 7 **sayeure**. [Altered form of SAWER, with assimilation of the ending to the Fr. suffix *-ier*. Cf. *bowyer, clothier, lawyer*.]

1. A workman whose business it is to saw timber, esp. in a saw-pit.

1350 in Riley *Mem. Lond.* (1868) 254 [Also, that the] sawiers [shall take in the same manner as the masons and carpenters take]. **1415** in *York Myst.* Introd. 22 Sirdellers, Naylers, Sawiers. **1497** *Naval Accts. Hen. VII* (1896) 143 Carpenters Sawyers Smythes laborers.. & other workemen. **1548** *Act 2 & 3 Edw. VI*, c. 15 §3 Any..joyner hardhewer sawyer tyler pavyer [etc.]. **1616** *Ms. Acc. St. John's Hosp., Canterb.*, Payd to the sayeures for honndred of bourdes. **1640** BROME *Antipodes* II. ii, With see saw sacke a downe, like a Sawyer. **1809** *Med. Jrnl.* XXI. 53 William Waters,.. a sawyer. **1886** *Encycl. Brit.* XXI. 344/2 The log being raised on trestle horses instead of one of the sawyers being sunk in the pit.

2. The name of a New Zealand beetle: see quots.

1789 ANBUREY *Trav.* II. 452 These insects, from the destruction as well as the noise they make, have the appellation of sawyers. **1898** MORRIS *Austral Eng.* 507 A huge, ugly grasshopper, *Deinacrida megacephala*, called by bush-men the Sawyer. **1890** *Sunday Mag.* July 488/2 The Sawyer is reported to saw the branches completely off the tree,.. the Sawyer beetle is the very largest insect known.

3. *U.S.* (See quots.)

1786 E. BEATTY *Diary* 6 Sept. in *Mag. Amer. Hist.* (1877) I. 312/2 Arrived at Guyandot this evening and lay all night off its mouth in rapid water—obliged to make fast to a sawyer. **1797** F. BAILY *Tour* (1856) 256 These sawyers are large trunks of trees, which are brought down by the force of the current. **1841** CATLIN *N. Amer. Ind.* xxxii. (1844) II. 1 We escaped snags and sawyers.. and arrived here safe from the Upper Missouri. **1882** *Society* 7 Oct. 8/1 'Snags' and 'sawyers', which mean trees swept away, the end of the 'snag' being fast in the mud of the river, and the 'sawyer' bobbing up and down.

sax (sæks), *sb.*[1] Forms: 1 **seax, sæx, sex**, 3 **seax, sax, sæx, sox**, 3–4 **sex**. In sense 2: 7 **sects**, 9 **saixe, sax(e, sex**, *s.w. dial.* **zax, zex**. [OE. *seax, sex, sæx* (also in comb. Northumb. *writsæx* 'writing-knife', i.e. pen) = OFris. *sax*, OS., MLG., OHG., MHG. *saks* (also in comb. OHG. *mezzisahs, mezzirahs*, MHG. *mezzeres, mezzer*, mod.G. *messer* knife = OE. *meteseax* 'meat-knife'), ON. *sax* (Sw., Da. *sax* scissors) :—OTeut. **sahsoᵐ*, f. root **sah-*, *sag-* to cut: see SAW *sb.*[1]

In the well-known story related by Geoffrey of Monmouth after 'Nennius', the signal given by Hengist to his Saxons for the treacherous slaughter of their British hosts appears in the form 'Nemet oure saxas'. The OE. form would be *Nimað éowre seax*, the sb. being uninflected in the plural. The two earliest MSS. of 'Nennius' (11th c.) have respectively *saxas* and *sexa*.]

†**1.** A knife; a short sword or dagger. *Obs.* exc. *Hist.*

Beowulf 1545 Heo..hyre seaxe ʒeteah brad brunecg. *a* **800** *Corpus Gloss.*, *Culter*, saex. *c* **1000** ÆLFRIC *Josh.* v. 2 Wirc þe nu stænene sex. *c* **1175** *Lamb. Hom.* 81 þet me sculde in þe ehtuþe dei þet knaue child embsniþen mid ane ulint sexe. *c* **1205** LAY. 4015 þe uniselie moder mid sexe hine to-snæde. *Ibid.* 22342 Mid swiðe scærpe sæxen. **1300–1400** *R. Glouc.* (Rolls) App. G. 40 Mid hare sexes hi corue þat bodi pece mele. **1968** *Medium Ævum* XXXVII. 130 The Hailfingen, Württemberg, sax. **1972** G. JONES *Kings, Beasts, & Heroes* I. i. 20 Wiglaf pierces the dragon's unarmoured under-belly, and..draws his sax and severs him at the middle.

2. A chopping-tool used for trimming slates.

1669 COLEPRESS in *Phil. Trans.* IV. 1009 If in hewing it does not break before the edge of the Sects (the hewing instrument of the Slatters) you may not much doubt of the firmness of the Slat. **1823** P. NICHOLSON *Pract. Build.* 400 The Saixe is of steel, and not unlike a large knife. **1842** GWILT *Encycl. Arch.* §1800 (*Slates*) It is thought to be a good sign, if, in hewing, it shatters before the edge of the zax. **1886** ELWORTHY *W. Somerset Word-bk.*, *Sex*, a tool used by slaters... It is a kind of straight chopper, with a bill or point projecting from the back for 'holing' the slates.

sax (sæks), *sb.*[2] Colloq. abbrev. of SAXOPHONE.

1. = SAXOPHONE 1. For *alto sax, tenor sax*, etc., see under first element.

1923 *N.Y. Times* 7 Oct. IX. 2 *Sax*, a saxophone. **1926** *Picture-Play Mag.* July 3/2 (Advt.), How I used to envy Laura playing beautifully mellow notes on her sax. **1931** *Amer. Mercury* Dec. 426/1 'Mom,' he said, 'is my old sax still around here?' **1943** J. B. PRIESTLEY *Daylight on Saturday* xi. 68 The works dance band, that *Elmdown Six* in which Jack Brimber played the tenor sax. **1955** L. FEATHER *Encycl. Jazz* 64 A bass sax might be used as a rhythm instrument. **1976** N. ROBERTS *Face of France* ix. 102 The moan and scream and shudder of sax and trumpet and drums in the band.

2. = SAXOPHONIST.

1926 *Melody Maker* Mar. 4 Then, for a certainty, you have heard some bad saxes! **1943** J. B. PRIESTLEY *Daylight on Saturday* iv. 21 In the canteen tomorrow..the Elmdown Six will perform. And I'm one of them. Jack Brimber—tenor sax. **1975** J. MCCLURE *Snake* vi. 86 I'm the tickler. Pianist... Drums and sax were here, but they've gone..to get pissed.

3. *attrib.* and *Comb.*, as ***sax-man, -player***; **sax section**, the wind section of a dance or jazz band.

1955 L. FEATHER *Encycl. Jazz* 118 Christy, June, *singer*... Married Kenton's tenor saxman, Bob Cooper. **1972** *Jazz & Blues* Sept. 10/1 Clarence Ford, sax-man with Fats Domino, is typical in this respect. **1926** WHITEMAN & MCBRIDE *Jazz* iii. 67 'Well,' said the biggest sax player, 'we didn't know what you would want us to do.' **1980** M. BOOTH *Bad Track* ix. 158 The sax-player could see a tired desperation..in her eyes. **1932** *Melody Maker* Jan. 11/2 Eddie Pratt, Sid Cole, and Stanley Quiddington, saxophones, the latter being previously together as Jay Whidden's sax section. **1977** J. WAINWRIGHT *Do Nothin'* viii. 124 The sax section—Ric.. fills it out, with the tenor..he doubles clarinet (like most sax men).

Hence **'saxist**, a saxophonist.

1939 *Melody Maker* 13 May 3 (*heading*) Dutch saxist collects band. **1952** B. ULANOV *Hist. Jazz in Amer.* (1958) xv. 178 Harry Carney joined the band..first as an alto saxist. **1969** *Guardian* 23 Aug. 6/4 No tenor saxist of the fifties would take the stand without a one-note stutter in his vocabulary. **1975** *Gramophone* Aug. 375/3 'The Foremost!' is devoted to three tenors and a baritone saxist from the bop era.

Sax, var. SAUK.

saxatile ('sæksətaɪl, -tɪl), *a.* Also 7 **saxatil**. [a. F. *saxatile* (16th c.) or ad. L. *saxātilis*, f. *saxum* rock, stone.]

†**1.** Of the nature of stone. *Obs. rare*⁻¹.

1651 BIGGS *New Disp.* ¶140 Gemmes, stones, and things of a saxatile substance.

2. *Zool.* and *Bot.* Living or growing among rocks.

1661 LOVELL *Hist. Anim. & Min.* 205 Saxatil fishes yeeld a dry aliment. *Ibid.* 238 Julis... Is a saxatile Fish. **1786** ABERCROMBIE *Gard. Assist.*, *Arrangem.* 48 Saxatile or rock yellow alysson. **1854** BADHAM *Halieut.* 42 Turdi and other saxatile fish of value.

saxaul ('sæksɔːl). Also **saksa(o)ul**. A shrub, *Anabasis* (or *Holoxylon*) *Ammodendron*, growing on the steppes of Asia.

1874 H. SPALDING *Khiva & Turkestan* 43 Scattered clumps of *saksaoul* and dwarf acacias. **1874** *Treas. Bot.* Suppl., *Saxaul*. **1882** *Encycl. Brit.* XIV. 64/2 (*Khiva*) Saksaul (*Holoxylon ammodendron*) is found in quantities, and furnishes excellent fuel.

'saxboard. *Boat-building.* [Cf. ON. *sax* (a use of *sax* = SAX *sb.*[1]) raised prow of a ship.] (See quots. 1891, 1898.)

1857 P. COLQUHOUN *Comp. Oarsman's Guide* 28 Above all [the straiks] comes the sax-board. **1891** WINN *Boating Man's Vade-m.* 60 *Saxboard* or *gunwalestrake*, the uppermost continuous strake or sideplank in a boat. **1898** ANSTED *Dict. Sea Terms* s.v. *Gunwale*, The gunwale strake (in open boats the *saxboard*) is the uppermost strake of a boat. To it the gunwale is fixed.

sax-cornet: see under SAX-HORN.

Saxe (sæks). Also **saxe**. [a. F. *Saxe* Saxony (G. *Sachsen*).] Used *attrib.* to designate articles which come from Saxony, as ***Saxe china***; **Saxe blue** (also *ellipt.*) = SAXONY *blue*; **Saxe paper** (also *ellipt.*), an albuminized paper used in photography.

1864 *Hardwich's Photogr. Chem.* (ed. 7) 304 Fifty whole sheets of Saxe paper, 18 × 22. **1866** J. HUGHES *Pract. Photogr.* (ed. 7) 26 Albumenized Paper... There are two principal kinds, known as *Rive* and *Saxe*. **1876** tr. *Tissandier's Hist. Photogr.* Advt. 5 Picked Rives and Saxes. **1881** ABNEY *Photogr.* 128 Good English paper of the consistency of medium Saxe answers every purpose. **1904** E. F. BENSON *Challoners* ii, A pale blue sunshade with a handle of Saxe china. **1905** *Westm. Gaz.* 2 Mar. 4/2 Bows of the new Saxe blue. **1908** *Ibid.* 29 Aug. 13/2 Saxe and turquoise-blue hinder each other. **1917** in G. Howell *In Vogue* (1975) 24/1 Afternoon Gown... In grey, saxe, navy, nigger, rose, and black. **1922** JOYCE *Ulysses* 441 In smart Saxe tailormade, white velours hat and spiderveil. **1939–40** *Army & Navy Stores Catal.* 607/3 Slippers... Red, Green, Saxe, Navy. **1959** G. D. PAINTER *Proust* I. vii. 87 Comparing the what-not on which she kept her Saxe figurines to an altar. **1974** *Harrods Christmas Catal.* 20 Cashmere cardigan... Natural, vicuna-colour, saxe, Harvard blue. **1980** *Radio Times* 29 Nov.–5 Dec. 34/1 Pyjamas... *Grey* trimmed *Wine*, *Saxe Blue* trimmed Navy.

†**saxeane**, *a.* *Sc. Obs. rare*⁻¹. [f. L. *saxe-us* (f. *sax-um* stone) + -ANE.] Made of stone.

1560 ROLLAND *Crt. Venus* II. 488 Ane Closter..Triangill maid, with craftie wark saxeane.

saxefras, obs. form of SASSAFRAS.

saxeous ('sæksɪəs), *a. rare.* [f. L. *saxe-us* of stone (f. *sax-um* stone, rock) + -OUS.] Of or pertaining to stone, stony. †***saxeous odour***, an exhalation supposed to be the cause of petrifaction.

1671 J. WEBSTER *Metallogr.* xxix. 362 That the petrifying seed doth consist alone in a saxeous or stony odour or steam [tr. Van Helmont *De Lithiasi* i. Quod semen petrificum consistat in solo odore saxeo]. **1845** FORD *Handbk. Spain* II. 664 Such a saxeous metamorphosis was an old story even in ..Ovid's time. *Ibid.* 875 The culprit in the saxeous change lost two-thirds of his original height.

sax-horn, saxhorn ('sæks,hɔːn). [f. the name *Sax*: see below.] The name given to a group of brass musical instruments of the trumpet kind, invented by a Belgian, Charles Joseph Sax (1791–1865), and improved by his son Antoine Joseph, known as Adolphe. Called also **sax-cornet**. Also **sax-tuba**, a brass instrument of this class. (Cf. SAXOPHONE *sb.*, SAXOTROMBA.)

1844 *Illustr. London News* 14 Dec. 384/2 The Sax Horn.. unites the powers of the French horn and those of the cornet-à-piston. **1852** *Crystal Palace* 285/1 The Sax-horns, which have become so popular..are also another modification of the cornopean. *Ibid.* 285/2 Sax-horns in alto, soprano, tenor, tuba, bass, &c. **1856** MARY C. CLARKE tr. *Berlioz' Mod. Instrum.* 234 M. Sax has also produced the family of sax-horns, of saxotrombas, and of sax-tubas,—brass instruments with a wide mouthpiece; and with a mechanism of three, four, or five cylinders. **1858** SIMMONDS *Dict. Trade*, *Sax-cornet*, *Sax-horn*, musical wind instruments usually made of brass. **1859** SALA *Gas-light & D.* xxv. 295 From David's harp to Mr. Distin's sax-horns. **1939** [see ALTHORN]. **1977** *Gramophone* May 1680/2 The piece works very well because the sax-horn family is able to offer a suitably mellifluous sound.

‖**Saxicava** (sæk'sɪkəvə). Pl. **-æ**. [mod.L., fem. of *saxicavus*: see next.] A genus of bivalve boring molluscs; a member of this genus. Also in anglicized form **'saxicave** (*rare*).

1826 E. OSLER in *Phil. Trans.* CXVI. III. 362 The Saxicava does not bore like the Pholas, by a rotatory motion. *Ibid.* 364 Where the Saxicavæ are numerous, their holes communicate very freely. **1835** KIRBY *Hab. & Inst. Anim.* I. viii. 248 The rugose Saxicave [note *Saxicava rugosa*].

saxicavous (sæk'sɪkəvəs), *a. Zool.* [f. mod.L. *saxicav-us* (f. *saxum* rock + *cavāre* to hollow, excavate) + -OUS.] Hollowing out rock or stone: epithet of certain molluscs.

1850 DANA *Geol.* ii. 122 They resemble, in fact, other saxicavous molluscs. **1882** GEIKIE *Text-bk. Geol.* 456 Saxicavous shells, by piercing stone and leaving open cavities for rain and sea-water to fill, promote its decay.

saxicole ('sæksɪkəʊl), *a. Bot.* [ad. mod.L. *saxicola*, f. *saxum* rock, stone + *colĕre* to inhabit.] = SAXICOLOUS.

1882 *Encycl. Brit.* XIV. 562/1 Saxicole lichens, which occur on rocks and stones.

saxicoline (sæk'sɪkəlaɪn), *a. Zool.* and *Bot.* [f. mod.L. *saxicol-a* SAXICOLE + -INE.] **a.** Living among rocks, growing on rocks (in recent Dicts.). **b.** *spec.* Pertaining to the subfamily *Saxicolinæ* of passerine birds (the stone-chats).

1899 A. H. EVANS *Birds* 516 As regards the Saxicoline and Ruticilline forms, attention should be drawn to [etc.].

saxicolous (sæk'sɪkələs), *a. Bot.* [f. mod.L. *saxicol-a* SAXICOLE + -OUS.] Growing on rocks.

1856 W. L. LINDSAY *Brit. Lichens* 104 In northern latitudes, Lichens are usually saxicolous. **1882** VINES tr. *Sachs' Bot.* 697 Saxicolous Lichens.

sa'xifical, *a. rare*$^{-0}$. [f. L. *saxific-us* (f. *saxum* rock, stone: see -FIC) + -AL[1].] (See quot.)

1656 BLOUNT *Glossogr.*, *Saxifical*, that turns into a stone, or is made stony.

saxifragaceous (sæksɪfrə'geɪʃəs), *a. Bot.* [-ACEOUS.] Belonging to the N.O. *Saxifragaceæ*.

1845 *Encycl. Metrop.* VI. 177*/1 Saxifragaceous shrubs. **1892** *Nation* 11 Aug. 114/3 A saxifragaceous tree.

saxifragal (sæk'sɪfrəgəl), *a.* and *sb. Bot.* [f. mod.L. *saxifraga* SAXIFRAGE + -AL[1].] Belonging to Lindley's 'alliance' *Saxifragales*, which comprises the *Saxifragaceæ* and four other orders. Hence as *sb.*, a member of this alliance.

1846 LINDLEY *Veget. Kingd.* 566.

sa'xifragant, *a. rare*$^{-0}$. [f. L. *saxifrag-us* (see SAXIFRAGE) + -ANT.] That breaks stones.

1656 BLOUNT *Glossogr.*, *Saxifragrant* [sic], that breaks stones, or is broken against stones. **1676** COLES, *Saxifragant*, breaking (or broken against) stones.

saxifrage ('sæksɪfrɪdʒ). Also 6 **saxfrage, saxefrage, sixfrag(e**, 7 **saxafrage, -phrage**, 8 **saxifrige**. [a. OF. *saxifrage*, *saxefrage*, *sassifrage* (13th c.), ad. L. *saxifraga* (sc. *herba*), in Pliny *saxifragum* (sc. *adiantum*): see next. Med.L. had also *saxifragia*, *-fragium* (It. *sassifraga*, *-fragia*).

The Latin name (= rock-breaking) was probably given because many species are found growing among stones and in the clefts of rocks. Pliny preferred to derive it from the supposed lithontriptic virtue of the plant (*H.N.* XXII. xxi. §64 *calculos e corpore mire pellit frangitque*), and this view has had great currency; but *saxum* is far from being synonymous with *calculus*.]

1. Any plant of the genus *Saxifraga*, esp. *S. granulata* (White Meadow Saxifrage). The numerous species are mostly dwarf herbs with tufted foliage and panicles of white, yellow or red flowers; many root in the clefts of rocks. Also applied to related plants, as the genus *Chrysosplenium* (Golden Saxifrage), *Pimpinella Saxifraga* (Burnet or Rough S.) and *P. magna* (Great S.), *Silaus pratensis* (Meadow or Pepper S.), the genus *Seseli* (Meadow S.).

c **1440** *Promp. Parv.* 442/1 Saxifrage, herbe, *Saxifragium*, *Saxifragia*. *c* **1450** *Alphita* (Anecd. Oxon.) 163 Saxifragia uel saxifraga similis est pimpinello, radice utimur, g^e. et a^e. saxifrage. **1526** *Grete Herball* ccccxxxviii. (1529) Z iij, *De Saxifraga minori*. The lesse saxifrage. **1548** TURNER *Names of Herbes* 87 The englishe mens Saxifragia, which they cal Saxifrage, hath leaues lyke smal perseley, & it groweth in middowes. *c* **1550** LLOYD *Treas. Health* N vij, Mingle it wyth Gillofloures and Sixfrag. **1551** TURNER *Herbal* I. O iiij, Pimpinell or roughe saxifrage. **1568** *Ibid.* III. 68 The white Saxifrage with the indented leafe is moste commended for the breakinge of the stone. **1578** LYTE *Dodoens* II. cii. 287 Of white Saxifrage or Stone-breake. *Ibid.* 288 Golden Saxifrage. **1597** GERARDE *Herbal* II. ccccciv. 887 Burnet Saxifrage. **1612** DRAYTON *Poly-olb.* xiii. 221 So Saxifrage is good, and Harts-tongue for the Stone. **1651** D. BORDER *Physitian* 139 The root of Saxafrage drunk with Wine and Vinegar cureth the Pestilence. **1683** RAY *Corr.* (1848) 132 Whether the Seseli..be a species distinct from our English Meadow Saxifrage? **1785** MARTYN *Rousseau's Bot.* xix. (1794) 270 Common White Saxifrage flowers early and in great quantities among the grass. **1796** WITHERING *Brit. Plants* (ed. 3) II. 295 *Peucedanum Silaus*..Meadow Saxifrage, or Sulphurwort. **1841** *Penny Cycl.* XX. 486/1 White or Granulated Meadow Saxifrage. **1846** *Ibid.* Suppl. II. 547/1 *Silaus pratensis*, Meadow Pepper Saxifrage. **1858** KINGSLEY *Miscell.* (1859) I. 164 The first stars of the white saxifrage,..which shine upon some green cushion of wet moss.

b. (with *pl.*) Any member of the genus *Saxifraga* or of the N.O. *Saxifragaceæ*.

1578 LYTE *Dodoens* II. ci. 286 The smal Saxifrages growe vnder hedges. **1785** MARTYN *Rousseau's Bot.* xix. (1794) 269 In the second [order] you have all the Saxifrages, forty-two in number. **1884** BOWER & SCOTT *De Bary's Phaner.* 53 The Saxifrages of the division Euaizonia.

†**2.** Applied to caraway-seed. *Obs.*

1696 *Phil. Trans.* XIX. 350 *Carum* grows plentifully in our Pastures; the seed they call Saxifrage, which they gather and send to London.

¶**3.** Misused for SASSAFRAS.

1670 D. DENTON *Descr. New York* (1845) 4 The greatest part of the Island is very full of Timber, as..Maples, Cedars, Saxifrage, Beach.

4. *attrib.*, as *saxifrage-root*, *-seed*, *-water*.

1547 BOORDE *Brev. Health* ccvii. (1557) 72 Putte thereto three vnces of Saxfrage rotes. *Ibid.* 72b, I did take..of Saxfrage sedes..an vnce. **1694** SALMON *Bate's Dispens.* (1713) 86/1 Strawberry or Saxifrage Water. **1841** *Penny Cycl.* XX. 486/1 The roots of this species [*Saxifraga granulata*], forming as they do little granular masses, were at one time sold in the shops under the name of saxifrage seed.

saxifragine (sæk'sɪfrədʒiːn). [a. F. *saxifragine* (Desorbiaux 1878), f. L. *saxifrag-us*: see next.] A species of gunpowder (see quot. 1889).

The statement in quot. 1881 is app. erroneous.

1881 GREENER *Gun* 320 Mataziette and Saxafragine [*sic*] are merely aliases for dynamite of different consistencies and strength. **1889** CUNDILL *Dict. Explosives* 16 Saxifragine consists of: Nitrate of baryta 77 parts, Charcoal 21 parts, Salt-petre 2 parts.

†**sa'xifragous**, *a. Obs. rare.* [f. L. *saxifrag-us* (f. *saxum* rock + *frag-*, *frangĕre* to break) + -OUS.] That has the property of 'breaking' or dissolving the stone in the bladder. Also *fig.*

1646 SIR T. BROWNE *Pseud. Ep.* II. v. 84 Saxifragous herbes, and such as are conceived of power to breake the stone. **1677** W. HUGHES *Man of Sin* III. iii. 98, I have six or seven Instances more,..which will make such a Saxifragous Dose, that no scruple can stand before it.

†**'saxify**, *v. Obs.*$^{-0}$ [f. L. *saxum* rock: see -FY. Cf. L. *saxificus* petrifying.] *trans.* To turn into rock or stone. In quot. **saxifying** *vbl. sb.*

1659 TORRIANO, *Lapificatióne*, a saxifying.

saxigenous (sæk'sɪdʒɪnəs), *a.* [f. late L. *saxigen-us*, f. *sax-um* rock + *-gen-us* begotten, sprung (from): see -OUS. The termination is here erroneously taken to mean 'producing', as in CORALLIGENOUS.] That produces (coral) rocks or reefs.

1842 DARWIN *Coral Reefs* iv. §1. 64 The saxigenous lithophytes. **1862** M. HOPKINS *Hawaii* 415 Saxigenous polypes or lithophytes.

Saxin ('sæksɪn). Also **saxin**. A proprietary name for artificial sweeteners and other products (see quots. 1897, 1964).

1897 *Trade Marks Jrnl.* 28 July 696 *Saxin*... Chemical substances prepared for use in medicine and pharmacy, but not including those prepared for use in the cure of corns and warts and not including any goods of a like kind to any of these excluded goods. Henry Solomon Wellcome,.. London, E.C.; manufacturing chemist. **1918** 'K. MANSFIELD' *Let.* 17 Feb. (1928) I. 130 I've just made myself a glass of boiling tea, very weak, with saxin. **1964** *Trade Marks Jrnl.* 19 Aug. 1366/2 *Saxin*... Flavourings and essences, none being essential oils; and sweetening materials included in Class 30.

†**'Saxish**, *a.* and *sb. Obs.* In 3 **Sax-, Sæx-, Sexisc, Saxiss, -ess.** [OE. *Seaxisc*, *Sęxisc*, f. *Seaxe* Saxons: see -ISH. Cf. OFris. *sassisk*, Du. *saksisch*, G. *sächsisch*, ON. *saxnesk-r*.] = SAXON *a.* and *sb.*

O.E. Chron. an. 1009, Brihtric..forwręgde Wulfnoð cild þone Suðseaxscian [*read* -seaxiscan] to þam cyning. *c* **1205** LAY. 7111 Seoððen comen Sæxisce [*c* **1275** Saxisse] men. *Ibid.* 14143 Ich wulle biliue senden after mine wiue, þat is a Sexisc wimmon. *Ibid.* 14979 Fortimer spæc Bruttisc & Rouuenne Saxisc [*c* **1275** Saxisse]. *Ibid.* 29963 Anglisce & Sexisce seouentene þusend mid machen weoren to-heowen. **1848** LYTTON *Harold* IX. iii. 305, I know well these Saxish men.

saxist: see SAX *sb.*[2]

saxitoxin (sæksɪ'tɒksɪn). *Biochem.* [f. mod.L. *Saxi-domus*, name of a genus of clams (f. L. *saxum* rock + -I- + *domus* home) + TOXIN.] A toxic alkaloid ($C_{10}H_{17}O_4N_7.2HCl$) synthesized by dinoflagellates of the genus *Gonyaulax* (which cause 'red tides') and accumulated by molluscs which feed on these, which thereby become toxic to man.

1962 *Jrnl. Amer. Chem. Soc.* LXXXIV. 2266/1 Saxitoxin, the paralytic poison isolated from toxic Alaska butter clams (*Saxidomus giganteus*),..is among the most toxic known substances. **1968** *New Scientist* 27 June 706/2 PSP [paralytic shellfish poison] is now known as saxitoxin and there is an extensive literature which dates back at least to the year 1778. *Ibid.*, It would appear that saxitoxin is a perhydropurine derivative into which are incorporated two guanidino moieties. **1977** *Sci. Amer.* Dec. 30/3 A tiny dose of saxitoxin—the 'red tide' toxin—can kill a man who weighs 500 million times as much as it does.

Saxo- ('sæksəʊ), combining form of SAXON *sb.* and *a.* [L. *Saxo-*], prefixed to ethnic adjs. in the sense 'Saxon and ——', as in ***Saxo-Danish***, ***-Norman*** adjs.

1798 tr. J. C. Adelung in A. F. M. Willich *Elem. Crit. Philos.* II. p. cxxiii, In the Saxon and Saxo-Danish periods, the national taste..was still much too rude to exhibit this corruption. **1932** C. J. W. MESSENT *City Churches of Norwich* 25 The base is supposed to be Saxon, or Saxo-Norman, that is built by Saxon labour under Norman direction. **1980** *Rescue News* No. 23. 2/3 A rim of Saxo-Norman pottery.

Saxon ('sæksən), *sb.* and *a.* Forms: 3-5 **Saxoyn(e**, 4-5 **Saxoun, Sessoyne**, 5-6 **Saxson(e**, 4- **Saxon.** [a. F. *Saxon*, ad. L. *Saxon-em* (nom. sing. *Saxo*, pl. *Saxonēs*, Gr. in Ptolemy *Σάξονες*), a. WGer. **Saxon-* (OE. *Seaxan*, *Seaxe* pl., OHG. *Sahsûn* pl., G. *Sachse*).

It has been conjectured that the name may have been derived from **sahso*^m SAX *sb.*[1], as the name of the weapon used by the Saxons; cf. the probable derivation of the German tribe-name *Cherusci* from OTeut. **heru* sword.]

A. *sb.*

1. a. One of a Germanic people which in the early centuries of the Christian era dwelt in a region near the mouth of the Elbe, and of which one portion, distinguished as *Anglo-Saxons* (see ANGLO-SAXON) conquered and occupied certain parts of South Britain in the 5th and 6th centuries, while the other, the ***Old Saxons*** (med.L. *Antiqui Saxones*, Beda; OE. *Ealdseaxe*) remained in Germany. Often, like *Anglo-Saxon*, applied indiscriminately to all the Germanic peoples that settled in Britain. Also, an Englishman who is presumed to be descended from this people.

1297 R. GLOUC. (Rolls) 2540 Hit was of grace þat þe saxoyns þus com verst to londe. **1390** GOWER *Conf.* I. 184 A Saxon and a worthi knyht. ?*a* **1400** *Morte Arth.* 3530 Sarazenes and Sessoynes. *c* **1420** *Chron. Vilod.* 99 Saxones were y-clepud Engestis men. *c* **1450** *Merlin* xii. 173 Oure werres a-gein the saxoyns. *Ibid.* xiii. 193 That day Gawein slowgh many a sarazin of the saxouns. **1547** BOORDE *Introd. Knowl.* xvi. (1870) 164, I do maruel greatly how the Saxsons should conquere Englonde. **1781** GIBBON *Decl. & F.* xxv. (1787) II. 522 The sea-coast of Gaul and Britain was exposed to the depredations of the Saxons. *Ibid.* xxxviii. III. 613 Three valiant tribes or nations of Germany; the *Jutes*, the *old Saxons*, and the *Angles*. **1856** EMERSON *Eng. Traits, Ability* Wks. (Bohn) II. 33 The Norman has come popularly to represent in England the aristocratic—and the Saxon the democratic principle. **1862** W. H. JERVIS *Hist. France* v. §6 (1872) 65 Divided into the three confederacies of Westphalians, Ostphalians, and Angarians, the Saxons occupied at this time the greater part of Northern Germany.

b. In mod. use *spec.* (primarily as the term used by Celtic speakers). An Englishman as distinct from a Welshman or Irishman, a Lowland Scot as distinct from a Highlander. Cf. SASSENACH. Also, an Englishman as distinct from a 'Latin'.

1810 SCOTT *Lady of Lake* IV. xxxi, He gave him of his Highland cheer..And bade the Saxon share his plaid. **1862** THACKERAY *Philip* xxx, Scores of [Irish] gentlemen..who would not object to take the Saxon's pay until they finally shook his yoke off. **1908** M. BEERBOHM *Let.* 23 Dec. (1964) 180 The Latins are born actors, while the Saxons have to train themselves up to the scratch. **1977** *Times Lit. Suppl.* 1 Apr. 394/3 In 1962 Ewart Milne returned to Ireland after more than twenty years in the land of the Saxon.

2. A native or inhabitant of Saxony in its modern German sense. (Saxony formerly included the kingdom of Saxony, the Prussian province of Saxony, and certain principalities; it existed as a state of the German Democratic Republic until 1952, when it was replaced as an administrative district by Leipzig, Karl-Marx-Stadt, and Dresden.)

1737 *Gentl. Mag.* VII. 4/1 The Saxons, who long since have done great damage to your coarser sorts of Cloths.

3. *Pyrotechnics.* (See quot. 1839.)

1839 URE *Dict. Arts* 480 The saxons are cartridges clayed at each end, charged with the brilliant turning fire, and perforated with one or two holes at the extremity of the same diameter. **1873** W. H. BROWNE *Pyrotechny* viii. 87 Saxons ..[are] used largely in the construction of set pieces; they are sometimes called Chinese flyers.

4. *Ent.* A night-moth, *Hadena rectilinea*.

1869 E. NEWMAN *Brit. Moths* 423.

B. *adj.*

1. a. Of or belonging to the Saxons (see A. 1). Formerly often used (like *Anglo-Saxon*) as the distinctive epithet of the Old English language, and of books written in it, and of the period of English history between the conquest of Britain by the Saxons, Angles, and Jutes, and the Norman Conquest. †*Saxon Angles* = Anglo-Saxons.

Old Saxon: pertaining to the Old Saxons or their language: see A. 1 and B. 2b.

1568 JEWEL *Let. to Abp. Parker* 18 Jan., Wks. 1848 VIII. 193, I..have found..one book, written in the Saxon tongue... It may be Alfricus for all my cunning. **1589** PUTTENHAM *Eng. Poesie* II. vi. (Arb.) 90 *Ryme* is a borrowed word from the Greeks by the Latines and French, from them by vs Saxon angles. **1605** CAMDEN *Rem., Languages* 24 The Saxon letter *Thorne*. **1781** GIBBON *Decl. & F.* xxv. (1787) II. 523 The Saxon pirates. *Ibid.* xxxviii. III. 610 The obscure hints of the Saxon laws and chronicles. **1819** SCOTT *Ivanhoe* xliii, The last scion of Saxon royalty. **1824** JOHNSON *Typogr.* II. 581 Greek, Hebrew, Saxon, &c., or any of the dead characters. **1840** *Rituale Eccl. Dunelm.* (Surtees) p. xii, An interlinear version into the Saxon language. **1849** MACAULAY *Hist. Eng.* vi. II. 130 In Ireland Scot and Southron were strongly bound together by their common Saxon origin. **1862** W. H. JERVIS *Hist. France* v. §6 (1872) 65 Witikind became the hero of the Saxon resistance.

b. Used to denote the element of the English tongue which is derived from Anglo-Saxon.

† *Saxon-English*, † *English-Saxon* = Anglo-Saxon.

1589 PUTTENHAM *Eng. Poesie* I. xxx. (Arb.) 72 This word (song) which is our naturall Saxon English word. *Ibid.* II. xiii. 126 Our vulgar Saxon English standing most vpon wordes monosillable. *Ibid.* 130 Not content with the vsual Normane or Saxon word. ? **1595–6** R. CAREW *Excell. Engl. Tongue* in G. G. Smith *Elizab. Crit. Ess.* II. 287 In our natiue Saxon language. **1840** CARLYLE *Heroes* v. (1841) 307 Wheresoever a Saxon dialect is spoken. **1849** F. W. NEWMAN *Soul* 71 Poetry must have Saxon vocables. **1860** WHYTE MELVILLE *Mkt. Harb.* 2 Mr. Sawyer's fluency in all Saxon expletives is undeniable.

c. Used (primarily by Celtic speakers: see A. 1 b) for 'English' in contradistinction to Welsh and Irish or Gaelic. Also, in wider sense, applied, like *Anglo-Saxon*, to the people of England and of the other English-speaking communities, chiefly in contradistinction to 'Latin'.

1787 BURNS '*When Guilford good*' vii, The Saxon lads, wi' loud placads, On Chatham's Boy did ca', man. *a* **1845** C. G. DUFFY in *Spirit of Nation* 3 Saxon wiles or Saxon powers Can enslave our land no longer Than your own dissensions wrong her. **1847** EMERSON *Repr. Men, Uses of Gt. Men* Wks. (Bohn) I. 282 Every child of the Saxon race is educated to wish to be first. **1862** CALVERLEY *Verses & Transl.* (1894) 49 Then nectar—was that beer, or whisky-toddy? Some say the Gaelic mixture, *I* the Saxon. **1893** LELAND *Mem.* II. 64, I never found a Saxon-Englishman who had this step.

d. *Arch.* Used to designate the special variety of Romanesque architecture used in England in the 'Saxon period'. (Formerly often misapplied to early Norman buildings.)

17.. WARBURTON *Note on Pope's Ep. Ld. Burlington* 29 This, by way of distinction, I would call the Saxon Architecture. **1762–71** H. WALPOLE *Vertue's Anecd. Paint.* (1786) I. 181 This Saxon style begins to be defined by flat and round arches. **1797** *Encycl. Brit.* (ed. 3) II. 222/1 Those arcades we see in the early Norman or Saxon buildings or walls. **1825** SCOTT *Betrothed* xiii, With doors and windows forming the heavy round arch which is usually called Saxon.

2. *absol.* (quasi-*sb.*). The language of the Saxons: **a.** = ANGLO-SAXON in its various applications. Often used for Modern English speech of Saxon or Anglo-Saxon origin; English diction derived chiefly from the Saxon stock, as distinct from the Latin and French elements.

† *English Saxon* = Anglo-Saxon.

1388 PURVEY *Prol. Bible* 59 Bede translatide the bible, and expounide myche in Saxon, that was English, either comoun langage of this lond. **1390** GOWER *Conf.* I. 206 For Couste in Saxoun is to sein Constance upon the word Romein. **1589** PUTTENHAM *Eng. Poesie* II. v. (Arb.) 90 For this purpose serue the monosillables of our English Saxons [*sic*] excellently well. *Ibid.* III. iv. (Arb.) 157 Neither shall he take the termes of Northern-men,.. nor in effect any speach vsed beyond the riuer of Trent, though no man can deny but that theirs is the purer English Saxon at this day. **1624** FLETCHER *Wife for a Month* I, A Letter, But 'tis a womans, Sir, I know by the hand, And the false Orthography, they write old Saxon. **1662** M. W. *Marriage Broaker* 72 He in olde Saxon's call'd a match-maker. **1819** SCOTT *Ivanhoe* xxvi, Here is a letter, and, if I mistake not, it is in Saxon. **1820** *Gentl. Mag.* Apr. 312/1 *Maund*. This word being derived from the Saxon, deserves to be in more frequent and general use.

b. *Old Saxon*: the language of the Old Saxons (see A. 1), especially as exemplified in the remains of 9th century poetry, including the *Heliand* and some fragments of paraphrases of the story of Genesis.

1841 R. G. LATHAM *Eng. Lang.* iii. 51 Grammatical Structure of Old Saxon, as compared with Anglo-Saxon. **1908** WRIGHT *O.E. Grammar* 2 Low German... Up to about 1300 it is generally called Old Saxon.

3. a. Of or belonging to Saxony in its modern German sense. (See A. 2.)

a **1634** CHAPMAN *Alphonsus* III. i. 271 With Saxon lans-knights and brunt-bearing Switzers. **1737** *Gentl. Mag.* VII. 3/1 The thriving.. Trade of all sorts of Saxon Cloths. **1842** MACAULAY *Ess., Fredk. Gt.* (near beginning), Even Frederic William, with all his rugged Saxon prejudices, thought it necessary that his children should know French. **1842** BISCHOFF *Woollen Manuf.* II. 363 The indigenous Saxon breed [of sheep] resembled that of the neighbouring states.

b. *Saxon blue* = *Saxony blue* s.v. SAXONY *sb.* 2. *Saxon green*: cobalt green.

1753 HANWAY *Trav.* (1762) I. VII. xciv. 432 The blues and greens, commonly called Saxon, are best dyed in this place. **1766** W. GORDON *Gen. Counting-ho.* 428, 2 Saxon-green durants. **1771** WOULFE in *Phil. Trans.* LXI. 127 Saxon blues ..are made by dissolving indigo in oil of vitriol. **1775** ROMANS *Hist. Florida* App. 19 The color of the water changes..to a beautiful saxon blue. **1804** tr. *Tingry's Painter & Varnisher's Guide* 302 Smalt, or the vitreous oxide of saffer, reduced to coarse powder, is distinguished by the name of coarse Saxon blue, or enamel blue. **1968** E. BRILL *Old Cotswold* v. 85 It is sometimes mixed with indigo, or in the old days with woad, to give what dyers call Saxon Green. **1976** *Southern Even. Echo* (Southampton) 12 Nov. (Advt. Suppl.) 14/3, 1973 Vauxhall Viva. Saxon blue... £1095.

Saxondom ('sæksəndəm). = ANGLO-SAXONDOM.

1840 CARLYLE *Heroes* iii. (1841) 184 East and west to the very Antipodes, there will be a Saxondom covering great spaces of the Globe. **1868** DILKE *Greater Brit.* I. Pref. 8 Sketches of Saxondom may be of interest. **1871** EARLE *Philol. Eng. Tongue* 24 The Anglian kingdom of Northumbria exhibited the first mature example of a Christian nation in Saxondom.

† **Sa'xonian**, *a.* and *sb. Obs.* [f. med.L. *Saxonia* SAXONY + -AN.] **a.** *adj.* = SAXON *a.* 3. **b.** *sb.* A Protestant of Saxony.

a **1600** HOOKER *Eccl. Pol.* VI. iv. §14 Saxonians and Bohemians in their Discipline constraine no man to open confession. **1761** SPENCE in *Epithal. Oxon.* Gj, Hail.., Saxonian plains! where deep Visurgis flows.

Saxonic (sæk'sɒnɪk), *a.* [ad. med.L. *Saxonic-us*, f. L. *Saxon-* SAXON.]

1. Of or belonging to Saxony.

c **1645** HOWELL *Lett.* (1650) II. xi. 23 They of the Anglican,.. Saxonick, Wirtinbergick, Palatin, and Belgick confessions.

2. Belonging to the Anglo-Saxons or their language.

1678 T. JONES *Heart & its Soveraign* 320 Their Saxonick letter, which much agrees with the character, the Irish still use. **1714** FORTESCUE-ALAND *Fortescue's Abs. & Lim. Mon.* I This Saxonick way of writing is to be found in Chaucer. **1888** EARLE (*title*) A Hand-Book to the Land-Charters, and other Saxonic Documents.

† **Sa'xonical**, *a. Obs.* = prec.

1577 DEE *Memor. Navig.* 57 King Edgar, that Saxonicall Alexander. **1617** MORYSON *Itin.* III. 211 The later Interpreters.. so interpret the Statute of the Saxonical Law.

sa'xonically, *adv. rare.* [f. prec. + -LY².] In the Saxonic manner.

1837 S. R. MAITLAND *6 Lett. Fox's A. & M.* 6 King Ina, ..[or,] as Fox more Saxonically called him, Ine.

Saxonish ('sæksənɪʃ), *a.* [f. SAXON + -ISH.] Belonging to the Saxons; resembling what is Saxon.

1549 BALE *Labor. Journ. Leland* Pref. B iij, A man lerned in many sondrye languages, as Greke, Latyne,.. Brittyshe, Saxonyshe, Walshe, Englyshe, and Scottyshe. **1577–87** HOLINSHED *Chron.* I. 126/2 Which terme being expired, the whole dominion of this realme was Saxonish. **1871** EARLE *Philol. Eng. Tongue* 16 The Welsh and the Gael, have still called us Saxons, and our language Saxonish.

Saxonism ('sæksənɪz(ə)m). [f. SAXON + -ISM.]

1. a. An Anglo-Saxon idiom or expression; Anglo-Saxon characteristics in speech.

1774 WARTON *Hist. Eng. Poetry* I. ii. 49 The language [of Robert of Gloucester].. is full of Saxonisms. **1845** KEMBLE in *Proc. Philol. Soc.* II. 121 How often have we not heard it asserted that particular districts were remarkable for the Saxonism of their speech, because they had retained the archaisms, *kine, shoon, housen*! **1851** H. MELVILLE *Whale* III. i. 10 *note*, Many other sinewy Saxonisms of this sort.

b. The doctrine or practice of employing English words of purely Anglo-Saxon derivation in preference to words of foreign origin.

1926 FOWLER *Mod. Eng. Usage* 514/2 Saxonism is a name for the attempt to raise the proportion borne by the originally & etymologically English words in our speech to those that come from alien sources. **1952** W. D. JACOBS *William Barnes Linguist* ii. 45 If Latinism had its failings, Saxonism manifested great excellences.

2. The characteristics of the Anglo-Saxon race; attachment to what is Anglo-Saxon.

1884 H. D. TRAILL in *Macm. Mag.* Oct. 443 Please to remember in abatement of your pride of Saxonism, that its moral association is not inherited but acquired. *a* **1894** C. H. PEARSON in Stebbing *Mem.* (1900) 92 The extravagant Saxonism of the present school [of historians].

Saxonist ('sæksənɪst). [f. SAXON + -IST.]

a. A Saxon scholar; one learned in Anglo-Saxon.

1599 THYNNE *Animadv.* (1875) 31 Vnleste a manne be a good saxoniste, frenche, and Italyane linguiste. **1770** *Archæologia* I. Introd. 25 Mr. Elstob the Saxonist. **1812** J. NICHOLS *Lit. Anecd. 18th C.* IV. 123 This ingenious Saxonist. **1847** *Blackw. Mag.* LXI. 80 Mr. Thorpe, so well known as one of the very few accomplished Saxonists of whom we can boast.

b. An advocate of the use of English words of purely Anglo-Saxon origin. Cf. SAXONISM 1 b.

1926 FOWLER *Mod. Eng. Usage* 228/1 While the plain Englishman is content that *events* should *happen*, the Saxonist..requires that there should be *happenings*, & the anti-Saxonist..that things should *eventuate*. **1934** J. J. HOGAN *Outl. Eng. Philol.* II. vii. 68 The Saxonists failed with *wheelman* 'cyclist'.

saxonite ('sæksənaɪt). *Geol.* [f. SAXON-Y + -ITE.] A name proposed for a group of peridotite rocks composed of olivine and enstatite.

1884 WADSWORTH *Lithol. Studies* 85 It is, then, proposed here to designate all these rocks by the term *saxonite*, from the country in which the terrestrial form was first so well described by Dathe.

Saxonize ('sæksənaɪz), *v.* [f. SAXON + -IZE.]

1. *trans.* To make Saxon or Anglo-Saxon.

1804 MITFORD *Inquiry* 405 The rest, French, Latin, and Greek, is little more than a magazine of words; rarely showing, except as in declension, comparison, or conjugation, they have been Saxonized, any relation to the rest of the speech. **1843** WORDSW. *Prose Wks.* (1876) III. 91 Saint Romualdo, (or Rumwald, as our ancestors saxonised the name). **1861** PEARSON *Early & Mid. Ages Eng.* vi. 55 Other invaders.. poured in.. till the island was Saxonized.

2. *intr.* To become Saxon (in quot., of Saxony).

1834 *Tait's Mag.* I. 440/1 Arthur is packed off to Saxonise at Weimar, to sigh at the feet of Goethe's handsome daughter-in-law.

Hence **'Saxonized** *ppl. a.*, **'Saxonizing** *vbl. sb.*

1867 SHAIRP *Sketches* (1887) 67 The decisive Saxonising of Scotland that took place under Margaret. **1886** *Encycl. Brit.* XX. 642 The Saxonized Britons of Wiltshire.

Saxonly ('sæksənlɪ), *adv.* [f. SAXON *a.* + -LY².] In a Saxon manner; in the Saxon tongue.

1387 TREVISA *Higden* (Rolls) II. 159 þe Flemmynges þat woneþ in þe weste side of Wales haueþ i-left her straunge speche and spekeþ Saxonliche i-now [L. *Saxonice satis proloquuntur*]. **1606** WARNER *Alb. Eng.* XV. xciii. 374 Of Britons (saxonlie calld Welsh, or Strangers). **1864** LOWELL *Fireside Trav.* 28 Insurgent after no mad Gallic fashion, but soberly and Saxonly discharging itself. **1870** —— *Study Wind., Chaucer* (1871) 195 He found our language lumpish, ..too apt to speak Saxonly in grouty monosyllables.

Saxony ('sæksənɪ), *sb.* [ad. late L. *Saxonia*, the country of the Saxons, f. *Saxon-* SAXON.

In ME. the name of the country appears in the forms *Saxon, Saxoyne, Sexone, Sessoyne* (after OF. *Saxoine, Sessoyne*); the similar use of *Saxon* in Chapman's *Alphonsus* (*a* 1634) may be from the mod.G. *Sachsen*.]

The name of a former kingdom of Germany (in Ger. *Sachsen*, in Fr. *Saxe*), used *attrib.* to designate products of the country: *esp.*

1. a. A fine kind of wool, and cloth made from it. Also *absol.* = *Saxony-cloth*.

Several distinct kinds of fabric are thus designated: ***Saxony coating***, Saxony wool made in coating styles; ***Saxony flannel***, Saxony wool in flannel weight and finish, usually scarlet; ***Saxony cord***, a black ribbed material with cotton warp and Saxony weft, used for cassocks and academic robes.

1842 *Punch* III. 74/2 House-painters, and others, will obstinately refuse to do their daily work in superfine Saxony. **1844** THACKERAY *Box of Novels* Wks. 1900 XIII. 412 His Saxony-cloth surtout. **1853** R. S. SURTEES *Sponge's Sp. Tour* (1893) 333 Mr. Sponge forthwith proceeded to put his brown boots,.. his dress blue saxony, his clean linen,.. into his solid leather portmanteau. **1888** *Encycl. Brit.* XXIV. 654/2 Specimens of the finest Saxony wools.

b. *spec.* This wool used in making carpets. Also, a synthetic material resembling Saxony used similarly.

1910 S. HUMPHRIES *Oriental Carpets* iv. 300 *Saxony Pile Carpets*.—Made in precisely the same way as the Brussels variety... The Saxony Brussels and Saxony Velvet yarns. **1924** R. BEAUMONT *Carpets & Rugs* viii. 298 Examples in Saxony or the longer variety of 'velvet' carpet... In.. Saxony velvets the design and colour element may be as clearly delineated as in Wiltons. **1933** *Heal & Son Catal.* Carpet..; seamless 'Saxony', various colours. **1976** *Daily Colonist* (Victoria, B.C.) 3 Oct. 3/3 (Advt.), A well-constructed, full-bodied saxony nylon that is versatile and long-wearing.

2. ***Saxony blue***: a solution of indigo in concentrated sulphuric acid, much used as a dye. Also *Saxon blue* (see SAXON *a.* 3 b).

1857 MILLER *Elem. Chem.* III. 616. **1863** *Chamb. Encycl.* V. 559/1.

† **'Saxony**, *a. Obs. rare*$^{-1}$. [? f. SAXON + -Y.] = SAXONISH.

1565 J. HALLE *Lanfranc's Cirurgia parua* Ded. ¶ j, Whiche was translated out of Frenche into the olde Saxony englishe, about two hundred yeres past.

saxophone ('sæksəfəʊn), *sb.* [f. the name *Sax* (see SAX-HORN) + Gr. -φωνος voiced, sounding.]

1. A brass wind-instrument with a clarinet mouthpiece, invented about 1840 by Adolphe Sax. Also preceded by qualifying adj. (or quasi-adj.), as ***soprano, alto*** (see ALTO *a.* b), ***tenor*** (see TENOR *a.* 1), ***baritone***, and ***bass saxophone***, in descending order of pitch. (The instrument is widely used in modern dance and jazz bands.) Cf. SAX *sb.*²

1851 *Catal. Gt. Exhib.* III. 1259/1 Sax, Adolphe & Co., Paris... Saxophone, and complete set of instruments for military bands, invented by the exhibitor. **1884** *Encycl. Brit.* XVII. 708/2 Adolphe Sax, a Belgian established in Paris, who invented the family of saxophones. **1927** *Melody Maker* Aug. 767/1 Then Mr. Billy Childs proved his excessive lung power by the force he put into blowing the soprano saxophone. **1934** S. R. NELSON *All about Jazz* ii. 57 The other saxophones in common use in the band are the tenor, baritone, soprano and bass. **1954** *Grove's Dict. Mus.* (ed. 5) VII. 434/2 Occasionally in the years just before 1917 the tenor saxophone did supplement the trombone and the soprano the clarinet, particularly in the rather larger and more highly organized bands on the Mississippi river boats. **1969** *Punch* 12 Feb. 245/3 A vaguely modal thrash headed by Lynn Dobson on flute and soprano saxophone. **1977** *Listener* 17 Feb. 215/3 Modern tenor-saxophone playing.

2. One who plays the saxophone; a saxophonist.

1929 H. MILES tr. *P. Morand's Black Magic* I. 48 The saxophone was a handsome tall fellow. **1938** D. BAKER *Young Man with Horn* III. i. 141 Rick met them... In the order of their presentation they were drums, saxophone, and trombone. 1949 N. Marsh *Swing, Brother, Swing* vi. 119 The first saxophone muttered something about hitting the high spots.

3. *attrib.* and *Comb.*

1927 *Melody Maker* May 489/2 Can you imagine anything worse than a saxophone section playing a nice legato movement and the banjo plonking away for all he is worth, ..and killing the good work of the saxes. 1954 *Grove's Dict. Mus.* (ed. 5) VII. 434/1 From time to time saxophone quartets..have appeared on the concert platform. 1973 *Advocate-News* (Barbados) 24 Feb. 3/6 (Advt.), Attention all musicians..Just arrived:..Trombone Stands..Saxophone Stands. 1976 A. White *Long Silence* i. 10 We'd ..have a jolly time dancing to saxophone music until the small hours.

Hence **saxo'phonic** *a.*, of or pertaining to a saxophone; **'saxophonist**, a saxophone-player.

1865 *Pall Mall G.* 28 Aug. 1/2 Hitherto we have had neither Zouaves, nor drummers, nor Turkish Saxophonists, nor Danish peasants, introduced into the orchestra. 1926 Whiteman & McBride *Jazz* ii. 34 Sleep for nights became a saxophonic mockery. *Ibid.* iii. 81 He noticed that a saxophonist was absent one night. 1958 *Times* 3 Dec. 14/6 The bassoon of Mr. Karl Kolbinger, which achieves an old fashioned diapason tone or a modern saxophonic reediness as he requires. 1970 *Daily Tel.* 19 May 16/4 Johnny Hodges, Duke Ellington's masterful alto saxophonist. 1976 *New Yorker* 15 Nov. 6/1 Alto saxophonist James Vass..will front his own quartet.

saxophone ('sæksəfəʊn), *v.* [f. the sb.] *intr.* To play on the saxophone. Also *fig.*, to produce a loud and raucous noise. Hence **'saxophoning** *vbl. sb.*

1927 *Sunday Express* 28 Aug. 5/2 America's noise was gramophoned everywhere, and bawled and saxophoned. 1928 *Daily Express* 17 Mar. 9/7 Ten pairs of Communist lungs gave vent to a chorus of as syncopated invectives as one could wish. The parties of the Centre and Right saxophoned back. 1952 B. Ulanov *Hist. Jazz in Amer.* (1958) xxi. 288 Other boppers' trumpeting or saxophoning just doesn't fit.

'saxotromba. [Formed as SAXOPHONE *sb.* + It. *tromba* trumpet.] (See quot. 1883.)

1856 [see SAX-HORN]. 1883 *Grove's Dict. Mus.* III. 232/1 In 1845 he [A. Sax] took out a patent..for a family of cylinder instruments called Saxo-trombas, intermediate between the Saxhorn and the cylinder trumpet.

†**'saxous,** *a. Obs. rare*⁻¹. [ad. L. *saxōs-us*, f. *saxum* rock, stone: see -OUS.] Rocky, stony.

1657 Tomlinson *Renou's Disp.* 309 It growes..on stone walls, old edifices, and rubbages, and other saxous and dry places [orig. *aliisque saxosis & aridis locis*].

saxoyne, saxsum: see SAXON, SIXSOME.

saxt(e, -ie, -en, -ine, -ieth, obs. Sc. ff. SIXTH, SIXTY, SIXTEEN, SIXTIETH.

†**'saxter aithe.** *Orkney* and *Shetland*. Refashioning, after Sc. *sax* 'six', of ON. *séttareiðr* 'an oath of six', i.e. of six compurgators.

1602 in Goudie *Diary J. Mill* (1889) 185 Jonat Archbald is dempt to quite hir selff with the saxter aithe for [etc.].

saxton, sax-tuba: see SEXTON, SAX-HORN.

‖**'saxum.** *Obs.* [L.] (See quot.)

1706 Phillips (ed. Kersey), *Saxum*, Stone or Rock-stone. 1776 G. Edwards *Elem. Fossilogy* 9 Class II. Stones... Order VI. Stone of a granulated structure, named Saxum. 1776 in *Phil. Trans.* LXVI. 525 The mass of native iron lay on the very ridge, without being fixed to the rock, which is a grey, stratified *saxum*.

say (seɪ), *sb.*¹ Forms: 5–6 **saye**, 6 **seeay, seye, see, sea,** 6–7 **saie,** 6–8 **sey,** 3– **say.** [a. F. *saie* fem. = Pr. *saia*, Sp. *saya*, Pg. *saia*, It. *saja*:—L. *saga* pl. of *sagum* military cloak.]

1. a. A cloth of fine texture resembling serge; in the 16th c. sometimes partly of silk, subsequently entirely of wool.

1297 R. Glouc. (Rolls) 8013 As is chanberlein him broȝte ar he aros aday Amorewe uor to werie a peire hosen of say. *c*1440 *Promp. Parv.* 440/2 Say, clothe, *sagum*. 1519 *Nottingham Rec.* III. 354 A kyrtylle of sylke seeay. 1538 Starkey *England* I. iii. 94 Fyne clothys, says and sylkys, bedys, combys, gyrdyllys and knyfys. 1590 Spenser *F.Q.* III. xii. 8 His garment nether was of silke nor say But [etc.]. 1659 *J. Cleaveland Revived* 68 Saw you the Cloak at Church to day, The long worne short Cloak lin'd with Say? 1728 Chambers *Cycl.* s.v., *Say*, or *Saye*,..a very light crossed stuff, all wool; much used abroad for linings, and by the religious for shirts; and with us, by the quakers, for aprons, for which purpose it is usually dyed green. 1778 *Eng. Gazetteer* (ed. 2) s.v. *Colchester*, It is principally noted for the manufacture of baizes and seys; for the support of which there is a corporation, called the governors of Dutch-baize-hall. 1862 *Catal. Internat. Exhib.* II. XXI. No. 3964 Worsted goods: merinos, says, shalloons, &c.

†**b.** The thread or yarn from which the material is woven. *Obs.*

1714 *Fr. Bk. of Rates* 85 Yarn ordinary *p.* 100 weight 07 00... Ditto Sayes per 100 weight 03 00.

¶**2.** In erroneous uses. **a.** Used by Wyclif to render the cognate L. *sagum*, in the Vulgate with the sense of curtain. **b.** Used to render F. *soie* silk.

*c*1380 *Sir Ferumb.* 213 Olyuer tok his mantel of say [Fr. *son bliaut de soie*]. 1388 Wyclif *Exod.* xxvi. 7 Also thou schalt make enleuene saies [Vulg. *saga cilicina undecim*] to kyuere the hilyng of the tabernacle; the length of o say schal haue thretti cubitis. 1601 Holland *Pliny* I. 323 This is the making of that fine Say, whereof silk cloth is made [Fr. version: *Et c'est comme se fait la soye*].

3. *attrib.* and *Comb.*, as ***say apron, curtain, doublet, petticoat; say-maker, -making, -mill, -weaver***; also **say-cast** = COW-TAIL 2; †**say man,** a maker or seller of say; †**say-thicker,** a fuller of say.

1724 Ramsay *Tea-t. Misc.* (1733) I. 89 And ye's get a green *sey apron And wastcoat of the London brown. 1940 *Chambers's Techn. Dict.* 742/2 *Say-cast, the coarse part of a fleece, at the tail end. 1945 [see COW-TAIL 2]. 1531 *Rec. St. Mary at Hill* 352 Paid for mending of the *Say Curtens in þe quere, ij d. 1541 *Test. Ebor.* (Surtees) VI. 144 One *say dublett. 1654 in *Cal. St. Papers, Irel., Adventurers* (1903) 333 Isaac Key..*say-maker [delivered] three pieces of coloured sayes. 1632 *Contin. Foxe's A. & M.* 32/2 Following the trade of *Say-making. 1488–9 in *Finchale Priory Charters*, etc. (Surtees) p. ccclxxxiii, Et solvit Johanni Francis, *sayman, pro lez hallyngs de sago viridi. 1904 *Essex Rev.* July 154 To the south of the Church [of Dedham] stands a picturesque old Bay and *Say mill. 1636 Davenant *Wits* v. i, I have nothing on my Bed at home, But a thin Coverlet, and my wives *Sey Petti-coat. 1641 *Short Relat. Soap-Business* 18 Diers, Wool-Combers, *Saye-Thickers, and the like. 1644 *Canterbury Marriage Licences* (MS.), Peter de Graue..*say-weaver.

†**say,** *sb.*² *Obs.* Forms: 4–9 **say,** 5–6 **saye,** 6 **saie, seye,** 6–8 **sey.** [Aphetic form of ASSAY *sb.* It is often uncertain whether the word intended was *assay* or *say* with indefinite article.]

1. The action of testing the quality, fitness of a person or thing; = ASSAY *sb.* 1. In later use only *Sc.*, a probation.

*a*1400 *R. Brunne's Chron. Wace* (Rolls) 4028 (Petyt MS.) [þe note he couþe of alle layes,] & mynstralcie all þe saies [*v.r.* al þer assayes]. *c*1400 *Destr. Troy* 8063 There is no hope so vnhappy, þat hastes to noght, Ne so vnsikur at a say, as to set vppon wemen! 1637–50 Row *Hist. Kirk* (Wodrow Soc.) 299, I have alreadie given him to the Duke of Bulloigne ..but if that had not been, it might have been that yee should had a sey of him, but now it cannot be helped. 1733 P. Lindsay *Interest Scot.* 59 The Publick can suffer little by his Admission without a Sey; if he does not work well and cheap he'll find no Business.

2. Trial; trouble; tribulation. = ASSAY *sb.* 2.

1568 *Satir. Poems Reform.* xxxi. 78 For than ȝe knew thay wer ȝour fais, Bot now thay cum in freindis clais, Quhilk is ane sairer sey.

3. Experiment. ***to set*** (something) ***in a say***, to make experiment of. = ASSAY *sb.* 3.

1390 Gower *Conf.* I. 229 Of suche men that now aday This vice setten in a say.

4. The testing of metals, in order to ascertain their standard of purity. = ASSAY *sb.* 6.

1577–87 Holinshed *Chron.* III. 1262/1 A piece of a blacke stone,..which being brought to certeine goldfiners in London to make a saie thereof, found it to hold gold. 1604 E. G[rimstone] *D'Acosta's Hist. Indies* IV. iv. 215 They cannot transport it [gold] from the Indies, for they can neither custome it, marke it, nor take say, vntill it be molten. 1669 Ld. Sandwich tr. *Barba's Metals* I. (1674) 121 All the Mines..in that Province have been found out, and first taken say of, by the Spaniards.

5. *Venery.* Trial of grease. = ASSAY *sb.* 9.

*c*1611 Chapman *Iliad* XIX. 246 There, hauing brought the Bore, Atrides with his knife tooke sey. 1686 Blome *Gentl. Recr.* II. 84 Then having sounded the Mot, or Morts, he that is to break him up (that is, to take say,) first, slits the Skin [etc.]. 1817 J. Mayer *Sportsman's Direct.* (ed. 2) 159 The first that is in cuts his throat, and takes say, which is, opening his belly, to see how fat he [a stag or buck] is.

b. *concr.* The cut in the flesh made in the process of taking say. ? Erroneous use: but cf. sense 9.

1855 Kingsley *Westw. Ho!* viii, You may lay your two fingers into the say there, and not get to the bottom of the fat.

6. A trial of food by taste or smell. = ASSAY *sb.* 10.

*c*1440 in *Househ. Ord.* (1790) 471 Take the laumpray, and wassh hym twyse or thries in lewe water,..sethe hym, and he schal be fresshe ynogh at a say. 1565 Cooper *Thesaurus, Degusto*,..to taste: to take a little saye. 1639 Massinger *Unnat. Combat* III. i, He ne're observ'd you..take A say of venison, or stale fowle by your nose.

7. The act of tasting food or drink before presenting it to a person of high rank. = ASSAY *sb.* 12.

1470 Henry *Wallace* VIII. 1274 A say scho tuk off all thyng at thai brocht. 1525 Ld. Berners *Froiss.* II. clxxxviii. 575 We toke the saye in the presence of the kinge. 1591 G. Fletcher *Russe Commw.* xxvi. 109 The taster..deliuereth it [*sc.* the cup] vnto him with a say, when hee calleth for it. 1647 Stapylton *Juvenal* 102 Let your wise guardians, e're you drink, take say. 1691 Wood *Ath. Oxon.* II. 519 The Kings dishes were brought up cover'd, the say was given, and all things were performed with satisfaction in that point.

b. *fig.*

1549 Coverdale, etc. *Erasm. Par. Heb.* vi. 1–6 Now (as it were) to take a saye & foretaste of the power of yᵉ worlde to come. 1600 Holland *Livy* V. xii. 188 Neither as yet is it for certaine knowne, why he..was counted a meet man to have handsell, or take sey of this new dignitie.

8. An attempt, an endeavour. = ASSAY *sb.* 13.

1568 T. Howell *Arb. Amitie* (1879) 45 Thus seeke all sayes hir sore to salue, by good and honest way. 1610 B. Jonson *Alch.* I. iii, This fellow, Captaine, Will come, in time, to be a great distiller, And giue a say..at the philosophers stone. 1637 C. Dow *Answ. to H. Burton* 212 To discover and prevent this their purpose before it had under-mined the present government of the Church, as no question it would have given a good say to it, if it had without controule proceeded as it began.

9. A trial specimen; a sample. = ASSAY *sb.* 17.

1530 Tindale *Answ. More* Wks. (1573) 279/2 To geue you a say or a taste what truth shall follow, he fayneth a letter sent from no man. 1656 in Irving *Hist. Dumbarton.* (1860) 535 Item, that neither prentis nor ither personne of the said craft be suffered to sett up ane bothe nor work in the said burgh till first he offers his sey to the said deacon and be fund worthy and able to be ane maister of the said craft.

10. Temper of metal. = ASSAY *sb.* 18.

1596 Spenser *F.Q.* VI. xi. 47 A sword of better say.

11. *attrib.* and *Comb.*, as (sense 7) ***say-taking***; **say-box,** the chest in which coins are deposited at the Mint for future examination at the Trial of the Pyx; **say-master** = ASSAY-MASTER; **say-piece,** anything chosen as an example of excellence.

1532 *Ld. Treas. Acc. Scotl.* VI. 103 To ane smytht for the of taking of the lok of the *say box. 1641 in R. W. Cochran-Patrick *Rec. Coinage Scotl.* (1876) I. Introd. 30 Item that the say box belong to him when it is broken vp quhich will not be much because that it conteins bot ane quartre of euerie say piece. 1721 Strype *Eccl. Mem.* II. II. iii. 266 The treasurer, comptroller and *seymaster of the late erected mints. 1680 Boyle *Scept. Chem.* VI. 401 This Gentleman having brought that Earth to the publick Say-Masters [etc.]. 1641 *Say piece [see above]. *a*1774 Fergusson *Ode to Gowdspink* Poems (1845) 20 Nae mair the rainbow can impart Sic glowin' ferlies o' her art, Whose pencil wrought its freaks at will On thee, the sey-piece o' her skill. 1788 in *Shirrefs's Poems* (1790) 341 With something of the comic vis, And, for a say-piece, not amiss. 1540 *St. Papers Hen. VIII*, VIII. 508 The Frenche King, and She also, was at the making seasoning and *saye taking of the said pasties. 1627 Hakewill *Apol.* IV. x. §2 (1630) 430 Dinner and supper was served in with all accustomed ceremonies, as sewing, water, grace, carving, say taking, &c.

†**say,** *sb.*³ *Obs.* exc. *dial.* Also 6, 9 **sey,** 8 **cea,** 9 **sae.** [Northern a. ON. *sá-r* cask (Sw. *så*, Da. *saa*, bucket), corresp. to OE. *saa* 'libitorium' (? read *libatorium*) in the Corpus Gloss. The midland form is SOE.] A bucket for domestic or other use, with two ears through which a pole may be passed as a handle.

1426 *Sc. Acts Jas. I* (1814) II. 12/2 Of þe samyn wyse [thair be ordanit] thre or four says to þe commoun vse. 1564 *Wills & Inv. N.C.* (Surtees 1835) 223, ij sayes & a chayre, xijᵈ. 1609 *Churchw. Acc. Pittington* (Surtees) 60 Item payed to James Rennet son for a say, iij s. 1752 *Rec. Elgin* (New Spald. Club 1903) I. 464 All tubs, ceas, kirns, kits, stoups, cogs and other cooper work. 1892 G. Stewart *Shetland Fireside Tales* (ed. 2) 247 She..set every tub an' sey 'at she could fin.

say (seɪ), *sb.*⁴ [f. SAY *v.*¹]

1. What a person says; words as compared with actions; also, a saying, dictum. *Obs.* exc. *poet.*

1571 *Satir. Poems Reform.* xxix. 30 ȝoʳ deid is not lyk ȝoʳ say. *a*1586 *Ibid.* xxxvii. 39 Bot, gif þei see ȝe sussie of þair sais, Blasone þai will, how ever ȝe behaue ȝou. 1644 Featly *Roma Ruens* 1 This hath been the say of all hereticks and schismaticks. 1741 Richardson *Pamela* (1824) I. 158 The poor woman has so little purity of heart, that it [the talk] is all say from her, and goes no farther than the ear. 1741 W. Wilson *Cont. Def. Reform. Ch. Scotl.* 87 The bare *Say* of Ministers..does not bind the Consciences of Church-members. 1872 Tennyson *Gareth & Lynette* 337 No boon is here, But justice, so thy say be proven true. 1885 Lyall *Anc. Arab. Poetry* 21 There rises a lord, to say the say, and do the deeds, of the noble. 1896 A. E. Housman *Shropshire Lad* lvii, You hearken to the lover's say, And happy is the lover.

2. A current saying, proverb, saw. Now chiefly *Sc.*

1602 Marston *Ant. & Mel.* III. Wks. 1856 I. 39 Tis an old say, Tis an old horse can neither wighy, nor wagge his taile. *c*1648–50 Brathwait *Barnabees Jrnl.* IV. (1818) 173 Now to Kirkland..May that say' be verified, 'Far from God, but neare the temple'. 1704 S. Knight *Jrnl.* 4 Oct. (1972) 14 So I remembered the old say, and suposed I knew Sarah's case. 1880 W. T. Dennison *Orcadian Sketch-Bk.* 7 A' to' hid's an' auld say an' a true say. 1923 R. L. Cassie *Heid or Hert* xii. 52 A' the says o' her deid midder wud come back tull her.

3. a. ***to have a say***: to have a 'voice' *in* a matter; to have the right to be consulted or the power to influence a decision.

1614 Jackson *Creed* III. 239 Shall they therefore haue no saye at all in deciding controuersies? 1823 'Jon Bee' *Dict. Turf* s.v., 'I have no say in the business'; no power one way or the other. 1865 *Pall Mall G.* No. 143. 5/1 You have no say in the matter. 1900 Gasquet *Eve of Reform.* iii. 52 Whether rightly or wrongly, those who found the money wished to have a say in its disposal. 1888 'R. Boldrewood' *Robbery under Arms* lii, One or two more people that had some say with the Government, was working back and edge for me.

transf. 1894 *Sat. Rev.* 17 Mar. 287 Buddha traditions had a good say in it.

b. ***to have the say***: to be in command. orig. *U.S.*

1838 *Jamestown* (N.Y.) *Jrnl.* 11 July 1/5 One thing I am determined on, and that is, that the folks who succeed best in hauling the Two Pollies in the stream shall have *the say* in rigging on her up for the voyage. 1902 Wister *Virginian* xiii, 'So you're acting foreman', said I. 'Why, somebody has to have the say, I reckon'. 1906 H. van Dyke *Ideals & Applic.* ii. 39 The men who have 'the say' about these subjects belong to the ruling classes. 1944 M. Paneth *Branch Street* 99, I had the 'say' now.

4. a. What one has intended or planned to say: chiefly in phrase ***to say*** (***out***) ***one's say.***

1692 R. L'Estrange *Fables* ci. 95 He had no sooner say'd out his Say, but [etc.]. 1768 Tucker *Lt. Nat.* (1834) I. 473 He would not interrupt me for fear I should not have time to say out all my say. 1782 Miss Burney *Cecilia* VI. i, For then we should have time to say all our say. **1808** Scott *Marm.* i. xxii, Well hast thou spoke: say forth thy say. **1816** Malcolm *Let.* in Smiles *Mem. J. Murray* (1891) I. 341, I have waited to the last, that I might condense all my *say* into one short sheet. **1819** Scott *Ivanhoe* xxxv, I have said my say. *a* **1843** Southey *Doctor* ccxxviii. (1848) 618, I shall say out my say in disregard of both. **1849** Thackeray *Pendennis* lxx, I have done my best, and said my say. **1859** Geo. Eliot *Adam Bede* xxxii, 'Yes, I know I've done it', said Mrs. Poyser; 'but I've had my say out, and I shall be th' easier for't all my life'. **1884** *Athenæum* 11 Oct. 461/1 [Professor Max Müller] has a knack of saying his say in a manner that renders the mere process of reading a pleasure.

b. *to have one's say*: to avail oneself of an opportunity of expressing one's views.

1858 Ruskin *Notes Royal Acad.* iv. 16, I merely pay tribute of admiration in passing, having had my say about Mr. Dobson's colour before. **1859** Meredith *R. Feverel* ix, Lobourne had its say on the subject. **1884** *Leeds Mercury* 24 Oct. 8/2 After one or two Peers had had their say on that subject, the Address was agreed to.

5. A talk *to* or *with* a person. Now *dial.*

1786 A. Gib *Sacr. Contempl.* II. i. vi. 206 The need of every perishing Sinner for whom he undertook had a Say to him before the Sinner's existence..; and to this Say he was most graciously attentive. **1894** Baring-Gould *Kitty Alone* I. 83 There's some one wants to have a say with you.

say (seɪ), *v.*[1] Forms: see below. [OE. *sęcgan*, pa. t. *sæȝde*, corresp. to OFris. *sega*, *sedza* (mod.Fris. *sizze*), OS. *seggian*, pa. t. *sagda* (MLG. *seggen*, MDu. *seggen*, *sagen*, Du. *zeggen*), OHG. *sagên*, pa. t. *sagita*, *segita* (MHG., mod.G. *sagen*), ON. *segja*, pa. t. *sagða*; repr. OTeut. **sagǣjan*, **sagjan*:—pre-Teut. **sokēi-*. The root is perh. WIndo-germanic **soq*^{u}*-*: **seq*^{u}, found in Lith. *sakýti*, OSl. *sočyti* to say, Gr. ἔννεπε imper. (:—**en-seq*^{u}*e* = OLatin *inseque*, *insece*), ἐνισπεῖν aorist inf., to tell, say, L. *inquam* I say (:—**in-squ-am*).

The normal mod.Eng. phonetic representative of the OE. inf. *sęcgan* (or the 1st sing. pres. *sęcge*) would have been **sedge*. As in the case of buy *v.*, lie *v.*[1], the mod. form comes from OE. forms which had *ȝ* (palatal) instead of *cg*, as imp. *seȝe*, *sæȝe*, 2nd sing. pres. ind. *seȝest*, *sæȝst*, 3rd sing. pres. ind. *seȝeð*, *sæȝð*. The *ȝ* represents WGer. *g*, and the *cg* WGer. *gg*; the OTeut. stem **sagj-* having become by phonetic law in W.Ger. **saggj-* before an inflexional suffix beginning with a vowel, and **sagi-* in any other position. In Middle English, alongside the tendency, which ultimately prevailed, to extend the stem *seȝ-*, *sei-*, *sai-* (:—OE. *seȝ-*) to all parts of the verb, there existed an opposite tendency to extend the stem *segg-* beyond its etymological limits. Hence most of the parts of the verb (though not the pa. t.) had two widely divergent forms, the distribution of which does not closely correspond to dialectal divisions. In some northern poetry the two forms occasionally occur in juxtaposition as distinct words (e.g. 'Tille I haue seggid and saide all my sawe', *York Myst.* xxxii. 16). In Robert of Brunne the form *segge*, **sedge* (implied in *sedgeyng*) seems to be appropriated to the sense 'recite' (as a minstrel): see sayer 1, saying 1.]

A. Inflexional Forms.

1. *Infinitive* **say** (seɪ). Forms: *α.* 1 secgan, secggan, -ean, sæcgan, sæcg(g)ean, 1–2 secgean, seggan, 2 seggon, secgen, -on, segcean, secgen, 2–4 segge(n, siggen, suggen, 2–5 sigge, 3 seuggen, sucgen, suge(n, seg, 3–4 sugge, *Kent.* zigge, zygge, 5 sygge, 6 *dial.* zedge. Also *Dative Infinitive* 1 to secgenne, -anne, 2 to seggan(n)e, 2–4 to seggen(e, *Kent.* to ziggene. *β.* 2 sæȝen, sæin, 2–3 seien, seȝen, 2–5 sei(e, 3 seiȝen, 3–5 sai, 4 seyen, saien, seiȝ(e, (? *erron.* sy), 4–5 seyn(e, sein, 4, 6 *Sc.* sa, 4–6 sayn, sey(e, saie, saye, 4–5, (6–7 *arch.* in rimes) sayne, saine, 4–5, (6, 9 *arch.*) sain, 6 sayen, (*erron.* sene), 8–9 *dial.* zay, 3– say. Also *Dative Infinitive* 4–5 to seyne, 4, 6 to saine, 5 to sane, to seinge, to sein, to seynt, 5–6 sayne.

α. *Beowulf* 880 þonne he swulces hwæt secgan wolde. *c* **1175** *Lamb. Hom.* 67 þenne muȝe we wenen and seggen þus. *c* **1205** Lay. 18377 þe king.. bad Gorlois suggen [*c* **1275** segge] his iwille. *c* **1250** *Kent. Serm.* in *O.E. Misc.* 28 We mowe sigge þet stor signefieþ þe herte. **1340** *Ayenb.* 134 þet is to ziggene. **1340–70** *Alisaunder* 1033 Now will I cease þis sawe & segge you more Of hym þat hight Alisaunder. **1393** Langl. *P. Pl.* C. xiii. 30 For to seggen as thei seen. *c* **1425** *Seven Sag.* (P.) 1708 To loke what he wolde sygge. **1553** *Respublica* v. vii. 14 (Brandl) Iche maie zedge to yowe, Is fearde pulling owte my throte.

β. *a* **1122** *O.E. Chron.* an. 1070 (Laud MS.) þa herdon þa munecas of Burh sæȝen þæt [etc.]. **1154** *Ibid.* an. 1137 ⁋ 5 Suilc & mare þanne we cunnen sæin. *c* **1250** *Gen. & Ex.* 2494 Vs he ðis bodewurd seiȝen bead. *a* **1300** *Cursor M.* 12813 Quat þan sal we sai to þaim? [*v.rr.* sayne; sai; sey]. *c* **1300** *Havelok* 2886 þe erl ne wolde nouth ageyn þe kinge be.., Ne of þe spusing seyen nay. *c* **1350** *Will. Palerne* 60 So, forto seiȝ al þe soþe so faire þei glosed, þat [etc.]. *c* **1368** Chaucer *Compl. Pite* 77 (Tanner MS.) Ther is no more to seyn [*v.rr.* seye, seyne]. *c* **1375** *Sc. Leg. Saints* xl. (*Ninian*) 276 For ocht þat he cuth sa ore do. *c* **1400** *Brut* lix. 55 The v kyng hade Merchemeriche, þat is to seynt, þe Erldome of Nichol. *c* **1420–30** ? Lydg. *Compleynt* 99 in *Temple Glas* (E.E.T.S.) 60 And of on thyng, soth for to seyne, I haue gret mater to compleyne. *a* **1450** *Knt. de la Tour* cxiii. (1906) 153 Syn the nwe testament, that is to sein, sen God was borne of the holy mayden Marie. **1513** Douglas *Æneis* i. Prol. 219 Eneuch thairof, now will I na mair sayne. *Ibid.* i. vi. 138 Venus na mair sufferit him plene nor sa. *a* **1547** Surrey in *Tottel's Misc.* (Arb.) 20, I dare well sayen. **1621** Bp. Mountagu *Diatribæ* 118 To say bo to a battledore. *a* **1643** Cartwright *Ordinary* ii. ii. (1651) 62 Ah benedicite I might soothly sayne. **1865** Swinburne *Poems & Ball.*, *Q. Bersabe* 345 Lord God, alas, what shall I sain?

2. *Indicative Present.* **a.** *1st pers. sing.* **say** (seɪ). Forms: *α.* 1 secge, (segce), secgge, sæcge, 2–5 segge, 3 sucge, seuge, sige, 3–4 sugge, 3–5 sigge, 4 suge, sege, sygge. *β.* 3 seie, 3–4 sai, 4 seiȝe, seȝe, 4–5 sey(e, sei, 4–6 saye, 5–6 saie, (*in rime pseudo-arch.* 5 sayne, 6 sane), 8–9 *dial.* zay, 3– say.

α. **971** *Blickl. Hom.* 69 Soþ is þæt ic eow secgge, þæt [etc.]. *c* **1200** Ormin 16632 To fulle soþ I segge þe. *c* **1205** Lay. 2979 Þis ich sucge [*v.r.* segge] þe to seoðe. *Ibid.* 2985 Ich þe Gornoille seuge. *c* **1250** *Kent. Serm.* in *O.E. Misc.* 30 Ine sigge nacht þet hi ne hedden þer before ine him beliaue. *a* **1275** *Prov. Ælfred* 706 ibid. 138 Hic ne sige nout bi þan, þat moni ne ben gentile man. *c* **1300** *Harrow. Hell* 171 (Digby MS.) Adam, nou i sege hit þe, To-day þou salt alesed be. *c* **1394** *P. Pl. Crede* 390 And þerfore, leue leel man leeue þat ich sygge. *c* **1400** *Solomon's Bk. Wisdom* 203 Riȝth to heuen ne segge ich nouȝth þat he euer come.

β. *a* **1300** *Cursor M.* 28036, I sai [*v.r.* say] noght þis þoqueþer of alle. **1362** Langl. *P. Pl.* A. i. 182 For-þi I seiȝe as I seide er be siȝte of þise tixtes. *c* **1374** Chaucer *Troylus* iv. 769 A by-word here I saye, That, 'rotelees, mot grene sone deye'. *c* **1400** *Gamelyn* 447 (Skeat), I say it for me,.. yuel mot I the! *a* **1450** *Knt. de la Tour* ix. (1906) 13 For y saie you alle, who that dothe a dedly synne [etc.]. *c* **1485** *E.E. Misc.* (Warton Club) 48 Furth he went, as y ȝow sayne. **1513** Douglas *Æneis* iii. ix. 96 For, quhow grislie and quhow greit I ȝow sane Lurkis Poliphemus. **1530** Palsgr. 696/2, I saye, I tell or speake a thyng.

b. *2nd pers. sing.* **sayest** ('seɪɪst), **sayst** (seɪst). Forms: *α.* 1 seȝst, saȝast, 2 sæȝst, 2–5 seist, 3 seiist, seiest, *Ormin* seȝȝst, 3–5 seyst, 3–6 seiste, 4 *Kentish* zayst, 4–7 saist, 5 (*erron.* seyth, seith), 3– sayst, 6– sayest. Also (*chiefly north.*) 3–5 sais, says, 4–5 seis, 5 sayes, seyes. *β.* 3 *Ormin* seggesst (*gg* = (dʒ)), 4 siggest, (seggez), 5 seggest, seggist.

α. **971** *Blickl. Hom.* 179 On þone þu leoȝende saȝast þæt þu sie þæt he is. *c* **1175** *Lamb. Hom.* 39 þenne þu seist *Dimitte* [etc.]. *c* **1200** Ormin 5188. *a* **1225** *Juliana* 11 (Bodl. MS.) Beo hit soð þat tu seiist [*v.r.* seist]. *a* **1250** *Owl & Night.* 1075 (Jesus MS.) Hwat seystu [*v.r.* seistu] þis for myne schome. **1297** R. Glouc. (Rolls) 10792 Wat seiste quaþ þis gode erl. *a* **1300** *Cursor M.* 965 He said, 'adam, now wel sais þou.' **1382** Wyclif *Mark* xv. 1 Thou seyst. **1432–50** tr. *Higden* (Rolls) I. 227 Alle thynges be to vs bare and open that thow seyes. *c* **1450** *Merlin* 17 We may neuer bileve that this be trewe that thow seiste. ? **1548** tr. *Viret's Expos. XII Art. Chr. Faith* A iv b, The thynge is euen as thou sayest. **1579** Lyly *Euphues* (Bond) I. 321 Moreouer thou saist that [etc.]. **1667** Milton *P.L.* v. 815 Unjust thou saist Flatly unjust, to bind with laws the free. **1741–2** Gray *Agrip.* 85 Say'st thou I must be cautious, must be silent. **1831** Scott *Ct. Robert* xix, 'Thou say'st a painful truth', said Count Robert.

β. *c* **1200** Ormin 1512. **13..** *E.E. Allit. P.* B. 621 'Fare forthe', quod þe frekez, '& fech as þou seggez'. **1402** *Jack Upland's Rejoinder* in *Pol. Poems* (Rolls) II. 72 The secte that thou seggist of.

c. *3rd pers. sing.* **says** (sɛz), *arch.* **saith** (sɛθ). Forms: *α.* 1 seȝ(e)þ, sæȝ(e)þ, sæiȝð, saȝað, 2 seȝð, sæȝð, 2 seigð, 2–3 sæið, seið, seieð (occas. written seid, seied), 2–5 seith, 3 sehð, sæið(e, *Ormin* seȝ(ȝ)þ, 3–4 seithe, 3–5 seyth, 4 *Kent.* zayþ, zaiþ, (2–3 seit, 3 seiet, 4 seyt), 4–5 seythe, 5–6 sayth, 6 saythe, saieth, 6–7 sayeth, 3– (now *arch.*) saith. Also (with ending orig. *north.*) 3–6 sais, 4 seys, (sas), 4–5 seis, sayse, saise, 4–7 sayes, 5 ? seysse, 5, 7 saies, 6 sayis, 9 *dial.* ses, sez, 4– says. *β.* 3 suggeð, 3–4 seggeþ. Also 4 sigges, 5 segges.

α. **971** *Blickl. Hom.* 27 Her saȝaþ Matheus se godspellere þætte [etc.]. *Ibid.* 55 Her seȝþ hu se æþela lareow wæs sprecende. *a* **1175** *Cott. Hom.* 239 þan seied ham god..ȝe senegeden an ȝeur ecenesse [etc.]. *c* **1175** *Lamb. Hom.* 45 Eft ure lauerd seolf seit. *Maledictus homo* [etc.]. *c* **1200** Ormin 10306 He seȝȝþ uss þatt [etc.]. *a* **1250** *Owl & Night.* 1072 (Jesus MS.) Wel viht þat wel spekþ seyþ in þe songe. *a* **1300** *Cursor M.* 8282 Als sais [*v.rr.* sas, saise, seiþ] þe stori. *c* **1320** *Sir Tristrem* 1545 He seyt he haþ don þis. *c* **1330** R. Brunne *Chron. Wace* (Rolls) 14779 But þat seynt Bede of þem alle seys, Elles schulde non haue knowe what weys. **1340** *Ayenb.* 134 Ase zaiþ zainte paul. **13..** *Seuyn Sag.* (W.) 2925 Opon the morn, the stori sayse, The knight toke horses and hernays. *c* **1500** *Melusine* vi. 28 Thystory saith, that [etc.]. **1508** Dunbar *Flyting* 133 He sayis [etc.]. **1523** Ld. Berners *Froiss.* I. ccclxxxvi. 661 If it be as he dothe, it is as he saythe. **1590** Greene *Orl. Fur.* (1599) B 2, What sayes the mightie Mandrecard? **1600** in *Shaks. Cent. of Praise* 35 He sayeth that [etc.]. *a* **1631** Donne *Poems* (1650) 9 Who saies my teares have overflow'd his ground? **1750** Gray *Long Story* 73 So Rumour says. **1819** Scott *Ivanhoe* xxxiv, For what saith holy writ.

β. **1205** Lay. 28818 Swa alse þe boc us suggeð. *c* **1275** *Ibid.* 10500 þe king þe greteþ Basan an seggeþ mid sore þat [etc.]. *a* **1375** *Joseph Arim.* 209 þenne spekes a vois and on heiȝ sigges, 'king [etc.]'. *c* **1440** *York Myst.* xxxiii. 98 Agayne Sir Cesar hym selfe he segges and saies [etc.].

d. *plural* **say** (seɪ). Forms: *α.* 1 secg(e)að, seggað, sæcg(e)að, secggaþ, 2–4 siggeþ, seggeþ, 3 sug(g)eð, segeþ, (segget); 1 segge (*we*), 2–4 segge, 4 *Sc.* sigge, 4–5 seggen. *β.* 4 seith, 4 seyth (occas. written seyt), seyithe. Also *north.* 3–6 sais, 4 seis, saise, 5 seise, 6 says, 6–7 sayes. *γ.* 3–4 seiȝen, 3–6 sey(e)n, 4 sein, 4–5 seyne, sain, 4–6 sayn(e, seien, 5 saien, 5 (6–7 *arch.*) saine, 5–6 sane, sayen, (9 *dial.* sen); 3–4 sai, seie, 4–5 sey, sei, 4–6 saye, 5–6 saie, (8–9 *dial.* zay), 4– say.

α. **971** *Blickl. Hom.* 125 Swylce eac we leorniaþ, men, þæt þa men secgaþ..þæt [etc.]. *a* **1175** *Cott. Hom.* 237 Of þe folce we siggeð þat hit cumþ fastlice fram middenardes. *c* **1205** Lay. 24275 Summe bokes suggeð [*v.r.* seggeþ] to iwisse þat [etc.]. *c* **1275** *Ibid.* 27480 For al so segge [*v.r.* suggeð] þe writes þat witty men dihte. **1377** Langl. *P. Pl.* B. xi. 425 'ȝe seggen soth', quod I.

β. *a* **1300** *Cursor M.* 343 Als clerkes sais þat are wis He wroght noght first wit partis. *Ibid.* 6697 Til hir husband men aght to giue Mendes þat men sais es right. *c* **1320** R. Brunne *Medit.* 675 Sum seyþ, 'saue þy selfe, ȝyf þou kunne'. **1563** Winȝet tr. *Vincentius Lirinensis* Wks. (S.T.S.) II. 76 We al says the samyn.

γ. *c* **1250** *Gen. & Ex.* 917 Ebruis seiȝen, wune hem wex [etc.]. *a* **1300** *Cursor M.* 14689 Gas lokes þe bokes o your lai, And vnderstandes quat þai sai. *c* **1320** *Sir Tristrem* 3220 þai leiȝen al bi dene þat sain he dar nouȝt fiȝt Wiþ his fo. **1362** Langl. *P. Pl.* A. vii. 122 ȝif hit beo soþ þat ȝe seyen. *c* **1400** *Destr. Troy* 277 Sum sayn full sure.. Hit was þe formast on flete þat on flode past. ? **1404** *26 Pol. Poems* 17/72 In sykernes may he go, and recche neuere what men say. **1422** tr. *Secreta Secret., Priv. Priv.* 196 Morouer hit is not to beleue to folys that Sayne that [etc.]. *c* **1460** Fortescue *Abs. & Lim. Mon.* xvii. (1885) 152 To this sane [*v.rr.* sayn, sayen] suche lordes on oþer men. *c* **1485** Caxton *Sonnes of Aymon* xxii. 481 Wene ye that I shall do that ye saye for fere of deth? **1504** in I. S. Leadam *Sel. Cases Crt. Requests* (1898) 9 And the saide Executours further seyen that [etc.]. **1513** Bradshaw *St. Werburge* i. 358 As dyuers auctours sayne. **1552** Lyndesay *Monarche* 6032 Than sall one Fyre, as Clerkis sane, Mak all the hyllis and valais plane. **1579** J. Stubbes *Discov. Gaping Gulf* C 5 b, A new match betweene hym and Marguerit daughter of a French Charles, as most men saien. **1581** Pettie tr. *Guazzo's Civ. Conv.* i. (1586) 11 What saie you of this? **1602** Breton *Mother's Blessing* B 4 b, But harken to the shepheards what they saine, Both of the Sunshine, and a showre of raine. **1614** B. Jonson *Barth. Fair* ii. ii, They say, a fooles handsell is lucky.

3. *Indicative past.* **a.** *1st and 3rd pers. sing.* **said** (sɛd). Forms: 1–2 sæȝde, (1 saȝode), 1–3 sæde, 2 saiȝde, sæide, 2–4 sede, sade, 2–5 seide, 2, 5–7 sed, 3 seaide, sæide, *Ormin* seȝȝde, 3–5 seyde, seid, 3–6 sayde, 3–7 saide, 4 seyede, seȝede, *Kentish* z(e)ayde, *Sc.* sad, 4–5 seyd, 4–7 sayd, 5 seyed, 5–7 saied, 5–7 sayed, 3– said.

c **1000** Ælfric *Saints' Lives* (1900) II. 322 þe þis gehyrde eall and hit eft sæde swa swa. *c* **1175** *Lamb. Hom.* 77 And þet hali meiden onswerede and seide [etc.]. *c* **1200** *Moral Ode* 131 (Trin.) Drihte self hit sade. *c* **1205** Lay. 1256 He þoute ..hou þe læfdi him sæide. *a* **1250** *Owl & Night.* 235 (Jesus MS.) For Alured king hit seyde [*v.r.* seide] & wrot. **13..** *K. Alis.* 1375 (W.) Yef ony saide no. *a* **1352** Minot *Poems* (ed. Hall) i. 46 Philip Valays..said he suld þaire enmys sla. *c* **1375** *Sc. Leg. Saints* i. (*Petrus*) 83 He sad, he subuertit nocht. *c* **1400** *Destr. Troy* 11259 þen þe traytur Antenor..to þe fre sayde. *c* **1400** Maundev. (1839) viii. 98 A chirche, where the Aungel seyde to oure Lady of hire Dethe. *c* **1440** *Generydes* 64 She seid he was welcome. *c* **1450** Myrc *Festial* 168 By vertu of þe holy wordys þat þe prest sayed þer. **1562** Winȝet *Cert. Tractates* Wks. (S.T.S.) II. 55 He sayd nocht, the thingis haldin of hald. *c* **1610** *Women Saints* 50 He..with execration sayed: 'If I haue committed this theft [etc.]'. **1611** Bible *Exod.* viii. 25 And Pharaoh..said, Goe yee [etc.]. **1632** Milton *L'Allegro* 103 She was pincht, and pull'd she sed. **1766** Gray *Kingsgate* 17 'Ah!' said the sighing peer, 'had Bute been true'.

b. *2nd pers. sing.* **saidest** ('sɛdɪst), **saidst** (sɛdst). Forms: 1 sæȝdest, sædest, 3 *Ormin* seȝȝdesst, (3–4 said, saide), 4–5 seidest, seydest, 5 seidist, saydes, 6–7 sayd'st, 6– saidst, 9– saidest.

c **1200** Ormin 8660 Acc do swa summ þu seȝȝdesst. *a* **1300** *Cursor M.* 15661 þou said [*v.rr.* saide, seidest] for me if mister war, to ded thole suld þou fight. *c* **1374** Chaucer *Troylus* i. 919 So seydestow ful ofte. *a* **1375** *Joseph Arim.* 224 þou..siþen seidest to me mi preyere scholde sitte. *c* **1450** Myrc *Festial* 19 Ryght as þou saydes, hit ys fallen! **1535** Coverdale *Ps.* lxxxix. 19 Thou..saydest [etc.]. **1596** Shaks. *1 Hen. IV*, ii. iv. 218 What, foure? thou sayd'st but two, euen now. **1850** Mrs. Browning *Felicia Hemans* ii, No need of flowers—albeit 'bring flowers', thou saidest.

c. *plural.* **said** (sɛd). Forms: 1 sæȝdun, seȝdon, 1–2 sæȝdon, sædon, -an, 2 saiȝden, sæden, sæidon, seidon, 2–3 seden, saden, 2–5 seiden, 3 sæiden, *Ormin* seȝȝdenn, 3, 5 sayden, 3–5 saiden, seyden, 4–5 saidon, 5 saydyn, -on; 3–4 sede, 3, 5 seyde, 3–5 seid(e, saide, 3, 5–6 sayde, 4 *Kentish* zede, 3– said.

c **900** tr. *Bæda's Hist.* v. x. (1890) 416 Seȝdon þæt hio hefdon nyt ærende. *c* **950** *Lindisf. Gosp.* Mark xiv. 57, & summ monn aras leas gecyðnise sæȝdon [*c* **975** *Rushw.* sæȝdun; *c* **1000** *Ags. Gosp.* sædon, *v.r.* sæȝdon; *c* **1160** *Hatton* saiȝden] wið him cuoeðendo. **1154** *O.E. Chron.* an. 1135, Men.. sæden ð[at] micel þing sculde cumen her efter. *c* **1175** *Lamb. Hom.* 89 þa seiden þa iudeiscen men a bismer. *c* **1205** Lay. 15600 þa cnihtes biliue comen to þan reue & þus him to sæiden. *c* **1340** *Ayenb.* 59 Ase we zede hyerbeuore. *a* **1352** Minot *Poems* (ed. Hall) i. 43 þai said it suld ful dere be boght. *c* **1386** Chaucer *Man of Law's T.* 113 Diuerse men diuerse thynges seyden. *c* **1400** *Destr. Troy* 12643 Yet thies lyghers.. Saidon the same kyng..þat [etc.]. *c* **1420** *Chron. Vilod.* 1713 þe lordus..saydon: Etheldrede oȝte not to be kynge. *c* **1449** Pecock *Repr.* ii. ix. 198 Thei maden hem a calf of siluer, and seiden that it was her God. **1470–85** Malory *Arthur* i. iii–v. 40 Letters there were wryten in gold aboute the swerd that saiden thus. **1662** J. Davies tr. *Olearius Voy. Amb.* 274 An accompt of what they said concerning [etc.].

4. *Subjunctive Present* **say.** Forms: *sing.* 1 secg(g)e, sæcge, 3 segge, sugge, sigge, 3, 6 saie, 4 sa, 4–5 sey(e, seie, 5– say. *Plural* 1 secg(g)an, secgen, secgeon, sæcgan, sæggon, 2–3 seggen, 3 sey, 4 sa, 5– say.

971 *Blickl. Hom.* 179 þa cwæþ Petrus, 'Secge Simon me nu, ȝif [etc.]'. *c* **1200** Ormin 9272, & lokeþþ wel þatt ȝure nan Ne segge þuss wiþþ worde [etc.]. *c* **1205** Lay. 13888 Ich ileue þe cniht þæt þu me sugge soð riht. *a* **1225** *Ancr. R.* 8 Sigge so monie [*sc.* beoden],..se heo euer wule. *c* **1275** *Passion our Lord* 523 in *O.E. Misc.* 52 þat his disciples..ne..seggen to þe volke.. He is aryse from deþe. **1390** Gower *Conf.* I. 103 What as evere that ye seie Riht as ye wole so wol I. *c* **1462** *Wright's Chaste Wife* 440 If he sey to the any þing He schall haue sorowe vn-sowte. **1513** DOUGLAS *Æneis* XI. ix. 36 Sytand at eys ilkane say his entent.

5. *Imperative* **say.** Forms: (*a*) *sing.* 1 **saᵹa, seᵹe, sæᵹe,** 2 **seȝe,** 3 **sæiȝe, sæi, saie, seiȝe,** *Ormin* **seȝȝ,** 3–4 **sei, sa,** 3–5 **sey(e, sai, seie,** 3–6 **saye,** 4 *Kentish* **zay,** (6 *pseudo-arch.* **saine),** 3– **say.**

971 *Blickl. Hom.* 233 Sæᵹe us þæt hrædlice. *a* **1000** [see B. 6]. *c* **1200** ORMIN 9299 Lef maȝȝstre, seȝȝ uss nu þin raþ. *c* **1205** LAY. 2269 Seie [*v.r.* sei] me Locrin, Saie me læðe mon. *Ibid.* 30283 Sæiȝe me biliue hu þe beon on siðe. *c* **1275** *Passion our Lord* 585 in *O.E. Misc.* 54 Saye heom þat ich astye to mynes vader riche. *a* **1300** *Cursor M.* 11964 Sai [*v.r.* say] þou; i der noght til him speke. **1340** *Ayenb.* 1 Zay þis þet uolȝeþ. **1513** DOUGLAS *Æneis* VI. v. 46 Say me, virgyne, quod Enee. *a* **1600** ? RALEIGH in *Eng. Helicon* L 3, Yet what is Loue, good Sheepheard saine? **1742** GRAY *Eton* 21 Say, father Thames! for thou hast seen Full many a sprightly race.

(*b*) *plural.* α. 1 **secg(g)að, seggað,** 2 **secgeð,** 2–3 **seggeð,** 3 **suggeð, siggeð, segget, segge.** β. 4 **seiȝth,** 4–5 **sayeth,** 5 **seith, seieþ, sayth(e.** Also *north.* 3–5 **sais,** 4 **saise, seys,** 5 **says.** γ. 3–4 **sai,** 4 *Sc.* **sa,** 4–6 **sey,** 5 **saie, seie,** 4, 6– **say.**

971 *Blickl. Hom.* 71 Secgaþ Siones dohtrun þæt heora cining cymeþ. *c* **1205** LAY. 865 Suggeð [*v.r.* Seggeþ] me to runun ræd þæt eou þunche. *a* **1250** *Owl & Night.* 116 (Jesus MS.) Seggeþ [*v.r.* Segge] me if ye hit wiste. *a* **1300** *Cursor M.* 5092 To fotte mi fader sal yee fund, And sais him i am hale and sund. *c* **1440** *York Myst.* xxxi. 146 Saie! beene venew in bone fay, Ne plesew et a parle remoy. **1450** FASTOLF in *Paston Lett.* I. 130 And sey hem on my half that they shall be qwyt. *c* **1728** EARL OF AILESBURY *Mem.* 626, I concluded with an old English term, 'Say, and keep to what you say'.

6. *Present Participle* **saying** ('seɪɪŋ). Forms: α. 1 **secg(g)ende,** 2–3 **seggende.** β. 2–4 **seinde,** 3–4 **saiand,** 4–6 **sayand(e,** 5 **seiand, sayn;** 4 **seyyng(e, seiynge, -enge,** 4–5 **seyinge,** 4–6 **saiyng, sayng, seying,** 5 **seiyng, seyng, seing, sainge, sayinge, saynge, saenge, saiynge, seyȝing,** 5–6 **saieng, seynge, seyenge,** 6 **say-, saieng(e, saing,** 7 *dial.* **zaying,** 3– **saying.**

α. **971** *Blickl. Hom.* 161 Hie pære soþfæstnesse spellodan & tacen secgende wæron, þa þe Drihten sylf getacnode. *c* **1200** *Trin. Coll. Hom.* 93 þus sit seggende, *Venite.*

β. *a* **1300** *Cursor M.* 17672 And als i stod saiand mi bede. *c* **1320** R. BRUNNE *Medit.* 228 He..cumforted hem ful feyre, seyyng [etc.]. *c* **1380** WYCLIF *Wks.* (1880) 3 Seiynge..þat crist tauȝte not his disciples..þe beste ordre and religioun. *c* **1400** *Rule St. Benet* (Prose) lxiv. 42 Sayng in þis wise [etc.]. **1426** LYDG. *De Guil. Pilgr.* 7008 Grace dieu seyng to me. *a* **1450** *Knt. de La Tour* viii. (1906) 11 A uoys come to her saieng [etc.]. **1460** CAPGRAVE *Chron.* (Rolls) 32 Josue..spak with God seiand swech wordes on to him. **1500–20** DUNBAR *Poems* xxviii. 3, I dremed ane angell came fra Hevin, With plesand stevin sayand [etc.]. **1535** COVERDALE *Zech.* iv. 4 So I..spake to the angel yᵗ talked with me, sayenge: O my lorde [etc.]. **1549** (Mar.) *Bk. Com. Prayer, Matins* A iv b, The priest standyng vp and saiyng. Let vs praye. **1664** J. WILSON *A. Comenius* v. vi, What was you saying?

7. *Past Participle* **said** (sɛd). Forms: α. 1 **(ᵹe-)sæᵹd, (ᵹe-)sæd,** 2 **ȝesed, iseȝd,** 2–3 **isæd, isæid(e, isait, i-, yseit,** 3–4 (6 *arch.*) **y-sed, i-sed,** (4 *Kent.* **y-zed),** 4 **ysade, y-sayd,** 2–5 **(y-, i-) seid(e,** 5–7 **sayed,** 6 **saied, say'd, seede,** 3–7 **sed,** 2– **said.** β. 5 **seggid.** γ. 6–7 (*chiefly in rimes*) **saine.** δ. 5 **seden, sadyn, saydyn.**

α. **971** [see B. 2 d]. *c* **1175** *Lamb. Hom.* 47 þeos ilke weord þe ic habbe her iseit. *c* **1200** *Trin. Coll. Hom.* 103 þus sit man on his sinne swo ich seid haue. *c* **1205** LAY. 11427 No here ich nenne godne ræd þe þe ȝet beo isæd. *c* **1250** *Owl & Night.* 395 (Jesus MS.) Vor heo ne myhte noht alegge þat þe vle hedde hire iseyd [*v.r.* ised]. **1297** R. GLOUC. (Rolls) 2126 As ichabbe ysed [*v.r.* yseit]. *a* **1300** *Cursor M.* 11261 Quen þai had sai(d) [*v.rr.* sayd, seid] þat þai wald sai. **13..** *E.E. Allit. P.* B. 353 Fro seuen dayez ben seyed I sende out bylyue. *c* **1330** *Arth. & Merl.* 525 (Kölbing) Mi deuise ich haue ysade. *c* **1386** CHAUCER *Knt.'s T.* 1010 If yow thynketh this is weel ysayd. **1390** GOWER *Conf.* I. 154 The king..hath al herd how sche hath said. *c* **1400** *Rule St. Benet* (Verse) 531 And when þai al þer sawes hafe saide [etc.]. **1432–50** tr. *Higden* (Rolls) VIII. 143 These wordes y-seide the develle evaneschede. *c* **1489** CAXTON *Sonnes of Aymon* xxvi. 560 All that they had sayed. **1515** in *Coll. Surrey Archæol. Soc.* (1858) I. 182, I will that there be seede..v masses. **1557** *Primer Sarum, Dirige* Ps. xxvi. I vij, My heart hath saied set vnto thee. **1560** DAUS tr. *Sleidane's Comm.* 94 b, The Ambassadours..were sayde naye. **1567** TURBERV. *Ovid's Ep.* 116 Alas, poore wretch, my Phaon I had very neare ysed. **1570** *Satir. Poems Reform.* xix. 99 Christ hes it sed,..That kingdome sall come to greit ruyne. **1637** [see 2 b *passive*]. **1648** in *Nicholas Papers* (Camden) 97 Very much hath beene sayed..to make the Prince jealous [etc.]. **1682** SIR T. BROWNE *Chr. Mor.* III. ii, Nothing can be said hyperbolically of God. *a* **1699** LADY HALKETT *Autobiog.* (1875) 49 To take that upon him hee had never Saied.

β. (See B. 2 g.)

γ. **1592** GREENE *Alphonsus* 583 Wks. (Grosart) XIII. 354 [You] Shall well repent the words which you haue saine. **1610** G. FLETCHER *Christ's Tri.* II. 9 O depth, without a depth farre better seene then saine.

δ. **1422** tr. *Secreta Secret., Priv. Priv.* 207 Of the vertu of Iustice afor in this boke Is largely Saydyn. *Ibid.* [see B. 2 e]. *Ibid.* 131 Seden.

B. Signification.

In Eng., as in other Teut. langs., *say* is an approximate synonym of *speak*, from which it differs in having normally as its object a particular word or series of words, or a sentence representing the meaning of a particular series of words. Cf. L. *dicere* and its representatives in Romanic (which, however, have also senses that are now expressed in Eng. by *tell*), and L. *aio, inquam.*

As the word designates not the action of speaking itself, but its relation to the object, its use with reference to written expression does not ordinarily, like the similar use of *speak*, involve any consciousness of metaphor.

1. *a. trans.* To utter or pronounce (a specified word or words, or an articulate sound). Also, in wider sense, used of an author or a book, with quoted words as object. Also *fig.*, of things: to suggest, to indicate. Phrs. ***I won't*** (or ***wouldn't***) ***say no to*** (something, usu. a food or drink): I would like; ***to say the word***: see WORD *sb.* 7; ***who says ——?***, with an item of food as object: who would like ——?

For various idiomatic collocations, as *to say nay, to say bo, to say farewell*, etc., see the conjoined words.

For *as who saith, as who should say*, see AS and WHO.

c **1000** *Ags. Gosp.* Mark xiv. 58 We ᵹe-hyrdon hine secgan ic to-wurpe þis hand-worhte tempel [etc.]. *c* **1175** *Lamb. Hom.* 35 Soðliche he walde seggen ȝif he mihte speken, wa is me þet ic efre dude swa muchele sunne. *Ibid.* 41 And eft þe boc seið, Ne scule ȝe neure god don unforȝolden. *c* **1200** *Trin. Coll. Hom.* 5 To þe oðer wurð iseid þat loðeliche word. ..*Ite maledicti* [etc.]. *c* **1200** ORMIN 149, & Godess enngell seȝȝde himm to..Ne dred te, Zacariȝe. *c* **1330** R. BRUNNE *Chron. Wace* (Rolls) 11399 At ilka mattyng þei seide 'chek'. *c* **1386** CHAUCER *Prioress' Prol.* 11 He sayde,..'My lady Prioresse [etc.]'. *c* **1449** PECOCK *Repr.* II. xviii. 258 In this maner of colourid speche we seien: 'This ymage is Seint Peter [etc.]'. **1535** COVERDALE *Ps.* cxvi. 11, I sayde in my haist: All men are lyers. **1611** BIBLE *Judg.* xii. 6 Then said they vnto him, Say now, Shibboleth: and he said, Sibboleth. *a* **1714** J. SHARP *Serm.* Wks. (1754) IV. xviii. 309 A man that swears and curses to add grace to his discourse, might as well serve his purpose by repeating a word or two out of *propria quæ maribus*, or saying any scrap of pedlars French. **1821** DE QUINCEY *Richter* Wks. 1863 XIII. 121 Not whilst you can say Jack Robinson. **1872** CALVERLEY *Fly Leaves* (1884) 64 Is it not—(never, Eddy, say 'ain't it') A marvellous sight? **1898** J. D. BRAYSHAW *Slum Silhouettes* 158 'Who says pudden? Mister What's It—a little piece?' **1910** H. G. WELLS *Hist. Mr. Polly* vi. 193 Sit down, everyone... Who says steak-and-kidney pie? **1939** A. THIRKELL *Before Lunch* iv. 85, I wouldn't say no to toast and honey. **1958** V. H. COLLINS *Second Bk. Eng. Idioms* 194, *I won't say no*, I won't refuse.. often only a genteel way of saying 'Thank you'. **1970** P. LAURIE *Scotland Yard* iii. 68 To me drugs say beatniks, layabouts..kids going to ruin. **1972** A. ROSS *London Assignment* 33 His shirt said custom-made silk even at that distance.

†**b.** In *passive*, of a word: To be derived. Const. *of. Obs.*

1340 *Ayenb.* 93 Vor of crayme is yzed crist and of crist cristendom. *c* **1440** LYDG. *Hors, Shepe & G.* 57 *Eques ab 'equo'* is seid..And cheualere is seid of cheualrye. **1597** G. HARVEY *Trim. Nashe* To Rdr., Lent (you know) is saide of leane, because it macerates & makes leane the bodye.

c. With an inanimate item as subject: to communicate or represent; *esp.* of a clock, calendar, etc., to show (a certain time or date); of a notice, to state (a certain message).

1930 W. FAULKNER *As I lay Dying* 237 The clock said twenty past twelve. **1944** M. LASKI *Love on Supertax* xi. 103 On the door..Clarissa found a notice saying, 'Welfare Officer. Knock and enter.' **1951** W. FAULKNER *Requiem for Nun* II. i. 112 A clock on the wall says two minutes past two. **1973** W. J. BURLEY *Death in Salubrious Place* v. 105 The perpetual calender said Wednesday August 25th. **1975** S. JOHNSON *Urbane Guerilla* I. 23 A sign said, 'Statue of Liberty—ticket office other side of building.' **1975** *Language for Life* (Dept. Educ. & Sci.) vi. 88 To teach a child that 'kuh-a-tuh' says 'cat' is to teach him something that is simply incorrect.

2. To declare or state in words (a specified fact, thought, opinion, or intention). Said of a speaker, writer; also of a literary composition, a proverb, etc. Const. *to* (†in OE. and ME. simple *dative*).

a. with obj. a clause (introduced by *that*, or with ellipsis of *that*). Also *fig.*, *spec.* with a sum of money as subject, used as a formula to bet or wager *that* (something is the case).

971 *Blickl. Hom.* 9 Se engel hire sæᵹde þæt heo sceolde modor beon hire Scyppendes. *c* **1175** *Lamb. Hom.* 15 Monimon seið þet þa weren strotige [? *read* stronge] laȝe. *c* **1200** ORMIN 255 þiss Goddspell seȝȝþ þatt Sannt Johan Wass [etc.]. *c* **1386** CHAUCER *Sqr.'s T.* 199 They..seyde that it was lyk the Pegasee. *c* **1450** *St. Cuthbert* (Surtees) 6185 Men saide him þat it was not sothe. *c* **1460** *Towneley Myst.* ix. 137 Go grete hym well,..say hym I com. **1561** *Reg. Privy Council Scot.* I. 181 Thair is na law that sayis that Frenchmennis gudis unmarkit shall pertene be escheit to the Lard of Bargany. **1577** KENDALL *Flowers of Epigrammes* 18 Thou saist thou art as much my frend as any man can be. **1617** MORYSON *Itin.* I. 178, I formerly said that I bought a horse at Paduoa. **1657** W. COLES *Adam in Eden* cviii, Some say, that it [*sc.* Sundew] is a searing or caustick Herb, and very much biting. **1673** WYCHERLEY *Gent. Dancing-Master* III. i, What I have said I have said. **1829** K. H. DIGBY *Broadstone of Honour* I. 272 Gibbon says that the French Monarchy was created by the bishops of France. **1833** TENNYSON *Lady of Shalott* II. i, She has heard a whisper say A curse is on her if she stay. **1859** GEO. ELIOT *Adam Bede* xlix, It's your kindness makes you say I'm useful to you.

fig. a **1340** HAMPOLE *Psalter* ii. 10 ȝoure consciens sais to þᵗ ȝe doe wrange. **1606** SHAKS. *Ant. & Cl.* II. i. 11 My powers are Cressent, and my Auguring hope Sayes it will come to'th' full. **1954** W. TUCKER *Wild Talent* xii. 184 A dollar says you won't come back. **1962** D. LESSING *Golden Notebk.* II. 230 The set of his shoulders said that he was listening, so she went on. **1974** L. DEIGHTON *Spy Story* xviii. 194 'A quid,' I said. 'You're on,' said Ferdy... 'And I've got a pound that says you're wrong,' said Schlegel. That's how I lost two quid. **1975** J. GORES *Hammett* iii. 28 I've got twenty at four-to-seven that says the semifinal is a draw. **1976** *Listener* 8 Apr. 427/3 This same man has since been in contact, and wants to go on another job with us.. —which, to me, says that he is happy that what could be done was done under the circumstances at the time.

b. with obj. a pronoun or quasi-pronominal word or phrase. Also *transf.* and *fig.*, to convey, communicate; to mean; to indicate.

c **1000** *Ags. Gosp.* Luke xxiii. 3 Ða andswarude he þu hit seᵹst. *a* **1122** *O.E. Chron.* an. 1083, Hwæt maᵹon we secgean buton þæt hi scotedon swiðe. **1154** *Ibid.* an. 1135, Durste nan man sei to him naht bute god. *c* **1205** LAY. 1164 Brutus hit herde siggen þurh his sæ-monnen. *a* **1250** *Owl & Night.* 60 (Jesus MS.) If ich me holde in myne hegge Ne recche ich neuer hwat þu segge. *a* **1300** *Cursor M.* 12293 And he said noiþer ill ne god. *c* **1485** *Digby Myst.* (1882) III. 893 Wher haue ȝe put hym? Sey me thys. **1611** BIBLE *Luke* xiii. 17 And when hee had said these things, all his aduersaries were ashamed. **1677** WOOD *Life* (O.H.S.) II. 395 Dʳ. Bathurst is no great freind to the Masters, and hath said it often that many of them deserve to be put out of the house. **1710–11** SWIFT *Jrnl. to Stella* 1 Jan., What say you to that? **1795** *Gentl. Mag.* 542/2 A good deal has been said already in your Magazine in praise of Dr. Berkeley. **1840** J. H. NEWMAN *Par. Serm.* V. iii. 51 Let us aim at meaning what we say, and saying what we mean. **1868** HELPS *Realmah* xv. (1876) 394 Mauleverer only said that to tease you. **1881** H. JAMES *Portrait of Lady* I. xviii. 222 I'm afraid there are moments in life when even Beethoven has nothing to say to us. **1893** E. SALTUS *Madam Sapphira* 57 What would a Scotch and soda say to you? **1932** J. BUCHAN *Sir W. Scott* xii. 333 Venice, Tirol, Munich, Heidelberg said nothing to him. **1932** R. CAMPBELL *Pomegranates*, They change and tremble As the lips they most resemble When one red kiss is all they say. **1951** M. MCLUHAN *Mech. Bride* (1967) 80/2 By juxtaposition and contrast he is able to 'say' a great deal. **1955** M. LASKI *Apologies* 14 No, not actually like it, but—.. it just doesn't say anything to me. **1966** *Listener* 10 Nov. 694/1 A Californian who knew the difference between summer and fall, no matter what the skies and the thermometer say. **1977** H. FAST *Immigrants* v. 302, I raised a hundred and sixty thousand dollars of San Francisco money that says so. **1977** *Jrnl. R. Soc. Arts* CXXV. 602/1 Titian, in the nature of what he can and does 'say' is at least as close to Cézanne or Francis Bacon..as he is to Sannazaro or Aretino.

Proverbial phrase. **1377** LANGL. *P. Pl.* B. XVII. 17 For þough I seye it my-self I haue saued with þis charme Of men & of wommen many score þousandes. *c* **1485** *Digby Myst.* (1882) I. 139 Though I sey it my-self I am a man of myght. *a* **1592** GREENE *Geo. a Greene* 397 Wks. (Grosart) XIV. 139 Though I say it that should not say it. **1606** HEYWOOD *2nd Pt. If you know not me* (1609) C 3, Shall a yong man as I am, and though I say it, indifferent proper, goe [etc.]. **1736** SHERIDAN in *Swift's Lett.* (1768) IV. 181, I have written a little pretty birth-day poem against St. Andrew's day... It is a very pretty thing (although I say it that shouldn't say it). **1736** GRAY *Let.* Dec. (1900) I. 4 Though I say it, that should not say it, there positively is not one that has a greater esteem for you. **1817** KEATS *Let.* 4 Sept. (1958) I. 150 This here Beast though I say it as shouldn't..can sing. **1818** *Blackw. Mag.* II. 214/2 My adversary might find it, however, (though I say it that shouldn't say it) in the vulgar phrase, rather a *tough job.* **1834** *Tracts for Times* No. 22. 3, I think you, Sir, will allow that it was not badly contrived, though I say it, who should not say it. **1842** DICKENS *Let.* 1 May (1974) III. 229, I do believe, though I say it as shouldn't, that they [*sc.* Dickens's children] *are* good 'uns. **1863** H. E. P. SPOFFORD *Amber Gods* 148 Though I say it thet shouldn't say it. **1889** E. DOWSON *Let.* 5 Mar. (1967) 45, I recognize in it, thou' I say it as shouldn't what Pater calls 'a delicate tact of omission'. **1892** C. M. YONGE *Cross Roads* i. 13 Ours is reckoned one of the best choirs..though I say it as should not say it.

passive. a **1175** *Cott. Hom.* 233 þa þis was iseȝd. **1387** TREVISA *Higden* (Rolls) VII. 145 þe whiche i-seide, þe emperour i-smyten aȝen promoted hym sone into a bisshop. **1637** MILTON *Lycidas* 129 Besides what the grim Woolf with privy paw Daily devours apace, and nothing sed.

c. *impers.* or with indefinite subject: *it says* = the author or the book referred to says. Now *colloq.*

The use with quoted words as obj. (belonging formally to 1) and the absolute parenthetic use (cf. 3 a, b) are for convenience included here.

971 *Blickl. Hom.* 41 þonne sæᵹþ on þissum bocum þæt Drihten sylf cwæde þæt [etc.]. *a* **1225** *Ancr. R.* 182 Vor hwon heo is ipreoued, hit seið, heo schal beon ikruned mid te crune of liue. *a* **1300** *Cursor M.* 8818 þus þai fanded it tre dais, Als it in þe stori sais. *c* **1400** *Rule St. Benet* (Prose) v. 9 Als yure maistiresse leris yu, als it sais: 'Qui uos audit [etc.]'. **1840**, etc. [see IT *pron.* 3 f]. **1894** 'R. ANDOM' *We Three & Troddles* xv. 130 Giants are always wicked people. It says so in the children's books. **1900** B. PAIN *Eliza* 54 'You told me it was port!' 'So it is.' 'It says tonic port on the label.' **1977** S. BRETT *Star Trap* xii. 134 'Christopher Milton is thirty-eight, at least.' 'But it says in the programme—' 'Charles, Charles, you've been in the business too long to be so naïve.'

d. quasi-*impers.* in *passive*, with clause (expressed or understood from context) as real subject: *it is* (*has been, will be*) *said.* In pres. tense now chiefly = 'it is commonly said', 'people say'.

After *as* the pronoun *it* is now commonly omitted.

971 *Blickl. Hom.* 65 Sæᵹd is þæt hit sy wyrtruma ealra oþerra synna. *a* **1225** *Ancr. R.* 274 Flesches lust is fotes wunde, ase was feor iseid þeruppe. **1258** *Procl.* in Rymer *Fœdera* (1816) I. I. 378 Alswo alse hit is biforen iseid. *a* **1300** *Cursor M.* 4507 For lang was said, and yeit sua bes, Hert sun for-gettes þat ne ei seis. **1390** GOWER *Conf.* I. 15 Bot it is seid and evere schal, Betwen tuo Stoles lyth the fal. *c* **1449** PECOCK *Repr.* I. v. 23 As it is bifore seid in the iiijᵉ. argument. **1549** COVERDALE, etc. *Erasm. Par. Heb.* vii. 1–3 Melchisedech..who as it is said had neyther father, nor mother. **1780** *Mirror* No. 75 (1787) III. 6 In the very next paragraph it is said, 'We have the pleasure of informing the Public [etc.]'. **1798** GARTHSHERE in *Paget Papers* (1896) I. 140 Lady Cahir off with Sʳ J. Shelley—Lady Assia (as is said) do. in Ireland. **1804** WORDSW. *Margaret* 20 If things ensued that wanted grace, As hath been said, they were not base. **1859** TENNYSON *Elaine* 148 We hear it said That men go down before your spear at a touch. **1861** M. PATTISON *Ess.* (1889) I. 48 It has been even said that this church was built by the Germans. **1881** BESANT & RICE *Chapl. Fleet* II. xx. 270 There had been found a man, it was said, to bell the cat.

†**e.** [After L. *dicere*, Fr. *dire*.] With complement: To speak of, call (by a specified name or designation): chiefly in *passive*. Also (and in later use exclusively) in *passive* with adj. or descriptive sb., = 'to be said to be', 'to be called'. *Obs.*

1382 WYCLIF *Bible* Prol. xiv. 55 Whanne the formere thingis ben set byhynde, it is seid recapitulacoun, either rehersing of thing doon bifore. *Ibid. Matt.* xxvi. 3 The prince of the prestis that was said Caiphas. **1390** GOWER *Conf.* I. 61 The ferste is seid Ypocrisie. *a* **1400–50** *Alexander* 1070 (Dubl. MS.) Sagittarius for soth men seggen it to name. *c* **1400** *Lanfranc's Cirurg.* 192 Forwhi impetigo serpigo & morphea ben seid in salerne diuers names. *c* **1400** tr. *Secreta Secret., Gov. Lordsh.* 52 Olde men louyn swylk a kynge, and he ys sayd vertuous, large and attempre. *c* **1420–30** *Wycliffite Bible* Pref. Ep. St. Jerom. i, Itali, the which sumtyme was seid Grete Grece. **1422** tr. *Secreta Secret., Priv. Priv.* 201 Prayer othyrwhyle is sadyn a good worke. **1450–1530** *Myrr. our Ladye* 267 The doughters of Syon have sene her, and they have sayde her blyssed. **1484** CAXTON *Fables of Æsop* v. xiv, None ought to say hym self mayster withoute that he haue fyrst studyed. **1526** *Pilgr. Perf.* (W. de W. 1531) 302 What wyll ye shall be done with Jesu that is sayd Chryst and Sauyour of the worlde. **1540–1** ELYOT *Image Gov.* 108, I saie you most victorious people, branches of Romulus, subduers of realmes. **1589** PUTTENHAM *Eng. Poesie* II. iii. (Arb.) 84 According to the number of the sillables contained in euery verse, the same is sayd a long or short meeter. *a* **1617** BAYNE *On Eph.* (1643) 66 Thus all things are said created in or by Christ. **1628** COKE *On Litt.* 69 What shall be said a voyage royall shall be adjudged by the judges. **1652** GAULE *Magastrom.* 277 And why must he needs make mention of the flesh, where as it was enough to say him mortall? **1690** LOCKE *Hum. Und.* II. xxv. §1 The Colour White, [is] the Occasion why he is said whiter than Freestone.

f. †(*a*) With direct object and inf. in lieu of clause. (A Latinism) (*obs.*). †(*b*) With ellipsis of reflexive obj. before the inf.: To allege oneself *to do* or *be* so and so (*obs.*). (*c*) In *passive* with following infinitive, *to be said to do* or *be* so and so.

The mod. passive use (*c*) has two different meanings: the predicate may denote an alleged or reported fact (as in quot. 1615), or a descriptive term used (as in quot. 1838).

(*a*) **1563** SHUTE *Architecture* F j, Whiche oure Author hath brought to a vniformity, saying the piller to be in height .9. Diameters. **1583** FULKE *Defence* vii. 224 Iacob, Ioab, and Shemei which none but madde men will say to haue descended into a receptacle of soules. **1639** LD. DIGBY *Lett. Conc. Relig.* (1651) 53 Papias, whom St. Jerome..sayes to have been the first Author of it [Millenarianism]. **1706** E. WARD *Wooden World Diss.* (1708) 42 It were great Malice, to say him to be a Man of no Principles.

(*b*) **1585** T. WASHINGTON tr. *Nicholay's Voy.* 111 Diuers of them doe say to be descended of the line of Mahomet.

(*c*) **1607** SHAKS. *Cor.* IV. v. 243 As warres in some sort may be saide to be a Rauisher, so [etc.]. **1615** G. SANDYS *Trav.* 152 This is said to haue hapned..about the time that the Judges began to governe in Israel. **1671** BLAGRAVE *Astrol. Pract. Physick* 165 A planet is said to be peregrine, when he is out of all essential dignities. **1803** DAVY in *Phil. Trans.* XCIII. 252 Catechu is said to be obtained from the wood of a species of the Mimosa. **1838** T. THOMSON *Chem. Org. Bodies* 980 The trees are then said to bleed. **1839** DE LA BECHE *Rep. Geol. Cornwall*, etc. iii. 72 This patch may be said to be dove-tailed into its highest part. **1846** LINDLEY *Veget. Kingd.* 727 The fruit of Rhizophora Mangle is said to be sweet and edible. **1878** HUXLEY *Physiogr.* ii. 21 Rocks which thus allow water to filter through them are said to be permeable.

g. With cognate obj. (See SAY *sb.*^{4} 4.)

c **1400** [see A. 7*a*]. *c* **1440** *York Myst.* xxxii. 16 Therfore take hede... þat none jangill nor jolle at my ȝate, Tille I haue seggid and saide all my sawe.

†**h.** *to say* (a person) *shame, scandal*, to make disgraceful accusations against. *Obs.*

a **1225** *Ancr. R.* 352 Preise him, laste him, do him scheome, seie him scheome al him is iliche leof. *a* **1250** *Owl & Night.* 50 (Jesus MS.) Ilome þu dest me grome & seist me boþe teone & schome. *a* **1300** *Cursor M.* 8914 'O godd', coth þai, 'said has sco scam.' **1828** SCOTT *F.M. Perth* xii, I will say them no scandal.

i. Phrase. *to have something* (*nothing*) *to say to* (or *with*): *fig.* to have (no) dealings with; of things, to have (no) connexion with or bearing upon.

1724 DE FOE *Mem. Cavalier* (1840) 267 We had nothing to say to him. **1780** *Mirror* No. 75 (1787) III. 5 Perhaps you have something to say with the gentlemen who make the news. **1844** W. G. TODD *Ch. St. Patrick* 27 All then that Rome had to say to the conversion of Ireland was simply this. **1871** EARLE *Philol. Eng. Tongue* (1887) 624 The imitation has nothing to say to the origin of the words. **1887** G. T. STOKES in *Dict. Chr. Biog.* IV. 202 The use of the word Roman here..has nothing to say to the Church of Rome. **1888** —— *Irel. & Celtic Ch.* 151 With that controversy the Irish Church had nothing to say. **1904** J. T. FOWLER *Durh. Univ.* 21 The Churchmen of the North would have nothing to say to a Puritan and intrusive foundation.

j. *to have* (*something, nothing*, etc.) *to say for oneself*: to be able to adduce (something, nothing) in defence or extenuation of one's conduct. Also (*colloq.*), *to have nothing to say for oneself*: to be habitually silent from a retiring disposition or lack of vivacity.

1779 MME. D'ARBLAY *Diary* (1891) I. 105 All that I can say for myself is, that I have always feared discovery [etc.]. **1850** J. H. NEWMAN *Difficulties Anglicans* I. vii. (1891) I. 221 Bishop Ken..could not take the oaths, and was dispossessed; but he had nothing special to say for himself.

k. Contrasted with *do*, in certain proverbial locutions.

Mod. colloq. That's easier said than done. No sooner said than done!

l. *when all is said and done* (and slight varr.): after all, in the long run, nevertheless, on balance.

c **1560** T. INGELEND *Disobedient Child* sig. A iii, Whan all is saide and all is done, Concernynge all thynges both more and lesse. **1583** B. MELBANCKE *Philotimus* sig. S iij, It must be as ye woman will, when all is said & done. *a* **1785** J. H. STEVENSON *Wks.* (1795) I. 137 And yet, when all is said and done, This something's nothing but a Pun. **1886** [see RUMOURER]. **1928** M. WILKINSON *Edict of Nantes* (C.T.S.) 29 When all is said Bâville was responsible for a good deal of cruelty. **1930** 'SAPPER' *Finger of Fate* 162 But when all is said and done, a prospective son-in-law is as important as any letter. **1937** 'G. ORWELL' *Road to Wigan Pier* iv. 73 When all is said and done, the most important thing is that people shall live in decent houses and not in pigsties. **1952** M. LASKI *Village* v. 98 After all, Friday's pay-day when all's said and done. **1981** R. BARNARD *Mother's Boys* iv. 49, I know. Still, when all's said and done—.

m. *what do you say to* ——?: what is your response to ——?; *fig.*, how would you like ——?, how would —— suit you?

1592 SHAKS. *Rom. & Jul.* III. iv. 28 But what say you to Thursday? **1833** J. CONSTABLE *Let.* 11 Jan. (1966) IV. 391 What do you say to all or any of Mr. White's 'says'—his dogmatical manner has force. **1851** MRS. STOWE *Uncle Tom's Cabin* (1852) II. xxiii. 77 What do you say to a game of backgammon? **1929** *Melody Maker* Jan. 20/2 What do you say to a beaker of 'the boy'? **1948** M. LASKI *Tory Heaven* vi. 84 I'm getting a bit peckish... What do you say to us going out and looking for a bite? **1980** M. GILBERT *Death of Favourite Girl* ii. 23 What do you say we go outside and get a breath of fresh air?

n. *that is saying* (*little, much, etc.*) (and varr.): that is to concede (little, much, etc.); used to qualify or intensify a previous statement; *it says much for* (and varr.): it is much to the credit of; *to say that* (or *one thing*) *for*: to concede (the previous or following statement) as one point in favour of.

1806 C. WILMOT *Let.* 23 Mar. in *Russ. Jrnls.* (1934) II. 223 Her Lenity makes their Lot better perhaps than that of others, but that's saying very little for the System. **1849** C. BRONTË *Let.* 5 Apr. in C. Shorter *C. Brontë & her Circle* (1896) xvi. 440, I cannot perceive that she is feebler now than she was a month ago, though that is not saying much. **1853** LYTTON *My Novel* III. IX. ix. 48 No, I will say one thing for English statesmen, no man amongst them ever yet was the richer for place. *Ibid.* X. xx. 202 They beat the New Yorkers in manners. I'll say that for them. **1876** J. BLACKWOOD *Let.* 18 May in *Geo. Eliot Lett.* (1956) VI. 253 She remarked that..if people were no wiser in their speculations about more serious subjects..it did not say much for human wisdom. **1917** E. FENWICK *Diary* 13 Nov. in *Elsie Fenwick in Flanders* (1981) 183 The worst and hardest day I've had for weeks and that's saying a good deal. **1942** E. PAUL *Narrow St.* vii. 59 He had with him a battery of the stuffiest lawyers in the Paris bar, and that is saying a lot. **1946** E. O'NEILL *Iceman Cometh* II. 138 Sure. Harry's the greatest kidder in this dump and that's saying something! **1956** B. HOLIDAY *Lady sings Blues* (1973) xix. 154 Fishman had been around before the concert was a sellout, you could say that for him. **1965** *New Statesman* 30 Apr. 670/1 It says a good deal for Mr Eyre that he..is the one Mr Powell himself seems to have favoured most. **1969** K. GILES *Death cracks Bottle* vi. 64 The most impecunious peer in Ireland, which is saying something. **1975** *New Yorker* 1 Dec. 47/3 Houtek was a Railroad Baron and acted the part, but he liked to make others feel important too, I will say that for him.

o. *you('ve) said it*: you are absolutely right; you have got the point completely; I agree with you entirely.

1919 C. H. DARLING *Jargon Bk.* 50 You said it, you said the right thing and I agree with you. **1925** E. HEMINGWAY *Undefeated* in *This Quarter* I. II. 208 'If you stand in with Retana..you're a made man.'.. 'You said it,' the other waiter..said. 'You said it then.' **1929** E. LINKLATER *Poet's Pub* ii. 34 'Peace is too exciting..' said Joan. 'You've said it, Miss Benbow.' **1947** 'N. BLAKE' *Minute for Murder* i. 9 'What do they find?' 'Chay-oh [i.e. chaos],' replied Nigel... 'You said it.' **1970** N. STREATFEILD *Thursday's Child* vii. 52 'It is a big place, there must be a lot of servants needed.'.. 'You've said it.'

p. *to say it with* (something): to express one's feelings, make one's point, etc., by the use of (that thing); *esp.* and orig. in phr. *say it with flowers*, advertising slogan of the Society of American Florists, freq. in general and *fig.* use.

1918 *Florists' Review* 3 Jan. 12/2 The slogan will be 'Say It With Flowers', and every florist who deals with the public should make that phrase a conspicuous feature of his advertising from the day the first S.A.F. page appears. **1921** I. BERLIN (*song-title*) Say it with music. **1925** *New Yorker* 21 Feb. 8 (*heading*) Say it with scandal. **1928** C. SANDBURG *Good Morning, America* 17 Behold the proverbs of a people, a nation... Say it with flowers. Let one hand wash the other. The customer is always right. **1932** WODEHOUSE *Hot Water* vi. 114 Here's this Gedge bird shoutin' about the plumbing of this Chatty-o and not saying it with flowers, neither. **1960** G. MIKES *How to be Inimitable* 33, I used to say it with flowers... More gallant, no doubt... But with *cognac* it is so much quicker. **1974** G. MITCHELL *Javelin for Jonah* xiv. 175 'Why did you knife your science master?' 'We disagreed... So I say it with knives.'

q. *you can say that again*, phr. expressing whole-hearted agreement with a previous speaker's statement. *colloq.* (orig. *U.S.*).

1942 *Richmond* (Va.) *Times-Dispatch* 29 Dec. 11/5 Arthur Murray keeps in step with his hobby, Broadway idiom... If you agree [to something said] you nod and add, 'You can say that again, brother.' **1950** *Sun* (Baltimore) 1 May 12/2 The Senator wrote..that he did not 'believe that savings caused by decreases in essential services constitute constructive economy.' Senator Lehman can say that again. **1960** *Observer* 20 Mar. 10/4 *Mary*:..Andy, it's serious! *Andy*: You can say that again! **1973** *Nature* 12 Oct. 339/2 'I feel that here is an area that has not been thought out completely', he writes; he can say that again. **1974** 'E. LATHEN' *Sweet & Low* xi. 102 'Everybody here is waiting for Dreyer..to put some support into this market.'.. 'You can say that again!' The fervent statement came from a total stranger. **1981** R. BARNARD *Mother's Boys* vii. 70 'These teenagers are all alike, aren't they?' 'You can say that again,' snarled Lill.

3. Absolute uses of senses 1 and 2. **a.** With adv. *so* or *thus* instead of pronominal obj. (cf. 2 b); also in clause introduced by *as*. *you don't say so!* a colloquial expression of astonishment at some statement; similarly *you don't say!* (orig. *U.S.*), occas. also used sarcastically; *as they say*: phr. used to mark a preceding or following expression as being proverbial or hackneyed; *if you say so*: phr. denoting acceptance of a statement or an order, usu. with grudging or placatory overtones.

c **1000** *Ags. Gosp.* Mark xiv. 16 His leorning cnihtas.. fundon hit eall swa he sæde. *c* **1200** ORMIN 463 þiss gode mann..Wass, alls I seȝȝde nu littlær, ȝehatenn Zacaryas. **1297** R. GLOUC. (Rolls) 8972 Wy seistou so. *c* **1320** R. BRUNNE *Medit.* 134 þey þat þe hous haue sey seyn ryȝt so. **1340** *Ayenb.* 96 þanne he openede his mouþ..and ham þus zeayde. *c* **1430** *Chev. Assigne* 162 Thus he seythe to his wyfe in sawe as I telle. *c* **1592** MARLOWE *Jew of Malta* (1633) H 3 b, Saist thou me so? **1611** SHAKS. *Wint. T.* II. iii. 138 If thou refuse, And wilt encounter with my Wrath, say so. **1644** MILTON *Areop.* (Arb.) 63 If he beleeve things only because his Pastor sayes so. **1662** STILLINGFL. *Orig. Sacræ* II. vi. §16. 202 Say you so? **1698** FRYER *Acc. E. Ind. & P.* 262 As we are wont to say, Well done. **1749** SMOLLETT tr. *Gil Blas* (1782) III. 7 So saying, he drew his long rapier. **1779** F. BURNEY *Diary* Feb. (1842) I. 183 No, you don't say so? **1814** SOUTHEY *Roderick* xxv. 378 Thus saying, they withdrew a little way. **1842** S. KETTELL *Quozziana* 14 'We shall have an explosion before long, that will shake the State of Massachusetts to its uttermost foundations.' 'You don't say so!' exclaimed I, in unfeigned alarm. **1873** MISS BROUGHTON *Nancy* xvi, 'You do not say so!' cry I, in some astonishment. **1875** JOWETT *Plato* (ed. 2) I. 386 Be persuaded by me, and do as I say. **1899** R. WHITEING *No. 5 John St.* xiv. 128 You don't say so; why, I'm going to a meeting at his mother's house. **1912** MULFORD & CLAY *Buck Peters, Ranchman* iv. 84 'An' I could never see how he done it.' 'You—don't—say,' was Buck's thoughtful comment. **1930** A. P. HERBERT *Water Gipsies* xxii. 321 Ernest, as they say, 'saw red'. **1932** L. GOLDING *Magnolia Street* I. x. 171 'Father, indeed!.. As much 'is father as I'm Queen Alexandra!' 'You don't say!' murmured Mr. Briggs. **1955** L. P. HARTLEY *Perfect Woman* xiii. 121 She lets me go, and then catches me again. It's a game, as they say. **1956** H. KURNITZ *Invasion of Privacy* iii. 30 'Okay. We've got a deal.'.. 'If you say so, George. Anything you say.' **1959** E. H. CLEMENTS *High Tension* iii. 49 'Didn't you have a lodger, though, some time last year?' The factor..was obviously..troubled at having told a lie. 'If you say so, Kilmorrin.' **1962** N. MARSH *Hand in Glove* ii. 67 'The Scorpion's not here, George.' 'You don't say,' Mr. Copper bitterly rejoined. **1976** J. BINGHAM *God's Defector* vii. 101 'You can..watch who goes in, can't you?' 'If you say so.' 'I do say so.' **1977** J. THOMSON *Case Closed* iii. 43 Water under the bridge, as they say. **1979** R. JEFFRIES *Murder begets Murder* xiii. 83 'Heard the latest, Bert?.. That young filly was murdered.' 'You don't say, sir!'

fig. **1613** SHAKS. *Hen. VIII*, IV. i. 54 All the rest are Countesses. 2 [*Gent.*] Their Coronets say so.

b. Used in parenthetic clause indicating the author of a quoted saying. (When the quotation purports to be exact, the order of verb and subj. is often inverted.) Also in parenthetic expressions like 'shall I say?', 'let us say': cf. 10. *says who?*: 'who says so?', used to challenge a previous speaker's remark. Occas. with retort ¶*says me*; cf. ¶*says you* below. *slang* (chiefly *U.S.*). Also parenthetic phr. *shall we say* (in quot. 1973, *attrib.* with ironic force).

c **1230** *Hali Meid.* 6 'I-her me, dohter', he seið. **1297** R. GLOUC. (Rolls) 921 Louerd he sede we beþ men wide idriue aboute. **1362** LANGL. *P. Pl.* A. I. 49 And he asked of hem of whom spac þe lettre..'Cesar', þei seiden, 'We seoþ wel vchone'. *c* **1386** CHAUCER *Shipman's Prol.* 17 'Nay, bi godis soule, that shal be nat,' Seide the Shipman. *a* **1529** SKELTON *Colyn Cloute* 1230 It is to drede, men sayes, Lest they be Saduces As they be sayd sayne. *a* **1585** POLWART *Flyting w. Montgomerie* 175 Thou was begotten, some sayes mee, Betwixt the deuil and a dun kow. **1590** SHAKS. *Mids. N.* II. ii. 62 Amen, to that faire prayer, say I. *Ibid.* III. ii. 277 Why then you left me..In earnest, shall I say? **1644** SYMONDS *Diary* (Camden) 48 A castle, belonging say they to a duke. **1692** R. L'ESTRANGE *Fables* lxxiii. 73 Shew me the Company (says the Adage) and I'll tell ye the Man. **1710** SWIFT *Jrnl. to Stella* 9 Sept., The Duke of Ormond, they say, will be Lieutenant of Ireland. **1798** WORDSW. *We are Seven* 6 She was eight years old, she said. **1882** W. S. GILBERT *Iolanthe* I. Ld. Chancellor's Song, I'll work on a new and original plan, (Said I to myself—said I). **1914** KIPLING *Let.* 15 Sept. in Ld. Birkenhead *Rudyard Kipling* (1978) xviii. 279 Much water, or shall we say much blood, has flowed under the bridges since they were written. **1931** M. GILMAN *Sob Sister* x. 143 We can park a car there and spoon—says who! **1932** 'SPINDRIFT' *Yankee Slang* 32 *Says who?*, challenge to a remark—what right have you to 'say so'? **1938** C. B. KELLAND *Dreamland* vii. 86 'Miss Higg, you are guilty of reprehensible waste.' 'Says Who?' 'Says me.' **1968** *Listener* 30 May 699/1, I think the play may, shall we say, amplify light which does already exist but doesn't seem to have been noticed. **1971** *Black World* June 81/2 'I just asked.' 'Had no business asking.' 'Says who?' 'Me, stupid!' **1973** E.-J. Bahr *Nice Neighbourhood* x. 104 Joe Walsh, Jack's shall-we-say housemate. **1977** J. Crosby *Company of Friends* viii. 116 It's not one [*sc.* a news story] of ours.. I read it with—shall we say, total astonishment. **1977** J. Porter *Who the Heck is Sylvia?* xvi. 151 'One should never break promises to children.' 'Sez who?'

¶ In this use, the 3rd sing. pres. is often substituted *colloq.* for the pa. t. *said*. Hence, in vulgar speech or jocular imitations of it, ***says I, says you*** = 'said I', 'said you'; ***says you*** is also (*slang* (orig. *U.S.*)) used in the present tense to convey doubt about, or contempt for, the remark of a previous speaker (freq. in form ***sez you***).

In uneducated use often with repetition: 'Says I to myself, says I'; 'Well, says Mr. Smith, says he'.

1682 Dryden & Lee *Dk. Guise* Epil., Jack Ketch, says I, 's an excellent Physician. **1700** Congreve *Way of World* III. v, Humh (says he) what you are a hatching some Plot (says he) you are so early abroad. **1700** Swift *Mrs. Harris' Petition* 30 Says Cary, says he,.. I never heard of such a thing. **1706** De Foe *True Relation* etc. Early Wks. (1889) 443 Mrs. Bargrave asked her whether she would drink some tea. Says Mrs. Veal, 'I do not care if I do'. **1712** Hearne *Collect.* (O.H.S.) III. 381, I ask you, says he, because I am sure, if any one, you can give me information. **1720** Gordon & Trenchard *Independ. Whig* (1728) 215 Says I to myself, This reverend ill-tongu'd Parson will certainly quarrel. **1784** Bage *Barham Downs* I. 79, I believe, says I, it has caught your sister's dejection. **1825** T. Hook *Sayings* Ser. II. *Doubts & F.* ii, Because, says I to myself, says I, it may save them there unfortunate, innocent people. **1848** Thackeray *Van. Fair* iii, 'I bet you thirteen to ten that Sophy Cutler hooks either you or Mulligatawney before the rains'. 'Done', says I. **1852** Dickens *Bleak House* v, That warn't Chancery practice though, says you. **1887** Henley *Culture in the Slums* i. 1 'O crikey, Bill!' she ses to me, she ses. **1927** Dunning & Abbott *Broadway* II. 108 Steve's a fine fellow and he's just out for some innocent fun—Says you—Says I—. **1931** *Amer. Speech* VI. 205 *Says you*, you say no, but I don't believe you. 'Says me' is the answer. **1931**, etc. [see sez]. **1932** J. Brophy *English Prose* v. 61 Oh yeah! Says you!—an expression of scornful disbelief. **1951** Wodehouse *Old Reliable* iv. 53 Says you, if I may use a homely phrase indicating doubt and uncertainty. **1981** M. C. Smith *Gorky Park* III. iii. 328 'He's a murderer.' 'Says you.'

†**c.** To speak or tell *of* something; to speak *for* or *against* a person or thing. *Obs.*

971 *Blickl. Hom.* 117 Þonne ȝehyrdon we ær on þas halȝan tide secgan be þære halȝan þrowunga ures Drihtenes. *a* **1175** *Cott. Hom.* 237 Of þeses fif ceþen.. we habbeð ȝeu ȝesed. *c* **1205** Lay. 13470 Ich wulle suggen eow uorð rihtes of mire muchele sorȝen. *a* **1300** *Cursor M.* 798 Her egain mai naman sai. **1340** *Ayenb.* 16 Uerst we willeþ zigge of þe zenne of prede. *a* **1352** Minot *Poems* (ed. Hall) iii. 36 And þare he made his mone playne þat no man suld say þare ogayne. **1377** Langl. *P. Pl.* B. v. 10 For I say [= saw] þe felde ful of folke þat I before of seyde. *c* **1400** Maundev. (Roxb.) ix. 37 A kirk whare þe aungell said to þe schephirdes of þe birth of Criste. *c* **1450** *St. Cuthbert* (Surtees) 1362 Bosyl come, and to him say Of cuthbert purpose and his will. *c* **1489** Caxton *Sonnes of Aymon* vii. 162 As he wolde have sayd agenst the duke Naymes, there cam a yonge gentilman [etc.]. **1523** Ld. Berners *Froiss.* I. xxx. 44 None durst say agaynst his opynion. **1534** —— *Gold. Bk. M. Aurel.* (1546) Hj, We haue saied of the hatred that this emperour had to trewandes. **1609** Skene *Reg. Maj.* 13 Alswa gif some of them sayes for ane partie, and some for ane other. **1709** Mrs. Manley *Secret Mem.* (1736) II. 175 My Lady herself can't say against it.

d. with certain advs., esp. *well*, also †*soothly*, *truly* (*true*), *wisely*, etc., the implied object being some particular saying. Somewhat *arch.*

1375 Barbour *Bruce* VII. 258 'Sa ȝhe suthly?' 'Ȝha, certis, dame'. **1387** Trevisa *Higden* (Rolls) III. 239 'Þou seist wel', quod þat oþer. *c* **1400** *Sowdone Bab.* 472 Beter myghte no man seyne. **1402** *Repl. Daw Topias* in *Polit. Poems* (Rolls) II. 49 Jak, thou seist ful serpentli. ? *a* **1425** *26 Pol. Poems* 103/1, I wole be mendid ȝif y say mys. *c* **1450** *Merlin* i. 5 Quod the gode man, 'Ye sey amysse'. *Ibid.* ii. 35 Thou seiste trewe. **1567** Harman *Caveat* xix. 73 And was not this a good acte? nowe, howe saye you? **1590** Marlowe *2nd Pt. Tamburl.* v. i, Wel said, let there be a fire presently. **1598** Shaks. *Merry W.* II. i. 226 Thou shalt haue egresse and regresse (said I well) and thy name shall be Broome. **1697** Dryden *Virg. Georg.* iv. 736 For sev'n continu'd Months, if Fame say true, The wretched Swain his Sorrows did renew. **1785** *Liberal Amer.* I. 47, I find Sir Edward Hambden is with you, and, if fame say true, a charming fellow he is. **1831** Scott *Ct. Robt.* xvi, The Immortal, so called, becomes now, if priests say true, an immortal indeed.

†**e.** In perf. (pluperf.) tense: ***when he has said*** = 'when he has finished speaking'. Also, in pa. t. *he said*, used in narrative poetry (after L. *dixit* or the Homeric ἦ ῥα) after the conclusion of a speech. *Obs.*

c **1205** Lay. 4150 Þe Dunewale hauede isæd al his folc luuede þene ræd. **1400** *Destr. Troy* 8916 When the souerain hade said, þen he sest here. **1525** Ld. Berners *Froiss.* II. ccxxxiii. 722 Whan he had sayd, then he was aunswered, howe the pope shulde take counsayle to answere. **1595** Shaks. *John* II. i. 231 When I haue saide, make answer to vs both! **1600** Nashe *Summers Last Will* I j, Loe, I haue said, this is the totall summe. **1667** Milton *P.L.* v. 869, IX. 664. **1697** Dryden *Virg. Georg.* IV. 722 She said, and from his Eyes the fleeting Fair Retir'd like subtle Smoke dissolv'd in Air. **1712–14** Pope *Rape Lock* I. 115 He said; when Shock, who thought she slept too long, Leap'd up, and wak'd his mistress with his tongue. **1738** Gray *Tasso* 39 Scarce had he said, before the warriors' eyes When mountain-high the waves disparted rise. **1757** W. Wilkie *Epigoniad* I. 24 He said. The chiefs with indignation burn'd; And Diomed submitting thus return'd.

f. *to say well, evil of*, † *by*: to speak well or evil of. Now *rare.* †Also in *indirect passive.*

a **1250** *Owl & Night.* 9 (Jesus MS.) And eyþer seyde of oþres custe þat alre wrste þat hi ywuste. **1445** tr. *Claudian* in *Anglia* XXVIII. 269 Thou seith of hem evir wele. **1470–85** Malory *Arthur* XIII. xix. 639 My name is sir Launcelot du lake that hath ben ryght wel said of. *Ibid.* XXI. i. 840 Thus was syr Arthur depraued and euyl sayd of. **1547** *Homilies* I. *Of Contention* I. T j b, Saie well by them, that saie euill by you. **1551–6** R. Robinson tr. *More's Utopia* Ep. (Arb.) 15 Them which can say well by nothing. **1713** Swift *Jrnl. to Stella* 16 May, Your new Bishop acts very ungratefully. I cannot say so bad of it as he deserved.

g. Contrasted with *do.* (Cf. 2 k.)

1382 Wyclif *Mat.* xxiii. 3 Sothely thei seien, and don nat. [So in the later versions.] *c* **1450** tr. *De Imitatione* III. xxxv. 103 Shal I be like a man þat saiþ & doþe not?

4. †**a.** Of words: To mean, signify. Also, *is (for) to say* = 'signifies'. *Obs.*

c **1000** Ælfric *De Vet. Test.* (Gr.) 7/42 *Cantica canticorum*, ðæt seȝþ on Englisc ealra sanga fyrmest. *c* **1230** *Hali Meid.* 6 Nim ȝeme hwet euch worð beo sunderliche to seggen. *c* **1350** *S. Ambrosius* 15 in Horstm. *Altengl. Leg.* (1878) 8/2 Oþer elles þou maiȝt sei þat Ambros Is seid of ambra and syos: Syos is to seyn 'God' riht, And ambrum good sauour pliht. *c* **1386** Chaucer *Prioress' T.* 71 Noght wiste he what this latyn was to seye, ffor he so yong and tendre was of age. **1450–1530** *Myrr. our Ladye* I These wordes are writen in holy scrypture & are thus to say in englyshe. **1541** Copland *Guydon's Quest.* K iij, Pigneum in Arabyke is to saye the ars hole. **1604** E. G[rimstone] *D'Acosta's Hist. Indies* v. xvii. 374 A lake.. which they call *Ezapangue*, which is to say, water of blood.

b. ***that is to say*** (orig. gerundial inf.): used to introduce a more explicit or intelligible re-statement of what immediately precedes, or a limiting clause necessary to make the statement correct. Sometimes used sarcastically to introduce a statement of the real fact which a quoted statement misrepresents or euphemistically veils. Cf. F. *c'est-à-dire*.

c **1175** *Lamb. Hom.* 123 Ðet is to seggane: Gif þa hefdmen of þissere worlde hefden icnawen crist. *c* **1200** *Trin. Coll. Hom.* 3 Aduent þat is seggen on englis ure louerd ihesu cristes tocume. *c* **1330** *Spec. Gy de Warewyke* 413 þis is to seie, i telle þe: 'þe clene of herte, blessed þeih be'. *a* **1340** Hampole *Psalter* iv. 1 þat is at say, fra anguys and sarynes þou has broght me in til brede of gastly ioy. *c* **1386** Chaucer *Prol.* 181 A fissh þat is waterlees, That is to seyn, a Monk out of his Cloystre. *c* **1391** —— *Astrol.* Prol. 26 Writen in hir owne tonge, that is to sein, in Latin. **1395** *E.E. Wills* (1882) 4, I bequethe to the same Thomas, the stoffe longyng therto, that is to seye, my beste fetherbed [etc.]. *a* **1400** in Halliwell *Rara Mathem.* (1841) 58 þe perpendicle þat es to say þe threde wheron þe plumbe henges. *c* **1400** *Rule St. Benet* (Prose) viii. 15 þat es hele of þa þat ere in sekenes, þat es at say in sinne. *c* **1440** *Gesta Rom.* xliii. 172 (Harl. MS.), Seing, thus, *Quomodo fiet istud?* this is to seye, how shulde this be I-done? **1471** Fortescue *Wks.* (1869) 530 His highnes hath now both titles, that is to saynge his auncient title,.. and this new title. **1486** *Bk. St. Albans, Hawking* b ij b, Bot it tempur yowre hawke that is to say ensayme yowre hawke. **1539** *Great Bible* title, The Byble in English; that is to saye, the Content of all the Holy Scripture. **1568** Grafton *Chron.* II. 130 Two Aldermen more.., that is to say, Arnold Thedmare, & Henry Walmode. **1677** Lauderdale in *L. Papers* (1885) III. lvii. 89 They pretend they cannot suppress these disorders, that is to say they will doe nothing towards it. **1687** A. Lovell tr. *Thevenot's Trav.* II. 25 Three hours after, that's to say, about eleven a Clock. **1864** Bryce *Holy Rom. Emp.* vi. (1875) 77 Francia Occidentalis, that is to say, Neustria and Aquitaine.

†**c.** *to say*: = 'namely', 'to wit'. *Obs.*

1547 Hooper *Declar. Christ & Office* v. D iij, Saint Paule callith Christ.. the minister and seruant of the saynctes to say of souche as be here lyuing in this troblyd and persecutyd churche. *Ibid.* vi. E viij, Hym that had the imperie and dominion of deathe to say the deuill.

5. a. With obj. an infinitive or a subjunctive clause and const. dative: To tell (a person) *to do* something. In modern *colloq.* use: (*a*) const. *for*; (*b*) without const., the personal object being understood from the context.

971 *Blickl. Hom.* 47 þæt hi secggan þæm Godes folce þæt hi Sunnandaȝum & mæssedaȝum Godes cyrican ȝeorne secan. *c* **1250** *Gen. & Ex.* 4114 Sey him on ðin stede to gon. *a* **1300** *Cursor M.* 6063 Says to mi folk on þiskin wis, þat þai me mak a sacrifice. *c* **1440** *Jacob's Well* xxxi. 203 þanne saye hem þat þei take of suche an hucche for þat is trewly gett, & do þat for me. *a* **1533** Ld. Berners *Huon* lxxxiii. 260 Say vnto hym that he drynke to you in the name of good peace. **1906** *Dialect Notes* III. 154 The doctor said for me not to eat a pickle. **1929** E. Hemingway *Farewell to Arms* xii. 87, I woke Georgetti, the other boy who was drunk, and offered him some water. He said to pour it on his shoulder and went back to sleep. **1934** D. L. Sayers *Nine Tailors* 72 'Why is that kept locked, Mr. Godfrey?'.. 'So Rector said to fix a lock the way they couldn't get the trap-door open.' **1946** *Publ. Amer. Dial. Soc.* VI. 26 She said for us to be there by eight o'clock. **1955** W. Denlinger *Complete Boston* I. 158 Without asking the price, the woman said to buy the dog. **1959** *Times* 20 June 7/7 Father said for Chris to take one of the lanterns. **1965** *New Statesman* 30 Apr. 687/1 On no other terms than as a parody could the book [*sc.* N. Mailer's *American Dream*] carry conviction. Its first sentence pals up with Jack Kennedy; its last paragraph includes a message from the grave from Marilyn Monroe ('Marilyn says to say hello').

b. In *passive*, of a person: To be ruled, submit to command or advice. Now *dial.*

1588 *Wills & Inv. N.C.* (Surtees 1860) 321 Whom I make my soule executors, equally together, wyllinge and commandinge them that they shalbe sayd and ruled by Ambrose Lancaster and Roger Megson, if [etc.]. **1643** Trapp *Comm. Gen.* xxxix. 10 Satan will not be said with a little. **1855** *Whitby Gloss.* s.v. *Sayed*, In spite of all I can do, she wont be sayed. **1888** 'R. Boldrewood' *Robbery under Arms* xxxix, Father didn't get well all at once. He went back twice.. and wouldn't be said by Aileen.

6. a. With obj. an indirect question: To declare or make known (*who, what, how, whether*, etc.). †In early use const. dat. of person (equivalent to the modern *tell* with direct obj.).

a **1000** *Riddles* xx. 9 Saȝa hwæt ic hatte. *c* **1175** *Lamb. Hom.* 3 þis godspel [for Palm Sunday] seð [*MS.* sed] hu þe helend nehlechede to-ward ierusalem þare burh to dei mid his apostles. *c* **1200** *Trin. Coll. Hom.* 21 We habbeð bigunnen to sege [? = seȝe] ou on englis hwat bitocneð þe crede [etc.]. *c* **1205** Lay. 4613 Ah ȝef ȝe wullen us seuggen ȝet ȝe mawen libben whonene ȝe beð icumene. *a* **1300** *Cursor M.* 3853 And siþen he did him for to sai Quat was þe chesiun of his wai. **1390** Gower *Conf.* I. 222 Bot of Envie, If ther be more in his baillie Towardes love, sai me what. *c* **1449** Pecock *Repr.* I. iii. 16 Seie to me also where is Holi Scripture is ȝouen the hundrid parti of the teching which [etc.]. *c* **1485** *E.E. Misc.* (Warton Club) 29 How ferful trowly there is no tong can saye. *a* **1529** Skelton *Agst. Garnesche* i. 13 But sey me yet, Syr Satropas, what auctoryte ye haue.. to calle me a knaue? **1667** Milton *P.L.* VII. 40 Say Goddess, what ensu'd. *a* **1771** Gray *Amatory Lines* 7 Ah! say, Fellow-swains, how these symptoms befell me? **1884** *Law Times* LXXVII. 369/2 It was not then necessary for the court to say authoritatively whether it was right or not. *Mod.* Did he say whether he had been successful? How far these figures can be trusted the writer does not say.

b. From the 18th c. often in expressions like 'it is hard to say', 'I cannot say', where the verb comes contextually to mean: To judge, decide.

1709 Pope *Ess. Crit.* I 'Tis hard to say, if greater want of skill Appear in writing or in judging ill. **1736** Butler *Anal.* I. iii. 52 No one can say, how considerable this Uneasiness and Satisfaction may be. **1891** 'J. S. Winter' *Lumley* x, What the end of it all would have been I really cannot say.

c. *absol.* In the imperative, introducing a direct question. In early use often const. *dative*; = 'tell (me, us)'. Now only *poet.*

The U.S. colloquial *say* seems, when introducing a question as well as when prefixed to a statement of fact, to be a shortening of *I say* (see 12 b).

c **1200** Ormin 10292 Seȝȝ uss, arrt tu profete. *a* **1225** *Leg. Kath.* 2241 Sei, þu Sathanesses sune,.. hwet constu to þeos men þet tu þus leadest? *a* **1300** *Cursor M.* 5005 'Sais me', coth iacob, 'how es þis, þat o mi childir an i misse?' *a* **1352** Minot *Poems* (ed. Hall) xi. 25 Say now, sir Iohn of France how saltou fare? **1387** Trevisa *Higden* (Rolls) IV. 303 Sey me, ȝonge man, was þy moder ever in Rome? *a* **1490** *Pope Gregory's Trental* 87 in *Minor Poems fr. Vernon MS.* 263 Sey me, modur, wiþ-outen feyne, Whi art þou put to al þis peyne? **1586** Marlowe *1st Pt. Tamburl.* II. v, Why say theridamas, wilt thou be a king? **1605** Shaks. *Lear* II. iv. 142 Say? How is that? **1741–2** Gray *Agrippina* 92 Tell me, say, This mighty emperor,.. Has he beheld the glittering front of war? **1814** F. S. Key *Star-spangled Banner* 7 O! say, does that star-spangled banner yet wave O'er the land of the free? **1896** A. E. Housman *Shropshire Lad* xxiv, Say, lad, have you things to do?

†**7.** To deliver (a speech, a discourse); to relate (a story); to express, give (thanks); to tell, speak (truth, lies); to express (one's opinion). *Obs.*

c **888** K. Ælfred *Boeth.* xxx. §1 þa ongon he eft seggan spell & cwæð. **971** *Blickl. Hom.* 103 On eallum tidum secggan we him þanc ealra his miltsa. *c* **1205** Lay. 3032 Cordoille iherde þa lasinge þe hire sustren seiden þon kinge. *Ibid.* 4620 We wullet soð sucgen. *a* **1250** *Owl & Night.* 98 (Jesus MS.) Hwar bi men seggeþ a vorbysne. *a* **1300** *Cursor M.* 4582 O þis ioseph sai me þi dome, And giue me þar-of god consail. *c* **1350** *Will. Palerne* 593 Seiȝth me al ȝour seknesse & what so sore ȝow greuis. *c* **1386** Chaucer *Man of Law's Prol.* 46 But nathelees certeyn I kan right now no thrifty tale seyn. *c* **1380** Wyclif *Wks.* (1880) 29 þus crist spekiþ to þe iewis & axeþ hem whi þei bileuen not to hym ȝif he seiþe trewþe. **1429** *Rolls of Parlt.* IV. 343/1 No persone of the seide Counseill, shall conceyve.. wrath, aȝeins any other of the seide Counseill, for saiying his advys or entent. **1463** *Bury Wills* (Camden) 17 Item I wyll that Maist[r] Thomas Harlowe sey the sermon at my interment. **1470** Henry *Wallace* XI. 1214 Master Barbour, quhilk was a worthi clerk, He said the Bruce amang his othir werk. *c* **1489** Caxton *Sonnes of Aymon* xxiv. 526 And whan the kyng simon herde mawgis speke so, he said him grete thanke. **1498** *Coventry Leet Bk.* (E.E.T.S.), There was a solempne sermon seyde, where the Maire there sette betwixt both presidentes. **1544** Patten *Exped. Scot.* Pref. a v, The whiche I had, or rather (to saie truth and shame the deuel, for out it wool) I stale. *a* **1568** Ascham *Scholem.* I. (Arb.) 81 Where they may freely say their mindes. **1657** *Burton's Diary* (1828) I. 334 Mr. Caryl only prayed, the other two preached, and very good sermons they said.

†**8.** To speak of, mention, enumerate, describe.

a **1225** *Ancr. R.* 346 Lihte gultes beteð þus anonriht, bi ou suluen and þauh siggeð ham ine schrifte. *a* **1375** *Joseph Arim.* 70, I am not worþi to seyn moni of his werkes. *a* **1400–50** *Alexander* 5551 And oþir sellis he saȝe at sai wald he neuir. *c* **1400** *Destr. Troy* 5204 The same yle I said you, Cicill is calt.

9. a. To recite or repeat (something that has a prescribed form); occas. to recite from memory, in contradistinction to reading. Often in traditional collocations, as ***to say grace, a lesson, (a) mass, a prayer, (one's prayers)***.

In ritual use *say* and *sing* are sometimes equivalent; but *say* is the wider term, and seems often to have been applied distinctively to recitation without note.

c **1200** *Trin. Coll. Hom.* 17 Ich wille.. segge ou þe crede word after word. *a* **1225** *Ancr. R.* 24 A þisse wise ȝe muwen, ȝif ȝe wulleð, siggen ower Paternostres. *a* **1300** *Cursor M.* 28248 My prayers say was me ful lathe. **1303** R. Brunne *Handl. Synne* 10429 Ȝyf one [*sc.* a mass] for me were specyale seyde. *c* **1330** *Chron. Wace* (Rolls) 93, I see in song, in sedgeyng tale of Erceldoun & of Kendale, Non þam says as þai þam wroght. *a* **1350** *Peter & Paul* 292 in Horstm. *Altengl. Leg.* (1881) 67 þan to þe body he made him boun

And sayd þore his coniurisoun. **1387** TREVISA *Higden* (Rolls) III. 7 Dauid..made..instrumentis of musik, in whiche þe dekenes schulde seie ympnes and songes. **1415** *E.E. Wills* (1882) 23 That ther be x. Ml. masses Isayde for me of gode prestes. *c* **1430** *Pilgr. Lyf Manhode* II. xviii. (1869) 82 The gospel that j haue herd seyd [Fr. *chanter*] in oure toun. *c* **1431** *Rec. St. Mary at Hill* 14 An honest Preest sufficiantly lerned in dyvynete to syng & sey dyuyne seruice in the said Chapell. *c* **1530** H. RHODES *Bk. Nurture* in *Babees Bk.* 81 And whyle that grace is saying, friend, looke that ye make no noyse. **1544** *Exhort. to Prayer* A ix b, That whyche is printed in blacke letters is to be sayde or song of the prieste. **1602** MARSTON *Ant. & Mel.* Induct., Faith, we can say our parts. *c* **1616** S. WARD *Coal from Altar* (1627) 74 Sermons..so deliuered, as if one were acting a part, or saying a lesson by heart. **1641** J. TRAPPE *Theol. Theol.* viii. 307 They could not say Psalmes..by heart. **1832** W. PALMER *Orig. Liturg.* I. 244 Collects to be said at matins and evensong. **1858** LONGF. *Birds of Passage* I. *Children* ix, Ye are better than all the ballads That ever were sung or said. **1861** M. PATTISON *Ess.* (1889) I. 48 The Germans..had their own masses said in it [this church] on special days. **1884** J. GILMOUR *Mongols* xviii. 212 In the act of disrobing, prayers are said most industriously.

†**b.** *absol.* with reference to church services.

c **1375** *Lay Folks Mass-bk.* (B.) 27 When þe preyst says, or yf he syng, To hym þou gyf gud herkenyng. **1439** in *Ancestor* July (1904) 16, I bequethe to the person for seying and syngynge atte my dirige viij d. **1558** KENNEDY in *Wodrow Soc. Misc.* (1844) 151 He can nolder sing nor say. **1607** TOPSELL *Four-f. Beasts* 106 Within a short space none of them were able either to say, reade, pray, or sing, in all the monastery. **1790** BURKE *Fr. Rev.* Wks. V. 291 They are as usefully employed as those who neither sing nor say.

10. On the analogy of expressions like 'let us say', 'shall we say?', etc. (referable to senses 1–3), where the verb has contextually the sense of 'suppose', 'assume', the imperative *say* is idiomatically used: **a.** to introduce a clause, with the sense 'supposing', 'on the assumption *that*'; **b.** parenthetically, to indicate that a preceding sentence expresses a supposition or a selected instance; **c.** prefixed to a designation of number, quantity, date, etc. to mark it as an approximate guess or as representing a hypothetical case; **d.** immediately following a word or phrase to show that it represents a supposition, an instance, an approximation, or the like.

In commercial documents *say* is also used, without any implication of inexactness, to introduce any varied repetition of a numerical or quantitative statement: e.g., 'a shipment of 215 (say two hundred and fifteen) tons of coal'; 'thirteen stones (say 182 pounds)'; 'four editions of 2000 copies each, or say in all 8000 copies'. Cf. Ger. *sage*, Da. *siger*, Sw. *säger*; the two last are indicative present, either 1st or 3rd pers. sing.; Du. has *zegge* (old form of *zeg*, 1st pers.), and Fr. has *je dis* similarly used.

c **1596** *Sir T. More* I. i. 159 Well, say tis read, what is your further meaning in the matter. **1601** SHAKS. *Twel. N.* I. iv. 23 Say I do speake with her (my Lord) what then? **1643** TRAPP *Comm. Gen.* xlvi. 1 But say it had been out of his way. **1656** EARL MONM. tr. *Boccalini's Advts. fr. Parnass.* II. lxxxvi. (1674) 238 When a Prince, say it be not out of private hatred, but justly doth vex any great Officer. **1736** BUTLER *Anal.* I. iii. 66 Pleasure and Pain are indeed to a certain Degree, say to a very high Degree, distributed amongst us without any apparent Regard to the Merit or Demerit of Characters. **1837** *Athenæum* No. 480, 6 A Venus—say of Parian marble in early Greek style. **1861** DICKENS *Gt. Expect.* lii, Early in the week, or say Wednesday. **1863** KINGSLEY in *Lett.* etc. (1877) II. 147 The wages of my people..average 11s. per week... Harvesting, say £5 more. **1875** CAYLEY in *Q. Jrnl. Pure & Appl. Math.* XIII. 321 Radius vectors belonging to the same angle (or say opposite angles). **1876** GLADSTONE *Homeric Synchr.* 143 But if the period of (say) 100 years subdivides itself. **1898** *Allbutt's Syst. Med.* V. 450 Equal volumes of, say, thirty and forty-fold diluted normal acid. **1927** *New Republic* 12 Oct. 208/1, I daresay the drummer sees no difference between Gary and, say, Newark. **1937** 'G. ORWELL' *Road to Wigan Pier* vi. 100 If he were, say, an Indian or Japanese coolie, who can live on rice and onions, he wouldn't get fifteen shillings a week—he would be lucky if he got fifteen shillings a month. **1938** W. STEVENS *Connoisseur of Chaos* in *Parts of World* (1942) 49 An upper, particular bough in, say, Marchand. **1940** W. FAULKNER *Hamlet* I. ii. 40 In Ratliff it was that hearty celibacy as of a lay brother in a twelfth-century monastery—a gardener, a pruner of vines, say. **1944** S. BELLOW *Dangling Man* 85 Little since then has worked upon me with such force as, say, the sight of a driver trying to raise his fallen horse. **1951** W. FAULKNER *Requiem for Nun* iii. 231 To boil for an instant to the surface like a chip or a twig—a match-stick or a bubble, say, too weightless to give resistance for destruction to function against. **1966** *Listener* 15 Sept. 388/3 A production volume of say, 20,000 units a year. **1977** L. MEYNELL *Hooky gets Wooden Spoon* iii. 40 Come in about six, say. **1977** *Proc. Classical Assoc.* LXXIV. 14 In very special circumstances, you might be pressured into parenthood; say, you came from a particularly respected royal line which your subjects felt should continue.

11. a. The inf. to say is used in parenthetic phrases with adv. or obj., as ***so to say, shortly to say, soothly to say; sooth*** or ***truth to say, to say (the) truth; shame to say***, etc. (Cf. senses 2, 3, 7.) †***to say better***: = 'more correctly speaking'.

a **1200** *Vices & Virtues* 11 Soþ to seggen, ic not ȝif ich auerȝete ani ðing dede ðat [etc.]. **1297** R. GLOUC. (Rolls) 3747 Bote to sigge [*v.rr.* segge, seye] ssortliche þer nas ver ne ner Of prowesse ne of corteisie in þe world is per. *a* **1352** MINOT *Poems* (ed. Hall) i. 81 þare dwelled oure king, þe suth to saine, With his menȝe a litell while. *c* **1386** CHAUCER *Prol.* 284 For sothe he was a worthy man with alle, But sooth to seyn, I noot how men hym calle. *Ibid.* 468 Gat tothed was she, soothly for to seye. *c* **1400** MAUNDEV. (1839) xvi. 176 And schortly to seye ȝou; thei suffren [etc.]. **1437** *Libel of Eng. Policy* in *Polit. Poems* (Rolls) II. 181 For here martis bene feble, shame to saye. **1484** CAXTON *Fables of Æsop* IV. viii, Oftyme for to saye trouthe men lese theyre lyues. **1577–87** HARRISON *England* II. i. 136/2 in *Holinshed*, And to saie truth, one..of these small liuings is of so little value, that [etc.]. **1585** T. WASHINGTON tr. *Nicholay's Voy.* IV. xv. 130 The auncient towne of the Sun called Heliopolis, or to say better, Solos or Soloe. **1601** SHAKS. *All's Well* II. ii. 12 And indeed such a fellow, to say precisely, were not for the Court. **1710** SWIFT *Jrnl. to Stella* 30 Nov., But, to say the truth, the present Ministry have a difficult task, and want me [etc.]. **1823** M. R. MITFORD in *Lady's Mag.* Sept. 501/2 My flowers..withered and faded and pined away; they almost, so to say, panted for drought. **1845** E. WARBURTON *Crescent & Cross* I. 311 We had been already five weeks in Savagedom,..and, to say the truth, we had had enough of it. **1886** C. E. PASCOE *London of To-day* xxvi. (ed. 3) 241 Having now, so to say, presented our humble duty to the Lord Mayor..let us retrace our steps. *Ibid.* xli. (ed. 3) 354 The investigation of this question, which, truth to say, was one of importance. **1966** *Listener* 10 Feb. 210/1 The part of the picture so to say nearest you, the foreground, the front plane, is painted to represent a doorway..which frames the main subject of the picture beyond.

b. ***not to say***...: used (*a*) to imply that the speaker is content with a more moderate statement than that which he might have made; (*b*) *colloq.* = 'not what one may call...', 'not..., properly speaking'.

1736 AINSWORTH *Lat.-Eng. Dict.*, *Nedum*, not to say. **1857** TROLLOPE *Barchester T.* xliv, 'Am not I [growing old], my dear?' 'No, papa, not old—not to say old'. *Mod.* His language was irreverent, not to say blasphemous.

c. ***to say nothing of***...: used to refer in passing to subjects that might be used to strengthen the speaker's case; cf. *not to mention* (*so-and-so*) (MENTION *v.* 1 a).

1934 WEBSTER, *Say nothing of*, not to take into consideration (something too important to be neglected). **1962** *Home Managem.* (Homecraft Ser.) 27 Much damage is caused to dressing-table and bed-side table tops by spilled cosmetics and perfumes, to say nothing of marks..caused by that early-morning cup of tea. **1966** *Listener* 28 July 126/1 In an industry that has experienced Northcliffe, Hearst, and Beaverbrook, to say nothing of Bartholomew and Cudlipp, this seems unlikely. **1976** J. CROSBY *Nightfall* xxxii. 191 Elf was her revolutionary sister-in-arms... To say nothing of her lover.

12. I say has various idiomatic uses. **a.** Introducing a word, phrase, or statement repeated from the preceding sentence (usually in order to place it in a new connexion). Now somewhat *rare*.

c **1220** *Bestiary* 680 After him prophetes alle miȝte her non him [Adam] maken on stalle, on stalle, i seie, ðer he er stod. **1540** *Great Bible, Ps.* cxxx. 6 My soule flyeth vnto the Lorde, before the mornyng watche (I saye) before the mornynge watche. **1563** WINȜET tr. *Vincentius Lirin.* To Q. Marie, Wks. (S.T.S.) II. 7 The mony diuerse..sectis, raigeing.. amangis the professouris of Christis name—raigeing I say, nocht only aganis..the haly, catholik Kirk, bot [etc.]. **1688** BOYLE *Final Causes* iv. 161 For this reason, I say, I thought it a part of my duty. **1719** DE FOE *Crusoe* I. (Globe) 94, I took out one of the Bibles..; I say, I took it out, and brought both that and the Tobacco with me to the Table. **1833** KEBLE *Serm.* vi. (1848) 134 The case is, I say, conceivable, of a government..deliberately throwing off the restraint. **1906** BELLOC *Hills & Sea* Introd. 11 They took a rotten old leaky boat (they were poor and could afford no other)—they took, I say, a rotten old leaky boat.

b. *colloq.* quasi-*int.* Used to call attention to what is about to be said. (In N. Amer. shortened to *say.*) Also, as a mere exclamation expressive of surprise, delight, dismay, or indignant protest. ***I say, I say, I say***, (theatr.) formula used to introduce a joke; also as *attrib. phr.*

1611 BEAUM. & FL. *Knt. Burning Pest.* III. v, I say, open the doore, and turne me out those mangy companions. **1830** F. TROLLOPE *Notebk.* in *Domestic Manners Americans* (1949) 427 Say! **1852** *Lantern* (N.Y.) I. 122/1 Say—d'you run with our machine? **1857** J. G. HOLLAND *Bay Path* xxvi. 336 Say! What are you laughing at? **1888** *Amer. Humorist* 5 May 72/1 Say, boys, let's climb the mountain. **1890** L. FALCONER *Mlle. Ixe* iii. 80, I say! won't it be glorious? **1913** J. LONDON *Let.* 20 Nov. (1966) 410 The galley stove kept going..and hot coffee—say! **1931** *Punch* 24 June 692 (*caption*) Patient (being shown into very modern consulting-room): 'I say, I didn't come to be operated on.' **1932** W. FAULKNER *Light in August* viii. 172 Well, say. Can you tie that. **1967** *Listener* 3 Aug. 154/3 The sort of performers who, every summer up and down the coasts of England, bounce cheerfully on to a number of creaking stages, shouting 'Hello, hello, hello!' or 'I say, I say, I say!' **1968** M. RICHLER in R. Weaver *Canad. Short Stories* 2nd Ser. 191 The middle-aged couple alighted from the car. 'Say,' Mr Cooper said, 'you've got quite a baby here.' **1968** in Partridge *Dict. Catch Phrases* (1977) 104/2 A character, mid-stage, is interrupted by a 'comic' rushing up to him yelling 'I say, I say, I say'. First character shushes him off with 'Kindly leave the stage'; intruder persists with some fatuous question. **1969** *Listener* 6 Mar. 314/1 Making idiotic jokes—'I say, I say' jokes. **1976** *Times* 3 Feb. 14/3, I say, I've been to the ballet. **1976** P. DICKINSON *King & Joker* viii. 114 They..grinned inanely with heads bent.. and legs in the pose of a comedy routine duo. 'I say I say I say,' said Louise, 'your public face isn't as good as mine, darling.'

†**c.** *Book-keeping.* Formerly used to introduce the correction of an error which the book-keeper perceives as soon as he has made it, but does not expunge, in order not to disfigure the page.

1793 NEMNICH *Comptoir-Lex.*, *Engl.* [with example 'Bought of M. N. *I say* Sold M. N.']

d. ***I'll say***: used to denote enthusiastic assent (either *absol.* or with object or dependent clause). Also ***I'll say so***.

1924 *Dialect Notes* V. 276 *Say*: I'd ——, I'll —— (both approv.). *Ibid.* 277 *So*:..I'll say —— (agreement). **1926** *S.P.E. Tract* XXIV. 123 *I'll say it is*, it's my opinion, certainly. **1926** MAINES & GRANT *Wise-Crack Dict.* 10/1 *I'll say so*, emphatic agreement. **1943** N. MARSH *Colour Scheme* vi. 99 'Does he want to keep him quiet?'.. 'I'll say! Too right he wants to keep him quiet.' **1945** P. CHEYNEY (*title*) I'll say she does. **1954** E. MCLEOD tr. *Colette's Vagabond* I. iv. 35 'Hullo, Stephen! Good house?' 'I'll say!' **1960** N. HILLIARD *Maori Girl* 93 'Do you miss home much?' 'I'll say. Not so much now, though.' **1972** G. DURRELL *Catch me a Colobus* v. 95 Would we, by any chance, be interested in a pair of leopards? 'I'll say we would! Why? Do you know where there are some?' **1974** S. WOODS *Done to Death* 218 'You've taken what might have been a knock down blow with a good deal of courage.' 'I'll say she has,' said Hugh. **1979** 'J. LE CARRÉ' *Smiley's People* (1980) iv. 53 'He was a declining asset, as all ex-agents are.'.. 'I'll say,' said Strickland *sotto voce*.

13. Combined with advs.

a. say away *intr.* = *say on. rare.*

1821 SCOTT *Kenilw.* viii, Say away, therefore, as confidently as if you spoke to your father.

†**b. say forth** *intr.* = *say on. Obs.*

1390 GOWER *Conf.* I. 47 'Sey forth', quod sche, 'and tell me how'. *Ibid.* 310 Thus have I, fader, said my wille; Say ye now forth, for I am stille. **1808** [see SAY *sb.*[4] 4].

c. say on. In the *imperative* = 'say what you wish to say'. Now only *intr.*; in early use also *trans.*

13.. *Seuyn Sag.* (W.) 1227 'Sei on dame!' and sche bigan To tellen als a fals wimman. **1375** BARBOUR *Bruce* XII. 199 Tharfor sais on ȝour will planly. *c* **1489** CAXTON *Sonnes of Aymon* vi. 146 'But here my wordes, yf it playse you'. 'saye on hardely', sayd the kynge. **1538** BALE *God's Promises* IV. (1744) 21, I wyll first conclude, and then saye on thy mynde. **1611** BIBLE *1 Kings* ii. 14 He said moreouer, I haue somewhat to say vnto thee. And she saide, Say on. **1667** MILTON *P.L.* VIII. 228 Say therefore on. **1851** TENNYSON *Edwin Morris* 57 Yet say on.

d. say out. *trans.* (*a*) To say openly. †(*b*) To finish saying, say to the end (*obs.*).

c **1407** LYDG. *Reas. & Sens.* 4583, I say yt out, me lyst nat rovne, Thus ye shuld hir name expovne. **1692** R. L'ESTRANGE *Fables* ci. 95 He had no sooner say'd out his Say, but [etc.]. **1768**, *a* **1843** [see SAY *sb.*[4] 4]. **1864** J. H. NEWMAN *Apol.* iv. (1904) 125/1, I apologize for saying out in controversy charges against the Church of Rome, which withal I affirm that I fully believed at the time when I made them.

e. say over. *trans.* To repeat from memory.

1560 DAUS tr. *Sleidane's Comm.* 231 Let the poorer sorte oftymes saye over theyr *Pater noster*, and after receyve the Sacrament. **1625** BACON *Ess.*, *Friendship* (Arb.) 177 Or that a Man in Anger is as Wise as he that hath said ouer the foure and twenty Letters. **1680** BAXTER *Answ. Stillingfl.* xxxvi. 60 It is lawful to hear an ignorant raw Lad, that saith over a dry Sermon as a Boy saith his Lesson. **1884** W. C. SMITH *Kildrostan* 47 Doris made a comic rhyme of it, And said it over to me.

14. *Comb.*: **say-grace**, one who says grace at meals; †**say-nay**, a refusal; **say-nothing** *a.*, silent. See also SAY-SO, SAY-WELL.

1688 C. HOOLE *School-Colloq.* 35 Perhaps you should have a Say-nay (or a Canvas). **1788** V. KNOX *Winter Even.* I. III. ii. 243 The race of formal spintexts and solemn say-graces is nearly extinct. **1838** LYTTON *Alice* v. v, She with her quiet, say-nothing manner slips through all my careless questionings. **1853** JAMES *Agnes Sorel* (1860) I. 98 One of your discreet, see-everything, say-nothing serving-men.

†**say**, *v.*[2] Forms: 4–6, 8 (9 *Sc.*) sey, 4–8 say, 4 saȝe, 5 saie. [Aphetic form of ASSAY *v.*] = ASSAY *v.* in various senses.

1. *trans.* To try, to put to the proof, to test the fitness of; = ASSAY *v.* 1.

c **1380** *Sir Ferumb.* 1093 Charlis clipede ys leches..þat þai scholde til him go is wounde to enserche & saye. **1382** WYCLIF *Eccl.* vii. 24 Alle thingis I saȝede [Vulg. *tentavi*] in wisdam. *a* **1440** *Found. St. Bart's* (E.E.T.S.) 51 He lost the light of boith yen; therfor he graspid abowte..sayynge his way with his stayff. *c* **1450** *Knt. de la Tour* (1868) 26 And thei ordeined amonges hem how thei shulde saie her wyfes. *a* **1578** LINDESAY (Pitscottie) *Chron. Scot.* (S.T.S.) I. 243 The blak knicht sayit thame all bot thair was nane that mycht war him. **1633** T. JAMES *Voy.* 7 We sayed the pumps, and found her stanch. **1725** RAMSAY *Gentle Sheph.* II. iv, I at ewe-milking first sey'd my young skill. *a* **1801** GALL *Poems* (1819) 12 Time in vain shall sey his rage To blot it frae the gilded page. **1813** HOGG *Queen's Wake* II. *Earl Walter* xlvi, Rise up, Lord Darcie, sey thy brand, And fling thy mail away.

2. *trans.*, also *intr.* with *of*. To try by tasting; = ASSAY *v.* 5.

c **1450** *Bk. Curtasye* 764 in *Babees Bk.*, When þe sewer comys vnto þe borde, Alle þe mete he sayes at on bare worde. *c* **1560** A. SCOTT *Poems* (S.T.S.) v. 34 Grene leikis and all sic, men may say. **1674** RAY *S. & E.C. Words* 75 Say of it: i.e. tast of it, *Suff.*

3. *trans.* To try (*on*) (clothes); = ASSAY *v.* 7.

1599 B. JONSON *Cynthia's Rev.* IV. i, *Phi.* Me thinkes, he lookes like a taylour alreadie. *Pha.* I, that had sayed on one of his customers sutes. **1625** —— *Staple of N.* I. ii. *Stage direct.*, He sayes his sute. **1630** —— *New Inn* IV. iii, She did but say the suit on.

4. To attempt, to try to do (anything difficult); = ASSAY *v.* 16.

? *a* **1550** *Freiris Berwik* 368 in *Dunbar's Poems* 297 On his feit he startis vp full sture, And come agane, and seyit all his cure. *a* **1585** MONTGOMERIE *Cherrie & Slae* 361, I was affrayd to mount sa hich, For feir to get ane fall: Affrayit to say it, I luikit vp on loft. **16..** *Childe Waters* XXX. in Child *Ballads* II. 87/1 For there is noe place about this house Where I may say a sleepe.

5. *intr.* or with *inf.* **a.** To apply oneself, to set oneself (*to do* something). = ASSAY *v.* 17.

c 1330 R. Brunne *Chron. Wace* (Rolls) 1826 Wyþ trip forsetten, ilk oþer to gyle, In lyft in wryþyng þey sayd vmwhile. 1412–20 Lydg. *Chron. Troy* 708/4906 (E.E.T.S.) Wherfore, þe kyng cast & wolde saie Shape a wei her malis to with-stonde. *c* 1475 *Partenay* 354 Sin Aforn vs thre ye apperen, lo! And without worde say for to make passage, It is noght the dede of gentil corage. *a* 1585 Montgomerie *Sonn.* vii. 6 Of mercy and of judgment sey to sing. 1601 B. Jonson *Poetaster, Apol. Dial.* Wks. 1616 I. 353 Once, I'le say, To strike the eare of time, in those fresh straines, As shall [etc.]. 1632 Heywood *2nd Pt. Iron Age* v. K 3 This Diomed? who..sayd to wound faire Venus in the hand. 1692 *Scarronides* II. 30 With trembling hands he 'says to pull at, And tear the throatling noose from gullet. 1790 A. Wilson *Poems & Lit. Prose* (1876) II. 95, I sey'd ance to cast off my coat.

say, obs. f. saw *sb.*[1]; obs. pa. t. and pa. pple. of see *v.*; obs. Sc. f. so *adv.* and *conj.*, sow *v.*

‖**saya** ('saja). [Sp.] In Spain and Spanish-speaking countries, a dress or outer garment worn by women (see quots.).

1841 G. Borrow *Zincali* I. II. v. 305 This female Gypsy fashion..is more properly the fashion of Andalusia, the principal characteristic of which is the saya, which is exceedingly short, with many rows of flounces. 1845 R. Ford *Hand-bk. Spain* I. ii. 196 This male *sagum* is the type of the modern *saya*, Arabic *sayah*, a long outer garment, which is always black, and is put over the indoor dress on going out. 1846 —— *Gatherings from Spain* xxiii. 323 The transparent, form designing *saya* of the lady, heightens the charms of a faultless symmetry which it fain would conceal. 1857 C. M. Yonge *Dynevor Terrace* II. ix. 132 A full dark purple satin skirt..was plaited low on the hips, and girded loosely with a brightly striped scarf. The head and upper part of the person were shrouded in a close hood of elastic black silk webbing, fastened behind at the waist, and held over the face by the hand... 'Ah, you found me out,' cried Rosita... 'I have the like *saya y manto* ready for you. Come, we will be on the Alameda [in Lima].'

sayable ('seɪəb(ə)l), *a.* and *sb.* [f. say *v.*[1] + -able.] **A.** *adj.* Capable of being said.

1856 Ruskin *Mod. Paint.* III. IV. viii. §9 What is suggested in times of play should be rightly sayable without toil. 1891 F. M. Wilson *Primer Browning* 132 Browning has said all that was sayable concerning the celebrated cause. 1902 *Month* Nov. 463 To him, nothing is sayable which has already been said.

B. *sb.* That which can be said; a statement which it is possible to make.

1937 *Essays & Studies* XXII. 136 The meanable crystallized and fixed in the sayable. 1957 G. Ryle in M. Black *Importance of Lang.* (1962) 169 It is the foreign relations, not the domestic constitutions of sayables that engender logical troubles and demand logical arbitration. 1969 J. S. Cunningham *Powers that Be* 3 Infant sayables Along the seamy permeable Undersides of words.

sayall, variant of seyal.

Saybolt ('seɪbɒlt). The name of George M. *Saybolt* (d. 1924), U.S. chemist, used *attrib.* to designate an apparatus he invented for measuring the kinematic viscosity of liquids, esp. oils, by measuring the time taken by a fixed quantity of liquid to pass through a standard capillary tube under specified conditions; so ***Saybolt viscosity***, the viscosity so measured, usu. expressed as ***Saybolt seconds***.

1886 B. Redwood in *Jrnl. Soc. Chem. Industry* 29 Mar. 124/2 The viscometer designed by Mr. G. M. Saybolt, inspector to the Standard Oil Company of New York, is before you... The Saybolt viscosimeter is not,..as at present constructed, suitable for use at very high temperatures. 1925 A. B. Thompson *Oil-Field Exploration & Development* I. xi. 520 The viscosity of oils is generally measured in one or other of three types of instruments, the Engler, Redwood and Saybolt viscosimeters, or viscometers. 1955 Kirk & Othmer *Encycl. Chem. Technol.* XIV. 763 Viscosity is normally reported simply as Saybolt Universal or Saybolt Furol seconds, but it may be converted to centistokes by means of appropriate tables. 1968 Snell & Hilton *Encycl. Industr. Chem. Analysis* VI. 295 The Saybolt Furol viscosity of a bituminous material is the time, in sec, that it takes 60 ml of sample to flow through the calibrated Furol orifice of the Saybolt viscometer tube, measured under carefully controlled conditions.

saycrying, saydly, obs. ff. sacring, sadly.

sayee (seɪ'iː). *rare.* [f. say *v.*[1] + -ee[1].] A person to whom something is said.

a 1902 S. Butler *Ess. Life* (1904) 183 It takes two people to say a thing—a sayee as well as a sayer... The belief on A.'s part that he had a *bonâ fide* sayee in B., saves his speech *quâ* him, but it has been barren and left no fertile issue.

sayer[1] ('seɪə(r)). Forms: 4–5 segger; 4 seiere, 4–5 seyere, 6 saier, 6 *Sc.* (9 *arch.*) sayar, 5– sayer. [f. say *v.*[1] + -er[1].] One who says.

†**1.** A professional reciter. Cf. disour. *Obs.*

c 1330 R. Brunne *Chron. Wace* (Rolls) 76, I mad noght for no disours, ne for no seggers, no harpours.

b. A poet, narrator. *arch.*

1513 Douglas *Æneis* IX. Prol. 27 The sayar eik suld weil consider this, His mater, and quhamto it entitillit is. 1806 W. Taylor in *Ann. Rev.* IV. 560 This is not a truth of nature; it is therefore not the meaning of Samund the sayer. 1819 W. Tennant *Papistry Storm'd* (1827) 17 Ilk comic scene of ilka age, Gleam'd out of ilka sayar's page.

2. One who says (something specified or implied).

1422 tr. *Secreta Secret., Priv. Priv.* 158 Lette not the autorie of the Seyere meve the; take no cure of the Seyere what Persone he is. *a* 1539 in *Archæologia* XLVII. 55 That by the hering of the same devocion may encrease aswell in the singers and sayers as in the herers. 1587 *Sc. Acts Jas. VI* (1814) III. 430/1 All sayaris and heiraris of messe. 1768 Boswell *Corsica* (ed. 2) 331, I cannot endure long the sayers of good things. 1779 Mme. D'Arblay *Let.* Dec. *Diary* (1891) I. 208, I never..have been a sayer of the thing that is not. 1838 Wilberforce in Ashwell *Life* (1880) I. 119 But merely saying a strong thing would..do them no good; they would only identify the sayer with a party. 1897 F. Thompson *New Poems* 136 Mother of mysteries! Sayer of dark sayings in a thousand tongues!

†**b.** With qualifying word, as ***false, ill, sooth sayer***: One who speaks falsely, ill, truly, etc. *Obs.*

1382 Wyclif *Job* xvi. 9 My ryuelis seyn witnesse aȝen me, and the false seiere is rered vp aȝen my face. *a* 1400 *Minor Poems fr. Vernon MS.* 524/33 Bettre is chidyng of a soþ seyere þen deceyuyng of a losyngere. *c* 1400 *title* (of 'Richard the Redeless') Mum, Soth-segger! 1533 More *Debell. Salem* Wks. 954/2 Lest men myghte thinke he fayned, he should seke out and bring furth some of those shrewd sayers himself. *a* 1533 Ld. Berners *Gold. Bk. M. Aurel.* (1546) N n iij b, The most vylanie in men, is to bee ylle saiers. 1588 A. King tr. *Canisius' Catech.* 40 We ar forbiddin be it to bear fals and deceptfull witnes..as verralie is doone be quhisperars, bakbytters, and euil sayers.

†**3.** A director. *Obs. rare*[−1].

1483 Caxton *Golden Leg.* 112/4 (Inv. St. Firmin) And the peple of thyse cytees meued them eche from his place.. wythout sayer or comander [L. *quasi ut unusquisque suum habuisset præceptorem et ducem*].

†'**sayer**[2]. *Obs.* [Aphetic var. of assayer. Cf. say *v.*[2]] One who assays or tests; an assayer of metals, a foretaster of food, etc.

? 1370 *Robt. Cicyle* 166 in Ellis *Metr. Rom.* (1805) III. 146 Thy 'sayer [*v.rr.* assayar, tastour] shall ben an hound, To assay thy meat before thee. *c* 1460 *Wisdom* 868 in *Macro Plays* 64 Wyth yow tweyn, wo ys replyede, He may sey he hathe a schrewde seyer. 1579 in R. W. Cochran-Patrick *Rec. Coinage Scotl.* (1876) I. Introd. 34 The generall of his cunyehous Mr. Cunyear Wardanis sinkar syer prentaris forgearis and vtheris. 1835 *App. Munic. Corpor. Rep.* IV. 2242 The Market Sayer, Corn Prizer, and all the other inferior officers mentioned above, are annually appointed by the alderman's court [at Grantham].

‖**sayer**[3] ('sɑːjə(r)). *India.* Also syre, sair. [Urdū, a. Arab. *sā'ir*, pres. pple. either of *sāra* to go or of *sā'ara* to remain. (For various proposed explanations see Yule.)] A general name for a class of imposts of the nature of transit and excise duties, originally levied by the zemindars within their own estates, and under the East India Company's rule chiefly collected by the government. Also *attrib.*

The sayer duties had been abolished in the three presidencies before the rule of the Company came to an end, and the term is no longer in official use.

1789 in *Cornwallis Corresp.* (1859) I. 557 What are called the Sayer collections. 1790 *Ibid.* II. 492 Our former despatches will have acquainted you that we had taken into the hands of Government the collection of the internal duties usually denominated the Sayer. 1811 Kirkpatrick *Nepaul* 103 The revenues of a village..consist principally in the rent of houses, and the Sair, or duties charged on salt, tobacco, pepper, beetle-nut [etc.]. 1850 *Directions Rev. Off. N.W. Prov.* 43 There are also other items, called Sayer or Sewaee collections, which are much prized by the proprietors, and which in some cases constitute a valuable property.

say'ette. *rare*[−0]. [a. F. *sayette*, dim. of *saie* say *sb.*[1]] (See quot.)

1858 Simmonds *Dict. Trade, Sayette*, a mixed stuff of silk and cotton, also called sagathy.

sayeure, obs. form of sawyer.

sayfe, obs. Sc. form of safe.

†**say-hand.** *Obs. rare*[−1]. [? From the phrase *to say* (= try) *one's hand.*] An attempt, experiment.

1712 Wodrow *Corr.* (1843) I. 362 Upon the 29th, there was a soldier buried in the High Church-yard with the English service. This is the first say-hand.

saying ('seɪɪŋ), *vbl. sb.*[1] Also *α.* 4–5 segg-, sedge, sigg-, sygg-, (4 *Kent.* zigg-); -ing(e, -yng(e; *β.* 4–6 sai-, sey-; -ing(e, -eng(e, -yng)e); 4–6 sayng(e, saing, seyng(e. [f. say *v.*[1] + -ing[1].]

1. The action of say *v.*[1]; utterance, enunciation; recitation. †*saying-again* = again saying.

Often (contrasted with *doing*) denoting a mere assertion or promise, as opposed to action or performance.

a 1300 *Cursor M.* 28581 On seuen maners ar þai [*sc.* sins] for-giuen,..Of hali water þe strenkling, And thoru þe pater noster saying. 1338 R. Brunne *Chron.* (1810) Pref. 99, I see in song in sedgeyng tale Of Erceldoun & of Kendale, Non þam says as þai þam wroght, & in þer sayng it semes noght. 1474 Caxton *Chesse* 134 Courtoyse langage and well sayinge is moche worth and coste lityll. *c* 1475 *Partenay* 3242 Geffray answered: 'wele saide here haue ye; Go forth,' said he, 'with-out sayng-Again'. 1562 J. Heywood *Prov. & Epigr.* R ij b, Saying and doyng, are two thinges, we say. 1582 Allen *Martyrdom Campion* (1908) 3 Saying of Masse, hearing of confessions, preaching and such like dueties and functions of Priesthod. 1845 W. Cory *Lett. & Jrnls.* (1897) 38 Saying by heart is a tiresome and unsatisfactory kind of teaching-work.

b. In phrase 'There is no saying' = it is impossible to say, there is no certainty attainable. Cf. the more usual 'there is no telling'.

1847 Marryat *Childr. N. Forest* xx, They won't come now..but there is no saying.

2. Something that is said; now chiefly, something that has been said by a (more or less distinguished) person, an apophthegm, a dictum.

1303 R. Brunne *Handl. Synne* 734 Þe caytyfe þat lay yn hys bedde, For here seyyng wax sore adredde. 1387–8 T. Usk *Test. Love* III. iv. (Skeat) 255 Certaynly, his noble sayinges can I not amende. 1463 in *Coventry Leet-bk.* 322 And þervppon the kyng, supposyng theyre seying to be trewe, sent his lettrez of priue sygnet to the Officers of this Cite. 1530 Palsgr. 427/2 Take no hede to his sayenges for he is madde. 1611 Bible *Ps.* xlix. 4, I will incline mine eare to a parable; I will open my darke saying vpon the harpe. 1671 Milton *P.R.* II. 104 My heart hath been a store-house long of things And sayings laid up, portending strange events. 1713 Steele *Englishm.* No. 52. 336 It is a Saying I have always admired in Monsieur Bruyere. 1849 Macaulay *Hist. Eng.* v. I. 660 The King read, and remained, according to the saying of Churchill, hard as the marble chimney-pieces of Whitehall. 1858 Lytton *What will He do* I. viii, Then came sayings of dry humour. 1871 Tennyson *Last Tourn.* 622 'May God be with thee, sweet, when old and gray, And past desire!' a saying that anger'd her. 1897 Grenfell & Hunt (*title*), *ΛΟΓΙΑ ΙΗΣΟΥ*, Sayings of our Lord.

b. Something commonly said; a proverb; *occas.* †a current form of speech.

c 1450 Myrc *Festial* 86 Ȝe haue a comyn sayng among you and sayn þat Godys grace ys worth a new fayre. 1480 Warkw. *Chron.* (Camden) 27 For ther is proverbe and a seyenge, that a castelle that spekythe, and a womane that wille here, thei wille be gotene bothe. 1530 Palsgr. 698/1 God save you, whiche sayeng we use whan we come firste to ones presence. *a* 1604 Hanmer *Chron. Irel.* (1633) 2 According to the common saying, Where God hath his Church, the Devill hath his Chappell. 1709 Steele *Tatler* No. 50 ¶8, I can see into a Mill-stone as far as another (as the Saying is). 1861 Max Müller *Chips* (1880) II. xxiv. 250 The name..was amplified into short proverbial sayings.

†**c.** ? = ditty 2. *Obs.*

1390 Gower *Conf.* VIII. 3081* It sit him wel to singe and daunce, And do to love his entendance In songes bothe and in seyinges After the lust of his pleyinges.

†**d.** Repetition of a spell or incantation. *Obs.*

1303 R. Brunne *Handl. Synne* 542 'Why', seyd he, 'wyl hyt nat ryse, And y haue do þe same wyse, And seyd þe wurdys, lesse ne mo, And for my seyyng wyl hyt nat go'? 1340–70 *Alisaunder* 531 With all þe wyle of his werk þe waie gon enchaunte, By segging of sorsery. *c* 1500 *Melusine* 296 So blynd ye are by her sayeng that ye dare not enquere nor knoweth wher she becommeth or gooth.

†**3.** *collect. sing.* General habit of speech; usual manner of speaking; the remarks of a person considered collectively. *Obs.*

c 1440 *York Myst.* xxx. 484 Nought so, sir, his seggyng is full sothly soth, It bryngis oure bernes in bale for to bynde. *c* 1570 W. Wager *The longer thou livest* 1774 (Brandl) But such fooles in their harts do say, That there is no God, neyther Heauen, nor Hell; According to their saying they follow that way.

†**4.** A right to speak; a 'voice' in an assembly. Also, ***to have a saying to*** = 'to have something to say to'. *Obs.* Cf. say *sb.*[4] 3.

1487 *Rolls of Parlt.* VI. 397/1 That no merchaunt..bere any voice, ne have saying in any Court. 1568 Grafton *Chron.* II. 131 These sixe Aldermen..knowyng that neither the Aldermen, nor the worshipfull of the Citie, should haue any saiyng in the matter, fearing their cause, went into a Canons house of Paules. 1568 C. Watson *Polyb.* 67 b, Of the contrary part the Carthaginenses ruled on the seas uncontrolled and hoped wel to have a saying by land. *c* 1592 Marlowe *Jew of Malta* II. (1633) E 1, For though they doe a while increase and multiply, I'le haue a saying to that Nunnery. 1607 B. Barnes *Divils Charter* v. ii. K 3, I must haue a saying to those bottels. (*He drinketh.*)

†'**saying,** *vbl. sb.*[2] *Obs.* [f. say *v.*[2] + -ing[1].] The action of say *v.*[2] in various senses.

1511–12 *Ld. Treas. Acc. Scotl.* IV. 274 Compt maid with William Striveling for expensis maid be him apone the sayng of the led mynd of Ilay.

b. *Comb.*: **saying-knife**, that with which the say of grease of a deer is taken.

a 1858 Kingsley *New Forest Ballad* 51 The young man drove his saying knife Deep in the old man's breast. 1865 —— *Herew.* xxxix, [He] pulled out a saying-knife, about half as long again as the said priest's hand.

saylch, sayll, obs. Sc. forms of seal.

saym(e, obs. forms of seam *sb.*, lard.

†'**sayment.** *Obs. rare*[−1]. [f. say *v.*[2] + -ment.] A trial, exploit.

c 1435 *Torr. Portugal* 50 Torrent sayd:..'An other sayment woll I see, Ore I take ordor of knyght'.

saymne, variant of samen *a. Obs.*, same.

sayn(e, obs. ff. s...nt, seine, see *v.*

saynd(e, sayndisman: see sand, sandesman.

saynite ('seɪnaɪt). *Min.* [a. G. *Saynit* (F. von Kobell 1853), after *Sayn*, Prussia, its locality: see -ite.] A synonym of grünauite.

1858 J. Nicol *Elem. Min.* 298.

saynsure: see sainse.

saynts-bell: see sanctus bell.

‖**sayon** (sɛjɔ̃). *Antiq.* [F., augm. of *saie*: see SAY *sb.*] A kind of sleeveless jacket, worn in the Middle Ages by men of the lower classes.

a **1843** SOUTHEY *Comm.-pl. Bk.* (1849) II. 342 Pietro della Valle describes the Aba as worn by the Persians and Arabs. He says it is a sayon open in front, and without sleeves.

‖**sayonara** (sajoːnara, saɪəˈnɑːrə). [Jap.] Good-bye. As *sb.*, a farewell, a leave-taking; also *attrib.* As *v. trans.*, to say 'sayonara' to.

1875 *Colburn's United Service Mag.* Oct. 185 'Sionara!' (good bye), is your answer. **1880** *Golden Days for Boys & Girls* 3 Apr. 71/4 After this speech they all cried: 'Sayonara (farewell), Momotaro!' **1892** KIPLING *Lett. of Travel* (1920) 51 A traveller who has been 'ohayoed' into half-a-dozen shops and 'sayonaraed' out of half-a-dozen more. **1908** LADY R. CHURCHILL *Reminiscences* (1973) xiii. 252 Many *sayonaras* were exchanged. **1910** *Pacific Monthly* XXIII. 259/2 He is a bad man. You go away! *Sayonara!* **1952** T. J. MULVEY *These are your Sons* vii. 146 The Sisters had arranged the children in the stiff and formal formation for the '*sayonara*'. **1965** *This is Japan 1966* 106 The Honourable Sex Shop then rescued me from an embarrassing and even disastrous *sayonara* at Kobe. **1972** *Mainichi Daily News* (Japan) 6 Nov. 7/4 The International Camera Club of Japan will hold a special Sayonara party for outgoing Chairman John Thorpe, Tues., Nov. 8. **1977** J. WAMBAUGH *Black Marble* (1978) iii. 25 If I ever knew for sure what I suspect about you, Philo, it'd be sayonara, baby.

sayr(e, obs. forms of SORE.

sayse, saysi, obs. forms of SEIZE.

saysine, saysing, obs. forms of SEISIN.

Say's law (seɪz lɔː). *Econ.* [f. the name of Jean Baptiste *Say* (see below).] The theory propounded by the French economist Jean Baptiste Say (1767–1832) that supply creates its own demand.

[**1817** D. RICARDO *Princ. Polit. Econ.* xix. 401 Is the following quite consistent with M. Say's principle?] **1934** *Encycl. Social Sciences* XII. 351/1 At any given time in one market area there could be only a single price relationship of each good to any other good there offered in exchange, so long as competition held sway. This tendency involved the fixation not only of an identity of offering price among different sellers of the given good to the same (prospective) buyer but also of an identity of the offering price to different (prospective) buyers of the given good from the same seller. This is the substance of what has been denominated Say's law. **1936** J. M. KEYNES *Gen. Theory Employment* iii. 26 Say's law, that the aggregate demand price of output as a whole is equal to its aggregate supply price for all volumes of output. **1969** *Daily Tel.* 21 Apr. 14/2 If Say's Law had been true there could have been no unemployment. **1972** T. SOWELL *Say's Law* i. 3 The idea that supply creates its own demand—Say's Law—appears on the surface to be one of the simplest propositions in economics.

say-so (ˈseɪsəʊ), *sb.* [f. SAY *v.*^{1} + SO *adv.*] (A person's) mere word or dictum. Also in extended senses: (*a*) an affirmation or assertion; (*b*) authority, authorization; (*c*) the right of consultation, a 'voice' (in some decision). ***upon my (your) say-so***, upon one's word; ***on the say-so of*** (a person): according to, on the authority of (that person); ***to have the say-so***: 'to have the say', to be the authority.

1637 HEYLIN *Antid. Lincoln.* i. 49 They are only say-soes, and no proofes at all. **1676** MOXON *Print Letters* 2 Their Say-so stands for no Proof. **1757** FOOTE *Author* II. Wks. 1799 I. 148 Do you love me?.. With all my soul... Upon your sayso?.. Upon my sayso. **1788** *Ann. Reg., Poetry* 185 On my Sayso, Miss, I'm turn'd thirteen. **1824** *Niles' Reg.* 10 Apr. 84/2 The whole number of republican members in 1824 (on the *say-so* of Messrs. Gales and Seaton) is 216. **1890** D. C. MURRAY *John Vale's Guardian* I. ix. 169 'Well, upon my sayso!' said Isaiah. **1896** *Harper's Mag.* XCIII. 33/2 It is just possible that I took him through from New York without a train, by the mere say-so of my pen. **1902** WISTER *Virginian* xvi, He was the cook that had the say-so in New York. **1902** W. N. HARBEN *Abner Daniel* 5, I think I've got a right.. to have a say-so in this kind of a trade. **1902** S. E. WHITE *Blazed Trail* 195 In questions of policy mine is the say-so every trip. **1924** 'W. FABIAN' *Sailors' Wives* xvi. 186 'Give 'em to me.' 'Not without Bob's sayso.' **1937** *N. & Q.* CLXXII. 305/1 The labour of scholars is nothing to them; they prefer the say-so of some casual maker of legend long since disproved. **1947** J. MULGAN *Report on Experience* v. 53, I expect major-generals and upwards have a good deal of say-so. **1956** D. MEADOWS *Eliz. Quintet* iii. 204 Perhaps he truly believed the rest of the story—on the say-so of his assistant. **1967** *Boston Sunday Herald* 30 Apr. (Bedding Suppl.) 9/1 Another place to give your husband more say-so is in the selection of a bed. **1978** S. BRILL *Teamsters* ii. 69 Giacalone and Provenzano had set up the meeting and the subsequent murder on the say-so of higher-ups in organized crime.

'**say-well**, *sb. Obs.* exc. *dial.* Also 4 seywel, seiwel. [f. SAY *v.*^{1} + WELL *adv.*] Approval expressed in words; verbal commendation. (Orig. as *personification.*)

1362 LANGL. *P. Pl.* A. x. 19 Þe Cunstable of þe Castel.. haþ fyue feire sones bi his furste wyf: Sire seowel and seywel [etc.]. **15..** *Six Ballads* (Percy Soc. 1844) 6 Say-well is good, but do-well is better. **1628** GAULE *Pract. Theorists Panegyr.* (1629) 9 He did not well to them, without their Say-well of him. **1876** *Whitby Gloss.* 52 'Say weel is good, but deea-weel is better', explained by what the pious matron remarked, 'I cannot talk my religion, but I can live it.'

‖**sayyid** (ˈseɪjɪd). Also seid, seyd, seyed, seyud, seyyad, seyyid, syed, syeud, syud. [Arab. *sayyid*, lit. 'lord', 'prince'. Cf. CID.] In Muslim countries, the title given to a man who is supposed to trace his descent from Husain, the elder grandson of the Prophet. Also *attrib.*

1788 BURKE *Sp. agst. W. Hastings* Wks. 1821 VII. 91 He was a Syed, that is to say, a descendant of Mahomed. **1799** EDMONSTONE in Owen *Wellesley's Desp.* (1877) 82 The respected and accomplished Syuds.. are now nominated and deputed with this friendly letter. **1811** tr. *Niebuhr's Trav. Arab.* in *Pinkerton's Voy.* X. 39 He looked with disdain upon the Turkish Sherriffes, and the Arabian Seids. *c* **1813** MRS. SHERWOOD *Ayah & Lady* v. 29 There is but one God, whatever you Hindoos may say. Our syeuds always say so. **1824** HEBER *Jrnl.* 20 July, Real Seyuds, descendents of the prophet. **1827** LADY H. STANHOPE *Mem.* (1845) I. ii. 56 A young *seyd*, a friend of mine. **1840** FRASER *Koordistan*, etc. I. iv. 99 All individuals of that order of Seyeds, called *Suggerân*,—that is, who can boast of an indisputable descent from the daughter of the prophet in the male line. **1849** *Dry Leaves* 22 A Seyyad by birth, he had killed his brother to obtain some property. **1850** *Directions Rev. Off. N.W. Prov.* 47 There is a great tendency.. to be more lenient towards the powerful or the indolent, such as Syuds, Bráhmans, or Goojurs. **1855** R. F. BURTON *Al-Medinah & Meccah* ii. (1893) 3 In Arabia.. the Sayyid is the descendant of Hosayn. .. In Persia and India, the Sharif is the son of a Sayyid woman and a common Moslem. **1912** *Scotsman* 5 Apr. 4 A seyyid.. and twenty-four other persons.. have been arrested.

‖**saz** (saz). [Turk., ad. Pers. *sāz* musical instrument.] A stringed instrument similar to the tamboura, found in Turkey, North Africa, and the Near East.

1870 C. ENGEL *Descr. Catal. Musical Instr. in S. Kensington Museum* 26 Saz, a small kind of *tamboura*... The *saz* is chiefly used by the *Sho'ara*, i.e. 'Poets', who are itinerant musicians and bands of the Mussulmans. *Double saz*, inlaid with various woods and mother-of-pearl. **1918** A. A. STANLEY *Catal. of Stearns Collection of Musical Instr.* IV. 150 *Saz*, tanbur type... Algeria... Slender neck with two flat heads. Wire strings. *Ibid.* 155 *Saz*... Egypt. Pear-shaped body of some soft wood. **1957** T. SLESSOR *First Overland* iv. 48 Umtaz played his *saz* and sang. It was an instrument like an Elizabethan mandolin, and gave a strumming, jangling accompaniment to the folk-songs. **1969** J. RATHBONE *With my Knives I know I'm Good* xiii. 103 We.. sang Turkish and Russian songs to a saz which he played well. **1977** *Early Music* July 437/1 The Early Music Consort of Melbourne (medieval harp, saz, lute, rauschpfeife, [etc.]). **1980** M. BAR-ZOHAR *Deadly Document* ix. 158 The music of the strolling accordion and *saz* players.

‖**saza** (ˈsaza). [ad. Luganda ˋ*ssaza*.] In Uganda: an administrative area; a county.

1950 *Times* 13 Feb. 3/2 Exempted from payment are those persons who, in the opinion of the Resident, are entirely free from blame—that is to say, non-natives and the inhabitants of eight sazas which throughout the disturbances were trouble-free. **1955** *Times* 25 Aug. 6/5 Mr. Kintu is a saza chief. **1958** E. WINTER in Middleton & Tait *Tribes without Rulers* 158 Toro as a whole, is divided into seven large administrative areas called sazas which may be translated as counties. **1964** C. WILLOCK *Enormous Zoo* iv. 58 The *saza* chief—an important man in the local [Ugandan] hierarchy—turned out a posse.

Sazarac (ˈsæzəræk). orig. and chiefly *U.S.* Also **Sazerac**. [Origin unknown.] A cocktail consisting of whisky, pernod or absinthe, bitters, and syrup, served usu. with a slice of lemon. Also *attrib.*, as ***Sazarac cocktail***.

1941 *Louisiana*: *Guide to State* (Writers' Program) 230 The most celebrated of New Orleans cocktails—the Sazerac—is a mixture of whisky, bitters, and sugar, served in a glass mixed with absinthe. **1946** C. H. BAKER *Gentleman's Compan.* II. 122 The best drinks produced in New Orleans stick to the ancient simple formula—and please, please, never try to vary it; for if you do you'll not be drinking a true Sazarac. **1958** E. DUNDY *Dud Avocado* I. i. 18 So many marvellous new drinks.. sazaracs and slings and heaven knows what else. **1961** F. CRANE *Reluctant Sleuth* viii. 66 Regan had liked Sazarac cocktails. **1963** M. MALIM *Pagoda Tree* xxii. 145 Then came the sazaracs. I remember having a word with Canthrop B beside the bar quite early on. He took charge of the bar, to superintend the mixing of this Fine Old Southern cocktail. 'I'm doubling up on the absinthe' he said gleefully. **1978** G. VIDAL *Kalki* iv. 93 We had each polished off a pair of Sazerac cocktails, a local killer [in New Orleans].

sazhen, variant of SAGENE^{1}.

‖**S-bahn** (ˈɛs baːn). [Ger., abbrev. of (*stadt*) *schnellbahn* (urban) fast railway.] In some German cities, a fast (sub)urban railway line or system.

1962 I. FLEMING *Living Daylights* in *Octopussy* (1966) 79 Feeling more encouraged, he took the S-Bahn back into the city. **1974** *Encycl. Brit. Macropædia* II. 851/2 East Berlin runs the S-Bahn.. elevated railway system started in 1871 as a connecting system to a rail net in and out of the city. **1976** P. R. WHITE *Planning for Public Transport* iv. 74 The creation of links across city centres.. to enable S-bahn trains to offer better accessibility within the central area. **1980** G. SEYMOUR *Contract* v. 63 We should take the U-Bahn to Alexander Platz, then the S-Bahn.

S-band: see S 12.

S-bend: see S 2 c.

sbirro (ˈzbirro). Pl. sbirri (ˈzbirri); also 7 *anglicized* sbirres, -is. [a. It. *sbirro*, whence F. *sbirre*; cf. Sp. *esbirro*.] An Italian police officer.

a **1668** LASSELS *Voy. Italy* II. (1670) 252 This Governour .. hath besides his own guards, a *Barigello* or Captain of the *Sbirri* or Sergeants. **1687** *Lond. Gaz.* No. 2224/1 The Sbirres or Officers of Justice. **1688** *Lett. conc. Present St. Italy* 119 The Sbiri (a sort of men like our Bailiffs) carried him to another [Judge]. **1693** *Lond. Gaz.* No. 2890/1 Sbirris or Officers of Justice. **1820** BYRON *Mar. Fal.* II. ii. 28 Had I been silent, not a sbirro but Had kept me in his eye, as meditating.. revenge. **1888** L. OLIPHANT *Episodes* 183, I rolled through Italy in a diligence, in company with sundry Papal *sbirri* as fellow-passengers.

'**Sblood** (zblʌd). *Obs.* exc. *arch.* Also 6 **zbloud, 'sblud, 7 s'bloud, slud, slood, 8** (*affected*) **s'blead.** A euphemistic shortening of ***God's blood*** (see GOD *sb.* 14), used as an oath or asseveration.

1598 SHAKS. *1 Hen. IV* (Qo. 1) I. ii. 82 Zbloud I am as melancholy as a gyb Cat. **1599** —— *Hen. V* (Fol. 1) IV. viii. 10 'Sblud. **1604** —— *Ham.* (Qo. 2) II. ii. 384 S'bloud. **1606** CHAPMAN *Gentl. Usher* I. i, Slud Aunt, what if my dreame had beene true. *Ibid.* II. i, Slood me thinks a man Should not of meere necessitie be an Asse. **1606** *Sir G. Goosecappe* V. i. in Bullen *O. Pl.* (1884) III. 89 Sblood what is learning? An artificiall cobwebbe to catch flies. **1705** VANBRUGH *Country House* II. iv, A parcel of Fellows swear they'll have our Venison, and s'blead I swear they shall have none on't. **1737** FIELDING *Hist. Reg.* I. i, 'Sblood, Sir, would it be in the Character of a Politician to make him a Conjurer? **1737** R. DRURY *Rival Milliners* II. xii, S'blud and Thunder, Give me the Settlement again. **1848** BOKER *Calaynos* V. ii. Poems (1857) I. 102 'Sblood! but they'd make you caper!

'**Sbobs.** An unmeaning oath: cf. prec. and *Od's bobs* under OD^{1}.

1694 ECHARD *Plautus* 170 'Sbobs, as I hope to breath, a smug-faced little Rogue! **1820** J. H. REYNOLDS *Fancy* (1906) 32 'Sbobs! I declare, it does not smack amiss.

'**Sbodikins** (ˈsbɒdɪkɪnz). A euphemistic shortening of *God's bodikins* (see GOD *sb.* 14 b, OD^{1} 2, and BODIKIN).

1676 DURFEY *Madam Fickle* I. i. (1677) 3 'Sbodikins, I am told in the Country there's not a true Wit in all the Fraternity but he. **1694** ECHARD *Plautus* 120 'Sbudikins, you've almost walk'd me off my Legs tho'. **1733** FIELDING *Intrig. Chamberm.* II. ix. S'bodikins! I am in a rage. **1733** —— *Quixote in Eng.* III. xiv, 'Sbodlikins! I find there's nothing in making love when a man's but once got well into 't. **1790** *Bystander* 183 'Sbodikins', cried Cozin, 'but I do tell ye I be not'. **1872** CALVERLEY *Fly Leaves* (1884) 115, I flopp'd forth, 'sbuddikins! on my own ten toes.

† '**'Sbody.** *Obs. rare*$^{-1}$. Shortened form of *God's body*, used as an oath.

1601 B. JONSON *Poetaster* II. i, S'body, giue Husbands the head a little more, and they'll be nothing but Head shortly.

† '**Sbores.** *Obs. rare*$^{-1}$. A euphemistic oath: cf. the preceding words.

1635 BROME *Sparagus Gard.* IV. iii, S'bores I bit my tongue too hard.

† '**Sbud(s.** *Obs.* = 'SBODIKINS.

1676 DURFEY *Madam Fickle* I. i. (1677) 3, I am heartily glad to see you, Good Mr. Harry. 'Sbud he sprouts up finely. **1682** SOUTHERNE *Loyal Brother* II. i, S'buds! a Months pay is Nothing to thee. **1733** FIELDING *Quixote in Eng.* II. v, 'Sbud! I'll beat your lanthorn jaws into your throat, you rascal. **1889** DOYLE *Micah Clarke* 305 S'bud, we had something better to do.

sca, obs. Sc. form of SCALL *sb.*

scab (skæb), *sb.* Forms: 4–6 **scabbe**, 4–7 **skab**, 5–6 **skabbe**, 6 **skabe**, **scappe**, 6–7 **scabb**, 3– **scab**. [a. ON. **skabb-r* (MSw. *skabb-er*, mod.Sw. *skabb*, Da. *skab* from the 13th c.), corresponding to OE. *sceabb* SHAB *sb.*, q.v. for cognate forms. With sense 4 cf. MDu. *schabbe*, applied to women with the senses 'slut' and 'scold'; possibly this word, used by foreign vagrants, may have helped the development of the sense in Eng.; its etymological relation to early mod.Du. *schabbe* (Kilian), Flem. dial. *schab* itch (= OE. *sceabb*) is not clear.

The occurrence of the word in Kentish of the 13th c. is a difficulty, as the Scandinavian form would be unlikely to be adopted in that dialect. Perh. the word may in this passage represent the OE. *sceabb*, with archaizing spelling due to the influence of the L. *scabies*, which it here renders (cf. Lev. xiii. 6, Vulgate). Association with the Latin word of similar sound has influenced the later medical use.]

† **1. a.** Disease of the skin in which pustules or scales are formed: a general term for skin diseases, but sometimes *spec.* = itch or scabies (also, *dry scab*), ringworm or tinea, syphilis; *wet scab*, eczema.

c **1250** *Kent. Serm.* in *O.E. Misc.* 31 Si lepre [signefieþ] þo sennen, þet scab bi-tokned þo litle sennen. *a* **1300** *Cursor M.* 11820 þe scab ouer-gas his bodi all. *a* **1366** CHAUCER *Rom. Rose* 553 Withoute bleyne scabbe or royne. **1398** TREVISA *Barth. De P.R.* VII. lxii. (Bodl. MS.), Wete scabbe [L. *scabies humida*] with quitter and scales. *Ibid.* lxiii, Drye scabbe.. somtyme.. comeþ of stronge colerike mater oþer melancolike.. and þis yuel hatte Impetigo. *c* **1400** *Lanfranc's Cirurg.* 191 Also scabbe, sum is drie & summe is wet. If it be drie, it schal propirli be clepid icche. And if it be moist, it schal be clepid scabbe. **1530** PALSGR. 265/2 Scabbe, *roigne*. **1563** T. GALE *Antidot.* II. 12 It healeth scabbes, and vlcers of the skinne. **1621** BURTON *Anat. Mel.* II. iv. I. v, It driues away Leaprosie, Scabbes, cleeres the blood. **1658** OSBORN *King James* Wks. (1673) 514 For (spight of his Tarbox) he died of the Scab. **1671** H. M. tr. *Erasm. Colloq.* 168, I think thou hast got the scab which they call Spanish. *a* **1682** SIR T. BROWNE *Tracts* (1683) 114 They commended Unguents of quick-silver against the Scab. **1742** tr. *Heister's Surg.* (1768) I. 279 The Term *Tinea* at present is applied to a large dry Scab, which Children and Infants are subject to upon the

Head. **1757** DYER *Fleece* I. 286 Th' infectious scab, arising from extremes Of want or surfeit.

†**b.** *fig.* Applied to moral or spiritual disease.

1529 S. FISH *Supplic. Beggers* (1871) 11 This is the great scabbe why they will not let the newe testament go a-brode yn your moder tong. **1567** PAULFREYMAN *Bauldwin's Mor. Philos.* VIII. ii, It is a scabbe of the world to be enuious at vertue. **1651** G. HERBERT *Jacula Prudentum* 1137 The itch of disputing is the scab of the Church [transl. of the saying *Disputandi prurigo est ecclesiæ scabies*]. **1791** WOLCOT (P. Pindar) *Rights of Kings* Wks. 1812 II. 429 O for an ointment to destroy the scab Call'd Envy.

2. a. A cutaneous disease in animals, esp. sheep, resembling the itch and the mange.

c **1386** CHAUCER *Pard. Prol.* 30 Of pokkes, and of scabbe, ..Shal euery sheepe be hool. **1523** FITZHERB. *Husb.* (1534) C 8 This maner of foldynge shall brede noo mathes nor scabbe. **1538** STARKEY *England* I. iii. 98 When they [*i.e.* sheep] are closyd in ranke pasturys and butful [? batful] ground, they are sone touchyd wyth the skabe. **1697** DRYDEN *Virg. Georg.* iii. 468 That free from Gouts thou mayst preserve thy Care [*viz.* sheep], And clear from Scabs. **1748** tr. *Vegetius' Distempers of Horses* 11 Some indeed have attempted to call the Scab the subtercutaneous Distemper. **1796** WITHERING *Brit. Plants* (ed. 3) III. 554 Swine that have the scab. **1863** BARING-GOULD *Iceland* 101 The sheep in the north are quite well—whilst the scab reappears yearly in the south.

b. A disease of cultivated plants, due to vegetable parasites, and causing scab-like roughness.

1750 W. ELLIS *Mod. Husbandm.* iv. iii. 27 (E.D.S.) **1790** *Trans. Soc. Arts* VIII. 39 The Potatoe is also liable to other disorders; in very dry seasons, excrescences will arise, vulgarly called the Scab. **1881** *Chicago Times* 11 June, The wet weather is likely to produce scab in growing wheat. **1908** *Daily Chron.* 30 Oct. 1/7 The disease of black scab is spreading alarmingly among potatoes.

3. a. The crust which forms over a wound or sore during cicatrization.

c **1400** *Lanfranc's Cirurg.* 185 Anoynte al his heed..til al þe scabbis þerof be wel tobroke. **1540** PALSGR. *Acolastus* Prol. B iij b, They clawe of their owne skabbe. **1581** MULCASTER *Positions* xxx. 110 The skinne being deuided and disvnited with scabbes. **1642** H. MORE *Song of Soul* III. III. xliii, Old fulsome hags with scabs and skurf bedight. **1710–11** SWIFT *Jrnl. to Stella* 23 Mar. My sore shin itched, and I forgot what it was, and rubbed off the scab, and blood came. **1799** *Med. Jrnl.* II. 371 An elevated smooth brown scab remained..upon each of the children's arms, after all discharge from the part had ceased. **1876** BRISTOWE *Theory & Pract. Med.* 316 Not unfrequently, when the scab seems fully formed, suppuration still goes on beneath and around it.

fig. **1599** SHAKS. *Much Ado* III. iii. 107 *Con.* Here man, I am at thy elbow. *Bor.* Mas and my elbow itcht, I thought there would a scabbe follow. **1607** —— *Cor.* I. i. 169. **1799** COLERIDGE *Lett.* 16 Sept. (1895) 306 Mere cutaneous scabs of loyalty which only ape the king's evil. **1893** F. ADAMS *New Egypt* 72 The great city seemed strangely squalid and mean, a sort of scab that had sprouted at the bosom of ancient and fertile nature.

b. *transf.* in *Iron-founding.* (See quot. 1884.)

1881 C. WYLIE *Iron Founding* 30 To avoid scabs and a bad casting. **1884** KNIGHT *Dict. Mech.* Suppl., *Scab*, a protuberance on a casting formed by the washing away of the mold-wall.

4. *slang.* A term of abuse or depreciation applied to persons: **a.** A mean, low, 'scurvy' fellow; a rascal, scoundrel. †*occas.* applied to a woman.

c **1590** R. GREENE *Fr. Bacon* i. (1630) 2 Loue is such a proud scab, that he will neuer meddle with fooles nor children. **1591** LYLY *Endym.* IV. ii, *Pages.* What are yee (scabs?) *Watch.* The Watch: This the Constable. [**1599**, **1607**: see 3 *fig.*] **1664** COTTON *Scarron.* I. 15 A vap'ring Scab, and a great Swearer. *a* **1700** B. E. *Dict. Cant. Crew, Scab*, a sorry Wench, or Scoundril-Fellow. **1701** DE FOE *Trueborn Eng.* I. 16 The Royal Branch from Pictland did succeed, With Troops of Scots and Scabs from North-by-Tweed. **1725** SWIFT *On Wood the Iron-monger* 9 This vap'ring Scab must needs devise To ape the Thunder of the Skies. **1735** SHERIDAN in *Swift's Lett.* 5 Oct., The devil take all the D's in Christendom, for a pack of saucy scabs. **1851** MAYHEW *Lond. Labour* I. 18 'There's a scurf!' said one; 'He's a regular scab,' cried another. **1899** KIPLING *Stalky* 71 You're three beastly scabs!

b. A workman who refuses to join an organized movement on behalf of his trade; in extended uses: a person who refuses to join a strike or who takes over the work of a striker; a blackleg; a strike-breaker. orig. *U.S.*

1777 *Bonner & Middleton's Bristol Jrnl.* 5 July, To the Public. Whereas the Master Cordwainers have gloried, that there has been a Demur amongst the Men's and Women's Men;—we have the Pleasure to inform them, that Matters are amicably settled... The Conflict would not been [*sic*] so sharp had not there been so many dirty Scabs; no Doubt but timely Notice will be taken of them. **1792** in A. Aspinall *Early Eng. Trade Unions* (1949) 84 What is a scab? He is to his *trade* what a traitor is to his *country*... He first sells the journeymen, and is himself afterwards sold in his turn by the masters, till at last he is despised by both and deserted by all. **1806** *Trial of Boot & Shoemakers* (Federal Soc. Journeymen Cordwainers, U.S.) 74, I concluded at that time I would turn a *scab*, unknown to them, and I would continue my work and not let them know of it. **1811** *Sel. Cases St. New York* I. 262 The offending member was then termed a *scab* and wherever he was employed no others of the society were allowed to work. **1881** *Standard* 3 Nov. 3/4 Mr. Abbott asked Passfield if he had not told him he heard Hall call Harris a '—— scab'. **1889** C. H. SALMONS *Burlington Strike* 259 The man who takes the place of another when that other engages in a struggle with a corporation, is a 'scab'. **1890** *Leeds Merc.* 1 July, Many of them acted as pickets with the object of preventing any strangers—commonly known as 'scabs', or 'blacklegs'..from entering the works. **1903** W. T. MILLS *Struggle for Existence* xxxv. 493 The 'scab' is no longer the unorganized and hungry worker, waiting at the factory gate. **1926** [see *bitter-ender* s.v. BITTER- *a.* and *adv.*]. **1938** *Sun* (Baltimore) 8 Sept. 3/1 He had instructed pickets not to call non-strikers 'finks' or 'scabs' or other epithets. **1974** *Socialist Worker* 26 Oct. 13/2, 180 women walked out. But 70 stayed in... The scabs soon found out what it was like to be hated.

attrib. and *Comb.* **1850** *Morning Chron.* 11 Feb. 5/6 Having thus given the characteristics and conditions of the 'legal', or honourable trade, I next turn my inquiry to the state of the labouring men, women, and children employed by the slop-masters, who are distinguished from the 'wages' (or legal) shops by the terms *'illegal'*, *'scab'*, or *'slaughtershop' keepers.* **1881** *Chicago Times* 11 June, It was decided to stop the purchase of what is termed 'scab beer' to-day. **1893** *Columbus* (Ohio) *Disp.* 27 Sept., Their rules prohibit them to work along with scab switchmen. **1926** *Socialist Rev.* June 10 The Labour Press..cannot descend to 'scab' printing. **1940** M. LOWRY *Let.* 7 May (1967) 31 Two years as a scab lavatory attendant in Saskatchewan. **1958** *Spectator* 15 Aug. 225/2 British writers, forced to become scab-labour, are undermining it, completely against their wishes. **1977** C. MCCULLOUGH *Thorn Birds* iii. 60, I suppose some scab contractor undercut me.

5. *attrib.* and *Comb.*, as ***scab-bringing*** adj.; **scab-mite** *U.S.*, the itch-mite, *Acarus scabiei*; †**scab-picker**, ? one who treats sheep for the scab; **scab weed** *N.Z.*, a low-growing plant of the genus *Raoulia*, adapted to poor conditions.

1499 *Exch. Rolls Scotl.* XI. 394 That na forestar hald undir him in his steid haggar, flegeour, turnour.., pelar of bark, scab pikar [etc.]. **1611** COTGR., *Escarotique*,..skab-bringing. **1927** L. COCKAYNE in R. Speight et al. *Nat. Hist. Canterbury* 143 *Raoulia lutescens*... Scabweed. **1933** *Discovery* Sept. 292/1 The bare land patchily covered by flat 'scab weed' looks horribly diseased. **1955** J. K. BAXTER *Fire & Anvil* iii. 78 It survives many droughts..like the scabweed in Central Otago.

scab (skæb), *v.* [f. SCAB *sb.*]

†**1.** *trans.* To form a scab or scabs upon. *Obs.*

1632 LITHGOW *Trav.* VIII. 376 Great drouth And fiery thirst, that scabbe my lips and mouth.

2. a. *intr.* and *pass.* To become encrusted with a scab or scabs. Also with *over.* † *to scab off*: to shed a scab.

1683 *Lond. Gaz.* No. 1864/8 A little Scar upon the Ribs of the fore-side scab'd. **1703** MEAD in *Phil. Trans.* XXIII. 1296 He pointed to a great many little Pustules not yet Scabb'd over. **1725** HUXHAM *ibid.* XXXIII. 394 Those Pustules arose, maturated, and scabb'd off. **1780** HUNTER *ibid.* LXX. 133 The sore being allowed to scab, the slough and scab unite and drop off together. **1843** R. J. GRAVES *Syst. Clin. Med.* xxix. 392 Thus forming two separate ulcers, which speedily scabbed. **1899** *Allbutt's Syst. Med.* VIII. 813 A slowly spreading infiltration of the skin, which tends to scab over.

b. *Iron-founding.* To form 'scabs'.

1881 C. WYLIE *Iron Founding* 58 A loam mould run at the top may scab.

3. a. *slang* (orig. *U.S.*). To behave as a 'scab' or 'blackleg'. Also with *it* as quasi-obj. and *trans.* in phr. *to scab a job*: to perform, or employ another to perform, the job of a striking worker.

1806 *Trial of Boot & Shoemakers* (Federal Soc. Journeymen Cordwainers, U.S.) 75 Their business was to watch the *Jers* [*sc.* journeymen] that they did not *scab* it. **1889** C. H. SALMONS *Burlington Strike* 357 The men.. declared that they had never scabbed a day in their lives. **1895** *Rep. on Chicago Strike June–July, 1894* (U.S. Strike Commission) 308 If there is a strike ordered I will be damned if I am going to scab. **1898** *Scribner's Mag.* Oct. 445/2, I won't scab any man's job. **1905** *Westm. Gaz.* 30 Sept. 10/2 A surplus army of labour which can be relied upon to 'scab' on their neighbours when these rebel against the capitalists. **1907** U. SINCLAIR in *Daily Chron.* 11 July 3/1 The starving workmen will scab. **1932** E. WILSON *Devil take Hindmost* xxi. 223 Several speakers protest..that the companies only want to get them out so that they can scab the job. **1969** *Times* 30 Oct. 10/7 Frantic calls to friends.. summoned..a driver who was prepared to scab as a special favour. **1969** *Daily Tel.* 16 May 27/7 Peaceful pickets outside all entrances will discourage all students from scabbing on the strike.

b. *trans.* To treat or label (a person or a firm employing scab labour) as a scab; to ostracize (a person who is a scab). *rare.*

1806 *Trial of Boot & Shoemakers* (Federal Soc. Journeymen Cordwainers, U.S.) 73 They told me if I did not come to the body, I was liable to be *scabb'd. Ibid.* 77 In a little time after this his shop was scabbed. **1888** *Montreal Daily Herald* 21 Feb. 1/5 Engineers and others who refused to hoist or handle coal during the late effort to 'scab' the collieries. **1922** F. B. YOUNG *Pilgrim's Rest* vi. 409 [The rioting strikers] went away, saying they'd come back again and scab us to-night.

scabard(e, -arge, obs. ff. SCABBARD *sb.*[1]

†**sca'bbado.** *Obs.* [f. SCAB *sb.* + -ADO. Cf. *scrubbado.*] Venereal disease, syphilis.

1651 *Pleas. Hist. Miller of Mansfield* 8 Or art thou not troubled with the Scabbado. **1680** R. L'ESTRANGE *Erasm. Colloq.* 62 Hot Baths..are found to be ill for the Scabbado. **1681** [see PSORA]. **1725** BAILEY *Erasm. Colloq.* (1878) I. 290 The new Scabbado.

scabbard ('skæbəd), *sb.*[1] Forms: *α.* 3 **scauberc,** 4 **scaberke,** 4–5 **scau-,** 5 **scaw-, s(c)kaw-, skau-, skaberk(e, skabrek.** *β.* 4–5 **scabarge, -erge,** 5 **skaberge,** 7 **sca(r)bridge.** *γ.* 4– 5 **scaubert,** 5 **scawbert, scaubart,** 6 **scaberth,** *Sc.* **scau-, scawbart, scaw-, skaw-, schawbert, scalbart, -bert,** 6–7 **scabbert.** *δ. Sc.* 5 **skawburn(e.** *ε.* 4 **skawbard,** *Sc.* **scalburde,** 4–5 **scauberd(e,** 5–6 **scabard(e,** 5–7 **-erd,** 6 **skabard, -ord,** 7 **scabbord, -erd,** 8 **-oard,** 6– **scabbard.** [a. AF. **escauberc* (recorded only in pl. *escaubers, -erz*, 'vaginas', 'dolones', Joannes de Garlandia, 13th c.), *escauberge* (13th c. in *Registr. Malmesb.*, Rolls Ser., I. 55), latinized *eschauberca* (an. 1204 in *Rot. Chart.* 134/1).

Evidence of the existence of the word in continental OF. has not yet been found, as J. de Garlandia, though resident in France, was an Englishman. The form represents an earlier **scalberc, -berge*, which must be an adoption of a Teut. compound, the last element of which contains the root **berg-* to protect (cf. HAUBERK). No such Teut. compound has, however, been found. As to the origin of the first element two suggestions have been made: (1) that it is OHG. *scala* shell, husk, which does not yield a very satisfactory sense; (2) that **scalberc* is altered by dissimilation from **scarberc*, from OHG. *scâr, scâra*, ordinarily meaning 'scissors', but occas. used as a designation for a sword. The Icel. *skálp-r* scabbard, *skálm* short sword (? a. Gr. σκάλμη), *skálm* 'one part of a cloven thing' (Vigf.), pl. bean-pods, have some resemblance in form and sense, but the possibility of etymological connexion is very doubtful.]

1. a. The case or sheath which serves to protect the blade of a sword, dagger, or bayonet when not in use. Also, a sheath in which a rifle, submachine gun, or similar firearm is kept.

Usually made of hide or leather, bound with metal; sometimes entirely composed of steel or more precious metals, and embroidered, inlaid, or decorated with precious stones and jewels.

α. **1297** R. GLOUC. (Rolls) 5538 To is scauberc he pulte is hond. *c* **1380** *Sir Ferumb.* 771 In-to is scaberke he potte his swerd. **1426** LYDG. *De Guil. Pilgr.* 2845 The swerd..was alway stylle cloos In the skawberk. *c* **1450** *Merlin* 118 Whan Arthur was releved, he drowgh his swerde oute of skabrek. *Ibid.* 347 He..yede firste to Calibourne and putte it in the skaberke whan he hadde dried it clene.

β. *c* **1380** WYCLIF *Sel. Wks.* III. 266 It is not liklyche þat Crist..schulde carie a swerd in a scaberge for to slee a sely lombe. *c* **1475** *Partenay* 2790 Then drawing his swerd the scaberge fro, The poynt gayn the dore put he ther-vnto. **1600–1** *Churchw. Acc. E. Budleigh* (Brushfield 1894) 19 Pd. for scabridges & for two swordes & a scabridge for a dager ij[s] vj[d]. **1673–4** *Totnes Rec.* in Jewitt & Hope *Corp. Plate* (1895) I. 162 Paid for a new Scarbridge for ye Town sword.

γ. *c* **1325** *Chron. Eng.* 628 in Ritson *Metr. Rom.* II. 296 The scaubert wes gold pur ant fin. *c* **1440** *Promp. Parv.* 443/1 Scawbert, or chethe (*S.* scawberk, *K.P.* scauberd), *vagina.* **1513** DOUGLAS *Æneis* IV. v. 160 The schawbert with broun jasp was picht. *Ibid.* XI. i. 27 Abowt hys gorget..Was hung hys suerd with evor scawbart fyne. **1535** STEWART *Cron. Scot.* (Rolls) I. 231 Ane scalbert also quilk was of purpure fine. **1600** J. LANE *Tom Tel-troth* (Shaks. Soc.) 127 Then..swords might in scabberts sleepe.

δ. **1474** *Acc. Ld. High Treas. Scot.* I. 25 Item a pirne of gold for a skawburne to the sammyn swerd.

ε. *c* **1375** *Cursor M.* 15791 (Fairf.) Of þe skawbard his suuerde he drogh. **14..** *Sir Beues* (M.) 688 The scabarde he ffound, the sword was away. **1456** SIR G. HAYE *Law of Arms* (S.T.S.) 110 Jhesu Crist..bad sanct Petir..that he suld put agayne the suerd in the scalburde. *a* **1548** HALL *Chron., Rich. III*, 25 b, After them folowed the newe erle of Surrey with the sword of estate in a riche skabard. **1601** SHAKS. *Twel. N.* III. iv. 303, I had a passe with him, rapier, scabberd, and all. **1617** MORYSON *Itin.* I. 111 The sword with the haft and scabbard of gold. **1675** HOBBES *Odyssey* (1677) 93 This My sword, with scabbord all of ivory. **1768** STERNE *Sent. Journ., The Sword*, He return'd his sword into its scabbard. **1802** C. JAMES *Milit. Dict.* s.v. *Unfix*, Unfix bayonet, on which the soldier disengages the bayonet from his piece, and returns it to the scabbard. **1834** MARRYAT *P. Simple* I. xix. 325 The officer..drawing his sword out of the scabbard, struck O'Brien with the flat of the blade. **1861** BRIGHT *Sp., Amer.* 4 Dec. (1876) 97 Every sword leaping from its scabbard. **1891** KIPLING *Light that Failed* xiii, The moonlight glittered on the scabbard of his sabre. **1923** *Dialect Notes* V. 220 *Scabbard*, holster, any leather sheath for a weapon. **1941** E. HEMINGWAY *For Whom Bell Tolls* xxi. 264 From the scabbard on the right of his saddle projected the stock and the long oblong clip of a short automatic rifle. **1979** *Navajo Times* (Window Rock, Arizona) 24 May 19/2 (Advt.), Truck seat cover. Rifle scabbard & map pouch!

b. *transf.* and *fig.* Often in context with *sword.*

c **1380** WYCLIF *Serm.* Sel. Wks. II. 368 Poul clepiþ þe sixte armure, swerd of þe Holy Goost..And þus þe tunge in mannis mouþe is a scaberke to þis swerd. **1589** NASHE *Almond for Parrat* 10 Whiles the sworde of iustice, slept in his scaberd. **1657** T. M. *Life Nim* 106 [That] if ever he met me, he would make my Heart the Scabbard of his Sword. **1671** CROWNE *Juliana* Prol., Whil'st tongue lyes still i' th' scabbard of his lips. **1895** WOLSELEY *Decl. & F. Napoleon* i. 2 He..so overstrained the machinery of his mind and body ..that both deteriorated... The sword as well as the scabbard showed unmistakable signs of wear-and-tear.

attrib. **1605** KYD *1st Pt. Jeronimo* I. iii. 105 What bloud sucking slaue Could choke bright honor in a skabard graue?

c. Used as a type of peace (opposed to *sword*).

1802 C. JAMES *Milit. Dict.* s.v., The favourite expression of the late Sir William Erskine—Some rise by the scabbard, and some by the sword! **1817** LADY MORGAN *France* I. (1818) I. 88 He sheathed her blood-stained sword in a scabbard of peace.

d. In proverbial uses.

1546 J. HEYWOOD *Prov.* (1867) 63 He that striketh with the swoorde, Shalbe strikyn with the scaberde. **1579** GOSSON *Apol. Sch. Abuse* (Arb.) 67 Considereth he now.. that hee which strikes with the sworde, shalbe beaten with the scabbarde? **1607** MIDDLETON *Fam. Love* v. i, Since he has strooke with the sword, strike you with the Scabbard: in plaine termes Cuckold him. **1823** LOCKHART *Reg. Dalton* III. vi, There is an old Scots saying..that 'the blade wears the scabbard'. **1874** MOTLEY *John of Barneveld* I. vii. 331 To throw away the sword and fight with the scabbard.

e. In fig. phrase, ***to throw away the scabbard***: to abandon all thought of making peace.

a **1674** CLARENDON *Hist. Reb.* x. §169 He who hath drawn his Sword against his Prince, ought to throw away the Scabbard. **1724** DE FOE *Mem. Cavalier* (1840) 196 The scabbard seemed to be thrown away on both sides. **1900** A. T. MAHAN *War S. Africa* v. (ed. 2) 200 Not the courage that throws away the scabbard, much less that which burns its ships.

†**2.** *transf.* Applied to various kinds of sheath or integument; a cocoon, etc. *Obs.*

[**1578** BANISTER *Hist. Man* VII. 90 It..prepareth way to the Nerues..as that it deduceth them, hid as it were in a scaberth, to it.] **1608** TOPSELL *Serpents* 103 They fold themselues into a..web. And thus beeing included in a greenish scabbard..they all die in Winter. **1713** A. VAN LEEUWENHOEK in *Phil. Trans.* XXVIII. 160 An Animalculum, that was fix'd in a little Scabboard or Sheath. **1753** *Chambers' Cycl. Supp.*, *Scabbard*,..is the skin that serves for a sheath or case to a horse's yard.

3. *attrib.* and *Comb.*, as ***scabbard-button, clasp, -maker***; **scabbard fish**, *Lepidopus caudatus*, a fish of long, compressed scabbard-like form and silvery-white colour; **scabbard razor-shell**, a razor-shell, *Solen vagina*, shaped like a scabbard.

1802 C. JAMES *Milit. Dict.* s.v., **Scabbard-button*, a brass button or hook by which the scabbard is attached to the frog of the belt. **1866** G. STEPHENS *Runic Mon.* I. 302 This runic *Scabbard-clasp. **1836** YARRELL *Brit. Fishes* I. 176 The *Scabbard-fish. *Lepidopus argyreus.* **1884** W. SAVILLE KENT *Fishes Brit. Isl.* (Fish. Exhib. Lit.) 123 The Scabbard-fish is distributed abundantly through the tropical waters of the Atlantic. **1611** COTGR., *Fourrelier*, a *scabberd maker. **1813** BINGLEY *Anim. Biog.* III. 448 The *scabbard razor-shell.

†**'scabbard,** *sb.*[2] *Obs. rare*$^{-0}$. Also 9 scalbert. [f. SCAB *sb.* + -ARD. Cf. Du. *schobberd* beggar, rogue.] A 'scabbed' person.

c **1440** *Promp. Parv.* 442/1 Scabbard, or he þat is scabbyd. **1824** MACTAGGART *Gallovid. Encycl.*, *Scalbert*, a low-lifed, scabby-minded individual.

scabbard ('skæbəd), *sb.*[3] Also 7 -erd, 7–8 -ord, -oard. [app. ad. MLG. *schalbort* thin board sawn off a length of timber in squaring it, f. *schale* shell, rind, etc. (see SCALE *sb.*[1]) + *bort* BOARD: = G. *schalbrett*. (Cf. SCALE-BOARD[1], which is recorded later.)] Thin board used in making splints, the scabbards of swords, veneer, etc., and by printers in making register (now called *scale-board*).

1635 *Patent Specif.* (1856) No. 87, p. 1 l. 9 Scabberds made of veneer. **1672** WISEMAN *Wounds* II. 123 Of these [splints] some are made of Tin, others of Scabboard [ed. 1676 Scabbard], Pastboard, and of wood... Those of Scabboards are apt to bow. **1683** MOXON *Mech. Exerc.*, *Printing* viii, Scabbord is that sort of Scale commonly sold by some Ironmongers in Bundles; And of which, the Scabbords for Swords are made: The Compositer cuts it Quadrat high. **1753** FRANKLIN *Let. to J. Bowden* 12 Apr. Wks. 1840 V. 299, I place them in loose rims of scabboard. **1771** LUCKOMBE *Hist. Printing* 312 The Ribs squeeze closer to the Winter one Scabbord. **1787** *Printer's Gram.* 116 In mixt matter, or Italic, a Scabbard at least is required before and after a thin Brass rule.

b. scabbard-plane = SCALEBOARD-*plane*.

1846 HOLTZAPFFEL *Turning* II. 504 The scale-board plane, abbreviated into scabbard-plane, for cutting off the wide chips used for making hat and bonnet boxes.

Hence †**'scabbarding**, the spacing of lines of type.

1786 M. CUTLER in *Life*, etc. (1888) II. 270 Scabbording of the lines,..scabbording of the prefaces.

'scabbard, *v.* [f. SCABBARD *sb.*[1]]

1. *trans.* To put (a sword) into its scabbard; to sheathe. Also *transf.* and *fig.*

1579–80 NORTH *Plutarch*, *Pyrrus* (1595) 446 For if any drewe out his sworde, or based his pike, he could neither scabarde the one againe, nor lift vp the other. **1679** CROWNE *Ambitious Statesman* III. 31 The shining Tongue of their chief leading Orator, Ha's neither edge nor point; but finely scabberded In Velvet Words [etc.]. **1812** W. TENNANT *Anster F.* IV. vii, Thus prepar'd To have their persons scabbarded in cloth. **1866** RUSKIN *Crown Wild Olive* (1873) 130 You find that you have put yourselves into the hand of your country as a weapon... You have vowed to strike, when she bids you, and to stay scabbarded when she bids you. **1898** *Chr. Herald* (N.Y.) 9 Mar. 200/2 Let the sword be scabbarded.

2. *Mil.* To punish with a scabbard (see quots.).

1802 C. JAMES *Milit. Dict.* s.v., Infantry soldiers are sometimes scabbarded under the sanction of the captains of companies, for slight offences committed among themselves. **1901** W. STARKE *Obs. Milit. Punishm.* 40 The common punishments..were scabbarding and cobbing, the former meaning to beat a man with a bayonet scabbard.

scabbarded ('skæbədɪd), *ppl. a.* [f. SCABBARD *sb.*[1] or *v.* + -ED.] **a.** Having a scabbard (of a specified kind). **b.** Sheathed.

1887 *Pall Mall G.* 21 June 3/2 A bright array of military and naval uniforms bristling with rich scabbarded swords and medals. **1888** KIPLING *Story of Gadsbys* L'Envoi, Tenderest voices cry, 'Turn again', Red lips tarnish the scabbarded steel.

'scabbardless, *a.* [-LESS.] Lacking a scabbard.

1577–87 HOLINSHED *Chron.* III. 1138/2 Had not a scaberdles sword about one of the souldiors..thrust him almost through the foot. **1823** SCOTT *Peveril* xxiii, The scabbardless sword which lay on the floor, and the empty sheath which hung by sir Geoffrey's side. **1870** E. PEACOCK *Ralf Skirl.* II. 3 His grandfather's scabbardless sword.

scabbed (skæbd, 'skæbɪd), *a.* Now *rare.* [f. SCAB *sb.* + -ED[2]. Cf. SHABBED.]

1. Having the scab or a similar skin-disease; covered with scab or scabs; = SCABBY 1.

a. Of human beings; (***scabbed head***, ringworm of the scalp, *tinea capitis*).

1338 R. BRUNNE *Chron.* (1810) 282 þou scabbed Scotte, þi nek þi hotte, þe deuelle it breke. *c* **1340** *Nominale* (Skeat) 206 W. hath the wriste scabbut. *c* **1400** *Lanfranc's Cirurg.* 186, & þus þou schalt do manie daies til þe skyn be more scabbid þan it was. **1483** CAXTON *Cato* f iv, A wonderful and foule woman ryghte olde that was scabbed. **1484** —— *Fables of Alfonce* vii, The porter..sawe his scabbed hede. **1542** *Rec. Elgin* (New Spald. Cl. 1903) I. 67 Calling of the said James scabbit lyþer carlle. **1621** BURTON *Anat. Mel.* I. ii. II. vi, Boyes in Germany are so often scabbed, because they vse exercise presently after meates. **1700** T. BROWN tr. *Fresny's Amusem.* iv. Wks. 1709 III. I. 41 Some of them having Scab'd or Pimpled Faces, wear a thousand Patches to hide them. **1772** W. BUCHAN *Dom. Med.* (ed. 2) 679 The most obstinate of all the eruptions incident to children are, the *tinea capitis*, or scabbed head, and chilblains.

b. Of animals.

c **1300** *Havelok* 2505 þei garte bringe þe mere sone, Skabbed, and ful iuele o bone. **1398** TREVISA *Barth. De P.R.* XVIII. xxvii. (1495) 788 The scabbyd hounde is drownyd at the laste wyth a rope..bounde abowte his necke. *c* **1430** *Pilgr. Lyf Manhode* II. civ. (1869) 114 For riht as a scabbed beste hateth hors comb,..riht so hate j techinge. **1534** FITZHERB. *Husb.* §42 If any sheepe be scabbed, the shepeherde maye perceyue it by the bytynge, rubbyng or scratchynge with his horne. **1679** *Lond. Gaz.* No. 1403/4 One gray Nag..having scabbed heels and malenders. **1709** STEELE *Tatler* No. 31 ¶3 This great Hero drooped like a scabbed Sheep. **1753** *Chambers' Cycl. Supp.*, *Scabbed heels* or *frush*, in the manege, is an eating putrefaction upon a horse's frush.

absol. **1484** CAXTON *Fables of Alfonce* vii, Of euery lame, scabbed, & of alle suche..he tooke a peny.

c. Of plants.

1693 W. BOWLES in *Dryden's Juvenal* v. (1697) 107 To you such scabb'd harsh Fruit is giv'n, as raw Young Souldiers at their Exercisings gnaw. *a* **1735** EARL HADDINGTON *Forest-Trees* (1756) 10 In bad soil, they [*sc.* elms] are nasty, scabbed, and hide-bound things.

d. Proverbially and allusively: see quots.

c **1450** in Aungier *Syon* (1840) 262 Leste one skabbed schepe infecte al the flokke. **1533** MORE *Debell. Salem* Wks. 938/2 The..putting the scabbed heretikes out of the clene flocke. **1562** J. HEYWOOD *Prov. & Epigr.* (1867) 153 A scabde horse is good enough, for a scalde squyre. **1596** NASHE *Saffron Walden* Wks. (Grosart) III. 71 O scabbed scald squire (Scythian Gabriell) as thou art. **1610** A. COOKE *Pope Joan* 5 Baronius brands him, not meerely for a skabd sheepe, but for an heretical skabby beast. **1651** G. HERBERT *Jacula Prudentum* 1113 A scabbed horse cannot abide the comb. **1798** W. HUTTON *Fam. Hutton* in *Life* (1816) 367 With all these qualifications she was tinctured with a most unaccountable species of paltry pride. Thus one scabbed sheep spoils the flock.

†**e.** *transf.* and *fig. Obs.*

1630 DAVENANT *Cruel Brother* v. K 2 b, Hide me swelling Hills! rough, and scabbed Rocks. **1674** MARVELL *Reh. Transp.* II. 72 In so rough and scabbed a Latine, that a man must have long nails..to distinguish betwixt the Skin and the Disease, the Faults and the Grammar.

f. *Iron-founding.* Blistered with 'scabs'.

1881 C. WYLIE *Iron Founding* 14 The casting is liable to be faulty, or 'scabbed'.

2. As a term of contempt: 'Scurvy', mean, contemptible. *Obs.*

1579 NORTHBROOKE *Dicing* 64 b, This scabbed and scuruie company of Dauncers. **1597** G. HARVEY *Trimming of Nashe* Wks. (Grosart) III. 25 Thou mayest well praye for the duall number, thou scabbed, scalde, lame, halting adiectiue. **1786** *Har'st Rig* cxxx, For our sma' wage, oh, wha wad bide—For scabbit aughtpence, woe betide That we should shear?

Hence †**'scabbedly** *adv.*, basely, meanly (with allusion to the scab in sheep).

a **1548** HALL *Chron.*, *Hen. VIII* (1550) 187 b, The great wether [*sc.* Wolsey] which is of late fallen..so craftely, so scabedly, ye & so untruly juggeled with the kyng.

†**'scabbedness.** *Obs.* [-NESS.] The condition of being 'scabbed' or suffering from 'scab'.

1483 *Cath. Angl.* 320/2 A scabbydness, *scabredo*, *scabritudo*. **1576** NEWTON *Lemnie's Complex.* II. iii. 116 It causeth no great ytch nor heat, as the skabbednes which commeth of salte Phlegme..doth. **1675** BROOKS *Gold. Key* 231 Though the *Psora* or scabbedness may be cured, yet that which is called *Lepra* Physicians acknowledg incurable.

scabberd, -ert, obs. ff. SCABBARD *sb.*[1], [3].

'scabbiness. [f. SCABBY + -NESS.] The condition or quality of being scabby, *lit.* and *fig.*

1584 COGAN *Haven Health* lix, Fumitorie..helpeth itching and scabbinesse. **1651** BIGGS *New Disp.* ¶77 Most of them have annexed their own cruelties, infamy, immaturities, scabbinesse, rottennesse. **1771** J. S. *Le Dran's Observ. Surg.* (ed. 4) Dict., *Psoriasis*, a Scurvy Scabbiness in the Body. **1816** J. SMITH *Panorama Sci. & Art* II. 614 It was observed, that whenever salt was used, this root was free from the scabbiness with which it is commonly infected.

scabbing ('skæbɪŋ), *vbl. sb.* [f. SCAB *v.* + -ING[1].]

1. The process of forming a scab.

1747 WALL in *Phil. Trans.* XLIV. 593, I now usually continue it..till, the Scabbing being perfected, I find it Time to cleanse the first Passages. **1805** *Med. Jrnl.* XIV. 507 The usual inflammation, vesication, and scabbing of the punctured part. **1876** *Trans. Clinical Soc.* IX. 161 The wound healed by scabbing.

2. *Iron-founding.* (See SCAB *sb.* 3 c.)

1883 T. D. WEST *Amer. Foundry Pract.* 246 Scabbing in loam and dry sand moulds.

3. a. The action of SCAB *v.* 3; refusal to strike on the part of a worker or employment of scab labour by a firm. Also *fig.*

1944 *Sun* (Baltimore) 28 Nov. 9/2 The worker who strikes while the war is on is guilty of scabbing. **1956** *Ibid.* 2 Feb. 18/1 Under a PSC order..the company would not be in a position of 'scabbing'. **1973** *Telegraph* (Brisbane) 28 July 5/2 In trades union circles the deadliest of sins is 'scabbing' while your union is on strike.

So **'scabbing** *ppl. a.* (orig. the *vbl. sb.* used *attrib.*), characterized by the formation of a scab.

1803 *Med. Jrnl.* X. 190 To shew..the progress of the inoculated cow-pock, through its stages of growing into a vesicle, constitutional disorder, scabbing process [etc.]. **1829** *Good's Study Med.* (ed. 3) III. 114 The progress of the disease has often been divided into four stages, an incursive, an eruptive, a maturing, and a declining or scabbing. **1872** T. BRYANT *Pract. Surg.* 483 Associated with a wound, punctured or open,..healing, or scabbing.

scabble ('skæb(ə)l), *v.* Also 7 **skable**, 7–9 **scable.** [Later variant of SCAPPLE.]

1. *trans.* To rough-dress (stone).

1620 BRENT tr. *Sarpi's Counc. Trent* II. 238 As the chezil is actiue, not onely in scabling the stone, but in giuing forme to the Statue. **1624** *Althorp MS.* in Simpkinson *Washingtons* (1860) App. p. lvi, To Blisse one daie scabling stone for the kitchen range att the stone pitts. **1833** LOUDON *Encycl. Archit.* §939 Stones are said to be scappled or scabbled when they are dressed with the pick end of the hammer. **1848** *Acc. Quarrendon Church* 7 The external walls are built with random-jointed squared ashlar, scabbled. **1852** T. WRIGHT *Celt, Roman, & Saxon* v. 154 The facings of the stones in Hadrian's Wall are sometimes roughly tooled, or, as it is technically termed, scabbled with the pick.

2. *Iron-manuf.* = CABBLE *v.*

1849, 1875 [see CABBLE *v.*].

Hence **'scabbler**, a workman whose occupation is scabbling; a hammer used in rough-dressing stone; **'scabbling** *vbl. sb.*, rough-dressing; *concr.* in *pl.*, chips of stone; *attrib.* in ***scabbling-axe, -hammer*** = SCABBLER.

1790 GROSE *Prov. Gloss.* (ed. 2), *Scablines*, chippings of stone. North. **1825** J. NICHOLSON *Operat. Mechanic* 537 The only preparation the stones undergo, is that of knocking off the sharp angles with the thick end of a tool called a scabling hammer. **1843** HOLTZAPFFEL *Turning*, etc. I. 171 The scabblers use heavy pointed picks. **1881** *Instr. Census Clerks* (1885) 86 Scabbler. **1881** *Leic. Gloss.* 231 *Scabblings*, the chips or refuse of stone made in scabbling it. *Ibid.*, *Scabble*, to rough dress stone with an axe for the purpose, called a Scabbling-axe. **1893–4** *Northumbld. Gloss.* II. 597 The tool used for the purpose [scabbling] is variously called a 'scaplar' or 'scabbler'.

scabbo(a)rd, obs. forms of SCABBARD *sb.*[1], [3].

scabby ('skæbɪ), *a.* [f. SCAB *sb.* + -Y.]

1. a. = SCABBED *a.* 1.

1526 *Grete Herball* ccccclxxiii. (1529) B b j b, It causeth also the skynne that is scabby to be fayre and clene. **1665** HOOKE *Microgr.* 122 Parts of the leaves grow scabby. **1674** J. SCHEFFER *Hist. Lapland* v. 15 They are nasty and scabby, and use not to comb their heads. **1742** tr. *Heister's Surg.* (1768) I. 288 There is still a worse kind of *Tinea*, or scabby Head, covering the whole hairy Scalp with an ash-coloured thick Crust. **1759** BROWN *Compl. Farmer* 86 Pigeons are sometimes apt to be scabby on the backs and breasts. **1801** WOLCOT (P. Pindar) *Tears & Smiles* Wks. 1812 V. 55 Thus scabby heads, the proverb says, For ever hate a comb. **1829** *Good's Study Med.* (ed. 3) V. 637 Ecpyesis porrigo. Scabby scall. **1883** SAYCE *Fresh Light Anc. Mon.* 81 Anything leprous or scabby or lean is forbidden.

Comb. *a* **1697** AUBREY in *Selden's Table-t.* (Arb.) 4 Selden was a long scabby-pol'd boy. **1695** *Lond. Gaz.* No. 3041/4 A middle sized man Scaby faced, with blotches.

b. Proverbially and allusively (cf. SCABBED 1 d). Also *scabby sheep*: a corrupt person, a moral leper.

1610 [see SCABBED 1 d]. **1728** EARL OF AILESBURY *Mem.* (1890) 176 At the Guildhall, those worthy Aldermen excluded were looked on as scabby sheep. **1861** MAYHEW *Lond. Labour* III. 99/1, I was the scabby sheep of the family, and I've been punished for it. **1894** HALL CAINE *Manxman* III. xviii, One scabby sheep infects the flock.

c. *Coal mining.* (See quots.)

1888 GREENWELL *Coal-trade Terms* s.v. *Claggy*, when the roof is..uneven or scabby. **1893–4** *Northumbld. Gloss.* s.v., A scabby-roof is when the coal does not part freely from the stone at the top.

d. *Iron-founding.* = SCABBED *a.* 1 e.

1883 T. D. WEST *Amer. Foundry Pract.* 246 Scabby castings in green and sand moulds.

e. *Printing.* Blotchy, through uneven inking.

1882 J. SOUTHWARD *Pract. Printing* xiii. 461 Dust..spoils the ink, surrounds the rollers and makes them work 'scabby'.

2. *fig.* Contemptible, mean, vile; stingy, 'shabby'. Now only *vulgar*.

1712 *Odes of Horace* VIII. 12/1 This scabby Lection has passed current in all the Editions. **1861** MEREDITH *Evan Harrington* I. vi. 92 A scabby sixpence?

3. Special collocations: ***scabby mouth*** (*Austral.* and *N.Z.*), a viral disease of sheep characterized by ulceration around the mouth; *scabby sheep*: see sense 1 b above.

1938 J. R. GREIG et al. *Hutyra's Special Path. & Therapeutics* (ed. 4) 579 (*heading*) Lip and leg ulceration, scabby mouth. **1950** *N.Z. Jrnl. Agric.* Aug. 100/2 On farms where scabby mouth occurs each new crop of lambs should be vaccinated, and this is most conveniently done at marking. **1966** V. G. COLE *Dis. Sheep* 217 Scabby mouth can be transmitted to the hands of persons handling affected sheep.

scaber (ˈskeɪbə(r)), *a.* Now *rare.* In 6 scabre. [a. F. *scabre* or L. *scaber.*] Scabrous.
1657 TOMLINSON *Renou's Disp.* 459 The shells wherewith they are tected,..are outwardly scabre and impolite. **1866** in *Treas. Bot.*

scaberd, -erge, etc., obs. ff. SCABBARD *sb.*[1]

scaberulous (skəˈbɛr(j)ʊləs), *a. Bot.* [f. mod.L. *scaberulus,* dim. of *scaber.*] Somewhat scabrous.
1870 HOOKER *Stud. Flora* 274 Stem..scaberulous.

scabia (ˈskeɪbɪə), dial. corruption of SCABIOUS *sb.*
1881 *Blackw. Mag.* Apr. 486/2 Purple scabias and pale pansies. **1886** BRITTEN & HOLLAND *Plant-n., Scabious*... Corrupted to *Scabia* in S. Cumb. **1903** *Westm. Gaz.* 26 Sept. 2/3 Still flowers the scabia, still the fuchsias rear Their purple bells above the tangled grass.

scabid (ˈskæbɪd), *a. rare.* [ad. late L. *scabidus,* f. *scabiēs* (see next).] Of the nature of scabies.
1829 *Good's Study Med.* (ed. 3) I. 637 Scabid, herpetic, and other cutaneous eruptions. **1834** J. HOUGHTON in *Cycl. Pract. Med.* III. 638 The cases in which much inflammation has attended the scabid eruption.

‖**scabies** (ˈskeɪbiːz, formerly ˈskeɪbɪiːz). *Path.* [L. *scabiēs,* f. *scabĕre* to scratch, scrape, prob. related ultimately to OE. *sceafan* (see SHAVE *v.*).]
†**1.** A general term for skin-diseases characterized by scabby or scaly eruption. *Obs.*
c **1400** *Lanfranc's Cirurg.* 248 Scabies is whanne þe iȝe liddis ben reed & to-swolle, & ful of reed pinplis. **1671** SALMON *Syn. Med.* I. xlviii. 114 Ψῶρα, Scabies, Scales or Tumours rising from corrupted blood. **1693** tr. *Blancard's Phys. Dict.* (ed. 2), *Scabies,* the Itch: 'Tis of two sorts, moist and dry. **1742** tr. *Heister's Surg.* (1768) I. 288 In the Pox you ..find both Head and Face..spread with dry Scabs, and scabby Ulcers, which is called a Venereal Scabies.
2. A contagious skin-disease, due to a parasite, *Sarcoptes scabiei*; the itch.
1814 T. BATEMAN *Synopsis* (ed. 3) 191 The Scabies, or Itch, is an eruption of pustules,..it is accompanied by constant..itching. **1834** *Cycl. Pract. Med.* III. 636 In whatsoever form scabies manifests itself, it is to be regarded entirely as a local affection. **1875** B. MEADOWS *Clin. Observ.* 23 Mr. R——, a farmer, of good constitution and quiet habits, is supposed to have had Scabies about twelve months ago.

†**scabiˈlonian.** *Obs.* [Cf. SCAVILONES.] A contemptuous term for some kind of garment.
1600 T. HILL *Quartron Reas. Cath. Relig.* xvi. 86 Did not all these new-fashioned attyres, come in with your new religion?..your Gallegascones, your Scabilonians..and a thousand such new deuised Luciferian trinckets.
So †**scabiˈlonious** (scabulo-) *a.*
1577 *Art Enq.* in J. Raine *Vestments,* etc. (1866) 15 Great bumbasted breches, skalinges, or scabulonious clokes or gownes after the laie fashion.

†**scabine.** *Obs.* Also -in. [ad. med.L. *scabīnus*: see ÉCHEVIN. Cf. OF. *scabin* 'a Iudge' (Cotgr.) and SCHEPEN.] = ÉCHEVIN.
1526 *Sc. Acts Jas. V* (1814) II. 305/1 þe burrow masteris, scabynis and consale of the toun of mydleburgh in Zeland. **1617** MORYSON *Itin.* III. 282 Such are the Scabines and the Bailies. Scabines are so called of a German word *Schaffen* (that is to despatch). **1673** RAY *Journ. Low C.* 42 The Government is by a Scout or Praetor, four Burgomasters, nine Scabins, and 36 Counsellors or Senators. **1678** PHILLIPS (ed. 4), *Scabine*..a Judge, Senator, or Alderman.

scabiˈosity. *rare.* [f. SCABIOUS + -ITY.] Scabious condition.
1608 MIDDLETON *Trick to Catch Old One* IV. v, Out you babliaminy..you cullisance of scabiosity!

scabious (ˈskeɪbɪəs), *sb.* Forms: 5 scabyouse, 5–8 -iose, 6 -yous, -iouse, skabious, 6–8 scabius, 6- scabious. [ad. med.L. *scabiōsa* (sc. *herba*), fem. sing. of *scabiōsus* (see next). Cf. F. *scabieuse.*]
1. Any of the herbaceous plants of the genus *Scabiosa* (N.O. *Dipsaceae*), formerly believed to be efficacious for the cure of certain skin-diseases.
blue scabious, *S. succisa.* **field** or **meadow scabious,** *S. arvensis.* **purple** or **sweet scabious,** *S. atropurpurea.* **small scabious,** *S. Columbaria.* **devil's bit scabious**: see DEVIL'S BIT. **musk scabious**: see MUSK *sb.* 4.
c **1400** *Lanfranc's Cirurg.* 213 Vpon þe enpostym..I leide scabiose grounden wiþ grese. *c* **1460** J. RUSSELL *Bk. Nurture* 993 Broke lempk Scabiose Bilgres wildflax is good for ache. **1526** *Grete Herball* ccccvii. (1529) Y ij b, Sethe the iuce of scabyous in oyle. **1578** LYTE *Dodoens* I. lxxiii. 109 The great Scabiouse and *Iacea nigra,* do grow in medowes and pastures. The smaller Scabious groweth in medowes and watery groundes that stande lowe. Sheeps Scabiouse groweth in the fieldes... All the Scabiouses are hoate and dry. **1579** LANGHAM *Gard. Health* (1633) 600 Skabious boyled by it selfe..doth cleanse the breast and lungs. **1605** TIMME *Quersit.* III. 175 Certaine droppes..of this being given..against the asthma or tissick, with the water of scabiose. **1713** PETIVER in *Phil. Trans.* XXVIII. 58 The Leaves next the Root are whitish and jagged like the small Field Scabiose. **1782** J. SCOTT *Poet. Wks.* 96 There Scabious blue and purple Knapweed rise. **1797** *Encycl. Brit.* (ed. 3) XVI. 687/1 The arvensis, or meadow-scabious. **1867** H. MACMILLAN *Bible Teach.* vi. 108 All the upland pastures are strewn thick with myriads of the purple scabious. **1882** *Garden* 18 Feb. 118/2 The dwarf Scabious is now used for pot culture in winter.
b. *U.S.* Applied to some species of *Erigeron.*
1830 LINDLEY *Nat. Syst. Bot.* 200 Erigeron philadelphicum and heterophyllum..are commonly sold under the name of Scabious.
c. *sheep's, sheep's bit scabious*: see SHEEP.
2. (See quot.)
1832 J. RENNIE *Consp. Butterfl. & Moths* 6 The Scabious (*Melitæa Artemis,* Leach) appears in the middle of May... Caterpillar..feeds on the devil's bit scabious.

scabious (ˈskeɪbɪəs), *a.* Now *rare.* [ad. F. *scabieux* or its source L. *scabiōsus,* f. *scabiēs*: see SCABIES.] Of the nature of or pertaining to scabies or itch; in early use = SCABBED, SCABBY.
1603 FLORIO *Montaigne* I. xxiv. 62 Hee..durst not dare to tell me that his posteriors are scabious, except he turne over his Lexicon to see what posteriours and scabious is. **1629** T. ADAMS *Soul's Sickn.* Wks. 472 If the humours be..thicker, they turne to a scabious matter in the skin. **1653** GAUDEN *Hierasp.* 504 Their illfed flocks and scabious Congregations. **1764** G. PSALMANAZAR *Mem.* 153 The scabious disease, which by that time had spread itself all over my skin. **1834** *Cycl. Pract. Med.* III. 639/1 The insects taken from the scabious vesicles.

ˈscabish. *U.S.* [? Corruption of SCABIOUS *sb.*] The Evening Primrose, *Œnothera biennis.*
1845–50 MRS. LINCOLN *Lect. Bot.* 159. **1846–50** A. WOOD *Class-bk. Bot.* 263.

scabland (ˈskæblænd). *U.S. Physical Geogr.* [f. SCAB *sb.* + LAND *sb.*] Flat, elevated land consisting of igneous rock with a patchy covering of poor, thin soil and little vegetation, and deeply scarred by channels of glacial or fluvioglacial origin; *spec.* that forming part of the Columbia Plateau, Washington State, U.S.A. Freq. *pl.*
1923 J. H. BRETZ in *Bull. Geol. Soc. Amer.* XXXIV. 577 The 'Scablands' are lowlands among the groups of 'Palouse Hills', plane in a general way, but diversified by a multiplicity of irregular and commonly anastomosing channels and rock-basins eroded in basalt, and containing meadows, swamps, and lakes... The local name refers to the absence of soil over much of these tracts, the basalt outcropping in ledges and over considerable level areas. **1923** —— in *Jrnl. Geol.* XXXI. 617 The terms 'scabland' and 'scabrock' are used in the Pacific Northwest to describe areas where denudation has removed or prevented the accumulation of a mantle of soil, and the underlying rock is exposed or covered largely with its own coarse, angular débris. *Ibid.* 620 The channeled scablands are the erosive record of large, high-gradient, glacier-born streams. **1943** *Science* 10 Sept. 229/1 The rock basins of the scablands are found in the wider channels particularly, and rock basins are an almost universal feature of glaciated regions. It is the channels with their included low mesas which are the unique feature of the scablands. **1956** C. RELANDER *Drummers & Dreamers* 235 The River People were virtually forgotten in their deep desolation of sagebrush, basaltic cliffs, raw umber hills and scabland. **1966** *N.Z. Jrnl. Geol. & Geophysics* IX. 130 (*heading*) Antarctic scablands. **1976** C. L. MATSCH *N. Amer. & Great Ice Age* vi. 74 At peak stage Lake Missoula had a surface area of about 7,500 km² and contained an estimated 2,000 km³ of water. All this water is thought to have discharged westward in a matter of a few days... This great flood moved boulders with diameters greater than 10 m and scoured a system of coulees across the Columbia Plateau. This great tract of flood-eroded topography is called the channeled scablands.

†**ˈscabness.** *Obs.* App. f. SCAB *sb.*[1] + -NESS, if not an error for SCABBINESS.
c **1450** *ME. Med. Bk.* (Heinrich) 222 Anoþer maner baþ for scabnesse & rownesse of body & of skyn.

scabrate (ˈskeɪbrət), *a.* [ad. late L. *scabrāt-us,* f. *scaber*: see -ATE[2].] = SCABROUS.
1890 BILLINGS *Med. Dict.*

scabre: see SCABER.

†**scaˈbredity.** *Obs.* [irreg. f. L. *scabrēdo* (f. *scaber* SCABROUS) + -ITY.] Roughness, scabbiness.
1624 BURTON *Anat. Mel.* III. ii. v. iii, Many faults in Physiognomie, and ill colour,..inequalities, roughnesse, scabredity, palenesse, yellownes.

scabrid (ˈskeɪbrɪd), *a.* [ad. late L. *scabrid-us,* f. *scaber* SCABROUS.] Somewhat scabrous.
1866 *Treas. Bot.* 1027/2 *Scabrid, Scabriusculous,* slightly rough to the touch. **1870** HOOKER *Stud. Flora* p. xv Borragineæ,..Hispid or scabrid herbs.

scabridge, obs. form of SCABBARD *sb.*[1]

scabridity (skəˈbrɪdɪtɪ). [f. SCABRID + -ITY.] Slight roughness.
1870 HOOKER *Stud. Flora* 474 Equisetum hyemale.. distinguished by its size, glaucous colour, scabridity, and stems.

scabriˈusculous, *a. Bot.* [f. mod.L. *scabriusculus,* irreg. dim. f. *scaber* SCABROUS.] = SCABRID.
1866 [see SCABRID].

scabro- (ˈskeɪbrəʊ), used as combining form of L. *scaber* SCABROUS in the sense of 'roughly', 'rough and...', as *scabro-striate.*
1848 DANA *Zooph.* 476 The lateral [calicles]..very finely scabro-striate.

scabrosely (skeɪˈbrəʊslɪ), *adv.* [f. **scabrose,* ad. late L. *scabrōsus,* f. *scaber* SCABROUS.] In a scabrous manner.
1848 DANA *Zooph.* 275 Lamellæ..scabrosely serrulate.

scaˈbrosity. *rare*[−1]. [ad. late L. *scabrōsitās,* f. *scabrōsus* (see prec.).] Roughness.
1657 TOMLINSON *Renou's Disp., Physical Dict.*

scabrous (ˈskeɪbrəs, now freq. ˈskæbrəs), *a.* [f. L. *scabr-, scaber* (related to *scabĕre* to scrape, scratch) + -OUS. Cf. also late L. *scabrōsus,* F. *scabreux.*]
1. a. Rough with minute points or knobs, as distinguished from unevenness of surface: esp. *Nat. Hist.* and *Physiol.*
1657 S. PURCHAS *Pol. Flying-Ins.* I. iii. 7 All her feet are scabrous, and rough, to take hold at the first touch. **1741** MONRO *Anat. Nerves* (ed. 3) 103 A scabrous bony Ridge. **1760** J. LEE *Introd. Bot.* III. v. (1765) 183 Scabrous, rugged; when the Disk is covered with Tubercules, little knobs. **1790** BEWICK *Hist. Quadrup.* 145 The surface of the skin was scabrous and knotty, of a close texture, and when dry extremely hard. **1803** HERSCHEL in *Phil. Trans.* XCVII. 215 A lens that had a very scabrous polish on one side. **1826** KIRBY & SP. *Entomol.* IV. xlvi. 273 *Scabrous*... Rough to the touch from granules scarcely visible. **1829** *Good's Study Med.* (ed. 3) III. 427 The alæ of the nose become swelled and scabrous. **1894** R. B. SHARPE *Birds Gt. Brit.* I. 4 [The Rook has] the forehead and sides of face bare, and covered with a white scabrous skin.
b. In fig. phr. with reference to caustic writing.
1862 M. HOPKINS *Hawaii* 275 He wrote with point and rapidity, and his pen had a scabrous edge.
c. Encrusted, begrimed. Chiefly *U.S.*
1939 *Listener* 19 Jan. 157/1 A once bewitching villa, now scabrous, awaits the knacker. *a* **1961** J. REYNOLDS in Webster s.v., [The] shell of the house is scabrous with lichen and mildew. **1962** P. H. JOHNSON *Error of Judgement* xxxiii. 240 In this early glow, the tattered and scabrous paintwork on the porticos looked like a covering of dead leaves, ivy, or virginia creeper, brittle at the end of autumn. **1967** T. KENEALLY *Bring Larks & Heroes* ii. 16 In its [*sc.* a hut's] bay of scabrous timber, it was altogether a poor comment on Halloran's vehemence. **1969** *N.Y. Rev. Books* 2 Jan. 14/1 Trudging over countless guts of cement that ran like slag in Gehenna; I stuffed my scabrous shoes with newspapers.
2. Of an author, his compositon or style: Harsh, unmusical, unpolished.
Cf. late L. *versus scabri* (Macrobius).
a **1585** POLWART *Flyting w. Montgomerie* 31 Thy ragged roundels,..some out of lyne, with scabrous colours. *a* **1637** B. JONSON *Discov.* Wks. II. 119 Virgill was most loving of Antiquity; yet how rarely doth hee insert *aquai,* and *pictai*! Lucretius is scabrous and rough in these. **1656** BLOUNT *Glossogr.* s.v., A Scabrous style, for an unpleasant kinde of writing. **1693** DRYDEN *Disc. Satire* Ess. (ed. Ker) II. 70 His [Persius'] verse is scabrous, and hobbling.
3. Full of obstacles, difficult, 'thorny'.
1646 R. BAILLIE *Lett. & Jrnls.* (1841) II. 349 We stick long sometymes upon scabrous questions. **1810** BENTHAM *Packing* (1821) 72 Whosoever would be saved from falling into error and heterodoxy on this scabrous ground. **1832** AUSTIN *Jurispr.* ii. 46 We must pick our scabrous way with the help of a glimmering light. **1904** *Times* 15 June 7/2 When this scabrous moment arrives the Russian defenders may remember Dragomiroff and his advice.
4. Risky, bordering upon the indelicate. Now freq. used in various extended senses: nastily abusive, disgusting, repulsive.
Cf. quot. 1862 under sense 1 b.
1881 MEREDITH *Tragic Com.* iv. 66 Sentiment, cynicism, and satin impropriety and scabrous, are among those verses where pure poetry has a recognized voice. **1882** *World* 1 Nov. 5 His scabrous novels. **1894** *Athenæum* 3 Mar. 275/3 Mr. Maude..has chosen to write about divorce and adultery,..and many other potentially scabrous topics. **1951** M. KENNEDY *Lucy Carmichael* II. i. 79 One shouldn't believe a word Emil says. I ventured to ask them..about Terrific Charles, because Emil is always particularly scabrous about him. **1969** *N.Y. Rev. Books* 16 Jan. 32/4 Without going into scabrous detail, might he not have given us just a teeny hint as to *why* 'the experience convinced me the union was indeed for decentralization'? **1973** *Times* 24 May 19/1 [Scandals] create hysteria because they appeal to a scabrous and irrational element in the human mind. **1979** *London Rev. Bks.* 25 Oct. 10/1 His propaganda pieces grow more outrageously scabrous.
Hence **ˈscabrously** *adv.,* in a scabrous manner, †harshly; **ˈscabrousness,** ruggedness, hardness.
1572 KNOX *Hist. Ref.* Wks. 1846 I. 10 Albeit that some thingis be obscurly, and some thingis scabruslie spokin. **1727** BAILEY vol. II, *Scabrousness,* Ruggedness, Roughness. **1847** *Fraser's Mag.* XXXVI. 519 What a contemporary of Shakspeare called the scabrousness of our elder literature. **1977** *N.Y. Rev. Books* 14 Apr. 8/2 The first of the book's three sections, in which a non-existent and uninhabited Ibansk is carefully and at times scabrously described.

†**ˈscab-shin,** *a. Obs.* [f. SCAB *sb.* + SHIN *sb.*[1]] Contemptuous epithet applied to friars.
1607 *Lingua* IV. i, Thou taugh'st a scab-shin frier the hellish inuention of pouder and gunnes. **1620** MELTON *Astrolog.* 59 These scab-shin Fryers.

†**ˈscabship.** *Obs.* [-SHIP.] Used with possessive as a mock title for a contemptible person.
1589 [? LYLY] *Pappe w. Hatchet* C iij, If that Martin could thatch vp his Church, this mans scabship should bee an Elder.

scabulonious: see SCABILONIOUS.

†**ˈscabwort.** *Obs.* [f. SCAB *sb.* + WORT. An old name of this plant was *Scabiosa major.*] The plant Elecampane, *Inula Helenium.*
c **1450** *Alphita* (Anecd. Oxon.) 83 *Iacea alba, scabiosa* id. g[e] *scabiose,* a[e] scabwort. **1526** *Grete Herball* clii. (1529) l v b, De Enula campana. Elfe docke, Scabwoort, or horshele. **1657** W. COLES *Adam in Eden* lxxix. 148 We in English call it

Elecampane generally, yet in some Countries of this Land, it is called Scabwort and Horse-heal.

scacchic ('skækɪk), *a. rare.* [f. It. *scacchi* chess + -IC.] Of or pertaining to chess.
1860 in W. Fiske *Chess Tales* (1912) 159 Stern old fellows were these scacchic sages! They considered the laws of chess as inviolable as those of the Medes and Persians. *Ibid.* 163 Since first the scacchic art was brought from the land of India. **1959** *Information Bull. Libr. Congress* 27 Apr. 238 The Chess Club has elected the following officers to guide its scacchic destinies during 1959.

scace, obs. form of SCARCE, SCATCH.

scach, scacite: see SCATCH, SCARCITY.

†**scad**[1]. *Obs. rare*—0. In 5 scadde. A corpse.
c **1440** *Promp. Parv.* 442/1 Scadde [*Winch. MS.* scaddo], *cadauer.*

scad[2] (skæd). Now *dial.* (Kent, Sussex, Lincs.: see E.D.D.). Also **skad.** [Cf. *scag*, SKEG.] A wild black plum; *esp.* the bullace, *Prunus insititia.*
1577 B. GOOGE *Heresbach's Husb.* II. 110 Okes, Mastholmes, Skaddes [orig. *pruno sylvestri*], Pine trees, and Fyrre. **1736** PEGGE *Kenticisms* (E.D.S.), *Scads*, black bullace; or a bastard damasin growing in the hedges. **1777** JACOB *Plantæ Faversh.* Index p. xxiii, Scad Tree, or Scad Plumb.

scad[3] (skæd). Also **skad.** [Source unknown; app. originally used in Cornwall.
Cf. Welsh *ysgadan* herrings, Norw. dial. *skad* gwyniad, Sw. *skädde* flounder.]
1. The fish *Caranx trachurus* (*Trachurus saurus*), characterized by having its lateral line armed with bony plates, found abundantly on the British coasts and used for bait; also applied to other fishes of the genus *Caranx* and related genera (cf. *mackerel-scad*); the horse-mackerel.
1602 CAREW *Cornwall* 30 Of round fish [there are] Brit, Sprat, Barne,.. Scad [etc.]. *Ibid.* 35 Some gutted and kept in pickle, as the lesser Whitings, Pollock, Eeles, and Squarie Scads. *a* **1672** WILLUGHBY *Hist. Pisc.* IV. xii. 290 *Cornubiensibus* a Scad. **1769** PENNANT *Brit. Zool.* III. 225. **1845** *New Statist. Acc. Scot.* XIV. (*Ross*) 190 The common mackerel is numerous as is also the scad or horse mackerel. **1888** GOODE *Amer. Fishes* 231 The Scads, known in England as the 'Horse-Mackerels', appear to occur in all temperate and tropical waters.
b. *attrib.*, as *scad mackerel, -net.*
1803 SHAW *Gen. Zool.* IV. 597 The Scad Mackrel. **1836** *1st Rep. Irish Fisheries* 167 The Skad-net is very similar to the Mackerel-net.
2. *U.S.* (See quot.)
1882 JORDAN & GILBERT *Synopsis Fishes N. Amer.* 432 *Decapterus punctatus*... Scad; Round Robin.

scad[4] (skæd). *Sc.* [Of obscure origin.] A faint appearance of colour or light; a reflexion; a faint gleam.
1640 RUTHERFORD *Lett.* (1664) 490 Yea it reflects a scad like the cross of Christ. **1788** PICKEN *Poems* 53 The wights, dispos'd for e'ening-fun, Flee frae the scad o' daylight. *a* **1800** *Lord Douglas* xii. in Child *Ballads* I. 102/2 It is but the scad of my scarlet cloak Runs down the water wan. **1824** MACTAGGART *Gallovid. Encycl.*, *Scades o' Licht*, flares, or flashes of light. **1890** SERVICE *Notandums* iv. 19, I took a veezy through the hoose by the scadd o' the lowe.

scad[5] (skæd). *local.* [Cf. SHAD-*salmon.*] The fry of the salmon.
1861 *Act 24 & 25 Vic.* c. 109 §4 All migratory fish of the genus salmon, whether known by the names.. shed, scad, blue fin, black tip, fingerling,.. or by any other local name.

scad[6] (skæd). *dial.* [Cf. Du. *schadde* grass, turf.] A slab of peat; a tuft of grass.
1880 F. M. PEARD *Mother Molly* iii, I kep un theer, and vather, he turned up the scads. **1906** PHILLPOTTS *Portreeve* I. iv, Two and two the scads stood propped in pairs to dry.

scad[7] (skæd). *colloq.* (orig. *U.S.*). Also **skad.** [Origin unknown.] **a.** A dollar. Usu. *pl.* in sense 'money'.
1858 *Hutching's Mag.* Aug. 85/2 Why he seed Bill and lifted him two scads. **1884** E. W. NYE *Baled Hay* 59 We have mercenary motives... We desire the scads. **1902** W. HARBEN *Abner Daniel* ix. 70 Ef he kin possibly raise the scads to pay the tax. **1909** *Amer. Mag.* Nov. 1 This land of our dads.. is a dinger at nailing the scads. **1933** J. V. ALLEN *Cowboy Lore* IV. 154 He would deal for you both day and night Or as long as he had a scad. **1959** E. POUND *Thrones* xcvii. 22 Canute opposing Byzantium, 20 scads to the dinar, 100 scads to the mark (of accountancy).
b. Chiefly *pl.* A large amount; 'heaps'.
1869 *Overland Monthly* III. 131 A Texan never has a great quantity of anything, but he has 'scads' of it.. or 'Scadoodles'. **1904** W. H. SMITH *Promoters* ii. 52 What did England do when she found she could raise scads of opium in India, but had no market for it? **1923** M. S. WATTS *Luther Nichols* II. iv. 214 The old girl surely did have it—scads of it. **1931** E. LINKLATER *Juan in Amer.* II. xvi. 176 And the pay? Skads of dough. Oodles and oodles of money. **1950** O. NASH *Family Reunion* 89 There's a scad o' things that to make a house a home it takes. **1956** 'N. SHUTE' *Beyond Black Stump* x. 297 It's water... Skads and skads of it, under Lucinda Station. Clear, cool water. **1977** D. BAGLEY *Enemy* xv. 121 He's installed a scad of microprocessors in that control board. **1980** *Telegraph* (Brisbane) 9 Apr. 53/6 They supply pay envelopes in scads to clients.

scad, obs. or Sc. form of SCALD.

scaddle ('skæd(ə)l), *a.* Now *dial.* Also 5 **skadylle,** 7 **skad(d)le.** [Later var. of SCATHEL.]
1. Wild; timid; shy.
1483 *Cath. Angl.* 341/2 Skadylle; *vbi* wylde. **1635** L. FOXE *North-West Fox* 203 There was fowle, but so skadle, as they would not abide them to come neere them. **1691** RAY *N.C. Words* 60 *Scaddle*, that will not abide touching: spoken of young Horses that fly out. **1862** [C. C. ROBINSON] *Dial. Leeds* 398 He's a scaddle horse to ride. **1876** *Mid-Yks. Gloss., Scaddle*, timid, usually applied to a horse.
2. Mischievous, troublesome; thievish; *esp.* of animals.
1589 [? LYLY] *Pappe w. Hatchet* 3 He shall knowe what it is for a scaddle pawne, to crosse a Bishop in his owne walke. **1674** RAY *S. & E.C. Words* 77 *Skaddle*: scathie, Ravenous, mischievous, Suss. **1736** LEWIS *I. Tenet* (ed. 2) 38 A Skaddle Cat, Boy, &c. **1847** BARHAM *Ingol. Leg.* Ser. III. *Jerry Jarvis's Wig*, Tib,.. the honestest, the least 'scaddle' of the feline race. **1887** *Kentish Gloss., Scaddle*, wild; mischievous; spoken of a dog that worries sheep; of a cat that poaches [etc.].

scade, obs. f. SCATHE; obs. pa. t. SHED *v.*

scadewe, obs. f. SHADOW.

scadling, variant of SCALDING *sb.*[1]

scadlips; see SCALD *v.* 1 d.

scælestious: see SCELESTIOUS.

scæn(e, -ical, obs. ff. SCENE, SCENICAL.

†'**scævity,** '**scevity.** *Obs.*—0 [ad. late L. *scævitās*, f. *scævus* left-sided, awkward, perverse, unlucky.]
1623 COCKERAM I, *Scæuitie*, vnluckinesse. **1656** BLOUNT *Glossogr.*, *Scevity*, unluckiness, lefthandedness. **1658** PHILLIPS, *Scævity.*

scaf. Also 4–6 **skaf(fe, scaff,** 5 **scaphe,** 6 **schaffe,** 7 *erron.* **scarfe,** 9– **scaffie, scaffy, scaph, skaffie.** [a. OF. *scaphe, scauphe, escaf(f)e*, ad. L. *scapha* light boat, skiff, a. Gr. σκάφη trough, tub, skiff, etc.]
1. A light boat, skiff. Also *attrib.* in *scaffy boat.* Chiefly *Sc.* Now *Hist.*
c **1375** *Sc. Leg. Saints* xxvi. (*Nycholas*) 274, & in a skaf a-pone þe se sayland. **1432–50** tr. *Higden* (Rolls) VII. 463 William.. was taken into an oþer scaphe. **1483** *Cal. Anc. Rec. Dublin* (1889) 364 All manner of men that occupieth shippes, piccardes, scaffes, and lighteres. **1512** *Acc. Ld. High Treas. Scot.* IV. 373 To Johnne of Newtoun and thre marinaris with him in the Inglis skaff. **1535** STEWART *Cron. Scot.* (Rolls) III. 287 Tha.. tuke the se thair in ane litill skaffe. **1576** FOXE *A. & M.* 183/2 Entring vpon a time with his Hauke into a certaine schaffe or cockbote alone. **1600** in *Rec. Convent. Roy. Burghs* (1870) II. 81 The brugh of Kinghorne.. is.. hewele trublit be the skaffis, skeldrykis and zowis of vnfre touns of Leith [etc.]. **1621** *Irish Act 5 Edw. IV*, c. 6 in Bolton *Stat. Irel.* 38 All other small vessells, as Scarfes or Boats, not hauing Drouer nor Lighter. **1781** *Aberdeen Jrnl.* 29 Oct., A large boat or scaff was put ashore two miles to the eastward of this place. **1877** E. W. H. HOLDSWORTH *Sea Fisheries* 168 The Buckie boats, known as 'Scaffs' or 'Scaffy boats', are of an entirely different build from the other Scotch craft. **1906** H. W. SMYTH *Mast & Sail* v. 100 From Portsoy westwards along the Banff and Moray coasts, and round the eastern seaboard of Ross-shire, until within the last forty years, the 'Skaffie' or 'Buckie Skaffie', as it was often known, was universally used in the herring fishing. *Ibid.* 436 *Skaffie, or scaith*, a type of Scotch lugger with raked stem and stern posts, used principally on the coastline between Frasersburgh and Dornoch, and apparently of Norse origin. **1914, 1927** [see FIFIE, FIFIE]. **1959** *Banffshire Jrnl.* 6 Jan. 4 Open sailing boats, lug-sail rigged, called herring luggers or more familiarly 'Scaffies'.
†**2.** [tr. L. *fiscella.*] An open basket. *Obs.*
1387 TREVISA *Higden* (Rolls) II. 319 Moyses.. was i-doo in a scaf of risshes i-schape as a litel boot.

scafe, variant of SCAIFE.

scaff (skæf), *sb. Sc.* Also **scauff.** [f. SCAFF *v.*]
1. Food, provisions. (Cf. RAFF *sb.*[1] 1.)
1768 ROSS *Helenore* II. 68 We'll ripe the pouch, an' see what scaff is there. **1806** [see RAFF *sb.*[1] 1]. **1819** W. TENNANT *Papistry Storm'd* III. (1827) 115 Weel you may see that siegin' host Had skaff and skink withouten Cost.
2. Scum, refuse (said of persons); riff-raff. (Cf. RAFF *sb.*[1] 2.) Also *scaff and raff, scaff-raff.*
1815 SCOTT *Guy M.* xxv, We wadna turn back, no for half a dizzen o' yon scaff-raff. **1816** —— *Old Mort.* v, Wi' a' the scaff and raff o' the water side. **1899** LUMSDEN *Edin. Poems & Songs* 54 Begone, ye scum and scaff!

scaff (skæf), *v.*[1] *Sc.* [Of obscure origin; cf. *skaigh*, which is used in Sc. with a similar though less emphatically contemptuous sense.
It has been conjectured that *scaff* may have been an adoption of the Du. and G. *schaffen* (whence MSw. *skaffa*) to provide or procure (food). The word might possibly have been brought over by soldiers who had served in the Continental wars; in military use it would naturally have a colouring that might account for the contemptuous sense of the verb in Sc.]
a. *trans.* To beg or ask for (food, etc.) in a mean or contemptible manner. Also *absol.* or *intr.* (Still in common use.) **b.** To sponge upon (a person). Now *rare* or *Obs.*
1508 DUNBAR *Flyting* 133 He sayis, thow skaffis and beggis mair beir and aitis, Nor ony cripill in Karrik land abowt. **15..** *Aberd. Reg.* (MS.) XV. (Jam.), Nae bygging of mair vittail nor sustenis thaim self, and topping of the samen, scaffyng thair nychtbouris. **1583** *Leg. Bp. St. Androis* 904 Ane scaffing warlot, wanting schame. **16..** *Lindesay's* (Pitscottie) *Chron. Scot.* (1814) 512 (Jam.) They scaffed throche all Scotland.. for thair particular commoditee.
Hence '**scaffing** *vbl. sb.* and *ppl. a.*
a **1568** *Ye Sonis of Men. be mirry and glaid* 30 in *Bannatyne MS.* (Hunter. Cl.) 59 Think that this lyfe is nocht the lent For skafing heir of scruf and skum. *c* **1600** ALEX. HUME *Poems* (S.T.S.) 73/163 Skaffing clarks with coueticе inspired. *Ibid.* 74/209 Skaffing scribes.

scaff, *v.*[2] *dial.* [Of obscure origin. Cf. SCOFF *v.*] *intr.* To eat voraciously.
1797 BRYDGES *Burlesque Homer* I. 53 But how the hungry whoresons scaff'd; How eagerly the beer they quaff'd. **1882** *Jamieson's Sc. Dict.*, *Skaff*.. 2. To eat greedily, Shetl.

scaffat, -ating, obs. ff. SCAFFOLD, -OLDING.

†'**scaffer.** *Sc. Obs.* [f. SCAFF *v.*[1] + -ER[1].] A parasite, sponger; an extortioner.
1500–20 DUNBAR *Poems* lxiii. 45 Scaffaris, and scamleris in the nuke. **1536** BELLENDEN *Cron. Scot.* (1821) II. 99 Juglaris, menstralis, bardis and scaffaris [orig. *Mimos, histriones, bardos, parasitos*]. **1598** *Aberd. Reg.* (1848) II. 167 A multitude of.. skafferis of the wymbes of the puir.

†'**scafferon.** Obs. variant of CHAFFRON.
a **1548** HALL *Chron.*, *Hen. IV*, 12 One band had the scafferon, the cranet, the bard of the horse all white. **1586** FERNE *Blaz. Gentrie* II. 67 The Bridle, Saddle, Scafferon, [etc.].

†**scaffery.** *Sc. Obs.* Also 6 **skafrie, skaif(f)ry,** 7 **scafferie.** [f. SCAFF *v.*[1] or SCAFFER: see -ERY.] Extortion; extortionate taking of perquisites.
1555 *Sc. Acts Mary* (1814) II. 500/1 The wemen perturbatouris for skafrie of money or otherwyse salbe [etc.]. **1561** *Aberd. Reg.* (1844) I. 335 Na skaiffry, sic as sampill and scheit schakin, to be tane thairof. **1606** *Act of Council* in *Sc. Acts Jas. VI* (1816) IV. 616/2 The with-gait and libertie grantit vnto Suche shamefull scafferie and extortioun. **1634** *Reg. Privy Council Scot.* Ser. II. (1904) V. 186 For componing.. with nombers of thame and taking of compositions frome thame.. quilk is a foule coosening scafferie. *a* **1651** CALDERWOOD *Hist. Kirk Scot.* (Wodrow Soc.) III. 662 Lyke as the poorer sort in the burrowes sould not have escaped the importable scafferie intended.

scaffle, variant of SCAVEL.

†'**scaffling,** *sb. Obs. rare*—0. [a. MDu. *sc(h)afteling(h, scaflingh.*] A kind of eel.
1589 RIDER *Bibl. Schol.* 1720/52 A grig, *minima.* A scaffling, *media.* **1611** COTGR., *Pimperneau*, a grig, scaffling, spitchcocke, fawson Eele.

'**scaffling,** *vbl. sb. local.* [app. variant of SCABBLING.] *pl.* Chippings of stone.
1747 HOOSON *Miner's Dict.* s.v., In Caukey Ore, the Scafflings are used to be beaten a little with some small Tool. **1886** *Cheshire Gloss.* 301.

scaffling, obs. form of SCAFFOLDING.

†'**scaffmaster.** *Obs.* In 6 **skafe-.** [ad. Du. *schaf-, scaffmeester*, f. *schaffen* to provide + *meester* MASTER *sb.*[1]] A steward.
1555 in *Hakluyt's Voy.* (1589) 298 All the said Agents, pilots, maisters, merchantes clerkes, boatswains, stewards, skafemasters, and all other officers.. of this present voyage.

scaffolage: see SCAFFOLDAGE.

scaffold ('skæfəld), *sb.* Forms: α. 4 **scaffot,** 5 **skaffaut,** 4, 6, 9 *dial.* **-at.** β. 4 **scaffalde,** 4–5 **skaf(f)ald,** 5 **scaffhold, skafold,** 5–6 **scaffolde, scafold(e,** 5–7 **skaffold,** 6 **scaffald, -ould, skefold, schapfold,** 4– **scaffold.** γ. 5 **schafhold, chaff-, schaffold, shaffolde.** δ. 6 **skaffell, -oll.** [a. NFr. forms corresponding to Central OF. *schaf-faut, eschaffaut, eschafal, eschaiphal*, earlier *escadafaut* = Pr. *escadafalc*, formed with prefix *es-* (:—L. *ex-* out) on the Com. Rom. word represented by OF. *chafau(l)t* (mod.F. *chafaud*), earlier *caafau-s, cadefaut*, Pr. *cadafalc*, OCat. *cadafal*, Sp. †*cadafalso*, now *cadahalso, cadalso*, Pg. *cadafalso*, It. *catafalco* (whence F. *catafalque* CATAFALQUE):—popular L. **catafalcum*, of uncertain formation: according to some scholars, f. Gr. prefix κατα- (see under CATAFALQUE) + *-falicum*, f. *fala, phala* wooden tower or gallery.
For other related forms see CATAFALQUE, and cf. med.Lat. *scadafale* (12th c.), *scadafaltum* (13th c.), *scafaldus, scalfaudus*, etc. (15th c.). The Romanic word has been adopted by continental Teut. langs.: (M)Du. *schavot*, G. *schavot(t*, Da. *skafot.* With the δ-forms in Eng. cf. SCAFFOLDAGE.]
A. Illustration of Forms.
α. **1349** Skaffotes [see B. 1]. **1375** BARBOUR *Bruce* XVII. 343 Scaffatis, ledderis, and coueryngis. *a* **1575** *Diurn. Occurr.* (Bannatyne Cl.) 68 Vpoun twa skaffattis. **1869** *Lonsdale Gloss.*, *Skaffat*, corr. of scaffold.
β. **1354** Skaffald [see B. 1]. **1435** *Contract Fotheringhay Ch.* (1841) 28 Ladderis, Tymbre, Scaffolds, Gynnes. *c* **1440** *Promp. Parv.* 442/1 Scafold, stage, *fala.* *c* **1450** *Cov. Myst.* (Shaks. Soc.) 298 Here Pylat syttyth in his skaffald. **1533** BELLENDEN *Livy* v. viii. (S.T.S.) II. 176 To be rehersit on scaffaldis for admiratioun and delite. **1536** KYNGSTON in Ellis *Orig. Lett.* Ser. I. II. 63 The preparacion of skefolds. **1570** LEVINS *Manip.* 219/10 A Scaffould, *theatrum, scena.* *c* **1618** MORYSON *Itin.* IV. (1903) 308 Mounting vpon stalls, or litle skaffolds.

γ. **1470–85** MALORY *Arthur* x. xliv. 484 They were set vpon schafholdes to gyue the Iugement of these two Knyghtes. **1514** *Acc. St. John's Hosp., Canterb.* (MS.), Payd for x naylls for þe chaffoldes. *a* **1552** LELAND *Itin.* (1769) IX. 140 Apon Schaffoldis yn the midle of the market place.

δ. **1581** *Sc. Acts Jas. VI* (1814) III. 197/1 Wpoun the skaffell the tyme of his executioun.

B. Signification.

1. a. A temporary platform usually supported on poles or (sometimes) trestles, but occasionally suspended, and designed to hold the workmen and materials employed in the erection, repairing, or decoration of a building. Also *pl.*, but now usually *sing.*, an assemblage of such platforms with their supporting poles, = SCAFFOLDING.

pl. **1349** *Acc. Exch. K.R.* Bundle 462 No. 16 lf. 7 In .xxvj. peciis maeremii emptis pro scaffotes ad idem opus. **1646** JENKYN *Ref. Remora* 30 The building's set up, let the scaffolds be pulld down. **1696** BENTLEY *Of Revel. & Messias* 32 They must needs be..abolished, like scaffolds that are removed when the buildings are finished. **1737** POPE *Hor. Ep.* II. i. 146 Away, away! take all your scaffolds down, For Snug's the word: My dear! we'll live in Town. **1849** MACAULAY *Hist. Eng.* iii. I. 351 The crowds of workmen, the scaffolds and the masses of hewn stone [etc.].

sing. **1354** *Mem. Ripon* (Surtees) III. 94 In mercede Laur. Wrigth sublevante le skaffald in choro. **1360–1** *Durham Acc. Rolls* (Surtees) 385 Cum cratis factis pro skafald. **1442** *Eton Coll. Acc.* in Willis & Clark *Cambridge* (1886) I. 387, v. dosyn of hyrdelez for skafold. **1691** *d' Emiliane's Frauds Romish Monks* 182 These Monks, out of Curiosity, whilst the Work-men were gone to get their Dinner, did climb up the Scaffold..to view their Work. **1724** DE FOE *Mem. Cavalier* (1840) 97 Bricklayers raise a low scaffold to build a brick wall. **1838** *Murray's Hand-Bk. N. Germany* 159 He was suspended by a scaffold, lying on his back, his eyes protected by a pair of glasses from the falling dust. **1841** *Penny Cycl.* XX. 497/2 As the building rises, the scaffold is strengthened by diagonal poles, the lower ends of which rest upon the ground, and which are tied to the vertical pieces wherever they intersect them. **1849** MACAULAY *Hist. Eng.* iii. I. 423 Every bricklayer who falls from a scaffold.

fig. **1641** DENHAM *Sophy* IV. i, These outward beauties are but the props and scaffolds On which we built our love. **1701** SWIFT *Contests Nobles & Comm.* iii. Wks. 1751 IV. 37 He [*sc.* Sylla] abolished the Office of Tribune, as being only a scaffold to tyranny, whereof he had no further use. **1768** TUCKER *Lt. Nat.* (1834) II. 408 Figure, parable, hypothesis ..serve as scaffolds in raising the building of righteousness in opinion and conduct. **1889** G. M. HOPKINS *Poems* (1967) 107 But man—we, scaffold of score brittle bones.

†b. A painter's easel. *Obs.*

1601 HOLLAND *Pliny* XXXV. x. II. 535 Zeuxis..brought upon the scaffold a table, wherein were clustres of grapes so lively painted, that the very birds of the aire flew flocking thither. **1638** JUNIUS *Paint. Ancients* 197 An old woman kept a large boord, alreadie fitted upon the Asse or scaffold, to have something drawne upon it.

c. *Mining.* (See quots.)

1860 *Eng. & For. Mining Gloss.* (ed. 2), *Derbysh. Terms* 43 *Scaffold*, in a mine, a platform made, where some miners work above the heads of others. *Ibid.*, *S. Staffs. Terms* 78 *Scaffold*, planking elevated by stays and ladders, in order to allow the miner to ascend and disengage the coal in the upper part of the seam. **1893–4** *Northumbld. Gloss.*, *Scaffold*, in mining, the platform at the top of a winning.

†2. A military engine for assailing a wall. *Obs.*

1375 BARBOUR *Bruce* XVII. 601 Syndry scaffatis thai maid vith-all That war weill hyar than the wall. *c* **1400** *Rom. Rose* 4176 They [ne] dredde noon assaut Of ginne, gunne, nor skaffaut. **1481** CAXTON *Godfrey* xxix. 63 They toke poles and made scaffholdes..whiche they sette to the walles. *c* **1520** BARCLAY *Jugurtha* (1557) 78 b, Afterwarde he commaunded scaffoldes to be made about the walles.

†3. A raised platform, seat, or stand, used for the purpose of exhibiting persons or actions to the public view, making proclamations, or the like.

c **1386** CHAUCER *Knt.'s T.* 1675 An heraud on a scaffold made an ho. *a* **1513** FABYAN *Chron.* VII. 506 The kynge.. causyd an hyghe scafolde to be made..where moch people beynge assemblyd, he shewyd vnto them a longe processe of his wrongefull enprysonement. **1523** LD. BERNERS *Froiss.* I. ccclxix. 606 The yonge kynge was..in a chayre lypt up on high,..and all yᵉ yong newe knyghtes on lower scaffoldes at his fete. **1535** COVERDALE *1 Esdras* ix. 42 Eszdras the prest & reder of yᵉ lawe stode vp vpon a scaffolde of wodd. **1590** GREENE *Mourn. Garm.* Wks. (Grosart) IX. 155 Rosamond set vpon a scaffold, to take view of all. **1611** BIBLE *2 Chron.* vi. 13 Solomon had made a brasen scaffold..and had set it in the midst of the Court, and vpon it hee stood. **1615** G. SANDYS *Trav.* 146 A scaffold, like those belonging to Queristers, in some of our Cathedrall Churches. **1687** A. LOVELL tr. *Thevenot's Trav.* I. 54 At the other end of the Hall ..there is a little Scaffold, on which are several Dervishes, that play on Flutes and Drums.

4. *spec.* A platform or stage on which theatrical performance or exhibition takes place; *esp.* in early use, a temporary stage on which a mystery play was performed. *Obs.* exc. *Hist.*

c **1386** CHAUCER *Miller's T.* 198 Somtyme..He pleyeth Herodes on a scaffold hye. **1507** in E. K. Chambers *Mediaeval Stage* (1903) II. 392 [A] schapfold [and] pagentts [are mentioned]. **1519–20** *Rec. St. Mary at Hill* (1905) 304 Paid for a quarter for the skaffold ouer þe porch ayenst palme-sonday. **1565** COOPER *Thesaurus* s.v. *Scena*, Orestes often-tymes represented on scaffoldes in playes. **1579** W. WILKINSON *Confut. Fam. Love* 47 Brought in lyke a mute vpon a scaffold, which departeth dumbe. **1599** ALEX. HUME *Poems* (S.T.S.) vii. 45 Make scaffalds clare for cumlie comedies. [**1801** STRUTT *Sports & Past.* III. ii. 143 The ecclesiastical plays..were usually performed in churches, or chapels, upon temporary scaffolds erected for that purpose.]

fig. **1594** T. B. *La Primaud. Fr. Acad.* II. 564 In the middest of such a..wonderfull scaffold and theatre. **1654–66** EARL ORRERY *Parthen.* (1676) 560 You ought to have so much respect, as not to be a publick Spectacle on an infamous Scaffold.

†5. A raised platform or stand for holding the spectators of a tournament, theatrical performance, etc. Also, a gallery in a theatre or church. *Obs.*

1470–85 MALORY *Arthur* VI. vi. 191 There were scaffoldis and holes that lordes and ladyes myghte beholde and to gyue the pryse. **1533** BELLENDEN *Livy* I. xxi. (S.T.S.) I. 119 þai war constrenit to mak public setis and scaffaldis in commoun placis quhare playis war devisit. **1597** HALL *Sat.* I. iii, Shame that the Muses should be bought and sold, For euery peasants brasse, on each scaffold. **1638** [see SCAFFOLD *v.* 1]. **1671** MILTON *Samson* 1610 The other side was op'n, where the throng On banks and scaffolds under Skie might stand. **1727** *MSS. Dk. Portland* (Hist. MSS. Comm.) VI. 19, I hope to get a good place in the Abbey for Lady Margaret Harley, though till the scaffolds are built I can't yet tell whereabouts it will be. **1770** LANGHORNE *Plutarch* (1879) II. 891/2 There was a show of gladiators to be exhibited..and most of the magistrates had caused scaffolds to be erected round the place, in order to let them out for hire.

fig. **1661** FELTHAM *Resolves* II. xxxviii. 259 By setting us upon an open and adjacent Scaffold, it gives us a view of the actions..that have sway'd the affairs of the World.

6. An elevated platform on which a criminal is executed. Phr. ***to go to the scaffold*** (= 'to be executed'), ***to bring*** or ***send to the scaffold***, etc. Hence ***the scaffold*** is often put for 'execution', 'capital punishment'.

1557 MORE *Rich. III* (1641) 307 He was at Salisbury..on a new skaffold beheaded. **1598** GRENEWEY *Tacitus, Ann.* XIV. iv. 204 He brought to the skaffold many descended of noble houses. **1602** WARNER *Alb. Eng.* VIII. xl. 196 She vnabashed, mounting now the Skaffold, theare attends The fatall Stroke. **1769** *Junius Lett.* xiv. 59 Paths which naturally conduct a minister to the scaffold. **1828** SCOTT *F.M. Perth* xxiv, I knew at Paris a criminal..who suffered the sentence ..showing no particular degree of timidity upon the scaffold. **1849–50** ALISON *Hist. Europe* III. xiii. §88. 92 We have..weighed the scaffold against the oppression of the Convention, and preferred the scaffold. **1871** FREEMAN *Norm. Conq.* IV. xviii. 256 The one man whom..William sent to the scaffold on a political charge.

7. A raised framework of wood used for other purposes; among the North American Indians, for the disposal of the dead (cf. SCAFFOLD *v.* 4). Also, a framework upon which tobacco is dried.

1534 FITZHERB. *Husb.* §32 It is better to laye thy pees and benes without vppon a reke, than other corne, and it is better vppon a scaffolde than vppon the grounde. **1634** W. WOOD *New Eng. Prosp.* (1865) 48 There was made here a ships loading of fish the last yeare, where still stands the stages, and drying scaffolds. *a* **1779** COOK *Voy. Pacific* III. ii. II. 35 The carcase of the dog, with what belonged to it, were laid on a whatta, or scaffold, about six feet high. **1784** J. SMYTH *Tour U.S.A.* II. 134 When the tobacco plants are cut and brought to the scaffolds. **1812** BRACKENRIDGE *Jrnl.* in *Views Louisiana* (1814) 203 A kind of scaffolds, ten or fifteen feet in height, which I was informed were erected..by the neighboring settlers for the purpose of shooting the deer by moon light... The hunter ascends the scaffold, and remains until the deer approaches. *Ibid.* 261 The scaffolds are supported with four forks, and sufficiently large to receive one or two bodies. **1886** C. G. W. LOCK *Tobacco* 75 Some prefer hanging the tobacco on scaffolds in the field until it is ready to be put in the barn and cured by the fire. **1888** *Encycl. Brit.* XXIII. 424/2 Red shipping qualities [of tobacco] are prepared by leaving the cut stems either in the field or hung on scaffolds in the barns for a few days to wilt and wither in the air.

8. *Iron-founding.* 'An obstruction in a blast furnace above the tuyeres caused by an accumulation or shelf of pasty, unreduced materials, adhering to the lining' (Raymond *Mining Gloss.* 1881).

1861 W. FAIRBAIRN *Iron* 48 So that the materials..may [not]..be so retarded as to adhere in a half-liquid state to the brick-work, and cool there, thus forming what are known by the name of scaffolds. **1884** W. H. GREENWOOD *Steel & Iron* vii. (ed. 2) 142 When a scaffold is discovered, the blast is eased so as to reduce the support from below due to the pressure of blast. **1892** *Min. Evid. Labour Comm.* Group A. II. 304 The variation of the temperature in the furnace itself would cause what are technically called scaffolds.

9. *attrib.* and *Comb.*, as (sense 1) ***scaffold board***, †***flake*** (see FLAKE *sb.*[1] 1), ***pole***, ***vantage***; **scaffold bracket** (see quot.); **scaffold hole**, a putlog-hole; (sense 4) †***scaffold pageantry***, †***wheel***; †**scaffold play**, a mystery play; so †**scaffold-player**; (sense 6) ***scaffold step***.

1592–3 *Act 35 Eliz.* c. 11 §1 So muche of *Shaffolde Borde in quantitye as the saide Clapborde amounteth unto. **1866** *Tomlinson's Cycl. Arts & Manuf.* II. 482/2 The scaffold boards are supported by the putlogs. **1875** KNIGHT *Dict. Mech.*, **Scaffold-bracket*, an implement to form a footing for a board to support a person in roofing. **1365–6** *Durham Acc. Rolls* (Surtees) 127, 20 *scaffalde flakes factis ad dictas fenestras. *c* **1568** in Swayne *Sarum Churchw. Acc.* (1896) 115 John clerke making *scaffold holes, 4 d. **1774** G. WHITE *Selborne, To Barrington* 26 Feb., Perhaps they nestle in the scaffold-holes of some old or new deserted building. **1687** *Refl. on Hind & P.* 24 No more than a Mountebank is to be credited, who after a deal of *Scaffold-Pageantry to draw Audience [etc.]. **1565** T. STAPLETON *Fortr. Faith* 138 As if in *scaffold plaies, he looked to haue napkins cast vp. **1559** in Strype *Ann. Ref.* I. II. IX. 436 The preachers and *scaffold players of this newe religion. **1798** W. HUTTON *Life* 7 If a straggling *scaffold pole could be found. **1862** *Sat. Rev.* 15 Mar. 298 The scaffold poles round the Guards Memorial. **1843** NEALE *Ball. & Songs for People* 21 So steadfastly the *scaffold-steps That good Archbishop trod. **1869** BROWNING *Ring & Bk.* XII. 167 Guido was last to mount the scaffold-steps..as atrociousest in crime. **1884** —— *Ferishtah's Fancies, A Camel-driver*, Reason aims to raise Some make-shift midway *scaffold-vantage, whence It may ..peer below. **1584** in *Coventry Corpus Christi Plays* (1902) 91 A iron pynne and a cotter for the *skaffolde whele.

scaffold ('skæfəld), *v.* Also 6 **scafold**, 7 **schaffold**, 7 **scaffole**. [f. SCAFFOLD *sb.* Cf. OF. *eschafauder*.]

†1. *trans.* To furnish with a platform, stand, or gallery. *Obs.*

a **1548** HALL *Chron., Hen. VIII*, 10 b, The Hall was scafolded and rayled on all partes. **1621** ELSING *Debates Ho. Lords* (Camden) 95 The Lower House desyre that the p[ainted] ch[amber] be scaffolde. **1636** PAGITT *Christianogr.* III. 101 The streets were scaffolded [*ed.* 1640 scaffoled] and covered with precious cloth. **1638** BP. MOUNTAGU *Art. Enq. Visit.* A 2 Is your Church scaffolded every where or in part? do those scaffolds so made, annoy any mans seat, or hinder the lights of any windows? **1650** R. STAPYLTON *Strada's Low C. Wars* I. 13 The Lists now set up, and scaffolded like a stage.

2. To put scaffolding up to (a building). Also *intr.* in indirect passive with *unto*.

a **1662** HEYLIN *Laud* (1668) 222 The Tower or Steeple [was] Scaffolded to the very top, with an intent to take it down to the very Arches. **1665** J. WEBB *Stone-Heng* 213 They must of necessity be scaffolded unto, or underpropt at least. *Ibid.* 230 Can..such stupendious Stones..be.. wrought, raised, scaffolded unto, set and finished in five Moneths? **1676** C. HATTON in *Hatton Corr.* (Camden) 134 The middle of Westminster Hall wase all schaffolded. **1836** E. HOWARD *R. Reefer* lxx, It was scaffolded to the very attics.

b. *transf.* To support with poles.

1884 *Harper's Mag.* 394/2 The apple-trees were scaffolded with great stakes to keep their branches from breaking.

c. *fig.* To prop up.

169. C. BLOUNT *Dial.* in *Coll. Poems* 24 New Titles may be Scaffolded with Laws.

†3. To send to the scaffold; to execute. *Obs.*

1716 *Mem.* in J. H. Burton *Lives of Forbes & Ld. Lovat* v. (1847) 116, I was sent to the castle, I believe, to be scaffolded next day if I had not been delivered.

4. To place (food) on a raised framework of wood, for the purpose of drying it or protecting it from animals; among North American Indians, to expose (corpses) on a scaffold (see SCAFFOLD *sb.* 7).

1775 ADAIR *Amer. Ind.* 323 *note*, They..scaffolded their dead kinsman. **1806** PIKE *Sources Mississ.* (1810) II. 155 In the afternoon we scaffolded some meat. **1862** D. WILSON *Preh. Man* II. xxii. 292 The remains of those whose bodies had been scaffolded.

5. *intr. Iron-founding.* To form a 'scaffold'.

1880 WRIGHT in *Encycl. Brit.* XIII. 296 When a furnace shows a tendency to 'scaffold' (by the fritting together of lumps which form a comparatively solid mass inside the furnace, preventing a charge from descending properly).

Hence '**scaffolded** *ppl. a.*

1862 D. WILSON *Preh. Man* II. xxii. 292 When the Mandans buried the remains of their scaffolded dead, they left the skull uninterred. **1871** E. B. TYLOR *Prim. Cult.* II. xii. 40 The Samoyed's scaffolded coffin.

scaffoldage ('skæfəldɪdʒ). *rare.* In 6 **scaffolage**. [f. SCAFFOLD *v.* + -AGE. Cf. F. *échafaudage*.] = SCAFFOLDING *vbl. sb.* 1.

1606 SHAKS. *Tr. & Cr.* I. iii. 156 To heare the woodden Dialogue and sound 'Twixt his stretcht footing, and the Scaffolage [*mod. edd.* scaffoldage]. **1889** FARRAR *Lives Fathers* II. xvi. 288 Their hair was elaborated into a scaffoldage of curls.

scaffolder ('skæfəldə(r)). [f. SCAFFOLD *sb.* and *v.* + -ER[1].]

†1. An occupant of the gallery at a theatre. *Obs.*

1597 BP. HALL *Sat.* I. iii If he can with termes Italianate ..Faire patch me vp his pure Iambick verse, He rauishes the gazing Scaffolders.

2. One whose business it is to erect scaffolding.

1864 *Law Times Rep.* X. (N.S.) 719/1 The plt. was in their employment as a scaffolder, and in raising the scaffolding he put his foot on a round putlog. **1901** *J. Black's Carp. & Build.*, *Scaffolding* 29 The operations of the scaffolder and builder must not interfere with the traffic of the town more than needful.

scaffolding ('skæfəldɪŋ), *vbl. sb.* Forms: 4 **skaf(f)aldyng**, 5 **scafaldynge**, 5–6 *Sc.* **scaffating**, 6 *Sc.* **scaffalding**, **scauffaulding**, **skaffeltein**, **skalfatting**, 6– **scaffolding**. Also β. 6 **skaffollyng**, 7, 9 (*dial.*) **scaffling**. [f. SCAFFOLD *sb.* and *v.* + -ING[1].]

1. The temporary framework of platforms and poles constructed to provide accommodation for workmen and their materials during the erection, repairing, or decoration of a building.

1347–8 *Durham Acc. Rolls* (Surtees) 546 In flakes et Skaffaldyng pro opere ejusdem capelle, 15 *d.* **1498** *Acc. Ld. High Treas. Scot.* I. 389 To mak scaffating for the masounis and holl barrowis. **1512** *Ibid.* IV. 279 Half ane hundretht rauchteris for skaffeltein. **1512** in Willis & Clark *Cambridge* (1886) I. 608 Lyme, sand, scaffoldyng,..and euery other thyng concernyng the same vawtyng. **1641** MILTON *Ch. Govt.* Wks. 1851 III. 129 Knowing that their high office was but as the scaffolding of the Church yet unbuilt. **1760** *Phil. Trans.* LI. 636 It burnt the wooden props or scaffolding which supported the column. **1816** J. SMITH *Panorama Sci. & Art* I. 214 In London,..the scaffolding for the workmen, in erecting the walls of a building, is external; but in Liverpool,..the scaffolding is wholly within the building. **1859** REEVE in Jephson *Brittany* xvi. 268 *note*, The large building..on the right,..is new, the scaffolding not yet taken down. **1901** *J. Black's Carp. & Build.*, *Scaffolding* 87

The old fashioned cradles, swing-boats, ladders, or pole scaffolding.

β. **1531** *Lett. & Pap. Hen. VIII*, V. 185 Cartes caryng of skaffollyng out of the Kinges storehouse. **1663** GERBIER *Counsel* 27 Never..suffer them to begin their Scafflings in the morning. **1886** *Cheshire Gloss.*, *Scaffling*, a scaffold for building.

fig. **1622** MASSINGER & DEKKER *Virg. Mart.* II. iii, The sight of whips, rackes, gibbets, axes, fires Are scaffoldings, by which my soule climbes vp To an Eternal habitation. **1697** C. LESLIE *Snake in Grass* (ed. 2) 241 That is but scaffolding to pull down our Church, and to build their own. **1712** POPE *Lett.* (1735) I. 182 Sickness, contributing..to the shaking down this Scaffolding of the Body. **1718** PRIOR *Knowledge* 478 New change of terms, and scaffolding of words. **1742** YOUNG *Nt. Th.* IX. 590 Teach me, by this stupendous scaffolding, Creation's golden steps, to climb to Thee. **1860** PUSEY *Min. Proph.* Introd. p. viii, My wish has been to give the results rather than the process by which they were arrived at; to exhibit the building, not the scaffolding. **1865** CARLYLE *Fredk. Gt.* XVIII. xiv. (1872) VIII. 58 That will be an excellent scaffolding for recapture of Silesia next year. **1874** SAYCE *Compar. Philol.* i. 9 Laws of phonology..forming the scaffolding of the higher and more comprehensive generalisations of the master-science itself.

†**b.** A wooden platform or framework; = SCAFFOLD *sb.* 3, 4, 7. *Obs.*

1537 LYNDESAY *Q. Magdalene* 106 Minor Poems (1871) 557 Rycht costlie scaffalding, Depayntit weill with Gold and asure fyne. **1732** LEDIARD *Sethos* II. VIII. 159 The lords and ladies were plac'd on scaffoldings behind the king. **1787** *Generous Attachment* III. 64 He ascended a small scaffolding, and from thence..harrangued them. **1789** MRS. PIOZZI *Journ. France* II. 27 Small calves dangle from a sort of neat scaffolding.

c. *Coal-mining.* (See quot.)

1839 URE *Dict. Arts* 980 The upper portion of the coal is first worked, then a scaffolding of coal is left, 2 or 3 feet thick, according to the compactness of the coal.

d. *transf.* A supporting framework.

1886 MIVART in *Encycl. Brit.* XX. 451/1 The skull of the Chamæleons has even more the aspect of an osseous scaffolding than has that of ordinary Lizards.

2. The action of the verb SCAFFOLD. **a.** The formation of 'scaffolds' in a blast-furnace; also *concr.* = SCAFFOLD *sb.* 8.

1864 PERCY *Metall., Iron & Steel* 491 The old method of blowing-in furnaces, called the 'scaffolding' system, is now seldom resorted to. **1880** WRIGHT in *Encycl. Brit.* XIII 299/1 If the hearth slopes too gently, the fall of the materials downwards as the reduced metal and cinder melt is apt to be retarded, and 'scaffolding' to be produced. **1883** *Science* I. 102 At the Durham furnace, a chill had caused a large scaffolding. **1884** W. H. GREENWOOD *Steel & Iron* (ed. 2) 139 Blowing in, blowing out, scaffolding, &c., of the blast furnace.

b. The action of placing on a scaffold.

1862 D. WILSON *Preh. Man* I. 366 The scaffolding and final sepulture of the bones of the dead, as practised among many of the Red Indian tribes.

3. *attrib.* and *Comb.* (cf. SCAFFOLD *sb.* 9), as *scaffolding* †*hole*, *pole*, *timber*, *work*.

1512–13 in Willis & Clark *Cambridge* (1886) I. 610 Olde scaffoldyng tymbre. **1663** GERBIER *Counsel* 27 Make small scaffling holes. **1759** MILLER *Gard. Dict.* s.v. *Pinus*, The Trees..will make good Putlocks for the Bricklayers, and serve for Scaffolding Poles. **1813** VANCOUVER *Agric. Devon* 89 The scaffolding-poles, planks, and ropes, are always provided by the employer.

†**'scaffoldize**, *v. Obs.* [f. SCAFFOLD *sb.* + -IZE.] *trans.* To convert into scaffolding.

1600 TOURNEUR *Transf. Metam.* xviii, Let Dodon's groue be lauish in expence, And scaffoldize her oakes for my defence.

scaffole, obs. var. SCAFFOLD *v.*

scaff-raff: see SCAFF *sb.*

scaffy ('skafɪ). *Sc. colloq.* Also **scavvy**. [dim. of SCAVENGER *sb.*] A street sweeper; a dustman. Also *attrib.*

1853 W. BLAIR *Chron. Aberbrothock* 19 Hecklers, an' wabsters, an' baxters, an' scaffies, an' wives, an' bairns, dowgs an' cats. **1876** J. SMITH *Archie & Bess* 25 Scaffies and leeries crackin' like pea-guns. **1892** W. M. ADAMSON *Betty Blether's Corr.* 74 Tin cans intendit for the scaffy cairt. **1918** *Kelso Chronicle* 1 Nov. 2 She often is too late for the Scaffy Bucket. **1931** J. HALL *Holy Man* iii. 37 Geordie, the road scavvy, was wearily trundling his little hand-cart up the steep slope of the village street. **1933** J. GRAY *Lowrie* 41 Dere's da scaffy fur takkin awa ony coarn o' bruck an' ess. **1967** *Buchan Observer* 7 Feb. 2 Not up in the morning early enough to catch the 'scaffy cairt'. **1978** *Scotsman* 30 June 10/7 The scaffies are now under the Environmental Health Department.

scaffy: see SCAF.

scaft(e, var. SHAFT *Obs.*, creature; obs. pa. t. of SHAVE.

scag (skæg). *U.S. slang.* Also **skag**. [Origin unknown.] **1.** A cigarette; a cigarette stub.

1915 *Dialect Notes* IV. 235 *Scag*, cigarette stub. **1928** *Amer. Speech* III. 454 *Skag*, a cigarette; to smoke. **1936** *Nat. Geogr. Mag.* LXIX. 778/2 A cigarette is a 'skag' (and cadets may not smoke in public).

2. Heroin.

1967 'G. BAGBY' *Corpse Candle* (1968) ix. 121 Acid, grass, skag? **1973** E. BULLINS *Theme is Blackness* 152 Most of the guys that we usta swing with are gone, man. In jail, on wine or scag. *Ibid.* 157 This scag they been sellin' me lately makes me hear funny. **1976** R. CONDON *Whisper of Axe* I. iv. 18 Addicts, prostitutes, skag merchants..the amoral and the lost. **1977** N. ADAM *Triplehip Cracksman* xiii. 138 I'm no junkie myself, never touched the scag, never even used the White Dragon Pearl.

scag, var. SKEG, wild plum.

scagger, var. SKEGGER, young salmon.

‖**scaglia** ('skɑːljə). *Geol.* [It. = scale, chip of marble: see SCALE *sb.*[2]] A local name in the Italian Alps for limestone of various colours.

1774 STRANGE in *Phil. Trans.* (1775) LXV. 34 This they call Scaglia, or Scagliola, from its being composed of thin slaty strata, which are of a yellowish colour. *Ibid.* 35 Sometimes an irregular mass of marble is found among the Scaglia. **1829** MURCHISON in *Phil. Mag.* June 406 The upper beds of the scaglia are red and fissile.

scagliola (skæl'jəʊlə). Also 6 **scaleola**, 8–9 **scagliuola**. [a. It. *scagliuola*, dim. of *scaglia* (see prec.).]

†**1.** = SCAGLIA. *Obs.*

1582 HESTER *Secr. Phiorav.* III. xcvii. 121 This Allum Scaleola or Gesso is vsed much in Italie to make Lyme of. **1774** [see prec.].

2. Plaster-work of Italian origin, designed to imitate kinds of stone.

1747 [see b]. **1787** P. BECKFORD *Lett. fr. Ital.* (1805) I. 298 John Hugford, an Englishman, Friar of this Convent [of Vallombrosa, Tuscany], was the inventor of the Scagliola. **1823** P. NICHOLSON *Pract. Build.* 369 The making and polishing the scagliola, now so much used for columns. **1870** F. HARRISON *Choice of Bks.* (1886) 170 Bepalaced for evermore in choice saloons resplendent with ormolu and scagliola.

b. *attrib.*

1747 H. WALPOLE *Let. to Mann* 28 July, The commission for the scagliuola tables. **1814** *Sporting Mag.* XLIV. 270 The basement is painted in rich Scagliola marble. **1859** GEO. ELIOT *Adam Bede* xvi, A scagliola pillar. **1859** SALA *Tw. round Clock* 245 Supported on the sham scagliola Corinthian columns, with the gilt capitals, is a trellised balcony.

Hence **scagli'olist**, a worker in scagliola.

1827 *Westm. Rev.* VII. 289 There is scarcely..a scagliolist, who is not an Italian.

scaife (skeɪf). *local.* Also **scafe**, **skief**, **skife**, **skeef** (see E.D.D.) [? a. Du. *schijf* (= G. *scheibe*), disk, wheel. Cf. SKEITH.]

1. A thin iron wheel, sharp at the edge, used in some ploughs in place of or in front of the coulter. Also *attrib.*

1793 G. MAXWELL *Agric. Huntingdon* 10 Instead of a foot or wheel, to support the beam of the plough, they use what is called a scaife, which is a circular plate of iron, turning constantly round. **1877** *N.W. Linc. Gloss.*, *Skief-plough*, a plough fitted with a skief. **1888** *Sheffield Gloss.*, *Scafe*, the little wheel which runs in front of the coulter of a plough. **1895** *E. Angl. Gloss.*, *Skife-nail*, a long nail, having its head formed so as to suit..the holes in the plat of a plough.

2. A revolving wheel used in polishing diamonds.

1887 *Horological Jrnl.* XXIX. 105 The ordinary workman puts his diamond on the scaife or cylinder without taking any particular pains.

scail(e, var. or obs. ff. SCALE, SKAIL, SQUAIL.

scailȝe(e, **-zie**, **scaillie**, obs. ff. SKAILLIE *Sc.*, slate.

scaily, obs. f. SCALY.

scain, obs. pa. t. of SHINE.

scaine, obs. f. SKEIN.

scaip(e, obs. Sc. ff. SCAPE.

scair, var. SKAIR *Sc.*, share.

scairce, **scairse**, obs. ff. SCARCE.

scait, obs. Sc. f. SKATE.

scaith: see SCATHE.

scak, obs. north. f. SHAKE.

scal, obs. f. SCALL, SHALL.

scala ('skeɪlə). *Anat.* [L., = 'ladder'.] Each of two passages (the ***scala tympani*** below and the ***scala vestibuli*** above) into which the spiral tube of the cochlea is divided by a bony spiral lamina and which communicate at the apex of the spiral; also, the ***scala media*** or central duct of the cochlea, situated between these two passages and shut off from them by two membranes.

1712 *Bibliotheca Anat., Med., Chir.* II. 214/2 We have discover'd two Channels into which the Cochlea is divided by the Septum, called Scalæ, or Ladders; one of which..is called the Scala Tympani: But the other..is called the Scala Vestibuli. **1803** C. BELL *Anat. Human Body* III. 430 Or it [*sc.* the vibrating motion] must pass from the scala vestibuli into the scala tympani. **1872** *Gray's Anat.* (ed. 6) 596 The space between the membrane of Reissner and membrana basilaris is generally described as the Scala media, Canalis membranacea, or Canalis cochleæ, and this is the nomenclature which will be used here. **1902** D. J. CUNNINGHAM *Text-bk. Anat.* 717 The two scalæ communicate with each other through the opening of the helicotrema at the apex of the cochlea. **1945** [see REISSNER]. **1974** *Encycl. Brit. Macropædia* V. 1123/2 The interior of the cochlea is divided longitudinally into three spiral ramps or scalae: the scala vestibuli,..the scala tympani,..and the scala media.

scalable ('skeɪləb(ə)l), *a.* [f. SCALE *v.*[3] + -ABLE.]

I. 1. Able to be scaled or climbed. *rare.*

1579–80 NORTH *Plutarch, Aratus* (1595) 1083 Without the wall the height was not so great, but that it was easily scalable with ladders. **1626** MINSHEU *Ductor* (ed. 2), *Scaleable.* **1839** *Fraser's Mag.* XIX. 632 Homer made..heaven scalable. **1903** QUILLER-COUCH *Adv. Harry Revel* xi, The cliff hereabouts was..scalable in a score of places.

II. 2. Able to be measured or graded according to a scale.

1936 *Psychol. Monogr.* XLVII. I. 15 A few [traits] seem common enough to be regarded as comparable from one individual to another. These might be called common or scalable traits. **1944** *Amer. Sociol. Rev.* IX. 147/1 The example..of desire to go to school is a fictitious version of data that have actually proved scalable for the Army. **1968** W. A. SCOTT in Lindzey & Aronson *Handbk. Social Psychol.* (ed. 2) II. xi. 222 A measure of the degree to which the set of items is scalable, that is, represents a unidimensional attribute. **1977** R. H. BROWN in Douglas & Johnson *Existential Sociol.* ii. 81 The questionnaire was particularly attractive as a measuring device because it standardizes responses, making them easily scalable and retrievable, in principle by anyone.

3. Able to be changed in scale. *rare.*

1977 *Jrnl. R. Soc. Arts* CXXV. 770/1 Such lasers are scaleable since large volumes could be pumped uniformly.

Hence **scala'bility**, the property of being scalable.

1944 *Amer. Sociol. Rev.* IX. 141/2 It may well be that the formal analysis for scalability may help clarify uncertain areas of content. **1959** *Psychol. Rev.* LXVI. 51/2 Ordinarily, when scalability is found, it is assumed that a unidimensional continuum exists. **1960** BROWN & GILMAN in J. A. Fishman *Readings Sociol. of Lang.* (1968) 270 We tested all 28 items for scalability and found that a subset of them made a fairly good scale. **1978** *Sci. Amer.* Nov. 44/2 It took demonstrations of the scalability of the technology and tests of improved beam focusing..to catalyze an effort that led to support by the AEC.

‖**Scala Cæli** ('skeɪlə 'siːlaɪ). Also 5–6 **scala cely**, **celi**, 6–9 **cœli**, 6 **scale**, **skaly celi**. [L. = ladder of heaven.]

1. The name of a church in the Tre Fontane, outside Rome, in which St. Bernard is related to have had a vision of souls for whom he was saying mass ascending by a ladder into heaven, and to which an indulgence is attached; hence, applied to chapels or altars in England and the masses said there to which the same indulgence was attached.

See Rymer *Fœdera* XII. 565, XIII. 102–3, Blomefield *Hist. Norfolk* (1745) II. 552.

c **1380** WYCLIF *Wks.* (1880) 102 Massis at rome, at scala celi. *Ibid.*, þat if a prest seye a masse at scala celi for a soule it schal onoon ben out of purgatorie. *a* **1400** *Stac. Rome* 118 (Vernon MS.), In þat place a Chapel is. Scala celi clepet hit is. *c* **1500** *God spede the plough* 74 Then commeth prestis that goth to rome For to haue silver to sing at *Scala celi.* **1515** in *Coll. Surrey Archæol. Soc.* (1858) I. 182, I will that there be seede..in the chapell of Skaly Celi at Westmynster v masses of the v wounds of our Lord God. **1519** *Churchw. Acc. St. Margarets, Westm.* (Nichols 1797) 8 To the Keeper of Scala Celi in the Abbey. **1534** HYLSEY in *Lett. Suppress. Monasteries* (Camden) 12 Massys off scale celi. **1536** *Articles devised by King* D iij b. *c* **1550** BALE *K. Johan* (Camden) 17 Legacyes, trentals, with scala cely messys. **1583** FOXE *A. & M.* (ed. 4) 1178/2 That all partakers of the same gylde [of our Lady in S. Botolph's, Boston],..which..shall say or cause to be sayde Masses for soules departed in paynes of Purgatory, shall..have the full remission due to them which visite the Chappell of Scala Cœli.

2. (With reference to the etymol. sense.) A ladder leading from earth to heaven; a means of attaining heaven or heavenly bliss.

1549 LATIMER *5th Serm. bef. Edw. VI* (Arb.) 139 *Scala cœli*, is a preachynge matter I tell you, and not a massyng matter. **1603** J. DAVIES in Sylvester *Du Bartas* (1621) 651 Making loose lines (forsooth) their Scala Cœli; A Tauerne for a Temple, to adore, Their only god, their guts. **1626** BACON *New Atl.* 15 The Magnificent Temple,..the seuerall Degrees of Ascent, wherby Men did climb vp to the same, as if it had bin a Scala Cæli.

scalade (skə'lɑːd), *sb.* Now *rare* or *Obs.* Also 7 **skal(l)ade**, **scallet**. [ad. It. *scalada* (Florio), now *scalata* (= Sp. *escalada*, whence F. *escalade* ESCALADE *sb.*), f. *scalare* to scale, f. *scala* ladder.]

1. = ESCALADE *sb.* 1.

1591 *Garrard's Art Warre* 63 A Wall, Trench, Scalade, Bulwarke. **1600** HOLLAND *Livy* XXVI. xlv. 620 The citie was tenable against all skalades. **1632** LITHGOW *Trav.* VIII. 349 The Ditch..is mainly pallasaded with wooden stakes, for preuenting of suddain Scallets. *a* **1639** SPOTTISWOOD *Hist. Ch. Scot.* III. (1677) 138 The Lords had resolved to enter the Town by scalade. **1761** HUME *Hist. Eng.* I. xii. 265 The English army..mounted the walls by scalade. **1858** CARLYLE *Fredk. Gt.* III. x. (1872) I. 195 He tried some small prefatory Siege or scalade of Pesth. **1859** THACKERAY *Virgin.* II. xxvi. 213 When we had made our famous scalade of the heights.

2. A scaling-ladder. *rare.*

1632 LITHGOW *Trav.* x. 502 Their Armes, a Crosse,..Limbd like a Scallet, trac'd with fleur du Luce. **1824** WIFFEN *Tasso* XVIII. xcv, Nor ceases to exhort Fresh knights to mount the tall scalades he bears.

Hence **sca'lade** *v. trans.*, to attack by escalade.

1729 SHELVOCKE *Artillery* v. 393 Places, when attacked or attempted to be stormed or scaladed.

†**sca'lado.** *Obs.* Also 6 **skallado, skallader,** 6–7 **scallado, scallada, scalada.** [a. It. *scalada*: see prec. and -ADO.]

1. = SCALADE *sb.* 1.

1585–6 EARL LEYCESTER *Corr.* (Camden) 429 We tooke another of the fortes..by a flat skallader. **1591** UNTON *Corr.* (Roxb.) 254 If it be taken by the enemy by scallado. **1610** HOLLAND *Camden's Brit.* II. 128 They that gave the Scallado were throwen downe headlong. **1629** MAXWELL *Herodian* App. 90 The whole Army beset the Towne, and made their Scaladaes on euery side. **1688** J. S. *Fortification* 129 The General..threatens several other places with the Scalado at the same instant. **1795** *Hist. Anecd. Her. & Chiv.* 22 Lloyd took the castle of Cardigan..by Scalado. **1847** THACKERAY in *Fraser's Mag.* Jan., Assaults, scaladoes, ambuscadoes,.. became the Captain's chief delight.

2. = SCALADE *sb.* 2.

1600 FAIRFAX *Tasso* XI. xxxiv, Adrastus..boldly gan a strong scalado reare. **1824** WIFFEN *Tasso* XI. xxxix, Some raise scalados, nor to mount decline.

scalage ('skeɪlɪdʒ). *Lumber-trade.* [f. SCALE *v.*[3] (sense 6 b) + -AGE.] The amount which a quantity of timber scales.

1878 *Michigan Rep.* XXXVI. 168 The total scalage of the logs to be delivered.

scalap, obs. form of SCALLOP.

scalar ('skeɪlə(r), formerly 'skeɪlɑː(r)), *a.* and *sb.* [ad. L. *scālār-is*, f. *scāla* ladder, SCALE *sb.*[3]]

A. *adj.* **1.** Resembling a ladder; *Bot.* = SCALARIFORM.

1656 BLOUNT *Glossogr.*, *Scalar, Scalary*, leaning one way, ladderwise, not bolt up right. **1880** *Linn. Soc. Jrnl.* XV. 92 Spire rather high, scalar.

2. *Math.* Of the nature of a scalar (see B).

1846 W. R. HAMILTON in *Phil. Mag.* XXIX. 26 The algebraically real part may receive, according to the question in which it occurs, all values contained on the one scale of progression of numbers from negative to positive infinity; we shall call it therefore the scalar part, or simply the scalar of the quaternion, and shall form its symbol by prefixing, to the symbol of the quaternion, the characteristic Scal., or simply S. **1853** HAMILTON in *Phil. Mag.* Ser. IV. V. 322 The two values of the vector ρ, which answer to the two values of the scalar coefficient *x*. **1853** —— *Elem. Quaternions* II. i. (1866) 175 The Scalar (or Scalar Part) of a Quaternion. *Ibid.* III. iii. 721 The scalar equation of the polar of the latter point. **1873** MAXWELL *Electr. & Magn.* I. 9 Scalar quantities do not involve direction. **1911** *Encycl. Brit.* XXVII. 962/2 The mass of a body, the pressure of a gas, the charge of an electrified conductor, are instances of scalar magnitudes. **1932** R. GANS *Vector Analysis* ii. 58 Let W..be a scalar.. property of a field, and let it be regarded as a function of the position and of the time. **1964** N. N. HANCOCK *Matrix Analysis Electr. Machinery* ii. 18 A 'scalar' matrix is a diagonal matrix in which all the elements on the principal diagonal are equal.

3. Of or pertaining to a musical scale (SCALE *sb.*[3] 4).

1928 G. COOKE *Theory of Music* ii. 18 One cannot..over-emphasise the importance of these groups of notes in the theoretic study of scalar development. *Ibid.* vi. 77 The variety inherent in modulation and scalar variety. **1946** R. BLESH *Shining Trumpets* ii. 25 The basic material is recast in its scalar compass and its tonal intervals. **1959** M. T. WILLIAMS *Art of Jazz* (1960) xi. 106 Sliding tones peculiar to the scalar and harmonic structure. **1966** *New Statesman* 11 Feb. 204/1 The integration of triadic and scalar elements within a serial or non-tonal field.

4. Of or pertaining to a graduated scale (SCALE *sb.*[3] 9).

1959 G. D. MITCHELL *Sociology* 130 Very often there is an identity of functional and scalar status. **1974** G. LEECH *Semantics* ii. 21 A selection from indefinitely many possible scales, which in any case would only provide for associative meaning in so far as it is explicable in scalar terms.

B. *sb.* **1.** *Math.* In quaternions, a real number. More widely, a quantity having magnitude but no direction, and representable by a single real number.

1846 [see sense A. 2]. **1853** HAMILTON *Elem. Quaternions* I. ii. (1866) 10 The..quotient..obtained by the division of two parallel vectors by another, including zero as a limit, may also be called a Scalar; because it can always be found ..by the comparison of positions upon one common scale (or axis)... Such Scalars are..simply the Reals..of Algebra. *Ibid.* 11 The combination, 'Scalar plus Vector,' is a Quaternion. **1882** MINCHIN *Unipl. Kinemat.* 260 The result of the operation ∇^2 on any scalar is purely a scalar. **1903** [see NON-DIRECTIONAL *a.* (*sb.*)]. **1932** R. GANS *Vector Analysis* i. 2 We shall denote scalars by ordinary type and vectors by heavy type. **1965** PATTERSON & RUTHERFORD *Elem. Abstr. Algebra* v. 145 By a scalar we shall mean an entity determined by a single real number and by a vector we shall mean an entity determined by both a positive real number, measuring magnitude, and a direction in space.

2. *attrib.* (some of the following may be regarded as collocations of the adj.): **scalar field**, a map from a space to the real line (see quot. 1932); **scalar function**, a function whose value is a scalar; **scalar multiplication**, multiplication of a vector by a scalar to give another vector; **scalar product** = *inner product* s.v. INNER *a.* (*sb.*[2]) 1 k; **scalar triple product**, a scalar function of three three-vectors $((a_1, a_2, a_3), (b_1, b_2, b_3), (c_1, c_2, c_3))$ which can be calculated as $(a_1 b_2 c_3 + b_1 c_2 a_3 + c_1 a_2 b_3 - a_1 c_2 b_3 - b_1 a_2 c_3 - c_1 b_2 a_3)$, being the volume of the parallelepiped which has the three vectors as three coincident edges.

1932 R. GANS *Vector Analysis* i. 1 The field is called a *scalar field or a vector field according as the quantity associated with the field is a scalar or a vector. **1959** M. R. SPIEGEL *Vector Analysis* i. 3 The temperature at any point within or on the earth's surface at a certain time defines a scalar field. **1974** G. REECE tr. *Hund's Hist. Quantum Theory* xv. 207 It was therefore a major advance when Pauli and Victor Weisskopf developed the quantum theory of a scalar field. **1956** A. A. TOWNSEND *Struct. Turbulent Shear Flow* iii. 35 The double-correlation function depends only on a single *scalar function. **1972** A. G. HOWSON *Handbk. Terms Algebra & Anal.* xxvi. 126 Functions such as *f* are often referred to as vector-valued functions and are denoted by symbols printed in bold type so as to distinguish them from real-valued or scalar functions. **1901** GIBBS & WILSON *Vector Analysis* i. 13 The laws which govern addition, subtraction, and *scalar multiplication of vectors are identical with those governing these operations in ordinary scalar algebra. **1968** A. P. ARMIT *Advanced Level Vectors* ii. 25 (*heading*) Scalar multiplication of a vector..in terms of cartesian components. **1878** *Scalar product [see VECTOR *sb.* 2]. **1932** R. GANS *Vector Analysis* i. 17 By the scalar product of two vectors A and B we mean a scalar of magnitude equal to the product of the absolute values and the cosine of the angle between the vectors. **1941, 1968** Scalar product [see INNER *a.* (*sb.*[2]) 1 k]. **1901** GIBBS & WILSON *Vector Analysis* ii. 68 The second triple product is the scalar product of two vectors, of which one is itself a vector product, as A · (B × C) or (A × B) · C. This sort of product has a scalar value and consequently is often called the *scalar triple product. **1959** M. R. SPIEGEL *Vector Analysis* ii. 17 The product A · (B × C) is sometimes called the scalar triple product or box product and may be denoted by [ABC]. **1964** E. Œ. WOLSTENHOLME *Elem. Vectors* ii. 38 If **a**, **b**, **c** are three vectors, any pair of them may be multiplied vectorially to form a new vector **d**, the third of the original vectors may then be multiplied by **d**, either scalarly to form what is known as a scalar triple product, or vectorially to form..the vector triple product.

scalarian (skə'lɛərɪən), *a.* and *sb.* [f. mod.L. *Scălāria*, f. *scāla* ladder, SCALE *sb.*[3]] **a.** *adj.* Belonging to the genus *Scalaria* of gasteropods. **b.** *sb.* A gasteropod of this genus.

1841 *Penny Cycl.* XX. 501/2 The Scalarians of Lamarck consist of the genera *Vermetus, Scalaria*, and *Delphinula*.

scalariform (skə'lærɪfɔːm), *a.* *Bot.*, etc. [ad. mod.L. *scălāriform-is*, f. L. *scālāris* SCALAR, SCALARY: see -FORM.] Of the form of, or resembling, a ladder; characterized by ladder-like formation, as cells or vessels of plants having the walls thickened so that they form transverse ridges.

1836 BUCKLAND *Geol. & Min.* xviii. §iii. I. 499 *note*, The presence of spiral, or scalariform vessels. **1848** LINDLEY *Introd. Bot.* I. 87 The pits extend into horizontal fissures resembling what are called Scalariform vessels. **1850** DANA *Geol.* App. I. 727 Spire scalariform. **1885** GOODALE *Physiol. Bot.* 30 When this kind of marking [in a cell-wall] becomes linear, or nearly so, it is termed scalariform.

scalarly ('skeɪləlɪ), *adv.* *Math.* [f. SCALAR *sb.* + -LY[2].] In such a way as to yield a scalar.

1964 [see *scalar triple product* s.v. SCALAR *sb.* 2].

'scalarwise, *adv.* [f. SCALAR *a.* + -WISE.] In the form of a ladder.

1816 R. JAMESON *Char. Min.* 129 *Scalarwise*, in which many tessular crystals are arranged like steps of a stair.

†**'scalary,** *a.* *Obs.* [f. L. *scālāris*: see SCALAR and -ARY.]

1. Having the form of a ladder or flight of steps.

1646 SIR T. BROWNE *Pseud. Ep.* v. xiii. 253 He made.. certaine elevated places, and Scalary ascents, that..they might with better ease..mount their horses. **1651** HOWELL *Venice* 23 Touching this kind of employment the Republic hath certain degrees, or Scalary ascents and rules of removall. **1656** [see SCALAR *a.* 1].

2. = CLIMACTERIC *a.* 1.

1588 J. HARVEY *Disc. Probl.* 25 The great Climactericall, Hebdomaticall, Scalary, Decretoriall yeere. **1635** HEYWOOD *Hierarchy* III. Comm. 167 The Scalary or Climatericall yeare consisteth of Seuen yeares nine times told or nine yeares Seuen times Multiplied.

3. Pertaining to masses of SCALA CÆLI.

1536 LATIMER *2nd Serm. bef. Convocation* i. 48 That satisfactory, that missal, that scalary.

scalawag, variant of SCALLYWAG.

scalbart, -bert, -burde, obs. ff. SCABBARD *sb.*[1]

scalc, variant of SHALK *Obs.*

†**scald,** *sb.*[1] *Obs.* Also 6 **skald.** [Alteration of SCALL *sb.* by association with SCALD *a.* (orig. *scalled*).] = SCALL *sb.*

1561 HOLLYBUSH *Hom. Apoth.* 2 The drye skaldes of it called in Latin *furfur*. **1590** SPENSER *F.Q.* I. viii. 47 Her crafty head was altogether bald, And..Was overgrowne with scurfe and filthy scald. **1648** HERRICK *Hesper.*, *Upon Blanch*, Blanch swears her Husband's lovely; when a scald Has blear'd his eyes. **1693** *Lond. Gaz.* No. 2930/4 Lately went from his Master one Martin Middleton... He hath a Scald behind in his Head.

fig. **1646** H. LAWRENCE *Comm. Angels* 104 The fire, the scald, the Itch of lusts.

scald (skɔːld), *sb.*[2] [f. SCALD *v.*]

1. An injury to the skin and flesh caused by hot fluid or steam.

1601 HOLLAND *Pliny* XXIX. xiii. II. 351 Say the place be blistered..with any burne or scald. **1749** BRACKEN *Farriery Impr.* (ed. 6) 301, I am satisfied that Spirit of Wine camphorated, is the very best Thing that can be applied to a Burn or Scald in Human Bodies. **1845** W. BOWMAN in *Encycl. Metrop.* VII. 865/2 A superficial scald of the whole body. **1879** *St. George's Hosp. Rep.* IX. 394 'Scald' of the air-passages. **1890** BOWLBY *Surg. Path.* (1900) 289 Scalds of the larynx..in children..commonly result from attempts to drink from a kettleful of boiling water.

b. *fig.* (*Sc.*) Disgust, aversion, vexation. See HEART-SCALD, -SCAD.

c. *transf.* Inflammation caused by heat; an inflamed part. Also, applied to diseases which produce a similar effect to that of scalding.

1882 *Jamieson's Sc. Dict.*, *Skaud, Scad*, a scald, or the mark of it; also, a galled or inflamed part of the body. **1886** C. SCOTT *Sheep-farming* 99 If manure is allowed to accumulate therein, it will get into the cleft of the foot and produce scald. **1895** *Funk's Stand. Dict.*, *Scald*, a destructive disease of cranberries,..applied also loosely..to any sudden wilting or decay..of leaves and fruit.

2. The action or an act of scalding articles of food, utensils, etc.

1661 RABISHA *Cookery Dissected* 5 You must give your Endive a scald. **1764** E. MOXON *Eng. Housew.* (ed. 9) 160 Put in your damsins, let them have one scald. **1869** MRS. WHITNEY *We Girls* vi, The coffee-pot and the two pans.. had their scald, and their little scour. **1894** *Times* 16 Apr. 7/3 The high scald to which the curd is subjected after breaking.

3. A hot liquor or solution used for scalding.

1684 HAN. WOOLLEY *Queen-like Closet* Suppl. 4 After the first ladder [= lather] let the other be very hot, and cast them into a Scald every time. **1741** *Compl. Fam.-Piece* I. ii. 110 Put your Fruit into boiling Water,..keep it in a scald till tender. **1780** A. YOUNG *Tour Irel.* I. 180 Next put it into a scald of soap.

4. A patch of land scorched by the sun. *local.*

1795 MARSHALL *Rur. Econ. Norf.* I. 14 'Scalds' are as pernicious in Norfolk, as quicksands and springy patches are in cold-soiled countries. **1853** R. S. SURTEES *Sponge's Sp. Tour* lxxi, The country..was all one dingy drab, with abundant scalds on the undrained fallows.

5. Dodder, *Cuscuta europæa*: cf. SCALDWEED. *local.*

1844 *Phytologist* I. 1140 *Cuscuta europæa*..is called 'scald' [in Cambridgeshire]; it may be presumed, on account of the scalded appearance which it gives to bean-crops.

scald, *sb.*[3]: see SKALD.

scald, *sb.*[4], northern form of SCOLD.

scald (skɔːld), *a.*[1] and *sb.*[5] *Obs.* exc. *arch.* and *dial.* Also 6 **scaulde,** *Sc.* **skawd, skaid,** 6–7 **scalde,** 7 **scal'd, scauld,** 8 *Sc.* **scaw'd,** 9 *dial.* **scalt, scaud.** [Later spelling of SCALLED.]

A. *adj.* **1.** Affected with the 'scall'; scabby.

In the 16th c. often in proverbial or allusive use: cf. SCABBED. (See also SCALD-HEAD.)

1529 MORE *Dyaloge* II. iv. Wks. 185 Than shall al these scalde & scabbed peces scale clene of, & the hole body of christes holy church remaine pure. **1535** COVERDALE *Lev.* xxi. 20 Whether he be blynde,..or is gleyd, or is skyrvye or scaulde. **1535** LYNDESAY *Satyre* 2485 Howbeit I se thy skap skyre skaid [*Bannatyne MS.* skawd], Thou art ane stewat, I stand foird. **1540** PALSGR. *Acolastus* II. iii. M ij b, He shall appoint him out for such a scald squier as he is. **1546** J. HEYWOOD *Prov. & Epigr.* (1867) 33 A scald horse is good inough for a scabde squyer. **1579** TOMSON *Calvin's Serm. Tim.* 474/2 Some murmure and snarle as soone as their scald backs are rubbed. **1639** O. WOOD *Alph. Bk. Phys. Secrets* 181 Scal'd head the cure. [**1808** JAMIESON, *Scaud-man's head*, the sea urchin.]

2. *fig.* 'Scurvy', mean, paltry, contemptible. (Cf. SCABBED *a.* 2.) **a.** Of persons.

c **1500** MEDWALL *Nature* I. 753 (Brandl) The scald capper sware..That yt cost hym euen as myche. **1595** PEELE *Old Wives Tale* 425 (Gummere) You whorson, scald Sexton and Churchwarden. **1606** SHAKS. *Ant. & Cl.* v. ii. 215. *a* **1625** FLETCHER *Bloody Brother* I. i, Your gravity once laid My head and heels together in the Dungeon, For cracking a scald Officers crown.

¶ *scald miserable*: a burlesque designation app. first used in 1742 in connexion with a procession of ragamuffins intended to ridicule the Freemasons. A print of 1771 representing this brought the expression into temporary currency with the sense 'despicable wretch'.

1742 (*title*) An Epistle from Dick Poney, Esq. Grand-Master of the Right Black-Guard Society of Scald-Miserable Masons. **1771** (*title of plate by Benoist*) A Geometrical View of the Grand Procession of the Scald Miserable Masons, Design'd as they were Drawn up over against Somerset House, in the Strand on the twenty Seventy of April, An°. 1742. **1772** NUGENT *Hist. Fr. Gerund* III. vi. 563 Our poor scald miserable of a Friar Gerund. **1773** BERRIDGE *Lett.* vii. (1864) 371, I am now, as the world accounts, a scold miserable. [**1828** ST. ANGELO *Remin.* I. 407 The print of the Scald Miserables..is by him [*sc.* Benoist]. *Ibid.* 408 The contrivers of the mock procession of scald masons, which actually took place in the year 1742.]

b. Of things.

1542 UDALL *Erasm. Apoph.* 260 If it chaunce a scalde cuppe of thyn to bee broken. **1592** NASHE *P. Penilesse* Ep. Printer, A scald triuiall lying Pamphlet, called *Greens groats-worth of wit*. **1609** B. JONSON *Sil. Wom.* IV. i, If [she have] a fat hand, and scald nailes, let her carue the lesse, and act in gloues. *a* **1627** MIDDLETON *Widow* IV. ii. Wks. (Bullen) V. 207 I'm rid of a sore burden, for my part, master, Of a scald little one. *a* **1774** FERGUSSON *Poems* (1807) 255 A scaw'd bit o' a penny note.

3. *Comb.*, as **scald-pate,** = SCALD-HEAD; **scald-pated** *a.* = SCALD-HEADED.

1611 COTGR., *Teigneux*, scuruie, scauld-pated. *Ibid.* s.v. *Teigneux*, No scauld-pate will the combe indure. **1653** URQUHART *Rabelais* II. xxx, Achilles was a scauld-pated maker of hay bundles. **1659** TORRIANO *Eng.-Ital. Dict.*, The scurfe or scauld pate, *tigna, pelarella*.

B. *sb.* **a.** A scurvy fellow. **b.** = SCALL.

1575 *Gamm. Gurton* III. iii. 26 Thou skald, thou bald, thou rotten, thou glotton! **1598** FLORIO, *Tegna*, the scurfe or scald that comes to some mens heades. **1909** G. B. SHAW *Press Cuttings* 37 G'lang, you young scald: if I had you here I'd teach you manners. **1919** —— *O'Flaherty V.C.* 179 What do you mean, you lying young scald, by telling me you were going to fight agen the English?

scald (skɔːld), *a.*[2] [pa. pple. of SCALD *v.*] = SCALDED *ppl. a.*[1]

scald cream: clotted or clouted cream. ***scald milk***: milk from which the cream has been skimmed after scalding.

1791 *Gentl. Mag.* LXI. II. 720/2 That cream termed scald, or clotted cream. *Ibid.* Those dairies that make scald-cream butter. **1796** MARSHALL *Rur. Econ. W. Eng.* I. 251 In 'scald cream dairies', no churn is in use. **1855** KINGSLEY *Westw. Ho!* viii, If it don't ate so soft as ever was scald cream, never you call me Thomas Burman. **1886** *All Year Round* 14 Aug. 34 Who in Cornwall ever thinks of drinking anything but 'scald' milk?

scald (skɔːld), *v.* Forms: 3–4 **schalde**, 4 **scalde**, **scolde**, 4–5 **skalde**, 4–6 **schald**, 5–6 **skald**, **scalde**, 6 **scaulde**, *Sc.* **scawde**, **skaude**, (7 **scal'd**, **scold**), 8–9 *Sc.* **scad**, **scaud**, 5– **scald**. *Pa. t.* 5 **skaldid**, 6 *Sc.* **scaldit**, 4– **scalded**; 6–7 **scalt**. *Pa. pple.* 4 **i-scalded** (**-sk-**), **skald**, 5 **skladdyt**, 4–6 **skaldyd**, **-id**, (etc.), 5–7, 9 *dial.* **scalt**, 6 *Sc.* **sc-**, **skaldit**, 9 *dial.* **scald**. [a. ONF. *escalder*, *escauder* = Central OF. *eschalder*, *eschauder* to burn, scald (mod.F. *échauder* to scald, earlier also to scorch), = Pr. *escaudar*, Sp., Pg. *escaldar* to burn, scald, make red-hot, It. *scaldare* to heat, warm:—late L. *excaldāre* to wash in hot water, f. *ex-* (see EX- *pref.*[1] 2. 2) + *cal(i)dus* hot, warm (see CALID and CHAUD).

The specific use referring to liquid agency, which is the prominent use in Fr. (and hence in Eng.), and is more or less represented in the other Rom. langs., is prob. to be accounted for by the fact that *excaldāre* could as well be referred to the *cal(i)da* sb., hot water, as to the adj. In Eng. this is the earliest sense of the word, which is first recorded in the Ancren Riwle (*a* 1225) both in its simple form (see quot. s.v. SCALDING *ppl. a.*) and in the compound *forsch(e)alde* (see FOR- *pref.*[1] 5).

The word entered at an early date into the Scandinavian languages: early MDa. *skolde*, MSw. *skalda*, *skolda*, *skolla*, Sw. *skålla* to scald.]

I. 'To burn with hot liquor' (J.).

1. *trans.* To affect painfully and injure with very hot liquid or steam.

1340 *Ayenb.* 66 Hare mouþ is ase þe wyȝte þet ualþ ine hot weter þet..scoldeþ alle þo þet byeþ þer aboute. *c* **1386** CHAUCER *Knt.'s T.* 1162 The Cook yscalded for al his longe ladel. *c* **1440** *Promp. Parv.* 442/2 Scalt, *estuatus.* **1601** HOLLAND *Pliny* II. 351 If one be scalded with hot water, lay ..an egg to the place. **1687** A. LOVELL tr. *Thevenot's Trav.* I. 33 They all drink it sipping, for fear of scalding themselves. **1786** ABERCROMBIE *Gard. Assist.* 302 For fear of.. steam scalding the plants. **1813** J. THOMSON *Lect. Inflam.* 605 Let a piece of linen dipt in brandy..be immediately applied to the parts scalded with hot water. **1822** SCOTT *Nigel* xxvii, Scalding yourself, as I may say, with your own ladle? **1849** MACAULAY *Hist. Eng.* iii. I. 285 Huge stones and boiling water were in readiness to crush and scald the plunderer.

b. *absol.* or *intr.* To be scalding hot.

a **1225** [see SCALDING *ppl. a.* 1]. *a* **1639** W. WHATELEY *Prototypes* I. xx. (1640) 20 Words of reviling scald as it were. **1642** FULLER *Holy & Prof. St.* II. xix. 127 Some excuse there is for bloud enraged, and no wonder if that scaldeth which boyleth. **1812** SIR H. DAVY *Chem. Philos.* 80 Water scalds at 150°.

c. *intr.* for *pass.* To become injured by hot liquid or steam.

1590 MARLOWE *2nd Pt. Tamburl.* II. iii, Now scalds his soul in the Tartarian streams. **1847** TENNYSON *Princess* v. 448 Those detestable That let the bantling scald at home, and brawl Their rights or wrongs like potherbs in the street.

d. *Comb.*: **scald-chops** (*humorous*), hot tea; **scald-lips** (Sc. *scadlips*), 'broth containing a very small portion of barley, and on this account more apt to burn the mouth' (Jam.).

a **1682** F. SEMPILL *Blythsome Wedding* 65 in *Poems of Sempills* (1849) 69 There will be..a haggize, And scadlips to sup till ye're fow. **1830** MARRYAT *King's Own* xl, It was the signal for tea. 'Hurra for Scaldchops!'

2. *trans.* To produce an injurious effect upon (something) similar to that produced by boiling water. **a.** Of tears, humours.

a **1225** [see SCALDING *ppl. a.* 2]. **1340** HAMPOLE *Pr. Consc.* 6576 Hate teres of gretyng, þat þe synful sal scalden in þe dounfallyng. **1605** SHAKS. *Lear* IV. vii. 48, I am bound Vpon a wheele of fire, that mine owne teares Do scal'd, like molten Lead. **1696** *Lond. Gaz.* No. 3240/4 The left side of his face burnt or scalded by some Humor. **1722** DOUGLAS in *Phil. Trans.* XXXII. 86 When the Urine begins to come the right way, it pains and scalds them much after the same manner. **1873** BRYANT *Living Lost* ii, The tears that scald the cheek. *absol.* **1692** DRYDEN *Cleomenes* I. i, And if a manly drop or Two fall down, It scalds along my Cheeks. **1835** TRENCH *Justin Martyr* 16 The tear which does not heal, will scald and sear.

b. *fig.* Of words, language.

1513 DOUGLAS *Æneis* I. Prol. 258 The quent and curious castis poeticall,..Caxtoun, for dreid thai suld his lippis scawde Durst neuer tuiche. **1847** J. MARTINEAU *Chr. Life* II. x. 170 He..grows glib in uttering falsehoods that should scald his lips.

3. To wash and cleanse with boiling water:

a. the carcasses of animals, esp. swine and poultry, in order to remove hair or feathers, etc.

a **1300** *Cursor M.* 15988 Ne sal he neuer vp-rise eft,..Ar sal þis cok vp-rise was skald yisternight! *c* **1420** *Liber Cocorum* (1862) 26 Take capons and schalde and pyke hom then. *c* **1430** *Two Cookery-bks.* 25 Fayre smal Chykenys wyl & clene skladdyd & drawe. **1565** COOPER *Thesaurus*, *Glabrare sues*, to scaulde hogges and take of their heare. **1607** SHAKS. *Timon* II. ii. 71 She's e'ne setting on water to scal'd such Chickens as you are. **1747** MRS. GLASSE *Cookery* ii. 32 Gut and scald your Pig. *Ibid.* viii. 72.

b. vessels, implements, clothes. (Also with *out.*)

1747 MRS. GLASSE *Cookery* xiii. 130 Scald the Pot clean. **1750** W. ELLIS *Country Housewife's Comp.* 308 To heat a good Quantity of Water..for scalding Pails. **1869** *Routledge's Ev. Boy's Ann.* 459 Preparing to scald out the frying-pan. **1897** *Allbutt's Syst. Med.* III. 339 All milk should be..boiled, and the bottle always scalded before use.

c. To take *off* (the hair or feathers of an animal) with hot water.

1387 TREVISA *Higden* (Rolls) I. 259 He gadereth water and heteþ it..þroweþ it vppon hunteres and houndes..and scaldeþ of þe heere of hem. **1481** CAXTON *Reynard* xlii. (Arb.) 113 The heer behynde was skalded of. **1617** MORYSON *Itin.* I. 26 The Marques Bath..is so hot, as it will scald off the haire of a Hogge.

d. To apply a hot lotion or solution to.

1753 J. BARTLET *Gentl. Farriery* xxxi. 260 If the matter flows in great abundance, and of a thin consistence, it must be scalded again. **1887** *Cassell's Encycl. Dict.*, *Scald*, to boil or buck cloth with white soap after bleaching.

4. *Cookery.* **a.** To heat liquid to a point just short of boiling point. Also *intr.* for *passive.*

1483 *Cath. Angl.* 320/2 To Scalde browes, *adipare.* **1692** TRYON *Good House-wife* iii. 45 If you take milk and scald it (but it must be done to a point, not to hot). **1725** RAMSAY *Gentle Sheph.* II. i, Our meikle pot that scads the whey. **1833** MRS. BRAY *Descr. Tamar & Tavy* xl. (1836) III. 290 There was a pan of milk..scalding over the embers of a wood fire. **1851** MAYHEW *Lond. Labour* I. 192/2 The milk is first 'scalded', the pan containing it being closely watched, in order that the contents may not boil.

b. To subject to the action of hot water; to pour hot liquid over.

c **1430** *Two Cookery-bks.* 24 Take fayre Bolasse..in Wyne boyle hem þat þey be but skaldyd bywese. **1591** COCKAINE *Treat. Hunting* C j, Ground Otes put in a tub and scalded with water. **1747** MRS. GLASSE *Cookery* xvi. 147 A Buttered Tort. Take eight or ten large Codlings and scald them. *c* **1830** *Glouc. Farm Rep.* 33 in *Libr. Usef. Knowl.*, *Husb.* III, It is customary with most dairy-maids to scald the curd with hot whey.

†**5.** *trans.* To boil to death. Also *absol.* *Obs.*

a **1536** in *Songs, Carols*, etc. (E.E.T.S.) 161 þer was on skaldyd in Smythfild, for poysenyng of dyueris men of þe Bisshop of Rochesters howse. **1552** LYNDESAY *Monarche* 4642 Peter, Andro, Iohne, Iames, and Paull,..To byrne and skald thay neuer pretendit. **1568** CHARTERIS *Pref. to Lyndesay's Wks.* ✠ iij b, To bruyle and scald quha sa euer suld speik aganis thame.

II. To burn.

6. *trans.* Of the sun or fire, etc.: To scorch, burn. Also said of certain soils. *Obs.* exc. *dial.*

a **1300** *E.E. Psalter* cxx. 6 Bi dai noght þe sunne skalde þe sal. *c* **1386** CHAUCER *Miller's T.* 667 And Nicholas is scalded in the toute. *c* **1460** *Towneley Myst.* xx. 4 Fro this burnyshyd brande..I red ye be shunand or els the dwill skald you. **1561** HOLLYBUSH *Hom. Apoth.* 25 b, Chafynge meates do scaulde the lyver. **1567** GOLDING *Ovid's Met.* VII. 89 b, Swelting heate that scalt their guts within. **1652–62** HEYLIN *Cosmogr.* II. (1682) 129 Blest with a sweet and temperate air, not over scalded with the Sun. **1785** BURNS *Addr. Deil* ii, I'm sure sma' pleasure it can gie, Ev'n to a deil, To skelp an' scaud poor dogs like me. **1793** *Trans. Soc. Arts* XI. 77 A heavy soil will..scald and starve any kind of grain. **1824** SCOTT *Redgauntlet* let. xi, That will be as bad as scauding your fingers wi' a redhot chanter. **1881** *Scribner's Monthly* XXII. 268 Not a leaf..burned or scalded during the hot, dry weather.

absol. *c* **1578** G. BEST in *Hakluyt's Voy.* (1600) III. 49 If any man say the Sunne may scalde a good while before and after it come to the Meridian. **1630** *R. Johnson's Kingd. & Commw.* 4 Fire, being invested in the body of..metals, scaldeth more furiously than in wood. **1686** tr. *Chardin's Trav. Persia* 413 The Reverberation of which [high mountain] so furiously heats the place in the dog-days, that it scalds again.

b. *intr.* for *pass.* To be scorched or burnt.

1513 DOUGLAS *Æneis* IV. x. 89 And all the cost belive of flambis scald [L. *iam fervere litora flammis*]. *c* **1520** M. NISBET *N.T. in Scots*, *Matt.* xiii. 6 Bot quhen the sonn was risen, thai scaldit. **1597** SHAKS. *2 Hen. IV*, IV. v. 31 Thou do'st sit Like a rich Armor, worne in heat of day, That scald'st with safetie. **1902** RIDER HAGGARD *Rural Eng.* II. 392 There the land was light and they scalded.

c. *transf.* To become inflamed, sore, or raw.

1580 BLUNDEVIL *Horsemanship, Horses' Dis.* xiv. 7 If you looke on his tongue, you shall see it almost rawe and scalte, with the heate that comes out of his bodie. **1808** JAMIESON, *To Skaude, Skad*, When any part of the body is galled and inflamed, in consequence of heat, it is said to *skad.*

†**7.** *trans.* Of desire, thoughts, etc.: To 'burn', inflame, irritate. Also *intr.*, to 'burn' or be fired with desire. *Obs.*

c **1375** *Sc. Leg. Saints* xviii. (*Egipciane*) 961 Quhene sick thocht can me schald. **1513** DOUGLAS *Æneis* VII. vii. 10 The byssy curis of Turnus mariage Skalding hir breist and mynd all in a rage. *Ibid.* XIII. vi. 104 In our [= over] ardent desyre Of the bargan he scaldit hait as fyre. **1595** SHAKS. *John* v. vii. 49, I am scalded with my violent motion And spleene of speede, to see your Maiesty. **1629** MASSINGER *Roman Actor* IV. ii, Would not a secret..Scald you to keep it? **1667** COTTON *Scarron.* IV. 65 For which she did so scald and burn That none but he could serve her turn.

III. 8. *Glass-making.* [after It. *scaldare*, F. *échauder.*] *trans.* ? To bring to a certain heat.

1662 MERRETT tr. *Neri's Art of Glass* 247 The Master workman, who..with his *ponteglo* sticks the Glass and scalds it. **1699** tr. *Blancourt's Art of Glass* iii. 27 With Blowing, Pressing, Scalding, Amplifying, and Cutting he forms it [glass] into what shape he pleases.

†‖**scalda'banco.** *Obs.* [a. obs. It. *scaldabanco*, f. *scaldare* to heat + *banco* bench.] A warm disputant or preacher.

a **1670** HACKET *Abp. Williams* II. (1693) 182 The Presbyterians, those Scalda-banco's, or hot Declamers, had wrought a great distast in the Commons at the King.

'scald-ˌberry. *dial.* [f. SCALD *sb.*[2] (see quot. 1838).] The bramble, *Rubus fruticosus.*

1726 THRELKELD *Syn. Stirpium Hib.* I. 5. **1750** W. ELLIS *Country Housewife's Comp.* 246 How to make Scald-berry Pies... Take ripe Scald-berries [etc.]. **1838** LOUDON *Arboretum* II. 743 The fruits..are called..scaldberries, from their supposed quality of giving scald heads to children.

scald-crow. Also **scalte-**, **scale-**, **scaul-** (see also E.D.D.). [? f. SCALD *a.*[1]] A name in Ireland for the Hooded Crow (*Corvus cornix*). Also *fig.*

1834 LOVER *Leg. & Stor. Irel.* Ser. II. 281 That one is for that poor scaldcrow there,..little Fairly. **1863** KINGSLEY *Water-Bab.* vii. 268 All the other scaul-crows set upon her, and pecked her to death there and then. **1879** O'DONOVAN *Merv Oasis* (1882) I. i. 8 We tear along,..scaring dozens of white-backed scald-crows.

scalded ('skɔːldɪd), *ppl. a.*[1] [f. SCALD *v.* + -ED[1].]

a. In various uses of SCALD *v.*

1494 *Act 11 Hen. VII*, c. 19 Pillows made of..scalded Feathers and dry pulled Feathers together. **1611** COTGR. s.v. *Chien*, ..The scaulded dog feares euen colde water. **1648** G. DANIEL *Eclog.* iii. 158 Scalded palats, who have lost their tasts. **1796** MARSHALL *Rur. Econ. W. Eng.* I. 250 The cream thus raised is termed 'scalded cream', or 'clouted cream'. **1825** JAMIESON, *Scadded beer*, or *ale*, a drink made of hot beer or ale... *Scadded whey*, a dish..made by boiling whey on a slow fire, by which a great part of it coagulates into a curdy substance. **1885** R. BRIDGES *Nero* I. ii. 4 Treat her eyes To hide these scalded rings.

(*b*) In proverbial phr. ***like a scalded cat.*** Hence ***scalded-cat raid*** (see quot. 1945).

1934 [see MARK *sb.*[1] 12 e]. **1943** *Times* 6 Nov. 2/1 The *Luftwaffe*..were now using a new type of twin-engine fighter-bomber... From the French coast to Westminster Bridge was a distance of 85 miles. In and out they flashed across it at their fastest speeds—like scalded cats. **1945** L. E. O. CHARLTON *Britain at War* IV. 80 When a small force of enemy raiders crossed the coast and penetrated towards London on November 8th, 1943,..three of them were destroyed. One of the aircraft brought down was..one of the new twin-engine fighter-bombers described by Sir Archibald Sinclair, Secretary of State for Air, a few days previously when he spoke of 'scalded cat' raids on London and the South Coast. **1977** *Hot Car* Oct. 75/3 We have driven a converted V6 and it certainly went like a scalded cat. **1977** C. MCCULLOUGH *Thorn Birds* ii. 45 Meggie hopped out like a scalded cat and dressed herself without even asking for help. **1980** *Herald* (Melbourne) 9 Apr. 7/4 How does it go, old boy? Like a scalded cat.

b. Inflamed or raw as if injured by hot water.

c **1450** *ME. Med. Bk.* (Heinrich) 76 For a man þat is scalded on his pintill [*v.r.* for a scaldid pintil]. **1818** *Art Pres. Feet* 206 The superabundant excretion produces langour and feebleness..; whilst the matter itself becomes so corrosive as to produce what is called scalded feet. **1846** J. BAXTER *Libr. Pract. Agric.* (ed. 4) II. 283 [In sheep] After the scalded parts have been rubbed off in the manner directed. **1851** H. STEPHENS *Bk. Farm* §3751 Scalded heads. —Sheep are much infested in summer with flies [etc.].

c. Of land: so poor as to support little if any vegetation. *Austral.*

1936 K. C. MCKEOWN *Insect Wonders of Australia* xx. 163 The eggs are deposited, as a general rule, upon the 'scalded plains' of the interior, but the insects will avail themselves of almost any area of hard bare ground. **1948** N. C. W. BEADLE *Vegetation & Pastures of Western New South Wales* vi. 58 Scalded surfaces are in general devoid of vegetation, even in the best seasons. **1977** *Weekly Times* (Melbourne) 19 Jan. 17/2 Deep gullies and scalded country are evidence of the worst abuses of valuable farming country.

†**'scalded,** *ppl. a.*[2] *Obs.* [f. SCALD *sb.*[2] + -ED[2].] = SCALD *a.*[1]

1508 KENNEDIE *Flyting w. Dunbar* 26 Pretendand the to wryte sic skaldit skrowis. *Ibid.* 37 Skaldit skaitbird. **1641** COWLEY *Guardian* v. vi, Give me the Periwig, boy. What? shall Empress Tabytha's husband go as if his head were scalded? *a* **1704** T. BROWN *Satire on Quack* Wks. 1730 I. 64 For scalded heads most learnedly advise.

'scalder, *sb.*[1] [f. SCALD *v.* + -ER[1].] One who scalds poultry, vessels, etc.

1536 in *Househ. Ord.* (1790) 237 The said..Clerke shall see that the said Poultry shall be dayly put into the Scalder's hands. **1612** *MSS. Dk. Rutland* (1905) IV. 488 Paid to a scallder from London, 16 dayes at v.s. the day. *a* **1625** FLETCHER & MASSINGER *Elder Brother* II. iii. (1637) D 3 b, Ralph [the cook] there with his kitchin boyes and scalders.

†**'scalder,** *sb.*[2] [ad. mod.L. *scalder* (Olaus Wormius 1633), f. ON. *skáld* SKALD.] = SKALD.

1765 BLAIR in Macpherson *Ossian* (1785) II. 290 *note*, An extract, which Dr. Hicks has given from the work of one of the Danish Scalders. *Ibid.* 291 This Lodbrog was a king of Denmark,..and at the same time an eminent Scalder or poet. **1774** WARTON *Hist. Eng. Poetry* I. Diss. i. e 4 b, In the place of their old scalders a new rank of poets arose, called Gleemen or Harpers.

scalder ('skɒldə(r)), *v. north. dial.* [? f. SCALD *v.* + -ER[5].] *trans.* To scald, scorch. Hence **'scaldered** *ppl. a.* (see quot. 1796).

1600 FAIRFAX *Tasso* XVIII. lxxxv. 332 The hardie Duke.. comforts those that from the scaldred hides, With water stroue th'approaching flames to chace. **1796** MARSHALL *Rur. Econ. Yorks.* (ed. 2) II. 341 *Scaldered*, chafed, blistered, or partially excoriated, whether by friction, heat, or corrosion. .. *Scalderings*, the under-burnt cores of stone lime: the surfaces of which peeling off, in scales or shells. **1804** R.

Anderson *Cumbld. Ball.* 51, I..scawder'd my fit. **1876** *Whitby Gloss., Scalder'd*, skin-chafed, leprous.

'scald-fish. [app. f. SCALD *a.*[1]: see quot. 1812.] The smooth sole, *Pleuronectes arnoglossus*.

1812 PENNANT *Brit. Zool.* III. 325 *Pleuronectes arnoglossus*... The scales are so deciduous that the friction of the trawl alone is sufficient to remove them; when taken out of the net, they are usually..in that bare state which gives some propriety to the name they are known by of Scald-fish. **1836** [see MEGRIM[2]]. **1876** SMILES *Sc. Natur.* xvi. (ed. 4) 346.

scald head, 'scald-head. [SCALD *a.*[1]]

1. A person's head diseased with ringworm or some similar affection.

1546 J. HEYWOOD *Prov.* (1867) 49 A scalde head is soone broken. **1615** G. SANDYS *Trav.* 53 Meane of stature he was, & euill proportioned: hauing euer a scald head. *a* **1756** ELIZA HEYWOOD *New Present* (1771) 247 An infallible Remedy for a Scald Head. **1826** HOOD *Irish Schoolm.* xix, The Pedagogue, with sudden drub, Smites his scald head, that is already sore. **1882** *Jamieson's Sc. Dict., Scaud-head, Scaut-head*, a head disfigured with patches of scrofula.

transf. **1808** MRS. KEMBLE *Day after Wedding* 12 I'll make you a toupee. I hate your scald-heads, all dragged up at the roots.

2. A popular term for tinea or other similar scalp affections.

1675 HAN. WOOLLEY *Gentlew. Comp.* 179 For a Scald head. Take a Candle, and let it drop upon it as hot as you can, in so doing it will scale off. **1725** *Bradley's Fam. Dict.* s.v., There are several sorts of Scald Heads, some resemble the Grains of Figs..; others are small bits of Flesh..and others are like Farinous Tetters. **1845** *Encycl. Metrop.* VII. 791/1 Porrigo is a generic term for an eruption of psydracious pustules, usually termed scald-head. **1871** NAPHEYS *Prev. & Cure Dis.* III. xiii. 1077 One of the forms of 'scald head'.

So **scald-headed** *a.*, having a 'scald head'; also *fig.*

1802 C. WILMOT *Let.* 19 Oct. in *Irish Peer on Continent* (1920) 102 Grim scaldheaded Mountains. **1837** CARLYLE *Fr. Rev.* III. vi, Is Royalty grown a mere wooden Scarecrow; whereon thou, pert scaldheaded crow, mayest alight at pleasure and peck? **1856** R. A. VAUGHAN *Mystics* I. III. iv. 103 Every humpbacked, one-eyed, scald-headed passenger had to pay a penny for each infirmity.

scald-hot, *a. Obs.* exc. *dial.* Also 5 schalde-, 9 scal-, scaul-. [f. SCALD *v.* + HOT *a.* Cf. Sw. *skållhet*, Da. *skoldhed.*] Scalding hot.

c **1425** *St. Christina* vi. in *Anglia* VIII. 122/25 She poured scalde-hoot watir on þos membrys þat were harmles withouten. *a* **1500** *E.E. Misc.* (Warton Club) 89 Whanne hit is more than schalde-hote, drawe owte ȝour fyre clene. **1858** N. HOGG *Poet. Lett.* (ed. 3) 52 Hur voun thare wis zummat scal hot to hur caf. **1867** POOLE & BARNES *Gloss. Wexford, Scaul, Scald*, e.g. 'Scaul hoate', scalding hot.

scaldic: see SKALDIC.

†**'scalding,** *sb.*[1] Chiefly *Sc. Obs.* Also 5 skalding(g), scaldyn, 6 schalding, 6–7 scadling. [? f. SCALD *a.* + -ING[1].] **a.** ? The carcass of a 'scald' sheep. **b.** A sheepskin of small value, ? one taken from a 'scald' sheep.

a. 1302–3 *Sacrist Rolls Ely* (1907) II. 17 Pro ij carcos. bouum et iij scaldyngis missis Episcopo. **1338** in Dugdale *Monasticon* (1819) II. 585/1 Vitulina et ij. skaldynges.

b. 1429 *Rolls of Parlt.* IV. 352/1 A nail of Lambeswolle, is at the value of ix *d.* or x *d.*, and a shorlyng feel or scaldyng, at ob. or I *d.* the best. **1442** *Aberd. Reg.* (1844) I. 397 That na man by woll skynnis derar than x d., schorlinges vi d., scaldynes iii d. **1538** *Ibid.* (MS.) XVI. (Jam.), Small wnwollit skynnis sic as hoyg schorlingis, scadlingis, and fuitfaill. **1661** *Sc. Acts Chas. II* (1820) VII. 253/2 Futfells & skaldings.

'scalding, *sb.*[2] *Hist.* (In 7–8 Often erron. stalding.) [Cf. OF. *eskallin, escalin, escarlin* (13–14th c.): see ESCALINE.] A Flemish coin introduced into England and Ireland in the 13th century.

[*c* **1285** in *Cal. Doc. rel. Irel.* (1879) III. 8 The bishop [of Waterford, Stephen de Fulborn]..caused new money to be made. It was called Scalding, Bishop's money, or Stephening, from the name of the bishop.] **1605** CAMDEN *Rem.* (1623) 176 Rosaries, Stepings, and Staldings. **1716** M. DAVIES *Athen. Brit.* III. 78 Pollards, Crocards, Staldings. **1866** ROGERS *Agric. & Prices* I. xi. 178 A considerable circulation of Flemish coins..was effected in England at the close of the thirteenth century. These pieces went by the name of Pollards, Crockards, Scaldings, Brabants, Eagles [etc.].

'scalding, *vbl. sb.* [f. SCALD *v.* + -ING[1].]

1. a. The act of burning with hot fluid or steam. Also, †a scalded part.

1398 TREVISA *Barth. De P.R.* XVII. cxix. (1495) 682 The rynde of the plane helpyth to ease scaldyng and brennynge yf it is layed therto. **1526** *Grete Herball* cxix. (1529) Hjb, Lay it vpon the scaldynge with a feder, and it wyll heale. **1578** LYTE *Dodoens* I. lxxxi. 121 The wilde Mulleyne stamped, is good to be layde vpon burnings and scaldings. **1605** SHAKS. *Lear* IV. vi. 131 There's hell,..there is the sulphurous pit; burning, scalding, stench. **1694** [see SANABLE 2]. **1742** tr. *Heister's Surg.* (1768) I. 240 The Burns ..which are occasioned by boiling Liquors (which we call Scalding).

b. *transf.* A hot sensation as of scalding.

1597 GERARDE *Herbal* III. xxxviii. 1174 The same is good ..against frettings of the bladder, and scalding of the vrine. **1709** *Brit. Apollo* No. 44. 2/2 A Scalding i' th' Urine.

†**c.** Inflamed or sore condition. (Cf. SCALDED *ppl. a.*[1] b.)

c **1450** *ME. Med. Bk.* (Heinrich) 76 Pro le scaldynge virge quod vocatur apegalle. **1597** GERARDE *Herbal* II. cccxiv. 745 Good medicines..for vlcerations and scaldings in the priuie parts.

d. *Horticulture.* Injury done to plants by the sun's heat after watering.

1865 *Trans. Illinois Agric. Soc.* V. 208 Here is no swaying of trees to the east, no scalding of the west side of the trunks in the sun. **1882** *Garden* 11 Mar. 169/2 The stem leaves.. which are subject to scalding, should never be syringed on bright mornings. **1890** *Daily News* 12 Sept. 2/3 There have been heavy dews and fogs, and as these have been followed by hot sun, it has caused what is known as scalding [in hops].

2. a. The use of boiling or hot liquid in the preparation of the carcasses of animals, etc. for food; the use of hot lotions (in farriery); the partial boiling of milk, etc.; a quantity of liquid thus heated.

139. *Earl Derby's Exp.* (Camden) 65/1 Pro skaldyng porcorum et porcellorum. *c* **1400** *Rom. Rose* 6820 Without scaldyng they hem pull. **1487** *Act 4 Hen. VII* c. 3 The Slaughter of Beasts, and Scalding of Swine, had and done in the Butchery. **1753** J. BARTLET *Gentl. Farriery* xxxi. 260 The manner of scalding is first to clean the abscess well with a piece of sponge dipped in vinegar; then put a sufficient quantity of the mixture into a ladle with a spout, and when it is made scalding hot, pour it into the abscess. **1875** KNIGHT *Dict. Mech., Scalding*, a. The last boiling or bucking of cloth with white soap after bleaching. b. The soap itself. **1882** *Jamieson's Sc. Dict.* s.v. *Scaudin*, 'I'll hae anither scaudin o' whey the day.'.. 'That's a big scaudin o' milk ye hae.'

b. *pl.* Scalding hot liquid. *to cry scaldings*: see quot. 1867.

1748 SMOLLETT *Rod. Rand.* xxv, He carried off a large wooden platter, and..returned with it full of boiled pease, crying 'scaldings' all the way. **1839** J. SNOWE *Leg. Rhine* I. 104 This temerarious lad was wont now and then to fling scaldings over him. **1867** SMYTH *Sailor's Word-bk., Scaldings!*, notice to get out of the way; it is used when a man with a load wishes to pass, and would lead those in his way to think that he was carrying hot water. **1878** H. C. ADAMS *Wykehamica* xxiii. 432.

3. *attrib.* (See also SCALDING-HOUSE.)

1608 H. CLAPHAM *Errour Left Hand* 34 The Pope hath a mighty allowance annually from the Courtizans scalding-tubs. **1753** J. BARTLET *Gentl. Farriery* xxxi. 259 Some make their scalding mixture milder. **1805** R. W. DICKSON *Pract. Agric.* II. 1023 The outside of the dairy or scalding-room. **1831** YOUATT *Horse* ix. 153 In extreme cases [of poll-evil], even the scalding mixture of the farrier may be called into requisition.

scalding ('skɔːldɪŋ), *ppl. a.* [-ING[2].]

1. That scalds; scalding hot.

a **1225** *Ancr. R.* 246 Þeo þet beoð wiðinnen heldeð schaldinde water ut, & werieð so þe walles. **1481** CAXTON *Reynard* xlii. (Arb.) 113 The cook..toke a grete bolle full of scaldyng water, and caste it on his hyppes behynde. **1590** MARLOWE *2nd Pt. Tamburl.* III. v, Searing thy hateful flesh with burning irons and drops of scalding lead. **1641** J. JACKSON *True Evang. T.* I. 27 He had caused him to be thrown into a Caldron of scalding oyle. **1755** HALES in *Phil. Trans.* XLIX. I. 339 To give the milk a scalding heat. **1816** SCOTT *Antiq.* xiv, He..drinks his tea scalding. **1853** KANE *Grinnell Exp.* xxx. (1856) 260 Some sugared cranberries, with a little butter and scalding water, and you have an impromptu strawberry ice.

†**b.** Of the sea, etc. [rendering L. *torrens*]: Boiling, seething. Also *subst.* = TORRENT. *Obs.*

a **1300** *Cursor M.* 20882 Apon þe skaldand see he [*sc.* St. Peter] yede. *a* **1300** *E.E. Psalter* cxxiii. 5 Oure saule overfore scaldand. *Ibid.* cxxv. 4 Turne, Laverd, our wrecchednesse, Als skaldand in south esse. **1513** DOUGLAS *Æneis* VI. iv. 59 Schaldand hellis flude, Flagiton.

†**c.** Of fire, the sun, etc.: Scorching. *Obs.*

1500–20 DUNBAR *Poems* xxvi. 23 Mony prowd trumpour with him trippit Throw skaldand fyre. **1577** tr. *Bullinger's Decades* II. ix. 210 Least..hee happ to fall into the scalding lyme kill. **1596** SHAKS. *3 Hen. VI*, v. vii. 18 In Summers scalding heate. **1621** BURTON *Anat. Mel.* II. ii. III. 335 Built, with high houses, narrow streets, to keep out these scoulding beames. **1697** DRYDEN *Virg. Georg.* IV. 32 The Banks of Brooks will make a cool retreat For the raw Soldiers from the scalding Heat. **1707** MORTIMER *Husb.* 63 They fallow it when the Sun is pretty high, which they call a scalding fallow. **1720** DE FOE *Capt. Singleton* vi. (1840) 98 A scalding sand, which..drove about in clouds.

2. *transf.* and *fig.* Producing an effect or sensation like that of scalding. **a.** Of tears, etc.

a **1225** *Ancr. R.* 246 Worpeð ut uppon him schaldinde teares. **1591** SYLVESTER *Du Bartas* I. i. (1621) 13 He, that in Sommer,..Scorched all day in his owne scalding sweat. **1667** MILTON *P.L.* x. 556 Parcht with scalding thurst. **1715** POPE *Iliad* II. 331 He..From his vile Visage wip'd the scalding Tears. **1829** *Good's Study Med.* (ed. 3) V. 469 [Paruria] Ardens. Scalding strangury. **1856** DOVE *Logic Chr. Faith* V. i. §2. 293 Where is the eye that has forgotten its scalding agonies. **1886** HALL CAINE *Son of Hagar* III. xix, Greta..wept scalding tears.

†**b.** Of desire, etc.: Burning, hot, fervent. *Obs.*

c **1375** *Sc. Leg. Saints* xxxvi. (*Baptista*) 81 In skaldand word luf god sal þay. *c* **1400** *Sc. Trojan War* II. 1674 A blynd fulische desyre..to pass into þar land With eger willis and scaldand. **1589** GREENE *Menaphon* (Arb.) 34 To breath out scalding sighes smothered within the fornace of his thoughts.

†**c.** Of utterances: Caustic, stinging. *Obs.*

1641 J. JACKSON *True Evang. T.* I. 74 Our venomous and scalding words, which burne like coals of Juniper.

scalding hot, *a.* Also 4 scladeng. [f. SCALDING *vbl. sb.* + HOT *a.*] Hot enough to scald.

1387 TREVISA *Higden* (Rolls) I. 259 Þeryn he gadereth water and heteþ it in his rennynge scladeng [*sic*; *Caxton* skaldyng] hoot. *c* **1430** *Two Cookery-bks.* 17 Whan þe Mylke his skaldyng hote, caste þe stuf þer-to. **1610** HOLLAND *Camden's Brit.* 233 They [*sc.* springs at Bath] are in maner skalding hote. **1707** MORTIMER *Husb.* 566 Put your first Wort into the Copper again, make it scalding hot. **1816** SCOTT *Old Mort.* xxxvi, Keep your ain breath to cool your ain porridge—ye'll find them scalding hot, I promise you. **1869** TOZER *Highl. Turkey* II. 302 A scalding-hot steam.

fig. **1562** COOPER *Answ. Priv. Masse* iii. 14b, Your scaulding hotte and firebourning charitee. **1679** ALSOP *Melius Inq.* Introd. 29 There's more danger of being lukewarm in Reforming than scalding-hot.

'scalding-house. [f. SCALDING *vbl. sb.* + HOUSE *sb.*[1]] A room in which utensils or the carcasses of animals are scalded.

1421 *Cov. Leet Bk.* 32 Allso-sone as the skaldyng-house.. be full fynyshid and redy that they skald þer swyne in the same house. **1577–87** HOLINSHED *Chron.* III. 920/1 In the scalding house, a yeoman and two groomes. **16..** MASSINGER, etc. *Old Law* III. ii. (1656) 39 And my three Court Codlings that looke parboyld, As if they came from Cupids scalding house. **1688** R. HOLME *Armoury* IV. xii. (Roxb.) 499/2 The Skalding house. **1805** R. W. DICKSON *Pract. Agric.* I. 56 The milk-house, the scalding and pressing house, and the salting-house.

†**b.** *fig.* Euphemistically for: Hell. *Obs.*

1549 LATIMER *7th Serm. bef. Edw. VI* (Arb.) 205 Even in the skaldinge house, in the vgsomnes of the place. *Ibid.* 208 You are lyke to go [to] ye Scalding house, and ther you shal haue two dishes, wepynge and gnashinge of teeth.

‖**scaldino** (skal'diːno). [It., f. *scaldare* to warm.] A small earthen brazier, used in Italy.

1866 HOWELLS *Venetian Life* iii. 35 The *scaldino* is a small pot of glazed earthenware, having an earthen bale: with this handle passed over the arm, and the pot full of bristling charcoal, [etc.]. **1873** 'OUIDA' *Pascarel* II. 23 She sat opposite me,..toasting her feet on an earthen *scaldino*.

†**'scaldness.** *Obs.* [f. SCALD *a.* + -NESS.] Scabbiness.

1527 ANDREW *Brunswyke's Distyll. Waters* T iij b, The same water heleth the scaldnes of the hede. **1562** TURNER *Herbal* II. 112 Radish..filleth vp with heyre agayne the places that were bared with scaldnes.

†**'scaldrag.** *Obs.* [f. SCALD *v.* + RAG *sb.*[1]] One who scalds or boils rags: a nickname for a dyer.

1630 J. TAYLOR (Water P.) *Wks.* II. 165 To cal a Justice of the Peace, a Beadle; a Dyer, a Scaldragge.

scaldricks: see SKELLOCH, wild mustard.

†**'scaldry.** *Sc. Obs.* [? f. *scald*, Sc. form of SCOLD *sb.* + -RY.] Abusive speech.

1502–3 *Burgh Rec. Edin.* (1869) 97 Personis convict for flyting and scaldrie.

'scaldweed. = SCALD *sb.*[2] 5.

1866 in *Treas. Bot.*

†**'scaldy,** *a.*[1] *Obs. rare*$^{-0}$. [f. SCALD *a.* + -Y.] Scalled.

1598 FLORIO, *Tegnoso*, scaldie, or scurfie, hauing a sore head.

scaldy ('skɔːldɪ), *a.*[2] *local.* [f. SCALD *sb.*[3] + -Y.] Of land: Containing 'scalds' (see SCALD *sb.*[3] 4); easily affected by drought.

1898 RIDER HAGGARD *Farmer's Year* (1899) 64 A good but rather scaldy piece of land. **1899** —— *Rural Eng.* 366 Forty-four coombs of oats..not a bad return from this scaldy soil.

scale (skeɪl), *sb.*[1] Forms: α. 3– scale; also 4–7, 9 skale, 5 skaylle, 9 scaile, skail. β. 3–7 (9 *dial.*) scole, 3, 6–7 scoale, 6–7 skole, 7 scoal, scowle, skoal(e. [a. ON. *skál* str. fem., bowl, *pl.* (weighing) scales (Sw. *skål*, Da. *skaal*: cf. SKOAL) = OHG. *scâla* (MHG. *schâle*, mod.G. *schale*):—OTeut. **skǣlā*, ablaut-var. of **skalā*, whence OE. *scealu* shell, husk, drinking cup, weighing scale (see SHALE *sb.*[1]), OHG. *scala* shell, husk (MHG., mod.G. *schale*); the quantity of the vowel is doubtful in OS. *skala* cup, and in the ODu. antecedent of MDu. *schale* (Du. *schaal*), though it is probable that in Du. as in Ger. two original forms, *skâla* cup, scales, and *skăla* husk, shell, have become phonetically coincident. For the OE. *scealu* the inflexion appears to attest the short vowel in all the senses. The WGer. **skăla* (:—OTeut. **skǣlā*, *skalā*) passed into OF. as *eschale*, *escale* cup (med.L. *scala* 'patera'), also husk (mod.F. *écale*). For the Teut. root **skel-*: *skal-*: *skǣl-* to separate, divide, cf. SHALE, SHELL, SKILL. See also SKELE.

Between the first quarter of the 13th c. and the 16th c. the α forms (containing the vowel *a*) represent the northern pronunciation, the β forms being midland and southern. In the 16th c., however, the northern *scale* seems to have found its way into the London dialect, being used by Palsgrave and later by Spenser and Shaks. In the 17th c. *scale* is the prevailing literary form, though *scole* (with other equivalent spellings) occasionally appears down to the middle of the century.]

I. 1. A drinking-bowl or cup. *Obs.* exc. *S. Afr.*

α. *c* **1205** LAY. 5368 Ælc mon nom an honde ane scale [*c* 1275 scele] of rede golde. *Ibid.* 14965 Heo fulde hir scale of wine. **1390–1** *Earl Derby's Exp.* (Camden) 100/21 Vasa Argentea..pro vj skales argenteis. *c* **1460** *Towneley Myst.* xii. 249 Ye hold long the skayll, Now let me go to. *c* **1475** *Cath. Angl.* (Addit. MS.) 320/2 A Scale of Ale. **1511–12** *Durham Acc. Rolls* (Surtees) 662 Pro 4 dd. Ciphorum et 2 dd. Scalez. **1616** in *N. Riding Rec.* (1884) II. 118 Geo.

Smales [presented] for..selling ale in scales and pottes not sealed. ?a 1800 *Jolly Hind's Squire* xi. in Child *Ballads* (1884) I. 429 There's ale into the birken scale, Wine in the horn green. 1946 P. Abrahams *Mine Boy* iii. 26 Joseph nodded, slapped Xuma heartily on the back and offered him a scale of beer... He smiled and took the scale. Xuma put the scale to his lips, then passed it to Daddy. 1953 P. Lanham *Blanket Boy's Moon* v. iii. 274 Drink a scale of fine home-brewed kaffir beer with us. 1969 *Post* (Golden City, S. Afr.) 6 Apr. 14 Gave her R1 and told her to buy a scale of KB from Mathebula. 1970 *Drum* Oct. 8, I found myself firmly grasping a plastic scale.

β. a 1225 *Ancr. R.* 214 A dischs ine his one hond, & a scoale [*v.rr.* schale, skale] in his oðer. c 1275 Lay. 1180 Ane scole he bar an honde al of rede golde milc was in þe scole. 13.. *E.E. Allit. P.* B. 1145 A bassyn, a bolle, oþer a scole.

II. Apparatus for weighing.

2. The pan, or each of the pans, of a balance. Also *fig.* † *to hold scale with*: to balance, to equal in weight.

α. c 1375 *Sc. Leg. Saints* xxii. (*Laurentius*) 739 Quhene we wald in skale put don his ewil consawit suspicione..& in-to þe tothyre skale his gud dedis ware al hale. c 1440 *Alphabet of Tales* 349 In þe to skale it weyed more þan all þat evur þai cuthe put in þe toder skale. 1483 *Cath. Angl.* 320/2 A Scale of a balañ, *lanx*. 1590 Shaks. *Mids. N.* iii. ii. 132 Your vowes to her, and me, (put in two scales) Will euen weigh, and both as light as tales. 1604 —— *Oth.* i. iii. 331 If the braine of our liues had not one Scale of Reason, to poize another of Sensualitie. 1654 Ambrose *Ultima* 193 This one sinne of refusing Christ may perhaps hold scale with the united horrours of all the rest whatsoever. 1687 Dryden *Hind & P.* ii. 624 Till when, your weights will in the balance fail A Church unprincipled kicks up the Scale. 1713 Steele *Englishm.* No. 55. 355 [They] made their Court by throwing themselves into the Scale of unlimited Loyalty. 1770 Burke *Pres. Discont.* Wks. II. 306 In a contest..where nothing can be put into their scale which is not taken from ours. 1842 *Penny Cycl.* XXII. 192/1 They [*sc.* the soils] are..placed in opposite scales of a balance, and poised. 1859 Tennyson *Geraint* 525 While slowly falling as a scale that falls, When weight is added only grain by grain. 1860 L. Harcourt *Diaries G. Rose* I. 179 He..would, Brennus-like, have thrown his sword into the scale of liberty. 1868 Browning *Ring & Bk.* v. 474 This time 'twas my scale quietly kissed the ground, Mere rank against mere wealth.

β. c 1440 *Jacob's Well* 4 Whanne þis smal precyous ston was leyd in a scole, it was so heuy, þat no-thing leyd in þe oþer scole, was it neuere so heuy, myȝte weyin it vp. 1594 T. B. *La Primaud. Fr. Acad.* ii. 183 The skoles in a payre of balance. 1601 Sir W. Cornwallis *Ess.* ii. xxvi. O 6 Iustice, which being the very soule and life of gouernment is oft time compelled to help the lightest scoale with her finger. 1611 Cotgr., *Bassin d'vne balance*, the scowle of a balance. 1648 Wilkins *Math. Magic* i. iii. 16 Both the scoles being empty shall hang in æquilibrio.

3. a. *pl.* (†In 16th c. rarely construed as *sing.*). A weighing instrument; *esp.* one (often called ***a pair of scales***) consisting of a beam which is pivoted at its middle and at either end of which a dish, pan, board, or slab is suspended. Also *fig.*

α. 1480 *Wardrobe Acc. Edw. IV* (Nicolas 1830) 131 Standisshes with weightes and scales iij. 1530 Palsgr. 182 *Vnes belances*, a payre of balans or scales to wey with. 1583 Golding *Calvin on Deut.* xciv. 56 Wee must not wey our own woorkes in our owne scales. 1592 Shaks. *Rom. & Jul.* i. ii. 101 In that Christall scales, let there be waid, Your Ladies loue against some other Maid. 1693 Bentley *Boyle Lect.* viii. 4 If we consider the Dignity of an Intelligent Being, and put that in the scales against brute inanimate Matter. 1697 Floyer *Eng. Baths* Pref. c 5 By Sanctorius's Scales he found the Body to weigh less after bathing in cold Water. 1719 D'Urfey *Pills* III. 83 Their Scales were false, their Weights were light. 1831 Scott *Ct. Rob.* ii, The goddess who had inclined the scales of battle in favour of Theodosius. 1872 Yeats *Techn. Hist. Comm.* 117 Public scales, at which citizens could weigh their corn food. 1884 Lowell *Democracy* (1887) 42 In the scales of the destinies brawn will never weigh so much as brain.

β. 1535 Coverdale *Ezek.* v. 1 Then take the scoales and the waight, and deuyde the hayre a sunder. 1571 Golding *Calvin on Ps.* xxvii. 1 As it were weying in a pair of skoles, whatsoever power is in the world and in hel. 1647 Ward *Simp. Cobler* 38 A sin..that seemes small in the common beame of the world, may be very great in the scoales of his Sanctuary. a 1825 Forby *Voc. E. Anglia*, *Scoles*, pl. scales.

b. as an attribute of Justice.

1593 Shaks. *2 Hen. VI*, ii. i. 204 And poyse the Cause in Iustice equall Scales, Whose Beame stands sure. 1604 [see baker 1]. 1610 G. Fletcher *Christ's Vict.* x, In one hand a paire of euen scoals she [Justice] weares. 1861 A. Leighton *Storied Trad. Sc. Life* Ser. ii. 71 We have left the heart-broken Ailsie suspended in the upper scale of justice.

c. ***to hold the scales even*** or ***equally***: to judge impartially. (Cf. 4 b.)

1648 Earl of Westmoreland *Otia Sacra* 118 [The King of Heaven] in his hands the Skoals doth hold so even, That [etc.]. 1692 Dryden *Eleonora* 108 Equally the scales to hold Betwixt the two extremes of hot and cold.

4. a. *sing.* = *pl.* (sense 3). Often *fig.*, esp. in ***to turn the scale***: said of an excess of weight on one side or the other.

c 1440 *Promp. Parv.* 449/2 Scole, to wey wythe,..*libra, balanx*. 1596 Shaks. *Merch. V.* iv. i. 330 If the scale doe turne But in the estimation of a hayre. a 1625 Fletcher *Nice Valour* i. i. (1647) 149 As even as the thirteenth of September, When day and night lye in a scale together. 1627 Speed *England* xxiv. §3 The Victor in Rome..with so equal an hand bare the Scoale of Resistance, that their owne Writers evermore terme it a dangerous Warre. 1674 Hickman *Quinquart. Hist.* (ed. 2) 137 He is..afraid to come either to the pole or to the scale; either to weigh, or to number authorities with us. 1720 De Foe *Capt. Singleton* vii. (1840) 119 We had..three pound and a half..according to..weight and scale. 1777 P. Thicknesse *Year's Journey* I. iii. 18 As he is a good seaman, and has a clean, convenient, nay an elegant vessel, I would rather turn the scale in his favour. 1814 Scott *Ld. of Isles* iii. x, And if my words in weight shall fail, This ponderous sword shall turn the scale. 1861 Flor. Nightingale *Nursing* (ed. 2) 41 When the scale was trembling between life and death. 1888 Bryce *Amer. Commw.* I. v. 62 The odd man whose casting vote would turn the scale as between the seven republican members of the Commission and the seven Democrats. 1902 *Daily Chron.* 7 Oct. 5/3 A cargo of Welsh coal..was put on the scale to-day at fifteen dollars per ton.

b. ***equal, even scale*** (poet.): a just balance; also, a condition of equilibrium or indecision.

1602 Shaks. *Ham.* i. ii. 13 In equall Scale weighing Delight and Dole. 1667 Milton *P.L.* vi. 245 Long time in eeven scale The Battel hung. 1671 —— *P.R.* ii. 173 Belial, in much uneven scale thou weigh'st All others by thy self. 1732 J. Hammond *Love Elegies* xi. 6 'Tis Gold o'erturns the even Scale of Life. 1781 Cowper *Table T.* 251 Kind Providence..weighs the nations in an even scale.

c. *spec.* in *Racing*. ***Clerk of the Scales***: the official who weighs the jockeys, etc. ***to ride*** or ***go to scale***: (of a jockey) to ride to the weighing-room before or after the race.

a 1837 [Apperley] *Turf* (1852) 37 Wright is..a steady..rider, and comes light to the scale. 1856 'Stonehenge' *Brit. Rural Sports* 364 In Catch Weights any person can ride without going to scale. 1857 G. A. Lawrence *Guy Liv.* iv, He would have dismounted before riding to scale, and so lost the stakes. 1877 Sayles *Law of Racing* 52 A horse shall not be qualified to run..unless his name has been notified as a starter to the clerk of the scales. 1894 Sir J. Astley *Fifty Yrs. Life* II. 201, I..could go to scale about 14 sts. 7 lb.

5. *Astr.* (*pl.* and †*sing.*) The sign of Libra. Chiefly *poet.*

1631 Heywood *London's Jus Hon.* B j b, Sayle By the signe Libra, that Celestiall scale. 1667 Milton *P.L.* x. 676 By Leo and the Virgin and the Scales. 1687 Dryden *Hind & P.* iii. 505 The Sun, already from the Scales declined. 1847 Barham *Ingol. Leg.* Ser. iii. *The Truants* iii, They filled the Scales with sulphur full, They halloed the Dog-Star on at the Bull. 1935 [see Algol[1]].

6. *attrib.* and *Comb.*, as ***scale balance***, ***baroscope***, ***instrument***, ***maker***, ***man***; **scale-beam**, (*a*) = beam *sb.*[1] 6; (*b*) a weighing instrument of the steelyard kind; **scale-box**, a box to contain a pair of scales; **scale house** *U.S.*, a place in which large scales, as for weighing animals, are kept; **scale-pan**, either of the dishes or pans of a balance.

1809 J. Hutchinson (*title*) The Spirometer, the Stethoscope, and *Scale-Balance. a 1691 Boyle *Hist. Air* (1692) 97 Bringing the *Scale-Baroscope to an exact equilibrium. 1723 *Lond. Gaz.* No. 6172/10 William White .., *Scalebeam-maker. 1789 C. Clarke (*title*) A new Complete System of Weights and Measures,..with considerable Improvements on the Scale-Beam. 1884 Knight *Dict. Mech.* Suppl. 782/1 The scale beam was still further relieved by the fifth lever. 1708 S. Sewall *Diary* 23 June (1879) II. 226 They..fin'd Mr. Tho. Banister..10s. Breach of the peace for throwing the pots and *Scale-box at the maid. 1881 *Instr. Census Clerks* (1885) 81 Scale Box Maker. 1754 *South Carolina Gaz.* 5 Feb. 3/1 A *Scale-House Beam, Scales and Weights, compleat. 1870 *Trans. Illinois Agric. Soc.* VII. 442 In this division of the stock yards there are three scale houses. 1885 *Rep. Indian Affairs* (U.S.) 80 To the southeast..is our large cattle corral..with scales and scale-house. a 1691 Boyle *Hist. Air* (1692) 98 Taking out my *scale-instrument, it appears to weigh precisely a drachm. 1655 in *Suffolk County* (Mass.) *Deeds* (1885) III. 209, I John Saers of Casco bay *scale maker.. Haue bargained & Sold..one Island. 1758 *Rep. Comm. Weights & Meas.* 57 They make use of single Weights made by their present Scale-maker, Mr. Freeman, and his Father, who was likewise Scale-maker to the Mint. 1894 *Daily News* 26 Feb. 7/1 Mr. Thomas Avery, formerly head of the well-known firm of scale-makers. 1783 in L. Chalkley *Chron. Scotch-Irish Settlement Virginia* (1912) I. 232 It is certified that the *scale man is Peter Hane. 1930 *Amer. Speech* VI. 13 [Sugar beets] first go to the washer man, then to the hopper which rests upon the weighing apparatus, operated by the scale man. 1830 Kater & Lardner *Mech.* xxi. 289 Place a weight in each *scale-pan.

scale (skeɪl), *sb.*[2] Forms: 4- scale; also 4-7 **skale** (4 **scaale**, 5 **scalle**, **skaylle**, 6 **skaile**, 7 **scail**, 8 **skeal**, 9 **scal**, **skail**, **skeel**). [aphetic a. OF. *escale* (12th c.), mod.F. *écale* husk, pod, chip of stone:—OTeut. **skalā* (see scale *sb.*[1], shale *sb.*). OF. had also *escaille* (13th c.), mod.F. *écaille* scale of fish, shell of oyster, etc. = It. *scaglia*:—Romanic (also med.L.) *scalia*, a. OTeut. **skaljā* (see shell *sb.*) from the same root; this is perh. the source of some of the ME. spellings.]

1. a. One of the small thin membranous or horny outgrowths or modifications of the skin in many fishes and reptiles, and some mammals, usually overlapping, and forming a complete covering for the body. Also applied to the minute structures forming the covering of the wings of butterflies, etc.

13.. *Guy Warw.* (A.) 7161 Þe smallest scale þat on him [*sc.* a dragon] is No wepen no may atame. c 1381 Chaucer *Parl. Foules* 189 Smale fischis lite With fynnys rede & skalis syluyr bryȝte. 14.. *Sir Beues* (M.) 2478 Upon the dragon he smote so fast, Where euer he hit, the skales brast. 1549 *Compl. Scotl.* vi. 37, I beheld the pretty fische..vitht..there skalis lyik the brycht siluyr. 1604 E. G[rimstone] *D'Acosta's Hist. Indies* iv. 313 Those which they call Armadillos are [defended] by the multitude of their scales. 1611 Cotgr., *Tablette*,..the scales of a Hawks legs. 1743 H. Baker *Microsc.* (ed. 2) 172 The Cuticula, Scarf-Skin, or outward Covering, of the Body, is remarkable for its Scales and for its Pores. 1784 Cowper *Task* ii. 324 Leviathan..Turns to the stroke his adamantine scales. 1826 Kirby & Sp. *Entomol.* III. 389 A vertical flat scale, observable on the footstalk of the genus *Formica*, &c. *Ibid.* 646 The gorgeous wings of these universal favourites [the Lepidoptera]..owe all their beauty..to an infinite number of little plumes or scales. 1834 McMurtrie *Cuvier's Anim. Kingd.* 186 Batrachians have neither scales nor shell; a naked skin invests their body. 1884 Day *Commercial Sea Fishes* 9 Scales may take on many characters, as denticles in the sharks, osseous plates in sturgeons.

b. *collect. sing.*

14.. *Sir Beues* (M.) 2537 Under the skale al on hyght The dragons hede he smote of ryght. 1665 Hooke *Microgr.* 184 The leggs..were all of them cover'd with a strong hairy scale or shel. 1820 Shelley *Prometh. Unb.* iv. 304 The anatomies of unknown wingèd things, And fishes which were isles of living scale. 1843 Marryat *M. Violet* xliv, Its body is covered with scale so hard as to be impenetrable. 1880 F. Francis *Angling* ix. (ed. 5) 306 They all began to change their scales and assume the silvery salmon scale.

†**c.** Used for: Kind or genus *of* fish. *Obs.*

1585 Jas. I *Ess. Poesie* (Arb.) 72 The Seas (which dyuers skaile Of fish contenis).

†**d.** *transf.* ? Surface, outside. *Obs.*

13.. *E.E. Allit. P.* A. 1005 Þe emerade..so grene of scale.

2. One of the small laminæ of epidermis which become detached from the tissue beneath in certain diseases of the skin; †hence, applied with or without qualification to various skin diseases.

(Cf. scall, with which it was probably confused in ME.)

14.. *Voc.* in Wr.-Wülcker 585/25 *Furfura*, the scales of the hede or berde. 14.. *Nom.* ibid. 675/33 *Hec glabra*, a scale. c 1450 in *Vicary's Anat.* (1888) App. ix. 228 His syght shall neuer fale, And heles of torne-seke, and of scale. 1597 Gerarde *Herbal* i. xxiv. 34 The ashes of them mixed with vineger helpeth the scales and scurfe of the head. 1609 Markham *Famous Whore* (1868) 30 Of french disease, of Leprous cureless skale. 1685 Jas. Cooke *Marrow Chirurg.* vi. ix. (ed. 4) 214 The Cuticula [in Scarlet-fever] falling off in Scales or great Fleaks. 1818–20 E. Thompson *Cullen's Nosologia* (ed. 3) 319 *Lepidosis*.—Scales. 1829 *Good's Study Med.* (ed. 3) III. 27 The spots fall off in branny scales. 1876 Duhring *Dis. Skin* 48 Scales are dry, laminated masses of epidermis which have separated from the tissues beneath.

3. a. A part (e.g. a husk) that may be peeled off or detached in flakes; a comparatively thin plate, lamina, or flake of any kind.

In Surgery, *scale* is used for 'an exfoliated lamina of bone'; in Anatomy for 'a thin scale-like bone'.

c 1450 *ME. Med. Bk.* (Heinrich) 208 Þe scales of notes ant ryndes. 1555 Eden *Decades* (Arb.) 131 An other frute browght from those landes beinge full of scales and with keys much lyke a pine apple. 1594 Blundevil *Exerc.* iii. i. viii. 141 The skales of an Onion. 1611 Coryat *Crudities* 363 [Hemp stripped] by certaine wooden instruments..that do very easily seuer the stranne from the scale. 1632 Sherwood s.v., Little scales of broken bones. 1739 Sharp *Surg.* Introd. 45 Every scale of a carious Bone is flung off by new Flesh generated between it and the sound Bone. 1759 Miller *Gard. Dict.* s.v. *Pirus*, The rigid Scale of the Cone. 1852 *Amer. Jrnl. Sci.* Ser. ii. XIV. 277 Iridosmine from the same locality occurs in lead-colored scales. 1875 *Encycl. Brit.* III. 707/2 (*Birds*) The main part of the frontal bone, covering the *hemisphere*, is a convex radiating scale. 1901 *Scotsman* 18 Sept. 7/8 The gold..was found in nuggets and scales.

†**b.** A slate. (Cf. skaillie.) *Obs. rare*[−0].

c 1481 Caxton *Dialogues* 40 Descailles de tieulles, With skaylles with tyles.

c. The tartar that collects on the teeth.

1594 [see scaly *a.* 1]. 1874 Salter *Dental Pathol. & Surg.* xxiv. 321 It [*sc.* salivary calculus] frequently affects a single tooth..in the form of a fast-growing scale.

d. *Bot.* A flattened, membranous, more or less circular plate of cellular tissue, usually a rudimentary or degenerate leaf, as the covering of leaf-buds of deciduous trees, the bracts of catkins, etc.

1776 J. Lee *Introd. Bot.* Explan. Terms 387 *Stipula*, a Scale at the Base of the Footstalk which it supports. 1787 tr. *Linnæus' Fam. Plants* I. 203 Nectaries five: each with an hearted concave scale. 1801 *Med. Jrnl.* V. 395 Lime-trees of America; petals provided with a scale, at their basis. 1830 Lindley *Nat. Syst. Bot.* 292 Flowers [of the Grass tribe] consisting of imbricated bracteæ, of which..the innermost at the base of the ovarium [are called] scales. 1856 Delamer *Fl. Gard.* 130 The undeveloped flower-buds are protected by membranous scales. 1884 Bower & Scott *De Bary's Phaner.* 93 The glandular scales of the Hop.

e. A mollusc of the genus *Terebratula* (†*Anomia*).

1784 G. Walker *Boys' Coll. Shells* 22 *Anomia*. The Scale. *Anomia Squammula*. The scale anomia.

f. The protective covering of insects of the family *Coccidæ*, which remains when they die and protects the eggs and afterwards the young beneath it; hence, = *scale-insect*; also, the diseased condition of plants caused thereby.

1822 *Trans. Hort. Soc.* (1826) VI. 117 Directions for destroying the Bug and Scale on Pine-apple plants. 1850 *Hooker's Jrnl. Bot.* II. 353 The 'Brown Scale' or Coccus, so injurious to the Coffee-plants in Ceylon. *Ibid.* 356 The number of eggs contained in one of these scales is prodigious. 1882 *Garden* 18 Feb. 117/1 Pines are subject to the attacks of mealy bug and brown and white scale. 1906 Marlatt (*title*) San Jose or Chinese Scale.

4. Taken (after *Acts* ix. 18) as a type of that which causes blindness (physical or moral).

a 1300 *Cursor M.* 19691 Skales fell fra his [*sc.* Saul's] eien a-wai, And had his sight forth fra þat dai. 1382 Wyclif *Acts* ix. 18 And anon ther felden from his yȝen as scalis [Vulg. *tanquam squamæ*; Gr. ὡσεὶ λεπίδες], and he receyuede siȝt. [So in later versions.] 1611 Bible *Transl. Pref.* ¶ 17 Hee remoueth the scales from our eyes, the vaile from our hearts. 1629 Sir W. Mure *True Crucifixe* 971 The skailes of darknesse which our eyes be-night. 1701 Stanhope *Aug. Medit.* iii. xv. 236 Command the Scales of my old Errors to fall off. **1732** W. ELLIS *Pract. Farmer* II. 20, I hope in time the Scales will be taken off the Eyes of the Landlord's Mind. **1896** N. MUNRO *Lost Pibroch*, etc. 83 One may look at a person for years and not see the reality till a scale falls from the eyes.

5. a. orig. *pl.* but now usually *collect. sing.* The film of oxide which forms on iron or other metal when heated and hammered or rolled.

1526 *Grete Herball* clxx. (1529) K v b, The scales of yren ..is that y^t fleeth of the yren whan it is forged. **1611** COTGR., *Escaille d'acier, de bronze, d'erain, de fer*, &c.; the Offalls of Steele, &c.; the skales that fly from them when they are hammered. **1796** KIRWAN *Elem. Min.* (ed. 2) II. 417 The Iron scales of a Smith's forge. **1800** tr. *Lagrange's Chem.* II. 100 Copper, in the state of scales, is not completely oxidated. **1831** J. HOLLAND *Manuf. Metal* I. 284 The act of forging produces a strong scale or coating which is spread over the whole of the blade [of the razor]. **1864** PERCY *Metall., Iron & Steel* 21 It is this oxide which is known as iron scale, or hammer slag. **1880** JEFFERIES *Hodge & M.* II. 72 As blow follows blow the red-hot 'scale' driven from the surface of the iron on the anvil by the heavy sledge, flies rattling against the window in a spray of fire.

b. *Salt-making.* An incrustation of dirt or lime on the pan bottoms. **c.** The hard deposit or 'fur' which gathers in boilers and other vessels in which water is habitually heated. (Rarely *pl.*)

1848 *Knapp's Chem. Technol.* I. 269 Some [brown scum] attaches itself to the bottom of the [salt] pans (the scale). **1875** KNIGHT *Dict. Mech.* [Of steam-boilers]. **1881** *Metal World* No. 18. 280 It is absolutely essential to the successful use of any boiler, except in pure water, that it be accessible for the removal of scale. **1883** R. HALDANE *Workshop Receipts* Ser. II. 48/1 Boiler 'scales' nearly everywhere are principally composed of sulphate of lime.

6. Thin board. [Cf. MDu. *schale.*] *Obs.* or *dial.*

1683 [see SCABBARD *sb.*^{2}]. **1707** MORTIMER *Husb.* 339 Of the thin Lamina or Scale of the Wood..they make Scabbards. **1847** HALLIWELL, *Scales*, the outermost cuts of a piece of timber with the bark on, not thick enough to be called planks. *Devon.*

7. a. Any of the thin pieces of metal composing scale-armour (see 12). Also *collect. sing.* (In poetry used vaguely.) **b.** See quot. 1853.

1809 T. HOPE *Costume Anc.* Plate 18 Dacian warrior.. with a coat of mail, or scales. **1820** SHELLEY *Ode to Naples* 68 Clothed in armour of impenetrable scale! **1847** TENNYSON *Princess* v. 39 Sheathing splendours and the golden scale Of harness. **1853** STOCQUELER *Mil. Encycl.*, *Scales*, a sort of armour consisting of brass plates, laid like scales one over the other, to defend the glandular parts, and the side-face of a dragoon. These scales are attached to the helmet, and can be buttoned up in front. **1875** J. ANDERSON in *Encycl. Brit.* II. 554/2 Cuirasses of bronze scales.

c. *U.S. slang.* A coin; money.

1872 SCHELE DE VERE *Americanisms* 296 Among the less generally known terms [for money] are..*wherewith*, *shadscales*, or *scales* 'for short'. **1874** B. F. TAYLOR *World on Wheels* 28 Promise him a 'scale'—scale, skilling, shilling. **1889** J. S. FARMER *Americanisms* 472/2 *Scales*, a common term for money; an abbreviation of Shadscales. **1929** *Amer. Speech* V. 152 The waitress received much scale at the hotel.

8. *Cutlery.* **a.** Each of the two plates of bone, horn, ivory, or wood which form the outside of the handle of a knife or razor.

1834–6 BARLOW in *Encycl. Metrop.* (1845) VIII. 650/1 The handle [*sc.* of a knife], consisting of two side pieces called scales, is rivetted through the tang on each side. **1877** *Encycl. Brit.* VI. 734/1. **1894** *Army & Navy Stores Circ.* Aug. 71 Toilet Knife. (Best Sheffield make and finish.) Pearl or tortoiseshell scales.

b. Each of the metal sides of the handle of a pocket knife on which such plates are riveted.

1834–6 BARLOW in *Encycl. Metrop.* (1845) VIII. 650/1. **1864** in WEBSTER; and in later Dicts.

9. A plate of metal worn instead of an epaulette by soldiers, sailors, and firemen. [F. *écaille.*]

1846 in E.E. Napier *Exc. Southern Afr.* (1849) I. 287 An old blue frock coat with large scales. **1852–63** BURN *Naval & Mil. Dict.* II. 227/1 Shoulder scale or strap. **1894** R. MANSFIELD *Chips* 54 The officers of the line wore blue frock coats with small brass epaulets, called 'scales'. **1894** C. N. ROBINSON *Brit. Fleet* IV. vii. 512 In 1846, scales, or epaulettes without bullion, were authorized for captains and commanders... The next year the scales..were abolished.

10. (See quots. 1860, 1880.)

1860 *Eng. & For. Mining Gloss., Cornwall Terms, Scal*, A shale or portion of earth, rock, &c., which separates and falls from the main body. **1880** *W. Cornwall Gloss.*, *Scal, Scale*, loose ground about a mine. **1884** *Falmouth & Penryn Weekly Times* 19 July 5/2 What is commonly known among miners as a 'jomb' or 'scale' of ground.

11. (See quot. 1885.)

1885 *Encycl. Brit.* XVIII. 242 The several kinds of crude paraffin extracted are classed as 'hard scale' or 'soft scale', according to their fusing points and consequent degrees of hardness [etc.]. **1889** *Pall Mall G.* 23 Jan. 7/3 The prices fixed on by the Association for burning oil and scale.

12. *attrib.* and *Comb.*, as (sense 1) ***scale-backed***, ***-bright***, ***-like***, ***-marked*** adjs.; ***scale-fashion*** adv.; (sense 2) ***scale-crust***; (sense 2 d) ***scale-leaf***; (sense 5) ***scale-cleaner***, ***-preventive***; **scale-armour**, armour consisting of small overlapping plates of metal, leather, or horn; **scale-back**, one of the family *Aphroditidæ* of scale-bearing annelids; **scale-bark**, bark which is shed in scale-like pieces, as that of the plane-tree; **scale-beetle**, a tiger-beetle (family *Cicindelidæ*); **scale-blight**, the disease caused by the scale-insect; **scale-blue**, the groundwork of royal blue with a scale-pattern characteristic of some Worcester china; **scale-borer**, 'an implement for removing the scale from boiler-tubes' (Knight *Dict. Mech.* 1875); **scale-bug** *U.S.* = *scale-insect*; **scale carp**, the common typical carp, *Cyprinus carpio*; **scale-fern** = CETERACH (q.v.), so called from the scales clothing the back of the fronds; **scale-fish**, (*a*) a fish armed with scales; (*b*) see quot. 1857; (*c*) the scabbard-fish (*Cent. Dict.*); **scale-foot**, the scabbard-fish; **scale-hair**, a short flattened hair resembling a scale (cf. *hair-scale*, HAIR *sb.* 9 a); **scale-insect** (see sense 3 f), any of the insects of the genus *Coccus* or family *Coccidæ*, which infest and injure certain plants, having the appearance of scales; **scale-moss**, a plant of the N.O. *Jungermanniaceæ*; †**scale-oyster**, a scallop; **scale-pad**, the part of the tail covered with scales in the *Anomaluridæ* (or scale-tailed squirrels); **scale-pattern**, a pattern having a representation of scales; an imbricated pattern; **scale-quail**, an American quail of the genus *Callipepla*, having scale-like plumage; **scale-reading**, the interpretation of the pattern of scales on a fish as an indicator of its age, history, etc.; an examination of scales for this purpose; so **scale-reader**; **scale-roof** = *scaled roof* (see SCALED *ppl. a.*^{1} 2 c); **scale-shell**, a name for various molluscs; **scale-shouldered** *a.*, ? wearing a 'scale' (sense 9) on the shoulder; **scale-skin**, a term including several scaly diseases; **scale-stone** *Min.*, (*a*) transl. of G. *schalstein* = tabular spar or wollastonite; (*b*) anglicization of LEPIDOLITE; **scale-tail**, a squirrel of the family *Anomaluridæ*, having scales on the under side of the tail; so **scale-tailed** *a.*; **scale-tang** (see quot.); **scale-wing**, a lepidopter; **scale-winged** *a.*, lepidopterous; **scale-work**, work, ornament, decoration, etc., of an imbricated pattern; **scale-worm** = *scale-back*; **scale-wort**, the plant *Lathræa squamaria*.

1842 W. C. TAYLOR *Anc. Hist.* xvii. §6 (ed. 3) 526 Both horses and men [of the Sarmatians] were covered with a curious kind of *scale armour formed of the sliced hoofs of animals. **1882** *Cassell's Nat. Hist.* VI. 330 *Scale-backs. **1803** SHAW *Gen. Zool.* IV. II. 539 *Scale-Backed Sciæna. **1859** K. CORNWALLIS *New World* I. 20 Scale-backed armadilloes. **1884** BOWER & SCOTT *De Bary's Phaner.* 558 [These] throw off the superficial periderm..in the form of *scale-bark. **1855** OGILVIE, Suppl., **Scale-beetles.* **1898** *Daily News* 5 July 6/4 Mr. W. M. Maskell..was considered the chief authority of the day on *scale-blight. **1906** *Westm. Gaz.* 5 May 9/3 A pair of handsome *scale-blue Worcester vases. **1555** PHAER *Æneid* II. 21 Their..*skalebright necks. **1883** *Century Mag.* Oct. 811/2 The orange's worst enemy is a curious insect, the *scale-bug. **1884** GOODE, etc. *Nat. Hist. Aquatic Anim.* 619 The '*Scale Carp'; with regular, concentrically arranged scales, being in fact the original species improved. **1881** *Instr. Census Clerks* (1885) 93 Wrought Iron Manufacture:..*Scale Cleaner. **1898** J. HUTCHINSON in *Arch. Surg.* IX. 308 A slight formation of exfoliative *scale-crust. **1611** COTGR. s.v. *Escaille*, a plated Corselet made *scale-fashion. **1548** TURNER *Names Herbes* (E.D.S.) 17 *Asplenum*... It mayе be called in englishe Citterach, or *Scaleferne, or Finger-ferne. **1862** D. T. ANSTED *Channel Isl.* II. viii. (ed. 2) 182 The scale-fern is met with, though rarely. **1601** HOLLAND *Pliny* I. Table, *Scale fishes have no ears. **1651** T. BARKER *Art of Angling* (1653) 8 This feed will gather the scale Fish together, as Carp, Tench, Roach, Dace and Bream. **1814** *Amer. Newsp.* in Byron *Corsair* III. xxiv *note*, The superior scale and shell fish with which its waters abound. **1856** J. REYNOLDS *Peter Gott* xix. 254 Four hundred quintals of fish, heavily salted, such as are in demand for the use of the negroes on the plantations. These fish are called scale fish; they consist of hake and haddock. **1857** PERLEY *Hand-Bk. New Brunswick* 24 The pollack, the hake, and the haddock, when dry-cured, are designated by dealers, 'scale-fish'. *Ibid.* 28 The torsk, or cusk, is..dry-cured as a 'scale-fish'. **1936** *Discovery* Jan. 16/1 The food of the natives consisted of various animals.. but never scale fish, which seem to have been the object of a curious taboo. **1967** *Nat. Fisherman* Nov. 11-C The term 'scalefish' is used in the Bahamas for fish proper as opposed to shellfish and crustaceans. **1828** FLEMING *Brit. Anim.* 205 Lepidopus. *Scale-foot... Two pointed scales in place of ventrals. **1898** PACKARD *Text-bk. Entom.* 198 Kellogg has detected these *scale-hairs, as he calls them, in Panorpa. **1840** *Cuvier's Anim. Kingd.* 572 The young *Scale-insects have the body oval, very flat. **1882** VINES tr. *Sachs' Bot.* 433 The buds produced on the leaf-stalks develope into long underground stolons furnished with *scale-leaves. **1611** COTGR., *Les Escaillons du palais*,..the skales, or *skale-like diuisions in the roofe..of the mouth of a horse. **1883** *Science* I. 150/2 The supposed scale-like nature of penguin-feathers. **1892** PATER *Emerald Uthwart* Wks. 1901 VIII. 228 Fritillaries..Snakes' heads, the rude call them, for their shape, *scale-marked too. **1846** LINDLEY *Veget. Kingd.* 59 These *Scalemosses differ from the Liverworts in the regularly valvate condition of the spore-cases. **1419** *Liber Albus* (Rolls) 275 *Scaleoisters, moules, welkes, et hanocynes. **1898** *Proc. Zool. Soc.* 17 May 451 Before the spot above the end of the lower *scale-pad is reached the tail is covered with long black hair. **1898** *Engineering Mag.* XVI. 145/1 Mineral Oils as *Scale-Preventives. **1930** G. H. NALL *Life Sea Trout* iii. 28 It is the business of the *scale reader to decipher how it [*sc.* the scale] reflects the growth, and to explain how this provides a clue to the life history of the individual fish. **1968** B. VESEY-FITZGERALD *World of Fishes* ii. 30 An expert scale-reader can tell the age of a fish accurately. **1912** *Salmon & Trout Mag.* No. 4. p. i (Advt.), The latest and most authoritative publication on the new science of *scale reading. **1938** B. CURTIS *Life Story Fish* iii. 29 Using scale-readings, he can construct the life-history of a species with far fewer specimens than he could in any other way. **1971** D. MILLS *Salmon & Trout* xii. 281 The data from such scale readings can then be incorporated into the construction of growth curves. **1862** H. MARRYAT *Year in Sweden* II. xliii. 83 The *scale-roof was struck by lightning. **1713** PETIVER *Aquat. Anim. Amboinæ* Tab. 16/30 *Auris marina*..*Scale-shell. *Ibid.* 16/31 *Operculum callorum*.. Scale-shell. **1891** *Century Dict.*, *Scale-shell*, a bivalve mollusk of the family Leptonidæ. **1893** R. S. SURTEES *Sponge's Sp. Tour* iv, Gigantic *scale-shouldered footmen. **1829** *Good's Study Med.* (ed. 3) V. 585 Lepidosis. *Scale-skin. **1819** BAKEWELL *Introd. Min.* II. 346 Lepidolite, or *Scale-stone..is composed of scales or minute laminæ. **1841** MAUNDER *Sci. & Lit. Treas.*, *Scale-stone*, or *Schaalstein.* **1888** *Riverside Nat. Hist.* V. 132 The technical characters..of *scale-tails are unmistakably sciurine. *Ibid.* 131 The..*Scale-tailed Squirrels. **1831** J. HOLLAND *Manuf. Metal.* II. 14 When the handles [of table knives] consist of sides, nailed upon a flat piece of iron, continued from the blade,..they are called *scale tangs. **1864** *Athenæum* 13 Feb. 228/3 Sixty very common species of *scale-wings. **1857** LARDNER *Anim. Phys.* §243 Lepidoptera. *Scale-winged. **1737** WHISTON *Josephus* XII. ii. 361 Of the cisterns of gold, there were two; whose sculpture was of *scale-work. **1875** FORTNUM *Maiolica* viii. 69 The ground..sometimes covered with scale work. **1882** *Cassell's Nat. Hist.* VI. 330 *Scale-worms. **1849** BALFOUR *Man. Bot.* §963 *Lathræa squamaria*, *Scale-wort, is parasitical upon the roots of Hazels, Cherry-laurels, and other trees.

scale (skeɪl), *sb.*^{3} Forms: 5–8 skale, 6 *Sc.* scaill(e, 5– scale. [ad. It. *scala* or its source L. *scāla*:—prehist. **scanslā* (*scand-* + *-tlā*), f. *scandĕre* to climb (see SCAND *v.*). Cf. Pr., Sp., Pg. *escala*, OF. *eschiele* (mod.F. *échelle*).]

I. †**1. a.** A ladder; in early use, a scaling-ladder.

1412–20 LYDG. *Chron. Troy* II. 7962 þay haue..Her wallis maskued, and ageyn oure skalis..made gret ordinaunce. **1426** —— *De Guil. Pilgr.* 566, I sawh..ffolkys, wych dyde entende To helpe her ffrendys to ascende..By scalys throgh the strong closure. *a* **1572** KNOX *Hist. Ref.* Wks. 1846 I. 452 Preparatioun of scailles and ledderis was maid for the assault. **1591** HARINGTON *Orl. Fur.* v. ix, I taught him by a scale of cord to clime. **1611** COTGR., *Eschellette*, a little ladder, or skale. *a* **1682** SIR T. BROWNE *Tracts* (1683) 33 A Scale or Ladder was made that reached unto the Roof.

†**b.** In figurative and allusive uses, freq. with reference to Jacob's ladder (*Gen.* xxviii. 12). *Obs.*

14.. LYDG. in *Tundale's Vis.* 123 Sython thou [the B.V.M.] of Jacob art the ryght scale..the laddur of holynes. **1494** *Hylton's Scala Perf.* (W. de W.) Envoy, This boke... Scale of perfeccion calde in euery place. **1605** BACON *Adv. Learn.* II. 24 b, All true and frutefull Natvrall Philosophie, hath A double Scale or Ladder, Ascendent and Descendent. *a* **1626** SIR J. DAVIES *Poems* (1876) II. 211 The Jacob's scales, whereby shee [Faith] clymes the skyes. **1667** MILTON *P.L.* IV. 354 In th' ascending Scale Of Heav'n the Starrs that usher Evening rose. *a* **1680** BUTLER *Rem.* (1759) I. 3 The lofty Tube, the scale With which they Heav'n itself assail, Was mounted full against the Moon. **1781** COWPER *Retirem.* 111 A scale by which the soul ascends From mighty means to more important ends. **1820** HAZLITT *Lect. Dram. Lit.* 14 They are the scale by which we can best ascend to the true knowledge and love of him.

†**2.** A rung or step of a ladder. Also *fig.* *Obs.*

c **1440** *Promp. Parv.* 442/1 Scale..of a leddur, *scalare.* **1530** PALSGR. 265/2 Scale of a ladder, *eschellon.* **1608** WILLET *Hexapla Exod.* 453 The steps or scales of wooden ladders. **1670** G. H. *Hist. Cardinals* I. III. 69 The Cardinalship being only a scale and step towards Episcopacy. *a* **1682** SIR T. BROWNE *Tracts* i. (1683) 5 Ladders signifie Travels, and the Scales thereof Preferment.

†**3.** A flight (of stairs); a staircase. *Obs.*

1592 R. D. *Hypnerotomachia* 9, I came by a long gallorie to a salying scale or downe going staire. **1658–9** in *N. Riding Rec.* (1888) VI. 16 No mariner..do moor, fesse or tye any ship etc. to the said bridge, the jewells, scales, or any part thereof. **1705** ADDISON *Italy*, *Caprea* 259 Several ancient Scales of Stairs, by which they us'd to ascend 'em [*sc.* mountains].

II. 4. *Mus.* **a.** A definite series of sounds ascending or descending by fixed intervals, *esp.* such a series beginning on a certain note (cf. KEY *sb.*^{1} 7 b) selected for the purposes of musical composition. **b.** Any of the graduated series of sounds into which the octave is divided, the sounds varying according to the system of graduation adopted.

For the various scales of ancient and modern music, see CHROMATIC *a.* 5, DIATONIC *a.* 1, 2, ENHARMONIC *a.* 1, 2, HARMONIC *a.* 4, MAJOR *a.* 4 c, MINOR *a.* 6 c, MELODIC *a.*, PYTHAGOREAN *a.*

1597 MORLEY *Introd. Mus.* 2 Here is the Scale of Musicke which wee terme the Gam. *Ibid.* 7 *Phi.* Why then was your Scale deuised of xx notes and no more? *Ma.* Because that compasse was the reach of most voyces: so that vnder *Gam vt* the voice seemed as a kinde of humming, and aboue *E la* a kinde of constrained shrieking. **1697** EVELYN *Numismata* viii. 285 Aretine..improved the Scale and set the first Gamut. **1710** J. HARRIS *Lex. Techn.* II, The Scale of Musick among the Greeks, consisted of fifteen Notes, or the Distances of two Octaves. **1777** SIR W. JONES *Ess. Imit. Arts* Poems, etc. 198 In the regular scale each interval assumes a proper character. **1818** BUSBY *Gram. Mus.* 362 The fifth of any Minor key is related to that key, because its scale, in order to be perfect, requires only one change in the octave of that key,—the sharpening of its sixth. **1866** ENGEL *Nat. Mus.* ii. 24 The musical scale varies in different nations, having in some instances more intervals than ours, in others fewer. **1876** STAINER & BARRETT *Dict. Mus. Terms* s.v., By starting from any note in the semitonal scale, we can have twelve minor modes. **1884** *Encycl. Brit.* XVII. 80/2 To this scale of four notes, G, A, ♭ B, C, were subsequently added a note below and a note above, which made the hexachord.

c. In particularized use (chiefly *pl.*): Any scale taken as a subject of instruction or practice.

1865 *Dublin Univ. Mag.* I. 267 She taught the very young collegians their 'scales'. **1870** MISS BRIDGMAN *R. Lynne* II. xiii. 285 She could just scamper through the scales. **1884** F. M. CRAWFORD *Rom. Singer* I. i. 11 We will try a scale. **1888** *Poor Nellie* II. i. 89, I do wish she would forget to play her scales some morning.

d. The compass or range of a musical instrument.

1818 BUSBY *Gram. Mus.* 484 The Violino, bulky in its mechanical construction, and deep in its scale. *Ibid.* 485 The Clarinett.. is an instrument of the reed species. Its scale extends from E below the F Cliff note to E in alt.

†**e.** The musical staff. *Obs.*

1598 *Riddles Heracl. & Democr.* Sol. 21 The scale of musicke is made with lines and spaces. **1609** DOWLAND *Ornith. Microl.* 83 It is necessary for yong beginners to make a Scale of ten lines. **1704** J. HARRIS *Lex. Techn.* I, *Scale of the Gamut*, or *Musical Scale*, is a kind of Diagram, consisting of certain Lines and Spaces drawn to shew the several Degrees, whereby a Natural or Artificial Voice or Sound may either ascend or descend.

5. a. A succession or series of steps or degrees; a graduated series, succession, or progression; *esp.* a graduated series of beings extending from the lowest forms of existence to the highest (***scale of being***(*s*, ***creatures***, ***existence***, ***life***, ***nature***, etc.).

1605 BACON *Adv. Learn.* II. 28 b, The speculation.. That all things by scale did ascend to vnitie. **1643** SIR T. BROWNE *Relig. Med.* I. §30 How so many learned heads should so farre forget their Metaphysicks, and destroy the Ladder and scale of creatures, as to question the existence of Spirits. **1712** *Spect.* No. 519 ¶8 If the Scale of Being rises by such a regular Progress, so high as Man. **1732** POPE *Ess. Man* I. 47 Then, in the scale of reas'ning life, 'tis plain, There must be, somewhere, such a rank as Man. *a* **1781** WATSON *Philip III*, VI. (1793) II. 183 A great addition to its power and importance in the scale of nations. **1855** BAIN *Senses & Int.* I. ii. 214 A scale of degrees from the most perfect opacity.. to the most perfect transparency. **1859** DARWIN *Orig. Spec.* ii. 54 Plants low in the scale of organisation. **1865** DICKENS *Mut. Fr.* IV. vii, I have made up my mind that I will become respectable in the scale of society. **1883** H. DRUMMOND *Nat. Law in Spir. W., Eternal Life* 211 As we ascend in the scale of Life we rise also in the scale of longevity.

b. A regular series of tones or shades of colour produced by mixing with different proportions of white or black. (Cf. It. *scala di colori*.)

1854 MARTEL tr. *Chevreul's Colours* (facing p. 308), Table of a classification of several varieties of dahlias by scales of colours. **1872** CHURCH *Colour* v. 41 Every colour admits of three scales.

c. *Psychol.* A graded series in terms of which the measurements of such phenomena as sensations, attitudes, or mental attributes are expressed; sometimes preceded by the name of the person to whom a particular scale is attributed (as *Binet scale*; cf. GUTTMAN SCALE), or some other qualifying word.

1898 G. F. STOUT *Man. Psychol.* I. ii. §5. 31 Thus, if we have a scale of increasing gradations of intensity, we may take as our point of departure any given intensity in the scale. We can then arrange other intensities in relation to this, proceeding by intervals which we judge to be equal. **1917** PINTNER & PATERSON (*title*) Scale of performance tests. *Ibid.* i. 11 The Stanford Revision adheres more closely to the original Binet Scale. **1929** THURSTONE & CHAVE *Measurement of Attitude* ii. 22 A list of 130 statements was prepared, expressive of attitudes covering as far as possible all gradations from one end of the scale to the other. *Ibid.* iv. 59 The scale-values represented by the 45 statements. **1960** *Jrnl. Pol.* XXII. 647 Scale analysis is now common enough in political science to justify omission of the details. **1966** T. M. NEWCOMB et al. *Social Psychol.* xiv. 429 The scale was a revision of the original Bogardus scale. *Ibid.* 498 The Likert scale may seem.. a natural way of drawing attitude measurements and combining them. *Ibid.* 523 'Neutral' items in Thurstone scales are a source of considerable nonvalidity. **1972** *Jrnl. Social Psychol.* LXXXVI. 105 The scale dimension of like–dislike was used as the source of names. **1977** K. G. SHAVER *Princ. Social Psychol.* v. 193 We have grouped the respondents in terms of a nominal scale: a scale of measurement by which the observations can be classified, but not ordered. *Ibid.* 194 Regardless of the distance between scores, when the data can be rank ordered (usually from the most favorable to the least favorable) they constitute what is known as an ordinal scale of measurement. *Ibid.* 196 When the numbers we assign to identify observations *do* tell us something about the distances between observations (while also providing us with a logical order), those numbers are said to constitute an interval scale of measurement. *Ibid.* 198 If an interval scale is constructed with an absolute zero point, rather than with an arbitrary one, that scale becomes.. a ratio scale.

6. *Math.* **a.** A number of terms included between two points in a progression or series.

1695 HALLEY in *Phil. Trans.* XIX. 59 A continued Scale of Proportionals infinite in Number between the two terms of the ratio... If there be supposed between 1 and 10 an infinite Scale of mean Proportionals, whose Number is 100000. **1785** HUTTON *Math. Tables* 22 There may be as many sets or scales of logarithms as we please, since they depend intirely on the arbitrary assumption of the first two arithmeticals. **1887** *Cassell's Encycl. Dict.*, *Scale of a Series*: In algebra, a succession of terms, by the aid of which any term of a recurring series may be found, when a sufficient number of the preceding ones are given.

b. *Arith.* Any of the various conceivable systems of notation which agree in the principle that the value of a figure varies in geometrical progression according to its serial place, but are distinguished according to the number chosen as the 'radix' or constant multiplier.

The 'scales' are usually designated by the adj. derived from the Latin distributive numeral, as *binary*, *ternary*, *denary*, *duodenary scale*, though *decimal* and *duodecimal scale* are sometimes substituted. In quot. 1797 *scale* seems to be loosely used for *radix*.

1797 *Encycl. Brit.* (ed. 3) II. 290 If eight were the scale, 6 times 3 would be two classes and two units, and the number 18 would be represented by 22. **1861** T. LUND *Wood's Elem. Alg.* §367 When the radix is 2, the scale is called Binary; when 3, Ternary; when 10, Denary or Decimal. **1875** [see DENARY].

c. ***scale of*** (***two***, etc.): a scale of arithmetical notation having as radix the number given, used *attrib.* and *absol.* to designate a form of scaler (see SCALER[3] 4) in which an output pulse is produced when a number of input pulses equal to the specified radix has been received.

1871 C. DAVIES *Metric Syst.* I. 18 The scale of tens was adopted. **1932** C. E. WYNN-WILLIAMS in *Proc. R. Soc.* A. CXXXVI. 318 As the recording.. values of the 'dial' units are, respectively, 2^0 or 1, 2^1 or 2, and 2^2 or 4, and since the meter indicates the total number of groups of 2^3 or 8, the counting is carried out according to a 'scale of two', the three thyratron dials recording 'units', 'twos' and 'fours' and the meter 'eights', instead of units, tens, hundreds, and thousands. **1933** *Ibid.* CXXXIX. 621 The impulses are then applied to a 'scale of two' thyratron counting circuit. **1948** *Nucleonics* Nov. 49/1 Scale-of-*N* circuits are important tools for counting radiations in nuclear physics, as well as for various other applications. **1950** *Progr. Nuclear Physics* I. 109 A scale of five can be made by the use of a form of ring circuit with five valves with their cathodes connected together. **1963** B. FOZARD *Instrumentation Nuclear Reactors* viii. 75 A cascade arrangement of six scales-of-two gives an over-all scale factor of 2^6 or 64.

7. a. A graduated table (of prices, charges, etc.).

1780 *Acts & Resolves Massachusetts* (1886) V. 1413 The following scale shall be the rule.. for settling the rate of depreciation on all contracts. **1788** JEFFERSON *Writ.* (1859) II. 360 A scale of their value for every month has been settled according to what they sold for at market. **1865** *Shareholders' Guardian* 8 Nov. 845/1 Reduction in Scale of Charges for Advertisements. **1895** *Law Times* XCIX. 544/1 The solicitor's own remuneration is in the main based upon a scale of allowances fixed in the year 1807.

b. *spec.* A graduated table of wage or salary rates; *transf.*, a wage or salary in accordance with such a table.

1921, etc. [see BURNHAM]. **1930** [see BEGGAR *v.* 3]. **1957** [see LABEL *sb.*[1] 7 c]. **1968** *New Yorker* 18 May 45/2 Pookie's Pub.. is not the highest-paying club in town. I make about scale, or about a hundred and fifty a week. **1977** *Times Educ. Suppl.* 21 Oct. 2/5 There seems to be a case for possible demotion from scales.

8. A metrical scheme. *rare.*

1835 ANTHON *Horatii Poëmata* p. xxiii, The scale of the mixed Iambic Trimeter is.. as follows.

III. 9. a. A set or series of graduations (marked along a straight line or a curve) used for measuring distances, registering the height of a liquid, mercury, etc., or determining amounts or quantities by inspection; a graduated line, arc, etc.; *spec.* the equally divided line on a map, chart, or plan which indicates its scale (sense 11), and is used for finding the distance between two points.

In quot. 1606 *pl.*, graduations.

c **1391** CHAUCER *Astrol.* I. §12 Next the forseide cercle of the A. b. c., vnder the cros-lyne, is Marked the skale, in Maner of 2 Squyres or elles in Manere of laddres. **1527** R. THORNE in *Hakluyt's Voy.* (1589) 253 Set the one foot of the compasse in the said transuersall line at the end of the nether scale, the scale of longitude, and the other foot sheweth the degree of longitude that the region is in. **1606** SHAKS. *Ant. & Cl.* II. vii. 21 They take the flow o' th' Nyle By certaine scales i' th' Pyramid. **1625** N. CARPENTER *Geog. Del.* II. iv. 65 The Distance of any two places set downe in the Chart, being taken and applyed to the scale, will shew how many miles it containes. **1652** (*title*) Posthuma [S.] Fosteri: the Description of a Ruler, Upon which is inscribed divers Scales and the Vses thereof. **1712** J. JAMES tr. *Le Blond's Gardening* 85 A small double Line divided.. which is called the Scale of the Plan, and is always at the Bottom of the Paper. **1728** CHAMBERS *Cycl.*, *Decimal Scales*,.. to expedite Decimal Arithmetic, by Shewing by Inspection the Decimal Fraction of any Part of Money, Weight, or Measure. **1735** MORTIMER in *Phil. Trans.* XLIV. 681 Fahrenheit begins his Scale from 0. the Point to which the Mercury hath been observed to fall by the greatest Cold in Ysland. **1873** *Act 36 & 37 Vict.* c. 85 §3 A scale of feet denoting her draught of water shall be marked on each side of her stem. **1889** WELCH *Text-bk. Naval Archit.* 12 Scale of tons per inch. Scale of mean drafts.

†**b.** ***scale of logarithms***, ***of numbers*** (see quots.).

1630 WINGATE *Arith.* II. iv. 291 The Line of Proportion consists of two scales, viz. the scale of Logarithmes, and the Scale of Numbers. *Ibid.*, The Scale of Logarithmes is, a scale of equall parts described vnder the common line, and abutting vpwards vpon the same line. *Ibid.* v. 299 The Scale of Numbers is a scale of Proportionall parts described aboue the common line, and abutting downwards vpon the same line. **1710** J. HARRIS *Lex. Techn.* II, *Proportional Scales*, sometimes also called Logarithmetical; are only the Artificial Numbers or Logarithms placed on Lines, for the ease and advantage of Multiplying, Dividing, Extracting Roots, &c. by the means of Compasses, or by Sliding-Rules.

c. ***diminishing scale***: see quot. 1842.

1753 F. PRICE *Brit. Carpenter* (ed. 3) 46 Make a diminishing scale, by setting that distance up, from t to l. **1842** GWILT *Archit. Gloss.*, *Diminishing Scale*, a scale of gradation used in finding the different points for drawing the spiral curve of the Ionic volute.

10. a. An instrument consisting of a strip or blade of wood, ivory, metal, or cardboard having graduated and numbered spaces upon it, used for measuring or laying down distances.

diagonal, ***Gunter's***, ***Marquois scale***: see the qualifying words. ***plane*** (†***plain***) ***scale***: see PLANE *a.* 3.

1607 NORDEN *Surv. Dial.* III. 125 By the plot which he so maketh, a stranger by scale and compasse may truly find the quantities of the particulars. **1660** J. MOORE *Arith.* I. Introd. 15 Those who use a decimall foot, yard or scale. **1701** [see REDUCING *vbl. sb.* 2]. **1758** WATSON *Milit. Dict.* (ed. 5), *A Scale*, a Rule used by Engineers to draw Fortifications on Paper, and another sort used by Gunners to take the Dimensions of their Guns. **1779** RAMSDEN *Descr. Engine for dividing Strait Lines* 3 Its uses for dividing all sorts of navigation scales, sectors, &c. must be obvious. **1840** BRUFF *Engin. Field-work* (ed. 2) 142 Press the rule gently, and move the slider on the scale. **1887** D. A. LOW *Machine Draw.* Introd. 5 The best scales are made of ivory, and are twelve inches long.

b. ***scale of equal parts*** = plane scale (PLANE *a.*[3]).

1630 [see 9 b]. **1777** WADDINGTON *Epit. Navig., Elem. Geom.* 85 To make a Mercator's Chart by Meridional Parts, to be set off from a Scale of Equal Parts. **1809** TROUGHTON in *Phil. Trans.* XCIX. I. 109 A finely divided scale of equal parts.

11. a. The proportion which the representation of an object bears to the object itself; a system of representing or reproducing objects in a smaller or larger size proportionately in every part. ***to scale***: with exactly proportional representation of each part of the model.

1662 J. GRAUNT *Bills of Mortality* xi. 61 The Map of London set out in the year 1658 by Richard Newcourt, drawn by a scale of Yards. **1681** RAY *Corr.* (1848) 130 To draw them *in piccolo*, using a small scale. **1682** GREW *Anat. Pl.* 2 As for their Figures, it were much to be wished, That they were all drawn by one Scale; or, at most, by Two; one, for Trees and Shrubs; and another for Herbs. **1793** SMEATON *Edystone L.* §97, I made some progress in laying down to a scale, the measures taken upon paper. **1801** *Farmer's Mag.* Aug. 270 The model of the best and cheapest cottage, on a scale of one inch to a foot. **1889** WELCH *Text-bk. Naval Archit.* i. 18 Construct to scale the curve of tons per inch immersion. **1895** *Bookman* Oct. 26/2 Single page plans of small districts on a fair scale.

in phr. used attrib. **1887** J. T. WALKER in *Encycl. Brit.* XXII. 709/2 For large scale work in plains. *Ibid.*, The smaller scale hill topography.

†**b.** A unit of dimension in a representation of an object, bearing the same proportion to the unit of dimension in the object itself, as the size of the object shown on the plan bears to the actual size of the object which it represents. *Obs. rare.*

1679 MOXON *Mech. Exerc.* 130 If you make every half quarter of an Inch to be a Scale for two Inches..: And if you make every half quarter of an Inch to be a Scale for four Inches.

12. a. Relative or proportionate size or extent; degree, proportion.

1607 B. JONSON *Volpone* Ep. Ded., With what ease I could haue varied it, nearer his scale (but that I feare to boast my owne faculty) I could here insert. **1813** WELLINGTON in Gurw. *Desp.* (1838) XI. 6 Castaños told me that he did not think the scale of command sufficient for him who had commanded in Catalonia. **1867** A. BARRY *Sir C. Barry* vi. 207 That practice,.. both in scale and area, began to diminish. **1877** FREEMAN *Norm. Conq.* (ed. 3) II. x. 515 Its scale no doubt far surpassed that of any church then standing in England. **1890** 'R. BOLDREWOOD' *Col. Reformer* (1891) 259 He.. adhered to the scale of non-expenditure which he found at Rainbar.

b. *Photogr.* The range of exposures (defined as the product of the light intensity and the time) over which a photographic material will give an acceptable variation in density. Also *transf.*

[**1891** *Jrnl. Soc. Chem. Industry* 28 Feb. 104/1 By variations in the time of development it is possible to produce secondary negatives in which the scale of tones is either contracted or extended. **1920** L. A. JONES in *Jrnl. Franklin Inst.* CLXXXIX. 480 If this scale of negative densities is too great for printing on the papers which are available, we can reduce the scale by lowering the contrast of the negative.] *Ibid.* 482 The total scale of the paper may be defined as the range of light intensities, expressed either in log exposure or exposure units, which can be reproduced by the paper as perceptibly different densities. **1942** C. E. K. MEES *Theory Photographic Process* xix. 736 If all different gradations on the negative are to be rendered as different gradations in the print, the scale of the paper must be at least as great as the difference between the maximum and minimum densities of the negative. **1967** *Electronics* 6 Mar. 127/1 The persistence of the scope that was necessary for a raster scan took five seconds from top to bottom, and did not have enough grey scale for good pictures. **1970** G. L. WAKEFIELD *Practical Sensitometry* viii. 83 A medium speed film is likely to have an exposure scale of at least 1,000 to 1 and it can be even bigger. On a log basis this is a range of 3·0 and higher. As a rule, the faster the material the larger the exposure scale.

c. ***economy*** (***economies***, ***economics***) ***of scale***, the relative gain in output or saving of costs derived from an increase in the size of plant or of a firm.

1944 A. CAIRNCROSS *Introd. Econ.* vi. 61 The economies of large-scale production—called for short 'economies of scale'—may be either 'internal' or 'external'. *Ibid.* xv. 195 Economies of scale, and economies of scale alone, make costs fall as output increases. **1953** STONIER & HAGUE *Textbk.*

Econ. Theory x. 221 Over relatively low levels of output it is likely that increasing returns to outlay will occur, because with larger output there are economies of scale to be reaped. **1966** A. Battersby *Math. in Management* ix. 220 A picture of the familiar 'economy of scale' which results from spreading the fixed costs over a large number of items. **1972** *Observer* 20 Aug. 9/7 The economics of scale, that much-abused phrase, used to justify any increase in size.

13. a. *fig.* A standard of measurement, calculation, or estimation.

1626 Bacon *Sylva* §835 Definite Axiomes are to be drawn out of Measured Instances: And so Assent to be made to the more Generall Axiomes, by Scale. **1651** Hobbes *Leviath.* II. xxvii. 157 The Degrees of Crime are taken on divers Scales. **1692** Ray *Disc.* ii. (1732) 91 Taking my Measures..by the Scale of the Eye. **1732** Pope *Ess. Man* II. 292 Ev'n mean Self-love becomes, by force divine, The scale to measure others' wants by thine. **1842** *Penny Cycl.* XXII. 192/1 A scale according to which the natural fertility of different soils can be classed.

b. Phr. ***on*** or ***upon a*** (***large, small, liberal,*** etc.) ***scale***. Also with ellipsis of *adj.*, and with *sb.*, as ***on a world scale***.

1784 Cowper *Tiroc.* 703 Were education..Conducted on a manageable scale. **1793** Burke *Let. to Sir G. Elliot* in *Corr.* (1844) IV. 151 On a far larger scale..than civil wars have generally extended themselves to. **1808** Scott *Autobiogr.* in *Lockhart* I. i. 49, I have all my life delighted in travelling, though I have never enjoyed that pleasure upon a large scale. **1843** Prescott *Mexico* I. ii. I. 35 His ordinary domestic expenditure..was certainly on no stinted scale. **1857** Buckle *Civiliz.* I. xiii. 739 It must be allowed that in his intellect, everything was on a great scale. **1904** H. James *Golden Bowl* I. I. ii. 26 Maggie's too wonderful—her preparations are on a scale! **1968** *Times* 15 Oct. 16/7 Possible arrangements on a world scale are affected by the telescopes available.

14. a. *Sculpture.* = *scale-stone* (see 16). **b.** *Painting.* 'A figure subdivided by lines like a ladder, which is used to measure proportions between pictures and the things represented' (*Cassell's Encycl. Dict.*).

1834-6 Barlow in *Encycl. Metrop.* (1845) VIII. 788/2 A wooden perpendicular rule the height of the work, which is movable from the strip of marble or scale under the model to that under the block of marble which is to be cut.

15. The ratio of the width of an organ-pipe to its length.

1881 Broadhouse *Mus. Acoustics* 78 A pipe of a large 'scale', by which organ builders mean a wide pipe, gives a much louder tone than a narrower one of the same length. **1884** Bosanquet in *Encycl. Brit.* XVII. 830/2 The scales..and voicing of the open diapason vary with fashion.

IV. 16. *attrib.* and *Comb.*, as (sense 9) ***scale-bar, -pipette, -reading***; (sense 4) ***scale degree, passage, singing***; (sense 11) ***scale drawing, model, plan***; (sense 7) ***scale charge, fee***; **scale effect**, an effect occurring when the scale of something is changed, as a result of contributory factors not all varying in proportion; *spec.* (see quot. 1940); **scale factor**, a numerical factor by which each of a set of quantities is multiplied; **scale height**, the vertical distance over which an atmospheric parameter or other quantity decreases by a factor *e* (= 2·718...); **scale-micrometer** (see quot.); **scale-paper**, paper having printed upon it divisions in eighths, tenths, &c. of an inch for drawing in proportion (*Dict. Archit. Publ. Soc.* 1881); **scale-stairs** *Sc.*, 'straight flights of steps, as opposed to a stair of spiral form' (Jam.); so **scale-staircase**; **scale-stone, -stool** (see quot. 1859).

1974 *Nature* 18 Oct. 647 (*caption*) Fully developed vegetative colonies (1 month old) on liquid surface (*scale bar, 0·5 cm). **1890** *Daily News* 5 Feb. 6/4 Each tenant has been black-mailed of eight guineas for a simple licence, in addition to the *scale charges for the conveyance of the house. **1889** *Century Dict.* s.v. *Degree*, To distinguish between degrees of the staff and degrees of the scale, the terms *staff-degree* and **scale-degree* are sometimes used. **1856** *Orr's Circ. Sci., Mech. Philos.* 260 In addition to the *scale-drawings of the whole, it is the practice of the best engineers to execute full-sized drawings of details. **1890** W. J. Gordon *Foundry* 153 A complete set of scale drawings, in which every detail is set out. **1917** *Rep. & Mem. Advisory Comm. Aeronaut.* (1921) No. 374 (*heading*) Report of the *scale effect sub-committee. **1930** *Engineering* 20 June 802/2 The skin friction of the plate gives a slightly erroneous velocity distribution under the model car... Still, the errors due to these imperfections are hardly likely to be so much greater than other unavoidable uncertainties, arising from scale effect and the varying conditions of full-scale operations. **1940** *Chambers's Techn. Dict.* 743/1 *Scale effect*, the effect of a change in Reynolds number upon the measured results in the performance of aerodynamic bodies. **1978** H. C. H. Armstead *Geothermal Energy* xv. 244 With conventional thermal power plants the capital cost per kilowatt installed is sensitive to what is generally known as the 'scale effect'; that is to say, a very large plant will tend to cost less per kilowatt than a small plant of similar type. **1979** *Daily Tel.* 15 Aug. 12/5 If you were trying to apply this concept to a Jaguar, you would need about a 20-litre engine—it only works because of the scale effect..on a very small car. **1948** *Electronics* Apr. 127/1 The corresponding initial voltages must be computed and the integrators set accordingly, using the correct *scale factor. **1963** [see sense 6c]. **1968** P. A. P. Moran *Introd. Probability Theory* v. 244 Thus S_n has the same distribution as the X_i but increased by the scale factor $n^{\frac{1}{2}}$. **1975** *Sci. Amer.* Nov. 120/2 The price paid for conformality is a distortion of the scale factor that increases with distance from the centre of the map. **1970** *Which?* Mar. 72/2 They saved the solicitor's *scale fee on the price of the house they were buying or selling. The higher the price of the house, the higher the fee. **1937** S. Chapman in *Rep. Progr. Physics* III. 44 *H* may then be interpreted as a unit of height-measurement relative to which, at the given level, the rate of upward decrease of log *p* is unity... The term 'height of the homogeneous atmosphere' is clearly not appropriate when *H* varies with height, and the name (local) '*scale-height' may be suggested. **1976** *Sci. Amer.* Mar. 53/1 In the sun or in the earth's atmosphere the size of the dominant energy-carrying cells is on the order of one scale height. **1978** *Nature* 26 Oct. 726/1 Suppose that 10^{38} ergs^{-1} of X rays are emitted by the pulsar... Assume the scale height of the photons is 3×10^8 cm. **1875** Knight *Dict. Mech.*, *Scale-micrometer, a graduated scale in the field of a telescope for measuring distances between objects. **1934** *Planning* I. xxii. 6 This is not, therefore, a scheme but a *scale model for one, intended to show precisely what is involved. **1952** 'T. Hinde' *Mr. Nicholas* v. 87 He had..small features..as neat as a scale model. **1907** *Daily Chron.* 16 Nov. 5/2 Her..facile execution of the *scale passages. **1875** Knight *Dict. Mech.*, *Scale-pipette, a tubular pipette having a graduated scale on the side. **1908** *Westm. Gaz.* 10 Aug. 3/1 All the old *scale plans and technical drawings. **1868** *Scale-reading [see electrometry]. **1873** Maxwell *Electr. & Magn.* II. 338 The scale-reading at certain definite times. **1962** L. S. Sasieni *Optical Dispensing* v. 110 A slight turn..will have the effect of moving both scale-readings in the same direction. **1890** *Daily News* 17 Feb. 3/2 Imperfect *scale singing. *c* **1730** Burt *Lett. N. Scot.* iii. (1754) I. 63 [In Inverness] a round Stair Case, [is called] a Turnpike; and a Square one goes by the Name of a *Skale Stair. **1821** Scott *Kenilw.* vi, Access was given to them [*sc.* apartments] by a large *scale staircase, as they were then called. **1841** *Penny Cycl.* XXI. 142/1 The whole instrument is then removed to the *scale-stone on which the rough block is placed. **1859** *Encycl. Brit.* (ed. 8) XIX. 868/2 If the model is to be copied in marble or stone, the first step is to procure a block of the required size. Two stones, called *scale-stones, are then prepared, upon one of which the model or plaster cast is placed, and upon the other the rough block of marble. The fronts of these stones have figured marks or 'scales' exactly corresponding. **1893** Symonds *Michel Angelo* I. 104 The ingenious process of 'pointing the marble' by means of the 'pointing machine' and 'scale-stones'. **1874** 'N. D'Anvers' *Elem. Hist. Art, Sculpture* (1889) 176 The cast and the marble are placed on two blocks, called *scale-stools, exactly alike.

scale (skeɪl), *sb.*[4] *dial.* Also 8 skell, 9 skeal(l. [a. ON. *skáli* wk. masc.:—OTeut. type **skǣlon-*, f. **skǣl-* (:**skal-*, **skel-*) to separate: see scale *sb.*[1], shale *sb.* Cf. sheal, shieling.] A hut, shed.

a **1300** *Cursor M.* 8592 For þai had husing nan to wale, þai lended in a littel scale. **1787** J. Clarke *Surv. Lakes* Introd. 30 The booths likewise, constructed for the watchers of cattle in summer,..were Skells or Scales. **1878** *Cumbld. Gloss.*, *Skeàll*, a scale; a shed or building on the fell. **1895** *Lakel. & Icel. Gloss.* s.v., Used of wooden huts put up as a temporary protection for turf, which are called 'peat scales'.

†**scale**, *sb.*[5] *Obs.* [ad. med.L. *scala*, whence OF. *eschiel(l)e*, *eskiele* (see eschele).] A maniple, squadron, or battalion.

c **1400** Maundev. (Roxb.) xxx. 135 Withouten þe principall oste..and also withouten certayne scales [orig. Fr. *escheles*] þat er ordaynd for forraying. **1591** *Garrard's Art Warre* 166 These bodies..are of many called maniples, or scales.

scale (skeɪl), *sb.*[6] [f. scale *v.*[3]]

†**1.** = escalade. *Obs.*

1577-87 Holinshed *Chron.* III. 1190/1 Diuerse bands..entring the ditches offered the scale. **1589** Ive *Pract. Fortif.* 3 The fort..will be free from surprise, skale, and myning. **1633** T. Stafford *Pac. Hib.* x. (1821) 121 Surprised by Scale, a Castle in the heart of the Countrie. **1667** Milton *P.L.* xi. 652 Others to a Citie strong Lay Siege, encampt; by Batterie, Scale, and Mine, Assaulting.

2. The estimation of an amount of timber standing or in logs; the amount of the estimate.

1877 *Mich. Reports* XXXIV. 376 To conclude the parties in that respect by his scale. *Ibid.* XXXV. 521 The scale bill showed four hundred and ninety three thousand five hundred and seventeen feet of white pine. **1880** *Northwest. Lumberman* 24 Jan., For punky knots the general rule is to allow the whole scale of the log for defects. *Ibid.*, A buyer should be allowed..one-half the scale of the punky log.

†**scale**, *sb.*[7] *Obs.* [ad. OF. *scal(l)e, escal(l)e* (mod.F. *escale*, esp. in phr. *faire escale* to go ashore) or its source It. *scala* = Sp., Pg. *escala* seaport, harbour:—L. *scāla* ladder (see scale *sb.*[3]).] **a.** A landing-place; *occas.* a custom-house. *rare.*

1682 Wheler *Journ. to Greece* III. 246 On the other side..is the Scale, or Custom-house for the Grand Signiors own Subjects. **1683** in *Misc. Curiosa* (1708) III. 49 Montanea..is the Scale or Landing-place for Prusa. **1813** J. C. Hobhouse *Journey* (ed. 2) 639 At the extremity of the inner bay there is a sort of scale or landing-place.

b. A seaport town; a trading port; a centre of trade or traffic; an emporium.

1613 Sir A. Sherley *Trav. Persia* 9 The Turke hauing giuen certaine scales to trade in. **1628** Digby *Voy. Medit.* (Camden) 42 The 24. the English Viceconsull att Scanderone came to me with a letter from the Aga there desiring me to be gone, for that I disturbed the Gran Signiors scale there. *c* **1645** Howell *Lett.* (1650) I. 38 A Maritim Town,..her chiefest Arsenal for Gallies, and the Scale by which she conveys her Moneys to Italy. **1682** Wheler *Journ. to Greece* I. 16 It [Spalato] being the chief Scale of Trade for Shipping of Goods from Turkey to Venice.

attrib. **1674** Evelyn *Navig. & Comm.* Misc. Writ. (1825) 648 Tripoly, and Alexandretta.., and..Aleppo..to which scale merchants came..from all the oriental countries.

scale (skeɪl), *v.*[1] Also 7 skale. [f. scale *sb.*[1]]

1. *trans.* To weigh in scales, find the weight of.

1691 *Virginia Stat. at Large* (1823) III. 76 That the court..appoint..fitt..persons..to..scale such leather as they shall find sufficiently curryed. **1883** *Harper's Mag.* Apr. 692/1 The cheeses go..to the..weigh-house to be scaled.

b. *Baking.* To weigh out (dough) in proper quantities for making up into loaves. Usually with *off*.

1841 *Guide to Trade, Baker* 40 The dough is pitched out of the trough on to the lid of the opposite trough, when it is cut into masses and weighed—technically *scaled off*. **1875** J. Paton in *Encycl. Brit.* III. 253/2 It [*sc.* dough] is then 'scaled off', *i.e.*, weighed on scales in pieces of 4lb. 4 oz., if 4 lb loaves are to be made. **1890** *Sci. Amer.* 1 Mar. 140/3 It [*sc.* the sponge] is..'scaled' into loaves, and baked.

†**2.** *fig.* **a.** To weigh as in scales; hence, to compare, estimate. *Obs.*

1603 Shaks. *Meas. for M.* III. i. 266 By this is your brother saued, your honor vntainted, the poore Mariana aduantaged, and the corrupt Deputy scaled. **1607** —— *Cor.* II. iii. 257 Skaling his present bearing with his past.

†**b.** With *up*: To compensate, balance. *Obs.*

1622 Callis *Stat. Sewers* (1647) 1, I put Charge and Care in one Scale, and Resolution in the other, which scaled them both up.

3. To weigh, have a weight of (so much).

1862 H. H. Dixon ('The Druid') *Scott & Sebright* 13 Eleven [stone] was his regular racing weight, and he scaled ten and a half at a pinch. **1867** Lowell *Study Wind., Gt. Public Char.* (1871) 68, I scale one hundred and eighty pounds, but when I'm mad I weigh two ton. **1888** Rider Haggard *Maiwa's Rev.* iv, The single tusk of the big bull [elephant] scaled one hundred and sixty pounds.

absol. **1869** 'Wat. Bradwood' *O.V.H.* xxix, At a weight to which Ralph could not scale. **1886** *Times* (weekly ed.) 6 Aug. 13/4 The deer..are sure to scale heavily when the stalking is in full swing.

b. *Racing.* To be weighed. ***to scale in***: to be weighed after the race, to 'weigh in'.

1859 H. H. Dixon ('The Druid') *Silk & Scarlet* 127 No welcome (1) was printed after his name till he scaled-in for Wanton. **1869** 'Wat. Bradwood' *O.V.H.* xviii, The open steeplechase, for which the jockeys had long ago scaled.

scale (skeɪl), *v.*[2] Also 6 scaale, 7 skale. [f. scale *sb.*[2] Cf. F. *écailler.*]

1. a. *trans.* To remove the scales from (fish, etc.).

c **1440** *Promp. Parv.* 442/1 Scalyn fysche, *exquamo*. **1530** Palsgr. 699/1 You are a cooke for the nones, wyll you sethe these roches or you have scaled them? **1598** *Epulario* F iv, The fish which you wil rost would not be scaled. **1674** tr. *Scheffer's Lapland* 98 A kind of glew made of Perches skin well scaled. **1747** Mrs. Glasse *Cookery* ix. 117 Scale, and clean your Salmon down the Back. **1800** *Phil. Trans.* XC. 163 Three herrings,..after being scaled and gutted.

b. In various technical uses:

(*a*) To remove the scale or film of oxide from the surface of (metal), esp. as a preparatory process for tinning. Also *absol.* (*b*) To clean the bore of (a gun or cannon) by firing off a charge of powder. (*c*) To remove tartar from (the teeth).

1702 Savery *Miner's Friend* 71 A red Heat, and sudden cooling it again, will Scale the Copper. **1728** Rutty *Tin-Plates* in *Phil. Trans.* XXXV. 633 If you scale with Vinegar..you need only plunge the Leaves once or twice at farthest. **1784** J. King *Voy. Pacific* v. x. 447 We unmoored, and scaled the guns. **1805** Pike *Sources Mississ.* (1810) 2 We..discharged our guns at a target, and scaled out our blunderbusses. **1823** Byron *Island* II. xxi, We have got some guns to bear, And scaled them. **1839** Ure *Dict. Arts* 1252 They [*sc.* iron plates] are..once more exposed to ignition in a furnace, whereby they are scaled, that is to say, cast their scales. **1840** De Loude *Dentistry* 97 The principal parts of operative dentistry..consist of scaling the teeth, lancing and scarifying the gums [&c.].

2. a. To remove as scale; to take *off* or *away* in scales. Also, to separate *into* layers. ***to be scaled***: to have the surface removed in scales or flakes.

a **1552** Leland *Itin.* (1768) I. 96 They be sore woren and scalid with wether. **1603** Holland *Plutarch's Mor.* 1187 This aire..forceth out of it a deale of rust, and skaleth as it were much terrestrial substance from it. **1611** Cotgr., *Rugine*, the Instrument wherewith a Surgeon scaleth bones. **1611** Bible *Tobit* iii. 17 To scale away the whitenesse of Tobits eyes. **1667** Waterhouse *Narr. Fire in London* 75 The Stones of the outside so scaled, as if the Fire was greedy to eat out all firmness in them. **1668** Culpepper & Cole *Barthol. Anat.* III. viii. 146 It may be scaled into four plates. **1754** J. Bartlet *Gentl. Farriery* (ed. 2) xxxv. 293 Taking care that it does not penetrate too deep, so as to scale off the thin bone. **1774** Goldsm. *Nat. Hist.* VII. 6 If the external coat be scaled off. **1843** *Civil Eng. & Arch. Jrnl.* VI. 161/1 The stones being..scaled by frost.

†**b.** ? To split off scales or flakes from (coin) for the purpose of fraud. *Obs.*

1576 *Act 18 Eliz.* c. 1. §1 Yf any person..deminishe falsefy skale or lighten the proper Moneys or Coignes of this Realme.

c. *Austral.* and *N.Z. slang.* To defraud or cheat (someone), to steal (something). In phr. ***to scale a train*** or ***tram***, to ride without paying on public transport; also *intr.*

1916 A. Wright *Under Cloud* 32 'How'd that happen,' asks Bill Odzon. 'Didn't think anyone could scale you.' **1941** Baker *N.Z. Slang* vii. 62 When we are taken down financially we are *scaled*. **1945** —— *Austral. Lang.* v. 103 A *steel jockey* is a tramp who scales a train or rides without paying. *Ibid.* 106 One can *get scaled*, in the sense of being done down, when overcharged for goods. **1953** 'Caddie' *Sydney Barmaid* xiv. 132 Better..than for them to be getting about the streets with snotty noses, and scaling trams. **1953** D. Cusack *Southern Steel* 3 Bumping in on the back of the old steam trams, too often scaling on the footboards because he hadn't the money to pay the penny fare.

3. *intr.* To come *off* (or *away*) in scales, flakes, or thin pieces; to flake or peel *off*. Also, of skin eruptions: To shed scales.

1529 [see SCALD *a.*[1] 1]. **1607** TOPSELL *Four-f. Beasts* 407 Annoint him..vntil the fiered place beginne to scale. **1675** HAN. WOOLLEY *Gentlw. Comp.* 179 It [*sc.* a scaldhead] will scale off. **1743** POCOCKE *Descr. East* I. 8 The pillar is well preserved, except that it has scaled away a very little to the south. **1752** HOLLIS in *Lett. Lit. Men* (Camden) 392 It is hoped the Voyage and Climate has not made it scale or fade. **1832** LYELL *Princ. Geol.* II. 220 Small angular fragments of limestone, which scale off under the influence of frost and rain. **1843** R. J. GRAVES *Lect. Clin. Med.* xxx. 385 Crops of pimples which scale away. **1884** HOWELLS *Silas Lapham* I. i, It ain't a-going to crack nor fade any; and it ain't a-going to scale.

4. *trans.* Of disease: To cover with scales. *rare.*

1889 TENNYSON *Happy* vii, The leper plague may scale my skin but never taint my heart.

scale (skeɪl), *v.*[3] Forms: 5 skayle, 5–7 skale, 6 scaile, skaille, 7 skaile, skall, scall, 5– scale. [f. SCALE *sb.*[3] Cf. OF. *escaller* (15th c.); also It. *scalare*, Sp., Pg. *escalar.*]

I. 1. a. *trans.* To attack with scaling ladders; to take by escalade.

?*a* **1400** *Morte Arth.* 3034 The kynge..Skyftis his skotiferis, and skayles the wallis. **1412–20** LYDG. *Chron. Troy* II. 6420 To skale þe wal after þei be-gonne. **1475** *Bk. Noblesse* (Roxb.) 16 To aproche the towne for to scale yt. **1587** GREENE *Euphues his Censure* Wks. (Grosart) VI. 220 Had not the citizens made as violent an intermedley,..the citty had bene scaled and sacked. **1617** MORYSON *Itin.* II. 24 Great multitudes of the assaylants..attempting to scale the fort. **1737** POPE *Hor. Ep.* II. ii. 40 He leap'd the trenches, scal'd a Castle-wall. **1838** THIRLWALL *Greece* xxxviii. V. 35 The assailants offered large rewards to the first who should scale the walls.

b. To climb, get over (a wall or the like); to ascend (a mountain); to get to or reach the top of.

1579 SPENSER *Sheph. Cal.* Dec. 31 How often have I scaled the craggie Oke, All to dislodge the Raven of her nest? **1605** *London Prodigal* III. iii. 255 That to him is as impossible As 'twere with me to scale the pyramids. **1669** STURMY *Mariner's Mag.* II. xvi. 94 To find the Height of an House,..and the length of the Ladder which will Scale it. **1680** OTWAY *Orphan* III. vii. (1705) 1301 I'll scale the Window and come in by force. **1762** GOLDSM. *Cit. W.* lvii. 256 She proposed that instant to scale the garden wall. **1860** TYNDALL *Glac.* I. vii. 50 It has long been the ambition of climbers to scale this peak. **1878** MACLEAR *Celts* i. 8 Scaling the mighty barrier of the Alps, they descended upon the fertile vales of Southern Europe.

c. *transf.* and *fig.* or in fig. context.

1557 *Tottel's Misc.* (Arb.) 172 When Cupide scaled first the fort, Wherin my hart lay wounded sore. **1563** SACKVILLE *Induct. Mirr. Mag.* xix, When sickenes seekes his castell health to skale. *a* **1625** FLETCHER *Wom. Pleased* I. i, Is your old Mistris growne so coy and cruell, She must be scal'd? **1755** YOUNG *Centaur* vi. Wks. 1757 IV. 245, I shall scale the summit of human nature. **1847** TENNYSON *Princess* VII. 245 She that out of Lethe scales with man The shining steps of Nature. **1908** *19th Cent.* Oct. 621 He has proved the value of attempting, at least, to scale the loftiest heights.

d. Of waves beating upon a ship or a cliff.

1401 *Pol. Poems* (Rolls) II. 109 ȝour brymme blastis awake the wilde wawlis, and scalen sely Peter ship. **1823** BYRON *Island* III. i, When scaling his enormous crag the wave Is hurl'd down headlong.

2. To 'mount' (the skies): to ascend or climb up into (heaven). Often *allusive.*

c **1380** WYCLIF *Sel. Wks.* II. 6 þus men moten nedis scale [*v.r.* stiȝe] heven. **1585** MONTGOMERIE *Sonnets* xiii. 3 Bright Apollo..Quhais glorious glance ȝit stoutly skaillis the skyis. **1614** CHAPMAN *Odyss.* IV. 57 Ile vtter truth in all; When heauens supremest height, the Sunne doth skall. **1762–71** H. WALPOLE *Vertue's Anecd. Paint.* (1786) IV. 6 He piles palaces on bridges, and temples on palaces, and scales Heaven with mountains of edifices. **1784** COWPER *Task* III. 221 God never meant that man should scale the heav'ns By strides of human wisdom. **1815** SHELLEY *Alastor* 278 [A swan] rose as he approached, and with strong wings Scaling the upward sky [etc.]. **1877** H. M. FIELD *Lakes of Killarney* 198 This is the highest pass in Europe..and on this day it seemed as if we were scaling heaven itself.

3. a. *intr.* To climb (*over*), ascend, mount.

a **1547** SURREY *Æneid* II. (1557) C j, The Grekes..rered vp ladders against the walles, Under the windowes scaling by their steppes. **1560** DAUS tr. *Sleidane's Comm.* 265 b, He..was avauncing his ladders to scale. **1593** SHAKS. *Lucr.* 440 Her bare breast,..Whose ranks of blue veins, as his hand did scale, Left their round turrets destitute and pale. **1601** HOLLAND *Pliny* I. 170 He..was honored with a murall crown of gold for skaling over the wall in an assault. **1645** SYMONDS *Diary* (Camden) 224 Our men alighted and with their pistolls scalld and gott in. **1760–72** H. BROOKE *Fool of Qual.* (1809) I. 171 Having scaled as far as the dining-room. **1843** TENNYSON *Two Voices* lix, That men with knowledge merely play'd, I told thee—hardly nigher made, Tho' scaling slow from grade to grade.

b. Of steps, etc.: To ascend, mount.

1667 MILTON *P.L.* III. 541 The lower stair That scal'd by steps of Gold to Heav'n Gate. **1861** LYTTON & FANE *Tannhäuser* 88 Flights of blinding brilliancy of stairs..that ..Scaled to the City of the Saints of God. **1863** P. S. WORSLEY *Poems & Transl.* 9 Far up the vault a dazzling pavement,..Scaled to the zenith.

c. Of the voice or a musical instrument: To rise high.

1859 TENNYSON *Elaine* 1013 Call and I follow, I follow! let me die. High with the last line scaled her voice. **1901** G. L. DICKINSON *Meaning of Good* 227 The rhythm grew more and more rapid, the instruments scaled higher and higher.

II. To measure or regulate by a scale.

4. a. *trans.* To fix the exact amount of. *U.S.*

1798 *Washington's Rep.* I. 130 Two accounts, in one of which he scales the credits, and in the other fixes them at their nominal amount.

b. With *down*: To reduce in amount according to a fixed scale or standard. Also *loosely*, to reduce. ? orig. *U.S.*

1887 *Pall Mall G.* 31 Oct. 6/1 There are several ways..in which boy and girl labour is utilized [in New York] to the disadvantage of adult labour, with the consequence of scaling down the adult's income. **1888** *Jrnl. Franklin Inst.* Oct. 340 At this rate it will require seventeen and one-half years, provided there be no failure of the bills during that period, and that the item be not scaled down. **1933** *Sun* (Baltimore) 5 Apr. 8/2 The indebted farmer gets his mortgage debt scaled down, but with that scaling down the payment of interest again becomes the vogue. **1934** [see next sense]. **1937** *Physical Rev.* LI. 1027/1 (*heading*) Vacuum tube circuits for scaling down counting rates. **1952** M. LASKI *Village* v. 95 Hospitality had been empirically scaled down to a universally possible level. **1979** *Daily Tel.* 19 May 2/1 The original pay claim for a 30 per cent. rise has been scaled down to 16 per cent.

c. With *up*: to increase in amount or size according to a fixed scale or standard; to increase from a small scale to a larger scale. Also *absol.*

1891 *Daily News* 17 Jan. 2/5 The scaling up instead of scaling down the London, Chatham, and Dover stock. **1934** W. NELSON *Seaplane Design* vi. 64 Scaling the size of existing floats and hulls up and down can be done to arrive at the dimensions of a new design. **1972** *Aquaculture* I. 182 During the summer of 1971, the project was scaled up in size and moved out-of-doors. **1973** *Times* 28 Nov. 19/5 If the pilot plant can be scaled up at this figure it offers great hopes for the development of these abundant fuel reserves. **1975** *Nature* 17 Jan. 149/3 There will probably be no need to scale up since the existing plant can cope with 50 tons every 24 hours. **1977** *Undercurrents* June–July 7/1 It remains doubtful whether the process..can work safely and effectively when 'scaled-up' to commercial size. **1979** *Sci. Amer.* Jan. 45/1 Several organizations are currently scaling up from laboratory-size cells to units of demonstration size.

d. To measure or represent (a quantity) in exact proportion to its absolute size or according to an arbitrary defined scale.

1885 W. PENMAN *Land Surveying* ix. 127 An area to the scale of 1 chain = 1 inch was scaled and found to give 12 ac. 1 ro. 01 pls. **1898** F. E. DIXON *T. Baker's Rudimentary Treat. Land & Engin. Surveying* (ed. 17) xii. 182 It sometimes happens that a distance is scaled on a plan using ..a wrong scale. **1923** *Rep. Internat. Air Congr., London, 1923* 63 Not only is it difficult to scale the printed forms with accuracy, but there is no assurance that the silhouette corresponds closely with the model tested in the wind channel. **1940** *Amer. Jrnl. Psychol.* LIII. 336 (*caption*) The curve shows how pitch, scaled in subjective units..varies with frequency. **1951** S. S. STEVENS *Handbk. Experim. Psychol.* i. 23/1 These operations are limited ordinarily by the peculiarities of the thing being scaled. **1951** H. P. BECHTOLDT in *Ibid.* xxxiii. 1240/2 Multiple-category qualitative variables representing intensive dimensions are 'scaled' in various ways, and numerical scores are determined. **1966** T. NEWCOMB et al. *Social Psychol.* (ed. 2) 506 In a most interesting approach to problems of scaling attitudes..Guttman..began to examine items apparently ordered on the basis of 'difficulty'. **1971** J. B. CARROLL et al. *Word Freq. Bk.* p. xxvii, The base line of Graph 1 is scaled, not in terms of ϕ, but in terms of a further transformation of ϕ to the Standard Frequency Index. **1976** B. S. PHILLIPS *Social Res.* (rev. ed.) ix. 211 Select or construct those items that you wish to scale.

e. To alter (a quantity or property) by changing the units in which it is measured; to change the size of (a system or device) while keeping its parts in constant proportion.

1954 *Computers & Automation* Dec. 20/2 *Scale*, computation. To change the scale (that is, the units) in which a variable is expressed so as to bring it within the capacity of the machine or program at hand. **1966** R. C. CARTER *Introd. Electr. Circuit Analysis* vii. 239 Once the desired design performance has been achieved in the low-frequency prototype laboratory model, all factors involving frequency and impedance may be scaled to the desired operating range. **1974** *Physics Bull.* Mar. 98/3 The symmetry transformation consists of scaling the physical dimensions d of the system according to $d \rightarrow \lambda d$. If the equilateral triangle of figure 1 is scaled then although the size is changed, the geometric shape and all the dimensionless properties of the triangle such as the angles remain unchanged. **1978** *Sci. Amer.* Dec. 128/2 The radio waves, completely unattenuated by the intervening dust, can be scaled several orders of magnitude in frequency to predict the true intensity of the optical radiation.

f. *intr.* Of a quantity or property: to vary according to a defined rule or principle.

1974 *Physics Bull.* Mar. 98/3 The invariance of all dimensionless properties can be used to determine whether the figure scales or not. **1978** *Nature* 20 Apr. 737/3 Surprisingly the limiting torque, even at optimised pressures, scales only at [*recte* as] T_i.

5. *Lumber-trade.* **a.** To measure (logs), or estimate the amount of (standing timber).

1867 LOWELL *Fitz Adam's Story* 526, I expect I can Scale a fair load of wood with e'er a man. **1873** *Wisconsin Rep.* XXXI, As soon as said logs shall be all rafted they shall be scaled. **1877** *Michigan Rep.* XXXV. 412 The logs were to be scaled by a scaler named.

b. Of timber: To produce or furnish (so much).

1853 LOWELL *Moosehead Jrnl.* Pr. Wks. 1890 I. 32 Their eye, accustomed to reckoning the number of feet a tree will *scale*. **1884** C. S. SARGENT *Rep. For. N. Amer.* 555 Trees which would scale from 1,000 to 3,500 feet of lumber each.

6. a. To estimate the proportions of.

1877 A. B. EDWARDS *Up Nile* vi. 144 In the absence of any near object by which to scale them. **1902** *Blackw. Mag.* June 865/2 The inability of the Australian labouring man to scale things correctly.

b. To provide a standard of proportion for.

1874 MICKLETHWAITE *Mod. Par. Churches* 29 Pews.. architects say, scale a building; that is, they give the eye a constant standard for judging of its size.

7. *trans.* Of a scaler (see SCALER[3] 4): to count (electrical pulses). Also *absol.*

1938 *Rev. Sci. Instruments* IX. 221/1 The circuit either scaled correctly or no counts were registered. **1947** *Ibid.* XXIV. 322/1 Although not developed as a high-frequency instrument, the model will scale a regular pulse input up to frequencies of the order of 100 kc/s.

'scale-board[1]. [f. SCALE *sb.*[2] + BOARD *sb.*[2] Cf. SCABBARD *sb.*[3]] Thin board used for hat-boxes, silk hats, veneer, etc., and by printers for justifying.

1711 *Act 10 Anne* c. 18 §62 To export such Paper Pastboard Mildboard or Scaleboard. **1821** J. SMYTH *Pract. Customs* (ed. 2) 202 Scaleboards, from Germany, are packed in Bundles, weighing 50 at each Draught. **1823** CRABBE *Technol. Dict.* s.v. *Printing*, To the furniture belong also scale-boards. **1855** OGILVIE Suppl., *Scale-board*, in *printing*, ..commonly pronounced scab'-board. **1874** *Spon's Dict. Engin.* VIII. 3091 In sawing veneers or scale-boards.

attrib. **1846** [see SCABBARD *sb.*[3] b]. **1875** KNIGHT *Dict. Mech.*, *Scaleboard-plane*, one for planing off wide chips, for fruit, hat, and bonnet boxes and other objects. **1881** *Instr. Census Clerks* (1885) 81 Scaleboard Box Maker.

'scale-board[2]. [f. SCALE *sb.*[1] + BOARD *sb.*[2]] A board used as one of the pans of a pair of scales.

1876 VOYLE & STEVENSON *Milit. Dict.*, *Beam-Scale*, a simple lever, the arms of which are equal. At the end of each arm a scale board is suspended by chains.

'scale-board[3]. [First element uncertain.] (See quot.)

1891 *Min. Evid. Labour Comm.* Group B. (1892) I. 54/2 Copper ore..is brought up on scale-boards or shoots. *Ibid.* Gloss., *Scaleboard*, a kind of large shovel, made of planks, which serves as a shoot and guide, down which goods are slid from ship to quay.

Scale Celi, obs. form of SCALA CÆLI.

scaled (skeɪld), *ppl. a.*[1] [f. SCALE *sb.*[2] + -ED[2].]

1. Having or furnished with scales, as a fish or a serpent; scaly. Now rare exc. as second element of comb., as ***silver-scaled***, and *Her.*

a **1400–50** *Alexander* 3865 Scalid neddirs. *c* **1420** LYDG. *Assembly of Gods* 614 Formyd lyke a dragon, scalyd harde as glas. **1586** FERNE *Blaz. Gentrie* I. 235 The creatures chelled, named *Conchilia*, and also of those that are scaled (called *insecta*). **1589** ELDRED in *Hakluyt's Voy.* 232 Euphrates.. hath diuers sorts of fish in it, but all are scaled. **1606** SHAKS. *Ant. & Cl.* II. v. 95 A Cesterne for scal'd Snakes. **1659** T. PECKE *Parnassi Puerp.* 155 The scal'd Crocodile, out-weep Thee can. **1688** HOLME *Armoury* II. 455/1 An Indian scaled Hedghog. **1868** CUSSANS *Handbk. Her.* vi. 91 Fish are described as being *Scaled* and *Finned* of whatever Tincture they may happen to be.

2. a. Of armour. Cf. *scale-armour*; SCALY *a.* 5.

1555 WATREMAN *Fardle Facions* II. vii. 160 A brestplate emboussed, of skaled woorke. **1657** G. THORNLEY *Daphnis & Chloe* (1893) 20 Their Scaled and nailed Corslets. **1825** FOSBROKE *Encycl. Antiq.* II. 782 Scaled Armour also occurs. **1834** *Penny Cycl.* II. 368/2 Whether this was the scaled-armour,..or that made of flat-rings..is not quite clear.

b. = IMBRICATED 2, 3.

1776 J. LEE *Introd. Bot.* Explan. Terms 392 *Imbricata*, scaled. **1872** COUES *Key N. Amer. Birds* 238 *Callipepla* [*squamata*]... Scaled Partridge. Blue Quail. **1884** *Ibid.* (ed. 2) 570 *Scardafella inca*... Inca Dove. Scaled Dove. **1884** *Fortn. Rev.* Apr. 533 The tear-bottle of scaled and iridescent glass. **1893** F. ADAMS *New Egypt* 97 The..date-palms, with their scaled trunks.

c. Covered with tiles in imitation of scales.

1862 H. MARRYAT *Year in Sweden* II. xliii. 80 The church boasts the loftiest scaled spire in Sweden. **1896** W. MORRIS in Mackail *Life* I. 231 The earlier house and its little gables and grey scaled roofs.

scaled (skeɪld), *ppl. a.*[2] [f. SCALE *v.*[2] + -ED[1].] From which scales have fallen or have been removed.

1599 H. C. in *Greenham's Wks.* (1601) Epigr. Rdr., From whose hie top thy scaled eyes may see, A glorious light that shall enlighten thee. **1601** HOLLAND *Pliny* XXVI. xiv. II. 265 The spills of broken and skaled bones. **1728** RUTTY *Tin-Plates* in *Phil. Trans.* XXXV. 636 To prevent this,..they might first make an Essay with small Pieces of the scaled Plates. **1840** BROWNING *Sordello* I. 503 A touch divine— And the scaled eyeball owns the mystic rod. **1873** J. & C. S. TOMES *Dental Surg.* (ed. 2) 560 In order to secure the smoothness of the scaled surface, they should be polished with pumice-powder on a piece of wood.

scaled (skeɪld), *ppl. a.*[3] [f. SCALE *sb.*[3] + -ED[2].] Provided or furnished with a graduated scale.

1900 *Daily News* 24 Aug. 5/1 Equipping the marksmen of every battalion with detachable scaled sights.

scaled, *ppl. a.*[4] [f. SCALE *v.*[3] + -ED[1].]

1. That has been taken by escalade.

1614 BRATHWAITE *Threnode* in *Poets Willow* 75 See how the Iuy twines Vpon the ruines of a skaled wall.

2. a. That has been measured by a scale or varied in a determined proportion.

1885 W. PENMAN *Land Surveying* ix. 127 The scaled area is less than the actual one, indicating shrinkage of the paper. **1938** *Rev. Sci. Instruments* IX. 221/1 The fluctuational analysis of the scaled counts occurring at an average rate of ten per minute indicated a scaling factor of 22 to 1. **1960** ROGERS & CONNOLLY *Analog Computation in Engin. Design* x. 261 The following scaled voltage equivalents are suitable for representing the variables of the problem; 2*x̄*, 20*ẋ*, 200*x*, 10*h*, 10*t*. **1976** Attewell & Farmer *Princ. Engin. Geol.* vii. 525 (*caption*) Scaled distance attenuation relationships for blasting in a rock.

b. ***scaled-up***: that has been increased proportionately in amount or size in all its parts. Similarly ***scaled-down***.

1944 P. Wilkinson *Aircraft Engines of World 1944* 38 The 12-cylinder 1,300 h.p. Jumo 211-J is a scaled-up version of the Jumo 210. **1947** A. E. Slater in A. C. Douglas *Gliding & Advanced Soaring* i. 12 The earliest recorded attempts to fly, as well as the legendary ones, usually began with an attempt to reproduce a scaled-up bird's wing, often to the extent of putting feathers on it, in the belief that such a structure was inherently able to keep itself up, once it got well aloft. **1953** *Trans. Soc. Instrument Technol.* V. 126/2 The pilot unit is not usually constructed unless the manufacturer is satisfied that he will eventually proceed to the erection of a full-scale plant. It is a scaled-down version of such a plant. **1963** Bird & Hutton-Stott *Veteran Motor Car* 49 B.S.A. cars..were virtually scaled-down Daimlers. **1973** *Lebende Sprachen* XVIII. 7/2 Go-ahead for a scaled-up version of the engine giving a 30 percent increase in original thrust. **1977** *Time* 19 Sept. 43/1 Anyone with a driver's license and a few dollars can safely savor some of the adrenaline-pumping, gut-clutching fever of Grand Prix racing on a minitrack, in a scaled-down Formula I speedster.

ˈscale-dish. *north. dial.* [? f. Scale *sb.*¹]

1. A shallow dish, esp. used for skimming milk.

1641 Best *Farm. Bks.* (Surtees) 18 Then putte it to the ale and make thereof two great possattes in two scale-dishes. **1787** J. Clarke *Surv. Lakes* Introd. 30 Every kind of dish likewise which is thin at the margin is a Scale-dish. **1829** Brockett *N.C. Gloss.* (ed. 2), *Scale-dish*, a thin dish used in the dairy for skimming milk.

2. (See quot.)

1828 [Carr] *Craven Gloss.*, *Scale-dish*, an implement made of tin with a short wooden handle for filling a scale with flour, &c.

†**ˈscaledness.** *Obs.* [f. Scaled *ppl. a.*¹] Scaly condition. (Cf. Scalledness.)

1530 Palsgr. 265/2 Scalydnesse, *escalerie*.

scaledrake (ˈskeɪldreɪk). Also 6–7 **skaildraik, -drake,** 9 **skale, skel-, skieldrake.** [The first element is of obscure origin: see Sheldrake. Cf. dial. *scale-*, *skell-duck*, and *skeel-*, *skeeling-goose*.] = Sheldrake.

1600 *Sc. Acts Jas. VI* (1816) IV. 236/2 Ony..skeldraikis herroun butter, or ony sic kynd of foullis. **1659** *Lady Alimony* ii. ii. B4, Who is she that looks like a mouted Scaledrake? **1813** Montagu *Ornith. Dict.* Suppl., Shieldrake..Scaledrake. **1885** Swainson *Prov. Names Birds* 153 Common Sheldrake (*Tadorna cornuta*)... Skeldrake or Scale drake (Orkney Isles). *Ibid.* 188 Oyster catcher (*Hæmatopus ostrilegus*)... Skeldrake or Skieldrake (Orkney Isles).

scaleful (ˈskeɪlfʊl). [f. Scale *sb.*¹ + -ful¹.] As much as a scale will hold.

1844 H. Stephens *Bk. Farm* III. 888 The weight of the number of scalefuls required to fill each pack.

scaleless (ˈskeɪllɪs), *a.* Also 7 **skalesse.** [f. Scale *sb.*² + -less.] Having no scales: chiefly of fish and reptiles.

1611 Cotgr., *Amie*, a certaine skalesse fish. *Ibid.*, *Gracieux seigneur*, a skalelesse fish, of a longe forme. **1803** Shaw *Gen. Zool.* IV. 370 Scaleless Chætodon. *Chætodon Alepidotus.* **1882** Huxley in *Nature* 9 Mar. 437/1 The scaleless parts of the body..of the fish. **1884** P. Robinson *Fishes of Fancy* in *Fish. Exhib. Lit.* III. 37 Egypt, where the scaleless fish were taboo in consequence of their.. unwholesomeness.

scalelet (ˈskeɪllɪt). *Bot.* [f. Scale *sb.*² + -let.] A small scale.

1787 tr. *Linnæus' Fam. Plants* I. 102 Asperugo... Cor[olla] one-petal'd... Throat closed: with Scalelets five.

scalene (ˈskeɪliːn, formerly skəˈliːn), *a.* and *sb.* [ad. late L. *scalēnus*: see Scalenus. Cf. F. *scalène*.] **A.** *adj.*

1. *Geom.* **a.** Of a triangle: Having three unequal sides.

1734 *Builder's Dict.* s.v., A scalene Triangle, scalenum Triangle. **1775** Harris *Philos. Arrangem.* xv. 377 The Genus, Triangle, being divided into equilateral, equicrural, and scalene. **1801** Bournon in *Phil. Trans.* XCI. 183 The crystal is often seen placed upon one of its scalene triangular sides. **1833** Dickens *Sk. Boz, Tales* ii, With one round and two scalene triangular beds, containing..an unlimited number of marigolds. **1854** H. Miller *Sch. & Schm.* v. 87 The sail itself..formed a scalene triangle.

b. *scalene cone, cylinder*: one of which the axis is not perpendicular to the base.

1684 Wallis *Angular Sections* i. 73 The Scalene Cone and Cylinder. **1807** T. Young *Nat. Phil.* II. 21 The sub-contrary section of a scalene cone is a circle.

c. *scalene cell*: see quot.

1875 Cayley in *Q. Jrnl. Pure & Appl. Math.* XIII. 321 The scalene cell is..a system of 3 pairs of equal rods *PA*, *QA*; *PB*, *QB*; *PC*, *QC* jointed together at and capable of rotating about the points *P*, *Q*, *A*, *B*, *C*; the three lengths *PA*, *PB*, *PC*..being all of them unequal.

2. *Anat.* *scalene muscle* = Scalenus.

scalene tubercle, an elevation on the upper edge of the first rib, from which the scalenus anticus muscle originates.

1827 Abernethy *Surg. Wks.* I. 133 The outer margin of the scalene muscles. **1934** [see Scalenotomy]. **1962** *Gray's Anat.* (ed. 33) 600 The scalene muscles, in particular the Scalenus medius, are important accessory muscles of inspiration.

B. *sb.* **1.** A scalene triangle. *rare.*

1642 H. More *Song of Soul* ii. i. ii. lvii, But if 't consist of points: then a Scalene I'll prove all one with an Isosceles.

2. *Anat.* = Scalenus.

1891 in *Century Dict.* **1978** [see Scalenotomy].

†**scaˈlenity.** *Obs.* [f. Scalene + -ity.] The quality of being scalene.

1788 T. Taylor *Proclus* I. Dissert. p. li, Do you by this means destroy the equality of its angles to two right ones? Certainly not;—take away its scalenity, yet this general affection remains.

scalenohedron (skəˌliːnəʊˈhiːdrən). *Cryst.* [mod.L., f. Gr. σκαληνός Scalene + ἕδρα seat, base.] A hemihedral form of the rhombohedral system in which the faces are similar scalene triangles.

1854 *Pereira's Polarized Light* (ed. 2) 199 Hemihedral Forms. 1. Rhombohedron. 2. Scalenohedron. **1878** Gurney *Crystallogr.* 48 A figure bounded by eight scalene triangles, which has been termed an octahedral scalenohedron.

So **scalenohedral** (-ˈhiːdrəl) *a.*, pertaining to, or having the form of, a scalenohedron.

1890 *Amer. Jrnl. Sci.* Ser. iii. XXXIX. 375 Scalenohedral, surrounded by..rhombohedral, depressions.

scalenoidal (ˌskælɪˈnɔɪdəl), *a.* *Cryst.* [f. Scalene + -oidal.] Having scalene faces.

1883 Heddle in *Encycl. Brit.* XVI. 354/2 Producing..in the dimetric system 'pyramidal' and 'scalenoidal' forms.

‖**scaˈlenon.** *Geom. Obs.* [a. Gr. σκαληνόν (sc. τρίγωνον triangle), neut. of σναληνός Scalenus.] = Scalenum.

1570 Billingsley *Euclid* i. def. xxix. 5 The angles of an Isosceles or a Scalenon, may diuersly vary. **1690** Locke *Hum. Und.* iv. vii. §9. 301 The general Idea of a Triangle,.. neither Equilateral, Equicrural, nor Scalenon; but all and none of these at once.

scalenotomy (skeɪlɪˈnɒtəmɪ). *Surg.* [f. Scalen(us + -o + -tomy.] Division or section of a scalene muscle.

1934 Romanis & Mitchiner *Sci. & Practice Surg.* (ed. 5) II. xi. 449 To produce further collapse of the apex, the operation of phrenic avulsion may be supplemented by a section of the scalene muscles. This is easily done through the same incision (scalenotomy). **1978** J. E. Bateman *Shoulder & Neck* (ed. 2) xv. 633/1 In some instances..the involvement of the paraspinal muscles, and the scalenes in particular, is prominent. Considerable relief..may be obtained by simple scalenotomy.

scalenous (skəˈliːnəs), *a.* Now *rare.* [f. L. *scalēn-us* + -ous.] = Scalene A. 1 a, b.

1656 Stanley *Hist. Philos.* v. xiii. (1687) 187/2 A Pyramid consisteth of four triangles,..each whereof is divided..into six scalenous triangles. **1710** J. Harris *Lex. Techn.* II, A Cone is called Scalenous when one side of it is longer than the other. **1728** Chambers *Cycl.* s.v. *Scalenum*, A Cylinder, whose Axis is inclined, is..said to be Scalenous. **1767** Ducarel *Anglo-Norman Antiq.* 5 The figure of this camp.. approaches nearly to that which mathematicians call a Scalenous Triangle. *c* **1850** *Rudim. Navig.* (Weale) 108 A scalenous or oblique cone.

Scalent (ˈskeɪlənt), *a.* and *sb.* *Geol.* [f. Scale *v.*³ + -ent.] Applied by H. D. Rogers to a series which with the Premeridian forms the upper part of the Silurian in the Appalachian chain.

1858 H. D. Rogers *Geol. Pennsylv.* I. 383 Scalent and Pre-Meridian Limestones of the General Tuscarora Synclinal. *Ibid.* II. ii. 754 Scalent Series, or Onondago Salt and Niagara Limestone Groups of New York.

‖**scaˈlenum,** *sb.* *Geom. Obs.* [L. (sc. *triangulum*), neut. of *scalēnus* (see next).] A scalene triangle. Also *predicatively* as *adj.* Cf. Scalenon.

1570 Billingsley *Euclid* i. def. xxvi. 4 Scalenum is a triangle, whose three sides are all vnequall. **1653** H. More *Schol. Antid. Ath.* Philos. Writ. (1712) 144 The rest of the scalenums which make up the Square. **1735** Berkeley *Def. Free-thinking* §45. 56 It [a triangle] must be neither oblique nor rectangular, neither equilateral, equicrural, nor scalenum. **1787** *Gentl. Mag.* LVII. ii. 1059/2 The true figure of the encampment is rather an isosceles than a scalenum.

‖**scalenus** (skəˈliːnəs). *Anat.* Pl. **scaleni** (-aɪ). [mod.L. (sc. *musculus*), a. Gr. σκαληνός uneven, unequal, odd (number), scalene.] One of a set of muscles of triangular form situated in the lower lateral region of the neck. Also *attrib.*

1704 J. Harris *Lex. Techn.* I, *Scaleni*, are three Muscles of the Thorax, so called from their Figure, having three unequal Sides. **1839–47** *Todd's Cycl. Anat.* III. 562/1 The *scaleni*..extending from the transverse processes to the first two ribs. **1873** Mivart *Elem. Anat.* ii. 71 In the Guinea Pig, ..the first rib bears a little spinous tubercle for the attachment of the scalenus muscle.

scalepp, obs. form of Scallop *sb.*

†**ˈscaler**¹. *Obs.* [f. Scale *sb.*¹ + -er¹.] A manufacturer of scales.

1415 in *York Myst.* Introd. p. xxiii, Cuttellers..Blade-smyth..Shethers..Scalers.

scaler² (ˈskeɪlə(r)). [f. Scale *v.*² + -er¹.]

1. One who removes scales or scale from fish, boilers, etc.

1611 Cotgr., *Escailleur*, a skaler, piller, shaler of. **1728** Rutty *Tin-Plates* in *Phil. Trans.* XXXV. 635 This..is kept as much a Secret by the Blancher, as the acid eroding Menstruum is by the Scaler. **1892** *Eastern Morn. News* (Hull) 1 June 4/8 Henry Toyne, boiler scaler.

2. An instrument for removing scales or scale.

1881 Coleman *Dental Surg. & Pathol.* xvi. 290 A.. removal of all salivary deposition from the exposed fangs of the teeth..can only be effected by very narrow sharp scalers. **1884** Knight *Dict. Mech.* Suppl., *Scaler*, a dentist's tool for removing scale or tartar from teeth. **1891** *Century Dict.*, *Scaler*, an instrument resembling a currycomb and usually made of tin, used for removing scales from fish.

3. *Austral.* and *N.Z. slang.* (See quots.)

1924 *Truth* (Sydney) 27 Apr. 6 Scaler, a fraud. *c* **1926** 'Mixer' *Transport Workers' Song Bk.* 5 (*title*) The Scaler... He waits until his dues are due, The bloke who does a scale. **1932** C. Wills *Rhymes of Sydney* (1933) 13 See the shoppers, toppers, tabs, Scalers by the score, Hopping off, Dropping off, Darting into shore. **1945** Baker *Austral. Lang.* v. 106 A *scaler* is a person who rides in a vehicle without paying, or one who decamps with money with which he has been entrusted.

scaler³ (ˈskeɪlə(r)). [f. Scale *v.*³ + -er¹.]

1. One who scales a wall or a mountain.

1568 Grafton *Chron.* II. 525 Martyn Godfrey called the scaler. **1591** Percivall *Sp. Dict.*, *Escalador*, a scaler, a pilferer, *Scalarum conscensor*. **1600** Fairfax *Tasso* xvii. xxxi, Brimarte the scaler [orig. *espugnator de le città*]. **1698** Fryer *Acc. E. India & P.* 99 Upon the Top they have piled spiked Timber to annoy the Scalers. **1862** Thornbury *Turner* I. 315 Jove hates the old scalers of heaven's walls. **1897** *Allbutt's Syst. Med.* III. 461 Nose-bleeding..which befell the first scalers of Mont-Blanc.

2. *Lumber-trade.* One who scales or measures logs.

1887 *Contemp. Rev.* May 762 Each district is supplied with its Corps of State inspectors, 'scalers', &c. **1893** *Scribner's Mag.* June 710/1 The logs..measured by the quick-witted scaler.

3. One who uses a scale in surveying.

1840 *Civil Eng. & Arch. Jrnl.* Dec. 406/1 By allowing two young hands to figure for each scaler, they check one another.

4. An electronic pulse-counter, suitable for high count-rates, in which a display or recording device is actuated after a fixed number of pulses has been received and added electronically.

1945 H. D. Smyth *Atomic Energy for Military Purposes 1939–45* 140 The scaler was set at zero. **1953** *Sci. Amer.* Mar. 105/3 As a series of pulses flows into the scaler a voltage builds up step by step... When the cut off point is reached, the tube begins to conduct and the condenser discharges, sending a single pulse from the tube's output. **1964** *Analytical Chem.* XXXVI. 2221/1 Development of the pipping scaler was stimulated by..experimental work in which it was necessary to determine time *vs.* concentration curves having a duration of a second or less. **1977** N. Freeling *Gadget* ii. 87 That's a PM—sorry, photo-multiplier tube... Sends signals here, to the amplifier, through here, that's the discriminator, to here, the scaler. **1980** J. W. Hill *Intermediate Physics* xxiii. 220 These are connected to about 400V obtained usually from a scaler, a piece of electronic apparatus which can count very rapidly using either 'dekatrons' or a digital display.

scalesman (ˈskeɪlzmən). [f. *scales*, pl. of Scale *sb.*¹ + Man *sb.*¹] A man who uses scales; a weigher.

1838 Arnold *Hist. Rome* I. xiv. 273 Five Roman citizens ..were to be present as witnesses, and a sixth, called the weigher or scalesman. **1881** *Instr. Census Clerks* (1885) 34 Railway Officials and Servants... Scalesman. **1889** *Star* 2 Jan. 4/6 Butchers.—Wanted first rate scalesman.

†**scalet.** *Obs.* [ad. It. *scaletta*, dim. of *scala* ladder. Cf. Sp. *escaleta*.] (See quot. 1876.)

1640 Hexham *Princ. Art Milt.* iii. 6 Because it may sometimes happen, that..you may be driven to dismount and remount your peece.., you must carry along with you a Fearne, a winch, or a Scalet. **1876** Voyle & Stevenson *Milit. Dict.*, *Scalet*, an ancient name given to a lifting-jack. It was chiefly used in extricating wheels from deep ruts and soft ground.

scaleton, scalfe: see Skeleton, Scalp *sb.*²

scale-up (ˈskeɪlʌp), *sb.* (*a.*) [f. vbl. phr. *to scale up* (Scale *v.*³ 4 c).] The action or result of increasing the scale of something. Also as *adj.*

1945 H. D. Smyth *Gen. Acct. Devel. Atomic Energy Mil. Purposes* viii. 82 Should the several steps in the separations process have to be developed partly by the empirical approach, there would be less risk in the scale-up of a precipitation process. **1953** *Industr. & Engin. Chem.* May 990/1 All the dimensions of the larger are *x* times those of the smaller. We call *x* the 'scale-up factor'. **1965** *Amer. Scientist* LIII. 280 These tanks are modeled..with a scaleup factor of about two. **1967** *Jane's Surface Skimmer Systems 1967–68* 49/1 In general layout, the craft represents a 'scale-up' of the configuration tested with the Raduga. **1979** *Sci. Amer.* July 79/3 The design of the 1899 kite was the basis for a scale-up version that was small enough to be flown as a kite but large enough to support a man.

scalewise (ˈskeɪlwaɪz), *a.* and *adv.* [f. Scale *sb.*³ 4 + -wise.] **A.** *adj.* = Scalar *a.* 3. **B.** *adv.* In the manner of a scale; in respect of a scale.

1931 G. Jacob *Orchestral Technique* ix. 81 Eighteenth-century trumpet parts were written very high because of the impossibility of obtaining scale-wise passages on the natural instrument except amongst the very high harmonics. **1959** *Listener* 8 Jan. 80/2 The opening cantabile theme, descending scalewise, continuously flows into more ornate melismata. **1977** *Early Music* Oct. 535/2 The interaction of *tirades* (scale-wise flourishes)..always requires some arbitrary adjustment by the player.

scaley, var. SCALY *sb.*

scalfer, scal-hot: see SKILFER, SCALD-HOT.

scalic (ˈskeɪlɪk), *a. Mus.* [f. SCAL(E *sb.*³ 4 + -IC.] = SCALAR *a.* 3.

1933 *Times Lit. Suppl.* 2 Mar. 139/1 'The Rebel Stranger'..shows in its seven versions how a tune may develop by blending scalic with figural features of melody. **1960** *Times* 5 Mar. 9/6 A scalic tune, that can sound quite unpromising. **1971** *Daily Tel.* 5 Apr. 10/3 Kempff will sometimes pedal scalic passages and is apt to be crowded out by violin accompaniments. **1979** *Early Music* Oct. 545/1 Babell's elaborations are always scalic, and on the first page of 51 the same passage, repeated sequentially, is embellished three times in an identical manner.

†**scalier.** *Obs.* [ad. F. *escalier.*] A staircase.

1652 URQUHART *Jewel* 120 A private passage, which led them to a Lanterne Scalier. **1653** —— *Rabelais* I. liii, In the midst there was a wonderful scalier or winding-staire.

scaliness (ˈskeɪlɪnɪs). [f. SCALY + -NESS.] The condition or character of being scaly.

1611 COTGR., *Tignon*, a scurfe, or scalinesse of the skin. **1818-20** E. THOMPSON *Nosologia* (ed. 3) 325 A thickened, hard, rough..texture of the integuments of the body with a tendency to scaliness. **1829** *Good's Study Med.* (ed. 3) V. 587 Red dandriff. Scaliness common to the body generally. **1899** *Allbutt's Syst. Med.* VIII. 661 Its excessive dryness, roughness, and scaliness.

†ˈ**scaling**, *sb. Obs.* [Of obscure origin; ? cf. SCAVILONES.] Some kind of garment.

1577 *Eccl. Proc. of Bp. Barnes* (Surtees) 17 Great britches gascogne hose, scalings, nor any other like monstrous and vnsemely apparell.

scaling (ˈskeɪlɪŋ), *vbl. sb.*¹ [f. SCALE *v.*¹ + -ING¹.] The action of weighing in scales; *esp.* in *Baking* and *Racing* (see SCALE *v.*¹ 1 b, 3 b).

1841 *Guide to Trade, Baker* 42 Engaged in pitching the dough, cutting, scaling off [etc.]. **1864** *Daily Tel.* 9 June, The large field anticipated [for the Hunt Cup] rendered it necessary that the business of weighing and scaling should be vigorously pushed forward.

scaling (ˈskeɪlɪŋ), *vbl. sb.*² Also 7 **skalling.** [f. SCALE *v.*² or *sb.*² + -ING¹.]

1. The action of SCALE *v.*²; the removal or peeling off of scales or scale.

1591 PERCIVALL *Sp. Dict., Escamadura*, scaling of fish. **1601** HOLLAND *Pliny* XXI. XXV. II. 141 The skalling and pilling of the face. **1686** GOAD *Celest. Bodies* I. ix. 30 The crumbling and scaling of Brick and Stone in Frosts that are extreme. **1899** *Allbutt's Syst. Med.* VIII. 553 As the spot [of psoriasis] enlarges..it often becomes very slightly raised above the surface, and the scaling is more marked.

b. In technical and manufacturing use.

1686 PLOT *Staffordsh.* 335 The plates..keeping each other also from scaleing, or being beaten..away into Cinders or wast. **1728** RUTTY *Tin-Plates* in *Phil. Trans.* XXXV. 633 The scaling will still be more expeditious, if you dissolve a little Sal-armoniack in the Vinegar. **1825** J. NICHOLSON *Oper. Mech.* 725 To prevent the copper from scaling. **1881** COLEMAN *Dental Surg. & Pathol.* xvi. 294 In the process of scaling, great care should be exercised to remove all fragmentary portions from between the teeth. *attrib.* **1840** DE LOUDE *Dentistry* 98 The dentist..will have a great number of those scaling instruments. **1853-62** BURN *Naval & Milit. Dict.* II. 227/1 Scaling oven (for tin), *fourneau à décaper.* **1875** KNIGHT *Dict. Mech Scaling-bar* (Steam.), a rod for detaching scale in boilers.

c. *concr.* That which scales off; scale, scales.

1651 FRENCH *Distill.* i. 4 To these adde the *Caput Mortuum*, of Vitriall, and Scaling of Iron. **1712** J. MORTON *Nat. Hist. Northampt.* 41 The Kealy Soil is such as is plentifully strewed with..a Stone in very small Masses... They have the Name of Keale, Kale, or Scale, for that they seem to have been Scalings of larger Masses. **1811** *Self Instructor* 534 Scalings of iron vitrified. **1894** BARING-GOULD *Deserts S. France* I. 143 Thin flakes..of the rock scale off.. and these scalings accumulate all along the foot of the escarpment.

2. Arrangement of scales.

1721 BRADLEY *Philos. Acc. Wks. Nat.* 72 To give my Reader the Satisfaction of observing..different Methods of their Scaling [*sc.* of serpents]. **1898** *Proc. Zool. Soc.* 17 May 451 On the upper side of the tail..only a few scattered hairs appear, barely hiding the rather coarse ordinary scales, but as the hair thickens the scaling becomes finer.

scaling (ˈskeɪlɪŋ), *vbl. sb.*³ [f. SCALE *v.*³]

1. a. Climbing, mounting; escalade.

*a***1513** FABYAN *Chron.* VII. ccxxx. 262 The castynge of stonys, or scalynge of the wallys, or fyllynge of the dyches. **1598** BARRET *Theor. Warres* II. i. 20 In the scaling and assaults of batteries or walles. **1655** FULLER *Ch. Hist.* I. i. §6 He daily walls them with his Providence, against the scaling of the swelling Surges. **1802** C. JAMES *Milit. Dict.* s.v. *Ladder*, The success of an attack by scaling is infallible, if they mount the 4 sides at once. **1832** G. DOWNES *Lett. Cont. Countries* I. 533 The scaling of the walls by the Duke of Savoy's troops.

†**b.** = SCALING-LADDER. *Obs. nonce-use.*

1582 STANYHURST *Æneis* II. (Arb.) 58 They clinge thee scalinges too wals.

2. In senses of SCALE *v.*³ II: Measurement or estimation of quantities; graduation (of charges, etc.); the construction of a scale. Also, measurement or grading of attributes; variation of size or scale; the action of a scaler. Also *attrib.*

*c***1710** CELIA FIENNES *Diary* (1888) 121 The scaleing hall where their stuffs are all measured. **1807** G. GREGORY *Dict. Arts & Sci.* II. 757/3 The plan being laid down, the content of the field may be found by scaling. **1875** KNIGHT *Dict. Mech., Scaling*,..the process of adjusting sights to the guns on shipboard was formerly so termed. **1877** *Michigan Rep.* XXXV. 506 The scaling at that mill would appear..to have been very carelessly kept. **1878** *N. Amer. Rev.* CXXVI. 159 Who threatened repudiation of the whole national debt if there should be resistance to such small scaling. **1899** *Westm. Gaz.* 11 Nov. 7/1 The scaling down of the fixed dividend from 7 to 6 per cent. **1929** F. N. FREEMAN in C. Murchison *Found. Experim. Psychol.* xviii. 721 The purpose of such scaling may be merely to secure items which are equally spaced in difficulty or it may also be to weigh the pupil's performance in terms of the difficulty of the items which he passes. **1938** *Rev. Sci. Instruments* IX. 221/1 No variations in the scaling factor were found for pulses varying in amplitude by a factor of six. **1949** *Nucleonics* Feb. 67/2 Several scale-of-2 circuits in tandem provide net scaling factors of 4-8-16-32-64, etc. Other designs, utilizing 'ring scalers' or modified scale-of-16 scalers yield decimal scaling ratios (10-100-1000). **1968** FOX & MAYERS *Computing Methods for Scientists & Engineers* v. 89 It is desirable that all rows and columns of [matrix] A, and also of **b**, should be of reasonable size... This can always be arranged..by appropriate scaling of the rows and columns. **1975** *IEEE Trans. Nuclear Sci.* XXII. 1580/1 Simple start-stop scaling, count = 8, frequency 53 MHz. **1979** *Sci. Amer.* July 120/3 One such manifestation of movement into a marginal niche is the scaling down of body size.

scaling (ˈskeɪlɪŋ), *ppl. a.*¹ [f. SCALE *v.*² + -ING².] That forms or sheds scales.

1897 *Allbutt's Syst. Med.* II. 219 The gradual appearance of copper-coloured scaling papules. **1898** P. MANSON *Trop. Diseases* xxxvii. 583 A ring of scaling epidermis.

scaling (ˈskeɪlɪŋ), *ppl. a.*² [f. SCALE *v.*³ + -ING².] That scales, in the senses of SCALE *v.*³ II.

1937 *Rev. Sci. Instruments* VIII. 414/1 The ultimate efficiency..is determined by the resolving power of the first stage of the scaling circuit. **1937** *Physical Rev.* LI. 1027/1 The ultimate efficiency that can be reached is fixed by the resolving power of the scaling down circuit. **1950** *Atomics* Sept. 255/1 The simplest scaling circuit is the 'scale of two'. **1961** G. R. CHOPPIN *Exper. Nuclear Chem.* iii. 43 The scaling system selects every *n*th pulse to pass on to the mechanical registers.

ˈ**scaling-ˌladder.** [SCALING *vbl. sb.*³] A ladder used in the assault of fortified places.

*c***1400** *Brut* II. 382/22 Bryggez of lethir, scaling laddres. **1412-20** LYDG. *Chron. Troy* II. 6442 Skalyng ladderis for sautis marcial. **1571** DIGGES *Pantom.* I. xxv. Hiij, You may in this manner..tell the iuste length of the scaling laders. **1697** DRYDEN *Æneid* II. 605 Some mount the scaling Ladders, some..by Posts and Pillars hold. **1739** tr. *Rollin's Anc. Hist.* III. i. I. 298 He caused rams, mantles, and scaling ladders to be got ready. **1802** C. JAMES *Milit. Dict.* s.v. *Ladder*, Scaling-ladders..are made..sometimes of flat staves, so as to move about their pins, and shut like a parallel ruler. **1893** FORBES-MITCHELL *Remin. Gt. Mutiny* 97 A number of men..carrying scaling-ladders.

b. A fireman's ladder used for scaling buildings.

1868 E. M. SHAW *Instr. Scaling Ladders* 4 The scaling ladders at present used by the Metropolitan Fire Brigade. **1888** MERRYWEATHER *Fire Brigade Handbk.* 106.

c. *Her.* A charge representing a ladder having two grappling-hooks at the top.

1780 EDMONDSON *Her.* II. Gloss., *Scaling-ladder*, in bend, between two caltraps.

scaliwag, variant of SCALLYWAG.

scall (skɔːl), *sb.* (and *a.*). *Obs.* exc. *Sc.* and *north. dial.* Also 4-6 **scalle, skalle,** 6-7 **scaul(e, skall,** 6, 9 **skal,** 7, 9 **scal.** *β. Sc.* and *north.* 4 **sca,** 6 **skaw,** 5, 7, 9 **scaw.** [prob. a. ON. *skalle* a (naturally) bald head (Sw. *skalle* skull; cf. *skallig* bald), app. a derivative of OTeut. **skal-* (whence SHALE *sb.*, SHELL *sb.*).] **A.** *sb.* A scaly or scabby disease of the skin, *esp.* of the scalp. ***dry scall***: psoriasis. ***humid*** or ***moist scall***: eczema.

honeycomb, milk, milky, ringworm scall: see the qualifying words.

α. *a***1300** *Cursor M.* 11819 In his heued he has þe scall. *c***1374** CHAUCER *To Scriv.* 3 Vnder þy long lokkes þowe most haue þe scalle. *c***1440** *Pallad. on Husb.* VI. 138 They wol been in good poynte Withouten scorf or scalle. **1526** *Grete Herball* cxxiii. (1529) Hij b, Agaynst scalles of the heed.. bruse grene camomyll. *a***1529** SKELTON *Howe the Douty Duke of Albany*, etc. 219 Wks. 1843 II. 74 Full of scabbes and scaules. **1598** SYLVESTER *Du Bartas* II. i. III. (1641) 99 Through their salt phlegms their heads were hid wth skalls. **1601** HOLLAND *Pliny* XX. ix. II. 52 It mundifieth the skurfe or dandruffe in the head, the running scalls likewise that are bred there. **1611** BIBLE *Lev.* xiii. 30 A dry skall, euen a leprosie vpon the head or beard. *Ibid.* xiv. 54 This is the law for all manner plague of leprosie and skall. **1694** SALMON *Bate's Dispens.* 157/1 The Leprosie, white Scall, and all sorts of Ulcers which are not corroding. **1829** *Good's Study Med.* (ed. 3) V. 641 The furfuraceous or branny scall..is often mistaken for a pityriasis or lepriasis, particularly where it appears in the scalp. **1833** TODD in *Cycl. Pract. Med.* I. 671 Ecthyma..papulous scall.

β. *c***1375** *Sc. Leg. Saints* xxxvi. (*Baptista*) 1067, & þar-to sic a sca had he þat of his body nocht was fre. *a***1450** *Ratis Raving* I. 182 The lypir and the faland Ill, Wild fyre and scaw. **1536** BELLENDEN *Cron. Scot., Descr. Alb.* x. Cj, This oulie hes ane singulare virtew aganis all maner of cankir and skawis. **1867** E. B. RAMSAY *Scot. Life & Char.* v. (ed. 15) 115, I've had..the scaw [*note*, The itch]. **1870** J. K. HUNTER *Life Studies* xxvi. 190 Brimstone and butter was..the great medium for curin' the scaw.

b. *attrib.*: **scall-bladder**, a vesicle of eczema (*Syd. Soc. Lex.* 1897).

B. *attrib.* or *adj.* = SCALLED. Also Comb., ***scall-patched*** adj.

1598 SHAKS. *Merry W.* III. i. 123 To be reuenge on this same scall-scuruy-cogging-companion the Host of the Garter. **1602** *Narcissus* (1893) 569 Goe to, y'are a scall scabbe. **1632** LITHGOW *Trav.* I. 3 Shallow scal-patch'd pates.

scall, obs. form of SCALE *v.*³

‖ˈ**scallag.** [Gael. *sgalag* = Ir. *sgológ.* Cf. SCOLOC.] A predial bondsman in the Hebrides.

1666 J. FRASER *Polichron.* (S.H.S.) 84 The very place named Bearn ni Scallag, that is, the Servants Gap, becaus the men who did the slaughter were servants and scallags. **1793** J. L. BUCHANAN *Trav. W. Hebrides* Introd. 6 The scallag, whether male or female, is a poor being, who, for mere subsistence, becomes a predial slave to another. **1807** J. HALL *Trav. Scot.* II. 549 The state of our negroes is paradise compared with that of the scallag.

†ˈ**scallard**, *sb.* (and *a.*) *Obs.* [f. SCALL + -ARD. Cf. SCABBARD *sb.*²] One who has the 'scall'.

*c***1440** *Promp. Parv.* 442/1 Scallarde (*S.* scallar), *glabrio.* **1530** PALSGR. 265/2 Scallarde, *tigneux.*

b. *attrib.* or *adj.* ? Wretched, mean.

*c***1580** J. HOOKER *P. Carew* in *Archæologia* XXVIII. 124 The saye syde, wheare as was a scallarde fysher boate provyded for theyme to carry theyme into Englande.

scallawag, variant of SCALLYWAG.

scalled (skɔːld), *a.* Now *rare.* Also 4 **scallede, scallid, scaled,** 5 **skallyd, skallid,** 5-6 **scallyd,** 6 **skalled.** [f. SCALL + -ED².] = SCALD *a.* ***scalled-head*** = SCALD-HEAD.

1340 *Ayenb.* (1866) 224 þe mezels, þe dyaue, þe doumbe, þe ssoruede, þe scallede. *c***1386** CHAUCER *Prol.* 627 With scaled browes blake and piled berd. **1426** LYDG. *De Guil. Pilgr.* 14676 And I kan sette (or folk take hed) A Coyffe vp-on a skallyd heed. **1530** TINDALE *Pract. Prel.* C, As the maner of scalled horses is, the one to clawe the other. **1546** PHAER *Regim. Life, Bk. Childr.* S vij, The heades of chyldren are oftentimes vlcered, & scalled. **1655** FULLER *Ch. Hist.* II. 97 A Dumb Youth, with a scalled head. **1829** *Good's Study Med.* (ed. 3) V. 637 *Ecpyesis Porrigo galeata.* Scalled head. **1871** NAPHEYS *Prev. & Cure Dis.* III. iv. 732 Scalled head and other troublesome skin diseases.

Hence †ˈ**scalledness**, scabbiness.

1398 TREVISA *Barth. De P.R.* VII. iii. (Bodl. MS.), Vnneþe suche skalles oþer schorfe is yheeled but somme for oþer skallednes oþer pillednes leue and beþ isene alwaye þerafter. **1530** PALSGR. 265/2 Scallydnesse, *roignevseté.*

scallet (ˈskælɪt). *local.* Also -ot. A bed of freestone in Wiltshire and Somerset.

1825 in Britton *Beauties Wilts.* III. 414 The upper beds [of the Portland series of oolitic rock] are known to the quarry-men by the name of the *Scallot beds.* **1839** *Civil Eng. & Arch. Jrnl.* Oct. 376/2 The scallet, which is the finest in grain, is used for ashlar.

scallet, obs. variant of SCALADE.

†ˈ**scalling**, *ppl. a. Obs.* [f. SCALL + -ING².] Producing 'scall' or scab.

1659 GAUDEN *Slight Healers* (1660) 93 To..infect the whole body with that itch, and scab, or scalling humor.

scallion (ˈskæliən). Forms: 4 **scalone, scaloun,** 5 **scalon, scalyone,** 5-6 **scalyon,** 6 **scallyon,** 6-7 **scalion,** 7 **skallion,** 6- **scallion.** [a. AF. *scal(o)un* = OF. *eschalo(i)gne*:—pop.L. **escalonia*, for class. L. *Ascalōnia* (sc. *cæpa* onion), f. *Ascalon*, name of a seaport of Palestine. Cf. Sp. *escalona*; also It. *scalogno* (:—*Ascalōnium*, sc. *allium*).]

a. The shallot. *U.S.* **b.** The Welsh onion or 'chibol'. **c.** An onion which fails to bulb but forms a long neck and strong blade; = *spring onion* s.v. SPRING *sb.*¹ 7 b. **d.** *U.S.* = LEEK 1.

13.. *Coer de L.* 6834 For thy lyff and thy barouns He wyl not geve two skalouns. **1393** LANGL. *P. Pl.* C. IX. 310 Perselye and scalones, Chiboles and chiruylles. *a***1400** *Octouian* 1313 He seyde hy ner worth a scaloun Alle y-fere. *c***1420** *Palladius on Husb.* IV. 635 In oil & Iuce of scalons longe With pepur mixt, ennoynte her pomys. **1547** BOORDE *Brev. Health* xv. 12 b, They muste eat no salades, garlyke, ramsons, onyons, chybolles, or scalyons. **1551** TURNER *Herbal* 96 A scalyon differeth from an onyon in that it hath a great deale lesse heade and a longer neck, and thycker. **1596** NASHE *Saffron Walden* F 2 Not content to..sustaine his hungry bodie with wythred scallions and greene cheese. **1620** VENNER *Via Recta* vii. 139 Scallions and Chibols are much of the nature of Onions. **1699** [see CIBOL]. **1786** ABERCROMBIE *Gard. Assist.* 9 Let such as have sprouted be planted for Spring scallions. **1855** DELAMER *Kitch. Gard.* 39 To supply..a substitute for scallions, whether the term is interpreted to mean the green tops of onions which do not bulb in the spring and the shoots from old bulbs of the preceding or former years, or the Welsh onion. **1882** *Garden* 30 Dec. 577/1 Scallions find favour with many who object to Onions generally. **1902** L. H. BAILEY *Cycl. Amer. Hort.* IV. 1622/2 Scallion, a name for the Shallot; also used for onions that do not make good bulbs but remain with thick necks. **1943** H. M. FOX *Gardening for Good Eating* ix. 135 When the [onion] seedlings are thinned, they can be eaten as scallions. **1963** [see *dandelion greens* s.v. DANDELION 3]. **1965** P. DE VRIES *Let me count Ways* xii. 159 Several stalks of crisp celery and a scallion or two left over from my lunch. **1969** *Yearbk. Agric.* (U.S. Dept. Agric.) 189/2 Green onions, shallots, and leeks are sometimes called 'scallions'. **1978** *Chicago* June 217/1 Other delicacies might be fresh crab legs

..and transparent noodles studded with shrimp, scallions, and black mushrooms.

attrib. and *Comb.* c**1550** LLOYD *Treas. Health* xiii. Fiij b, Put oyle & scalion seed together. **1580** BARET *Alv.*, A Scallion onion, *Ascalonia.* a**1625** BEAUM. & FL. *Love's Cure* II. i, What a scallion fac'd-rascall 'tis!

ˈscallom, *v. Basket-making.* Also **scallum**. [Of obscure origin.] *trans.* (See quot.) Hence **ˈscallomed** *ppl. a.*, **ˈscalloming** *vbl. sb.*

1875 *Encycl. Brit.* III. 423/1 These [*sc.* the stout osiers that are to form the ribs of the basket] are forced or plaited, 'scallumed', between the rods of the bottom from the edge to the centre, and are turned up, 'upset', in the direction of the sides. **1912** T. OKEY *Art of Basket-Making* vii. 80 When the side stakes are scallomed on. **1929** A. G. KNOCK *Fine Willow Basketry* 61 To the curved part of the hoop, eight stakes are now scallomed. *Ibid.* 62 In scalloming a long tongue is formed at the butt-end of the stake. **1959** D. WRIGHT *Baskets & Basketry* ii. 45 The sticks are scallomed, that is: thinned down to a long, flat point and taken round the frame... Scalloming is easier to work with willow than with cane because the rods kink and stay rigid when dry. *Ibid.* iv. 114 This basket and its lid are made on a scallomed base.

scallom (ˈskæləm), *sb. Basket-making.* [Of obscure origin: see SCALLOM *v.*] A stake or rod, of which a thin or spliced end is wrapped round another stake to form a base or frame of a basket; the method of weaving baskets thus.

1912 T. OKEY *Art of Basket-Making* vii. 75 Bottoms and covers may also be made on hoops and scalloms. *Ibid.* Gloss. 154 *Scallom*, a method of forming the rigid inner frame of a bottom or cover, or of staking up a basket. **1929** A. G. KNOCK *Fine Willow Basketry* 18 *Scallom*, a stake, or the equivalent of a bottom-stick or lid-stick which has been affixed by looping its thinned end round a hoop or the outside stick of a bottom. **1959** *Gloss. Terms Packaging* (*B.S.I.*) 16 *Scallom*, the spliced end of a stake which is wrapped round the bottom outside stick and woven into the next two scalloms. **1959** D. WRIGHT *Baskets & Basketry* iv. 115, 5 scalloms of No. 12 cane run from end to end. *Ibid.* vi. 136 *Scallom*, method of fixing stakes to a ring of willow or cane.

scallop, scollop (ˈskɒləp, ˈskæləp), *sb.* Forms: α. 5 **scalap, -opp**, 5, 7 **scalop, skalop**, 6 **scalepp, -oppe, scallopp(e, skallap, -op**, 9 **scallope, scallap**, 6– **scallop**. β. 7 **s(c)kollop**, 7–8 **scollup**, 7– **-op.** [aphetic a. OF. *escalope*: see ESCALLOP.

While the pronunciation (ˈskɒləp) is still common in all uses, the spelling *scollop* appears now to be confined to sense 2, and even in that application is less usual than *scallop*.]

1. a. A shell-fish of the genus *Pecten*.

α. c**1440** *Promp. Parv.* 442/2 Scalop, fysche [*Winch. MS.* Scalap]. **1530** PALSGR. 265/2 Scaloppe a fysshe. **1601** HOLLAND *Pliny* XI. li. I. 353 The great Scallops make a certaine noise as they shoot out of the water. **1617** MORYSON *Itin.* I. 70 The skalops which they call holy cockels, twelue for a lire. **1626** BACON *Sylva* §747 No Liuing Creatures, that haue Shells very hard; (As Oysters, Cockles, Mussles, Scallops). c**1711** PETIVER *Gazophyl.* vii. 62 Madras spotted Scallop. **1716** GAY *Trivia* II. 417 And luscious 'scallops, to allure the tastes Of rigid zealots to delicious fasts. **1802** BINGLEY *Anim. Biog.* (1813) III. 454 The Scallop has the power of progressive motion upon land, and likewise of swimming on the surface of the water. **1841** T. R. JONES *Anim. Kingd.* xxii. 391 In the Scallops (*Pecten*) the edges of the mantle are studded with..pearl-like points.

β. **1630** J. TAYLOR (Water P.) *Wks.* I. 117/1 The blushing Prawne, the well-armed Oyster, the Scollop, the Wilke. **1646** SIR T. BROWNE *Pseud. Ep.* v. i. 234 Oysters, Cochles, Sckollops, and other testaceous animals. **1661** RABISHA *Cookery Dissected* 125 First boyl your Scollups, then take them out of the shells and wash them. **1705** *Phil. Trans.* XXV. 2160 (2), I took this..Scollop and Sea Horn.

b. A scallop-shell; a vessel resembling one, used in baptism, etc.

α. **1401** *Durham Acc. Rolls* (Surtees) 452 Item j scalap et j navis argent' deaurat'. **1408** *Ibid.* 402 Et in I scalopp argent. pro sale benedicendo. **1639** T. HEYWOOD *Londini Status Pacatus* A4b, A person representing the ancient River Nilus, mounted in a Sea-Chariot, and seated upon a silver Scallop. **1796** MORSE *Amer. Geog.* I. 357 A lump, taken fresh from the stratum,..exhibits, in perfect shape, innumberable muscle shells, scallops, &c.

β. **1752** POCOCKE *Tour* (1891) 87 The woman also melted tallow in a scollop and dipt the rushes in it.

c. A pilgrim's cockle-shell worn as a sign that he had visited the shrine of St. James at Compostella.

?a**1400** *Morte Arth.* 3474 With scrippe, ande with slawyne, and skalopis i-newe, Both pyke and palme, alles pilgram hym scholde. **1501** *Bury Wills* (Camden) 83 The stooll..coloord and garnyschyd wt scalepps and othyr sygnys of Seynt Jamys. **1532** in Weaver *Wells Wills* (1890) 186 My bedes with scallopps. **1710** PARNELL *Hermit* 25 The pilgrim-staff he bore, And fix'd the scallop in his hat before. **1871** LOWELL *Study Wind., Pope* 291 As little typical of the inward man as the scallop of a pilgrim.

2. a. An object of the shape of a scallop-shell; a part or formation resembling a scallop-shell.

1609 *Test. Ebor.* (Surtees) V. 5, I will have my *Derege* in my house,..and at Mr. Perot be at the same dener; and at tharbe skallapis of mayne breid. **1629** DEKKER *London's Tempe* (Percy Soc.) 43 Bases and buskins cut..at the top into silver scollups. **1668** CULPEPPER & COLE *Barthol. Anat.* I. xiv. 32 A Mans Liver is not divided into Laps or Scollops. **1688** HOLME *Armoury* III. 374/1 The Scallop, as covers the Winding hole [in a watch].

b. *esp.* One of a series of convex rounded projections forming the scalloped edge of a garment or other object. Also, a scalloped form, a scalloping.

This use prob. has a double origin; a 'scalloped' edge may be compared either to a row of scallop-shells, or to the edge of a scallop-shell.

1612 BEAUMONT *Masque of Inner Temple* D b, The hinder part cut into Scallops, answering the skirts of their doublets. c**1710** CELIA FIENNES *Diary* (1888) 16 All of them gather'd up ye upper peticoate in little scallops. **1713** *Guardian* 1 Sept., The Men have contented themselves with the Retrenchment of the Hat, or the various Scallop of the Pocket. **1768** PENNANT *Brit. Zool.* (1776) II. 414 Four scollops on the exterior toe..each finely serrated on their edges. **1839–47** BOWMAN in *Todd's Cycl. Anat.* III. 508/1 Thus giving a slight scallop, or regular indentation, to the edge. **1867** AUGUSTA WILSON *Vashti* iv, The girl sewed on, working scallop after scallop, and flower after flower. **1886** MISS C. F. WOOLSON *East Angels* ix, The beach waved in and out in long scallops.

†**c.** Lace or edging of a scalloped pattern; a scalloped lace band or collar. *Obs.*

1603 in *38th Rep. Dep. Kpr. Rec.* App. 444 Stamells, stanimes, scallops, tapessary or tapestry. **1661** PEPYS *Diary* 7 Dec., My wife and I were talking about buying of a fine scallop..which is to cost her 45*s*.

3. *attrib.* and *Comb.*, as (sense 1) ***scallop-bank, bed, boat, dredge, -fishery, net***; (sense 2) ***scallop-wise*** adv.; quasi-adj. = 'scalloped', as ***scallop capital, lace, moulding, tile, top; scallop-edged, -leaved, -necked, -shaped, -striped, -tailed, -toed, -winged*** adjs.; **scallop budding** (see quot.); **scallop crab**, a pea-crab inhabiting scallops; **scallop hook tip** (see quot.); †**scallop-iron** (see quot.); †**scallop slate**, ? shale containing fossil scallops; †**scallop-stone**, ? a fossil pecten.

1851 WOODWARD *Mollusca* iii. 12 *Scallop-banks at twenty fathoms. **1977** *N.Z. Herald* 8 Jan. 1-2/3 *Scallop beds around the Coromandel Harbour could be wiped out within five years if the onslaught of spiked dredges used mainly by holiday-makers continued. **1977** *New Yorker* 15 Aug. 46/1 The Sniktaw III, a forty-foot **scallop boat*, is moving rapidly south-ward down the channel. **1825** *Greenhouse Comp.* I. 234 The *scallope or French mode of budding, in which a section or scallope of bark and wood containing a bud is taken from one tree, and applied to a part of the stem of another tree, where a similar scallope had been removed. **1862** *Rickman's Archit.* (ed. 6) 138 The *scollop capitals are..frequently used. **1884** *U.S. National Mus. Bull.* No. 27. 268 Implements [used in shellfish fishery include]..*Scallop-dredge. **1887** GOODE, etc. *Fisheries U.S.* v. II. 571 The ordinary scallop dredge holds from one to two bushels. **1856** W. WHITMAN *Leaves of Grass* (ed. 2) xi. 214, I saw..the *scallop-edged waves in the twilight. **1967** R. S. CHURCHILL *Winston S. Churchill* II. viii. 274 A splendid scallop-edged silver tray presented by all his colleagues in the Government. **1886** *Amer. Naturalist* XX. 1001 It is only between Cape Cod and New Jersey that any commercial *scallop-fishery exists. **1829** J. F. STEPHENS *Catal. Brit. Insects* II. 156 *Platypteryx..lacertula*..*Scallop Hook-tip. **1688** HOLME *Armoury* III. 397/1 Sadlers Tools..a Larg *Scallop Iron,..being a kind of Punch to cut Leather Scallop wise. **1706** *Hudibras Rediv.* (Nares), Pinners.. Edg'd round with ancient *scollop laces. **1822** *Hortus Anglicus* II. 76 *Scollop-leaved Iron Wort. **1848** *Rickman's Archit.* (ed. 5) p. xx, Two varieties of *scallop mouldings. **1783** LATHAM *Synopsis Birds* IV. 643 *Scallop-necked Pigeon. **1881** E. INGERSOLL *Oyster-Industry* 247 **Scallop Net*, the small dredge used in catching scallops. **1843** R. J. GRAVES *Syst. Clin. Med.* xxvi. 334 *Scollop-shaped condylomata. c**1711** PETIVER *Gazophyl.* vi. 51 Flat thin *Scallop Slate. **1668** CHARLETON *Onomast.* 267 *Pectinitis* ..*Scollop-stone. **1873** BROWNING *Red Cott. Nt.-cap* 567 One level, *scallop-striped With bands of beet and turnip and luzern. **1802** SHAW *Gen. Zool.* III. 276 *Scollop-tailed Gecko. **1728** CHAMBERS *Cycl.* s.v. *Tyle*, *Scallop or Astragal Tyles,..their lower Ends are in Form of..a Semicircle, with a Square on each Side. **1674** RAY *S. & E.C. Words* 92 A bird of the Coot kind, *scollop-toed. **1843** YARRELL *Brit. Birds* I. Index p. xxvii, Scallop-toed Sandpiper. **1711** ADDISON *Spect.* No. 128 ¶10 A Pair of Shoes with high *Scollop Tops. **1749** B. WILKES *Eng. Moths & Butterflies* 39 The *Scallop wing'd Moth laid her Eggs on the 5th of August. **1829** J. F. STEPHENS *Catal. Brit. Insects* II. 97 *Cymatophora..Oo*..Scallop-winged Oak M[oth]. **1558** in Feuillerat *Revels Q. Eliz.* (1908) 38 Greane vellvet cutt in leaves *scallopwise. **1688** [see *scallop-iron*].

ˈscallop, ˈscollop, *v.* [f. SCALLOP *sb.*]

1. *trans.* To shape or cut (*out*) in the form of a scallop-shell; to ornament or trim with scallops.

1749 SHENSTONE *Irreg. Ode after Sickness* 100 To fence for you my shady grove And scollop ev'ry winding shore. **1760–72** H. BROOKE *Fool of Qual.* (1809) IV. 155 A vest of silver brocading, scalloped over a petticoat of the same fabric. **1771** SMOLLETT *Humph. Cl.* 26 June (1815) 197 This fellow..having no inclination to curry any beast out of the stable, was at great pains to scallop his nails in such a manner that the blood followed at every stroke. **1809** PINKNEY *Trav. France* 203 It fits closely, and is scolloped round the neck, arms, and at the bottom. a**1810** J. HENRY *Camp. agst. Quebec* (1812) 21 The face of the rock was, as it were scalloped out, down to the water's edge. **1836** HOR. SMITH *Tin Trump.* I. 44 The bow windows and balconies that scallop the narrow side streets. **1908** *Blackw. Mag.* July 101/2 Their edges are elaborately scalloped with a drop of clear water lodged in each rounded notch.

b. *Mining.* (See quot.)

1883 GRESLEY *Gloss. Coal-mining*, *Scallop*, to cut..the sides of a heading without holing them, or using powder.

2. *Cookery.* To bake (oysters, etc.) in a scallop-shell or similar-shaped pan or plate with bread crumbs, cream, butter, and condiments.

1737 [see SCALLOPED 2]. **1769** MRS. RAFFALD *Eng. House-kpr.* (1778) 287 To scollop Potatoes. Boil your potatoes, then beat them fine [etc.],..put them into scollop shells,.. put them in a Dutch oven [etc.]. **1841** J. T. HEWLETT *Parish Clerk* II. 75 Lobsters, boiled, scalloped, and hot-buttered. **1885** E. P. WRIGHT *Anim. Life* 555 The shell [of the scallop *Pecten maximus*] is often used for 'scalloping' oysters.

scalloped, scolloped (ˈskɒləpt, ˈskæləpt), *ppl. a.* Also α. 8 **scallaped**, 9 **scallopped, scallopt.** β. 8 **scollopt**, 9 **scoloped.** [f. SCALLOP *sb.* or *v.* + -ED.]

1. Having the border, edge, or outline cut into a series of segments of circles resembling a scallop-shell. **a.** *Nat. Hist.* (Sometimes the specific name of an animal or plant: see quots.)

α. **1682** GREW *Anat. Pl.* III. I. i. 105 A scalloped Parenchymous Ring, or a Ring of many short and slender white Arches. **1778** M. HARRIS *Aurelian* p. xvii, Inferior Wing scallaped. **1793** MARTYN *Lang. Bot.*, *Scalloped leaf*, this term may be applied to the *folium Repandum*. **1819** J. F. STEPHENS in *Shaw's Gen. Zool.* XI. 43 The feathers that cover the sides of the neck are scalloped in the centre. **1821** CLARE *Vill. Minstr.* II. 111 Scallop'd briony. **1869** [see *hook-tip*, HOOK *sb.*[1] 19]. **1900** B. D. JACKSON *Gloss. Bot. Terms*, *Scalloped*, crenate.

β. **1768** PENNANT *Brit. Zool.* (1776) II. 414 The toes extremely singular, being edged with scolloped membranes like the coot. **1819** SAMOUELLE *Entomol. Compend.* 423 Geometra emarginata. The scolloped Double-line. **1872** COUES *N. Amer. Birds* 51 The lobation may be either scolloped, or cut out at the joints, as in the coot, or plain.

Comb. [cf. SCALLOP *sb.* 3]. **1832** J. RENNIE *Consp. Butterfl. & Moths* Index, Scolloped Winged Broad Bar.

b. Of articles of dress.

1687 *Lond. Gaz.* No. 2234/4 A brown colour close-bodied Coat, with scollop'd Pockets. **1716** GAY *Trivia* I. 32 The wooden Heel may raise the Dancer's Bound, And with the scallop'd Top his Step be crown'd. **1863** LONGF. *Wayside Inn, Sicilian's T.* 83 The King's Jester, thou Henceforth shalt wear the bells and scalloped cape. **1888** *Lady* 25 Oct. 378/1 Cloth hats and bonnets, with scalloped edges.

c. Of utensils, architectural features, etc.

1766 *Compl. Farmer* s.v. *Mole* 5 O 4/2 Scoop them out at once, with what Mr. Bradley calls a scolloped mole-hill plough. **1840** BUEL *Farmer's Comp.* 150 The concave, or scolloped roller, is adapted to the form of ridges. **1870** F. R. WILSON *Ch. Lindisf.* 176 The caps of the columns..are scalloped. **1881** YOUNG *Every Man his own Mechanic* §9/2 Leather edging with scalloped edges or strips of American leather cloth should be attached to the shelves.

2. *Cookery.* (See SCALLOP *v.* 2.)

1737 *Ochtertyre House Bk. Acc.* (1907) 3 Scollopt oysters. **1791** HUDDESFORD *Salmag.* 93 And shoals of bawling choristers He ate, like scallop'd oysters. **1827** HONE *Every-day Bk.* II. 58 Stewed oysters! I ordered scolloped! **1877** *Home Keeper's Guide* 45 Scalloped tomatoes. **1884** *New Kentucky Home Cook Bk.* 157 Scalloped potatoes. **1925** W. G. R. FRANCILLON *Good Cookery* (ed. 3) 435 *Scalloped Oysters*... Butter a scallop shell. Arrange layers of crumbs, oysters, and butter alternately... Bake. **1936** *Farmhouse Fare* 10 *Scalloped Meat with Macaroni*... Arrange..cooked macaroni, meat, and gravy in alternate layers...cover the top with browned breadcrumbs...bake. **1960** *Woman* 23 Apr. 51/1 Scalloped Ham... Layer potatoes, onions and ham in the casserole... Pour in milk... Bake in moderate oven. **1975** B. WOOD *Killing Gift* (1976) v. iv. 243 Scalloped potatoes..next to the roast.

3. Wearing a scallop-shell. *rare.*

1832 G. DOWNES *Lett. Cont. Countries* I. 324 A pilgrim regularly scalloped.

scalloper (ˈskɒləpə(r)). [f. SCALLOP *v.* and *sb.* + -ER[1].] **a.** One who makes scalloped ornament, etc. **b.** One who gathers scallops.

1881 *Instr. Census Clerks* (1885) 70 Lace Finishing... Scolloper. *Ibid.* 89 Glass Scolloper. **1887** GOODE, etc. *Fisheries U.S.* v. II. 577 At Wickford, R.I., there live a few scallopers, and three boats are owned.

ˈscalloping, ˈscolloping, *vbl. sb.* [f. SCALLOP *sb.* or *v.* + -ING[1].] The action of the vb. SCALLOP. Also *concr.*, scalloped ornament, edging, marking, or the like.

a**1800** *Peggy Irvine* iv. in Child *Ballads* V. 301/2 Her petticoats was of the silk so fine, set out with the silver and scolloping. **1889** A. R. WALLACE *Darwinism* 255 Minute examination detects differences in form and scalloping of the wings.

attrib. **1875** KNIGHT *Dict. Mech.*, *Scalloping-tool* (*Saddlery*), a tool for giving an ornamental edge to leather straps.

So **ˈscalloping** *ppl. a.*, forming 'scallops'.

18.. WHITTIER *Prose Wks.* (1889) II. 381 A long scalloping range of hills.

scallopini (skæləʊˈpiːnɪ). Also in It. form ‖**scaloppine.** [ad. It. *scaloppine*, pl. of *scaloppina*, dim. of *scaloppa* ESCALOPE.] A dish consisting of very thin slices of meat (esp. veal) sautéed or fried.

1950 E. HEMINGWAY *Across River & into Trees* 103 The scaloppine with Marsala. **1957** F. & R. LOCKRIDGE *Tangled Cord* (1959) vi. 73 The waiter..heated and served scallopini. **1975** *Times* 6 Sept. 9/1 In Cardiff..it is easier to find well-cooked scaloppine and cannelloni than anything in the native tradition. **1977** J. WAMBAUGH *Black Marble* (1978) iv. 46 Sal Moroni got arrested for throwing a Sicilian cook out the window of an Italian restaurant for overcooking his scallopini.

ˈscallop-shell. Cf. ESCALLOP-SHELL.

1. The shell of the scallop, or, more usually, one valve of it: freq. with reference to its being a pilgrim's badge. (Cf. note s.v. ESCALLOP-SHELL.)

1530 PALSGR. 265/2 Scaloppe shell, *quocquille de saint Jacques.* **1562** *Inv. St. Margaret's Westm.* in *Malcolm's Londinium* IV. 137 One Cope of crimson velvet with scallop shells of silver. a**1618** RALEIGH *Pilgrimage* 1 Give me my

Scollap-Shell of Quiet, My Staff of Faith to lean upon. **1747** MRS. GLASSE *Cookery* ix. 95 Put your Oysters into Scollop-shells for that purpose. **1819** SCOTT *Ivanhoe* xxviii, By the scallop-shell of Compostella, I will make a martyr of him. *attrib.* **1807** W. IRVING *Salmag.* (1811) II. 102 The outside of the boxes inlaid with scallop shell-work.

2. Collectors' name for the moth *Triphosa* (*Eucosmia*) *undulata*.

1829 J. F. STEPHENS *Catal. Brit. Insects* II. 140.

scallum, var. SCALLOM *v.*

†**'scally**, *a. Obs. rare.* [f. SCALL + -Y.] = SCALLED. Cf. SCALY *a.* 4.

1530 PALSGR. 323/1 Scally or scourfy, *roigneux.* **1699** DAMPIER *Voy.* II. II. 74 Over its [the Alligator's] Eyes there are two hard scally Knobs, as big as a Mans Fist.

Hence †**'scalliness.** (Cf. SCALINESS.)

1610 MARKHAM *Masterp.* I. xcv. 189 Any drynesse or scallynesse of the skinne.

scallywag, scallawag ('skælɪwæg, -əwæg). *slang* or *colloq.* (orig. *U.S.*) Also 9 scal(l)i-, scala-, scallo-, skalle-. [Origin obscure.]

1. A disreputable fellow; a good-for-nothing; a scapegrace, blackguard; in *Trade Union slang*, a man who will not work. Also *attrib.*

1848 BARTLETT *Dict. Amer.*, *Scalawag*, a favorite epithet in western New York for a mean fellow; a scape-grace. **1855** HALIBURTON *Nature* I. 112 You good-for-nothing young scallowag. **1885** G. B. SHAW *Let.* 4 Sept. (1965) I. 138 Any socialist of the plentiful 'scallawag' type. **1893** LELAND *Mem.* II. 178 There are so many scallawags from the East come here, that we are obliged to be a little particular. **1891** *Labour Commission* Gloss., *Scalliwags*, an opprobrious term, equal to scamp or villain, applied to men who will not work. **1926** *Glasgow Herald* 10 Sept. 11 Go back to your scallywag union. **1957** *Listener* 17 Oct. 608/2 Voyez, that rather scallywag wanderer who was dismissed by Wedgwood.

2. An impostor or intriguer, esp. in politics; in *U.S. Hist.*, a native white of the southern states who was willing to accept the reconstructionary measures. Also *attrib.*

1862 *Charleston* (S. Carolina) *Mercury* 9 Aug. 1/3 This invaluable class is composed..of ten parts of unadulterated Andy Johnson Union men, ten of good lord and good devilites, five of spuss and seventy-five of scallowags. **1864** SALA in *Daily Tel.* 27 Sept., The councilmen too often belong to the comprehensive genus 'scallywag'. They have intrigued and speechified, and stumped their ward. **1867** *Nation* (N.Y.) 12 Dec. 470/1 The Macon *News* has to print in full the names of thirteen persons..described (as having 'voted the Scalawag ticket'). **1879** TOURGEE *Fool's Err.* (1883) 111/25. **1885** *Times* (weekly ed.) 29 May 12 Our correspondent tells us that the new system [*i.e.* of Mental Healing] has not yet fallen into the hands of the 'Scalawags'. **1886** *Forum* Apr. 128 Then came the absurd process called Reconstruction, with its swarm of leeches, carpet-baggers and Scalawags. **1888** J. BRYCE *Amer. Commonwealth* II. II. xliv. 164 A group of such 'scallawag' members..increase their legislative income.

3. *U.S.* A name for undersized or ill-conditioned cattle. Perhaps the original use of the word.

1854 *New York Tribune* (Cattle Rep.) 24 Oct. (Cent. Dict.), The number of miserable 'scallawags' is so great that ..they tend to drag down all above themselves to their own level. **1868** *Daily News* 18 Sept., Wade Hampton explained the origin of the term..by saying that 'scalawag' was the name applied by drovers to lean and ill-favoured kine.

Hence **scally'waggery**, (*a*) roguery, (*b*) political opportunism; **'scallywagism** = *scally-waggery* (*a*); **'scallywagging** *vbl. sb.*, *ppl. a.*

1897 *Daily News* 9 Dec. 7/1 The stages of accumulating merit for the fighting man, as Lord Charles gives them, appear to be first robbing orchards, next hatred of a life at the desk, and finally scallywagism. *Ibid.*, Robbing orchards and general scallywaggery is not within them [*sc.* disqualifications for military service]. **1911** H. S. HARRISON *Queed* iv. 45 The morning *Post* was an old paper... It had crucified carpet-baggism and scalawaggery upon a cross of burning adjective. **1915** W. J. LOCKE *Jaffery* xii. 158 He was fed up with scalliwagging all over the place. He wanted a season in town! **1962** *Punch* 9 May 735/1 Wilkes is worth writing about..for all his scallywaggery. **1977** *Times* 18 Aug. 6/1 Mr. Frank Johnson..has unimpeachable credentials as a civil rights defender. Governor George Wallace of Alabama once denounced him as 'a scallywaggin', integratin', carpet-baggin' liar'.

scalmuse, scalop(e, scalo(u)n, scalour: see SHAWM, SCALLOP, SCALLION, SQUALOR.

scalogram ('skeɪləʊgræm). *Psychol.* [f. SCAL(E *sb.*[3] 6 + -O + -GRAM (perh. by analogy with *cardiogram* s.v. CARDIO-).] A diagram showing the numerical values assigned to responses and persons in an attitude test, designed esp. to analyse whether the questions relate to the same factor and the results are scalable. Also *attrib.* and *Comb.*: **scalogram analysis**, the analysis of results revealed by a scalogram; **scalogram board**, a board with movable slats on which the results are recorded.

1944 L. GUTTMAN in *Amer. Sociol. Rev.* IX. 139/2 The results of the analysis are presented and easily assimilated in the form of a 'scalogram', which at a glance gives the configuration of the qualitative data. *Ibid.* 144/1 The scalogram boards used in practical procedures are simply devices for shifting rows and columns to find a scale pattern if it exists. **1950** S. A. STOUFFER *Measurement & Prediction* i. 9 The approach which was developed in the Research Branch under..Louis Guttman has been named scalogram analysis. *Ibid.*, The scalogram hypothesis is that the items have an order such that, ideally, persons who answer a given question favorably all have a higher rank on the scale than persons who answer the same question unfavorably. **1970** E. J. WILKINS *Introd. Sociol.* v. 81 The items in this type of scalogram are accorded points, both positive and negative, and they are also of a cumulative nature. **1973** *Times Lit. Suppl.* 2 Nov. 1332/2 The second [kind of historical explanation] sublimates personality, thrives upon roll-call votes and produces a scalogram to measure regularity or deviance as its finest achievement. **1978** T. H. POISTER *Public Program Anal.* x. 362 The development of the coefficient of reproducibility (also referred to as scalogram analysis) is useful for assessing the..internal consistency of a Guttman scale.

scaloppine, var. SCALLOPINI.

scalp (skælp), *sb.*[1] Also 4–7 **skalp**, 5–7 **scalpe**, 6 **skalpe**; (chiefly *Sc.*) 5, 8 **skap**, 6 **scawpe**, **skape**, 7 **scop**, 8–9 **scaup**, **scawp**, 9 **scap**. [Northern ME. *scalp*; presumably of Scandinavian origin, though the Eng. senses are not found in any Scandinavian or Teut. language. Cf. ON. *skálp-r* sheath, Da. dial. *skalp* shell, husk, MLG. *schulpe*, *scholpe*, MDu. *schelpe* (Du. *schelp*) shell; the sense of these words suggests derivation from OTeut. **skal-*, **skel-* (see SCALE *sb.*[1]), but a Teut. *p-* suffix is not known.

The It. *scalpo*, given by Oudin 1540 with the rendering *le test*, and by Florio 1611 with the rendering 'scalp', seems to be of doubtful genuineness. The Eng. word in sense 3 has passed into several European langs.: F. *scalpe*, G., Sw. *skalp*.]

1. a. The top or crown of the head; the skull, cranium. Now only *Sc.* and *north. dial.* (*scaup*, *scap*).

a **1300** *E.E. Psalter* vii. 17 His wiknes in his scalp doune falle. *c* **1400** MAUNDEV. (Roxb.) xxxiv. 153 Of þe scalpe [*v.r.* brayn panne] of þe heued he gers make him a coppe. *c* **1460** *Towneley Myst.* xvi. 353 Then thi scalp shall I clefe. *c* **1480** HENRYSON *Mor. Fab.*, *Trial of Fox* 1026 (Charteris MS.) With bludie skap, and cheikis bla and reid. **1508** DUNBAR *Test. Kennedy* 52 To hede of kyn, bot I wait nought Quis est ille, than I schrew my scawpe [*Bann. MS.* skape]. **1535** COVERDALE *Ps.* lxvii[i]. 21 The God that smyteth his enemies vpon the heades & vpon the hayrie scalpes. [Similarly **1611.**] **1541** R. COPLAND *Guydon's Quest. Chirurg.* D iij b, What is the skull or scawpe of the heade? Answere. It is that parte of the heade that is full of heare, wherin the anymal membres are conteyned. **1590** SHAKS. *Mids. N.* IV. i. 69 Take this transformed scalpe, From off the head of this Athenian swaine. **1598** STOW *Surv.* 270 In digging the foundation of this newe woorke..there were founde more then an hundred scalpes of Oxen, or Kine. **1607** TOPSELL *Four-f. Beasts* 124 [Their] hornes..grow.. not to their bones or skalps, but to their skin. **16..** *Robin Hood & Tanner* ix, If I get a knop upon the bare scop thou canst as well shite as shoote. **1650** G. P. *Comenius' Janua Ling.* xxiv. 297 If the skull [*marg.* scalp, brainpain] bee one entire bone. **1724** RAMSAY *Vision* iii, To..skonce my skap and shanks frae rain. **1899** J. LUMSDEN *Edin. Poems & Songs* 198, I wat for't sune his Scotch scap reissils.

fig. **1596** NASHE *Saffron Walden* F 2 Not content to haue the naked scalp of his credit new couered with a false periwig of commendations.

b. The head or skull of a whale exclusive of the lower jaw.

In recent Dicts.

2. a. The integument of the upper part of the head, usually covered with hair and moving freely over the underlying bones.

Formerly often †*hairy scalp*; cf. quot. 1535 in sense 1. Possibly this Bible phrase (a literal rendering of the Heb.) may have caused the development of sense 2 a.

1616 BULLOKAR *Eng. Expos.*, *Scalpe*, the haire skinne of the head. **1651** BIGGS *New Disp.* ¶259 Those fained vapours ..stirre up the tempest of the diseases causation, before they can come to the hairy scalp. **1656** BLOUNT *Glossogr.*, *Scalp* (*pericranion*), the skin compassing and covering all the skull. **1676** WISEMAN *Chirurg. Treat.* v. ix. 374 The Hairy scalp. **1725** *Bradley's Fam. Dict.* s.v. *Turning-Evil*, Then take a long sharp Knife and a Hammer, and cut the Scaup two Inches square, and turn it up. **1800** *Med. Jrnl.* III. 444 Five or six small spiculæ of bone worked themselves through the scalp, (the wound being healed). **1872** DARWIN *Emotions* xiv. 352 The naked scalp of a very young infant reddens from passion. **1894** H. DRUMMOND *Ascent Man* 117 Every one has met persons who possess the power of moving the whole scalp to and fro.

Phrase. **1842** TENNYSON *St. Sim. Styl.* 2 From scalp to sole one slough and crust of sin. **1890** TALMAGE *From Manger to Throne* 78 Christian infidels..who are from scalp to heel surcharged with unbeliefs.

transf. **1658** SIR T. BROWNE *Gard. Cyrus* iii. 47 He that inquireth into the little bottom of the globe-thistle, may finde that gallant bush arise from a scalpe of like disposure.

b. *Her.* The skin of the head of an animal.

1688 HOLME *Armoury* II. 166/1 The Horns of a Bull fixed upon the curled Skalp..with two Ears, Sable. **1722** NISBET *Syst. Her.* II. iv. 337 The Attirings of a Stag fixed to the Scalp.

c. *U.S.* The skin from the head of an animal preserved as proof of its death (usu. in order to obtain a bounty).

1703 *Narragansett Hist. Reg.* (1884–5) III. 162 All persons who shall kill any Sheep or Lambs..shall be obliged to carry in the Skalp with Ears of the same. **1847** J. S. ROBB *Streaks of Squatter Life* 80 He can git a bonus for wolf-scalps. **1890** *Stock Grower & Farmer* 22 Feb. 3/1 The bounty law must be fixed up so that scalps will be paid for. **1901** DUNCAN & SCOTT *Hist. Allen & Woodson Counties, Kansas* 15 [The county board] offered a bounty of twenty-five cents for wolf scalps.

3. a. The scalp with the hair belonging to it cut or torn from a man's head: prized by American Indians as a battle trophy.

1601 HOLLAND *Pliny* VII. ii. I. 154 The former Anthropophagi..whom we have placed about the North pole,..use..to weare the scalpes, haire and all, in steed of.. stomachers before their breasts. **1677** W. HUBBARD *Narrative* I. 19 Two or three miles further they came up with some Heads, Scalps, and Hands cut off from the bodies of some of the English. **1748** WASHINGTON *Jrnl.* 23 Mar., Writ. 1889 I. 3 We were agreeably surprized at ye sight of thirty odd Indians coming from war with only one scalp. **1781** GIBBON *Decl. & F.* xxvi. II. 24 The scalps of their enemies formed the costly trappings of their horses. **1817** J. BRADBURY *Trav. Amer.* 42 The dance of the scalp. **1837** W. IRVING *Capt. Bonneville* I. iv. 76 The chief..had his scalps to show and his battles to recount. **1867** PARKMAN *Jesuits in N. Amer.* xix. (1875) 282 Eleven fresh scalps fluttered in the wind.

b. *fig.* as the symbol of a victory gained.

1759 W. MASON *Let.* 25 Jan. in *Corr. of Thomas Gray* (1935) II. 612 Criticks like Indians are proud of the number of scalps they make in a Manuscript. **1828–40** BERRY *Encycl. Her.* II, *Dymock...* Crest..the skalp of a hare, the ears erect sa. **1870** M. D. CONWAY *Earthward Pilgr.* xxiii. 276 The savage creed that wears the scalp of Shelley at its belt. **1902** C. N. & A. M. WILLIAMSON *Lightning Conductor* 141 If I had been, that girl wouldn't have got back into the house without being proposed to, and having another 'scalp' to count, as they say American beauties do. **1928** T. E. LAWRENCE *Lett.* (1938) 571 It riles me unbearably to lose my scalp to a lot of fellows round whom I can make rings. **1977** *R.A.F. News* 11–24 May 19/1 Convincing wins..for the RAF under-21 hockey team... The Navy provided the first scalp.

4. A wig made to cover a part of the scalp.

1801 *Chron.* in *Ann. Reg.* 458 [Patent] for a method of making perukes and scalps. **1843** THACKERAY *Ravenswing* i, Mr. Eglantine, the celebrated perruquier..whose..patent ventilating scalps are known throughout Europe.

5. a. A bare piece of rock or stone standing out of water or surrounding vegetation (thus resembling a hairless skull). *Sc.* and *north. dial.* (pronounced and often written *scaup*).

1721 RAMSAY *Prospect of Plenty* 215 (1877) I. 52 Plenty shall cultivate ilk scawp and moor. **1722** *Newcastle Courant* 1 Sept. Advt. (E.D.S. 71) The Ship called the John and Margaret,..now lying upon the Scalp against Mr. Jennison's Key, North Shields. **1865** G. TATE in *Hist. Berw. Nat. Club* (1868) V. 151 On the scalp of the rock where it dips into the hill, four figures are traceable. **1871** *Daily News* 21 Aug., There there is a bare 'scaup' of boulders and scanty turf. **1903** *Expositor* Jan. 11 The grey argillaceous soil is shallow, stony and constantly interrupted by scalps, ledges and knolls of naked limestone.

b. The cap of a mountain. Chiefly *poet.*

1810 SCOTT *Lady of L.* III. ix, Ben-an's grey scalp the accents knew. **1816** BYRON *Ch. Har.* III. lxii, The Alps,.. whose vast walls Have pinnacled in clouds their snowy scalps. **1848** CLOUGH *Bothie* I. 58 The frosty scalp of the Cairn-Gorm. **1875** J. GRANT *One of the 600* III. xxi. 290 When the snows of Christmas whiten the scalps of Largo and the Lomond Hills.

6. *attrib.* and *Comb.* **a.** (sense 1) **scalp-house** *dial.*, a charnel house.

1890 *Murray's Handbk. Lincolnshire* 113 Below is a groined undercroft, known as the 'scaup (skull-) house'.

b. (sense 2), as ***scalp hair***, ***knot***, ***length***, ***-massage***, ***muscle***, ***wound***.

1805 SOUTHEY *Madoc* II. xvi, On the front it [the spear] met him, and plough'd up The whole scalp-length. **1851** H. MELVILLE *Whale* iii. 24 There was no hair on his head.. nothing but a small scalp-knot. **1868** DARWIN in *Life & Lett.* (1887) III. 99, I believe all anatomists look at the scalp-muscles as a remnant of the *Panniculus carnosus*. **1879** *St. George's Hosp. Rep.* IX. 237 Forty cases of simple scalp-wounds. **1890** BILLINGS *Med. Dict.*, *Scalp-tumor*, caput succedaneum; cephalhæmatoma. **1930** A. BENNETT *Imperial Palace* xxiii. 143 An electric scalp-massage. **1977** J. AIKEN *Last Movement* vii. 125, I always gave her scalp massage in the evenings..her shaved hair was taking its time about growing back.

c. (sense 3), as ***scalp-bearer***, ***-dance***, ***-hunter***, ***-mark***, ***-merchant***, ***-trophy***, etc.; **scalp-knife** = *scalping-knife*; **scalp-lock**, a long lock of hair left on the head (the rest being shaved) by North American Indians as a challenge to their enemies; **scalp-money**, money paid as a reward for 'bringing in' scalps of men or animals; **scalp ticket** orig. *U.S.*, a ticket sold by a scalper (see SCALPER[2] 2 a); **scalp yell**, a shout celebrating the taking of a scalp.

1878 C. TUTTLE *Border Tales* 18 One by one the squaws fell in behind the *scalp-bearer. **1791** J. LONG *Voyages* 35 The dances among the Indians are many and various, ..[including] the *scalp dance. **1878** C. TUTTLE *Border Tales* 17 The weird music of the scalp-dance. **1835** R. M. BIRD *Hawks of Hawk-Hollow* I. 79 He acquired a singular reputation as a bold and successful *scalp-hunter. **1851** MAYNE REID *Scalp Hunt.* xvii. 121, I became a scalp-hunter. **1937** T. RATTIGAN *French without Tears* II. i. 37, I can't quite see what my novel has got to do with the machinations of a scalp-hunter. **1975** *Observer* (Colour Suppl.) 23 Nov. 25/3 Once the scalp-hunters get the word that such-and-such a diplomat wants to defect or to become an out-and-out agent they enjoy priority over the sanctifiers and all the other categories of black operations people. **1807** J. BARLOW *Columb.* v. 52 Ax, quiver, *scalpknife on the girdle hung. **1827** J. F. COOPER *Prairie* II. i. 5 His head was shaved to the crown, where a large and gallant *scalp-lock seemed fearlessly to challenge the grasp of his enemies. **1877** G. GIBBS *Tribes of W. Wash.* 222 A figure of a man, with a long queue, or scalp-lock, reaching to his heels. **1866** WHITTIER *Snow-Bound* 261 How the Indian hordes came down..And how her own great-uncle bore His cruel *scalp-mark to four-score. **1795** COLERIDGE *Conciones ad Pop.* 46 In

America the recent enormities of their *Scalp-Merchants. **1704** in G. Sheldon *Hist. Deerfield, Mass.* (1895) I. 299 That the sum of Sixty Pounds be allowed and Paid to the Petitioners..as *Scalp money. **1712** S. Sewall *Diary* 13 June (1879) II. 351 Council would have had subsistence and £100 Scalp-money. **1880** G. A. Sala *Amer. Revisited* 201/1 There are 'round trip' tickets which are something more than return, tickets; and finally, there are '*scalp' tickets, which you can deal in and discount. **1941** Baker *Dict. Austral. Slang* 68 *Scalp ticket*, the return half of a train ticket. **1792** H. H. Brackenridge *Mod. Chivalry* I. v. ii. 113 A warrior..separates it [*sc.* a scalp] from the head, giving, in the mean time, what is called the *scalp yell. **1913** J. London *Valley of Moon* 465 He drew his finny prize to the bank..with the scalp-yell of a Comanche. **1947** *National Geogr. Mag.* July 108/1 The hundreds of scientists being marshaled there are pioneers more potent than any who fought when war drums rolled along the Mohawk, scalp yells quivered on the valley air, and the frontier was aflame.

scalp (skælp), *sb.*[2] Chiefly *Sc.* and *north.* Forms: 6 **skap, scawip, skalp, scalfe, scalph,** 7 **scap,** 7, 9 **scaup,** 6- **scalp.** [Perh. a specific use of prec. (cf. sense 5), but the forms with *f, ph* point to the possibility of a different origin. Cf. SHELP.] A bank providing a bed for shellfish, *esp.* oysters and mussels; an oyster or mussel bed or colony. (Often ***mussel-, oyster-scalp.***)

1521 *Aberdeen Reg.* (1844) I. 98 Nane of the mussillis..now begingin to gader one ane now skap at the northt watter, besyd the Cunningar hillis. ?**15..** *Aberd. Reg.* (Jam.), The scawip of mussillis & kokilliss. **1552** Huloet, Muskleskalp. *Ibid.*, Oyster scalph, *ostrifer*. [Cf. Elyot *Dict.*, *Ostrifer*, the place in the sea, whiche is apte to ingender oysters.] **1557** *Sel. Pleas Crt. Admiralty* (Selden Soc.) II. p. lxvii, Mussel scalfe. **1587** *Burgh Rec. Edin.* (1882) 488 To caus brek the swame of the mvssill scalp in the heavin of Leyth. **1593, 1879, 1896** [see MUSSEL *sb.* 4]. *a* **1672** Willughby *Ornith.* III. (1676) 279 Avis hæc *the Scaup-duck* dicta est, quoniam scalpam [Ray (1678) 365 *Scaup*] i.e. pisces testaceos fractos seu contritos esitat. **1793** *Statist Acc. Scot.* VIII. 461 A *scalp* of a small kind of mussels. **1862** *Macm. Mag.* Oct. 503 There used to be great battles between the men of Newhaven and the men of Fisherrow, principally about their rights to certain oyster-scalps. **1882** *Standard* 26 Sept. 2/1 Boston Deep, which is admirably suited for mussel culture, returns, now that the 'scalps' are protected, over 5000*l.* per annum.

†**scalp,** *v.*[1] *Obs.* [ad. L. *scalpĕre.*] *trans.* To cut, carve, engrave; to scrape, scratch.

1552 [implied in SCALPING *vbl. sb.*[1]]. **1662** Evelyn *Chalcogr.* i. 9 With the..stile, we only cut the Vernish, razing, and Scalping as it were, the Superficies of the Plate. *a* **1764** R. Lloyd *Poet. Wks.* (1774) I. 95 Critics..Should..not, unskilful, yet with lordly air, Read Surgeon's lectures while they scalp and tear. **1802** M. Moore *Lascelles* II. 23 The points of their swords scalped off their noses.

scalp, *v.*[2] Also 7 **skulp** (?). [f. SCALP *sb.*[1]

From Eng. are F. *scalper*, G. *skalpiren*, Du. *scalpeeren*, Sw. *skalpera.*]

1. a. *trans.* To cut off the scalp of (a person): chiefly said of the North American Indians.

1676 N. S. *Narrat. New-Eng.* 14 Laying him for dead, they flead (or skulp'd) his head of skin and hair. **1697** S. Sewall *Diary* 13 Sept. (1878) I. 459 Indians shot and scalped him about noon. **1754** H. Walpole in *World* III. 285 The Chippoways and Orundaks are still very troublesome. Last week they scalped one of our Indians. **1867** Parkman *Jesuits in N. Amer.* xix. (1875) 281 They sought out the bodies, carefully scalped them, and set out in triumph on their return. **1877** G. Gibbs *Tribes of W. Wash.* 192 None of the western tribes within my observation have pursued the practice of scalping the slain.

absol. **1759** W. Mason *Let.* 25 Jan. in *Corr. of Thomas Gray* (1935) II. 612 If you don't let them [*sc.* critics] scalp they'll do you no service. *c* **1778** *Conquerors* 61 Whose Indians scalp'd and carry'd desolation..to christian nation.

fig. **1849** N. Hawthorne *Let. to H. Mann* 8 Aug., I shall do my best to kill and scalp him in the public prints. **1856** Ferrier *Inst. Metaph.* xi. ix. (ed. 2) 298 Dr. Reid and his followers, instead of scalping a doctrine, have merely tomahawked a word. **1939** 'A. Bridge' *Four-Part Setting* ii. 16 Henry is plain sailing, of course—he's quite simply scalped... He's always being scalped. It's his own fault—he will chase women so. **1973** D. Kyle *Raft of Swords* (1974) x. 99 Calder took a taxi to Heathrow airport. Inevitably he would be scalped on the cab fare.

b. *U.S. political slang.*

1891 *Century Dict.*, *Scalp*,..to destroy the political influence of, or punish for insubordination to party rule.

2. *transf.* **a.** *U.S.* (See quot. 1895.)

1825 J. Lorain *Pract. Husb.* 335 The Yankee farmer first chops the fallen timber, then scalps off the grubs level with the ground. **1895** *Funk's Stand. Dict.*, *Scalp*, to level by cutting off, as the tops of cradle-knolls and the knobs of logs laid in corduroy roads; as, to scalp a road.

b. *dial.* To strip off (the turf or upper soil).

1806 Forsyth *Beauties Scot.* IV. 524 Unmerciful destroyers of all the grounds around them, scalping and tearing up every bit of better soil. **1866** Edmondston *Shetland & Orkney Gloss.*, *Scalp*; 'To scalp the land'—to pare off the surface of the soil, S.

c. *Metallurgy.* To remove the surface layer of (metal); to remove (the surface) *from* metal.

1922 *Brass World & Plater's Guide* XVIII. 96 After the slabs are cooled they are sent to the overhauling machines where a thin layer of metal is scalped from the surface. **1922, 1949** [implied in SCALPING *vbl. sb.*[2] 2]. **1958** A. D. Merriman *Dict. Metallurgy* 305/1 Other methods used to scalp the ingot are by chipping, milling, planing or by means of the oxyacetylene torch.

3. *Milling.* **a.** To separate the 'hair' or 'fuzz' from (wheat, etc.) by attrition and screening. **b.** To separate the different sizes of wheat, etc. from one another by means of sieves or screens.

1883 Neftel *Rep. Flour-Milling* (10th Census U.S.) 16 The wheat is scalped in four reels. **1884** [see SCALPING *vbl. sb.* 2, 3].

4. *Stock Exch.*, etc. To buy at very low rates so as to be able to sell at less than official rates. Also *absol.*

1886 *Harper's Mag.* July 213/2 [The scalper buys] any quantity of grain that may be offered, sells it at an advance of 1/8 cent per bushel, thus scalps the market. **1888** *Pall Mall G.* 15 Oct. 12/1 A professional speculator, who 'scalped' the market on a big scale for a small profit per bushel. **1891** *Century Dict.* s.v., To scalp railway-tickets. **1897** *Boston Globe* 29 Aug. 39/5 The broker himself would be selling the stock at 104 in New York, thereby 'scalping' one-fourth and making a handsome profit at no risk. **1902** G. H. Lorimer *Lett. Merchant* 201, I saw what looked like a safe chance to scalp the market for a couple of cents a bushel. **1948** *Sun* (Baltimore) 26 Nov. 18/2 The Stadium attendants told me they are the same men..who scalp at other games,..selling 60-cent tickets for $1. **1977** *Time* 19 Dec. 66/1 The generous benefactor to down-and-out friends wore the same loud waistcoats as the pinchpenny negotiator who scalped outmatched publishers.

scalp, *v.*[3] *rare.* = SCAPPLE *v.*

1725 *J. Webb's Stone-Heng* 88 They were scalped [*ed.* 1665 scapled] at the Quarries. **1883** *Stonemason* Jan., It is then trimmed (or scalped) into shape by men called block-choppers.

scalped (skælpt), *ppl. a.*[1] [f. SCALP *v.*[2] + -ED[1].] **a.** Having the scalp torn off. **b.** Of a mountain: Having a naked summit. Of land: Having the turf stripped off.

1754 Shebbeare *Matrimony* (1766) II. 275 A long list of ruined Virgins by means of this Act will undoubtedly be as acceptable to its Abettors as a Number of scalped Christians to an Indian Chief. **1855** Browning *Childe Roland* xxx, A tall scalped mountain. **1890** *St. Nicholas* May 556/2 Many a good in-field [for base-ball] has no turf on it, and is called a 'scalped' field.

c. *Metallurgy.* Having had the surface layer removed.

1958 *Times Rev. Industry* June 53/1 Scalped wire bars..seen in the place of the familiar round extrusion billet. **1965** *Gloss. Terms Copper, Zinc & Alloys* (*B.S.I.*) 15 *Scalped stock* (*for other than tube*), stock intended for further fabrication from which the surface has been removed by machining to improve the quality of the final product.

scalped, *ppl. a.*[2] *dial.* In quot. **scauped.** [f. SCALP *sb.*[2] + -ED[2].] Cultivated on a 'scalp'.

1894 *Standard* 10 Feb. 6/7 'Scauped', or cultivated mussels.

scalpeen (skæl'piːn). *Anglo-Irish.* [Of obscure origin: cf. SCALPIN.] (See quot.)

1834 Lover *Leg. & Stories Irel.* Ser. ii. 18 Peter..determined on a cargo of scalpeens. *Ibid.* 55 Scalpeens is pickled mackerel.

scalpel ('skælpəl), *sb.* [ad. L. *scalpell-um, -us*, dim. of *scalper, scalprum.* Cf. F. *scalpel* (in 16th c. *scalpelle*), G. *skalpel.*] A small light knife used in surgical and anatomical operations.

1742 Simson in *Edin. Med. Ess.* V. i. 445 The Scalpel is about an Inch in length, and a third in Breadth. **1879** T. Bryant *Pract. Surg.* II. 5 Shaving the redundant mass off the cartilage with a scalpel. **1893** W. R. Gowers *Man. Dis. Nerv. Syst.* (ed. 2) II. 333 If a scalpel be passed over the surface, it removes a little pyo-lymph.

attrib. **1742** Simson in *Edin. Med. Ess.* V. i. 447, I contrived the Scalpel-ring I have sent you the draught of, which may be used safely with the Uterus at any Distance.

b. *fig.*

1818 Scott *Rob Roy* xxi, Whoever should happen to overhear their character discussed in their own servants'-hall, must prepare to undergo the scalpel of some such anatomist. **1851** H. Reed *Lect. Eng. Lit.* xi. (1855) 339 It demands, too, for this serious service the most acute intellectual scalpel which the metaphysician can handle.

Hence **'scalpel** *v. trans.*, to cut with a scalpel; **scal'pellic** *a.*, involving the use of the scalpel.

1748 tr. *Vegetius' Distempers of Horses* 53 Let the whole Circumference of the Soal of the Hoof be scalpelled or cut with a Lancet. **1877** Ruskin *Wks.* IV. 155 *note*, Ocular and passionate study of nature [as opposed to] telescopic, scalpellic and dispassionate.

scal'pelliform, *a.* *Bot.* [ad. mod.L. *scalpelliformis*: see prec. and -FORM.] 'Having the form of a common penknife-blade, but planted vertically on a branch' (*Treas. Bot.* 1866).

scalper[1], **scauper** ('skælpə(r), 'skɔːpə(r)). [Partly a. L. *scalper*, by-form of SCALPRUM, partly f. SCALP *v.*[1] + -ER[1].]

†**1.** *Surg.* = SCALPRUM 1. *Obs.*

1656 Blount *Glossogr.*, *Scalper* or *Scalping Iron* (*scalprum*), a Surgeons Instrument, to scrape or take away corrupt flesh from the bones; a Lance to let blood with.

2. *Engraving.* A kind of graver used for hollowing out the bottom of sunken designs.

1688 Holme *Armoury* iii. 308/1 The Scalper, is a kind of Graver with a flat point; its use is to clear the bottoms of broad Letters or Escochions sunk into the Metal. **1821** Craig *Lect. Drawing*, etc. vii. 377 A large square tool, called a scawper. **1855** tr. *Labarte's Arts Mid. Ages* iv. 122 With scalpers he tooled or hollowed out all the spaces. **1869** *Eng. Mech.* 10 Dec. 298/3 Scaupers are used for cutting out the white parts of the block.

scalper[2] ('skælpə(r)). [f. SCALP *v.*[2] + -ER[1].]

1. One (esp. an American Indian) who removes scalps.

1760 S. Niles in *Mass. Hist. Soc. Coll.* (1837) 3rd Ser. VI. 174 This reminds me of an account we had of a notable old scalper among [the Indians]. **1795** Coleridge *Conciones ad Pop.* 45 Did not this employment of merciless Scalpers rouse the indignation of Britons? **1807** J. Barlow *Columb.* vi. 371 Scalpers and ax-men rush from Eerie's shore. **1884** E. P. Roe in *Harper's Mag.* Mar. 617/2 This treacherous scalper of birds.

fig. **1904** *Sat. Rev.* 29 Oct. 536 The scalpers of the yellow press had not time to put on their war-paint.

2. a. *U.S. slang.* One who buys and sells at a profit, but at a price lower than the official one, unused portions of long-distance railway tickets.

1875 *Chicago Tribune* 8 Dec. 12/3 The new town grew up to be..the great commercial centre of rail-road 'scalpers'. **1882** *Nation* 5 Oct. 276 (Cent. Dict.) The eternal quarrel between railroads and scalpers. **1891** C. Roberts *Adrift Amer.* 51, I went round to all the railroad ticket agents, called scalpers, in the city, and at last decided to go down as far as Topeka in Kansas, as that was the cheapest journey I could pick out for the distance.

b. *Stock Exch.* One who sells stock at lower than the offical rates.

1886 *Harper's Mag.* July 213/2 The 'Pit' is the scalper's delight. **1888** *Pall Mall G.* 15 Oct. 12/1 'Old Hutch,' by which title B. P. Hutchinson has been known on the Chicago Board of Trade for years as the champion scalper and speculator. **1891** *Times* 8 Oct. 11/1 Late trading was dull, but steady, on moderate covering by 'scalpers'.

c. *slang* (orig. *U.S.*). A speculator who obtains tickets for a popular entertainment and sells them for more than their face price.

1869 *Harper's Mag.* Sept. 623/2 Where theatres are all the run, And bloody scalpers come to trade. **1948** *Sun* (Baltimore) 26 Nov. 18/2 Since these 60-cent tickets are sold, or supposed to be sold, only to students, the question is how the scalpers obtained them. **1969** *Truth* (Melbourne) 12 July 24/7 I'm sure scalpers wouldn't buy lottery tickets. **1977** *Rolling Stone* 16 June 12/2 The Palladium shows sold out in a few hours and scalpers have been getting up to $75 per ticket. **1978** G. Vidal *Kalki* vi. 137 One-third of the tickets for the rally..are now in the hands of scalpers who are selling the most desirable seats..for as high as one thousand dollars a-piece!

d. *U.S.* (See quots.)

1874 J. G. McCoy *Hist. Sketches Cattle Trade* 292 So soon as an incoming train is announced nearing the stock yards, the hurrying tramps of solicitors, called 'Scalpers', may be heard hustling toward the unloading platform. If there is a shipper on the train whose stock is not consigned, they..[present] the business cards of the commission firms which have the Scalpers employed. **1930** *Amer. Speech* X. 271/2 *Scalper*, one who buys feeder cattle and resells to farmers and feeders at a profit. A speculator.

3. A scalping-knife. *rare.*

1837 R. M. Bird *Nick of Woods* II. xviii. 245 Captain Ralph Stacpole did..meet another Injun-savage in the woods..with gun, axe, and scalper. **1893** Leland *Mem.* II. 297 A tussle *à la Choctaw*, with biting, gouging, tomahawk and scalper. **1947** B. De Voto *Across Wide Missouri* 32 The Company is sending..100 dozen 'common scalpers' and 55 dozen more expensive knives for murder with style.

4. A 'scalping' machine: see SCALP *v.*[2] 3.

1886 W. A. Harris *Techn. Dict. Fire Insur.* 251 *Scalpers*, or *Scalping Reels*, the simple hexagon dressing-reels with iron shaft, iron arms, and iron rails clothed with tin or steel-wire cloth. *Ibid.* 252 Wheat is partially crushed by rollers, and afterwards passed through the scalpers and the silk dressing-machines. **1950** *Engineering* 13 Jan. 30/1 [In flour milling] the endosperm released..and sifted out in the scalpers consists of particles of various sizes.

scalpette (skæl'pɛt). [f. SCALP *sb.*[1] + -ETTE.] (See quots. 1887, 1960.)

1881 in J. Lichtenfeld *Princ. Mod. Hairdressing* 35 (Advt.), J. Lichtenfeld's Illustrated Catalogue contains Illustrations and Description of..Invisible Scalpette Fringes, Bébé Scalpette, [etc.]. **1887** E. Creer *Board-Work* vii. 97 What is a scalpette?.. I..consider it to signify an artificial covering for concealing a deficiency of hair, or to cover a bald place upon the female head—but not a wig. **1924** *Chambers's Jrnl.* Oct. 669/1 Skilled hair-workers who will make up wigs, scalpettes. **1960** C. W. Cunnington et al. *Dict. English Costume* 190/1 *Scalpette*,..a false front of invisible net to which luxuriant tresses are attached. **1961** E. S. Turner *Phoney War* vii. 54 My private drill consists of taking off my scalpette, putting it into the sponge bag and then slipping the latter with its closed outlet downwards into the hip pocket.

scalph, obs. form of SCALP *sb.*[2]

†**'scalpin.** *Obs.* Also 5–6 **scalpyn,** 6 **scalphyn,** 7 **scalpion.** [Of obscure origin: cf. SCALPEEN.] The whiting.

c **1400** *Little Red Bk. Bristol* (1900) II. 72 Toutz maners grociz pissouns, cestassauoir Samoundes, Congres, Melewels, Lenges, Hakes, Scalpyn et Harrynges venauntz au dite ville de Bristuyt hors del meer. **1548** (30 June) *Admiralty Court Oyer & Terminer* 35 Departyd therewithe [i.e. with a fishing boat] from Poole towards Wynchelsey on Scalpyn fare. **1549** in *Pat. & Close Rolls, Irel.* (1861) I. 196 [For every cwt. of] scalphyn [or other fish 1 *d.*]. **1602** Carew *Cornwall* 35 Whitings (in the East parts named Scalpions).

†**'scalping,** *sb. Obs.* [? f. SCALP *sb.*[1] + -ING[1].] (See quot.)

1746 Catesby in *Phil. Trans.* XLIV. 126 Mr. Joice, in digging the Foundation of an House..found, at the Depth of 6 Feet, a Part of a Jaw-bone..; then one Foot of Scalping or Sand-bed; then eighteen Inches of Stone.

'scalping, *vbl. sb.*[1] [f. SCALP *v.*[1] + -ING[1].] In †scalping iron = SCALPER[1] I.

1552 HULOET, Scalping yron for a surgeon, *scalpellum, scalprum.* [Also in later Dicts.]

'scalping, *vbl. sb.*[2] [f. SCALP *v.*[2] + -ING[1].]

1. a. *Surg.* The laying bare of the bone of the skull by cutting and raising the scalp.

1739 SHARP *Surg.* xxvii. 139 For it never happens that we inquire for a Fracture of the Scull by scalping, but that the Scalp itself is contus'd. **1787** *Med. Commun.* II. 153 Which he had experienced before the scalping and trepanning. **1897** *Syd. Soc. Lex.*

b. The tearing off of the scalp of an enemy.

1747 *Gentl. Mag.* 43 Scalping is cutting the skin from the eyebrows round the head and peeling it off. **1876** BANCROFT *Hist. U.S.* VI. xxiv. 3 He taunted Burgoyne with the murders and scalpings by the Indians in his employ.

2. In technical and slang uses (see the vb.).

1871 COWIE *Shetland* viii. 158 (E.D.D.) The ruinous process of 'scalping', or removing the turf of the commons for manuring the farms. **1882** *Nation* 5 Oct. 276 (Cent. Dict.) A corporation like the Pennsylvania Railroad must protect itself against loss through scalping. **1884** KNIGHT *Dict. Mech.* Suppl., *Scalping* (*Milling*), brushing the hair or fuzz from the ends of wheat grain to prevent its getting into the flour. **1894** *Standard* 3 May 7/1 (Farmer) A scalping of the Stock at the expense of the genuine investor. **1901** *Dundee Advertiser* 23 Apr. 4 Numbers of crofter grazings have been spoiled..by 'scalping', irregular peat cutting,.. and careless heather burning. **1922** *Jrnl. Inst. Metals* XXVIII. 881 Rolling data for brass and bronze, scalping, annealing, and pickling. **1949** J. E. GARSIDE *Process & Physical Metall.* viii. 123 It is becoming general practice in the case of non-ferrous alloys to subject slabs and billets to a surface machining operation known as 'scalping' prior to cold-rolling. **1960** *New Scientist* 19 May 1269/2 The machine..is used for scalping. By scalping, the quarryman means separating the dirt from the mine output before the stones are passed into the crusher. **1967** *Gloss. Highway Engin. Terms* (*B.S.I.*) 25 *Scalpings*, hard material extracted as being unsuitable for crushing and screening. **1975** *Bristol Evening Post* 19 Feb. 1/4 The firm plan to protect Portway and services underneath from impact, possibly with a blanket of steel plating topped by scalping and sand.

3. *attrib.* and *Comb.*, as ***scalping act, party***; fig. in ***scalping measure***; **scalping-machine** (see quot.); **scalping-tuft**, a scalp-lock.

1750 in Temple & Sheldon *Hist. Northfield* (1875) 381 Our Men will not venture out after the Enemy on any Scalping Act whatsoever. **1757** WASHINGTON *Lett.* Writ. 1889 I. 454 *note*, They have detached their principal force into many scalping parties. **1777** FOX in *Hansard's Parl. Hist.* (1814) XIX. 523 The most violent, scalping, tomahawk measures. **1826** J. F. COOPER *Mohicans* iii, The well-known and chivalrous scalping-tuft. **1883** NEFTEL *Rep. Flour-milling* (10th Census U.S.) 9 The resultant 'chop' is separated into..flour, middlings, and bran, by means of bolts technically called 'scalping-reels'. **1884** *Bath Herald* 27 Dec. 6/5 A 'scalping' machine..separates the 'middlings' from the larger pieces of wheat.

'scalping, *ppl. a.* [f. SCALP *v.*[2] + -ING[2].] That scalps (in various senses).

1762–71 H. WALPOLE *Vertue's Anecd. Paint.* (1786) V. 75 A scalping Indian. **1903** *Times* 3 Mar. 9/2 Chicago, March 2. Wheat... Scalping traders were moderate buyers.

'scalping-knife. [SCALPING *vbl. sb.*[2]] A knife such as that used by the North American Indians in scalping their enemies.

1759 JOHNSON *Idler* No. 40 ¶7 A..Mohawk Indian warrior,..with his scalping-knife, tom-ax and all other implements of war! **1825** MACAULAY *Ess.*, *Milton* (1843) I. 8 The Mohawk hardly feels the scalping-knife while he shouts his death-song. **1867** PARKMAN *Jesuits in N. Amer.* xxii. (1875) 328 They had no motive for exchanging the comforts of home..for..the scalping-knives of the Iroquois.

b. *fig.* and allusively.

1764 CHURCHILL *Gotham* I. 5 Whilst her brave rage, not satisfied with life, Rising in blood, adopts the Scalping-Knife. **1831** SCOTT *Ct. Robt.* Introd. Addr. ¶37 Peter Pattison's last labours shall now go down to posterity unscathed by the scalping-knife of alteration.

scalpless ('skælplɪs), *a.* [f. SCALP *sb.*[1] + -LESS.] Without a scalp.

1756 J. CLUBBE *Misc. Tracts, Physiognomy* (1770) I. 17 The scalpless musty skull of the famous Helen. **1850** KINGSLEY *Alton Locke* I. vi. 90 A tall cast of Michael Angelo's well known skinless model—his pristine white defaced by a cap of soot upon the top of his scalpless skull.

scalpriform ('skælprɪfɔːm), *a.* [f. L. *scalprum* (see next) + -FORM.] Chisel-shaped: applied to the incisors of rodents.

1828 *Lancet* 3 May 130/2 These chisel or scalpriform teeth. **1839** *Penny Cycl.* XIV. 454 Rhizophaga. Two scalpriform incisors in both jaws. **1870** ROLLESTON *Anim. Life* 6.

‖**scalprum** ('skælprəm). Also 7 *erron.* **scalpra.** [L., f. *scalpĕre* SCALP *v.*[1]]

1. *Surg.* A rasping instrument; a raspatory.

1688 HOLME *Armoury* III. xx. (Roxb.) 235/2 The Scalpra or Scraping Toole; it is to scrape or shave bones with all. **1767** GOOCH *Treat. Wounds* I. 303 With the knife appropriated to this use and the scalprum, a piece of the scalp is to be removed. **1858** MAYNE *Expos. Lex.*, *Scalprum* ..Name for a denticular raspatory used in trepanning.

2. *Anat.* The cutting edge of an incisor. Also, a scalpriform incisor.

1842 BRANDE *Dict. Sci.*, etc., *Scalprum*, in Mammalogy, the cutting edge of the incisor teeth.

†**'sculptize**, *v. burlesque nonce-wd.* [f. L. *scalpt-*, *scalpĕre* SCALP *v.*[1] + -IZE.] *trans.* To scratch.

1708 MOTTEUX *Rabelais* v. xx. 60 You have..sculptiz'd your Heads with frequent Applications of your Ungicules.

'scalpture. *rare.* [ad. L. *scalptūra*, f. *scalpt-*, *scalpĕre* SCALP *v.*[1]] Carving, graving.

1656 BLOUNT *Glossogr.*, *Scalpture*,..a graving in Mettal, a cutting or scratching. **1850** LEITCH tr. *C.O. Müller's Anc. Art* Introd. §27 (ed. 2) 10 Scalpture (the art of cutting stones and dies).

scalpy ('skælpɪ), *a. dial.* [f. SCALP *sb.*[1]] Having a thin covering of soil suggesting a scalp.

1621 BRATHWAIT *Omphale* in *Nat. Emb.* 222 Where scalpie hils and sandie vales imply, The ploughmans toile's requited slenderly. **1808** JAMIESON, *Scalpy* (pron. *Scaupy*), a term applied to ground, when the soil is thin. **1877** *N.W. Linc. Gloss.* s.v., Some's so near th'rock it's scalpy, and, in a way o' speakin', good to nowt.

scalt: see SCALD *a.*[2] and SCALD *v.*

scalter, scaltre, var. ff. SHALTREE *Obs.*

scaly ('skeɪlɪ), *a.* Also 6–7 **skaly**, 6–7, 9 **scalie**, 7 **scaily**, *Sc.* **skailly**, 7–9 **scaley.** [f. SCALE *sb.*[2] + -Y.]

1. Abounding in, covered with, or consisting of scales; having a surface that peels off in thin plates or layers.

1538 ELYOT *Dict.*, *Squammosus*, skaly. **1594** PLAT *Jewellho*, III. 74 If your teeth be verie scalie, let som expert Barber first take off the scales. **1615** CROOKE *Body of Man* 442 The scalie Sutures of the Temple-bones. **1682** WHELER *Journ. to Greece* I. 14 The surface..is covered with a scaly rock. **1793** *Gentl. Mag.* May 422/1 An altar-tomb, or altar, of scaly stone. **1857** MILLER *Elem. Chem.*, *Org.* III. 82 A scaly, sweetish, gummy mass. **1892** E. LAWLESS *Grania* ii. 7 The wind..tearing off fragments of scaly stone from the rocks.

2. a. Of fishes, serpents, and other animals; freq. in poetry = pertaining to or consisting of fish (*scaly flock, herd, nation, tribe*).

1528 PAYNELL *Salerne's Regim.* O ij b, The more skaly that fishe is, the better hit is. **1595** SPENSER *Epithal.* 57 The silver scaly trouts. *c* **1614** SIR W. MURE *Dido & Æneas* III. 127 The skailly squadrones of the liquid lakes. **1629** MILTON *Hymn Nativ.* xviii, The scaly Horrour of his foulded tail. **1666** DRYDEN *Ann. Mirab.* xv, So hear the scaly herd when Proteus blows. **1704** POPE *Windsor For.* 139 The patient fisher takes his silent stand,.. With looks unmov'd, he hopes the scaly breed. **1741** *Compl. Fam.-Piece* I. ii. 108 Season the Scaley Side first. **1828** STARK *Elem. Nat. Hist.* I. 450 The body of these fishes is scaly. **1857** J. HAMILTON *Less. from Gt. Biogr.* (1859) 278 His own line quivered with a scaly captive. **1872** BAKER *Nile Trib.* viii. 115 A strip of the scaly hide of a crocodile.

b. In specific names, usu. repr. L. *squamosus, squamatus*, or *squameus*: see quots. ***scaly ant-eater, scaly lizard***, names for the pangolins.

1681 GREW *Musæum* I. iii. 46 The Scaly-Lizard..is a yard and ½ long. **1774** GOLDSM. *Nat. Hist.* (1862) I. vi. iii. 468 The Pangolin, which has been usually called the scaly lizard. **1802** SHAW *Gen. Zool.* III. 74 Scaly Tortoise. *Testudo Squamata.* **1812** *Ibid.* VIII. 463 Scaly Lory. *Psittacus squameus.* **1840** *Penny Cycl.* XVII. 186/1 Pangolins, a name in common use to designate the Scaly Ant-eaters. **1872** COUES *Key N. Amer. Birds* 227 Genus *Scardafella* Bonaparte. Scaly Dove.

c. ***scaly fish*** (*slang*): see quot.

1796 GROSE *Dict. Vulgar T.* (ed. 3), *Scaly Fish*, an honest, rough, blunt sailor.

3. a. Of plants and their parts: Covered with scales or consisting of scale-like elements.

1597 GERARDE *Herbal* II. ccxxxviii. 588 Small scaly knops, like to the knops of Corne flower. **1688** HOLME *Armoury* II. 80/2 The Arbor Vitæ, or Tree of Life hath a small scaly leaf. **1786** ABERCROMBIE *Gard. Assist.* 242 The main bulbs of lilies, of the scaly tribe, will not keep good so long out of the ground as the solid bulbous kinds. **1839** LINDLEY *Introd. Bot.* III. (ed. 3) 470 *Scaly*.., covered with minute scales, fixed by one end; as the young shoots of the Pine tribe. **1857** A. GRAY *First Less. Bot.* (1866) 46 When the scales are narrow and separate, as in the Lily, the bulb is said to be scaly. **1884** BOWER & SCOTT *De Bary's Phaner.* 622 Rhizomes with scaly leaves.

b. ***scaly fern*** or ***spleenwort***, the ceterach. ***scaly water-moss***, *Fontinalis squamosa.*

1796 WITHERING *Brit. Plants* (ed. 3) III. 789 Scaly Water-moss. **1859** MISS PRATT *Brit. Grasses* 224 Common Ceterach, or Scaly Spleenwort.

4. a. Of skin diseases. ***scaly ringworm***, tinea imbricata. ***scaly tetter***, psoriasis.

1575 TURBERV. *Venerie* lxxix. (1908) 228 The skaly Mange, which..taketh off the skinne where it goeth. **1796** MORSE *Amer. Geog.* I. 112 Those who make a free use of it, ..have a scaly appearance, not unlike the leprosy. **1799** *Med. Jrnl.* II. 112 Scaly Tetter. **1826** S. COOPER *First Lines Surg.* (ed. 5) 194 In the majority of cancerous diseases, the skin has a yellowish or lead-coloured tinge, and is dry and scaly. **1898** P. MANSON *Trop. Dis.* Introd. p. xiii, Tropical scaly ringworm.

b. *transf.* Of trees: Infested with the scale insect.

1894 *Times* 14 May 3/4 This [wash] is strained before being sprayed upon the scaly trees.

5. Of armour. Cf. *scale-armour* s.v. SCALE *sb.*[2] and SCALED. Chiefly *poet.*

1597 SHAKS. *2 Hen. IV*, I. i. 146 A scalie Gauntlet now, with ioints of Steele, Must gloue this hand. **1747** GRAY *Cat* 16 Their scaly armour's Tyrian hue. **1781** GIBBON *Decl. & F.* xviii. II. 120 His cuirassiers..glittering with their scaly armour. **1791** COWPER *Iliad* xv. 641 His corslet thick With plates of scaly brass.

6. *Min.* (See quots.)

1796 KIRWAN *Elem. Min.* (ed. 2) II. 339 Brown Scaly Iron Ore. **1815** AIKIN *Man. Min.* (ed. 2) 200 *Scaly Talc*,..an aggregate of minute scales of a greenish colour. *Ibid.* 202 *Scaly Chlorite*,..composed of glimmering scaly particles. **1816** R. JAMESON *Min.* (ed. 2) III. 243 Red Ironstone. This species is divided into four subspecies, viz. Scaly Red Ironore [etc.].

7. *slang.* Poor, shabby, despicable; *esp.* (of persons) mean, stingy; occas., in poor health, 'seedy'.

1793 SOUTHEY *Lett.* (1856) I. 19 Poor Anax! he was quite scaly before his departure, but is now recovering apace. **1821** EGAN *Life in London* II. iii. (Farmer), If you are too scaly to tip for it, I'll shell out, and shame you. **1823** *Spirit Publ. Jrnls.* 233 They had proved themselves so very scaley, by forgetting to remember the waiter. **1844** DICKENS *Mart. Chuz.* xxviii, A reg'lar scaly old shop, warn't it? **1875** BESANT & RICE *Harp & Cr.* I. x. 206 If I were an author —they are a scaly lot, and thank Heaven I am not one.

8. *Comb.*, chiefly parasynthetic. **scaly-bark (hickory)**, the shagbark hickory, *Carya ovata*, or its edible nuts; cf. HICKORY 1; **scaly-tail** = *scale-tail* s.v. SCALE *sb.*[1] 12; so **scaly-tailed** *a.*

1634 MILTON *Comus* (Facsimile MS. 1899, 13), The scalie-harnest dragon. *c* **1711** PETIVER *Gazophyl.* vii. 64 Scaly-like Fruit. **1775** J. ADAIR *Hist. Amer. Indians* 360 Filberts..are as sweet and thin-shelled, as the scaly bark hiccory-nuts. **1781** LATHAM *Gen. Syn. Birds* I. 246 Scaly-breasted Parrakeet. **1785** T. JEFFERSON *Notes on Virginia* vi. 63 Scaly bark hiccory. **1803** SHAW *Gen. Zool.* IV. 400 Scaly-tailed scarus. **1814** F. PURSH *Flora Amer.* II. 637 This useful tree is known by the name of..Scaly-bark Hickory, on account of its bark, which is torn in loose fragments. **1816** R. JAMESON *Char. Min.* (ed. 2) 237 Scaly foliated, when the folia cover each other only partially. **1836** *Penny Cycl.* VI. 332/1 *Carya alba*, white-shell-bark, shag-bark, scaly-bark hickory (*Juglans squamosa*, Michaux). **1852** MAYNE REID *Desert Home* 198 The tree is known among backwoodsmen as the 'scaly bark'. **1859** MISS PRATT *Brit. Grasses* 21 Scaly-stalked Club-rush. **1893** *Advance* (Chicago) 23 Mar., A pretty young woman rings your bell to ask, 'You all buy some scaly-barks?' **1906** 'O. HENRY' *Rolling Stones* (1912) 8, I saw..a little flaxen-haired man with a face like a scaly-bark hickory-nut. **1921** *Brit. Mus. Return* 97 in *Parl. Papers* XXVII. 651 A West African Scaly-tail (*Anomalurus erythronotus*), and an Ituri Scaly-tail (*Anomalurus pusillus*). **1964** L. S. CRANDALL *Management of Wild Mammals in Captivity* 229 The life-histories of the scaly-tails are not well known. **1962** M. BURTON *Syst. Dict. Mammals of World* 121 Scaly-tailed Flying Squirrels..not related to true squirrels. **1964** E. P. WALKER et al. *Mammals of World* II. 750/2 Scaly-tailed squirrels den in hollow trees. **1975** P. W. HANNEY *Rodents* ii. 30 There are no flying squirrels in Africa, but in the west of the continent their niche is filled by ..the Anomaluridae or scaly-tailed squirrels.

scaly ('skeɪlɪ), *sb. S. Afr.* Also **scaley.** [f. the adj.] A large yellow-fish, *Barbus natalensis*, of the family Cyprinidæ, found in certain rivers in Natal.

1947 K. H. BARNARD *Pict. Guide S. Afr. Fishes* 56 The well-known Scaley..of Natal is a near relative of the Yellow-fish. **1971** *Rand Daily Mail* (Johannesburg) 27 Mar. 23/3 An interesting observation last week was the presence of shoals of scalies in the Bushmans river. **1975** *Stand. Encycl. S. Afr.* XI. 563/1 The Natal scaly..reaches 5 kg and is restricted to the Pongola system and the rivers of Natal.

scalyon, obs. form of SCALLION.

scam (skæm), *sb. slang* (orig. and chiefly *U.S.*). [Origin obscure.] **1. a.** A trick, a ruse; a swindle, a racket. Also *attrib.*

1963 *Time* 28 June 48/2 He..worked..as a carny huckster... 'It was a full scam.' **1971** *Harper's Mag.* Feb. 89 A gambling house is a sitting duck to every con man or outlaw who comes through; he is invariably convinced that he has a scam that you have never seen before. **1972** *Sunday Mail* (Brisbane) 2 July 19/6 It was necessary to the success of the latest 'scam' that it be worked in places where $25 chips were constantly in play. **1975** J. F. BURKE *Death Trick* (1976) iv. 64 Hustling of any kind he could live with in his hotel, dope-dealing, selling ass, almost any scam, even burglary. **1976** M. MACHLIN *Pipeline* v. 58 Gamblers, pimps, whores, conmen, and scam artists of every persuasion were drawn to the scene like sharks. **1978** M. PUZO *Fools Die* xii. 131 The bribe-taking scam had been going on for nearly two years without any kind of hitch.

b. *spec.* A fraudulent bankruptcy (see quot. 1966). Also *attrib.*

1966 *Wall Street Jrnl.* 9 Sept. 1/1 (*heading*) 'Fat Man' Scolnick & 'scams'... They're known as 'scam' operators, promoters who set up ostensibly legitimate businesses, order large amounts of merchandise on credit, sell it fast and strictly for cash—and then go 'bankrupt', leaving their creditors unpaid. **1968** J. M. ULLMAN *Lady on Fire* (1969) xiv. 181 'The main plan's to go bankrupt... The suppliers will be stuck with unpaid bills for millions. There's a name for that—' 'Scam game,' Forbes said. **1974** *N.Y. Times* 8 July 26/1 Organized crime is stealing millions of dollars from the public through planned fraudulent bankruptcies, called 'scams' by the underworld.

2. A story; a rumour; information.

1964 *Guardian* 8 July 7/6 'People want the 1930s all over again: a thousand naked chorus girls dancing in a pink smog under crystal chandeliers on a revolving staircase on an Alp.' .. 'Didn't someone tell us once that Hollywood went bust with that scam?' **1966** *Amer. Speech* XLI. 281 *Lowdown, scam, the word*, information. **1972** W. MCGIVERN *Caprifoil* (1973) viii. 137 There's been a security break... He's scheduled a press conference... The scam is he's going to break what we know on Spencer. **1972** J. WAMBAUGH *Blue Knight* (1973) i. 28, I paid them [*sc.* informers] from my pocket, and when I made the bust on the scam they gave me, I made it look like I lucked on to the arrest. **1976** *New*

Musical Express 17 Apr. 10/2 No, still no scam on Donny and Marie.

scam (skæm), *v. slang* (orig. and chiefly *U.S.*). [Origin obscure: cf. prec.] *intr.* and *trans.* To perpetrate a fraud; to cheat, trick, or swindle. Hence **'scamming** *vbl. sb.* (in sense 1 b of SCAM *sb.*).

1963 *Time* 28 June 48/2 My boss was scammin' from the public, and I was scammin' from him. **1966** *Wall Street Jrnl.* 9 Sept. 1/1 'Scam' originally was a carnival term meaning 'to fleece the public'. **1974** *Whig-Standard* (Kingston, Ont.) 9 Apr. 4/1 Scamming..is a form of criminal bankruptcy in which a front man buys out a legitimate firm and then uses the credit rating of the firm to buy large quantities of merchandise. *Ibid.* 4/3 Scamming, he said, ranks second only to bookmaking in financial importance to criminals. **1977** *New Yorker* 30 May 96/2 Local citizens..try to avoid being scammed by the familiar tergiversations of city politicians.

scam, obs. form of SHAME; var. SCAUM *v.*, *Sc.*

scamandee, variant of SCAMATO *Obs.*

scamander (skəˈmændə(r)), *v.* [app. f. the name of the river *Scamander* (Σκάμανδρος Homer), in imitation of MEANDER *v.*

Cf. Yorks. dial. '*skimaundering*, hanging or hovering about' (*Almondbury Glossary*).]

intr. To wander about, take a devious or winding course. Hence **sca'mander** *sb.*, devious progress.

1864 *Hotten's Slang Dict.* (ed. 3) 220 *Scamander*, to wander about without a settled purpose. **1868** M. COLLINS *Sweet Anne Page* II. 195 Isola had given up 'scamandering'. **1873** —— *Miranda* II. 247 When he got into an unknown town, it was his wont to sinuously scamander through it. **1873** *St. Paul's Mag.* Feb. 133 His two..doggish friends.. made miles of scamander for his every furlong.

†**'scamato.** *Obs.* Forms: 6 **scamato**, 7 **scammatie, scamoty, scamandee.** [app. repr. some mod.Gr. corruption of med.Gr. ἐξάμιτον SAMITE.

Cf. mod.Chios dialect σκαμάγκι and σκαμάνδρα, σκάμανδρον 'spun cotton' (Paspates Χιακόν Γλωσσάριον, 1888; in a quot. there given the latter is associated with δίμιτον: cf. quots. below).]

Some kind of textile fabric.

1570 CAMPION in *Hakluyt's Voy.* (1599) II. I. 115 For we do vse to buy..of their Scamato and Dimite, that the poore people make in that towne [*sc.* Chio]. **1625** PURCHAS *Pilgrimes* II. 1812 The downie or woolly substance..of which the Ilanders doe make a certaine stuffe called Dimitie, and another called Scammatie. **1660** *Act 12 Chas. II*, c. 4 Scamoty the peece containing seven yardes & ½..vij s. vj d. **1687** A. LOVELL tr. *Thevenot's Trav.* I. 99 In most of these Villages are made the Stuffs, which they call Dimite, and Scamandee.

'scamble, *sb.*[1] *Sc.* and *north.* Forms: 5 **skamyll**, 9 **skemmel**; 6 *pl.* **skaymlis, scamles, scamells, scambills, skemlis**, 7 **skemmillis.** [Northern var. of SHAMBLE *sb.*; prob. due to Scandinavian influence; cf. ON. *skemill*, Da. *skammel* footstool.]

1. A bench; now, 'a kind of long form used in a farm-house kitchen' (E.D.D.).

c **1470** HENRY *Wallace* XI. 1352 Thai xxx^{ty} dayis his band thai durst nocht slaik, Quhill he was bundyn on a skamyll off ayk. **1885** HALL CAINE *Shadow of a Crime* x, [He] had placed the benches called skemmels down each side.

†**2.** *pl.* (const. as *sing.*). A slaughter-house (also *fig.*); a meat or fish market; a shambles. *Obs.*

1549–50 *Stirling Burgh Rec.* (1887) I. 58 To brek fischis apon the skemlis of the foirgate. **1561** *Aberdeen Reg.* (1844) I. 334 For makking of ane skaymlis of tre at the fysche cors, for laying of the quhyt fysche tharupoune. **1570** BUCHANAN *Admonit.* Wks. (1892) 23 Sum convoyaris of him to ye scamles that slew his guidschir. **1572** *Satir. Poems Reform.* xxxv. 94 We sall avenge it on that clan, ȝour freind that to the scambills sauld. **1582–8** *Hist. Jas. VI* (1804) 195 They marchit..to Edinburgh, and plantit a gairdhous at the comon scamells. **1607** *Stirling Burgh Rec.* (1887) I. 116 The fische skemmillis.

†**'scamble**, *sb.*[2] *Obs. rare.* [f. SCAMBLE *v.*] A scramble, confused struggle.

1609 J. DAVIES *Humours Heau'n on Earth* I. clxxxiii. (Grosart) 23/1 Here Bugs bestirre them, with a bellowing rore, As at a Scamble we see Boyes to sturre, Who for Soules scamble on a glowing flore; Biting and scratching, like the Cat and Curre. **1664** H. MORE *Myst. Iniq.* I. xvi. 320 This pretended Triumvirate is no Supreme Magistracy, but a Political Scuffle or Scamble or transient Shuffle betwixt these three men, Octavius, Antony and Lepidus.

scamble (ˈskæmb(ə)l), *v.* Also 6 **skamble**, 9 *Sc.* and *dial.* **skammel, skemmel, -il, skemmle, skemble.** [Of obscure origin; app. related both to SHAMBLE and SCRAMBLE *vbs.*, which are not recorded until much later.]

†**1.** *intr.* To struggle with others for money, fruit, sweetmeats, etc. lying on the ground or thrown to a crowd; hence, to struggle in an indecorous and rapacious manner in order to obtain something. Const. *for*, *after*. *Obs.* (now superseded by SCRAMBLE).

1539 TAVERNER *Erasm. Prov.* (1545) 22 b, The apes.. skambled and went together by ye eares for the nuttes. **1553** *Respublica* I. iii. 176 *Avar*... Therefore catche that catche maye, hardely, & spare not,..the Devyll ys a knave an I catche not a flyce,..I doubte not to skamble and rake as well as one. **1589** PUTTENHAM *Eng. Poesie* I. xxvi. (Arb.) 66 Ladies and gentlewomen..with their handes wantonly scambling and catching after the nuttes. **1595** SHAKS. *John* IV. iii. 146 England now is left To tug and scamble, and to part by th' teeth The vn-owed interest of proud swelling State. **1600** HOLLAND *Livy* XLIV. xlv. 1199 The king,..laid out fiftie talents among them upon the river side to skamble for. **1609** [see SCAMBLE *sb.*]. **1621** BURTON *Anat. Mel.* I. ii. III. xv. 178 *margin*, I had no money, I wanted impudence, I could not scamble, temporise, dissemble. **1636** SIR T. WENTWORTH *Let.* in *Carte's Coll.* (1735) 6 Every man had his money at a day, not scambling one before another without so much as giving of thanks. **1668** J. OWEN *Expos. Ps. cxxx.* 68 This may consist with an obstinate resolution to scamble for something upon the account of self endeavours. **1687** WOOD *Life* 5 Sept. (O.H.S.) III. 237 After the king had don his breakfast, they began to scramble [MS. 19 D (3) fol. 90 scamble]. [In Wood's MS. drafts of this portion of the *Life* the word occurs several times, variously written *scramble* and *scamble*.]

†**b.** To struggle wildly. *Obs.*

1591 LYLY *Sapho & Phao* IV. iii, He [a stockdoue].. scambling to catch hold to harbor in the house hee had made,..sodainely fell.

2. *trans.* To scatter (money, food) for a crowd to scramble for. *Obs.* exc. *dial.*

Also Sc. (Roxb.) '*Skemmel*, *skammel*, to throw things hither and thither in a slovenly and careless way' (Jam.).

1573–80 TUSSER *Husb.* (1878) 112 Keepe threshing..to haue to be suer fresh chaffe in the bin. And somewhat to scamble, for hog and for hen. **1600** HOLLAND *Livy* LXIX. 1246 C. Marius..had purchased a sixth Consulship by a largesse of money skambled amongst the tribes. **1894** *Northumbld. Gloss.* s.v., At weddings it is customary to scammle money after leaving the church.

†**3.** To seize in a scuffle; hence, to take in a rapacious or unscrupulous manner. Const. *away*. *Obs.*

1599 SANDYS *Europæ Spec.* (1629) 150 Hee will not be a raiser of new stirrs in Italy; as divers of them to scamble somewhat for theyr owne haue beene. **1638** FORD *Fancies* I. iii, Perhaps The scambling halfe a duccat now and then To rore and noyse it with the tatling hostesse. **1695** WOOD *Life* 9 Nov. (O.H.S.) III. 495 There were only some gentlemen and ordinary people..in the Area who [after the king's departure] rudely scamb[l]ed away all the banquet.

4. *intr.* To make one's way as best one can; to stumble along. *lit.* and *fig.* Now only *dial.*

Also Sc. 'to climb or walk over slight or loose obstacles, to climb over rocks or walls' (Jam. s.v. *Skemmel*).

1571 CAMPION *Hist. Irel.* To Rdr. (1633), From thence to Henry the Eight, because nothing is extant orderly written, ..I scamble forward with such records as could be sought up. **1579** GOSSON *Sch. Abuse* 23 b, I haue in my voyage suffred wrack with Vlisses, & wringing-wett scambled with life to the shore. **1621** BURTON *Anat. Mel.* I. ii. III. xv. 181 When they contemne Learning, & think themselues sufficiently qualified, if they can write & read, or scramble at a piece of Evidence. **1685** H. MORE *Cursory Refl. Baxter* 8 Having scambled through a multitude of Authors carelesly and superficially, he was [etc.]. **1706** PHILLIPS (ed. Kersey), *To Scamble*, to rove or wander up and down. **1901** MISS HAYDEN *Trav. round Village* ii. 42 You had best try an' scamble through the water afoor 'tis too late. *Ibid.* xv. 254 How do 'ee manage to scamble along wi'out Kizzy?

†**b.** To make shift, find means somehow. *Obs.*

1608 *Merry Devil Edmonton* D 4 b, Be ready but to take her at our hands, Leaue vs to scamble for her getting out.

†**c.** To make shift for a meal. *Obs. rare*$^{-1}$. (Cf. SCAMBLING *vbl. sb.* b.)

1591 LYLY *Sapho & Phao* III. ii, *Molus*. I am in the deapth of my learning driuen to a muse, how this lent I shall scamble in the court, that was woont to fast so oft in the Vniuersitie. *Criti*. Thy belly is thy God.

†**d.** quasi-trans. *to scamble out*: to get through (a period of time) in a haphazard way. *Obs.*

1571 CAMPION *Hist. Irel.* xi. (1633) 34 In this division they scambled out a few yeares, untill the malice of Carassus a Britaine forced a quietnesse betweene them.

5. To throw out the limbs in a loose and awkward manner in walking; to shamble. *Obs.* exc. *dial.*

1633–1852 [see SCAMBLING *ppl. a.*]. **1825** JAMIESON, *Skemmel*, *skemble*, *skammel*.

6. *trans.* To collect in a haphazard or irregular manner; to 'scrape' *together*, *up*. Now *dial.*

1577 HARRISON *England* Ep. Ded., It may be..that your Honour will take offence at my rashe and rechlesse behauiour vsed in the composition of this volume, and much more that being scambled vp after this maner, I dare presume [etc.]. *c* **1592** MARLOWE *Jew of Malta* I. i. (1633) B 3, They say we are a scatter'd Nation: I cannot tell, but we haue scambled vp More wealth by farre then those that brag of faith. **1603** KNOLLES *Hist. Turks* (1621) 541 Before the enemie should perceive the weaknesse of his power, which was not great, and scambled up upon the suddain. **1638** WOTTON *Let. to Bacon* 6 Nov. in *Reliq. W.* (1672) 471 With this dispatch I will intermingle no other vulgar subject, but hereafter I will entertain you with as jolly things as I can scamble together. **1834** *Tait's Mag.* I. 544/2 Each might, without much difficulty, 'scamble up some sort of husband' from among the corps.

7. To remove piecemeal; to cut *away*.

1707 MORTIMER *Husb.* 426 Finding my Wood cut in patches, and other parts of it scambled and cut before it was at its Growth. **1888** *Athenæum* 11 Feb. 186/2 This band.. was left untouched when the sculptor scooped or scambled away the substance to give depth of space for the relief of the two figures.

Hence **'scamble-shamble** *v.* (*nonce-wd.*) *intr.*, to lounge or shamble.

1887 RUSKIN *Præterita* II. 332 He went scamble-shambling on, a plague to the end.

scambler (ˈskæmblə(r)). *Sc.* Also 6 **scamler, skam(e)lar.** [app. f. SCAMBLE *v.* + -ER[1].

The vb., however, is app. not recorded in Sc. before the 19th c., and derivation from SCAMBLE *sb.*[1], a bench, would not be inconsistent with the sense. Cf. Gael. *sgimilear*.]

A parasite, sponger.

1500–20 DUNBAR *Poems* lxiii. 45 On ȝour hienes follows eik..Scaffaris, and scamleris in a nuke, And hall huntaris of draik and duik. **1508** KENNEDIE *Flyting w. Dunbar* 37 Skaldit skaitbird, and commoun skamelar. **1533** BELLENDEN *Livy* v. iii. (S.T.S.) II. 153 þe maist parte of þe knichtis.. war passand like skamlars throw þe cuntre. **1721** J. KELLY *Sc. Prov.* 274 It is well ken'd your Father's Son was never a Scambler. [*Foot-note*. One that goes about among his Friends for Meat.] **1755** JOHNSON *Scambler* (Scottish), a bold intruder upon one's generosity or table.

scambling (ˈskæmblɪŋ), *vbl. sb.* [-ING[1].] The action of the vb. SCAMBLE.

c **1538** R. COWLEY in Ellis *Orig. Lett.* Ser. II. II. 98 Such havok and skameling as they make was never seen, to the utter pilling and beggering of the land. **1584** *Leycesters Commonw.* 106 And how so euer thes two conioyned Earles, do seeme for the tyme to draw together, and to playe bootie: yet..Hastings for ought I see, when he commeth to the scambling, is like to haue no better luck by the Beare, then his auncestor had once by the Boare. **1599** SHAKS. *Hen. V*, v. ii. 218. **1659** GAUDEN *Serm.* etc. (1660) 9 Whatever scambling and confusion in Civil and Regular Magistracy mens ambition brought on the state of the Jews, yet [etc.]. **1878** GROSART *H. More's Poems*, Mem. Introd. 10/1 Those noble old folios, matterful and painstaking, and putting to shame the literary scambling of to-day.

b. †The action of making shift for a meal or for meals. *scambling day*: see quot. (*obs.*). Also, a makeshift or informal meal. Now only *dial.*

c **1512** *Regul. Northumberld. Househ.* (1770) 80 This is the ordre of the Service of Meat and Drynk to be servyd upon the Scamlynge Days in Lent Yerely as to say Mondays and Setterdays thrughe out Lent and what they shall have att the said Scamlyngs. **1563** PILKINGTON, etc. *Burnynge Paules Ch.* I iiij, Some..eat more at that one dynner, than the poore man can get at three scamlinges on a day. **1606** MARSTON *Parasitaster* II. i, Come Sir, a stoole boy, the Court Feasts are to vs Seruitors Court Fasts, such scambling, such shift for to eate and where to eate. **1873** W. P. WILLIAMS & W. A. JONES *Somerset. Gloss.*, *Scamblin*, irregular meal.

scambling (ˈskæmblɪŋ), *ppl. a.* [-ING[2].]

†**1.** Contentious, rapacious. *Obs.*

1599 SHAKS. *Much Ado* v. i. 94, I know them,..Scambling out-facing, fashion-monging boyes. **1599** —— *Hen. V*, I. i. 4 The scambling and vnquiet time. *a* **1639** WOTTON *Life Buckingham* (1642) 29 He was no sooner entred into the Town, but a scambling Souldier clapt hold of his bridle. **1691** *New Disc. of Old Intreague* xvi. 28 Whose regular noise, ..Some dreadful scambling combate did present.

2. Clumsily or carelessly executed; slipshod, slovenly; makeshift. Also of a person: Blundering, bungling.

1589 NASHE *Anat. Absurd.* C j, Who is it, that reading Beuis of Hampton, can forbeare laughing, if he marke what scambling shyft he makes to ende his verses a like. **1599** HARSNET *Discov. Fraud. Darrel* 275 It is not likelie that the Diuell coulde bee dispossessed, by such almost priuate, slender, interrupted, and scambling prayers. **1653** H. MORE *Antid. Ath.* II. vii. §5 (1712) 61 Or if you will say, that there may some scambling shift be made without them [etc.]. **1856** P. THOMPSON *Hist. Boston* 721 [Provincialisms.] You've made a scambling dinner, I fear. **1884** ROGERS *Six Cent. Work & Wages* II. 412 The establishment of a rule that members of such unions would denounce and expose dishonest and scambling work.

3. Irregular, rambling, scattered.

1592 WYRLEY *Armorie* 67 The scambling chace eight leags endurd right, Ending almost at the gate of Reans. **1657** OWEN *Review Nat. Schism* ix. 141 To declare the way of his exerting his Authority..is not a matter to be tossed up and down in this scambling chase. **1658** EVELYN *Diary* 27 Sept., To Bedington,..a fine old hall, but a scambling house. **1680** MORDEN *Geog. Rect.*, *Ganges Penins.* 404 Her Capital City, which is large but scambling. **1702** D. GRANVILLE *Rem.* (Surtees) 241 Letters..to my scatter'd, scambling, and sometimes scabby sheep. **1786** tr. *Sparrman's Voy.* 324 Being..upon a plain under the shelter of a few scambling thorntrees. **1891** *Reports Provinc. Dev.* (E.D.D.) There wad'n on'y two or dree scamlin ones [*sc.* pheasants] down thick way.

4. Straddling, shambling.

1633 FORD *Love's Sacr.* v. i, Can you imagine, Sir, the name of Duke Could make a crooked leg, a scambling foot, ..fit for a Ladies pleasure, no. **1658** ROWLAND tr. *Moufet's Theat. Ins.* 952 The Gnat..hath six long crooked scambling legs..growing from his prominent breast. **1852** R. S. SURTEES *Sponge's Sp. Tour* viii. 33 On horseback, Tom was a..hard-bitten little fellow.., while on foot he was the most shambling, scambling, crooked-going crab that ever was seen.

Hence **'scamblingly** *adv.*

1611 COTGR. s.v. *Griffe*, *Griffe graffe*, by hooke or by crooke,..scamblingly, catch that catch may. **1755** in JOHNSON.

scame, variant of SCAUM; obs. form of SHAME.

†**'scamel.** *Obs. rare*$^{-1}$. Meaning uncertain: the statement in quot. 1866 is of doubtful value. Some have proposed to read *staniel*.

1610 SHAKS. *Temp.* II. ii. 176 And sometimes I'le get thee young Scamels from the Rocke. [**1866** H. STEVENSON *Birds of Norfolk* II. 260 At Blakeney Mr. Dowell states that bar-tailed godwits are known to the local gunners by the singular appellation of 'Picks' and 'Scamells'... He believes by 'Scamells' are meant the females and those found singly in autumn.]

scamely, obs. form of SCAMMONY.

scamler, scamles: see SCAMBLER, SCAMBLE *sb.*[1]

scammatie, variant of SCAMATO *Obs.*

†**'scammel,** *a. Obs. rare*⁻¹. [Perh. connected with SCAMBLE *v.*: cf. Sc. *skemmel* 'a tall, thin, ungainly person' (Jam.); also dial. *scrammel* 'a lean, gaunt, ill-favoured person or animal' (E.D.D.).] Lean, scraggy.
1658 tr. *Porta's Nat. Magic* II. ix. 39 That [mule] which is begotten of the wilde Asse, cometh nothing behind the other, but only that it is unruly and stubborn, and somewhat scammel, like the Sire [L. *nisi, quod..strigosum patris proferet habitum*].

†**sca'mmonial,** *a. Obs. rare*⁻¹. [f. L. *scammōni-um* + -AL[1].] = SCAMMONIATE *a.*
1657 TOMLINSON *Renou's Disp.* v. xiii. 167 Rhabarb or some scamoniall Medicine is often added to Cassia.

†**sca'mmoniate,** *a.* and *sb. Obs.* [ad. mod.L. *scammōniātus* (neut. *-ātum* as used subst.), f. L. *scammōnium* SCAMMONY.] **A.** *adj.* Made with or containing scammony; hence, purgative. Also *fig.*
1620 BP. ANDREWES *Serm., Holy Ghost* xiii. (1629) 740 Neither Scammoniate, tormenting the conscience; nor yet Opiate stupifying it. **1651** BIGGS *New Disp.* §113 A Scammoniate medicine. **1725** *Phil. Trans.* XXXIII. 389 The hot, scammoniate, aloetic Purgers seem not so proper.
B. *sb.* A medicine containing scammony; a purgative medicine.
1665 M. N. *Med. Medicinæ* 389 Ill-corrected Scammoniates.

scammonic (skə'mɒnɪk), *a. Chem.* [f. L. *scammōn-ium* SCAMMONY + -IC.] ***scammonic acid*** = jalapic acid: see JALAPIN.
1864 WATTS tr. *Gmelin's Handbk. Chem.* XVI. 408.

scammonin ('skæmənɪn). *Chem.* [Formed as prec. + -IN.] = JALAPIN.
1868 WATTS *Dict. Chem.*

†**scammonite,** *a. Obs. rare*⁻¹. [ad. L. *scammōnītes*, a. Gr. σκαμμωνίτης, f. σκαμμωνία SCAMMONY.] Medicated with scammony.
1601 HOLLAND *Pliny* XIV. xvi. I. 421 In like maner also is made the Scammonite wine.

scammony ('skæmənɪ). Forms: 1 scamonie, (-am, Lat. *accus.*), 3 scamoi(e)ne, 5 scamely, 5–6 scamonie, scammonye, 5–7 scamony, 5 skamonye, 7 -ony, 6–7 scammonie, 6– scammony. [ad. L. *scammōnia, scammōnium* (also *scammōnea*), a. Gr. σκαμμωνία, -ώνιον. Cf. OF. *scamonee, escamonie* (mod.F. *scammonée*), Pr., Sp., Pg. *escamonea*, It. *scammonea*.]
1. A gum-resin obtained from the tuberus roots of *Convolvulus Scammonia* (see sense 2) used in medicine as a strong purgative; also, the dried tuberous root from which the drug is prepared.
Also with qualifying word indicating the place of export, esp. in ***Aleppo, Smyrna scammony.***
c **1000** *Sax. Leechd.* II. 272 Nim scamoniam þæt peniȝ ȝeweȝe & ȝeȝnid smæle. *Ibid.*, Wyrtdrenc scamonian ȝeceos þus. *c* **1205** LAY. 17740 Appas..dude þer to atter þa scamoiene [*c* **1275** scamoine] hatte. **1436** *Libel Eng. Policy* in *Pol. Poems* (Rolls) II. 173 That wee shulde have no nede to skamonye, Turbit, euforbe [etc.]. *c* **1475** *Non-Cycle Mystery Pl.* (E.E.T.S.) 73/506, I haue gyven hyr a drynke made.. wyth scamely. **1526** *Grete Herball* ccccciii. (1529) Cc iij b, Scamony is often contrefayted with mylke of yᵉ herbe of catapucie. **1626** BACON *Sylva* §19 You may make it as strong a Purging Medicine, as Scammony. **1875** H. C. WOOD *Therap.* (1879) 470 Scammony acts upon the system like jalap, but is somewhat more irritating.
fig. **1678** B. R. *Let. Pop. Friends* 4 What Protestant Scammony is strong enough to make a thorough-pac'd Catholick Disgorge Infallibility?
b. (See quot.)
1849 BALFOUR *Man. Bot.* §956 A spurious kind of Scammony has been prepared from the root of *Convolvulus* (*Calystegia*) *sepium*; and several plants belonging to the order Asclepiadaceæ yield a purgative exudation which has been used under the names of Montpellier and Bourbon Scammony.
2. The plant *Convolvulus Scammonia*, native in Syria and Asia Minor, having a fleshy root which furnishes the scammony (sense 1) of commerce.
1567 MAPLET *Gr. Forest* 61 Scammony..hath a leafe like Iuie. **1597** GERARDE *Herbal* II. cccv. 716 Of Scammonie, or purging Bindweed. **1785** MARTYN *Rousseau's Bot.* xvi. 191 This genus contains several remarkable plants; as Scammony..and Jalap.
3. *attrib.*
1871 GARROD *Mat. Med.* (ed. 3) 282 Compound Scammony Powder...Scammony Mixture. *Ibid.* 283 Scammony resin also forms an important ingredient in extractum colocynthidis compositum. **1887** BENTLEY *Man. Bot.* (ed. 5) 627 This Scammony as also Scammony Root, and Scammony Resin, are official in the British Pharmacopœia.

scamoniall: see SCAMMONIAL.

scamoty, variant of SCAMATO *Obs.*

scamp (skæmp), *sb.* Also 9 *Sc.* **skemp.** [f. SCAMP *v.*[1]]
1. A highway robber. *arch.*
1782 MESSINK *Choice of Harlequin* (Farmer), Ye scamps, ye pads, ye divers. **1785** GROSE *Dict. Vulgar Tongue, Scamp*, a highwayman; royal scamp, a highwayman who robs civilly; royal foot scamp, footpads who behave in like manner. **1809** G. ANDREWES *Dict. Slang, Scamp-foot*, a street robber, a foot pad, spicer. **1834** H. AINSWORTH *Rookwood* III. v, A rank scamp!
†**b.** Highway robbery. *Obs.*
1786 *Life Miss Davies* 11 He resolved to go upon the scamp. **1812** J. H. VAUX *Flash Dict.* s.v., The game of highway robbery is called *the scamp*... *Done for a scamp* signifies convicted of a highway robbery.
2. A good-for-nothing, worthless person, a ne'er-do-well, 'waster'; a rascal. Also *playfully* as a mild term of reproof.
α. **1808** JAMIESON, *Scamp*, a cheat, a swindler; often used as to one who contracts debt, and runs off without paying it, *Loth., Perths.* **1825** BROCKETT *N.C. Gloss., Scamp*, a mean rascal, a fellow devoid of honour and principle. **1833** MARRYAT *P. Simple* xxix, He was a sad scamp. **1837** DICKENS *Pickw.* xlvii, Those are the cleverest scamps I ever had anything to do with. **1844** LOCKHART *Let.* 13 May in *Life & Lett.* (1897) II. 199 Ben Disraeli, the Jew scamp, has published a very blackguard novel. **1874** L. STEPHEN *Hours in Libr.* (1892) II. vi. 181 The prodigal who has been with scamps in gambling-houses. **1878** BROWNING *Poets Croisic* 133 This scamp Voltaire!
β. **1818** HOGG *Brownie of Bodsbeck* I. 110 Ye're surely some silly skemp of a fallow, to draw out your sword on a puir auld woman. **1824–7** MOIR *Mansie Wauch* xxii. (1828) 339 Skemps that had not wherewithal to pay lawful debts.
3. *U.S.* (See quots.)
1882 JORDAN & GILBERT *Synopsis Fishes N. Amer.* 538 *Trisotropis falcatus* Poey.—Scamp. **1884** G. B. GOODE, etc. *Nat. Hist. Aquatic Anim.* 413 Another fish..*Mycteroperca falcata*, is called at Pensacola by the name 'Scamp'.

scamp (skæmp), *v.*[1] [app. cogn. with SCAMPER *v.*, which occurs earlier. An earlier evidence of the word may exist in the mock-heraldic SCAMPANT (*c* 1585).] *intr.* †**a.** *cant.* (See quot. 1753). **b.** *Sc.* With advs. *about, off.* (See quot. 1867).
1753 *Disc. John Poulter* (ed. 2) 39 I'll scamp on the Panney; [=] I'll go on the Highway. **1867** GREGOR *Banffsh. Gloss., Scamp*, to go about in an idle manner; often with the idea of mischief; followed by *aboot* and *through*.

scamp (skæmp), *v.*[2] [Prob. of dialectal origin; cf. SKIMP *v.*, used *dial.* in the same sense; the source may possibly be ON. *skemma* to shorten, f. *skamm-r* short: see SCANT *a.*]
1. *trans.* To do (work, a task, etc.) negligently or hurriedly. Also ***to scamp off, over.*** Cf. SKIMP *v.*
1837 WHITTOCK *Bk. Trades* (1842) 392 (*Printer*) The best work which cannot be 'scamped' over. **1861** SMILES *Engineers* I. 11 From the very earliest times the tendency to 'scamp' work seems to have existed. **1867** G. MUSGRAVE *Nooks in Old France* I. ii. 80 A perilous mode of scamping off their work. **1888** W. P. FRITH *Autobiog.* III. v. 112 A portrait, in which..the man's figure had been what we call 'scamped'.
absol. **1859** SMILES *Self-Help* viii. 211 There are tradesmen who adulterate, contractors who 'scamp' [etc.].
2. *U.S. intr.* (in quot. quasi-*trans.*) To be stingy or excessively economical. Cf. SKIMP *v.*
1894 C. MERIWETHER in *Nation* 16 Aug. 116/2 If three or four dollars more are added for rent, the tenant either scamps the life out of himself and family, or crops the land to death.
3. *Comb.*: **scamp-work,** scamped work.
1840 MARRYAT *Olla Podr.* xxviii, To use a joiner's phrase, everything abroad is comparatively scamp-work. **1884** E. H. PLUMPTRE in *Expositor* Apr. 275 What we call 'scamp-work' in building was as common..in Ezekiel's time, as it is with us.
Hence **scamped** *ppl. a.*
1871 CARLYLE in Mrs. Carlyle *Lett.* III. 198 The house was..misbuilt..a despicable, cockney, scamped edifice. **1885** J. G. WOOD *My Garden Wall* in *Longm. Mag.* VI. 518 This one little bit of 'scamped' brickwork is almost the only part that is worth watching.

†**'scampant.** *Obs. nonce-wd.* [quasi-*Her.* after RAMPANT; cf. SCAMP *v.*]
c **1585** in *Rel. Ant.* II. 122 [Burlesque coat of arms] A lyther lad scampant, a roge in his ragges.

‖**scampavia** (skampa'via). Also 8 **scampavie.** [It., f. *scampare* to run off, decamp (see DISCAMP *v.*) + *via* way, away.] A swift sailing vessel used in the Mediterranean.
1723 *Pres. St. Russia* I. 35 Three Russian Scampavies full of Russian Soldiers. **1802** *Naval Chron.* VIII. 122 Quick sailing little vessels called scampavias. **1867** SMYTH *Sailor's Word-bk., Scampavia*, a fast rowing war boat of Naples and Sicily.

scamper ('skæmpə(r)), *sb.*[1] [f. SCAMPER *v.*] The action of scampering, in the senses of the vb.; also, an instance of this. Also in the phrases ***to be on*** or ***upon the scamper, to put to the scamper.***
1697 VANBRUGH *Æsop* Pref., The first day it [*sc.* this Play] appear'd, 'twas routed.., the fourth it gave a vigorous Attacque, and the fifth put all the Feathers in Town to the scamper. **1766** COLMAN & GARRICK *Clandestine Marr.* v. ii, If we had not watch'd them and call'd up the fammaly, they had been upon the scamper to Scotland by this time. **1809** MALKIN *Gil Blas* IV. xi. ¶4 Those who are always on the scamper see a great deal of the country. **1885** *Field* 7 Feb. 147/3 A fox..led hounds a short but merry scamper over a stiff country. **1888** BURGON *12 Gd. Men* II. v. 4 He loved.. a scamper round the garden.

scamper ('skæmpə(r)), *sb.*[2] [f. SCAMP *v.*[2] + -ER[1].] One who scamps work.
1851 MAYHEW *Lond. Labour* II. 199 To a notorious 'scamper', he one morning sent three cart-loads of 'mac' at 1s. a load, all to be used in the erection of..one..house. **1884** C. GIBBON *By Mead & Stream* II. xxxii. 144 Work was scamped: he detected it, and dismissed the scampers.

scamper ('skæmpə(r)), *v.* [Of uncertain origin.
In our quots. first recorded in 1687, but very common between that date and 1700. Not improbably the word was originally military slang, either from obs. Du. *schampen* 'to escape or flie, or to be gone' (Hexham 1660), which is a. OF. *escamper* to decamp, or from It. *scampare* to decamp, run away: see DISCAMP *v.* A less likely, though possible, supposition is that it represents a ME. derivative of the OF. word, preserved in some non-literary dialect.]
†**1.** *intr.* To run away, decamp, 'bolt'. *Obs.*
1687 T. BROWN *Saints in Uproar* Wks. 1720 I. 89 It rejoices me to consider, with what wonderful Alacrity you [*sc.* St. Ursula and her Virgins] scamper'd over the Alps, and without a Farthing of Money in your Pockets. **1688** in Ellis *Orig. Lett.* Ser. II. IV. 144 Upon beat of drum..[they] have scampered away, and by flight provided for their safety. **1693** DENNIS *Impartial Critick* iii. 18 *Beaum...* But whose are those Verses? If they are thine, I scamper immediately. **1697** DAMPIER *Voy.* I. 189 We were forc'd to cut our Cables in all haste, and scamper away as well as we could. *a* **1700** B. E. *Dict. Canting Crew, Scamper*, to run away, or Scowre off, either from Justice, as Thieves, Debtors, Criminals, that are pursued; or from ill fortune, as Soldiers that are repulsed or worsted. **1788** FRANKLIN *Autobiog.* Wks. 1840 I. 191 The wagoners took each a horse out of his team and scampered. **1822** BYRON *Juan* VIII. lxxv, The Turks at first pretended to have scamper'd. **1833** M. SCOTT *Tom Cringle* ix, The few of the Pirates who had escaped having scampered into the woods.
2. To run or caper about nimbly; to go or journey hastily from place to place. Also with advs. *about, away, off*, etc.
1691 [see SCAMPERING *vbl. sb.*]. **1697** DAMPIER *Voy.* I. 517 For which reason, I suppose, they represented so many Serpents scampering about in the printed Picture that was made of him. **1760–20** GOLDSM. *Cit. W.* Pref., I have been set up for half-pence, to fret and scamper at the end of my chain [like a dancing bear]. **1833** HT. MARTINEAU *Manch. Strike* i. 3 Barefooted children were scampering up and down these stairs at play. **1835** WILLIS *Pencillings* II. xlvi. 63 The current scampers through between the two castles. **1873** HOLLAND *A. Bonnic.* iii. 60 A black fox dashed across our way, and, giving us a scared look, scampered into cover. **1882** MISS BRADDON *Mt. Royal* II. i. 3 He is devoured by impatience to be scampering off again.
fig. **1870** MISS BRIDGMAN *R. Lynne* II. xiii. 285 She could just scamper through the scales.
Hence **'scampered** *ppl. a.*
1894 MRS. DYAN *Man's Keeping* (1899) 249 After a scampered-through breakfast. **1906** *Daily News* 21 Mar. 6/5 The usual scampered mid-day meals.

scamperer ('skæmpərə(r)). [f. SCAMPER *v.* + -ER[1].] One who scampers; †? a street ruffian.
1712 STEELE *Spect.* No. 276 ¶3 A very gay..old Man.. who has been, he tells me, a Scowrer, a Scamperer, a Breaker of Windows [etc.]. **1802** MISS EDGEWORTH *Manœuvring* vi. (1809) 149 This ever idle, ever busy scamperer. **1804** *Hull Advertiser* 4 Feb. 3/3 A gang of scamperers. **1871** TYNDALL *Forms of Water* §14 ¶123 They were no idle scamperers on the mountains that made these wild recesses first known.

scampering ('skæmpərɪŋ), *vbl. sb.* [f. SCAMPER *v.* + -ING[1].] In the senses of the verb.
1691 MOUNTFORT *Greenwich Park* II. iii. 22 *Sir Tho...* Let's have a Dance... *La. Haz.* I think we had better Dance at Home... *Sir Tho.* Agreed, then we'll first to Supper, and then for a Rubbers at scampring. **1765** TUCKER *Lt. Nat.* II. 677 Nobody else can know in what instances I have restrained its [*sc.* a horse's] scamperings. **1843** MACAULAY *Ess., Mme. D'Arblay* ¶40 A cry of 'The King!' was set up. A general scampering followed. **1865** G. MACDONALD *A. Forbes* 25 A terrible noise of scrambling and scratching and scampering in the very room beside her.

scampering ('skæmpərɪŋ), *ppl. a.* [f. SCAMPER *v.* + -ING[2].] In senses of the verb.
1859 K. CORNWALLIS *Panorama of New World* I. 199 A scampering crowd of agile young runners. **1876** BESANT & RICE *Gold. Butterfly* Prol. i In these days of Pacific Railways and scampering Globe Trotters.

scamphood ('skæmphʊd). *rare.* [f. SCAMP *sb.* + -HOOD.] The quality of being a scamp.
1845 J. S. LE FANU *Cock & Anchor* I. xvii. 257 He was ripe for the domestic virtues, and ought to renounce scamphood. **1866** CARLYLE *E. Irving* in *Remin.* (1881) I. 205 Hazlitt,..a fine talent too, but tending towards scamphood.

scampi ('skæmpɪ), *sb. pl.* [a. It. *scampi.*]
1. Also in *sing.* **scampo.** = *Dublin Bay prawn* s.v. DUBLIN.
1928 RUSSELL & YONGE *Seas* xiv. 316 It is extremely plentiful in the Adriatic and is sold in the Italian ports under the name of 'Scampo'. **1953** P. BONNER *SPQR* viii. 70 Those little *scampi* are not enough for hungry fishermen. **1966** *Punch* 28 Sept. 483/3 The mysterious scampo which we see in this country, an animal which appears to have no head, is in fact the tail of the Dublin Bay Prawn. **1972** *Daily Tel.* 5 May 2/6 Scampi..make deep burrows in the mud.. and thus easily escape the trawling nets of fishermen.
2. a. (A dish of) these prawns eaten as a delicacy, usu. coated with breadcrumbs and fried in oil, or boiled and served with (garlic) sauce.

1930 E. WAUGH *Labels* vi. 158, I ate *scampi* at Cavaletto and felt no ill effects. **1951** N. BALCHIN *Way through Wood* xii. 176 You look like a man who's been gazing on the scampi when they're brown. **1958** A. WILSON *Middle Age of Mrs Eliot* II. 268 It's sure to be scampi or snails or some-thing I couldn't eat. **1962** D. LESSING *Golden Notebook* II. 244 This theme takes us through scampi and the main course. **1978** *Times* 11 Apr. 16/4 Bartolomeo Calderoni..introduced scampi to Britain. *Ibid.* 16/5 As for the scampi, he imported them from Venice's Grand Hotel..when he was head chef at Quaglino's in the 1930s.

b. *attrib.* and *Comb.*

1959 *Good Food Guide* 46 Scampi Provençales and duck Grand Marnier can be arranged to order. **1960** *House & Garden* July 60/3 Such memorable dishes as scampi risotto. **1966** D. SKIRROW *It won't get You Anywhere* vi. 32 What about a little schmaltzy restaurant down the King's Road? Or..maybe further up the river in the scampi belt? **1977** *Chicago Tribune* 2 Oct. VI. 19/1 The scampi marsala and the baked clams also were worthy antipasti choices as was the cannelloni bechamel. **1980** *West Lancs. Evening Gaz.* 7 Jan. 11 (Advt.), Vacancies for full-time/part-time scampi processors.

scamping ('skæmpɪŋ), *vbl. sb.* [f. SCAMP *v.*[2] + -ING[1].] The action of the vb. SCAMP.

1862 SMILES *Engineers* III. 467 He did all thoroughly and honestly. There was no scamping with him. **1890** W. J. GORDON *Foundry* 150 A scamping in the work,..a flaw in the metal, may mean the destruction of the train.

scamping ('skæmpɪŋ), *ppl. a.*[1] [f. SCAMP *v.*[1] or *sb.* + -ING[2].] That behaves as a scamp, good-for-nothing.

1832 W. STEPHENSON *Gateshead Poems* 63 The scamping, filthy loon. **1839** STONEHOUSE *Axholme* 244 *note*, You are not one of these scamping Dutchmen, but one of the original.. inhabitants of the country.

scamping ('skæmpɪŋ), *ppl. a.*[2] [f. SCAMP *v.*[2] + -ING[2].] Of a workman, etc.: That scamps work.

1851 MAYHEW *Lond. Labour* II. 199 One man..informed me that 'mac' was most in demand among scamping builders.

scampish ('skæmpɪʃ), *a.* [f. SCAMP *sb.* + -ISH.] Having the character or disposition of a scamp; characteristic of a scamp.

1847 DE QUINCEY *Sp. Mil. Nun* xxiii. Wks. 1854 III. 76 The alcade personally renewed his regrets for the ridiculous scene of the two scampish oculists. **1892** *Nation* 28 Apr. 325/3 His temporary religious fervor is a scampish aberration.

Hence **'scampishly** *adv.*, **'scampishness**.

1858 S. BROOKS *Gord. Knot* ii. (1860) 16 But he did his best for Arundel, alternately dilating upon the scampishness of Robert Spencer and the vulgarity of his wife [etc.]. **1880** MISS BRADDON *Just as I am* ix, Vargas had been scampishly disposed at his best.

†**'scampsman.** *Obs.* [f. *scamp's*, SCAMP *sb.* 1 b + MAN *sb.*] A highwayman.

1799 *Spirit Publ. Jrnls.* (1805) III. 352 Memorandum.—If any thing done by scampsmen on the Fulham road, send the traps to pull up Bounce and Blunderbuss. **1834** H. AINSWORTH *Rookwood* III. v, 'The Game of High Toby', Forth to the heath is the Scampsman gone.

scampy ('skæmpɪ), *a.* [f. SCAMP *sb.* + -Y.] = SCAMPISH.

In some recent Dicts.

scan (skæn), *sb.* [f. SCAN *v.*] **1. a.** The action of scanning; close investigation or scrutiny; perception, discernment; a scanning look.

1706 *Col. Rec. Pennsylv.* II. 266 May bear the scan of our superiors. **1775** WASHINGTON 28 Nov. in Sparks *Writings* (1834) III. 178 (Funk) What will be the end of these manœuvres is beyond my scan. **1827** HARE *Guesses* (1859) 215 The princes and lords of thought shoot forth their winged words into regions beyond the scan of the people. **1828** COLERIDGE *Gard. Boccaccio* 33 All spirits..that..lent a lustre to the earnest scan Of manhood, musing what and whence is man. **1903** *Blackw. Mag.* Apr. 480/1 A curious watchfulness pervades every man—a quick scan of every rock and bush on walking abroad. **1970** O. DOPPING *Computers & Data Processing* xvii. 277 If the computer were to continue the forward scanning, four scans would be needed. **1973** W. MCCARTHY *Detail* ii. 90 The air marshals scanned their bodies with their eyes. Ben passed through. I guess this scan works, he thought.

b. The action or practice of scanning with a beam, aerial, or detector. Cf. SCAN *v.* 6 f.

1937 *Discovery* Nov. 330/1 This..scheme is modified by leaving out alternate lines during alternate scans, a technique which improves the definition and reduces flicker. **1955** *Sci. Amer.* June 41/1 When Hey published his discovery after the war, radio astronomers began an intensive radio scan of the Sun. **1958** *Times* 2 May 7/2 One of these provided the long-range warning, while the others made a coordinated scan of various sections of the target area as the structure rotated. **1966** M. WOODHOUSE *Tree Frog* xxi. 155 Say that echo's your drone up there... Then you get your vertical scan radar for altitude. **1972** *Sci. Amer.* Jan. 57/1 The rate of scan that produces a micrograph is often much lower than the scanning rate in television.

2. A single line or sweep produced by or in a scanning action (cf. SCANNING *vbl. sb.* 2 b); also, an entire raster.

1934 J. H. REYNER *Television* ix. 103 The separation between the centres of the lenses was equal to the width of the picture scan. **1945** *Electronic Engin.* XVII. 689 The scan to fly-back ratio is constant for all time base velocities. **1952** *Jrnl. Lab. Clin. Med.* XXXIX. 153 The counter is moved alternately back and forth, with an $\frac{1}{8}$ inch vertical displacement for each sweep or scan over the area occupied by the thyroid gland. **1966** *Electronics* 17 Oct. 114 The large spike at the beginning of each scan is a turnaround transient. **1967** [see FIELD *sb.* 16 d]. **1975** D. G. FINK *Electronics Engineers' Handbk.* xx. 7 The half line, left over at the end of the field scan, displaces the next field downwards by a full line, and interlacing is achieved.

3. An image, diagram, etc., obtained by scanning; *spec.* in *Med.* = SCINTISCAN.

1953 *Nucleonics* Nov. 45/1 Fig. 13 presents the coincidence scan and unbalance scan of a patient who showed a regrowth of tumor beneath an area of previous resection. **1956** *Jrnl. Neurosurg.* XIII. 347 (*heading*) This scan is in the posterior-anterior orientation of the head. **1969** M. CRICHTON *Andromeda Strain* I. 22 We'll want a flyby over that town... And a complete scan. **1971** *Guardian* 6 Feb. 1/7 There were, as the first scan of the [lunar] landscape showed, a few very large boulders. **1976** *Woman's Day* (U.S.) Nov. 164/2, I might ask for bone, liver and brain scans to make sure there had not been any metastasis to other parts of my body. **1978** *Nature* 14 Dec. 733/2 (*caption*) Absorbance scans of..SDS-polyacrylamide gels.

4. Special Comb.: **scan-column index**, a tabular representation of coded information concerning or contained in a set of documents, for use in information retrieval.

1962 J. O'CONNOR in *Amer. Documentation* XIII. 205/1 Place the document number in the left-hand column. Then, for each indexing term assigned to that document, look up the column and character abbreviation for the term, and in that column enter that character. I call an index of this form a Scan Column index. **1965** M. E. STEVENS *Automatic Indexing* vi. 118 Tabledex, the Scan-column Index, and similar tools provide to some extent a display of prior associations between index terms. **1971** A. GILCHRIST *Thesaurus in Retrieval* 140 The scan-column index. This is another book-form coordinate information retrieval system ..in which all the item numbers are listed numerically in the first column, the other columns containing descriptors, allotted to those items. A separate table indicates which column would be searched for a particular descriptor. To facilitate searching, descriptors have been reduced to symbols.

scan (skæn), *v.* Also α. 4-7 scanne, 6-7 scann, skan(ne. β. 5-8 scand. [ad. L. *scandĕre*, lit. to climb, in late L. to 'scan' verses. Cf. F. *scander* (perh. the source, but in Fr. dicts. first cited from the 16th c.), Sp. *escandir*, It. *scandere* (also to climb), G. *skandiren*, Du. *skandeeren*.

The Latin word is cogn. w. Sk. *skand* to leap and Gr. σκάνδαλον stumbling-block, SCANDAL; derivatives in Eng. are SCANSION, SCANSORY etc., SCALE *sb.*[3]; also, from L. compounds, the vbs. *ascend, descend, transcend.*]

1. a. *trans.* To analyse (verse) by determining the nature and number of the component feet or the number and prosodic value of the syllables; to indicate the structure or test the correctness of (a verse) by reciting it with metrical emphasis and pauses, or by counting on the fingers the feet as they occur in recitation. Also *occas.* to describe prosodically (a word or sequence of words); to find (a particular kind of foot) in a given portion of a verse.

α. **1398** TREVISA *Barth. De P.R.* XVII. lxxxv. (Bodl. MS.), & who kanne scanne [in 1495 *printed* scand] a verse may knowe þ[t] þe myddel silable stondeþ for a schorte silable in þe secunde verse. *c* **1440** *Promp. Parv.* 442/2 Scanne verse (*P.* scannyn versis), *scando.* **1567** DRANT *Horace, Ep.* B ij, Those verses..Whiche longe deliberation..hath not..on the fingers scande. *a* **1613** OVERBURY *A wife*, etc. (1638) 93 He treads in a rule, and one hand scannes verses, and the other holds his scepter. **1638** H. RAINSFORD in *G. Sandys' Div. Poems* To Author, Thy Lines I weigh not by th'Originall; Nor skan thy Words how evenly they fall. **1706** W. WALSH *Let. to Pope* 9 Sept., P.'s Wks. (1736) V. 51 They scan their verses upon their fingers. **1874** SYMONDS in *Fortn. Rev.* Dec. 769 But a trochee in the fourth place! (for so he [Johnson] scanned the lines), O Milton and Cowley! shame upon your ears! *Ibid.* 770 Critics like Todd think nothing of scanning an anapæst in the place of one of Johnson's feet. **1900** SKEAT *Chaucer Canon* §15 It is impossible to scan the Ormulum until one has learnt the grammar.

transf. **1791-2** WORDSW. *Descr. Sk.* 147 There an old man an olden measure scanned On a rude viol.

β. **1495** [see quot. 1398 in α]. **1642-53** LEIGHTON *Comm. 1 Pet.* ii. 12 (1693) 306 The word is *My Observers*, or those that scand my wayes every foot of them, that examine them as a Verse,..if there be but a wrong measure in them, they will ..mark it. **1729** MANDEVILLE *Fab. Bees* II. 416 The manner of scanding and chanting those Verses.

b. *absol.*

1642 MILTON *Apol. Smect.* Wks. 1851 III. 292 An eare that could measure a just cadence, and scan without articulating. **1735** POPE *To Arbuthnot* 165 Each Wight, who reads not, but who scans and spells. *a* **1740** J. WARTON *Sappho's Advice* 30 A pen I handled for a fan, And learnt not how to dance but scan.

c. *intr.* (for *pass.*). To admit of being scanned, to be found metrically correct.

1857 HUGHES *Tom Brown* II. iii, Martin..proceeded..to convert these..into Latin that would scan. **1865** F. A. PALEY tr. *Æschylus* 184 *note*, The lines will neither scan nor construe like ordinary verses.

†**2. a.** *trans.* To criticize; to test or estimate the correctness or value of; to judge *by* a certain rule or standard. Sometimes with allusion to sense 1.

c **1540** tr. *Pol. Verg.* I. (Camden) 95 Constantinus..did banishe Arrius,..bie cause hee went abowte to skanne the Christian religion with mischevus lies and glosinges [*quod Christiana dogmata nefariis commentis metiri est impie conatus*]. **1584** COGAN *Haven Health* ccxviii. (1636) 252 If a man would exactly scanne the temperature of beere. **1607** HIERON *Wks.* I. 179 The loue of fathers toward their children,..of egles to their young ones, of hens to their chickens, all these haue beene but shadowes to it, but no sufficient measures by which to skanne it [*sc.* God's mercy]. **1618** NAUNTON in *Fortescue Papers* (Camden) 64 For to write I had neither leysure, nor lyst to have my lines scanned by any equivocating preists. **1672** DRYDEN *Conq. Granada* II. i, The Rule of Happiness by Reason scan. **1732** POPE *Ess. Man* II. 1 Know then thy self, presume not God to scan. **1754** SHERLOCK *Disc.* (1759) I. i. 64 We attempt to scan the divine Justice by our narrow conceptions of it. **1764** GOLDSM. *Trav.* 333, I see the lords of human kind pass by. .. True to imagin'd right, above control, While e'en the peasant boasts these rights to scan, And learns to venerate himself as man. **1817** JAS. MILL *Brit. Ind.* II. v. iv. 428 The feeble discernment which has generally scanned the proceedings of the East India Company.

β. **1585** J. NORDEN *Sinfull Man's Solace* 161 b, If thou, oh sillie booke, doe chaunce To light into the hand Of any such as takes delight Ech others worke to scand.

†**b.** *intr.* To pass judgement *on, upon*; to form an opinion *of*. Often in indirect passive. *Obs.*

1582 A. MUNDAY *Eng. Romayne Lyfe* i. 10 But when the Pope had scanned on this hasty business..they were denyed their request. **1583** GOLDING *Calvin on Deut.* v. 26/1 By these wordes he betokeneth, that wee must rest wholely vppon that which God saith, and not stande scanning after our owne fancies. *Ibid.* xiii. 76/1 When men will needes scanne of Gods workes and prouidence according to their owne reason: they shall finde thinges to grudge at. **1587** TURBERV. *Trag. Tales* 42, I leaue for you to scan, Both of the maydens rich attyre, and iewels of the man. **1589** PUTTENHAM *Eng. Poesie* (Arb.) 132, I intend not to proceed any further in this curiositie..nor..to haue it put in execution in our vulgar Poesie, but to be pleasantly scanned vpon. **1602** ROWLANDS *Tis Merrie*, etc. 23 And when they meete, they do discourse and scan About whose choyce hath got the kindest man. **1610** HEALEY *St. Aug. Citie of God* III. xvii. 132 If this hadde hapened in our times, Lord how it would haue beene scanned vppon.

3. a. *trans.* To examine, consider, or discuss minutely. †*to scan out*: to discover by examination.

1550 CROWLEY *Inform. & Petit.* 706 Scan the wordes of the Psalmist concernyng this mattier. **1586** *Let. to Earl Leicester* 16 But you Lawyers are so nice in sifting and skanning euery woorde and letter. **1596** BABINGTON *Notes upon Genesis* xi. 82 The time of this tower built, and speech confounded, may be asked...I stand not vpon coniectures to scan it out. **1604** SHAKS. *Oth.* III. iii. 245 My Lord, I would I might intreat your Honor To scan this thing no farther. **1674** *Essex Papers* (Camden) I. 166 Whoever scanns y[e] words of y[e] Adress cannot..putt any other construction upon them then such as we have done. **1770** GOLDSM. *Des. Vill.* 161 Careless their merits or their faults to scan, His pity gave ere charity began. **1828** J. W. CROKER in *C. Papers* 11 July (1884), It is wonderful with what facility and accuracy he scanned all those facts. **1871** DARWIN *Desc. Man* II. xxi. 402 Man scans with scrupulous care, the character and pedigree of his horses..before he matches them. **1886** BOWEN in *Law Rep. 31 Chanc. Div.* 379 We ought not, I think, to scan the pleadings too narrowly upon a question of the right to discovery.

β. *a* **1635** RANDOLPH *Poems* (1638) 11 The smooth Viper every member [of sleeping Lycoris] scands.

†**b.** With clause as obj. *Obs.*

1558 PHAER *Æneid* III. F iv b, And what those walls shuld be we skanne, & councel great we take. **1594** CAREW *Huarte's Exam. Wits* v. 55 There riseth a like difficultie, in skanning whence it commeth that nature made two eyes, and two eares. **1621** T. WILLIAMSON tr. *Goulart's Wise Vieillard* 189 It belongs to some god, to scan and to see which of all these opinions is true.

†**4.** To interpret, assign a meaning to. *Obs.*

1562 HEYWOOD *Prov.* O iij, This woord *enough* twoo waies we may skan. Thone much enough, thother littell enough. **1602** SHAKS. *Ham.* III. iii. 75 And now Ile doo't, and so he goes to Heauen, And so am I reueng'd: that would be scann'd, A Villaine killes my Father, and for that I..do this same Villaine send To heauen. **1608** WILLET *Hexapla Exod.* 463 But concerning the limiting of the space of sixe yeares for seruice,..what might bee the reason thereof, thus it is diuersly scanned. 1. Some do thus moralize it [etc.]. **1611** HEYWOOD *Gold. Age* V. i, The Fates..Haue summon'd Saturnes three sonnes to the Tower, To them the three Dominions to assure Of Heauen, of Sea, of Hell. How these are scand, Let none decide but such as vnderstand. **1641** MILTON *Reform.* I. 4 Hence men came to scan the Scriptures by the Letter.

5. To perceive, discern. Now *rare.*

1558 PHAER *Æneid* II. F j b, Whan sodenly the sound Of feete we heare to tread, and men full thicke my father skand. **1605** *Hist. Capt. Stukeley* C 4, My meaning had you beene but heere euen now, you might haue scand without my vtterance. **1768** BEATTIE *Minstrel* I. l, One part, one little part, we dimly scan Through the dark medium of life's feverish dream. **1792** COWPER *Stanza for* 1792 ii, Man..not wise enough to scan His best concerns aright, Would gladly stretch life's little span To ages, if he might. **1808** SCOTT *Marmion* III. xii, His thoughts I scan not; but I ween, That [etc.]. **1868** TENNYSON *Lucretius* 192 A satyr..draws Nearer and nearer, and I scan him now Beastlier than any phantom of his kind.

6. a. To look at searchingly, examine with the eyes.

1798 SOPHIA LEE *Canterb. T., Young Lady's T.* II. 251 His wild..eyes now scanned heaven impatiently. **1810** SCOTT *Lady of L.* II. xxi, While Roderick scann'd, For her dear form, his mother's band. **1840** DICKENS *Barn. Rudge* ii, 'Humph', he said, when he had scanned his features, 'I don't know you'. **1853** KINGSLEY *Hypatia* x, She..sat scanning him intently from head to foot. **1861** J. H. BENNET *Shores of Medit.* II. xii. (1875) 412 The lost dog will scan the features of those who pass him in the street. **1893** F. C. SELOUS *Trav. S.E. Africa* 375, I climbed to the top of the hill in order to scan the country on ahead.

b. To search (literature, a text, a list, etc.) quickly or systematically for particular information or features.

1926 *Rec. Geol. Surv. India* LIX. 202 On scanning this table it will be observed that the pyrope molecule is present in quantity..only in one garnet. **1950** *Amer. Documentation* I. 81 The rapid selector employs an optical-electronic system for scanning a reel of motion picture film on which are entered both abstracts and corresponding index entries. **1966** *Computers & Humanities* I. 12 Some [articles] are so superficial that the reader for whom the volume is designed would do better to scan the most recent ACLS list of computerized research projects in the humanities. **1967** C. Berners-Lee in Wills & Yearsley *Handbk. Management Technol.* 7 Some computer manufacturers supply.. suites of statistical programs for scanning files to accumulate the required statistics and then to analyse them in one of a number of ways. **1967** *Times Rev. Industry* July 89/2 Without guide lines as to where the company wants to go, scanning environmental information becomes directionless. **1970** O. Dopping *Computers & Data Processing* xvii. 277 The computer first scans the table from the beginning to the end comparing the first record with the second, the second with the third, etc. **1972** *Computers & Humanities* VII. 19 Dilligan examines the extent to which linguistic orientation toward prosody serves as the basis for computer programs to scan large bodies of English verse. **1973** *Nature* 31 Aug. p. xiii/1 (Advt.), He or she will be required to scan incoming literature, undertake literature searches.

c. To cause (an area, object, or image) to be systematically traversed by a beam or detector; to convert (an image) into a linear sequence of signals in this way for purposes of transmission or processing; *spec.* in *Med.*, to make a scan of (the body or part of it); to examine (a patient, etc.) with a scanner.

1928 *Television* Nov. 9/1 One feature which is wrongly quoted by critics relates to how a scene is scanned. **1933** *Proc. Wireless Section Inst. Electr. Engineers* VIII. 219/2 Nipkow in 1884 proposed.. to transmit the picture point by point, or to scan the picture. **1953** Amos & Birkinshaw *Television Engin.* I. iv. 52 The electron beam is made to scan the target in a series of nearly horizontal lines. **1953** *Amer. Jrnl. Roentgenol.* LXX. 605/1 These instruments have been used to scan the thyroid gland of human patients in vivo. *Ibid.*, It becomes practical to scan a patient from head to toe in a routine manner. **1954** *Nucleonics* Jan. 60/1 By placing tracing paper and carbon paper between the stylus and the drawing table, the distribution of radioactivity in an area being scanned is recorded. **1962** A. Nisbett *Technique Sound Studio* iv. 81 A replay head scans a slightly greater length of tape than would be suggested by the size of the gap. **1966** *Sci. News* 3 Sept. 166 An improved way of scanning the brain for tumors has been reported by two California scientists. **1967** *Nursing Times* 18 Aug. 1093/1 Not so well known is the use of radio-isotopes in radiography, to enable various organs of the body to be 'scanned' to investigate function, or the presence of tumours. **1968** *Brit. Med. Bull.* XXIV. 191/2 Radiographs.. and so on.. can also be digitally structured for insertion in a computer... They are scanned line by line (television-wise) by a 'flying-spot scanner', and passed through an analogue-to-digital converter which.. encodes the contrast level of each point, as a row of holes. **1969** *Times* 15 Mar. 7/8 The photographs are scanned point by point by a photoelectric device. **1975** D. G. Fink *Electronics Engineers' Handbk.* xx. 79 Hard-copy facsimile systems generate a signal by systematically scanning the subject copy and producing a current corresponding to its light-intensity variations. **1986** *Acta Obstetr. & Gynecol. Scand.* LXV. 147/1 One hundred and fifteen women were considered to be at risk of cervical incompetence... They were scanned serially from the first trimester to 32 weeks of gestation.

d. *intr.* To carry out scanning. Const. various preps.

1934 J. H. Reyner *Television* viii. 95 By causing the spot on the cathode ray screen to scan over a suitable area the image of the spot traverses the whole of the film. **1948** 'N. Shute' *No Highway* v. 147 What interested me most, however, as in every technical paper that one scans through quickly, was the paragraph headed 'Conclusions'. **1953** A. T. Starr *Radio & Radar Technique* i. 46 For the purpose of homing on a ship or aircraft, it is sufficient to scan through a relatively small angle in azimuth, say ±30°. **1961** G. Millerson *Technique Television Production* ii. 20 A gun in the picture-tube.. produces such a stream of electrons, and this is made to scan over the powdered screen in a regular series of sweeps. **1965** 'J. le Carré' *Looking-Glass War* xviii. 204 He may start with the wrong crystal... It's safest for base to scan with so many crystals. **1975** *Physics Bull.* July 327/1 As the beam repeatedly scans across the faceplate, charge is accumulated. **1979** *Sci. Amer.* Mar. 82/1 Given a source of light that is monochromatic but tunable, an absorption spectrum can be measured by passing the light through a sample of the gas and scanning continuously through the frequencies surrounding a line in the spectrum.

e. *trans.* To traverse or light upon (a constituent element) as part of the scanning of the larger whole.

1937 A. M. Turing in *Proc. London Math. Soc.* XLII. 233 The machine moves so that it scans the square immediately to the right of the one it was scanning previously. **1937** *Discovery* Nov. 329/1 When the dots are being scanned, the transmitted signal depends on the relative brightness of the dots in turn. **1961** G. Millerson *Technique Television Production* ii. 19 As each element is scanned and gives up its information, it becomes 'wiped clean'.

f. To cause (a beam, etc.) systematically to traverse an area; to cause (an aerial) to rotate or oscillate to this end.

1960 E. V. Truefitt in R. F. Hansford *Radio Aids to Civil Aviation* v. 328 The nodding heightfinder is so called because the aerial performs a nodding motion which scans the radar beam in elevation. **1972** *Sci. Amer.* Nov. 40/3 The beam is positioned and focused by scanning the beam over the sample surface and detecting the change in the emission of secondary and reflected electrons as the beam passes over surface detail. **1973** Meyer & Mayer *Radar Target Detection* i. 15/1 If the antenna is scanned sufficiently slowly, more than one pulse may be transmitted and received while the antenna beam sweeps across a given reflecting point. **1976** *Physics Bull.* Oct. 437/1 The proton beam was scanned right across the annulus and hole. **1977** *Sci. Amer.* Sept. 123/3 A much smaller area.. is exposed, and the exposure is repeated by either stepping or scanning the image over the wafer.

†**7.** To climb. *Obs. rare*$^{-1}$. [A latinism.]

1596 Spenser *F.Q.* vii. vi. 8 Whose silver gates.. she entred,.. Ne staide till she the highest stage had scand.

Hence **'scanned** *ppl. a.*

1567 Drant *Horace, Ep.* ii. ii. Hiiij, As thou in lawfull scanned vearse canste well descryue a thinge. **1598** Marston *Pygmal.* iv. 154 When once they can in true skan'd verses frame A braue Encomium of good Vertues name. **1937** *Proc. London Math. Soc.* XLII. 231 We may call this square the 'scanned square'. **1953** Amos & Birkinshaw *Television Engin.* I. iv. 52 To avoid keystone effect and obtain a true rectangular scanned area, the line saw-tooth current is modulated by the field saw-tooth current so that the angular sweep in the horizontal plane is decreased as the beam moves up the mosaic. **1975** D. G. Fink *Electronics Engineers' Handbk.* xx. 8 Color television standards use the back porch to position the color burst, an eight-cycle burst of color subcarrier.. that synchronizes the color-subcarrier oscillator at the end of each scanned line.

scance (skæns), *sb. Sc.* Also 7–9 **skance.** [f. scance *v.*^{2}] **a.** A glance; a glimpse. **b.** A gleam (of light).

a. 1787 J. Skinner *Misc. Poetry* (1809) III. 108 O happy hour.. That.. gae him.. Sae braw a skance Of Ayrshire's dainty Poet. **1871** W. Alexander *Johnny Gibb* (1873) 66 Then they stumbled on a field of the laird's.. and took a 'skance' of what was going on there.

b. 1819–20 'Antiquary' *St. Patrick* 168 (Jam.), I looket up amang the craigs an saw a red scance o' light beekin' on the taps o' the highest o' them.

scance (skɑːns, -æ-), *v.*^{1} Chiefly *Sc.* Also 6–7, 9 **skance,** 7–8 **scanse.** [app. f. L. *scans-*, ppl. stem of *scandĕre* to climb, to scan.]

†**1.** *trans.* To examine critically, to scrutinize; to turn over in one's mind, to reflect on; also (with indirect question as obj.), to debate with oneself, 'wonder'. Cf. scan *v.* 2, 3. *Obs.*

1597 Montgomerie *Cherrie & Slae* 1357 Give him ȝour gude advyce; And panse not, nor skance not, The perril nor the pryce. **1603** *Philotus* ci, Full oft this mater did I skance, Bot with my self befoir. **1638** H. Adamson *Muses Threnodie* (1774) 161 How that can be forgote I greatlie scance.

2. *intr.* To reflect, comment, descant. Const. *of, on, upon.* Cf. scan *v.* 2b.

1606 Rollock *Lect. 2 Thess.* 28 (Jam.) To scanse of these things ouer far it is but vaine curiositie. **1739** A. Nicol *Nature without Art* 69 Oh my Muse, I want Engine To scance upon the Ancient Name. *Ibid.* 80, I ne'er admire the Learned, tho' they Scance On Stile and Numbers. **1806** A. Douglas *Poems* 151 (Jam.) Now round the ingle in a ring On public news they're scancin'.

†**3.** = scan *v.*^{1} *Obs. rare*$^{-1}$.

1704 T. Watt *Gram. made easy* (1742) 78 To know how to Scanse the 10 Ode of the first Book [of Horace].

4. *trans.* To climb. (Cf. scan *v.* 7.)

1714 R. Smith *Poems* (1853) 112 His Pious Soul did Jacob's Ladder scanse. **1861** R. W. Dixon *To Shadow* viii, If ever thou didst scance In a wayward wistful dance Up and down.. On the wall with giant scrawl.

scance (skɑːns, -æ-), *v.*^{2} Chiefly *Sc.* [Of obscure origin; cf. askance.]

1. *intr.* To glance, look with disdain.

1611 *Coryat's Crudities* Panegyr. Verses hjb, The Country Boores dasht with the matter Beganne on him to skance awry. **1883** R. Cleland *Inchbracken* xiv. 113 Cockin' her neb at decent folk, an' scancin' at my tuscan bonnet.

2. To make a display or show.

1813 Picken *Poems* I. 123 (Jam.) In silk an' sattin ilk ane scances, An' gawze beside.

Hence **'scancing** *ppl. a.*

a **1774** Fergusson *Poems* (1807) 344 Where now cou'd shine The scancin glories o' carmine?

scance, obs. form of sconce (fort).

Scand (skænd). Colloq. abbrev. of Scandinavian *sb.*

1930 J. Masefield *Wanderer of Liverpool* 14 The others, all Scands, from North Europe, not knowing a word Of English. **1965** *Sun* 28 Sept. 4/5 She is still reckoned a world beauty. How does she do it, this middle-aged Scand? **1973** H. Miller *Open City* ix. 87 She had spent four days among the stodgy, unsubtle Scands on his behalf.

scand, rare obs. form of sand *sb.*^{2}

scandal ('skændəl), *sb.* Forms: α. 3 **scandle, schandle, schaundle;** β. 6–7 **scandale, scandall,** 7 **skandall,** 6– **scandal.** [Early ME. *scandle*, *scha(u)ndle*, a. ONF. *escandle*, Central OF. *eschandle*, semi-popular ad. eccl. L. *scandalum* cause of offence or stumbling, ad. Gr. σκάνδαλον, recorded only in Hellenistic literature, in the fig. sense 'snare for an enemy, cause of moral stumbling', but certainly an old word meaning 'trap' (cf. the derivative σκανδάληθρον spring of a trap), believed to be f. the Indogermanic **skand-* to spring, leap: cf. L. *scandĕre* to climb, to scan.

Before the 16th c. the word occurs only in the *Ancren Riwle*, exc. in the forms treated s.v. slander *sb.* (from the OF. variants *escandre, esclandre*). In the 16th c. it was re-adopted from the Latin in the form *scandal*, possibly after the Fr. learned form *scandale*, which had been introduced to represent the strict sense of eccl. L. *scandalum*, as distinguished from the senses that had been developed by F. *esclandre*. Cf. Sp. *escándalo*, Pg. *escandalo*, It. *scandalo*, G. *skandal* (which has developed the sense 'up-roar'), Du. *schandaal*.]

1. In religious use. **a.** Discredit to religion occasioned by the conduct of a religious person; †conduct, on the part of a religious person, which brings discredit on religion. Also, perplexity of conscience occasioned by the conduct of one who is looked up to as an example.

α. *a* **1225** *Ancr. R.* 12 Auh hwarse wummon liueð oðer mon bi him one, eremite oðer ancre, of þinges wiðuten hwarof scandle ne kume: nis nout muche strencðe. *Ibid.* 108 Auh er þen þet biddunge arere eni schaundle, er heo ouh for to deien martir in hire meseise. *Ibid.* 380 ȝe nowen nout unnen þet eni vuel word kome of ou: uor schandle is heaued sunne.

β. **1581** Pettie tr. *Guazzo's Civ. Conv.* iii. (1586) 135 A punishment of her lightnesse and vanitie, by meanes whereof she hath giuen occasion of scandale and offence. *a* **1633** G. Herbert *Priest to Temple* xxiv, So for Scandall: what scandall is, wher given or taken; whether, there being two precepts, one of obeying authority, the other of not giving scandall, that ought not to be preferred, especially since in his obeying there is scandall also. **1740** C. C. Graves in *Wesley's Jrnl.* 1741–3 (1749) 68, I am heartily sorry, that I have given offence and scandal, by frequenting the meetings and attending the expositions of the persons commonly call'd Methodists. **1863** Froude *Hist. Eng.* VII. 24 Catholics.. could not appear in Protestant assemblies without causing scandal to the weaker brethren.

b. Something that hinders reception of the faith or obedience to the Divine law; an occasion of unbelief or moral lapse; a stumbling-block; = offence 2.

The New Testament phrase †*the scandal of the Cross* (Gr. τὸ σκάνδαλον τοῦ σταυροῦ, Vulg. *scandalum crucis*) seems to have been used by some writers with a colouring derived from sense 2.

1582 N. T. (Rhem.) *Matt.* xiii. 41 They shal gather out of his kingdom al scandals. —— *Gal.* v. 11 Then is the scandal [1611 offence; 1880 (*Revised*) stumbling-block] of the crosse euacuated. **1607** B. Barnes *Divils Charter* i. i. A3b, Since all skandalls are remou'd and cleer'd. **1619** Sanderson *Serm.* i. (1689) 3 Despising is both a grievous sin in the despiser, and a dangerous scandal to the despised. **1625** Bacon *Ess., Unity in Religion* (Arb.) 423 Heresies and Schismes, are of all others, the greatest Scandals. **1689** Hickeringill *Modest Inq.* iii. 28 Are not they that thus Excommunicate, the Schismaticks, by laying a Scandal in their Brothers way. **1754** Sherlock *Disc.* I. vii. 214 The Resurrection.. has wiped away the Scandal and Ignominy of the Cross. **1846** Keble *Lyra Innoc.* (1873) 107 Then, heavenly calmness, lest thou fall, Where scandals line the way. **1872** A. de Vere *Leg. St. Patrick* 117 That Crown of Truths, Scandal of fools, and conqueror of the world. **1908** Tyrrell in *Hibbert Jrnl.* Jan. 247 As a shock and scandal to the religious imagination of the masses, the thesis of Darwin is insignificant beside that of Galileo.

c. ***scandal of particularity*** [tr. Ger. (see quots. 1930, 1936)], the difficulty of seeing the particular man, Jesus, as the universal Saviour. Cf. particularity 1.

1930 tr. G. Kittel in Bell & Deissmann *Mysterium Christi* ii. 31 The scandal of particularity.. is the problem of history. Can a particular historical happening be peculiar? Can it be significant *sub specie aeternitatis*? And above all, can this particular occurrence be either peculiar or significant? **1936** C. H. Dodd *Apostolic Preaching & its Development* iv. 219 'Like a strange people left on earth After a judgment day.' This view of the historical status of the events comprised in the coming of Christ introduces us at once to what Professor Gerhard Kittel, in *Mysterium Christi*, calls '*das Ärgernis der Einmaligkeit*', 'the scandal of particularity'. **1961** *Listener* 9 Mar. 435/2 We do no service to religion by reducing either term of the problem, the total mystery of the Godhead or the scandal of particularity. **1979** C. F. D. Moule in M. D. Goulder *Incarnation & Myth* iv. 86 The 'scandal of particularity' is by no means a denial but rather a confirmation of the ubiquity and continuity of God's activity.

2. a. Damage to reputation; rumour or general comment injurious to reputation.

1590 Shaks. *Com. Err.* v. i. 15, I wonder much That you would put me to this shame and trouble, And not without some scandall to your selfe, With circumstance and oaths, so to denie This Chaine, which now you weare so openly. **1611** —— *Wint. T.* i. ii. 330 Giue scandall to the blood o' th' Prince, my Sonne,.. Without ripe mouing to't? **1615** W. Lawson *Country Housew. Gard.* (1626) A2, I could.. so shroud my selfe from scandall vnder your honourable fauour. **1643** Sir T. Browne *Relig. Med.* i. §1 For my Religion, though there bee severall circumstances that might perswade the world I have none at all, as the generall scandall of my profession [etc.]. **1687** A. Lovell tr. *Thevenot's Trav.* i. 102 A Stranger who had never seen them before, may without scandal, stop and talk to her he likes best. **1694** Penn *Rise & Progr. Quakers* i. 17 Persecuting one another, to the shame and scandal of their common Christianity. **1706** E. Ward *Wooden World Diss.* (1708) 42 Get drunk like a Gentleman, with no Scandal. **1798** in *Spirit Publ. Jrnls.* (1799) II. 259, I have practised levities for the sake of disrepute—and have written lampoons to be involved in the scandal. **1828** Scott *F.M. Perth* xii, The ill consequences or scandal which might arise from such a measure. **1856** Kane *Arct. Expl.* I. xxix. 387 To the scandal of our domestic regulations, the guns were all impracticable.

†**b.** A disgraceful imputation. In later use, a baseless imputation, a slander. *Obs.*

1602 Shaks. *Ham.* ii. i. 29 You must not put another scandall on him That hee is open to Incontinencie. **1621** T. Williamson tr. *Goulart's Wise Vieillard* 114 Cleansing vs from the filth of so many scandalls and imputations wherewith we haue beene disgraced and diffamed. **1708** Swift *Sentim. Ch. Eng. Man* Wks. 1751 IV. 93 To affirm that he [James II] had any cause to apprehend the same treatment with his Father, is an improbable scandal flung upon the nation by a few bigotted French scribblers. **1725** *Pope's Odyss.* ii. Notes I. 104 Eustathius.. quotes Herodotus, as affirming that she [*sc.* Penelope] had a son, named Pan, by Hermes; but the Bishop declares it is all a scandal. **1814** SCOTT *Swift's Works, Right of Preced. betw. Physicians & Civilians* (1824) VI. 326 *note*, Even Father Chaucer alludes to this scandal upon the medical faculty.

3. a. A grossly discreditable circumstance, event, or condition of things.

1591 SHAKS. *1 Hen. VI*, III. i. 69 Oh, what a Scandall is it to our Crowne, That two such Noble Peeres as ye should iarre? **1613** PURCHAS *Pilgrimage* (1614) 225 A scandall are the alterations which they are forced by the Inquisitors to make in their Authors and Monuments of Antiquitie. **1853** J. H. NEWMAN *Hist. Sk.* Ser. II. III. vi. 142 There were great scandals among the Bishops and Priests, as well as heresy. **1878** LECKY *Eng. in 18th C.* I. iii. 490 Those Fleet marriages which had become one of the strangest scandals of English life. **1885** *Law Times* LXXIX. 37/2 The thousand and one scandals of metropolitan misgovernment.

b. *concr.* A person whose conduct is a gross disgrace to his class, country, position, or the like.

1634 FORD *Perk. Warbeck* III. iv, What shall I call thee, thou grey-bearded scandal, That kick'st against the sovereignty to which Thou owest allegiance? **1683** WOOD in *Life* (O.H.S.) III. 60 Duncombe, a drunken M.A. of St. Marie Hall, a scandall to his profession. **1725** POPE *Odyss.* VIII. 387 But say, if that lewd scandal of the sky, To liberty restor'd, perfidious fly. **1743** FRANCIS tr. *Hor., Odes* II. xiii. 4 Thou bane and scandal of my land. **1814** SCOTT *Ld. of Isles* v. xxiv, So let it be, with the disgrace And scandal of her lofty race! **1889** *Spectator* 28 Dec., A Prime Minister nowadays is under no temptation to nominate men who will be either drones or scandals.

4. Offence to moral feeling or sense of decency.

1622 MABBE tr. *Aleman's Guzman d'Alf.* II. 273 The people take great scandall thereat. **1712** STEELE *Spect.* No. 546 ¶1 It gives me very great Scandal to observe, wherever I go, how much Skill, in buying all manner of goods, there is necessary to defend yourself from being cheated. **1821** BYRON *Two Foscari* v. i, Why So rashly? 'Twill give scandal. **1848** THACKERAY *Van. Fair* xxxiii, That old wretch had given himself up entirely to his bad courses, to the great scandal of the county. **1849** MACAULAY *Hist. Eng.* vi. II. 43 The disclosure, indeed, could not be made without great scandal. **1893** LELAND *Mem.* I. 160 The injured husband came raging on board and tried to shoot the captain, which made a great scandal.

5. The utterance of disgraceful imputations; defamatory talk. Now often playfully in milder sense, talk that is concerned with the faults or foibles of others, malicious gossip.

The word differs from the etymologically identical SLANDER in not implying the falsity of the imputations made.

1596 LODGE *Wits Misery* 17 The next Harpie of this breed is Scandale and Detraction. **1692** R. L'ESTRANGE *Fables* xxxi. 31 Those Liberties in Conversation... When they Exceed these Limits, they Degenerate into Scurrility, Scandal, and Reproach. **1716** ADDISON *Freeholder* No. 32 ¶11 Secret History and Scandal have always had their Allurements. **1779** SHERIDAN *Critic* II. i, *Sneer.* No scandal about Queen Elizabeth, I hope? **1867** FREEMAN *Norm. Conq.* (1876) I. vi. 411 Scandal affirmed that neither of them was really of kingly birth. **1886** WELLDON *Serm. Harrow* x. (1887) 148 Even in the worst courts there have been ladies upon whom the breath of scandal has never passed.

6. a. *Law.* Any injurious report published concerning another which may be the foundation of legal action.

1838 BELL *Dict. Law Scot.* s.v., All actions upon scandal, ..although competent in inferior courts, may also be brought before the Court of Session.

b. An irrelevancy or indecency introduced into a pleading to the derogation of the dignity of the court.

1750 *Vesey's Chanc. Cases* (1773) II. 24 The single question is, whether these charges, referred for scandal and impertinence, may be relevant to the merits. **1801** *Ibid.* (1827) VI. 514 It is not to be called scandal, if material, and relevant to the justice of the case. **1835** J. S. SMITH *Chanc. Pract.* (1837) I. 567.

7. *Comb.*, chiefly objective, as *scandal-bearer*, *-bearing* adj., *-monger*, *-mongering*, *monging* sb. and adj., *-mongery*; **scandal-broth**, **-potion**, **-water**, humorous names for tea; **scandal-crimp**, an agent for collecting scandal; **scandal-proof**, †*sb.* see quot.; *adj.*, unable to be touched by scandal; **scandal sheet**, a newspaper that is notorious for publishing scandalous or sensational stories.

1712 STEELE *Spect.* No. 427 ¶1 The Unwillingness to receive good Tidings is a quality as inseparable from a *Scandal-Bearer, as the Readiness to divulge bad. **1790** BURNS *Let. to Cunningham* 13 Feb., The *scandal-bearing help-mate of a village priest. **1795** POTTER *Dict. Cant* (ed. 2), **Scandal broth*, tea. **1798** WOLCOT (P. Pindar) *Tales Hoy* Wks. 1812 IV. 389 Even Rose's News-hunters, his *Scandal-crimps Are changed to wits. **1721** AMHERST *Terræ Fil.* xxxiii. 173 There is no society in the world without *scandal-mongers and tale-bearers. **1899** WATTS-DUNTON *Aylwin* v. II. 216 A man may be a scandal-monger without being really malignant. **1865** *Cornh. Mag.* Nov. 579 The infernal *scandal-mongering in the neighbourhood. **1874** HELPS *Soc. Press.* xii. 158 The grander vices of calumny and scandal-mongering. **1902** *Westm. Gaz.* 12 Mar. 2/1 A scandalmongering old lady. **1838** CARLYLE *Misc.* (1857) IV. 186 Are there not dinner-parties, 'æsthetic teas', *scandal-mongeries? **1801** COL. G. HANGER *Life* II. 109 Gossiping, *scandal-monging, and sweethearting. **1904** EDITH RICKERT *Reaper* 57 Get you home for a scandal-monging body! **1786** BURNS *Twa Dogs* 224 Whyles, owre the wee bit cup an' platie, They sip the *scandal potion pretty. *a* **1700** B. E. *Dict. Cant. Crew*, **Scandal-proof*, a thorough pac'd Alsatian, or Minter, one harden'd or past shame. **1904** SLADEN *When we were Lovers in Japan* II. viii, Their friendship was still recognised as scandal-proof. **1904** ADE *True Bills* 110 The *Scandal Sheets never show up my Family History. **1939** R. CHANDLER *Big Sleep* xi. 82 The deal has to be closed to-night or they give the stuff to some scandal sheet. **1974** M. HOUSE et al. *Lett. Charles Dickens* III. 363/2 The *Age* and *Satirist*, though infamous indeed, were mere weekly scandal-sheets of no influence or political import. **1981** C. R. LAJEUNESSE *Dead Man Running* xi. 33 Nobody pays attention to that scandal sheet, let alone reads it. **1873** LELAND *Egypt. Sketch-Bk.* 234 The Tabbies [kill their neighbours' reputations] with '*scandal-water'.

scandal ('skændəl) *v.* Forms: 6–7 **scandall, scandale,** 7– **scandal.** [f. SCANDAL *sb.*]

†**1.** *trans.* To disgrace, bring into ill repute or obloquy. *Obs.*

1592 *Nobody & Someb.* E2b, O God, that one borne noble should be so base, His generous blood to scandall all his race. **1615** CHAPMAN *Odyss.* XXII. 586 Scandalling the Court, With men debaucht, in so abhorr'd a sort. **1662** J. WILSON *Cheats* II. iii, Lest the Profession should be scandal'd by it, we hold it better, to trust Providence, by forswearing the Fact. **1684** BUNYAN *Holy Life* 99 If you will not leave off to name the name of Christ, nor yet depart from iniquity, you also scandal the sincere professors of Religion.

2. a. To spread scandal concerning (a person); to defame. Now *arch.* and *dial.* (see E.D.D.). †**b.** To vituperate, revile. *Obs.*

1601 SHAKS. *Jul. C.* I. ii. 76 If you know That I do fawne on them [*sic*], and hugge them hard, And after scandall them ..then hold me dangerous. **1632** LITHGOW *Trav.* VI. 245, [I] intreat you..onely to abstaine from scandalling and mocking our Rites. **1700** DRYDEN *Flower & Leaf* 607 She.. gave me Charms and Sigils, for Defence Against ill Tongues that scandal Innocence. **1894** F. S. ELLIS *Reynard the Fox* 79 And Reynard's crimes were finely handled; Well he and Ermelyne were scandalled.

†**3.** To be a cause of stumbling to; to injure by evil example. *Obs.*

1632 STRAFFORD in Browning *Life* (1892) 301 As for his example of life, itt was soe vertuouse, or so viciouse, as I beleeue wee might finde hundreths scandalled sooner, then one betterd by it.

†**4.** To shock the feelings of; to scandalize. *Obs.*

1643 CHAS. I in Clarendon *Hist. Reb.* VI. §346 To the great danger of scandaling of our well affected Subjects. **1701** STEELE *Chr. Hero* (1711) 60 There are Earthly and Narrow Souls, as deeply Scandal'd at the Prosperity the Professors and Teachers of this Sacred Faith enjoy.

†**'scandalist.** *Obs.* [f. SCANDAL *sb.* + -IST.] One who causes scandal.

a **1706** EVELYN *Hist. Relig.* (1850) II. 262 That public scandalists should be suspended the Eucharist.

scandalization (ˌskændəlaɪ'zeɪʃən). [f. SCANDALIZE *v.* + -ATION.] The action of scandalizing; the condition or fact of being scandalized.

1530 *Dial. Gent. & Husb.* in Roy *Rede me* (Arb.) 168 Let one lyue neuer so wyckedly In abhominable scandalisacion ..They shall make of him no accusacion. **1881** *Daily Tel.* 14 Feb., The Prince and his wife, to the amusement of some and the scandalisation of others, indulged in a violent bout of fisticuffs in open court. **1883** *Harper's Mag.* Dec. 90/1 State of scandalization and outraged proprieties.

scandalize ('skændəlaɪz), *v.*[1] [a. F. *scandaliser* (OF. *escandalisier*), ad. eccl. L. *scandalizāre*, ad. late Gr. σκανδαλίζειν, f. σκάνδαλον: see SCANDAL *sb.* and -IZE. Cf. Sp. *escandalizar*, Pg. *escandalisar*, It. *scandalizzare*, *scandalezzare*.]

†**1.** *trans.* To bruit abroad, make a public scandal of (a discreditable secret). *Obs. rare*⁻¹.

c **1489** CAXTON *Blanchardyn* 44 Ye wyll scandalyze & vttre your mysfal that is now happed to you of one man.

2. To be the occasion of stumbling to; to injure spiritually by one's example. Now *rare*.

1538 POLE *Let.* 1 Aug. in Strype *Eccl. Mem.* I. App. lxxxiii. 214 But they that scandalize a whole Nation, what shal follow? **1609** DOWNAM *Chr. Libertie* 78 Thou doest scandalize..thy weake brethren.

3. To utter false or malicious reports of (a person's) conduct; to slander, to charge slanderously (†*with*). Now somewhat *rare*. In early use also †to insult, treat with contempt.

1566 in Strype *Ann. Ref.* (1709) I. xlviii. 486 He came thither..to embrace the Truth, which he had for a long time scandalized and rejected. **1606** G. W[OODCOCKE] *Hist. Ivstine* XX. 77 Let Iustice carry his ballance neuer so euen, the gouernment shall be dispised, the lawes scandalised, religion disdained, authority slandered. **1631** HEYWOOD *London's Jus Hon.* Ded. to Sheriffs, The Tribunes of the people..are cal'd Sacro Sancti, whose persons might not be iniured, nor their names any way scandaliz'd. **1705** VANBRUGH *Confederacy* IV. 53 We'll read Verses,..tell Lies, scandalize our Friends. **1790** PENNANT *London* (1813) 499 He was scandalized with suicide. **1819** SCOTT *Ivanhoe* xxxvi, To tell his tale might be interpreted into scandalizing the Order. **1840** DICKENS *Old C. Shop* iv, The company being accustomed to scandalise each other in pairs. **1865** *Intell. Observer* No. 42. 412 Scandalise or malign the owl's character.

b. *absol.* and *intr.* To talk scandal.

1745 FRANKLIN *On Scandal* Wks. 1887 II. 27 If to scandalize be really a crime, what do these puppies mean? **1888** HENLEY *Bk. Verses* 122 Saving to scrub, to bake, to brew, Nurse, dress, prattle, and scandalize, Nothing is left for the men to do.

4. *trans.* To bring shame or discredit upon; to disgrace. *Obs.* exc. *poet.*

1583 STUBBES *Anat. Abus.* II. (1882) 91 Nor yet any church scandalized with the wicked liues of their pastors. **1631** GOUGE *God's Arrows* I. §45. 78 To live under the Gospell of Christ, and to live in sinne is..to scandalize the Word of Grace. **1659** *Burton's Diary* (1828) IV. 438 The Committee thought it reasonable to..adjourn to the Inner Court of Wards, he being scandalized to stand at that bar where he had been judge of the Court. **1700** T. BROWN *Amusem. Ser. & Com.* 32 There's a Beau..going to sell himself to Barbadoes, to keep himself..from Scandalizing his Relations at Tyburn. **1880** TENNYSON *Columbus* 189 We, who bore the Cross Thither, were excommunicated there, For curbing crimes that scandalised the Cross.

5. To horrify or shock by some supposed violation of morality or propriety.

1647 CLARENDON *Hist. Reb.* I. §42 Others..were more scandalized at so precipitate a Promotion of a person of Such an Education. **1676** *North's Plutarch, Add. Lives* 90 The Spaniards..had by their filthy behaviour scandalized all the chief inhabitants of the Island. **1706** E. WARD *Wooden World Diss.* (1708) 14 He is much scandaliz'd to find any in his Ship out-witting him. **1779** GIBBON *Misc. Wks.* (1814) IV. 623 The critic is scandalized at the epithets of scanty and suspicious. **1849** JAMES *Woodman* v, You will scandalise our reverend friend here. **1873** SYMONDS *Gk. Poets* iii. 79 The prudes of antiquity were scandalized at Solon, for having penned some amorous verses of very questionable character.

scandalize ('skændəlaɪz), *v.*[2] *Naut.* [Alteration of SCANTELIZE, assimilated to prec. Cf. SCANTLE *v.* 4.] *trans.* To reduce the area of (a sail) by lowering the peak and tricing up the tack.

1862 'VANDERDECKEN' *Yacht Sailor* 18 Keep your peak standing, or scandalise the mainsail. **1867** *N. & Q.* 28 Sept. 260/2 *Scandalising a Sail.* This phrase is neither very new, nor confined to Thanet. It was in common use among Cornish sailors fully forty years ago.

Hence **'scandalized** *ppl. a.*

1893 CLARK RUSSELL *Ida Noble* 205 We reduced the schooner down to what is termed a scandalised mainsail and a jib.

scandalized ('skændəlaɪzd), *ppl. a.* [f. SCANDALIZE *v.*[1] + -ED[1].] In senses of the verb; now only, Horrified, shocked.

1664 H. MORE *Myst. Iniq.* I. II. vii. 130 By their absence and silence will they preach and inculcate Atheism and Infidelity into their scandalized Clergie. **1861** LYTTON *Str. Story* xxvi. (1864) 82 My eye turned in scandalized alarm towards Mrs. Poyntz. **1890** S. J. DUNCAN *Soc. Departure* 305 Mrs. Fitzomnipo..smoketh cigarettes..under the very noses of the scandalised.

scandalizer ('skændəlaɪzə(r)). [f. SCANDALIZE *v.*[1] + -ER[1].]

1. One who slanders; a libeller.

1632 LITHGOW *Trav.* IX. 409 A damnable scandalizer of the Church. **1680** J. PHILLIPS *Dr. Oates's Narrat. Vind.* 52 The Scandalizer of the Presbyterians, and the Vindicator of the English Catholicks. **1865** *Cornh. Mag.* Nov. 484 The assembled fathers decreed that the corpse of the scandaliser of women should forthwith be exhumed.

2. One who places a moral stumbling-block in the way of another. ? *Obs.*

1680 BAXTER *Cath. Commun.* I. xi. (1684) 28 Even those little ones of whose scandalizers and neglecters Christ spake so terribly, were none of them without some Sin.

scandalizing ('skændəlaɪzɪŋ), *vbl. sb.* [f. SCANDALIZE *v.*[1] + -ING[1].] The action of the verb SCANDALIZE in various senses.

1575 GASCOIGNE *Posies* Ep. to Rev. Divines ¶¶j, [They] haue presumed to thinke that the same was indeed written to the scandalizing of some worthie personages. **1637** GILLESPIE *Eng. Pop. Cerem.* II. ix. 39 They are rather to be thought obstinate in scandalizing, who..take not away the occasion of the scandall. **1709** STRYPE *Ann. Ref.* I. xxiii. 237 It was thought fit that the Scandalizing of such a Person should not be passed over without publick Satisfaction. **1816** W. DUNCAN *Sel. Orat. Cicero* x. 311 Scandalising has nothing in view but contumely.

scandalizing ('skændəlaɪzɪŋ), *ppl. a.* [f. SCANDALIZE *v.*[1] + -ING[2].] That scandalizes.

1. Causing offence.

1594 HOOKER *Eccl. Pol.* IV. xii. §2 Good things haue no scandalizing nature in them. **1661** GURNALL *Chr. in Arm.* III. Ep. Ded., Neither have you in this scandalizing Age laid a stone of offence before others, but admirably vindicated the honour of Religion.

2. Uttering malicious and false reports.

1646 'ALETHEGRAPHUS' *Let. to G. Wither* 1 Being stigmatized, at least with the name of lying and Scandalizing Bard. **1847** *Mischief of the Muses* 45, I bear the jokes Of cruel scandalizing folks. **1876** CLARK RUSSELL *Is he the Man?* II. 226, I would..wash my hands of this unjust scandalizing neighbourhood.

†**'scandalled,** *ppl. a. Obs.* Also 7 scandald. [f. SCANDAL *v.* + -ED[1].]

1. Disgraced, shameful.

1610 SHAKS. *Temp.* IV. i. 90 Since they did plot The meanes, that duskie Dis, my daughter got, Her, and her blind-Boyes scandald company, I haue forsworne.

2. Slandered, falsely accused.

a **1639** T. CAREW *Fem. Honour* 3 When scandall'd vertue might be bold, Bare foot, upon sharp Cultures spread O'r burning coles to march. **1660** *Plea for Ministers in Sequestr.* 3 What with him was the highest cognizance of (not the scandalous but scandeled) Puritan Ministers, but the brand of Raschals?

†**'scandaller.** *Obs.* [f. SCANDAL *v.* + -ER[1].] One who utters scandal; one who slanders.

c **1620** W. HUDSON in *Intell. Observer* (1867) XI. 107 Libellers, scandalors of the state, and such like. **1684** 'PHILO PATER' *Observator Reproved* 5 The first step to it in Petitioning against the Observator, for a Common Scandaler of the Church and Church-men.

scandalous ('skændələs), *a.* (and *sb.*). Also 6 scandelouse, 7 scandolous, scandelous. [a. F. *scandaleux* = Sp., Pg. *escandaloso*, It. *scandaloso*, med.L. *scandalōsus*, f. eccl. L. *scandalum*: see SCANDAL *sb.* and -OUS.]

A. *adj.* †**1.** Of the nature of, or causing, a 'stumbling-block' or occasion of offence; also, bringing discredit on one's class or position. *Obs.*

1592 *Maldon (Essex) Borough Deeds* Bundle 149 No. 13 Hereby you are growen verie scandalouse and offensive vnto many. **1649** MILTON *Eikon.* xxvii. 216 Many Laws..may be found both scandalous and full of greevance to their Posterity that made them. **1670** WALTON *Lives* I. 47 He was enabled..to make such provision for his children that they were not left scandalous, as relating to their or his Profession and Quality.

†**b.** In the 17th century applied to ministers of religion who were regarded as unfit for their office on the ground of heresy or unbecoming conduct.

1631 *High Commission Cases* (Camden) 219 That such were scandalous and fitt to be therfore removed from the ministry. **1647** CLARENDON *Hist. Reb.* III. §56 Who were quickly taught, to call all those against whom such Petitions and Articles were exhibited the Scandalous Clergy; which appellation was frequently applied to men of great Gravity and Learning, and the most Unblemish'd lives. **1667** MARVELL *Corr.* Wks. (Grosart) II. 242 Yesterday was the debate concerning..the punishing of scandalous Clergymen.

2. Of the nature of a scandal; grossly disgraceful. Also (now *rarely*) of a person: Guilty of grossly disgraceful conduct, infamous.

1611 SHAKS. *Wint. T.* II. iii. 121 But this most cruell vsage of your Queene..somthing sauors Of Tyrannie, and will ignoble make you, Yea, scandalous to the World. **1681** FLAVEL *Meth. Grace* xxxv. 588 The scandalous falls of good men are like a bag of poison cast by Satan into the spring whence the whole town is supplied with water. *a* **1704** T. BROWN *Eng. Sat.* Wks. 1730 I. 28 Domitian, the most scandalous emperor, and most infamous of men. **1720** HEARNE *Collect.* (O.H.S.) VII. 91 The most scandalous Election that ever was in Oxford. **1769** *Junius Lett.* lxviii. 348 Scandalous traffic..is introduced into the administration of justice. **1770** BURKE *Pres. Discont.* 52 Persons not only generally scandalous in their lives, but the identical persons who [etc.]. **1828** SCOTT *F.M. Perth* xxv, I ..was this instant setting forth to Kinfauns, to plead my innocence of this scandalous charge. **1849** MACAULAY *Hist. Eng.* vi. II. 96 The worst that can be said of him is that he was indolent, luxurious, and worldly: but such failings..are scandalous in a prelate. **1868** E. EDWARDS *Ralegh* I. xx. 445 The great extent to which they [bribes] were accepted has long been one of the foulest scandals of a scandalous reign.

3. Of words and writing: Defamatory, libellous. Of persons: Addicted to or loving scandal.

1603 SHAKS. *Meas. for M.* v. i. 122 Shall we thus permit A blasting and a scandalous breath to fall, On him so neere vs? **1617** MORYSON *Itin.* II. 167 They were not content to returne a resolute answere, but added scandalous words, terming us *meschini.* **1642** (*title*) An Ordinance..for prohibiting the printing..of any Lying Pamphlet scandalous to His Majestie. **1646** H. MARKHAM *Let.* in *12th Rep. Hist. MSS. Comm.* App. v. 2, I shall not trouble your Ladyship with her scandelous and sawcy language of my Lorde or yourselfe. **1700** CONGREVE *Way of World* II. ii, He ..will willingly dispence with the hearing of one scandalous Story. **1749** FIELDING *Tom Jones* II. vii, The most scandalous tongues have never dared censure my reputation. **1821–22** SHELLEY *Chas. I*, III. 48 In distraining for ten thousand pounds Upon his books and furniture at Lincoln, Were found these scandalous and seditious letters. **1875** TENNYSON *Q. Mary* v. ii, But I am small and scandalous, And love to hear bad tales of Philip.

4. Of a statement, etc.: Not pertinent to the case, irrelevant.

1750 *Vesey's Chanc. Cases* (1773) II. 24 Nothing pertinent to the cause can be said to be scandalous. **1809** *Ibid.* (1827) XV. 477 The introduction of irrelevant and scandalous matter upon affidavits. **1835** J. S. SMITH *Chanc. Pract.* (1837) I. 567.

†**5.** *Path.* ? Putrid, offensive. *Obs.*

1676 WISEMAN *Chirurg. Treat.* VII. vi. 66 These are the Ulcers which render *fistulæ ani* Scandalous. **1694** SALMON *Bate's Dispens.* (1713) 183/1 It cures the Scurvy, (even when it is become scandalous).

B. *sb. slang.* A periwig.

a **1700** in B. E. *Dict. Cant. Crew.*

scandalously ('skændələslı), *adv.* [f. SCANDALOUS *a.* + -LY[2].] In a scandalous manner.

1602 in Moryson *Itin.* (1617) II. 252 Some seditious persons..speak scandalously. **1631** GOUGE *God's Arrows* Treat. III. §39 Provided that the good lawes..be not herein scandalously violated. **1756** BURKE *Vind. Nat. Soc.* 51 So scandalously debauched a People as that of Venice, is to be met with no where else. **1810** SCOTT *Let.* in *Lockhart* (1837) II. viii. 302, I have been scandalously lazy in answering your kind epistle. **1895** *Law Times* XCIX. 499/2 The number of convictions is so scandalously out of proportion to the number of crimes committed.

'scandalousness. [f. SCANDALOUS *a.* + -NESS.] The quality of being scandalous.

1646 P. BULKELEY *Gospel Covt.* v. 383 If we open the mouthes of men against our profession, by the reason of the scandallousness of our lives, we shall have the greater sinne. **1818** COBBETT *Pol. Reg.* XXXIII. 462 They even surpassed the Pittites in the prodigality and scandalousness of their giants [etc.].

‖**'scandalum mag'natum.** *Law.* Pl. scandala magnatum. *Obs.* exc. *Hist.* [med.L., 'scandal of magnates': *scandalum* SCANDAL *sb.*, *magnātum* gen. pl. of *magnās* MAGNATE.

The term was suggested by the wording of the statute *2 Ric. II* stat. 1 c. 5, which provides penalties for the offence; the Anglo-Fr. text of the statute, however, does not contain any literally equivalent expression.]

The utterance or publication of a malicious report against any person holding a position of dignity. (In popular writings, the plural was sometimes misused as a sing.) Also *transf.* in jocular use, something scandalous.

1607 MIDDLETON *Phoenix* F j b, A Writ of Delay, Longsword. *Scandala Magnatum*, Backesword. **1632** MASSINGER *City Madam* I. i, 'Tis more punishable in our house Then Scandalum magnatum. **1682** N. O. *Boileau's Lutrin* II. 14 Venturing at last on *Scandalum Magnatum*, Two thousand more; yet still the Jade did rate 'um. **1692** R. L'ESTRANGE *Fables* clvi. 141 A *Scandala Magnatum*, or a Libel upon his Superiors. **1713** ADDISON *Trial Count Tariff* 9 He in the First Place accused his Adversary of *Scandalum magnatum.* **1771** BURKE *Sp. Powers Juries* (1816) I. 83 The statute of *scandalum magnatum* is the oldest that I know. **1850** SMEDLEY *Frank Fairlegh* iv, *Scandalum magnatum!* not a true bill.

scandaroon (skændə'ru:n). Also 7 skanderoun. [Presumably from *Scanderoon*, *Iskanderūn*, the name of a seaport in Syria.]

†**1.** ? A swindler, fraudulent dealer. *Obs.*

1631 WEEVER *Anc. Funeral Mon.* 342 There are a company of notable Skanderouns which greatly desire to be stiled Merchants, and these are such as runne from house to house, from Market to Market,..with packs and Fardels vpon their backes, filled with counterfeit and adulterate wares..: and these are called Pedlers.

2. A variety of Carrier Pigeon.

Perh. so called from the fact that 'formerly the Pigeon was employed by the English Factory at Scanderoon to carry intelligence of the arrival of their ships in that port to Aleppo' (*Encycl. Metrop.* XVII. 37).

1860 BRENT *Pigeon Bk.* 21 The Scandaroon, or Great Horseman (*Columba tuberculosa*)... This is another breed of the Wattled Pigeons. **1879** L. WRIGHT *Pract. Pigeon Keeper* 80 We should..be very much inclined to try a cross with a white Scandaroon.

scandent ('skændənt), *a. Zool.* and *Bot.* [ad. L. *scandent-em*, pr. pple. of *scandĕre* to climb: see SCAN *v.*] Climbing; ascending.

a **1682** SIR T. BROWNE *Tracts* (1683) 7 Hedera or Ivy, which notwithstanding, except in its scandent nature, agreed not fully with the other. *c* **1711** PETIVER *Gazophyl.* ix. 84 A scandent Plant with long opposite Leaves, and a Melon-like Root. **1821** W. P. C. BARTON *Flora N. Amer.* I. 38 Root perennial, stem scandent, red. **1847** HODGSON in *Jrnl. Asiatic Soc. Bengal* XVI. II. 700 The Goats have callosities on the chest and knees... Eminently bold, saucy, and scandent. **1879** M. COLLINS *Pen Sketches* I. 116 Covered by blossoming wistaria and other scandent plants.

†**'Scanderbeg,** *sb.* and *a. Obs.* Also 6–7 scanderbag. [A use of the Turkish appellation (*Iskander* = Alexander, with the title BEG *sb.*[1]) of George Castriotes, who led a successful revolt of the Albanians against the Turks in the 15th c.] **a.** *sb.* The proper name used allusively: One resembling Scanderbeg. **b.** *adj.* Used as an epithet of abuse: Rascally.

1598 B. JONSON *Ev. Man in Hum.* I. ii. (1601) B 4, Horson Scanderbag rogue. *a* **1635** RANDOLPH *Hey for Honesty* III. i. (1651) 21 And I will be the Scanderbeg of the Company, The very Tamberlane of this ragged rout. **1684** OTWAY *Atheist* I. i, The Scanderbeg-monkey has not behav'd himself unhandsomely.

Hence †**scanderbegging** *ppl. a.*

1593 G. HARVEY *New Letter* D 3 b, Haue you forgot the Scanderbegging wight?

Scandian ('skændıən), *a.* [f. L. *Scandia* (app. a synonym of *Scandinavia*) + -AN.] = SCANDINAVIAN; *subst.* an inhabitant of Scandinavia.

1668 WILKINS *Real Char.* I. i. §3. 3 The Danish, Scandian, or perhaps the Gothic [dialect], to which belongs the Language used in Denmark, Norway, Swedeland, and Island. **1708** CHAMBERLAYNE *St. Gt. Brit.* I. III. iii. (1743) 162 Norway, inhabited by the Progeny of the old Scandians. **1887** SKEAT *Princ. Engl. Etymol.* 454 The only objection to the title 'Scandinavian' is its length, on which account I shall take the liberty to shorten it to 'Scandian'.

†**'Scandic,** *a. Obs.* [f. *Scandia* (see prec.) + -IC.] = SCANDINAVIAN *a.*

1708 CHAMBERLAYNE *St. Gt. Brit.* I. III. iii. (1743) 162 Their Christian names were generally Scandic. **1808** FINLAY *Sc. Hist. & Rom. Ballads* I. p. xxix, The Scandic scholars, we know, lay claim to an extravagant antiquity for their Edda.

Scandihoovian (,skændı'hu:vıən), *sb.* (and *a.*) *slang* (chiefly *N. Amer.*). Also -huvian. Arbitrary jocular alteration of SCANDINAVIAN *sb.* Also as *adj.*

1929 F. BOWEN *Sea Slang* 117 *Scandihoovian*, any Scandinavian; used as an alternative to *Scandiwegan* or *Scowegian*, but generally in mild contempt. **1966** *Publ. Amer. Dial. Soc. 1964* XLII. 39 Applied to all Scandinavians ..were *scoop, Scandihuvian*, and *Scandie.* **1968** *Amer. Speech* XLIII. 303 There's plenty of color in his [*sc.* the logger's] language too... His 'snuff' is *Scandihoovian dynamite.* **1973** B. BROADFOOT *Ten Lost Years* xi. 120 Salt cod! Ugh! Even a Scandihoovian couldn't take that.

Scandiknavery (,skændı'neıvərı). *nonce-wd.* [Fanciful blend of SCANDINAVIAN *a.* or *sb.* and KNAVERY.] Deceit or trickery by Scandinavians.

1939 JOYCE *Finnegans Wake* 47 We'll have a free trade Gaels' band and mass meeting For to sod the brave son of Scandiknavery. **1971** S. E. MORISON *European Discovery Amer.: Northern Voy.* iii. 72 Michael A. Musmanno's *Columbus was First* (1966) is an amusing, emotional assault on what he calls 'Scandiknavery'.

Scandinavian (,skændı'neıvıən), *a.* and *sb.* [f. L. *Scandinavia* + -AN.

The name *Scandinavia*, which appears in the existing text of Pliny, is a mistake for *Scadinavia*, a. Teut. **Skadinaujā*, whence by normal phonetic development OE. *Scędeniᵹ* (Beowulf 3336) = ON. *Skáney* (adopted in OE. as *Scōnéᵹ*), the name of the southern extremity of Sweden; the terminal element is **aujā*, OE. *éᵹ*, *íᵹ*, island.]

A. *adj.* **1.** Of or pertaining to Scandinavia, a geographical term including the three countries Norway, Sweden, and Denmark.

1784 JERNINGHAM (*title*) The Rise and Progress of the Scandinavian Poetry. **1864** D. COOK in *Once a Week* 26 Nov. 627/2 The flowing flaxen Scandinavian locks which Mr. Fechter's picturesque *Hamlet* has brought upon the boards.

2. Applied to a style of furnishing, etc., in a Scandinavian manner, esp. as characterized by simplicity of design and the use of pine-wood.

1959 R. CONDON *Manchurian Candidate* ii. 19 All of the furniture was made of blond wood in mutated, modern Scandinavian design. **1964** L. DEIGHTON *Funeral in Berlin* vi. 42 There was Scandinavian-style East German furniture in the room. **1968** S. B. HOUGH *Sweet Sister Seduced* xxviii. 163 He looked around the room, at the Scandinavian chairs, at the window curtains, and the Hi-fi in the corner. **1972** C. FREMLIN *Appointment with Yesterday* xi. 83 Visions of colourful teenage rooms in the Sunday colour-supplements, with Scandinavian wood window-seats, and bright cushions. **1979** M. EDEN *Document of Last Nazi* xxix. 171 A neat, cold-looking room, with..Scandinavian furniture.

B. *sb.* **1.** One connected ethnographically with one of the Scandinavian countries.

1830 SCOTT *Ivanhoe* xlii. *note*, The architecture of the ancient Scandinavians.

2. The various languages of the Scandinavian peoples considered as a unit; *spec.* North Germanic, a subdivision of the Germanic group of Indo-European languages spoken principally in Scandinavia.

1766 J. CLELAND *Way to Things by Words* 63 A sense which it also specifically has in the old Scandinavian. **1822** tr. *Malte-Brun's Universal Geogr.* I. 568 The Mœso-Gothic, ..the Icelandic and modern Scandinavian, in its two principal dialects the Swedish and the Danish, constitute the Gothic branch. **1888** J. WRIGHT tr. *Brugmann's Elem. Compar. Gram. Indo-Gmc. Lang.* I. 10 Norse (or Scandinavian)..down to the Viking period (800–1000 A.D.) was practically a single language. **1933** L. BLOOMFIELD *Language* iv. 59 While the language of the Lombards seems to have been of the West Germanic type, the others, including Gothic, were closer to Scandinavian. **1954** PEI & GAYNOR *Dict. Linguistics* 148 *North Germanic*, a branch of the Germanic group of the Indo-European family of languages; it comprises Icelandic, Swedish, Danish, Norwegian, Faroese and Gotlandic (or Gutnian). Also called *Scandinavian.* **1966** W. P. LEHMANN in Birnbaum & Puhvel *Anc. Indo-Europ. Dial.* 18 The occurrence of a third singular form without *-t* in the three coastal dialects of West Germanic and in Scandinavian gives evidence of interrelations between these dialects subsequent to the earliest dialect division of Proto-Germanic. **1978** W. WHITE in W. Whitman *Daybooks & Notebooks* I. 69 Rasmus B. Anderson..Professor of Scandinavian at the University of Wisconsin.

Hence **Scandi'navianism**, the characteristic ideas of the Scandinavian people.

1864 *Daily Tel.* 11 May, During the first quarter, however, of the present century, there was a national reaction in favour of Scandinavianism. **1907** *Academy* 5 Oct. 962/1 In plastic art there is a certain Scandinavianism visible, which has lasted longest in Iceland.

Scandinavianize (,skændı'neıvıənaız), *v.* [f. SCANDINAVIAN *a.* + -IZE.] *trans.* To render (place-names, etc.) Scandinavian in form or character. So ,**Scandi'navianized** *ppl. a.*; hence ,**Scandi,naviani'zation.**

1924 MAWER & STENTON *Introd. to Survey of Eng. Place-Names* iv. 60 English names often appear in a Scandinavianised form. **1933** *Times Lit. Suppl.* 20 Apr. 271/3 The distribution of place-names..is conclusive proof that all but the south-western Corner of Northamptonshire was Scandinavianized to a far greater extent than has been realized. **1937** *Harvard Stud. & Notes in Philol. & Lit.* XX. 155 *Cyninges-clif*, High Coniscliffe... The modern form shows adaptation of the first el[ement] to ON *konungr* for OE *cyning*; for further examples [of] a similar Scandinavianization see..'Connington'. **1956** I. S. MAXWELL in D. L. Linton *Sheffield* 131 Those settlements sited somewhat farther from the rivers whose names also contain Scandinavian elements or have been Scandinavianized. **1959** C. L. WRENN *Word & Symbol* (1967) 24 It would seem..that the Irish word [*cros*] came into Old English rather through Scandinavianised Irish settlers than direct. **1962** H. R. LOYN *Anglo-Saxon England* (1963) i. 60 Only occasionally, as in the Wreak valley..is there overwhelming Scandinavianization of the place-name structure. **1970** *Jrnl. Eng. Place-Name Soc.* II. 12 Rudston YE 98 (originally OE **rōd-stān*) appears in the Bruce fief with the second element scandinavianised to *-stein*, *Rodestein* 332v beside DB *Rodestan. Ibid.*, The second element has probably been scandinavianised to *-heim.* **1981** *N. & Q.* Apr. 177/1 In the Danelaw the Grimston(e) names have been taken to be partial scandinavianizations of earlier English names.

† **'scandiscope.** *Obs.* [irreg. f. L. *scandĕre* to climb + -SCOPE (used unmeaningly).] A machine for cleaning chimneys, invented by G. Smart.

1825 HONE *Every-day Bk.* II. 617 Pray order maids the Scandiscope And not the climbing boy.

scandium ('skændɪəm). *Chem.* [f. *Scandia*: see SCANDIAN and -IUM; *scandium* first formed in Sw. (L. F. Nilson 1879, in *Öfversigt af K. Vetenskaps-Akad. Förh.* XXXVI. III. 47).] A silvery white metallic element, the 'eka-boron' of Mendeleev, which is found in small quantities in association with rare-earth metals (among which it is often classified) and in some tin and tungsten ores, and forms colourless salts in which it is trivalent. Symbol Sc; atomic number 21. Hence '**scandia**, the white oxide, Sc_2O_3.

1879 *Academy* 13 Sept. 198 P. T. Cleve has isolated the metal scandium. **1880** *Jrnl. Chem. Soc.* XXXVIII. 7 Scandium forms but one oxide, scandia, Sc_2O_3. **1887** *Athenæum* 3 Sept. 299/3 Three recognized gaps have been filled by the discovery of the elements gallium, scandium, and germanium. **1905** *Ibid.* 22 July 118/2 Sir Norman Lockyer has also observed in the chromosphere of the sun the spectrum of the rare element scandium, the predicted discovery of which was one of the crowning triumphs of Mendeléeff's Periodic Law. **1922** *Nature* 17 June 799/1 The extraction and purification of scandium from thorveitite of Madagascar. This mineral, which contains 42 per cent of scandium oxide, is fused with soda and the silica removed by washing. **1955** *Sci. News Let.* 11 June 374/3 Studies made by Britain's Hydraulics Research Station and the Atomic Energy Research Establishment have shown that very finely ground glass containing radioactive scandium oxide moves with the mud when mixed with it in the River Thames. **1974** *Encycl. Brit. Micropædia* VIII. 944/3 Nilson discovered.. its oxide, scandia, in the rare-earth minerals gadolinite and euxenite. *Ibid.*, Scandium is now produced on a small scale mostly as a by-product of uranium extraction from the mineral davidite (about 0·02 percent scandium oxide). Very few uses.. have been developed.

scandle, obs. form of SCANDAL.

† **'scandular.** *Obs. rare*$^{-0}$. [ad. late L. *scandulāris*, f. *scandula* a roofing shingle.]

1656 BLOUNT *Glossogr.*, *Scandular*, that is of wooden Tiles, or Shingles.

scane, obs. form of SKEIN.

Scanian ('skeɪnɪən), *a.* (*sb.*) [f. med.L. *Scania*, ad. ON. *Skáni* or *Skáney*, the province of Skane in south Sweden + -AN.] **1.** Of or pertaining to the province of Skåne.

1895, etc. [see below]. **1932** *Times Lit. Suppl.* 28 Apr. 306/3 The unrounded *o*, which sometimes becomes the 'sorry caterwaul' of Scanian Swedish. **1963** J. SAHLGREN in Brown & Foote *Early Eng. & Norse Studies* 176 The formation of Scanian place-names.

2. a. Designating the first glaciation of the Pleistocene in northern Europe, roughly corresponding to the Günz glacial in the Alps. Also as *sb.* Now *rare.*

1895 J. GEIKIE in *Jrnl. Geol.* III. 246 *Scanian.* The earliest glacial deposits of northern Europe occur in Skåne—the old division of southern Sweden—hence the provisional name I suggest. *Ibid.* 263 Not a trace of the Scanian bowlder-clay has been recognized in Britain. **1903** A. GEIKIE *Text-bk. Geol.* (ed. 4) II. 1313 Scanian or 1st Glacial Epoch, represented only in the south of Sweden (Scania), which was overridden by a large Baltic glacier. To this period may belong.. the oldest terminal moraines and fluvio-glacial gravels of the Arctic lands. **1910** *Encycl. Brit.* XII. 59/1 Although it is admitted that no strict correlation of the European and North American stages is possible, it has been suggested that.. the Kansan may represent the Saxonian;.. the Jerseyan, the Scanian; [etc.]. **1957** J. K. CHARLESWORTH *Quaternary Era* II. xxxvi. 921 J. Geikie, a constant advocate of multiplicity, postulated six glaciations, named Scanian, Saxonian, Polandian, [etc.]. **1972** R. G. WEST *Pleistocene Geol. & Biol.* (ed. 2) xi. 219 (*table*) Scanian.

b. Designating a stade in the retreat of the ice-sheet at the end of the last Pleistocene glaciation in northern Europe (corresponding to the end of the Würm glacial in the Alps), and the resulting stadial moraines. Also as *sb.*

1937 WOOLDRIDGE & MORGAN *Physical Basis Geogr.* xxiii. 413 The retreat [of the Scandinavian ice-sheet] was punctuated by pauses, marked by well-developed stadial moraines. We have thus the Pomeranian Moraine, the Scanian Moraine (13,700 B.C.) and the Salpausselka of Finland. **1963** R. A. DALY *Changing World of Ice Age* ii. 54 During the third substage, which will be referred to as the Scanian, the front retreated to the position of one of the strong moraines in central Finland, where it bears the name 'First Salpausselkä Moraine'.

† **'scanic,** *a. Obs. rare*$^{-1}$. [f. *Scania* (latinized form of ON. *Skáney*: see SCANDINAVIAN) + -IC.] = SCANDINAVIAN *a.*

1665 J. WEBB *Stone-Heng* (1725) 192 The Scanick, of old the Gothick.

scanke, obs. form of SHANK *sb.*

scanklyone, variant of SCANTILLON.

scanlot, obs. form of SCANTLET.

scanmag ('skæn,mæg). *slang.* The abbreviated form (*scan. mag.*) of SCANDALUM MAGNATUM, used jocularly as a word in the sense of 'scandal'.

1779 SHERIDAN *Critic* I. ii, The publisher.. threatening himself with the pillory, or absolutely indicting himself for Scan. Mag. **1826** T. HOOK *Sayings* Ser. II. *Man of Many Fr.* (Colburn) 124 I can give you a daily abstract of fashionable scan-mag. **1841** W. H. MAXWELL *Scotland* (1855) 17 *Scan-mag* is never heard of. **1859** SALA *Twice round Clock* (1861) 135 The swarms of flies.. noisily buzzing their scan-mag in private parlours.

scannable ('skænəb(ə)l), *a.* [f. SCAN *v.* + -ABLE.] That can be scanned.

1828 *Blackw. Mag.* XXIII. 751 Sonnets.. which are not even scannable nonsense verses. **1936** W. DE LA MARE *Wind blows Over* 37 How narrow a circle of its waters was actually scannable from where she stood. **1975** *Nature* 28 Aug. 703/1 The charges can be liberated optically, in which case the device acts as a scannable photo-detector array, already on the market in the form of hand-held TV cameras.

scanner ('skænə(r)). [f. SCAN *v.* + -ER^1.]

1. One who scans or examines critically.

1557 R. RECORDE *Whetstone* b iiij, [*Lines.*] To the curiouse scanner. **1575** *Recorde's Gr. Arts* CC vij, Suche scanners [*sc.* cunning Lawyers] shoulde seeme to cunning, and yet not so cunning as cruell. **1604** BABINGTON *Comf. Notes Levit.* xiii. 110 Beware euer to be a curious scanner of other mens liues, or a rash iudge. **1834** F. MAHONY *Reliq. Father Prout* iv. (1836) 170 The keen and scrutinizing philosopher, the scanner of whate'er lies hidden in the folds of the human heart. **1967** *Times Rev. Industry* July 89/2 A really sensitive scanner can pick up a bit of information which to most people would be.. irrelevant but which to him assumes significance.

2. One who scans verse.

1800 W. TAYLOR in *Monthly Mag.* X. 317 The scanner has to consider neither the articulation of the vowels, nor the position of the consonants. **1906** H. VAN DYKE *Ideals & Applic.* xi. 237 We are spending infinite toil and money to produce spellers and parsers and scanners.

3. a. Any device for scanning or systematically examining all parts of something.

1927 *Public Opinion* 18 Feb. 152/3 Place the 'telegraph card' on an endless band passing at a fixed rate under the 'scanner', while at the other end a reproduction soon tumbles into a basket. **1952** *Progress* Spring 34 The Time-Springdale electronic scanner was used to make, from an Ektachrome transparency, the negatives needed for the colour reproduction. **1958** *Times Rev. Industry* July 25/3 A beam-scanner with an output window of pure aluminium foil is fitted to the accelerator. **1970** *New Scientist* 27 Aug. 420/3 Trials with an airborne infrared scanner over the leaking oil well.. demonstrated that oil shows up clearly on the scanner. **1977** *Time* 27 June 25/3 Using elaborate 'scanners' to monitor police radio channels, reporters were often at the spot of a reported sighting before the guards and dogs.

b. *Television.* Any of several devices that permit the sequential transmission of an image or its subsequent reconstruction in a receiver.

1929 SHELDON & GRISEWOOD *Television* xiv. 162 Another decided advantage of the drum-scanner is its compactness. **1958** *Observer* 12 Oct. 1/3 There is.. a television-type scanner which can transmit pictures of the perpetually unseen far side of the moon. **1975** D. G. FINK *Electronics Engineers' Handbk.* xx. 31 Flying-spot scanners are used in broadcast stations in Europe for both color and monochrome film reproduction.

c. A transmitting and receiving radar aerial, usu. one that rotates or oscillates in order to scan a large area.

1946 *Electronic Engin.* XVIII. 360/2 The speed of rotation of the scanner when manually controlled can be varied from 0 to 4 r.p.m. in either direction. **1965** *New Scientist* 15 July 130/1 The radar scanner continuously sweeps the sky, sending out its impulses and receiving back the reflected impulses. **1970** H. A. TAYLOR *Airspeed Aircraft since 1931* 172 The raised fuselage also permitted the aircraft to be loaded with the retractable air-to-surface-vessel (ASV) scanner, below and aft of the control cabin.

d. *Med.* A machine for scanning the body and measuring the intensity of the radiation from different areas as a diagnostic aid, e.g. after administration of a radio-isotope; *spec.* = *body scanner* s.v. BODY *sb.* 30. Also, a machine for directing ultrasound into the body and obtaining a visual representation of the reflections from different internal areas, analogous to a radar display or radiograph.

1951 *Nucleonics* Aug. 50/2 The first tests of the scanner were made with filter paper wetted with a solution containing radioiodine. **1953** *Amer. Jrnl. Roentgenol.* LXX. 605/2 The scanner produces a picture of the distribution of the gamma-emitting activity present in a small area. **1960** *McGraw-Hill Encycl. Sci. & Technol.* XIV. 8/2 Scanners have been devised which can accurately fix the size of the thyroid gland and determine the presence of nodules or abnormalities in the shape of the gland. **1975**, etc. [see CAT *sb.*^{5}]. **1977** *Listener* (N.Z.) 15 Jan. 10/1 Scanners are an important innovation because of their superior diagnostic capabilities over alternative techniques, and the enhanced degree of patient safety and comfort they offer. **1986** *Daily Tel.* 28 July 11/1 Modern scanners are accurate to $\frac{1}{25}$ inch. **1987** *Oxf. Textbk. Med.* (ed. 2) I. XII. 5/2 Ultrasound. High definition sector scanners provide an excellent real-time image of the gall-bladder.

e. *fig.*

1959 *Listener* 8 Jan. 83/2 The selectivity of your mind—your mental scanner—will quickly reveal what there is to be thought about. **1964** *Ann. Reg. 1963* 403 Work by an Oxford psychologist.. suggested that the mechanism.. involved the use of a 'scanner' in the brain which sifted through a large number of possible names.

4. Special Comb.: **scanner fo(u)nt**, a typewriting fount that can be read by an optical character-recognition device.

1968 *Amer. Documentation* Jan. 74/2 A secretary types each record for scanner input, using a standard typewriter fitted with an ASA scanner font golfball. *Ibid.*, The optical character reader.. reads standard ASA scanner font: 26 alphabetic characters (all upper case), 10 digits, and 25 punctuation and special characters. **1969** *Computers & Humanities* III. 132 Each item to be entered into the file is coded; typed in ASA scanner font; read by an optical scanner.. onto magnetic tape; and, finally, entered into an INFOL file.

scanning ('skænɪŋ), *vbl. sb.* [f. SCAN *v.* + -ING^1.] The action of the vb.

1. a. *Pros.* = SCANSION 2.

c **1440** *Promp. Parv.* 442/2 Scannynge, of verse, *scansio.* **1586** W. WEBBE *Eng. Poetrie* (Arb.) 69 All quantities necessary to the skanning of any verse. **1676** MARVELL *Mr. Smirke* 6 This Scanning was a liberal Art that we learn'd at Grammar-School. **1797** *Monthly Mag.* III. 258 It will be verse only to the scanning, and neither verse nor prose to the ear. **1886** J. B. MAYOR *Eng. Metre* iv. 54 We come now to the lines which are said to be beyond the reach of analysis by feet. I give what I consider the true scanning of each.

b. *Path.* (Cf. SCANNING *ppl. a.* 2.)

1887 *Brit. Med. Jrnl.* 2 Apr. 732/2 A case of locomotor ataxy.. with 'scanning' of speech.

2. a. Close investigation or consideration, critical examination or judgement; discussion, comment, perception, discernment. Cf. SCAN *v.* 2 b. Phrases, † *to have* (a matter) *in scanning*, † *to come, fall to scanning.*

1560 DAUS tr. *Sleidane's Comm.* 238 Therfore muste prynces and noble men be at the skannyng therof. **1575** *Recorde's Gr. Arts* Cc vj b, If some cunning Lawyers had this matter in scanning, they would determine this Testament to be quite voide. **1576** GASCOIGNE *Spoyle of Antwerp* C vij, But I leaue the skanning of theyr deedes vnto God. **1602** CAREW *Cornwall* 57 Another question falleth sometimes into scanning, namely [etc.]. **1611** SPEED *Hist. Gt. Brit.* VII. xliii. (1632) 411 It was therefore instantly desired, that the cause might once more come to scanning. **1670** HOBBES *Behemoth* (1840) 167 The private interpretation of the Scripture, exposed to every man's scanning in his mother-tongue. **1699** POMFRET *Marr. Earl of A——* 76 Ev'ry teeming thought, Is to the scanning of her judgment brought. **1704** HEARNE *Duct. Hist.* (1714) I. 413 They used a sweet fluent kind of Rhetorick.. which.. serv'd only to put a present good Face upon an Argument, but would not bear Scanning. **1840** CARLYLE *Heroes* iii. (1841) 165 The 'Tree Igdrasil' buds and withers by its own laws,—too deep for our scanning.

b. The action of systematically traversing with a beam or detector, as in *Television.* In *Med.*, the process or action of making a scan of the body or part of it; cf. *brain scanning* s.v. BRAIN *sb.* 6.

1927 *Bell System Technical Jrnl.* VI. 552 We have thus available in television the same artifice.. that is, of scanning, or running over the elements of the image in sequence. **1933** *Discovery* May 156/2 As much as 120-line scanning was used, thus permitting very fine detail indeed. **1936** *Electr. Commun.* XV. 187/1 The most recent demonstration of television in Italy was at Milan in April, 1936. The equipment employed electronic scanning for transmission. **1951** *Nucleonics* Aug. 46/2 The results indicated the desirability of an automatic scanning and recording device. **1956** *Radiology* LXVI. 730/1 During the past four years.., external scintillation counter scanning has been used to provide information relative to the distribution of radioactive isotopes in patients. **1968** *Sci. News* 6 Apr. 333/1 In scanning, a radioactivity compound is administered to the patient, after which the compound's distribution is mapped out by a scintillation camera that detects gamma rays coming from the child. **1971** *Amat. Photographer* 13 Jan. 65/2 The system [for reading videotape] was later superseded by transfer scanning, using four magnetic heads on a 2 in diameter drum rotating at 14,400 rpm almost at right angles across 2 in tape, pulled past at 15 ips. **1975** D. G. FINK *Electronics Engineers' Handbk.* xx. 7 Interlaced scanning is achieved by making the horizontal (line-scanning) rate an odd multiple of one-half the vertical (field-scanning) rate. **1987** *Oxf. Textbk. Med.* (ed. 2) II. XVIII. 138/1 If obstruction is detected pelvic scanning may reveal the cause and drainage can be effected.. by.. nephrostomies performed under ultrasound control.

c. The rapid or systematic searching of textual material for particular information or features.

1937 *Discovery* Sept. 256/2 A random scanning of the list reveals many names familiar to the British Association. **1954** *Amer. Documentation* V. 18/2 Speeds of operation are such as to permit scanning and correlating of generic and specific aspects of indexes in a reasonable time. **1967** *English Studies* XLVIII. 60 (*heading*) An archive of older Scottish texts for scanning by computer. **1970** O. DOPPING *Computers & Data Processing* xvii. 277 The misplaced record has only been moved one step, and if the computer were to continue the forward scanning, four scans would be needed. **1975** *Language for Life* (Dept. Educ. & Sci.) viii. 115 The intermediate skills, so essential in word attack in the early stages, are at work in skimming, scanning, and the extraction of meaning in the more complex reading tasks of the later stages.

3. *auditory scanning*: the emission of short pulses of sound and detection of echoes from nearby objects, thought to be used by dolphins for the location and ranging of submerged objects.

1960 W. N. KELLOGG in *Psychol. Record* X. 26 Since the noises which make up the echoes are emitted by the dolphin itself, the activity as a whole amounts to a kind of scanning by sound. We suggest the term *auditory scanning*, therefore, as a good name for both the acoustic and the general behavior comprising this elaborate pattern of activity. **1963**

Language XXXIX. 464 The dolphin's auditory scanning is shown to consist of the emission of a continuous series of sound signals for echolocation plus binaural localization.

4. *attrib.* and *Comb.*, as *scanning movement, speed*; **scanning coil**, any of four coils arranged in pairs around the neck of a cathode-ray tube, the magnetic field of which is varied so as to cause the electron beam to trace out a raster pattern on the screen of the tube; **scanning disc**, a rotating disc having a spiral of holes near the edge, used in mechanical systems of television to provide a sequential scan of a scene by optical means for transmission and to permit reconstruction of the scene at the receiver; **scanning electron microscope**, a form of electron microscope in which an electron beam is scanned in a raster pattern across the specimen; an electrical signal is obtained by collecting and amplifying secondary electrons emitted by the specimen and is applied to a cathode-ray tube scanned in synchronism with the electron beam; hence *scanning electron micrograph, microscopy*; **scanning field** = RASTER *sb.*[2] a; **scanning line** = LINE *sb.*[2] 7 i; **scanning raster** = RASTER *sb.*[2] a; **scanning spot**, the spot where an incident beam (usu. of electrons or light) strikes the surface it is scanning.

1938 J. H. REYNER *Testing Television Sets* iv. 41 The function of the transformer is to step-down the voltage applied to the *scanning coil which operates with a correspondingly larger current. **1978** *Broadcast* 27 Nov. 15/2 Camera heads are still stuck with bulky camera tubes, scanning coils, splitter blocks and such paraphernalia. **1927** *Wireless World* 20 Apr. 685/1 This film was then repeated for an observer by means of a receiving equipment involving the use of a suitable neon tube and a *scanning disc. **1975** D. G. FINK *Electronics Engineers' Handbk.* xx. 82 An exciter lamp illuminates the subject copy via a curved mirror, and an objective lens images the reflected light to an aperture plate in front of a scanning disk. The scanning disk is opaque except for a transparent spiral, which curves outward from the center of the disk. **1962** *Nature* 6 Oct. 82/1 Figs. 1 and 2 are *scanning electron micrographs. **1979** *Sci. Amer.* Sept. 30/3 Wonderful drawings..complemented by scanning electron micrographs. **1953** *Proc. Inst. Electr. Engineers* C. II. 246/2 The main advantage of the *scanning electron microscope for transparent specimens is that the resolution is not affected by energy losses of the electrons in the specimen, which in the conventional electron microscope give rise to chromatic aberration. **1972** *Sci. Amer.* Jan. 55/2 The scanning electron microscope is capable of a range of magnifications that overlaps the range of the light microscope or hand magnifying glass at the low end and the range of the transmission electron microscope at the high end. **1966** D. G. BRANDON *Mod. Techniques Metallogr.* 51 Image formation by..*scanning electron microscopy. **1975** J. I. GOLDSTEIN et al. in Goldstein & Yakowitz *Practical Scanning Electron Microsc.* i. 3 The purpose of this brief historical introduction is to point out the pioneers of scanning electron microscopy and in the process trace the evolution of the instrument. **1935** *Television Today* I. 247/1 Such a *scanning field is known as a 'raster'. **1975** D. G. FINK *Electronics Engineers' Handbk.* xx. 5 The lines of the second scanning field fall between the lines of the first field. **1929** *Scanning line [see LINE *sb.*[2] 7 i]. **1933** *Discovery* Oct. 318/1 The new German standard picture, consisting of 180 scanning lines, is officially considered sufficient for the opening of regular transmissions. **1960** in *Rep. Comm. Broadcasting* 334 in *Parl. Papers 1961–2* (Cmnd. 1753) IX. 259 There was..a significant difference in the visibility of the scanning lines — the 625-line pictures being..noticeably better than the 405-line pictures. **1958** *Observer* 12 Oct. 15/4 Every few minutes, the radio telescope makes small *scanning movements, up and down and from side to side. This helps to fix the direction of the radio signals from the rocket to within half a degree. **1935** *Television Today* I. 247/2 The production of a *scanning raster on the cathode-ray tube of a television receiver by electrical means involves the application of two voltages of saw-tooth wave form to the two pairs of deflecting plates of a cathode-ray tube. **1975** D. G. FINK *Electronics Engineers' Handbk.* xx. 33 The starting point for generating color pictures is the optical and electronic superposition of the red-, green-, and blue-tube scanning rasters. **1929** SHELDON & GRISEWOOD *Television* xii. 126 The *scanning speed may be greatly increased by use of a series of oppositely rotating lens-discs. **1934** *Sun* (Baltimore) 20 Aug. 2/3 A tiny metal mirror, mounted on a slender rod and vibrated at scanning speeds, was presented ..as..the solution of one of television's major problems. **1929** SHELDON & GRISEWOOD *Television* xiii. 139 Since the *scanning spot has finite dimensions, its response to an abrupt change in the surface being viewed will be less sharply defined than the original. **1975** D. G. FINK *Electronics Engineers' Handbk.* xx. 5 The electron beams that create the scanning spots are approximately circular, but their intensity is not uniform.

scanning (ˈskænɪŋ), *ppl. a.* [f. SCAN *v.* + -ING[2].]

1. That scans or examines closely; critical, searching.

1863 GEO. ELIOT *Romola* I. iii, When his eyes fell again they glanced round with a scanning coolness. **1881** E. F. POYNTER *Among the Hills* I. 196 She hated to meet her neighbours and feel their scanning glances.

2. *Path.* Epithet applied to a measured manner of speaking or utterance, with more or less regular pauses, characteristic of certain nervous diseases.

1866 FLINT *Princ. & Pract. Med.* (1880) 740 The patient speaks in a slow, monotonous manner, with intervals between syllables, as in scanning. The peculiarity is known as the 'scanning speech'. **1899** *Allbutt's Syst. Med.* VII. 58 A peculiar defect of speech described as a scanning utterance. *Ibid.* 382.

Hence **ˈscanningly** *adv.*

1876 GEO. ELIOT *Dan. Der.* IV. xxxiv, Jacob looked up into his face scanningly for a moment or two. **1884** E. FAWCETT *Rutherford* ix. 96 He looked down for a moment scanningly at..his delicate filbert-shaped nails.

scans, obs. form of SCONCE, fort.

scanse, obs. var. SCANCE *v.*[1]

scansion (ˈskænʃən). [ad. L. *scansiōn-em*, n. of action f. *scandĕre* to climb, SCAN. Cf. F. *scansion* (G. *scansion*), It. *scansione.*]

†**1.** The action of climbing up. *Obs. rare*$^{-1}$.

1654 Z. COKE *Logick* 200 Ascension is the scansion or moving from an inferior place to a superior.

2. *Pros.* The action or the art of scanning verse; the division of verse into metrical feet; also, an example of this.

1671 in PHILLIPS. **1779** LOWTH in *Serm. & Rem.* (1834) 387 The author..only intended, that we should give him credit awhile for the truth of his scansion. *a* **1849** POE *Rationale of Verse* Wks. 1864 II. 249 The object of what we call scansion is the distinct marking of the rhythmical flow. **1874** SYMONDS in *Fortn. Rev.* Dec. 772 In this prosody [of blank verse] scansion by time takes the place of scansion by metrical feet. **1894** SALA *London up to Date* ii. 30 He is an amiable poet..and does not bite, unless the accuracy of his scansion be impeached. **1900** SKEAT *Chaucer Canon* §37 Chaucer has certain peculiarities of grammar, upon which the scansion of his lines largely depends.

scansionist (ˈskænʃənɪst). [f. SCANSION + -IST.] One who is versed in the art of scansion.

1849 *Fraser's Mag.* XXXIX. 106 The scandalised scansionist stumbles at occasional trochees. **1907** T. S. OMOND *Eng. Metrists* ii. 60 All musical scansionists of prose seem to me apt to read into it a factitious regularity.

†**ˈscansive**, *a. Obs. rare*$^{-1}$. [f. L. *scandĕre* (ppl. stem *scans-*) + -IVE.] = SCANDENT *a.*

1657 TOMLINSON *Renou's Disp.* 279 Both [black and white pepper plants] are scansive [L. *scansilis est*].

‖**Scansores** (skænˈsɔəriːz), *pl. Ornith.* [mod.L., pl. of *scansor*, agent-n. of *scandĕre* to climb.] The name given by Illiger (1811) to his first Order of birds, comprising the Climbers (see CLIMBER *sb.* 3).

1835–6 OWEN in *Todd's Cycl. Anat.* I. 268/1 Order III. Scansores... The disposition of the toes..gives the *Scansores* great facility in climbing the branches of trees. **1872** NICHOLSON *Palæont.* 395.

scansorial (skænˈsɔərɪəl), *a.* and *sb.* [a. L. *scansōri-us*, used for climbing (f. *scandĕre* to climb: see SCAN *v.*) + -AL[1].] **A.** *adj.*

1. Of or pertaining to climbing; *spec.* of the feet of birds and animals, adapted for climbing.

1806 TURTON tr. *Linn. Syst. Nat.* VII. Expl. Terms, *Scansorial*, formed for climbing: Applied to the feet of birds which have two toes before and two behind. **1837** *Penny Cycl.* VIII. 146/2 In the *Certhiadæ* the foot is not strictly scansorial. *Ibid.* 206/2 Birds which have..three anterior toes and one posterior scansorial one. **1877** COUES *Fur-Bearing Anim.* vii. 215 A tardy terrestrial animal..lacking.. the scansorial ability of the Martens. **1884** —— *Key N. Amer. Birds* (ed. 2) 130 The zygodactyle or yoke-toed modification..was formerly made much of, as a scansorial or climbing type of foot.

2. That climbs or is given to climbing; spec. of a bird, belonging to the Order SCANSORES.

scansorial barbet, a barbet of the family *Capitonidæ* or Barbets proper as distinguished from the Puff-birds.

1835–6 OWEN in *Todd's Cycl. Anat.* I. 268/2 The scansorial families are the..Parrots..Woodpeckers, Wry-necks..Cuckoos..Toucans. **1837** *Penny Cycl.* VIII. 146 The Scansorial birds. **1841** SELBY in *Proc. Berw. Nat. Club* I. 253 Of the Scansorial tribe, the *Picus major* (great spotted woodpecker) is the only species. **1871** C. H. T. & G. F. L. MARSHALL (*title*) A Monograph of the Capitonidæ, or Scansorial Barbets. **1875** BLAKE *Zool.* 19 The scansorial Ape of the Old World.

B. *sb.* A bird of the Order SCANSORES.

1842 in BRANDE *Dict. Sci.*, etc. In recent Dicts.

scansorious (skænˈsɔərɪəs), *a. rare.* [f. L. *scansōri-us* (see prec.) + -OUS.] = prec. A. 1.

1814 W. E. LEACH *Zool. Misc.* I. 71 Cuckow... The feet are generally considered as scansorious, or formed for climbing (*pedes scansorii*). **1815** J. F. STEPHENS in *Shaw's Zool.* IX. 66 *note*, The Parrot genus (*Psittacus*) affords a good example of true scansorious feet.

scansory (ˈskænsərɪ), *a. rare.* [ad. mod.L. *scansōri-us* of or for climbing, f. *scandĕre* to climb.] Of or pertaining to climbing; given to climbing.

1657 TOMLINSON *Renou's Disp.* 264 Scammony..is a lacteous, volvulous, scansory, and smooth Plant. **1826** KIRBY & SP. *Entomol.* III. xxxv. 546 They are eminently the *scansory* or climbing legs in almost all insects.

scant (skænt), *sb. Obs.* exc. *dial.* Also 4–7 **skant**, 5–6 **scante**, 6 **skaunte**. [a. ON. *skamt* (neut. adj. used *absol.*): see SCANT *a.*]

1. Scanty supply; dearth, scarcity.

a **1350** *S. Andrew* 274 in Horstm. *Altengl. Leg.* (1881) 7 When þai saw it skarsli spring, þan hopid þai to haue skant of corn And of fruyt. *c* **1460** *Towneley Myst.* iii. 198 Yit of mete and of drynk haue we veray skant. *c* **1475** *Rauf Coilȝear* 273 The King buskit him sone with scant of Squyary. *c* **1565** ABP. PARKER *Ps.* xxiii, How can I want, or suffer scant, whan he defendth my side. *a* **1599** ROLLOCK *Serm.* xiii. (1616) 255 There is no want nor scant of mercy in Him. *a* **1639** T. CAREW *To A. L.* 54 Like the ant In plenty hoord for time of scant. **1721** RAMSAY *Keitha* 77 Hynds and herds whase cheeks bespake nae scant. **1757** J. H. GROSE *Voy. E. Indies* 360 If there is a scant of wood, or rain intervenes to damp it. **1823** GALT *Entail* I. ix. 66 There was neither scant nor want at his burial.

†**2.** Want, need, requirement. *Obs. rare*$^{-1}$.

c **1550** *Songs & Poems Costume* (Percy) 82 With meate before the set, Suffise but nature's scant.

†**3.** *Naut.* The action of SCANT *v.*; the drawing ahead (of wind). *Obs.*

1595 *Drake's Voy.* (Hakl. Soc.) 19 The scant of winde we had on Wednesday.

scant (skænt), *a.* and *adv.* Now mainly *arch.* or *literary*. Forms: 4–8 **skant**, 5 **skantt**, (**schante**, 6 **skaunte**), 5–6 **scante**, **skante**, 5– **scant**. [a. ON. *skamt*, neut. of *skamm-r* short, brief (= OHG. *scamm*). For the retention of the neuter ending cf. THWART and QUART *a.* See also SCANT *sb.*]

A. *adj.*

1. Existing or available in inadequate or barely sufficient amount, quantity, or degree; stinted in measure, not abundant. Said of commodities, esp. provisions; also of immaterial things, actions, qualities, etc.

a **1400** *Minor Poems fr. Vernon MS.* 501 He wrot so faste til þat he want, For his parchemyn-skin was so scant, To speken þei hedde such space. **1428** in *Surtees Misc.* (1890) 3 Iren waxed skant and dere. *c* **1449** PECOCK *Repr.* v. viii. 530 Thei lyueden streitli and in scant mete and drinke. **1513** DOUGLAS *Æneis* I. Prol. 307 Thocht in my translatioun eloquence skant is. **1548** HALL *Chron., Edw. IV* (1550) 41 b, If vrgent necessitie should expostulate, he wer of scant abilitie, to conscribe and set furthe a newe armie. **1550–3** *Decaye Eng.* in S. Fish *Supplic. Beggers* (1871) 96 The more shepe, the skanter is the whit meate. **1624** FLETCHER *Rule a Wife* III. (1640) 39 She had but a scant fame. **1632** LITHGOW *Trav.* I. 29 Deuotion waxed scant amongst the Christians. **1636** HEYWOOD *Chall. Beauty* III. F 1, They are full of large promises outward, but lin'd with narrow and scant-performance within. **1714** PRIOR *Viceroy* xiv, By which provisions were so scant, That hundreds there did die. *a* **1771** GRAY *Dante* 23 What scant Light That grim and antique Tower admitted. **1818** SCOTT *Heart Midl.* viii, Doctor, my breath is growing as scant as a broken-winded piper's. **1842** BORROW *Bible in Spain* xlii, In the country money is rather scant. **1879** FARRAR *St. Paul* (1883) 250 The notices of this part of their journey are scant.

b. Preceding a sb. without article or other qualifying word: Very little, less than enough.

1852 DICKENS *Lett.* (1880) I. 279 You do scant justice to Dover. **1855** M. ARNOLD *Balder Dead* ii. 90 Scant space that warder left for passers by. **1898** RIDER HAGGARD *Dr. Therne* 7 This country is too full; there is scant room for the individual.

†**c.** Limited in numbers, numerically rare. *Obs.*

1581 PETTIE *Guazzo's Civ. Conv.* II. (1586) 55 b, Philosophers and Oratours, who are very scant in the world.

†**d.** *to come scant of*: to fall short of. *Obs.*

1607 DEKKER & WEBSTER *Northw. Hoe* I. A 2, True, but yet it comes scant of the Prophesy: Lincolne was, London is, and Yorke shall-be.

2. Of a quantity or amount of anything: Limited, stinted; not full, large, or copious.

1556 LAUDER *Tractate* 260 Than can ȝe be no maner want Gold, thocht ȝour pose wer neuer sa skant. **1598** BARNFIELD *'As it fell vpon a Day'* 35 But if store of Crownes be scant, No man will supply thy want. **1611** BIBLE *Micah* vi. 10 The scant measure that is abominable. **1624** SANDERSON *Serm.* (1689) 264 Many others that have a scanter Portion. **1634** MILTON *Comus* 308 In such a scant allowance of Star-light. **1766** GOLDSM. *Hermit* iv, And tho' my portion is but scant, I give it with good will. **1885** *Manch. Exam.* 16 May 6/1 The attendance..was..so scant as to suggest that many members must have anticipated the holiday. **1891** F. THOMPSON *Sister-Songs* (1895) 19 And of her own scant pittance did she give, That I might eat and live.

b. Barely amounting to, or hardly reaching (a specified number or amount). Chiefly *U.S.*; cf. SCANT *adv.* 1 b.

1856 KANE *Arct. Expl.* II. vi. 70 We have just a scant two day's allowance of meat for the sick. **1895** *Funk's Stand. Dict.*, *Scant*, a. 2. (Colloq.) Being just short of the measure specified: often with the indefinite article even with a plural noun; as, a scant half-hour; a scant five yards.

3. Limited in extent; not wide or spacious.

a **1533** LD. BERNERS *Gold. Bk. M. Aurel.* (1546) H vij b, Though the realme of Italy was scant, their hertes were grette. *a* **1639** SPOTTISWOOD *Hist. Ch. Scot.* v. (1677) 255 By reason of the skant and narrow passage many were killed. **1665** GLANVILL *Scepsis Sci.* v. 23 And lye in as narrow a room as their images take up in our scanter Craniums. **1743** BLAIR *Grave* 219 The petty Tyrant Of scant Domains Geographer ne'er notic'd. **1863** KINGLAKE *Crimea* II. xvi. 407 The curt, red shell-jacket he wore was as though it were a world too scant for the strength of the man.

4. Having a scanty or limited supply; poorly furnished. Const. *of*.

1577–95 *Descr. Isles* in Skene *Celtic Scotl.* III. App. 436 Quhairthrow thai are scant of fire. **1602** SHAKS. *Ham.* v. ii. 298 He's fat, and scant of breath. **1642** *Declar. Lords & Comm. to Gen. Assembly Ch. Scot.* 13 You were scant of furniture of this kind your selves. **1789** BURNS *To Dr. Blacklock* ix, But to conclude my silly rhyme (I'm scant o' verse, and scant o' time). **1833** TENNYSON *Two Voices* 397 'Tis life whereof our nerves are scant. **1856** KANE *Arct. Expl.* II. App. II. 311 We were scant of fuel. **1879** STEVENSON *Trav. with Donkey* 72 Cold, naked, and ignoble, scant of wood, scant of heather, scant of life.

5. Deficient or lacking in quality; poor, meagre, not full or rich. Chiefly of immaterial things. Const. *in*.

a **1631** DONNE *Ecstasie* 39 Poems (1633) 279 A single violet transplant, The strength, the colour, and the size, (All which before was poore, and scant) Redoubles still, and multiplies. **1633** G. HERBERT *Temple, True Hymn* iv, Whereas if th' heart be moved, Although the verse be somewhat scant, God doth supplie the want. **1850** BLACKIE *Æschylus* I. 26 Hence it spread Not scant in strength, a mighty beard of flame.

†**6.** Sparing, parsimonious, not liberal. Also in good sense: Chary, not lavish. Const. *of*. *Obs.*

c **1366** CHAUCER *A.B.C.* 175 Sithe he his merci mesured so large, Be ye not skant. *c* **1440** *Promp. Parv.* 442/2 Scant, *parcus*. *c* **1550** H. RHODES *Bk. Nurture, For the Wayting Seruaunt* 41 Be not to liberall nor to scant, vse measure in eche thing. **1602** SHAKS. *Ham.* I. iii. 121 For this time, Daughter, Be somewhat scanter of your Maiden presence. *a* **1631** DONNE *Serm.* lxxii. (1640) 727 God in his owne behalfe complaines of the scant and penurious Sacrificer. *a* **1639** T. CAREW *To A. L.* 21 Did the thing for which I sue Only concern myself, not you.. Then had you reason to be scant. **1649** [cf. *scant-handedness* in 8]. **1651** DAVENANT *Gondibert* II. i. 2 When Infant Morn.. With a scant face peep'd shylie through the East.

7. *Naut.* Of wind: Too much ahead, so that the ship has to sail very close. Cf. SCANT *v.* 2. (Opposed to *large* or *free*.)

1600 E. BLOUNT tr. *Conestaggio* 276 The winde grew scant [orig. *scarso*] to approch to land. *a* **1642** SIR W. MONSON *Naval Tracts* II. (1704) 255/1 We ply into the Bay with a scant Wind. **1793** RENNELL in *Phil. Trans.* LXXXIII. 189 Yet the wind, being both scant and light, we could never overcome the tendency of the current. **1867** SMYTH *Sailor's Word-bk.*, *Scant*, a term applied to the wind when it heads a ship off, so that she will barely lay her course when the yards are very sharp up.

8. *Comb.*, as *scant-feathered* adj.; †**scant-brain**, one lacking in wits; †**scant-handedness**, niggardliness; **scant-of-wind** *a.*, causing shortness of breath; **scant o' grace** *Sc.*, a graceless fellow.

1864 A. LEIGHTON *Myst. Leg. Edinb.* (1886) 122 Those *scant-brains who deny ghosts. **1872** COUES *Key N. Amer. Birds* 201 Tarsi long, *scant-feathered. **1649** W. SCLATER *Comm. Malachy* (1650) 161 To what cause should we impute the *scant-handedness of men professing of Religion, and the fear of God; that they, notwithstanding, should so niggardly contribute? **1718** RAMSAY *Christ's Kirk Gr.* III. xvii, Your tippanizing *scant o' grace, Quoth she, gars me gang duddy. **1818** SCOTT *Rob Roy* xxviii, I ken'd that Scant-o'-grace weel eneugh frae the very outset. **1823** —— *Quentin D.* xiv, I never love a man better than when I have put my *scant-of-wind collar about his neck.

B. *adv.*

1. Hardly, scarcely; barely. Now *dial.* (see E.D.D.).

? *c* **1450** *Compend. olde Treat.* in Roy *Rede me* (Arb.) 175 Other Gospels ben yet in many places of so olde englishe that scant can anye englishe man reade them. **1492** *Paston Lett.* III. 376 Hors flesche is of suche a price here that my purce is schante able to bye one hors. **1562** COOPER *Answ. Priv. Masse* vii. 47 b, I thinke you wyl scant affirme it, although ye be ready to affirme straunge thinges. **1586** W. WEBBE *Eng. Poetrie* (Arb.) 29 He would haue a cast at some wanton and skant comely an Argument. **1587** FLEMING *Contn. Holinshed* III. 1982/1 His lordship himselfe scant with sixteene horses.. returned towards the passage. **1592** BACON *Wks.* (1862) VIII. 198 It was wont to be a token of scant a good liegeman, when the enemy spoiled the country and left any particular mans houses or fields unwasted. *a* **1661** FULLER *Worthies, Surrey* (1662) III. 82 Some who could scant brook the name of Bishop were content to give .. him a good Report.

b. qualifying a numeral (which sometimes precedes). Now *arch.* (? *U.S.*)

c **1400** MAUNDEV. (1839) xxiii. 252 And whan thei wil fighte, thei wille schokken hem to gidre in a plomp; that ȝif there be 20000 men, men schalle not wenen, that there be scant 10000. **1466** *Mann. & Househ. Exp.* (Roxb.) 362 The ij[de]. federbed conteynethe of lengthe iij. Flemyshe stykes, iij. quarters and more, and in brede iij. Flemyshe stykes scant. **1502** *Will of Somer* (Somerset Ho.), A mast of Corall weyng vj[th] skant. **1601** R. JOHNSON *Kingd. & Commw.* 55 Of ten thousand rowers.. scant the fourth part returneth againe. **1604** E. G[RIMSTONE] tr. *Acosta's Hist. Indies* III. iv. 128 They have scant any neede to touch their sailes in the whole voiage. *c* **1715** RAMSAY *Vision* iv, A man.. With baird thre quarters skant. **1808** SCOTT *Marm.* v. xxxiii, Scant three miles the band had rode. *a* **1849** HAWTHORNE *Twice-told T., Gt. Carbuncle*, While scant a mile above their heads, was that bleak verge where the hills throw off their shaggy mantle of forest trees. **1867** HOWELLS *Ital. Journeys* ii. 12 At the rate of five miles scant an hour.

†**c.** with superfluous negative. *Obs.*

c **1400** [see b]. **1508** FISHER *Ps.* li. Wks. (1876) 133 He sholde.. not leue scante a dogge. **1515–20** *Vox populi* 24 in Hazl. *E.P.P.* III. 269 Thei be not able to feade In theire stable scant a steade. **1552** LATIMER *Serm. Bexterly* (1584) 271 Many of vs.. are so slouthfull that we will not scant abide one houre to heare the word of God. **1583** L. M. tr. *Bk. Dyeing* (1588) 39 Warme it over the fire, so that you may not skant suffer your hand therein.

†**d.** Used with a following *when* (*but, but that*) to indicate immediate succession of events. *Obs.*

1551 T. WILSON *Logike* (1580) 58 b, In this worlde a childe shall scant be out of his shell, but [etc.]. **1560** ROLLAND *Crt. Venus* II. 648 Skant was he vp, quhen at the eird was he. *c* **1610** *Women Saints* 95 She had scant thrice repeated these wordes, but that the mayd came oute of the water with the booke. *a* **1718** PARNELL *Fairy Tale* 31 But scant he lays him on the floor, When hollow winds remove the door.

†**2.** Scantily. *Obs. rare.*

c **1440** *Pallad. on Husb.* v. 18 And fodder for thi beestes therof make First scant [orig. *Sed primo parcius præbenda est nouitas pabuli*]. *c* **1620** Z. BOYD *Zion's Flowers* (1855) 153 A heart couragious never breathed scant.

scant (skænt), *v.* Also 6–7 **skant**. Now mainly *arch.* [f. SCANT *a.*]

I. *intr.*

†**1. a.** To become scant or scarce. *Obs.*

1436 *Pol. Poems* (Rolls) II. 189 Allas! fortune begynneth so to stant [*read* scant?], Or ellis grace, that dede is governaunce. **1470** HENRY *Wallace* XI. 35 In Wallace ost so scantyt the wictaill, Thai mycht nocht bid [na] langar till assaill. **1586** BRIGHT *Melanch.* x. 45 Spirit.. is either plentifull, or scanteth, as it hath want, or.. nourishment. **1611** SPEED *Hist. Gt. Brit.* IX. xxiii. 94 Where.. they continued till their maintenance began to scant. **1624** 'R. JONES' (T. Lushington) *Resurr. Serm.* (1659) 77 Of these in their order, as the time hath scanted.

†**b.** To be diminished. Const. *of*. *Obs.*

1607 *Relat. Disc. River* in *Capt. Smith's Wks.* (Arb.) Introd. 42 The Ryver skantes of his breadth .2. mile before we come to the Ilet mentyoned.

2. *Naut.* Of the wind: To become unfavourable, to draw too much ahead. Const. *upon, with*. (Cf. SCANT *a.* 7.) ? *Obs.*

c **1553** J. LOCKE in *Hakluyt's Voy.* (1599) II. I. 104 About the third watch the winde scanted, so that we bare with the shore. **1628** DIGBY *Voy. Medit.* (1868) 15 The wind scanted much vpon vs, so that wee had much adoe to double the point. **1769** [see SCANTING *vbl. sb.*]. **1823** W. SCORESBY *Jrnl. Whale Fish.* 392 The wind declined and scanted during the night, so that we could not fetch our port.

II. *trans.*

3. a. To furnish (a person, etc.) with an inadequate supply; to stint or limit in respect of provision; to put or keep on short allowance. In *pass.*, to be restricted in the matter of supply, to be straitened (*for*). ? *Obs.* (cf. 3 b).

1606 SHAKS. *Tr. & Cr.* IV. iv. 49 He.. scants vs with a single famisht kisse. **1607** HIERON *Wks.* I. 230 They are neither scanted for victuals, nor straitened for lodging. **1613** F. ROBARTES *Revenue Gosp.* 135 These wil be glad to scant the Minister, that they may haue the more for their owne luxurie. **1626** BACON *New Atl.* 17 [He] bad us not to scant our selves; For he would procure such time as wee desired. **1692** R. L'ESTRANGE *Josephus, Antiq.* XIII. xvi. (1733) 347 The Camp was for some short Time scanted for Water. **1719** D'URFEY *Pills* I. 243 The Germans bemoaned their Condition, Squadrons were scanted, Officers wanted.

b. with *of*: To put or keep on short allowance of; to keep (one) short of; to abridge or deprive of. In *pass.*, to be in want of, have only a scant supply of, be badly off for. Now *rare*.

1565 JEWEL *Repl. Harding* XVI. vi. 552 M. Harding is much scanted of good Authorities, when he is thus driuen by Tales, & Fables, to countreuaile the Tradition of the Apostles. **1597** SIR R. CECIL in Ellis *Orig. Lett.* Ser. I. III. 42 A man, whose fortune scants him of meanes to do you service. **1616** R. COCKS *Diary* (Hakl. Soc.) I. 134 They skanted him of victuells. **1670** *Lond. Gaz.* No. 517/3 The other Yacht happening to be scanted of Water near Flaerding. **1861** TRENCH *Ep. 7 Churches Asia* 125 This promise.. is misunderstood, or at any rate is scanted of its full meaning, unless [etc.]. **1877** PATMORE *Unknown Eros* (1890) 115 She scants me of my right. **1888** LOWELL in *Even. Post* 17 Apr., I.. shall not allow myself to be circumscribed and scanted of elbow room.

c. To limit or restrict *in* (a supply, endowment, etc.). ? *Obs.*

1600 HOLLAND *Livy* XXI. xvii. 402 In the number of ships especially was Cornelius skanted. **1611** W. SCLATER *Key* (1629) 129 Howsoeuer the Lord hath scanted thee in the things of this life. **1723** WILLIAMS in *Phil. Trans.* XXXII. 266 Had I not been scanted in Time. **1788** CLARA REEVE *Exiles* I. 190, I was so scanted in my allowance, that I dared not make acquaintance where I had not the power to make suitable returns. **1836** LANE *Mod. Egypt.* II. xii. 228 Miserable, or unfortunate, or scanted in my sustenance.

†**d.** with subject a thing. *Obs. rare.*

1628 GAULE *Pract. Theories* (1629) 21 Time would long fayle me, ere the Truth would here scant mee. *Ibid.* 61 What weake notions straighten our harts? What imperfect sounds and syllables scant our mouths? While we labour to apprehend his Nature, Person, and Acts.

4. a. To make scant or small; to reduce in size, cut down; to diminish the amount of. ? *obsolescent.*

c **1590** E. WRIGHT in *Hakluyt's Voy.* (1599) II. ii. 163 Hereupon also our allowance of drinke, which was scant ynough before, was yet more scanted, because of the scarcitie thereof in the shippe. **1606** SHAKS. *Ant. & Cl.* IV. ii. 21 Scant not my Cups. **1661** GLANVILL *Van. Dogm.* 120 The wrong end of the Perspective, which scants their dimensions. **1668** H. MORE *Div. Dial.* ii. I. 221 The Generations of men being not considerably scanted for all these four greedy devourers of them. **1870** LOWELL *Study Wind.* 92 As the clearing away of the woods scants the streams. **1880** *Sat. Rev.* No. 1291. 118 He has not hesitated to expand rather than scant the meaning of the original. **1886** *Field* 13 Feb. 204/2 Having had to scant the printer's bill to the lowest penny.

†**b.** *absol.* Cf. SCANTING *ppl. a.* *Obs.*

1577 TUSSER *Husb.* (1878) 184 Ill huswiferie wanteth with spending too fast. Good huswiferie scanteth the lenger to last. **1611** BIBLE *2 Kings* iv. 5 Borrow not a few. Marg. *Or,* scant not.

5. To stint the supply of; to refrain from giving, to withhold; to be niggardly of. Now *rare*. †*to scant out*: to dole out sparingly.

1573–80 TUSSER *Husb.* (1878) 10 This tree.. whose fruite to none is scanted, in house or yet in feeld. **1590** SHAKS. *Com. Err.* II. ii. 81 What he hath scanted them in haire, hee hath giuen them in wit. **1599** —— *Hen. V*, II. iv. 47 Doth like a Miser spoyle his Coat, with scanting A little Cloth. *c* **1603** HEYWOOD & ROWLEY *Fortune by Land & Sea* I. ii. (1655) 8 What age doth scant me In sprightly vigour, Ile make good in wealth. **1605** SHAKS. *Lear* I. i. 281 You haue obedience scanted. **1630** DAVENANT *Just Italian* v. i. H 3, Th'obedience which I scanted to his life, Vnto his memory I'le strictly pay. *a* **1654** SELDEN *Table-T.* (Arb.) 48 When Constantine became Christian, he so fell in love with the Clergy, that he let them be Judges of all things, but that continued not above three or four Years,.. and then.. all Jurisdiction belonged to him, and he scanted them out as much as he pleased. **1768** H. WALPOLE *Myst. Mother* v. i. (1791) 74 Oft as they scant obedience to the church. **1846** BROWNING *Lett.* (1899) I. 392, I cannot undervalue my own treasure and so scant the only tribute of mere gratitude which is in my power to pay.

†**6.** *gen.* To confine within narrow bounds, deprive of free scope; to limit, restrict, hedge in.

1596 SHAKS. *Merch. V.* II. i. 17 If my Father had not scanted me And hedg'd me by his wit to yeelde my selfe [etc.]. **1621** BP. MOUNTAGU *Diatribæ* 174 If Christ in Melchisedec, shall be so scanted, as to be tyed vnto onely Spoyles. *a* **1628** PRESTON *Effect. Faith* v. (1637) 248 Wee scant God according to our measure; we square Gods mercy according to our owne thoughts. *a* **1631** DONNE *Serm.* xlv. (1640) 455 Though there be no.. imminent danger.. of inhibiting or scanting the liberty of the Gospel.

7. To treat slightingly or inadequately; to neglect, do less than justice to. Now chiefly *U.S.*

1604 SHAKS. *Oth.* I. iii. 268 And Heauen defend your good soules, that you thinke I will your serious and great businesse scant When she is with me. **1644** J. FARY *Gods Severity* (1645) 27 How are our devotions scanted and slubbered over? **1851** NEALE *Mediæval Hymns* 101 Letter held by, spirit scanted, Saw the Synagogue supplanted. **1969** *New Yorker* 6 Sept. 111/1 Several thousand.. men were on duty in the streets that day, while, presumably, Securitate was not scanting its duties elsewhere. **1977** *N.Y. Rev. Books* 14 Apr. 5 (Advt.), No thinker or movement is dismissed as too radical, no issue is scanted as too controversial.

†**8.** *Naut.* In *passive*, of a ship: To be impeded by the 'scanting' of the wind. Cf. sense 2. *Obs.*

1555 (16 Oct.) *Admiralty Court* Exam. x, The Pellican being a myle.. behind thother shipps was scanted with the wind.

Hence **'scanting** *vbl. sb.*

1625 PURCHAS *Pilgrims* II. 1696 They sayled for certaine dayes with aforewind till it came upon the skanting. **1626** B. JONSON *Staple of N.* II. i, Your macerating of your body thus with cares and scantings of your dyet, and rest. **1672** DRYDEN *Conq. Granada* I. *Heroic Plays* a 3 b, And, therefore, in the scanting of his Images, and design, he comply'd not enough with the greatness and Majesty of an Heroick Poem. **1769** FALCONER *Dict. Marine* (1780), *Scanting*, the variation of the wind by which it becomes unfavourable to a ship's course, after having been *fair* or *large*. It is distinguished from a foul wind, as in the former a ship is still enabled to sail on her course, although her progress is considerably retarded.

scanted ('skæntɪd), *ppl. a.* [f. SCANT *v.* + -ED[1].] In senses of the verb: Made scant or small, stinted, diminished, restricted, etc.

1594 MARLOWE & NASHE *Dido* I. A 4, And euery beast the forrest doth send forth, [shall] Bequeath her young ones to our scanted foode. **1605** SHAKS. *Lear* III. ii. 67 While I to this hard house.. returne, and force Their scanted curtesie. *a* **1635** NAUNTON *Fragm. Reg.* (Arb.) 53 Wherein my Lord of Essex so wrought, by despising the number and quality of Rebels, that Norris was sent over with a scanted force. **1865** SWINBURNE *Poems & Ball., Two Dreams* 112, I have no wit to shape in written rhymes A scanted tithe of this great joy they had.

†**'scantelize**, *v.* *Obs.* [f. SCANTLE *sb.* + -IZE. Cf. SCANDALIZE *v.*[2]] *trans.* To shorten, curtail.

1611 SPEED *Hist. Gt. Brit.* v. iii. §22. 18 By which account the great supposed antiquity of Brute, is now lessened by seuen hundred fiftie and two yeares; and the time so scantelized betwixt his and Cesars entrance, that two hundred forty six yeares onely remaine.

†**'scanten**, *v.* *Obs. rare* [f. SCANT *a.* + -EN[5].] *intr.* To wax scant, diminish.

1585 T. WASHINGTON tr. *Nicholay's Voy.* I. xix. 22 The diminishing of our victuals, which began to scanten. **1613** F. ROBARTES *Revenue Gosp.* 113 [They] will not be found so vnfaithfull, as to neglect their workes for the scantning of their temporarie hyre.

†**scantillon.** *Obs.* Forms: 3 schauntillun, 3–4 scantliun, -lion, -lyoun, 3–5 -lyon, scantilon, 4 -ioun, 4–5 -ilone, -elon(e, -eloun, -ylloun, -il(l)ioun, 5 -ylyon, -ylone, -eleon, -ulon, skantulon, -yllȝon, skanklyon(e, scanklyone, 5–6 scantlon, 7 scantillon. See also SCANTLING. [Aphetic f. OF. *escantillon*, *eschantillon* (mod.F. *échantillon*), of uncertain etymology.

According to Hatz.-Darm., an alteration (influenced by *cantel* CANTLE) of **esc(h)andillon*, related to Pr. *escandith* gauge, It. *scandaglio* sounding-line; commonly regarded as f. L. *scandĕre* to climb, to SCAN.]

1. A tool used by masons and carpenters for measuring the thickness of anything; a gauge.

a **1300** *Floriz & Bl.* 325 Ber wiþ þe squire and schauntillun, Also þu were a gud Mascun. *a* **1300** *Cursor M.* 2231 And do we wel and make a toure, Wit suire and scantilon [*Gött.* scantlion, *Trin.* scanteloun] sa euen, þat may reche heghur þan heuen. *Ibid.* 8775 þe king did cast wit scantliun [*Gött.* scantlyon, *Fairf.* scantilioun, *Trin.* scanteloun], And did mak al þe timber bun. *c* **1400** *Rom. Rose* 7064 Though it were of no vounde stone Wrought with squyre and scantilone. **15..** *Debate Carpenter's Tools* 107 in Hazl. *E.P.P.* I. 83 Soft, ser, seyd the skantyllȝon.

2. Dimension, measured size; in carpenters' and masons' work chiefly sectional dimension, thickness.

c **1400** *Master of Game* (MS. Digby 182) xxv, þen shulde þe lymmer go þeder as þe hert yede in, and take þe scantelon of þe trace, þe whiche he shulde kutte of his roddes ende, and ley it in þe talon of þe trace. **1452** in Willis & Clark *Cambridge* (1886) I. 282, iij sengulere Principalls..in Scantlyon accordyng to the Principalls. *a* **1513** FABYAN *Chron.* VI. clxi. 154 Theyse .ii. storyes..occupy in Frenshe, of leuys of great Scanteleon ouer .lxiiii.

3. ? A stick cut to record a certain measurement.

c **1400** *Master of Game* (MS. Digby 182) xxv, Ley it in þe talon of þe trace þer as he yede in hardest grounde euen in þe botome þerof, so þat þe scanteloun vnneth touche at neiþer ende þe erth. And þat done, he shulde hewe a bough of grene leues and ley it þer as þe hert yede in and kutte an oþer scantelon þer after to take to þe hunter.

4. A strip or piece serving as a specimen; a sample.

1465 *Mann. & Househ. Exp.* (Roxb.) 492 My master bout of Barthelmew Syates a short goune clothe of cremysen velvet... And a short goune clothe of tawny velvet... And the said Barthelmew hathe it to kepe, and my master hathe sealed it at bothe endes, and take a scantylone of eche of them. **1530** PALSGR. 265/2 Scantlon of a clothe, *eschantillon*. **1603** HOLLAND *Plutarch's Mor.* 403 This booke, wherein their words are gathered, and comprehended together by themselves, as the verie scantillons (as I may so say) and seeds extracted a part from their lives.

scantily ('skæntɪlɪ), *adv.* [f. SCANTY *a.* + -LY[2].] In a scanty manner or measure.

1774 GOLDSM. *Nat. Hist.* (1776) III. 5 That nourishment which their vegetable food so scantily supplies. **1840** DICKENS *Old C. Shop* i, Though more scantily attired than she might have been, she was dressed with perfect neatness. **1897** D. LYALL in *Brit. Wkly.* 7 Jan. 214/5, I knew nothing but my medical work—and that but scantily.

scantiness ('skæntɪnɪs). [f. SCANTY *a.* + -NESS.] The quality or fact of being scanty.

1567 *Reg. Privy Council Scot.* I. 571 Considdering that victualis ar cariit furth of this realme be marchantis and utheris..to the greit incres of derth and skantines. *a* **1695** J. SCOTT *Chr. Life* III. [IV.] iii. Wks. 1718 I. 673 Such is the Scantiness of Sensual Goods, that we not being able to content our selves with any one of them, are fain [etc.]. **1745** *Life Bampfylde-Moore Carew* 71 The..frugal Way of Life to which the Scantiness of their Pay obliges those Military Gentlemen to live. **1824** L. MURRAY *Eng. Gram.* (ed. 5) I. 198 The too frequent use of such words tends to breed a suspicion, that one labours under a scantiness of ideas. **1848** DICKENS *Dombey* i, Miss Tox's dress,..had a certain character of angularity and scantiness. **1888** BURGON *Lives 12 Good Men* II. x. 253 The scantiness of manuscript authority under which the text..labours.

'scanting, *ppl. a.* [f. SCANT *v.* + -ING[2].]

†**a.** Inclined to be sparing or niggardly; chary in giving or bestowing. *Obs.*

1613 *Uncasing of Machiav.* 22 At such a time of care friends are scanting. **1674** J. B[RIAN] *Harv. Home* iv. 25 Gods hand in pouring forth will not be scanting.

b. Decreasing, diminishing. *rare.*

1916 KIPLING *Tales of 'The Trade'* 107 It was necessary to go down at once and waste whole minutes of the precious scanting light.

Hence †**'scantingly** *adv.*

1627 W. SCLATER *Exp. 2 Thess.* (1629) 261 Scantingly, it should seeme, the Lord had distributed to these poore Artisans..the good things of this life. *a* **1661** FULLER *Worthies, Wilts* (1662) III. 148 Richard Smart..but once, and that scentingly [? *read* scantingly] mentioned by Mr. Fox.

'scantity. *rare.* [irreg. f. SCANT *a.* + -ITY, perh. after *quantity*.] Scantiness; scarceness.

c **1386** CHAUCER *Parson's T.* ¶357, I sey nat that honestitee in clothynge of man or womman is vncouenable, but certes the superfluitee or disordinat scantitee [*v.rr.* skantite(e, scantite] of clothynge is repreuable. **1550–3** *Decaye Eng.* in S. Fish *Supplic. Beggers* (1871) 95 Shepe & shepemasters doeth cause skantyte of corne. **1577–87** HARRISON *England* III. iv. 225/2 Such is the scantitie of them here in England, in comparison of the plentie that is to be seene in other countries. **1839** J. H. NEWMAN *Paroch. Serm.* IV. xv. 265 At least there are cases where this wavering of mind does arise from scantiness of prayer; and if so, it is worth a man's considering..whether this scantity be not perchance the true reason of such infirmities in his own case.

'scantle, *sb.* Also 6 skantell. [? f. SCANTLE *v.*]

1. = SCANTLET 1, SCANTLING *sb.* 2 b.

c **1525** *Contract* in Gage *Hengrave* (1822) 43 All man[r] of tymber, hewyn and sawyn, of all manner of skantells, y[t] shall be nedeful and redy to y[e] worke.

2. A small piece or portion, a scantling.

In 1596 'scantle' of the Qq. is perh. simply an error for 'cantle', the reading of the Ff.

1596 SHAKS. *1 Hen. IV*, III. i. 100 (1st Qo.) See how this riuer comes me cranking in, And cuts me from the best of all my land, A huge halfe moon, a monstrous scantle out. **1654** VILVAIN *Theorem. Theol.* vii. 194 The future cannot be confined to so short a scantle.

3. *Slate-making.* See quots. (two distinct senses).

1850 OGILVIE, *Scantle*, among slaters, a gauge by which slates are regulated to their proper length. **1865** J. T. F. TURNER *Slate Quarries* 15 There are, in addition to these 'size slate'..a small, irregular sort, called 'scantle', made of pieces too small to make 'size slate'. This last kind is in great request in west Cornwall, and forms a very strong roof... All scantle is cut by boys. **1887** *Dict. Arch. Publ. Soc.*, *Scantle*, a gauge for regulating the proper length of slates. 'Scantle slates' are squared slates as opposed to rag slates.

†**'scantle,** *v. Obs.* Also 6 skantle, 7 scantel. [? dimin. of SCANT *v.*: see -LE 3. In sense 3 perh. a back-formation from SCANTLING.]

1. *trans.* To give scant provision to, stint, put on short allowance; = SCANT *v.* 3.

1581 RICH *Farewell* (Shaks. Soc.) 184 There to be fedd with bread and water, (and yet to be scantled with suche short alowance, as it was not able to suffice nature). **1630** BRATHWAIT *Eng. Gentlem.* 220 Besides, you should be sometimes so scantled, for want of subjects, that [etc.].

b. with a thing as subject: To be wanting to, fail to supply. Cf. SCANT *v.* 3 d.

1641 BRATHWAIT *Turtle's Triumph* 15 Time would sooner faile me, then this subject scantle me.

2. To make scant or small; to diminish, cut down, curtail; to limit, restrict.

1596 HARINGTON *Ulysses upon Ajax* B 7 b, Loosing his repose, and scantling his repaste. **1596** LODGE *Wit's Miserie* 14 The chines of Beefe in great houses are scantled to buie chains of gold. **1611** SPEED *Hist. Gt. Brit.* VII. xii. §7. 275 Vortiporus..succeeded him in the Kingdome of the Britains, which then was much scantled by the intrusions of the Saxons. *a* **1641** BP. MOUNTAGU *Acts & Mon.* (1642) 40 Enlarged mercies must not be cooped up, or scantled.

b. To narrow the meaning or application of.

1644 BP. MAXWELL *Prerog. Chr. Kings* v. 56, I shall give thee the heathen for thine inheritance [etc.]: which is not to be scantled by conceiving it onely of the calling of the Gentiles to the communion of his Church. *Ibid.* 65 This is not to be so scantled, as if there were no more influence from Kings upon the Church but by honour and riches.

3. To adjust to a required measure; to make proportionate *to*.

1621 BP. MOUNTAGU *Diatribæ* 110–111 We are not to expect a like exactnesse and accurate handling in all passages. But it sufficeth to be scantled according to the Subject. **1625** J. ROBINSON *Ess.* iii. (1638) 18 How graciously our wise and good God provides for our slipperie state, in scantling his promise of good things of that kinde to our Spirituall skill, and care of using them. **1711** W. SUTHERLAND *Shipbuild. Assist.* 62 The Knee being scantled to suit the Stem as far as 'tis join'd to it.

4. To shorten (sail); similarly of a bird, to draw in (its wings). Cf. SCANDALIZE *v.*[2]

a **1592** LODGE & GREENE *Looking-glass* (1598) F 2 b, Then scantled we our sailes with speedie hands. **1630** DRAYTON *Noah's Flood* in *Muses Eliz.* 100 The soaring Kyte there scantled his large wings.

5. To parcel *out*.

1749 CHESTERF. *Let. to Son* 9 Oct., The Pope's.. territories..will, most undoubtedly, within a century, be scantled out among the great Powers, who have now a footing in Italy.

6. *intr.* Of wind: To become 'scant'. (But app. here taken to mean 'to become light'.)

1627 DRAYTON *Moon-calf* in *Agincourt*, etc. 173 She could sell windes to any one that would,..Which euer as the Seafarer vndid They rose or scantled, as his Sayles would driue, To the same Port whereas he would ariue.

Hence †**'scantled** *ppl. a.*, made scant, limited.

1604 DRAYTON *Owle* 1294 This small Portion of my scantled Store! **1622** —— *Poly-olb.* xxiv. 12 [Welland] in her scantled banks, though wandring long inclos'd. *a* **1641** BP. MOUNTAGU *Acts & Mon.* (1642) 33 This was their pittance, and scantled allowance in those dayes.

†**'scantlet.** *Obs.* Also 6 scanlot. [? f. SCANTLE *sb.* + -ET[1]; or f. SCANTLING by substitution of the suffix -LET for *-ling*.]

1. Prescribed size, scantling.

1502–3 (4 Jan.) *Office of Augment.* Miscell. Bk. xxxvi. No. 146, iiij[c]. M[l]. of goode lawfull & sufficiant breke [= bricks] & thurgh & suerly to be brent and after the Scanlot of ix ynches & a halfe of lengthe large & in brede & thyknes accordynge to the same lengthe.

2. ? A limit, boundary.

1547 SALESBURY *Welsh Dict.*, *Ystordyn* ['a trigger in bowling; a mark to jump from' (Owen Pugh)], scantlet.

3. A limited quantity, small portion.

a **1642** SUCKLING *Lett. to Sev. Persons of Honor* (1659) 9, I have been something curious to consider the scantlet of ground that angry Monsieur would have had in. [Allusion to Shaks.: see quot. 1596, SCANTLE *sb.* 1.] *a* **1676** HALE *Prim. Orig. Man.* (1677) 226 As the World grew by that means fuller, so their Lives were successively reduced to a shorter scantlet, till they came to that ordinary Age..which now they have.

scantling ('skæntlɪŋ), *sb.* Also 6–7 scantlin, skantling, 7 scantelinge. [Etymologizing alteration of SCANTILLON, after -LING[1]. The development of some of the senses appears to have been influenced by association with SCANT *a.*]

†**1. a.** A builder's or carpenter's measuring-rod. Cf. SCANTILLON 1. *Obs. rare*[−1].

1556 J. HEYWOOD *Spider & F.* xvii. 27 Whiche sqwyre shall sqware me, a scantlin well bent, For a right rewle, to show me innocent.

†**b.** *fig.* A rule or standard of measurement or estimation.

1587 GOLDING *De Mornay* x. 156 That nothing in al the Worlde is made of nought,..is a measuring of the builder and his building by one rule or skantling. **1678** *Lively Oracles* iii. §19. 269 To mesure immensity and omnipotence by our narrow scantling.

2. Measured or prescribed size, dimensions, or calibre. †**a.** with reference to material objects generally.

1526 *Househ. Ord.* (1790) 215 They shall neither send nor bring into the Court...any Pike of less scantling than eighteen inches long. **1588** *Acts Privy Council* (1897) XVI. 171 Provyde bullettes of all scantelins to be sent to the Lord Admirall, and two last of poulder. **1607** TOPSELL *Four-f. Beasts* 148 Dogs of a middle scantling beetwixt the first and the second. **1683** PETTUS *Fleta Min.* II. 15 The water..keeps at one scantling, neither swelling higher nor decreasing. **1686** PLOT *Staffordsh.* 390 Having several holes of different Sizes fit for the scantlings of all fingers. **1708–9** PRIOR *The Mice* 100 A coat not of the smallest scantling. **1725** BRADLEY *Fam. Dict.* s.v. *Elm*, Truncheons of the Boughs cut to the Scantling of a Man's Arm.

b. *techn.* with reference to the measurement of timber and stone, and of ships or other vessels and of aircraft.

As applied to timber, the word usually denotes the sectional dimensions (thickness and breadth) of a beam etc., in contradistinction to the length. The scantling of a block of stone is its measurement in all three dimensions. In Shipbuilding, used in *sing.* and *pl.* for the dimensions of the various parts of a vessel, regarded collectively.

1555 *Act 2 & 3 Philip & Mary*, c. 16 §5 Any Whirye or Boate..which shall not bee..according to thold quantitie, scantlyng, thicknes of boorde, goodnes & good proportyon, heretofore had & used. **1608** WILLET *Hexapla Exod.* 605 That is the vsuall scantling for the thicknes of planke boord. **1615** E. S. *Britain's Buss* in Arber *Garner* III. 625 A Buss of thirty-five Last, that is, of seventy Tons, is of a very good and meet size or scantling, wherewith [etc.]. **1673** TEMPLE *Ess. Ireland* Wks. 1731 I. 120 Forbidding any Man to cut down any Oak..unless it be of a certain Scantling. **1792** *Trans. Soc. Arts* X. 31 Young oaks and chestnuts of the same age and scantling. **1793** SMEATON *Edystone L.* §91 The harder the quality of the moorstone, the more exactly..it could be split to the size or scantling required. **1812** CAPT. CARDEN *Let.* 28 Oct. in *Examiner* (1813) 4 Jan. 6/2 The United States is built with the scantling of a seventy-four gun ship. **1829** P. NICHOLSON *Carp.* in *Encycl. Metrop.* (1845) VI. 235/1 In regard to squared stones the term [scantling] is applied to the three dimensions of length, breadth, and thickness. **1837** *Civil Eng. & Arch. Jrnl.* I. 6/2 The piles are from twelve to twenty-five feet long, and eight by six inches and a half scantling, shod with iron. **1874** POLLEN *Anc. & Mod. Furniture* Introd. 34 Veneers of well mottled wood or of precious wood, small in scantling, were glued on pine, cedar, &c., as a base. **1888** *Daily News* 17 Oct. 4/7 A fine twin screw steamship, built of steel to the same scantlings as if of iron. *a* **1895** LD. C. E. PAGET *Autobiog.* vi. (1896) 196 Our armour-clads were on the scantling of line-of-battle ships, but with the addition of considerable beam or width. **1933** [see FRAME *sb.* 11 i]. **1978** *Jrnl. R. Soc. Arts* CXXVI. 681/2 Figure 3 indicates the comparative scantlings for compression structures having the same load carrying capacity.

†**c.** of immaterial things. In the 17th c. often, the measure or degree of (a person's) capacity or ability. *Obs.*

1586 FERNE *Blaz. Gentrie* 94 If it can be so, that our Gentle-man before proposed, the scantling and measure of his liuing considered. **1600** SURFLET *Country Farm* III. xlix. 530 When..the apples shall be well prepared, and come to a good scantling of ripenes. **1624** BP. MOUNTAGU *Immed. Addr.* 144 The Angels behold what they can behold and see, and Archangels as much as they are capable of, each according vnto his owne measure and scantling. **1654** H. L'ESTRANGE *Chas. I* (1655) 74 The Rochellers perceived by the scantling and grandure of this preparation, the natural issue could be no other than their ruine. **1692** R. L'ESTRANGE *Fables* cxli. 129 Though 'tis a Hard Matter to find out a Woman, even at the Best, that's of a Just Scantling for her Age, Person, Humour, and Fortune to make a Wife of. **1716** J. SHARPE *12th Serm.* 3 Oct., We then according to our scantlings return glory to Him when we serve those purposes He made us for. *a* **1734** NORTH *Exam.* II. iv. §143 (1740) 307 We may propose the Extremes to shew the Scantling of the Author's false and inveterate Malice. **1756** *Monitor* No. 39 I. 381 There are many others, whose abilities are of the same scantling; that have large salaries too.

†**d.** *of one* (or *a*) *scantling*: of the same size; hence, much alike, 'much of a muchness'. (*of* is sometimes omitted.) *Obs.*

1551 EDW. VI *Jrnl.* in *Lit. Rem.* (Roxb.) II. 337 My lord marcus' reward was delivered at Paris, worth 500 pound, my lord of Ely's 200, mr. Hobbies 150, the rest al about on scantling. **1633** SHIRLEY *Bird in Cage* I. i, Your Lordships wisedome and mine is much about a scantling then. **1679** ALSOP *Melius Inq.* Pref., That there can be No Unity hoped for,..nor peace maintained, unless all men be of a scantling in their judgments.

†**e.** *to take a scantling of*: to measure or estimate the size or amount of; hence, to judge of, estimate. So *to have a scantling of*. *Obs.*

1585 PARSONS *Chr. Exerc.* I. iii. 15 By this now may a carefull Christian take some scantling of his own estate with God. **1607** TOPSELL *Four-f. Beasts* 655 If you take their scantling and length as they crooke a little, then are they about three foot long. **1647** TRAPP *Comm. 2 Cor.* vi. 11 We pour forth our selves in this flood of speech, that thereby ye may take a scantling of our over-abundant love to your souls. **1657** SANDERSON *Serm.* Pref. §15 (1689) 74 From hence chiefly..we are to take our best scantling, whereby to judge what is, and what is not, to be esteemed Popery. **1674** *Govt. Tongue* ix. §15. 154 We have not so just a scantling of our selves, as to know to a grain what will level the scales, and place us in the right mediocrity.

†**3. a.** Limited measure, space, amount, etc.: a limit.

1597 BACON *Ess., Hon. & Reput.* (ad. fin.), Such as exceede not this scantling [L. *qui non ultra hoc potes sunt*] to bee sollace to the Soueraigne and harmelesse to the people. **1600** SURFLET *Country Farm* II. lxvi. 414 The butterflies.. are forciblie kept within a narrow scantling, the pot it selfe being not wide, but narrow. **1617** HIERON *Wks.* II. 281 Wo to them that ayme at the cherishing of the people in a kind of formall Religion, and would haue none to exceede their owne Laodicean scantling! **1621** BP. MOUNTAGU *Diatribæ* 2 Because it farre exceeded the scantling of their Poore Vnderstandings, and Vndertakings. **1650** BULWER *Anthropomet.* xx. (1653) 331 Which when they are too strictly swathed with Bands, reduce the Breast to so narrow a scantling as is apt to endanger..the life of Children. **1678** BUTLER *Hud.* III. ii. 1046 And setting all the Land on fire, To burn t' a Scantling, but no higher. **1691** SIR T. P. BLOUNT *Ess.* 74 But this certainly is to measure Truth by a wrong Standard, and to Circumscribe her by too narrow a Scantling.

†**b.** *spec.* in *Archery*, applied to the distance from the mark, within which a shot was not regarded as a miss. Also *fig. Obs.*

1577–87 STANYHURST *Descr. Ireland* i. 11/2 If I may craue your patience till time you see me shoot my bolt, I hope you will not denie, but that as neere the pricke as you are, and as verie an hagler as I am, yet the scantling shall be mine. **1584** W. E[LDERTON] '*Yorke, Yorke for my Monie*' in Halliw. *Yorksh. Anthol.* (1851) 4 And then was shooting out of crye, And skantling at a handfull nie. **1591** G. FLETCHER *Russe Commw.* xix. 72 b, Not suffering them to eate, til they haue shot neere the marke within a certein scantling. *a* **1661** FULLER *Worthies, Lond.* (1662) II. 191 A poor Blew Cap.. played so well thereon [*sc.* a fire-engine], that..he could hit within the scantling of a Shilling.

4. A portion, allotted quantity, allowance. *arch.*

1659 *Gentlem. Calling* VI. x. 432 Nor is their pride so affronted, as to be forgot in the distribution of their time, a good scantling of it is cut out to its use. **1765** STERNE *Tr. Shandy* VII. xxi, The muleteer..thought not of to-morrow .., provided he got but his scantling of Burgundy. **1835** THIRLWALL *Greece* I. vi. 171 The practice of burying criminals alive, with a scantling of food by their side.

5. a. A small or scanty portion or amount, a modicum (of things material or immaterial).

1585 HIGINS *Junius' Nomencl.* 412 *Ramentum*,..a fragment, remnant, scantling, or litle peece of marble, or other thing. **1607** TOPSELL *Four-f. Beasts* 537 The former hoofes of a horse being scraped, and the same fragmentes or scantlinges thereof being beaten in the duste. **1665** BRATHWAIT *Comment Two Tales* (1901) 24 One now resolved to sleep out that small scantling of time which is left him. **1743** H. WALPOLE *Let. to Mann* 4 Apr., I am really ashamed to send this scantling of paper by the post, over so many seas and mountains. **1760–72** H. BROOKE *Fool of Qual.* I. p. iv, I cannot find about me the smallest scantling of veneration for your virtues. **1849** C. BRONTE *Shirley* III. iv. 89 But a scantling of apples enriched the trees. **1858** CARLYLE *Fredk. Gt.* IX. xi. (1872) III. 190 You shall get back your Lombardy,—all but a scantling which we fling to the Sardinian Majesty. **1876** PAGE *Adv. Text-bk. Geol.* i. 26 Some scantling of geological knowledge will be of advantage.

†**b.** An epitome, abridgement; also, a small remnant. *Obs.*

1576 FLEMING tr. *Caius' Dogs* To Rdr. (1880), The booke ..being but a pamphlet or skantling. **1693** J. EDWARDS *Auth. O. & N. Test.* I. 425 Velleius Paterculus..is an Epitomizer, a Scantling of an Historian. **1708** HUDSON in Hearne *Coll.* 3 Aug. (O.H.S.) II. 123 Thetford..is nothing but ye poor scantling of an ancient spatious town.

†**6.** A sample, pattern, specimen. Hence, a sketch, outline, rough draft. *Obs.*

1567 GOLDING *Ovid's Met.* Epist. 379 How Ovids scantlings with the whole true patterne doo agree. **1597** BEARD *Theatre God's Judgem.* (1612) 539 This is but a tast and scantling of those torments and punishments which are prepared and made ready for them in the world to come. **1606** SHAKS. *Tr. & Cr.* I. iii. 341 For the successe (Although particular) shall giue a scantling Of good or bad, vnto the Generall. **1663** MARQ. WORCESTER (*title*) A Century of the Names and Scantlings of such Inventions, as at present I can call to mind to have tried and perfected. *a* **1668** LASSELS *Voy. Italy* I. (1670) 82 And all the way long we saw such a continual Suburbs of stately Villas and Villages, that these scantlings made us in love with the whole Piece it self, Genua. **1679** C. NESSE *Antid. agst. Popery* 104 To give but a scantling and landskip of some of them. *a* **1680** BUTLER *Rem.* (1759) I. 108 Had you sent a Scantling of your Wit, You might have blam'd us, if it did not fit. **1704** SWIFT *Tale of Tub* xi. 201 This I have produced, as a Scantling of Jack's great Eloquence. **1838** T. MITCHELL *Clouds of Aristoph.* 113 The slight tests to which Strepsiades is put in the verses following, are of course but a dramatic scantling of those probations to which candidates were often put before admission into the philosophic schools of antiquity.

7. *concr.* in technical use (see 2 b). **a.** A small beam or piece of wood; *spec.* one less than five inches square.

1663 GERBIER *Counsel* 42 The cutting of their Scantlings. **1683** MOXON *Mech. Exerc., Printing* xxii. ¶1 The Composite sends..for..good strong Wast-Paper, and cuts it into so many several Scantlins as the number of each Scantlin of his Boxes in his Case are. **1704** *Lond. Gaz.* No. 4002/4 A Good quantity of..Oak Timber, fit to be cut for Planks and Scantlings for Shipping,.. is to be sold. **1784** COWPER *Task* III. 753 He that saw His patrimonial timber cast its leaf, Sells the last scantling, and transfers the price To some shrewd sharper. **1829** P. NICHOLSON *Carp.* in *Encycl. Metrop.* (1845) VI. 235/1 In the construction of naked flooring and roofing the small timbers which are used are called by the general name of scantlings. **1889** 'MARK TWAIN' *Yankee at Crt. K. Arthur* xxiii. 257 About two hundred yards off..we built a pen of scantlings. **1958** *Chambers's Techn. Dict.* 743/2 *Scantling*.., a piece of timber of thickness from 2 to 4 in. and of width from 2 to 4½ in. **1965** 'LAUCHMONEN' *Old Thom's Harvest* ii. 15 The young girl walked round the pickets that had fallen off the rotten scantling runners of the wooden part of the fence. **1972** *Gloss. Terms Timber* (*B.S.I.*) 21 *Scantling*. 1. *Softwood.* A piece of square-sawn timber 50 mm to under 100 mm thick and 50 mm to under 125 mm wide. 2. *Hard-wood.* Timber converted to an agreed specification such as waggon oak scantlings. Otherwise any squared-edged piece of dimensions not conforming to other standard terms.

b. *collect. sing.* Timber in the form of scantlings.

1703 tr. *H. van Oosten's Dutch Gardener* IV. xii. 225 You must keep your Scantling or Boares whereon your Pots stand very neat. **1743** *Colonial Rec. Georgia* (1906) VI. 68 The Reverend Mr. Bolzius [petitioned] this Board to allow him a Quantity of Boards, Planks, and Scantling. **1785** T. JEFFERSON *Notes on Virginia* xv. 279 The private buildings are very rarely constructed of stone or brick; much the greatest portion being of scantling and boards. **1794** MORSE *Amer. Geog.* 520 Boards, scantling, staves, shingles. **1901** *J. Black's Carp. & Build., Scaffolding* iii. 32 If it is decided to use scantling [for ladder-sides] the two pieces should be tapered from about 3½ in. by 2 in. at the bottom end.

c. A block or slice of stone of a fixed size; also *collect. sing.* stone cut into scantlings.

1726 LEONI *Alberti's Archit.* I. 38/1 Whether square Stone, or uneven Scantlings. *Ibid.* II. 16/1 The method of cutting Marble into thin scantlings..scarce half an inch thick. *Ibid.* 41/2 The Ancients.., instead of panes of glass, made use of thin transparent scantlings of Alabaster. **1824** *Fowler Corr.* (MS.) 482 Account of stone..sawn into scantling at Quarry. **1825** J. NICHOLSON *Operat. Mechanic* 622 The blocks [of slate]..are, by the application of wedges, reduced into layers, called scantlings, from four to nine inches in thickness, and of any required length and breadth. **1842** GWILT *Encycl. Arch.* §1799, §1909.

8. (See quot.) Cf. CANTLING 2.

1632 in E. B. Jupp *Carpenters' Co.* (1887) 301 The making and layeing of all manner of beare Joysts Stillings and Scantlyngs for Vinteners, Brewhouses [etc.]. **1875** KNIGHT *Dict. Mech., Scantling*,..a trestle or horse in a cellar for holding casks on tap.

9. *attrib.*, as ***scantling board, piece, prop***; **scantling stick** *Shipbuilding* (see quot. 1874).

1883 *Daily News* 17 Sept. 8/1, 150 Standards of Timber, consisting of deals, battens, *scantling boards. **1584** in Feuillerat *Revels Q. Eliz.* (1908) 368 For ii *scantling peeces. **1853** KANE *Grinnell Exp.* xxi. (1856) 164 The *scantling props still stuck in the frozen soil. **1874** THEARLE *Naval Archit.* 55 A stick is provided for each head and sirmark, and upon this stick are marked the mouldings of all the square body frames measured square to the surface at that head or sirmark. These sticks are known as *scantling or moulding sticks.

†**'scantling**, *a. Obs.* [f. SCANTLING *sb.*]

1. Very small, insignificant in size or extent.

1652 BENLOWES *Theoph.* I. xliv, Heav'ns Glorie to atchieve, what scantling Span Hath the frail Pilgrimage of Man! Which sets, when risen; ends, when it but now began. *a* **1763** SHENSTONE *Elegies* x. 30 How would some flood with ampler treasures blest, Disdainful view the scantling drops distil! **1788** BURNS *Let. to Clarinda* 6 Mar. (Globe) 402 How little of that scantling portion of time, called the life of man, is sacred to happiness.

2. *techn.* Cut into 'scantlings' or thin slices.

1726 LEONI *Alberti's Arch.* II. 46/1 The Window must be ..paned with scantling talc.

'scantling, *v.* ? *Obs. rare.* [f. SCANTLING *sb.*] *trans.* To construct (a ship) of a certain scantling.

1780 CAPT. W. YOUNG *Let. to Comptroller* 24 July (Ld. Barham Papers), Small 20-gun ships who were only scantlined to carry six pounders, might very well bare twelve-pound carronades.

'scantlins, *adv. Sc.* [f. SCANT *a.* + *-lin(g)s*, -LING².] Scarcely, hardly.

a **1774** R. FERGUSSON *Poems* (1807) 235 When merry Yule-day comes, I trow, You'll scantlins find a hungry mou.

†**scant'lometer.** *Obs.* [f. SCANTL(ING) + -(O)METER.] (See quot.)

1844 *Rep. Brit. Assoc.* II. 99 The Scantlometer. The instrument thus named, the invention of Mr. Wylson, determines the scantlings of joists and rafters, the former level, the latter sloped to any pitch not exceeding sixty degrees.

scantly ('skæntlı), *adv.* [f. SCANT *a.* + -LY².]

1. Scarcely, hardly, barely. *arch.*

Exceedingly common from the 15th to the middle of the 17th c.; in the 18th c. it had app. become obsolete; revived in literary use by Scott.

c **1375** *Sc. Leg. Saints* xvii. (*Martha*) 111 Scantly þe todir day fand þai quhare þe body lay. *c* **1440** *Ipomydon* 1228 Scantly had they the mete corvyn, That in comyth the kyngis messyngere, And grette the lady in thys manere. *c* **1449** PECOCK *Repr.* I. iii. 15 ȝit of thilk vertu or gouernaunce scantli is writen in al Holi Writt ten lynes. *c* **1489** CAXTON *Sonnes of Aymon* xxi. 460 Ye can scantly heve up your staff. **1520** NISBET *N.T., Luke* ix. 50 And scantlie [*Wycl.* vnnethe; Vulg. *vix*] he gais away al to drawand him. **1565** COOPER *Thesaurus*, s.v. *Cerrus*, The maste rough like a chesten, scantly holsome for swyne. **1575–85** ABP. SANDYS *Serm.* x. 153 Wee are hearers of the woord, and yet skantly that. **1627** HAKEWILL *Apol.* (1630) 221, I say it is scantly foure inches long. **1805** SCOTT *Last Minstr.* III. xvii, His kirtle..Reach'd scantly to his knee. *a* **1844** CAMPBELL *Napoleon & Brit. Sailor* 65 Our sailor oft could scantly shift To find a dinner, plain and hearty. **1859** TENNYSON *Marr. Geraint* 287 We hold a tourney here tomorrow morn, And there is scantly time for half the work.

†**b.** with superfluous negative. *Obs.*

1585 PARSONS *Chr. Exerc.* I. viii. 87 For scantly, there is not a seuere saying of God..which commeth not now to his mind.

†**2.** Sparingly; at little cost. *Obs.*

c **1440** *Alphabet of Tales* ix. 8, I liff als skantlie as I can, & diligentlie I kepe all my merchandise.

3. In scant measure; inadequately; scantily. Also *rarely* †grudgingly.

1509 BARCLAY *Shyp of Folys* (1874) I. 223 And where as the angels ar ther with reuerence..worshyppynge our holy sauyour These vnkynde caytyfs wyll scantly hym honour. *a* **1585** MONTGOMERIE *Cherrie & Slae* 1058 For all the proverbs they perusit, ȝe thocht them skantly skild. **1606** SHAKS. *Ant. & Cl.* III. iv. 6 He hath..spoke scantly of me. *a* **1631** DONNE *Serm.* vii. (1640) 70 Indeed, God can doe nothing scantly, penuriously, singly. **1817** KEATS *Sonn.* i, Cynthia is from her silken curtains peeping So scantly, that it seems her bridal night. **1840** HOOD *Kilmansegg, Birth* xvi, Tables sprang up all over the lawn; Not furnish'd scantly or shabbily. *a* **1859** DE QUINCEY *Posth. Wks.* (1891) I. 50 On that ground, agreeably to the logic I have so scantly expounded.

b. Curtly. ? *rare.*

1884 HOWELLS *Silas Lapham* (1891) I. 133 'How?' asked the Colonel scantly.

scantness ('skæntnıs). [f. SCANT *a.* + -NESS.]

1. The condition of being scant or insufficient in quantity.

c **1386** CHAUCER *Parson's T.* ¶415 The synful costlewe array of clothynge, and namely in to muche superfluite, or elles in to desordinat scantnesse [*v.r.* skarsenesse]. *c* **1412** HOCCLEVE *De Reg. Princ.* 1243, I am so drad of monyes scantnesse, That myn hert is al makid of lightnesse. **1574** DEE in *Lett. Lit. Men* (Camden) 33 Considering your mervailous skantnes of leysor from very waighty matters. **1608** R. DOBSON in *Lismore Papers* Ser. II. (1887) I. 124 As for the skantness of it, I know it is as full of stuffe as any gowne you haue..worn. **1609** SKENE *Reg. Maj., Stat. David II*, 45 There is great raritie, and skantnes within the Realme, ..of silver. **1661** GLANVILL *Van. Dogm.* 193 The miserable scantness of our capacities. **1684** BAXTER *Twelve Arg.* i. 2 Tho the scantness of History..tell us not what words were then used. **1846** TRENCH *Mirac.* Introd. iii. 30 All scantness and scarceness, such as this lack of bread in the wilderness, ..belonged not to man as his portion at the first.

†**b.** Penury, lack of comforts or necessaries.

c **1400** MAUNDEV. (Roxb.) xxvi. 124 þai liffe with grete wricchedness and scantness. *c* **1440** *Promp. Parv.* 442/2 Scantnesse, *parcitas, parcimonia*.

†**c.** = SCARCITY 3. *Obs.*

1543 *Aberdeen Reg.* (1844) I. 190 The grit dartht and skantnes in the contray.

†**2.** Of the wind (cf. SCANT *a.* 7). *Obs.*

1574 W. BOURNE *Regiment for Sea* xix. (1577) 50 b, Tydes, currentes, or the scantnesse of the wynde, which may put the ship vnto the leewardes of his course.

scanty ('skæntı), *a.* and *sb.* [f. SCANT *sb.* or *a.* + -Y.]

A. *adj.* **1.** Of a quantity, store, supply, or any collective unity: Meagre, slender, not ample or copious.

1660 HARRINGTON *Prerog. Pop. Govt.* II. v. Wks. (1700) 379 Clemens says they were very few, their Assemblys privat, and very scanty things. **1668** CULPEPER & COLE *Barthol. Anat.* Man. III. i. 323 More plentiful or scanty influx of the Spirit. **1690** LOCKE *Hum. Und.* III. v. §8 The terms of our law..will hardly find words that answer them in the Spanish or Italian, no scanty languages. **1791** COWPER *Iliad* XIX. 259 Me, in no scanty measure, thou excell'st. **1836** LD. ST. HELENS in *Croker Papers* (1884) 2 Nov., [The] King ..used to dispatch his solitary and scanty meal in a very short time. **1838** LYTTON *Alice* III. i, Proud aristocrats began to recollect that a mushroom peerage was supported but by a scanty fortune. **1866** GEO. ELIOT *F. Holt* i, Since her early gladness in this best-loved boy, the harvests of her life had been scanty. **1907** A. LANG *Hist. Scotl.* IV. xviii. 465 Congregations were scanty.

2. Deficient in extent, compass, or size.

1701 STANHOPE tr. *Augustine's Medit.* II. ii. 115 They proportion their Regard to Him according to their own Scanty Notions of His goodness toward them. **1709** STEELE *Tatler* No. 128 ¶4 You appear to my Imagination more agreeable in a short scanty Petticoat, than the finest woman of Quality in her spreading fardingal. *a* **1721** SHEFFIELD (Dk. Buckhm.) *Wks.* (1753) I. 264 This scanty road bears us not both together; And we must once divide, to part no more. **1725** WATTS *Logic* I. vi. §9 Our Minds are narrow and scanty in their Capacities. **1873** DIXON *Two Queens* III. iii. I. 129 They sailed from Harfleur in the scantiest craft that ever ventured for a crown. **1874** WHYTE MELVILLE *Uncle John* xiv. II. 95 Scanty trousers..and a forward set of the hat.

3. Existing or present in small or insufficient quantity; not abundant. †Of wind: = SCARCE *a.* 1 b.

1674 JOSSELYN *Two Voy.* 196 The wind was scanty all along. **1705–6** PENN in *Pa. Hist. Soc. Mem.* X. 107 My paper is scanty and time more so. **1732** BERKELEY *Alciphr.* VI. §30 If our scanty experience were made the rule and measure of truth. **1770** GOLDSM. *Des. Vill.* 304 He drives his flocks to pick the scanty blade. **1801** *Med. Jrnl.* V. 409 Breath very short, urine scanty. **1804** *Naval Chron.* XI. 80 Wind scanty, but fair. **1839** JAMES *Louis XIV*, I. 221 Forage and provisions beginning to grow scanty, and the winter approaching. **1849** MACAULAY *Hist. Eng.* iii. (*init.*), Such a description, composed from scanty and dispersed materials, must necessarily be very imperfect. **1871** FREEMAN *Norm. Conq.* (1876) IV. xviii. 173 With regard to Worcestershire our knowledge is in one way still scantier, while in another it is much fuller. **1884** *Manch. Exam.* 20 May 5/2 He pegged away, however, with his scanty dollars until he came into alliance with Jay Gould.

†**4.** Parsimonious. Of soil: Yielding little. *Obs.*

1692 DRYDEN *Eleonora* 105 She..Ascribed above their due to every one, Unjust and scanty to herself alone. **1794** BURKE *Pref. to Brissot's Addr. Constituents* ¶21 He allows a space of time for the duration of these agitations: and least he should be thought rigid and too scanty in his measure, he thinks it may be long. **1796** COLERIDGE *Ode Depart. Yr.* ix, With..daily toil Soliciting for food my scanty soil.

B. *sb.* Now only *pl.* Underwear, esp. short knickers or panties for women. *colloq.* (orig. *U.S.*).

1928 J. P. MCEVOY *Show Girl* (*title-page*), The hottest little wench that ever shook a scanty at a tired business man. **1929** M. LIEF *Hangover* 269 There's no law in New Jersey forcing a husband to look at his wife's scanties, is there? **1934** T. SMITH *Bishop's Jaegers* 5 Whereas men..still struggle along with the old-fashioned..name of drawers.. women have far outstripped them. Theirs must be known now by such frivolous..appellations as panties, scanties.. step-ins..and other similar..terms. **1944** E. CARR *House of All Sorts* 101 A puff of wind from the open door caught and ballooned the scanties. **1951** M. DICKENS *My Turn to make Tea* iv. 73 No don't go, dear. You've seen me in my scanties, anyway. **1959** 'O. MILLS' *Stairway to Murder* vii. 75 'Now you've got some midnight-blue scanties.' He held up Charles's underpants apologetically. **1964** J. HALE *Grudge Fight* I. i. 22 Bennet, who always looks after number one, is wearing Scapa scanties next to the skin. Long underpants and a long-sleeved vest made of thick, oily wool. **1977** *Time* 24 Jan. 46/1 Maddie's blue scanties emerge from the M.P.s' briefcases at inauspicious moments and whip through the air like naval pennants.

scap: see SCALP, SCAPE *v.*, SHAPE.

scapa, var. SCARPER *v.*

scape (skeɪp), *sb.*[1] Also 4 **schap**, 4–6 **skape**. [Aphetic var. of ESCAPE *sb.*[1]]

1. An act of escaping; = ESCAPE *sb.*[1] *arch.* Now chiefly in ***hairbreadth scape***, after Shakspere: see HAIRBREADTH. (Often written *'scape.*)

a **1300** *Cursor M.* 23730 All sal we rin into his rape, we wat þat þar mai li na scape. **13..** *K. Alis.* 4273 (Bodl. MS.), He haþ ylore his foo..And bymeneþ his skape sore. *a* **1500** *Arnolde's Chron.* (1502) B ij, That the sherefs of london bee amerced for a scape of thefes at C. s. only. **1591** G. FLETCHER *Russe Commw.* xiii. 48 You shall seldome see a Russe a traueller, except he be with some Ambassadour, or that he make a scape out of his Countrie. **1653** DOROTHY OSBORNE *Lett. to Sir W. Temple* (1888) 51 But *à propos* of Monsr. Smith what a scape has he made of my Lady Barbury. **1658** SIR T. BROWNE *Hydriot.* v. 29 To hold long subsistence seems but a scape in oblivion. **1739** G. OGLE *Gualtherus & Griselda* 77 How great our Scape, who never yet knew Man! **1897** *Church Quarterly* 11 The romantic scapes..of St. Athanasius gave birth to no literature of song and legend like the wanderings of Prince Charlie.

†**2.** A transgression due to thoughtlessness; also, with different notion, a breaking out from moral restraint, an outrageous sin; often applied to a breach of chastity. Cf. ESCAPE *sb.*[1] 7. *Obs.*

c **1440** *Found. St. Bartholomew's* (E.E.T.S.) 3 He, wepynge hys dedis and reducyng to mynde the scapis of his yougth and ignoraunces. **1553** T. WILSON *Rhet.* 60 b, Maydens that haue made a scape are commonly called to bee nurses. *c* **1590** GREENE *Fr. Bacon* vii. 136 My Lord, pardon vs, we knew not what you were: But Courtiers may make greater scapes than these. **1592** —— *Disput. Hee & Shee Connycatchers* C 1 b, The old Croane..sayd the childe was hers, and so saued her daughters scape. **1599** MARSTON *Pygmal., Sat.* v, Slight scapes are whipt, but damned deeds are praised. *a* **1656** HALES *Golden Rem.* I. (1673) 91 Men are universally more apt from the errours and scapes of good men to draw apologies for their own. **1671** MILTON *P.R.* II. 189 Then lay'st thy scapes on names ador'd, Apollo, Neptune, Jupiter, or Pan. **1681** W. ROBERTSON *Phraseol. Gen.* (1693) 560 One miscarriage, one scape in bad company, will not quite undo me.

†**3.** An inadvertent mistake; *esp.* a slip of the tongue or a clerical error, a 'fault escaped'; = ESCAPE *sb.*[1] 6. *Obs.*

1565 JEWEL *Repl. Harding* To Rdr. ¶3 b, To consider better the ouersightes, and scapes of his former Booke. **1586** HOOKER *Learned Disc.* §39 (1612) 68 Let no man..thinke himselfe..alwaies freed from scapes and oversights in his speech. **1613** SIR E. HOBY *Counter-snarle* 33 Such scapes oftentimes happen, when the Author himselfe cannot attend the presse. **1669** STURMY *Mariner's Mag., Penalties & Forf.* 11 Such As poyson all they see, foul all they touch, And on Mechanick Scapes forge Arts detraction. **1705** J. BLAIR in W. S. Perry *Hist. Coll. Amer. Col. Ch.* I. 153 Involuntary Scapes of Transcription excepted.

†**4.** ***to let a scape***: to break wind. (See also ESCAPE *sb.*[1] 4 b.) *Obs.*

1549 CHALONER *Erasm. on Folly* N iv, I for my parte, through laughter, had almost let goe a skape, as Priapus did. **1577** KENDALL *Flowers of Epigr.* 104 She would not misse her fistyng curre for any thyng: and why? Forsothe when so she letts a scape, she cries me, fie curre, fie. **1618** *Barnevelt's Apol.* B 2 b, This is the language of dissimulation, with whom a scape passes for currant, vnder the name of coughing. **1681** W. ROBERTSON *Phraseol. Gen.* (1693) 584 To let a fart or let a scape.

†**5.** *pl.* ? Grapes that have been left ungathered.

1607 TOPSELL *Four-f. Beasts* 667 In some Countries they also giue them [*sc.* swine] the scapes or refuse Grapes of Vintage.

6. = SCAPEMENT. Cf. SCAPE *v.*[2] and *scape-wheel.*

1798 *Trans. Soc. Arts* XVI. 312 Exactly like those of a common clock with the dead scape.

7. *Comb.*: † **scape-door**, a door through which to escape, a means of escape; **scape-pipe** *U.S.* = *escape pipe* s.v. ESCAPE *sb.*[1] 8; **scape-spring**, a spring that is automatically liberated when its action is required; **scape-wheel**, = *escape-wheel.*

1607 HIERON *Defence* I. 44 To himselfe a *scapedoore to flie out at. **1838** E. FLAGG *Far West* I. 51 The stern roar of the *scape-pipe, gave evidence of the fearful power summoned up to overcome the flood. **1949** E. HUNGERFORD *Wells Fargo* 22 This craft, in her neat coat of immaculate white, and her yellow stacks, 'scape pipes and upper works, and her gayly striped paddle-houses, was a pretty sight. **1825** J. NICHOLSON *Operat. Mechanic* 512 Fig. 518 represents a side view of the *scape-spring which locks the wheel. **1822** IMISON *Sci. & Art* I. 85 Thus the motion begun by the weight is transported to the *scape wheel. **1877** *Encycl. Brit.* VI. 18/2 The scape-wheel tooth does not overtake the face of the pallet immediately.

scape (skeɪp), *sb.*[2] [ad. L. *scāpus*, a. Gr. (Doric) σκᾶπος (Hesych.), cogn. w. σκῆπτρον SCEPTRE. Cf. F. *scape*, Sp. *escapo*. See also SCAPUS.]

1. *Arch.* The shaft of a column. (With reference to the alleged sense = APOPHYGE, see ESCAPE *sb.*[2])

1663 CHARLETON *Chor. Gigant.* 20 From the third part of their Scape, or lower part, upward. **1842** GWILT *Archit.* Gloss., *Scape* or *Scapus*, the shaft of a column; also the little hollow, above or below, which connects the shaft with the base, or with the fillet under the astragal.

†**2.** The tongue of a balance. *Obs.*

[So L. *scapus trutinæ* is explained by Cooper 1565; Lewis & Short render it 'beam'.]

1633 G. HERBERT *Temple, Justice* ii, The beam and scape Did like some tott'ring engine show.

3. *Bot.* A long flower-stalk rising directly from the root or rhizome; †*gen.*, a stem or stalk.

1601 HOLLAND *Pliny* XIII. xi. I. 392 The scape or stalke that ariseth from it hath three sides with three corners triangle-wise. **1785** MARTYN *Rousseau's Bot.* xv. (1794) 166 Ribwort Plantain has..the scape angular and twisted. **1824** J. BARNET in *Trans. Hort. Soc.* (1826) VI. 152 The scapes are short, generally half the length of the leaf-stalk. **1885** GOODALE *Physiol. Bot.* (1892) 384 The scapes of many plants develop at a rapid rate.

attrib. **1870** HOOKER *Stud. Flora* 32 Draba rupestris.. scape-leaf 1 or 0.

4. *Ornith.* (See quot.)

1872 COUES *Key N. Amer. Birds* 2 A perfect feather consists of a main stem, or scape (*scapus*..), and a supplementary stem or aftershaft.

5. *Ent.* (See quots.)

1826 KIRBY & SP. *Entomol.* xxxiii. III. 366 Scapus (the Scape). The first and in many cases the most conspicuous joint of the *Antennæ*. It includes the *Bulbus*. *Ibid.* xxxiv. 515 The scape, or first joint, by means of the bulb inosculates in the torulus, or is suspended to it. **1898** PACKARD *Text-bk. Entomol.* 57 In the more specialized forms it [the antenna] is divided into the *scape*, the *pedicel*, and a *flagellum* (or *clavola*).

scape (skeɪp), *sb.*[3] [Back-formation from LANDSCAPE *sb.*] A view of scenery of any kind, whether consisting of land, water, cloud, or anything else. Also as the second element of combs. formed in imitation of *landscape*, as SEA-SCAPE, *cloud-scape*, and various nonce-words. See also CITYSCAPE, LUNARSCAPE, MOONSCAPE, ROOFSCAPE, etc.

1773 G. WHITE *Selborne, Let. to Barrington* 9 Dec., Mr. Ray..was so ravished with the prospect from Plumpton-plain, near Lewes, that he mentioned these scapes in his 'Wisdom of God in the Works of the Creation' with the utmost satisfaction. **1776** —— *Let. to J. White* 9 Aug., He first of all sketches his scapes with a lead pencil. **1796** CHARLOTTE SMITH *Marchmont* IV. 339 My simile..brings me to remark on the landscape, or rather the prison-scape around me. **1853** WARTER *Paroch. Fragments W. Tarring* 362 During the ten years I have lived hard by the Downs, I have never seen a single dotterel on their scapes, much less a trip of them. **1868** *Daily News* 3 Sept., Some of these cloud-scapes are extremely grand. **1885** [W. H. WHITE] *Mark Rutherford's Deliv.* ii. (1892) 18 Some relief from the contemplation of the landscape or brick-scape. **1907** E. W. COLERIDGE *Christabel* 3 Here was one of those moon-scapes which the poet should depict in verse. **1908** 'O. HENRY' *Gentle Grafter* 6 The third day of the rain it slacked up awhile in the afternoon, so me and Andy walked out to the edge of the town to view the mud-scape. **1930** *Sat. Rev. Lit.* 27 Dec. 486/3 One may..strive to..obtain a meager impression—starved, wry glimpses—of the private mindscape beyond. **1972** G. S. FRASER in Cox & Dyson *20th-Cent. Mind* II. xi. 382 Stephen's associations [in Joyce's *Ulysses*] are not really loose, he composes elaborate moodscapes in sub-Paterian prose. **1973** *Art Internat.* Mar. 49/2 Raffael's minutely dabbed garnish color..has more in common with the jungle-scapes and frottages of Max Ernst. **1975** *Times Lit. Suppl.* 28 Nov. 1409/3 The 'largest oil painting in the world' (a sea-cum-strandscape by the rightly overlooked Jacob Mesdag). **1977** 'J. MCVEAN' *Bloodspoor* xvii. 208 The two figures..were as much part of the desert winterscape now as the thorn barbs or the wheeling constellations in the sky above.

scape (skeɪp), *sb.*[4] [Origin unknown: perh. f. SCAPE *sb.*[3] (see INSCAPE *sb.*).] In the terminology of G. M. Hopkins: a reflection or impression of the individual quality of a thing or action. Hence **scaped**, **'scapish** adjs.; **'scaping**.

1868 G. M. HOPKINS *Jrnls. & Papers* (1959) 170 The types of the two thieves..were in the wholeness and general scape of the anatomy original and interesting. (The prominence of the peculiar square-scaped drapery etc. in Holbein and his contemporaries is remarkable.) **1869** *Ibid.* 194 It is just the things which produce dead impressions, which the mind..has made nothing of and brought into no scaping, that force themselves up in this way afterwards. **1874** *Ibid.* 245, I saw also a good engraving of his *Vintage Festival*, which impressed the thought one would also gather from Rembrandt..of a master of scaping rather than of inscape. For the vigorous rhetorical but realistic and unaffected scaping holds everything but no arch-inscape is thought of. *Ibid.* 247 W. L. Wylie—*Goodwin Sands*—Fiery truthful rainbow-end; green slimy races of piers; all clean, atmospheric, truthful, and scapish. **1883** —— *Sermons & Devotional Writings* (1959) II. ii. 136 Our action leaves in our minds scapes or species, the extreme 'intention' or instressing of which would be painful. *Ibid.*, The soul then can be instressed *in* the species or scape of any bodily action ..and so *towards* the species or scape of any object, as of sight, sound, taste, smell. **1948** W. A. M. PETERS *Gerard Manley Hopkins* i. 2 The suffix 'scape' in 'landscape'..posits the presence of a unifying principle which enables us to consider part of the countryside..as a unit..but so that this part is perceived to carry the typical properties of the actually individed whole... 'Scape' comes to stand for that being which is an exact copy or reflection of the individual whole on which it is dependent for its existence.

scape (skeɪp), *v.*[1] Forms: 3 **scapie**, 4 **scap, skape**, 4–5 **skap, schap(e**, 4–6 **skape**, 5 **scappe, sckap, shape, skapp(e**, 5–6 *Sc.* **schaip**, 6–7 **scaipe**, 9 *dial.* **sceape**, 4– **scape**. Also 4–6 *str. pa. t.* **scope, skope**, 4 **skepe**. [Aphetic var. of ESCAPE *v.* Frequent in prose use till near the end of the 17th c.; subsequently only *arch.* and *poet.*, and often written *'scape.*]

1. = ESCAPE *v.* in its various senses. **a.** *intr.*

c **1275** LAY. 826 Ne lete ȝe nanne cwicke scapie to felde. *a* **1300** *Cursor M.* 5009 For þar vs tok þe hei baili, To scap [*Gött.* schap, *Trin.* skape] wit gisel war we fain. **1303** R. BRUNNE *Handl. Synne* 10667 For he ne shulde skape by þe weye, He dyd on hym, bondes for to leye. **13..** *Gosp. Nicod.* 240 (Add. MS.) Pilate saide: 'is þis he þat herode pursewed soo?' '3ha', þai saide, 'pardye, and ȝit he skappid hym fro'. **13..** *E.E. Allit. P.* C. 155 Mony ladde þer forth-lep to laue & to kest, Scopen out þe scaþel water, þat fayn scape wolde. *c* **1450** *Cov. Myst.* (Shaks. Soc.) 141 Yf thou be gylty thou mayst not schape. *c* **1489** CAXTON *Blanchardyn* xlvii. 181 He was ryght wrooth and sory that she was scaped soo from hym. **1506** *Kal. Sheph.* (Sommer) 159 She shall be syke in the age of .v. yere she shallbe in daungere of dethe: and yf she skape she may leue tyll .xliij. yere. **1526** TINDALE *Matt.* v. 18 One tytle of the lawe shall not scape tyll all be fulfilled. [So **1557** (Geneva).] **1540** *Cranmer's Bible, 1 Sam.* xiv. 41 Saul and Jonathas were caught, but the people skaped free. **1573** *Satir. Poems Reform.* xl. 163 Thay fryit in furie that he schaipit quick. *c* **1630** MURE *Ps.* cxxxix. 7 Where from thy spirit shall I scaipe? Where from thy presence flee? **1634** MILTON *Comus* 814 What, have you let the false enchanter scape? **1665** HOOKE *Microgr.* Pref., How difficult it will be for any..to scape from being discover'd. **1692** R. L'ESTRANGE *Fables* lxxi. 70 In the case of a Battle, where the Soldier grows Every day less apprehensive of the Hazzard, by seeing so many People Scape. **1744** ARMSTRONG *Art Preserv. Health* III. 583 Of many thousands few untainted 'scaped; Of those infected fewer 'scap'd alive. **1784** COWPER *Task* II. 831 The croaking nuisance lurk'd in ev'ry nook; Nor palaces, nor even chambers, 'scap'd. **1814** CARY *Dante, Par.* I. 89 Lightning, scaped from its own proper place. **1814** SCOTT *Ld. of Isles* III. iv, In hurry of the night, Scaped noteless, and without remark, Two strangers sought the Abbot's bark.

β. strong pa. t.

c **1400** *Destr. Troy* 13541 Thus I skope fro the skathe with skyrme of my hondes. *Ibid.* 13616 Aschatus þen skepe furth with his skire wordis. *c* **1450** *Mirk's Festial* 257 So þat noþyng lafte saue þe kyng, þat vnneþe scope, and a ȝeong sonne of his wyfe. **1480** CAXTON *Trevisa's Higden* (Rolls) VIII. 534 But he scope fro hem in to his lordes place. **1536** *St. Papers Hen. VIII* (1834) II. 352 They scaled the bridge, which thothers perceyvyng, scope oute at thother ende therof. **1538** *Ibid.* III. 19 Your son Bartholomew scope then hapy, for he was with Aylmer.

b. *trans.*

a **1300** *Cursor M.* 29260 þe man..mai noght þis cursing scape. **13..** *K. Alis.* 7735 (Bodl. MS.), Myne honde ne skapeþ he neuermore. *c* **1386** CHAUCER *Man of Law's T.* 1151 Now is she scaped al hire auenture. **1387** TREVISA *Higden* (Rolls) IV. 295 No day schulde hym scape þat he nolde rede, write, oþer declare riȝtwisnesse. *c* **1440** *Generydes* 2849, I see noo cause, for we shall do right wele And skape ther handes, doughte ye neuer a dele. *c* **1450** *Cov. Myst.* (Shaks. Soc.) 223 For trewly I am so woundyrly seke I may nevyr schape this grett seknes. **1547** *Bk. of Marchauntes* b j, Nothynge scapeth them, but at their plasures [*sic*] they occupi it. **1577** B. GOOGE *Heresbach's Husb.* I. (1586) 37 b, It is sowed in April or later, in May, to scape the frostes. **1593** *Udalls' Key of Holy Tongue* Note by Printer, The Typographical faultes, which perhaps haue scaped us. **1596** DANETT tr. *Comines* (1614) 130, I maruelled to heare such a word scape him. **1600** SHAKS. *Sonn.* xc, Ah doe not, when my heart hath scapte this sorrow Come in the rereward of a conquerd woe. **1693** LOCKE *Educ.* §93 (1699) 148 Courage in an ill-bred Man, has the Air, and scapes not the Opinion of Brutality. **1710** SWIFT *Jrnl. to Stella* 14 Dec., If Patrick had been at home, I should have 'scaped this; for I have taught him to deny me almost as well as Mr. Harley's porter. **1784** COWPER *Task* IV. 185 While we retrace with mem'ry's pointing wand,..The dangers we have 'scaped. **1859** TENNYSON *Guinevere* 345 Pray for him that he scape the doom of fire. **1878** BROWNING *La Saisiaz* 75 Ye mounts Where I climb to 'scape my fellow.

2. The verb-stem occurs in objective combinations, as **scape-gallows**, one who has escaped the gallows though deserving it; so † *scape-Tyburn*; † **scape-sermon**, an excuse for not preaching a sermon. Also SCAPEGRACE, SCAPETHRIFT.

1799 WASHINGTON *Writ.* (1893) XIV. 154 The *scape-gallowses of the large cities. **1838** *Blackw. Mag.* XLIII. 520 The Whigs now support all the scape-graces, and sometimes scape-gallowses. **1654** GAYTON *Pleas. Notes* III. xiii. 167 Thirdly, I believe that Mr. Curate was not provided, and that's enough at any time, for a *scape Sermon. **1602** F. HERING *Anat.* 4 *Scape-Tibornes, Dog-leeches, and such like baggage.

scape (skeɪp), *v.*[2] *Horology.* [Back-formation from SCAPEMENT.] *intr.* Of an escapement or one of its parts: To perform its function (in a certain manner).

1739 [see ESCAPEMENT 2]. **1761** [see DEAD *a.* 24 b]. **1884** F. J. BRITTEN *Watch & Clockm.* 141 The pallets 'scape' over three teeth of the wheel.

scape (skeɪp), *int.* A conventional imitation of the cry of the snipe when flushed (also used for the brambling's call). Hence used *subst.* as a nickname for the snipe.

1862 G. H. KINGSLEY *Sport & Trav.* (1900) 380 The.. half-frozen sedges in which one kills friend Scape at home. **1870** H. STEVENSON *Birds Norf.* II. 324 Its warning cry of 'scape, scape' on rising attracted my notice. **1903** *Westm. Gaz.* 25 Nov. 2/3 Sceape! Sceape! a sudden gleam of mottled grey Rising from nowhere wings its wizard flight. **1962** *Times* 6 Nov. 14/4 The bramblings' harsh and nasal call-note, usually written 'scape'.

scapegoat ('skeɪpgəʊt), *sb.* [f. SCAPE *sb.*[1] or *v.*[1] + GOAT.

App. invented by Tindale (1530) to express what he believed to be the literal meaning of Heb. *ʕăzāzel*, occurring only in Lev. xvi. 8, 10, 26. (In verse 10 he renders: 'The goote on which the lotte fell to scape'.) The same interpretation is expressed by the Vulgate *caper emissarius* (whence the Fr. *bouc émissaire*), and by Coverdale's (1535) rendering 'the fre goate', but is now regarded as untenable. The word does not appear in the Revised Version of 1884, which has 'Azazel' (as a proper name) in the text, and 'dismissal' in the margin as an alternative rendering.]

1. In the Mosaic ritual of the Day of Atonement (Lev. xvi), that one of two goats that was chosen by lot to be sent alive into the wilderness, the sins of the people having been symbolically laid upon it, while the other was appointed to be sacrificed.

1530 TINDALE *Lev.* xvi. 8 And Aaron cast lottes ouer the .ii. gootes: one lotte for the Lorde, and another for a scape-goote. (So **1537**, **1539**, **1560** (Geneva), **1568**, **1611**.) **1651** HOBBES *Leviathan* xli, Our Saviour Christs sufferings seem to be here [*sc.* in Lev. xvi] figured..: He was both the sacrificed Goat and the Scape Goat.

2. One who is blamed or punished for the sins of others. (So F. *bouc émissaire.*)

1824 MISS MITFORD *Village* Ser. I. 204 Country-boys.. are patient, too, and bear their fate as scape-goats, (for all sins whatsoever are laid as matters of course to their door, ..), with amazing resignation. **1867** FREEMAN *Norm. Conq.* I. vi. 416 He has been made the scape-goat for many of the sins both of other individuals and of the whole nation. **1888** BRYCE *Amer. Commw.* v. lxxxviii. III. 193 The leaders of Tammany undertook to make a scapegoat of Conolly—the least respected and most unpopular of their number.

attrib. **1877** TENNYSON *Harold* I. ii, A scape goat marriage —all the sins of both The houses on mine head. **1895** J. MORLEY in *Daily News* 3 Dec. 3/2, I for one am not going to launch scapegoat Bills. I am not going to say this Bill or that Bill was wrong, and that, therefore, we deservedly lost the elections.

¶ The formation of the word has been imitated in nonce-combinations (chiefly jocular) in which the name of some other animal is substituted for 'goat' (cf. the quots.).

1765 H. WALPOLE *Let. to Earl of Hertford* 12 May, That scape-goose, Lord Halifax. **1783** JUSTAMOND tr. *Raynal's Hist. Indies* I. 86 They have a scape-horse, analogous to the scape-goat of the Jews. **1831** SOUTHEY in *Q. Rev.* XLIV. 286 To place himself in so prominent a position that he was noted for a scape-rat.

scapegoat ('skeɪpgəʊt), *v.* [f. the sb. or back-formation from SCAPEGOATING.] *trans.* To make a scapegoat of (someone); to subject to scapegoating. Hence **'scapegoated** *ppl. a.*; **'scapegoater.**

1943 *Jrnl. Abnormal & Social Psychol. Clin. Suppl.* XXXVIII. 143 Persons who had been inclined to scapegoat him originally. *Ibid.* 151 The immediate and desired objective of the scapegoaters was to relieve their feelings of frustration, of fear [etc.]. **1972** *Guardian* 27 Dec. 12/3 We either scapegoat the individual..or we scapegoat society. **1974** S. G. SHOHAM *Society & Absurd* IV. iv. 162 The child becomes a receptacle for the ressentiment of the scapegoater. **1976** *Child's Guardian* Winter 13/3 Oliver's problems illustrate one of the great difficulties in trying to help a scapegoated child. Often the parent/child relationships are so complicated that they seem to need each other in order to continue hurting each other. **1977** R. L. DUNCAN *Temple Dogs* (1978) I. ii. 55 A company is really too large to scapegoat.

scapegoating ('skeɪpgəʊtɪŋ). [f. SCAPEGOAT + -ING[1].] The action or practice of making a scapegoat of someone; *spec.* in *Psychol.*, aggressively punitive behaviour directed for whatever reason against other (weaker) persons or groups.

1943 VELTFORT & LEE in *Jrnl. Abnormal & Social Psychol. Clin. Suppl.* XXXVIII. 138 Scapegoating is a phenomenon wherein some of the aggressive energies of a person or group are focused upon another individual, group, or object. **1950** T. ADORNO et al. *Authoritarian Personality* xi. 409 Lack of insight into one's own short-comings and the projection of one's own weaknesses and faults onto others..probably represents the essential aspect of..scapegoating. **1962** *Listener* 7 June 1002/2 Speaking of scapegoating in new housing blocks, she tells of patients who have actually been robbed finding it difficult to obtain a hearing because they were suspected of paranoid delusions. **1977** C. HUSBAND in H. Giles *Lang., Ethnicity & Intergroup Relations* ix. 234 The intervention of Powell at a singularly propitious moment.. propelled the already vigorous scapegoating process into an unmanageable level.

scapegrace ('skeɪpgreɪs), *sb.* and *a.* [f. SCAPE *v.* + GRACE *sb.*, the etymological notion being 'one who escapes the grace of God'. Cf. the older *scapethrift* and *want-grace.*] **A.** *sb.* **1.** A man or boy of reckless and disorderly habits; an incorrigible scamp. Often used playfully.

1809 MALKIN *Gil Blas* V. i. ¶ 3 That scape-grace Leganez had incurred the penalty of the rod. **1819** SCOTT *Let.* in *Lockhart* (1839) IV. 294 Most of the Irish of that class are scapegraces—drink, steal, and lie like the devil. **1852** THACKERAY *Esmond* III. i, He..was the most charming young scapegrace in the army. **1897** MEREDITH *Amazing Marriage* I. xv. 168 Mention of her old scapegrace of a father lit her up again.

¶ Applied to a female. *rare.*

a **1847** ELIZA COOK *Rory O'More* iii, Hebe, that teasing young scapegrace.

2. *N. Amer.* The red-throated loon or diver, *Gavia stellata.*

1835 J. J. AUDUBON *Ornith. Biogr.* III. 24 In the neighbourhood of Boston, and along the Bay of Fundy, they are best known by the names of 'Scape-grace' and 'Cape-racer'. **1917** T. G. PEARSON *Birds Amer.* I. 15 Red-throated Loon..Cape Racer; Scape-grace. **1957** W. L. MCATEE *Folk-Names Canad. Birds* 2 Red-throated Loon..scape-grace (Rationalization of Cape Race [where it is often seen]).

B. *adj.* That is a scapegrace; characteristic of a scapegrace.

1830 *Forrester* I. 202 A warrant, sir, to bind over your scapegrace friend there to keep the peace. **1836** T. HOOK *G. Gurney* II. 189 After a sort of scape-grace acquaintance with the maddest wag of London. **1856** MASSON *Ess.* iv. 120 The scapegrace young earl.

'scapel. *Bot. rare.* [ad. mod.L. *scāpellus* (Lindley 1839), dim. of *scāpus* SCAPE *sb.*[2]] 'The caulicle, or neck formed between the root and cotyledon at the time of germination' (*Treas. Bot.* 1866).

scapelar, -eler, obs. forms of SCAPULAR *sb.*

scapelarie, -y, obs. ff. SCAPULARY.

scapeless ('skeɪplɪs), *a.*[1] *Bot.* [f. SCAPE *sb.*[2] + -LESS.] Destitute of a scape.

1828–32 in WEBSTER.

scapeless ('skeɪplɪs), *a.*[2] [f. SCAPE *sb.*[1] or *v.*[1] + -LESS.] Not to be escaped from; inevitable.

1850 BLACKIE *Æschylus* I. 164 My fate is fixed and scapeless. **1883** R. BRIDGES *Prometheus* 1227 The scapeless net spread in thy sight around thee.

scapeless ('skeɪplɪs), *a.*[3] [f. SCAPE *sb.*[4] + -LESS.] In the terminology of G. M. Hopkins: lacking scape, without distinctive and individual quality.

1874 G. M. HOPKINS *Jrnls. & Papers* (1959) 245 Scapeless aimless background of tapestry, a cannon, and so on. *Ibid.* 248 The feet not inscaped but with a scapeless look they sometimes no doubt have..and veined too, which further breaks their scaping.

scapellar, scapelor, obs. ff. SCAPULAR.

scapelori, -y, -elry, obs. forms of SCAPULARY.

scapement ('skeɪpmənt). [Aphetic form of ESCAPEMENT.] = ESCAPEMENT 2.

1755 [see ESCAPEMENT 2]. **1789** *Trans. Soc. Arts* II. 245 A Scapement, for the use of clock-makers. **1822** SCOTT *Nigel* ii, They..have no more regularity in them than a watch without a scapement. **1879** *Cassell's Techn. Educ.* I. 190/2 The mechanism by which these numbers are counted is technically called a scapement.

scaper, obs. form of SHAPER.

'scapethrift. *Obs.* exc. *arch.* [f. SCAPE *v.* + THRIFT.] A spendthrift.

c **1460** *Towneley Myst.* ii. 384 How, pyke-harnes, scape-thryft! how, pike-harnes, how! **1526** SKELTON *Magnif.* 761 Howe be it, of Scape Thryfte your clokes smelleth musty. **1577–87** HOLINSHED *Hist. Scot.* 263/1 He gathered a power of wicked scapethrifts..burnt the towne [etc.]. **1656** EARL MONM. tr. *Boccalini's Advts. fr. Parnass.* I. i. 3 Scape-thrifts, who have but the purse of a private man, yet will spend like a Prince. **1838** *Gentl. Mag.* CVIII. II. 71 A scape-thrift laid his hand on his father's plough.

scaph, var. SCAF.

†**'scaphage.** *Obs. rare*$^{-1}$. [app. f. Gr. σκάφ-ος act of digging + -AGE.] (See quot.)

1610 W. FOLKINGHAM *Art of Survey* I. vii. 14 Scaphage is the digging, deluing, and preparing of the Soile with Spades or other handie-tooles for the sowing, setting, planting, and propagating of..Plants, Trees, &c. [Hence **1688** in HOLME *Armoury* III. 333/2, misspelt *Scaphiage.*]

scaphander (skæ'fændə(r)). [ad. F. *scaphandre* (so named by La Chapelle, the inventor, 1775), f. Gr. σκάφη boat + ἀνδρ-, ἀνήρ man.] A cork belt used as a support in swimming.

1825 CLIAS *Gymnastics* 165 A third..follows behind.. with the scaphander. [In later Dicts. with erroneous explanation: a water-tight suit for a diver.]

scaphe, variant of SCAF.

scaphite ('skæfaɪt). [ad. mod.L. *scaphītēs* (Parkinson 1804–11), f. Gr. σκάφη boat (with reference to the boat-shaped form of the shell): see -ITE.] A cephalopod of the fossil genus *Scaphites.*

1822 CONYBEARE *Outl. Geol.* II. ii. §9. 162 Turrilite. Scaphite [etc.]. **1835** KIRBY *Hab. & Inst. Anim.* I. i. 20 The Baculites, Hamites, Scaphites.

scapho- ('skæfəʊ), comb. form of Gr. σκάφη boat, in many scientific terms (of which the most important will be found as main words). **scapho-cal'caneal** *a.*, pertaining to the scaphoid and calcaneum (in recent Dicts.). **scapho-'cuboid** *a.*, pertaining to the scaphoid and cuboid bones. **scapho-cuneiform** *a.*, pertaining to the scaphoid and cuneiform bones. **sca'phognathite** [Gr. γνάθος], a flat oval plate in the gill chamber of fishes, which by movement promotes a constant flow of water through the gill; hence **,scaphogna'thitic** *a.*, pertaining to a scaphognathite (*Cent. Dict.* 1891). **scapho-'lunar** *a.* [cf. LUNAR B. 3], the epithet of a small bone in the carpus of some animals; also *ellipt.* as *sb.* **,scapho-tra'pezium,** a bone in the carpus of the sloth tribe, corresponding to the scaphoid and the trapezium united.

1876 *Quain's Elem. Anat.* (ed. 8) I. 177 *Scapho-Cuboid Articulation. *Ibid.* 178 *Scapho-Cuneiform Articulation. **1870** ROLLESTON *Anim. Life* 104 The branchia..act mainly as the *scapho-gnathite does. **1854** R. OWEN in *Orr's Circ. Sci., Org. Nat.* I. 252 The..end of the *scapho-lunar bone. **1870** FLOWER *Osteol. Mammalia* xvi. 279 The first row consists of a scapho-lunar and a cuneiform. **1854** R. OWEN in *Orr's Circ. Sci., Org. Nat.* I. 246 The *scapho-trapezium is characteristic of the sloth-tribe.

‖**scaphocephalus** (,skæfəʊ'sɛfələs). *Path.* [mod.L., f. Gr. σκάφη boat + κεφαλή head: after *hydrocephalus.*] 'Boat-shaped head'; a condition of the skull (caused by premature ossification of the sagittal suture preventing transverse development), in which the length greatly exceeds the breadth.

1865 THURNAM in *Nat. Hist. Rev.* Apr. 247 In the Negro ..the more marked features of true scaphocephalus are more rarely seen.

Hence **scaphoce'phalic, scapho'cephalous** *adjs.*, of or pertaining to scaphocephalus; **scapho'cephalism, scapho'cephaly** = SCAPHOCEPHALUS.

1863 D. WILSON *Preh. Ann.* I. I. ix. 236 Professor v. Baer ..proposes the term scaphocephalic to indicate the same boat-like head-form. **1888** *Amer. Naturalist* July 614 Scaphocephalism..occurs from defective parietal bone formation. **1889** *Mayne's Med. Voc.* (ed. 6), Scaphocephalous. **1899** *Allbutt's Syst. Med.* VIII. 240 There are other types [of idiots] of less importance, such as the amaurotic, syphilitic, choreic, scaphocephalic [etc.]. **1901** *Nature* 12 Sept. 490/2 Two..papers..on deformed heads of living subjects; the one in a case of oxycephaly or acrocephaly and the other of scaphocephaly.

scaphocerite (skə'fɒsəraɪt). [f. Gr. σκάφ-η boat + κέρ-ας horn + -ITE.] The third section of the antenna of an arthropod.

1877 HUXLEY *Anat. Inv. Anim.* vi. 314 Next, a basicerite, to the outer portion of which a flattened plate..here called the scaphocerite, is articulated. **1893** STEBBING *Crustacea* iv. 38 A thin plate, known as the antennal scale.., while those who love long words are privileged to call it the scaphocerite.

scaphoid ('skæfɔɪd), *a.* and *sb.* [ad. mod.L. *scaphoīdēs*, a. Gr. σκαφοειδής, f. σκάφ-η boat: see -OID. Cf. F. *scaphoïde.*] **A.** *adj.* Shaped like a boat. Chiefly *Anat.* and *Zool.* ***scaphoid bone*** = B. ***scaphoid fossa***: the fossa of the helix of the ear. ***scaphoid tubercle***: the short process of the malleus.

1741 A. MONRO *Anatomy* (ed. 3) 51 The Ligaments stretching from the Heel-bone to the Scaphoid Bone. **1858** H. GRAY *Anat.* 35 A small, oval, shallow depression, the scaphoid fossa. **1876** *Trans. Clinical Soc.* IX. 72 The hollow which should exist between the internal malleolus and the scaphoid tubercle was entirely obliterated. **1884** COUES *Key N. Amer. Birds* (ed. 2) 118 Where the lateral feathers slant upward from the lowermost central pair, like the sides of a boat from its keel, this is the scaphoid..or carinate..tail. **1901** OSLER *Pract. Med.* (ed. 4) I. 26 Peritonitis may occur.. with an abdomen flat or even scaphoid.

B. *sb.* [Short for *scaphoid bone*; in mod.L. *scaphoides.*] The first proximal carpal bone in Mammalia, or the corresponding bone in the foot. See NAVICULAR A. 1.

1846 BRITTAN tr. *Malgaigne's Man. Oper. Surg.* 249 One inch in front of the malleolus you feel the projection of the scaphoid; the joint is one inch beyond it. **1873** MIVART *Elem. Anat.* 151 A concavity on the radial side to receive a prominence of the scaphoid.

†**sca'phoidal,** *a. Obs. rare*$^{-1}$. [Formed as SCAPHOID + -AL[1].] Boat-shaped, hollowed out.

1681 WHARTON *Eclipses* Wks. (1683) 102 The Earth is not Cubical, nor Pyramidal, Scaphoidal, or otherwise Hollow, ..but on every side perfectly round.

scaphopod ('skæfəʊpɒd). *Zool.* [ad. mod. L. class name *Scaphopoda* (H. G. Bronn *Klassen & Ordnungen des Thier-reichs* (1862) III. II. 524), f. SCAPHO- + Gr. πούς, ποδ- foot.] (See quot. 1935); = *tusk-shell* s.v. TUSK *sb.*[1] 3. Also *attrib.*

1913 B. B. WOODWARD *Life of Mollusca* iii. 47 A true Scaphopod (*Dentalium*) and representatives of the more primitive Ammonoidea..likewise came into existence in the Devonian epoch. **1935** TWENHOFEL & SHROCK *Invertebr. Paleontol.* ix. 360 Scaphopods are small, marine, bilaterally symmetrical mollusks with an external, curved and tapering tubular shell open at each end. *Ibid.* 362 The scaphopod shell is composed of aragonite. **1975** *Nature* 11 Dec. 555/3 Molluscs, primarily bivalves but also scaphopods and various gastropods, .. progress through soft substrates.

scapiform ('skeɪpɪfɔːm), *a.* [f. L. *scāp-us* SCAPE *sb.*² + -FORM.] Having the form of a SCAPE (in various senses).

1796 KIRWAN *Elem. Min.* (ed. 2) II. 338 Scapiform Iron Ore. **1857** A. GRAY *First Less. Bot.* 229 *Scapiform*, scape-like. **1900** B. D. JACKSON *Gloss. Bot. Terms* 232 *Scapiform*, .. resembling a scape, a stem wanting leaves.

scapigerous (skə'pɪdʒərəs), *a. Bot.* [f. L. *scāp-us* SCAPE *sb.*² + -GEROUS.] Bearing a scape; having a stalk devoid of leaves.

1859 D. BUNCE *Travels with Dr. Leichhardt* 29 *Xanthoria*, or grass-tree, three species of which enlivened the landscape with their scapigerous white blossoms. **1870** HOOKER *Stud. Flora* 215 Taraxacum, Dandelion. Perennial, scapigerous herbs.

scapiller, obs. form of SCAPULAR.

† '**scaping**, *vbl. sb. Obs.* [f. SCAPE *v.*¹ + -ING¹.] The action of the verb SCAPE; escaping.

c **1374** CHAUCER *Boeth.* IV. Pr. iv. (1868) 135 They wene that either the leve or the mowinge to don wikkednesse, or elles the scapinge withoute peyne, be weleful. *c* **1450** tr. *De Imitatione* II. xii. 59 It must be so, for þere is no remedie of scapyng fro tribulacion of euel men & sorowe, but þat þou suffre. **1526** *Pilgr. Perf.* (W. de W. 1531) 20 b, Fewe there be that gothe safely by this waye, but with great difficultye and hard scapynge.

scaple, scapler, obs. ff. SCAPPLE, SCAPULAR.

scaplerie, -erye, -ory, obs. ff. SCAPULARY.

scapolite ('skæpəlaɪt). *Min.* [ad. G. *skapolith* (D'Andrada 1800), f. Gr. σκᾶπο-ς rod (see SCAPE *sb.*²) + λίθος stone: see -LITE.] One of a group of minerals (including dipyre, ekebergite, marialite, etc.) composed of silicates of aluminium, calcium, and sodium.

1802 T. THOMSON *Syst. Chem.* III. 480 Scapolite. **1879** RUTLEY *Study of Rocks* x. 111.

scapolitization (ˌskæpəlɪtaɪ'zeɪʃən). *Geol.* [f. SCAPOLITE + -IZE + -ATION.] The alteration of alumino-silicate minerals of igneous rocks into, or their replacement by, minerals of the scapolite group. Also **sca'politize** *v. trans.*; **sca'politized** *ppl. a.*

1909 A. HARKER *Nat. Hist. Igneous Rocks* xii. 302 (*caption*) Apatite vein with scapolitized borders. *Ibid.* 383/1 (Index), Scapolitization. **1924** *Mineral Abstr.* II. 227 Chemical analyses by Pisani on fresh and scapolitized material from Pouzac show that the alteration is accompanied only by addition of sodium chloride. **1932** A. HARKER *Metamorphism* xvi. 255 This widespread scapolitization .. is doubtless related to the mechanical conditions proper to regional metamorphism, which facilitate the permeation of the rocks by volatile bodies. **1936** *Nature* 29 Feb. 366/2 Gabbroid rocks were intruded .. and were followed by late-stage solutions which scapolitised the sediments, turned the gabbro into epidiorite and chloritised the Basement schists. **1954** *Jrnl. Geol. Soc. Australia* I. 6 The current-bedded sediments are scapolitized calcareous rocks. *a* **1965** A. W. G. WHITTLE in G. J. Williams *Econ. Geol. N.Z.* (1965) xiv. 227/1 A large amount of titanite was introduced as anhedra during scapolitization, commonly aggregated to form elongated veins within the rock.

scappe: see SCAB *sb.*, SCAPE *v.*, SHAPE, SKEP.

scappel, obs. form of SCAPPLE *v.*

† **scapperboiling**, *a. Obs.* ? Hotheaded.

1673 KIRKMAN *Unlucky Citizen* 53 Who would trust such a Scapperboyling young Giddy-braind Coxcomb as I was?

scappiller, obs. form of SCAPULAR *sb.*

† '**scapple**, *sb. Obs.* Also scaple. Anglicized form of SCAPULA.

1578 BANISTER *Hist. Man* I. 2 Some great bones haue no manifest hollownes, as the .. Scapple bones. *Ibid.* 25 b *marg.*, The shoulder blades or scaple bones. *Ibid.*, The vse of yᵉ cartilage in yᵉ vniting of the shoulder to the scaple.

scapple ('skæp(ə)l), *v.* Forms: (4 ? scorpil), 5–7 scaple, 8 scappel, 9– scapple. See also SCABBLE *v.*, SCALP *v.*³ [Aphetic a. OF. *escapeler, eschapeler* to dress timber.] *trans.* To reduce the faces of (a block of stone; †in 15th c. also of timber) to a plane surface without working them smooth.

1443 *Contract* in Willis & Clark *Cambridge* (1886) I. 386, xvj fote of Seuerant table scapled with poynts. **1479** W. WAYNFLETE ibid. 410 He .. shalle dygge and reyse and scaple the best stone yn the same quarrey. **1587** HOLINSHED *Chron.* III. 1538/1 And there was for this purpose alreadie perfectlie hewed of the same stone seuen thousand foot, and six thousand foot more was scapled. **1665** J. WEBB *Stone-Heng* 88 They [many of the upright Stones] were scapled at the Quarries. **1793** SMEATON *Edystone L.* §113 The best way to get our stone rough scappelled, nearly to the shape I required. **1842** *Civil Engin. & Arch. Jrnl.* V. 320/1 The face stones should be roughly squared on the beds and joints, or what is called in the North 'scappled' to the form of the curve. **1845** PARKER *Gloss. Archit.* (ed. 4), *Scapple*, .. the term is now used exclusively (or nearly so) in reference to stone, but was formerly applied to timber also, and must have signified the barking of a tree, or, more probably, squaring it with the axe. **1849** E. DOBSON *Masonry & Stonecutting* 89 The block being roughly scappled to its shape. **1904** GRIFFITHS *50 Years Public Life* xxii. 333 His brother, in a Portland Quarry, scappling a block of stone, presents a family likeness.

Hence '**scappled** *ppl. a.* '**scappling** *vbl. sb.*, the action of the vb. (also *attrib.*); in dialectal use *concr.* in *pl.*, fragments of stone chipped off in scappling.

[**1399** in *Fabric Rolls York Minster* (Surtees) 15 Pro scorpillyng lapidum.] **1473–4** in Swayne *Sarum Churchw. Acc.* (1896) 15 Item in hewinge and scapelynge of j elme viij d. **1793** SMEATON *Edystone L.* §107 The stone .. had always been shipped off in .. what is called rough scappelled blocks; to be sawn and fair wrought to the particular purposes, where wanted. **1890** *Archæol. Jrnl.* XLVII. 162 Of the tools it is clear the scappling hammer and small axe were the chief.

Also **scapple-dress** *v. trans.*, in the same sense.

1840 *Civil Engin. & Arch. Jrnl.* III. 30/1 All the front stones of the foundation were laid with a lewis of this kind, as well as the backing of squared stones, which were previously scapple-dressed at the quarry.

‖**scapula** ('skæpjʊlə). Pl. **scapulæ**. [L. *scapula*, in class. Latin only pl. *scapulæ* the shoulders, shoulder-blades. Cf. SCAPPLE *sb.*]

1. *Anat.* **a.** The shoulder-blade, blade-bone, or omoplate (in man and other animals).

1578 BANISTER *Hist. Man* I. 26 In the toppe of the shoulder blade, betwene the Processe *Acromion*, and the supreme part of *Scapula*. **1615** CROOKE *Body of Man* x. xxiii. (1631) 772 Of the muscles of the Shoulder-blade called Omoplata or Scapula. **1672** WISEMAN *Wounds* I. viii. 72 The other wound under the Scapula was painful. **1808** BARCLAY *Muscular Motions* 380 When the scapula is meant to form a steady support for the humerus, its antagonist muscles are made to act with an equal force, or to moderate one another with the steadiness required. **1876** BRISTOWE *Theory & Pract. Med.* (1878) 361 All that part of the back of the chest situated below the lower angle of the scapula.

† **b.** ***scapulæ of the nose*** = mod.L. *scapulæ nasi*, 'the lateral portions of the nose' (*Syd. Soc. Lex.*).

1650 BULWER *Anthropomet.* vii. (1653) 118 The Elegancy of the Scapula of the Nose, .. and that beauty which so manifestly appears in the wings of the Nose.

2. *Ent.* (See quot.)

1826 KIRBY & SP. *Entomol.* III. 369 *Scapula* (the Scapula). The second joint of the Brachium, answering to the Trochanter in the legs.

‖**scapulalgia** (skæpjuː'lældʒɪə). *Path.* Also anglicized '**scapulalgy** (Mayne's *Med. Voc.*, 1889). [mod.L., f. SCAPULA + Gr. -αλγία, ἄλγος pain.]

1855 DUNGLISON *Med. Lex.*, *Scapulalgia*, arthralgia of the shoulder-joint. **1901** *Brit. Med. Jrnl.* 23 Feb. *Epitome* 29 Hysterical Scapulalgia.

scapular ('skæpjʊlə(r)), *sb.* Forms: 5 scapelar, scapulare, 6 scap(e)ler, -uler, -iller, -ellar, skappler, 7, 9 scapulaire, 7 -air, 6– scapular. [ad. med.L. *scapulāre* (whence It. *scapulare*), f. *scapula* shoulder; for the formation cf. L. *collāre* COLLAR *sb.* and -AR. For the earlier forms in Eng. (and for F. *scapulaire*, whence some of the forms above), see SCAPULARY *sb.* (In senses 3 and 4 properly a distinct word, subst. use of SCAPULAR *a.*)]

1. *Eccl.* **a.** A short cloak covering the shoulders; prescribed by the Rule of St. Benedict to be worn by monks when engaged in manual labour, and adopted by certain religious orders as a part of their ordinary costume.

In later times often confounded with the cowl.

[*c* **960** ÆTHELWOLD *Rule St. Benet* (Schröer 1885) 89 Hæbban hy eac mid to wyrcenne scapulare, þæt is ȝehwæde cuȝelan and slyflease.] **1483** *Cath. Angl.* 321/1 Scapulare. **1499** *Promp. Parv.* (Pynson) O iij, Scapelar. **1509** BARCLAY *Ship of Fools* (1874) II. 324 Hange vp the scapler: the amys cowle and frocke Or other habyte of eche relygyon Vpon a tre clene dede or rottyn stocke. **1546** LANGLEY tr. *Pol. Verg. de Invent.* VII. iii. 134 The Chanons Clothyng was a white Cote, and a linnen rochet under a blacke Cope, with a Scapuler to couer their hed and shoulders. **1547** *Injunct. Visitors Windsor* ii, in Wordsw. *Tracts of Clem. Maydeston* 234 *note*, Wee require you .. that all Prebendaries .. doe surcease from useing or wairing any blacke cope or Scapuler of Cloath above their surplises. **1653** H. COGAN tr. *Pinto's Trav.* xxxii. 129 The Chaem was apparelled in a long Gown of violet Satin, .. with a kind of Scapulair about his neck. **1698** FRYER *Acc. E. India & P.* 297 We Housed ourselves Cap-a-pee under Felts, .. with a Scapular to pull over our Heads and Face. **1814** SCOTT *Ld. of Isles* VI. ii, The rule that bid thee wear Dim veil and woollen scapulaire. **1908** *Blackw. Mag.* Dec. 808/1 His hands were clasped under his white scapular.

b. An article of devotion composed of two small squares of woollen cloth, fastened together by strings passing over the shoulders, worn as a badge of affiliation to the religious order which presents it.

1870 *Daily News* 5 Sept. 6 The old lady was working a scapular for a second youth who had gone to the front. **1884** *Catholic Dict.* (1897) 821/2 There are four other scapulars [besides that of the Carmelites] used in the Church: that of the Trinity, of white linen with a red cross, given by the Trinitarians .. ; the Servite scapular of the Seven Dolours .. ; that of the Immaculate Conception .. given by the Theatines .. ; the red scapular of the Passion .. given by the Vincentian Fathers.

attrib. **1854** FABER *Growth in Holiness* xv. (1872) 282 World-wide devotions as the rosary, and scapular-prayers.

† **c.** One who wears a scapular. *Obs. rare*⁻¹.

a **1550** *Image Ipocr.* iv. 211 in *Skelton's Wks.* II. 441/2 Some be Vitlers, Some be Scapelers, And some Cubiculers.

† **2.** *Surg.* A bandage passing over and around the shoulders to support other bandages, etc. upon the lower parts of the body. *Obs.*

1754–64 SMELLIE *Midwifery* I. 161 Sometimes a bandage applied round the lower part of the belly, and supported with the Scapular is of singular service. **1758** J. S. tr. *Le Dran's Observ. Surg.* (1771) 109 Compresses, which were secured by a Napkin round the Body and the Scapular.

3. *Ornith.* [Elliptical for *scapular feather*: see SCAPULAR *a.* 2.] Any feather which grows from the *pterylæ humerales* or scapular region.

1768 PENNANT *Brit. Zool.* (1776) II. 440 The back, coverts of the wings, and scapulars, are black. **1884** J. H. GURNEY *Diurnal Birds Prey* 151 In No. 1 the scapulars had become slightly paler.

4. *Ent.* (See quots.)

1826 KIRBY & SP. *Entomol.* III. 378 *Scapularia* (the Scapulars). Two pieces, one on each side the *Medipectus*, which succeed the *Peristethium*, and lie between the mid-legs and the *Pteropega*, or wing-socket. *Ibid.* IV. 494 The South American species (*Goliath micans*, &c.) have not this projection of the scapulars.

scapular ('skæpjʊlə(r)), *a.* [ad. mod.L. *scapulāris*, f. L. *scapula*: see SCAPULA and -AR. Cf. SCAPULARY *a.*]

1. Of or pertaining to the scapula.

1713 DERHAM *Phys.-Theol.* v. ii. (1727) 286 The Viscera of the Belly counterpois'd with the Weight of the scapular Part, and that useful Cushion of Flesh behind. **1847–9** *Todd's Cycl. Anat.* IV. 438/1 The scapular region is sometimes the seat of furuncular inflammation. **1848** *Quain's Elem. Anat.* (ed. 5) I. 517 The scapular arteries. **1880** GÜNTHER *Fishes* 59 The scapular or humeral arch is suspended from the skull by the post-temporal.

2. *Ornith.* Applied to any feather which grows upon the *pterylæ humerales*.

1688 HOLME *Armoury* II. 264/2 The Craker, or Sea-Pheasant .. the scapular feathers are black. **1768** PENNANT *Brit. Zool.* (1776) II. 435 The scapular feathers black and white. **1872** COUES *Key N. Amer. Birds* 16 The scapular feathers or scapulars.

3. *Ent.* Pertaining to the scapular in insects; see SCAPULAR *sb.* 4.

1826 KIRBY & SP. *Entomol.* III. 379 *Spiracula Scapularia* (the Scapular Spiracles). Two spiracles observable, one in each scapular, in *Acrida laurifolia*, &c.

4. In names of birds: **scapular crow** = *scapulated raven* (*Corvus scapulatus*); **scapular wagtail** (see quot.).

1823 J. LATHAM *Gen. Hist. Birds* VI. 336 Scapular Wagtail. *Jora scapularis.*

scapulary ('skæpjʊlərɪ), *sb.* Forms: 3 scapelori, 4 scapelry, chapolory, 5 scapelerey, scaplerie, -erye, -or(e)y, scapelarie, -ory, (kapelary), skaplorie, 5, 7 scapelary, scapularie, 6 skapellarye, 5– scapulary. [ad. med.L. *scapulārium*, a var. of *scapulāre* SCAPULAR *sb.* (the pl. *scapulāria* being common to the two sing. forms). Cf. F. *scapulaire*, Sp., Pg. *escapulario*. The confusion of the ending with L. *-ōrium*, -ORY, appears in the AF. *eschapeloyre* (J. de Garlandia, 12th c.), whence app. the 14th c. form *chapolory*.

The 15th c. form *kapelary*, if not a mere scribal error, may be compared with med.L. *capulāre*, *capulārium*, OF. *capillaire*, which seem to be etymologizing alterations of *scapulārium* (as if derived from *caput* head).]

1. *Eccl.* **a.** = SCAPULAR *sb.* 1.

[*a* **1030** *Rule St. Benet* lv. (E.E.T.S.) 91 Culam on wintre þicce on sumere þinne oððe ealdnesse & scapularian for weorcum.] *a* **1225** *Ancr. R.* (Cleop.) 424 Inwið þe wanes ha muhe werie scapeloris hwen mantel ham heueges. *c* **1290** *S. Eng. Leg.* I. 287/330 Al bi-neoþe sat a frere in is scapelori ȝwijt, his hod i-drawe ouer is eiȝen. *c* **1375** *Sc. Leg. Saints* xxxi. (*Eugenia*) 672 With þat scho kest þe cule away & scapelry but delay. *c* **1394** *P. Pl. Crede* 550 Þei schapen her chapolories & streccheþ hem brode. **1402** *Pol. Poems* (Rolls) II. 69 Thou axist me, Jacke, of my grete hood, what that it meneth, my scapelarie and my wide cope, and the knottide girdil. *c* **1440** *Alphabet of Tales* 341 He doffid his cowle & did on his skaplorie, and so he dyed. *c* **1474** *Inventory* in *Paston Lett.* III. 410 Item, a scapelerey with an hodde. *c* **1485** *Frere & Boy* in *E.E. Misc.* (Warton Club) 56 The bramblys .. rent hys [the friar's] kyrtyll and his kapelary, And all hys other wede. **1552** LYNDESAY *Monarche* 5858 Gyf ȝe tuk the Skapellarye, That ȝe mycht leif more plesandlye. **1687** *Lond. Gaz.* No. 2282 The Commissary of the Inquisition .. put on him the Habit of Penance, which is a Yellow Scapulary with a Red Cross, before and behind. **1875** W. MᶜILWRAITH *Guide Wigtownshire* 87 They [*sc.* Cistercian monks] wore white robes with black scapularies.

b. = SCAPULAR *sb.* 1 b.

1674 BREVINT *Saul & Sam.* xiii. 277 The Badg it [*sc.* this Confraternity] gives which is call'd the Holy Scapulary, is made of two small Pieces of woollen Stuff [etc.]. **1699** BURNET *39 Art.* xxii. 228 They [*sc.* indulgences] are also affixed to .. Rosaries and Scapularies. **1903** MORLEY *Gladstone* x. iii. III. 407 They found on his corpse the scapulary worn by devout catholics.

† **2.** *Anat.* (See quot.) *Obs.*

1615 CROOKE *Body of Man* VIII. i. (1631) 533 The double Scapulary, or the veines of the shoulder-blade. **1668** WILKINS *Real Char.* II. vi. §1. 178 The upper Convexity of Breast and Back .. Shoulder, Scapulary.

† **3.** *Surg.* = SCAPULAR *sb.* 2. *Obs.*

1754–64 SMELLIE *Midwifery* III. 427, I applied a large compress, and over all the napkin and scapulary. **1879**

STORMONTH *Man. Sci. Terms, Scapulary*, a broad bandage with two flaps passed over the shoulders.

4. = SCAPULAR *sb.* 3.

1854 OWEN in *Orr's Circ. Sci., Org. Nat.* I. 223 Those [feathers] which lie over the humerus are called 'scapulariæ', or scapularies. **1874** WOOD *Nat. Hist.* 261 On the neck, the back, the shoulders, and the scapularies, the black hue is shot with bronze, green, and purple.

scapulary ('skæpjʊlərɪ), *a.* In 6 scopelary. [ad. F. *scapulaire* and mod.L. *scapulārius*, f. *scapula*: see SCAPULA and -ARY.]

†**1.** ***scapulary mantle***: a cloak covering the shoulders. *Obs.* [Cf. OF. *cote eschapulaire*.]

a **1548** HALL *Chron., Hen. VIII* 46 b, The kynge was in a scopelary mantel, and hatt of clothe of syluer.

2. = SCAPULAR *a.* 1.

1785 J. LUCAS in *Med. Commun.* II. 92 The canula was secured in the wound by a bandage, with scapulary straps. **1880** GÜNTHER *Fishes* x. 150 The Heart is situated.. between the two halves of the scapulary arch.

scapulated ('skæpjʊleɪtɪd), *a.* [f. mod.L. *scapulāt-us* (see SCAPULA and -ATE[2]) + -ED[1].] ***scapulated raven***: the book-name of *Corvus* (*Pterocorax*) *scapulatus* distinguished by a patch of pure white feathers upon the scapular region.

1869-73 T. R. JONES *Cassell's Bk. Birds* I. 260 Throughout the whole of the Soudan and the lower parts of Abyssinia the Scapulated Raven is found living in pairs.

scapulette ('skæpjʊlɛt). *Zool.* Also scapulet. [a. G. *scapulette* (Haeckel): see SCAPULA and -ETTE.] (See quots.)

1887 *Amer. Jrnl. Sci.* Ser. III. XXXIII. 123 The smaller appendages to the oral cylinder are sixteen in number, and are known as the scapulettes or upper leaf-like appendages. **1894** GOULD *Illustr. Dict. Med.* etc., *Scapulet, Scapulette*, in biology, one of the leaf-like appendages of the manubrium of certain *Cnidaria*.

scapulimancy ('skæpjʊlɪˌmænsɪ). Also scapulomancy. [Hybrid f. L. SCAPULA + -MANCY.] Divination by means of the cracks in a shoulder-blade put into the fire.

1871 TYLOR *Prim. Cult.* I. 112 Divination by a shoulder-blade, technically called scapulimancy or omoplatoscopy. **1911** J. HASTINGS *Encycl. Relig. & Ethics* IV. 817/1 Scapulomancy is mentioned by Jāḥiẓ together with palmistry and another mode of augury.., viz. divination by the gnawing of mice. **1937** R. H. LOWIE *Hist. Ethnol. Theory* xi. 184 Speck and Cooper have traced scapulimancy from northern Europe through Asia to Eastern North America. **1961** G. CLARK *World Prehistory* viii. 199 It will be recalled that the practice of scapulomancy.. can be traced back to the 'Neolithic' Lung-shan culture. **1973** T. R. TREGEAR *Chinese* i. 19 The bones used in their scapulimancy were incised by markings which are the earliest form of Chinese writing.

Hence **scapuli'mantic** *a.*, pertaining to scapulimancy (*Cassell's Encycl. Dict.* Suppl. 1902).

scapulo- ('skæpjʊləʊ), used as combining form of L. *scapula*, the shoulder, in many scientific terms. **scapulo-a'xillary** *a.*, **-'brachial** *a.*, defining particular dorsal areas. **scapulo-cla'vicular** *a.*, of or belonging to the scapula and the clavicle; also *sb.*, the scapulo-clavicular joint. **scapulo-'coracoid** *a.*, of or belonging to the scapula and the coracoid. **scapulo'dynia** [Gr. ὀδύνη pain], pain in the muscles of the shoulder. **scapulo-'humeral** *a.*, of or belonging to the scapula and the humerus. **scapulo-'radial** *a.*, of or belonging to the scapula and the radius. **scapulo-'ulnar** *a.*, of or belonging to the scapula and the ulnus. **scapulo-'vertebral** *a.*, of or belonging to the scapula and the spine.

1899 *Allbutt's Syst. Med.* VI. 865 *Scapulo-brachial or 3rd dorsal area... *Scapulo-axillary or 5th dorsal area. **1858** H. GRAY *Anat.* 158 *Scapulo-Clavicular Articulation. The Scapulo-Clavicular is an arthrodial joint, formed between the outer extremity of the clavicle, and the upper edge of the acromian process of the scapula. **1854** OWEN in *Orr's Circ. Sci., Org. Nat.* I. 210 The *scapulo-coracoid arch.. is applied.. over the anterior thoracic hæmal arches. **1870** FLOWER in *Jrnl. Anat.* May 242 Superior border, anterior in most animals, with scapulo-coracoid notch. **1866** FLINT *Princ. Med.* 835 Valleix entitles the affection here situated *scapulodynia. **1840** W. J. E. WILSON *Anat. Vade M.* (1842) 114 The *scapulo-humeral articulation is an enarthrosis. **1899** *Syd. Soc. Lex.*, *Scapulo-radial... *Scapulo-ulnar... *Scapulo-vertebral.

‖**scapus** ('skeɪpəs). Pl. scapi ('skeɪpaɪ). [L.: see SCAPE *sb.*[2]]

1. *Arch.* = SCAPE *sb.*[2] 1. ? *Obs.*

1563 SHUTE *Archit.* B iv b, Vpon the foote of the pillor, directly & vpright set Scapus,.. the which Scapus, is the boddy of the pillor. **1598** HAYDOCKE tr. *Lomazzo* I. xxiv. 85 The Scapus or shafte with his base and capitel. **1664** EVELYN tr. *Freart's Archit.*, etc. 139 The Rings.. begirting the Scapus of a Column near the Apophyges. *a* **1728** WOODWARD *Nat. Hist. Fossils* I. I. (1729) 20 The slender round Scapi of the Pillars of the Abbey-Church in Westminster.

†**2.** *Bot.* = SCAPE *sb.*[3] 3. *Obs.*

1704 J. HARRIS *Lex. Techn.* I, *Scapus*, the strait Stalk or Shaft of a Plant, standing upright like a Pillar or Column. **1762** EHRET *Ophrys* in *Phil. Trans.* LIII. 81 These encompass a triquetrous scapus.

3. *Ornith.* = SCAPE *sb.*[2] 4.

1882 H. GADOW in *Proc. Zool. Soc.* 420 Fig. 1.. *s*, scapus or shaft. **1883** MARTIN & MOALE *Vertebr. Dissect.* 95 It possesses a main stem or *scapus* composed of quite different proximal and distal portions.

†**4.** *Ent.* = SCAPE *sb.*[2] 5. *Obs.*

1826 KIRBY & SP. *Entomol.* III. 323 To begin with the first joint, or scapus.

scar (skɑː(r)), *sb.*[1] Forms: 4-5 **skerre** (5 **sckerre**), **skarre**, 4-6 **skar**, 4-5, 7 **scarre**, 5 **skyrre**, 7 **scarr**, 7- **scar**, (8-9 *dial.* **skeer**, 9 *Sc.* **skair**). Also SCAUR. [App. a. ON. *sker* neut. (Da. *skjær*, Sw. *skär*) recorded only in the sense of a low reef in the sea, a SKERRY (cf. sense 3). Cf. Gael. *sgeir* a rock in the sea (from ON.), f. OTeut. **sker-* to cut: see SHEAR *v.*]

†**1.** A rock, crag. *Obs.*

13.. *St. Cristofer* 135 in Horstm. *Altengl. Leg.* (1881) 456 He loked abowte; þane was he warre Of an ermytage vndir a skerre. **1387** TREVISA *Higden* (Rolls) I. 99 Þe mount of Oreb is a partie of þe mounte of Synay,.. but hit is harde to come þerto for hiȝe rokkes and skarres [L. *propter scopulos præruptos*]. **1388** WYCLIF *1 Sam.* xiv. 4 Scarris brokun bifore [Vulg. *scopuli prærupti*]. *a* **1400-50** *Alexander* 4865 Rochis & rogh stanes rokkis vnfaire, Scutis to þe scharpe schew sckerres a hundreth. *c* **1450** *Mirks Festial* 206 For þer was non erþe to make a graue, he layde hit vndyr a honging skyrre. **1535** STEWART *Cron. Scot.* (Rolls) II. 415 Ane fair castell standand on the se skar, Is callit now the castell of Dumbar Efter his name.

2. A lofty, steep face of rock upon a mountainside; a precipice, cliff.

1673 *Depos. Cast. York* (Surtees) 196 She and Jane Makepeace of New Ridly had trailed a horse of the said Geo. downe a great scarr. **1721** RAMSAY *Ode to the Ph*—— i, O'er ilka cleugh, ilk scar, and slap. **1776** PENNANT *Tour in Scot.* II. 347 Wensley-dale, a beautiful and fertile vale.. in many parts cloathed with woods, surmounted by long ranges of scars, white rocks, smooth and precipitous in front, and perfectly even at their tops. **1833-4** J. PHILLIPS *Geol.* in *Encycl. Metrop.* (1845) VI. 703/2 The magnificent ranges of scars which begird the hills of Derbyshire and Westmoreland. **1847** TENNYSON *Princess* IV. (Song), O sweet and far from cliff and scar The horns of Elfland faintly blowing! **1888** HENLEY *Bk. Verses* 157 And in the silver dusk you hear, Reverberated from crag and scar, Bold bugles blowing points of war.

3. A low or sunken rock in the sea; a rocky tract at the bottom of the sea.

a **1712** HALYBURTON *Memoirs* ii. (1824) 74 We were in imminent danger of shipwreck on the scars of England. **1791** 'G. GAMBADO' *Ann. Horsem.* ix. (1809) 106 My horse .. ran straight on for the cliffs above the Scar. **1823** W. SCORESBY *Jrnl. Whale Fish.* 6 A bank or 'scar' stretches from Kirkholm Point on the west side. **1882** J. B. BAKER *Hist. Scarborough* 329 The bottom [of the sea] from hence all the way to the edge of the Dogger Bank is a scarr.

4. The rough burnt-out cinder left in a furnace; = CLINKER *sb.*[1] 3.

1852 *Eng. & Foreign Mining Gloss.* 62 *Scars*, clinkers. **1893-4** *Northumbld. Gloss.*

5. *attrib.*, as **scar-limestone**, a carboniferous rock occurring in the Pennine Range.

1831 A. SEDGWICK in *Trans. Geol. Soc.* (1836) Ser. II. IV. 70 Great scar limestone.

scar (skɑː(r)), *sb.*[2] Forms: 5-7 **scarre**, 6 **scare**, 6-7 **skar**(re, 7 **scarr**, 4, 6- **scar**. [Prob. aphetic a. OF. *escare* (F. *escarre*, now written *eschare*), = Sp., Pg., It. *escara*, ad. late L. *eschara*, an ESCHAR or scab formed in the healing of a burn or wound, a. Gr. ἐσχάρα lit. 'hearth'. The Eng. sense has prob. been influenced by association with SCAR *sb.*[3]]

1. a. The trace of a healed wound, sore, or burn; = CICATRIX 1.

1388 WYCLIF *Lev.* xxii. 22 If it is blynd, if it is brokun, if it hath a scar [Vulg. *cicatricem*]. (*Gloss in 5 MSS. c* **1420-30**: that is a notable fouleness dwellinge after the helinge of a woundis). **1530** PALSGR. 265/2 Scarre of a wounde, *covsture .., trasse.., cicatrice*. **1559** *Mirr. Mag., Salisb.* xii, Of cured woundes beset with many a skarre. **1576** FLEMING *Panopl. Epist.* 307 That wound neuer groweth to a skarre, which is not plyed with playsters. **1601** SHAKS. *All's Well* IV. v, A scarre nobly got, Or a noble scarre, is a good liu'rie of honor. **1633** G. HERBERT *Temple, Ch. Mil.* 63 The Warrior his deere skarres no more resounds, But seems to yeeld Christ hath the greater wounds. **1658** A. FOX *Wurtz Surg.* II. x. 87 At the Throat usually happen gross scarrs. **1672** WISEMAN *Wounds* I. viii. 73 He presently stript himself of his shirt, and shewed the Doctor, who both see and felt their scars [1676 the Cicatrices] and replied they are well. *a* **1701** MAUNDRELL *Journ. Jerus.* (1732) 70 A great scar upon his Arm, which he told us was the mark of a wound. **1785** BURNS *Jolly Beggars* Air i, I am a son of Mars, who have been in many wars And show my cuts and scars wherever I come. **1810** SCOTT *Lady of L.* III. iv, His naked arms and legs, seamed o'er, The scars of frantic penance bore. **1875** MANNING *Mission Holy Ghost* viii. 216 If you had ever been wounded, there would be a scar left behind.

transf. **1742** YOUNG *Nt. Th.* I. 430 As from the wing no scar the sky retains. **1884** 'MARK TWAIN' *Huck. Finn* (1885) ii. 24 We.. pulled down the river.. to the big scar on the hillside, and went ashore. **1929** W. FAULKNER *Sartoris* IV. 305 He sat his horse in the faint scar of the road. **1946** *R.A.F. Jrnl.* May 172 Their repair work had been so rapid that we could find few scars in the main part of the city.

b. *fig.* A fault or blemish remaining as a trace of some former condition or resulting from some particular cause.

1583 BABINGTON *Commandm.* ix. (1590) 404 Let no proofe be brought for it, and neuer so much against it, yet stickes the scarre of suspition still. **1634** W. TIRWHYT tr. *Balzac's Lett.* I. 169 There is now no longer meanes to cover this skarre which dishonoureth the face of State. **1710** SACHEVERELL *Sp. Impeachment* 57 The Prosecution wou'd leave a Scar upon his good Name. **1820** SHELLEY *Fragm. Satire* 19 The leprous scars of callous Infamy. **1860** EMERSON *Cond. Life, Worship* Wks. (Bohn) II. 397 Another scar of this scepticism is the distrust in human virtue.

†**c.** In phrases ***to bring, to draw, to cure to a scar***, to treat a wound until it cicatrizes; to induce healing. Also *fig. Obs.*

1532 MORE *Confut. Tindale* Wks. 440/1 Penaunce.. plastereth and patcheth vp, and maketh muche woorke to cure the wound and bring it to a scarre. **1578** LYTE *Dodoens* I. xxxix. 57 The leaues.. doth cure and heale olde woundes, that are harde to close or drawe to a Scarre. **1629** GAULE *Holy Madn.* 285 Bold Heart and Braue! that hath already curbed his Passions and cured them to a skarre.

2. *Nat. Hist.* A mark or trace indicating the point of attachment of some structure that has been removed; *Bot.* and *Conch.* = CICATRIX 2 and 3.

1793 MARTYN *Lang. Bot.* (1796), *Hilum*... The external mark or scar of the umbilical chord on some seeds, where they adhere to the pericarp. **1836** BUCKLAND *Geol. & Min.* xviii. §2 I. 475 Scars of leaves small. **1861** BENTLEY *Man. Bot.* 97 The outside of the stem of a Fern is marked with a number of scars. **1870** H. A. NICHOLSON *Man. Zool.* xlvi. (1875) 338 The 'foot'.. is essentially a muscular organ,.. its retractor muscles usually leaving distinct impressions or scars (the 'pedal impressions') in the interior of the shell.

3. *attrib.* and *Comb.*, as ***scar-bearer***; ***scar-clad***, ***-seamed*** adjs.; **scar-edge** = HILUM; **scar tissue**, the fibrous connective tissue of which scars are formed; also *fig.*; **scar-wort**, ? some species of *Lepidium*.

a **1701** SEDLEY *Tyrant of Crete* I. ii, Sure, he was *scar-bearer to some army. **1792** J. WOLCOT (P. Pindar) *Ep. to Ld. Macartney* 59 And lo! The *scar-clad Veteran adores! **1887** *Amer. Naturalist* XXI. 576 Four out of the twenty with the *scar-edge up, after exhausting the nourishment stored in the cotyledons, perished in their attempts to make a successful growth. **1813** SCOTT *Rokeby* IV. iii, There rose the *scar-seam'd Veteran's spear. **1875** T. HOLMES *Treat. Surg.* xxi. 386 When the *scar-tissue remains permanent, although the scar is ugly and of lower organisation than the natural parts, yet it causes no important inconvenience. **1932** F. BEEKMAN *Office Surg.* xii. 291 Keloids appear most frequently in individuals of races who have a predisposition for the formation of excessive scar tissue. **1957** A. HUXLEY *Let.* 12 Jan. (1969) 815, I have just embarked on a new treatment aimed at getting rid of some of the scar tissue on my corneas. **1975** *New Yorker* 1 Dec. 55/2 'It leaves scar tissue,' one former campaign manager said. 'There's no way it can't have a deep impact on the candidate's psyche and physical condition.' **1978** J. IRVING *World according to Garp* iii. 53 The brave face was naked, the eyes clear and challenging, the scar tissue every-where. **1657** W. COLES *Adam in Eden* cccxvi. 588 Of Pepperwort or Dittander... There is a kinde hereof called '*Scarrewort, after the Greek name, either because it maketh a marke in the hand of him that shall hold it, or because it taketh away all manner of Scarres.

scar (skɑː(r)), *sb.*[3] [Perh. an altered form of SCARTH (a. ON. *skarð*), the loss of the *th* (ð) may have taken place in the plural: cf. *clo'es* (kləʊz) for *clothes*. Cf. also *ON. skor* SCORE *sb.*]

†**1.** A crack, chink; a cut, incision. *Obs.*

1390 GOWER *Conf.* I. 20 And ek fulofte a litel Skar Upon a Banke, er men be war, Let in the Strem. *c* **1407** LYDG. *Reas. & Sens.* 5427 The tother [bow], hydouse and ryght blak,.. Ful of knottys and of skarrys, The tymber is so ful of warrys. *c* **1440** *Promp. Parv.* 442/2 Scarre, or brekynge, or ryvynge. *c* **1440** CAPGRAVE *Life St. Kath.* v. 712 (Arund.) Thei myght see light as it gan creepe Thurgh-oute the scarres. **1653** WALTON *Angler* vii. 150 You must take your knife.. cut or make an insition, or such a scar as you may put the arming wyer of your hook into it.. and.. draw out that wyer or arming of your hook at another scar neer to his tail.

2. A fragment, 'shard'. *Obs.* exc. *dial.* (see E.D.D. s.v. *Scard*).

1698 THORESBY in *Phil. Trans.* XX. 311, I got also some Scars of broken Urns,.. which are of the finest blew Clay I have seen.

scar (skɑː(r)), *sb.*[4] See also SCARE *sb.*[3], SCARO. [ad. L. *scarus*.] = SCARUS. Also ***scar-fish***.

1748 tr. *Horace, Sat.* II. ii. (ed. 3) 117 Those who gorge and cloy themselves by over-eating, can relish neither Oysters, Scar, no, nor the Lagois itself. **1828-32** WEBSTER, *Scar*, a fish of the Labrus kind. **1883** *Fisheries Exhib. Catal.* 380 Zanzibar has a large import trade of dry and salt fish, principally shark and scar-fish.

scar (skɑːr), *a.* *Sc.* and *north.* (see E.D.D.) Also 5-6 **skar**, 6 **sker**, 8-9 **scaur**. [a. ON. *skiarr* (Norw. *skjerr*), whence *skirra* to SCARE.]

1. Shy, afraid; scrupulous.

1530 LYNDESAY *Test. Papyngo* 126 That daye Neptunus hid hym, lyke one sker. *c* **1560** A. SCOTT *Poems* i. 211 Quhilkis ar noᵗ skar to bar on far fra bawrdis. **1573** *Satir. Poems Reform.* xlii. 61 The vther sayis: 'thocht ȝe wes skar, Me think that now ȝe cum ouir nar'. **1785** BURNS *Addr. to Deil* iii, An' faith! thou's neither lag nor lame, Nor blate nor scaur.

b. Of a horse: Shy, easily scared, restive. Of sheep: Wild. [So ON. *skiarr*.]

1508 DUNBAR *Tua Mariit Wemen* 357 The cappill.. is nought skeich, na ȝit sker, na scippis nought on syd. **1679** FOUNTAINHALL *Decisions* (1759) I. 59 The horse being scar, he twice threw him off, and so he broke his neck. **1714** in Shirreff *Agric. Shetld.* (1814) App. 61 That such as had scar sheep might be appointed to tame them.

†**2.** ? Easily provoked. [Cf. Norw. *skjerresinnad* (Aasen) in the same sense.] *Obs. rare.*

c **1460** *Towneley Myst.* xxi. 301 Ye ar bot to skar, good sir abate.

scar (skɑː(r)), *v.* [f. SCAR *sb.*²]

1. *trans.* To mark with a scar; to disfigure by inflicting a wound.

1555 EDEN *Decades* (Arb.) 164 A certayne well learned phisytion of Ciuife, was scarred with lyghtnynge in the nyghte season. **1604** SHAKS. *Oth.* v. ii. 4 Yet Ile not shed her blood, Nor scarre that whiter skin of hers then Snow. **1737** [S. BERINGTON] *G. di Lucca's Mem.* (1738) 32 One of the Balls went thro' my Hair, and the other scarr'd the side of my Neck. **1757** BURKE *Abridgm. Eng. Hist.* Wks. X. 262 In the same design of barbarous ornaments, their faces were generally painted and scarred. **1834** MARRYAT *P. Simple* xli, She was scarred with the small-pox. **1852** MITCHELL *Dream Life* 219 The old maples are even now scarred with the rude cuts you gave them. **1884** *Punch* 13 Sept. 122/1 I'm.. scarred with brambles from head to foot.

b. *transf.*

1697 DRYDEN *Virg. Georg.* I. 100 But if the Soil be barren, only scar The Surface, and but lightly print the Share. **1850** MRS. BROWNING *Crowned & Buried* xviii, I would that hostile fleets had scarred Torbay. **1871** L. STEPHEN *Playgr. Eur.* x. (1894) 241 It is scarred and gashed by some of the.. gullies of the Dolomite mountains. **1908** *Outlook* 10 Oct. 460/2 Durham has been scarred and blackened by modern industrialism.

c. *fig.*

1593 NASHE *Christ's T.* 81 Chastitie being once scarred is neuer salued.

2. a. *trans.* with *up.* To heal, cover with a scar. **b.** *intr.* with *over.* To heal; to become covered with a scar as a sign of healing.

1609 [BP. W. BARLOW] *Answ. Nameless Cath.* 266 This Antilogie the Antapologer..would salue by a figure in Grammar called Acyrologie, and would scarre vp the wound by an improprietie of speech. **1888** BRYCE *Amer. Commw.* III. cix. 577 Wounds which were just beginning to scar over were reopened by the war of 1812.

scar, obs. form of SCARE *sb.* and *v.*, SHEAR.

scarab ('skærəb). Also 6 **scarabb(e**, 6–7 **scarabe**, 7 **scarrab**, **-ubb.** [ad. F. *scarabée*, SCARABEE (= Pr. *escaravai*, Sp. *escarabajo*, Pg. *escarabeo*, *scaraveo*, also dim. *escaravelho*, It. *scarabeo*, also *scarafaggio*), ad. L. *scarabæus*, SCARABÆUS. Cf. Gr. κάραβος, dim. κᾱράβιον, also κᾱραβίς, horned beetle, stag-beetle, also sea crayfish.]

1. a. In early use, a beetle of any kind (chiefly referred to as supposed to be bred in and to feed upon dung). Now *rare* exc. (also ***scarab beetle***) as applied to the scarabæid beetle, *Ateuchus sacer*, reverenced by the ancient Egyptians (cf. sense 2).

1579 GOSSON *Sch. Abuse* (Arb.) 19 The *Scarabe* flies ouer many a sweete flower, and lightes in a cowshard. **1615** MARKHAM *Pleas. Princ.* ii. (1635) 15 A hollow Cane in which he may put them [Maggots, etc.], and Scarrabs. **1681** in *Phil. Collect.* XII. 54 A large Scarabe, I found among Goods brought from the Indies. **1776** G. WHITE *Selborne*, *To Barrington* 3 Apr., This stomach was..stuffed..with.. various insects, such as small scarabs, spiders, and dragonflies. **1845** BROWNING *Glove* 34 An Arab As glossy and black as a scarab. **1904** BUDGE *3rd & 4th Egypt. Rooms Brit. Mus.* 187 A deceased king is said to have entered the boat of the Sun in the form of the scarab.

attrib. **1582** LYLY *To Author* in *T. Watson's Poems* (Arb.) 29 Not vnlike vnto..the Scarab flies, which enter into the roote and neuer touch the rinde. **1921** C. A. EALAND *Insect Life* vi. 179 We do not possess in this country [*sc.* Great Britain] any of the Scarab Beetles, sacred to the ancient Egyptians. **1958** 'W. HENRY' *Seven Men at Mimbres Springs* vii. 73 Young Sanchez [packed] a cottonwood slingshot and six or eight smooth stones suitable for anything up to bullfrogs or scarab beetles.

†**b.** *transf.* and *fig.* esp. as a term of abuse for a man. *Obs.*

c **1600** *Distr. Emperor* II. i. in Bullen *Old Pl.* (1884) III. 195 But be assurd I am no scarabb for a castrells breakfast. **1601** B. JONSON *Poetaster* IV. vii, They are the moths, and scarabes of a state. **1610** —— *Alch.* I. i, *Fac.* You might talke softlier, raskall. *Svb.* No, you scarabe, I'll thunder you, in peeces. **1676** DURFEY *Madam Fickle* II. i. (1677) 11 Must a Man of honour wait your leisure, you Dog, and miss his necessary diversion, through the negligence of such a Scarab.

2. *Antiq.* A gem (of carnelian, emerald, obsidian, etc.) cut in the form of a beetle (*scarabæus*), having on the flat under-side a design in intaglio.

Scarabs were worn either as signet-rings or attached on a chain hung round the neck. They were common among the Egyptians, Etruscans, and the peoples of Western Asia.

1878 A. S. MURRAY in *Encycl. Brit.* VIII. 640/2 But excepting the form there is singularly little in common between the scarabs of Etruria and of Egypt. **1900** PETRIE *Dendereh* 7 From a scarab found in this tomb it is probably of the XIIth Dynasty.

scarabæan (skærə'biːən), *a.* *rare.* Also **scarabean.** [f. SCARABÆ-US + -AN.] Of, pertaining to, or characteristic of, a scarabæus or scarab.

1631 R. H. *Arraignm. Whole Creature* xiv. §1. 227 As the Scarabean Flea, or Wag-taile, that skips from place to place. **1837** *Fraser's Mag.* XVI. 404 On the opposite face is the same boat and globe, without the scarabæan symbol. **1867** F. FRANCIS *Angling* vi. (1880) 231 Folding up its wings [it] resumes its scarabean appearance.

scarabæid (skærə'biːɪd), *a.* and *sb.* *Ent.* [f. mod.L. *scarabæid-æ* (Leach 1817), f. L. *scarabæus*: see SCARABÆUS and -ID.] **a.** *adj.* Of or pertaining to the *Scarabæidæ*, a large family of lamellicorn beetles, including cockchafers, stag-beetles, dung-beetles, etc. **b.** *sb.* A scarabæid beetle. So **scara'bæidan**, a beetle of the family *Scarabæidæ*. **scara'bæidoid** *a.*, resembling a scarabæid; used by C. V. Riley to denote the third stage in the larval development of hypermetamorphic beetles, as oil-beetles (*Meloidæ*). **scara'bæidous** *a.* = SCARABÆID *a.*

1842 BRANDE *Dict. Sci.*, etc., *Scarabæidans.* **1884** *Science* 1 Feb. 127/2 The ordinary hairs of scarabaeidous beetles. **1891** *Century Dict.*, *Scarabæid* [*a.* and *sb.*]. **1898** PACKARD *Text-bk. Entomol.* 692 This Riley denominates the scarabæidoid stage of the second larva.

scara'bæist. Also **scarabe(e)ist.** [f. SCARABÆUS + -IST.] One who studies the *Scarabæidæ*.

See quot. 1872; in allusion to this passage the word is sometimes used derisively for a narrow specialist.

1872 O. W. HOLMES *Poet Breakf.-t.* ii, 'I suppose you are an entomologist?'.. 'Not quite so ambitious as that, sir... I am often spoken of as a Coleopterist,..but I have no right to so comprehensive a name... Call me a Scarabeeist if you will.' **1883** *Athenæum* 24 Mar. 380/1 If only it can convince the 'scarabæist' that there are realms of wonder and of interest beyond the limits of his own domain.

scarabæoid (skærə'biːɔɪd), *a.* and *sb.* [f. SCARABÆUS + -OID.] **A.** *adj.* **a.** *Ent.* = *scarabæidoid* (Cent. Dict.). **b.** *Antiq.* Resembling a scarab.

1889 *Athenæum* 11 May 602/3 A collection of early Greek scarabæoid gems.

B. *sb.* **a.** *Ent.* = SCARABÆID *sb.* (1895 in *Funk's Stand. Dict.*). **b.** *Antiq.* (See quot. 1887.)

1887 AMELIA B. EDWARDS tr. *Maspero's Egypt. Archæol.* v. 242 Others [*sc.* scarabæi] again but vaguely recall the form of the insect, and are called scarabæoids. **1888** *Athenæum* 16 June 765/1 The collection of Phœnician scarabs and scarabæoids of hard stones is large and curious.

‖**scarabæus** (skærə'biːəs). Pl. **scarabæi** (-'biːaɪ). Also 6, 7–9 **-beus.** [L.: see SCARAB.]

1. *Ent.* A beetle of the genus *Scarabæus*, formerly a very large genus corresponding to some extent with the modern family *Scarabæidæ*; now an Old World genus (Linnæus 1767) of lamellicorn beetles typical of the *Scarabæidæ* (see SCARABÆID). Sometimes used loosely = SCARABÆID *sb.*

[**1432–50** tr. *Higden* (Rolls) II. 209 Somme thynges goe in to other kyndes by corrupcion, as bees of roten calfes, and vermyn callede scarabei [L. *scarabæi*] of corrupte horses.] **1664** HUBERT *Catal. Rarities* (1665) 39 A great Scarabeus of the Amazons. *Ibid.* 41 A little brown Scarabeus of East India. **1741** WARBURTON *Div. Legat.* IV. iv. 112 To signify the Sun, they sometimes painted a Hawk,..sometimes a Scarabæus with a round Ball in its Claws. **1876** *Van Beneden's Anim. Parasites* viii. 167 The larva of the large scarabæus (*Oryctes nasicornis*), which is found in tan.

2. *Antiq.* = SCARAB 2.

1775 *Tassie's Catal. Impress. Gems* 4 Reverse of Scarabeus. **1860** C. W. KING *Antique Gems* 123 This manner of mounting the scarabeus was often used by the Egyptians. *Ibid.*, Some early Etruscan scarabei. **1886** *Guide Exhib. Galleries Brit. Mus.* 54 Agate scarabæus... Inscribed in Phœnician with the name Yesha-el.

scarabean, variant of SCARABÆAN *a.*

scarabee ('skærəbiː). *arch.* Also (9 **scaribee**), *pl.* 6–7 **scarabies.** [a. F. *scarabée*: see SCARAB.] = SCARAB 1.

1591 SPENSER *Vis. Worlds Vanitie* iv, The kingly Bird, that beares Joves thunder-clap, One day did scorne the simple Scarabee. **1599** DRAYTON *Idea* No. 31 Vnto my pitch no common iudgement flies, I scorne all earthlie dung-bred scarabies. **1665** NEEDHAM *Med. Medicinæ* 197 Horses generate Wasps and Scarabees. **1820** SHELLEY *Œdipus* I. 157 The beast Has a loud trumpet like the scarabee.

attrib. **1830** MARRYAT *King's Own* xx, Little animals of the scaribee tribe, denominated weevils.

b. *transf.* and *fig.* = SCARAB 1 b.

1615 BRATHWAIT *Strappado* (1878) 102 Let mee vnrippe my sorrowes, that my brest May void such Scarabees, that vse to sit Vpon each vlcer. **1677** *2nd Packet of Adv. to Men of Shaftesbury* 15 Some few Scarabees of the Law.

scarabeus, variant of SCARABÆUS.

scaraboid ('skærəbɔɪd), *sb.* and *a.* [f. SCARAB + -OID. Cf. Gr. καραβοειδής, also κᾱραβώδης like a κάραβος (see SCARAB).] **A.** *sb.*

1. *Antiq.* = SCARABÆOID *sb.* b.

1879 A. S. MURRAY in *Encycl. Brit.* X. 137/1 Four porcelain scaraboids from Camirus. **1886** *Guide Exhib. Galleries Brit. Mus.* 54 Jasper scaraboid..[with] Phœnician inscription. *Ibid.* 190 The Greeks..had no favour for finger-rings with a beetle on the back of them. They preferred the scaraboid, with its plain, smooth back, for gems that were to be worn as swivel rings.

2. A scarabæid.

1891 in *Century Dict.*

B. *adj.* Resembling a scarab or scaraboid.

1888 A. S. MURRAY *Brit. Mus. Catal. Engr. Gems* Introd. 17 Gems of the true scaraboid form.

scaramoche, -osh, obs. ff. SKIRMISH.

scaramouch ('skærəmaʊtʃ, -muːtʃ, -mɑːʃ), *sb.* Forms: α. 7 **scaramuzza, scaramoucha, -ouchi(o, -ouchè, -oche, scaramuccio, -uccie, -uchi(o, -ucha, scarramuccio,** 7–8 **scaramouchi;** β. 7 **scharamouch,** 7– **scaramouch.** [ad. It. *Scaramuccia* (see sense 1); the name is a use of *scaramuccia* SKIRMISH *sb.*, in allusion to the character of the personage. The β form, which now alone survives, comes through the F. *Scaramouche* (Molière); the α forms represent corruptly the Italian original.]

1. (As proper name, with capital S.) A stock character in Italian farce, a cowardly and foolish boaster of his own prowess, who is constantly being cudgelled by Harlequin.

The character was intended in ridicule of the Spanish don, and was dressed in Spanish costume, usually black; the costume was often adopted in masquerades.

The clever impersonation of the part by Tiberio Fiurelli, who brought his company of Italian players to London in 1673, rendered the word very popular in England during the last quarter of the 17th c.

α. **1662** J. DAVIES tr. *Olearius' Voy. Amb.* VI. 380 Such distorted Countenances and Postures, as Scaramuzza himself would be much troubled to imitate. **1673** WYCHERLEY *Gentl. Dancing-Master* III. i. 39, I diddè go to the Italian Academy at Paris thrice a week to learn to play de Fool of Signior Scaramouchè. **1673** DRYDEN *Epil. to Univ. Oxon.* 15 Stout Scaramoucha with Rush Lance rode in, And ran a Tilt at Centaure Arlequin. **1673** A. MARVEL *Rehearsall Transp.* II. 60 There were no less than six Scaramuccios together upon the Stage. **1676** SHADWELL *Virtuoso* v. 88 Entry of Scaramonchi [sic] and Clowns. *Ibid.* 89 Enter Sir Formal in Scaramoucha's habit. **1696** V. ALSOP *God in Mount* 13 Where are the Jesters, the Buffoons, the Scarramuccioes? Will not these afford a more pleasing entertainment?

β. **1677** E. RAVENSCROFT (*title*) Scaramouch. *Ibid.*, The Persons Names. Scaramouch, a Philosopher... Harlequin. **1678** DRYDEN *Kind Kpr.* I. i. (1680) 10 But I speak no Italian, a few broken scraps which I pick'd from Scaramouch and Harlequin at Paris. **1749** H. WALPOLE *Let. to Mann* 3 May, A troop of harlequins and scaramouches. **1771** T. HULL *Sir W. Harrington* (1797) I. 143 Mrs. Granville a nun, myself a shepherdess, Lord S. a scaramouch [at the Masquerade]. **1855** W. IRVING *Tour Prairies* xix, Like a posture-master or scaramouch at a circus. **1876** 'OUIDA' *Winter City* x. 315 She was silent watching the whirling of the pierrots..scaramouches and dominoes.

b. A puppet representing Scaramouch.

1816 J. SCOTT *Vis. Paris* (ed. 5) 98 He gave motion to a small wooden scaramouch that danced well in tune. **1819** S. ROGERS *Human Life* 492 The booths whitening the village-green, Where Punch and Scaramouch aloft are seen. **1851–61** MAYHEW *Lond. Lab.* III. 52 This here is the Scaramouch that dances without a head.

2. *transf.* and *fig.* In later use often employed loosely as a term of contempt: A rascal, scamp.

α. **1676** DURFEY *Madam Fickle* II. i. (1677) 11 *Tob.* Hoy; Scaramouchi, Rascal, Poltron, Popinjay!..must a Man of honour wait your leisure. *a* **1683** OLDHAM *Rem.* (1684) 113 Without doubt he was..design'd for the Scaramuchio of Mankind.

β. **1694** JER. COLLIER *Miscell.*, *Of Duelling* 32 It makes the Laws cheap and ridiculous, the Solemnities of Justice a piece of Pageantry, the Bench a few Reverend Poppets, or Scharamouches in Scarlet. **1716** in W. W. Wilkins *Polit. Ballads* (1860) II. 175 The scaramouches everywhere With open throats bawl'd out. **1824** W. IRVING *T. Trav.* II. 141 He swore no scaramouch of an Italian robber would dare to meddle with an Englishman. **1865** MEREDITH *Rhoda Fleming* x, Once I was an idle young scaramouch.

3. *attrib.*

1870 DISRAELI *Lothair* lvii, The Sicilian with his scaramouch tricks got on very well with the gentle and polished Tuscan. **1906** *Athenæum* 10 Mar. 294/3 Irresponsible Kitty..lived merrily throughout her scaramouch childhood and flirting girlhood.

Hence **'scaramouch** *v. intr.*, to act the part of a scaramouch, or to behave like a scaramouch.

1834 BECKFORD *Italy* I. 119 The rabble were gathered in knots round the strollers and mountebanks, singing and scaramouching in the middle of the square. **1864** MRS. LLOYD *Ladies of Polcarrow* 134 Didnt he use to scaramouch up over-stairs just the like o' that, when he was a purty little fellow!

scaramouch, obs. form of SKIRMISH *sb.*

scarbabe: see SCAREBABE.

Scarborough ('skɑːbərə). Also 6 **Scar-, Skarboro(w, Scarbrough,** 7 **Scarburg, Scarreborough.** The name of a town on the coast of Yorkshire, used *attrib.*

1. Scarborough warning. Very short notice, or no notice at all; a surprise.

The statement of Fuller, that the phrase originated in an allusion to the surprise of Scarborough by Thomas Stafford in April 1557, is disproved by the earlier example below.

1546 J. HEYWOOD *Prov.* (1562) E ij, A daie er I was wedde, I bad you (quoth I) Scarbrough warnyng I had (quoth he) wherby, I kept me thens. *a* **1561** T. MOUNTAIN in Strype *Eccl. Mem.* (1721) III. 189 Your friendship, Mr. Charlys, is but hard and scarce, in giving me this Scarborow Warning [viz. the notice that he was to be hanged 'even this Foornoon']. **1592** LYLY *Sp. to Eliz. at Quarrendon* i. Wks. 1902 I. 455 The Knight wisheth it may be a watch (better than Scarborows warning) to the Noble Gentelmen of your Courte. **1603** BP. T. MATTHEW *Let.* 19 Jan. in Cardwell *Confer.* (1840) 166, I received a message..that it was his Majesty's pleasure that I should preach before him upon Sunday next; which Scarborough warning did not only perplex me, but [etc.]. **1697** DE LA PRYME *Diary* (Surtees)

125 'Scarburg Warning' is a proverb in many places of the north, signifying any sudden warning given upon any account. **1832** SCOTT *Redgauntlet* ch. xix, The true man for giving Scarborough warning—first knock you down, then bid you stand. **1890** P. H. EMERSON *Wild Life on Tidal Water* 8 Tha wind wos werry moderate, but that shifted an' come round strong from the norrawest, an' hove her ashore; 'twos a Scarboro' warnin'.

†**b.** Hence in *nonce-uses*. *Obs.*

1577 STANYHURST *Descr. Irel.* iii. 12 in *Holinshed*, And withall, as far as their scarborrough leasure coulde serue them, they ransacke the Prince his thesaure. **1582** —— *Æneis* IV. (Arb.) 116 Al they the lyke poste haste dyd make, with scarboro scrabbling [L. *rapiuntque ruuntque*].

2. Scarborough lily, *Vallota purpurea*.

1882 *Garden* 9 Sept. 224/2 A correspondent sends us two blooms of the Scarborough Lily.

†**scarbot(e.** *Obs.*$^{-0}$ Also **scharabot.** [Aphetic a. F. *escarbot*, in OF. also *escharbot(e*, f. L. *scarabæus* with Fr. dim. suffix *-ot.* (Cf., however, late OE. *scearn-budda*, SHORN-BUD, dung-beetle, which, or some equivalent continental form, may have influenced the Fr. word.)] A beetle.

c **1440** *Promp. Parv.* 442/2 Scarbot [*Winchester MS.* scarbote], flye, *scabo.* **14..** *Voc.* in Wr.-Wülcker 609/47 *Scarabo, anc*e a scharabot (*et anc*e a bytylle).

†**scarboyle,** *v.* *Obs. rare*$^{-1}$. [ad. F. *escarbouiller* (16th c. in Littré), OF. *escarbellier.*] *trans.* To smash, to break in pieces.

1502 *Star Chamber Cases* No. 1, They ryvefilled, spoyled, scarboyled and made havokk of her said goods.

scarbridge, obs. form of SCABBARD *sb.*[1]

scarbroite ('skɑːbrəʊaɪt). *Min.* [f. *Scarbro*' a form of SCARBOROUGH + -ITE[1].] A hydrous carbonate of alumina, formerly regarded as a silicate, found near Scarborough.

1829 W. V. VERNON in *Philos. Mag.* Ser. II. V. 180 It.. may be distinguished by the appellation of Scarbröite. **1883** M. F. HEDDLE in *Encycl. Brit.* XVI. 424/2. **1960** *Mineral. Mag.* XXXII. 353 Scarbroite, a fine-grained but compact deposit obtained from fissures in the sandstone on the north Yorkshire coast, is shown by chemical analysis to have an idealized formula $Al_2(CO_3)_3 \cdot 12Al(OH)_3$.

scarce (skɛəs), *a.* and *adv.* Forms: α. 3–7 **scars, skars(e,** 4–8 **scarse,** (5 **scarske),** 5–7 **skarce,** 6 *Sc.* **skairs(e, skarss, skeis(s, skaris, skairce,** 7 *Sc.* **schairce,** 5- **scarce;** β. 5–6 **scace,** 6 **scas(e, skace, skase,** *Sc.* **scaysse.** [ME. *scars*, a. ONF. *scars, escars, escas* (Central OF. *eschars*, mod.F. *échars*, now only said of coin, with the sense 'below standard value', and of wind, in sense 1 b below) = Pr. *escars, escas*, Sp. *escaso*, Pg. *escaço, escasso*, It. *scarso*:—popular L. **scarsus* (med.L. *scarsus* from It. and Fr.), prob. repr. an older **excarpsus*, pa. pple. of **excarpĕre* (= class. L. *excerpĕre* to select out, EXCERPT), f. *ex* (see EX-) + *carpĕre* to pluck. Cf. MDu. *schaers* (Du. *schaars*) from Fr.] **A.** *adj.*

†**1. a.** Restricted in quantity, size, or amount; scanty. *Obs.*

α. **1297** R. GLOUC. (Rolls) 6862 His moder he dude ek in warde & scars liflode ire found. **1340** *Ayenb.* 53 Nou behoueþ to habbe tuo mesures ane little and ane scarse, þet he useþ touore þe uolke. And anoþre guode and large, þet he useþ þet non ne y-zyȝþ. **1387** TREVISA *Higden* (Rolls) III. 457 Vile cloþinge and scars [L. *vilis et rara vestis*] we haveþ in stede of gold and of greet array. *c* **1412** HOCCLEVE *De Reg. Princ.* 478 His hous in london is to streyt & scars To doon his craft. **1596** DALRYMPLE tr. *Leslie's Hist. Scot.* I. I. 90 Bot at evin only they first prepaired the table, and that verie scharpe and skairs.

β. **1509** BARCLAY *Ship of Fools* (1874) II. 103 Than was theyr fode scas, theyr lyuynge lyberall Theyr labour comon, they knewe no couetyse.

†**b.** Of wind: Slight in force or strength; almost calm. *Obs.*

c **1400** *St. Alexius* (Laud 622) 560 Þe wynde was gret, & nothing skars, þonder dyned shille. **1511** *Guylforde's Pylgr.* (Camden) 11 How be it ye wynde was so scarce and calme that we coude not come to the towne of Corfona tyll Monday ayenst nyght. **1600** HAKLUYT *Voy.* III. 401 Wee sayled neere to the coast on the same side, with very scarce winde, and in a manner calme.

†**c.** Of the water of a river, etc.: Low. *Obs.*

1732 EARL OF OXFORD in *Portland Papers* (Hist. MSS. Comm.) VI. 150 This year has been very bad for them [the boats], the water is very scarce.

2. †**a.** Of persons, their attributes and actions: Stingy, sparing, niggardly, parsimonious, penurious. Also, sparing or chary *of*. *Obs.*

α. *c* **1330** *King of Tars* 92 Sire, the kyng of Tars Of wikked wordes nis not scars. **13..** *Seuyn Sag.* (W.) 1244 Bothe he was scars and chinche. *c* **1386** CHAUCER *Melib.* ¶633 Ye shul vse the richesses,.. in swich a manere, that men holde nat yow to scars, ne to sparynge, ne to fool large. *c* **1400** *Cato's Morals* 211 in *Cursor M.* App. IV. 1672 Be scarske of þi louing. **1483** CAXTON *Golden Leg.* 128b/1 And gaf to them largely to ete suche as they asked but to herself she was hard in her sekeness & skarce. *c* **1500** *Three Kings Sons* 78 The sone of a mighti kynge hath delyuerd a felaw that he knew not, which hath not ben scars, nor of so pore corage, but that he hath wele to his knowlage delyuerd the sone of the grettist kynge that leuyth. *c* **1510** BARCLAY *Mirr. Gd. Manners* (1570) Gj, Men oft haue repented of wordes superflue, But seldome of scilence doth any man repent, Wherfore scarce of wordes is counted great vertue. **1531** ELYOT *Gov.* III. xxvii, Superfluous in wordes, or els to scarse. *a* **1539** in *Archæologia* XLVII. 54 Wee.. aduertise you all to be contented to lyue under a scarcer manour for a tyme then ye haue doon in tymes past. **1562** SHUTE *Cambine on Turkish Aff.* 52b, They knewe him to be of nature scarse, and not liberal. **1605** VERSTEGAN *Dec. Intell.* viii. (1628) 244 Whereas many haue written of these Etymologies, yet are all of them very scarse in shewing the reasons of many their interpretations. *a* **1639** T. CAREW *To A. L.* 12 And 'twere a sin There to be scarce, where she hath bin So prodigal of her best graces.

β. **1414** BRAMPTON *Penit. Ps.* (Percy Soc.) 21 To synfull man thou were nevere scace Of 'Ne reminiscaris, Domine!' *a* **1550** *Vox Populi* 740 in Hazl. *E.P.P.* III. 293 By cause thei be so base, Thei wylbe neadye and scase [*Harl. MS.* skarsse].

b. Of a period of time: Characterized by scarcity. ? *Obs.*

c **1290** *All Saints' Day* 41 in *S. Eng. Leg.* I. 419 Ech man .. made þane day feste, And in a skars tyme of þe ȝere ase we wyten, it was in May. **1624** CAPT. SMITH *Virginia* II. 31 Powhatan.. and some others that are provident, rost their fish and flesh vpon hurdles.. and keepe it till scarce times.

3. Of food or other commodities, rarely of immaterial things: Existing or accessible in deficient quantity.

α. *c* **1374** CHAUCER *Former Age* 36 Ther as vitaile is eek so skars and thinne That noght but mast or apples is therinne. *c* **1450** *Brut* 448 In þat tyme money was skarse. **1593** SHAKS. *Rich. II*, II. i. 7 Where words are scarse, they are seldome spent in vaine, For they breath truth, that breath their words in paine. **1697** DAMPIER *Voy.* I. 301 The Padre told Capt. Swan that Provision was now scarce on the Island. **1842** TENNYSON *Audley Crt.* 31 Then touch'd upon the game, how scarce it was This season. **1878** STUBBS *Const. Hist.* III. xviii. 90 Money was scarce. **1896** *Law Times* C. 488/2 Like most other lawyers, Inglis had his probationary period when work was scarce.

β. **1414** BRAMPTON *Penit. Ps.* (Percy Soc.) 37 For my tyme is lytel here; My dayes be waxen wonder scace. *a* **1548** HALL *Chron., Hen. VIII*, iv. 153 All thyng there was scace, by reason of the continuall warres.

4. a. Existing in limited number; seldom seen or met with; rare. Said chiefly of things that are sought after by collectors, e.g. a book, coin, engraving, a species of plant or animal.

1398 TREVISA *Barth. De P.R.* XVI. xlviii, [Gems] ben preciouse for þey ben scars and diuerse; for all þat is scars and selden hadde [L. *omne enim rarum*] is clepid gret and preciouse. **1705** ADDISON *Italy, Bolonia* 434 The scarcest of all is a *Pescennius Niger* on a Medallion well preserv'd. **1710** HEARNE *Coll.* (O.H.S.) III. 41 A scarse Book. **1844** DICKENS *Mart. Chuz.* xvi, You will not find it a scarce quality here. **1858** HAWTHORNE *Fr. & It. Note-bks.* II. 219 Good bakers were as scarce in ancient Rome as in the modern city. **1873** *Chamb. Jrnl.* 27 Dec. 821/2 The wood-cock.. is much scarcer than it used to be. **1884** *Chr. World* 31 July 583/3 Knowledge is scarce, wisdom is scarcer.

b. in collectors' names of butterflies and moths.

1832 J. RENNIE *Butterfl. & Moths* 1 The scarce Swallow Tail. *Ibid.* 2 The scarce Clouded Yellow. **1884** *Leisure Hour* Jan. 48/1 The rarest is one of the fen-country butterflies, known as the 'Scarce Copper'.

†**c.** said of a disease. *Obs. rare.*

1528 PAYNELL *Salerne's Regim.* b iij, Pontike melancolye is very scarse.

5. *scarce of*: poorly or scantily supplied or provided with; deficient in; not having much of, short of. Now *rare* or *Obs.*

1541 R. COPLAND *Guydon's Quest. Chirurg.* O ij b, In places drye and scarce of flesshe, as the fyngers and ioyntes. **1547** BOORDE *Introd. Knowl.* xxx. (1870) 198 These countreys be baryn of wine and corne, and skarse of vitels. **1667** MILTON *P.L.* III. 433 Dislodging from a Region scarce of prey To gorge the flesh of Lambs. **1681** W. ROBERTSON *Phraseol. Gen.* (1693) 1098 We are very scarce of such citizens. **1808** PIKE *Sources Mississ.* (1810) III. 253 This route.. is very scarce of water. **1847** MARRYAT *Childr. N. Forest* xiii, We are scarce of provisions.

6. Phr. ***to make oneself scarce***: to absent oneself, go away, keep away. *colloq.*

1809 MALKIN *Gil Blas* x. i. ¶2 My liberty was granted only on condition of making myself scarce in the two Castiles. **1826** SCOTT *Jrnl.* (1890) I. 169 Rose late in the morning, past eight, to give the cold and toothache time to make themselves scarce, which they have obligingly done. **1860** THACKERAY *Lovel* i, When Lovel's wife began to show me that she was tired of my company, I made myself scarce. **1895** MRS. H. WARD *Bessie Costrell* iv, Just mek yourselves scarce, all the lot o' yer.

7. Qualifying a noun of action, forming a phrase equivalent to the gerund qualified by *scarcely*. *rare.*

1841 LEVER *C. O'Malley* lxxvii, She.. with a half smile of scarce recognition passed by me.

B. *adv.*

†**1.** Scantily, sparsely. Cf. SCARCELY *adv.* 1. *Obs. rare.*

c **1300** *Beket* 274 (Percy Soc.) 13 And of the beste him silve he at swithe scars and lute. *c* **1450** *Mirk's Festial* 9 For when hit schall be dere, hit walleth scarse; and when hit schall be gret schep, hit walleþe plentwysly ynogh.

2. Now *arch.* or *literary.* **a.** Barely, only just; not quite; = SCARCELY *adv.* 2. Also †*full scarce.*

See the remarks under SCARCELY 2, which apply also to the uses of this word. Before advs. in *-ly* the form *scarce* is often adopted instead of *scarcely*, to avoid the iteration of the suffix.

α. **1413** *Pilgr. Sowle* (Caxton 1483) IV. xvi. 71 A litel hows whiche hath in euery side skars a mannes lengthe. **1558** BP. WATSON *Sev. Sacram.* xii. 73 All wee haue done, is but our dutie and skarse that. **1565** *Reg. Privy Council Scot.* I. 402 Skairis aneuch to sustene this thair realme. **1577** KENDALL *Flowers of Epigrammes* 4b, With worldly cares he was so toste, that scarse he tooke his reste. **1591** SHAKS. *1 Hen. VI*, I. i. 112 Retyring from the Siege of Orleance, Hauing full scarce six thousand in his troupe. **1621** BP. MOUNTAGU *Diatribæ* 40 The blinde may Judge as well of colours, as may Master Selden of a deceiving argument, who hath saluted Logick scarce along. **1644** MILTON *Areop.* (Arb.) 54 In a hand scars legible. **1671** —— *P.R.* III. 85 Till Conquerour Death discover them scarce men, Rowling in brutish vices. **1676** PRIDEAUX *Lett.* (Camden) 54, I scarce think she would marry on [= one] with nothing. *a* **1699** LADY HALKETT *Autobiog.* (1875) 44 They were so shaken they could skarce hold there feett. *a* **1715** BURNET *Own Time* (1766) I. 188 He scarce ever went to their meetings. **1720** WATERLAND *Eight Serm.* 119 The other Construction.. is scarce Sense. **1862** TENNYSON *Idylls of K.* Ded. 6 And indeed He seems to me Scarce other than my own ideal knight. **1886** C. E. PASCOE *Lond. of To-day* xx. (ed. 3) 200 A sleepy little town scarce bigger than a village. **1886** STEVENSON *Treas. Isl.* xiv, I ran as I never ran before, scarce minding the direction of my flight, so long as it led me from the murderers.

β. **1526** TINDALE *Acts* xiv. 18 With these sayings scase refrayned they the people. **1548** in *Cal. Scott. Pap.* (1898) I. 91 Her ovarlope ys so sanke, scaysse abull to bere her ordynans. **1568** GRAFTON *Chron.* II. 470 The stowte Souldiour for faintnesse could scase welde his weapon.

†**b.** with pleonastic negative. Cf. SCARCELY 2 b, SCANT *adv.* 1 c. *Obs.*

1591 HARINGTON *Orl. Fur.* Pref. ¶8 For the verse I do challenge none, being a thing that euery body that neuer scarce bayted their horse at the Vniuersitie take vpon them to make. **1624** LD. KENSINGTON in Ellis *Orig. Lett.* Ser. I. III. 177 They will not conceive mee nor scarse receive mee but as a publike instrument for the service of an alliance. **1685** J. DUNTON *Lett. fr. New-Eng.* (1867) 13 Not Heljogabalus himself could scarce boast a more delicious table.

c. with reference to time. Cf. SCARCELY 2 c.

α. **1513** DOUGLAS *Æneis* XII. iii. 90 Scars had Juno thir wordis brocht to end, Quhen [etc.]. *a* **1547** SURREY *Æneid* II. (1557) B iij, Scarse spake I this, when wailing thus he sayd. **1665** BOYLE *Occas. Refl.* IV. ii. (1848) 173 We had scarce entred those Fields, when our Ears were saluted with [etc.]. **1667** MILTON *P.L.* IX. 850 There he her met, Scarse from the Tree returning. **1799** S. TURNER *Hist. Anglo-Sax.* 352 Scarce had they submitted, but the Huns were invading him [Charlemagne].

β. *a* **1548** HALL *Chron., Hen. VI* 90 He had skace ended his exhortacion, but the Englishmen beyng encouraged with his prudent persuasion, sette on their enemies.

d. Qualifying a ppl. adj. used attributively. Commonly hyphened.

1591 SHAKS. *1 Hen. VI*, IV. iii. 50 Our scarse-cold Conqueror,.. Henrie the fift. **1594** KYD *Cornelia* III. i. 86 His iawes.. slyghtly couer'd with a scarce-seene skyn. **1607–12** BACON *Ess., Fortune* (Arb.) 376 A number of litle and scarce discerned vertues. **1631** MILTON *Epit. March. Winch.* 20 He at their invoking came But with a scarce-wel-lighted flame. *c* **1665** BP. KING *Let. to Walton*, The scarce-closed wounds of a newly bleeding State and Church. **1814** BYRON *Lara* II. xix, The accents his scarce-moving pale lips spoke. **1868** FITZGERALD tr. *Omar* xc, And once again there gather'd a scarce heard Whisper among them. **1899** H. WRIGHT *Depopulation* 102 The pair rose from the scarce-tasted breakfast. **1915** G. FRANKAU *Tid'apa* ii. 14 A scarce-breathed, flickering soul-wave, discoded but conscience-deep. **1921** W. DE LA MARE *Veil* 35 There came, scarce-heard, Claws, fluttering feathers, Of deluded bird. **1922** BLUNDEN *Shepherd* (ed. 2) 53 In the scarce-glimmering boles. **1935** C. DAY LEWIS *Time to Dance* 33 Like a bird scarce-fledged they flew, whose flying-hours are few. **1951** W. DE LA MARE *Winged Chariot* 57, I match that child with this scarce-changed old man.

†**3.** Seldom, scarcely ever, rarely. *Obs.*

1596 DALRYMPLE tr. *Leslie's Hist. Scot.* I. Prol. 40 The turtle dwe, the feldifare, the nichtingale, with vthiris natiounis ar frequent bot skairs with us ar fund. **1600** SHAKS. *A.Y.L.* I. ii. 41 For those that she makes faire, she scarce makes honest. **1663** WOOD *Life* (O.H.S.) I. 479 Never or scarse was the like seen.

4. Used (after L. *vix*) for: With difficulty. *rare.*

1667 MILTON *P.L.* VII. 470 Scarse from his mould Behemoth biggest born of Earth upheav'd His vastness. **1819** SHELLEY *Prometh.* II. v. 17 How thou art changed! I dare not look on thee;.. I scarce endure The radiance of thy beauty. **1883** R. W. DIXON *Mano* I. xv. 49 For a brass demon .. Leaped on him, and he scarce departed thence, Leaving the riches o'er the cavern strewn.

†**scarce,** *v.* *Obs. rare.* Forms: 4 **skarse,** 5 **scarce,** 5, 7 **scarse.** [f. SCARCE *a.* Cf. SCARCEN.]

1. *intr.* **a.** To become less, diminish. **b.** To become scarce.

1390 GOWER *Conf.* III. 313 The wyndy Storm began to skarse. *a* **1500** *Brut* 400 (MS. Galba), By that tyme her vitailis scarsid sore with-ynne the Cite.

2. *trans.* To make less; to rarefy.

c **1440** *Promp. Parv.* 442/2 Scarsyn, or make lesse, *minoro.* **1598** FLORIO, *Scarsare*, to scarce, to spare, to pinch, to cut off, to scant. **1603** PLATT *Fire of Cole-balles*, When the smoke doth passe and become scarsed through the lome.

†'**scarcehead.** *Obs. rare.* [f. SCARCE *a.* + -HEAD.] Stinginess, niggardliness.

Cf. dial. *scarceheed* 'scarcity, want' (Elworthy *W. Somerset Word-bk.* 1886).

1420–2 LYDG. *Thebes* III. in *Chaucer's Wks.* (1561) 369/1 But in his Courte let him first deuise To exile Scarcehed and Couetise. **1566** DRANT *Horace, Sat.* I. i. A iiij, A niggerde cloune, At whose scarceheade and couetyce the worlde did outas make.

†'**scarceler.** *Obs.* [ad. some derivative (? Fr. Sp., or It.) of F. *escarcelle* (16th c. in Hatz.-Darm.), Sp. *escarcela*, It. *scarsella*, pouch carried at the girdle.] A kind of courier: see quot.

14.. *Direct. Travellers* in *Eng. Stud.* VIII. 278 Who-so woll ride faste and with-oute hevy cariage, good were to fynde atte Brigges suche a scarceler as bereth marchauntes lettres; which will fayne ride with men for fyndyng of hym and his hors, w^{t}oute eny other wages.

scarcely ('skɛəslɪ), *adv.* Forms: see SCARCE *a.*; also α. 4 **skarschliche**, 6 (**charsely**), *Sc.* **scairslie**, **skarslie**, **skirslie**, **skayirslye**, 6, 8 *Sc.* **skairslie**, 7 *Sc.* **skaircelie**; β. 6 **skacely**. [f. SCARCE *a.* + -LY[2].]

†**1.** Scantily, in small quantities; inadequately, sparingly, niggardly, parsimoniously. *Obs.*

13.. *K. Alis.* 1011 (Bodl. MS.), In a castel she was yshett And was assigned lyueresoun Skarslich [*Weber* Skarschliche] & nouȝth a foysoun. **1340** *Ayenb.* 34 Auarice is disordene loue zuo disordene him ssewеþ..ine spendinge scarsliche. *a* **1400** *Cato* 569 in *Minor Poems fr. Vernon MS.* 603 Preise a mon so scarsliche, Whom þat þou wolt him proue. *c* **1440** *Gesta Rom.* xxxvi. 147 (Harl. MS.), Bryng home thi grehounde,..and fede it so scarsly, that hit breke no more loos. **1540–1** ELYOT *Image Gov.* (1556) 15 He dranke wine not scarcely, not to muche, but competently. **1613** PURCHAS *Pilgrimage* (1614) 718 It was verie scarcely inhabited, of few and small Nations. **1669** MILTON *Acced. Grammar* To Rdr., It hath been long a general complaint.. that the tenth part of mans life..is taken up in learning, and that very scarcely, the Latin Tongue.

2. Originally used to express a restrictive qualification, = 'barely', 'only just'; hence also, = 'barely, or not quite', 'only just, if at all'. In mod. use the original sense survives only in definite statements of fact. In sentences relating to belief, expectation, or estimation, the word now (as occas. in ME.) serves as a restricted negative (= 'not quite'). Often, however, the qualification really relates, not to the contents of the sentence in which the adv. occurs, but to the degree of the speaker's belief: thus 'You will scarcely maintain this proposition' is equivalent to 'I cannot quite believe that you will maintain', etc. Cf. SCARCE *adv.* and HARDLY *adv.*

The adv. qualifies verbs, adjs., advs., and advb. phrases, and esp. numerals (sbs., adjs., and advs.), designations of quantity, and indefinite pronouns. In many cases it may most correctly be regarded as qualifying the whole predication, though placed in proximity to the word in the sentence to which the qualification chiefly relates.

α. **1297** R. GLOUC. (Rolls) 10614 Þe sink pors scarseliche mid ssipes eiȝtetene. *c* **1374** CHAUCER *Tr. & Cr.* II. 43 Eek scarsly been ther in this place three That han in love seyd lyk and doon in al. *c* **1386** —— *Pars. T.* ¶927 And if he abide to his laste day scarsly may he shryuen hym or remembre hym of hyse synnes. **1387** TREVISA *Higden* (Rolls) I. 17 Knowleche of greet dedes is so nyh loste and forȝet, þat skarsliche [**1527** charsely, Caxton **1482** scarsely] bare names of places we haueþ now in mynde. *c* **1430** *Pilgr. Lyf Manhode* I. lxxxiii. (1869) 47 Serteyn, quod he, a kyte a litel enfamined shulde skarsliche be ful sauled ther with; For it is litel. **1576** FLEMING *Panoplie Epist.* 205 Somewhat there is in them, wherewith I am skarcely pleased. **1596** DALRYMPLE tr. *Leslie's Hist. Scot.* II. x. 294 About this tyme the pest was ryfe in Scotland, cheiflie in Dundei, Abirdine, and in sum vtheris tounes and dorpes, quhilkes a hail ȝeir skirslie [*sic*] culd be clinsed. **1605** SHAKS. *Macb.* I. v. 37 One of my fellowes had the speed of him; Who almost dead for breath, had scarcely more Then would make vp his Message. **1713** STEELE *Englishm.* No. 40. 259 In Paris..there are scarcely six Streets wider than the narrow End of St. Martin's-lane. **1781** SIR J. REYNOLDS *Tour Flanders* Wks. 1797 II. 122 It [the drapery] is scarcely ever cast with any choice or skill. **1825** MACAULAY *Ess., Milton* ¶19 The genius of Petrarch was scarcely of the first order. **1857** T. MOORE *Handbk. Brit. Ferns* (ed. 3) 4 Sometimes it [the Caudex] is scarcely or not at all lengthened. **1860** TYNDALL *Glac.* I. x. 65 The rain continued with scarcely any pause. *a* **1885** 'H. CONWAY' *Living or Dead* viii, He..blamed my partner, who could scarcely believe his ears.

β. **1542** *Lament. & Piteous Treatise* in *Harl. Misc.* (1809) IV. 541 That skacely ther remayned ynough [grain] to serue us in our journeye homeward. **1551** ROBINSON tr. *More's Utopia* II. vii. (1895) 239 But in that newefonnde parte of the worlde, whiche is scaselye so farre from vs beyonde the lyne equinoctiall, as [etc.].

†**b.** With pleonastic negative, or in an implied negative context. *Obs.* (Cf. SCARCE *adv.* 2 b.)

c **1369** CHAUCER *Dethe Blaunche* 289 Ne [coude] nat scarcely Macrobeus..I trowe arede my dreames even. *c* **1400** *Rom. Rose* 5460 Than shulde they seen who freendis ware For of an hundred, certeynly, Nor of a thousand ful scarsly, Ne shal they fynde unnethis oon, Whan povertee is comen upon. *c* **1570** W. WAGER *The longer thou livest* 177 (Brandl), Not one good man is scarsly among ten. **1795** *Fate of Sedley* II. 158 Recollection, however, returned before I had scarcely written a line.

c. With reference to time: Barely, only just. Chiefly with pluperfect tense, before a clause introduced by *when* or *before*.

1542 UDALL *Erasm. Apoph.* 231 Augustus beeyng scacely come to mannes state was putte to haue dooynges in the commenweale. **1766** GOLDSM. *Vic. W.* i, I had scarcely taken orders a year before I began to think seriously of matrimony. **1779** *Mirror* No. 1, He is scarcely seated before every body present begins to form some notion of his character. **1848** THACKERAY *Van. Fair* lxvii, In old-fashioned days,..when you were scarcely born. **1875** JOWETT *Plato* (ed. 2) I. 10 He had scarcely said the word, when Charmides entered.

†**3.** Used (after L. *vix*) for: With difficulty. *Obs.*

1697 DRYDEN *Virg. Past.* I. 19 This you see I scarcely drag along, Who yeaning on the Rocks has left her Young. *Ibid.*, *Georg.* III. 167. *Ibid.*, *Æneid* VI. 558.

scarcement ('skɛəsmənt). *Sc.* and *north.* Also 6 *Sc.* **skarsment**, 9 **scarsement**. [app. f. SCARCE *v.* + -MENT.] **a.** *Building.* A plain flat set-off or rebate in a wall, or in a foundation or bank of earth. Also *transf.* a flat ledge projecting from the face of a rock. **b.** *Mining.* A ledge left projecting into a mine-shaft.

a. [**1398** in *Hist. Dunelm. Script. tres* (Surtees) p. clxxx, Erit eciam planus murus et in fundamento spissitudinis sive latitudinis duarum ulnarum, cum quatuor bonis et securis scarcementis.] **1501** DOUGLAS *Pal. Hon.* III. xvii, Skarsment, reprise, corbell, and battellingis. **1824** MACTAGGART *Gallovid. Encycl.*, *Scarcement*, a shelf amongst rocks; a shelf leaning out from the main face of a rock; on scarcements, build sea-fowl. **1833** LOUDON *Encycl. Archit.* §1073 The foundations to be laid with flat-bedded stones laid in regular courses, and to be taken in by regular scarsements (sets back) as shown in the sections. **1844** H. STEPHENS *Bk. of Farm* I. 170 The outside walls should be founded with stones..so laid, in reference to the line of foundation, as to form a scarcement of 6 inches on each side of the wall above them. **1899** MUNRO *Preh. Scot.* x. 393 A scarcement or ledge, nearly a foot in width, ran round the entire inner court.

b. **1839** URE *Dict. Arts* 971 If a strong bed of sandstone occurs, a scarcement of it is left projecting about 3 feet into the shaft. **1881** in RAYMOND *Mining Gloss.*

'**scarcen**, *v.* Now *dial.* (see E.D.D.). Also 6–7 **scarsen**. [f. SCARCE *a.* + -EN[5]. Cf. SCARCE *v.*]

1. *trans.* To make meagre or lean.

1594 CAREW *Huarte's Exam. Wits* (1616) 329 These three things..scarsen and drie vp the flesh, and their contraries, fatten and enlarge the same.

2. *intr.* To become scarce.

1803 W. TAYLOR in *Ann. Rev.* I. 387/2 If drafts abound on a particular place, they tend to sink in value. If drafts scarcen on a particular place, they tend to rise in value.

scarceness ('skɛəsnɪs). Now *rare.* Forms: see SCARCE *a.*; also α. 6 **charsnes**, *Sc.* **scaircenes**, 7 *Sc.* **scairsenesse**; β. 6 **skasenes**; γ. 5 **skarnes**, **scarnes**, 6–7 **scarnesse**. [f. SCARCE *a.* + -NESS.

The γ forms are not easy to account for, but they occur so frequently that it is difficult to regard them as due to misprints or scribal errors.]

†**1.** Niggardliness, stinginess. Of soil: infertility. *Obs.*

a **1300** *Cursor M.* 28628 Gain pride þat orisun mai rise, And fast gain flesli couetis, Almus gain scarsnes wit-stand. **1390** GOWER *Conf.* II. 286 And thus be cause of my scarsnesse Ye mai wel understonde and lieve That I schal noght the worse achieve The pourpos which is in my thoght. **1482** *Monk of Evesham* l. (Arb.) 100, Y knowe not onethe any prelate in thys dayes, that vsyd so grete scarsnes to her kynnys folke as sche me semyd dydde to her cosynis. **1509** BARCLAY *Ship of Fools* (1874) II. 97 Theyr scarsnes nowe is tournyd to couetyse. **1678** DRYDEN *All for Love* I. i, Ægypt is doom'd to be A Roman Province; and our plenteous Harvests Must then redeem the Scarceness of their Soil.

†**2. a.** Of diet: Scantiness, meagreness. **b.** Of persons: Abstemiousness. *Obs.*

c **1380** WYCLIF *Wks.* (1880) 316, & so scarsnesse of heere foode tellith to men þat þei ben hooly. **1451** CAPGRAVE *Life St. Gilbert* (E.E.T.S.) 97 What schuld we speke of his diete, with what scarsnesse of mete & drynk he was fed? **1526** *Pilgr. Perf.* (W. de W. 1531) 47 Wede them out by abstinence, chastite, hardnes in weryng, scarsnes in fedyng.

3. Deficient supply, scarcity.

1387 TREVISA *Higden* (Rolls) I. 251 Neuerþeles in Hannibals tyme þey were i-constreyned for to goo out of skarsnesse of knyȝtes. *c* **1450** tr. *De Imitatione* II. Contents (1893) 39 Of skarsenes of louers of the crosse of crist. **1508** FISHER *7 Penit. Ps.* cii. Wks. (1876) 173 For in so grete charsnes [ed. 1555 skaresnes] of ryghtwyse people, tyme is to shewe mercy vpon it. **1526** *Grete Herball* xci. (1529) F ij, Agaynst cough & scarcenesse of breth caused of cold take [etc.]. **1553** EDEN *Treat. New Ind.* (Arb.) 21 Yet hath it wheate and fleshe; but greate scarcenesse of wood. **1651** *Reg. Commission Gt. Assemb.* 3 Jan. (S.H.S.) III. 176 It shall be a shame for any in this land..becaus of the scairsenesse of men, to make use of such. **1812** G. CHALMERS *Dom. Econ. Gt. Brit.* 30 Nor, need you fear this scarceness of money.

β. **1538** STARKEY *England* I. ii. 47 Ther schal also sprynge therof grete penury and scasenes of al thyngys necessary for mannys lyfe.

γ. *c* **1400** *Apol. Loll.* (Camden) 109 Þat is, as þe Glose seiþ, þat I falle not in to forgeyting of euer lasting, for nede, or scarnes of passing þingis. **1535** COVERDALE *2 Sam.* iii. 29 And in the house of Ioab there ceasse not one to haue a renninge yssue..and to haue scarnesse of bred.

†**b.** *absol.* Scarcity of food or provisions. *Obs.*

1481 CAXTON *Godfrey* xciii. 144 And was grete suffrete and scarsenes in thoost. **1530** PALSGR. 266/1 Scarsnesse or hungre, *famine.* **1533–4** *Act 25 Hen. VIII*, c. 4 By reason whereof a great scarsenes and derthe doeth insue to the kinges subiectes. **1538** BALE *God's Promises* v. (1744) 26 A scarsenesse vii. years, or else iii. monthes exyle. **1555** EDEN *Decades* I. III. (Arb.) 78 They are content with soo lyttle, that in soo large a countrey, they haue rather superfluitie then scarsenes.

†**4.** Want, poverty. *Obs.*

α. **1535** COVERDALE *Ps.* lxvii. 6 He is the God y^{t}..bryngeth ye presoners out of captiuite in due season, but letteth ye rennagates continue in scarcenesse [So **1611**]. **1581** STYWARD *Mart. Discipl.* II. 162 [He] pittied in his heart the scarsenesse or pouertie of an expert man of warre.

β. **1528** ROY *Rede me* (Arb.) 79 They flye diligently all excesse Livynge in poverte and scasnes With smale dryncke and browne breade.

γ. *c* **1400** *Apol. Loll.* (Camden) 26 For wan þei prey for plentey, and pees,..he wil send hem skarnes & noiȝes. *c* **1650** *Earl of Westm.* 178 in *Percy's MS. Ball. & Rom.* (1867) I. 308 For thé haue knowen me in wele and woe, in neede, scarnesse & pouertye.

5. Uncommonness, rarity.

1672 BOYLE *Ess. Gems* ii. 113 The Rarity of transparent Gems,..and the great Value, which their Scarceness and mens Folly sets upon them. **1744** BERKELEY *Siris* §22 The folly of man rateth things by their scarceness. **1871** FREEMAN *Norm. Conq.* (1876) IV. xvii. 66, I have already spoken of the scarceness of Castles in England before the Norman Conquest.

scarch, obs. form of SCRATCH.

scarcht, obs. form of SCRAT, hermaphrodite.

scarcity ('skɛəsɪtɪ). Forms: 4–5 **scarsete(e**, **skarsete**, **-cete**, **scharsete**, (**scarestee**), 5 **scarcete**, **-ie**, 6 **-sety**, **-cety**, *Sc.* **skaircetie**, 7 **skarsety**; 4–5 **scarste(e**, 5 **skarste**; 4–6 **scarsitee**, 4–5 **-citee**, **-site**, **skarsytee**, 5 **skersytye**, **scarcyte**, **-sytie**, 5–6 **-cite**, **-scitie**, **-ssite**, 6 **skarsyte**, **-sitie**, **-citie**, **scacity**, 6–7 **scarcitie**, 5–7 **-sitie**, 6– **scarcity**. [a. ONF. *escarceté*, Central OF. *escharseté*, f. *esc(h)ars*: see SCARCE *a.* and -ITY.] The quality, condition, or fact of being scarce.

†**1.** Frugality, parsimony; niggardliness, stinginess, meanness. *Obs.*

1340–70 *Alex. & Dind.* 871 For almus-dede do ȝe non as ȝe demen alle, But skarsete & skaþe vn-skilfully fonden. *c* **1386** CHAUCER *Melib.* ¶634 For right as men blamen an Auaricious man by cause of his scarsetee and chyngerie, In the same wise [etc.]. **1484** CAXTON *Fables of Æsop* v. xii, Thow dyest for honger by cause that thy mayster gyueth the no mete by his grete scarcyte. **1531** ELYOT *Gov.* III. xxii, Althoughe I dispraysed nygarshyp and vicious scarsitee.

2. a. Insufficiency of supply; smallness of available quantity, number, or amount, in proportion to the need or demand.

13.. *K. Alis.* 54795 (Bodl. MS.), Wexe to bygge in þis Cite, Of whiche hij hadden scarsete. *c* **1450** *Brut* 436 And tho was..grete scarste of corne and of othir vitaill. **1571** *Act 13 Eliz.* c. 14 §1 The excessive pryce of Bowe Staves wch groweth principally by the Scarcitie of Bowe Staves brought into this Realme. **1599** NASHE *Lenten Stuffe* 26 Of leade and tinne is the most scarsity in forraine dominions, and plenty with vs. **1651** *Reg. Commission Grt. Assemb.* 5 Jan. (S.H.S.) III. 189 The scarsitie of ministers in Cathness and Orkney. **1760** JOHNSON *Idler* No. 103 ¶2 Value is more frequently raised by scarcity than by use. That which lay neglected when it was common, rises in estimation as its quantity becomes less. **1833** HT. MARTINEAU *Fr. Wines & Pol.* v. 80 Now tell me..whether you think it a good thing or not that there should be a scarcity of wine? **1881** W. NEWTON *Serm. Boys & Girls* 108 There was one year a great scarcity of rain.

b. *attrib.*: **scarcity value**, an enhanced value due to scarcity. So ***scarcity price***, ***rent***, etc.

1848 MILL *Pol. Econ.* III. iv. §6 (1876) 283 Things which cannot be increased *ad libitum* in quantity, and which therefore, if the demand goes beyond a certain amount, command a scarcity value. **1883** Scarcity value [see *monopoly value* s.v. MONOPOLY 8]. **1904** *Daily Chron.* 8 Oct. 3/3 The taxability of scarcity rents and profits. **1920** *Times* 5 June 15/3 Profits made on selling commodities at scarcity prices since then would escape the levy. **1936** J. M. KEYNES *Gen. Theory Employment* xxiv. 377 Our aim of depriving capital of its scarcity-value. **1972** 'G. BLACK' *Bitter Tea* (1973) x. 162 She was a blonde. They have a great time in the Orient, scarcity value.

¶ **c.** Comparative fewness, small number (of something not desirable). *rare.*

1663 GERBIER *Counsel* 93 The Hollanders..Vant of their scarcity of theeves..but attribute the same scarcity to that defence they..make against Theeves.

3. *absol.* Insufficiency of supply, in a community, of the necessaries of life, dearth. Also an instance of this, a period of scarcity, a dearth.

c **1450** *Brut* ccxxiv. 292 Þer folwyd in Engelond good chepe, and wonder grete plente of chaffaree, vitaile and marchaundice, and þere aȝens, honger, scrafte [? *read* scarste], mischif, and nede of money. **1584** POWEL *Lloyd's Cambria* 71 After such a famine there followed a Scarsitie in South Wales. **1686** J. SCOTT *Chr. Life* II. iv. §2 Wks. 1718 I. 271 All Hands are at work,..to store them [*sc.* apartments] all with Provision against the ensuing Time of Scarcity. **1781** GIBBON *Decl. & F.* xxxi. III. 220 That unfortunate city gradually experienced the distress of scarcity, and at length the horrid calamities of famine. **1801** *Farmer's Mag.* Jan. 23 It is short allowance alone that can then prevent a scarcity from ending in absolute famine. **1803** MALTHUS *Popul.* III. v. 399 These general reasonings have been strikingly confirmed during the late scarcities. **1908** *Q. Rev.* July 224 Lesser visitations of scarcity have occurred in various provinces.

†**4.** Scantiness (of diet). *Obs.*

1398 TREVISA *Barth. De P.R.* VI. xx. (1495) 207 In scarsetee of dyetes seke men fayllen moost. **1526** *Pilgr. Perf.* (W. de W. 1531) 82 b, Scarcite in meate, and the bely alway somwhat hungry, is..praysed.

†**5.** Deficiency, shortcoming. *Obs.*

c **1380** WYCLIF *Wks.* (1880) 364 In full euydence and open tooknynge þat god takiþ þis ordenance in his chirche as full sufficient, and in no wise fawtye in scarste or excesse þer-of. *c* **1392** CHAUCER *Compl. Venus* 80 And ekke to me it is right gret penaunce Sith ryme in englisshe haþe suche skarsytee [*v.rr.* scarstee, scarestee, etc.] To folowen word by word þe curyosytee Of Graunsone flour of hem þat make in ffraunce. **1412–20** LYDG. *Troy Bk.* II. 168 Preying þe reder, wher any word myssit, Causyng þe metre to be halte or lame, For to correcte, to saue me fro blame: Late hym nat wayte after coryouste, Syth þat in ryme ynglysch hath skarsete [*v.r.* skersytye]. *c* **1450** —— *Secrees* 872 Set in A meene of prudent governaunce, That ther be nouthir skarsete nor excesse, But a ryght Rewle of Attemperaunce.

†**6.** The condition of being slenderly or inadequately provided (const. *of*). Also *absol.*, straitened condition with regard to means of living or comfort; penury, hardship. *Obs.*

1387 TREVISA *Higden* (Rolls) III. 465 Þerfore it is good to lyve in good rule and in plente, and nouȝt in streiȝtnesse, scarsite, and meschief [*Caxton*, in strayte skarste and meschyef]. **1528** Roy *Rede me* (Arb.) 93 Soche poverte is plente, For by it avoydynge scacite All welthynes they have. **1596** Dalrymple tr. *Leslie's Hist. Scot.* I. II. 145 This king commandet to bring vpe the 3outh wt al hardnes and skaircetie. **1599** Hakluyt *Voy.* I. 599 Gunne-powder, whereof they were in great skarcitie. **1607** Shaks. *Timon* II. ii. 234 When he was poore, Imprison'd, and in scarsitie of Friends, I cleer'd him with fiue Talents. **1610** —— *Temp.* IV. i. 116 Scarcity and want shall shun you, Ceres' blessing so is on you.

7. In full, ***root of scarcity***: the mangel-wurzel. Also *scarcity plant, root*.

For the origin of the name see MANGEL-WURZEL.

1787 J. Woodforde *Diary* 29 June (1926) II. 330 Sr. Willm Jernegan sent me by Mr. Custance a Treatise on the Plant called Scarcity Root. **1787, 1789** [see ROOT *sb.*[1] 3b]. **1800** [see MANGEL-WURZEL β]. **1803** *A. Hunter's Georg. Ess.* III. 109 Another new article which has been very lately introduced, is the Mangel Wurzel, or Scarcity Plant. **1856** A. Gray *Man. Bot.* (1860) 367 *Beta vulgaris*, the Beet, with its varieties, the Scarcity and Mangel Wurtzel.

'scarcy, *a. Obs.* exc. *dial.* (see E.D.D.). [f. SCARCE *a.* + -Y.] = SCARCE.

1677 Plot *Oxfordsh.* 51 Now 'tis so scarcy, that 'tis a common thing to sell it by weight.

†**scare**, *sb.*[1] *Obs.* [a. ONF. *escar*, var. of *escarn* (Central OF. *eschar(n)*, vbl. sb. f. *escarnir* to deride. Cf. SCORN *sb.* and *v.* The final *e* may be the ending of the dative case.] Scorn, derision, contempt.

c **1205** Lay. 5835 Þanne we heonne i-funde farren ure frenden to scare. *Ibid.* 20746 Iswenched us sære folke to scare. *Ibid.* 29548 He talde heom godes leore and duden him to scare.

scare (skɛə(r)), *sb.*[2] Also 6–7 **scarre**, 7 **skar(e**, 9 *dial.* **scar**. [f. SCARE *v.*]

†**1.** Fear, dread. *Obs.*

a **1400–50** *Alexander* 4731 And þai for skere of þe skrike into þe schaw fledd. **1578** T. N. tr. *Conq. W. India* 21 They would sell him no provision for scare of the Governour Velasques. **1616** T. Scot *Philomythie* I. (ed. 2) C4b, The night is come, the Shepheard soundly sleeps As he had wont, no skar his conscience keeps.

2. An act of scaring or a state of being scared; a sudden fright or alarm; *esp.* a state of general or public alarm occasioned by baseless or exaggerated rumours; *occas.* in generalized use, panic.

a **1548** Hall *Chron., Rich. III*, 39 They were sodaynely amased and striken with a soden scare. **1600** Holland *Livy* VIII. xxxvii. 308 At Rome there happened a scare by night, which raised euery man so suddainely out of their first sleepe. *c* **1610** Sir J. Melvil *Mem.* (1683) 70 This I said by the way to give her a little scare from marriage. **1664** Pepys *Diary* 25 Nov., God knows this is only a scare to the Parliament, to make them give the more money. **1721** Hearne *Collect.* (O.H.S.) VII. 280 He was seiz'd upon the Scare of the Popish Plot. **1844** G. W. Kendall *Santa Fé Exped.* I. 97 Nothing can exceed the grandeur of the scene when a large *cavallada*, or drove of horse, takes a 'scare'. **1881** *Standard* 4 Jan., We are evidently to have another Fenian scare. **1887** Fenn *Master Cerem.* xiv, You did give me a scare. **1898** *Westm. Gaz.* 22 Feb. 8/1 The time to buy stocks is when prices are depressed by scare.

†**3.** Something that scares or frightens; *spec.* a scarecrow. *Obs.*

1530 Palsgr. 265/2 Scarre to scar crowes. **1607** Markham *Caval.* II. (1617) 12 When you make an old ridden horse lead you the way where there bee manie Scarres and Boggards. **1620** —— *Farew. Husb.* (1625) 96 The nearer that these Blinkes or Scarres come to the ground.. so much the better it is, lest the fowle finding a way to creep under them, begin not to respect them. **1824** Loudon *Encycl. Gard.* (ed. 2) §1483 *Engines of alarm*, or scares, are the bell or gong alarm for man; and the rattle-engine driven by hand, or a small wind-engine for herds. **1828** M'Dowall *Poems* 71 Rather hold him up a bug-bear or scare.

4. *attrib.* and *Comb.*: **scare-buying** *U.S.* = *panic buying* s.v. PANIC *sb.*[2] 3b; **scare-head, -heading**, a heading to a column of newspaper matter written in extravagant language to produce a 'scare'; hence as *v. trans.*, to furnish with a scare-head; to display as a scare-headline; **'scare-headed** *ppl. a.*; **scare-line**, a sensational announcement upon a newspaper poster; similarly in ***scare-headline, -letter, -novel, -politics, -report, -story***, etc.; **scare-string**, an arrangement of twine on and about seed-plots and fruit-trees to frighten away birds; **scare tactic**, a stratagem or ruse which seeks to manipulate public reaction by the exploitation of fear; usu. *pl.*

1944 *Sun* (Baltimore) 23 Nov. 15/3 The sharply restricted supply of cotton goods.. comes at a time when so-called '*scare' buying of such commodities is in boom proportions. **1959** *Wall St. Jrnl.* 4 May 1/1 Steel customers have been buying heavily for weeks, in anticipation of a strike... This 'scare buying'.. boosted steel-making to a scheduled 94·4% of the industry's rated capacity last week. **1887** *Courier-Jrnl.* (Louisville, Kentucky) 15 Feb. 6/4 The '*scare' head which follows.. is an evidence that the country paper tries hard to keep pace with the times and its metropolitan contemporary. **1888** *Pall Mall G.* 29 Oct. 3/1 A Japanese newspaper.. has no such thing as head lines or scare heads. **1894** Stead *If Christ came* 104 The sensationalists who manufacture scare heads for the Chicago papers. **1902** F. Norris *Responsibilities of Novelist* (1903) 300 The name of the leading lady or leading man is 'scare-headed' [on theatre bills]. **1911** H. S. Harrison *Queed* xviii. 219 The.. penny evening paper.. scare-headed a jaundiced account of the affair. **1926** *Scribner's Mag.* Sept. 251/1 If he is at all impressionable, a glance at the scare-heads will utterly ruin what otherwise might have been a successful day. **1951** E. Paul *Springtime in Paris* v. 95 Metal workers were uneasy, having been stamped with scareheads against the Marshall Plan. **1971** *Sci. Amer.* May 10/2 Professor Reuterdahl's recent article in the *Dearborn Independent* is given its real place by the scare-head of the cover, which asks, in 3/4-inch letters, 'Is Einstein a Plagiarist?'. **1889** W. D. Howells *Hazard of New Fortunes* II. 281 He read.. the deeply *scare-headed story of Conrad's death. **1894** *Daily News* 15 Mar. 5/8 The men who manufacture *scare headings for the paper saw the chance, and they worked up a great sensation. **1892** J. Kirkland *Story of Chicago* I. xxxii. 381 The newspapers blazed with what are technically called '*scare headlines'. **1912** Kipling *Uses of Reading* in *Book of Words* (1928) 87 The other made bad worse by shouting what was no better than a newspaper scare head-line. **1907** *Westm. Gaz.* 25 Mar. 9/3 When we members want to stimulate our jaded senses we go into the street and read the *scare-lines on some of the posters. **1960** *Guardian* 11 Apr. 1/1 Rumours circulated.. that the Government might introduce martial law, but this appeared to have been purely a *scare story. **1977** P. Johnson *Enemies of Society* vii. 94 The technique of the lobby is to put out a scare-story, and then move on quickly to a fresh one when scientific investigation proves the first one unfounded. **1979** *Time* 8 Jan. 40/1 The scare stories are based on phony evidence or plain prejudice. **1889** Pask *Eyes of Thames* 151 The young birds pay little heed to the *scare strings, and pull up the seedlings to their heart's content. **1967** *Punch* 8 Nov. 719/1 This alleged address from Zinoviev, the President of the Comintern.. left an *Angst* about Tory *scare-tactics from which Transport House has never recovered. **1973** *Black Panther* 17 Mar. 8/1 (*caption*) Boxes of poisoned lettuce have had to be destroyed. This is no 'scare tactic', it is for real. **1976** *Survey* Summer-Autumn 191 The slickers in the Pentagon are using their annual scare tactics in support of bigger budgets.

†**scare**, *sb.*[3] *Obs. rare.* See also SCAR *sb.*[4] [a. F. *scare*, ad. L. *scarus*.] = SCARUS.

1706 Phillips (ed. Kersey), *Scare*, a sort of Fish. **1803** Shaw *Gen. Zool.* IV. 488 Scare Labrus.. Labrus Scarus.

scare (skɛə(r)), *sb.*[4] *Golf.* [orig. Sc. dial., a joint or splice (e.g. of a fishing-rod: see E.D.D.), a. ON. *skǫr* (:—**skaru*:—OTeut. **skarā*).] The part of a golf club where the head joins the handle.

1881 Forgan *Golfer's Handbk.* 35 *Scare*, the narrow part of the club-head by which it is glued to the handle. **1897** *Encycl. Sport* I. 473/1 (Golf) *Scare*, the part of the club where the head and shaft are joined.

scare (skɛə(r)), *a. rare.* [modernized form of SCAR *a.*, after SCARE *v.*] Timid, frightened.

1885–94 R. Bridges *Eros & Psyche* Dec. iii, But ere Her tale was done resumed his manner scare, Ran down, and on his way in darkness kept.

scare (skɛə(r)), *v.* Pa. t. and pa. pple. **scared** (skɛəd). Forms: α. 3–6 **skerre**, 4 *Sc.* **sckir**; β. 6–7 **scarre**, 5–7 **skar**, 5–8 **scar**, 6–7 **skarre**, 7 *Sc.* **scarr, skarr**, 7–9 *Sc.* **scaur**; *Pa. t.* and *pa. pple.* 4 *Sc.* **schard**, 4, 6–9 **scarred**, 5 **scharid**, 5–7 **skard**, 6 **scard**, *Sc.* **skarred, skarrit**, 9 *dial.* **scart**; γ. 4–5 **scere**, 5 **skere**, 6 **skeare**; 9 *dial.* (and *U.S. vulgar*) **skear, skeer**; δ. 4–5 **skayre**, 5–7 **skare**, 6– **scare**; *Pa. pple.* 7 **skaerd**. [ME. *skerre*, a. ON. *skirra* (Icel. only in phr. *skirra vandrædum* to avoid strife, and refl. *skirra-sk* with accus. to shrink from; but cf. Norw. *skjerra*, Sw. dial. *skjarra* to scare), f. *skiarr* (:—**skerro-*) shy, timid, startled: see SCAR *a.*

The ME. *skerre* normally became *skarre*; the form *scar*, now dialectal, is therefore regular. The phonology of the δ type (represented by the mod. standard form), and of the γ type (represented by the dialectal *skeer*) is obscure.]

1. a. *trans.* To frighten, terrify.

α. *c* **1200** *Ormin* 676 He [*sc.* the devil] wile himm færenn, 3iff he ma33, & skerrenn mare & mare. *c* **1375** *Sc. Leg. Saints* xxv. (*Julian*) 595 Þat takine þe feyndis sckiris, & of þar mycht & purpos merrys.

β. **1508** Dunbar *Flyting* 214 Cum thow agane to skar us with thy strais, We sall gar scale our sculis all the to scorne. **1568** Grafton *Chron.* II. 90 King Richard so scarred the French kinges host, that he tooke the kinges Sumpter horse and parte of his treasure. **1606** Shaks. *Tr. & Cr.* v. x. 21 There is a word will.. Scarre Troy out of it selfe. **1671** Flavel *Fount. Life* xi. 31 When they should find themselves more skarred than hurt by His Threats. **1721** Ramsay *Concl.* 6 Daft, giddy thing! to.. spang o'er dykes that scar the blate. **1901** G. Douglas *Ho. Green Shutters* 279 He never met what scaured him!

γ. *a* **1400–50** *Alexander* 3865 Þan comes þare-out creuesses of manykins hewis, Scorpions þaim to scere & scalid neddirs. *c* **1440** *Promp. Parv.* 457/2 Skeryn' a-wey, *abigo*. **1558** Phaer *Æneid* Y 4b, Now gastly sights mens hearts to skeare, In forgyng fire they shope. **1845** Judd *Margaret* II. v. (1874) 254 Don't be so despit skeered, Mr. Hadlock.

δ. **1591** Shaks. *1 Hen. VI*, II. ii. 28 My selfe, as farre as I could well discerne,.. Am sure I scar'd the Dolphin and his Trull. **1596** Warner *Alb. Eng.* XII. lxix. (1612) 291 At first she feares, but lastly finds the Armor was vn-man'd: When skaerd, and cheerd, with Dorcas she did enter, theare at hand. *a* **1639** W. Whateley *Prototypes* I. xi. (1640) 107 Let not every shew of danger skare you. **1686** tr. *Chardin's Trav. Persia* 165 Such dreadful Precipices, that scar'd me to look down. **1700** T. Brown *Amusem. Ser. & Com.* 37, I that am always more scared at the sight of a Sergeant, or Bayliff, than at the Devil and all his Works. **1738** Gray *Propertius* III. 44 The triple dog that scares the shadowy kind. **1810** Scott *Lady of L.* II. xxx, A thousand villages in flames Shall scare the slumbers of King James! **1825** J. Neal *Bro. Jonathan* I. 104 Ye wasn't skeered, nor nothin' was ye tho'? *a* **1839** Praed *Poems* (1864) II. 12 Who scared me with that Gorgon face? **1864** Blackmore *Clara Vaughan* (1872) 50 Turning to me, 'Doon'e be skeared, Miss Clerer.' **1875** Jowett *Plato* (ed. 2) V. 505 Such practices.. scare the multitude out of their wits.

†**b.** ? To alarm, put on the alert (a sentry). *Obs.*

13.. *E.E. Allit. P.* B. 838 In grete flokkez of folk, þay fallen to his 3atez, As a scowte wach scarred, so þe asscry rysed. *a* **1400** *Morte Arth.* 2468 Discoueris of schottemene, and skyrmys a lyttille; Skayres thaire skottefers, and theire skowtte-waches. *c* **1425** *Cast. Persev.* 1907 in *Macro Plays* 134 Schapyth now 3oure scheldys schene, 3ene skallyd skoutis for to skerre up-on 3one grene grese!

c. To frighten away, drive off. Now chiefly with adv., exc. with reference to keeping off birds from corn, etc.

c **1400** *Destr. Troy* 13404 This Ascatus with skathe skerrit of his rewme Pelleus. *c* **1450** *Mankind* 800 in *Macro Plays* 29 He skaryth vs with a bales; we may no lengere tary. **1573** Tusser *Husb.* (1878) 125 Keepe cart gap weele, scare hog from wheele. **1641** Milton *Reform.* I. 4 Being scarr'd from thence by the pangs, and gripes of a boyling conscience. **1660** F. Brooke tr. *Le Blanc's Trav.* 237 They were soon scared away, when we assured them we were Christians. **1785** Burns *Death & Dr. Hornbook* xiii, Mony a scheme in vain's been laid To stap or scaur me. **1816** Scott *Antiq.* xxvi, Ou, that wad be the lights and the noise that scarr'd us awa. **1851** D. Jerrold *St. Giles* xii. 114 A chap, with rags on him, not fit to scare birds in a bean-field.

d. scare out, up. orig. and chiefly *U.S.* To frighten (game) out of cover. Hence *fig.* to bring to light, to discover; to procure, obtain, 'rustle up'. *colloq.*

1846 *Spirit of Times* 25 Apr. 97/1 He is also to send us the rattles of the biggest snake ever scared up in 'Old Norf Caline'. **1852** H. C. Watson *Nights in Block-House* 169 Ad was equal to two or three common men in scarin' up and shootin' red-skins. **1853** *Putnam's Mag.* Sept. 304/2 A great man.. does not make the noodles and nobodies that he may scare up any where, his chief agents. **1857** *The States* (*Washington*) (Bartlett 1860), A very useful bag in a family, in scaring up eggs for breakfast. **1862** Lowell *Biglow P.* Ser. II. iii, Where can you scare up names like them among your mudsill folks? **1874** Long *Amer. Wild-fowl Shooting* 142 We probably won't scare out any very large batches of ducks. **1890** *Stock Grower & Farmer* 1 Feb. 4/2 A country the like of which can not be 'scared up' in many thousands of miles travel. **1913** J. London *Night-Born* 262 Los Angeles must be on the dink when this is the best you can scare up. **1922** Galsworthy *Loyalties* II. ii. 71 Let's cut it and get out to Nairobi. I can scare up the money for that. **1940** *New Yorker* 13 Jan. 31/2 A young woman who had somehow contrived to scare up a permit to leave the country. **1952** J. Jones *From Here to Eternity* xii. 145 Maybe I can scare you up some [work]. **1961** *Listener* 2 Nov. 738/1 Professor Ford has always managed to scare up a few distinguished contributors. **1976** H. Nielsen *Brink of Murder* ii. 21 Why don't you relax.. and then we'll scare up some dinner.

†**2.** *intr.* To take fright; to be scared (at). *Obs.*

β. **13..** *E.E. Allit P.* B. 598 Bot of þe dome of þe douþe for dedez of schame He is so skoymus of þat skaþe, he scarrez bylyue. *c* **1470** Henryson *Mor. Fab.* IX. (*Wolf & Fox*) iii, I am rad, gif thay me se on far, That at my figure beist and bird will skar. **1500–20** Dunbar *Poems* xxx. 6 With him and with his abbeit bayth I skarrit, Lyk to ane man that with a gaist wes marrit. *a* **1605** Montgomerie *Devot. Poems* vi. 62 Then prayers, almesdeids, and tearis, Vhilks 3it to skorne 3ee skantly skar, Sall mair availl than jaks and spearis. **1629** Sir W. Mure *True Crucifixe* 1775 Thou must not skarre vpon thy Soares to looke, To read thy dittay in that sacred Booke. **1682** Peden *Lord's Trumpet* 30 Scar not at the cross for it is the way to the crown. **1710** in Calderwood *Dying Testim.* (1806) 157 What ails poor harlot Scotland to scar so much at that noble gift. **1721** Wodrow *Hist. Suff. Ch. Scot.* (1829) I. I. iv. 358 He cried with a loud voice, 'I beseech you .. not to scar at sufferings for the interests of Christ.'

δ. **1699** T. Boston *Art of Man-fishing* (1900) 52 Every parish will scare at thee as a monster of men. **1731** —— *Mem.* (1899) 48 Being everywhere scared at by some. **1869** 'Mark Twain' *Innoc. Abr.* 440 This creature has scared at everything he has seen to-day.

3. To take a scare (see SCARE *sb.*[2]); to be alarmed by rumours or the like. Freq. in negative, esp. with *easily* or *easy*.

1900 *Academy* 8 Sept. 194/1 The big depositors wouldn't scare. **1941** *Sun* (Baltimore) 4 Jan. 6/2 Whatever else they do or fail to do, the Irish don't scare easily. **1951** 'M. Spillane' *One Lonely Night* iv. 61 They're the kind of people who scare easily. **1967** O. Ruhen in *Coast to Coast 1965–6* 192 The horse won't scare, but take it easy. **1972** *Village Voice* (N.Y.) 1 June 5/2 'We don't scare easy,' his cousin said as I went out the door.

4. *Comb.* with an object-sb., forming sbs. with the sense 'one who or something which scares', as ***scare-bear, -beggar, -bullfinch, -christian, -goose, -sinner, sleep***.

1843 *P. Parley's Ann.* IV. 216 Logs hung vibrating from the branches of trees, and other *scare-bears. **1806** *Sporting Mag.* XXVII. 186 He.. is the *scare-beggar of the parish. **1849** *Zoologist* VII. 2568 A stuffed cat.. has been found a capital *scare-bullfinch. **1772** Nugent tr. *Hist. Friar Gerund* I. 455 Whom he esteemed the most redoubted *Scare-christian that dignified the pulpit in that age. **1887** R. Garnett *Carlyle* iv. 67 Letters poured in, countermanding subscriptions until the *scaregoose should be removed. **1765** Sterne *Tr. Shandy* VII. vii, Do stop that death-looking, long-striding scoundrel of a *scare-sinner, who is posting after me. **1817** Kirby & Sp. *Entomol.* (1818) II. 401 The great lantern-fly.. from its noise in the evening .. is called *Scare-sleep by the Dutch in Guiana.

scare, obs. form of SHEAR.

†**'scare-babe.** *Obs.* Also 7 **scarbabe, scarrebabe.** [f. SCARE *v.* + BABE *sb.*] Something to frighten children; a bugbear, bogy.

a **1591** H. Smith *Serm.* (1594) 279 Therfore take heed of hell, for Purgatorie is but a scarre babe. *a* **1606** *Wily*

Beguiled (1623) E 2, Ile.. come like some Hob-goblin.. And like a Scarbabe make him take his legges. **1621** A. CAVE *Serm.* 16 They become scarre-babes and bugbeares to their innocent neighbours.

attrib. **1594** *Epit. of 'Old Scarlett' in Peterb. Cath.*, A Scarebabe mighty voice with visage grim.

So †**'scare-bairn.**

1681 W. ROBERTSON *Phraseol. Gen.* (1693) 495 An Hagg or scare-barn, a bug-bear to frighten children.

†**'scare-bug,** *sb. Obs.* Also 6 scare-bugge, 7 scarbug, scarbugg(e, skar-bugg. [f. SCARE *sb.*[2] + BUG *sb.*[1]] = BUGBEAR.

1583 GOLDING *Calvin on Deut.* cxciv. 1204 All those which nowadayes doe name themselues Bishops and Prelates, are but scarebugs set vp by the diuell. **1601** DENT *Pathw. Heaven* (1603) 345 For sinne is no scar-bugge. **1618** S. WARD *Jethro's Just. Peace* 18 These complements without the substance are but empty gulls and scarbuggs of maiestie. **1642** D. ROGERS *Naaman* 536 Haue made his solemne Commands, idle scare-bugs, and haue turned them into shadowes. **1657** TRAPP *Comm. Ps.* lii. 5 Think not that these things are spoken on *in terrorem*, for a Scarebug, for they shall all be surely fulfilled upon thee.

attrib. **1616** *Manifest. Abp. of Spalato's Motives* 5 Surely (in the scare-bug feares, which from my tender yeeres haue possessed mee) I haue held them detestable.

†**'scare-bug,** *v. Obs.* Also 6 scarrebugge. [f. prec.] *trans.* To frighten with idle terrors.

1594 NASHE *Unfort. Trav.* I. 1 b, Now thinkest thou that I.. can be scare-bugd with the plague? **1596** —— *Saffron Walden* 134 She.. scarrebugges me with a Comedie, which shee hath scrawld and scribeld vp against mee.

scarecrow ('skɛəkrəʊ), *sb.* Forms: 6 scarre-crowe, skar-crowe, 6–7 scarrecrow, scarcrow(e, 7 skar-crow, 7- scarecrow (formerly often written with hyphen). [f. SCARE *v.* + CROW *sb.*[1]]

1. A person employed in scaring birds.

1553 T. WILSON *Rhet.* 47 b, Plaie as young boyes or scarre crowes do, whiche showte in the open and plaine feldes at all aventures hittie missie. **1908** E. C. PALMER in *Daily Mail* 11 Apr. 6/5 He is not ashamed of being a scarecrow.

2. a. A device for frightening birds from growing crops, usually a figure of a man dressed in old and ragged clothes.

1592 *Nobody & Somebody* H 4, Let me be hangd vp sunning in the ayre, And made a scarr-crow. **1637** HEYWOOD *Royall King* III. ii, Wots thou who's returnd, The unthrift Bonvile, ragged as a scarre-crow. **1726** DE FOE *Hist. Devil* II. iii. (1840) 202 We set the devil up like a scarecrow to frighten children and old women. **1762** LLOYD *Nightingale* Poems 96 Critics, who like the scarecrows stand Upon the poet's common land. **1874** GEO. ELIOT *Coll. Breakf. P.* 427 Can you.. Frighten the blind with scarecrows? **1887** BESANT *The World went* xx, No scarecrow in the fields ever had such clothes.

b. *fig.* Something (not really formidable) that frightens or is intended to frighten: a 'bogy'.

1589 *Marprel. Theses Martin.* D ij, All the bishops of England are too weake to deale with a scarre-crowe, that hath but the name of reuerend Martin written vppon it. **1591** SHAKS. *1 Hen. VI*, I. iv, Here, sayd they, is the Terror of the French, The Scar-Crow that affrights our Children so. **1642** HALES *Schism* 1 Heresie and Schisme as they are commonly used, are two Theological scar-crows. **1686** T. BROWN *To Ld. Chancellor* Wks. 1709 III. III. 99 So grisly Comets from the Dung-hills rise, Those upstart Scare-crows of the wond'ring Skies. **1746** WESLEY *Princ. Methodist* 23, I should wonder if the Scarecrow of sinless Perfection was not brought in some way or other. **1812** *Examiner* 12 Oct. 653/2 That idle scarecrow,—the Bribery Act. **1870** THORNBURY *Tour round Eng.* I. iv. 89 What a scarecrow to a blushing curate that stiff old lady.. must have been.

c. *Mil. slang.* Used in the war of 1939–45, to designate weapons or manœuvres which had a purely deterrent effect (see quots.).

1943 T. DUDLEY-GORDON *Coastal Command at War* iv. 41 This was the squadron.. which flew the Scarecrow Control... No one knows how many times a U-Boat captain was forced to keep submerged because a Tiger Moth, which *might* be dangerous, was doing a scarecrow on him. **1952** M. TRIPP *Faith is Windsock* ii. 41 Two daylight attacks on Solingen... Gigantic blobs of oily smoke hung in the sky... It was their first experience of the German terror weapon, the scarecrow. **1966** L. MIALL *Richard Dimbleby, Broadcaster* 39 A great gush of flame and smoke showed the bursting of a 'scarecrow', the oddity designed by the Germans to simulate a heavy bomber being shot down, and so to put any of our less experienced pilots off their stroke.

3. A person whose appearance causes ridicule; a lean, gaunt figure; one who resembles a scarecrow in his dress, 'a guy.'

1590 SPENSER *F.Q.* II. iii. 7 Thereat the Scarcrow wexed wondrous prowd. **1596** SHAKS. *1 Hen. IV*, IV. ii. 41. **1625** B. JONSON *Staple of N.* IV. iv, A true Souldier.. runnes those vertuous hazards, that this Scarre-crow Cannot endure to heare of. **1672** MARVEL *Reh. Transp.* I. 50 You never saw such a Scarcrow as he makes him. **1711** ADDISON *Spect.* No. 9 ¶2 In Opposition to this Society [of Fat-men], there sprung up another composed of Scare-Crows and Skeletons. **1749** BERKELEY *Word to the Wise* Wks. III. 441 People well fed, and well clad, instead of famished, ragged scarecrows. **1838** DICKENS *Nich. Nick.* viii, In front of the schoolmaster's desk, half a dozen scarecrows out at knees and elbows. **1874** L. STEPHEN *Hours in Library* (1892) I. v. 192 A grim and ugly scarecrow, on whom every buffoon may break his jest. **1881** W. S. GILBERT *Foggerty's Fairy* 11, I was sorry to see a fine young man throw himself away upon such a scarecrow. **1932** E. MUSPRATT *Wild Oats* v. 96 He was a great gaunt scarecrow, bent and crippled by disease. **1959** I. & P. OPIE *Lore & Lang. Schoolch.* ix. 169 Thin people inspire almost as many names and jokes as fat people, but.. the names.. are merely descriptive, as:.. scarecrow, scraggy, skin and bones.

†**4.** An alleged name of the Black Tern, *Hydrochelidon nigra*, and of the Hooded Crow, *Corvus cornix. Obs.*

a **1672** WILLUGHBY & RAY *Ornith.* (1676) 269 Larus niger Gesneri... The Scar-crow. **1802–33** *Montagu's Ornith. Dict.* 258 Hoody, Dun Crow, Scare Crow.

5. *attrib.* (quasi-*adj.*)

1602 *2nd Pt. Return fr. Parnass.* I. vi. 498 Hang him,.. That when the cloud of his inuention breakes, Cannot out-cracke the scarr-crow thunderbolt. **1644** MILTON *Divorce* Introd. 4 The greatest burden in the world is superstition; not only of Ceremonies in the Church, but of imaginary and scar-crow sins at home. **1663** COWLEY *Verses & Ess.*, *To Royal Soc.* iii, The Orchard's open now, and free; Bacon has broke the Scar-crow Deitie. **1761** WESLEY *Jrnl.* 19 Feb. (1827) III. 40 Many may forget my scarecrow name. **1837** LOCKHART *Scott* VI. 68 He was a scarecrow figure—attired much in the fashion of the *strugglers*. **1894** JEAFFRESON *Bk. Recoll.* II. xxv. 223 Wearing a scarecrow hat.. in his rural walks.

Hence **'scarecrowish, 'scarecrowy** *adjs.*

1862 THORNBURY *Turner* I. 277 All through the 'Liber the figures are admirable, except the larger ones in the home pastoral scenes, and they are rather weak, sketchy and scarecrowy. **1892** MAR. NORTH *Recoll. Happy Life* I. 94, I found his worship in an extra scarecrowish costume.

scarecrow ('skɛəkrəʊ), *v.* Also 6 scarrecrow. [f. SCARECROW *sb.*]

†**1.** *trans.* To frighten, as with a scarecrow. *Obs.*

1593 G. HARVEY *Pierce's Super.* 69 That old acquaintance, ..is neither lullabied with thy sweete Papp, nor scarre-crowed with thy sower hatchet. **1675** DUFFETT *Mock Tempest* I. 42 Yea, I will scare-crow thee, I will top and scourge thee.

2. To dot and disfigure as scarecrows do.

1853 *Fraser's Mag.* XLVIII. 471 Yet wilder specimens of the human race.. here and there scare-crow the broad, sadly picturesque expanse.

scared (skɛəd), *ppl. a.* [f. SCARE *v.* + -ED[1].] Frightened, startled.

1725 POPE *Odyss.* XI. 782 Sad groans and dismal sounds Stun my scar'd ears. **1802** COLERIDGE *Picture* 6 Hurrying along the drifted forest-leaves, The scared snake rustles. **1833** J. H. NEWMAN in *Lyra Apost.* lxxx. (1836) 96 Let your words be strong, Your cry be loud, till each scared boaster flies. **1907** A. C. BENSON *Altar Fire* 266 The Master has a very scared and dull pupil alas!

'scare-devil. [f. SCARE *v.* + DEVIL *sb.*]

†**1.** A name for plants of the genus *Hypericum*, formerly supposed to possess the power of curing persons possessed with devils. *Obs. rare*$^{-1}$.

1751 LAVINGTON *Enthus. Meth. & Papists* III. (1754) 178 Such is the herb Hypericum, called also St. John's-Wort, and Scare-Devil.

2. *dial.* A name for the Swift (*Cypselus apus*), perh. with reference to its dark colour and rapid flight.

1831 *Montagu's Ornith. Dict.* 462 Skeer devil.. Skir devil. A name for the swift. **1886** ELWORTHY *W. Som. Word-bk.*, *Scare-devil*, the swift.

scaredly ('skɛədlɪ), *adv.* [f. SCARED *ppl. a.* + -LY[2].] In a scared manner.

1901 G. B. SHAW *Devil's Disciple* I, in *Three Plays for Puritans* 18 To Essie. Essie: did you say amen? *Essie* (scaredly). No. **1978** G. VAUGHAN *Belgrade Drop* xi. 74 Savka said suddenly, scaredly: 'I hope to God you're sure!'

scaredy-cat ('skɛədɪkæt). *slang.* [f. SCARED *ppl. a.* + -Y[6] + CAT *sb.*[1]] A timorous person, a coward; = *fraidy cat* s.v. 'FRAID *a.* Also as *adj.*, scared. Also *ellipt.*, as *scaredy*.

1933 D. PARKER *After Such Pleasures* (1934) 86 It's so nice to meet a man who isn't scaredy-cat about catching my beri-beri. **1948** D. BALLANTYNE *Cunninghams* 173 Sydney called them scaredy-cats because they wouldn't run like he had. **1959** I. & P. OPIE *Lore & Lang. Schoolch.* x. 185 The boy.. who will not take part in a prank.. is a 'scaredy', a 'scare-baby'. **1965** 'LAUCHMONEN' *Old Thom's Harvest* xii. 149 You can play hard-to-get but don't look so scaredy-cat. **1980** H. R. F. KEATING *Murder of Maharajah* iii. 57 You know your mother, always was a scaredy-cat.

†**'scare-fire.** *Obs.* Also 6 skarifyer, 7 scar-, scarre-, skare-, skar-. [Prob. a corruption of SCATHEFIRE, as if f. SCARE *sb.*[2]] A sudden conflagration.

1572 *Nottingham Rec.* (1889) IV. 143 Payd to Thomas Clarke for his payns at the skarifyer at Mr. Burtons. **1600** HOLLAND *Livy* XXVI. xxvii. 604 These speeches.. were interrupted and stayed by occasion of a Scare-fire, that began in sundrie places together about the Forum. **1637** POCKLINGTON *Altare Christ.* 132 We reject private Masses ..to be a remedy against Pestilence, inundation, tempest, scare-fire, &c. **1648** HERRICK *Hesper.*, *Bell-man*, From noise of Scare-fires rest ye free, From Murders Benedicitie. **1684** S. G. *Angl. Spec.* 479 Of Manufactures, the greatest is the Engine, for quenching of Scare-fires.

fig. **1642** FULLER *Holy & Prof. St.* III. xxv. 230 The Priests melted mens hearts into Charity with the Scare-fire of Purgatory.

†**'scare-fly.** *Obs.* [f. SCARE *v.* + FLY *sb.*]

1. One who drives away flies: used to render Gr. ἀπόμυιος as an epithet of certain deities. *rare*$^{-1}$.

1587 GOLDING *De Mornay* xxiii. 402 And hereof it came that the Chananites called their Belzebub, and the Greekes their Iupiter, by the name of Scarefly.

2. A device for frightening away flies.

1862 *All Year Round* 13 Sept. 9 An ingenious Florentine gentleman has communicated to the world, a scare-fly.

scareful ('skɛəfʊl), *a.* Now *rare* exc. *dial.* [f. SCARE *sb.* + -FUL.] Terrifying, alarming.

1567 GOLDING *Ovid's Met.* VI. (1593) 144 The scarefull erne With hooked talents trussing up a hare. **1655** GURNALL *Chr. in Arm.* I. verse 13, vii. (1656) 370 The evil day is not such a scareful thing to thee that art a Christian, as thou shouldest start for it. **1841** J. F. COOPER *Deerslayer* iii, It's skearful to think for how many causes one gets to be your inimy.

scaremonger ('skɛəˌmʌŋgə(r)). [f. SCARE *sb.* + -MONGER[1].] One who occupies himself in spreading alarming reports; an alarmist. Hence as *v. intr.*, to spread alarming reports; **'scaremongering** *vbl. sb.*, the action of a scaremonger; the spreading of alarming reports; also as *ppl. a.*

1888 *Pall Mall G.* 23 May 4/1 Neither the scaremongers nor the peacemongers will feel any security whatever that the Cabinet is taking the country into its confidence. **1907** *Standard* 25 Nov. 6/6 To dismiss as 'scaremongering', and the like, criticism founded upon facts of common knowledge. **1966** *New Statesman* 14 Jan. 38/3 The new Home Secretary, Roy Jenkins, commented on TV that the *Express* story was 'premature and slightly scaremongering'. **1976** 'D. HALLIDAY' *Dolly & Nanny Bird* ii. 28 You scaremongered all the way through. You created panic.

scarer ('skɛərə(r)). [f. SCARE *v.* + -ER[1].] One who or something which scares. *spec.* (usu. as *bird-scarer*) a person or thing (other than a traditional scarecrow) for frightening birds away from crops.

1740 RICHARDSON *Pamela* I. Introd. 30 Till the Ghost of Lady Davers, drawing open the Curtains, scares the Scarer. **1820** *Examiner* No. 621. 154/1 Like a scarer away of birds from the grapes. **1865** DICKENS *Mut. Fr.* I. v, To a old bird like myself these are scarers. **1879** ESCOTT *England* I. 299 When he commences life as an agricultural labourer, it will probably be, not in the capacity of scarer—bird-scaring is now generally done by inanimate scarecrows. **1930** H. H. THOMAS *Pop. Gardening Ann.* 24 A good cheap scarer on the market is obtainable in the shape of a black cat's head. **1953** R. GODDEN *Kingfishers catch Fire* xiii. 157 The bird-scarers had come to watch over the cherry crop. **1961** *Times* 7 Jan. 8/6, I could not make out whether the contents were a bird-scarer or a child's rattle. **1971** *Country Life* 16 Sept. 682/1 We were much troubled by an explosive bird-scarer in a field of barley adjoining our house.

scarestee, obs. form of SCARCITY.

scarey, variant of SCARY *a.*

scarf (skɑːf), *sb.*[1] Pl. scarfs, scarves. Forms: 6–7 scarfe, scarff(e, scarph(e, skarf(e, 7 skarffe, 6– scarf. [Of obscure history; not recorded before the middle of the 16th c., but prob. a. ONF. *escarpe* = Central OF. *escharpe*, mod.F. *écharpe* sash, sling for a wounded arm, etc. (whence It. *sciarpa*, *ciarpa*, Sp. *charpa*, G. *schärpe*, MDu. *scharpe*, and mod.Du. *sjerp*), prob. the same word as OF. *escharpe*, *escarpe*, *esquerpe*, *escreppe*, etc., a pilgrim's scrip suspended from the neck; of Teut. origin: cf. ON. *skreppa* SCRIP *sb.*[1]

The more normal form *scarp* is found (almost as early as *scarf*) in the heraldic sense 5 a; possibly, though unrecorded, it may have been the original Eng. form in all senses. It is noteworthy that all the words of the form *scarp* have variants with *f*: for the change of final *p* into *f* after liquids cf. SCALP *sb.*[2] Various Ger. dialects have *scherf(e*, *scharfe* (whence Russian *sharf*) for the literary Ger. *schärpe*, but this coincidence with Eng. seems to be merely accidental.

The original plural form *scarfs* has never gone out of use; but from the beginning of the 18th c. the form *scarves* (on the analogy of *halves*, etc.) has been common, and in London commercial use it appeared to have become universal in the early 20th c. No other sb. of other than native origin had this change of *f* into *v* in the plural.]

1. A broad band of silk or other material, worn (chiefly by soldiers or officials) either diagonally across the body from one shoulder to the opposite hip, or round the waist; = SASH *sb.*[1] 2.

The purpose of the military 'scarf' or 'sash' is now merely decorative or significant of rank or the like. Originally, it served for carrying things, and some references to this use occur in the early quots. below.

1555 [? alluded to in quot. for sense 2]. **1566** PAINTER *Pal. Pleas.* I. 51 His wife Panthea brought him an armure of golde,.. and a crimsen skarfe. **1585** T. WASHINGTON tr. *Nicholay's Voy.* IV. xiii. 126 b, The target.. hee carryed in a scarfe about his shoulders. **1594** NASHE *Unfort. Trav.* 20 Flourishing entred Iohn Leiden the Botcher into the field, with a scarffe made of lysts like a bow-case. **1599** SHAKS. *Much Ado* II. i. 198 What fashion will you weare the Garland off?.. vnder your arme, like a Lieutenants scarfe? **1644** SYMONDS *Diary* (Camden) 41 A man in compleate coloured armour and scarfe. **1660** F. BROOKE tr. *Le Blanc's Trav.* 350 The men wear apparel of Deer-skins.., one arm uncovered, and so they wear their garment like a scarf. **1660** TATHAM *Roy. Oak* 2 Eight other Gentlemen carrying Banners in Plush Coats, and Skye coloured Scarffs about their Shoulders. **1689** *Lond. Gaz.* No. 2445/4 Lost.., an Officers Scarf with four gold Fringes round the Wast, set on Crimson Silk, and a very deep Fringe at each end. **1732** POPE *Ess. Man* II. 279 Scarfs, garters, gold, amuse his riper age. **1762–71** H. WALPOLE *Vertue's Anecd. Paint.* (1786) V. 130 Cromwell, half-length in armour, page tying his scarf. **1823** SCOTT *Quentin D.* ii, Over his left shoulder hung an embroidered scarf, which sustained a small pouch of scarlet velvet. **1837** CARLYLE *Fr. Rev.* XIII. iii, Municipality and

Mayor have on their scarfs. **1874** MOTLEY *Barneveld* I. ii. 126 Forty-eight pages in white, yellow, and red scarves. **1902** AMERY *War S. Africa* II. 189 Their colonel..had led waving his silk scarf to his men.

2. *Eccl.* A band of silk or other material worn round the neck, with the two ends pendent from the shoulders in front, as a part of clerical costume. In the 18th c. *spec.* the scarf worn by a nobleman's chaplain (cf. quot. 1866); hence, a chaplaincy.

1555 LADY VANE *Let. to Philpot* in Foxe *A. & M.* (1583) 1829/1, I will supply your request for the Scarfe yee wrote of, that ye may present my handy worke before your Captayne. **1555** PHILPOT *Let. to Lady Vane* 10 Dec. *ibid.* 1837/2 You haue so armed me to the Lordes battell both inwardly and outwardly... You haue appointed me to so good and gracious a General of the field,.. that [etc.]... The Scarffe I desire as an outward signe to shew our enemies. **1710** SWIFT *Jrnl. to Stella* 11 Dec., I dined with Mrs. Vanhomrigh, to desire them to buy me a scarf; and lady Abercorn is to buy me another, to see who does best; mine is all in rags. **1712** BUDGELL *Spect.* No. 539 ¶3, I yesterday heard a young Gentleman, that look'd as if he was just come to the Town, and a Scarf, upon Evil-speaking. **1738** MRS. DELANY *Life & Corr.* (1861) II. 35 The Duke of Portland is very sorry not to be able to grant a scarf to our acquaintance —his are all filled up. **1844** *Life C'tess Huntingdon* I. 132 The excellent Lady Huntingdon..invited him to her house.., gave him her scarf, and as her chaplain, he continued long to preach to the poor in her kitchen unmolested. **1866** *Direct. Anglic.* (ed. 3) 359 Scarf worn by Chaplains; it is made of silk of the colour of the nobleman's livery to whom the cleric is chaplain... The Black Scarf is worn over the Gown by Doctors in Divinity, Cathedral Dignitaries and Bishops' Chaplains. **1903** *Church Times* 11 Dec. 748/4 A deacon is entitled, like any other clergyman, to wear the broad black tippet, or scarf, over his surplice.

3. a. A broad strip of silk, gauze, or other fine material, worn hung loosely over the shoulders or otherwise as an ornamental accessory to the costume.

1562 J. HEYWOOD *Prov. & Epigr.* Bbjb, When do mothers fray their babes most from duggis. When they put on blacke scrafs [sic], and go like beare buggis. **1583** GREENE *Mamillia* II. Wks. (Grosart) II. 220 Needlesse noughts, as crisps and scarphes worne Alla Morisco. **1583** STUBBES *Anat. Abuses* I. Gjb, Then must they haue their silk scarffes cast about their faces, & fluttering in the winde with great tassels at euery end, either of gold, siluer or silk. **1592** MARLOWE *Massacre Paris* I. A7b, They that shalbe actors in this Massacre Shall..tye white linnen scarfes about their armes. **1600** ROWLANDS *Lett. Humours Blood* xxvii. 33 Why in the Stop-throate fashion doth he go, With Scarfe about his necke? Hat without band? **1601** SHAKS. *Jul. C.* I. ii. 289 Marcellus and Flauius, for pulling Scarffes of Cæsars Images, are put to silence. **1624** *Skelton's E. Rummyng* Prol. 82 Scarfs, feathers, and swords, And thin bodkin-beards. **1631** HEYWOOD *Fair Maid of West* I. Wks. 1874 II. 264 Trickt in skarffe and feather. **1713** *Lond. Gaz.* No. 5173/4 A black Gause Scarf;..a blue Lustring-Scarf with a Gause Body. **1748** RICHARDSON *Clarissa* (1811) IV. xlii. 282 What a pretty show they will make, with their white hoods, white gowns, white petticoats, white scarves! **1766** *Lond. Mag.* July 335 The new thing called a Scarf, with its depending tassels, looks so much like an advertisement that if the place of abode was added, there is no doubt, but that it would draw in custom. **1837** DICKENS *Pickw.* iv, Two young ladies in scarfs and feathers. **1859** TENNYSON *Marr. Geraint* 169 A purple scarf at either end whereof There swung an apple of the purest gold Sway'd round about him. **1863** GEO. ELIOT *Romola* Introd., His..cap, with its..long hanging strip of drapery, to serve as a scarf in case of need. **1887** BOWEN *Virg. Æneid* IV. 138 Dressed in a Tyrian scarf with a fringe of broidery gay.

†**b.** used as a bandage for the eyes, or a veil.

1587 GOLDING *De Mornay* xx. (1617) 349 His [God's] spiritual nature, which we cannot possibly comprehend, but as it were through a glasse, or a scarfe. **1611** CHAPMAN *May Day* Plays 1873 II. 349 My assurance is that Cupid will take the scarfe from his owne eyes and hoodwinke the old buzzard. **1642** R. CARPENTER *Experience* II. vii. 170 And if anything slip under the rehearsall it is to be a scarff over the face, and to shew, the griefe could not be expressed. *a* **1656** BP. HALL *Rem. Wks.* (1660) 232 They have but a maske or scarfe over their faces.

c. *transf.* and *fig.*

1610 SHAKS. *Temp.* IV. i. 82 And with each end of thy blew bowe do'st crowne My boskie acres, and my vnshrubd downe, Rich scarph to my proud earth. **1614** DRUMM. OF HAWTH. *Poems* (1616) Fj, Among the lesser Lights as is the Moone, Blushing through Scarfe of Clouds on Latmos Mountaine. **1822** SHELLEY *Triumph* 357 Still before me on the dusky grass, Iris her many-coloured scarf had drawn. **1867** AUGUSTA WILSON *Vashti* xxvii, The moon had risen slowly, breaking through a rent scarf of cloud that barred her solemn, white disc. **1880** STEVENSON *Across the Plains* ii. (1892) 89 The fogs are in possession of the lower levels; they crawl in scarves among the sandhills.

d. *spec.* The scarf of black crape or silk worn over the shoulder by mourners at funerals.

1739 *Will* in Payne *Engl. Cath.* (1889) 53 No scarves, gloves, nor hat-bands. **1842** TENNYSON *Morte Arth.* 194 A dusky barge, Dark as a funeral scarf from stem to stern. **1850** G. J. FRENCH *Tippets* 8 *note*, The modern custom of wearing at funerals both a hatband and a scarf over the shoulder, curiously marks the extravagance which has crept into such ceremonies.

e. A band of warm and soft material worn round the neck in cold weather; = COMFORTER 6.

1823 C. MATHEWS *Let.* 17 Feb. in A. Mathews *Mem. C. Mathews* (1839) III. 368 And also two scarfs, I think they are called. **1844** MRS. GAUGAIN *Knitting*, etc. II. Accomp. 37 Warm Crochet Scarf. Worked in eight-ply Berlin wool.

f. A necktie or cravat that more or less covers the bosom of the shirt.

1865 MORLEY *Mod. Characteristics* 79 Gorgeous scarves which have been long superseded by white ties. **1886** PASCOE *Lond. of To-day* (ed. 3) xli. 355 Most gentlemen are now content with the made-up scarves of all sizes, colours, and materials, which [etc.].

†**4.** A sling for an ailing limb. *Obs.*

1597 A. M. tr. *Guillemeau's Fr. Chirurg.* 29/2 He must weare his arme before on his breste in a scarfe. **1600** SHAKS. *A.Y.L.* V. ii. 23 Oh my deere Orlando, how it greeues me to see thee weare thy heart in a scarfe. *c* **1645** HOWELL *Lett.* (1650) I. 260 Lesly..carried his foot in a scarf for a wound he had received at Buckstobo. **1656** RIDGLEY *Pract. Physick* 165 The arm must be carried in a Scarf. **1828** SCOTT *F.M. Perth* xxi, His wounded arm was supported by a scarf, or sling of crimson silk.

5. *Her.* **a.** = SCARP *sb.*[1]

1688 HOLME *Armoury* I. 30/1 He beareth Argent, a Scarpe Purpure, of some termed a Scarf. **1738** CHAMBERS *Cycl.* (ed. 2) s.v. *Bend-sinister*, The bend-sinister is subdivided into the *scarf*, or *scarp*, and the *battoon*. **1823–4** *Encycl. Metrop.* (1845) XV. 431 The *Bend sinister* consists of similar lines drawn in an opposite direction from the *sinister chief* to the *dexter base* of the shield. Its diminutive is the *scarf* occupying one half of its breadth.

b. = BANDEROLE 2.

1780 EDMONDSON *Her.* II. Gloss., *Scarf*, a small ecclesiastical banner, hanging down from the top of a crosier.

†**6.** A scroll or plate bearing an inscription.

1655 FULLER *Ch. Hist.* XI. x. §49 The Vault thus prepared, a scarfe of lead was provided some two foot long,..therein to make an inscription.

7. *attrib.* and *Comb.*, as ***scarf-end***, ***-maker***, ***-tie***, ***-veil***; ***scarf-like*** adj. and adv.; **scarf cloak**, a light narrow cloak or tippet; **scarf-loom**, a loom for weaving figured fabrics of moderate breadth (Knight *Dict. Mech.* 1875); †**scarf-man**, a clergyman of rank entitling him to wear a scarf; †**scarf-officer**, an officer who is entitled to wear a scarf; **scarf-pin**, a pin for fastening a scarf, or worn for ornament in a scarf (sense 3f); **scarf-ring**, a ring for holding a scarf (sense 3f) in position.

1804 *Jackson's Oxford Jrnl.* 4 Aug. 2/3 *Scarf cloaks of leno or worked muslin over coloured silks, are universally worn. **1868** G. M. HOPKINS *Note-bks. & Papers* (1937) 115 Fine afternoon with snow-white flying *scarf-ends in the clouds. **1611** COTGR., *Escharpeux*,..*scarfe-like. **1852** *Meanderings of Memory* I. 109 Scarf-like and ethereally slight. **1874** BOUTELL *Arms & Armour* iv. 67 Suspended from a baudrick, or scarf-like shoulder-belt, this sword reached from the hollow of the back to about the middle of the thigh. **1725** *Lond. Gaz.* No. 6403/4 Anne Howard, ..*Scarf-maker. **1711** P. H. *Impartial View of 2 late Parlts.* 23 The inferior Priests and Deacons, and all under the Degree of *Scarf Men were made to understand. **1710–11** ADDISON *Spect.* No. 21 ¶2 We may divide the Clergy into Generals, Field-Officers, and Subalterns. Among the first we may reckon Bishops, Deans, and Arch-Deacons. Among the second are Doctors of Divinity, Prebendaries, and all that wear Scarfs... It is found that there has been a great Exceeding of late Years in the Second Division, several Brevets having been granted for the converting of Subalterns into *Scarf-Officers. **1859** *Habits of Gd. Society* iii. (new ed.) 142 A *scarf-pin which is neither large nor showy. **1922** JOYCE *Ulysses* 440 In an oatmeal sporting suit .., tony buff shirt, shepherd's plaid Saint Andrew's cross *scarftie. **1976** *Billings* (Montana) *Gaz.* 16 June 9-c/5 (Advt.), This dress is a breeze—buttons up one side to the flutter of a scarf tie. **1907** *Westm. Gaz.* 12 Dec. 4/3 A useful *scarf-veil.

scarf (skɑːf), *sb.*[2] Also 5 **scarffe**, 6 **skarfe**, 8 **scarfe**, 8–9 **scarph**, 9 **skerf**. [Words of related form and identical meaning (chiefly belonging to the nautical vocabulary) are found in several mod. langs., but recorded much later than in English: F. *écart* (:—**escarf*) a scarf, vbl. noun from *écarver* (:—**escarver*) to scarf; Sp. *escarba*, Pg. *escarva* a scarf; Du. *scherf* a scarf, *verscherven* (whence G. *verscherben*) to scarf; Sw. *skarf*, Norw. *skarv* piece added to lengthen a board or a garment, also the joint or seam by which this is effected; Sw. *skarfva*, Norw. *skarva*, *skjerva* to lengthen by joining or sewing on an additional piece (Da. has in this sense *skarre*, the relation of which to the Sw. form is obscure).

The relation of these words to each other and to the English sb. and vb. is uncertain. The fact that the Sw. words are not, like those in the other langs., exclusively technical, but have a wider meaning, seems to afford a slight presumption in favour of Scandinavian as the ultimate source. But even assuming this, it remains doubtful whether the Eng. sb. comes from Sw. (or some other Scandinavian dialect) directly or through the medium of OF. **escarf*.

The Sw. *skarf* has commonly been referred to the Teut. root **skerƀ-*, *skarƀ-*, represented by OE. *scearfian* (= OHG. *scarpôn*, G. *scharben*) to cut into shreds, OE. *sceorfan* str. vb., to gnaw, bite, scarify, Du. *scherf* (= OHG. *scirbi*, G. *scherbe*) potsherd; but affinity in meaning seems wanting.]

1. a. *Carpentry* and *Shipbuilding*. A joint by which two timbers are connected longitudinally into a continuous piece, the ends being halved, notched, or cut away so as to fit into each other with mutual overlapping.

1497 [see *scarf-timber* in 3]. *c* **1580** H. SMITH in *Hakluyt's Voy.* (1599) I. 453 Wee haled aground to stoppe a leake, which we found to be in the skarfe afore. **1626** CAPT. SMITH *Accid. Yng. Seamen* 8 Next your Nauell timbers, and bind them all with sixe foote Skarfe at the least. **1691** T. H[ALE] *Acc. New Invent.* 47 The Scarfs of her Keel and Stern. **1769** FALCONER *Dict. Marine* (1780) s.v. *Apron*, The scarf thereof should be at some distance from that of the stern. **1779** BARNARD in *Phil. Trans.* LXX. 108 Pl. 3, Beams of Fir 12 inches square, put across in halves, with 12 feet scarph. **1823** P. NICHOLSON *Pract. Builder* 280 In each piece of timber to be joined, the parts of the joints that come in contact are called scarfs. **1842** *Civil Eng. & Arch. Jrnl.* V. 362/1 The scarf of the poles is shown in Fig. 3. **1889** WELCH *Text Bk. Naval Archit.* viii. 109 The ends of these planks are supported on the frames, adjacent ones being formed into a scarph.

†**b.** *Shipbuilding*. The overlapping of adjacent timbers in a ship's frame, in order to secure continuity of strength at the joints. Phrase, *to give scarf*. *Obs.*

1711 W. SUTHERLAND *Shipbuild. Assist.* 39 Let the Top-timber be placed..that they may give Scarf to the Port-holes. **1769** [see SCARF *v.*[2] 1b]. **1797** *Encycl. Brit.* XVII. 379/2 These represent the length and scarf of the several timbers in the midship frame. *c* **1850** *Rudim. Nav.* (Weale) 141 The lower..riders..fay alongside the floor riders, and give scarph above them.

2. *Metal-working*. (See quots.)

1843 HOLTZAPFFEL *Turning*, etc. I. 220 In smith's work likewise, the joinings are called scarfs... The scarfs required for the shut, are made by first upsetting or thickening the iron... It is next rudely tapered off. **1875** KNIGHT *Dict. Mech.*, *Scarf*, the flattened or chamfered edges of iron prepared for welding. **1884** C. G. W. LOCK *Workshop Rec.* Ser. III. 297/2 The point of the scarf is farthest into the fire.

3. *Comb.*: **scarf-joint** = senses 1 and 2; hence **scarf-jointing**, the process of joining timbers by means of a scarf; † **scarf-timber**, timber in short lengths for scarfing; **scarf-weld** (see quot.).

1791 SMEATON *Edystone L.* §252 The four stones..were.. to be united to each other by Hook-*Scarf-Joints. **1851–4** *Cycl. Useful Arts* (ed. Tomlinson) I. 329 The common scarf joint is made by merely halving each piece of timber for a certain length, and then bolting or strapping the two pieces together. **1919** S. F. WALKER *Electr. Mining Machinery* xx. 154 A scarf joint is..good if it is well made and very carefully bound. **1948** F. WIGHTMAN *Wind is Free* ii. 33 It had to be hoisted with a block & tackle on sheerpoles to bring it up to where its scarph joint fitted into the one cut on the forward end of the keel timber. **1907** *Proc. Soc. Antiq.* 14 Feb. 349 The method of construction is that known technically as *scarf-jointing. **1497** *Naval Acc. Hen. VII* (1896) 312 Certeyn *Scarffe Tymbre price—viij^{s} vj^{d}. **1882** OGILVIE, **Scarf-weld*, a peculiar joint made in welding two pieces of metal, as iron, together.

†**scarf**, *sb.*[3] *Mil.* [Alteration of SCARP *sb.*] = SCARP *sb.*[2]

1591 PERCIVALL *Sp. Dict.*, *Coraxa entre dos muros*, a scarfe between wals, *Musculus*. **1598** BARRET *Theor. Warres* V. i. 126 These Caualleres..haue also their Scarphe or Alambor [Sp. *alambor* declivity of a ditch]. **1603** *Court Roll* in *Athenæum* 21 Nov. (1885) 668/3 Euerie man shall make vpe sufficiently all the Scarfes betwixt the milne & Restone Inges betwene this & Christmas next. **1645** *Enchir. Fortif.* 6 The Talud, or Scarfe, of the outside of the Rampart. **1656** EARL MONM. tr. *Boccalini's Advts. fr. Parnass.* II. xlii. 297 Ditches, Ravelins, Scarfes, & Counter-scarfes.

scarf (skɑːf), *sb.*[4] *Orkn.* and *Shetl. dial.* Also 7, 9, **scarfe**, 9 **scarff**; and see SCART. [a. ON. *skarf-r*, Norw., Sw. *skarf*.] A cormorant or a shag.

1668 F. JESSOP in *Philos. Lett. Ray* (1718) 38, I have procured the Skin of a great Bird which he that gave it me call'd a Scarfe. *a* **1693** *Urquhart's Rabelais* III. xiii. 107 The sussing of Kitnings, clamring of Scarfes, whimpring of Fullmarts. **1744** PRESTON *Zetland* in *Phil. Trans.* XLIII. 61 (2) Whaps, Toists,..Plovers, Scarfs, &c. **1805** G. BARRY *Orkney Isl.* 300 The Shag (*pelecanus graculus*), so well known by the name of Scarf, is very frequently seen. *Ibid.*, The Cormorant..our great Scarf, is a species not so numerous as the former. **1868** D. GORRIE *Summers & Winters in Orkneys* v. 153 A lazy scarff here and there raised himself up at length over the surface.

scarf (skɑːf), *sb.*[5] **1.** *Whaling* A longitudinal cut made in a whale's body.

1851 H. MELVILLE *Whale* II. xxv. 181 As the blubber in one strip uniformly peels off along the line called the 'scarf'. **1874** C. M. SCAMMON *Marine Mammals* 63 (Cent.) A scarf is cut along the body and through the blubber, to which one end of a tackle is hooked.

2. *Forestry*. A V-shaped incision cut in a trunk during felling, to govern the direction in which the tree is to fall; also, the sloping surface left by such an incision.

1863 *8th Ann. Rep. Maine Board Agric.* 36 The bark of the stock opposite the scarf with a thin sliver of wood is cut down. **1887** J. D. BILLINGS *Hardtack & Coffee* (1888) 180 When an army first went into camp trees were cut with the scarf two or three feet above the ground. **1903** R. J. CLOW *Pillar of Salt* iii. 55 It meant a bit of work to cut down a tree seven feet in diameter... Stello cut in the inside scarf and I put in the back chip. **1926** K. S. PRICHARD *Working Bullocks* xxxii. 296 Half-dozen men..stood on their rough-barked logs... The scarf showed ruddy as a wound in the logs. **1962** J. N. WINBURNE *Dict. Agric. & Allied Terminology* 673/1 *Scarf*,..the beveled cut on a log or stump which results from undercutting a tree in felling.

scarf (skɑːf), *sb.*[6] U.S. slang var. SCOFF *sb.*[2]

1932 *Evening Sun* (Baltimore) 9 Dec. 31/5 *Scarf*, food. **1944** D. BURLEY *Orig. Handbk. Harlem Jive* 81 'Pick up on the scoff, cherub.'.. The 'scoff' or 'scarf' in the above simple statement is dinner food, meals. **1961** RIGNEY & SMITH *Real Bohemia* p. xvi, *Scarf*, food; eat, believed to have come from a French chef, Scarfannelli. **1973** L. SNELLING *Heresy* II. iv. 89 How's for a bit of scarf, my tummy's anguished.

scarf (skɑːf), *v.*[1] Also 7 **scarfe**, **skarfe**, 9 **skarf**. [f. SCARF *sb.*[1]]

1. *trans.* To clothe, cover, or wrap with or as with a scarf or scarves; to invest with a scarf; †to blindfold.

1598 BP. HALL *Sat.* IV. vi. 46 The sturdy Plough-man doth the soldier see, All scarfed with pide colours to the knee. **1613** HEYWOOD *Brazen Age* II. ii. C 3, Why doth Adonis..shun this Iuory girdle of my armes? To be thus scarft the dreadfull God of warre Would giue me conquered kingdomes. **1632** SIR T. HAWKINS tr. *Mathieu's Unhappy Prosperitie* 95 Claudius caused that of Augustus to be taken from the Theater of the Gladiators, that it might not ever be present at murther, or be alwayes scarfed. *a* **1640** J. DAY *Peregr. Schol.* (1881) 48 Slitely shadowed or scarft with a thin tinsell or Tirean vaile. **1805** SOUTHEY *Madoc* II. xix, Bare Of foot, of limb, scarfed only round the loins. **1849** M. ARNOLD *Resignation* 5 Warriors..Scarf'd with the cross. **1894** DU MAURIER *Trilby* VI. (1895) 280 Our three friends.. duly scarfed and scarfpinned [etc.].

b. *transf.* and *fig.*

1605 SHAKS. *Macb.* III. ii. 47 Come, seeling Night, Skarfe vp the tender Eye of pittifull Day. **1630** DRUMM. OF HAWTH. *Flowres of Sion* 18 Scarff'd in a rosie Cloud, Hee doth ascend the Aire. *c* **1640** ROWLEY, etc. *Witch of Edmonton* II. ii, Blushing Adonis scarft in modesties. **1814** CARY *Dante, Hell* xxxiii. 92 Others skarf'd in rugged folds of ice. **1876** FARRAR *Marlb. Serm.* xxxi. 309 The great sun is still shining, though it be scarfed by earthly vapours. **1897** F. THOMPSON *New Poems* 112 Who scarfed her with the morning?

2. To wrap (a garment) *about* or *around* a person in the manner of a scarf. Also *transf. rare.*

1602 SHAKS. *Ham.* V. ii. 13 Vp from my cabin My sea-gowne scarft about me in the darke, Grop'd I to finde out them. **1613** HEYWOOD *Silver Age* III. I. 3 b, My fingers Il'e intangle in these curles, And scarfe my Iuory arme about thy necke. **1795** SOUTHEY *Joan of Arc* IX. 256 On the earth the chieftain slept, His mantle scarft around him. **1807** —— *Espriella's Lett.* II. 252 They..had a large mantle of gray checquered cloth scarft round them.

†**3.** To bind up (wounds) with, or as with a scarf; ? to place (a limb) in a sling. *Obs.*

1601 BP. W. BARLOW *Defence* 161 Wee scarifie them, we scarfe them not. **1605** A. WOTTON *Answ. late Popish Articles* 25 Let them shift themselues, as they list, and skarfe their soares, according to their fancies. **1643** TRAPP *Comm. Gen.* xliv. 1 Had it been fit for him to scarfe their bones before they were set.

scarf (skɑːf), *v.*[2] Also 7 scarfe, scarff, skarf, 8 scarph. [f. SCARF *sb.*[2]]

1. a. *trans.* To join by a scarf-joint.

1627 CAPT. SMITH *Seaman's Gram.* ii. 3 Those are skarfed into the ground timbers. **1643** HORN & ROB. *Gate Lang. Unl.* xlviii. §530 The Joyner plaineth plankes..he skarfeth and ioyneth them close with culver-tailes. **1704** J. HARRIS *Lex. Techn.* I. s.v., Thus they say the Stem of a Ship is *Scarfed* into her Keel; and they imply by it, That the two Peices are shaped away slanting, so as to join with one another close and even. **1791** SMEATON *Edystone L.* §42 Timbers, properly scarphed together. **1841** *Civil Eng. & Arch. Jrnl.* IV. 285/1 Tye-beams..were formed almost wholly of short lengths, averaging not more than 20 feet, lapped and scarfed. **1850** LONGF. *Building Ship* 137 The keel of oak for a noble ship, Scarfed and bolted. **1860** *Encycl. Brit.* (ed. 8) XX. 186/1 The several pieces are scarphed together. **1976** *Yankee* Apr. 109/1 He forced me to scarph the keel timbers in watertight sections.

b. (See quot.)

1769 FALCONER *Dict. Marine* (1776) s.v. *Scarf*, But when the ends of the two pieces [of timber] are cut square, and put together, they are said to *butt* to one another; and when another piece is laid upon, and fastened to both, as in the case in all frame timbers, this is called scarfing the timbers; and half the piece which fastens the two timbers together is reckoned the length of the scarf.

2. *Metal-working.* To bevel or flatten (the ends or edges of the pieces of metal to be welded).

1831 J. HOLLAND *Manuf. Metal* I. 188 The extremities of each bar are scarfed. **1861** FAIRBAIRN *Iron* 211 Mr. Bertram scarfs the edges of the plates, places them together [etc.]. **1884** C. G. W. LOCK *Workshop Rec.* Ser. III. 303/1 Scarf it for welding.

3. *intr.* To be joined with a scarf. Const. *to.*

1794 *Rigging & Seamanship* I. 35 The inner end of the boom, to which it scarfs with a tongue. **1860** *Encycl. Brit.* (ed. 8) XX. 185/2 The foremost end of the keelson scarphs to the stemson.

scarf (skɑːf), *v.*[3] [f. SCARF *sb.*[5]] **1.** *trans. Whaling.* To make a 'scarf' or incision in the blubber of (a whale). Also *absol.*

1851 H. MELVILLE *Whale* II. xxv. 182 The heavers singing, the blubber-room gentlemen coiling, the mates scarfing, the ship straining, and all hands swearing occasionally. **1887** GOODE, etc. *Fisheries U.S.* v. II. 278/1 The second mate 'scarfs', or cuts the body blubber.

2. *N.Z. Forestry.* To cut a scarf in (timber). Also *back-*, *belly-scarf* (see quot. 1928). Cf. SCARF *sb.*[5]

1899 J. BELL *Shadow of Bush* xiv. 83 The smaller trees.. had been 'scarfed', or cut partly through in readiness, and skilfully, so that each, when struck, might again in its turn strike and bring down another. **1904** 'G. B. LANCASTER' *Sons o' Men* 164 He..scarfed the timber for the saw. **1928** P. T. KENWAY *Pioneering in Poverty Bay* v. 38 He will 'belly-scarf' and 'back-scarf' the lot, that is to say he will cut about a third through on both the lower and higher sides.

scarf (skɑːf), *v.*[4] U.S. slang var. SCOFF *v.*[2] 1. Also *absol.* and const. *up* and *down.*

1960 R. G. REISNER *Jazz Titans* 164 *Scarf*, eat. **1968** C. ARMSTRONG *Balloon Man* viii. 98 They don't want to faint from hunger, so..they scarf up what they call a bite before they go. **1974** *Black World* June 77/1 King Dust would sit there, 'scarfing', as he called it, in silence. **1975** *High Times* Dec. 80/3, I can pick jimsonweed and chop it up and scarf it down as well as the next guy. **1976** R. CONDON *Whisper of Axe* II. xviii. 265 Let's..scarf up some of that osso bucco.

scarf-bolt, incorrect form of SCARP-BOLT.

scarfe: see SCAFF.

scarfed (skɑːft; *poet.* 'skɑːfɪd), *ppl. a.*[1] Also scarved. [f. SCARF *v.*[1] + -ED[2].] Invested with a scarf; wearing a scarf; also, decorated with or as with scarfs. Cf. SCARVED *ppl. a.*

1596 SHAKS. *Merch. V.* II. vi. 15 The skarfed barke puts from her natiue bay. **1837** CARLYLE *Fr. Rev.* II. v. xii. 356 Scarfed tricolor Municipals. **1863** KINGLAKE *Crimea* (1876) I. xiv. 269 Their fire pelted straight into the group of the scarfed Deputies. **1920** BLUNDEN *Waggoner* 53 The lispering aspens and the scarfed brook grasses With wakened melancholy writhe the air. **1967** *Boston Sunday Herald* 30 Apr. v. 5/1 (Advt.), Shaped and scarfed for cool summer perfection in rayon and silk.

1885 PERRING *Hard Knots* 81 The noted beauty—she who was admired, courted, beautifully scarved and apparelled. **1958** M. STEWART *Nine Coaches Waiting* v. 54 Philippe and I went out..coated and scarved against the breeze. **1972** F. WARNER *Lying Figures* III. 21 Scarved, laughing children, scuffing the leaves! **1976** *New Yorker* 8 Mar. 41/2 The lottery sellers were gloved and scarved.

scarfed ('skɑːft), *ppl. a.*[2] Also scarphed. [f. SCARF *v.*[2] + -ED[1].] Joined by means of a scarf. *scarfed joint* = SCARF *sb.*[2] 1.

1704 J. HARRIS *Lex. Techn.* I, *Skarfed*, the Sea Term, when one Peice of Timber is let and fastned into another. **1801** *Encycl. Brit.* Suppl. I. 170/2 Scarfed tie-beams. **1805** SOUTHEY *Madoc* II. xxv, Tear up the deck, the severed planks bear off, Disjoin the well-scarfed timbers. **1825** J. NICHOLSON *Operat. Mechanic* 652 The joint is what is denominated a half-lap, or scarfed joint. **1975** *Anglo-Saxon England* IV. 187 D. M. Wilson has noted that long ships with scarphed keels were built in Scandinavia in the thirteenth century.

†**'scarfing**, *vbl. sb.*[1] *Obs.* [f. SCARF *v.*[1] + -ING[1].] *concr.* A covering network.

1613 CHAPMAN *Maske Inns Court*, To euery one of which, was tackt a Scarffing of Siluer; that ran sinuously in workes ouer the whole caparison.

scarfing ('skɑːfɪŋ), *vbl. sb.*[2] [f. SCARF *v.*[2]]

1. The action of joining by means of scarfs.

1644 MANWAYRING *Sea-mans Dict.* 89 So when the stem or any other timber..is too short, it is peeced in this manner, and that they call scarffing. **1769** FALCONER *Dict. Marine* II. (1780), *Assembler*, to unite the several pieces of a ship, as by ..scarfing, scoring, tenenting, &c. **1823** P. NICHOLSON *Pract. Build.* 280 Scarfing, is..the art of connecting two pieces of timber together, in such a manner as to appear like one piece. **1894** C. N. ROBINSON *Brit. Fleet* 247 To Sir Robert Seppings we owe the device known as 'scarphing'.

b. *concr.*

1671 PHILLIPS, *Skarfing*, (in Navigation) is one piece of wood let into another, or so much wood cut away from the one as the other. **1791** SMEATON *Edystone L.* §54 *note*, A.. draught..in which..the places and nature of the scarfing or joinings [could be] distinguished. **1847** G. A. SMEATON *Builder's Man.* 79, Fig. 17 is a representation of a scarfing, which is very simple. **1908** CRADOCK *Whispers fr. Fleet* 108 The fore and aft thwarts that strengthen the sailing thwart are called scarping [*sic.*].

†**'scarfing**, *vbl. sb.*[3] [f. SCARF *sb.*[3] + -ING[1].] = SCARPING.

1721 PERRY *Daggenh. Breach* 129 He will..repair with good Scarfing the Walls or Banks belonging to the Levels.

scarfing ('skɑːfɪŋ), *ppl. a.*[1] [f. SCARF *v.*[1] + -ING[2].] Enveloping like a scarf.

1897 F. THOMPSON *New Poems* 48 For Earth's bosom pants, and heaves her scarfing sea.

'scarfing, *ppl. a.*[2] [f. SCARF *v.*[2] + -ING[2].] That scarfs, or serves as a longitudinal tie.

1869 SIR E. REED *Shipbuild.* i. 9 The builders afterwards applied a short scarphing keelson-piece. *Ibid.*, The side keelsons..had to be strengthened in a similar manner, except that the scarphing angle-irons had no plate between them.

'scarf-skin. [SCARF *sb.*[1], in the sense of light outer covering.] The outer layer of the skin; the epidermis, cuticle.

1615 [see CUTICLE 1]. **1774** GOLDSMITH *Nat. Hist.* (1862) I. xi. 215 The blackness lay in the epidermis, or scarf-skin, which was burnt up like leather. **1864** TENNYSON *Aylmer's F.* 660 Not a hair Ruffled upon the scarf-skin. **1882** *Encycl. Brit.* XIV. 383/2 The first operation to which they [*sc.* hides] are subjected is depilation, which removes, not only the hair, but also the scarf-skin.

b. *transf.*

1669 *Addr. Young Gentry of Eng.* 53 Raise up but the skarfe skin which covers this fine mould. **1796** *New Ann. Reg.* 144 By making four or five small longitudinal incisions with a sharp-pointed knife..on one side only of the head or pod, just through the scarf-skin. **1847** H. MILLER *First Impr. Eng.* xi. (1857) 175 Let us..strip the vast landscape here of its upper integuments,..beginning first with the vegetable mould—the scarf-skin of the country.

†**'scarfways**, *adv. Obs. rare*[−1]. [f. SCARF *sb.*[1] + WAY *sb.* with adverbial *s.*] = next.

1653 URQUHART *Rabelais* I. xxvii, Thus went he out in a faire long-skirted jacket, putting his frock scarfewayes athwart his breast.

'scarf-wise ('skɑːfwaɪz), *adv.* [f. SCARF *sb.*[1] + -WISE.] In the manner of a scarf; passing from the shoulder across the breast and tied beneath the arm. Cf. F. *en écharpe.*

1581 GOLDWEL in Nichols *Progr. Eliz.* (1788) II. 129 A scrowle or band of silver, which came scarfe-wise over the shoulder, and so downe under the arme. **1601** HOLLAND *Pliny* XXXIII. iii. II. 462 Let them have their chains of gold as large as they list under their arms or crosse over their sides, scarfe-wise. **1653** H. COGAN tr. *Pinto's Trav.* xl. 160 Great chains of gold scarf-wise about them. **1900** *Daily News* 26 Nov. 7/4 A wide red ribbon with green edges athwart his chest scarfwise.

†**'scarfy**, *a. Obs.* [f. SCARF *sb.*[1] + -Y.] Resembling a scarf. *scarfy skin* = SCARF-SKIN.

1611 COTGR., *Escharpeux*, scarfie. **1621** LADY M. WROTH *Urania* 511 Alasse you frowne, and pull a scarfie Clowd ouer your diuine face to hide your fauour from me. **1744** tr. *Boerhaave's Inst.* III. 295 Over all these is extended the Cuticle or scarfy Skin.

scarfyre, obs. variant of SCAREFIRE.

scarification (ˌskærɪfɪ'keɪʃən). Also 5 scarificacioun, 6 scaryfycacyon, skarificacion, 7 scarrification. [ad. late L. *scarīficātiōn-em*, n. of action f. *scarīficāre* to SCARIFY. Cf. F. *scarification* (1314 in Hatz.-Darm.).]

1. The action of scarifying; an instance of this.

c **1400** tr. *Secreta Secret., Gov. Lordsh.* 86 Latynge of blood, noght by openynge of veynes, but by scarificacioun of fflesch. **1533** ELYOT *Cast. Helthe* III. viii. (1541) 61 In what member the bloud is gathered, the body being fyrst pourged by scarification, the grefe maye be cured. **1601** HOLLAND *Pliny* XVII. xxvii. I. 545, I cannot omit one manner of cure by way of Scarification. For when the bark is poore and leane [etc.]. **1672** WISEMAN *Wounds* I. x. 101 Also cupping with scarification of the Neck and Shoulders. **1758** J. S. *Le Dran's Observ. Surg.* (1771) 47 These Scarifications procured..a Discharge of Serum. **1822** SCOTT *Nigel* xxi, While his chin sustained from the razor literal scarification. **1899** *Allbutt's Syst. Med.* VIII. 496 In massive swellings of the tongue and throat relief has been given by scarification.

fig. **1881** J. H. INGRAM *Poe's Wks.* I. Mem. 34 He began that system of literary scarification—that crucial dissection of bookmaking mediocrities, which [etc.].

2. *concr.* A slight incision or a number of slight incisions made by scarifying.

1541 R. COPLAND *Guydon's Quest. Chirurg.* O j b, Ye ought to make certayne scaryfycacyons very depe with the rasour. **1562** BULLEIN *Dial. Sorenes & Chir.* 17 Laie upon the same skarificacion baie Salte. **1599** A. M. tr. *Gabelhouer's Bk. Physicke* 363/2 Therby shall the scarifications be kept open. **1660** F. BROOKE tr. *Le Blanc's Trav.* 350 They..make incisions in their face, then laying gum on a fire, hold over their faces that smoak may colour the scarifications. **1782** ELIZ. BLOWER *Geo. Bateman* II. 138 Whose..face was rendered more disagreeable..by deep scarifications of the small-pox.

scarificator ('skærɪfɪˌkeɪtə(r)). [a. mod.L. *scarīficātor* (F. *scarificateur*, Paré 16th c.), f. late L. *scarīficāre* to SCARIFY.]

1. *Surg.* An instrument used in scarification, for making several incisions simultaneously.

1611 COTGR., *Scarificateur*, a Scarificator, or Scarifier; an Instrument wherein there are 18 sharpe wheeles, the which let goe at once doe scarifie, and make incision, in as many seuerall places. **1634** H. CROOKE *Expl. Instr. Chirurg.* xxxii. 54 For this purpose Pareus hath an instrument which he calleth the Scarificator. It is a box wherein are fastened many rownd wheeles as it were, sharpe as phlegmes, which [etc.]. **1742** tr. *Heister's Surg.* (1768) II. 402 This Eyebrush, or Scarificator. **1875** tr. *von Ziemssen's Cycl. Med.* X. 115 The useful scarificators devised by C. Mayer.

b. (See quot.)

1858 MAYNE *Expos. Lex.*, *Scarificator*,..an instrument with a blunt edge, used chiefly in the operation of tooth-extraction, for separating the gum from the tooth.

c. A lancet for scarifying the skin.

1861 BUMSTEAD *Ven. Dis.* (1879) 434 The scarificator may be contaminated by contact with one person under the influence of syphilis and convey the disease to the next.

†**2.** *Agric.* = SCARIFIER 3. *Obs.*

1776 BOWDEN *Farmer's Director* 12 By cutting the surface of the meadow with an instrument called a scarificator. **1814** SHIRREFF *Agric. Orkney* 67 The scarificator being afterwards, at seed time, used to loosen the soil, if necessary.

3. One who scarifies; = SCARIFIER 1.

1748 RICHARDSON *Clarissa* IV. 84 What tho' the scarificators work upon him [a man mortally ill] day by day?

scarified ('skærɪfaɪd), *ppl. a.*[1] [f. SCARIFY *v.*[1] + -ED[1].] In senses of the vb.

1607 TOPSELL *Four-f. Beasts* 126 As a cupping-glasse draweth blood out of a Scarified place of the body. **1654** GAYTON *Pleas. Notes* 67 With a face and skinne as scarrified as that body before an Almanack. **1797** *Encycl. Brit.* (ed. 3) XVIII. 120/1 These [glasses] being placed upon the scarified parts. **1879** ATCHERLEY *Trip Boërland* 185 Some soothing ointment applied to my scarified limbs.

scarified, *ppl. a.*[2]: see SCARIFY *v.*[2]

scarifier ('skærɪfaɪə(r)). [f. SCARIFY *v.*[1] + -ER[1].]

1. One who or something which scarifies. *lit.* and *fig.*

1566 SECURIS *Detection* D ij b, Playster makers, clyster geuers, scarifiers, letters out of bloud, &c. **1683** SALMON *Doron Med.* I. 79 Cicatrizers, or 'Scarrifyers'. **1855** DICKENS *Lett.* (1880) I. 403, I have almost finished No. 3, in which I have relieved my indignant soul with a scarifier. **1862** THACKERAY *Philip* XVI, There is an air of fashion in everything which Digges writes,..which makes me pretty certain that D. was my scarifier.

2. = SCARIFICATOR 1.

1611 in COTGR.; and in later Dicts.

3. *Agric.* An implement for loosening the soil.

1797 BILLINGSLEY *View Agric. Somerset* 278, His [Rev. J. Cooke's] instruments called the scuffler, and scarifier, are the best contrivances I ever beheld, for the pulverization of the soil. **1880** J. W. HILL *Guide Agric. Implements* 472 Improved four-wheel wrought iron lever Scarifiers.

4. *Road-making.* A machine used for breaking up a road. Cf. SCARIFY *v.*[1] 3 b.

1892 *Daily News* 21 Oct. 5/5 Our new acquaintance 'the scarifier', whose operations when the roadway of the Thames Embankment is remaking attract so much attention. **1901** *Athenæum* 1 June 697/2 Scarifiers..appear to have been first introduced in England in 1884; and these machines form very valuable adjuncts to steam rolling.

scarify (ˈskærɪfaɪ), *v.*[1] Also 6–8 scarrify. [a. F. *scarifier* (13–14th c. in Hatz.-Darm.), ad. late L. *scarīficāre*, altered form of *scarīfāre* to scarify, ad. Gr. σκαρῑφᾶσθαι, recorded in the senses 'to scratch an outline, sketch lightly, to do anything slightly or slovenly' (L. & Sc.), f. σκάρῑφ-ος pencil, stilus.]

1. a. *trans.* (chiefly *Surg.*) To make a number of scratches or slight incisions in (a portion of the body, a wound). Hence *gen.* to cover with scratches.

1541 R. COPLAND *Galyen's Terap.* F iv, Yf it appere pale, ..it must be scarified and made to blede. **1582** STANYHURST *Æneis* II. (Arb.) 43 You me byd, O Princesse, to scarrify a festered old soare. **1601** HOLLAND *Pliny* XXXII. vii. II. 440 Divers..with foure..teeth of this serpent, scarifie the gums of the upper chaw, in case the teeth therein doe ake. **1604** R. CAWDREY *Table Alph.*, *Scarifie*, to launce, or open a sore. **1662** EVELYN *Chalcogr.* 19 By Insculping, Scarrifying, and making a kind of Incision into it. **1749** FIELDING *Tom Jones* II. ix, The captain..had his veins scarified. **1751** SMOLLETT *Per. Pic.* xxxix. (1779) II. 28 Fixing her nails in his antagonist's face, she scarified all one side of his nose. **1788** GIBBON *Decl. & F.* lv. V. 552 They shaved their hair, and scarified their faces. **1865** LUBBOCK *Preh. Times* xiii. (1878) 459 The body was scarified in horizontal bands. **1876** *Trans. Clin. Soc.* IX. 169 These places were accordingly scarified under the ether spray. **1908** H. D. ROLLESTON *Dis. Liver* 118 The local pain..[should be] relieved by cold applications, poultices, scarifying the skin [etc.].

transf. **1861** GEO. ELIOT *Silas M.* xi. 198 If I offend her, she's sure to scarify my throat with black pepper the next day.

b. *fig.* To make sore, wound. Also, in mod. use, to subject to merciless criticism.

1582 STANYHURST *Æneis* II. (Arb.) 55 Theese woords theyre valiant courradge dooe scarrifye deeply. **1714** *Spect.* No. 595 ¶6 You have Quartered all the foul Language upon me, that could be raked out of..Billingsgate, without knowing..whether I deserve to be Cupped and Scarified at this rate. **1721** *(title)* Medicina Flagellata, or the Doctor scarify'd. **1844** DISRAELI *Coningsby* I. ii, There..he..cut up a rising genius..or scarified some unhappy wretch. **1884** *West. Morn. News* 13 Sept. 4/4 Next week he will be heard at Northampton, whither he goes to scarify the Tories.

c. *transf.* (? Associated with SCAR *sb.*) To cover with scars, to scar.

1687 *Lond. Gaz.* No. 2271/4 A Chesnut Gelding.., scarrified with the Farcie in both his hind Legs. **1697** *Ibid.* No. 3318/4 A Bay Nag with the near Flank a little Scarrified with some former hurt. **1862** DANA *Man. Geol.* 540 Mount Monadnock..is scarified from top to bottom on its northern and western sides.

¶**d.** App. misused for: To anoint (a wound).

1596 WARNER *Alb. Eng.* IX. xlix. (1612) 226 Which had scarrifide our woundes, if wounded, with the Balme Of her sweete Presence. **1607** TOPSELL *Four-f. Beasts* 78 Then scarifie the wound with that oyntment, till it be wrought in.

2. To make incisions in the bark of (a tree).

c **1440** *Pallad. on Husb.* IV. 601 The turgent trunk let scarifie, That humour effluent out of hit hie. **1658** tr. *Porta's Nat. Magic* III. xvii. 98 Boring the stock, or scarrifying it round about. **1824** LOUDON *Encycl. Garden.* §7455 As the trees get old..or infected with canker,..or rottenness, they are scarified. **1856** OLMSTED *Slave States* 326 Every tree.. was scarified for turpentine. **1887** LADY BRASSEY *Last Voy.* xiii. (1889) 300 The vineyards [Australia]..were not in their best looks, having only just been scarified, as the process is called. It means cutting off the branches and reducing the vines to small and ugly bushes, destitute of leaves at this season.

3. a. *Agric.* To break up or loosen (ground) with a scarifier. **b.** *Road-making.* (Cf. quot. 1817 and SCARIFIER 4.)

1805 R. W. DICKSON *Pract. Agric.* I. 21 Instruments..for scarifying and stirring the earth between the rows of drilled crops. *Ibid.* 468 Scarifying the corn, first operation. **1817** in *Repert. Arts*, etc. XXXII. 132 Secondly, a harrow, which is intended to scarify the uneven parts of any road, leaving it even after the operation, previous to the use of the great roller. **1893** *Jrnl. R. Agric. Soc.* Dec. 822 Scarify or cultivate the stubble as soon as possible.

absol. **1829** *Glover's Hist. Derby* I. 196 Skerrify [*sic*] and harrow two or three times over each field.

Hence **ˈscarifying** *vbl. sb.*; **ˈscarifyingly** *adv.*[1]

1533 ELYOT *Cast. Helthe* (1541) 53 b, Letting of bloude, scarifieng callid cupping, sweating, &c. **1667** *Decay Chr. Piety* Pref. §10 It being too probable that this is Gods last experiment upon us, like the causticks and scarifyings to a lethargic patient. **1783** CULLEN *First Lines Physic* §ccxcv. Wks. 1827 II. 32 To draw blood..by cupping and scarifying. **1865** W. WHITE *Eastern England* xvi. 222 The engine..is ready for ploughing, scarifying or drain-cutting. In working the scarifier, the large iron pully is anchored on the edge of the ditch. **1880** JEFFERIES *Hodge & M.* II. 74 He contracts to do their ploughing and scarifying at so much per acre. **1921** D. CANFIELD *Brimming Cup* II. xi. 182 How scarifyingly he would laugh at me.

attrib. **1599** A. M. tr. *Gabelhouer's Bk. Physicke* 363/2 Scarifye the skinne of the tumor with scarifyinge instrumentes. **1865** *Morn. Star* 15 Mar., To try whether the scarifying process may not do more to bring South Carolina back to the Union than [etc.].

scarify (ˈskɛərɪfaɪ), *v.*[2] *slang* (orig. *dial.*). Also scarrify. [Irreg. f. SCARE *v.* + -IFY, perh. after TERRIFY *v.*] *trans.* To scare, frighten; to terrify.

1794 A. THOMAS *Newfoundland Jrnl.* (1968) 107 If a Clergyman was to make his appearance in his Canonical Robes at one of the Outharbours I have little doubt but the Weomen and Children would be scarified out of part of their senses. **1897** G. FORD *Larramys* xxxii. 231 Vine rider! Scarify mos' volks to death, 'er wüd, I reckon. **1901** 'A. FORBES' *Odd Fish* 149 It will be more likely to scarrify 'er if I tells 'er nigh twelve o'clock. **1961** 'F. O'BRIEN' *Hard Life* vii. 53 You want to scarify the divils in the town of Kinnegad? **1966** *New Statesman* 14 Jan. 51/3 There are almost forgotten casualties like *disinterested* and *jejune* and *scarify* (which was once used to mean *to wound*, not as a smart synonym for *to scare*).

Hence **ˈscarified** *ppl. a.*[2], **ˈscarifying** *ppl. a.*; **ˈscarifyingly** *adv.*[2]

1895 MEREDITH *Amazing Marriage* II. xxix. 330 Here I'm like a cannon for defending the house, needs be, and all inside flies off scarified. **1916** M. WEBB *Golden Arrow* iv. 26 Fixing a scarifying gaze on the truant. **1924** N. COWARD *Rat Trap* I. 12, I suppose it's silly nerves, but to be on the brink of a great happiness is a scarifying feeling. **1963** *Times* 13 June 16/7 A comic role (scarifyingly overdone). **1973** *Times* 17 Jan. 17/5, I would support the comparison with a historical rationale which may be deeply disturbing, even scarifying, but it is certainly not motivated by sensationalism or propaganda.

ˈscarily, *adv.* [f. SCARY *a.* + -LY[2].]

1. Timidly.

1845 W. G. SIMMS *Wigwam & Cabin* 1st Ser. 107 My heart as cold as ice, and jumping up and down as scarily as a rabbit's. **1880** HOWELLS *Undisc. Country* ix. 133 The light ..was held scarily aloft above the head of an elderly woman.

2. Frighteningly, unnervingly.

1967 *Economist* 19 Aug. 664/2 Shell is running a scarily fine operation with a smaller proportion than most companies of its tanker needs provided by its own fleet and with relatively short charters. **1978** L. BLOCK *Burglar in Closet* xi. 94 He'd come scarily close to the truth.

scaring (ˈskɛərɪŋ), *vbl. sb.* [f. SCARE *v.* + -ING[1].] The action of the vb. SCARE.

1573–80 TUSSER *Husb.* (1878) 32 No scaring with dog. **1580** *Reg. Privy Council Scot.* III. 295 Scarring and debarring of the salmound fischeis. **1611** COTGR., *Espoventement*..a frighting, fraying, skaring. **1852** G. W. JOHNSON *Cottage Gard. Dict.* s.v. *Scares*, It is best to employ boys for the short time scaring is required.

scaring (ˈskɛərɪŋ), *ppl. a.* [f. SCARE *v.* + -ING[2].] That scares; terrifying.

1641 MILTON *Reform.* ii. Wks. 1851 III. 64 As a tender Mother takes her Child and holds it over the pit with scarring words that it may learne to feare, where danger is. **1764** GOLDSM. *Trav.* 205 As a child, when scaring sounds molest, Clings close and closer to the mother's breast. **1813** COLERIDGE *Night-Scene* 37 A rude and scaring note, my friend! **1879** BARING-GOULD *Germany* II. 207 Let not women be frightened by the scaring name.

†**ˈscariole.** *Obs.* Also 5 skariole, 6 scaryole. [ad. (through med.L.) It. *scariola* (whence F. *escarole, scarole.*] Broad-leaved endive.

c **1400** tr. *Secreta Secret., Gov. Lordsh.* 73 Wylde letus þat feldmen clepyn skarioles. **1422** *Ibid., Priv. Priv.* 244 Letus sauage, that is y-callid scariole. **1526** *Grete Herball* cl. (1529) 1 v, Endiuia is endyue... It is otherwyse called scaryole. **1597** GERARDE *Herbal* II. xxvii. 222. **1658** PHILLIPS, *Scariole*, a kind of herb otherwise called broad leaved endive. **1725** *Bradley's Fam. Dict.* s.v. *Syrup*, Two Leaves of Succory, Dandelion, Endive or Scariole.

scariose (ˈskɛərɪəʊs), *a.* *Bot.* [ad. mod.L. *scariōsus*, of obscure origin.] = SCARIOUS 1.

1785 MARTYN *Rousseau's Bot.* xxvi. (1794) 383 The scales in the Artichoke are scariose or ragged. **1806** GALPINE *Brit. Bot.* 21 Glumes scariose. **1881** BAKER in *Jrnl. Linn. Soc.* XVIII. 279 Stipules large, brown, deltoid, scariose.

†**Scariot(h.** *Obs.* Aphetic forms of ISCARIOT.

c **1380** WYCLIF *Wks.* (1880) 49 þei leden wiþ hem a scarioth stolen fro is eldris by þefte to robbe pore men bi beggynge. *c* **1550** R. BIESTON *Bayte Fortune* B iij b, Great cause hath now the Scariot to wepe & to bewaile it.

scarious (ˈskɛərɪəs), *a.* [ad. F. *scarieux*, ad. mod.L. *scariōsus* SCARIOSE *a.*]

1. *Bot.* Having a dry and shrivelled appearance.

1806 TURTON tr. *Linn. Syst. Nat.* VII. Expl. Terms, *Scarious*, dry and rigid, as if dead. **1819** *Pantologia*, *Scarious leaf*, in botany. **1872** OLIVER *Elem. Bot.* II. 261 The scarious perianth by which the Order [*Juncaceæ*] is distinguished from Liliaceæ. **1882** G. ALLEN in *Nature* 17 Aug. 372 The corolla is thin and scarious.

2. *Zool.* Dry, not fleshy.

1861 HULME tr. *Moquin-Tandon* I. 49 In some animals.. the tongue is scarious cartilaginous, or provided with a corneous investment. **1872** COUES *Key N. Amer. Birds* 47 When the harder sorts of either scutella or plates are roughened without obvious elevation, the leg is said to be scabrous or scarious.

scaritid (ˈskærɪtɪd), *a.* [f. mod.L. *Scarītēs*: see below.] Pertaining to the *Scaritini*, a tribe of ground-beetles of the family *Carabidæ*, typified by the genus *Scarites*. So **scaˈritidan**, a beetle of this tribe.

1837 KIRBY *Richardson's Fauna Bor.-Amer.* IV. 6 *Oxygnathus* De Jean, and some of the other Scaritidans. **1890** *Century Dict.* s.v. *Morio*, The genus pertains to the scaritid section of *Carabidæ*.

†**ˈscarkle**, *v.* *Obs.* *rare*$^{-1}$. [Cf. DISPARPLE, DISPARKLE *vbs.*] *trans.* To scatter, disperse.

c **1450** *Roll* in *3rd Rep. Hist. MSS. Comm.* (1872) 280/1 For therby be the Frensshemenne riched, the Englishmenne povered; they mightly recured of men & peple, we distroied; they to gader, we assundred scarkeled.

scarlad, scarlat, obs. ff. SCARLET *sb.* and *a.*

†**scarˈlatical**, *a.* *nonce-wd.* Having the prejudices characteristic of those who wear the 'scarlet' of a doctor of divinity or law.

1672 WOOD *Life* (O.H.S.) II. 243 Dr. Clerk..lazy and idle, scarlaticall.

scarlatina (skɑːləˈtiːnə). *Path.* Also 9 scarlet(t)ina. [a. mod.L. *scarlatina* (Sydenham 1676), a. It. *scarlattina* (used by Lancelotti in 1527), fem. of *scarlattino* adj., dim. of *scarlatto* SCARLET. Cf. F. *scarlatine*, Sp., Pg. *escarlatina.*] = SCARLET FEVER. (Popularly often misapprehended as denoting a milder form of the disease than that designated by the vernacular term.)

1803 *Med. Jrnl.* X. 455 Several children were..seized with the measles and scarlatina. **1813** WILBERFORCE *Let.* in *Life* (1838) IV. 131 One of our children having had the Scarlettina. **1845** G. E. DAY tr. *Simon's Anim. Chem.* I. 300 Persons suffering from scarlatina. **1863** MISS BRADDON *Eleanor's Victory* III. i. 16 She looks as if she were going to a ball; or going to have the scarlatina.

allusively **1823** MOORE *Fables Holy Alliance* 49 Woe to Kings when Freedom's fever Once turns into a Scarletina!

scarlatinal (skɑːləˈtiːnəl), *a.* [f. prec. + -AL[1].] Belonging to, or resulting from, scarlatina.

1861 GRAHAM *Pract. Med.* 683 Hence, for want of caution at this time we may have the scarlatinal dropsy. **1878** L. BROWNE *Throat & Dis.* 137 In scarlatinal sore throat the local differences are not so well marked.

scarlatiniform (skɑːləˈtiːnɪfɔːm), *a.* [f. SCARLATIN-A + -(I)FORM.] Resembling the rash or eruption of scarlatina.

1866 FLINT *Princ. Med.* (1880) 1042 A scarlatiniform eruption. **1899** *Allbutt's Syst. Med.* VIII. 65 Eruptions of toxic character, erythematous, scarlatiniform [etc.].

scarlatinine (skɑːləˈtiːnɪn). [f. SCARLATIN-A + -INE.] The hypothetical infectious principle of scarlatina.

1864 FARR in *Rep. Reg. Gen.* Suppl. 34 When any zymotic matter such as varioline, scarlatinine or typhine finds its way into a village or street, it is more likely to pass from house to house. **1897** *Allbutt's Syst. Med.* II. 164 A toxine has been extracted from the urine, of which the chemical composition has been ascertained, and to which the name Scarlatinine has been given.

scarlatinoid (skɑːləˈtiːnɔɪd), *a.* and *sb.* [-OID.]

a. *adj.* Having the appearance of scarlatina. **b.** *sb.* One of a group of Erythemas which closely resemble scarlatina.

1886 FAGGE *Princ. Med.* (1888) I. 172 A diffused scarlatinoid eruption. **1899** *Allbutt's Syst. Med.* VIII. 464 The first group which they call Puteoloids and Scarlatinoids comprises the erythemas which simulate the erythematous eruptive fevers in all their stages.

scarlatinous (skɑːləˈtiːnəs), *a.* [f. SCARLATIN-A + -OUS.] Affected with scarlatina.

1878 T. BRYANT *Pract. Surg.* I. 141 Scarlatinous tonsils.

scarlatte, obs. form of SCARLET *sb.* and *a.*

†**scarle.** *Obs.* Also 5 skerel(e. [Earlier *skerel*, f. *skerre* SCARE *v.*: see -EL.] A scarecrow.

c **1440** *Promp. Parv.* 457/2 Skerel, *larva* [*c* **1460** Winch., skerele]. **1483** *Cath. Angl.* 321/2 A scarle or visern, *larua*.

scarless (ˈskɑːlɪs), *a.* [f. SCAR *sb.*[1] + -LESS.]

1. Showing no scar; lacking blemish.

1630 DRUMM. OF HAWTH. *Flowres of Sion* D 2, Amidst that Masse of Ruines they did make, Safe and all scarrelesse yet remaines my Minde. **1863** *Possib. Creation* 103 The living canvass..is..as scarless and unsullied, as if it had never been touched by the burning pencils of the sun. **1891** MEREDITH *One of our Conq.* I. xii. 226 His pride in appearing woundless and scarless.

2. Leaving no scar.

1823 BYRON *Juan* XIII. lxxxii, Escaping with a few slight scarless sneers.

scarlet (ˈskɑːlɪt), *sb.* and *a.* Forms: 3–7 scarlat, skarlet, 4 scarleit, scharlette, 4–6, 8 scarlett, 5 scarlatte, scarlad, skarlot, 5–6 scarlot, skarlat, 5, 8 skarlett, 6 scarlette, skarlette, skarlote, skerlyt, 3– scarlet. [Aphetic a. OF. *escarlate* sb. fem. (mod.F. *écarlate*) = Pr. *escarlat* masc., *-ata* fem. In Fr. and Pr. recorded from the 12th c.; the other Rom. forms are later: Sp., Pg. *escarlate, -ata*, It. *scarlatto*, med.L. *scarlat(t)um, -a, scarlettum* (1204 in *Excerpta Historica* 393). In Teut. the word appears as ON. *skarlat, skallat*, MHG. *scharlât*, early mod.Flem. *schaerlat*; also, with etymologizing alteration (cf. LAKE *sb.*[5]), MHG. *scharlach(en*, MLG., Du. *scharlaken* (whence Da. *skarlagen*, Sw. *skarlakan*, Icel. *skarlak, skarlakan*). From It. are prob. mod. Gr.

σκαρλάτον, Church Slav. *skrŭlato*, Serbian *skrlet*, Turk. *iskerlet*.

If the OHG. *scarlahhan*, in a gloss explained as 'shorn cloth' (*rasilis*) be identical with this word (the interpretation as well as the form being due to popular etymology), it is the earliest evidence of its existence. It is hardly possible that this OHG. word can be the source of the Rom. forms. The prevailing view is that OF. *escarlate* is an alteration of Pers. *saqalāt, siqalāt, suqlāt*, a kind of rich cloth, a derivative of which appears as CICLATOUN. (The form *saqirlāt*, given in some Arabic dictionaries, is modern and prob. adopted from some European language.)]

A. *sb.*

1. † **a.** In early use, some rich cloth, often of a bright red colour, but (according to Fr., MDu., and med.L. sources) also sometimes of other colours, as 'pers', blue, green, brown. *Obs.* **b.** In later use, cloth or clothing of the colour described in 2.

† *scarlet in grain* (*s. engreyned, grayned s.*, etc.): cloth fast dyed of a scarlet colour (cf. GRAIN *sb.*[1] 10 and INGRAIN *a.*). It is doubtful whether 'scarlet and grene', frequently occurring in ME. poetry in descriptions of splendid attire, originated in a misunderstanding of this phrase.

c **1250** *Death* 10 in *O.E. Misc.* 168 Ȝe þat sittet i-schrud wið skarlet and wið palle. **1297** R. GLOUC. (Rolls) 6390 A robe he let him ssape uerst of blod red scarlet þere. **13..** *K. Alis.* 4987 Hy clothen hem with grys and ermyne With golde and siluer and skarlet pers fyne. **13..** *Reinbrun* v, Scarlet and grene wel y-wrouȝt. *c* **1375** *Cursor M.* 25463 (Fairf.) Nauþer aske I skarlet ne grene Ne purtraied stede. *c* **1380** *Sir Ferumb.* 4464 And we han her scarletes & grene, & cloþes of tarse. *c* **1386** CHAUCER *Sir Thopas* 16 His rode is lyk scarlet in grayn. *a* **1400** *Morte Arth.* 3459 And one he henttis a hode of scharlette fulle riche. **14..** *Guy of Warw.* 8996 Hys lymmes were bare and euyll beseyn, That some tyme were clad in scarlet in greyne. *a* **1420** *Wyclif's N.T., Rev.* xviii. 16 Wo! wo! thilke greet citee, that was clothid with bijs and purpur, and reed scarlet. **1480** *Coventry Leet-bk.* 438 The seid Recordor answered & saide that they shuld not be relesed þerof for þe best peice of scarlet in Englond. *a* **1533** LD. BERNERS *Huon* ix. 23 Huon toke hys cloke of skerlat & wrappyd it about hys arme. **1545** *Rates Custom ho.* d vj b, In primus a brode cloth payeth xii. A scarlette xxxiiii. *a* **1548** HALL *Chron., Hen. V*, 52 b, The Mayre of London.. appareled in orient grayned Skarlet. **1588** HICKOCK tr. *Frederick's Voy.* 31 Ships bring cloth of Wooll, Scarlets, Veluets, Opium and Chickenes. **1649** J. MASTER *Daily Expense-bk.* 4 Aug., For 4 ya & half of right french scarlet at 45[s]. **1662** *Comenius' Janua Ling. Triling.* 96 Sattins, damasks, scarlets, cobweb-lawns [etc.]. **1796** BURKE *Regic. Peace* iv. Wks. IX. 123 An Ambassador, whose robes are lined with a scarlet dyed in the blood of Judges. **1859** TENNYSON *Elaine* 501 Then the trumpets blew Proclaiming his the prize, who wore the sleeve Of scarlet, and the pearls.

2. a. A brilliant vivid red colour, inclining to orange.

c **1440** *Promp. Parv.* 442/2 Scarlet, colowre, *lutus.* **1530** PALSGR. 265/2 Scarlet a reed colour. **1648** HERRICK *Hesper.*, *Weeping Cherry*, Which rubies, corals, scarlets, all For tincture, wonder at. **1690** LOCKE *Hum. Und.* III. iv. §11 His Friend demanding what Scarlet was? the blind Man answered, It was like the sound of a Trumpet. *a* **1734** R. NORTH *Life John North* (1742) 237 Scarlet was commonly called the King's Colour. **1788** COWPER *Gratitude* 29 This moveable structure of shelves,.. Where flaming in scarlet and gold My poems enchanted I view. **1856** RUSKIN *Mod. Paint.* IV. v. iii. §24. 53 In this chord the scarlet is the most powerful colour. **1894** K. GRAHAME *Pagan P.* 68 A riot of scarlet on gold, the red poppy of our native fields tosses heavy tresses with gipsy *abandon*.

b. A pigment or dye of this colour. In recent use also *spec.*, any one of a certain group of coal-tar colouring matters used in scarlet pigments and dyes.

1653 JER. TAYLOR *Serm. for Year* (1678) 333 A ship laden with Persian Carpets, and the ingredients of the rich Scarlet. **1672** W. S. *Polygraphice* 178 For a Scarlet. Take Vermilion, and deepen it with Lake or Indian Red. **1859** GEO. ELIOT *Adam Bede* xxi, He had already a high reputation in the district for his dyes, and he was bent on discovering some method by which he could reduce the expense of crimsons and scarlets. **1862** O'NEILL *Dict. Calico Print. & Dyeing* 61 The best scarlets are still obtained from cochineal alone as colouring matter. **1886** tr. *Benedikt's Chem. Coal-tar Colours* 198 The scarlets have replaced cochineal to a considerable extent in wool-dyeing.

3. Official or ceremonial costume of scarlet, as the uniform of a soldier, the gown or robe of a doctor of divinity or law, a judge, a cardinal, etc.; also, the scarlet coat worn in the hunting field (= PINK *sb.* 6). Hence *occas.* the rank, dignity, or office signified by a scarlet robe.

1496 in *Rep. Hist. MSS. Comm. Var. Coll.* (1907) IV. 212 All they of the xxiiij that hath be maire shall ride in scarlett ayenste the Kynge. **1568** T. HOWELL *Arb. Amitie* (1879) 81 For Fortune may as then, make kings as pleaseth her: Since she the riche and noble men, to scarlets can prefer. **1610** B. JONSON *Alch.* I. iii, This Summer He will be of the Clothing of his company. And, next spring, call'd to the Scarlet. **1654** H. L'ESTRANGE *Chas. I* (1655) 110 The Lord Maior with his confraternity of Aldermen also mounted and in their Scarlets. **1685** RYCAUT *Contn. Lives Popes* 16 After this he made little account of his Scarlet, or degree of Cardinal. **1706** HEARNE *Collect.* (O.H.S.) I. 311 White Kennett.. sometimes waited on Dr. Wallis to Church with his skarlett. **1764** *Oxf. Sausage* 38 The splendid Fortunes and the beauteous Face.. Too soon are caught by Scarlet and by Lace. **1885** *Field* 7 Feb. 147/3 A good man in scarlet is down at the first fence. **1891** MORRIS *Poems by the Way* (1896) 17 What mayor shall rule the hall we built? Whose scarlet sweep the floor?

4. † **a.** One who wears a scarlet uniform or insignia; e.g. a judge. *Obs.*

c **1610** BEAUM & FL. *Philaster* v. i. (1622) 70 Doe the Lords bow, and the regarded scarlets, Kisse their gumd gols, and cry we are your seruants? **1628** FELTHAM *Resolves* I. viii. 18 Open Rebukes are for Magistrates, and Courts of Iustice: for Stelled Chambers, and for Scarlets, in the thronged Hall.

b. *occas.* Persons clothed in scarlet; men in the hunting field (cf. PINK *sb.* 6 b) or on the golf links; also soldiers in red uniform.

1827 *Sporting Mag.* XIX. 353 The whole field was fairly pounded: I was one among the number, and consider myself a good bit of scarlet too. **1842** G. F. CARNEGIE *Golfiana* in R. Clark *Golf* (1875) 150 He whirls his club to catch the proper swing, And freely bets round all the scarlet ring. **1896** A. E. HOUSMAN *Shropshire Lad* xxxv, Gay the files of scarlet follow.

† **5.** ? An aristocratic street ruffian, a Mohock.

1755 J. SHEBBEARE *Lydia* (1769) II. 437, I expected to have seen her.. encouraging the young bloods, bucks and scarlets at a riot in Drury-lane.

6. Short for *scarlet strawberry* (see B. 4 c).

1815 SIR JOS. BANKS in *Trans. Hort. Soc.* I. 55. **1824** J. BARNET *Ibid.* (1826) VI. 155 Princess Charlotte's Strawberry.. is perhaps the richest of all the Scarlets. **1828** *Trans. Hort. Soc.* (1830) VII. 345 Old Scarlet.

7. A small moth, *Erastria ostrina.*

1832 J. RENNIE *Consp. Butterfl. & Moths* 97 The Scarlet (*E. ostrina*, Curtis) appears in June.

B. *adj.* (Originally the sb. used attrib.)

1. a. Having, or pertaining to, the colour scarlet (see A. 2).

c **1386** CHAUCER *Wife's Prol.* 559 Therfore I made my visitacions,.. And wered vpon my gaye scarlet gytes. **1436** in *E.E. Wills* (1882) 107 All-so I wol that Iohn Melbourne haue my scarlet goune furred with martrouns. **1479** in *Eng. Gilds* (1870) 415 He to come in.. his Skarlat cloke furred. **1501** DOUGLAS *Pal. Hon.* I. xlvi, Purpour colour, punik and skarlote hewis. *a* **1586** SIDNEY *Arcadia* III. (Sommer) 248 Sixe maides, all in one liuerie of skarlette petticotes. *a* **1633** T. TAYLOR *God's Judgem.* II. vii. (1642) 110 He kept two or three tall fellowes in Skarlet Liveries. **1677** WOOD *Life* (O.H.S.) II. 386 The chancellour,.. and the rest of his retinew, put on scarlet habits. **1717** LADY M. W. MONTAGU *Let. to Mrs. T.* 1 Apr., Mine [*sc.* a sofa] is of scarlet cloth, with a gold fringe. **1784** COWPER *Task* I. 320 The sycamore, capricious in attire, Now green, now tawny, and ere autumn yet Have chang'd the woods, in scarlet honours bright. **1816** KEATS *To my Brother George* 130 The poppies show their scarlet coats. **1879** *St. George's Hosp. Rep.* IX. 722 She also now had a scarlet eruption.

b. Clothed in scarlet, wearing a scarlet uniform or distinguishing dress.

1591 SHAKS. *1 Hen. VI*, I. iii. 56 Out Tawney-Coates, out Scarlet Hypocrite. **1642** MILTON *Apol. Smect.* Wks. 1851 III. 280 The invincible warriour Zeale shaking loosely the slack reins drives over the heads of Scarlet Prelats and such as are insolent to maintaine traditions. **1902** *Words of Eyewitness* 3 There is no more universally beloved individual in the world than this same scarlet Atkins.

c. Red with shame or indignation. †Also *transf.* blushing, indignant.

1865 BARING-GOULD *Werewolves* xii. 222 Several times his face had become scarlet, and his eyes had fallen. **1881** W. H. MALLOCK *Rom. 19th Cent.* II. 120 She flushed scarlet.

transf. **1593** SHAKS. *Rich. II*, III. iii. 99 But ere the Crowne he lookes for, liue in peace, Ten thousand bloody crownes of Mothers Sonnes Shall ill become the flower of Englands face, Change the complexion of her Maid-pale Peace To Scarlet Indignation.

2. *fig.* **a.** Of an offence (after Isa. i. 18), hence *occas.* of an offender: Heinous, deep-dyed.

[**1613** SHAKS. *K. Hen. VIII*, III. ii. 255 (To Wolsey) Thou scarlet sinne.] **1641** J. SHUTE *Sarah & Hagar* (1649) 206 Who doth forgive..even foul sins, crimson, scarlet iniquities, upon humiliation. **1656** SIR G. WHARTON *Hemerol., Proanaph.* 30 The Final cause [of earthquakes], is a sign of an Angry God, justly provoked by the Scarlet crimes of a sinful People. **1709** MRS. MANLEY *Secret Mem.* (1720) IV. 97 How precipit up, as thou dost, Vertue and Moderation, when thy self art Scarlet deep tinged with the highest Crimes?

b. in allusions to the glaring effect of the colour.

1820 HAZLITT *Lect. Dram. Lit.* 16 The deathblow which had been struck at scarlet vice and bloated hypocrisy.

3. General combinations: **a.** parasynthetic, as *scarlet-barred, -blossomed, -breasted, -circled, -coated, -coloured, -crested, -flowered, -haired, -moustached* adjs.; frequent in specific names of animals and plants. **scarlet-chested (grass) parrakeet, parrot**, a small blue and green parrot with a red breast, *Neophema splendida*, found in parts of southern Australia.

1832 J. RENNIE *Consp. Butterfl. & Moths* 227 The *Scarlet Barred Gold (*Lampronia sanguinella*, Stephens). **1845** *Florist's Jrnl.* 178 The well-known *scarlet-blossomed currant. **1822** LATHAM *Gen. Hist. Birds* II. 121 *Scarlet-breasted Parrot... Inhabits New-Holland. **1901** A. J. CAMPBELL *Nests & Eggs Austral. Birds* II. 654 (*heading*) *Scarlet-chested Grass Parrakeet. **1931** N. W. CAYLEY *What Bird is That?* 152 Scarlet-chested Parrot... Rarely recorded, then only as isolated pairs. **1938** —— *Austral. Parrots* 283, I had the pleasure of seeing the Scarlet-chested Parrakeet living happily and breeding freely. **1977** *Weekly Times* (Melbourne) 19 Jan. 23/3 Mrs Jones (West Hobart) would be interested to hear from any reader who would exchange orange-breasted wax-bills for scarlet-chested parrots. **1704** POPE *Windsor For.* 116 His purple crest, and *scarlet-circled eyes. **1693** R. DUKE in *Dryden's Juvenal* iv. (1697) 78 So many Sesterces were swallow'd down, To stuff one *Scarlet-coated Court Buffoon. **1617** HIERON *Wks.* (1619) II. 317 The citie of Rome.. may shew her selfe to bee indeed that *Scarlet-coloured Harlot, described by John in his Reuelation. **1753** CHAMBERS *Cycl. Supp.* s.v. *Lychnis*, The lesser *scarlet flowered Constantinople lychnis. **1872** *Routledge's Ev. Boy's Ann.* 419/1 The *Scarlet-Haired Poppy. **1872** COUES *Key N. Amer. Birds* 192 Bill dark; *scarlet-crested, *scarlet-moustached.

b. qualifying the name of a colour, as *scarlet-crimson, -red, -vermilion.*

1882 *Garden* 7 Oct. 312/2 Of older self-flowers.. Joseph Green, bright *scarlet-crimson. *c* **1386** CHAUCER *Prol.* 456 Hir hosen weren of fyn *scarlet reed. **1590** SPENSER *F.Q.* I. ii. 13 A goodly Lady clad in scarlot red. *a* **1711** KEN *Christophil* Poet. Wks. 1721 I. 510 She saw the Place where Jesus bled, And dy'd the Turff of Scarlet-red. **1882** *Garden* 29 July 104/2 It has flowers.. of bright scarlet-red hue. *Ibid.* 25 Mar. 196/2 Many drooping flowers.. of a brilliant *scarlet-vermilion hue.

4. a. Special collocations: **scarlet-day**, † **scarlet-gown day**, an occasion in university or civic life observed by the public wearing of state or official robes of scarlet; † **scarlet-grain**, = ALKERMES 1, cf. KERMES; **scarlet lady**, an abusive epithet applied to the Church of Rome in allusion to Rev. xvii. 1-5; **Scarlet Lancers**, nickname for the 16th Lancers, from their distinctive red tunic; **scarlet letter** chiefly *U.S.*, a representation of the letter *A* in scarlet cloth which persons convicted of adultery were condemned to wear, as described in the novel by Hawthorne (see quot. 1850); also in *fig.* and allusive use (cf. BRAND *sb.* 4 b); **Scarlet Pimpernel** (see also sense 4 c), the name assumed by the hero of a series of novels by Baroness Orczy (1865–1947), a dashing but elusive Englishman who rescued potential victims of the French Reign of Terror, used allusively; also *attrib.*; cf. PIMPERNEL 4; **scarlet rash**, a scarlet eruption, symptomatic of certain diseases; † **scarlet runner** *Obs. Mil. slang*, a soldier, with reference to his scarlet jacket; also *pl.*, a scarlet military uniform; **scarlet ward**, a part of a fever hospital reserved for patients suffering from scarlet fever; **scarlet whore** = *scarlet lady* above; **scarlet woman**, orig. = *scarlet lady* above; now used to mean: a notoriously immoral woman; a prostitute.

1632–33 in *Publ. Colon. Soc. Mass.* VIII. 361 [That the lecturer should preach on all the] *scarlet days, as they name them. **1721** AMHERST *Terræ-Fil.* No. 39 (1726) II. 51 He preached it upon a scarlet day, when the vice-chancellor and all the doctors go to church in red. **1888** *Daily News* 11 June 5/7 In University parlance it was a Scarlet Day. **1710** J. CHAMBERLAYNE *St. Gt. Brit.* II. III. (ed. 23) 663* The *Scarlet-Gown Days in the University of Oxford. **1597** GERARDE *Herbal* III. xxx. 1158 The Oke which beareth the *scarlet graine is a small tree. **1601** HOLLAND *Pliny* XXVII. ix. II. 280 The berrie Coccum Gnidium, in colour resembleth the Scarlet graine. **1807** SYD. SMITH *Peter Plymley's Lett.* ii, I will not dispute with you whether the Pope be or be not the *Scarlet Lady of Babylon. **1873** *Punch* 23 Aug. 72/2 Let us be just even to the Scarlet Lady. **1885** 'J. S. WINTER' (*title*) Bootles' Baby: a story of the *Scarlet Lancers. **1850** N. HAWTHORNE (*title*) The *scarlet letter. **1872** *Cincinnati* (Ohio) *Times & Chron.* 28 May 2/1 A grand mass meeting in Gotham the other night consecrated Apollo Hall by unfurling therein the scarlet letter—we mean banner—of Woodhull and Free Love. **1882** *Internat. Rev.* Mar. 301 Polygamy is the scarlet letter upon the brow of this young commonwealth which proclaims her deep shame and forbids her entrance into the sisterhood of States. **1944** W. J. CARRINGTON *Safe Convoy* 112 However, a few minutes later when the unwanted visitor arrived, she directed her venomous tongue against the daughter whom she branded from head to foot with verbal scarlet letters. **1965** M. DRABBLE *Millstone* 20, I walked around with a scarlet letter embroidered upon my bosom.. but the A stood for Abstinence, not for Adultery. **1977** D. ANTHONY *Stud Game* xxi. 132 You hard-shelled Baptist prig. You can't see past the scarlet letter, can you? **1958** E. H. CLEMENTS *Uncommon Cold* vii. 178 As for cloak-and-dagger work on the moor, what price your family of *Scarlet Pimpernels? **1958** *Observer* 25 May 15/5 George Baker.. appears as a Scarlet Pimpernel type. **1961** *Guardian* 24 May 11/3 A war-time Scarlet Pimpernel organisation which rescued thousands of East European Jews from the Nazis. **1977** M. DRABBLE *Ice Age* III. 287 The image of Anthony as Scarlet Pimpernel, flying out to rescue stepdaughter in distress. **1822–29** *Good's Study Med.* (ed. 3) III. 16 The *angina gangrænosa* (sore throat with *scarlet-rash) usually commences in the winter or the spring. *c* **1864** BROUGH & HALLIDAY *Area Belle* 7 Who are you calling bluebottle?—you *scarlet runner! **1920** G. FRANKAU *Peter Jackson* VII. 78 'A few of our old militia uniforms.' 'Not the old scarlet-runners?'... 'The identical, sir, with the old white facings.' **1888** HONNOR MORTEN *Sk. Hosp. Life* 51 The laconic order, 'To the *Scarlet Ward', is given. **1590** SPENSER *F. Q.* I. viii. 29 Forthwith he gaue in charge vnto his Squire, That *scarlot whore to keepen carefully. **1648** WINYARD *Midsummer-Moon* 1 The Scarlet-whore of Babylon spawn'd it with her menstruous profluviums. **1709** *Tatler* No. 190 ¶2 Nor yet did that Epistle at all come unto thee from the Mansion-House of the Scarlet Whore. **1816** SOUTHEY *Poet's Pilgr.* II. iii. 10 *note*, I have seen her somewhere called the *Scarlet Woman. **1853** T. PARKER *Theism, Atheism, & Popular Theology* 131 Atheism turns the soul out of doors, and the flesh has no better time of it; no, has a worse time, with its scarlet woman 'tinging the pavement with proud wine too good for the tables of pontiffs'. **1867** LOWELL *Gt. Publ. Char.* Wks. 1890 II. 274 The latter old lady [*sc.* the Church of Rome] may be the Scarlet Woman, or the Beast with ten horns, if you will. **1924** in H. Havelock Ellis *Stud. Psychol. Sex* (ed. 3) II. 124, I sought out a scarlet woman in the streets of —— and went home with her. **1977** M. KENYON *Rapist* x. 115 'Is this me?' She was holding.. a turtle-neck jersey dress... 'Or would you hazard it's.. old-fashioned for the scarlet woman of the bogs?'

b. In names of birds, insects, etc.: **scarlet cantharis**, a beetle, *Cantharis cardinalis*; **scarlet finch**, *Fringilla coccinea* (Shaw); **scarlet**

grosbeak, the Cardinal-bird; **scarlet ibis**, *Eudocimus ruber*, a bird congeneric with the typical Ibis, native in tropical America; **scarlet lory**, a name given to several birds of the Parrot-tribe; **scarlet macaw**, *Psittacus macao*, a parrot native in S. America and the West Indies; **scarlet mite**, *Trombidium holosericeum*; **scarlet mussel**, a shell-fish (see quot.); **scarlet rose-finch**, *Carpodacus erythrinus* (cf. *rose-finch* s.v. ROSE *sb.* 24 b); **scarlet snake**, a name applied to two colubriform snakes of tropical America (see quot.); **scarlet sparrow**, *Tanagra rubra*; **scarlet spoonbill**, *Platalea ajaja*; **scarlet tanager**, the RED BIRD, *Pyranga rubra*; **scarlet tiger (moth)**, *Hypercampa dominula*.

1806 SHAW *Gen. Zool.* VI. 81 One of the most elegant insects of this genus is the *Scarlet Cantharis. **1783** LATHAM *Synopsis Birds* III. 270 *Scarlet Finch... Inhabits Sandwich Islands. **1837** GOULD *Birds of Europe* III. Pl. 206 *Scarlet Grosbeak. **1785** PENNANT *Arctic Zool.* II. 458 *Scarlet Ibis. **1835** J. J. AUDUBON *Ornith. Biogr.* V. 62, I have found the Scarlet Ibis less numerous than even the Glossy Ibis. **1971** *Country Life* 22 July 220/1 The vivid colouring of the scarlet ibis is as expressive of the South American tropics as the bright colours of macaws and toucans. **1751** G. EDWARDS *Nat. Hist. Birds* IV. 172 The *Scarlet Lory. **1811** SHAW *Gen. Zool.* VIII. 533 *Psittacus grandis*..Scarlet Lory. *Ibid.* 386 The *Scarlet Maccaw. **1826** KIRBY & SP. *Entomol.* III. 492 The little *scarlet mite ..(*Trombidium holosericeum*). **1672** *Phil. Trans.* VII. 5022 The *Scarlet-Mustle, having a purple-vein, which being prickt with a needle yeilds a perfect Purple or Scarlet Juyce that will not be washt out of the Linnen died therewith. **1884** H. SEEBOHM *Hist. Brit. Birds* II. 47 The *Scarlet Rose-finch is not particularly interesting at its breeding-grounds. **1976** J. T. R. & E. M. SHARROCK *Rare Birds in Britain & Ireland* 284 Scarlet Rosefinch..breeds from Germany and southern Sweden eastwards to Kamchatka. **1842** HOLBROOK *N. Amer. Herpet.* III. 127 *Rhinostoma coccinea*... The *Scarlet Snake. *Ibid.*, The 'Couleuvre écarlate' (Scarlet Snake) of Bosc is quite another animal, doubtless the *Calamaria elapsoidea*. **1764** G. EDWARDS *Glean. Nat. Hist.* III. 278 The *Scarlet Sparrow. **1819** SHAW *Gen. Zool.* XI. 642 *Scarlet Spoonbill. **1808–13** A. WILSON *Amer. Ornith.* (1831) II. 226 *Scarlet Tanager. **1832** J. RENNIE *Consp. Butterfl. & Moths* 42 The *Scarlet Tiger (*Hypercampa Dominula*, Stephens) appears in June.

c. In names of plants and fruits: **scarlet banana**, *Musa coccinea*; **scarlet-bean** = *scarlet runner* below; **scarlet cardinal-flower**, **scarlet lobelia**, *Lobelia cardinalis* (see CARDINAL-FLOWER); **scarlet convolvulus**, *Ipomæa coccinea*; **scarlet geranium**, a pelargonium with scarlet blossoms, largely used as a bedding-plant (see GERANIUM 2 and PELARGONIUM); **scarlet maple**, *Acer rubrum*; **scarlet oak**, *Quercus coccinea* (see OAK 1 b); also †the Holm Oak, *Quercus Ilex*; **scarlet painted-cup** (see PAINTED *ppl. a.* 4); **scarlet pea** (see quot.); **scarlet pimpernel**, *Anagallis arvensis* (see PIMPERNEL 3 and 3 b); **scarlet runner (bean)**, a red- or white-flowered climbing bean, *Phaseolus coccineus*, or its edible pods; **scarlet sage**, *Salvia fulgens*, a native of Mexico (Miller *Plant-n.* 1884, 245); also *S. splendens*, a native of Brazil (*Cent. Dict.* 1891); **scarlet seed**, a name of two tropical trees (see quot. 1866); **scarlet strawberry**, any cultivated variety of the Virginian Strawberry, *Fragaria virginiana*, having scarlet 'fruit'; **scarlet thorn**, *Cratægus coccinea*.

1885 LADY BRASSEY *The Trades* 29 The *scarlet banana. **1731** MILLER *Gard. Dict.* s.v. *Phaseolus*, The *Scarlet Bean. **1852** MRS. CARLYLE *Lett.* II. 168 Some scarlet beans that were growing in his own piece of garden. **1698** *Scarlet Cardinal-Flower [see CARDINAL-FLOWER]. **1856** O. W. HOLMES *Aut. Breakf.-t.* x. (1895) 253 Dream of that winding shore Where scarlet cardinals bloom—for me no more. **1823** CRABB *Technol. Dict.* s.v. *Scarlet*, *Scarlet-Convolvulus. **1760** *Scarlet geranium [see GERANIUM 2]. **1870** RUSKIN *Lect. Art* vi. 162 There are few flowers of which the impression on the eye is more definitely of flat colour, than the scarlet geranium. **1874** *Scarlet lobelia [see LOBELIA]. **1768** P. MILLER *Gardeners Dict.* (ed. 8) s.v. *Acer.* I have observed, upon cutting off branches from the *scarlet Maple in February, a great quantity of a very sweet juice hath flowed out. **1813** H. MUHLENBERG *Catal. Plant. Amer. Sept.* 95 Scarlet, white, red, or soft maple. **1833** *Penny Cycl.* I. 79/2 The nursery-men usually call this species the cut-leaved scarlet maple. **1916** E. T. SETON *Woodcraft Man. for Girls* 292 Red, Scarlet, Water, or Swamp Maple... Noted for its flaming crimson foliage in fall, as well as its red leaf-stalks, flowers, and fruit earlier. **1597** GERARDE *Herbal* III. xxx. 1159 For want of a fit English name, we haue thought good to christen it by the name of *Scarlet Oke, or Scarlet Holme Oke: for Ilex is named of some in English Holme. **1712** J. JAMES tr. *Le Blond's Gardening* 148 The Scarlet-Oak, or Holm. **1882** *Garden* 13 May 323/3 A specimen of the Scarlet Oak. **1753** CHAMBERS *Cycl. Supp.* App. s.v. *Pea*, *Scarlet Pea,..the English name of a genus of plants, called by Linnæus *Glycine*. **1855** MISS PRATT *Flower. Pl.* IV. 238 *Scarlet Pimpernel. **1786** J. ABERCROMBIE *Gardener's Daily Assistant* p. vii, A list of kitchen-garden plants... Kidney Bean (Dwarf)..*Scarlet Runner. **1806** B. MCMAHON *Amer. Gard. Cal.* 580 Bean, The Dwarf Kidney... Running kinds ..Scarlet Runners. **1824** LOUDON *Encycl. Gard.* (ed. 2) §3634 The scarlet runner ranks first for its prolific property and long continuance in fruit. **1908** *Garden* 25 Apr. 205/2 Possibly there is not a vegetable grown that is a more general favourite among amateurs than the climbing bean known as the Scarlet Runner. **1969** *Oxf. Bk. Food Plants* 36/1 The Scarlet Runner is by far the most popular green bean in Britain. **1756** P. BROWNE *Jamaica* 368 The *Scarlet-seed. **1866** *Treas. Bot.*, Scarlet-Seed. *Ternströmia obovalis*, and *Lætia Thamnia*. **1786** ABERCROMBIE *Gard. Assist.* 256 The *scarlet strawberry. **1882** *Garden* 12 Aug. 145/3 The *scarlet Thorn..is a bold, vigorous-growing American species.

Hence **ˈscarletness.** *rare.*

1611 FLORIO, *Scarletezza*, rednesse, scarletnesse.

†**ˈscarlet,** *v. Obs.* [f. SCARLET *sb.*] *trans.* To clothe in scarlet; to colour scarlet. Chiefly *passive*. Hence **ˈscarleted** *ppl. a.*, in quot. tinged with scarlet.

1553 BALE *Vocacyon* 10 The Idolatour, the tyraunt, and the whoremonger are no mete mynisters for hym, though they be neuer so..fynely forced, pylyoned, and scarletted. **1641** J. JACKSON *True Evang. T.* I. 49 The whole earth is almost a purple Island, scarletted and redded with the bloud of Martyrs. **1685** SIR G. MACKENZIE *Religious Stoic* ii. 23 At which we should scarlet our cheeks with blushes. **1688** R. HOLME *Armoury* IV. ix. (Roxb.) 382/1 Fine scarletted murrey.

†**ˈscarleˌteer.** *Obs.* [f. SCARLET *sb.* + -EER[1].] One clothed in scarlet, as a soldier in uniform, or a doctor in the gown of his degree.

1637 N. WHITING *Albino & Bellama* 142 Then say (faire Lady) truth I doe not jeere, Will you be wedded to a scarleteere? **1677** WOOD *Life* (O.H.S.) II. 386 The chancellour, with the bedells before him and the scarleteers after him.

ˈscarlet ˈfever. a. A contagious febrile disease, distinguished by a scarlet efflorescence of the skin and of the mucous membrane of the mouth and pharynx. Also known as SCARLATINA.

1676 JAS. COOKE *Marrow Chirurg.* VI. ii. (1685) 214 The first and last [*i.e.* Small-Pox and Rossalia] of these were in Warwick at the writing hereof; the last going under the name of Scarlet Fever. **1799** M. UNDERWOOD *Dis. Childhood* (ed. 4) I. 227 Whenever the Scarlet-fever becomes epidemic among adults, children rarely fail being attacked by it in great numbers. **1848** THACKERAY *Van. Fair* i, Poor Miss Birch died of the scarlet fever. **1876** BRISTOWE *Theory & Pract. Med.* (1878) 156 Down to the sixteenth or seventeenth century scarlet fever was confounded with measles.

b. An instance or an attack of this disease. *rare.*

1775 SHERIDAN *St. Patr. Day* I. i, He had rather see his daughter in a scarlet fever than in the arms of a soldier. **1870–2** LIDDON *Elem. Relig.* iv. §1, [He] will be..as well as another who may have happily survived a scarlet fever.

†**c.** *joc.* A passion for soldiers, with reference to their scarlet uniforms. *Obs.*

1861 B. HEMYNG in H. Mayhew *London Labour* (1862) Extra vol. 235 Nurse-maids..are always ready to succumb to the 'scarlet fever'. A red coat is all powerful with this class. **1890** BARRÈRE & LELAND *Dict. Slang.* II. 206/1 Ladies who run after military society are said to have *scarlet fever*.

†**ˈscarletite.** *nonce-wd.* [f. SCARLET *sb.* + -ITE[1].] One who hunts in scarlet (see SCARLET *sb.* 3).

1829 *Sporting Mag.* XXIII. 426 The wagons..were.. some of them occupied by scarletites from Melton.

ˈscarlety. *nonce-wd.* [f. SCARLET *sb.* + -Y.] Having a tinge of scarlet.

1840 RUSKIN *Diary* 23 Aug. in *Harrison* (1902) 53 Note the intense scarletty purple of the shattered larch stems.

scarling, scarlot: see SKIRLING, SCARLET.

scarmesh, -mige, -moge, -m(o)uch(e, etc., obs. forms of SKIRMISH *sb.* and *v.*

scarn, scarnes(se, obs. ff. SCORN, SCARCENESS.

†**ˈscaro.** *Obs.* It. form of SCARUS.

1722 DIAPER tr. *Oppian's Halieut.* I. 215 Here Scaro's feed. *Ibid.* I. 219, II. 1078, IV. 58, 61.

†**scaˈrotique.** *Obs. rare*$^{-1}$. = ESCHAROTIC.

1673 *Phil. Trans.* VIII. 6054 The touch of an hot Iron, the application of Vitriol or other Scarotiques.

scarp (skɑːp), *sb.*[1] *Her.* Also scarpe. [a. ONF. *escarpe* = Central OF. *escharpe* (mod.F. *écharpe*), lit. sash: see SCARF *sb.*] A diminutive of the bend sinister, one-half its width, crossing the shield diagonally from the sinister chief to the dexter base. (Cf. SCARF *sb.*[1] 5 a.)

1562 LEGH *Armory* (1597) 64 b, Knowe that this [bende sinyster] conteineth as much in breadth as a dexter bende doth. The halfe whereof is called a Scarpe, and no bastard's mark, neither may it be charged with any thing. **1610** GUILLIM *Heraldry* II. v. (1611) 52. **1780** EDMONDSON *Her.* II. Gloss. s.v. *Scarpe*, In blazon, it should be named Scarp, without mentioning the word sinister. The French call it a Bar. **1868** CUSSANS *Her.* (ed. 4) 58.

scarp (skɑːp), *sb.*[2] Also 6–7 **scarpe**; and see SCARF *sb.*[3] [ad. It. *scarpa*, whence F. *escarpe* ESCARP.]

1. *Fortif.* = ESCARP *sb.* 1.

1589 IVE *Pract. Fortif.* 10 The scarpe that the Curtin will make may bee some 28. foote, or more or lesse. **1654** COKAINE *Dianea* IV. 280 On the top they [the walls] are made after the fashion of a scarpe. **1709** LUTTRELL *Brief Rel.* (1857) VI. 471 The enemy..lye 2 leagues off behind the scarp. **1876** BANCROFT *Hist. U.S.* III. xiii. 199 The left extended to a scarp surmounted by an abattis.

†**b.** The total pitch or 'batter' of a bank. *Obs.*

1639 R. NORWOOD *Fortif.* 113 If the ditch be dry it must be the deeper, and have the lesse scarpe. **1669** STAYNRED *Fortif.* 7 The Inward Scarp of the Parapet... The outward Scarp of the Rampire... The Scarp of the Ditch.

2. The steep face of a hill; = ESCARP *sb.* 2.

1802 PLAYFAIR *Illustr. Huttonian Theory* 410 The scarps of the hills face indiscriminately all points of the compass. **1901** H. TRENCH *Deirdre Wed* 32 Far up, where darkling copses over-grow Scarps of the gray cliff from his river'd base.

scarp (skɑːp), *v.*[1] [f. SCARP *sb.*[2]] *trans.* To cut to a steep face, to slope; also *to scarp away, down*; = ESCARP *v.*

1803 WELLINGTON *Let.* in Gurw. *Desp.* (1837) II. 584 The rock is scarped on each side. **1807** G. CHALMERS *Caledonia* I. I. iv. 157 The top of the bank..was artfully scarped away, to augment the strength of the defences. **1829** SCOTT *Anne of G.* iii, The elevation of the site..was on this side a steep eminence, which had been scarped like a modern glacis, to render the building more secure. **1865** GEIKIE *Scen. & Geol. Scot.* iii. 66 The result has been..to scarp the coasts of the Shetlands into the most rugged and fantastic cliffs. **1894** WOLSELEY *Marlborough* II. 173 The rock on which this fort stands was scarped towards the city. **1905** R. HAGGARD in *Windsor Mag.* Jan. 244 The rock upon one side of it had often been scarped by the hand of man.

Hence **scarped** *ppl. a.*, reduced to a steep face, laid bare, cut away, steep.

1823 *Treat. Field Fortif.* 26 When the earth scarped off is used to encrease the height, the original surface should be cut [etc.]. **1837** CARLYLE *Fr. Rev.* III. v. vi, Redoubts are carried, and Passes and Heights of the most scarped description. **1850** TENNYSON *In Mem.* lvi, 'So careful of the type?' but no. From scarped cliff and quarried stone She cries 'a thousand types are gone: I care for nothing, all shall go'. **1877** L. MORRIS *Epic of Hades* II. 102 Once the waters Broke louder on the scarped reefs.

scarp (skɑːp), *v.*[2] *Agric.* [Of obscure origin; possibly the same word as prec.] *intr.* Of land: To be torn up irregularly.

1843 *Jrnl. R. Agric. Soc.* IV. II. 563 The land is not liable to scarp, as after the common roller. **1866** BLACKMORE *Cradock Nowell* xi, His mighty forehead would scarp and chine like the headland when the plough turns.

scarp-bolt (ˈskɑːpbəʊlt). *Shipbuilding.* Also *erron.* scarf-. [App. a. Da. *skarpbolt* lit. 'sharp bolt'.] (See quot. 1852.)

[**1852** J. FINCHAM *Outl. Ship Build.* (ed. 3) 26 The long bolts, through the knee of the head, and the deadwood, are pointed bolts (Swedish, *skarpbultar*; Danish, *skarpbolte*; Dutch, *puntbout*; German, *scharf-bolzen*..).] **1867** SMYTH *Sailor's Word-bk.* s.v. *Bolt*, Scarp-bolts and keel-bolts, pointed, not clinched, used for false keel or temporary purposes. **1875** KNIGHT *Dict. Mech.* 2051 Scarf-bolt.

scarper (ˈskɑːpə(r)), *v. slang.* Also **scapa, scarpa.** [Prob. ad. It. *scappare* to ESCAPE, get away; reinforced during or after the war of 1914–18 by *scapa* from Cockney rhyming slang *Scapa Flow*, to go.] **a.** *intr.* To depart hastily, run away; to escape, make one's get-away.

1846 *Swell's Night Guide* 43 He must *hook it* before 'day-light does appear', and then scarper by the back door. **1861** H. MAYHEW *London Labour* III. 48/1 When I was scarpering with my culling in the monkey. **1931** M. ALLINGHAM *Look to Lady* xxiv. 253 Round up this lot now and scarpa yourselves. **1933** G. INGRAM '*Stir*' iii. 45 'I'll be punching you up the belly if you don't scarper,' threatened Smith. **1954** M. PROCTER *Hell is City* II. i. 44 Wi' my record I thought I'd better scarper before I got dragged into trouble. **1970** *Private Eye* 27 Feb. 16 Take this lolly and scarpa for lawd's sake. **1972** A. DRAPER *Death Penalty* v. 37 Ben..shouted, 'Scapa. Everyone scapa.' **1974** *Sunday Post* (Glasgow) 21 July 16/4 His panic became unbearable. He jumped out of bed and scarpered! **1977** 'E. CRISPIN' *Glimpses of Moon* vii. 111 He's downstairs now with the others—and they're keeping a sharp eye on him; he won't have a chance to scarper again.

b. *trans.* To depart or escape from (a place); usu. in phr. *to scarper the letty*, to leave one's lodgings without paying the rent (cf. LETTY *sb.*).

1937 PARTRIDGE *Dict. Slang* 731/2 *Scarper*,..to decamp from... *Scarper the letty*, to leave one's lodgings without paying. **1957** [see LETTY *sb.*].

Hence as *sb.* in phr. *to do a scarper*, to run away, 'do a bunk'.

1958 F. NORMAN *Bang to Rights* 63 We had all planned to do a scarper.

‖**scarpetti** (skɑːˈpɛtiː), *sb. pl.* [It., pl. of *scarpetto*, a small shoe.] Rope-soled shoes worn for rock-climbing, esp. in the North Italian Alps. Cf. KLETTERSCHUH.

1897 O. G. JONES *Rock-Climbing in Engl. Lake District* p. xxiv, The Cumberland crags are too smooth to make *scarpetti* (*Kletterschuhe*) worth trying. **1907** G. D. ABRAHAM *Compl. Mountaineer* xxviii. 463 If the conditions become wet or icy, rubber soles are a snare and a delusion; scarpetti should be carried as a reserve. **1923** —— *First Steps to Climbing* vi. 71 They [*sc.* rubber-soled shoes] were preferable to the scarpetti, or rope-soled boots, which are the standard Dolomite wear. **1931** *Times Lit. Suppl.* 19 Feb. 129/3 On it [*sc.* Mount Blanc], climbing guideless, they practise every modern refinement, the use of crampons, scarpetti and the rappel. **1941** C. KIRKUS *Let's go Climbing!* vi. 96 Scarpetti—rope soled shoes used in the Dolomites —are coming into favour in this country. **1956** C. EVANS *On Climbing* II. 32 In the Alps there have been other kinds of friction footwear... The rag-soled scarpetti of the Dolomites.

scarph(e, obs. forms of SCARF *sb.* and *v.*

scarpine (ˈskɑːpiːn). Also 6 *Sc.* **scarpene**. [ad. It. *scarpino* (dim. of *scarpa* shoe), whence F. *escarpin*, Sp. *escarpino*.]

†**1.** A light shoe. *Obs. rare*$^{-1}$.

a **1586** in Pinkerton *Anc. Sc. Poems* (1786) 184 Thair dry scarpenis..; Thair mullis glitteran on thair feit. **1611** FLORIO, *Scarpini*, Scarpines, Pumps, or Sockes.

2. *Hist.* An instrument of torture for the feet. (Cf. BOOT *sb.*^{3} 3.)

1855 KINGSLEY *Westw. Ho!* vii, I was put to the scarpines, whereof I am.. somewhat lame of one leg to this day.

scarping (ˈskɑːpɪŋ), *vbl. sb.* [f. SCARP *v.*^{1} + -ING^1.] A steep slope; the rocky face of a hill. †Also *pl.* the amount of slope or batter in an escarp.

1639 R. NORWOOD *Fortif.* 105 The scarpings thereof [*sc.* of the Rampire] within and without are [etc.]. **1909** *Contemp. Rev.* Apr. 478 The scarpings of an overhanging cliff.

ˈscarpment. *rare*$^{-1}$. [Aphetic for ESCARPMENT, after SCARP *v.*^{1}] = ESCARPMENT I.

1861 LEWIN *Jerusalem* 223 The foundations of the Temple were.. formed by scarping the sides of the rock and carrying up a wall upon the scarpment.

scarpyn, obs. form of SCORPION.

scarr(e, obs. forms of SCAR, SCARE.

scarred (skɑːd), *ppl. a.* [f. SCAR *v.* + -ED^1.]

1. Of a human or animal body or its parts: Bearing scars or traces of wounds or sores.

c **1440** *York Myst.* xxxiii. 35 Ȝaa, and with schath of skelpys yll scarred. **1872** L. P. MEREDITH *Teeth* 176, I have seen the scarred hero of many battles cry like a child when called upon to have a tooth extracted. **1899** *Allbutt's Syst. Med.* VI. 22 Especial attention was directed to the exclusion of cases of scarred kidneys, of which there were many.

2. *transf.* Of inanimate objects: Bearing traces of injury, weathering, or the like. Often of rocks, etc.: Broken as by a convulsion of nature.

1600 MARLOWE *Lucan* I. Cj, Headles darts, olde swords With vgly teeth of blacke rust fouly scarr'd. **1816** SHELLEY *Mont Blanc* 71 How hideously Its shapes are heaped around! rude, bare, and high, Ghastly, and scarred, and riven. **1877** BLACK *Green Past.* xxxvii, In the sheer precipices.. scarred with ruddy rocks and sunless woods.

3. *Bot.* (See quot.)

1793 MARTYN *Lang. Bot.*, *Cicatrisatus truncus s. caulis.* A scarred stem. Marked with the remains of leaves that have fallen off. **1839** LINDLEY *Introd. Bot.* III. (ed. 3) 468.

scarre-fire, obs. variant of SCARE-FIRE.

scarrify(e, var. forms of SCARIFY.

scarring (ˈskɑːrɪŋ), *vbl. sb.* [f. SCAR *v.* + -ING^1.] The action of the vb. SCAR in various senses; an example of this; *concr.* an assemblage of scars.

1816 J. SCOTT *Paris Revisited* (ed. 3) 221 The charges of the cavalry had trampled deep scarrings into the ground. **1898** *Allbutt's Syst. Med.* V. 327 [There was] slight scarring in the right bronchus. **1906** *Q. Rev.* Jan. 151 The results in regard to scarring were good.

scarring (ˈskɑːrɪŋ), *ppl. a.* [f. SCAR *v.* + -ING^2.] That scars, in various senses of the verb; causing a blemish; undergoing cicatrization.

1833 J. H. NEWMAN '*Latest born of Jesse's race*' 28 Strange, that guileless face and form To lavish on the scarring storm! **1899** *Allbutt's Syst. Med.* VIII. 771 In scarring lesions the [hair] follicles are destroyed.

scarrubb, obs. form of SCARAB.

scarry (ˈskɑːrɪ), *a.*^{1} [f. SCAR *sb.*^{1} + -Y.] Precipitous, rocky.

1382 WICLIF *Job* xxxix. 28 In heȝe sett scarri flintis [Vulg. *in præruptis silicibus*] he [*sc.* the eagle] bideth. **1577** HARRISON *England* I. xi. [xv.] 31 b, in *Holinshed*, The Ure.. receyueth the Burne, by south west (as it dyd the Wile, from very deepe scarry rockes, before at Askaran). **1853** G. JOHNSTON *Nat. Hist. E. Bord.* I. 80 A high, steep, scarry, and partially wooded bank. **1901** H. TRENCH *Deirdre Wed* 32 Many a mountain's scarry flank.

†**ˈscarry**, *a.*^{2} *Obs.* [f. SCAR *sb.*^{2} + -Y.] Of the nature of a scar; also, marked with scars.

1653 URQUHART *Rabelais* I. ii, If they might be reduc'd t'a scarry stuffe [F. *à cicatrice*]. **1695** *Lond. Gaz.* No. 3113/4 The Hair wanting on the Rump, a gall'd scarry back. **1894** *Monthly Packet* Christmas No. 193 Scarry indentations [in buns] made by small dried currants.

†**ˈscarry**, *a.*^{3} *Obs. rare*$^{-1}$. ? Thin, meagre.

1422 tr. *Secreta Secret., Priv. Priv.* 239 But thay men wych haue the body more scarry, and the ouertures streyte, shulde vse Sotille diet and in lytill quantite.

scars(e, scarsement, obs. ff. SCARCE, -MENT.

scarsitee, obs. form of SCARCITY.

scart (skɑːt), *sb.*^{1} *Sc.* Forms: 5, 9 **scarth**, 6 **skarth**, 8–9 **skart**, 7– **scart**. See also SCRATH. [The forms *scarth*, *scart*, are successive corruptions of SCARF *sb.*] The Cormorant, *Phalocrocorax carbo*. Also applied to the Shag, *P. graculus*.

c **1450** HOLLAND *Howlat* 181 The Scarth a fische fangar, And that a perfyte. **1513** DOUGLAS *Æneis* v. iii. 49 A standand place quhar skarthis with ther beikis.. glaidlie thaim pronȝe and bekis. **1710** SIBBALD *Hist. Fife & Kinross* 45 The Fowls which most frequent the Bass are the.. Scarts [etc.]. **1816** SCOTT *Antiq.* viii, D'ye think ye'll help them wi' skirling that gate like an auld skart before a flaw o' weather? **1852** J. WILSON in *Blackw. Mag.* LXXII. 395 He sits a cormorant on the tree of life... A scarth—not an eagle—not a swan. **1892** BLACK *Three Feathers* 183 The black rocks basked in the sunlight, the big skarts standing on their ledges, not moving a feather.

scart (skart), *sb.*^{2} *Sc.* [Metathesis of SCRAT *sb.*]

1. A scratch.

a **1585** POLWART *Flyting w. Montgomerie* 555 With scartes and scores, athort his frozen front. **1718** RAMSAY *Christ's Kirk Gr.* III. xvii, Wi' her nails she rave his face, Made a' his black baird bloody Wi' scarts that day. **1871** C. GIBBON *Lack of Gold* xi, Folk never see a scart on their ain backs. **1897** CROCKETT *Lad's Love* xxvii. 266 It never does to mislippen the scart o' a pin on the thickest skull.

2. A mark made by a pen.

1824 SCOTT *St. Ronan's* iii, What signified, she said, a wheen bits of paper, wi' black and white scarts upon them, that he ca'd bushes, and trees, and craigs? **1861** RAMSAY *Remin.* Ser. II. 122 He has naything comed himsel', nor had the ceevility tae sen' us the scart o' a pen.

scart (skɑːt), *sb.*^{3} *rare.* [? var. of SCAT *sb.*] A gust, puff (of wind); a strip (of cloud).

1860 G. H. KINGSLEY in F. Galton *Vac. Tour* 127 Donald, who assures me that some day a scart of wind will snatch the paper out of my hand. **1899** *Pall Mall Mag.* Apr. 568 The gusty wind blew thin wisps and scarts of cloud athwart the sharp hooks of the crescent moon.

scart (skart), *v. Sc.* Also, 4, 6, 9 **skart**. [Metathesis of SCRAT *v.*]

1. *trans.* To scratch, scrape. Also *absol.*

c **1375** *Sc. Leg. Saints* xxvii. (*Machor*) 249 With hyre handis [she] skartyt hir face. **1508** DUNBAR *Tua Mariit Wemen* 93 To see him scart his awin skyn grit scunner I think. **1560** ROLLAND *Seven Sages* 36 With skarting [scho] causit hir face to bleid. **1821** SCOTT *Pirate* xv, Ye scart the land with a bit thing ye ca' a pleugh. **1893** CROCKETT *Stickit Minister* 75, I fand the hoose, by scartin' a match an' readin' the plate on the gate.

†**2.** To gather together carefully. Also *absol.*

1629 MURE *True Crucifixe* 2573 If Loue of Money,.. Moue thee to scrape, to scart, to pinch, to spare. **1725** RAMSAY *Gentle Sheph.* I. ii, And syne the fool-thing is obliged to fast, Or scart anither's leavings at the last.

†**3.** *trans.* To scribble. *Obs. rare*$^{-1}$.

1826 J. WILSON *Noct. Ambr.* Wks. 1855 I. 144 I've skarted some odds and ends wi' the keelivine on brown paper.

Hence **ˈscarted** *ppl. a.*, scribble over.

1814 SCOTT *Wav.* lxv, And what use has my father for a whin bits o' scarted paper?

scartch, obs. form of SCRATCH.

scarth (skɑːθ), *sb.*^{1} Also 4–5 **skarth**. [a. ON. *skarð* neut., notch, cleft, mountain pass (MSw. *skardh* neut., notch, diminution, ruin, *skardher* masc., broken piece) = OE. *sceard* SHARD, SHERD.]

†**1.** A fragment, sherd. *Obs.*

a **1340** HAMPOLE *Psalter* xxi. 15 My vertu.. is wex vile as a pot scarth. **13..** *Childh. Jesus* 340 in *Archiv Stud. neu. Spr.* LXXIV. 331 His pechere he brake.. And Jhesu gadirde þe skarthes. *c* **1460** *Towneley Myst.* xii. 160 The mylk pycher was layde, The skarthis was the tokyn.

fig. **1482** CAXTON *Trevisa's Higden* III. xviii. 132 b, Both the wyues.. chidden him alto scarthes by one assente.

2. A cliff, a bare rock. *dial.*

1863 BARING-GOULD *Iceland* iii. 45 To our right was a bold scarth of dark rock thronged with ravens. **1869** *Lonsdale Gloss.*, *Scar, Scarth*, a line of rock bare of vegetation.

†**scarth**, *sb.*^{2} *Obs.* [Altered form of SCRAT *sb.*] An abortion, monster; a hermaphrodite.

1508 DUNBAR *Flyting* 58 Revin, raggit ruke, and full of rebaldrie, Scarth fra scorpione, scaldit in scurrilitie. **1508** —— *Tua Mariit Wemen* 92 Ane skabbit skarth, ane scorpioun. *a* **1578** LINDESAY (Pitscottie) *Chron. Scot.* (S.T.S.) I. 145 Of the skartht [*c* **1603** scratche (MS. B.), *c* **1598** scarcht (MS. I.)] yat was born of baith the kyndis maile and female.

scartling (ˈskɑːtlɪŋ). *Sc.* [f. SCART *sb.*^{1} + -LING^1.] A young scart or cormorant.

1893 *Blackw. Mag.* Sept. 444 In several nests were found young scartlings—fluffy, dull-grey, ungainly creatures.

‖**Scarus** (ˈskɛərəs). Pl. **scari** (ˈskɛəraɪ). [L. *scarus*, a. Gr. σκάρος.] A fish described by ancient writers; in mod. use, the name of the typical genus of the family *Scaridæ*; a fish of this genus, a PARROT-FISH. Cf. SCAR *sb.*^{4}, SCARE *sb.*^{3}, SCARO.

1601 HOLLAND *Pliny* IX. xvii. I. 245 The fish called Scarus .. is said to chew cud. **1774** GOLDSM. *Nat. Hist.* III. 6 The salmon also is said to be of this number [ruminants]: and, if we may believe Ovid, the scarus likewise. **1803** SHAW *Gen. Zool.* IV. II. 394 Green Scarus [etc.]. **1848** DICKENS *Dombey* xii, The sounds of the fish called scari. **1885** *Encycl. Brit.* XVIII. 324 Ever since the time of Aristotle it has been maintained that the Scarus ruminates.

scarved (skɑːvd), *ppl. a.*: see SCARFED *ppl. a.*^{1}

scary (ˈskɛərɪ), *a.*^{1} Also 6 (9 *vulgar*) **skeary**, 9 *vulgar* **skeery**, 9– **scarey**. [f. SCARE *sb.*^{2} + -Y^1.]

1. Terrifying, frightful.

1582 STANYHURST *Æneis* IV. (Arb.) 109 But toe the, poore Dido, this sight so skearye beholding, What feeling creepeth? **1827** J. F. COOPER *Prairie* II. v. 68 If any can pretend to know the world, or to have seen scary sights, it is myself! **1854** 'MARION HARLAND' *Alone* xiii, A Giant Grim, who frequents places of amusement to corner children, and relate scary stories to them. **1894** D. C. MURRAY *Making Novelist* 29 Whatever the miners thought about it, it was rather a scarey business for me. **1938** J. STEINBECK *Long Valley* 14 It would be a lonely life for a woman, ma'am, and a scarey life too, with animals creeping under the wagon all night. **1955** E. COXHEAD *Figure in Mist* iv. 123 We're over the scary part now. **1960** *Guardian* 27 Oct. 9/5 This is real scarey. **1961** G. GREENE *Burnt-Out Case* VI. iii. 237 Goodness, I'm glad to be here. It was really scary driving all the way alone. **1975** *New Yorker* 21 Apr. 105/1 It's something scary you don't have to believe in. **1975** *University* (Princeton Univ.) Winter 9/1 The latter showed that energy consumption, per person, could easily double by 2000. That's pretty scary, with energy resources almost sure to decline. **1977** *Times Lit. Suppl.* 11 Feb. 145/4 (Advt.), Set against a background of sinister ritual, vengeance and murder, a novel to be read at one scarey sitting. **1978** *Nature* 20 July 199/1 The procession was headed by figures dressed in radioactive protection gear, clearly intended to be scary. **1981** *Listener* 1 Jan. 23/3 The threat.. is pretty scary.

2. Frightened, timorous. orig. and chiefly *N. Amer.*

1800 M. L. WEEMS *Let.* 29 Dec. in *Works & Ways* (1929) II. 160, I have always been very scary about our monies. **1827** J. F. COOPER *Prairie* II. vi. 92 A skeary comrade in the woods is apt to make a short path long. **1842** in *Coquet-Dale Fishing Songs* (1852) 104 The scary trout glides swiftly out. **1887** I. R. *Ranche Life Montana* 137 My mount was a young 'scarey' horse. **1873** CARLETON *Farm Ball.* 8 Women are skeery critters. **1894** FENN *Real Gold* 138, I want to talk. It keeps one from feeling a bit skeary. **1903** J. VAIZEY *Pixie O'Shaughnessy* ix. 107 She was too frightened to own up last night—you know what a scarey little thing she is. **1907** J. M. SYNGE *Let.* 25 Apr. (1971) 128, I have been getting a little bit scary about your extravagance. **1951** L. CRAIG *Singing Hills* vi. 45 He'd a been right smart proudified of your not being scary. **1970** N. STREATFEILD *Thursday's Child* xxxii. 218 He was as scary of being seen as a wild deer.

scas(e, obs. forms of SCARCE.

†**scat**, *sb.*^{1} *Obs.* (*rare* after OE.). Also 3 **sat**. [OE. *sceat* masc., = OFris. *sket*, OS. *skat* (MLG., Du. *schat*, whence next), OHG. *scaz* (MHG. *schaz*, mod.G. *schatz*), treasure, ON. *skatt-r* tribute (whence SCAT *sb.*^{3}; Da. *skat*, Sw. *skatt*), Goth. *skatt-s* piece of money, money:—OTeut. **skatto-z*. Cf. SCEAT.

The *sc* stands for (ʃ); if the word had survived its form would be **shat*.]

Treasure, money; in ME. only in phr. *scat and s(c)rud*.

a **1122** *O.E. Chron.* (Laud MS.) an. 1070, Swa manega ȝersumas on sceat & on scrud & on bokes swa nan man ne mæi oðer tællen. *a* **1200** *Moral Ode* 367 Ne sal þer ben naðer scat ne srud ne wereldes wele none. *c* **1250** *Gen. & Ex.* 795 God gaf him ðor siluer and gold, And hird, and orf, and srud and sat. *Ibid.* 3169 Quat-so he boden, srud or sat, Egipte folc hem lenen ðat.

†**scat**, *sb.*^{2} *Obs. rare*$^{-1}$. In 5 **scatte**. [a. Du. *schat*: see prec.] Treasure.

1481 CAXTON *Reynard* xvi. (Arb.) 35, I haue so grette scatte and good of syluer and of gold that seuen waynes shold not conne carye it away.

scat (skæt), *sb.*^{3} Also 5 **skatte**, 5–6 **skait**, 6–9 **scatt, skat(t**. [a. ON. *skatt-r*: see SCAT *sb.*^{1}]

1. a. *gen.* A tax, tribute. Now only *Hist.* with reference to countries under Scandinavian rule.

1502 *Reg. Privy Seal Scot.* I. 116/1 The rasing of al unlawis, eschetis, proffittis, skattis and dewiteis according to the said regalite. **1506** *Exch. Rolls Scot.* XII. 703 That the fredome and privelege of halikirk be observit.. without ony scatt, stent, taxation, or extortion to be maid in tyme cuming. **1513** DOUGLAS *Æneis* Prol. 24 Wrangys to redres suld weyr be vndertane, For na conquest, reif, skat nor pensioun. **1863** LONGF. *Wayside Inn, K. Olaf* XVI. xii, Laying waste the kingdom, Seizing scatt and treasure. **1886** J. CORBETT *Fall of Asgard* ii. 22 He will not be content with setting his men over us and taking scatt.

b. In Orkney and Shetland, the land-tax paid to the Crown by a udal tenant. †Also, in certain parts of Scotland and the north of England, the designation of various local imposts in the 15–17th c.

1577 in D. Balfour *Oppressions in Orkney & Zetld.* (1859) 18 Ane dewtie thai pay to the Kingis Majestie for thair scat and landmales zeirlie. **1598** *Aberdeen Reg.* (1848) II. 172 Ilk howsholder in Futtie.. to pay the skait vsid and wont. **1612** *Sc. Acts Jas. VI* (1816) IV. 481/2 Toillis, anchorages.. scattis, land maillis [etc.]. **1814** SHIRREFF *Agric. Orkney* 30 Subject only to the tax of scat and tithe. **1821** SCOTT *Pirate* xviii, We must pay scat and wattle. **1838** BELL *Dict. Law Scot.*, *Udal Right* is that right in land, which though dependent on the Crown as superior, for payment of a tribute called Skat, is completed [etc.]. **1859** in D. Balfour *Oppressions in Orkney & Zetld.* 128 *Skat*, the Tax upon all land occupied by Odal-red, for the support of the Crown, and expense of government.

2. *attrib.*, as *scat-field*, *scat tax*; † **scat gild**, the payment or tax of 'scat'; † **scat haver, malt**, oats, malt, taken in payment of 'scat'; **scat land**, land subject to 'scat'.

14.. *Customs of Malton* in *Surtees Misc.* (1890) 60 For sellyng of the same [heryng] thay schall gyffe to yᵉ *skatte-gyld iiij d. **1483** in R. Davies *York Records* (1843) 175 In esyng of the tolls, murage, bucher penys & skaitgyld. **1344–5** *Durham Acc. Rolls* (Surtees) 172 Decem boll avene que vocatur *Scathaver de bondis de Heworth. **1450–51** *Ibid.* 187 Et de vs. rec. pro xij bollez de Scathaver. **1502** in Peterkin *Rentals of Orkney* (1820) 12 Item wᵗ flawis j d terre *scatland anᵗ in butter scat vij d. **1438–9** *Durham Acc. Rolls* (Surtees) 63 Pro 7 bondis antedictis in precio 7 quar. de

*Scatmaltez sic sibi vend. hoc anno. **1868** D. GORRIE *Summers & Winters in Orkneys* v. 158 Ruga who collected the King of Norway's corn, or the *Scatt-tax in Orkney. **1881** *Standard* 26 July 5 [Shetland] The sheep and ponies run on the 'Scatfield', or common; and the 'Scat tax' is not a popular impost.

scat (skæt), *sb.*[4] *dial.* (See E.D.D.) [Perh. onomatopœic; the identity of the word in the various senses is uncertain. Cf. SQUAT *sb.*]

1. A blow or buffet.

1872 MRS. LYNN LINTON *Joshua Davidson* 6 It was a laugh..that seemed to mean the same thing as 'scat',—our Cornish word for a blow. **1901** MRS. E. L. VOYNICH *Jack Raymond* 173 The soft and pitying eyes seemed to shame him 'like a scat in the face'.

2. 'Anything burst or broken open; the sound of a rent; the sharp sound of a bullet' (E.D.D.). Cf. SCAT *v.*[3] and *adv.*

1895 CROCKETT *Bog-Myrtle* 294 A shot rang out, followed immediately by the 'scat' of a bullet against the rock.

3. A brief spell of weather; a short turn of work.

1880 *Cornwall Gloss.* s.v., A scat of fine weather. **1882** F. W. P. JAGO *Anc. Lang. Cornwall* 256 A scat of frost. **1895** E. M. STOOKE *Not Exactly* i. 24 An' cashionally 'e dooes a scat to gardenin'.

4. A sudden or passing shower of rain.

17.. *Prov.* in Brice *Gazetteer* (1759) s.v. *Haldon*, When Haldon hath a Hat, Kenton beware a Skat [Risdon (1714) 47 Squatt]. **1834** G. ROBERTS *Lyme Regis* 252 *Scatt*, a shower. **1897** E. PHILLPOTTS *Lying Prophets* II. vi. 187 Presently a scat of heavy rain on a squall of wind shut out the harbour for a time.

scat (skæt), *sb.*[5] *U.S. slang.* [Origin obscure.] Whisky.

1914 JACKSON & HELLYER *Vocab. Criminal Slang* 73 *Scat, noun*, general circulation. Whiskey. Derived by suggestion from 'skey' (skee), the termination of 'whiskey'. **1949** PARTRIDGE *Dict. Underworld* 597/2 *Scat*, whiskey... Perhaps proleptic: it causes intelligence to *scat*, to scatter, to vanish. **1955** *Publ. Amer. Dial. Soc.* XXIV. 161 Peter men don't punch much guff as a rule, but sometimes the scat will loosen them up for some good yarns.

scat (skæt), *sb.*[6] (and *a.*) *Jazz.* [Prob. imitative: see quot. 1929.] **a.** A style of improvised singing in which meaningless but expressive syllables, usu. representing the sound of a musical instrument, are used instead of words. Freq. *attrib.* passing into *adj.* (see also b below).

1929 *Melody Maker* Apr. 369/1 This particular type of vocalism is known as 'Scat' singing. This name undoubtedly owes its origin to the almost inevitable way of starting any line with 'Scat-da-doo'. A very fine example of this 'Scat Singing' is in 'Candy Lips' by Louis Armstrong's Wash-board beaters.., the label rightly describing it as 'Scat' chorus by Clarence Williams. **1933** D. RUNYON in *Collier's* 28 Jan. 41/1 She has to play against a scat band. **1937** *Amer. Speech* XII. 182/2 *Scat*, a style of singing in which the vocalist scorns the lyrics, substituting meaningless but expressive syllables of his own improvisation. **1946** R. BLESH *Shining Trumpets* x. 229 The pattern..was derived..from attempts of white singers of popular tunes to imitate the rhythmic Negro scat song. **1963** *Times* 27 Dec. 4/7 The exhilarating and often quasi-instrumental vocal duetting, sometimes in scat or in falsetto, behind the melodic line. **1977** *Rolling Stone* 24 Mar., Jarreau is a sophisticated cabaret artist whose vocal mimicry and jazz-man scat account for much of his onstage success.

b. *Comb.*, as **scat-singing** *sb.*, singing in this style; also as adj.; hence **scat-singer** and (as a back-formation) **scat-sing** *v. trans.* and *intr.*

1929 [see above]. **1934** A. BOWLLY *Modern Style Singing* xxiv. 118 Current records should be the best guide of how.. to 'scat' sing. **1936** *Amer. Mercury* May p. x/2 *Scat singer*, a hi-de-ho shouter. **1949** L. FEATHER *Inside Be-Bop* v. 39 The swing era produced such notable 'scat' singers as Leo Watson. **1952** B. ULANOV *Hist. Jazz in Amer.* (1958) xx. 252 She pressed the full impact of her scat-singing personality into record grooves. **1957** *Amer. Speech* XXXII. 275 Many bop phrases seem to derive from the nonsense syllables of scat-singing, which, in turn, is simply the voice imitating the sound of an instrument, the first known instance of which, so the story goes, occurred when Louis Armstrong dropped his lyric sheet in the middle of a 1926 recording date and was forced to improvise the words. **1962** 'K. ORVIS' *Damned & Destroyed* iv. 29 A hot-jazz man..with..a misplaced confidence in his ability as a scat-singer. **1968** P. OLIVER *Screening Blues* vi. 205 With a fierce line in 'scat' singing which had the 'dirty tone' of a muted trumpet, Mary Dixon sang with no apparent restraint. **1974** *New Yorker* 29 Apr. 73 Scat-singing Ella Fitzgerald doesn't just see an audience. **1976** *National Observer* (U.S.) 20 Nov. 24/3 He didn't invent scat singing any more than Louis Armstrong did, but it's a technique he perfected. **1978** *Fanfare* (Toronto) 10 May 11/2 She sings Twisted, scat sings it, tosses her head back, shakes her lion's mane, pushes her voice into a falsetto that does no little damage to the eardrums. **1978** *Maledicta* 1977 I. 222 *Fang Dang* would *scat-sing* the melody (i.e. using nonsensical words or 'vocalese' to 'sing' the parts of the instrumentation).

scat (skæt), *sb.*[7] [ad. Gr. σκατ-, σκῶρ dung.]

1. Dung; (*pl.*) droppings.

1950 in WEBSTER Add. **1959** E. COLLIER *Three against Wilderness* xx. 207 Whenever I travelled the game trails, my eyes were alert for any coyote scat (manure) deposited on them. **1966** C. SWEENEY *Scurrying Bush* iv. 48 The speculation when finding a spoor or scat. **1977** *Devon Wetlands* (Devon County Council) xix. 74 The two signs of Otters most likely to be found are their footprints and their droppings (usually known as scats or spraints)... Recognising spraints requires some practice particularly to avoid confusing them with Mink scats. **1977** *New Yorker* 27 June 70/3 We avoid a mound of bear scat.

2. *slang.* Heroin. Cf. SHIT *sb.*[1] 1.

1970 *Lebende Sprachen* XV. 103/2 *Scat*, heroin. **1972** D. E. WESTLAKE *Cops & Robbers* (1973) ii. 39 You're dealing in machismo, man, just like I'm dealing in scat.

†**scat**, *v.*[1] *Obs.* In 5–6 scatte. [In Caxton, a. MDu. *schatten*, f. *schat* SCAT *sb.*[2]; in the Sc. use perh. a. ON. *skatta*, f. *skatt-r* SCAT *sb.*[3]] *trans.* To oppress by exactions.

1481 CAXTON *Reynard* xlii. (Arb.) 114 Whan they be myghty and doubted thenne ben they extorcionners and scatte and pylle the peple. **1543** *Aberdeen Reg.* (1844) I. 191 The toune is hauely murmurit be the landmen, that the vittell hyaris of the merkat, scattis thame grytlie in taking of sampills, scheyt-schakkingis, and sic oder ewill vsit custum. *a* **1578** LINDESAY (Pitscottie) *Chron. Scot.* (S.T.S.) I. 67 He conselled thame [to] exerceis skarting [*v.r.* scatting] and oppressioun wpoun the realme.

†**scat**, *v.*[2] *Obs.* In 6 skatt, 6–7 scatt. [Alternation of SCOT *v.*, due to association with SCAT *sb.*[3]] *intr.* In phrase *to scat and lot* (later *to scat or contribute*) = 'to scot and lot', i.e. to contribute equally to the defraying of some charge or cost.

1560 *Burgh Rec. Edin.* (1875) III. 87 Personis..quhilkis ..nother scattis lottis extentis walkis nor wardis nor yit beris na portable charges within this burgh. **1581** in *Rec. Convent. Roy. Burghs* (1870) I. 117 The acts of burrowes maid anent the scatting and lotting for pilleit and cassin guids. **1594** *Ibid.* 449 Nather skatt and lott with thame. **1612** *Ibid.* II. 340 That no monye sould scatt or contribute with onye goods castin or pilleyit.

scat (skæt), *v.*[3] *dial.* [Cf. SCAT *sb.*[4]] *trans.* To break in pieces, shatter.

1837 J. F. PALMER *Dial. Devonsh. Dial.* 79 To *Scat*, to dash any fragile body on the ground. **1893** 'Q.' (Quiller-Couch) *Delect. Duchy* 306 The van..scat itself to bits against the bridge.

scat (skæt), *v.*[4] *Jazz* (chiefly *U.S.*). [f. SCAT *sb.*[6]] **a.** *intr.* To perform scat-singing; to sing or improvise with meaningless syllables.

1935 *Metronome* Apr. 54/3 Cab scats through this pair in his best Harlem manner. **1941** *Daily News* (Chicago) 11 June 24/1 Johnny..didn't know the words to the second verse. Instead he sang 'sho-ho-ho', and discovered he liked it that way. Since his audience liked it too, he.. has been 'scatting' ever since. **1975** *New Yorker* 26 May 6/1 He and Buddy Rich..launch a series of fusillading four-bar breaks, in which..Torme scats in the Ella Fitzgerald mode.

b. *trans.* To sing or improvise (a song) by replacing the words by meaningless syllables.

1946 MEZZROW & WOLFE *Really Blues* (1957) 104 Louis Armstrong riffed and scatted them. **1958** *Gramophone* Dec. 331/2 Only a couple of songs are scatted. **1973** *Black World* Aug. 58/1 Could scat all Prez's solos note for note in the right key.

Hence **'scatting** *vbl. sb.*

1946 MEZZROW & WOLFE *Really Blues* (1957) viii. 119 The first time Old Gatemouth ever put his scatting on wax. **1952** B. ULANOV *Hist. Jazz in Amer.* (1958) xx. 252 In 1946 she coined the whole new scatting vocabulary. **1973** S. HENDERSON *Understanding New Black Poetry* 57 The most interesting technical feature of the poem, however, is the singing and scatting of two songs connected with Coltrane.

scat (skæt), *adv. dial.* Also **skat, scatt.** [Prob. onomatopœic: cf. SCAT *sb.*[4]] *to go scat*: to fall down; to break in pieces; to become bankrupt.

1867 ROCK *Jim an' Nell* xxix. (E.D.S. No. 76), I've trad upon a patch, I'm veared a shall go scat. **1887** 'Q.' (Quiller-Couch) *Dead Man's Rock* 7 Finally my father's bank broke —or, as we say in the West 'went scat'. **1887** BARING-GOULD *Gaverocks* xxxiii, Little Ruth wiped up the mess made by the broken eggs. Poor Ruth was sore distressed at their 'going scatt' on the floor.

scat, *int. colloq.* [? identical with 'ss cat!' (i.e. a hiss followed by the word *cat*) used in driving away cats.] Begone! Hence used as verb (*intr.*). Also in phr. ***quicker than scat.***

1838 'T. TITTERWELL' *Yankee Notions* 52 Drive her away! 'scat her away! *Ibid.* 56 Stop, there! whisht! scat! **1860** J. S. JONES *Green Mountain Boy* I. iii. 13 I'll have the square discharge him quicker than s'cat. **1869** MRS. WHITNEY *We Girls* x. (1874) 218 'Scat!' cried Stephen. And Ruth scatted. **1880** J. C. HARRIS *Uncle Remus* xxii. (1883) 110 W'en ole man Rabbit say 'scoot', dey scooted, en w'en ole Miss Rabbit say 'scat', dey scatted. **1896** J. F. B. LILLARD *Poker Stories* ix. 210 We chucked him two watches and 380 dollars in cash quicker'n scat. **1917** D. CANFIELD *Understood Betsy* x. 229 Ann and I hitched up quicker'n scat. **1931** M. ALLINGHAM *Look to Lady* xiv. 145 Shoo! Shoo! Scat! We've got a policeman coming. **1950** 'D. DIVINE' *King of Fassarai* xviii. 147 Get the hell out of it!.. I told you kids to scat. **1977** H. GREENE *FSO-1* xvii. 152 Set the breakfast table out here in the drawing room. And then, scat!

scatald, obs. form of SCATTALD.

scatback ('skætbæk). *U.S. Football.* [BACK *sb.*[1] 21: see SCAT *int.*] A fast-running backfield player.

1946 *Sun* (Baltimore) 16 Dec. 15/1 They made it 14-0.. with an intercepted pass by Dante Magnani, the scatback from St. Mary's of California. **1948** *Sport Life* Nov. 70/1 The Bears have signed scatback J. R. Boone. **1976** *National Observer* 13 Nov. 1/1 He is slim and muscular-looking—a scatback set to run for daylight.

scatch[1] (skætʃ). Forms: 5–6 **scache**, 6 **skache**, 7 **skatch**, 6–8 **scatch**, 9 *dial.* **sketch.** [a. ONF. *escache* = Central OF. *eschasse* (mod.F. *échasse*), whence Du. *schaats* SKATE *sb.*[2]]

1. A stilt; usually pl. *scatches. Obs.* exc. *dial.*

1545 ELYOT *Dict.*, *Grallatores*, they which dooe goe on styltes or skaches. **1570** LEVINS *Manip.* 5/44 A Scache, *grallus.* **1653** URQUHART *Rabelais* II. i, Others grew in the legs, and to see them, you would have said they had been.. men walking upon stilts or scatches. **1681** W. ROBERTSON *Phraseol. Gen.* (1693) 915 Never,..till geese go on scatches. **1730** BAILEY (fol.), *Scatches*, Stilts to put the Feet in to walk in dirty Places. **1893** BARING-GOULD *Cheap Jack Zita* xii, Sketches?—does that word puzzle you..? They are what some folk call stilts.

2. ? A scaffold-pole. [So. F. *échasse.*]

1420 *Searchers Verdicts* in *Surtees Misc.* (1890) 15 William of Alne..sall fynde the brygges, the scaches, nayles, and all the tymbre that sall ga un to the gutter.

†**scatch**[2]. *Obs.* Also 5–6 **scache.** [ad. It. *scaccia* ('skatʃa), whence F. *escache.*] An oval bridle-bit. Also *scatch-mouth.*

1565–80 BLUNDEVIL *Art Riding* III. xxiii. 51 Some are called Canon bits, some scatches. **1598** FLORIO, *Scaccia*, the mouth of a bit called a scache. **1607** MARKHAM *Caval.* II. (1617) 56 The next bytt you shall vse after the Cannon, shall bee the plaine Scatch. **1611** COTGR., *Scace*, a Scatch bit. **1704** *Dict. Rust.* (1726) s.v. *Bit*, The ends of a Scatch-mouth can never fail, by reason of their being over-lapped.

Scatchard ('skætʃɑːd). *Biochem.* [The name of George *Scatchard* (1892–1973), U.S. physical chemist, who published a form of such analysis in 1949 (*Ann. N.Y. Acad. Sci.* LI. 660–72).] ***Scatchard plot***, a graph of the concentration of a solute absorbed by a protein, membrane, cell, or the like against its concentration in the surrounding medium; ***Scatchard analysis***, the use of such graphs to deduce the number and nature of the binding sites on the protein, etc.

1958 EDSALL & WYMAN *Biophys. Chem.* I. xi. 617 (*heading*) The Scatchard plot of $\bar{v}/(A)$ against $\bar{v}$. **1970** *Arch. Biochem. & Biophysics* CXLI. 623/2 (*caption*) Scatchard plot for binding of cytochrome *c* to normal rat liver mitochondria. **1975** *Nature* 13 Nov. 154/2 (*caption*) Scatchard plot of insulin-membrane interaction in two representative preparations from 10 control..and 10 diabetic..animals. *Ibid.* 27 Nov. 339/2 Scatchard analysis of the binding data revealed a class of receptors for 5-α-dihydro-testosterone of uniform affinity. **1978** *Ibid.* 12 Oct. 553/2 (*caption*) Scatchard analysis of interaction between diazepane and 'endogenous inhibitor' of Na^+-independent ^{3}H-GABA binding.

scate, obs. form of SKATE.

†**'scatebrous**, *a. Obs. rare*⁻⁰. [f. L. *scatebra* a gushing forth, f. *scatēre* to gush, spring forth: see -OUS.] (See quots.) Hence †**scate'brosity.**

1721 BAILEY, *Scatebrosity*, a flowing or bubbling out. *Scatebrous*, bubbling out like Water out of a Spring, abounding. **1755** JOHNSON, *Scatebrous*, abounding with springs.

scater, obs. form of SCATTER *v.*

scathe (skeɪð), *sb.* Now *arch.* and *dial.* (see E.D.D.). Forms: 3– **scathe, scath,** 3–4 **sckathe,** 3–7 **skathe,** 3–8 **skath,** (4 **skade,** 5 **scade**); *Sc.* and *north.* 4–9 **scaith, skaith,** 4–7 **skaithe,** 5 **scaythe,** 5–6 **skaitht,** 6 **skayth(t, scaithe, skeath.** Also 3–5, 7 **schath,** 3–6 **schathe,** 4 **schatht.** [The existing word is a. ON. *skaðe* wk. masc., harm, damage (Sw. *skada* fem., Da. *skade*) = OE. *sc(e)aða* masc., one who injures, malefactor, also (rarely) hurt, injury, OFris. *skatha, skada* injury, OS. *skaðo* masc., malefactor, MDu. *schade* masc. and fem. (Du. *schade* fem.), injury, OHG. *skado* masc. (MHG., mod.G. *schade*):—OTeut. **skaþon-*, f. root **skaþ-*, whence Goth. *skaþis* harm, *skaþjan* = SCATHE *v.*; the ablaut-var. **skōþ-* is represented in ON. *skóð* neut., that which harms, *skǿð-r* harmful. On the other hand, Layamon's *scaðe* in sense 1 almost certainly had (ʃ), and represents the OE. *sceaða* (the mod. form of which would have been **shathe*). The ME. spelling with *sch-* is of doubtful phonetic interpretation: in most of the verse examples the word thus written alliterates with *sk-*, and must therefore be regarded as of Scandinavian etymology; but some of the other instances may possibly (though there is no definite evidence) represent the native word.

The Teut. root **skaþ-* is believed to represent an Indo-germanic **skath-*: *skēth-*; cf. Gr. ἀ-σκηθής unscathed.]

†**1.** One who works harm; a malefactor; a wretch, fiend, monster. *Obs.*

Beowulf 274 Sceaða ic nat hwylc, deogol dædhata. *c* **1000** *Ags. Gosp.* Matt. xxvii. 38 Ða wæron a-hangen mid hym twegen sceaþan. *c* **1205** LAY. 1923, & þus þe hæȝe scaðe ferde to helle. *Ibid.* 14945 He wende þat hit weore soð þat þeo scaðe sæide. *Ibid.* 25877 For nu anan cumeð þe scaðe þe alle þine leomen wule to-draȝen.

2. Hurt, harm, damage.

Usually sing. and without article; but also occasionally with *a* (etc.) or in pl.

a **1000** *Cædmon's Gen.* 549 Cwæð, þæt sceaðena mæst eallum heora eaforum æfter siððan wurde on worulde. *c* **1250** *Gen. & Ex.* 2314 Ðis sonde hem ouertakeð raðe, And bi-calleð of harme and scaðe. *a* **1300** *Cursor M.* 6686 þe smiter sal quite his lechyng And þe scath [*Gött.* skade] of his liging. *c* **1325** *Metr. Hom.* 4 Hou thai mai yem thaim fra schathe. **1377** LANGL. *P. Pl.* B. III. 57 Who may scape þe sklaundre þe skaþe is sone amended. *c* **1440** *York Myst.* xviii. 77, I praye þe lorde, kepe us fro skathe. *Ibid.* xxxiii. 35 With schath of skelpys yll scarred. **1450** in *Charters*, etc. *Edinb.* (1871) 71 We ar informit..þat þai dreid the evil and skath of oure enemeis of England. **1527** ANDREW *Brunswyke's Distyll. Waters* K iv, For all that it muste be knowen for the great schathe that therof myght come. *a* **1578** LINDESAY (Pitscottie) *Chron. Scot.* (S.T.S.) I. 22 It sall redound to his avantage and to our gret skaith and schame. **1606** DRAYTON *Ode written in the Peak* 30 Strong Ale and Noble Cheare, T'asswage breeme Winters scathes. *a* **1670** SPALDING *Troub. Chas. I* (1829) 2 To the great hurt and skaith of the king's lieges. **17..** RAMSAY *Falling of a Slate* v, Watching sylphs flew round, To guard dear Madie from all skaith. **1785** BURNS *Death & Dr. Hornbook* ix, I red ye weel, tak care o' skaith, See, there's a gully! **1874** SYMONDS *Sk. Italy & Greece* (1898) I. xvi. 355 Round them [obstacles]..he passed nimbly, without scar or scathe. **1895** HUXLEY in *Life* (1900) II. xxiii. 401 It was cheering..to hear that you had got through winter and diphtheria without scathe.

b. Phr. ***to do*** (***work***, †***make***) ***scathe***, to do harm. *Const.* indirect (dative) object, with or without *to*. † ***to wait*** (one) ***scathe*** [= Icel. *veita einhverjum skaða*], to inflict injury upon.

c **1205** LAY. 12026 Mælga wes inne Scise þer he scaðe makede. *Ibid.* 15784 Ne doð heo noht muchel scaðe. *c* **1250** *Gen. & Ex.* 850 An ðere he werken scakðe and bale. *c* **1300** *Havelok* 1352 Dwelling haueth ofte scaþe wrouth. **1303** R. BRUNNE *Handl. Synne* 5987 Or ouþer skaþe he wyl hym weyte. *c* **1350** *Will. Palerne* 4051 þat no burn nere so bold.. to wait þe werwolf no maner schaþe. *c* **1470** HENRY *Wallace* I. 111 Is nayne in warld, at scaithis ma do mar, Than weile trastyt in borne familiar. *c* **1489** CAXTON *Sonnes of Aymon* xiii. 308 Grete hurte & scathe was there made of bothe partes. **1588** SHAKS. *Tit. A.* v. i. 7 And wherein Rome hath done you any scathe, Let him make treble satisfaction. **1595** *Locrine* v. ii. 33 Nor can I finde in heart to worke his scathe. **1632** T. TAYLOR *God's Judgem.* I. I. xvi. (1642) 57 His owne side came to the worse, doing more scath to themselves, than to their enemies. **1715** *Wodrow Corr.* (1843) II. 114, I cannot tell particularly what skaith they did. **1834** H. MILLER *Scenes & Leg.* xxii. (1850) 316 They were doing great skaith, it was said, to victual and drink. **1865** J. M. NEALE *Hymns on Paradise* 68 If manifold temptations Of the fiend should work thee scathe.

c. The corresponding passive notion is expressed by ***to get, have, take scathe***. †Also, ***to catch, find, hent, kep, thole***, etc., ***scathe***.

1303 R. BRUNNE *Handl. Synne* 10648 Sey me þe soþe, and, as y am knyȝt, þou ne shalt haue for me skaþe ne plyȝt. **1362** LANGL. *P. Pl.* A. IV. 65 Withouten gult, god wot gat I þis scaþe. **13..** *E.E. Allit. P.* B. 151 Lest he skaþe hent. **1375** BARBOUR *Bruce* VIII. 358 Menand the scath that he had tane. *c* **1400** *Destr. Troy* 5103 Hit is skille for his skorne, þat he scathe thole. *c* **1420** *Avow. Arth.* xvi, He began to dotur and dote Os he hade keghet scathe. **1470–85** MALORY *Arthur* x. xxx. 464 To redresse the harmes and the scathes that he had of them. **1513** DOUGLAS *Æneis* III. v. 116 How grete harme and skaith..That childe hes caucht throw lossing of his modir! **1549** *Compl. Scot.* vi. 60 The fyir slaucht vil consume the vyne vitht in ane pipe..& the pipe vil resaue na skaytht. **1572, 1721** [see KEP *v.* 2 b]. **1586** WARNER *Alb. England* I. vi. (1589) 20 He tolde what skath the Centaures late..had found. **1642** in Row *Hist. Kirk* (Wodrow Soc.) p. xvii, Suche personis as had cum from Irland, and had gottin great skaithe thair. **1730** T. BOSTON *View this & other World* 263 He could not miss to catch skaith, if all the better care were not taken to prevent it. **1839** HARR. CAMPBELL *Only Daughter* iii, The Laird of Kilmore..took no scaith from the ..attractions of the Misses Sibellas, and Miss Anabels of the county, and at the age of forty he was still a bachelor.

d. Alliteratively coupled with *scorn*. Chiefly *Sc.*

a **1300** *Cursor M.* 23338 For þair misfair suld þai not murn, Ne ans for þair skathes skurn [*Gött.* schathes schurn]. *c* **1400** *Destr. Troy* 1874 For to wreke vs of wrathe, & the wegh harme Bothe of skathe & of skorne. **1508** DUNBAR *Tua Mariit Wemen* 358 And thus the scorne and the scaith scapit he nothir. **1674** RAY *N.C. Words* 41 One doth the skath, and another hath the scorn. Prov. **1755** JOHNSON, *Scath* in Scotland denotes spoil or damage: as, he bears the scath and the scorn. A proverb. **1864** CARLYLE *Fredk. Gt.* xv. iv. (1865) V. 308 Let us take the scathe and the scorn candidly home to us.

e. *quasi-concr.* A physical hurt or damage.

c **1440** *Pallad. on Husb.* I. 1116 Conuenyent hit is to knowe, of bathis Whil speche is mad, what malthis hote & colde Are able, ther as chynyng, clift, or skathe is, To make hit hool and watir wel to holde.

f. Something which works harm.

1579 GOSSON *Sch. Abuse* (Arb.) 46 The Adders death is her own broode, the Fencers scath, his own knowledg. **1795** MACNEILL (*title*) Scotland's Skaith. **1888** HENLEY *Bk. Verses* 102 The pride I trampled is now my scathe, For it tramples me again.

g. *spec.* 'Injury supposed to proceed from witchcraft' (Jam.).

1795 *Statist. Acc. Scot.* XVI. 122 This is done with a view to prevent skaith, if it should happen that the person is not cany. **1899** J. SPENCE *Shetland Folk-Lore* 111 The person who attempted to cross a fisherman's path when on his way to the boat, intended to do him scathe.

3. Matter for sorrow or regret. In various phrases, as ***it is scathe***, it is a pity. ***it is*** (***great***) ***scathe of him***, he is a great loss. ***to think*** (***no***) ***scathe of***, ***think*** (***it***) ***no scathe***, (not) to regret, think (it) no harm. [Cf. G. *schade*.]

c **1250** *Gen. & Ex.* 2298 In fulsum-hed he wurðen glaðe, Iosep ne ðoht ðor-of no scaðe. *c* **1300** *Havelok* 2006 But it is of him mikel scaþe: I woth þat he bes ded ful raþe. **13..** *Guy Warw.* 1542 Sir, in þe sond he liþe, & þat is scaþe. **13..** *Gaw. & Gr. Knt.* 674 Bi Kryst, hit is scaþe, þat þou, leude, schal be lost. *c* **1386** CHAUCER *Prol.* 446 But she was som del deef, and þat was scathe. *c* **1450** *Merlin* xxxiii. 678 And that was grete scade that thei sholde die so soone. **15..** *Christ's Kirk Gr.* viii, Grit skayth wes'd to haif skard him. **1787** W. TAYLOR *Scots Poems* 11 (E.D.D.) To cheat the rich some think nae skaith. **1870** MORRIS *Earthly Par.* III. IV. 57 They deemed it little scathe indeed That her coarse homespun ragged weed Fell off from her round arms.

†**4.** An injury, damage, or loss for which legal compensation is claimed. In pl. = damages; also, costs or expenses incurred by the claimant. Chiefly *Sc. Obs.*

1456 SIR G. HAYE *Law Arms* (S.T.S.) 136 He may demaund his scathis at the lord, be way of accioun of dett. *a* **1500** ARNOLDE *Chron.* (1811) 118, I promyse to make good all costis and scathes that may growe therby for defaute off payment. **1504** in Littlejohn *Aberd. Sheriff Crt.* (1904) 48 Thomas Leslie..protestit for thar costs skaithts and expenses. **1678** SIR G. MACKENZIE *Crim. Laws Scot.* I. xix. §xv. (1699) 104 The Unlaw to be ten Pound, and mends to the Party, conform to the skaith.

5. *attrib.* and *Comb.*, as ***scathe-deed***, ***-work***; objective, as ***scathe-causer***, ***scathe-taking*** vbl. sb.

c **1205** LAY. 1547 Swa þe rimie wulf þane he wule on scheapen scaðe were wrchen. *Ibid.* 29578 þa hine isend hafden mid heore scaðe deden. *a* **1300** *Cursor M.* 28161 Quen i sagh oþer men mistad, of his fare wald i be gladd, for his ded and his vn-hele, for skath takyng of his catell. **1559** *Mirr. Mag., Hen. VI* xiii, If likewise such as say the welken fortune warkes, Take Fortune for our fate, and sterres therof the markes, Then destiny with fate, and Gods wil al be one: But if they meane it otherwise, skath causers skyes be none.

scathe (skeɪð), *v.* Forms: 2–5 **skathe**, 4–9 **scathe**, **scath**, (4 **sckathe**); chiefly *Sc.* 5–6 **skayth**(**e**, 6 **ska**, 5–9 **scaith**, 8–9 **skaith**. [a. ON. *skaða* impers., it hurts (Sw. *skada*, Da. *skade* to hurt, injure); corresponding to OE. *sc*(*e*)*aðian* to injure, rob, OFris. *skathia* to injure, OS. *scaðon* (Essen Gl.) to slander, Du. *schaden* to injure, OHG. *skadôn* (MHG., mod.G. *schaden*):—OTeut. **skaþōjan*, f. **skaþon-* SCATHE *sb.*

ON. had also another verb from the same root, *skeðja* (pa. t. *skadde*), corresponding to OE. *sceððan* (orig. strong, pa. t. *sceód*, pa. pple. (*ȝe*)*sceaðen*, whence by analogy an inf. form *sceaðan*; commonly weak, pa. t. *scęðede*), Goth. *skaþjan* (pa. t. *skōþ*). There is no evidence, however, that the ON. *skeðja* was adopted in English, or that either of the OE. vbs. (with initial (ʃ)) survived into ME.]

1. *trans.* To injure, hurt, damage. Now *arch.* and *Sc.*

c **1200** ORMIN 4468–9 Forr ȝiff þu skaþesst aniȝ mann þu skaþesst firrst te sellfenn. *c* **1380** *Sir Ferumb.* 759, Y schal scaþye hem niȝt & day þat bileueþ on Mahounde. *a* **1400** *Relig. Pieces fr. Thornton MS.* 26 He þat will noghte sckathe his euencristyn, he sall noghte consente ne na consaile gyffe to do hym ill. *c* **1460** *Towneley Myst.* xxii. 365 Syrs, I haue a greatt Iornay That must be done this same day, Or els it will me skathe. **1470–85** MALORY *Arthur* II. xii. 90 That wille I not, sayd the knyghte, for hit wylle scathe me gretely and now do yow none auaylle. **1566** *Reg. Privy Council Scot.* I. 468 Throw the quhilk [false coin]..this commoun weill hes bene greitlie hurt, and oure Soveranis and thair trew subjectis defraudit and skaythit. **1592** SHAKS. *Rom. & Jul.* I. v. 86 This tricke may chance to scath you. **1728** RAMSAY *Last Sp. Miser* xvi, But that ne'er skaith'd or troubled me, Gin I grew rich. **1784** BURNS *Ep. J. Rankine* iv, Think, wicked Sinner, wha ye're skaithing. **1829** H. MILLER *Lett. on Herring Fish.*, I manna skaith the rape. **1840** BARHAM *Ingol. Leg.* Ser. I. *St. Nicholas*, Holy Church..the wolves doth mock who would scathe her flock.

†**b.** *spec.* To subject to pecuniary loss. (The amount is expressed by a second object or introduced by *of*.) *Obs.*

1456 SIR. G. HAYE *Law Arms* (S.T.S.) 167 He aw to be payit of the baroune of all his soume of lenth that he war scathit of. ? **1496** in *Lett. Rich. III & Hen. VII* (Rolls) II. 69 Ther entred neuer a straunger ship here sithins Midlent, and that hath skathed the Kinges grace c. li. **1600** DARRELL *Detect. Harsnet's Lying Disc.* 202 The poore man..had as liue she had so kindly imbraced another as him, for the louing salutation..scathed him 4. nobles. **1602** *How Man may chuse Good Wife* C 1, Ile crosse thy name quite from my reckoning booke: For these accounts, faith it shall skathe thee somewhat.

†**c.** *absol.* To do harm. *Obs.*

1470 HENRY *Wallace* VIII. 1132 It ma nocht scaith, suppos it do na waill.

2. To injure or destroy by fire, lightning, or similar agency; to blast, scorch, sear. *poet.* and *rhet.*

This, and the derived sense 3, appear to have been developed from the Milton passage (quot. 1667), perh. partly through sound-association with *scorch*.

[**1667** MILTON *P.L.* I. 613 As when Heavens Fire Hath scath'd the Forrest Oaks,..With singed top their stately growth though bare Stands on the blasted Heath.] **1810** SCOTT *Lady of L.* III. x, The monk resumed his mutter'd spell:..The while he scathed the Cross with flame. **1813** —— *Rokeby* IV. iii, The pine-tree scathed by lightning-fire. **1814** —— *Ld. of Isles* IV. viii, Seek not the giddy crag to climb, To view the turret scathed by time. **1831** CARLYLE *Sart. Res.* II. viii, The fire-baptised soul, long so scathed and thunder-riven, here feels its own Freedom. **1844** THIRLWALL *Greece* VIII. lxiii. 240 The flames that scathed Thermus. **1882** FARRAR *Early Chr.* II. 213 The whole country had been scathed with fire and drowned in blood.

fig. **1842** MANNING *Serm.* (1843) I. vi. 83 Familiar consent to evil..scathes and deadens the spiritual sense.

3. *fig.* To sear or 'wither' with fierce invective or satire. Cf. SCATHING *ppl. a.*

1852 ROBERTSON *Serm.* Ser. III. (1857) 152 At the same time that He scathed with indignant invective the Pharisees. **1867** FROUDE *Short Stud.* Ser. I. I. 77 (*Erasmus & Luther* ii.) His satire flashed about,..scathing especially his old enemies the monks.

Hence **scathed** *ppl. a.*

1791 GILPIN *Forest Scenery* II. 71 Many of the oaks are scathed, and ragged. **1831** SCOTT *Ct. Robt.* xxix, The hulk of the Grecian Admiral, burnt to the water's edge, and still sending forth a black smoke from its scathed beams and planks. **1842** BORROW *Bible in Spain* vi, Its scathed and gigantic crags. **1873** MISS BROUGHTON *Nancy* III. 152 Is that one withered scathed little stick to be our sole protection against the storm?

†**'scathefire.** *Obs.* Also 7 **scath-**, **skath-**, **schath-**, 8 *dial.* **scale-**. See also SCAREFIRE. [f. SCATHE *sb.* + FIRE *sb.* Cf. G. *schadenfeuer*, Da. *skadeild*, Norw. *skadeverme*.] A destructive fire or conflagration.

1632 HEYWOOD *2nd Pt. Iron Age* v. i. I 4, These horrid sights Lighted by scathe-fires. **1658** W. BURTON *Itin. Anton.* 155 Her frequent Schathfires have rendred her not less magnificent, but more famous. *a* **1663** BRAMHALL *Vind. fr. Popery* vi. (1672) 115 In a great Scathfire it is wisdom not only to suffer those Houses to burn down which are past quenching, but [etc.]. **1796** PEGGE *Derbicisms* Ser. I. 60 (E.D.S.) *Scale-fire*, when a house or town is on fire.

scatheful ('skeɪðfʊl), *a. arch.* Forms: see SCATHE *sb.* [f. SCATHE *sb.* + -FUL. Cf. Ormin's *unnskaþefull*.] Hurtful, harmful, injurious.

c **900** tr. *Gregory's Dial.* 209 Swa þonne ȝeweorðeð þæt we becumað þonne fram þam idlan wordum to þam sceaðfullum. **1375** BARBOUR *Bruce* v. 249 Gif the hapnys ony thing, That anoyus or scathfull be. **1513** DOUGLAS *Æneis* II. i. 34 And sum, wondring, the skaithfull gift beheld. **1527** ANDREW *Brunswyke's Distyll. Waters* B j b, This water.. withdryveth the scadefull swellyng in the bely. **1586** WARNER *Alb. Eng.* I. v. (1589) 15 Hercules..with skathfull strokes bestird his Club so well,..that [etc.]. **1601** SHAKS. *Twel. N.* v. i. 59 With which such scathfull grapple did he make With the most noble bottome of our Fleete. **1855** SINGLETON *Virg., Georg.* I. I. 80 That scathful rust should prey upon its stalks.

†**scathel**, *a. Obs.* Forms: 4 **scathel**, **-ylle**, 5 **skethill**, **skathil**(**l**, **-ell**, 6 **skatell**. *β.* 5 **schatell**, **schathill**. See also SCADDLE *a.* [a. ON. **skǫþull* = OHG. *scad*(*h*)*al*, *scadel*, *scatal*, *-el*, Goth. *skaþuls*:—OTeut. **skaþulo-*, f. **skaþ-*: see SCATHE *sb.*] Injurious, harmful, dangerous. Also *absol.* as *sb.*

a **1300** *Cursor M.* 28773 Almus askes to be wroght o rightwis aght,..for elles vnmedi sal it be, scathel and wrangwise als to þe. **13..** *E.E. Allit. P.* C. 155 Mony ladde þer forthlep to laue & to Rest, Scopen out þe scaþel water, þat fayn scape wolde. *a* **1400** *Morte Arth.* 32 Scathylle Scottlande by skylle he skyftys as hym lykys. *Ibid.* 1642 That no skathelle in the skroggez skorne vs here-aftyr. *c* **1400** *Destr. Troy* 4067 Ascalaphus, a skathil duke & skant mon in wer. *Ibid.* 13442 There were sones vpposyde,..To Askathes full skete, skethill of hor hond. *a* **1400–50** *Alexander* 2992 þat skapid..skatheles fra all his schathill dukis [*Dubl.* scapett..schatheles..schatell]. **1515** *Scot. Field* 342 in *Chetham Misc.* (1856) II, Those skatell Scotts, that all the skath diden.

scatheless ('skeɪðlɪs), *a.* Forms: see SCATHE *sb.* [f. SCATHE *sb.* + -LESS. Cf. ON. *skaðlauss*.] Without scathe; unharmed. †Const. *of*.

c **1200** ORMIN 12038 ȝiff þatt he lupe dun All skaþelæs till eorþe. *c* **1350** *Will. Palerne* 1855 To a-schape schaþles fram þat schamful best. *a* **1366** CHAUCER *Rom. Rose* 1550 That scathles, fulle sykerly, I myght unto the welle goo. *a* **1400–50** [see SCATHEL]. **1563** *Reg. Privy Council Scot.* I. 241 To keip him skaithless of the samyn [penalty]. **1818** SCOTT *Hrt. Midl.* xv, 'I wad ware the best blood in my body to keep her skaithless,' said Jeanie. **1865** TROLLOPE *Belton Est.* xxviii. 341 It is a game from which you will come out scatheless, but I have been scalded. **1884** *Law Times* LXXVIII. 57/1 The wife and the fortunate individual who shared her indictment escaped scatheless.

Hence **'scathelessly** *adv.*

1844 TUPPER *Heart* xi. 121 In the hope..of ruining him, if not of getting scathelessly off themselves. **1858** J. H. BENNET *Nutrition* vi. 209 The soldier who..passes scathlessly through twenty campaigns.

†**'scathely**, *adv. Obs.* [f. SCATHE *sb.* + -LY².] With damage or injury. Only in allit. phr. ***to scape*** (or ***aschape***) ***scathely***.

c **1350** *Will. Palerne* 2794 þat we so scaþli ar a-schaped god mowe [we] þonk. *a* **1400–50** *Alexander* 642 If any scolere in þe scole his skorne at him makis, He skapis him full skathely bot if he skyp better.

scathing ('skeɪðɪŋ), *ppl. a.* [-ING².]

1. That scathes or blasts (see SCATHE *v.* 2).

1794 COLERIDGE *Monody Death Chatterton* 51 The scathing lightning. **1813** BYRON *Corsair* I. x, Mark how that lone and blighted bosom sears The scathing thought of execrated years! **1858** GLADSTONE *Homer* II. 180 He launches the scathing thunderbolt.

2. Of invective, etc.: Very sharp and damaging; searing, 'withering', cutting.

1865 LECKY *Ration.* (1878) I. 251 Week after week he launched from the pulpit the most scathing invectives. **1893** *Times* 28 Apr. 9/4 Mr. Goschen's speech was a scathing exposure of the contrast between promise and performance.

Hence **'scathingly** *adv.*

1847 *Tait's Mag.* XIV. 238 A feeling of his insignificance flashed scathingly on the quivering pride of Robert Anderson. **1868** E. EDWARDS *Ralegh* I. xxii. 497 That Duke of Savoy whom Milton has made scathingly famous.

scatire, obs. form of SCATTER *v.*

scatol, variant of SKATOL *Chem.*

scatologic (skætəˈlɒdʒɪk), *a.* [f. SCATOLOG(Y + -IC.] Of or pertaining to scatology (sense 1).

1891 J. G. BOURKE (*title*) Scatalogic [*sic*] Rites of all Nations. **1897** in *Syd. Soc. Lex.*

scatological (ˌskætəˈlɒdʒɪkəl), *a.* [f. as prec.: see -ICAL.] Of or pertaining to scatology (senses 1 and 3); characterized by a preoccupation with obscenity.

1924 F. M. FORD *Some do Not* II. ii. 237 The late Mr. Duchemin was a scatological—afterwards a homicidal—lunatic. **1959** J. KIRKUP tr. *S. de Beauvoir's Mem. Dutiful Daughter* I. 82 There was one phrase grown-ups were always using: 'It's not proper!'.. At first I had taken it to have a scatological connotation. **1960** G. MAXWELL *Ring of Bright Water* IX. 123 As a useful by-product of his [*sc.* the otter's] impish sense of humour, the cattle tended to keep farther from the house, thus.. reducing the number of scatological hazards to be skirted at the door. **1969** *Daily Tel.* 13 Mar. 23/2 The scatological streak in the man, his disgusted-disgusting jokes about excreting nymphs. **1979** *London Rev. Bks.* 25 Oct. 8/2 One might almost assume from a few of these scatological diatribes that he thought there was something intrinsically disgusting about physical love.

scatology (skəˈtɒlədʒɪ). [f. Gr. σκατ-, σκῶρ dung + -(O)LOGY.]

1. That branch of science which deals with diagnosis by means of the fæces.

1897 in *Syd. Soc. Lex.*

2. That branch of palæontology which treats of fossil excrement or coprolites.

In recent Dicts.

3. Filthy literature.

1876 *N. & Q.* Ser. v. V. 31 Mr. Swifte's suggestion that *scatology* may be derived from *scateo*. **1887** SAINTSBURY *Elizab. Lit.* x. 370 A large quantity of mere scatology and doggerel. **1936** R. QUINTANA *Mind & Art of Jonathan Swift* VI. ii. 360 From scatology one turns with relief to the careful verses entitled *Helter Skelter*. **1959** N. O. BROWN *Life against Death* xiii. 179 The most scandalous pieces of Swiftian scatology are.. *The Lady's Dressing Room, Strephon and Chloe, Cassinus and Peter*. **1975** *Publishers Weekly* 22 Sept. 134/1 Funny, albeit unintentional scatology in the [zodiacal] Sign abbreviations.

scatomancy (ˈskætəʊmænsɪ). [ad. mod.L. *scatomantīa*: see prec. and -MANCY.] Divination or diagnosis based on the examination of the fæces.

1569 J. SANFORD tr. *Agrippa's Van. Artes* lxxxiii. 145 b, For this cause Scatomancie, Oromancie, Drymimancie, be called the diuinations or Prognostications of Phisitians, gathered by ordures and vrines. **1861** READE *Cloister & H.* xxvi, I studied at Montpelier... There learned I Dririmancy, Scatomancy, Pathology [etc.]. **1897** in *Syd. Soc. Lex.*

†**scatomanter.** *Obs. rare*⁻¹. [irreg. ad. mod.L. *scatomantis*, f. Gr. σκατ(o)- dung + μάντις prophet.] One who practises scatomancy.

1569 J. SANFORD tr. *Agrippa's Van. Artes* lxxxiii. 145 b, [The name *Scatophagos*] afterwards was deriued to all Phisitions, in suche wise, that wee call them Scatophagians and Scatomanters, that is, ordure eaters, and lookers on ordure.

scatophage (ˈskætəʊfeɪdʒ). [ad. mod.L. *scatophag-us*, a. Gr. σκατοφάγος: see SCATOPHAGOUS *a.* Cf. F. *scatophage* adj.] A scatophagous insect or animal; esp. a dung-fly.

In recent Dicts.

†**scatoˈphagian.** *Obs. rare*⁻¹. [f. mod.L. *scatophag-us* (see next) + -IAN.] One who feeds on dung.

1569 [see SCATOMANTER].

scatophagous (skəˈtɒfəgəs), *a.* [f. mod.L. *scatophag-us*, a. Gr. σκατοφάγος, f. σκατ(o-), σκῶρ dung: see -PHAGOUS.] Feeding upon dung.

1891 in *Century Dict.* **1896** *Nature* 16 July 247/2 In *Stomoxys*,.. the larvæ are normally scatophagous.

scatoscopy (skəˈtɒskəpɪ). *rare*⁻⁰. [Cf. prec. and -SCOPY.] Inspection of the fæces for the purpose of divination or diagnosis.

In recent Dicts.

scatses, obs. pl. form of SKATE *sb.*²

scattald (ˈskætəld). *Orkney* and *Shetl.* Also 7 scat(t)ell, 8 scatald, scatteld, scat(t)hold, scattald, -old, scathald, skattald. [ad. local Scandinavian **skatthald* (= ON. *skatt-r* SCAT *sb.*³ + *hald* HOLD *sb.*] The common ground for pasture or furnishing fuel, etc. of a district. Hence **ˈscattalder**, one who shares in the scattald. Also *in-scattalder* = 'scattalder'; *out-skattalder*, a resident in the district who has no share in the scattald.

1615 *Acts* etc. *Orkney & Shetl.* (Maitl. Cl. 1840) II. 174 Anent going throuch thair nychtbours scattell... It sall not be lesum to ony persone.. to go throuch his nychtbouris scatell or comontie with ane scheip dog Except [etc.]. *a* **1733** *Shetland Acts* 32 in *Proc. Soc. Ant. Scot.* (1892) XXVI. 201 That every scatald have a sufficient pund. *Ibid.* 35 ibid., All horses belonging either to outscattalders or inscattalders. *Ibid.* 39 ibid., That the Sheriff.. ride the marches of the parish.. when required thereto by the scattalders. **1809** A. EDMONSTON *Pres. St. Zetland* I. 148 The uncultivated ground, outside of the enclosure [or town], is called the Scatthold, and is used for general pasture, and to furnish turf for firing. **1883** *Chamb. Jrnl.* 211 Beyond the turf dikes is the scattald or common.

scatter (ˈskætə(r)), *sb.* [f. SCATTER *v.*]

1. a. The action or an act of scattering; wide or irregular distribution; dispersion. Now chiefly with reference to shot.

1642 J. W[EALL] *Prepar. Fast* 4 We are exposed aswell to Forraigne and intestine mischiefes. This divide and scatter, if it be not prevented, will be no small curse. **1650** T. VAUGHAN *Anthroposophia* 68 Advt. to Rdr., Let Them [*sc.* the Galenists] not mangle, and discompose my Book with a scatter of Observations, but proceed Methodically to the Censure of each part. **1893** *Westm. Gaz.* 14 Dec. 5/1 Had there been no deflection from the hard skull the shot.. would have been smaller in scatter than it is.

b. *transf.* in Linguistics.

1934 J. R. FIRTH *Papers in Linguistics 1934–51* (1957) ii. 4 All the common phonetic contexts of each phoneme should be stated, and the contextual spread or 'scatter' of the phonemes compared. This knowledge of the contextual scatter of a phoneme will be found of the greatest importance for the statement of our future sound laws. **1935** —— in *Trans. Philol. Soc.* 45 The frequency of reference to sex had necessarily extended what I term the formal scatter of the word, and we now have *sexed, sexless, sexy, sexiness*, even *sexology*. **1963** J. LYONS *Structural Semantics* vii. 178 One point that seemed to be of relevance in the inquiry was the defective formal 'scatter' of the lexeme εἰδέναι.

2. A quantity loosely distributed or interspersed; a scattering, sprinkling. Also *spec.* in *Archæol.*

1859 R. F. BURTON *Centr. Afr.* in *Jrnl. Geog. Soc.* XXIX. 158 Its sole displays quartzose sand, with scatters of granite. **1888** *Daily News* 17 May 5/8 The bodice, too, had a scatter of diamonds and pearls. **1943** V. SACKVILLE-WEST *Eagle & Dove* iii. 17 A sick woman with a scatter of high-spirited children to control would welcome any method of keeping them quiet. **1954** J. B. MITCHELL *Historical Geogr.* iii. 73 A scatter of Scandinavian settlers in a district primarily English. **1959** *Listener* 12 Mar. 449/2 The ascendancy of the U.S.A., along with that of the U.S.S.R., has relegated the scatter of European nations to subsidiary status. **1974** C. TAYLOR *Fieldwork in Medieval Archaeol.* ii. 27 Much of it [*sc.* the information] will probably be vague, such as notes of pottery scatters, low banks, water-filled ditches and possible old quarries. **1977** *Christian* IV. 109 The human race is not a scatter of individuals.

3. *Statistics.* The degree to which repeated measurements or observations of a quantity differ; that which is measured by the variance.

1921 R. S. WOODWORTH *Psychol.* (1922) xii. 273 Usually there is some 'scatter' in the child's successes. **1923** *Proc. R. Soc.* A. CII. 357 The question arises as to how much of the 'scatter' of the Gaussian curve is due to error of observation, inexperience in making the readings, accidental variations, etc., and how much is due to a real difference in the physiological equipment of the observer. **1934** *Brit. Jrnl. Psychol.* XXIV. 344 The I.Q.'s of the boys showed a wider scatter than those of the girls. **1963** B. FOZARD *Instrumentation Nucl. Reactors* vii. 70 A commonly used measure of the dispersion or scatter of a number of observed values about the central values is the standard deviation. **1968** *Brit. Med. Bull.* XXIV. 246/2 Most observations are subject to considerable scatter, especially where mammalian systems are used, and statistical procedures of varying complexity are called for.

4. a. The scattering of light or other radiation.

1942 *Tee Emm* (Air Ministry) II. 145 Preventing the 'light scatter' which comes from scratched Perspex or slightly dirty windscreens. **1962** H. C. WESTON *Sight, Light & Work* (ed. 2) vi. 206 It is better that the increased illumination required by older eyes should be provided by 'warmer' illuminants so that 'hazing' due to scatter within the eyes is minimised.

b. *spec.* with reference to radio waves, freq. denoting the use of scattering within the atmosphere to extend the range of radio communication. Freq. *attrib.*

1950 *Proc. IRE* XXXVIII. 412/2 For two-directional antennas of beam width θ facing one another, the greatest angle of scatter that need be considered is θ. **1956** *Ann. Reg. 1955* 155 It was announced that a revolutionary new system of communications, known as 'scatter', which was not susceptible to jamming,.. would be introduced. **1958** *Times* 30 Apr. 6/6 A range of tropospheric scatter transmitting and receiving equipment. **1966** *McGraw-Hill Encycl. Sci. & Technol.* XIII. 439/1 Radio relay systems are usually more suitable than the scatter systems for overland use where intermediate radio relay stations can be constructed. **1977** *Lancs. Life* Nov. 83/2 On the radar screen shown here, Manchester is permanently blacked-out because of 'scatter' from buildings and nearby high ground, to avoid masking approaching precipitation.

5. *Comb.* **scatter diagram, plot** *Statistics*, a diagram having two variates plotted along its two axes and in which points are placed to show the values of these variates for each of a number of subjects, so that the form of the association between the variates can be seen.

1925 F. C. MILLS *Statistical Methods* x. 366 The equation to a straight line, fitted by the method of least squares to the points on the scatter diagram, will express mathematically the average relationship between these two variables. **1937** YULE & KENDALL *Theory of Statistics* (ed. 11) xiv. 275 The scatter diagram in two dimensions may be generalised to three dimensions, and may also be used as a mental construct for higher dimensions, though no actual model can of course be made. **1960** [see KARYOGRAM b]. **1971** *Nature* 9 Apr. 390/2 Scatter diagrams were drawn to show mean concentrations of albumin, γ-globulin, fibrinogen and cholesterol against age. **1971** *Jrnl. General Psychol.* LXXXV. 266 Inspection of the scatter plot.. indicates that any index of relationship would be misleading. **1973** *Jrnl. Genetic Psychol.* CXXII. 45 Guilford's triangular scatterplot conceptualization of intelligence-creativity relationship seemed most congruent with the present.. data.

scatter (ˈskætə(r)), *v.* Forms: 2 scatere, 3–6 scater, skater, 4 schatre, scatir(e, 4–5 scatre, 5 skatre, (schatir), 6 scattre, skattir, sketer, 7 skatter, 6– scatter. [Early ME. (12th c., Midland); of obscure origin; formed with iterative suffix (see -ER⁵).

This and SHATTER *v.* (which appears much later) are commonly regarded as respectively northern and southern representatives of an OE. **sc(e)aterian*, which is referred to a supposed Teut. root **skat-* cogn. w. Gr. σκεδ-αννύναι to scatter. The etymological identity of the two vbs. seems, however, doubtful, although they have some affinity of sense. It is true that in ME. *scatter* occurs only in northern and midland texts, with one exception (quot. 1330, sense 3); and that in this sole southern instance the MS. spells it with *sch*, which should normally stand for (ʃ). But initial (sk) from OE. *sc* in a native word would be no less abnormal in northern and midland than in southern English. The alleged cognates in Du. and LG. are questionable. Two instances are cited of MDu. *schaderen*, with the senses 'to squander (money)', 'to shed (blood)'; but this does not agree in form. The sense 'to scatter' assigned to early mod.Du. *schetteren*, rests on the authority of Kilian, whose citation of the Eng. word renders his testimony suspicious. The Du. and MLG. *schateren* to resound, to laugh uproariously (MLG. once, to be shattered by an explosion) would seem to be onomatopoeic; at least their sense cannot easily be derived from that assigned to the alleged Teut. root. Cf. SCAT *v.*² and SQUATTER *v.*]

1. *trans.* To dissipate, squander (goods or possessions). *Obs.* or *arch.*

1154 *O.E. Chron.* an. 1137, He hadde ȝet his tresor ac he to deld it & scatered sotlice. *c* **1380** WYCLIF *Serm.* Sel. Wks. II. 78 For ȝif þes ordres geten nevere so myche good, þei seien þat al is þer ordris, and it were a deedli synne to scatire þes goodis in þe world. **1522** MORE *De quat. Noviss.* Wks. 94 They would.. neuer be so mad, gredily to gather together that other men shal merely sone after scatter abrode. *c* **1645** HOWELL *Lett.* VI. xvii. (1650) I. 204, I leave the rest of all my goods to my first-born Edward, to be consum'd or scatterd (for I never hoped better). *a* **1716** SOUTH *Serm.* (1744) VIII. 326 And was it not worth the.. seeing his substance scattered, his children struck dead [etc.].

absol. **1879** G. CAMPBELL *White & Black* 243 Mr. J—— says the Germans are the only men who are saving; all the rest scatter.

2. a. To separate and drive in various directions (a body of men or animals, a collection of things); to disperse, dissipate (a quantity of matter); to dispel (clouds, mists).

a **1300** *E.E. Psalter* xvii. 16 [xviii. 14] And he sent his arwes, and skatered þa. **1382** WYCLIF *Matt.* xxvi. 31, I shal smyte the sheperde, and the sheep of the floc shulen be scatered. **1582** STANYHURST *Æneis* I. (Arb.) 19 Duck downe theire fleete with a tempest, Or ships wyde scatter. **1594** SHAKS. *Rich. III*, IV. iv. 513 Buckingham's Armie is dispers'd and scatter'd. **1596** —— *Merch. V.* I. i. 33 Dangerous rocks, Which touching but my gentle Vessels side Would scatter all her spices on the streame. **1596** DALRYMPLE tr. *Leslie's Hist. Scot.* II. x. 453 Lyk a certane sone, new risen to skail and skattir the Cloudis of al tumulte. **1657** W. COLES *Adam in Eden* xxiii. 49 The Leaves of wild Clary.. put into Pottage.. scatter congealed blood. *c* **1788** BURNS *Ep. to R. Graham* 26 Some spumy, fiery, *ignis fatuus* matter, Such as the slightest breath of air might scatter. **1860** TYNDALL *Glac.* I. iii. 30 A breeze.. keen and hostile, scattering the snow. **1871** FREEMAN *Norm. Conq.* IV. xviii. 117 The terrible name of Odo scattered them in all directions. **1879** MISS BRADDON *Clov. Foot* xxviii, 'What has become of all the photographs?'.. 'Given to Tom, Dick and Harry—scattered to the four winds. I have not kept one of them.'

absol. **1594** T. B. *La Primaud. Fr. Acad.* II. 283 It is the nature of this enemy of mankind [*sc.* the Devil] to scatter, to disioyne and separat.

fig. **1613** PURCHAS *Pilgrimage* (1614) 45 So doth God scatter the counsells of his enemies. [Cf. *Vulg.* Ps. xxxii[i]. 10 *Dominus dissipet consilia gentium.*] **1822** SHELLEY tr. *Calderon* iii. 145 So that Heaven May scatter thy delusions. **1869** LECKY *Europ. Mor.* I. iii. 430 No one did more to scatter the ancient superstitions than did Cicero.

b. *intr.* for *refl.* To separate and disperse; to go dispersedly or stragglingly. †Also of a hawk: To go to a distance.

c **1430** *Syr Gener.* (Roxb.) 158 And kepe we vs to-gedre trew That we skater not a-sondre. **1486** *Bk. St. Albans* b iij b, When thay [a Couy of partrichys] be putt upp, and begynne to scatre, ye most haue markeris to marke some of thaym. **15..** *Scot. Field* 513 in *Chetham Misc.* II, When the Skottes.. seen our men sketer They.. came downwarde. **1593** SHAKS. *2 Hen. VI*, III. ii. 126 The Commons like an angry Hiue of Bees That want their Leader, scatter vp and downe. **1610** GUILLIM *Heraldry* II. v. (1611) 46 The Fillet is shaped long and narrowe for the more commodious vse of women in.. restraining of their haire from scattering about theire browes. **1626** BACON *Sylva* §138 Sound diffuseth it selfe in round..; But if the Sound, which would scatter in Open Aire, be made to goe all into a Canale; It must needs giue greater force to the Sound. **1771** *Encycl. Brit.* II. 541/2 She [the falcon] must also have two good bells, that she may be found when she scattereth. **1795** SOUTHEY *Joan of Arc* VI. 309 Aright, aleft, The affrighted foemen scatter from his spear. **1796** WITHERING *Brit. Plants* II. 74 The stems generally decline and scatter from each other, instead of being upright and close together. **1817** SHELLEY *Rev. Islam* VI. xix, When on my foes a sudden terror came, And they fled, scattering. **1909** *Blackw. Mag.* Aug. 230/2 The fugitives scattered for miles, bearing appalling tales of massacre.

c. *refl.* Now *rare* or *Obs.*

1535 COVERDALE *1 Chron.* xv. [xiv.] 9 The Philistynes came, and scatered them selues beneth in yᵉ valley of Rephaim. **1579** TOMSON *Calvin's Serm. Tim.* 128/2 They be enimies to the Churche, and scatter themselues farre from vs. **1625** B. JONSON *Staple of N.* IV. ii. 175 *Shr.* He'll let you ha' your liberty—. *Alm.* Goe forth, Whither you please, and to what company—. *Mad.* Scatter your selfe amongst vs.

†**d.** *trans.* To separate, drive apart (one or more individuals *from* the main body). *Obs.*

1588 EARL OF LEICESTER in *Defeat Sp. Armada* (Navy Rec. Soc.) II. 35 Two of the greatest carracks that the King of Spain had in his fleet, being scattered from the rest. *a* **1661** FULLER *Worthies, Derbysh.* (1662) I. 234 Their ships with the violence of the wind were much shattered, and the Bonaventure, scattered from the other two ships.

†**e.** *fig.* To dissipate, distract (the mind, etc.).

1450–1530 *Myrr. Our Ladye* 122 A warnynge to take hede that yf the mynde were eny thynge scatered before, then to gather yt ageyne to gyther. **1625** B. JONSON *Staple of N.* IV. ii, Look, look, how all their eyes Dance i' their heads (obserue) scatter'd with lust! **1715** tr. *T. à Kempis' Chr. Exerc.* III. xv. 138 If thou art hereby scattered in thy Mind.

3. a. *trans.* To throw about in disorder in various places.

c **1330** *Arth. & Merl.* (Kölbing) 553 Ac þo þai come þider eft, Her werk was al vp aleft & yschatred here & þere. *c* **1386** CHAUCER *Can. Yeom. Prol. & T.* 361 The pot to-breketh.. And somme [of the metals] are scatered al the floor aboute. **1860** TYNDALL *Glac.* I. xx. 142 The fragments of rock scattered about were..polar.

†**b.** To throw down (a thing) negligently; to drop. *Obs. rare*$^{-1}$.

a **1640** *Wizard* (MS.) (Nares), It is directed to you; some love-letter, on my life, that Luce hath scattered.

4. a. To distribute to various positions; to place here and there at irregular intervals. Chiefly in *pa. pple.*

c **1380** WYCLIF *Sel. Wks.* III. 445 Mykel more if newe religious be skaterud in Cristendome. **1549** ALLEN *Par. Leo Jude upon Rev.* 8 These are ye messengers of Antichrist, scattrid thoroweout the whole worlde. **1712** SWIFT *Let. Eng. Tongue* Wks. (1755) II. 184 William the Conqueror proceeded much further; bringing over with him vast numbers of that nation, scattering them in every monastery. **1837** LOCKHART *Scott* I. x. 326 Many tributes to his memory are scattered over his friend's other works. **1868** RUSKIN *Pol. Econ. Art* ii. 130 So long as works of art are scattered through the nation, no universal destruction of them is possible. **1882** P. G. TAIT in *Encycl. Brit.* XIV. 583/1 If stars be scattered through infinite space, with average closeness.

†**b.** *intr.* in pres. pple. used with a vb. of rest (= 'scattered'). *Obs.*

1555 WATREMAN *Fardle Facions* Pref. 6 From Adam to the floud..when men liued skateryng on the earthe. **1716** CHURCH *Philip's War* (1867) II. 149 He answered, there were several Families, but they liv'd scattering. **1726** LEONI *Alberti's Archit.* I. 66/2 Laying all the..earth into the furrow again inward, so that none might lie scattering outward.

c. *trans. Baseball.* Of a pitcher: to yield (hits) only at intervals and so restrict scoring.

1892 *Chicago Herald* 25 May 6/1 Young kept the hits well scattered. **1954** *Post-Herald* (Birmingham, Alabama) 7 June 7/2 Winning pitcher was Dave Benedict, who relieved in the first inning and scattered four hits the rest of the way. **1976** *Billings* (Montana) *Gaz.* 27 June 2-F/4 Joaquin Andujar scattered 10 hits Saturday to pace the Houston Astros to a 3–0 victory over the Cincinnati Reds.

5. a. To throw or send forth so that the particles are distributed or spread about; to sow or throw (seed, money, etc.) broadcast; to sprinkle, strew; to diffuse (fragrance).

c **1450** *St. Cuthbert* (Surtees) 4682 Molle on þair heueds þai scaterd. **1530** PALSGR. 699/1, I scatter small thynges abrode, as peasyn, or beanes. **1535** COVERDALE *Ps.* cxlvii. 16 He..scatereth ye horefrost like ashes. **1606** SHAKS. *Ant. & Cl.* II. vii. 25 As it [*sc.* the Nile] ebbes, the Seedsman Vpon the slime and Ooze scatters his graine. **1644** SYMONDS *Diary* (Camden) 54 Some of our men by the King's command scattered some papers, that if any would come in..they should be pardoned. **1698** FRYER *Acc. E. India & P.* 107 The Governor..bestows his Largess..liberally scattering Rupees. **1821** SHELLEY *Ginevra* 126 The matin winds from the expanded flowers Scatter their hoarded incense. **1861** MISS J. M. CAMPBELL in Bere *Garland of Songs* 61 We plough the fields and scatter The good seed on the land.

absol. **1748** GRAY *Alliance* 17 Scatter with a free, though frugal, Hand.

b. *transf.* and *fig.* Also, †to spread (reports, a prophecy).

1576 FLEMING *Panopl. Epist.* 118 O ioyfull report, and most acceptable rumour, which was scatered abroade. **1601** SHAKS. *All's Well* I. ii. 54 His plausiue words He scatter'd not in eares, but grafted them To grow there and to beare. *a* **1662** HEYLIN *Laud* II. (1671) 251 The Lady Davies.. scatters a Prophesie against him. *a* **1771** GRAY *Birds* 2 The song-thrush there Scatters his loose notes. **1858** LONGF. *M. Standish* IV. 74 A hand-grenade, that scatters destruction around it.

c. *intr.* for *refl.*

1577 B. GOOGE *Heresbach's Husb.* I. (1586) 35 When it [Pulse] is rype it must be geathered..for it scattereth very soone. **1642** JER. TAYLOR *Episc.* (1647) 233 The Bishop should separate the scabbed sheep from the sound, least their infection scatter. **1720** DE FOE *Capt. Singleton* v. (1840) 93 The small shot..scattered among them. **1817** SHELLEY *Rev. Islam* VI. xlvi, A wood Whose bloom-inwoven leaves now scattering fed The hungry storm.

d. Of a gun, a cartridge: To distribute (the shot). Chiefly *absol.*

1741 *Compl. Fam.-Piece* I. ii. 320 You must also be well acquainted with the Condition of the Gun, whether it be apt to scatter, or carry the Shot round within Compass. **1823** J. F. COOPER *Pioneers* i, The gun scatters well. **1881** GREENER *Gun* 439 Cartridge loaded to scatter the shot.

e. *Physics.* Of a surface, semi-opaque substance: To throw back (light) brokenly in all directions. More widely, to deflect, diffuse, or reflect (radiation, particles, or the like) in a more or less random fashion. Also *absol.*

1833 HERSCHEL *Astron.* §45 (1839) 32 The sun.. illuminates the atmosphere and clouds, and these again disperse and scatter a portion of its light in all directions. **1878** LD. RAYLEIGH *Theory of Sound* II. xv. 139 If the primary sound be a compound musical note, the various component tones are scattered in unlike proportions. **1882** P. G. TAIT in *Encycl. Brit.* XIV. 583/2 In order that a surface may be illuminated..it must be capable of scattering light. **1891** HURTER & DRIFFIELD in W. B. Ferguson *Photogr. Res. F. Hurter & V. C. Driffield* (1920) 146 Captain Abney has discovered that negatives 'scatter' so much light that our instrument cannot possibly measure all the light which a negative transmits. **1911** *Phil. Mag.* XXI. 675 In these calculations, it is assumed that the α particles scattered through a large angle suffer only one large deflexion. **1938** R. W. LAWSON tr. *Hevesy & Paneth's Man. Radioactivity* (ed. 2) vii. 75 Hydrogen nuclei alone behave differently, for they scatter [neutrons] very much more strongly than would be expected from the magnitude of the cross-section of hydrogen nuclei. **1955** HUETER & BOLT *Sonics* vi. 232 This limits the sound pressure that can be transmitted beyond the point where cavitation first occurs since the bubbles present will scatter and dissipate a part of the sound energy. **1955** C. G. DARWIN in W. Pauli *Niels Bohr* 6 There were a few α-particles scattered through such broad angles, even right backwards, that no conceivable compound effect could possibly explain them. **1959** *Listener* 18 June 1057/1 The distortions introduced by scattering a signal from such a surface might not be too serious. **1971** *Sci. Amer.* June 61/2 Since the neutron and the proton respond to the electromagnetic force, they scatter electrons aimed at them.

f. *intr. Physics.* Of radiation, particles, etc.: to undergo scattering.

1971 *Nature* 16 July 167/2 The double reflexion mechanism gives way to multiple reflexions, that is, a ray is trapped in surface cavities before scattering out, randomizing the polarization. **1975** *Ibid.* 25 Sept. 275/1 The majority of the energy is carried by phonons which inelastically scatter at the interface. **1980** *Sci. Amer.* July 57/1 Inside it an entering gamma-ray photon typically scatters off several electrons in succession.

6. *trans.* To sprinkle or strew *with* something.

1590 SPENSER *F.Q.* I. x. 35 A narrow way, Scattred with bushy thornes and ragged breares. **1667** MILTON *P.L.* XI. 649 Now scatter'd lies With Carcasses and Arms th' ensanguind Field Deserted. **1720** DE FOE *Capt. Singleton* vi. (1840) 106 The ground was scattered with elephant's teeth. **1902** E. PHILLPOTTS *River* i, Where the desert spread, all scattered with great stones.

7. a. *Comb.*: **scatteraway** *rare*, dispersion; **scatter bomb**, a bomb that scatters its material over a wide area; also *fig.*; **scatter bombing** *vbl. sb.*, bombing carried out haphazardly over an area; **scatter-charge, load**, a charge for a gun, made to distribute the shot when fired; **scattershot** orig. and chiefly *N. Amer.*, the shot contained in a scatter-charge; also used *fig.* (chiefly *attrib.*) to designate something of a random, haphazard, or indiscriminate character (cf. SCATTER-GUN 2); **scatter-site** *a. U.S.* = *scattered-site* s.v. SCATTERED *ppl. a.* 2b; †**scatter-story**, one who 'spreads' a report or story; **scatter-tuft**, the genus *Sporochnus*, one of the algals (*Cassell's Encycl. Dict.*, 1887); †**scatter-wise** *adv.*, in straggling order.

1851 SIR F. PALGRAVE *Norm. & Eng.* I. 325 So complete was the *scatteraway, that one of the brethren never stopped till he reached Saint-Gâll. **1961** WEBSTER, *Scatter bomb. **1973** J. QUICK *Dict. Weapons & Mil. Terms* 386/1 Fragmentation bombs or fragmentation clusters, as well as certain incendiary bombs equipped with bursters, are scatter bombs. **1977** *Rolling Stone* 16 June 43/2 Okay, Scorsese is a violent scatter-bomb. **1977** *Daily Tel.* 3 Aug. 5/5 West Germany's new scatter bomb..comprises more than 1,000 mini-bombs which can be fired in different patterns by rockets triggered from the cockpit. **1940** *Aeroplane* 13 Sept. 314/1 The *scatter-bombing..must at times have sorely tried pilots who had seen the effects of it. **1881** GREENER *Gun* 439 The *scatter-charge has good penetration at 30 and 40 yards. **1901** *Ibid.* (ed. 8) Index, *Scatter loads. **1961** WEBSTER, *Scattershot. **1965** *Economist* 19 June 1393/2 The President's..scatter-shot efforts to reduce the government's spending. **1967** *Boston Globe* 5 Apr. 51/2 Jack Nicklaus is more concerned over his scattershot driver than the threat of mumps. **1972** *Publishers' Weekly* 10 July 42/2 Shirley Green brings more scattershot curiosity than serious learning to her 'history'. **1974** *State* (Columbia, S. Carolina) 27 Feb. 18-A/6 When demagogic politicians ride the land firing scatter shot, nobody..is safe unless he shares their prejudices. **1978** R. STEVENS *Law & Politics* 505 The future of the judicial role in England..may lie far more with subtle use of judicial restraint than with scattershot judicial activism. **1972** *N.Y. Times* 3 Nov. 16/2 The *scatter-site housing dispute in Forest Hills. **1977** *New Yorker* 27 June 85/2 Jimmy Carter's mention of his belief in ethnic purity..in response to a *News* reporter's question about scattter-site housing. *a* **1670** HACKET *Cent. Serm.* (1675) 734 Ælian, and some other such *scatter-stories as himself, do make more reports of.. unreasonable creatures, than of reasonable men. **1875** DASENT *Vikings* III. xviii. 278 They sail very *scatter-wise in coming back, if, indeed, these few ships be part of the host.

b. *attrib.*, passing into *adj.* Designating one of a number (intended to be) scattered decoratively here and there, as *scatter cushion, pin, rug*, etc. orig. *U.S.*

1933 'E. QUEEN' *Siamese Twin Mystery* I. ii. 30 A living-room..dotted with armchairs and small scatter-rugs. **1946** *Negro Digest* Aug. 51/1 Its large living room has a vaulted ceiling and arched beams, and the floor is covered with deer skins and scatter rugs. **1957** J. D. SALINGER in *New Yorker* 4 May 123/1 Three domestic Oriental scatter rugs, extremely worn, were on the floor. **1960** *Woman* 5 Mar. 19/1 Scatter cushions have become a favourite furnishing accessory. **1960** I. WALLACH *Absence of Cello* 13 She stopped first at the jewelry counter where she sneered at some scatter pins. **1966** T. PYNCHON *Crying of Lot 49* ii. 36 Bracelets then, scatterpins, earrings, a pendant. **1974** J. IRVING *158-Pound Marriage* 104 The bed..had pitched the mattress and us across the scatter rug. **1976** L. DEIGHTON *Twinkle, twinkle, Little Spy* xviii. 185 There [were].. scatter-cushions on the floor. **1980** P. HARCOURT *Tomorrow's Treason* I. i. 31 The floor was..wood with a couple of bright scatter mats.

scatterable ('skætərəb(ə)l), *a.* [f. SCATTER *v.* + -ABLE.] That may be scattered.

1800 HERSCHEL in *Phil. Trans.* XC. 523 The rays of heat are..less refrangible than those of light; and..they are also, if I may introduce a convenient term, less scatterable.

scatteration (skætə'reɪʃən). [f. SCATTER *v.* + -ATION.] The action of scattering. Also, the fact or condition of being scattered.

1776 MRS. A. GRANT *Lett. fr. Mountains* (1806) I. 212 After the dissolution and scatteration of last year's happy trio. **1865** *N.Y. Times* 25 Feb., The scatteration of Cobb's forces. **1880** 'MARK TWAIN' *Tramp Abroad* xix. 183 A raft.. hit the pier in the center and went all to smash and scatteration like a box of matches struck by lightning. **1892** KIPLING *Lett. of Travel* (1920) 40 A household spreads itself over plots, maybe, a quarter of a mile apart. A revenue map of a village shows that this scatteration is apparently designed. **1900** *Engineering Mag.* XIX. 750/2 Scatteration of effort is dissipation of energy. **1910** *Blackw. Mag.* July 24/1 Here there is a scatteration, but the tufters..are stopped and laid on to the line of a single stag. **1930** R. FRASER *Rose Anstey* xlix. 328 At night she stared from her bed at a great scatteration of stars. **1936** *Burlington Mag.* June 261/1 The gilt frame of the mirror is not a strong enough colour to correct the consequent scatteration. **1965** *Economist* 6 Feb. 509 A growing desire to end what Mr Walter Lippmann calls 'globalism and scatteration' in foreign policy in favour of a concentration on America's 'primary vital interests'. **1965** D. OWEN *Eng. Philanthropy* IV. xx. 559 'Scatteration' philanthropy—spending too small amounts on too many agencies or individuals.

scatteraway: see SCATTER *v.* 7.

scatter bomb, bombing: see SCATTER *v.* 7a.

'scatter-brain. [f. SCATTER *v.* + BRAIN *sb.* Cf. the earlier SHATTERBRAIN.] One who is incapable of serious connected thought; a thoughtless, giddy person.

1790 COWPER *Let.* 31 July *Wks.* 1836 VI. 324 Though I have seen you but once,.. I have found out that you are a scatter-brain. **1898** BARING-GOULD *Old Eng. Home* xii. 284 The generality of these scapegraces are simply scatter-brains.

So **'scatter-brained** *a.*, that is a scatter-brain; characteristic of a scatter-brain.

[**1747**: cf. *scattered-brained*, SCATTERED *ppl. a.* 6.] **1804** CURRIE in *Creevey Papers* (1904) I. i. 30 A scatter-brained fellow. **1866** CARLYLE *Remin.* I. 122 A cheerful scatter-brained creature.

scattered ('skætəd), *ppl. a.* [f. SCATTER *v.* + -ED^{1}.] In senses of the verb.

1. a. Of a flock, tribe, company of persons, troops, etc.: Disunited and dispersed; disorganized; also, spread out in all directions.

1388 WYCLIF *Jer.* l. 17 Israel is a scaterid flok. **1593** SHAKS. *3 Hen. VI*, II. vi. 93 And hauing France thy Friend, thou shalt not dread The scattred Foe, that hopes to rise againe. **1786** BURNS '*The gloomy night*', The Hunter now has left the moor, The scatt'red coveys meet secure. **1855** MACAULAY *Hist. Eng.* xx. IV. 412 From the field of battle he made his way..to the neighbourhood of Louvain, and there began to collect his scattered forces.

b. *fig.* Of feelings, thoughts, etc.: Distracted, discomposed; vagrant. Now *rare* or *Obs.*

1638 JUNIUS *Paint. Ancients* 26 It doth require..some labour to settle our wild scattered thoughts. **1667** MILTON *P.L.* XI. 294 Adam..his scatterd spirits returnd, To Michael thus his humble words addressd. **1819** SCOTT *Ivanhoe* xlv, One word from Isaac..recalled her scattered feelings.

2. a. Widely separated one from another; placed here and there; spread over a wide area; straggling.

1595 *Polimanteia* in Brydges *Brit. Bibl.* I. 281 Mourne for the trulie Hon. Ferdinandos death: whom though scattered teares haue honoured in some few sonnets, yet [etc.]. **1617** MORYSON *Itin.* I. 112 Having passed long suburbs and scattered houses we came within a Musket shot to the mountaine. **1715** POPE *Iliad* I. *Ess. on Homer* 18 Some other scatter'd Stories of Homer. **1791** BURNS *Lament for Earl Glencairn* iii, Ye scatter'd birds that faintly sing. **1828** SCOTT *F.M. Perth* xxvii, A few aged and scattered yew trees. **1845** BUDD *Dis. Liver* 175 Ulceration of the gall-bladder..may lead to scattered abscesses in the substance of the liver. **1897** *Westm. Gaz.* 11 Mar. 2/1 The Poor-law Conference.. showed a remarkable consensus of opinion in favour of the substitution of the boarding-out and scattered home system for the present barrack schools.

b. *scattered-site* (U.S.), used *attrib.* to designate public housing (esp. for low-income families) distributed throughout a city rather than concentrated in a few areas. Also *absol.* in *pl.* (unhyphenated) as *sb.*

1956 *Jrnl. Housing* May 163/1 (*heading*) Scattered site projects. *Ibid.* 'We have inaugurated a new policy that not only permits but encourages the use of small scattered sites,' PHA Commissioner Charles E. Slusser told delegates. **1958** *Ibid.* Jan. 11 (*caption*) Diagrammatical sketch of the City of Cedartown, showing the seven sites on which the Cedartown Housing Authority constructed..the first scattered-site project in the nation. 1959 *Ibid.* Nov. 359/2 In many areas the row house has been adapted for scattered-site use. 1966 *Daily Progress* (Charlottesville, Va.) 12 Aug. 10/1 'Scattered-site' housing is an alternative to high-rise, low-income apartments.

3. a. Cast or driven about loosely in all directions; thrown broadcast. †Of the hair: Disordered.

1667 MILTON *P.L.* I. 304 His Legions..lay..Thick as..scattered sedge Afloat, when with fierce Winds Orion arm'd Hath vext the Red-Sea Coast. 1785 COWPER *Task* IV. 121 Oh Winter, ruler of th' inverted year, Thy scatter'd hair with sleet like ashes fill'd..I love thee! *Ibid.* v. 67 The sparrows peep... Well they eye The scatter'd grain. 1839 J. MAIN *Abercrombie's Ev. Man his own Gard.* 40 Let grass be rolled with a wooden roller, to which all the scattered worm-cast earth will readily adhere.

†b. Of a single thing: Cast off; thrown negligently, let drop. *Obs.*

1596 SPENSER *F.Q.* v. ii. 3 Whom having lost,..And finding in the way the scattred scarfe, The fortune of her life long time did feare. 1600 SHAKS. *A.Y.L.* III. v. 104 Loose now and then A scattred smile, and that Ile liue vpon. 1781 COWPER *Table-T.* 674 [He], like a scatter'd seed at random sown, Was left to spring by vigour of his own.

4. *spec.* **a.** *Bot.* Occurring at wide and irregular intervals (see quots.).

[1640: cf. SCATTEREDLY.] 1796 WITHERING *Brit. Plants* I. 225 Cal. none, (except some scattered sheaths). *Ibid.* III. 176 Root-leaves on leaf-stalks, somewhat toothed, beset with scattered hairs. 1839 LINDLEY *Introd. Bot.* III. (ed. 3) 492 Scattered (*sparsus*); used in opposition to whorled, or opposite, or ternate, or other such terms. 1872 H. C. WOOD *Fresh-w. Algæ* 54 Filament single, mostly scattered.

b. *Ent.* (See quot.)

1826 KIRBY & SP. *Entomol.* IV. 313 Scattered (*Sparsi*). When simple eyes are separate from each other and not arranged in a certain order.

c. *Physics.* Of light: Refracted and dispersed in all directions. More widely, of electromagnetic radiation generally and sub-atomic particles: subjected to scattering.

1808 HERSCHEL in *Phil. Trans.* XCIX. 280 The [prismatic] bows are formed by scattered light. 1878 ABNEY *Treat. Photogr.* xii. 88 The blurring caused by the reflection of the scattered rays from the plate. 1878 LD. RAYLEIGH *Theory of Sound* II. xv. 139 If a number of small bodies lie in the path of waves of sound,..the exaltation of the higher harmonics in the scattered waves involves a proportional deficiency of them in the direct wave after passing the obstacles. 1906 *Phil. Mag.* XII. 144 From measurements of the width of the band due to the scattered α rays, it is easy to show that some of the α rays in passing through the mica have been deflected from their course through an angle of about 2°. 1926 R. W. LAWSON tr. *Hevesy & Paneth's Man. Radioactivity* iii. 39 The whole of the scattered radiation also enters the electroscope. 1966 *McGraw-Hill Encycl. Sci. & Technol.* XIII. 438/2 Although radio waves at these frequencies are not reflected by the ionosphere, it has been found that if large amounts of power are radiated, scattered energy will be received over relatively long distances beyond the horizon. 1970 I. E. MCCARTHY *Nuclear Reactions* i. 5 In addition to elastically scattered α particles, two groups of protons..were observed. 1978 P. W. ATKINS *Physical Chem.* xvii. 546 If the molecules are excited by the light during the collision they withdraw some energy from the photons, and so the scattered light emerges with a lower frequency than the incident light.

5. Covered with scatterings; strewn or littered with something. *rare.*

1798 BLOOMFIELD *Farmer's Boy, Winter* 56 [He] Fills the tall racks [with hay] and leaves a scatter'd road.

6. *Comb.*: **†scattered-brained** = SCATTER-BRAINED.

1747 *Mem. Nutrebian Crt.* II. 14 [Expressions] such as easy fool, scattered-brained madman.

scatteredly ('skætədlɪ), *adv.* [f. SCATTERED *ppl. a.* + -LY².] In a scattered manner; disorderedly, irregularly; †intermittently.

1611 SPEED *Theatre Gt. Brit.* i. §3 All other Ilands and Ilets, which doe scatteredly inuiron it. 1640 PARKINSON *Theat. Bot.* 283 Sometimes also growing scatteredly on the stalks. 1684 H. MORE *Answ. Remarks upon More's Expos.* 275 What is more scatteredly and interruptedly done as to time, and place,..is..represented as done at one time, and in one place. 1847 HARDY in *Proc. Berw. Nat. Club* II. No. 5. 252 Elytra..minutely and scatteredly punctulate. 1882 R. A. PROCTOR in *Knowledge* No. 41. 176 Meteors of the Perseid system may..be seen..in greater number, but with shorter paths near Perseus; more scatteredly, but with longer paths at a distance from that constellation.

scatteredness ('skætədnɪs). *rare.* [Formed as prec. + -NESS.] Scattered condition.

1667 H. MORE *Div. Dial.* v. iv. (1713) 408 The Defectuousness and Scatteredness of the Prophecies.

scatterer ('skætərə(r)). [f. SCATTER *v.* + -ER¹.]

1. One who scatters, in the senses of the verb. Also, something which scatters; a device for broadcasting seed.

1535 COVERDALE *Nahum* ii. 1 The scaterer shal come vp agaynst the, & laye sege to the castell. 1555 PHILPOT *Apol. for Spitting upon Arrian* A 8 b, Least you might appeare to be scatterers wᵗ heretiks, rather than gatherers together with Christ. 1616 T. SCOT *Philomythie* I. (ed. 2) F 2, There be few scraping fathers, but their children prooue witty scatterers, or foolish retainers. 1738 WESLEY *Hymns, 'The Sun of Righteousness appears'* i, Adore the Scatterer of your Fears, Your Rising Sun adore! 1868 *Rep. Iowa State Agric. Soc. 1867* 227 The seed is scattered by a vibrating scatterer. 1872 SPURGEON *Treas. Dav.* Ps. lix. 11 He who is the shield of his people is the scatterer of their enemies.

2. *Physics.* Anything which scatters radiation, particles, or the like.

1930 A. B. WOOD *Textbk. Sound* III. 282 The amplitude of the secondary waves varies directly as the volume of the 'scatterer'. 1931 [see IMPURITY 3 b]. 1936 *Nature* 1 Feb. 185/2 The product of the 140 sec. half-period is enhanced in the case of all scatterers [of neutrons] investigated except carbon and aluminium. 1959 *Listener* 18 June 1057/1 If it [*sc.* the moon] were behaving as a uniform scatterer of radio waves. 1973 *Nature* 7 Sept. 38/2 The beam [of protons]..is made to strike a scatterer of lead or copper. 1977 R. KATZ *Ziggurat* (1978) vi. 59 Beryllium..was an excellent reflector, or 'neutron scatterer', because it had an atomic structure more dense than any other element. 1977 *Sci. Amer.* Oct. 90/2 In synthetic-aperture radar the interference pattern from each scatterer on the terrain is recorded..as a narrow broken line parallel to the edge of the data film.

scattergood ('skætəgʊd). [f. SCATTER *v.* + GOOD *sb.* (sense 7).] One who dissipates or squanders goods or possessions; a spendthrift.

1577 KENDALL *Flowers of Epigr.* 56 A mery iest of a scattergood. 1659 W. BROUGH *Sacr. Princ.* 220 If the first heire be not a scatter-good, the third is commonly a lose-all. 1818 SCOTT *Br. Lamm.* v, That young scattergood, the Laird of Bucklaw. 1884 BLACKMORE *Tommy Upmore* II. 178 You have heard what careless scattergoods all honest sailors are.

scattergram ('skætəgræm). *Statistics.* A contraction of *scatter diagram* s.v. SCATTER *sb.* 5.

1938 A. E. WAUGH *Elem. Statistical Method* ix. 235 This is the method of plotting the data on a scatter diagram, or scattergram, in order that one may see the relationship. 1966 *Jrnl. Neurophysiol.* XXIX. 812 To see how latencies and phases change with frequency, scattergrams can be made comparing each interval with the latency or phase of the spikes that occur during the interval. 1973 B. J. WILLIAMS *Evolution & Human Origins* xii. 215/2 In Figure 5.1 we saw a scattergram of a spurious correlation between R_o and heart disease. 1980 *Amer. Speech* LV. 226 The reader is told to calculate..z's for inter-group differences, scattergrams, and correlation coefficients.

'scatter-gun. orig. and chiefly *N. Amer.* [f. SCATTER *v.* + GUN *sb.*] **1.** A shot-gun.

1836 H. R. HOWARD *Hist. V. A. Stewart* 140, I have a choice scatter-gun. 187. G. H. KINGSLEY *Sport & Travel* v. (1900) 142, I take up my scattergun and wander away. 1891 C. ROBERTS *Adrift Amer.* 237 A 'double-pronged scatter gun'. 1910 *Blackw. Mag.* Feb. 285/1 All round Muttra shooting with a scatter-gun is varied and good. 1923 J. H. COOK *Fifty Years on Old Frontier* i. 4 Pigeon shooting was good..for anyone who owned or could borrow a 'scatter-gun'. 1932 'D. YATES' *Safe Custody* ix. 198 We've thirteen men, and between us we've got six pistols and three scatter-guns. 1968 *Punch* 1 May 624/1 He hands his trunk to this Puerto Rican who's carrying..a sawn-off scatter-gun. 1973 R. D. SYMONS *Where Wagon Led* i. iv. 51 Once in a while one of us would pack a scatter gun and get a brace or two of prairie chicken.

2. *fig.* (*attrib.* in quots.). Cf. *scattershot* s.v. SCATTER *v.* 7.

1952 J. STEINBECK *East of Eden* II. xiv. 150 A scattergun method for dealing with unpleasant facts. 1963 *Daily Progress* (Charlottesville, Va.) 6 Feb., Republicans agreed..to a 'scattergun plan'. Each representative wrote the name of his choice..on a secret ballot. There were no nominations and no debate. 1974 *Publishers Weekly* 4 Feb. 70/1 Farson sets it all down with a scattergun assertiveness that inevitably turns up contradictions. 1980 *Times Lit. Suppl.* 15 Aug. 913/1 Stuart Holland's scatter-gun polemic embodies many of the misconceptions which now threaten to dominate the Labour Party's attitude to Europe.

Hence as *v. intr.* (*fig.* in quot.) and **'scatter-gunner.**

1968 R. M. NIXON in W. Safire *Before the Fall* (1975) I. vi. 72 If we scatter-gun too much we are not going to have an impact. 1969 *Daily Colonist* (Victoria, B.C.) 8 Nov. 20/1 Two traps will be in operation and all scattergunners are invited to compete. 1980 *Outdoor Life* (U.S.) (Northeast ed.) Oct. 104/2 Scatter-gunners bag approximately 50 million of them each hunting season.

scatterheaded, *a. rare*⁻¹. = SCATTER-BRAINED.

1867 E. FITZGERALD *Lett.* (1889) I. 308 A scatterheaded Paddy like myself.

scattering ('skætərɪŋ), *vbl. sb.* [-ING¹.]

1. The action of the verb SCATTER, in various senses; also, an instance of this.

1382 WYCLIF *Jas.* i. 1 James..to the twelue kynredis, that ben in scateringe abrood, helthe. *a* 1425 *Cursor M.* 15541 (Trin.) þis nyȝt shal ben a scateryng [*v.rr.* sculd, skaile, parting] bitwene ȝou and me. 1545 JOYE *Exp. Dan.* xii. 121 There muste nedis folowe..skaterings and dissipacions of nacions. 1588 SIR J. HAWKINS in *Defeat Sp. Armada* (Navy Rec. Soc.) I. 359 By the occasion of the scattering [*MS.* schateringe] of one of the great ships from the fleet. 1662 STILLINGFL. *Orig. Sacræ* III. i. §1 By reason of the promiscuous scatterings of good and evil in this life.

attrib. 1833 HERSCHEL *Astron.* §45 (1839) 33 Were it not for the reflective and scattering power of the atmosphere, no objects would be visible to us out of direct sunshine... This scattering action of the atmosphere [etc.].

(*b*) *spec.* in *Physics*: cf. SCATTER *v.* 5 e.

1866 B. STEWART *Heat* §189 (1876) 186 As in the case of light.., so also with regard to heat there is a diffuse reflection or scattering about of the rays. 1911 *Proc. Manchester Lit. & Philos. Soc.* LV. p. xviii (*heading*) The scattering of the α and β rays and the structure of the atom. 1942 J. D. STRANATHAN *'Particles' Mod. Physics* xi. 405 On the theory of multiple scattering an entirely negligible number of particles should be scattered at large angles. 1950 *Nature* 30 Dec. 1103/2 It is..probable that turbulent scattering..plays an important part in determining the signals received from high-power metre-wave transmitters at distances greater than about 100 miles. 1955 HUETER & BOLT *Sonics* iii. 85 Scattering at the grain boundaries is one important cause for the absorption of ultrasonic waves in metals. 1974 G. REECE tr. *Hund's Hist. Quantum Theory* iv. 56 In 1903 J. J. Thomson worked out from the intensity of scattering of X-rays that the number of electrons must be roughly equal to the atomic weight. 1975 D. G. FINK *Electronics Engineers' Handbk.* XVIII. 91 At frequencies in the 30- to 100-MHz region, regular but weak propagation by ionospheric scattering is obtained.

2. a. *concr.* That which is scattered.

a 1340 HAMPOLE *Psalter* cxlvi. 2 *Dispersiones israelis congregabit*... þe scatiryngis of israel he sall gadire. 1546 *Supplic. of Poore Commons* (E.E.T.S.) 71 They..must leue the latward fruit, with the scateryng of theyr corne, for the poor to gather. *a* 1662 HEYLIN *Laud* I. (1671) 156 Which alone will be able to bind up the scatterings of divided affections into strength. 1692 SOUTH *12 Serm.* (1697) II. 455 The former Instances of Temporal Prosperity, which are but (as it were) the promiscuous Scatterings of his Common Providence. 1747 W. GOULD *Ants* 36 A white Substance, not altogether unlike the Scatterings of fine Sugar. 1908 *Betw. Trent & Axeholme* 107 On the grass..lies a thick scattering of petals.

b. A sparse number or amount; a small proportion (of persons) interspersed.

1628 EARLE *Microcosm.* xxxii. G, He has his sentences for Company, some scatterings of Seneca and Tacitus. 1690 C. NESSE *Hist. O. & N.T.* I. 180 The gentile world wherein God had some scatterings of holy ones. 1896 *Strand Mag.* XII. 348/1 There is a scattering of Europeans among the divers.

3. Special Comb.: **scattering angle** *Physics*, the angle through which a scattered particle or beam is deflected.

1913 *Phil. Mag.* XXVI. 711 It is a different matter..when the scattering angle is only about $\frac{1}{10}$ of a degree, as in the present experiment. 1950 *Nature* 30 Dec. 1102/2 A great simplification of the results is effected by restricting the discussion to small angles (beam-widths and scattering angles). 1970 I. E. MCCARTHY *Nuclear Reactions* I. i. 9 We see that for a given scattering angle particles of higher energy come closer to the nucleus.

scattering ('skætərɪŋ), *ppl. a.* [f. SCATTER *v.* + -ING².]

1. In intransitive senses. **a.** That disperses in all directions; hence vagrant, roving, stray. †Of action: Erratic.

c 1450 *Brut* I. 191 Thus staterand [? *read* scaterand] Scottes, holde y for sottes, of wrenches vnwar. [Cf. Skiterende Scottes *v.r. c* 1330 in Langtoft *Chron.* (Rolls) II. 252.] 1555 EDEN *Decades* (Arb.) 121 The naked seely sowles were slayne for the most parte lyke scaterynge sheepe. 1604 SHAKS. *Oth.* III. iii. 151 Nor build your selfe a trouble Out of his scattering, and vnsure obseruance. 1691 RAY *Creation* I. (1692) 36 The scattering Spirits remaining in the Heart may for a time being agitated by heat, cause these faint Pulsations. 1718 ROWE tr. *Lucan* IV. 190 The scatt'ring clouds disclos'd the piercing light. 1724 DE FOE *Mem. Cavalier* (1840) 122 They sent about twenty scattering troopers.

b. Lying scattered or spread out over a comparatively wide area; occurring sparsely or irregularly; sporadic; of a composite thing, having its parts so spread out; straggling. Now chiefly *U.S.*

Of votes (*U.S.*): Miscellaneous, cast for candidates whose poll is too small to call for separate enumeration.

1610 HOLLAND *Camden's Brit.* I. 439 A small village it is in these daies, inhabited in scattering wise. 1642 FULLER *Holy & Prof. St.* v. xiv. 414 Then first he sells..some stragling mannour..as counting the gathering of such scattering rents rather burdensome then profitable. 1677 HUBBARD *Indian Wars* (1865) II. 256 Many of these scattering Plantations in our Borders..were contented to live without..Yoake of Government. 1697 DRYDEN *Virg. Georg.* IV. 192 Yet, lab'ring well his little Spot of Ground, Some scatt'ring Potherbs here and there he found. 1709 STRYPE *Ann. Ref.* xxxii. 325 Now to gather up a few more scattering passages that happened this year. *c* 1710 CELIA FIENNES *Diary* (1888) 164 They being scattering houses, here one, there another. 1828–32 WEBSTER, *Scattering*, not united; divided among many; as, scattering votes. 1856 OLMSTED *Slave States* 642 Washington is a mean, scattering village. 1875 WHITNEY *Life Lang.* xiii. 266 When the Etruscans were Latinized, but for the scattering words which they had written down, their speech passed out of all reach of knowledge. 1879 A. JOHNSTON *Hist. Amer. Politics* (1884) 221 The Electoral votes..were found to be, for President, Grant, 286, T. A. Hendricks, of Indiana, 42, and 21 scattering. 1888 *Amer. Jrnl. Psychol.* I. 408 Letters appearing in the record less frequently than five per cent of these numbers have been regarded as scattering errors.

c. That scatters or falls here and there.

1761 WESLEY *Jrnl.* 20 June (1827) III. 61 We had only some scattering drops [of rain]. 1794 NELSON 21 Jan. in Nicolas *Disp.* (1845) I. 364 They only got a few scattering shot at us.

2. a. *Physics.* That causes scattering (of light, radiation, particles or the like).

1808 HERSCHEL *Col. Rings* in *Phil. Trans.* XCIX. 280 A scattering glass applied to the incident ray, had no other effect than to diminish the brightness of the [prismatic] bow. 1911 *Phil. Mag.* XXI. 675 It is essential that the thickness of the scattering material should be so small that the chance of a second encounter involving another large deflexion is very small. 1938 R. W. LAWSON tr. *Hevesy & Paneth's Man. Radioactivity* (ed. 2) ix. 95 A strong pencil of α-particles of definite velocity is allowed to strike a thin sheet of the scattering substance. 1958 *Times* 30 Apr. 6/6 The forward scatter technique..in this case uses the troposphere as the scattering medium. 1970 D. W. TENQUIST et al. *University Optics* II. ii. 84 If the incident light photon of energy $h\nu$ impinges upon a molecule of the scattering medium and the energy state of this molecule changes from E_1 to E_2, the energy of the Raman scattered photon is given by $h\nu - (E_2 - E_1)$.

b. *scattering layer* (Oceanogr.), any of a number of layers in the sea which give rise to strong acoustic echoes owing to the presence of a high concentration of living organisms.

1942 *Reverberation Stud. at 24 Kc* (Univ. Calif. Div. War Res. Rep. U7) 48 (*heading*) Deep scattering layers. *Ibid.* 49 Observations indicate that deep scattering layers, in a given area, may appear and disappear and yet persist for periods as long as a month or perhaps even longer. **1948** *Nat. Geogr. Mag.* Sept. 277/2 So incredibly numerous are such sea creatures that this layer of ocean life actually returns an echo of the sound sent down by the Fathometer. The echo from this so-called 'scattering layer' is sometimes so strong that it causes navigators to think they are sailing over a shoal. **1972** J. WILLIAMS *Oceanogr.* 53 At night this deep scattering layer ..is centered near the sea surface... In the morning it moves down into the depths again. **1977** CLAY & MEDWIN *Acoust. Oceanogr.* vii. 237 A great deal of data, particularly the frequency dependence of scattering layers, are obtained by using explosive sources.

Hence † **'scatteringness**. *Obs. rare*$^{-1}$.

1747 in *Col. Rec. Pennsylv.* V. 102 The scatteringness of the Settlements..must ever render them liable to Depredations.

scatteringly (ˈskætərɪŋlɪ), *adv.* [f. SCATTERING *ppl. a.* + -LY^{2}.] In a scattering manner; so as to disperse in all directions; not compactly and in a body; irregularly; intermittently.

1570 FOXE *A. & M.* (ed. 2) 250/1, I thought here good to packe them all in one general heape together, as I finde them in Malmesbery, and in other sondry autors scateryngly recited. **1597** GERARDE *Herbal* I. ci. 163 The Humble Bee Orchis hath..leaues, which growe scatteringly about the stalke. **1652** HEYLYN *Cosmogr.* IV. 127 The Houses scatteringly built amongst Hills and Gardens. *c* **1680** SIR T. BROWNE *Tracts* 126 Some [Gradual Verses] are scatteringly to be found in Homer. **1746** S. SIMPSON *Agreeable Historian* I. 300 This town..consists of one Street, lying scatteringly almost a Mile in Length. **1880** W. G. T. SHEDD *Homiletics* v. 118 Too many sermons are composed scatteringly all along through the week.

scatterling (ˈskætəlɪŋ). [f. SCATTER *v.* + -LING^{1}.] A wandering or vagabond person; a vagrant. Also *transf.* Now *arch.*

1590 SPENSER *F.Q.* II. x. 63 Yet oft annoyd with sondry bordragings Of neighbour Scots, and forrein Scatterlings. **1611** SPEED *Hist. Gt. Brit.* IX. ix. §8. 510/2 But God was no better pleased with these, then with the other scatterlings at Lincolne. **1824** *Blackw. Mag.* XVI. 517 From mossy hillock, and tremulous stalk, We gather'd the lovely scatterlings.

attrib. **1880** BLACKMORE *Mary Anerley* II. iv. 62 The four ..had nothing to do with, and little to say to, any of the scatterling folk about them.

scattermouch (ˈskætəmaʊtʃ). [Alteration of SCARAMOUCH after SCATTER *v.*] (See quot. 1892 and cf. SCARAMOUCH 2.)

1892 STEVENSON & L. OSBORNE *Wrecker* 194 *note*, In sea lingo (Pacific) Dutchman includes all Teutons and folk from the basin of the Baltic; Scattermouch, all Latins and Levantines. **1894** CROCKETT *Raiders* (ed. 3) 360 Scattermouches and ruffians from the four seas.

scatterometer (skætəˈrɒmɪtə(r)). [f. SCATTER *sb.* + -OMETER.] A radar designed to provide information about the roughness or the profile of a surface from the way it scatters the incident microwaves.

1966 *Electronics* 14 Nov. 44 A spacecraft, using a Scatterometer, has to fly over a pock-marked area of the lunar surface only once to get a detailed profile of the terrain. **1978** *Nature* 22 June 586/2 Seasat-A is primarily a 'proof of concept' mission designed primarily to discover how effectively the microwave equipment which it carries—a scanning radiometer, a radar scatterometer, a synthetic aperture radar, and a radar altimeter—can provide useful scientific information for oceanographers, meteorologists and commercial sea-users.

scattershot, -site: see SCATTER *v.* 7.

scattery (ˈskætərɪ), *a.* [f. SCATTER *v.* + -Y.]

a. Characterized by scattering; scattered; sparse; straggling.

1816 L. HUNT *Rimini* I. 4 And the far ships, lifting their sails of white Like joyful hands, come up with scattery light, ..true to the wished-for day. **1847** LD. JEFFREY *Let.* 20 Apr. in Ld. Cockburn *Life* (1852) II. 413 The village is very small and scattery, and all mixed up with trees. **1877** BLACKMORE *Erema* xvi. (1880) 96 Not to benefit the world in general, in a large and scattery way—but to right the wrong of my own house.

b. Scatter-brained. *rare.*

1924 J. GALSWORTHY *White Monkey* I. v. 33 The scattery enthusiasm of the sucking publisher. **1928** —— *Swan Song* III. i. 226 He himself knew how to wait, but did this modern young man, so feather-pated and scattery?

scattiness (ˈskætɪnɪs). [f. SCATTY *a.*^{2} + -NESS.] The quality or condition of being scatty or scatter-brained.

1959 S. GIBBONS *Pink Front Door* iv. 52 For all her scattiness, Daisy was a good child. **1959** A. BUCHAN *Spare Chancellor* v. 118 Catherine Gladstone with the characteristic scattiness of the Glynnes and the Lytteltons always referred to Lowe's followers as 'The Dolomites'. **1976** E. BERCKMAN *Be All & End All* v. 62 A peculiar combination of scattiness accompanied by a desperate concentration. **1977** 'M. INNES' *Honeybath's Haven* viii. 82 The spectacle of [Hamlet's] random and intermittent scattiness is confusing.

scatty (ˈskætɪ), *a.*^{1} *U.S. Underworld slang.* [Of unknown origin; cf. SCOTTY *a.*] Bad-tempered.

1909 W. H. DAVIES *Beggars* xxvi. 205 Nearly all men that live in common lodging-houses..are..more or less short-tempered, or as they say—'scatty'. **1927** *Dial. Notes* V. 461 *Scatty*, ill-natured.

scatty (ˈskætɪ), *a.*^{2} *colloq.* [Prob. f. SCATT(ER-BRAINED *a.* + -Y^{1}.] Of a person: scatter-brained; driven distracted, mad; of a story, etc.: illogical and absurd.

1911 J. W. HORSLEY *I Remember* xi. 254 Cockney slang was far more familiar to me than most..'scatty' for mad. **1934** *Punch* 17 Jan. 74/1 Simpson, who lives opposite, says it [*sc.* the house] was preying on his mind... 'Another week and I should have been scatty,' he explained. **1951** M. KENNEDY *Lucy Carmichael* II. i. 83 She is amusing in a breathless, scatty sort of way. **1956** J. DICKSON CARR *Patrick Butler for Defence* iii. 26 If we tell this scatty story about an impossible murder, they won't believe one word we say. **1972** 'J. BELL' *Death of Poison-Tongue* i. 11 Do you mean you know who the person is who spreads wicked lies about the neighbours? Don't the ones attacked do anything if they know the person? It sounds utterly scatty. **1977** *News of World* 17 Apr. 16/7 My scatty friend..had later gone into the butchers and loudly asked for a shepherd to make a pie with. **1980** J. MCCLURE *Blood of Englishman* i. 11 The scatty receptionist had looked at him with twinkling eyes.

†**sca'turiency.** *Obs. rare*$^{-1}$. [f. next: see -ENCY.] The condition of being scaturient.

1667 H. MORE *Div. Dial.* III. xlv. (1713) 544 Is it so difficult to determine, whether is more expedient,.. Fruitfulness or Sterility, or if you had rather, Aridity or Scaturiency?

scaturient (skəˈtjʊərɪənt), *a.* [ad. L. *scatūrient-em*, pr. pple. of *scatūrīre*, f. *scatēre* to flow out.] That flows out or gushes forth.

1684 tr. *Bonet's Merc. Compit.* VI. 221 The glandulous substance of the Paps is a little contracted, so that they do not so readily receive the milky humour, that very scaturient. **1805** *Edin. Rev.* VII. 214 He wielded..a pen so scaturient and unretentive, that..he himself must have been often astonished..at the extent of his lucubrations. **1831** LAMB *Elia* Ser. II. *Newspapers 35 yrs. ago*, We well remember.. sallying forth..to trace the current of the New River..to its scaturient source. *a* **1876** M. COLLINS *Pen Sketches* (1879) I. 150 The drip and tinkle of its scaturient waters.

†**scatu'riginous**, *a. Obs. rare.* [f. L. *scatūrīgin-ōsus*, f. *scatūrīginēs* pl. gushing waters, f. *scatūrīre*: see SCATURIENT and -OUS.] Full of or abounding in springs. In quots. *fig.*

1656 BLOUNT *Glossogr.*, *Scaturiginous*,..that bursts out, or runs over, out of which water riseth. **1708** *Brit. Apollo* No. 36. 2/1 Our Querist..has exhausted his Scaturiginous Brains, to explore Epithets. **1709** *Ibid.* II. No. 64. 2/2 Thou ..from whose Scaturiginous Inventive Faculty, such a Multiplicity of Horisonant Phrases arise.

scaubard, -art, -erc, etc., obs. ff. SCABBARD *sb.*^{1}

scaud, variant form of SCALD *a.*^{1} and *v.*

scauff, obs. Sc. form of SCAFF *sb.*

scaul, obs. f. SCALL *sb.* and Sc. f. SCOLD.

scaulde, var. f. SCALD *a.*^{1}; obs. f. SCALD *v.*

scaum (skɑm), *sb. Sc.* and *dial.* Also **scam, scame, skaum.** [Belongs to SCAUM *v.*]

1. A burn or scorch; 'the act of singeing clothes by putting them too near the fire, or by means of a hot iron' (Jam.); also, a mark of burning.

1813 PICKEN *Poems* I. 132 (Jam.) But ay whan Satan blaws the coal, I find it's best the scaum to thole. **1874** G. MACDONALD *Malcolm* II. xix. 260 To hide a scaum she had taen for a' her pride.

2. A thin haze or mist; a light, misty vapour.

1824 MACTAGGART *Gallovid. Encycl.* 421 There is red scaum, white scaum, and many others. By the colour or hue of the scaum do Watherwiseakers guess about coming weather. **1825** JAMIESON, *Scaum o' the sky.* **1877** J. VEITCH *Hist. & Poet. Sc. Border* xii. 426 A wide-spreading web of greyish cloud, the skaum of the sky.

scaum (skɑm), *v. Sc.* and *dial.* Also **scam(e, skaum.** [Of obscure origin.]

1. *trans.* To burn slightly, scorch, char. Also, 'to bespatter' (Brockett *N.C. Gloss.*, ed. 2, 1829).

a **1670** SPALDING *Troub. Chas. I* (Bannatyne Club) II. 247 Ane fyrie cros of tymber, quhairof everie point of the cros was scamit and brynt with fyre. **1808** JAMIESON *App.*, *To Scam*, to scorch. **1825** —— *To Scaum, Scame*, v.a. to burn slightly; to singe. **1841** W. AITKEN *Poet. Wks.* 53 Some had their claes tied in a clout To keep them frae be'n scaumed. **1882** *Pall Mall G.* 26 July 4/2 Then comes a bitter March wind, with snow and sleet, which 'scam' the soft plants, and leave them withered as if they had been touched by fire.

2. 'To envelope in a mist or haze, to shade' (E.D.D.).

1871 P. H. WADDELL *Ps.* lxxx. 10 The heights they were scaumed wi' her shadow.

scaumpioun, obs. form of CHAMPION.

†**scaunt**, *a. Obs. rare*$^{-1}$. [Aphetic form for *ascaunt.* See ASKANT *adv.*] Oblique.

1741 *Betterton's Eng. Stage* v. 66 The Contraction of the Lips and the Scaunt Look of the Eyes, expresses the Gesture of a deriding and malicious Person.

scaup (skɔːp). Short for SCAUP-DUCK. Also Comb. *scaup-pochard* (rare) = scaup-duck.

1797 LATHAM in *Trans. Linnean Soc.* IV. 116 The trachea of the Pochard, at first sight, seems to be similar to that of the Scaup. **1824** J. F. STEPHENS in Shaw's *Gen. Zool.* XII. II. 198 Scaup pochard (*Fuligula Marila*). *Ibid.* 200 The Scaup..inhabits Iceland, and the more northern parts of the continents of Europe and America. **1905** *Blackw. Mag.* June 768/2 A small party of scaup..next came into focus.

scaup, variant form of SCALP *sb.*^{1} and *sb.*^{2}

scaup-duck (skɔːpdʌk). [? f. *scaup* SCALP *sb.*^{2}: see quot. *a* 1672.

The Icel. *skálphœna* (*hœna* = hen), occurring once as the nickname of a man, is prob. unconnected.]

A duck of the genus *Fuligula*, esp. *Fuligula marila*, inhabiting the seas of northern Europe, Asia, and America.

a **1672** WILLUGHBY & RAY *Ornith.* III. (1676) 279 Avis hæc *the Scaup-duck* dicta est, quoniam scalpam i.e. pisces testaceos fractos seu contritos esitat. **1785** PENNANT *Arctic Zool.* II. 565 Scaup Duck. **1797** *Encycl. Brit.* (ed. 3) I. 661/1 The maula, or scaup-duck, is less than the common duck. **1886** NEWTON *ibid.* (ed. 9) XXI. 378/2 The female Scaup-Duck can be readily distinguished from the Dunbird or female Pochard by her broad white face.

scauper, variant form of SCALPER^{1}.

scaur (skɔː(r)). Chiefly *Sc.* [dial. var. of SCAR *sb.*^{1}] A precipitous bank; a cliff; the ridge of a hill.

1805 SCOTT *Last Minstr.* I. xii, Is it the roar of Teviot's tide, That chafes against the scaur's red side? **1834** H. MILLER *Scenes & Leg.* iv. (1857) 45 Its place on the rock has ever since remained as undistinguishable as the scaurs and cliffs around it. **1859** TENNYSON *Elaine* 54 Down the shingly scaur he plunged. **1871** M. COLLINS *Marq. & Merch.* II. i. 6 Hesper shone Like a beacon over the mountain scaurs. **1883** STEVENSON *Silverado Sq.* 243 Dwarf pines..grew thinly among loose stone and gravel scaurs. **1897** KIPLING *Capt. Cour.* ix. 193 Scaur and ravine changed and rolled back to jagged mountains.

scaur, var. SCAR *a.*; obs. Sc. f. SCARE *v.*

scaurie (ˈskɔːrɪ). *Orkney* and *Shetland.* Also **scorey, scory, scourie, scowry, scurrie, skoray, scorie, sko(r)rie, skory.** [Scandinavian: cf. Norw. *skaare* (Aasen), ON. *skáre.*] The young of any kind of gull.

a **1795** G. LOW *Fauna Orcadensis* (1813) 122 The Brown and White Gull..Orc. Scory..is the scarcest of the Gull-kind in Orkney. **1805** G. BARRY *Orkney Isl.* 303 The Brown and White Gull..which the people here call the scorey, is much more rarely met with than most others. **1806** P. NEILL *Tour Orkney & Shetland* 25 The Brough..is the resort and nursery of hundreds of scauries, or herring-gulls (*larus fuscus*). I believe the Orkney name scaurie is applied to this gull only while it is young and speckled; and it loses its speckled appearance after the first year. **1821** SCOTT *Pirate* v, For your harvest on the crag, I suppose you mean these scowries, or whatever you call them. **1822** [see ICELAND]. **1844** W. H. MAXWELL *Sports & Adv. Scot.* xxxviii. (1855) 300 A skoray, or young kittiwake. **1899** J. SPENCE *Shetland Folk-Lore* 14 The plee o' the skorie, the birr o' the snipe. **1918** T. MANSON *Humours of Peat Commission* I. 125, I mind haein a tame scorie..whin I wis a boy. **1960** *People's Jrnl.* (Dundee) 12 Mar. 9/2 Ah'm fair deav't wi' the awfa scraichin' o' the scurries.

†**scaut**, *v. Obs.*$^{-0}$ [Origin obscure; connexion with mod. dial. *scaut*, to push with the feet, is unlikely.] *intr.* ? To dart. Hence **scautand** *ppl. a.*

a **1400–50** *Alexander* 4200 þire Cocatricesse in creuessis þar kindiles þai brede, Scorpions many score scautand neddirs.

scavage (ˈskævɪdʒ), *sb.* Also 5 **scawage**, 6 **skawage, skavag(e**, 7 **scavadge.** [a. AF. *scawage*, *schawage* (*Rolls of Parlt.* an. 1402), = North-Eastern OF. *escauwage*, f. *escauwer* to inspect, ad. Flemish *scauwen* = OE. *scéawian* SHOW *v.*

The OE. synonym was *scéawung* (see SHOWING *vbl. sb.*), the ME. form of which was adopted into AF. as *scawenge* (1419 in *Liber Albus* 223). In the 15th c. lawyers were aware of the etymological meaning, and invented the word SHEWAGE as an explanatory synonym.]

1. A toll formerly levied by the mayor, sheriff, or corporation of London and other towns on merchant strangers, on goods offered for sale within their precincts. The toll was prohibited by Act 19 Hen. VII, c. 8. Also *attrib. Obs.* exc. *Hist.*

1474 CAXTON *Chesse* III. vii. (1481) h vij b, And by the purse been signefyed them that receyue the costumes, tolles, scawage, peages and duetees of the cytees and townes. *a* **1500** ARNOLDE *Chron.* (1811) p. xiv, The marchaundyses wherof skauage ought to be taken in London, and how meche. **1502** in I. S. Leadam *Star Chamber Cases* (1903) 90 He was Skavage gatherer in London, both to the maire and Shreves there. *Ibid.* 92 There was skavage askyd by oone James skavage gatherer then of oone Skrevener Freman of Excestre for cloth bi him brought to London by water, and he refusid to pay it. *a* **1513** FABYAN *Chron.* VII. 338 This yere [1252] the cytezyns [of London] had graunted of ye Kyng, y^{t} no cytezyns shulde paye scauage or tolle for any bestis by them brought, as they before tymes had vsed. **1530–1** *Act 22 Hen. VIII*, c. 8 §4 The tables so to be sette upp in the Cytie of London touchynge Scavage. **1583** *Rates Custom ho.* g iij, *heading*, Scauadge. **1641** W. HAKEWILL *Libertie of Subject* 123 There are other duties then Customes and Subsidies due upon the landing of wares; for example Wharfage, Cranage, Scavage and such like. **1676** MOLLOY *De Jure Marit.* II. xiv. (1688) 325 Scavage is an ancient Toll or Custom exacted by Mayors, Sheriffs, &c. of Merchant-Strangers for Wares shewed or offered to sale within their Precincts. **1800** COLQUHOUN *Comm. Thames* xi. 332 Of

Scavage (i.e. Shewage or Surveying) of certain Goods imported by Foreign Merchants.

†**2.** The fulfilment of the duties of a scavager.

1547 in E. B. Jupp *Carpenters' Co.* (1887) 386 Item payd to the skavynger for hys hole yeres skavag, .. ij[s].

†**3.** Refuse, etc. scavenged from the roads. *Obs.*

1706 in J. E. Cox *Ann. St. Helen's Bishopsgate* vii. (1876) 127 Mr. Chewter had leave to sink a place for laying in of dung or scavage.

'scavage, *v. rare.* [Back-formation from SCAVAGER.] *trans.* = SCAVENGE *v.* Also *intr.* for *refl.* (*fig.*). Hence **'scavaging** *vbl. sb.*

1851 MAYHEW *Lond. Labour* II. 222/1 The scavaging work, moreover, was 'scamped'. *Ibid.* 252/2 The general depreciation of wages in the scavaging trade. *Ibid.* 259 The street-orderly system of scavaging the metropolitan thoroughfares. **1852** *Meanderings of Mem.* I. 56 The brain will scavage and the breast unstuff.

'scavager. Also skavager. [a. AF. *scawager*, f. *scawage* SCAVAGE *sb.*: see -ER[2].

1307 in R. R. Sharpe *Cal. Lett. Bk. C. City of London* (1901) 151 *note*, Pro curia de scawageriis. **1419** *Liber Albus* (Rolls) 333 Lez scawageours averont iiii deniers pur chescun tile nusance issint remoez ou debrusez.]

†**1.** An officer whose duty it was to take 'scavage', and who was afterwards also charged with the duty of keeping the streets clean. *Obs.*

1477–9 *Rec. St. Mary at Hill* (1905) 89 Item, paid to the Skauagers for the pament endited. viij d. **1536** *City of Lond. Rep.* ix. 183 b, in *Vicary's Anat.* (1888) App. III. 171 Item, for by cawse compleynt was made by one of þe scavagers of ye Warde of Faryngdon, for kepyng of the stretes there vnclene. **1835** *App. Munic. Corpor. Rep.* II. 845 Searchers for unwholesome Meat. Scavager to gather the Money. Gaoler.

2. Used for SCAVENGER 2. *rare.*

1851 MAYHEW *Lond. Labour* II. 218 The nominal wages of the scavagers. *Ibid.* 221, 252.

'scavagery. *rare*[−1]. [f. SCAVAGE *sb.* + -ERY.] = SCAVENGERY.

1851 MAYHEW *Lond. Labour* II. 217/2 In scavagery, the average hours of daily work are twelve. *Ibid.* 259/2 When the sages of the city sewers did not consider any proposed improvement in scavagery worthy their attention.

scavan(t: see SAVANT.

scavel ('skævəl). *dial.* Also 5, 7 **scavell,** 6–7 **skavell,** 6 **skavel,** 7 ? **skeval,** 9 **skafell, skaffel, scaffle.** [? f. ON. *skafa* to scrape, SHAVE *v.*] A small spade (see quot. 1823).

c **1440** *Jacob's Well* xxvii. 178 Now schal I telle ȝou, how ȝe schal caste out þe hard wose of ȝoure synne .. wyth a scauel of confessioun. *Ibid.* 179 A scauel, in þe heued beforn, hath a scho of yren, scharp & myȝti, & an heued, hole & narow, & a long stele, an handyll. **1559** in Boys *Sandwich* (1792) 737 One workeman with a spade or skavell may digg in one howre C. foote. **1573** TUSSER *Husb.* (1878) 38 With skuppat and skauel, that marsh men alow. *c* **1613** SPELMAN *Relat. Virginea* 47 They digg many holes which before the English brought them scauels and spades they used to make with a crooked peece of woode. **1823** MOOR *Suffolk Wds.* 352 *Skaffel*, a small spade or skuppet used in draining... It differs from a spade in not tapering toward the edge, and in having its sides slightly turned up.

b. *attrib.*, as *scavel work*; **scavel-man, scavel spitter** (see quots.).

1581 in C. Welch *Tower Bridge* (1894) 103 [A number of] showtmen, now called *scavelmen. **1584** *Faversham Parish Reg.* (MS.), John Price a scauelman or dicker. **1587** FLEMING *Contn. Holinshed* III. 1544/2 A great manie marshmen were assigned to laie the fleech vpon the sides of the wals, and were called scauelmen. **1803** *Naval Chron.* XV. 58 The scavelmen are a description of labourers .. who attend to clean and pump the docks, and in general assist the ship-wrights. **1750** BLANCKLEY *Nav. Expositor*, **Scavel Spitters*, are a small Spade, only shod half way, and are used for digging Clay. **1642** *Burghmote Book B, Canterb.* (MS.), Which persons are appointed for the *Scavell work and are disired to digge Turf and earth for the fortification.

scavenage ('skævənɪdʒ). [Irreg. f. SCAVEN(GE) + -AGE.] The action or work of scavenging.

1878 *Lancet* 12 Jan. 64 The system of scavenage for the borough. **1885** *Scientific American* 9 May, The Jewish priests maintained a system of scavenage, themselves supervised the cleansing of cities and habitations.

scavenge ('skævəndʒ), *v.* [Back-formation from SCAVENGER.]

1. *trans.* To clean *out* (dirt, etc.).

a **1644** QUARLES *Sheph. Orac.* ii. (1646) 22 Should I but name The Tithe of that base dunghill trash, brought in By your Dominicans, scaveng'd out agin By worse Franciscans.

2. a. To scrape dirt from (the streets); also, to cleanse (the surface of a river).

1851 MAYHEW *Lond. Labour* II. 197/2 In wet weather there is at least twenty times more 'mac' than dung scavenged. **1866** *Act 28 & 30 Vict.* c. 89 §52 The Conservators shall cause the Surface of the Thames to be effectually scavenged, in order to the Removal therefrom of Substances liable to Putrefaction.

transf. **1858** KINGSLEY *Misc., Chalk-Stream* I. 182 They are Vorticellæ; and every one of those bells, by the ciliary current on its rim, is scavenging the water—till a tadpole comes by and scavenges it.

b. To extract and collect (anything that can be used or eaten) from discarded material.

1922 JOYCE *Ulysses* 158 Saw her in the viceregal party when Stubbs the park ranger got me in with Whelan of the *Express*. Scavenging what the quality left. High tea. Mayonnaise I poured on the plums thinking it was custard. **1971** J. S. WEINER *Man's Natural History* v. 199 Big-game hunters, living by means of scavenging dead mammoths. **1977** *Times Lit. Suppl.* 7 Jan. 9/5 In Kingston [Jamaica] .. 'scuffling' (dealing in whatever can be scavenged).

3. *absol.* or *intr.* **a.** In sense 2 a. **b.** *transf.* To borrow; to thieve; to search through rubbish *for* (left-overs or unwanted objects).

In quot. 1960 simply 'to search thoroughly'.

1883 *Harper's Mag.* Mar. 528/1 We saw fleeting glimpses of working-women scavenging, hanging out clothes, huckstering. **1894** *Daily News* 26 Apr. 2/4 Mr. Milvain .. objected to the Conservancy being released .. of their power to scavenge eastward. **1938** *Sun* (Baltimore) 17 June 3/4 A woman relief investigator said aged men whom she recognized as relief clients were 'scavenging' at a market for discarded sprigs of celery. **1941** BAKER *Dict. Austral. Slang* 63 *Scavenge, to*, to borrow: to act the petty thief. **1960** P. S. BEAGLE *Fine & Private Place* xiv. 252 She .. scavenged frantically in her purse, trying to hold back a sneeze until she found a handkerchief. **1978** S. TENNENBAUM *Rachel, the Rabbi's Wife* (1979) x. 340 Rachel worked hard to refurbish her studio... She scavenged for pieces of furniture, and found an old armchair, a small table, and a low couch without a cushion.

4. a. *trans.* To remove (the combustion products) from the cylinders of an internal-combustion engine. Also *absol.*, and with the engine or cylinder as object. Cf. SCAVENGING *vbl. sb.* 2.

1894 [implied in SCAVENGING *vbl. sb.* 2 a]. **1903** *Amer. Inventor* 15 Aug. 78/3 The engine under description scavenges thoroughly and completely upon the return stroke of the pistons. **1954** E. J. KATES *Diesel & High-Compression Gas Engines* ii. 23 Just as before, this helps to get the exhaust gases out, or scavenges them. **1961** K. ČÁSLAVSKÝ tr. *Mackerle's Air-Cooled Motor Engines* xviii. 376 With a mixing ratio $\lambda > 1$ the cylinder charge is increased by the amount of air contained in the exhaust gas not scavenged from the cylinder. **1966** *McGraw-Hill Encycl. Sci. & Technol.* VII. 208/2 Most medium and large two-cycle diesel engines are usually equipped with blowers to scavenge the cylinders after the working strokes and to supply the air required for the subsequent cycles. **1975** M. J. NUNNEY *Automotive Engine* x. 246 The development of the two-stroke cycle of operation is generally attributed to Dugald Clerk who, in 1878, adopted this principle for a successful design of engine that was scavenged by a separate pumping cylinder.

b. *Chem.* To combine with or remove (free radicals, electrons, or other species).

1955 *Jrnl. Amer. Chem. Soc.* LXXVII. 3245/2 This would mean that all of the radicals which are being scavenged are swept from the solution by the mercaptan. **1966** W. A. PRYOR *Free Radicals* xxi. 324 An added free radical species will inhibit the process .. if it scavenges S· but does not react with S to convert it to S·. **1974** *Sci. Amer.* Dec. 71/1 Z is eventually restored to neutrality by scavenging four electrons from two water molecules. **1978** *Nature* 1 June 374/1 Newly formed amorphous iron hydroxides seem to scavenge phosphate and silicate from solution.

Hence as *sb.*, = SCAVENGING *vbl. sb.* 2 a. Freq. *attrib.*

1912 A. P. CHALKLEY *Diesel Engines* vi. 156 On the up stroke the scavenge ports .. are closed before the exhaust ports. **1925** *Glasgow Herald* 1 Apr. 11/2 This new type of engine, with its straight through scavenge and absence of air and exhaust valves. **1930** *Engineering* 21 Nov. 645/3 The scavenge pumps for the Junkers engine are mounted on the locomotive frame. **1949** T. D. WALSHAW *Diesel Engine Design* xviii. 338 Typical figures for an engine supercharged to give 50 per cent. increase in available B.H.P. are: 30 per cent. through scavenge (i.e. a volume of air equal to 30 per cent. of the cylinder volume is swept through the exhaust valve), and the amount of overlap would be about 135°. **1955** *Know your Tractor* (Shell) i. 11 The air for combustion assists removal of the exhaust gases; it is therefore known as 'scavenge' air, and its admission to the engine as 'scavenging'. **1957** [see LUBE *sb.* & *v.*]. **1975** A. J. WHARTON *Diesel Engines: Questions & Answers* 19 Even in slow running engines, this allows only a very short period of time for scavenge to be completed.

scavenger ('skævəndʒə(r)), *sb.* Also 6 **skavinger, -ynger, scavengere,** 6–8 **scavinger,** 7 **skavenger.** [Altered form of SCAVAGER, with intrusive *n* as in *passenger, messenger.*]

1. a. = SCAVAGER 1. Now only *Hist.*

1547 [see SCAVAGE *sb.* 2]. **1598** STOW *Surv.* 328 In Sepulchers parish common Counsaile six, Constables foure, Scauengers foure [etc.]. **1638** *Tarlton's Jests* C 1 b, When Tarlton dwelt in Gracious street .. he was chosen Scauenger, and often the Ward complained of his slacknesse, in keeping the streets cleane. **1677** THOROTON *Nottinghamsh.* 492 There is an Officer of the Town called the Scavenger, that looks to the Pavement and Streets of the Town, and attends upon the Majors wife. **1695** *Lond. Gaz.* No. 3053/2 An Act for Exempting Apothecaries from Serving the Offices of Constable, Scavenger, and other Parish and Ward-Offices. **1766** ENTICK *London* IV. 4 The government of this ward is in one alderman, .. seven scavengers, and a beadle. **1835** *App. Munic. Corpor. Rep.* I. 172 (Aberystwith), The Scavengers are appointed in the same manner. The persons usually selected for this office are the churchwardens and overseers of the poor, and they employ the paupers in sweeping the streets.

†**b.** As the title of an official under the East India Company. *Obs.*

1702 *MS. list* in Yule s.v., John Butt, Scavenger and Cornmeeter, Tevenapatam, Merchant. **1760** *Fort William Cons.* in Long *Sel. Rec. Gov.* (1869) 245 (Yule) Mr. Handle, applying to the Board to have his allowance of Scavenger increased .. we allow him Rs. 20 per month more than before.

2. a. A person whose employment is to clean streets, by scraping or sweeping together and removing dirt. †Also, a person employed to keep clean a church.

1530 PALSGR. 266/1 Scavenger that clenseth stretes, *bovevr.* **1563–83** FOXE *A. & M.* 19/2 And as in the other vnder wardens cometh the order of Scauingers: so neither doth the Popes Monarchy lacke his kaynilrakers. **1598** BP. HALL *Sat.* VI. ii. 99 To see .. a cloked Frere Sweating in the channell like a Scauengere. **1642** *Laws of War Army Earl Essex* 21 The rest [shall] serve for Pioners and Scavengers, till a worthy exployt take off that Blot. **1690** C. NESSE *Hist. & Myst. O. & N. Test.* I. 101 The sorry scavengers who live honestly by emptying privies. **1696** *Act 8 & 9 Will. III*, c. 37 §1 To the end the Dirt and Soyl may be heaped ready for the Scavenger to carry away. **1714** MANDEVILLE *Fab. Bees* (1733) I. p. xi, Now would I ask if a good citizen .. might not assert that dirty streets are a necessary evil inseparable from the felicity of London, .. without any prejudice either to the blackguard or the scavingers. **1725–6** in J. L. Chester *Westm. Abbey Reg.* (1876) 316 John Chittham, Scavenger to this Church: in the South Cloister. **1802** MAR. EDGEWORTH *Moral T.* (1816) I. xvi. 136 The scavenger, with his broom .. was clearing away a heap of mud. **1865** DICKENS *Mut. Fr.* IV. xiv, A scavenger's cart happening to stand unattended .. Mr. S. found it impossible to resist the temptation of shooting Mr. Silas Wegg into the cart's contents.

b. *transf.* One who or something which removes dirt or putrid matter. Applied to various animals that feed on decaying matter, esp. the scavenger beetle.

1596 NASHE *Saffron Walden* I Chiefe scauinger of chins. **1614** MARKHAM *Cheap Husb.* I. *Swine* i. 87 The Swine .. is the Husbandmans best scauenger, .. for his food and liuing is by that which would else rot in the yard. **1648** WINYARD *Midsummer-Moon* 4 Thus sinkes and common shoares are the best scavengers. **1719** BAYNARD *Health* (ed. 2) 6 And Fasting's Nature's Scavenger. **1845** DARWIN *Voy. Nat.* i. (1879) 10 Numerous spiders, which I suppose prey on these small attendants and scavengers of the waterfowl. **1854** OWEN in *Orr's Circ. Sci., Org. Nat.* I. 164 The sturgeons may be called the scavengers of the great rivers which they frequent. **1858** BAIRD *Cycl. Nat. Sci.* 48/1 The argala .. is extremely useful in removing noxious animals, and devouring all sorts of carrion. It is called the scavenger in Calcutta. **1868** *Rep. U.S. Commissioner Agric.* (1869) 307 The *Silphidæ* (burying or sexton beetles, scavengers, &c.). **1899** *Allbutt's Syst. Med.* VII. 719 The spider-cells .. act as phagocytes or 'scavengers', multiplying upon and removing the degenerate nerve-elements.

c. *fig.* in various uses: One who collects filth; one who does 'dirty work'; a dishonourable person. Also, in favourable sense, one who labours for the removal of public evils.

1562 PILKINGTON, etc. *Burnynge Paules* A vij, In like maner where thys scauenger sweping the stretes with his bookes .. hais spoken the truth, not trulye .. I shal passe ouer it with silence. **1582** STANYHURST *Æneis* Ded. (Arb.) 9 Are there not diuerse skauingers of draftye poetrye in this oure age, that bast theyre papers with smearie larde [etc.]. **1598** B. JONSON *Ev. Man in Hum.* II. ii, The gentleman-citizen hath satisfied me, Ile talk to no scauenger. **1642** MILTON *Apol. Smect.* Wks. 1851 III. 265 That Suburbe sinke, as this rude Scavinger calls it, .. shall be in my account a more honourable place then his University. **1767** A. CAMPBELL *Lexiph.* (1774) Pref. 30, I am no other than a literary scavenger. **1771** *Junius Lett.* lxvii. (1788) 340 *note*, In the senate, their abilities have confined them to those humble, sordid services, in which the scavengers of the ministry are usually employed.

3. A child employed in a spinning-mill to collect loose cotton lying about the floor or machinery. Also, a roller used to collect the loose fibres or fluff; also called *scavenger-roll.*

1833 LYTTON *England & Engl.* (ed. 2) I. 201 My children shall never go into a factory, more especially as scavengers and piecers. **1835** URE *Philos. Manuf.* 289 The masters paid the spinners the full allowance of wages for these piecers and scavengers, as they are called. **1853** —— *Dict. Arts* (ed. 4) II. 831 In the mules we notice a peculiar arrangement of 'scavenger' is applied. The object of this apparatus is to clear particles of waste from the top of the carriage, and the operation is effected by means of a roller.

4. *Chem.* A substance or species which scavenges (sense 4 b) free radicals or other species.

1955 *Jrnl. Amer. Chem. Soc.* LXXVII. 3244 The demonstration that various radical scavengers such as butyl mercaptan, α, α-diphenyl-β-picrylhydrazyl .., iodine and oxygen do not capture the decomposition products quantitatively. **1961** G. R. CHOPPIN *Exper. Nuclear Chem.* xii. 196 The presence of even small amounts of impurity, especially if it has a high affinity for radicals (a scavenger), causes decomposition. **1970** *Financial Times* 13 Apr. 20/4 Manganese is probably the most important 'minor' metal used in the steel industry, being used as a de-oxidiser and scavenger to combine with sulphur. **1974** C. C. PATTON in P. L. Moore et al. *Drilling Practices Manual* xv. 397 Scavengers can also be added to a drilling fluid to remove small amounts of hydrogen sulfide. **1978** *Nature* 23 Nov. 347/2 Hydroxyl is the most reactive trace species in the troposphere and is therefore the dominant scavenger of many anthropogenic substances.

5. a. *attrib.* and *Comb.*, as *scavenger duck, shovel, work*; *scavenger-like* adj. and adv.; **scavenger-cell** = PHAGOCYTE *sb.*; **scavenger hunt** orig. *U.S.*, a game in which people try to collect certain miscellaneous objects from the neighbourhood; **scavenger-roll** (see sense 3); †**scavenger-stuff** (see quot. 1787).

1899 *Allbutt's Syst. Med.* VIII. 324 In the lowest layer '*scavenger' cells and nuclei cover the spindle cells. **1884** *Good Words* Nov. 746/2 A band of *scavenger ducks picking up the garbage. **1940** *Sun* (Baltimore) 1 Nov. 7/3 Eight young persons on a *scavenger hunt sponsored by a Westport High School sorority went to the Sixty-third street police station willingly to obtain signatures of policemen. **1963** 'E. MCBAIN' *Ten Plus One* xi. 136 We're two college kids on a scavenger hunt... We're supposed to bring back a hibernating bear. **1977** *Times* 24 Dec. 10/2 The outdoors scavenger hunt is a good exercise after overeating. **1980** *Jewish Chron.* 18 July 25/5 Sunday, July 27. Car Rally/Scavenger Hunt. **1611** COTGR., *Voyer*, a Surueyer.. of highwayes.. who..*Scauinger-like, giues order that they be made cleane. **1890** *Spectator* 28 June, When such scavenger-like work is thus forced upon a man of letters, it is [etc.]. **1611** COTGR., *Paelle à bourbe*, a *Scauingers shouell; ..such a one as durt is vsually remoued, or taken vp, with. **1787** WINTER *Syst. Husb.* 332 *Scavenger stuff, is a mixture of coal ashes and street dirt. **1835** URE *Philos. Manuf.* 312 There is so little *scavenger work required in fine spinning, on account of the small quantity of waste from the long-stapled cotton.

b. In designations of certain animals (see 2 b): **scavenger-beetle**, a necrophagous beetle, especially one of the family *Scaphidiidæ*; **scavenger-crab**, any crab which feeds on dead animal matter; **scavenger-vulture** (see quot.).

1854 A. ADAMS, etc. *Man. Nat. Hist.* 182 *Scavenger-Beetles (*Scaphidiidæ*). **1857** A. WHITE *Pop. Hist. Brit. Crust.* Index, *Scavenger-crab. **1894** *19th Cent.* XXXVI. 436 Scavenger crabs line this coast in myriads. **1885** HORNADAY *2 Yrs. in Jungle* vi. 61 No wonder the builder of such a nest is called the *scavenger vulture [*Neophron percnopterus*].

'scavenger, *v. rare.* [f. SCAVENGER *sb.*]

1. *trans.* To remove dirt from, chiefly *fig.*; also, to make dirty with scavenging.

a **1644** QUARLES *New Distemper* (1645) 3 All the Romish Rubbish and Trumpery was scavengerd out of this [the new Reformed] Church. **1806-7** J. BERESFORD *Miseries Hum. Life* (ed. 3) II. x, After having scavengered your hands and gloves in slaving to drag up each [shoe out of the quagmire].

2. *intr.* To work at scavenging.

1843- [implied in SCAVENGERING *vbl. sb.*]. **1894** *Season* X. 71/3 Scavengering with bent spine in the gutter.

scavengering ('skævəndʒərɪŋ), *vbl. sb.* [f. SCAVENGER *v.* + -ING[1].] The action or work of removing filth, etc. from the streets. Also *attrib.*

1841 *Literary Gaz.* 11 Dec. 801/3 M. de Lucy.. recommended that steam should be used for melting the snow.., in order to facilitate the process of scavengering. **1843** *Penny Cycl.* XXVI. 472/2 In Cairo these vultures are ..prized for their scavengering services. **1860** *All Year Round* No. 72. 510 The..management of a barrow, as applied to scavengering, is a matter of serious moment. **1885** *Daily News* 31 Jan. 5/1 The scavengering alone costs 1,300*l.* a year.

fig. **1869** *Echo* 26 Aug. 4 It is..a sort of moral scavengering to which the Commissioners are condemned.

Scavenger's daughter. Also Skevington's, Skeffington's daughter. [From a jocular perversion of the name *Skevington*. See DAUGHTER 6 c.] An instrument of torture (invented in the reign of Hen. VIII by Leonard Skevington or Skeffington, Lieutenant of the Tower), which (bringing the head to the knees) so compressed the body as to force the blood from the nose and ears. Also † *Skevington's gyves, irons.*

1564 in Coverdale *Lett. Martyrs* 686 *marg.*, Thys Engine is called Skeuyngtons Giues, wherein the body standeth double, the head being drawen towardes the feete. **1580** RISHTON *Diarium* in Sanders *De Schism. Angl.* (1586) I i 5, 10 [Dec.] Thomas Cotamus & Lucas Kirbeus presbyteri, Scauingeri filiam ad vnam horam & amplius passi, ex quo prior copiosum sanguinem e naribus emisit. **1580-1** in D. Jardine *Use Torture Eng.* (1837) 84 We have made triall of hym by the torture of Skevington's Yrons. **1604** *Jrnls. Ho. Commons* I. 209/1 An Engine devised by Mr. Skevington, some time Lieutenant of the Tower, called Skevington's Daughters, or Little Ease. **1826** W. E. ANDREWS *Review Fox* II. 369 One of the instruments of torture, called the Scavenger's daughter, employed in the Tower on Catholics. **1897** *Dict. Nat. Biog.* LII. 325/1 Leonard [Skeffington].. the inventor of an instrument of torture, known as 'Skevington's irons' or 'Skevington's daughter'.

scavengery ('skævəndʒərɪ). [f. SCAVENGER *sb.* + -Y.] The municipal or state arrangements for cleaning and removing dirt, refuse, etc.; the action of collecting and removing dirt from the streets.

1656 EARL MONM. tr. *Boccalini's Polit. Touchstone* 449 Since Tuscany did breed a numerous rascallity of turbulent mad-caps..he had yet farther very great need of those Gallies, which were as the scavengery of his State, by which he kept it cleanly. **1663** ROLLOCK in *Marq. Worcester's Exact Def. Water Engine* 6 Whole Cities may be kept clean,.. needing no other Scavengery than by means thereof [i.e. of the Water Engine] to void their Dirt, and avoid Noisomness. **1715** M. DAVIES *Athen. Brit.* I. Pref. 56 The Brutal Scavengry of *Cacarello's Modus*. **1851** MAYHEW *Lond. Labour* II. 207/2 By one or other of these modes of scavengery all the public ways of the metropolis are cleansed.

scavenging ('skævəndʒɪŋ), *vbl. sb.* [f. SCAVENGE *v.* + -ING[1].]

1. Street-cleaning; removal of filth; also, the cleaning of a river, etc.

1851 MAYHEW *Lond. Labour* II. 208/1 The private scavenging of the metropolitan mews. **1883** *Summary* 26 July 6/4 He considers..that nothing short of a daily scavenging [of the Regent's Canal] will be satisfactory.

transf. **1862** *Sat. Rev.* XIII. 618/2 He was accustomed to cut a number of sermons out of the volumes in order to carry on his scavenging in his own garret.

2. a. Removal of combustion products from the cylinders of internal-combustion engines. Also as *ppl. a.*

1894 *Work* 17 Feb. 73/3 Questions such as late ignitions, scavenging, varying explosive charges [etc.]. **1896** B. DONKIN *Text-bk. Gas, Oil, & Air Engines* (ed. 2) I. xix. 269 The increase in economy obtained with the new (1894) 'scavenging' Crossley-Atkinson engine. **1915** *Illustr. London News* 13 Mar. 340 Scavenging-pump for expelling used gases at the end of each stroke. **1924** *Times Trade & Engin. Suppl.* 29 Nov. 250/3 As is usual with large Sulzer engines the scavenging air is supplied from electrically driven turbo blowers installed in the engine-room. **1954** E. J. KATES *Diesel & High-Compression Gas Engines* ii. 24 Instead of rotary blowers, many two-cycle diesels employ what is called crankcase-scavenging. *Ibid.* 25 The outside atmospheric pressure then pushed open the scavenging valve and permitted a fresh supply of air to enter the crankcase. **1962** J. M. DOHERTY *Diesel Locomotive Practice* ii. 25 To obtain efficient scavenging in two-stroke engines, the air is always admitted to the cylinder under pressure. **1975** M. J. NUNNEY *Automotive Engine* x. 248 The mean effective pressures developed by a two-stroke engine.. depend upon its scavenging efficiency.

b. *Chem.* The action of SCAVENGE *v.* 4 b.

1955 *Jrnl. Amer. Chem. Soc.* LXXVII. 3245/2 There must be two reactions which produce the dinitrile, one which is subject to scavenging by the mercaptan and one which is not. **1978** *Nature* 1 June 374/1 Lal *et al.* have shown that from 12 to 15% of dissolved silicate can be removed from seawater by scavenging during precipitation of finely dispersed ferric hydroxide.

†**scavilones,** *sb. pl. Obs. rare.* [Of obscure origin: cf. SCABILONIAN.] 'Long drawers worn under the hose by men in Queen Elizabeth's time' (J. R. Planché *Cycl. Costume* 1876, I. 447).

1577 HOLINSHED *Chron.* II. 1859/2 Nayler put off hys nether stockes, and so bare foote and bare legged saue hys silke scauilones to the ankles..came in.

scavinger, obs. form of SCAVENGER *sb.*

scavvy, var. SCAFFY.

scaw (skɔː). Also **skaw.** [Shetland dial., repr. ON. *skage.*] A promontory.

1821 SCOTT *Pirate* viii, A child might travel with a purse of gold from Sumburgh-head to the Scaw of Unst, and no soul would injure him. **1842** LONGF. *Skeleton in Armor* xiv, Yet we were gaining fast, When the wind failed us; And with a sudden flaw Came round the gusty Skaw.

scaw, var. Sc. f. SCALL *sb.*; obs. f. SHOW *v.*

scawage, obs. form of SCAVAGE.

scawbard, -art, -ert, obs. ff. SCABBARD *sb.*[1]

scawde, Sc. form of SCALD *a.* and *v.*

†**scawe.** *Obs. rare*[−1]. [Of obscure origin and meaning: cf. s.w. dial. *scovy, scawvy*, 'uneven in colour, blotched, streaky, mottled' (*E.D.D.*), also *squally* in quot. 1552 s.v. BANDY *a.* 2.

The mod. Sc. *scaw*, 'a faded or spoilt mark' (Jam.) is a form of SCALL *sb.*, and is prob. unconnected.]

Some kind of defect in cloth.

1463-4 *Rolls of Parlt.* V. 501/2 In case that eny such diversite, or rawe, scawe, kokell, or fagge happen to be in any part of the seid clothes.

†**scawed,** *a. Obs.* [? f. prec. + -ED[2].] Spotted.

1398 TREVISA *Barth. De P.R.* XVIII. lxxv. (Bodl. MS.), Some Catte is white and some is reed and some is blacke and some is specked and scawed [orig. *maculosum*].

scawip, obs. Sc. form of SCALP *sb.*[2]

scawl, Sc. form of SCOLD.

scawp(e, obs. and var. ff. SCALP *sb.*[1]

scawtite ('skɔːtaɪt). *Min.* [f. the name *Scawt* (see quot. 1930) + -ITE[1].] A hydrated carbonate and silicate of calcium which occurs as minute, colourless, monoclinic crystals.

1929 *Nature* 7 Dec. 896/1 C. E. Tilley: On scawtite... This new monoclinic mineral, with composition $6CaO.4SiO_2.3CO_2$, occurs in the contact zone between the chalk and the dolerite. **1930** C. E. TILLEY in *Mineral. Mag.* XXII. 224 It is proposed to designate this new mineral scawtite, from the original locality, Scawt Hill, Co. Antrim. **1957** *Amer. Mineralogist* XLII. 387 A zone about ten inches thick between the larnite zone and the limestone consists essentially of scawtite. The scawtite rock is greyish-white, dense and flinty. **1973** *Acta Crystallographica* B. XXIX. 73 Scawtite contains 2 units of $Ca_7(Si_6O_{18})(CO_3).2H_2O$ in a monoclinic cell.

scaymes, variant of SQUEAMOUS, squeamish.

scayne, variant of SKEAN, obs. form of SKEIN.

scayse, obs. Sc. form of SCARCE *adv.*

‖**scazon** ('skeɪzɒn). *Prosody.* Pl. scazons, also **scazontes** (skə'zɒntiːz). [L., a. Gr. σκάζων, sb. use of pres. pple. of σκάζειν to limp, halt.] A modification of the iambic trimeter, in which a spondee or trochee takes the place of the final iambus; = CHOLIAMB. Also *scazon iambic.*

The name was also applied by some ancient metrists to a similar modification of the trochaic tetrameter catalectic, and to various other metres which are variations of some common type of verse produced by a change in the last foot.

1673 O. WALKER *Educ.* xi. 124 Archilochus and Hipponax two very bad Poets..invented those doggrel sorts of Verses, Iambics and Scazons. **1806** C. SYMMONS *Life of Milton* (1810) 138 On the occasion of Salsilli's illness Milton sent to him those scazons, which are rich in poetic imagery, though inaccurate in their metrical construction. **1869** H. SNOW *Theocritus, Epigr.* xix. Notes (1873) 221 The..catalectic scazon iambics. *Ibid.* xxi. 221 The metre is scazon iambic. **1889** J. JACOBS *Caxton's Æsop* 21 the Babrian scazon is.. influenced by Latin metre.

Hence †**sca'zontian** *a.*, **sca'zontic** *a.*, consisting of, written in, scazons; *sb.* = SCAZON.

1782 ELPHINSTON tr. *Martial* Pref. 3 He [Martial] some-times..chooses the Iambic stanza..and often the Scazontian. **1845** H. THOMPSON in *Encycl. Metrop.* X. 412/1 Cneius Matius..wrote Mimiambics, which differed from the Mimes of the two former authors only by being written in scazontics. **1898** R. ELLIS in *Class. Rev.* Mar. 121/2 There is a semblance here of a scazontic original.

sceane, variant of SENE, synod, visitation.

scear, variant of SEAR *sb.* (of a gun).

scearche, obs. form of SEARCH.

sceat. *Hist.* and *Numism.* Pl. sceattas. Also written 8-9 **skeat** (*pl.* **skeats, skeattas**), 9 **scaett** (*pl.* **scaettas**); 9 *erron. forms* **sceatta, skeatta,** *pl.* **sceattæ, skeattæ.** [a. OE. *sceat, scætt* (see SCAT *sb.*[1]). The OE. pronunciation was (ʃat) or (ʃæt).] **a.** *Hist.* A coin or denomination of money mentioned in OE. documents, app. of somewhat different values in the different kingdoms. (In Mercia 250 *sceattas* are mentioned as equivalent to a 'pound'; in Kent the value seems to have been $\frac{1}{20}$ of a 'shilling'). **b.** *Numism.* Adopted by modern writers as the name for a small Old English silver coin, about 15 grains in weight, the examples of which belong to the 7th and 8th c. Also occas. applied to an Old English gold coin of similar size.

[*c* **970** *Merc. Laws* ii. (Lieb. 462), Ðonne bið cynges anfeald werȝild six þeȝna wer be Myrcna laȝa, þæt is xxx þusend sceatta, & þæt bið ealles cxx punda. *a* **1000** *Laws Æthelb.* xxxiii. (Lieb. 5), Gif feaxfang ȝeweorð, L sceatta to bote. *Ibid.* lxxii. (7), Gif þare mycclan taan næȝl of weorþeð, xxx scætta to bote. Et þam oþrun ȝehwilcum x scættas ȝebete.] **1720** J. JOHNSON *Collect. Eccl. Laws etc. Ch. Eng.* Laws Ethelstan an. 926 No. 2, The King's single Weregild is..thirty Thousand Skeats, in all, 120 Pound. **1817** RUDING *Ann. Coinage* I. 203 Sceattæ are known of the early Kings of Kent. *Ibid.* 217 The Sceatta. **1845** PETRIE *Eccl. Archit. Ireland* 224 The skeattas or English pennies. **1853** HUMPHREYS *Coin Collect. Man.* II. 410 Many skeattæ are with-out inscription at all. **1860** C. R. SMITH in *Archæol. Cantiana* III. 39 The earliest Anglo-Saxon silver coins, commonly called sceattas. **1887** C. F. KEARY *Catal. Ags. Coins Brit. Mus.* Introd. 22 The immense difference in character between the sceattas and the pennies.

sceau, erron. form of SEAU.

‖**Sceaux** (səʊ). The name of a town near Paris used *attrib.* and *absol.* to denote tin-enamelled faience made there in the latter part of the eighteenth century, often painted with floral and figure subjects and modelled in the form of figures.

1884 GASNAULT & GARNIER *French Pottery* 182 (Index), Sceaux mark on faïence. **1903** M. L. SOLON *Old French Faïence* 125 An anchor, in allusion to the dignity of the Duke de Penthièvre, High Admiral of France, or the stencilled name: 'Sceaux', are the marks of the productions. **1948** A. LANE *French Faïence* x. 40 In the 1770's the factory apparently looked for inspiration to Sceaux faïence and Sèvres porcelain. *Ibid.* 42 The Sceaux faïence-painting was of a very high quality. **1960** R. G. HAGGAR *Conc. Encycl. Continental Pott. & Porc.* 421/1 Enamelling..gives a distinctive quality to Sceaux faience. **1971** L. A. BOGER *Dict. World Pott. & Porc.* Pl. 283 (*caption*) Cruet frame and two cruets, enameled faïence. French, Sceaux, c. 1760. **1974** *Country Life* 24 Jan. 129/3 (*caption*) Sceaux faience duck tureen.

†**scede.** *Obs. rare*[−1]. [ad. L. *sceda*, var. spelling of *scheda*: see SCHEDE.] A strip of papyrus.

1628 BURTON *Anat. Mel.* Democr. To Rdr. (ed. 3) 50 Like that scede or Scytala Laconica, so much renowned of old in all contracts, which Tully so earnestly commends to Atticus.

scedula, scedule, scedull, obs. ff. SCHEDULE.

sceg(g, scegger: see SKEG, SKEGGER.

‖**scelalgia** (skɛ'lældʒɪə). *Path.* Also in anglicized form **sce'lalgy.** [mod. L., f. Gr. σκέλ-ος leg + -αλγία, ἄλγος pain.] Neuralgia in the leg.

1855 DUNGLISON *Med. Lex.*, *Scelalgia*, pain of the leg. **1858** MAYNE *Expos. Lex.*, *Scelalgia*,..scelalgy.

scelerate ('sɛlərət), *a.* and *sb.* Also 6-9 **scelerat,** 6 *Sc.* **scelerait.** [ad. L. *scelerātus*, pa. pple. of *scelerāre*, f. *sceler-, scelus* wickedness: see -ATE[2]. Cf. F. *scélérat* (in Cotgr. 1611; OF. had *sceleré*), It. *scellerato*, Pg. *scelerado.*]

†**A.** *adj.* Atrociously wicked. *Obs.*

a **1513** FABYAN *Chron.* VII. 675 And fledde is now clerely the scelerat flokke. *a* **1548** HALL *Chron., Rich. III* 29 b, His myscheuous actes and scelerate doynges. **1560** ROLLAND *Crt. Venus* II. 296 So scelerait, and ingrait for to chois. **1613** SIR A. SHERLEY *Trav. Persia* 8 The scelerat treason conspired against vs. **1625** PURCHAS *Pilgrims* II. 1845 There was resistance against such a scelerate Prince. **1665**

WINSTANLEY *Loyal Martyrol.* 102 Such a Scelerate Villaine. *a* **1734** NORTH *Exam.* I. iii. §98 (1740) 191 The most scelerate Plot that ever was heard of.

B. *sb.* An atrociously wicked person, a villain, wretch. *Obs.* exc. *arch.*

The spelling *scelerat* is after the F. *scélérat*; the word has been occasionally used by Eng. writers with italics and accents as a foreign word.

1715 CHEYNE *Philos. Princ. Relig.* II. 88 Hence it is, that Scelerats, can by no Arts, nor any Amusements how violent soever, stifle the Cries of a wounded Conscience. **1728–31** *Lett. fr. Fog's Jrnl.* (1732) I. 15 That honourable Prison [the Tower of London] is reserv'd for illustrious Scelerates. **1790** BURNS *Let. to* (? *G. Hamilton*), Creation-disgracing scelerats such as they, God only can mend, and the devil only can punish. **1880** SHORTHOUSE *J. Inglesant* xxii. 295 He was, and is, a scelerat and a coward.

Hence †**'scelerately** *adv.*; †**'scelerateness.**

1613 SIR A. SHERLEY *Trav. Persia* 5 The punishment was nothing proportionable to the sceleratnesse of the fact. **1632** LITHGOW *Trav.* v. 188 My companion fled, and escaped the sceleratnesse of their hands. *Ibid.* x. 493 The peruerted policy of subtile Serpents, had sceleratly suggested my concealment.

†**'scelerous,** *a. Obs.* Also 6 scelorous. [f. L. *scelerōs-us* full of wickedness, f. *sceler-*, *scelus*: see SCELERATE and -OUS.] Wicked, villainous.

1534 *Act 26 Hen. VIII*, c. 6 §1 Wilfull burninge of Houses, and other scelerous Dedes and abhominable malifactes. **1567** HARMAN *Caveat* Epist. (1869) 20 Not one amongst twenty [of these vagabonds] wyll discouer eyther declare there scelorous secretes. **1657** W. MORICE *Coena quasi Κοινὴ* i. 31 Lest the city..be as Philip styled one in Greece, that fostered all scelerous persons. *a* **1660** *Contemp. Hist. Irel.* (Ir. Archæol. Soc.) I. 277 Come on then, blinde beetles,..lett apeere your scelerous acte, your inimitable foperie.

†**sce'lestic,** *a. Obs. rare*⁻¹. In 7 -ique. [f. L. *scelest-us* wicked, villainous (f. *sceles-*, *scelus*: see SCELERATE) + -IC.] Wicked.

1628 FELTHAM *Resolves* I. v. 12 The World hath not better men, then some, that suffer vnder that name [of Puritan]: nor withall, more Scelestique Villaines.

†**sce'lestious,** *a. rare*⁻¹. In 7 scælestious. [f. L. *scelest-us* (see prec.) + -IOUS.] Wicked.

1608 HEYWOOD *Salust* 13 This scælestious match.

scelet(on, obs. forms of SKELET(ON.

scelidate ('sɛlɪdeɪt), *a.* [f. mod. L. *scelid-* (see next) + -ATE.] Having legs.

1877 LE CONTE *Elem. Geol.* II. (1879) 328 It is a true scelidate, or legged fin.

‖**scelides** ('sɛlɪdiːz), *pl.* [mod.L., pl. of **scelid-*, *scelis*, f. Gr. σκέλος leg.

The formation was perh. suggested by Gr. περισκελίς leg-band. The Gr. σκελίς rib of beef is a later form for σχελίς.]

The posterior or pelvic extremities of mammals.

1842 in BRANDE *Dict. Sci.*, etc. And in later Dicts.

scelidosaur ('sɛlɪdəʊsɔː(r)). *Palæont.* [ad. mod.L. *scelidosaur-us*, f. *scelid(o)-* (see SCELIDES) + Gr. σαῦρ-α, σαῦρ-ος lizard (see SAURIA).] A dinosaur of the genus *Scelidosaurus*, the typical genus of the family *Scelidosauridæ* of stegosaurian herbivorous dinosaurs. Hence ˌ**scelido'saurian** *a.*, of or pertaining to the *Scelidosauridæ*; *sb.*, a scelidosaurian reptile. ˌ**scelido'sauriform** *a.* = next. ˌ**scelido'sauroid** *a.*, pertaining to or characteristic of the *Scelidosauridæ*; *sb.*, a scelidosauroid reptile.

1861 OWEN *Monogr. Fossil Reptilia Liassic Format.* I. 5 It most probably formed part of a very young or fœtal Scelidosaur. **1869** HUXLEY in *Q. Jrnl. Geol. Soc.* XXVI. 44, I think it will be proper to restrict the name *Palæosaurus* to the latter (or Megalosauroid) form of tooth, and to use *Thecodontosaurus* for the former (or Scelidosauroid) type. *Ibid.* 45 On the other hand, the teeth of *Thecodontosaurus* are Scelidosaurian in character. **1885** LYDEKKER *Rept. & Amphibia Maleri & Denwa Groups* 29 Scelidosauriform teeth. **1891** *Century Dict.*, *Scelidosauroid* [a. and *sb.*].

‖**Scelidotherium** (ˌsɛlɪdəʊ'θɪərɪəm). *Palæont.* [mod.L. (Owen 1840), f. *scelid(o)-* (see SCELIDES) + Gr. θηρίον wild animal.] A genus of megatherioid edentate mammals. Also anglicized **'scelidoˌthere**, an animal of this genus.

1840 OWEN in *Zool. Beagle* I. 75 The teeth, however, are fewer in the Scelidothere than in any Armadillo. **1847** ANSTED *Anc. World* xv. 369 The Scelidotherium..differs rather more from the Megatheroid type than either the Mylodon or Megalonyx... In all important points however ..the Scelidothere and the Megatherium are so closely analogous that they hardly admit of a separate description.

scellat, obs. Sc. form of SKILLET.

scelleton, scellum: see SKELETON, SKELM *sb.*

scelp, sceme, scemiter: see SKELP, SCHEME *sb.*¹, SCIMITAR.

scemmel, obs. form of SHAMBLE *sb.*¹

‖**scena** ('ʃena). [It., ad. L. *scēna* SCENE.]

1. a. A scene in an Italian opera; the words and music of the scene. **b.** A composition consisting largely of recitative of a dramatic and impassioned character, for one or more voices with accompaniment; either forming part of an opera, or composed separately for the concert-room.

1819 T. HOPE *Anast.* (1820) III. 323 This gentleman.. wondered he should have inspired me..with the *scenas* of a pastoral. **1825** [see SCENE 5 d]. **1842** LYTTON *Zanoni* I. iii, The applause with which they had hailed the overture and the commencing scenas. **1845** *Athenæum* 22 Feb. 204 A beautiful *scena* by Romberg. **1862** MISS BRADDON *Lady Audley* xxxii, My lady's piano was..covered with scattered sheets of music and exquisitely-bound collections of scenas and fantasias. **1886** MRS. CRAIK *King Arthur* vi. 232 She placed the trio before him. It was one of those dashing operatic scenas of the last generation, full of show and difficulty.

2. Used jocularly = SCENE 11.

1847 J. G. LOCKHART in *Croker Papers* (1884) III. xxv. 103, I hear there was a very hot little *scena* at a late Carlton Club dinner between Stanley and Lord George Bentinck.

scenario (sɪ'nɑːrɪəʊ, sɪ'nɛərɪəʊ, older ʃe'nario), *sb.* [It., f. *scena* SCENA.]

1. a. A sketch or outline of the plot of a play, ballet, novel, opera, story, etc., giving particulars of the scenes, situations, etc. Also *transf.* and *fig.*

1878 G. H. LEWES *Jrnl.* 28–29 Apr. in *Geo. Eliot Lett.* (1956) VII. 13 Schemed a scenario from *Daniel Deronda*. **1880** STEVENSON *Let. to Henley* Feb. *Lett.* (1899) I. iv. 167, I shall make you a full scenario as soon as the *Emigrant* is done. **1883** GROVE *Dict. Music* III. 241 *Scenario*, an Italian term, meaning a sketch of the scenes and main points of an opera libretto, drawn up and settled preliminary to filling in the detail. **1884** P. SIMPSON in *Pall Mall G.* 19 May 1/2 As the next step, I write an elaborate scenario..minutely setting down, not only the scenes as they follow, the action of the personages engaged, the sense of all they have to say, but even the 'stage business'. **1903** A. M. BINSTEAD *Pitcher in Paradise* ii. 51 The small card of *data* which forms the 'scenario' from which these stories are being constructed. **1911** O. ONIONS *Widdershins* 279, I myself have drafted a rough scenario of the form it appeared to me the 'Life' might with advantage be cast in. **1923** WODEHOUSE *Inimitable Jeeves* xviii. 250 'Jeeves!' 'Sir?' 'I'm in the soup.' 'Indeed, sir?' I sketched out the scenario for him. 'What would you advise?' **1924** —— *Bill the Conqueror* ix. 159 A young man in a vivid check suit came out, a small young man with close-set eyes and the scenario of a moustache. **1929** C. K. S. MONCRIEFF tr. *Proust's Captive* iii. 493 No doubt the scenario [of a series of events in the narrator's life] was not merely different but almost opposite. **1947** A. EINSTEIN *Music in Romantic Era* xvi. 284 He outlined a scenario, and ..obtained a completed libretto from Somma. **1953** WODEHOUSE *Performing Flea* 69 Today I reached page 254 and have a very detailed scenario of the rest. **1955** W. DEAN in H. Van Thal *Fanfare for Ernest Newman* 59 Trianon..an inveterate compiler of librettos and ballet scenarios for all three Paris opera houses. **1977** *Dædalus* Summer 73 Thus the dramatic scenario—frequently the enactment of a sacred narrative—now becomes a performative mode sui generis.

b. *Cinemat.* A film script with all the details of scenes, appearances of characters, stage-directions, etc., necessary for shooting the film.

1911 [see *picture-play* s.v. PICTURE *sb.* 6 a]. **1919** F. HURST *Humoresque* 184 So many times it comes up in the scenarios and the picture-plots..how money don't always bring happiness. **1922** WODEHOUSE *Girl on Boat* ix. 144 Fate, thought Sam, had constructed a cheap, mushy..five-reel film scenario. **1926, 1930** [see CONTINUITY 6]. **1934** *Punch* 18 Apr. 426/2 The film is still full of real characters, not the pasteboard subsidiaries we meet so often in modern American scenarios of love and murder. **1937** A. HUXLEY *Let.* 15 Dec. (1969) 429 Unless in the interval I get any news about a scenario I wrote while out in Hollywood. **1941** *Spectator* 10 Oct. 355/1 Miss Bette Davis..has proved her genius for breathing life into scenarios which have been synthesized from the more extravagant..of ancient theatrical situations. **1950** T. S. ELIOT *Cocktail Party* I. i. 14 They did a film But they used a different scenario. **1969** M. STEINBECK *On Stage* 165 Strictly speaking a scenario is a film script. It is not used very much. Usually one hears..film script.

2. A sketch, outline, or description of an imagined situation or sequence of events; esp. (*a*) a synopsis of the development of a hypothetical future world war, and hence an outline of any possible sequence of future events; (*b*) an outline of an intended course of action; (*c*) a scientific model or description intended to account for observable facts. Hence, in weakened senses (not easily distinguishable from sense 1 a *transf.* and *fig.*): a circumstance, situation, scene, sequence of events, etc.

The over-use of this word in various loose senses has attracted frequent hostile comment.—R.W.B.

1962 H. KAHN *Thinking about Unthinkable* v. 143 A scenario results from an attempt to describe..some hypothetical sequence of events... Scenarios may explore and emphasize an element of a larger problem such as..the process of 'escalation' of a small war. *Ibid.*, The scenario is an aid to the imagination. *Ibid.* 146 The scenario begins by assuming a crisis; everybody is on edge. A Soviet missile is accidentally fired. **1965** 'R. L. PIKE' *Police Blotter* xi. 185 If you hadn't tried to build up a big scenario with that self-defense crap, if you had just kept your big mouth shut, it might have held us up. **1966** 'W. COOPER' *Memoirs of New Man* I. viii. 103, I admired the beauty and simplicity of his plan—or 'scenario', as the case might be. **1968** *Guardian* 21 Feb. 7/1 Germany then plans to produce a so-called 'scenario' for arriving at an arrangement with Britain. **1968** *Listener* 20 June 791/1 The Hudson Institute..is an organisation largely devoted to preparing what it likes to call 'scenarios of the future'. **1969** M. CRICHTON *Andromeda Strain* viii. 87 The President would face four circumstances (scenarios) in which he might have to issue the Cautery order. **1971** *Observer* 27 June 1/3 Several of the computer 'scenarios' include a catastrophic and sudden collapse of population. **1974** *Nature* 15 Feb. 445/2 As a possible scenario we assume the previously reported pulses to be the chance superposition of more frequent, randomly occurring subpulses. **1975** *Sci. Amer.* Jan. 29/2 Some meteoriticists boldly construct multistage scenarios of condensation, agglomeration, accretion, heating, metamorphism and differentiation to explain the accumulated facts. **1975** *N.Y. Times* 29 Mar. 11/1 There is a certain narrative element in this whacky art, but it would be a brave man who tried to extract a single coherent scenario from any single picture or construction. **1976** *Daily Tel.* 13 Feb. 1/8 Speculation.. about the likely scenario when the Cuban-armoured units reach the point..when they will encounter South African forces. **1976** *Sci. Amer.* Oct. 79A/2 Many of the models we have mentioned here are better characterized by the term scenario... There is so little detailed information that the proposals should not be dignified by the term model. Nevertheless, a good scenario can sometimes lead to a good model. **1977** C. MCCARRY *Secret Lovers* ix. 112 I'll give you the scenario... You're free to modify it..in the light of conditions in the field. **1977** *Time* 18 Apr. 46/2 By escaping from the lab and multiplying, their scenario goes, it could find its way into human intestines. **1978** J. IRVING *World According to Garp* viii. 157 The good-byes that Garp imagined conducting with Alice were violent scenarios. **1980** *Jrnl. R. Soc. Arts* July 474/2 The best scenario..that we can envisage is one in which all those who want to do formal work will have an opportunity of doing two or three days a week.

3. *attrib.* and *Comb.* in sense 1, as ***scenario department, editor, picture, production, sketch, writer, writing.***

1921 B. TARKINGTON *Let.* 2 July in *On Plays* (1959) 65 About your scenario dep't [*sic*] friend's suggestion. **1959** W. S. SHARPS *Dict. Cinematogr.* 127/1 *Scenario Editor*... The title usually applied to the person in charge of the story department of a film producing company. **1929** W. S. CHURCHILL *World Crisis* V. vii. 122 Mr. Baker detracts from the vindication of his hero by the absurd *scenario* picture which he has chosen to paint. **1945** *Amer. Cinematographer* Mar. 122 (*heading*) Trials of making a scenario production. **1921** B. TARKINGTON *Let.* 30 Mar. in *On Plays* (1959) 50, I am sending you the scenario sketch for a picture of 'Beaucaire'. **1914** R. GRAU *Theatre of Science* 224 We have seen the last of the amateur scenario writer. **1939** C. ISHERWOOD *Goodbye to Berlin* 101, I thought you took an interest in the cinema? He's miles the best young scenario writer. **1976** BOTHAM & DONNELLY *Valentino* xi. 82 The woman considered to be the best scenario writer of the day, June Mathis. **1928** H. CRANE *Let.* 27 Mar. (1965) 321 Maybe scenario writing eventually.

Hence **sce'nario** *v. trans.*, to make a scenario of (a story, book, or idea); to sketch *out*; also **sce'narioˌize, 'scenarize.**

1918 *Dial. Notes* V. 13 'The *scenarioizing* of a drama.' Moving Picture advertisement. **1922** A. BENNETT *Let.* 17 Jan. (1966) I. 300, I had attempted to scenario-ize the story and had failed to do it properly. **1922** *Moving Picture Stories* 14 July 26/3 'Clarence'..is already scenarioized and requires only the producer's final approval. **1927** *Sunday Express* 21 Aug. 4 The films were scenarioised, directed, cut, edited, distributed, and exploited by him. **1946** *Amer. Speech* XXI. 304/2, 1946 Press-sheet of RKO Radio Pictures, Inc. Geoffrey Homes is now at the RKO studios scenarizing his best seller, 'Build My Gallows High'. **1953** WODEHOUSE *Performing Flea* 23 So far I have scenarioed it out to about the 40,000 word mark. **1974** *Daily Tel.* (Colour Suppl.) 6 Dec. 42/1 Tonight's entertainment is a fashion show. 'I hear they've got it all scenarioed out,' says Bernie.

scenarist (sɪ'nɑːrɪst). *Cinemat.* [f. SCENAR(IO + -IST.] A scenario writer.

1920 *N.Y. Times* 24 May 20/4 'Old Lady 31', taken by June Mathis as scenarist and John E. Ince as director from Rachel Crother's play. **1925** *New Yorker* 28 Nov. 26/2 You never can tell just what happened to the tale when it fell into the hands of the gifted scenarists. **1932** A. BUCHANAN *Films* v. 92 Every shot..is recorded by the scenarist in his script. **1941** B. SCHULBERG *What makes Sammy Run?* vii. 153 Sammy Glick, prominent scenarist and playwright. **1958** *Times Lit. Suppl.* 15 Aug. p. xxviii/1 The opening passages of *Bleak House* are a supreme evocation of atmosphere which no contemporary scenarist could equal. **1966** *New Statesman* 30 Sept. 488/2 Miss McCarthy could yet prove to be a born scenarist. Film largely robs her work of its overbearing, destructive omniscience. **1977** *Times* 10 June 15/4 Wenders explains that he and his scenarist, the playwright Peter Handke, both happened to read the book at the same time. **1977** *Time* 12 Sept. 60/1 Can an English playwright turned Hollywood scenarist find, in his late 40s, happiness and the right woman?

†**'scenary,** *sb. Obs.* [ad. It. *scenario*: see SCENARIO *sb.* and -ARY¹ B. 2.]

1. 'The disposition and consecution of the scenes of a play' (J.); = SCENARIO *sb.*

1695 DRYDEN *Dufresnoy's Art Paint.* Pref. 44 To make a Sketch, or a more perfect Model of a Picture, is in the Language of Poets, to draw up the Scenary of a Play. **1719** BOYER *Eng.-Fr. Dict.*, Scenary (the ordering of the Scenes of a Play) *Arrangement des Scenes d'une Piece de Theatre*. **1736** POPE *Dunc.* III. 328 *note*, The Edition of Shakespear..took up near two years more, in the drudgery of comparing Impressions, rectifying the Scenary, &c.

2. 'The representation of the place in which an action is performed' (J.).

1729 POPE *Dunc.* II. 262 *note*, The progress of the sound.. and the scenary here of the bordering regions,..are imitated from Virg. Aen. 7 on the sounding the horn of Alecto. **1808** *Ramsay's Gentle Shepherd* I. 109 The plot, characters, and scenary of this exquisite transcript from nature.

3. = SCENERY 3.

1712 ADDISON *Spect.* No. 417 ¶3 A Poet..must gain a due Relish of the Works of Nature, and be thoroughly conversant in the various Scenary of a Country Life. **1748** *Anson's Voy.* III. ii. (ed. 4) 415 The fortunate animals too.. partake in some measure of the romantic cast of the Island, and are no small addition to its wonderful scenary. **1808** *Ramsay's Gentle Shepherd* I. p. x, The minute coincidence between its natural scenary, and his descriptions.

†**'scenary**, *a. Obs.* [ad. L. *scēn-, scænārius* scenic, f. *scēna, scæna* SCENE: see -ARY[1] A.] Scenic, theatrical.

1730 A. GORDON *Maffei's Amphith.* 18 In the Morning Scenary Diversions were exhibited. **1758** BORLASE *Nat. Hist. Cornwall* 298 The scenary part of these performances [Miracle Plays] was much worse than the composition.

scence, obs. form of CENSE *v.*[1]

scend, 'scend, var. ff. SEND *sb.*[2] and *v.*[2] (*Naut.*).

scene (siːn). Also 6 sean, 6–7 seane, scæne, 6, 8 schene, 7 scæn, sceane(e. [a. F. *scène* (14th c. in Hatz.-Darm.), ad. L. *scēna, scæna* stage, scene, a. Gr. σκηνή tent or booth, stage, scene.

Dryden (*Virg. Georg.* III. 38) rimes the word with *train*.]

I. With reference to the theatre.

1. *Antiq.* The stage of a Greek or Roman theatre, including the platform on which the actors stood, and the structure which formed the background (usually representing the outside of a house or temple). Also *transf.*

1612 W. STRACHEY *Trav. Virginia* (1953) I. vi. 78 By their howses, they have sometymes A Scæne or high Stage raised like a Scaffold.. covered with Matts, which.. is a Shelter and serves for such a covered place, where men vsed in old tyme to sitt and talke. **1638** JUNIUS *Paint. Ancients* 241 Apaturius Alabandeus made.. a scene [= *scenam*, Vitruv.] with a neat hand, wherein he made images instead of columnes... He made moreover an upper-scene [= *episcenium*, Vitruv.], wherein the seelings of the porches, the halfe-house-tops were diversly adorned by the Painter. **1682** WHELER *Journ. Greece* v. 365 The Scene is oblong, jetting out six Paces more forward in the Front, than the Seats of the Spectators. **1734** tr. *Rollin's Anc. Hist.* Pref. (1827) I. 125 The division for the actors was called in general the scene, or stage. **1924** A. HUXLEY *Let.* 29 Apr. (1969) 229 A Palladian theatre with fixed scene and various other delights.

2. [= F. *scène*.] The stage or theatre taken as standing for either the dramatic art or the histrionic profession. Now only *arch.*

1682 WHELER *Journ. Greece* 370 For [athletic] games had such an officer belonging to them... But whoever heard of such an officer belonging to the Scene? **1697** DRYDEN *Æneis* Ded (a) 3, I have more than once already maintain'd the Rights of my two Masters [Homer and Virgil] against their Rivals of the Scene, even while I wrote Tragedies my self. **1713** POPE *Prol. to Cato* 41 Our Scene precariously subsists too long On French Translation, and Italian Song. **1761** CHURCHILL *Rosciad* 475 Giddy with praise, and puff'd with female pride, She quits the tragic scene.

†**3. a.** The action or representation of a piece upon the stage; a stage-performance; a play or drama in representation. *Obs.* exc. as in b.

1592 KYD *Sp. Trag.* IV. iv. 79 To die to day for fashioning our Scene.. And in a minute starting vp againe, Reuiue to please too morrowes audience. **1599** SHAKS. *Hen. V*, Prol. 4 A Kingdome for a Stage, Princes to Act, And Monarchs to behold the swelling Scene. **1608** *Merry Devil of Edmonton* Prol. 3 Your silence and attention, worthy friends, That your free spirits may with more pleasing sense Relish the life of this our actiue sceane. **1634** HEYWOOD & BROME *Late Lancashire Witches* Prol., We are forc'd from our owne Nation To ground the Scene that's now in agitation. **1679** DRYDEN *Troilus & Cr.* Pref. b 3, And now behold King Richard entring upon the Scene. **1697** —— *Æneis* Ded. (a) 2 b, The Poet who Flourish'd in the Scene is damn'd in the *Ruelle*. **1814** *Orpheus* I. ii, They crowd the trembling poet's scene.

b. ***the scene opens*** or ***is opened***: a phr. used to express the beginning of the action of a play, or of an act or scene. Cf. F. *ouvrir la scène*, 'commencer la représentation' (Littré).

1673 SETTLE *Empress of Morocco* I. i, Scene opens, Muly Labas appears bound in Chains. *Ibid.* II. i, The Scene opened, is represented the Prospect of a large River. **1693** RYMER *Short View Trag.* i. 14 The Scene opening presents 15 Grandees of Spain.

4. The place in which the action of a play, or part of a play, is supposed to occur. Hence also, the setting of a dialogue, novel, etc. Phr. ***to lay the scene*** (see LAY *v.*[1] 20 b); ***to change, shift the scene.***

1592 KYD *Sp. Trag.* IV. iii. 18 Well doon, Balthazar, hang up the Title: Our scene is Rhodes. **1592** SHAKS. *Rom. & Jul.* Prol. 2 In faire Verona, where we lay our Scene. **1599** —— *Hen. V*, II. Prol. 42 Vnto Southampton do we shift our Scene. **1611** B. JONSON *Catiline* I. i, As soone.. As is a vaile put off, a visor chang'd, Or the scene shifted in our theaters. **1668** DRYDEN *Ess. Dram. Poesy* 43 He has remov'd the Scene in the same Act from Rome to Catiline's Army, and from thence again to Rome. **1712** ADDISON *Spect.* No. 357 ¶7 Asia, Africk, and Europe are the several Scenes of his [Virgil's] Fable. **1725** *Pope's Odyss.* III. Notes I. 157 The Scene is now remov'd from Ithaca to Pylos. **1875** JOWETT *Plato* (ed. 2) V. 5 The scene is laid in Crete.

5. a. A subdivision of an act of a play (or of a short play which is not divided into acts), marked by the entrance or departure of one or more actors (and, in romantic or non-classic drama, often by a change of *locale*). Hence, the action and dialogue comprised in any one of these subdivisions; a situation *between* certain actors.

In editions of the Roman dramatists, and of the French classic dramatists, the entrance or exit of any actor makes a new numbered 'scene'. In the English drama, on the other hand, the 'scene' is a distinct subdivision of the act, marked by the fall of the curtain or the leaving of the stage empty; even when the *locale* and the actors remain the same in two consecutive 'scenes', the stage is not supposed to have been occupied continuously through the interval.

1540 PALSGR. *Acolastus* I. i. C iij b, All the versis of this scene be *Senarii*. **1562** J. HEYWOOD *Prov. & Epigr.* (1867) 147 In volewmes full or flat, There is no chapter, nor no seane, That thou appliest like that. **1592** KYD *Sp. Trag.* IV. i. 187 And all shalbe concluded in one Scene, For there's no pleasure tane in tediousness. **1611** FLORIO, *Scena*... Also any one scene or entrance of a Comedie or Tragedie. **1665** SIR R. HOWARD *Four New Plays* To Rdr. b, The Spanish Plays.. being nothing but so many Novels put into Acts and Scenes. **1668** DRYDEN *Ess. Dram. Poesy* 20 [In the ancient drama] it is to be accounted a new Scene, not [1684 p. 14 not only] every time the Stage is empty, but every person who enters, though to others, makes it so; because he introduces a new business. **1678** —— *All for Love* Pref. (end), I prefer the Scene betwixt Antony and Ventidius in the first Act, to any thing which I have written in this kind. **1756** FOOTE *Engl. ret. fr. Paris* Epil., Does not this poisoning scene The sacred right of Tragedy profane. **1783** BLAIR *Lect.* xlv. II. 496 The entrance of a new personage upon the Stage, forms what is called a New Scene. **1865** T. W. ROBERTSON *Society* Act I. Scene I.—Sidney Daryl's Chambers, in Lincoln's Inn.

b. The pl. is sometimes put for 'a play', 'dramatic writing'.

1664 DRYDEN *Rival Ladies* Ep. Ded. A 3 b, Following the New way, I mean, of writing Scenes in Verse. **1710** GRANVILLE *Epil. for 'Brit. Enchanters'* 27 Our Author wou'd excuse these youthful Scenes, Begotten at his Entrance in his Teens.

c. *fig.*

1577 WHETSTONE *Life & Death of Gaskoigne* B iij b, His Sean is played, you folowe on the act. **1592** GREENE *Philomela* (1615) E 4, Till Fortune.. entred into the Theatre of Philomelaes life and beganne to acte a balefull Sceane in this manner. **1594** SHAKS. *Rich. III*, II. ii. 38 *Dut.* What meanes this Scene of rude impatience? *Qu.* To make an act of Tragicke violence. **1595** LODGE *Fig for Momus* G 1 b, In that shamefull schene of treasons play. **1596** LAMBARDE *Peramb. Kent* (ed. 2) 407 At this place of the Bishop in Halling, I am drawing on the last Scæne of my life. **1638** SIR T. HERBERT *Trav.* (ed. 2) 72 We are now to present you upon the Asiatique stage, various Scænes compos'd of a miscelany of subjects. **1648** HERRICK *Hesp.*, *To Mistress Amie Potter*, Nature has pre-compos'd us both to Love; Your part's to grant; my Scean must be to move.

d. *Mus.* = SCENA 1 b.

1825 DANNELEY *Encycl. Mus.*, *Scena* or *Scene*, a piece of music composed of a *recitative*, an *andante* or a *largo*, a *larghetto*, and an *agitato* or *allegro*. The *cavatine*, or first air, is often separated by a *couplet de recitatif*. A scene may be for one or more voices.

6. a. The material apparatus, consisting chiefly of painted hangings, slides, etc., set at the back and sides of the stage, and intended to give the illusion of a real view of the *locale* in which the action of a play takes place; the view thus presented to the spectators at any time during the action of a play. Also, any one of the painted hangings, slides, etc. used for this purpose.

On the Elizabethan stage, the curtain or hanging at the back of the stage, concealing the vestry or green-room, stood in lieu of scenery. Painted scenes and elaborate machinery, the representation of buildings or landscape in perspective, etc., were a principal feature of the privately-produced masques of Jas. I and Chas. I and, later, of the operatic play (see OPERA 1).

1540 [see SCENISH]. **1605** B. JONSON *Masque of Blackness*, First, for the Scene, was drawne a *Landtschap*, consisting of small woods,.. which falling, an artificiall sea was seene to shoote forth. **1608** —— *Masque at Ld. Hadington's Marr.*, The scene to this Masque, was a high, steepe red cliffe, aduancing it selfe into the cloudes. **1618** HOLYDAY *Technogamia* Prol. *marg.*, Here the vpper part of the Scene open'd, when straight appear'd a Heauen [etc.]. **1625** BACON *Ess.*, *Masques*, And let the Masquers, or any other, that are to come down from the Scene, have some Motions, vpon the Scene it selfe, before their Comming down. **1633** SHIRLEY *Tri. Peace* 7 A Curtaine being sodainly drawne up, the Sceane was discovered representing a large streete with Sumptuous Pallaces. **1656** DAVENANT (*title*), The Siege of Rhodes Made a Representation by the Art of Prospective in Scenes. And the Story sung in Recitative Musick. **1667** FLECKNOE *Damoiselles à la mode*, Of Persons represented, Any Italian Scænes with four Doors serving. *a* **1693** AUBREY *Lives* (1898) II. 244 He has some scaenes to it, which in those dayes were only used at masques. **1719** YOUNG *Busiris* IV. (Stage-dir.), The back scene opens. *Ibid.*, Scene shuts on them. **1737** POPE *Hor. Ep.* II. i. 315 Back fly the scenes, and enter foot and horse. *a* **1814** *Gonzanga* V. v. in *New Brit. Theatre* III. 161 All the characters appear lost in astonishment and terror as the scene closes them in. **1904** *Westm. Gaz.* 4 Jan. 9/1 The opening of the doors at the back of the stage caused a draught which blew over a large fan-scene containing a number of incandescent lights.

fig. **1748** HUME *Philos. Ess. Hum. Underst.* vii. (1751) 104 The Scenes of the Universe are continually shifting.

†**b.** *pl.* ? A succession of realistically-lighted stage-pictures, telling their story without words or action. *Obs.*

1625 BACON *Ess.*, *Masques*, The Alterations of Scenes, so it be quietly, and without Noise, are Things of great Beauty, and Pleasure: For they feed and relieue the Eye, before it be full of the same Obiect. Let the Scenes abound with Light, specially Coloured and Varied. **1650** DAVENANT *Pref. to Gondibert* 8 Painted History, when with the cousenage of lights it is represented in Scenes, by which we are much lesse inform'd then by actions on the Stage. **1657** —— *Entert. Rutland-Ho.* 17 Would you meet to be delighted with Scænes? which is, to be entertain'd with the deception of motion, and transposition of Lights; where, whilst you think you see a great Battel, you are sure to get nothing by the Victory.

c. *transf.* A curtain or veil; also, a decorative hanging on a wall.

1638 SIR T. HERBERT *Trav.* (ed. 2) 138 When the greene and crimson scænes [ed. 1677 p. 132 curtains or scenes] of silke were drawne, from this Apollo, wee lookt into a great square court. **1648** HERRICK *Hesper.*, *Upon some women* 8 Out-side silk, and out-side Lawne; Sceanes to cheat us neatly drawne. **1662** J. DAVIES tr. *Mandelslo's Trav.* 194 Instead of Tapistry, they have a kinde of Scenes or Shutters, which serve them also for Pictures.

†**d.** *pl.* Used to describe the appearance of strata or clusters of clouds, piled one above another.

1686 GOAD *Celest. Bodies* I. xv. 83 Frosty, mist, fair; clouds in scenes. *Ibid.* II. ii. 162 We often times see Clouds as in several Stories, Lofts or Scenes, one over another.

7. a. ***behind the scenes***: amidst the actors and stage-machinery, where ordinary spectators are not admitted.

1668 DRYDEN *Ess. Dram. Poesy* 32 Things hapning in the Action of the Play, and suppos'd to be done behind the Scenes. **1672** —— *Assignation* Epil. 21 His Nuns are good, which on the Stage are shown, And, sure, behind our Scenes you'll look for none. **1791** BOSWELL *Johnson* an. 1749, She was carried off to be put to death behind the scenes. **1890** *All Year Round* 29 Mar. 302 (art.), Behind the Scenes at the Lane.

b. *fig.* Also (with hyphens) as *attrib. phr.*

1748 CHESTERF. *Lett.* 16 Feb., I, who have been behind the scenes, both of pleasure and business. **1812** MAR. EDGEWORTH *Absentee* v, Miss Pratt.. had obtained the *entrée* to a number of great houses, and was behind the scenes in many fashionable families. **1869** TOZER *Highl. Turkey* I. 158 Another personage of greater importance was behind the scenes in this movement. **1955** H. ROTH *Sleeper* ix. 69 His behind-the-scenes directors must have trusted him. **1959** *Manch. Guardian* 23 July 6/6 One version of the behind-the-scenes interview. **1959** 'S. RANSOME' *I'll die for You* xii. 134 He was quietly directing his official resources into a wide, behind-the-scenes investigation.

II. In various established metaphorical uses.

Sense 8 is developed from 4; senses 9–11 from 5, though in sense 9 there is some mixture of sense 6.

8. a. The place where an action is carried on and people play their parts as in a drama. Phr. ***to enter*** or ***appear on the scene, to quit the scene. the scene of action***, the place where events are actually happening or business being done.

1594 CONSTABLE *Diana* VIII. iv, Meeting Heroick feete in euery line, That tread high measures on the Scene of Fame. **1608** D. TUVIL *Ess. Pol. & Mor.* 125 True vertuous actions, are neuer seene vpon the Scene, but when by the necessitie of Lawes, they are enforced to show themselues. **1648** *Petit. Eastern Assoc.* 8 Awakening endlesse war upon our Brittish Scenes. *a* **1658** J. CLEVELAND *Wks.* (1687) 100 The Sand was always the Scene of Quarrelling. **1659** *Clarke Papers* (Camden) IV. 294 The persones in the proclamacion mencioned having made this citty parte of their scene to act their designe upon. **1673** DRYDEN *Marr. à la Mode* III. i, But though these are not My Province, I have Scene enough within To exercise my vertue. **1677** MIEGE *Eng.-Fr. Dict.* s.v., There will be the Scene of Action this Campaigne, *ce sera là le Theatre de la Guerre.* **1685** SOUTH *Serm.* (1727) I. 388 The viith of the *Romans* (which has been made the unhappy Scene of so much Controversy about these Matters). **1704** *Royal Let.* 25 June in *Lond. Gaz.* No. 4037/1 To render that.. Kingdom a Schene of Blood and Disorder. **1705** ADDISON *Italy* Pref., There is [not].. so much as a Mountain or River that has not been the Scene of some extraordinary Action. **1721** DE FOE *Mem. Cavalier* (1840) 37 The part I acted on this bloody scene. **1791** MRS. RADCLIFFE *Rom. Forest* i, Paris, the scene of her former happiness. **1833** T. HOOK *Parson's Dau.* I. vii, It was clear *she* could not quit the scene of action. **1857** LIVINGSTONE *Trav.* ix. 181 My arrival on the scene was felt to be so much weight in the scale. **1884** *Manch. Exam.* 16 Feb. 4/6 West Somerset was the scene, yesterday, of the first contested county election under the provisions of the Corrupt Practices Act. **1889** *Field* 19 Jan. 67/3 Whereupon Mr. Calvert's solicitor came upon the scene, with a demand for an undertaking not to offend again. **1926** *Melody Maker* Sept. 61 Since 'Nelly Kelly's Cabaret' came on the scene, it's put fresh kick into dancing. **1936** W. H. SAUMAREZ SMITH *Let.* 26 June in *Young Man's Country* (1977) ii. 11, I rode out after breakfast to the scene of action. **1946** ROSENTHAL & ZACHERY *Jazzways* 16 By 1907, Bolden had disappeared from the scene, confined to an insane asylum. **1963** D. OGILVY *Confessions Advt. Man* (1964) ii. 26 By the time I came on the scene, the big advertisers had grown more cautious. **1968** *Jazz Monthly* Apr. 8/1 People like Buddy Collette, Red Callender,.. were the big time musicians on the scene then. **1979** 'E. FERRARS' *Witness before Fact* xv. 150, I don't know what things were like for you before he arrived on the scene, perhaps not so good.

b. The world in which man is an actor; the theatre of this life. Often in phr. (*this*) ***scene of things. to quit the scene***, to die.

1662 H. MORE *Philos. Writ.* (1712) Pref. 25 Which makes .. the whole scene of things evidently to begin from Adam. **1681** S. PARKER *Demonstr. Law of Nature* 112 Who would enter upon this tragical Scene of things onely to appear and so return into dust and silence? **1736** BUTLER *Anal.* I. iii. 61 The known Course of human Things, the Scene we are now passing through. *a* **1822** SHELLEY *Ess.*, *Lett.* etc. (1840) I. 225 Life.. strips, as it were, the painted curtain from this scene of things. **1870** J. H. NEWMAN *Gram. Assent* II. viii. 261 This universal living scene of things is after all as little a logical world as it is a poetical.

c. ***the scene of the crime***, the place where a crime has been committed. Also *attrib.*, as ***scene(s)-of-crime***, used *esp.* to designate (a member of) a civilian branch of the police force concerned with the collection of forensic evidence.

1923 A. CHRISTIE *Murder on Links* iv. 51 Now, Monsieur Poirot, you would without doubt like to visit the scene of the crime. **1931** D. L. SAYERS *Five Red Herrings* xvi. 175 He didn't take the body with him... Now he's got to get back to the scene of the crime. **1943** G. GREENE *Ministry of Fear* I. v. 67 A few elderly men in the C.I.D... might..visit the scene of the 'crime'. **1954** F. CHERRILL *Cherrill of the Yard* iii. 38 Scenes of Crime prints. *Ibid.* 39 By this arrangement it became much easier to carry out a search with a single Scenes of Crime mark which had been classified in accordance with the single fingerprint system. **1961** *Observer* 21 May 5/3 The War Office have placed an order ..for thirty-eight 'Scene of Crime Kits', to issue to their security-men. **1971** R. LEWIS *Error of Judgment* i. 38 The scene-of-crime unit upstairs have discovered nothing, but one of the constables..came up with a glove. **1972** *Police Rev.* 8 Dec. 1601/2 Certain duties such as those of scenes-of-crime officers..were not performed by the R.U.C. **1977** P. HILL *Liars* iii. 33 The Scene of Crime man went over..the cottage for fingerprints.

d. Some portion of human activity (as delimited by a preceding *adj.* of place, time, etc.); the realm or sphere (of an activity or interest indicated by a preceding *attrib. sb.*).

1931 *Times Lit. Suppl.* 15 Oct. 786/3 Mr. Masters..is no optimistic observer of the contemporary American scene. **1938** D. BAKER *Young Man with Horn* I. v. 52 If Rick had grown up in the present scene he'd probably have had his head perpetually inside a walnut radio cabinet listening to this one or that one playing a tea dance. **1943** H. READ *Politics of Unpolitical* vii. 98 There have been times when he was bored with the social scene, and 'doodled' while he stared hopelessly into the future. **1949** *Ebony* Nov. 24 (*heading*) The jazz scene. **1959** L. LIPTON *Holy Barbarians* I. i. 40 Something was happening on the poetry scene in Venice West. **1970** *Daily Tel.* 9 Jan. 3/6 Wilson was not mixed up with the drug scene. **1974** *Howard Jrnl.* XIV. 108 (Advt.), One of the most forceful and controversial writers on the magisterial scene. **1977** *Listener* 17 Feb. 214/2 Without that little building at Swiss Cottage..London's theatre scene would be much duller.

e. *slang* (orig. *U.S. jazz* and *beatniks'*). A place where people of common interests meet or where a particular activity is carried on. Hence, more loosely, an activity or pursuit (esp. a fashionable or superior one); a situation, event, or experience; a way of life. Freq. in phrases, as ***a bad scene***, an unpleasant experience; ***to make the scene***, to participate in an event or activity; to arrive (somewhere); (***to go***) ***on the scene***, (to become) involved in some activity, esp. drug-taking; (***not***) ***one's scene*** (and varr.), (not) what one enjoys or finds interesting.

There is some overlap with sense d above.

1951 E. PAUL *Springtime in Paris* vi. 125 'Nobody comes on this scene wearin' any green,' said another taller Negro. **1957** *N.Y. Times Mag.* 18 Aug. 26/3 *Scene*, any place where musicians play or gather; by extension, any place where people meet or any event they attend. Thus, 'Let's make the country scene this week-end.' **1958** G. LEA *Somewhere there's Music* xxi. 179 Something on the scene you don't dig. *Ibid.*, It was a bad scene. It scared me, man. **1958** *Look* 19 Aug. 65/2 The regulars who 'make the scene'. 'The scene', geographically, is a narrow area running about four blocks along Grant Avenue in San Francisco's North Beach district. *Ibid.* 67/1 Like many on 'the scene', she is attracted to Zen Buddhism. **1964** *New Society* 20 Feb. 8/2 What happens to the young drug taker? It can be described..by actually going through the experience, going 'on the scene'. **1966** *New Statesman* 1 July 26/2 Her final surrender to Clive Francis seems unlikely: his jeans are too baggy for her scene. **1966** *Melody Maker* 15 Oct. 6/6, I decided I wanted to play jazz more than any other scene. **1967** *Punch* 18 Oct. 574/3 They come here to work because it's exciting and new and because it's the scene. **1968** M. RICHLER *Cocksure* xiii. 74 Like we're having a scene on Saturday night. At Timothy's pad. **1969** *Oz* Apr. 32/1 We've all got different scenes. The whole thing is to get to know each other's trips... Are you on an acid scene? **1970** [see MAKE *v.*[1] 65 b]. **1975** D. LODGE *Changing Places* ii. 84 Washing up was more his scene than body language. **1977** I. SHAW *Beggarman, Thief* I. viii. 101 He could take a look at the scene and blow if he didn't like it.

9. a. A view or picture presented to the eye (or to the mind) of a place, concourse, incident, series of actions or events, assemblage of objects, etc.

1653 JER. TAYLOR *Serm. for Yr.* i. 11 This is the greatest Scene of Majesty that shall be in that [*i.e.* the last] day, till the Sentence bee pronounced. **1660** F. BROOKE tr. *Le Blanc's Trav.* 249 At last all vanished, leaving a scene of.. lovely trees. **1667** MILTON *P.L.* XI. 637 But now prepare thee for another Scene. **1704** POPE *Summer* 59 See what delights in sylvan scenes appear! **1705** ADDISON *Italy, Antiq. near Naples* 216 About Eight Miles Distance from Naples lyes a very noble Scene of Antiquities. **1715** POPE *Iliad* XVI. 360 The smiling Scene wide opens to the sight. **1781** GIBBON *Decl. & F.* xxx. (1787) III. 171 This scene of peace and plenty was suddenly changed into a desert. **1797** MRS. RADCLIFFE *Italian* xiii, The travellers stopped to admire the scene. **1797** SOUTHEY *Lett. Resid. in Spain* xiii. 240 A most curious scene did our dressing-room exhibit. *a* **1828** H. S. VANDYK *The Light Guitar* (Bartlett's *Fam. Quots.*), Oh, leave the gay and festive scenes, The halls of dazzling light. **1848** THACKERAY *Van. Fair* xxxii, We of peaceful London City have never beheld..such a scene of hurry and alarm, as that which Brussels presented. **1860** TYNDALL *Glac.* I. xi. 72 The scene outside was at once wild, grand, and beautiful.

b. *fig.* A vista or prospect of something expected or to come.

1762 T. MORTIMER *Ev. Man his own Broker* (ed. 5) 173 Light Horse [otherwise called 'scrip']..is the Commodity to Jobb with, and opens a most extensive scene of it.

10. a. An action, episode, complication of events, or situation, in real life.

1679 *Season. Adv. Protest.* 3 The Roman Party was never wanting in any bloudy Scene to destroy Christ's Disciples. **1692** R. L'ESTRANGE *Fables* xlii. 44 And 'tis a Pleasant Scene enough, when Thieves fall out among themselves, to see the Cutting of One Diamond with Another. **1766** in *3rd Rep. on E. India Comp.* App. No. 74 *H. of C. Rep. Comm.* III. 400 We think the vast Fortunes acquired in the inland Trade have been obtained by a Scene of the most tyrannic and oppressive Conduct that ever was known in any Age or Country. **1766** FORDYCE *Serm. Yng. Wom.* (1767) II. xiii. 224 You were not made for scenes of danger. **1833** T. HOOK *Parson's Dau.* I. vii, A scene followed, the like of which is often enacted in higher places and by more important personages. **1845** M. PATTISON *Ess.* (1889) I. 18 Not at all disconcerted by the scene that had just occurred, the wily Roman undertook to justify himself. **1878** SIMPSON *Sch. Shaks.* I. 29 Then he disappears from this scene in his career.

b. An episode, situation, etc., forming a subject of narration or description.

c **1630** MILTON *Passion* 22 These latter [*ed.* 1673 latest] scenes confine my roving vers. **1704** PRIOR *Celia to Damon* 112 Say, Shepherd, say: Are these Reflections true? Or was it but the Woman's Fear, that drew This cruel Scene, unjust to Love and You? **1850** SMEDLEY (*title*) Frank Fairlegh, or Scenes from the Life of a Private Pupil. **1858** GEO. ELIOT (*title*) Scenes of Clerical Life.

11. An exhibition of excited or strong feeling between two or more persons; a stormy encounter or interview. ***to make*** (***create, have***) ***a scene***, to make a disturbance, 'kick up a row'. [Cf. F. *faire une scène* (*à quelqu'un*).]

1761 FOOTE *Lyar* III. (1786) 65 My father has got to the bottom of the whole Abington business. *Pap.* The deuce! *Y. Wild.* We parted this moment. Such a scene! **1787** MME. D'ARBLAY *Diary* Aug., She counselled me..to avoid complaints that led to scenes of such violence and impropriety. **1804** G. ROSE *Diaries* (1860) II. 169 The reconciliation should be accompanied with *éclat*, and..it was intended to make a scene of it. **1831** *Society* I. 252 Aubrey.. had just sense enough to see the folly of making a scene. **1844** DISRAELI *Coningsby* VIII. vii, From an anticipatory horror of something like a scene. **1848** THACKERAY *Van. Fair* lxiv, Madame de Belladonna made him a scene about you, and fired off in one of her furies. **1887** *Spectator* 10 Sept. 1202 One of those scenes in the House of Commons which now occur once or twice in the week. **1888** *Poor Nellie* 34 You made a regular scene. **1957** *Sunday Mail* (Glasgow) 10 Feb. 11 *Kick up a storm*—to cause trouble, or create a scene. **1958** [see BRACE *v.*[1] 5 c]. **1959** T. S. ELIOT *Elder Statesman* II. 61 I've made him understand That the doctors want you to be free from worry. He won't make a scene. **1970** G. F. NEWMAN *Sir, You Bastard* viii. 255 Two of them rose and followed him out. 'Don't let's have a scene,' one of the Rubber Heels said... The other ran his hands over Sneed's jacket.

† **III. 12.** A screen for the reception of images projected from a lens. Also ***scene-plate***.

1706 *Phil. Trans.* XXV. 2237 A Sevenfoot Telescope was fitted up with a Scene to receive the Species of the Sun cast through it. *Ibid.* 2239 Mr. Abr. Sharp cast the Species of the Sun on a Scene-plate, behind his Seven foot Glass.

IV. 13. *attrib.* and *Comb.*, as (sense 11) ***scene-making***, (senses 5 and 6) ***scene-change***; **scene-dock** [DOCK *sb.*[3]], the place in which scenes are stored in a theatre; † **scene-drawer** = SCENE-SHIFTER; † **scene-keeper**, one who has charge of the scenes in a theatre; † **scene-man** = SCENE-SHIFTER; **scene-painted** *a.*, painted with scenes; **scene-painter**, one who paints scenes or scenery for the theatre; also *transf.*; **scene-painting**, the art of painting scenes according to the rules of stage-perspective; *fig.* descriptive writing in a bold and vivid style; also *attrib.*; **scene-plate** (see sense 12); **scene-plot**, the list and description of the scenes in a play; **scene-room**, a room where scenes are stored (in quot. *fig.*); **scene-setting**, *vbl. sb.* and *ppl. a.*, setting a scene; usu. *transf.* and *fig.*; so ***scene-setter***; **scene-steal** *v.*, to appropriate more than one's fair share of attention by one's performance in a scene; so ***scene-stealer*** (also *transf.*), ***scene-stealing*** ppl. adj.; † **scene-work**, dramatic representation; stage-scenery. Also SCENE SHIFTER.

1952 W. GRANVILLE *Dict. Theatrical Terms* 158 **Scene-change*, the striking of one scene and the erection of another. **1962** A. NISBETT *Technique Sound Studio* ix. 153 When a situation calls for a scene change the simplest form that this can take is a slow fade to silence over about ten seconds, a pause of three or four seconds, and an equally slow fade in. **1871** E. L. BLANCHARD *Diary* Mar. in Scott & Howard *Life E. L. Blanchard* (1891) II. 395 Then to Standard [Theatre] ..go behind the scenes and see the wonderful *scene dock. **1885** J. K. JEROME *On the Stage* iii. 29 Piled up at the back, in what was called the 'scene dock'. **1916** [see BACK STAGE, BACKSTAGE *sb.* and *adv.*]. **1977** *Times* 1 Nov. 14/6 The [Wexford] Opera House..[has] no scene-dock, no workshops, no adequate dressing-rooms. **1709** STEELE *Tatler* No. 99 ⁋3 Door-Keepers came out clad like Cardinals, and *Scene-Drawers like Heathen Gods. **1669** E. CHAMBERLAYNE *Pres. St. Eng.* 280 *Scene-keeper, Coffer-Maker, Wax-Chandler,..one of each. **1876** GEO. ELIOT *Dan. Der.* xxx, Not molesting him with passionate appeals and *scene-making. **1737** FIELDING *Eurydice Hissed* Wks. 1903 III. 409 His levee is compos'd of..box-keepers, *scene-men, fiddlers, and candle-snuffers. **1918** W. OWEN *Lett.* (1967) 558 *Scene-painted boulders, and all the arts and deceitful devices of Victoria. **1749** SMOLLETT *Gil Blas* VII. viii. (1782) III. 67, I was obliged to undergo the civilities of the *scene-painter, the music [etc.]. **1824** Scene-painter [see MASTER *sb.*[1] 25 d]. **1853** [see CHURRIGUERESQUE *a.*]. **1882** *Illustr. Lond. News* 16 Dec. 619/3 Scene-painters and scene-shifters. **1754** KIRBY *Perspective* II. vi. 76 The Design of *Scene-Painting, is not only to decorate the Theatre, but to make that Part of it which lies beyond the Stage, appear much longer than it really is. **1821** H. C. ROBINSON *Diary* 2 Dec. (1967) 71, I have finished *Waverley*... Its merit lies in portrait and scene painting. **1825** J. NEAL *Bro. Jonathan* II. 251, I know my propensity for scene-painting. **1838** MACAULAY in Trevelyan *Life* (1880) II. 11 A bold,..scene-painting manner is that which..succeeds best in periodical writing. **1859** GULLICK & TIMBS *Paint.* 305 Scene Painting is an extensive and peculiar walk of art, with its own laws and practical and scientific rules. **1847** W. C. MACREADY *Diary* 20 Oct. (1912) II. 375 Made one *scene plot of 'Van Artevelde', and sent it with note to Stanfield. **1933** P. GODFREY *Back-Stage* i. 19 The stage-manager, with every detail of the scene-plot in his head, stands directing the whole. **1737** *Daily Advertiser* 4 Feb., And the *Scene-Rooms, Green and Dressing Rooms, to be on the outside of the last mention'd Measure. **1826** J. O'KEEFFE *Recoll.* II. 39 The author is often brought into the scene-room to give his opinion on the progress of their work. **1859** E. FITZBALL *35 Yrs. Dram. Author's Life* II. 124 The celebrated Mr Grieve, and his two sons, Thomas and William, the most perfect scene painters in the world..in their scene-room, genius always found a welcome footing. **1881** STEVENSON *Virg. Puerisque* (1895) 232 That stage-wardrobe and scene-room that we call the memory. **1974** *Times* 16 Apr. 16/3 Miss Tanburn will kick-off one of the panel discussions with a half-hour *scene-setter. **1978** *Language* LIV. 353 Only three functions—*subject*, *topic*, and *relator*—are assigned by the rules of H's sample and DDG of English, although a fourth (*scene-setter*) is mentioned in the text. **1963** *Times Lit. Suppl.* 17 May 358/3 A biographer with a sense of character, an eye to *scene-setting. **1968** P. FOOT *Politics of Harold Wilson* 11 The two most important scene-setting subjects are food and the weather. **1972** M. GILBERT *Body of Girl* xx. 183 With a little care and scene-setting it could be made to look very convincing. **1977** D. WILLIAMS *Treasure by Degrees* iii. 34 The Prince's finery and the size of his entourage—natural scene-setting for an important Arab. **1976** *Woman's Weekly* 6 Nov. 6/2 Trish Van Devere, who not only plays Beauty in the movie (and guess who *scene-steals as the Beast!) but in real life also happens to be Mrs George C. Scott. **1978** *Radio Times* 18–24 Mar. 16/3 Director Jules Dassin's wife Melina Mercouri turns every trick to scene-steal from Morley and Ustinov. **1955** T. STERLING *Evil of Day* xviii. 193 These lousy actors are all *scene-stealers. **1960** *Vogue Pattern Book* No. 4. 51 The addition of demure puffed sleeves makes it the scene-stealer of more sedate occasions. **1977** M. HINXMAN *One-Way Cemetery* xiii. 94 It's not the leading role, but it's a scene-stealer. **1963** *Times* 29 Jan. 11/1 Mr. Craig's is a good, workmanly Cavaradossi, a little stiff and never *scene-stealing. **1980** *Times Lit. Suppl.* 21 Mar. 323/2 A small but scene-stealing knockabout part. **1642** MILTON *Apol. Smect.* Wks. 1851 III. 261 Likening those grave controversies to a piece of Stagery, or *Scene-worke where his owne Remonstrant..must of all right be counted the chiefe Player. **1728** CHAMBERS *Cycl.* s.v. *Architecture*, Counterfeit Architecture, which we otherwise call Scene-Work.

Hence † **scened** *pa. pple.*, displayed or set as in a stage-scene, staged. **'scening** *vbl. sb.*, furnishing with stage-scenery.

1691 SANCROFT in D'Oyly *Life* (1821) II. 17 Our course of employment and action [continues] the very same, only not scened so illustriously; nor set off with so good company and conversation. *a* **1750** A. HILL *Wks.* (1753) I. 105 It were a downright shame, if these good people, who gave the Tragedy all its merit, of fine dressing and sceneing, should be suffered to lose their money.

scene, obs. form of SEINE.

‖**scène à faire** (sɛn a fɛr). *Theatr.* Pl. **scènes à faire.** [Fr., lit. 'scene for action'.] The most important scene in a play or opera, made inevitable by the action which leads up to it. Also *transf.*

1893 *Manch. Guardian* 24 Oct. 8/3 The subject of the 'Dame aux Camellias' trying to begin life over again, and to live as if the past had never been, has often been essayed, and the *scène à faire* of her confrontation..with the inexorable reality of things has been often and sometimes admirably composed. **1921** P. LUBBOCK *Craft of Fiction* vii. 102 Thackeray's skill betrays him... His climax, his *scène à faire*, has been insufficiently prepared for. **1922** W. S. MAUGHAM *On a Chinese Screen* xlviii. 188 He was asking for the *pièce bien faite*, the *scène à faire*, the curtain, the unexpected, the dramatic. **1948** F. R. LEAVIS *Great Tradition* ii. 112 The brilliant art with which James, choosing his *scènes à faire*, works in terms of dramatic presentation. **1965** *New Statesman* 10 Dec. 943/2 A big added *scène à faire* in the council chamber gave Verdi a chance for the creation of an ensemble that looks forward very clearly to the third act of *Otello*. **1969** *Listener* 13 Feb. 220/2 Robert Hoffman acts badly, and the *scène à faire* in a wobbling rowing boat..is a triumph of embarrassment. **1980** *Times* 14 Mar. 13/8 They do, eventually, get a *scène à faire* (which, so often, proves to be a *scène à ne faire*) in which she tries to treat him as Louis XV.

'sceneful, *a. rare*$^{-1}$. [-FUL.] Abounding in scenes or scenery.

1746 COLLINS *Ode, Manners* 78 O Nature boon,..The Sports and I this hour agree, To rove thy scene-full world with thee.

scenery ('siːnərɪ). [Alteration of SCENARY, as if f. SCENE + -ERY. The word is not in Johnson, who gives only SCENARY.]

† **1.** Dramatic action; a moving exhibition of feeling. *Obs.*

1748 RICHARDSON *Clarissa* VII. 213 When he opened it, never was such a piece of scenery. He trembled like a devil at receiving it: Fumbled at the seal, his fingers in a palsy. **1808** SYD. SMITH *Peter Plymley's Lett.* iii. Wks. 1859 II. 144/2 If there were any great scenery, and heroic feelings, any blaze of ancient virtue, any exalted death, any termination of England that would be ever remembered, ever honoured in that western world, where liberty is now retiring, conquest would be more tolerable, and ruin more sweet.

2. a. The decoration of a theatre-stage, consisting of painted hangings, slides, etc., representing the scene of the action; theatre-scenes collectively. Also, that used in film and television.

1774 *Lond. Mag.* Nov. 518/2 It is said that the scenery only, which has been painted on purpose for the *Maid of the Oaks*, cost 1500 l. **1789** TWINING *Aristotle's Treat. Poetry* I. 72 Sophocles increased the number of actors to three, and added the decoration of painted scenery. **1837** J. F. COOPER *England* (ed. 2) III. 97 The chief merit [of the play] was the scenery. **1890** *All Year Round* 29 Mar. 306 The dangers of flying flats and rolling scenery. **1959** W. S. SHARPS *Dict. Cinematogr.* 127/1 *Scenery*, the various parts and accessories used on the set to represent the actual scene of an action. **1960** O. SKILBECK *ABC of Film & TV* 11 Scenery which may be viewed in close-up must be more convincing than that of the theatre. **1961** G. MILLERSON *Technique Television Production* 142 By special electronic equipment, we can place one camera's performers and/or scenery in the background picture provided by another picture source.

b. *transf.* and *fig.* So phr. ***part of the scenery***.

1770 BURKE *Pres. Discont.* 12 To recommend this system to the people, a perspective view of the Court, gorgeously painted,..was exhibited to the gaping multitude... The whole scenery was exactly disposed to captivate those good souls, whose [etc.]. **1774** J. ADAMS *Diary* 9 Oct., Wks. (1850) II. 395 Went..to the Romish chapel... The scenery and the music are so calculated to take in mankind, that I wonder the Reformation ever succeeded. **1835** DICKENS *Sk. Boz, Tales, Mr. W. Tottle* ii, 'Take off the covers, Martha,' said Mrs. Parsons, directing the shifting of the scenery with great anxiety. **1867** F. D. MAURICE *Patriarchs & Law-givers* vi. (ed. 4) 120 However shifting the scenery of a man's life may have been. **1876** GEO. ELIOT *Dan. Der.* xxix, Gwendolen was just then enjoying the scenery of her life. **1970** N. MARSH *When in Rome* viii. 221 He..must often hang about the premises... Part of the scenery as it were. **1971** 'H. CALVIN' *Poison Chasers* v. 65 Dai had mentioned her to me as an interesting part of the local scenery. **1977** *Times* 4 July 12/4 Inexperienced Mabel..was allowed to sing the old things in harmony. I was, at first, only part of the scenery.

3. a. The general appearance of a place and its natural features, regarded from the picturesque point of view; the aggregate of picturesque features in a landscape.

1784 COWPER *Task* v. 741 He looks abroad into the varied field Of nature, and..Calls the delightful scen'ry all his own. His are the mountains, and the vallies his. **1801** CAMPBELL *Hohenlinden* 8 But Linden saw another sight When the drum beat at dead of night, Commanding fires of death to light The darkness of her scenery. **1837** LOCKHART *Scott* I. viii. 265 He was so enraptured with the scenery of the lakes as to take a house in Keswick. **1871** MOZLEY *Univ. Serm.* vi. (1876) 124 A kind of passion for scenery and natural beauty..has..gained an extraordinary power over people's minds. **1881** FROUDE *Short Stud.* (1883) IV. II. iii. 194 Anyone with a well-stored memory is affected by historical scenery.

b. with defining word prefixed. Also applied to the varied aspect of clouds and sky.

1820 W. IRVING *Sketch Bk.* I. 124 The magnificence of English park scenery. **1858** HAWTHORNE *Fr. & It. Note-bks.* II. 48 The entire cloud and sun scenery was fully presented to us. **1897** *Outing* (U.S.) 440/2 One of the most impressive pictures of tree-scenery that man ever beheld.

†**c.** Picturesqueness. *Obs. rare.*

1786 SIR J. REYNOLDS *Disc.* xiii. Wks. 1797 I. 287 As such buildings depart from regularity, they now and then acquire something of scenery by this accident.

4. (With *a* and *pl.*) A landscape or view; a picturesque scene; also, the pictorial representation of a landscape. Now *rare*.

1777 J. FORSTER *Voy. round World* II. 367 The pleasure of contemplating a great variety of rich sceneries, made us some amends for the wretchedness of our diet. **1794** A. YOUNG *Trav. France* I. 83 A very little cleaning would make here a delicious scenery. **1814** *Sporting Mag.* XLIV. 66 Beautiful Indian sceneries from the skilful hand and unsophisticated pallet of this worthy academician. **1851** CARLYLE *Sterling* III. iv, At Naples next,..was due admiration of the sceneries and antiquities. **1879** DIXON *Windsor* I. i. 3 The houses of famous men, the sceneries of great events.

'scene-shifter. One who shifts and arranges the scenes during the performance of a play.

1752 JOHNSON *Adventurer* No. 3 ¶9 Half a dozen scene-shifters. **1760-2** GOLDSM. *Cit. W.* xcvii, The scene-shifter's whistle. **1887** 'EDNA LYALL' *Knt.-Errant* (1889) 144 Behind the scenes the very scene-shifters and carpenters were eager to congratulate him. **1908** [see LEGIT., LEGIT]. **1957** L. DURRELL *Justine* II. 102 Quick as a scene-shifter the station packs away advertisement after advertisement. **1978** *Lancashire Life* Apr. 35/3 A saviour came in the shape of little Alfie Gee—part-time electrician and scene-shifter... 'Shuffle off the stage sideways,' he whispered, 'and don't drop it, man.'

fig. **1903** LD. R. GOWER *Rec. & Remin.* 92 When once the Great Scene-Shifter has made his final call, which none can disobey.

So **'scene-shifting** *vbl. sb.*

1818 LADY MORGAN *Autobiog.* (1859) 212 The.. mechanical aids of science and scene-shifting. **1882** *Macm. Mag.* XLVI. 330/2 The unwonted silence of the scene-shifting.

scenic ('siːnɪk, 'sɛnɪk), *a.* Also 7 **scenicke, schenick, 7–8 scenick.** [a. F. *scénique* (14th c.), ad. L. *scēnic-us*, *scænic-us*, a. Gr. σκηνικός belonging to the stage, theatrical, f. σκηνή SCENE.]

1. a. Of or belonging to the stage, dramatic, theatrical.

scenic poet = L. *poeta scenicus*. *scenic games* = L. *ludi scenici* (dramatic entertainments, as distinguished from athletic sports).

1623 H. HOLLAND in *Shaks. fol.*, Upon the Lines and Life of the Famous Scenicke Poet, Master William Shakespeare. **1640** R. BAILLIE *Canterb. Self-convict.* Postscr. 3 Any who had perused your former schenick writs, that comedie of your seven Sages. **1728** CHAMBERS *Cycl.*, *Scenic Games* or *Representations*. **1781** WARTON *Hist. Eng. Poetry* III. 200 The ridicule of scenic exhibition. **1796** MORSE *Amer. Geog.* II. 186 Ireland now produces a catalogue of celebrated scenic writers. **1809** MALKIN *Gil Blas* XII. ii. (Rtldg.) 425 She is all that..veteran managers seek when they sign articles, in scenic qualifications. **1869** TOZER *Highl. Turkey* II. 201 These scenic edifices are amongst the most interesting..remains that have come down..from antiquity. **1879** H. PHILLIPS *Addit. Notes Coins* 18 A scenic mask of Pan.

b. Represented on the stage.

1747 JOHNSON *Prol. Opening Drury Lane* 61 Bid scenick virtue form the rising age, And truth diffuse her radiance from the stage. **1838** T. MITCHELL *Clouds of Aristoph.* 360 (note) The scenic Socrates here folds his arms. **1868** WHYTE MELVILLE *White Rose* lix. III. 237 The long-drawn aisles of its scenic cathedral had been darkened so skilfully, as to convey an idea of dim religious grandeur, and vast architectural space.

c. Fitted for the stage.

1857 DE QUINCEY *Bentley* Wks. VI. 176 *note*, The most popular and *scenic* of the Shaksperian dramas.

d. Of or belonging to stage-scenery or stage effect.

1824 R. HUMPHREYS *Mem. J. Decastro* 16 It is that [part] of the scenic department from whence the borders of chambers or clouds drop, to complete each different scene. **1827** J. BOADEN *Mem. Mrs. Siddons* II. xix. 292 A benefit proportioned to the pains that have been taken in the scenic department of our stages. **1854** C. A. MOWATT *Autobiography of Actress* 48 Costumes and rehearsals and scenic effects. **1868** WHYTE MELVILLE *White Rose* lviii. III. 230 It is the great scenic triumph of the play, and a burst of grand music appropriately heralds its exhibition to the audience. **1882** FARRAR *Early Chr.* 9 The Drama had degenerated into a vehicle for the display of scenic splendour or ingenious machinery. **1889** HAIGH *Attic Theatre* iii. §7. 139 As changes of scene were almost unknown in the Greek drama, the scenic appliances were of the simplest character.

e. ***scenic artist***, a painter or designer of scenery for the stage. orig. *U.S.*

1840 *Spirit of Times* 21 Nov. 456/3 C. L. Smith..is the scenic artist of the Theatre. **1877** W. R. ALGER *Life Edwin Forrest* II. 581 John Wiser, a scenic artist, arranged and painted it. **1919** G. B. SHAW *Great Catherine* 114 It was quite easy for Patiomkin to humbug Catherine as to the condition of Russia by conducting her through sham cities run up for the occasion by scenic artists. **1930** SELDEN & SELLMAN *Stage Scenery & Lighting* ii. 31 Before the scenic artist can start to make scenery it is necessary that he learn thoroughly the form of scenery. **1971** BURRIS-MEYER & COLE *Scenery for Theatre* (rev. ed.) ii. 22 The designer is a member of the scenic artists' union.

2. *fig.* Resembling, or likened to, stage representation and stage effect; dramatic or theatrical in style.

1857 MRS. MATHEWS *Tea-Table Talk* I. 85 Her charities were wide,..often spontaneous, though perhaps somewhat scenic. **1863** KINGLAKE *Crimea* (1876) I. xiv. 226 He was impelled to be contriving scenic effects and surprises. **1870** J. H. NEWMAN *Gramm. Assent* I. iv. 93 Christianity is a history supernatural, and almost scenic. **1878** R. H. HUTTON *Scott* ii. 19 The lad began his study of the scenic side of history.

3. a. Of or belonging to natural scenery. In recent use: Abounding in fine scenery, affording landscape views. Also, of a window or the like: designed to afford a landscape view. Now chiefly *N. Amer.*

1842 DICKENS *Amer. Notes* xv, The country round this town being very flat, is bare of scenic interest. **1906** *Scribner's Mag.* July 87/1 The Grand Trunk Pacific..will be a scenic line. **1937** *Discovery* Oct. 306/2 Small-holders in scenic areas. **1967** *Boston Sunday Herald* 26 Mar. VI. 3/1 (Advt.), See the scenic glories of our great continent. **1970** *Globe & Mail* (Toronto) 26 Sept. 30/1 (Advt.), The Canadian, one of the world's great trains... Soft music. Air conditioning... Scenic Domes.. all the way. **1971** *New Yorker* 9 Oct. 170/3 (Advt.), Golf on scenic course. **1978** *N.Y. Times* 30 Mar. B17/2 (Advt.), Floor to ceiling scenic windows.

b. Applied to a road that has been planned and landscaped so as to provide fine views. orig. and chiefly *N. Amer.*

1914 H. MACNAIR (*title*) Scenic motorway; a motor tour de luxe. **1916** *Road Maps & Tour Bk. Western N. Carolina* (N. Carolina Good Roads Assoc.) 149 The Asheville–Murphy Scenic Highway through Swain County will afford scenery unsurpassed by any section of the country. **1934** *Popular Mechanics* Aug. 238/1 The modern de luxe highway cruiser..may take you and your baggage safely and inexpensively anywhere along historic and scenic highways. **1935** *Nature Mag.* Mar. 101 Let us hope that there will be a policy of scenic road construction. **1943** J. S. HUXLEY *TVA* ix. 60 The Norris Freeway..is a scenic highway on which access is limited to a very few points, and where no building is allowed within several hundred yards on either side. **1959** W. B. SNOW *Highway & Landscape* 111 For specialized types of highway, scenic parkways particularly, the national standards may not always be entirely appropriate. **1967** *Boston Sunday Herald* 26 Mar. II. 9/1 A 7·4-mile Appleton Ridge Scenic Drive became a women's project in 1966. The women got the town to bulldoze the rough spots on a dirt road, cut bushes to open up magnificent views, and provide a stretch for 'slow drivers who really want to enjoy the scenery'. **1979** D. CLARK *Heberden's Seat* i. 7 Masters had suggested that they should find a scenic route and take their time.

4. a. With reference to painting or sculpture: Representing a 'scene' or incident in which several persons are concerned.

1845 *Punch* VIII. 247/1 To criticise a Picture by Stanfield. —Begin by unqualified praise; then commence detracting, ..on the score of..'scenic effect of the figures'; and conclude by a wish he had never been a scene-painter. **1848** MRS. JAMESON *Sacr. & Leg. Art* II. 159 The 'Martyrdom of St. Laurence' by Baccio Bandinelli the sculptor, is arranged as a scenic bas-relief. **1850** —— *Leg. Monast. Ord.* 390 The most perfect scenic picture in the world. **1890** C. H. MOORE *Gothic Archit.* x. 307 There is far less antagonism between what is decorative and what is scenic in painting than is sometimes supposed.

b. With reference to wallpaper: creating a continuous scene or landscape on the walls of a room.

1924 N. MCCLELLAND *Historic Wall-Papers* xii. 279 (*heading*) Some famous scenic papers and their owners. **1929** C. C. OMAN *Victoria & Albert Museum: Catal. Wall-Papers* 63 The earliest scenic wall-papers..were produced by hand-painting. **1951** L. & W. KATZENBACH *Pract. Bk. Amer. Wallpaper* vi. 61 This scenic wallpaper pictures a tropic Haiti. **1976** *National Observer* (U.S.) 25 Sept. 9/1 Now about all that remains is the neon-red carpet and 'scenic' wallpaper that once surrounded a bathtub.

scenic ('siːnɪk), *sb.* [f. the adj.] **1.** = SCENE 6 *fig.* *rare*[−1].

1891 G. MEREDITH *One of Our Conquerors* III. vi. 125 She passed into music, as she always did under motion of carriages and trains, whether in happiness or sadness: and the day being one that had a sky, the scenic of music swung her up to soar.

2. A scenic film or photograph; a film or photograph the subject of which is natural scenery.

1918 *N.Y. Times* 25 Nov. 11/3 Robert C. Bruce has a scenic at the Rivoli entitled 'A Wee Bit Odd', which is entertaining pictorially in spite of labored wit in the subtitles. **1922** *Ibid.* 2 July VI. 3/3 The short comedies, scenics, travel films and other so-called non-dramatic productions are so much better than the photoplays when they are at all good. **1971** *Amateur Photographer* 3 Mar. 23/1 A cine columnist's thoughts thankfully turn from the interiors he had intended to shoot..to the spring scenic he has for years been intending to make... I like scenics and am not put off by objections that they are old-fashioned... So are trees and meadows. **1979** *SLR Camera* June 56/2 Scenics, particularly townscapes, at night are best shot while there is still some tone in the sky.

3. Short for 'scenic wallpaper' (see SCENIC *a.* 4 b).

1951 L. & W. KATZENBACH *Pract. Bk. Amer. Wallpaper* vi. 65 While the composition of this scenic is traditional, it is executed in a technique that is distinctly modern. **1966** M. M. PEGLER *Dict. Interior Design* (1967) 393 *Scenic*, a wallpaper mural usually made up of three or four panels that create a continuous scene, vista, or design. **1972** E. A. ENTWHISTLE *French Scenic Wallpapers 1800–1860* v. 35 *Les Monuments de Paris*..was different from most of the other scenics. **1976** B. GREYSMITH *Wallpaper* 92 The most striking examples of the new French manner were the 'scenics', the term used to describe *trompe l'oeil* landscapes on a grand scale, not repeating but creating a complete scene around the walls of a room.

4. Short for SCENIC RAILWAY.

1968 D. BRAITHWAITE *Fairground Architecture* viii. 125 In structural form there was little difference between the 'Scenic' and the earlier switchback.

5. A scenic pattern or design.

1977 *Chicago Tribune* 2 Oct. v. 9 (Advt.), Make slipcovers, draperies of 100% cotton prints in florals, scenics, geometrics.

scenical ('siːnɪkəl, 'sɛnɪkəl), *a.* Also 5 **scenicalle**, 6–7 **scenicall**, 7 **scænical(l**, **scenecal**. [f. L. *scēnic-us* SCENIC + -AL[1].]

1. Of or belonging to the stage; = SCENIC *a.* 1.

scenical games, plays, †*disports* = L. *ludi scenici* (see SCENIC *a.* 1).

1432-50 tr. *Higden* (Rolls) IV. 101 This..institucion off disportes scenicalle [L. *Ista institutio ludorum scenicorum*]. **1579** NORTHBROOKE *Dicing* (1843) 97 Your bishops.. hath forbidden and prohibited those kynde of scenicall and enterlude playes. **1621** BURTON *Anat. Mel.* II. ii. VI. iv. (1624) 251 Vse honest and chast sports, scenicall shewes, playes. **1623** MIDDLETON & ROWLEY *Sp. Gipsy* III. i. 57 The scenical school Has been my tutor long in Italy. **1749** FIELDING *Tom Jones* VII. i, Those scenical representations, which Thespis is first reported to have invented. **1823** DE QUINCEY *Lett. on Educ.* iv. Wks. 1860 XIV. 75 Each steps forward as a scenical person, to play a distinct part or character. **1890** *Spectator* 2 Aug., If scenical representation affects us more powerfully than actual suffering, must not the influence of the theatre be, on the whole, harmful to character?

b. with special reference to stage-scenery.

1791-1823 D'ISRAELI *Cur. Lit.* (1858) III. 9 These scenical effects existed in great perfection in the Masques. **1884** SYMONDS *Shaks. Predec.* viii. (1900) 233 The absence of scenical appeals to the sense of sight.

2. *fig.* **a.** (Chiefly in bad sense.) Resembling, or likened to, stage-representation and stage-illusion; theatrical in style.

a **1563** BECON *Compar. Lord's Supper & Mass* Wks. III. 97 b, The Massemonger handlyng hys scenicall and stage-lyke Supper, calleth vpon the dead very busyly. **1622** PEACHAM *Compl. Gent.* vi. (1634) 42 That same ampullous and scenicall pompe, with empty furniture of phrase, where-with the Stage, and our petty Poeticke Pamphlets sound so big. **1833** COLERIDGE *Table T.* 15 Aug., In Gibbon ..nothing is real, vivid, true: all is scenical, and, as it were, exhibited by candlelight. **1845** J. MARTINEAU *Ess.* (1890) I. 235 If the universe and God set the example of being scenical, what shall hinder religion from becoming histrionic?

†**b.** Fictitious, pretended; illusory, imaginary; not real or genuine. *Obs.*

(Cf. Florus II. xiv. §4 *Invictusque a veris regibus, ab illo imaginario et scenico rege superatur.*)

1610 HEALEY *St. Aug. Citie of God* VI. vii. 245 Therefore this fabulous, scænicall, filthy and ridiculous diuinity [orig. *theologia fabulosa, theatrica, scenica*] hath al reference vnto the ciuill. **1643** SIR T. BROWNE *Relig. Med.* II. (near end), These scenical and accidental differences between us, cannot make me forget that common and untoucht part of us both. **1660** FULLER *Mixt Contempl.* II. xli. 60 King Hen. the seventh was much troubled (as he was wont to say) with Idols, Scenecal Royaletts, poor petty, pittifull Persons, who pretended themselves Princes. **1709** STEELE *Tatler* No. 167 ¶4, I..who look upon the Distinctions amongst Men to be meerly Scenical.

c. Resembling a stage-scene.

a **1706** EVELYN *True Relig.* (1850) I. vii. §2. 363 Many things and actions they speak of as having done, which they did no otherwise than in prophetic vision and scenical imagery. **1741** WARBURTON *Div. Legat.* II. 485 The scenical image of Job and his friends sitting together on the ground seven days and seven nights without a word speaking. **1832** DE QUINCEY *Charlemagne* Wks. V. 354 The second form [of History] is that which may be styled the Scenical.

scenically (ˈsiːn-, ˈsɛnɪkəlɪ), *adv.* [f. prec. + -LY².] In a scenic or scenical manner.

1650 A. B. *Mutat. Polemo* 2 He must now act a Kings part more Scenically. **1689** J. HOWE in H. Rogers *Life* (1836) 384 The prayers were also read but carelessly, sleepily, or scenically, flauntingly, and with manifest irreverence. **1890** H. ELLIS *Ibsen's Pillars of Soc.*, etc. Pref. 7 They [the Scandinavians] possess..a stage on which great literary works may be performed, and the burning questions of the modern world be scenically resolved.

scenic railway (ˈsiːnɪk ˈreɪlweɪ). [f. SCENIC *a.* + RAILWAY *sb.*] A switchback or miniature railway running through artificial representations of beautiful or spectacular scenery, as an attraction at fairs, etc.

1894 *Official Guide Calif. Midwinter Exposition* 130 (*heading*) Scenic railway. *Ibid.*, It must not be supposed that gravity alone is the motive power in the Scenic Railway. **1908** *Westm. Gaz.* 6 July 2/2 The Scenic Railway at the Exhibition. **1917** *Jrnl. Exper. Psychol.* II. 158 The popularity of such amusements as 'scenic railways', the sole attraction of which lies in the fright on the steep inclines, suggests that fear may be pleasant—at least retrospectively. **1923** H. C. WITWER in *Cosmopolitan* Aug. 46/1 You're a woman, a good looker with more curves than a scenic railway. **1926** T. E. LAWRENCE *Seven Pillars* (1935) III. xxxii. 184 About their crests ran narrow veins of granite-coloured stone, generally in pairs, following the contour of the skyline like the rusted metals of an abandoned scenic railway. **1930** E. WAUGH *Labels* 200 There were switch-backs and scenic railways on which empty cars swooped and swerved through breath-taking descents. **1968** [see GALLOPER 1 b]. **1973** 'M. INNES' *Appleby's Answer* iii. 33 Shaftesbury Avenue..was like going through a 'scenic' railway in a Brobdingnagian fun-fair. **1980** *Times* 4 Oct. 12/8 One of the sights worth seeing was the drunks on the new 60 mph 'Super-looping' scenic railway.

Scenicruiser (ˈsiːnɪˌkruːzə(r)). *U.S.* Also with small initial. [f. SCENI(C *a.* + CRUISER.] The proprietary name of a line of luxury coaches equipped for long-distance travel, esp. for touring areas of scenic beauty.

1954 *Business Week* 17 July 33/2 Greyhound is wagering heavily that the Scenicruiser will rejuvenate its business. **1955** *American Mag.* Jan. 92/2 We were riding in a new Greyhound 'Scenicruiser'. **1959** *Official Gaz.* (U.S. Patent Office) 13 Jan. TM77/2 The Greyhound Corporation, Chicago...Scenicruiser. **1965** M. BRADBURY *Stepping Westward* viii. 403 They ate fast..and returned to the scenicruiser. **1974** *Encycl. Brit. Macropædia* XVIII. 721/2 The Sceni cruiser introduced in the United States in 1954 for trans-continental use..utilizes air suspension and has six wheels. **1976** *Yellowstone Explorer* July 8/1 (*heading*) Scenicruiser mini voyages. *Ibid.*, Your captain will keep you posted as the scenicruiser glides along.

†**'scenish**, *a. Obs.* [f. SCENE + -ISH.] Scenic.

1540 PALSGR. *Acolastus* Prol. Bij, In this scenyshe apparaylynge [L. *In apparatu scaenico*], i. the settying forth or trymming of our scenes, that is to saye (our places appoynted for our players to come forth of).

scenist (ˈsiːnɪst). ? *Obs.* [f. SCENE + -IST.] One who has to do with stage-scenery: **a.** A scene-shifter; **b.** a scene-painter.

1803 *Pic Nic* No. 8 (1806) II. 43 The scenists and machinists are their patrons. **1826** *Blackw. Mag.* XX. 57 The reader must make the same allowances for such deficiency, as are granted to the scenist, or decorator of the drama.

scenite (ˈsiːnaɪt). *rare.* [ad. L. *scēnītes*, a. Gr. σκηνίτης, f. σκηνή tent: see -ITE. Cf. F. *scénite* (adj.).] One who dwells in a tent; a member of a nomad tribe dwelling in tents.

1607 TOPSELL *Four-f. Beasts* 678 The Arabian Scenites neuer eate hereof. **1728** MORGAN *Algiers* I. i. 10 The Sabæan Arabs, like all other Nomades or Scenites.

b. *attrib.* or *adj.*

1752 CHAMBERS *Cycl.* s.v. *Ambulatory*, The itinerant or scenite life is the life of nature. **1844** G. S. FABER *Eight Dissert.* (1845) II. 370 A scenite breeder of cattle.

scenograph (ˈsiːnəʊgrɑːf, -æ-). *rare*⁻¹. [ad. Gr. σκηνογράφ-ος, f. σκηνή SCENE + γράφ-ειν to write, draw, paint.] = next.

1842 WORNUM in *Smith's Dict. Grk. & Rom. Antiq.* s.v. *Painting* §10 Clisthenes of Eretria is mentioned as architect and scenograph.

scenographer (siːˈnɒgrəfə(r)). [Formed as prec. + -ER¹.] A scene-painter; one who draws buildings, etc. in perspective.

1598 R. HAYDOCKE tr. *Lomazzo* II. 199 Astronomers, Scenographers, Makers of glasses. **1669** E. CHAMBERLAYNE *Pres. St. Eng.* (ed. 2) 267 Scenographer, or Designer of Prospects. **1850** LEITCH tr. *C.O. Müller's Anc. Art* §107 (ed. 2) 75 An architect and scenographer called Cleisthenes.

scenographic (siːnəʊˈgræfɪk), *a.* Also 8 scheno-. [a. F. *scénographique* or ad. Gr. σκηνογραφικ-ός, f. σκηνογράφ-ος SCENOGRAPH.] Of or belonging to scenography, scene-painting, or drawing in perspective.

1670 MOXON *Pract. Perspective* 2 There be two sorts of Ichnographies named in this Book, viz. the Geometrick Ichnographie, and the Scenographick Ichnographie. **1704** J. HARRIS *Lex. Techn.* I. s.v. *Scenography*, The Scenographick appearance of any Figure, Body, or Building. **1719** B. TAYLOR *Princ. Linear Perspective* 6 The Representation of any Object is no other than its Schenographic Projection on the Plane of the Picture. *c* **1780** BARRY *Lect. Art* v. (1848) 202 The scenographic part of optics examines how the drawings of edifices should be drawn. **1813** T. BUSBY *Lucretius* II. IV. *Comm.* p. xxi, The information of the sense goes no further than to the scenographic existence of the object. **1850** LEITCH tr. *C.O. Müller's Anc. Art* §184 (ed. 2) 167 Scenographic pictures, in which illusion was the highest aim, were also employed at the games.

b. quasi-*sb.* in *pl.* The principles of perspective.

1761 KIRBY *Persp. Archit.* I. i. 2/1 The doctrine of projection may..be considered as consisting of three distinct branches,..viz. Orthographics, stereographics, and scenographics, commonly stiled Perspective.

Hence **sceno'graphical** *a.* = SCENOGRAPHIC. **sceno'graphically** *adv.*

1703 T. N. *City & C. Purchaser* 60 More than one Face may be represented in one Diagram Scenographically. **1729** SHELVOCKE *Artillery* IV. 207 The oblique lines, upon the one and the other Scenographical Figure.

scenography (siːˈnɒgrəfɪ). Also 7 **-graphie, senography,** 8 **scheno-,** 9 **skenography.** [a. F. *scénographie* (16th c. *schenographie* in Littré) or ad. L. *scēnographia*, a. Gr. σκηνογραφία, f. σκηνή: see SCENE and -GRAPHY.]

†**1.** The representation of a building or other object in perspective; a perspective elevation.

Distinguished from ICHNOGRAPHY and ORTHOGRAPHY.

1645 *Enchir. Fortif.* Table (at end), *Scenographie*, is the modell or draught of any work presented with its shadowes, ..with its dimensions according to the Rules of Prospective. **1659** LEAK *Waterwks.* 33 The Senography or Perspective. **1705** GREENHILL *Embalming* 203 We shall..here only represent to you the Ichnography and Schenography of the antient Burial-Places of the Egyptians. **1843** *Civil Eng. & Arch. Jrnl.* VI. 131/1 The idea of the scenography, or view in perspective, taken on the angle.

2. Scene-painting (in ancient Greece).

1738 J. HAMILTON *Stereogr.* I. VII. ii. 370 Scenography is the Art of Painting on several Planes or Scenes at different Distances, and in various Positions with respect to the Eye, in such Manner, that all those different Scenes..may.. represent one intire View. Let *QYSZ* represent the Room intended for a Theatre. **1848** WORNUM *Lect. Paint. Barry*, etc. 201 *note*, Perspective scenery (scenography) was introduced on the Greek stage as early as the time of Æschylus. **1903** tr. *Mantzius Hist. Theat. Art* I. 131 Aristotle states..that Sophocles introduced skenography.

‖**Sceno'pegia.** In 4 s(c)eno-, **synofegia.** Also 8 anglicized **scenopegy.** [L. *scēnopēgia*, a. Gr. σκηνοπηγία, f. σκηνή SCENE + πηγνύναι to fix. Cf. F. *scénopégie.*] The Jewish Feast of Tabernacles.

c **1380** WYCLIF *Sel. Wks.* II. 103 A feste of Jewes, þat þei clepen Senofegia [*v.r.* synofegia]. **1382** —— *John* vii. 2 Scenofegia [**1388** Senofegia]. **1728** CHAMBERS *Cycl.* s.v. *Tent*, The Scenopegy or Feast of Tabernacles.

scent (sɛnt), *sb.* Forms: 4–7 (9 *rare*) sent, 5–6 sente, 6 cent, 7– scent. [ME. *sent*, f. *sent* SCENT *v.*

Orig. a term of hunting. It is possible that there may have been an AF. *sent, verbal noun from *sentir* to scent.]

1. a. The faculty or sense of smell. Chiefly, and now exclusively, with reference to animals (esp. dogs) which find their prey or recognize objects by this sense.

c **1470** HENRY *Wallace* v. 26 In Gyllisland thar was that brachell brede, Sekyr off sent to folow thaim at flede. **1596** DALRYMPLE tr. *Leslie's Hist. Scot.* I. 20 Fisches lurking amang the stanes thay [*sc.* dogs] seik out with thair sent. **1642** JER. TAYLOR *God's Judgem.* II. vii. 110 He had all the Aromaticks and Odoriferous Perfumes to delight his sent in smelling. **1735** SOMERVILLE *Chase* I. 94 The perfect Hound, in Scent and Speed Unrivall'd. **1784** COWPER *Task* III. 621 The sight is pleas'd The scent regal'd. **1875** JOWETT *Plato* (ed. 2) IV. 277 The dog, having the help of scent as well as of sight, is superior to the savage.

b. *fig.*

1590 NASHE *Pasquil's Apol.* I. Wks. (Grosart) I. 218 It may be I am of some better sente then you take me for, and finding a Machiauellian tricke in this plot..I was [etc.]. **1812** *Sporting Mag.* XXXIX. 237 An eminent Evangelical Divine..long celebrated for the keenness of his scent in 'legacy hunting'. **1838** PRESCOTT *Ferd. & Is.* (1846) I. i. 104 The courtiers, with the quick scent of their own interest,.. soon turned their attention to the same polite studies. **1857** J. G. HOLLAND *Bay Path* xxvi. 315 All of them had a scent for heresy so subtle and acute that [etc.].

¶**c.** In etymological sense: Perception by the senses, feeling. *Obs.* (? *nonce-uses.*)

14.. HOCCLEVE *Jereslaus' Wife* 850 And ther-to eek as sharp punisshement As þat dyuyse ther kowde any wight, Thow sholdest han y-preeued by the sent. **1590** SPENSER *F.Q.* I. i. 43 He bids thee to him send for his intent A fit false dreame, that can delude the sleepers sent.

2. a. The odour of an animal or man as a means of pursuit by a hound; hence a track or trail as indicated by this odour.

cold scent: see COLD *a.* 12. *hot scent*: see HOT *a.* 8 a.

1375 BARBOUR *Bruce* VI. 500 [The sleuthhund] hym luffit swa, That fra he mycht anys feill The kyngis sent..he vald change it for na thyng. *c* **1400** *Master of Game* (MS. Digby 182) i. 7 b, For the fous of somme hares is of hotter sent thenne some. *c* **1470** HENRY *Wallace* v. 141 The sloith stoppyt..Rycht wa thai [*sc.* the Englishmen] war that losyt was thair sent. **1576** TURBERV. *Hunting* xiv. 36 When they haue well beaten and founde the tracke or sent of the Harte. **1596** SHAKS. *Tam. Shr.* Induct. i. 24 He [*sc.* a hound]..twice to day pick'd out the dullest sent. **1686** BLOME *Gentl. Recr.* II. 88/2 When one or more of them [*sc.* foxhounds] opens, 'tis a sure sign that he is upon the Scent. **1693** *Humours Town* 8 It would be to as little purpose to seek you, as to follow the Chace upon a wrong Scent. **1726** DEFOE *Hist. Devil* II. ii. (1840) 190 We can follow as hounds do a fox upon a hot scent. **1774** GOLDSM. *Nat. Hist.* (1776) III. 329 What adds to this entertainment is the strong scent which the fox leaves, that always keeps up a full cry. **1885** *Field* 7 Feb. 147/2 Once in the open, it was obvious that there was only half a scent. **1897** *Encycl. Sport* I. 583/1 *Scent*—The odour given off by the fox... It is *burning* if..strong; *breast-high*, if so good that the hounds do not stoop to it; *moving*, if it is so fresh that it must be recent..; *flighty* or *catchy*, if variable; *holding*, if good enough, but not very strong.

b. *fig.*

1601 SHAKS. *Twel. N.* II. v. 134 He is now at a cold sent. **1605** VERSTEGAN *Dec. Intell.* ii. 30 His tale..hath as plain a sent as a man need to wish, to fynd out a fable by. **1656** HEYLIN *Extran. Vapulans* 15 Follow this Game a little further, now we are on the sents. *a* **1715** BURNET *Own Time* (1766) II. 144 The scent of preferment will draw aspiring men after it. **1765** STERNE *Tr. Shandy* IV. xviii, Trim found he was upon a wrong scent. **1872** *Q. Rev.* Jan. 267 Another false scent by which the Proletariat have long been led astray is that [etc.].

c. *transf.* in the game of *Hare-and-hounds*: Fragments of paper scattered on the ground by the 'hares' to serve as a track for the 'hounds'.

1857 HUGHES *Tom Brown* I. vii, It's the turn of our house to find scent for..Hare-and-Hounds.

d. Phrases. ***to follow*** (or rarely ***pursue***) ***the scent, to get*** (***a*** or ***the***) ***scent of, to have*** (***a***) ***scent of,*** lit. and fig. ***to lay, put*** (hounds) ***on or upon the scent;*** hence fig. ***to put*** (a person) ***on*** or ***off the scent,*** also ***on a false, wrong scent. to lose, recover the scent,*** lit. (of hounds) and fig.; also, ***to lose the scent,*** (of the game) to baffle the hounds by passing through water. ***to carry a*** or ***the scent,*** (of ground) to retain the scent of the game; also (of fox-hounds) to follow the scent. †***full scent*** (advb.): ? of a hound, excited by the perception of the scent (in quot. *transf.*).

? *a* **1400** *Morte Arth.* 1040 Bot thow moste seke more southe..ffor he [*sc.* the giant] wille hafe sent hym selfe sex myle large. **14..** HOCCLEVE *Jereslaus' Wife* 272 [There was] An Erl..Beforn whos howndes was a fox rennynge,..And as þat they ran they hadden a sent Of the lady and thidir be they went. **1655** *Nicholas Papers* (Camden) II. 350 This is to let my Sec. Ni. know that I am still close following the same sent. **1683** TEMPLE *Mem.* Wks. 1731 I. 399 All further Thoughts of a present Peace ended, and left me only to pursue the cold Scent of a Mediation in the common Forms. **1688** in *Phil. Trans.* XVII. (1693) 784 One day there came three or four full sent to tell me they were certain they smelt the Pines. **1711** *Spect.* No. 116 ¶5 He immediately called in the Dogs, and put them upon the Scent. **1722** DE FOE *Col. Jack* (1840) 51 He had got a scent of it. **1730–46** THOMSON *Autumn* 446 Oft in the full-descending flood he [the stag] tries To lose the scent. **1781** [see LAY *v.*¹ 15 h]. **1821** SCOTT *Kenilw.* vii, 'Thou hast lost the scent, said Varney, 'of thy comrade Tressilian.' **1832** *John Bull* 26 Nov. 379/2 The hounds were for some time at fault. They soon, however, recovered the scent. **1832** 'NIMROD in *Q. Rev.* Mar. 219 The scent being seldom sufficient to enable the hound to carry it up to his [*sc.* the fox's] kennel. **1862** MISS BRADDON *Lady Audley* xxx, How if she..wished to throw my poor friend off the scent by this false announcement? **1878** 'BROOKSBY' *Hunting Countries* I. 8 The surrounding country being strongly fenced, and carrying a good scent, a bad hunter is of little use here. **1882** AINGER *Lamb* vi. 116 Lamb had a love of..putting his readers on a false scent. **1884** L. J. JENNINGS *Croker Papers* I. iii. 77 The police..had got scent of the intended affray.

3. In wider sense: Distinctive odour. Now almost exclusively applied to agreeable odours, e.g. those of flowers.

1471 CAXTON *Recuyell* (Sommer) I. 41 Every man rose fro the table abhorryng & eschewyng the sente and sauour of the dede man. **1509** HAWES *Past. Pleas.* IV. iv. (1555) C ij b, And in my mouthe, it had a marueylous cent Of dyuers spyces. **1591** SYLVESTER *Du Bartas* I. v. 148 The fragrant sents of flowry banks. **1635** STAFFORD *Fem. Glory* (1869) 116 It is impossible to handle perfumes, without bearing away part of their sent. **1718** POPE *Iliad* VI. 359 Her rich Wardrobe.. Where treasur'd Odors breath'd a costly Scent. **1774** GOLDSM. *Nat. Hist.* (1776) II. 226 The Negroe nations..of Guinea..have an insupportable scent. **1826** KIRBY & SP. *Entomol.* IV. 140 There is scarcely a scent odious or agreeable that may not be met with in the insect world. **1862** LONGF. *Wayside Inn* I. Prol. 195 His garments breathed a spicy scent Of cinnamon and sandal blent.

fig. *a*1586 SIDNEY *Arcadia* III. (Sommer) 266 One.. would haue iudged that his eies would haue run into him & his soule out of him; so vnkindly did either take a sent of danger. 1590 NASHE *Pasquil's Apol.* I. Wks. (Grosart) I. 212 When I see the theefe, and the sente of Church-robbers is in my nosthrils. 1868 FREEMAN *Norm. Conq.* (1876) II. viii. 252 Perhaps some scent of the coming danger reached him.

4. An odoriferous liquid prepared by distillation from flowers, etc.; a perfume.

1750 *Leonardus' Mirr. Stones* 74 It has the smell and colour of myrrh, and is used as a scent. 1898 *Cassell's Mag.* June 42 A certain celebrated scent, made from the original recipe.

5. *attrib.* and *Comb.*: simple attrib., as ***scent-ball, -casket, -sachet***; instrumental, as ***scent-laden*** adj.; objective, as ***scent-snuffing*** adj.; special comb.: **scent-bag**, (*a*) a pouch, sac, or gland found in some animals, containing a secreted odoriferous substance; (*b*) a bag containing a strong-smelling substance drawn over ground to make an artificial scent for hounds; (*c*) = SACHET 3; **scent-bean**, an aromatic bean carried with the snuff in a snuff-box; **scent-bottle**, (*a*) a bottle of scent; spec., an ornamental bottle containing scent, smelling-salts, etc. for the toilet-table or pocket; (*b*) a bottle designed to contain scent; **scent-box**, (*a*) a box for carrying scent; (*b*) *Pugilistic slang*, the nose; **scent-dog** *Sc.*, a pointer; **scent-gland**, a gland which secretes an odoriferous substance; **scent-holder, -jar**, an ornamental vase or jar, usually with perforated top, in which odorous substances are kept to perfume an apartment; **scent-organ** *Ent.* and *Zool.*, an organ that secretes scent, a scent-bag, scent-gland; **scent-scale** *Ent.*, a perfumed scale found on the males of some Lepidoptera; **scent-spray**, an ornamental scent-bottle with apparatus for distributing the scent; † **scent-strong** *a.*, having great scenting powers; **scent-tuft** *Ent.*, a brush-like scent-bearing organ (Webster *Suppl.* 1902); **scent-vase** = *scent-jar*; **scent-wood**, a Tasmanian evergreen shrub, *Alyxia buxifolia* (Treas. Bot. 1866).

1682-3 E. TYSON in *Phil. Trans.* XIII. 38 Two Baggs which I have taken the liberty to call the *Scent-baggs [in a viper]. 1889 C. D. WARNER in *Harper's Mag.* Oct. 726/2 The young men.. expended an immense amount of energy .. in riding at fences after the scent-bag. 1892 *Cooley's Cycl. Pract. Receipts* 1487/1 Scent-bags. See Sachets. *Ibid.*, *Scent-balls. 1892 H. AINSLIE *Pilgr. Land of Burns* 85 Their mouths were dry as snuff-boxes, and their tongues rattled therein like unto *scent beans. 1833 T. HOOK *Parson's Dau.* I. iv, Cut-glass *scent bottles. 1856 C. M. YONGE *Daisy Chain* I. xxv. 262 She flew for the scent-bottle, while her father bent over Margaret. 1895 *Army & Navy Co-op. Soc. Price List* 714/2 Scent Bottles—Fancy,—A large assortment in Stock. 1917 *Harrods Gen. Catal.* 219 Sterling silver and cut glass scent bottle. 1930 T. S. ELIOT tr. *St.-J. Perse's Anabasis* 37 And a man strode forth at the threshold of the desert—profession of his father: dealer in scent-bottles. 1975 J. O'FAOLAIN *Woman in Wall* iii. 55 Translucent scent-bottles of glass and alabaster. 17.. in Ashton *Social Life* (1882) I. 158 A Cane with a Silver Head and *Scent Box. 1826 *Sporting Mag.* XVIII. 315 Pat napped him on the scent-box. 1879 PIESSE *Perfumery* (ed. 4) Index, *Scent-casket. 1894 CROCKETT *Raiders* 29 Nosing them for myself like a *Scent-Dog after birds. 1683 E. TYSON in *Phil. Trans.* XIV. 377 Those scent-bags, or *scent-glands, I have formerly mentioned to be in other Animals. 1866 OWEN *Anat. Vertebr.* I. 615 [During the breeding-season] the anal scent-glands are in active function in both groups [*sc.* Lizards and Serpents]. 1832 G. R. PORTER *Porcelain & Gl.* 22 A *scent-jar, forty-four inches high... The scent is allowed to escape through hexagonal openings in the neck. 1816 KIRBY & SP. *Entomol.* xxi. (1818) II. 245 Another insect.. furnished with osmateria, or *scent-organs. 1892 B. HINTON *Lord's Return* 206 A silken coverlet, quilted and perfumed like a *scent-sachet. 1898 PACKARD *Text-bk. Entomol.* 198 To these *scent-scales is applied the term *androconia*. 1592 SHAKS. *Ven. & Ad.* 692 For there his smell with others being mingled, The hot *sent-snuffing hounds are driuen to doubt. 1897 *Daily News* 9 July 6/3 A silver and Venetian glass *scent spray. 1591 SYLVESTER *Du Bartas* I. v. 660 The *sent-strong Swallow sweepeth to and fro.

scent (sɛnt), *v.* Forms: 5–7 (9 *rare*) sent, 6–7 sente, (7 cent), 7– scent. [ME. *sent*, a. F. *sentir* to feel, perceive, spec. to smell; = Pr., Sp., Pg. *sentir*, It. *sentire*:—L. *sentīre* to feel, perceive. The spelling *scent* (for this and the sb.) does not occur in our material until the 17th c. A revival of the etymological spelling *sent* was attempted by A. and J. C. Hare (*Guesses at Truth*, ed. 1838).]

1. *trans.* Of a hound or other animal: To find or track (game, prey, etc.) by the smell; also, *to scent out*. In later use said also, with wider application, of persons and animals: To become aware of the presence or approach of, or to recognize at a distance, by the sense of smell; also (*rarely*), to inhale the smell of, to smell at.

*c*1400 *Master of Game* (MS. Digby 182) I. 7 b, Whan hares be ygete with the kynde of a conynge.. the houndes lust nor sentith hem nought so wele. 1575 TURBERV. *Venerie* 117 By that time he have gone xx or xxx paces, the slot is better, and the hounds shall sent him much better. 1602 SHAKS. *Ham.* I. v. 58 *Ghost.* But soft, me thinkes I sent the Mornings Ayre; Briefe let me be. 1638 SIR T. HERBERT *Trav.* (ed. 2) 179 Let us goe cent the Caspyan ayre. 1721 R. KEITH tr. *T. à Kempis' Soliloquy of Soul* x. 177, I myself have even scented from afar the celestial Spices. 1822-34 *Good's Study Med.* (ed. 4) III. 200 The refreshment which is felt on scenting the pungent vapour of carbonate of ammonia. 1834 PRINGLE *Afr. Sk.* ix. 307 Our oxen had scented the water at a distance. 1853 KANE *Grinnell Exp.* xxix. (1856) 239 A bear and two cubs, that had.. been scenting our foot-marks of the day before. 1871 L. STEPHEN *Playgr. Eur.* IV. 230 These animals [*sc.* sheep-dogs] scent the traveller from an incredible distance. 1878 BOSW. SMITH *Carthage* 295 Like vultures scenting their prey afar.

b. *fig.* To perceive as if by smell; to find out instinctively; to detect.

1553 *Respublica* 164 Nowe a wheale on suche noses.. That so quicklie canne sente where hidden golde dothe lye. *c*1620 FLETCHER & MASS. *Double Marriage* I. ii, *Fer.* Is Virolet in [the conspiracy]? *Ron.* The head of all, he onely scented me. 1658 CLEVELAND *Rustick Rampant* (1687) 416 Perhaps not senting the Design of the Clowns. 1833 I. TAYLOR *Fanaticism* ii. 26 The religious classes who.. will scent a heresy in every such definition. 1870 A. R. HOPE *Schoolboy Fr.* xiv. 182, I thought he would scent us out. 1897 L. J. TROTTER *John Nicholson* xix. 227 Chamberlain, scenting possible mischief, made a forced march to Amritsar.

†c. In etymological sense: To discern, perceive. *Obs. rare.*

1586 BRIGHT *Melanch.* xix. 115 Soules haue sense of things without organicall senses: and when they bee but fancies, yet that which ministreth the object.. is sensed with the minde only. 1609 C. BUTLER *Fem. Mon.* (1623) B 4, Hir horns.. are the proper organum of the sense of feeling; by which, with the least touch, the Bee sodainely senteth any tangible object.

2. *intr.* Of a hound or other animal: †a. To perceive the smell *of* (the quarry). *Obs.* b. To hunt by the sense of smell; also, to 'smell about', sniff the air for a scent.

*c*1400 *Master of Game* (MS. Digby 182) ii. 11 And he shall kepe hym.. always in þe myddell of the water for cause that the houndes shall not sent of hym. 1598 MARSTON *Pygmal.* IV. 151 But Grillus subtile-smelling swinish snout Must sent, and grunt, and needes will finde it out. 1667 MILTON *P.L.* x. 279 So sented the grim Feature, and upturn'd His Nostril wide into the mirky Air. 1730 SWIFT *Answ. Delany's Fable* 8 The hound would scent; the wolf would prowl.

fig. *a*1641 BP. MOUNTAGU *Acts & Mon.* (1642) 20 But at length they began to sent after the Egyptians gods.

3. To exhale an odour, to smell. [So F. *sentir.*] Now *rare* or *Obs.*

*c*1400 *Beryn* 2765 This gardeyn is.. ful of may flouris,.. The wich been so redolent, & sentyn so a boute. 1578 LYTE *Dodoens* I. xliii. 63 The seede is small and black, and senting like Rosin. 1664 HUBERT *Catal. Rarities* (1665) 66 A stone that smells only when it is blown on, and the harder one blowes, the stronger it sents. 1698 FRYER *Acc. E. India & P.* 182 The Fruit when Green scents like Turpentine. 1843 tr. *Custine's Empire of Czar* I. 125 This perfumed Cerberus, for he scented of musk at the distance of a league, released us.

fig. 1632 MASSINGER & FIELD *Fatal Dowry* IV. i, Season now your youth With one braue thing, and it shall keep the odour.. and on your Tombe Sent like sweet oyles and Frankincense. 1642 FULLER *Holy & Prof. St.* IV. xvi. 321 Such is the fresh nature of some Embassages, if not spent presently, they sent ill. 1826 LAMB *Elia* Ser. II. *Genteel Style in Writing*, They [*sc.* Sir William Temple's essays] scent of Nimeguen, and the Hague. 1831 *Fraser's Mag.* IV. 584 The very air scents of knavery.

4. *trans.* [From the sb.] To impregnate with an odour; to perfume.

1697 DRYDEN *Virg. Georg.* III. 636 With Smoak of burning Cedar scent thy Walls. 1725 POPE *Odyss.* VIII. 398 An hundred altars rise, And breathing odours scent the balmy skies. 1792 BELKNAP *Hist. New-Hampsh.* III. 147 To decoy him, the hunters scent the ground with a drug. 1837 DICKENS *Pickw.* vii, The hundred perfumes of the little flower-garden.. scented the air around. 1899 *Allbutt's Syst. Med.* VIII. 762 The ointment may be scented with any essential oil.

scent, obs. form of SAINT.

scented ('sɛntɪd), *ppl. a.* [f. SCENT *v.* and *sb.*]

†1. With prefixed adv.: Endowed with the power of tracking by sense of smell. *Obs.*

1579 E. K. *Spenser's Sheph. Cal.* Ep. Ded., So Marot, Sanazarus, and.. other.. Poetes, whose foting this Author every where followeth; yet so as few, but they be wel sented, can trace him out. 1656 EARL MONM. tr. *Boccalini's Advts. fr. Parnass.* I. lii. 104 There were.. Beagles which were very well sented to find out wild beasts.

2. Impregnated with perfume; perfumed.

scented caper, tea: see CAPER *sb.*[1] 4.

1740 C. PITT *Æneid* IV. 318 Paris.. In scented tresses and a mitre gay. 1839 URE *Dict. Arts* 1149 The scented soap being put into the frames, speedily consolidates. 1879 PIESSE *Perfumery* (ed. 4) 316 Scented shells. Venetian Shells.. are .. steeped into the scent... When dry these shells will serve for perfuming jewel-cases and work-boxes.

3. That has a scent or perfume; exhaling a scent.

1666 BOYLE *Orig. Formes & Qual.* 276 One of the subtlest and strongest sented Drugs. 1784 COWPER *Task* VI. 151 The scentless and the scented rose. 1849 M. ARNOLD *Obermann* xlii, The scented pines of Switzerland. 1886 BRITTEN & HOLLAND *Plant-n.*, Scented Fern. *Nephrodium Oreopteris*, Desv.

scenter ('sɛntə(r)). [f. SCENT *v.* + -ER[1].] One who or that which scents, in the senses of the vb. Also ***scenter out***.

1611 COTGR., *Flaireur*, a senter, smeller, venter. 1838 HARE *Guesses* Ser. II. (1866) 307 The senters-out [*sic*] of allegories. 1977 *Islander* (Victoria, B.C.) 13 Nov. 3/1 And now, in November, the rain is.. a scenter of soil, a painter of stones.

scentful ('sɛntfʊl), *a.* [f. SCENT *sb.* + -FUL.]

1. Full of or abounding in perfume; fragrant.

1612 DRAYTON *Poly-olb.* xv. 196 The scent-full Camomill. 1732-3 SAVAGE *Volunteer Laureat* II. 34 Ye blossoms,.. send your scentful tribute to the skies.

†2. Having keen scent or sense of smell. *Obs.*

1616 W. BROWNE *Brit. Past.* II. iii. 55 For whom (had she not so beene nourished).. The sentfull Osprey by the Rocke had fish'd.

scenting ('sɛntɪŋ), *vbl. sb.* [f. SCENT *v.* + -ING[1].] The action of the verb.

1580 HOLLYBAND *Treas. Fr. Tong*, *Flairement*, smelling, senting. 1855 BAIN *Senses & Int.* II. ii. §3 (1864) 166 In scenting, a pointer keeps his nose close to the ground. 1855 PIESSE *Perfumery* 100 The perfumer uses musk principally in the scenting of soap. 1890 'R. BOLDREWOOD' *Col. Reformer* (1891) 209 An unusually difficult tract of country .., where 'scenting' was slow.

†b. Sensation. *Obs. rare*[−1].

1657 S. PURCHAS *Pol. Flying-Ins.* 22 Bees have all the five senses, though there do not appear all those outward Organs of senting, which some other Animals have.

'**scenting**, *ppl. a.* [f. SCENT *v.* + -ING[2].]

1. That exhales an odour or perfume.

1577 KENDALL *Flowers of Epigr.* 22 b, Strong sentyng Leekes of Tarentine. 1595 P. T. G. *Blanchardyn* (1890) 216 All costly odors and sweet senting spices. 1772 T. SIMPSON *Vermin-Killer* 10 The senting oils may be used as mentioned for rats.

2. Of or pertaining to hunting by scent. Of a hound: That hunts by scent. *Sporting.* Of a day, country: Characterized by the prevalence of a (good, bad, etc.) scent.

1577 KENDALL *Flowers of Epigr.* 51 The sentyng hounds pursude the hastie Hare of foote. 1749 FIELDING *Tom Jones* VII. iv, When any thing in the least soured him, as a bad scenting day, or a distemper among his hounds. 1897 *Encycl. Sport* I. 543/1 It will be well to select a good scenting covert.. for the first morning.

[**scentingly**: see SCANTINGLY *a.* (quot. *a* 1661).]

scentless ('sɛntlɪs), *a.* [f. SCENT *sb.* + -LESS.]

†1. Without the faculty of smell. *Obs. rare*[−1].

1605 SYLVESTER *Du Bartas* II. iii. III. *Law* 1473 Their deaf, dull Idols, sent-lesse, sight-lesse, dumb.

2. Without odour or perfume.

*a*1618 SYLVESTER *Tri. Faith* IV. xv. Wks. (Grosart) I. 18 By Faith three Hebrews.. escape the raging Fire: (Their very garments sent-lesse and entire). 1756 C. LUCAS *Ess. Waters* I. 98 Each ingredient before mixture was scentless. 1813 T. MOORE *Last Rose of Summer* 16 Where thy mates of the garden Lie scentless and dead. 1870 HOOKER *Stud. Flora* 44 Flowers.. scentless.

3. *Hunting.* Of ground: That does not carry scent. Also of a day on which there is no scent for the hounds to follow.

1880 'BROOKSBY' *Hunting Countries* II. 218 Foxes occasionally travel on to these scentless heights from the Vale. 1885 *Field* 4 Apr. 428/1 That dry, scentless cycle of days. 1921 *Ampleforth Jrnl.* Jan. 137 On October 16th we hunted the high country, after a scentless day at Tom Smith's Cross on the previous Wednesday. 1976 *Horse & Hound* 3 Dec. 30/3 They had an exciting, if rather scentless, morning, catching a brace of foxes, the last one within 20 yards of the kennel gates!

4. **scentless mayweed**, a perennial herb, *Tripleurospermum maritimum* (formerly *Matricaria inodora*), belonging to the family Compositæ and bearing white, yellow-centred flowers and finely divided leaves.

1800 J. E. SMITH *Eng. Bot.* X. 676 (*heading*) Corn feverfew. Scentless may-weed. 1857 A. PRATT *Flowering Plants & Ferns Gt. Brit.* III. 315 Scentless Mayweed.. puzzles the young botanist by belying its name, and having an odour which, though not aromatic, is powerful and unpleasant. 1914 A. R. HORWOOD *Story of Plant Life Brit. Isles* I. 140 The Scentless Mayweed.. has a larger flower and a generally darker green colour [than the stinking mayweed]. 1931 M. GRIEVE *Mod. Herbal* II. 524/1 The Scentless Mayweed owes its generic name to its reputed medicinal properties. 1975 E. J. GIBBONS *Flora of Lincolnshire* 232 Scentless Mayweed... Native. Weed of cultivation.

scenty ('sɛntɪ), *a. rare.* [f. SCENT *sb.* + -Y[1].] Smelling of scent; scented.

1937 G. FRANKAU *More of Us* x. 111 Yet, ere he handed scenty lace-edged flax back, Long to his seat in knightly honour rooted The hero cleaved. 1963 D. BALLANTYNE *And the Glory* 148 There was the warm and scenty smell of her body.

scep, obs. form of SHEEP, SKEP, SKIP.

sceppe, scepper, variants of SKEP, SKEPPER.

scepsis ('skɛpsɪs). [a. Gr. σκέψις inquiry, hesitation, doubt, f. σκέπ-τεσθαι: see SCEPTIC.] Sceptical attitude in philosophy.

1876 J. MARTINEAU *Ess. & Addr.* (1891) IV. 94 Among their products were the system of Locke, the scepsis of Hume, the critical philosophy of Kant.

sceptic, skeptic ('skɛptɪk), *a.* and *sb.* [ad. F. *sceptique* adj. and sb., or its source late L. *scepticus* (*Scepticī* sb. pl., the Sceptics), lit. inquiring, reflective, assumed by the disciples of Pyrrho as their distinctive epithet; f. σκεπ- in σκέπτεσθαι to look out, consider, ablaut-var. of σκοπ- in σκοπεῖν to look, σκοπός watchman, mark to aim at, etc.: see SCOPE *sb.* Cf. Sp. *escéptico*, Pg.

sceptico, It. *scettico*, G. *skeptiker* sb., *skeptisch* adj.

In Fr. the *sc* is pronounced (s) as in *sceptre*. In Eng. direct recourse to Greek produced the pronunciation with (sk). The spelling with *sk-*, for which cf. SKELETON, occurs in the earliest instance, and has been used occas. by later writers. It is adopted without comment or alternative in Johnson's Dictionary, but did not become general in England; in the U.S. it is the ordinary form. Now usually spelt *sceptic* in the U.K. and British Commonwealth and *skeptic* in the U.S. Similarly all the derivatives, *scepticism/skepticism*, etc.]

A. *adj.* = SCEPTICAL *a.* Now *rare* exc. as the epithet of a school of philosophers (see B. 1).

c **1575** G. BUCHANAN *Let. to Randolph* Vernac. Writ. (S.T.S.) 57, I can not tak you for ane Stoik philosopher..or ane cairless [*margin* skeptik] hart that taks cuccaldris as thyng indifferent. **1598** MARSTON *Sco. Villanie* I. i. 174 Fye Gallus, what, a Skeptick Pyrrhomist [*sic*]? **1654** WHITLOCK *Zootomia* 221 Calling..humble Ductility after further Reason, and Discovery, Sceptick Inconstancy. **1709** SHAFTESB. *Moralists* I. ii. 27 Using a known Sceptick Privilege, and asserting strenuously the Cause I have hitherto oppos'd. **1839** *Morn. Herald* 14 Sept., The sceptic geologists of the British Association. **1865** W. G. PALGRAVE *Arabia* II. 3 Free from the sceptic distrustfulness..so common.

B. *sb.*

1. *Philos.* One who, like Pyrrho and his followers in Greek antiquity, doubts the possibility of real knowledge of any kind; one who holds that there are no adequate grounds for certainty as to the truth of any proposition whatever. Also, often applied in a historically less correct sense, to those who deny the competence of reason, or the existence of any justification for certitude, outside the limits of experience.

1587 GOLDING *De Mornay* i. (1592) 10 There was in deede a kinde of Philosophers called Scepticks..(that is to say Doubters) which did rather suspend their Judgements concerning the Godhead then call it in question. **1608** BP. HALL *Charact.* 151 Hee is a Scepticke, and dare hardly giue credit to his senses. *a* **1631** DONNE *Paradoxes* (1652) 22 The Skeptike, which doubts all, was more contentious then either. **1633** MASSINGER *Guardian* III. vi, And I have eyes too... If I have no belief in their assurance, I must turn sceptick. **1661** GLANVILL *Van. Dogm.* Ep. Ded., Confidence in uncertainties is the greatest enemy to what is certain; and were I a Sceptick, I'de plead for Dogmatising. **1768–74** TUCKER *Lt. Nat.* (1834) II. 576, I am apt to think there never yet has really been such a monster in the world as a thorough sceptic. **1781** COWPER *Conversat.* 138 Howe'er ingenious on his darling theme A sceptic in philosophy may seem [etc.]. **1872** MORLEY *Voltaire* (1886) 11 The old-fashioned nomenclature puts him down among sceptics. **1893** J. OWEN (*title*) The Skeptics of the Italian Renaissance.

2. One who doubts the validity of what claims to be knowledge in some particular department of inquiry (e.g. metaphysics, theology, natural science, etc.); *popularly*, one who maintains a doubting attitude with reference to some particular question or statement. Also, one who is habitually inclined rather to doubt than to believe any assertion or apparent fact that comes before him; a person of sceptical temper.

1615 CROOKE *Body of Man* 48 The Philosopher..calleth the head, the chest, and the belly, principall Organs, because the most irresolute Scepticke, cannot but acknowledge their action and diuerse composition. **1650** BAXTER *Saints' R.* I. iii. (1662) 14 In the meantime I am a Sceptick, and know little in this whole doctrine of Spirits, and spiritual workings, further than Scripture clearly revealeth. **1657** *Treat. Conf. Sin* 342 If we still continue Scepticks in the settlement of Church and Doctrine. **1725** WATTS *Logic* II. iii. §3 The Dogmatist is in haste to believe something... The Sceptick will not take Pains to search Things to the Bottom, but when he sees Difficulties on both Sides resolves to believe neither of them. **1779** JOHNSON *L.P., Milton* 102 If every sceptick in Theology may teach his follies, there can be no religion. **1820** BYRON *Mar. Fal.* I. ii. 154 Tis the first time that honour has been doubted, And were the last, from any other sceptic. **1848** LYTTON *Harold* XI. i, But one smile of the sceptic or the world-man was seen on the paling lips of those present. **1887** *Pall Mall G.* 7 Nov. 2/2 Who says there is no romance in food? Let the sceptic turn to 'Lorna Doone'.

3. *spec.* One who doubts, without absolutely denying, the truth of the Christian religion or important parts of it; often *loosely*, an unbeliever in Christianity, an infidel.

1638 CHILLINGW. *Relig. Prot.* I. Pref. §8 So an Atheist or a Sceptique may not conclude as well. **1674** T. SMITH (*title*) Christian Religion's Appeal from the groundless prejudices of the Sceptick to the Bar of Common Reason. **1711** G. HICKES *Two Treat. Chr. Priesth.* (1847) II. 154, I wish.. such men would..not give such advantage to deists and sceptics. **1781** CRABBE *Library* 261 There sceptics rest, a still-increasing throng. **1863** R. B. GIRDLESTONE *Anat. Scepticism* 100 In listening to the arguments of a sceptic you are breathing a poisonous atmosphere.

4. Occas. used with reference to the etymological sense: A seeker after truth; an inquirer who has not yet arrived at definite convictions.

a **1618** RALEIGH *Sceptick* (1651) 1 The Sceptick doth neither affirm, neither denie any Position: but doubteth of it, and opposeth his Reasons against that which is affirmed, or denied to justifie his not Consenting. **1653** GAUDEN *Hierasp.* 96 Which temerity..hath, we see, made some poor souls turn Scepticks and Seekers after true Religion. **1865** GROTE *Plato* I. vi. 212 Several critics of antiquity considered Plato as essentially a sceptic—that is, a Searcher or Enquirer, not reaching any assured or proved result. **1870** M. D. CONWAY *Earthw. Pilgr.* xxi. 248 A Sceptic, then, is one who shades his eyes in order to look steadfastly at a thing.

5. *attrib.* and *Comb.*, as *sceptic-Christian*, *-friend*; *sceptic-like*, *-ridden* adjs.

1709 SHAFTESB. *Moralists* I. iii. 38 But..bore with me when I treated all his Thoughts as visionary; and when *Sceptick-like I unravel'd all his Systems. **1711** —— *Charac.* III. *Misc. Refl.* II. ii. 72 The best Christian in the World, who..depends only on History and Tradition for his Belief in these Particulars, is at best but a *Sceptick-Christian. *Ibid.* v. ii. 288 To deal the better with his *Sceptick-Friend, he falls again to personating. **1711** HICKES *Two Treat. Chr. Priesth.* (1847) I. 267 He may.. regale his atheist-ridden, or theist-ridden, or *sceptic-ridden..or devil-ridden mind.

sceptical, skeptical ('skɛptɪkəl), *a.* [f. SCEPTIC + -AL[1].] **a.** Of persons: Inclined to or imbued with scepticism (in the various senses of that word); in modern use often, dubious or incredulous. **b.** Of doctrines, opinions, etc.: Characteristic of a sceptic; of the nature of scepticism.

1639 FULLER *Holy War* IV. v. (1640) 176 Desiring rather to be scepticall then definitive in the causes of Gods judgements. **1660** PEPYS *Diary* 15 May, My Lord and I walked together..talking together upon..religion, wherein he is, I perceive, wholly sceptical, saying, that indeed the Protestants as to the Church of Rome are wholly fanatiques. **1736** BUTLER *Anal.* I. ii. 42 There is no Sort of Ground for being thus presumptuous, even upon the most sceptical Principles. **1788** BURKE *Sp. agst. W. Hastings* Wks. 1821 VII. 82 There were at that time, it seems, in Calcutta a wicked sceptical set of people, who somehow or other believed, that human agency was concerned in this elective [? *read* electric] flash, which came so very opportunely. **1840** WHEWELL *Philos. Induct. Sci.* (1847) II. 465 The Catastrophist's dogmatism is undermined by the Uniformitarian's skeptical hypotheses. **1870** BALDW. BROWN *Eccl. Truth* 231 There is a sense in which every age is..bound to be sceptical. **1884** RYLE *Princ. Churchmen* (ed. 2) 435 Many a sceptical saying is nothing more than a borrowed article, picked up and retailed by him who says it, because it seems clever. **1885** PATER *Marius* I. 157 He continued the sceptical argument he had commenced.

sceptically, skeptically ('skɛptɪkəlɪ), *adv.* [f. SCEPTICAL + -LY[2].] In a sceptical manner; like a sceptic.

[**1633**: see SCEPTICLY *adv.*] **1671** J. WEBSTER *Metallogr.* v. 84 Things being yet so far from being certainly known that I dare but Sceptically treat of them. **1709** SHAFTESB. *Charac.* (1711) III. *Misc. Refl.* II. ii. 74 He condescended still, on many occasions, to speak sceptically, and with some Hesitation and Reserve, as to the Certainty of these Divine Exhibitions. **1839** HALLAM *Lit. Eur.* III. iii. III. 203 Even this [the atomic theory] has been sceptically accepted by our cautious school of philosophy. **1884** *Harper's Mag.* May 908 'Where did they get the banjo?' asked..Jones, skeptically.

†'scepticalness, 'skepticalness. *Obs. rare.* [f. SCEPTICAL + -NESS.] The quality or condition of being sceptical.

1633 FULLER *Serm. Assurance* (1647) 4 Continuall wavering, or Scepticalness concerning our Calling and Election.

scepticism, skepticism ('skɛptɪsɪz(ə)m). [ad. mod.L. *scepticismus*, f. late L. *sceptic-us*: see SCEPTIC and -ISM. Cf. F. *scepticisme*.]

1. *Philos.* The doctrine of the Sceptics; the opinion that real knowledge of any kind is unattainable.

1652 N. CULVERWEL *Light of Nature* 150 He [*sc.* Pyrrho] perswades men to encline to his Scepticisme. **1661** BLOUNT *Glossogr.* (ed. 2), *Scepticism*, the Doctrine or opinion of the *Scepticks*. **1672** *Phil. Trans.* VII. 5081 Here he taketh occasion to examine Pyrrhonisme or Scepticisme, professed by a Sect of men that speak otherwise than they think. **1768–74** TUCKER *Lt. Nat.* (1834) II. 576 There is an air of positiveness in all scepticism, an unreserved confidence in the strength of those arguments that are alleged to overthrow all the knowledge of mankind. **1840** WHEWELL *Philos. Induct. Sci.* (1847) II. 655 There is by no means any ground of general skepticism with regard to truth involved in the doctrine of the necessary combination of two elements in all our knowledge. **1908** *Hibbert Jrnl.* Oct. 82 Consistent rationalism always in the end collapses into scepticism.

2. Sceptical attitude in relation to some particular branch of science; doubt or incredulity as to the truth of some assertion or supposed fact. Also, disposition to doubt or incredulity in general; mistrustfulness; sceptical temper.

1646 T. EDWARDS *Gangræna* I. 156 First bring in Scepticism [*sic*] in Doctrine and loosenesse of life, and afterwards all Atheism. **1661** GLANVILL *Van. Dogm.* Ep. Ded., Scepticism is less reprehensible in enquiring years. **1776** GIBBON *Decline & F.* xv. (1782) I. 602 A state of scepticism and suspense may amuse a few inquisitive minds. **1822** *Retrosp. Rev.* V. 103 He was a little tainted with the scepticism of that Irish prelate who qualified his admiration of Gulliver's Travels by hinting, that there were some things in them of which he had his doubts. **1880** DISRAELI *Endym.* xlviii, Endymion had often listened, half with fondness and half with skepticism, to Waldershare dilating..on the character and qualities of Imogene.

3. Doubt or unbelief with regard to the Christian religion. Cf. SCEPTIC B. 3.

1800 *Med. Jrnl.* III. 227 The general prevalence of infidelity and scepticism has been, with some degree of justice, attributed to enthusiasm in religion. **1836** HOR. SMITH *Tin Trumpet* (1876) 322 Scepticism may be assumed as an excuse for immorality. **1884** RYLE *Princ. Churchmen* (ed. 2) 433 A vague kind of scepticism or agnosticism is one of the commonest spiritual diseases in this generation.

†scep'ticity. *Obs. rare*[−1]. [f. SCEPTIC + -ITY.] The quality of being sceptical.

1650 CHARLETON *Paradoxes* Ep. Ded. 5 Whether my Scepticity, even in such Notions..be not evidence strong enough.

scepticize ('skɛptɪsaɪz), *v.* [f. SCEPTIC + -IZE.]

†1. *trans.* With *away*: To remove (a certainty) by casting doubt upon its proofs. *Obs.*

1681 GLANVILL *Sadducismus* II. Introd. 2 The more subtle [unbelievers] are ready to Scepticize away those grounds.

2. *intr.* To play the sceptic; to take up the position of a philosophical doubter.

1698 H. B. *Free but Modest Cens.* 6 He hath a great mind to Scepticize, and to maintain Paradoxes. **1709** SHAFTESB. *Moralists* II. i. 44 You can afford to scepticize where no one else will so much as hesitate. **1840** TENNYSON in *Mem.* (1897) I. 178 You used to scepticize till we both ran away. **1893** *Nat. Observer* 25 Nov. 44/1 Mr. Owen is best described as scepticising *pour encourager les autres*.

†'scepticly, *adv. Obs.* = SCEPTICALLY.

1633 JAMES in *Hearne's Collect.* (O.H.S.) I. 9, I, who skeptiklye scarce dare..speake.

sceptire, obs. form of SCEPTRE *sb.*

†'sceptism. *Obs. rare.* Also 6 sceptisme. [Badly formed on SCEPT(IC) + -ISM.] = SCEPTICISM.

1652 N. CULVERWEL *Light of Nature* 153 *Des-Cartes* the French philosopher..will be fain to stop and stay in Sceptisme... He that will not cast Anchor upon these, condemnes himself to perpetual Sceptisme. **1658** J. ROBINSON *Stone to Altar* 96 Without subscribing to a Protagorean Sceptism, That which is true in one place, may be false in another. **1737** A. BAXTER *Enq. Hum. Soul* (ed. 2) II. 21 That kind of Sceptism called Egomism.

sceptral ('sɛptrəl), *a.* [f. SCEPTRE *sb.* + -AL[1].] Pertaining to a sceptre; serving as a sceptre.

1838 *Fraser's Mag.* XVIII. 447 Zeus grasps the sceptral lightnings of the air. **1877** BLACKMORE *Cripps* xxxviii, The Carrier..bore with a bent arm and set muscle the sceptral whip of the family. **1884** SWINBURNE *Midsummer Holiday* 12 Sceptral stems bore stars whose reign endures, not flowers that fall.

sceptre ('sɛptə(r)), *sb.* Forms: 3–6 ceptre, 4 ceptire, 5 ceptur(e, ceptyr, 5–6 ceptour, 6 cepter; 4 septir, 4–6 septor, septre, septur(e, 4–7 septer, 5 seipter, septere, 5–6 septour(e, 6 septar; 4 sceptir(e, sceptree, 5 sceptoure, 5–6 scepture, 6 sceptar, 6–9 scepter, 4– sceptre. [ME. *ceptre*, *septre*, *sceptre*, a. OF. *ceptre*, *sceptre* (mod.F. *sceptre*) = Sp. *cetro*, Pg. *sceptro*, It. *scettro*, *scetro*, ad. L. *scēptrum*, *scæptrum*, a. Gr. σκῆπτρον staff, sceptre, f. root of σκήπτεσθαι to prop oneself, lean on something.]

1. An ornamental rod or wand (often of gold and jewelled) borne in the hand as a symbol of regal or imperial authority.

In England the royal assent to a bill passed by Parliament is signified by the sovereign's touching it with a sceptre.

a **1300** *Cursor M.* 7863 Þai sett a ceptre in his hand, Þat man clepes kyngs wand. *a* **1340** HAMPOLE *Psalter* Cant. 511 Sceptire is þe kyngis wand, þat bitakyns his pouste. *c* **1386** CHAUCER *Monk's T.* 3564 And she that bar the ceptre ful of floures Shal bere a distaf hire costes for to quyte. *a* **1400–50** *Alexander* 502 Þe king was sett in his sale with septer in hand. **1430–40** LYDG. *Bochas* VIII. xiii[i]. (1494) Dij b, Swerde, sceptre [**1554** scepter, **1558** seipter] crowne and state Imperiall. *c* **1485** in *Rutland Papers* (Camden) 10 A septre with the dowe, and a rodd of gold for the King, and with a septre of iuere also with a dove and an other rodd of gold also, for the Quene. **1513** BRADSHAW *St. Werburge* I. 151 Duke Engystus in honour excellent, With septre and crowne fyrst reygned royally. **1555** EDEN *Decades* (Arb.) 124 She appeared to them shakynge a septer in her hande. **1596** SHAKS. *Merch. V.* IV. i. 190 His Scepter shewes the force of temporall power, The attribute to awe and Maiestie. **1613** —— *Hen. VIII*, IV. i. 38 Who's that that beares the Scepter? Marquesse Dorset. **1689** *Lond. Gaz.* No. 2461/3 This Act being touched with the Scepter, the President..Adjourned the Parliament to the 17th of this instant June. **1756–7** tr. *Keysler's Trav.* (1760) IV. 353 The figure of a sceptre inclosed within a wreath of crowns and sceptres interwoven. **1813** SCOTT *Trierm.* II. vii, I swear by sceptre and by sword, as belted knight and Britain's lord. **1871** B. TAYLOR *Faust* (1875) I. vi. 105 So sit I, like the King upon his throne: I hold the sceptre, here,—and lack the crown alone. **1882** 'OUIDA' *Maremma* I. 147 The eagle with spread wings upon his ivory sceptre.

b. *Her.* A representation of this.

1610 GUILLIM *Heraldry* III. i. (1611) 191 The Field is Iupiter, a Scepter Roiall in Pale. **1831** H. THOMPSON *Heraldry* in *Encycl. Metrop.* V. 614/2 It is not usual, but Heraldic and allowable, to marshal behind the Arms of the Sovereign the different Sceptres to which he is entitled. **1909** FOX-DAVIES *Compl. Guide to Heraldry* 298 The other chief emblem of sovereignty—the Sceptre—is occasionally met with, as in the Whitgreave crest of augmentation.

c. In figurative context.

1750 JOHNSON *Rambler* No. 3, ¶9 When her examination had convinced her [*sc.* Criticism], that the laws of just writing had been observed, she touched it with the amaranthine end of the sceptre, and consigned it over to immortality. **1813** SHELLEY *Q. Mab* v. 176 Though they [*sc.* Tyranny and Falsehood] wield With blood-red hand the sceptre of the world.

¶ **d.** Used to render Gr. σκῆπτρον staff.

1526 TINDALE *Heb.* xi. 21 By fayth Iacob when he was a deyinge, blessed both the sonnes of Ioseph, and worshipped on the toppe of his Ceptre.

2. *fig.* Taken as the power or authority symbolized by a sceptre; hence, royal or imperial dignity, sovereignty, supremacy.

1382 Wyclif *Gen.* xlix. 10 The septre fro Juda shal not be takun awey. *c* **1400** *Destr. Troy.* 119 Of Septur and soile he sesit his brothir, And hym crownede as kyng in þat kithe riche. **1535** Coverdale *Ps.* xliv. 6 Thy seate (o God) endureth for euer: the cepter of thy kyngdome is a right cepter. *a* **1586** Sidney *Arcadia* iii. (Sommer) 303 b, She (in whose mind Vertue gouerned with the scepter of Knowledge). *c* **1620** A. Hume *Brit. Tongue* (1865) 3 Your Majesties self noe less, commanding, at your first entrie to your Roial scepter, to reform the grammar, and to teach Aristotle in his aun tongue. **1781** Logan in *Sc. Paraphr.* xviii. iv, His sceptre shall protect the just. **1788** Gibbon *Decl. & F.* xlvi. IV. 504 The Persian conqueror governed his new subjects with an iron sceptre. **1820** Byron *Mar. Fal.* i. ii. 269 Could I not shatter the Briarean sceptre Which in this hundred-handed senate rules. **1865** Ruskin *Sesame* ii. §90 Before the myrtle crown, and the stainless sceptre, of womanhood. **1902** Fuller-Maitland *Oxf. Hist. Music* IV. Introd. 4 The student of history watches the sceptre of musical supremacy passing, as it were, from England to the Netherlands.

3. A popular name of the sceptred gold unite first coined in 1604; also, †the name suggested for a silver coin in 1695.

1695 Lowndes *Rep. Ess. Amend. Silver Coins* 62 One Piece which may be called the Sceptre or the Silver-Unite. **1736** Folkes *Gold Coins* 6, 2 Ja. I. Sovereigns or Units, vulgarly called Scepters. **1763** Snelling *Gold Coin* 22 The Unitie or Unite..is also frequently called a scepter, from the scepter in the king's hand, in distinction to those..called Laurels, from the laureated head. **1870** Henfrey *Eng. Coins* i. 56.

†4. A constellation in the southern hemisphere.

1728 Chambers *Cycl.*, *Scepter, Sceptrum*, in astronomy, one of the six new constellations of the southern hemisphere, consisting of 17 stars. **1837** *Penny Cycl.* VII. 476 There are many other constellations formed by different individuals; but these are not now generally admitted. Such are..the Sceptre of Brandenburgh [etc.]. **1850** in Ogilvie.

5. *attrib.* and *Comb.*, as ***sceptre-bearer***, †***-holder***, †***-staff***, †***-wand***; ***sceptre-bearing*** adj.; †**sceptre broad-piece, -piece,** †**-unite** = sense 3; **sceptre-flower** (see quot. 1866); †**sceptre-rule** (see quot.); †**sceptre-state**, a king.

1598 Florio, *Scetrigero*, a ruler, a *scepter-bearer, a sergeant at armes. *c* **1611** Chapman *Iliad* ii. 69 The other *scepter-bearing States..obeyd The peoples Rector. **1625** K. Long tr. *Barclay's Argenis* ii. viii. 88 Restore them; or no reverence shall withstand Of thy crown'd head, or scepter-bearing hand. **1701** *Lond. Gaz.* No. 3739/4 A striped Silk Spring-Purse with *Scepter Broad Pieces of Gold and others, Guineas, Pistols, &c. **1866** *Treas. Bot.*, *Sceptre-flower. *Sceptranthus. a* **1653** Gouge *Comm. Heb.* i. 81 A Scepter..is so proper to a King, as he is called a *Scepter-holder. **1695** Locke *Further Consid. Value Money* 86, 1 Crown or *Scepter piece 0 6 3. **1736** Folkes *Gold Coins* (1745) 12 A unit of his [Jas. I] 2[d] year, called a scepter piece. **1611** Florio, *Scetro*,..a Kingdome or *Scepter-rule. **1832** Tennyson *Œnone* 124 Till thy hand Fail from the *sceptre-staff. **1598** Chapman *Iliad* ii. 83 The other *scepter-states Rose and obayde the Generall. **1853** Humphreys *Coin-Coll. Man.* xxxii. 464 After the coining of the units—coins of similar value—these pieces were sometimes called *sceptre units. **1456** Sir G. Haye *Law Arms* (S.T.S.) 189 The *scepter wand suld nocht be away tane fra the princis of Jowry.

sceptre (ˈsɛptə(r)), *v.* [f. sceptre *sb.*]

1. *trans.* To furnish with a sceptre.

1526 *Pilgr. Perf.* (W. de W. 1531) 260 When he was..crowned with thornes, Sceptred with a rede in derysyon and scorne. **1634** Bp. Hall *Contempl. N.T., Christ bef. Pilate* 263 Thy head smitten, thy hand sceptred with a reed. *a* **1711** Ken *Hymns Evang.* Poet. Wks. 1721 I. 156 Jesus..Crown'd with sharp Thorns, and scepter'd with a Reed. **1870** Morris *Earthly Par.* III. iv. 223 Most like a mighty king was he, And crowned and sceptered royally.

2. To touch (with a sceptre) as a sign of royal assent or ratification. (Cf. sceptre *sb.* 1, quot. 1689.)

1851 Miss Strickland *Queens of Eng.* I. Introd. 18 William III..arrogated exclusively to himself the privilege of sceptering or rejecting bills.

Hence ˈ**sceptring** *vbl. sb.*

1821 *Examiner* 449/1 The real meaning of scepterings and anointings.

sceptred (ˈsɛptəd), *ppl. a.* Also 6 cepturyt, 7 sceptered. [f. sceptre *v.* + -ed[1].] Bearing a sceptre; invested with regal authority. ***sceptred unite*** = sceptre *sb.* 3.

1513 Douglas *Æneis* xi. vi. 25 Thys ancyent kyng dyd set hym dovn amyd The cepturyt men, as first and principall. **1596** Shaks. *Merch. V.* iv. i. 193 But mercy is aboue this sceptred sway, It is enthroned in the hearts of kings. **1632** Milton *Penseroso* 98 Som time let Gorgeous Tragedy In Scepter'd Pall com sweeping by. **1667** —— *P.L.* ii. 43 And next him Moloc, Scepter'd King Stood up. **1754** Gray *Progr. Poesy* 20 Perching on the scept'red hand Of Jove. **1806** Landor *Rose Aylmer*, Ah, what avails the sceptred race? **1816** Byron *Ch. Har.* iii. xli, For sceptred cynics earth were far too wide a den. **1817** Ruding *Ann. Coinage* II. 221 Scotland, where the Scepter'd Unit..still continued to be coined as before. **1894** Boyd Carpenter *The Son of Man* ii. 36 We see beneath the sceptred symbols of earthly power an unexpected feebleness.

ˈ**sceptredom.** [f. sceptre *sb.* + -dom.]

†1. Period of sceptred rule; reign (of a king).

1599 Nashe *Lenten Stuffe* 9 In a faire text hand texting vnto vs how in the Scepterdome of Edward the Confessor, the sands first began to growe into sight at a low water.

2. Sovereign authority.

1878 Boardman *Creative Week* 251 (Cent.) The Sabbath comes down to us..imperial with all the sceptredom of the Creator's example.

ˈ**sceptreless,** *a.* [f. sceptre *sb.* + -less.] **a.** Obeying no sceptre. **b.** Wielding no sceptre.

1820 Shelley *Prometh. Unb.* iii. iv. 194 The man remains Sceptreless, free, uncircumscribed. **1838** Talfourd *Athen. Captive* i. i, Sceptreless, uncrown'd, Unheeded.

†**scepˈtriferous,** *a. Obs. rare*[−0]. [f. sceptre *sb.* + -iferous.] Bearing a sceptre.

1656 in Blount *Glossogr.* **1658** in Phillips.

†ˈ**sceptrous.** *nonce-wd.* [f. sceptre *sb.* + -ous.] Of the nature of a sceptre.

1822 T. G. Wainewright *Ess. & Crit.* (1880) 270 The sceptrous wand of fairy Oberon, the lily.

†ˈ**sceptry,** *a.* [f. sceptre *sb.* + -y.] Sceptred.

1819 Keats *Otho* i. i. 107 E'en for his highness Ludolph's sceptry hand, I would not Albert suffer any wrong.

scepture, scer, obs. ff. sceptre, shear.

scere, scerge, obs. ff. scare *v.*, search *v.*

†**scerne,** *v. Obs. rare*[−1]. [Aphetic for discern *v.*, after It. *scernere.*] *trans.* with *obj. clause.* To perceive, discover.

1590 Spenser *F.Q.* iii. x. 22 But, as he nigher drew, he easily Might scerne that it was not his sweetest sweet.

sceselle, obs. form of chisel.

scevity, var. scævity.

scew, obs. f. skew.

sch. This sequence of letters corresponds in present or past English spelling to the various sounds or combinations of sounds (ʃ, tʃ, sk, s, stʃ).

In ME. it was one of several modes of expressing the sound (ʃ), represented in OE. by *sc*, and in mod.E. normally by *sh*. With this value it continued to be used in Sc. down to the beginning of the 17th c. In ME. *sch* was sometimes miswritten for *ch*, pronounced (tʃ). In this Dictionary the words occurring in early texts spelt with initial *sch* which are not entered with this spelling will ordinarily be found under *sh* or *ch*.

In modern spelling *sch* has the value (ʃ) only in a few alien words from German (e.g. *schnapps*), in *schist* (of Gr. origin, influenced in pronunciation by German) and its derivatives, and in the abnormal (British) pronunciation of *schedule*. Formerly *sch* was often used for (ʃ), after German and French example, in transliterations of Oriental words, as in *schekinah, schah, haschisch*; but in these *sh* is now almost universally used instead. In words derived from Yiddish in which initial (ʃ) precedes a consonant, there is much variation in written English between *sch-* and *sh-*; however (following the German usage) *sch-* seems to be the prevailing spelling, except before *t*, where German would use simple *s-*: here *sh-* is the usual form, as it is before vowels. For the two main types see schlemiel, schmo, schnook, etc., and shtik. Such words are extremely common in the U.S. but are rarely encountered in Great Britain.

In mod.E. (sk) is the normal pronunciation of *sch* in words of classical derivation, where it represents L. *sch*, Gr. σχ. (The only exceptions are *schist* etc. and *schedule*, mentioned above, and *schism* etc. for which see below.) *Sch* is also pronounced (sk) in Italian words, e.g. *scherzo*. In Du. words the native pronunciation of *sch* is (sx) initially and (s) finally; but in the few Du. words with initial *sch* that are used in English without change of spelling the English custom is to substitute (sk).

In ME. texts initial *sch* sometimes occurs where the alliteration or the etymology shows that it is to be pronounced (sk). This probably arose from the fact that many Teut. words existed in two dialectal forms, one from OE. with (ʃ), and the other from ON. with (sk), and as both forms were used by the West Midland and Northern alliterative poets, they were often confused by the scribes. The existence of etymological spellings like *schole* for *scole* (school *sb.*[1]), which occur sporadically from the 13th c., may have had some effect in suggesting the use of *sch* as a symbol for (sk).

The only words in which *sch* now represents (s) are *schism* and its derivatives, the pronunciation of the ME. form *cisme* (from OF. *cisme*) having survived although the spelling has been altered in accordance with the ultimate etymology. A similar explanation applies to the now obsolete pronunciation of *schedule* as (ˈsɛdjuːl).

The pronunciation of *sch* as (stʃ) occurs only medially in words like *escheat, eschew, discharge*, where the *s* and the *ch* belong to different syllables.

scha, schach, obs. forms of shah.

schaalstein, schalstein (ˈʃɑːlʃtaɪn). *Geol.* Also **schaallstein**, and partly translated as **schaalstone** (ˈʃɑːlstəʊn). [Ger., f. *schale* (formerly *schaale*) skin, shell + *stein* stone. See also shale *sb.*[2] and scale *sb.*[1]] †**a.** = wollastonite. *Obs.*

1804 R. Jameson *Syst. Min.* I. 519 (*heading*) Schaalstein.—Werner. *Ibid.* 520 It is named schaalstone, which in German intimates that it is composed of lamellar distinct concretions. I have not been able to find any English word synonymous to the German, so that I am under the necessity of adopting it. **1819** W. Phillips *Elem. Introd. Mineral.* (ed. 2) 300/1 (Index), Schaallstein. **1836** T. Thompson *Outl. Min., Geol.* I. 129 Bisilicate of Lime. Table spar, schaalstein, grammite, wollastonite of Hauy.

b. Any of several basic or calcareous tuffaceous rocks, usu. laminated in structure, affected by low-grade metamorphism; a slaty or sheared greenstone.

1866 P. H. Lawrence tr. *von Cotta's Rocks classified & Described* ii. iv. 311 Some part at least of what has been called schalstein belongs to the tufa formation. **1882** A. Geikie *Text-bk. Geol.* 165 Schalstein.—Under this name German petrographers have placed a variety of rocks which consist of green, grey, red, or mottled diabase-tuff impregnated with carbonate of lime and mixed with calcareous and argillaceous mud. **1897** —— *Ancient Volcanoes of Gt. Brit.* II. xxix. 36 Some layers of this tuff assume a finely foliated appearance by the development of pale leek-green folia, which show slickensided surfaces parallel with the bedding. The rock then presents one of the usual appearances of schalstein. **1909** W. A. E. Ussher et al. *Geol. Country around Bodmin & St. Austell* vi. 44 North of Bury Down..the Middle Devonian Slates are associated with schalsteins. **1974** E. Lehmann in G. C. Amstutz *Spilites & Spilitic Rocks* 23 In the Lahn syncline..of Western Germany, the central rock complex, of upper Middle Devonian and lower Upper Devonian age, consists of so-called 'schalstein'. Any consistency, however, suggested by that old miner's term, is not reflected in the petrographic character of the rock.

schaapsteker, var. skaapsteker.

Schabzieger (ˈʃaptsiːgər). Also **Chapsager, -ziger, Schabzeiger, Schabziger,** etc. [ad. G. *schabziger*, f. *schaben* to grate + *ziger* a kind of cheese.] A kind of hard green cooking cheese made in Switzerland from curds, and flavoured with melilot. In full, **Schabzieger Käse**. Cf. sapsago.

1837 *Penny Cycl.* VII. 15/2 The green Swiss cheese, commonly called *Schabzieger*, which is made in the canton of Glarus. **1846** Worcester, *Chapsager*. **1866** Lindley & Moore *Treas. Bot.* s.v. *Melilotus*, Schabzieger or Chapziger. **1879** *Encycl. Brit.* X. 636/1 *Glarus*... The *Schabzeiger, Schotter Käse, Kräuterkäse*, or 'green cheese', made of skim milk, whether of goats or cows, mixed with butter-milk and coloured with powdered *steinklee* (*Melilotus cœrulea*), is still largely manufactured. **1887** R. Bentley *Man. Bot.* (ed. 5) 534 They [*sc.* flowers and seeds of *Melilotus officinalis*] are used to give flavour to the 'Schabzieger'. **1892** *Mrs. Beeton's Bk. Househ. Managem.* xli. 894 Shabzieger is a cheese exceedingly strong both in smell and taste. **1950** *Chamber's Encycl.* VI. 371/1 *Glarus*... The green cheese called Schabziger is wholly made here. **1955** *Times* 10 May 12/4 Schabzieger, a Swiss green cheese, may well be considered regional by virtue of its limited appeal. **1958** *Catal. County Stores, Taunton* June 9 *Cheese*..Schabzieger, for grating—each 1/6. **1969** R. & D. De Sola *Dict. Cooking* 202/1 *Schabzieger Käse* (German—scraped whey cheese), hard greenish cheese used in cooking and somewhat like sapsago, its American counterpart.

schadchen, var. shadchan.

‖**Schadenfreude** (ˈʃɑːdənfrɔɪdə). Also with small initial. [Ger., f. *schaden* harm + *freude* joy.] Malicious enjoyment of the misfortunes of others.

[**1852** R. C. Trench *Study of Words* (ed. 3) ii. 29 What a fearful thing is it that any language should have a word expressive of the pleasure which men feel at the calamities of others; for the existence of the word bears testimony to the existence of the thing. And yet in more than one such a word is found... In the Greek ἐπιχαιρεκακία, in the German, 'Schadenfreude'. **1867** Carlyle *Shooting Niagara: & After?* iii. 12 Have not I a kind of secret satisfaction, of the malicious or even of the judiciary kind (*schadenfreude*, 'mischief-joy', the Germans call it, but really it is *justice*-joy withal), that he they call 'Dizzy' is to do it.] **1895** C. Lowe *German Emperor William II* ix. 256 But the *Schadenfreude*, or malicious joy, of the French was premature. **1901** *Q. Rev.* CXCIII. 316 Sometimes it [*sc.* Queen Victoria's smile] would be coyly negative, leading the speaker on, the lips slightly opened, with a suggestion of kindly fun, even of a little innocent *Schadenfreude*. **1902** *Contemp. Rev.* May 662, I am persuaded that what (no doubt by a slip of undesigned candour) is described in the recent *Life of Claude Bernard* by an eminent English physiologist as the '*Joys* of the Laboratory', are very real 'joys' to the vivisector; that is, *Schadenfreude*,—Pleasure in the Pain he witnesses and creates. **1902** C. Hague tr. *Brentano's Origin of Knowledge of Right & Wrong* 85 Pleasure at the misfortunes of others (Schadenfreude) is bad on the first ground. **1920** F. Hamilton *Days before Yesterday* iv. 118 The particular sentiment described in German as 'schadenfreude' 'pleasure over another's troubles' (how characteristic it is that there should be no equivalent in any other language for this peculiarly Teutonic emotion!) makes but little appeal to the average Briton except where questions of age and of failing powers come into play. **1939** *Palestine Post* 31 Aug. 6/3 There appears to be a certain amount of 'Schadenfreude' in London.. at Germany's failure to get the German-Soviet Pact ratified. **1947** AUDEN *Age of Anxiety* (1948) I. 14 The *Schadenfreude* of cooks at keyholes. **1974** K. CLARK *Another Part of Wood* i. 8 Arthur Rackham.. certainly had a vein of *schadenfreude* (what is now misleadingly described as sadism) and took an intense delight in scraggy fingers. **1977** 'E. CRISPIN' *Glimpses of Moon* iv. 62 Solidarity or no solidarity, Widger was not wholly without *Schadenfreude* at seeing his informative colleague discomfited for once. **1978** 'A. STUART' *Vicious Circles* 15 For a Russian.. there is a curious fascination, mixed with *Schadenfreude*, about.. titles and honours lists.

† **'schadon.** *Obs.* Also 8 skaddon. [a. Gr. σχάδων (Aristotle).] The larva of a bee.

1609 C. BUTLER *Fem. Mon.* (1623) I 3, The weather keeping them [*sc.* Bees] in, they can do nothing but breed and hatch their schadons. **1657** S. PURCHAS *Pol. Flying-Ins.* 71 That no schadon.. can break through into a cell on the other side. **1736** BAILEY *Househ. Dict.* 93 The skaddons or young bees that are in the combs.

schafarzikite (ʃə'fɑːzɪkaɪt). *Min.* [ad. G. *schafarzikit* (J. A. Krenner 1921, in *Zeitschr. f. Kristallogr.* LVI. 198), f. the name of Ferenc *Schafarzik* (1854–1927), Hungarian mineralogist: see -ITE[1].] A tetragonal antimonite of iron, first found as red to red-brown prismatic crystals with a metallic lustre in a stibnite mine in Slovakia.

1922 *Mineral. Mag.* XIX. 348 Schafarzikite... Red, tetragonal crystals found with kermesite (and resembling this in appearance) at Pernek, Hungary, contain iron and phosphorus. **1955** M. H. HEY *Index Min. Species* (ed. 2) 271 Schafarzikite... Isostructural with artificial tetragonal $FeSb_2O_4$, but the one analysis approaches $Fe_5Sb_4O_{11}$. **1975** *Tschermaks Mineral. und Petrogr. Mitteilungen* XXII. 236 The crystal structure of schafarzikite, $FeSb_2O_4$,.. has been refined... The Fe atoms are surrounded octahedrally by six oxygen atoms, the Sb atoms form with three oxygen atoms a flat trigonal pyramid.

schagh, obs. f. SHAW.

schairerite ('ʃɛərəraɪt). *Min.* [f. the name of John F. *Schairer* (1904–70), U.S. geochemist + -ITE[1].] A sulphate and fluoride of sodium, Na_3FSO_4, usu. also containing chlorine, first found as colourless rhombohedral crystals in the salt crust of Searles Lake, San Bernardino Co., California.

1931 W. F. FOSHAG in *Amer. Mineralogist* XVI. 134 For this new species, a sulfate and fluoride of soda, the name schairerite is proposed in honor of Dr. J. F. Schairer of the Geophysical Laboratory of the Carnegie Institution, who studied the quaternary system $Na_2SO_4-NaF-NaCl-H_2O$, in which this compound plays a prominent part. **1963** *Doklady Earth Sci.* CXXXIX. 839/1 We succeeded in discovering schairerite in totally different conditions—nepheline syenite pegmatites of Alluayv Mountain in the Lovozero massif (Kola Peninsula). **1971** *Amer. Mineralogist* LVI. 177 All but the smallest and most perfect schairerite crystals are affected by voids or imperfections.

schako: see SHAKO.

schalde, obs. f. SCALD.

‖**schalet(e** ('ʃalɪt, ʃa'lɛt). *Jewish Cookery.* Also schaleth. [app. a Ger. variant of Yiddish *tsholnt.*] **a.** A kind of baked fruit pudding. **b.** A Sabbath dish of meat, potatoes, and vegetables, prepared on a Friday and baked slowly overnight.

1943 A. SIMON *Conc. Encycl. Gastronomy* IV. 27/1 *Schaleth* is an old favourite among Jewish cookery recipes.. a pudding made of.. apples.. raisins and sultanas.. spices.. and baked under a cover of a hard wheat paste. **1949** *Housewife* May 2/2 The traditional Saturday lunch-dish is the Schalet, a stew of meat and beans, prepared on the Friday and left to cook at the back of the stove. **1956** L. BLANCH *Around World in Eighty Dishes* 99 Schalète (from Israel)... An apple and raisin cake. **1966** J. GARDNER *Amber Nine* iii. 40 'Best Schalete I've ever tasted.'.. 'Kosher, of course.' **1970** L. M. FEINSILVER *Taste of Yiddish* ii. 172 Heine, in discussing the merits of *schalet,* or *tsholnt,* expressed regret that 'the Christian Church, which borrowed so much that was good from ancient Judaism, should have failed to adopt *schalet* as its own'.

‖**Schallanalyse** ('ʃalana,lyːzə). *Philology.* [Ger., lit. 'sound analysis'.] (See quot. 1931.)

1930 [see MOTORIC *a.* a]. **1931** *Year's Work Mod. Lang. Studies* I. III. 126 Siever's 'Schallanalyse'.. is a method of restoring the accentuation of a given textual record by registering and analyzing the reaction of a trained observer, who responds instinctively and directly to the psychological compulsion exerted by the text on any one who reads it aloud. **1939** L. H. GRAY *Found. Lang.* ii. 44 One must exclude from linguistics proper all consideration of rhythm (including the so-called *Schallanalyse*). **1947** C. L. WRENN *Poetry of Cædmon* 3 But it is made very clear at the outset of this [*sc.* Sievers's] exposition of *Schallanalyse* that only those who possess certain qualities in their motor nerves can participate in such experiments or judge of their effects. **1953** K. SISAM *Studies in Hist. of Old Eng. Lit.* vi. 103 Sievers, using arguments from 'Schallanalyse' which I cannot follow, concludes that the translator of *Genesis B* produced the whole work *Genesis A* and *B* by a process of compilation and revision.

schallemele, schalme, -muse, etc.: see SHAWM.

schallerite ('ʃæləraɪt). *Min.* [f. the name of Waldemar T. *Schaller* (1882–1967), U.S. mineralogist + -ITE[1].] A reddish-brown basic silicate, arsenate, and chloride of iron and manganese crystallizing in the rhombohedral system.

1925 R. B. GAGE et al. in *Amer. Mineralogist* X. 9 The name schallerite is proposed for the mineral after Dr. Waldemar T. Schaller, of the United States Geological Survey, Washington, D.C. *Ibid.*, Schallerite occurs in seams or on cleavage faces in the massive zinc ore. **1970** *Soviet Physics: Crystallogr.* XV. 40/1 This has made it possible to carry out a systematic derivation of the possible polytype modifications of pyrosmalite and to determine the structures of schallerite and friedelite.

schalstein, var. SCHAALSTEIN.

schamatize: see SHAMMATIZE *v.*

schamel, obs. f. SHAMBLE.

‖**schanse** (skans), *sb. S. Afr.* Also schanze, schantze, schans, schanz, skans. [Du. *schans* (Cape Du. *skans*) = G. *schanze.* Cf. SCONCE.] A heap or breastwork of stones used as a protection against rifle fire.

1880 *Times* 18 Oct. 4/3 Some of these paths are.. barred by lines of schanzes, or stone barricades. **1885** J. NIXON *Complete Story Transvaal* xi. 200 They found the Boers intrenched in a series of *schanses* (stone-works, breast high), along the northern ridge of the valley. **1894** B. MITFORD *Renshaw Fanning's Quest* xxii. 177 Lucky, I took the precaution of building a *schanz,*—eh? **1896** *St. James's Gaz.* 10 Jan. 4/1 Wherever there was a decent lot of rocks and schantzes.. to hide behind. **1899** G. H. RUSSELL *Under the Sjambok* ii. 25 The ruined kraals and schanses were the abodes of innumerable serpents. **1900** *Daily News* 15 Jan. 5/5 The first line of schanzes, or stone breastworks,.. were promptly occupied by the Boer sharpshooters. **1929** D. REITZ *Commando* ix. 75 We were sustaining heavy casualties from the English *schans* immediately in front of us. **1969** J. SELBY *Boer War* 15 Boers digging defense works and building stone schanzes. **1974** in J. Branford *Dict. S. Afr. English* (1978) 218/1 The British thought the Boers would be hiding behind these skanses or heaps of stone.

Hence **schanze** *v. trans.*, to fortify or protect with a schanse or schanses. *rare.*

1901 *Contemp. Rev.* Dec. 888 The English had schanzed the long ridge for a long distance.

schape, schapfold, obs. ff. CHAPE *sb.*, SCAPE, SCAFFOLD.

schappe (ʃæp, ‖'ʃapə). [a. G. *schappe* silk waste.] A fabric or yarn made from waste silk (orig. by removal of the gum by fermentation). Hence **schappe** *v. trans.*, to ferment (waste silk) in order to remove gum; **'schapping** *vbl. sb.*

1885 *Harper's Mag.* July 246 Now they [*sc.* waste cocoons] are spun into yarn,.. and made into *schappe* or 'spun silk' fabrics, not as lustrous as reeled silk goods, but stronger and cheaper. **1909** WEBSTER, Schapping, n. **1921** BEAUMONT & HILL *Dress, Blouse, & Costume Cloths* 94 The 'Schappe' or 'steeping practice' consists in placing the supply of waste silk in jacketed pans. **1957** *Textile Terms & Defs.* (*Textile Inst.*) (ed. 3) 124 *Schapping,* a continental method of degumming, applied to silk waste, that removes part of the gum by a fermentation process. Up to 10 per cent of gum may remain on the fibre. **1969** A. J. HALL *Stand. Handbk. Textiles* (ed. 7) iii. 129 Spun or schappe yarns which are short fibred and free or partly free from silk-gum are made from silk waste.

schapps: see SHAPS.

schapska ('ʃæpskə). Also chapska. [Fr. *chapska, schapska,* ad. Pol. *czapka* cap.] A flat-topped cavalry helmet.

1894 *Daily News* 27 Mar. 5/4 Helmets, shakos, chapskas, and other head coverings were to be had in great profusion. **1909** WEBSTER, Schapska. **1918** E. S. FARROW *Dict. Mil. Terms* 536 *Schapska,* a military helmet or shako, first worn by the Polish lancers. **1930** *Times Educ. Suppl.* 19 July (Home & Classroom Section) p. iv/2 Spahis, in their baggy trousers, their burnouses,.. their chapskas, their boléros, and all the other items of equipment,.. followed. **1936** C. S. FORESTER *General* ii. 16 Put on again the glories of blue and gold, schapska and plume, lance pennons and embroidered saddlecloths. **1951** J. MASTERS *Nightrunners of Bengal* xxiv. 331 A horseman galloped up... He wore.. a black schapska with a gold bag tied to its side.

scharabot, var. SCARBOT.

schat(e, obs. ff. SKATE.

schatchen, var. SHADCHAN.

schathill, schathles: see SCATHEL, SCATHELESS.

‖**Schatz** (ʃats). Also schatz. [Ger., lit. 'treasure'.] In Germany: a term of endearment for a woman; a (German) girl-friend or female companion. Also dim. **Schätzi, Schatzi(e.**

1907 M. A. VON ARNIM *Fräulein Schmidt & Mr. Anstruther* xlii. 174 The trumpeter and his *Schatz* sat quietly in the kitchen. **1956** *Amer. Speech* XXXI. 142 A sizable body of German words and idioms has entered the lingo of Army troops in Germany and Austria... *Schatzi,* or sometimes *shots* (= German *Schatz*), is a sweetheart. **1966** E. WEST *Night is Time for Listening* vi. 190 He sat at a table in Pommler's.. the place bulging with GI's, *Schatzis,* and miscellany. **1970** L. SANDERS *Anderson Tapes* xi. 30 Oh, *Schatzie,* I stopped wanting many years ago. Now I just accept. **1971** D. MACKENZIE *Sleep is for Rich* vi. 198 We've been through all this before, *schatz.* **1972** L. P. BACHMANN *Ultimate Act* xxiii. 209 'Are you all right, *Schätzi?*' she asked... 'What's *Schätzi?*' 'You. It's an old-fashioned translation of 'chéri' into German.' **1976** P. HENISSART *Winter Quarry* viii. 83 *Schatz,* I know my business.

schauld, schaule, var. ff. SHALD.

Schaumann ('ʃaʊmən). *Med.* [Name of J. *Schaumann* of Stockholm, who described them (*Acta Med. Scand.* (1941) CVI. 239, etc.).] *Schaumann('s) body*: a rounded, laminated body containing iron and often calcium, numbers of which are common inside giant cells in sarcoidosis tissue.

1955 P. A. HERBUT *Pathology* xii. 342 Schaumann bodies are deeply bluish staining, concentric, lamellated, multiple contoured, iron- and calcium-positive concretions of variable sizes. **1976** ROBBINS & ANGELL *Basic Path.* (ed. 2) xii. 421/1 The distinctive.. morphologic feature of sarcoidosis.. is the noncaseating granuloma... In 80 to 90 per cent of these granulomas, laminated concretions of calcium and proteins, known as Schaumann's bodies, can occasionally be found within giant cells.

schaundle, schauntillun: see SCANDAL, SCANTILLON.

schawage, schawbert, schawd: see SCAVAGE, SCABBARD, SHALD.

schawnter, schayle, -lle, obs. ff. CHANTRY, SKAIL.

scheam, obs. f. SCHEME.

schec(h: see SHEIKH.

schecina: see SHEKINAH.

schecon, obs. f. CHICKEN *sb.*[1]

sched (ʃɛd, skɛd), colloq. abbrev. of SCHEDULE *sb.* 4 b.

1958 R. STOW *To Islands* iv. 88, I took your telegram.. to send to the doctor, but it was too late for the sched... I felt the wireless and it was cold. **1963** L. DIACK *Labrador Nurse* III. xviii. 91 There was the radio-telephone.. and there was always a daily 'sched' at twelve noon.

schedare, schedaw, obs. ff. SHEATHER, SHADOW.

† **schede.** *Obs.* Also 7 skead(e. Cf. SCEDE. [ad. L. *scheda* (whence med.Gr. σχέδη), also *sceda* or *scida.*] A written paper.

1566 in C. Plummer *Elizab. Oxford* (O.H.S.) 200 There were divers schedes of verses in Greek, Latin, and Hebrew, set upon the doore. **1609** HEYWOOD *Troia Brit.* VII. Argt., Iasons rich Fleece, and proud Troy once more racst By Hercules, in our next skeades are placst. *Ibid.* XII. iii, And all thy skeads Achilles Fame display.

schede, obs. form of SHEATH.

† **'schediasm.** *Obs.* Also in Gr. form schediasma. [a. Gr. σχεδίασμα, f. σχεδιάζειν: see next.] An extemporized work, a jotting.

1656 BLOUNT *Glossogr.*, *Schediasm,* a sudden invention, or a work extempore. **1716** M. DAVIES *Athen. Brit.* I. Pref. 83 The best Collections of Historical Schediasma's and Memoirs that ever were publish'd. **1787** S. PARR *Let.* Aug., Wks. (1828) VII. 403, I beg of you to print the Schediasm, for it is extremely useful.

† **schedi'astic,** *a. Obs. rare*[−1]. [ad. Gr. *σχεδιαστικός (implied in -τικῶς *adv.*), f. σχεδιάζειν to do a thing off-hand.] Off-hand, superficial.

a **1640** JACKSON *Creed* x. viii. Wks. 1654 IX. 44 Such schediastic surveyors of the book of grace.

schedulate ('ʃɛdjuːleɪt), *a. rare*[−1]. [ad. mod.L. **schedulāt-us,* f. *schedula*: see next and -ATE[2].] Specified in a schedule; scheduled.

1811 W. SCOTT in *Dodson's Rep.* (1815) I. 39 Mr. Hansen has, by his act in paying the wages schedulate, waved all objection to the informality of the proceedings.

schedule ('ʃɛdjuːl, 'ʃɛdʒəl; *U.S.* 'skɛdjuːl), *sb.* Forms: 4–6 cedule, sedule, 5–6 cedull, sedull, 6–7 cedul, scedull, scedule, shedule, 6 schedul(l, (chedull, seadule, 7 shedulle), 6– schedule. Also 7 in Latin form scedula. [ME. *cedule, sedule,* a. OF. *cedule* (mod.F. *cédule*), ad. late L. *scedula* (in med. and mod.Latin also written *schedula*), dim. of L. *sceda* (med.L. also *scheda*): see SCEDE, SCHEDE *sbs.* The word has passed from Latin into most of the Rom. and Teut. langs.: Pr. *cedula, cedola,* Sp. *cédula,* Pg. *cedula,* It. *cedola*; MHG. *zedele, zetele* (mod.G. *zettel*), MLG. *sedele,* MDu. *cedule, cedele* (Du. *cedel, ceel*), Sw. *sedel,* Da. *seddel,* Icel. *seðill.*

In the 16th c., both in Fr. and Eng., the spellings *scedule* and *schedule,* imitating the contemporary forms of the Latin word, were used by a few writers. In Fr. this fashion was transient, but in Eng. *schedule* has been the regular spelling from the middle of the 17th c. The original pronunciation ('sɛdjuːl) continued in use long after the change in spelling; it is given in 1791 by Walker without alternative; in his second ed. (1797) he says that it is 'too firmly fixed by custom to be altered', though on theoretical grounds he would prefer either ('skɛdju:l), favoured by Kenrick, Perry, and Buchanan, or—'if we follow the French'—('ʃɛdju:l). The latter he does not seem to have known either in actual use or as recommended by any orthoepist. Smart, however, in 1836 gives ('ʃɛdju:l) in the body of his Dictionary without alternative, although in his introduction he says that as the word is of Gr. origin the normal pronunciation would be with (sk). Several later Dicts. recognize ('sɛdju:l) as permissible, but it is doubtful whether this was really justified by usage. In England the universal pronunciation at present seems to be with (ʃ); in the U.S., the authority of Webster has secured general currency for (sk).]

†**1.** A slip or scroll of parchment or paper containing writing; a ticket, label, placard; a short note. *Obs.*

1397 *Rolls of Parlt.* III. 378/2 [He] hathe..confessyd..alle the matiere and poyntz i wrete in this grete roule annexid to this sedule. *c* **1440** *Alphabet of Tales* 58 He prayed hym write his confession in a scrow, and at he wold giff it vnto þe bisshopp... And þe preste offerd þis cedull vnto þis bisshopp. *c* **1465** *Plumpton Corr.* (Camden) 14 Scribled in hast with mine owne hand..the 21 of June, which day your dayly Bedewoman..desired that by this rude sedule, she may humblie be recommended to your..mastership. *c* **1470** HENRY *Wallace* II. 216 Compleyn, Sanctis thus, as your sedull tellis; Compleyn to hewyn. **1483** CAXTON *Golden Leg.* 114/2 He had in hys honde a cedule wherein was wreton the oryson of our lord. *a* **1513** FABYAN *Chron.* (1811) 548 The cedule or byll of renouncement, sygnyd with Kynge Rychardes hande. **1523** LD. BERNERS *Froiss.* I. cclxxii. 408 Writynges and seadules to be set vp on the pales,..sayeng thus [etc.]. *a* **1533** —— *Gold. Bk. M. Aurel.* (1546) M iiij, Cedules to hange aboute the peoples necke, to heale the feuer quartayne. **1560** ROLLAND *Seven Sages* 36 Als sone as scho the Chedull had out red, Under hir feit incontinent it tred. **1584** R. SCOT *Discov. Witchcr.* XIV. iv. 300 A Schedull or Scroll, containing the names. **1598** BARCKLEY *Felic. Man* (1631) 225 About the pigeon's necke they had fastned a little schedule wherein was written [etc.]. **16..** BEAUMONT & FL. *Tri. Love* ii. Four Plays (1647) 33/2 The States advise, that Letters missive be straight dispatcht..And Schedules too divulg'd on every post, to enquire the lost Duke forth. **1612** W. PARKES *Curtaine-Dr.* (1876) 8 Fixed a copious Scedule ore his head, Where all his mischiefes are inregistred. **1615** T. BEDWELL *Arab. Trudg.* L 2 b, Lawes written by Mohammed, as they say, in schedules & litle scroles. **1635** PAGITT *Christianogr., Relig. Brit.* 56 As Pope Urban sent his Bull to Eve, so he sent her a Schedule, or booke of the office or service for that day. **1650** FULLER *Pisgah* IV. vi. 107 Phylacteries..being schedules, or scrouls of parchment..wherein the Decalogue, and..four other sections of the Law were written.

2. †**a.** Originally (as specific use of sense 1), a separate paper or slip of parchment accompanying or appended to a document, and containing explanatory or supplementary matter; in 16–17th c. sometimes used for a codicil to a will. *Obs.* **b.** Hence (without material reference) an appendix to an Act of Parliament or a legal instrument, containing (often in tabular form) a statement of details that could not conveniently be placed in the body of the document. **c.** In wider sense, any tabular or classified statement, esp. one arranged under headings prescribed by official authority, as, e.g. an insolvent's statement of assets and liabilities, a return of particulars liable to income or other tax, and the like. Also occas. a blank form to be filled up by the insertion of particulars under the several headings.

With reference to the British Income Tax, 'Schedule A,' 'Schedule B,' etc., are the official names for the forms of return applicable severally to the various classes into which sources of taxable income are divided.

c **1420** HEN. V. in Ellis *Orig. Lett.* Ser. III. I. 72 We sende yow closed wiyin yis lettre a Cedule contenyng ye names of certein maistres for owr grete shippes. **1429** *Rolls of Parlt.* IV. 346/2 Aftre the fourme and effect of the Cedule annexed to this Bille. **1478** *Bury Wills* (Camden) 80 The same cedule is annexid to myn testament. **1516** *Nottingham Rec.* III. 349 The cedule of the yerely rentes. **1531–2** *Act 23 Hen. VIII*, c. 4 This Acte of Brewers and Coupers whereunto this Cedule is annexed. **1560** Q. ELIZ. in Ellis *Orig. Lett.* Ser. II. II. 265 We will that you shall from time to time address several Schedules containing the names of all such hable Scholers. **1601** SHAKS. *Twel. N.* I. v. 263, I will giue out diuers scedules of my beautie. It shalbe Inuentoried and euery particle and vtensile labell'd to my will. **1607** COWELL *Interpr.* s.v. *Clerk of the extreates*, He also maketh ceduls of such summes extreated, as are to be discharged. **1625** *Maldon* (Essex) *Documents* (Bundle 201. no. 2), The trained men within the sayd parish (whose names are specified in a Scedula heerevnto annexed). **1626** B. JONSON *Staple of N.* I. vi, Your father..Left it in writing in a Schedule here, To be annexed to his Will; that you..should take [etc.]. **1735** BERKELEY *Querist* §179 Whether there should not be published yearly schedules of our trade. **1788** J. POWELL *Devises* (1827) II. 277 Certain acts on the part of the insolvent are necessary, as the delivery of a petition and schedule, constituting it a voluntary alienation, as distinguished from a bankruptcy. **1803** WELLINGTON in Gurw. *Desp.* (1837) II. 612 Of which territories, etc. a detailed list is given in the accompanying schedule. **1803** *Income Tax Act 43 Geo. III* c. 122 s. 1 in *Statutes United Kingdom* (1804) I. 1012 During the Term herein mentioned, there shall be raised, levied, collected, and paid, throughout Great Britain, the several Duties and Contributions in the Schedules contained in this Act, marked (A) (B) (C) (D) and (E). **1824** *Saunders' K.B. Rep.* I. 308 a, *note*, When an inferior court, in obedience to the writ of certiorari, returns an indictment to the K.B. it is annexed to the caption, then called a schedule, and the caption concludes with stating, that 'it is presented in manner and form as appears in and by a certain indictment annexed to this schedule'. **1831** J. MACINTOSH *Sp. Ho. Commons* 4 July, Wks. 1846 III. 538 It does not only itself exhibit the principle of the schedules of this Bill, but [etc.]. **1838** BELL *Dict. Law Scot.* s.v. *Schedule of poinding*, When a poinding is completed, the messenger or officer who executes it, leaves a schedule for the debtor, of the particulars of the effects taken. **1852** MᶜCULLOCH *Taxation* II. iii. (ed. 2) 288 The head of settlements in the stamp-duty schedule. **1863** KINGSLEY *Water-Babies* iv, The Chancellor of the Exchequer..jumped at the notion; for he saw in it the one and only plan for abolishing Schedule D. **1873** *Daily News* 12 Sept. 4/5 Both schedules show a rapid increase in the number of persons assessed. **1882** A. MACFARLANE *Consanguinity* 13 He took for the basis of his schedule of questions the Roman method of denoting relationships. **1887** *Live Stock Jrnl.* 1 July 21/3 The schedule of the annual [agricultural] show..to be held at Ormskirk on July 20th. has been received. **1902** KIPLING *Traffics & Discoveries* (1904) 29 'You'll only be an additional expense to me as a taxpayer. Think of Schedule D,' he says, 'and take parole.' **1966** B. E. V. SABINE *Hist. Income Tax* ii. 35 The tax was for the first time divided up into the well-known five schedules. Schedule A charged tax on the amount of land and buildings; Schedule B covered farming profits; Schedule C taxed fundholders in respect of annuities payable out of any public revenue... Schedule D was divided into the six cases which are still familiar today and brought into charge various forms of profit and interest ..and Schedule E embraced the charge on income from offices and employments of profit and annuities and pensions. **1970** *Money Which?* Mar. 4/2 Schedule A. Income from rents and other receipts from property which is unfurnished (formerly Case VIII of Schedule D, but reclassified as Schedule A as from 6 April 1970).

transf. and *fig.* *c* **1630** DONNE *Serm.* ix. (1640) 95 Then the Accuser will be ready to interline the schedules of thy debts, thy sins, and insert false debts. **1649** JER. TAYLOR *Great Exemp.* I. 118 He gave particular schedules of duty to several states of persons. **1653** —— *Serm. for Yr.* ii. 27 The Devill shall accuse the Brethren..and shall tell..the long schedule of omissions of duty. **1654** tr. *Scudery's Curia Pol.* 4 Hedin ..desired permission to be inserted in the Schedule of my Triumphs. **1659** *Gentl. Calling* (1696) 17 Having given this Schedule of undeniable Priviledges they enjoy.

3. *U.S.* (See quot.)

1860 BARTLETT *Dict. Amer.* (ed. 3), *Schedule*, in the State of Rhode Island, the printed 'Acts and Resolves' of the General Assembly.

4. a. A time-table. Orig. *U.S.* (but cf. SCHEDULE *v.*). Also *transf.* Also in extended sense, a programme or plan of events, operations, etc. Freq. in phrs. ***according to, before, behind, on,*** etc., ***schedule*** (***time***).

In the sense 'a printed time-table of arrivals and departures of trains, buses, aeroplanes, etc.', the use remains chiefly *N. Amer.*

1863 O. W. NORTON *Army Lett.* (1903) 282 That is all that ever caused the name to be printed on anything but time-tables and schedules of a one-horse railroad. **1866** C. H. SMITH *Bill Arp* 21 We tried our durndest to comply with your schedule. **1873** HALE *In His Name* vi. 47 Halting was not in John of Lugio's schedule for that afternoon. **1881** A. A. HAYES *New Colorado* vii. 94 As he [*sc.* the engineer] rounded the curves in about half of schedule time. **1883** C. D. WARNER *Roundabout Journey* 2 We travel fast and we reach places at the time named on the schedule. **1884** J. G. BOURKE *Snake Dance Moquis* i. 6 There was no probability of trains running on schedule time for several days. **1891** *Scribner's Mag.* Sept. 270/1 A steamer to-day leaves her wharf at the moment of time set forth in her schedule. **1901** O. WISTER in *Lippincott's Monthly Mag.* Aug. 193 As a delayed train makes the last few miles high above schedule speed. **1902** *Munsey's Mag.* XXVI. 606/2 A regular train schedule was established between Caloocan and Manila. **1904** *Newark Evening News* 13 June 6 It is on the schedule for the new Equal Taxation Commission to organize to-morrow. **1906** 'O. HENRY' *Rolling Stones* (1912) 22 Tuesday, the day set for the revolution, came around according to schedule. **1909** *Springfield* (Mass.) *Weekly Republican* 19 Aug. 10 The train was running exactly on schedule when the party left it. **1911** C. E. PERSONS *Labor Laws & their Enforcement* 109 Most important of these enforced concessions was the temporary reduction to a ten-hour [factory] schedule at Fall River. **1927** *Daily Tel.* 1 Mar. 6/4 The material must be finished on time, routed on schedule, and delivered at exactly the psychological moment. **1961** *Lancet* 29 July 230/1 In investigations into new treatment schedules, close co-operation between the clinician and the laboratory is essential. **1968** *Globe & Mail* (Toronto) 3 Feb. 35/9 The standing in the Metro Junior B Hockey League is beginning to appear like a jig-saw puzzle as the schedule enters its final week. **1975** M. RUSSELL *Murder by Mile* ix. 93 How far behind schedule are you now? **1977** I. SHAW *Beggarman, Thief* II. i. 119 He looked up the schedule of the planes flying out of Brussels to New York. **1980** *Nature* 24 Apr. 654/1 Preparations for the launch, begun on 2 April, are going ahead on schedule following the arrival of the Lo2 launcher at Kourou.

b. An agreed period of time during which a radio transmission may be made; time allocated to listening for transmissions.

1958 'N. SHUTE' *Rainbow & Rose* i. 9, I should say they've closed down for the night. They'll be speaking on the morning schedule, at seven o' clock. **1974** D. KYLE *Raft of Swords* xiii. 143 We'd better watch this six o'clock schedule like hawks.

†**5.** Used to render Sp. *cédula* and It. *cedola*: **a.** A royal writ or permit; **b.** A bond or promissory note. *Obs.*

1622 MABBE tr. *Aleman's Guz. d'Alf.* II. 357 The Captaine ..gaue me leaue to goe at libertie vp and downe the Gally, till his Majesties Royall Scedula should be sent for my absolute discharge. *c* **1645** HOWELL *Lett.* (1650) I. II. xiv. 125, I have procur'd a Royal Cedule..by which Cedule I have power to arrest his very person. **1668** *Lond. Gaz.* No. 278/2 He presented the Pope with..a Cedule of 7000 Ducats, as a Tribute. **1761** *Ann. Reg.* 290/1 Heavy penalties contained in the..royal cedules issued on like occasions in times past.

schedule ('ʃɛdju:l, *U.S.* 'skɛdju:l), *v.* [f. prec.]

1. *trans.* To enter in a schedule or list. In railway use: To enter (a train) in the time-table (cf. SCHEDULE *sb.* 4). Hence, in extended uses: to place (something) on a programme of future events; to arrange for (a person or thing) to do something or *for* an event.

1862 SHIRLEY *Nugæ Crit.* §7. 303 The mind is not incessantly watched; its most flimsy experiences are not officially scheduled. **1869** *Daily News* 31 Aug., He was told that he would be scheduled as a briber. **1883** *Act 46 & 47 Vict.* c. 52 §122 (10) Any creditor of the debtor..shall be entitled to be scheduled as a creditor of the debtor for the amount of his proof. **1887** JESSOPP *Arcady* ii. 31 To have one's career in a manner cut short by being scheduled with the infirm, is really too bad. **1891** *Law Times* XC. 376/2 The liabilities he had scheduled amounted to nearly £2500. **1897** *Daily News* 13 Sept. 7/6 Trains which are scheduled to run have to get through some time. **1898** T. N. PAGE *Red Rock* 478 The trial would come off as already scheduled. **1904** *N.Y. Even. Post* 30 Sept. 1 The archbishop is scheduled to speak this afternoon at the Academy of Music. **1922** JOYCE *Ulysses* 313 It was a historic and a hefty battle when Myler and Percy were scheduled to don the gloves for the purse of fifty sovereigns. **1931** H. F. PRINGLE *Theodore Roosevelt* I. xiv. 190 The advance took place as scheduled. **1958** 'N. SHUTE' *Rainbow & Rose* i. 7 There was a Dakota freighter scheduled to leave for Hobart..at one o'clock. **1968** *Globe & Mail* (Toronto) 17 Feb. B 7 (Advt.), *Wanted* Masonry Superintendent, to take complete charge of a young masonry construction firm. Must be able to..schedule jobs, assist in bidding etc. **1976** *Columbus* (Montana) *News* 3 June 2/3 Kristy McFarland..is scheduled for back surgery June 4. **1976** *Sunday Times* (Lagos) 1 Aug. 22/2 Two top Nigerian lawn tennis players..are scheduled for the Zambian Open Championships. **1979** *Tucson* (Arizona) *Citizen* 20 Sept. 3A/1 A spokesman for St. Paul [Hospital] said an autopsy was scheduled.

2. To affix as a schedule (*to* an Act of Parliament).

1885 J. PEARSON in *Law Times' Rep.* LIII. 385/1 A certain number of these are scheduled to the Act. **1908** *Act 8 Edw. VII*, c. 20 §3 (4) The letter addressed by senate of the University to the corporation..which is scheduled in an appendix to this Act.

3. To include (a building, etc.) on a list of buildings that are to be preserved and protected for architectural or historic reasons.

1921 *Report of Ancient Monuments Advisory Committee* 5 The Commissioners of Works are bound to prepare and publish a list of all monuments the preservation of which is reported by any of the three Ancient Monuments Boards to be of national importance, and to inform the owners of their intention to include them and of the penalties herein-after mentioned. This is called scheduling a monument. **1960** *Twentieth Century* Nov. 480 A decaying polygon.. scheduled as being of architectural or historical interest. **1971** P. GRESSWELL *Environment* 23 Ancient Monuments are 'scheduled' by the Department of the Environment.

'**scheduled,** *ppl. a.* [f. SCHEDULE *v.*] **a.** Entered on a schedule or list; included in a schedule.

1881 *Daily News* 21 Jan. 2/1 Antrim was not in the scheduled district. **1888** *Ibid.* 5 Nov. 5/2 Students..must make up their minds for which particular competition they shall enter, and..must..waste no time by straying from the scheduled path. **1911** G. B. SHAW *Doctor's Dilemma* p. xx, Treatment varies widely from doctor to doctor, one practitioner prescribing six or seven scheduled poisons for so familiar a disease as enteric fever. **1921** *Report of Ancient Monuments Advisory Committee* 6 A scheduled monument.. whether public or private may not be in any way damaged. **1931** H. F. PRINGLE *Theodore Roosevelt* III. v. 568 He insisted..upon making a scheduled speech. **1952** 'J. TEY' *Singing Sands* ix. 130 Most of us fly scheduled routes, but some fly tramps. **1970** *Guardian* 31 Dec. 18/3 BEA will be able to offer seats on scheduled flights to package tour holidaymakers..at knock-down prices. **1976** *Southern Even. Echo* (Southampton) 16 Nov. 3/7 A scheduled meeting with Mr. Ford will not take place until the following week.

b. In specific collocations: **Scheduled Caste** (or **class**), in India, a category of persons in the lowest castes, or Untouchables; **scheduled territory**, between 1947 and 1972, any of a group of countries, mostly within the British Commonwealth, with currencies linked to sterling; the sterling area; after 1972 (see quot. 1977; the Republic of Ireland has now ceased to be part of the sterling area); **Scheduled Tribe**, in India, a group of aborigines who do not observe the taboos of caste.

1935 *Government of India Act 25 & 26 Geo. V* c. 42 1st. sched. §26 The 'scheduled castes' means such castes, races or tribes or parts of or groups within castes, races or tribes, being castes, races, tribes, parts or groups which appear to His Majesty in Council to correspond to the classes of persons formerly known as 'the depressed classes'. **1943** B. R. AMBEDKAR *Mr. Gandhi & Emancipation of Untouchables* iii. 15 Under the Government of India Act of 1935 the Untouchables are designated as 'Scheduled Castes'. **1975** Y. B. DAMLE in H. M. Patel et al. *Say not the Struggle Nought Availeth* 143 Students belonging to the scheduled and backward classes tend to be less than ten per cent of the total students in most of the states. **1947** *Act 10 & 11 Geo. VI* c. 4 §1 (3) In this Act..the expression 'the scheduled territories' means the territories specified in the First Schedule to this Act, so, however, that the Treasury may at any time by order amend the said Schedule, either by the additon or exclusion of territories. **1964** *Financial Times* 12 Mar. 19/5 The Scheduled Territories are the British Commonwealth (except Canada), the Irish Republic, British Trust Territories, British Protectorates and Protected States, Burma, Iceland, the Hashemite Kingdom of Jordan, Kuwait, Lybia, South Africa and South West

Africa, Western Samoa. **1972** *Statutory Instruments* II. I. 2926 The Scheduled Territories now consist only of the United Kingdom, the Channel Islands, the Isle of Man, and the Republic of Ireland. **1977** *Guide to United Kingdom Exchange Control* (Bank of England) 6 The Scheduled Territories at present comprise the United Kingdom, including the Channel Islands and the Isle of Man, the Republic of Ireland and Gibraltar. **1957** G. S. GHURYE *Mahadev Kolis* i. 4 Many sections of Kolis describe themselves as Mahadev Kolis in order to be able to claim the special benefits of the Scheduled Tribes. **1972** *Times of India* 28 Nov. 13/2 (Advt.), This post is unreserved, however, preference will be given to Scheduled Caste|Scheduled Tribe candidates.

scheduler ('ʃɛdjuːlə(r), *U.S.* 'skɛdjuːlə(r)). [f. SCHEDULE *v.* + -ER[1].] **1.** One who draws up a schedule or arranges activities in accordance with one.

1952 *Antioch Rev.* Dec. 426 After school there are music lessons, skating lessons, riding lessons, with mother as chauffeur and scheduler. **1957** *Electronic Engin.* XXIX. 179/1 The two schedulers interpret the required data-processing operations in terms of machine functions. **1978** *Sci. Amer.* Mar. 124/2 The priority list *L* is an ordering of the tasks according to the preferences of the scheduler. **1979** H. KISSINGER *White House Years* xxii. 923 The schedulers had arranged for a visit to the Vatican in the afternoon. **1980** *Daily Tel.* 18 June 8/7 So far the Radio 3 schedulers have mostly been able to replace these concerts with records of the works that would have been played.

2. a. A machine, esp. a computer, that can arrange a number of planned activities into the order in which they should take place.

1962 *Times* 26 Oct. (Spencer Steelworks Suppl.) p. xiv/3 The finishing end scheduler is the coordinating and planning authority for the whole finishing process. *Ibid.*, The finishing end scheduler prepares and revises production schedules.

b. *Computers.* Any of several control programs that arrange jobs or the computer's operations into an appropriate sequence; also, a part of the hardware designed to perform a similar function.

1966 C. J. SIPPL *Computer Dict. & Handbk.* 279/2 The scheduler is called at regular intervals to decide which program in memory is to be run... A program may be terminated temporarily by user intervention to the scheduler, or it may suspend its own operation. **1968** *Communications Assoc. Computing Machinery* XI. 349/1 The part of the system responsible for handling block and wakeup instructions will be called the scheduler. *Ibid.* 357/2 All the external interrupt lines are directed into the scheduler, which..loops constantly, examining them. **1973** C. W. GEAR *Introd. Computer Sci.* iv. 168 When a job is terminated, the scheduler uses the space for another job and puts the output on a work list for the output processor.

'scheduling, *vbl. sb.* [f. as prec. + -ING[1].] The action of entering in or drawing up a schedule; *esp.* the preparation of a timetable for the completion of the various stages of a complex project; the co-ordination of many related actions or tasks into a single time-sequence.

1894 *Times* (weekly ed.) 9 Feb. 108/1 The Scheduling of Canadian cattle..may prove..a blessing in disguise. **1957** *Proc. Conf. Operations Res., Computers, & Management Decisions* (Case Inst. Technol.) 63/1 A minimum of constraints were used to define the models of the cut-and-fill operation and of construction scheduling. **1959** *Naval Research Logistics Q.* (U.S.) VI. 131 There is an indication of the possibility of constructing special algorithms to exploit the structure of certain of the 'classical' scheduling problems. **1964** A. BATTERSBY *Network Analysis* ix. 138 A fairly simple arrow diagram..usually contains about 150 to 200 activities and forms the basis for the overall scheduling. **1967** *Times Rev. Industry* Mar. 15/1 Scheduling times on much plant and equipment are long and one can do little about rephasing such spending in the short term. **1976** P. R. WHITE *Planning for Public Transport* viii. 170 A graphic timetable of this type can be used for scheduling purposes. **1977** *Rep. Comm. Future of Broadcasting* iv. 35 To our mind an executive Broadcasting Commission..would be bound to be drawn into the details of scheduling..in making decisions about individual programmes. **1978** *Sci. Amer.* Mar. 129/3 In critical-path scheduling the tasks are assigned to processors according to the length of the various precedence chains they head in the diagram of precedence constraints. **1980** *Times* 29 Nov. 5/8 The scheduling of an interim stop in Athens after the airliner took off.

schedulize ('ʃɛdjuːlaɪz), *v. rare*[−1]. [f. SCHEDULE *sb.* + -IZE.] *intr.* To make schedules.

1832 J. WILSON in *Blackw. Mag.* XXXII. 407 We shall either have it in our power to cancel the Whig schedules *in toto*—or be convinced..that, schedulize to the end of the chapter, the national heart is Tory.

scheele, obs. form of SHEAL *v.*

Scheele's green ('ʃeɪləz griːn). *Chem.* [f. the name of Karl Wilhelm *Scheele* (1742–1786), German-born Swedish chemist, who first prepared it.] A hydrated form of copper arsenite, $Cu_3(AsO_3)_2.xH_2O$, formerly used as a pigment in calico printing and wallpaper manufacture.

1819 W. T. BRANDE *Man. Chem.* v. 274 Mixed with a solution of sulphate of copper, a precipitate of a fine apple-green colour falls, called from its discoverer, Scheele's green, and useful as a pigment. **1935** *Discovery* Sept. 261/2 The dark green background of a so-called Holbein portrait was recently found, on..analysis.., to consist of Scheele's green, a copper arsenate discovered in 1778. **1967** *Jrnl. Colour Group* 92/2 Scheele's green and emerald green, both copper arsenates, lost their popularity [with artists] because of their poisonous effects. **1973** J. D. SMITH in J. C. Bailar et al. *Comprehensive Inorg. Chem.* II. xxi. 609 Yellow silver arsenite..and copper arsenite (Scheele's green) may be precipitated from neutral solutions.

scheelite ('ʃiːlaɪt). *Min.* [f. the name of K. W. *Scheele*, the discoverer of tungstic acid + -ITE.] Tungstate of calcium, found in brilliant crystals of various colours.

1837 DANA *Min.* 208. **1878** H. P. GURNEY *Crystallogr.* 79.

scheelitine ('ʃiːlɪtɪn). *Min.* Also **scheeletine.** [f. SCHEELITE from its resemblance to that mineral + -INE.] An obsolete synonym of stolzite.

1843 CHAPMAN *Pract. Min.* 41 Scheelitine. **1849** NICOL *Man. Min.* 386. **1854** DANA *Syst. Min.* (ed. 4) 349 Scheeletine.

scheererite ('ʃɪərəraɪt). *Min.* [Named after von *Scheerer*, its discoverer: see -ITE.] A solid hydrocarbon, found in pearly, tabular crystals.

1836 T. THOMSON *Min., Geol.*, etc. I. 59 Scheererite... Observed in the year 1822. **1883** *Encycl. Brit.* XVI. 429/1.

scheete, obs. f. SHOOT, SKATE.

schefe, obs. f. SHEAF, SHEAVE.

scheff: see CHIEF *a.*

schefferite ('ʃɛfəraɪt). *Min.* [Named 1862 after H. T. *Scheffer*, a Swedish chemist: see -ITE.] A manganese pyroxene, of yellowish or reddish-brown colour.

1868 in DANA *Syst. Min.* (ed. 5) 215.

schefflera ('ʃɛflərə). [mod.L. (J. R. & G. Forster *Characteres Generum Plantarum* (1776) 45), f. the name of J. C. *Scheffler* of Danzig + -A 2.] An evergreen shrub or small tree of the genus so called, belonging to the family Araliaceæ, native to many tropical or subtropical regions, and bearing large compound leaves and clusters of small white, greenish, or red flowers, followed by small berries.

1954 F. KINGDON-WARD *Berried Treasure* xviii. 164 The slim rigid spikes of Schefflera, like tall black candles, give a Gothic dignity to this little palm-like tree. **1976** *National Observer* (U.S.) 25 Sept. 9/2 We couldn't buy a schefflera that big for $50. **1978** *Homes & Gardens* Apr. 32/1 Some philodendrons and schefflera..do well in most places, given reasonable light.

Scheherazade (ʃəˌhɛrəˈzɑːd, ʃəˌhɪər-, -ˈzɑːdə). The name of the female narrator of the *Arabian Nights*, used allusively as the type of a (usu. young and attractive female) teller of long or numerous stories.

1851 DICKENS *Let.* 25 Oct. in W. Gérin *E. Gaskell* (1976) xii. 123 My dear Scheherazade,—For I am sure your powers of narrative..must be good for at least a thousand nights and one. **1872** O. W. HOLMES *Poet at Breakfast-Table* iii. 87, I had noticed that the Young Girl—the story-writer, our Scheherazade, as I called her—looked as if she had been crying or lying awake half the night. **1896** G. B. SHAW *Let.* 5 July (1965) I. 634 Or are you only a flattering storytelling Scheherezade? **1946** L. P. HARTLEY *Sixth Heaven* i. 4 'I'm afraid it will be a long story,' he said... 'Waste no time in self-depreciation, Scheherazade, but..take up your tale.' **1973** G. BUTLER *Coffin for Pandora* viii. 192 You're a teller of tales, young lady... Quite a Scheherazade. **1978** M. PUZO *Fools Die* xxix. 343 During that happy time, a blond Scheherazade, she told me the story of her life. **1981** A. FRASER *Splash of Red* i. 11 That's *another* story I shall tell you... I shall be Scheherazade.

schei(c)k: see SHEIKH.

scheild, obs. f. SHIELD.

schein, obs. Sc. f. SHEEN *a.*

scheind, obs. f. SHEND *v.*

Scheiner ('ʃaɪnə(r)). *Photogr.* The name of Julius *Scheiner* (1858–1913), German astrophysicist, used, usu. *attrib.*, with reference to a way of measuring and expressing the speed of photographic emulsions that he devised, as ***Scheiner degree, scale, sensitometer, speed, system***; **Scheiner number**, a number depending on the logarithm of the least exposure that will give a visible image on development.

1900 *Astrophysical Jrnl.* XI. 91 In a simple experiment with the aid of Scheiner's sensitometer equal degrees of blackening were produced by continuous exposures of 96, 72, 48, 24, 12 secs. *Ibid.* 98 Remarks on the Scheiner sensitometer. **1911** A. WATKINS *Photography* iii. 47 In the case of Wynne, Scheiner, and Warnerke numbers..there is not the same direct proportion between the numbers. *Ibid.* 332 (Index), Scheiner speeds. **1918** J. R. ROEBUCK *Science & Practice of Photogr.* 225 'n' is the Scheiner degree and 'A' has the value in this case of about 4·4. **1936** *Discovery* June 192/2 The rating [of the exposure meter] agreeing more or less with the Scheiner system. **1938** S. G. B. STUBBS et al. *Modern Encycl. Photogr.* II. 1105/1 The so-called 'Scheiner speeds' quoted by Continental manufacturers are in reality not Scheiner speeds at all, as all 'Scheiner' measurements are now carried out by the Eder-Hecht method. **1942** C. B. NEBLETTE *Photography* (ed. 4) xiii. 419 The ratio of the exposures between consecutive steps on the Scheiner sensitometer is as 1:1·27. **1962** *Ibid.* (ed. 6) xx. 267/1 The Scheiner speed number was obtained originally by exposing the negative material in a sensitometer with a sector wheel having exposure steps numbered from 1 to 20, with a log exposure difference of 0·15. *Ibid.* 267/2 In 1931, the German photographic industry replaced the then meaningless Scheiner numbers by a new German standard (DIN) speed. **1963** JERRARD & MCNEILL *Dict. Sci. Units* 106 The Scheiner scale was devised in 1898..and was first used commercially by the Secco Film Company of Boston, Mass. in 1899. **1973** *Focal Dict. Photogr. Technol.* 544 Scheiner speed was expressed in degrees, every increase of 3° corresponding to a doubling of the working speed.

scheip, obs. f. SHEEP, SHIP.

scheir, obs. f. SHEER *a.*

‖**Scheitholt** ('ʃaɪthɔlt). [Ger., f. *scheit* log + dialectal *-holt* wood.] A former stringed instrument of central Europe, a precursor of the zither.

1961 A. BAINES *Musical Instr. through Ages* 210 The simplest forms [of zither], as Alpine *Scheitholt, épinette des Vosges*, and the Dutch *hummel*..have a long narrow hollowed-out sound-box, placed on the knees or on a table. **1976** D. MUNROW *Instr. Middle Ages & Renaissance* 33/4 Various names have been used for the string drum including *Scheitholt* and *tambourin*.

schek, scheke, schekinah, schekkar: see SHEIKH, SHAKE, SHEKINAH, SHAKER.

scheker, schekyn, obs. ff. CHEQUER *sb.*[1], CHICKEN *sb.*[1]

†**schelchene.** *Obs. rare.* Also 3 -ine. [OE. *scielcen, scylcen*:—OTeut. **skalkinjā*, fem. of **skalko-z* (OE. *scealc*) servant.] A female servant.

c **1000** ÆLFRIC *Hom.* (ed. Thorpe) II. 162 þæt heora mod wurde ontend to ȝalnysse, þurh ðæra scylcena pleȝan. *a* **1225** *Ancr. R.* 12 Al nis bute ase a schelchine to seruien þe leafdi to riwlen ðe heorte. *Ibid.* 390. *c* **1275** *Passion our Lord* 279 in *O.E. Misc.* 45 Þer com o schelchene gon þat wes myd kayphas.

scheld, scheldbrede: see SHIELD, -BOARD.

scheldroun, -dtrome: see SHELTRON.

scheldur, etc.: see SHOULDER.

schele: see SHELL, SHEAL.

schellam, -um: see SKELM *sb.*

‖**schelling** ('skɛlɪŋ, in Du. 'sxɛlɪŋ). *Obs.* exc. *Hist.* Also 6 **shylyng,** 7 **skilling, schilling,** 7, 8 **skelling.** [Du.: see SHILLING. Cf. SCHILLING[1], SKILLING.] A silver coin formerly current in the Low Countries, of the value of 6 stivers or from 5*d.* to 7½*d.* sterling.

1535 JOYE *Apol. Tindale* (Arb.) 22 In al I had for my labour but xiiij shylyngis flemesshe. **1692** *Lond. Gaz.* No. 2829/3 After which time such Skellings are only to pass for five Stivers and a half each. **1693** DRYDEN *Persius* VI. (1697) 485 And prize a hundred Zeno's just as much As a clipt Sixpence, or a Schilling Dutch. **1700** S. L. tr. *Fryke's Voy. E. Ind.* 6 The Cash-keeper paid us..three Dutch Skillings every day while we stayed on shoar. **1706** PHILLIPS (ed. Kersey), *Schelling*, a Coin in Holland and Flanders, containing 12 Groots or 6 Stivers and equal to 6⅔ of our English Money. **1772–84** COOK *Voy.* (1790) 1252 At the Cape..it was discovered that a number of counterfeit schellings..had been circulated. **1785** G. FORSTER tr. *Sparrman's Voy. Cape G. Hope* (1786) I. 68 Eighteen China oranges I had bought in Paarl for one skelling Dutch.

schelling: see SCHILLING[1].

Schellingian (ʃɛ'lɪŋɪən), *a.* [f. *Schelling* (see below) + -IAN.] Of or pertaining to the German philosopher, F. W. J. von Schelling (1775–1854), or to his doctrines. Hence as *sb.*, a follower of Schelling. Also **Schellingism** ('ʃɛlɪŋɪz(ə)m) [ad. G. *Schellingismus*], the system of philosophy taught by Schelling; **'Schellingist**, a disciple of Schelling.

1865 tr. *Strauss's New Life of Jesus* I. 190 Similar instances may be brought forward from the history of the Schellingian philosophy. **1865** J. H. STIRLING *Secret of Hegel* I. I. v. 275 Once in Jena, we have to see him a declared Schellingian. **1865** W. PATER *Appreciations* (1889) 75 Schellingism, the 'Philosophy of Nature', is indeed a constant tradition in the history of thought. **1874** MORRIS & PORTER tr. *Ueberweg's Hist. Philos.* II. 114 Kantism, the renewed Spinozism (Schellingism), and Herbartism lay conjoined and undeveloped in the doctrine of Leibnitz. **1894** C. S. PEIRCE *Let.* 28 Jan. in R. B. Perry *Tht. & Char. of W. James* (1935) II. 416 If you were to call my philosophy Schellingism transformed in the light of modern physics, I should not take it hard. **1895** C. GARNETT tr. *Turgenev's On the Eve* iv. 30 My father was a learned man, a Schellingist. **1967** *Encycl. Philos.* VII. 260/2 The most important of the Russian Schellingians were Professor D. M. Vellanski..and Prince V. F. Odoyevski. *Ibid.* 261/2 In his early Schellingian period he [*sc.* Belinski] stressed aesthetic activity.

schelly: see SKELLY.

‖**schelm** (ʃɛlm). *arch.* Also 6–7 **shelm(e.** [Ger.; for forms repr. the equivalent Du. *schelm* ('sxɛləm), see SKELM *sb.*] A rascal. (A term of abuse or contempt, attributed to German speakers.)

1584 ? SIDNEY *Disc. Def. Earl Leicester* Misc. Wks. (1829) 272 An evil tongued shelm, as the Germans especially call such people. **1603-5** J. MELVIL *Mem.* (1735) 23 The Land-grave called him Shelm, Pultroon, Traitor [etc.]. *a* **1634** CHAPMAN *Alphonsus* II. ii. 62 Thou art a schelm. *Ibid.* II. iii. 109 Call you me shelme? **1823** SCOTT *Q. Durward* ii, The rascally schelm shot my bird with an arrow. **1889** DOYLE *Micah Clarke* 202 Some rascally schelm..stabbed my horse.

Hence †'**schelmish** *a.* [G. *schelmisch*], rascally.

a **1634** CHAPMAN *Alphonsus* III. i. 173, I highly do mistrust this schelmish bowr.

schelm, var. SKELM.

scheltopusik: see SHELTOPUSIK.

schema ('skiːmə). Pl. **schemata** ('skiːmətə), **schemas**. [a. Gr. σχῆμα, form, figure: see SCHEME *sb.*[1]]

1. a. *Philos.* In Kant: Any one of certain forms or rules of the 'productive imagination' through which the understanding is able to apply its 'categories' to the manifold of sense-perception in the process of realizing knowledge or experience.

1796 F. A. NITSCH *View of Kant's Princ.* 103 The Schema of a Category is no picture of anything. **1839** *Penny Cycl.* XIII. 176 To the subsumtion of an object under a category, a schema, 'time', is indispensable, and, apart from all sensation, this schema itself does not subsist. **1877** E. CAIRD *Philos. Kant* II. x. 408 The schema in itself is nothing but a product of imagination. **1880** ADAMSON *Kant* in *Encycl. Brit.* XIII. 852 The specific forms of productive imagination are called *schemata*. **1961** B. M. MILMED *Kant & Current Philos. Issues* iv. 81 For both Kant and Lewis.. the image is empirical, a reproduction of past experience, while the schema, through which the image becomes part of a criterion of empirical meaning, is a priori in its role as a definition of the experience to be interpreted by it. **1963** A. PAP *Introd. Philos. of Sci.* vi. 102 The schemas correspond to the following principles of logic: the principle of the hypothetical syllogism..; a statement implied by a true statement is true [etc.]. **1966** E. S. CASEY tr. *Dufrenne's Notion of A Priori* viii. 156 Now, if the schema is the *a priori* in its original state, is it not the *a priori* in its corporeal state as well?

b. *Neurol.* and *Psychol.* An automatic, unconscious coding or organization of incoming physiological or psychological stimuli, giving rise to a particular response or effect.

1920 H. HEAD *Stud. in Neurol.* II. IV. v. 605 For this combined standard, against which all subsequent changes of posture are measured before they enter consciousness, we propose the word 'schema'. **1926** M. GABAIN tr. *Piaget's Lang. & Thought of Child* v. 236 This schema may be thought to apply only to 'whys', but it is obvious that other types of question..are more or less incorporated in it. **1932** —— tr. *Piaget's Moral Judgment of Child* ii. 20 The child is undoubtedly trying..to understand the nature of the marbles and to adapt its motor schemas to this novel reality. **1950** W. R. BRAIN in D. Richter *Perspectives in Neuropsychiatry* 138 The schema would then develop by becoming a resonator to a pattern received from any part of the corresponding sensory cortex and 'learned' by repetition, and would thus be the basis both of simple recognition and of abstraction. *Ibid.* 139 The schema is a neurophysiological disposition..which plays an essential part in perception and action, speech and thought... It may prove to be the bridge between body and mind. **1964** *Listener* 25 June 1029/1 Again, Koestler uses the idea of the 'schema' to discuss memory, but he does not mention that Bartlett..wrote a whole book..precisely to develop that very idea. **1971** J. Z. YOUNG *Introd. Study Man* xxi. 277 Many, however, are very useful, especially the concept of a 'schema'. In Piagetian language this is described as a 'cognitive structure which has reference to a class of similar action sequences'. **1978** HOCHBERG & BROOKS in J. W. Senders et al. *Eye Movements & Higher Psychol. Functions* v. iv. 295 If visual momentum is the impetus to obtain sensory information, and to formulate and test a schema, it should be reflected by the frequency with which glances are made.

2. a. A diagrammatic representation. Also in extended use.

1890 GOULD *New Med. Dict.*, *Schema*, figure or design made by the abstraction of certain exceptions or peculiarities, in order to show the general law or type. **1895** J. SULLY *Stud. of Childhood* x. 353 Number is here as little attended to as in the radial arrangements. It is worth noting that this *schema* seems to be widely diffused among children of different nationalities. **1943** H. READ *Educ. through Art* v. 121 All previous writers on the subject have attempted to trace the evolution of the schema, from the first chance recognition of a resemblance in the child's..scribblings..to an outline or two-dimensional schema. **1960** E. H. GOMBRICH *Art & Illusion* v. 168 We shall never know what Rubens' children 'really looked like', but this need not mean we are forever barred from examining the influence which acquired patterns or schemata have on the organization of our perception. **1971** E. KRAMER *Art as Therapy* vi. 127 A five- or six-year-old child who is in the process of discovering various schemata that unmistakably denote for him men, women,..or animals is..enormously increasing his power of expression. **1981** *Times Lit. Suppl.* 10 July 783/2 He painted what the schemata of Rembrandt and J. R. Cozens enabled him to see.

b. In *gen.* use, a hypothetical outline or plan; a theoretical construction; a draft, design.

1939 E. MUIR *Present Age* i. 30 When he [*sc.* H. G. Wells] tried to reinstate society again his society was a schema, not an actual society such as Fielding described. **1947** *Partisan Rev.* XIV. 231 In the countries where capitalism really triumphed, it has yielded with far better grace..than the Marxist schema predicted. **1978** N. MARSH *Grave Mistake* iv. 123 The gardens today bear little resemblance in concept to this exquisite *schema*.

3. *Eccl.* A draft canon or decree submitted to either of the Vatican Councils for discussion.

1870 T. MOZLEY *Let.* 24 Mar. (1891) II. 273 The Council has been sitting on three successive days... Today makes the fourth given to the amended *Schema* on matters of faith. **1930** E. C. BUTLER *Vatican Council* I. x. 199 Two months elapsed during which the deputation worked at the remodelling of the schema. **1963** *Ann. Reg. 1962* 370 The first schema presented for discussion, Liturgy, seemed relatively innocuous.

schematic (skiː'mætɪk), *a.* and *sb.* [ad. mod.L. *schēmaticus*, f. *schēmat-* SCHEMA, SCHEME *sb.*[1] Late Gr. had σχηματικός in the sense 'false, pretended', from σχῆμα in the sense 'appearance' (see SCHEME *sb.* 8 c). Cf. G. *schematisch*.]

A. *adj.* **1.** Pertaining to a scheme or schema; of the nature of, or resembling, a diagrammatic representation; †corresponding (to something else) according to a scheme.

1701 BEVERLEY *Grand Apocal. Question* 6, I shall, by applying each portion of Time to its proper Schematick Prophecy, Justify this Plan of Time. **1856** DOVE *Logic Chr. Faith* II. ii. 110 He must confine himself to a..schematic mensuration of the changes. **1882** W. P. MEARS (*title*) Schematic Anatomy; or, Diagrams, tables and notes treating of the association and systematic arrangement of structural details of human anatomy. **1890** GOULD *New Med. Dict.*, *Schematic*, pertaining to or of the nature of a schema. *S. eye*, one showing the proportions of a normal or typical eye. **1902** W. JAMES *Var. Relig. Exper.* 209 It seems to me a true account—so far as conceptions so schematic can claim truth at all.

2. Pertaining to logical 'figure'.

1838 SIR W. HAMILTON *Logic* xxii. (1866) I. 446 That a hypothetical reasoning was exposed to the schematic modifications of the categorical.

3. Suggested or modified by a preconceived system.

1894 R. V. FRENCH *Lex Mosaica* 174 What is said of him is made up merely of the schematic devices of the redactor.

4. *Fine Art.* Following a conventional type.

1868 GEO. ELIOT in Cross *Life* III. 45 Their art symbolised these in grand schematic forms. **1907** *Westm. Gaz.* 13 July 2/1 The drawing of the features and of the hands (which is less schematic than is customary with Van Dyck).

B. *sb.* A schematic representation; a diagram.

1929 R. T. A. DENNISON *Private Automatic Branch Exchanges* vii. 187 In Fig. 5, a general P.A.B.X. schematic is given. **1949** *Electronic Engin.* XXI. 366/1 The amplifier, the schematic of which is shown here, consists of a two-stage unit in which the pulses are indicated by flashes on a neon light. **1961** *New Scientist* 16 Mar. 684/2 (*caption*) A schematic of a rotary copying machine working on the distillation principle. **1971** H. A. WHITAKER in W. O. Dingwall *Survey Linguistic Sci.* 154 Further differentiation ..may be seen in the schematic of the pyramid and extra-pyramid motor systems in Figure 3. **1978** R. LUDLUM *Holcroft Covenant* v. 68 It was not out of the ordinary for long-range projects in faraway places to employ consulting architects, men whose names would not appear on schematics or blueprints but whose skills would be used.

†**sche'matical**, *a. Obs.* [Formed as prec.: see -ICAL.]

1. Pertaining to rhetorical figures.

1679 J. GOODMAN *Penitent Pardoned* I. i. (1713) 6 Touching the ancient use of this schematical and figurative way of expression.

2. Pertaining to or founded on a scheme or methodical arrangement.

1701 BEVERLEY *Grand Apocal. Question* Pref. a 2 b, I may shew; That there is strength in Schematical Arguments from, and according to the Laws of a Mystic Prophecy.

3. ? Statistical. *rare*$^{-1}$.

1762 tr. *Busching's Syst. Geog.* V. 462 The new genealogical, schematical, Imperial and political manual mentions by name the present provincial-commendator thereof.

schematically (skiː'mætɪkəlɪ), *adv.* [f. as prec. + -LY[2].] **a.** By means of a tabular arrangement. **b.** In a definite pattern; according to a symmetrical plan.

1881 *Amer. Naturalist* July 514 Which can be represented schematically. **1892** SYMONDS *Michel Angelo* (1899) I. iv. 170 These [figures] are schematically arranged in three planes.

schematism ('skiːmətɪz(ə)m). [ad. mod.L. *schēmatismus*, a. Gr. σχηματισμ-ός the assumption of a certain form or appearance, f. σχηματίζειν: see SCHEMATIZE *v.* Cf. G. *schematismus*.]

†**1.** The use of a 'scheme' or rhetorical figure.

1617 COLLINS *Def. Bp. Ely* II. x. 446 By tongues, we may understand *omne prodigiosum*, euen all miracles, the *genus* by the *species*, no vnusuall schematisme.

2. Mode of arrangement of parts or particles; inner structure. Now *rare*.

1660 H. MORE *Myst. Godl.* VII. xiv. 336 Not any Bustles or Counter-blasts of various Aspects of the Heavenly bodies, that do and undo according to the diversities and contrarieties of their Schematisms and Configurations. **1664** EVELYN *Sylva* (1679) 8 Some haply might here recommend to us a more accurate Microscopical examen, to interpret their most secret Schematismes, which were an over nicety for these great Plantations. **1665** HOOKE *Microgr.* 109 The pores or interstitia, which may, perhaps, be even in the texture or Schematism of that part of the Wood. **1686** J. GOAD *Celest. Bodies* I. 39 Planetary Aspects are no vain Terms of a Bawbling Art, but are Mysterious Schematisms of a secret Force. **1846** LEWES *Hist. Philos.* III. iii. 42 The latent schematism [Bacon's *latens schematismus*] is that invisible structure of bodies on which so many of their properties depend. **1860** DORA GREENWELL *Patience of Hope* 24 The structure, the schematism of our faith.

3. A schematic arrangement; a set form for classification or exposition. Also, the schematic method of presentation, or excessive addiction to this.

1701 BEVERLEY *Grand Apocal. Question* 21, I shall therefore compare Three Schematisms of Prophecy, and one Great Apostolic Scripture to Clear this. **1828** PUSEY *Hist. Enq.* I. 47 Homiletic consists only in a philosophical schematism, how a sermon is logically to be arranged. **1887** *Pall Mall G.* 23 June 3 There are pages and pages of this sort of thing, chock-full of schematism and mathematical symbols. **1902** DENNEY *Death of Christ* 211 One could not go to the New Testament with a more misleading schematism in his mind. **1905** SANDAY *Crit. Fourth Gospel* 131 Here we have a 'schematism', a stereotyped formula, which shows poverty of invention.

4. *Philos.* 'Schematizing' action (of the intellect). In Kant: The application of the categories, by means of schemata (see SCHEMA 1), to the data of sense-perception. Also in *Psychol.* (cf. SCHEMA 1 b).

1796 F. A. NITSCH *View of Kant's Princ.* 103 Our conceptions of figures and pictures originate in the schematism of the pure intellect. **1839** *Penny Cycl.* XIII. 176/1 (art. *Kant*). **1865** GROTE *Plato* II. xxiv. 259 Indispensable to the exigencies and consistent schematism of the theorising intelligence. **1951** GATTEGNO & HODGSON tr. *Piaget's Play, Dreams & Imitation* viii. 220 Two peculiarities..remind us once again of the sensori-motor schematism of stage VI, but this time on the new plane of concepts in the process of formation. **1974** *Nature* 8 Mar. 177/1 This kind of knowledge (or understanding) is conceptualised as being based on a hierarchy of operative schemes (Piaget calls it 'schematism').

schematist ('skiːmətɪst). [f. Gr. σχηματ-, σχῆμα SCHEME *sb.* + -IST.]

1. The framer of a 'scheme' or system of doctrine.

1693 CHAUNCY *Rej. to Williams* 13 You are sure I am against all the Confessions of Faith that are orthodox (but indeed you say, which we call orthodox) that we, I suppose, are, you and your Schematists. **1906** *Expositor* Aug. 163 The Christian schematists adjusted to the theogony of the Neoplatonists the Scripture doctrine of God.

†**2.** One who propounds a scheme, a projector.

1710-11 SWIFT *Exam.* No. 31 ¶4 He fill'd the Antichambers with a Crew of his Dependants and Creatures, such as Projectors, Schematists, Occasional Converts to a Party. **1711** —— *Let. to Abp. King* 26 Aug., The treasurer..makes little use of those thousand projectors and schematists, who are daily plying him with their visions. **1716** M. DAVIES *Athen. Brit.* III. *Diss. Drama* 4 Astrology..allegorizes the discontented Schematists of all States and Churches; such as Jacobites, Non-Jurors,..&c. **1718** *Free-thinker* No. 64 Some of our Schematists might be able to project a Form of Law &c. which, abstractedly considered, may appear as useful as that, which we enjoy. **1739** CIBBER *Apol.* (1756) I. 294 As much if not more in favour with their chief manager as a schematist than as an actor.

schematization (ˌskiːmətaɪ'zeɪʃən). [f. SCHEMATIZE *v.* + -ATION.] **1.** The act or process of reducing to a scheme or formula; formulation in a regular order, organization according to a conventional pattern or preconceived system.

1904 W. JAMES *Let.* 31 July in R. B. Perry *Tht. & Char. of W. James* (1935) II. 151 To me the whole Munsterbergian Circus seems a case of the pure love of schematization running mad. **1937** *Proc. Prehistoric Soc.* III. 36 A natural tendency towards schematisation accounts for the rendering of the lowest zone. **1953** *Trans. Philol. Soc. 1952* 16 Over-schematization..has also left its mark on the study of Old English. **1962** W. NOWOTTNY *Lang. Poets Use* vi. 123 'Formal relationships' have already appeared..in connection with verse structure, not with schematization at the level of diction. **1979** *London Rev. Books* 25 Oct. 21/4 It is a curiously French combination: on the one hand, a Cartesian..sense of schematisation, [etc.].

2. A hypothetical organization of schemata; an analytical or tabular representation of data.

1940 *Mind* XLIX. 320 The schematization of our primitive space to the more precise form is evidently correlated in some way with the conformation, structure, and distribution of our sense-organs. **1956** *Scottish Jrnl. Theol.* IX. 399 The sharply hostile and antithetic presentation of the debates [of Jesus with the Jewish authorities], where a dualistic schematisation points to a presupposition other than the relativism of merely human squabbles. **1973** A. J. POMERANS tr. *Piaget & Inhelder's Memory & Intelligence* xix. 341 It seems clear that the 'raw' memory plays no more than a limited role in these responses while schematizations are of considerable importance. **1979** *Amer. Pol. Sci. Rev.* Mar. 168/1 It rests on images, predicative assimilations, schematizations and imaginative illustrations of various sorts.

schematize ('skiːmətaɪz), *v.* [ad. Gr. σχηματίζειν, f. σχηματ-, σχῆμα SCHEME *sb.*[1] Cf. G. *schematisiren*.]

1. *intr.* To assume new forms or shapes. *Obs.*

1650 BULWER *Anthropomet.* Pref., I have observ'd thy Nature-scoffing Art Wherewith th'ast Schematiz'd in every part.

2. *trans.* To formulate in regular order; to reduce to a scheme or formula.

a **1866** J. GROTE in *Jrnl. Philology* (1872) IV. 56 The *phonism* of one language differs from that of another in, 1st. The different radical phones used in it. 2nd. The different distribution of these among the noems, and 3rd. The different laws and ways in which the phones are schematized. **1878** E. Jenkins *Haverholme* 84 If the Benjingo ideas were to be schematised you see that they might lead to prodigious consequences. **1886** Mayor *Eng. Metre* vii. 117 The refrain..(thus schematized ∪-∪∪-∪-∪-∪∪-∪-). **1913** A. S. Pringle-Pattison *Idea of God* (1917) 293 When we do try to schematize the fact [*sc.* that there can be no barrier between the finite consciousness and the Being in which its existence is rooted] for ourselves, we either eliminate the characteristics of selfhood..or..lose hold of the creative unity. **1954** *Circulation* X. 14/2 These reactions which seem to be enzymatic transformations may be schematized as follows.

3. To give conventional form to.

1908 A. Lang *Orig. Religion* 4 The tendency of representative art to 'schematise' its designs into what seem mere geometrical patterns.

4. *Kantian Philos.* To apply the categories, by means of schemata, to the data of sense-perception.

1839 *Penny Cycl.* XIII. 176 The notion of substance is said to be schematised, when it is not conceived of absolutely as a self-subsisting thing, but as one which persists in time. **1877** E. Caird *Philos. Kant* II. x. 407 To ask how the categories are schematised, is simply to ask how they are applied to the form of inner sense, that through it they may be applied to the matter of all sense.

Hence **'schematized** *ppl. a.*; **'schematizing** *vbl. sb.* and *ppl. a.*

1828 De Quincey in *Blackw. Mag.* XXIV. 900 To say, therefore, that a man is a great thinker..is but another expression for saying that he has a schematizing..understanding. **1893** W. G. Collingwood *Ruskin* I. 96 The details of schematised Aristotelianism. **1903** *Hibbert Jrnl.* Mar. 603 The charge of schematising may be brought with more justice against M. Loisy himself. **1946** R. G. Collingwood *Idea of Hist.* 109 The whole world of events in time is thus a schematized representation of the world of logical or conceptual relations.

schematologetically, *adv. nonce-wd.* [f. Gr. σχῆμα scheme *sb.*[1] I.] By means of figured language.

1652 Urquhart *Jewel* Wks. (1834) 292 Schematologetically adorning the proposed theam with the most especial and chief flowers of the garden of rhetorick.

'schemato,mancy. *rare.* [f. Gr. σχηματ(ο)-, σχῆμα form + -mancy.] A form of divination, by which the personal history of a man is inferred from his form and appearance.

1826-7 *Encycl. Metrop.* (1845) XVIII. 175 [Modes of divination among the Arabs.] Schematomancy (*kiyáfah*).

scheme (skiːm), *sb.*[1] Forms: 7 **skeme, sceme, ?sceame,** 7-8 **scheam,** 6- **scheme.** [a. med.L. *schēma*, a. Gr. σχῆμα form, figure, f. root σχ-:—pre-Hellenic *zgh-*, zero-grade of Indogermanic *segh-, whence Gr. ἔχ-ειν to have, hold, be in such or such a condition. Cf. F. *schéma, schème*, It., Pg. *schema*, G. *schema*. The earlier uses in Eng. show direct influence from Gr.; the usual med.L. rendering of σχῆμα being *figura*, the Eng. *scheme* was in the 16-17th c. a synonym of figure *sb.* in several technical senses.]

†**1.** *Rhet.* Any of the recognized modes of deviating from the ordinary use and arrangement of words for the sake of effectiveness or beauty of expression: = figure *sb.* 21. *Obs.*

1553 T. Wilson *Rhet.* 94, I might tary a longe time in declaryng the nature of diuerse Schemes, whiche are woordes or sentencies altered..contrarie to the vulgare custome of our speache. **1617** Collins *Def. Bp. Ely* II. viii. 304 By a scheme of speach they are made to be casters on of the perfume. **1684** Tillotson *Serm.* (1714) III. xlix. 586 In the Text, by a very elegant Scheme of Speech he does, as it were, once more set them at liberty; and, as if they had never engaged themselves to God by Covenant before, he leaves them to their free choice.

†**2. a.** A diagram showing the relative positions, either real or apparent, of the heavenly bodies.

1638 Burton *Anat. Mel.* II. ii. III. (ed. 5) 257 [They] are all so confident, that they have made skemes and tables of their motions. **1665** *Phil. Trans.* I. 107 Amongst his Observations and Schemes of this Comet. **1755** B. Martin *Mag. Arts & Sci.* 23 What do you intend by those small Stars round Jupiter and Saturn, in the Scheme? **1774** J. Bryant *Mythol.* I. 341 They borrowed all the schemes under which the stars are comprehended, from the Egyptians. **1824** J. Johnson *Typogr.* I. 419 The volume is decorated with schemes of spheres and the signs of the Zodiac.

†**b.** *esp.* in *Astrology*, a diagram representing the position of the planets at the hour of a person's birth, a horoscope; = figure *sb.* 14. *Obs.*

1610 B. Jonson *Alch.* IV. iv, My most honor'd ladie, (For so I am now to stile you, hauing found By this my scheme, you are to vnder-goe An honorable fortune, very shortly). **1647** Lilly *Chr. Astrol.* title, The first [Book] containing the use of an Ephemeris, the erecting of a Scheam of Heaven. **1708** Swift *Predict.* Wks. 1751 IV. 188 Upon reviewing my Schemes, I quickly found the cause of that Error. **1770** Langhorne *Plutarch* (1851) I. 472/2 A Chaldean scheme was found in his bosom as he lay. **1815** Scott *Guy M.* iv.

†**3. a.** In wider sense: A diagram; a figure drawn to illustrate a mathematical proposition, or to elucidate descriptions of natural phenomena, machinery, etc.; a map or plan of a town; an architect's designs for a building; and the like. *Obs.*

1649 J. Ellistone tr. *Behmen's Epist.* vi. §81 (1886) 100 Like as my writings do sufficiently and largely show, and here only is represented briefly in a figure or scheme. **1660** Boyle *New Exp. Phys. Mech.* Proem 9 The shape of the Glass, you will find express'd in the first Figure of the annexed Scheme. **1665** *Phil. Trans.* I. 28 The Author hath ..drawn all the Schemes of these 60 microscopical objects with his own hand. **1674** Ray *Coll. Words, Wire-Working* 134 The Description whereof would be tedious and difficult to understand without a Scheme and therefore I shall omit it. **1682** *Weekly Mem.* 214 In the next place he gives us a scheme of the city of Lepanto. **1695** Alingham *Geom. Epit.* 117 The delineating of any Geometrick Scheme or Figure. **1703** T. N. *City & C. Purchaser* 60 Unless the Schemes be very large, it will be very difficult to take the Dimensions nicely. **1704** J. Harris *Lex. Techn.* I, *Scheme*, is the representation of any Geometrical or Astronomical Figure or Problem, by Lines sensibly to the Eye; and these are otherwise called Diagrams. **1771** Luckombe *Hist. Print.* 89 He used a great variety of mathematical schemes, maps, and other useful devices to embellish his works. **1826** Scott *Woodst.* xxxii, 'This,' said he, 'is a scheme of the citadel, as I call it, which may hold out long enough'.

†**b.** *fig.*

1646 Crashaw *Sospetto d'Herode* xlvi, What ever Schemes of Blood, fantastick-frames Of Death Mezentius, or Geryon drew. *a* **1701** Sedley *Tyrant of Crete* v. i, Look upon my misfortunes, and you shall find A perfect scheme of all your saddest evils. **1717** De Foe *Ch. Scot.* (1844) 6, I shall give it [the Particulars] at large in the Scheme I purpose to draw of the State of these Judicatories.

4. An analytical or tabular statement. **a.** A conspectus, exposition in outline; an epitome exhibiting the structure of a book, passage, argument, etc.; also an outline draft of a projected literary work.

1647 Clarendon *Hist. Reb.* II. §68 [Mr. Pym said] that he had only laid that scheme [*sc.* the enumeration of grievances] before them, that they might see how much work they had to satisfy their country. **1652** Needham tr. *Selden's Mare Cl.* 16 Having given you a plain scheme of the Law. **1685** Baxter *Paraphr. N.T.* Matt. vi. 9 So perfect is the method of the Lord's Prayer, that I had thought to have Anatomized it and set it before thee in a Scheme. **1695** Woodward *Nat. Hist. Earth* (1723) 2, I intend this but for a Scheme of a larger Design. **1878** Dale *Lect. Preach.* iii. 75 You may occasionally find it necessary to make a 'scheme' of an argument in order to grasp it. **1882** Farrar *Early Chr.* II. 394 The student who reads it [*sc.* the First Epistle of St. John] in the light of some well considered scheme will gain more advantage from it than others, even if details of his scheme be untenable.

b. A table, a methodical list; a prearranged system of classification. †In *University slang*: see quot. 1780.

Perh. *obs.* exc. as reintroduced from German; cf. G. *schema* blank form to be filled up.

a **1677** Hale *Prim. Orig. Man.* II. ii. 132, I shall prefix a short Chronological Scheme of Times. *a* **1715** Burnet *Own Time* (1766) II. 218 He desired me to give him a scheme of heads fit to be spoken to, and of the order in which they should be laid. **1780** *Gentl. Mag.* L. 278 He provides what is here called a scheme, which contains a collection of all the questions, which will probably be asked him in each science. **1868** Bain *Mental & Moral Sci., Ethics* II. 546 In Chapter ix. is given his [Hobbes'] Scheme of Sciences. **1884** tr. *Lotze's Logic* 188 The difference or the kinship between any two conceptions *M* and *N* should be exactly indicated by their position in the universal scheme. **1895** *Daily News* 14 Sept. 2/4 In the majority of the programmes the chief orchestral work will be Tschaïkowsky's 'Symphonie Pathétique'..while the rest of the schemes will be devoted to Wagner.

c. *Pros.* A tabular analysis of the admissible varieties of structure in a particular kind of verse or stanza; the structure of a verse or a stanza as represented by such an analysis.

1838 T. Mitchell *Clouds of Aristoph.* 120 The following scheme of the metre in which this Address is written..is given by the learned editor of Hephæstion.

5. a. A plan, design; a programme of action; the designed scope and method of an undertaking or a literary work, etc. Phrases, *to †cast, lay a scheme.*

1647 Clarendon *Hist. Reb.* III. §254 To lay the scheme [*MS.* sceme] how the next year should be spent. **1704** Addison *Campaign* 64 Our god-like leader, ere the stream he past, The mighty scheme of all his labours cast. **1718** *Col. Rec. Pennsylv.* III. 59 That first fframed the Scheme and then Laid the Solid ffoundation of this fflourishing Colony. **1726** Shelvocke *Voy. round World* (1757) 5, I also reminded them of the scheme of the voyage. **1727** Gay *Begg. Op.* I. x, That is the whole scheme and intention of all marriage-articles. **1738** Wesley *Ps.* cxxxix. iii. 3 Thine Eye with tender Care survey'd The Growth of every Part, 'Till the whole Scheme thy Thoughts had laid Was copy'd by thy Art. **1754** Shebbeare *Matrimony* (1766) I. 22 The one laid the scheme, and the other took the Town. **1756** Burke *Subl. & B.* Introd. (end), It is the nature of our particular scheme, and the single point of view in which we consider it, which ought to put a stop to our researches. **1775** —— *Corr.* (1844) II. 53 This is no time for taking public business in their course and order, and only as a part in the scheme of life, which comes and goes at its proper periods. **1848** Thackeray *Van. Fair* xlvii, It forms no part of our scheme to tell what became of the remainder. **1859** Jephson *Brittany* x. 162 For us they are things of the past, they find no place in our scheme of life. **1883** Froude *Short Stud.* IV. II. ii. 179 The scheme of teaching for the higher class of men was essentially good.

b. Hence, A plan of action devised in order to attain some end; a purpose together with a system of measures contrived for its accomplishment; a project, enterprise. Often with unfavourable notion, a self-seeking or an underhand project, a plot (cf. scheme *v.*, scheming *ppl. a.*), or a visionary or foolish project. Phrase, *to lay a scheme.*

This is now the most prominent use, and in some degree colours the other senses so far as they survive.

1718 *Free-thinker* No. 90. 249 This was the Scheme which the Heads of the Parliament-Party pursued. **1719** De Foe *Crusoe* II. (1858) 333 The scheme hit so exactly with my temper. **1746** *Col. Rec. Pennsylv.* V. 51 It is no new thing for Arbitrary Princes to contrive and promote Schemes for the subversion of a Government. **1750** Johnson *Rambler* No. 73 ¶4 Plans of elegance and schemes of pleasure. **1759** Robertson *Hist. Scot.* III. Wks. I. 243 But this deep-laid scheme was in a moment disconcerted. **1775** A. Burnaby *Trav.* 23 Some few, indeed, have been rather more enterprising, and have endeavoured to improve their estates by raising indigo, and other schemes. **1776** Adam Smith *W.N.* II. ii. I. 384 The idea of the possibility of multiplying paper money to almost any extent, was the real foundation of what is called the Mississippi scheme. **1814** Jane Austen *Mansfield Park* viii, Her opposition to Edmund now, arose more from partiality for her own scheme, because it was her own, than from anything else. **1826** Scott *Woodst.* xxxii, Men come and go, lay schemes, and alter them, in my house, without deigning to consult me! **1832** Ht. Martineau *Ireland* iii. 36 Dan proposed a grand scheme to his father-in-law. **1857** *Act 20 & 21 Vict.* c. 84 Preamble, The Charity Commissioners..have provisionally approved and certified (among other Schemes for the Application and Management of Charities) a Scheme for the College of God's Gift in Dulwich. **1863** Geo. Eliot *Romola* xxiii, He never thought of any scheme for removing his enemy. **1868** J. H. Blunt *Ref. Ch. Eng.* I. 353 The end of this vast scheme of spoliation. **1888** J. Inglis *Tent Life* 306 The great irrigation schemes of the North-West Provinces. **1895** *Bookman* Oct. 22/2 At the Congress of Ryswick..Louis placed his own dynastic schemes above the interests of the nation.

c. In generalized sense: 'Scheming', contrivance, design. *rare*[−1].

1790 Paley *Horæ Paul.* i. 4 A coincidence which shows, by its very obliquity, that scheme was not employed in its formation.

d. An escapade of a humorous character, a 'spree'; an outing or excursion. Now only *dial.*

1758 Johnson *Idler* No. 33 All the provisions bespoke by some rakish fellow-commoner in the next room, who had been on a scheme to Newmarket. **1762** Foote *Orators* I. (1780) 6 Will and I are here upon a scheme from Oxford. **1764** *Oxf. Sausage* 26 Woodstock, farewell! and Wallingford adieu! Where many a Scheme reliev'd the lingering Day. **1789** Jane Austen in *Loiterer* 12 Sept. 6 That glorious achievement, A Scheme to Town. **1813** —— *Pride & Prejudice* III. ix. 166, I did not once put my foot out of doors... Not one party, or scheme, or any thing. **1904** *Eng. Dial. Dict.* s.v., [Camb.], I never used to have such schemes when I was young.

Comb. **1764** *Oxf. Sausage* 44 No scheme-enamour'd Youth.

6. †**a.** A hypothetical construction, a theory. *Obs.* **b.** A body of related doctrines, a speculative system.

a. 1675 Baxter *Cath. Theol.* I. i. 58 Many Arminians write as if the order of Intention and of Execution were the same, and so begin at the other end, and give us a Scheme just contrary to the first sort. **1682** Creech *Lucretius* v. (1683) 162 And this the later Babylonian Sect Doth hold, and the Chaldean Schemes reject. **1709** Steele *Tatler* No. 69 ¶4 Eboracensis has read all the Schemes which Writers have formed of Government and Order. **1725** Watts *Logic* II. iii. §3 Thro' the Influence which our own Schemes or Hypotheses have upon the Mind, we sometimes become so sharp-sighted as to find these Schemes in those Places of Scripture where the holy Writers never thought of them.

b. 1685 Temple *Ess. Learning* Wks. 1731 I. 291 Des-Cartes was the next that would be thought to excel the Ancients, by a new Scheme or Body of Philosophy. **1754** Sherlock *Discourses* (1759) I. i. 12 Complete Schemes of Natural Religion drawn from Principles and Axioms of Reason. **1858** Sears *Athan.* III. viii. 324 His comprehensive scheme of theology.

7. a. A complex unity in which the component elements co-operate and interact according to a definite plan; a system of correlated things, institutions, arrangements, etc.; also, the manner in which such a system is organized.

1736 Butler *Anal.* I. vii. 121 (*chapter-heading*), Of the Government of God, considered as a Scheme or Constitution, imperfectly comprehended. **1772** Priestley *Inst. Relig.* (1782) I. 39 Evil..is a necessary part of the whole scheme. **1791** Burke *Corr.* (1844) III. 278 He then asked me whether I had seen that scheme of absurdity, the French constitution, and what I thought of it. **1820** Shelley *Sensit. Pl.* II. 4 There was a Power in this sweet place, An Eve in this Eden; a ruling Grace Which to the flowers, did they waken or dream, Was as God is to the starry scheme. **1833** T. Hook *Parson's Dau.* I. i, To this disadvantage (the only one, perhaps, of the scheme of society to which it belongs) may be attributed many of those ill-assorted matches made by ladies of quality. **1836** J. Gilbert *Chr. Atonem.* iii. (1852) 69 In the present scheme of things, man is so closely linked with his fellow man,..that in a thousand instances the moral exchange is both required and made. **1840** S. Wilberforce *Sp. Missions* (1874) 89 But it must be that a little while longer, and this nation, aye, and all the great scheme of nations, of which it is part, will have passed utterly away, and be no more. **1859** FitzGerald tr. *Omar* lxxiii, Ah Love! could thou and I with Fate conspire To grasp this sorry Scheme of Things entire, Would not we shatter it to bits! **1878** Browning *La Saisiaz* 41 From thine apprehended scheme of things deduce Praise or blame of its contriver. **1888** Henley *Bk. Verses* 121 Pulpit and platform overflowing, Ready the scheme of things to revise.

b. Painting. *scheme of colour*: the system of selection and arrangement of colours characteristic of a particular painter or school, or adopted in a particular picture; now chiefly = *colour scheme* (in both senses) s.v. COLOUR *sb.*[1] 19. Freq. *ellipt.* Also *transf.*

1884 *Sat. Rev.* 7 June 745/1 We wish that this artist would abandon the chocolate-like scheme of colour in which he has indulged for the last few years. **1897** *Private Life of Queen* ii. 15 The general scheme of colour is crimson and cream and gold. This scheme of paint prevails throughout the suite. **1905** P. WHITE *Patient Man* vii. 67 Mrs. Dacre was proud of the 'scheme' of the dining-room, although she admitted it was a little trying to the complexion by daylight. **1925** R. W. G. HINGSTON in E. F. Norton *Fight for Everest: 1924* 265 Certain of the little birds are decidedly conspicuous, and in some cases we see the obvious reason why they do not require a protective scheme. *Ibid.* 267 Its [*sc.* a locust's] scheme of colour was grey and black with delicate transverse bands across its thighs. **1969** J. CHEEVER *Bullet Park* ii. 31 Nubbly stretchy reps look completely out of place in my decorating scheme.

†**8.** In certain senses of Gr. σχῆμα. **a.** = FIGURE *sb.* 10. **b.** Stateliness, pomp. **c.** Form, aspect, appearance. *Obs.*

a. 1638 JUNIUS *Paint. Ancients* 311 Every picture consisting of many figures must needs have some historicall part in it, seeing it is but a dull and unprofitable thing when many schemes are heaped up together without either sense or learning.

b. 1647 H. MORE *Poems* Pref., So high confidence might become the heat and scheme of Poetry much better than sober Philosophy.

c. 1654 H. L'ESTRANGE *Chas. I* (1655) 125 The Nation and race of men were.., under the scheme of.. specious plain-dealing, most perfidious. **1664** H. MORE *Myst. Iniq.* vii. 21 It is likely the imposing Priests would pretend either of these to the people (though not in that odious scheme) as persuasions of the presence of the Dæmons themselves in these consecrated Places and Images. **1677** GALE *Crt. Gentiles* III. 84 For they had the scheme of truth not the substance. **1682** SIR T. BROWNE *Chr. Mor.* IV. §14 (1756) 99 Be not under any brutal metempsychosis while thou livest, and walkest about erectly under the scheme of man. **1743** N. APPLETON *Serm.* 13 Contending for the same Thing ultimately, but in a different Scheme.

†**9.** *Ancient Music.* (See quot. 1753. Cf. 4 c.)

1721 A. MALCOLM *Treat. Mus.* 534 The mutual Distances of these *Meses potestate* are expressed in the Scheme by (:) which signifies a Tone, (.) a Semitone or Limma. **1753** *Chambers' Cycl. Supp.*, *Scheme*.. in the antient music, is used for the varieties arising from the different positions of the tones and semitones in a consonance. **1811** T. BUSBY *Dict. Mus.* (ed. 3).

scheme (skiːm), *sb.*[2] ? *Obs.* Forms: 8 **scheam, skeen,** 9 **skene,** 8– **scheme.** [Of obscure origin. Some etymologists have conjectured that *scheme-arch* is an adaptation of a hypothetical It. *arco scemo*, 'imperfect arch'; but this seems very unlikely.]

The arc of larger radius in the middle of a three-centre arch or elliptical arch; chiefly *attrib.*, in **scheme-arch**, an arch of this kind (but by various writers defined as an arch of the form of a circular segment less than a semicircle).

1703 MOXON *Mech. Exerc.* 273 Let the length given be AB,.. describe the *Hanse* AG;.. then.. describe a part of the *Ellipsis* BH, which is called the *Hanse*: The other part to be described from G to H, is called the *Scheam.* **1725** W. HALFPENNY *Sound Building* 2 To describe a Scheme-Arch. **1772** HUTTON *Bridges* 78 A scheme or skeen arch is a segment less than the semicircle. **1842** *Civil Eng. & Arch. Jrnl.* V. 251/2 Scheme or Skene, or Imperfect Arch, less than semicircle.

b. quasi-*adj.* Constructed with a 'scheme'.

1703 T. N. *City & C. Purch.* 8 Of Circular Arches, there are 3 Kinds; Semicircular, Scheme, or Skeen, and Arches of the 3d. and 4th. Point. **1715** LEONI *Palladio's Archit.* (1721) I. 71 The Ceilings are either made semi-circular, or scheme [orig. *a schiffo*], that is, so flat as to have in height only one third of the breadth of the Room.

scheme (skiːm), *v.* [f. SCHEME *sb.*[1]]

1. *trans.* To devise as a scheme; to lay schemes for; to effect by contrivance or intrigue.

1767 LEWIS *Statius' Thebaid* II. 320 For useless lay the now-neglected Chain; Threats fail'd, and Punishments were schem'd in vain. **1831** SCOTT *Ct. Robt.* xxxiii, Offences which were wilfully and maliciously schemed. **1868** F. E. PAGET *Lucretia* 180, I resolved to adopt both plans, and if possible, scheme a mode of escape. **1893** MCCARTHY *Red Diamonds* I. 3 That modern travel.. which has schemed out its great scheme of the Euphrates Valley railroad.

b. *intr.* To lay schemes; to use ingenuity, resort to contrivance; to devise plans, esp. underhand or with sinister motive.

1842 BROWNING *Count Gismond* ii, And doubtlessly ere he could draw All points to one, he must have schemed. **1851** HAWTHORNE *Ho. Sev. Gables* x. (1852) 117 You may scheme for me as much as you please; but I'm not going to give up this one scheme of my own. **1865** CARLYLE *Fredk. Gt.* XXI. iv. X. 27 It is not true that Friedrich had schemed to send Henri round by Petersburg. **1866** KINGSLEY *Herew.* xix, Half-a-dozen plans suggested themselves to his crafty brain as he sat brooding and scheming.

2. *trans.* To reduce to a scheme or formula. Also, to *scheme out*: to plan methodically. *rare.*

1716 M. DAVIES *Athen. Brit.* II. 19 The King's having the Opinion or Endeavour of.. any Body.. in Scheming out the rough Draft.. of the Treatise.. can't be any Argument that the King was not the Author of it. **1858** BUSHNELL *Nat. & Supernat.* xii. (1864) 400 It may scheme out a system or hypothesis. **1865** —— *Vicar. Sacr.* I. ii. (1866) 21 Every such attempt to scheme the work of Christ, and put Him in the terms of the understanding.

3. *intr.* To go on the spree. Also *trans.* to play truant from (school). ? *dial.* Cf. SCHEME *sb.*[1] 5 d.

1738 MRS. MONTAGU *Lett.* (1809) I. 32 We all came croaking down to breakfast the next morning, and said we had caught no cold, as one always says when one has been scheming. **1905** *Blackw. Mag.* Oct. 510/1 He would be leathering me for scheming school.

†**schemed,** *a. Obs.* [f. SCHEME *sb.*[2] + -ED[2].] Constructed with a SCHEME (*sb.*[2]).

1715 LEONI *Palladio's Archit.* (1721) I. 80 The Arches are schem'd [orig. *sono a schiffo*].

schemeless ('skiːmlɪs), *a.* [f. SCHEME *sb.*[1] + -LESS.] Destitute of plan; lacking a plot.

1877 BROWNING *Agamemnon* 118 Since I'm schemeless [Gr. δυσμηχανῶ] How to raise up again by words—a dead man! **1887** *Pall Mall G.* 28 Dec. 11/1 He began to turn to account an old inherited habit of sending himself to sleep by making up fanciful, schemeless stories.

schemer ('skiːmə(r)). [f. SCHEME *v.* + -ER[1].]

1. One who devises or enters into schemes.

1724 LADY M. W. MONTAGU *Let. to C'tess. Mar* Feb. (1893) I. 477 They call themselves Schemers; and meet.. three times a week, to consult on gallant schemes. **1760** C. JOHNSTON *Chrysal* I. iv. (1822) I. 29, I therefore immediately became a Schemer. **1831** LYTTON *Godolphin* xxii, I was born a schemer. **1875** LONGF. *Masque Pandora* III, Tempt no more the noble schemer.

2. One who plots, or lays plans in an underhand manner.

1849 MARRYAT *Valerie* vii, Lady M—— is a schemer, always plotting. **1884** *Chr. Commonw.* 14 Feb. 416/2 England has always been too much the prey of fanatics and schemers in matters of this kind.

3. (Cf. SCHEME *v.* 3.) One who plans methods for evading duties; a shirker.

1843 GAVIN *Feigned or Factitious Dis.* 32 The—regiment .. were all schemers and malingerers.

4. (See quot.)

1867 SMYTH *Sailor's Word-bk.*, *Schemer*, one who has charge of the hold of a North Sea ship.

schemer, obs. form of SHIMMER.

schemery ('skiːmərɪ). *rare.* [f. SCHEME *sb.*[1] + -ERY.] Scheming practices.

1822 *Examiner* 273/1 The long-expected Ministerial Schemery for the Relief.. of the People. **1828** *Ibid.* 184/2 The hollow schemery of Prince Metternich.

scheming ('skiːmɪŋ), *vbl. sb.* [f. SCHEME *v.* + -ING[1].] The action of the vb. SCHEME; planning, contrivance.

1813 SHELLEY *Q. Mab* v. 163 Blunting the keenness of his spiritual sense With narrow schemings and unworthy cares. **1843** MRS. CARLYLE *Lett.* I. 246 It needed a deal of scheming .. to make them fit our high room. **1884** CHURCH *Bacon* ii. 32 Essex.. drifted into discontent,.. into questionable schemings for the future of a reign that must shortly end.

scheming ('skiːmɪŋ), *ppl. a.* [f. SCHEME *v.* + -ING[2].] That schemes; contriving, plotting.

1838 LYTTON *Alice* I. i, An artful, scheming, almost heartless man. **1884** *Contemp. Rev.* Oct. 514 This class is.. recruited.. from voluble, scheming men and zealous charlatans.

schemist ('skiːmɪst). [f. SCHEME *sb.*[1] + -IST.]

†**1.** A framer of 'schemes' or horoscopes; an astrologer. *Obs.*

1641 BROME *Joviall Crew* I. (1652) B 1 b, Another Schemist Found, that a squint-ey'd boy should prove a notable Pick-purse.

†**2.** One who is concerned with intrigues; a plotter. *Obs.*

1724 BP. DOWNES in Nicolson *Epist. Corr.* 581 The schemists have laid out Armagh for the Archbishop of Dublin. **1825** G. MCCANN *Right Private Judgem.* 266 Manes was an arrogant philosopher and a great schemist.

3. One who forms a scheme; a projector.

1753 A. MURPHY *Gray's Inn Jrnl.* No. 42 Her Undertaking is more likely to do Honour to our Country, than that of any other Schemist now in being. **1769** BURKE *Late St. Nat.* Wks. 1842 I. 112 Are not these schemists well apprised, that the colonists.. import more from Great Britain, ten times more than they send in return to us? **1875** JEVONS *Money* (1878) 246 A number of Schemists have urged from time to time, that.. there ought to be an interest-bearing currency.

schemozzle, schepsel, varr. SHEMOZZLE, SKEPSEL.

schene, obs. form of CHAIN, SCENE.

schenick, schep, obs. ff. SCENIC, CHEAP.

‖**schepen** ('skeɪpən, in Du. 'sxeːpən). Forms: 5–6 **skepyn,** 6 **skepon,** 7 **skepen,** 8 **schepin,** 9 **schepen.** [Du. *schepen* = OS. *scepino*, OFris. *sceppena*, OHG. *sceffin, scaffin, sceffino* (MHG. *schepfe, scheffe*, mod.G. *schöffe*):—OTeut. types **skapino-z*, **skapinon-*. Cf. ECHEVIN, SCABINE, SKEVIN.] A Dutch alderman or petty magistrate.

c **1481** CAXTON *Dialogues* 43 Somme of the skepyns Ryde with [the condemned] There as they be put to death. **1587** FLEMING *Contin. Holinshed* III. 1341/1 The amptman, boroughmaisters, and skepons of Antwerpe came to the said palace of S. Michaell the next thursdaie. **1681** H. NEVILE *Plato Rediv.* 77 For Form sake [they] defer something to him as the Approbation of their Skepen and other Magistrates, and some other Matters. **1756** NUGENT *Gr. Tour, Netherlands* I. 222 The city magistrates consist of two .. burgomasters, and seven schepins or aldermen. **1809** W. IRVING *Knickerb.* III. ii. (1820) 163 This potent body consisted of a schout or bailiff,.. five burgermeesters.. and five schepens.

scher, obs. form of SIR.

scherald, var. SHIRREL *Sc. Obs.*

†**scherand.** *Sc. Obs.* [Origin unknown: ? a form of the name of the French river *Gironde.*] The designation of a kind of wine.

1536 *Elgin Rec.* (New Spald. Club, 1903) I. 30 The pynt of fine Scherand or Amzerk vyne x d. **1564** *Reg. Privy Council Scot.* I. 299 The tun of Scherand wyne.. and the pynt of Scherand wyne.

scherat, -att, -et(t: see CHARIOT *sb.*, SHIRREL.

Scherbius ('ʃɜːbɪəs). *Electr.* The name of Arthur *Scherbius* (*fl.* 1906), German engineer, used *attrib.* with reference to a method which he devised for regulating and changing the speed of large a.c. induction motors, in which the voltage applied to the rotor is altered according to the load by means of a separate commutator motor and flywheel assembly wired in series with it.

1910 *Electrician* 8 July 513/2 In the Scherbius motor the compensating winding is connected to the brushes in opposition to the armature. **1928** *Engineering* 24 Aug. 247/2 The speed regulation of the motors is controlled by a Scherbius set. **1962** *Newnes Conc. Encycl. Electr. Engin.* 515/1 A considerable number of variable-speed induction motors with Scherbius control has been built in the past for outputs up to several thousand horse-power, particularly for steel-mill drives. **1973** J. M. D. MURPHY *Thyristor Control of A.C. Motors* x. 160 In the Scherbius system.. a rotary converter rectifies the slip power, and the rectified output drives a d.c. motor which is mechanically coupled to a squirrel-cage induction generator.

schere, obs. f. CHEER, SIR.

Schering ('ʃɛərɪŋ). *Electr.* The name of Harald Ernst Malmsten *Schering* (1880–1959), German engineer, used *attrib.* and in the possessive with reference to an alternating-current bridge circuit which he devised for measuring the capacitance and power factor of insulating materials.

1926 *World Power* V. 238/2 Of the many bridges so far developed, the Schering bridge is the most suitable for high voltage work. **1928** *Engineering* 13 Jan. 50/1 The Schering bridge is operated by a fixed-frequency valve oscillator, with a frequency of 800 periods per second. **1958** J. SHEPHERD et al. *Higher Electrical Engin.* iii. 64 The Schering bridge was developed to measure the loss resistance of dielectrics, line insulators, cables and high voltage capacitors under high voltage conditions (up to 100kV). **1975** D. G. FINK *Electronics Engineers' Handbk.* XVII. 29 Schering's bridge is widely used for measuring capacitance and dissipation factors.

scherk, obs. f. SARK.

scherm, var. SKERM.

Schermuly ('ʃɜːmuːliː). The name of William *Schermuly* (1857–1929), English inventor, used *attrib.* and *absol.* as proprietary names of apparatus comprising a line-carrying rocket fired from a pistol, used in life-saving at sea.

1922 *Life-Boat* Feb. 243/1 The Line-Throwing Gun... The two appliances to which chief attention was given were the Coston gun, an American invention.. and the Schermuly Portable Rocket Apparatus. **1933** R. B. CHENEVIX-TRENCH *Jrnl.* 28 Sept. in *Mariner's Mirror* (1979) LXV. 274 One line was fired by a Schermuly pistol. **1947** *Trade Marks Jrnl.* 30 July 443/2 *Schermuly*... Pyrotechnic articles, cartridges, and apparatus for firing rockets. The Schermuly Pistol Rocket Apparatus Limited,.. Newdigate, Surrey; Manufacturers. **1960** E. L. DELMAR-MORGAN *Cruising Yacht Equipment & Navigation* ix. 111 The Schermuly.. are of sealed metal case construction and embody a sealed-in mechanical ignition device. **1973** B. CALLISON *Web of Salvage* x. 134 With the Schermuly pistol angled upward and to windward. **1979** P. FERRIS *Talk to Me about England* II. 103 Jarre picked his way aft... Hansen [was] tearing the wrapper from a Schermuly rocket.

schertelite ('ʃɜːtəlaɪt). *Min.* [f. the name of Arnulf *Schertel* (1841–1902), Bavarian chemist: see -ITE[1].] A hydrated acid phosphate of ammonium and magnesium, $(NH_4)_2Mg_3H_4(PO_4)_4.8H_2O$, found as small water-soluble orthorhombic crystals in deposits of bat guano in caves near Ballarat, Victoria.

1902 R. W. E. MACIVOR in *Chem. News* 9 May 217/1 To prevent all future confusion, I have now decided to call this interesting mineral Schertalite [*sic*]. **1963** *Amer. Mineralogist* XLVIII. 639 Schertelite dissolves rapidly and incongruently in water with the formation of struvite. Exposure of schertelite to the atmosphere for several months results in alteration of the surface of the crystals, apparently to an intimate mixture of struvite and monoammonium phosphate.

scherv-, scherw-, obs. Sc. spelling of SERV-.

‖**scherzando** (sker'tsando), *adv. Mus.* [It., gerund of *scherzare* to sport, play, f. *scherzo*: see SCHERZO] Playfully, sportively; used to indicate that a movement or passage is to be rendered in a lively manner. Also *attrib.* (quasi-*adj.*), and *ellipt.* as *sb.*, a 'scherzando' movement. So (*rarely*) **scherzan'dissimo** (It. superlative).

1811 BUSBY *Dict. Mus.* (ed. 3), *Scherzando*, or *Scherzo*, in a sportive, playful manner. **1876** STAINER & BARRETT *Dict. Mus. Terms, Scherzando, Scherzandissimo*... (1) Playful, lively, jokingly, merry. (2) A movement of a lively and droll character. **1881** FULLER-MAITLAND in *Grove's Dict. Mus.* III. 245/2 The phrasing of a *scherzando* passage is of paramount importance.

scherzetto, scherzino: see next entry.

||**scherzo** ('skɛərtsəʊ, ||'skertso). *Mus.* [It., *lit.* sport, jest; of Teut. origin: cf. MHG., mod.G. *scherz* sport.] A movement of a lively character, occupying the second or third place in a symphony or sonata. Also *Comb.*, as ***scherzo-like*** adj.

1852 GEO. ELIOT *Let.* 13 Nov. (1954) II. 67, I went to one of Jullien's concerts.. and endured the Polkas for the sake of Zampa and Mendelssohn's Scherzo. **1862** E. PAUER in *Programme* 8 Mar., Scherzo, a piece of jocular and cheerful character. **1891** PROUT *Counterpoint* (ed. 2) 69 It is comparatively seldom that a long passage of double counterpoint is to be found in a scherzo. **1931** *Times* 19 Feb. 10/1 The contrasts of solemnity and recklessness in the slow movement and scherzo were made particularly vivid. **1962** *Times* 20 June 15/2 The scherzo-like middle movement. **1976** *Scotsman* 20 Nov. 9/5 It was an exquisitely controlled and subtle performance,.. delightfully airy in the scherzo-like variation.

fig. **1907** *Q. Rev.* Apr. 411 Shall we dwell.. on the scherzo in the suite, that.. comic exposure of the fantastic enigma called the 'Mirror of Justices'? **1911** O. ONIONS *Widdershins* 265 'Scherzos in Silver and Grey!' he chuckled. **1955** *Sci. News Let.* 25 June 411/3 The mockingbird [will].. ring in bits from the repertories of other birds, with catcalls and rusty-hinge squeaks by way of scherzo interludes. **1964** *Listener* 12 Mar. 447/1 The play is a ruthless little fantasia (well named a *scherzo*).

Hence in dim. forms **scherzetto** (-'ɛtəʊ), **scherzino** (-'i:nəʊ), a short passage or piece of music with the character of a scherzo.

1884 F. NIECKS *Conc. Dict. Mus. Terms* 273 *Scherzino*, a short or light scherzo. **1907** T. S. WOTTON *Dict. Foreign Mus: Terms* 169 *Scherzettino, scherzetto*.., a little scherzo. **1954** *Grove's Dict. Mus.* (ed. 5) VII. 480/2 *Scherzino* or *Scherzetto*... The words are occasionally used for a short or very slight piece in the character of a scherzo. **1961** *Times* 3 Jan. 3/4 Fricker's octet.. was well chosen.. for the sociability of its scherzetto. **1963** *Times* 28 Jan. 5/2 Nothing could have been.. more playful than the little scherzino movement in the *faschingsschwank aus Wien*. **1978** *Gramophone* June 95/2 There is quite a well articulated performance of the Mab *scherzetto* by Rémy Corazza.

schese, var. *chese*, obs. f. CHOOSE *v.*

scheselle, obs. form of CHESIL[1], CHISEL *sb.*[1]

||**'schesis.** *Obs.* [mod.L., a. Gr. σχέσις relation, state, condition (in medical writers = sense 2 below), root σχ-:—pre-Hellenic *zgh-, weak grade of *segh-, whence Gr. ἔχειν to have, hold, etc.: see SCHEME *v.*]

1. The manner in which a thing is related to something else; relation.

1678 CUDWORTH *Intell. Syst.* I. v. 723 The Idea of God or an absolutely Perfect Being including in it.. a necessary schesis or relation to existence, it follows.. that He doth exist. **1678** NORRIS *Miscell.* (1699) 160 If that mind which has existing in itself from all Eternity, all the simple Essences of things, and consequently, all their possible Scheses or Habitudes, should ever change, there would arise a new Schesis in this Mind that was not before.

2. *Phys.* A temporary habit or state of the body.

Cf. SCHETIC *a.*; the explanation in quot. 1706 is erroneous. **1684** tr. *Blancard's Phys. Dict.*, *Schesis* is the Disposition of the Body. **1706** PHILLIPS (ed. Kersey), *Schesis*, the Habit or Constitution of the body; accordingly as it is fleshy or lean, hard or soft, thick or slender.

schesse, obs. f. CHESS *sb.*[1]

schet, obs. ff. SHEET, SHOOT *v.*, SHUT, SKEET *adv.*

schetare, obs. f. SHOOTER.

schete, obs. ff. SHEATH, SHEET, SHOOT, SKEET *adv.*

schetel, obs. f. SHUTTLE.

scheten, obs. f. SHOOT, SHUT.

scheter, obs. f. SHOOTER.

scheth(e, -are, -ere, obs. ff. SHEATH, SHEATHER.

†**'schetic**, *a. Path. Obs.* [a. mod.L. *scheticus* (in *schetica febris*), ad. Gr. σχετικός (taken in the etymologically admissible sense 'related to a σχέσις SCHESIS 2, or temporary condition of the body'; the classical senses are 'holding firm, holding back, retentive'), f. σχ-, ἔχειν: see SCHESIS.] Of diseases: see quots.

1706 PHILLIPS (ed. Kersey), *Schetick-Feaver*, a Feaver so call'd because it is chiefly seated in the Blood, and may be easily cur'd; upon which account it is oppos'd to a Hectick Feaver, that is fixed in the Very Habit of the Body, and not to be remov'd without great Difficulty. **1753** *Chambers' Cycl. Supp.*, *Schetic diseases*, a term used by the old writers in medicine to express such diseases as were not deeply rooted in the constitution, but might be easily removed.

†**'schetical**, *a. Obs.* [See prec. and -ICAL.]

1. *Path.* = SCHETIC *a.*

1666 G. HARVEY *Morb. Angl.* ii. 14 A feavor that's grown habitual, in opposition to a Schetical or moveable feavor.

2. Relative.

a **1688** CUDWORTH *Immut. Mor.* I. ii. (1731) 158 Moral Good and Evil are Schetical and Relative Things.

Hence †**'schetically** *adv.*, in a relative sense.

1678 CUDWORTH *Intell. Syst.* I. iv. 188 Images, Statues and Symbols.. are only Schetically Worshipped by them, the Honour passing from them to the Prototype.

schett(e, obs. ff. SHEET, SHUT *v.*

schetylle, schever(e, obs. ff. SHUTTLE, SHIVER.

scheulie, var. SCHOOLIE.

†**schew**, *v.* Aphetic variant of ESCHEW *v.*

c **1500** MEDWALL *Nature* (Brandl) I. 346 To hawnt vertue and schew all vyce.

schew(e, obs. ff. SHE, SHEAF, SHOW *v.*, SKY.

schewill, var. SHEWEL *Obs.*

schey, obs. form of SHY *a.*

scheyff, Sc. aphetic var. of ESCHEW *v.*

c **1470** HENRY *Wallace* III. 264 My lorde, my consaill will I giff; Bot ye do it, fra scaith ye may nocht scheyff.

scheyl, schi, obs. ff. SHAIL *v.*, SKY.

schiacciato, var. STIACCIATO.

schiatica, schiaticke, obs. ff. SCIATICA, SCIATIC.

schich, obs. form of SHEIKH.

Schick (ʃɪk). *Med.* The name of Bela *Schick* (1877-1967), Hungarian-born U.S. pædiatrician, used *attrib.* and *absol.* to designate a test he devised consisting in the intradermal injection of diphtheria toxin: the absence of an erythematous reaction indicates previously acquired immunity to diphtheria. [Described by Schick in *Münchener med. Wochenschr.* (1908) LV. 504-6.]

1916 *Jrnl. Immunol.* I. 203 This principle is applied today in the so-called Shick [*sic*] test of immunity to diphtheria. **1927** R. MUIR et al. *Man. Bacteriol.* (ed. 8) xvii. 478 If a positive Schick is present in addition, the reaction due to the unheated toxin will be more marked. **1955** *Sci. News Let.* 9 Apr. 229/3 The Schick test, familiar to many school children, tells whether or not 'shots' to protect against diphtheria have been effective. **1971** D. LAMBERT in C. Bonington *Annapurna South Face* 290 A test known as the Schick Test may have to be done beforehand.

Hence **Schick-positive (-negative)** *adjs.*, showing (failing to show) an erythematous reaction in the Schick test.

1927 R. MUIR et al. *Man. Bacteriol.* (ed. 8) xvii. 476 If the suspected carrier is Schick-positive, i.e. non-immune, the organism is likely to be non-virulent. **1932** *Ibid.* (ed. 9) xvii. 507 The proportion of Schick negative reactions increases with age much as in Europe; also the blood of Schick negative reactors contains diphtheria antitoxin. **1944** L. E. H. WHITBY *Med. Bacteriol.* (ed. 4) xiii. 237 Hospital nurses should always be actively immunized if they are Schick-positive. **1951** WHITBY & HYNES *Ibid.* (ed. 5) xiii. 239 Infants born of Schick-negative mothers are themselves immune to diphtheria for the few months during which maternal antibodies persist in the circulation.

||**schiedam** (ski:'dæm). Also **schiedamm, sk(i)edam.** A variety of gin, so called from the town in Holland where it is distilled.

1821 SCOTT *Pirate* xvii, There was the potent Irish Usquebaugh—right Nantz—genuine Schiedamm. **1831** TRELAWNY *Adv. Younger Son* I. 291 A dusty-looking stone bottle of the right bamboo-coloured skedam. *Ibid.* II. 35 To take a glass of skiedam. **1833** HOOD To *Adm. Gambier* vi, Consider, too—before all Eau-de-vie, Schiedam or other drinkers, you rebut. **1891** KIPLING *Light that Failed* xv, A bottle of peculiarly strong Schiedam.

Comb. **1834** *Tait's Mag.* I. 542/1 Schiedam-punch.

schieferspar ('ʃi:fəspɑ:(r)). *Min.* [Half-translated ad. Ger. *schieferspath* (1789 C. A. S. Hoffmann in *Bergmännisches Jrnl.* I. 187), f. *schiefer* slate + *spath* spar.] = SLATE-SPAR.

1807 J. MURRAY *Syst. Chem.* III. 672 The Schiefer Spar, or Argentine,.. occurs always massive. **1836** T. THOMSON *Min., Geol.*, etc. I. 114 Calcereous Spar... Schiefer spar.

schiende, var. SHEND.

Schiff (ʃɪf). *Chem.* The name of Hugo *Schiff* (1834-1915), German chemist, used *attrib.* and in the possessive to designate things he devised or investigated, as **Schiff('s) base**, any organic compound having the structure $R^1R^2C{=}NR^3$; **Schiff('s) reaction**, the action of aldehydes of restoring the magenta colour to Schiff's reagent; **Schiff('s) reagent**, an acid solution of fuchsin (magenta, rosaniline) decolorized by sulphur dioxide or potassium metabisulphite; **Schiff('s) test**, the Schiff reaction employed as a test for aldehydes.

1892 *Jrnl. Chem. Soc.* LXII. II. 1189 Schiff's bases, derived from aromatic aldehydes, have a similar constitution to benzylidenaniline, PhN:CHPh, which serves as the type of these compounds. **1915** P. E. SPIELMANN tr. *V. von Richter's Org. Chem.* 383 Hydrocyanic acid attaches itself similarly to the oximes.. and to the Schiff bases. **1951** I. L. FINAR *Org. Chem.* I. xiii. 257 Primary amines combine with aromatic aldehydes to form Schiff bases. **1971** *Nomencl. Org. Chem.* (I.U.P.A.C.) (ed. 2) 258 Compounds $R^1R^2C{=}NR^3$ have the class name 'azomethines'. When the nitrogen atom is substituted, this class of compound has the generic name 'Schiff's bases'. **1975** *Nature* 30 Oct. 823/2 In visual pigments, retinal is bound by way of a Schiff base linkage to the protein. **1894** PERKIN & KIPPING *Org. Chem.* I. viii. 122 Aldehyde may be detected.. by the 'magenta' or 'rosaniline test' (Schiff's reaction). **1897** *Chem. News* 9 July 23/2 (*heading*) Schiff reaction applied to acid fuchsine. **1951** I. L. FINAR *Org. Chem.* I. viii. 123 Ketones do not give Schiff's reaction. **1897** *Jrnl. Chem. Soc.* LXXII. II. 468 The author [*sc.* B. von Bittó] has also studied the behaviour of Schiff's reagent (a 0·025 per cent. solution of magenta decolorised by passing sulphurous anhydride through it).. with a number of aldehydes and ketones. **1929** EVERS & ELSDON *Analysis of Drugs & Chemicals* 279 The proportion of formaldehyde may be determined by the use of Schiff's reagent. **1964** M. HYNES *Med. Bacteriol.* (ed. 8) xxvii. 412 Schiff reagent. **1902** J. B. COHEN *Theoret. Org. Chem.* ix. 128 A further reaction for aldehydes is known as Schiff's test. **1949** ENGLISH & CASSIDY *Princ. Org. Chem.* xi. 202 Advantage is taken of the greater reactivity of aldehydes toward bisulfite in the Schiff test for aldehydes. **1972** NORMAN & WADDINGTON *Mod. Org. Chem.* xii. 174 The addition of an aldehyde to this colourless solution restores the pink colour of the dye (Schiff's test).

schiff(e, obs. ff. SKIFF.

schil, obs. f. CHILL *a.*, SKILL; var. SHILL, shrill.

schild, obs. form of CHILD.

c **1450** *Mirk's Festial* (1905) 205 For wondyr sory he was for his wyfys deth, and nedys he most se his schild dye.

Schilder's disease ('ʃɪldəz). *Path.* [The name of Paul Ferdinand *Schilder* (1886-1940), U.S. neurologist and psychiatrist, who described the disease in 1912 (*Zeitschr. f. die gesammte Neurol. u. Psychiatrie* X. 1-60).] A disease characterized by degeneration of the neurones of the brain, esp. in the occipitotemporal lobes, leading to blindness, deafness, and death.

1940 HINZIE & SHATZKY *Psychiatric Dict.* 475/1 Schilder's disease or encephalitis periaxialis diffusa, is a slowly progressive degenerative disease of the brain occurring mainly in children and young people. **1961** R. D. BAKER *Essent. Path.* xxii. 599 Diffuse cerebral sclerosis, one form of which has been called Schilder's disease, is a widespread demyelination of the cerebral hemispheres alone. **1966** WRIGHT & SYMMERS *Systemic Path.* II. xxxiv. 1284/2 A feature of Schilder's disease is that the subarcuate fibres are spared, as in some cases of multiple sclerosis.

||**schill** (ʃɪl). Also **schiel.** [Ger. *schill.*] A European pike-perch; the ZANDER.

1885 *Encycl. Brit.* XIX. 89/1 In Europe two species occur, the more celebrated being the 'Zander' of North Germany or 'Schiel' of the Danube (*Lucioperca sandra*). **1888** GOODE *Amer. Fishes* 14 In the Old World, as in the New, there are two well marked species, the Zander, or Schill, *Stizostedion lucioperca*, and the Berschick, or Sekret, *S. volgensis*.

schill, schille, obs. ff. CHILL *a.*, SHELL.

||**schiller** ('ʃɪlə(r)). *Min.* [Ger., play of colours, glistening brightness.

The Ger. word has been used by English entomologists in the literal sense: **1835** J. DUNCAN *Beetles* 87 The elegant tribe of *Cetonidæ*.. are generally of a fine green, often accompanied with a delicate schiller or play of colour.]

1. In certain terms adapted from Ger., denoting minerals or rocks having a shining surface, as ***schiller asbestos, rock, -stone***; also SCHILLER-SPAR.

1804 JAMESON *Syst. Min.* I. 428 Schiller Stone. Schiller-stein.—*Werner*. **1862** DANA *Man. Min.* 146 *Picrolite*, Schiller asbestus. A fibrous serpentine, of an olive-green color, constituting seams in serpentine. **1862** Schiller rock [see SCHILLERITE].

2. A peculiar lustre characteristic of certain minerals, as hypersthene. Also *attrib.*

1885 JUDD in *Q. Jrnl. Geol. Soc.* XLI. 383 The peculiar phenomenon expressed by the term 'Schiller'. **1888** TEALL *Brit. Petrogr.* 446 *Schiller-plane*, a plane in a crystal in which occur the enclosures giving rise to the phenomenon of schiller.

schillerite ('ʃɪləraɪt). *Min.* [f. SCHILLER + -ITE.] An aggregate of anorthite and enstatite, allied to diallage.

1862 DANA *Man. Geol.* vii. 82 Schillerite or Schiller rock, Diallage rock. A dark green to greenish-black rock made up of Schiller spar.

schillerization (ˌʃɪləraɪ'zeɪʃən). [f. SCHILLERIZE + -ATION.] A process of change in crystals, giving rise to a 'schiller' appearing when the crystal is turned in various directions.

1885 JUDD in *Q. Jrnl. Geol. Soc.* XLI. 383 It will be convenient to have a general name for this kind of change, and I propose to employ the term 'Schillerization' to express it. *Ibid.* 385 The phenomena of Schillerization. **1888** HUTTON *Ibid.* XLIV. 746 Some of these crystals show traces of schillerization in one direction.

schillerize ('ʃɪləraɪz), *v.* [f. SCHILLER + -IZE.] *trans.* To subject (a crystal) to the change known as schillerization. Hence **'schillerized** *ppl. a.*, **'schillerizing** *vbl. sb.* (in quot. *attrib.*).

1885 JUDD in *Q. Jrnl. Geol. Soc.* XLI. 383 Thus I shall call diallage and pseudo-hypersthene 'Schillerized augites', bronzite and the typical hypersthene of Labrador 'Schillerized ferriferous enstatites'. *Ibid.* 384 All Schillerized minerals on analysis yield a small but notable proportion of water. **1886** —— in *Mineral. Mag.* Dec. 88 The Schillerizing process. **1890** COLE & GREGORY in *Q. Jrnl. Geol. Soc.* XLVI. 310 The augite is not schillerized.

schiller spar ('ʃɪləspɑː(r)). *Min.* [ad. G. *schillerspath* (1786 Heyer in *Chemische Annalen* I. 335): see SCHILLER and SPAR *sb.*] = BASTITE.

1796 KIRWAN *Elem. Min.* (ed. 2) I. 221 Schiller Spar. **1813** BAKEWELL *Introd. Geol.* 79 Shining laminæ of schiller spar or crystallized serpentine. **1854** DANA *Syst. Min.* (ed. 4) 160 Diallage..includes Schiller spar (in part) and Bronzite. **1879** RUTLEY *Stud. Rocks* x. 120 Enstatite becomes altered to Schiller-spar or bastite, talc, etc.

‖**schilling**[1] ('ʃɪlɪŋ). Also 8 shilling. [Ger.: see SHILLING. Cf. SCHELLING, SKILLING.] A silver coin and money of account formerly in use in North Germany, of the value of $\frac{1}{16}$ mark or 12 pfennigs; (in 1910 slightly over 1*d.* sterling). Now, an Austrian unit of currency, equivalent to 100 groschen; a coin or note of (multiples of) this value.

In some parts of Germany, where coins of various states circulated freely, the names *schilling* and *groschen* were till about 1870 treated as synonymous.

1753 HANWAY *Trav.* (1762) I. VII. lxxxviii. 407 [*Dantzig*], 3 Shillings, or 18 phennigen..1 grosch. *Ibid.* II. I. iii. 17 [*Hamburg*], They keep their accounts in marks and schillings, sixteen schillings to a mark. **1838** *Murray's Handbk. N. Germ.* 299/2 Warm sea-baths..cost 24 schillings. **1924** *Times* 23 June 11/1 The Austrian new Schilling..which is being issued to the public over the counters of the Austrian National Bank since Monday last [*sc.* 16 June]. **1932** *Daily Tel.* 8 Oct. 2/3 New bonds will not be issued for a smaller amount than 50 schillings. **1948** G. CROWTHER *Outl. Money* (ed. 2) ix. 312 In the countries that suffered the worst inflation, entirely new currencies were introduced (the reichsmark in Germany, the schilling in Austria, the pengö in Hungary, in place of marks and crowns). **1978** J. IRVING *World according to Garp* v. 94 'It costs five hundred schillings,' the whore said.

Schilling[2] ('ʃɪlɪŋ). *Med.* The name of Victor *Schilling* (1883–1960), German hæmatologist, used *attrib.* and in the possessive to designate a method of classifying and counting white blood cells, and the results so obtained; (proposed by Schilling in *Deutsch. med. Wochenschr.* (1911) XXXVII. 1159).

1922 *Jrnl. Amer. Med. Assoc.* 11 Mar. 769/2 (*heading*) The Schilling differential blood count. **1924** *Ibid.* 20 Dec. 2055/1 (*heading*) Schilling's hemogram. **1927** A. PINEY *Rec. Adv. in Hæmatol.* 276/1 (*Index*), Schilling index. **1935** WHITBY & BRITTON *Disorders of Blood* iv. 77 In Schilling's method all the data of an ordinary total and differential leucocyte count, as well as a simplified nuclear count, are correlated and considered in the form of a 'hæmogram'. **1972** F. NOUR-ELDIN *Haematol.* iv. 20/2 In practice, this method is more useful than the Schilling haemogram which is based on dividing the granulocytes into four groups.

Schilling[3] ('ʃɪlɪŋ). *Med.* [The name of Robert Frederick *Schilling* (b. 1919), U.S. physician, who described the test in 1953 (*Jrnl. Lab. & Clin. Med.* XLII. 946–7).] *Schilling test*, a test, used esp. for pernicious anæmia, in which a small oral dose of radioactively labelled vitamin B_{12} is followed by a much larger unlabelled dose administered intramuscularly: subsequent excretion of the label in the urine is reduced if there is malabsorption by the gut.

1955 *Gastroenterol.* XXIX. 654 The radioactive material ..which appears in the urine under the conditions of the Schilling test has the same distribution coefficient between ammonium sulfate saturated urine and *n*-butanol as pure vitamin B_{12}-Co^{60}. **1976** *Lancet* 13 Nov. 1087/2 The Schilling test was repeatedly normal.

schilteroun, -thrum, etc., var. ff. SHELTRON *Obs.*

‖**'schimmel.** Chiefly *S. African.* [Ger. ('ʃɪməl) and Du. ('sxɪməl, Cape Du. 'skɪməl)] A roan horse.

1848 THACKERAY *Van. Fair* lxvi, 'There's..Kunz.. coming down the market with three schimmels. *Ibid.*, Up sprang Francis to the box, away went the schimmels, and Dobbin with his head on his breast. **1899** RIDER HAGGARD *Swallow* v, You may take my best horse..the thorough-bred schimmel. **1905** *Blackw. Mag.* Sept. 393/2 Saddle the blue schimmel and ride hard after Baas Hartley.

‖**Schimpfwort** ('ʃɪmpfvɔrt). Pl. Schimpfwörter (-vœrtər). [Ger., f. *schimpf* insult + *wort* WORD.] An insulting epithet, a term of abuse.

1949 R. K. MERTON *Social Theory & Social Structure* v. 153 The community at large, however, evidently emphasizes the imperfections of bureaucracy, as is suggested by the fact that the 'horrid hybrid', bureaucrat, has become an epithet, a *Schimpfwort*. **1974** *Amer. Speech 1971* XLVI. 84 Reinhold A. Aman..lists under *Schimpfwörter*: emotive language and verbal aggression, including cuss words, swear words, terms of abuse, insults, [etc.]. **1978** *Verbatim* Winter 3/2 For the Nazis, the word provided a wonderfully Protean term of abuse, a *Schimpfwort* of unparalleled virtuosity.

schin, obs. form of SKIN.

‖**schindylesis** (skɪndɪ'liːsɪs). *Anat.* [mod.L., a. Gr. σχινδύλησις (Hippocrates cited by Galen).] An articulation formed by the reception of a thin plate of one bone into a fissure or groove in another.

1830 R. KNOX *Béclard's Anat.* 280 Schindylesis is a synarthrosis which results from the reception of the crest or ridge of a bone into the groove of another. **1889** LEIDY *Human Anat.* (ed. 2) 50.

attrib. **1840** W. J. E. WILSON *Anat. Vade M.* (1842) 42 The schindylesis suture is the reception of one bone into a sheath or fissure of another.

†**schine.** *Obs. rare*⁻¹. [ad. L. (Vulgate) *schīnus*, a. Gr. σχῖνος the mastic-tree. Cf. CHINA[2].] *schine-tree* = MASTIC *sb.* 2.

1609 BIBLE (Douay) *Susanna* 54 Under a schine tree.

‖**'schinkel.** *Obs. rare.* [Du. *schinkel* knuckle, shinbone, *schink* gammon, ham; cf. G. *schinken* ham.] A ham, gammon.

a **1634** CHAPMAN *Alphonsus* III. (1654) 33 He and his fellow bowrs..Have brought a schinkel of good raw Bacon.

‖**schinken** ('ʃɪŋkən). [Ger.; cf. SCHINKEL.] German ham. Also in *Comb.*, as **'schinkenwurst** (-vʊrst), ham sausage.

1848 THACKERAY *Van. Fair* lxii. 563 The little boy.. consumed schinken, and braten, and kartoffeln, and cranberry jam. **1957** S. STRONG *Good Food from Vienna* 89 (*heading*) Baked ham (Gebackener Schinken). **1962** [see PICON]. **1967** M. WALDO *Internat. Encycl. Cooking* II. 549/1 *Schinkenwurst*.., ham sausage. **1978** *Sunday Times* (Colour Suppl.) 21 May 78/2 Schinkenwurst, fleischwurst and herb leberwurst will provide a wealth of tastes. **1979** P. FRIEDMAN *Termination Order* (1980) viii. 129 He got a plate of *schinken* and salad.

Schiötz (ʃjɜːts). *Ophthalm.* Also **Schiøtz**. The name of Hjalmar *Schiøtz* (1850–1927), Norwegian physician, used *attrib.* and in the possessive to designate a type of tonometer he devised for measuring the tension of the sclera, and to denote readings made with such a tonometer.

1913 TÖRÖK & GROUT *Surg. of Eye* vi. 173 More accurate information can be had by the use of a Schiötz tonometer. **1917** A. DUANE *Fuchs's Text-bk. Ophthalm.* (ed. 5) II. i. 83 In Schiötz's tonometer a collar..bears at its lower end a concave plate..which is fitted to the curvature of the cornea. **1918** [see HYPOTONIC *a.* 1 b]. **1964** [see LACHRYMATE *v.*]. **1964** S. DUKE-ELDER *Parsons' Dis. of Eye* (ed. 14) x. 113 The type of tonometer should always be cited and the reading expressed in this form—20 mm. Hg (Schiötz).

schip, -ard, obs. forms of SHEEP, SHEPHERD.

schiph, obs. form of SKIFF.

schippe, obs. f. SHAPE *v.*, SHIP, SKIP.

schipper: see SKIPPER (of a ship).

‖**schipperke** ('sxɪpərkə, 'ʃɪpəkɪ). [Du. dial., *lit.* 'little boatman'.] A small black dog belonging to the breed so called, distinguished by pointed, erect ears, a large ruff of longer fur on neck and chest, and usually a docked tail.

1887 *Field* 2 July 7/2 The Schipperkes..little black dogs, born without tails, some 10 lb. in weight or so,..are bred by the boatmen in Holland..and..are said to be excellent hands at killing rats. **1895** 'F. ANSTEY' *Lyre & Lancet* XI. 111 Ought a schipperke to have meat? **1912** 'SAKI' *Unbearable Bassington* xiv. 263 A small black dog, something like a schipperke,..ran from behind my chair. **1950** A. C. SMITH *About our Dogs* xxii. 327 The Schipperke Club standard states that the head is of the foxy type. **1976** A. POWELL *Infants of Spring* iii. 56 The 'odd' lady..used to breed schipperkes, small black dogs from the Netherlands, with sharp ears and curly tails.

schir, obs. form of SHEER, SIR.

†**schirk**, *v. Obs. rare*⁻¹. [f. *schir*, SHIRE *a.* + *-k* as in LURK, TALK *vbs.*] *trans.* To brighten.

a **1400–50** *Alexander* 4816 Þe schaftis of þe schire son schirkind þe cloudis.

schirme, var. SKIRM *Obs.*

Schirmer ('ʃɜːmə(r)). *Ophthalm.* [The name of Otto *Schirmer* (1864–1917), German ophthalmologist, who proposed the test in 1903 (*Archiv f. Ophthalm.* LVI. 197).] *Schirmer('s) test*: a test in which the end of a strip of filter paper is placed on the surface of the eye over the lachrymal duct: the rate at which it is moistened indicates the rate of lachrymal secretion.

1935 *Trans. Amer. Ophthalm. Soc.* XXXIII. 428 Schirmer's test read 3 mm. O.S., 5 mm. O.D., in five minutes. **1941** *Amer. Jrnl. Ophthalm.* XXIV. 21/1 The Schirmer test shows zero to 6–8 mm. in 5 minutes, whereas the lower limit of the normal is 15 mm. according to Schirmer. **1977** *Lancet* 12 Nov. 1027/2 Schirmer's test, which is often reported in the assessment of eye complaints in patients who are taking beta-adrenergic-receptor blocking drugs, is misleading and inaccurate.

schirra, obs. f. SHERIFF.

schirrhus, etc.: see SCIRRHUS, etc.

schirryve, obs. Sc. form of SHRIVE.

schism (sɪz(ə)m, skɪz(ə)m), *sb.* Forms: 4–7 scisme, 5 cisme, cissime, 5–6 sisme, sysme, scysme, 6 scissym, sciseme, cysme, *Sc.* scisma, 6–7 schisme, 7 scism, shism, 7– schism. [ME. *scisme, cisme, sisme*, a. OF. *scisme, cisme* (mod.F. *schisme*) = Pr. *scisma*, Sp. *cisma*, Pg. *scisma* (masc. schism, fem. whim), It. *scisma* schism, *cisma* discord, ill-will, ad. eccl. L. *schisma* neut., a. Gr. σχίσμα rent, cleft (in the N.T. applied fig. to division in the church), f. σχιδ-, σχίζειν to split, rend.

In the 16th c. the spelling was altered in Eng. (as also in Fr.) to *schisme* by assimilation to the late L. and Gr. form.

The pronunc. (skɪz(ə)m), though widely regarded as incorrect, is now freq. used for this word and its derivatives both in the U.K. and in North America.]

1. In the versions of the New Testament, used to represent the Gr. σχίσμα in some passages, where the sense is that of a (metaphorical) rent or cleft.

1382 WYCLIF *1 Cor.* i. 10, I biseche ȝou..that ȝe alle seye the same thing, and that scismes, or dyuysiouns, dissenciouns, or discordis, be not among ȝow. **1552** ABP. HAMILTON *Catech.* (1884) 4 Lat na scismes discord or divisioun be amangis yow. **1582** BIBLE (Rheims) *1 Cor.* xii. 25 That there might be no schisme in the body. [So **1611**.]

2. *Eccl.* **a.** A breach of the unity of the visible Church; the division, either of the whole Church or of some portion of it, into separate and mutually hostile organizations; the condition of being so divided, or an instance of this. Also *transf.* with reference to other religious communities.

According to the definition given repeatedly in various forms by Augustine and other Fathers, the term has reference to outward separation, not to inward divergence of belief. Hence a 'schism' does not necessarily proceed from heresy; indeed the most prominent application of the word is to separations caused by disputes on matters of discipline, the validity of an election to a bishopric or of a sentence of deprivation, or the like.

1390 GOWER *Conf.* I. 15 And so to speke upon this branche, Which proud Envie hath mad to springe, Of Scisme. [The reference is to the Papal schism: see b.] *c* **1400** *Apol. Loll.* (Camden) 29 þe seedis of scysmis schuld be tan a wey. **1440** in *Wars Eng. in France* (1864) II. 453 Goddes chirche [was] supported, and thestate and oonhede thereof observed; scismes, like elles to have growed thereinne, letted and thoo that were growen letted and ceassed. **1456** SIR G. HAYE *Law Arms* (S.T.S.) 25 The kirk..was all..in obscuritee of scisme and of weris. **1549** *Compl. Scot.* xix. 160 Doutles thy abusione, and the sinister ministratione of thy office, is the special cause of the scisma and of diuers sectis that trublis al cristianite, and quhou beit that the rute of thir scismes and sectis be in germane, denmark and ingland. **1558** Q. MARY *Will* in J. M. Stone *Mary I Engl.* (1901) 508 In the tyme of the late Scisme within this Realme. *a* **1600** HOOKER *Serm. Jude* i. §11 (1614) 18 If they breake the bond of vnitie, whereby the body of the Church is coupled and knit in one,..this is to separate themselues by schisme. **1630** PRYNNE *Anti-Armin.* 175 By which words he doth reiect the Scisme of the Donatists. **1678** CUDWORTH *Intell. Syst.* 231 Faustus..took up this conceit—That both the Christians and Jews..were no other than schisms or subdivided sects of paganism. **1689** POPPLE tr. *Locke's 1st Let. Toleration* 61 Schism then..is nothing else but a Separation made in the Communion of the Church, upon account of something in Divine Worship, or Ecclesiastical Discipline, that is not any necessary part of it. **1782** BURNEY *Hist. Mus.* II. 46 The schism between the Greek and Latin churches, which happened in the ninth century. **1831** SCOTT *Ct. Robt.* vii, In order to compel the Patriarch to submit himself to the Pope, adopt the Latin form of the cross, and put an end to the schism.

b. *spec.* A state of divided spiritual allegiance in Western Christendom (or, at an earlier period, in Christendom generally) caused by a disputed election to the Papacy; esp. ***the Great (Western) Schism*** (1378–1417); other 'schisms' arose from the claims of the rivals of Alexander III (1159–1177) and of the antipope Felix V (1432–1448).

1460 CAPGRAVE *Chron.* (Rolls) 88 In his tyme was a scisme betwix him [Symmachus] and on Laurens. *c* **1460** *Brut* 507 This yere þe general Counsel of Basile deposed Pope Eugeny; & þei chese Felix..; & þan began þe Scisme which endured vnto þe yere of oure Lord Ihesu Crist M[l] iiij[c] xlviij. *a* **1513** FABYAN *Chron.* VII. ccxxxvi. 273 The sisme, y[t] after fell amongis the cardynallys, for eleccion of the pope Alexander the .iii.: which sysme, by mean of the first Frederike than emperoure, endured almooste .xx. yeres. *a* **1548** HALL *Chron., Hen. V*, 34 The long scisme and devision sprong & continued in the catholike church. **1651** N. BACON *Disc. Govt. Eng.* II. vi. (1739) 34 The Popedom was now under a Schism between two Popes, Clement and Urban. **1761** HUME *Hist. Eng.* I. viii. 167 The schism of the Papacy between Alexander and Victor. **1845** *Encycl. Metrop.* XII. 182/1 The death of Gregory was followed by serious difficulty respecting the choice of his successor, which gave rise to the long-continued dissension in the Church, commonly called *the Great Western Schism.* **1885** MULLINGER in *Encycl. Brit.* XIX. 502/1 The outbreak of the great schism struck no less deeply at those sentiments of veneration and deference which had been wont to gather round the pontiff's chair.

c. The offence of promoting the formation or contributing to the permanence of 'schisms' or divisions in the Church or a portion of it; the state of being culpably separated from the Church. Phrase, ***in schism.***

1402 *Repl. Friar Topias* in *Pol. Poems* (Rolls) II. 41 Now is that seed of cisme sowen in the chirche; the whete fadith with the floure, oure fode is for to feche. **1551** CROWLEY *Pleasure & P.* 359 You layde to theyr charge herecie, Sisme, and Sedicion also. **1557** CARD. POLE in Strype *Eccl. Mem.* (1721) III. App. lxviii. 254 And for theyr remayninge in Schisme, great Plages of God remayninge styll upon them. **1567** in Ellis *Orig. Lett.* Ser. III. III. 324 That doth not comply with the orders of the Church, lately purged or clensed from Sisme and Idolatry. **1571** CAMPION *Hist. Irel.* xii. (1633) 36 That the onely report of his holynesse and cunning, excited the Scotts (late christened, but abiding in scisme). **1662** *Bk. Com. Prayer, Litany*, From all false doctrine, heresy, and schism. **1670** WALTON *Lives* I. 13 There could be no such sin as Schism, if an adherence to some visible Church were not necessary. **1689** POPPLE tr. *Locke's 1st Let. Toleration* 61 Use, which is the Supream Law in matter of Language, has determined that Heresy relates to Errors in Faith, and Schism to those in Worship or Discipline. **1704** NELSON *Fest. & Fasts* II. x. (1705) 512 Till our refractoriness degenerates into the grievious Sin of Schism. **1769** BLACKSTONE *Comm.* IV. iv. 52 The sin of schism..is by no means the object of temporal coercion and punishment. **1819** SHELLEY *Peter Bell* Prol. 11 Shielding from the guilt of schism The orthodoxal syllogism. **1842** TENNYSON *Epic* 16, I heard The parson..Now harping on the church-commissioners, Now hawking at Geology and schism. **1856** R. A. VAUGHAN *Mystics* (1860) I. 113 And then, despite all heresy and schism, theocracy will flourish.

d. A sect or body formed by division within the Church; a body which, either in Christendom generally or in some portion of it, maintains an ecclesiastical organization distinct from that of the Catholic Church; a schismatic sect.

c **1511** *1st Eng. Bk. Amer.* (Arb.) 290 They doo therfore with a more constante mynde perseuer in theyr fyrst fayth.. than doo manye of vs beinge diuided into scismes and sectes whiche thynge neuer chaunceth amonge them. **1577** tr. *Bullinger's Decades* III. vi. 366 Neither Christ nor our saluation is to bee found without the church, in the sects or schismes of wicked heretikes. *c* **1645** HOWELL *Lett.* (1650) II. 9 Hence comes it that the earth is rent into so many religions, and those religions torn into so many schismes, and various forms of devotion. **1649** MILTON *Eikon.* xxvii. 215 That Church that from the name of a distinct place takes its autority to set up a distinct Faith or Government, is a Scism and Faction, not a Church. **1840** MACAULAY *Ess., Ranke* (1850) II. 143 If a noble lady is moved..she will end by giving her name to a new schism. **1884** TENNYSON *Becket* I. iii, And that I cannot sign: for that would make Our island-Church a schism from Christendom.

fig. **1640** HABINGTON *Q. Arragon* IV. i, If your designe Be to convert me; for I know you hold All Ladies in a Schisme, who are young and proud.

†**e.** ? A schismatical opinion. *Obs. rare*$^{-1}$.

1644 MILTON *Areop.* (Arb.) 55 Not to count him fit to print his mind without a tutor and examiner, lest he should drop a scism, or something of corruption.

3. a. *gen.* In early use, a state of disunion, dissension, or mutual hostility. Now with more restricted meaning (influenced by sense 2 and the Gr. etymology), a division into mutually opposing parties of a body of persons that have previously acted in concert. Also, in recent use, a severance of unity, a discord, breach (between persons or things).

c **1425** LYDG. *Assembly of Gods* 411 The goddys remembryd the scisme odyous Among the three goddesses that she [Discord] had wrought At the fest of Peleus. *c* **1440** CAPGRAVE *Life St. Kath.* II. 454 (MS. Arund.), 'It is ful perillous, he seyde, 'to be a mayde And eke a qveen; ȝe may be ful sone afrayde If ony rysynge or ony sisme [*MS. Rawl.* scisme] be sterde.' *c* **1440** *Gesta Rom.* xxviii. 196 (Add. MS.) Where that was cissime and debate amonge any, he labored for to make accorde, that good acorde shold be had. **1447** BOKENHAM *Seyntys* (Roxb.) 36 But whan that cyte [Antioch] wyth scysme was ner nowt Oon Austyn to Tuskayne from thens me [St. Margaret] browt. **1477** *Coventry Leet Bk.* 420 Eny persone..that haue eny seducious langage, which myght sowe eny sysme betwixt the kynges goode grace and eny his lordez. *a* **1674** CLARENDON *Hist. Reb.* x. §110 But this Schisme carried all the Reputation and Authority to the Army, and left none to the Parliament. **1783** BURKE *Indian Committee* Wks. II. 216 An open schism instantly divided the Council. **1834** MACAULAY *Ess., Pitt* ¶10 The schism which had divided the Whig party was now completely healed. **1839** *Blackw. Mag.* XLV. 460 The eternal and inevitable schism between the Romanticists and the Classicists. **1851** M. HOPKINS *Strength & Beauty* xiv. 261 (Funk) It is a prejudice, as disastrous as it is unfounded, that there can be a schism between the heart and the intellect to the advantage of either. **1852** T. PARKER *Ten Serm. Relig.* iii. (1863) 42 Attraction is the most general law in the material world, and prevents a schism in the universe. **1872** H. T. BUCKLE *Misc. Wks.* I. 252 The schism between literature and the government was aided by another schism between literature and religion.

b. *nonce-uses.* A faction, party; a set or class of people.

1819 SHELLEY *Peter Bell* II. v, He had on an upper Benjamin (For he was of the driving schism). **1820** —— *Witch of Atlas* lxxv, In a band The gaolers sent those of the liberal schism Free through the streets of Memphis.

†**4.** *Mus.* = SCHISMA. *Obs. rare.*

1653 LD. BROUNCKER tr. *Des Cartes' Compend. Mus.* 30 A certaine Fraction, which may be the difference betwixt a Tone major and a Tone minor, which we nominate a Schism [orig. *quam schisma nominamus*]. **1694** W. HOLDER *Harmony* 86, *Note*, whenever I mention Diesis without Distinction; I mean Diesis *Minor*, or Enharmonic: and when I so mention Comma; I mean Comma *Majus*, or Schism.

¶ **5.** Used *jocularly* in the etymological sense: A rent or tear (in a garment).

1767 STERNE *Tr. Shandy* IX. xxiv, My shirts! see what a deadly schism has happen'd amongst 'em. **1772** R. GRAVES *Spir. Quixote* (1783) II. 140 He..levelled his needle at the schism in his Master's trousers.

6. *attrib.* and *Comb.*, as *schism-sower*, *time*; **Schism Act**, the statute 13 Anne c. 7 (1714; repealed in 1719 by 5 Geo. I, c. 4), requiring all teachers to conform to the Established Church; so **Schism Bill**; **schism-house, -shop**, a contemptuous term for a nonconformist place of worship (occasionally also applied to a proprietary chapel licensed for Church of England services).

1733 *Free-Briton* No. 200 ¶6 This was the Act which repealed the *Schism-Act. *Ibid.* ¶1 The *Schism-Bill. **1814** W. WILSON *Dissent. Ch. Lond.* IV. 533 The schism bill received the royal assent June 25, 1714. **1843** MIALL in *Nonconf.* III. 607 What the vicar calls '*schism-houses'. **1893** *Church Times* 21 July 757/4 In Romish schism-houses in this country. **1801** COL. G. HANGER in *Life* II. 404 You might travel 60 or 70 miles and not see a church, or even a *schism-shop. **1823** SOUTHEY *Let. to Mrs. Southey* 30 Dec. in *Life* (1850) V. 154, I recollected that in most schism shops the sermon is looked upon as the main thing for which the congregation assemble. *c* **1449** PECOCK *Repr.* II. ii. 139 Therfore the aȝenseiers her of ben to be reiated and rebukid as..*scisme sowers and disturblers of the peple. **1589** NASHE *Martins Months Mind* Ep. to Rdr. D 1, Al such vntractable and seditious scisme sowers. **1539** WRIOTHESLEY *Chron.* (1875) I. 107 The great studie and stedfastness that he had taken and contynued in all the *scysme and division tyme.

†**schism**, *v. Obs. rare.* [f. SCHISM *sb.*] *intr.* To separate schismatically.

1604 H. JACOB *Reasons taken out* 77 He that differeth from the Gospell ioyneth not to the Church, but schismeth from it. **1610** J. ROBINSON *Justif. Separation* Wks. 1851 II. 293 It is necessary that he which thinks it a true church return unto it, from which he hath wickedly schismed. **1645** KIFFEN in R. Baillie *Anabaptism* (1647) 69 The notorious guilt of schisming from Rome.

‖**schisma** ('skɪzmə). *Acoustics.* Pl. **schismata**. Also 9 **skhisma**. [late L. *schisma* 'dimidium commatis' (Boëthius, quoting Philolaus), a special use of Gr. σχίσμα division: see SCHISM *sb.*] A term denoting a small interval of musical pitch. †**a.** In ancient Greek use, the half of a comma. *Obs.* †**b.** By Descartes and some later writers applied to the difference between a major and a minor tone; = COMMA 3 (1). *Obs.* **c.** The difference between a diaschisma and a syntonic comma, represented by the ratio 32.805:32.768.

1653 [see SCHISM *sb.* 4]. **1753** *Chambers' Cycl. Supp.* **1875** ELLIS *Helmholtz' Sensat. Tone* III. xiv. 431 *note*, This substitution..amounts to a temperament with perfect Fifths, and major Thirds too flat by a skhisma, or nearly the eleventh of a comma. **1876** C. BROWN *Mus. Common Things* II. 38 Between all enharmonic changes,..the interval of the schisma always occurs, 32,768: 32,805, the difference being 37. **1876** STAINER & BARRETT *Dict. Mus. Terms, Schisma* (Gk.), an approximate half of a Pythagorean comma, that is, half of the difference between twelve fifths and seven octaves. **1885** ELLIS *Helmholtz' Sensat. Tone* Addit. (ed. 2) 432 Twelve Fifths up and seven Octaves down give the sum of a Comma and a Skhisma, known as the Pythagorean Comma.

†'**schismacy.** *Obs.* In 4 scismacye, cismacie. [f. SCHISMAT(E: see -ACY.] = SCHISM *sb.* 2.

1387 TREVISA *Higden* (Rolls) VII. 149 In tyme of þis Henry, so moche scismacye [L. *tantum schisma*] was in þe chirche of Rome, þat þre men were chosen popes. *Ibid.*, þis Henry comynge to Rome for to cese þe cismacie [L. *pro schismate sedando*].

†'**schismarch.** *Obs.* [ad. med.L. *schismarcha*, f. *schisma* SCHISM *sb.* + *-archa*, a. Gr. -άρχης ruler. Cf. *heresiarch.*] A founder of a schism.

1657 J. WATTS *Dipper Sprinkled* 31 Your own original Authors and Scismarchs.

†**schismat(e.** *Obs. rare.* [In 15th c. *scismat(e*, a. OF. *scismat* (Godefr.), app. a back-formation from *scismatique* SCHISMATIC.] = SCHISMATIC *sb.*

c **1450** *St. Cuthbert* (Surtees) 3702 ȝe assent to sin or to scismates. *Ibid.* 4598 To bow þaim to scismats. *c* **1450** *Mirk's Festial* 123 Yn þes orisons, holy chyrch prayth for all maner folke, for lewes,..for herytykys, for scismatys.

schismatic (sɪz'mætɪk, sk-), *a.* and *sb.* Forms: 4–6 **scismatik**, 5 **cysmatyke, scismattike**, 5–6 **sys-, scismatyk**, 6 **scysmatik, -yk(e, schismatik, sys-, scismatick**, 7 **scismatique**, 6–7 **schismatike, -ique, icke**, 7 **schismatick**, 7– **schismatic**. [ME. *cysmatyke, scismatik*, etc., a. OF. *cis-, scismatique* (mod.F. *schismatique*, after Gr.; the altered spelling came in both in Fr. and Eng. near the end of the 16th c.), ad. eccl. L. *schismaticus*, a. eccl. Gr. σχισματικός, f. σχισματ-, σχίσμα SCHISM *sb.* Cf. Pr. *sismatic*, Sp. *cismático*, Pg. *schismatico*, It. *scismatico*.

Johnson, Walker, Todd, and Smart (1836–48) have the stress '*schismatic*, which appears in many early verse examples. The accentuation now current is given by Webster in 1828; cf. quot. 1822 (Byron).]

A. *adj.* Of or pertaining to schism or schismatics; of the nature of schism; guilty of the offence of schism.

c **1440** *Promp. Parv.* 78/2 Cysmatyke, *cismaticus, cismatica. Ibid.* 456/2 Sysmatyk, *scismaticus.* **1456** SIR G. HAYE *Law Arms* (S.T.S.) 109 The subjectis of the Emperour suld kepe thair obedience till him alset he war scismattike. **1512** *Act 4 Hen. VIII*, c. 19 Preamble, Whiche Scismatyk demeanure of the seid Frensche King ys and hathe ben parlyous and terrible example to all Cristen fayth. **1534** in *Lett. Suppress. Monasteries* (Camden) 8 Yn the whych sermondes he prechyd dyvers sysmatyke and yronyous opinions. **1543** BALE *Yet a Course at Rom. Foxe* 98 b, Hontyngton..can not amonge all hys heretyques fynde..one scysmatyk Prest. **1645** EVELYN *Diary* ? July, I went over to St. George's to the ceremonie of the schismatic Greekes, who are permitted to have their Church, tho' they are at defiance with Rome. **1728** MORGAN *Algiers* I. iii. 59 The Schismatick Mahometans..employed their utmost malice against that unhappy City. **1818** SCOTT *Hrt. Midl.* viii, It was to be hoped, that, though she was the widow of an enthusiastic corporal of Cromwell's dragoons, her grandson might be neither schismatic nor anti-national. **1822** BYRON *Werner* IV. i, Though the schismatic Swede, Gustavus, is Gone home. **1864** PUSEY *Lect. Daniel* (1876) 258 The schismatic kingdom of Israel. **1865** —— *Truth Eng. Ch.* 65 There may be schismatic acts, which have not the deadliness of the sin of schism. **1887** RUSKIN *Præterita* II. 312 The..Modern Painters were..more startled than flattered by my schismatic praise.

B. *sb.* One who promotes or countenances schism or breach of external unity in the Church; one who is guilty of the sin of schism; a member or adherent of a schismatical body.

1377 LANGL. *P. Pl.* B. XI. 115 For cryste cleped vs alle come if we wolde, Sarasenes and scismatikes. *c* **1440** *Jacob's Well* iv. 28 Alle, þat kepyn holy cherch-godys, or wyth-holdyn þat arn alyenyd awey be sysmatykes..& noȝt wyln restoryn þe godys aȝen [etc.]. **1460** CAPGRAVE *Chron.* (Rolls) 242 And because that the Spaynardis were scismatikes, the Pope Urban graunted [etc.]. **1526** *Pilgr. Perf.* (W. de W. 1531) 218 b, Malicyous lyuers, as moost specially ben these heretykes and scismatykes. **1579** W. WILKINSON *Confut. Fam. Love* 2 Whosoever doth cut a sunder the unitye, and disturbe the peace of the Church,..is a Schismatique. **1600** *Sir John Oldcastle* IV. iii. 134 Old Ruffian past-grace, vpstart schismatike. **1621** BURTON *Anat. Mel.* III. iv. I. i. 715 Enthusiasts, Diuinators, Prophets, Sectaries, Scismaticks. **1642** CHAS. I *Declar. to County York* 3 June 2 Separatists and Shismaticks. **1650** HUBBERT *Pill Formality* 34 Are they not still called Roundheads, Sectaries, Schismaticks, and what not? **1678** EVELYN *Diary* 22 Feb., Dr. Pierce preach'd at White-hall on 2 Thessal. 3. 6 against our late Schismatics. *a* **1680** BUTLER *Rem.* (1759) I. 230 Support all Schismatics and Sects. **1688** *Answ. Talon's Plea* 16 There is none but the Greek Schismaticks that reject the Councill of Florence. **1726** AYLIFFE *Parergon* 480 By the Laws of England a Schismatick is one that divides and separates himself from the Establish'd Church of the Realm, not on Fundamentals of Faith, but on some Points of Religion relating to Church Discipline and external Worship. **1769** BLACKSTONE *Comm.* IV. iv. 52 Papists and protestant dissenters..were supposed to be equally schismatics in departing from the national church. **1849** MACAULAY *Hist. Eng.* ii. I. 164 Both [the puritans and quakers] were schismatics. Both hated episcopacy and the liturgy. **1859** JEPHSON *Brittany* vi. 73 Fleury was no longer read by the young clergy, being considered a Gallican and a schismatic. **1866** GEO. ELIOT *F. Holt* xxiii, The wretched cavils of the Nonconformists, and the noisy futility that belongs to schismatics generally.

loosely. **1535** STEWART *Cron. Scot.* 29455 Schort quhill befoir his dais war compleit, The scismatik callit wes Mohomeit, In Arrabie closit his latter dayis.

Comb. **1577** tr. *Bullinger's Decades* III. viii. 422 They saide that Paule..did schismatiquelike sowe in the churches a certeine doctrine peculiar to him selfe.

b. *spec.* In Roman Catholic use, one of those Roman Catholics who in the reign of Elizabeth conformed by occasionally attending the services of the Church of England, in order to avoid the penalties denounced against recusants.

1584 in Foley *Rec. Eng. Prov. S.J.* (1880) VI. 726 The schismatics who come to church, and yet in heart are Papists, they do most mischief. **1600** in Morris *Troubles Cath. Foref.* I. iv. (1872) 194 And this doth touch chiefly schismatics, whose wives for the most part are all recusants, and many Protestants, besides Catholics. **1877** FOLEY *Rec. Eng. Prov. S.J.* I. 147 His friends and relations were Protestants, but his parents and brothers schismatics.

c. *transf.* and *fig.*

a **1652** BROME *Mad Couple* Addr. to Stationer, But 'tis the Custome, and who won't submit, Must be esteem'd a Schismatick in wit. *a* **1704** T. BROWN *Sat. upon Fr. King* Wks. 1730 I. 60 My breeches too..I found grown Schismaticks, and fall'n asunder. **1834** MACAULAY *Ess., Pitt* ¶19 Pulteney..was the schismatic; they [the Whigs] were the true Catholics, the peculiar people, the despositaries of the orthodox faith of Hampden and Russell.

schismatical (sɪz'mætɪkəl, sk-), *a.* [Formed as prec. + -AL[1].] = SCHISMATIC *a.*

a **1548** HALL *Chron., K. Hen. V*, 34 b, Gregory the xij was one of the Scismatical numbre. **1558–9** *Act 1 Eliz.* c. 1 §19 Any Error, Heresie, Scisme or Scismaticall Opinion. **1613** PURCHAS *Pilgrimage* (1614) 589 Peucerus maketh the Egyptian Caliphs to be Schismaticall from their first entrance, which was (as he saith) in Anno 703. **1614** RALEIGH *Hist. World* II. xxvi. 600 Syracon, Captain of the Turkes, that had beene in Aegypt, goes to the Caliph of Baldach, offering his best meanes for the extirpation of the Schismaticall Caliph. **1637** *Decree Star-Chamb. concern. Printing* §1 in Milton *Areop.* (Arb.) 9 That no person..shall presume to print..any seditious, scismaticall, or offensive Bookes or Pamphlets. **1642** *Compl. to Ho. Comm.* 15 Schismatical men addicted to Anabaptisme and Brownisme. **1659** BP. WALTON *Consid. Considered* 190 That Manasseh.. built a temple on Mount Gerizim,..and there worshipped God, and offered sacrifices, (though in a schismatical way,) is out of doubt. **1680** BAXTER *Rep. Stilling fleet's Let.* vi. 16 And therefore your accusation of us thus grounded is Shismatical and unjust. **1686** *Answ. to Printed Paper* 16 Then the Church of Rome is the most Schismatical in the World, that denies Communion with all Churches that are not in all Tridentine points one with her. **1738** *Gentl. Mag.* VIII. 18/1 The Prophets of the Grove, were not indeed Prophets of the Lord, as Elijah was, but they were the only Prophets of the Schismatical Jewish Church at Samaria. **1761** HUME *Hist. Eng.* II. xxvii. 123 He put Pisa under an interdict, and all the places which gave shelter to the Schismatical Council. **1826** SCOTT *Woodst.* x, But what are these schismatical proceedings to our present purpose? **1879** R. T. SMITH *Basil the Great* x. 124 The passage above quoted in respect to baptism, concerning the failure of the gifts of the spirit in schismatical bodies after the first generation, shows how strongly Basil held the doctrine of Apostolical Succession. **1882–3** *Schaff's Encycl. Relig. Knowl.* I. 204/2 One who has received heretical or schismatical baptism when he might have had the Catholic.

b. *spec.* in Roman Catholic use. (See SCHISMATIC *sb.* b.)

1582 ALLEN *Martyrdom Campion* (1908) 108 This blessed man..had an old schismaticall priest to his uncle.

schismatically (sɪzˈmætɪkəlɪ, sk-), *adv.* [f. SCHISMATICAL *a.* + -LY[2].] In a schismatic manner.

1554 BONNER *Art. Visit.* B ij, Item, whether any such, as were ordered scismatically and contrary to the olde order & custome of the catholike churche, or being vnlawfully and scismaticallye married after the late innouation and maner. *a* **1600** HOOKER *Eccl. Pol.* VII. ix. §2 Aërius, so Schismatically and stifly maintaining it, must even stand where Epiphanius and Augustine have placed him. **1661** *Terms of Accomm.* 9 It was done schismatically. **1683** *Addr. fr. Sudbury* in *Lond. Gaz.* No. 1847/3 Those People who in their Fanatick Zeal have Schismatically divided from the best constituted Church in the World. **1691** WOOD *Ath. Oxon.* II. 256 He..preached very schismatically. **1871** FREEMAN *Norm. Conq.* IV. xvii. 94 With what eyes..did Stigand look on the works of the predecessor whom, in Norman belief, he had unjustly and schismatically driven from his throne.

schisˈmaticalness. *rare.* [f. SCHISMATICAL *a.* + -NESS.] The quality of being schismatic.

1664 H. MORE *Myst. Iniq., Apol.* x. 562 Your mere Schismaticalness and Contumacy against the Church is so. **1637** H. STUBBE *Further Justif. War Neth.* 47 Their Bishops were recalled, and a plenary toleration granted unto them; their Madness, or Schismaticalness being left to the immediate punishment of God. **1681** H. MORE *Expos. Dan.* Pref. 90 We are to..repent us..of our Schismaticalness and Rebelliousness. **1718** HICKES & NELSON *J. Kettlewell* III. lxix. 362 The Schismaticalness of the Congregations.

†**schismaticating,** *ppl. a.* *Obs.*[−1] [f. SCHISMATIC + -ATE[3] + -ING[2].] = SCHISMATIZING *ppl. a.*

1712 M. HENRY *Nat. Schism* (1886) 5 Some of the schismaticating doctors the Church has known.

schisˈmatico-, combining form of SCHISMATIC.

1689 *Apol. Fail. Walker's Acc.* 25 It being Canonico-Prelatically impossible, tho Schismatico-Presbyterially certain. **1818** G. S. FABER *Horæ Mosaicæ* I. 315 Their Schismatico-political mode of worship.

ˈschismatism. *nonce-wd.* [f. SCHISMAT-IC + -ISM.] Schismatic principles.

1859 MRS. GASKELL *Round the Sofa* 223 But, at any rate, he is a Baptist, and has been in trade. What with his schismatism and Mr. Gray's methodism, I am afraid all the primitive character of this place will vanish.

schismatist (ˈsɪzmətɪst, ˈsk-). *rare.* [Formed as next + -IST.] A schismatic.

1754 *Let. fr. Member of Ch. of Scot. to Elder of Seceders* 52 He says not to these schismatists you are not a Member of the Church. **1852** *Blackw. Mag.* LXXI. 750 [He] hopes the best for Schismatists, but can't See aught for them within the covenant. **1895** *Cath. News* 12 Oct. 7/5 It would be one of the greatest triumphs of Leo's sovereignty if he succeeded in winning back the Alexandrian schismatists to the true faith.

schismatize (ˈsɪzmətaɪz, ˈsk-), *v.* [a. OF. *scismatiser* (Cotgr.), f. Gr. σχίσματ-, σχίσμα SCHISM + -IZE.]

1. *intr.* To behave as a schismatic; to favour or advocate schismatic principles; to lead or belong to a schismatic body.

1601 W. WATSON *Sparing Discov.* A 3 b, The Secular priests haue only..Schismatiz'd and rebelled against M. Geor. Blackwell and his Jesus Masters. **1611** COTGR., *Scismatiser*, to Scismatise it, or play the Scismatick. **1657** J. SERGEANT *Schism Dispatch't* 89 Therefore to schismatize is to divide himself voluntarily from the Church. *Ibid.* 382 Which being too weak a ground in the judgment of every prudent Conscientious man to hazard his Soul upon, as he must if he begin to Schismatize upon no better Grounds. **1659** GAUDEN *Tears Ch.* I. ii. 42 From which [Church] I rather chose boldly to separate than poorly to *schismatise* in it. **1689** HICKERINGILL *Ceremony-Monger* Concl. iv. Wks. 1716 II. 488 Must we Schismatize from Scripture, and from all the Protestants in the World, to follow a Custom they got into the Greek Church? **1705** —— *Priest-cr.* I. ibid. III. 13 If [the Church of England] say true, then it is impossible.. to Schismatize from her. **1716** M. DAVIES *Athen. Brit.* III. 11 All Foreign Calvinists..disown and condemn our Dissenters for Idiotizing as well as Schismatizing in their Uncivil as well as Unchristian Obstinacy. **1833** J. H. NEWMAN *Arians* I. i. (1876) 6 His intimate friend..Lucian, who schismatized or was excommunicated on his deposition. **1864** —— *Apol.* 239 It may be the providential means of uniting the whole Church in one, without fresh schismatizing or use of private Judgment.

b. *transf.* To make a division in a political party.

1793 JEFFERSON *Writ.* (1859) IV. 52, I am not sure whether some of the more furious republicans may not schismatize with him.

2. *trans.* **a.** To lead into schism. **b.** To divide into parties. *rare.*

1645 *Liberty of Conscience* 35 We must distinguish the persons who are in the error, whether Heresiarchs and ring-leaders, or whether followers only,..whether schismatizing, or schismatized. **1813** JEFFERSON *Writ.* (1830) IV. 202 They [these questions] now schismatize every people whose minds and mouths are not shut up by the gag of a despot.

Hence **ˈschismatizing** *ppl. a.*

1657 J. SERGEANT *Schism Dispach't* 559 To reunite..a schismatizing Congregation to the Body it broke from. **1712** M. HENRY *Nat. Schism* (1886) 9 The great schismatizing principle which has been so much the bane of the Christian Church.

†**ˈschismic,** *a. Obs. rare*[−1]. [f. SCHISM *sb.* + -IC.] Schismatic.

1608 SYLVESTER *Du Bartas* II. iv. III. *Schisme* 525 Then to Carmel's top The Schismick Priests were quickly called up. **1614** —— *Little Bartas* 1047 Vouchsafe our souls rest, without Schismick strife.

†**ˈschismless,** *a. Obs. rare*[−1]. [f. SCHISM *sb.* + -LESS.] Without or free from schism.

1641 MILTON *Ch. Govt.* I. vi. 22 The peace and good of the Church is not terminated in the schismelesse estate of one or two kingdomes.

schismogenesis (sɪzməʊˈdʒɛnɪsɪs). *Anthrop.* [f. SCHISM *sb.* + -O + -GENESIS, after *biogenesis*, *parthenogenesis*, etc.] A term proposed for the origin of differentiation between groups or cultures caused by the reciprocal exaggeration of behaviour patterns and responses that may result in the destruction of social balance. Hence **schismoˈgenic** *a.*

1935 G. BATESON in *Man* XXXV. 181 A position is set up in which the behaviour X, Y, Z, is the standard reply to X, Y, Z. This position contains elements which may lead to progressive differentiation or *schismogenesis*. **1936** R. FIRTH *We, the Tikopia* p. vii, Attempts are made to analyse cultures in terms of Schismogenesis. **1940** *Brit. Jrnl. Psychol.* Oct. 133 The growth or divergence between the two kinds of game [*sc.* rugby football]..is an excellent example of what Bateson has called 'schismogenesis'—the development of cultural traits in opposition and divergence. **1949** G. BATESON in M. Fortes *Soc. Structure* 47 In schismogenic theory it was tacitly assumed that the individuals would maximize intangible..variables such as prestige, self-esteem, or even submissiveness. **1969** B. MCLAUGHLIN *Stud. in Soc. Movements* 477 Norman Miller, 'Formal Organization and Schismogenesis', unpublished paper.

schist[1] (ʃɪst). *Geol.* Also 8 **shist**; and see SCHISTUS. [a. F. *schiste* (in 16th c. *scisth*, in 18th c. occas. *chite*, in accordance with the then usual pronunciation), a. L. *schistos* adj., fissile, readily splitting (*lapis schistos*, a kind of stone mentioned by Pliny), a. Gr. σχιστός (σχ. λίθος, 'probably talc', L. & Sc.), f. σχιδ-, σχίζειν to split: see SCHISM *sb.*] A crystalline rock whose component minerals are arranged in a more or less parallel manner.

Some continental writers call any fissile rock a 'schist', prefixing the word 'crystalline' to denote the rocks described in the above definition. The parallel structure in schists is independent of original stratification, being due to metamorphic action; indeed, many schists are modified igneous rocks.

1795 MILLS in *Phil. Trans.* LXXXVI. 41 A thin stratum of vegetable soil lies uppermost; then clay, mingled with fine sand, composed of small particles of quartz, mica, and shist. **1832** DE LA BECHE *Geol. Man.* (ed. 2) 309 The schist, and its accompanying clays, contain an abundance of fossils. **1885** TEALL (*title of paper*) On the Metamorphosis of Dolomite into Hornblende-Schist. **1886** BONNEY *Pres. Addr. Geol. Soc.* 57 Again in the mouth of one geologist a 'schist' will mean any rock that has a rough fissility,..while another restricts the term to the foliated rocks. **1903** A. GEIKIE *Text-bk. Geol.* 246 A rock possessing a crystalline arrangement into separate folia is in English termed a Schist. **1904** VAN HISE *Treat. Metamorphism* (U.S. Geol. Survey) 780 Illustrations of the use of the term Schist both as the name of a definite rock and with a structural signification are furnished by the terms mica-schist, chlorite-schist, and hornblende-schist as generally used.

b. *attrib.*

1839 URE *Dict. Arts* 36 The evaporation of the Schist Lixivium. *Ibid.* 39 For evaporating the schist liquors. **1878** *Schiller's Technol. Dict.*, Schist-oil. **1903** GEIKIE *Text-bk. Geol.* IV. VIII. §1 (ed. 4) 782 The schist district of the Elbe valley hills in Saxony.

schist[2] (skɪst). *Acoustics. rare.* In quot. **skhist**. [ad. Gr. σχιστόν, neut. of σχιστός divided: see SCHIST[1].] A small interval equal to one-eighth of a schisma.

1875 [see SCHISTIC *a.*[3]].

schiˈstaceous, *a. Bot.* [f. SCHIST[1] + -ACEOUS.] Having the colour of schist or slate, blue-grey.

1900 B. D. JACKSON *Gloss. Bot. Terms.*

†**ˈschistic,** *a.*[1] *Obs. rare*[−1]. In 8 *erron.* **schystic.** [ad. assumed Gr. *σχιστικός, f. σχιδ-, σχίζειν to split: see SCHISM *sb.*] Dividing, analytical. (In quot. *humorously pedantic.*)

1742–3 FIELDING *Phil. Trans.* Wks. 1771 VI. 500 We are forced to proceed..by the metabolic or mutative [method], not by the schystic or divisive.

ˈschistic, *a.*[2] *Geol. rare.* [f. SCHIST[1] + -IC.] Pertaining to, resembling a schist: = SCHISTOID.

1806 *Gazetteer Scot.* (ed. 2) 259 The rocks in the parish are mostly whinstone, and schistic strata. **1807** HEADRICK *Arran* 50 Masses of schistic rock. **1931** *Discovery* Nov. 355/2 Around the melting snow in schistic soil *Androsace hedreantha* was flowering in hundreds.

schistic (ˈskɪstɪk), *a.*[3] *Acoustics.* In 9 **skhistic.** [See quot.] Of a system of musical temperament, or tones as tempered on this system: Based on an allowance for the difference of a 'schist'.

1875 ELLIS tr. *Helmholtz' Sensat. Tone* App. XIX. 652 Skhistic, or Helmholtzian [temperament] as it may be called... The name Skhistic is derived from skhist..which I use for the small interval that is one-eighth of the Greek skhisma. *Ibid.*, The complete series of skhistic tones. *Ibid.* 764 If skhistic intonation could be easily produced in practice.

ˈschistify, *v. Geol.* [f. SCHIST[1] + -IFY.] *trans.* To develop a schistose structure in, to change into schist. Hence **ˈschistified** *ppl. a.*

1890 COLE & GREGORY in *Q. Jrnl. Geol. Soc.* XLVI. 301 Some of this rock is fine-grained, and some schistified with large diallage- and felspar-eyes. *Ibid.* 305 This rock was described..as a schistified serpentine.

schistoid (ˈʃɪstɔɪd), *a. Geol.* [f. SCHIST[1] + -OID.] Having the nature of, or resembling, schist.

1852 TH. ROSS tr. *Humboldt's Trav.* II. xxiv. 398 We saw in the mountains of Upper Orinoco,..granites passing into gneiss, and schistoid hornblendes. **1858** MAYNE *Expos. Lex.*

schistoscope (ˈskɪstəʊskəʊp). *Chromatics.* [f. Gr. σχιστό-ς divided, divisible (see SCHIST[1]) + -SCOPE.] An optical instrument producing complementary colours side by side.

1874 *S. Kens. Mus. Catal. Sci. Apparatus* No. 3678 (1877) 935 Rose's Schistoscope, for the physiology of colour. **1879** ROOD *Mod. Chromatics* xi. 161 Perhaps the..best [instrument] is that which was contrived by Brücke..and called by him a schistoscope... This..is merely a combination of a low-power simple microscope with a polariscope.

schistose (ˈʃɪstəʊs), *a.* Also 8–9 **shistose.** [f. SCHIST[1] + -OSE[1].]

1. *Geol.* Laminated; having a formation resembling a schist.

1794 KIRWAN *Elem. Min.* (ed. 2) I. 182 Shistose Clay... 1st variety, Slate Clay, Shale. **1821** *Tales My Landlord, Fair Witch Glas Llyn* II. 353 A conical hill, called Cerrig Tym, composed of a schistose rock. **1838** W. F. AINSWORTH *Res. Assyria*, etc. 337 With a foliated or shistose fracture in one direction. **1879** *Cassell's Techn. Educ.* IV. 255/2 The ores are rich, and are found in pockets in a schistose rock.

†**2.** Cleaving after the manner of a schist. *Obs.*

1831 MACCULLOCH *Syst. Geol.* I. 158 A soft claystone, with a schistose tendency on exposure.

†**3.** Abounding in, characterized by schist. *Obs.*

1843 PORTLOCK *Geol.* 175 Quartz veins are abundant in many parts of the schistose country.

4. *Bot.* 'Slaty, as to tint' (B. D. Jackson, 1900).

schiˈstosity. *Geol.* [f. SCHISTOSE + -ITY.] The direction or line of cleavage in a rock of crystalline formation.

1885 *Nature* 8 Oct. 558/2 The Arnaboll (Hebridean gneiss) can be traced..from spots where it retains its original strike and petrological characters, to others where it acquires the normal strike and mineralogical features of the ordinary Sutherland schists. The old planes of schistosity become obliterated, and new ones are developed. **1888** TEALL *Brit. Petrogr.* 446 *Schistosity*,..denotes the fissility of the crystalline schists. **1901** J. HORNE in *Nature* 19 Sept. 513/2 Before the planes of schistosity were developed in these Dalradian schists. **1908** *Mineral. Mag.* XV. 145 To the imperfect substitution of dissolved kaolin by mica and secondary quartz and resultant gravitation under the pressure of superincumbent masses may, in like manner, be attributed schistosity in Zinnwald greisen. **1919** *Amer. Jrnl. Sci.* XLVII. 203 Geinitz called attention to the delicate ruffling of the surface of schistosity of many slates, which may represent an analogous phenomenon of friction. **1951** *Jrnl. Geol.* LIX. 68 The ice..forms along joints, planes of schistosity, or any other available fractures. **1977** A. HALLAM *Planet Earth* 175/3 Deformation and the development of schistosity may result in the complete obliteration of primary planar features such as sedimentary bedding.

schistosome (ˈskɪstəʊsəʊm). *Zool.* [ad. mod.L. *Schistosoma* (D. F. Weinland *Tapeworms in Man* (1858) 87), f. Gr. σχιστό-ς divided + σῶμα body; cf. -SOME[4].] Any member of the trematode genus *Schistosoma* (formerly *Bilharzia*), of which the cercariæ are parasitic on fresh-water snails and the adults of certain species are parasitic in man, inhabiting the blood vessels; a blood fluke.

1905 *Brit. Med. Jrnl.* 7 Jan. 11 (*caption*) Two male schistosomes. *Ibid.* 12/1 A distinctive feature of this schistosome is the absence of ciliated warts on the integument. *Ibid.* 12/2 The habitat of the new schistosome is mainly arterial. **1931** BLACKLOCK & SOUTHWELL *Guide to Human Parasitol.* xvii. 144 Unlike all other digenetic trematodes, no rediae are produced at any time of the life history of the schistosomes, the asexual multiplication taking place in the sporocyst stage. **1955** *Nature* 19 Nov. 981/2 An important snail host in one country may be refractory or only slightly susceptible to the same species of schistosome from another region. **1968** *Sci. Jrnl.* Oct. 7/1 An infected human excretes anything from a few to a million schistosome eggs a day. **1970** G. R. TAYLOR *Doomsday Bk.* 92 The high schistosome infection rate in Lower Egypt.

Hence **schisto'somal** *a.*; also **schisto'somicide** *Pharm.* [-CIDE], a substance which kills schistosomes; **,schistosomi'cidal** *a.*

1931 BLACKLOCK & SOUTHWELL *Guide to Human Parasitol.* iii. 13 Protozoal, e.g. amoebic, and helminthic, e.g. schistosomal, dysenteries, are not the only forms which may occur in the tropics. **1954** *Trans. R. Soc. Tropical Med. & Hygiene* XLVIII. 446 (*heading*) A new series of schistosomicides. *Ibid.*, No other known schistosomicide shows a corresponding degree of activity. *Ibid.*, During the last seven years a search for drugs with schistosomicidal activity has been carried out in these laboratories. **1965** *Ann. Trop. Med. & Parasitol.* LIX. 304 (*heading*) Bacteriological and immunological findings in the presence of schistosomal infection. **1978** *Nature* 22 June 628/1 Despite the efforts ever since in the search for more effective schistosomicides, few drugs can be considered as antischistosomal agents of proven value. *Ibid.* 628/2 Although further studies are needed, oxamniquine seems to be an effective schistosomicidal oral drug suitable for use in endemic areas.

schistosomiasis (ˌskɪstəʊsəʊ'maɪəsɪs). *Path.* [f. mod.L. *Schistosoma* (see prec.) + -IASIS.] Disease caused by infection with parasites of the genus *Schistosoma*, characterized by chronic symptoms esp. of the digestive and urinary systems, and sometimes by fever.

1906 *Philippine Jrnl. Sci.* I. 89 A second Chinese case of schistosomiasis has been recorded. **1963** O. BRELAND *Animal Life & Lore* ii. 110 The parasite causing snail fever (or schistosomiasis) must pass through stages in freshwater snails before it can attack man. **1977** J. DIDION *Bk. Common Prayer* I. iv. 25 Isabel's children suffered gastrointestinal bleeding from..schistosomiasis. **1979** *Jrnl. R. Soc. Arts* Dec. 51/2 Zinc losses from the body are abnormally high due to a high incidence of hookworm infestation and schistosomiasis causing bleeding and excessive losses of sweat.

Hence **schisto'somial** *a.*, pertaining to or characteristic of schistosomiasis.

1934 R. GIRGES *Schistosomiasis* v. ii. 194 It [*sc.* bladder irritability] may be mistaken for enlargement of that gland and remain undiagnosed as schistosomial for a considerable period.

schistosomulum (skɪstəʊ'sɒmjʊləm). *Zool.* Pl. **-somula**. Also anglicized as **-somule**. [mod.L., f. as prec. + L. *-ulum*, neut. of *-ulus*, diminutive ending.] A parasite of the genus *Schistosoma* which has entered its adult host but is not yet mature. Cf. prec.

Also erroneously used as *schistosomula* sing., *schistosomulæ* pl.

1924 FAUST & MELENEY *Studies on Schistosomiasis* I. 4 To test his hypothesis he attempted to recover schistosomula from the peripheral vein. **1934** R. GIRGES *Schistosomiasis* II. ii. 56 Entering the lymphatics or blood-vessels, schistosomula proceed..to the liver of the host. **1961** *Exper. Parasitol.* XI. 209/2 The gland cells appeared to collapse after exhaustion of their contents and no replacement of secretion was encountered even in schistosomules which had been in skin for as long as 11 days. **1961** *Jrnl. Parasitol.* XLVII. 891/2 This interval..allowed the schistosomulae to reach the hepatic portal system. **1975** *Nature* 6 Mar. 17/3 The stage in the life cycle most susceptible to the immune response is the schistosomula, the young form that penetrates the skin and migrates to the blood vessels in which the adult develops. **1975** *Jrnl. R. Soc. Arts* May 363/2 The cercaria..then penetrate the skin, lose their tails and change to yet another stage called a schistosomule, which is much like an adult worm but smaller. **1978** *Parasitology* LXXVII. 282 The number and location of schistosomulum deaths will have a considerable influence on the pattern of migration out of the skin.

Hence **schisto'somular** *a.*

1975 *Nature* 28 Aug. 727/1 Sera from five patients infected with *S*[*chistosoma*] *mansoni* were used as sources of anti-schistosomular antibody in different experiments.

schistous ('ʃɪstəs), *a.* [f. SCHIST[1] + -OUS.]

1. *Geol.* = SCHISTOSE *a.* 1.

1802-3 tr. *Pallas's Trav.* (1812) II. 115 It is scarcely ever observed in thin layers between schistous minerals. **1833** L. RITCHIE *Wand. by Loire* 122 An immense schistous rock. **1875** *Wonders of Phys. World* I. i. 29 The schistous slate separates readily into leaves.

2. Formed of schist.

1829 PEACOCK *Misfort. Elphin* xi. 139 Prince Rhun being safe in schistous bastile, Taliesin commenced his journey. **1835** BROWNING *Paracelsus* I. 812 In the steady, rolling Mayne..is mixed its mass of schistous ore. **1840** ARNOLD *Jrnl.* in Stanley *Life* (1858) II. 351 Bare schistous hills.

3. *Nat. Hist.* = SCHISTOSE *a.* 4.

1858 MAYNE *Expos. Lex.*, *Schistosus*..sometimes applied the same as *Ardisiaceus*, to indicate a shade of blue, as the *Coluber schistosus*: schistous.

‖**'schistus.** *Obs.* Also 9 **shistus**, 7 in Gr. form **schistos**. [mod.L.; see SCHIST[1].] = SCHIST[1].

[**1601** HOLLAND *Pliny* XXXV. xv. II. 558 Of alume..there is one kind which the Greeks call Schistos, and the nature thereof is to cleave along into certaine filaments or threads like haires. **1623** COCKERAM III, *Schistos*, a stone of Saffron colour, easie to be cleft into thin plates.] **1775** MASSON in *Phil. Trans.* LXVI. 306 A kind of rotten schistus or slate. **1799** *Monthly Rev.* XXX. 12 Micaceous shistus, granite, gneiss, chlorite-shistus, sand-stone, and lime-stone. **1831** BREWSTER *Optics* xiv. 115 Take a plate of regularly formed mother-of-pearl, with its surfaces nearly parallel, and grind these surfaces upon a hone or upon a plate of glass with the powder of schistus.

schiz (skɪts), *sb.* and *a. slang* (chiefly *N. Amer.*). Also **schitz**. [Abbrev. of SCHIZOID *a.* and *sb.* or SCHIZOPHRENIC *a.* and *sb.*]

A. *sb.* A schizophrenic person; *spec.* one who experiences a drug-induced hallucination.

1955 [see NEEDLE *sb.* 3 b]. **1967** A. LURIE *Imaginary Friends* xii. 174 How can you tell what a schiz like her is going to do? **1973** T. PYNCHON *Gravity's Rainbow* 131 There's a long-time schiz..who believes that *he* is World War II.

B. *adj.* Schizophrenic.

1960 A. HUXLEY *Let.* 28 July (1969) 894, I imagine you cd find out a great deal—given your special knowledge of schiz symptoms. **1964** C. HODDER-WILLIAMS *Main Experiment* II. xvi. 207 Typically schitz, you know. They never can resist symbolic compulsions. **1969** —— *98·4* xii. 155, I took their damn drugs and..I nearly went schitz.

Hence **'schitzy**, **'schiz(z)y** *a.*, schizophrenic; *spec.* exhibiting or suffering from the effects of hallucinogenic drugs.

1968 'R. MACDONALD' *Instant Enemy* xxv. 157 What's the matter with her? Schitzy? **1972** D. ANTHONY *Blood on Harvest Moon* xxvii. 237, I feel schitzy. The grieving widow's mask—well, sometimes it's no mask. **1975** *New Yorker* 20 Jan. 31 This friend of mine—a bit of a schizzy dude, to be sure—has been telling me that if we go on muddying up the ecosphere, [etc.]. **1975** SHEA & WILSON *Golden Apple* 142 The awkwardness of their first efforts would be published in all the psychiatric journals as proof of the regressive and schizzy nature of their unsocial and unnatural impulse toward walking. **1977** *Time* 3 Jan. 56/2 So does Director Pierson, as he captures the schizzy, druggy, enclosed, exploding tension of rock superstardom. **1979** D. ANTHONY *Long Hard Cure* xvi. 130 If you stay here long enough, you can get too dependent on the Retreat... You become a little schitzy yourself.

schizanthus (skɪt'sænθəs). [mod.L. (H. Ruiz & J. Pavon *Floræ Peruvianæ et Chilensis Prodromus* (1794) 6), f. SCHIZO- + Gr. ἄνθος flower.] = *poor man's orchid* s.v. POOR MAN 5 a.

1823 *Curtis's Bot. Mag.* I. 2404 (*heading*) Wing-leaved Schizanthus. **1908** *Garden* 30 May 263/3 Much has been done in the way of improving the Schizanthus. **1931** *Daily Tel.* 21 May 17/1 The pansy-flowered schizanthus. **1959** [see *poor man's orchid* s.v. POOR MAN 5 a]. **1963** *Times* 1 May 14/4 The County Borough of East Ham occupies the middle of the hall with a group of schizanthus varieties and sweetly scented stocks. **1979** *Daily Tel.* 19 May 15/5 It is schizanthus, a thick bushy plant with leaves like parsley and a riotous show of flowers, pink, crimson, white and purple.

†**schize**, *v. Obs. rare*[−1]. [ad. Gr. σχίζειν, after the derivative SCHISM *sb.*] *intr.* To separate from, to commit schism. Cf. SCHISM *v.*

1596 H. CLAPHAM *Briefe Bible* I. 80 As they had schized from the true Church, so now likewise from the true worship to a false.

schizo ('skɪtsəʊ), *sb.* and *a.* Slang abbrev. of SCHIZOPHRENIC *a.* and *sb.* **A.** *sb.*

1945 N. BALCHIN *Mine Own Executioner* vi. 92 He just sank back into that queer not-really-there mood that schizos have. **1955** 'E. C. R. LORAC' *Ask Policeman* vii. 87 Let's assume a split personality..a schizo, as they say nowadays. **1961** J. I. M. STEWART *Man who won Pools* III. 203 He might have been a schizo..for all the tie-up there seemed to be between the Phil of this rational conversation and the Phil who wanted Jean Canaway. **1972** 'L. EGAN' *Paper Chase* xii. 194 He had a long history of violence and was diagnosed as a schizo.

B. *adj.*

1957 M. GAIR *Sapphires on Wednesday* x. 120, I think he must have a split mind—be schizo or something. **1958** A. HUXLEY *Let.* 16 Dec. (1969) 858 I'm glad to hear that your schizo research goes forward satisfactorily. **1960** *Harper's Bazaar* Aug. 50/2 He had gone stereo in April... Cheaper than going schizo. **1977** J. AIKEN *Last Movement* v. 89 Gertrude was a kind of belle Otèro-cum-Phaedra..and Hamlet perfectly epicene and schizo.

schizo- ('skaɪzəʊ, skaɪ'zɒ, 'skɪtsəʊ, skɪt'sɒ, -ɪdz-).

1. irreg. representing Gr. σχίζειν to split, combining with other words of Greek origin in various scientific terms. **'schizocarp** (-kɑːp) *Bot.* [Gr. καρπός fruit], a term applied to dry fruits which break up into two or more one-seeded mericarps without dehiscing. Hence **schizo'carpic, schizo'carpous** *adjs.*, 'resembling or belonging to a schizocarp' (*Cent. Dict.* 1891). **schizo'chroal** *a. Palæont.* [Gr. χρώς skin], applied to certain trilobite eyes in which the cornea is divided to form several discrete lenses. **'schizocœle** (-siːl) *Zool.* [Gr. κοῖλον a hollow], a perivisceral cavity formed by a splitting of the mesoblast. Hence **schizocœlic, schizo'cœlous** *adjs.* **'schizocœly** (-siːlɪ) *Zool.*, schizocœlic mode of formation (of a cœlom). **schizo'dinic** *a. Zool.* [Gr. ὠδῖνες birth-pains + -IC], belonging to a group of Mollusca, in which a temporary rupture of the body-wall takes place for the extrusion of the genital products. ‖**'Schizodon** *Zool.* [mod.L.; Gr. ὀδοντ- tooth], a genus of rodents, distinguished by having a molar with single internal and external folds, which meet in the middle of the tooth. ‖**schizo'genesis** *Biol.* [mod.L. (Haeckel, 1866); Gr. γένεσις reproduction], fissiparous generation. **schizoge'netic** *a. Bot.* [-GENETIC] = *schizogenic*; hence **schizoge'netically** *adv.* **schizogenic** (-'dʒɛnɪk) *a. Bot.* [-GEN 2 + -IC], formed by cleavage; applied to cavities formed by the splitting of the common wall of contiguous cells. **schizogenous** (-'ɒdʒɪnəs) *a. Bot.* [-GEN 2 + -OUS] = *schizogenic*. **schizognathism** (-'ɒgnəθɪz(ə)m) *Ornith.* [Gr. γνάθ-ος jaw + -ISM], a condition in which the bony palate is cleft from the posterior nares to the end of the beak. Hence **schi'zognathous** *a.*, having a cleft palate. **schizogony** (-'ɒgənɪ) *Zool.* [ad. mod.L. *schizogonia* (Haeckel); Gr. -γονία, reproduction] = *schizogenesis*. Hence **schizo'gonic** *a.*, pertaining to schizogony; spec. ***schizogonic cycle***, the second of the two stages in the life-history of a Coccidian. ‖**schizomycetes** (-maɪ'siːtiːz) *sb. pl. Biol.* [see MYCETES], a group of microscopic, rod-like, unicellular organisms, multiplying by fission, variously known as *bacteria*, *microbes*, etc.; *rarely* in sing. **schizomycete**. Hence **schizomy'cetic, -my'cetous** *adjs.* **'schizophyte** (-faɪt) *Biol.* [-PHYTE], a microscopic organism multiplying by fission, akin to *Schizomycetes*. **'schizopod** (-pɒd) *Zool.*, a member of the ‖**schi'zopoda** *sb. pl.* [Gr. ποδ- foot], a sub-order of crustaceans, named from the apparent splitting of the thoracic limbs produced by the great development of the exopodites; hence **schi'zopodous** *a.* **schizo'rhinal** *a. Ornith.* [Gr. ῥίν-, ῥίς nose], having each nasal bone deeply cleft or forked. **schizo'thecal** *a. Ornith.* [Gr. θήκη a case], having the podotheca divided by scutellation or reticulation.

1870 *Henfrey's Bot.* §247 In such a case the term **schizocarp* is employed to designate the whole fruit. **1905** BALFOUR tr. *Goebel's Organogr. Plants* II. 160 Andreaea..is an exception, and its sporogonia are *schizocarpous, for no lid is produced. **1889** J. M. CLARKE in *Jrnl. Morphol.* II. 254 The character of the visual area in the trilobites is twofold; (*a*) it may be covered by a smooth, continuous epithelial film or cornea, through which the lenses of the ommatidia are visible by translucence, and (*b*) the cornea may be transected by the protrusion of the sclera and limited to the surfaces of the ommatidia... The first group may be designated by the term Holochroal; the second group by the term *Schizochroal. *Ibid.* 266 The schizochroal eyes of the Trilobites are aggregated and not properly compound eyes. **1976** *Nature* 13 May 130/1 Trilobites of the suborder Phacopina had schizochroal eyes, in which comparatively few large separate lenses are distributed over the eye surface. **1877** HUXLEY *Anat. Inv. Anim.* i. 51 That form of perivisceral cavity which I have termed a *schizocœle. **1888** ROLLESTON & JACKSON *Anim. Life* Introd. 30 The well-known term schizocoele may be retained for them [the coelomic cavities of *Vertebrata*]. **1900** *Lankester's Treat. Zool.* III. 26 Formerly the system was supposed to develop as a cleft in the mesenchyme, and therefore was called the '*schizocoelic system'. **1875** HUXLEY in *Encycl. Brit.* II. 53/1 In the Lamellibranchiata and Odontophora, there is every reason to believe that the perivisceral cavity is formed by splitting of the mesoblast, or that they are *schizocœlous. **1962** D. NICHOLS *Echinoderms* i. 14 A coelom..can arise as a split in the mesoderm (*schizocoely) or as an outgrowth of the gut cavity or enteron (enterocoely). **1978** *Nature* 4 May 23/2 In this context, the mode of formation of the coelom (enterocoely, schizocoely, gonocoely) is of secondary importance. **1883** E. R. LANKESTER in *Encycl. Brit.* XVI. 682/1 Cœlomate animals are, according to this nomenclature, either *Schizodinic or Porodinic. **1848** WATERHOUSE *Nat. Hist. Mammalia* II. 265 *Schizodon fuscus*. The Brown *Schizodon. **1891** *Century Dict.*, **Schizogenesis*.., fission as a mode of reproduction; generation by fission. **1884** BOWER & SCOTT *De Bary's Phaner.* 213 To the first, *schizogenetic, category belong the larger air-spaces in stem, roots, and leaves of many marsh and water-plants. *Ibid.* 209 The reservoirs arise *schizogenetically. **1885** GOODALE *Physiol. Bot.* 99 *note*, The first mode of development of intercellular spaces has been termed *schizogenic. **1883** *Athenæum* 29 Dec. 870/3 [Mr. J. R. Green concludes] that, at least in some species [of Hypericaceæ], there is also a series of *schizogenous ducts. **1884** COUES *Key N. Amer. Birds* (ed. 2) 170 *Schizognathism is the kind of 'cleft palate' shown by the columbine and gallinaceous birds. **1872** COUES *Key N. Amer. Birds* 229 The palate is *schizognathous. **1902** *Encycl. Brit.* XXXII. 816/1 The *schizogonic cycle..occurs in human blood, giving rise to malarial fever. **1887** HUBRECHT in *Q. Jrnl. Microsc. Sci.* Mar. 613 *Schizogony having once been established, it must have been further beneficial to the species. **1880** A. FLINT *Princ. Med.* 96 The living organisms to which the advocates of the germ theory attribute the causation of the infectious diseases, are embraced under the name **schizomycetes*. **1898** SALTER tr. *Lafar's Techn. Mycol.* I. title, *Schizomycetic Fermentation. **1902** *Cassell's Encycl. Dict.* Suppl., *Schizomycetous. **1880** *Libr. Univ. Knowl.* (N.Y.) XII. 229 **Schizophyte*, a microscopic organism belonging to Cohn's order schizoporeae, and allied to bacteria..regarded as a variety of bacillus. **1887** GARNSEY & BALFOUR tr. *De Bary's Bacteria* 37 This group has received the name of Fission-plants or Schizophytes. **1840** *Cuvier's Anim. Kingd.* 422 *note*, The *Schizopoda..have been found to be more nearly allied to the order Stomapoda. **1842** BRANDE *Dict. Sci.* etc., *Schizopods. **1877** HUXLEY *Anat. Inv. Anim.* vi. 348 This may be termed the Schizopod stage. **1858** MAYNE *Expos. Lex.*, *Schizopodus*, applied..to a tribe of the *Crustaceæ*..the feet of which are deeply divided into slender branches: *schizopodous. **1877** HUXLEY *Anat. Inv. Anim.* vi. 367 The Schizopodous *Podophthalmia*. **1884** COUES *Key N. Amer. Birds* (ed. 2) 165 In the Columbidæ,..the nasal bones are *schizorhinal. **1896** NEWTON *Dict. Birds* Introd. 91 Herein he [Garrod] strove to prove that Birds ought to be divided into two Subclasses—one, called Holorhinal,..and the other, called Schizorhinal. **1884** Coues *Key N. Amer. Birds* (ed. 2) 125 Such a podotheca is holothecal... The generic opposite is *schizothecal.

2. *Psychol.* With pronunc. (skɪtsəʊ, skɪdzəʊ). Used to repr. SCHIZOPHRENIA, as in **schizo'taxia** [Gr. τάξις order, arrangement], a genetically determined defect in the functioning of the nervous system which has been suggested as predisposing to schizophrenia; hence **schizo-'taxic** *a.* and *sb.*; **'schizothyme** *sb.* and *a.* [Gr. θυμός mind, temper], (characteristic of) a person who is introverted and imaginative, and so regarded as tending to schizophrenia rather than to manic-depressive illness; hence **schizo'thymic** *a.*; also **schizo'thymia**, schizothymic constitution or temperament; **'schizotype**, a personality type in which schizophrenia is potentially or actually present; hence **schizo'typal**, **-'typic** *adjs.*; **'schizotypy**.

1962 P. Meehl in *Amer. Psychologist* XVII. 830/1 This neural integrative defect, which I shall christen schizotaxia, is all that can properly be spoken of as inherited. *Ibid.*, The imposition of a social learning history upon schizotaxic individuals. *Ibid.* 831/1 All schizotaxics become, on all.. existing social learning regimes, schizotypic in personality organization. **1966** I. B. Weiner *Psychodiagnosis in Schizophrenia* i. 7 Persons with schizotaxia acquire a personality organization called schizotypy that is characterized by four core behavior traits... These schizotypic traits are universally learned by all schizotaxic persons... Whereas most schizotypes remain compensated, those who are confronted with certain causal environmental influences..are likely to decompensate into clinical schizophrenia. **1974** S. Arieti *Interpretation of Schizophrenia* (ed. 2) xlv. 697 A minority of schizotaxics.. are 'potentiated into clinical schizophrenia'. *Ibid.*, Schizotaxia is a necessary but not sufficient condition in the etiology of schizophrenia. **1925**, **1932** Schizothyme [see *cyclothyme* adj. and sb. s.v. CYCLO-]. **1936** A. Huxley *Eyeless in Gaza* viii. 87 'What a lot of ribs you've got!' she said at last. 'Schizothyme physique,' he answered. **1952** H. Read *Philos. Mod. Art* iv. 84 If in the end we describe.. Michelangelo as a typical 'schizothyme', the common reader is not much the wiser. **1964** I. M. Smith *Spatial Ability* vii. 229 He found the creative significantly more schizothyme, self-sufficient, withdrawn, sophisticated, desurgent and radical. **1972** *Encycl. Psychol.* III. 180/1 The schizothyme is characterized by..'a conscious contrast between the ego and the outside world', 'a touchy or indifferent withdrawal from the mass of his fellow men', the predominance of 'dreams, ideas or principles'. **1940** H. G. Wells *Babes in Darkling Wood* iv. ii. 335 Schizothymia, the psychoanalysts would have called this sort of dreaming. **1964** I. M. Smith *Spatial Ability* ix. 287 The hyperactivity.., nervousness and anxiety seem..more closely related to introversion or schizothymia than to extraversion. **1925** W. J. H. Sprott tr. *Kretschmer's Physique & Char.* xiii. 223 The group of wits.. ironists and satirists whose nature is indicated by the names, Heine, Voltaire,..Nietzsche. This group belongs quite decidedly to the schizothymic side. **1951** *Mind* LX. 287 The ethical question is not whether one should be cyclothymic like Goering or schizothymic like Himmler in one's destructiveness; rather it is whether one should be destructive at all, and, if so, towards what. **1961** *Lancet* 23 Sept. 712/1 Hereditary factors were more important for excitability, the cyclothymic-schizothymic scale, and super-ego strength. **1953** S. Rado in *Amer. Jrnl. Psychiatry* CX. 409/2 In this sense the patient suffering from an open schizophrenic psychosis is a schizophrenic phenotype, engendered by a schizophrenic genotype in its interaction with the environment... For psychodynamic purposes I shall abbreviate the term schizophrenic phenotype to schizotype. *Ibid.* 410/1 The ensemble of psychodynamic traits peculiar to the schizotypes may be called schizotypal organization. **1962**, **1966** Schizotypic, -typy [see *schizotaxia* above]. **1962** *Amer. Psychologist* XVII. 830/2 The most important research need here is development of high-validity indicators for compensated schizotypy. **1965** G. E. Daniels et al. *New Perspectives in Psychoanal.* 109 Variants of the schizophrenic disorders like—schizoid personality, schizotypal,..and pseudo-neurotic schizophrenia. **1974** S. Arieti *Interpretation of Schizophrenia* (ed. 2) xlv. 697 All schizotaxics become schizotypic in personality organization, but most of them do not decompensate and never develop a psychosis. **1978** P. O'Brien *Disordered Mind* iv. 75 Such syndromes are now officially classified as Schizotypal

schizo-a'ffective, *a.* (*sb.*) *Psychol.* Also without hyphen. [f. SCHIZO- + AFFECTIVE *a.*] Exhibiting symptoms of both schizophrenia and manic-depressive psychosis. Also as *sb.*, a schizo-affective person.

1933 I. L. Polozker in *Amer. Jrnl. Psychiatry* XC. 123 We have been in the habit of labeling these cases as psychopathic personalities with schizoid make-up... I think the name of schizoaffective is more appropriate. **1933** J. Kasanin in *Ibid.* 126 My cases are not necessarily schizo-affective psychoses but schizoaffective personalities. **1965** J. Pollitt *Depression & its Treatment* iii. 38 Another criterion of schizo-affective disorder is the appearance of typical features of schizophrenia in circumscribed episodes. **1974** *Nature* 18 Jan. 160/2 All of the schizo-affectives had a history of at least five episodes of mania, hypomania or depression. **1976** Smythies & Corbett *Psychiatry* x. 185 Cases of schizoaffective psychosis where there is much admixture of depressive symptoms may require a tricyclic anti-depressant in addition. **1979** *Daily Tel.* 19 May 3/6 Dowdeswell had had a schizo-affective psychosis which had been cured but could recur.

schizoid ('skɪtsɔɪd, skɪdz-), *a.* and *sb. Psychol.* [a. G. *schizoid* (E. Kretschmer *Körperbau und Charakter* (1921) ix. 96): see SCHIZO- 2 and -OID.] **A.** *adj.* Resembling or tending towards schizophrenia, but with milder or less developed symptoms, e.g. an absence of delusions.

1925 W. J. H. Sprott tr. *Kretschmer's Physique & Char.* xii. 208 One may for convenience call the transitional stages between illness and health, and the pathological abortive forms, 'schizoid' and 'cycloid'. **1931** *Times Lit. Suppl.* 17 Sept. 692/4 Professor Kretschmer manages to convey the impression that all philosophers and tragedians are schizophrenic, or at least 'schizoid'. **1938** *Oxford Times* 8 Apr. 23/5 He said Phillips was of what would be called 'schizoid type' but he could not agree that in the case of a split mind the subject could not distinguish between right and wrong. **1949** Koestler *Insight & Outlook* xxiv. 343 The frequent occurrence of infantile and schizoid features in the psychic make-up of poets. **1957** A. Huxley *Let.* 18 Nov. (1969) 830 Dr. Abram Hoffer..has treated several hundred patients under his care with 3 to 4 grammes of niacin—with striking success in many cases of schizoid neurosis. **1960** R. D. Laing *Divided Self* ix. 149 It is..not always possible to make sharp distinctions between sanity and insanity, between the sane schizoid individual and the psychotic. **1964** M. Argyle *Psychol. & Social Probl.* iii. 35 Withdrawn, schizoid people..produce a tense, uneasy atmosphere. **1976** Smythies & Corbett *Psychiatry* vi. 95 The 'schizoid' individual has usually been a lone wolf since childhood. **1977** A. Sheridan tr. *Lacan's Écrits* i. 5 The schizoid and spasmodic symptoms of hysteria.

b. *transf.* and *fig.*, freq. = SCHIZOPHRENIC *a.* b.

1955 G. S. Fraser in J. Wain *Interpretations* 233 It is a kind of poem which could only have been written in the age that invented the phrase 'dissociation of sensibility' and that thought of the schizoid state as the typical occupational risk of intellectuals. **1959** *Times* 20 Feb. 14/5 It was a schizoid programme... On the one hand Daniel Jones's new fifth symphony..; on the other, a bizarre coupling of two..sets of variations on Paganini's celebrated A minor caprice. **1959** N. Mailer *Advts. for Myself* (1961) 173 'It's all schizoid,' Sam said. 'Modern life is schizoid.' **1960** *Spectator* 6 May 652 (*heading*) The schizoid state [*sc.* South Africa]. **1964** J. Jackson et al. *Rayden's Practice & Law of Divorce* (ed. 9) iii. 155 Such schizoid situations reflect little credit on the law. **1974** 'R. Tate' *Birds of Bloodied Feather* ix. 176 He was schizoid..partly clever, partly stupid... I think he wanted to be found out. **1977** *Ripped & Torn* vi. 10/1 The best track .. is 'Energy', a piece of schizoid trash. **1977** *Proc. R. Soc. Med.* LXX. 398/1 The principle..serves to emphasize that, if the tumour is to be cured, the surgeon must approach the problem in an almost schizoid frame of mind.

B. *sb.* A schizoid person; also *loosely*.

1925 W. J. H. Sprott tr. *Kretschmer's Physique & Char.* x. 149 We sometimes find schizoids, who look just as if they had already been through a schizophrenic psychosis before they were born. **1938** S. Beckett *Murphy* ix. 168 An emaciated schizoid..his left hand rhetorically extended.., his right, quivering and rigid, pointing upward. *a* **1941** F. Scott Fitzgerald *Tender is Night* (rev. ed., 1953) i. ix. 48 She's a schizoid—a permanent eccentric. *a* **1957** J. Cary *Captive & Free* (1959) xii. 57 Preedy has been taken to pieces by experts. They say, 'The typical schizoid—a little Hitler. You find him everywhere—the village boy who goes from Mass to do murder is the basic type.' **1970** *Science* 16 Jan. 251/1 Though unsatisfactory, the only means of identifying many—perhaps most—schizoids remains genealogical, and a clinical understanding of the schizoid can best be gained by reading descriptions of abnormal relatives of schizophrenics. **1975** D. Lodge *Changing Places* i. 6 Flown by pilots long gone over the hill, alcoholics and schizoids.

Hence **schi'zoidal** *a.*

1938 S. Beckett *Murphy* iv. 49 'That long hank of Apollonian asthenia,' groaned Neary, 'that schizoidal spasmophile.' **1973** F. Johnson *Alienation* ii. 63 The discovery of latent schizoidal themes can be found routinely in individuals whose functioning would in no way suggest.. the existence of such 'splitting'.

schizoidia (skɪt'sɔɪdɪə, skɪdz-). *Psychol.* [ad. G. *schizoidie* (E. Bleuler 1922, in *Zeitschr. f. die gesammte Neurol. u. Psychiatrie* LXXVIII. 373), f. *schizoid* SCHIZOID *a.* and *sb.*: see -IA[1].] The schizoid state, esp. when regarded as caused by the same genetic disorder as schizophrenia.

1940 in Hinsie & Shatzky *Psychiatric Dict.* 475/1. **1970** *Science* 16 Jan. 253/1 By including schizoid disease (schizoidia), this hypothesis extends that of Slater... The view that schizoidia and schizophrenia are a single disease genetically is supported by their clinical similarity. **1973** McClearn & DeFries *Introd. Behavioral Genetics* xi. 275 Twin data are utilized to support the hypothesis that schizoidia and schizophrenia are manifestations of the same underlying genetic disease. **1976** Ehrman & Parsons *Genetics of Behav.* xi. 276 Schizoidia may be defined as a pre- or potentially schizophrenic mental state.

schizont ('skaɪzɒnt). *Zool.* [a. G. *schizont* (F. Schaudinn 1900, in *Zool. Jahrb., Abt. f. Anat. u. Ontogenie* XIII. 213), f. Gr. σχίζ-ειν to split (cf. SCHIZO-) + ὀντ-, ὤν, pres. pple. of εἶναι to be, exist.] In Protozoa, a cell that divides asexually to form daughter cells; *esp.* in Sporozoa, a multinucleate cell that divides asexually to form merozoites.

1900 *Jrnl. R. Microsc. Soc.* June 336 In the author's [*sc.* Schaudinn's] nomenclature this process of asexual multiplication is known as schizogony, the mother cells are schizonts, and the daughter cells merozoites... They may grow rapidly.., and become converted into schizonts. **1912**, **1957** [see GAMONT]. **1974** *Nature* 22 Nov. 268/1 Three different sorts of vaccine are at present being investigated: irradiated sporozoites from the mosquito, extracts from schizonts (developing stages in the blood) and emulsified merozoites (the stages which pass between blood cells).

schizonticide (skaɪ-, skɪ'zɒntɪsaɪd). *Pharm.* Also schizonto-. [f. prec. + *-icide*, as in *parricide*, *tyrannicide*, etc., or + -O + -CIDE.] A substance that kills schizonts.

1943 *Jrnl. Infectious Dis.* LXXIII. 11/2 In textbooks.. quinine and atabrine are considered to be 'schizonticides', whereas plasmochin is called a 'gametocide'. **1944** W. N. Bispham *Malaria* x. 133 Quinine is not as satisfactory as atabrine as a schizonticide in the treatment of *P[lasmodium] falciparum*. **1963** E. Pampana *Textbk. Malaria Eradication* viii. 211 Drugs that act on the asexual forms, as schizontocides. **1970** W. Peters *Chemotherapy & Drug Resistance in Malaria* v. 139 The main outcome of this investigation was to pinpoint mepacrine as a safe and potent schizontocide, superior to quinine against all human malaria species. **1977** *Martindale's Extra Pharmacopoeia* (ed. 27) 343/2 The 8-aminoquinolines..have a marked effect on gametocytes..but are not effective blood schizonticides.

Hence **schizonti'cidal**, **-o'cidal** *adjs.*

1963 P. F. Russell et al. *Pract. Malariol.* (ed. 2) xix. 503 Recent trials with relatively non-toxic schizonticidal drugs ..have had some more promising results. **1963** *Terminol. Malaria* (World Health Organization) iv. 66 Schizontocides or blood schizontocides ('schizontocidal drugs'..) act on asexual erythrocytic stages of the parasite. **1979** *Amer. Jrnl. Trop. Med. & Hygiene* XXVIII. 937/1 By the early 1970's over 200,000 compounds had been screened for blood schizonticidal activity.

schizophrene ('skɪtsəʊfriːn, 'skɪdz-). *Psychol.* [ad. G. *schizophren*, f. *schizophrenie* SCHIZOPHRENIA.] A schizophrenic, or a person with a predisposition towards schizophrenia. Also *attrib.* and *loosely*.

1925 W. J. H. Sprott tr. *Kretschmer's Physique & Char.* x. 147 In the schizophrene group, still less than in the circular, can we separate the healthy from the diseased. **1936** *Scrutiny* V. 248 Comparing the psychology of the schizophrene with that of the modern artist. **1945** *Times* 26 Apr. 6/5 No one would claim Beethoven as an example of the highly integrated personality but he is no schizophrene, as Dr. Carner calls Mahler outright. **1968** *Listener* 29 Aug. 260/2, I have heard a saloon-bar customer, a postman by profession, address the barmaid as: 'You dreamy schizophrene.' **1977** 'D. Cory' *Bennett* ii. 76 Schizophrenes are often held to be people of exceptional charm.

schizophrenese (ˌskɪtsɒfrə'niːz, skɪdz-). *Psychol.* [f. next + -ESE.] Disordered speech as manifested by a schizophrenic.

1964 *Internat. Psychiatry Clinics* I. 829 The speech deficiencies are not consistent from one schizophrenic child to another. One is thus not justified in referring to 'schizophrenese'—that is, a specific and positive schizophrenic speech pattern. **1976** Smythies & Corbett *Psychiatry* v. 67 It is helpful to do an amytal or pentothal interview. The schizophrenic patient often loosens up and talks 'schizophrenese' (the typical speech disorder of schizophrenia).

schizophrenia (skɪtsəʊ'friːnɪə, skɪdz-). *Psychol.* [ad. G. *schizophrenie* (E. Bleuler 1910, in *Psychiatrisch-Neurol. Wochenschr.* XII. 171), f. Gr. φρήν mind: see SCHIZO- and -IA[1].] A mental disorder occurring in various forms, all characterized by a breakdown in the relation between thoughts, feelings, and actions, usu. with a withdrawal from social activity and the occurrence of delusions and hallucinations.

Used in the U.S. with a broader meaning than in Britain (cf. quots. 1979, 1980).

The pronunc. (skɪts-), i.e. with short (ɪ) and with (ts), is prob. influenced by the Ger. pronunc. (sçɪts-).

1912 *Lancet* 21 Dec. 1730/1 This little volume is a translation of a series of articles by Professor Bleuler which appeared..during 1910 and 1911, in which he advances a theory of the negativism so frequently met with in dementia praecox or schizophrenia. **1925** J. Riviere tr. *Freud's Unconscious* in *Collected Papers* IV. 129 In schizophrenia a great deal is consciously expressed which in the transference neuroses can be demonstrated to exist in the Ucs only by means of psycho-analysis. **1944** E. A. Strecker *Fund. Psychiatry* vi. 123 In spite of the fact that schizophrenia and manic-depressive are divergent and alien to each other in psychopathology, there are clinical situations in which the differential diagnosis is difficult. **1945** W. Sadler *Mod. Psychiatry* xxxix. 464 Among the trends of schizophrenia is the persistent tendency to shun reality. **1958** M. Argyle *Relig. Behaviour* ix. 107 By the psychoses we mean the clinical conditions of schizophrenia, mania and depression, paranoia, epilepsy, together with certain organic states. **1964** *Internat. Psychiatry Clinics* I. 743 While many of these cases can be grouped into the classic forms of schizophrenia, such as simple, catatonic, hebephrenic, or paranoid, others cannot be so classified and will, therefore, be diagnosed as mixed or undifferentiated types of schizophrenia. **1979** *Internat. Rehabilit. Med.* I. 79/1 It was found that hospital psychiatrists in New York included under 'schizophrenia' part of what British hospital psychiatrists diagnosed as mania, psychotic depression, and personality disorder. **1980** J. Ashton *Everyday Psychiatry* v. 33 His [*sc.* Bleuler's] use of the word in a wide sense has influenced the practice of Swiss and American psychiatry to the present day, so that 'American schizophrenia' ranges from apparently minor personality disorders with a range of emotional reactions, through to the major deterioration of personality that is recognized as schizophrenia by British psychiatrists.

b. *transf.* and *fig.*

1933 T. S. Eliot *Use of Poetry & Use of Criticism* v. 99 For a poet to be also a philosopher he would have to be virtually two men; I cannot think of any example of this thorough schizophrenia, nor can I see anything to be gained by it. **1945** 'G. Orwell' in *Polemic* I. 40 Some nationalists are not far from schizophrenia, living quite happily amid dreams of power and conquest which have no connection with the physical world. **1949** *Here & Now* (N.Z.) Oct. 32/2 There are few alien hills in Mr Witheford's poems and he is not preoccupied with cultural schizophrenia. **1958** *Listener* 9 Oct. 557/1 They admire big dams and high buildings..

and the *contrast* these afford to the familiar buildings... It may occur to you that the character of our environment is likely to be split in two by this schizophrenia. **1969** *Daily Tel.* 6 Oct. 9/5 Bristol's Little Theatre illustrates the same provincial schizophrenia, with the farce 'One for the Pot' next in the bill after Ibsen's 'Master Builder'.

schizophrenic (skɪtsəʊ'frɛnɪk, skɪdz-), *a.* and *sb.* [f. prec. + -IC.] **A.** *adj.* **a.** *Psychol.* Characteristic of or having schizophrenia.

1912 [see AUTISM]. **1927** HENDERSON & GILLESPIE *Text-bk. Psychiatry* ix. 218 It is now generally recognised that although a schizophrenic type of disturbance is always most serious, there are certain cases which can, and do, readjust themselves. **1931** [see SCHIZOID *a.* a]. **1945** *Times* 28 Sept. 7/5 He was schizophrenic long before the thing became fashionable, half of him being entirely rational, the other half living in a world in which it was taken for granted that pigs have wings. **1973** I. L. CHILD *Humanistic Psychol.* ix. 137 Laing and Esterson.. argue that schizophrenic behavior appears in these patients as a somewhat sensible response to an extremely difficult situation. **1974** PASSMORE & ROBSON *Compan. Med. Stud.* III. xxxv. 55/2 Other examples are the 'schizophrenic smile', which appears without obvious external cause and is presumed to be a response to an internal hallucinatory stimulus, and the 'schizophrenic handshake', the patient's hand when grasped remaining limp. **1981** *Brit. Med. Jrnl.* 24 Jan. 313/3 While drugs have certainly facilitated the extramural care of schizophrenic patients the minimisation of prolonged inpatient treatment has, to a large extent, been due to social measures and to changes in attitude within the psychiatric services.

b. *transf.* and *fig.*, freq. with the implication of mutually contradictory or inconsistent elements.

1955 *Sci. Amer.* Oct. 113/1 The behavior of the puzzled Board reflected its schizophrenic task. The members performed as part jury, part judge, and then as part administrative agency, engaged in a part rule-making, part quasi-judicial proceeding. **1960** *Times* 13 June 14/1 It was a schizophrenic day when nearly every player seemed to live two lives. **1962** A. LURIE *Love & Friendship* viii. 155 You're not living two different lives that don't match... For me it's absolutely impossible. It's schizophrenic. *a* **1974** R. CROSSMAN *Diaries* (1977) III. 71 We are all deeply schizophrenic on this Bill, hate the interference, hate the break with the trade unions, yet we can see that without it there must be a higher level of unemployment than we can tolerate. **1978** M. SHANKS *What's Wrong with Mod. World?* iii. 45 In their reaction to inflationary pressures government have been.. schizophrenic. On the one hand they have sought.. to fight them. On the other hand they have felt obliged to compensate the victims. **1980** *Daily Tel.* 24 July 11/5 The work is schizophrenic in its switches of style from geniune opera-drama to operetta and then to the typical vehicle for a soprano anxious and able to sing Ophelia's mad scene.

B. *sb.* A person with schizophrenia.

1926 W. McDOUGALL *Outl. Abnormal Psychol.* xxiii. 384 The delusions and hallucinations of the schizophrenic so commonly concern his body. **1953** W. BURROUGHS *Junkie* (1972) x. 111 One young schizophrenic had both hands fastened in front with a bandage so he could not bother the other patients. **1956** A. HUXLEY *Heaven & Hell* 84 Many schizophrenics pass most of their time.. in a shadowy world of phantoms and unrealities. **1958** M. ARGYLE *Relig. Behaviour* ix. 109 Schizophrenics.. are more chaotic and harbour a number of unrelated fantasies and identifications simultaneously. **1979** N. SCHEPER-HUGHES *Saints, Scholars & Schizophrenics* iii. 69/1 Interviews with Irish schizophrenics support the hypothesis that the later age of onset of the disease in rural Ireland is related to the postponed adulthood.. of the Irish bachelor.

Hence **schizo'phrenically** *adv.*, in a manner suggestive or characteristic of schizophrenia.

1963 *Times* 23 Apr. 16/1 Ionesco's hero—perpetually exhausted, always eating, schizophrenically incapable of action. **1975** *Gramophone* Nov. 790/1 Then there's what one might call a strange psychological world in which almost schizophrenically Sibelius uses brightness and lightness juxtaposed with the darkest and most ferocious gestures. **1979** *Times* 27 Dec. 11/5 Schizophrenically Janus-like, we offer at least two different faces towards a policeman.

schizophreniform (skɪtsəʊ'frɛnɪfɔːm, skɪdz-), *a. Psychol.* [f. as prec. + -FORM.] Resembling schizophrenia.

1937 G. LANGFELDT *Prognosis in Schizophrenia* i. 17 The author.. is of opinion that it will be advantageous to separate *atypical* conditions, and give them their own description, such as 'Schizofreni-form' (or 'Schizophrenic reaction types'). **1951** *Practitioner* Aug. 135 Schizophreniform conditions.—Usually acute, dramatic and often running a benign course, even without much active treatment. **1976** SMYTHIES & CORBETT *Psychiatry* iv. 37 Even normal people can experience a short-lived schizophreniform psychosis as the result of unbearable stress—as in battle exhaustion—or severe sleep deprivation. **1978** P. O'BRIEN *Disordered Mind* ii. 35 If the disorganized state of mind lasts.. less than 6 months, but more than one week, it is called a schizophreniform disorder.

schizophrenogenic (ˌskɪtsəʊfriːnəʊ'dʒɛnɪk, ˌskɪdz-), *a. Psychol.* [f. as prec. + -O + -GENIC.] Tending to give rise to schizophrenia.

1949 F. FROMM-REICHMANN in *Psychiatry* XI. 265/2 The schizophrenic is painfully distrustful and resentful of other people, due to the severe early warp and rejection he encountered in important people of his infancy and childhood.. mainly in a schizophrenogenic mother. **1956** *Behavioral Sci.* I. 263/1 Whenever the system is organized for hospital purposes and it is announced to the patient that the actions are for *his* benefit, then the schizophrenogenic situation is being perpetuated. **1975** HIRSCH & LEFF *Abnormalities in Parents of Schizophrenics* vi. 95 This study provides somewhat stronger evidence against the concept of the cold, aloof, hostile schizophrenogenic mother. **1979** B. INEICHEN *Mental Illness* 41 The question of whether schizophrenics are downwardly mobile socially, or whether lower-class culture is schizophrenogenic, remains an open one.

schizostylis (skɪzəʊ'staɪlɪs). Pl. **-stylis.** [mod.L. (Backhouse & Harvey 1864, in *Curtis's Bot. Mag.* XC. 5422), f. SCHIZO- + L. *stilus* (*stylus*) (see STYLE *sb.* 8), in allusion to the split styles of the plant.] A rhizomatous herb of the genus so called, belonging to the family Iridaceæ, native to South Africa, and bearing linear leaves and spathes of red or pink flowers. Cf. *Kaffir lily* s.v. KAFFIR 4.

1864 *Curtis's Bot. Mag.* XC. 5422 Crimson Schizostylis. .. This lovely Iridaceous plant.. inhabits eastern rivers of South Africa. **1961** *Amateur Gardening* 16 Sept. 7/4 Less romantic in association but flowering later and valuable for October and November colour, are the Caffre lilies, or schizostylis. **1979** *Daily Tel.* 27 Oct. 31/2 Earlier flowering herbaceous plants, which the schizostylis have outshone.. with the onset of autumn.

‖ **'schizzo.** *Obs.* Also **skizzo**; *pl.* **schizzos, scizzi, scizzis.** [It.: see SKETCH *sb.*] A sketch.

1686 AGLIONBY *Painting Illustr.* Explan. Terms s.v., The Schizzos are ordinarily reduced into Cartoons in Fresco Painting, or Copyed and Enlarged in Oyl-Painting. *Ibid.* iii. 117 He seldom Designed a Story in his first Schizzos, that he did not do it four or five several ways, to choose at last the best. *a* **1734** NORTH *Exam.* II. iv. §6 (1740) 234 The Crafts-masters of that Plot, from the very first *Scizzi* of the Design, considered [etc.]. **1736** LEDIARD *Life Marlborough* I. Ded. 5, I have aim'd at no more than a brief *Skizzo* of it in my Preface. **1793** SIR E. HARINGTON (*title*) A Schizzo on the Genius of Man.

schizzy, schizy: see SCHIZ *sb.* and *a.*

‖ **schlafrock** ('ʃlaːfrɔk). [G., f. *schlaf-en* to sleep + *rock* coat, gown.] A dressing-gown.

1836 LONGF. in *Life* (1891) I. 248 One nasty little professor in a dirty *schlafrock* took the pipe out of his mouth and kissed me on the lips. **1848** THACKERAY *Van. Fair* lxv, A student, in jack-boots and a dirty *schlafrock*, was lying on the bed smoking a long pipe.

‖ **schlag** (ʃlaːg, ʃlaːk). Abbrev. of SCHLAGOBERS or SCHLAGSAHNE.

1969 A. ARENT *Laying on of Hands* xii. 138 She debouched at Demel's for pastry and *Schlag.* **1977** *Time* 24 Oct. 44/3 A slavic sour cream lay over the proceedings in place of Viennese *schlag.*

schlag, var. SCHLOCK.

‖ **schlagobers** ('ʃlaːgoːbɛrs). [Ger. dial., f. *schlagen* to beat + *obers* cream.] Whipped cream; coffee with whipped cream. Also *fig.*

1938 J. FLANNER in *New Yorker* 10 Sept. 55/1 You can now get a seat and *Schlagobers* on Tomaselli's terrace. **1967** *Listener* 27 July 123/3 This *Schlagobers* made one thirsty for pop. **1969** *Harper's Bazaar* Oct. 12/1, I consumed huge quantities of their *Torte* heaped high with *Schlagobers.*

‖ **schlagsahne** ('ʃlaːgzaːnə). [Ger., f. *schlagen* to beat + *sahne* cream.] Whipped cream.

1907 M. A. VON ARNIM *Fräulein Schmidt & Mr. Anstruther* 9 We are poor... If we were not.. we should have different sorts of puddings.. with *Schlagsahne* on their tops. **1936** D. BARNES *Nightwood* i. 12 The inevitable arc produced by heavy rounds of burgundy, schlagsahne, and beer. **1972** J. EASTWOOD *Henry in Silver Frame* xviii. 155 The delicious fraulein.. become[s] a devotee of *schlagsahne.*

‖ **schlamperei** ('ʃlampəraɪ). [Ger.] Indolent slovenliness, muddleheadedness; esp. designating a supposed south German and Austrian characteristic.

1961 *Economist* 30 Dec. 1282/2 A horrific picture of Austrian *Schlamperei* in a provincial court. **1966** F. SPIEGL in F. Shaw et al. *Lern Yerself Scouse* 12 Here the Scouser's sense of humour outweighs his *Schlamperei*, for he will never use a single word when he can think of some more or less long-winded picturesque phrase in its place. **1974** *Times Lit. Suppl.* 28 June 687/3 Surely it was not all *sachertorte* and *schlamperei* among the villas of Gringing?

schlemazl, var. SCHLIMAZEL.

schlemiel (ʃlə'miːl). *colloq.* Also **schlemihl, shlemiel.** [Yiddish, possibly ad. Heb. *Shelumiel*, name of a person in the Bible (Num. i. 6) said by the Talmud to have met with an unhappy end; perh. influenced by the name of the eponymous hero of A. von Chamisso's *Peter Schlemihls wundersame Geschichte* (1814).] An awkward, clumsy person, a blunderer; a 'born loser'; a 'dope' or 'drip'. Also *attrib.*

1892 I. ZANGWILL *Childr. Ghetto* I. I. i. 30 The withered old grandmother.. cursed her angrily for a *Schlemihl.* **1898** A. M. BINSTEAD *Pink 'Un & Pelican* xi. 247 He also was what the Yids call a shlemiel; no matter what he turned his hand to, nothing ever came of it. **1932** *N.Y. Times* 10 Nov. 23/7 If they expect to beat me by having their names writ in, they're schlemiels—saps, if you get me. **1941** B. SCHULBERG *What makes Sammy Run?* iv. 68 Don't talk like a schlemiel, you schlemiel. Sounds like you're letting them push you around. **1959** *Times Lit. Suppl.* 6 Nov. p. xxxv/2 Bellow's.. free-swinging translation of 'Gimpel, the Fool'—probably the best *schlemiel* story in the literature. **1963** T. PYNCHON *V.* i. 37 Only something that, being a schlemihl, he'd known for years: inanimate objects and he could not live in peace. **1969** L. MICHAELS *Going Places* 21 A hundred fifty-five pounds of stomping shlemiel. **1972** *Listener* 14 Sept. 339/3 A schlemiel is a man who falls on his back and breaks his nose. Or you can say 'When a schlemiel leaves the room, you feel as if someone came in.' **1973** *New Society* 11 Oct. 95/1 The choice of making a fool of himself or being made a fool of by others, being a schmuck or a schlemihl. **1978** I. B. SINGER *Shosha* iii. 50 You should have taken the whole five hundred. To him that's a trifle. He'll think you're a shlemiel.

schlemozzle, var. SHEMOZZLE.

schlenter ('ʃlɛntə(r)), *sb.* and *a.* Also **schlanter, shlanter, shlenter, shlinter, sl-.** [Poss. ad. Afrikaans or Du. *slenter* knavery, trick.

The history of this word is obscure; the Austral. and N.Z. forms are possibly borrowed from S. Afr. English, but by what route is not clear.]

A. *sb.* **1.** *Austral.* and *N.Z. colloq.* A trick.

1864 C. R. THATCHER *Invercargill Minstrel* 15 'Twas a 'shlinter' for the tenant one morning departed Without paying his rent. **1919** W. H. DOWNING *Digger Dial.* 45 *Slanter* (or *schlanter*), a trick. 'To run a schlanter'—to make no genuine effort to win a game. **1925** A. WRIGHT *Boy from Bullarah* 133 'A shlanter' he bellowed. **1934** *Bulletin* (Sydney) 20 June 47/1 'You worked a schlenter on me, laddie,' he said, grinning at me in the wings, 'but you're forgiven.' **1945** *N.Z. Geographer* I. I. 24 Most [shearing] sheds have somebody articulate to voice their worries if any slinters are feared. **1959** G. SLATTER *Gun in Hand* xii. 166 Wilkinson.. worked a slinter at the end. Ref shoulda penalised him. **1965** F. HARDY *Yarns of Billy Borker* 70 (*title*) The greatest slanter in the history of the racing game.

2. *S. Afr.* Something counterfeit; *spec.* a counterfeit diamond.

1892 J. R. COUPER *Mixed Humanity* 263 A new branch of industry had started in Kimberley, the manufacture of 'schlenter' stones, a name given to diamonds made of glass. **1898** *Cape Argus* (Weekly ed.) 16 Mar. 35 (Pettman), A small sack containing bars of gold or schlenter. **1937** H. KLEIN *Stage-Coach Dust* x. 112 Schlenters were also useful to the individual digger to drop into the pans of their rotating washing machine, to test the honesty of their native boys; and they were also useful to a more unscrupulous class to 'salt' diamondless claims. **1946** L. G. GREEN *So Few are Free* ix. 127 That is the trade in 'schlenters', bits of glass shaped roughly from bottle stoppers to resemble diamonds. They have none of the peculiar soapy feel of the geniune diamond, but they pass muster sometimes in a hurried deal at night. **1969** J. M. WHITE *Land God made in Anger* 131 *Schlenters*, or *slenters*, are false diamonds. The best Schlenters in South West are made from the marbles in the necks of the lemonade or mineral-water bottles that can be found in dozens at the old German diggings.

B. *adj.* Dishonest, crooked; pretended, counterfeit, fake. *Austral.*, *N.Z.* and *S. Afr. colloq.*

1889 WILLIAMS & REEVES *Colonial Couplets* 51 Broke! Broke! Broke! At the will of the C.J.C. For the slenter race with the favourite dead Will never come back to me. **1891** A. DE BRÉMONT *Gent. Digger* viii. 99 'Of course,' whispers the seller who had pushed his way to the side of the buyer, 'this sale was only *shlenter.*' **1900** J. SCOTT *Tales Colonial Turf* 35 [These race-course rogues] can draw deductions so beautifully, piecing together imaginary 'schlenter goes', and 'put-up jobs' with the cleverness of a whole courtful.. of lawyers. **1916** C. J. DENNIS *Songs Sentimental Bloke* 55 The slanter game I'd played wiv my Doreen—.. I seen wot made me feel fair rotten mean. **1924** L. COHEN *Reminiscences of Johannesburg & London* viii. 166 Confidence men found customers in plenty for schlenter gold bricks and amalgam. **1932** *Zionist Record* 25 Our courts employ schlenter as a word requiring no further definition, in the sense of fake when applied to mineral products. **1974** *Sunday Times* (Johannesburg) 24 Nov. 4 What makes the event more gratifying still is the fact that they sold schlenter uranium.

schlep (ʃlɛp), *v. colloq.* Also **schlepp, shlep.** [Yiddish *shlepn*, ad. G. *schleppen* to drag.]

a. *trans.* To haul, carry, drag. Also *transf.* and *fig.*

1922 JOYCE *Ulysses* 48 She trudges, schlepps, trains, drags.. her load. **1931** L. STEFFENS *Autobiogr.* I. xix. 137 By this means the tuglike *Schlepper* schlepped a string of cargo boats up the Neckar to Heilbronn. **1966** *New Statesman* 19 Aug. 261/3, I have a dread of being a martyr. Let them *schlep* Sonny Liston instead. **1973** *Jewish Chron.* 19 Jan. 11/1 The first thing you remember to do when shown the studio floor is to schlepp the book—out of the briefcase.. and at a right moment casually hold up the volume. **1973** *Publishers Weekly* 26 Feb. 125/1 The one thing you would not want to schlep along on a backpacking trip is this book, which runs to over 340 pages. **1975** *New Yorker* 11 Aug. 32/1 When her husband, Sidney, was alive he sustained a rupture, and Mrs. Singer says she had to schlepp him in and out of bed several times a day. **1975** R. H. RIMMER *Premar Experiments* (1976) i. 68 Merle schleps cocktails at the Persian Room in the Sheraton between six and midnight. **1977** G. MARTON *Alarum* 189 The CIA schlepped you from Moscow to Washington.

b. *intr.* To toil, to 'slave'; to go or travel with effort, to traipse. Also with quasi-*obj.*

1963 'R. L. PIKE' *Mute Witness* x. 172, I waste a whole evening *schlepping* around with him. **1964** W. MARKFIELD *To Early Grave* iii. 54 My destiny, my fate.. to *shlepp* for her. **1964** S. BELLOW *Herzog* 136 Why should I *schlepp* out my guts? **1972** D. E. WESTLAKE *Cops & Robbers* (1973) 137 We don't both have to hang around. Why don't you shlep on back to the station. **1978** J. PASCALL *Illustr. Hist. Rock Music* 15 As he schlepped his weary way from date to date.

Hence **'schlepping** *vbl. sb.*

1977 *New Society* 3 Mar. 454/3 The endless flat-footed *schlepping* you have to do at Gatwick or Chicago O'Hare.

schlep (ʃlɛp), *sb.*[1] *U.S. colloq.* Also **schlepp, shlep.** Abbrev. of SCHLEPPER.

1939 *News Letter & Wasp* 23 June 13 The name of the radio character known to thousands, Schlepperman, is evidently a personification of 'schlep', which means a poor slob. **1963** T. PYNCHON *V.* iv. 104 'Quiet, shlep,' said the doctor, scrubbing. **1977** *New Yorker* 19 Sept. 80/3 My teacher can just zero in on one phrase, and it's immediately obvious that what I've done is so immature it makes me feel like an absolute schlepp.

schlep (ʃlɛp), *sb.*[2] *colloq.* (chiefly *U.S.*). Also schlepp. [Yiddish, prob. f. SCHLEP *v.*] A troublesome business, a piece of hard work.

1964 *Economist* 1 Aug. 449/3 It was a schlep to find out. **1973** L. SNELLING *Heresy* II. ii. 68 Who thought up this *schlepp* with the sign, anyway? **1976** *National Observer* (U.S.) 4 Dec. 19-B/3 Anybody who has ever tried to make even a small amount of a classic brown sauce from scratch would probably agree with Liederman's assessment that 'it's the ultimate schlep'.

schlepper (ˈʃlɛpə(r)). *colloq.* (chiefly *U.S.*). Also shlepper. [Yiddish, f. SCHLEP *v.*: see -ER[1].] A person of little worth, a fool, a 'jerk'; a pauper, a beggar, a scrounger; an untidy person; (see also quot. 1934).

1934 *Amer. Speech* IX. 284/1 A customer who shops from store to store continually trying on shoes but not buying is known as a *shlepper*. **1949** S. J. PERELMAN *Westward Ha!* i. 13 In vain I protested that my dependents would be reduced to beggary; the editor's face remained flinty. 'About time those *schleppers* went to work,' he grunted. **1950** G. MARX *Let.* 20 Mar. (1967) 72 The paupers, or schlepper crowd, still hang on to their portable radios, but unfortunately they're not the ones who buy Chryslers. **1954** *Ibid.* 4 Aug. 59 Women always seem so much more joyous than men when another schlepper gets hooked. **1968** L. ROSTEN *Joys of Yiddish* 346 Hike up your slip; straighten your seams; you look like a shlepper. **1973** *Jewish Chron.* 19 Jan. 10/4 A 'star', you should pardon the expression, is never short of schleppers. And schleppers are like the tides of the ocean. If you make a hit film, they come in and almost drown you. If you make a flop, they recede into the distance. **1977** *Rolling Stone* 24 Mar., I've got a message for the Penelopes of this world. It's high time they say to their Ulysseses, 'Okay Schlepper, you've been around the world, your turn to keep the home fires burning, I'm splitting on my own trip for a while.'

schlich (ʃlɪç). *Metallurgy.* [Ger.: see SLIKE *sb.*] = SLICK *sb.*[2]

1677 E. BROWNE *Travels Germany* 135 They have also ..*slich*, or pounded and washed ore. **1757** tr. *Keysler's Travels* IV. 65 This method of burning of the *Schlich* saves considerable charges. **1839** URE *Dict. Arts* 814 Water..is made to flow with greater or less velocity and abundance over the schlich or pasty mud spread on a table of various inclination. **1855** J. R. LEIFCHILD *Cornwall* 207 Should the product (called *schlich*) seem tolerably rich, the operative turns the table round its axis. **1920** A. H. FAY *Gloss. Mining & Mineral Industry* 595/1 Schlich, finely pulverized ore; mud.

schlicht (ʃlɪçt), *a. Math.* [a. G. *schlicht* simple, plain.] (See quot. 1944.)

1944 J. E. LITTLEWOOD *Lect. Theory of Functions* i. 120 A function is called 'schlicht' in *D* if $f'(z) \neq 0$ in *D*, and $f(z_1) \neq f(z_2)$ for distinct points z_1, z_2 of *D*. Or: if $f(z) - a = 0$ has never more than one solution (counting multiplicities) for *z* of *D*. **1968** E. T. COPSON *Metric Spaces* vii. 86 An important instance of a bijection is the schlicht function of complex variable theory.

Schlieffen (ˈʃliːfən). The name of Alfred, Graf von *Schlieffen* (1833–1913), German general, used *attrib.* of a plan for the invasion and defeat of France that was formulated by him before 1905 and applied, with modifications, in 1914.

1919 A. P. F. VON TIRPITZ *My Memoirs* II. xvii. 289 The Schlieffen plan of attacking France through Belgium was intended to stave off from Germany the first vital danger. **1926** *Encycl. Brit.* Suppl. III. 479/1 How armies are to be handled in the Schlieffen spirit the war on the Eastern front showed. **1931** W. S. CHURCHILL *World Crisis* VI. vi. 89 He drew up the celebrated 'Schlieffen Plan' in which the whole strength of Germany was to be directed from the outset with the utmost rapidity upon France by means of a wheeling movement through Belgium. **1965** A. J. P. TAYLOR *Eng. Hist. 1914–45* xiv. 484 He planned to attack on the extreme right, according to the Schlieffen model. **1977** *Listener* 4 Aug. 140/2 In the Schlieffen plan, the railways..took troops to Belgium and northern France.

schliere (ˈʃlɪərə). *rare* in *sing.* Also Schliere. Pl. -n, and erron. schliere, schlierin. [Ger., f. regional *schliere* (fem.) striæ, streaks, corresp. to *schlier* (masc.) marl, f. early new HG. *schlier* (masc. and neut.), f. MHG. *slier* mud, related to MHG. *slier*, *sliere* ulcer, f. OHG. *sclierrun* (dat. pl.).]

1. a. *Petrol.* An irregular streak or mass in igneous rock differing transitionally from its surroundings in texture or composition, and usu. elongated by flow.

[**1885** A. GEIKIE *Text-bk. Geol.* (ed. 2) 94 Streaked, arranged in streaky inconsistent lines (Germ. Schlieren), either parallel or convergent, and often undulating.] **1888** J. J. H. TEALL *Brit. Petrogr.* ii. 40 The differential motion of the lava will tend to drag out any parts of exceptional composition into the form of streaks or elongated lenticles (schliere). **1898** *Jrnl. Geol.* VI. 794 In the granites of Essex county are found in abundance streaks (Schlieren) and rounded rock masses of darker color and of finer grain than the surrounding rock. **1937** *Mem. Geol. Soc. Amer.* No. 5. 25 Sheet-like bodies, in which certain minerals appear in abnormal proportions, are called flow layers, or schlieren. **1966** *McGraw-Hill Encycl. Sci. & Technol.* VII. 15/2 Schlieren may represent early segregation drawn out by magma flow. Some may be xenoliths more or less digested and reworked by magma. Others may represent residual magmatic liquors of different composition injected into already crystallized portions. Schlieren formed in solid rocks are more properly metamorphic or metasomatic features.

b. A zone or stratum in a transparent medium whose density differs sufficiently from that of the surrounding medium for it to be detectable by refraction anomalies, usu. in consequence of pressure or temperature differences or composition inhomogeneities.

1895 C. S. PALMER tr. *Nernst's Theoret. Chem.* I. v. 121 If one adds, by means of a capillary pipette, a drop of a strong solution of potassium ferro-cyanide to a moderately strong solution of copper sulphate, one can see with the naked eye that a *schliere* (i.e. thin layer) of concentrated solution of copper sulphate flows downwards. **1946** F. SCHNEIDER *Qualitative Organic Microanalysis* ii. 22 The appearance of schlieren indicates the presence of impurities. **1949** *Proc. R. Soc.* A. CXCVII. 485 However imperfect an electron lens may be from the point of view of theoretical optics, it can contain neither dust nor 'schlieren', as the electromagnetic field smoothes itself out automatically. **1965** G. J. WILLIAMS *Econ. Geol. N.Z.* x. 149/1 The chromite occurs as..sporadic small narrow schlierin paralleling the enstatite crystal lamination... 1 to 3 mm schlierin in dunite show a local concentration of chromite. **1967** *Oceanogr. & Marine Biol.* V. 107 These variations may appear as 'Schlieren', that is, as thin bands of water at the surface or at any depth.

2. *attrib.* uses of pl. *schlieren*, with reference to an experimental method for the observation and recording of schlieren in transparent media, in which the specimen is illuminated with a collimated beam of light, and the diffraction pattern resulting from localized refraction of light rays by the schlieren is photographed or displayed on a screen, as ***schlieren apparatus*** [ad. G. *schlieren-apparat* (A. Töpler *Beobachtungen nach einer neuen optischen Methode* (1864) 16)], ***illumination***, ***method***, ***photograph***, ***photography***, ***picture***, ***system***, ***technique***.

1895 C. S. PALMER tr. *Nernst's Theoret. Chem.* I. v. 121 Tammann observed the osmotic stream produced by the changes of concentration by means of a so-called *schlieren* apparatus. [*Translator's note*] This term, for which I find no concise English equivalent, is in common use in Germany to denote a delicate apparatus of Töpler used to detect small differences in the refractive power of the different layers ('schlieren') of heterogeneous media. **1933** *Jrnl. Scientific Instr.* X. 381 (*caption*) General arrangement of 'schlieren' apparatus set up for photographic or screen observation. **1971** *Sci. Amer.* May 118/1 In its simplest form the schlieren apparatus consists of a light source, two lenses, a pair of knife-edges and a sheet of photosensitive film. **1966** D. G. BRANDON *Mod. Techniques Metallogr.* 18 Some increase in sensitivity can be obtained if the stop is displaced from the image of the condenser aperture, so that the direct beam is merely reduced to the same intensity as the diffracted beam and not completely eliminated. This system is known as schlieren illumination and can be used to give accurate information on surface tilt. [**1899** *Phil. Mag.* XLVIII. 218 (*heading*) Photography of sound-waves by the 'Schlieren-Methode'.] **1933** *Jrnl. Scientific Instr.* X. 378 The 'Schlieren' method is an old but little-known method of rendering visible either colourless fluids, which have a different refractive index from their surrounding medium, or variations of refractive index or thickness of transparent solids. **1940** *Nature* 29 June 1021/1 The differentiation of the native proteins in the [egg] white was attempted on the basis of ionic mobilities by the method of Tiselius. The migration of the boundaries was followed optically by the 'schlieren' method using a sodium vapour lamp. **1962** *New Scientist* 6 Dec. 576/1 The effects that make optical schlieren methods feasible become negligible in gases at very low pressures. **1953** *Proc. Inst. Mech. Engineers 1951–2: Automobile Div.* 97/2 Observations by Miller of schlieren photographs taken during a very violent knocking combustion show a normal progression of the flame about three-quarters of the way across the combustion chamber. **1970** *New Scientist* 18 June 581/1 Ultrasonic frequencies up to 40kHz radiated at the base of a roaring jet of burning gas have a marked effect on the flame, altering its appearance and cutting down the noise produced. This is clearly illustrated in the two sets of spark schlieren photographs of town gas diffusion flames... An acoustic frequency of 38kHz is responsible for the remarkable alteration seen in the schlieren pictures. **1931** *Trans. Inst. Mining Engin.* LXXX. 18 Experiments carried out with Schlieren photography at Buxton are being supplemented at the U.S. Bureau of Mines Explosives Station at Pittsburgh. **1937** *Jrnl. R. Aeronaut. Soc.* XLI. 621 By using 'Schlieren' photography the air flow, fuel injection and flame formation were recorded simultaneously. **1979** *Nature* 29 Mar. 384/2 Drs Clark and B. J. Mullan used Schlieren photography to look at the air flow in and around cabinets running with and without an operator. **1957** LIEPMANN & ROSHKO *Elem. Gasdynamics* vi. 161 Schlieren pictures are seldom used for a quantitative evaluation of density. They are, however, indispensable for obtaining qualitative understanding of flows. **1966** *McGraw-Hill Encycl. Sci. & Technol.* XII. 68/1 Numerical values of density can be obtained only from schlieren pictures of airflow about two-dimensional models or about simple axisymmetric models. **1970** Schlieren picture [see *schlieren photograph* above]. **1949** O. G. SUTTON *Science of Flight* 203 Two other methods, the schlieren system and the interference method, are also in common use... The schlieren system uses either lenses alone or in combination with a concave mirror. **1956** *Nature* 10 Mar. 485/1 A schlieren system has been combined with a rotating mirror camera so that the shock propagation can be recorded in the regions outside the arc as well as in the arc channel. **1966** *McGraw-Hill Encycl. Sci. & Technol.* XII. 67/2 The schlieren system is used particularly in supersonic wind tunnels because it clearly shows the density gradients created by the shock and expansion waves of the airflow around the wind tunnel model. **1962** *New Scientist* 6 Dec. 576/1 The Schlieren technique is an optical method of studying changes of density, and hence of refractive index, in transparent media.

Hence **'schlieric** *a.*

1921 *Geol. Mag.* LVIII. 550 *Mixed rocks*, rocks which must be regarded as mixtures of carbonate magma of sövite type, and of the silicate rocks already enumerated are developed as schlieric intrusions, or as dykes cutting other members of the Fen group.

schlimazel (ʃlɪˈmɒz(ə)l). *colloq.* (chiefly *U.S.*). Also schlimazzel, schlimazl, shl-, etc. [Yiddish, f. MHG. *slim* crooked + Heb. *mazzāl* luck.] A consistently unlucky, accident-prone person, a 'born loser'. Hence as *v. trans.*, to make a schlimazel of (a person) (*nonce-use*).

1948 N. AUSUBEL *Treasury of Jewish Folklore* III. i. 344 Sholom Aleichem drew endless amusement out of the misadventures of his irrepressible, daydreaming *schlimazls*. **1960** *Encounter* May 84/1 In the *schlimazl* of Jewish tradition, I found the ancestors of Bellow's 'Angie March'. If the *schlimazl* went into the hat business, babies would be born without heads. **1962** J. ISH-KISHOR *Tales from Wise Men of Israel* 199 She shrugged. What could one make of such a *shlimmazzel*? **1963** T. PYNCHON *V.* i. 24 It seemed sometimes that he put himself deliberately in the way of hostile objects, as if he were looking to get schlimazzeled out of existence. **1968** L. ROSTEN *Joys of Yiddish* 347 A *shlimazl* wryly sighed: 'From *mazel* to *shlimazl* is but a tiny step; but from *shlimazl* to *mazel—oy*, is that far!' **1972** J. WAMBAUGH *Blue Knight* (1973) i. 15 Just bring me a cold drink, you old schlimazel. **1980** *Times* 12 June 16/8 When a waiter spills soup on a customer, the waiter is a *shlemiel* and the customer is a *shlemazl*.

schlock (ʃlɒk). *colloq.* (chiefly *N. Amer.*). Also schlag, shlock. [Yiddish, app. f. *shlogn* to strike.] Cheap, shoddy, or defective goods; inferior material, junk, 'trash' (freq. applied to the arts or entertainment). Also *attrib.* or as *adj.*, and *Comb.* in **'schlockmeister, -master** [G. *meister* master], a purveyor of cheap merchandise, 'special offers', and the like.

1915 *N.Y. Tribune* 25 July 12/1 Damaged articles..are sold..to the..'schlock' store proprietors. **1916** *Ibid.* 10 Jan. 14/1 There is nothing 'schlock' about the Goodell method. **1939** *Amer. Speech* XIV. 80/2 Schlag describes a skirt which has scant length, tightness where it should be full, is off size, has many loose threads, defective buttons, and off size button-holes. **1963** T. PYNCHON *V.* iv. 110 She loves my rhinoplasty But the others are schlock. **1965** J. M. ULLMAN *Good Night, Irene* i. 20 Public relations, an elastic term that encompasses everything from crude schlockmeisters operating out of phone booths to high-powered representatives of billion-dollar corporations. **1966** L. DEIGHTON *Billion-Dollar Brain* xv. 142 The schlock-shops were afire with sale signs and smiling suckers. **1970** *Toronto Daily Star* 24 Sept. 30/1 The most successful..have substituted sociological satire for sentimental schlock. **1972** *Publishers Weekly* 21 Aug. 71/3 Shlock fiction with all the necessary ingredients, the result is mindlessly entertaining, if rather tasteless. **1976** *New Mus. Express* 31 July 37/1 Presley was already showing..an inclination to go in for schlock rather than rock. **1978** M. PUZO *Fools Die* xii. 131, I knew it [*sc.* magazine writing] was schlock, but still I loved it. *Ibid.* xxxiii. 388 He had signed a long-term contract with Tri-Culture and become the ace schlockmaster for Jeff Wagon. **1981** *Listener* 26 Feb. 294/1 Atkinson is more fun away from showbiz schlock.

Hence **'schlocky** *a.*, characterized by schlock; that is schlock; shoddy, trashy.

1968 *N.Y. Times* 25 July 26 Playing the 'special guest star' in a series of schlocky European films. **1970** *Wall St. Jrnl.* (Eastern ed.) 10 Sept. 1/6 The schlocky corner gas station import dealer is gone. **1975** *Publishers Weekly* 1 Dec. 67/2 Just what the marketplace doesn't need, one more schlocky Gothic series. **1981** *Spectator* 24 Jan. 7/2 The concentration on Sinatra arises out of the suspicion that the Reagan entourage of friends and hangers-on is loaded with shabby, shady, schlocky, smarmy, shyster millionaires.

‖**schloss** (ʃlɔs). [Ger.] A (German) castle.

[**1617** MORYSON *Itin.* I. 202 A Castle (which the Dutch call *Schlosse*).] **1820** D. WORDSWORTH *Jrnl.* 29 July (1941) II. 74 The rest of the company had proceeded..to the Schloss.. to be spectators of the moonlight festivities of the ruined castle. **1855** GEO. ELIOT in *Fraser's Mag.* LI. 700/1 We saw the Schloss, and discovered the labyrinthine beauties of the park. **1883** 'OUIDA' *Wanda* I. 61 She had a beautiful little *schloss* on the green Ebensee. **1896** *Strand Mag.* XII. 282 Virginia creeper draped the quaint grey schlosses with crimson cloaks. **1974** *Times Lit. Suppl.* 23 Aug. 894/1 The incessant cold, the huge, half-ruinous, unheated schloss. **1980** *Early Music* Jan. 136 (Advt.), Our inclusive prices provide the course, room and board at Breiteneich, use of the facilities at the schloss.

schlub (ʃlʌb). *U.S. slang.* Also shlub. [Yiddish, perh. ad. Pol. *żłób* blockhead.] A worthless person, a 'jerk', an oaf.

1964 'E. MCBAIN' *Ax* viii. 149 'Kaplowitz,' I say, 'are you a janitor or a schlub? I'm a janitor... And such a dirty basement I can't stand.' **1969** D. E. WESTLAKE *Up your Banners* (1970) v. 39 When a man..doesn't know the facts and nobody will tell him..and people keep throwing apples and unkind remarks at him, he has no choice but to look like a *shlub*. **1970** R. H. GREENAN *Nightmare in Colour* (1971) xxxii. 114 He backed out—can you imagine? Hired a couple of college shlubs. **1978** *N.Y. Times Book Rev.* 2 Apr. 22 After bearing two children of the real-estate shlub, Earl Jr.

schm- *colloq.* (chiefly *U.S.*). Also shm-. An element, derived from the numerous Yiddish words that begin with this sequence of sounds, fused with or replacing the initial letter(s) of a word, so as to form a nonsense-word which is added to the original word in order to convey disparagement, dismissal, or derision.

1929 I. Goller *Five Bks. of Mr. Moses* v. ii. 215 'I know he made Davy go to the Palace to-day with the idea of hastening on the crisis in his illness.'.. '*Crisis-shmisis!*' mocked Barnett disparagingly. **1935** A. Kober *Thunder over Bronx* 28 Now alluva sudden is fency-shmency with forks. *Ibid.* 48 So who you rushing to see, Miss Hurry Shmurry? **1952** *Jrnl. Eng. & Gmc. Philol.* LI. 226 The morphological pattern of the jocular repetition of a word or word-ending prefixed by the cluster ʃm- seems to have become quite generalized... I have heard..moon-schmoon, etc. **1953** I. Asimov *Second Foundation* xviii. 183 'Time; schmime,' said Pappa irritably. **1963** T. Pynchon *V.* xii. 354 'It's murdering your own child, is what it is.' 'Child, schmild. A complex protein molecule, is all.' **1966** *N.Y. Herald Tribune* 20 Mar. (Sunday Mag.) 33/3 Trotsky-shmotsky, Lesbian- or adultery-wise—any way you slice *The Group* on screen it's the same old baloney about The Girls. **1967** *New Yorker* 28 Oct. 105/2 Two early Christians chanced to meet in Heaven. .. 'Saul of Tarsus, yet!' cried one. 'What are *you* doing here?' 'Tarsus-Schmarsus,' replied the other, 'I'm Paul already.' **1969** *Listener* 24 Apr. 569/1, I was surprised to find René Cutforth retelling the old story of the psychiatrist and the fond mother without specifying that she's a *Jewish* mother. ('I have to tell you, madam, that your son is suffering from an Oedipus complex.' 'Oedipus, Schmoedipus! What does it matter so long as he loves his mother?') **1971** D. Heffron *Nice Fire & Some Moonpennies* xv. 140 Gods, schmods! You can have them. **1978** F. Ross *Sleeping Dogs* 110 'Listen, honey—' 'Listen schmisten! I tell you I won't be here.'

schmagagi, var. SCHMEGEGGY.

schmaltz (ʃmɒlts, ʃmalts), *sb.* Also **schmalz, shmaltz**, etc. [a. G. and Yiddish *schmalz* fat, dripping.] **1.** Melted chicken fat; ***schmaltz herring***, a form of pickled herring.

1935 L. Zara *Blessed is Man* II. ii. 232 Two or three other kegs of *schmalz* herring and such for pickling. **1951** L. W. Leonard *Jewish Cookery* vi. 42 (*heading*) Rendering chicken or goose fat (schmaltz). **1959** *20th Cent.* June 583 Shops all choked with..schmaltz herring. **1960** A. Wesker *I'm talking about Jerusalem* I. 13 All right, so it's shmultz herring and plum pudding. **1968** M. Richler *Cocksure* viii. 46, I don't want this apartment stinking of schmaltz herring. **1974** *New Yorker* 3 June 80/2 If a diner thinks the mashed potatoes might be improved by a bit of schmalz—liquid chicken fat—he pours some out of a dispenser. **1976** *Ibid.* 16 Feb. 58/1 The newest supermarket in Washington Avenue specializes in Cuban food instead of schmalz herring and stuffed kishke.

2. *colloq.* Sentimentality, emotionalism; excessively sentimental music, writing, etc. Also *attrib.*

1935 *Vanity Fair* (N.Y.) Nov. 71/2 *Schmaltz* (cf. the German *schmalz*, meaning grease) is a derogatory term used to describe straight jazz. **1938** *Manch. Guardian Weekly* 2 Sept. 188/3 Sometimes they play 'schmaltz' or 'salon' (ordinary jazz). **1944** [see HAM *sb.*[1] B. 1]. **1950** *Here & Now* (N.Z.) Nov. 27/2 Howard Wyatt has an impressive technique for his age, and his greatest lack is what has come to be known as schmalz. A certain amount..of this quality is necessary, and..I'd recommend a serious study of the 'white' jazz exponents. **1956** [see Disneyesque *a.*]. **1957** J. D. Salinger *Zooey* in *New Yorker* 4 May 37/1 Will you be content with that standard box-office schmalz? **1960** *Guardian* 7 July 6/3 A purveyor of 'Schmalz' in long-winded repetitive symphonies. **1967** *Spectator* 24 Nov. 634/2 Some Presidents could turn..these frustrations to good account by retailing their moral and physical struggles... Lyndon Johnson spares us none of this schmaltz. **1977** *Spare Rib* June 46/4 She..is saying with appalling schmaltz that 'Josh's warm, funny smile was where I lived now'. **1978** *Observer* 19 Nov. 31/1 'What we call honest sentiment,' he says in equally honest puzzlement, 'you call schmaltz.'

schmaltz (ʃmɒlts, ʃmælts), *v. colloq.* Also **schmalz, shmaltz.** [f. prec.] *trans.* To impart a sentimental atmosphere to; to play (music) in a 'corny' or sentimental manner. Also with *up*.

1936 *Amer. Mercury* May p. x, *Schmalz it*, play it long-haired. **1966** D. Skirrow *It won't get you Anywhere* xxxi. 143 She was like the white light of early morning, before the hot sun schmalzes up the scene. **1968** L. Rosten *Joys of Yiddish* 351 To *shmaltz* ('to *shmaltz* it up'): to add 'corn', pathos, mawkishness. **1969** A. Laski *Dominant Fifth* ii. 41 He..tried to lighten his touch; no use giving this—visitor—the notion that they schmaltzed it up.

schmaltzy ('ʃmɒltsɪ, 'ʃmæltsɪ), *a. colloq.* Also **schmalzy.** [f. as prec. + -Y[1].]

Sentimentalized, over-emotional; 'corny'. Hence **'schmal(t)ziness.**

1935 [see GROOVE *v.* 5]. **1949** L. Feather *Inside Be-Bop* iii. 22 Edgar Hayes, a pianist whose schmaltzy record of *Stardust* had made him a Harlem juke box favorite. **1952** B. Malamud *Natural* 170 A heavy-set German with a schmaltzy accent. **1959** *Guardian* 27 Oct. 7/6 I'm working on something real schmaltzy for one of your women's magazines. **1962** *John o' London's* 5 July 19/1 A few weeks ago she [*sc.* the All-American Mum] turned up in *All Fall Down*, embodied with searing schmalziness by Angela Lansbury. **1974** T. P. Whitney tr. *Solzhenitsyn's Gulag Archipelago* I. I. v. 218 Yuri painted for nothing schmaltzy pictures such as *Nero's Feast* and the *Chorus of Elves* and the like for the German officers on the commandant's staff. **1978** P. Griffiths *Conc. Hist. Mod. Music* vii. 101 In the opera *Lulu* the effect of Berg's half-tonal serialism is an over-ripe schmalzy quality. **1980** [see SCHMUTZIG *a.*].

schmatte ('ʃmætə). *U.S. colloq.* Also **shmatte, schmottah**, etc. [a. Yiddish *schmatte*, ad. Pol. *szmata* rag.] A rag, a ragged garment; any garment. Also *fig.*

1970 L. M. Feinsilver *Taste of Yiddish* ii. 121 A 1969 sale catalog of the Ktav Publishing Company, New York book dealers, listed Philip Roth's licentious novel *Portnoy's Complaint* with the comment: 'A shmatte.' **1972** H. Kemelman *Monday Rabbi took Off* xxii. 144, I mean when they wear those checkered *shmattes* around their heads, then they're Arabs. Right? **1973** J. Marks *Mick Jagger* 128, I ran away from home in San Bernardino when I was fifteen... All I took was this *schmottah* I wore Halloween. **1977** *New Yorker* 24 Oct. 39/2 A young woman, pale, in a Victorian schmotta.

schmeck (ʃmɛk). *slang.* Also **smeck.** Pl. **'schmecken.** [a. Yiddish *schmeck*, sniff.] A drug; *spec.* heroin.

1932 *Evening Sun* (Baltimore) 9 Dec. 31/5 *Smeck*, dope. **1941** M. U. Schappes *Lett. from Tombs* 104 'Shmeck'—dope, a drug. **1966** *Sunday Times* (Colour Suppl.) 13 Feb. 35/4 *Schmeck*, heroin. **1967** M. Calpan *In Deadly Vein* ix. 196 'He was always wild... Anything for kicks... In the end it was schmeck.' 'Heroin?' 'Yes. Hooked.' **1970** L. Sanders *Anderson Tapes* xxxi. 86 She's hustling right now—schmeck, tail, abortion—the whole lot. *Ibid.* xcii. 218, I have some drugs. Some schmeck. Do you want a shot? **1971** *Oz* No. 36. 40/1 Shoot enough schmeck into them and they won't even *think* of burning and looting.

Hence **'schmecker**, a drug-addict, esp. one who takes heroin.

1953 W. Burroughs *Junkie* (1972) viii. 77 He went on talking about some old acquaintances who got their start in junk and later turned respectable. 'Now they say, "Don't have anything to do with Sol. He's a *shmecker*".' **1955** *Publ. Amer. Dial. Soc.* XXIV. 193 If they are all schmeckers, or narcotic addicts, they have a prearranged time to fix or take a bang. **1966** C. Himes *Heat's On* xix. 145 The skin-poppers and the schmeckers (those who used the needle and those who sniffed the powder).

schmeer (ʃmɪə(r)). *N. Amer. colloq.* Also **shmear, shmeer.** [ad. Yiddish *schmirn* to smear, grease, flatter.] **1.** Bribery, corruption, flattery.

1961 A. Berkman *Singers' Gloss. of Show Bus. Jargon* 78 *Shmear*,..payola; graft. **1962** E. Lacy *Freeloaders* ii. 42 Our lad didn't want the *shmear* to start with, so he ain't greedy. **1978** *Amer. Film* Apr. 57/2 He knew the *shmeer* was on when the producer invited him to lunch..and began the meal by ordering caviar and champagne.

2. ***the whole schmeer***, everything, everything possible or available, every aspect of the situation.

1969 E. Stewart *Heads* 48 Why couldn't you burrow around and ferret out the whole shmear yourself? **1970** L. Sanders *Anderson Tapes* v. 23, I want a complete list... Any thing and everything... The whole shmear. **1971** K. Wheeler *Epitaph for Mister Wynn* (1972) xxix. 374, I picked you because you know the whole schmeer. **1972** H. Kemelman *Monday Rabbi took Off* xxii. 146 Some special kind of prayer maybe where you could ask for the success of our enterprise...especially the financing, but I was thinking of the whole *shmeer*. **1978** *Maledicta 1977* I. 282 Eventually, the whole schmeer was declared a Mexican stand-off.

schmegeggy (ʃmə'gɛgɪ). *U.S. slang.* Also **schmagagi, shmegegge**, etc. [Origin obscure; see quots. 1968, 1970 for sense 1.]

1. A contemptible person, an idiot.

1964 S. Bellow *Herzog* 29 He better get it this afternoon, that ludicrous schmegeggy! **1968** L. Rosten *Joys of Yiddish* 353 *Shmegegge*,..Ameridish slang. Origin: unknown; probably, a dazzling onomatopoetic child of the Lower East Side. 1. An unadmirable, petty person. 2. A maladroit, untalented type. 3. A sycophant, a *shlepper*, a whiner, a drip. **1970** L. M. Feinsilver *Taste of Yiddish* 121 *Shmegegge* (*or shmegeggi*), a galoot, a bird-brain, a stupid character... The disdain involved prompts me to suggest that the term may be a combination of two other words for 'fool': the vulgar *shmok*..and *yeke* or its German antecedent *Gecke*. **1971** *Observer* 23 May 36/3 He says he's a schlemiel which is.. better than being a schmagogy... Schlemiels..drop things and..they drop on schmagogys.

2. Rubbish, nonsense.

1968 L. Rosten *Joys of Yiddish* 353 *Shmegegge*,..a lot of 'hot air', 'baloney', a *cockamamy* story. 'Don't give me that *shmegegge*!' **1970** L. M. Feinsilver *Taste of Yiddish* 121 *Schmegegge* (*or shmegeggi*),..as picked up in American theatrical circles, this is sometimes used in the sense of 'malarkey' or 'bushwa'. **1973** Boyd & Parkes *Dark Number* ii. 23 There was a bunch of students... They had the lot, the full schmagagi: girls got up like camp grannies..boys in kaftans.

Schmeisser ('ʃmaɪsə(r)). The name of Louis and Hugo *Schmeisser*, German small-arms designers, used *attrib.* or *absol.* to designate various German types of submachine gun, in use from 1918 onwards.

1950 G. Wilson *Brave Company* 7, I saw that he [*sc.* a German] carried a Schmeisser. **1963** D. Bagley *Golden Keel* ix. 268, I opened the locker under my berth and took out the Schmeisser machine pistol and all the magazines. **1976** *Valiant* 8 May 3 (*caption*) In the United States, gun shops sell every kind of weapon, from shotguns to schmeissers. **1981** E. Ward *Baltic Emerald* xiv. 117 Modern Schmeissers..the most reliable..of all the medium-range killing devices.

schmelz (ʃmɛlts). Also erron. **schmel(t)ze.** [a. G. *schmelz* enamel.] Any one of several varieties of decorative glass; *spec.* a variety coloured red with a metallic salt, used to flash white glass. Also *attrib.*

[**1854** C. Tomlinson *Cycl. Useful Arts* I. 784/1 Smetz [*sic*: ? *read* Smelz] glass is formed by fusing lengths of coloured glass into each other, so that the section shall resemble carnelian and the agates.] **1859** R. Hunt *Guide Museum Pract. Geol.* (ed. 2) 111 The Bohemian ruby is thus prepared:—a preparation called schmelze is made; it is composed of silica 500, minium 800, nitre 100, calcined potash 100. **1866** *Christie, Manson & Woods Sale Catal. 9 Feb. 1867* 65 A vase, on foot, of tortoiseshell Schmeltze... A green basket, mounted with or-molu; and a Schmeltze ditto. .. A ball of variegated Schmeltze. **1879** *Encycl. Brit.* X. 652/1 That peculiar kind of glass usually called schmelz, an imperfect imitation of calcedony, was also made at Venice in the 15th century. **1882** *Hamilton Palace Collection Catal.* No. 846 A Fluted Tumbler, of red and white schmelz. **1907** E. Dillon *Glass* xii. 207 There are a few exceptionally fine early examples of this schmelz at South Kensington. **1961** E. M. Elville *Collector's Dict. Glass* 183/1 Variegated or marbled opaque glass, commonly known by the German word *schmeltz*.

Also ‖**Schmelzglas.**

1935 W. A. Thorpe *English Glass* v. 148 Measey and Greene ordered and sold the following lines, but the list applies generally to the members of the Company, and excepting the items of opaque-white and *calcedonic* (marbled glass or *Schmelzglas*) it may be taken as a production list. **1960** H. Hayward *Antique Coll.* 10/2 '*Agate*' *glass*, a glass of several colours which have been allowed to mingle before the vessel is formed, in imitation of agate. This type of glass was popular during the Renaissance.., particularly in Venice and Germany, and is sometimes known as *Schmelzglas*. **1975** *Oxf. Compan. Decorative Arts* 398 Not only did they [the Venetians] reproduce the Roman 'mosaic' and *millefiori* glass and the material made of blended opaque colours in imitation of natural stones (*calcedonio*, sometimes miscalled *Schmelzglas*), but they seem even to have copied..typical Roman shapes.

schmendrik ('ʃmɛndrɪk). *U.S. slang.* Also **schmendrick, shmendrik.** [The name of a character in an operetta by Abraham Goldfaden (1840–1908).] A contemptible, foolish or immature person; an upstart, a 'sucker'.

1944 M. Samuel *Harvest in Desert* xii. 115 The colonists called the workers *Shmendriks*, tatterdemalions, n'er-do-wells. **1951** A. Hirschfeld *Show Business is No Business* 47 A schmendrick with a noodle for a brain. **1970** S. Ellin *Bind* xxx. 151 This boy is no *shmendrik*... Believe me, he knows from the real thing. **1976** L. Deighton *Twinkle, twinkle, Little Spy* x. 93 Maybe if I'd been at college with Andrei Bekuv, I could even feel sorry for *that* schmendrik.

‖**schmerz** (ʃmɛrts). Also **Schmerz.** [a. G. *schmerz* pain.] Grief, sorrow, regret, pain.

1911 'P. Harding' *Corner of Harley Street* xxx. 260 So white-coat gives him a swiftly helping hand, and within five minutes is removing a decayed semitic molar that has been giving its owner *schmerz* indescribable. **1925** R. Frost *Let.* 20 June (1964) 174 What lies at the bottom of your *Schmerz* is your own dereliction. **1977** *Times* 13 July 11/8 There is much more to Schiele than terrified mirror-gazing and sexual *Schmerz*. He was a splendid..portraitist.

Schmidt[1] (ʃmɪt). *Org. Chem.* [The name of Karl Friedrich *Schmidt* (b. 1887), German chemist, who first employed a reaction of this kind in 1923 (*Zeitschr. f. angew. Chem.* XXXVI. 511).] ***Schmidt('s) reaction***: a widely-used synthetic method in which a carbonyl compound is treated with hydrazoic acid in the presence of mineral acid, the product(s) depending on the kind of carbonyl compound used (e.g. an aldehyde gives a mixture of a nitrile and a formyl derivative of an amide, a ketone gives an amide, and a fatty acid gives an amine).

[**1936** *Proc. R. Soc.* A. CLIV. 54 The introduction of the Schmidt method leaves the Hofmann method of great historical interest but deprives it of importance for costly and delicate synthetic work.] **1937** *Jrnl. Amer. Chem. Soc.* LIX. 2658/1 Although the Schmidt reaction has been used in a few instances it has never been extensively studied. **1963** I. L. Finar *Org. Chem.* (ed. 4) I. ix. 178 Schmidt's reaction with acids is a modification of the Curtius reaction. **1967** L. F. & M. Fieser *Reagents for Org. Synthesis* I. 447 Application of the Schmidt reaction to cyclohexanone effects ring enlargement to ϵ-caprolactam. **1976** Streitwieser & Heathcock *Introd. Org. Chem.* xxviii. 825 The Schmidt reaction may also be used for the synthesis of simple amino acids if it is applied to an alkylated malonic acid.

Schmidt[2] (ʃmɪt). *Astr.* The name of Bernhard Voldemar *Schmidt* (1879–1935), Estonian-born German optician, used *attrib.* with reference to an optical system invented by him, as **Schmidt camera**, an astronomical telescope, used exclusively for wide-field photography at the primary focus, in which a Schmidt correcting lens is placed at the centre of curvature of a spherical primary mirror, the combination having no spherical aberration and little chromatic aberration; **Schmidt correcting lens, corrector, (correcting) plate**, an aspheric lens of complex figure used in the Schmidt camera and other catadioptric systems that utilize the same principle; **Schmidt telescope** = *Schmidt camera*. Also *ellipt.*, = *Schmidt camera*.

1939 Skilling & Richardson *Astron.* iii. 82 The great advantages of the Schmidt telescope are that it can photograph a very large area in the sky, giving sharp focus clear to the edge of the picture; and that it is very fast. *Ibid.*, These telescopes are sometimes called Schmidt cameras, for they cannot be used visually. **1946** *Nature* 17 Aug. 222/1 A Schmidt plate presents a very different problem, since the highest optical homogeneity is required for this, and a low-expansion glass has never yet been produced in the requisite optical quality. **1961** Miczaika & Sinton *Tools of Astronomer* iii. 99 (*caption*) Possible shapes of Schmidt correcting lenses. *Ibid.* 100 Such solid Schmidts, as they are called, may be made with *f*-numbers as small as *f*/0·6. **1964** *Listener* 21 May 831/1 The Armagh Schmidt is employed mainly on variable star research. **1966** *McGraw-Hill Encycl. Sci. & Technol.* XIII. 452/1 A similar correction of the principal defects of the paraboloidal reflector can be obtained by replacing the thin Schmidt correcting plate with a weakly diverging meniscus lens. **1973** *Sci. Amer.* Aug. 111/1 Schmidt correctors and other aspheric surfaces are sold by the tens of thousands in quality zoom lenses for film and television. **1978** PASACHOFF & KUTNER *University Astron.* iv. 90 The 1·2-meter Schmidt has been used to map the entire sky that is visible from Palomar. *Ibid.*, The new 1-meter Schmidt camera at the European Southern Observatory and the British 1·2-meter Schmidt camera at Siding Spring, Australia, are now being used in a joint project to extend the survey to incorporate the one-quarter of the sky that cannot be seen from Palomar. **1978** *Sci. Amer.* Dec. 90/3 The lens of the scallop eye appears to perform much the same function as the corrector plate of the Schmidt telescope.

Schmidt number (ʃmɪt). *Physics.* [Named after Ernst Heinrich Wilhelm *Schmidt* (b. 1892), German engineer.] A dimensionless number, analogous to the Prandtl number, used in the study of convective mass transfer and evaluated as the ratio of kinematic viscosity to mass diffusivity.

1955 D. B. SPALDING *Some Fundamentals of Combustion* vi. 239 Other experimental procedures can easily be conceived with various advantages or disadvantages, the guiding principle being that the Peclet numbers based on flow velocity and on flame speed must be kept constant, and that if possible the Mach number, Prandtl number and Schmidt number.. should all have equal values in the model and the original. **1957** JAKOB & HAWKINS *Elements of Heat Transfer* (ed. 3) xvi. 293 The heat transfer equation may be altered to represent the mass transfer equation by replacing the Nusselt number by the corresponding Nusselt number for mass transfer, and replacing the Prandtl number by the Schmidt number. **1975** CROOME-GALE & ROBERTS *Airconditioning & Ventilation of Buildings* iii. 92 It can be shown that the well-known result expressing *Nu* [*sc.* the Nusselt number] as a function of the Reynolds and Prandtl numbers, i.e. $Nu = f(Re, Pr)$, has an analogous form in mass transfer $Sh = f(Re, Sc)$ where *Sc* is the Schmidt number.

‖**schmierkäse** (ˈʃmiːrkɛːzə). Also **Schmierkäse.** [G.: see SMEAR-CASE.] = SMEAR-CASE. Also *fig.*

1905 W. WITTIGSCHLAGER *Minna* 104 She carried some schmierkase (cream cheese), and butter that smelt so oily.. I had to turn my head away. **1931** F. HURST *Back Street* i. 13 Sturdy, unstylish women with enormous busts, who ate and drank with relish, but knew, to the penny, for how much less they could spread their groaning home-table with these luxuries of *Schmierkäse.* **1949** *Sat. Even. Post* 23 Apr. 80/3, I took large helpings of ham and potatoes, *schmierkase*, and green salad with tomatoes. **1955** H. KURNITZ *Let.* Dec. in G. Marx *Groucho Lett.* (1967) 249, I am..whipping up a schmierkase about light love and dark doings. **1969** R. & D. DE SOLA *Dict. Cooking* 202/2 *Schmierkäse,* (German—soft cheese). To Germans, any soft cheese; to Pennsylvania-Germans, cottage cheese.

Schmitt (ʃmɪt). *Electronics.* The name of Otto Herbert *Schmitt* (b. 1913), American biophysicist and electronics engineer, used *attrib.* and *absol.* to designate a bistable circuit devised by him, in which the output increases to a steady maximum when the input rises above a certain threshold, and decreases almost to zero when the input voltage falls below another threshold (usu. lower than the first).

1946 *Jrnl. Inst. Electr. Engineers* XCIII. IIIA. 306/1 Positive feedback can be used to reduce the effective grid base, or even to make it negative; an example is shown. [*Note*] This is the 'Schmitt circuit'. **1953** VON TERSCH & SWAGO *Recurrent Electr. Transients* viii. 272 If both plate-to-grid coupling and cathode coupling are utilized another trigger circuit is obtained. This circuit is called the Schmitt trigger circuit. **1962** SIMPSON & RICHARDS *Physical Princ. Junction Transistors* xvi. 418 The Schmitt trigger is neither bistable nor monostable in the ordinary sense. Its behaviour is similar to that of a non-regenerative switch but it has the advantages that it switches regeneratively at very high speed and can be designed with an accurate adjustable trigger threshold. **1967** *Electronic Engin.* XXXIX. 752/1 A theory was required to account for the existence of a minimum ionization current below which the Schmitt fails to trigger, and a maximum above which the Schmitt fails to reset. **1975** D. G. FINK *Electronics Engineers' Handbk.* XVI. 45 Schmitt bistables, also called Schmitt triggers, are suitable for detecting the moment when an analog signal crosses a given dc level. They are widely used in oscilloscopes to provide time-base synchronization pulses... In some Schmitt trigger circuits it is possible to modify the switching level by electrically changing the operating points of the transistors.

schmo (ʃməʊ). *U.S. slang.* Also **shmo(e).** [f. SCHMUCK.] An idiot, a fool.

1948 *Life* 15 Mar. 23/2 Schlump is a friendlier, more sympathetic term than 'schmo', which has completely replaced 'jerk'. A schmo, of course, is a person who stands watching a machine make doughnuts, and 1) cannot understand the process, 2) cannot get up will power to leave. **1955** 'H. ROBBINS' *Stone for Danny Fisher* I. vii. 56 Let some other shmoe wet-nurse a bunch of kids. **1957** S. J. PERELMAN *Road to Miltown* 125 A couple of shmos like you and me, we can't even get up our rent, whereas them dukes and earls..are rolling in dough. **1970** D. FRANCIS *Rat Race* ii. 27 'Who,' he said crossly, 'is going to give that schmo a thousand quid for breaking his ankle?' **1979** 'H. HOWARD' *Sealed Envelope* xi. 159, I was feeling like a shmoe... Paul Ingram had outsmarted me.

schmock, var. SCHMUCK.

schmoll (ʃmɒl). *slang.* [app. ad. Yiddish *shmol* narrow.] An idiot, a fool.

1967 J. WAINWRIGHT *Worms must Wait* xl. 101 Let's say ..he was killed by some *schmoll* who wanted to rob him. **1973** —— *Pride of Pigs* 103 These hot-shot scientists... They're schmolls—every last one of 'em..but they get away with it.

schmooze (ʃmuːz, ʃmuːs), *v. U.S. colloq.* Also **schmoos(e), schmuss, shmooz,** etc. [ad. Yiddish *shmuesn* to talk, converse, chat, f. as next.] *intr.* To chat, gossip, engage in a long and intimate conversation. Hence **ˈschmoozer; ˈschmoozing** *vbl. sb.*

1897 *N.Y. Times Weekly Mag.* 14 Nov. 4/1 He loves dearly to stop and chat (*Schmoos,* he calls it). **1921** J. ANTHONY *Gang* 28 When Mrs. Sinbaum comes, we *schmoos.* **1928** *Amer. Speech* III. 364 The presence of a Jewish contingent of 'producers' and managers is responsible for such New York expressions as 'mazuma' (money), 'schmuss' (talk). **1939** *New Yorker* 4 Feb. 30/1 'Schmooze' (pronounced 'shmooss') is related to the Yiddish verb 'schmooze', which means 'to talk'. But schmoozing in the garment district is more than just a lot of idle chatter. Schmoozing is a careful tradition, dear to the hearts of everyone in New York's most thickly populated business section. *Ibid.* 30/2 Everybody in the district eats fast, the better and more to schmooze. **1939** *Reader's Digest* May 106/1, The schmoozers gulp down lunch in 15 minutes and then arrange themselves according to caste and craft. **1966** H. KEMELMAN *Saturday Rabbi went Hungry* x. 60 On Friday nights or Saturdays, don't we stand around after the services and *schmoos* a while? **1973** *New Yorker* 3 Feb. 56/2 We would schmoose all afternoon, with her talking in that funny, high Pennsylvania Dutch voice: 'Dat's gute,' or 'Dat's humbug.' **1977** *Time* 25 Apr. 47/2 Neil Diamond's beach house, Linda Ronstadt's $325,000 clapboard and the sprawling nine-bedroom house Guitarist Robbie Robertson took over from Carole King are all within schmoozing distance. **1977** *New Yorker* 27 June 29/1 Had she worked here part time, returning today out of sentimentality to schmooze with the boss? **1980** W. SAFIRE in *N.Y. Times Mag.* 18 May, A 'stoop', from the Dutch word for 'step', is a description of the porch and front steps on which Brooklynites sit and schmooze.

schmooze (ʃmuːz, ʃmuːs), *sb. U.S. colloq.* Also **shmoos.** [ad. Yiddish *shmues* chat, gossip, ad. Heb. *shĕmūʿah* rumour.] Chat; gossip; a long and intimate conversation.

1939 *Reader's Digest* May 106/2 Because of schmooze, the garment district is the most hypersensitive city of 200,000 in the world. **1956** B. HOLIDAY *Lady sings Blues* (1973) xix. 156 [Lena Horne] insisted on taking me out with her and bought me lunch, and we had a wonderful schmooze about the old days in Hollywood. **1970** S. ELLIN *Man from Nowhere* (1971) xxxix. 194 Ready to order now..or do I wait until the end of the *shmoos*? **1977** *Zigzag* Aug. 24/1 The general demeanor and schmooze level of the crowd indicates it's a predominantly invitational radio/press group, more disposed to be open-minded.

schmottah, schmozzle, varr. SCHMATTE, SHEMOZZLE.

schmuck (ʃmʌk). *slang.* Also **schmock** (ʃmɒk), **shmock, shmuck.** [Yiddish; originally a taboo-word meaning 'penis'.] A contemptible or objectionable person, an idiot. Hence **ˈschmucky** *a.*, objectionable, obnoxious.

1892 I. ZANGWILL *Childr. of Ghetto* II. I. xvi. 45 Becky's private refusal to entertain the addresses of such a *Shmuck.* **1945** G. MARX *Let.* 16 Feb. in *Groucho Lett.* (1967) 51 He doesn't know I can write, in fact, he thinks I'm a complete schmuck. **1958** F. NORMAN *Bang to Rights* III. 132 But as I'm no shmock I deside to play along with her. **1963** *Globe & Mail* (Toronto) 10 July 9/1 Only the pay-TV concept.. can break the hold of the 'Madison Ave. schmucks, the Gestapo of the television industry'. **1967** D. SKIRROW *I was following this Girl* xxxix. 241, I know that one schmucky swallow doesn't have to spoil the barrel. **1971** B. MALAMUD *Tenants* 50 Art is the glory and only a shmuck thinks otherwise. **1972** J. CAINE *Hamlet, My Boy* xi. 161 As soon as the *shmock* of a witness offered to testify on television. **1975** *Harpers & Queen* May 128/3 Schmucky agents and flacks and show-biz parasites. **1978** M. PUZO *Fools Die* xxi. 239 Cully felt some anger that this guy was treating Merlyn like such a schmuck. **1981** *Times* 2 July 15/2 Mary Gordon is extremely funny about the beautiful Robert..and about the Woody Allen-like schmuck in the apartment below whom she sleeps with.

schmutter (ˈʃmʌtə(r)). *colloq.* Also **shmuter, shmutter.** [ad. Yiddish *schmatte,* rag; cf. SCHMATTE.] Clothing; also *fig.*, rubbish. Also *attrib.*, esp. in ***schmutter trade, business,*** etc.

1959 C. MACINNES *Absolute Beginners* 138 Coming down the steps, wearing some very fancy schmutter: mauve, button-two tuxedo, laced shirt, varnished pumps with bows, and, on his arm, a nameless dame. **1962** F. NORMAN *Guntz* i. 9 There ain't all that many birds who are loaded in the shmuter trade. **1965** *New Statesman* 30 July 152/2 Jews ..may prefer their son to go into the family schmutter business. **1967** G. SIMS *Last Best Friend* xiii. 114 They said it was like Buck House but it was a right load of old schmutter! You see, everyone's an antique dealer today. **1972** *Bookseller* 27 May 2358/1 Several dresses (at trade terms) were bought for Mrs. Wolfe..from small shmutter merchants. **1980** *Times* 22 July 10/6 You can always dump a load of old schmutter destined for the California leisure set onto the unsuspecting women of Nottingham.

schmutz (ʃmʊts). *slang.* Also **shmutz.** [Yiddish or Ger.] Dirt, filth, rubbish. Also *fig.* So **ˈschmutzig, -ik** *a.*, filthy.

1967 P. WELLES *Babyhip* xxiv. 161 She was the one at your party wearing the *schmutzik* suit. **1968** M. RICHLER *Cocksure* xix. 116 'Of my son's ability there is no question.' '—and, em, the contents of your son's novel. You see—' '*Shmutz,*' Daniels shouted at Katansky. 'Pardon?' 'Filth. Today nothing sells like filth.' **1971** O. NORTON *Corpse-Bird Cries* vi. 113 It means dropping this driver in the *schmutz* insurance-wise. I was trying to avoid that. **1972** *Last Whole Earth Catalog* 178/1 It delights them to watch us rummaging around in the schmutz. **1980** *Times Lit. Suppl.* 5 Sept. 968/3 His [*sc.* Kurt Weill's] jazz is *schmutzig*, not *schmalzy*.

schnapper (ˈsnæpə(r)). Formerly also **snapper.** [An alteration, after the equivalent G. *schnapper,* of SNAPPER (f. SNAP *v.* + -ER[1]), a name which has been given independently in various parts of the world to many different fishes.]

a. A valuable sparoid food-fish (*Chrysophrys guttulatus* or *C. auratus*), abundant upon the coasts of South Australia and New Zealand.

1827 P. CUNNINGHAM *N.S. Wales* I. 68 Snappers, bream, flat-heads, and various other descriptions of fishes, are all too found plentifully about. **1850** CLUTTERBUCK *Port Phillip* iii. 44 Besides the fish above numerated, are the Schnapper, black-fish and eel. **1890** 'R. BOLDREWOOD' *Col. Reformer* (1891) 171 The first fish, a twelve-pound schnapper. **1908** E. J. BANFIELD *Confessions of Beachcomber* II. i. 243 When maybe they have caught schnapper..they drift among the turtle. **1917** *Chambers's Jrnl.* Apr. 237/2 The schnapper, a sea-bream, is a splendid fish. **1947** K. TENNANT *Lost Haven* vi. 89 The deck was littered with the pink-bronze bodies of schnapper. **1971** *Sunday Australian* 8 Aug. 5/6 Sir Henry's best catch this time was a 10 lb schnapper.

b. *attrib.* and *Comb.*

1859 *All Year Round* No. 4. 80 We had been accustomed to..fish..for Schnapper-fish weighing from seven to twenty-five pounds. **1883** E. P. RAMSAY *Food Fishes N.S. Wales* 31 Schnapper-fishing. **1944** *Living off Land* vii. 133 Cotton schnapper line. **1947** K. TENNANT *Lost Haven* i. 14 The schnapper boat moored beside..the grey skeleton of the half-built ship.

‖**schnapps, schnaps** (ʃnæps). [Ger.] An ardent spirit resembling Hollands gin.

1818 *Blackw. Mag.* III. 403 Enjoy your schnaps, give sorrow to the wind. **1823** BYRON *Juan* x. lxxi, Not like slow Germany wherein they muddle Along the road,..and also pause besides, to fuddle, With 'schnapps'. *a* **1848** O. W. HOLMES *On Lend. Punch-bowl* 16 He went to Leyden, where he found conventicles and schnaps. **1885** C. LOWE *Bismarck* II. 488 A General, talking of drinks, had laid down the principle: 'Red wine for children, Champagne for men, *Schnaps* for Generals'.

schnauzer (ˈʃnaʊtsə(r)). [G.] A black or pepper-and-salt wire-haired terrier belonging to the breed so called, which includes large, standard, and miniature dogs distinguished by a stocky, robust build, docked tail, blunt, bearded muzzle, and ears that droop forwards; formerly called the wire-haired pinscher.

1923 *Dog World* Aug. 14/2 A new breed has come to America—the Schnauzer. **1930** *Observer* 9 Feb. 13/2 The German Schnauzers have sterling qualities, though they may not be particularly showy in their close wiry coats. **1957** *New Yorker* 5 Oct. 34/1 For rainy weather, this miniature schnauzer is wearing our ready-made gabardine rain-coat. **1968** [see PINSCHER]. **1970** *Manch. Guardian Weekly* 14 Mar. 4/4 She bought a schnauzer, a placid beast with large brown eyes and a yelp like a police car siren. **1977** *Time Out* 28 Jan.–3 Feb. 64/2 (Advt.), Has own home, Central London and owns beautiful little schnauzer.

schnebelite (ˈʃneɪbəlaɪt). [f. the name *Schnebelin* (see below) + -ITE.] An explosive principally composed of specially treated chlorate of potash, invented by the brothers Schnebelin *c* 1893.

1893 *Daily News* 22 Sept. 6/6 L'Abbé Schnebelin, who was illustrating by a series of experiments the advantages of Schnebelite gunpowder. **1894** *Westm. Gaz.* 25 June 6/2 Though the base of the Schnebelite..is chlorate of potash, the..powder seems to be less dangerous to handle than any other.

schneider[1] (ˈʃnaɪdə(r)). *Skat.* Also **Schneider.** [G., lit. 'tailor'.] (See quots.) Also as *adj.* and *v. trans.*

1886 E. E. LEMCKE *Skat* 7 With 60 points only he loses; with 30 points he is '*Schneider*' or '*geschnitten*' (cut); with no count at all he is '*Schwarz*' (black = whitewashed). Consequently the two hands in opposition to the 'player', scoring jointly 60 points, win the game from player; scoring 30 are out of *Schneider*, but are *Schwarz* with no count. **1909** R. F. FOSTER *Foster's Compl. Hoyle* 420 If he can get 91 points, he wins a double game, which is called *schneider.* *Ibid.* 437 It may be played out to see if he can make schneider or schwarz. **1935** *Encycl. Sports, Games & Pastimes* 553/1 If he scores 91 points he makes his opponents schneider. **1947** *New Compl. Hoyle* 385 If the player wins 91 or more points in play, he is said to *schneider* the opponents and the value of his game is increased. **1949** A. A. OSTROW *Compl. Card Player* 645 Official laws of American skat... The player to be out of schneider must have at least 31 points, the opponents 90. **1975** *Way to Play* 109/1 If the bidder has named suits or grand, he may before the opening lead, declare: a) schneider, ie he aims to win at least 91 trick points; or b) schwarz, ie he aims to take every trick. **1976** *National Skat & Sheepshead Q.* Mar. 18 A grand scores 80 points and possibly 100 if the hand is schneidered.

Schneider[2] (ˈʃnaɪdə(r)). The name of Jacques *Schneider* (1879–1928), French flying enthusiast, used *attrib.* in ***Schneider trophy, cup***: the Jacques Schneider Maritime Cup, presented in 1913 by Schneider to the winner of an international competition for seaplanes comprising an air race and seaworthiness trials, and contested annually (with certain exceptions) until won outright by Great Britain in 1931.

[**1912** *Flight* 14 Dec. 1182/1 M. Schneider has offered for international competition a trophy of the value of £1,000, to go to the club which the winning pilot represents.] **1913** *Ibid.* 5 Apr. 395/1 The French team for the forthcoming international contest for the Schneider Cup at Monaco. **1927** A. HUXLEY *Let.* 8 Oct. (1969) 291 Time rushes past as though it were trying to win the Schneider Cup. **1929** *Radio Times* 8 Nov. 395/3 We were testing all the arrangements for the Schneider Trophy relay, making sure that the loudspeaker system at various points round the coast could pick up our broadcast. **1933** *Ann. Reg. 1932* I. 24 After paying a tribute to all who had been concerned in the winning of the Schneider trophy, [the minister] remarked that though in size the Royal Air Force took only fifth place . . there was no other better equipped. **1977** *Times* 23 Sept. 12/4, I hope the Schneider Trophy will be given an extra loving dust down at its home in the Science Museum.

Schneiderian (ʃnaɪˈdɪərɪən), *a. Anat.* [f. the name of C.V. *Schneider* of Würtemberg (1610–80), who investigated this structure.] ***Schneiderian membrane***, the mucous membrane of the nose.

1803 *Med. Jrnl.* X. 115 The inflammation of the Schneiderian membrane, and that of the mucous membrane of the bronchiæ were much more frequently absent than present. **1899** *Allbutt's Syst. Med.* VI. 753 Situated in the Schneiderian mucous membrane is a large number of bipolar cells.

schnitzel (ˈʃnɪtzəl). [G.] A veal cutlet, esp. in ***Wiener*** (ˈviːnə(r)) ***schnitzel***, one coated with egg and breadcrumbs, fried and often garnished with lemon, capers, anchovies, etc., in the Viennese style.

1854 *Pioneer* (San Francisco) Nov. 318 Eggs, coffee, toast, and now and then, a chop or a 'snitzel' is the order given for thousands of people. **1862** *Temple Bar* Nov. 63 After a dinner such as Vienna only can furnish; *e.g.* a delicate soup . . a *Wiener Schnitzel* (a savoury cutlet greatly to be recommended) . . we take rail at half-past two p.m. **1904** *Adventures of Elizabeth in Rügen* 262 Her eyes were discreetly fixed on a *Wiener Schnitzel* that she was eating with a singular mincingness. **1911** A. FILIPPINI *International Cook Bk.* 144 Arrange a thin slice of lemon, with a twisted anchovy in oil placed over each slice of lemon, on top of each schnitzel. **1936** E. AMBLER *Dark Frontier* vii. 114 They do know how *wiener schnitzel* should be cooked. **1956** [see ESCALOPE]. **1960** *News Chron.* 23 Feb. 3/2 Swop the porridge and oatcakes for schnitzel and strudel. **1978** *Chicago* June 210/2 The entrées perk one up immediately, though. The schnitzel à la Holstein came with a perfect fried egg and a golden puff of crust.

schnockered (ˈʃnɒkəd), *ppl. a. U.S. colloq.* Humorous var. of SNOCKERED *ppl. a.*

1955 *Amer. Speech* XXX. 303 *Schnockered; way up*, . . drunk. **1976** *Verbatim* Feb. 15/1 George really got schnockered at Judy's party. **1977** B. GARFIELD *Recoil* iii. 45 Bradleigh took the empty glass. 'That's probably enough. You don't want to get schnockered.'

schnook (ʃnʊk). *U.S. colloq.* Also **schnuck**, **shnook**. [app. Yiddish: perh. repr. Yiddish *shnuk* snout, or f. G. *schnucke* a small sheep.] A dupe, a sucker; a simpleton, a 'dope'; a pitiful wretch.

[**1943** S. J. PERELMAN *Let.* 7 Apr. in G. Marx *Groucho Lett.* (1967) 190 It's the story of a small schnükel of a barber who accidentally brings a statue of Venus to life.] **1948** H. L. MENCKEN *Amer. Lang.* Suppl. II. 757 *Schnuck* . . , a customer easily persuaded, a sucker. **1955** N. MAILER *Deer Park* xii. 136 I'd be making a stinking seven hundred and fifty a week now like all those poor exploited schnooks. **1959** R. CHANDLER in Gardiner & Walker *R. Chandler Speaking* (1962) 262 Why does he want to see me so badly that he has to send a couple of shnooks after me? **1964** S. BELLOW *Herzog* 29 This shnook of a chiropodist—what a hellcat *he* married. **1975** A. BERGMAN *Hollywood & Le Vine* xiii. 187 It was all pretty fascinating for a Sunnyside schnook like me. **1980** W. SAFIRE in *N.Y. Times Mag.* 2 Aug. 8 To be self-conscious about the possibility of error . . is to be a nerd, a schnook and a wimp.

Schnorchel, **schnorkel**, **Schnorkel**, varr. SNORKEL.

schnorrer (ˈʃnɒrə(r)). *Jewish.* Also **shnorrer**. [Yiddish var. of G. *schnurrer*, f. *schnurren* (slang) to go begging.]

A Jewish beggar. Now in extended *U.S.* use, a beggar, layabout, scrounger, good-for-nothing.

1892 ZANGWILL *Childr. Ghetto* i. 4 The Schnorrer felt no false shame in his begging. **1899** *Daily Chron.* 10 Mar. 3/4 The crowd of half-starved immigrants, consisting of street hawkers and schnorrers, who are the plague of the Jewish Board of Guardians. **1934** E. POUND *Eleven New Cantos* xxxv. 24 The tale of the perfect schnorrer. **1959** [see LAYABOUT]. **1962** J. D. SALINGER *Franny & Zooey* 136, I had lunch with him one day a couple of weeks ago. A real schnorrer, but sort of likable. **1977** *New Yorker* 24 Oct. 38/3 Investigate your own pants, you schnorrer. **1981** J. BARNETT *Firing Squad* xiv. 190 A right pair of miserable schnorrers I've got here.

So **s(c)hnorr** *v. trans.* and *intr.*, to obtain by begging; to beg, sponge (*off*).

1892 I. ZANGWILL *Childr. Ghetto* III. II. vii. 125 Your father . . stood in the Lane with lemons, and *schnorred* half-crowns of my father. *Ibid.* xii. 221 But isn't it *schnorring* to be dependent on strangers? **1894** —— *King of Schnorrers* iii. 67 Even if you can prove you can *schnorr* enough to keep a wife, I do not bind myself to consent. **1964** W. MARKFIELD *To Early Grave* iv. 76 Box after box. *Shnorred*, with cunning and craft, from tough-minded Cousin Schmeilick. **1968** *Encounter* Sept. 30/1, I can go out and within an hour *shnorr* the entire amount I owe you. **1975** *Publishers Weekly* 19 May 90/1, I hope to shnorr off a couple of Scottish landowners I've met here.

schnozz (ʃnɒz). *U.S. slang.* Also **schnoz**. [app. Yiddish: cf. G. *schnauze* snout, and see next.] **a.** The nose, nostril.

1942 A. KOBER in *New Yorker* 13 June 19/1, I see she's not occupied excep' she's powderin' her schnoz. **1940** L. SHELLY *Hepcats Jive Talk Dict.* 17/1 *Schnozz*, . . the nose. **1967** P. WELLES *Babyhip* xx. 131 Mr Cox stuffed a rusty paper clip up his schnozz and broke his nose. **1973** R. HAYES *Hungarian Game* iii. 28 'You remember what our boy looks like?' 'Gray hair, widow's peak, big schnozz, red ski parka and no luggage.'

b. In fig. phr. (***right***) ***on the schnozz***, precisely, exactly, on the dot (of time).

1949 W. R. BURNETT *Asphalt Jungle* xx. 130 Headlights flashed into the parking-lot, and then went out. 'This is us, I think,' said Louis, 'and right on the schnoz.' **1967** 'E. QUEEN' *Face to Face* xxx. 140 Twenty minutes to twelve on the schnozz.

schnozzle (ˈʃnɒz(ə)l). *U.S. slang.* [pseudo-Yiddish: cf. Yiddish *shnabl* beak, and see prec.] The nose. Similarly (*joc.*) **s(c)hnoˈzzola** [cf. -OLA].

Esp. applied as a nickname to the U.S. entertainer James Francis ('Jimmy') Durante (1893–1980).

1930 *Variety* 26 Feb. 24/5 It's the medium for the screen debut of Jimmy Durante, he of the large schozzola [*sic*.]. *Ibid.* 56/2 'Roadhouse Night' . . . brings Jimmy Durante to the screen. Admirers of his peculiar madness usually fear for its reception by a general public . . but the Schnozzle's first screen appearance removes any doubts that might have been entertained. **1937** J. DURANTE in *Amer. Mag.* May 61/1 A youngster like me whose schnozzle could be seen two blocks away. *Ibid.* 61/2 When we admit our schnozzles . . we begin to laugh. **1937** in Wentworth & Flexner *Dict. Amer. Slang* (1960) 448/1 A broken nose epidemic hit Dennison. In early contests 5 players broke their schnozzolas. **1959** J. LUDWIG in *Tamarack Rev.* Summer 24 What a way to louse up this new magenta outfit—streaming eyes, a shiny shnozzola! **1977** *Listener* 9 June 746/2 Hebrew amens are breathed through Yiddish schnozzles. **1981** *Times Lit. Suppl.* 15 May 535/2 He is sunk in the multiplied particularities of his vivid surroundings. Not least, in the pongs to which his great schnozzle . . is peculiarly susceptible.

‖**Schnurkeramik** (ˈʃnuːrkeˌraːmɪk). *Archæol.* Also with small initial. [G., f. *schnur* string, cord + *keramik* ceramics, pottery.] = *corded ware* s.v. CORDED *ppl. a.* 3 b.

1902 J. ABERCROMBY in *Jrnl. Anthrop. Inst.* XXXII. 391 In Germany, there is a class of ceramic which goes by the name of *Schnurkeramik*, from its being almost exclusively ornamented by cord-impressions. **1928**, **1950** [see CORDED *ppl. a.* 3 b]. **1954** S. PIGGOTT *Neolithic Cultures* xi. 344 Comparable ornament appears on pots in a *schnurkeramik* context from Switzerland.

scho(e, obs. form of SHE, SHOE, SHOW.

schoche: see SCOTCH *v.*, SOUCH *v.*

†**schœnanth.** *Obs.* Also (erron.) **schæ-**, **scæ-**. [ad. mod.L. *schœnanthus*, a. late Gr. σχοίνανθος (also σχοινάνθη, σχοινάνθιον), f. σχοῖν-ος rush + ἄνθος flower.] A sweet-scented grass of Asia, *Andropogon Schœnanthus*, formerly used in medicine; camel's-hay.

1702 PETIVER in *Phil. Trans.* XXIII. 1257 This is easily known from the other Schænanths in having hollow Oat-like husks. **1712** tr. *Pomet's Hist. Drugs* I. 110 Schœnanth. **1753** *Chambers' Cycl.* Suppl., *Scænanth*, or *Schænanth* . . , the dried stalk of a plant brought to us from Arabia.

Schoenbergian (ʃœnˈbɛːgɪən), *a.* and *sb.* Also **Schönbergian**. [-IAN.] **A.** *adj.* Of, pertaining to, or characteristic of the Austrian composer Arnold *Schoenberg* (1874–1951) or his music. **B.** *sb.* An admirer or adherent of Schoenberg; an exponent of Schoenberg's music. Hence **ˈSchoenbergism** *rare*, the advocacy or practice of Schoenbergian techniques of musical composition.

1922 C. GRAY in *Mus. & Lett.* III. 79 Side by side with a daring experiment like Op. 6, No. 1, *Traumleben*, with its characteristic late-Schönbergian voice part. **1931** [see DIATONICISM]. **1934** C. LAMBERT *Music Ho!* v. 330 His earlier works . . show signs of a Schönbergian ruthlessness. **1947** *Penguin Music Mag.* Dec. 21 An extraordinary combination of the traditional Italian lyrical *cantilena* writing with the Schönbergian technique. **1951** Schoenbergism [see DODECAPHONIC *a.*]. **1959** *Times* 13 Feb. 13/4 Other names in these programmes are those of Egon Wellesz, a lapsed Schönbergian . . and Karlheinz Stockhausen. **1976** *Gramophone* Aug. 324/1 He had been taking a crash course in early Schoenbergian expressionism. **1978** P. GRIFFITHS *Conc. Hist. Mod. Music* iv. 46 Apart from that the work is not at all Schoenbergian.

†**schœne.** *Obs.* Also **schene**. [ad. L. *schœnus*, a. Gr. σχοῖνος, commonly believed to be a use of σχοῖνος rush, rope, but possibly a foreign word. Cf. F. *schène*.] An ancient measure of distance mentioned by Gr. writers and Pliny (chiefly as in use among the Persians); the length is variously stated at from 30 to 60 stadia (= $3\frac{1}{2}$ to 7 miles).

1555 EDEN *Decades* (Arb.) 300 Islande . . is extended betwene the south and the north almost two hundreth schoenes in longitude. **1603** HOLLAND *Plutarch's Mor.* 274 Measure not wisedome by the Persian Schœne. **1615** G. SANDYS *Trav.* 132 Three Schœnes aboue the South angle of the Delta, (each Schœne containing fiue miles at the least, and sometimes seuen and a half). **1674** JEAKE *Arith.* (1696) 112 In Aegypt they reckon by Schœnes of various Magnitude, some 60, some 40, some 20 Furlongs.

Schoenflies (ˈʃøːnfliːs). *Cryst.* The name of Arthur *Schoenflies* (1853–1928), German mathematician, who listed the 230 space groups in 1891 (*Krystallsysteme und Krystallstruktur*), used *attrib.* with reference to the system of nomenclature which he devised for them.

1934 W. P. DAVEY *Study of Crystal Struct.* viii. 222 Of the four sets of symbols listed in the table it is recommended that only the Schoenflies and the Wyckoff be used . . . The Schoenflies symbols have the great advantage of world-wide use. **1961** TERPSTRA & CODD *Crystallometry* iv. 132 The symbol $\bar{1}$ thus corresponds to the Schoenflies C_i. **1970** A. J. WILSON *Elem. X-Ray Crystallogr.* 225 For space groups the Schoenflies symbols are quite inconvenient. *Ibid.*, There is also a Schoenflies notation for the Bravais lattices, which is used even less than the symmetry notation.

schœnobatic (skiːnəʊˈbætɪk), *a. rare*⁻¹. [ad. Gr. σχοινοβατικ-ός, f. σχοινοβάτης (L. *schœnobatēs*) rope-dancer, f. σχοῖνο-ς rope + βα-, βαίνειν to walk.] Pertaining to rope-walking. So **schœˈnobatist**, a rope-walker, rope-dancer.

1839 *Blackw. Mag.* XLVI. 21 A troop of young schoenobatists. **1862** *London Rev.* 23 Aug. 160 Scænobatic [*sic*] or acrobatic feats.

schoepite (ˈsxɜːpaɪt). *Min.* [f. the name of Alfred *Schoep* (1881–1966), Belgian mineralogist + -ITE[1].] A hydrated form of uranium trioxide found as yellow to brown tabular or prismatic orthorhombic crystals as an alteration product of uranium ore; three phases (schoepite I, II, and III) are known, differing slightly in composition, colour, and morphology.

1923 T. L. WALKER in *Amer. Mineralogist* VIII. 69 As this mineral appears to be quite distinct in optical and crystallographic properties from all known uranium minerals, the writer proposes to name it schoepite in honor of Professor Alfred Schoep, of the University of Ghent, who has contributed so much to our knowledge of the secondary uranium minerals from the Congo. **1960** *Ibid.* XLV. 1034 Crystals of schoepite that are apparently single yield multiple diffraction patterns . . . These . . correspond to the presence of two out of three possible distinct orthorhombic phases in parallel intergrowth in the crystal. The three phases are designated schoepite I, II and III. **1965** *Ibid.* L. 236 Crystals of schoepite commonly occur with an amber-brown core completely or partially surrounded by a derivative golden-yellow rim which retains the morphology of the original crystal . . . The brown part consists chiefly of schoepite I, and the yellow part mostly of schoepite II or schoepite III.

schofeet, obs. form of SOFFIT.

schoff, var. SCOFF *sb.*[2]

schoffe, obs. form of SCOFF, SHOVE.

schoind, variant of SCHYND *Obs.*

schoir, **-ling**, Sc. forms of SHORE, SHORLING.

schol (skɒl). Colloq. abbreviation of SCHOLARSHIP (sense 2).

1899 *Captain* Nov. 115/2 Wardour had licked Eccles and forfeited the 'schol'. **1958** B. HAMILTON *Too Much of Water* xi. 247, I won a schol to the House. **1965** J. SYMONS *Belting Inheritance* ii. 35 'The old thing's *delighted* about the schol,' Uncle Miles had written.

‖**schola cantorum** (ˈskəʊlə kænˈtɔːrəm). [med.L. = school of singers.] **a.** The choir-school attached to a cathedral or monastery (orig. the Papal Choir at Rome, established by Gregory the Great (*c* 540–604)). **b.** Used as the title of various groups of singers.

1782 C. BURNEY *Gen. Hist. Mus.* II. i. 16 Fleury, in his *Hist. Eccl.* . . . gives a circumstantial account of the *Scola Cantorum*, instituted by St. Gregory. **1887** E. L. TAUNTON *Hist. & Growth Church Music* iv. 39 The elder members of the Schola Cantorum, as it was called, had the title of Subdeacons. **1902** E. DICKINSON *Music in Hist. of Western Church* v. 181 The Schola Cantorum of Paris . . is exerting a strong influence upon church music. **1929** E. C. THOMAS *Lay Folks' Hist. Liturgy* II. xiv. 223 The members of the schola cantorum to which the lectors belonged had no other function than that of singing. **1941** G. CHASE *Music of Spain* xi. 168 Morera . . has written . . choral arrangements of Catalan folk songs, some of which have been performed by the Schola Cantorum of New York. **1964** P. F. ANSON *Bishops at Large* x. 475 The ladies of the *schola cantorum* looked fetching in their red gowns and caps.

scholar (ˈskɒlə(r)). Forms: 1 scolere, scoliere, 3–7 scholer, 4–5 scolere, 4–6 scoler, 5 scolare, skolere, scolier, (*Caxton* escolyer), 5–6 scolar, 5–7 scoller, 6 scolear, -eir, scollar, skoller, skolar, 6–7 scholler, -ar, schooler, 7 schoolar, skooller, skollar, (sholar), 6–9 *vulgar* schollard, 9 scholard,

6- scholar. [OE. *scolere, scoliere* (= OHG. *scuolari*, MHG. *schuolære*, early mod.G. *schuler*, now *schüler*), ad. late L. *scholār-is* (f. *schola* SCHOOL), with substitution of the native ending -ER[1]. The word is rare in OE., and the ME. *scoler(e* may be wholly or in part a. OF. *escoler, escolier* (mod.F. *écolier*). Cf. Du. *scholier* (? from Fr.), MDu. also *scholare, scholer*.]

1. a. One who is taught in a school; *esp.* a boy or girl attending an elementary school. Often qualified by prefixed word, as *Sunday, infant scholar*, DAY-SCHOLAR. Now somewhat *arch.*

c **1055** *Byrhtferth's Handboc* in *Anglia* VIII. 308 Seo ræding pingð þæne scoliere. **1389** in *Eng. Gilds* (1870) 51 A fraternite was begonne..of ȝonge scolers. *a* **1400-50** *Alexander* 641 If any scolere in þe scole his skorne at him makis. **1402** HOCCLEVE *Let. Cupid* 211 That boke scolers lerne in hir chyldehede. **1538** STARKEY *England* I. i. 3 He was neuer gud mastur that neuer was scoler. **1596** SHAKS. *Tam. Shr.* III. i. 18, I am no breeching scholler in the schooles. **1610** HOLLAND *Camden's Brit.* I. 266 Two Schoole maisters and threescore and ten schoolers. *a* **1656** BP. HALL *Rem. Wks.* Special. Life 8 Some unwise friends..perswaded him [my Father] to fasten me upon that School as Master, whereof I was lately a Scholler. **1820** SOUTHEY *Wesley* II. 162 In two or three months there were twenty-eight scholars, notwithstanding the strictness of the discipline. **1843** (*title*) The Sunday Scholar. **1888** J. RUNCIMAN in *Contemp. Rev.* LIV. 39 An accurate inquiry disclosed the fact that 38 per cent. of these poor scholars were breakfastless every morning.

b. One who is receiving, or has received, his instruction or training from a particular master; a pupil (*of* a master). Now *arch.* or *rhetorical.*

c **1000** *Canons of Edgar* 10 in Thorpe *Laws* II. 246/14 þæt ænig preost ne underfo oþres scolere. *c* **1305** *St. Edm. Conf.* 247 in *E.E.P.* (1862) 77 His scolers þat ihurde of him gode men were ynouȝ. **1340** *Ayenb.* 39 Ine þis clergie heþ dame auarice uele scolers. **1387** TREVISA *Higden* (Rolls) III. 195 Pictagoras hadde þis manere by seuene sciences: non of his scoleres schulde to fore þe seuenþe ȝere axe resoun noþer skile of his lore. **1471** CAXTON *Recuyell* (Sommer) II. 396 Hys escolyers that lerned of hym. *a* **1590** *Marr. Wit & Wisd.* viii. (Shaks. Soc.) 56 *Wit.* Your most vnworthy schollard Giues to you immortall thainks. **1606** SHAKS. *Ant. & Cl.* IV. xiv. 102 Thy Master dies thy Scholler; to do thus I learnt of thee. **1644** MILTON *Areop.* (Arb.) 68 We are become..the backwardest Schollers, of whom God offer'd to haue made us the teachers. **1699** BENTLEY *Phal.* ii. 57 While young, he was Scholar to Thales. **1745** J. HAMMOND *Love Elegies* xiii, And teach my lovely scholar all I know. **1869** TENNYSON *Coming of Arthur* 153 Merlin's master (so they call him) Bleys, Who taught him magic; but the scholar ran Before the master. **1896** BESANT *Master Craftsman* (1897) 67 It looks like Grinling Gibbons..or perhaps one of his scholars.

c. *transf.* One who acknowledges another as his master or teacher; a disciple.

1577 VAUTROULLIER *Luther on Ep. Gal.* 10 That they were the ministers of Christ and the Apostles scholers. **1597** HOOKER *Eccl. Pol.* v. vii. §3 To professe themselues therein schollers and followers of the auncient. **1606** B. BARNES *Offices* II. 50 Gower and his Scholler Chaucer. **1759** JOHNSON *Idler* No. 68 ¶4 The Romans confessed themselves the scholars of the Greeks. **1791** BURKE *Let. Memb. Nat. Assembly* Wks. VI. 37 Your masters, who are his [Rousseau's] scholars. **1842** J. H. NEWMAN *Par. Serm.* V. viii. 127 They think it a fine thing to..profess themselves the devil's scholars.

d. With qualifying adj.: One who is quick (or the reverse) at learning.

c **1605** ROWLEY *Birth of Merlin* II. iii. 232 *Prince.* Dost think thy Lady is of thy opinion? *Gent.* She's a bad Scholar else; I have brought her up, And she dares owe me still. **1719** DE FOE *Crusoe* I. (Globe) 214 He was the aptest Scholar that ever was. **1733** in *Swift's Lett.* (1766) II. 177, I am conscious of only one [good quality], that is, being an apt scholar.

2. a. One who studies in the 'schools' at a university; a member of a university, esp. a junior or undergraduate member. Now only *Hist.* and in official use.

1303 R. BRUNNE *Handl. Synne* 7999 Þe fourþe sone was a scoler, To lerne more he dyde hys power. *c* **1340** HAMPOLE *Prose Treat.* 7 A scolere at pares had done many full synnys. *c* **1386** CHAUCER *Miller's T.* 4 With hym ther was dwellynge a poure scoler, Hadde lerned Art, but al his fantasye Was turned for to lerne Astrologye. **1472-3** *Rolls of Parlt.* VI. 33/2 Your humble Oratours and Subgiettes, the Chaunceler and Scolers of the Universite in your Toune of Oxonford. **1572** *Act 14 Eliz.* c. 5 §5 All Scollers of the Universityes of Oxford or Cambridge yᵗ goe aboute begginge, not beinge aucthorysed under the Seale of the said Universities. **1579** LYLY *Euphues* (Arb.) 139 Such a confusion of degrees, that the scholler knoweth not his dutie to the Bachelor, nor the Bachelor to the Master. **1596** DALRYMPLE tr. *Leslie's Hist. Scot.* II. 247 The Burgesses and skolleris [at Aberdeen]. **1613-14** *Aberd. Acc.* in *Spalding Club Miscell.* V. 94 Gave to ane Hungarian scoller for his supporte..3 lib. **1632** LITHGOW *Trav.* II. 43 The Schollers here in the night commit many murthers. **1681** *Lond. Gaz.* No. 1656/2 At the very Entrance whereof, the Scholars were placed; First, the Under-Graduates, then the Batchelors of Arts. **1868** *Local Act 31 & 32 Vict.* c. 59 Preamble, The Chancellor, Masters, and Scholars of the University of Oxford.

†**b.** In the Elizabethan period, often applied to one who had studied at the university, and who, not having entered any of the learned professions or obtained any fixed employment, sought to gain a living by literary work. *Obs.*

1597 *Pilgr. Parnassus* I. 74 (Macray) Let schollers be as thriftie as they maye, They will be poore ere theire last dyinge daye.

3. a. One who has acquired learning in the 'Schools'; a learned or erudite person; esp. one who is learned in the classical (i.e. Greek and Latin) languages and their literature.

13.. *E.E. Allit. P.* B. 1554 Scoleres skelten þeratte þe skyl forto fynde, Bot þer was neuer on so wyse couþe on worde rede. **1540-1** ELYOT *Image Govt.* (1549) 80 In the habite of a schooler of philosophie. **1599** SHAKS. *Much Ado* II. i. 264, I would to God some scholler would coniure her. **1607** *Peele's Jests* (*c* 1620) 11 He goes directly to the Mayor, tels him he was a Scholler and a Gentleman. **1621** BP. MOUNTAGU *Diatribæ* 181 As becommed a Gentle-man and a Scholer. **1779-81** JOHNSON *L.P.*, *Akenside* Wks. 1787 IV. 290 A very conspicuous specimen of Latinity, which entitled him to the same height of place among the scholars as he possessed before among the wits. **1820** LAMB *Elia* I. *Christ's Hospital*, Matthew Field belonged to that class of modest divines who affect to mix in equal proportion the gentleman, the scholar, and the Christian. **1856** EMERSON *Eng. Traits, Religion* Wks. (Bohn) II. 97 Thus the clergy for a thousand years have been the scholars of the nation. **1886** R. C. CHRISTIE in *Encycl. Brit.* XXI. 362/2 Joseph Justus Scaliger (1540-1609), the greatest scholar of modern times.

b. with qualifying word indicating the degree of one's attainment.

c **1290** *St. Francis* 154 in *S. Eng. Leg.* I. 58 Bernard, þat was a guod scholer, formest to him cam. **1598** SHAKS. *Merry W.* IV. i. 82 He is a better scholler then I thought he was. **1629** LENTON *Yng. Gallants Whirligigg* in *Marr. Wit & Wisdom* (Shaks. Soc.) 125 His Childhood next..Required them to put him unto schoole, Where in processe of time he grew to bee A pretty scholler. **1649** JER. TAYLOR *Gt. Exemp.* II. Disc. vi. 11 An ignorant mans faith..may be as strong as the faith of the greatest Scholler. **1717** LADY M. W. MONTAGU *Let. to Pope* 12 Feb., I pass for a great scholar with him, by relating to him some of the Persian tales. **1719** DE FOE *Crusoe* I. (Globe) 224 He..made me..a much better Scholar in the Scripture Knowledge, than I should ever have been by my own private meer Reading. **1820** LAMB *Elia* I. *Christ's Hospital*, Under him were many good and sound scholars bred.

c. In illiterate use, one whom the speaker regards as exceptionally learned. Often merely, one who is able to read and write. Freq. in vulgar or dial. form *scholard, schollard*, etc.

1644 QUARLES *Judgem. & Mercy* Wks. (Grosart) I. 79 The Vicar of our Parish..being so good a Churchman, and so great a Schollard, and can speake Latine too. **1667** DRYDEN & DK. NEWCASTLE *Sir M. Mar-all* II. ii, Nay, faith, sir, I am not so good a schollard to say much. **1678** *Quack's Acad.* in *Harl. Misc.* (1809) II. 33 The admiring patient shall certainly cry you up for a great schollard, provided always your nonsense be fluent. **1824** MISS MITFORD *Village* Ser. I. 207 He [*sc.* a lad of thirteen] is a great 'scholar', too, to use the country phrase. **1853** LYTTON *My Novel* I. iii, You know Mark was a schollard, sir, like my poor, poor sister. **1893** PEEL *Spen Valley* 274 When the paper was bought by Law's work-people, they had to seek up John Jowett, or some other scholar to read it aloud to them.

4. A student who receives emoluments, during a fixed period, from the funds of a school, college, or university, towards defraying the cost of his education or studies, and as a reward of merit.

At the colleges of Oxford and Cambridge and in the University of Durham such students wear a distinctive academic dress, and have special seats in hall and chapel.

1511-2 *Act 3 Hen. VIII*, c. 22 §5 Any particular persone being fellowe or scoler of any of the said Colleges or Halles. **1584** POWEL *Lloyd's Cambria* 400 The Warden and Scholers of new College in Oxenford. **1693** DRYDEN *Persius* iii. (pref. note), I remember I Translated this Satyr, when I was a Kings-Scholar at Westminster-School, for a Thursday-Nights Exercise. **1831** *Oxf. Univ. Herald* 19 Feb. 3/3 The election for a Vinerian Scholar, in the room of Mr. Giles, will take place on Thursday. *Ibid.* 11 June 3/2 On Monday last, Mr. Spranger, commoner of Exeter Coll. was elected a Scholar of that Society. **1853** 'C. BEDE' *Verdant Green* I. v, A scholar's gown was accordingly produced. **1857** *Act 20 & 21 Vict.* c. 84 Sched. §71 The foundation scholars at the lower school [Dulwich] shall be appointed by the governors.

5. *attrib.* and *Comb.*, as ***scholar-craft, -part, phrase***; appositive, as ***scholar-official, -performer, -poet, -printer, publisher, -saint***; †***scholar-respecting*** adj.

1820 SCOTT *Monast.* xi, And since you like *scholarcraft so well, Mary Avenel, you shall see whether Edward or I have most of it. **1978** *Nagel's Encycl.-Guide: China* 323 All the prestige and importance of the *scholar-officials came from their knowledge of characters. **1711** SHAFTESB. *Charac.* I. 333 *note*, The full advantage of a just and liberal Education, by uniting the *Scholar-part with that of the real Gentleman and Man of Breeding. **1978** C. HOGWOOD in J. M. Thomson *Future of Early Music in Britain* 16 Much of the scholarly evidence is so easily assimilated by the performer that you have to invent a halfway category of the *scholar-performer or the research-performer. **1599** PORTER *Angry Wom. Abingt.* (Percy Soc.) 27 That womans will borne, common, *scholler phrase. **1928** J. BAILEY *Let.* 23 July (1935) 289 Do you know Hölderlin, the *scholar-poet? **1979** R. P. GRAVES (*title*) A. E. Housman: the scholar-poet. **1902** M. R. JAMES in *Camb. Mod. Hist.* I. xvii. 619 The sixteenth century was the age of publication. What had been recovered was given to the world by the great *scholar-printers. **1963** *Times Lit. Suppl.* 26 Apr. 312/2 Dr. Mardersteig's position in typographical history as at once an artist-printer and a *scholar-publisher. **1595** *Polimanteia* in Brydges *Brit. Bibl.* I. 275 A *scholar-respecting honor. **1894** *Dublin Rev.* Oct. 340 The serene *scholar-saint, the Benedictine, Jean Mabillon.

b. ***scholar's mate***: see MATE *sb.*[1] b. Also †***scholar's check.***

1656 tr. *Biochimo's Chesse-Play* 17 The Schollers Mate. **1688** HOLME *Armoury* III. v. 264/1 Scholars Check.

Hence **'scholar** *v.* (*nonce-wd.* in pa. pple. and gerund), *intr.* to act the scholar or learner; *trans.* ? to educate as a scholar.

1793 MME. D'ARBLAY *Lett.* (1843) V. 402, I have been scholaring all day, and mastering too; for our lessons are mutual. **1836** MAHONY *Reliques* I. 309 (tr. Gresset) Thus for a time did Vert-Vert dwell Safe in this holy citadelle; Scholared like any well-bred abbé, And loved by many a cloistered Hebé.

scholarch ('skəʊlɑːk). *Hist.* [ad. Gr. σχολάρχ-ης (mod.L. *scholarcha*, G. *scholarch*), f. σχολή SCHOOL + -αρχης ruler.] The head or ruler of a school: *spec.* **a.** The head of an Athenian school of philosophy. **b.** In certain parts of Germany, Switzerland, and France, an official, or one of a body of officials, formerly charged with the inspection of the schools within a city or district.

1863 DOWDING *Life G. Calixtus* 145 'I will not deny,' he tells the Scholarchs of Nürnberg, 'that' [etc.]. *a* **1871** GROTE *Aristotle* (1872) I. ii. 52 The Scholarchs, successors of Theophrastus at Athens. **1875** M. PATTISON *Casaubon* 260 Laurence, the scholarch, Casaubon's successor as classical professor. **1884** *Ch. Quarterly* XIX. 227 The first Scholarch after the fall of Constantinople was Matthew the Camariot. **1888** *Encycl. Brit.* XXIV. 718/2 Xenocrates.., scholarch or rector of the Academy from 339 to 314 B.C.

Hence **'scholarchate** [= G. *scholarchat*], the office of a scholarch; the body of scholarchs.

1762 tr. *Busching's Syst. Geog.* V. 514 The greatest part of the clergy in the town are referred to the scholarchate and the ecclesiastic office, and those who officiate at the spital to the upper administrator thereof.

'scholardom. *rare.* [-DOM.] The realm of scholars or scholarship; scholars collectively.

1882 *Fraser's Mag.* Oct. 440 Under the new secretary [of the Philological Society]..scholardom was ruled to admirable effect. **1907** T. C. MIDDLETON *Geog. Knowl. Time Discov. Amer.* 18 *note*, A most damaging blunder in scholardom.

'scholarhood. *rare.* [-HOOD.]

a. The body of scholars, the learned world. **b.** The condition of being a scholar or learner.

1837 *Tait's Mag.* IV. 726 The whole scholarhood of England consented to kiss the toe of William Gifford. **1880** J. ROSS *Hist. Corea* x. 306 He is entirely ignorant of their meaning for at least two years of his scholarhood.

†**scho'larian.** *Obs. rare*$^{-1}$. [? f. L. *scholāri-s* SCHOLAR + -AN; or f. SCHOLAR + -IAN.] ? A scholar.

1647 BOYLE *Let.* 8 May, Wks. 1772 I. p. xli, I am confident ..that those elevated spirits will not prove half so costive and pedantical, as the great scholarians of our colleges.

'scholarism. Now *rare.* [f. SCHOLAR + -ISM.] The learning of the 'schools'; scholarship. Sometimes used disparagingly.

1588 GREENE *Perimedes* To Gentl. Rdrs. A 3 b, If there be anye in England that set the end of scollarisme in an English blanck verse. *c* **1590** MARLOWE *Faustus* Chorus (1604) A 2, So soone hee profites in Diuinitie, The fruitfull plot of Scholerisme grac't, That shortly he was grac't with Doctors name. **1611** G. H. *Anti-Coton* 64 [He] hath a purpose to erect a new Colledge in the Vniuersitie, where he will raise the study of good letters, which are falne, sith these men have soyled them, by reducing them vnto a miserable kinde of Schollerisme. **1878** DORAN *Mem. Gt. Towns* 225 There was an impression that this new-fangled scholarism was a very sad matter indeed.

†**scho'larity.** *Obs. rare.* [ad. med.L. *scholāritāt-em*, OF. *sc(h)olarité*, f. *scholār-is* SCHOLAR: see -ITY.] The status of a scholar.

1599 B. JONSON *Cynthia's Rev.* v. iv. Wks. 1616 I. 251 Content, I'le pay your scholaritie. Who offers? **1895** RASHDALL *Univ. Europe Mid. Ages* II. II. 505 The certificate of 'scholarity' was to be refused if the applicant's Latinity proved unequal to the strain.

'scholarize, *v. rare*$^{-1}$. [f. SCHOLAR + -IZE.] *intr.* To study at a university.

1894 J. H. WYLIE *Hist. Eng. Hen. IV*, II. 359 Thomas Gascoigne, a sickly youth then scholarizing at Oriel.

'scholarless, *a. rare*$^{-1}$. [-LESS.] Without scholars or pupils.

1887 RUSKIN *Præterita* II. 310 Turner being..lawless alike and scholarless.

'scholarlike, *a.* and *adv.* [-LIKE.] **A.** *adj.*

†**1.** Pertaining to scholars or 'the schools'; scholastic. *Obs.*

1577 tr. *Bullinger's Dec.* v. iv. 895 We do not meane a childlike and scholerlike examination [orig. *examen..puerile et scholasticum*]. **1580** HOLLYBAND *Treas. Fr. Tong, Scholastique*, scholerlike. **1592** NASHE *Strange Newes* D 3, They..bad him performe all the Schollerlike ceremonies and disputatiue right appertaining thereto.

2. Resembling or befitting a scholar or learned man; scholarly.

1589 *Marprel. Epitome* B 1 b, What cannot a smooth tongue, and a schollerlike wit bring to passe? **1672** DRYDEN *Def. Epil.* in *Conq. Granada* II. 172 Truewit was a Scholar-like kind of man. **1734** A. A. SYKES *2nd Defence, Dissert. Phlegon* 6, I shall always acknowledge the schollarlike manner in which they have both wrote. **1858** MOTLEY *Let.* 28 May, *Corr.* (1889) I. 227 Stirling..is mild, amiable, bald-headed, scholarlike. **1862** MAX MÜLLER *Chips* (1880) I. ix. 195 He set to work in a more scholarlike spirit.

†**B.** *adv.* Like a scholar or learned man; in a manner befitting a scholar. *Obs.*

1551 T. WILSON *Logike* Bj b, Euery mans wit, can geue lightly a reason of diuers thinges,..& yet not be able to set the same in order Scholerlike, either to proue, or to confute. **1589** *Marprel. Epitome* B 1 b, Wherein he hath behaued himselfe verye scholerlike. **1627** ABP. ABBOTT *Narr.* in Rushw. *Hist. Coll.* (1659) I. 441, I pray you tell his Majesty that I am dealt with neither Manly nor Scholar-like.

So †**scholar-likely** *adv.*

1599 H. BUTTES *Dyets Drie Dinner* To Rdrs. Aa 2 b, Thus very rudely, I obtrude vnto thee not a banquet, but a byt rather of each dish Scholler-likely, that is, badly carued. For Schollers are bad Caruers.

scholarliness ('skɒləlɪnɪs). [f. SCHOLARLY + -NESS.] Scholarly quality or character.

1611 COTGR., *Scholarité*, schollership, schollerlinesse. **1868** MISS YONGE *Cameos* (1877) I. xviii. 132 That mixture of scholarliness and high spirit that was inherent in the Norman and Angevin princes. **1906** *Hibbert Jrnl.* Oct. 54 The writer's argumentative force and facile scholarliness.

scholarly ('skɒləlɪ), *a.* [f. SCHOLAR + -LY^1.]

Not in Johnson or Todd.

Pertaining to, or characterizing, a scholar; befitting, or natural to, a scholar; learned, erudite.

1638 PEACHAM *Valley of Variety* Ep. Ded., They are compact of rarieties, to enable ingenious and schollerly discourse. **1821** SCOTT *Kenilw.* xii, And learned Master Mumblazen, too, can say scholarly things of their inferiority. **1863** GEO. ELIOT *Romola* vii, The scholarly poet's temper [got] more and more venomous. **1908** R. BRIDGES *Sel. Poems R. W. Dixon* (1909) p. xix, A tallish elderly figure, its litheness lost in a slight, scholarly stoop.

scholarly ('skɒləlɪ), *adv. rare.* [f. SCHOLAR + -LY^2.] As befits a scholar.

1598 SHAKS. *Merry W.* I. iii. 2 What saies my Bully Rooke? speake schollerly, and wisely. **1868** *Contemp. Rev.* IX. 287 The revision is carefully and scholarly done. **1903** KIPLING *5 Nations* 50 We shall harness horses (Death's own pale horses) and scholarly plough the sands.

scholarment ('skɒləmənt). *nonce-wd.* [-MENT.] Scholardom; scholars collectively.

1922 JOYCE *Ulysses* 416 Toil on, labour like a bandog and let scholarment and all Malthusiasts go hang.

scholarship ('skɒləʃɪp). Forms: see SCHOLAR. [-SHIP.]

1. a. The attainments of a scholar; learning, erudition; esp. proficiency in the Greek and Latin languages and their literature. Also, the collective attainments of scholars; the sphere of polite learning.

1589 NASHE *Pref. Greene's Menaphon* (Arb.) 16–17 [T. Atchelow] hath more than once or twise manifested his deepe witted schollership in places of credit. **1624** GATAKER *Transubst.* 75 He hath a singular piece of Schollership by himselfe to justify his Exposition. **1784** COWPER *Tiroc.* 280 Ye once were justly fam'd for bringing forth Undoubted scholarship and genuine worth. **1823** D'ISRAELI *Cur. Lit.* Ser. II. (1851) 313 Scholarship has hitherto been a term reserved for the adept in ancient literature. **1887** RUSKIN *Præterita* II. 18 His memory (the necessary instrument of great scholarship) errorless and effortless.

b. Applied, by unlearned speakers, etc., to educational attainments of a more modest character.

1620 ROWLANDS *Nt. Raven* 8 Then for my schollership a gentleman, Both reade and write, and cast a count I can. **1650** COWLEY *Guardian* I. iii, Hast thou scholarship enough to make a Brewers clerk? **1758** JOHNSON *Idler* No. 26 ¶6 My reputation for scholarship..was..considered as a crime. **1860** WARTER *Sea-board* II. 30, I did not tell you what the lady said to me on my telling her I was no scholar. 'Never mind that,' said she... 'Your no scholarship is no hindrance if you are only faithful.'

†**c.** 'Literary education' (J.). *Obs. rare.*

1644 MILTON *Educ.* 3 This place should be at once both School and University, not needing a remove to any other house of Schollership, except it be some peculiar Colledge of Law, or Physick.

2. a. The status or emoluments of a scholar (see SCHOLAR 4) at a school, college, or university.

1535–6 *Act 27 Hen. VIII*, c. 42 §1 The..Felowshippes Scolershippes Dimishippes..within the said Universities. *a* **1583** SIR H. GILBERT *Q. Eliz. Achad.* (1869) 10 And also the other vniuersities shall then better suffize to releive poore schollers, where now the youth of nobility and gentlemen, taking vp their schollarshippes and fellowshippes, do disapoincte the poore of their livinges and avauncementes. **1746** T. WARTON *Progr. Discontent* 23 A Scholarship but half maintains, And College Rules are heavy Chains. **1829** R. GILBERT *Liber Scholast.* 3 Craven Scholarships. *Ibid.* 5 Dean Ireland's Scholarships. **1857** HUGHES *Tom Brown* I. vi, I know I'd sooner win two School-house matches running than get the Balliol scholarship any day. **1884** J. F. MOSS *Handbk. New Code* 78 What are called Elementary School Scholarships. **1861** J. S. WATSON *Life Porson* xx. 239 He was sent, on a scholarship, to Jesus College, Cambridge.

b. *spec.* (though *loosely*) The 'eleven-plus' examination or the entrance to a grammar school made possible by reaching a satisfactory standard.

1959 in I. & P. Opie *Lore & Lang. Schoolch.* xi. 227 On the day I went to sit the scholarship I took the little owl and wrapped it up in a handkerchief in my pocket for luck. **1959** I. & P. OPIE *Ibid.* xvi. 356 Today the sharpest feeling is between the grammar schools and the secondary moderns, that is, between those who have gained a scholarship and those who have not in the eleven-plus examination. **1966** J. PARTRIDGE *Middle School* iv. 59 In Middle School the eleven plus is still viewed as 'the scholarship'.

3. *attrib.* and *Comb.*, as (sense 2) ***scholarship boy, -candidate, child, class, exam, kid, paper, system***; **scholarship level** = *S-level* s.v. S I. 4 a.

1959 T. S. ELIOT *Elder Statesman* I. 31 A scholarship boy from an unknown grammar school. **1980** R. F. FOSTER in Lyons & Hawkins *Ireland under Union* 254 'Scholarship boys' in politics. **1965** N. COGHILL in J. Gibb *Light on C. S. Lewis* 65 What it was learned to know in 1950 will be expected of scholarship-candidates in 2000. **1964** D. HOLBROOK *English for the Rejected* 4 The attempt to turn every child into a 'scholarship child' fit for academic education. **1966** J. PARTRIDGE *Middle School* v. 79 In the Junior School a 'scholarship' class soon emerges. **1959** in I. & P. Opie *Lore & Lang. Schoolch.* xi. 227, I took it to the scholarship exam for the grammar school and I passed. **1977** M. WALKER *National Front* 8 My education as a scholarship kid who went to grammar schools and won a scholarship to Oxford. **1947, 1963** Scholarship level [see ORDINARY *a.* 5 e]. **1832** J. ROMILLY *Diary* 26 Apr. (1967) 11 Worked at the Scholarship papers all day. **1927** CARR-SAUNDERS & JONES *Social Structure Eng. & Wales* xi. 119 We must also attempt to analyse the working of the free-place and scholarship system.

†**scho'laster.** *Obs.* [a. med.L. *scholaster*, ad. OF. *scolaistre, escolastre* (mod.F. *écolâtre*), altered form of *escolaste*, a. L. *scholasticus*: see next.] The holder of a prebend in a cathedral, to which certain teaching duties were attached.

In quot. 1793 app. used loosely for a scholastic divine.

1732 *Hist. Litteraria* IV. 298 The old Translators..have render'd it [*Ecolâtre*] by a very unusual term, viz. the Scholaster Anselm. **1793** D'ISRAELI *Cur. Lit.* II. 63 The inexpugnable ignorance and superstition of the ancient heathens,..and of the popish scholasters and canonists.

scholastic (skəʊ'læstɪk, skɒ-), *a.* and *sb.* [ad. L. *scholasticus*, a. Gr. σχολαστικός studious, learned, subst. a learned man, scholar, f. σχολάζειν to devote one's leisure (to learning), orig. to be at leisure, f. σχολή leisure: see SCHOOL *sb.*

Cf. F. *scolastique*, Pr. *escolastic*, Sp. *escolástico*, It. *scolastico*, G. *scholastisch* adj., *scholastiker* sb.]

A. *adj.*

†**1.** Of persons: Having the characteristics of the scholar or student, as distinguished from the man of affairs. *Obs.*

1641 MILTON *Reform.* II. 72 Then shall the Nobles possesse all the Dignities and Offices of temporall honour to them-selves, sole Lords without the improper mixture of Scholastick, and pusillanimous upstarts, the Parliament shall void her Upper House of the same Annoyances [etc.].

2. Of or pertaining to the teaching or methods of the Schoolmen.

1596 DALRYMPLE tr. *Leslie's Hist. Scot.* II. 13 This man [Duns Scotus] meruellouslie amplifiet and helpet the scholastik Theologie. **1644** MILTON *Educ.* 2, I deem it to be an old errour of universities not yet well recover'd from the Scholastick grosnesse of barbarous ages, that..they present their..novices at first comming with the most intellective abstractions of Logick and metaphysicks. **1712** S. CLARKE *Script. Doctr.* II. 349 The Scholastick Writers in later Ages, have generally put this matter upon another Foot. **1759** GOLDSM. *Pres. State Pol. Learn.* xi. Wks. (Globe) 443/2 The absurdities of scholastic philosophy. *Ibid.* 444/1 This slowness of conferring degrees is a remnant of scholastic barbarity. **1770** BURKE *Pres. Discont.* Wks. II. 340, I remember an old scholastick aphorism, which says, 'that the man who lives wholly detached from others, must be either an angel or a devil'. **1842** *Penny Cycl.* XXIV. 329/2 Those of the former class [of active mind] sought for satisfaction in the scholastic philosophy... It was for the most part a revival of the philosophy of Aristotle. **1873** W. G. WARD *Ess. Philos. Theism* (1884) I. 160 On this particular there is no difference of doctrine, but only of words, between other writers of the scholastic following and the philospher of Königsberg. **1884** PENNINGTON *Wiclif* iii. 120 He is answering in a scholastic manner those who had attacked him with the weapons of the schoolmen.

3. Pertaining to schools or school education.

1647 CLARENDON *Hist. Reb.* I. §96 The Bishop of Lincoln ..a man of great wit, and good Scholastick learning. **1691** LUTTRELL *Brief Rel.* (1857) II. 241 The queen has sent a letter to the vicechanceller of Cambridge, to have an account what persons in any scholastick preferments have not taken the oaths. **1751** JOHNSON *Rambler* No. 137 ¶11 It is too common for those who have been bred to the scholastick profession..to disregard every other qualification. **1791** BOSWELL *Johnson* an. 1759 I. 190 *note*, Mr. Muller, of Woolwich Academy, the scholastick father of all the great engineers which this country has employed for forty years. **1845** R. W. HAMILTON *Pop. Educ.* vii. (ed. 2) 157 Bavaria.. has reached the eighth of its people in the number of its scholastic youth. **1855** MACAULAY *Hist. Eng.* xiii. III. 297 Carstairs..united great scholastic attainments with great aptitude for civil business. **1870** DICKENS *E. Drood* iii, A dainty room, with nothing more directly scholastic in it than a terrestial and a celestial globe.

4. Following the methods of the 'schools'; befitting the school; in bad sense, 'pedantic, needlessly subtle' (J.).

1779 JOHNSON *L.P., Cowley* Wks. II. 28 The following lines of Donne..have something in them too scholastick. **1820** HAZLITT *Lect. Dram. Lit.* 266 It [Sidney's *Arcadia*] is not romantic, but scholastic; not poetry, but casuistry. **1869** J. MARTINEAU *Ess.* II. 56 The perspicuous good sense and scholastic precision of Whately. **1871** EARLE *Philol. Eng. Tongue* §251 The modifying words especially..look very much like scholastic products.

B. *sb.*

1. A Schoolman or a disciple of the Schoolmen; a representative or adherent of the scholastic philosophy.

1644 MILTON *Divorce* Introd. 5 Doubt not, worthy Senators, to vindicate the sacred honour and judgment of Moses your predecessor, from the shallow commenting of Scholasticks and Canonists. **1794** SULLIVAN *View Nat.* I. 97 Aristotle, Gassendus, Des Cartes, with the numerous family of the scholastics, all ran into the same trackless error. **1818** HALLAM *Mid. Ages* (1872) III. 426 It was not only a knowledge of Aristotle that the scholastics of Europe derived. **1875** LONGF. *Monte Cassino* vi, In its streets The Angelic Doctor as a school-boy played, And dreamed perhaps the dream that he repeats In ponderous folios for scholastics made. **1907** *Academy* 30 Nov. 184/2 In the year 1907..one must hesitate to discuss Antonio Rosmini—the last of the Scholastics.

†**2.** A scholar, man of learning; *occas.* a mere scholar, as opposed to a man of the world. *Obs.*

1657 *Idiota's Div. Love* Ded. 2 They perswade themselues ..that hee hath taught you more high, and euident truths,.. then all the subtile Scholasticks and subtle politicks put together could haue done. **1710** STEELE *Tatler* No. 244 ¶2 The Town Orators..despise all Men as unexperienced Scholasticks who wait for an occasion before they speak. **1748** HUME *Ess. Mor. & Polit.* (ed. 3) 223, I..am in Danger ..of passing for a Pedant and Scholastic.

†**3.** = SCHOLASTER. *Obs. rare*$^{-1}$.

1844 CRAIK *Sk. Hist. Lit. Eng.* I. 49 In 1179 it was ordered ..that in every cathedral there should be appointed and maintained a head teacher, or scholastic.

4. *Hist.* (repr. Gr. σχολαστικός). In the Byzantine Empire, an advocate.

1846 *Penny Cycl.* Suppl. II. 558/1 Socrates, the ecclesiastical historian..followed the profession of scholastic or advocate.

5. *R.C. Ch.* A member of the third grade in the organization of the Society of Jesus.

1876 J. MORRIS in J. H. Pollen *Life* (1896) 181 Three different communities under one Rector—the novices, scholastics, and Tertian Fathers. **1881** *Memorials Stonyhurst College* iii. 21 The English Jesuits had another College in Belgium, at Liège. This was for the higher studies of their own scholastics.

6. An artist who adheres to 'scholastic' or academic methods.

1892 *Daily News* 30 Apr. 6/2 Idealists and naturalists, scholastics and impressionists, were necessarily exclusive when each was struggling for the ascendant, and claiming for its school the possession of the truth.

†**scho'lastical,** *a.* and *sb. Obs.* Also 5–6 sco-, 6 sko-. [Formed as prec. + -ICAL.] **A.** *adj.*

1. *Story Scholastical*: tr. med.L. *Historia Scholastica*, the title of a work by Petrus Comestor.

1432–50 tr. *Higden* (Rolls) IV. 367 Also hit is redde in the story scolasticalle, that [etc.].

2. Following the teaching of the Schoolmen; pertaining to Scholasticism. = SCHOLASTIC A. 2.

1551 CRANMER *Answ. to Gardiner* III. 73 So you condemn of madnes not onely al yͤ scholastical doctors..but also your own former saieng. **1599** SANDYS *Europæ Spec.* (1632) 155 Which scholasticall subtilities plaine suiteres doe not love. **1639** ROUSE *Heav. Univ.* ii. (1702) 18 The Scholastical Commentators living in those which are called the dark ages of the Church. **1669** BARROW *Expos. Creed* (1697) 14 *margin*, This scholastical acception is not ancient.

3. Following the methods of the 'schools'; befitting the school, academic; in bad sense, pedantic, unduly formal or subtle.

1531 FRITH *Judgm. Tracy* Wks. (1573) 79 A proper distinction, by the whiche you may escape the scholasticall snares and mases. **1538** STARKEY *England* I. iii. 69 Thys vnyuersal and scolastycal consyderatyon of a veray and true commyn wele lytyl schal profyte. *a* **1583** SIR H. GILBERT *Q. Eliz. Achad.* (1869) 2 For of what Comodity such vse of arte wilbe in our tounge may partely be seene by the scholasticall rawnesse of some newly Commen from the vniuersities. **1614** RALEIGH *Hist. World* IV. vii. §2. 298 A matter of such consequence, as was not to bee omitted, in regard of any scholasticall disputation. *a* **1626** BACON *Controv. Ch. Eng.* Resuscit. (1657) 177, I speak not of the vain, Scholasticall, Manner of Preaching. **1679** EVELYN *Diary* 4 Apr., The Bishop of Gloucester preach'd, in a manner very like Bishop Andrews, full of divisions, and scholastical, and that with much quicknesse. **1793** D'ISRAELI *Cur. Lit.* II. 37 Terms of art and scholastical expressions.

4. Belonging or attached to a place of learning; academic. = SCHOLASTIC A. 3.

1536 BOORDE *Let.* in *Introd. Knowl.* (1870) 59 In the partes þat I am yn, þe kynges grace hath many, ȝe, (& in maner) all maner of persons (exceppt some skolastycall men) þat be hys aduersarys. **1594** HOOKER *Eccl. Pol.* Pref. v. §1 The fauour of proposing there in conuenient sort whatsoeuer ye can obiect (which thing my selfe haue knowen them [*sc.* the schools in universities] to graunt of Scholasticall courtesie vnto strangers) neither hath (as I thinke) nor euer will (I presume) be denied you. **1612** BRINSLEY *Lud. Lit.* xiii. 174 And the rather haue I bin careful to seek out the easiest and plainest way, that I might allure & draw on my schollars in this exercise,..to proceed as in a scholasticall play, with vnderstanding, loue and delight. *a* **1672** WOOD *Life* (O.H.S.) I. 129 A. W...did never afterwards care to hear of New Coll. school to have given him scholastical education but applied all that he had to that of Thame. **1673** RAY *Journ. Low C.* 36 No Scholastical Habits as Gowns or Caps worn by the Students [in Leyden].

†**B.** *sb.* = SCHOLASTIC B. 1. *Obs. rare*$^{-1}$.

1565 JEWEL *Repl. Harding* 259 There is Scotus againste Thomas:..the Nominales against the Reales: the Scholasticalles against the Canonistes.

scholastically (skəʊ'læstɪkəlɪ, skɒ-), *adv.* [f. SCHOLASTICAL + -LY^2.] In a scholastic manner; like a Schoolman; in the manner characteristic of the schools or of schoolmasters.

1559 BERCHER *Nobility Women* (Roxb. Club 1904) 114 Ye muste geve me leave to speake a lyttle Scolastycallye. *a* **1619** FOTHERBY *Atheom.* Pref. 8 Dealing onely Scholastically, by way of Logicall Arguments. **1711** SHAFTESB. *Charac.* Misc. III. i. 141 When our Princes and Senators became Scholars, they spoke scholastically. **1812** L. HUNT in *Examiner* 9 Nov. 716/1 Poets and others who have been scholastically brought up. **1882–3** *Schaff's Encycl. Relig. Knowl.* III. 2221 The old-fashioned, scholastically developed Lutheran orthodoxy.

scholasticate (skəʊ'læstɪkeɪt, skɒ-). *Eccl.* [ad. mod.L. *scholasticātus* (*u* stem), f. *scholastic-us* SCHOLASTIC *a.*: see -ATE[1].] A house of studies for members of the third grade in the Society of Jesus.

1875 J. MORRIS *Troub. Cath. Forefathers* Ser. II. 280 Wherever he went he found the fathers who had been with him in the Novitiate or Scholasticate, now Rectors and Superiors. **1895** *Month* July 101 Let it be placarded in the novitiates and colleges and scholasticates the world over.

†**scho'lasticated,** *a.* *Obs.* *rare*$^{-1}$. [f. SCHOLASTIC + -ATE[3] + -ED[1].] Filled with subtleties.

1772 NUGENT tr. *Friar Gerund* II. i. 270 Seeing Friar Toribio so scholasticated with these vain sophistries.

scholasticism (skəʊ'læstɪsɪz(ə)m, skɒ-). [f. SCHOLASTIC + -ISM.]

1. The doctrines of the Schoolmen; the predominant theological and philosophical teaching of the period A.D. 1000–1500, based upon the authority of the Christian Fathers and of Aristotle and his commentators.

1756–82 J. WARTON *Ess. Pope* (ed. 4) I. vi. 313 But the talents of Abelard were not confined to theology, jurisprudence, philosophy, and the thorny paths of scholasticism. **1854** MILMAN *Lat. Chr.* VI. ii. (1864) III. 389 Erigena.. the parent of scholasticism.. as a free discursive Speculative Science, before it had been bound up with rigid orthodoxy.

2. Servile adherence to the methods and teaching of the schools; narrow or unenlightened insistence on traditional doctrines and forms of exposition.

1861 HOLLAND *Lessons in Life* x. 146 He found his county tied up in formalism, scholasticism, and tradition, and by strokes as remarkable for boldness as strength he set it free. **1878** BAYNE *Purit. Rev.* ii. 47 This argument.. was quite in the manner of seventeenth century scholasticism. **1879** FARRAR *St. Paul* I. 127 Contact with the world had.. enabled them so far to raise their heads out of the heavy fog of Jewish scholasticism. **1884** HUNTER tr. *Reuss' Hist. Canon* 341 The unattractive form of the works it produced has in general the stamp of a dull, dry scholasticism.

scholasticized (skəʊ'læstɪsaɪzd, skɒ-), *ppl. a.* [f. as next: see -ED[1].] Imbued with or influenced by scholasticism.

1923 C. SINGER in *Edin. Rev.* Jan. 101 Dioscorides, the drug-monger, appealed to scholasticised minds for centuries. **1927** W. R. INGE *Protestantism* 12 This philosophy, already scholasticised by Proclus, became.. a coherent body of doctrine.

scholasticizing (skəʊ'læstɪsaɪzɪŋ, skɒ-), *ppl. a.* [f. **scholasticize* vb. (f. SCHOLASTIC + -IZE) + -ING[2].] Inclining to or favouring scholastic principles.

1857 BADEN-POWELL in *Oxford Ess.* 174 The lingering remains of the old scholasticizing spirit. **1908** *Contemp. Rev.* Aug. 187 These and other baleful consequences of the scholasticising and centralising tendencies inaugurated by Pope Pius IX.

†**scho'lasticly,** *adv.* = SCHOLASTICALLY.

1597 JAS. VI *Dæmonol.* To Rdr., But onelie, to speak scholasticklie.. I reason vpon *genus*, leauing *species* and *differentia* to be comprehended therein.

schold, obs. form of SCOLD *sb.*

schold(e, obs. pa. t. of SHALL *v.*, obs. ff. SHOAL.

†**schole.** *Obs.* *rare*$^{-1}$. Anglicized form of SCHOLIUM. (Cf. SCHOLY).

1565 W. ALLEN *Def. Purgatory* x. 98 Aske theime where these prety scholes were first picked.

schole, obs. form of SCHOOL, SHOVEL.

†**'scholian.** *Obs.* *rare*$^{-1}$. [? f. SCHOLI-UM + -AN.] = next.

1610 HEALEY *St. Aug. Citie of God* XIX. xii. Vives 768 Our scholians say that wee must neuer respect words in matter of diuinity or Philosophy.

scholiast ('skəʊlɪæst). [ad. late L. *scholiasta*, a. late Gr. σχολιαστής, f. σχολιάζειν (see SCHOLIAZE *v.*), f. Gr. σχόλι-ον SCHOLIUM. Cf. F. *scoliaste* (16th c. *scholiaste*), It. *scoliaste*.] One who writes explanatory notes upon an author; esp. an ancient commentator upon a classical writer.

In quot. 1820 perh. misused in the sense of 'schoolman' or 'scholastic' (as if = G. *scholast*). The mistake is not uncommon: cf. Funk's *Stand. Dict.* s.v., where the sense is recognized (with a quot. from C. Bucke 1837).

1583 FULKE *Def. Tr. Script.* iv. 137 They [the General Epistles] are not sent to any particular Church or persons, but to all in general, as the Greeke scholiast truly noteth. **1642** MILTON *Apol. Smect.* Wks. 1851 III. 282 Which the Masoreths and Rabbinicall Scholiasts not attending, have often us'd to blurre the margent with *Keri* instead of *Ketiv.* **1770** LANGHORNE *Plutarch* (1879) I. 143/2 The scholiast upon Thucydides tells us, Themistocles served the people of Corcyra. **1820** SCOTT *Monast.* xxxi, This is no vain question, devised by dreaming scholiasts, on which they may whet their intellectual faculties until the very metal be wasted away. **1837** HALLAM *Lit. Eur.* I. iv. §20 In this academy a Greek press was established, where the scholiasts on Homer were printed. **1866** GEO. ELIOT *F. Holt* Introd., He let it pass, with all the discreetness of an experienced theologian or learned scholiast, preferring to point his whip at some object which could raise no questions. **1880** SWINBURNE *Stud. Shaks.* 5 Least of all will the method of a scholiast be likely to serve him as a clue to the hidden things of Shakespeare.

fig. **1864** LOWELL *Fireside Trav.* 41 With what pride did we hail her [the ship's] return! She was our scholiast upon Robinson Crusoe and the Mutiny of the Bounty.

scholiastic (skəʊlɪ'æstɪk), *a.* and *sb.* *rare.* [f. SCHOLIAST + -IC.] **a.** *adj.* Of or pertaining to a scholiast. †**b.** *sb.* ? A scholiast (*obs.*).

1684 N. S. *Crit. Enq. Edit. Bible* App. 292 There is nothing that Simon has written concerning the public Notaries of the Hebrew Nation, but what these Diminitive Saints and nice Stomack'd Scholiasticks are extreamly offended at. **1891** SAINTSBURY *Polit. Verse* Introd. 15 They require.. a rather unusual amount of scholiastic annotation to render them intelligible to generations not their own.

†**'scholiˌasting.** *Obs.* *rare*$^{-1}$. [f. **scholiast* vb. (f. SCHOLIAST) + -ING[1].] The action of making a scholium; a commentary, annotation.

1678 CUDWORTH *Intell. Syst.* 212 The ancient Scholiasting upon him [*sc.* Hesiod], writ thus, that Hesiods Love was ὁ οὐράνιος ἔρως, ὅς καὶ Θεός.

†**'scholiaze,** *v.* *Obs.* *rare*$^{-1}$. [ad. late Gr. σχολιάζειν, f. σχόλι-ον SCHOLIUM.] *intr.* To write scholia, comment.

1645 MILTON *Tetrach.* 64 He.. who thinks to Scholiaze upon the Gospel.

†**'scholical,** *a.* *Obs.* *rare*$^{-1}$. [f. L. *scholic-us*, Gr. σχολικός (f. Gr. σχολή, L. *schol-a* SCHOOL *sb.*) + -AL[1].] Pertaining to schools, scholastic.

a **1656** HALES *Golden Rem.* (1688) 351 It is a common scholical error to fill our papers and note-books with observations of great and famous events.

†**scholi'ographer.** *Obs.* *rare*$^{-1}$. [f. late Gr. σχολιογράφ-ος, f. σχόλιον SCHOLIUM: see GRAPHER.] A writer of scholia.

1710 *Lond. Gaz.* No. 4656/3 Corrected.. by the help of ancient MSS. the best Editions, Scholiographers, &c.

‖**scholion** ('skəʊlɪən). Now *rare.* [Gr.: see SCHOLIUM.] = SCHOLIUM I.

1579 E. K. *Spenser's Sheph. Cal.* Ded., Hereunto haue I added a certain Glosse, or scholion, for thexposition of old wordes. **1616** T. BRIGHTMAN (*title*) The Revelation of S. Iohn illustrated with an Analysis and scholions. **1706** PHILLIPS (ed. Kersey). **1858** GLADSTONE *Homer* I. 53 An ancient Scholion, recently discovered, names four poets who worked under that prince [Pisistratus]. **1882** FARRAR *Early Chr.* II. 487 *note*, The opinion that the Lady is a Church is mentioned.. by an ancient scholion.

†**'scholist.** *Obs.* [? f. L. *schola* SCHOOL *sb.* + -IST. (But perh. an error for *sciolist*.)] ? One who has nothing but school training, a mere theorist.

1618 W. LAWSON *New Orch. & Gard.* (1623) 1 A Gardner... Concerning his skill, hee must not be a Scholist, to make shew of or take in hand that, which he cannot performe. **1671** PANTON *Spec. Juv.* 104 To breed Gentlemen at Schools, and in Learning, is the way to make them meer Scholists and Pedants.

‖**scholium** ('skəʊlɪəm). Pl. **scholia** ('skəʊlɪə); also 8 scholiums, 6–7 *erron.* scholias. [med.L., ad. Gr. σχόλιον SCHOLION, f. σχολή SCHOOL *sb.*[1] Cf. F. *scolie* fem. (from the med.L. plural) in sense 1, *scolie* masc. in sense 1 b.]

1. An explanatory note or comment; *spec.* an ancient exegetical note or comment upon a passage in a Greek or Latin author.

1535 JOYE *Apol. Tindale* (Arb.) 23 And when I shulde make scholias, notis, and gloses in the margent as himself and his master doith. **1660** HEYLIN *Hist. Quinquart.* II. 42 Mr. Fox was fain to make soom Scholia's on it, to reconcile a gloss like that of Orleance, which corrupts the Text. **1760–2** GOLDSM. *Cit. W.* cxiii, Almost every word admits a scholium, and a long one too. **1799** *Monthly Rev.* XXX. 136 Short Scholia are added to almost every chapter, containing various readings, or various translations, selected with much judgment and critical acumen. **1866** G. MACDONALD *Ann. Q. Neighb.* ix, Judy, however, did not choose to receive the laugh as a scholium explanatory of the remark. **1904** R. C. JEBB *Bacchylides* (Proc. Brit. Acad.) 9 From a scholium on the *Iliad* (24. 496) we know that Bacchylides spoke of Theano as having borne fifty sons to Antenor.

b. In certain mathematical works (e.g. Newton's *Principia*): A note added by the author illustrating or further developing some point treated in the text.

1704 J. HARRIS *Lex. Techn.* I, *Scholium*, is a remark made leisurely, and as it were by the by, on that Proposition, Subject or Discourse before advanced, treated of, or delivered. **1715** tr. *Gregory's Astron.* (1726) I. 23 Which is evident likewise concerning the Orbits of Mars, Jupiter and Saturn, from the Scholium to Prop. 9. **1741** WATTS *Improv. Mind* I. xiv, Some.. cast all their.. metaphysical and.. moral learning into the method of mathematicians, and bring every thing relating to those abstracted or those practical sciences under theorems, problems, postulates, scholiums, corollaries, &c. **1824–5** BARLOW in *Encycl. Metrop.* I. 314/2 A scholium is a remark applied to some preceding propositions, in order to point out their relative connection, or general utility and application.

¶**2.** ? A 'copy-book maxim', trite saying.

1830 MARRYAT *King's Own* xix, The old scholium, that 'too much familiarity breeds contempt'.

scholl, dial. var. SCHOOL *sb.*[2]

scholtrum, variant of SHELTRON.

†**'scholy,** *sb.* *Obs.* Also 6–7 scholie; 6 *pl.* schollies. [Anglicized form of SCHOLIUM. Cf. F. *scolie* (in 16th c. *scholie*).] = SCHOLIUM.

1549 BECKE *Bible* (1551) Ded., One.. commodious Byble is put furth wyth certayn sundry Prologues, schollies, or briefe Annotations. **1570** BILLINGSLEY *Euclid* title, Whereunto are annexed certaine Scholies, Annotations, and Inuentions, of the best Mathematiciens, both of time past, and in this our age. **1594** HOOKER *Eccl. Pol.* III. viii. §2 That Scholie had neede of a verie fauourable Reader and a tractable. *a* **1697** AUBREY *Lives* (1898) I. 100, I have added plaine declarations and examples, manifold additions, scholies, annotations, and inventions which I have gathered.

†**'scholy,** *v.* *Obs.* [f. SCHOLY *sb.*]

1. *trans.* To write scholia upon; to annotate.

1594 HOOKER *Eccl. Pol.* III. viii. §16 The dutie of their teachers.. must needes be somewhat more, then only to read the sentences of scripture, and then paraphrastically to scholie them. **1612** T. JAMES *Corrupt. Scripture* IV. 51 His Epistles are likewise censured and scholied in 2. places.

2. *intr.* To comment.

1597 HOOKER *Eccl. Pol.* V. xxii. §7 The very chiefest cause of committing the sacred word of God vnto bookes, is surmised to haue bene, least the Preacher should want a text whereupon to scholie. **1641** J. JACKSON *True Evang. T.* I. 7, I have prefaced and scholied sufficiently unto the Text, I come now to seek out [etc.].

scholzite ('ʃɒltsaɪt). *Min.* [ad. G. *scholzit* (H. Strunz 1948: see H. Strunz *Mineralogische Tabellen* (ed. 2, 1949) 164, and in *Fortschritte der Mineral.* (1950) XXVII. 31), f. the name of Adolf *Scholz*, 20th-cent. German mineral collector and industrialist: see -ITE[1].] A hydrated basic phosphate of calcium and zinc, $Ca_2Zn(PO_4)_2(OH)_2.H_2O$, occurring as a secondary mineral in colourless to greyish monoclinic crystals.

1950 *Chem. Abstr.* XLIV. 9306 (*heading*) Scholzite, a new mineral. **1974** *Mineral. Mag.* XXXIX. 686 Scholzite.. is the most common and conspicuous phosphate mineral in the mineralized zones at Reaphook Hill [in the Flinders Ranges, South Australia]. It occurs in voids as sprays of radiating white to colourless prismatic needles up to 3 cm long.. or as interpenetrating groups of white fibres.

schomache, schom(e, obs. ff. SUMACH, SHAME.

Schönbergian, var. SCHOENBERGIAN *a.* and *sb.*

schone, obs. pres. pl. of SHALL.

Schönlein ('ʃøːnlaɪn). *Path.* The name of Johann Lucas *Schönlein* (1793–1864), German physician, used in the possessive and occas. *attrib.* to designate a form of purpura associated with arthritis (described by him in 1837 (*Path. und Therapie* II. 48–49)); also used in combination with the name of *Henoch* (see HENOCH).

Schönlein's disease is now regarded as one form of Henoch-Schönlein purpura.

1892 W. OSLER *Princ. & Pract. Med.* ii. 318 The diagnosis of Schönlein's disease offers no difficulty... Schönlein's peliosis is thought by most writers to be of rheumatic origin. **1937** *Arch. Dermatol. & Syphilol.* XXXV. 847 (*caption*) Photomicrograph of a section from a lesion of purpura affecting the leg only of a patient with Schönlein-Henoch's purpura. **1943** ORMSBY & MONTGOMERY *Dis. Skin* (ed. 6) ii. 501 Peck describes the histological changes of four cases of Schönlein-Henoch's purpura as resembling those produced by venom. **1948**, etc. [see HENOCH]. **1974** *Encycl. Brit. Micropædia* VIII. 972/1 He [*sc.* Schönlein] was the first to describe the minute hemorrhages of the skin occurring in cases of anaphylactoid (allergic) purpura (Schönlein-Henoch purpura) and purpura rheumatica (Schönlein's disease; 1837), characterized by the appearance on the skin of small purple spots, by swelling pain, and tenderness of joints, and frequently by swelling of the hands, feet, or eyelids.

Schoodic ('skuːdɪk). The name of a lake on the borders of Maine and New Brunswick; used *attrib.* in ***Schoodic salmon*** or ***trout***, the name of a variety of salmon (*Salmo salar*, var. *sebago*) which inhabits landlocked lakes.

1883 G. B. GOODE *Rev. Fish. Industr. U.S.* (Fish. Exhib.) 69 Station for collecting eggs of the Schoodic salmon. **1884** —— *Nat. Hist. Aquatic Anim.* 470 The.. 'Fresh-water' Salmon, known.. in different parts of Maine as 'Schoodic Trout'.

school (skuːl), *sb.*[1] Forms: 1 scól (? scolu), 2–7 scole, 3–6 (in Comb.) scol, 3–7 schole, (4 cole), 4–5 skule, 4, 6 scoole, 4–6 skole, *Sc.* scule, 5 skoole, (scwylle), *Sc.* sculle, 5–6 scoll, *Sc.* scoulle, 6 skoll, scolle, *Sc.* scoile, scwle, scuil(l, schuill, schuile, scoill, skuil(l, 6–7 schoole, schoule, (scool), (7 *Sc.* scoull, scooll), 6– *Sc.* schule, 7– school. [OE. *scól* str. fem., a. L. *schola* (in Rom. pronunciation *scōla*) school, a. Gr. σχολή, orig. leisure, hence employment of leisure, study, and (in later use) a school. The L. word has been adopted in nearly all the Rom., Teut., and Celtic langs.: OF. *escole* (mod.F. *école*), Pr., Cat., Pg. *escola*, Sp. *escuela*, It. *scuola*, Romanian *şcoală*; OHG. *scuola* (MHG. *schuole*, mod.G. *schule*), MDu. *schole* (Du. *school*, mod.Fris. *skoalle*),

ON., MSw. *skóle* wk. masc. (Sw. *skola* fem., Da. *skole*); OIrish *scol* (mod.Ir., Gael. *sgoil*), Welsh *ysgol*, Breton *skol*; also Russ. *shkola*.

An OE. form *scolu* occurs once in the *OE. Chron.* (Parker MS.) an. 816. It is doubtful whether this is to be read as *scólu*, with irregular *u* due to some analogy, or as *scōlu*, which might be an adoption of L. *schŏla* with original short vowel (perhaps from the pronunciation of Britons: cf. Ælfric *Gramm.*, Præfatio). The OE. *scolu* troop (see SHOAL) which is often confused with this word, is certainly unconnected. The curious 14th. c. form *cole* is perh. aphetic from OF. *escole*.]

I. Place or establishment for instruction.

1. a. An establishment in which boys or girls, or both, receive instruction.

See also BOARDING-, CHARITY-, GRAMMAR-, INFANT-, PUBLIC, SUNDAY-SCHOOL; also *free school* (FREE *a.* 32b), *normal school* (NORMAL A. 3), etc.

c **1000** ÆLFRIC *Saints' Lives* (Skeat) I. 50 Eac þær leornode on þære ylcan scole se æðela Gregorius. *a* **1225** *Ancr. R.* 422 Ancre ne schal nout forwurðen scolmeistre, ne turnen hire ancre hus to childrene scole. *c* **1386** CHAUCER *Prioress' T.* 43 A litel scole of cristen folk ther stood.. in which ther were Children an heepe. *c* **1440** *Alphabet of Tales* 475 When he was a child and went vnto þe skule. **1512–13** *Acc. Ld. High Treas. Scotl.* IV. 404 Maister David Vocat, maister of the scule of Edinburgh. **1577** M. LOK in *Frobisher's Voy.* (Hakl. Soc.) 87 My late father.. kept me at scholes of grammer in England till I was xiij yeres olde. **1707** J. CHAMBERLAYNE *Pres. St. Gt. Brit.* III. xi. 386 There are in London divers endowed Schools, which in France would be stiled Colleges. **1784** COWPER (*title*) Tirocinium: or, A Review of Schools.

b. Used, without article, to mean: Instruction in, attendance at, a school. Chiefly in set phrases, as ***to be at school, to go to school, to put, send,*** † ***set to school***.

c **1000** *Sax. Leechd.* III. 184 Cildru on scole betæcen. *c* **1205** LAY. 9897 He wes isende to Rom to leornien in scole. ? *a* **1300** *Oxf. Student* 19 in *E.E.P.* (1862) 41 þis child was siþþe ido to scole. **13..** *S.E. Legendary* (MS. Bodl. 779) in *Archiv Stud. neu. Spr.* LXXXII. 337/17 Crissaunt.. to cole [so often in this MS.] gan to go. *c* **1430** LYDG. *Min. Poems* (Percy Soc.) 255, I hadde in custom to come to scole late. **1470–85** MALORY *Arthur* I. ii. 38 The thyrd syster.. was put to scole in a nonnery. *a* **1533** LD. BERNERS *Huon* cxvii. 419 He set me to scole to Parys. **1590** SHAKS. *Mids. N.* III. ii. 324 She was a vixen when she went to schoole. **1596** —— *Merch. V.* III. iv. 75 That men shall sweare I haue discontinued schoole Aboue a twelue moneth. **1751** JOHNSON *Rambler* No. 141 ¶5 From school I was dismissed to the University. **1846** DICKENS *Cricket on Hearth* i. 25 She and I were girls at school together. **1848** J. H. NEWMAN *Loss & Gain* I. xii, Some say that school is the pleasantest time of one's life. **1857** HUGHES *Tom Brown* II. v, The stock contrivances of boys for wasting time in school.

c. *fig.* in various phrases. ***to go to school*** **(*to*,** (now *rare*) ***with*)**: to submit to be taught (by). † ***to hold at school***: to have under one's control, to keep in tutelage. ***to put***, †***set to school***: to subject to teaching; often, to presume to correct (one's superior).

? **1404–8** *Man know thy self* 9 in 26 *Pol. Poems* 27 Lerne to dye, and go to skole, Siþ þou fro deþ may not fle. **1426** LYDG. *De Guil. Pilgr.* 16990 Tyl I hadde gone to Scole with Trybulacion. **1546** J. HEYWOOD *Prov.* (1867) 97 Why sonne thinkst thou me such a foole? That my childe shall set his mother to scoole? **1570–6** LAMBARDE *Peramb. Kent* (1826) 301 Wee must give these good fellowes leave (after their woonted manner) to set the Holy Ghost to schoole. **1605** SHAKS. *Lear* II. iv. 68 Wee'l set thee to schoole to an Ant, to teach thee ther's no labouring i' th' winter. **1643** SIR T. BROWNE *Relig. Med.* I. §15. 30 What reason may not goe to Schoole to the wisedome of Bees, Aunts, and Spiders? **1647** N. BACON *Disc. Govt. Eng.* I. vi. (1739) 14 Rome held now the most part of the Churches of Europe at School. **1697** DRYDEN *Virg. Georg.* III. 261 The Calf, by Nature and by Genius made To turn the Glebe, breed to the Rural Trade. Set him betimes to School. **1708** MOTTEUX *Rabelais* IV. xlvi, You must e'en go to School yet, you are no Conjurer, for ought I see. **1883** M. PATTISON *Milton's Sonnets* 46 Milton had put his poetical genius to school to the Italians, Dante, Petrarch, and the rest. **1959** *Listener* 3 Dec. 1005/1 Even those who cannot accept it entirely must assuredly go to school with him.

d. ***to*** †***hold, keep (a) school***: to be the master or mistress of a school. ***to teach (a) school*** (now *dial.* and *U.S.*): to teach in a school.

1390 GOWER *Conf.* II. 114 For whanne I schal myn yhen close, Anon min herte he wole oppose And holde his Scole in such a wise, Til it be day that I arise. **1426** LYDG. *De Guil. Pilgr.* 21105, I lernede my konnyng off Sathan, Wych halt hys scole nat hennys ffer. **1487** CAXTON *Bk. Gd. Manners* I. xvii. (W. de W. *c* 1515) E vj b, He became so poore that for to gete his lyuynge he taught the lesson and held scole to smale chyldren of Corynthye. **1565** COOPER *Thesaurus*, *Ludum aperire*, to beginne to keepe a schoole. **1590** C. OCKLAND in *Lett. Lit. Men* (Camden) 74, I teach schole at Grenewych. **1686** PARR *Life Usher* 75 Forbidding them, under great penalties to teach Schools. **1715** POPE *Iliad* I. *Ess. on Homer* 14 Phemius.. taught a School in Smyrna. **1740** J. CLARKE *Educ. Youth* (ed. 3) 169 The Business of Teaching School.. leaves but little Time for Study. **1770** GOLDSM. *Des. Vill.* 196 There.. The village master taught his little school. **1821** COMBE *Syntax, Wife* III. 47 An Elephant might keep a school. **1828–30** GODWIN in C. K. Paul *Life* (1876) II. 304 [Eugene Aram] keeps school at Netherdale. **1883** *Harper's Mag.* July 226/1 By keeping school.. she strove to provide for her.. family. **1891** J. F. KIRK *Suppl. to Allibone's Dict. Eng. Lit.* s.v. *Emerson*, He taught school for three years. **1893** LELAND *Mem.* I. 21 An infant school.. kept by the Misses Donaldson.

e. Proverbial phrases. ***to tell tales out of school*** (or †***the school***), †***forth of school***: said *lit.* of children (now *rare* or *obs.*); hence *fig.*, to betray damaging secrets. Also, † ***to tell out of school***.

1546 J. HEYWOOD *Prov.* (1867) 19 To tell tales out of schoole, that is hir great lust. **1579** GOSSON *Sch. Abuse* (Arb.) 24, I shoulde tel tales out of the Schoole, and bee Ferruled for my faulte, or hyssed at for a blab, yf I layde al the orders open before your eyes. **1629–30** in *Crt. & Times Chas. I* (1848) II. 65 We have some news at Cambridge, but it is too long to relate; besides, I must not tell tales forth of school. **1662** STILLINGFL. *Orig. Sacræ* I. iv. §10. 70, I am very prone to think that the ground of the great pique in some of the Greek writers against Herodotus, was, that he told too many tales out of School, and had discovered too much of the Infancy of Greece. **1679** C. NESSE *Antichrist* 221 Which book, were it extant.. would tell tales out of the school. **1690** J. NORRIS *Refl. Cond. Hum. Life* Ep. Ded. (1691) A 6 b, 'Tis well if I do not.. make them Angry with me for telling out of School. **1887** T. A. TROLLOPE *What I remember* II. vi. 102 A very handsome.. supper, at which, to tell tales out of school,.. the guests used to behave abominably. **1894** SIR J. ASTLEY *Fifty Yrs. Life* I. 31 Possessing a slight failing in the shape of 'telling tales out of school' as the saying is.

f. Used, without article, for: A session of school; the set time of attendance at school.

1598 SHAKS. *Merry W.* IV. i. 10 How now Sir Hugh, no Schoole to day? **1797** F. REYNOLDS *The Will* v. (ed. 3) 57 *Alb.* School's up! School's up! **1834** *Tracts for Times* No. 22. 5 It still wanted a considerable time to school. **1857** HUGHES *Tom Brown* II. iv, About ten minutes before school Martin and Arthur arrived in the quadrangle. **1881** O'SHAUGHNESSY *Songs of a Worker* 176 In yonder quiet ground against the church Where between schools the children play with flowers. **1893** LELAND *Mem.* I. 42 Keeping me in after school to study.

g. Those who are present in, or are attending, a school; the scholars of a school.

a **1300** *Cursor M.* 12476 All þe scole on him can wonder. **1857** HUGHES *Tom Brown* I. v, The whole school of three hundred boys swept into the big school to answer to their names.

h. Applied (with defining word, as ***upper, lower school***) to a division of a large school, comprising several forms or classes. Also, in Jesuit schools, a form or class.

1629 WADSWORTH *Pilgr.* iii. 15 The Students of the three under schooles, go up to those of the upper. **1857** HUGHES *Tom Brown* I. viii, The lower-fourth form.. was the largest form in the Lower school. **1857** *Act 20 & 21 Vict.* c. 84 Sched. §45 There shall be two schools, viz. an 'Upper School', and a 'Lower School' [at Dulwich]. **1880** *Macm. Mag.* No. 245. 423 The general students, or boys at Stonyhurst, are.. divided into seven forms, or, as they are called there, 'schools'.

i. The building in which a school is carried on. At Rugby, a school-house; also, the large classroom of a school-house.

1843 DICKENS *Christm. Carol* ii, The school is not quite deserted... A solitary child.. is left there still. **1857** HUGHES *Tom Brown* I. viii, There was another large unoccupied desk in the corner of the great school. *Ibid.* I. ix, They saw five or six nearly new balls hit on the top of the School. *Ibid.*, After one or two attempts, [they] scaled the schools.

j. high school. A designation applied (with some variety of use) to certain classes of schools for secondary education in the British Islands and the United States. Also *attrib.* Cf. -SCHOOLER.

The first school known to have been so designated in Great Britain is that established in Edinburgh in 1519. In the year of its foundation this is referred to in the records of the Town Council as 'the principale schule' and 'the principall gramer schule', and it had by municipal enactment the exclusive privilege of teaching the higher branches of school learning within the burgh. In 1531 it is mentioned as 'the hie schule' (see below); this appellation occurs frequently in the 16th c., and from the 17th c. onwards has continued to be the official name of the institution. About the middle of the 19th c. the name of 'High School' was given, in imitation of the example of Edinburgh, to the principal secondary school in many Scottish burghs; these schools having been for the most part either founded or reconstituted about that time. In the United States, the term seems to have come into use about 1824, and is applied to a class of schools to which pupils are admitted when they have completed their course in the elementary school, and which afford preparation for the college, the university, or the technical school. In England, when used without qualification, the designation 'High School' is understood to refer to the schools established and managed by the Girls' Public Day-school Company (founded 1874) and to some other schools similar to these in the method and character of the instruction given. The few schools for boys and co-educational schools in England that are known as 'High Schools' are chiefly of recent foundation. While a 'high school' in the American sense of the term gives advanced instruction only, the schools so designated in Britain usually include elementary classes.

1531 *Edinb. Town Council Rec.* 19 Mar., I. 38 a, Maister Adam Melvil maister of the hie Schule oblist him to mak the bairnys perfyte gramarians within thrie ȝeires. **1818** SCOTT *Hrt. Midl.* iii, The old Town-Guard of Edinburgh, who.. were, in my boyhood, the alternate terror and derision of the petulant brood of the High-school. **1826** *Acc. High School for Girls* (Boston, U.S.) 3 The English High School [for boys] has been in successful operation since 1821; and the satisfactory result of this experiment prepared the way for the establishment of the High School for Girls. **1844** EMERSON *Lect. New Eng. Reform.* Wks. 1884 I. 262 In a hundred high-schools and colleges. **1875** A. McDOWALL *Let.* 9 Oct. in V. E. Stack *Oxford High School* (1963) I. 1 At a special Council meeting.. it was resolved.. to open the Oxford High School on Wednesday November 3rd. **1893** WYLIE & BRISCOE *Popular Hist. of Nottingham* xii. 122 In.. 1868, the Free Grammar School was removed.. to.. Arboretum Street, and its designation was changed to that of 'The High School'. **1901** E. NESBIT *Wouldbegoods* i. 4 After the holidays the girls went to the Blackheath High School. **1933** V. BRITTAIN *Testament of Youth* I. i. 37 In the months before I went up to Oxford,.. I often privately condemned my parents for not sending me to Cheltenham, or Roedean, or even to an ordinary High School, where practised authorities would have saved me from the fret of wrestling with academic mysteries. **1970** G. TREASE *Nottingham* xviii. 213 The High School governors seemed boldly original in choosing a scientist,.. an appointment for a long time almost unique among schools represented on the Headmasters' Conference. **1974** M. SPACKMAN *Hist. Oxford Central Girls' School & Cheney Girls' Grammar School* iii. 43 In most years, two or more girls.. entered for and gained one of these places at either the High School or Milham Ford.

2. The place in which an ancient Greek or Roman philospher taught his hearers.

c **1375** *Sc. Leg. Saints* xxi. (*Clement*) 154 He.. ȝed full of[t].. to þe scule of phylosophy. **1549** *Compl. Scot.* Prol. 13 He persauand thir tua princis entir in his scule, he changit the mater of that present lecture. **1594** ASHLEY tr. *Loys Le Roy* 67 b, Alexander.. gaue to the Philosopher Anaxarchus to set vp his Schoole, a hundred talents. **1634** MILTON *Comus* 439 Or shall I call Antiquity from the old Schools of Greece To testifie the arms of Chastity? **1651** HOBBES *Leviath.* IV. xlvi. 369 Also the Philosophers them-selves had the name of their Sects, some of them from these their Schools. **1781** GIBBON *Decl. & F.* xvii. II. 40 The most famous school [of jurisprudence] was that of Berytus, on the coast of Phœnicia.

3. a. *gen.* An institution in which instruction of any kind is given (whether to children or adults). Often with defining word indicating the special subject taught, as *dancing, music, riding school*. In recent use, after French example, employed as the official title of various institutions for superior technical or scientific instruction, e.g. *The School of Mines, The School of Economics*, etc.

Also in the names of certain organizations established by various nations for the systematic prosecution of archæological research, as the British School at Athens and at Rome.

c **1440** *Promp. Parv.* 449/2 Scole, of pleyynge gamys, or werre, or other lyke.., *gignasium*. *c* **1570** *Pride & Lowl.* (1841) 48 Then to the Master of the daunsing schoole. **1565** COOPER *Thesaurus*, *Ludus gladiatorius*, a schoole of fence. **1579** GOSSON *Sch. Abuse* (Arb.) 46 The Senators of Rome.. caused Schooles of Defence to be erected in Capua. *a* **1583** SIR H. GILBERT *Q. Eliz. Achad.* (1869) 5 The.. Mathematician.. shall haue in his Schole a shippe and gallye, made in modell. **1641** EVELYN *Diary* 5 Oct., To this school join the music and mathematical schools. **1683** *Col. Rec. Pennsylv.* I. 93 Proposed that care be Taken, about the Learning and Instruction of Youth, to Witt, a scool of Arts and Siences. **1802** C. JAMES *Milit. Dict.* s.v., Royal Military School or College. **1816** J. SCOTT *Vis. Paris* (ed. 5) 232 The school of mines [in Paris]. **1835** *Rep. Sel. Committee on Arts & Manuf.* 35 They prayed for assistance towards establishing a school of design. **1845** DISRAELI *Sybil* III. viii, Lady Maud.. longed to teach in singing schools. **1886** C. E. PASCOE *Lond. of To-day* xxxvi. (ed. 3) 315 At Chatham.. is the School of Military Engineering.

b. *fig.*

1579 GOSSON (*title*) The Schoole of Abuse. **1589** R. HARVEY *Pl. Perc.* 10 Or else a free schoole of skolds shalbe set vp for the nonce. **1596** SHAKS. *Tam. Shr.* IV. i. 54 *Tra.* Faith he is gone vnto the taming schoole. *Bian.* The taming schoole: what is there such a place? **1605** *1st Pt. Jeronimo* I. iii. 23 From drinking schooles.. From dicing houses. **1690** (*title*) The School of Politicks; or the Humours of a Coffee-house. A poem. **1777** SHERIDAN (*title*) The School for Scandal. **1788** GIBBON *Decl. & F.* l. V. 190 The science of astronomy was cultivated at Babylon; but the school of the Arabs was a clear firmament and a naked plain. **1832** THIRLWALL in *Philol. Mus.* I. 495 The ancient rhetoricians were a class of babblers, a school for lies and scandal.

c. Formerly often adopted in the titles of manuals of instruction in particular subjects. Now only *Mus.*, as the title of an instruction-book dealing with a particular instrument.

1696 R. H. (*title*) The School of Recreation: or a guide to the most ingenious exercises of Hunting, Riding, Racing, Fireworks [etc.]. **1733** (*title*) The School of Miniature, erected for the instruction of the ignorant. **1845** E. HOLMES *Mozart* 7 The system of fingering laid down in this violin school.

d. *spec.* = *riding-school*. Hence [after F. *école*], the exercises or system of training for horses and riders practised in the schools. ***high school*** [= F. *haute école*]: the more difficult class of exercises taught in the schools.

1850 WAYTE *Equestrian's Man.* 5 Tuition, in the school alone, can seldom make a good rider. **1881** E. L. ANDERSON *How to Ride*, etc. Introd. 5 It is to be regretted that, in this nation of horsemen, riding as practised in the schools, should have fallen into disuse; for the *manège* is the foundation of horsemanship. **1884** —— *Mod. Horsemanship* 143 (*title of chapter*) The High School.

4. *fig.* **a.** A place, environment, etc., where one gains instruction or training in virtue, accomplishments, or the like; a person or thing regarded as a source of instruction or training.

c **1000** ÆLFRIC *Saints' Lives* (Skeat) I. 38 Her synd eac þa cnihtas.. mid ðam ic becom to cristes scole. *c* **1314** *Guy Warw.* 384 (Auchin. MS.) þou art y-tauȝt to a liþer scole. *c* **1374** CHAUCER *Troylus* I. 634 And þere thow wost þat I haue out myswent, Eschewe þou þat, for swych þyng to þe scole is. **1390** GOWER *Conf.* I. 174 As he which of the Scole of helle Is tawht. **1579** W. WILKINSON *Confut. Fam. Love* 1 b, Whether this family haue bene taught in the schole of the holy ghost, or in the schole of the Anabaptistes. **1583** BODY in J. H. Pollen *Acts of Engl. Martyrs* (1891) 55 From our school of patience, the 16th Sept., 1583 [i.e. from prison]. **1605** BACON *Adv. Learn.* I. 29 The Ægyptians; which Nation we know was one of the most ancient Schools of the world. **1656–63** DAVENANT *Siege of Rhodes* v. (1672) 64, I was bred in Natures simple School. **1671** MILTON *P.R.* III. 238 Empires, and Monarchs, and thir radiant Courts,

Best school of best experience. **1705** ADDISON *Italy* Pref., Italy..is the great School of Musick and Painting. **1759** GOLDSM. *Pres. St. Pol. Learn.* xi. Wks. (Globe) 443/2 They keep the student from the world, which, after a certain time, is the only true school of improvement. **1813** BYRON *Corsair* I. xi, Warp'd by the world in Disappointment's school. **1833** E. EVERETT *Orat.* (1850) I. 395 The men of 1776 were trained in the strictest school of British military discipline and conduct. **1840** MACAULAY *Ess., Clive* (1897) 534 A succession of commanders, formed in the school of Clive. **1849–50** ALISON *Hist. Eur.* xlix. §4 VIII. 3 The best of all schools—that of great operations and adverse fortune. **1856** EMERSON *Eng. Traits, First Visit* Wks. (Bohn) II. 5 He [Coleridge] said..that Sicily was an excellent school of political economy.

b. ***the school of hard knocks***, the experience of a life of hardship, considered as a means of instruction. *U.S. slang.*

1912 ADE *Knocking Neighbors* 24 They had been brought up in the School of Hard Knocks. **1931** *Kansas City Star* 23 Oct. 36/5 Fraternity brothers in the school of hard knocks. **1953** *Sun* (Baltimore) 5 Sept. 10/6 He has been through the school of hard knocks, and battled his way up with his fists to the top of fistiana. **1980** G. V. HIGGINS *Kennedy for Defense* xx. 178, I learned my business in the school of hard knocks.

5. a. The body of persons that are or have been taught by a particular master (in philosophy, science, art, etc.); hence, in wider sense, a body or succession of persons who in some department of speculation or practice are disciples of the same master, or who are united by a general similarity of principles and methods. Also, in descriptions of works of art, in phr. *school of* (an artist), used to designate an anonymous work produced in the school of a particular artist.

Sometimes (e.g. in *Roman, Venetian, Tuscan School*; *British, French, Flemish School*; with reference to painting), the term denotes in the first place those whose training was obtained in the same locality; but in the main this local association is understood to imply more or less community of doctrines or style.

1612 BACON *Ess., Atheism* (Arb.) 330 Most of all, that schoole which is most acused of Atheisme, doth demonstrate Religion. That is, the Schoole of Leusippus, and Democritus, and Epicurus. **1660** JER. TAYLOR *Worthy Communic.* i. §4. 66 If by faith we eat the flesh of Christ; as it is confessed by all the Schooles of Christians; then [etc.]. *a* **1680** BUTLER *Rem.* (1759) I. 217 A peripatetic Cobler scorn'd to soal A pair of Shoes of any other School. **1728** CHAMBERS *Cycl.*, *School*, in Painting, is a Term used to distinguish the different Manners of Places, and Persons: As, the Roman School, the Venetian School, the Flemish School, &c. **1771** SIR J. REYNOLDS *Disc.* iv. Wks. 1797 I. 61 The Roman, the Florentine, the Bolognese schools... These are the three great schools of the world in the epick stile. **1849** MACAULAY *Hist. Eng.* vii. II. 195 William Wycherley, the most licentious and hardhearted writer of a singularly licentious and hardhearted school. **1891** R. FRY *Let.* 17 May (1972) I. 145, I find..the Venetian School of painting far more instructive than the Florentine. **1903** *Ibid.* 16 Mar. 207 This, which was called 'School of Lorenzo', is Piero all over. **1958** *Spectator* 15 Aug. 219/2 An American school-of-Chayevsky drama about a jailbird's wife. **1976** D. FRANCIS *In Frame* ix. 135 Although they were original oil paintings, they were basically second rate. The sort sold as 'school of' because the artists hadn't bothered to sign them. **1981** M. SPARK *Loitering with Intent* ii. 56 She said, 'Is that a real Degas you have in your room?' 'School of,' I said.

b. *fig.* A set of persons, who agree in certain opinions, points of behaviour or the like. Cf. OLD SCHOOL.

1827 SCOTT *Chron. Canongate* vi, She did not hesitate to admit him to her boudoir, after the privilege of the French and the old Scottish school. **1844** THIRLWALL *Greece* lxiv. VIII. 295 He was a Roman of the new school, which studied to soften the homely roughness of the old Italian character.

c. In extended use of sense 5 a, in phr. ***school of thought*** (also †*opinion*). Also used (freq. *absol.*) with 'school' considered impersonally, a particular type of doctrine or practice as followed by such a body of persons.

1864 J. H. NEWMAN *Apol.* v. (1904) 173/1 There are various schools of opinion allowed in the Church: and on this point I follow others. **1873** *Illustr. London News* 26 July 70/2 It will not be necessary to utter a single word that need occasion offence to either of those 'schools of thought' into which The Church of England is divided. **1892** *New Review* May 571 He is a 'gentleman and scholar',..'trained in a liberal school of thought'. **1909** A. BERGET *Conquest of Air* II. v. 230 We are confronted by two schools of aviating apparatus: the American school..which demands everything of the aviator, and the French school..which requires..the minimum from the pilot. **1927** *Public Opinion* 28 Feb. 179/1 There is in philosophy a school of thought christened by Professor William James with the name Pragmatism. **1940** *Manch. Guardian Weekly* 5 Apr. 270 With two schools of thought existing in France on the subject of Russia, Molotoff's speech,..has produced two different sets of reactions. **1977** R. WILLIAMS *Marxism & Lit.* II. iv. 97 The theory became at once a cultural programme and a critical school. **1979** L. KALLEN *Introducing C.B. Greenfield* xii. 148 There's a school of thought that considers benevolent paternalism a little sick.

6. *slang.* **a.** (See quot. 1812.) **b.** A company of thieves or beggars working together.

1812 J. H. VAUX *Flash Dict.*, *School*, a party of persons met together for the purpose of gambling. **1842** *Impositions practised by Vagrants* 12 These lurkers generally go in schools, (companies) and will obtain from One to Two Pounds daily. **1851** MAYHEW *Lond. Labour* I. 244 He scraped acquaintance with a 'school of shallow coves'; that is, men who go about half naked, telling frightful tales about shipwrecks [etc.]. **1856** WYNTER *Cur. of Civ.* xii. (1860) 478 Inferior classes of thieves work in smaller 'schools,' say of a couple of women and a boy. *Ibid.* 481 What is called a 'school' of boys, who pick pockets in concert, under the eye of a master. **1859** *Slang Dict.*, *School*, or *Mob*, two or more 'patterers' working together in the streets. **1882** *Sydney Slang Dict.* 7/2 *School*, company of gamblers, mob of sharpers, and those who prey on the public. **1911** L. STONE *Jonah* II. vi. 213 He could think of nothing but the two-up school, which had swallowed all his spare money before he was married. **1946** A. MARSHALL *These are my People* 83 If I got into a school with some of the mugs round here they'd be penniless in two hours. **1952** H. INNES *Campbell's Kingdom* II. 230 Four of the boys had started a poker school. **1976** J. R. L. ANDERSON *Death in Desert* v. 87 Sometimes a few of the chaps would get a card school going after supper.

c. A group of persons drinking together in a bar or public house, and taking turns to buy the drinks.

1890 BARRÈRE & LELAND *Dict. Slang* II. 206/2 *School*,.. any small gathering of people generally bent on pleasure, as a school of drinkers in a public house or canteen. Much used by soldiers. **1911** R. MACAIRE *Disease & Remedy* 11 A 'school' got more from those that did not drink. **1951** *Landfall* V. 22 [She] goes across to join another school by the wall. **1963** W. H. PEARSON *Coal Flat* i. 21 He came up to the school Rogers was drinking with. **1971** D. LEES *Rainbow Conspiracy* v. 72, I..ordered a pint of bitter for myself. I didn't want to get into a school and I needed to think.

II. Senses of mediæval academic origin.

7. a. An organized body of teachers and scholars in one of the higher branches of study cultivated in the Middle Ages; *esp.* one of the various bodies of this kind which jointly constituted a university; a faculty. †In early use the article is commonly omitted after a preposition. Now in revived use within U.S. and some British universities (esp. those of recent foundation), a department, faculty, or course of study in a college or university. (Perh. influenced by senses 9 and 10.)

In the U.S. *school* is often used to designate either a department devoted to one subject or a grouping of several subject departments. It is also the standard designation for an institution providing postgraduate instruction in a particular subject (as *law school, medical school*, etc.). In recently founded universities in the U.K. *school* has been used to designate a department teaching a range of subjects traditionally taught separately.

c **900** *Bæda'a Hist.* III. xiii. (1890) 190 Sum leornungmon in scole [L. *scolasticus quidam*]. *c* **1380** WYCLIF *Sel. Wks.* I. 93 Siche doutes we shulden sende to þe scole of Oxenforde. *c* **1386** CHAUCER *Sompn. T.* 478 No maister, quod he, but seruitour, Thogh I haue had in scole swich honour. *c* **1440** *Alphabet of Tales* 105 He lefte þe logykk skule, & made hym a monk of Ceustus ordur. *c* **1449** PECOCK *Repr.* I. xvi. 88 Summe werers of pilouns in scole of dyuynyte han scantli be worthi for to be in the same scole a good scoler. **1617–20** MORYSON *Itin.* (1903) 319 The publike schoole at Strasburg was not reputed an universitie yet gave the degrees of Bachelors and Masters of Artes. **1651** HOBBES *Leviath.* IV. xlvi. 370 That which is now called an University, is..an Incorporation under one Government of many Publique Schools, in one and the same Town or City. In which, the principall Schools were ordained for the three Professions, that is to say, of the Romane Religion, of the Romane Law, and of the Art of Medicine. **1727** *Statutes Wm. & Mary Coll.* in Hofstadter & Smith *Amer. Higher Educ.* (1961) I. I. x. 43 Let there be four schools assigned within the college precincts. *Ibid.* 44 In the philosophy school we appoint two masters or professors. **1772** J. WITHERSPOON *Address Inhabitants Jamaica* in *Ibid.* II. x. 144 Two at least of the Professors of the justly celebrated Medical School lately founded in Philadelphia. **1835** J. MARTIN *Descr. of Virginia* 82 The different branches of science and literature..taught [at the University of Virginia] are styled *schools*. **1871** L. H. BAGG *Four Years at Yale* 32 Connected with the college are four professional 'schools' or 'departments', of which..the oldest is the Theological. **1894** *Rep. Commissioners Gresham Univ. London* p. xix, in *Parl. Papers 1893–4* (C. 7259) XXXI. 807 We propose that each of the teaching institutions which complies with the necessary conditions shall be admitted, either as a whole or in certain departments, as a School of the University [of London], that is as a School at which University courses of instruction are to be pursued. **1910** *Encycl. Brit.* XIII. 39/1 The medical school [of Harvard University]..dates from 1782, the law school from 1817, the divinity school..from 1819, and the dental school..from 1867. **1949** *Cavalier Daily* (Univ. of Va.) 22 Oct. 1/3 Williams graduated from the University in 1949 and is now in his second year of medical school at Johns Hopkins University in Baltimore. **1964** A. BRIGGS in D. Daiches *Idea of New University* iv. 62 The Schools [of the University of Sussex] were envisaged not as super-departments, to which 'subjects' were attached, but as centres of linked studies, some of which would be shared with other Schools. **1971** E. ASHBY *Any Person, any Study* ii. 71 Some British universities, in their enthusiasm to 'redraw the map of knowledge', have abolished departments and put in their place 'schools of study' (e.g. European studies, African studies, which include the history, economics, politics, language and literature, and geography of these regions). **1972** J. BEN-DAVID *Amer. Higher Educ.* vi. 87 Intellectually the graduate school had become the decisive influence in higher education by the beginning of this century. **1976** *Bull. Yale Univ.* 30 Dec. 163 The courses of study in Yale University are offered in twelve schools, as follows. Yale College (1701), which is the undergraduate school, the Graduate School (1847), School of Medicine (1810), Divinity School, [etc.].

b. *collect. plural.* (In later use always ***the schools.***) The faculties composing a university; universities in general; the sphere or domain of academic discussion or traditional academic doctrines and methods.

a **1400–50** *Alexander* 4610 Is þar na lare in ȝoure land, labour of scolis, Fesike, ne no philosofy. *c* **1449** PECOCK *Repr.* I. xvi. 89 Manye, whiche neuere leerned ferther in scolis than her grammer. **1535** STEWART *Cron. Scot.* (Rolls) I. 103 He..haittit all that cunnyng wer in scuillis. **1596** DALRYMPLE tr. *Leslie's Hist. Scot.* II. 111 That sik frehalderis..sulde susteine thair eldest sones at the schuilis, quhill perfytlie tha vndirstude the Canon lawis. *a* **1628** PRESTON *Breastpl. Love* (1631) 199 We learne at Schooles what to say in such a controversie, how to dispute rather than how to live. **1634** T. JOHNSON *Parey's Chirurg.* III. x. (1678) 62 Which I have sometimes shewed in the Physick Schools, at such times as I there dissected Anatomies. **1638** CHILLINGW. *Relig. Prot.* I. v. §63. 279 Boyes in the Schooles know, that *a Posse ad Esse*, the Argument followes not. **1644** DIGBY *Two Treat.* Ded. a iv, I haue not endeauoured to expresse my conceptions eyther in the phrase, or in the language of the schooles. **1649** LOVELACE *Lucasta* 84 And henceforth..Be able to dispute ith' field, And Combate in the Schooles. **1690** LOCKE *Hum. Und.* III. iii. §9. 192 This whole mystery of Genera and Species, which make such a noise in the Schools. **1701** SWIFT *Contests of Nobles & Comm.* Wks. 1755 II. I. 12 A mixed government partaking of the known forms received in the schools. **1774** BURKE *Sp. Amer. Tax.* (1775) 52 These are the arguments of states and kingdoms. Leave the rest to the schools; for there only they may be discussed with safety. **1785** COWPER *Task* II. 534 Is Christ the abler teacher or the schools?

†**c.** In various phrases, as ***to go to school***, to study at a university; ***man of school***, one who is versed in the learning of the schools; ***degree of school(s, in schools***, a university degree. *Obs.*

1377 LANGL. *P. Pl.* B. xx. 271 Enuye..heet freres to go to scole, And lerne logyk and lawe. *c* **1380** WYCLIF *Eng. Wks.* (1880) 427 Degre takun in scole makiþ goddis word more acceptable. *Ibid.* 428 So prestis wiþ-oute degre of scole may profite more þan don þes maystris. *Ibid.*, & þus men of scole trauelen veynly for to gete newe sutiltees. **1426** LYDG. *De Guil. Pilgr.* 11477 Thogh a man wer neuere so wys, And hadde lernyd at Parys, Thys thyrty yer at scole be In that noble vnyuersyte. **1451** *Rolls of Parlt.* V. 222/2 After the degrees in Scoles singulerly of the seide Scolers. **1513** DOUGLAS *Æneis* I. Prol. 381 Amange clerkis in scule. **1591–5** SPENSER *Col. Clout* 702 A filed toung, furnisht with tearmes of art, No art of schoole, but Courtiers schoolery. **1611** CORYAT *Crudities* 392 Though it be no Vniuersitie to yeeld degrees of Schoole to the students. **1638** BP. MOUNTAGU *Art Enq. Visit.* A 4, Of what degree in schools is he?

†**d.** ***to hold*** or ***keep schools***: to engage in academic disputation or discussion. *Obs.*

c **1460** SIR R. ROS *La Belle Dame* 329 In fayre langage,.. which ye and mo holde scoles of dayly. **1533** MORE *Debell. Salem* Wks. 949/2 We wyl in this matter keepe no longe scholes. **1567** JEWEL *Def. Apol.* III. 345 Wherefore doo your Doctours keepe sutche hote Schooles emongst them selues.

†**e.** *pl.* with sing. construction: An assembly of the 'schools' of a university, a public disputation.

c **1470** GREGORY in *Hist. Coll. Cit. Lond.* (Camden) 229 Mayster Halden kept the scholys with in the Fryers and dysputyd a gayne a Gray Fryer..; and at that scholys were many grete docters and clerkys to geve hym audyens.

f. *U.S.* A college or university. Also in phrases *to go* (†*put*) *to school*, to attend (send to) college or university.

1767 P. V. FITHIAN *Jrnl. & Lett.* (1900) 1 A letter to my Father, begging him to put me to School. **1904** *Delineator* Oct. 657 College pillows..of crimson, with 'Harvard', in white letters; of orange, with 'Princeton' in black, and similarly with the names and colours of other schools. **1957** A. BUCHWALD *Brave Coward* 54, I am more American than you are. I even went to school on the GI Bill of Rights, in Rome. I got an honorable discharge from the Army. **1962** —— *How much is that in Dollars?* p. ix, When friends.. assured me the streets of Paris were paved with mattresses, I decided to finish up my last year of schooling there... But while we were going to school..Congress passed the monumental Marshall Plan. **1967** *Boston Sunday Herald* 26 Mar. II. 5/6 (*caption*) Oxford crewman J. K. Mullard waves jubilantly after victory over traditional rival Cambridge... Oxford won by three lengths in 113th meeting between the schools. **1977** I. SHAW *Beggarman, Thief* I. vi. 76 The proms at which he played the trumpet in the band, to help pay his way through school. **1978** *Sci. Amer.* July 15/2 The latter experience convinced him that his interest lay in research; he therefore went back to school, acquiring his Ph.D. from Stanford University in 1965.

8. ***the School, the Schools***: the Schoolmen, the scholastic philosophers and theologians collectively. Now *rare* or *Obs.*

a **1614** DONNE *Βιαθανατος* (1644) 127 Many of the Schoole, as Aquinas Fra. Victoria, Sotus, Bannes. **1651** HOBBES *Leviath.* IV. xlvi. 374 A *Nunc-stans* (as the Schools call it). **1662** STILLINGFL. *Orig. Sacræ* II. vi. §3. 181 The spirit of Prophecy came upon them *per modum impressionis transeuntis*, as the Schools speak. **1683** J. NORRIS *Parting* 3, Poems (1684) 20, I now believe the Schools with ease,.. That should the sense no torment seize, Yet Pain of Loss alone would make a Hell.

9. a. *sing.* The building or room set apart for the lectures or exercises of a particular 'school' (in a university). **b.** *pl.* A building belonging to a university, containing rooms serving in some cases originally for lectures in the several faculties, in later times chiefly for the disputations and exercises for degrees, and for meetings of the academic body or of portions of it. Hence, in modern Oxford use: The building in which most of the university examinations are held.

c **1590** MARLOWE *Faustus* (1604) A 3 b, Ile haue them fill the publike schooles with skill [*mod. edd.* silk] Wherewith the students shalbe brauely clad. **1644** EVELYN *Diary* Jan., We went into some of the Scholes [of the Sorbonne], and in that of Divinity we found a grave Doctor in his chaire, with a multitude of auditors, who all write as he dictates. *a* **1674** CLARENDON *Hist. Reb.* VIII. §120 They caused provisions of corn to be laid in,..assigning the public schools to that purpose. **1697** EVELYN *Acc. Archit.* Misc. Writ. (1825) 366

Or compare the Schools and Library at Oxford with the Theatre there. **1706** T. HEARNE *Collect.* 3 Oct. (O.H.S.) I. 292 Forreigners..frequently go to ye Schools to hear Lectures. **1751** WESLEY *Wks.* 1872 II. 222, I went to the Schools, where the Convocation was met. **1861** HUGHES *Tom Brown at Oxf.* xxiv, There is no more characteristic spot in Oxford than the quadrangle of the schools. **1873** *Students' Handbk. Univ. Oxf.* 151 A copy of it must be deposited in the Music School.

10. In modern Oxford use. **a.** *pl.* The periodical examinations for the degree of B.A.

1828 J. H. NEWMAN *Lett.* (1891) I. 180. I am going out of the Schools, and Dornford (I fancy) will supply my place for the ensuing examination. **1861** HUGHES *Tom Brown at Oxf.* xxiv, The row of victims..'sitting for the schools' as it is called. **1868** FREEMAN *Norm. Conq.* II. App. 581 A former colleague of mine in the Oxford Schools. **1882** *Society* 18 Nov. 11/2 The schools at Oxford are 'on' once more, and white ties are again the order of the day.

b. Each of the several courses of study, in any of which an 'honours' degree in Arts may be taken: corresponding to the Cambridge 'Tripos'.

In 1910 the 'Schools' were as follows: '*Literæ Humaniores*' (i.e. classics), Mathematical and Physical Science, Natural Science, Jurisprudence, Modern History, Theology, Oriental Languages, English Language and Literature, Modern Languages.

1873 *Students' Handbk. Univ. Oxf.* 110 Those who have obtained Honours in the School of Theology.

†**III. 11. a.** The doctrine or teaching of a master; the lore or knowledge of a subject imparted by teaching. *Obs.*

1390 GOWER *Conf.* III. 84 As thou hast preid above That I the Scole schal declare Of Aristotle. *Ibid.* III. 139 Ther mai a man the Scole liere Of Rethoriqes eloquences. **1423** JAS. I. *Kingis Q.* vii, Quhich to declare my scole is ouer ȝong. *c* **1460** *Wisdom* 86 in *Macro Plays* 38 Teche me þe scolys of yowur dyvynyte. **15..** *Piers of Fullham* 3 in Hazl. *E.P.P.* II. 2 A man, that lovyth fyscheng and fowlyng bothe, ofte tyme that game schall hym be lothe, of that crafte all thoghe he can the scole, yn the see, in rever, in ponde, or yn pole. **15..** *Mayd Emlyn* 128 ibid. IV. 87 Thus by her scole Made hym a fole, And called hym dodypate.

†**b.** A particular method or discipline taught.

c **1386** CHAUCER *Prol.* 125 Frenssh she spak ful faire and fetisly, After the scole of Stratford atte Bowe. —— *Miller's T.* 143 In twenty manere koude he trippe and daunce After the scole of Oxenforde tho. *c* **1400** *Beryn* 2403 So yee aftir my scole Wol do, & as I rede ȝew. *c* **1400** *Sowdone Bab.* 1141, I shall the lerne a newe scole, If thoue so hardy to fighte be. *c* **1440** *Pallad. on Husb.* II. 14 At the wendyng slake The yoke, thyne oxen neckes forto cole: But drawing by the horne is noo goode scole. *a* **1529** SKELTON *P. Sparowe* 117 It wold syt on a stole, And lerned after my scole For to kepe his cut.

†**c.** Schooling, discipline. *Obs.*

1449 PECOCK *Repr.* III. viii. 328 Certis the freelnes of the wil is to be kutt awei and to be leid aside with greet bateil, greet scole, and greet craft.

IV. Repr. L. *schola*, Gr. σχολή, in late senses.

†**12.** A hostelry at Rome for the reception of pilgrims. *Obs.*

O.E. Chron. an. 816, þy ilcan ȝeare forborn Ongolcynnes scolu. ? *a* **900** in Thorpe *Diplomat. Anglicum* (1865) 116 Ic [Æthelwulf] on Rome..Englisce scole ȝesette. *c* **1450** *Brut* 316 Seynt Peters pens,..þe whiche Kyng Iva [*sic*]..ferst graunted to Rome, for þe scole of Engelond ther to be continued.

†**13.** A public building, gallery, or the like. *Obs.*

c **1400** MAUNDEV. (Roxb.) xi. 44 A kirk theked with leed, þat es called þe Scole of Salomon. **1534** WHITINTON *Tullyes Offices* I. (1540) 33 Solon fyrste edifyed the schole of Areopagus in Athenes. **1601** HOLLAND *Pliny* XXXVI. v. II. 568 In the same place, and namely in the schoole or gallerie of learned men, there be many more images highly commended.

14. *Hist.* One of the cohorts or companies into which the Imperial guard was divided.

1776 GIBBON *Decl. & F.* xiii. I. 388 The avenues of the palace were strictly guarded by the various schools, as they began to be called, of domestic officers. *Ibid.* xvii. II. 57 The whole number consisted of three thousand five hundred men, divided into seven schools, or troops, of five hundred each.

V. 15. [f. SCHOOL *v.*] A cross-country ride.

1892 *Field* 9 Apr. 512/2 Then began a cheery 'school' over some scrubby hills.

VI. *attrib.* and *Comb.*

16. Simple attributive.

a. Pertaining to a school (sense 1) or schools, as ***school-age, assembly, atlas, bag, beret, blazer, blouse, bus*** (also ***-busing***), ***curriculum, -desk, dinner, education, eleven, -fee, -French, -friendship, holiday, -hours*** (HOUR 2 b), † ***law, librarian, -life, lunch, mag, magazine, meal, nurse, party, play, -poem, -prank, prefect, prize, reader,*** † ***-recess, register, rule, satchel, scarf, secretary, slang, song, subject, system, -teacher*** (hence ***-teacherish*** adj.), ***tie, treat, trunk, uniform, -vacation, warden, wear, -work, -year,*** etc. See also *school cap* at sense 19 below, SCHOOL-BOARD, -BOOK, -DAY, -MA'AM, -MASTER, -MISTRESS.

1741 S. RICHARDSON *Familiar Lett.* cxxx. 168 Nor is the Consequence of this Defect confin'd to the *School-age, as I may call it. **1879** *St. George's Hosp. Rep.* IX. 716 So soon as children have passed school-age, they [etc.]. **1939** M. S. RICE *Working-Class Wives* iii. 66 The children of school age come under the School medical services. **1972** G. SERENY *Case M. Bell* II. i. 80 Fernwood Reception Centre..is used for children of school age who come there primarily because of sudden family emergencies. **1974** *Sat. Rev. World* (U.S.) 2 Nov. 24/3, 95 per-cent of school-age Eskimos are in school. **1932** MRS. J. MURRAY (*title*) Incidental music for use at *school assembly. Arranged by I. R. Davies. **1977** J. AIKEN *Last Movement* ix. 166 Opera and large gatherings ran each other close for first place among her dislikes. How did she stand school assemblies? **1815** J. A. CUMMINGS (*title*) A *school atlas, accompanying ancient and modern geography. **1885** C. M. YONGE *Two Sides of Shield* I. vi. 100 The elder boys' old school atlases. **1979** H. MCLEAVE *Borderline Case* xvi. 155 On a school atlas Dr. Li charted the progress of the disease. **1895** *Montgomery Ward Catal.* Spring & Summer 118/3 Water-proof *School Bags; made of enameled cloth, with flap and leather shoulder strap. **1913** P. GEDDES *Masque of Anc. Learning* 3 Boy enters, swinging his school-bag. **1977** C. FREMLIN *Spider-Orchid* xiii. 90 She'd dumped her school bag on the floor. **1967** M. DRABBLE *Jerusalem the Golden* iii. 51 The girls in her class.. regarded her as relatively plain..with no notion of how to twist a *school beret or hitch a school skirt. **1975** 'J. BELL' *Victim* xiii. 140 A small girl stepped out. She held a school beret in one hand. **1913** J. VAIZEY *College Girl* v. 62 The boys wore flannel trousers with *school blazers and caps. **1978** A. PRICE *'44 Vintage* vi. 74 His school blazer..had been too small for him. **1932** D. C. MINTER *Mod. Needlecraft* 253/1 **School or Gym Blouse*... Long sleeves for school type, short for gym blouse. **1979** K. CONLON *Move in Game* I. i. 14 Mrs Brennan wrote: 'butter, eggs, shoe polish, school blouse, [etc.].' **1908** *Suburban Life* July 48/1 (*caption*) The *school bus. **1939** G. HOUSEHOLD *Rogue Male* 110, I saw the school-bus and an occasional car. **1976** P. R. WHITE *Planning for Public Transport* i. 25 A local authority..may also be an important customer in its own right, by allocating subsidies, and contracts for school bus services. **1974** *Times* 25 Oct. 10/5 The sensitive issue of *school busing in Boston. **1913** C. MACKENZIE *Sinister St.* I. II. i. 156 He taught Geography and English History and English Literature, so far as the *school curriculum allowed him. **1981** *Listener* 1 Jan. 22/3 His comments on the school curriculum contain a germ of truth. **1842** DICKENS *Amer. Notes* I. iii. 75 A little enclosure, made of *school-desks and forms. **1953** A. CLARKE *Moment next to Nothing* I. ii. 29 I'll clear the table, have our school-desk ready. **1835** DICKENS *Sk. by Boz* (1836) 1st Ser. I. 26 They were three long graces in drapery, with the addition—like a *school-dinner—of another long grace afterwards. **1963** *New Society* 22 Aug. 5/1 That inevitable horror, the school dinner. **1973** J. BURROWS *Like Evening Gone* x. 115 She used to help with school dinners.. serving and washing up. **1731** J. CREICHTON *Mem.* 10 Having lost the Benefit of a thorough *School-Education.. the Reader cannot reasonably expect to be much pleased with my Style. **1848** MILL *Pol. Econ.* I. II. xiv. 463 The earnings of..any labour which requires school education, are at a monopoly rate. **1857** HUGHES *Tom Brown* II. viii, The Captain of the *School eleven..accompanied them. **1511–12** *Acc. Ld. High Treas. Scot.* IV. 242 In haill payment of half ane ȝeris burd and *scoile fee. **1870** *Act 33 & 34 Vict.* c. 75 §25 The school board may, if they think fit,..pay the whole or any part of the school fees payable at any public elementary school by any child [etc.]. **1873** C. M. YONGE *Pillars of House* I. iii. 64 The school-fee was a mere trifle, but Mr. Ryder would willingly have boarded and lodged the boy. **1958** 'CASTLE' & 'HAILEY' *Flight into Danger* 17 Pay off the bills—the new water tank, school fees, instalments on the Chev. **1973** J. LEASOR *Host of Extras* ii. 32 He'd be selling the car to pay his son's school fees. **1837** [MISS MAITLAND] *Lett. fr. Madras* xv. (1843) 145 About half of them know the language well, and the rest speak it like *school-French. **1784** COWPER *Tiroc.* 436 *School-friendships are not always found..permanent and sound. **1939** *School holiday [see *nursery tea* s.v. NURSERY 8 a]. **1981** J. ROBIN *Elmdon* xi. 224 A private house, occupied in the school holidays by the wife of a business-man in Baghdad. **1740** J. CLARKE *Educ. Youth* (ed. 3) 137 Out of *School-Hours. **1848** THACKERAY *Van. Fair* ii, Surreptitiously nursing it [a doll] in school hours. **1650** J. M. (*title*) *School-Laws, or Qui Mihi in English. **1920** B. M. PEACOCK (*title*) A *school and club librarians' handbook. **1978** J. IRVING *World according to Garp* ii. 28 It was a habit among the school librarians, upon recognizing that they didn't have a book which someone sought, to say, 'Perhaps the infirmary has it.' **1721** M. CAVE *Let.* 27 Nov. in M. M. Verney *Verney Lett. of Eighteenth Cent.* (1930) II. xxiii. 71 The apprehension of Tommy's weak Constitution I find very grevious, inferring that he is unable to undergo a *School Life. **1857** HUGHES *Tom Brown* II. viii, The care with which he has watched over every step in your school lives. **1885** WELLDON *Serm. Harrow* i. (1887) 6 In a few days perhaps..you will feel the continuity of your school-life; but for the present it seems to you to have been broken. **1949** M. MEAD *Male & Female* xvi. 330 As *school-lunches develop, the home with school-age children is deserted all day long. **1980** *Times* 10 Sept. 8/1 Changes [are] taking place in the school meals service... Many parents are weighing up the relative merits of school lunches versus packed ones. **1960** L. DURRELL *Let.* in *Spirit of Place* (1969) 153 The boys of King's School..asked for an article for the *school mag. **1976** *Listener* 8 Apr. 452/4 It is very difficult to write about school, and the tone of the school mag is not wholly avoided. **1856** C. M. YONGE *Daisy Chain* II. v. 383, I got leave to send a ballad..to that *school magazine... It was actually inserted. **1939** C. ISHERWOOD *Goodbye to Berlin* 311 The newspapers are becoming more and more like copies of a school magazine. **1963** A. HERON *Towards Quaker View of Sex* iii. 23 The occasional poems which seek entry in the columns of the school magazine. **1948** F. LE G. CLARK (*title*) The social history of the *School Meal service. **1973** *Times* 5 Oct. 4/5 A [parliamentary] resolution called for..free school meals. **1912** *Q. Rev.* July 57 Enormous improvements..have been effected in the environment of the nation since that time. A full account of these is here impossible but it may be said that they include..the appointment of..district and *school nurses. **1976** J. PHILIPS *Backlash* (1977) III. i. 122 If..the school nurse.. came, I was to tell her to give me some first aid. **1803** T. LAWRENCE *Let.* 28 Jan. in D. E. William *Life & Corr. Sir T. Lawrence* (1831) I. 231 We all sat down like a Rugby *school party, but rather more vociferous. **1968** J. SANGSTER *Touchfeather* ii. 11, I went [to Berlin] with a school party... We stayed for five days..visiting the museums. **1976** H. TRACY *Death in Reserve* xviii. 136 He was told that there were parties of Boy Scouts..and a school party due next week. **1933** E. K. CHAMBERS *Eng. Folk-Play* 187 It is not to be supposed that, after the Reformation and the growth of the professional travelling companies, local plays..ceased to be performed... Some are *school-plays produced by the local Holophernes. Some are May games. **1972** *Guardian* 17 Aug. 10/6 It is impossible not to wish him well..like you would a child on sports day or in a school play. **1973** J. R. L. ANDERSON *Death on Rocks* iii. 62 She's gone with the kids to a school play. **1922** JOYCE *Ulysses* 167 That last pagan king of Ireland Cormac in the *schoolpoem choked himself. **1933** R. TUVE *Seasons & Months* iii. 75 *Cuculus*, above all *Philomela* (familiar as the subject of various 'school-poems'). **1799** HT. LEE *Canterb. T., Poet's T.* (ed. 2) I. 48 Playing *school-pranks with his companions. **1949** E. COXHEAD *Wind in West* vii. 178 He who had been the naughty child was now the *school prefect. **1975** P. D. JAMES *Black Tower* ii. 35 The old insistent arguments spoken in that confident school prefect's voice. **1853** C. BRONTË *Villette* I. iii. 54 Graham, it chanced, was at that time greatly preoccupied about some *school-prize, for which he was competing. **1904** 'E. NESBIT' *Phœnix & Carpet* xi. 206 Its conversation..was entertaining and instructive—like school prizes are said to be. **1835** H. A. HANSARD (*title*) Souter's second *school reader. **1940** J. BUCHAN *Memory Hold-the-Door* 194 *Prester John*..has since become a school-reader in many languages. **1981** E. HAY *Sambo Sahib* viii. 110 Helen [Bannerman]..was delighted ..that some of her books had been selected as school readers. **1795** *Jemima* I. 63 A pressing invitation that she would spend the next *school recess at the Hall. **1973** J. BURROWS *Like Evening Gone* vi. 73 There were forty-three names on the *school register. **1943** G. GREENE *Ministry of Fear* III. ii. 192 Excited like a boy breaking a *school rule. **1978** F. WELDON *Praxis* vii. 36 School rules forbade conversation between girls of different age groups. **1907** *Yesterday's Shopping* (1969) 325/2 *School Satchels. Waterproof Brown Canvas. **1972** J. FLEMING *Alas Poor Father* i. 7 Picking up the school satchel, he hooked it over his arm. **1907** E. NESBIT *Enchanted Castle* iii. 90 The crimson *school-scarf that had supported his white flannels. **1971** A. PRICE *Alamut Ambush* x. 119 Carelessly hung coats and school scarves on the row of wooden pegs. **1958** J. TOWNSEND *Young Devils* vi. 52, I was shown into his room by a cheerful middle-aged *school secretary. **1977** J. AIKEN *Last Movement* i. 24 Mother..had asked if Gina would be interested in the job of school secretary. **1900** FARMER *Public School Word-Bk.* p. v, It would, however, seem almost necessary to emphasise that this Word-Book is not, *per se*, a dictionary of *school slang. **1934** PRIEBSCH & COLLINSON *German Lang.* II. v. 263 A word or two may be added on German school-slang (*Pennälersprache*). **1975** D. DURRANT *With my Little Eye* xviii. 181 Patty's coarse, cruel, school slang bitchery. **1934** M. V. HUGHES *London Child of Seventies* vi. 68 Another treat to me was the *school song ('Homo plantat'). **1974** *Listener* 17 Jan. 84/1 E. E. Bowen and John Farmer started the collection of Harrow School Songs, in the 1870s. **1922** H. E. PALMER *Everyday Sentences in Spoken Eng.* p. v, English is no longer either an abhorred *school-subject nor a fascinating literary hobby. **1977** *Grimsby Even. Tel.* 5 May 5/2 She said..that it could easily be possible to make road safety a school subject on its own merit. **1814** JANE AUSTEN *Mansfield Park* III. iii. 63 Common neglect of the qualification..in the ordinary *school-system for boys. **1869** C. L. BRACE *New West* 79 The general school system of California..is more centralized. **1911** C. E. PERSONS et al. *Labor Laws & their Enforcement* 218 We should know how many children..the school system could no longer control, as well as those it still retains. **1976** *National Observer* (U.S.) 1 May B4/4 In America, school systems have expanded in the atmosphere of an anticipated tug-of-war with parents. **1847** WEBSTER, **School-teacher*, one who teaches or instructs a school. **1932** G. GREENE *Stamboul Train* I. i. 6, I see his passport. Richard John. Schoolteacher. **1950** C. S. BELSHAW *Island Admin. in S.W. Pacific* xii. 122 In one or two cases Councils unofficially..levied their own funds, which were to be put to such purposes as paying school-teachers [etc.]. *a* **1930** D. H. LAWRENCE *Phoenix* (1936) 361 The heroine being one of the old-fashioned *school-teacherish sort. **1978** H. WOUK *War & Remembrance* xiii. 126 She shook a schoolteacherish finger at him. **1932** *School tie [see OLD SCHOOL TIE]. **1937** G. BARKER *Poems* 24 O long lost upward in the dream descending, The flying pig and the school-tie anaconda! **1977** *Times* 23 Nov. 12/8 Western society..puts children.. in school uniform and school ties to make them conform. **1888** MRS. H. WARD *Robert Elsmere* II. III. xxv. 274 Counting up the engagements of the next few weeks—the *school-treat, two club field-days, a sermon. **1934** D. L. SAYERS *Nine Tailors* 121 An importunate child at a school treat. **1915** KIPLING *Diversity of Creatures* (1917) 429 We'll get his old *school trunk to-morrow and pack his civilian clothes. **1978** *Times* 3 Aug. 9/2 Cash's name-tapes are very widely available... But get a move on if..the first school trunk is looming. **1933** A. WHITE *Frost in May* ii. 47 She trotted sedately behind the lay-sister, wearing her *school uniform. **1976** W. TREVOR *Children of Dynmouth* ii. 37 They were still in their school uniforms—Stephen's grey with touches of maroon, Kate's brown and green. **1787** HAWKINS *Life Johnson* 471 Whose son in his *school-vacation was come home. **1835** *App. Munic. Corpor. Rep.* IV. 2897 The two *School Wardens [at Kingston-upon-Thames] are elected in like manner. Their duty is to visit and superintend the school. **1939–40** *Army & Navy Stores Catal.* p. lv/1 *School wear. **1976** *Evening Post* (Nottingham) 14 Dec. 15/8 (Advt.), Derby's leading boyswear and schoolwear specialists. **1857** HUGHES *Tom Brown* ii. vi, There could be no reason for stopping the *school work at present. **1857** *Ibid.* II. ii, There were thirty-eight weeks in the *school year. **1961** *Guardian Jrnl.* (Nottingham) 14 Nov. 4 The intention here is to reduce these dates in the school year from three to two. **1965** *New Society* 16 Sept. 4/2 The new school year has begun and millions of parents have heaved a sigh of relief. **1975** *Language for Life* (Dept. Educ. & Sci.) xx. 293 An additional benefit was the informal contact between teacher and parent, a valuable foundation for the coming school year.

b. Taught in or attending school, as ***school bully, -child, -chum, -companion,*** † ***-fere, friend, -kid, -maid, -miss, -urchin,*** etc. Also SCHOOL-BOY, -FELLOW, -GIRL, -MATE.

1907 'MARK TWAIN' in *N. Amer. Rev.* Jan. 7, I had had a quarrel with a big boy who was the *school-bully. **1956** 'C.

BLACKSTOCK' *Dewey Death* vii. 154 Mark..had something of the school bully in him... It seemed he derived a cruel satisfaction from the young man's palpable fear. **1840** CARLYLE *Heroes* iv. (1841) 207 He [Luther] had to beg, as the *school-children in those times did. **1879** *St. George's Hosp. Rep.* IX. 705 The first case of illness was a school-child. **1846** MRS. GORE *Eng. Char.* (1852) 149 The stupid *school-chum of his private secretary! **1771** SMOLLETT *Humph. Cl.* 31 May (1815) 108 The departure of your *school-companions. **1387** TREVISA *Higden* (Rolls) III. 449 One Calistenes, Alisaundre *scolefere under Aristotil. *Ibid.* VII. 397 He..went to Rome at þe laste wiþ oon of his scole feres. **1853** C. BRONTË *Villette* I. iii. 43 Graham is busy with his school-friends. **1973** 'M. INNES' *Appleby's Answer* x. 97 He recalled Judith's school friend as soon as he set eyes on her. **1938** *School-kid [see FEIS 2]. **1976** J. WAINWRIGHT *Who goes Next?* 164 He went to live with his boy-friend—little more than a schoolkid. **1603** SHAKS. *Meas. for M.* I. iv. 47 Is she your cosen? *Isa.* Adoptedly, as *school-maids change their names By vaine, though apt affection. **1873** BLACK *Pr. Thule* ii, I take her to be an affected *school-miss. **1922** JOYCE *Ulysses* 201 Antiquity mentions that Stagyrite *schoolurchin and bald heathen sage.

c. Belonging to or connected with the school as a building (cf. 1), as ***school-bell, building, -chapel, -door, gate, library, -roof, -yard***, etc. See also *school hall* at sense 19 below, SCHOOLHOUSE.

1702 S. SEWALL *Diary* 9 Aug. (1879) II. 61 Set out from Salem as the *School-Bell rung. **1779** J. WEDGWOOD *Let.* 23 Nov. (1965) 247 Rise at 7 in winter, when I shall ring the school bell. **1862** CALVERLEY *Verses & Transl.* (1894) 12 When the school-bell cut short our strife. **1976** C. DEXTER *Last seen Wearing* xvii. 136 The school bell rang at 4.00 p.m., and the last lesson of the day was over. **1829** R. GILBERT *Liber Scholast.* 167 The *school buildings are well adapted [etc.]. **1975** *Language for Life* (Dept. Educ. & Sci.) xix. 280 The class is likely to be held in a school building. **1884** *Tablet* 11 Oct. 591/2 The erection of a *school-chapel was immediately begun. **1641** MILTON *Ch. Govt.* II. Concl. 62 There is not that sect of Philosophers among the heathen so dissolute..but would shut his *school dores against such greasy sophisters. **1847** C. M. YONGE *Scenes & Characters* xxiii. 280 William walked to the *school gate with them. **1973** J. MANN *Only Security* iii. 23 When she left the school gates behind her, she was finished with the problems for the day. **1854** *Rep. Trans. Pennsylvania State Agric. Soc.* 276 Another great reform would be the introducing of a *school library into every district school. **1860** J. A. SYMONDS *Let.* 18 Aug. (1967) I. 260, I shall..get to Shrewsbury at about half past one. That will allow me time to see the MS in the School Library. **1941** M. TREADGOLD *We couldn't leave Dinah* i. 20 A discerning headmaster..had directed..her vivid imagination to the excellent school library. **1971** J. B. CARROLL et al. *Word Freq. Bk.* p. vi, Some of these publications are normally found in the classroom, others in the school library. *c* **1340** *Hampole's Wks.* (1895) I. 140 An Abbot þat..neuer lift vp his heued to see þe *scole-rouf. **1870** EMERSON *Soc. & Sol.* v. 99 The warm sympathy with which they kindle each other in *school-yard, or in barn or woodshed.

d. Pertaining to the Schoolmen (cf. sense 8), or to the 'schools' of universities (cf. sense 7 b), scholastic, academic, as in ***school-account***, †***-amorist, -argument, author, -clerk***, †***dispicion, -ethics, -exercise***, †***implement, -language, -logic, -manner, matter, -medicine, moralist, morality, name, -opinion, -pedantry, philosopher, philosophy, -phrase, -question, quiddity, -subtilty, -syllogism, term, -theology, trick***, etc.; ***school-like*** adj. and adv. See also SCHOOL-CRAFT, -DIVINE, -DIVINITY, -DOCTOR, -MAN, -POINT.

1701 NORRIS *Ideal World* I. vii. 408 To lay open the *school-account of this matter, and unravel it through all its abstrusities. **1644** BULWER *Chirol.* 163 Thus the *Schoole-Amorist [= Ovid]. **1587** GOLDING *De Mornay* xv. (1592) 225 The holy Scripture..vseth no *schoole arguments to make vs beleeue that there is a God. **1551** CRANMER *Answ. Gardiner* III. 90 It is not plainly written of all the Papists, both lawyers and *schole authors, that [etc.]. *a* **1583** SIR H. GILBERT *Q. Eliz. Achad.* (1869) 3 The greatest *Schole clarkes are not alwayes the wisest men. **1600** W. WATSON *Decacordon* (1602) Pref. A 2, Arguments of proofe in shew holden on a whole day by fine wits, in a *schoole despicion. **1710** BERKELEY *Princ. Hum. Knowl.* I. §100. 145 One may make a great progress in *School-Ethics without ever being the wiser or better Man for it. *c* **1425** *Orolog. Sapient.* i. in *Anglia* X. 327/43 Hem þat in *scole-excersyse..sechene þoo þinges þat bene nedefulle to sowle-hele. **1586** HOOKER *Answ. Travers* xvi. (1612) 19 These *schoole implements are acknowledged by graue and wise men not vnprofitable to haue beene inuented. **1639** DRUMM. OF HAWTH. *Disc. Impresa's* Wks. (1711) 229 For ladies, who understand not the *school languages. **1840** CARLYLE *Heroes* v. (1841) 289 Eagerly devouring what spiritual thing he [Johnson] could come at; school-languages and other merely grammatical stuff, if there was nothing better! **1563–87** FOXE *A. & M.* (1596) 14/2 Such as more distinctlie and *schoolelike discusse this matter. **1601** B. JONSON *Poetaster* v. i. 129 His learning labours not the schoole-like glosse. **1645** MILTON *Tetrach.* 23 Such a methodical and School-like way of defining. **1818** HALLAM *Mid. Ages* ix. II. (1819) III. 538 Philology..degenerated through the prevalence of *school-logic. **1560** DAUS tr. *Sleidane's Comm.* 229 b, He discourseth at large the article of Justyfication after the *scoole maner [orig. *more scholastico*]. *c* **1386** CHAUCER *Friar's Prol.* 8 Ye han heer touched al so moot I thee In *scole matere greet difficultee. **1447** in *Epist. Acad. Oxon.* (O.H.S.) I. 260 All his buks of study, also oder boks longyng to scole mater. **1731** *Hist. Litteraria* III. 260 The Venereal Disease had just then made its appearance, which the common *School-Medicine was not able to cure. **1710** NORRIS *Chr. Prud.* iv. 149 This the *School-Moralists..have abundantly proved. *Ibid.* iii. 125 The *School Morality. **1581** SIDNEY *Apol. Poetry* (Arb.) 41 Who thinke vertue a *schoole name. **1751** WARBURTON *Pope's Ess. Man* II. 81 *note*, For this dangerous *school-opinion gives support to the Manichean or Zoroastrian error. **1704** NORRIS *Ideal World* II. Pref. 16 Which..would perhaps savour a little too much of *school-pedantry. *a* **1704** T. BROWN *Dial. Dead, Reas. Oaths* Wks. 1711 IV. 96 A *School-Philosopher with his newest set of Distinctions. **1701** NORRIS *Ideal World* I. ii. 72 It agrees not with the principles of the *School-Philosophy, that will by no means allow the essences of things to be eternal. **1759** GOLDSM. *Pres. State Pol. Learn.* xi. Wks. (Globe) 443/2 Universities..where the pupils..support every day syllogistical disputations in school philosophy. **1668** HOWE *Blessedn. Righteous* xii. 218 *Servato ordine finis*, as the *School-phrase is. **1586** HOOKER *Answ. Travers* xvi. (1612) 18 If..it were a *schoole question. *a* **1625** E. CHALONER *Six Serm.* (1629) 30 The husbandman..vsed not..those *schoole quiddities to simple labourers. **1629** H. BURTON *Truth's Tri.* 67 No Romish sophistrie, or *schoole-subtilty can inuent any probability. **1709** SHAFTESB. *Moralists* i. 4 Her *School-Syllogism and her Elixir, [are] the choicest of her [Philosophy's] Products. *c* **1386** CHAUCER *Mech. T.* 325, I counte nat a panyer ful of herbes Of *scole termes. **1825** SOUTHEY in *Q. Rev.* XXXI. 380 It is (to use a school term) an inseparable accident of Lisbon. **1591** SPENSER *M. Hubberd* 512 And if one could, it were but a *schoole trick.

e. Produced by the pupils or assistants of a master of a school of art (see sense 5 a), as ***school painting, -piece, -work***.

1903 R. FRY *Let.* 16 Mar. (1972) I. 207, I have found..a tondo..which I can't help still fancying a schoolpiece. Anyhow this, which was called 'School of Lorenzo', is Piero all over. **1905** MRS. H. WARD *Marriage of William Ashe* I. ii. 31 It was an old low-ceiled room, panelled in white and gold, showing here and there an Italian picture—Saint, or Holy Family, agreeable school-work. **1937** *Burlington Mag.* Feb. 77/1 The accidental meeting of northern and southern art-forms, as it were, in a school-piece. **1979** R. COX *Auction* iii. 58, I would certainly not say priceless. As School paintings go, yes, it's valuable.

17. locative, in sense 'at school', with ppl. adjs., as ***school-based, -bred, -made, -taught, -trained***, etc.

1975 *Language for Life* (Dept. Educ. & Sci.) xxiii. 339 Up to a third of the time is normally given to *school-based teaching practice. **1977** *Times Educ. Suppl.* 21 Oct. 7/1 Many people..believe school-based assessments are important in giving a comprehensive picture of the candidates' achievements. **1784** COWPER *Tiroc.* 840 And if it chance..That though *school-bred, the boy be virtuous still. **1899** *Allbutt's Syst. Med.* VII. 870 As in chorea, so in tic, there are cases which appear to be *school-made. **1765** GOLDSM. *Trav.* 41 Let *school-taught pride dissemble all it can, These little things are great to little man. **1897** MARY KINGSLEY *W. Africa* x. 214 Boys trained in the mission school and married to *school-trained girls.

18. objective and obj. gen., as ***school desegregation, -drilling, governor, -leaving, management, manager, -teaching***, etc.

1961 J. W. PELTASON (*title*) Fifty-eight lonely men: Southern federal judges and *school desegregation. **1976** *Billings* (Montana) *Gaz.* 20 June 11-E/6 President Ford heard pro and con views on busing as a remedy for school desegregation from school superintendents and principals Saturday. **1822–29** *Good's Study Med.* (ed. 3) IV. 347 The whole system of *school-drilling education. *Ibid.* 349 Such and a thousand similar recreations..should enter into the school-drilling of the day. **1976** L. HENDERSON *Major Enquiry* xvii. 116, I was attending a meeting of the Branton Education Committee, I am one of the *school governors. **1901** *Daily Chron.* 21 Nov. 3/6 A..*school-leaving certificate. **1883** J. LANDON (*title*) *School management. **1975** *Language for Life* (Dept. Educ. & Sci.) xii. 193 It would not be easy to argue for another post to be added to the senior level of the school management structure. **1862** *Edin. Rev.* Apr. 415 That fortunate individual has dined at the house of a *school manager. **1888** *Pall Mall G.* 12 Jan. 4/1 The celibacy of the 'school marm' is a heresy which as yet only exists in the pious dream of school managers and school boards. **1847** WEBSTER, **School-teaching*, the business of instructing a school. **1854** C. M. YONGE *Castle Builders* v. 65 The example of their sister..made them think *school-teaching the most dignified and delightful of tasks. **1950** *Sport* 7–11 Apr. 14/1 Defensive stability has been added by the signing of schoolteaching goalkeeper, Alec Grant. **1981** E. NORTH *Dames* vi. 101 You did the right thing getting out of schoolteaching when you did.

19. Special Combinations: **school air** *Horsemanship*, an 'air' (AIR *sb.* 17) which horses are taught in the school; **school attendance**, attendance at a school, used *attrib.* of persons or things involved in the enforcement of compulsory school attendance; **school(s) broadcast**, a radio or television broadcast for the instruction of children in school; also **school broadcaster, broadcasting**; **school-butter**, (*a*) cf. quots. 1584–93 (sense obscure); (*b*) *slang*, a flogging; (*c*) *U.S.* 'a teasing call to school children' (Payne *Wordlist East Alabama*); **school-cap**, (*a*) *Geol.* (see quot. 1829); (*b*) a cap worn as part of a school uniform (hence ***-capped*** adj.); **School Cert.**, abbrev. of next; **School Certificate**, in one of several (public) examination systems, a certificate of proficiency in subjects learned at school; **school colours**, the distinctive colours of a school, esp. as conferred as a sign of sporting achievement (see COLOUR *sb.*[1] 6 c); **school committee**, (*a*) *U.S.* = SCHOOL BOARD 2; (*b*) *N.Z.*, a group of the parents of primary school-children elected to assist the headmaster of that school; **school crossing**, a supervised road-crossing for school-children near the entrance to a school; **school-dame**, an old woman who keeps a small school for young children; **school district** *N. Amer.*, a unit for the local administration of schools; †**school-feast**, a tea-party or picnic for village school-children; **school-gait** (see sense 3 d); **school-gallop** (see quot.); **school-going** *sb.*, attendance at school; **school-going** *a.*, that goes, or is suitable to go, to school; †**school-hall**, (*a*) the room or building in which university disputations were held; (*b*) the assembly hall of a school; †**school-hire**, = *school-wage*; **school inspector**, an officer appointed to inspect and report on the condition of schools and the teaching therein; hence **school-inspectorship**; **school journal** *N.Z.*, a booklet prepared by the Department of Education and issued to all primary schools at regular intervals; **school land** *N. Amer.*, land set apart for the financial support of schools (cf. *school section*); **school-learning**, †(*a*) the learning of 'the schools' (7 b), (*b*) education at school; **school-leaver**, one who is about to leave or has just left school (cf. LEAVER); **school leaving age** = *leaving age* s.v. LEAVING *vbl. sb.*; **school-mamma, -mother**, an elder girl at a girls'-school who acts as a protectress of one or more younger ones; **school method**, the teaching system to be followed by a teacher in training; the practice or theory of school-teaching; **school milk**, milk provided at reduced cost or free of charge to children in school; †**school-pace**, = *school-gait*; **school-pence**, a small weekly sum of money paid for tuition in elementary schools; **school phobia** *Psychol.*, excessive anxiety about or fear of attending school; so **school-phobic** *a.* and *ellipt.* as *sb.*; **school report** = REPORT *sb.* 2 e; **school-rider**, a school-trained horseman; so **school-riding**; †**school-rod** [cf. G. *schulrute*], a birch-rod or cane; †**school-scholar**, one who has the learning taught at school (sense 1); **school section** *U.S.* and *Canad.*, 'a section of land set apart for public schools' (Bartlett 1860); **school-ship**, a ship used for the instruction and training of boys in practical seamanship; **schools programme** = *school broadcast*; **schools television**, a television broadcast for schools; **school story**, a story treating of life in a school; **school-tide** = *school-time* (b); **school-time**, (*a*) the time at which school commences, or during which school continues; (*b*) that period of life which is passed at school; **school-wage** (now *dial.*), the periodical payment made for tuition at school; **school-years** = *school-time* (*b*).

1885 DODGE *Patroclus & Penelope* 58 Horses educated in all the *School airs which are applicable to road-riding. **1876** *Act 39 & 40 Vict.* c. 79 §7 The provisions of this Act ..shall be enforced— (1.) In a school district within the jurisdiction of a school board, by that board; and (2.) In every other school district by a committee (in this Act referred to as a *school attendance committee). **1911** G. B. SHAW *Getting Married* Pref. 185 If you pay less than £40 a year rent, you will sometimes feel tempted to say to the.. school attendance officer, and the sanitary inspector: 'Is this child mine or yours?' **1944** *Act 7 & 8 Geo. VI* c. 31. 252 The authority shall serve upon the parent an order in the prescribed form (hereinafter referred to as a 'school attendance order') requiring him to cause the child to become a registered pupil at a school named in the order. **1971** *Reader's Digest Family Guide to Law* 219/2 The education authorities sent the school attendance officer to the home and..he found that the child had received no tuition that day. **1931** *4th Ann. Rep. B.B.C.* in *Parl. Papers 1930–31* (Cmd. 3863) X. 291 It is believed that 5,260 schools followed the *school broadcasts in the year. **1949** *Radio Times* 15 July 6/1, I asked the Chief Wireless Operator if it would be possible for me to listen to the Schools Broadcast. **1962** A. NISBETT *Technique Sound Studio* 246 The BBC permits the recording of schools broadcasts. **1974** *School broadcaster [see *school broadcasting* below]. **1927** *B.B.C. Handbk. 1928* 138/1 Many thousands have their school set with its loud-speaker, and *School Broadcasting has become a subject for educational research. **1928** *1st Ann. Rep. B.B.C.* 6 in *Parl. Papers* (Cmd. 3123) VII. 121 The Kent Education Committee undertook an enquiry into the efficacy of schools broadcasting. **1974** *Time* 8 Apr. 13/1 This autumn radio will celebrate 50 years of school broadcasting... School broadcasters use much more sophisticated material to complement the work of the teacher. **1584** A. MUNDAY *Fidele & Fortunio* 1473 in *Archiv. Stud. neu. Spr.* CXXIII. 76 O that I had some of Pediculus [*i.e.* Pedante's] *Schoole-butter to make me a lip salue. **1593** G. HARVEY *Pierces Super.* Wks. (Grosart) II. 231 Should the Butterwhore..try all the conclusions of her cherne, she might peradaunture in some sort pay thee home with Schoole-butter: but vndoubtedly she should haue much adooe, to stoppe thy Ouen-mouth with a lidde of Butter. **1618** FLETCHER *Loyal Subj.* v. iv, *Anc.* He was whipt like a top, I never saw a whore so lac'd: Court schoole-butter? Is this their diet? *a* **1700** B. E. *Dict. Cant. Crew*, *School-butter*, a Whipping. **1912** *Dialect Notes* III. 588 When he yelled *school butter* at us, we yanked him off the wagon and blacked his eyes. **1935** A. B. LONGSTREET *Georgia Scenes* 84, I fell down.., running after that fellow that cried 'school-butter'. **1829** *Trans. Geol. Soc.* Ser. II. II. 42 The bed below this is called the Top Cap... The next bed is called the *School Cap..; it consists of a compact limestone extremely cellular [etc.]. **1908** *Magnet* I. 1, His hair was thick and curly, and there was a school-cap stuck on the back of his head. **1930** AUDEN *Poems* 18 The rest as jury, wearing school caps. **1975** *Listener* 4 Dec. 747/3 Tell us that story about going to St John's Wood. Well, I had a letter, and went up wearing a school cap. **1933** M. Lowry *Ultramarine* ii. 97 Mothers with warm-smelling furs are fussing with their *school-capped sons. **1973** M. Russell *Double Hit* ii. 15 A school-capped boy bicycled out of the main gates. **1937** *Discovery* Jan. p. ii/1 (Advt.), **School Cert.* and *Army*. Quick easy way if *Latin* taken for former only. **1967** H. W. Sutherland *Magnie* vii. 92 She could have taken the one year course herself, but she thought you'd need a school cert. at least. **1977** D. May in P. Collenette *Winter's Tales 23* 90 We were doing a run-through of School Cert. **1888** Kipling *Wee Willie Winkie* 75 They were an educated regiment, the percentage of *school-certificates in their ranks were high, and most of the men could do more than read and write. **1911** *Rep. Consultative Comm. Exam. Secondary Schools* 106 in *Parl. Papers* (Cd. 6004) XVI. 159 We would suggest that the examination should be called the examination for the Secondary School Certificate. **1931** 'G. Trevor' *Murder at School* ii. 36 He was in my junior form. .... I expect he'd have taken his School Certificate. **1948** *Min. of Educ. Circular* No. 168. 23 Apr. 3/1 In 1951 the Minister proposes that the existing School and Higher School Certificate examinations should be discontinued and that in their place there should be introduced an examination for the 'General Certificate of Education'. **1966** G. W. Turner *Eng. Lang. in Australia & N.Z.* viii. 173 He [[*sc.* a New Zealander] is likely to sit School Certificate (approximately equivalent to English GCE Ordinary Level). **1978** A. Price *'44 Vintage* iv. 46 The acquisition of School Certificate German had been the limit of his ambition. **1913** C. Mackenzie *Sinister St.* I. ii. xiv. 382 He respected the quest of *School Colours. **1924** A. Huxley *Little Mexican* 3 Holding to my head..a speckled straw [hat], gaudy with the school colours. **1972** L. P. Davies *What did I do Tomorrow?* v. 63 A scarf in the school colours of narrow emerald and gold stripes on black. **1787** in C. O. Parmenter *Hist. Pelham, Mass.* (1898) 226 Voted Not to Devid the School Quarter where Dea. John Crawford is *School Committee Man. **1877** *Statutes N.Z.* xxi. §58. 122 For every school district constituted under this Act there shall be a School Committee consisting of seven householders within the school district, to be elected as hereinafter provided. **1945** *Suburban List* (Essex Junction, Vermont) 8 Feb. 10/3 The school committee could not keep the buses running. **1947** 'A. P. Gaskell' *Big Game* 87 To crown it all the damned School Committee had to pick on this Saturday for their school picnic. **1951** *Sunday Pictorial* 21 Jan. 4/3 The warning signs brandished by Bristol's *school-crossing wardens are so large that wardens find it hard to keep both feet on the ground in a strong wind. **1979** *Hampstead & Highgate Express* 22 June 10/3 Most of the school crossings in the borough were without lollipop men and women. *a* **1652** J. Smith *Sel. Disc.* iv. 101 We could suppose our senses to be the *school-dames that first taught us the alphabet of this learning. **1852** T. Parker *Ten Serm. Relig.* i. (1863) 10 He must study the anicular lines on the school-dame's slate. **1809** E. A. Kendall *Travels through Northern Parts U.S.* I. 128 There are thirteen *school districts [in Berlin, Conn.]. **1876** [see *school attendance* above]. **1903** A. B. Hart *Actual Govt.* 542 The smallest unit of school administration is the school district, which in many States has its own board, raises its own taxes, and appoints its own teachers. **1978** *N.Y. Times* 29 Mar. A13/1 In Duarte,..the school district and a medical center are the two major employers. **1849** C. Brontë *Shirley* II. vi. 137 (*heading*) The *school-feast. **1879** M. E. Braddon *Vixen* I. xvii. 325 The school-feast was fixed..for the Wednesday in Whitsun week. **1753** *Chambers' Cycl.* Suppl., A **school pace* or *gate* denotes the same with *ecoute*. **1885** Dodge *Patroclus & Penelope* 130 The traverse is a School gait rarely needed on the road. **1884** E. L. Anderson *Mod. Horsemanship* 148 The *School Gallop is a pace of four beats, and is procured from the ordinary gallop by demanding a close union, and by sustaining the forehand with the reins [etc.]. **1896** A. Morrison *Child of Jago* 78 *School-going was a practice best never begun. **1884** *Athenæum* 15 Mar. 347/3 According to these statistics 1 out of 4 boys and 1 out of 89 girls of school-going age are under instruction. **1900** *Daily News* 1 June 6/4, 93,000 school-going children. **1509** *Parlt. Devylles* xl, I wyst hym [Jesus] neuer go to scole, And yet I sawe hym dyspute in the *scole hall. **1933** A. Thirkell *High Rising* viii. 161 Amy took Laura over to the school hall. **1980** J. Thomson *Alibi in Time* viii. 104 The school hall opened off the entrance foyer. *c* **1440** *Promp. Parv.* 449/2 *Scole hyre, *scolagium*. **1588** *Wills & Inv. N.C.* (Surtees 1860) I. 182 For schole heir of the childer, for twoe wekes, 1s. 2d. More paid to Mr. Turpen, that was owne for Abraham schole heir, 8s. **1681** W. Robertson *Phraseol. Gen.* (1693) 1099 Schooling or school-hire, *minerval*. **1822** *Missionary Reg.* Dec. 501/2 (*heading*) *School inspectors and village readers. **1873** C. M. Yonge *Pillars of House* IV. xli. 192 He's a school inspector! Don't you have inspections here? Not under Government? O thrice happy people! **1924** M. Kennedy *Constant Nymph* xiv. 190 He knows too much about everything..being a school inspector. **1979** D. Cook *Winter Doves* I. 26 The School Inspectors came round..and they saw the state of the house, so they sent someone from the Council. **1911** H. S. Walpole *Mr. Perrin & Mr. Traill* iii. 47 He saw himself at Eton or Harrow, or a *school-inspectorship. **1907** *Append. Jrnls. House Reps. N.Z.* E.1E. 6, I might mention..the **School Journal*, because it will give an opportunity of explaining the place it should occupy in the school system. **1935** J. Guthrie *Little Country* v. 102 The word [*sc.* Australasia] was expurgated from school journals. **1648** *Suffolk Co.* (Mass.) *Deeds* (1880) I. 91 Humphrey Johnson of Roxbury granted unto William Chenie of Roxbury twenty Acres of land in Roxbury bounded with..the *school lands & Richard Peacocks northwest. **1775** *Let.* 28 Feb. in *Coll. New Hampshire Hist. Soc.* (1889) IX. 89, I might..lay out for the Clearing the School Lands to the amount of £500 Sterlg. **1885** *Rep. Indian Affairs* (U.S.) 147 Others claim they have purchased their lands from the State of Nevada under the school-land grant. **1952** D. F. Putnam *Canad. Regions* 372/2 Another factor in the land pattern was the reservation of certain parcels as school lands. *a* **1583** Sir H. Gilbert *Q. Eliz. Achad.* (1869) 10 In the vniuersities men study onely *schole learninges. **1751** Eliza Heywood *Betsy Thoughtless* I. 8 He having finished his school-learning, and was soon to go to the university. **1840** Carlyle *Heroes* ii. (1841) 84 Mahomet ....had no school-learning, of the thing we call school-learning none at all. **1925** *Contemp. Rev.* May 634 The problem of the unemployed '*school-leaver' complicates in many ways the problem of the boy at work. **1955** *Times* 14 July 2/6 The Student Training Scheme is designed to enable public and grammar school-leavers to qualify professionally, having particularly in view careers in design, development, production, or commercial engineering. **1980** *Listener* 19 June 803/1 Wakefield was a miner's son and his parents did not expect him to be a late school-leaver. **1920** *Circular* (Board of Educ.) No. 1180. 12 Oct. 3 The Board are prepared to consider proposals for making a byelaw under the subsection raising the *school leaving age to 15. **1946** *Ann. Reg. 1945* I. iii. 75 On September 28 the Minister of Education announced that the school-leaving age would be raised to 15 on April 1, 1947, and that no attempt would be made to postpone the change beyond that date. **1955** *Times* 9 July 2/6 Many people thought that fewer pupils were now staying after school-leaving age, but that was not so. **1972** *Times* 15 Jan. 2/5 Mrs Thatcher, Secretary of State for Education and Science, said in London last night that she had signed the order-in-council to raise school-leaving age to 16 in September. **1876** Miss Yonge *Womankind* v. 31 The institution of '*school mammas' may secure a protector for each. **1877** F. J. Gladman (*title*) *School method. **1917** Beresford & Richmond *W. E. Ford* ix. 194 A description of a typical staff-meeting discussion of school method. **1927** J. Adams *Errors in School* 35 School-method books. **1934** *Milk-in-Schools Scheme* (Milk Marketing Board) 6 Communications should be addressed to the '*School Milk' Dept., Thames House, Millbank. **1964** L. Lee *Firstborn* 11 I'd ask her to accept her faults..and not blame them..on..school-milk, or the British Railways. **1977** *Times* 10 May 4/3 Ministers will consider claiming an EEC grant worth 3p a pint on school milk. **1826** Miss Mitford *Village* II. 30, I..provided myself with a *school-mother, a fine tall blooming girl. **1753** *School pace [see *school gait* above]. **1889** *19th Cent.* Oct. 741 The parents are to pay *schoolpence. **1941** A. M. Johnson in *Amer. Jrnl. Orthopsychiatry* Oct. 702 The syndrome, often referred to as '*school phobia', is recognizable by the intense terror associated with being at school. **1959** *Times* 24 Nov. 13/3 Wherein is school-phobia different from the traditional reluctance which was met by old-fashioned compulsion? **1980** *Daily Tel.* 19 Nov. 15/5 By that time, the more timid boy had been brought to the verge of school-phobia by it all. **1977** *Daily Colonist* (Victoria, B.C.) 22 Oct. 28/7 A psychiatrist..said mothers of *school-phobic children are over-protective. **1981** *Lancashire Life* Jan. 25/2 We now have a new word for it... The 'school-phobic' says Lancashire Education Authority, is clearly intimidated by being required to attend school. **1874** C. M. Yonge *Lady Hester* ix. 205 Feeling very happy over the best **school report of our boy we had ever had. **1958** J. Cannan *And be a Villain* iv. 109 As his school reports revealed..he was useless at games. **1975** T. Allbeury *Palomino Blonde* xi. 71 There were a few school reports showing that Kristina was doing average well. **1882** E. L. Anderson *School-training for Horses* 75 A distinguished *school-rider, who gave me my first practical lessons in this movement. **1897** Ld. Ribblesdale *The Queen's Hounds* 264 He was probably not so good a school rider as the Prince Imperial. **1881** E. L. Anderson *How to Ride*, etc. Introd. 6 *School-riding, in one form or another, is used in all armies, and, indeed, wherever the horse must be under command. **1633** Ford *'Tis Pity* v. iii, A *Schoole-rod keepes a child in awe. *a* **1697** Aubrey *Lives* (1898) I. 328 At fourteen, he went away [from school] a good *schoole-scholar to Magdalen-hall in Oxford. *a* **1734** North *Life Sir D. North* (1744) 2 In the End, he came out a moderate School-scholar. **1835** *Indiana Mag. Hist.* XXII. 438 This was an action brought by the Trustees of a *school Section for money due on two years rent. **1849** *Rep. of Com. of Gen. Land Office* (Bartlett 1860), School-section. **1881** *Edmonton Bull.* 5 Nov. 3/2 As the surveys in Manitoba are made it is found that sections which should be available for school sections are already occupied..by the Syndicate for station grounds and other purposes. **1891** C. Roberts *Adrift Amer.* 37 A school section is a section of land..set apart by the Government for the purpose of raising funds for building and maintaining schools. **1841** *Southern Lit. Messenger* VII. 7/2 The means of creating officers [for the navy]..are to be derived from the *school-ship. **1867** Longf. in *Life* (1891) III. 89 We stopped near the school-ship, which was crowded with boys. **1971** C. Storr *Thursday* viii. 92 'Heaps of people do say it [*sc.* 'bloody']. Even on television.' 'But not on *schools programmes.' **1973** *Listener* 31 May 707/1 Of the 30 channels in the system, three are to be made available..for *schools television. **1974** Schools television [see pip *v.*³ 1 c]. **1895** C. M. Yonge *Long Vacation* vii. 66 He had heard enough *school stories to be wary of boasting of his title. **1914** 'I. Hay' *Lighter Side School Life* vi. 151 Whereas school stories were formerly written to be read by schoolboys, they are now written to be read..by grown-up persons. **1971** 'S. Smith' *Grave Affair* iv. 52 'Some boys from the Fifth. I don't know their names,' he lied in the best tradition of school stories. **1808** Scott *Autobiog.* in Lockhart *Life* (1839) I. 63 My greatest intimate from the days of my *school-tide was Mr. John Irving. **1740** J. Clarke *Educ. Youth* (ed. 3) 191 Such Boys..will be at Liberty out of *School-time. **1848** Thackeray *Van. Fair* lvi, The introduction of crackers in school-time. **1890** *Lancet* 4 Oct. 708/1 Life here is but the school-time of eternity hereafter. **1542** *Richmond Wills* (Surtees) 36 To finde John Fell meate and drinke, clothing, boks, and *scolewaige to go to the scole..to he be xxvi yeares of aige. **1864** Carlyle *Fredk. Gt.* xv. iii. IV. 30 He is now about to be taught several things;—and will have to pay his school-wages as he goes. **1922** Joyce *Ulysses* 669 Moral apothegms (e.g. *My Favourite Hero* or *Procrastination is the Thief of Time*) composed during *schoolyears.

school (skuːl), *sb.*² Forms: 5 scoll, 5–7 scole, scul(le, 6 skoole, *Sc.* scuill, 6–7 skul, skole, 6–9 scull, skull, 7 skoule, scoale, schole, 7–9 scool, 8–9 schull, 9 *dial.* schule, scholl, 9– school. [a. Du. *school* troop, multitude, 'school' of whales :—MDu. *schole*, OS. *scola* troop = OE. *scolu* :—OTeut. **skulā* str. fem., perh. orig. 'division', f. **skel-*, *skal-*, *skul-* to divide: see skill, shell.]

1. A shoal or large number of fish, porpoises, whales, etc. swimming together whilst feeding or migrating. Also *in a school*, *in* or *by schools*.

c **1400** *Laud Troy Bk.* 14205 Thei falle thikkere than heryng fletes In-myddes the se In here scole. *c* **1440** *Promp. Parv.* 450/2 Sculle, of a fysshe (scul of fysh, *S.*), *examen.* **1486** *Bk. St. Albans* f vij, A scoll of ffysh. *a* **1552** Leland *Itin.* (1769) V. 70 They [bream] appere in May in mightti Sculles, so that sumtime they breke large Nettes. *a* **1578** Lindesay (Pitscottie) *Chron. Scot.* (S.T.S.) II. 317 Thair come in our firth ane scuill of heirinng. *c* **1585** Janes in *Hakluyt's Voy.* (1600) III. 102 We saw to the West of those Isles three or foure whales in a skull. **1599** Hakluyt *Voy.* II. ii. 108 And this skole of fish continued with our ship for the space of fiue or sixe weekes. **1603** Owen *Pembrokeshire* (1891) 121 They swymme in great scooles together. **1606** Shaks. *Tr. & Cr.* v. v. 22 And there they flye or dye, like scaled sculs, Before the belching Whale. **1615** G. Sandys *Trav.* 100 He saw at the mouth of Nilus..a scole of dolphins rushing up the river. **1641** S. Smith *Herring Buss Trade* 25 According to the conveniency of the Skoles and places of fishing. **1655** Walton *Angler* x. (1661) 173 Repaire to the River, where you have seen them to swim in skuls or shoales in the Summer time. **1667** Milton *P.L.* vii. 402 Shoales of Fish that..Glide under the green Wave, in Sculles that oft Bank the mid Sea. **1673** H. Stubbe *Further Justif. War Netherl.* Apol., etc. 127 The latter should not fish within eighty miles of the Coast, least the Scholes of Herrings should be interrupted. **1769** *De Foe's Tour Gt. Brit.* (ed. 7) I. 380 A great Shoal, or, as they call it, a Scool of Pilchards, came swimming..into the Harbour. **1791** Lincoln in Belknap *Hist. New-Hampsh.* (1792) III. 456 These fish..take each schull its proper river. **1819** W. Tennant *Papistry Storm'd* (1827) 36 Great skulls o' haddock, cod and ling. **1839** Beale *Sperm Whale* 20 The groups, herds, or 'schools', which are formed by the sperm whale, are of two kinds. **1863** Pennell *Angler-naturalist* 285 The smolts assemble in sculls of from forty to seventy together. **1884** *Leisure Hour* Jan. 64/1 A 'school' of porpoises gambolling in mid ocean.

2. *transf.* †**a.** A troop, crowd (of persons); a large number, mass (of inanimate things). *Obs.* **b.** A flock, company (of animals).

1555 Phaer *Æneid* ii. (1558) D ij b, About him ronnes of boyes & girles yᵉ skull [*Lat.* 238–9 *Pueri circum innuptæque puellae Sacra canunt*]. *Ibid.* ix. (1584) O vj, Go fisgigs, frisk your woods in double pype in skipping skooles [*Lat. 617 Ite per alta Dindyma, ubi adsuetis biforem dat tibia cantum*]. **1563–87** Foxe *A. & M.* (1596) 83/2 A scull of pictured boies did band, about that lothsome sight. *Ibid.* 85/1 The youth in skuls flocke and run togither. **1567** Drant *Horace, Epist.* To Rdr., So greate a scull of amarouse Pamphlets haue so preoccupyed the eyes, and eares of men, that [etc.]. **1592** Lyly *Midas* iv. iii, Ile warrant hee hath by this started a couey of Bucks, or roused a scull of Phesants. **1665** Boyle *Occas. Refl.* vi. iii. (1848) 348 When we dip them [oysters] in Vinegar, we may, for sauce to one bit, devour alive a schole of little Animals. **1858** K. H. Digby *Children's Bower* II. 13 Sitting on their heels by the margin of a pond to feed what they call the school of ducks that gathers round them. **1861** Du Chaillu *Equat. Afr.* xiii. 194 A school of hippopotami. **1880** *Times* 24 Nov. 10/3 The Macclesfield tipplers [pigeons], which fly in schools or 'kits' for hours against another school. **1894** R. Leighton *Wreck Golden Fleece* 189 Look at that school of gulls yonder.

3. *attrib.*: **school-bass**, the *Sciæna ocellata*; **school-cod**, a cod inhabiting the open sea, opposed to *shore-cod*; **school-fish** *U.S.*, any fish which usually appears in schools or shoals, also one of a school of fish; *spec.* the menhaden. So **school-schnapper**, **-shark**, **-whale**.

1884 Goode, etc. *Nat. Hist. Aquatic Anim.* 372 The smaller fish of the species [*Sciæna ocellata*] are called simply 'Bass' or '*School Bass'. *Ibid.* 201 Still another class of fish is known..as 'Deep-water Cod', 'Bank Cod', and '*School Cod'. **1876** Goode *Fishes of Bermudas* 11 The smaller *school-fishes. **1882** Tenison-Woods *Fish N.S. Wales* 40 The time of the appearance of the '*school schnapper' is the early part of summer. **1852** Mundy *Antipodes* viii. (1855) 198 The '*school-shark' is dealt with as above. But if the 'grey-nurse' or old solitary shark be hooked, the cable is cut [[etc.]. **1840** F. D. Bennett *Whaling Voy.* II. 176 A *School Whale, upon being attacked by the boats, rejected from her stomach a bony fish.

school (skuːl), *v.*¹ Forms: see school *sb.*¹ [f. school *sb.*¹ Cf. G. *schulen*.]

1. a. *trans.* To put or send to school; to educate at school.

1577 Stanyhurst *Descr. Irel.* vii. 24 b in *Holinshed*, Schooled in the vniuersitie of Parise. **1600** Shaks. *A.Y.L.* i. i. 173 Yet hee's gentle, neuer school'd, and yet learned, full of noble deuise. **1846** *Eng. Rev.* VI. 138 The number actually schooled in the State schools was no less than 2,021,421. **1850** Lynch *Theo. Trinal* xi. 211 How he was born, cradled, schooled, tailcoated, colleged, and the like. **1869** Blackmore *Lorna D.* i, My father..being a great admirer of learning sent me to be schooled at Tiverton. **1884** G. Allen *Philistia* II. 13 Eight children to be washed and dressed and schooled daily.

b. *intr.* To attend school. *rare.*

1934 in Webster. **1972** *Straits Times* 23 Nov. 15/4 'It's incredible,' says the amiable 32-year-old Globe Silk Store proprietor who has schooled in England.

†**2.** To have as a member of one's school or sect.

c **1570** L. Gibson in *Collect. B.L. Ball. & Broadsides* (1867) 115 It seemes, by your doynges, that Cressed doth scoole ye,—Penelopeys vertues are cleane out of thought. **1577** Hanmer *Anc. Eccl. Hist.* (1619) 73 This man was first schooled by Valentinus.

3. a. 'To teach with superiority, to tutor' (J.); †in early use, to 'lecture', admonish reprimand.

1573 G. Harvey *Letter-bk.* (Camden) 10 This is the wai that thes fellonli men have taken to school and coole me, silli soul. *c* **1586** C'TESS PEMBROKE *Ps.* L. v, Mildly the good, God schooleth in this wise. **1592** in Fowler *Hist. C.C.C.* (O.H.S.) 160 She [Q. Eliz.] schooled Dr. John Rainolds for his obstinate preciseness. **1606** J. CARPENTER *Solomon's Solace* xxii. 91 He hearkened to.. his mother when shee schooled him. *c* **1610** HEYWOOD & ROWLEY *Fortune by Land & Sea* I. i, Nay school us not old man, some of us are too old to learn. **1622** FLETCHER *Span. Curate* I. i, *Arsen.* Fy upon thee. This is prophane. *Mil.* Good Doctor, doe not schoole me, For a fault you are not free from. **1624** *Visibility of True Ch.* 91 He schooleth and lessoneth the Pope plainly. *a* **1657** R. LOVEDAY *Lett.* (1663) 272 That's my Landlord's fault, for which I shall school him. **1687** DRYDEN *Hind & P.* III. 306 It now remains for you to school your child, And ask why God's anointed he reviled. **1691** —— *K. Arthur* III. ii, My former Lord, Grim Osmond, walks the Round: Calls o'er the Names, and Schools the tardy Sprights. *a* **1700** B. E. *Dict. Cant. Crew, I school'd him,* I chid him severely. **1710** CONGREVE *Poems, Of Pleasing* Wks. 1720 II. 426 So Macer and Mundungus school the Times, And write in rugged Prose the Rules of softer Rhymes. **1746** SMOLLETT *Rod. Random* xlv, The doctor.. was infinitely surprized to find himself schooled by one of my appearance; and.. cried, 'Upon my word! you are in the right, Sir! **1818** SCOTT *Hrt. Midl.* xviii, 'I ken a' that as weel as—I mean to say,' he resumed, checking the irritation he felt at being schooled,—a discipline of the mind, which those most ready to bestow it on others, do themselves most reluctantly submit to receive. **1865** LIVINGSTONE *Zambesi* Introd. 13 Many will prefer to draw their own conclusions from them rather than to be schooled by us.

†**b.** To give a lesson to (a person) by punishment; to chastise. *Obs.*

a **1592** GREENE *Jas. IV,* III. ii, I say thou art too presumptuous, and the officers shall schoole thee. **1595** *Locrine* III. iii. 25 Then wil we schoole you, ere you and we part hence. [They fight.] **1628** FORD *Lovers Melancholy* v. i, Take hence the wag, and school him for't.

4. a. To educate, train (a person, his mind, powers, tastes, etc.); to render wise, skilful, or tractable by training or discipline. Often *transf.*, said of God, the experiences of life, surrounding influences, etc.

a **1591** H. SMITH *Serm.* (1594) 385 Now, Salomon, full of wisdome, and schooled with experience, is licensed to giue his sentence of the whole world. **1591** SPENSER *M. Hubberd* 855 For he was school'd by kinde in all the skill Of close conveyance. **1657** J. WATTS *Dipper Sprinkled* 59 Visited of God with sickness, and so scholed, and enlightned by him therein and thereby. **1755** SMOLLETT *Quix.* (1803) IV. 169 A teacher of the Gentiles, schooled by Heaven, and whose professor and master was Jesus Christ himself. **1762** GOLDSM. *Nash* 174 A mind neither schooled by philosophy, nor encouraged by conscious innocence. **1826** DISRAELI *Viv. Grey* III. i, Having schooled his intellect in the Universities of two nations. **1838** LYTTON *Leila* I. iv, Leila, thou hast been nurtured with tenderness, and schooled with care. **1856** FROUDE *Hist. Eng.* (1858) II. vii. 229 They were too well schooled in the tricks of reservation. **1878** BOSW. SMITH *Carthage* 114 Among these was Xanthippus,.. one who had been well schooled in war by the admirable training which the Spartan discipline still gave. **1888** BRYCE *Amer. Commw.* xcv. III. 337 But the ambition of American statesmen has been schooled to flow in constitutional channels.

b. To discipline, bring under control, correct (oneself, one's mind, feelings, thoughts, etc.).

1579 GOSSON *Sch. Abuse,* etc. *To Gentlew. Citizens* (Arb.) 58, I haue seene many of you whiche were wont to sporte your selues at Theaters, when you perceiued the abuse of those places, schoole your selues, and of your owne accorde abhorre Playes. **1605** SHAKS. *Macb.* IV. ii. 15 My deerest Cooz, I pray you schoole your selfe. **1657** TRAPP *Comm. Ps.* xlii. 6 Though before he had schooled himself out of his distempers. **1813** SCOTT *Rokeby* IV. xiv, Now must Matilda stray apart, To school her disobedient heart. **1837** DISRAELI *Venetia* V. v, She had too long and too fondly schooled herself to look upon the outraged wife as the only victim. **1844** KINGLAKE *Eothen* xxi. 326 After the first half hour I so far schooled myself to this new exercise [riding a dromedary] that [etc.]. **1865** TROLLOPE *Belton Est.* x, Clara schooled herself into a resolution to bear it with good humour. **1876** GEO. ELIOT *Dan. Der.* VI. xlviii, No wonder that Deronda now marked some hardening in a look and manner which were schooled daily to the suppression of feeling.

c. With advs. *to school away*: to remove by instruction or discipline (*rare*). *to school down*: to subdue by training.

1833 CHALMERS *Const. Man* I. v. (1834) I. 194 It may at least school away those prepossessions of the fancy or of the taste that would lead us to resist or to dislike such evidence when offered. **1863** KINGLAKE *Crimea* (ed. 3) II. ii. 63 Lord Raglan.. was so schooled down by long years of flat office labour that it shocked him to see a man bearing no uniform, yet warlike, and armed to the teeth. **1867** TROLLOPE *Chron. Barset* II. lii. 90 At home she had schooled herself down into quiescence.

d. *passive.* To be educated *in* (certain beliefs, sentiments, habits). Also const. *inf.*

1841 MIALL in *Nonconf.* I. 529 We.. have been so schooled in modern ecclesiastical phraseology that we cease to regard it as singular. **1862** LYTTON *Str. Story* 10 Their seniors are cramped by the dogmas they were schooled to believe when the world was some decades the younger.

5. To instruct or inform (a person) how to act; to teach (a person) his part.

1579 SPENSER *Sheph. Cal.* May 227 So schooled the Gate [goat] her wanton sonne, That answerd his mother, all should be done. **1587** HOOKER *Ir. Hist.* 79/1 in *Holinshed,* Wherefore it was blazed in Ireland, that the king [Hen. VII] .. had schooled a boie to take vpon him the earle of Warwikes name. **1596** SHAKS. *Tam. Shr.* IV. iv. 9 But sir here comes your boy, T'were good he were school'd. **1874** H. R. REYNOLDS *John Bapt.* vii. 440 Herodias schooled Salome in the part she was to play. **1883** S. C. HALL *Retrospect* II. 271 Schooled by my guide, it was not difficult to realise the scene [etc.].

6. a. To train or exercise (a horse) in movements.

1869 'WAT. BRADWOOD' *The O.V.H.* xix, The way you had schooled him [a horse]. **1890** *Daily News* 23 Dec. 2/4 Some well-known horses on the flat are being schooled for hurdle jumping. **1881** E. L. ANDERSON *How to Ride,* etc. 60 Part II, How to School a Horse. The Early Education of the Horse.

b. *intr.* To ride straight across country.

1885 *Field* 4 Apr. 428/2 We schooled back to the Poorhouse Gorse, and a couple of fences of the order intricate had to be jumped, under the penalty of a long round. **1892** *Ibid.* 9 Apr. 512/2 Let me draw a discreet veil over sundry acts of renaging and recusancy on the part of good hunters and good riders, for in every country it will be found that some few celebrities of the hunting field have a rooted antipathy to 'schooling'.

7. *trans.* To rear (a plant) in a nursery.

1902 CORNISH *Naturalist Thames* 122 The young osiers.. should be taken from a nursery in which they have been 'schooled' for one year.

8. *intr.* To gamble in a 'school' (cf. SCHOOL *sb.*[1] 6a). *slang.*

1935 A. J. CRONIN *Stars look Down* I. ii. 17 Some colliers .. that made up the gambling school in ordinary times—squatted upon their hunkers against the wall. They were not schoolin' now, they had no coppers for schoolin'.

school (sku:l), *v.*[2] Forms: see SCHOOL *sb.*[2] [f. SCHOOL *sb.*[2]] *intr.* To collect or swim together in 'schools' or shoals (of fish). *to school up*: to collect or crowd close together at or near the surface of the water, said of fishes.

1597 BRETON *Wits Trenchmour* (Grosart) 10/1 The Herings seldom scull, but on a thick misty morning. **1606** S. GARDINER *Bk. Angling* 45 Fishes of each kind skull togeather. **1725** DUDLEY in *Phil. Trans.* XXXIII. 264 Let the Wind blow which Way it will, that Way they [*sc.* dead whales] will scull a Head, tho' right in the Eye of the Wind. **1873-** [see SCHOOLING *ppl. a.*[2] and *vbl. sb.*[2]]. **1884** GOODE, etc. *Nat. Hist. Aquatic Anim.* 375 Yellow-tails.. do not school, but swim singly or in pairs. **1891** *Century Dict.* s.v., Menhaden do not school up until the beginning of the summer. **1897** KIPLING *Capt. Cour.* viii. 154 The caplin schooled once more at twilight.

schoolable ('sku:ləb(ə)l), *a. rare.* [f. SCHOOL *sb.*[1] + -ABLE.]

†**1.** Capable of being schooled or trained. *Obs.*

1594 CAREW *Huarte's Exam. Wits* iv. (1596) 38 Amongst beasts of one kind, he which is most Schooleable and skilfull is such because he hath his braine better tempered.

2. Of proper age to attend school.

1846 *Eng. Rev.* VI. 138 In 1831 the number of children between the ages of 7 and 14, the approved schoolable period, was 2,043,030. **1869** *Echo* 15 Mar., 250,000 children of 'schoolable' age. **1888** *Rep. U.S. Commissioner Educ.* 1886–87, 59 Each tax-payer.. would have a far less burden to bear in the work of getting all the 'schoolable' children within the schools.

†**'schoolage.** Forms: 6 scolage, 7 scollage, scholage, schoolage. [f. SCHOOL *sb.*[1] + -AGE. Cf. med.L. *scolagium*, OF. *escolage.*]

1. *Sc.* The fee paid for tuition at school. Also *schoolage-fee.*

1511–12 *Acc. Ld. High Treas. Scot.* IV. 242 Item the xxviij day of Januar, send with William Alresky to Maister David Wocat for half ane ȝeris burd and his scolage fee at his entre this day to the scoile. **1602** *Stirling Burgh Rec.* (1887) I. 101 And thrie pundis vjs. viijd. to be payed to ilk ane of thame be the maister of the scole furth of the excres of his scollage mair nor wes first conditionate to him be his contract. **1607** in J. Grant *Burgh. Sch. Scot.* II. xiii. (1876) 467 Bringing with them [to school] their quarter's scholage. **1662** *Stirling Burgh Rec.* (1887) I. 238 And it salbe be lawchfull for the said maister Thomas to take for ilk townes bairn in schooleage, each quarter of the yeare, six shilling eight pennyes Scotts money.

2. Instruction in school; the services of a schoolmaster.

1603 HOLLAND *Plutarch's Mor.* 454 You are well enough served and receive a due Minervall for your schoolage.

schoolar, obs. form of SCHOLAR.

†**schoo'lation.** *Obs.*[−1] [f. SCHOOL *v.*[1] + -ATION.] Schooling, education at school.

1575 LANEHAM *Let.* (1871) 22 That throogh good scoolation becam az formall in his action az had he been a bride groom indeed.

school board. [BOARD *sb.* 8b.]

1. In England and Wales from 1870 to 1902, and in Scotland from 1872 to 1918, a body of persons elected by the rate-payers of a 'school district', and charged by statute with the provision and maintenance of sufficient accommodation in public elementary schools for all the children of the district.

In England school boards were established only in districts in which either a majority of the ratepayers approved, or the existing accommodation in public elementary schools was considered by the Education Department to be insufficient. The Education Act of 1902 abolished school boards in England, and transferred their duties and powers to the County Councils.

In Scotland there was a school board in every school district (which was usually a burgh or a parish). By the Act of 1872 the control of the burgh and parish schools established by previous Acts, was vested in the school boards, which were also required to establish and maintain such additional schools as might be needed.

The Education (Scotland) Act of 1918 abolished school boards in Scotland, and transferred their duties and powers to burgh or county education authorities.

1870 *Act 33 & 34 Vict.* c. 75 §10 If.. the Education Department are satisfied that all the public school accommodation required.. has not been so supplied.. the Education Department shall cause a school board to be formed for the district. **1872** *Act 35 & 36 Vict.* c. 62 §8 A school board shall be elected in and for each and every parish and burgh [in Scotland]. **1876** FAWCETT *Pol. Econ.* II. viii. (ed. 5) 234 A school board is very rarely established in a country parish. **1882** M. ARNOLD *Ir. Ess.,* etc. 131 You often see the School Boards.. making the programme of their elementary schools too ambitious.

attrib. **1891** KIPLING *Light that Failed* xiv, Alf was not a nice child, being puffed up with many school-board certificates for good conduct.

2. In countries other than Great Britain, a board charged with the provision and maintenance of schools.

1836 *Chambers's Edin. Jrnl.* 27 Aug. 244/2 Over these provinces [in Prussia] is placed a consistory, or council, divided also into three sections, one of which is termed the school-board. **1838** F. B. HAWKINS *Germany* xii. 201 Every circle and parish has also its school-board. **1857** *Harper's Mag.* Sept. 571/2 Can you inform me where the president of your school board resides? **1911** *Daily Colonist* (Victoria, B.C.) 11 Apr. 7/3 The school board which recently submitted its estimates for the year to the city council will have to revise them. **1972** *Even. Telegram* (St. John's Newfoundland) 24 June 6/1 The government.. tried to save a few dollars on the busing of children to school. There were immediate cries of pain from the Opposition and from some school boards. **1976** *National Observer* (U.S.) 2 Oct. 15/1 It was my job to cover the.. school-board meetings of several communities.

'school-book. [Cf. G. *schulbuch.*]

1. a. A book of instruction used at school.

1745 B. FRANKLIN *Let.* 11 Dec. in *Writings* (1905) II. 296 At present I only send for a few school books, and books of navigation. **1771** LUCKOMBE *Hist. Print.* 103 A patent [was] granted him to print Latin School-books. **1848** THACKERAY *Van. Fair* l, His bundle of school-books hanging by a thong. **1855** TENNYSON *Brook* 9 In our school-books we say,.. They flourish'd then or then.

b. *attrib.*

1751 *Pope's Wks., Epil. Sat.* i. 76 *note,* Full of school-book phrases and Anglicisms. **1821** C. SIMEON *Let.* 27 Nov. in Carus *Life* (1847) 558 The abundance of your own personal labours, and of those engaged in the School-book Society, amazes me.

2. An account-book, register, etc. belonging or relating to a particular school.

1870 *Act 33 & 34 Vict.* c. 75 §72 If the managers or teacher of any school refuse.. to allow the inspector to.. examine the school books and registers.

schoolboy ('sku:lbɔɪ). [f. SCHOOL *sb.*[1] + BOY.]

1. a. A boy attending or belonging to a school.

1588 SHAKS. *L.L.L.* v. ii. 403 O! neuer will I trust to speeches pen'd, Nor to the motion of a Schoole-boies tongue. **1599** B. JONSON *Cynthia's Rev.* IV. v, Death, what talke you of his Learning? he vnderstands no more then a schoole-Boy. **1600** SHAKS. *A.Y.L.* II. vii. 145. **1788** BURKE *Sp. agst. W. Hastings* Wks. XIII. 37 School-boys without tutors, minors without guardians. **1813** SOUTHEY in *Croker Papers* (1884) I. 49, I should go to the task like a schoolboy. **1881** CROWEST *Phases Mus. Eng.* 164 The merest schoolboy, it would be thought, could have detected the absurdity of such a musical passage.

b. In phr. ***every schoolboy knows***, referring to a matter of factual information, supposed to be elementary and generally known.

1654 JER. TAYLOR *Real Pres.* 80 Every Schole-boy knows it. **1721** SWIFT *Poems* (1958) I. 281 How haughtily he lifts his Nose, To tell what ev'ry School Boy knows. **1840** MACAULAY in *Edin. Rev.* Jan. 295 Every schoolboy knows who imprisoned Montezuma, and who strangled Atahualpa. **1966** *Listener* 8 Sept. 365/3 Tallis's motet *Spem in alium nunquam habui* was for years more often written about than heard. A *tour-de-force* in forty voice-parts: so much every schoolboy knew. **1977** *Times* 15 Oct. 2/8 Every schoolboy knows that the No. 3 bus from Piccadilly Circus comes to Valley Fields, Wodehouses's familiar pseudonym for Dulwich.

2. *attrib.* and *Comb.*, passing into *adj.* as ***schoolboy code*** (***of honour***), ***English***, ***French***, ***honour***, ***humour***; also ***schoolboy-like*** adj.

1874 C. M. YONGE *Lady Hester* vii. 169 The boy endured all the rage and scorn that a threat so contrary to all schoolboy codes of honour and friendship might deserve. **1977** P. G. WINSLOW *Witch Hill Murder* II. xviii. 248 His blue gaze fell on Capricorn expecting him to understand and accept his schoolboy code. **1798** SOUTHEY *Autumn* 18, I call to mind The school-boy days. **1835** J. ROMILLY *Diary* 6 July (1967) 82 P. George of Camb. delighted me by his returning thanks, because it was good simple schoolboy English. **1955** E. BLISHEN *Roaring Boys* III. 158 He delighted in mimicking my schoolboy French. **1977** J. CLEARY *High Road to China* ii. 41 A six months' affair with a girl in Auxi had improved his schoolboy French. **1848** THACKERAY *Van. Fair* xxx, In his big schoolboy hand-writing. **1876** C. M. YONGE *Womankind* xviii. 138 To keep up a standard of real honour, above schoolboy honour, is most needful. **1970** P. Y. CARTER *Mr Campion's Falcon* xxii. 166 He has a sense of schoolboy honour, a perfectly straightforward code. **1962** G. K. HUNTER *John Lyly* iv. 237 The inane schoolboy humour of his part, and the tradition of Ralph Roister Doister to which it belongs, both point to a juvenile rather than an adult actor. **1977** R. PERRY *Dead End* viii. 99 Just forget the schoolboy humour and do as you're told. **1802** H. MARTIN *Helen of Glenross* III. 74, I cannot help laughing at his schoolboy-like joy in his new play-things. **1812** BYRON *Ch. Har.* II. xviii, Or schoolboy Midshipman that.. Strains his shrill pipe as good or ill betides. **1687** SETTLE *Refl. Dryden* 6 This great pretender to Learning has not wit enough to make an Allegory, but violates the common

School-boy Rules of sence. **1712** ADDISON *Spect.* No. 523 ¶2 A parcel of School-Boy Tales. **1887** *Spectator* 15 Oct. 1380 This curiously school-boy way of insulting a foreign nation.

Hence **ˈschoolboydom, ˈschoolboyhood,** the state or condition of being a schoolboy; also, schoolboys collectively. **ˈschoolboyism,** action or conduct characteristic of a schoolboy.

1836 E. HOWARD *R. Reefer* xxi, The pedantic schoolboyism of calling a house-keeper a nymph. **1854** WHEWELL in *Life* (1881) 436 The recollections of schoolboyhood. **1880** R. G. WHITE *Every-Day English* 277 The first great English grammar, the one by which school-boydom has been chiefly oppressed, was written by an American. **1893** *Temple Bar* XCVIII. 139 Schoolboyhood whispers derision.

schoolboyish (ˈskuːlbɔɪɪʃ), *a.* [f. SCHOOLBOY + -ISH.] Schoolboy-like. Hence **ˈschoolboyishly** *adv.*, in the manner of a schoolboy; **ˈschoolboyishness,** the conduct or manner of a schoolboy.

1831 *Fraser's Mag.* IV. 278 All this being not particularly new, and rather schoolboyish withal. **1888** *Academy* 18 Feb. 112 An eminently schoolboyish story. **1898** G. B. SHAW *Let.* ? 2 May (1972) II. 39 Irving & I are too eminent to indulge in such schoolboyishness in public. **1901** W. J. LOCKE *Usurper* xviii. 247 He..was so schoolboyishly happy the next morning on starting for his holiday. **1972** J. POTTER *Going West* 159 His step was jaunty and his manner schoolboyishly affable. **1976** *Daily Tel.* 9 Sept. 13/1 As an example of the schoolboyishness, I would cite the fact that Ransome and a friend..had coded signals which they displayed on their respective houses..to give notice when they were going fishing.

schoolcraft (ˈskuːlkrɑːft, -æ-). *arch.* [f. SCHOOL *sb.*[1] + CRAFT.] Knowledge taught in the schools.

1629 B. JONSON *New Inn* II. ii, He has met his parallel in wit and school-craft. **1832** W. IRVING *Alhambra* II. 187 Take care how you play off your schoolcraft another time upon an old soldier. **1862** LYTTON *Str. Story* II. 271 Had I been less devoted a bigot to this vain school-craft, which we call the Medical Art..I might [etc.]. **1865** KINGSLEY *Herew.* xv, Schoolcraft and honesty never went yet together.

schoold, variant of SHALD, shallow.

schoolday (ˈskuːldeɪ). [f. SCHOOL *sb.*[1] + DAY.]

1. *pl.* The days or period (of one's life) at which one is at school.

1590 SHAKS. *Mids. N.* III. ii. 202 O, is all forgot? All schooledaies friendship, child-hood innocence? **1594** —— *Rich. III*, IV. iv. 169 Tetchy and wayward was thy Infancie. Thy School-daies frightfull,..Thy prime of Manhood, daring. **1798** LAMB *Old Familiar Faces* i, In my joyful school-days. **1885** LD. BLACKBURN in *Law Rep. 10 App. Cases* 388 In his schooldays or in his grown up days.

attrib. **1844** DISRAELI *Coningsby* VII. ii, When two school-day friends..meet at the close of their college careers.

2. A day on which there is school.

1852 WALCOT *William of Wykeham* 233 On whole school-days, morning school lasts from 7 till 8 A.M.; middle school from 9 until noon; evening school begins at 2, and ends at 6. **1857** HUGHES *Tom Brown* II. v, It is a whole school-day. **1873** *Routledge's Young Gentl. Mag.* Dec. 101/1 During the holidays, or on a school-day.

ˈschool-diˈvine. = SCHOOLMAN 1.

1594 HOOKER *Eccl. Pol.* III. ix. §2 The greatest amongst the Schoole diuines studying how to set downe by exact definition the nature of an humaine lawe..found not which way better to do it then in these words [following]. **1613** SALKELD *Treat. Angels* title-p., Collected out of the holy Scriptures, ancient Fathers, and Schoole-Divines. **1737** POPE *Hor. Epist.* II. i. 102 In Quibbles Angel and Arch-angel join, And God the Father turns a School-divine. **1865** PUSEY *Truth Eng. Ch.* 214 What school-Divines call 'Potentia proxima'.

ˈschool-diˈvinity. The religious principles and doctrines maintained and taught in the Schools, or by the mediæval moralists and divines.

1594 CAREW *Huarte's Exam. Wits* ix. (1596) 124 The truth of schooldivinity abhorreth many words. **1616** S. PRICE *Ephesus Warning* 48 It is a true axiome in schoole-Diuinity, that..whatsoeuer is spoken of God bodily, must be vnderstood figuratiuely. **1710** ADDISON *Whig-Examiner* No. 4 ¶1 The most abstruse and profound tract of school-divinity. **1840** CARLYLE *Heroes* iii. (1841) 140 His [Dante's] education was the best then going; much school-divinity, Aristotelean logic, some Latin classics.

school doctor.

†**1.** = SCHOOL-DIVINE.

1528 TINDALE *Obed. Chr. Man* 40 b, Marke here how past all shame oure scole doctours are. **1565** JEWEL *Repl. Harding* 259 The Schoole Doctours canne in no wise agree; there is Scotus agamste Thomas [etc.]. **1609** BIBLE (Douay) *1 Kings* viii. Annot. 587 Who so desireth, may search the iudgement of ancient Fathers, and see S. Thomas, and other schole Doctors.

†**2.** The teacher of a school. *Sc. Obs. rare.*

1730 T. BOSTON *My Life* (1908) 7 The school-doctor's son put a pipe-stopple in each of his nostrils.

3. The medical attendant of a school; esp. a medical practitioner who receives a fixed salary for his services in attending the pupils when ill.

1906 R. BROOKE *Let.* 1 Apr. (1968) 47 Dukes, the school doctor, was paying us his hurried visit. **1933** A. WHITE *Frost in May* xiii. 333 The school doctor..told them..they were now perfectly well. **1963** M. KENDON *Ladies College, Goudhurst* 19 Dr. Mapleton, the school doctor,..would drive up in his dog-cart, with his wooden stethoscope inside his silk hat. **1976** J. PHILIPS *Backlash* (1977) III. ii. 148 He had a sinecure for me. School doctor.

schooldom (ˈskuːldəm). [f. SCHOOL *sb.*[1] + -DOM.] The domain or world of school or schools; the persons, things, and conditions concerned in the affairs of schools.

1826 MISS MITFORD *My Godfather* in *Lit. Souvenir* 393 A young girl, just freed from the trammels of schooldom. **1854** MARION HARLAND *Alone* iv, A summons to 'the study' was an event of rare occurrence..in the annals of schooldom. **1902** *Spectator* 26 July 110 The sense of injustice in this particular has permeated the ranks of schooldom.

schooled (skuːld), *ppl. a.* [f. SCHOOL *v.*[1] + -ED[1].] Taught, trained, or disciplined.

1821 Joanna Baillie *Metr. Leg.*, *Columbus* xl, This all-schooled forbearance would surpass. **1877** BLACK *Green Past.* iv, Forgetting indeed in this one outburst all his schooled reticence. **1882** E. L. ANDERSON *School-training for Horses* 120 It is not necessary to use a sharp spur upon a schooled horse.

schooler, obs. form of SCHOLAR *sb.*

-schooler (ˈskuːlə(r)). *U.S.* [f. SCHOOL *sb.*[1] + -ER[1].] As the second element in Combinations, designating a pupil at a specified type of school, or stage of school-life, as ***grade, high schooler***. See also PRE-SCHOOLER.

1971 *Sci. Amer.* Dec. 114/3 Martin Gardner's well-known learning and mathematical depth are worn lightly in this friendly, comical book for grade schoolers. **1972** *Newsweek* 25 Sept. 106/2 (*caption*) Harvard tutor..and high schoolers. **1973** *Black World* June 44/1 Ronald and Wayne are high schoolers. **1977** *Rolling Stone* 30 June 60/2 High schoolers will dye their hair gray, and buy iron-on wrinkles, and yearn for the day when their bodies begin to sag.

ˈschoolery. *rare.* [f. SCHOOL *sb.*[1] + -ERY.] That which is taught in a school, or as in a school.

1591-5 SPENSER *Col. Clout* 702 A filed toung, furnisht with tearmes of art, No art of schoole, but Courtiers schoolery. **1807** [IRELAND] *Mod. Ship of Fools* 266 Rear'd in folly's ideot schoolerie, Every age thus boasts its foolerie. **1894** W. S. GILBERT *His Excellency* I. 12 Oh you may laugh at our dancing-schoolery, It's all very well, it amuses you.

schoolfellow (ˈskuːlfɛləʊ). [f. SCHOOL *sb.*[1] + FELLOW *sb.*] One who is or formerly was at the same school at the same time with another.

In early use sometimes applied to one's contemporary at a university.

1440 SIR R. LAIDAMIS *Let.* in *Athenæum* (1864) 10 Sept. 340/2 Ye and Y where scollfelaus sumtyme at Hylmyster. **1551** ROBINSON *More's Utopia* Epist. (1895) 19 The old acquayntaunce, that was betwene you and me in the time of our childhode, being then scolefellowes togethers. **1581** PETTIE tr. *Guazzo's Civ. Convers.* I. (1586) 11 A Gentleman sometime my Schoolefellowe at Pad. who in learning was not inferiour to anie Scholler in the Uniuersitie. **1602** SHAKS. *Ham.* III. iv. 202 (1604 Qo.) My two Schoolefellowes. **1669** R. MONTAGU in *Buccleuch MSS.* (Hist. MSS. Comm.) I. 425 Mr. Vernon, who was a schoolfellow of mine. **1690** LOCKE *Educ.* §70 (1699) 97 The emulation of Schoolfellows often puts Life and Industry into young Lads. **1783** COWPER *Valediction* 35 Thy schoolfellow, and partner of thy plays. **1848** THACKERAY *Van. Fair* xlix, The Colonel's countenance..wore as many blushes as the face of a boy of sixteen assumes when he is confronted with his sister's schoolfellows.

Hence **school-fellowship.**

1722 WODROW *Corr.* (1843) II. 628 It seems there are some secret remains of what we call school-fellowship, that have led him to a better opinion of my book than it deserves. **1844** S. R. MAITLAND *Dark Ages* 128 Who was perhaps bound to him by what is often the closer and stronger tie of school-fellowship.

schoolful (ˈskuːlfʊl). [f. SCHOOL *sb.*[1] + -FUL.] As much or as many as a school will hold.

1881 *Academy* 22 Oct. 307 Such a monster may perchance exist,..but surely not a whole schoolful of them. **1900** *Daily News* 16 Aug. 6/7 We enjoyed it like a schoolful of children.

schoolgirl (ˈskuːlgɜːl). [f. SCHOOL *sb.*[1] + GIRL.]

1. A girl attending school.

1777 E. DRAPER *Let.* 10 July in *N. & Q.* (1944) CLXXXVII. 12/2 The pertness, of the consequential School Girl, has given place to softer Manners. **1778** F. BURNEY *Evelina* I. xi. 36, I did not choose to tell him it [*sc.* my fear] was owing to my never before dancing but with a school-girl. **1809** MALKIN *Gil Blas* VII. ii, Fortune, wearied out with the school-girl's tricks she had been playing me. **1831** MACAULAY *Ess.*, *Boswell's Johnson* ¶5 Every school-girl knows the lines: 'Scarce had lamented Forbes paid..'. **1847** C. BRONTË *Jane Eyre* xiii, You play a little, I see; like any other English school-girl.

2. *attrib.* and *Comb.*, passing into adj. as ***schoolgirl complexion, crush, English, French, passion.***

1922 *Woman's Home Compan.* Oct. 35 (Advt.), Better than jewels——that schoolgirl complexion... Choose Palmolive, because its action is soothing. **1924** WODEHOUSE *Ukridge* x. 241 A man like myself, who finds at least eight hours of sleep essential if that schoolgirl complexion is to be preserved. **1938** G. GREENE *Brighton Rock* v. ii. 196 The long parade of posters..Guinness is Good for You, Try a Worthington, Keep that Schoolgirl Complexion. **1973** A. MACVICAR *Painted Doll Affair* iii. 39 She was an enthusiast for soap and water, as her schoolgirl complexion showed. **1952** Schoolgirl crush [see CRUSH *sb.* 2 d]. **1963** P. MOYES *Murder à la Mode* iv. 69 Olwen had a sort of schoolgirl crush on her. **1978** C. STORR *Winter's End* xiii. 143 Bran..wondered what she'd..meant when she'd told Rosey that she loved Philip. A schoolgirl crush? A romantic fantasy? **1939** C. ISHERWOOD *Goodbye to Berlin* 32 Frl. Hippi..speaks schoolgirl English with a slight American accent. **1967** W. G. CORP tr. *L. Oriol's Short Circuit* ii. 11 She spoke a schoolgirl English which nobody could understand. **1909** W. J. LOCKE *Septimus* iv. 49 'Will a hundred francs be of any use to you?' she asked, in her schoolgirl French. **1977** J. CLEARY *High Road to China* iv. 119 Mustafa Kemal said in French,..'I apologize for not speaking English.' Eve said..'I speak only schoolgirl French.' **1847** C. BRONTË *Jane Eyre* xiv, Not three in three thousand raw school-girl-governesses would have answered me as you have just done. **1936** M. MITCHELL *Gone with Wind* xvii. 312 You still cherish a romantic schoolgirl passion for him. **1832** L. HUNT *Sir R. Esher* (1850) 87 A proper school-girl tone.

Hence **ˈschoolgirlhood,** the state or condition of being a schoolgirl. **ˈschoolgirlism,** the action or conduct of a schoolgirl. **ˈschoolgirly** *a.*, like a schoolgirl, schoolgirlish.

1885 *Spectator* 1010/2 It is all absurdly missish and school-girly. **1889** 'F. ANSTEY' *Pariah* I. ii, It isn't nearly so school-girly as it used to be, is it? **1893** COLLINGWOOD *Life Ruskin* I. 60 Emancipated from schoolgirlhood. **1901** *Academy* 8 June 495/2 Southport, with its sponge-cakeyness and school-girlism is surely worth study.

schoolgirlish (ˈskuːlgɜːlɪʃ), *a.* [-ISH.] Resembling or characteristic of a schoolgirl.

1867 MISS BROUGHTON *Cometh up as Fl.* I. i. 9 So school-girlish as if you had never seen a man before! **1881** MISS BRADDON *Asphodel* III. 8 What a romantic schoolgirlish notion!

Hence **schoolgirlishness.**

1886 *Pall Mall G.* 12 Oct. 5/2 That rather objectionable quality..'school-girlishness', sentimentality, or 'gush'.

ˈschool-house.

1. A building appropriated for the use of a school; also, the dwelling-house provided by the school authorities for the use of the schoolmaster or schoolmistress, usually attached to or adjoining a school.

1429 *Nottingham Rec.* II. 122 Unam domum vocatam 'Scolehous'. **1523-4** *Rec. St. Mary at Hill* 321 Paid for makyng clene of a chambre in the Abbottes yn for to be a skole howse for Northfolkes children. **1583** *Leg. Bp. St. Androis* 40 in *Satir. Poems Reform.* xlv, Maitland, Melwill, and Matchevellous, Learned never mair knaifrie in a scholehous. **1590** SPENSER *F.Q.* I. x. 18 To haue her knight into her schoole-house plaste That of her heauenly learning he might taste. *a* **1610** HEALEY *Cebes* (1636) 156 It is an easie thing for one to be a deepe scholer, & yet bee as prone to drunkenness [etc.] as hee that neuer saw the inside of a school-house. **1673** *Essex Papers* (Camden) I. 115 In the Diocesse of Raphoe there is a freeschoole..but there is noe publicke schoolhouse built there or elsewhere in the Diocesse. **1818** SCOTT *Hrt. Midl.* ix, But when, seated on the benches of the school-house, they began to con their lessons together, Reuben [etc.]. **1870** *Act 33 & 34 Vict.* c. 75 §72 If the managers or teacher of any school refuse..to allow the inspector to inspect the schoolhouse or examine any scholar. **1875** MᶜILWRAITH *Guide Wigtownshire* 45 Here are the school-house, play-ground, and teacher's dwelling.

b. *transf.* and *fig.*

c **1440** *Jacob's Well* xxii. 147 þe tauerne is welle of glotonye, for it may be clepyd þe develys scolehous & þe deuelys chapel. **1541** (*title*) Here begynneth a lytle boke named the Scole house of women. *a* **1568** ASCHAM *Scholem.* I. (Arb.) 62 Erasmus..saide wiselie that experience is the common schole house of foles, and ill men. **1607** HIERON *Wks.* I. 252 He doth first traine them vp in the schoole-house of His church.

c. *attrib.*

c **1440** *Alphabet of Tales* 426 Hym happend se þe scole-howse dure oppyn. **1679** *First Cent. Hist. Springfield, Mass.* (1898) I. 427 To Sam: Ely..for entertaining the schoole house raisers..I. 05. 00. **1841-4** EMERSON *Ess.*, *Love* Wks. (Bohn) I. 73 The rude village boy teases the girls about the school-house door.

2. At some public schools, the name given to the headmaster's house. Also, the boys belonging to the 'school-house'.

1857 HUGHES *Tom Brown* I. v, The long line of grey buildings, beginning with the chapel, and ending with the school-house, the residence of the head-master. *Ibid.*, The School-house are being penned in their turn, and now the ball is behind their goal. **1887** *Spectator* 25 June 859/2 When the sixth form, or the School House, played against the rest of the school.

schoolie (ˈskuːlɪ). Also **scheulie.** [f. SCHOOL *sb.*[1] + -IE.] **a.** *north. dial.* and *Austral.* A schoolteacher.

1901 in *Eng. Dial. Dict.* (1904) V. 250/2 That only three children out of a hundred have been absent on an average throughout twelve months will strike the ordinary scheulie ..with astonishment. **1907** N. SPIELVOGEL *Cocky Farmer* 33 The prettiest of all the girls was the schoolie, and didn't she lead the lads a dance. **1951** E. COXHEAD *One Green Bottle* vii. 179 'What a lot I've got to teach you!' said Christopher smiling. 'Schoolie.' 'Well, of course I'm a schoolie. What else could you expect?' **1960** S. H. COURTIER *Gently dust Corpse* xiii. 189 She was away at college, being taught to be a schoolie all that time. **1980** *Globe & Laurel* July/Aug. 198/2 At Lydd and Hythe, we enjoyed such epics as the formation of the Nelson brick (Doctor, Dentist, Padre and Schoolie).

b. *slang.* In the Navy, a classroom instructor.

1946 J. IRVING *Royal Navalese* 151 *Schoolie*, a naval schoolmaster. **1964** J. HALE *Grudge Fight* vii. 97 The E.R.A. instructors, the P.T. instructors, the gunnery instructors, the schoolies began to..brace themselves for another day of ramming drill and P.T. and lathe work and chipping and filing and maths., mechanics, machine drawing, naval history..into the minds and bodies of eight divisions of apprentices. **1977** *Navy News* Dec. 12/2 The official announcement says that in meeting the needs of the Navy during the past 20 years the role of instructor officers—the schoolies—has changed significantly.

schooling ('skuːlɪŋ), *vbl. sb.*^{1} [f. SCHOOL *v.*^{1} + -ING^1.]

1. The action of teaching, or the state or fact of being taught, in a school; scholastic education.

c **1449** PECOCK *Repr.* I. xvi. 90 But certis her withal y wolde that profound and groundli scoling in logik, philsophi, and dyuynyte, and lawe were not left bihinde. **1579** NORTHBROOKE *Dicing* (1843) 121 All the world seeth so many small children, that are orphans, lacking schooling for want of helpe. **1588** W. KEMPE *Educ. Children* F 3 b, He shall proceede to the second degree of Schooling, which consisteth in learning the Grammar. **1599** HEYWOOD *1st Pt. Edw. IV*, III. ii, That halfyear's schooling at Lichfield was better to thee than house and land. **1766** ENTICK *London* IV. 422 There is a charity-school.. for 36 boys,.. for schooling only. **1783** WESLEY *Wks.* 1872 XIII. 93, I will give you a year's schooling and board at Kingswood School. **1820** SCOTT *Monast.* Introd. Ep., Whose sons he had at bed, board, and schooling, for twenty pounds per annum a-head. **1837** HT. MARTINEAU *Soc. Amer.* III. 138 To give her Sunday-schooling, and a certain amount of weekday schooling in the year. **1844** THACKERAY *Barry Lyndon* i, Six weeks' was all the schooling I got. **1894** MRS. OLIPHANT *Hist. Sk. Q. Anne* vii. 337 The son.. after sundry local schoolings went to Charterhouse. **1904** R. C. JEBB *Bacchylides* (Proc. Brit. Acad.) 17 The man of mere lore and schooling.

b. *transf.* and *fig.*

1540 PALSGR. *Acolastus* II. i. H iij b, Suerly it shulde not greue me so moche, so it myghte be lefull for me, nowe to folowe thy dyscipline .i. to be one of thy scoolynge. **1561** T. NORTON *Calvin's Inst.* IV. xx. (1634) 740 The ceremoniall law was the schooling of the Jewes. **1813** SCOTT *Trierm.* Introd. iv, Then, Lucy, hear thy tutor speak, For Love, too, has his hours of schooling. **1838** PRESCOTT *Ferd. & Is.* II. ix. III. 53 The severe schooling of these wars had prepared it for entering on a bolder theatre of action. **1851** THACKERAY *Eng. Hum.* i. (1876) 158 His mind had had a different schooling. **1870** LOWELL *Among my Bks.* Ser. I. (1873) 12 But perhaps there is no schooling so good for an author as his own youthful indiscretions. **1899** H. LATHAM (*title*), Pastor Pastorum, or the Schooling of the Apostles of our Lord.

c. The maintenance of a child at school, considered as involving expense; hence, cost of school education.

1563 *Haddington Council Rec.* in J. Miller *Rem. Old Haddington* (1883) 183 Ilk bairn [was to pay] ilk term xij of skoilings silver alanerlie. *c* **1610** LADY COMPTON in Grose *Antiq. Rep.* (1808) III. 438 Find my Children Apparel and their Schooling. **1681** W. ROBERTSON *Phraseol. Gen.* (1693) 1099 Schooling or school-hire, *minerval*. **1727** *Philip Quarll* (1816) 34 His parents.. being no longer able to continue his schooling. **1802** MAR. EDGEWORTH *Moral T.* (ed. 2) I. iv. 25 She could not afford to pay for her little lass's schooling. **1848** THACKERAY *Van. Fair* xlvi, She would.. pay his half-year's schooling. **1885** *Law Rep., Weekly Notes* 150/2 The husband refused to pay for the schooling of one of the two youngest daughters.

fig. **1577** *F. de L'isle's Legendarie* B v, In deede during the raigne of Francis the second they were euen with him, and paid for their scholing, as hereafter more at large wil appeare.

d. The employment or profession of teaching in school; 'schoolmastering'. *rare.*

1837 [MISS MAITLAND] *Lett. fr. Madras* (1843) 149 They had not much of a school, only five or six boys; I do not think that schooling will ever be their vocation.

attrib. **1784** COWPER *Tiroc.* 621 For such is all the mental food purvey'd By public hacknies in the schooling trade.

e. *slang.* A term of confinement in a reformatory.

1879 HORSLEY *Jottings fr. Jail* i. (1887) 8 'This is young ——, just come home from a schooling' (a term in a reformatory).

†**2.** Disciplinary correction, chastisement; also, admonition, reproof, scolding. *Obs.*

1557 N. T. (Genev.) *2 Cor.* Argt., Albeit certeyn wicked persones abused his afflictions to condemne therby his autoritie, yet they were necessarie schollings, and sent to hym by God for their bettering. **1590** SHAKS. *Mids. N.* I. i. 116 But Demetrius come, And come Egeus, you shall go with me, I haue some priuate schooling for you both. **1601** J. CHAMBERLAIN in *St. Papers, Dom.* 1598–1601 (1869) 544 The Lord Keeper has had some schooling about it [the vacant Mastership of the Rolls], and is much troubled, but only cares that Hele may miss it. **1703** QUICK *Serious Inquiry* 32 And she would be there in her stead to give him such a Schooling.., as he never had in all his Life. **1818** SCOTT *Rob Roy* xiii, I confess I thought the schooling as severe as the case merited.

†**b.** *to have in schooling*: to be engaged in tutoring or admonishing. *Obs.*

1553 *Respublica* v. vi. 1537 Ah, in feith, dame Veritee hath had youe in scooling of late. *a* **1591** H. SMITH *Serm.* (1592) 597 Because ther is such warning before vs, now we haue the drunkard in schooling, I will spend the time that is left to shew you the deformity of this sinne.

3. a. The training or exercising of horse and rider in the riding-school. **b.** The exercising of horses in the hunting field. Also *attrib.*, as ***schooling-match***.

1753 *Chambers' Cycl.* Suppl., *School*, or *Schooling*, in the manege, is used to signify the lesson and labour both of the horse and horseman. **1860** TROLLOPE *C. Richmond* iii, In Ireland a schooling match means the amusement of teaching your horses to jump. **1869** 'WAT. BRADWOOD' *The O.V.H.* xxvii, Ralph had gone.. to improve the occasion by testing the schooling of the four-year-old filly.. over the timber obstacles. **1890** *Daily News* 2 Dec. 3/7 The schooling of horses over hurdles and fences. **1893** *Star* 24 Dec. 3/6 Alec Taylor has had schooling hurdles put up.

4. *slang.* (See quots.)

1859 *Slang Dict.*, *Schooling*, a low gambling party. **1883** *Pall Mall G.* 10 Dec. 1/1, I saw no 'schooling' or gambling groups.

'schooling, *vbl. sb.*^{2} [f. SCHOOL *sb.*^{2} and *v.*^{2} + -ING^1.] The action of swimming together in schools or shoals.

1880 *Rep. Roy. Comm. Fishing N.S. Wales* 12 [The schnapper] has its periods of migration and accumulation in shoals, a movement so well expressed by the term 'schooling' that we shall adopt the phrase for the future. **1884** GOODE, etc. *Nat. Hist. Aquatic Anim.* 374 In November, when schooling begins, the fish are full-roed.

attrib. **1883** E. P. RAMSAY *Food Fishes N.S. Wales* 12 The schooling-season is midsummer.

'schooling, *ppl. a.*^{1} [f. SCHOOL *v.*^{1} + -ING^2.]

1. That schools, instructs or educates; also, †admonishing, reproving.

1753 RICHARDSON *Grandison* (1781) II. v. 73 Let me reckon with you, Harriet, said Miss Grandison (taking my hand with a schooling air). **1839–52** BAILEY *Festus* 333 All the schooling spheres he had passed through. **1896** KIPLING *Seven Seas* 65 And the schooling bullet leaped across and showed them whence they came.

2. Attending school.

1890 *Star* 15 Dec. 4/3 We have over 1,000 schooling children.

'schooling, *ppl. a.*^{2} [f. SCHOOL *sb.*^{2} or *v.*^{2} + -ING^2.] That swim together in 'schools'.

1873 S. POWEL in *Rep. U.S. Fish Commission* 1871–2, 74 The scup are known to be schooling, wandering fish of the high seas; and come from the Gulf Stream and from the Florida Cape. **1888** GOODE *Amer. Fishes* 189 Mackerel, mullet, silversides and all our other schooling species contribute also a share to its support.

'schoolingly, *adv. nonce-wd.* [f. SCHOOLING *vbl. sb.*^{1} + -LY^2.] So as to afford a lesson.

1871 MEREDITH *H. Richmond* lv, The end.. came abruptly, and was schoolingly cold and short.

†**'schoolish,** *a. Obs. rare*$^{-1}$. [f. SCHOOL *sb.*^{1} + -ISH.] Savouring of the 'schools', scholastic.

c **1618** BOLTON *Hypercrit.* iv. §5 In this fine and meer schoolish Folly.. George Buchanan is often taken.

'school-keeper, 'schoolkeeper.

1. One who 'keeps school'; applied to a school-master or mistress. So **school-keeping.**

1651 *Early Rec. Dedham, Mass.* (1892) III. 191 The time of covenant in ye schoole keepeing being expired. **1829** A. SHERWOOD *Gazetteer Georgia* (ed. 2) 193 Why is it that school-keeping is so disreputable an employment in our State? **1854** C. M. YONGE *Castle Builders* v. 70 All we have ever had to do with school-keeping, was in that short visit to my sister. **1857** H. MORLEY *Gossip* 183 After two years of school-keeping. **1871** M. COLLINS *Marq. & Merch.* I. iv. 126 God is too strong for City men and school-keepers. **1885** [W. H. WHITE] *M. Rutherford's Deliv.* iv, He was tired of school-keeping in England.

2. The caretaker of a school building.

1889 *Daily News* 28 Nov. 3/6 A small room in the school-keeper's house. **1898** *Ibid.* 10 Sept. 3/6 Making it requisite for the schoolkeepers to undertake the arduous work of carrying up the water for flushing these closets.

schoolless ('skuːllɪs), *a.* [f. SCHOOL *sb.*^{1} + -LESS.] Having no school, or attending no school.

1614 SYLVESTER *Little Bartas* 1009 [The Holy Spirit enables] Som (School-lesse, Schollers; Learned, studi-lesse) To understand and speak all Languages. **1848** *Blackw. Mag.* LXIV. 151 Our schoolless art.. has wandered into strange and lower lands. **1861** M. ARNOLD *Pop. Educ. France* 101 The 21,025 schoolless children of Glasgow. **1904** J. WELLS *Life J. H. Wilson* xiv. 119 The Saltmarket.. was swarming with school-less arabs.

schoolman ('skuːlmən). [SCHOOL *sb.*^{1} Cf. G. *schulmann*, a man belonging to the scholastic profession.]

1. One of the succession of writers, from about the 9th to the 14th century, who treat of logic, metaphysics, and theology as taught in the 'schools' or universities of Italy, France, Germany, and England; a mediæval scholastic.

a **1540** BARNES *Art.* xvii. Wks. (1573) 213/1 Your owne scholemen say, the popes power is so greate, that no man can, nor may discusse it. **1561** T. NORTON *Calvin's Inst.* II. 76 Peter Lombard and the other scholemen. *a* **1591** H. SMITH *God's Arrow* v. (1614) 87 Thomas Aquinas, a school-man of the Papists. **1651** HOBBES *Leviath.* IV. xlvii. 383 The frivolous Distinctions, barbarous Terms, and obscure Language of the Schoolmen. **1690** LOCKE *2nd Let. Toleration* 38 And the Artisan must sell his Tools, to buy Fathers and School-men, and leave his Family to starve. **1751** HUME *Enq. Princ. Morals* vi. 120 He would stand, like the Schoolman's Ass, irresolute and undetermin'd, betwixt equal Motives. **1817** COLERIDGE *Biog. Lit.* xii. (1907) I. 170 The substantial forms and entelechies of Aristotle and the schoolmen. **1869** LECKY *Europ. Mor.* I. i. 17 This opinion which was propounded by the schoolman Ockham.

2. One who is versed in the traditional learning of the 'schools', *esp.* (cf. sense 1) one who is expert in formal logic or school-divinity. ? *Obs.*

a **1550** *Image Ipocr.* 103 in *Skelton's Wks.* (1843) II. 434 It is no play.. for lay men; But only for schole men For they be witty men. **1571** CAMPION *Hist. Irel.* II. ix. (1633) 115 Wonderfully courteous, a ripe Schooleman. **1590** NASHE *Pref. to Greene's Arcadia* (1616) 2 Some deepe-read Schoole-men or Grammarians. **1622** BACON *Hen. VII* 202 The King had (though hee were no good Schooleman) the Honour to conuert one of them [*sc.* heretics] by Dispute at Canterburie. *a* **1625** FLETCHER *Women Pleas'd* IV. i, To absolve this Riddle? Diviners, Dreamers, Schoolemen, deep Magitians, All have I tride, and all give severall meanings. *a* **1631** DONNE *Poems, The Will* 30 To Schoole-men I bequeath my doubtfulnesse. **1690** LUTTRELL *Brief Rel.* (1857) II. 134 In the schools at Rome.. it was held by the majority of the school men to be lawfull. **1732** POPE *Ess. Man* II. 81 Let subtle schoolmen teach these friends to fight, More studious to divide than to unite.

3. One engaged in scholastic pursuits; a professional teacher or student.

1712 STEELE *Spect.* No. 278 ¶1 Of late she has got acquainted with a Schoolman, who values himself for his great Knowledge in the Greek Tongue. **1756** TOLDERVY *Hist. 2 Orphans* IV. 110 These quotations are made use of.. to deter certain schoolmen whom they have been concerned to see employing their hours in censuring, or rather abusing those literary personages. **1870** DISRAELI *Lothair* Pref. 15 These great matters fell into the hands of monks and school-men. **1884** *Congregational Year Bk.* 80 The schoolman was greater than the warrior.

4. *slang.* A fellow-member of a 'school' or gang.

1834 AINSWORTH *Rookwood* III. v. 'Jerry Juniper's Chaunt', The knucks in quod did my schoolmen play.

'school-marm. orig. *U.S.* Also **ma'm, -ma'am.**

1. A schoolmistress. Now freq. implying the conventionally prim and correct behaviour of a school-mistress. Also *fig.*

1831 *Ladies' Mag.* (Boston) IV. 557 [It] obliged me to stay the longest in the houses where.. there was the most work to do, and the least time to make the school Ma'am comfortable. **1840** *Spirit of Times* 8 Aug. 276/2 Them mirrors.., why what you got agin 'em? Cost me twenty-five dollars for the set—they be busters! open like a School-marm, by Jerusalem! **1841** *Picayune* (New Orleans) 23 Feb. 2/1 What will the 'school marm' say when she reads the following extract of a letter? **1845** S. JUDD *Margaret* II. viii, She is the best School-ma'am I ever went to. **1886** STEVENSON *Silverado Sq.* 82 The school-ma'am.. walking thence to the.. shanty where she taught the young ones. **1888** C. M. YONGE *Our New Mistress* xii. 107 He said he supposed he should be a startling visitor for the school marm. **1897** GUNTER *Susan Turnbull* xi. 131 In this cheerful way the Schoolmarm runs on for over an hour, the sky looking very dark for poor Irene. **1924** A. E. HOUSMAN *Let.* 10 Mar. (1971) 218 A French school-ma'm wrote to me wanting to translate *A Shropshire Lad.* **1929** D. H. LAWRENCE *Phoenix II* (1968) 579 Now the funny thing is that nobody, not even the most conscientious father, ever questions the absolute rightness of these school-marms. **1951** M. MCLUHAN *Mech. Bride* (1967) 69/2 Rigid with the social cocksureness of the schoolmarm. **1974** *Times* 14 Mar. 16/1 Mrs Margaret Thatcher.. had the bearing of a school ma'am, an inability to suffer fools. **1977** M. EDELMAN *Political Lang.* v. 90 Schoolmarms of both sexes behave like teachers in the living room and when reacting to novels or to public affairs.

attrib. **1965** *New Statesman* 7 May 719/1 The schoolma'am tone that husbands are quick to notice. **1972** WODEHOUSE *Pearls, Girls, & Monty Bodkin* xii. 181 Less than the dust beneath his chariot wheels, if he remembered the quotation correctly from his school-marm days. **1978** M. PUZO *Fools Die* xxix. 333 Going through a bedroom, I saw a couple head to toe and I heard a woman's very schoolmarm voice say, 'Get *up* here.'

2. *N. Amer. slang.* (See quots.)

1939 H. O'HAGAN *Tay John* 217 It was a pine. Long ago its trunk had been broken off by a slide or by the wind. Two stout branches had grown up instead, lightly tufted, to form a crotch. It was what the men there call a 'school-marm tree'. **1958** *Scope Weekly* 22 Oct. 7/1 The same situation may occur in felling a 'schoolma'am' which is essentially a forked tree, having two main trunks. **1965** M. MCINTYRE *Place of Quiet Waters* iv. 82 The 'schoolmarm' turned out to be a tree that had branched out into two separate trunks.

Hence as *v. trans.*, to treat (someone) in the manner of a school-marm, to instruct or guide patronizingly; **'school-marming** *vbl. sb.*, the occupation of being a school-marm; **'school-marmish, 'school-marmy** *adjs.*, like or suggestive of a school-marm; **'school-marmishly** *adv.*, in the manner of a school-marm.

1887 H. FREDERIC *Seth's Brother's Wife* 24 She was held to be too serious and 'school-ma'am-ish' for pleasant company. **1914** KIPLING *Egypt of Magicians* iv, in *Cosmopolitan* Sept. 458/1 Our trouble in America is we're being school-marmed to death. **1920** 'O. DOUGLAS' *Penny Plain* xii. 124 Heaps of girls would think school-marming very dull, but Elspeth makes it into a sort of daily entertainment. **1921** R. MACAULAY *Dangerous Ages* vii. 132 The W.E.A. was a practical body... Dowdy, schoolmarmish, extension-lecturish, it might be. **1941** *Scrutiny* X. 115 The priggishness of the book [sc. *Mansfield Park*] is of a special kind, not just the occasional schoolmarmy effects of *Sense and Sensibility* which there are only the result of artistic inexperience. **1943** W. S. CHURCHILL *Second World War* (1951) IV. 824 Considering .. that it was the Americans.. who led the world astray, it is pretty good cheek of them now coming to school-marm us into proper behaviour. **1945** R. HARGRAVES *Enemy at Gate* 234 The Radicals' itch to continue 'school-marming' the native populations of the former Boer territories. **1959** K. VONNEGUT *Sirens of Titan* (1967) x. 174 'This way, please, We haven't got all day, you know,' said Rumfoord school-marmishly. **1967** *Economist* 15 Apr. p. xvii/1 Typical of all her encounters was her inability to find the disapproving school-marmy guide, Miss Tsu, anything but likeable. **1977** N. FREELING *Gadget* II. 83 Prissy, schoolmarmish, but a good schoolmarm. **1979** *Guardian* 23 Oct. 8/1 The remarks tend to sound school-marmy and pontifical.

schoolmaster ('skuːlmɑːstə(r), -æ-), *sb.*^{1} Forms: see SCHOOL *sb.*^{1} and MASTER *sb.*^{1} [f. SCHOOL *sb.*^{1} + MASTER *sb.*^{1} Cf. G. *schulmeister*, Du. *schoolmeester*, Sw. *skolmästare*, Da. *skolemester*.]

1. a. The master of a school, or one of the masters in a school.

†*schoolmaster of grammar*: a teacher of Latin in a school.

a **1225** *Leg. Kath.* 522 þes sondes mon..brohte wið him fifti scolemaistres. **1429** *Coventry Leet Bk.* 118 Mayster John Pynchard, skolemayster of Grammer, shall haue the place that he duelleth Inne for xl s. ye yere, whyles that he duellithe In hit & holdythe gramer skole hym-self ther-Inne. **1480** Caxton *Descr. Brit.* xv. 18 Othir scolemaiestres vse the same way now. **1531** Elyot *Gov.* i. xv. (1880) I. 166 If the name of a schole maister were nat so moche had in contempte. **1546** in *Eng. Gilds* (1870) 198 For the meyntenaunce of a scolemaster of Gramer. *a* **1583** Sir H. Gilbert *Q. Eliz. Achad.* (1869) 2 First, there shalbe one Schole-maister, who shall teach Grammar, both greke and latine. **1596** Dalrymple tr. *Leslie's Hist. Scot.* II. 465 [He and] Robert Maxual baith scuil maisteris. **1610** Holland *Camden's Brit.* 254 Master Lilye Schoole-maister of Paules. *Ibid.* 761 Reginold Bainbrig..head schoolemaster of Applebey. **1690** Locke *Hum. Und.* iii. x. §16. 245 'Twould be a hard Matter, to persuade any one, that the Words which his Father or School-Master..used, signified nothing that really existed in Nature. **1722** De Foe *Col. Jack* (1840) 173 Every good scholar is not fitted for a schoolmaster, the art of teaching is quite different from that of knowing the language taught. **1815** Elphinstone *Acc. Caubul* (1842) I. 249 The sum commonly paid to a schoolmaster in Peshawer, is about fifteen pence a month. **1815** *Falconer's Dict. Marine* (ed. Burney) *s.v.*, The heads of the examination of a schoolmaster for the Royal Navy, are as follows.

b. *the schoolmaster is abroad*: a saying of Ld. Brougham (see quot. 1828) which became proverbial, at first in its original meaning as expressing exulting confidence in the results of the spread of popular education, afterwards chiefly in derisive use.

Sometimes jocularly misapplied, as if *abroad* meant 'not at home', 'gone out of the country'.

1828 Brougham in *Times* 30 Jan. 3/3 Let the soldier be abroad, in the present age he could do nothing. There was another person abroad... The schoolmaster was abroad.. and he trusted more to him, armed with his primer, than he did to the soldier in full military array, for upholding and extending the liberties of his country. **1831** Praed *Why & Wherefore* in *Pol. & Occas. Poems* (1888) 138 The school-master's abroad, you see; And, when the people hear him speak, They all insist on being free, And reading Homer in the Greek; The Bolton weavers seize the pen, The Sussex farmers scorn the plough. **1836** Haliburton *Clockmaker* Ser. i. xv, Well, they've got a cant phrase here, 'the school-master is abroad', and every feller tells you that fifty times a day. **1853** Lytton *My Novel* i. x, In those dark days, before the schoolmaster was abroad. **1857** Trollope *Three Clerks* ii, 'Well, I believe it's quite a new thing,' said Marie Tudor. 'The school-master must be abroad with a vengeance, if he has got as far as that.' [**1886** Minchin *Growth Freedom Balkan Penin.* 53 The progress of education in Bosnia and Herzegovina since the Austrian occupation has been immense. The schoolmaster has crossed the Save. Since 1878, no less than forty schools have been established under Government auspices.]

c. *transf.* and *fig.*

1526 Tindale *Gal.* iii. 24 The lawe was oure scolemaster vnto the tyme of Christ. **1550** Coverdale *Spir. Perle* vi. 51 Therefore the heauenly scholemaster knappeth vs on the fingers, tyll we apprehende and learne his wyll more perfitely. **1605** Camden *Rem., Inhabitants* 10 Our countrimen have twice beene scholemaisters to France. First when they taught the Gaules the discipline of the Druides; and after [etc.]. **1678** J. Browne *Disc. Wounds* 51 Anatomy..is an excellent Schoolmaster, the which perfectly learneth us to know how the Nerves which are sprinkled about the Face [etc.]. **1875** Jowett *Plato* (ed. 2) II. 506 The sailors of Salamis became the schoolmasters of Hellas, teaching the Hellenes not to fear the barbarians at sea.

†**d.** Used for the later schoolmistress. *Obs.*

Quot. *c* 1460 perhaps hardly belongs here, as the poet seems to be comparing the lover's timidity in the presence of his lady to a boy's dread of his schoolmaster. The alteration in the Trinity MS. removes the awkwardness of the expression, but destroys the point.

a **1225** *Ancr. R.* 422 Ancre ne schal nout forwurðen scolmeistre, ne turnen hire ancre hus to childrene scole. *c* **1460** Sir R. Ros *La Belle Dame* 137 His scole-maister [*MS. Trin.* scolemaystress] had suche auctorite That.. Speke coude he nat, but upon her beaute.

†**e.** Applied to a private tutor. *Obs.*

c **1510** *Robt. Deuyll* in Thoms *Prose Rom.* (1827) I. 10 My sone me thyncke it necessary and tyme, for me to gete you a wyse scole mayster, to lerne vertues and doctrine. **1565** Cooper *Thesaurus* s.v. *A, A studiis*,..a princes schole maister or instructour in learnyng. **1596** Shaks. *Tam. Shr.* i. i. 94 And for I know she taketh most delight In Musike, Instruments, and Poetry, Schoolemasters will I keepe within my house, Fit to instruct her youth. *Ibid.* i. ii. 133. **1645** Symonds *Diary* (Camden) 226 Dr. Dereham.. received one Horner to be a schoole-mr. to some youthe in his howse. **1654** Gataker *Disc. Apol.* 45 A yong Scholar, who was then School-master in his Familie.

f. An experienced horse used to train horses or riders at a riding-school.

1937 in Partridge *Dict. Slang.* **1938** H. Wynmalen *Equitation* ix. 40 Moving away from other horses must be taught him. To this end we shall ride him beside another horse, a schoolmaster. **1976** *Horse & Hound* 10 Dec. 68/4 (Advt.), This pony is one of the finest schoolmasters jumping in 12 hands 2 in. classes.

2. Used as a name for certain species of fishes. Also *attrib.*

1734 Mortimer *Nat. Hist. Carolina & Bahamas* in *Phil. Trans.* XXXVIII. 316 *Perca marina, pinnis branchialibus carens.* The School-master. **1876** Goode *Fishes of Bermudas* 55 The School-master Snapper and Silk Snapper of the fishermen probably belong to this genus.

3. a. *attrib.* and *Comb.*

1642 J. Eaton *Honey-c. Free Justif.* 103 The school-master-like governement began to slacke and cease. *Ibid.* 104 Schoole-master-like whippings inflicted in former times. **1898** A. D. Coleridge *Eton in Forties* 401 Okes was conscious of a difficulty in divesting himself of a schoolmaster manner. **1898** *Academy* 5 Nov. 189/1 Thring was the most original and striking figure in the schoolmaster world of his time.

b. Special Comb.: **schoolmaster studentship**, in Oxford colleges, a studentship tenable by schoolmasters; hence **schoolmaster student**.

1957 *Oxf. Univ. Gaz.* 20 June 1142/1 Balliol College Elections. *To Schoolmaster Studentships.* For Michaelmas Term. **1978** *Times Educ. Suppl.* 3 Feb. 68/3 (Advt.), Merton and St. Peter's Colleges Schoolmaster Studentships 1978/79... The two colleges above intend to elect four *schoolmaster students* between them.

Hence (*nonce-wds.*) ˈ**schoolmasterhood**, the state or condition of a schoolmaster. ˈ**schoolmasterism**, the action of a schoolmaster. ˈ**schoolmastery** *a.* = schoolmasterish *a.*

1861 E. Steere in *Mem.* (1888) 400 Dry schoolmasterism is a dreary thing, but dry formal office-saying and Bible-reading is a great deal worse. **1887** *Spectator* 29 Oct. 1452 With no more knowledge of actual schoolmasterhood than such as he had gained in organising the squire's school. **1928** *Observer* (Apr. 7) In the earlier days the Staff College did not justify the expectations founded on it. It was unreal, academic, and 'schoolmastery'. **1942** J. Lees-Milne *Ancestral Voices* (1975) 17 What an unattractive, schoolmastery fellow.

ˈ**schoolmaster**, *sb.*^{2} [f. school *sb.*^{2}, after schoolmaster *sb.*^{1}] The leader of a 'school' of fishes, etc.; esp. a bull whale.

1839 Beale *Sperm Whale* 178 The old 'schoolmaster' had outwitted those in the boats. **1848** *Chamb. Inform. People* I. 692/1 The sailors call a herd [of whales] a 'school', and the old bulls the 'schoolmasters'. **1851** H. Newland *The Erne* 181 Your honour might have landed a school-master [*i.e.* salmon] with it ten minutes afterwards. **1851** H. Melville *Whale* III. ii. 25 Now, as the harem of whales is called by the fisherman a school, so is the lord and master of that school technically known as the schoolmaster.

ˈ**schoolmaster**, *v.* [f. schoolmaster *sb.*^{1}]

1. *trans.* To govern, regulate, or command in the manner of a schoolmaster. *rare.*

1850 J. Oxenford tr. *Eckermann's Conversations of Goethe* I. 377 [Schlegel] is permitted, upon such high authority, to fall foul of this mighty ancient [*sc.* Euripides], and to schoolmaster him as much as he can. **1891** *Chamb. Encycl.* VII. 611 Opitz, originally a schoolmaster, schoolmastered poetry into lifeless imitation of pseudo-classical models. **1893** G. B. Shaw in *Fortn. Rev.* Feb. 279 He [Gladstone] so towers above them..that he is able to schoolmaster them into grudging submission.

2. *intr.* To be a schoolmaster. *rare.*

1908 *Daily Chron.* 18 June 4/6 Carlyle and Edward Irving, who schoolmastered together in the same Kirkcaldy Academy for a couple of years. **1966** *Listener* 5 May 659/2 Nicholas Urfe is schoolmastering on a Greek island, seeking escape from..an oppressive love affair. **1977** *Times* 15 Nov. 14/6 Mr Rogers..schoolmastered for a time.

ˈ**schoolmastering**, *vbl. sb.* [f. schoolmaster *sb.*^{1} + -ing^1.] The occupation or profession of a schoolmaster; also, an education in school.

1844 Craik *Sk. Hist. Lit. Eng.* II. 221 His son, though born to the throne..received a schoolmastering fit for a bishop. **1845** H. Rogers *Ess.* (1874) I. iii. 100 The native bias is so strong, that it is beyond the art of all the schoolmastering in the world to alter it. **1859** Shairp in W. A. Knight *Shairp & his Friends* (1888) 200 As to schoolmastering..all the best comes first. **1864** Carlyle *Fredk. Gt.* xvi. v. IV. 301 A *Candidatus*, say Licentiate,.. Subsists, I should guess, by schoolmastering..in the Villages about. **1894** Parry *Stud. Gt. Composers, Schubert* 227 Schoolmastering was a characteristic occupation of the family.

ˈ**schoolmastering**, *ppl. a.* [f. schoolmaster *sb.*^{1} + -ing^2.] Like, or acting as, a schoolmaster.

1831 Trelawny *Adv. Younger Son* vii, You don't take me for that lubberly school-mastering parson on board, do you? **1893** *Times* 13 Feb. 5/3 Its artificial schoolmastering tone.

ˈ**schoolmasterish**, *a.* [f. schoolmaster *sb.*^{1} + -ish.] Like, or characteristic of, a schoolmaster.

1866 *Pall Mall G.* 15 Dec. 1 The duke of Argyll's presence and address are hard, rigid, schoolmasterish. **1883** Black *Yolande* II. ix. 157 He claimed a sort of schoolmasterish authority over her. **1896** *Nation* (N.Y.) 3 Dec. 421/2 At the risk of seeming schoolmasterish.

Hence ˈ**schoolmasterishness**.

1789 Bentham *Mem. & Corr.* Wks. 1843 X. 217 Your age and character fit you better for intimacy with him: the schoolmasterishness of mine acting naturally as a repellant.

ˈ**schoolmasterly**, *a.* [-ly^1.] Characteristic of or resembling a schoolmaster.

1865 *Sat. Rev.* 15 July 77/1 With a masterly knowledge of his subjects, the member for Lynn never seems to get beyond the schoolmasterly way of treating them. **1880** Miss Broughton *Second Th.* i. xii, Still speaking in that rather harsh and schoolmasterly tone.

ˈ**schoolmastership.** [-ship.] The office or work of a schoolmaster; a post as schoolmaster.

1561 T. Norton *Calvin's Inst.* iv. 49 He [God] did in dede in fewe wordes sette oute hys [Christ's] scholemaistership vnto vs, when he said, heare him. **1642** J. Eaton *Honey-c. Free Justif.* 105 Not needing that legall schoolemastership. **1892** *Times* 15 Feb. 5/4 Schoolmasterships are likely to be bestowed in future on local candidates. **1894** *Athenæum* 14 July 57/1 He..left his parish schoolmastership at Ruthven.

schoolmate. [f. school *sb.*^{1} + mate *sb.*^{2}] A friend or companion at school.

1563 *Homilies* II. *Place & Time of Prayer* i. 141 Shewe you to be like them, whose schole mates you take vppon you to be, that is, the Apostles and Disciples of Christ. **1810** *Sporting Mag.* XXXV. 303 One of her school-mates, who was priding herself over the rest of the scholars. **1894** S. Fiske *Holiday Stories* (1900) 206 They had been playmates and schoolmates..as long as they could remember.

schoolmistress (ˈskuːlmɪstrɪs). Forms: see school *sb.*^{1} and mistress. A woman who teaches in a school; a mistress in a school. †In early use with wider sense, a female teacher, governess. Also *transf.* and *fig.*

a **1500** *Sir R. Ros's La Belle Dame* 137 (MS. Trin.), [see quot. *c* 1460, schoolmaster *sb.*^{1} 1 d]. **1535** Coverdale *Wisd.* viii. 4 For she [wisdom] is ye scolemastresse of ye nurtoure of God, & ye choser out of his workes. **1560** Becon *Catech.* vi. Wks. I. 537 b, Al that they [*sc.* nuns] were commaunded to do of their scholemastresses and gouernesses. **1598** Grenewey *Tacitus, Ann.* xii. xiii. (1604) 176 A schoole-mistris of such practises was chosen of purpose, called Locusta of late condemned of empoisoning. **1639** Fuller *Holy War* ii. xii. (1640) 59 Phenicia was the schoolmistresse of Grecia, and first taught her her alphabet. **1726** Swift *Gulliver* iv. vii, But Nature, it seems, hath not been so expert a School-mistress. **1865** Dickens *Mut. Fr.* i. vi, She had more of the air of a schoolmistress than Mistress of the Six Jolly-Fellowship-Porters.

Hence **schoolmistressy** *a.*, characteristic of or resembling a schoolmistress.

1915 D. H. Lawrence *Rainbow* x. 251 Miss Grey..had a certain silvery, school-mistressy beauty of character. *a* **1974** R. Crossman *Diaries* (1975) I. 339 In that grating voice, she gave her clear, schoolmistressy, common-sense view of the White Paper.

†ˈ**school-point.** *Obs.* [f. school *sb.*^{1} + point *sb.*] A point taught or debated in the schools.

1571 Golding *Calvin on Ps.* xxxiv. 20 It is needful for them to be exercised with sundry scholepoints. **1587** —— *De Mornay* ix. (1592) 113 It is also a schoolepoint of Platoes teaching, That in these high matters of the Godhead,..and such other like, we must giue credit..to the sayings of men of most antiquitie, as folke that were..nearer to God than we. **1589** Puttenham *Eng. Poesie* iii. xii[i]. (Arb.) 180 We are to teache Ladies and Gentlewomen to know their schoole points and termes appertaining to the Art. *a* **1653** Gouge *Comm. Heb.* v. 12 They stuff their Sermons with.. obscure comparisons, and curious School-points.

attrib. *a* **1568** Ascham *Scholem*, ii. (Arb.) 131, I neuer saw yet any Commentarie vpon Aristotles Logicke..that euer I lyked, bicause they be rather spent in declaryng scholepoynt rules, than in gathering fit examples for vse and vtterance.

†ˈ**schoolric.** *Obs.*$^{-1}$ *U.S.* [? f. school *sb.*^{1} + *-ric*, after *bishopric*.] ? A school district.

1789 *Hist. Pelham, Mass.* (1898) 227 That Each School Rick Shall Build and Maintain their own School Houses. **1797** *Ibid.* 228 District Lists of the Assesment of every School Rick.

schoolroom (ˈskuːlruːm). [f. school *sb.*^{1} + room *sb.*]

1. A room in which a school is held. Also, a room in a pivate house, in which the children of the family receive instruction or prepare their lessons. Also, in *fig.* phr. ***in the schoolroom***: of a young lady, not yet 'out' (cf. out *adv.* 26 b (a)).

1773 P. V. Fithian *Jrnl. & Lett.* (1900) 61, I have to myself in the Evening..my Liberty, either to continue in the School room, in my own Room, or to sit over at the great House. **1775** Ash, *Schoolroom*, a room in which a school is kept. **1812** E. Weeton *Let.* July (1969) II. 58, I breakfast with Mr. & Mrs. Armitage, and then return again to the children till 9, we go into the school-room till 12. **1817** Shelley *Rev. Islam* Ded. iii, Until there rose From the near schoolroom, voices. **1837** H. Pidgeon *Mem. Shrewsbury* 144 The school rooms are in the rear of the buildings, in which twenty-five boys and as many girls receive their education. **1848** Thackeray *Van. Fair* viii, We have a schoolroom on the second floor, with my bed-room leading into it on one side, and that of the young ladies on the other. **1857** C. M. Yonge *Dynevor Terrace* i. viii. 126 'I suppose her daughters are not come out yet?' 'Her own are in the school-room; but there is a step-daughter who is much admired.' **1860** M. Arnold *Rep. Elem. Schools* (1889) 86 This..may excuse individual managers for the dirty and unhealthy state of their school-rooms. **1867** W. L. Collins *Public Schools* 176 The noble schoolroom [at Westminster], nearly a hundred feet in length. **1952** M. Laski *Village* ii. 35 The younger daughter in the schoolroom, the elder about to blossom forth. **1977** C. Fremlin *Spider-Orchid* vii. 51 She's not 'out' yet, she's only in the schoolroom still.

2. Accommodation for teaching.

1891 *Century Dict.* s.v., The city needs more school-room.

3. *attrib.*

1814 Jane Austen *Mansfield Park* I. xviii. 353 Very good school-room chairs, not made for a theatre, I dare say. **1847** A. Brontë *Agnes Grey* xv. 242 There was the bell—the odious bell for the school-room dinner. **1857** C. M. Yonge *Dynevor Terrace* I. xiv. 227 The school-room maid..was busy unpacking in a corner of the room. *Ibid.* xv. 238 She repaired to the school-room tea. **1875** L. Troubridge *Jrnl.* 25 Dec. in J. Hope-Nicholson *Life amongst Troubridges* (1966) 133, I..found everyone congregated round the school-room table. **1923** W. J. Locke *Moordius & Co.* ii. 17 The family can always come up if it likes for schoolroom tea. **1948** F. Thompson *Still glides Stream* iv. 91 They should have heard the music, the schoolroom piano and two violins. **1959** I. & P. Opie *Lore & Lang. Schoolch.* xvi. 343 Children whose schoolroom attitude to history is antipathetic. **1969** D. Holman-Hunt *My Grandfather* xviii. 232 She would get rid of the schoolroom maid and order some new dresses. **1972** W. Labov *Lang. in Inner City* i. 30 The subjects are asked to change certain sentences to correct schoolroom

English. **1975** R. PLAYER *Let's talk of Graves* iv. 118 We had schoolroom tea in deathly silence.

Hence **'schoolroomy** *a.*, characteristic of or resembling a schoolroom.

1895 W. S. CHURCHILL *Let.* 3 Aug. in R. S. Churchill *Winston S. Churchill* (1967) I. Compan. I. viii. 581 A very lovely—but stupid and school roomy girl—to whom I talked a good deal. **1975** D. DANIELL *Interpreter's House* ii. 20 A bit schoolroomy, possibly, and a little too much the work of a *belle-lettrist*.

schoolt, variant of SHALD, shallow.

schoolward ('sku:lwəd), *adv.* and *a.* [f. SCHOOL *sb.*¹ + -WARD.] **A.** *adv.* Towards school; in the direction of school.

[*c* **1386** CHAUCER *Prioress' T.* 97 To scoleward and homward whan he wente. **1451** CAPGRAVE *Life St. Gilbert* (E.E.T.S.) 118 This clerk in his weye to skoleward fell in grete heuynesse.] **1801** WORDSW. *Prioress' T.* 98 Homeward and schoolward whensoe'er he went. **1848** LOWELL *Biglow P.* Ser. I. Introd., Poems 1890 II. 24 The ramble schoolward through dew-sparkling meads. **1886** A. WINCHELL *Geol. Talks* 47 This mill-pond was dear to every school-ward trudging urchin that had to pass it.

B. *adj.* Directed or going toward school.

1888 *Daily News* 13 Sept. 4/7 By the time a boy reaches the first big station on his schoolward road. **1898** *Blackw. Mag.* Aug. 271 The depression of the schoolward journey.

So **'schoolwards** *adv.*

1859 J. C. ATKINSON *Walks & Talks* (1892) 86 Away they went schoolwards, as hard as they could.

schooly ('sku:lɪ). *U.S.* [Cf. SCHOOL *sb.*²] The menhaden.

1891 in *Century Dict.*

schoon (sku:n), *v. rare.* [See etym. note at SCHOONER *sb.*¹ The modern examples represent a fanciful back-formation from this sb.] **a.** *intr.* To sail or skim over the water, esp. in the manner of a schooner. **b.** *trans.* To run or glance (one's mind) *over* (something). Hence **'schooning** *vbl. sb.*

With quot. 1836 cf. etym. note s.v. SCHOONER *sb.*¹

1836 J. R. NEWHALL *Essex Memorial* 100 Capt. R[obinson] had constructed a vessel which he masted and rigged in the manner that schooners at this day are, and on her going off the stocks into the water, a bystander cried out, 'O how she scoons!' Robinson instantly replied, 'A schooner let her be.' **1937** O. NASH in *New Yorker* 13 Feb. 20/2 Where the schooner schoons, I schoon. **1959** I. JEFFERIES *13 Days* ix. 115, I spent my time schooning my mind over the calculations.

schooner ('sku:nə(r)), *sb.*¹ Forms: 8 **scooner, skooner,** 8– **schooner.** [Of uncertain origin; recorded early in the 18th c. as *skooner, scooner*; the present spelling, which occurs only a few years later, may be due to form-association with *school*, or with Du. words having initial *sch*. The word has passed from English into most of the European langs.: Du. *schooner, schoener*, G. *schoner, schooner, schuner* (recorded 1786), F. *schooner, schoaner*, Da. *skonnert*, Sw. *skonare, skonert*.

The story commonly told respecting the origin of the word is as follows. When the first schooner was being launched (at Gloucester, Mass., about 1713), a bystander exclaimed 'Oh, how she scoons!' The builder, Capt. Andrew Robinson, replied, 'A scooner let her be!' and the word at once came into use as the name of the new type of vessel. The anecdote, first recorded, on the authority of tradition, in a letter of 1790 (quoted in Babson *Hist. Gloucester*, p. 252), looks like an invention. The etymology which it embodies, however, is not at all improbable, though there seems to be a lack of evidence for the existence of the alleged New England verb *scoon* or *scun*, 'to skim along on the water'. Cf. Sc. (Clydesdale) *scon*, 'to make flat stones skip along the surface of the water', also *intr.* 'to skip in the manner described' (Jam.). The early examples afford strong ground for believing that the word really originated about 1713 in Massachusetts, and probably in the town of Gloucester. The evidence of two or three old prints seems to prove that the type of vessel now called 'schooner' existed in England in the 17th c., but it app. first came into extensive use in New England.]

1. a. A small sea-going fore-and-aft rigged vessel, originally with only two masts, but now often with three or four masts and carrying one or more topsails.

The rig characteristic of a schooner has been defined as consisting essentially of two gaff sails, the after sail not being smaller than the fore, and a head sail set on a bowsprit.

1716 in *Hist. Rec.* (Boston) XXIX. 231 Yᵉ Skooner Mayflower from North Carolina. **1721** MOSES PRINCE *Let.* in J. J. Babson *Hist. Gloucester* (Mass.) (1860) 252 Went to see Capt. Robinson's lady. This gentleman was the first contriver of schooners, and built the first of the sort about eight years ago. **1724** *Boston (Mass.) News-Letter* 16 Apr., Upon the 4th instant Benjamin Chadwell in the Scooner Good-Will, of Marblehead, was taken by a private sloop. **1725** *Ibid.* 22 Apr., The Schooner Swallow. **1741** in Bulkeley & Cummins *Voy. S. Seas* (1743) 126 Witness our Hands, on Board the Speedwell Schooner, in the latitude 50: 40 S. this 8th Day of November, 1741. **1774** T. HUTCHINSON *Diary* I. 336 We are in pain for Cap. Dundass and passengers in a scooner sent Express from Gen. Gage, and spoke within Scilly the 16th. **1840** LONGF. *Wreck of Hesperus* i, It was the schooner Hesperus, That sailed the wintry sea. **1908** *Toilers of Deep* Sept. 178/2 Both the warship and the fishing schooner were sounding fog-alarms.

b. *schooner on the rocks* (see quots.). *Naut. slang.*

1916 'TAFFRAIL' *Carry On!* 28 A 'schooner on the rocks' does not refer to a nautical disaster, but to meat and potatoes baked in a peculiar way. **1922** *Mariner's Mirror* VIII. 222/1 *Schooner on the Rocks*. This dish consists of a joint baked in a sea of batter. **1927** P. RILEY *Memories* ii. 11 Dinner.. varied from salt beef,.. 'Schooner on the Rocks', i.e., joint of meat roasted on potatoes, or 'toad in the hole'.

2. *U.S.* (See quot. 1904).

1858 [see PRAIRIE SCHOONER]. **1882** B. HARTE *Flip* i, The blinding white canvas covers of mountain schooners. **1891** E. ROPER *By Track & Trail* xii. 174 Goods and passengers are delivered by the railway to be conveyed by 'prairie schooners' over this road. **1904** P. FOUNTAIN *Gt. North-West* xxviii. 342 A prairie schooner is a waggon furnished with all sorts of stores likely to be required in outlying stations and farms.

3. *attrib.* and *Comb.*, as ***schooner-rigged*** adj.; ***schooner-man, -sail*** [tr. G. *schonersegel* foresail]; **schooner barge**, (*a*) *U.S.*, a short-masted vessel designed to be towed; (*b*) a flat-bottomed vessel rigged as a topsail schooner; **schooner-frigate, -gun-vessel, -yacht**, vessels of various classes resembling a schooner in build or rig; **schooner yawl**, a variety of two-masted schooner.

1819 *Western Rev.* I. 361 The River is navigated by steam boats, barges, keel boats, *schooner barges. **1867** *Mitchell's Maritime Reg.* 1620 On Monday the fine schooner-barge Edith was launched. **1900** *Bath* (Maine) *Daily Times* 22 May 5/3 The new three-masted schooner barge *Flora* for the Commercial Towboat Co. of Boston was launched yesterday. **1945** *Amer. Neptune* V. 139 In the East Coast schooner-barge fleet, only a few have been built with five masts. **1951** F. G. C. CARR *Sailing Barges* 126 As far as the hulls of these big barquentine and schooner barges were concerned, they were like very large boomies. **1799** *Naval Chron.* II. 271 Admiral Knowles constructed.. a *schooner frigate, that carried twenty twelve-pounders on the main-deck, and two eighteen-pounders on her fore-castle. **1806** A. DUNCAN *Life of Nelson* 136 The..*schooner gun-vessels made their escape. **1914** W. D. STEELE *Storm* 270 Then he scrutinized the rank of *schooner-men flanking me. **1972** F. E. BOWKER *Blue Water Coaster* 30 We thought that he had picked up an old schoonerman, but it wasn't long before we discovered that he was an unemployed shoemaker. **1769** *Schooner-rigged [see RIGGED *ppl. a.* 1 b]. **1812** *Examiner* 7 Sept. 576/1 A large schooner-rigged canoe. **1895** *Oracle Encycl.* I. 503/2 *Brigantine*, a small vessel, partly square-rigged and partly schooner-rigged. **1924** R. CLEMENTS *Gipsy of Horn* iii. 47 All hands were working schooner-rigged, going at it with their blood up. **1935** *Amer. Speech* X. 79/1 *Schooner rigged*, unequipped with proper clothes or other necessities. **1946** R. E. HIGGINBOTHAM *Wine for My Brothers* vi. 126 The Dane travelled schooner-rigged, and philosophically heaved his mail overboard. **1930** D. MARTIN *Boy Scout with Sea Devil* 48 We hoisted up the Fores'l and the *Schooners'l. **1952** G. COWAN *Log of Pelican* vi. 41 We cleaned out lockers,..bent the schooner sail and got the fore-canvas up in stops, and found a place for everything. **1876** T. HARDY *Ethelberta* xxxv, A *schooner-yacht, whose sheets gleamed like bridal satin. **1889** *Forest & Stream* 4 Apr. 227/3 Adding a jigger mast..cuts off the nasty big boom and large mainsail..making the yacht a *schooner yawl. **1970** *Amer. Neptune* XXX. 196 Not counting the schooner-yawl *White Cap*, which was discussed among the schooners, yawls made up 8.7 percent of American sailing yachts in 1902.

schooner ('sku:nə(r)), *sb.*² [Of obscure origin; perh. a fanciful use of prec.]

1. a. *U.S.* 'A tall glass, used for lager-beer and ale, and containing about double the quantity of an ordinary tumbler' (Webster, Suppl. 1879). **b.** Hence, in British use, a customary measure (see quot. 1896) by which beer is sold by retail in various places.

1886 *Boston (Mass.) Jrnl.* 21 July 2/4 Scene: A beer garden. Mr. Schweitzer (referring to the music): 'Dot vos Meyerbeer.' Mr. Hooligan (excitedly, in view of the fact that only one schooner stands on the table between the two gentlemen): 'Ye're a liar, it's *my* beer'. **1895** *N.B. Daily Mail* (Glasgow) 23 Sept. 4 He..had two glasses of whisky and a schooner of beer. **1896** *Ibid.* 7 Mar. 2 Of these [local measures] 'the schooner' containing 14 fluid ounces, or 2 4-5ths imperial gills, occupied perhaps the most prominent place..., being found in everyday use, under various names, in London, Glasgow, Aberdeen, and elsewhere.

c. *Austral.* and *N.Z.* A large beer-glass of locally variable capacity (see quots. 1966 and 1973); the (measure of) beer contained in such a glass.

1934 *Bulletin* (Sydney) 21 Feb. 10/1 In Brisbane, a standard pint served in a long glass is a 'schooner'. **1947** D. M. DAVIN *Gorse grows Pale* 126 Sitting in the pub with a schooner under his nose. **1966** G. W. TURNER *Eng. Lang. in Austral. & N.Z.* viii. 163 A *schooner* in New South Wales is a fifteen-ounce glass, in Adelaide a nine-ounce glass. **1969** *Advertiser* (Adelaide) 12 May 5/4 Just because someone wants to spend an arvo sinking a few schooners in his own way. **1973** *Courier-Mail* (Brisbane) 1 Dec. 17/7 The traveller finished up at the Federal with 128 schooners (the local term for an eight ounce glass). **1977** *Bulletin* (Sydney) 22 Jan. 27/2 He calculated he would consume eight schooners (15oz glasses) of beer, plus some spirits, over three hours. **1981** *Advertiser* (Adelaide) 2 July 6/6 Mr Connelly and Mr McKenzie said the second stage of the change was planned for October when the 285 ml (10 oz) glass would be introduced to replace the 255 ml (9 oz) schooner.

d. *Comb.*: **schooner-house**, a place for the sale of schooners of liquor.

1893 E. M. WHITTEMORE *Delia* ix. 59, I was having a big time sporting round schooner houses.

2. A tall, waisted sherry glass; the measure contained by this.

1967 J. POTTER *Foul Play* xvii. 204 What about joining me in a schooner of sherry? **1973** *Times* 20 Oct. 14/3 The abominably proportioned waisted Elgin glass, sometimes used for sherry, or its vulgar outsize version, the schooner. **1975** [see NOSHERY]. **1977** *Habitat 1977/78 Catal.* 121 *Elgin schooner*. For large sherries. 3½ oz.

schoot, obs. f. SCHUYT.

Schopenhauer ('ʃəʊpənhaʊə(r), 'ʃɒp-). The name of the German philosopher, Arthur *Schopenhauer* (1788–1860), used allusively, esp. for the pessimism and concept of will for which his philosophy is noted. Hence **'Schopenhaueresque** *a.*, resembling, of the same type as, the ideas of Schopenhauer; **'Schopenhauerian** (also as *sb.*), **'Schopenhauerish** *adjs.*, characterized by the doctrines or ideas of Schopenhauer; **'Schopenhauerism**, the pessimistic and atheistic philosophy of Schopenhauer, according to which the world is governed by a blind cosmic will entailing suffering from which man finds release only through knowledge, contemplation, and compassion; **'Schopenhauerist, 'Schopenhauerite**, a follower of Schopenhauer or his doctrines.

1882 W. S. LILLY in *19th Cent.* May 713 Schopenhauerism..is little more than Buddhism vulgarized. **1882** *Mind* VII. 561 Thought, with Hegel, stands for something objective and unconscious (like the Schopenhaurian Will). **1891** G. B. SHAW *Let.* 25 Oct. (1965) I. 317 This does not make me a Schopenhaurist, or Ibsen one. **1898** —— *Perfect Wagnerite* 101 Wagner's determination to prove he had been a Schopenhaurite all along. **1906** *Academy* 10 Mar. 233/1 It is a shallow philosophy that issues in Schopenhauerism. **1906** *Daily Chron.* 26 Sept. 4/4 You would say at one glance that he is a pessimistic ass, a Schopenhauer of donkeys. **1908** *Edin. Rev.* Apr. 423 He is a Schopenhauerian. **1928** C. E. M. JOAD *Diogenes* 96 We shall all be living Schopenhauerian lives. **1959** K. F. LEIDECKER tr. *Nietzsche's Lett.* (1960) 50 To infuse into my presentation of the science this new blood, to transfer to my hearers that Schopenhauerian seriousness which is impressed on the forehead of this grand man,—this is my desire, my audacious hope. **1965** *New Statesman* 18 June 971/1 The shuddering Schopenhaueresque preoccupation with personal annihilation. **1968** *Guardian* 30 July 4/1 The Schopenhauerish misanthropy of the essays. **1976** *Amer. N. & Q.* XV. 57/1 A rather gloomy Schopenhauerian melancholy and despair in *The White Peacock* and *The Trespasser*.

schoppe, obs. f. CHOP *v.*, SHOP; obs. pa. t. of SHAPE *v.*

schor(e, schorch, schorchattis: see SCORE, SHORE, SCORCH, SCROCHAT.

schorer, obs. f. *chorer* charwoman (see *E.D.D.*).

c **1638** EARL CORK in Dor. Townshend *Life & Lett.* (1904) 303 That all the Women Servants under the Degree of Chambermaids be certainly known by their names to the Steward,..and no Schorers to be admitted in the house.

schorge, obs. f. SCORCH *v.*¹, SCOURGE *sb.*

schorl (ʃɔ:l). *Min.* Forms: 8 **schoerl,** 8–9 **shirl, shorl, schorl.** [a. G. *schörl*, in the 18th c. also *schierle, schirl, schürl, schurl, schurell, schirlich, schörlich, schorlet*, in 16th c. *schrul*; of obscure origin. From Ger. are F. *schorl*, Sw. *skörl*, Da. *skjørl*.] Tourmaline, esp. the black variety.

Formerly applied loosely to various other minerals, esp. with prefixed adj., as in ***white schorl***, a name for albite, ***blue schorl***, hauyne, etc.

[**1761** DA COSTA *Tourmalin* in *Phil. Trans.* LII. 446 The miners of Germany vulgarly call them Schirl, and sometimes our English miners name them Cockle and Call.] **1779** *Phil. Trans.* LXIX. 24 It is evident that skirl contains nearly as much earth of allum as the Cornish porcellane clay. **1784** CULLEN tr. *Bergman's Phys. & Chem. Ess.* II. 125 A form which, even among the schoerls themselves, is extremely rare. **1811** PINKERTON *Petral.* II. 132 This rock is chiefly composed of the common black shorl, the black tourmaline of Haüy. **1855** LEIFCHILD *Cornwall* 72 Schorl may be observed between and approaching the joints of granite in many places, as, for example, near the Logan stone. **1894** BARING-GOULD *Deserts S. France* I. 106 These are sandstone, schorls, and clays.

b. *Comb.*, as **schorl-rock** (see quot. 1882); so **schorl-schist.**

1811 PINKERTON *Petral.* II. 132 *Shorl rock. **1838** LYELL *Elem. Geol.* 201 Schorl rock and schorly granite. **1882** GEIKIE *Text Bk. Geol.* II. ii. §6. 134 Tourmaline rock or schorl-rock, is a crystalline aggregate of quartz and black tourmaline or schorl. **1885** *Ibid.* II. ii. §7 (ed. 2) 131 Tourmaline-schist (*Schorl-schist).

schorlaceous (ʃɔ:'leɪʃəs), *a. Min.* Also 8 **sh-.** [f. SCHORL + -ACEOUS.] Of the nature of schorl.

1794 KIRWAN *Elem. Min.* (ed. 2) I. 89 A fibrous or striated limestone..which consists of asbestine or shorlaceous particles. **1839** DE LA BECHE *Rep. Geol. Cornwall*, etc. vi. 157 It is very frequently porphyritic and here and there schorlaceous. **1886** F. H. BUTLER in *Mineral. Mag.* Dec. 79 The black highly schorlaceous rock.

†**'schorlite.** *Min. Obs.* Also 8 **shorlite.** [ad. G. *schorlit* Klaproth 1788): see SCHORL and -ITE¹ 2 b.] = PYCNITE.

1794 KIRWAN *Elem. Min.* (ed. 2) I. 286 Siliceous genus.. Shorlite... Infusible at 168°, and no way altered by heat. **1821** JAMESON *Man. Min.* 189 Schorlite, or Schorlous

Topaz. **1836** T. Thomson *Min. Geol.*, etc. I. 254 Pycnite, or Schorlous Beryl. Schorlite, *stangenstein*.

schorlomite (ˈʃɔːləmaɪt). *Min.* Also *erron.* **schorlamite, schorlemite.** [irreg. f. SCHORL; named by Shepard 1846 from its resemblance to that mineral.] A vitreous black silicate of titanium, iron and calcium, resembling garnet.

1846 C. U. Shepard in *Amer. Jrnl. Sci.* Ser. II. II. 252 Fragments of pure schorlomite an inch in diameter.. may be detached from this skeleton-crystal. **1858** J. Nicol *Elem. Min.* 275 Sphene, Titanite... Schorlamite, black shining.. from Arkansas, is related. **1883** *Encycl. Brit.* XVI. 426/1 Schorlomite (Ferrotitanite)... Perhaps a titaniferous garnet.

† **ˈschorlous,** *a. Min. Obs.* [f. SCHORL + -OUS.] Resembling or having the nature of schorl.

1816 Jameson *Syst. Min.* (ed. 2) I. 61 This substance.. might then be named schorlous topaz. **1836** [see SCHORLITE].

† **ˈschorly,** *a. Min. Obs.* [f. SCHORL + -LY[1].] Containing schorl; chiefly in ***schorly granite***.

1838 Lyell *Elem. Geol.* 201 When felspar and mica are also present, it may be called schorly granite.

schorn(e, schorte, obs. ff. SCORN, SHIRT.

schorters(s, schortschettis: see SCROCHAT.

‖ **schottische** (ʃɒˈtiːʃ, ˈʃɒtɪʃ), *sb.* [a. G. (*der*) *schottische* (*tanz*), the Scottish dance.

The quasi-Fr. pronunciation given above is the prevailing one, but has no justification; the form used in Fr. is *scottish*, regarded as Eng. and pronounced (skɔtiʃ); Littré gives also the semi-German spellings *schottish, schotisch*, but with the same pronunciation. In German the pronunciation is (ˈʃɔtɪʃə).]

a. A dance of foreign origin resembling the polka, first introduced in England in 1848. Also the music for such a dance.

1849 *Theatrical Programme* 9 July 48 The aim of whose existence appears to be that of rattling through the polka or schottische with the velocity of a spinning jenny. **1855** J. E. Cooke *Ellie* 151 This abominable German usage we have imported—the polka and the schottish too. **1859** Sala *Tw. round Clock* (1861) 299 An adept in the *Schottische*. **1862** *Athenæum* 25 Jan. 111/3 The 'Polka tremblante', or Schottisch, is also a Bohemian national dance, and was brought out in Paris by Cellarius in 1844. **1892** E. Scott *Dancing as an Art* 168 The Schottische is very seldom danced now in its original form... The dance consists of two distinct parts... The first part may appear to bear a certain resemblance to the polka; but there is a considerable difference in the nature of the movements.

b. ***Highland*** or ***Balmoral Schottische***: a lively dance resembling the Highland fling. ***Military Schottische***: a dance of American origin.

1882 *Society* 21 Oct. 5/2 There were a couple of reels, a Highland Schottische [etc.]. **1894** E. Scott *Dancing* 134 The Military Schottische or Barn Dance was known to and danced by the Americans long before it became generally popular over here. *Ibid.* 137 Scotch music is naturally the music most suitable for the Highland Schottische.

schottische (ʃɒˈtiːʃ), *v.* [f. prec.] *intr.* To dance a schottische.

1865 O. W. Norton *Army Lett.* 27 Aug. (1903) 277, I could only schottische a little. **1872** 'Mark Twain' *Innoc. at Home* xiii. in *Roughing It*, etc. (1882) 340, I polked and schottisched with a step peculiar to myself—and the kangaroo.

Schottky (ˈʃɒtkɪ). [The name of Walter *Schottky* (1886–1976), German physicist.]

1. Used *attrib.* in *Electr.* and *Electronics*: **Schottky barrier**, an electrostatic depletion layer formed at the interface of a metal and a semiconductor in contact, causing the junction to act as an electrical rectifier; freq. *attrib.*; **Schottky diagram** = *Schottky plot*; **Schottky diode**, a solid-state diode having a metal-semiconductor junction, used in fast switching and voltage-clamping applications; **Schottky effect**, the increase in thermionic emission of a solid surface resulting from the lowering of its work function by the presence of an external electric field; *esp.* the increase in anode current in a thermionic valve beyond that predicted by the Richardson equation because of the electric field produced by the anode at the surface of the cathode; **Schottky line**, the straight line on the Schottky plot predicted by the Schottky theory; **Schottky plot**, a diagram used to illustrate the Schottky effect, obtained by plotting the logarithm of the current density against the square root of the applied electric field at constant emitter temperature; **Schottky slope**, the gradient of the Schottky line; **Schottky theory**, the theoretical basis of the Schottky effect.

1949 *Proc. Inst. Electr. Engineers* XCVI. I. 258, F_0 is the field of the Sc[h]ottky barrier at the contact with the metal. **1957** H. K. Henisch *Rectifying Semi-Conductor Contacts* vii. 195 It is desirable to examine to what extent tunnel penetration near the top of a Schottky barrier (where the barrier is thin) determines the effective barrier height. **1964** *Bell System Technical Jrnl.* XLIII. 215 GaAs Schottky barrier varactor diodes constructed on epitaxial films may be designed to yield a high cutoff frequency. **1975** Schottky barrier [see *Schottky diode* below]. **1967** *Brit. Jrnl. Appl. Physics* XVIII. 629 The saturation values were obtained from Schottky diagrams in which the logarithm of the current is plotted against the square root of the anode voltage. **1968** *Proc. Inst. Electr. & Electronics Engineers* LVI. 232/2 (*heading*) Integrated Schottky-diode clamp for transistor storage time control. **1969** *Electronics* 21 July 76/2 The Schottky diode storage time is effectively zero, in contrast to typical values of 6 nsec for the gold-doped junction diode and 30 nsec for the junction diode without gold doping. **1975** D. G. Fink *Electronics Engineers' Handbk.* VIII. 39 In Schottky barrier diodes current flow is by majority carriers, rather than by minority carrier diffusion. Thus switching speeds of Schottky diodes are not limited by storage-time delays. **1925** J. B. Johnson in *Physical Rev.* XXVI. 71 When current is limited by space charge the Schottky effect decreases because of the interaction of the electrons. **1949** *Rev. Mod. Physics* XXI. 226/2 Theory and the periodic Schottky effect both indicate at most a small reflection effect for clean tungsten. **1975** D. G. Fink *Electronics Engineers' Handbk.* I. 34 The increase in current as the anode voltage is increased beyond the value at which the normal saturation value of emitted current occurs (the Schottky effect) results from reduction by the applied field of the work function. **1930** *Rev. Mod. Physics* II. 151 A quantitative estimate of the field strength that is needed to cause the emission to depart appreciably from the Schottky line.. may be made by considering the.. simplified case. **1949** *Ibid.* XXI. 200/1 The well-established low voltage deviation from the Schottky line for thermionic emission from polycrystal surfaces of clean metals indicates a variation in thermionic properties of the various surfaces of crystals. *Ibid.* 204/1 Generally, the experimental Schottky plots deviate from the theory.. in the low voltage region. **1967** *Brit. Jrnl. Appl. Physics* XVIII. 629 The zero-field emission is obtained by prolonging the straight asymptote of the Schottky plots to the $V = 0$ line. **1939** *Physical Rev.* LVI. 664/2 The slope of the reference line.. was the Schottky slope. **1963** J. J. Brophy *Electr. Processes in Materials* xi. 317 At the larger fields, the data points fall on a straight line having the Schottky slope.., and extrapolation of this line to zero field gives the value of *J*. **1930** *Rev. Mod. Physics* II. 155 Reynolds.. found a variation with voltage in excellent agreement with the Schottky theory for field strengths exceeding about 10,000 volts/cm. **1958** Condon & Odishaw *Handbk. of Physics* VIII. vi. 77/2 The small periodic deviations of the emission current from that predicted by the Schottky theory are.. a field effect but come about through the interference effect of electron waves as the shape of the barrier is changed by means of the applied field.

2. Used *attrib.* and in the possessive with reference to the **Schottky defect**, a vacancy in a crystal lattice in which the missing atom is not an interstitial one and the number of anion and cation vacancies is such as to preserve electrical neutrality; also, the smallest possible group of such vacancies that preserves neutrality.

1938 *Trans. Faraday Soc.* XXXIV. 861 In the case of Schottky-disorder an equivalent number of anions and cations have been removed from normal lattice positions leaving holes of both 'signs'. **1940** Mott & Gurney *Electronic Processes in Ionic Crystals* ii. 26 There are two ways in which.. vacant lattice points and interstitial atoms or ions can arise; we shall call them 'Frenkel defects' and 'Schottky defects'. *Ibid.* 30 We now consider a crystal containing *n* Schottky holes. **1958** K. M. Hornsby tr. *P. Glafkides's Photographic Chem.* iii. 25 Schottky's defects consist of shallow vacant sites of Br^- and Ag^+ ions, in equal quantity. **1958** Condon & Odishaw *Handbk. of Physics* VIII. iii. 48/2 In a crystal containing a divalent cation impurity,.. there will be a temperature below which the number of Schottky cation vacancies will be smaller than the number of additional free cation vacancies. **1966** *McGraw-Hill Encycl. Sci. & Technol.* III. 583/2 In $CaCl_2$, the Schottky defect is one positive-ion vacancy and two negative-ion vacancies. **1966** C. R. Tottle *Sci. Engin. Materials* iv. 90 The Schottky defect.. is not limited to the migration of an atom to the surface, but refers to the production of a vacancy whenever a migrating atom moves to some position that does not create disturbance in the remaining lattice, i.e. the surface of a void or other sink of disordered atoms. **1967** F. C. Brown *Physics of Solids* x. 303 By comparing the lattice parameter.. with the observed mass and volume of the sample, it is possible to distinguish between Frenkel and Schottky disorder. **1972** B. Henderson *Defects in Crystalline Solids* i. 11 The change in thermal entropy favours the formation of Schottky vacancies.

schoul, schourge: see SCHOOL, SCOWL, SCOURGE.

‖ **schout** (skaʊt, in Du. sxout). Also 5–6 scoute, 6 scowte, 7–9 scout. [Du. *schout*, MDu. *schout, schoutet, schoutheet*, corresponding to OS. *sculthêto* (Essen Gl.), MLG. *schultête, schulte* (mod.LG. *schulte*), OE. *sculthéta* (Corpus Gl.), *scyldhǽta, -háta*, OFris. *skeldata, skelta*, OHG. *scultheizo, -heizo* (MHG. *schultheize, -heitze*, mod.G. *schultheiss, schulz, schulze*):—OTeut. type **skuldi-, skuldohaiton-, -tjon-*, f. **skuldi-z, skuldā* obligation, duty, + **hait-* to command (see HIGHT *v.*). Cf. med.L. *scultetus*.] A municipal or administrative officer in the Low Countries and in Dutch colonies.

Originally the *schout* was the lord's bailiff in a subject town or village. In later use the functions and status of the officers so named have varied according to time and place as widely as have those of the English *bailiff*, the term sometimes denoting a municipal dignitary of high rank, and sometimes a mere police officer.

c **1481** Caxton *Dialogues* 43 Bayllyes, scoutes, Some of the skepyns, Ryde with. *a* **1500** *Arnolde's Chron.* (1811) 230 We late you weten in beryng witnesse and certifiyng for troueth that yᵉ day of the date of these presentis before oure scoute and vs and appered these persones. **1533** J. Coke in Ellis *Orig. Lett.* Ser. II. II. 44, I resorted to the Scowte, borowmaisters, and skepyns of the said towne of Barowe. **1617** Moryson *Itin.* III. 285 Ten Judges of criminall causes (vulgarly called Skout). **1670** Temple *Let. to Sir J. Trevor* 15 Aug., Wks. 1720 II. 233 They said the Magistrates did not know the Man, nor any of their Officers. But if I could send some body that did to the Town-house, they would send their Scout with him to execute what I desired. **1673** —— *Obs. United Prov.* ii. 82 The Scout, who takes care of the Peace, seizes all Criminals, and sees the Sentences of Justice executed, and whose Authority is like that of a Sheriff in a County with us, or a Constable in a Parish. **1809** [see SCHEPEN]. **1867** Smyth *Sailor's Word-bk.*, *Schout*, a water-bailiff in many northern European ports, who superintends the police for seamen.

schout, obs. form of SCOUT *sb.*[3]

schow(e, obs. ff. SHE, SHOE *v.*, SHOVE.

schowhe, obs. variant of CHOUGH.

c **1440** *Promp. Parv.* 84/2 Coo, birde, or schowhe, *monedula, nodula*.

schownd, schowne: see SCHYND, SOON.

schoy(e, schoyne, obs. forms of SHE, SHOE.

schrad, obs. form of SHRED.

schradan (ˈʃrɑːdən). Also **Schradan.** [f. the name of Gerhard *Schrader* (b. 1903), German chemist, who first prepared it + -AN.] A viscous liquid organophosphorus compound, bis(bisdimethylamino)phosphonous anhydride, $((CH_3)_2N)_2PO.O.PO(N(CH_3)_2)_2$, used as a systemic insecticide in the form of an aqueous solution.

1951 *Jrnl. Sci. Food & Agric.* II. 310 The systemic insecticide Schradan is slowly broken down in the plant by enzymic reaction. **1953** *New Biol.* XIV. 108 Schradan.. renders plants highly toxic to sucking insects but has no appreciable effect on bees. **1964** A. H. Burgess *Hops* i. 17 Systemic insecticides, such as schradan, which was first introduced for commercial use on hops in 1949, have revolutionized the control of pests on hops. **1977** M. B. Green et al. *Chemicals for Crop Protection & Pest Control* vii. 54 The only other compound with.. any commercial utility was schradan, but this.. is not now used because of its high mammalian toxicity.

Schrader (ˈʃreɪdə(r)). The name of George H. F. *Schrader* (fl. 1895), of New York, used as a proprietary term to designate air valves of a type introduced by him and used esp. on tyres.

1895 *Official Gaz.* (U.S. Patent Office) 30 Apr. 750/2 Pneumatic and tire valves. George H. F. Schrader, New York, N.Y... Essential feature.—The words 'Schrader Universal'. Used since February 12, 1895. **1920** R. T. Nicholson *Bk. of Ford Van* xvi. 100 (*caption*) Section of the Schrader tyre valve. **1921** —— *Bk. of Ford* (ed. 6) xi. 252 Most tyres fitted to the Ford have Schrader valves, which want understanding. **1940** E. Molloy *Landing Legs, Wheels, & Brakes* i. 8 (*caption*) The cap of the special Schrader valve is screwed on in reverse to release the air pressure. **1950** C. A. H. Pollitt *Air Systems for Aircraft* iv. 38 The valve has the usual Schrader-type screwed fixing sleeve. **1967** *Trade Marks Jrnl.* 10 May 588/1 Schrader. **1977** *Lancet* 23 July 175/1 Thinking, reasonably, that this was a colour-coding marker indicating nitrous oxide, she reconnected this hose to the spigot of the blue-painted nitrous-oxide Schrader valve.

Schrage (ˈʃrɑːgə). *Electr.* The name of H. K. *Schrage* (fl. 1914), Swedish engineer, used *attrib.* and in the possessive to designate a type of three-phase a.c. motor invented by him, in which a commutator motor is combined with an induction motor to provide speed variability at high torque.

1919 R. M. Walmsley *Electr. in Service of Man* (rev. ed.) II. II. v. 780 (*caption*) Connections of Schrage's three-phase shunt commutator motor. *Ibid.*, The brush mounting.. of a Schrage motor. **1927** V. Karapetoff *Exper. Electr. Engin.* (ed. 3) II. 439 The Schrage motor belongs to the class of adjustable-speed compensated polyphase induction motors. **1945** E. Molloy *'Electr. Engineer' Ref. Bk.* viii. 51 The Schrage system of speed control requires that the primary winding (which is connected to the supply system) shall be on the rotor and the secondary winding on the stator. **1962** G. A. T. Burdett *Automatic Control Handbk.* i. 12 A Schrage motor operates on the moving brush or rotor fed principle.

Schrammel (ˈʃræməl). Also with small initial. The name of Johann (1850–97) and Josef (1852–94) *Schrammel*, Austrian musicians, used *attrib.* in **Schrammel quartet** [G. *Schrammel-quartett*, also used], a Viennese light-music ensemble comprising two violins, guitar, and accordion (orig. clarinet) popularized by the Schrammels. Also ‖ **Schrammel-musik** [G. *Schrammelmusik*], music played by or arranged for a Schrammel quartet or orchestra; so **Schrammel band, orchestra.**

1924 E. Wellesz in A. Eaglefield-Hull *Dict. Mod. Music & Musicians* 445/2 Nearly all the comp[ositions] of popular Viennese comp[osers], especially operetta-comp[osers] are arr[anged] for this combination which is called *Schrammel quartet*. **1938** *Oxf. Compan. Music* 848/2 *Schrammel quartet*, this is a popular Viennese type of instrumental quartet for light music... Sometimes the combination expands somewhat, into a 'Schrammel Orchestra'. **1963** E.-L. Wuorio *Woman with Portuguese Basket* xix. 167 We can go to a 'nobelheurige' which is a big place with schrammel band and singers. **1967** R. M. Stern *Kessler Legacy* ii. 24 In one corner.. a stringed orchestra played *Schrammel-musik*. **1969**

A. ARENT *Laying on of Hands* xii. 138 The new wine and *Schrammelmusik* were available in Grinzing. **1974** P. GORE-BOOTH *With Great Truth & Respect* 72 We sought a '*Heuriger*', a traditional garden restaurant in Grinzing, where people drink new wine to the sound of the Schrammel-Quartett, a small ensemble with violin and harmonica.

schreame, schreape, obs. forms of SCREAM, SCRAPE.

‖**Schrecklichkeit** ('ʃrɛklıçkaıt). [Ger., = 'frightfulness'.] = FRIGHTFULNESS 2 b. Also *transf.* and *fig.*

1917 G. B. SHAW in *New Republic* 6 Jan. 274/1 As to the deliberate *Schrecklichkeit* of the Germans in Belgium..no man should judge unless he knows the military history of all invasions, and of that very British institution, the punitive expedition. **1944** —— *Everybody's Political What's What?* xxxv. 307 The British frightfulness of 1943 has left the German Schrecklichkeit of 1915 far behind. **1969** R. LOWELL *Notebk. 1967–68* 96 Mohammed..smashed the celibates..Changed their non-activist Buddhistic rote to his clans' strict laws of *schrecklichkeit* and honor. **1972** K. BONFIGLIOLI *Don't point that Thing at Me* ii. 10, I embarked on the quotidian *schrecklichkeit* of getting up. **1976** *Listener* 6 May 588/3 The *Schrecklichkeit* in which the relations between parents and children are so often conducted in Britain.

schreen(e, obs. form of SCREEN.

schreibersite ('ʃraıbəzaıt). *Min.* [Named after von *Schreibers*, of Vienna.]

†**a.** A chromium sulphide, Cr_2S_3, supposed to have been found in a meteorite. *Obs.*

1846 C. U. SHEPARD in *Amer. Jrnl. Sci.* LII. 383 Schreibersite, (Shepard).—Named in honor of the late Carl von Schreibers, Director of the Imperial Cabinet at Vienna, and a well known author on meteorites.

b. A strongly magnetic phosphide of iron and nickel, $(Fe,Ni)_3P$, usu. with small amounts of cobalt, that is present in iron meteorites and forms lustrous white tetragonal crystals that tarnish to yellow or brown. Cf. RHABDITE 3. [ad. G. *schreibersit* (A. Patera 1847, in *Österreichische Blätter f. Lit. und Kunst* 23 July 694/2).]

1849 *Amer. Jrnl. Sci.* LVIII. 440 Something..similar is found in the meteoric iron of Arva. Patera was enabled to collect a sufficient quantity of it to make three analyses... As Berzelius had given no name to this substance, Haidinger, in concurrence with M. Patera, proposed for it the specific name of Schreibersite. At a subsequent session..Haidinger ..says he has since learned that the American mineralogist and chemist, Prof. Shepard,..had given..*this same name* to a mineral, also of meteoric origin, which occurs in small brown striated prisms in the meteoric stone of Bishopsville, S.C., which fell in March, 1843... Haidinger.. would be pleased to continue the name of Schreibersite to the Arva Species, and would propose for Shepard's new species, the name of Shepardite. **1868** LOCKYER *Elem. Astron.* §318 Besides these substances, a compound of iron, phosphorus and nickel, called schreibersite, is generally found: this compound is unknown in terrestrial chemistry. **1968** *Jrnl. Geophysical Res.* LXXIII. 6963/2 The most notable feature of schreibersite is its compositional variability. **1975** *Sci. Amer.* Feb. 35/1 At 1,294 degrees gaseous molecular phosphorus reacted with the surface of the metal grains, thus forming the mineral schreibersite. **1977** A. HALLAM *Planet Earth* 27/3 Other highly significant features which must be explained are the presence within some tektites of minute grains of the meteoritic minerals kamacite, troilite and schreibersite, [etc.].

‖**schreierpfeife** ('ʃraıərp,faıfə). Also Schreierpfeife. Pl. **schreierpfeifen**. [G., lit. 'screamer pipe'.] A musical instrument of the variety collectively known as SCHRYARI.

1939 [see SCHRYARI]. **1957** A. BAINES *Woodwind Instr. & their Hist.* x. 258 Several German inventories..mention a consort of *Schreierpfeifen* or *Schryari* ('crying' or 'screaming' pipes..). These do not seem to occur in any known account of a musical performance, but Praetorius says that they could be used either alone or with other instruments. **1976** D. MUNROW *Instr. Middle Ages & Renaissance* 51/1 The origin of the name *Schreierpfeife* (Italian *schryari*) is unclear: perhaps it had something to do with the instrument's 'screaming' tone quality.

schreik, var. SKRIK.

Schreiner ('ʃraınə(r)). *Textiles.* Also **schreiner**. The name of Ludwig *Schreiner* (fl. 1900), German textile manufacturer, used *attrib.* with reference to a method of finishing mercerized fabrics by passing them through a calender, one of whose rollers has engraved upon it many fine, evenly-spaced, parallel lines which are impressed on to the fabric imparting lustre to the material.

1904 *Dyer & Calico Printer* XXIV. 9 The Schreiner finish is daily growing in importance and will..become of vaster importance than is at present dreamt of. **1946** A. J. HALL *Stand. Handbk. Textiles* iv. 241 Whilst quite a high lustre can be secured in this way there is another kind of calender which can achieve even more. It is the Schreiner calender. **1960** *Times Rev. Industry* Nov. 46/2 Among the ways of finishing a standard grey rayon material of this type are durable schreiner finishes, permanent glazed finishes, and embossed finishes. **1962** J. T. MARSH *Self-Smoothing Fabrics* xiii. 201 For the schreiner effect, pressures of 20 tons or so are commonly utilised and a temperature of 170 to 180° C; many finishers calender the impregnated and dried goods before putting them through the schreiner machine. **1963** A. J. HALL *Textile Sci.* v. 257 A light Schreiner calendering can very effectively and desirably make more opaque the gossamer sheer and transparent knitted nylon nightwear fabrics... The passage of this fabric through a Schreiner calender..just flattens the thermoplastic nylon threads so as to fill out the interstices in the fabric yet without..impairing the fabric lustre.

Hence **'Schreiner** *v. trans.*, to finish (fabric) by this method; also *absol.*; **'Schreinered** *ppl. a.*; **'Schreinering, 'Schreinerizing** *vbl. sbs.*

1905 BEAN & MCCLEARY *Chem. Finishing* 375 When the 'schreinering' process is combined with 'mercerising', it gives the nearest approach to silk ever obtained. *Ibid.* 376 Plain woven Calico goods may also be 'schreinered' with advantage. **1906** *Dyer & Calico Printer* XXVI. 17 During the last few years Schreinerising has made rapid strides, and is now a very general method of finishing dyed cotton piece goods. **1929** E. MIDGLEY *Finishing of Woven Fabrics* xii. 160 The type of lustre or reflection obtained from a broken surface, such as in the case of..schreinered sateens, is shown in Fig. 51. **1945** M. D. POTTER *Fiber to Fabric* v. 96 Schreinerizing is an inexpensive method for imparting luster to low-priced cottons. **1946** A. J. HALL *Stand. Handbk. Textiles* iv. 242 The method of schreinering fabric is comparatively simple. **1962** J. T. MARSH *Self-Smoothing Fabrics* xiii. 198 The general method is to impregnate the fabric, dry to definite requirements of moisture content, and then glaze, emboss, or schreiner, before completing the final condensation of the resin. *Ibid.* 202 The final handle of the goods is affected by the amount of moisture in the fabric at the moment of schreinering.

schrepe, obs. form of SCRAPE.

schrich-owl, obs. form of SCREECH-OWL.

‖**Schriftsprache** ('ʃrıft-ʃpraːxə). *Philol.* [G., = literary or standard language.] The conventional and standardized written variety of a given language (or occas. a dialect).

1931 K. MALONE in *Mod. Lang. Notes* XLVI. 8 Caxton's importance for the English language lies chiefly in the part which he played in the standardization of our *schriftsprache*. **1934** C. L. WRENN in *Trans. Philol. Soc. 1933* 85 There was a common and universally used West-Saxon *Schriftsprache* in the late tenth and early eleventh centuries, as well known in York as in Canterbury. **1935** *Ess. & Stud. in Eng.* (Univ. Michigan Publ. Lang. & Lit. XIII) 281 The rise of a literary language, divorcing to some degree spelling and pronunciation, arouses our curiosity in regard to the extent of adoption of these voiceless inflections within the *Schriftsprache*. **1959** A. CAMPBELL *Old Eng. Gram.* 11 The vernacular ninth-century charters show a steady tendency towards the development of a local *Schriftsprache*, with increasing avoidance of Anglian spellings, and care to express local sound-changes.

schrijk, schrik, varr. SKRIK.

schrippe, obs. form of SCRIP *sb.*[1]

schröckingerite ('ʃrɜːkıŋəraıt). *Min.* Also **schroeckingerite**. [ad. G. *schröckingerit* (A. Schrauf 1873, in *Mineral. Mitt.* 137), f. the name of Baron J. von *Schröckinger*, 19th-cent. Austrian mineralogist: see -ITE[1].] A hydrated carbonate, sulphate, and fluoride of uranyl, calcium, and sodium found as greenish-yellow scales, usu. as an alteration product of uraninite.

1875 G. J. BRUSH *Dana's Syst. Min.* (ed. 5) App. II. 50 Schröckeringite [*sic*]... Occurs at Joachimsthal on uraninite, in small, six-sided tabular crystals. **1921** *Bull. U.S. Geol. Survey* No. 679. 131 A number of other specimens labeled 'schroeckingerite' were examined, but they proved to be uranothallite, or some other uranium mineral. **1967** *Mineral. Abstr.* XVIII. 247/1 The uranium is located only in a small mineralization zone and is primarily in pitchblende form. Secondary uranium minerals are: schröckingerite, Ca-nováčekite, and meta-zeunerite.

Schröder ('ʃrøːdə(r)). Also **Schroeder**. The name of H. G. F. *Schröder* (1810–85), German mathematician and physicist, used *attrib.* and in the possessive to designate an optical illusion described by him (see *Ann. der Physik und Chem.* (1858) CV. 307), in the form of a line drawing of a staircase drawn without convergence of receding parallel lines, so that one appears successively to look down at the top and up at the underside of the staircase as the perspective reverses.

1898 E. C. SANFORD *Course in Exper. Psychol.* II. vii. 256 'Schröder's Stair Figure'..generally appears first as the upper flight of steps. **1901**, etc. [see NECKER[1]]. **1925** J. P. C. SOUTHALL tr. J. von Kries in tr. *Helmholtz's Treat. Physiol. Optics* III. 597 A similar reversal of the impressions of distance occurs in looking at Schroeder's 'staircase' diagram .., especially if it is turned round. **1957** *Acta Psychologica* XIII. 86 With the Schröder stairs, now, a new means was found to ask the subject without using the words 'Up' or 'Down'. The S was simply asked: 'From which end would you approach the stairs in order to mount them, from Right or from Left?' **1974** *Sci. Amer.* July 101/1 The Schröder stairs, another 19th-century reversible-perspective illusion, ..is the theme of Escher's 1953 lithograph *Relativity*.

Schrödinger ('ʃrøːdıŋə(r)). *Physics.* Also **Schroedinger**. The name of Erwin *Schrödinger* (1887–1961), Austrian-born physicist, used *attrib.* and in the possessive to designate concepts developed by him, as **Schrödinger('s) (wave) equation**, a differential equation whose solution is the Schrödinger function; this equation became the basis of the quantum-mechanical description of matter; **Schrödinger (wave, ψ-) function**, a complex function ψ of space and time such that the square of its absolute value is a measure of the local spatial probability density for a particle in the state (or with the probability amplitude) ψ, i.e., $|\psi|^2$ represents the average particle density at a given location in space and time.

1927 *Proc. R. Soc.* A. CXIV. 251 The Hamiltonian function will now provide a Schrödinger wave equation. **1935** PAULING & WILSON *Introd. Quantum Mechanics* iii. 53 The function $\Psi(x, t)$ is called the Schrödinger wave function including the time. **1938** R. W. LAWSON tr. *Hevesy & Paneth's Man. Radioactivity* (ed. 2) viii. 90 In wave mechanics a vibration law is formulated for the atom which is quite similar to the law of the mechanical vibrations of strings. But here we are not dealing with the motion of material particles, but with that of an abstract quantity called the Schrödinger ψ-function, which is only mathematically intelligible. **1955** W. HEISENBERG in W. Pauli *Niels Bohr* 23 His point of attack is..the fact that the wave function representing the system changes discontinuously when the observer takes cognizance of a result of measurement. Janossy asserts that this reduction cannot be deduced from Schrödinger's equation. **1961** POWELL & CRASEMANN *Quantum Mechanics* ii. 59 Many of the properties of ψ which are of physical interest are brought out more clearly by the Schrödinger equation than by the direct representation of ψ in terms of its harmonic components. **1968** M. S. LIVINGSTON *Particle Physics* iii. 51 The Schrödinger wave equation is based on the well-known differential equation for a traveling wave in a homogeneous medium. **1968** G. LUDWIG *Wave Mech.* I. iii. 42 Hence..the Schrödinger functions $\phi(x)$ are nothing other than the representation of the Hilbert space corresponding to the position operator. **1974** GILL & WILLIS *Pericyclic Reactions* i. 17 Now the energy can be calculated by substitution into the Schrödinger equation appropriate to the system.

schrole, obs. form of SCROLL *sb.*

schronch, var. SCRONCH.

†**schrötterite**. *Min. Obs.* [ad. G. *schrötterit* (E. F. Glocker, *Grundr. d. Mineralogie* (1839) 536), f. the name of Anton *Schrötter* (1802–75), German chemist and mineralogist: see -ITE[1].] A name formerly applied to greenish opaline specimens of allophane.

1844 J. D. DANA *Syst. Mineral.* (ed. 2) 531 Schrötterite. Resembles allophane, and has been called opal allophane. **1858** *Amer. Jrnl. Sci.* LXXVI. 79 The fragment of rock upon which the Schrötterite occurs is a dark-colored bituminous slate. **1934** *Prof. U.S. Geol. Survey* No. 185. 146/2 The analyses reported in this paper and earlier studies by others have discredited all the known reported occurrences of schrötterite, including the type material... Schrötterite should be entirely discarded as a mineral name.

schrozatis: see SCROCHAT *Sc. Obs.*

schrund (ʃrʊnt). [Ger.] A crevasse; *spec.* = BERGSCHRUND. ***schrund line, schrundline***: (see quot. 1904[2]).

1870 A. G. GIRDLESTONE *High Alps without Guides* ii. 36 We could see into the great blue 'schrunds', in which innumerable and gigantic icicles depended from the roof. **1871** E. WHYMPER *Scrambles amongst Alps* xiv. (1900) 263 A schrund is simply a big crevasse. **1884** —— in *Good Words* Feb. 101/1 Schrunds or great crevasses. **1904** G. K. GILBERT in *Jrnl. Geol.* XII. 573 Among the numerous crevasses or schrunds of several diverse systems sharply lining the snow surface.., one master opening, the *Bergschrund* of the Swiss mountaineers, paralleled the amphitheater wall... My instant surmise..was that this curving great schrund penetrated to the foot of the wall. *Ibid.* 582 Usually in viewing a cirque it is possible to trace about its wall a somewhat definite line separating a cliff or steeper slope above from a gentler, usually scalable, slope below. This line I conceive to mark the base of the bergscrhund [*sic*] at a late stage in the excavation of the cirque basin. I have called it in my notes 'the schrund line'. **1938** *Geol. Mag.* LXXV. 262 This scarp..passes into the great vertical cliffs below Y Lliwedd so that the schrundline was present only on the side wall. **1939** *Geogr. Jrnl.* XCIV. 462 Above the crevasse the surface of the glacier was covered by scree; and the material embedded in the ice, as seen in the bergschrund, is probably derived in some way from this surface material... A snow-bridge occurred 25 feet below the surface in the open part of the schrund. **1968** R. W. FAIRBRIDGE *Encycl. Geomorphol.* 741/2 Below the schrund line, where there is one, the cirque floor begins as a slope that bears marks of glacial abrasion. **1971** C. BONINGTON *Annapurna South Face* xii. 152 They were both worried by the huge overhang of snow that reared over the schrund like a breaking wave.

‖**schryari** (ʃrı'ɑːrı). Usu. *collect.* [Of uncertain origin (see note below).] A variety of wooden double-reed wind instrument used in the sixteenth and seventeenth centuries and recently revived for the playing of early music.

Our knowledge of the *schryari* comes principally from descriptions and drawings furnished by Praetorius, who regards the term as a plural form related to SCHREIERPFEIFE. Later authorities have suggested an Italian or Oriental origin, but satisfactory evidence is lacking.

[**1618–20** M. PRAETORIUS *Syntagma Musicum* II. xviii. 42 Schryari (Auff deutsch Schreyerpfeiffen) sennd starck vnnd frisch am Laut/können vor sich alleine/vnd auch zu andern Instrumenten gebraucht werden [etc.].] **1939** A. CARSE *Musical Wind Instr.* xi. 129 Still more shadowy are the *schryari* or *schreierpfeifen* of which Praetorius gave a brief description... Not a single specimen is known. **1940** C. SACHS *Hist. Mus. Instr.* xv. 322 *Schryari* were loud, shrill, double-reed instruments with a tapering bore and a reed-concealing cap; they had seven fingerholes in front and two in back for the two thumbs. **1964** S. MARCUSE *Mus. Instr.*

463/1 Schryari were made in consorts of soprano, alto/tenor, and bass; they had conical tubes with double reed protected by a reed cap, 7 front fingerholes, and 2 rear thumbholes. **1976** D. MUNROW *Instr. Middle Ages & Renaissance* 52/2 The most surprising feature however is that the exterior of the schryari is conical.

schryche, obs. form of SCREECH.

schtick, var. SHTIK.

schtschi, var. SHCHI.

Schubertiad (ʃuːˈbɜːtɪæd). Also ‖Schubertiade (ʃuːbɛtɪˈɑːdə), pl. -n. [ad. G. *Schubertiade*: see next and -AD.] A concert party or recital devoted solely to the performance of music and songs by Schubert.

1869 A. D. COLERIDGE tr. *K. von Hellborn's Life F. Schubert* I. ix. 223 The 'Schubertiaden',—social unions of Schubert's friends, where..Schubert's own compositions formed the staple of the entertainment. **1905** E. DUNCAN *Schubert* 93 Many of Schubert's friends and acquaintances ..banded together in a kind of social union, which became known by the name of *Schubertiaden*. Games were played, dancing and speech-making were cultivated, while the heart of the whole entertainment was discovered in the performance of Schubert's latest songs, and others of his compositions. **1945** A. HUTCHINGS *Schubert* iv. 39 Netty Hönig, in whose home so many happy Schubertiads had been held. **1963** *Times* 12 Mar. 14/4 Last night he and Mr. Gerald Moore gave us a Schubertiad in the Festival Hall. **1967** M. J. E. BROWN *Schubert Songs* v. 40 His [*sc.* Schubert's] time was occupied in Vienna by..the increasing demands of the very popular *Schubertiaden*—evenings devoted to the performance of his songs. **1977** *Times* 1 Feb. 9/2 Yesterday was Schubert's birthday..suitable occasion for a Schubertiad.

Schubertian (ʃuːˈbɜːtɪən), *a.* and *sb.* Also Schubertean. [f. the name of Franz Peter *Schubert* (1797–1828), Austrian composer + -IAN.] **A.** *a.* Of, pertaining to, or characteristic of Schubert or his music. **B.** *sb.* An admirer or adherent of Schubert; a (skilled) exponent of Schubert's music.

1866 E. WILBERFORCE *Franz Schubert* iv. 83 The present biographer discovered it in a pile of Schubertian MSS. **1911** J. A. FULLER-MAITLAND *Brahms* iv. 90 The fourth ballade, after its Schubertian waverings between minor and major, strikes the same mysterious note. **1927** *Observer* 2 Oct. 14/4 The work was well chosen to follow the Schubert Quintet, for in its trio there is the germ from which sprang what is now recognised as a truly Schubertian progression. **1928** B. MARSHALL tr. *K. Kobald's F. Schubert* 276 In the streets of the city the faithful Schubertians followed their adored genius to the grave. **1945** A. HUTCHINGS *Schubert* iii. 28 Anselm had two brothers, Josef and Heinrich, who were ardent Schubertians. **1959** *Times* 9 Nov. 6/4 The long, smooth lines of the allegretto were clouded by no more than a Schubertian wistfulness. **1971** *Daily Tel.* 25 Jan. 6/2 He [*sc.* Wilhelm Kempff] plays a lovely short A-major sonata.. but he cannot, I conclude, be counted among the true-blue Schubertians.

schuce, var. SCUSE.

schuchardtite (ˈʃuːxətaɪt). *Min.* [ad. G. *schuchardtit* (A. Schrauf 1882, in *Zeitschr. für Krist.* VI. 386), f. the name of Theodor *Schuchardt*, 19th-cent. mineral dealer: see -ITE[1].] An ill-defined green hydrated silicate of nickel, resembling chlorite.

1885 *Jrnl. Chem. Soc.* XLVIII. I. 32 Schuchardtite... This mineral is of an apple-green colour, soft, and is disintegrated by water. **1966** *Amer. Mineralogist* LI. 292 The analytical data for schuchardtite are inconclusive; they do not fall near to the composition of the serpentine group where they would be expected to be situated but suggest admixture with pimelite. **1975** *Mineral Mag.* XL. 152 We hesitate to label the Jacupiranga minerals as schuchardtites mainly because the type material was insufficiently defined.

schuche, obs. f. SUCH.

schucheon, -ion, obs. forms of SCUTCHEON.

‖**Schuhplattler** (ˈʃuːplatlər). Also schuh- and erron. Schuplaettler, -platter, etc. [G., f. *schuh* shoe + south G. dial. *plattler* (f. *platteln* to slap).] A lively Bavarian and Austrian folk-dance, characterized by the slapping of the thighs and heels. Also 'Schuhplattltanz (*irreg.*); 'Schuhplatteln [G. *schuhplatteln*, to perform this dance].

1874 K. STIELER in Schmid & Stieler *Bavarian Highlands* 108 The idea of the 'Schuhplattltanz' is taken from hunting-life—from the movements of the moor-cock and wood-grouse. **1895** L. GROVE *Dancing* ix. 317 An old German dance..called the 'Schuhplatteln'. **1905** W. D. McCRACKAN *Tyrol* x. 82 The dancer extemporized as he threw down his money for the musicians. This pay gave him the privilege of the floor for his *Ländler* (waltz), or his *Schuhplattler*. **1920** D. H. LAWRENCE *Women in Love* xxix. 456 They were dancing all together, dancing the Schuhplatteln. **1958** M. WEST *Second Victory* i. 5 The orchestras played Strauss waltzes and the peasant troupes came in to dance the *Schuhplattler* and play the zither for local colour. **1960** *Guardian* 12 Apr. 8/7 Besides the yodelling..there are the frolicsome Schuplaettler dances. **1962** *Times* 10 Nov. 11/7 The dancing of the *schuhplattler* forms a cheerful accompaniment to a stein of beer. **1976** *Michigan Holiday News* (West Michigan Tourist Assoc.) May 11/1 The Schuhplatter Dancers, the Bavarian contribution to the art of dance, occupy a unique place in the central Michigan area.

‖**schuit** (skɔɪt, Du. sxœɪt). Also 7 scuit, 9 schuyt. [Du. *schuit*, earlier *schuyt*:—MDu. *schûte*, adopted in Eng. as *scute*, *scoute*, etc. (see SCOUT *sb.*). Cf. SHOUT *sb.*[1]] A Dutch flat-bottomed river-boat.

1666 *Lond. Gaz.* No. 28/2 There were seven or eight hundred Seamen sent from Rotterdam, with sixteen or twenty Scuits, and two Men of War. **1833** MARRYAT *P. Simple* xxvii, He's built like a Dutch schuyt, great breadth of beam, and very square tuck. **1899** *Academy* 18 Nov. 567/1 The Dutch eel schuyt is familiar to Londoners.

schul, schulde, obs. ff. SHALL, SHIELD.

†**schuldere.** *Obs. rare*[−1]. Given as a synonym of COLDER *sb.*[1]

c **1440** *Promp. Parv.* 86/2 Coolder, schuldere,..*petrosa*.

schuldi, variant of SHILDY *a.*, guilty.

†**schule**, *v. Obs. rare.* [ME. *schüle*, repr. OE. **scȳlan*, **scīelan* (only in comb. *bescȳlan*), f. *sceolh* awry, oblique. Cf. OHG. *scilihen* (MHG. *schilhen*, mod.G. *schielen*).] *intr.* To look obliquely.

a **1225** *Ancr. R.* 210 Summe iuglurs beoð þet ne kunnen seruen of non oðer gleo, buten makien cheres, & wrenchen mis hore muð, & schulen mid hore eien. *Ibid.* 212, & ȝif þer is out to eadwiten, oðer lodlich, þiderward heo schuleð mid eiðer eien.

schule, schull: see SCHOOL, SHALL, SHOVEL.

†**schulle.** *Obs. rare*[−1]. [ME. = MDu., MLG. *schulle*, *scholle* (mod.Du. *schol*), whence mod.G. *scholle*. Cf. Da. *skulle*, *skulde*, Norw. *skuldra* (Aasen).] A plaice.

a **1300** *Havelok* 759 þe Butte, þe schulle, þe þornebake.

schulle: see SHALL, SHELL, SHILL *a.*, SKULL.

Schüller-Christian (ˈʃʊlə ˈkrɪstɪən). *Path.* The names of Artur *Schüller* (1874–1958), Austrian neurologist, and Henry Asbury *Christian* (1876–1951), U.S. physician, who each described the condition (in *Fortschritte a.d. Geb. d. Roentgenstrahlen* (1916) XXIII. 12 and *Contrib. Med. & Biol. Res.* (1919) I. 390 respectively), used *attrib.* to designate a pathological condition, often associated with diabetes insipidus, in which masses of lipid-laden histiocytes develop, usu. in the bones. Also in comb. with the name of Alfred *Hand* (1868–1949), U.S. pædiatrician.

[**1925** C. Q. THOMPSON et al. in *Arch. Internal Med.* XXXVI. 650 As Christian's excellent paper has formed and will continue to form the basis for studies of this baffling syndrome, it is suggested for the sake of simplicity the name Christian's syndrome be used.] **1935** *Brit. Jrnl. Surg.* XXII. 810 It is that which is known to the medical profession as Schüller-Christian's syndrome. *Ibid.* 811 An excess of cholesterol in certain body tissues is the primary factor in the production of the clinical syndrome of lipoid granulomatosis (Schüller-Christian's disease). **1953** Schüller-Christian disease [see HISTIOCYTOSIS] **1960** Hand-Schüller-Christian disease [see *lipid storage* s.v. LIPID 2]. **1974** R. M. KIRK et al. *Surgery* vii. 151 Schuller-Christian disease. Histiocytes contain cholesterol.

schultenite (ˈʃʊltənaɪt). *Min.* [f. the name of August Benjamin Friherre at *Schultén* (1856–1912), Finnish chemist and mineralogist: see -ITE[1].] A native lead hydrogen arsenate, $PbH(AsO_4)$, found as colourless, transparent monoclinic crystals.

1926 L. J. SPENCER in *Mineral. Mag.* XXI. 149 His 'monétite arséniée de plomb' is the subject of the present note, and for it, as a mineral, the name schultenite is suggested. **1968** I. KOSTOV *Mineralogy* 467 Schultenite is found in gypsum-like crystals with distinct {010} cleavage.

Schultz-Charlton (ʃʊlts ˈtʃɑːltən). *Med.* The names of Werner *Schultz* (1878–1948) and Willy *Charlton* (b. 1889), German physicians, together used *attrib.* to denote the test made by intradermal injection of antibody to scarlet fever toxin, or of serum containing this; and to denote the phenomenon, characteristically diagnostic of scarlet fever, whereby such an injection causes local extinction of a rash.

1922 *Jrnl. Amer. Med. Assoc.* 12 Aug. 594/1 Rojo's experience has confirmed the specific and reliable nature of the Schultz-Charlton phenomenon in the differential diagnosis of scarlet fever. **1925** *Jrnl. Clin. Invest.* I. 275 (*heading*) The Schultz-Charlton phenomenon. *Ibid.* 293 Serum from convalescent scarlet fever patients produced the Schultz-Charlton rash extinction phenomenon in twenty-four of twenty-seven cases tested. **1974** *Encycl. Brit. Micropædia* VIII. 948/1 When an injection of a small amount of immune serum..is made into the skin while the rash is at its height, a blanched area results at the point of injection within 18 hours if the rash in question is caused by scarlet fever toxin. This reaction is known as the Schultz-Charlton test.

Schultze (ˈʃʊltsə). [The name of Eduard *Schultze*, the inventor, used attrib.] ***Schultze*** (also *Schultze's*) ***gunpowder, powder***: an explosive having nitrolignin as its chief constituent, first made in England in 1863; hence ***Schultze cartridge***, one charged with this powder.

1881 GREENER *Gun* 321 Schultze powder... Schultze gun-powder..is manufactured from light fibrous woods. **1885** *Field* 31 Jan. 139/2, I have used a large quantity of Schultze cartridges during the past season.

schulzite (ˈʃʊltsaɪt). *Min.* [Named after its discoverer W. *Schulz*: see -ITE.] = GEOCRONITE.

1849 J. NICOL *Man. Min.* 483 Geokronite occurs..at Mérédo in Galicia..with galena (*Schulzite*).

Schumannesque (ʃuːməˈnɛsk), *a.* [f. the name of Robert Alexander *Schumann* (1810–1856), German composer + -ESQUE.] Resembling the compositions or technique of Schumann. So **Schumannism**, a musical element in the style of Schumann; **Schumannite**, an admirer or interpreter of Schumann.

1901 G. B. SHAW in *Anglo-Saxon Rev.* Mar. 229, I doubt whether even Puccini really studies Schumann, in spite of his harmonic Schumannisms. **1947** A. EINSTEIN *Music in Romantic Era* xiv. 191 Another follower of Schumann was Robert Franz (1815–1892), a pure specialist in song—a 'Schumannite'. *Ibid.* 196 It is significant that his first, Schumannesque songs were composed to German texts. **1958** *Listener* 18 Sept. 441/2 The richly coloured, evocative scores of Lalo are few. The 'Symphonie espagnole' is among them but not his Schumannesque symphony. **1961** *Times* 20 Feb. 6/1 His account of the first movement of Beethoven's Waldstein Sonata seemed wayward and at times almost Schumannesque in its fluctuations of tempo. **1977** *Gramophone* Sept. 503/3 Several passages, in particular the long, Schumannesque interlude before the eighth (of twelve) song, that add something to our knowledge of Strauss's abilities.

Schu mine (ʃuː maɪn). [App. an Eng. shortening of G. *Schützenmine* S-MINE, but see quot. 1945[2].] A type of German anti-personnel mine used in the war of 1939–45.

1945 *Finito! Po Valley Campaign* (15th Army Group) 41 The 10th Mountain Division pushed forward..across a valley studded with Teller mines, Schu mines and the glass-topped Topf mines that fooled the mine-detectors. **1945** [see *anti-personnel* s.v. ANTI-[1] B. 4 (iii)]. **1961** W. VAUGHAN-THOMAS *Anzio* ix. 209 The Germans..discovered the path ..and sowed it with *Schu* mines—those vicious, light-weight, anti-personnel mines, cased in plastic.

Schumpeterian (ʃʊmpəˈtɪərɪən), *a. Econ.* [f. the name of the Moravian-born economist, Joseph Alois *Schumpeter* (1883–1950) + -IAN.] Applied to the economic doctrines put forward by Schumpeter, esp. those dealing with the rôle of the entrepreneur, interest, and business cycles in the capitalist system. Hence as *sb.*, an advocate of these doctrines.

1950 CLEMENCE & DOODY *Schumpeterian System* vii. 57 The innovation of mild prosperity is the innovation of the Schumpeterian System. **1970** C. FURTADO in I. L. Horowitz *Masses in Lat. Amer.* ii. 32 These urban elements were indeed the Schumpeterians of the development, 'the forward marchers' of Latin America. **1975** *New Society* 2 Oct. 28/1 The negative, Schumpeterian defence of democracy stresses the political skills of the leaders rather than the rank and file..but sees that being chosen by an appropriate constituency is the great source of legitimacy in the modern world. **1976** *Times Lit. Suppl.* 20 Feb. 206/4 Japanese businessmen have not been typical exponents of the Weberian 'spirit of capitalism' or even Schumpeterian individualists.

schunder, -ir, obs. Sc. forms of SUNDER.

schungite, var. SHUNGITE.

schup(e, obs. forms of SHAPE *v.*, SHIP.

Schuplaettler, ¶ var. SCHUHPLATTLER.

‖**Schupo** (ˈʃuːpo). Also schupo. [G., colloq. abbrev. of Schu*tzpo*lizei and Schu*tzpo*lizist security police(man).] In Germany, a policeman; also *collect.*, the police force.

1923 *Glasgow Herald* 20 Mar. 9/5 In the events which are taking place in the Ruhr daily there is hardly one in which the schupos or green police are not concerned. **1934** *New Republic* 18 July 249/2 Similar to the *Gestapo* was the *Schupo*, the former municipal police forces of Germany. **1966** *Economist* 5 Nov. 568/1 Many of these former 'schupos' hold fairly prominent positions in the Austrian police and gendarmerie today. **1979** G. MARKSTEIN *Traitor for Cause* 14 As usual, two green-uniformed Schupos were at their post, the token presence..of West German authority.

†**schur.** *Obs. rare.* [= MLG. *schûr*, OHG. *scûr*; cf. the derivative OHG. *scûra*, LG. *schüre*, mod.G. *scheuer* barn.] A shed, hovel.

a **1400–50** *Alexander* 4049 And þar þai schewid him in schurrys [orig. *tuguria*] to schellis & to caues. **1455** in Stevenson *Rental of Houses in Gloucester* 18 Ric. Hanley, cuttelar, tenet..unum curtilagium cum schura.

schurge, schurgynge, schurling: see SCOURGE, SHRUGGING, SHORLING.

‖**schuss** (ʃʊs), *sb. Skiing.* [G., lit. 'a shot'.] A straight, downhill run; the slope on which such a run is executed. Also *transf.* and *attrib.*

1937 O. LANG *Downhill Skiing* ii. 19 The straight running, or 'schuss', position should be very elastic. **1947** F. A. SMYTHE *Again Switzerland* 37 Down to the broad-backed ridge beneath..the last hundred feet in a glorious 'schuss'.

1958 L. Whishaw *As Far as you'll take Me* iii. 31 Jack [*sc.* a lorry driver] started us on another downhill schuss. **1961** *Times* 10 Jan. 14/7 There is then a final *schuss*, which will provide sufficient speed to make the bumps before the finish. **1966** M. Catto *Bird on Wing* iv. 62 Skis close—the whang of the wind eddying in a blast up the *Schuss*. **1977** C. Wood *James Bond* ii. 21 He.. dropped to the schuss position as soon as he began to pick up speed.

‖**schuss**, *v.* *Skiing.* [f. prec.]

1. *trans.* To ski down (a slope, etc.) or cover (a certain distance) by means of a schuss.

1937 O. Lang *Downhill Skiing* v. 27 In practice you will find that it is impossible to take everything 'straight' or to 'schuss' it as we express it. **1947** *Sun* (Baltimore) 28 Mar. 13/3 In April, 1939, in the annual 'inferno' races from the summit, Toni 'schussed' 3.8 miles with a vertical drop of 4,300 feet in 6½ minutes. **1972** T. McHugh *Time of Buffalo* xii. 147 Within minutes we were schussing cornices. **1976** *National Observer* (U.S.) 20 Nov. 15/1 Schussing the Italian Alps is the newcomer on many skiers' dream list.

2. *intr.* To effect a schuss; to ski downhill. Also with *down*.

1963 I. Fleming *On H.M. Secret Service* xvii. 188 Bond schussed easily downwards.. resting his limbs. **1969** R. Petrie *Despatch of Dove* xii. 181 Would she.. assume Zoë had *schussed* down on her own? **1973** *Times* 28 Sept. 36/5 Forty miles of pistes where you can schuss, trek, slalom, langlauf. **1979** N. Slater *Falcon* ix. 160 When he *schussed* down the shallower *pistes*, his skis were closely parallel.

Hence '**schussing** *vbl. sb.*, the action of the vb.

1961 R. Skepper *Tackle Ski-ing this Way* vi. 74 Schussing is probably where the pleasure skier and the racer come into closest contact. Everybody enjoys trying a schuss. **1969** R. Petrie *Despatch of Dove* xii. 176 The Grand Finale will be mass *schussing*. **1977** *Time* 21 Feb. 52/2 He gave up downhill schussing, lest an accident keep him away from the boardroom, but enjoys cross-country skiing.

‖**schussboomer** ('ʃuːsbuːmə(r)). *U.S.* [f. as prec. + boom *v.*[1] + -er[1].] A fast downhill skier. Also *attrib.* Hence '**schussbooming**, fast downhill skiing.

1959 *Washington Post* 11 Dec. c6/4 Expert schussboomers appear to be coming down the slopes in effortless motion. **1961** *Ski* Nov. 33 (*heading*) Can schussbooming be stopped? *Ibid.* 34/2 The various solutions proposed for the 'schussboomer problem' in the past have tended to place most of the burdens on the ski area operators. **1967** *N.Y. Times* 20 Jan. 33/6 Cervenia continues to be the schussboomer's paradise.

schut, obs. form of scout *sb.*[3]

schute, variant of chute *sb.*[1]

1817 J. Bradbury *Trav.* 317 They pass betwixt two rocks in the Indian schute.

schute, obs. form of shit, shoot.

‖**Schutzbund** ('ʃʊtsbʊnt). [G., lit. 'defence alliance'.] In full ***Republikanischer Schutzbund***, an Austrian Social Democratic paramilitary organization, dissolved in 1933. Also *attrib.* Hence '**Schutz͵bündler**, a member of the Schutzbund.

1927 *Daily Tel.* 19 July 11/5 In an encounter between the Schutzbund and Communists and criminals six persons were killed. **1955** Koestler *Trail of Dinosaur* 44 The few thousand foreign workers—mainly Austrian *Schutzbund* people and German Communists—who were admitted into Soviet Russia. **1973** E. Osers tr. *K. Waldheim's Austrian Example* ii. 27 From them [*sc.* workers' militias] grew the *Republikanischer Schutzbund*, the army of the Social-Democratic Party. **1974** T. P. Whitney tr. *Solzhenitsyn's Gulag Archipelago* I. i. ii. 59 There were Schutzbündlers who had lost the class battles in Vienna and had come to the Fatherland of the world proletariat for refuge.

Schutzstaffel ('ʃʊtsʃtafəl). Also pl. Schutzstaffeln, and with lower-case initial. [G., lit. 'defence squadron'.] The internal security force of the Nazis in Germany, more usually known by its initials S.S. (see S 4 a). Also *transf.* and *attrib.*

1930 *Times* 18 Sept. 11/1 If the Storm detachments form the potential army of an imaginary Hitler State, the defence squads (Schutzstaffeln) are its police. **1932** [see S.S. s.v. S 4 a]. **1946** E. Linklater *Private Angelo* iv. 40 The Count was a prisoner of the Schutzstaffel. **1968** *Punch* 26 June 939/3 Certainly Richelieu was both cruel and sinister... But then, nobody runs a country for 18 years—single-handed except for cronies, spies and *schützstaffel* [sic]—without being ruthless. **1974** F. Nolan *Oshawa Project* xv. 94 The black *Schutzstaffel* uniforms.

schvartze, schvartzer ('ʃvaːtsə, -ə(r)). *slang.* Also schw-, shv-, -ze(r), -tza, etc. [Yiddish, f. *shvarts* black: cf. swart *a.* (*sb.*).

Strictly, Yiddish *shvartser* represents the masculine, and *shvartse* (occas. written *schvartza*, etc.) the feminine form, but these distinctions have become blurred. The pl. *schvartzes* could, in English, correspond to a sing. form *schvartz*, but there is no evidence for the latter.]

A Negro, a Black; *spec.* (with the ending *-a* or *-e*) a black maid (in the U.S.).

Somewhat derogatory.

1961 A. Smith *East-Enders* vi. 92 All der young generation flocks rahnd de Schwarzers. **1963** *Spectator* 19 July 79 Where Perec Rachman gained his first experience of putting in the schwarzes. **1967** P. Roth in *Esquire* Apr. 191/4 She [*sc.* my mother] sews, she knits, she darns—she irons better than the *shvartze*. **1967** P. Welles *Babyhip* xvi. 114 Imagine those *schvartzas*. Pretty soon they'll be living next door. *Ibid.* 115 'She's just the *schwartza*,' Mrs Green said, 'I don't call her a nigger, it isn't nice.' **1967** *Times* 11 Nov. 17/3 Marrying a girl he hardly knew, an honest-to-god peasant, and a Haitian one at that, a schvartsa yet. **1969** L. Greenbaum *Out of Shape* xii. 78 I'm not robbing Wheeler of his civil rights or picking on him because he's a *shwarze*. **1971** B. Malamud *Tenants* 213 An irritable old man.., says to his sweating son: 'You should be ashamed to dance like a shvartzer, without any clothes on.' **1975** R. H. Rimmer *Premar Experiments* i. 140, I couldn't forget the whole mad business of bringing a black girl home to my unsuspecting parents. If I arrived with one who stank of sweat, it would only prove what they already suspected about *schvartzers*, that they not only look different, but they smell different too. **1976** R. B. Parker *Promised Land* xvii. 102 'Were you aiming at an exclusive Jewish clientele?' 'Huh? Jewish? Why Jewish? Anybody was welcome. I mean we wouldn't be thrilled if the Shvartzes moved in, but we didn't care about religion.' **1979** *Guardian* 17 Mar. 13/1 'The schwartzes can't spell,' he lapsed into Yiddish, 'but.. the schwartzes have good taste.'

schw, obs. form of she, show.

schwa (ʃwɑː). Also **shwa**. [G.: see sheva.] The central vowel sound (ə), typically occurring in weakly stressed syllables, as in the final syllable of 'sofa' and the first syllable of 'along'; = sheva 2. Occas., the symbol of an inverted 'e' used to represent this sound. Also *attrib.* and *Comb.*

1895 P. Giles *Compar. Philol.* 134 Indo-G. ə 'schwa' or the neutral vowel. **1933** Bloomfield *Language* 519 Linguists sometimes speak of this phoneme by the name *shwa*, a term taken from Hebrew grammar. **1934** Priebsch & Collinson *German Lang.* i. iii. 51 These overshort vowels are called 'Schwa-vowels' (from the Hebrew *ševa*). **1954** W. F. Leopold in Saporta & Bastian *Psycholinguistics* (1961) 354/1 Central [ə] (schwa) was learned in unstressed syllables during the second half of the second year, because its neutral character made it suitable in such a position. **1956** D. Jones *Outl. Eng. Phonetics* (ed. 8) viii. 30 The sound known as the 'neutral vowel' or 'schwa'. **1963** *English Jrnl.* May 393/1 The inverted *e* or schwa for the neutral vowel used in weakly stressed syllables. **1964** D. Ward in D. Abercrombie et al. *Daniel Jones* 393 The plosives and j being registered with a following shwa vowel for present purposes. **1973** A. H. Sommerstein *Sound Pattern Anc. Gr.* iii. 87 Though Greek has had a stress accent for about 1,600 years, unstressed vowels have firmly resisted reduction to schwa. **1975** *Language* LI. 265 The syncope of a penultimate unaccented vowel and the deletion of final shwa lead to a system in which stress invariably falls on the last syllable. **1978** *Canada. Jrnl. Ling.* 1977 XXII. 226 In the treatment of German phonology.. shwas (in, e.g., *Zunge, geöffnet*, etc.) are phonemicized as /e/ with no explanation. **1979** T. Burrow (*title*) The problem of shwa in Sanskrit. **1980** *Amer. Speech* 1976 LI. 272 The schwa some speakers have in the third syllable of *medicine* is produced by a low-level phonetic rule that reduces unstressed short vowels.

Schwabacher ('ʃvaːbaːxə(r)). [G., f. *Schwabach*, name of a town in central Bavaria.] A German black-letter type-face, a simplified, lighter version of bastarda, used in the late fifteenth and sixteenth centuries. Also *attrib.*

[**1910** *Encycl. Brit.* VII. 723/2 For these scanty writings the German so-called 'Schwabach' characters were used.] **1922** D. B. Updike *Printing Types* i. iv. 62 The smaller type of the Indulgences, which is a rounder black-letter, has certain peculiarities later found in 'schwabacher' fonts. **1926** [see fraktur]. **1934** A. F. Johnson *Type Designs* i. 31 Schwabacher has the usual Bastarda characteristics, the closed, one-storeyed a, and pointed descenders to s and f; the tail of the g is open. **1969** [see fraktur]. **1972** P. Gaskell *New Introd. Bibliogr.* 18 The Schwabacher group .. tended towards the rotundas.

schwaerm, ¶ var. schwarm *sb.*

Schwann (ʃvæn). *Anat.* The name of Theodor *Schwann* (1810–82), German physiologist, who described the neurilema in 1839 (*Mikroskop. Untersuchungen ü. d. Uebereinstimmung in d. Strukt. u. d. Wachsthum d. Thiere u. Pflanzen*), used *attrib.*, in the possessive, and with *of*: **a.** as ***sheath of Schwann, Schwann's sheath***: = neurilema, neurilemma c.

1874 A. E. J. Barker tr. *Frey's Histol. & Histochem. of Man* 680/1 (Index), Schwann's sheath of nerve fibre. **1882** T. E. Satterthwaite *Man. Histol.* (ed. 2) ix. 110 A delicate membrane or envelope, the sheath of Schwann or primitive sheath. *Ibid.*, The neurilemma, which by some is spoken of as synonymous with Schwann's sheath (Frey). **1892**, etc. [see neurilema, neurilemma c]. **1898** *Jrnl. Compar. Neurol.* VII. 183 The terminal branches of the axis cylinder are not invested with a continuation of the sheath of Schwann. **1925** Elwyn & Strong *Bailey's Test-bk. Histol.* (ed. 7) viii. 197 (*caption*) Ring-like thickening of Schwann's sheath at node of Ranvier. **1972** Matzke & Foltz *Synopsis of Neuroanat.* (ed. 2) ii. 11 The axon may have one or two coverings: myelin and sheath of Schwann.

b. to designate the cells which enwrap the axons of peripheral nerve fibres and form the myelin sheath (when it is present); formerly, the parts of these cells containing the nucleus and cytoplasm.

1904 *Amer. Jrnl. Anat.* III. 261 [He] referred to them as 'nerve corpuscles' and 'half-moon cells', and they have since been called 'Schwann's corpuscles' from their relation to the sheath of Schwann and their supposed identity with the nucleus of that sheath in the adult peripheral nerve. **1906** *Ibid.* V. 121 If one examines a developing nerve, one sees that there are numerous spindle shaped cells (cells of Schwann, sheath cells) throughout its course. **1931** W. Bloom *Maximow's Text-bk. Histol.* xii. 254 The nuclei of the Schwann cells usually are flattened and oval. **1960** G. Causey *Cell of Schwann* i. 5 The differentiation between Schwann membrane and Schwann cell that has been made by many histologists since 1839 is not a distinction that existed in Schwann's original description. *Ibid.* iv. 45 The term Schwann cell will be now used for any cell that enfolds a nerve fibre within its cytoplasm, whether.. in the somatic or visceral parts of the peripheral nervous system. **1966**, etc. [see neurilema, neurilemma c]. **1967** Matzke & Foltz *Synopsis of Neuroanat.* ii. 11 The Schwann cell contains a scanty amount of cytoplasm but a prominent nucleus. **1976** *Path. Ann.* XI. 355 Studies of regenerating nerve provided morphologic data suggesting that Schwann cells are capable of manufacturing fibrillar collagen.

Schwannoma (ʃvæ'nəʊmə). *Path.* Also **schwannoma**. [f. prec. + -oma.] A tumour derived from a Schwann cell.

1932 P. Masson in *Amer. Jrnl. Path.* VIII. 367 (*heading*) Experimental and spontaneous schwannomas. **1948** [see neurilemoma, neurilemmoma]. **1961** R. D. Baker *Essent. Path.* xxii. 604 Neurilemmomas (neurinomas, Schwannomas) are tumors which arise from the nerves and are composed of tissue like that of the sheath of Schwann. **1976** J. H. Lizuka in G. Berci *Endoscopy* lix. 756/1 Schwannomas arising from the peripherial nerve sheath.. can be stereoencephaloscopically diagnosed.

‖**schwarm** (ʃvarm), *sb.* Also erron. **schwaerm, schwärm.** [G.: see swarm *sb.*] An enthusiasm, a 'craze'; *spec.*, an erotic attachment, as of one woman or adolescent girl for another; a 'crush'.

1926 F. M. Ford *Man could stand Up* i. iii. 58 Your *schwaerm* for my father's memory and all. **1931** E. F. Benson *Mapp & Lucia* vi. 151 Irene.. had developed a violent *schwärm* for Lucia. *a* **1956** F. Lawrence *Mem. & Corr.* (1961) 121 The adoration, the *Schwarm*, for somebody or other exclusively. **1968** N. Marsh *Clutch of Constables* iv. 87 The wretched woman.. had developed a *schwarm* for Troy herself.

‖**schwärm** (ʃvɛrm), *v.* [ad. G. *schwärmen*: see next.] *intr.* To feel or display enthusiasm or passion. Also '**schwärmer**, (fem.) '**schwärmerin**, an enthusiast, a zealot.

1884 G. Meredith *Let.* 17 Sept. (1970) II. 745 The enclosed, from a Wagner Schwärmer, may induce you to visit Munich. **1913** R. Brooke *Let.* 17 Dec. (1968) 553 They dance so well, the Fijians... I *schwärm* for it; and no white in or near Fiji cares twopence for anything except money-making. **1927** M. Sadleir *Trollope* 211 Kate Field.. developed first into a *Schwärmerin* for all the arts, then into a blue-stocking, and finally into a champion of woman's rights. **1946** J. Cary *Moonlight* xxxiv. 276 'Oh, I saw it, a great bare barrack, and not even allowed to speak to other girls in the passages, or, walk arm-in-arm, and nowhere to go by yourself...' Amanda, mildly surprised by this explosion of anger, said, 'It's true we weren't allowed to schwärm—.'

‖**schwärmerei, Schwärmerei** ('ʃvɛrməraɪ). [G., f. *schwärmen* to swarm, to display enthusiasm, to rave: see swarm *v.*[1]] Religious zeal, fanaticism, extravagant enthusiasm for a cause or a person; an erotic attachment, esp. of one woman or adolescent girl for another; a 'crush'.

1845 *Edin. Rev.* LXXXII. 453 His [*sc.* Lessing's] mind is both clear and strong, free from *schwärmerei*, (a word untranslatable, because the thing itself is un-English,) free from cant and affectation of all kinds. **1857** G. H. Lewes *Biogr. Hist. Philos.* (ed. 2) ii. 531 Kant's.. energetic contempt for Swedenborgianism and all other *Schwärmerei* is unequivocally expressed. **1863** Crown Princess of Prussia *Let.* 21 Mar. in R. Fulford *Dearest Mama* (1968) 183, I did wrong in allowing my feelings vent in writing to you about England; I thought afterwards it would bore you and my 'schwarmerei' would make you impatient. **1880** G. Gissing *Workers in Dawn* I. xii. 261 He has no belief whatever in the heroic woman, laughing to scorn women's rights, and speaking almost as disrespectfully of that *schwärmerei* of which you are yourself such an exalted instance. **1886** *Athenæum* 3 Apr. 451/3 A few hours' *schwärmerei* over what Joan [of Arc] must have felt under certain circumstances. **1927** F. B. Young *Portrait of Clare* i. vi. 63 The expression of liberty and exultant youth that her mother's mid-Victorian fantasias and Miss Boldmere's *Schwärmerei* denied her. **1930** E. Scott *Forgotten Image* xiii. 98 Her idiotic, schoolgirlish schwärmerei attachment. **1937** *Times Lit. Suppl.* 8 May 358/2 It would be easy to dismiss her account of how she 'read Schopenhauer and was blissfully happy' as the Schwärmerei of a pretentious blue-stocking. **1958** *Observer* 26 Jan. 16/6 Philhellenism, when it is not a mere student Schwärmerei, may sometimes develop along much the same lines as a certain type of love affair. **1971** *Times Lit. Suppl.* 23 Apr. 470/1 There were two Watts sisters, the husband of one of them and a young son for whom Swinburne had at one time a *schwärmerei*. **1976** W. Gérin *Elizabeth Gaskell* x. 92 Mr. Gaskell shielded himself as best he could from the Miss Winkworths' *schwärmerei*.

‖**schwärmerisch** ('ʃvɛrmərɪʃ), *a.* [Ger.: see prec.] Extravagantly enthusiastic; infatuated.

1894 Mrs. H. Ward *Marcella* III. iv. iii. 295 Betty.. wrote.. wild, '*schwärmerisch*' letters. **1927** D. L. Sayers *Unnatural Death* ii. xvi. 179 It is natural for a schoolgirl to be *schwärmerisch*—in a young woman of twenty-two it is thoroughly undesirable. **1933** J. Buchan *Prince of Captivity* iv. i. 321 The type of American whose mind had two compartments, realistic business and *schwärmerisch* dreams. **1980** *Country Life* 10 Dec. 2278/1 Many had adored her [*sc.* George Eliot], and not only the *schwärmerisch* women she so forcefully attracted.

schwartz (ʃvaːts). *Skat.* Also **Schwartz, schwarz.** [a. G. *schwarz* black.] (See quot. 1880.) Also as *adj.* and *v. trans.*

1880 W. B. Dick *Amer. Hoyle* (ed. 13) 103 If he should propose to make no less than a hundred and twenty points, he would call his bid a *Schwartz*. *Ibid.*, With a very strong hand, a player may bid to *Schwartz* his opponents, that is, prevent them from making a single point. **1886** E. E. LEMCKE *Skat* 7 With no count at all, he is '*Schwarz*' (black = whitewashed). **1908** A. D. GRANGER *Skat & How to play It* i. 35 All the ten tricks must be taken to score Schwarz. *Ibid.* 36 Some authorities consider that in Schwarz if a trick which contains no points is lost by the player it ought not to count against him. **1949** A. A. OSTROW *Compl. Card Player* 628 If declarer wins every trick, opponents are said to be 'schwarz'. *Ibid.* 645 To make schwarz, he must take every trick. **1975** *Way to Play* 109/1 If the bidder has named suits or grand, he may before the opening lead, declare:.. schwarz, ie he aims to take every trick. **1976** *National Skat & Sheepshead Q.* Mar. 18 The correct answer is to declare a club solo schwartz announced which scores 96 points.

schwartza, schwartze: see SCHVARTZE, SCHVARTZER.

schwartzembergite ('ʃwɑːtsəmbɜːgaɪt). *Min.* [Named by Dana, 1868, after *Schwartzemberg*, its discoverer: see -ITE.] Oxy-chloro-iodide of lead, found in small yellow crystals.

1868 DANA *Min.* (ed. 5) 120. **1883** *Encycl. Brit.* XVI. 385.

Schwarz (ʃvɑːts). *Math.* Also (*erron.*) Schwartz. The name of Hermann Amadeus *Schwarz* (1843–1921), German mathematician, used *attrib.* and in the possessive to designate the various forms of the theorem which states that the square of the sum of a set of products of two quantities cannot exceed the sum of the squares of the first terms multiplied by the sum of the squares of the second terms.

1955 M. LOÈVE *Probability Theory* ix. 156 Hölder's inequality with $r = s = 2$, is called the Schwarz inequality: $E^2|XY| \leqslant E|X|^2.E|Y|^2$. **1962** W. B. THOMPSON *Introd. Plasma Physics* viii. 222 This makes use of the Schwartz inequality $\int f^2 dx \int g^2 dx \geqslant [\int fg dx]^2$. **1964** MCCORD & MORONEY *Introd. Probability Theory* ix. 155 Let X_1 and X_2 be any two jointly distributed random variables which have finite, positive variances... If a and b are any real constants deduce that $[E(X_1 - a)(X_2 - b)]^2 \leqslant [E(X_1 - a)^2][E(X_2 - b)^2]$, which is a form of Schwarz's inequality. **1965** PATTERSON & RUTHERFORD *Elem. Abstr. Algebra* v. 176 In a unitary space $\|a\| \|b\| \geqslant |a \cdot b|$... The inequality is known as Schwartz's inequality. **1975** KARLIN & TAYLOR *First Course Stochastic Processes* (ed. 2) ix. 452, $E[|YZ|] \leqslant \sqrt{(E[Y^2]E[Z^2])} = \|Y\| \|Z\|$. This is known as Schwartz' inequality.

schwarze, schwarzer: see SCHVARTZE, SCHVARTZER.

‖**schwarzlot** ('ʃvartsloːt). Also with capital initial. [G., lit. 'black lead'.] A type of decoration used on Dutch and German glass of the seventeenth century, and subsequently on German and Austrian pottery and porcelain, consisting wholly or chiefly of black enamel.

1925 B. RACKHAM tr. *E. Hannover's Pottery & Porcelain* I. IV. iii. 357 At Nuremberg and Augsburg,..there lived enamel-painters who had white wares delivered to them from the factories to be decorated by them at home.., designs in purple or pictures in the so-called *Schwarzlot*. *Ibid.*, The glass and *Schwarzlot* painter *Johann Schaper*.. lived at Nuremberg between 1640 and 1670. **1952** J. F. HAYWARD *Viennese Porcelain of Du Paquier Period* ix. 107 The combination of hunting subjects and schwarzlot decoration must have been one of the more successful ventures of the [Vienna] factory. *Ibid.* xi. 123 The big schwarzlot-decorated services date from the 1730s. **1954** G. SAVAGE *Porcelain through Ages* v. 172 Daniel Preussler and his son Ignaz, were Bohemian decorators whose work was principally executed in black enamel—*Schwarzlot*—which was a characteristically Bohemian practice. **1971** *Daily Tel.* 6 Apr. 10/4 An early Meissen Hausmaler coffee pot and cover... It was decorated in schwarzlot by J. Auffenwerth at Augsburg. **1975** *Oxf. Compan. Decorative Arts* 335/2 Johann Anton Carli of Andernach (d. 1682), painted in schwarzlot a fine goblet bearing a view of Andernach and a beautifully rendered hunting scene.

Schwarzschild ('ʃvɑːtsʃiːlt, 'ʃwɔːtstʃaɪld). The name of Karl *Schwarzschild* (1873–1916), German astronomer, used *attrib.* and in the possessive to designate various concepts developed by him or arising from his work.

1. *Photogr.* Used with reference to a quantitative law of reciprocity failure in emulsions.

1920 *Jrnl. Optical Soc. Amer.* IV. 272 If Schwarzschild's law is correct, the reciprocity law does not hold for any value of the intensity, the error being the same in percentage amount for all intensities. **1942** C. E. K. MEES *Theory of Photographic Process* vi. 236 Schwarzschild (1899) confirmed Abney's results that the reciprocity law is not valid and concluded that a constant effect is produced so long as the condition It^p = constant is satisfied, in which p is constant and equal to about 0.8. This relation, with p constant, came to be generally known as Schwarzschild's law and is frequently referred to by this name today. **1960** G. E. LOCKIE tr. *K. S. Lyalikov's Chem. of Photographic Mechanisms* I. i. 58 The Schwarzschild equation is not valid for the range of exposures used in this investigation.

2. *Physics.* Denoting concepts arising out of the exact solution of Einstein's field equations described by Schwarzschild soon after the publication of the general theory of relativity (*Sitzungsber. der k. preuss. Akad. der Wissensch.* (1916) 189, 424), as ***Schwarzschild coordinate, field, geometry, horizon, solution, space-time, surface***; **Schwarzschild black hole**, a static, non-rotating, and uncharged black hole, i.e., an object postulated to result from the complete gravitational collapse of an electrically neutral and non-rotating body, and which has a physical singularity at the centre of its Schwarzschild sphere to which the infalling matter inevitably proceeds and at which the curvature of space-time is infinite; **Schwarzschild line element**, (*a*) a scalar representation of the Schwarzschild metric, being an expression for the separation of two adjacent points in the space-time of Schwarzschild geometry; (*b*) *loosely* = *Schwarzschild metric* (*a*); **Schwarzschild metric**, (*a*) a mathematical description of the geometry of space-time exterior to a non-rotating body, usu. expressed as a tensor in differential geometry; (*b*) *loosely* = *Schwarzschild line element* (*a*); **Schwarzschild radius**, the radius of the Schwarzschild sphere; **Schwarzschild singularity**, a singularity in coordinates, but not a physical singularity in space-time, occurring at the Schwarzschild radius; **Schwarzschild sphere**, the effective boundary or horizon of a Schwarzschild black hole, which infalling matter reaches in an infinite time as seen by an external observer but a finite time in the reference frame of the matter, and at which the escape velocity is infinite, so that the escape of matter or radiation from the inside is impossible except by a postulated quantum-mechanical process.

1927 G. D. BIRKHOFF *Relativity & Mod. Physics* (ed. 2) xv. 255 The most general solution can be obtained from the Schwarzschild solution by a proper choice of coördinates. **1934** R. C. TOLMAN *Relativity, Thermodynamics & Cosmology* 208 There are..three consequences which can be obtained from the Schwarzschild line element which can be used to distinguish between the relativistic and Newtonian theories of gravitation. **1939** *Ann. Math.* XL. 924 In the case of a Schwarzschild field a particle is bound to follow a path with a radius greater than $(2 + \sqrt{3})$ times the radius of the Schwarzschild singularity. **1957** *Physical Rev.* CVIII. 1067/2 This transformation is not acceptable..because it assumes Euclidean rather than Schwarzschild geometry for the displacement. *Ibid.*, We get the difference between the Schwarzschild metrics for the two reduced masses. *Ibid.* 1068/2 The effective potential starts from 0 at the Schwarzschild radius, rises to a maximum and then falls off again to zero at very large r. **1965** B. K. HARRISON et al. *Gravitation Theory & Gravitational Collapse* 157 Introduce Schwarzschild coordinates ds^2 = [etc.]..as well as the baryon number coordinate. **1966** R. AKERIB tr. *M. A. Tonnelat's Einstein's Unified Field Theory* v. 82 This is the Schwarzschild solution of the field equations. It defines completely the gravitational field in the neighborhood of attractive masses and permits the determination of the trajectories of particles moving in it. **1968** ROBERTSON & NOONAN *Relativity & Cosmology* ix. 236 The Schwarzschild line element has at the radius 2μ a singularity known as the Schwarzschild singularity. **1968** SEARS & BREHME *Introd. Theory of Relativity* xi. 200 If the Schwarzschild singularity did exist, the Schwarzschild radius would be the radius of a spherical surface which separates the universe into two parts which are isolated from one another by the fact that local time does not elapse at the bounding surface. **1968** *Commun. Math. Physics* VIII. 245 In the special case where the gravitational coupling of the electromagnetic energy density is neglected..all solutions are computed explicity, thus extending an earlier result of Ginzburg for a magnetic dipole in Schwarzschild's space-time. **1969** *Nature* 16 Aug. 690/1 Nothing can ever pass outwards through the Schwarzschild sphere of radius $r = 2GM/c^2$. **1970** *Ibid.* 4 Apr. 64/2 The metric used to describe the geometry of space-time in the vicinity of the collapsed object in this and other papers..has been the spherically symmetric Schwarzschild metric, which is valid only if the collapsed object has zero angular momentum. **1971** *Jrnl. Math. Physics* XII. 1846/1 We consider the problem of a point charge slowly lowered into a Schwarzschild black hole as a simple example where the final outcome can be investigated. **1973** C. W. MISNER et al. *Gravitation* xxiii. 597 The above discussion identifies the Schwarzschild coordinates..by their intrinsic geometric properties. Not only are r and t radial and time variables, respectively (in that $\partial/\partial r$ and $\partial/\partial t$ are spacelike and timelike, respectively..), but they have particular properties..that distinguish them from other possible coordinate choices... No claim is made that they are the only coordinates that might reasonably be called r and t. **1973** *Physics Bull.* Nov. 654/3 An observer falling with the surface of the collapsing star has his light cones squashed as he reaches the Schwarzschild surface of radius $2GM/c^2$; he finds it ever more difficult to signal to distant observers as collapse proceeds. He will appear to them to fall ever more slowly as he approaches the critical surface, and never actually reach it. **1974** *Nature* 5 July 37/2 There is no creation of massless particles in the exterior region of a Schwarzschild black hole, which is the static end state reached as a result of spherically symmetric gravitational collapse. *Ibid.* 17/1 In essence the significance of the Schwarzschild surface at $r = R_s$ must have been known to Eddington, certainly by the early 1930s. *Ibid.*, Once inside the Schwarzschild sphere, one cannot communicate with the world outside; and moreover, one would inexorably be propelled towards the centre: not all the King's horses nor all the King's men can prevent it from happening. **1974** *Encycl. Brit. Macropædia* XV. 587/1 The most conspicuous feature of the Schwarzschild field is that if the total mass is thought of as concentrated at the very centre, then at a finite distance from that centre, the Schwarzschild radius, the geometry of space-time changes drastically from that to which we are accustomed. **1977** *Sci. Amer.* Jan. 34/3 For a star of about 10 solar masses the Schwarzschild radius is about 30 kilometres.

schwassle: see SWATCHEL.

schwatzite ('ʃwætsaɪt). *Min.* Also erron. schwartzite. [Named in 1853, f. *Schwaz*, Tyrol + -ITE.] A mercurial variety of tetrahedrite.

1887 DANA *Man. Min. & Petrogr.* 150 *Schwatzite.* **1891** T. E. THORPE *Applied Chem.* II. 97/1 Mercurial fahl-ore has been named Schwatzite, from Schwatz in Tyrol.

Schweik (ʃwaɪk). A character in *The Good Soldier Schweik* by Jaroslav Hašek (1883–1923), Czech writer, pictured as an unlucky and simple-minded but resourceful little man oppressed by higher authorities; a person of this type. Hence **Schweik** *v. intr.*, to behave in the deferential, crafty manner of Schweik; '**Schweikism**, behaviour characteristic of a Schweik; '**Schweikist** *a.*, typical of a Schweik.

1952 M. MCCARTHY *Groves of Academe* vi. 128 They're the expression of a certain reactionary Schweikism which we've seen also in faculty meetings. **1965** *New Statesman* 7 May 708/1 The Berlin Battle Groups..paraded in Bebel Square to be given their medals—a bored and happy collection of shuffling, grumbling Schweiks. **1968** *Economist* 14 Sept. 27 Censorship is now operating... In a somewhat Schweikist manner, the Czech papers succeeded in getting around this by reporting, poker-faced and without comment, what the 'socialist' press is saying, trusting to their own readers' ability to read between the lines. **1973** *Libertarian Education* XI. 17/2 They will make some kind of bitter psychological adjustment and Schweik their way to retirement.

‖**schwein(e)hund** ('ʃvaɪn(ə)hʊnt). Also **schwine-, -hundt** and with capital initial. [G. *schweinehund*, f. *schwein* pig + *hund* dog: cf. *pig-dog* s.v. PIG *sb.*[1] 14.] A German term of abuse: filthy dog, 'swine', 'bastard'.

1941 [see KNOB *sb.* 1 e]. **1959** B. MATHER *Achilles Affair* I. ix. 105, I heard a curt command in German—'Spread out, you *schwinehund*—spread out.' **1975** I. MELCHIOR *Sleeper Agent* III. vii. 154 Himmler had turned traitor!.. That back-stabbing *Schweinehund*! **1978** T. L. SMITH *Money War* I. 67 He farted long and loud. Mundt giggled, 'Schweinhundt!'

‖**Schweinerei** ('ʃvaɪnəraɪ). Also with small initial. [G., lit. 'piggishness'.] Obnoxious behaviour, a repulsive incident or object, a scandal.

1906 G. B. SHAW *Let.* 7 May (1972) II. 620 Reinhardt took not the smallest notice of either your letter or Barker's. Barker naturally regards this as a Schweinerei of the first order. **1938** L. BEMELMANS *Life Class* I. vi. 98 Whenever a student brought in a reproduction of one of her paintings, Thaddeus would..shout: 'Take it out, out with this *Schweinerei*'! **1965** *Economist* 25 Dec. 1433/3 Some Japanese producers were discovered selling out of line at the recent Canton Fair. But this *schweinerei* was swiftly stamped on. **1975** *Times* 7 Oct. 12/8 India..will outline the petty *Schweinerei* of Mrs. Gandhi.

schweinfurt green ('ʃvaɪnfʊət). *Chem.* [f. *Schweinfurt*, name of a city in Germany.] A toxic green pigment that is a mixed acetate and arsenite of copper, $Cu_3(AsO_3)_2.(CH_3COO)_2Cu$, and was formerly used as an insecticide. Also called *Paris green, Vienna green.*

1852 [see *Vienna green* s.v. VIENNA a]. **1874** W. CROOKES *Dyeing & Calico-Printing* II. ii. 156 Schweinfürt green or aceto-arsenite of copper. **1879** H. CARR *Our Domestic Poisons* 7 Experiments were made on a paper coloured with Schweinfurt-green, an aceto-arsenate of copper. **1930** I. J. KLIGLER *Epidemiology & Control of Malaria* vii. 147 Paris green or Schweinfurt green (copper aceto-arsenite) used so much as an insecticide is an efficient larvacide.

‖**Schweizerdeutsch** ('ʃvaɪtsərdɔɪtʃ), **Schwyzertütsch** ('ʃviːtsərtyːtʃ). Also **Schwei(t)zer-Deutsch, Schwyzerdütsch,** etc. [G. *Schweizerdeutsch*, Swiss G. *Schwyzertütsch.*]

a. Swiss German dialect. **b.** A Swiss German; also *collect.*

1934 PRIEBSCH & COLLINSON *German Lang.* vii. 326 The Alemannic group includes Swabian..; High Alemannic (with 'Schwyzerdütsch' and the dialects of the southern parts of the Black Forest and Vorarlberg)..; Low Alemannic. **1953** U. WEINREICH *Languages in Contact* ii. 14 Schwyzertütsch, an Alemannic dialect,..spoken in the village of Thusis. **1961** [see LUXEMBURGISCH]. **1963** I. FLEMING *On H.M. Secret Service* xxiv. 257 Swiss Air Control, in thick Schwyzerdütch, asked them politely to identify themselves. **1963** *Guardian* 22 Aug. 6/6 The cast of the Zurich opera doing 'Porgy and Bess' in black faces *and* Schweizerdeutsch. **1963** *Punch* 18 Sept. 399/2 Your single word of Schwyzertütsch will trigger a multitude of pleased smiles. **1964** 'P. QUENTIN' *Family Skeletons* II. 61 The pleasure steamer on Lac Leman..the drunken Schweizer-Deutsch trying to get fresh with her. **1969** *Beaver* Summer 6/2 Three of the sailors come in and talk the harsh Schweitzer-Deutsch of Basle. **1974** F. NOLAN *Oshawa Project* xxxi. 186 You speak Schweizer-Deutsch very well. **1978** LD. HAILSHAM *Dilemma of Democracy* xxv. 163 Schwyzer Dütsch, Suisses Romands, and Ticinese can form one Switzerland.

schweizerite ('ʃwaɪtsəraɪt). *Min.* [Named in 1847 after M. E. *Schweizer*, its discoverer: see -ITE.] = ANTIGORITE.

In some recent Dicts.

Schwendenerism ('ʃwɛndənərɪz(ə)m). [f. *Schwendener* + -ISM.] The theory of S. Schwendener, a German botanist (b. 1829) that lichens are parasite fungi growing upon algæ (see quot.).

1882 *Encycl. Brit.* XIV. 556/2 Not being able otherwise to account for the origin of the gonidia, and following up one or two alternatives put forward by De Bary..he [*sc.* Schwendener] promulgated the hypothesis now familiarly known as Schwendenerism.

‖**'Schwenkfelder.** Also **Schwenckfelder, Schwenkfeldter.** [Ger.] = SCHWENKFELDIAN *sb.*

1882-3 *Schaff's Encycl. Relig. Knowl.* III. 2404 The Schwenckfelders do not observe the sacraments. **1884** *American* VIII. 280 There are Germans, also, who are Schwenkfeldters.

Schwenkfeldian (ʃwɛŋk'fɛldɪən), *sb.* and *a.* Also 6 **Zuenk-, Swenk-, Suengfeldian, Schuenkfildian.** [f. the name *Schwenkfeld* + -IAN.] **a.** *sb.* One of a sect founded by Caspar Schwenkfeld, a Silesian Protestant mystic (1490-1561). **b.** *adj.* Belonging to this sect.

1562 tr. *Jewel's Apol.* 19b, Certen newe sectes..as Anabaptistes,..Zuenkfeldians. **1564** HARDING *Answ. Jewel's Challenge* xv. 154 The Swenkfeldians. **1587** T. ROGERS *Eng. Creed* II. 41 Who wil not vse the Sacraments at al, but contemne them, as the Schuenkfildians. **1876** R. BARCLAY *Inner Life Relig. Soc.* 243 In 1734, forty Schwenkfeldian families travelled to England, and finally emigrated to Pennsylvania. **1886** *Encycl. Brit.* XXI. 463/2 Schwenkfeld left behind him a sect (who were called subsequently by others Schwenkfeldians, but who called themselves 'Confessors of the Glory of Christ').

Hence **Schwenkfeldianism.**

1579 *St. Papers, Foreign 1579-80*, 81 Nestorianism, Eutychianism, Suengfeldianism and the like damnable heresies.

schwinehund, var. SCHWEIN(E)HUND.

schwlis, obs. Sc. pl. f. SHOVEL.

schwne, schwt: see SHUN, SHOOT.

schwyne, obs. Sc. f. *shoon*: see SHOE.

schye, schyffe, schygge, obs. ff. SKY, SHEAVE, SHIG.

schyld, -er, schyl(e, schylle, schyn, obs. ff. CHILD, SHOULDER, SKILL, SHELL, CHAIN.

schynbalde, -band, -bawde: see SHIN-.

†**schynd, skynd.** *Orkney* and *Shetland*. *Obs.* Also **schoind, schownd, shynd.** [repr. ON. *skyn* perception, in MSw. examination, inquiry.] See quot. 1859. Also *attrib.*

1576 in *Oppress. Orkney & Zetld.* (1859) 58 For making of the divisioun of the said airschip, callit ane Scheind. *Ibid.*, The Laird compellit him to pay ane ox pryce, viz.—thre dolouris, for his scheind fee. **1592** *Ibid.* 102 Ane breiff of divisioun, callit in Denmark and Norroway ane Shownd Bill. **1809** A. EDMONDSTON *View Zetl. Isl.* I. iii. 130 Documents..established by what is called a *Shynd* or *Soind Bill.* **1859** D. BALFOUR *Ibid.* Gloss. 128 *Schynd, Schoind, Schownd*, an Inquest of Thingmen to examine, sanction, and confirm all procedure respecting the Succession, Impignoration, or Alienation of Heritage; anciently by a *vivâ voce* doom, but frequently (after the accession of the Scottish Jarls) by a Skynd-bref or 'Schynd Bill'. **1866** T. EDMONSTON *Shetl. Gloss* 101 *Shynd*, a court of law. **1883** J. R. TUDOR *Orkneys & Shetl.* ii. 18 If disputes arose as to the due division of the property, it was settled by a *Schynd*, or inquest held by the Odallers who constituted the local *Thing* or court of the district.

schyp, obs. f. SHEEP, SHIP.

schyppune: see SHIPPEN.

schyr(e, schyrray, schyrreff, obs. ff. SHIRE, SHERIFF.

schyrche, obs. f. CHURCH.

schytle, -ttyl, schytte, obs. ff. SHUTTLE, SHUT.

schytylle, var. SHITTLE *a.*

schytz, obs. f. SKETCH.

schyver, -vyr, obs. ff. SHIVER.

schyyd: see SHIDE.

†**scia.** *Obs. rare.* Also 5 **scie.** Cf. SCIAT. [med.L., app. aphetic for the pl. *ischia* (see ISCHIUM) taken as sing.] The hip.

c **1400** *Lanfranc's Cirurg.* II. x. 176 þe place of þe coniuncioun of þese boones is clepid þe scie. *Ibid.* 177 þat oon veyne þerof is clepid sciatica, & þat oþere is clepid renalis, &..oon veyne serueþ for þe scie, & þat oþer for þe reynes. **1541** R. COPLAND *Guydon's Quest. Chirurg.* Kiij b, The great fote lasteth fro the ioynt of the huckle called scia, vnto the ferdest parte of the toes.

‖**sciæna** (saɪ'iːnə). [L., a. Gr. σκίαινα a fish, perh. the meagre.] †**a.** In the 18th c. a name of the MAIGRE. *Obs.* **b.** In mod. scientific use, the name of the genus to which the meagre (*S. aquila*) belongs; also a fish of this genus.

1774 GOLDSMITH *Nat. Hist.* (1824) III. 62 The Sciæna.

sciænoid (saɪ'iːnɔɪd), *a.* and *sb. Ichth.* [f. SCIÆN-A + -OID. Cf. F. *sciénoïde.*] **a.** *adj.* Belonging to, characteristic of or resembling a sciænoid or the sciænoids. **b.** *sb.* A fish of the family *Sciænidæ* (of which SCIÆNA is the type).

1840-5 OWEN *Odontogr.* I. 100 Sciænoids [etc.]. **1863** T. GILL in *Proc. Acad. Nat. Sci. Philad.* 28 Catalogue of the North American Sciænoid Fishes. **1880** GÜNTHER *Study of Fishes* 427 To this fish (*Pogonia chromis*) more especially is given the name of 'Drum', from the extraordinary sounds which are produced by it and other allied Sciænoids.

‖**sciage** (sjaʒ). [Fr., f. *scier* to saw.] A sawing movement of the hand used in massage.

1885 D. MAGUIRE *Massage* (ed. 4) 46 Sciage is a pressure of a come-and-go movement, similar to the action of a saw, and is practised with the hard side of the hand. **1900** in GOULD *Dict. Med.*

[**sciagram, -grammatic**, etc. These forms, which the prevailing rules for the treatment of words of Greek etymology would require instead of SKIAGRAM, etc., do not appear to have been in actual use. The words are therefore given in this Dictionary with the spelling *sk-*. The forms SKIAGRAPH, -GRAPHER, etc., which are almost universally adopted for the terms relating to the production of pictures by means of the Röntgen rays, are given in their alphabetical place, though etymologically identical with SCIAGRAPH, etc.]

sciagraph ('saɪəgrɑːf, -æ-). Forms: 7 **sciograph**, 7, 9 **sciagraph.** [Formed (as if on Gr. type *σκιάγραφον) after SCIAGRAPHY.]

†**1.** A representation of the section of a building. *Obs.* So F. *sciagraphie.* (Cf. SCIAGRAPHY 2 b.)

1656 BLOUNT *Glossogr.*, *Sciagraph* (*schigrapha*) a description of the whole frame and contrivance of every room. **1855** in OGILVIE, Suppl.

†**2.** A diagram. *Obs. rare*$^{-1}$.

1657 J. B[EALE] *Herefordsh. Orch.* 17, I did..set kernels of the finest sort of apples, with delineating in a sciograph the several kinds in severall places.

3. A picture obtained by means of the Röntgen rays. See SKIAGRAPH.

1898 *Daily News* 1 Apr. 6/7 The visible effect of the X Rays is only..a shadow... It is not enough for the surgeons to have a fine 'sciagraph'. **1901** *Nature* 24 Oct. 625/1 A sciagraph exhibited before a meeting of the Zoological Society.

sciagrapher (saɪ'ægrəfə(r)). *rare.* Also 7 **scio-.** [f. Gr. σκιᾱγράφ-ος, later σκιογράφος (f. σκιά shadow + -γράφος depicting, etc.) + -ER[1]: see -GRAPHER.] One who practises sciagraphy.

1690 LEYBOURN *Curs. Math.* 205 The complete Sciographer can cause the Sun to trace out his way upon the Earth; and by the Shadow of an Axis, to point out to us those Atomes of Time into which our artificial Day is..divided. **1850** LEITCH tr. *C. O. Müller's Anc. Art* §136. 113 Apollodorus of Athens, the sciagrapher, was the first who directed a deeper study to the gradations of light and shade.

sciagraphic (saɪə'græfɪk), *a.* Also **scio-** and see SKIAGRAPHIC. [f. G. σκιᾱγράφ-ος (see prec.) + -IC.] Of or pertaining to sciagraphy.

1815 R. BROWN *Princ. Pract. Perspective* 2 Sciagraphic Perspective is the art of projecting shadows of objects from a luminous body. **1867** BARRY *Life C. Barry* ix. 308 Sciographic and orthographic rules and systems.

sciagraphical (saɪə'græfɪkəl), *a.* Also 7-8 **scio-.** [Formed as prec. + -ICAL.] Of or pertaining to sciagraphy; of the nature of a sciagraph.

1690 LEYBOURN *Curs. Math.* VIII. 698 This Sciographical Art [*sc.* Dialling]. **1716** M. DAVIES *Athen. Brit.* II. 76 These Sciographical Pamphlets [*sc.* on Dialling] were writ at the desire of William Tyler. **1892** *Cornhill Mag.* June 633 A shadowy cross, cast by crosslights, on the shaft of the central pillar of the Lady Chapel, which is surely a sciagraphical curiosity.

Hence **scia'graphically** *adv.*

1727 in BAILEY vol. II.

sciagraphy (saɪ'ægrəfɪ). Forms: 6-9 **sciography**, 7, 9 **sciagraphy.** See also SKIAGRAPHY. [a. F. *sciagraphie, sciographie*, ad. L. *scia-, sciographia*, a. Gr. σκιᾱ-, σκιογραφία, f. σκιᾱ-, σκιογράφος: see SCIAGRAPHER.]

1. That branch of the science of Perspective which deals with the projection of shadows; also, the delineation of an object in perspective with its gradations of light and shade. Cf. SCENOGRAPHY 1.

1598 R. HAYDOCKE tr. *Lomazzo* IV. xxii. 173 Sciographie is..the second part of Perspective; considering the self same reasons of the shaddowes of bodies, which Delineation or drawing doth. **1664** EVELYN tr. *Freart's Archit.* 122 Scenography, or (as some) Sciagraphy, which is the same object elevated upon the same draught and center in all its optical flexures, diminutions and shadows, together with a fore shortning of a third side, so as the whole solid of the edifice becomes visible in perspective. **1788** T. TAYLOR tr. *Proclus* I. 78 [Optics] is divided into that which is properly called optics..; and into universal catoptrics..: as also into that which is called sciography, or the delineation of shadows. **1789** SMYTH tr. *Aldrich's Archit.* I. I. i. 2 Let the Architect first make a draught on paper of the intended work: 1. the Ichnography..; 2. Orthography..; 3. Sciagraphy, or Scenography, which exhibits the front and the sides retiring in a perspective view. **1822** GWILT (*title*), Sciography; or Examples of Shadows, and Rules for their Projection. **1868** R. C. PUCKETT *Sciography* Introd., This..book does not treat upon..Linear Perspective; but is limited to the perspective projection of shadows.

b. = SCENOGRAPHY 2.

1850 LEITCH tr. *C. O. Müller's Anc. Art* §324. 380 This..gave rise to a separate branch of perspective painting, scenography or sciagraphy, in which..more careful and delicate design was sacrificed to the attainment of illusive effects for distant beholders unskilled in art.

¶**c.** In allusion to the etymology: The depicting of shadows.

1639 FULLER *Holy War* III. ii. 111 Let those who are delighted with Sciographie paint out (if they please) these shadow-Patriarchs.

†**2.** A sciagraphic delineation or picture. *Obs.*

1611 CORYAT *Crudities* 486 Plate, A Sciographie or Modell of that stupendious vessell which is at this day shewed in the Palace..in..Heidelberg. **1648** HERRICK *Hesper., On Julia's Picture*, How am I ravisht! when I do but see The Painter's art in thy Sciography?

†**b.** = SCIAGRAPH 1. *Obs.*

The only sense of F. *sciographie* given by Littré; it would appear to have arisen from some misunderstanding of the statements of ancient writers respecting σκιαγραφία.

1704 J. HARRIS *Lex. Techn.* I, *Sciography*,..in Architecture,..is sometimes taken for the Draught of a Building cut in its Length or Breadth, to show the Inside of it; as also the Thickness of the Walls, Vaults, &c. **1755** in JOHNSON, *Sciagraphy*.

†**3.** An outline, draught, rough sketch. Chiefly *fig. Obs.*

[**1624** WOTTON *Elem. Arch.* 65 Let no man that intendeth to build, setle his Fancie vpon a draught of the Worke..or ..vpon a bare Plant thereof, as they call the Schiographia or Ground lines.] **1678** CUDWORTH *Intell. Syst.* 146 The first sciography and rude delineation of atheism. **1683** *Weekly Memorials* 22 Hereto is added Dr. Slades Sciagraphy of the Nutrition of Animals. **1686** GOAD *Celest. Bodies* I. ix. 32 Nature being nothing else but a Sciagraphy of Divinity. **1721-31** BAILEY, *Sciagraphy*, a profile or platform; the first rude draught of a thing. **1738** RAY *Coll. Travels* (ed. 2) II. 445 And thus much of the Sciography, or of the artificial and architectonical part [of the Pyramids].

†**4.** The art or practice of finding the hour of the day or night by observation of the shadow of the sun, moon or stars upon a dial. *Obs.*

[**1635** J. W[ELLS] (*title*) Sciographia, Or the Art of Shadowes.] **1651** HOBBES *Leviath.* 40 Table, Consequences from the Light of the Starres. Out of this, and the Motion of the Sunne is made the Science of Sciography. **1679** MOXON *Math. Dict., Sciography*..is the Art of Shadows, comprehending Dialling, and part of Astronomy, as far as serves for finding out the hour of the Day or Night, or other Question, by the Shadow of the Sun, Moon, or Stars. **1721** BAILEY, *Sciagraphy*,..the Art of Dialling.

sciamachy (saɪ'æməkɪ), **skiamachy** (skaɪ-). Also 7 **sciamachie**, 7-9 **scio-**, 8-9 **skio-**, 9 **skiamachy.** [ad. Gr. σκιᾱμαχία, f. σκιά shadow + μαχ-, μάχεσθαι to fight.

The Gr. word is explained as having originally meant 'a fighting in the shade', i.e. in the school; cf. L. *umbratilis exercitatio* (Cic.). It was, however, also used in the sense of 'a fighting with shadows'.]

A sham fight for exercise or practice; also, the action of fighting with a shadow. Often *fig.*

1623 COCKERAM, *Sciamachie*, counterfeit fighting. **1637** IRONSIDE *Seven Quest. Sabbath* To Rdr. Biij b, Least thou shouldst perhaps think I affected a Sciomachy or Umbratilous skirmish. **1657** W. MORICE *Coena quasi Κοινή* xv. 187 Their arguing against it is but a Sciamachy. **1748** *Answ. Scurrilous Libel* 12 But enough of this skiomachy. **1833** THIRLWALL in *Philol. Museum* II. 170 A great part of Cotta's argumentation becomes a mere sciomachy. **1862** *Chr. Remembrancer* Apr. 446 As we have no taste for skiomachy, we leave the fuller exposure of this portentous mare's nest to other hands. **1895** MEREDITH *Amazing Marriage* I. viii. 88 It was a piece of skiamachy, difficult to render clear to the defeated.

sciamancy, obs. form of SCIOMANCY.

Scian ('saɪən), *a.* [f. *Scio*, mod. It. name of *Chios*, the reputed birthplace of Homer.] Chian.

1820 BYRON *Don Juan* III. lxxxvi. Isles of Greece ii, The Scian and the Teian muse,..Have found the fame your shores refuse.

scians, obs. form of SCIENCE.

‖**Sciapodes** (saɪ'æpədiːz), *pl.* In 6 *erron.* **Siopodes.** [L., a. Gr. σκιάποδες pl., f. σκιᾱ shadow + ποδ-, πούς foot.] A fabulous people of Libya 'with immense feet which they used as sunshades' (Liddell & Scott). Hence **sci'apodous** *a.*

1581 J. BELL *Haddon's Answ. Osor.* 267 Seeing that the very poreblinde do see it,..yea wherewith the Siopodes are so well acquainted also:..that it is merueile that any man could be so shameles to deny it to be true. **1798** FERRIAR *Varieties of Man* 200 The people were..sciapodous, having feet so large as to shelter the whole body.

†**sciat.** *Obs. rare*$^{-1}$. The sciatic vein.

1503 *Kal. Sheph.* (Sommer) h iij, The wayn qwych ys wnder the anthleht of the fowt & yt ys namyt scyat [ed. 1506 sciat].

†**scia'theric**, *a.* and *sb. Obs. rare.* In 7 **scioterique**, 8 **scio-**, **sciatherick.** [ad. late Gr. σκιᾱθηρικός, f. σκιᾱθήρας (also σκιάθηρον, σκιόθηρος), sun-dial, lit. 'shadow-catcher', f. σκιά shadow + θηρᾶν to catch. Cf. L. *sciothēricon* (Pliny), a sun-

dial.] **a.** *adj.* = SCIATHERICAL *a.* **b.** *sb.* in pl. form **sciatherics**, the art of dialling.

1677 CARY *Chronology* I. I. §1. ii. 6 The marking out the Time of the day in such a way as in the Scioteriques, or Art of Dialling,..was rightly imputed to Anaximines. **1721** BAILEY, *Sciotherick*, investigating Shadows. *Sciotherick Telescope*, a Mathematical Instrument for observing the True Time for adjusting Pendulum-Clocks, Watches, &c. **1755** JOHNSON, *Sciatherick*, belonging to a sun-dial.

†**scia'therical**, *a. Obs.* Forms: 7 (sciofericall), scia-, sciotherical, -tericall. [Formed as prec. + -AL[1].] Concerned with the recording of the shadows cast by the planets, esp. that of the sun as a means of finding the hour of the day.

1614 TOMKIS *Albumazar* I. vii, With Sciofericall instrument, By way of Azimuth and Almicantarath I'le seeke some happy point in heauen for you. **1646** SIR T. BROWNE *Pseud. Ep.* v. xviii. 259 There were also.. Sciotericall or Sun Dialls. **1656** BLOUNT *Glossogr.*, *Sciatherical. Ibid.*, *Sciotherical.* **1755** JOHNSON, *Sciatherical.* .. This should be written *skiatherical*.

Hence †**scia'therically** *adv.*, after the manner of a sun-dial.

a **1646** J. GREGORY *Posthuma* (1650) 37 Let the Plane bee sciaterically prepared, and it shall bee necessarie for the shadow of the Sun to go back.

sciatic (saɪ'ætɪk), *a.*[1] and *sb.* Forms: 6 scyatyke, sc(h)iaticke, syaticke, 7 sciatique, (seatick), 7–8 sciatick, 8– sciatic. [a. F. *sciatique*, ad. med.L. *sciatic-us*, corrupt form of L. *ischiadic-us* (see ISCHIADIC). Cf. Pr. *sciatic*, Sp. *ciático*, Pg., It. *sciatico*.] **A.** *adj.*

1. Affecting the hip or the sciatic nerves.

[**1398** TREVISA *Barth. De P.R.* VII. lvii. (1495) 271 It helpith them moche that haue this euyll that hyghte *Sciatica passio*. **1547** BOORDE *Brev. Health* xxiii. 9 A gout or a syaticke passion. **1552** LYNDESAY *Monarche* 4926 Off Malideis it generis mony mo,..As, in the theis, Siatica Passio.] **1586** T. B. *La Primaud. Fr. Acad.* I. 225 Sciaticke goutes. **1788** GIBBON *Decl. & F.* xlvi. IV. 429 His body was tortured with sciatic pains.

2. Of or belonging to the ischium or hip.

sciatic artery, the larger of the two terminal branches of the internal iliac; it is distributed to the muscles of the back part of the pelvis. *sciatic nerve*, each of the two divisions of the sacral plexus, esp. the ***great sciatic nerve***, which is the largest nerve in the human body; it emerges from the pelvis and passing down the back of the thigh extends to the foot. *sciatic notch*, each of the two notches on the posterior border of the hip bone. *sciatic vein*, †(*a*) the sciatic artery (*obs.*); (*b*) ? each of the companion veins of the sciatic artery.

[*c* **1400** *Lanfranc's Chirurg.* II. x. 177 þat oon veyne þerof is clepid sciatica, & þat oþere is clepid renalis.] **1597** A. M. tr. *Guillemeau's Fr. Chirurg.* 30/1 The third is the Schiaticke vayn, which externallye demonstrateth her selfe above the ankle. **1656** BLOUNT *Glossogr.* s.v. *Vein*, *Sciatique vein*..is a branch of the thigh vein, which descends down the leg to the outward ankle. **1741** MONRO *Anat. Nerves* (ed. 3) 69 The largest Nerve..of the Body..is..known by the Name of *Sciatic* or *Ischiatic* Nerve. **1780** *Phil. Trans.* LXX. App. 32 Having laid bare the sciatic nerve of a rabbit. **1828** R. KNOX *Cloquet's Anat.* 117 The other two notches are situated.. between the sciatic tuberosity and the sacrum. They are named the Sciatic notches. **1836–9** *Todd's Cycl. Anat.* II. 250/1 The alteration in the condition of the sciatic artery.. caused by ligature of the femoral..artery presents.. remarkable results..: its branch to the sciatic nerve becomes greatly enlarged. **1881** MIVART *Cat* 213 The sciatic artery, which passes out of the pelvis at the great sciatic notch.

B. *sb.*

†**1.** The ischium or hip. *Obs.*

1541 R. COPLAND *Guydon's Quest. Chirurg.* L j b, That [*sc.* the joint] of the lytell fote is moste dyffycyll [to set], & that of the kne is more, and the scyatyke is meane. **1565** COOPER *Thesaurus*, *Coxa*, the hippe or huckle bone..Sometime the sciatike.

†**2.** = SCIATICA. *Obs.*

1656 COWLEY *Davideis* I. Note 32 Baptista Porta..says, that..Sciatique [is to be cured] by a Musical Instrument made of Poplar. **1678** JAS. DK. OF ALBANY in *15th Rep. Hist. MSS. Comm.* App. VIII. 232 The fitt of the seatick came so violently on me, that I am forced to make vse of my wifes hand, not beein able to writ myselfe. **1737** POPE *Hor. Ep.* I. vi. 54 Rack'd with Sciatics, martyr'd with the Stone. **1801** RANKEN *Hist. France* I. I. v. 76 Marcellus the empiric.. mentions with distinction a remedy for the sciatic, or hip-gout.

3. Short for *sciatic nerve, vein.*

1541 R. COPLAND *Guydon's Quest. Chirurg.* M iij, And there be .viij. [veynes to be let blode] in the fete, two on the knees, two sopheynes, two scyatykes, [etc.]. **1741** MUNRO *Anat. Nerves* (ed. 3) 70 The two Crurals, with the Sciatic.. are distributed to the inferior Extremities. **1899** *Allbutt's Syst. Med.* VI. 667 If one sciatic is paralysed alone, the patient can still walk.

sciatic (saɪ'ætɪk), *a.*[2] *Naut.* ? *Obs.* Also 8 **skiatic.** [Of obscure origin: cf. TRIATIC *a.*] Only in *sciatic stay* (see quot. 1805).

Not known to the English nautical experts consulted.

1794 *Rigging & Seamanship* I. 175 *Skiatic-stays* are ropes used for hoisting or lowering burdens in or out of ships. **1805** *Mariner's Dict.* (Washington, U.S.), *Sciatic Stay*, a strong rope fixed from the main to the foremast heads in merchant ships; when loading or unloading it serves to sustain a tackle, which, travelling upon it, may be shifted over the main or fore hatchways. [Hence **1815** in *Falconer's Dict. Marine* (ed. Burney), and in some later Dicts.]

sciatica (saɪ'ætɪkə). Forms: 5 cyetica, sytyca, seyetyka, ciatica, 5–6 siatica, 6 seattica, schiatica, 6–7 cyatica, 7 sciathica, scyatica, sciattica, 6– sciatica. [a. med.L. *sciatica* (*passio*), fem. of *sciaticus* SCIATIC *a.* Cf. F. *sciatique*.] A disease characterized by pain in the great sciatic nerve and its branches.

In the first quot. misapplied, perh. with jocular intention.

a **1450** *Mankind* (Brandl) 484 Remembre my brokyne hede..ȝe, goode ser, & þe sytyca in my erme. **1477** *Paston Lett.* III. 215 Elisabet Peverel hath leye sek xv or xvj wekys of the seyetyka. *c* **1520** SKELTON *Magnyf.* 1956 Allasse, I haue the cyatyca full euyll in my hyppe! **1543** TRAHERON *Vigo's Chirurg.* v. v. 169 Nowe we wyll come to the cure of the goute (called sciatica) of the huckel bones. **1603** SHAKS. *Meas. for M.* I. ii. 59 How now, which of your hips has the most profound Ciatica? **1607** —— *Timon* IV. i. 23 Thou cold Sciatica, Cripple our Senators. **1687** JENNER in *Magd. Coll. & Jas. II* (O.H.S.) 211 The Bishop ill of his sciatica. **1839** BARHAM *Ingol. Leg.* Ser. I. *St. Gengulphus*, Rheumatics,— sciatica,—tic-doloureux! **1860** EMERSON *Cond. Life* v. *Behaviour* Wks. (Bohn) II. 392 If you have headache, or sciatica, or leprosy,..I beseech you, by all angels, to hold your peace. **1866** A. FLINT *Princ. Med.* (1880) 801 Sciatic neuralgia, or sciatica. **1871** NAPHEYS *Prev. & Cure Dis.* III. iv. 701 A victim to sciatica, or neuralgic pain in the hip.

fig. **1596** NASHE *Saffron Walden* Ep. Ded. B 3, They are the verie botts & the glanders to the gentle Readers,..the Sarpego and the Sciatica of the 7. Liberall Sciences.

b. An attack of this disease.

1444 *Paston Lett.* I. 50 He hath hadde a cyetica that hath letted hym a gret while to ride. **1606** [see LIME-KILN b]. **1641** BROME *Jovial Crew* I. (1652) C 4, He..was taken lame with lying in the Fields by a Sciatica. **1682** N. O. *Boileau's Lutrin* IV. 83 He curst an old Sciatica that Stop'd him. **1697** SIR J. FLOYER *Enq. Baths* Pref. b 7 Erysipela's, Sciatica's, Fluxes. **1722** *Hearne's Collect.* (O.H.S.) VII. 384 For a Sciatica. A Catskin tann'd with the Fur on, and layd upon the Part affected. **1759** STERNE *Tr. Shandy* I. iv, He was all that time afflicted with a Sciatica. **1831** SCOTT *F.M. Perth* Introd., Well, enough that I awake without a sciatica.

†**c. sciatica cress, grass** (see quot. 1886).

1562 TURNER *Herbal* II. 20 Of Sciatica cresse or wilde cresse. *Iberis. Ibid.* 20 b, It may be called in Englishe.. sciatica cresses, because the herbe is good for the sciatica. **1597** GERARDE *Herbal* II. xiv. 197 Sciatica Cresses hath many slender braunches..with small, long, and narrowe leaues, like those of garden Cresses. The flowers be very small, and yellow of colour. *Ibid.* Table Eng. Names, Sciatica grasse, that is wilde Cresses. **1886** BRITTEN & HOLLAND *Plant-n*, *Cress, Sciatica*. A name invented by Turner (Herb.) for a cruciferous plant (which Prior identifies with *Iberis amara*, L., but which seems to us a species of Lepidium).

sciatical (saɪ'ætɪkəl), *a.* [f. SCIATIC + -AL[1].]

†**1.** = SCIATIC *a.* 2. *Obs. rare*⁻¹.

1597 A. M. tr. *Guillemeau's Fr. Chirurg.* 12/2 The Sciaticalle vayne in the externalle anckle.

2. Pertaining to or of the nature of sciatica. Of a person: Affected with sciatica. Now *rare*.

1657 TOMLINSON *Renou's Disp.* 202 Empasms are used.. to help the Hydroptical, or Sciatical..Patients. *c* **1714** POPE, etc. *Martinus Scriblerus* vi. (1756) 28 Whence is it that I daily deplore my sciatical pains? **1765** STERNE *Tr. Shandy* VII. xxi, Overlooking a sciatical old nun..Margarita, the little novice, was elected as the companion of the journey. **1886** *Times* 13 Apr. 10/1 The [Canadian] Premier continues to improve in health, the sciatical pains are diminishing daily.

Hence **sci'atically** *adv.*, 'with or by means of sciatica' (Webster 1864).

†**sci'bility.** *Obs.* [f. L. *scībilis* knowable (here taken in the active sense = able to know), f. *scīre* to know: see -BLE and -ITY.] Power of knowing.

1677 GALE *Crt. Gentiles* IV. II. v. 332 That God doth not know things future by the Infinitie or Immensitie of his own Scibilitie or Scientivitie.

scien, obs. form of SCION.

science ('saɪəns). Forms: 4 sienz, cience, ciens, 4–5 siens, syence, syense, 4–6 scyence, sciens(e, 4, 6–7 sience, 5 scians, 5–6 syens, 6 sienc, scyens, 6–7 scyense, 4– science. [a. F. *science* = Pr. *sciensa*, Sp. *ciencia*, Pg. *sciencia*, It. *scienza*, ad. L. *scientia* knowledge, f. *scient-em*, pr. pple. of *scīre* to know.]

1. a. The state or fact of knowing; knowledge or cognizance *of* something specified or implied; also, with wider reference, knowledge (more or less extensive) as a personal attribute. Now only *Theol.* in the rendering of scholastic terms (see quot. 1728), and occas. *Philos.* in the sense of 'knowledge' as opposed to 'belief' or 'opinion'.

a **1340** HAMPOLE *Psalter* Cant. 500 Ald thyngis deport fra ȝowre mouth: for God of sciens is lord, and till him ere redyd the thoghtis. *c* **1374** CHAUCER *Boeth.* II. pr. vii. (1868) 59 þe soule whiche þat haþ in it self science of goode werkes [L. *sibi mens bene conscia*]. **1426** LYDG. *De Guil. Pilgr.* 2697 Therfor ye trewly ber the name Cherubin, fful of scyence And of dyvyne sapyence. **1532** MORE *Confut. Tindale* Wks. 361/2 Whereof saynt Paule cryeth hymself, *O altitudo diuitiarum sapientie & scientie dei*. O the heyght and depenes of the ryches of the wysedome and scyence of god. **1601** SHAKS. *All's Well* v. iii. 103 Plutus himselfe,..Hath not in natures mysterie more science, Then I haue in this Ring. **1667** MILTON *P.L.* IX. 680 O Sacred, Wise, and Wisdom-giving Plant, Mother of Science. **1678** GALE *Crt. Gentiles* IV. III. 36 Some of our Opponents resolve Gods certain prescience of sin into the infinitude of his science. **1697** tr. *Burgersaicius' Logic* II. xx. 99 The word science is either taken largely to signifie any cognition or true assent; or, strictly, a firm and infallible one; or, lastly, an assent of propositions made known by the cause and effect. **1700** ROWE *Amb. Step-Mother* II. ii. 852 What makes Gods divine But Power and Science infinite. **1725** POPE *Odyss.* II. 198 For lo! my words no fancy'd woes relate: I speak from science, and the voice is Fate. **1728** CHAMBERS *Cycl.* s.v. *Science*, Divines suppose three kinds of Science in God: The first, Science of mere Knowledge... The second, a Science of Vision... The third, an intermediate Science. **1753** JOHNSON *Adventurer* No. 107 ¶ 18 Life is not the object of Science: we see a little, very little; and what is beyond we can only conjecture. **1882** SEELEY *Nat. Relig.* 260 Though we have not science of it [supernaturalism] yet we have probabilities or powerful presentiments.

†**b.** Contrasted or coupled with *conscience*, emphasizing the distinction to be drawn between theoretical perception of a truth and moral conviction. *Obs.*

1620 T. SCOTT *God & King* (1623) 84 This my Sermon.. is perhaps tost by censure and science for a while, but scarce touched by conscience, or drawne into practise. **1637** ABP. LAUD *Sp. Star-Chamber* 14 June 62 The Author is clearely conceived..to have written this Book wholly..against both his science and his conscience. **1654** OWEN *Doctr. Saints' Persev.* xi. 249 A wilfull perverting of it, contrary to his own science & conscience.

2. a. Knowledge acquired by study; acquaintance with or mastery of any department of learning. Also †*pl.* (a person's) various kinds of knowledge.

13.. *E.E. Allit. P.* B. 1289 Wyth alle þe coyntyse þat he cowþe..De-uised he [salomon] þe vesselment,..Wyth slyȝt of his ciences, his souerayn to loue. **1390** GOWER *Conf.* II. 82 And Heredot in his science Of metre, of rime and of cadence The ferste was of which men note. *c* **1400** *Destr. Troy* 5524 Epistaphus..a discrete man of dedis, dryuen into age, And a sad mon of sciens in the seuyn artis. *c* **1440** *Gesta Rom.* xxxiv. 132 (Harl. MS.) No man myght be likenid to him in no kynne sciens. **1456** SIR G. HAYE *Law Arms* (S.T.S.) 16 Clerkis of hye science, the quhilkis had the grete dignities in haly kirk. *c* **1475** *Partenay* 107 As rose is aboue al floures most fine So is science most digne of worthynesse. **1538** BALE *John Baptist* in *Harl. Misc.* (1744) I. 105 You boast your selues moch, of ryghteousness and scyence. **1557** NORTH *Gueuara's Diall Pr.* II. xxx. (1568) 138 b, The auncient women were more esteamed for their sciences, then for their beauties. **1562** WINȜET *Cert. Tractates* I. 16 Giue Johne Knox and ze affirmis zour selfis lauchful be ressoun of zour science [etc.]. **1738** GRAY *Propertius* II. 52 Be love my youth's pursuit, and science crown my Age. **1781** COWPER *Conversation* 14 As alphabets in ivory employ, Hour after hour, the yet unletter'd boy, Sorting and puzzling with a deal of glee Those seeds of science call'd his A B C.

b. Trained skill. Now *esp.* (somewhat jocularly) with reference to pugilism (cf. 3 c); also to horsemanship and other bodily exercises.

1785 MRS. BELLAMY *Apol.* (ed. 3) IV. 156 She could by no means be said to surpass Mrs. Yates, who joined hard-earned science to her other great qualifications. **1793** W. ROBERTS *Looker-on* No. 33 (1797) II. 111 Mr. Powell, the fire-eater, is a singular genius; and Mendoza has more science than Johnson. **1812** *Sporting Mag.* XXXIX. 22 Molineux sparred neatly early in the fight, but he lost his science after he had been a good deal punished. **1889** *Field* 12 Jan. 41/2 It was most disappointing to their huntsman to have the cup thus dashed from his lips when it only required a kill to render complete as fine an exhibition of science as could possibly be seen.

c. *fig.* ***to blind with science*** (*slang*): to confuse by the use of polysyllabic words or involved explanations (see also quot. 1937).

1937 PARTRIDGE *Dict. Slang* 64/2 *Blinded with science*. A catch-phrase applied by brawn defeated by brains: Australian and New Zealand: C. 20. **1948** —— *Dict. Forces' Slang 1938–45* 18 *Blind with science*, to explain away an offence, a mistake, by talking at great length and very technically, thus dazzling one's interlocutor into non-pursuance of the matter. (Mostly Army.) **1973** *Daily Tel.* 17 Oct. 14/6 We are also more familiar..with the tendency for people to be blinded by science and to succumb to 'expert' medical opinion, however quackish. **1977** *Time Out* 17–23 June 11/3 It's very easy to coast and blind the office with science.

3. a. A particular branch of knowledge or study; a recognized department of learning.

In the Middle Ages, 'the seven (liberal) sciences' was often used synonymously with 'the seven liberal arts', for the group of studies comprised by the *Trivium* (Grammar, Logic, Rhetoric) and the *Quadrivium* (Arithmetic, Music, Geometry, Astronomy).

13.. *Seuyn Sag.* (W.) 48, I wil that ye teche him euyn The sutelte of science seuyn. *c* **1386** CHAUCER *Frankl. T.* 1122 As yonge clerkes..Seken in euery halke and euery herne Particuler sciences for to lerne. *c* **1400** *Lanfranc's Cirurg.* 7 Therfore he þat wole knowe what siurgie is, he most vndirstonde, þat it is a medicinal science. **1421** *Rolls of Parlt.* IV. 158 Thre Sciences that ben Divinite, Fisyk, and Lawe. **1486** *Bk. St. Albans, Her.* e iv b, Bott in thes borduris ther is a grete differens emong men pretendyng theym experte and wyse in thys sciens. **1509** WATSON *Ship of Fools* ii. (1517) A iij, It is they the whiche ben yᵉ leest experte in scyences, as in lawe. **1542** UDALL *Erasm. Apoph.* 61 A philosopher of Athenes excellyng in all the mathematical sciencies. **1553** EDEN *Treat. Newe Ind.* (Arb.) 5 The good affeccion whyche I haue euer borne to the science of Cosmographie. **1596** SHAKS. *Tam. Shr.* II. i. 57, I do present you with a man of mine Cunning in Musicke, and the Mathematickes, To instruct her fully in those sciences. **1613** PURCHAS *Pilgrimage* (1614) 795 Mexico is now an Vniuersitie, and therein are taught those Sciences which are read in our Vniuersities of Europe. **1662** STILLINGFL. *Orig. Sacræ* II, vi. §3 The right understanding of the principles of a science, is the ground why all things belonging to that science are understood. **1683** *Col. Rec. Pennsylv.* I. 93 To Witt: a scool of Arts and Siences. **1727** DE FOE *Syst. Magic* I. ii. (1840) 59 And thus you have an honest system of the science called Magic. **1794** GODWIN *Caleb Williams* 1, I was taught the rudiments of no science, except reading, writing, and arithmetic. **1864** TENNYSON *Aylmer's F.* 435 So Leolin went; and..toil'd Mastering the lawless science of our law. **1892** WESTCOTT *Gospel of Life* 89 Theology is the crown of all the sciences, and Religion the synthesis of all.

transf. **1752** *Adventurer* No. 9 ⁋10 Give us..that master of the science the celebrated Hoyle, who has composed an elaborate treatise on every fashionable game. **1770** Burke *Pres. Discont.* 66 Underhand and oblique ways would be studied. The science of evasion, already tolerably understood, would then be brought to the greatest perfection. **1794** Godwin *Caleb Williams* 20 Unpardonably deficient in the sciences of anecdote and match-making. **1810** Syd. Smith *Public Schools* Wks. 1859 I. 188 His sister, who has remained at home at the apron-strings of her mother, is very much his superior in the science of manners. **1826** Lamb *Elia* II. *Pop. Fallacies* xvi, But facts and sane inferences are trifles to a true adept in the science of dissatisfaction. **1837** Lockhart *Scott* I. iv. 128 Scott did not pursue the science of chess after his boyhood.

b. Contradistinguished from *art*: see art *sb.* 8.

The distinction as commonly apprehended is that a science (= ἐπιστήμη) is concerned with theoretic truth, and an art (= τέχνη) with methods for effecting certain results. Sometimes, however, the term *science* is extended to denote a department of practical work which depends on the knowledge and conscious application of principles; an *art*, on the other hand, being understood to require merely knowledge of traditional rules and skill acquired by habit.

1678 Moxon *Mech. Dyalling* 4 Though we may justly account Dyalling originally a Science, yet..it is now become to many of the Ingenious no more difficult than an Art. **1712** Budgell *Spect.* No. 307 ⁋5 Without a proper temperament for the particular Art or Science which he studies, his utmost Pains and Application..will be to no purpose. **1796** Kirwan *Elem. Min.* (ed. 2) I. Pref. 11 Previous to the year 1780, mineralogy, though tolerably understood by many as an art, could scarce be deemed a Science. **1834** Southey *Doctor* cxx. (1862) 294 The medical profession..was an art, in the worst sense of the word, before it became a science, and long after it pretended to be a science was little better than a craft. **1907** Hodges *Elem. Photogr.* 58 The development of the photographic image is both an art and a science.

c. ***the noble science*** (***of defence***): the art of boxing or that of fencing. Now *jocular.* Also, in mod. slang, ***the science.*** (Cf. sense 2 b).

c **1588–1839** [see noble A. 9]. **1837** Dickens *Pickw.* xlix, Up to that time he had never been aware that he had the least notion of the science [*sc.* fencing].

†**d.** A craft, trade, or occupation requiring trained skill. *Obs.*

c **1480** *Childe of Bristowe* 78 in Hazl. *E.P.P.* I. 114 He gaf hym gold gret plenté, the child hys prentys shuld be, his science for to conne. **1526** *Pilgr. Perf.* (W. de W. 1531) 67 Whan a virgyn begynneth fyrst to lerne to sewe in the samplar, that scyence to her as than semeth very harde. **1530–1** *Act 22 Hen. VIII*, c. 13 That no..persones..shalbe enterpret or expounded hande craftesmen, in, for, or by reason of usyng any of the sayde mysteryes, or scyens, of bakyng, bruyng, surgery or wrytyng. **1551** Robinson tr. *More's Utopia* III. iv. (1895) 139 Husbandrye is a scyence common to them all ingenerall, both men and women, wherin they be all experte and cunnynge. **1576** *Lichfield Guilds* (E.E.T.S.) 26 The Master, Wardens and Combretheren of the mystery, crafte, and Scyence of the Taylers of the Citie of Lichffelde. **1600** Dekker *Gentle Craft* (1610) B 1 b, My iolly coze..Became a Shoomaker in Wittenberg, A goody science for a gentleman. **1660** *Boston Rec.* (1877) II. 156 No person shall henceforth open a shop in this Towne, nor occupy any manufacture or Science, till hee hath compleated 21 years of age.

4. a. In a more restricted sense: A branch of study which is concerned either with a connected body of demonstrated truths or with observed facts systematically classified and more or less colligated by being brought under general laws, and which includes trustworthy methods for the discovery of new truth within its own domain.

1725 Watts *Logic* II. ii. §9 The word science, is usually applied to a whole body of regular or methodical observations or propositions,..concerning any subject of speculation. **1794** Hutton *Philos. Light*, etc. 117 Philosophy must proceed in generalising those truths which are the object of particular sciences. **1860** Abp. Thomson *Laws Th.* §131 (ed. 5) 281 Classification of the Sciences. Mathematics... Astronomy... Physics [etc.]. **1882** Adamson in *Encycl. Brit.* XIV. 781/2 It may be said that in all sciences there are implied clearly defined notions, general statements or judgments, and methodical proofs.

b. with defining word.

The many conflicting systems proposed in recent times for the classification of the sciences, and the need frequently arising (apart from any formal classification) for a common designation applicable to a group of sciences that are related by similarity of subject or method, have given currency to a large number of expressions in which the word *science* is qualified by an adj. The application of these collocations, so far as it is not obvious, is explained under the adjs. Among the most prominent of the adjs. designating particular classes of sciences are: *abstract, concrete, biological, descriptive, exact, experimental, historical, mathematical, mechanical, moral, mixed, pure, natural, physical.* Also with preceding sb., as *life science*, and combined with a prefix, as *bio-, geo-, neuroscience.* (See under the first element.)

1795 Burke *Let. to Earl Fitzwilliam* Wks. IX. 1, I am not sure, that the best way of discussing any subject, except those, that concern the abstracted sciences, is not somewhat in the way of dialogue.

c. In phrases: ***science of art, of expression, of mind, of religion***(***s***), denoting esp. the application of scientific methods in fields of study previously considered open only to theories based on subjective, historical, or undemonstrable abstract criteria.

1828 J. S. Mill in *Westm. Rev.* IX. 140 The impugners of the school logic, as they term it, may be divided into two classes. The first class consists of men not untinctured with philosophy, including even some writers of considerable eminence in the science of mind. **1869** W. James *Let.* 21 Jan. in R. B. Perry *Tht. & Char. W. James* (1935) I. 291 Some weeks ago I read the three last articles on 'Science of Religions' by Emile Burnouf in the *Revue des deux mondes.* **1886** T. Paterson *Mental Sci.* 4 This confusion of opinion has led many to deny the possibility of any science of mind, beyond the physical or material facts of life. **1902** W. James *Var. Relig. Exper.* xviii. 433 Of late, impartial classifications and comparisons have become possible... We have the beginnings of a 'Science of Religions', so-called. **1909** D. Ainslie tr. *Croce's Aesthetic* (*subtitle*), As science of expression and general linguistic. **1933** *Burlington Mag.* May 248/2 The great problem as to whether the science of art really is a science in the sense that the word is used in relation to natural science remains, however, unsolved. **1937** H. Read *Art & Soc.* vii. 233 Though based on the science of art and a deduction from the whole range of relevant material, the facts in question are relative to the aesthetic sensibility. **1944** J. S. Huxley *On Living in Revol.* iv. 45 The science of mind developed later than biological science. **1973** N. Smart (*title*) The science of religion and the sociology of knowledge. **1976** F. McDonagh tr. *Pannenberg's Theol. & Philos. of Sci.* iv. 256 Theology then comes under the general heading of a science of religion.

5. a. The kind of knowledge or of intellectual activity of which the various 'sciences' are examples. In early use, with reference to sense 3: What is taught in the schools or may be learned by study. In mod. use chiefly: The sciences (in sense 4) as distinguished from other departments of learning; scientific doctrine or investigation. Often with defining adj. as in 4 b.

In the 17th and 18th c. the notion now usually expressed by *science* was commonly expressed by *philosophy.*

1387 Trevisa *Higden* (Rolls) I. 3 After solempne and wise writeres of arte and of science. *c* **1400** Maundev. (1839) xiv. 159 And ȝif ȝou lyke to knowe the Vertues of the Dyamand ..I schalle telle ȝou: as thei beȝonde the See seyn and afferme of whom alle Science and alle Philosophie comethe from. *c* **1440** *Gesta Rom.* xxxiv. 112 He also hade a sone passyngly wyse ande witty,..ande no man myght be likenide to him in no kynne sciens. **1651** Hobbes *Leviath.* II. xxxi. 191 The Principles of naturall Science. **1668** Dryden *Ess. Dram. Poesy* 9 Nothing spreads more fast than Science, when rightly and generally cultivated. **1744** Akenside *Pleas. Imag.* II. 127 Speak ye the pure delight, whose favoured steps The lamp of Science through the jealous maze Of Nature guides. **1759** Goldsm. *Bee* No. 3 ⁋2 Nature was never more lavish of its gifts than it had been to her [Hypatia], endued as she was with the most exalted understanding and the happiest turn to science. **1857** Henfrey *Bot.* §1 Botany is that department of Natural Science which deals with Plants. **1859** Ruskin *Arrows of Chace* (1880) I. 194 How strange it seems that physical science should ever have been thought adverse to religion! **1864** Cobbold *Entozoa* 298 This species is new to science.

Comb. **a 1628** F. Grevil *Treat. Hum. Learn.* xxvii, Strong instances to put all Arts to schoole, And proue the science-monger but a foole. **1857** Reade *Course of True Love* 151 Casenower, the science bitten, had read all the books.

b. In modern use, often treated as synonymous with 'Natural and Physical Science', and thus restricted to those branches of study that relate to the phenomena of the material universe and their laws, sometimes with implied exclusion of pure mathematics. This is now the dominant sense in ordinary use. Also *attrib.*, as in ***science-class, -master, -teacher, -teaching.***

1867 W. G. Ward in *Dubl. Rev.* Apr. 255 *note*, We shall.. use the word 'science' in the sense which Englishmen so commonly give to it; as expressing physical and experimental science, to the exclusion of theological and metaphysical. **1870** Yeats *Nat. Hist. Comm.* Introd. 14 An acquaintance with science or with the systematised knowledge of matter and its properties. **1895** *Educat. Rev.* Sept. 25 Science-teaching is nothing, unless, it brings the pupil in contact with nature. **1913** C. Mackenzie *Sinister St.* I. II. vii. 253 Science is all the go nowadays... And Science is what we want. Science and Religion. **1946** R. J. C. Atkinson *Field Archaeol.* 12 One more problem.. remains to be mentioned, the problem of co-operation between archaeologists and workers in other sciences. **1955** *Bull. Atomic Sci.* Apr. 141/1 Science has become a major source of the power of civilized man. **1976** *Norwich Mercury* 17 Dec. 3/8 Second year prizes—English,..mathematics,.. science,..history,..geography,..music. **1978** *Nature* 10 Aug. 522/1 Funds for lunar sample analysis have remained roughly constant over the past few years and the programme has received praise for the high quality of the science conducted.

†**c.** *Oxford University.* Formerly applied to the portions of ancient and modern philosophy, logic, and cognate subjects, included in the course of study for a degree in the school of Literæ Humaniores. *Obs.*

1831 Gladstone *Diary* in Morley *Life* (1903) I. 78 Examined by..Hampden in science. **1848** J. H. Newman *Loss & Gain* III. iv, Our men know their books well, but I should not say that science is their line. **1855** M. Pattison *Oxf. Studies* in *Oxf. Ess.* 290 A new element of uncertainty came in, in the difference between taste and scholarship on the one hand, and attainment in Aristotle (science, it was called) on the other. **1884** E. A. Freeman *Let.* (MS.) 10 Feb., I remember him years ago as a logic and science coach. I don't mean for cutting up cats, but what science meant then, Ethics, Butler, and such like. **1903** *Athenæum* 7 Feb. 176/3 He had none of his brother's love for the Greek philosophy, then known as 'science'.

d. Personified.

1742 Gray *Eton* 3 Where grateful Science still adores Her Henry's holy Shade. **1862** G. H. Lewes *Let.* 30 Aug. in *George Eliot Lett.* (1955) IV. 52 If the passions and impertinences of public speakers, and newspaper writers on *both* sides of the Atlantic are madly widening the wounds which each ought to strive to heal, it is some comfort to reflect that Science keeps aloof from such misplaced and unjustifiable criticisms. **1894** A. Lang *Cock Lane & Common-Sense* 328 It is in this way that Science makes herself disliked. **1975** J. Plamenatz *K. Marx's Philos. Man* viii. 218 Science recognizes that its hypothesis and theories are provisional and has criteria for deciding whether or not they should be discarded for better ones.

e. (Usually with capital initial.) *U.S.* = Christian Science.

1902 'Mark Twain' in *N. Amer. Rev.* 768 Does the Science kill a patient here and there? **1915** E. B. Holt *Freudian Wish* 21 The 'Science' healer was immediately consulted. **1916** H. Crane *Let.* 26 Jan. (1965) 3 Carry the *science* as far as you can. **1919** —— *Let.* 2 Apr. (1965) 15 Concerning me and my attitude toward Science. **1946** *Christian Sci. Jrnl.* Dec. 616 We called on a practitioner to learn what this Science was. **1980** A. Wilson *Setting World on Fire* II. i. 51 Servants..live in a world of doctors and illnesses and death... Of course I wasn't in Science then. I believed all their nonsense.

6. man of science. †**a.** A man who possesses knowledge in any department of learning, or trained skill in any art or craft. *Obs.* **b.** In modern use, a man who has expert knowledge of some branch of science (usually, of physical or natural science), and devotes himself to its investigation.

1552 in *Vicary's Anat.* (1888) App. ii. 119 Here after is declared the names of all suche officers, men of Scyence, Artyficers, Craftismen, and other mynistres. **1562** Winȝet *Cert. Tractates* I. 16 Sen the saidis lordis and gentilmen being men of science [etc.]. **1759** Johnson *2nd Let. to Gazetteer* 8 Dec., No man of science will deny that architecture has..degenerated at Rome to the lowest state. **1819** Shelley *Peter Bell 3rd* IV. xix, It was his fancy to invite Men of science, wit, and learning, Who come to lend each other light. **1855** Tennyson *Maud* I. IV. vii, The man of science himself is fonder of glory, and vain, An eye well-practised in nature, a spirit bounded and poor. **1890** Le Gallienne *G. Meredith* 71 The man of science is nothing if not a poet gone wrong.

7. *attrib.* and *Comb.*, as (sense 5 b) ***science-based*** adj.; **science park** orig. *U.S.*, an area of land devoted to scientific research or to industrial enterprises connected with the physical sciences.

1962 *Economist* 14 Apr. 187/1 An industry can be science-based, said Lord Hailsham, and yet do little or no actual research. **1965** A. Farrer in J. Gibb *Light on C. S. Lewis* 28 Scientific formulae may be empirically verified, but no science-based picture of the sum of things is better than a symbol. **1970** *Daily Tel.* 27 Apr. 3/8 Trinity College, Cambridge, is proposing to create a 'science park' on the north-east outskirts of the city. **1973** *Nature* 22 June 430/2 In the United States, there are over 80 science parks,..but 27 of them are wholly limited to science-based industry. **1981** *Daily Tel.* 31 July 8/3 A 116-acre science park to attract high technology-based firms, and provide hundreds of jobs, is to be established in Peterborough. Lynch Wood Science Park will also include conference and sports centres and a hotel.

scienced ('saɪənst), *a.* [f. science + -ed[2].]

†**1.** Possessed of science, learned. *Obs.*

1656 Earl Monm. tr. *Boccalini's Advts. fr. Parnassus* 53 Other Scienced men were served with all the delicacies of Learning. **1743** Francis *Horace, Odes* I. xxxiv. 3, I mock'd at all religious Fear, Deep scienc'd in the mazy Lore Of mad Philosophy. **1746** —— *Horace, Ep.* I. xviii. 165 Enquire of every scienc'd Sage. **1836** R. Furness *Astrologer* III. Wks. (1858) 161 Beyond the scienced reach of ought refined In Herschell's mighty ken, or Newton's mind.

2. Trained, well versed, in the knowledge of the art of self-defence.

1820 *Blackw. Mag.* VI. 613 He was a stronger and taller man than Mendoza..full of pluck, and fine scienced.

'science 'fiction. [f. science + fiction.] Imaginative fiction based on postulated scientific discoveries or spectacular environmental changes, freq. set in the future or on other planets and involving space or time travel. Also *attrib.*

Quot. 1851 shows an isolated use. The expression did not come into general use until the end of the 1920s.

1851 W. Wilson *Little Earnest Bk. upon Great Old Subject* x. 137 (*heading*) Science-Fiction. *Ibid.*, We hope it will not be long before we may have other works of Science-Fiction, as we believe such works likely to fulfil a good purpose, and create an interest, where, unhappily, science alone might fail. *Ibid.* 139 Campbell says that 'Fiction in Poetry is not the reverse of truth, but her soft and enchanting resemblance.' Now this applies especially to Science-Fiction, in which the revealed truths of Science may be given, interwoven with a pleasing story which may itself be poetical and *true*—thus circulating a knowledge of the Poetry of Science, clothed in a garb of the Poetry of Life. **1929** *Science Wonder Stories* June 89 The editor of this publication [*sc.* H. Gernsback] addressed a number of letters to science fiction lovers. The editor promised to pay $50.00 for the best letter each month on the subject of 'What Science Fiction Means to Me.' **1933** *Astounding Stories* Dec. 142/1 The..science-fiction fan does not care for stories of the supernatural... Intelligent people, as a rule, will read science fiction. **1949**, etc. [see fantasy, phantasy *sb.* 4 f]. **1954** A. Huxley in *Encounter* Feb. 5/1 These make up a tale which no self-respecting reader, even of Science Fiction, should be asked to swallow. **1958** *Listener* 20 Feb. 334/3 *The Naked Sun* is a happy wedding of the two great pseudo-literary forms of the century—science fiction and the 'tec. **1964** C. S. Lewis *Discarded Image* vii. 142 The theory of the Four Zones taught that the equatorial region was too hot for life. The other hemisphere of the Earth was to us wholly inaccessible. You could write science-fiction about it, but not geography. **1972** *Sci. Amer.* Sept. 38/2, I for one would rather command a computer through a keyboard than talk to it, even if that science-fiction dream were possible. **1977** *N.Y. Rev. Bks.* 13 Oct. 13/4 The mind produces meaning like a plant branching out in a science-fiction movie. **1979** *Guardian* 18 Aug. 10/1 Science Fiction fans..have chosen April 1926 as their sacred date and nominated Hugo Gernsback for the title of Father of Science Fiction. **1980** N. BABSON *Dangerous to Know* viii. 56 The long open-plan Newsroom..always gave me a science-fiction feeling of being the last man alive.

Hence **science-fictional, science-fictive** *adjs.*, pertaining to or characteristic of science fiction; **science-fictionalized** *a.*, made into science fiction; **science-fictioneer, science-fictionist**, a writer or connoisseur of science fiction; **science-fictioner**, a film script upon a science-fictional theme.

1939 *Astounding Science-Fiction* Oct. 155 The Jekyll-science-fictionist stands for experimental truth, for logic, for *proof*. **1950** *Jrnl. Brit. Interplanetary Soc.* IX. 197 In a 'science-fictionalized' review of Arthur Clarke's book 'Interplanetary Flight', the *Daily Mirror* gave the astonishing news that British atomic scientists are now waiting for the go-ahead..to build an atomic engine which could be used as a rocket propulsion unit. **1953** C. RYAN *Conquest of Moon* i. 3 The ships the explorers will use for the long journey through space will bear little resemblance to those depicted by the science-fictionists. **1954** J. W. CAMPBELL in *Astounding Science Fiction* Aug. 5 That science-fictional device 'the planet-wrecker' bomb. **1955** *Britannica Bk. of Year* 490/1 *Science Fictioner* was coined to describe a film play of the science fiction type. **1959** C. FADIMAN in A. C. Clarke *Across Sea of Stars* p. ix, Some science fictioneers are plain old-style typewriter hacks. **1960** K. AMIS *New Maps of Hell* v. 129 That science-fictional uneasiness appears, attaching itself to an existent or incipient neurosis about overcrowded streets and buildings as well as to the rational fear of global overpopulation. **1976** I. MURDOCH *Henry & Cato* II. 222 The glossy hexagonal glasses which looked here like the appurtenances of some science fictional spaceman. **1977** *Times Lit. Suppl.* 14 Jan. 26/1 Put one science-fictioneer on a desert island and he will start a magazine. **1980** *Ibid.* 7 Nov. 1265/4 Yet Silverberg's Majipoor, where humanity..finds its future home, is about as science-fictional as Tolkien's Middle Earth.

†'sciencer. *Obs.* [f. SCIENCE + -ER^1.] A professor of a particular science.

1547 BALDWIN *Mor. Philos.* I. vii. (1550) B v, Whan it was asked hym what sciencer he was, he [*sc.* Pythagoras] answered, a Philosopher. **1630** WESTCOTE *View Devonsh.* (1845) 301 The other two, with their protector the mystical sciencer, proceed.

sciencial, obs. form of SCIENTIAL.

†'sciencist. *Obs. rare*$^{-1}$. [f. SCIENCE + -IST.] One who works on scientific principles.

1778 [W. MARSHALL] *Minutes Agric., Digest* 8 This is the money-getting Farmer, whose Agriculture the Sciencist ought to endeavour to excel.

†'sciency. *Obs. rare.* [ad. L. *scientia*: see SCIENCE and -ENCY.] The condition or fact of knowing; = SCIENCE I.

1642 H. MORE *Song of Soul* I. II. xxvi, His name is Dæmon, not from Sciency, Although he boasteth much in skilfull pride. *Ibid.* II. iii. I. vi, My hackney fails, not I; my pen, not sciencie.

sciens(e, obs. forms of SCIENCE.

scient ('saɪənt), *a.* and *sb.* [ad. L. *scient-em*, pr. pple. of *scīre* to know.] **A.** *adj.* Having science, knowledge, or skill. Now *rare*.

c **1430** LYDG. *Min. Poems* (Percy Soc.) 27 The clerk that I of tolde, Which was ful fayne feithful counsel to make, For he was scient, expert, and ful bolde. **1597** J. KING *On Jonas* (1618) 156 Of what people? The most scient and skilfull in the seruice of God. **1626** CORNWALLIS *Disc. Prince Henry* (1641) 7 To this so rare a disposition, which being by a Prince entertained, cannot but make him..scient of the Offices appertaining to his high estate,..is to be added [etc.]. **1798** LANDOR *Gebir* v. Wks. 1846 II. 498 Together these her scient hand combined and more she added. **1820** T. G. WAINEWRIGHT *Ess. & Crit.* (1880) 24 Watching with scient eye the number of aureate particles.

B. *sb.* A man of science, scientist. *rare.*

1889 *Harper's Mag.* Feb. 383/1 Philosophers, historians, and scients. **1894** *Ibis* Oct. 555 The contributors to the Tromsö Museum's Annual may be called 'scients' or 'savants', but, please, Mr. Cocks, not 'scientists'.

scientaster (saɪən'tæstə(r)). *rare.* [f. SCIENT(IST + -ASTER after POETASTER.] A petty or inferior scientist.

1899 M. FOSTER *Claude Bernard* ix. 232 We may recognise a salient difference between..the false scientaster and the true inquirer. **1969** *Sci. Jrnl.* Sept. 91/1 Zahlen made the neat distinction that in Lebanon most advisory scientists were 'not scientists at all but just had some scientific education'. Michael Foster coined the word 'scientaster' for such people; it deserves reintroduction.

‖**scienter** (saɪ'ɛntə(r)), *adv. Law.* [L., f. *scient-em*: see SCIENT.] Knowingly. Often as *sb.* in the phr. ***to prove (a) scienter***, etc., to prove that the act complained of was done knowingly; ***law of scienter***, the law with regard to the neccessity of 'proving a scienter' in order to obtain damages.

1824 STARKIE *Evidence* II. 469 The plaintiff must prove not only the falsity of the representation, but also the *scienter*, the knowledge of the defect on the part of the defendant. **1879** *Cassell's Techn. Educ.* IV. 252/2 The use, therefore, of the name of another manufacturer, whether done scienter or not, is an interference with his business. **1897** *Daily News* 15 Dec. 5/4 In this case the plaintiff stood in a lucky position in regard to the law of scienter. **1898** *Westm. Gaz.* 23 Nov. 3/2 When the injury is to cattle or sheep, the necessity of proving 'the scienter' was abolished by the Dogs Act, 1865.

sciential (saɪ'ɛnʃəl), *a.* Forms: 5 sciencial, 7 scientiall, 7- sciential. [ad. med.L. *scientiālis*, f. L. *scientia*: see SCIENCE.]

1. Of or pertaining to knowledge or science. †***sciential faith***: faith resting on demonstrative evidence.

c **1456** PECOCK *Bk. of Faith* (1909) 141 The more cleer, sure, and expert evydencis ben had for a sciencial feith, the more is thilk sciencial feith. **1605** B. JONSON *Masque Blackness* Wks. (1616) 898 His light scientiall is, and (past mere nature) Can salue the rude defects of euery creature. **1645** MILTON *Tetrach.* 23 Those Sciential rules which are the implements of instruction. **1667** —— *P.L.* IX. 837 The power..whose presence had infus'd Into the plant sciential sap. **1680** I. C. *Vind. Oaths & Swearing* (ed. 2) 3 An oath hath place but in such things as depend upon testimony, and the speakers credit and honesty, and is not to be used in things purely sciential and probable by demonstration. **1788** T. TAYLOR *Proclus* I. 19 He ascended to the greatest and most consummate or telestic virtues; employing for this purpose, the felicity of his nature, and a sciential institution. **1820** LAMB *Elia* I. *Oxf. Vac.*, The odour of their old moth-scented coverings is fragrant as the first bloom of those sciential apples which grew amid the happy orchard. **1827** COLERIDGE *Lit. Rem.* (1838) IV. 423 Their entire consonance with..the Scriptures and with the sciential and the practical reason. **1834** WHEWELL in Todhunter *Acc. Writ.* (1876) II. 186 Modes of conception, sciential conditions, or whatever else you can help me to call them.

2. Endowed with knowledge.

1477 EARL RIVERS (Caxton) *Dictes* 17 The wiese man knoweth the prouffit of the riche & the riche knoweth not the prouffit of the sciencial wiese man. **1646** GAULE *Cases of Consc.* 28 That is the Magicall, Speculative, Scientiall, or Arted Witch. **1820** KEATS *Lamia* I. 191 Not one hour old, yet of sciential brain To unperplex bliss from its neighbour pain. **1891** MEREDITH *One of our Conq.* I. xiv. 265 A sciential rascal.

Hence **†'scientialness.** *Obs. rare*$^{-1}$.

1579 W. WILKINSON *Confut. Familye of Love* 39 b, Onely the taking on knowledge which is learned out of the scientialnes of the letter..is blamed by HN.

†'scientiate. *Obs. rare*$^{-1}$. [f. L. *scientia* SCIENCE + -ATE^1.] An adept in a science.

1647 tr. *Malvezzi's Pourtract* 100 Such as will learne an Art or a Science, the first object that they set before them, is not immediately that of the Art, or that of the Science, but an Artist, or a Scientiate.

†'scientic, *a. Obs.* In 6 scyentyke. [irreg. f. L. *scient-ia* SCIENCE + -IC. (Unless it be a mistake for *scientific*, of which in that case this would be the earliest example in Eng.)] = SCIENTIFIC *a.* Also **†'scientical** *a.*

1541 R. COPLAND *Guydon's Quest. Chirurg.* Pref., There be ryght many and sondry sortes, aswell of very good and scyentyke bokes, as of ryght expert men within this Realme in the scyentycall arte of Cyrugery. *Ibid.*, Your scyentycall beneuolence.

scientician (saɪən'tɪʃən). [f. *scient-* (see SCIENTIST) after *physician*, etc.] = SCIENTIST.

1885 J. S. GRIMES *Geonomy* 49 in *Science* 13 Feb. 142/1 The reason why scienticians have neglected to investigate the laws of the currents thoroughly,..is that [etc.].

scientific (saɪən'tɪfɪk), *a.* and *sb.* [ad. late L. *scientificus*, f. *scient-em*, pr. pple. of *scīre* to know (or perh., less regularly, f. *scienti-am* knowledge: see SCIENCE) + *-ficus* making, f. *facĕre* to make. Cf. F. *scientifique*, Sp. *científico*, Pg., It. *scientifico*.

The ultimate source of the word is to be sought in Aristotelian expressions like that in *Post. Anal.* I. ii. (71 b), where it is said that unless certain essential conditions are fulfilled, a syllogism will not be demonstrative, 'for it will not produce knowledge' (οὐ γὰρ ποιήσει ἐπιστήμην, rendered in the translation attributed to Boethius 'non enim *faciet scientiam*'). In pursuance of the suggestion of this phrase, the translator in the same chapter renders συλλογισμὸν ἐπιστημονικὸν by 'syllogismum epistemonicon, *id est facientem scire*', and in I. vi. uses 'scientificæ demonstrationes' for αἱ ἐπιστημονικαὶ ἀποδείξεις. In this application the word survived in Latin text-books of logic down to Aldrich, though some of them have instead *scientiam pariens* or *faciens scire*.

From having been thus employed as a contextual interpretation of ἐπιστημονικός (pertaining to science or knowledge; = med.L. *scientialis*), the L. *scientificus* was afterwards used inappropriately (instead of *scientialis*) in the 13th c. translation of Aristotle's Ethics (VI. i. §6) to render this Gr. word where it designates the theoretic as opposed to the deliberative faculty of the soul. This use was followed by Aquinas; it is in this application that the It. *scientifico* is used by Dante, and the F. *scientifique* by Oresme (14th c.). Hence the prevailing sense of the adj. in subsequent Latin, in the Rom. langs., and in English, has been 'pertaining to science'; it is merely by a contextual accident that in phrases like 'scientific investigation' the word admits of being interpreted in its etymological meaning. Aquinas also uses *scientificus* for 'expert in science, learned', a sense which still survived in 16th c. Latin. The lateness of the first appearance of the word in English is remarkable.]

A. *adj.*

†1. Of a syllogism, a proof: Producing knowledge, demonstrative. Cf. SCIENTIFICAL *a.* I. *Obs.*

To be distinguished from the mod. use in phrases like 'scientific proof', 'scientific evidence', where the adj. has the sense 3 or 4 below.

1637 GILLESPIE *Eng. Pop. Cerem.* III. ix. 198 Aquinas..maketh the Law of Nature to containe certaine principles, having the same place in practicall reason, which the principles of scientifike demonstrations have in speculative reason. **1667** SOUTH *Serm.* (1823) I. 360 No man who first trafficks into a foreign country has any scientific evidence that there is such a country, but by report, which can produce no more than a moral certainty.

2. a. Of persons, books, institutions, etc.: Occupied in or concerned with science or the sciences. In early use, † concerned with the 'sciences' or 'liberal arts', opposed to *mechanical*.

1589 PUTTENHAM *Eng. Poesie* I. i. (Arb.) 19 The premises considered, it giueth to the name and profession no smal dignitie and preheminence, aboue all other artificers, Scientificke or Mechanicall. **1815** BANKS in *Fragm. Rem. Sir H. Davy* (1858) 208 By the more brilliant discoveries you have made, the reputation of the Royal Society has been exalted in the opinion of the scientific world. **1822** LAMB *Elia ii. Detached Th. on Bks. & Reading*, In this catalogue of books which are no books..I reckon Court Calendars,..Scientific Treatises, Almanacks, Statutes at Large. **1884** F. TEMPLE *Relat. Relig. & Sci.* i. (1885) 4 The scientific man often asserts that he cannot find God in Science. **1888** ROLLESTON & JACKSON *Anim. Life* Pref. 7, I may mention that scientific periodicals on the general subject and its branches have since 1870 been almost doubled.

¶**b.** Having scientific knowledge or given to scientific study *of* something. *nonce-use.*

1877 RUSKIN *Fors Clavig.* No. 75 VII. 63 Behold, there is the Universe; and here are we, the British public, in the exact middle of it, and scientific of it in the accuratest manner. **1884** *Ibid.* No. 95 VIII. 257 Most men are not intended to be any wiser than their cocks and bulls—duly scientific of their yard and pasture, peacefully nescient of all beyond.

3. Of or pertaining to science or the sciences; of the nature of science.

1722 WOLLASTON *Relig. Nat.* iii. 50 Who by a proper exercise of his mind in scientific studies first opens and enlarges its capacity. **1812** SIR H. DAVY *Chem. Philos.* 2 Analogy confirmed by experiment becomes Scientific truth. **1859** DARWIN *Orig. Spec.* xiv. 485 It is quite possible that forms now generally acknowledged to be merely varieties may hereafter be thought worthy of specific names,..and in this case scientific and common language will come into accordance. **1871** MORLEY *Carlyle* in *Crit. Misc.* Ser. I. (1878) 163 The familiar distinction between the poetic and the scientific temper is another way of stating the same difference. **1902** *Encycl. Brit.* XXVIII. Pref. 15 To study religions in a scientific spirit is to admit that all religions, if not equally good, spring at least from a common source.

4. a. Of an art, practice, operation, or method: Based upon or regulated by science, as opposed to mere traditional rules or empirical dexterity. So of a worker or agent: Guided by a knowledge of science, acting according to scientific principles.

1678 MOXON *Mech. Dyalling* 3 Scientifick Dyalists..have found out Rules, to mark out the irregular motion of the Shaddow... And these Rules of adjusting the motion of the Shaddow to the motion of the Sun may be called Scientifick Dyalling. **1903** CHAMBERLAIN *Sp. Glasgow* 6 Oct. 42 The one is profitless taxation, the other scientific taxation.

b. Devised on scientific principles. Also, more loosely: systematic, methodical.

1794 SULLIVAN *View Nat.* II. 320 Had the Romans any thing so scientific as a sun-dial, even during the second Punic war? **1863** GEO. ELIOT *Let.* 18 July (1956) IV. 94 He [*sc.* Renan] has always seemed to me remarkable as a French mind that is at once 'scientific' (in the German sense) and eminently tender and reverent towards the forms in which the religious sentiment has incarnated itself. **1878** BEACONSFIELD in *Times* 11 Nov. 10/4 But our North-Western frontier [of India] is a haphazard and not a scientific frontier. **1976** *National Observer* (U.S.) 13 Mar. 1/6 The Observer tally on abortion, however, is consistent with the findings of other recent, more 'scientific' polls.

c. Characterized by 'science' or trained skill.

1792 in G. B. Buckley *Fresh Light on 18th Cent. Cricket* (1935) 231 Brighton v. Lord Winchilsea, Hon. Mr. Bligh, Mr. Smith & Mr. Hale with 7 approved scientific men from the County of Hants. *a* **1817** JANE AUSTEN *Persuasion* (1818) IV. viii. 155 She had feelings for the tender, spirits for the gay, attention for the scientific, and patience for the wearisome; and had never liked a concert better. **1833** J. NYREN *Young Cricketer's Tutor* 29 In this accomplishment lies the distinction between the scientific player and the random batsman. **1851** H. MELVILLE *Moby Dick* II. xxv. 181 This accomplished swordsman..once more makes a scientific dash at the mass. **1862** *Lillywhite's Cricket Scores & Biogr.* I. 440 William Searle..was..as a batsman..steady and scientific. **1885** *Field* 17 Jan. 82/3 A strong wind and a spongy ground were against a scientific display [of football]. **1891** W. G. GRACE *Cricket* xi. 300 From that year [*sc.* 1859] until 1876 he [*sc.* R. Daft] was the most scientific batsman amongst the professionals.

5. Of, pertaining to, or inspired by Christian Science. *U.S.*

1875 M. B. EDDY *Science & Health* viii. 428 The spirituality that abstracts all attention from the body, never manipulates and is the only positive position of scientific healing. *Ibid.* 429 To be able to discern the cause of sickness after the scientific mode of our Master, depends on your spirituality. **1919** H. CRANE *Let.* 7 Mar. (1965) 13, I feel quite certain that Mrs. Brooks is afflicted with consumption against which she is doubtless putting up a strenuous Scientific fight.

6. Special collocations: **scientific farming**, farming conducted according to theories based on science rather than on tradition; also **scientific farmer**; **scientific fiction** now *rare* = SCIENCE FICTION; **scientific humanism**, a theory that humanism should be based on scientific empiricism (see quot. 1909); a doctrine that man should direct the future and the welfare of the human race by using the scientific methods he applies to other species and to the material environment; so **scientific humanist**; **scientific management** orig. *U.S.*, management of a business, industry, etc., according to principles of efficiency derived from experiments in methods of work, production, payment, etc., and esp. from time-and-motion studies; **scientific method**, a method of procedure that has characterized natural science since the 17th century, consisting in systematic observation, measurement, and experiment, and the formulation, testing, and modification of hypotheses; **scientific notation**, a system of representing numbers as a product of a number between 1 and 10 (or 0·1 and 1) and a power of 10; **scientific revolution**, a rapid and far-reaching development in science; *spec.* the developments occurring in the twentieth century that have involved the introduction of automation, atomic energy, electronics, etc.

1850 C. Kingsley *Alton Locke* II. iv. 43 He had one scientific farmer after another, staying in his house as a friend. **1789** A. Young *Jrnl.* 19 June in *Trav. France* (1792) I. 115, I wish my brethren to stick to their *scientific* farming, and leave the practical to those that understand it. **1886** C. M. Yonge *Chantry House* I. xvii. 159 [He] worked off his superfluous energy in scientific farming. **1902** A. Bennett *Anna of Five Towns* ix. 205 A great landowner is exhibiting the beauties of scientific farming for the behoof of his villagers. **1876** W. H. L. Barnes in W. H. Rhodes *Caxton's Book* 7 The great master of scientific fiction, Jules Verne. **1937** *Discovery* Oct. 318 'The Man in the Moone', the fantasy of Bishop Godwin.., is an early excursion into the realms of scientific fiction. **1909** W. James *Meaning of Truth* iii. 59 'Energetics', measuring the bare face of sensible phenomena so as to describe in a single formula all their changes of 'level', is the last word of this scientific humanism. **1931** J. S. Huxley *What dare I Think?* iv. 148 The only way in which the conflict between science and human nature can be ended is by combining science and the other fruits of the human spirit in a new alliance, a new attitude, to which we may give the name of Scientific Humanism. **1941** —— *Uniqueness of Man* xiii. 274 Scientific humanism.. insists that the same scientific procedure can be applied to human life as has been applied to lifeless matter and to animals and plants—scientific survey, study, and analysis, followed by increasing practical control. **1963** V. Brome *Problem of Progress* vii. 144 If the modern scientific humanist would have no truck with the religious tinge in Huxley's creed he equally rejects any divine inspiration in Buddhism, Christianity, [etc.]. **1903** F. W. Taylor in *Trans. Amer. Soc. Mech. Engineers* XXIV. 1366 The choice must be made between some of the types of management in common use.. and the more modern and scientific management based on an accurate knowledge of how long it should take to do the work. **1910** L. D. Brandeis in *N.Y. Times* 22 Nov. 8/2 As an alternative to the practice of combining to raise rates and hence to increase prices, we offer cooperation to reduce costs... This can be done through the introduction of scientific management. **1911** F. W. Taylor in *Amer. Mag.* Mar. 571/2 The best management is a true science, resting upon clearly defined laws, rules, and principles, and.. these fundamental principles of Scientific Management are applicable to all kinds of human activities. **1949** Gilbreth & Carey *Cheaper by Dozen* i. 1 Dad always practised what he preached and it was just impossible to tell where his scientific management company ended and his family life began. **1972** *Scientific Management in American Industry* (Taylor Soc.) i. 2 The body of interlocking procedures which resulted from these investigations came to be known as the 'Taylor System', and to the doctrine and principles later derived from them was given the name 'Scientific Management'. **1854** T. H. Huxley *Educational Value of Nat. Hist. Sciences* 13 The man of business must as much avail himself of the scientific method.. as the veriest bookworm. **1871** J. A. Froude *Short Studies on Great Subjects* (ser. 2) 485 Neither history, nor any other knowledge, could be obtained except by scientific methods. **1889** 'L. Carroll' *Sylvie & Bruno* xviii. 255 That, I believe, is the true Scientific Method. **1908** W. McDougall *Introd. Soc. Psychol.* i. 4 When.. the modern principles of scientific method began to be generally accepted. **1927** J. S. Huxley *Relig. without Revelation* iii. 83 There was a great outcry when scientific method was applied, in the form of the so-called 'Higher Criticism'. **1955** *Bull. Atomic Sci.* Oct. 295/1 Scientists possess a technique which they call the scientific method of thought, and they are impelled by circumstances to use it with the force of a new inspiration. **1959** L. W. H. Hull *Hist. & Philos. Sci.* vii. 194 The subtle blend of observation, hypothesis, mathematics and planned experiment in the Scientific Method is a more effective procedure than that of Bacon. **1961** Webster, Scientific notation. **1963** W. H. Ware *Digital Computer Technol. & Design* I. ii. 22 The power of the base appearing in an expression which is in scientific notation in effect indicates the position of the point. **1973** C. W. Gear *Introd. Computer Sci.* ii. 61 The number ·00000001 is represented as ·1 × 10^{-7}... We call this floating-point or scientific notation for numbers. **1975** *Physics Bull.* Mar. 135/3 The most important [feature of the calculators].. is the provision of exponential or 'scientific' notation. **1803** S. Miller *Brief Retrospect of Eighteenth Cent.* I. II. 416 The frequency and rapidity of scientific revolutions may be accounted for in various ways. **1946** *Amer. Jrnl. Sociol.* Jan. 267/1 The use of atomic energy appears to be a beginning of the 'scientific revolution'. **1959** C. P. Snow in *Encounter* July 22/2, I believe the industrial society of electronics, atomic energy, automation, is in cardinal respects different in kind from any that has gone before... It is this transformation that, in my view, is entitled to the name of 'scientific revolution'. **1977** G. Clark *World Prehistory* (ed. 3) ii. 41 A Neolithic Revolution comparable in importance with the Industrial and Scientific Revolutions.

B. *sb.*

1. A man of science. *colloq.*

1830 Lyell *Let.* in Smiles *Mem. J. Murray* (1891) II. xxxii. 391 The scientifics having at last a government to which they are not ashamed to turn courtiers. **1853** De Morgan in Graves *Sir W. R. Hamilton* (1889) III. 464 This meeting of literaries and arts—not a scientific among them but myself. **1883** Black *Shandon Bells* xxi, Some of the scientifics, as she calls them, are very fond of shooting.

2. *pl.* [See -ic 2, -ics.] Scientific matters. *nonce-use* or *vulgar*.

1842 Lover *Handy Andy* v, 'Leave off your confounded scientifics, there,' shouted Murphy, from the head of the table, 'and let us have a song.'

C. quasi-*adv.*, as ***scientific-minded*** adj.

1946 J. Cary *Moonlight* xxiii. 179 Our admirals are uneducated men who despise science, and the Germans are really scientific-minded men. **1976** I. Levin *Boys from Brazil* iii. 78 He's hardly a scientific-minded man.

scientifical (saɪənˈtɪfɪkəl), *a.* Also 6–7 -all. [f. late L. *scientific-us* + -al[1]: see scientific.]

†**1.** Of a syllogism, proof, evidence: 'Producing knowledge', demonstrative. Also, of a conclusion: Demonstratively proved. *Obs.*

1588 J. Harvey *Disc. Probl.* 30 But in the meanwhile they presume that this point of philosophy is Scientificall: and doth it indeed *Sub scientiam cadere*, as they presuppose? **1628** T. Spencer *Logick* 282 Our next labour must be, to set out these scientificall Syllogismes by other properties. **1658** Baxter *Saving Faith* viii. 62 But multitudes.. discern not this evidence so clearly, as may make it scientifical to them. **1732** Berkeley *Alciphr.* vi. §31 Who ever supposed that scientifical proofs were necessary to make a Christian?

†**2.** Designed for the furthering of knowledge.

1597 Beard *Theatre God's Judgem.* (1612) 143 This is the diuinitie and goodlie instruction that commeth.. from that scientificall Vniuersitie and Colledge of the right reuerend Masters. **1640** Howell *Dodona's Gr.* 42 She is alwaies furnished with nurseries of scientificall graffes, which she disperseth up and downe to unfold the sacred Oracles. **1642** T. Taylor *God's Judgem.* I. I. xxii. (1642) 89 This is the Divinity.. that commeth.. from that scientifical University.

3. Expert in science; occupied in or concerned with science; treating of science. Now *rare*.

c **1645** Howell *Lett.* (1655) III. ix. 18 And in these modern times, the most speculative and scientificallest men, both in Germany and Italy, seem to adhere to it. **1756–82** Warton *Ess. on Pope* I. §iii. 177 No author ever adorned a scientifical treatise with so many beautiful metaphors. **1793** Smeaton *Edystone L.* §61 *note*, Consulting my scientifical friends respecting this fact. **1827** Hood *Craniology* 36 Those scientifical hotch-potch men. **1840** Thackeray *Paris Sk. Bk.* I. 169 Works political, philosophical,.. scientifical, theological.

4. Of or pertaining to science. *rare.*

1777 Priestley *On Air* Pref. 16 It is rather to be regretted, however, in such a number of nobility and gentry, so very few should have any taste for scientifical pursuits. **1783** Blagden in *Phil. Trans.* LXXIII. 372 This was the period of scientifical enterprise. **1796** Wansey *Jrnl.* 268 Sense of security, which scientifical pursuits require. **1855** Milman *Lat. Chr.* xiv. viii. (1864) IX. 300 Under a guild,.. there had been.. more close adherence to rule in the scientifical and technical parts.

scientifically (saɪənˈtɪfɪkəlɪ), *adv.* [f. scientifical + -ly[2].]

1. In a scientific manner; according to the laws of science; †by means of 'scientific' or demonstrative reasoning.

1640 J. Stoughton *Def. & Distrib. Div.* i. 18 Many things he did know then scientifically, which now he doth so much as opinionatively. *a* **1688** Cudworth *Immut. Mor.* (1731) 227 Consider what the Subject of it is, Scientifically comprehended. **1796** Morse *Amer. Geog.* I. 217 The tortoises of the northern states are of several species but have not been scientifically designated. **1855** Kingsley *Glaucus* 69 A party of genera and species which connect families scientifically far apart. **1876** E. R. Lankester *Hist. Creat.* I. i. 6 We are now in a position to establish scientifically the groundwork of a non-miraculous history of the developement of the human race. **1885** FitzGerald in *Law Rep. 10 App. Cases* 227 The law upon this subject has been properly and scientifically put in a later case.

2. Systematically, methodically, thoroughly.

1922 Wodehouse *Jill Reckless* i. 28 Freddie poked the fire scientifically, and assisted it with coal. **1965** *Listener* 30 Dec. 1077/2 Three friends scientifically mete out to a bully the same bullying he administered to a small boy.

3. *Comb.*, as ***scientifically-minded*** adj.

1927 B. Russell *Analysis of Matter* xiv. 130 Levers and pulleys, falling bodies, collisions of billiard balls, etc., are all familiar in everyday life, and it is a pleasure to the scientifically minded youth to find them amenable to mathematical treatment. **1931** H. N. Shenton et al. *Internat. Communication* i. 63 Associations of scientifically-minded persons can continually bring to the problem of verbal communication the rapidly growing possibilities of social engineering. **1959** I. & P. Opie *Lore & Lang. Schoolch.* ix. 174 Wisecracks which.. scientifically minded boys indulge in when, at about twelve years old, they begin to take up their subject in earnest. **1977** P. Fitzgerald *Knox Brothers* iv. 107 It was neither weakness nor compromise to try to reach this kind of unity with millions of the half-persuaded and the scientifically-minded.

scientificalness (saɪənˈtɪfɪkəlnɪs). [f. scientifical + -ness.] The quality of being scientific.

1866 *Reader* 24 Feb. 206/3 Though markedly deficient in scientificalness. **1876** Morley *Comte* in *Crit. Misc.* (1886) III. 365 The whole of our knowledge will be impressed with .. the character of positivity or scientificalness.

†**scientiˈficiall**, *a. Obs. rare.* [Bad form of scientifical, after *artificial*.] = scientifical.

1646 Sir T. Browne *Pseud. Ep.* I. vii. 26 In naturall Philosophy,.. is expected a satisfaction from scientificall progressions, and such as beget a sure and rationall beleefe. **1649** Jer. Taylor *Gt. Exemp.* Disc. iii. §21 In other sciences the terms must first be known and then the rules, and conclusions scientificiall.

scienˈtificism. *rare.* [f. scientific *a.* + -ism.] Analysis or explanation which only admits what is considered to be scientifically demonstrable.

c **1875** W. James in R. B. Perry *Tht. & Char. of W. James* (1935) I. 523 In a rough way materialism or 'scientificism' gratifies no. (1) [*sc.* an explanation of things by their cause]. **1884** —— *Will to Believe* (1897) 165 Subjectivism has three great branches,—we may call them scientificism, sentimentalism, and sensualism, respectively.

scientificity (saɪəntɪˈfɪsɪtɪ). [f. scientific *a.* + -ity.] The quality of being scientific; scientific character.

1970 B. Brewster tr. *Althusser & Balibar's Reading Capital* I. 49 The form of order required at a given moment in the history of knowledge by the existing type of scientificity, or, if you prefer, by the norms of theoretical validity recognized by science.. as scientific. **1973** *Screen* Spring/Summer 209 Science.. in its efforts to set itself off from *opinion* (the act of break which is scientificity itself).. is led to criticise most often the opinions which it meets most often. **1976** T. Eagleton *Crit. & Ideology* i. 32 A mistaking of scientificity for positivism.. links him.. with the Romantic 'anti-scientism' of Lukács and the Frankfurt school.

scientifico-, used as comb. form of scientific *a.*, in hyphened nonce-formations with adjs., expressing the sense 'scientific and (something else)'.

1882 *Times* 21 Apr. 5/4 Erasmus Darwin,.. known.. by his scientifico-poetic work 'The Botanic Garden'. **1884** *Contemp. Rev.* Mar. 395 The novelist proceeds with that scientifico-historical conscience. **1887** *Ibid.* May 715 He [Sardou] attempted to dethrone Jules Verne in the realm of the scientifico-geographical spectacular piece.

scientifiction (saɪəntɪˈfɪkʃən). [Blend of scientific *a.* and *sb.* + fiction.] Science fiction. Hence **scientiˈfictional** *a.*

1916 H. Gernsback in *Electr. Experimenter* Jan. 474/1, I am supposed to report Münchhaussen's doings; am supposed to be writing fiction, *scientifiction*, to be correct. **1929** *Amazing Stories Q.* Fall 575, I wish to compliment you on your choice of 'scientifictional' stories. **1930** *N. & Q.* 10 May 339/1 This class of literature is having a tremendous vogue in America just now. Quite a number of popular magazines are devoted to what they have dubbed 'Scientifiction'. **1940** *Illustr. London News* CXCVII. 32/3 'Dr. Cyclops', at the Carlton, applies Technicolor to what is called 'scientifiction'. **1940** 'G. Orwell' in *Horizon* I. 191 H. G. Wells.. is the father of 'Scientifiction'. **1943** C. S. Lewis *Perelandra* vi. 91 He was a man obsessed with the idea which is at this moment circulating all over our planet in obscure works of 'scientifiction', in little Interplanetary Societies and Rocketry Clubs. **1955** —— *Surprised by Joy* ii. 41 That the ordinary interest in scientifiction is an affair for psychoanalysts is borne out by the fact that all who like it, like it thus ravenously. **1970** *New Scientist* 5 Feb. 264/2 In this scientifictional milieu I can still sit on the lakeshore and rationally speculate that sounds heard across the water are messages from the past.

scientintically, *adv.* A burlesque nonce-word, formed by a blending of *scientifically* and *tint*.

1761 Sterne *Tr. Shandy* III. v, He must have redden'd, pictorically and scientintically speaking, six whole tints and a half.. above his natural colour.

†**ˈscientious**, *a. Obs.* [ad. late L. **scientiōsus* (implied in *scientiōsē* adv.), f. *scientia* knowledge, science: see -ous. Cf. OF. *sciencieux*.] Full of knowledge, knowing. Hence † **scientiously** *adv.*

1651 Biggs *New Disp.* §76 There is none amongst all of them that hath scientiously describ'd the properties of simples. **1654** Vilvain *Theorem. Theol.* Suppl. 239b, Serjeant Glyn.. can scientiously satisfy any Man, that ther be such impious confederats with Satan. **1657** W. Morice *Coena quasi Κοινη* Def. xxi. 200 Ministers.. must be obeyed by more scientious auditors when they speak in his name.

scientism (ˈsaɪəntɪz(ə)m). [f. *scient-* (see scientist) + -ism.]

1. The habit and mode of expression of a man of science.

1877 *Fraser's Mag.* XVI. 274 Its dogmatism on the one hand,.. and its 'scientism' on the other, even when most atheistic, are tempered with mutual civility. **1895** *Daily News* 14 Nov. 6/5 By scientism he meant to express that change which had come over the thought of the world in consequence of the wonderful additions to the common stock of knowledge. **1903** *Contemp. Rev.* May 727 What modern Scientism knows as the Supersensuous Consciousness.

2. A term applied (freq. in a derogatory manner) to a belief in the omnipotence of scientific knowledge and techniques; also to the view that the methods of study appropriate to physical science can replace those used in other fields such as philosophy and, esp., human behaviour and the social sciences.

1921 G. B. Shaw *Back to Methuselah* p. lxxviii, The iconography and hagiology of Scientism are as copious as they are mostly squalid. **1937** J. Laver *French Painting in Nineteenth Cent.* i. 73 It really appeared to many educated people that at last all the secrets of the universe would be discovered and all the problems of human life solved. This superstition.. we may call 'Scientism'. **1938** G. Reavey tr. *Berdyaev's Solitude & Society* i. 12 Science has not only progressively reduced the competence of philosophy, but it has also attempted to suppress it altogether and to replace it by its own claim to universality. This process is generally known as 'scientism'. **1942** F. A. von Hayek in *Economica* IX. 269 We shall wherever we are concerned, not with the general spirit of disinterested inquiry but with that slavish imitation of the method and language of science, speak of 'scientism' or the 'scientistic' prejudice. **1953** A. H. Hobbs *Social Problems & Scientism* ii. 17 Scientism, as a belief that science can furnish answers to all human problems, makes science a substitute for philosophy, religion, manners, and morals... It is a pattern of beliefs.. a creed that shapes thinking and affects behavior. **1956** E. H. Hutten *Lang. Mod. Physics* vi. 273 This belief in the omnipotence of science is.. making a mockery of science: for this scientism represents the same, superstitious, attitude which, in previous times, ascribed such power to a supernatural agency. **1957** W. H. Whyte *Organization Man* iii. 23 *Scientism*,.. the promise that with the same techniques that have worked in the physical sciences we can eventually create an exact science of man. **1969** *Encounter* Jan. 23/2 There is an aberration of science.. which has come to be known as 'scientism'... It stands for the belief that science knows or will soon know all the answers. **1972** K. R. Popper *Objective Knowl.* iv. 185 The term 'scientism' meant originally 'the slavish imitation of the method and language of (natural) science', especially by social scientists. *Ibid.* 186 But I would go even further and accuse at least some professional historians of 'scientism'. **1977** A. Sheridan tr. *J. Lacan's Écrits* iii. 76 The early development of psychoanalysis.. expresses.. nothing less than the re-creation of human meaning in an arid period of scientism. **1980** *Times Lit. Suppl.* 26 Sept. 1072/2 Naturalism, in David Thomas's usage, is equivalent to what many know as scientism: the doctrine that there is no reason to think that the study of human agents, and the study of the social systems to which human agents give rise, cannot be pursued according to a methodology drawn from natural science.

†**scien'tissimous**, *a.* *Obs.* *rare*$^{-1}$. [f. L. *scientissim-us*, superl. of *sciens* knowing + -ous.] Very learned.

1650 J. Jones *Judges Judged* 88 The Wise, Learned,.. Scientissimous Interpreters of the Laws of England.

scientist ('saɪəntɪst). [f. *scient-* (in L. *scientia* science, and in scientific) + -ist.]

1. A person with expert knowledge of a science; a person using scientific methods.

1834 *Q. Rev.* LI. 59 Science.. loses all traces of unity. A curious illustration of this result may be observed in the want of any name by which we can designate the students of the knowledge of the material world collectively. We are informed that this difficulty was felt very oppressively by the members of the British Association for the Advancement of Science, at their meetings.. in the last three summers... *Philosophers* was felt to be too wide and too lofty a term,..; *savans* was rather assuming,..; some ingenious gentleman proposed that, by analogy with *artist*, they might form *scientist*, and added that there could be no scruple in making free with this termination when we have such words as *sciolist*, *economist*, and *atheist*—but this was not generally palatable. **1840** Whewell *Philos. Induct. Sci.* I. Introd. 113 We need very much a name to describe a cultivator of science in general. I should incline to call him a Scientist. **1840** *Blackw. Mag.* XLVIII. 273 Leonardo was mentally a seeker after truth—a scientist; Coreggio was an assertor of truth—an artist. **1853** F. Hall in *Leslie's Misc.* II. 169 Atrabilious scientists. **1878** T. Sinclair *Mount* 13 They know that the sun is better where it is than under the scalpel or other instruments of the intense scientists.

2. (Usu. with capital initial.) A Christian Scientist.

1875 M. B. Eddy *Science & Health* viii. 428 The Scientist sees more clearly the cause of disease in mind, than the anatomist can in body; the latter examines the body to learn how matter is committing suicide, and the former reads the mind to find what beliefs are destroying the body. **1902** 'Mark Twain' in *N. Amer. Rev.* CLXXV. 763 Where can you purchase it, at any outlay of any sort, in any Church or out of it, except the Scientist's? **1903** —— in *Ibid.* CLXXVI. 509 The Scientist hastened to Concord and told Mrs. Eddy what a disastrous mistake had been made. **1938** M. Muggeridge *In Valley of this Restless Mind* ii. 8 'There's a Congregational Chapel.. and a Church of England third on the right.'.. 'Do many people go to them?' 'Not many, I think... We're Scientists.' **1980** *Country Life* 17 July 243/1 There is the dowager, American.. a Scientist (of the Christian kind).

3. Appositively in *Comb.*, as ***scientist-administrator***, ***-astronaut***, ***-dietician***, ***-philosopher***.

1964 M. Gowing *Britain & Atomic Energy 1939–1945* iii. 106 The two most influential American scientist-administrators.. were positively anxious to have a joint Anglo-American project. **1965** M. Stone *Man in Space* (rev. ed.) 15 A second large group of astronauts.. are a different breed. These newcomers are scientists... Some of these scientist-astronauts will go along on trips to the moon with the pilot-astronauts. **1971** *New Scientist* 18 Mar. 596/1 Dr Philip Chapman, the scientist-astronaut who served as mission scientist for Apollo 14. **1961** *Ann. Reg. 1960* 14 A 'scientist-dietician' and fanatical vegetarian, she believed that if we could discover the right diet we should live for ever. **1943** Blunden *Return to Husbandry* 32 Whitehead, A.N... The most eloquent of modern scientist-philosophers. **1977** *Dædalus* Fall p. v, The contributors were humanists, natural scientists, and social scientists who had met to present their papers in homage to the work of two distinguished colleagues, the scientist-philosophers P. W. Bridgman and Philipp Frank.

scientistic (saɪən'tɪstɪk), *a.* [f. scientist + -ic.]

1. Characteristic of, or having the attributes of, a scientist. (Used depreciatively). *rare.*

1878 T. Sinclair *Mount* 105 'The more the worse', is the fearful political fact of the coming time; and it will by and bye be seen that scientific free-trade is responsible for it. **1892** *Sat. Rev.* 6 Aug. 160/1 The most conscientiously scientistic of scientists.

2. Of or pertaining to scientism (sense 2).

1942 [see scientism 2]. **1943** [see historicism 3]. **1952** K. R. Popper *Open Society & its Enemies* (ed. 2) I. 286 A typical and influential scientistic argument in favour of historicism is, in brief, this: 'We can predict eclipses; why should we not be able to predict revolutions?' **1969** *Nature* 2 Aug. 541/1 We must apply scientific method to social studies without being besotted by a scientistic philosophy and pragmatism. **1972** *Observer* 30 Apr. 36/6 They regard his [*sc.* Russell's] kind of piecemeal, logically technical, scientistic philosophy as a covert ideological support for technological civilisation. **1980** *Times Lit. Suppl.* 26 Sept. 1072/5 My remarks.. should be put down to my own lack of sympathy with the scientistic vision which Thomas upholds.

Hence **scien'tistically** *adv.*

1883 Wright *Dogm. Scepticism* 12 All that may be scientifically true or scientistically false in connexion with bioplasmic theories.

†'**scientive**, *a.* *Sc.* *Obs.* [a. OF. *scientif*, f. *scient* scient *a.*: see -ive.] Well-versed, learned.

1560 Rolland *Crt. Venus* ii. 536 Then Desperance deliuerit his missiue Vnto thir ten, so sweit and scientiue. **1560** —— *Seven Sages* 10 Within ȝeiris fiue He sall be mair cunning and Scientiue Nor I. **1596** Dalrymple tr. *Leslie's Hist. Scot.* II. 44 He was sa weil instructed,.. and in al sciences was sa scientiue and cunning, that in quhat science he was cunningest culd na man tel.

†**scien'tivity.** *Obs.* *rare*$^{-1}$. [f. scientive + -ity.] The power or faculty of knowing.

1677 Gale *Crt. Gentiles* iv. ii. 331 The Scientivitie of God and his Intellect is never satisfied with any finite or infinite number of existent singulars of any one species or al. *Ibid.* 332 [see scibility].

scientize ('saɪəntaɪz), *v.* *rare.* [f. *scient-* (as in scientist) + -ize.] **a.** *intr.* To lay down scientific propositions, to theorize. **b.** *trans.* To make scientific; to give (something) a scientific character, basis, or rationale; to organize on scientific principles.

1890 *Murray's Mag.* May 697 Some few of your philosophers.. have scientised over it. **1921** M. Corelli *Secret Power* ix. 104, I was just crazy to help all the scientists.. and started 'scientising' myself. **1957** W. H. Whyte *Organization Man* iii. 29 If ethics is to be scientized, some specific people will have to do it. **1969** H. Daalder in R. A. Dahl *Political Oppositions* vi. 209 Marxism.. 'scientized' hope, and thus made life more bearable in what was otherwise a relatively weak social and political position. **1976** *Survey* Spring 75 The hitherto forbidden fields of cybernetics and sociology were called upon to improve and scientize the management of Soviet society.

Hence '**scientized** *ppl. a.*; also **scienti'zation**, the action or result of scientizing.

1971 J. J. Shapiro tr. *Habermas's Toward Rational Society* v. 62 The scientization of politics is not yet a reality, but it is a real tendency. *Ibid.* 66 The decisionistic model.. approximates the actual procedures of scientized politics. **1976** *Amer. Speech 1973* XLVIII. 288 As occupations become more mechanized and scientized, folk terms are often displaced by standard ones.

†'**scientman.** *Obs.* *rare*$^{-1}$. [? f. scient + man *sb.*] A man of knowledge.

1636 Prynne *Unbish. Tim.* (1661) 127 Therefore these Elders, must certainly be the better, the most eminent Scientmen, and so Paramount the Angel-Bishops in all these respects.

Scientologist (ˌsaɪən'tɒlədʒɪst). Also with small initial. [f. Scientology + -ist.] An adherent or practitioner of Scientology; a member of the 'Church of Scientology'. Also *attrib.* and *appositively.*

1952 L. R. Hubbard *Scientology: 8–80* vi. 24 The E-Meter is available from The Hubbard Association of Scientologists. **1954** *Notes on Lectures given by L. Ron Hubbard* iv. 22 A scientologist is expected to be able to resolve problems in a great many specialized fields, of which auditing is the first field he addresses. **1956** J. F. Horner *Summary of Scientology* i. 9 Scientologists work toward a world in which men cheerfully and willingly work together as fully free individuals able to co-operate toward the increased understanding and improvement of themselves, the race and the universe. **1965** L. R. Hubbard *Scientology Abridged Dict.* 30 *Scientologist*, one who knows he has found the way to a better life through Scientology and who, through Scientology books, tapes, training and processing, is actively attaining it. **1968** *Time* 23 Aug. 40/3 By watching the fluctuations of a needle, Scientologist 'auditors' can supposedly discern when a student has become 'clear' and has attained 'total awareness and freedom'. **1971** *Times* 20 Nov. 3/2 After Mr Vosper had left the institution he was declared to be in a condition of enemy and fair game for scientologists. **1977** *Daily Colonist* (Victoria, B.C.) 7 Aug. 9/2 Scientologists.. can hardly be termed medical researchers. **1978** G. Vidal *Kalki* i. 18 They were perfect 'clears', to use Scientologist jargon.

Scientology (ˌsaɪən'tɒlədʒɪ). Also s-. [f. *scient-* (in L. *scientia* knowledge) + -ology.] A system of beliefs based on the study of knowledge and claiming to develop the highest potentialities of its members, founded in 1951 by L. Ron Hubbard (b. 1911).

Scientology is registered in the U.S. as a proprietary term.

[**1937** A. Nordenholz *Scientologie* 7 Die Scientologie oder Eidologie, als eine Wissenschaft vom Wissen selbst, stellt sich ihrer Anlage nach in einen Gegensatz zu den Wissenschaften von den Dingen, die ins Wissen eingehen.] **1951** L. R. Hubbard (*title*) Handbook for Preclears: Scientology. **1952** —— *Scientology: 8–80* 8 Scientology means knowing about knowing, or science of knowledge. **1960** *Daily Tel.* 29 Nov. 13/2 Meanwhile, I toured the town trying to discover the meaning of 'scientology' and 'creative learning', the system under which the children were instructed to imagine they were dead. **1965** L. R. Hubbard *Scientology Abridged Dict.* 30 *Scientology*, an applied religious philosophy dealing with the study of knowledge, which, through the application of its technology can bring about desirable changes in the conditions of life. **1969** *Wall St. Jrnl.* 30 July, The Court of Claims ruled that the Founding Church of Scientology failed to show its net income didn't benefit private individuals. **1970** *Official Gaz.* (U.S. Patent Office) 1 Sept. TM 52/2 [Reg. no.] 898,018. L. Ron Hubbard, Washington, D.C... *Scientology*. For Bulletins, Books and Newsletters (Int. Cl. 16). First use Nov. 21, 1951. **1971** J. G. Foster *Enquiry into Pract. & Effects Scientology* iv. 42 in *Parl. Papers 1971–2* XXXVI. 917 Scientology departs from the mechanistic psychology of Dianetics by introducing a new causative agent... More usually.. and especially in recent works.. it is called the 'spirit' or 'thetan'... Among the goals of Scientology processing are to increase the beingness of the thetan and thus increase the creative potential of the individual personality and its analytical mind. **1973** *Daily Tel.* 31 Oct. 14/4 There was Lord Soper grudgingly admitting that Scientology was entitled to be called a religion even if it was the worst one he had come across. **1975** D. Lodge *Changing Places* v. 176 A young man distributing, without conviction, leaflets about courses in Scientology. **1980** *Daily Tel.* 14 July 3/1 A Scientology spokesman said the removal of the ban would be 'in keeping with Mrs Thatcher's beliefs in individual freedom and human rights'.

scieve, obs. f. sieve.

sci. fa., abbrev. f. scire facias.

sci-fi (saɪ faɪ). Also **scifi**, **sci fi**. Colloq. abbrev. of science fiction.

1955 *Britannica Bk. of Year* 490/1 The popularity of science fiction was reflected in the contracted form Scifi. **1957** *MD Medical Newsmag.* June 62/1 Modern sci-fi writers follow an honorable tradition. **1961** B. Wells *Day Earth caught Fire* viii. 123 'I'm not up on my sci-fi,' hesitantly. 'So we're orbiting to the sun.' **1974** *Observer* 27 Oct. 1/7 The SF fan world abounds in language.. that can baffle the novice... Most important of all, you must not say 'sci fi'—it's always SF. **1978** *N.Y. Times* 30 Mar. C 22/3 A 10-part series based on what Mr. Kotlowitz called 'speculative fiction', stories that go beyond sci-fi and deal with 'ethical and moral demands' made in new worlds to come. **1980** *Verbatim* Autumn 10/1 'Sci fi' is a term used to describe bad Hollywood science fiction movies, trashy science fiction novels, and bad science fiction written by mundane writers. **1981** 'D. Jordan' *Double Red* xiv. 61 There was a sci-fi film we didn't watch.

sci-fic (saɪ fɪk). *rare.* = prec.

1963 *Guardian* 4 Jan. 5/3 (*heading*) Psychic sci-fic. **1979** *Now!* 14 Sept. 6/4 Arthur C. Clarke is first of five sci-fic writers to talk about their work.

scift(e, obs. ff. shift.

scil., abbrev. f. scilicet.

scild, obs. f. shield.

scilence, obs. f. silence.

scilfisc, obs. f. shellfish.

‖**scilicet** ('saɪlɪsɛt), *adv.* (*sb.*). [L. *scīlicet* = *scīre licet* 'it is permitted to know'.] To wit; that is to say; namely. Abbreviated *scil.* or *sc.*

1387 Trevisa *Higden* (Rolls) II. 335 Looke to fore in þe firste book Capitulo Grecia, scilicet El[l]adia. **1547** Hooper *Declar. Christ & Off.* xii. L vij b, God sentithe an other mystres to scole man, scilicet aduersitie. **1601** [W. Watson] *Dial. Sec. Priest & Lay Gentl.* Pref. *iij b, Vntill they heare the case decided: and who they are, *scil.* the secular priests or the Iesuits. **1643** in J. Simon *Ess. Irish Coins* (1749) 120 They.. shall stamp the same on the one side with these letters (*scilicet*) C.R. for *Carolus Rex*. **1652** Gaule *Magastrom.* xviii. 160 The ultimate end of the universe, *sc.* to know, and love God. **1855** J. S. Watson tr. *Xenophon's Anab.* i. x. §3 *note*, [For πρὸς τῶν Ἑλλήνων] Brodæus suggested πρὸς τὸ τῶν Ἑλλήνων, scil. στρατόπεδον.

†**b.** Used ironically: Forsooth.

1539 Cromwell in Merriman *Life & Lett.* (1902) II. 207 That holy (scilicet) father of R[ome].

c. as *sb.* The word 'scilicet' or its equivalent, introducing a specifying clause.

1650 *Hobart's Rep.* 171 Now I come to the use of a (viz.) or (sc.) or in english (that is to say) and the nature and force of it. **1669** *Croke's Rep. Jas. I* (ed. 2) 429 But it was adjudged, that *postea convertit*, is sufficient, and the *scilicet* is void. **1805** *East's Rep.* V. 253 Where that which comes under a *scilicet* is consistent with what went before.

‖**scilla** ('sɪlə). [L. = Gr. σκίλλα.] **a.** *Bot.* A genus of liliaceous plants; a plant of this genus, a squill. **b.** *Pharmacy.* The bulb of *Urginea Scilla* (formerly called *Scilla maritima*).

1824 Loudon *Encycl. Gard.* §6502 Some species of scilla, muscari, iris, allium, oxalis. **1880** *Echo* 4 Oct. 4/1 Hardy bulbs, tulips, crocus, and scillas for example.

scilling, obs. form of shilling.

sci'llitic, *a.* *Pharmacy.* *rare*$^{-0}$. [ad. L. *scillīticus*: see next.] (See quot.)

1876 Dunglison *Med. Lex.*, *Scillitic* containing squill.

scillitin ('sɪlɪtɪn). *Chem.* Also -ine [a. F. *scillitine*, f. *scillit-ique* obtained from squills, ad.

L. *scillīticus*, a. Gr. σκιλλιτικός, f. σκιλλίτης of the same meaning, f. σκίλλα SCILLA, SQUILL: see -ITE and -IN.] (See quot. 1819.)

1819 CHILDREN *Chem. Anal.* 288 Scillitin is the bitter principle of the scilla maritima or squill. **1850** *Chem. Gaz.* VIII. 276 The author [Bley] has obtained scillitine in a crystalline state. **1875** H. C. WOOD *Therap.* (1879) 479 Scillitin has been asserted to be the active principle of squill; but the scillitin of different authors is diverse.

Scillonian (sɪ'ləʊnɪən), *a.* and *sb.* [f. *Scilly* + -*onian* (? after *Devonian*; but cf. *Islonian*, 'a native of the Isle of Axholme', Peacock *Manley & Corringham Gloss.*).] **a.** *adj.* Pertaining to the Scilly Isles or their inhabitants. **b.** *sb.* An inhabitant of the Scilly Isles.

1794 A. THOMAS *Newfoundland Jrnl.* (1968) ii. 19 The Scillonians (as they call themselves) have very little to fear as to a viset from a foreign power. **1822** WOODLEY *Scilly Isl.* I. v. 108 The majority of the Scillonians.. are very exemplary. **1884** *Pall Mall Gaz.* 2 Aug. 4/1 The dominant..idea in every Scillonian breast. **1896** BESANT *Armorel* I. iv, 'Now to a Scilly boy—' 'A Scillonian,' the girl corrected him. **1976** *Sunday Post* (Glasgow) 26 Dec., The council are determined to protect Scillonians against the tourist element!

scilocco, scilwis: see SIROCCO *sb.*, SKILLWISE.

scim, scima, obs. forms of SKIM, CYMA.

scimble-scamble, obs. f. SKIMBLE-SKAMBLE.

scimitar ('sɪmɪtə(r)). Forms: α. 6 cimitarie, -erie, 7 -ary, -ery; 6 semeterrie, -iterie, -orie, 6–7 -arie, scimitarie. β. 6 cemiterre, -are, cimyter, 6–7 cimiterre, cymiter, 6–9 cimiter, 8 -etar, 7 cymitar, -et(t)er, -etre, cemiter, -ar, -eter, 7–9 cimeter. γ. 6 semitor, symitare, 6–7 semitar, 7 -iter(e, -yter, symeter, 8–9 simitar. δ. 7 scindifer, skimiter, scemiter, 7–9 scimiter, scimeter, scymitar, -etar, -iter, -eter, scimetar, 6– scimitar. [Adopted in the 16th c. in various forms from different Rom. langs. The word appears as F. *cimeterre* (15th c. in Hatz.-Darm.; also ? *sanneterre*, ? *sauveterre*, and 16th c. *cimiterre*), It. *scimitarra* (formerly also *cimitara*), Sp. *cimitarra*, Pg. *cimitarra*, *semitierra*, *samitarra*. A Turkish origin would be expected, but no likely etymon has been found in that language; the Persian *shamshīr*, formerly pronounced *shamshēr* (whence Gr. σαμψήρα 'a barbarian sword', Suidas) agrees in sense but is unsatisfactory as to form. The Basque **cimeterra* 'sharp-edged', has been suggested as the source, but this appears unlikely, and recent Basque dicts. do not give the adj.

In Chr. Richerius Thorigneus *De Rebus Turcarum* (1540), *cymitharra* is given as the name by which the Janizaries called their weapon; but this does not prove that the word was Turkish.]

1. a. A short, curved, single-edged sword, used among Orientals, esp. Turks and Persians.

α. *a* **1548** HALL *Chron., Hen. VIII*, 6b, Appareled after Turkey fashion..girded with two swordes, called Cimiteries. **1596** NASHE *Saffron Walden* 8 A trenchant Turkish semitorie. **1603** FLORIO *Montaigne* II. xxvii. 403 By one onely blow of a Cimitary or broade Persian Sword. **1623** BINGHAM *Xenophon* 79 With the stroke of a Cimitery. **1623** COCKERAM I, *Semitarie*, a crooked Sword or Faulchion.

β. **1579** NORTH tr. *Plutarch, Alexander* (1595) 751 He.. ran sodainly to him with a cimiter drawen in his hand. **1596** SPENSER *F.Q.* V. v. 3 Vppon her thigh her Cemitare was tide. **1615** G. SANDYS *Trav.* 28 The Patrone..drawing a Turkish Cymiter, beginneth to lay about him. **1781** GIBBON *Decl. & F.* III. xxxiv. 266 They worshipped their tutelar deity under the symbol of an iron cimeter. **1838** LYTTON *Leila* I. ii, The curving cimiter. **1886** *Harper's Mag.* Feb. 467/2 Shemr raised his glittering cimeter.

γ. **1588** SHAKS. *Tit. A.* IV. ii. 91 He dies vpon my Semitars sharpe point. **1592** KYD *Sol. & Pers.* I. iii. 100 With this Semitor I..Endured some three or foure howers combat. **1634** SIR T. HERBERT *Trav.* 53 An vnexpected Semiter..cut off his head. **1662** EVELYN *Chalcogr.* Table, Damascus Symeters. **1690** *Gt. Scanderberg* 78 His Semitar had cleaved so fast to his hand in the heat of the Fight, that it could not be pluck'd off.

δ. **1562** J. SHUTE tr. *Two Comm.* II. 43 The sworde that Scanderberg strake the beste with was a Scimitar bending lyke vnto a falchion. **1621** BURTON *Anat. Mel.* I. ii. IV. vii, If they haue a good skimiter, [they] had rather haue a blow on their arme, then their weapon hurt. **1669** DAVENANT *Man's the Master* IV. 57 Suppose that with a Syrian Scemiter,..I were minc'd into a Py. **1750** JOHNSON *Rambler* No. 82 ⁋10 A Scymitar once wielded by a soldier. **1788** GIBBON *Decl. & F.* lxvii. VI. 441 In the hands of the Turks, the scymetar was the only instrument of conversion. **1813** BYRON *Corsair* III. 8 Therefore came I..To smite the smiter with the scimitar. **1832** W. IRVING *Alhambra* II. 64 His scymetar and dagger were of the workmanship of Fez. **1870** LUBBOCK *Orig. Civiliz.* vi. (1875) 310 The Scythians worshipped an iron scimetar as the symbol of the war-god.

b. *transf.* and *fig.*

1689 COTTON *Winter* xxxv, And Pendant by their brawny Thighs, Hang Cimetars of burnisht Ice. **1825** SCOTT *Talism.* iii, To raise up the scimitar of resistance.

2. Short for *scimitar razor-shell* (see 3).

1855 KINGSLEY *Glaucus* (1878) 70 The grey scimitars are Solens.

3. *attrib.* and *Comb.*, as *scimitar-horned*, -*shaped* adjs.; **scimitar-babbler**, a northern Indian or Australian bird belonging to the genus *Pomatorhinus* or *Pomatostomus*, and distinguished by a long curved bill; **scimitar-pea**, a variety of pea (named from the shape of the pod); **scimitar-pod**, the woody legume of the tropical climber *Entada scandens*; **scimitar razor-shell**, the *Solen Ensis*; **scimitar-tree**, an evergreen tree of the genus *Harpephyllum*.

1863 T. C. JERDON *Birds of India* II. 31 (*heading*) The Southern *Scimitar-babbler. **1928** H. WHISTLER *Pop. Handbk. Indian Birds* 38 This Scimitar-Babbler is a gregarious species going about in small parties. **1964** R. PERRY *World of Tiger* iv. 58 Such small pests as scimitar-babblers, whose clear ringing cries are audible half a mile away in the hills. **1895** J. G. MILLAIS *Breath fr. Veldt* (1899) 145 The noble presence of the *scimitar-horned sable antelope. **1844** STEPHENS *Bk. Farm* II. 550 The Carolina, blue *scimitar, and blue and green tall and dwarf imperial [peas]. **1856** MORTON *Cycl. Agric.* II. 576 The blue scimitar pea. **1871** J. SMITH *Domestic Bot.* 432 *Scimitar Pods (*Entada scandens*)... Its large hard-wooded flat pods.. resemble a sword or scimitar. **1819** TURTON *Conchol. Dict.* 160 *Solen Ensis*, *Scimitar Razor-shell. **1776** J. LEE *Introd. Bot.* Expl. Terms 386 Acinaciforme, *scymitar-shaped. **1850** R. G. CUMMING *Hunter's Life S. Afr.* (1902) 142/2 Knotted, scimitar-shaped horns.

Hence **'scimitared** *a.*, (*a*) bearing or armed with a scimitar; (*b*) 'scimitar-shaped, acinaciform' (*Cent. Dict.* 1891).

1845 E. WARBURTON *Crescent & Cross* II. 280 Turbaned and scimitared servants. **1885** MEREDITH *Diana* xxxv, The scimitared Mesrour.

scin, scinc, obs. forms of SKIN, SKINK.

scincidoid ('sɪnsɪdɔɪd). [f. mod.L. *Scincidæ* pl., f. L. *scinc-us* SKINK: see -ID and -OID.] A lizard of the family *Scincidæ*.

1841 *Penny Cycl.* XXI. 73/1 Scincidoïds.

scincle, obs. form of SHINGLE.

scincoid ('sɪŋkɔɪd), *a.* and *sb.* [ad. mod.L. *scincoīdēs* (neut. pl. -*oīdea*), f. *scinc-us* SKINK: see -OID.] **a.** *adj.* Resembling a skink; belonging to the group *Scincoidea* or the family *Scincidæ* of skink-like lizards. **b.** *sb.* A skink-like lizard.

1790 J. WHITE *Jrnl. Voy. N.S. Wales* 242 The Scincoid, or Skinc-formed Lizard. **179.** G. SHAW *Naturalist's Misc.* Pl. 179 The Scincoid Lizard is a native of New Holland. **1841** *Penny Cycl.* XXI. 72/2 Oppel included under his Scincoïds ..the Scinks, the genus *Seps*, the Scheltopusiks, the genus *Anguis*, and the Orvets. **1870** GILLMORE tr. *Figuier's Reptiles & Birds* ii. 40 The smooth scales of various Scincoid Lizards.

scincoidian (sɪŋ'kɔɪdɪən), *a.* and *sb.* Also -**ean.** [f. as prec. + -IAN.] = SCINCOID.

1840 *Penny Cycl.* XVIII. 258/2 Scincoidian Lizards, or Lepidosauri. **1841** *Ibid.* XXI. 74/1 There is not a single Scincoidian whose geographical range is confined to Europe. **1870** H. A. NICHOLSON *Man. Zool.* lxiv. (1875) 481 The Scincoidean Lizards.

scind (sɪnd), *v. rare.* [ad. F. *scinder*, or its source L. *scind-ĕre*: see SCISSION.] *trans.* To divide, make a scission in.

1870 BARING-GOULD *Orig. & Dev. Rel. Belief* II. ii. 25 A fatal mistake to scind what is by its nature indivisible.

scind, variant of SYND *v. dial.*, to rinse.

†**scindapse.** *Obs. rare*⁻¹. [ad. Gr. σκινδαψός a 'thingumbob', a what-d'ye-call-it.]

a **1641** BP. MOUNTAGU *Acts & Mon. Ch.* (1642) 211 So might the Sibyls be Scindapses, Counterfaits, *Entia rationis*, no such creatures.

scindapsus (sɪn'dæpsəs). [mod.L. (H. W. Schott *Meletemata Botanica* (1832) 21), f. Gr. σκινδαψός a plant resembling ivy.] A tropical climbing plant of the genus so called, belonging to the family Araceæ and native to Malaysia, esp. *Scindapsus pictus*, which has large variegated leaves and is often cultivated as a house plant. Cf. POTHOS, the former name of the genus *Scindapsus*.

1946 M. FREE *All about House Plants* xiii. 103 Scindapsus, Hoya, and others..attach themselves to supports by aerial roots. **1959** *Listener* 17 Dec. 1094/3 Variegated scindapsus must have plenty of light. **1980** A. HUXLEY *Huxley's House of Plants* 102/1 Philodendrons, and scindapsus (devil's ivy), will do better growing around a moss cylinder.

scinder, obs. f. SUNDER *v.*

scine, obs. f. SHINE.

†**'sciniphes.** *Obs.* (See CINIPHES.)

1607 R. C[AREW] tr. *Estienne's World of Wonders* Ep. Ded. ⁋5 Whose prouidence reacheth from the Center to the Circumference; from the silliest Scyniph to the highest Seraphin. **1609** BIBLE (Douay) *Exod.* viii. comm., *Sciniphes*, smale flying beastes, especially molesting mens eyes.

scink: see SKINK.

scintigram ('sɪntɪgræm). *Med.* Also scinto-. [f. SCINTI(LLATION + -GRAM.] An image or other record of part of the body obtained by measuring radiation from an introduced radioactive tracer by means of scintillation or an analogous detection method.

1952 F. K. BAUER et al. in *Jrnl. Lab. Clin. Med.* XXXIX. 153 It is suggested that this type of picture or visualization of a radioactive area be called a 'scintigram' and that specifically in this case they be called 'thyroid scintigrams'. **1963** LEADER & STELL in M. F. Campbell *Urol.* (ed. 2) I. vii. 238 The renal scintogram does not distinguish cyst from tumour, and lesions smaller than 3 cm. in diameter cannot be picked up. **1971** EMMETT & WITTEN *Clinical Urogr.* (ed. 3) III. xx. 2041/1 To localize radioactivity graphically by moving external counting probes or by scintillation camera-type detectors, producing a cartographic image known as a scintigram or scintiscan. *Ibid.* 2064/2 The hippurate scintigram reveals the presence of abnormal kidneys. **1974** R. M. KIRK et al. *Surgery* iv. 66 A scanner or gamma camera may be used to map out the distribution of radio-activity in a body, producing a diagram or 'scintigram'. **1980** *Brit. Med. Jrnl.* 29 Mar. 883/2 Bone metastases may be detected early as areas of increased isotope uptake ('hot spots') on scintigrams.

Hence **'scintigraph,** (*a*) a device for producing scintigrams; (*b*) a scintigram; **scinti'graphic** *a.*, of, done by, or pertaining to scintigraphy; **scinti'graphically** *adv.*, by means of scintigraphy; **scin'tigraphy,** the production and use of scintigrams.

1958 *Strahlentherapy* CV. 257 Scintigraphy and the use of collimaters provide the means of portraying true size and form of the thyroid. **1960** *Radiology* LXXIV. 913/1 (*caption*) X-ray exposure is made during the scintigraphic procedure. *Ibid.* 914/1 Metastases in the right hepatic lobe can be scintigraphically demonstrated with only slightly less definition than in the left. **1961** *Med. Radiol.* VI. x. 76 Scintigraph. *A. Stefanovich.* Summary. A short description is given of a design of the apparatus used to investigate the localisation of radioactive isotopes in the human body. **1975** *Sci. Amer.* July 42/3 A scintigraph is an image constructed by a computer from the signals of many scintillation detectors arranged to detect the annihilation gamma rays in coincidence. For example, a patient can inhale nitrogen containing the positron-emitting isotope nitrogen 13. The scintigraphs clearly show how the gas enters the wind-pipe, passes through the bronchi and finally reaches the alveoli..in the lung. **1976** *New England Jrnl. Med.* CCXCV. 1/1 We have previously reported on scintigraphic visualization of myocardial infarction in man with use of thallium-201. **1977** *Lancet* 8 Jan. 92/2 (*caption*) Scintigraphs of left thigh showing localisation of Tc-99 diphosphonate in soft tissue. *Ibid.* 7 May 1012/2 Amyloidosis should be suspected when scintigraphy with Tc-99m diphosphonate shows a positive activity of soft tissues. **1978** *Jrnl. R. Soc. Med.* LXXI. 39 Lesions in the pubis and ischium may be very difficult to detect scintigraphically.

†**scintill,** *sb. Obs.* or *arch.* Also 7 **syntille,** 7, 9 **scintil.** Anglicized form of SCINTILLA.

1599 in *Archpriest Controv.* (Camden) I. 158 This gentleman, in whome..neuer scintill of disloyalty..did once lurke. **1644** BP. MAXWELL *Prerog. Chr. Kings* xiii. 128 The scintil from the flint-stone. **1653** A. WILSON *Jas. I*, 55 Some little scintils of Love. **1860** SANGSTER *Hesperus*, etc. 26 No scintil of their [the stars'] jewelled flame.

†**scintill,** *v. Obs.* [ad. F. *scintiller* or L. *scintillāre*, f. *scintilla* (see next).] *intr.* To sparkle.

1681 COLVIL *Whigs Supplic.* (1751) 150 His breast so filled was with ire, That's eyes both sparkled and scintilled.

‖**scintilla** (sɪn'tɪlə). [L.] A spark; always *fig.*, a minute particle, an atom.

1692 T. WATSON *Body of Div.* 434 God takes notice of the least scintilla, the least spark of grace in his Children. *a* **1734** NORTH *Examen* III. ix. §11 (1740) 655 Such was the Disposition..in most People, upon a Scintilla of Evidence, to conclude the King was a Papist. **1851** HELPS *Comp. Solit.* xii. (1874) 229 They are daring words,..but they have a scintilla of truth in them. **1887** T. A. TROLLOPE *What I remember* III. xxii. 324 She expressed herself..accurately.. but without a scintilla of animation.

scintillant ('sɪntɪlənt), *a.* Also 8 **scintilant.** [ad. L. *scintillant-em*, pres. pple. of *scintillāre* to SCINTILLATE. Cf. F. *scintillant*.] Scintillating.

1737 M. GREEN *Spleen* 219 Who can view the pointed rays, That from black eyes scintillant blaze? **1790** R. KERR tr. *Lavoisier's Elem. Chem.* 497 Red scintilant zeolite from Edelfors. **1806** TURTON tr. *Linn. Syst. Nat.* VII. Expl. Terms, *Scintillant*, emitting sparks of fire when burnt. **1864** G. MUSGRAVE *Ten Days in Fr. Parsonage* II. ii. 53 Cloth of gold,..silk, and other scintillant adornments. **1890** CLARK RUSSELL *Shipmate Louise* III. xli. 289 By this time the island had melted into the scintillant dusk of the sky.

b. *Her.* Emitting sparks.

1610 GUILLIM *Heraldry* III. iv. (1611) 95 He beareth seven Firebrands flammant and Scintillant proper. **1868** CUSSANS *Handbk. Her.* viii. (1893) 130.

c. *fig.*

1794 MRS. PIOZZI *Brit. Synon.* I. 400 Hudibras too, of all books perhaps most dazzling with scintillant brightness. **1828** D'ISRAELI *Chas. I*, viii. I. 249 His scintillant wit. **1880** RUSKIN *Notes on Prout & Hunt* 9 Genius..scintillant enough to be made more vivid by contraction.

scintillantly ('sɪntɪləntlɪ), *adv.* [f. SCINTILLANT *a.* + -LY².] In a scintillating manner.

1900 H. HARLAND *Cardinal's Snuff-Box* xix. 191 The.. buildings stood out..the white marble, palely, scintillantly amethystine. **1928** A. L. FLEMING *Dwellers in Arctic Night* 151 Flashes of light from the Aurora Borealis move scintillantly in the sky.

scintillate (ˈsɪntɪleɪt), *v.* [f. L. *scintillāt-*, ppl. stem of *scintillāre*, f. SCINTILLA. Cf. F. *scintiller* (13th c. in Hatz.-Darm.).]

1. a. *intr.* To send forth sparks or little flashes of light; to sparkle, twinkle.

1623 COCKERAM I, *Scintillate*, to sparkle or leape vp. **1789** MASKELYNE in *Phil. Trans.* LXXIX. 262 They appear to cast out rays of a determinate figure,..and to scintillate a little, if the air be not very clear. **1824** GALT *Rothelan* I. II. ix. 226 Now and then the glancing of armour scintillated out from the grey. **1840** BARHAM *Ingol. Leg., Lady Rohesia*, Her eyes..scintillating like flint and steel. **1869** DUNKIN *Midnight Sky* 191 The latter [planets] have been known to scintillate more or less. **1894** MRS. F. ELLIOT *Roman Gossip* xv. 319 Her dark eyes scintillating with fury.

b. *fig.*

1864 *Reader* 23 Apr. 515 A work scintillating throughout with wit and humour. **1899** ELLEN T. FOWLER *Double Thread* vii. 93 My wit is all of the p.m. variety, and never scintillates in the morning.

c. *intr. Nucl. Physics.* Of a phosphor: to fluoresce momentarily when struck by a charged particle or high-energy photon.

1958 O. R. FRISCH *Nuclear Handbk.* xiv. 20 The recent discovery that some gases scintillate will undoubtedly have many future applications. **1966** *McGraw-Hill Encycl. Sci. & Technol.* XII. 76/1 The liquid organic solvent scintillates satisfactorily. **1971** *Sci. Amer.* June 61/2 The box was.. provided with a zinc sulfide screen that would scintillate when it was struck by an alpha particle.

2. *trans.* To emit as a spark or sparks; to send forth (sparkles of light); to flash forth.

1809 W. IRVING *Knickerb.* I. ii. (1820) 46 That this globe was originally a globe of liquid fire, scintillated from the body of the sun, by the percussion of a comet. *a* **1864** N. HAWTHORNE *Mother Rigby's Pipe* ii, The star on Feathertop's breast had scintillated actual flames. **1866** *Pall Mall Gaz.* 13 Oct. 1 A little too much given to scintillate bitter epigram.

3. *pass.* To be ornamented with bright specks.

1851 TURNER *Dom. Archit.* II. iii. 87 Painted of a green colour, scintillated or starred with gold.

scintillating (ˈsɪntɪleɪtɪŋ), *ppl. a.* [-ING[2].] That scintillates; sparkling. *lit.* and *fig.* ***scintillating scotoma*** (Path.), hallucinatory flickering patterns and gaps in the visual field as seen in migraine.

1775 ASH, *Scintillating*, sending forth sparks, sparkling as the stars. **1789** E. DARWIN *Bot. Gard.* I. (1791) 33 Cold from each point cerulean lustres gleam, Or shoot in air the scintillating stream. **1810** SHELLEY *Zastrozzi* i. Pr. Wks. 1888 I. 6 A scintillating flame darted from the ceiling to the floor. **1883** F. HARRISON *Choice of Bks.*, etc. (1886) 401 It is a very inferior task to extract statements from a thousand writers, and then to piece them together into a sort of scintillating mosaic. **1883** W. B. HADDEN tr. *J. M. Charcot's Lect. Localisation of Cerebral & Spinal Dis.* xi. 122 A particular form of megrim..characterised especially by the co-existence of scintillating scotoma. **1918** J. H. PARSONS *Diseases of Eye* (ed. 3) xix. 384 Scintillating scotomata of various kinds occur in migraine... A positive scotoma appears in the field of vision; while obscuring sight it has a peculiar shimmering character. **1950** BERENS & SIEGEL *Encycl. of Eye* 37 Visual hallucinations, such as scintillating scotoma.

scintillatingly (ˈsɪntɪleɪtɪŋlɪ), *adv.* [f. SCINTILLATING *ppl. a.* + -LY[2].] In a scintillating manner; sparklingly.

1927 *Sunday Express* 6 Feb. 4 A scintillatingly funny burlesque.

scintillation (sɪntɪˈleɪʃən). [ad. L. *scintillātiōn-em*, n. of action f. *scintillāre* to SCINTILLATE. Cf. F. *scintillation* (Cotgr., 1611).]

1. a. The action of scintillating; emission of sparks or spark-like flashes of light.

1623 COCKERAM I, *Scintillation*, a sparkling. **1656** BLOUNT *Glossogr., Scintillation*, a sparkling up of fire, or new wine leaping in the glass. **1671** J. WEBSTER *Metallogr.* vi. 96 Coruscation, or scintillation, is a certain sign of Metals that are unripe. **1836** MACGILLIVRAY *Trav. Humboldt* x. 125 The fire-balls seemed to explode, but the largest disappeared without scintillation. **1847** DE QUINCEY *Sp. Mil. Nun* §19 (1853) 59 The sudden scintillation from Kate's dress played upon by the morning sun. **1862** MILLER *Elem. Chem., Org.* 686 The red prussiate burns with scintillation when introduced into the flame of a candle.

b. An instance of this; a flash, a spark.

1643 SIR T. BROWNE *Relig. Med.* I. §32 That is the Spirit of God, the fire and scintillation of that noble and mighty Essence, which is the life and radical heat of spirits. **1646** —— *Pseud. Ep.* v. ix. 247 Our Saviour, and the Virgin Mary ..are commonly drawne with scintillations, or radiant Halo's about their head. **1791–2** COWPER tr. *Milton's Ode to his Father* 22 Some scintillations of Promethean fire. **1866** TYNDALL *Fragm. Sci.* iii. (1876) 83 The heat there is competent to raise iron to a temperature at which it throws off brilliant scintillations. **1869** ROSCOE *Elem. Chem.* 39 Iron wire held in the flame burns with beautiful scintillations.

c. *spec.* The twinkling or tremulous motion of the light of the fixed stars.

1652 GAULE *Magastrom.* xiii. 115 About the magnitude of the Stars... About their scintillation or their trepidation. **1789** MASKELYNE in *Phil. Trans.* LXXIX. 261 When I look at the brighter fixed stars, at considerable elevations,..they appear to me without scintillation. **1873** HERSCHEL *Pop. Lect. Sci.* vii. §101. 317 The twinkling of the stars and the changes of colour they exhibit during the different phases of their scintillations.

d. of the flashing of the eyes.

1838 *J. M. Wilson's Tales Borders* IV. 175/1 While the fire flashed frae his ee in almost palpable scintillations o' fury. **1867** MISS BROUGHTON *Cometh Up* xxxvi, An angry scintillation flashes from Dolly's superb black eyes.

e. *Nucl. Physics.* A small flash of visible or ultraviolet light emitted by fluorescence in a phosphor when it is struck by a charged particle or high-energy photon.

1903 W. CROOKES in *Science* 26 June 1002/1 Bringing the radium nearer the screen the scintillations become more numerous and brighter. **1915** *Arch. Radiol. & Electro-therapy* XX. 183 The phosphorescence observed by the naked eye is..found to consist of individual instantaneous flashes or 'scintillations', each produced by the impact of a single α particle. **1963** B. FOZARD *Instrumentation Nuclear Reactors* vi. 68 The scintillations must pass from phosphor to photocathode with minimum absorption at intervening surfaces. **1971** *Sci. Amer.* June 61/2 The screen could be moved to intercept particles scattered at any angle, and the scintillations were counted one at a time with the aid of a low-power microscope.

2. *fig.* A flash, a brilliant display (of wit, of thought).

1751 JOHNSON *Rambler* No. 141 ¶7 A man who..dazzles the attention with sudden scintillations of conceit. **1821** V. KNOX *Grammar Sch.* 77 Displaying..scintillations of great genius. *a* **1864** FERRIER *Grk. Philos.* (1866) I. xii. 349 Every time his pages are turned they throw forth..new scintillations of thought. **1867** LYDIA M. CHILD *Rom. Republ.* xxiii. 282 These small scintillations of wit.

¶ Misused for SCINTILLA.

1654 H. L'ESTRANGE *Chas. I* (1655) 5 Had he had the least scintillation of animosity, or majestick indignation. **1862** GOULBURN *Pers. Relig.* I. iii. (1871) 32 If the soul has the least scintillation of a desire to be holy. **1883** S. C. HALL *Retrospect* I. 240 He..had not a scintillation of eloquence, and his manner was brusque.

3. *attrib.* and *Comb.* in *Nucl. Physics*, as ***scintillation fluid, method, screen***; **scintillation counter**, a particle counter consisting of a scintillation detector and an electronic counting circuit; hence **scintillation counting** *vbl. sb.*; **scintillation detector**, a detector for charged particles and gamma rays in which scintillations produced in a phosphor are detected and amplified by a photomultiplier, giving an electrical output signal; **scintillation spectrometer**, a form of scintillation counter with which the incident energy of the particle or gamma ray may be determined.

1948 *Physical Rev.* LXXIII. 1406/1 We have prepared some transparent crystalline slabs of both materials, and their behavior as scintillation counters has been compared. **1968** *New Scientist* 15 Aug. 338/2 The receiver consists of four scintillation counters, each shielded from the others and each covering a quadrant of the azimuth circle. **1975** K. H. GOULDING in Williams & Wilson *Biologist's Guide to Princ. & Techniques Pract. Biochem.* vi. 180 The fact that the pulse is directly related to the energy of the original radioactive event is a considerable advantage of scintillation counters over Geiger counters. **1949** *Nucleonics* Oct. 30/2 During the past year the technique of scintillation counting has been considerably advanced and the applications to nuclear research have become widespread. **1979** *Nature* 29 Mar. 410/1 Individual wood samples were finely chipped in preparation for chemical pretreatment and subsequent conversion to benzene for liquid scintillation counting. **1955** A. E. S. GREEN *Nuclear Physics* v. 133 In recent scintillation detectors a photomultiplier is used to change the light pulse into a large burst of electrons. **1977** *Dædalus* Fall 42 The detectors used in the balloon flights were mainly scintillation detectors, which are particularly useful for the detection of photons with energies greater than about 15 kev. **1979** Scintillation fluid [see *scintillation spectrometer* below]. **1909** *Proc. R. Soc.* A. LXXXII. 496 For the observation of the reflected particles the scintillation method was used in all experiments. **1929** *Ibid.* CXXIII. 375 An intense beam of α-particles of definite speed falls on a thin sheet of matter and the number of α-particles scattered through an angle of about 135° is counted by the scintillation method. **1953** GAYNOR & ZEPPELIN tr. *Heisenberg's Nuclear Physics* vii. 141 We shall begin with the instruments of detection and study. The oldest method is the scintillation method. **1938** R. W. LAWSON tr. *Hevesy & Paneth's Man. Radioactivity* (ed. 2) ii. 31 If we allow the α-particles from a point source to pass in a narrow pencil through thin metal foils,..and then to fall on a scintillation screen.., we find that a fraction of the α-rays is deflected through a small angle from their original direction. **1955** W. HEISENBERG in W. Pauli *Niels Bohr* 24 Schrödinger cannot hereby remove the element of discontinuity from the world, which is found everywhere in atomic physics (very obviously, for instance, on the scintillation screen). **1949** JORDAN & BELL in *Nucleonics* Oct. 38/1 The..fact that the amount of light emitted in each flash is very nearly proportional to the energy of the particle opens up the possibility of using the instrument for measurement of gamma- and beta-ray energies. We have developed such an instrument and call it a scintillation spectrometer. **1952** *Ann. Rev. Nucl. Sci.* I. 226 A γ-ray scintillation spectrometer, in conjunction with a magnetic lens spectrometer, has proven very valuable in determining decay schemes and beta-gamma angular correlations. **1979** *Nature* 25 Jan. 313/1 (*caption*) Radioactivity was assayed in a scintillation spectrometer after addition of 5 ml ACS scintillation fluid.

scintillator (ˈsɪntɪleɪtə(r)). [f. SCINTILLATE *v.* + -OR.]

1. A scintillating star.

1872 PROCTOR *Ess. Astron.* xxi. 256 Capella is another notable scintillator.

2. *Nucl. Physics.* **a.** A material that fluoresces when struck by a charged particle or high-energy photon.

1950 *Physical Rev.* LXXVIII. 81/2 Terphenyl crystals.. appear to be among the most durable of presently known organic scintillators. **1955** *Nucleonics* Feb. 10/1 (*heading*) Gaseous scintillators. **1963** B. FOZARD *Instrumentation Nuclear Reactors* vi. 63 Even in crystalline or liquid scintillators of high transparency it is usual to surround the phosphor with a reflecting surface. **1971** *Nature* 20 Aug. 574/2 Cosmic ray muons..were selected by a counter telescope consisting of one or two 2·5 cm diameter disks of plastic scintillator and a 58 cm diameter tank of liquid scintillator placed approximately 90 cm below. **1975** DAVIS & SIMPKINS in Williams & Wilson *Biologist's Guide to Princ. & Techniques Pract. Biochem.* iv. 112 The supporting medium may be cut into small sections which are then immersed in a suitable scintillator solution.

b. = *scintillation detector* s.v. SCINTILLATION 3.

1952 *Ann. Rev. Nuclear Sci.* I. 188 The increase in scintillator signal when the plate is grounded is a measure of the beam which travels more than once around the orbit before being lost. **1958** *Times* 28 July 8/5 The radiation counters comprise two geiger counters and two scintillators, the geiger counters recording radiation within the satellite and the scintillators measuring exterior intensities. **1964** J. A. RANSOM *Range Guide to Mines & Min.* ii. 26 Anomaly maps were made originally by..flying airplanes over regions of suspected radioactivity with scintillators on long cables below the planes registering areas of abnormal gamma-ray count. **1977** *Kuwait Times* 1 Nov. 9/5 (Advt.), On display: Diagnostic and therapeutic X-ray equipments. Surgical steel instruments. Scintillators.

scintiˈllescent, *a.* [irreg. f. L. *scintillāre* to SCINTILLATE + -ESCENT.] ? Scintillating feebly.

1860 LD. LYTTON *Lucile* II. iii. §13. 13 One pale, Minute, scintillescent, and tremulous star.

†**ˈscintillize**, *v. Obs.* [f. L. *scintillāre* to SCINTILLATE + -IZE.] *intr.* To scintillate.

1694 MOTTEUX *Rabelais* v. xx. (1737) 89 The Probity that scintillizes in the Superficies of your Persons.

scintillogram (sɪnˈtɪləʊgræm). *Med.* [f. SCINTILL(ATION + -O + -GRAM.] A scintigram.

1958 *Proc. 2nd U.N. Internat. Conf. Peaceful Uses of Atomic Energy* XXVI. 245/1 Indefiniteness can be eliminated by making scintillograms in three mutually perpendicular planes. **1966** G. M. BERLYNE *Course in Renal Dis.* xvii. 348 The scintillogram using [203]Hg labelled mercurial diuretics is a useful way of diagnosing small infarcted areas of the kidney.

Hence **scinˈtillograph**, a scintigraph; **scintilloˈgraphic** *a.*, **scintiˈllography**.

1958 *Proc. 2nd U.N. Internat. Conf. Peaceful Uses of Atomic Energy* XXVI. 243/1 Scintillography is principally used to examine objects of which the shapes and location are approximately known. *Ibid.* 245/2 A systematic search for thyroid tissue precedes all scintillographic examination. *Ibid.* 248/1 The scintillograph reveals only lesions with a diameter greater than 2 or 3 centimetres, unless they are confluent. **1965** *Biol. Abstr.* XLVI. 4558/1 (*heading*) Scintillographic study of the spleen. **1975** *Nature* 2 Oct. 426/1 The possibility that the phenomenon was due to physical migration of isotope was investigated by serial gamma camera scintillography of two specially prepared T tubes.

scintillometer (sɪntɪˈlɒmɪə(r)). [f. L. *scintilla* spark + -(O)METER.]

1. An instrument invented by Montigny for measuring the intensity of the scintillation of the stars.

1877 *Monthly Notices Astron. Soc.* XXXVII. 204 A scintillometer, formed of a circular plate of thick glass, was mounted obliquely in the tube of the telescope.

2. A device containing a scintillator for detecting and measuring low intensities of ionizing radiation.

1955 *Times* 17 Aug. 7/6 An R.A.A.F. spokesman said today that Beaver aircraft with scintillometer and other radio gear would fly from Mawson early next year to search for a radioactive minerals map of the Antarctic coastline. **1956** *Proc. Internat. Conf. Peaceful Uses of Atomic Energy* VI. 660/1 An efficient scintillometer is about 50 times more sensitive to terrestrial gamma rays than a Geiger-Müller counter. **1977** A. HALLAM *Planet Earth* 111 The most useful geophysical surveys for mineral deposits are magnetic.., radiometric (the main prospecting tool for uranium deposits, using Geiger counters, scintillometers and gamma-ray spectrometers), electromagnetic, electrical, gravitometric, and seismic.

Hence **scintiˈllometry**, study by means of the scintillometer (sense 2).

1960 *Los Alamos Sci. Lab. Rep.* LAMS 2445. 337 (*heading*) Clinical applications of whole body scintillometry. **1974** *Nature* 15 Mar. p. xvi/2 (Advt.), The department has excellent modern facilities for work on tissue and organ culture, including..scintillometry.

scintilloscope (sɪnˈtɪləʊskəʊp). Also **scintillascope, scintilliscope**. [f. L. *scintill-a* spark + -O + -SCOPE.] An instrument in which alpha rays are detected by the flashes of light which are emitted when they strike a fluorescent screen.

1904 *Nature* 29 Sept. 535 The little instrument, which is called the 'Scintilloscope', consists of a simple magnifier of adjustable focus, as in the spinthariscope, but instead of the fixed screen and particle of radio-active substance a small double plate of glass is used. **1906** *Nature* 1 Nov. Advts. p. vii/2 Glew's Scintilloscope..Shows a magnificent display of scintillations, showers of sparks, direct from the mineral Pitchblende, Radium,..Thorium, or any radio-active substance. **1916** *Yukon Territory* (Canada Dept. Interior) 173 The scintilliscope is a much more convenient instrument. **1949** *New Gould Med. Dict.* 912/2 *Scintillascope*, an instrument for observing minute flashes of light upon a fluorescent screen struck by alpha particles, emitted from a small source of radioactive material. **1951** I. L. IDRIESS *Fortunes in Minerals* (ed. 2) xxxix. 250 These tiny flashes are known as scintillations, and can be seen through a magnifying glass. This is best done by a simple little instrument called a scintilliscope or spinthariscope. It is merely a small tube, probably of brass. In one end is fitted a glass prism. The outer side of the glass is coated with zinc sulphide powder... At the other end of the tube is fixed an eyepiece, which is a small magnifying glass.

scin'tillose, *a. rare*$^{-0}$. [f. L. *scintilla* spark + -OSE.] 'Full of sparks' (Bailey, vol. II, 1727).

scin'tillous, *a. rare.* [f. L. *scintilla* spark + -OUS.] Scintillating.

1826 MOORE *Mem.* (1854) V. 49 The grand march of the line,..coming after the broken and scintillous verses that precede it. **1837** RICHARDSON, *Scintillant,.. Scintillous.*

So †**scin'tillously** *adv.*, so as to produce sparks.

a **1529** SKELTON *Bk. 3 Foles* Wks. 1843 I. 203 Wyth theyr eyen beholdinge a trauers, of stomackes chaufed syntillously.

scintiscan ('sɪntɪskæn). *Med.* [Back-formation from next.] An autoradiograph obtained with a scintiscanner.

1960 *Radiology* LXXV. 821/1 (*caption*) Bilateral renal scintiscan superimposed on abdominal radiograph. **1971** [see SCINTIGRAM]. **1977** *Lancet* 6 Aug. 261/2 Liver scintiscans with ^{99m}Tc sulphur colloid were performed in 52 patients.

scintiscanner ('sɪntɪskænə(r)). *Med.* [f. SCINTI(LLATION + SCANNER.] A radiosensitive device which scans the body or part of it and creates an image of the distribution of radioactivity therein.

1953 *Radiology* LXI. 88/1 The point-by-point technique of plotting the frontal area occupied by the thyroid gland.. has been simplified by the introduction of the 'scintiscanner' for obtaining an actual size scintigram of the gland. **1956** *Jrnl. Neurosurg.* XIII. 345 (*caption*) Scintiscanner showing patient beneath the focusing collimator. **1968** *New Scientist* 12 Dec. 617/1 The computer is connected 'on-line' to a scintiscanner instrument, which measures radiation intensities as it is moved over a patient who has ingested a weakly radioactive isotope.

So '**scintiscanning** *vbl. sb.*, the production and use of scintiscans.

1954 *Amer. Jrnl. Roentgenol.* LXXII. 881/2 One tube stand suspends a shielded Geiger tube for uptake studies, the other tube stand supports the scintiscanning device. **1967** *Nursing Times* 18 Aug. 1095/2 The diagnostic uses of scintiscanning are extending rapidly with technical advances in radiobiology. **1980** *Nature* 17 Apr. 619/1 When bonded to the γ-emitter technetium-99..it is used clinically for scintiscanning of functioning renal cortex.

scintle, variant of SKINTLE *v.*

†'**scio**[1]. *Obs.* [Subst. use of L. *scio* I know.] At Oxford University: The formal testimony, by a member of the faculty, to the fitness of a candidate for a degree. Also, a person who gives this testimony.

Before a candidate could proceed to a degree, a certain number of members of his faculty had to 'depone' secretly to the Vice-Chancellor in favour of his fitness with regard to conduct and learning. Nine were required in Arts, three in the other faculties. The Vice-Chancellor put the question to each in Latin, and the answer was given in the word 'Scio', 'Credo', or 'Nescio'.

1664 WOOD *Life* (O.H.S.) II. 16, I gave a scio for Sr. Boen and Sr. [Henry] Knap of Merton Coll. **1681** *Ibid.* 518 The scio's taken in Adam Brom's chapel. **1711** HEARNE *Collect.* (O.H.S.) III. 278 His Scios were Dr Turner [etc.].

Scio[2] (ʃiːəʊ). [Modern name of the island of Chios (see CHIAN).] In full *Scio turpentine*: turpentine obtained from *Pistacia terebinthus*.

1830 LINDLEY *Nat. Syst. Bot.* 129 Scio turpentine is yielded by Pistacia Terebinthus. **1837** R. ELLIS *Laws & Regul. Customs* III. 482 Scio or Cyprus is obtained from the *Pinus Pistacia.*

scio- (saɪəʊ-), comb. form of Gr. σκιά shadow, as in **sci'ophilous** *a. Bot.* [-PHILOUS], thriving best in shade; '**sciophyte** *Bot.* [-PHYTE], a plant that thrives best in shade; hence **scio'phytic** *a.* Also SCIOMANCY etc.

1905 F. E. CLEMENTS *Res. Methods Ecol.* iii. 140 The slight development of hairs in sciophilous plants is an advantage. **1932** FULLER & CONARD tr. *Braun-Blanquet's Plant Sociol.* v. 107 In general the lower layers of stratified communities.. are designated as sciophilous. **1905** F. E. CLEMENTS *Res. Methods Ecol.* iii. 144 (*heading*) Heliophytes and sciophytes. **1947** R. F. DAUBENMIRE *Plants & Environment* v. 234 Sciophytes may be at a disadvantage in full sunlight if they cannot manufacture chlorophyll at a rapid rate. **1974** *Nature* 23 Aug. 623/1 For many years it has been conventional to classify plants into sun-demanding (heliophytes) and shade-requiring (sciophytes). **1976** *Ibid.* 22 July 281/1 We provide evidence for the existence of 'sun' (heliophytic) and 'shade' (sciophytic) differences in the net photosynthesis-radiant flux intensity response of individuals of one coral species.. on the same lagoon.

sciofericall, variant of SCIATHERICAL *Obs.*

sciograph, -er, etc., obs. ff. SCIAGRAPH, -ER, etc.

sciolism ('saɪəlɪz(ə)m). [f. next: see -ISM.] The character or qualities of a sciolist; pretentious superficiality of knowledge.

1816 COLERIDGE *Statesm. Man.* App. 31 That epidemic of a proud ignorance occasioned by a diffused sciolism. **1855** KINGSLEY *Glaucus* 44 The tendency to shallow and conceited sciolism, engendered by hearing popular lectures on all manner of subjects. **1876** FARRAR *Marlb. Serm.* xvi. 148 The empty sciolism of much that calls itself criticism.

sciolist ('saɪəlɪst). [f. late L. *sciol-us* (see SCIOLOUS *a.*) + -IST.] A superficial pretender to knowledge; a conceited smatterer.

1615 BRATHWAIT *Strappado* (1878) 20 The Generall Sciolists or Poettasters of Britannie. **1656** BLOUNT *Glossogr.* To Rdr. A 4, Every..homebred Sciolist being at liberty..to coyn and innovate new Words. **1782** V. KNOX *Ess.* cx. (1819) II. 264 Contemptible sciolists who called themselves theatrical critics. **1817** COLERIDGE *Biogr. Lit.* I. iii. 58 In proportion as a still greater diffusion of literature shall produce an increase of sciolists. **1880** SWINBURNE *Stud. Shaks.* 18 The last resource of an empiric, the last refuge of a sciolist.

Hence **scio'listic** *a.*, characteristic of a sciolist.

1831 W. GODWIN *Thoughts Man* 369 Must there not be in this subtle distribution much of what is arbitrary and sciolistic? **1870** LOWELL *Among my Bks.* Ser. II. (1873) 298 Sciolistic theorizing and dogmatism.

sciolous ('saɪələs), *a.* Now *rare.* [f. late L. *sciol-us* smatterer (dim. of L. *scius* knowing, f. *scīre* to know) + -OUS. Cf. It. *sciolo.*] Having a smattering of knowledge, sciolistic.

1639 LD. DIGBY *Lett. conc. Relig.* (1651) 18 Only sciolous wits float onely in uncertainty. **1640** HOWELL *Dodona's Gr.* 87, I could wish, that these sciolous Zelotists had more Judgement joynd with their Zeale. **1836** D. HOFFMAN *Course Legal Study* (1846) 794 The elaborated works of ignorance,..the speculations of the sciolous. **1861** *Temple Bar* IV. 114 Legros was not the superficial, supercilious, sciolous man many of his countrymen are.

‖'**sciolus.** *Obs.* Pl. scioli. [L.: see prec.] A smatterer, sciolist.

1612 T. JAMES *Corrupt. Script.* v. 7 Certaine *Scioli*, or cunning men, which tooke vpon them..to mend the old Bookes vpon coniecture. **1658** BURTON *Comment. Itin. Antoninus* 34 Camden..advises to exclude these words,..as a *glossema* foisted in by some *sciolus.*

sciomachy, variant of SCIAMACHY.

sciomancy ('saɪəmænsɪ). Also 7 -mantie, 8 scia-. [ad. mod.L. *sciomantīa*, f. Gr. σκιο-, σκιά shadow + μαντεία: see -MANCY. Cf. F. *sciomance* (Cotgr. 1611).] Divination by communication with the shades of the dead.

1623 COCKERAM, *Sciomancie*, diuination by shadowes. **1647** A. ROSS *Mystag. Poet.* xii. (1675) 307 This..was but Sciomancy, or a sight of shadows only, not Necromancy. **1656** BLOUNT *Glossogr.*, *Sciomantie*,..the part of Necromancy, practised by shadows. *a* **1693** *Urquhart's Rabelais* III. xxv, If you be afraid of the Dead,..I will make use of the Faculty of Sciomancy. **1728** CHAMBERS *Cycl.* s.v. *Sciomantia*, The Witch who conjured up the Soul of Samuel ..did it by Sciomancy. **1752** *Ibid.* (ed. 7), Sciamantia, Sciamancy, or Sciomancy. **1852** ROGET *Thesaurus* §511 Divination... By ghosts; Psychomancy. By shadows or manes; Sciomancy.

Hence **sciomantic** *a.*, pertaining to sciomancy.

1859 *Mem. E. Henderson* vi. 378 The actual not sciomantic appearance of Samuel at Endor.

scion ('saɪən). Forms: α. 4 si-, syoun, 5-6 syon, syun, 6-7 si-, syen, 6 sion, 7 seyon. β. 5 cyun, 6-9 cion, 7-8 ci-, cyen, cyon. γ. 6 scyence, 6-7 science, 6-7 siens, sient, 7 sience, cions, cyons, -ens, sciance, cyence, scient. δ. 4, 8-9 scyon, 5 scioun, 7 sci-, scyen, 5- scion. [a. OF. *cion, ciun, cyon, sion*, mod.F. *scion* (Picard *chion*), of obscure origin.

The early forms in OF. are inconsistent with the commonly assumed derivation from *scier* to saw.]

1. † **a.** *gen.* A shoot or twig; also, a sucker. *Obs.* exc. *fig.* **b.** *spec.* A slip for grafting, a graft.

α. *c* **1305** *Land Cokayne* 74 in *E.E.P.* (1862) 158 þe siouns beþ al sedwale. *c* **1380** WYCLIF *Serm.* Sel. Wks. I. 166 As a sioun mai not bere fruyt but if it stonde stable in þe vyne. **1388** —— *Num.* xiii. 24 Thei..kittiden doun a sioun with his grape, which twei men baren in a barre. *c* **1440** *Promp. Parv.* 457/2 Syvn, of a tree. **1483** *Cath. Angl.* 341/2 A Syon or A twige. **1513** DOUGLAS *Æneis* III. i. 71 The thrid syon of treis [L. *tertia hastilia*]. **1590** GREENE *Neuer too late* Wks. (Grosart) VIII. 97 A crooked sien will proue a straight tree. **1615** BRATHWAIT *Strappado* (1878) 170 Seyons young tender plants Where the quire of woodbirds chants. **1642** D. ROGERS *Naaman* 843 The graffing of a sien into the stocke. **1693** EVELYN *De la Quint. Compl. Gard.* Refl. Agric. 75 Young Siens growing out at the Roots.

β. *c* **1440** *Promp. Parv.* 79/1 Cyvn' of a tre, *surculus, vitulamen.* **1572** MASCALL *Plant. & Graff.* (1592) 14 When trees shall be thus proined, they shall bring great Cions from their rootes, which shall be frank & good to replant. **1697** DRYDEN *Virg. Georg.* ii. 92 From Roots hard Hazles, and from Cyens rise Tall Ash. *a* **1722** LISLE *Husb.* 441 Cyons grafted upon suckers. **1796** C. MARSHALL *Gardening* vii. (1813) 85 Proper stocks being ready, and cions or buds procured. **1802** W. FORSYTH *Fruit Trees* xxii. (1824) 304 The cion preserves its natural purity and intent, though it be fed and nourished by a mere crab.

γ. **1523** FITZHERB. *Husb.* (1525) 46 The scyences growynge aboute the tree of the same. **1577** B. GOOGE *Heresbach's Husb.* II. (1586) 76 The yoong sciences plucked from the rootes of the trees will growe. **1597** GERARDE *Herbal* I. xxv. 34 The roote..from the which there doth shoote foorth manie yoong sciences. **1600** SURFLET *Country Farm* III. v. 431 The litle sciences of cherry trees growne thick with hairie roots..being remooued [etc.]. **1612** T. TAYLOR *Comm. Titus* ii. 14 No more than a sient can bring forth fruit which is not set into a stocke. **1626** BACON *Sylva* §453 If you can get a Cions to grow vpon a Stocke of another kinde. **1657** AUSTEN *Fruit Trees* I. 48 Graft every Cyence into its own kind. **1688** HOLME *Armoury* II. v. 87/1 Suckers,..sprouts: some call them Sciences.

δ. **1398** TREVISA *Barth. De P.R.* XVII. cxviii. (Tollem. MS.), *Propago* is a ȝonge spray of a vyne, þat spryngeþ of a scyon. *c* **1440** *Pallad. on Husb.* II. 89 Lest the sciouns crokidly vp crepe. **1619** T. TAYLOR *Comm. Titus* Ded., Not tied to it as scion to a tree. **1791** E. DARWIN *Bot. Gard.* I. 104 Emerging scion, or awaken'd seed. **1814** SOUTHEY *Roderick* xix. 78 Ne'er shall it clothe its boughs Again, nor push again its scyons forth. **1849** H. MILLER *Footpr. Creat.* xii. (1874) 217 The species propagated itself by seed, bud, or scion. **1882** *Garden* 25 Mar. 200/1 In making the scions only the well ripened portions of such shoots are used.

c. *fig.* and in *fig. context.*

1590 LODGE *Rosalynde* (1592) A 4 b, Shewe your selues siens worthie of so florishing a tree. **1596** SPENSER *F.Q.* v. i. 1 Some of the vertuous race Rose up..That cropt the branches of the sient base. **1611** SHAKS. *Wint. T.* IV. iv. 93 You see (sweet Maid) we marry A gentler Sien, to the wildest Stocke. **1658** MILTON *Lett. State* Wks. 1851 VIII. 404 To prevent the extirpation of this most antient Scien of the purer Religion. **1684** T. HOCKIN *God's Decrees* 161 To be really in Christ, is to be grafted into him with the Cyon of divine grace. **1790** BURKE *Fr. Rev.* 45 Upon that body and stock of inheritance we have taken care not to inoculate any cyon alien to the nature of the original plant. **1818** BUSBY *Gram. Mus.* 429 Imitation, a scion of which the Fugue is the parent-tree. **1821** LAMB *Elia* I. *Imperf. Sympathies*, An humble and secular scion of that old stock of religious constancy.

2. An heir, a descendant.

1814 MRS. J. WEST *Alicia de Lacy* IV. 248 To guard the precious scion of a noble house. **1816** BYRON *Dream* ii, Herself the solitary scion left Of a time-honour'd race. **1817** MALTHUS *Popul.* I. 135 Young scions are then pushed from the parent stock, and instructed..to gain happier seats for themselves by their swords. **1869** FREEMAN *Norm. Conq.* III. 22 No son of a kingly father, no scion of legendary heroes. **1871** DIXON *Tower* III. vi. 51 A scion of the imperial Hapsburg line.

scioness ('saɪənɛs). *joc. rare.* [f. SCION 2 + -ESS[1].] A female heir or descendant.

1928 'BRENT OF BIN BIN' *Up Country* xi. 36 Harriet Mayborn, scioness of the English aristocracy, was dumb-founded, but kept her head. **1969** T. SOUTHERN *Magic Christian* (ed. 2) xv. 120 A venerable scioness of Roman society.

scioptic (saɪ'ɒptɪk), *a.* and *sb.* [f. Gr. σκιά shadow + ὀπτικός pertaining to vision: see OPTIC *a.*

From the dates of our examples, it would appear to be a correction of the less regularly formed SCIOPTRIC.]

= SCIOPTRIC.

1738-52 CHAMBERS *Cycl.*, *Scioptic* [ed. 1728 *Scioptrick*], a sphere or globe of wood, with [etc.]. **1775** ASH, *Scioptic*, belonging to an instrument used in the camera obscura. **1794** G. ADAMS *Nat. & Exp. Philos.* II. xv. 178 The scioptic ball..may be considered as a kind of artificial eye. **1828-32** WEBSTER, *Scioptics*, the science of exhibiting images of external objects, received through a double convex glass into a darkened room. [App. an error: cf. quot. 1706 s.v. SCIOPTRIC B.] **1842** [see SCIOPTRIC *a.*].

sciopticon (saɪ'ɒptɪkən). [Formed as prec. with Gr. neuter ending.] 'A magic lantern adapted for the exhibition of photographed objects' (Knight *Dict. Mech.* 1875).

1876 *S. Kens. Mus. Catal. Sci. Apparatus* No. 964 a (1877) 245 Sciopticon. **1879** *Nature* 16 Oct. 204/2 Advt. **1883** *Eng. Mech.* 6 Apr. 104 Of the oil-lanterns it will be supposed that I prefer the sciopticon. **1885** C. G. W. LOCK *Workshop Rec.* Ser. IV. 401/2 To make an enlargement on a 12 by 10 opal, using a sciopticon burning paraffin.

scioptric (saɪ'ɒptrɪk), *a.* and *sb.* Now *rare* or *Obs.* [f. Gr. σκιά shadow, after *catoptric, dioptric.* Cf. SCIOPTIC.] **A.** *adj.* ***scioptric ball***: a ball of wood with a hole made through it in which a lens is placed, used in the camera obscura.

a **1764** J. HARRIS *Treat. Optics* (1775) 269 For holding the lens, there is a little convenient apparatus to be had ready in the shops, called a Scioptric-ball. **1783** *P. Fletcher's Purple Isl.* v. xxxvi. *note*, Herein is described the *Camera Obscura*, ..which exhibit the pictures of external objects in their proper colours, by means of a convex glass, or Scioptric Ball, either in a darkened chamber, or portable box. *c* **1790** IMISON *Sch. Arts* I. 270 A scioptric ball and socket being fastened against a hole in the window-shutter in a darkened chamber. **1797** *Encycl. Brit.* (ed. 3) VI. 36/1 Put the object-glass of a 10 or 12 feet telescope into the scioptric ball. **1842** BRANDE *Dict. Sci.* etc., *Scioptic Ball* or *Scioptric Ball.*

B. *sb.* = *scioptric ball*: see A.

1704 J. HARRIS *Lex. Techn.* I. s.v. *Obscura Camera*, Such ready fitted are now commonly sold..on Ludgate-hill, and are called Scioptricks. [**1706** PHILLIPS (ed. Kersey), *Scioptricks*, a part of Optics. See *Obscura Camera.*] **1721** in BAILEY.

Sciote ('ʃiːəʊt), *a.* and *sb.* [f. It. *Scio* SCIO[2] + -OTE] **a.** *adj.* = CHIAN *a.* **b.** *sb.* A native or inhabitant of Chios.

1718 M. WORTLEY MONTAGU *Let.* 31 July (1965) I. 419 The ruins of this great City is now inhabited by poor Greek peasants who wear the Sciote habit. **1837** H. MARTINEAU *Jrnl.* 8 Sept. in *Autobiogr.* (1877) III. 190 Eastlake..must be a metaphysician to have painted his Sciote picture. **1866** *Chambers's Encycl.* VIII. 549/1 A number of the Sciotes having, in 1822, joined the Samians,..the inhabitants.. were indiscriminately massacred... Subsequently..many of the Sciote families returned.

sciotericall, -ique: see SCIATHERICAL, -THERIC.

scio'theism. [f. Gr. σκιο-, σκιά shadow + θε-ός god + -ISM.] A proposed term for the form of religion in which ghosts take the place of gods.
1886 HUXLEY in *19th Cent.* Apr. 493 This sciotheism, as it might be called. **1886** *Blackw. Mag.* CXL. 794 She has been discoursing.. upon sciotheism.

sciotherical, -therick: see SCIATHERICAL, -IC.

scious ('saɪəs), *a. rare*$^{-1}$. [f. L. *sci-us* (see SCIOLIST) + -OUS.] Having knowledge.
a **1834** COLERIDGE *Lit. Rem.* (1839) IV. 428 Brutes may be, and are scious.

scip, scipper, scipple, obs. ff. SHIP, SKIPPER, SIPPLE.

scir(e, obs. ff. SHEER *a.*, SHIRE.

‖**scire facias** ('saɪəri: 'feɪʃɪæs). *Law.* [Subst. use of the Law Latin phrase *scīre facias*, 'do (him) to wit', the characteristic words of the writ.] A judicial writ, requiring the sheriff to do the party concerned to wit that he should come before the Court to 'show cause' why execution should not be taken against him, or why letters patent, such as a charter, should not be revoked. Often abbreviated *sci. fa.*
In England now practically superseded by other forms of procedure for most purposes, except the revocation of royal charters.
144. *Rolls of Parlt.* V. 111/1 And he.. be admitted therto, and have for his action in this case, a scire fac' ayenst hym that offendith ayenst this Ordenaunce. **1456** *Coventry Leetbk.* 295 And thei to haue for the seid forfatores seueral Scire facias vpon this mater ayenst suche as offenden. **1544** tr. *Nat. Brevium* 176 In these cases a man shal haue a scire facias within the yere. **1641** *Argts. Hutton & Croke* title-p., A Scire facias brought by the Kings Majesty, in the Court of Exchequer, against John Hampden Esquire. **1688** SHADWELL *Sq. Alsatia* I. 5 Put the Case you are indebted to me 20l. upon a *Scire facias*. **1768** BLACKSTONE *Comm.* III. 48 It's jurisdiction is to hold plea upon a *scire facias* to repeal and cancel the king's letters patent [etc.]. **1818** CRUISE *Digest* (ed. 2) II. 73 He may recover the debt out of the goods of the cognizor, by a *scire facias*, or take his body. **1876** BANCROFT *Hist. U.S.* II. xxxi. 279 The power.. to bring a chartered colony, by a scire facias, before the English tribunals.

scirmige, -yssh, obs. forms of SKIRMISH.

sciroc(co: see SIROCCO *sb.*

†**scirpean,** *a. Obs.*$^{-0}$ [f. L. *scirpe-us* (f. *scirpus* bulrush) + -AN.] 'Of or belonging to bulrushes' (Blount *Glossogr.* 1656).

scirra, scirreve, obs. ff. SIERRA, SHERIFF.

†**scirrhe.** *Obs.* Also 7 schirrh, schirr(h)e, schyrrhe, skirrh, 8 schir. [a. F. *scirre*, *scirrhe* (16th c.; now *squirre*, *squirrhe*), ad. Gr. σκίρρος SCIRRHUS.] = SCIRRHUS.
1598 SYLVESTER *Du Bartas* II. i. *Furies* 486 Phlegmons, Oedems, Schyrrhes, Erysipiles. **1608** *Ibid., Index Hardest Words, Schirrhes*, a kinde of hard (yet paine-lesse) swellings in the flesh. **1601** HOLLAND *Pliny* XXIV. xix. II. 207 Whether the matrice haue a schirre in it and be hard or swolne. *Ibid.* XXX. xiv. II. 397 Hard tumors, schirrhs, and impostumations of the matrice. **1606** —— *Sueton.* Annot. 15 These Cancers be certain tumors or swellings,.. which he called Scirrhes. **1659** MACALLO *Can. Physick* 66 The latter declares an intemperature, that is, an inflammation, a skirrh or wind to be in those parts [liver and stomach, etc.]. **1761** tr. *Störck's 2nd Ess. Hemlock* 3 Fifteen schirs, the smallest of which was equal to a hen's egg. [In a footnote, the translator says he has chosen this form to avoid 'the disagreeable hissing of the word *schirusses*'.]

scirrho- ('sɪrəʊ, sk-), used as combining form of SCIRRHUS, in *scirrho-contracted* adj.
1829 *Good's Study Med.* (ed. 3) I. 385 What is usually called a scirrho-contracted rectum. **1835** *Cycl. Pract. Med.* IV. 578/1 It has been clearly proved.. that scirrho-contracted rectum.. is of not infrequent occurrence.

scirrhoid ('sɪrɔɪd, sk-), *a.* [f. SCIRRHUS + -OID.] Resembling scirrhus.
1855 DUNGLISON *Med. Lex.*

‖**scirrhoma** (sɪ'rəʊmə, sk-). *Path.* [mod.L. (in tr. *Blancard's Phys. Dict.* 1684, Phillips, ed. Kersey, 1706), f. Gr. σκίρρωμα, σκίρωμα, f. σκίρρος, σκῖρος SCIRRHUS: see -OMA.] A schirrous tumour.
1834 *Cycl. Pract. Med.* III. 657/2 Carcinoma may be divided into two species, the first of which we have called *scirrhoma*, the second *cephaloma*.

†**scirrhose,** *a. Obs.*$^{-1}$ In 8 schirrose. [ad. mod.L. *scirrhōsus*: see -OSE.] = SCIRRHOUS.
1725 ROBINSON *Th. Physick* 159 Schirrose Tumours.

scirrhosity (sɪ'rɒsɪtɪ, sk-). Also 6 schirrositye, 7 scirrosity, 7–8 schirrosity, 8 scyrrhosity, schirrhosity. [ad. mod.L. *scirrhōsitās*, f. late L. *scirrhōs-us* SCIRRHOUS: see -ITY.] A morbid hardness or scirrhous condition of an organ or a part; the quality or state of being scirrhous.
1599 A. M. tr. *Gabelhouer's Bk. Physicke* 363/1 First on the schirrositye, be it wher it will, you must applye a little Sheepes-woolle dipped in Oyle of Lillyes. **1601** HOLLAND *Pliny* XXX. iii. II. 406 They breed obstructions and schirrhosities in the bellie. **1669** *Phil. Trans.* IV. 980 In diseases of.. Spleen Liver and Mesentery; and the scirrosity and hardness of those parts. **1730** STUART ibid. XXXVI. 346 In Scyrrhosities of the Liver. **1733** CHEYNE *Eng. Malady* II. vii. §1 (1734) 184 A discoverable.. Schirrosity, or Cancer already extant in it [the Stomach]. **1762** R. GUY *Pract. Obs. Cancers* 30 They often produce Schirrhosities which have afterwards proved cancerous. **1776–84** CULLEN *First Lines Physic* §258 Wks. 1827 II. 12 It is in glandular parts chiefly that scirrhosity is observed. **1822–29** *Good's Study Med.* (ed. 3) I. 387 The existence of transverse filaments [in the gut] is generally preceded by scirrhosity.

scirrhous ('sɪrəs, sk-), *a.* Also 6 schirrhouse, 7 skirrous, skyrrhus, 7, 9 scirrous, 7–9 schirrous, 8 skirrhous. [ad. F. *scirr(h)eux* (16th c.; now *squirreux*), ad. mod.L. *scirrhōsus*, f. L. *scirrhus*: see SCIRRHUS and -OUS. Cf. Sp. *escirroso*, Pg. *scirrhoso*, It. *scirroso*.] Proceeding from, of the nature of, or resembling a scirrhus.
1563 T. GALE *Antidot.* I. 4 These medicines.. make softe bodyes whiche bee scirrhous and harde. **1599** A. M. tr. *Gabelhouer's Bk. Physicke* 362/2 For harde knobbes, and Schirrhouse tumefactiones. **1615** CROOKE *Body of Man* 183 The substance of the spleene is more rare and open then that of the Liuer, but yet is oftner afflicted with scirrhous tumors. **1666** J. SMITH *Old Age* 186 The entrails of man.. become far harder and faster, and more Schirrous than they were before. **1674–7** J. MOLINS *Anat. Obs.* (1896) 23 The Liver preternaturally large and Skyrrhus. **1754–64** SMELLIE *Midwifery* I. 132 The parts will grow schirrous and a cancer ensue. **1776** *Trial of Nundocomar* 33/1, I believe he has a scirrhous liver. **1790** J. C. SMYTH in *Med. Commun.* II. 481 A.. tumor of the indolent or skirrhous kind. **1855** RAMSBOTHAM *Obst. Med. & Surg.* 227 Skirrhous glands may be detected by their being more or less firmly attached to the surrounding structures. **1878** BRYANT *Pract. Surg.* I. 119 Scirrhous cancer.
b. *transf.* Indurated; covered with hard excrescences. Also *fig.*
1658 FRANCK *Northern Mem.* (1821) 299 Worms that are taken and drag'd forth out of a hard and skirrous earth. **1781** SIR J. REYNOLDS *Tour Flanders* Wks. 1797 II. 97 A fine portrait of Vesalius the Anatomist, when young, by Tintoret. He has a skirrous bone in his left hand, the other holds a compass. **1816** SOUTHEY in *Q. Rev.* XVI. 512 In attempting to produce an effect upon scirrhous hearts and distempered intellects. **1842** TENNYSON *Amphion* 64 Blow, flute, and stir the stiff-set sprigs, And scirrhous roots and tendons. **1845** S. JUDD *Margaret* I. ii. (1874) 7 The father disclosed a merry expression of face, shining, scirrhous skin, and a plump, ruby head.
Hence **'scirrhousness** (Bailey vol. II, 1727).

‖**scirrhus** ('sɪrəs, sk-). *Path.* Pl. scirrhi, also anglicized scirrhusses. Also 7 skyrrhus, schirrous, 7–8 schirrhus, 8–9 schirrus, *pl.* 7 scirri, 8 schirri. [mod.L., a. Gr. σκίρρος, properly σκῖρος a hard coat or covering, a hardened swelling or tumour, related to σκῖρός hard. Cf. F. *scirre* (16th c.; now *squirre*), Sp. *escirro*, Pg. *scirrho*, *scirro*, It. *scirro*.]
1. A hard, firm, and almost painless swelling or tumour; now *spec.* a hard cancer.
1615 CROOKE *Body of Man* 460 In this place sayth Bauhine ..I found a scirrhus or hard tumor. **1658** ROWLAND tr. *Moufet's Theat. Ins.* 1000 For a Schirrous of the womb he useth a Bupretis. **1660** JER. TAYLOR *Worthy Commun.* ii. §3. 140 The Priest.. thrusts his hand into the region of the lower belly, and looks if there be an ulcer, or a scirrhus. **1674–7** J. MOLINS *Anat. Obs.* (1896) 20 The weaknesse of the Liver caused by a Skyrrhus. **1681** tr. *Willis' Rem. Med. Wks.* Vocab., *Schirri* and *scirri* are hard swellings in the flesh, without pain, but hardly curable. **1684** BOYLE *Porousn. Anim. & Solid Bodies* vi. 55 The outward Medicine resolved the scirrhus. **1766** *Gentl. Mag.* Dec. 578/2 A schirrus in the right breast.. had considerably encreased, looked livid, oozed a little, and was painful. **1782** HEBERDEN *Comm.* iii. (1806) 13 Dropsy.. or scirrhi of some of the viscera. **1866** A. FLINT *Princ. Med.* (1880) 46 A scirrhus is a hard cancer in which the fibrous stroma predominates.
b. *fig.*
1646 FULLER *Wounded Consc.* (1647) 22 And when that Callum, Schirrus or Incrustation drawn over it by nature.. is once fleyed off, the Conscience becomes so pliant and supple, that the least imaginable touch is painfull unto it.
2. The disease of having a scirrhus (sense 1); an instance or attack of this disease.
1605 TIMME *Quersit.* III. 161 Of the congelations of these salts comes goutes stones, scirrhus, hardnesse, and divers kinds of obstructions. **1651** BIGGS *New Disp.* §155 The dysentery, Colick or nephritick Convulsions, schirrhus, &c. **1719** QUINCY *Compl. Disp.* 121 It somewhat inclines by Urine, and is reckon'd good in Schirri. **1732** ARBUTHNOT *Rules of Diet* in *Aliments*, etc. 323 And many chronical Distempers, as Jaundice, Dropsy, Schirrus's and Scurvies. **1813** J. THOMSON *Lect. Inflam.* 126 To regard schirrus as one of the usual effects of ordinary inflammation. **1872** PEASLEE *Ovar. Tumors* 20, I also think a single ovary to be more frequently affected by scirrhus than both. **1899** *Allbutt's Syst. Med.* VI. 97 According to Douglas Powell, scirrhus is the most frequent form [of mediastinal cancer].

sciruy, obs. form of SCURVY.

†**'sciscitation.** *Obs. rare.* [f. L. *sciscitātiōn-em* inquiry, f. *sciscitārī* to ask, inquire, question, f. *scisc-ĕre* search, seek to know, inceptive of *scīre* to know.] Questioning.
1634 BP. HALL *Contempl., N.T.* I. *Annunc.* 8 There is not a more noble proofe of our faith, then.. without all sciscitation, to goe blindfold whither he will lead us. **1646** TRAPP *John* ix. 7 He believeth and doth as he was bidden, without sciscitation. **1656** —— *Heb.* xi. 8 He is to be obeyed without sciscitation, with a blinde obedience. **1690** C. NESSE *Hist. & Myst. O. & N. Test.* I. 132 Abraham.. immediately departed without sciscitation or carnal reasonings.

[**scise** *v.* Explained in 1864 WEBSTER, *Cassell's Encycl. Dict.*, etc. as: To cut, penetrate; and etymologized as from L. *scissus*, pa. pple. of *scindere* to cleave. Inferred from *scis'd*, misreading for *seiz'd* (early edd. *seaz'a*) in: 1600 FAIRFAX *Tasso* VII. xli. 125 The wicked steele seaz'd deepe in his right side. [See SEIZE *v.* 9 b, 'to penetrate deeply'.]]

sciseme, obs. form of SCHISM.

scism(a, -e, etc., obs. forms of SCHISM, etc.

scissel ('sɪsəl). Also 7 scizell, 9 sizel, scissil(e. [a. F. *cisaille* 'the clipping of coyne presently after the stampe' (Cotgr. 1611), verbal noun from *cisailler* to clip with shears.] (See quot. 1842.)
1622 MALYNES *Anc. Law-Merch.* 282 The wast of Copper, which commeth by melting of Bullion, remelting of the Brocage and Scizell, and by working, hammering, often nealing and blaunching of the moneys. **1834–6** BARLOW in *Encycl. Metrop.* (1845) VIII. 613/2 The remainder of the plate between the holes left by the blank was remelted again, under the denomination of *sizel*. **1842** BRANDE *Dict. Sci.*, etc., *Scissel*, the clippings of various metals produced in several mechanical operations concerned in their manufacture. The slips or plates of metal out of which circular blanks have been cut for the purpose of coinage are called *scissel* at the Mint. **1864** *Chamb. Encycl.* VI. 481/2 The scrap left after the blanks are cut out, called *scissel*, is sent back to be remelted. **1868** SEYD *Bullion & Foreign Exch.* 273 The perforated ribbons.. called Scissel go back to the Melting Room.

[**scissible:** see SCISSILE *a.*, quot. 1626.]

scissile ('sɪsaɪl, -ɪl), *a.* [ad. L. *scissilis*, f. *scindĕre* to cut or divide. Cf. F. *scissile* (1611 Cotgr.), It. *scissile*.] Capable of being cut or divided; *spec.* in *Min.*, that splits into laminæ, esp. of alum; in *Chem.*, capable of being broken (cf. SCISSION 3 a.)
1621 WYDOWES *Nat. Philos.* 30 Hard Allome or Allome Scissile is thicke, and cleaueth. **1626** BACON *Sylva* §846 The Differences of.. Scissile and Not Scissile [1635 Scissible and Not Scissible]; and many other Passions of Matter are Plebeian Notions. **1670** *Phil. Trans.* V. 2040 We found it [a stone] somewhat scissile and reducible by a knife into thin lamina's or plates. **1731** ARBUTHNOT *Aliments* vi. (1735) 194 Animal Fat.. is scissile like a Solid. **1753** *Chambers' Cycl. Suppl.* s.v. *Alum*, Scissile or fossile Alum. **1967** *Listener* 10 Aug. 187/2 The first [play] in the series.. was.. as scissile by commercials as anything on ITV. **1978** *Nature* 5 Jan. 94/3 The scissile bond in a peptide substrate.

scission ('sɪʃən). [a. F. *scission* (14th c. in Hatz.-Darm.) (= It. *scissione*), ad. late L. *scissiōn-em* a cleaving or dividing, f. L. *scindĕre* (ppl. stem *sciss-*) to cut or divide.]
1. The action, or an act of cutting or dividing, as with a sharp instrument.
1676 WISEMAN *Chirurg. Treat.* V. iii. 357 Nerves may be many ways wounded, viz. by Scission or Puncture. **1835** KIRBY *Hab. & Inst. Anim.* I. Introd. 25 Mix them, and you have an animal which begins to absorb fluid, and.. multiplies itself by scissions or germes.
2. *fig.* Division, separation; in early use = SCHISM.
1443 *Sc. Acts Jas. II* (1814) II. 33/1 Alsua at ferme & faste obedience be kepit til our haly fadir the pape Eugene.. And at rigorouss processis be maid agaynis þe fauoraris of scissione, & the agaynstandaris of þe said obedience. **1736** HERVEY *Mem. Geo. II*, 252 A scission (which is the term the Poles have to express an election decided by arms and not by voices). **1789** JEFFERSON *Writ.* (1853) II. 561 The Princes of the blood.. presented and published a memoir, threatening a scission. **1798** *Ibid.* IV. 246 If on a temporary superiority of the one party, the other is to resort to a scission of the Union, no federal government can ever exist. **1837** CARLYLE *Fr. Rev.* II. III. iii. (1872) 97 Things ripen towards downright incompatibility and what is called 'scission'. **1870** BARING-GOULD *In Exitu Israel* I. xiv. 185 The Church was divided into two classes,.. and the scission between them was almost as sharp as that between the noble and the roturier. **1887** STEVENSON *Merry Men*, etc. (ed. 2) 123 He feared.. some scission in the continuity of man's experience.
3. a. *Chem.* Breakage of a bond, esp. in a long chain polymer such that two smaller chains result.
1923 *Jrnl. Chem. Soc.* CXXIII. I. 85 The scission of the ring.. with elimination of nitrogen seems possible. **1944** *Jrnl. Appl. Physics* XV. 389/2 For the case of Hevea and GR-S, the number of places along the chain that are subject to scission is not very large. **1952** TURNER & HARRIS *Org. Chem.* xxvii. 524 Another apparently reasonable alternative is that hydrazobenzene undergoes scission at the N—N link. **1975** *Nature* 1 May 31/2 mRNA was treated with 0.M NaOH for 4 min at 0°C, which gave on average about one scission per molecule.
b. *Nuclear Physics.* The event of separation of the parts of a nucleus undergoing fission, as opposed to the process as a whole.
1956 *Physical Rev.* CII. 440/1 The corresponding deformed shape roughly approximates the egg-shaped fragment resulting from scission of a dumbbell-shaped parent nucleus. **1958** *Rev. Mod. Physics* XXX. 555/1 The separation of charge centers at the moment of scission. **1964** L. WILETS *Theories Nuclear Fission* ii. 21 Of greater relevance to the fission process is the energy release to the point of scission, the time at which the fragment masses are unalterably determined. **1975** *Physics Bull.* July 307/1 Dr Specht.. concentrated on a description of those fission phenomena which seem to be decided by conditions in the

nucleus at the time of scission rather than at the saddle point.

scissiparity (sɪsɪˈpærɪtɪ). *Biol.* [f. L. *sciss-* ppl. stem of *scindĕre* to cut or divide + *par-ĕre* to produce, bring forth + -ITY. Cf. PARITY².] Reproduction by fission, fissiparity, schizogenesis.

1877 BATEMAN *Darwinism* 32 This most simple mode of reproduction by scissiparity or self-division is the same by which cells are reproduced. **1901** *Nature* 12 Sept. 496/2 On scissiparity in the Hydroides, by M. Armand Billard.

So **sciˈssiparous** *a.* = FISSIPAROUS.

1900 B. D. JACKSON *Gloss. Bot. Terms.*

scissor (ˈsɪzə(r)), *v.* Also 7 cizar, 9 scissar. [f. SCISSORS *sb.*]

1. *trans.* To cut with scissors, to cut *up*, *off*, or *into* pieces with scissors. Also, †to prepare or trim (the beard) with scissors.

1612 *Two Noble K.* I. ii. 59 My poore Chinne too, for tis not Cizard iust To such a Favorites glasse. **1840** L. HUNT *Seer* ix. 21/2 The young shoots of it [*sc.* ivy]..point in a most elegant manner over the edge of a glass or decanter, seeming to have been newly scissared forth by some fairy hand. **1885** FENN *Brownsmith's Boy* 24, I scissored off two or three berries in the way he had taught me. **1886** *Pall Mall Gaz.* 2 Sept. 1 When the luckless Abdul Aziz was scissored into a bloody grave. **1894** D. C. MURRAY *Making of Novelist* 31 Each folio being scissored into half a dozen pieces.

2. a. To clip out (extracts) from newspapers or the like. Also *absol.*

1865 *Dubl. Univ. Mag.* I. 146 Lucy surreptitiously scissored these charming songs, and kept them in a little volume. **1893** LELAND *Mem.* II. 133, I had for a long time, at intervals, been at work on a book to be entitled the 'Origin of American Popular Phrases'. I had scissored from newspapers, collected from negro minstrels [etc.].

b. *fig.* To excise.

1890 G. B. SHAW in *Star* 19 Apr. 2/6 The first act was vigorously scissored. **1968** *Listener* 10 Oct. 462/1, I was invited by the BBC to cut a single sentence from a broadcast talk I had recorded previously... I refused to do this, and accordingly the talk was hastily scissored out of the Third Programme. **1977** *Time* 24 Oct. 23/3 The Finance Committee scissored the entire wellhead tax scheme out of the bill.

3. a. To cause (one's legs) to move like scissors. **b.** To fix (a person) in the scissors hold or with a grip resembling it (cf. SCISSORS *sb. pl.* 2 a).

1961 *Rogue* May 14 Feathertop watched the smooth scissoring of her slim, trim legs as she walked to the bags. **1968** A. KEITH *Compl. Guide to Championship Wrestling* v. 76 Scissoring the bottom leg frees the hips. *Ibid.* 77 A scissors his right leg through underneath the left. **1973** *Funk & Wagnalls New Encycl.* XXII. 366 The legs are then scissored while the upper arm pushes toward the feet and the lower arm returns to the chest. **1974** J. IRVING *158-Pound Marriage* i. 12 When he rode you with a cross-body ride—your near leg scissored, your far arm hooked—Severin said Jones cut off your circulation somewhere near your spine. **1975** R. H. RIMMER *Premar Experiments* (1976) ii. 162 With her legs scissored around me, I found it impossible not to pat her smooth black behind.

4. *intr. Rugby Football.* To execute a scissors movement. Cf. SCISSORS *sb. pl.* 2 d.

1970 *Financial Times* 23 Mar. 3/8 Robertson and Turner scissored impeccably for Turner to score a try that Brown converted. **1975** *Sunday Times* 23 Feb. 28/2 Smaje scissored with Aitchison to get the Lancashire try, converted by Gullick.

scissorer (ˈsɪzərə(r)). *U.S.* [f. SCISSOR *v.* + -ER¹.] One who uses scissors; hence, a compiler.

1878 *Cornell Rev.* Feb. 188 Ye scissorers of the college press! **1898** *Pall Mall Gaz.* 26 Sept. 4/1 He certainly does show..considerable ability and discrimination as a scissorer.

scissoring (ˈsɪzərɪŋ), *vbl. sb.* Also scissorsing. [f. SCISSOR *v.* + -ING¹.] The action of cutting with scissors.

1822 *Blackw. Mag.* XII. 111 He may have written some pretty things, but he is taken now to slum, scissorsing, namby pamby, and is quite spoiled. **1892** MRS. SALA *Famous People* 4 By half-past ten or so his task of scissoring is over.

b. *pl.* Clippings made with scissors.

1890 *Bradford Observer* 6 Jan. 8/3 Is it [the Review of Reviews] not all made up of scissorings from the magazines?

scissors (ˈsɪzəz), *sb. pl.* Forms: α. 4–5 sissoures, sisours, 5 sesours, syssoris, sysors, -our(e)s, -owrys, *sing.* -owre, 6 scycers, sysers, syzers, sis(z)ers, 6–8 sissars, siz(z)ers, 7 sizars, sizzors, sissers, sissors, *sing.* sizar. β. 5 cysors, *sing.* cysowre, 5–6 cysars, 6 cysers, -ours, cyzers, cycers, cyssers, cisars, *sing.* cizar, 6–7 ciz(z)ers, 7 cizars, cissours, cis(s)ers, cissars. γ. 6 scissoures, 7 scisers, scizars, scizzers, 7–8 scissers, scizzars, 7–9 scizzors, scissars, 7– *dial.* scithers (see also E.D.D.), 8 scizers, 7– scissors. [ME. *sisours*, *cysowres*, a. OF. *cisoires* (mod.F. only in the sense 'large shears'; the sense 'scissors' is expressed by the cognate *ciseaux*, pl. of OF. *cisel*, mod.F. *ciseau*: see CHISEL *sb.*) = It. *cesoje* (rare; the usual word is *forbici*), a fem. pl. ad. late L. **cīsōria* (neut.) pl. of *cīsōrium* cutting instrument (Vegetius, 4–5th c.), f. *-cīs-*, *-cīdĕre*, the form assumed in prepositional compounds by *cæs-*, *cædĕre* to fell, strike, beat, slay, cut. The last sense, rare in the simple vb., is prominent in most of the compounds (as *abscīdĕre*, *concīdĕre*, *incīdere*, *excīdĕre*); hence the late L. use of *cīs-* instead of *cæs-* in derivatives related to this sense.

The spelling with *sc*, first found in the 16th c., appears to be due to etymologizing confusion with L. *scissor*, agent-n. f. *scindĕre* to cut, split, rend. (Cf. also *scythe*.) There appears to be no evidence of this confusion at an earlier date, though in Eng. mediæval documents *scissor* (written also *cissor*, *cisor*) was the usual Latin word for a tailor.]

1. A cutting instrument consisting of a pair of handled blades, so pivoted that the instrument can be opened to a shape resembling that of the letter X, and the handles then brought together again so as to cause the edges of the blades to close on the object to be cut.

The larger instruments of this kind, especially those which are too large to be manipulated with one hand, are called *shears*. Tailors call the large size *shears*, the medium size *trimmers*, and the small size *scissors* or *cuts*. In Sc. dialects all sizes of the article are called *shears*, the word *scissors* not being in use.

a. in *pl.* form with plural construction, either in singular or plural sense. When qualification by a numeral or an indefinite article is required, ***pair of scissors*** is used.

α. *c* **1384** CHAUCER *H. Fame* 690 (Fairf.) And moo berdys in two oures Withoute Rasour or Sisoures Y-made then greyndes be of sondes. *c* **1400** *Beryn* 2916 Getith a peir sisours, sherith my berd a-noon. *Ibid.* 2917 Som went to with sesours. *c* **1450** *Bk. Curtasye* 830 in *Babees Bk.*, þe snof of hom dose a-way With close sesours, as I ȝow say; þe sesours ben schort and rownde y-close, With plate of irne vp-on bose. **1483** *Act 1 Rich. III*, c. 12 §2 No Merchant Stranger..shall bring into this Realm..Tailors Shears, Sysors. **1530** PALSGR. 251/1 Payre of sycers, *ciseletz*, *forces*. *c* **1580** TUSSER *Husb.* (1878) 36 A buttrice and pincers, a hammer and naile, an aperne and siszers for head and for taile. **1592** GREENE *Quip Upst. Courtier* D 3 b, Then begins he to take his sissars in his hand and his combe. **1617** MORYSON *Itin.* II. 45 The haire on his chin..he used almost daily to cut it with his sizers. **1650–63** COWLEY *Cutter Coleman Street* I. vi, He..had neither mony enough to hire a Barber, nor buy Sizars. **1682** SHADWELL *Lanc. Witches* II. 22 Out upon that filthy visage, My maid with her Sizars in two minutes shall Cut me a Better in brown paper. **1706** VANBRUGH *Mistake* IV. 45 And there's thy pretty Pocket-Sissars thou hast honour'd me with. **1719** DE FOE *Crusoe* I. (Globe) 57, I found..one Pair of large Sizzers.

β. **1483** *Cath. Angl.* 65/1 A Pare of cysors. **1487** *Ann. Barber-Surg. Lond.* (1890) 530 My plaster box..and the cysars therein. **1590** SHAKS. *Com. Err.* V. i. 175 His man with Cizers nickes him like a foole. **1599** HAKLUYT *Voy.* II. II. 87 A paire of sharpe cyzers. **1600** J. PORY tr. *Leo's Africa* VIII. 304 They..shaue off their haires to the very bones without any cizzers or rasors. **1673** E. BROWNE *Trav. Germ.*, etc. (1677) 161 Cut in pieces with large Cissars. **1686** PLOT *Staffordsh.* 391 In the management of her Cisers. *a* **1697** AUBREY *Brief Lives* (1898) II. 21 He would bring a paire of cizers in his muffe.

γ. **1568** *Gonsalvio's Sp. Inquis.* Pref. *B iij b, This gentleman..toke a paire of scissoures, and pared his maker where he was ouergrowne. **1612** WOODALL *Surg. Mate* Wks. (1653) 17 Two pair of good Scissers for to cut hair. **1664** WOOD *Life* (O.H.S.) II. 8 For grinding my scithers, 2*d.* **1673** RAY *Journ. Low C.* 460 They take the fairest bunches, and with a pair of scissers snip off all the faulty grapes. **1785** J. COLLIER *Mus. Trav.* (ed. 4) 104 Clipping my beard with a pair of scissars. **1815** ELPHINSTONE *Acc. Caubul* (1842) I. 103 Their beards..are never touched by scissors. **1832** G. R. PORTER *Porcelain & Gl.* iv. 172 Any superabundance of material is cut away by the scissors while the glass is red-hot. **1856** *Orr's Circ. Sci.*, *Mech. Philos.* 99 Scissors and carpenters' pincers are examples of double levers of the first kind. **1886** H. C. DENT *Yr. Brazil* 409 My men advocated ..cutting them [*sc.* ticks] in two with scissors.

†**b.** in sing. form, = pair of scissors. *Obs.*

c **1440** *Promp. Parv.* 78/2 Cysowre, *forpex*. *Ibid.* 456/2 Sysowre, schere, *forpex*. **1611** COTGR., *Ciselet*, a little sizar, or chisell. *Ibid.*, *Forcette*, a cizar, a small paire of sheeres.

¶ **c.** in *pl.* form construed as *sing. rare.*

1843 GRAVES *Syst. Clin. Med.* xxix. 390, I removed the callous edges with a scissors. **1847** EMILY BRONTË *Wuthering Heights* ix, Now don't you think the lad would be handsomer cropped?..get me a scissors. **1849** MISS WARNER *Wide Wide World* iv, What a lovely scissors! did you choose it, mamma, or did it belong to the box? **1906** *Westm. Gaz.* 21 Mar. 12/1 Which is easily removed with a scissors. **1976** *National Observer* (U.S.) 29 May 11/1 Each without the other is only half a scissors.

d. *transf.* and *fig.* (Cf. *shears*, which is more common in dignified metaphor.)

1655 tr. *Com. Hist. Francion* III. 75 This good Servant.. somewhat courtailed our Commons, and for this reason we gave him the nick-name of being Hortensius his Sissors. **1742** YOUNG *Nt. Th.* v. 698 Aid me, to keep pace With destiny; and ere her scissars cut My thread of life, to break this tougher thread Of moral death, that ties me to the world. **1770** tr. *Mme. Du Bocage's Lett.* II. 211 The scissars of time cut their [Alps'] summits into a thousand strange forms. **1843** CARLYLE *Past & Pr.* II. xvi. 169 And Jocelin's Boswellean Narrative suddenly shorn through by the scissors of Destiny, ends. **1883** *Sat. Rev.* 13 Oct. 464/2 A Life of Gargantua on which he has plied the not unnecessary scissors.

e. ***scissors and paste*** (†***paste and scissors***): proverbially referred to as the instruments used by the newspaper sub-editor or the mere mechanical compiler. Also *transf.* and *attrib.*

1809 *Monthly Pantheon* Apr. 266 He was to..take the scissors and paste brush in hand. **1817** SCOTT *Let.* 16 June in *Lockhart* (1837) IV. 65 The incidents selected should have some reference to amusement as well as information, and may be occasionally abridged in the narration; but, after all, paste and scissors form your principal materials. **1826** F. REYNOLDS *Life & T.* II. 408, I hastily commenced an alteration, and as hastily concluded it, aided with those two effective co-operators, paste and scissors. **1867** *Chamb. Jrnl.* 14 Dec. 785/1 (*title of article*) Scissors and Paste. **1925** T. E. LAWRENCE *Let.* 21 Apr. (1938) 475, I haven't much desire to undertake so difficult a scissors and paste job. **1936** [see COLLAGE]. **1946** R. G. COLLINGWOOD *Idea of Hist.* 257 History constructed by excerpting and combining the testimonies of different authorities I call scissors-and-paste history. **1951** [see CRADLE *sb.* 2]. **1977** A. GIDDENS *Stud. in Social & Polit. Theory* ii. 97 'Scissors and paste' ethnology of the sort which..assembled together examples from numerous different societies without regard to the social context in which they were embedded.

2. a. *Wrestling.* A grip with the legs or ankles (formerly, the wrists) crossed like a pair of scissors. Also *attrib.* and ***body scissors***.

1904 SKINNER *Jiu-Jitsu* 117 Hasami Shime, or Scissors Grip. **1909** *Daily Chron.* 10 Feb. 8/1 At the second meeting Crozier quickly fixed his favourite scissors hold. *Ibid.* 8/2 In the second bout Crozier, after a few minutes, again put the scissors on, and this time pinned his man down after using the double nelson. **1909** WEBSTER, *Scissors*, a hold in which one contestant clasps the other's head or body with his legs. **1921** *Daily Colonist* (Victoria, B.C.) 13 Oct. 10/7 He [*sc.* a wrestler] took the..second [fall]..with a body scissors. **1940** R. CHANDLER *Farewell, my Lovely* 173 The Indian threw me sideways and got a body scissors on me as I fell. **1961** J. S. SALAK *Dict. Amer. Sports* 381 *Scissors hold* (wrestling), a hold which is secured by locking the legs at the ankles around a part of the opponent's body, pressure being applied. It formerly meant a grip with the wrists crossed like a pair of scissors.

b. *High jumping.* (See quots. 1961, 1976.) Also *attrib.* as ***scissors jump***.

1897 *Encycl. Sport* I. 50/2 The methods of jumping are various, but two main types predominate—viz., the straight jump, and the side-way or scissors jump. **1959** *Times* 1 Oct. 3/3 Her legs..flashed over the bar in the old-fashioned scissors style. **1961** F. C. AVIS *Sportsman's Gloss.* 61/2 *Scissors jump*, in high jumping, that method in which the body is in a virtually upright sitting position, and the legs move in an up-and-down motion. **1964** M. WATMAN *Encycl. Athletics* 79/2 There are four basic styles of high jumping: scissors, eastern cut-off, western roll and straddle... The ordinary scissors, which is taught to most schoolchildren, is the least effective of the four styles. **1976** *Webster's Sports Dict.* 371/1 *Scissors*,..a method of high jumping in which the jumper leads with the leg nearest the bar, crosses the bar in a sitting position, and then brings the trailing leg up over the bar as the lead leg is brought down on the other side.

c. *Swimming.* A movement in which the legs, held rigid, are parted slowly and brought together forcefully. Usu. *attrib.*

1904 R. THOMAS *Swimming* 418/1 The simile of the scissors clip is accurate..for the breast stroke (and would be also for the English sidestroke). **1973** *Funk & Wagnalls New Encycl.* XXII. 367/1 Sidestroke. This stroke, employed on either the right or left side with a scissors kick, ..is of particular value for lifesaving technique, but is not used in competition. **1974** 'G. BLACK' *Golden Cockatrice* xii. 200, I saw their legs..the girl doing a scissors kick that seemed to weaken as I swam towards them.

d. *Rugby Football.* (See quot. *c* 1915.) Also *attrib.* and *transf.*

c **1915** R. A. LLOYD in E. B. Poulton *Life R. Poulton* (1919) 218 The 'Scissors' trick was this: when I had the ball, and Ronald was running beside me just as if he was going to take an ordinary pass, he would suddenly change his direction and come racing straight across at me and practically take the ball out of my hands, and breaking clean through would run right across to the opposite wing. **1927** WAKEFIELD & MARSHALL *Rugger* 229 The two [*sc.* a centre and wing three-quarter] may also combine when the centre still has the ball, when.. they exploit the scissors movement. *Ibid.* 230 This scissors, and dummy scissors, attack may be tried also by two centres or by a centre and stand-off half. **1960** V. JENKINS *Lions down Under* 106 One forty yards' run of his, after he and Malcolm Thomas had worked a perfect dummy scissors, was a gem. **1976** *Wymondham & Attleborough Express* 3 Dec., They worked one of their excellent set pieces including two dummies, a well taken scissors and a Gary Owen.

e. *fig.* A progressive divergence between two kinds of price or income, so called from the appearance of a graph of the two indices plotted against each other; *orig.* and *spec.* used *attrib.* of a crisis in the Soviet Union in 1923 (see quots. 1926, 1965).

1924 M. FARBMAN *After Lenin* vii. 125 The economic crisis of the autumn and winter of 1923–24 is known as the crisis of the scissors. **1926** *Encycl. Brit.* III. 425/1 The first of these was a crisis which from an image used by Trotsky came to be known as the crisis of the 'scissors'. The two blades of the scissors represented the prices of agricultural products and the price of manufactured goods. **1965** A. NOVE in B. Pearce tr. *Preobrazhensky's New Economics* p. xi, In 1923 the Soviet economy faced the so-called 'scissors crisis': the terms of trade between town and country had become so unfavourable to the latter that the peasants were reluctant to sell their produce. **1974** J. WHITE tr. *Poulantzas's Fascism & Dictatorship* IV. ii. 193 The index of labour income shows that the scissors between the income of skilled and semi-skilled workers widened considerably. **1979** *China Now* Mar./Apr. 25/1 The closing of the price scissors (the gap between the price paid for agricultural foods and the prices paid by the peasants for manufactured goods) has not gone far enough.

f. In phr. ***scissors and stones***, ***scissors cut paper***, ***scissors game***, a game for two players using three postures of the right hand (see quot. 1934).

Or the left hand if one is left-handed.

1934 P. FLEMING *One's Company* II. ii. 198 From a room downstairs came that sound which so often accompanies meals in China—the staccato, competitive ejaculations of a party playing the 'scissors' game. In this you and your opponent shoot out your right hands at each other simultaneously, the fingers being arranged in one of three postures. A clenched fist means 'stone'; two fingers extended mean 'scissors'; all five fingers extended mean 'paper'. Scissors cut paper but are broken on stone, and paper wins against stone because stone can be wrapped up in paper. **1952** J. B. PICK *Phoenix Dict. Games* 291 Scissors and stones. **1964** I. FLEMING *You only live Twice* i. 18 It was the old game of Scissors cut Paper, Paper wraps Stone. Stone blunts Scissors, that is played by children all over the world. **1976** *Times* 2 Dec. 16/5 The Chinese hand-game Scissors Cut Paper.

3. A mechanical contrivance for gripping a block of stone.

1892 STEVENSON *Across the Plains* 198 That two men should handle a stone so heavy, even swinging in the scissors.

4. *slang.* An exclamation of disgust or impatience.

1843 SELBY *Ant. & Cl.* (Farmer), Oh, scissors; insinuate that it takes nine of us to make a man! **1893** MILLIKEN *'Arry Ballads* 33/1 Oh, scissors! jest didn't we give 'em tantivy.

5. *attrib.* and *Comb.* (chiefly in form *scissor-*), as ***scissor-blade, -case, -leg, -maker, -smith***; ***scissor-cut, -legged, -like, -tailed, -winged*** adjs.; ***scissor(s-fashion, -wise*** advs.; **scissor(s)-beak, -bill**, (*a*) a skimmer or shearwater, esp. *Rhynchops nigra*; (*b*) *slang* in various senses; *esp.* a foolish, incompetent, garrulous, or objectionable person; **scissor bird** = *scissor-tail*; **scissor-cut** [tr. G. *scherenschnitt*], a silhouette that has been cut freehand with scissors; also as vb.; **scissor(s)-grinder**, (*a*) a man who grinds scissors; (*b*) a dial. name for the nightjar, *Caprimulgus europæus*; **scissor-hold** = SCISSORS 2 a; **scissor(s)-lift**, a surface that is raised or lowered by the closing or opening of crossed supports pivoted like the two halves of a pair of scissors; **scissor-man**, a man who wields scissors, *spec.* a censor, a surgeon, or a tailor; **scissor-tail**, either of two American birds of the family *Tyrannidæ*, *Milvulus forficatus* and *M. tyrannus*; **scissor-tooth**, the sectorial or carnassial tooth of a carnivore.

1839 DARWIN *Voy. Nat.* vii. (1845) 137, I here saw a very extraordinary bird, called the *Scissor-beak (*Rhynchops nigra*). **1839** BEALE *Sperm Whale* 212 The large grey pelican, the *scissors-bill and diver. **1869–73** T. R. JONES *Cassell's Bk. Birds* IV. 185 The Scissor-bills (*Rhynchopes*) constitute a group of night birds. *Ibid.*, The Indian Scissor-bill (*Rhynchops orientalis*). **1871** *Atlantic Monthly* Nov. 566/2 Pootiest band of hogs in Tulare County! There's littler of the real sissor-bill nor Mexican racer stock than any band I have ever seen in the State. **1913** *Industrial Worker* (Spokane, Washington) 1 May 5/3 Scissorbill is a localized slang term. Here it refers to the 'home-guard' worker, who is filled with bourgeoise [*sic*] ideas and ethics. It ordinarily describes a worker who has some source of income other than his wages. **1926** J. BLACK *You can't Win* x. 129 When a bums' 'convention' is to be held, the jungle is first cleared of all outsiders such as 'gay cats',..'jungle buzzards', and 'scissors bills'. **1931** B. STARKE *Touch & Go* xvi. 259 Dick praised me for not saying anything. 'You're not a scissor-bill.' A scissor-bill was a woman who gossiped and nagged and was bad generally. **1931** 'D. STIFF' *Milk & Honey Route* xiv. 163 The line in waiting [for prostitutes] is usually monopolised by the village scissorbills. *a* **1944** J. CONROY in B. A. Botkin *Treas. Amer. Folklore* (1944) IV. 548 Some sign painters couldn't dot the letter 'i' without a pounce to go by. It was enough to make a dog laugh to see some poor scissorsbills wrastling around with a pounce. **1961** R. P. HOBSON *Rancher takes Wife* iii. 56 The hell you did, you big scissorbill, you stepped on my bum leg and my hand both. **1869–73** T. R. JONES *Cassell's Bk. Birds* II. 161 The *Scissor Bird of the Brazilians (*Milvulus tyrannus*),..is occasionally met with in the United States. **1879** *St. George's Hosp. Rep.* 514 After closure of the *scissor-blades. **1706** *Lond. Gaz.* No. 4234/5 Two *Scisser Cases.., both of Silver. **1931** *Times Lit. Suppl.* 25 June (Suppl.) p. iii/2 His many brilliant students have perhaps done more service to the book-jacket than to the page by some of their shadow, *scissor-cut and engraved letter forms. *Ibid.* p. iv/2 Professor D. P. Sterenberg portrays objects of daily life in flat lithographs that resemble scissor-cuts. **1931** V. WOOLF *Waves* 126, I see ..Neville, scissor-cutting, exact. **1960** *Times* 11 Feb. 3/4 The graceful and elegant animated scissor-cuts of Lotte Reiniger. **1976** *Times* 26 Nov. 4/7 An octagonal scissor-cut emerald is set in a gold and enamel ring. **1895** *Outing* (U.S.) XXVI. 68/2, I..worked my long legs *scissors-fashion through the water. **1841** N. HAWTHORNE *Amer. Notebks.* (1932) 88 The squirrel..frequently uttered a sharp, quick, angry noise, like that of a *scissors-grinder's wheel. **1855** 'Q. K. P. DOESTICKS' *Doesticks* 155 The loving accents of the scissor-grinder's wheel. **1869** LOWELL *Under the Willows* 227 Here The Scissors-grinder, pausing, doffs his hat. **1893** in Cozens-Hardy *Broad Norfolk* 50 The Nightjar [is known as the] 'Scissor-grinder'. **1974** D. SEARS *Lark in Clear Air* iii. 43 She pulled my head down close, jimmied her knees around my leg so that she had a *scissor hold. **1923** W. DE LA MARE *Riddle & Other Stories* 178 Before him stood a kind of gaping wallet, of cracked American cloth, held yawningly open by its *scissor-legs. **1947** —— *Collected Stories for Children* 26 His lank scissor-legs. **1967** FLAKOLL & ALEGRIA tr. *M. A. Asturias' Cyclone* ii. 22 The *scissor-legged cot. **1961** *Aeroplane & Astronautics* CI. 568/2 The mobile *scissor-lift intermediate-base loading platform developed by Canadair is seen here being demonstrated with a Seaboard World Airways' CL-44. **1970** *Times* (Aviation Suppl.) 4 Sept. p. xiv/8 Ready-prepared meals for the galleys on board the aircraft are..loaded by mobile scissors-lift vehicles direct to the galley hatches. **1980** *BSI News* June 5/3 Most types of scissor lift present trapping hazards to persons employed on or about them. **1868** *Rep. U.S. Comm. Agric.* (1869) 316 It [*sc.* the instrument] consists of a *scissor-like frame. **1886** GÜNTHER in *Encycl. Brit.* XXI. 775/2 They [the piked dog-fish] cut the lines with their scissors-like teeth. **1704** *Lond. Gaz.* No. 4082/4 *Scizer or Knife-maker. **1848** tr. *Hoffmann's English Struwwelpeter* (ed. 4) 16 The door flew open, in he ran, The great, long, red-legged *scissar-man. Oh! children, see! the tailor's come. **1932** AUDEN in *Rev. Eng. Stud.* (1978) Aug. 301 The hump-backed surgeons And the scissor-man. *a* **1953** DYLAN THOMAS *Quite Early One Morning* (1954) 22 Struwelpeter—oh! the baby-burning flames and the clacking scissorman! **1968** *Listener* 5 Sept. 292/1 Arts censorship in Britain lives on mainly through the sheer personality of its few remaining scissormen. **1623–4** *Act 21 Jas. I*, c. 31 §6 The Occupacion of a Cutler, *Scissorsmith, Shearsmith or Sicklesmith. **1813** *Examiner* 10 May 294/2 S. Broadhead and E. Gurney, Sheffield, scissor-smiths. **1839** DARWIN *Voy. Nat.* vii. (1845) 138 A bird with a forked tail, terminated by two long feathers (Tyrannus savana) and named by the Spaniards *scissor-tail, is very common near Buenos Ayres. **1872** COUES *Key N. Amer. Birds* 169 Swallow-tailed Flycatcher. Scissor-tail. **1894** NEWTON *Dict. Birds* III. 816 Scizzors-tail, *Milvulus forficatus*, one of the most beautiful of the *Tyrannidæ*. **1823** LATHAM *Gen. Hist. Birds* VII. 348 *Scissars-tailed Goatsucker... Inhabits Paraguay. **1811** SHAW *Gen. Zool.* VIII. I. 280 Scissars-tailed humming-bird. *Trochilus Furcifer*... Native of Paraguay. **1840** *Cuvier's Anim. Kingd.* 151 The *carnassier*, or *scissor-tooth. **1894** *Outing* (U.S.) XXIV. 53/1 A short..column of *scissor-winged birds. **1873** C. W. THOMSON *Depths of Sea* v. 214 A pair of scoops..close upon one another *scissorwise on a hinge.

scissure ('sɪʃjʊə(r)). ? *Obs.* Also 6 scissur. [a. F. *scissure* (16th c. in Hatz.-Darm.), ad. L. *scissūra*, f. *scindĕre* (pa. pple. *scissus*) to cut, divide: see SCISSION.]

1. A longitudinal cleft or opening made by cutting or separation of parts; a rent, fissure.

1511 *Guylforde's Pilgr.* (Camden) 26 Therby also..is a scissure or clyfte in the stone rok, so moche that a man almoste may lye therin. **1616** S. PRICE *Ephesus Warn.* 37 Like an earthquake,..whose rent & scissure is the breaking of the heart. **1633** T. ADAMS *Exp. 2 Pet.* iii. 9 A robe that is thus artificially mangled, if the scissures and breaches be reconciled with 'borders of Gold and studdes of Silver',.. appeares more glorious, than the former continuity could have made it. **1656** BLOUNT *Glossogr.*, *Scissure*, a cleft, a cut or rent; the division or parting of a river. *a* **1660** HAMMOND *Serm.* ii. (1664) 20 As when the Body is torn asunder, the Soul is without any farther act of violence forced out of its place, that it takes its flight home to Heaven, being thus let out at the Scissure, as at the Window. **1681** H. MORE *Exp. Dan.* 6 As if a Clayie ground should cleave with a wide scissure and swallow down a sudden Torrent. **1759** tr. *Duhamel's Husb.* (1762) I. viii. 37 And divides it, by making in a manner a scissure. **1822** T. TAYLOR *Apuleius* 169 He thought that the wounds which he had made with his lance would resemble the scissures of teeth.

b. *fig.* A split, division, schism.

[**1634** M. WILSON *Charity Maintained* I. v. §3. 152 Contrary to which, is *Schisme*, from the Greeke word signifying *Scissure*, or *Diuision*.] **1643** HOWELL *Tru Informer* (1661) 22 To proceed in the true discovery of these Domestick scissures. **1644** —— *Engl. Tears* 181 Torn and rent into so many scissures and Sects. *c* **1645** —— *Lett.* (1655) III. iii. 6 To this Sect [the Presbyterians] may be imputed all the scissures that have happen'd in Christianity. **1647** HAMMOND *Power of Keys* iv. 67 It would both unpeople their assemblies, and necessarily cause a dangerous scissure in the multitude. **1654** BRAMHALL *Just Vind.* ii. (1661) 14 Schisme signifies a criminous scissure, rent, or division in the Church.

2. *Anat.*, etc. A natural cleft or opening in an organ or part.

c **1400** *Lanfranc's Cirurg.* 263 Scissure is a passioun in a mannes tunge þat is as it were kutting. **1607** TOPSELL *Four-f. Beasts* (1658) 340 In the male [hyæna, under the tail] there is a scissure like the secrets of a female. **1642** H. MORE *Song of Soul* (1647) Notes 138/2 It being a round fruit, and representing the seminall fullnesse of the Earth, by its scissure in the side, full of kernells or seeds. **1658** A. FOX *Wurtz' Surg.* II. viii. 71 If you find after the opening of the skin, neither fracture nor scissure. **1668** WILKINS *Real Char.* II. vii. 177 That Scissure of the Face through which we breath and receive our nourishment. **1725** *Bradley's Fam. Dict.* s.v. *Liver*, These two Lobes [of the Liver] are separated by a Scissure or Cleft through which the Umbelical Vein enters. **1822–29** *Good's Study Med.* (ed. 3) IV. 633 Whether the blood occupy the great interlobular scissure, and thus lie upon the corpus callosum.

†**b.** A segment. *Obs.*

1662 H. STUBBE *Indian Nectar* iii. 20 It is..divided into several scissures, and pieces, as is a cow's kidney.

3. The action of cutting.

1509 BARCLAY *Shyp of Folys* (1570) 8 Socrates with many mo in wisedome excellent,..Let growe their here without cutting or scissure.

scissym, obs. form of SCHISM.

†**scitament.** *Obs.*$^{-0}$ [ad. L. *scītāmenta* neut. pl., f. *scītus* elegant, dainty, pa. pple of *sciscĕre*: see SCISCITATION.] (See quot.)

1656 BLOUNT *Glossogr.*, *Scitament*, a kind of meat having a very pleasant taste; Also pleasantness, or a fine or witty thing set to adorn ones talk.

scitamineous (sɪtə'mɪnɪəs), *a.* *Bot.* Also **scitaminous**. [f. mod.L. *Scitamineæ* (1810 R. Brown *Prodr.* 305, altered form of *Scitamina* neut. pl., the name given to this order by Linnæus 1751, suggested by L. *scītāmenta*: see prec.) + -OUS.] Of or pertaining to the *Scitamineæ*, a former order of monocotyledonous tropical plants, including the present orders *Musaceæ* and *Zingiberaceæ*.

1806 TURTON tr. *Linn. Syst. Nat.* VII. Expl. Terms, *Scitamineous*, of a spicy taste and odour. **1818** COLEBROOKE *Import Colonial Corn* 130 It is to be had..from yams, potatoes, arrow-roots,..orchideous roots and scitamineous. **1824** LOUDON *Encycl. Gard.* (ed. 2) 930 Scitaminous, or Reedy Stove Plants. **1851–9** HOOKER in *Man. Sci. Enq.* 426 Nothing is known of the origin of the scitamineous fruit to which the name Large Round China Cardamom has been given. **1851** RICHARDSON *Geol.* (1855) 175 Palms and scitamineous plants.

scitation, obs. form of CITATION.

†**scite.** *Obs.*$^{-0}$ [ad. L. *scītum* (*plēbis*) a decree or ordinance (of the people), neut. pa. pple. of *sciscĕre* to accept, approve, hence to appoint, decree, ordain.] (See quot.)

1656 BLOUNT *Glossogr.*, *Scite*, an Ordinance, Decree, or Statute.

scite, obs. form of CITE *v.* and CITY.

scithers, obs. and dial. form of SCISSORS.

scitie, obs. Sc. form of CITY.

†'**sciture.** *Obs.*$^{-1}$ [f. L. *scīt-*, ppl. stem of *scīre* to know + -URE.] Knowledge.

c **1540** *Privy Seal of Hen. VIII* Miscell. Bk. (A.O.) xxx. 18 Know ye that we of our certen Sciture and mere mocion.. haue given licence [etc.].

sciurine ('saɪjʊərɪn), *a.* and *sb.* [f. L. *sciūr-us*, ad. Gr. σκίουρος squirrel (f. σκιά shadow + οὐρά tail) + -INE.] **a.** *adj.* Of or pertaining to the genus *Sciurus* or subfamily *Sciurinæ* of squirrels. **b.** *sb.* A sciurine rodent; a squirrel.

1842 BRANDE *Dict. Sci.* etc., *Sciurines*... The name of a family of Rodents of which the genus *Sciurus* is the type. **1859–62** SIR J. RICHARDSON, etc. *Mus. Nat. Hist.* (1868) I. 212 The Sciurine Petaurist (*Petaurus sciureus*) or Sugar Squirrel. **1877** COUES & ALLEN *N. Amer. Rodentia* 830 It is at once recognizable by..its general Sciurine form. **1883** *Encycl. Brit.* XV. 416/2 In the Sciurine and Hystricine Rodents the tibia and fibula are distinct.

sciuroid (saɪ'jʊərɔɪd), *a.* [f. L. *sciūr-us* (see prec.) + -OID.]

1. *Zool.* Of or pertaining to the *Sciuridæ*, or squirrel-family.

1891 in *Century Dict.*

2. *Bot.* 'Curved and bushy, like a squirrel's tail' (B. D. Jackson *Gloss. Bot. Terms* 1900).

1895 in *Funk's Stand. Dict.*

sciuromorph (saɪ'jʊərəʊmɔːf), *a.* [ad. mod.L. *Sciuromorph-a* neut. pl., f. Gr. σκίουρος (see SCIURINE) + μορφή form.] A rodent of the superfamily *Sciuromorpha*, comprising the *Sciuridæ*, *Anomaluridæ*, etc.

1882 *Pop. Sci. Monthly* XX. 423 The sciuromorphs (squirrels and marmots). **1891** in *Century Dict.*

Hence **sciuro'morphic**, **sciuro'morphine** *adjs.*, of, pertaining to, or resembling the *Sciuromorpha*.

1891 *Century Dict.* s.v. *Sciuridæ*, A family of sciuromorphic simplicident rodent mammals. **1894** *Athenæum* 31 Mar. 415/3 Mr. F. G. Parsons read a paper on the myology of the hystricomorphine and sciuromorphine rodents.

sck-, an occasional ME. spelling for SC- or SK-.

scl-: ME. and Sc. variant of SL-.

sclaff (sklæf), *v.* *Golf.* [A use of Sc. *sclaff* 'to strike with the open hand or with anything having a flat surface', 'to walk in a clumsy way without properly lifting the feet, to shuffle along'. Prob. of onomatopœic origin; cf. *sclaff* sb., 'the noise made by a slight blow' or 'in shuffling the feet' (E.D.D.).] **a.** *intr.* (See quot. 1897.) **b.** *trans.* To scrape (the ground) behind the ball in striking; also, to hit (a ball) after having scraped the ground with the club. Hence **sclaffed** *ppl. a.*, '**sclaffing** *vbl. sb.*

1893 A. LANG in *Longm. Mag.* Apr. 651 That they might toe or heel the ball And sclaff along like me. **1896** W. PARK Jr. *Game of Golf* 269 In baffing a ball the stroke is played with the intention of lofting it high in the air, whereas a sclaffed ball is not necessarily lofted high. **1897** *Encycl. Sport* I. 473/1 (Golf) *Sclaff*, to scrape the surface of the ground with the sole of the club head before striking the ball. *Ibid.* 469/2 Sclaffing is also the result of striking the ground behind the ball. **1904** *Westm. Gaz.* 13 May 3/1 An uncertain proportion are shorter, in consequence of sclaffing the ground, than the players had intended.

sclaff (sklæf), *sb.* *Golf.* [See SCLAFF *v.*] A stroke in which the club scrapes the ground before hitting the ball. Hence '**sclaffy** *a.*

1893 H. HUTCHINSON *Golfing* 82 'Tops', and 'sclaffs', and misses. **1896** W. PARK *Game of Golf* 91 The sight of bare earth..gives the impression that contact between it and the club-head, which might happen with a sclaffy shot, would inevitably result in damage to the club. **1903** W. J. TRAVIS *Pract. Golf* 20 If..the head is allowed to move, the chances are that a sclaff or a top will result. **1948** DANTE & DIEGEL *Nine Bad Shots of Golf* x. 104 There is one other swing that will produce a sclaff. **1973** A. MACVICAR *Painted Doll Affair* vii. 84 My drives would be hooks and slices, my irons sclaffy travesties.

sclareol ('sklɛərɪɒl). *Chem.* [ad. F. *sclaréol* (Volmar & Jermstad 1928, in *Compt. Rend.* CLXXXVI. 519), f. *sauge sclarée* CLARY *sb.*²

(mod.L. *Salvia sclarea*): see -OL.] A colourless crystalline diterpenoid alcohol, $C_{20}H_{36}O_2$, found in the leaves of clary; also, one of the two constituent epimers of this.

1928 *Chem. Abstr.* XXII. 1828 The essence [of clary].. contains 42·2% of crystallizable sclareol. **1959** *Chem. & Industry* 1379/1 Since sclareol has been dehydrated to a mixture of manool and manoyl oxide, all three compounds must have the same absolute configuration at C(13). **1975** *Nature* 22 May 328/2 An epimeric mixture of the diterpenes sclareol and 13-epi-sclareol (sclareol)..has been shown to constitute 10% of the surface exudate on leaves of *Nicotiana glutinosa*. *Ibid.*, In replicate experiments, applications of.. sclareol consistently gave good control of rust on French bean, broad bean and wheat, reducing infection to less than 10% of control.

Sclave, Sclavic, Sclavonian: see SLAV, etc.

‖**sclera** ('sklɪərə). [mod.L. f. Gr. σκληρός hard.] The sclerotic coat of the eyeball.

1888 J. M. CLARKE in *Jrnl. Morphol.* II. 261 Immature eyes, in which the sclera has attained no excessive growth.

scleractinian (ˌsklɪəræk'tɪnɪən), *sb.* and *a.* [f. mod.L. order name *Scleractinia* (coined as *Scleractineae* by G. C. Bourne, in E. R. Lankester *Treat. Zool.* (1900) II. vi. 55), f. Gr. σκληρ-ός hard + ἀκτῖν-, ἀκτίς ray + IA^1, -AN: cf. ACTINIA, ACTINIAN.] **A.** *sb.* A coral of the order Scleractinia or Madreporaria, which is characterized by compact calcareous skeletons and includes all living true corals. **B.** *adj.* Of or pertaining to such a coral or the group as a whole.

1900 G. C. BOURNE in E. R. Lankester *Treat. Zool.* II. vi. 61 The anatomy of any Scleractinian resembles, in essential points, that of an Actinia. *Ibid.* 80 In *Heliopora* the skeleton is not spicular but lamellar, resembling in structure that of the Scleractinian corals. **1943** *Spec. Papers Geol. Soc. Amer.* No. 44. 1 This revision is the result of a study of the genotype species..of nearly every described scleractinian genus... The distribution of fossil and recent scleractinian faunas is broadly analyzed. *Ibid.* 90 The forerunners of most of the groups of the scleractinians are found in the Middle and Upper Triassic rocks. **1952** R. C. MOORE et al. *Invertebrate Fossils* iv. 143/2 The scleractinians differ from rugose corals chiefly in the mode of addition of new septa. **1973** *Nature* 27 July 201/1 The thirty-six scleractinian species of coral found on the actively growing, fringing reefs along the western coast of Barbados are complemented by varied populations of sponges, anemones,..and cucumbers.

† '**scleragogist**. *Obs.*$^{-1}$ [f. next + -IST.] One who practises 'scleragogy', a rigorous ascetic.

a **1641** BP. MOUNTAGU *Acts & Mon. Ch.* (1642) 403 Ascetæ and Scleragogists they were in most..rigid manner.

† '**scleragogy**. *Obs.* [ad. Gr. σκληραγωγία hardy training, f. σκληρ-ός hard, harsh + ἀγωγ-ή conducting, guiding.] Severe discipline or training; hard treatment of the body; mortification.

1621 BP. MOUNTAGU *Diatribæ* 379 Amongst Christians, that Scleragogie of the ancient Monks and Ascetæ was in feeding vpon those λάχανα. **1659** H. L'ESTRANGE *Alliance Div. Off.* 149 Godly sorrow or contrition, which the Scleragogy..was most like to create. **1680** *Counterplots* 15 We have heard from St. Jerome of the abstinence and Scleragogy of Montanus.

scleral ('sklɪərəl), *a.* [f. SCLERA + -AL^1.] Of or pertaining to the sclera or sclerotic.

1869 G. LAWSON *Dis. Eye* (1874) 139 The blade is now pushed on a little way in the scleral plane. **1888** J. M. CLARKE in *Jrnl. Morphol.* II. 266 The scleral portion of the visual surface is of the same structure as the test. **1890** *Amer. Jrnl. Sci.* Ser. III. XXXIX. 410 In the compound eye of Phacops are continuous patches of scleral integument between the ommatidia.

scleranth ('sklɪərænθ). *Bot.* [Shortened ad. mod.L. *Sclērantheæ*, f. *Sclēranthus* (see below), f. Gr. σκληρ-ός hard + ἄνθος flower.] A plant belonging to the N.O. *Scleranthеæ*, of which the typical genus is *Scleranthus* or Knot-grass.

1846 LINDLEY *Veget. Kingd.* 513 Those perigynous plants which are stationed with Scleranths in Ficoidals.

sclere (sklɪə(r)). *Zool.* [ad. Gr. σκληρόν, neut. of σκληρός hard.] A hard siliceous or calcareous body forming an element in the skeleton of a sponge.

1887 SOLLAS in *Encycl. Brit.* XXII. 413/1 The walls of *Ascetta* are strengthened by calcareous scleres, more especially designated as spicules.

sclereid ('sklɪəriːɪd). *Bot.* Also **sclerid**, **scler(e)ide**. [a. G. *sclereïd* (A. Tschirch 1885, in *Jahrb. f. Wissensch. Bot.* XVI. 308), irreg. f. Gr. σκληρ-ός hard: see -ID^2.] = *stone cell* s.v. STONE *sb.* 20.

1896 *Ann. Bot.* X. 11 The walls of the sclereids..acquire during the ripening an increasingly dark brown colour. **1900** B. D. JACKSON *Gloss. Bot. Terms* 233/2 *Sclereid*, a sclerotic or stone-cell, a strongly thickened or lignified cell; it is sometimes spelled *Sclerid*. **1914** M. DRUMMOND tr. *Haberlandt's Physiol. Plant Anat.* iv. 160 The coarse villi or shaggy hairs of the Melastomaceae often contain whole bundles of sclereides, which penetrate below into the mesophyll. **1919** F. O. BOWER *Bot. of Living Plant* ix. 145 Such stone-cells or sclereids, give a hard gritty texture to the parts where they occur, as in the bark or pith of various woody plants. **1934** *Jrnl. Arnold Arboretum* XV. 247 Clusters of sclerides or stone cells..are of not infrequent occurrence in the pith of the redwood. **1969** E. G. CUTTER *Plant Anat.* I. vi. 57 Sclerenchyma may be sub-divided into sclereids and fibres.

‖**sclerema** (sklɪə'riːmə). Also **scleremia**. [mod.L. form of F. *sclérème*, f. Gr. σκληρ-ός hard, on the supposed analogy of *œdème* ŒDEMA. The form in *-ia* is due to assimilation to other names of diseases.] (See quot. 1858.) Also ***sclerema neonatorum*** [gen. pl. of mod.L. *neonātus* (cf. NEONATE)].

1858 MAYNE *Expos. Lex.*, *Sclerema*, *Scleremia*, term for the hardening of the cellular tissue of new-born infants. **1879** KHORY *Digest Med.* 60 The skin has a peculiar marble-like feel in sclerema and in morphœa. **1889** J. E. GRAHAM in J. M. Keating *Cycl. Diseases Children* II. I. 90 Sclerema neonatorum..is distinguished by a peculiar, œdematous, corpse-like hardening of the skin. **1899** *Allbutt's Syst. Med.* VIII. 675 The genus 'scleremia', in which he included also the œdematous sclerema of infants. **1962** *Lancet* 27 Jan. 226/1 Pneumonia, hæmorrhagic disease of the new-born, or sclerama neonatorum may be diagnosed. **1974** PASSMORE & ROBSON *Compan. Med. Stud.* III. xlv. 31/1 The baby's rectal temperature..falls... He becomes less active, less hungry and less vocal. The skin reddens and grows cold and the subcutaneous tissue slowly becomes hard... This state is known as sclerema.

‖**sclerenchyma** (sklɪə'rɛŋkɪmə). Also anglicized **scle'renchym**. [mod.L., f. Gr. σκληρ-ός hard + ἔγχυμα an infusion, after *parenchyma*.]

1. *Zool.* The hard substance of the calcareous skeleton of sclerodermic corals.

1861 J. R. GREENE *Cœlent.* 161 The 'sclerenchyma' or coral tissue.

2. *Bot.* (See quot. 1900.)

1875 BENNETT & DYER tr. *Sach's Bot.* 106 The sclerenchyma in the carpel of stone-fruits (the tissue of the stone in Prunus, Cocos, &c.) forms closed massive layers. **1881** *Encycl. Brit.* XII. 15/2 De Bary includes under the name of sclerenchyma all the hard thickened cells of plants, whether long or short, which have become greatly thickened, and whose cavity is nearly if not quite obliterated. **1883** HUXLEY *Pract. Biol.* 57 The dark-brown bands..consist of cells which are so much elongated as almost to deserve the name of fibres and constitute what is termed sclerenchyma. **1900** B. D. JACKSON *Gloss. Bot. Terms*, *Sclerenchyma*, (1) formerly applied to stone-cells, sclereids; (2) afterwards proposed for bast or liber cells, which are immensely thickened, with their protoplasm lost.

attrib. **1881** *Encycl. Brit.* XII. 16/1 The wall of the sclerenchym fibre often exhibits peculiar split-like pitted markings. **1882** BOWER in *Q. Jrnl. Microsc. Sci.* XXII. 287 Long unbranched sclerenchyma fibres with smooth walls.

sclerenchymatous (sklɪərɛŋ'kɪmətəs), *a.* [f. mod.L. *sclērenchymat-*, SCLERENCHYMA + -OUS.] Consisting of, or containing sclerenchyma.

1861 J. R. GREENE *Cœlent.* 215 The numerous laminæ of a sclerenchymatous deposit. **1881** BOWER in *Q. Jrnl. Microsc. Sci.* XXI. 20 Scattered irregularly through the cortical tissue..are sclerenchymatous cells.

‖**scleriasis** (sklɪə'raɪəsɪs). *Path.* [mod.L., f. Gr. σκληρ-ός hard, after *elephantiasis*.] A hard tumour or induration; a scirrhus.

1684 tr. *Blancard's Phys. Dict.*, *Scleriasis*, is a Hardness of any part. **1849** in CRAIG. **1869** *Lancet* 18 Dec. 842/2 Dr. Fagge brought to the Society a living specimen of Scleriasis or Scleroderma. **1872** J. L. MILTON *Dis. Skin* 333 Diffused scleroderma (*scleriasis*).

sclerid, variant of SCLEREID.

sclerite (sk'lɪəraɪt). *Zool.* [f. Gr. σκληρ-ός hard + -ITE.] In the anatomy of invertebrates, each of the definite component portions into which the hard portion of the substance of certain animals is divided.

1861 J. R. GREENE *Cœlent.* 161 Five kinds of these spicules, or 'sclerites'. **1877** HUXLEY *Anat. Inv. Anim.* vii. 410 [In the cockroach.] On the under side of the lingua are two broader sclerites, which also unite and form an arch. **1888** ROLLESTON & JACKSON *Anim. Life* 141 *note*, In the neck there are certain chitinous pieces, or cervical sclerites. **1894** *Athenæum* 10 Feb. 184/1 He [M. Laurie] considered the first two ventral sclerites of the abdomen to be appendages and not sternites.

Hence **scle'ritic** *a.*, pertaining to sclerites; of the nature of a sclerite.

scleritis (sklɪə'raɪtɪs). [f. SCLERA + -ITIS.] Inflammation of the sclera, sclerotitis.

1861 BUMSTEAD *Ven. Dis.* (1879) 703 Affections..due to parenchymatous scleritis are rarer still.

sclero- ('sklɪərəʊ), occurring in scientific terms.

1. As combining form of Gr. σκληρό-ς hard. ˌ**sclerobla'stema** *Anat.* [BLASTEMA], the embryonic tissue which gives rise to bone. ˌ**sclero'brachiate** *a.* [L. *brāchium* arm], the distinctive epithet of those brachiopods in which the arms are supported by a hard plate. ˌ**sclero'dactyle** *a. Path.* [Gr. δάκτυλος finger], suffering from ˌ**sclero'dactyly** [mod.L. *sclerodac'tylia*], a form of sclerodermia affecting the fingers and toes. **sclerœ'dema** (also **scleredema**) *Path.* (see quot. 1976). **sclero'protein** *Biochem.*, any insoluble structural protein. ˌ**sclero'skeletal** *a.*, pertaining to or of the nature of the ˌ**sclero-'skeleton**, the hardened or ossified fibrous and tendinous tissues which enclose organs. **sclero'therapy**, the treatment of varicosities by the injection of a substance which induces clotting.

1934 WEBSTER, *Scleroblastema. **1968** PASSMORE & ROBSON *Compan. Med. Stud.* I. xviii. 11/2 Each vertebra is laid down as a densely cellular mesenchymal precursor, the scleroblastema; this transforms into a cartilage model which is subsequently replaced by bone by the process of endochondral ossification. **1854** A. ADAMS, etc. *Man. Nat. Hist.* 163 *Sclerobrachiate-Brachiopods (*Sclerobrachiata*). **1899** *Allbutt's Syst. Med.* VIII. 676 The fingers [may become] 'clawed' (*sclerodactyle, acroscleroderma). **1897** *Ibid.* II. 74 Well-advanced cases [of leprosy] have frequently been confounded with..*sclerodactyly [etc.]. **1932** *Jrnl. Amer. Med. Assoc.* 3 Sept. 822/1 *Scleredema adultorum is characterized by progressive induration and swelling of the deeper portions of the skin and subcutaneous tissues. *Ibid.* 825/1 Scleredema always involutes spontaneously without subsequent atrophy of the affected tissues. **1946** *New England Jrnl. Med.* 15 Aug. 209/1 The appearance of a patient with scleredema is so striking as to suggest the diagnosis immediately. **1976** *Proc. R. Soc. Med.* LXIX. 844/2 Sclerœdema is characterized by sudden onset of diffuse symmetrical hardening of the skin of the face, neck and upper arms. **1907** HALLIBURTON & HOPKINS in *Jrnl. Physiol.* XXXV. p. xix, *Sclero-proteins. This new word takes the place of the word albuminoid... It includes such substances as gelatin and keratin; the prefix indicates the skeletal origin and often insoluble nature of its members. **1958** *Immunology* I. 49 Some of the scleroproteins comprising the scale plate are antigenic, but are only slowly digested by homologous recipients. **1970** R. M. BLACK *Elements Palaeont.* ii. 8 The matrix of bone consists mainly of collagen (a fibrous scleroprotein) hardened by mineral salts. **1977** A. HALLAM *Planet Earth* 241 More usually, however, only the most resistant and stable organic materials can survive long after death, as with the lignified tissues of fossil land plants and the scleroprotein skeleton of the extinct fossil graptolites. **1884** COUES *Key N. Amer. Birds* (ed. 2) 134 Certain bones developed apart from the systematic endo-skeleton, in fibrous tissue, are called *scleroskeletal. **1854** OWEN in *Circ. Sci., Org. Nat.* I. 163 Those [bones] developed in tendons, ligaments, and aponeuroses, [form] the '*sclero-skeleton'. **1944** *Amer. Jrnl. Surg.* LXVI. 363 The advantages of *sclerotherapy are low morbidity, almost no mortality and no necessity for hospitalization... The disadvantage is the very high incidence of recurrence. **1977** *Lancet* 25 June 1343/1 F. Bezzouni of Russia has an approach similar to that of most surgeons in Britain—injection sclerotherapy for small, below-knee varices and high ligation and stripping for gross main-stem incompetence.

2. As combining form of SCLERA (chiefly written with hyphen). ˌ**sclero-'corneal** *a.*, pertaining to the sclerotic coat and the cornea. ˌ**sclero-i'ritis**, inflammation of the sclerotic coat and the iris.

1876 *Clin. Soc. Trans.* IX. 3 The plan I now adopt is to make a very small incision in the sclero-corneal junction.

3. Used (after SCLEROTIUM, SCLEROTIC *a.*^{2}) to form the names of a number of chemical substances obtained from ergot, e.g. **scle'rerythrin**, a red colouring matter; **sclero'mucin**, a gummy nitrogenous substance.

1876 *Pharm. Jrnl.* 17 June 1001/1 Scleromucin. *Ibid.* 1001/2 Sclererythrin. Scleroiodin. *Ibid.* 1002/1 Scleroxanthin. Sclerokrystallin. **1878** F. H. BUTLER in *Encycl. Brit.* VIII. 521 [Ergot contains] minute quantities of sclererythrin, scleroiodin, with sclerokrystallin, scleroxanthin, and other substances.

sclerobase ('sklɪərəʊbeɪs). *Zool.* Also in mod.L. form **scle'robasis**. [f. Gr. σκληρό-ς hard + βάσις BASE *sb.*, BASIS.] The axis or stem of a compound actinozoan when forming a horny or calcareous skeleton. Hence **sclerobasic** *a.*, pertaining to or consisting of a sclerobase; also as the epithet of those corals (in mod.L. *Sclerobasica*) which have a sclerobase.

1861 J. R. GREENE *Cœlent.* 153 The 'sclerobasic' corallum, a true tegumentary excretion, formed by the conversion of successive growths from the outer surface of the ecderon. *Ibid.* 154 Section of a sclerobasis shows it to be, in some cases, solid or nearly so. *Ibid.* 156, Fig. 28 Θ, epitheca; I, sclerobase. **1870** H. A. NICHOLSON *Man. Zool.* I. xiii. 99 There may be no corallum, or rarely a 'sclerobasic' one. **1877** HUXLEY *Anat. Inv. Anim.* iii. 161 It is in these Octocoralla that the form of skeleton which is termed a sclerobase..occurs. **1879** STORMONTH *Man. Sci. Terms* s.v. *Sclerobasic*, Forming a solid axis invested by the soft parts of the animal—called the sclerobase.

scleroblast ('sklɪərəʊblæst). [f. Gr. σκληρό-ς hard + -BLAST.]

1. *Bot.* A stone-cell or sclereid.

1882 VINES tr. *Sachs' Bot.* 125 Of very common occurrence are, moreover, groups or layers of scleroblasts (especially in the cortex of many woody plants and the juicy flesh of pears). **1884** MASTERS *Henfrey's Bot.* (ed. 4) 461 The term..scleroblast or stone-cell.

2. *Zool.* A spicule-forming cell in sponges.

1887 SOLLAS in *Encycl. Brit.* XXII. 417/2 (*Sponge*) The sigmaspire is formed as a superficial spiral thickening in the wall of a spicule cell or scleroblast. **1909** J. W. JENKINSON *Experim. Embryol.* 3 In some Sponges the scleroblasts begin to secrete spicules in the larval period.

sclerocele ('sklɪərəʊsiːl). *Path.* ? *Obs.* [f. Gr. σκληρό-ς hard + κήλη tumour.] A hard tumour.

1811 RAMSDEN (*title*), On Sclerocele, Hydrocele [etc.].

scleroclase ('sklɪərəʊkleɪs). *Min.* [f. Gr. σκληρό-ς hard + κλάσις fracture.] (See quot. 1896.)

1868 DANA *Syst. Min.* (ed. 5) 88 As the name Scleroclase is inapplicable, and the mineral was first announced by Sartorius v. Waltershausen, the species may be appropriately called Sartorite. **1896** CHESTER *Dict. Min.* 244 *Scleroclase*, a syn. of sartorite. Sometimes used as a syn. of dufrenoysite.

scleroderm ('sklɪərəʊdɜːm), *sb.* and *a.* [ad. mod.L. *sclērodermus*, a. Gr. σκληρόδερμος, f. σκληρός hard + δέρμα skin.] **A.** *sb.*

1. a. A fish of the group *Sclerodermi*, which have the skin covered with hard scales. **b.** A polyp of the division *Sclerodermata*.

1840–5 OWEN *Odontogr.* I. 82 Sclerodermes. **1842** BRANDE *Dict. Sci.*, etc., *Scleroderms*, a name given by Cuvier to his family of Plectognathic fishes, comprehending those which have the skin covered with hard scales. **1896** H. WOODWARD *Guide Fossil Rept. & Fish Brit. Mus.* 121 Fossil Scleroderms, in an excellent state of preservation, are found in the Eocene Slates of Glaris.

2. 'The hard or stony external skeleton of sclerodermatous zoantharians, or corals in an ordinary sense; corallum; coral' (*Cent. Dict.* 1891).

B. *adj.* 'Of or pertaining to the *Sclerodermi*; sclerodermous' (*Cent. Dict.* 1891).

‖**scleroderma** (sklɪərəʊ'dɜːmə). *Path.* [mod.L., formed as prec.] A chronic hardened condition of the skin, resulting from hypertrophy of connective tissue.

1866 A. FLINT *Princ. Med.* (1880) 763 The affection called scleroderma or sclerema, also sclerodermia and scleremia, may be here noticed. **1876** DUHRING *Dis. Skin* 69 Hypertrophy of the connective tissue is noted in scleroderma.

sclerodermatous (sklɪərəʊ'dɜːmətəs), *a.* [f. Gr. σκληρό-ς hard + δερματ-, δέρμα skin + -OUS.] Having a hard skin.

1. *Zool.* Belonging to the division *Sclerodermata* of zoantharian polyps.

In recent Dicts.

2. *Path.* Pertaining to scleroderma.

1899 *Allbutt's Syst. Med.* VIII. 494 Unusual forms of wheals..may simulate..gummata or sclerodermatous patches.

‖**sclerodermia** (sklɪərəʊ'dɜːmɪə). *Path.* [mod.L., f. SCLERODERMA: see -IA[1].] = SCLERODERMA.

1866 [see SCLERODERMA]. **1899** *Allbutt's Syst. Med.* VIII. 675 In sclerodermia the most marked character is a peculiar hard stiffening and immobility of the skin.

sclerodermic (sklɪərəʊ'dɜːmɪk), *a.* [f. SCLERODERM + -IC.]

1. *Zool.* **a.** = SCLERODERMATOUS *a.* 1.

1861 J. R. GREENE *Cœlent.* 187 Basal gemmation, among sclerodermic Corals, affords very different products. **1875** BLAKE *Zool.* 365 The sclerodermic corallum differs altogether from the corallum. **1879** STORMONTH *Man. Sci. Terms, Sclerodermic*, applied to the corallum deposited within the tissues of certain Actinozoa.

b. Of or pertaining to the order *Sclerodermi* of fishes.

2. *Path.* = SCLERODERMATOUS 2.

1899 *Allbutt's Syst. Med.* VIII. 677 Parts at some distance from the sclerodermic integument.

sclerodermite (sklɪərəʊ'dɜːmaɪt). [f. SCLERODERM + -ITE.] One of the hard bodies of which the skeleton of Crustacea is composed; also, one of the hard skeletal parts in certain Actinozoans.

1877 HUXLEY *Anat. Inv. Anim.* vi. 308 The sides only being strengthened by calcareous plates extending inwards from the dorsal hard skeletal element, or sclerodermite. **1884** SEDGWICK, etc. tr. *Claus' Text-bk. Zool.* I. 231 In all cases definite calcareous bodies, the sclerodermites, form the foundation of the skeleton.

sclerogen ('sklɪərəʊdʒɛn). *Bot.* [f. Gr. σκληρό-ς hard + -GEN.] The hard lignified matter on the sides of some cells, which gives hardness to wood, fruit-stones, etc.

1835 LINDLEY *Introd. Bot.* (1839) 4 Turpin has remarked that this thickening of the membranous sides of cells by means of a hard sedimentary matter, called by him *sclerogen*, is what causes the grittiness of the pear. **1861** BENTLEY *Man. Bot.* 11 It is these deposits which give hardness and firmness to the wood of plants and to the stones of fruits, and hence the name of Sclerogen..has been given to them.

sclerogenic (sklɪərəʊ'dʒɛnɪk), *a.* *Phys.* and *Path.* [f. Gr. σκληρό-ς hard + -GEN + -IC.] Tending to produce hardening (of animal tissues).

1892 *Brit. Med. Jrnl.* 17 Sept. 653/1 In this way the creasote treatment of tuberculosis was combined with the 'sclerogenic' method introduced by M. Lannelongue. **1905** H. D. ROLLESTON *Dis. Liver* 184 It [i.e. alcohol] gives rise to cirrhosis in a secondary manner, either by leading to the production of sclerogenic poisons [etc.].

sclerogenoid (sklɪə'rɒdʒɪnɔɪd), *a.* and *sb.* *Zool.* [f. mod.L. *Sclērogen-idæ* (f. Gr. σκληρός hard + γέν-υς cheek) + -OID.] **a.** *adj.* Belonging to the family *Sclerogenidæ* or mail-cheeked fishes. **b.** *sb.* A fish of this family.

1861 T. GILL *Catal. Fishes Eastern N. Amer.* 5 The Cottoids and other Sclerogenoids..are now placed after the Scombroid and before the Blennoid group.

sclerogenous (sklɪə'rɒdʒɪnəs), *a.*[1] [f. Gr. σκληρό-ς hard + -GEN + -OUS.]

1. = SCLEROGENIC.

1847–9 *Todd's Cycl. Anat.* IV. 456/1 The filling up of their cavities [i.e. those of the cells] with..sclerogenous secretions. **1878** BELL tr. *Gegenbaur's Comp. Anat.* 28 Apparently indifferent cells, which secrete a sclerogenous substance. **1891** *Pall Mall Gaz.* 8 July 6/2 Dr. Lannelongue calls his method the sclerogenous method—that is to say, a method destined to render the flesh and fibres attacked capable of being cicatrized.

2. Consisting of sclerogen.

1856 W. L. LINDSAY *Brit. Lichens* 40 The thick sclerogenous cell-wall of the seed of the..Ivory Palm.

sclerogenous (sklɪə'rɒdʒɪnəs), *a.*[2] *Zool.* [Formed as SCLEROGENOID + -OUS.] = SCLEROGENOID.

In some recent Dicts.

scleroid (sk'lɪərɔɪd), *a.* [f. Gr. σκληρό-ς hard + -OID.] **a.** *Bot.* 'Having a hard texture, as the shells of nuts'. **b.** *Zool.* 'Hard, as a sclere or sclerite; scleritic; sclerous' (*Cent. Dict.* 1891).

1856 in HENSLOW *Dict. Bot. Terms* 166.

‖**scleroma** (sklɪə'rəʊmə). *Path.* Also anglicized sclerome. [mod.L., a. Gr. σκλήρωμα, f. σκληροῦν to harden, f. σκληρό-ς hard: see -OMA.] = SCLERIASIS 1.

[**1684** tr. *Blancard's Phys. Dict., Scleroma*, the same (as *Scleriasis*). **1823** CRABB *Technol. Dict., Scleroma (Med.)* or *scleromis*,..a hard tumour, or induration.] **1857** GOODSIR in *Edinb. New Philos. Jrnl.* V. 122 For the entire frame-work of an Entomasome..I employ the term Sclerome. *Ibid.* 123 The source and mode of origin of the Sclerome in the Vertebrate Embryo. **1858** MAYNE *Expos. Lex., Scleroma*,.. a sclerome. **1874** BUCKNILL & TUKE *Man. Psych. Med. Insanity* 530 The term scleroma or scleriasis has indeed very properly been substituted for that of cirrhosis, which refers to the colour of the diseased liver, and is obviously inappropriate to designate an analogous change in the brain or spinal cord. **1899** *Allbutt's Syst. Med.* VIII. 889 Hence the name rhinoscleroma is not strictly correct, and some authors, as Paultof, speak of scleroma simply.

sclerometer (sklɪə'rɒmɪtə(r)). [f. Gr. σκληρό-ς hard + -METER. Cf. F. *scléromètre*.] An instrument for measuring the hardness of crystals.

1879 in WEBSTER, Suppl. **1886** JUDD in *Mineral. Mag.* Dec. 85 A means of expressing the cohesive force in different parts of a crystal mass as determined by the sclerometer. **1895** STORY-MASKELYNE *Crystallogr.* i. §9 The hardness of crystals in different directions has been estimated by means of an instrument termed a sclerometer.

scleromyxœdema (ˌsklɪərəʊmɪksiː'diːmə). *Path.* Also -myxedema. [ad. G. *skleromyxödem* (H. H. Gottron 1954, in *Arch. f. Dermatol. u. Syphilis* CXCIX. 71): see SCLERO- and *myxœdema* s.v. MYXO-.] A disease characterized by the extensive proliferation of fibroblasts and deposition of mucopolysaccharides in the skin, causing distortions of the features and lichenous eruptions.

1964 *Arch. Dermatol.* LXXXIX. 446/1 Lichen myxedematosus, also known as..scleromyxedema, is a well-known clinical entity. **1968** R. J. CAIRNS in A. Rook et al. *Textbk. Dermatol.* II. lv. 1621/2 A variant of lichen myxoedematosus is scleromyxoedema..—the Arndt-Gottron syndrome—in which diffuse thickening of the skin underlies the papules... The features may be distorted by the exaggeration of the facial ridges and flexion of the fingers may be limited. **1977** *Lancet* 4 June 1208/2 Ten years previously this patient has been treated for scleromyxœdema..with melphalan.

‖**sclerophthalmia** (sklɪərɒf'θælmɪə). ? *Obs.* Also 8 anglicized sclerophthalmy. [mod.L., ad. late Gr. σκληροφθαλμία, f. Gr. σκληρό-ς hard + ὀφθαλμός eye.] (See quots.)

[**1693** tr. *Blancard's Phys. Dict.* (ed. 2), *Scleropthalmia*, a hard Blearedness of the Eyes accompanied with Pain, a slow Motion of the Eyes, with redness and dryness of 'em.] **1704** J. HARRIS *Lex. Techn.* I. *Scleropthalmy* [with definition from Blancard]. **1728** CHAMBERS *Cycl., Sclerophthalmia*, a kind of Ophthalmia wherein the Eye is dry, hard, red, and painful.

sclerophyll ('sklɪərəʊfɪl), *sb.* and *a.* *Bot.* [ad. G. *sklerophyll* (A. F. W. Schimper *Pflanzengeographie* (1898) v. 538: see next word.]

A. *sb.* A sclerophyllous plant.

1911 J. M. COULTER et al. *Textbk. Bot.* II. iii. 710 In the inclement period they [*sc.* the leaves of deciduous trees] are as well protected as are the cacti and better protected than are the sclerophylls. **1923** *Jrnl. Ecol.* XI. 287 Northwards.. the forest becomes more important, but is soon supplanted by conifer forest.. into which many of the sclerophylls, both shrubs and trees, pass as subordinate members. **1939** *Nature* 11 Mar. 412/2 The 'rhenosterbush'..represents the most arid kind of sclerophyll. **1975** *Sci. Amer.* Jan. 133/1 The text itself considers one by one the 10 vegetational zones, from the evergreen tropical forests to the regions of winter-rain sclerophylls.

B. *adj.* = SCLEROPHYLLOUS *a.*

1926 TANSLEY & CHIPP *Aims & Methods in Study of Vegetation* vi. 99 Where the rain mainly falls in the late autumn and winter, but is sufficient in quantity, and there is a hot dry summer, the vegetation is of the evergreen sclerophyll type—trees or shrubs with rather small leathery leaves. *Ibid.* 100 Sclerophyll regions always abut on desert regions. **1970** GAY & CALABY in Krishna & Weesner *Biol. Termites* II. ix. 413 Symmetrical dome mounds..are found only occasionally in the sclerophyll woodland and mallee. **1978** *Nature* 9 Mar. 160/1 A general and sustained increase in sclerophyll vegetation at the expense of drier rain forest types, probably a result of aboriginal man's activities, can explain some..of the evolutionary changes.

So **scle'rophylly**, the fact of being sclerophyllous.

1903 W. R. FISHER tr. *Schimper's Plant-Geogr.* i. 9 With increasing physiological dryness, the leaves become smaller in surface but proportionally thicker, more leathery (sclerophylly). **1909** E. WARMING *Œcol. Plants* xlvi. 194 Sclerophylly is frequent and is due to thickness of the epidermal wall, as in Adromeda polifolia. **1973** J. WIESER tr. *Walter's Vegetation of Earth* IV. iii. 121 The ecological significance of sclerophylly is..to be seen in the ability of sclerophyllous species to conduct active gaseous exchange.. in the presence of an adequate water supply, but to cut it down radically by shutting the stomata when water is scarce.

sclerophyllous (sklɪə'rɒfɪləs), *a.* *Bot.* [f. Gr. σκληρός hard + φύλλ-ον leaf + -OUS.] Pertaining to or designating woody evergreen plants having leaves that are hard and tough, and usu. small and thick, so reducing the rate of loss of water; characterized by such plants.

1903 W. R. FISHER tr. *Schimper's Plant-Geogr.* v. 507 The mild temperate districts with winter rain and prolonged summer drought are the home of evergreen xerophilous woody plants, which, owing to the stiffness of their thick, leathery leaves, may be termed sclerophyllous woody plants. *Ibid.* 516 The best known districts inhabited by sclerophyllous woods are the coasts of the Mediterranean Sea. **1926** TANSLEY & CHIPP *Aims & Methods & Study of Vegetation* ii. 26 The dominance of [s]clerophyllous trees or shrubs (rather small hard evergreen leaves) indicates a moderate rainfall mainly concentrated in the winter half of the year, which is mild, and a hot dry summer. **1961** *Times* 12 Apr. 3/2 (Advt.), The Department is noted for its research in..plant ecology (with emphasis on sclerophyllous and arid plants). **1973** J. WIESER tr. *Walter's Vegetation of Earth* IV. iii. 127 The roots of sclerophyllous species reach far down into the ground because the upper soil layers are usually completely dried out in summer.

sclerosant (sklɪə'rəʊzənt, sklər-), *sb.* and *a.* *Med.* [f. SCLEROS(IS + -ANT[1].] **A.** *sb.* A sclerosant agent. **B.** *adj.* Producing sclerosis or hardening of tissue.

1956 *New Gould Med. Dict.* (ed. 2) 1076/1 *Sclerosant*, a chemical irritant producing an inflammatory reaction and subsequent fibrosis. **1962** *Lancet* 8 Dec. 1221/2 McEvedy seems to have had good results after the injection of a *sclerosant* solution such as ethanolamine. **1977** *Brit. Med. Jrnl.* 12 Feb. 434/2 When ligamentous pain and tenderness seem to dominate, 'sclerosant' mixtures of phenol, dextrose, and glycerine may be injected into the tender area. **1979** *Ibid.* 22 Sept. 704/2 We used two sclerosants—namely, phenol..and tetradecyl sulphate.

Scleroscope ('sklɪərəskəʊp). Also scleroscope. [f. SCLERO- + -SCOPE.] An instrument for measuring the hardness of a material, this being indicated by the height of rebound of a small diamond-tipped hammer dropped from a standard height on to the material. Also *attrib.* Hence **sclero'scopic** *a.*

Scleroscope is a proprietary term in the U.S.

1907 A. F. SHORE in *Amer. Machinist* 14 Nov. 748/1 The instrument was named scleroscope, from the Greek words *sclerotus*, meaning hardness, and *scope*, because it is direct reading. **1908** [see SHORE *sb.*[5]]. **1915** [see BRINELL]. **1921** *Glasgow Herald* 23 Sept. 9 The use of the scleroscope on light specimens of metals. **1936** P. F. FOSTER *Mech. Testing of Metals & Alloys* viii. 143 A dynamic hardness test is provided by the Shore scleroscope in which a small pointed tup weighing about 0·0052 lb. is allowed to fall freely from a height of 10 in. on to the test piece. **1950** *Engineering* 31 Mar. 371/2 Scleroscopic hardness values are approximately 85 and 65. **1961** *Official Gaz.* (U.S. Patent Office) 29 Aug. TM 149/1 The Shore Instrument & Mfg. Company, Inc.,.. N.Y...*Scleroscope*... For instruments used to test hardness of metals and other substances. **1977** R. B. ROSS *Handbk. Metal Treatments & Testing* 166 The Scleroscope test is of limited use and accuracy but, because of its extreme portability, has certain advantages over other more conventional tests.

sclerose (sklɪə'rəʊs), *v.* [Back-formation from next.] *trans.* To affect with sclerosis; to harden.

1899 *Allbutt's Syst. Med.* VII. 599 The long-continued deep seated inflammation has sclerosed the bone.

sclerosed (sklɪə'rəʊst), *ppl. a.* [f. SCLEROS-IS + -ED[1].] **a.** *Path.* Affected with sclerosis; rendered abnormally hard.

1878 A. McL. HAMILTON *Nerv. Dis.* 100 Separated from the brain-tissue in the vicinity by a sclerosed mass. **1896** *Allbutt's Syst. Med.* I. 382 No power can renew sclerosed nerve-cells. **1898** J. HUTCHINSON in *Arch. Surg.* IX. 292, I had removed by superficial excision some sclerosed patches.

b. *Bot.* Hardened; lignified.

1881 SHATTOCK in *Linn. Soc. Jrnl.* XIX. 6 In the case which I have described the sclerosed tissue is formed of the indifferent cells of the pith. **1887** GARNSEY tr. *De Bary's Fungi* 499 *Sclerosed*, exhibiting sclerosis.

sclerosic (sklɪə'rəʊsɪk), *a. Path.* [f. SCLEROS-IS + -IC.] = SCLEROTIC *a.* 3.

1889 W. B. LEWIS *Mental Dis.* 464 We regard these multiple lesions not as a primary sclerosic change, but [etc.].

sclerosing (sklɪə'rəʊsɪŋ), *ppl. a.* [f. SCLEROSE *v.* + -ING².] Becoming affected with sclerosis.

1894 *Educator* (Philad.) Sept. 118 The most common lesions which appear to have caused loss of hearing are to be classified under the term sclerosing processes of the middle ear. **1897** *Allbutt's Syst. Med.* IV. 425 Perinephritis, either of the sclerosing or suppurative variety.

sclerosis (sklɪə'rəʊsɪs). Also 4–7 sclirosis. [med.L. (written *sclirosis* in *Alphita*, 15th c.), a. Gr. σκλήρωσις, f. σκληροῦν to harden, f. σκληρός hard: see -OSIS.]

1. *Path.* †**a.** A hard external tumour. *Obs.* **b.** A morbid hardening of any tissue or structure.

1398 TREVISA *Barth. De. P.R.* VII. lix. (1495) 274 Of melancolia comyth a postume, and yf the matere is all wythout the postume highte Sclirosis. *c***1400** *Lanfranc's Cirurg.* 222 Ofte þer comeþ þerof sclirosis or a festre. **1543** TRAHERON *Vigo's Chirurg.* 7 And there is a pannicle compouned in yᵉ eye called sclirosis. *Ibid.*, Table, Sclerosis. **1846** G. E. DAY tr. *Simon's Anim. Chem.* II. 411 *Sclerosis.* Ragsky has analysed bone in several cases of this affection. **1861** BUMSTEAD *Ven. Dis.* (1879) 593 Sclerosis of the tongue is most frequent about the fifth year of syphilis. **1879** KHORY *Digest Med.* 111 This inflammation occurs in the liver or the kidneys where it is known as cirrhosis, when in the brain or cord, it is called sclerosis. **1899** *Allbutt's Syst. Med.* VIII. 642 There was diffuse sclerosis [of the spinal cord].

2. *Bot.* (See quot. 1887.)

1884 BOWER & SCOTT *De Bary's Phaner.* 28 When..a hardening of the wall thus occurs, this process will for the future be indicated by the term *Sclerosis.* **1887** GARNSEY & BALFOUR tr. *De Bary's Fungi* 499 *Sclerosis*, induration of a tissue or a cell-wall either by thickening of the membranes or by their lignification.

3. *fig.* Rigidity, excessive resistance to change.

1954 B. & R. NORTH tr. *M. Duverger's Pol. Parties* I. ii. 89 Such a drying-up of new recruits is the symptom of a serious sclerosis. **1958** *Times* 11 Aug. 2/5 All the world knows that he was faced with the problem of revitalizing a good tradition that was beginning to suffer from sclerosis. **1966** S. H. BEAVER tr. *J. Beaujeu-Garnier's Geogr. Population* x. 228 Research work..has shown the parallelism that exists between the sclerosis of social structures and the high proportion of marriages between first cousins. **1977** *N.Y. Rev. Bks.* 14 July 35/2 Popovic saw his harassment as a symptom of the ideological sclerosis which is increasing with Tito's age.

sclerotal (sklɪə'rəʊtəl). *Anat.* [f. SCLEROT-IS + -AL¹.] Any of the component plates of the bony ring which protects the sclerotic coat of the eyeball in certain birds and reptiles.

1854 OWEN in *Orr's Circ. Sci., Org. Nat.* I. 179 An ossified part of the eye-capsule, commonly in two pieces, 'sclerotals'. **1884** COUES *Key N. Amer. Birds* (ed. 2) 182 It is reinforced by a circlet of bones, the sclerotals.

sclerotic (sklɪə'rɒtɪk), *a.*¹ and *sb.* In 7 sclero-, sclirotyke, -tike. [a. med. and mod.L. *sclērōticus* (med.L. in fem. form SCLEROTICA), a. late Gr. *σκληρωτικός having the property of hardening, pertaining to sclerosis or hardening, f. σκληροῦν: see SCLEROMA.] **A.** *adj.*

1. *Anat.* In *sclerotic coat, membrane, tunic* = B. 1. Cf. SCLEROTICA.

1543 TRAHERON *Vigo's Chirurg.* Interpr., Sclirotike. The fyrst skynne of the eye, which conteyneth vnder hym all the other skinnes, & coueretb, in yᵉ hinder the glassye, and crystalline humour, is called in Greke Scleros, and barbarouslye sclirotike, that is to saye, harde. **1691** RAY *Creation* II. (1692) 26 The ciliary processes, or rather the ligaments, observed in the inside of the Sclerotick Tunicles of the Eye,..do serve instead of a Muscle. **1741** A. MONRO *Anat. of Nerves* (ed. 3) 44 After piercing the sclerotick Coat. **1842** BRANDE *Dict. Sci.*, etc. s.v. *Eye*, The internal parts of the eye are, the sclerotic membrane, which is the hard outer case of the globe [etc.]. **1882** NEWTON in *Encycl. Brit.* XIV. 244/1 The irides are of a light orange, and the sclerotic tunics,—equivalent to the 'white of the eye' in most animals, ..are in this [the Lämmergeyer] very conspicuous.

b. Of or pertaining to, or connected with the sclerotic coat of the eye.

sclerotic bone, plate = SCLEROTAL; *sclerotic ring*, the ring formed by the sclerotic bones of the eyeball.

1822–29 [see SCLEROTITIS]. **1840** MACGILLIVRAY *Brit. Birds* III. 150 The Sclerotic Bones..are in this eye fifteen in number. **1851** MANTELL *Petrifactions* iii. §3. 160 The bony sclerotic plates of the organs of vision. **1883–4** *Medical Ann.* 13/1 Less likely to be followed by complications than sclerotic..incisions. **1896** H. WOODWARD *Guide Fossil Rept. Brit. Mus.* 8 A genus of Crocodiles remarkable for the presence of a sclerotic ring in the eye and the absence of bony scutes.

†**c.** See quot. (? A misapprehension.)

1681 tr. *Willis' Rem. Med. Wks.* Vocab., *Sclerotick*, that is troubled with some tumor in the third panicle of the eye, called the cornea membrana, or somewhere thereabouts.

2. Of medicines: Adapted to harden the tissues.

1696 PHILLIPS (ed. 5), *Sclerotic* Medicines, such as unite the parts more firmly amongst themselves. **1858** MAYNE *Expos. Lex.*, *Sclerotic*, applied to drying medicines.

3. *Path.* Of or pertaining to sclerosis; affected with sclerosis.

1543 TRAHERON *Vigo's Chirurg.* 78 Apostemes sclerotyke, of the fyngers and toes. *Ibid.*, Table, Sclirotyke aposteme. **1897** *Allbutt's Syst. Med.* II. 521 The lesion invariably consists of a nodule or mass of hard sclerotic tissue with a calcified centre. *Ibid.* 864 Alcohol is usually said to..lead to sclerotic changes in the valves of the heart.

4. *Bot.* Hardened, stony in texture.

sclerotic cells, grit-cells or sclereids; *sclerotic parenchyma*, grit-cells or stone-cells in pears, etc.

1884 BOWER & SCOTT *De Bary's Phaner.* 330 A sheath composed of sclerotic lignified elements goes all round the bundle. *Ibid.* 419 The outer layer of the cortex of the root is often sclerotic in a high degree.

5. *fig.* Unmoving, unchanging, rigid.

1965 *Listener* 20 May 737/2 Why is it, I asked myself, that so many theatre people in Russia call the Moscow Arts old-fashioned and sclerotic? **1968** *Daily Tel.* (Colour Suppl.) 13 Dec. 61/1 The sidewalks of New York seem to get harder year by year, the skyscrapers more inhumanly overbearing, the traffic more sclerotic. **1979** *Washington Star* 8 May A15/7 She [*sc.* Margaret Thatcher] has to deal with tacky little things like the secondary boycotts, repealing sclerotic tax laws, [etc.].

B. *sb.*

1. The hard outer coat of the posterior part of the eyeball, forming the white of the eye.

1690 J. EDWARDS *Demonstr. Exist. God* II. (1696) 30 It is the foremost part of this skin which hath the epithet of corneous, and the hinder is properly the sclerotick. **1751** SPRY *Morbid Eye* in *Phil. Trans.* XLIX. 19 Yet the bloodvessels of the conjunctive were no way enlarged, nor in the least redder than that and the sclerotic were before. **1872** HUXLEY *Physiol.* ix. 225 The eyeball is composed..of a..case consisting of fibrous..tissue the greater part of which is white and opaque, and is called the sclerotic. **1900** J. HUTCHINSON in *Arch. Surg.* XI. 42 He is a pale sallow man with very white sclerotics.

2. A medicine for hardening the flesh, etc.

1728 in CHAMBERS *Cycl.*; and in later Dicts.

sclerotic (sklɪə'rɒtɪk), *a.*² [f. SCLEROT-IUM + -IC.] *sclerotic acid*, one of the two most active constituents of ergot.

1876 *Pharm. Jrnl.* 17 June 1001/1 In ergot there also occurs from 2 to 3 per cent. of a substance similarly soluble in water,..this..we have named Sclerotic Acid.

‖**sclerotica** (sklɪə'rɒtɪkə). Also 6 slirotiqua. [med.L. *sclērōtica* (written *sclirotica* in Lanfranc *c* 1300), fem. (with ellipse of *tunica* tunic) of *sclērōticus*, a. Gr. *σκληρωτικός: see SCLEROTIC *a.*

The form in Lanfranc represents the late Gr. pronunciation of η as *i*; cf. OF. *sclirotique* (mod.F. *sclérotique*), Sp. *esclirótica*.]

= SCLEROTIC *sb.* 1.

1541 R. COPLAND *Guydon's Quest. Chirurg.* E iij b, In the inwarde party it is called slirotiqua and in the outwarde cornea. **1667** *Phil. Trans.* II. 536 the Sclerotica formed like a Cup. *c* **1790** IMISON *Sch. Arts* I. 196 It is contained in three membranes; the outermost is the *Sclerotica*; the second the *Tunica Choroides.* **1880** GÜNTHER *Fishes* vii. 113 The sclerotica is cartilaginous in Chondropterygians.

sclerotical (sklɪə'rɒtɪkəl), *a.* [f. SCLEROTIC + -AL¹.] = SCLEROTIC.

1897 in WEBSTER.

sclerotin ('sklɪərətɪn). *Biol.* [f. SCLERO- + *-tin* after CHITIN, KERATIN, etc.] Any of a class of structural proteins which form the exocuticles of insects and harden and darken by a natural tanning process in which protein chains become cross-linked by quinone groups.

1940 M. G. M. PRYOR in *Proc. R. Soc.* B. CXXVIII. 391, I therefore propose the name 'sclerotin' as a general term to describe proteins such as that of the cockroach ootheca, which owe their stability to a process of natural tanning. **1957** RICHARDS & DAVIES *Imms's Textbk. Ent.* (ed. 9) I. 11 Polyphenols..are the precursors of the quinones which link the arthropodin molecules to form sclerotin. **1969** R. F. CHAPMAN *Insects* xxii. 434 Part of the protein may later be tanned.., stabilised by cross-linkages between the molecules, to form a hard, inflexible and usually darkened structure. Such tanned arthropodin is called sclerotin, and this produces the hardness of the sclerites. **1976** *Sci. Amer.* Apr. 134/3 Such quinone-linked proteins, called sclerotins, are usually coloured brown or black, accounting for the hard beetle look we all know.

sclerotinia (sklɪərəʊ'tɪnɪə). [mod.L. (L. Fuckel 1870, in *Jahrb. d. Nassauischen Vereins f. Naturk.* XXIII–XXIV. 330), f. SCLEROTIUM + *-inium*, arbitrary suffix.] The name of a genus of parasitic fungi, used *attrib.* and *absol.* to designate plant diseases caused by them.

1926 *Misc. Publ. Min. Agric. & Fish.* LII. 26 Sclerotinia disease..reported from Lancashire [potatoes]. **1950** *N.Z. Jrnl. Agric.* July 79/2 Causing rapid decay, sclerotinia rot (*Sclerotinia* spp.) attacks many plants, including petunias, zinnias, stocks, and wallflowers. Dead plants are usually black, but are covered by a white growth. **1976** E. SCARROW *N.Z. Veg. Gardening Guide* 64 Fungal diseases include early and late blight sclerotinia (or white mould disease) and various other stem and leaf blights.

sclerotioid (sklɪə'rəʊtɪɔɪd), *a.* Also sclerotoid. [f. SCLEROTIUM + -OID.] Resembling a sclerotium.

1857 M. J. BERKELEY *Cryptog. Botany* §405 A large stipitate species with a sclerotoid rooting base. **1874** COOKE *Fungi* 102 Ergot, which is the sclerotioid condition of a species of Claviceps. **1900** B. D. JACKSON *Gloss. Bot. Terms*, *Sclerotioid, sclerotoid*, like a sclerotium.

†**scle'rotis.** *Obs.* [mod.L.] = SCLEROTICA.

1670 *Phil. Trans.* V. 1042 The Optique nerve after its insertion into the Eye is inflected, and extends it self on the Concavity of the Sclerotis about the breadth of 2 or 3 lines.

‖**sclerotitis** (sklɪərəʊ'taɪtɪs). *Path.* [mod.L., f. prec.: see -ITIS.] Inflammation of the sclerotica.

1822–29 *Good's Study Med.* (ed. 3) II. 550 Sclerotic inflammation, or *sclerotitis*, as it is frequently termed. **1897** *Allbutt's Syst. Med.* III. 68 The affections of the eye in gonorrhœal rheumatism..take the form of conjunctivitis, or sclerotitis, and iritis.

‖**Sclerotium** (sklɪə'rəʊtɪəm). Pl. sclerotia. [mod.L. (Tode 1790), f. Gr. σκληρός hard.]

†**1.** A former genus of *Cryptogamia*, comprising small, hard black bodies producing smut in wheat and ergot in rye; now known to be a particular stage of growth of the mycelium of certain fungi.

1819 *Pantologia*, *Sclerotium*, in botany, a genus of the class cryptogamia, order fungi. **1845** *Encycl. Metrop.* VI. 51/1 The spur, or ergot, is by some considered as a fungus, a species of sclerotium.

2. A tuberous body forming on the mycelium of a fungus, from which it becomes detached when its growth is complete. (See quot. 1879.)

1871 GARROD *Mat. Med.* (ed. 3) 350 Ergot. The sclerotium (compact mycelium or spawn) of Claviceps purpurea, produced within the paleæ of the common rye, Secale cereale. **1879** G. MURRAY in *Encycl. Brit.* IX. 828 Sclerotia are tuberous bodies composed of densely interwoven mycelial hyphæ enclosed by a layer of pseudo-parenchyma... They were long regarded as independent forms of fungi, but it has been discovered that they are only resting states in which nourishment is stored up.

3. *Zool.* In *Mycetozoa*, a cyst-like growth enclosing a portion of the plasmodium in its dormant stage.

1885 E. R. LANKESTER in *Encycl. Brit.* XIX. 841/2. **1888** ROLLESTON & JACKSON *Anim. Life* 909 But if the plasmodium is ripe for sporulation, its resting-phase, the sclerotium, has a different character.

sclerotized ('sklɪərəʊtaɪzd), *ppl. a. Zool.* [f. SCLEROT(IC *a.*¹ and *sb.* + -IZ(E + -ED¹.] Hardened by conversion into sclerotin.

1928 FERRIS & CHAMBERLIN in *Entomol. News* XXXIX. 215 We might very logically extend the use of the root which appears in the word 'sclerite'. This word alone is hardly sufficient to meet all our needs and we could speak of 'sclerotic areas' or of 'sclerotized areas'. **1955** P. A. BUXTON *Nat. Hist. Tsetse Flies* iii. 53 The upper wall of the labium is also sclerotized and forms the labial gutter. **1975** *Nature* 8 May 142/2 A sclerotised edge of the left wing [of the tree cricket] serves as the scraper.

So ˌ**scleroti'zation**; '**sclerotize** *v. trans.*

1957 RICHARDS & DAVIES *Imms's Textbk. Entomol.* (ed. 9) I. 9 In most insects..the greater part of the cuticle undergoes a process of sclerotization whereby it becomes hardened and darkened to form more or less tough, rigid sclerites separated from each other by membraneous zones of unchanged soft cuticle. **1963** R. P. DALES *Annelids* ii. 41 The cuticle of the earthworm gizzard is like that of the epidermis and is simply collagenous, but in polychaetes the stomodeal cuticle may be sclerotized to form teeth or jaws. **1974** *Nature* 30 Aug. 799/2 An early effect of ecdysoids at metamorphosis in some caterpillars is conversion of tryptophane into red ommochrome pigments; in fly larvae, the conversion of tyrosine into quinones to sclerotize the puparium. *Ibid.* 20 Dec. 710/2 The sclerotisation and tanning of insect cuticles is generally thought to result from a crosslinking of the cuticular proteins by quinonoid derivatives of tyrosine.

sclerotome ('sklɪərəʊtəʊm). *Anat.* Also sk-. [f. Gr. σκληρό-ς hard + τομή section, and -τόμος cutter: see -TOME.]

1. A sclerous element intervening between successive myotomes.

1857 GOODSIR in *Edinb. New Philos. Jrnl.* V. 122 To a segment of the sclerome I apply the designation Sclerotome. **1872** HUMPHRY *Myology* 98 A piece of the lateral muscle with one of the myotomes dissected out to shew the sclerotome, or intermuscular septum.

2. A knife used in incising the sclerotic.

1885 *Lancet* 11 July 56/1 The eyeball is then rotated..and a lance-pointed sclerotome passed through the sclerotic.

Hence **sclero'tomal, sclero'tomic** *adjs.*, of or pertaining to a sclerotome.

1890 WEBSTER, Sclerotomic. **1894** [see MYOTOME 1]. **1925** J. S. KINGSLEY *Vertebrate Skeleton* 21 There is one great difference between Elasmobranches and higher Vertebrates; in the former cells from the sclerotomic elements..break through the elastica externa.., invade the notochordal sheath, and may chondrify there. **1971** A. J. WATERMAN *Chordate Struct. & Function* vi. 211 The sclerotomic cells form the perichordal tube. In addition, a mass of sclerotomic tissue migrates to the myoseptum to form the neural and haemal arch anlagen. *Ibid.* (*caption*) Precartilage stage; further compaction of sclerotomal tissue with establishment of basic vertebral shape... Sclerotome stage; sclerotomal cells migrate from somite and form sclerotome. **1974** D. & M. WEBSTER *Compar. Vertebr. Morphol.* v. 87 The posterior half of one sclerotomal segment and the anterior half of the segment just behind it join together, so that each presumptive vertebra forms on a level overlapping two somites.

sclerotomy (sklɪə'rɒtəmɪ). *Surg.* [f. Gr. σκληρό-ς hard (here repr. its derivative SCLEROTIC) + -τομία cutting.] Incision into the sclerotic coat of the eye-ball; an operation of this kind.

1876 *Clin. Soc. Trans.* IX. 139 The operation of sclerotomy, as performed in the following cases, is a modification of that proposed by M. Quaglino of Pavia. **1879** *St. George's Hosp. Rep.* IX. 535 A late sufferer from glaucoma, for whom two sclerotomies had been done elsewhere.

sclerous (ˈsklɪərəs), *a.* [f. Gr. σκληρ-ός hard + -OUS.] **a.** *Phys.* Of animal tissue: Hard, bony. **b.** *Path.* Indurated, affected by sclerosis.
1845 TODD & BOWMAN *Phys. Anat.* I. 48 The sclerous tissue contains a large proportion of inorganic material, to which it owes its hardness. **1876** DUNGLISON *Med. Lex.*, *Tissue, Sclerous.* This name has been used collectively for the cartilaginous, osseous, and fibrous tissues. **1897** *Allbutt's Syst. Med.* II. 863 The cord changes are due to slowly encroaching sclerous changes. **1899** *Ibid.* VI. 486 In so far as the sclerous condition of the skin acts as an impediment.

scleuthe, scleve, obs. ff. SLOTH, SLEEVE.

scley, obs. f. SLY.

scleyre, var. SKLEIR *Obs.*

sclinder, obs. Sc. f. SLENDER.

sclink, obs. f. SLINK, a kind of leather.

sclirosis, sclondre, obs. ff. SCLEROSIS, SLANDER.

‖**scloˈpeta.** *Antiq.* [? Pl. of med.L. *sclopētum* (see next), or perh. an incorrect sing.: cf. Sp. *escopeta.*] = SCLOPETTE.
1709 STEELE *Tatler* No. 34 ¶5 His [*sc.* the antiquary 'Don Saltero's'] double-barrelled Pistols, Targets, Coats of Mail, his Sclopeta, and Sword of Toledo.

sclopette (skləʊˈpɛt). *Antiq.* [ad. med.L. *sclopettum, sclopētum*, f. *sclopus*: see ESCLOPETTE, ESCOPETTE.] 'A hand-culverin of the end of the fourteenth century' (*Cent. Dict.* 1891).

scluse, scnorte, obs. forms of SLUICE, SNORT.

sco, obs. form of SHE, SHOE.

scoad (skəʊd), *v. s.w. dial.* Also 7–8 scode. *trans.* To scatter (ashes or other agricultural dressing). Hence ˈ**scoading** *vbl. sb.*
1602 CAREW *Cornwall* 20 The charges of this Beating, Burning, Scoding and Sanding,..amounteth to..twentie shillings for euerie Acre. **1787** GROSE *Provinc. Gloss.*, *Scode*, to scatter. Cornw. **1864** T. QUILLER-COUCH *E. Cornw. Words* in *Jrnl. R. Inst. Cornw.* Mar., *Scoad*, to scatter, spill. 'To scoad dressing'. *a* **1870** J. COUCH *Hist. Polperro* vi. (1871) 118 The turf is collected into separate 'burrows' or heaps, burnt, and the ashes 'scoaded', or scattered over the field.

scoal(e, scoale, obs. ff. SCALE *sb.*[1], SCHOOL *sb.*[2]

scoar(e, scoase, scoat: see SCORE, SCORSE, SCOTE *v.*

†**scob**[1] (skɒb). *Obs.* Also 5 scobe, 5–6 skobbe, 7 scobb. [Of obscure etymology.] A box, a chest.
1469–70 in Swayne *Sarum Churchw. Acc.* (1896) 13 Pro ij^bus clauibus..vnum..pro parua skobbe in Vestibulo. **1481–2** *Ibid.* 368 A lytell key to the scobbe by fore the Rood Awt'. **1507–8** *Ibid.* 261, j skobbe pro ornamentis Altaris predicte imponend'. **1521–2** *Ibid.* 65 A loke to the sextens scobe. **1550–51** *Ibid.* 91 Sold' to Xpōfer tucker a skobbe wch we Receyued therfor xxd.
b. *Winchester School* (see quots. 1862 and 1891).
c **1615** in Walcott *William of Wykeham* (1852) 167 Item, for a scobb to hold his books 0 3 6. **1862** H. B. WHEATLEY *Anagrams* 141 At Winchester School the boys are in the habit of calling the huge old boxes that serve them for desks, skobs; skob being box (or rather boks) spelt backwards. **1891** WRENCH *Winchester Word-bk.*, *Scob*, or *Scobb*, an oak box with a double lid, set at the angles of the squares of wooden benches in School. It is used as desk and bookcase. **1893** *Q. Rev.* Oct. 382 Here stood the 'Scobs' or oak boxes which contained all that a boy could call his own.

scob[2] (skɒb). *Weaving.* (See quots.)
1863 J. WATSON *Art Weaving* 141 When the weft passes over a portion of the warp without being interwoven with it, the defect is that the yarn hangs loose at that part, and it is called a Scob, Float, or Flow. *Ibid.*, Scob or Float Preventer. **1878** BARLOW *Weaving* 442 *Scobs* (Scotch term), the warp and weft not properly interwoven.

scobberlotcher. Also scobolotcher. [Cf. SCOPPERLOIT.] An idler. (So explained in context of quot. *a* 1697.)
a **1697** AUBREY *Lives* (1898) II. 26 Dr. Kettle, when he scolded at the idle young boies of his colledge, he used these names,..Rascal-Jacks, Blindcinques, Scobberlotchers. **1933** C. DAY LEWIS *Dick Willoughby* 10 Thou bed-worm, thou scobberlotcher! **1956** *Bournemouth Daily Echo* 21 Apr. 10/4 A scobolotcher, said Mr. Moore, was an undergraduate walking around a quadrangle hands in pockets and deep in thought.

scobby (ˈskɒbɪ). Also scobbie, skobby. A north-country name for the chaffinch, *Fringilla cœlebs.*
1800 D. WORDSWORTH *Jrnl.* 17 May (1941) I. 39 The Skobby sate quietly in its nest. **1813** MONTAGU *Ornith. Dict.* Suppl. **1852** F. O. MORRIS *Hist. Brit. Birds* II. 236. **1976** *Jrnl. Lakeland Dial. Soc.* No. 38. 39 She wes gitten weel on afoor she kent et a scobbie wes oot but a scobbie.

†**scobe,** *sb. Obs.* [a. L. *scob-em, scobs.*] Sawdust.
c **1440** *Pallad. on Husb.* III. 901 Ek populer or fir is profitabull To make & lye among hem scobes abull. *Ibid.* IV. 491 Hem summe in cedur scobe..wel witholde.

†**scobe,** *v. Obs. trans.* To gag.
1652 *Nocol's Diary* 30 Sept. (MS.) (Jam.), One of them had his mouth scobit. *a* **1657** SIR J. BALFOUR *Ann.* Hist. Wks. 1825 III. 316 [General Monk] in a rage commandit Mr. Jo. Robertsone not to speake one word, wich if he presumed to doe, he wold scobe his mouthe.

scobiform (ˈskəʊbɪfɔːm), *a. Bot.* [f. L. *scob-s* sawdust, filings + -(I)FORM.] Like sawdust or filings in appearance.
1760 J. LEE *Introd. Bot.* II. xxiii. (1765) 129 The seeds are scobiform. **1830** LINDLEY *Nat. Syst. Bot.* 52 Seeds scobiform, subulate, smooth.

‖**scobina** (skəʊˈbaɪnə). *Bot.* [mod.L., use of L. *scobīna* rasp.] 'The zigzag rachis of the spikelets of grasses' (*Treas. Bot.* 1866).
1839 LINDLEY *Introd. Bot.* I. ii. (ed. 3) 153 In the spikelets of Grasses the rachis has an unusual, toothed, flexuose appearance, and has received the name of *scobina* from Dumortier.

scochen, -eoun, -ynne, etc.: see SCUTCHEON.

scode, variant of SCOAD *v. dial.*

scodgy (ˈskɒdʒɪ). *Sc.* Also 8–9 scogie, scougie, scudgie, skodge, skodgie, skudgy. [Of obscure origin.] 'A boy or girl who cleans boots, or does the dirty work of the kitchen; a drudge' (E.D.D.). Also *attrib.*
1786 *Har'st Rig* xci, The Scogie lass does rin wil haste And bring the *kale.* **1850** A. McGILVRAY *Poems* 208 Look after cleaning pans and tins, And all the scudgie matters. **1895** P. H. HUNTER *Jas. Inwick* x. 124 Misca'in me for a turncoat, an' a rinawa, an' scodgy to the laird.

scoff (skɒf), *sb.*[1] Forms: 4 skof(f, (*pl.* scoffes), 4–6 scof, 6 *Sc.* skwff, skuf, 6–7 scoffe, skoffe, 7 (schoffe), *Sc.* skuff, 6– scoff. [ME. *scof, skof*, of obscure origin.
In sense the word agrees with ON. *skop* neut. (the ablaut-variant *skaup* is more common), corresp. to OHG. *scoph, scopf* and prob. cogn. w. OE. *scop* poet: see SCOP. It is possible that there was a cognate and synonymous form **skof* of which the Eng. word may be an adoption; cf. early mod.Da. *skuf, skof*, jest, mockery, *skuffe* to jest, mock, also (as now) to deceive, disappoint, MLG. *schoven*; Richthofen cites a single instance of OFris. *schof*, which he interprets 'mockery'.]
1. a. 'Contemptuous ridicule; expression of scorn; contumelious language' (J.); mockery. Phrase, *to make scoff.* Now *rare* or *Obs.*
13.. *K. Alis.* 667 (Laud MS.) This nis nouȝth romaunce of skof [*Lincoln's Inn MS.* scof]. *Ibid.* 5461 Nov it is ypassed, hij ne don þerof Bot gamenen togedres, & ek scoff. *c* **1330** R. BRUNNE *Chron. Wace* (Rolls) 7586 'Drynk hail', he seyþ, & drynkeþ þer-of, Kyssyng hym in bourde & scof. **1340** *Ayenb.* 128 Do away þe scoffes and þe scornes. *a* **1450** MYRC What maner þynge þou art gulty of, Telle me boldely & make no scof. *c* **1530** *Crt. Love* 1185 'Bereve me, goddesse', quod he, [of] thy might, My skornes all and skoffes, that I have No power forth, to mokken any wight That in thy service dwell. **1538** BALE *Brefe Comedy Tempt. Chr.* D iv, If ye do beleue, that ye are the sonne of God, Beleue thys also, if ye leape downe here in scoff, From thys hygh pynnacle, ye can take no harme theroff. *a* **1572** KNOX *Hist. Ref.* Wks. 1846 I. 49 The Bischope was heightly offended, asweill at the skwff and bitter mock, as at the bold libertie of that learned man. **1588** SHAKS. *L.L.L.* v. ii. 263 By heauen, all drie beaten with pure scoffe. **1596** DALRYMPLE tr. *Leslie's Hist. Scot.* II. 188 Doubtles gif we returne, we sal vndirly a perpetual skuf and shame. **1598** GRENEWEY *Tacitus, Ann.* I. iii. (1622) 6 [Augustus] asked the opinion of the Pontife in a scoffe, whether there might be a lawfull marriage betwixt them. **1612** T. TAYLOR *Comm. Titus* i. 1 As in nicknames taken up in scoffe. **1617** MORYSON *Itin.* I. 205 Being to receive the Sacrament he demaunded in scoffe a great piece of bread. *a* **1854** H. REED *Lect. Brit. Poets* (1857) 360 It was a piece of scoff at his political foes.'
b. A derisive jest, an expression of mockery.
1573 G. HARVEY *Letter-bk.* (Camden) 14 And now he was thurrouly furnisshid with a cumpani of gud lusti cuts and stateli scofs. **1604** HIERON *Wks.* I. 502 The schoffes of Ismalitish papists. **1610** HEALEY *St. Aug. Citie of God* XIII. xvi. (1620) 456 But the Philosophers..thinke they giue vs a witty scoffe for saying that [etc.]. **1660** F. BROOKE tr. *Le Blanc's Trav.* 313 We..telling him of these spirits, being a Protestant, he made a scoffe at it. *c* **1665** MRS. HUTCHINSON *Mem. Col. Hutchinson* (1885) I. 37 He detested all scoffs at any practice of worship. **1741** WATTS *Improv. Mind* I. xiv, Some little souls..for want of a due acquaintance with other sciences make a scoff at them all in comparison of their favourite science. **1751** EARL ORRERY *Remarks Swift* (1752) 124 The scoffs and sarcasms of Swift, like the bite of the rattlesnake, distinguish themselves more venomously dangerous, than the wounds of a common serpent. **1818** SHELLEY *Rev. Islam* XII. iii, Yet none do wreak their scoffs on him. **1827** COLERIDGE *Lit. Rem.* (1839) IV. 319 Why, this is the very scoff of a late Unitarian writer. **1842** J. H. NEWMAN *Par. Serm.* VI. xvii. 258 Worldly men have their scoff at our failure of discernment now. **1877** FROUDE *Short Stud.* (1883) IV. I. xi. 130 With the scoffs came tales of the retribution which instantly over-took the scoffers.
†**c.** *transf.* A mere jest. *Obs.*
1594 NASHE *Unfort. Trav.* K 4 b, Day by day he disgested his meate with leading her the measures [making her 'dance', by flogging]... The ballet of the whipper of late days here in England, was but a scoffe in comparison of him.
2. An object of contempt or scorn; a mark for derision or scoffing.
1640 SIR W. MURE *Counter-Buff* 382 Then with a daring boldenesse, thou reviles That sacred name, and with base skurill stiles..Thus makes of it a sesam, a skuff, a sport. **1660** N. INGELO *Bentiv. & Ur.* I. (1682) 77 Is not he the common scoff of all beholders? **1668–9** PEPYS *Diary* 31 Jan., Dr. Waterhouse..was mighty passionate against people that make a scoff of religion. **1672** VILLIERS (Dk. Buckhm.) *Rehearsal* III. ii, How has my passion made me Cupid's scoff! **1733** SWIFT *Apol.* 55 And since I 'scap'd being made a Scoff, I think I'm very fairly off. **1781** COWPER *Hope* 743 These are thy glorious works, eternal truth, The scoff of wither'd age and beardless youth. **1817** KEATINGE *Trav.* I. 215 Ancient history, even where only founded on tradition, so long the scoff of shallow ignorance, pseudo-philosophy, and sordid indolence. **1825** MACAULAY *Ess., Milton* ¶77 The principles of liberty were the scoff of every grinning courtier. **1855** —— *Hist. Eng.* xvi. III. 623 But the rest of his army was the scoff of all Europe.

scoff (skɒf, -ɔː-), *sb.*[2] *colloq.*, orig. *S. African.* Also schoff, skoff. [Cape Du., repr. Du. *schoft*, quarter of a day, hence each of the four meals of the day.] Food; also a meal. (Cf. SCAFF *sb.*) Also *attrib.*
1846 *Swell's Night Guide* 51 It vas hout-and-hout good scoff, and no flies. **1855** J. W. COLENSO *Ten Weeks in Natal* 54 The *meat* and other *scoff* (food), which the Kafirs are so fond of. **1863** J. S. DOBIE *Jrnl.* 6 Jan. (1945) 60 The best one was consigned to the Kafirs for 'scoff'. **1879** ATCHERLEY *Trip Boërland* 101 Kafirs..get wages varying from 15*s.* to £1, besides their food, or 'scoff'..Indian or mealie flour. **1892** LD. R. CHURCHILL *Men, Mines, & Anim.* ix. (1895) 132 They were stranded without any skoff. **1899** FLYNT *Tramping with Tramps* II. iii. (1900) 251 Scoff's always more plenty than money. **1900** S. CHAMBERS *Rhodesians* 63 The bones left over from the Boss's skoff. **1902** 'COLDSTREAMER' *Ballads of Boer War* vii. 66 They gives 'im 'schoff' an' treats 'im kind, Instead o' striking 'im be'ind. **1926** *Variety* 29 Dec. 5/3 Slang, in addition to providing me with seven flops weekly and three scoffs daily, has saved me from night school. **1928** *Daily Express* 14 May 10/6 While you've had me locked up, I've eaten your scoff! **1934** *Detective Fiction Weekly* 21 Apr. 109/2 Where the criminal eats he says he scoffs, and if he goes to a restaurant it is called a beanery, chow joint or scoff joint. **1955** J. COPE *Fair House* v. 62 He treated them familiarly, shared his skoff-tin with them. **1960** [see BEVVY]. **1969** in Halpert & Story *Christmas Mumming in Newfoundland* 84 One of the men might suggest to those in his group that everyone come over to his house for a 'scoff'. **1976** *Australasian Express* 11 June 25/3 A particularly memorable scoff was had on Colitzani beach. **1977** J. WAINWRIGHT *Do Nothin'* xi. 182 A dance, all of her own, with guests and scoff and booze of her own choice. **1981** *Guardian* 24 Aug. 8 Ah! Scoff ahoy! I spy Florida Cocktail and Gammon Steak Hawaii!

scoff (skɒf, -ɔː-), *v.*[1] Also 4 scof, 6–7 scoffe, skoffe. [f. SCOFF *sb.*[1]]
1. *intr.* To speak derisively, mock, jeer. Const. *at*, †*of*, †*over*, †*upon*, †*with.* Chiefly implying unworthy derision, as of something deserving reverence or consideration.
a **1380** *St. Savina* 255 in Horstm. *Altengl. Leg.* (1878) 97 Hit neodeþ not to þe forte scof. **1530** PALSGR. 706/1, I scoffe, I bourde or jest with one, *je me bourde.* I scoffe with hym, *je me bourde a luy. Ibid.*, I scoffe, I jest upon one, *je jonche* and *je larde.* Hast thou naught els to do but scoffe upon me. **1560** JEWEL *Reply to Cole* Wks. (1609) 37 The Councell of Paris was scoft at, and iested out of all parts. **1570** LEVINS *Manip.* 156/39 To skoffe, *scommari. a* **1572** KNOX *Hist. Ref.* I. (1586) 163 In this disputation manie other thinges were merily skoft ouer. **1590** SPENSER *F.Q.* III. vi. 21 Thereat Diana gan to smile, in scorne Of her vaine plaint, and to her scoffing sayd. **1591** SHAKS. *1 Hen. VI*, III. ii. 45 *Burg.* [to Joan of Arc] Scoffe on vile Fiend, and shamelesse curtizan. **1611** BIBLE *Transl. Pref.* ¶2 And yet for as worthy an acte as euer he [David] did..he was scorned and scoffed at by his owne wife. *a* **1643** LD. FALKLAND, etc. *Infallibility* (1646) 94 There is a difficulty which may exercise you instead of scoffing of his Lordship in the close of the Chapter. **1655** WALTON *Angler* i. (1661) 4 'Tis an easie thing to scoff at any Art or Recreation; a little wit mixt with ill nature, confidence, and malice, will do it. **1667** MILTON *P.L.* VI. 629 So they among themselves in pleasant veine Stood scoffing. **1758** JOHNSON *Idler* No. 18 ¶3 Among the numbers whom you have taught to scoff at the retirement of Drugget, there is one who offers his apology. **1770** GOLDSM. *Des. Vill.* 180 And fools who came to scoff, remain'd to pray. **1821** SHELLEY *Song, 'Rarely, rarely, comest thou'* ii, With the joyous and the free Thou wilt scoff at pain. **1859** TENNYSON *Marr. Geraint* 58 And by and by the people..Began to scoff and jeer and babble of him As of a prince whose manhood was all gone. **1886** G. ALLEN *Darwin* xii. 201 Harvey's grand discovery..was scoffed at for nearly a whole generation.
2. a. *trans.* To scoff at, deride, ridicule irreverently. ? *Obs.* exc. *U.S.*
1579 LYLY *Euphues* (Arb.) 170 Such grosse questions are to be aunswered with slender reasons, and such idle heads should be scoffed with adle aunsweres. *c* **1592** MARLOWE *Massacre Paris* (? 1600) B 3, Was it not thou that scoftes [*sic*] the Organon, And said it was a heape of vanities? **1593** SHAKS. *Rich. II*, III. ii. 163. **1607** B. BARNES *Divils Charter* I. v. C 2, Scoffst thou me Gismond with continuall taunts? **1624** QUARLES *Job Militant* xi. 39, I would not scoffe you, nor with taunts torment ye. **1643** TRAPP *Comm. Gen.* xxxvi. 24 This same foolish wittiness Alexander wittily scoffed, when he gave [etc.]. **1676** GLANVILL *Seasonable Reflect.* 35 To Scoff Religion is ridiculously proud and immodest. **1733** SWIFT *Apol.* 148 To see th' important Man of Dress Scoffing my College Aukwardness. **1795** SOUTHEY *Joan of Arc* x. 319 He..scoff'd their easy fears. **1891** MARY A. DODGE *Washington Bible Class* ii. 48 (Funk) The men who are increasing the sum of the world's knowledge are studying, not scoffing the Bible. **1892** GUNTER *Miss Dividends* (1893) 210 Oh, how I have scoffed them in my heart.
†**b.** *to scoff out*: to dismiss or put aside scoffingly. *Obs. rare.*
1549 LATIMER *7th Serm. bef. Edw. VI* (Arb.) 200 They that be called to aunswere wyll not aunswere directlye, but skoffe the matter out. **1551** CRANMER *Answ. Gardiner* I. 10 And so scoffe out both these hygh mysteries of Christe.
c. To utter in a scoffing manner (with the spoken words as obj.).
1862 MRS. H. WOOD *Channings* I. v. 70 'A senior do it!' scoffed Roland Yorke. **1894** E. FAWCETT *New Nero* v. 66 'I no more ruined her,' scoffed Egerton, 'than the Sultan of Turkey did!' **1898** SKEEL & BREARLEY *King Washington* xxv. 155 'Not I,' scoffed Anne, shaking her taffeta flounces. **1921**

[see POOF *int.* A]. **1976** J. WAINWRIGHT *Bastard* i. 23 'In *this* weather?' I scoff. **1977** P. G. WINSLOW *Witch Hill Murder* II. xvii. 219 'Oh, come on, Supe,' Jed scoffed. 'You're really not trying to pin that murder on me, are you?'

scoff (skɒf, -ɔː-), *v.*^{2} *slang* and *dial.* Also scorf, skoff. [app. orig. a variant of SCAFF *v.*, taken into slang from dialectal use; latterly associated with the orig. South African SCOFF *sb.*^{2}]

1. a. *trans.* To eat voraciously, devour; also *gen.* to eat. Also with *up*, *down*. Also *fig.*

1846 *Swell's Night Guide* 48 He scoffed weed; that is, chewed tobacco. *Ibid.* 50 You must grub with the grunters, and scoff cabbage without salt. **1864** *Hotten's Slang Dict.*, *Scorf*, to eat voraciously. **1876** *Whitby Gloss.*, *Skoff*, to eat with audible voracity. **1883** CLARK RUSSELL *Sailors' Lang.*, *Scoffing*, eating. To *scoff* a thing is to eat it. **1886** W. H. LONG *Dict. Isle Wight Dial.* 61 They zet down and scoffed every bit o' grub there was on the taable. **1895** A. PATTERSON *Man & Nature in Broads* 122 A bunch of grey lag-geese as wor scoffin' (eating) the young wheat in a field up hinder. **1901** W. S. WALKER *In the Blood* iv, Those birds kill snakes do they?.. Rather... They goes down themselves and scoffs them. **1942** *Tee Emm* (Air Ministry) II. 148 Fluorescence which he said tasted horrible, and of which he scoffed quite a fair amount while he was waiting to be lifted out of the water. **1956** I. MURDOCH *Flight from Enchanter* 125, I wonder what happens to it [*sc.* a magazine]. Fay must scoff it up in her room. **1967** E. GILZEAN *Murder on Sundays* ii. 33 Come on, Janet. They'll have scoffed all the beer and cider if we don't hurry. **1972** R. K. SMITH *Ransom* v. 231 Scoff it up, chillun..and you'll grow up big and strong. **1973** J. PORTER *It's Murder with Dover* v. 45 In the dining room the reporters..were..noisily scoffing down everything that was put in front of them. **1979** *Daily Tel.* 13 Oct. 12/3 Should the farmer wish to supplement the rations of his cattle or sheep in bad weather then he must stand guard over the feeding trough to stop the horses scoffing the lot.

b. *intr.* To eat or feed; to have one's food *with*.

[Cf. Du. *schoften* to take one's meals.]

1798 A. BARNARD *Jrnl.* 24 May in A. W. C. Lindsay *Lives of Lindsays* (1849) III. 464 [The Boer] concludes of course that the passengers want to *scoff* (to eat). **1850** H. MELVILLE *White-Jacket* xv. 73 Bear a hand, and '*scoff*' (eat) away... Some of you fellows keep *scoffing* as if I had nothing to do but..look on. **1855** G. H. MASON *Life with Zulus of Natal* xvi. 193 A Caffre..entered our service... It soon became manifest that our new servant was a madman... He would commence a war-song, or call for us to get up and 'scoff' (eat) *with him*. **1899** LOWTH *Dau. of Transvaal* xi. 191, I say, here come those three, still skoffing. **1900** S. CHAMBERS *Rhodesians* 18 I'll 'skoff' with Achille this month. **1926** *Clues* Nov. 158/2 Let's scoff. Get the duffer. **1931** 'D. STIFF' *Milk & Honey Route* 213 *Scoffing*, to eat. *To scoff regularly* means to miss no meals. **1944** D. BURLEY *Orig. Handbk. Harlem Jive* 70 Really knock yourself out as you scoff. **1965** R. ERSKINE *Passion Flowers in Business* xiii. 164 Can we please go and scoff? **1973** C. HIMES *Black on Black* 133 Go on, baby, you can be back in an hour with 'nuff bread so we can scoff.

2. *trans.* To seize, plunder.

1893 KIPLING *Many Invent.*, *Judson & the Empire*, Are we a set of hairy pirates to scoff the storeroom of a painted Levantine bumboat? *Ibid.*, There's enough [gold-leaf] for two first-rates, and I've scoffed the best half of it. **1898** HYNE *Capt. Kettle* xi. 289 Some of those lousy Portuguese have been on board and scoffed all the money. **1903** B. MITFORD *Veldt Vendetta* 122 Why the Kafirs'd have skoffed the whole span long before and started out to rake in more.

†'**scoffage.** *Obs. rare*$^{-1}$. [f. SCOFF *v.*^{1} + -AGE.] The action or fact of scoffing.

a **1639** WHATELEY *Prototypes* I. xix. (1640) 222 These gracelesse young men think the threats but words of sport, counterfeit words which have no truth nor substance in them, but were very mockery and scoffage.

scoffer^{1} ('skɒfə(r), -ɔː-). Also 6 scoffar. [f. SCOFF *v.*^{1} + -ER^{1}.]

1. One who scoffs. Const. *at*; also (now *rarely*) *of*. Often *spec.*, one who scoffs at religion or morality.

1470–85 MALORY *Arthur* x. xlvii. 488 He was a good knyȝt but he was a scoffer and a Iaper. **1540** PALSGR. *Acolastus* IV. ii. S ij, The order or felowshyp of scoffers, or common gesters. *a* **1568** ASCHAM *Scholem.* I. (Arb.) 33 In yougthe also they be readie scoffers. **1600** SHAKS. *A.Y.L.* III. v. 62 Cry the man mercy, loue him, take his offer, Foule is most foule, being foule to be a scoffer. **1611** BIBLE *Transl. Pref.* ¶ 16 We might also be charged (by scoffers) with some vnequall dealing towards a great number of good English wordes. **1630** *R. Johnson's Kingd. & Commw.* 190 It is also naturall to the French, to be a great scoffer; for men of light and unsteady braines, have commonly sudden and sharpe conceits. **1691** WOOD *Ath. Oxon.* II. 195 He closed with the Presbyterians, notwithstanding he had before..been a scoffer of them. *a* **1768** SECKER *Serm.* (1770) I. 209 They have..become Railers and Scoffers at it [Christianity]. **1790** G. WALKER *Serm.* II. xxx. 327 The impious scoffer of his Maker, of providence, of religion and of a future world. **1814** WORDSW. *Excurs.* II. 484 This dull product of a scoffer's pen. **1852** T. PARKER *Ten Serm. Relig.* iv. (1863) 76 The long line of scoffers from Lucian..down to Voltaire. **1853** HERSCHEL *Pop. Lect. Sci.* ii. §5 (1873) 52 What would Anaximander or the scoffer of Anaxagoras have said, could he have known what we now know. **1855** MACAULAY *Hist. Eng.* xiv. III. 445 To put any other interpretation on his words would be..to give an occasion of triumph to scoffers. **1869** FREEMAN *Norm. Conq.* III. xii. 80 The subject of foolish and brutal jests among the profligate scoffers of his Court.

†**2.** A jester, buffoon. *Obs.*

1530 PALSGR. 268/1 Scoffer or jestar, *gaudissevr.* **1540** —— *Acolastus* II. i. H iij b, Take me hardely in all the hast to be bounde prentyse to thy felowshyp or craftes men of scoffars. **1568** WITHALS *Dict.* 65 a/2 A scoffer, *histrio*. **1623** COCKERAM I, *Mimicke*, a scoffer, a iester.

scoffer^{2} ('skɒfə(r), -ɔː-). *colloq.* [f. SCOFF *v.*^{2} + -ER^{1}.] One who eats greedily.

1935 *Amer. Speech* X. 20/1 *Scoffer*, a glutton; one who has no control over his appetite. (Obs.) **1959** I. & P. OPIE *Lore & Lang. Schoolch.* ix. 154 A pair of Hertfordshire 14-year-olds,..when asked about their classmates and invited to set down their epithets for them, promptly came to life and wrote: 'Phumph, lumber bontts [bonce],..hog, scoffer, flippin kid [etc.]'. **1976** *Times* 21 Aug. 12/6 The scoffers of doughnuts, bananas and raw eggs.

†'**scoffery.** *Obs. rare.* [f. SCOFF *v.*^{1} + -ERY, after *mockery*.] **a.** A mockery, ridiculous proceeding. **b.** Mockery, jeering, derision.

1577 HARRISON *England* III. vii. 108 b, King Henrye.. thought it a mere scoffery to pursue any fallow Deare with hounds or greyhounds. **1589** PUTTENHAM *Eng. Poesie* I. xxxi. (Arb.) 76 Skelton a sharpe Satirist, but with more rayling and scoffery then became a Poet Lawreat. **1836** *Fraser's Mag.* XIV. 507 With..a scowling scoffery of all the principles which those who gathered together the National Assembly had contemplated.

†'**scoffic,** *a. Obs. rare*$^{-1}$. In 7 scophick. [f. SCOFF *sb.*^{1} + -IC.] Resembling, or of the nature of, a scoff. So also †'**scoffical** *a.*

1653 R. BAILLIE *Dissuas. Vind.* (1655) 86 You must make me a forger of meer reproachful, and scoffical calumnies. **1654** HAMMOND *Answ. to Animadv.* v. § 1. 118, I must in the same Scophick [*sic; but in Wks.* 1684 Scoptick] humour, be styled a learned man.

scoffing ('skɒfɪŋ, -ɔː-), *vbl. sb.* [f. SCOFF *v.*^{1} + -ING^{1}.] The action of SCOFF *v.*^{1}; †a scoff.

1377 LANGL. *P. Pl.* B. XIII. 277 Of scornyng and of scoffyng and of vnskilful berynge. **1529** MORE *Supplic. Soulys* Wks. 332/1 He laith agaynst it nothing but skoffing. **1530** PALSGR. 268/1 Scoffynges or tryfles, *fredaynes*. **1723** SWIFT *Epitaph Judge Boat* 2 Pray, Gentle-folks, forbear your Scoffing. **1820** BYRON *Mar. Fal.* v. i. 425 Men whose vice is to start at vice's scoffing. **1883** R. W. DIXON *Mano* IV. xv. 188 He bitter jests and filthy scoffing made.

b. *Comb.*: **scoffing-stock** [cf. LAUGHING-STOCK], an object of scoffing.

1571 GOLDING *Calvin on Ps.* lxix. 13 Hee was a scoffing-stock to yᵉ very princes. **1662** BARGRAVE *Pope Alex. VII* (1867) 96 The other Cardinals do but make him their scoffing-stock to laugh at. **1870** F. JACOX *Recr. Recluse* I. iv. 86 This same scoffing-stock of the school..displayed the energetic originality of genius.

scoffing ('skɒfɪŋ, -ɔː-), *ppl. a.* [f. SCOFF *v.*^{1} + -ING^{2}.] That scoffs; contemptuous, derisive.

1538 ELYOT *Dict.*, *Scurriliter*, in raylynge or scoffyng facion. **1540** PALSGR. *Acolastus* II. i. H ij b, Dysours or skoffyng fellowes. *a* **1586** SIDNEY *Arcadia* II. (Sommer) 184 b, And so in this iollie scoffing brauerie he went ouer vs all, saying [etc.]. **1592** GREENE *Upst. Courtier* B 3, Questioning with one that I met why these women were so cholericke, he, like a skoffing fellow, pointed to a bush of nettles. **1610** HOLLAND *Camden's Brit.* I. 534 Niele, a scoffing Poet in those daies,..wrot thus of them. *a* **1637** B. JONSON *Discov.*, *Nil gratius* (1640) 91 Indeed..nothing is of more credit, or request now, then a petulant paper, or scoffing verses. **1683** SOAME & DRYDEN tr. *Boileau's Art Poet.* III. 771 A Socrates himself in that loose age, Was made the pastime of a scoffing stage. *a* **1859** MACAULAY *Hist. Eng.* xxiii. V. 70 The people of the capital had been annoyed by the scoffing way in which foreigners spoke of the principal residence of our sovereigns.

scoffing ('skɒfɪŋ, -ɔː-), *sb. U.S. Tramps' slang.* [f. SCOFF *v.*^{2}] Usu. *pl.* Food, something to eat.

1907 J. LONDON in *Cosmopolitan* May 17/1 A hard town for 'scoffings', was what the hoboes called it [*sc.* Reno] at that time. **1914** *Sat. Even. Post* 4 Apr. 11/3 Got to throw your feet if yuh want scoffin's. *Ibid.*, You'll have to batter for handouts this mornin'. I'll get my own scoffin's.

scoffingly ('skɒfɪŋlɪ, -ɔː-), *adv.* [f. SCOFFING *ppl. a.* + -LY^{2}.] In a scoffing manner.

1538 ELYOT *Dict.*, *Ironice*, mockyshly, scoffyngly. **1560** DAUS tr. *Sleidane's Comm.* 32 b, To this decree of theyrs aunswereth Philip Melancthon, and after that Luther him selfe, but skoffyngly. **1641** *Pet. Istleworth* 4 He had rather hear an Organ..than singing of Psalmes, which scoffingly he called Hopkins his jigges. **1725** *Pope's Odyss.* III. Notes I. 167 What the Suitors had spoken scoffingly in the preceding book,..appears in this not to be impracticable. **1870** R. C. JEBB *Sophocles' Electra* (ed. 2) 126/1 Clytaemnestra says scoffingly..'now by *thy* favourite goddess'.

†**scoffion.** *Obs. rare*$^{-1}$. [a. F. *scoffion* (Du Bellay, 16th c.), *escoffion* (Molière), a. Sp. *escofion* or It. *scuffione* augmentative of Sp. *escofia*, It. *scuffia*, synonymous and cogn. w. Sp. *cofia*, It. *cuffia*: see COIF *sb.*] A kind of head-dress.

1604 E. G[RIMSTONE] *D'Acosta's Hist. Indies* IV. xiv. 249 Lelia a Romane Dame bestowed vppon a scoffion [orig. *tocado*] and a garment embroidered with pearle and emerald 400000. ducats.

scofflaw ('skɒflɔː). Chiefly *U.S.* [f. SCOFF *v.*^{1} + LAW *sb.*^{1}] One who treats the law with contempt, esp. a person who avoids various kinds of not easily enforceable laws. Also *attrib.*

1924 *Boston Herald* 16 Jan. 1/2 Delcevare King of Quincy last night announced that 'scofflaw' is the winning word in the contest for the $200 he offered for a word, to characterize the 'lawless drinker' of illegally made or illegally obtained liquor. 'Scofflaw' was chosen from more than 25,000 words, submitted from all the states and from several foreign countries. The word was sent by two contestants, so the prize will be equally divided between Henry Irving Dale.. and Miss Kate L. Butler. **1936** MENCKEN *Amer. Lang.* (ed. 4) 174 The announcement that *scofflaw*..had won was made on Jan. 15, 1924. The word came into immediate currency, and survived until the collapse of Prohibition. **1956** *N.Y. Times* 17 Jan. 27/3 The maximum fine of $50 a ticket was imposed yesterday upon a woman scofflaw who had accumulated fifty-one parking tickets. **1961** *Observer* 1 Oct. 30/6 An unenforceable law which automatically transformed every wet citizen into a scofflaw. **1965** P. DE VRIES *Let Me count Ways* iv. 57 A scofflaw in such a jam could easily insist that the facts in his possession during his lifetime justified his unbelief. **1971** J. GRAY *Red Lights* iii. 78 Moose Jaw became the happy hunting ground for Regina gamblers, philandering husbands..and unclassified scofflaws. **1973** D. E. WESTLAKE *Cops & Robbers* 25 He had New York plates. Good. If I gave him a ticket he couldn't be a scofflaw, fade away into some other state and thumb his nose at me. **1977** *Sat. Rev.* (U.S.) 3 Sept. 6/1 The illegal phone-dialing devices called 'blue boxes' are about to be put out of business... By..pressing its rewired dial-tone buttons, a scofflaw could bypass phone company billing systems.

†'**scofting.** *Obs. rare*$^{-1}$. [? f. Du. *schoft* blackguard.] A term of contempt for a person.

1514 BARCLAY *Cit. & Uplondyshm.* (Percy Soc.) 16 This scorfy scoftynge declareth openly Agaynste rurall men, rebuke and iniury.

scog, variant of SCUG *v. Sc.* and *dial.*

†'**scoggan.** *Mech. Obs.* Also 8 scoggen. [Of obscure origin; as it was a quasi-personal name, it may have been an application of SCOGGIN.

Commonly alleged to be from a dialect verb *scog*, to idle, loiter; but no such sense of the verb is known to exist. Desaguliers, the sole authority for the 'Humphrey Potter' story, does not say that the boy invented 'Scoggan' to save himself labour; he merely substituted one automatic contrivance for another less efficient. But the truth of the whole story has been questioned: see the art. *Newcomen* in *Dict. Nat. Biog.*]

An automatic contrivance for opening valves in Newcomen's steam engine *c* 1713. (See quot. 1744.)

1719 *Plate repr. Newcomen's engine* (*Dict. Nat. Biog.* art. Newcomen), Scoggen and his mate that do more work than the boy [? = buoy]. **1744** DESAGULIERS *Exper. Philos.* II. 533 They used before to work with a Buoy in the Cylinder.., which Buoy rose when the Steam was strong, and open'd the Injection,..thereby they were capable of only giving six, eight, or ten Strokes in a Minute, 'till a boy, Humphry Potter, who attended the Engine, added (what he call'd Scoggan) a Catch that the beam Q always open'd: and then it would go 15 or 16 Strokes in a Minute.

scogger ('skɒgə(r)). *north. dial.* Also skogger, scugger. [Cf. *cogger* COCKER *sb.*^{1} 2.] A footless stocking, or a knitted article of similar form, worn either as a gaiter or as a sleeve to protect the arm; also the foot of a stocking worn over the boot to prevent slipping on ice.

1615 BRATHWAIT *Strappado* 130 Fute-sare I was, for Bille shoon had neane, Nor hose-legs (wele I wate) but skoggers aud, That hardly hap't poore Billes legs fra caud. **1820** SOUTHEY *Wesley* I. 51 *note*, So the word [snuffers]..may possibly be a misprint for scoggers, as such sleeves are called in some parts of England. **1829** BROCKETT *N.C. Gloss.* (ed. 2), *Skogger*, the leg of an old stocking; used by countrymen to keep the snow out of their shoes. **1887** D. DONALDSON *Suppl. to Jamieson*, Scoggers, Scuggers. **1899** *Cumberld. Gloss.*, *Scogger*.

†'**scoggery.** *Obs. rare.* [App. for *scogginry: see next and -RY.] Buffoonery, scurrility.

1600 W. WATSON *Decacordon* (1602) 95 Villanie, scoggerie, and popularitie. *Ibid.* 266 You might haue left such scoggerie as Parsons hath set out in Greenecoate, to Tarleton, Nashe, or else to some Puritane Martin Mar-prelate.

†'**scoggin.** *Obs.* The name of John *Scoggin* (or Scogan), court fool to Edw. IV, used allusively for: A coarse jester, buffoon.

The allusion is to a fictitious compilation entitled Scoggin's Jests, licensed for printing in 1566; the 17th c. editions attribute the work to Andrew Boorde.

Shakspere (2 Hen. IV, III. ii.) confused the jester with Chaucer's friend Henry Scogan.

1579 G. HARVEY *Three Proper Lett.* (1580) 55 Some wordes we haue indeede, as for example..*ayer*, both *pro aere*, and *pro hærede*, for we say not *Heire*, but plaine *Aire* for him to, (or else Scoggins Aier were a poore iest) whiche are commonly, and maye indifferently be vsed eyther wayes. **1593** —— *Pierce's Super.* 2 Malice was neuer such an hypocrite, as now; and the world neuer such a Scoggin, as now. **1597** GERARDE *Herbal* I. xlii. 258[Stinking Orach] is of a most lothsome sauour.., vpon which plant if any should chaunce to rest and sleepe, he might very well report..that he had reposed himselfe amongst the chiefe of Scoggins heires. **1607** R. C[AREW] tr. *Estienne's World of Wonders* 253 Playing the Scoggins with the Scripture; a common thing at this day euen among the Laity. **1625** HART *Anat. Ur.* I. ii. 26 Hauing discoursed a little with this Scoggin concerning the errand he came for. **1653** R. SANDERS *Physiogn.* etc. 67 He that hath such a thing, deserves to be a Scoggin, an Vlespiegle, for he knows all the Tricks of knavery.

Comb. **1607** R. C[AREW] tr. *Estienne's World of Wonders* 281 Ridiculous and Scoggin-like speeches.

Hence '**scogginism** (also 7 scoganism), scurrilous jesting. '**scogginist**, a scurrilous jester. '**scogginly** *a.* (in 7 scoganly), scurrilous.

1593 G. HARVEY *Pierce's Super.* 17 The Ciceronian may sleepe, til the Scogginist hath plaid his part. One sure Conny-catcher, woorth twenty Philosophers. *Ibid.* 149 They..may peruse his guegawes with indifferency: and finde..no honesty, but pure Scogginisme; no Religion, but precise Marlowisme. **1620** BP. HALL *Hon. Marr. Clergy* I. viii. 46 But what doe I trouble my Reader with this idle

Scoganisme? Scolds or Iesters are onely fit for this combat. *Ibid.* III. iii. 269 Where is the shame of this Romane Priest, whiles he so manifestly belies our holy, reuerend, worthy Master Foxe, whom this Scoganly Pen dare say playes the Goose in the inconstancie of his Relation of this Nicholas?

† **scogh.** *Obs. rare.* Also **skowe, skuwe, scoe.** [a. ON. *skóg-r.*] A wood.

a **1375** *Cursor M.* 15826 (Fairf.) Baþ ouer hil & scogh. *a* **1400–50** *Alexander* 3915 And many scopid into þe scoghe without scath mare. *Ibid.* 5157 Scho gaffe skirmand skrikis at all þe skowis range. *c* **1420** *Anturs of Arth.* 53 (Irel.) Alle dyrkyns the dere, in the dym scoghes [*v.r.* skuwes], For drede of the dethe droupus the doe. *Ibid.* 129 The bryddus in the boes That of the gost gous Thay scryken in the scoes [*v.r.* skowes].

scoile, scoill, obs. Sc. forms of SCHOOL *sb.*[1]

scoinson (ˈskɔɪnsən). *Arch.* [Refashioned form of SCUNCHEON, after its source, OF. *escoinçon.*] Used *attrib.* in *scoinson arch* = REAR-ARCH; also in *scoinson shaft.*

1842 WILLIS *Arch. Nomencl. Mid. Ages* 57 The 'pilastres des écoinsons' of Roubo, correspond exactly in position to the mediæval 'scoinson shaft (or rear-shaft) above described. **1849** E. SHARPE *Decor. Window Tracery* v. 28 In Windows which are placed in walls of considerable thickness, or where the Tracery lies near the outer surface, ..there frequently occurs an arch which is not to be confounded with the Window-Arch... The object of this Arch, to which Professor Willis was the first to call attention, and which he has named the Scoinson-Arch, appears to have been twofold. **1851** TURNER *Dom. Archit.* II. 166 The scoinson arch is trefoiled. **1887** *Archit. Publ. Soc. Dict., Scoinson arch...* Also *rere* and *rear arch.* The interior edge of a window side.

scoir, scoit, scok: see SCORE, SHOOT, SHAKE.

scoke (skəʊk). *U.S.* [Of obscure origin.] The poke-weed, *Phytolacca decandra.*

1794 MORSE *Amer. Geog.* 145 Gargit or Skoke. **1856** A. GRAY *Man. Bot.* (1860) 361 *Phytolacca decandra,* (Common Poke or Scoke. Garget. Pigeon-Berry). **1866** *Treas. Bot.* s.v.

scol, -age, -ar, etc.: see SCHOOL *sb.*[1], SKOAL, SCHOOLAGE, SCHOLAR, etc.

scolay: see SCOLEYE.

scolcurye, obs. form of SKULKERY.

scold (skəʊld), *sb.* Forms: α. *north.* (now *north. dial.* and *Sc.*) 3–4, 8–9 **scald,** 4–6 **skald,** 5 **skawde, scawde, skalde, scalde,** 9 **scauld, scaad.** β. 3–7 **scolde,** 4–6 **skolde,** 5–7 **skold,** 6 **schold, skould,** 6–7 **scould,** 7 **scowld,** 3– **scold.** γ. *north.* 6 **scolle, skol, scaule, scoule,** 8 **scaul, scawl.** [App. a. ON. *skáld* neut. (see SKALD), originally meaning a poet; the sense-development postulated is strange, but the probability of a sense 'lampooner' as an intermediate stage seems to be indicated by the fact that the derivative *skáldskapr,* lit. 'skaldship', poetry, has in the Icel. law-books the specific sense of libel in verse.]

1. In early use, a person (esp. a woman) of ribald speech; later, a woman (rarely a man) addicted to abusive language.

In the example from Ormin, the sense may be 'minstrel'.

α. *c* **1200** ORMIN 2192 Full wel birrþ ure maȝȝdenn ben Forrshamedd, ȝiff mann brinngeþ Biforenn hire unnþæwfull word & wælinng word þurrh scaldess. *a* **1300** *Cursor M.* 22030 [Anticrist] sal be born..of bismer brem and bald And geten of a glotun scald [*Gött.* of glotun and skald] Þat þar may be na fuler tuin. *Ibid.* 29342 Womman commun and alsua scald, Alle ar suilk for cursd tald. *c* **1400** *Ywaine & Gaw.* 69 He was of his tong a skalde, And for to boste was he ful balde. *c* **1460** *Towneley Myst.* xiii. 596 Lett bren this bawde and bind her fast. A fals skawde hang at the last; so shall thou. **1483** *Cath. Angl.* 322/1 A Scawde, *barda, vt supra vbi* scalde. **1508** KENNEDIE *Flyting w. Dunbar* 322 And knaw, kene skald, I hald of Alathya. **1825** JAMIESON, *Scald,* 1. A scold; applied to a person.

β. *c* **1275** *Prov. Ælfred* 412 in *O.E. Misc.* 127 Be þu neuere to bold, to chiden agen oni scold. *Ibid.* 705 He is cocker, þef, and horeling, scolde, of wrechedome he is king. *c* **1325** *Poem temp. Edw. II* (Percy) li, As wel wol a knyȝt chide As eny scold in a toun. **1362** LANGL. *P. Pl.* A. XII. 34 And when scripture þe skolde hadde þus wyt y-sheued, Clergie in-to a caban crepte anon after. **1377** *Ibid.* B. XIX. 279 Ne sholde no scorner ne scolde oute of skyl hym brynge. *c* **1450** *Mirk's Festial* 229 A claterer, a ianguler, a flyter, a curser, a swerer, and a skold of hur mowþe. *a* **1529** SKELTON *Agst. Venemous Tongues* Wks. 1843 I. 132 A sclaunderous tunge, a tunge of a skolde, Worketh more mischiefe than can be tolde. **1565** *Child-Marriages* 127 She takes her for no schold, nor an vnhonest woman. **1577** HARRISON *England* III. vi. 108/1 Scoldes are ducked vpon cuckingstooles in the water. *a* **1586** SIDNEY *Arcadia* III. (1598) 345 Miso interrupted his tale, with rayling at Damætas, with all those exquisite termes, which I was neuer good skold inough to imagine. **1596** SHAKS. *Tam. Shr.* I. ii. 188, I know she is an irkesome brawling scold. **1611** BIBLE *Ecclus.* xxvi. 27 A loude crying woman, and a scolde, shall be sought out to driue away the enemies. **1611** COTGR., *Causeresse,* a scowld, a brabling woman. **1640** in *10th Rep. Hist. MSS. Comm.* App. IV. 433 For leading scoldes bridled along the Town at Mr. Bayliffes commaund, 6*d.* **1642** FULLER *Holy & Prof. St.* III. xxiii. 218 Fame hath much of the scold in her; the best way to silence her is to be silent. **1713** SHAFTESB. *Judgm. Hercules* iii. Charac. (1723) III. 368 The Painter..will doubtless beware of representing his Heroine as a mere Scold. **1782** MRS. H. COWLEY *Bold Stroke for Husband* I. ii, Every body supposes my lady an arrant scold. **1817** COLERIDGE *Biog. Lit.* xxiii. (1907) II. 206 The Prior was one of the many instances of a youthful sinner metamorphosed into an old scold. **1842** MRS. GORE *Fascination* 15 'If you only manage to drink the wine *I* send to fetch for you,' said the scold of a wife, 'you won't be much the worse for it.' **1863** P. BARRY *Dockyard Econ.* 67 Too often he is under the dominion of a forbidding scold, who, in addition to her other bad qualities, is slovenly and unthrifty.

γ. **1569** scolle, **1572** skol [see *scold-cart,* below]. **1570** LEVINS *Manip.* 43/45 A Scaule, *rixosa mulier. Ibid.* 218/15 A Scoule. **1718** RAMSAY *Christ's Kirk Gr.* III. xvi, Ye's thole for this, ye scaul. **1785** BURNS *Addr. Deil* xviii, His ill-tongu'd, wicked Scawl [*sc.* Job's wife].

b. *common scold*: a woman who disturbs the peace of the neighbourhood by her constant scolding.

1467 *Crt. Rolls Maldon, Essex* (Bundle 43 no. 1), Eadem Katerina est communis scolde. **1581** J. BELL *Haddon's Answ. Osor.* 500 Lyke a common skold in a Cage. **1769** BLACKSTONE *Comm.* IV. xiii. 169 A common scold, *communis rixatrix,* (for our law-latin confines it to the feminine gender,) is a public nusance to her neighbourhood. **1858** J. P. BISHOP *Comm. Crim. Law* II. §147 A common scold is one, who, by the practice of frequent scolding, disturbs the repose of the neighborhood.

c. *Comb.*: **scold's bit, bridle** = BRANKS[1] 1; † **scold-cart,** a cart used for the public exposure of common scolds.

1569 *Nottingham Rec.* IV. 135 Mendyng of the scolle kart. **1572** *Ibid.* IV. 145 Mendyng the skolcart. **1604** *Ibid.* IV. 265 Wee desire we may haue a scould carte for scoulds, and to carye criples in. **1858, 1869** Scold's bridle [see BRANKS[1] 1]. **1884** *Chr. World* 4 Sept. 661/5 Then came Walton, where the famous scold's bit is preserved in the church.

2. [From the verb.] An act of scolding; a scolding rebuke. ? *Obs.* exc. *Sc.*

α. **1773** FERGUSSON *Farmer's Ingle* 54 The waefu' scald o' our Mess-John to bide. **1831** R. SHENNAN *Tales, Songs,* etc. 65 (E.D.D.) Whiles they got a skelp or scauld. **1871** W. ALEXANDER *Johnny Gibb* iv. 33 Aw doot Gushetneuk cam' in for a bit scaad yon'er.

β. **1726** LADY M. W. MONTAGU *Let. to C'tess Mar* Apr. (1893) I. 495 Mamma and I were in an actual scold when my poor father expired. *a* **1774** GOLDSM. tr. *Scarron's Com. Romance* (1775) II. 133 The Lady Abbess had already put him in an ill humour by the scold she gave him for overturning her. **1778** JOHNSON *Let. to Mrs. Thrale* 31 Oct., To-day Mrs. Williams and Mrs. Desmoulins had a scold. **1807** WILLIAMS *Let. to Parr* 28 Dec. in *Parr's Wks.* (1828) VIII. 293, I should not have been so long in answering your sharp scold and soothing invitation had I not [etc.]. **1847** MRS. CARLYLE *Let.* Dec. in *New Lett.* (1903) I. 237, I have not had to transact one scold since this girl came to me. **1854** H. MILLER *Sch. & Schm.* (1858) 91 His scold died out good naturedly enough in the end, and I saw him laugh as he turned away. **1891** 'L. KEITH' *My Bonnie Lady* ix. 93 Now that I have given you your scolds we'll say no more about it.

scold (skəʊld), *v.* Forms: α. 4–6 **scolde,** 5 **scoolde,** 5–6 **skolde,** 6 **scoulde, skowlde, scowde, skoolde,** 6–7 **scould,** 7 **scowlde,** (9 *dial.* **scoud**), 6– **scold.** β. *north.* and *dial.* 6 **scaule, scoule,** 9 **scall.** γ. *Sc.* 8 **scald, scauld.** [f. SCOLD *sb.*

Notwithstanding the close resemblance in form and meaning with the WGer. str. vb. OFris. *skelda,* OS. *sceldan* (in a gloss), Du., MLG. *schelden,* OHG. *sceltan* (MHG., mod.G. *schelten*), there appears to be no etymological connexion.]

1. *intr.* † **a.** Originally, to behave as a scold; to quarrel noisily, to brawl; to rail *at* or wrangle *with* some one; to use violent or unseemly language in vituperation; said chiefly of women. *Obs.* **b.** Now with milder sense (partly as absol. use of sense 3): To use undignifed vehemence or persistence in reproof or fault-finding; *colloq.* often merely, to utter continuous reproof.

α. **1377** LANGL. *P. Pl.* B. II. 81 To scorne and to scolde sclaundere to make. **1398** TREVISA *Barth. De P.R.* VI. xiii. (1495) 197 Noo man hath more woo than he that hath an euyll wyfe, cryenge and janglynge, chydynge and skoldynge. **1526** TINDALE *N.T.* Prol. A ij b, Lest we..fall from meke lernynge into ydle despiciouns, braulinge and scoldynge aboute wordes. **1530** PALSGR. 706/2, I scoulde, as a man or woman dothe that chyde, *je tence...* They scolde togyther lyke two women. *a* **1548** HALL *Chron., Hen. VIII,* 160 b, Every day almost they would bryng them furth openly and scolde and chyde with them, and make them beleve that they woulde hange them if they were not payed. **1584** in D. Fenner *Def. Ministers* (1587) 43 Let him goe home and skoolde with his wife. **1596** SHAKS. *Tam. Shr.* I. i. 177 Mark'd you not how hir sister Began to scold, and raise vp such a storme, That mortal eares might hardly indure the din. **1607** —— *Cor.* v. vi. 106 Pardon me Lords, 'tis the first time that euer I was forc'd to scoul'd. *c* **1618** MORYSON *Itin.* IV. (1903) 239 Some runn out to braule and scowlde like women with the next enemyes. **1673** WOOD *Life* (O.H.S.) II. 265, I told her I came to be merry and not to be scolded at. **1675** ALSOP *Anti-Sozzo* III. ii. 193 Therefore go scold with the Apostle: that which will bring him off will bring off the Doctor. **1713** SWIFT *Cadenus & Vanessa* 287 For Gods, we are by Homer told, Can in Celestial Language scold. **1722** DE FOE *Col. Jack* vii, I scolded heartily at him when he came back. **1764** WESLEY *Jrnl.* 21 June, A woman had 'scolded with her neighbour'. **1771** SMOLLETT *Humph. Cl.* 24 Apr. (1815) 37 He might harp as long as he pleased upon her scolding; but she never scolded, except for his advantage. **1822** A. CUNNINGHAM *Tradit. Tales, Death of Laird of Warlsworm* (1887) 273 All women love to be married, were it only for the sake of having somebody to scold at. **1833** T. HOOK *Parson's Dau.* II. iii, I have no doubt that Lady Frances will, at first, look grave, and even perhaps scold, but it will wear off. **1847** C. BRONTË *Jane Eyre* iv, I just put my two arms round her, and said, 'Come, Bessie! don't scold.'

β. **1570** LEVINS *Manip.* 44/2 To Scaule, *rixari. Ibid.* 218/24 To Scoule. **1820** J. JOHNSTONE *Poems* 127 (E.D.D.) I'm sure that ye a' got a part o't, And needna scall oft sae at me.

2. quasi-*trans.* with complementary adj., adv., or phrase expressing the result of scolding. Also † *to scold it out*: to continue wrangling to the end.

c **1590** GREENE *Fr. Bacon* xiii. 48 Stand on thy guard, I cannot scold it out. **1613** SHAKS. *Hen. VIII,* v. i. 173 *Lady.* An hundred Marks? By this light, Ile ha more... I will haue more, or scold it out of him. *c* **1645** HOWELL *Lett.* (1655) IV. vii. 18 She had scolded her Husband one day out of doores. **1650** B. *Discolliminium* 10 Meer morall prudence might suffer wise men to stand still.., and such shallow heads as I am, to scould themselves quiet. **1754** WARBURTON *View Bolingbr. Philos.* I. 34 My Master is not a man to be scratched and scolded out of his Kingdom. **1783** COWPER *Let.* 17 June, No man was ever scolded out of his sins. **1887** R. N. CAREY *Uncle Max* v. 42, I scolded back the foolish thoughts, and felt ashamed of myself for entertaining them.

3. *trans.* To address (esp. an inferior or a child) with continuous and more or less angry reproach; to chide.

This construction is prob. of late introduction from northern dialects. Johnson does not mention it in his Dictionary (1755), though Boswell reports him as having used it orally in 1763. In the 19th c. the use was still colloquial rather than literary, and its associations were somewhat undignified; but it is now quite free from the discreditable implications which the intransitive use (sense 1) has not yet wholly lost.

1715 RAMSAY *Christ's Kirk Gr.* II. xxiii, Auld nick Should tempt their wifes to scald Them for't. **1763** JOHNSON in *Boswell* (1831) I. 418 You may scold a carpenter who has made you a bad table, though you cannot make a table. **1771** SMOLLETT *Humph. Cl.* 2 June (1815) 120 She has left off scolding the servants. **1781** COWPER *On Madan's Answ. Newton* 12 But the strife is the strangest that ever was known, If a man must be scolded for loving his own [wife]. **1832** LYTTON *Eugene A.* I. v, Well, Walter, I feel, for the first time these ten years, that I have a right to scold you. **1848** THACKERAY *Van. Fair* lxi, She scolds the servants from morning till night. **1865** LIVINGSTONE *Zambesi* xix. 398 The headman scolded the fellow for his meanness. **1889** MRS. OLIPHANT *Poor Gentl.* xlii. III. 173 She scolded Anne,..but so softly that Anne fell asleep in the middle of the little lecture.

scoldable (ˈskəʊldəb(ə)l), *a. nonce-wd.* [f. SCOLD *v.* + -ABLE.] Fit or suitable to be scolded.

1857 MISS MULOCK *Woman's Th.* iii. (1858) 44 A kissable, scoldable, sugar plum-feedable plaything. **1903** *Westm. Gaz.* 22 May 3/2 The small caddie is a defenceless, a scoldable thing.

scolde, obs. form of SCALD *v.*

scolder[1] (ˈskəʊldə(r)). [f. SCOLD *v.* + -ER[1].] One who scolds. Formerly, †a common scold.

1423 *Coventry Leet-bk.* 59 A Cookestowle..to punysche skolders and chidders as þe law wyll. **1497** *Will* in Strype *Stow's Surv.* (1754) I. 573/2 Provyded that al Vacabonds, Scowldars, and Brawlers be rewarded after the Mind and Discretion, and good Conscience of mine Executors. *c* **1510** BARCLAY *Mirr. Gd. Manners* (1570) G iij, Heare not that scolder and brauling hounde of hell. **1595** KATH. OLIVER *Conf.* in *Trans. Roy. Hist. Soc.* Ser. III. (1907) I. 273, I have bene a scoulder and a slaunderouse person, and a source of strife amongst my neighbors. **1673** H. STUBBE *Further Justif. War Netherl.* 70 A Scoulder and a Taunter is reckoned..with Thieves and Idolaters. **1794** COLERIDGE *Robespierre* I. 183 The cool ferocious Robespierre turn'd scolder! **1875** M. COLLINS *Sweet & Tw.* I. I. vii. 102 Betty Carr was a finer scolder..than you will easily meet with.

scolder[2] (ˈskəʊldə(r)). *Orkneys.* Also 8 **sceolder.** The oyster-catcher, *Hæmatopus ostralegus.*

a **1795** G. LOW *Fauna Orcad.* (1813) 91 The Sea-Pie.. Orc. Sceolder. **1805** G. BARRY *Orkney Isl.* 306 The Sea Pie ..in some places here gets the name of the scolder.

scolding (ˈskəʊldɪŋ), *vbl. sb.* [f. SCOLD *v.* + -ING[1].] The action of the verb SCOLD; vituperation, angry reproach, reproof.

1486 *Bk. St. Albans* f. vij, A scoldyng of kemsteris. **1547** *Nottingham Rec.* (1889) IV. 92 We presentt Anes Fylldyng for okypying of comyn skowdyng. *a* **1586** SIDNEY *Arcadia* I. (Sommer) 59 He fell to a fresh scolding, in such mannerlie manner, as might well shewe he had passed thro' the discipline of a Tauerne. **1596** SHAKS. *Tam. Shr.* I. ii. 109 And she knew him as wel as I do, she would thinke scolding would doe little good vpon him. **1651** BAXTER *Inf. Bapt.* 239 And then they make Religion the pretence for all their scoldings. **1755** J. SHEBBEARE *Lydia* (1769) II. 33 Mrs. Clench, as I am informed, was obliged to turn her and her mother out of doors, they kept such an eternal scolding together. **1877** O. W. HOLMES *How not to Settle it* 12 A page of Hood may do a fellow good After a scolding from Carlyle or Ruskin. **1875** W. S. HAYWARD *Love agst. World* 38, I shall give him a good scolding after dinner.

b. *attrib.* and *Comb.*, as *scolding-match*; † **scolding cart** = *scold-cart* (SCOLD *sb.* 1 c); **scolding-stock** *nonce-wd.*, an object for scolding; † **scolding stool,** a cucking stool.

1474 in *Jrnl. Chester Arch.* etc. *Soc.* (1861) VI. 216 Costes doon in makyng of the scooldyng stoole. **1629** in W. Kelly *Anc. Rec. Leicester* (1855) 78 Paid to Frauncis Pallmer for making two wheeles and one barr for the Scolding-Cart ij[s]. **1754** FIELDING *Voy. Lisbon* Wks. 1882 VII. 65 She played on two instruments..; these were two maids, or rather scolding-stocks. **1855** MACAULAY *Hist. Eng.* xv. III. 548 Report indeed spoke of some scolding matches between the Chancellor and his friend.

scolding (ˈskəʊldɪŋ), *ppl. a.* [f. SCOLD *v.* + -ING[2].] That scolds.

? **1533** FRITH *Another Bk. agst. Rastell* B iij, He..calleth them raylynge gestynge and scoldinge wordes. **1577** KENDALL *Flowers of Epigr.* 95 b, But Molzus..caste in his wife, and saied, Naught heauier than a skoldyng wife, I deme there can be waied. **1596** SHAKS. *Tam. Shr.* I. ii. 100 Her name is Katherina Minola, Renown'd in Padua for her scolding tongue. **1638–56** COWLEY *Davideis* III. note 37 Juvenal says of a loud scolding woman, that she alone was able to relieve the Moon out of an Eclipse. **1719** D'URFEY *Pills* II. 324 Think what lives Some of you daily Live with Scolding Wives. **1844** MRS. CARLYLE *Lett.* I. 298, I have written Jeannie a very scolding letter.

transf. and *fig.* **1601** SHAKS. *Jul. C.* I. iii. 5, I haue seene Tempests, when the scolding Winds Haue riu'd the knottie Oakes. **1855** TENNYSON *Brook* 84 The gate Half-parted from a weak and scolding hinge, Stuck.

Hence **'scoldingly** *adv.*

1548 ELYOT *Dict., Rixose*, scoldynglie. **1912** J. STEPHENS *Crock of Gold* v. xiv. 208 As they approached the door the sound of a female voice came to them scoldingly. **1933** E. O'NEILL *Ah, Wilderness!* IV. iii. 152 She goes on scoldingly.

†**'scoldster.** *Obs. rare*$^{-1}$. In 7 skolster. [f. SCOLD *sb.* + -STER.] A scold.

c **1600** in A. H. A. Hamilton *Quarter Sessions* (1878) 85 [By the entry in the Sessions Book, it appears that Agnes Pringe was indicted for a] Skolster.

scole, obs. f. SCALE *sb.*[1]; SCHOOL; SHOAL; SKULL.

scolear, obs. form of SCHOLAR.

scoleces, pl. of SCOLEX.

scolecid (skəʊ'liːsɪd). [ad. mod.L. *Scōlēcida* neut. pl., f. Gr. σκώληξ SCOLEX: see -ID.] An animal of the class *Scolecida* of *Annuloida*.

1864 HUXLEY *Elem. Comp. Anat.* 76 The ciliated larvæ of some Scolecids and Echinoderms.

scoleciform (skəʊ'lɛsɪfɔːm), *a.* [f. mod.L. *scōlēc-*, SCOLEX + -(I)FORM.] Resembling or having the character of a scolex.

1891 *Century Dict.* s.v., The measles of pork is the scoleciform stage of *Tænia solium*.

scolecite ('skɒlɪsaɪt). Formerly skol-, scolezite. [f. Gr. σκωληκ-, σκώληξ SCOLEX + -ITE[1].

The name in sense 1 was given because the mineral sometimes curls up when heated. The orig. form *scolezite* is f. Ger. *scolezit* (1813, see Chester *Dict. Min.* 1896).]

1. *Min.* Hydrous silicate of aluminium and calcium, found in needle-shaped crystals and fibrous or radiated masses.

1823 W. PHILLIPS *Min.* (ed. 3) 40 Skolezite. **1829** *Nat. Philos., Optics* xviii. 61 (U.K.S.) Scolezite. **1857** DANA *Man. Min.* (1862) 167 Scolecite resembles natrolite.

2. *Bot.* The vermiform carpogonium of certain fungi.

1875 COOKE & BERKELEY *Fungi* 173 Tulasne observes that this 'scolecite' or ringed body can be readily isolated in Ascobolus furfuraceus. **1882** VINES tr. *Sachs' Bot.* 310 The adjacent threads put out small branches, pollinodia, the terminal cells of which attach themselves firmly to the anterior part of the scolecite.

†**scolecobrotic.** *Obs.*$^{-1}$ [f. Gr. σκωληκ(ο)-, σκώληξ SCOLEX + βρωτικός inclined to eat. Cf. σκωληκόβρωτος worm-eaten.] A vermifuge.

1661 LOVELL *Hist. Anim. & Min.* 369 Ascarides [are killed] by suppositories, clysters, with scolecobroticks, &c.

scolecoid (skəʊ'liːkɔɪd), *a.* Also *erron.* scolicecoid. [ad. Gr. σκωληκοειδής, f. σκωληκ-, σκώληξ worm, SCOLEX: see -OID.] Resembling a worm or a scolex.

1858 MAYNE *Expos. Lex., Scolecoides*, resembling a worm; vermiform: scolecoid. **1864** [see SCOLEX]. **1891** in *Century Dict.*

scolecology (skɒlɪ'kɒlədʒɪ). [ad. mod.L. *scōlēcologia*, f. Gr. σκωληκ(ο)-, σκώληξ worm, SCOLEX + -λογία -LOGY.] A treatise on worms.

1858 in MAYNE *Expos. Lex.* **1895** in *Funk's Stand. Dict.*

scolecophagous (skɒlɪ'kɒfəgəs), *a.* [f. mod.L. *scōlēcophagus*, a. Gr. σκωληκοφάγος f. σκωληκ(ο)-, σκώληξ worm (see SCOLEX) + -φάγος: see -PHAGOUS.] 'Worm-eating, as a bird' (*Cent. Dict.* 1891).

scoleir, -er(e, obs. forms of SCHOLAR.

†**scoleryng.** *Obs. rare*$^{-1}$. [f. *scolere* SCHOLAR.

The sense seems to require a fem. rather than a dim. formation, but it is not easy to explain *-ing* as a fem. suffix, as *carling* (CARLINE[1]), the only example of the fem. ending *-ing*, is purely northern. But Chaucer or his scribe may have been familiar with the Du. and LG. suffix *-in*.]

? A female scholar.

14.. *Chaucer's Wife's Prol.* 44–45 Diverse scoles maken parfyt clerkes..; Of five husbondes scoleryng am I.

‖**scolex** ('skəʊlɛks). Pl. scoleces (skəʊ'liːsiːz), also *erron.* scolices ('skəʊlɪsiːz). [mod.L., a. Gr. σκώληξ (*pl.* σκώληκες) worm.] The larva or embryo produced directly from the egg in metagenesis; esp. the larva or head of a tapeworm or other parasitic worm.

1855 T. R. JONES *Anim. Kingd.* (ed. 2) 135 The Scolex, therefore, in this stage of development is synonymous with 'the head', or, as it might as well be called, the 'root' of the worm. **1864** COBBOLD *Entozoa* 265 These thickened portions, in their turn, become true scolices, or, in some cases, scolicecoid formations. **1888** ROLLESTON & JACKSON *Anim. Life* 233 Van Beneden's discovery of proscolices with scolices in all stages of growth in the intestine of the Lump-fish.

attrib. **1857** tr. *von Siebold's Tape & Cystic Worms* (Syd. Soc.) 87 This worm [*bothriocephalus latus*] is never met with amongst our cattle in a scolex condition. **1865** *Nat. Hist. Rev.* July 349 A small scolex-cyst.

†**sco'leye**, *v. Obs. rare.* Also (*v.rr.*) scolay, scoleie, scholey, schole heye, skole-aye. [? a. AF. *escoleier, f. OF. *escole* SCHOOL.] *intr.* To attend school; to study as a scholar.

c **1386** CHAUCER *Prol.* 302 But al þat he myghte of his freendes hente, On bookes and his lernynge he it spente, And bisily gan for the soules preye Of hem þat yaf hym wher with to scoleye. *a* **1400–50** *Alexander* 645 þus skilfull lange he scolaid & þe scole vsed. **1430–40** LYDG. *Bochas* IV. ix. (1494) o vj, Calistenes was in his youth put for to scoleye [*MS. Rawl.* scoleie, 1554 scoleye, 1558 scholey] In the two scoles of prudent Socrates And of plato.

scolezite, obs. form of SCOLECITE.

scolicecoid, erron. form of SCOLECOID.

scolices, pl. (*erron.*) of SCOLEX.

scolier, obs. form of SCHOLAR.

Scoline ('skəʊliːn). *Pharm.* Also scoline. [f. S(UCCINYL)C(H)OLINE.] A proprietary name for succinylcholine.

1952 *Trade Marks Jrnl.* 30 Jan. 89/2 *Scoline*... Pharmaceutical preparations and substances. Allen & Hanburys Ltd, Three Colts Lane, Bethnal Green, London, E.2; wholesale Chemists and Druggists. **1952** *Lancet* 21 June 1226/2 Succinylcholine chloride ('Scoline') was given intravenously. **1965** J. POLLITT *Depression & its Treatment* iv. 50 A modern relaxant such as succeryl choline (Scoline) is given intravenously. **1965** *Daily Express* 14 Oct. 5/7 The two-inch long ampoules of scoline and of distilled water.. were kept together in a plastic bowl in a refrigerator. **1976** SMYTHIES & CORBETT *Psychiatry* xvii. 291 American psychologists treated some criminals in jail by asking them to imagine themselves reliving the circumstances of their criminal activities and then giving an injection of scoline.

scoliograptic, *a. nonce-wd.* [f. Gr. σκολιόγραπτ-ος marked with oblique lines (f. σκολιό-ς bent, crooked + γραπτός marked as with letters, f. γράφ-ειν to write, mark) + -IC.] Obliquely marked.

1853 *Fraser's Mag.* XLVII. 257 All mackerel are nearly similar in form, hue, and the scoliograptic markings of their sides and backs.

scolion ('skəʊlɪən). *Gr. Antiq.* Also skolion, scolium, *erron.* scholion. [Gr. σκόλιον.] A song sung in turn by the guests at a banquet.

1603 HOLLAND *Plutarch* 1257 Terpander was the inventour of those songs called *Scolia*, which were sung at feasts. **1656** STANLEY *Hist. Philos.* VI. iv. 7 Which Athenæus, proveth against the Calumiations of Demophilus not to be a sacred hymne or Pæan, but a *Scolion* or Festivall Song. **1776** BURNEY *Hist. Mus.* I. 467 In the following Scolium, Timocreon gives his opinion of riches. **1850** MURE *Lit. Greece* III. 101 The celebrated scolion, or series of scolia, addressed to Harmodius and Aristogiton. **1874** MAHAFFY *Soc. Life Greece* x. 296, I mean the *Scolia*, when one guest commenced a sentence in verse, and handed a branch to any other he chose, who was compelled to finish the verse in the cleverest way he could.

‖**scoliosis** (skɒlɪ'əʊsɪs). Pl. scolioses (-'əʊsiːz). *Path.* [mod.L., a. Gr. σκολίωσις, f. σκολι-ός bent, curved, crooked: see -OSIS.] Lateral curvature of the spine; distinguished from *lordosis* and *cyphosis*. Hence **scoli'otic** *a.* [see -OTIC], pertaining to scoliosis.

1706 PHILLIPS (ed. Kersey), *Scoliosis*. **1849–52** *Todd's Cycl. Anat.* IV. 949/1 The vertebral column misformed by *scoliosis*. **1858** MAYNE *Expos. Lex., Scoliotic*. **1875** KNIGHT *Dict. Mech., Scoliosis Brace*, a brace for treating lateral curvature of the spine. **1899** *Allbutt's Syst. Med.* VI. 555 The arguments centering round the nature of the scoliosis which is so common. **1939** H. H. JORDAN *Orthopedic Appliances* iii. 90 A group of scolioses which are suitable for treatment by forces which we can introduce by means of an active correcting brace. **1958** *Jrnl. Bone & Joint Surg.* XLA. 553 Correction and fusion of the scoliotic spine. **1976** *Lancet* 4 Dec. 1234/1 In the causation and progression of scoliosis spinal muscles may have a major role. *Ibid.*, On electronmicroscopy there are signs of dystrophy and atrophy in the spinal muscles of scoliotic patients.

scolk, scolker: see SKULK, SKULKER.

scoll, obs. form of SCHOOL; variant of SKOAL.

scollage, scollar: see SCHOOLAGE, SCHOLAR.

†**scollardicall**, *a. Obs. rare.* [f. *scollard* (see SCHOLAR 3 c) + -ICAL.] A supposed illiterate epithet for a man of learning.

1654 WHITLOCK *Zootomia* 69 These peevish Scollardicall Doctors (that will not let people beleive Lies quietly).

scolle, obs. f. SCHOOL *sb.*[1], SCOLD, SKULL.

scoller, scollerie, obs. ff. SCHOLAR, SCULLERY.

scollop, *sb.*[1] and *v.*: see SCALLOP.

scollop ('skɒləp), *sb.*[2] *Irish.* Also scolp. [a. Irish *sgolb.*] A thatch-peg.

1813 MAR. EDGEWORTH *Early Lessons* (1829) III. 107 The thatcher.. fastens them down with bent twigs which he calls scollops. Here is a scollop: you see it is sharpened at both ends that it may stick in the roof. **1873** O'CURRY *Manners Anc. Irish* III. 32 The house.. was thatched with straw, rushes, or sedge, and neatly fastened down with what are now Anglicised 'scollops'. **1888** LAWS *Little Eng.* 421 [Pembrokeshire word] *Scolps*, thatch pegs.

scollup, obs. form of SCALLOP *sb.*

‖**scoloc** ('skɒləʊk). *Hist.* Also scoloch, scolog. [OIrish *scolóc*, f. *scol* SCHOOL; cf. mod.Irish *scológ, scalóg* farmer, rustic, and SCALLAG (though these may be of different origin).] (See quots.)

Cf. Reg. Dunelm. *De Cuthberti Vita* (Surtees), p. 179: Clerici illi..qui Pictorum lingua Scollofthes cognominantur.

1852 J. ROBERTSON in *Spalding Club Miscell.* V. Pref. App. 56 Three offices or grades of a scholastic kind—the Scolocs, the Master of the Schools, and the Ferleiginn—obtained in the ancient Scottish Church. *Ibid.* 59 The Lord Bishop protested..that the heir of every Scolog ('*cujuslibet Scolgi*', '*cuius Scolagij*') should enter to his heritage by inquest and seisin. **1873** BURTON *Hist. Scot.* (ed. 2) I. 399 Researches through the records show that among the Culdees there was a grade of churchman—the humblest, apparently—who was called the scholar. In the Pictish language, as we are told, he was called Scoloch. **1888** W. LOCKHART *Ch. Scot. 13th c.* 122 There had been..a deadly feud between two Scolocs or Scologs (*clerici scholares*).

scolopaceous (skɒləʊ'peɪʃəs), *a. Ornith.* [f. mod.L. *scolopāceus*, f. L. *scolopax* snipe, woodcock, a. Gr. σκολόπαξ: see -ACEOUS.] Resembling a snipe; *spec.* used as epithet of a species of courlan, *Aramus scolopaceus*. Also = next.

1785 LATHAM *Gen. Synopsis Birds* V. 102 Scolopaceous Heron..inhabits Cayenne. **1819** J. F. STEPHENS in *Shaw's Gen. Zool.* XI. II. 540 Scolopaceous courlan (*Aramus Scolopacea*). **1835** KIRBY *Hab. & Inst. Anim.* II. xxiii. 454 The plumage of others, especially of some of the scolopaceous tribe, is beautifully mottled. **1841** SELBY in *Proc. Berw. Nat. Club* I. No. 9. 254 Of the Scolopaceous family, there are two..residents.

scolopacine ('skɒləʊpəsɪn), *a.* and *sb.* [ad. mod.L. *scolopacinus*, f. L. *scolopac-em, scolopax*: see prec. and -INE[1].] **a.** *adj.* Belonging to the sub-family *Scolopacinæ* or the family *Scolopacidæ*, typified by the genus *Scolopax*, and including the woodcock, redshank, etc. **b.** *sb.* A scolopacine bird.

In recent Dicts.

scolopale ('skɒləpeɪl). *Ent.* Formerly also **-pala** (pl. **-palæ**). [ad. G. *scolopal* adj. (in *scolopale körperchen*) (V. Gräber 1882, in *Arch. f. mikrosk. Anat.* XX. 516), f. Gr. σκολοπ-, σκόλοψ spike + *-al* -AL.] The rod-like structure inside the sheath of a scolopidium; also, the sheath itself.

1912 J. H. COMSTOCK *Spider Bk.* iii. 169 The failure of other observers to discover scolopalæ or auditory pins..has made this conclusion doubtful. **1917** *Ann. Entomol. Soc. Amer.* X. 69 Its distal portion penetrates the center of the enveloping cell into the proximal end of the cap cell, where the nerve enlarges to form the peg-shaped body or scolopale. **1925** [see SCOLOPOPHORE]. **1932** *Parasitology* XXIV. 457 These cells are connected with the main antennal nerve, whereas the other end gives off a long scolopala, or the sense rod. **1948** *Sci. News* VII. 19 One finds in all insects structures which consist of parallel elements—elongated spindle-shaped sensory cells whose axes are prolonged into nerve fibres on the central side while on the other side they are in contact with the so-called 'scolopales' (pointed stakes). **1964** [see SCOLOPOPHORE]. **1969** R. F. CHAPMAN *Insects* xxx. 630 The most fully studied contact chemoreceptors are the trichoid sensilla on the legs and mouth-parts of *Phormia*. They are from 30 to 300 μ long. From the tip the scolopale is invaginated. **1978** H. V. DALY et al. *Introd. Insect Biol. & Diversity* vi. 107/2 In the usual arrangement [of sensilla], the dendrite of a single bipolar neuron is attached to a movable part of the body, often by a minute cuticular sheath called a scolopale.

scolopender (skɒləʊ'pɛndə(r)). Also 6–8 scolopendre. [a. F. *scolopendre*, ad. L. *scolopendra*.]

1. = SCOLOPENDRA 2.

1562 TURNER *Herbal* II. 55 The same [leaves of wild mint] ..are dronken..agaynst scolopendres & styngynges of serpentes. **1569** J. SANFORD tr. *Agrippa's Van. Artes* 138 Serpents, Salpeges, Scolopenders. **1597** GERARDE *Herbal* II. ccxv. 553 Mint..is taken inwardly against Scolopenders. **1610** MARCELLINE *Tri. Jas. I* 5 His Squadrons are prepared, and consiste of Furyes, Scolopenders, Stellions, Phalanges, and Philemons, more mad and enraged then those of Orestes. **1658** ROWLAND tr. *Moufet's Theat. Ins.* 1045 The great earth Scolopender. **1759** *Phil. Trans.* LI. 35 This creature, in its figure, is like the Land Scolopendre. *Ibid.* 37 Having put these Sea Scolopendres upon my fingers, they thrust a great number of their prickles into the skin, and caused a sharp pain for some hours. **1867** *Morn. Star* 29 Jan., The body and tail of a monster scolopender. **1881** DARWIN *Veg. Mould* ii. 62 Can the plugs aid in concealing the burrows from scolopenders,..the bitterest enemies of the worms?

†**2.** = SCOLOPENDRA 1. *Obs.*

1658 PHILLIPS, *Scolopender*,..also a certain fish, which having swallowed a hook vomited up its entrails, and rid of it sucketh them in again.

†**3.** = SCOLOPENDRIUM. *Obs.* [Cf. Gr. σκολόπενδρα used by Galen for σκολοπένδριον.]

1696 PHILLIPS (ed. 5), *Scolopender*... Also a certain Medicinal Herb, vulgarly call'd Harts-Tongue, in Latin

Scolopendria, such as Sea-green, Nightshade, Water Lentils, &c.

‖**scolopendra** (skɒləʊˈpɛndrə). Also 7 *erron.* scolopendria. [L., a. Gr. σκολόπενδρα.]

†**1.** A fabulous sea-fish which 'feeling himselfe taken with a hooke, casteth out his bowels, vntill hee hath vnloosed the hooke, and then swalloweth them vp againe' (Bullokar *Eng. Expos.* 1616).

1590 SPENSER *F.Q.* II. xii. 23 Bright Scolopendraes, arm'd with siluer scales. **1591** SYLVESTER *Du Bartas* I. v. 278 But, if the Scolopendra have suckt-in The sowr-sweet morsell with the barded Pin, She hath as rare a trick to rid her from it: For, instantly, she all her guts doth vomit; [etc.]. **1635** SWAN *Spec. M.* (1670) 342 The Scolopendra is a fish.. which refuseth not the bait, but [etc.].

2. A centipede or millipede. Also, a Linnean genus of myriapods, including the largest and most formidable of the centipedes.

1608 TOPSELL *Serpents* 31 There are Scolopendraes Vipers, and Slow-wormes in Creete, yet.. they are without venome. **1611** COTGR., *Scolopendre*, the Scolopendria, a reddish, many-legd, and venomous worme. **1646** SIR T. BROWNE *Pseud. Ep.* III. xv. 142 Upon the same ground hath arisen the same mistake concerning the Scolopendra or hundred footed insect. **1673** E. BROWN *Trav. Germ.*, etc. (1677) 17 An Indian Scolopendra, or Forty-foot. **1751** CHAMBERS *Cycl.* s.v. *Dying* [*Advancement of*], The amber-coloured scolopendra will give, with lye, a most beautiful and pleasant azure. **1796** STEDMAN *Surinam* II. xxiii. 167 We discovered some scolopendras, or centipedes, no less than eight or ten inches in length. **1829** H. MURRAY *N. Amer.* I. xi. 516 Rattlesnakes and scolopendras crawled about. **1861** HULME tr. *Moquin-Tandon* v. ii. 265 The Scolopendra are insects belonging to the order Myriopoda and to the family Chilopoda. They are commonly termed Millipedes.

†**3.** Applied in reproach to a woman. *Obs.*

1633 SHIRLEY *Gamester* II. ii, More wine, you varlets! And call your mistress up, you scolopendra. *a* **1668** DAVENANT *Siege* v. (1673) 83 Go bring a Barrel hither; why? when you Scolopendra.

scolopendre, obs. form of SCOLOPENDER.

scolopendria, obs. erron. f. SCOLOPENDRA; obs. f. SCOLOPENDRIUM.

scolopendriform (skɒləʊˈpɛndrɪfɔːm), *a. Ent.* [f. mod.L. *Scolopendra* (see SCOLOPENDRA 2) + -(I)FORM.] Resembling a centipede; *spec.* applied to the larvæ of certain water beetles.

1828 KIRBY & SPENCE *Entomol.* xxx. III. 167 [The larva of Gyrinus] appears to be the most perfectly Scolopendriform of any yet known.

scolopendrine (skɒləʊˈpɛndrɪn), *a.* [f. mod.L. *Scolopendrinæ*, f. *Scolopendra* (the Linnean genus: see SCOLOPENDRA 2) + -INE.] Resembling or related to the centipedes. **scolopendrine scale-back**, a polychætous marine annelid of the genus *Polynoë*, as *P. scolopendrina*; a kind of sea-centipede. Also *fig.*

1882 *Cassell's Nat. Hist.* VI. 230 This Scolopendrine Scale-back [*Polynoe scolopendrina*] is four inches in length. **1963** V. NABOKOV *Gift* iv. 257 He left a scolopendrine trace in literature as the translator of foreign poets.

‖**scolopendrium** (skɒləʊˈpɛndrɪəm). Also 7–8 scolopendria. [mod.L., ad. L. *scolopendrion* = Gr. σκολοπένδριον a hart's-tongue fern, so called from a fancied resemblance to the scolopendra.] A genus of ferns; a fern of this genus; = HART'S-TONGUE.

1611 COTGR., *Scolopendrie vraye*,.. called *Vraye*, to make it differ from Harts-tongue, or stone Harts-tongue, which is also (falsly) tearmed *Scolopendria.* **1621** BURTON *Anat. Mel.* II. iv. I. iii. 439 Scolopendria, Cuscuta, Ceteratche, Mugwort. **1729** in *Dampier's Voy.* (ed. 3) III. 428 The Flat-ring'd Scolopendria. Is black, with yellow Edges on the Rings. **1882** GEIKIE *Geol. Sketches* 9 Not a vestige of vegetation could we see save.. some dwarfed scolopendriums.

scolopendroid (skɒləʊˈpɛndrɔɪd), *a.* [f. SCOLOPENDRA + -OID.] Resembling a scolopendra.

1839–47 *Todd's Cycl. Anat.* III. 548/1 In the Scolopendroid races, the rings are flattened.

scolophore, var. SCOLOPOPHORE.

scolopidium (skɒləˈpɪdɪəm). *Ent.* Pl. -idia. [mod.L., coined in Ger. (F. Eggers 1923, in *Zool. Anzeiger* LVII. 239), f. Gr. σκολοπ-, σκόλοψ spike, after OMMATIDIUM.] An elongated sensory end-organ in insects consisting chiefly of the nucleus and dendrite of a sensory nerve cell and a tubular sheath enclosing the dendrite; *spec.* each of those that compose a chordotonal organ.

1939 V. B. WIGGLESWORTH *Princ. Insect Physiol.* vii. 135 Chordotonal sensilla or scolopidia—These sensilla are generally believed to be derived from campaniform sensilla through their component parts becoming elongated and deeply sunk within the body. **1957** *New Biol.* XXIII. 38 Applied to the inside of the membrane [of a locust's tympanal organ] are the ends of a number of special sense cells, or scolopidia, which transmit the movements of the membrane as impulses along the auditory nerve. **1971** [see SCOLOPOID *a.*]. **1978** H. V. DALY et al. *Introd. Insect Biol. & Diversity* vi. 107/2 Chordotonal organs are completely internal and formed by units or scolopidia consisting of three cells: a bipolar neuron, a scolopale cell, and an attachment cell.

scolopoid (ˈskɒləpɔɪd), *a. Ent.* [f. Gr. σκολοπ-, σκόλοψ spike + -OID.] = SCOLOPOPHOROUS *a.*

1963 V. G. DETHIER *Physiol. Insect Senses* ii. 19 (*caption*) Different forms of scolopoid sensilla. A. Terminal peg from a grasshopper sensillum. [Etc.] **1971** E. O. WILSON *Insect Societies* (1972) xi. 202/2 Typical chordotonal sensilla—or scolopoid sensilla, or scolopidia as they are often alternatively labelled.

scolopophore (ˈskɒləpəfɔə(r)). *Ent.* Also scolophore. [ad. G. *scolopophor* (V. Graber 1881, in *Zool. Anzeiger* IV. 452), f. Gr. σκολοπ-, σκόλοψ spike + -PHORE.] The sheath enclosing the terminal rod of certain cells in insects. Also, the sensory end-organ of which this sheath is part, comprising in addition the enclosed rod and neurone.

1888 ROLLESTON & JACKSON *Anim. Life* 503. **1917** *Ann. Entomol. Soc. Amer.* X. 66 Schwabe (1906).. first showed that the nerve end-organ or scolopophore is composed of three cells with definite boundaries. **1925** A. D. IMMS *Gen. Textbk. Entomol.* I. 82 An auditory or chordotonal sensilla consists of a nerve end-organ or scolophore, enclosing a hollow peg-like structure or scolopale. **1933** *Jrnl. Cellular & Compar. Physiol.* IV. 80 The scolophores are either directly connected with the tympanum or lie on a secondary membrane so situated as to move with it. They contain a chitinous rod or scolopale, one end of which projects from the cell body into one or more supporting cells which abut against the body wall. **1964** R. M. & J. W. FOX *Introd. Compar. Entomol.* vi. 193 The unit of the chordotonal organ is the scolopophore.., composed of an apical cap cell attached to the body wall and an envelope cell; in the central part of the cap cell is a terminal ligament which forms a functional extension of the sensory rod (scolops or scolopale) in the envelope cell. **1967** C. P. HICKMAN *Biol. Invertebrates* xxv. 459/1 Many Orthoptera.. have sound receptors, which are spindle-shaped bundles of chordotonal sensilla attached to the integument and called scolophores.

scolopophorous (ˌskɒləˈpɒfərəs), *a. Ent.* [f. prec. + -OUS, after G. *scolopofer* (V. Graber 1881, in *Zool. Anzeiger* IV. 450).] Of a sensory end-organ: having the elongated tubular form of a scolopidium.

1935 R. E. SNODGRASS *Princ. Insect Morphol.* xviii. 527 Scolopophorous sense organs are widely distributed in insects, but until recently they have not been reported in other arthropods. **1973** W. S. ROMOSER *Sci. of Entomol.* v. 122 A type of sensillum that is rather dramatically different from those already described is the scolopophorous or chordotonal organ.

scolops (ˈskɒləps). *Ent.* [a. Gr. σκόλοψ spike, adopted in this sense in Ger. by F. Eggers 1923, in *Zool. Anzeiger* LVII. 239.] The rod-like structure inside the sheath of a scolopidium.

1935 R. E. SNODGRASS *Princ. Insect Morphol.* xviii. 526 The distinguishing feature of sensilla scolopophora is the presence of a well-differentiated, peg-shaped 'sense rod', or scolops, at the apex of each cell. **1964** [see SCOLOPOPHORE].

scolping, scolyon, obs. ff. SCULPIN, SCULLION.

scolytid (ˈskɒlɪtɪd), *sb.* [ad. mod.L. *Scolytid-æ*, f. *Scolytus* (E. L. Geoffroy *Hist. Insectes de Paris* (1762) I. 309), f. Gr. σκολι-ός bent, curved: see next and -ID.] A small cylindrical bark- or wood-boring beetle of the family Scolytidæ; of or pertaining to a beetle of this kind or the family as a whole.

1890 *Proc. Entomol. Soc. Washington* II. 77 (*title*) Notes on the breeding habits of some Scolytids. **1899** D. SHARP *Insects* II. (Camb. Nat. Hist.) 295 The work of particular Scolytids can be recognised by the initiated. **1909** *Bull. U.S. Bureau Entomol.* LXXIII. 1 (*title*) Practical information on the Scolytid beetles of North American forests. **1925** A. D. IMMS *Gen. Textbk. Entomol.* III. 510 Scolytid larvæ are apodous. **1959** E. F. LINSSEN *Beetles Brit. Isles* II. 256 The best-known scolytid is probably.. the Large Elm Bark Beetle. **1972** *Oxf. Univ. Gaz.* CII. No. 3496 (Suppl.* 2) 22 Investigations on Scolytid beetles of timber. **1976** *Nature* 24 June 696/2 Most scolytids.. occupy temporary habitats.

scolytoid (ˈskɒlɪtɔɪd), *a. Ent.* [f. mod.L. (Geoffroy, 1762) *Scolyt-us* + -OID.]

a. Pertaining or resembling the coleopterous family *Scolytidæ*. **b.** *spec.* A term used by C. V. Riley to denote the sixth and final larval stage of insects which undergo hypermetamorphosis.

1883 C. V. RILEY in *Amer. Naturalist* XVII. 790 We would propose, therefore, the following arrangement. Triungulin = first larval stage... Scolytoid = sixth larval stage. **1899** D. SHARP *Insects* II. (Camb. Nat. Hist.) 272 Scolytoid larva.

scom, obs. form of SCUM *v.*

‖**Scomber** (ˈskɒmbə(r)). Pl. Scombri (ˈskɒmbraɪ). [L. *scomber*, ad. Gr. σκόμβρος tunny or mackerel.] A mackerel. In mod. use only as the L. name of the genus.

1623 J. WEBSTER in *Cockeram* To Author, Thy leaues shall scape the Scombri, and be read. **1772–84** *Cook's Voy.* (1790) I. 217 Oysters of different sorts, cavalhe or scomber, flat fish. **1854** BADHAM *Halieut.* 193 Here, accordingly, the thunny fishery is exclusively carried on, nor was one of these scombers, he says, ever known to visit the opposite shore of Chalcedon.

scombre, obs. form of SCUMMER.

scombroid (ˈskɒmbrɔɪd), *a.* and *sb.* Also (earlier) scomberoid. [f. Gr. σκόμβρ-ος SCOMBER + -OID. Cf. F. *scombéroïde* (Cuvier).] **A.** *adj.* Resembling the mackerel; belonging to the family *Scombridæ*.

1841 *Penny Cycl.* XX. 462/1 They much more closely resemble the teeth of certain Scomberoid fishes. **1880** GÜNTHER *Fishes* 294 The Scombroid genus, *Gastrochisma.*

B. *sb.* A scombroid fish.

1842 BRANDE *Dict. Sci.*, etc., *Scomberoids*... The name of the family of fishes of which the genus *Scomber* is the type. **1849–52** OWEN *Teeth* in *Todd's Cycl. Anat.* IV. 874/2 As in *Trichiurus*, and some other Scomberoids. **1877** STREETS *Contrib. Nat. Hist. Hawaiian Isl.* 58 The Carangoids and Scombroids.

scome, scomer, obs. ff. SCUM, SCUMMER.

scomfish (ˈskʌmfɪʃ), *v. Sc.* and *north.* Also 8 sconfice, 8–9 scumfish; *pa. pple.* 4 sconfyste, 8 scunfest. [Shortened f. DISCOMFISH.] *trans.* †**a.** = SCOMFIT *v. Obs.* **b.** To suffocate, stifle, choke (with heat, smoke, a bad smell). Also, to injure, 'do for'. (See E.D.D. s.v. *Scumfish.*)

a. *c* **1375** *Sc. Leg. Saints* xvii. (*Martha*) 67 And as sconfyste stil he stud.

b. **1768** ROSS *Helenore* 30 Her stinking breath Was just enough to sconfice ane to death. **1787** GROSE *Prov. Gloss.*, *Scumfish'd*, smother'd. N. **1818** SCOTT *Hrt. Midl.* xxxix, A' thing is sae poisoned wi' snuff, that I am like to be scomfished whiles. **1819** —— *Montrose* iv, Without scomfishing them with so much smoke. **1853** MRS. GASKELL *Ruth* xviii, I'll scomfish you if ever you go for to tell.

†**ˈscomfit**, *sb. Obs.* Forms: 4 scoumfyt, sconfit, scumfite, 4–5 scom-, skomfite, 6 skumfite. [f. SCOMFIT *v.*; cf. DISCOMFIT *sb.*] Defeat, discomfiture.

13.. *K. Alis.* 959 Ac the scoumfyt, and the damage, Feol on heom of Cartage. *c* **1320** *Beues* 890 Iosian lai in a castel & seȝ þat sconfit euerich del. *c* **1330** *Arth. & Merl.* 6445 (Kölbing) After þis bataile & scumfite. **1422** tr. *Secreta Secret., Priv. Priv.* 129 How youre Same graunde Syre wyth few Pepill Arthure Macmurgho wyth myche pepill to scomfite sette. **1540** *St. Papers Hen. VIII*, III. 173 At the skumfite gyven upon ONeyle and ODonell at the laste insurreccion.

†**ˈscomfit**, *v. Obs.* Forms: 4 scum-, scoom-, scoum-, scounfit(e, -fyt, -phit, -fithe, 4–5 skom-, sconfit(e, -fyt, 4–6 scomfit(e, -fyt(e, 5 -fet(t, scum-, scowmfet(e, skunfit, schomfyt. *Pa. t.* and *pa. pple.* 4 scumfyghte, scoum-, skoumfit, -fyt, 4–5 scum-, skomfit(e, -fyt(e, -fet, 5 sckonfet, scoumfyght, (scomfede, -fide), 4–6 scomfyt(e; also regularly scomfited, etc. [Shortened f. DISCOMFIT *v.*] *trans.* To defeat, vanquish, discomfit.

1303 R. BRUNNE *Handl. Synne* 4980 þe folk of Isrel had þoght, and syghte, For þey were twyys scumfyghte. **13..** *Coer de L.* 3777 Yiff he scounfithe us in bekyr. **1340** HAMPOLE *Pr. Consc.* 2269 And when þe devel herd hym þus say, Alle skomfit he vanyst oway. **13..** *Cursor M.* 7799 (Gött.) þai er scumphited wid þair fas. *c* **1380** WYCLIF *Sel. Wks.* III. 147 By þat þei wan þo world and scounfitiden þo fende. *c* **1420** *Chron. Vilod.* 3440 He.. scomfede his enymes & droff hem ouȝt. **1435** MISYN *Fire of Love* 39 All þinge he scumfetis, all þinge he ouercomys. *c* **1440** *Generydes* 570 So rebukyd and skomfite as he was. *c* **1470** in *Three 15th Cent. Chron.* (Camden) 20 Kynge Edward was scomfide and put to flight. **1503** HAWES *Examp. Virt.* XII. 214 Whan I had scomfyte this serpent venymous. *Ibid.* 226 How.. Haue ye scomfyted.. The.. dragon. *a* **1513** *Fabyan's Chron.* VII. 324, & gaue to hym batayll, & scoumfyght hym at lengthe. **1530** PALSGR. 706/1, I scomfyte, or I overcome, *je vayncs*... He hath scomfyt all his ennemyes.

Hence †**scomfit** *ppl. a.* (in quot. *absol.*), †**scomfiting** *vbl. sb.*

c **1333** in *Minot's Poems* (ed. Hall) App. i. 26 So þere itte was welle semyng, þatte with multitude is no scomfiting. *c* **1450** LOVELICH *Grail* lii. 738 For it is A ful gret Merveyl to Me, the Conqwerour to þe scomfyt ȝolden to be. **1483** *Cath. Angl.* 323/2 A scomfetynge, *superacio, triumphus.*

†**ˈscomfiter.** *Obs. rare*$^{-1}$. In 5 skomfitoure. [Shortened f. *descomfitour* DISCOMFITER.] A discomfiter, victor.

a **1400** *Morte Arth.* 1644 Loke ȝe skyfte it so that vs no skathe lympe, ffor na skomfitoure in skoulkery is skomfite euer.

†**ˈscomfiture.** *Obs.* Forms: 4 scomfitour, 5 scom-, skomfiture, -fyture, -fytour, -fertour, scumfetore. [Shortened f. DISCOMFITURE.] Discomfiture, defeat.

13.. *Guy Warw.* 5235 Wel gret it was þe scomfitour. ? *a* **1400** *Morte Arth.* 1561 Skilfulle skomfyture he skiftez as hym lykez. *c* **1450** *Brut* 439 But God was lord and maistir of that victorie and scomfiture. *c* **1471** in *Pol. Poems* (Rolls) II. 278 When the comens the skomfertour did understonde, Thay seuyd owte freshly, thay kepud none araye. *a* **1513** *Fabyan's Chron.* v. cxi. 84 He made a newe voyage ageyne theym, & made of theym a nother scomfiture.

†**scomm.** *Obs.* Also 7 scomme, scom. [ad. L. *scōmma* (Macrobius), a. Gr. σκῶμμα (σκωμματ-), f. σκώπ-τειν to jeer, scoff.] A flout or scoff.

The sense 'a buffoon', by which J. explains a mutilated version of quot. 1692, is recorded in all subsequent Dicts.

a **1619** FOTHERBY *Atheom.* II. i. §8 (1622) 189 Whose vaine ostentation is worthily scoffed with scomme of the Orator. **1628** W. SCLATER *Three Serm.* (1629) 6 Enough of this, least

I incurre the prouerbiall scomme; *Sus Mineruam.* **1692** R. L'Estrange *Fables* ccccx. 386 The Scomms of Great Men, or Buffoons of Quality, are every jot as Wolvish in Conversation, as they are here in the Fable. **1711** Puckle *Club* (1723) 8 Scomms and derision unbridle fear, and make the peasant brave the prince.

Hence †**sco'mmatic** [Gr. σκωμματικ-ός], †**sco'mmatical** *adjs.*, characterized by gibe or scoff. †**sco'mmatically** *adv.* †**'scommatism**, scoffing. †**'scommatizing** *ppl. a.*, derisive.

1601 Bp. W. Barlow *Defence* 88 This imputation scommaticall of faithlesse fidelitie. **1613** Sir E. Hoby *Counter-sn. Ishmael Rabshacheh* 8 Those vniust Cauills and scomatizing imputations. **1650** Hobbes *Answ. Davenant* ¶3 From hence have proceeded three sorts of Poesy, Heroique, Scommatique, and Pastorall.. The Heroique Poem Dramatique is Tragedy. The Scommatique Narrative is Satyre. **1656** —— *Six Lessons* vi. 55 Whatsoever is added of contumely, either directly or scommatically, is want of Charity and uncivil. **1664** H. More *Myst. Iniq.* xviii. 67 As he that has been casting his angle a good part of the day into the river, and brings home no fish, may yet be rightly saluted *Mr. Fisherman* or *Mr. Angler* at his return, though not without some kind of Scommatism at the bottom. *Ibid.*, By way of Scommatical reproach. **1668** E. Howard *Usurper* Epist. A 3, The other extream.. is that of Farce or Scommatick Plays. **1671** Shadwell *Miser* i. (1672) 6, I know as well as you that I depend (*Scommatically*) upon a Father.

scommar, scomme, obs. ff. scummer, scum.

scommer, scomor, -our, -ur, obs. ff. scummer.

scon, variant of scone *sb.*

sconce (skɒns), *sb.*¹ Forms: 4–6 skonse, 5–6 skonce, scons(e, (5 sconsce, 7 skons, 8 *dial.* scoance), 5– sconce. [Aphetic a. OF. *esconse* lantern (also hiding-place), ad. monastic L. *sconsa*, shortened f. *absconsa*, fem. of L. *absconsus*, pa. pple. of *abscondĕre* to hide. Cf. OIcel. *skons*, ? lantern, candlestick (1397 in a church inventory).]

†**1.** A lantern or candlestick with a screen to protect the light from the wind, and a handle to carry it by (as distinguished from a lantern carried suspended from a chain). *Obs.*

c **1392** in *Fabric Rolls York Minster* (Surtees) 129 Pro reparacione de iij skonses fractis in vestiario, 12 d. **14..** *S. Etheldred* 351 in Horstm. *Altengl. Leg.* (1881) 290 And in a sconsce he hadde hurre candelle with hurre lyȝt. **1434** *E.E. Wills* (1882) 102, Y bequethe.. to.. sir Iohn Russhebrok a skonce. **1450** *Pol. Rel. & L. Poems* 11 It wexyth derke, thou nedyst A scons. **1486** *Bk. St. Albans* d ij b, Clymbe to her with a sconce or a lanterne that hath bot oon light. **1530** Palsgr. 268/1 Scons to sette a candell in, *lanterne a mayn.* **1602** Middleton *Blurt* iv. iii, *Wood.* Yonder's a light, Master Constable. *Blu.* Peace, Woodcocke, the sconce approaches. **1644** Evelyn *Diary* 22 Nov., The windows of the whole city were set with tapers put into lanterns, or sconces, of several coloured oiled paper. *c* **1746** J. Collier (Tim Bobbin) *View Lanc. Dial.* (1787) 10 It begun t' be dark, on I'r beawt Scoance in a strawnge Country.

transf. and *fig.* **1532** More *Confut. Tindale* Wks. 445/1 Tindal.. hydeth himself in the darkenesse of the deuill, walking with a sconse of a dimme light, to make men wene he would shewe them the way. **1747** Hervey *Medit.* II. 85 The moon is of signal service.. to the Mariner.. to explore his way and under the influence of this beaming Sconce, to avoid the fatal rock.

b. A flat candlestick with a handle for carrying.

1834 Lover *Leg. & Stor. Irel.* Ser. ii. 190 Put a candle in the tin sconce. **1858** Mrs. Oliphant *Laird of Norlaw* I. v. 55 Taking the candle.. she stood with the little flat brass sconce in her hand. **1897** Barrère & Leland *Slang, Sconce* (public schools), a tin candlestick.

2. A bracket-candlestick, usually of brass or iron, to fasten against a wall; esp. an ornamental bracket for holding one or more candles, often fitted with a mirror. Also, a candle-bracket for a piano, etc.

c **1450** in Aungier *Syon* (1840) 363 The mynyster of hyghe masse schal.. lyght the quyer sconses.. as ofte as nede is. **1509–10** *Rec. St. Mary at Hill* 270 Paid for iij plattes with nosis for þe skonsis ij d. **1662** Pepys *Diary* 4 Jan., Seeing how my pewter sconces that I have bought will become my stayres and entry. **1685** Dryden tr. *Lucretius* ii. 28 If Golden Sconces hang not on the Walls, To light the costly Suppers and the Balls. **1688** Holme *Armoury* iii. 381/2 The forms.. of these.. Sconces, are numberless; some having them with Faces, others with Birds, Beasts, Fish, Trees and Flowers; some with round or oval imbossed works. **1706** Hearne *Collect.* 4 Dec. (O.H.S.) I. 310 Mr. Thomas Cherry was buried on Wednesday... The Rooms were very handsomely set out wᵗʰ black sconces &c. proper for such occasions. **1729** Swift *Direct. Serv.* i. (1751) 22 You may likewise stick the Candle so loose, that it will fall upon the Glass of the Sconce, and break it into Shatters. **1755** Johnson, *Sconce*, a pensile candlestick, generally with a looking-glass to reflect the light. **1821** Scott *Kenilw.* vi, The dark colour.. was relieved by the number of lights in silver sconces, which hung against the walls. **1859** W. Collins *Q. of Hearts* (1875) 41 This strange scene was lighted up by candles in high and heavy brass sconces. **1881** Besant & Rice *Chapl. of Fleet* ii. iv, Wax candles, arranged upon the walls on sconces. **1908–9** *Civil Service Supply Assoc. Catal.* 1212 Piano Candle Sconces. *Ibid.* 1241 Adjustable shaving stand.. with.. Sconces and best mirror.

3. A street-lamp or lantern attached to a wall. Only in descriptions of Continental life.

1849 James *Woodman* ii, A sconce was lighted on the side of the nunnery. **1873** 'Ouida' *Pascarel* I. 176 The oil wicks were lighted in the iron sconces of the streets.

4. The tube in an ordinary candlestick in which the candle is inserted.

1850 in Ogilvie.

5. *attrib.*, as *sconce candlestick, light, maker.*

1455 in Anstey *Munim. Acad.* (Rolls) II. 664, j. *scons candelstik of latone. **1479** in *Eng. Gilds* (1870) 427 *Skonce light. **1530** Palsgr. 268/1 *Sconsmaker, *lanternier.* **1688** Holme *Armoury* iii. 381/2, S. the like O. with a Candle burning in the Socket proper, is the Badge of the Sconce-makers.

sconce (skɒns), *sb.*² *arch.* Also 6–7 sconse, skonce. [Of obscure origin; possibly a slang use of sconce *sb.*¹ or of sconce *sb.*³ (though in our quots. recorded earlier than the latter).] A jocular term for: The head; esp. the crown or top of the head; hence, 'head', ability, sense, wit. †Also put for the person himself.

1567 Turberv. *Epit.*, etc. 105 A curled Sconce he hath, with angrie frowning browe. **1577** Kendall *Flowers of Epigr.* 94 b, Bartlet a pleasant sconse, whose mirthe all men did muche delight. **1586** A. Day *Eng. Secretary* ii. (1625) 47 Master B. found Socrates in my Letter, and sent to seeke out your well reputed skonce to expound it. **1593** G. Harvey *New Let. Notable Contents* C 2 b, The Princock.. that can play vpon his warped sconce, as vpon a tabor. **1621** Burton *Anat. Mel.* Democr. to Rdr. 64 Much learning.. hath crackt their skonces. **1645** Milton *Colast.* 25 How many are there .. who have such a Fee simple in their sconse, as to take a Leas of their own Lands from another? **1651** Cleveland *Poems* 20 Who swears &c., swears more oaths at once Than Cerberus out of his triple Sconce. **1771** Smollett *Humph. Cl.* 15 Sept., He.. running into the house, exposed his back and sconce to the whole family. **1809** W. Irving *Knickerb.* vi. viii. (1849) 370 As he stooped.. Peter Stuyvesant dealt him a thwack over the sconce. **1883** *Century Mag.* XXVI. 915/2 To put it [the sum] up to twelve dollars.. if she.. showed any sconce for the business. **1888** J. Inglis *Tent Life in Tigerland* 197 He had received a crack on the sconce.

sconce (skɒns), *sb.*³ Forms: α. 6–7 skonce, sconse, (7 sconch), 6– sconce. β. 6 scance, skance, 7 skants, scans. [a. Du. *schans* (in early mod.Du. also written *schantze, schentze*), with assimilation of form to sconce *sb.*¹ and *sb.*²

The word (of which the synonymous early mod.Du. *schranse, schrantze,* seems to be a variant) is found also in late MHG. and mod.G. *schanze* fem.; in the 16th c. it had in Du. the senses 'brushwood', 'bundle of sticks', 'screen of brushwood for soldiers', 'earthwork made with gabions' (cf. Du. *schanskorf* gabion). The ultimate origin is obscure; the late appearance of the word in Teut. would suggest the probability of some Romanic source, but neither form nor sense supports the hypothesis of adoption from OF. *esconse* hiding-place (cf. sconce *sb.*¹) which app. does not occur in any military application.]

1. *Fortif.* A small fort or earthwork; esp. one built to defend a ford, pass, castle-gate, etc., or erected as a counter-fort.

α. **1571** Digges *Pantom.* 54 To make Plattes, and set downe the proportion of anye Sconces, Fortes, Bulwarkes, or Townes. **1586** J. Hooker *Hist. Irel.* 178/2 in *Holinshed*, Caluerleigh.. went vnto that end of the towne where the seneschall scaled the wals, & there he made a sconse, or a little bulworke, and.. saued the towne. **1599** Shaks. *Hen. V*, iii. vi. 76 They will learne you by rote where Seruices were done; at such and such a Sconce, at such a Breach. **1611** Speed *Hist. Gt. Brit.* ix. xv. §39. 630/1 And raising the rampier to a great thicknes whereon he erected many sconces of earth like vnto Castles. **1639** R. Norwood *Fortif.* 134 Of small Forts or Field Skonces, and marking them out Mechanically, and first of a Skonce of foure sides. **1656** Heylin *Surv. France* 11 Neither is there any of the least Sconces or Blockhouses, on the shore-side of that Countrey [Hampshire]. *a* **1668** Davenant *Siege* (1673) 67 The Out-works are made perfect, and our River Guarded by a Sconce. **1673** Sir J. Moore *Mod. Fortif.* 94 Of small Forts or Skonces, which are built for Defence of some Pass, River, or other place. **1727** A. Hamilton *New Acc. E. Ind.* I. xiii. 147 The Citizens built Sconces in convenient Places, about half a Mile without the Wall, to protect the Suburbs. **1755** Carte *Hist. Eng.* IV. 288 They had raised two sconces or breast-works over against two fords passable at low water. **1821** Scott *Kenilw.* i, [He] was shot at the head of his regiment at the taking of a sconce near Maestricht. **1849** [J. Grant] *Mem. Kirkaldy* xxi. 246 The Earl of Morton and his troops.. threw up a battery on the southern part of Calton Hill... This sconce they hoped would command the Canongate.

β. **1598** Barret *Theor. Warres* v. i. 141 To carrie victuals or munition.. to a distressed Scance. *Ibid.* Gloss. 252 *Skance*, a Dutch word: and is a small fortresse built of turffe and earth, commonly vsed in the low countries. **1632** Holland *Cyrupædia* 115 To the end it might be, as a warlike and defensive fortresse for themselves, so a strong skants, and offensive to the Assyrians. **1675** *Lond. Gaz.* No. 1017/1 They had beaten the Indians from a certain Scans, on the foresaid Promontory of Land.

†**b.** *fig.*

1590 Shaks. *Com. Err.* ii. ii. 37 And you vse these blows long, I must get a sconce for my head, and Insconce it to. *c* **1592** Bacon *Conf. Pleasure* (1870) 23 It is her govermᵗ and her gvermᵗ alone that hath (bene yᵉ) sconse and forte of all Europe. **1598** Sylvester *Du Bartas* ii. iv. ii. *Magnificence* 337 Honour is but a puffe.. Health but a sconce of paper. **1615** T. Adams *Blacke Devill* 55 If he loose the sconce of the understanding, yet give him the citadell of the affections. **1633** —— *Exp. 2 Peter* i. 6 All sins break in at the loss of the sconce, or capitol, reason. **1633** G. Herbert *Temple, Ch. Porch* xxii, Look to thy mouth: diseases enter there. Thou hast two sconses, if thy stomach call; Carve, or discourse. **1647** Ward *Simple Cobler* 6 To authorise an untruth.. is to build a Sconce against the walls of heaven. **1655** Fuller *Ch. Hist.* iv. 148 This was one of the best bulwarks and sconces of Soveraignty. *a* **1670** Hacket *Abp. Williams* ii. (1693) 166, I spend too much time to pull down a Sconce of Sand. **1676** Hobbes *Iliad* iii. 221 Great Ajax, Who of the Argives is the Sconce [ἕρκος Ἀχαιῶν]. **1711** in *10th Rep. Hist. MSS. Comm.* App. v. 198 Flanders was.. to be garrisoned, to the end that it might be a sconce between them and France.

c. slang. † *to build a sconce* (see quot. 1730).

1640 Nabbes *Bride* iii. i, By battering downe with th'engine of their purse Some sconch your drunken valour in a taverne Hath built with sack. **1641** Brathwait *Eng. Gentlem.* 23 These have beene Men in their time,.. but now their fortunes falling to an ebbe,.. they are enforced.. to erect a Sconce whereto the Roarers make recourse, as to their Rendevous. **1649** Dk. Newcastle *Country Capt.* i. i. 7 *Vnd.* Hee shall read warrs to me and fortification. *Tho.* For a neede I could teach you to build a sconce Sir. **1687** [see *sconce-building* in 5]. *a* **1700** B. E. *Dict. Cant. Crew* s.v., *To build a large Sconce*, to run deep upon Tick, or Trust. *a* **1704** T. Brown *Lett. fr. Dead* iii. Wks. 1730 II. 282 A lieutenant and ensign whom once I admitted upon trust,.. built a sconce, and left me in the lurch. **1730** Bailey (fol.), *To build a Sconce*, to run a Score at an Ale-house, Tavern, &c. so as to be afraid to go there, for fear of being dunn'd. **1760** C. Johnston *Chrysal* (1822) I. 174 Cribbing from the till, and building sconces, and such-like tricks. **1765** Goldsm. *Ess.* viii. Wks. (Globe) 307/2 He ran into debt with everybody that would trust him, and none could build a sconce better than he.

2. *transf.* A protective screen or shelter (from fire or the elements).

1591 R. Bruce *Serm.* R 3, We ar no more bot as stubble is to the fyre, so ar we in the presence of God, who is consuming fyre, except we haue a sconce, except wee haue Christ Iesus to gang betuixt vs and him. *a* **1616** Beaum. & Fl. *Scornf. Lady* v. I 3 b, I am.. a rascal: one that vpon the next anger of your brother, must raise a sconce by the high way, and sel switches. *a* **1670** Hacket *Cent. Serm.* (1675) 454 He would make small Sconces or Tabernacles upon the top of the Hill. **1688** Holme *Armoury* iii. 449/1 Some call it [*sc.* an Umbrella] a Skonce, which Gentlewomen.. beare up .. to keep and shadow them from heat. **1730** A. Gordon *Maffei's Amphith.* ii. xiv. 348 The fervent Heat of the Sun made some kind of Sconce or other necessary at the Games.

3. *dial.* **a.** A screen, partition.

1695 Kennett *Paroch. Antiq.* s.v. *Helowe-wall, Hollen* in the North is a wall.. to secure the family from the blasts of wind rushing in when the *heck* or door is open: to which wall on that side next the hearth is annext a sconce or screne of wood or stone. **1829** Brockett *N.C. Wds.* (ed. 2), *Sconce*,.. a short partition near the fire upon which all the bright utensils in a cottage are suspended. **1863** J. C. Atkinson *Danby Gloss., Sconce*, a screen.. lined with some reflecting metal, which is set before the fire when a joint is roasting. **1876** *Whitby Gloss., Sconce*, a screen or partition.

b. (See quots.) [Perhaps a different word.]

1781 Hutton *Tour to Caves* (ed. 2) Gloss., *Sconce*, a fixed seat by the side of a fire place. **1829** Brockett *N.C. Wds.* (ed. 2), *Sconce*, a seat at one side of the fire-place in the old large open chimney. **1885** Hall Caine *Shadow of Crime* vi, She cleared the sconce and took down the flitches that hung from the rannel tree to dry. **1886** Alice Rea *Beckside Boggle* 4 A long freestone slab, or sconce, as dale folk call it, firmly fixed into the wall by the fireplace, which must have made a comfortable fireside couch in olden times.

4. (Also *sconce-piece.*) A low water-washed iceberg (see quot. 1856).

1856 Kane *Arct. Expl.* I. vii. 72 Just then, a broad sconce-piece or low water-washed berg came driving up... As the sconce moved rapidly close alongside us, McGary managed to plant an anchor on its slope. **1889** R. Collinson *Jrnl. H.M.S. Enterprise* 294 We.. were.. unable to see our way among the sconces, and.. I hove-to for daylight.

5. *Comb.*: **sconce-battle**, a particular mode of drawing up troops in the field; †**sconce-building** *a.*, that 'builds a sconce' (see 1 b); †**sconce-korf** [Du. *schans-korf*], a gabion.

1635 W. Barriffe *Mil. Discipl.* xcv. (1643) 273 The *Sconce Battell is a Figure most properly fit for a whole Regiment. **1687** T. Brown *Saints in Uproar* Wks. 1730 I. 80 Thou huffing, puffing, *sconce-building ruffian. **1629** tr. *Pelegromius' Shertogenbosh* 41 Our Land-souldiers.. did set on fire some *Sconce-kornes [? *read* -korues = -korves].

sconce (skɒns), *sb.*⁴ [f. sconce *v.*²]

1. At Oxford (? formerly also at Cambridge): †**a.** A fine imposed for a breach of university or college discipline (*obs.*). **b.** A fine of a tankard of ale or the like, imposed by undergraduates on one of their number for some breach of customary rule when dining in hall.

1650 in Rashdall & Rait *New College* (1901) 176 Taking off the sconce [*misprinted* scoure] which, for their absence from prayers, was laid upon them by the said Warden. **1653** in *4th Rep. Hist. MSS. Comm.* (1874) 456/1 In the case of neglect thereof they shall be punished by sconce, or imposed exercises, as to the officers of the said Colleges.. shall seeme meete. **1691** Wood *Ath. Oxon.* I. 521 Upon the hearing of one of Sir Hen. Savile's mathematic lectures by accident, or rather to save the sconce of a groat, if he had been absent. **1707** in Hearne *Collect.* 23 Dec. (O.H.S.) II. 83 The Dean put yᵉ usual Sconce for missing Prayers upon his Name. **1763** Colman *Terræ-Filius* No. 1 ¶10 If I fine them for their Irregularities, it shall be in a much more moderate Sum than Forty Shillings, or any other Sconce imposed by the Proctors. **1885** *N. & Q.* Ser. vi. XII. 523/2 When I was at Oriel,.. sconces were the fines.. inflicted in the 'gate-bill'... Sconces, as fines for offences in hall *contra bonos mores*, were in vogue in other colleges but not with us.

attrib. **1885** *N. & Q.* Ser. vi. XII. 449/1 The sconce-tankards held about two quarts.

†**2.** In extended application: A mulct, fine (exacted, e.g. from a member of a society, from a servant). *Obs.*

1683 Barnard *Life Heylin* 112 The exacting of Sconses or perdition mony, which he [as Treasurer of Westminster] divided among them that best deserved it. **1703** *MS. Bk. of Receipts Ashm. Museum* 2 b, Gilacholuim's sconces or Forfeits out of his wages, Beginning Oct. 22, 1703.

† **sconce**, *v.*[1] *Obs.* [f. SCONCE *sb.*[3] Cf. Du. *(be)schansen*.]

1. *trans.* To fortify, entrench; in later use, to shelter, protect. ***to sconce away*** Sc., to ward off.

1598 W. PHILLIP tr. *Linschoten* I. 153/2 They set vppon the towne of Ioor, that was sconsed [orig. *beschanst*] and compassed about with woodden stakes. **1620** BRATHWAIT *Five Senses* 75 Long time, therefore, haue I resolued to sconce my selfe betwixt these two. **1621** G. SANDYS *Ovid's Met.* XIV. (1626) 282 A little Bay, by Scylla haunted, lies.. sconst from the Seas and skies Distemper. **1690** C. NESSE *Hist. & Myst. O. & N. Test.* I. 208 A screen to sconce and shelter us from consuming fire. **1706** E. WARD *Wooden World Diss.* (1708) 65 He's pretty well sconc'd against Bullets. *c* **1715** RAMSAY *Vision* iii, To.. skonce my skap and shanks frae rain. **1746** D. GRAHAM *Hist. Rebell.* x. Writ. 1883 I. 178 Confin'd into a stinking stye, And 'bove his head two hydes of kye, To skonce away the sooty rain.

2. [? By etymological association with F. *esconser* (Cotgr.).] To hide, screen from view.

1652 URQUHART *Jewel* 122 With so close and secret a minde did he harbour in his heart, that new love,.. remotely skonsing it from the knowledge of all men. **1663** SIR G. MACKENZIE *Religious Stoic* xiii. (1685) 146 As if a thicket of trees could have sconced him from his all-seeing Maker.

sconce (skɒns), *v.*[2] [Of obscure origin. As a term of University slang, it may have arisen from some far-fetched reference to SCONCE *sb.*[1], *sb.*[2], or *sb.*[3] Our first two quots. refer it to SCONCE *sb.*[2]; so app. also quot. 1641 in sense 2.]

1. *trans.* At Oxford (? formerly also at Cambridge): To fine, mulct; often with the penalty as second object. Formerly said of university and college officials, with reference to fines inflicted for breaches of discipline. Now only of undergraduates when dining in hall: To fine (one of their number) a tankard of ale or the like, as a penalty for some breach of good manners or conventional usage.

1617 MINSHEU *Ductor* s.v., Wherevpon comes the terme in Oxford to sconce one, Lat. *Mulctare pecunia*, i. to set vp so much in the butterie booke vpon his head to pay for his punishment. **1628** SHIRLEY *Witty Fair One* IV. ii, I have had a head in most of the butteries of Cambridge, and it has been sconced to purpose. **1687** *Magd. Coll. & Jas. II* (O.H.S.) 224 The said persons entering the Buttery, and taking out their crosses, M[r]. Charnock thereupon sconced the Butler ten shillings each. **1687** SETTLE *Refl. Dryden* 11 The poorest Freshman in the University would be sconced for half so great a blunder. **1688** WOOD *Life* Apr. (O.H.S.) III. 265 The vicechancellor told him the Coll. was to be sconced: Charnock said he had provided a peancer. **1706** HEARNE *Collect.* (O.H.S.) I. 238 D[r] Mill.. saying.. that no Master of Arts in the Hall should for y[e] future have any Privilege of sconsing or otherwise punishing the Servants in the Hall. **1707** *Ibid.* II. 9 Yesterday the Vice-Chaunc. scons'd all that were without their Hoods at S[t] Marie's. **1728** JOHNSON in J. Hawkins *Life* (1787) 9 [He said to Jordan] Sir you have sconced me two-pence for non-attendance at a lecture not worth a penny. **1821** *Etonian* II. 391 Hall dinner. Was sconced in a quart of ale for quoting Latin. **1853** 'C. BEDE' *Verdant Green* III. xi, There was a shout of indignation and he [the punster] was sconced by the unanimous vote of the company.

2. In extended application (cf. SCONCE *sb.* 2).

1641 MILTON *Ch. Discipl.* II. 85 We must of duty still appear before them once a year.. to be taxt by the poul, to be scons't our head money.. in their Chaunlerly Shop-book of Easter. **1755** *Connoisseur* No. 57 ¶7 [The toast-master of a drinking society] punishes an offender by sconcing him a bumper. **1849** ROCK *Ch. of Fathers* IV. xi. 107 A theft committed on any one of these three [Rogation] days, was, by Alfred's laws, sconced in a two-fold 'bot' or fine. **1869** GLADSTONE *Sp. Ho. Comm.* 18 June, This superstition.. by which every officer.. who only had the good fortune to tie himself to the tail of some Judge,.. had built up around him this sanctity of tenure, by which the public had been sconced generation after generation. **1892** SYMONDS *Life in Swiss Highl.* xvi. 346 He who comes last is sconced three litres of Veltliner for the company. **1901** *Speaker* 27 Apr. 99/1 Why should a small village public-house be sconced five or six times as much as one of the great gin-palaces. **1903** MORLEY *Gladstone* IV. ii. I. 471 A new minister, who.. did not shrink from sconcing the powerful landed phalanx like other people.

† **b.** ***to sconce off***: to take off, rebate. *Obs.*

1768 FOOTE *Devil* II. Wks. 1799 II. 260 The widow.. paid my bill.. without sconcing off sixpence.

Hence '**sconcing** *vbl. sb.* (Also *attrib.*)

1695 KENNETT *Paroch. Antiq.* App. 688 Neither are any polling Officers to draw fees and sconcing money to enrich themselves. **1885** *N. & Q.* Ser. VI. XII. 448/2 Sconcing was a privilege possessed by the senior scholar or commoner dining in hall of fining any delinquent.

sconce, *v.*[3] *nonce-wd.* Aphetic form of EN-SCONCE *v.*

1841 BARHAM *Ingol. Leg.* Ser. II. *Auto-da-fé*, All, save Privy-purse Humez, Who sconced in his room is.

sconce, dial. form of SCUNCH.

sconcer[1] ('skɒnsə(r)). *north.* [f. SCONCE *sb.*[1] + -ER[1].] ? = SCONCE *sb.*[1] I.

1731 *Inv. G. Bamforth, Sheffield*, A large glass, six sconcers.

sconcer[2] ('skɒnsə(r)). [? f. SCONCE *v.*[1] + -ER[1].] A malingerer.

1843 G. HECTOR *Feigned Dis.* 43 One was pronounced by the surgeon an imposter, the other was admitted. It is probable he had received a hint that one of them was a sconcer.

sconch, sconcheon, obs. forms of SCONCE *sb.*[3], SCUNCHEON.

scond(e, obs. forms of SHAND, shame.

scone (skəʊn, skɒn), *sb.* Orig. *Sc.* Also 6–9 **scon, skon**, (8 **sconn**). [Perh. a shortened adoption of MDu. *schoonbrot*, MLG. *schonbrot* 'fine bread'.

The LG. word is explained in the Bremen glossary (1771) as a sort of white loaf with two acute and two obtuse angles, and the similar *schönroggen* ('fine rye') in the Hamburg dialect denoted 'a seed-cake with three rounded corners'. (See Grimm's *Deutsches Wb.* s.v. *Schön.*) From the latter word are MSw. *skanroggä*, MDa. *skonroggen*, Icel. *skonrok* 'a biscuit' (Vigf.).]

1. A large round cake made of wheat or barley-meal baked on a griddle; one of the four quadrant-shaped pieces into which such a cake is often cut; more generally, a soft cake of barley- or oatmeal, or wheat-flour, baked in single portions on a griddle or in an oven. Also with defining words, denoting varieties of this cake, as ***butter, potato, soda, treacle scone***; **brown scone**, one made of whole meal; **drop-, dropped scone**, one made of a small portion of batter dropped on the griddle or on a tin and baked; **fried scone**, one in which the ingredients are made into a batter and fried; **sweetie scone** *Sc.* (see quot. 1808).

The *Eng. Dial. Dict.* has an 18th c. quot. for 'three nucket scons' (three-cornered scones). The context of quot. 1513 below shows that a four-cornered cake was meant.

1513 DOUGLAS *Æneis* VII. iii. 15 The flour sconnis war sett in, by and by, Wyth wther mesis. **1549** *Compl. Scot.* vi. 43 Thai hed na breyd bot ry caikis and fustean skonnis maid of flour. **1744** in *Scottish Jrnl. Topogr.* (1848) I. 334/2, 3 Pyes and Bread and a Currand Scone. **1787** BURNS *Scotch Drink* iv, On thee [*sc.* John Barleycorn] aft Scotland chows her cood, In souple scones, the wale o' food! **1808** JAMIESON s.v. *Yule* §4 What the vulgar call a sweetie-skon, or a loaf enriched with raisins, currants, and spiceries. **1818** SCOTT *Br. Lamm.* xxvi, Never had there been such.. making of car-cakes and sweet scones. **1886** STEVENSON *Kidnapped* xx, We lay on the bare top of a rock, like scones upon a girdle. **1899** E. HEDDLE *Marget at Manse* 100 She.. would bake drop-scones, and carry in my tea with her own hands. **1899** R. WALLACE *Country Schoolmaster* 20 Potato scones, soda scones, 'droppet' scones, treacle scones. **1942** C. SPRY *Come into Garden, Cook* xv. 213 Most people have a good recipe for dropped scones... Drop the batter from a spoon on the hot girdle and turn once. **1956** E. GRIERSON *Second Man* ii. 44 Some tea-cake and drop scones and jam. **1977** *Age* (Melbourne) 18 Jan. 13/4 The cheese soufflé looked more like a cheese drop-scone.

2. (More fully ***scone cap***.) 'The old broad bonnet of the Lowlands' (Jam.).

1820 *Blackw. Mag.* Dec. 322 From the shepherd's shealing.. to the pillared palace..—from the scone cap, to the jewelled bonnet. **1826** G. R. GLEIG *Subaltern* xvii, The Lowland bonnet, or scone.

3. a. (Always with pronunc. skɒn) ***to do one's scone***, to lose one's head, temper. Hence ***scone-doer, -doing***. *N.Z. slang.*

1942 *2nd N.Z.E.F. Times* 20 Apr. 6 Scone-doer. A person subject to sudden fits of excitement and irritation. *Ibid.* 19 Oct. 5 'Don't do your plurry scone, Dig!'.. 'Who's sconing?' **1944** F. I. COOZE *Kiwis in Pacific* i. 8 The camp at Pahantanui was much as all military camps. Tedious training, fatigues, and 'scone-doing' from 6 a.m. to 4 p.m. **1952** *Here & Now* (N.Z.) II. IV. 20 Everyone question Rangi. Everyone do the Scone. **1957** M. K. JOSEPH *I'll Soldier no More* (1958) ix. 167 Gillies finds him a bit of a nagger, but likes him for being efficient and not doing his scone.

b. The head. *Austral. slang.*

c **1945** in S. J. Baker *Austral. Lang.* (1966) viii. 172 *Scone*, head. **1957** D. NILAND *Call Me when Cross turns Over* v. 138, I can just see you running a house. I'd give you a week before you went off your scone. **1968** D. O'GRADY *Bottle of Sandwiches* 58 He reckoned we weren't right in the scone to be travelling so far on a Sunday just to chase a ball around a paddock.

4. *Comb.*, as **scone-hot** *a. Austral. slang*, in phr. ***to go*** (someone) ***scone-hot***, to reprimand (someone) severely, to lose one's temper at (someone); see also quot. 1941.

1938 X. HERBERT *Capricornia* 530 Halfcaste Shillingsworth goes Copra Co scone-hot! **1941** BAKER *Dict. Austral. Slang* 63 *Scone-hot*, an intensive to describe great vigour of attack, scolding or speed, e.g., 'Go for someone scone-hot', to reprimand severely. (2) Exorbitant, unreasonable. (3) Expert, proficient, e.g., 'He's scone-hot at shearing'. **1944** *Coast to Coast 1943* 116, I don't want Reg going me scone hot because his wife's not capable of looking after herself. **1967** K. TENNANT *Tell Morning This* (1968) xvii. 139 When my big brother Jim come home from work, he went Dad scone hot. **1974** D. IRELAND *Burn* 136 When he finds out he'll go me scone-hot.

scone (skɒn), *v. Austral.* and *N.Z. slang.* [f. dial. *scon, scun*: see *Eng. Dial. Dict.*] *trans.* To hit.

1948 *Coast to Coast 1947* 187 The bottle broke. Damn! he hadn't meant to scone the bottle first go-off. **1958** I. CROSS *God Boy* iv. 30 Joe was worried in case he had really sconed the girl.

sconfice, obs. form of SCOMFISH *v. dial.*

sconn, obs. f. SCONE *sb.*

sconner, var. SCUNNER.

sconscyence, rare obs. form of CONSCIENCE.

scontion, variant of SCUNCHEON.

† '**scontre**, *v. Obs. rare*[−1]. [app. ad. It. *scontrare*. Cf. RESCOUNTER *v.*] *intr.* = ENCOUNTER I b.

1545 *St. Papers Hen. VIII*, X. 515 It is raported that Barbarossa is going to Alger with 10 or 12 galeis, and that thImperial galeis are departid to scontre with him.

scoochion, obs. form of SCUTCHEON.

scool(e, scoolde, obs. ff. SCHOOL, SCOLD *v.*

scoomfit(e, -phit, etc., obs. ff. SCOMFIT *v.*

scoomme, obs. form of SCUM.

scoop (skup, locally skoup), *sb.*[1] Forms: 4–6 **scope**, *Sc.* and *north.* **skowp**, 5 **scowpe**, 6 **skop(e, scoupe, skoupe**, *Sc.* **skwpe, skupe**, *north.* **skoppe**, 6–7 **scoope**, 7 **skoope, scowp**, 7– **scoop**. [App. of twofold origin (which is reflected in the diversity of pronunciation): (1) a. MLG. *schôpe* fem. (whence prob. MSw. *skôpa*) or MDu. *schôpe, schoepe* (mod.Du. *schoep*) vessel for drawing or bailing out water, bucket of a water-wheel, corn-scoop = MHG. *schuofe* (early mod.G. *schufe*, mod.HG. dial. *schuffe*) :—W.Ger. **skōpōn-*, f. **skōp-* ablaut-var. of **skap-*, root of **skappjan* to draw water (OS. *sceppian*, LG., Du. *scheppen*, OHG. *scephan*, MHG. *schepfen*, mod.G. *schöpfen*); (2) MDu. *schoppe* fem. (mod.Du. *schop*) = MLG. *schuppe* shovel (whence mod.G. *schüppe*):—OTeut. type **skuppōn-*, prob. repr. an older **skubnó-*, f. root **skub-*: *skeub-*: see SHOVE *v.*

The two words, though etymologically quite distinct, have, owing to their close resemblance in form and sense, been to some extent confused in continental Teut. The senses of both are represented in the Fr. adoption *écope* (*c* 1413 *escope*, mod. dial. *escope, escoupe, écoupe*) vessel or ladle for bailing out water, large shovel, skimming-dish. It is possible that the word may have come into Eng. through Fr.; but the Fr. word is first found nearly a century later than the Eng., and as the term was in nautical use immediate adoption from Du. or LG. is not improbable.]

1. a. A utensil for bailing out, ladling or skimming liquids; usually in the form of a ladle or a concave shovel with a straight handle. Now chiefly *Naut.* and *dial.*

c **1330** R. BRUNNE *Chron. Wace* (Rolls) 8168 Folk.. þat þe water wiþ scopes vp drowe. *c* **1362** *Durham Acc. Rolls* (Surtees) 566 In emendacione unius scope pro aqua evacuanda in quarera, ij d. *c* **1440** *Jacob's Well* x. 65 A scope is deep & hool to resceyue watyr. **1512** *Acc. Ld. High Treas. Scotl.* IV. 454 Item, for vj greit skowpis for the greit schip to cast the watter, iij s. **1594** in *Archæologia* XLVIII. 133 Item one mashefatt,.. iij sooes and ij scopes. **1600** SURFLET *Country Farm* III. li. 546 Be furnished of.. scoopes of iron, to draw and emptie out the oiles. **1668** CHARLETON *Onomast.* 96 The long crooked scoop with which Dutch Mariners throw up water to wet their sails. **1725** BRADLEY *Fam. Dict.* s.v. *Coal*, Water.. is dash'd on with a great Dish or Scoop. **1769** FALCONER *Dict. Marine* (1780), *Scoop*, a little hollowed piece of wood, employed to throw water out of a boat. **1844** H. STEPHENS *Bk. Farm* II. 417 The scoop best adapted to this purpose [*i.e.* lifting liquid manure] is a small wooden pitcher,.. the helve passing through its sides in an oblique direction. **1867** SMYTH *Sailor's Word-bk.*, *Scoop*, a long spoon-shaped piece of wood to throw water, when washing a ship's sides in the morning. **1886** *Cheshire Gloss.*, *Scope*, a bowl with a straight wooden handle fixed to it. Used for baling or skimming... In salt making a scope is a wooden bowl used for skimming the scum from brine.

b. *transf.* and *fig.*

c **1440** *Jacob's Well* i. 2 Watyrs of cursyng.. muste be cast out of ȝoure pytt with a scope of penaunce. **1589** R. HARVEY *Pl. Perc.* 3 They had neede be large long Spoons (say you) if I come to feed with such whipsters. Let me alone, for my actiuity, at the dish meat, and a long arme, though my scoope be the shorter. **1859** DICKENS *T. Two Cities* I. v, Some men kneeled down, and made scoops of their two hands joined, and sipped.

c. The bucket of a water-wheel or of a dredging or draining machine. [So Du. *schoep*.]

1591 PERCIVALL *Sp. Dict.*, *Alcaduz*, the scoope in a water wheele. **1875** KNIGHT *Dict. Mech.*, *Scoop* (Hydraulic Engineering), the bucket of a dredging-machine. **1888** W. H. WHEELER *Drainage Fens* v. 73 The scoops beat or lift the water from the lower to the upper side.

d. Applied to a mechanical contrivance for drawing water.

1580 HOLLYBAND *Treas. Fr. Tong*, *Bascule à tirer l'eau*.. a scoupe to drawe water out of a shallow well. **1851–4** *Cycl. Useful Arts* (ed. Tomlinson 1867) I. 516/2 Mr. W. Fairbairn.. has contrived a new form of scoop or alternating trough [for drainage purposes].

2. a. A kind of shovel (varying greatly in size and shape according to its special purpose), used for dipping out or shovelling up and carrying materials of a loose nature; usually an implement of iron, tin, etc. with a short handle and a broad, concave, or curved blade, the part of which next the handle is often covered over to form a receptacle for the material scooped up.

1487 *Naval Acc. Hen. VII* (1896) 63 Shovills.. iij dd j, Scopis.. j. **1495** *Ibid.* 203 Skoopes for pitche. **1581** J. BELL *Haddon's Answ. Osor.* 478 His accusations.. are throwen together in an heape with full skoupes. **1678** *Phil. Trans.* XII. 1070 Brewers use to keep their Barly.. laid about a foot in depth, and so turned over now and then with Scoops. **1839** URE *Dict. Arts* 549 The charge of coals is most conveniently introduced [into the gas retort] in a tray of sheet iron, made somewhat like a grocer's scoop. **1844** H. STEPHENS *Bk. Farm* II. 284 A couple of wooden scoops, .. to shovel up the corn in heaps, are useful implements in a corn-barn. **1851-4** *Cycl. Useful Arts* (ed. Tomlinson 1867) I. 739/2 [Gas-making.] Each retort is recharged by means of a long curved tray of sheet-iron, .. called a scoop. **1906** *Daily News* 16 Sept. 6 Huge canvas scoops were used to shovel the dried hops into .. heaps.

†**b.** A gunner's ladle = LADLE *sb.* 2a. *Obs.*

1525 *Acc. Ld. High Treas. Scotl.* V. 258 Skupis for the artalȝere. **1635** *Phil. Trans.* XV. 1092 The Gunners in charging her, wet not at all the scoop, or spunge.

3. An instrument with a spoon-shaped or gouge-shaped blade, used for cutting out a piece from some soft material, or for removing a core or an embedded substance. **a.** Applied to various small utensils in domestic use: chiefly short for *apple-scoop, cheese-scoop, potato-scoop*, for which see the first element.

1747 MRS. GLASSE *Cookery* xiv. 134 With a small Scoope very carefully take off the Eye [of the Codling] as whole as you can, and scoope out the Core. **1774** MRS. DELANY *Lett.* Ser. II. II. 81, I have not been able to get your silver scoop yet... I could not wait for it, as I thought you might want the fruit. **1805** R. W. DICKSON *Pract. Agric.* II. 612 The eye or root-bud of the potatoe .. is usually cut out of it by a scoop .. to the thickness of about half a crown.

b. A similar instrument for surgical purposes.

1739 SHARP *Surg.* xviii. 86 It is much safer to .. lay hold of it [the Stone] with the Forceps, than endeavour with the Scoop .. to force it outwards. **1895** *Arnold & Son's Catal. Surg. Instruments* Index, Acne, aural, gallstone, lithotomy, lupus scoops [etc.].

c. (See quot.)

1862 PIESSE *Perfumery* (ed. 3) 254 Balls are cut by hand, with the aid of a little tool called a 'scoop', made of brass or ivory, being, in fact, a ring-shaped knife.

d. Applied to certain tools used in excavation of soil; hence, the quantity of earth taken up at once by a scoop. †Also in *Gardening*, a hollow trowel.

1706 LONDON & WISE *Retir'd Gard'ner* I. vi. 254 The Displanting Scoop is made use of to take up some Sorts of Plants with the Earth about them. **1844** H. STEPHENS *Bk. Farm* I. 503 The scoop .. is then employed to cut under the last narrow spit. **1846** J. BAXTER *Libr. Pract. Agric.* (ed. 4) I. 238 Now take a navigator's scoop, that will measure three and a half inches from edge to edge, taking straight across the front or hollow side. With this instrument commence digging another ditch... After the first few scoops have been taken out of the lower ditch .. the covering in should commence. **1881** YOUNG *Ev. Man his own Mech.* §1100 The bottom [of a drain] being made smooth and level by means of the scoop.

†**4.** A kind of basket. Cf. SKEP, and MDu. *schoepe* winnowing-basket (= FAN *sb.*[1] 1 a). *Obs.*

1546 in Ellis *Orig. Lett.* Ser. II. II. 174 A thirde q[r]. a scope of Olyves cost vj[d]. **1641** BEST *Farm. Bks.* (Surtees) 103 To take the same bushell or scopp that wee measured the corne in. **1673** O. HEYWOOD *Diaries* (1883) III. 204 They let him down in a scoop or basket.

5. A variety of coal-box, somewhat resembling a flour-scoop in shape; short for *coal-scoop*.

1850 in OGILVIE; and in later Dicts.

6. Short for *scoop-net*.

1865 LUBBOCK *Preh. Times* xiv. (1869) 513 The fish nets .. are of two kinds, the scoop and the seine.

7. *attrib.* and *Comb.*, as ***scoop-load, -spade, -tool***; ***scoop-like, -shaped*** adjs.; **scoop bonnet**, a woman's bonnet shaped like a scoop; also ***scoop-shovel bonnet***; **scoop driver** (see quot.); **scoop wheel** [cf. 1 c], a wheel driven by wind or steam for lifting water.

1846 E. W. FARNHAM *Life in Prairie Land* 102 Sometimes her *scoop bonnet covered half my field of vision. **1901** W. CHURCHILL *Crisis* I. iv. 40 Her face was in that most seductive of frames, a scoop bonnet of dark green velvet. **1905** J. C. LINCOLN *Partners of Tide* 30 [Portraits] of ladies in flowered scoop bonnets .. gazed down upon him with rigid disapproval. **1941** L. I. WILDER *Little Town on Prairie* xix. 222 She wore a sweeping black gown and a scoop bonnet. **1892** *Labour Commission Gloss.* s.v., The *scoop driver .. guides the scoop into the [gas] retort, turns it over, and then brings it back again for filling. **1676** WISEMAN *Chirurg. Treat.* III. v. 240 A Scoop-like Instrument. **1883** F. DAY *Indian Fish* 64 A scoop-like net for catching small fish. **1841** *Jrnl. Franklin Inst.* Oct. 233 A *scoop load may be taken at one tenth of a cubic yard. **1844** H. STEPHENS *Bk. Farm* II. 302 The buckets .. are .. *scoop-shaped. **1884** 'MARK TWAIN' *Huck. Finn* xvii. 154 One was a woman in a slim black dress .. and a large *scoop-shovel bonnet. **1844** H. STEPHENS *Bk. Farm* I. 601 Any loose soil .. should be .. taken out by a *scoop spade. **1800** *Trans. Soc. Arts* XVIII. 153 An iron-edged *scoop-tool. **1838** *Civil Eng. & Arch. Jrnl.* I. 90/1, I have always used *scoop-wheels, the float-boards of which dip 5 feet below the water's surface.

scoop (sku:p), *sb.*[2] [f. SCOOP *v.*[1]]

1. a. The action or an act of scooping. Also, a quantity scooped up.

1742 YOUNG *Nt. Th.* IX. 910 Excavated grots .. yawning wide From Nature's structure, or the scoop of Time. **1832** J. P. KENNEDY *Swallow Barn* I. iii. 34 Nine scoops of water in the hollow of the hand, from a sycamore spring .., will break an ague. **1851** W. BOLLAND *Cricket Notes* 13 That runs were obtained more readily .. by off hitting than by the old scoop to leg. **1908** *Edin. Rev.* Apr. 396 He makes wild scoops at the fighting fish.

b. *Mus.* = PORTAMENTO.

1911 W. K. SMITH *Training Village Choirs* 8 The scoop is made on the commencing note of a tune or phrase. It consists in attacking it by way of a chromatic slide from the 'fourth' below. **1967** A. L. LLOYD *Folk Song in Eng.* i. 64 The sundry ways the folk singer has of passing from note to note by means of scoops, slides, hovers and such. **1975** *Gramophone* Aug. 316/1 He pulls the *Rosamunde* 'Entr'acte' about horribly and there are all sorts of period scoops that modern listeners will find intolerable. **1977** *Early Music* July 343/2 Special techniques and playing styles that can be developed are .. 'scoops' on a note, e.g. D–C♯–D completely slurred and glided simply by relaxing the breath pressure and increasing it again, keeping the fingering for the upper note held all the time.

2. a. *concr.* A place scooped or hollowed out; also, a natural concavity or hollow resembling this; *rarely*, an artificial basin for water. Also ***scoop-out***.

1762-71 H. WALPOLE *Vertue's Anecd. Paint.* (1786) IV. 289 He felt the delicious contrast of hill and valley changing imperceptibly into each other, tasted the beauty of the gentle swell, or concave scoop. **1821** CLARE *Vill. Minstr.* I. 115 Here a knoll and there a scoop. **1871** ROSSETTI *Poems, Dante at Verona* xxviii, The conduits round the gardens sing And meet in scoops of milk-white stone. **1874** T. HARDY *Far from Mad. Crowd* II. ii. 21 All foot and horse tracks made previous to the storm had been abraded and blurred by the drops, and they were now so many little scoops of water. **1884** *Milit. Engineering* II. 33 Most of the pieces would be fired through countersloping scoops. **1900** *Daily News* 1 June 3/1 Lying in a shallow scoop-out among the hills.

b. *Film* and *Television*. (See quots.)

1940 *Chambers's Techn. Dict.* 747/2 *Scoop*, one or more suspended broadsides, which are special types of incandescent flood-lights for use in motion-picture studios. **1974** *Some Technical Terms & Slang* (Granada Television), *Scoop*, 500 watt lamp suspended from studio ceiling.

3. In various slang uses. **a.** ***on the scoop***, 'on the drink, or a round of dissipation' (Farmer).

1871 F. C. BURNAND *More Happy Thoughts* xxxiv. 248 'Both the nautical Cockalorums have been going on the scoop, and are slightly moppy.' By which we understand him to mean, that the two naval officers have had as much as is bad for them. **1884** *Graphic* 30 Aug. 223/2 A young stockbroker .. who, in the absence of his wife, has gone on the scoop with his father-in-law. *a* **1893** MILLIKEN *'Arry Ballads* 47 An English Milord on the scoop carn't be equalled at blueing a quid.

b. orig. *U.S.* (See quots. 1886, 1906.) Cf. SCOOP *v.*[1] 5 b. Also *transf.*

1874 *Macomb* (Illinois) *Eagle* 23 Nov. 1/2 Owing to a slight misunderstanding, the *Sentinel* found itself without a copy of the decision, and for a time a terrible scoop seemed imminent. **1886** *Phonetic Jrnl.* 6 Feb. 63/1 In American newspaper offices an item of news is valued largely according to the likelihood of its being an exclusive piece of information, or a 'scoop'. *Ibid.* 63/2 'Has the *Herald* got that water-pipe contract paragraph in its City Hall column?' 'No,' answers the *Tribune* city editor, .. 'It's a scoop'. **1892** HOWELLS *Mercy* 113 'Any scoops?' asked Pinney, warily—'Anything exclusive?' **1892** *Nation* (N.Y.) 29 Dec. LV. 487/3 Is there one of us .. who would not .. conceal one [*sc.* a reporter] of his own in the shrubbery .. so as to get 'a scoop' on his contemporaries? **1906** *Daily Chron.* 29 Jan. 4/6 The feat escaped the notice of the representatives of all other newspapers; so the item is what in Fleet-street language is styled an 'exclusive' or 'scoop'. **1913** E. POUND *Let.* Mar. (1971) 16 It's our second scoop, for I only found the man [*sc.* Robert Frost] by accident and I think I've about the only copy of the book that has left the shop. **1917** CHESTERTON *Short Hist. Eng.* xiv. 181 One of these scares and scoops (not to add the less technical name of lies) was the Popish Plot. **1920** *Times* 25 Oct. 15/3 The edition would have been on the streets .. leaving the heartbroken editor to bewail the death of his great 'scoop'. **1930** 'SAPPER' *Finger of Fate* 127 The first thing to do was to get on the 'phone to his editor, because he had intended returning to London that night. He knew there would be no difficulty—especially if he gave a hint over the wire that he was on a scoop. **1940, 1969** [see BEAT *sb.*[1] 15 c]. **1973** D. BARNES *See the Woman* 75 We've got some scoop that our outstanding suspect is holed up in the Rocket Motel.

c. *U.S.* 'A sudden breaking down of prices for the purpose of buying stocks at cheaper rates followed by a rise'.

1879 in WEBSTER, Suppl.; and in later Dicts.

d. A lucky stroke of business, a 'haul'.

1893 KIPLING *Many Invent.* 166 You'll see how I work a big scoop when I get it. **1909** *Daily Chron.* 27 July 1/6 Her engagement .. at the Palace is a big 'scoop'.

4. *attrib.* and *Comb.*, as **scoop neck**, a rounded, low-cut neck on a garment; also (with hyphen) *attrib.*; so ***scoop-necked*** adj.; **scoop neckline** = *scoop neck*.

1953 *New Yorker* 20 June 64/2 At Rosette Pennington, 20 East 56th Street, there's a cool little sleeveless black cotton dress with a scoop neck and a full, flounced skirt. **1956** *Ibid.* 28 Jan. 68/3 There are short beach coats and scoop-neck dresses, all of the same material. **1972** *Vogue* Jan. 22 Bell sleeves, scoop neck, pintucks on jacket. **1978** *Detroit Free Press* 16 Apr. D 14 (Advt.), The tab-closing jacket with a skirt and scoop-neck shell in pink or beige. **1955** *New Yorker* 17 Sept. 96/1 De Pinna has acquired another sleeveless, scoop-necked Trigère dress. **1977** *Daily Tel.* 4 Apr. 15/4 The scoop-necked three-quarter mohair-knit coat over scooped-necked long-torso fine-knit sweater. **1959** *Times* 21 Sept. 12/4 A gown of deep cream satin with a fitting bodice, a scoop neckline, and a full skirt.

scoop (sku:p), *v.*[1] Also 4-5 scope, 4, 6 scoupe. [f. SCOOP *sb.*[1]]

1. *trans.* To lade or bail out (water) with or as with a 'scoop'. Also with *out*. Now *rare*.

c **1330** R. BRUNNE *Chron. Wace* (Rolls) 8164 Do scope þis water, & turn þe borne. **13..** *E.E. Allit. P.* C. 155 Scopen out þe scaþel water. *c* **1440** *Jacob's Well* i. 2 Vnder þis watyr in ȝoure pytt, whan þis watyr is scopyd out, is deep wose benethe. *Ibid.* x. 65 ȝow nedyth .. to scopyn out þis corrupte watyr of curs wyth þe scoope of penauns. **1530** PALSGR. 699/2 Let us scoupe out the water out of this ponde. *a* **1625** FLETCHER *Woman's Prize* I. ii, Tis as easie with a Sive to scoope the Ocean, as To tame Petruchio. **1697** DRYDEN *Æneid* IX. 26 He scoop'd the water from the crystal flood. **1773** MME. D'ARBLAY *Early Diary* July (1889) I. 226 The waves seemed to redouble their violence, and the boat scooped one fairly over us.

absol. *c* **1440** *Jacob's Well* x. 66 þe scope of þi penaunce .. muste be deep in sorwe, .. & ellys thou scopyst in veyn.

2. a. To remove or detach (a portion of friable or soft material, or part of a heap of objects) by passing a scoop or concave instrument obliquely through the mass, so as to leave a rounded hollow; to rake in as with a scoop. Chiefly with *away, out, up*. Also, to take *out* (a core, some embedded object) with or as with a scoop.

1622 MABBE tr. *Aleman's Guzman d'Alf.* II. 135 There are some kinde of people so cruell and vnconscionable, that they thinke of nothing but deceit and cozenage, scooping like shouels all to themselues. **1653** H. MORE *Antid. Ath.* II. x. §5 (1712) 71 Her Forefeet are broad, that she may scoop away much Earth at a time. **1718** POPE *Iliad* XIV. 578 Full in his Eye the Weapon chanc'd to fall, And from the Fibres scoop'd the rooted Ball. **1747** [see SCOOP *sb.*[1] 3]. **1807** G. CHALMERS *Caledonia* I. I. iv. 161 It was plainly formed by scooping the earth from the sides. **1836** W. IRVING *Astoria* I. 164 The Indians .. scoop them [*sc.* fish] up with small nets. **1867** HOWELLS *Ital. Journeys* iii. 16 The name of Byron .. had been scooped away by the Grand Duke of Tuscany. **1871** ROSSETTI *Poems, Last Confession* 546 She .. fell, and her stiff bodice scooped the sand Into her bosom.

absol. **1705** ADDISON *Italy, Sienna*, etc. 393 Whatever part of the Harbour they scoop in, it has an Influence on all the rest; for the Sea immediately works the whole Bottom to a Level.

b. To heap *up*, or collect *together* as by means of a scoop; *fig.* to obtain by effort from various quarters.

1855 MACAULAY *Hist. Eng.* xx. IV. 503 The government, instead of laboriously scooping up supplies from numerous petty sources, could now draw whatever it required from an immense reservoir.

c. *U.S.* To take (oysters) with a dredge. Also *intr.*

1891 in *Century Dict.*

3. a. *trans.* To hollow out with or as with a scoop; to form a concavity or depression in. Also with *out*.

1708 PHILIPS *Cyder* I. 396 The little Race of Birds, that hop from Spray to Spray, scooping the costliest Fruit. **1711** ADDISON *Spect.* No. 50 ¶3 As soon as this Rock was thus curiously scooped to their Liking. **1726** *Whole Art Gaming* 31 Such as Quatre-Trois .. are made new by the Die-maker .. whereas Loaded Dice are easy to Scoop or Load. **1731** POPE *Ep. Burlington* 60 Consult the Genius of the Place in all; That .. scoops in circling theatres the Vale. **1801** MOLLARD *Art of Cookery* 127 Take clean turnips and carrots, and scoop or cut them into shapes. **1871** L. STEPHEN *Playgr. Eur.* iii. (1894) 88 The rocks below having been scooped out by the glacier in old days. **1880** MISS BIRD *Japan* II. 84 The posts are scooped at the top, and heavy poles, resting on the scoops, are laid along them.

b. *intr.* To make a hollow as with a scoop. (In quot. *indirect passive*.)

1863 BARING-GOULD *Iceland* 189 A pitch black rock, scooped into by the stream.

4. To form by scooping or as if by scooping. Also with *out*.

1730-46 THOMSON *Autumn* 740 These .. The mountain-cisterns fill,—those ample stores Of water, scooped among the hollow rocks. *c* **1750** SHENSTONE *Elegy* xx. 10 See the wild Sons of Lapland's chill domain, That scoop their Couch beneath the drifted Snows! **1760** GOLDSM. *Trav.* 290 The firm connected bulwark [*sc.* the dikes of Holland] .. Spreads its long arms amidst the wat'ry roar, Scoops out an empire, and usurps the shore. *a* **1813** A. WILSON *Foresters* Poet. Wks. 217 Scooped from the woods unnumbered spots were seen, Embrowned with culture. **1816** BYRON *Prisoner of Chillon* vii, He died, and they .. scoop'd for him a shallow grave. **1827** HOOD *Mids. Fairies* 433 Sometimes we scoop the squirrel's hollow cell. **1841** B. HALL *Patchwork* I. vii. 107 Vaults scooped out by the running water. **1856** STANLEY *Sinai & Pal.* i. 60 One of us scooped out a horse, more complete than any of these sculptured animals, in ten minutes. **1877** A. B. EDWARDS *Up Nile* xviii. 484 The path was scooped out to a depth of four feet like a miniature railway cutting.

5. *slang.* **a.** To take or take up in large quantities; to appropriate (something) in advance of or to the exclusion of other competitors. Chiefly ***to scoop in*** (or ***up***). Also in various extended uses; *esp.* to defeat, destroy, get the better of. Phr. ***to scoop the kitty*** (or ***pool***), in *Gambling*, to win all the money that is staked; also *transf.*, to gain everything, to be completely successful.

In some uses difficult to distinguish from sense 6.

1850 W. COLTON *Three Years in Calif.* xxxiii. 440 A faith that could scoop up whole tribes of savages, .. impressing them with the conviction that submission to the padres was obedience to God. **1866** *Harper's Mag.* Oct. 680/1 Tell him he'll have to send this other fellow some more beans, for I've got him scooped [at draw-poker]. **1867** A. D. RICHARDSON *Beyond Mississippi* xi. 134 'Scooped' was an importation from Wall Street. 'I am badly scooped' meant [in Kansas]: 'I am used up' or 'defeated'. **1872** 'MARK TWAIN' *Roughing It* xlvii. 333 'It ain't no use. They've scooped him.' 'Scooped him?' 'Yes—death has.' **1882** J. D. MCCABE *New York* 160 (Farmer) He runs seventy 'busses on this line, and scoops in three 'r four hundred a day. **1888** HOWELLS *Annie Kilburn* xi. 118 The Irish are spreading out into the country and scooping in the farms that are not picturesque enough for the summer folks. **1901** G. DOUGLAS *House with Green Shutters* 11 They felt it .. a .. personal defeat that he .. should scoop every chance that was going. **1903** A. BENNETT *Leonora* vii. 194 Milly had shown a straight flush and scooped the kitty. **1903** KIPLING *Stellenbosh* in *Five Nations*

195 The Boojers scooped the crowd, To the last survivin' bandolier an' boot. **1916** J. Buchan *Greenmantle* xxii. 297 We have won any way; and if Peter has had a slice of luck, we've scooped the pool. **1929** H. Maclaren *Private Opinions of Brit. Blue-Jacket* 100, I haves everey intentuons to make a short spich, as scoops in the old man also a fairly wheard tipe of two passingers. *Ibid.* 101 This phrase from 'scoops in the old man' is plainly to be interpreted, by any one familiar with the ways of the fo'c'sle, as 'we have persuaded the captain to come, also two weird passengers'. **1937** H. C. Bailey *Clunk's Claimant* xlvi. 315 A million to one some side-line of a next of kin would bob up and pinch their share. Josh wouldn't scoop the pool. **1939** Wodehouse *Uncle Fred in Springtime* v. 70 There was a bit of unpleasantness at the Ball, and they scooped me in. **1944** *Jrnl. R. Aeronaut. Soc.* XLVIII. 363 De Havilland engines—the Gipsy, Gipsy Six and Gipsy Twelve..—together with the Cirrus, have almost completely 'scooped the pool' for light aircraft. **1953** K. Tennant *Joyful Condemned* viii. 69 There wasn't a girl..to touch her. She could walk right in and scoop the pool. **1959** *Encounter* Aug. 37/2 The rest of them were struggling..with razors and stakes... And soon I got scooped into the thing. **1972** Wodehouse *Pearls, Girls, & Monty Bodkin* ii. 27 You will give your consent to my scooping in the girl I love. **1973** 'P. Malloch' *Kickback* xxv. 164 You've scooped the pool. If you watch your step, you shouldn't have any more worries. **1976** *Evening Post* (Nottingham) 15 Dec. 23/9 Radford Swimming Club ended the 1976 season in fine style by scooping all but one award at the Notts. ASA Medley Team Swimming League. **1978** G. Mitchell *Mingled with Venom* iii. 23 Unless we all take care, that black boy the other lot adopted is going to scoop the pool.

b. *In journalistic use.* (Orig. *U.S.*) To 'cut out' a rival reporter or editor, or his paper, by obtaining and publishing exclusive or earlier news. Also *transf.* Also with the news as object, and occas. the person from whom information is derived.

1884 *Christian World* 5 June 421/2 He said he was not going to be scooped out by the other fellow. **1886** *Phonetic Jrnl.* 6 Feb. 63/1 The ever-gnawing anxiety of the city editor [in America] is to 'scoop' the opposition papers. **1902** Eliz. Banks *Newspaper Girl* 38 Miss Jackson across the way has got it, and she's going to print it in to-morrow's paper, and I shall be scooped. **1937** *Printers' Ink Monthly* May 42/1 *Scoop*, to gainfully outwit a rival network or station in the broadcasting of a special event or public interest program. **1938** E. Waugh *Scoop* I. v. 88 He told..how Wenlock Jakes, highest paid journalist of the United States, scooped the world with an eye-witness story of the sinking of the *Lusitania* four hours before she was hit. **1939** R. Campbell *Flowering Rifle* vi. 143 Then if some British pressman should be handy—From a safe distance, priming him with brandy, To scoop their story in his red receivers. **1948** G. V. Galwey *Lift & Drop* v. 88 The *Voice* must scoop you when you retire from Scotland Yard. **1968** J. M. Ziman *Public Knowledge* v. 98 Many scientists are so obsessed with the fear of being 'scooped'..that they issue a long succession of scrappy communications instead of waiting until the work is complete. **1974** *Times* 17 Apr. 16/7 The Israeli press..is sometimes scooped by the foreign press... The scooping.. often results from ministerial indiscretions overseas. **1978** G. McDonald *Fletch's Fortune* vi. 49 Do you realize what it would be worth to a person's career to scoop the murder? ..A handful of Pulitzer Prizes.

c. *intr.* Of a right whale: To feed by taking in large mouthfuls of brit. *U.S.*

1887 Goode, etc. *Fish. Industr. U.S.* v. II. 264 Again the whale may be 'scooping' or feeding.

6. To propel or to take by or as by a scooping movement. Also with *up*.

1867 *Australasian* 19 Jan. 76/3 Davis scooped a slow to Dan Wilkie, who..held it. **1882** *Sat. Rev.* 2 Sept. 313/1 The last comer scooped his first ball round to leg for 2. **1886** F. R. Stockton *Casting away of Mrs. Lecks & Mrs. Aleshine* 50 I'll never leave this place if I have to scoop myself out to sea with an oar. **1910** *Blackw. Mag.* Feb. 269/1 A very dark-coloured little man, with his arms and legs cut off, short at the knees and elbows,..scooping himself along on his stumps. **1916** 'Boyd Cable' *Action Front* 257 And he moved as if to scoop the German's head under his arm again. **1960** *Daily Tel.* 6 Dec. 1/1 Helicopters flew to the rescue of villagers trapped by floods at Hampton Bishop, near Hereford, last night. Forty men, women and children were 'scooped' from their cottages as swirling water crept towards their upstairs rooms. **1961** 'E. Lathen' *Banking on Death* xiii. 104 'I have a dinner date.' 'So do I,' replied Nicolls, hastily scooping up the letter. **1963** G. H. Thomson *Crocus Country* xix. 127 Mother never allowed anyone to 'scoop' the ball, that is, push it ahead with the mallet. **1966** *Listener* 17 Mar. 384/2 When she moves off, either she scoops the infant up to help him cling to her or else he springs to catch hold of her. **1973** N. Graham *Murder in Dark Room* ix. 60 The phone rang and I scooped up the receiver and said, 'Solo Malcolm here.' **1978** H. Wouk *War & Remembrance* ii. 20 We'd be scooped up as we stepped off the gang-plank.

7. *Mus. intr.* To perform a scoop (scoop *sb.*[2] 1 b).

1927 H. J. Wood *Gentle Art of Singing* 35 They are very apt to make a slow slur, to connect the notes by scooping and dragging the voice. **1958** A. Jacobs *New Dict. Music* 333 *Scoop*, in singing, to glide up to a note disagreeably from below instead of attacking it cleanly. **1975** *Gramophone* Nov. 846/3 In the thirties Busch was frequently praised because he scooped so rarely; as opposed to Lener who did it all the time. **1977** *Ibid.* Jan. 1154/2 Both violin and cello scoop heavily from note to note.

†**scoop**, *v.*[2] *Obs. rare.* In 7 scoup, scoope. [Cf. swoop *v.*[1]] *intr.* Of a bird: To swoop *at*. Also *trans.* To take (something) with a swoop.

1605 Chapman *All Fooles* III. G, Like a Iacke-daw that when he lights vpon A dainty morsell, kaas and makes his brags, And then some kite doth scoope it from him straight. **1611** Speed *Hist. Gt. Brit.* vi. xlvi. §12. 160 Whiles they were measuring out the circuit, an Eagle scouping at the line, flew with it ouer the Sea.

scooped (sku:pt), *ppl. a.* [f. scoop *v.*[1] + -ed[1].]

1. a. In various senses of the verb. Also *scooped-out*.

1726 *Whole Art Gaming* 28 The Three first Frauds... 1. Loaded and Scooped Dice. **1775** Adair *Amer. Ind.* 425 On the point of them [*sc.* the arrows] is fixed..a scooped point of buck-horn. **1805** R. W. Dickson *Pract. Agric.* II. 612 The scooped sets [of potatoes], though they grew, continued in a perfectly dwarfish state. **1862** S. Lucas *Secularia* 137 Philip of Spain..comes out after this test little better than a scooped turnip. **1886** *Phonetic Jrnl.* 6 Feb. 63–4 'How did you let the *Tribune* man "get away with you" again yesterday?' inquires the excited city editor... Then away the 'scooped' reporter goes to study the *Tribune* file... But a 'scooped' city editor is a disagreeable man to argue with. **1897** Anne Page *Afternoon Ride* 61 Round scooped-out spaces. **1907** *Westm. Gaz.* 24 Aug. 13/1 Venetian lace bordering the scooped-out front.

b. *scooped neck, neckline* = *scoop neck*(*line*) s.v. scoop *sb.*[2]

1956 *New Yorker* 14 Jan. 53 The scooped neckline blouse has a soft bow and short sleeves. **1959** *Harrods News* Summer 5 A matalessé cocktail frock with scooped neck. **1969** *Sears Catal.* Spring/Summer 3 Long, full skirt gathered at waistline, scooped neckline on bodice.

2. [f. scoop *sb.*[1]] Of the hands: Hollowed and joined so as to form a scoop. *rare.*

1860 Sala *Badd. Peerage* i, She stooped..and plunged her scooped hands into the kennel.

scooper ('sku:pə(r)). [f. scoop *v.*[1] + -er[1].]

1. One who or that which scoops.

1668 [implied in b]. **1755** in Johnson. *a* **1861** T. Winthrop *Canoe & Saddle* iii. (1883) 27 The Indians.. sweep down stream with a scoop-net. Salmon..are taken twenty an hour by every scooper. **1897** *Syd. Soc. Lex.*, *Scoopers' Pneumonia*, a form of chronic *Pneumoconiosis* occurring among grain-scoopers. **1908** *Speaker* 1 Aug. 633/2 The custom was for the steamboat company to go to a 'boss shoveller' and hire his gang of 'scoopers'.

b. A name for the avocet (see quot. 1668).

1668 Charleton *Onomast.* 96 *Avosetta*,..the Scooper (because his long narrow beak, arched upward, resembles the long crooked scoop). **1768** Pennant *Brit. Zool.* II. 399. **1856** Morris *Nests & Eggs Brit. Birds* III. 15.

2. A tool used for hollowing out portions of the surface worked upon; esp. in *Engraving*.

1837 *Penny Cycl.* IX. 437/2 Other lines being of the same width through their whole depth, must have been produced with that species of graver called a scooper. **1839** Chatto *Wood Engraving* 653 Gravers; tint-tools; gouges or scoopers; and flat tools or chisels. **1872** *Spon's Dict. Engin.* v. 1817 [Engravers' tools] A flat scooper;..a round scooper. **1884** *Cassell's Family Mag.* Feb. 152/2 [Modelling in clay] A scooper and two or three..scrapers will be..required.

scooper, scoopet: see scupper, scuppet.

scoopful ('sku:pfʊl). Also -full. [f. scoop *sb.*[1] + -ful.] A quantity that fills a scoop.

1725 De Foe *Voy. round World* II. 94 The Water falling thus hard, every Scoop-full upon the Sand..wash'd a great deal of it away. **1881** *Scribner's Mag.* XXII. 217/1 They throw rapid scoopfuls..over their shoulders.

scooping ('sku:pɪŋ), *vbl. sb.* [f. scoop *v.*[1] + -ing[1].] **a.** The action of the vb., in various senses.

1841 *Jrnl. Franklin Inst.* Oct. 233 For successful scooping [in excavation] the ground usually requires loosening. **1865** C. Geikie *Scenery & Geol. Scotl.* iv. 80 The scooping out of hollows in solid rock. **1960** C. Day Lewis *Buried Day* ii. 38 She sang her favourite arias..with much *portamento*, or luscious scooping. **1978** *Amer. Speech* 1975 L. 301 *Scooping*, sliding into a tone, hitting a note on the flat side and sliding up to the proper pitch, an undesirable practice on the part of one voice in a quartet.

attrib. **1871** Tyndall *Fragm. Sci.* (1879) I. ix. 301 The scooping power of a glacier. **1895** *Daily News* 23 Nov. 5/6 Scooping and boring tools.

b. *concr.* A concavity, hollow.

1862 Ansted *Channel Isl.* I. ii. (ed. 2) 27 Two or three such scoopings out of the surface are passed on the south-east coast. **1894** Baring-Gould *Deserts S. France* I. 141 There are..the same caves and scoopings.

scooping ('sku:pɪŋ), *ppl. a.* [-ing[2].] That scoops, in the senses of the verb. Of a rock, the sea: That forms hollows or depressions.

1821 Clare *Vill. Minstr.* I. 79 The shepherd leaves his unprotected flock, And flies for shelter in some scooping rock. **1828** Hood *Poems, To Tom Woodgate* xiv, Be mine the swelling, scooping sea, That is both hill and dale! **1864** J. C. Atkinson *Stanton Grange* 44 The poor trout were flung out with scooping hands.

b. *scooping avocet* = scooper 1 b.

1768 Pennant *Brit. Zool.* (1776) II. 425 Scooping Avoset. **1828** Fleming *Brit. Anim.* 101.

Hence '**scoopingly** *adv.*, so as to resemble a scoop.

1750 G. Hughes *Barbados* 232 These leaves turn very scoopingly inward on the upper side.

'**scoop-net.** [f. scoop *sb.*[1] or *v.*[1]] A small long-handled net; a dip-net.

1792 Belknap *Hist. New Hampsh.* III. 90 The Indian scoop-net is shaped like a pocket. **1883** Goode *Fish. Industr. U.S.* 51 The ordinary scoop or dip net, also called crab-net.

fig. **1895** Crockett *Men Moss-Hags* xxiv, The townsfolk stood about, but not too near..lest they should be called in question for compliance with the deed,..for the King's scoop-net gathered wide.

scoopy ('sku:pɪ), *a. Fashion slang.* [f. scoop *sb.*[2] or *v.*[1] + -y[1].] Of the neck of a garment: rounded and low-cut. Cf. scoop *sb.*[2] 4, scooped *ppl. a.* 1 b.

1970 *Daily Tel.* 1 June 13 This summer's dresses are heaven-sent for this event. The voiles are in full swing, the necks are scoopy. **1974** *Country Life* 17 Jan. 107/1 A range of knitwear..that incorporates low, scoopy necklines. **1976** *Ibid.* 22 Feb. 377/1 Evening dresses have scoopy or draw-string necklines.

scoore, obs. form of score, scour.

scoorse, scoory: see scorse *v.*[1], scoury *a.*[1]

scoot (sku:t), *sb.*[1] *Sc.* Also **scout.** [f. scoot *v.*[1]] (See quots.)

1825 Jamieson, Suppl., *Scout*, a syringe. **1880** *Jamieson's Dict.*, *Scoot*, 1. A gush or flow of water; also, the pipe or opening from which it flows. Clydes. **1887** Service *Dr. Duguid* III. iv. 259 Stottin' up the gate like a haw from a callan's gulshock scoot.

scoot (sku:t), *sb.*[2] *dial.* or *slang.* [f. scoot *v.*[1]]

1. The action or an act of 'scooting'.

1864 *Morning Star* 2 Feb., House-rent, too, as it elegantly expresses it, is on the 'same scoot upwards'. **1884** F. R. Stockton *Lady or Tiger?* 95 Ev'ry dog an' man an' nigger made one skoot fur that tree.

2. A bout of drunkenness, a drunken spree; chiefly in phr. ***on the scoot.*** *Austral.* and *N.Z. colloq.*

1924 *Truth* (Sydney) 27 Apr. 6 *Scoot*, to clear out; also continued bout of drunkenness. **1936** I. L. Idriess *Cattle King* xiv. 131 'He's a man who likes his meat raw, he chews his glass when he empties it.' 'I'm sorry to hear Eureka is on the scoot.' 'He's not. They don't go on the scoot out there. They drink dynamite and bust.' **1959** G. Slatter *Gun in Hand* iii. 42, I suppose you left the wife up there [on the farm] and you're down on the scoot. **1962** S. Gore *Down Golden Mile* vi. 120 Make mine a glass this time, seein' I have to go on the scoot with you booze artists to-night. **1975** X. Herbert *Poor Fellow My Country* 1019 We could've.. gone on a proper scoot.

scoot (sku:t), *sb.*[3] *slang.* [Abbrev. of scooter *sb.*] A motor-cycle or motor-car (see also quot. 1943).

1943 *Amer. Speech* XVIII. 169/1 *Scoot*, shuttletrain. **1968–70** *Current Slang* (Univ. S. Dakota) III–IV. 105 *Scoot*, *n.* A motorcycle, the type often used by the Hell's Angels Motorcycle Club. **1977** *Custom Car* Nov. 64/1 For this season he's gone over to a radical Volvo-engined scoot.

scoot (sku:t), *v.*[1] Also 9 **skute, skewt,** 8–9 scout. [In sense 1, which is purely Sc., the word prob. represents a ME. **skūte*, of Scandinavian origin, cogn. w. ON. **skióta* to shoot. The identity of the word in senses 2 and 3 is not quite certain.]

1. *Sc.* **a.** *trans.* 'To eject, jerk, or squirt' (Jamieson, 1880).

1805 J. Nicol *Poems* I. 155 (Jam.) An' gut an' ga' he scoutit. **1897** C. Grey *Misanthrope's Heir* xv, Naebody kent he was there till he scootit the water on Maister Ogilvy.

b. *intr.* (See quot.)

1880 *Jamieson's Dict.* s.v., To *scoot*,..to flow or gush out with force. Clydes.

2. *Sc.* and *U.S.* To slide suddenly, as on slippery ground.

1838 J. C. Neal *Charcoal Sk.*, 'Pair of Slippers' (Farmer), Notwithstanding his convulsive efforts to clutch the icy bricks he skuted into the gutter. **1851** H. Melville *Whale* III. xii. 79 The enormous casks..scoot across the slippery decks, like so many land slides.

3. *slang* or *colloq.* **a.** To go suddenly and swiftly, to dart; to go away hurriedly. Often with advs.

The (? originally nautical) slang word, written *scout* and prob. pronounced (skaʊt), seems to have become obsolete early in the 19th c. The modern *scoot* was app. imported into general British use from the U.S.

1758 Capt. Tyrrell *Let.* 9 Nov. in *Ann. Reg.* II. (1759) 61 The largest frigate being troublesome, I gave him a few of my lower deck pills and sate [= set] him a scouting like a lusty fellow, and he never returned to the action again. **1780** Capt. Young *Let.* 3 June in *Barham Papers* (MS.), They had rigged out the fore topmast studding-sail booms to scout for it. **1805** J. Nicol *Poems* II. 103 (Jam.) Wi' arm raxt out, awa' she scouted. **1810** *Splendid Follies* II. 28 Sponge was actually obliged to scout out of the room to conceal his risible muscles. **1847** Lowell *Biglow Papers* Ser. I. ii, An' th' Cunnles, tu, could..send the insines skootin' to the bar-room with their banners. **1856** *Knickerbocker Mag.* Mar. (Bartlett 1860), When he goes skewtin about, buying goods in business hours. **1882** B. Harte *Flip* ii, Yer had better drop that axe and scoot round getting the stranger some breakfast. **1892** *Sat. Rev.* 27 Feb. 244/1 He scoots off like a rabbit in the opposite direction. **1897** Olive Schreiner *Peter Halket* 66 A nigger man met them twenty miles off, and he said they were skooting up for Lo-Magundi's country as fast as they could go. **1904** J. Sweeney *At Scotl. Yard* xiii. 339 Forster always got wind of the warrant's being drawn out and..conveniently scooted.

b. *trans.* To move or convey suddenly or swiftly.

1905 *Automobile Topics* 27 May 462 Basle's engine had all the power necessary to scoot him up the hill on his fourth speed. **1947** J. Steinbeck *Wayward Bus* ii. 22 Juan put his little platform behind the bus and he lay on it on his back and scooted himself under with his feet. **1968** *Globe & Mail* (Toronto) 5 Feb. 22/1 Larush scooted his charge to the front from the outset to reach the quarter pole in a swift 0:30 2–5. **1975** N. Freeling *What are Bugles blowing For?* vi. 35 She scooted her wheelchair across the room.

scoot (sku:t), *v.*[2] Colloq. abbrev. scooter *v.*

1951 N. Mitford *Blessing* I. vii. 72 The happy crowd of scooting, skating children in the Tuileries gardens. **1962** A.

HUXLEY *Island* ix. 140 'Scooters are going to become a major political issue.' Vijaya laughed. 'To scoot or not to scoot, that is the question.'.. 'Wherever I've been.. they've opted wholeheartedly for scooting.'

scoot, variant of SCOUT.

scooter ('sku:tə(r)), *sb.* [f. SCOOT *v.*[1] + -ER[1].]

1. One who 'scoots' or goes hurriedly.

a **1825** FORBY *Voc. E. Anglia* s.v., 'To run like scooter,' i.e. very nimbly. **1893** *Blackw. Mag.* Sept. 367/2 We do not.. curse the harmless Saxon... If he is circling the coast of Antrim on mail-cars, we call him a 'Scooter'—nothing worse.

2. *Sc.* and *north.* A syringe, squirt.

1829 in BROCKETT *N.C. Words.* **1882** in JAMIESON.

3. *U.S.* [Perh. a different word: cf. *cooter* dial. form of COULTER.] A simple plough with a single handle used for marking furrows, making drills, breaking up the soil in furrows or between rows of plants. In full *scooter plough.*

1820 in *Henderson's North Carolina Almanack* (1823) 25 The ridges are opened with a small plough called a scooter, something like a shovel plough. **1842** in J. A. Turner *Cotton Planter's Manual* (1857) 55 The next operation to be performed.. is to plough out the middles well, the wide way, with a good shovel-plough, having first run around the young plant with a scooter-plough. **1868** *Rep. U.S. Commissioner Agric.* (1869) 414, 100 bushels of cotton seed were turned under with a Brinley plow, followed in the same furrow by a scooter, breaking the soil six or seven inches. **1895** *Rural World* 14 Dec. 867/2 If there is no proper subsoil plough, then run a.. scooter in the furrow. **1905** *Times*, Engineering Suppl. 9 Aug. 189/3 As soon as the tobacco plants are firmly set, a 'scooter' is run between the rows, which throws up a flat-bottom furrow. **1938** M. K. RAWLINGS *Yearling* xxx. 385 He brought old Caesar and the scooter plow and turned in to the field, laid off and bedded up ready for the corn, to open the furrows for the planting. **1944** T. D. CLARK *Pills, Petticoats & Plows* 281 By colloquial designations the various strange shapes were known to the trade as sweeps, shovels, scooters, twisters,.. scrapers and subsoilers.

4. a. A boat, propelled by sails, capable of being used both on ice and in water. *N. Amer.* **b.** A fast motor-boat, used in the war of 1914–18. **c.** A motorized pleasure boat resembling a motor-scooter. In full, ***sea scooter, water scooter.***

1903 *N.Y. Times* 13 Dec., The 'scooter'.. is built with a bottom and a deck which are duplicates of each other. **1909** *Cent. Dict.* Suppl. s.v. *Ice-scooter.* These scooters may be run alternately through water and over ice. **1919** *Times* 21 Feb. 11/2 The war has produced 'P' boats and 'Q' boats and 'U' boats, but the wildest of all wild things is the 'scooter', professionally known as the coastal motor-boat. **1927** G. BRADFORD *Gloss. Sea Terms* 151/1 *Scooter*, an amphibious craft, shallow and beamy, equipped with runners beneath and rigged with a jib and mainsail. It is used as an ice boat, particularly on Great South Bay, Long Island. It is capable of crossing patches of open water. **1929** F. C. BOWEN *Sea Slang* 118 *Scooter*, a coastal motor boat in the war. **1948** J. STEINBECK *Russian Jrnl.* vi. 116 There were boat races on the river, little water-scooters with outboard motors. **1958** *Times* 21 Jan. 8/5 (*heading*) Man on sea scooter believed drowned. *Ibid.*, Mr. John Penn..., believed to have been drowned.. while testing a water scooter at West Mersea, Essex. **1966** *Kingston* (Ont.) *Whig-Standard* 13 Jan. 2/6 A provincial police diver today located an ice-scooter owned by a local insurance agent who vanished here last night. **1976** *Vacation Fun in Dearborn* (Dearborn, Mich., Times-Herald) Summer, Pedal boats and water scooters on Lakes Three and Six.

5. a. A child's toy consisting of a footboard mounted between two tandem wheels with a long handle attached to the front wheel, operated by resting one foot on the footboard while pushing with the other and steering by the handle.

1919 *Times* 21 Feb. 11/2 The 'scooter' we knew before the war was a new terror to the pavement. **1921** *Spectator* 2 July 8/1 Must you not use first one foot then another on your scooter, lest you get 'scooter leg'. **1939** JOYCE *Finnegans Wake* 191 A youth those reporters so pettitily wanted as gamefellow that they asked his mother for ittle earps brupper to let him tome to Tindertarten, pease, and bing his scooter 'long. **1943** D. POWELL *Time to be Born* iv. 79 The first twenty years of their existence which had been wasted in marbles, dolls, hoop-rolling, and scooter-racing. **1961** *Toys & Fancy Goods* Aug. 22 Two pavement scooters.. with red frame, yellow wheels and white grips.

b. = *motor-scooter* s.v. MOTOR *sb.* 6.

1917 *Autocar* 20 Jan. 60/1 For some months past it has been known in this country that the 'scooter' in America has developed into something rather beyond the child's plaything so popular in the British Isles. Until quite recently, however, the American motor-driven 'scooter' has not been seen in London. **1919** *Model Engineer & Electrician* 27 Feb. 142/1 A scooter of this type can cover 100 miles on a gallon of petrol. **1944** R. CHANDLER *Lady in Lake* v. 30 An anxious-looking bird thumped past on a power-scooter. **1957** *Times* 19 Nov. 11/3 The rising popularity of new types of machines—the scooter and the moped. **1971** *Daily Tel.* 16 Dec. 1/3 Safety helmets are to be made compulsory for riders and passengers of solo motor cycles, scooters and mopeds.

c. In various extended and slang uses: see quots.

1917 *Little Folks* Sept. p. vi. (Advt.), The free-wheel auto-scooter propelled by pedal. **1919** I. F. MARCOSSON *S.O.S.: America's Miracle in France* vi. 154 The vastness of these Depots is such that an inspection on foot.. is out of the question. They are so criss-crossed with rails that you must use a 'Scooter', which is a motor-driven hand-car fitted for standard-gauge tracks... Every important official has his own 'Scooter' and you can see them scooting over the place at all hours of the day and night. **1930** A. ARMSTRONG Taxi! v. 48 There were still a large number of two-cylinder Renaults (called 'scooters') plying for hire. **1935** N. ERSINE *Underworld & Prison Slang* 64 *Scooter*, a rum-running car. **1948** 'J. EVANS' *Halo for Satan* vi. 78 'We'll use your scooter, Mac... Where's she parked?'.. I wondered how they knew I had a car. **1953** *Sun* (Baltimore) (B ed.) 15 June 4/2 A new $1,000 'flying scooter' powered by a 12-horse-power engine for the 'people's car' (*Volkswagen*), has been making test flights from a forest clearing south of Hamburg. *Ibid.*, The scooter has five or eight vanes, radiating from a circular passenger cabin which stands on three wheels. **1961** PARTRIDGE *Dict. Slang* Suppl. 1261/1 *Scooter*.., a single-deck bus; a driver-only bus: busmen's: since ca. 1945. **1963** *Daily Progress* (Charlottesville, Va.) 28 June 1/6 An aerospace firm has come up with something it calls a space scooter, a one-man platform with handlebars designed for crater hopping and crag climbing on the moon. **1971** A. DIMENT *Think Inc.* iv. 70 A scooter truck, that strange bastard little vehicle with a bulbous cab married to a small, pick-up body. **1972** *N.Y. Times* 3 Nov. 14/4 Fleets of flag-bedecked scooter-buses.

6. *attrib.* and *Comb.* (sense 5b), as ***scooter-man, rider, -traffic.*** (See also senses 3 and 5c.)

1960 *Guardian* 12 Dec. 2/4 The irresponsible way in which many scootermen (and ladies) wind their way through traffic. **1959** *Times* 16 May 7/6 As a scooter-rider of some seniority I ventured to write to you some months ago about the apparent disinterest of the authorities in the parking of scooters. **1976** *Daily Mail* (Hull) 16 Dec. 1/4 Scooter-rider J. B... was admitted to Hull Royal Infirmary.. after his vehicle was involved in an accident with a car. **1960** *Daily Tel.* 14 June 1/1 Accidents involving motor-scooters showed the greatest percentage increase, 61 per cent, but the scooter traffic was estimated to have gone up by 64 per cent. during the year.

'scooter, *v.* [f. the sb.] *intr.* To travel by scooter (senses 4 and 5). Hence **'scootering** *vbl. sb.*

1911 WEBSTER, *Scooter*.., a strongly built sailboat... Hence: *scootering, n.* **1957** C. BROOKE-ROSE *Languages of Love* 15 He climbed on to his Lambretta and scootered off towards Oxford Street. **1957** *New Yorker* 26 Oct. 35/3 Scootering is the most economical and practical form of transportation available in New York today. **1960** *Housewife* May 46/1 When scootering, slacks are just about permissible. **1961** *Times* 9 Mar. 21/3 Scootering in Great Britain has also become a hobby.

scooterist. [f. SCOOTER + -IST.] One who drives, or travels on, a scooter (sense 4 or 5).

1919 *Model Engineer & Electrician* 27 Feb. 142/1 The 'scooterist' is Mr. Franklin Gunther, First Secretary U.S. Diplomatic Service. **1956** *New Yorker* 8 Dec. 44/3 One of the owners.. was a young man wearing a white crash helmet and lying supine on the pavement under his blue Vespa... As each new scooterist arrived, he would extend an arm upward to shake hands. **1959** *Times* 16 May 7/6 Does a scooterist pay his sixpence or a shilling and take up the space that will hold a mammoth Cadillac? **1976** R. HILL *Another Death in Venice* I. ii. 31 A flotilla of motor-scooters went by. .. There was something so utterly careless about the scooterists that he felt a pang of envy. **1981** *Times* 27 July 26/2 They withstood extreme provocation by large numbers of these scooterists.

scop (ʃɒp, skɒp). *Hist.* Also (erroneously) scóp or scôp. [OE. *scop, sceop* = OHG. *scoph, scof* masc., cogn. w. OHG. *scoph* (? neut.) poetry, fiction ('commentum'), sport, jest, derision ('ludibrium'), ON. *skop* railing, mocking: see SCOFF *sb.*[1]] An Old English poet or minstrel.

Beowulf 496 Scop hwilum sang hador on Heorote. *c* **888** K. ÆLFRED *Boeth.* xli. § 1 Omerus se goda sceop. *c* **1205** LAY. 22705 Scopes þer sungen of Arðure þan kingen. **1774** R. HENRY *Hist. Gt. Brit.* II. 437 Whether this similarity was owing to the Welsh bards having imitated the Saxon scops and Danish scalds,.. it is not easy to determine. **1826** J. J. CONYBEARE in W. D. Conybeare *Illustrations of Anglo-Saxon Poetry* 245 The following lines [from The Exile's Complaint] may therefore be considered as an unique specimen of an original attempt of this kind [*sc.* elegiac] by an Anglo-Saxon Scop. **1839** T. WRIGHT *Ess. Lit. & Learning under Anglo-Saxons* 1 The heroic song in which the *scóp* or poet told the venerable traditions of the foreworld to the chieftains assembled on the 'mead-bench'. **1848** LYTTON *Harold* VI. i, I have heard scops and harpers sing [etc.]. **1860** G. STEPHENS *King Waldere's Lay* 27 The less remarkable Hero names more or less connected with this Legend which may be found in Beowulf, the Scóp's Song, the Traveler's Lay, the Codex Dipl. and elsewhere. **1887** MORLEY *Introd. to A. Cunningham's Tradit. Tales* 8 The recitations of the Scóp and gleeman. **1892** BROOKE *Early Eng. Lit.* I. 12 The Scôp and the gleeman were professional persons. **1893** *Trans. Philol. Soc. 1891–4* 379 To compose with such a Prosody would imply at once the greatest crudity and the greatest subtlety in the ancient 'scop'. **1898** T. ARNOLD *Notes on Beowulf* ii. 16 Hroðgar.. gives rich gifts to Beowulf, and his *scóp*, or poet, recites the lay of Hnæf and Hengest, and their great fight in Friesland. **1903** L. F. ANDERSON *Anglo-Saxon Scop* 5 The poem itself is an aggregation of several interesting specimens of the scop's art. **1928** W. W. LAWRENCE *Beowulf & Epic Trad.* 281 What, in a Christian era, were the court-poets, the *scops*, to do, except to fall in with the new ways? **1948** K. MALONE in *English Studies* XXIX. 164 The scops kept the old ideals strong by singing the heroes of the past. **1968** E. B. IRVING *Reading of Beowulf* iv. 169 The story of Finn, which Hrothgar's scop tells at the Great Banquet.

scop, obs. f. SCALP *sb.*[1]; obs. pa. t. of SHAPE.

‖**scopa**[1] (skəʊpə). *Ent.* [L. *scōpa*, in class. use only in pl. *scōpæ* twigs, shoots, a broom or brush.] A bundle or tuft of bristly hairs on the legs of bees, used for collecting pollen; a pollen-brush.

1802 KIRBY *Monogr. Apum Angliæ* I. 109 *Scopa.* This term, which is used by Schrank to denote another part, to which I have given its diminutive [i.e. *scopula*] as a name, I have adopted to signify the thick coat of hairs which externally covers the posterior tibiæ of many of these insects, by means of which they probably brush the pollen from the flowers. **1840** WESTWOOD *Introd. Classif. Insects* II. 260 The other instruments consist of bundles of hairs, whence they have been termed the scopa or scopula by Mr. Kirby, 'la brosse' by the French, and which we may call the pollen brushes.

‖**scopa**[2] ('skopa). *rare.* [It.] An Italian card-game.

1965 'W. HAGGARD' *Hard Sell* iii. 26 There were cafés and men inside them. They were playing *scopa.* **1977** *Time* 3 Jan. 40/3 Premier Giulio Andreotti's Christmas gift to his staff last week was a single playing card—the seven of diamonds, which in the Italian game of *scopa* is worth double and thus is considered the luckiest card in the deck.

scoparin ('skəʊpərɪn). Also -ine. [f. SCOPARIUM + -IN.] A diuretic principle found in the common broom.

1850 STENHOUSE in *Phil. Trans.* CXLI. 422 This very impure jelly consisted chiefly of a crystalline yellow colouring matter (scoparine). **1862** MILLER *Elem. Chem.*, *Org.* (ed. 2) 479 Scoparin.

scoparious (skəʊ'pɛərɪəs), *a.* [f. mod.L. *scōpārius*, f. *scōpa*: see SCOPA[1] and -ARIOUS. Cf. late L. *scōpārius* a sweeper.] Broom-shaped, scopiform.

In recent Dicts.

‖**scoparium** (skəʊ'pɛərɪəm), **scoparius** (skəʊ'pɛərɪəs). [Use of mod.L. specific name: see below.] Pharmacopœial names for the tops of the common broom, *Spartium scoparium* or *Cytisus* (*Sarothamnus*) *scoparius.*

1871 GARROD *Mat. Med.* (ed. 3) 411 Diuretics.. Digitalis. Squill. Scoparium [etc.]. **1875** H. C. WOOD *Therap.* (1879) 483 Scoparius.. is a most efficient hydragogue diuretic.

scopate ('skəʊpeɪt), *a. Ent.* [ad. mod.L. *scōpāt-us*, f. *scōpa*: see SCOPA[1], -ATE[2].] (See quot.)

1826 KIRBY & SP. *Entomol.* IV. xlvi. 347 Scopate (*Scopata*). When it [the tibia] is quite covered with a brush of hairs with which it brushes off the gross pollen, and in which it carries it.

†**scope**, *sb.*[1] *Obs. rare.* In 4 scoppe. [Related to SCOPE *v.*[1]] A leap or skip.

13.. *K. Alis.* 5777 Tho hy seighe that folk, I wys, Hy plumten doune, as a doppe, In the water at on scoppe. **1688** HOLME *Armoury* III. xix. (Roxb.) 184/1 Scop of an horse, is the distance of his treat vpon the ground from the fore-feete to the hinder feete, in his full speed.

scope (skəʊp), *sb.*[2] Also 6 scoope, skoape, 6–7 skope, *Sc.* scop. [ad. It. *scopo* aim, purpose, ad. Gr. σκοπός mark for shooting at, aim, f. σκοπ- ablaut-variant of σκεπ-, σκέπτεσθαι to look out.]

†**1. a.** A mark for shooting or aiming at. Chiefly in figurative context, and tending to coincide with sense 2 or 3. *Obs.*

1562 *Aberd. Kirk Sess. Rec.* (Spalding Club) 4 Seing also the haill scripture of God to tend and shote at this scope and mark. **1579** SPENSER *Sheph. Cal.* Nov. 155 O!.. slipper hope Of mortal men, that swincke and sweate for nought, And, shooting wide, doe misse the marked scope. *a* **1602** W. PERKINS *Cases Consc.* (1619) 24 The sinner makes an abberration from the scope or marke that is set before him. **1670** MILTON *Hist. Eng.* v. Wks. 1851 V. 223 The Saxon Annalist,.. runs on a sudden into such extravagant fansies and metaphors, as bare him quite beside the scope of being understood. **1673** O. WALKER *Educ.* I. vi. 49 From want of such a scope or marke it comes that most men shoot under, employ their minds in little by-businesses. **1677** GALE *Crt. Gentiles* IV. 170 This is the primary end of our life, unto which al our actions ought to collime, as arrows to their scope. **1683** D. A. *Art Converse* 54 He shall be a scope to envy in all future times.

†**b.** The goal or terminal point of a race, a journey, etc. *Obs. rare.*

c **1611** CHAPMAN *Iliad* XXIII. 301 He better skild, that rules worse horse, will all obseruance bend Right on the scope still of a Race [323 αἰεὶ τέρμ' ὁρόων]. *a* **1628** PRESTON *New Covt.* (1634) 182 Every step a man takes tends to some scope or other East or West or North or South.

2. a. Something aimed at or desired; something which one wishes to effect or attain; an end in view; an object, purpose, aim. Now *rare.*

c **1555** HARPSFIELD *Divorce Hen. VIII* (Camden) 229 The seventh Counsell of Carthage and the Milevitane Counsell, which both tend to one end and scope, that there should be no appellations made out of Affricke. **1559** tr. *Geminus' Anat.* 4/1 If there be 300 scopes or endes of the vse of the partes of the bodie. **1584** *Reg. Privy Council Scot.* III. 645 His Majestie hes thocht it maist convenient to mak manifest the cours and scope of the dangerous and indirect dealing pretendit. **1606** WARNER *Alb. Eng.* xv. xcvi. (1612) 383 A mortall Man, sinfull as ye, or worser is the Pope, Your Coyne of all his Practises and Pedlaries the scope. **1622** MALYNES *Anc. Law-Merch.* 60 Gaine being the scope of all merchants. **1669** BOYLE *Contn. New Exp.* I. (1682) 95 One of the scopes I propos'd to my self in this experiment was to discover [etc.]. **1671** MILTON *P.R.* I. 494 Thy coming hither, though I know thy scope, I bid not or forbid. **1731** SWIFT *On Death of Swift* 499 Alas, poor Dean! his only Scope Was to be held a Misanthrope. **1736** BERKELEY *Disc.* Wks. 1871 III. 422 Plato.. even maintains religion.. to be the chief aim and scope of human life. **1774** J. Bryant *Mythol.* I. 171 Truth was the scope, at which they aimed. **1853** M. Arnold *Scholar Gipsy* xvii, O Life unlike to ours! Who fluctuate idly without term or scope. **1869** Mozley *Univ. Serm.* i. (1876) 8 These societies have two distinct scopes and ends.

†**b.** A person who is an object of desire or pursuit. *Obs.*

1590 Spenser *F.Q.* iii. iv. 52 He..cursed night, that reft from him so goodly scope. **1594** T. B. *La Primaud. Fr. Acad.* ii. 10 God, who is the scope, which we desire & shal one day attaine vnto. **1624** Sir J. Davies *Ps.* xxxix, Of my desires Thou art the only scope. **1707** tr. *Wks. C'tess D'Anois* (1715) 646 Being impatient to see the Princess, who was the only Scope of his hopes and desires.

†**c.** *to scope*: to the purpose. *Obs.*

1607 Shaks. *Timon* i. i. 72 'Tis conceyu'd, to scope.

†**d.** Degree of excellence to be aimed at. *Obs.*

1674 Playford *Skill Mus.* Introd. A4b, Musick..hath been the study of Millions of Men for many thousand years, yet none ever attained the full scope and perfection thereof.

3. a. The object which a writer or speaker has in view, that which he wishes to express or enforce; the main purpose, intention, or drift of a writer, a book, etc.; †the subject, theme, argument chosen for treatment. Now *rare*: cf. sense 6b.

1536 Cranmer in Ellis *Orig. Lett.* Ser. iii. III. 24 The scope and effecte of both my sermons stode in three thyngs. **1549** Latimer *5th Serm. bef. Edw. VI* (Arb.) 134 *marg.*, The scope or state of the boke, tendes to dysuade the kinge from hys supremycye. **1552** —— *Serm. Septuag. Sunday* (1584) 323 Euery parable hath *certum statum*, a certayne scope,..it is enough for vs when we haue the meaning of the principall scope, and more needeth not. **1581** R. Goade in *Confer.* ii. (1584) I iiij, Out of the whole scope and drift of the place, it is euident to be spoken onely of the Apostles. *a* **1591** H. Smith *Serm.* (1594) 127 The scope of the Euangelist is this: First, that Christ would not hinder his doctrine for mother, or brethren, or any kinsman. **1612** Brinsley *Lud. Lit.* x. (1627) 157 To consider well the scope and drift of the Author. **1617** Moryson *Itin.* iii. 5 This is the scope of all I say: That by this course the good become best, the bad prove worst. *a* **1703** Burkitt *On N.T.* Mark xii. 8 The design and scope of the parable, is to discover to the Jews..their obstinate impenitency under all the means of grace. **1709–11** Pope *Ess. Crit.* 120 Know well each Ancient's proper character; His fable, subject, scope in ev'ry page. **1776** Sir J. Reynolds *Disc. Roy. Acad.* vii. (1778) 322 It has been the main scope and principal end of this discourse to demonstrate [etc.]. **1866** Felton *Anc. & Mod. Gr.* II. i. xii. 227 In its scope and substance the argument of Demosthenes may be compared [etc.].

b. The intention or tendency of a law; the drift or meaning of a proposal.

1647 Sprigge *Anglia Rediv.* iii. vi. 155 No sooner did the General satisfie himself in the scope of these Overtures from the Prince and the Lord Goring; but [etc.]. **1674** Allen *Danger Enthus.* 32 According to those plain Precepts of the Gospel which answer the Spirit and Scope of the Law. **1696** Bentley *Serm. Of Rev. & Messias* 14 The scope and tendency of the Law it self is always mine and every man's advantage.

†**c.** A person who is a subject or theme of discourse. (Cf. 2b.) *Obs.*

1659 Pearson *Creed* (1839) 134 All which had respect unto the Messias, as the scope of all the prophets, and the complement of their prophecies.

†**4.** *Med.* A plan or method of treatment; = intention 10, 10b. *Obs.*

1590 Barrough *Meth. Physick* v. xvii. (1596) 312 By this cataplasme you shall very well accomplish the second intention or scope of curing herpes. **1625** Hart *Anat. Ur.* Pref. A iv b, Afterwards also were set downe diuerse scopes and indications requisite for the cure of the disease. **1634** T. Johnson *Parey's Chirurg.* xviii. xiv. (1678) 422 The Palliative cure of that Gout..is performed by four scopes. **1690** Blancard *Lex. Med.* 234 Endeixis est morborum indicatio, qua demonstratur, quid sit faciendum... A[ngl.] A scope.

5. †**a.** ? Skill in aiming. *Obs. rare.* **b.** The range of a missile weapon; also *fig.* Cf. 8.

a **1548** Hall *Chron., Hen. V*, 65 He knewe that he was nether free from disdain nor yet deliuered from the scope of malice. **1594** *2nd Rept. Dr. Faustus* in Thoms *E. Eng. Prose Rom.* (1858) III. 397 With great scope throwing his launce forwards just upon the Turks face. **1830** Galt *Lawrie T.* i. i, My infirmity..led me to ettle at butts far beyond the scope of the spring that was thought to be in my bow.

6. a. The distance to which the mind reaches in its workings or purpose; reach or range of mental activity; extent of view, outlook, or survey.

c **1600** Shaks. *Sonn.* xxix. 7 Desiring this mans art, and that mans skope. **1775** Mason *Mem. Gray* 5 These papers.. will ascertain, not only the scope and turn of their genius, but of their temper. **1807–8** Wordsw. *White Doe* iii. 57 With wishes of still bolder scope On you we look, with dearest hope. **1836** *Random Recoll. Ho. Lords* xvi. 404 He is ..a man of very limited scope of mind. **1850** Ht. Martineau *Hist. Peace* v. ii. (1877) III. 205 No one doubted his patriotism: the question was of its scope and enlightenment. **1861** Buckle *Civiliz.* II. i. 46 In the progress of civilization, the scope of the intellect is widened; its horizon is enlarged. **1862** Miss Braddon *Lady Audley* xxxix, Her intellect was rather limited in its scope.

b. The sphere or area over which any activity operates or is effective; range of application or of subjects embraced; the reach or tendency of an argument, etc.; the field covered by a branch of knowledge, an inquiry, concept, etc.

1830 Herschel *Stud. Nat. Phil.* 305 Like particular theorems in geometry, which..have..their several scopes and ranges of extensive application. **1844** H. H. Wilson *Brit. India* iii. vi. III. 247 An arrangement of a more deliberate and comprehensive scope was at the same time adopted. **1855** Lynch *Rivulet* lxxx. iv, And teach how great our treasure, How great salvation's scope. **1857** Gladstone *Glean.* VI. i. 47 He may accuse us of incapacity even to measure the scope of our own arguments. **1874** Green *Short Hist.* vi. §4 (1882) 304 Art, if it lost much in purity and propriety, gained in scope. **1875** Stubbs *Const. Hist.* III. xviii. 53 The deliberations of the parliament almost immediately took a much wider scope. **1895** *Bookman* Oct. 25/2 This history..is not dissimilar in scope to Bright's well-known History of England.

c. In phrases, as ***within, beyond*** (one's) ***scope***.

1661 Glanvill *Van. Dogm.* xii. 107 Every thing that falls within the scope of our enquiry. **1789** Burke *Corr.* (1844) III. 105 Things, indeed, have already happened so much beyond the scope of all speculation. **1808** Wellington in Gurw. *Desp.* (1835) IV. 169 They did not come regularly within the scope of a military dispatch. **1854** 'C. Bede' *Verdant Green* ii. xi, [He] soon saw that the questions were within his scope, and that he could answer most of them. **1858** Hawthorne *Fr. & It. Note-bks.* (1871) II. 240 We were above the scope of many of the showery clouds that haunt a hill-country. **1868** M. Pattison *Acad. Org.* v. 121 An historical enquiry into what Oxford was is beyond the scope of this memoir. **1884** *Law Times Rep.* L. 367/2 At the time of the accident, Moore clearly was not acting within the scope of his employment.

†**d.** ***to have the right scope of***: ? to take the right view of. *Obs.*

1563–83 Foxe *A. & M.* II. 1861/1 Well sayde the king, I well perceiue that you haue the right scope of this matter.

7. a. Room for exercise, opportunity or liberty to act; free course or play. Often in phrases, ***to give scope*** (*to* a person or thing); ***to have*** or ***take scope***. Also followed by defining inf., or by *for*.

1534 *Act 26 Hen. VIII*, c. 13 (§1) To great a scope of vnreasonable libertie should be giuen to all cankarde and traiterous hartes. **1553** T. Wilson *Rhet.* 17 Wherein we might take a large scope if we would fully speake of all thynges that are comprehended vnder honestie. **1567** Fenton *Trag. Disc.* 139b, The dames of Myllan haue a more skoape of libertie then the reste of the Ladies in any part in Italie. **1576** E. Waterhouse *Let. to Sir H. Sidney* in Collins *Lett. State* (1746) I. 147 Because I wold give free Scope to all Men to utter their Opinions concerning my Behaviour. **1601** Shaks. *Jul. C.* iv. iii. 108 Be angry when you will, it shall haue scope. **1602** W. S. *Cromwell* i. iii. 99 Giue not such cruell scope vnto your hart. **1610** J. Robinson *Justif. Separat.* 171 With their transcendent jurisdiction in their..Diocesan Churches [they] take their scope without orb, or order. **1625** Bacon *Ess., Simulation* (Arb.) 509 So that no man can be secret, except he giue himselfe a little Scope of Dissimulation. **1647** Clarendon *Hist. Reb.* i. §129 As his person and parts were such as are before mentioned, so he gave them full scope, without restraint. **1678** Sir G. Mackenzie *Crim. Laws Scot.* i. xix. §viii. (1669) 101 Which is much safer than that they should be allowed Scop, to break out into the Extreams of either Cruelty or Cowardliness. **1765** Blackstone *Comm.* I. 43 Here the inferior legislature has scope and opportunity to interpose. **1768** Sterne *Sent. Journ., The Captive*, I gave full scope to my imagination. **1809** *Med. Jrnl.* XXI. 188 On this, he pitched on Bristol, where..there appeared to be full scope for an honourable and successful career. **1855** Prescott *Philip II*, i. i, The more adventurous found a scope for their prowess in European wars. **1876** Miss Braddon *J. Haggard's Dau.* II. 72 Perhaps you have too much common sense, Naomi. You will not give your fancies scope.

†**b.** An instance of liberty or licence. *Obs.*

1603 Shaks. *Meas. for M.* i. ii. 131 As surfet is the father of much fast, So euery Scope by the immoderate vse Turnes to restraint.

8. a. (With more reference to *literal* space or motion). Room to move in; space or range for free movement or activity. (Phrases as in prec. sense.)

1555 Eden *Decades* iii. vi. (Arb.) 163 The sea is here very large, so the waters haue their full scoope. **1555** W. Watreman *Fardle Facions* Pref. 7 Walking at free skope emong the wanderyng beastes of the fielde. **1591** Savile *Tacitus, Hist.* iii. xxiii. 128 To haue an open passage and free scope to shoote out. **1600** Fairfax *Tasso* xx. xii, Then through his hoast, that tooke so large a scope, He road. **1600** Surflet *Country Farm* i. xxi. 119 They be very fierce, and in that respect they are not accustomed to haue either so much scope or light as other birdes. **1601** R. Johnson *Kingd. & Commw.* (1603) 184 In no place plants may take larger scope to spread their branches..then in this countrie. **1614** Raleigh *Hist. World* ii. i. §9. 229 Amraphel who held Babylonia it selfe, seemeth at this time to haue had no great scope or large dominion. **1615** Crooke *Body of Man* 368 The heat when it hath too much scope or roomth..is easily dissipated and vanisheth. *a* **1616** B. Jonson *Hymenæi, Barriers* Wks. I. 930 And to their wiues men giue such narrow scopes, As if they meant to make them walke on ropes. **1653** Urquhart *Rabelais* i. xlviii, To give the ordnance leave to play and range with the larger scope [orig. *pour mieux donner lieu à l'artillerie*]. **1790** Burke *Fr. Rev.* Wks. V. 403 Publick virtue..requires abundant scope and room, and cannot spread and grow under confinement. **1809** Campbell *Gertrude* ii. ii, Yet wanted not the eye far scope to muse, Nor vistas open'd by the wand'ring stream. **1871** R. Ellis *Catullus* lxviii. 67 He in a closed field gave scope of liberal entry.

b. The ability of a horse to extend its stride or jump.

The semantic resemblance to scope *v.*[1] must be coincidental in view of the chronologies of the words.

1970 A. Fielder *Vibart & Friends* xiv. 115 Britain has got to produce horses of scope over big courses..if we want to bring home more Olympic medals. **1971** Broome & Murphy *Jump-Off* x. 79 Sunsherpa..had a big jump in him ..but, unfortunately, he was nothing like his half-brother as far as style and scope were concerned. **1975** B. Froud *Better Show Jumping* viii. 63 The average horse with reasonable scope can clear a low fence of say three feet high from two feet or twelve feet away from the base. **1980** *Times* 11 July 11/1 The final Liverpool fence of sloping poles at 6ft required more scope than most of the contenders possessed.

9. Extent in space, spaciousness; a (large) space, extent, tract, or area.

1590 Spenser *F.Q.* iii. ix. 46 So huge a scope at first him seemed best, To be the compasse of his kingdomes seat. **1600** Sir F. Vere *Comm.* 93 They would the rather attend the growing of the tide..that the scope of the sands might be less spacious and serviceable for horsmen. ? **1601** Bacon *Let.* in Spedding *Life* (1862) II. 369 The land is good land, and well countenanced by scope of acres, woods and royalties. **1834** Disraeli *Rev. Epick* ii. v. 63 Of adamant That mighty reservoir: its scope secure Might screen a navy. **1904** A. L. Salmon *Pop. Guide to Devonsh.* 59 The moormen may fish and dig turf, and use the infinite scope for pasturing their cattle.

†**10.** A tract (of land); esp. a piece of land belonging to an individual owner. ? *Anglo-Irish. Obs.*

1569 *Irish Act Eliz.* (1621) 313 The whole North of Ireland..wherein he had a scope of a hundred and twentie miles long, and a hundred and odd miles broade to runne and roome himself. **1577** Stanyhurst *Descr. Irel.* iii. 11 in *Holinshed*, The paroche was meared from the Crane castle, to the fishambles, called the cockehil with Preston hys Innes, and the lane thereto adioyning, which scope is now vnited to S. Iohn hys paroche. **1612** Davies *Why Ireland*, etc. 133 The Scopes of Land which were granted to the first Aduenturers were too Large. **1659** *Burton's Diary* (1828) IV. 470, 3. That he had gotten vast sums of money and scopes of land, by fraud. *a* **1687** Petty *Pol. Arith.* i. (1690) 11 Shall not much more time be spared if they [1000 men] lived all upon a Thousand Acres, then if they were forced to live upon ten times as large a Scope of Land. *a* **1691** Boyle *Hist. Air* (1692) 164 The Czar's chief physician confirmed to me..that in the year 1664, or 65, extraordinary dry and great scopes of land were set on fire, and miserably wasted by the great heat of the sun.

11. *Naut.* The length of cable at which a ship rides when at anchor. Also ***riding-scope***.

1697 Dampier *Voy.* I. 437 This obliged us to let go our Sheet Anchor, veering out a good scope of Cable. **1726** Shelvocke *Voy. round World* 265 Having our yaul in tow, and having but a short scope of boat rope for her. **1841** Riding scope [see riding *vbl. sb.* 7]. **1868** *Nat. Encycl.* I. 691 At long scope, Rodgers' [anchor] dragged 7 feet $8\frac{1}{2}$ inches. **1885** *Law Times Rep.* LIII. 53/2 A tow which is being towed with a long scope of hawser by night. **1893** Clark Russell *Ida Noble* 98 We'll..ride to a short scope.

scope (skəʊp), *sb.*[3] *colloq.* Also 'scope.

a. A shortened form of many words terminating in -scope, as *cystoscope, horoscope, microscope, periscope, telescope*, etc.

1603 B. Jonson *Sejanus* iv. v, Casting the Scope of mens Natiuities. **1872** O. W. Holmes *Poet Breakf.-t.* v. 123, I hope you won't lose any patients by my making a little fun of your meters and scopes. **1914** *Dialect Notes* IV. 131 *Scope*, from *microscope*. Student slang. 'Have you a slide in your scope?' **1933** Partridge *Slang To-day & Yesterday* iii. iii. 190 *Scope*, the cystoscope, an instrument used for examining the bladder. **1937** V. Woolf *Let.* 17 Aug. (1980) VI. 159 Now I must..have out the scope and see if I can pry into your bedroom. **1968** C. Helmericks *Down Wild River North* i. ii. 32, I selected a good four-power scope and a carrying sling. **1976** J. F. Panish in G. Berci *Endoscopy* xxi. 296/2 We lubricate the scope with mineral oil. If examination is going to include the right side of the colon, we begin with the longer colonoscope. **1978** W. F. Buckley *Stained Glass* xxi. 206 They can peer into the bowels of the scope all they want to.

b. Also *scope sight.* A telescopic sight for a gun.

1934 in Webster. **1966** 'A. Hall' *9th Directive* x. 96 The dealer had sent it [*sc.* a rifle]..with the scope-sight already mounted. **1968** K. Weatherly *Roo Shooter* 93 All he had to do was put on the 'scope off the ·303. **1976** *Shooting Times & Country Mag.* 16–22 Dec. 7 (Advt.), The BSA Scorpion is a super accurate air pistol even without its 'scope sight. **1978** R. Ludlum *Holcroft Covenant* xxxi. 366 Automatic repeating rifle and scope are sewn into the mattress of the bed nearest the window.

c. An oscilloscope or visual display unit; *spec.* a radar screen.

1945 *Army & Navy Jrnl.* 18 Aug. 1534/1 In using the PPI, the operator knows that the plane is the center of the circular scope and that the map which forms shows by the intensity of its light the terrain below and buildings or other targets. **1948** M. H. Nicolson *Voyages to Moon* 3 Two and one-half seconds later a returning pulse was clearly detected on a radar scope. **1958** P. Bryant *Two Hours to Doom* 106 Goldsmith peered closely at his scope. **1960** *Practical Wireless* XXXVI. 401/1 (Advt.), Compact portable 'scope ideal for servicing and general work. **1964** *Ann. N.Y. Acad. Sci.* CXV. 659 There are two distinct display channels which may be connected either to the display scope..or else to remote standard oscilloscopes. **1965** *Wireless World* July 359/1 The oscilloscope (or 'scope' as it is now commonly called) is an instrument that lets you see what is going on inside an electrical circuit. **1968** *Amer. Documentation* Jan. 72/1 Editing will be done on-line with a display scope and keyboard. Information from the central file will be retrieved, displayed on the scope, edited, and then stored in a new file which will go directly to a printer for publication. **1970** *Times Lit. Suppl.* 23 July 821/3 With his text stored on magnetic tape, the linguist can..have printed out on paper or displayed on a visual display unit (a 'scope'), the parts of the text that he wants to inspect. **1971** R. Sale *Man who raised Hell* i. i. 16 A big fat green carnation popped up on the scope where the blip had been. **1974** *Sci. Amer.* Sept. 18/2 (Advt.), Its flexible controls allow the cardiologist to keep a waveform on the scope for as long as 40 seconds.

†**scope**, *v.*[1] *Obs.* Also 4, 7 scop, 4 schope. [a. ON. *skopa* (in phr. *skopa skeið* to take a run); cf. MSw., Norw. *skopa* to skip, leap. Cf. SCOUP *v.*]

1. *intr.* To leap, skip. In later use only of horses.

13.. *Cursor M.* 19080 (Gött.) Þe propheci was þan fild sua, þat said þe halt suld scope [*c* 1400 *Edinb.* scop] as ra. *Ibid.* 23569 Mani thinges mai we do, þat forto do war littel fro, Als forto schope and forto rin, Quen it war better for to blin. **1483** *Cath. Angl.* 323/2 To Scope, *vbi* to rynne or lepe. **1567** DRANT *Horace, Ep.* I. xiv. E iiij b, Yet thither-warde assuredlye my harte, and mynde is bente. And burnes, and burnes to braste the bondes which doe inclose it so, That it ne can goe scope abrode where it woulde gladly goe. **1572** *Satir. Poems Reform.* xxxiii. 140 Wer not thir thingis that maks me leif in hope, At libertie to se this Lyoun scope, One day to Rore and Ramp vpon his fois. **1607** MARKHAM *Caval.* I. 2 That your Mares and Colts may not bee throng'd vp,.. wanting libertie to scope and runne vp and downe at pleasure. *Ibid.* 5 That a Foale may.. by scoping or galloping vp and downe the hill, come to a purenes of winde, and a nimblenes of bodie. **1639** T. DE GRAY *Compl. Horsem.* 5 Grounds.. are very profitable for your colts to scope, run, and play in.

2. *trans.* To make (a horse) leap for exercise.

1607 MARKHAM *Caval.* VI. 29 Then you shall gallop and scope him gently vp and down to keep him warme. **1688** HOLME *Armoury* III. xix. (Roxb.) 184/2 Termes used about dressing and feeding of horses... Scop or aire him.

†**scope**, *v.*[2] *Obs. rare.* [f. SCOPE *sb.*[2]]

1. *intr.* To aim *at* (see quot.). *nonce-use.*

1668 HOWE *Blessedn. Righteous* xv. 267 And the word [σκοπούντων *2 Cor.* iv. 18] here rendred (*look*).. doth not import.. a taking notice, or assenting onely, that there is such things, but a designing or *scoping* at them (which is the very word) with an appropriative eye.

2. *trans.* ? To calculate the scope or range of.

1807 J. BARLOW *Columb.* v. 608 Lincoln.. Scoped the whole war and measured well the foes.

scope, obs. form of SCALP *sb.*[1]

1578 BANISTER *Hist. Man* I. 16 In the head and scope of the scull are yet diuerse and sundry little Perforations.

scope, obs. form of SCOOP *sb.* and *v.*

scope, scopid, obs. pa. t. of SCAPE *v.*[1]

a **1400-50** *Alexander* 3915 And many scopid in þe scoghe without scath mare.

-scope, an ending representing mod.L. *-scopium* (f. Gr. σκοπεῖν to look at, examine) in MICROSCOPE and TELESCOPE. Hence used, by addition to Greek stems, to form many words denoting scientific instruments or contrivances for enabling the eye to view or examine or make observations: as *autoscope*, *baroscope*, *chronoscope*, *dynamoscope*, *gyroscope*, *helioscope*, *laryngoscope*, *ophthalmoscope*, *periodoscope*, etc. (Cf. F. *-scope*, It. *-scopio*, etc.) Also added to L. stems, as in *fluoroscope*, *oscilloscope*, and to Eng. words, as in *radarscope*, *sniperscope*.

scopeboard, obs. (perverted) var. of SCUPPER.

†'**scopeful**, *a. Obs.* In quots. -full. [f. SCOPE *sb.*[3] + -FUL.] Having or affording large scope.

1598 FLORIO, *Ampio*, ample, large, scopefull. **1603** —— *Montaigne* II. xii. 315 Giving them that were disposed to mock at him, a pleasant and scopefull occasion to doe it. **1611** COTGR., *Ample*,.. wide, large, scopefull, spacious. *a* **1618** SYLVESTER *Posthumi*, *Sonn.* vii. Wks. (Grosart) II. 322/1 Sith round beleaguer'd by rough Neptune's legions Within the straite-nookes of this narrow Ile; The noblest volumes of our vulgar style Cannot escape unto more scopefull Regions.

†'**scopel, 'scopple.** *Farriery. Obs.* [? contraction of SCOPPERIL.] A seton: = SCOPPERIL 3.

1737 BRACKEN *Farriery Impr.* (1757) I. 337 Scopels or round Pieces of Leather with Holes in the Middle, lap'd round with Tow, are the most fit and proper in these Cases. *Ibid.* II. 17 They can only bleed a Horse, draw a Sole, put in a Rowel or Scopple, cut for the Lampers.

scopeless ('skəʊplɪs), *a.* [f. SCOPE *sb.* + -LESS.] **a.** Having no purpose or aim; objectless (? *Obs.*). **b.** Not affording scope or opportunity.

1666 BP. S. PARKER *Free & Impart. Censure* (1667) 81 Which scopeless desire of searching into things exempt from humane Inquisition, is that which renders Curiosity Criminal. **1866** J. H. NEWMAN *Gerontius* §1 And drop from out this universal frame Into that shapeless, scopeless, blank abyss, That utter nothingness, of which I came. **1882** *Society* 7 Oct. 12/2 Mr. E. H. Sothern acted well in the scopeless character of the Squire's son.

Scopelid ('skɒpɪlɪd). [ad. mod.L. *Scopelid-æ*, f. SCOPEL-US: see -ID.] A fish of the group *Scopelidæ*.

1882 JORDAN & GILBERT *Synopsis Fishes N. Amer.* 279 Family XLII.—Scopelidæ. (The Scopelids.) **1887** HEILPRIN *Distrib. Animals* 297 Among the better known bony-fishes.. are the.. scopelids.

scopelidan (skəʊ'pɛlɪdən). [f. mod.L. *Scopelid-æ* (see prec.) + -AN.] = SCOPELID.

1859-62 SIR J. RICHARDSON, etc. *Mus. Nat. Hist.* (1868) II. 149 Scopelidans.

scopeliform (skəʊ'pɛlɪfɔːm), *a.* [f. mod.L. SCOPEL-US + -(I)FORM.] = SCOPELOID *a.*

In some recent Dicts.

scopeloid ('skɒpɪlɔɪd), *sb.* and *a. Zool.* [f. SCOPEL-US + -OID.] **A.** *sb.* A fish of the family *Scopelidæ* (see SCOPELID).

1880 GÜNTHER *Fishes* 42 In addition to the rayed dorsal fin, many Malacopterygian fishes (as the Salmonoids, many Siluroids, Scopeloids, etc.) have another of greater or lesser extent. **1896** H. WOODWARD *Guide Fossil Reptiles Brit. Mus.* 112 Herrings, Scopeloids, etc., occur abundantly in association with these.

B. *adj.* Like or pertaining to the *Scopelidæ*.

In recent Dicts.

‖**Scopelus** ('skɒpɪləs). *Zool.* [mod.L.; introduced (along with the Fr. form *scopèle*) in 1817 by Cuvier, who gives the etymon as 'σκόπελος, Greek name of an unknown fish'; the Gr. word, however, app. means only a rock.] The typical genus of the family *Scopelidæ*: see SCOPELID.

1840 *Cuvier's Anim. Kingd.* 320 *Scopelus*, have the gape and the gill openings very deep. **1880** GÜNTHER *Fishes* 585 Some species never rise to the surface; indeed, Scopeli have been brought up in the dredge from almost any depth to 2500 fathoms.

scoper, obs. form of SCUPPER.

†'**Scopetine.** *Obs. rare.* [ad. med.L. *Scopetīnī* pl., one of the religious orders following the Augustinian rule (Du Cange).] (See quot.)

1537 *Orig. & Sprynge of Sectes* 27 The Scopetines or S. Saluators order. The yeare after Christes byrth .Mccclxvii. dyd thys order begynne by certayne spirituall fathers of saynt Austins order.

scopett, obs. form of SCUPPET.

scopey, var. SCOPY *a.*

Scophony ('skɒfənɪ). *Television.* [Perh. f. Gr. σκο-πεῖν to look at, examine + *-phony*, after *telephony*, etc.] A proprietary name for a television system employing an optical and mechanical method of picture scanning. Freq. *attrib.*

1932 *Trade Marks Jrnl.* 20 Apr. 488/2 *Scophony*... Philosophical instruments, scientific instruments and apparatus for useful purposes; instruments and apparatus for teaching. Scophony Limited,.. London W.1.; Manufacturers. **1934** J. H. REYNER *Television* xi. 135 One of the most ingenious alternative methods proposed is the Scophony system devised by G. W. Walton. **1935** *Television Today* I. 197/1 In the Scophony system the image to be transmitted is reflected on to a special stepped prism or reflector which so displaces the image laterally that the picture is spread out into a continuous line. The line is then scanned by a vibrating light spot. **1940** D. G. FINK *Princ. Television Engin.* x. 511 The heart of the Scophony system is the so-called 'supersonic light valve'. **1957** —— *Television Engin. Handbk.* iii. 49 The Scophony system employs a liquid cell containing a piezoelectric quartz crystal as the light modulator.

†**sco'piferous**, *a. Obs.* [f. mod.L. *scōpifer* (f. L. *scōp-a* SCOPA[1] + *-fer* bearing) + -OUS.] (See quot.)

1826 KIRBY & SP. *Entomol.* IV. 324 Scopiferous (*Scopiferæ*). When they [the antennæ] are furnished with one or more dense brushes of hair.

scopiform ('skəʊpɪfɔːm), *a. Nat. Hist.* [f. L. *scōp-a* SCOPA[1] + -(I)FORM.] Arranged in bundles; broom-shaped, fascicular.

1794 KIRWAN *Elem. Min.* (ed. 2) I. 278 [Zeolyte] Its texture.. either stelliform or scopiform. **1852** DANA *Crust.* II. 1034 Of the two setiform processes, one is closely ciliate, and the other has a short scopiform extremity.

Hence '**scopiformly** *adv.*, in a scopiform manner.

1804 JAMESON *Syst. Min.* I. 589 Their cross fracture exhibits a scopiformly diverging aspect.

scopine ('skɒpiːn). *Chem.* [ad. G. *scopin* (J. F. Eijkman 1892, in *Ber. der Deut. Chem. Ges.* XXV. 3078), f. L. *Scop-olia* (see SCOPOL-) + *-in* -INE[5].] A colourless crystalline alkaloid, $C_8H_{13}NO_2$, formed by hydrolysis of scopolamine (a tropyl ester of scopine) and yielding scopoline on further hydrolysis.

1923 *Chem. Abstr.* XVII. 3189 According to the investigations of Gadamer & Hammer.. and of Hess and Wahl.. the basic component (I) of scopolamine (II) (which, following a suggestion of Eykman, is designated scopine) is yet unknown, the known scopoline (III) being formed from it by rearrangement of the α-oxide into a γ-oxide ring. **1957** K. W. BENTLEY *Alkaloids* I. i. 20 Scopine, which is optically inactive and cannot be resolved, is readily converted into oscine by acids or alkalis. **1960** A. R. PINDER in E. H. Rodd *Chem. Carbon Compounds* IVc. xxiii. 1857 Scopolamine.. is the (−)- or (±)-tropyl ester of scopine.

†'**scopious**, *a. Obs.* [f. SCOPE *sb.* + -(I)OUS.] Wide, spacious.

1599 T. M[IDDLETON] *Micro-cynicon* vi. C 7, Streames y[t] are bard their course Swel with more rage, & far more greater force, Vntill there full stuft gorge a passage makes Into the wide mawes of more scopious lakes. **1612** HOOKER *Serm.* III. iii. Wks. 1888 III. 623, I should have a large and scopious field to walk in, if I did here endeavour [etc.].

scopol- (skɒ'pɒl), used *Chem.* and *Pharm.* to form names of certain extractive principles obtained from *Scopolia Japonica* (Japanese belladonna), as ***scopolenin***; †**sco'poleine** [ad. G. *scopoleïn* (A. Langgaard 1876–80, in *Mitth. der Deutsch. Ges. für Natur- und Völkerkunde Ostasiens* II. (Beilage III) 267)], a crystalline alkaloid said to have the formula $C_{17}H_{21}NO_4$; **scopoletin**, [ad. F. *scopolétine* (J. F. Eijkman 1884, in *Rec. des Trav. chim. des Pays-Bas* III. 171)], 7-hydroxy-6-methoxycoumarin, $C_{10}H_8O_4$; '**scopolin**, a glycoside of scopoletin; '**scopoline**, an alkaloid, $C_8H_{13}NO_2$, obtained from scopolamine on hydrolysis; also called *oscine*.

The genus *Scopolia* was named after *Scopoli*, an Italian naturalist of the 18th c.

1885 *Jrnl. Chem. Soc.* XLVIII. I. 404 The author has isolated three principles from the root: skopoletin, $C_{12}H_{10}O_5$,.. skopoleïne, a crystalline alkaloid;.. skopolin, $C_{24}H_{30}O_{15}$ + $2H_2O$, the glucoside of skopoletin. **1911** *Chem. Abstr.* V. 2155 Halogen alkylates and alkyl nitrates of the alkaloids of the tropeine and scopoleine series are obtained by forming addition products.. of the bases of the tropeine and scopoleine series with the sulfurous acid dialkyl esters. **1893** R. H. HARTE, etc. *Local Therap.* 399 Scopolenine. An alkaloid present in Japanese belladonna. **1885** Skopoletin [see *scopoleine* above]. **1899** CAGNEY tr. *von Jaksch's Clin. Diagn.* (ed. 4) 397 In cases of poisoning with deadly nightshade berries.. the urine has a peculiar fluorescence.., due to the presence of scopoletin. **1931** *Jrnl. Chem. Soc.* 1244 On cooling, the dark bluish solution deposited scopoletin in pale yellow needles. **1959** N. CAMPBELL in E. H. Rodd *Chem. Carbon Compounds* IVB. viii. 881 Scopoletin.. occurs in the free state and as the glucoside scopolin, $C_{22}H_{28}O_{14}$.. in *Solanaceae* and *Scopolia* species. **1963** T. ROBINSON *Org. Constituents of Higher Plants* iv. 51 Scopoletin is the most common coumarin of higher plants. **1885** Scopolin [see *scopoleine* above]. **1933** *Chem. Abstr.* XXVII. 2685 Methylated with CH_2N_2, cichorün yields a Me ether identical with scopolin. **1959** Scopolin [see *scopoletin* above]. **1892** *Jrnl. Chem. Soc.* LXII. II. 1255 The identity of scopoline is somewhat uncertain; its boiling point agrees with that of oxytropine. **1919** *Ibid.* CXV. 476 Oscine (or scopoline).. is capable of resolution into its constituents *d*- and *l*-oscine. **1960** A. R. PINDER in E. H. Rodd *Chem. Carbon Compounds* IVc. xxiii. 1856 Scopoline, $C_8H_{13}O_2N$, contains an N-methyl group and is a secondary alcohol.

scopolamine (skə'pɒləmiːn). *Chem.* and *Pharm.* Formerly also -in. [ad. G. *skopolamin* (E. Schmidt 1891, in *Apotheker Zeitung* VI. 522): see SCOPOL- and AMINE.] A syrupy liquid alkaloid, $C_{17}H_{21}NO_4$, having powerful narcotic and sedative properties, which is found in plants of the family *Solanaceæ*, notably the thorn-apple, *Datura stramonium*; hyoscine.

1892 *Jrnl. Chem. Soc.* LXII. II. 1255 Inasmuch as the name hyoscine has been misapplied to tropine, it has become somewhat ambiguous, and the author [*sc.* E. Schmidt] proposes to call the hyoscine from hyoscyamus, scopolamine, a name which is in accord with the recent isolation of this alkaloid from *Scopolia atropoïdes*. **1899** *Allbutt's Syst. Med.* VI. 837 Dilatation of the pupil.. dependent.. upon.. the application of some drug (atropine, ..scopolamine, etc.). **1925** F. J. REYNOLDS *Marvels of 1924* 44 Dr. R. E. House has experimented with inmates of prisons, who were reduced by scopolamin to a state in which only their memories functioned. **1940** R. CHANDLER *Farewell, My Lovely* xxxiii. 156 There's a drug called scopolamine, truth serum, that sometimes makes people talk without their knowing it. **1945** A. HUXLEY *Let.* 13 Oct. (1969) 535 The adumbrations of future possibilities are to be seen in the practices of contemporary dictatorships—.. use of scopolamine and other drugs to extract confessions and make people more susceptible to propaganda, [etc.]. **1976** SMYTHIES & CORBETT *Psychiatry* vii. 140 Many proprietary sleeping pills.. contain small doses of scopolamine. **1977** LEWIS & ELVIN-LEWIS *Med. Bot.* ix. 223/2 *Datura fastuosa* and *D. metel* are abundant sources of scopolamine. **1981** T. BARLING *Bikini Red North* v. 114 Sedating her with enough scopolamine to keep her comatose.

†**sco'polian.** *Ent. Obs.* [ad. mod.L. *Scopoliān-us*, app. f. the name of *Scopoli*, an Italian naturalist of the 18th c.] A collector's name for a small brownish-red moth, *Semasia scopoliana*.

1829 STEPHENS *System. Cat. Brit. Insects* II. 180 *Semasia Scopoliana*... Scopolian. **1832** J. RENNIE *Butterfl. & Moths* 169 The Scopolian.

†**sco'pology.** *Obs. rare*[−1]. [f. Gr. σκοπό-ς aim, end (see SCOPE *sb.*[2]) + -LOGY.] A (suggested) name for a science of the 'ends' of human conduct.

1730 CHAMBERLAYNE *Relig. Philos.* Pref. 34 A Scopology, or Study of Ends, would prove one of the most exalted Parts of Philosophy.

scopophilia (skɒpəʊ'fɪlɪə). *Psychol.* Also **scoptophilia** (but see quot. 1968), **skoptophilia**. [A formative element f. Gr. -σκοπία observation (cf. -SCOPY) + -PHILIA.] Sexual stimulation or satisfaction derived principally from looking; voyeurism. Hence **scopo-, scopto'philiac** *a.* and *sb.*, **scopo-, scopto'philic** *a.* and *sb.*; also '**scoptophile** *a.*; **scop'tophilist**.

1924 J. RIVIERE tr. *Freud's Psychogenic Visual Disturbance* in *Coll. Papers* II. 111 The obscure psychical processes implicit in the repression of scoptophilia and in the outbreak of psychogenic visual disturbance. **1928** H. H. ELLIS *Stud.*

in Psychol. of Sex VII. vi. 362 The failure to react to sex attractions..is a well-defined sexual perversion, with relationships to other perversions, especially scoptophilia. **1930** W. EMPSON *Seven Types of Ambiguity* ii. 69 Shakespeare's partly scoptophile desire to see him settled in love. **1931** *Times Lit. Suppl.* 21 May 402/3 An eventual future in which..nobody will wear anything at all;..and the scoptophilists will have their day. **1931** J. C. FLÜGEL in W. Rose *Outl. Mod. Knowl.* ix. 374 Those [*sc.* component instincts] connected with the activities of vision..the active or 'scoptophilic', and the passive or 'exhibitionistic'. **1937** M. HIRSCHFELD *Sexual Anomalies & Peversions* xxviii. 621 One of the principal criteria of pathological scopophilia is the *dominant* character of the urge. **1940** C. ALLEN *Sexual Perversions* iv. 75 The scoptophiliac pervert may occur in two varieties. **1957** J. STRACHEY tr. *Freud's Instincts & Viciss.* in *Compl. Wks.* XIV. 129 The instincts whose respective aim is to look at and to display oneself (scopophilia and exhibitionism, in the language of the perversions). *Ibid.* 130 For the beginning of its activity the scopophilic instinct is auto-erotic. **1960** R. HEPPENSTALL *Four Absentees* xxiii. 198 Gill was a bit of a scopophiliac, a 'voyeur'. **1960** *Spectator* 8 Apr. 506/3 Perhaps I am going ga-ga through skoptophilia. **1960** *Times Lit. Suppl.* 24 June 394/2 There appears to be a..scopophiliac streak in both. **1968** C. RYCROFT *Crit. Dict. Psychoanal.* 148 Scopophilia.., the spelling 'scop*t*ophilia' dates from a mistake made by Freud's first translators. **1971** *Psychol. Abstr.* XLV. June 1131/2 A sexually inhibited male scopophilic.

scopperil ('skɒpərɪl). Forms: 5 scop(e)relle, 5, 7, 9 scopperell, 6 scopperelle, 7–9 scop(p)eril(l), scop(p)ril, scop(p)erel, scoprel. See also SCOPEL. [Of obscure origin; a remarkable similarity of form is presented by mod.Icel. *skoppara-kringla* spinning-top, f. *skoppa* to spin like a top; cf. MSw. *skoppa* to jump, run about, MDu., mod.Du. *schoppen* to swing, sea-saw; also SCOPE *v.*[2]]

1. A kind of teetotum or small top (spun with the thumb and finger) made by passing a pointed peg through the centre of a disc (often a flat button or button-mould). Now *dial.* (see *Eng. Dial. Dict.*).

In some dialects applied to a small disc (as a button-mould) apart from its application.

c **1425** *St. Christina* xxiv. in *Anglia* VIII. 128/35 Alle hir body was..turnyd in to a whirlynge about as a scoprelle or a toppe þat childer playe with. **1483** *Cath. Angl.* 324/1 A scoperelle, *giraculum*. **1621** G. MARKHAM *Hunger's Prevent.* 117 Vpon the least touch it will twerle and tourne as round as any Scopperill. **1636** W. SAMPSON *Vow Breaker* I. i. B 2, If once we creepe out o' th shells, we run from our ould loves like Scopperells, weomens minds are planetary.

b. *transf.* Applied to an active, restless child; also to a squirrel. *dial.* (See *Eng. Dial. Dict.*)

†**2.** *Her.* A badge in the form of a disc. *Obs.*

1486 *Bk. St. Albans, Her.* b iv b, Diaclys be called in armys scopprellys. **1562** LEGH *Armory* (1597) 37 The sixt badge are Diacles, commonly called Scopperelles.

3. *dial.* A seton: = SCOPEL.

1855 ROBINSON *Whitby Gloss.*, A *Scopperil*, a plug put into an issue or seton made in the diseased part of an animal to drain off the humours. **1878** *Cumberld. Gloss.* 82 Scopperel. **1893–4** *Northumbld. Gloss.* II. 603 *Scopper, scopperalt, scoperal*, a seton.

'scopperloit. *dial.* Also 7 skoppoloit, -lot. [Of obscure origin: cf. SCOBBERLOTCHER and SCOTERLOPE *v.*] (See quots.)

1691 RAY *S. & E.C. Wds.* 111 A *Scopperloit*, a time of idleness, a play-time. **1787** in GROSE *Prov. Gloss.* **1878** S. H. MILLER & SKERTCHLY *Fenland* iv. 131 *Skoppolot, Skoppoloit*, romping, rude, indelicate play.

scoppet, obs. form of SCUPPET.

scopple, variant of SCOPEL *Obs.*

scops (skɒps). [a. mod.L. *Scōps* (generic name), a. Gr. σκώψ the little horned owl.] A genus of *Strigidæ* containing nearly forty species distinguished by plumicorns upon the head; now usually *scops owl*. Also a member of this genus, a horn-owl.

1706 PHILLIPS (ed. Kersey). **1781** LATHAM *Synopsis Birds* I. 129 Scops. E.O. [i.e. belonging to the division 'Eared Owls'.] **1809** SHAW *Gen. Zool.* VII. I. 234 The Scops is a native of the warmer parts of Europe, and is of a migratory nature. **1825** *Sporting Mag.* XV. 271 The scops or little horned owl. **1887** *Atheæum* 19 Mar. 387/2 The little scops owl.

b. *Comb.* **scops-eared** *a.*, having plumicorns upon the head, the characteristic feature of *Scops*.

Prob. arising from a misunderstanding of quot. 1781 above.

1825 SELBY *Illustr. Brit. Ornith.* I. 56 Scops-eared Owl. **1870** GILLMORE tr. *Figuier's Reptiles & Birds* 551 The Scops-eared Owl..is remarkable for its diminutive size.

'scoptic, *a.* and *sb. rare.* [ad. Gr. σκωπτικός, f. σκώπτειν to mock, jeer.]

A. *adj.* Mocking, satirical.

1670 S. WARD *Serm. agst. Anti-Script.* 57 Julian and Lucian and other Scoptick wits. **1972** P. M. FRASER *Ptolemaic Alexandria* I. x. 571 The last of the trio, Hedylus, seems to have specialized particularly in scoptic epigrams on gluttons.

†**B.** *sb. pl.* Mocking or satirical writings. *Obs.*

a **1644** QUARLES *Sheph. Orac.* i. (1646) 9, I fear'd thy game-some wit began to paint, In shadow'd Scopticks some that beare the Crook In our blest Island. **1656** BLOUNT *Glossogr.*, *Scopticks*, Jests, Jeers, Flouts, Cavils.

†**'scoptical,** *a. Obs.* [f. prec. + -AL[1].] = prec. *a.*

c **1611** CHAPMAN *Iliad* XVI. Comm. 235 It flies all his Translators and Interpreters; who take it meerely for serious, when it is apparantly scopticall and ridiculous. **1684** H. MORE *Answer* 59 The Remarker here is very Magisterial and somewhat Scoptical.

†**'scoptically,** *adv. Obs.* [f. SCOPTICAL + -LY[2].] In a scornful, satirical manner.

c **1611** CHAPMAN *Iliad* II. Comm. 35 In this first and next verse, Homer (speaking scoptically) breakes open the fountaine of his ridiculous humor following. **1647** R. STAPYLTON *Juvenal* 114 Jove's secret springs: scoptically spoken, as if the astrologers were inspired by Jupiter [etc.]. **1686** H. MORE *Real Pres.* 55 Not as one scoptically would make us to profess, that this real participation of the Body and Blood of Christ, has no reality any where but in our phancy.

scoptophile, -philia, -philiac, -philic, -philist: see SCOPOPHILIA.

‖**scopula** ('skɒpjʊlə). *Ent.* [late L. *scōpula*, dim. of *scōpa* a broom.] A small brush-like group of hairs upon the tarsus of bees and spiders.

1802 KIRBY *Monogr. Apum Angliæ* I. 110 *Scopula*. This is the name by which I denominate the hairs which cover the inside of the plantæ, called by Schrank *scopa*, and by Reamur 'la brosse'. **1816** KIRBY & SP. *Entomol.* xix. (1818) II. 127 *note*, Underneath they [the posterior plantæ] are furnished with a *scopula* or brush of stiff hairs set in rows. **1844** BLACKWALL in *Rep. Brit. Assoc.* I. 62 Those remarkable appendages termed *scopulæ* or brushes, with which the tarsi of numerous species of spiders are provided.

'scopulate, *a.* [ad. mod.L. *scōpulātus*: see prec. and -ATE[2].] (See quot. 1826.)

1826 KIRBY & SP. *Entomol.* IV. xlvi. 348 Scopulate... When the first joint [of the tarsus] on the under side is covered with a dense brush of rigid hairs. **1901** *Proc. Zool. Soc.* I. 212 Both tarsi and protarsi scarcely scopulate in the middle.

scopulipede ('skɒpjʊlɪpiːd), *a. Ent.* [ad. mod.L. *scōpuliped-*, *-pēs*, f. *scōpula* (see SCOPULA) + *ped-*, *pēs* foot.] Of certain bees: Having the feet furnished with scopulæ.

1881 *Cassell's Nat. Hist.* V. 367 The Scopulipede Solitary Apidæ, or those furnished, like the Hive Bee and the Humble Bee, with an apparatus for the conveyance of pollen on the hind legs. *Ibid.* 368 Closing our account of the Scopulipede Bees with this brilliant foreigner, we must now proceed [etc.].

†**'scopulous,** *a. Obs.* [ad. L. *scopulōsus* craggy, f. *scopul-us* a rock.] Abounding in rocks, rocky. Hence †**'scopulousness,** †**scopu'losity** (*rare*[−0]).

1596 DALRYMPLE tr. *Leslie's Hist. Scot.* I. 261 How Scopulous, stendirrie, or stanie, was the stedd..quhairon thay than stude. **1658** FRANCK *Northern Mem.* (1694) 211 Edinburgh..stands on a mighty scopulous Mountain. **1721** BAILEY, *Scopulosity*, Abundance of Rocks. **1727** —— vol. II, *Scopulousness*.

scopy ('skəʊpɪ), *a.* Also **scopey**. [f. SCOPE *sb.*[2] + -Y[1].] Having or displaying plenty of scope (SCOPE *sb.*[2] 8 b).

1976 *Horse & Hound* 21 May 44/4 (Advt.), This very attractive pony has a big scopey jump. **1976** *Sunday Times* 30 May 31/7 Her big, scopy Mr Vee..has shown himself a bit strong for a woman rider. **1977** *Horse & Hound* 14 Jan. 37/2 (Advt.), Bay mare..proving to be fast and exceptionally bold with a big scopy jump.

-scopy, a formative element f. Gr. -σκοπία observation (f. σκοπεῖν to examine, look at: see -Y[3]), used to form sbs. denoting: (*a*) (formerly) divination by inspection of something (*ooscopy, ornithoscopy*); (*b*) scientific examination by means of some instrument (*stethoscopy, telescopy*); (*c*) medical examination of some part of the body (*gastroscopy, peritoneoscopy*).

scor, obs. form of SCORE.

scorable ('skɔərəb(ə)l), *a.* [f. SCORE *v.* + -ABLE.] Capable of being scored; from which a score may be made.

1964 J. JAFFE in Rioch & Weinstein *Disorders Communication* xxvii. 389 All the indices used are completely scorable by the computer. **1977** *Linlithgowshire Jrnl. & Gaz.* 15 Apr. 16/5 Each time the threat of a scorable free kick came about, they were watching for the curve shot.

scorar, obs. form of SCOURER.

‖**'scorbuch, -buicke.** *Obs.* [Du.: see next.] = SCURVY.

1598 W. PHILLIP tr. *Linschoten* I. iii. 8 With sicknes and diseases, as swellings of the legs, and the scorbuicke. **1601** HOLLAND *Pliny* XXV. iii. II. 212 *marg.*, Some thinke this disease to bee the Schorbuck or Scorbute. **1613** PURCHAS *Pilgrimage* VIII. iv. (1614) 748 The Scuruie or Scorbuch much consumed the French in these partes.

†**'scorbut(e.** *Path. Obs.* [a. F. *scorbut*, whence Sp. *escorbuto*, Pg. *escorbut*, *scorbuto*, It. *scorbuto*, mod.L. *scorbūtus* (whence G. *scorbut*).

The Fr. word is app. ad. MLG. *schorbûk*, early mod.Du. *schorbuyck, scheurbuik* (now *scheurbuik*), whence G. *scharbock*, Da. *skørbug*, MSw. *skörbiug* (Sw. *skörbjugg*), OIcel. (14th c.) *skyrbjúg-r*. If the word be orig. LG. or Du., and not an adoption from some foreign source, the etymological sense must be 'disease that ruptures or lacerates the belly' (MLG., MDu. *schoren*, Du. *scheuren* to break, lacerate, MLG. *bûk*, Du. *buik* belly). Cf. early mod.Du. *scheurmond* (*mond* = mouth) scurvy of the gums, *scheurbeen* (*been* = bone) scorbutic affection of the bones.] = SCURVY.

1597 GERARDE *Herbal* II. xvii. 201 Water Cresse..is verie good against the scuruie or scorbute. **1611** in Birch *Crt. & Times Jas. I* (1848) I. 137 His disease proves..to be nothing but the scorbut, or, as we term it, the scurvy. **1634** SIR T. HERBERT *Trav.* 5 The Calenture, Scorbute or Scuruie, Feauers [etc.]. **1665** J. GADBURY *London's Deliv.* vii. 24 His frivolous supposition of the Plague its taking beginning from the disease called the Scorbute.

attrib. **1665** E. MAYNWARING *Treat. Scurvy* 65 The Scorbute Pills are efficacious against the defects and errors of digestion in the first, second and third Office.

scorbutic (skɔː'bjuːtɪk), *a.* and *sb. Path.* Also 7–8 scorbutick, 8 scurbutick. [ad. mod.L. *scorbūticus*: see prec. and -IC. Cf. F. *scorbutique*.]

A. *adj.* **1.** Of or pertaining to scurvy; symptomatic of or proceeding from scurvy; of the nature of scurvy. Of a patient: Affected with scurvy.

scorbutic gums, a condition of the gums induced by scurvy, characterized by swelling and a tendency to bleed.

1655 CULPEPER, etc. *Riverius* I. v. 19 This is very manifest from the Scorbutick Palsey, or that which is joyned with the Scurvy. **1665** E. MAYNWARING *Treat. Scurvy* 51 The colour of scorbutick spots declaring this Disease, is to be regarded. **1694** tr. *Marten's Voy. Spitzbergen* in *Acc. Sev. Late Voy.* II. 194 Plenty of Vetches, which recover'd our Scorbutick Men. **1748** *Anson's Voy.* III. ii. 311 Vegetables extremely conducive to the cure of..scorbutic disorders. **1835–6** *Todd's Cycl. Anat.* I. 425/1 No attempt..at any chemical examination of the properties of scorbutic blood. **1837** DICKENS *Pickwick* xxxii, A renewal of hostilities between the scorbutic youth and the gentleman in the sanguine shirt. **1853** KANE *Grinnell Exp.* xxxi. (1856) 267 Eight cases of scorbutic gums were already on my black-list. **1897** *Allbutt's Syst. Med.* III. 128 Rickets is produced as certainly by rhachitic diet, as is scurvy by a scorbutic diet. **1898** *Ibid.* V. 589 Very frequently the first manifestations of a scorbutic taint are excited by extreme cold.

†**2.** Of articles of diet, remedies, etc.: Good against scurvy, anti-scorbutic. *Obs.*

1696 SALMON *Fam. Dict.*, Scorbutic-Syrup. *Ibid.*, Scorbutick-Water. **1710** T. FULLER *Pharm. Extemp.* (1719) 17 A sweetning Scorbutic Ale. *Ibid.* 187 A Scorbutic Foment. **1789** BUCHAN *Dom. Med.* App. (1790) 705 *Scorbutic Whey*. This whey is made by boiling half a pint of the scorbutic juices in a quart of cow's milk... The scorbutic plants are, bitter oranges, brooklime, garden scurvy-grass, and water-cresses.

B. *sb.*

†**1.** The scurvy. *Obs. rare*[−1].

1676 LADY FANSHAWE *Mem.* (1830) 118 He was advised to go to Bath for his scorbutic, that still hung on him.

†**2.** A remedy for the scurvy, an anti-scorbutic.

a **1774** HARTE *Eulogius* 85 Spoon-wort was there, scorbutics to supply.

3. 'One affected with scurvy'.

1855 DUNGLISON *Med. Lex.*

†**scor'butical,** *a. Obs.* [f. SCORBUTIC + -AL[1].] Relating to, characterized by scurvy.

1656 RIDGLEY *Pract. Physick* 181 Also there is a Gangreen Scorbutical which beginneth commonly from an internal cause. **1676** WISEMAN *Chirurg. Treat.* II. iv. 177 A Person.. of a full and scorbutical Body. **1753** MAITLAND *Hist. Edin.* (1768) 507 An unctuous substance wherewith it is covered is said to be good for scorbutical disorders.

Hence †**scor'butically** *adv.*

1665 NEEDHAM *Med. Medicinæ* 393 Persons that are.. Scorbutically inclined. **1676** WISEMAN *Chirurg. Treat.* II. iv. 178 Thus in scorbutically-habited ill Bodies..we frequently see these simple Ulcers afflicted with sharp Humours.

†**scor'buticism.** *Obs. rare*[−1]. [f. SCORBUTIC + -ISM.] A general tendency to develop scurvy, a scorbutic habit of body.

1665 NEEDHAM *Med. Medicinæ* 86 There are but few Cases wherein there is not somwhat of Scorbuticisms mixt.

'scorbutized, *ppl. a. nonce-wd.* [f. SCORBUT-IC + -IZE + -ED[1].] Affected with scurvy.

1856 KANE *Arct. Expl.* II. vii. 83 Yesterday's walk makes my scorbutized muscles very stiff.

‖**scorbutus** (skɔː'bjuːtəs). *Path.* [mod.L.: see SCORBUTE.] Scurvy.

1866 A. FLINT *Princ. Med.* (1880) 1121 Scorbutus..is frequently combined with other diseases. **1876** tr. *Wagner's Gen. Path.* 235 To the cachectic dropsies belong also those of scorbutus and conditions resembling it.

scorce, obs. variant of SCORSE *sb.* and *v.*

†**scorch,** *sb.*[1] *Obs.* Forms: 5 scorche, skorch, scorce, 6 scorch. [a. OF. *escorche*, *escorce* (mod.F. *écorce*).] Rind, bark.

1480 CAXTON *Ovid's Met.* x. viii, The chylde, of whiche Mirra was grete, grewe, wt payne under the scorche & rynde. **1481** —— *Myrrour* II. x. 90 Other trees there growe ..that bere notemygges, And of the rynde and scorce is the canell or synamome. **1579** W. LANGHAM *Gard. Health* (1633) 15 Make..Almond milke.., and eate it with Sugar, and powder of the ryndes and scorches of a Pomegranate.

scorch (skɔːtʃ), *sb.*[2] Also 7 scortch. [f. SCORCH *v.*[1]]

1. a. A mark or impression produced by scorching; a superficial burn. Also *fig.*

1611 COTGR., *Maquereaux*, red scorches, or spots on the legs of such as vse to sit neere the fire. **1872** CUYLER *Heart-Thoughts* 38 The ugly scorch upon the commercial integrity of the merchant.

b. A scorched appearance of foliage, symptomatic of various plant diseases.

1906 *Misc. Publ. Board Agric. & Fisheries Dis. Fruit* 13 Cherry leaf-scorch. A disease which every now and then proves destructive to the cherry crop. The leaves are attacked by a minute fungus, which causes them to turn brown and die, often quite early in the season. **1926** *Misc. Publ. Min. Agric.* LII. 63 Leaf scorch (physiological) [of apple trees]... In Lancashire the trouble appeared largely to be due to lack of potash, which is a contributory factor in many cases. **1933** *Discovery* Nov. 350/1 Scorch, due to the fungus *Kabatiella caulivora*, a disease which has come into prominence in recent years, causes considerable destruction in pure stands of red clover. **1974** *Nature* 8 Feb. 338/1 An experimental pirimiphos-methyl formulation produced localised scorch on citrus fruit.

2. a. Scorching effect (of the sun or fire).

1646 SIR T. BROWNE *Pseud. Ep.* VI. x. 330 Not onely their legitimate and timely births, but their abortions are also duskie, before they have felt the scortch and fervor of the Sun. *c* **1790** COWPER *Wks.* (1837) XV. 318 When he calls it a *balm to heal the scar of these corrosive fires* [Milton *P.L.* II. 401], we almost feel the scorch, and the pleasure of the remedy. **1862** LADY DUFF-GORDON in F. Galton *Vac. Tourists* (1864) 162 They said the thermometer was at about 130° where I was walking yesterday, but (barring the scorch) I could not have believed it.

b. *fig.*

1626 BP. H. KING *Serm. Deliv.* 9 Which.. shelters vs from the scorches of the last Iudgement. **1672** W. PENN *Spir. Truth Vind.* 52 Persecution comes, with the Scorch of which they are wont to singe and wrap up like a Scrole. **1859** I. TAYLOR *Logic in Theol.* 212 Profligate magnates quailed.. whenever this scorch of eternal reason was sent in upon their conscience.

3. [From SCORCH *v.*[1] 3.] An act of 'scorching'; a rapid run on a cycle or a motor-car.

1885 *Cyclist* 19 Aug. 1084/1 Another 24 hours scorch! **1890** *Polytechnic Mag.* 13 Mar. 161/1 An impromptu scorch was started by the members trying to keep behind a really fast cabby to obtain shelter from the wind.

4. *attrib.*: as ***scorch-mark***; **scorch-patch** (see quot.); **scorch pencil**, a tool used in 'poker-work'.

1897 J. HUTCHINSON in *Archives of Surg.* I. 62 'Scorch-patches' is, I think, the best descriptive epithet to apply to the brown patches which occur in the macular stage of leprosy. **1903** *Daily Mail* 21 Aug. 9/2 The chief instrument used is a 'scorch pencil', so called because with it the required design is burnt upon the prepared wood surface that is to be decorated. **1952** 'M. COST' *Hour Awaits* 112 She would.. wash this scorch-mark off her thumb. **1974** M. BIRMINGHAM *You can help Me* ii. 38 The whole landmark came down in spectacular flames. There is still rubble and scorch marks. **1978** R. BARNARD *Unruly Son* viii. 83 If she has her eyes on someone, they show the scorch-marks pretty fast.

scorch (skɔːtʃ), *v.*[1] Forms: (? 5 schorge), 5–6 skorch, scorche, (6 schorch, 7 scorge, *Sc.* scrotch), 6–8 scortch, 6– scorch. [Related to the earlier synonyms SCORKEN, SCORKLE.

The formation is obscure. It has been supposed that the word is identical with SCORCH *v.*[2] to skin, the sense being altered by association with *scorken*, *scorkle*. Against this is the fact that *scorch*, to skin, occurs only in a few translations from Fr. (where the original has *escorchier*), and is therefore not likely to have had any real currency.]

1. a. *trans.* To heat to such a degree as to shrivel, parch, or dry up, or to char or discolour the surface; to burn superficially.

14.. *Chaucer's Boeth.* II. metre vi. (*Addit. MS.*) (1868) 55 Alle þe poeples þat þe violent wynde Nothus scorchiþ [*Camb. MS.* scorklith; *orig. has* torret]. **1430** LYDG. *St. Margaret* 415 This gemme of maydenhede Was brent with brondes.. Hir sydes skorched. **1471** CAXTON *Recuyell* (Sommer) I. 43 Whan the pelagyens sawe this dede man of whom the skyn was scorched the ffllesh rosted the senewes shronken [etc.]. **1511** *Guylforde's Pilgr.* (Camden) 11 An hande with parte of the arme of seynt John Baptyste, some what scorcherde [*sic*] with the fyre as it was brente. **1553** EDEN *Treat. Newe Ind.* (Arb.) 14 The bodyes of men begin to waxe blacke and to be scorched. **1560** DAUS tr. *Sleidane's Comm.* 118 They.. wer after let downe into the fyre from on hyghe, and there synged and skorched. **1611** BIBLE *Rev.* xvi. 8 Power was giuen vnto him to scorch men with fire. **1634** MILTON *Comus* 929 Summer drouth, or singed air Never scorch thy tresses fair. **1697** DRYDEN *Virg. Georg.* IV. 616 'Twas Noon; the sultry Dog-star from the Sky Scorch'd Indian Swains, the rivell'd Grass was dry. **1748** *Anson's Voy.* II. vi. 279 He did not awake till the fire came near enough to scorch him. **1764** HARMER *Observ.* i. §20. 45 He had many times his forehead so scorched as to swell exceedingly. **1781** COWPER *Expost.* 15 Fiery suns, that scorch the russet spice Of eastern groves. **1813** SHELLEY *Q. Mab* VII. 9 His resolute eyes were scorched to blindness soon. **1830** M. DONOVAN *Dom. Econ.* I. 49 Her skeleton.. remained entire in the chair, which was only a little scorched. **1882** 'OUIDA' *Maremma* I. 18 Much beaten about by sea-winds and scorched by poisonous suns.

absol. **1576** TURBERV. *Venerie* 138 They quenche the skaldyng fire, which skorched with his heate.

b. *fig.*

c **1586** C'TESS PEMBROKE *Ps.* LXXXIX. xxxi, Scorcht with Thy wrath is Thy anointed one. **1620** SANDERSON *Serm.* 27 Feb. (1632) 307 Take Truth without Mercy; as an hot poyson it scaldeth vs, and scortcheth vs in the flames of restlesse Despayre. **1702** PRIOR *Song to his Mistress* I Whilst I am scorch'd with hot Desire. **1882** 'MARK TWAIN' *Prince & Pauper* 225 An' I tell him this, he will scorch thee finely for it. **1884** —— *Huck. Finn* xvi. 135 It hadn't ever come home to me before, what this thing was that I was doing. But now it did; and it staid with me, and scorched me more and more. **1934** ADE *Let.* 22 June (1973) 183 To me he continues to be a revelation and a marvel although he would scorch anyone who tried to put either of those labels on him. **1965** M. SPARK *Mandelbaum Gate* v. 122 Gardnor's hushed confidence continued to scorch Freddy's ear-drums.

absol. **1851** WHITTIER *Chapel of Hermits* 178 The fame that crowned him scorched and burned.

c. with *away*, *up*.

1598 SHAKS. *Merry W.* I. iii. 74 The appetite of her eye did seeme to scorch me vp like a burning-glasse. *a* **1691** BOYLE *Hist. Air* (1692) 165 The weather being very dry and hot, the grass and other vegetables were scorched up. **1697** DRYDEN *Virg. Georg.* II. 516 Whose Leaves are not alone foul Winter's Prey, But oft by Summer Suns are scorch'd away.

d. *transf.* To shrivel up as if by heat.

1607 TOPSELL *Four-f. Beasts* 274 If a mans feete be scorched with cold, the powder of a Hares Wooll is a remedy for it. **1905** RIDER HAGGARD *Gardener's Year* Oct. 333 Even the hardy Sea-Buckthorns.. have been sadly scorched by the spray brought up in the recent gales.

e. *intr.* for *refl.*

Quot. *c* 1430 may belong to SCORCH *v.*[2]; the form in any case is irregular, and may be due to misreading.

c **1430** *Two Cookery Bks.* 42 With a lytil Watere, late hem seþe til þey ben drye, & þat þey schorge. **1896** A. AUSTIN *England's Darling* I. iii, And then together we will watch the cakes, Nor let them scorch.

f. *trans.* Esp. in phr. ***to scorch the earth***, to subject (an area) to a scorched earth policy (see SCORCHED *ppl. a.*[1] 1 b). Also *transf.*

1941 H. G. WELLS *You can't be too Careful* v. ii. 245 The Russians, falling back slowly upon their main line of defence, 'scorching the earth' before this last convulsive thrust of the Nazi. **1943** *Ann. Reg. 1942* I. 193 Enormous quantities of petrol, which could not be made available until the Russian oil wells, also 'scorched', produced again. **1944** *Return to Attack* (Army Board, N.Z.) 9/2 There were neither women nor children, neither villages nor farms to be destroyed. Long ago nature had scorched the earth. **1945** *Yorkshire Post* 19 Apr. 1/1 The Germans are scorching towns in the way of the great armoured thrusts now threatening Hamburg.

†**2.** *trans.* To burn, consume by fire. *Obs.*

c **1475** *Partenay* 3412 Ther o soule man escapid noght, But scorched and brend were to Askes small. **1582** STANYHURST *Æneis* I. (Arb.) 18 As thogh that Pallas could not bee fullye reuenged, Thee Greek fleete scorching. **1624** MIDDLETON *Game at Chess* II. i. D 1, Here (wench) take these papers, Scorch 'em me soundly; burne 'em to French-russet.

3. *intr.* To cycle or motor at high speed. Also in extended use, and with *away*, *up*.

[Cf. F. *brûler le pavé*, lit. 'to burn the pavement', said of a furious driver.]

1891 *Wheeling* 25 Feb. 405 Be wise in time, and do not 'scorch' while you are out of condition. **1898** *Allbutt's Syst. Med.* V. 852 The father.. with his nervous system corroded by drudgery and care is determined to scorch on his bicycle or to climb the Alps with any of them. **1906** SOMERVILLE & 'ROSS' *Irish Yesterdays* 150 The priest who was to have performed the Funeral Office scorched up on his bicycle, scarlet-faced, and half an hour late. **1957** A. C. CLARKE *Deep Range* iv. 48 By keeping the torp tail-heavy and nose-up he was able to scorch along on the surface like a speed-boat. **1972** *Shooting Times & Country Mag.* 27 Mar. 22/2 The favourite scorched away to win by four lengths.

†**scorch**, *v.*[2] *Obs.* (Only in translations from Fr.) In 5 skorche. [a. OF. *escorchier* (mod.F. *écorcher*):—popular L. **excorticāre*, f. *ex-* (see ES-) + *cortic-*, *cortex* bark. Cf. ESCORSE *v.*] *trans.* To strip off (skin or bark), to flay. Also *fig.*

c **1430** *Pilgr. Lyf Manhode* I. xx. (1869) 15 Shere yow youre shepherde may at his neede but to skorche yow is not yiue him leeue. *Ibid.* III. xvi. 143 Whan the poore ben skorched thus and to pulled and that alle here goodes ben thus shaken and drawen out and arased. *a* **1450** *Knt. de la Tour* (1868) 6 Her fader.. made cast her in-to the Riuer, and drenche her and her childe, And made to scorch [orig. *escorchier*] the knight quicke.

†**scorch**, *v.*[3] *Obs.* Also 6 skorch, schortch, 6–7 scortch(e. [An alteration of SCORE *v.*; perh. after *scratch*. Cf. SCOTCH *v.*] *trans.* To slash with a knife.

c **1550** H. RHODES *Bk. Nurture* B ij, Afore dyner nor after, with thy knyfe scorche [1577 scortche] not the borde. **1597** J. PAYNE *Royal Exch.* 23 Baulls preists.. skorched there fleshe to the bones with there knyves. **1605** SHAKS. *Macb.* III. ii. 13 We have scorch'd the snake, not kill'd it. **1656** COWLEY *Misc.*, *Duel* 20 The Living and the Killing Arrow ..broke the Bones, and scortcht the Marrow. **1823** [see SCORCHED *ppl. a.*[2]].

scorchanarrow, obs. form of SCORZONERA.

scorcheatis: see SCROCHAT *Sc. Obs.*

scorched (skɔːtʃt), *ppl. a.*[1] [f. SCORCH *v.*[1] + -ED[1].]

1. a. Burnt and discoloured by heat, touched by fire.

1595 SHAKS. *John* III. i. 278 And falshood, falshood cures, as fire cooles fire Within the scorched veines of one new burn'd. **1639** G. DANIEL *Ecclus.* xxxviii. 81 The Smith.. To apt the Mettall; thrusts his scorched Browes Into the flames. **1715–20** POPE *Iliad* XXI. 14 As the scorch'd Locusts from their Fields retire, While fast behind them runs the Blaze of Fire. **1817** SHELLEY *Rev. Islam* III. 1365 My scorched limbs he wound In linen moist and balmy. **1897** MARY KINGSLEY *W. Africa* 397 'People should be careful with fire', I say sententiously and they all agree with me, the scorched ones enthusiastically.

b. *scorched earth*: used *attrib.* of a policy of destroying all means of sustenance or supply in a country that might be of use to an invading enemy, or of orders, operations, etc., designed to effect this policy; also *transf.* and *fig.*, and *absol.*

Apparently a translation of Chinese *jiāotǔ* (*zhèngcè*) scorched earth (policy).

1937 C. MCDONALD in *Times* 6 Dec. 12/2 The populace.. are still disturbed, in spite of official denials, by wild rumours of a 'scorched earth policy' of burning the city before the Japanese enter. **1938** *Times* 21 Feb. 15/6 (*heading*) Scorched earth. **1941** *Hutchinson's Pictorial Hist. of War* I Oct.–23 Dec. 115 The Soviet have left nothing but scorched earth and derelict, burned-out buildings to the invaders. **1941** E. SNOW *Scorched Earth* II. iv. 60 The 'scorched-earth' policy was credited to General Pai Tsung-hsi, the ablest strategist on Chiang's staff. **1945** *Daily Herald* 20 Apr. 1/3 A special 'scorched earth' order issued by Hitler. **1959** *Listener* 12 Nov. 818/2 Remember the scorched earth, too. How can Russia forget the menace of Germany? **1960** *Twentieth Century* July 63 The so-called concentration camps.. were part of Kitchener's 'scorched earth' strategy. **1963** WODEHOUSE *Stiff Upper Lip, Jeeves* xvii. 135 The kitchen maid.. always adopts the scorched earth policy when preparing a meal. **1976** H. WILSON *Governance of Britain* iii. 44, I was announcing in Parliament the discovery of documents envisaging an IRA offensive and virtual 'scorched earth' policy.

2. a. Parched by the sun.

a **1593** MARLOWE *Lucan* I. 208 Like to a Lyon of scortcht desart Affricke. **1600** J. PORY tr. *Leo's Africa* Descr. Places 43 Thither do the people resort, partly for the watring of their scorched grounds. **1707** MORTIMER *Husb.*, *Kalendar* July, The Earth now would be glad of refreshing showers to moisten the scorched Vegetables. **1817** SHELLEY *Rev. Islam* x. iv, Like the roaring Of fire, whose floods the wild deer circumvent In the scorched pastures of the South.

b. *Comb.*, as ***scorched-looking*** adj.

1970 T. HUGHES *Crow* 11 Who owns this bristly scorched-looking face?

3. *Nat. Hist.* †**a.** Having an appearance as if shrivelled by heat (*obs.*). **b.** Having colouring resembling a scorch.

1682 LISTER *Gœdart of Insects* 33, I could never Observe from these kind of Catterpillars a perfect and compleat Butterfly, but with contracted, and as it were scorched Wings, not to be expanded, or fit for flight. **1832** J. RENNIE *Butterfl. & M.* 162 The Scorched Blunt-wing. *Ibid.* Index 276 Scorched Carpet. Scorched Wing. **1845** LINDLEY *Sch. Bot.* vi. (1858) 84 The scales scorched at the apex. **1859** MISS PRATT *Brit. Grasses* 37 *Carex ustulata* (Scorched Alpine Sedge).

†**scorched**, *ppl. a.*[2] *Obs. rare*[−1]. [f. SCORCH *v.*[3] + -ED[1].] Slashed, divided.

1823 SCOTT *Quentin D.* i, The members of the League.. like a scorched snake might re-unite.

scorcher ('skɔːtʃə(r)). [f. SCORCH *v.*[1] + -ER[2].] One who or something which scorches.

1. *colloq.* A very hot day.

1874 M. C. *Explorers* 25 One regular scorcher we camped before noon. **1899** F. V. KIRBY *Sport E.C. Africa* xxiii. 259 A heavy mist.. gave promise of a hot day, and it turned out a 'scorcher'.

2. *colloq.* One who cycles or motors furiously.

1885 PENNELL *Canterb. Pilgr.* Pref., Nor does it seem to us worth while.. to record our time, since we were pilgrims, and not scorchers. **1901** *Daily Tel.* 7 Jan. 8/3 (Farmer), As a result of complaints as to the excessive speed at which motor-cars are driven.. the police have been keeping a sharp look-out for scorchers.

3. *slang.* **a.** Something scorching or stinging; a scathing rebuke or attack.

1842 R. W. GRISWOLD *Let.* 7 Sept. (1898) 120 The review in The Examiner.. is a 'scorcher'. **1869** 'MARK TWAIN' *Innocents Abroad* 453 Every time they read me a scorcher of a lecture I mean to talk back in print. **1888** *Pall Mall Gaz.* 27 Jan. 1/1 We have no doubt that his 'letter, in the strongest Saxon I could command', about the Intelligence Department was, as the schoolboys would say, 'a regular scorcher.'

b. One who causes a 'sensation'. *spec.* a very attractive girl or woman, a 'smasher'.

1881 *Punch* 29 Oct. 204/2 She was 'a Scorcher', was Lady O. **1898** [see HOT *a.* 6 c]. **1899** DOYLE *Duet* (1909) 44 A perfec' pair of scorchers. **1935** WODEHOUSE *Luck of Bodkins* ix. 88 When I'd had a look at the young lady next door and seen what a scorcher she is.

c. In *Sport*, an extremely fast shot or hit.

1900 *Dialect Notes* II. 57 *Scorcher*,.. a swiftly batted ball. **1943** *Amer. Speech* XVIII. 104 A batter who hits a line drive (also called a *liner* or a *scorcher*..) is said to *line it out*. **1977** *Belfast Tel.* 14 Feb. 21/8 He.. diverted a scorcher from Pat Spence later in the game.

d. Something licentious or risqué (esp. a book or play).

1942 BERREY & VAN DEN BARK *Amer. Thes. Slang* §281/6 *Risqué joke or story*,.. scorcher. *Ibid.* §590/4 *Scorcher, sexer*, a risqué play. **1974** P. CAVE *Dirtiest Picture Postcard* ii. 12 Then he produced a scorcher which managed to get itself banned by the country's leading booksellers and nominated for public prosecution at the Old Bailey. **1978** *Morecambe Guardian* 14 Mar. 15/3 (*heading*) It's a scorcher at the Duke's. A scorching new show opened at Lancaster's Duke's Playhouse on Friday.

†'**scorcheresse**. *Obs. rare*[−1]. [a. OF. *escorcheresse*, fem. agent-n. f. *escorchier* to flay, SCORCH *v.*[2]] A female flayer; in quot. *fig.*

c **1430** *Pilgr. Lyf Manhode* III. xvi. (1869) 143 This hand is a skorcheresse and a baconresse of poure folk.

scorchet(t)is: see SCROCHAT *Sc. Obs.*

scorching ('skɔːtʃɪŋ), *vbl. sb.* [f. SCORCH *v.*[1] + -ING[1].]

1. The action or an act of burning superficially, or of parching or shrivelling up by intense heat.

1563 HYLL *Art Garden.* (1593) 16 And if.. you dout either the coldnes or hotnes of the season, in the scorching or burning of your seedes, then couer your beddes with the chaffe of corne. **1649** BP. REYNOLDS *Hosea* v. 22 Those parts of the world which are under.. perpetuall scortchings. **1699** EVELYN *Kal. Hort., June* (ed. 9) 74 The excessive Scorchings of this, and the two following Months.. do frequently indanger the untimely falling both of Blossom and Fruit before their maturity. **1768** TUCKER *Lt. Nat.* (1834) I. 641 The scorchings of unextinguishable flames and gnawings of the never dying worm.

†**b.** *pl.* Fragments detached by scorching. *Obs.*

1607 TOPSELL *Four-f. Beasts* 253 Goates Horne being burned at the end, and the pieces or scorchinges that rise thereof, must be shaken into a new vessel vntill the horne be quite consumed. **1676** T. MACE *Musick's Monum.* 59 Then with your Working-knife, or Chizzel, take off the Scorchings to the clean Wood.

2. The action of riding a cycle or driving a motor-car at a furious pace.

1891 *Wheeling* 4 Mar. 422 We are.. in a strong position to denounce the abuse of 'scorching' through inhabited parts of the country. **1898** *Daily News* 22 July 8/2 Do you ever scorch?—I do not know what you call scorching.

scorching ('skɔːtʃɪŋ), *ppl. a.*[1] [f. SCORCH *v.*[1] + -ING[2].] **1. a.** That scorches, burning, withering.

1563 B. GOOGE *Eglogs*, etc. (Arb.) 87 The Body dryed by broylyng blase Of preuy schorchyng Flame. **1628** MURE *Doomsday* 206 There, to the drunkard's parched throate, Justice doth scrotching drought allote, In floods of fire. **1667** MILTON *P.L.* x. 691 How had the World Inhabited, though sinless, more then now, Avoided pinching cold and scorching heate? **1697** DRYDEN *Virg., Past.* II. 11 While in the scorching Sun I trace in vain Thy flying footsteps. **1745** *Watts' Hymn, 'How bright these glorious spirits shine,'* Hunger and Thirst are felt no more, Nor Suns with scorching Ray. **1812** BYRON *Ch. Har.* I. vi, He.. from his native land resolved to go, And visit scorching climes beyond the sea. **1875** JOWETT *Plato* (ed. 2) III. 299 Under the heat of a scorching sun.

fig. **1646** CRASHAW *Steps, Charity* 43 No more shalt thou .. on Gods Altar cast two scorching [1648 scortching] eyes. **1666** BUNYAN *Grace Abound.* §294, I have been about to preach upon some smart and scorching portion of the word. **1895** LD. ACTON *Study Hist.* 59 After looking about for a scorching imprecation, he [Titus Oates] began to call them Tories.

b. *transf.* Causing a burning sensation, irritant.

1768 MILLER *Gardener's Dict.* (ed. 8), *Thapsia*... The deadly Carrot, or scorching Fennel.

c. Applied *transf.* to a period of excessive sunshine and heat.

1940 'GUN BUSTER' *Return via Dunkirk* II. xix. 220 It is a pale, steady dawn, breaking with a slight haze that presages another scorching day. **1962** A. WESKER *Chips with Everything* I. i. 12 This hut.. is going to be your home for the next eight scorching weeks.

2. *colloq.* Astounding, sensational; licentious, risqué; in *Sport*, of a shot or hit: exceedingly fast, 'blistering'.

1890 *St. Nicholas* Sept. 945/1 The first senior to the bat made first-base on a scorching grounder past third. **1896** A. BEARDSLEY *Let. c* 20 Sept. (1970) 167 Your joke is charming and I shall do you some scorching drawings for No. 8 [of *The Savoy*]. **1897** *Referee* 24 Oct. 3/1 A said-to-be 'scorching' play entitled 'At the Foot of the Altar'. **1963** A. ROSS *Australia 63* iii. 88 The two scorching catches by Cowdrey and Jarman. **1976** *Ilkeston Advertiser* 10 Dec. 18/2 Garbett scored with a scorching left foot drive. **1978** [see SCORCHER 3 d].

3. quasi-*adv.*, in ***scorching cold, hot.***

1873 E. HOOPER *Nurseries & School Rooms* 197 The sand so scorching hot that one could not bear one's hand upon it. **1876** E. W. HEAP *Diary* 8 Sept. in *Publ. Amer. Dial. Soc.* (1969) LII. 54 Another scorching cold morning. **1883** *Century Mag.* July 428/1 The sun was scorching hot and the shade chilly.

Hence '**scorchingly** *adv.*, '**scorchingness**.

1593 NASHE *Christ's T.* 70b, Hauing naturally cleere beauty, scortchingly blazing, which enkindles any soule that comes neere it. **1775** ASH Suppl., *Scorchingness.*

†'**scorching**, *ppl. a.*[2] *Obs.* [f. SCORCH *v.*[2] + -ING[2].] Cutting, slashing.

1570 in *B.L. Ballads* (1867) 179 The sister dire, fearce Atropos, with schortchyng cuttynge knyfe, Hath shred the threede that longe dyd holde this godly ladies lyfe.

†'**scorchvillein.** *Obs.* [a. AF. **escorche-villein*, f. OF. *escorchier* (mod.F. *écorcher*) to flay + *villein*.] A 'flay-villein'; an oppressive lord.

1577–87 STANYHURST *Descr. Irel.* v. 32/1 in *Holinshed*. [The nickname of Abp. Henry de Loundres; Stanyhurst tells a story to connect it with SCORCH *v.*[1]]

‖**scordatura** (skorda'tura). *Mus.* [It. *scordatura*, f. *scordare* to be out of tune, short for *discordare* DISCORD *v.*[1]] A term used for the alteration in the manner of tuning some stringed instruments in order to produce particular effects.

1876 STAINER & BARRETT *Dict. Mus. Terms, Scordatura* (It.) the mis-tuning of an instrument. When a violinist alters the *accordatura* of his instrument for a special purpose, he is sometimes said to make a *scordatura*. **1888** *Encycl. Brit.* XXIV. 245 The violoncello is less amenable to the scordatura than the violin.

‖'**scordium.** *Bot. Obs.* Also 6 scordion. [mod.L. (cf. L. *scordion*, Pliny), a. Gr. σκόρδιον a plant that smells like garlic. Cf. G. *skordien*, MDu. *scordioen*.] A name for the Water-Germander, *Teucrium Scordium*, a plant formerly in use in medicine as a sudorific, an antidote for poisons, etc.

[*c* **1050** *Herb. Apuleii* in Cockayne *Sax. Leechd.* I. 174 Wið nædran slite ȝenim þas wyrte þe man scordean.. nemneð.] **1548** TURNER *Names Herbes* (E.D.S.) 71 Scordium groweth in diuerse places of Germany,.. & I heare saye that it groweth also besyde Oxforde. **1578** LYTE *Dodoens* I. lxxv. 111 Scordion is hoate and dry in the thirde degree. **1597** GERARDE *Herbal* II. cciv. 535 Called in English Scordium, Water Germander & Garlicke Germander. **1757** A. COOPER *Distiller* III. xv. (1760) 169 Of the Leaves of Scordium one Pound and a Half. **1866** *Treas. Bot.* 1040/1 Scordium, *Teucrium Scordium.*

score (skɔə(r)), *sb.* Forms: 1 scoru, 3–6 scor, 4–5 schore, 4–6 skor, 4–7 skore, 5 *Sc.* scoyr, skowre, 5, 7 scoure, 6 scoore, *Sc.* scower, skoir, 6–7 scoare, *Sc.* scoir, 3– score. [Late OE. *scoru* str. fem. (sense 16), a. ON. *skor* str. fem., notch, tally, the number of twenty (cf. *skora* wk. fem., notch):—OTeut. type **skurā*, f. **skur-*, wk. grade of **sker-* to cut: see SHEAR *v.*]

I. A cut, notch, mark.

1. a. †A crack, crevice (*obs.*); a cut, notch, or scratch; a line drawn with a sharp instrument.

c **1400** *Rom. Rose* 2660 Than shal thou go the dore bifore, If thou maist fynde any score, Or hole, or reft, what ever it were. **1570** LEVINS *Manip.* 174/11 A skore, *crenale*. *a* **1585** POLWART *Flyting w. Montgomerie* 555 With scartes and scores, athort his frozen front. **1792** BELKNAP *Hist. New-Hampsh.* III. 113 To procure the sap, an incision is made by two scores, an inch and a half, or two inches deep. **1884** KNIGHT *Dict. Mech.* Suppl. 783/2 To make a score on the future angles of the box in order to make the stuff bend readily.

b. *Naut.* and *Mech.* (*a*) The groove of a block or dead-eye round which the rope passes; (*b*) a notch or groove made in a piece of timber or metal to allow another piece to be neatly fitted into it.

1794 *Rigging & Seamanship* I. 29 The cross-trees are let into the trestle-trees, with scores. **1815** *Falconer's Dict. Marine* (ed. Burney), *Score of a Dead-Eye*, is the hole through which the rope passes. *c* **1850** *Rudim. Navig.* (Weale) 155 *Tabling*, letting one piece of timber into another by alternate scores or projections. **1874** THEARLE *Naval Archit.* 16 A score, the width of which is equal to the siding of the post. **1901** *J. Black's Carp. & Build., Scaffolding* 89 This is called the 'strap' and lies in the 'score', or channelled part of the block.

c. *local.* 'A vertical indentation in a hill; a gangway down a cliff; a cutting through a ridge of hills' (E.D.D.); *spec.* in East Anglia, a narrow, steep path or street leading to the sea. Used esp. in place-names. Cf. ON. *skor* in sense 'a rift in a rock or precipice'.

The place-names *Syrithescore* and *Scourton* are recorded from the 13th century and *c* 1550 respectively (A. H. Smith, *Place-Names of East Riding of Yorkshire* (1937) 328; E. Ekwall, *Place-Names of Lancashire* (1922) 164).

1790 E. GILLINGWATER *Hist. Acct. Lowestoft* viii. 356 There are several of these passages in Lowestoft called scores, leading from the High-Street to the sea side, such as the Swan Score, Salter's Score, Rant's Score, &c. **1807** J. GRIERSON *Delineations of St. Andrews* iii. 104 That space of ground which is now converted into a public walk, and known by the name of the *Scores*. **1835** J. D. CARRICK *Laird of Logan* II. 271 The hail place was in a perfect fizz.. frae the head of the Causeyside till the Score. **1858** *Hist. & Topogr. Handbk. Lowestoft* i. 3 On the land side are many narrow streets or lanes branching off into the country; whilst seaward there are, at short intervals, steep and narrow passages down the cliff, formed into steps, and leading to the *Denes*. These passages are known locally and technically as *Scores*. **1929** H. MEREDITH *E. Anglia* iii. 95 The Scores are Lowestoft's counterpart of Yarmouth's more famous Rows. **1958** *E. Anglian Mag.* Feb. 193/1 East Anglian cities and towns have each and all their picturesque narrow ways... The scores of Lowestoft have a unique character added to their picturesqueness in that they are steep as well as narrow. **1961** *Scottish Studies* V. 14 The Score is the downfall of the west edge of Edinburgh Castle.

2. a. A line drawn; a stroke, mark; a line drawn as a boundary.

The sense, though in our examples not found in literal use earlier than the 16th c., seems to be old, as the fig. phrases in b apparently belong to it.

1501 DOUGLAS *Pal. Hon.* III. lxxviii, Prosperitie in eird is bot a dreme, Or like as man war steppand ouir ane scoir. **1603** *Philotus* cxxv, Trowis thow to draw me ouir the scoir, Fals feind with thy alluring. **1681** GIB in Wodrow *Hist. Suff. Ch. Scot.* (1722) II. App. lxxiii. 80 Drawing Scores betwixt the Books of the Bible. **1688** HOLME *Armoury* III. iii. 144/2 Feathers of a Ducks Wing, or such like.. to wipe off a superfluous score made in a draught by the Charcoal. **1710–11** SWIFT *Jrnl. to Stella* 9 Feb., It was that ugly score [*foot-n.* A crease in the sheet] in the paper that made me mistake. **1783** BURNS *Rantin', Rovin' Robin* v, I see by ilka score and line, This chap will dearly like our kin'. **1818** SCOTT *Rob Roy* i, Draw a score through the tops of your t's. **1836** *Comic Almanack* Sept. (1870) 63 We've chalked a score on every door Of publican or sinner. **1859** DARWIN *Life & Lett.* (1887) II. 171, I hope you will mark your copy with scores.

b. Phrases. † ***out of score***, beyond the mark, excessively, unreasonably (frequent in R. Brunne); † ***over score***, over the mark, aside.

1303 R. BRUNNE *Handl. Synne* 6872 Þe aumenere was wroth þerfore, Þat he asked so oute of skore. *Ibid.* 11225 But leuer ys me my mouþe to steke Þan y spak oȝ t oute of skore. **1513** DOUGLAS *Æneis* I. Prol. 496 As now war tyme to schift the wers ouer scoir.

†**c.** ? A track, trace of footsteps. *Obs.*

c **1330** R. BRUNNE *Chron. Wace* (Rolls) 3377 To trauersen hem al ouer þere score, & passe þe Romayns wel byfore. *Ibid.* 13694 After hym his folk held wel þe score.

3. a. *spec.* The 'scratch' or line at which a marksman stands when shooting at a target, or on which the competitors stand before beginning a race.

1513 DOUGLAS *Æneis* v. vi. 70 He suld full sone haue skippit furth befoir And left in dowt quha first coyme to the scoir. **1570** *Satir. Poems Reform.* xx. 69 Stand to, thair-foir, fyle not the scoir, But all togidder draw. *c* **1880** in Greener *Gun* (1881) 506 In case of breech-loaders, the party called to the score shall not place his cartridge in the gun until he arrives at the score.

b. Phrases. ***to go off*** (***set off, start***) ***at score***, of a horse, to make a sudden dash at full speed; *fig.* of a person, to break out suddenly into impetuous speech or action. So ***to go off full score, to keep on at a score.***

c **1800** R. CUMBERLAND *John De Lancaster* (1809) II. 95 John and his steed were in the same humour for a start at score. **1807** [E. GOULBURN] *Epwell Hunt* 117 Resolv'd at all Hazards to follow Bob Canning; To accomplish which End he kept on at a Score. **1818** SCOTT *Hrt. Midl.* xvii, Madge no sooner received the catch-word, than she vindicated Ratcliffe's sagacity by setting off at score with the song: 'O sleep ye sound, Sir James, she said'. **1833** MOORE *Mem.* (1854) VI. 309 Talking of a paragraph lately which stated that all the Church dignitaries meant to resign.., he went off at score on the sad state we should be reduced to by such a resignation. **1834** J. WILSON in *Blackw. Mag.* XXXV. 1016 Start at score and make play we must, if we were now to resume the contest. **1848** DICKENS *Dombey* vi, Lest the black-eyed should go off at score and turn sarcastic. **1863** W. C. BALDWIN *Afr. Hunting* iii. 64 His horse, Blesbok, went off at score, and followed the spoor as accurately as any dog. **1867** M. ARNOLD *Celtic Lit.* 71 After the mediæval touch of the visit to the buttery in the land of the Trinity, he goes off at score: 'I have been instructed in the whole system of the universe [etc.]'. **1869** 'WAT. BRADWOOD' *The O.V.H.* xxxiv, The slackened rein.. encouraged the gray to take a final kick and fling, and then set off at score up the slope. **1900** POLLOK & THOM *Sports Burma* iii. 99 The bull picked himself up and went off full score.

c. *Curling.* = HOG-SCORE.

1862 *Chamb. Encycl.* III. 368/2 (*Curling*), At a certain distance from each of the tees, a score—the hog-score—is drawn across the ice. **1877** *Encycl. Brit.* VI. 713/2 (*Curling*), Every stone to be a hog which does not clear this score.

4. A line that crosses out or cancels something.

a **1756** *Pennecuik's Collect. Sc. Poems* 120 A roll of sins hath got the clergy's score.

†**5.** *pl.* as the name of a game. *Obs.*

1710 RUDDIMAN *Gloss. to Douglas' Æneis* s.v. *Skore*, The word score, is.. most used at the long Bowls, which are sometimes call'd the Scores, because they make draughts or impressions in the ground where they are to begin and leave off.

6. *Mus.* A written or printed piece of concerted music, in which all the vocal and instrumental parts are noted on a series of staves one under the other.

Commonly stated to be so called from the practice (not now always followed) of connecting the related staves by 'scores' or lines continuing the bars.

1701 *Lond. Gaz.* No. 3748/4 The Score of Musick for the Fairy Queen. **1752** AVISON *Mus. Express.* Advt., Music is said to be in Score, when all the Parts are distinctly wrote and set under each other, so as the Eye, at one View, may take in all the various Contrivances of the Composer. **1784** COWPER *Task* II. 360 He.. sells accent, tone And emphasis in score. **1785** GEO. III in Mrs. Delany *Life & Corr.* (1862) III. 247 The King has just received the copies of the three operas M[rs]. Delany so obligingly borrow'd for him. He therefore returns the three scores. **1845** E. HOLMES *Mozart* 13 This concerto was written with a full score of accompaniments, and even trumpets and drums. **1883** ROCKSTRO in *Grove's Dict. Mus.* III. 427/1 The most important varieties [of scores] are (I.) the Vocal Score; (II.) the Orchestral, or Full Score; (III.) the Supplementary Score, or Partitino; (IV.) the Organ, Harpsichord, or Pianoforte Score; (V.) the Compressed Score; and (VI.) the Short Score. *Ibid.* 434/1 The term *Short Score* is indiscriminately applied to Organ and Pianoforte Scores of works originally written with Orchestral Accompaniments; to Compressed Scores; and to maimed transcriptions, in which the leading Parts only are given *in extenso*.

b. A musical composition with its distribution of parts.

1881 CROWEST *Phases Mus. Eng.* 295 The London Musical Society has set itself the task of familiarising English people with those scores which are either little known, or which have not had a hearing in this country.

c. *spec.* (A piece of) music composed for a film; the musical part of the sound-track of a film; formerly, the background music and effects of a silent film.

1927 *Kinematograph Year Book* 32 Scores to films can be recorded by the world's greatest orchestras, under the baton of conductors impossible to obtain for motion picture houses. **1935** R. SPOTTISWOODE *Grammar of Film* v. 191 The score composed by Edmund Meisel for *Ten Days*. **1957** MANVELL & HUNTLEY *Film Music* i. 23 Among the more celebrated film score.. are those by Edmund Meisel for Eisenstein's films *The Battleship Potemkin* and *October*. **1965** *Movie* Summer 40/2 Jerry Bresler had re-edited the film.. adding a score that was far from Peckinpah's choosing. **1976** R. SANDERS in D. Villiers *Next Year in Jerusalem* 212 Irving Berlin.. wrote the best over-all score of his career, *Annie Get Your Gun*.

7. *Weaving.* = BEER *sb.*[3]

1712 [see BEER *sb.*[3]]. **1726** *Act 13 Geo. I*, c. 26 §13 So as to distinguish the Number of biers or scores of Threads in the breadth of the said Cloth.

8. A cut or slash, as with a whip.

1882 J. T. MORSE JR. *John Q. Adams* iii. (1885) 230 There was scarce a back in Congress that did not at one time or another feel the score of his cutting lash.

II. Notch cut for record, tally, reckoning.

†**9. a.** A notch cut in a stick or tally, used to mark numbers in keeping accounts; also the tally itself.

c **1460** *Launfal* 419 All that Launfal had borwyth before Gyfre, be tayle and be score, Yald hyt well and fyne. *c* **1460** *Bk. Curtasye* 416 in *Babees Bk.*, Yf þo koke wolde say þat were more, þat is þo cause þat he hase it in skore. **1530** PALSGR. 268/1 Score on a tayle, *taylles.* **1538** ELYOT *Dict.*, *Crene* [1545 *Crenæ*],..the scores whiche men vnlerned do make on styckes for their remembrance. **1565** COOPER *Thesaurus, Crena*, a notche in a skore. *Ibid.*, *Tessera*,..a tayle or score, wheron the number of thynges deliuered is marked. **1593** SHAKS. *2 Hen. VI*, IV. vii. 38 Whereas before, our Fore-fathers had no other Bookes but the Score and the Tally, thou hast caused printing to be vs'd.

b. *Games.* A mark made for the purpose of recording a point or the like. Cf. CHALK *sb.* 5.

1680 COTTON *Compl. Gamester* (ed. 2) 102 Lanterloo... Having dealt set up five scores or chalks; and then proceed forwards in your Game. *Ibid.*, Every deal rub off a score, and for every trick you win set up a score by you till the first scores are out, to remember you how many tricks you have won in the several deals in the Game. **1801** STRUTT *Sports & Past.* II. iii. 84 It is called a run, and one notch or score is made upon the tally towards the game. *Ibid.* III. vii. 203 One chalk, or score, is reckoned for every fair pin; and the game of skittles consists in obtaining thirty-one chalks precisely.

10. a. A record or account (of items of uniform amount to be charged or credited) kept by means of tallies, or (in later use) by means of marks made on a board (with chalk), on a slate, or the like. Now chiefly, the row of chalk marks on a door, or of strokes on a slate, which in rural alehouses used to serve to record the quantity of liquor consumed on credit by a regular frequenter. Hence occas. *transf.*, a customer's account for goods obtained on credit.

a **1400** in *Eng. Gilds* (1870) 362 ȝif þat þe axkere bryngeþ skore oþer wryt, and aske þe berynge y-hole-cheche... Whos paye y-maked by skore oþer by scryt oþer by sywete, so þ[t] he bere tayle oþer scryt, to preue hit vp-on hure nature. *c* **1421** *26 Pol. Poems* 119 þe fendes redy my rolle to rede, þe countretayle to shewe, þe score. *c* **1450** *Mirk's Festial* 255 And he anon radly laft all his scores, and cownturs, and his bokes, and suet Cryst forþe. **1483** *Cath. Angl.* 324/1 A score, *epimeridia.* **1591** R. PERCIVALL *Sp. Dict.*, *Tablilla*, writing tables, a score. **1593** SHAKS. *2 Hen. VI*, IV. ii. 80 There shall bee no mony, all shall eate and drinke on my score. **1614** RAVENSCROFT in *Festive Songs* (Percy Soc.) 40 When all is gone we have no more, Then let us set it on the score, Or chalke it up behinde the dore. **1648** CRASHAW *Steps to Temple* Matt. xxiii, The stones that on his Tombe doe lye Keep but the score of them that made him dye. *a* **1704** T. BROWN *Laconics* Wks. 1711 IV. 20 He ought to have preach'd against..rubbing out of Ale-house Scores. **1837** HAWTHORNE *Twice-told T.* (1851) II. i. 9 A familiar visitor of the house, who might be supposed to have his regular score at the bar. **1867** LOWELL *Fitz Adam's Story* 388 These paid no money, yet for them he..chalked behind the door With solemn face a visionary score. **1887** JESSOPP *Arcady* i. 19 Formerly every man had a score at the village shop.

†**b.** *in, upon, on (the) score*: in debt. *to run into scores* or *in score*, *to run* or *go on* or *upon (the) score*: to incur debts. *upon the score of*: indebted to. Also *on score, upon the score*: on credit. *Obs.*

1568 FULWELL *Like will to like* E ij, But now my masters you are on the score. **1577** STANYHURST *Descr. Irel.* iii. 11 in *Holinshed*, The citie merchants not vttering their wares, but to such as had not redy chinkes, and therevpon forced to run on y[e] score, were very much empouerished. **1592** GREENE *Upst. Courtier* G j, If any chance to go on the skore, you skore him when he is a sleepe. **1596** SHAKS. *Tam. Shrew* Induct. ii. 25 If she say I am not xiiii d on the score for sheere Ale, score me vp for the lyingst knaue in Christendome. **1602** ROWLANDS *Tis Merrie* 11 There's many deale vpon the score for wine, When they should pay forget the Vint'ners Syne. **1615** R. COCKS *Diary* (Hakl. Soc.) I. 57 He had stolne and pawnd his companions aparell,..and was gon upon the score in divers howses. **1633** G. HERBERT *Temple, The Size* iv, Those have their hopes: these what they have renounce, And live on score. **1649** MILTON *Eikon.* v. 42 He had.. begger'd both himself and the Public; and besides had left us upon the score of his needy Enemies, for what it cost them in thir own defence against him. **1649** BP. HALL *Cases Consc.* I. vii. 66 Seneca reports of a Pythagorean Philosopher at Athens, who having run upon the score for his shoos at a shop there [etc.]. **1658** H. CROMWELL in Thurloe *St. Papers* VI. 820 The country, to whom the army is in score, will be all in a flame. **1659** *Gentl. Calling* (1696) 75 'Tis become so fashionable a thing to run into Scores, and so unfashionable to pay them [etc.]. **1667** PEPYS *Diary* 30 Dec., I perceive he is known there, and do run upon the score for plays. **1685** EVELYN *Mrs. Godolphin* 195 Every Saturday she used to sum up, and never went on score. **1702** YALDEN *Æsop at Crt.* iii. 43 See, injur'd Britain, thy unhappy case,..If fond of the expensive pain, When eighteen millions run on score: Let them clap mufflers on again, And physick thee of eighteen more. **1760** GOLDSM. *Cit. W.* lxv, I..drank while I had money left, and ran in score when anybody would trust me.

c. In *colloq.* phrases, as *to go over the score* (chiefly *Sc.*): to act (esp. drink) immoderately; *to have a few over the score* (see FEW *a.* 2 f): to drink more at one time than one should.

1768 A. ROSS *Fortunate Shepherdess* II. 100 She thinks ye hae ga'en o'er the score. **1851** W. ANDERSON *Rhymes, Reveries, & Reminiscences* 50 Lest some o' the nickums should gang owre the score. **1915** J. L. WAUGH *Betty Grier* 157 He gangs fairly ower the score baith wi' drinkin' himsel' an' treatin' ithers. **1951** N. M. GUNN *Well at World's End* xviii. 145 'You know how, when you have had a few over the score and you may not trust your legs, your brain remains as clear—' 'I know,' said Peter.

11. a. The sum recorded to a customer's debit in a 'score' (sense 10); the amount of an innkeeper's bill or reckoning. Also, †a debt due to a tradesman for goods obtained on credit (*obs.*).

1600 *Ball. Coll. Acc.* (*MS.*), Item, paid to Warde the Baker for 2 skores dewe in Mr. More's yeare, 8 li. 18 s. 9 d. **1601** SHAKS. *All's Well* IV. iii. 253 After he scores, he neuer payes the score. **1615** BRATHWAIT *Strappado* 133 Chauke me on Vinters, and for aw thy skore, Let great words pay for aw, still run on more. **1648** HERRICK *Hesper.*, *Country Life* 14 Or how to pay thy hinds and clear all scores. **1667** PEPYS *Diary* 6. Apr., Away to the Exchange, and mercers and drapers, up and down to pay all my scores. **1675** KIDDER *Charity Directed* 31 How often do men contend at a Tavern who shall pay the score. **1677** OTWAY *Cheats of Scapin* II. i, Some Scores that are due to the Landlady. **1687** SEDLEY *Bellamira* v. i. 53, I have been in the Country, and have brought wherewith to pay old Scores, and will deal here-after with ready Mony. **1701** *Pennsylv. Hist. Soc. Mem.* IX. 79 Hasten over rents, and all thou canst, for many call upon me for old scores. **1715** PRIOR *Down-Hall* 96 When in the morning Matt ask'd for the score, John kindly had paid it the evening before. **1748** SMOLLETT *Rod. Rand.* ix, After having paid our score. **1761** *Brit. Mag.* II. 626 He had run a score at the public house, which he had no mind to discharge. **1766** COWPER *Wks.* (1837) XV. 9 If..you think I can afford to quit scores with the little Doctor, I shall be obliged to you if you will do it forthwith. **1807** [IRELAND] *Mod. Ship of Fools* 236 Or, when in school, neglecting book, Or, running scores with pastry cook, That breech should feel the twitch of birch. **1824** W. IRVING *T. Trav.* I. 230, I agreed that he should pay the score at our next meeting. **1886** *Contemp. Rev.* July 80 The week's score at the public-house is paid up and a fresh one started.

b. *fig.*, esp. in certain phrases. ***to clear, pay, quit a score*** or ***scores***: to requite an obligation; sometimes, to revenge an injury, to 'be even *with*' some one. † ***to cut the score, cut scores***: to forgive a debt. Also ***to pay off, rub out,*** etc., ***old scores.***

a **1617** BAYNE *On Eph.* (1658) 170 God cuts all scores betwixt him and his children. **1634** H. SYDENHAM *Serm.* (1637) 70 That that Justice which is conferr'd on them, consists rather in the participation of Christs merits, who cut the score, than in any perfection of Vertues. **1672** DRYDEN *2nd Pt. Conq. Granada* v. ii, Yet, forced by need, ere I can clear that score, I like ill debtors, come to borrow more. **1690** LOCKE *Govt.* I. ix. §90 To the Grandfather, there is due a long Score of Care and Expences laid out upon the Breeding and Education of his Son. **1707** NORRIS *Treat. Humility* vi. 252 Which she readily accepts, and perhaps does not make so much haste to quit scores, as Pride does. **1775** SHERIDAN *St. Patrick's Day* I. i, Are you sure you do nothing to quit scores with them? **1787** 'P. PINDAR' *Ode upon Ode* (ed. 5) 25 A pretty Way of rubbing out old Scores! *c* **1863** T. TAYLOR *Ticket-of-Leave Man* III. 56 There's the satisfaction of doing one's duty..but there's something better than that... Paying off old scores. **1913** E. PHILLPOTTS *Widecombe Fair* xxx. 236 This evening.. promised good opportunity to pay off old scores. **1918** L. STRACHEY *Eminent Victorians* 67 The old scores, they found, were not to be paid off, but to be wiped out.

12. [Originally a figurative use of sense 10.] Account, reason, ground, sake, motive. In phrases ***on, upon the score (of)***: by reason of, for the sake of, with regard to.

1651 BAXTER *Inf. Bapt.* 346, I presume not to expect this for my own sake and meerly upon the score of Christian love. **1651** EVELYN *Diary* 6 Sept., He..embark'd for Scotland with some men he had raised, who..were all.. imprison'd on y[e] Marq. of Montrose's score. *a* **1654** SELDEN *Table Talk* (Arb.) 70 By reason..their great Grandfather did not do it, upon that old Score they think they ought not to do it. **1654** DICKSON *Explic. Ps.* cxxix. 1 (1655) 263 The persecution of former enemies is imputed and put upon the score of present persecutors. **1655** *Clarke Papers* (Camden) III. 3 The House of Peeres was never yet denied by them to be dissolved upon the like scoare. **1661** BOYLE *Style of Script.* (1675) 244 Divers that first believe the Scripture but upon the Church's score, are afterwards by acquaintedness brought to believe the Scripture upon its own score. **1667** DRYDEN *Ind. Emp.* I. ii, I could not do it on my Honour's score. **1722** DE FOE *Plague* (1884) 250 Men..began to be over-easie upon that Score. **1751** *Affecting Narr. Wager* 47 The Crew..were however on that Score implacably incensed against the Captain. **1769** BLACKSTONE *Comm.* IV. 51 All persecution and oppression of weak consciences, on the score of religious persuasions, are highly unjustifiable. **1802** MRS. J. WEST *Infidel Father* I. 231 An eminent solicitor ..whom it was fashionable to consult on the score of settlements. **1827** HALLAM *Const. Hist.* x. (1876) II. 269 It was necessary to summon a parliament on the usual score of obtaining money. **1847** MARRYAT *Childr. N. Forest* xviii, Master Heatherstone knows more on that score than any one. **1859** MILL *Liberty* iv. 165 Other countries are not asked to..release any portion of their inhabitants from their own laws on the score of Mormonite opinions. **1883** F. M. CRAWFORD *Dr. Claudius* iv. 59 You have some right to flatter yourself on that score. **1888** BRYCE *Amer. Commw.* xlvi. II. 198 This state of things..disposes the men on one side to reject a proposal of the other side on the score, not of its demerits, but of the quarter it proceeds from. **1907** HODGES *Elem. Photogr.* 13 Much trouble on this score will be avoided.

†**13.** A list, enumeration; number as counted. Also ***by score***: (after a numeral) by tale, precisely so many. *Obs.*

c **1325** *Chron. Eng.* 253 (Ritson), That were sixti yer by score Er then Crist were ybore. **1577** tr. *Bullinger's Decades* (1592) 1052 So that hereby wee may iudge what great store the Lorde setteth by Infantes, and learne not to wype them out of the skore of Gods people. *a* **1586** SIDNEY *Ps.* xxx. iii, Thou would'st not sett me in their score, Whom death to his cold boosome drawes. **1596** SPENSER *F.Q.* VI. ix. 21 My lambes doe every yeare increase their score.

14. *Games.* The record or register of points made by both sides during the progress of a game or match; also the number of points made by a side or individual. ***to get the score***: to obtain the highest number of runs (in a cricket-match).

1742 HOYLE *Whist* 8 If a Revoke happens to be made, the adverse Party may take down 3 Points from the Scores, or add 3 Points to his own Score, or take 3 of his Adversary's Tricks; the Revoke takes place of any other Score of the Game. *Ibid.* 68 This Method of Play may be made use of at any Score of the Game, except at 4 and 9. **1778** —— *Games* 74 Score of the Game is the Number of Points set up, ten of which make a Game. **1825** T. HOOK *Sayings* Ser. II. *Sutherl.* (Colburn) 33 The care of the score [at billiards] was solely confided to the charge of the tall gentleman in the stockinet pantaloons. **1837** DICKENS *Pickw.* vii, The score of the Dingley Dellers was as blank as their faces. **1850** 'BAT' *Cricketer's Man.* 98 It was on this occasion..that Mr. Ward obtained the unprecedented score of 278 runs in one innings. **1861** HUGHES *Tom Brown at Oxf.* xxx, It was true that she liked keeping the score at cricket. **1862** *Lillywhite's Cricket Scores & Biogr.* I. 20 Hogsflesh (by the score) bowled in the second innings of Kent, but he is not inserted among the batsmen on the Hambledon side. *Ibid.* 225 John Small, sen. who got the score in the second innings of Hampshire. **1876** GEO. ELIOT *Dan. Der.* x, The belief in both naturally grew stronger as the shooting went on, for she promised to achieve one of the best scores. **1877** *Encycl. Brit.* VI. 578/2 (*Cricket*), The score was kept by notching each individual run on a stick. **1883** R. W. DIXON *Mano* II. viii. 95 The town in this game made the losing score.

b. Phr. ***to make a score off one's own bat***: see BAT *sb.*[2] 3 c.

1869 TROLLOPE *He knew*, etc. xii. (1878) 67 Do you know the meaning of making a score off your own bat, Martha?

c. *transf. Psychol.* A numerical record of the marks allotted to individuals in the measurement of abilities, capacity to learn, or in the assessment of personality.

1910 E. L. THORNDIKE in *Amer. Jrnl. Psychol.* XXI. 485 (*caption*) Scores reduced to single variables by allowance for examples wrong. **1929** F. N. FREEMAN in C. Murchison *Found. Exper. Psychol.* xviii. 722 These two measures..do not give the same learning curve, or the same curve when the scores are plotted by ages or grades. **1951** T. HUNT in J. S. Gray *Psychol. in Use* (rev. ed.) x. 421 This test underwent extensive validation by study of the relationship between the test scores of students and their subsequent performance in the medical schools. **1977** P. J. DUNHAM *Exper. Psychol.* ix. 240 A score of 10 representing a very anxious individual.

d. *fig.* The essential point or crux of a matter; the state of affairs, the (present) situation; how matters stand; the full facts (*about, on*, etc. someone or something); freq. in phrases, as ***to know the score***; ***to ask, realize***, etc., ***what the score is***; ***what's the score***; etc. *colloq.*

1938 D. NOWINSON in *Better English* Oct. 8/1 Dope..a guy who doesn't know the score. **1939** *Time* 16 Oct. 101/2 But when Holger begins to long for home and daughter, Anita, realizing what the score is, runs off to Paris to study. **1948** G. H. JOHNSTON *Death takes Small Bites* i. 16 Why don't you speak to some people who can really tell you the score? **1950** E. HEMINGWAY *Across River* xxxiii. 250 It leaves a core of certain un-killed characters who know what the score is. **1953** W. BURROUGHS *Junkie* xii. 121, I asked Ike what the score was on pushing in Mexico city. He said it was impossible. **1958** P. KEMP *No Colours or Crest* iv. 68 You were fully justified in breaking off the action when you did, in view of the score at the time. **1958** P. SCOTT *Mark of Warrior* II. 176 'What's the score about Havildar Baksh?' 'He's a prisoner.' **1959** N. MAILER *Advts. for Myself* iii. 234, I was out of fashion and that was the score; that was all the score. **1962** J. D. SALINGER *Franny & Zooey* 167 You've been around schools long enough to know the score. **1971** N. STACEY *Who Cares?* xvii. 284 At least he had the courage to tell me the score as far as I was concerned, so that I did not waste time yearning and hoping. **1977** A. SCHOLEFIELD *Venom* III. 86 You didn't ask the Boss what the score was, he told you.

15. *colloq.* [From the verb.] **a.** *lit.* in games: An act of 'scoring' or gaining a point or points. **b.** *fig.* A successful 'hit' in debate or argument.

1844 MARDON *Billiards* 94 For should he play it slowly and miss the score, he will..leave a certain canon for his opponent. **1873** BENNETT & 'CAVENDISH' *Billiards* 301 This position gives the striker such command over the balls that it is almost impossible not to leave a score. *Ibid.* 386 A miss should be given so as to leave a difficult score for the adversary. **1875** *Encycl. Brit.* III. 675/2 (*Billiards*), No score can be reckoned for a foul stroke. **1901** *Scotsman* 15 Mar. 7/4 A loud cheer signified that..this was a distinct score. **1901** S. PAGET *Mem. Sir J. Paget* II. 407 An admirable 'score' that he made at Harewood Place.

c. The money or goods obtained by means of a successful crime. *Criminals' slang.*

1914 in JACKSON & HELLYER *Vocab. Criminal Slang* 74. **1930** D. RUNYON in *Collier's* 13 Sept. 7/4 We have a business proposition for Big Butch. It means a nice score for him. **1936** [see HAVE *v.* 14 l]. **1956** H. KURNITZ *Invasion of Privacy* xi. 76 He's just a few months out of the jug and he hasn't turned a trick or made a score anywhere. **1977** *New Yorker* 22 Aug. 38/1 A million dollars from a computer crime is considered a respectable but not an extraordinary score.

d. The action or process of obtaining a supply of narcotic drugs; a supplier of narcotic drugs. Cf. SCORE *v.* 16 d. *slang* (orig. *U.S.*).

1951 [see HIT *sb.* 1 b]. **1953** W. BURROUGHS *Junkie* x. 97 'It's hard to find a score now,' I said. 'Most of them have gone away.' **1976** DEAKIN & WILLIS *Johnny go Home* ii. 47

The whole day passes..going from fix to score, to ripping off enough money to support the habit.

e. A prostitute's client (cf. SCORE *v.* 16 f); also in homosexual use. *slang.*

1961 J. RECHY in *Evergreen Rev.* July–Aug. 15, I could spot the scores easily—the men who paid other men sexmoney. **1969** *Jeremy* I. III. 23/1 The boy will then deliberately reveal and manipulate his erect penis, thereby exciting the score. **1972** G. BAXT *Burning Sappho* ix. 153, I ..got my hot tail out of there. I heard the score yelling. **1976** 'TREVANIAN' *Main* iv. 66 She won't be able to make a score until dark, if then.

III. A group of twenty.

[Presumably from the practice, in counting sheep or large herds of cattle, of counting orally from 1 to 20, and making a 'score' (sense 9) or notch on a stick, before proceeding to count the next twenty.]

16. a. A group or set of twenty. Primarily a sb., const. *of* (in OE. *gen. pl.*), but owing to ellipsis and loss of inflexions often serving (when preceded by *a*, or in uninflected pl. by a numeral) as a numeral adj. (Cf. *dozen*, *hundred*, *thousand*, etc.)

The combinations THREESCORE and FOURSCORE are common as mere archaistic synonyms for sixty and eighty; the similar combinations with other numerals are rarely used exc. when there is intentional division into groups of 20.

[*a* **1100** *Bury St. Edm. Rec.* in Napier *Contrib. OE. Lexicogr.* 56 Ðæt is..v scora [glossed *quinquies uiginti*] scæp ..& viii score [*octies uiginti*] æcere ȝesawen.] *c* **1290** *S. Eng. Leg.* I. 101/13 Folke..bi manie scor to-gadere. *a* **1300** *Cursor M.* 3209 Sex scor and seuen yeir liued sarra. *c* **1330** *Arth. & Merl.* 3099 (Kölbing) Wiþ him he brouȝt þritti score Wiȝt kniȝtes him bifore. **1340** HAMPOLE *Pr. Consc.* 3492 Bot yhit þar er ful many ma Of veniel syns, be many a score. **1362** LANGL. *P. Pl.* A. III. 118 Heo makeþ men misdo moni score tymes. *c* **1375** *Sc. Leg. Saints* xvii. (*Martha*) 52 Sewyne schore of fute & na ma. *a* **1400** *Morte Arth.* 2344 The taxe and the trebutte of tene schore wynteres. *c* **1400** *Destr. Troy* 2638 My fader was a philisofer, & of fele yeres, To the nowmber of nene skowre. *c* **1470** *Gol. & Gaw.* 483 Seuyne score of scheildis thai schew at ane sicht. **15..** *Scot. Field* 231 in *Chetham Soc. Misc.* II, There were killed of the Scottes moe than xij scower. **1583** BP. MIDDLETON *Injunct.* in *2nd Rep. Ritual Comm.* (1868) 426/2 Excepte there bee at the leaste, three for euery score communicantes that bee in the Parishe. **1596** SHAKS. *Tam. Shrew* I. ii. 111 Shee may perhaps call him halfe a score knaues, or so. **1611** —— *Cymb.* III. ii. 69 How many score of Miles may we well rid Twixt houre, and houre? **1645** *Shetland Witch Trial* in Hibbert *Descr. Shetl. Isl.* (1822) 600 At your returne they continuit with you, and conversit *ut supra*, als far back agane as scoir and threttein. *a* **1649** WINTHROP *New Eng.* (1825) I. 286 They chose divers scores men, who [etc.]. **1696** *Lond. Gaz.* No. 3190/4, 41 stout Cambridgeshire Wethers, worth about 14l. a Score. **1734** tr. *Rollin's Anc. Hist.* (1827) I. 340 Six score thousand. *a* **1742** SOMERVILLE *Yeom. Kent* 82 Neighbours around, and cousins went By scores, to pay their compliment. **1768** STERNE *Sent. Journ.* (1778) I. 69 (*In the Street*), I form'd a score different plans. **1775** C. JOHNSTON *Pilgrim* 273 He taught him to..bend his body into half a score antic postures. **1800** LD. KEITH in *Paget Papers* (1896) I. 223 The inhabitants of Genoa Die by Scores of hunger. **1810** CRABBE *Borough* v, Till he had box'd up twelve score pounds at least. **1842** MACAULAY *Lays, Lake Regillus* xxviii, And still stood all who saw them fall While men might count a score. **1848** THACKERAY *Van. Fair* xxxiv, There were a score of generals now round Becky's chair. **1883** STEVENSON *Treas. Isl.* vii, I wished a round score of men.

b. with ellipsis of *years* (referring to age). Now *rare* exc. in THREESCORE and FOURSCORE.

13.. *Seuyn Sag.* (W.) 1019 He thoughte wel, at a score, He sscholde passi him before. **1900** H. SUTCLIFFE *Shameless Wayne* viii. (1905) 101 He died at two-score.

17. A weight of twenty or twenty-one pounds, esp. used in weighing pigs or oxen.

c **1460** *Towneley Myst.* xiii. 631 As a shepe of sevyn skore he weyd in my fyst. **1766** *Museum Rust.* I. 475 To kill several hogs in a season, which shall weigh from eight to ten score. **1825** COBBETT *Rural Rides* 274 The thousands of scores of bacon and thousands of bushels of bread that have been eaten from the long oak table. **1829** *Glover's Hist. Derby* I. 217 At fifteen months old, they weigh about 28 score. **1858** *Ulster Jrnl. Archæol.* VI. 361 The meal came down to three thirteens the score. **1885** W. WESTALL *Old Factory* xix. 134, I'll send them a score of meal and half a score of flour and some milk.

†**18.** A distance of twenty paces. *Obs.*

1545 ASCHAM *Toxoph.* II. (Arb.) 157 For I should se one streame wyth in a score on me. **1577–87** HOLINSHED *Chron.* III. 1142/1 The trees were pulled up by the roots and cast twelve score off. **1588** SIR W. WYNTER in *Defeat Sp. Armada* (Navy Rec. Soc.) II. 10 My fortune was to make choice to charge their starboard wing without shooting of any ordnance until we came within six score of them. **1591** LYLY *Entert. Elvetham* Proeme, Wks. 1902 I. 432 Other such buildings..fourteene score off from the house on a hill side. **1598** SHAKS. *Merry W.* III. ii. 34 As easie, as a Canon will shoot point-blanke twelue score. **1622** DRAYTON *Poly-olb.* xxvi. 331 At Markes full fortie score they vs'd to Prick and Roue. **1646** ELDRED *Gunners Glasse* 71 Foure Demi-Culverings to the moule Rod or Pole, distant 53 score. **1672** H. MORE *Brief Reply* Pref. *a* 4 b, Wherein the Authors fancy ..leaping over all boundaries of Church-Authority,..runs on at eleven-score, as if he were upon a warm scent, giving chase to some of his Platonical Idea's [*sic*].

19. *Coal mining.* (See quot. 1851.)

1754 T. GARDNER *Dunwich* 216 This Port [Southwold] is of singular note in merchandizing Corn and Coals, where twenty-one is deemed a Score. **1789** BRAND *Hist. Newcastle* II. 681 The wages of hewers 2s. 8d. for hewing every score or twenty corves of coals. **1812** HODGSON in Raine *Mem.* (1857) I. 98 Persons who..wrought 624 scores of coal, equal to 1300 Newcastle chaldrons. **1851** GREENWELL *Coal-trade Terms, Northumb. & Durh.* 46 *Score*, a standard number of tubs or corves of coals at each colliery, upon which the hewers' and putters' prices for working are paid. It varies, in different localities, from 20 to 26 tubs.

20. (See quot.) ? *Obs.*

1854 *Househ. Words* IX. 88 Strips [of straw plait] are.. sold in scores, or pieces twenty yards long.

21. *Criminals' slang.* **a.** Twenty dollars; a twenty-dollar bill. *U.S.* **b.** Twenty pounds sterling (esp. in banknotes).

1929 G. L. HOSTETTER *It's a Racket!* 237 *Score*, twenty dollar bill, or units thereof—hundred, two hundred. **1933** G. INGRAM *Stir* xiv. 231, 'I got about £10 out of the first, then £2 and then another "score".' 'That makes £32.' **1941** *Coast to Coast 1941* 225 They only owe me a couple of quid since Christmas now. I was holdin' a score but I dropped most of it. **1958** F. NORMAN *Bang to Rights* III. 152 When they turned me over I had about a score on me. **1979** K. BONFIGLIOLI *After you with Pistol* vii. 39 You'll have to give me a score to buy an old throwaway shooter.

IV. 22. *attrib.* and *Comb.*, as ***score-keeping***; (sense 15 d) ***score dough*** (DOUGH *sb.* 2 b), ***money***; **score-bid** *Contract Bridge*, a bid by a player whose side has a part-score, sufficient to give his side game; **score-board,** (*a*) a blackboard in a public house, on which debts are chalked up; (*b*) in *Cricket*, a large board erected so as to be seen by the onlookers, on which the score of the game is kept; also *gen.*, a master board displaying the score of any contest; also *fig.* and *attrib.*; **score-book,** a book for preserving the scores of games; a scoring-book; **score-box** *Cricket*, a room or hut in which the official scorers work and (usu.) the telegraph is operated; **score-card,** (*a*) a printed card with a blank form on which spectators may enter the score in a game of cricket or baseball; also in extended uses, esp. a card issued to a competitor before a contest, on which his score (or that of his opponent) is to be recorded, or one held by a referee or judge for the same purpose; (*b*) *U.S.*, 'in exhibitions of poultry, a rating card' (*Funk's Stand. Dict.* 1895); (*c*) see quot. 1909; (*d*) *U.S. slang.*, a menu; **score draw,** a non-goalless draw (DRAW *sb.* 5) counting for three points on a football-pool coupon; **score-game** *Golf*, a game in which the player's object is to obtain the highest score possible (opposed to *match game*); so **score-play; scoreline,** (a line, or part of one, in a newspaper, etc., giving) the intermediate or final score in a sports contest between two persons or team; **score-paper** = *score-sheet*; **score-reading,** the action or process of reading a musical score; hence ***score-reader***; **score-sheet** (see quot. 1895); also *transf.* and *fig.*, esp. in phrases, as ***to add one's name to the score-sheet***, to score a goal (in Association Football and the like).

1928 M. C. WORK *Contract Bridge* (ed. 2) IV. 76 If my side has a contract score of 60, I must put a construction on my partner's minor two bid different from the construction put upon such a bid at no score... '*Score-bids' are exceptions to the general rules. **1826** HOR. SMITH *Tor Hill* (1838) I. 90 A species of desk on which was lying a black *score-board and a lump of chalk. **1884** *Harper's Mag.* Jan. 299/1 The club has its own score-board. **1904** *Daily Chron.* 26 July 7/1 The score-board showed Somerset 147 up for the loss of four wickets. **1936** F. D. ROOSEVELT in *N.Y. Herald Tribune* 2 Oct. 10/2 From where I stand it looks as if the game was pretty well in the bag... It's just plain scoreboard arithmetic... Now, when the present management of your team took charge in 1933 the national scoreboard looked pretty bad. **1963** J. JOESTEN *They call it Intelligence* I. v. 51 What kind of record has the CIA?..The scoreboard: 'Soviet satellites—Excellent'...'Missiles—Good.' **1977** *Rolling Stone* 13 Jan. 43/3 There were shouts of delight as Texas lit up in red on one of the network's scoreboards, but it was still a close race. **1977** J. LAKER *One-Day Cricket* 72 A few narrow escapes kept the scoreboard officials busy. **1851** J. PYCROFT *Cricket Field* iv. 69 'Seventy-two runs,' said Fennex, and the *score-book attests his accuracy, 'was Beldham's first and only innings.' **1862** *Lillywhite's Cricket Scores & Biogr.* I. 191 In Britcher's printed score-book, Mr. J. Tufton is..put down as bowled merely. **1902** W. J. FORD *Hist. Camb. Univ. C.C.* Pref. 9 The C.U.C.C. has but..two scorebooks. **1921** P. F. WARNER *My Cricketing Life* vi. 111 Sixteen centuries stand to his credit in the Middlesex score-book. **1977** J. LAKER *One-Day Cricket* 113 Gone are the days of the old green bound Club scorebook. **1890** in W. A. Bettesworth *Walkers of Southgate* (1900) xvi. 335 Pressmen were expected to..keep running to the *score-box to ask for any information they required. **1934** W. J. LEWIS *Lang. Cricket* 226 Underneath (the score-box was) a room for the printers. **1877** C. BOX *Eng. Game of Cricket* xxvi. 459 **Score card*, a printed card, with the names of the players and the results of each person's innings. **1903** *Daily Chron.* 4 July 5/7 For without stop-watches, score-cards, and constant figuring, one had no idea where the contestants were. **1905** *McClure's Mag.* June 125/2 The football score-card privilege is 'sold to a New York expert'. **1909** EASTWOOD *Rep. to L.G.B. on Amer. Methods Milk Supply* 69. Most of the cities which I visited have adopted the score card system of inspection. When examining a place where milk is..sold, the inspector fills up a card containing a printed list of the details on which he is required to report. For each detail a maximum score of a certain number of points is assigned. **1918** E. S. FARROW *Dict. Mil. Terms* 538 *Score cards*, pasteboard cards issued to competitors at competitions, giving the number of the target of each competitor firing,.. and containing a blank space for the record of the shots fired. **1930** J. DOS PASSOS *42nd Parallel* 160 He handed her the menu. 'Here's the scorecard.' **1958** *People* 4 May 19/7 How much is a quarter of a point worth on a fight referee's score-card? **1976** *Cumberland & Westmorland Herald* 4 Dec. 13/6 The other [*sc.* dart-players'] score cards were not in at the time of writing. **1978** *Cornish Guardian* 27 Apr. 23/5 (Advt.), When you call in at our showrooms and test drive the Austin Morris range, we'll provide a detailed scorecard. First test our cars then try to match them against the competition. **1942** BERREY & VAN DEN BARK *Amer. Thes. Slang* §510/1 *Connection* or **score dough*, the price of a 'bindle' of narcotics. **1970** *Sporting Life* 2 Nov. 12 Percentage is based on three points for a correct *score draw and two for a correct no-score match against the total number of points possible. **1977** *Daily Mirror* 15 Mar. 27/1 Plan 6..guarantees a line of at least seven score draws if any eight of your selections result as score draws. **1905** *Daily Chron.* 19 Aug. 9/7 The amateurs like match play best because they do better in it than they do at the *score game. *Ibid.* 20 Dec. 3/4 Many witty things he has to say, as, for instance, on *score-keeping. **1969** B. JAMES *England v Scotland* iii. 64 The *score line was a far from accurate guide to the run of play. **1971** *Rand Daily Mail* 27 Mar. 23/6 Had Arcadia grabbed their chances the scoreline could have been reversed. **1977** *Sunday Times* 9 Jan. 30/6 It was only when he..scored three times, that the scoreline became slightly more respectable. **1953** W. BURROUGHS *Junkie* vi. 61 Nick had just arrived at my apartment with some *score money when I was called to the hall phone by the buzzer. **1847** W. DENISON *Cricketer's Comp.* p. xv, [Such runs] ought in fairness not to be placed on the *score-paper as single byes. **1862** *Lillywhite's Cricket Scores & Biogr.* I. 315 Scorers, or those who copied the score papers into the book, must have been very careless. **1902** *Westm. Gaz.* 2 Jan. 2/1 In *score play..the same argument does not apply. **1946** *Penguin Music Mag.* Dec. 75 Music does not exist until it is *performed*, whatever our armchair *score-readers may say to the contrary. **1961** J. A. MACGILLIVRAY in A. Baines *Musical Instruments through Ages* 247 Music is written for the player, not for the score-reader. **1909** *Cent. Dict.* Suppl. II. 1183/2 *Score-reading. **1931** G. JACOB *Orchestral Technique* i. 4 To facilitate score-reading we give below the English, Italian, French, and German names for the instruments. **1977** *Listener* 23 June 822/2 Score-reading involves two quite different activities. First, you must learn to read music... The second element..is the ability to hear in imagination, in the mind's ear. **1859** in W. A. Bettesworth *Walkers of Southgate* (1900) v. 54 (*plate*) 'Bell's Life in London' *Score Sheets, &c. &c., may be had at the Tent. **1895** *Funk's Stand. Dict.*, *Score-sheet*, a sheet ruled or designed for scoring; specifically, in baseball and cricket, a sheet ruled for recording all the features of the game. **1944** W. W. ELTON et al. *Guide Naval Aviation* iv. 73 Dive bombers caused much of the Jap grief at Midway, where the score sheet revealed four Jap carriers sunk and other craft damaged and sunk. **1976** *Cumberland & Westmorland Herald* 4 Dec. 12/6 Ullswater managed to keep the score sheet blank up to half-time. **1976** *Norwich Mercury* 10 Dec. 8/3 They..made sure of the points when Stew Reynolds added his name to the scoresheet.

score (skɔə(r)), *v.* Also 5–7 skore, 6 scoore, 6–7 scoure, 7 scoar. [a. ON. *skora* to make an incision, to count by tallies, f. *skor*: see SCORE *sb.* The Eng. development of senses has been largely influenced by the sb., and in some senses the vb. may be regarded as an Eng. formation on this.]

I. To cut, mark with incisions.

1. a. *trans.* To cut superficially; to make scores or cuts in; to mark with incisions, notches, or abrasions of the skin. Also, † *to score away*, to remove by cutting.

c **1400** *Lanfranc's Cirurg.* 231 If þou desirist to cure glandulas & scrophulas..kutte þe skyn endelongis þe necke, ..& þane score [Latin *discarnare*] him & drawe him out al hool with þe cloop. *c* **1440** *Pallad. on Husb.* VI. 119 Have a thing therfore Made like a swerde this folk [*sc.* the testicles] away to score. **1500–20** DUNBAR *Poems* lxxii. 55 His feit with stanis war rewin and scorde. *a* **1529** SKELTON *Agst. Garnesche* iv. 34 Thow wolde haue scoryd hys habarion. **1570** LEVINS *Manip.* 174/27 To score, *crenare, incidere.* **1622** FLETCHER *Prophetess* IV. v, Scoring a man ore the cox-comb is but a scratch with you. **1748** *Anson's Voy.* II. i. 124 She with her teeth scored his skull in notches in many places. **1794** J. CLARK *Agric. Heref.* 44 When the trees are unkindly 'hide-bound', they are 'scored' by cutting the bark with the point of a knife. **1807** J. BARLOW *Columb.* v. 615 Here stood stern Putnam, scored with ancient scars. **1824** W. IRVING *T. Trav.* (1850) 380 He..found most of the tall trees..more or less scored by the axe. **1845** DARWIN *Voy. Nat.* v. (1879) 84 The elephant..deeply scores with its tusks the trunk of the tree. **1851** MAYNE REID *Scalp Hunt.* x. 75 We see the primitive plough of the forking tree-branch, scarcely scoring the soil. **1852** M. ARNOLD *Tristram & Iseult* III. 172 A briar in that tangled wilderness Had scor'd her white right hand. **1872** BAKER *Nile Trib.* xi. 186 Young infants are scored with a razor. **1891** *Century Dict.*, *Score*, to make a long shallow cut in (cardboard or very thick paper), so that the card or paper can be bent without breaking, as for book-covers or folded cards. **1896** A. E. HOUSMAN *Shropshire Lad* lxii, Out of a stem that scored the hand I wrung it in a weary land.

b. *spec.* in *Cookery.* To make long parallel cuts upon (meat, etc.).

c **1460** *Towneley Myst.* xii. 236 A calf lyuer skorde with the veryose. **1747** MRS. GLASSE *Cookery* ix. 87 To Roast a Cod's Head. Wash it very clean and score it with a Knife. **1771** MRS. HAYWOOD *New Present* 95 The skin [of a loin of pork] must then be scored cross-wise. **1844** H. STEPHENS *Bk. Farm* II. 168 Some butchers in the north country score the fat of the closing of the hind quarter. **1853** SOYER *Pantropheon* 138 Having previously scored the back of the animal [to be baked].

c. To mark by cuts of a whip. Also *transf.* and *absol.*

1606 SHAKS. *Ant. & Cl.* IV. vii. 12 Let vs score their backes. **1785** BURKE *Sp. Nabob of Arcot's Debts* Wks. IV. 286 The remaining miserable last cultivator, who grows to the soil, after having his back scored by the farmer, has it again flayed by the whip of the assignee. *c* **1806** SIR R. WILSON *Cape of Good Hope* in *Life* (1862) I. 362 It is not pretended ..that the lash never scores at the caprice of ill temper.

†**d.** Sc. ***to score aboon the breath***: to gash the forehead of (a suspected witch) with a knife or a rusty nail, in order to render her incapable of mischief. *Obs.*

1787 W. TAYLOR *Poems* 93 (Jam.) A witty wife did than advise Rob to gang to Maukin Wise, An' score her over, ance or twice, Aboon the breath. **1807** HOGG *Mountain Bard* Note xi, He seized her forcibly, and cut the shape of the cross on her forehead. This they call *scoring aboon the breath.*

e. *Geol.* To mark with scratches or furrows; said esp. with reference to glacial action.

1862 TYNDALL *Mountaineer*. iii. 19 All around the rocks are carved, and fluted, and polished, and scored. **1878** HUXLEY *Physiogr.* 161 These stones, pressed by the weight of ice above, scratch and score the rocky bed in the direction of the ice-flow. **1879** LE CONTE *Elem. Geol.* I. ii. 66 If the water be not sufficiently deep, they ground, and being swayed by waves and tides they [*sc.* icebergs] chafe and score the bottom in a somewhat irregular manner.

†**2.** To fracture, wreck (a ship). *Obs.*

1504 in *Charters*, etc. *Edinb.* (1871) 188 The schip callit the Litill Martin latlie skorit or brokin in tha partis. **1513** DOUGLAS *Æneis* v. iv. 91 Hir foirschip hang, and sum deill scorit throwout [orig. *inlisaque prora pependit*]. **1513** *Acc. Ld. High Treas. Scot.* IV. 482 Item, for the mendyng of the said boit, scho beand skorit with greit artailyery passand to the schippis. **1546** [see SCORING *vbl. sb.* 1].

3. To produce (marks, figures, etc.) by cutting. Also (with allusion to sense 10), to record or express by cuts or notches.

1590 SPENSER *F.Q.* I. i. 2 And on his brest a bloodie crosse he bore,..Upon his shield the like was also scor'd. **1592** SHAKS. *Com. Err.* I. ii. 65 She will scoure your fault vpon my pate. **1605** B. JONSON *Volpone* III. ii, Draw your iust sword, And score your vengeance, on my front, and face. **1616** R. C. *Times' Whistle* (1871) 81 My pen shall point thee out, And thy lewde actes vpon thy forehead score. **1824** W. IRVING *T. Trav.* (1850) 380 On the bark of the tree was scored the name of Deacon Peabody. **1869** FROUDE *Short Stud.* Ser. II. (1871) 325 If we except the Athenians and Jews, no people so few in number have scored so deep a mark in the world's history as you [Scots] have done. **1889** —— *Two Chiefs of Dunboy* xxvii. 415 They shall..score such marks on you as the quarter-master leaves on the slaves that you hire to fight your battles.

4. *Naut.* To make a 'score' or groove in; to fix by means of a 'score'.

1779 BARNARD in *Phil. Trans.* LXX. 108 Pl. 3, E. Pillars in hold about which every half Beam was scored. **1845** *Encycl. Metrop.* VIII. 298/1 These brass wheels..are fixed over the centre of each block that is to be scored. **1869** SIR E. REED *Shipbuild.* ii. 27 This bulb-iron is scored down between the floors sufficiently deep to lay hold of the Keelson-pieces with a double row of rivets.

5. *N. Amer.* [? fig. use of 1 c.] To rate, scold severely. Now esp. used in newspaper headlines.

1812 J. K. PAULDING *John Bull & Brother Jonathan* xiv. 102 She..fell upon Beau Napperty, and scored him at such a rate, that if poor Beau had heard her, he would have been mad enough I warrant you. **1891** LOUNSBURY *Studies Chaucer* III. vii. 223 Even poor Lipscomb..was soundly scored for his grossness and vulgarity. **1896** *Nation* LXIII. 37/2 He does not hesitate to score the Germans for their obstinate adherence to their own language and manners. **1912** J. SANDILANDS *Western Canad. Dict. & Phrase-Bk.* s.v. *Scored*, An Opposition newspaper came out with the heading 'Government Legislation Scored'. **1930** *Publishers' Weekly* 8 Mar. 1331/2 (*heading*) Smoot's secret session scored. **1967** *N.Y. Times* (Internat. ed.) 11–12 Feb. 3/3 (*heading*) Professor scores Reagan.

II. 6. a. To mark with a line or lines.

1398 TREVISA *Barth. De P.R.* XVI. vii. (1495) 555 Thouh syluer be white, yet it makyth blacke lynes and strakes in the body that it is scoryd therwyth or rulyd therwyth. **1530** PALSGR. 706/2 Whan your tymber is well scored, you can never fayle to sawe it right. **1602** *2nd Pt. Return fr. Parnassus* III. iii. 1326 Then with his nayle score the margent as though there were some notable conceit. **1632** MARMION *Holland's Leaguer* I. v, No name or title but on posts and trenchers, And doors scored with a coal instead of chalk. **1672** *Essex Papers* (1890) 18, I desire his Maj[tie] would bee pleasd to review y[e] sevrall clauses w[ch] for his greater ease I have scored with a pen in the severall copys here transmitted. **1784** W. KING *Cook's 3rd Voy.* v. vii. III. 151 They have likewise a method of scoring them [*sc.* gourds] with a heated instrument. **1833** LOUDON *Encycl. Archit.* §185 Covered with cement, scored (lined) in imitation of stone, and white-washed. **1848** THACKERAY *Van. Fair* l, Passages had been scored in his favourite books. **1869** PARKMAN *Discov. Gt. West* xiii. (1875) 154 The plains were scored with their pathways. **1872** BLACK *Adv. Phaeton* ii. 20 Fields and meadows, scored with hedges. **1878** BOSW. SMITH *Carthage* 384 A votive tablet covered with Punic characters and scored with rude figures of a triangle and an uplifted hand. **1881** FROUDE *Short Stud.* (1883) IV. II. 1. 163 We had found ..a copy of the once famous Tract 90..scored over with pencil marks.

b. *absol.* To make marks.

1698 *Phil. Trans.* XX. 272 Upon Torrefaction it was all become a Yellow Ochre, and would score like it.

†**c.** To mark *out* (a path, a boundary, etc.).

1608 DAY *Hum. out of Breath* II. i, Giue me money, ile be thy snaile and score out a siluer path to his confusion. **1610** G. FLETCHER *Christ's Tri.* IV. 20 Acquieting the soules that newe before Their way to heav'n through their owne blood did skore. **1633** G. HERBERT *Priest to Temple* xiii, These Two Rules..excellently score out the way, and fully, and exactly contain..what course is to be taken. **1638** G. SANDYS *Paraphr. Job* 55 Hast thou..Scor'd out the bounded Suns obliquer wayes? **1652** NEEDHAM tr. *Selden's Dominium Maris* Advt., The limits thereof, being a fluent element, could not bee scored out, or certainly determined. **1712** J. JAMES tr. *Le Blond's Gardening* 84 Never to take up the Stakes till the Track be scored out very plain upon the Ground.

†**d.** *to score out*: to sketch in outline, adumbrate. *Obs.*

1615 CROOKE *Body of Man* 265 Almost in the same instant the first threds of the spermaticall partes are together and at once skored or shaddowed out with rude lines.

7. To draw a line through (writing, etc.) in order to cancel. Often with *out*.

1687 JOHNSTON in *Magd. Coll. & Jas. II* (O.H.S.) 154 In the..Paper I found it scored out. *a* **1722** FOUNTAINHALL *Decis.* (1759) I. 10 Where the penalty in a bond was left blank, and the said blank scored, the Lords refused to modify any expences. **1832** HT. MARTINEAU *Ireland* iii. 42 Scoring the lease from corner to corner, with his newly-mended pen. **1872** BLACKIE *Lays Highl.* 184 His full Mercy's gracious store With liberal dash thy guilt shall score And blot the sentence. **1879** *Daily Tel.* 29 May, The passage in the will containing the bequest of the annuity to the noble Lord and his Lady was scored out.

†**8.** *trans.* To stripe, braid. *Obs. rare.*

1604 T. M. *Black Bk.* D 3 b, A payre of Veluet slops, scored thicke with Lace.

9. *Mus.* **a.** To write down in score. **b.** To compose or arrange for orchestral performance.

1839 HOOD *Storm at Hastings* xvi, Handel would make the gusty organs blow Grandly, and a rich storm in music score us! **1850** W. IRVING *Goldsmith* xxxiv. 326 He pretended to score down an air as the poet played it. **1871** R. BROWNING *Prince Hohenstiel-Schwangau* 1813 Who scores a septett true for strings and wind Mulcted must be. **1884** *American* VIII. 94 Mr. Gilchrist skilfully scored the cantata for full orchestra. **1885** *Manchester Exam.* 9 Jan. 5/6 The Adagio is scored with great beauty, the treatment of the wood instruments and horns being especially effective.

c. To write the score for (a film). Cf. SCORE *sb.* 6 c.

1934 WEBSTER, *Score*,..to add music to a picture that already has sound effects. **1967** H. HARRISON *Technicolor Time Machine* (1968) xv. 156 'Is it true you scored a couple of films?' 'It is true I did the music for a ragged piece of class-X crap.' **1969** *Daily Progress* (Charlottesville, Va.) 15 May 1-C/7 Poet-singer-composer Rod McKuen has scored three movies.

III. To record by scores.

10. a. To record (debts) by means of notches on a tally; hence to write down as a debt. Also with *up*.

c **1386** CHAUCER *Shipman's T.* 416 And, if so be I faille, I am your wyf; score it vp-on my taille, And I shal paye, as soone as euer I may. *c* **1460** *Bk. Curtasye* 407 in *Babees Bk.*, Þer-fore on his ȝerde skore shalle he Alle messys in halle þat seruet be. **1530** PALSGR. 706/2, I score, I marke upon a tayle or score, *je marque*. Score it, I pray you, for forgettyng. **1596** SHAKS. *1 Hen. IV*, II. iv. 29 Score a Pint of Bastard in the Halfe Moone. **1600** ROWLANDS *Lett. Humours Blood* viii. 14 He..scores his dyet on the Vitlers post. **1631** HEYWOOD *Fair Maid of West* II. 15 When I brought them a reckoning, they would have had me to have scor'd it up. **1669** ETHEREDGE *Love in Tub* I. ii, The Chandler refus'd to score a quart of Scurvy-grass. **1719** D'URFEY *Pills* IV. 184 Let's ..keep drinking and scoring brisk Claret. **1749** FIELDING *Tom Jones* VIII. xii, He answered: 'That signifies nothing: Score it behind the door'. **1840** DICKENS *Barn. Rudge* lxxxii, Joe provided him with a slate, upon which the old man regularly scored up vast accounts. **1860** SALA *Badd. Peerage* iv, Pleading some ridiculous three-and-ninepence scored against me on the slate.

fig. **1600** HOLLAND *Livy* xxx. 760 And certes you also.. may skore up this for none of the least. *c* **1600** SHAKS. *Sonn.* cxxii, Nor need I tallies thy dear love to score. **1647** N. BACON *Disc. Gov. Eng.* I. lxiv. (1739) 133 The Subject must be contented rather to score it up against the future, than require present pay. **1852** MRS. STOWE *Uncle Tom's C.* xxxvi, I won't deal with you now,..I'll score it against ye, and some time I'll have my pay out o' yer old black hide. **1883** TYNDALL in *Contemp. Rev.* XLIV. 39 His [Rumford's] inference from his experiments was scored in favour of those philosophers who held that heat is a form of motion.

†**b.** *to score* (something) *on* a person or thing: to lay to the charge of, to impute to. *Obs.*

1645 MILTON *Colasterion* 3 Bearing us in hand as if hee knew both Greek and Ebrew, and is not able to spell it; which had hee been, it had bin either writt'n as it ought, or scor'd upon the Printer. *a* **1661** FULLER *Worthies, Surrey* (1662) III. 96 This was the true Cause of his Execution, though in our Chronicles all is scored on his complying in a Plot.

†**11. a.** *intr.* To run up a score; to obtain drink, goods, etc. on credit. *Obs.*

1594 NASHE *Unfort. Trav.* K 1 b, Pitch and pay, they will pray all day: score & borrow, they will wish him much sorrow. **1631** HEYWOOD *Fair Maid of West* I. 12 It is the commonest thing that can bee for these Captaines to score and to score, but when the scores are to be paid, *Non est inventus*. **16..** CLEVELAND *May Day* xiv. Wks. (1687) 253 Then lose the Flood-gates George, we'll pay or score. **1727** *Philip Quarll* 83 Being as welcome to score, as with ready Money. **1779** *Mirror* No. 23 ¶ 3 Which title [*sc.* of an honest fellow] he continued to enjoy..while he had credit to score for his reckoning.

b. *trans.* To add (an item) to one's score; to incur (a debt). In quot. *fig.*

1681 DRYDEN *Sp. Fryar* I. i. 3 It seems the holy Stallion durst not score Another Sin before he left the world.

12. a. *trans.* To enter as a debtor. Also with *up*.

1592 GREENE *Upst. Courtier* G j, If any chaunce to go on the skore, you skore him when he is a sleepe, and set vp a grote a daye more than he hath. **1596** NASHE *Saffron Walden* L 4 b, He stood noted or scoard for it in their bookes manie a faire day after. **1639** FULLER *Holy War* v. ix. (1640) 244 By dying for the Crosse [they did] crosse the score of their own sinnes and score up God for their debtour. **1801** HUNTINGTON *God Guardian of Poor* 64 Thus I scored up my blessed Master, who, in his own time, always discharged my debts with honour. **1809** MALKIN *Gil Blas* x. x. ¶ 17 You may earn your board easily enough, by scoring up the customers, and keeping my ledger.

†**b.** *to score up*: to placard as an offender.

1581 PETTIE tr. *Guazzo's Civ. Conv.* I. (1586) 38 b, I thinke good they [flatterers] were scored up among the intollerable. **1596** SHAKS. *Tam. Shr.* Induct. ii. 25 If she say I am not xiiii. d. on the score for sheere Ale, score me vp for the lyingst knaue in Christendome.

13. a. To record the number of (anything) by notches or marks; to keep an account of; to count and set down the number of (e.g. sheep). Also with *up*.

a **1400** *Quatrefoil of Love* in *Furnivall Miscell.* 128 Oure werkes are wretyn and scorde, In a role of recorde. **1571** CAMPION *Hist. Irel.* II. ix. (1633) 119 Wherein the age to come may skore him among the auncient Princes. **1609** ROWLANDS *Whole Crew* 7 When I was Maid, with Chalke behind our doore, Some fiue and forty Suitors I did score. **1621** T. WILLIAMSON tr. *Goulart's Wise Vieillard* 40, I haue not taken vpon mee to score vp all the accidents and occasions to further old age. **1631** A. WILSON *Swisser* III. ii, Wee will score vp Summs Of our embraces. **1633** G. HERBERT *Temple, Good Friday* iii, Or shall each leaf, Which falls in Autumne, score a grief? **1656** COWLEY *Anacreontics* vi. Poems 34 An hundred Loves at Athens score, At Corinth write an hundred more. **1681** DRYDEN *Sp. Fryar* I. i. 6 We were in hast; and cou'd not stay To score the men we kill'd: But there they lye. **1681** —— *Abs. & Achit.* I. 542 Such were the tools; but a whole Hydra more Remains of sprouting heads too long to score.

b. *Biol.* and *Med.* To examine (experimentally treated cells, bacterial colonies, or the like), making a record of the number showing some character.

1964 *Virol.* XXIII. 118/1 Subconfluent monolayers were infected with 0·5 ml of virus and transferred the following day at an inoculation density of 100 and 500 cells per plate. Transformed colonies were scored 14 days later. **1971** *Nature* 20 Aug. 559/1 After 2–3 weeks the plates were fixed, stained and the colonies scored.

14. a. In a game or contest: To set down in the score: often with *complementary obj.* Chiefly in *passive*.

1742 HOYLE *Whist* i. 15 If your Game is scored 1, 2, or 3, you must play the Reverse. **17..** in *Lillywhite's Cricket Scores & Biogr.* (1862) I. Pref. 10 Y[e] Umpires..in case of hindrance may order a Notch to be Scored. **1862** *Lillywhite's Cricket Scores & Biogr.* I. 22 Leg-before-wicket was also introduced about this time [1775], but at first simply scored down as bowled. *Ibid.* 191 [Aug. 12–15, 1795] In this match 'leg-before-wicket' is found scored for the first time. **1892** *Hurlingham Club Rules* 241 If a bird that has been shot at perches or settles on the top of the fence,..it is to be scored a lost bird.

b. *absol.* or *intr.* To record the points in a game or contest, to act as scorer.

1846 W. DENISON *Sk. Players* 11 Mr. Whittaker.. accompanied Mr. Mynn, and scored for him. **1862** *Lillywhite's Cricket Scores & Biogr.* I. 244 No one was bowled out on the England side, therefore (owing to the imperfect way of scoring at this period [1798]) it is impossible to say who got the wickets. **1891** W. G. GRACE in *Outdoor Games* 14 The great thing in keeping score, after keeping it correctly, is to score neatly.

15. a. *trans.* Of a player or competitor: To add (so many points) to one's score. Also said of an incident in the game: To count for (so many points) in a player's score. Phr. ***to score a miss***: see MISS *sb.*[1] 7 b.

1742 HOYLE *Whist* 8, A and B are to score 10 Points. **1782** BURNBY in *Kentish Gaz.* 20–3 Nov., Now the Batsman.. Sends the Ball Over all Scores six Notches for the feat. **1833** NYREN *Yng. Cricketer's Tutor* 81 When a batter..was scoring more runs than pleased our general, he would put Mann in to give him eight or twelve balls. **1850** 'BAT' *Cricketer's Man.* 100 Pilch scored sixty-one. **1856** 'CAPT. CRAWLEY' *Billiards* (1859) 33 My first stroke scored three. **1862** 'CAVENDISH' *Whist* (1879) 2 To score honours is not sufficient; they must be called at the end of the hand. **1869** TROLLOPE *He knew*, etc. xxii. (1878) 125 On the present occasion a great many sixpenny points [at whist] were scored. **1885** *Manchester Exam.* 13 July 5/5 Two batsmen of the Harrow eleven..scored respectively 100 and 135. **1897** *Encycl. Sport* I. 264/2 (Curling) *Souter*, to score a love game; not to allow the opponents to score. **1898** *Ibid.* II. 262/2 (Ringoal) If the ring hit the goal-post and glance off it through the goal, it shall score a point to the server.

b. *intr.* To make points in a game or contest: said of a player or competitor; also, of a card or an incident in the game.

1844 MARDON *Billiards* 115 But, should the striker not score, it is at the option of the opponent to break them or not. *Ibid.* 116 If either of the balls lodge on a cushion, it is off the table; and should a canon or hazard be made, it does not score. **1853** LYTTON *My Novel* IX. xi, It might score well in the game. **1862** *Lillywhite's Cricket Scores & Biogr.* I. 440 William Beldham was now fifty-five years of age, and still continued to score largely. **1873** BENNETT & 'CAVENDISH' *Billiards* 417 Sometimes it is advisable to combine safety with an attempt to score. **1875** *Encycl. Brit.* III. 676/1 The player whose ball is in hand cannot score, unless he play his ball out of baulk before striking the object-ball. **1889** *Field* 12 Jan. 47/3 Spit drew out three lengths, scored thrice, and after a few exchanges with Gradation, picked puss up.

c. To count or be reckoned in a score.

1885 *Field* 19 Dec. 847/1 The hazard scores to the striker.

d. *trans. Baseball.* To cause (a team-mate) to score.

1912 C. MATHEWSON *Pitching in Pinch* v. 109 Schlei made a base hit..and scored both men. **1976** *Billings* (Montana) *Gaz.* 17 June 2-H/4 Mark Belanger singled to score May before DeCinces' fourth home run of the season.

e. *Psychol.* To obtain (results in a test designed to measure abilities, capacities, or personality traits); to record results in (a test). Also *intr.* Cf. SCORE *sb.* 14c.

1922 *Jrnl. Experim. Psychol.* V. 101 College students scoring 88 to 195 in the first trial. **1952** A. G. WESMAN in N. E. Gronlund *Readings in Measurement* (1968) xx. 201 It is important to know the extent of agreement between the persons who score them [*sc.* tests]. *Ibid.*, Such a correlation coefficient yields important information—it tells us how objectively the test can be scored. **1968** P. MCKELLAR *Experience & Behaviour* xi. 277 Engineers tend to score highly on the economic (applied science) value trait. **1977** P. J. DUNHAM *Experim. Psychol.* ix. 240 We will not deal with the details of how the TAQ is scored. *Ibid.*, The calm collected type of person who would score around 1 on the TAQ measure.

16. *transf.* and *fig.* (chiefly *colloq.*) **a.** *trans.* To gain, win (a success, etc.). ***to score a point*** (or ***points***) ***off*** (a person) = *to score off* (see sense 16b).

1883 J. HAWTHORNE *Dust* xv. 124 She felt that she had scored the first success in the encounter. **1884** *Athenæum* 24 May 658 Occasionally the latter editor scores a point. **1884** *Manchester Exam.* 12 May 5/3 Last year he scored two unequivocal successes. **1885** *Ibid.* 13 Jan. 5/1 Prince Bismarck has at length scored a victory in his impracticable Reichstag. **1908** *Athenæum* 27 June 786/2 Though never exactly profound, Macaulay invariably scores his point. **1956** R. BRADDON *Nancy Wake* xiii. 140 Fournier was ecstatic with pride and pleasure—and with delight at having scored a point off Gaspard! **1957** *Practical Wireless* XXXIII. 558/1 The episode I heard, 'Rumour is a Lying Jade', proved very amusing, with both stars scoring points off each other with satisfactory frequency.

b. *intr.* To achieve a success; to make a hit. ***to score off*** (a person): to gain a triumph over, to make a point at the expense of.

1882 'LUCAS MALET' *Mrs. Lorimer* I. xiii, For once she felt she had scored off her adversary. **1884** *Illustr. Lond. News* 29 Nov. 522/1 The hat was cut and smashed, the lord's head was uninjured; so that, happily, the lord may be said to have 'scored'. **1887** DOYLE *Study in Scarlet* (1892) 87, I told you that, whatever happened, Lestrade and Gregson would be sure to score. **1890** SAINTSBURY in *New Rev.* Feb. 143 The Republic scores by its appeal to..the most widely diffused of human weaknesses. **1891** *Spectator* 1 Aug. 148/1 Boys home for the holidays delight in 'scoring off' their most beloved friends and relatives.

c. *trans.* and *intr.* To make a (freq. dishonest) gain; spec. *Criminals' slang*, to commit a theft or robbery; to steal, filch, or purloin (something), esp. from an open counter or display. orig. *U.S.*

1914 JACKSON & HELLYER *Vocab. Criminal Slang* 74 *Score*, ..to successfully negotiate; to 'make a touch'... 'We scored seven times in the same joint by ringing up,' i.e., disguising. **1926** J. BLACK *You can't Win* xiv. 191 [The thief] throws a few dollars on the bar just to..let them guess where he 'scored' and how much he got. **1930** [see PLAY *sb.* 10g]. **1942** BERREY & VAN DEN BARK *Amer. Thes. Slang* §490/8 *Steal*,.. salvage, score, shark. **1972** *Last Whole Earth Catalog* 49/3 She was already plotting in her mind to stash part of their supper in her bag so they'd have something to eat the next day. She'd already scored a can of beer and a handful of cashew nuts. **1976** D. TOPOLSKI *Muzungu* vi. 99, I spotted a sugar factory, drove in, and scored a couple of kilos. **1977** D. MACKENZIE *Raven & Kamikaze* xii. 146 'Where did you get it [*sc.* a newspaper]?'.. 'Nicked it... It was too early to score any milk.'

d. *intr.* and *trans.* To buy or otherwise obtain a narcotic drug; by extension, to take a narcotic drug. *slang* (orig. *U.S.*). Cf. SCORE *sb.* 15d.

1935 A. J. POLLOCK *Underworld Speaks* 101/2 *Scored*, made a purchase of dope. **1953** W. BURROUGHS *Junkie* 9 Junk wins by default. I tried it as a matter of curiosity. I drifted along taking shots when I could score. **1959** *Alfred Hitchcock's Mystery Mag.* Feb. 68/1 To get you out of my pad I'll let you score for a low, low forty. **1969** *Guardian* 3 Dec. 9/1 She had needed the money to score H up in the West End. **1972** J. BROWN *Chancer* ii. 30 The weekend ravers and joy-poppers..who maybe score half a pill of H for kicks. **1972** *Daily Tel.* 25 Feb. 17/3 Mick the Pimp asked me if I wanted to 'score' and gave me a tablet from a matchbox and I gave him £1. **1977** *It* June 18/1 (*caption*) I can score better shit in Hendon on an off night!

e. *intr.* Of a racehorse: to win a race.

1941 *Sun* (Baltimore) 13 June 21/1 Their choice scored by a head from Epindel. **1977** *Evening Gaz.* (Middlesbrough) 11 Jan. 13/4 Shifting Gold had gone on to score again in the Tote Northern Chase at Haydock Park.

f. *intr.* and *trans.* Of a man: to achieve intercourse (*with* a woman); to have (casual) intercourse with (a woman); also occas. of a prostitute: to obtain (a client). *slang* (chiefly *U.S.*).

1960 R. G. REISNER *Jazz Titans* 164 *Score, to*, to attain success, to get what you want. Example: I scored with that chick. **1961** J. RECHY in *Evergreen Rev.* July–Aug. 19 You wanna score?.. See that old cat over there... He wants us both to come over to his house. **1970** G. GREER *Female Eunuch* 249 The boys used to go to the local dance halls and stand around..until the..sexual urge prompted them to *score a chick*. **1973** W. H. CANAWAY *Harry doing Good* I. 36 They might begin to ball later on... He would like to score with the Cheryl chick. **1976** D. CRAIG *Faith, Hope & Death* ix. 42 They talk about 'taking' a woman... Or, 'Did you score last night?'—like some great goal, scheming and forcing. **1976** 'TREVANIAN' *Main* (1977) ii. 39 He feels particularly sorry for the whores..who can only score drunks.

IV. 17. *intr.* To 'go off at score' (see SCORE *sb.* 3b).

1858 R. S. SURTEES *Ask Mamma* xxxviii. 160 They [the hounds] score away full cry on getting upon more propitious ground. **1897** *Encycl. Sport* I. 583/1 (Fox-hunting) *Scoring*. Hounds 'score' when the whole pack speak to a strong scent.

scored (skɔəd), *ppl. a.* [f. SCORE *v.* + -ED¹.]

1. In senses of the vb.: Marked with lines, furrows, or grooves.

1535 in Weaver *Wells Wills* (1890) 208 To henry my son, a red scoryd cow. **1775** SCHUYLER in Sparks *Corr. Amer. Rev.* (1853) I. 41, I..beg you to erase the scored part of the letter after perusal. **1793** MARTYN *Lang. Bot.* s.v., Scored stem, *exaratus caulis*, marked deeply with parallel lines, or rather grooves. **1796** WITHERING *Brit. Plants* (ed. 3) I. 210 Seeds 2, egg-oblong, convex and scored on one side. **1854** HOOKER *Himal. Jrnls.* II. xviii. 45 With ragged bark, and scored timbers. **1875** KNIGHT *Dict. Mech.*, *Scored pulley*, a pulley grooved around its perimeter for a round band. **1897** *Bookseller's Catal.* Oct. 10/1, 4 vols in 2, cr. 8vo, full bound scored russia.

2. *Mus. rare.* Of a film, or part of a film: provided with a score (see SCORE *sb.* 6c); of a piece of music: written down in a score.

1957 MANVELL & HUNTLEY *Technique Film Music* i. 21 Cueing was unusually elaborate and some of the more closely-scored scenes began to approach the techniques later developed in sound film recording. **1962** *Observer* 27 May 27/1 By the late 1920s Henderson was learning how to blend scored passages into a succession of solos.

†**'scorel, 'skorrell.** *Obs.* ? Loppings of trees.

1671 *Maldon* (Essex) *Borough Deeds* (Bundle 97. no. 2), To John Wright for one load of skorrell and three load of slag wood to make a groyn. **1817** J. MAYER *Sportsman's Direct.* (ed. 2) 128 To take the mantle off the water, lash bits of scorels, about four feet long, to each other [etc.].

scorel, obs. form of SQUIRREL.

scoreless ('skɔəlɪs), *a.* [f. SCORE *sb.* + -LESS.]

1. Making no 'score' or mark.

1611 J. DAVIES *Rights Living & Dead* (Grosart) 69 Thy patient bearing this thy Scourge (or Crosse) Doth make it scorelesse.

2. In a game: Having no score. Also, of a game, a period of play, etc.: from which no score results; involving no score. Phr. ***to hold*** (a person or team) ***scoreless***: to prevent (a stronger opponent) from scoring.

1885 *Field* 4 Apr. 447/1 When both their hands had been disposed of they were still scoreless. **1890** *Times* 20 May 11/1 Three Notts batmen had been got out scoreless. **1961** *Sun* (Baltimore) 18 Mar. 18/4 Hartman..allowed no hits in his scoreless three-inning appearance. **1972** J. MOSEDALE *Football* iii. 41 The team that had held them scoreless was weak against counterplays. **1974** *Sumter* (S. Carolina) *Daily Item* 23 Apr. CA/1 Bill Paschall..stretched his scoreless string to 23 innings. **1977** *Arab Times* 13 Dec. 9/1 N.C.C. started the first inning against Foster Wheeler with two runs but then were held scoreless throughout the remainder of the game. **1978** *Rugby World* Apr. 25/1 France..have never held Wales to a scoreless draw in the championship.

scorer ('skɔərə(r)). [f. SCORE *v.* + -ER¹.]

1. One who marks trees for felling.

1394 in *Archæologia* XXIV. 310 Et sic deficiunt ij lodes xij pedes [meremii] unde respondent le scorer et le carier et alii ministri ibidem. **1880** *Lumberman's Gaz.* 7 Jan. 28 The scorers and liner fell the trees and roughly trim the two opposite sides.

2. Any instrument used for scoring (see quots.).

1688 HOLME *Armoury* III. vi. 290/2 The Scorer is a round piece of Iron-plate fixed in another long piece,..with this Taylors score, or make a mark on Cloth before they venture to cut it. **1831** LOUDON *Encycl. Agric.* (ed. 2) 374 The scorer is a well known instrument used by woodmen in marking numbers on timber trees. **1875** KNIGHT *Dict. Mech.* 2056 *Scorer* (*Joinery*), an instrument employed to cut transversely the face of a board to enable it to be planed without slivering.

3. a. In a game or contest: One whose duty it is to keep a record of the score.

1732 *Applebee's Orig. Weekly Jrnl.* 16 Sept. 3/3 There wanted six Minutes of the Time by the Scorer's Watch. **1773** *Kentish Cricketers* in *Canterbury Jrnl.* 21–8 Sept., And underneath the shady tree The Scorer's fix'd the Runs to see. **1833** NYREN *Yng. Cricketer's Tutor* 65 The whole eleven, with the umpire and scorer, were conveyed in one caravan. **1837** DICKENS *Pickw.* vii, The umpires were stationed behind the wickets; the scorers were prepared to notch the runs. **1890** W. CAMP in *Century Mag.* June 206 There is one scorer, who records the order in which contestants finish, as well as their time.

b. One who allots marks or records the scores obtained in the measurement of ability, capacity, or personality traits.

1922 *Jrnl. Exper. Psychol.* V. 107 Provision must be made to free the results from the personal equations of the scorers. **1952** A. G. WESMAN in N. E. Gronlund *Readings in Measurement* (1968) xx. 201 The scorer is required to make a judgment as to the correctness or quality of the response. *Ibid.*, Two scorers should agree perfectly..in assigning scores.

4. a. One who makes a score.

1884 *Pall Mall Gaz.* 16 July 8/2 The highest scorer in the first stage of the Queen's Prize. **1901** *Scotsman* 11 Mar. 4/8 Credit must be given to Bell, to whom the scorer was indebted for getting the ball.

b. A winner, esp. of a horse-race. Cf. SCORE *v.* 16e.

1974 *Marlboro Herald-Advocate* (Bennettsville, S. Carolina) 18 Apr. 5/7 After dinner six tables of bridge were played. Scorers for the ladies, Mrs. Richard Fletcher..and Mrs. Robert Lockey. **1976** *Scottish Daily Express* 27 Dec. 10/3 I'm Alright Jack..a smooth Devon and Exeter scorer last month, can put up a repeat performance in the opener at Newton Abbot.

5. One who scores (i.e. composes a score for) a film. Cf. SCORE *v.* 9c. *rare.*

1969 *Daily Progress* (Charlottesville, Va.) 15 May 1-c/6 The talkies brought a demand for 'scorers', composer-orchestrators of background music to enhance scenic mood.

scorey, variant of SCAURIE.

scorf, scorfy, obs. ff. SCURF, SCURVY *a.*

scorge, obs. var. SCOURGE *sb.*¹, *sb.*², and *v.*

‖**scoria** ('skɔərɪə). Pl. **scoriæ** ('skɔərɪiː) and (rarely) **'scorias.** Cf. SCORIUM, SCORY. [L. *scōria* dross, a. Gr. σκωρία, f. σκῶρ dung. Cf. F. *scorie.*]

1. The slag or dross remaining after the smelting out of a metal from its ore. Also *transf.*

1398 TREVISA *Barth. De P.R.* XVI. xliv. (1495) 568 Syndre hyght Scoria and is the fylth of yren that is clensyd therfro in fyre. **1601** HOLLAND *Pliny* XXXIII. iv. II. 467 The grosse substance cast up from the pot or vessell & swimming aloft ..is named Scoria. **1683** DIGBY *Chym. Secrets* 105 See that you do not cast away the *Scoria*. **1758** REID tr. *Macquer's Chym.* I. 146 These floating matters take the name of *Scoriæ*. **1878** NEWCOMB *Pop. Astron.* III. ii. 245 Dark patches, like scoria, floating on the molten surface of the photosphere. **1887** A. M. BROWN *Anim. Alkaloids* 144 Those alkaloids and extractive matters..must be regarded as veritable scoria, resulting in the processes of physiological combustion of the elements of the organic tissues.

fig. **1808** BENTHAM *Sc. Reform* 41 So redundant is the population of the Inner House found to be,..so large the proportion of the mass that runs into *scoriæ* [etc.]. **1836** EMERSON *Nature, Lang.* Wks. (Bohn) II. 154 'Material objects', said a French philosopher, 'are necessarily kinds of *scoriæ* of the substantial thoughts of the creator'.

2. Rough clinker-like masses formed by the cooling of the surface of molten lava upon exposure to the air, and distended by the expansion of imprisoned gases.

1792 BELKNAP *Hist. New Hampsh.* III. 37 A company of persons..have found further evidences of internal fires; particularly a large quantity of *scoriæ*. **1830** HERSCHEL *Stud. Nat. Phil.* 294 The ejected scoriæ of volcanoes are receptacles in which mineral products previously unknown are constantly discovered. **1896** F. M. CRAWFORD *Corleone* ii. (1898) 16 A barren stretch of burnt lava and scoriæ, which had descended..from some lower crater of the volcano.

attrib. **1872** C. KING *Sierra Nevada* xi. 235 The further ascent lies up along scoria ridge of loose, red, pumiceous rock.

scoriac ('skɔərɪæk), *a.* [f. prec. + -AC.] = next.

a **1849** POE *Ulalume* 15 These were days when my heart was volcanic As the scoriac rivers that roll. **1878** LANGLEY in Newcomb *Pop. Astron.* 280 Views which regard..the spots as analogous..to scoriac matter.

fig. **1870** FRISWELL *Mod. Men of Lett.* xvi. 275 There is something scoriac about the face, as if the fires of a volcano had nearly burnt themselves out. **1876** FARRAR *Marlb. Serm.* iii. 26 They rush madly to the 'scoriac fire of passion' and consume their very beings with draughts of its liquid fire.

scoriaceous (skɔərɪ'eɪʃəs), *a.* [f. SCORIA + -ACEOUS. Cf. F. *scoriacé.*] Having the nature of scoria.

1776 *Phil. Trans.* LXVI. 527 Since it has no one character of scoriaceous matters melted by artificial fire. **1821** H. E. LLOYD tr. *Kotzebue's Voy.* III. 352 Scoriaceous Lava, resembling the dross of a forge. **1882** GEIKIE *Text Bk. Geol.* II. ii. §3. 89 Portions..are called scoriaceous, this being the character of the rough clinker-like scoriæ of a recent lava stream.

scoriated ('skɔərɪeɪtɪd), *ppl. a.* [f. SCORIA + -ATE³ + -ED¹.] Reduced to scoria, scorified.

1891 *New Rev.* Oct. 325 Hideous tracts of scoriated refuse.

†**scori'ation.** *Obs. rare.* [Aphetic form of EXCORIATION.] = EXCORIATION 3.

1582 HESTER *Secr. Phiorav.* III. li. 73 The oyle of Vitrioll healeth all the Scoriaciones of the mouth.

scorie, variant of SCAURIE.

scorification (ˌskɔərɪfɪ'keɪʃən). [f. SCORIFY; see -FICATION.] The process of reducing to scoria; formation of scoria or slag; *spec.* as a method of refining or assay.

1754 LEWIS in *Phil. Trans.* XLVIII. 683 The scorification and dissipation, which most of the metals suffer in the fire. **1825** J. NICHOLSON *Oper. Mech.* 762 If..the extremity of the hook..is covered with a thin, shining, smooth crust, the scorification is perfect. **1881** RAYMOND *Mining Gloss.* s.v., The operation involves roasting, fusion, and scorification proper, or the formation of a slag.

attrib. **1877** GEE *Silversmith's Handbk.* 18 The scorification process..is..applicable to the assay of all kinds of argentiferous ores.

b. *transf.* (Cf. SCORIA 2.)

1867 W. W. SMYTH *Presid. Addr. Geol. Soc.* 72 We may conclude that the peridotic rocks are the most direct products of a scorification which took place at an enormously remote epoch. *Ibid.* 73 Such is the metallurgical sense in which the scorification of the globe is intended to be understood.

scorified ('skɔərɪfaɪd), *ppl. a.* [f. SCORIFY + -ED¹.] Reduced to the form of scoria.

1815 *Edin. Rev.* XXV. 99 The scorified remains of a current of lava. **1878** RAMSAY *Phys. Geol.* 614 The scorified ramparts of the forts in Bohemia.

scorifier ('skɔərɪfaɪə(r)). [f. SCORIFY + -ER¹.] A vessel of fire-clay used in the process of the purification of metals in assaying.

1758 REID tr. *Macquer's Chym.* I. 177 These vessels are called Tests, or Scorifiers: they are scarce ever used but in the Docimastic art, that is, in making small Assays of ores. **1861** J. PERCY *Metallurgy, Fuel*, etc. 456 Scorifiers or roasting dishes. **1881** *Metal World* No. 6. 83 The scorifier must be large enough to admit the charge without filling it.

scoriform ('skɔərɪfɔːm), *a.* [f. SCORIA + -FORM.] Having the form of scoria, resembling scoria.

1794 KIRWAN *Elem. Min.* (ed. 2) I. 169 The substance.. melts into a scoriform mass. **1862** G. P. SCROPE *Volcanoes* 23 Instantaneously congealed into a thick scoriform crust. **1871** *Hartwig's Subterr. World* vi. 62 The black chaotic rocks of scoriform lava which form the floor of the crater.

scorify ('skɔərɪfaɪ), *v.* [f. SCORIA + -FY.]

1. *trans.* To reduce to scoria or slag.

1754 LEWIS in *Phil. Trans.* XLVIII. 686 Mixtures of platina with bismuth.. were.. scorified in assay-crucibles. **1822** IMISON *Sci. & Art* II. 214 The lead which in this operation is scorified, and scorifies along with it the imperfect metals. **1864** *Q. Jrnl. Sci.* I. 492 The iron is fused under an oxidizing flame, by which about 10% is scorified.

2. To convert (lava) into scoria.

1852 T. ROSS tr. *Humboldt's Trav.* I. ii. 115 Wherever these lavas are scorified, and where they have a shining surface,.. the development of vegetation is extremely slow.

scoring ('skɔərɪŋ), *vbl. sb.* [f. SCORE *v.* + -ING[1].]

1. The action of the verb SCORE in various senses; an instance of this.

1546 *St. Papers Hen. VIII*, XI. 145 Mr Seymour who landed here yesternyght.., scapyng a scoryng, beyng chased furst by that knave cowerd Burley, and put in gret dawnger with the shot of a sacre. **1592** GREENE *Disput. Hee & Shee Conny-c.* F 4, Hearing how that poore woman did finde fault with his scoring, the Gentleman not only put her out of doores with-out wages, but would haue arrested her. **1698** PLOT *Black-lead* in *Phil. Trans.* XX. 183[Called] by Dr. Merret, *Nigrica Fabrilis*, from its use in Scoring. **1769** FALCONER *Dict. Marine* II. (1780), *Assembler*, to unite the several pieces of.. a ship, as by.. scarfing, scoring, tenenting, &c. **1801** T. BUSBY *Dict. Mus.*, *Scoring*, the art of forming a score by collecting and properly arranging under each other the several detached parts of any composition. **1851** C. BOX *Cricketer's Man.* (ed. 5) 51 Printed forms.. for scoring are not procurable. *Ibid.* 53 The annexed score will serve to illustrate the principles of scoring. **1876** GEO. ELIOT *Dan. Der.* I. II. xi. 201 Shall we go now and hear what the scoring says? **1885** *Athenæum* 4 Apr. 446/1 The bold drawing and emphatic scoring of the graver. **1893** F. F. MOORE *I Forbid Banns* (1899) 109 Julian did not admire this 'scoring' on Bertha's part. **1904** *Daily Chron.* 21 Nov. 7/2, I viewed the match from the pavilion behind the goal where all the scoring was done. **1922** *Jrnl. Experim. Psychol.* V. 107 The scoring requires judgment. **1940** *Chambers's Techn. Dict.* 747/2 *Scoring*,.. the preparation of the sound-script, in which are described all music and noises to be introduced into a motion-picture. **1952** A. G. WESMAN in N. E. Gronlund *Readings in Measurement* (1968) xx. 201 Many objective tests.. are not very reliable, yet the scoring is by definition objective. **1967** *Daily Mirror* 14 Aug. 9/1 This buying of heroin ('scoring' in junkie language) is being watched closely by London Drug Squad detectives. **1978** *Time* 3 July 45/1 Warren stays with a picture through editing, mixing and scoring.

2. *concr.* Lines or figures scored.

1688 HOLME *Armoury* III. iii. 94/1 Scoreing or Strick lines on the Canvice to sow straight. **1864** *Reader* 13 Feb. 209/3 Sir Charles Nicholson.. referred to the scorings of human or animal forms on rocks. **1890** *St. Nicholas* Nov. 66/2 In the sandstone.. the deep, broad scorings can be plainly seen.

3. *attrib.*: **scoring block** *Card-playing*, a pad of printed score-sheets; **scoring board**, a board on which the state of the score at a match or contest is shown; **scoring-book**, a book in which the scores of games are entered; **scoring-booth, -box** *Cricket* = *score-box* s.v. SCORE *sb.* 22; **scoring-card** = *score-card (a)* s.v. SCORE *sb.* 22; **scoring engine** *Naut.*, a machine for scoring blocks; **scoring iron** (see quot. 1688); **scoring-knife**, a knife for marking turf; **scoring machine** = *scoring engine*; also, a machine for scoring cardboard for making boxes (Knight *Dict. Mech.* 1884); **scoring-paper**, *(a)* = *score-paper* s.v. SCORE *sb.* 22; *(b) Mus.* printed paper on which a musical score may be entered; **scoring-sheet** = *score-sheet*; **scoring stroke** *Golf*, a stroke in score-play; **scoring-table** *Cricket*, the table at which the scorer or scorers sit.

1907 *Yesterday's Shopping* (1969) 375/2 *Table*.. with drawer divided to take cards and bridge *scoring blocks, whist cards and markers, piquet scoring blocks and cards. **1933** G. D. H. & M. COLE *End of Ancient Mariner* ii. 18 On the table stood a decanter, flanked with packs of cards and scoring-blocks. **1882** *Bell's Life* 20 May 5/1 An excellent novelty was exhibited on the ground during the Oxford Match, and that was a patent *scoring board. **1894** *Times* 16 July 8/1 The Scottish eight was at least nine points better than the scoring boards gave them credit for being. **1904** P. F. WARNER *How We recovered Ashes* iv. 60 The Melbourne Cricket Ground, with its.. huge scoring-board. **1851** F. LILLYWHITE *Guide to Cricketers* 71 'Lillywhite's Registered *Scoring Book' will be found extremely useful to Clubs, for the purpose of keeping the exact averages of all the members. **1856** 'STONEHENGE' *Brit. Rural Sports* III. I. i. 490/2 (*Cricket*), Scoring-books (Lillywhite's). **1883** F. M. CRAWFORD *Dr. Claudius* vii, The little card-box and the scoring-book of the players. **1867** F. GALE *Public School Matches* 29 And now let us go to the *scoring booth and get a 'true and correct score to the end of the first innings'. **1960** *Cricketer Spring Annual* 58/2, 1851 A scoring booth was on view in the Great Exhibition. **1877** C. BOX *Eng. Game Cricket* xxvi. 459 **Scoring box*, a small enclosure, so situated as to command a full view of the play. **1908** W. E. W. COLLINS *Leaves from Old Country Cricketer's Diary* xii. 201 When.. I passed the scoring-box, *en route* for the pavilion, I found the small telegraph boy in the act of returning my score as sixty-nine. **1891** W. G. GRACE *Cricket* iii. 94 We kept in constant touch.. posting the *scoring-card at the end of every day's play. **1907** *Yesterday's Shopping* (1969) 386/1 Whist scoring cards. **1912** A. A. LILLEY *Twenty-four Years of Cricket* 124 No scoring-card could be invented to equal it in its completeness. **1839** URE *Dict. Arts* 147 The *scoring engine receives two blocks.. and forms the groove round their longest diameters for the reception of their ropes or straps. **1688** HOLME *Armoury* III. ix. 397/1 A *Scoaring Iron... With this.. they Scoare and run Veines on the Leather. **1725** *Bradley's Fam. Dict.* s.v. *Green-plot*, After the Lines are thus scored out with a sharp *Scoring-knife. **1845** *Encycl. Metrop.* VIII. 298/1 Scoring the blocks.. is performed by the *scoring Machine. **1851** C. BOX *Cricketer's Man.* (ed. 5) 53 Some clubs make it a rule to mark the number of 'overs' that each bowler gives, at the foot of the *scoring papers. **1851** F. LILLYWHITE *Guide to Cricketers* 79 Scoring Papers, per dozen... 2/6. **1908** G. B. SHAW *Let.* 27 May (1972) II. 788 You will only waste a good deal of scoring paper which you might employ far better by trying to deal, as Strauss does,.. with the modern world in a crisp and powerful style. **1859** in W. A. Bettesworth *Walkers of Southgate* (1900) v. 54 (*caption*) *Scoring Books and Sheets. **1891** W. G. GRACE in *Outdoor Games* 15 Scoring-sheet. Match played at Bilbery. **1857** HUGHES *Tom Brown* II. viii, 'How many runs?' Away scamper three boys to the *scoring-table.

scorious ('skɔərɪəs), *a.* [f. SCORIA + -OUS.] Of the nature of scoria; abounding in scoria.

1646 SIR T. BROWNE *Pseud. Ep.* II. ii. 59 By the fire they omit.. many drossie and scorious parts. **1676** BOYLE in *Phil. Trans.* XI. 808 The other part of the Cone.. is of a more scorious Nature. **1816** P. CLEAVELAND *Min.* 256 In porous or scorious lavas, the crystals are more friable and opaque, than those in more compact lavas. **1852** TH. ROSS tr. *Humboldt's Trav.* I. ii. 73 These débris form a wall of scorious rock. **1862** MRS. SPEID *Last Yrs. India* 34 Aden —shrubless, flowerless, dusky, grim, and scorious.

†'scorium. *Obs.* Erroneously formed sing. to SCORIA, mistaken for a neut. pl.

1681 GREW *Musæum* III. §ii. i. 325 The Scorium of the Freybergick S[ilver] Ore. **1705** ADDISON *Italy, Antiq. near Naples* 237 As we see the *Scorium* of Metals always gathers into a solid Piece.

†'scorken, *v.* In 3 (Ormin) scorrcnenn. [? a. ON. *skorpna* to be shrivelled, f. *skorpenn* shrivelled.] In *passive*: To be scorched or parched.

c **1200** ORMIN 1474 Þe rihhte dom iss starrc & harrd & all þe rihhte wræche, Swa summ itt wære scorrcnedd laf þatt iss wiþþutenn crummess. *Ibid.* 8626 Forr þatt te land wass driȝȝedd all & scorrcnedd þurrh þe druhhþe.

†'scorkle, *v. Obs. rare.* [? Altered form of prec.] *trans.* To scorch.

c **1374** CHAUCER *Boeth.* II. met. vi. (Camb. MS.) (1886) 43 And ek nero gouernede alle þe poeples þat the vyolent wynd nothus scorklith [*Addit. MS.* scorchiþ; *orig. has* torret], and bakyth the brennyng sandes by hys drye hete. *c* **1440** *Promp. Parv.* 450/1 Scorklyd, *ustillatus.* Scorkelyn, *ustulo.* Scorklynge [*v.r.* Scorkelyng], *ustillacio.*

scorn (skɔːn), *sb.* Forms: α. 2–3 **skarn**, 3 **scarn**, **scharne**. β. 2–7 **scorne**, 3–4 **schorn**, 3–7 **skorn**, 4 **schorne**, 4–7 **skorne**, 6 *Sc.* **scrone**, 2– **scorn.** [Early ME. *skarn*, *scharne*, aphetic a. OF. *escarn*, *escharn* = Pr. *esquern-s*, Sp. *escarnio*, Pg. *escarnho*, It. *scherno*; a Com. Rom. word of Teut. origin: cf. OHG. *skern*, MHG. *schern*, OS. *scern*, early mod.Du. *scherne* mockery, sport.

The β forms, which both in the sb. and in the vb. appear equally early with the α forms, are not easy to account for. The remarkable similarity of form and sense with It. *scornare*, lit. to deprive of the horns (:—popular L. **excornāre*, f. L. *cornū* horn), hence to disgrace, slander, deride, *scorno* (vbl. sb.) dishonour, insult, contempt, has given rise to the suggestion that the form of the Eng. words may have been influenced by OF. *escorner* (mod.F. *écorner*) to deprive of horns. But although the Fr. verb occurs (rarely) in the 16th c. with the sense 'to put to confusion', 'to mock', this seems to be a late adoption from Italian; OF. *escorner* has, besides its literal meaning, only the transferred sense to despoil. In the 16th and 17th c. the It. word may perh. have influenced the Eng. literary use.]

1. Mockery, derision, contempt; in mod. use, indignant or passionate contempt.

α. *c* **1200** ORMIN 4402 Þatt tu ne take nohht wiþþ skarn, Wiþþ hæþinng, ne wiþþ idell, Þe name off ure Laferrd Crist. *Ibid.* 4876, & all onn hæþing & o skarn Off me gaþ eȝȝwhær spæche. *c* **1205** LAY. 17307 Þa þe king Gillomar makede mucchel hoker & scarn.

β. *c* **1200** *Trin. Coll. Hom.* 169 Þo ne mihte no man for stenche cumen him enden.. ac mest manne gremede him mid scorne. *a* **1225** *Ancr. R.* 106 Amid þe muðe me gurde him sume cherre, inoh reðe, ase me to beot his cheoken, & spette him a schorn [*v.r.* o scharne]. *c* **1290** *S. Eng. Leg.* I. 255/8 Gret scorn heo hadden of alle þulke: þat icristnede were. **1303** R. BRUNNE *Handl. Synne* 12495 With skorne wenest þou þe quyte As a fals ypocryte. **1340** *Ayenb.* 22 Þe vifte out-kestinge of þe ilke stocke is scorn. **1377** LANGL. *P. Pl.* B. x. 304 In scole þere is scorne but if a clerke wil lerne. *c* **1400** *Destr. Troy* 5557 Hit is heghly to haue, & of hert dryue Soche sklaundur & skorne, þat skathis to mony. *c* **1450** *Mirk's Festial* 147 Þen was he for scorne lad to þe ȝate of þe cyte of Rome. **1526** *Pilgr. Perf.* (W. de W. 1531) 259 The vestymentes [betokeneth] the garmentes in ye whiche our Sauyour was clothed in scorne. **1528** LYNDESAY *Dreme* 2132 Quhilk bled with effusioun, With scrone and derisioun, And deit with confusioun, Confirmand our peace. **1599** SHAKS. *Much Ado* II. iii. 133 Shall I, saies she, that haue so oft encountred him with scorne, write to him that I loue him? **1616** T. SCOT *Philomythie* II. C 3, As when laden gun Spits forth its load, in scorne to be restraind. *a* **1645** WALLER *To A.H.* 12 Till my just disdain Of her neglect above that Passion born, Did pride to pride oppose, and scorn to scorn. **1719** OZELL tr. *Misson's Mem. & Observ.* 25 The Bull, immoveable, looks down upon the Dog with an Eye of Scorn. **1781** COWPER *Table-T.* 201 Or tell me, if you can, what pow'r maintains A Briton's scorn of arbitrary chains? **1866** SWINBURNE *Select. fr. Byron* Pref. 15 Scorn is brief or silent: anger alone finds vent in violent iteration and clamorous appeal. **1882** 'OUIDA' *Maremma* I. 25 His great black eyes blazing in a scorn he strove to assume.

b. Alliteratively coupled with *scathe*. *Sc.* and *arch.*

a **1300** [see SCATHE *sb.* 2 d]. *c* **1375** *Sc. Leg. Saints* xxxii. (*Iustin*) 767 Iustine & cypriane of þe caldrone son wes tane als hale & fere, but schath & schorne, as þai ware of þare modir borne! *c* **1400** [see SCATHE *sb.* 2 d]. *a* **1585** MONTGOMERIE *Cherrie & Slae* 211 As skorne cummis commonlie with skaith. **1819** SCOTT *Leg. Montrose* iv, And at the best I shall be ill enough off, getting both the scaith and the scorn. **1864** [see SCATHE *sb.* 2 d].

c. *personified.*

1500–20 DUNBAR *Poems* xlii. 81 Thrucht Skornes noss thai put a prik, This he wes banist and gat a blek. **1599** SHAKS. *Much Ado* III. i. 51 Disdaine and Scorne ride sparkling in her eyes, Mis-prizing what they looke on. **1613** J. DAVIES *Muses Teares* (Grosart) 5 For Hate, by feare, is held from bold Attempt: But, Scorne doth make it daring. **1742** GRAY *Eton* 73 Ambition this shall tempt to rise, Then whirl the wretch from high, To bitter Scorn a sacrifice. **1833** T. HOOK *Parson's Dau.* II. vi, The mark for scorn to point his finger at.

2. A manifestation of contempt; a derisive utterance or gesture; a taunt, an insult. *arch.*

c **1275** LAY. 29564 And suþþe ȝ[eiden] hine on mid hire foule scornes. *a* **1330** *Otuel* 1316 Þo otuwel sauȝ is cheke bon, He ȝaf clarel a skorn a non. *c* **1410** *Sir Cleges* 393 He cam anon, and teryde natt, Wythout any skorn. **1523** SKELTON *Garl. Laur.* 1382 Also a deuoute Prayer to Moyses hornis, Metrifyde merely, medelyd with scornis. **1604** SHAKS. *Oth.* IV. i. 83 Do but encaue your selfe, And marke the Fleeres, the Gybes, and notable Scornes That dwell in euery Region of his face. **1692** R. L'ESTRANGE *Fables* xi. 12 What Man then that is not stark Mad, will Voluntarily Expose himself to the.. Scorns of Great Men! **1850** TENNYSON *In Mem.* lxix. 9, I met with scoffs, I met with scorns From youth and babe and hoary hairs.

3. **†a.** Matter for scorn, something contemptible. (Cf. *to think scorn* in 4.) *Obs.* **b.** An object of mockery or contempt.

c **1350** *Leg. Rood* (1871) 81 Scho.. trowed no vertu in þe tre; Hir thoght it was scorne in hir wit þat oþer men so honord it. **1535** COVERDALE *Ps.* xxi. 6 But as for me, I am a worme and no man: a very scorne of men and the outcast of the people. **1590** SHAKS. *Com. Err.* IV. iv. 106 Thou.. art confederate with a damned packe, To make a loathsome abiect scorne of me. **1671** MILTON *Samson* 34 Made of my Enemies the scorn and gaze. **1692** R. L'ESTRANGE *Fables* ccxxiii. 195 But in a Dead Calm, a Man loses his Spirits, and lies in a Manner Expos'd, as the Scorn and Spectacle of Ill Fortune. **1718** *Free-thinker* No. 57. 29 Let him live to be the Scorn of every Honest Man. **1870** BRYANT *Iliad* I. III. 82 A scandal and a scorn To all who look on thee.

4. Phr. **†** *to bring*, **†** *drive to scorn*, to shame, disgrace; **†** *to do* (a person) *scorn*, to insult; **†** *to get the scorn* (Sc.), to be treated with contumely; **†** *to hold*, **†** *have scorn at, of*, to entertain a feeling of contempt for; *to laugh to scorn*, now *arch.* and *literary* (see LAUGH *v.* 3); **†** *to make scorn at, to*, to mock, deride; **†** *to put a scorn on, upon*, to offer indignity to; *to speak scorn of*, to revile, speak opprobriously of; **†** *to take scorn at*, to despise; **†** *to take scorn*, to be indignant *that*, to disdain *to* do something; **†** *to take at* or *in scorn*, to feel as an indignity; *to think scorn of*, to despise; *to think (it) scorn*, to disdain (const. *that* or *inf.*), now *arch.* and *literary*.

In the 16–17th c. *foul* often appears as an intensive qualification of *scorn* in these phrases. Cf. quot. *c* 1275 in 2.

a **1300** [see DRIVE *v.* 17]. *c* **1320** *Beues* 1357 Beues.. louȝ hem alle þer to scorn. *c* **1330** R. BRUNNE *Chron. Wace* (Rolls) 5391 Scorn hym þought, & swor his heued þer truage schold nought so be leued. *c* **1375** *Cursor M.* 16701 (Fairf.) To hym mekyll scorne they made. *a* **1400–50** *Alexander* 641 If any scolere in þe scole his skorne at him makis, He skapis him full skathely bot if he skyp better. *c* **1400** MAUNDEV. (Roxb.) xxii. 103 Þise smale men hase als grete scorne at þe grete men. *c* **1430** *Chev. Assigne* 264 And he of suche one gret skorne he þowte. **1470–85** MALORY *Arthur* VIII. xvi. 297 Syre Sagramore loked vpon syre Tristram and hadde scorne of his wordes. *Ibid.* X. iii. 417 That strong knyght toke his wordes at scorne and said he said it for mockery. **1523** CROMWELL in Merriman *Life & Lett.* (1902) I. 38 They wold thynck grete skorne, to take lether for our prynce. **1535** COVERDALE *Ps.* cv[i]. 24 Yee they thought scorne of yt pleasaunt londe. *c* **1560** A. SCOTT *Poems* (S.T.S.) ii. 94 Thay wist not how to get him pynd, That thame had drevin to skorne. **1561** T. HOBY tr. *Castiglione's Courtyer* IV. (1577) V vj, Neyther can I think that Aristotle and Plato tooke scorn at the name of a perfect Courtier. **1568** GRAFTON *Chron.* II. 213 Thus he passed.. with Trumpes and Pipes of Reedes blowen before him, to do him the more scorne and despight. **1575** tr. *Marlorat's Apocalips* 49 In Dathan, Core, Abyron: and in the Prophetes of Baal: all whych perished miserably for taking skorne to amend. **1577** HANMER *Anc. Eccl. Hist.* (1619) 228 Neither took I in scorne that I coupled myself with you in those affaires. **1579** [see HOLD *v.* 12]. **1581** HANMER *Jesuites Banner* A 1 b, Yee take scorne that I tearme him a cripled soldiour. **1593** ABP. BANCROFT *Dangerous Positions* IV. i. 137 They doe take it in scorne to be thought so weake. **1601** DENT *Pathw. Heauen* 309 They hold scorn to be taught. **1611** BIBLE *Esther* iii. 6 Hee thought scorne to lay hands on Mordecai alone. **1615** BRATHWAIT *Strappado* 222 The God of heauen, Who in his great compassions, thought 't no scorne, That the Creator take the creatures forme. **1622** MABBE tr. *Aleman's Guzman d'Alf.* I. 248 So his Steward.. turn'd me out of doores. Which I tooke in that foule scorne..that in a kind of sullen and dogged fashion.. I left the house. **1633** [see PUT *v.* 23 b]. **1653** HOLCROFT *Procopius, Goth. Wars* II. 53 All sat and ate with him, and put licentious scornes on him. **1738** WESLEY *Ps.* II. iv, The Lord ..Shall..laugh to Scorn their furious Pride. *a* **1850** ROSSETTI *Dante & Circle* I. (1874) 7 Messer Corso spoke great scorn of Messer Vieri, calling him 'the Ass of the Gate'. **1856** F. E. PAGET *Owlet of Owlst.* 227 The worst manager among them thinks scorn of wastefulness in a superior. **1866** [see LAUGH *v.* 3]. **1876** FREEMAN *Norm. Conq.* V. xxii. 35 The straightforward and business-like writs which did not think it scorn to speak to Englishmen in the English tongue.

5. *Comb.*, as *scorn-blighted*, *-pointing*, *-worthy* adjs.

1819 SHEIL *Evadne* II. ii. 33 Be all who bear Colonna's name *scorn-blighted. **1898** ARCH *Story Life* xi. 253, I made myself as blind as I could to the *scorn-pointing finger pointed it ever so scornfully. **1602** CAREW *Cornwall* I. 66 To make great prouision vpon small hope of vtterance were to incurre a *skorne-worthy losse. **1859** W. ANDERSON *Discourses* (1860) 19 It makes a most scorn-worthy exhibition of itself.

scorn (skɔːn), *v.* Forms: α. 2–3 skarne, 3 scarne, (scærn). β. 3–5 schorn, 3–6 skorn, 4 scornie, 4–7 scorne, skorne, 6 *Sc.* scowrn, 7 *vulgar* squorn, 3– scorn. [Early ME. *scarne, schorne*, aphetic a. OF. *escarnir, escharnir, eschernir* = Pr. *esquernir, escarnir*, Sp., Pg. *escarnir* (more commonly *escarnecer*), It. *schernire*:—Com. Rom. **skernīre*, of Teut. origin; cf. OHG. *skernôn, skirnôn* (MHG. *schernen*), MDu. and early mod.Du. *schernen* to ridicule, treat with contumely, f. the sb. represented by OHG. *skern*, OS. *scern*: see SCORN *sb.*

With regard to the vowel of the β. forms see the remarks under the sb.]

†**1.** *intr.* To speak or behave contemptuously; to use derisive language, jeer. Const. *at, with*. *Obs.*

α. *c* **1200** ORMIN 7397 Þa beþ hemm ȝarrkedd mare inoh & werrse pine inn helle, Þann iff þeȝȝ haffdenn herrd itt nohht Ne skarnedd tær onnȝæness.

β. **1303** R. BRUNNE *Handl. Synne* 12481 Skorne nat, and seye þou wylt forsake þy synne, and eft aȝen hyt take. **1362** LANGL. *P. Pl.* A. XI. 221, 'I nile not scorne', quod scripture 'but scryueyns liȝe'. *c* **1400** MAUNDEV. (1839) xvii. 178 Thei scornen, whan thei seen ony strange Folk goynge clothed. **1449** *Paston Lett.* I. 85 And dey bade me do my wurst, bycause I had so fewe schyppys and so smale, that they scornyd with me. *c* **1520** NISBET *N.T.* Matt. xxvii. 29 Thai knelit before him, and scornit, and said, Haile, king of Jewis. **1565** JEWEL *Repl. Harding* (1611) 302 And in like sort Iuuenal an Heathen Poet, scorneth at this folly. *c* **1660** WOOD *Life* (O.H.S.) I. 297 Scorning at anything that seemed formall. **1816** SCOTT *Antiq.* xxxiii, She gecked and scorned at my northern speech and habit.

†**2.** *trans.* To treat with ridicule, to show extreme contempt for, to mock, deride. *Obs.*

a **1225** *Ancr. R.* 248 And hweðer so he deð, hokereð & schorneð, & lauhweð þe olde ape lude to bismare. *a* **1300** *E.E. Psalter* ii. 4 Þat wones in heuen scorne þam salle, And lauerd sal snere with-alle. **1340** HAMPOLE *Pr. Consc.* 1189 Bot þa þat wille him folow, he ledes And þam scornes and taries in his nedes. *c* **1386** CHAUCER *Sec. Nun's T.* 506 It is a shame that the peple shal So scorne thee and laughe at thy folye. **1421** *Coventry Leet-bk.* 27 Allso that no man throw ne cast at noo straunge man, ne skorn hym. *c* **1440** *Ipomydon* 323 That they hym scornyd wist he noght. **1470** HENRY *Wallace* VI. 133 'Quhom scornys thow?' quod Wallace. **1500–20** DUNBAR *Poems* xxxiii. 98 The ja him skrippit with a skryke, And skornit him as it was lyk. **1577** KENDALL *Flowers of Epigr.* 52 b, Replide the Goddesse: what? skornste thou in armour me? **1631** *High Commission Cases* (Camden) 208 He that in the two former partes of his life mocked and scorned all both the message and messengers of God.

3. To hold in disdain, to contemn, despise.

α. *a* **1275** *Prov. Ælfred* 238 in *O.E. Misc.* 117 Bi-foren he þe bimened, bi-hindin he þe scarned.

β. *c* **1375** *Sc. Leg. Saints* xxxiii. (*George*) 417 Nocht-þane, þo þu oure godis skorne, þu tellis ws first quhar þou wes borne. *c* **1500** *Young Childr. Bk.* 57 in *Babees Bk.*, Scorne not þe pore, ne hurte no mane. *c* **1590** MARLOWE *Faustus* iii. (1604) B 2 b, Learne thou of Faustus manly fortitude, And scorne those ioyes thou neuer shalt possesse. **1600** in T. Stafford *Pac. Hib.* I. xiv. (1633) 87 Hee must be maintained with a conuenient attendance, that they may not scorne him. **1669** DRYDEN *Wild Gallant* III. 37 *Franc.* Come, come, you'r a slanderful huswife, and I squorn your hallottry trick. **1697** —— *Virg. Past.* II. 43 Nor scorn the pipe: Amyntas, to be taught, With all his kisses would my skill have bought. **1697** CONGREVE *Mourning Bride* III. viii, Heav'n has no Rage, like Love to Hatred turn'd, Nor Hell a Fury, like a Woman scorn'd. **1742** YOUNG *Nt. Th.* I. 411 'Tis not in folly, not to scorn a fool. **1813** SCOTT *Rokeby* I. viii, Death had he seen .., Knew all his shapes, and scorn'd them all. **1827** WORDSW. *Miscell. Sonn.* II. i. 1 Scorn not the Sonnet. **1855** TENNYSON *Maud.* I. XIII. 1 To be scorn'd by one that I scorn.

b. *fig.* Of things: †To defy, be secure against (*obs.*); also *poet.* to be immeasurably superior to.

1648 GAGE *West Ind.* xviii. 130 Such is this Golfe, whose entrance is straitned with two rocks or mountains on each side (which would well become two great Peeces and so scorne a whole fleet). **1764** GOLDSM. *Trav.* 319 Where lawns extend that scorn Arcadian pride.

4. With *inf.* as object. To feel it beneath one, to disdain indignantly *to* do something.

1605 [WAYER?] *Dick Bowyer* C 2, I scorne to humble the least part about me. **1701** DE FOE *Trueborn Eng.* 36 They scorn their Laws or Governours to fear. **1780** BURKE *Sp. Bristol* Wks. III. 373 We were saved the disgrace of their formal reception, only because the congress scorned to receive them. **1837** LOCKHART *Scott* (1839) II. 104 He scorned for a long while to attach any consequence to this complete alternation of habits. **1885** E. ARNOLD *Secret of Death* 23 Thou Scorned'st to tread the path of wealth, wherein The foolish perish.

†**5.** *Comb.*: **scorn-book**, an unwilling learner; **scorn-gold** *a.*, out-vying gold in colour. *Obs.*

a **1586** SIDNEY *Arcadia* I. Ecl. i. (1598) 86 Braue crest to him her scorn-gold haire did yeeld. **1682** N. O. *Boileau's Lutrin* I. Argt., St. George oth' back-side of the Horn-book, The Dragon kills, to Humour Scorn-book.

scorned (skɔːnd), *ppl. a.* [f. SCORN *v.* + -ED¹.] Despised, contemptible.

1598 Q. ELIZ. *Horace* 151 The hilz ther frute do yeld, a skorned mouse is born. **1616** T. SCOT *Philomythie* II. C 1, The crested Horse..with head Tost in the ayre his hardned hoofes doth tread The scornd earth with contempt. *a* **1625** FLETCHER *Knt. Malta* I. i, The wages of scorn'd Love is baneful hate. *a* **1704** T. BROWN *Satire on Quack* Wks. 1730 I. 64 Be the most scorn'd Jack-pudding in the pack. *a* **1882** CHR. G. ROSSETTI *Poems* (1904) 176/2 The scorned thief who hangs by Thee.

scorner ('skɔːnə(r)). [f. SCORN *v.* + -ER¹.]

1. One who scorns, derides, mocks or contemns; esp. one who scoffs at religion.

1303 R. BRUNNE *Handl. Synne* 4934 Lyers, robbours, and lechours, Skorners, and also auoutours. *c* **1381** CHAUCER *Parl. Foules* 357 The fesaunt skornere of the cok be nyghte. *c* **1440** *Promp. Parv.* 450/1 Scornare, *derisor*. **1500–20** DUNBAR *Poems* xx. 35 Be nocht in countenance ane skornar, nor by luke. **1596** SPENSER *State Irel.* Wks. (Globe) 640/1 Very present in perrills, very great scorners of death. **1657** *Penit. Conf.* ix. 291 As Apes are inimical imitators of mens actions, so do skorners usually act. **1651** BAXTER *Saints' Rest* III. (ed. 2) 43 The vilest..scorner at Godliness. **1713** BERKELEY *Guardian* No. 3 ¶1 Whatever one of these Scorners may think, they certainly want Parts to be Devout. **1817** COLERIDGE *Biog. Lit.* ii. (1907) I. 24 From others only do we derive our knowledge that Milton, in his latter day, had his scorners and detractors. **1820** SHELLEY *To Skylark* 100 Thou scorner of the ground! **1847** TENNYSON *Princess* IV. 402 Not a scorner of your sex But venerator.

b. Phr. *seat* (*chair, stool*) *of the scorner*, the position of a mocker (a reminiscence of Ps. i. 1).

1589 NASHE *Pasquil's Ret.* C iij, He roares and he fomes, and sets himselfe downe in the Scorners Chayre. **1596** SPENSER *F.Q.* VI. viii. 21 Thus I triumphed long in lovers paine, And, sitting carelesse on the scorners stoole, Did laugh at those that did lament and plaine. **1788** V. KNOX *Winter Even.* (1790) I. xliv. 377 The frontispiece to the *Rules of holy dying* cannot but excite mirth even in those who do not habitually sit in the seat of the scorner.

¶**2.** As a proposed term of rhetoric: see quot.

1589 PUTTENHAM *Eng. Poesie* III. xix. (Arb.) 219 Yee haue another figure much like to the *Sarcasmus*, or bitter taunt.. and is when with proud and insolent words, we doo vpbraid a man, or ride him as we terme it: for which cause the Latines also call it *Insultatio*, I choose to name him the *Reprochfull* or *scorner*.

scornful ('skɔːnfʊl), *a.* [f. SCORN *sb.* + -FUL.]

1. Full of scorn, contemptuous, derisive.

a **1400** *Morte Arth.* 1840 Thow skornede vs lang ere with thi skornefulle wordez. **1480** CAXTON *Chron. Eng.* ccxxx. 244 And whan he had of hem but a short and a scornefull ansuere he told it to the kyng. **1596** SHAKS. *Tam. Shrew* V. ii. 137 And dart not scornefull glances from those eies. **1667** MILTON *P.L.* x. 625 To gratifie my scornful Enemies. **1712** STEELE *Spectator* No. 272, I offered..to each of them a Kiss; but, one, more scornful than the rest, turned her Cheek. **1848** DICKENS *Dombey* liv, The same defiant, scornful woman still.

quasi-*adv.* **1667** MILTON *P.L.* IV. 536 So saying, his proud step he scornful turn'd.

b. *absol.* (Cf. SCORNER 1 b.)

1535 COVERDALE *Ps.* i. 1 O blessed is yᵉ man, yᵗ..sytteth not in yᵉ seate of the scornefull. **1894** K. GRAHAME *Pagan P.* 73 Did they..sit at the table of the scornful and learn, with Dante, how salt was alien bread?

c. Const. *of*.

1704 PRIOR *Let. to Boileau* 180 The English Muse.. Scornful of Earth and Clouds, should reach the Skies. *a* **1763** SHENSTONE *Elegies* x. 22 Honorio built, but dar'd my laws defy; He planted, scornful of my sage commands.

†**2.** Regarded with scorn, contemptible. *Obs.*

1570 LEVINS *Manip.* 187 Scornful, *ridiculus*. *a* **1586** SIDNEY *Apol.* (Arb.) 66 But I speake to this purpose, that all the end of the comicall part, bee not vpon such scornefull matters, as stirreth laughter onely. **1592** GREENE *Upst. Courtier* D 2, Of a scornefull Taylor, he sets up an vpstart scuruy Gentleman. **1593** SHAKS. *Lucr.* 520 So thy suruiuing husband shall remaine The scornefull marke of euerie open eye. **1596** *Edw. III*, I. ii. 7 Thou dost not tell him, what a griefe it is To be the scornefull captiue to a Scot. **1618** WITHER *Motto* (1621) C 2, To whom the riches of the minde, doe seeme A scornefull pouerty. **1624** DONNE *Devot.* (ed. 2) 277 And wee haue heard of death, vpon small occasions, and by scornfull instruments; a pinne, a combe, a haire, pulled, hath gangred, and kild.

scornfully ('skɔːnfʊlɪ), *adv.* [f. SCORNFUL *a.* + -LY².] In a scornful manner.

c **1380** *Sir Ferumb.* 356 Fyrumbras on him glente ys eyȝe scornfullich & low. **1447** BOKENHAM *Seyntys* VII. 156 (Horstm.) Oon Theophyl preyid hyr schornfully..That she sum rosys wold hym sendyn hastyly From hyr spousys gardyn. **1533** BELLENDEN *Livy* III. 242 And in þe mene tyme ane of þe equis cryit skornefully, It was propir to romanis erare to mak ane vane manassing, þan to gif batall. **1599** SHAKS. *Hen. V*, IV. ii. 42 Their ragged Curtaines poorely are let loose, And our Ayre shakes them passing scornefully. **1661** COWLEY *Vis. Cromwell* 55 It is bold to violate so openly and so scornfully all Acts and Constitutions of a Nation, and afterwards even of his own making. **1783** W. THOMSON *Watson's Philip III* (1839) 367 He scornfully declined to solemnize the double marriages. **1835** W. IRVING *Tour Prairies* xxiv, 'Bread,' he would say, scornfully, 'is only fit for a child.' **1906** H. VAN DYKE *Ideals* viii. 153 It is the fashion nowadays to speak scornfully of a book religion.

'scornfulness. [f. SCORNFUL *a.* + -NESS.] The quality or state of being scornful; contemptuousness; †contemptibleness.

1535 COVERDALE *Job* xxxiv. 7 Where is there soch one as Iob, that drinketh vp scornefulnes like water? **1581** SIDNEY *Apol. Poetry* (Arb.) 66 The scornefulnes of the action, stirreth laughter. **1606** HOLLAND *Sueton.* 203 Hee exacted also with great skornefulnesse and extremitie, good money rough and new coyned. **1665** J. FRASER *Polichron.* (S.H.S.) 315 Montrose..receaved no answer from him but what relisht of scornfullness. **1727** BAILEY vol. II, *Scornfulness*, contemptuousness.

scorning ('skɔːnɪŋ), *vbl. sb.* [f. SCORN *v.* + -ING¹.] The action of the verb SCORN.

a **1205** LAY. 2791 Nefden heo of heore kinge buten heora scærninge. *a* **1240** *Lofsong* in *Cott. Hom.* 207 Bi his scornunge and bi his spotlunge and bufettunge. **1303** R. BRUNNE *Handl. Synne* 12484 Ȝyt wyl y warne þe of o þyng, Yn shryfte make þou no skornyng. *c* **1386** CHAUCER *Pars. T.* 635 Afterward speke we of scornynge which is a wikked synne. *c* **1460** J. RUSSELL *Bk. Nurture* 291 in *Babees Bk.*, Speke not lowd be war of mowynge & scornynge. **1526** *Pilgr. Perf.* (W. de W. 1531) 250 b, And here consyder with thankes, the paynes & illusyons or scornynges that he suffred. **1641** J. JACKSON *True Evang. T.* II. 152 Breaches of charity..by the wincking and scorning of our eyes. **17..** RAMSAY *Throw the Wood* iii, I'm fash'd wi' their scorning. **1833** TENNYSON *Goose* 42 He took the goose upon his arm, He utter'd words of scorning.

†**b.** Phr. *to laugh* or *take to scorning*. *Obs.*

13.. *Cursor M.* 1830 (Gött.) Quen þai forsoke his sarmoning And toke his speche to scorning. *Ibid.* 2028 Cam ..was vnkind enogh, To skorning he his fader logh.

scorning ('skɔːnɪŋ), *ppl. a.* [f. SCORN *v.* + -ING².] That scorns; scornful, contemptuous.

c **1325** *Lei le Freine* 62 A proude dame..Squeymous and eke scorning. *c* **1381** CHAUCER *Parl. Foules* 346 The skornynge Iay. **1483** *Cath. Angl.* 324/1 Scornande, *deridens, illudens*. **1582** STANYHURST *Æneis* I. (Arb.) 18 And Paris his scorning iudgement dooth burne in her entrayls.

Hence **'scorningly** *adv.*

c **1440** *Gesta Rom.* xxiii. (Add. MS.) 80 The Porter toke all his wordes in scorne; neverthelesse scornyngly he went to the Emperesse,..and told her all the prive tokens that he had herd.

†**'scorning-stock.** *Obs. rare*⁻¹. [f. SCORNING *vbl. sb.* + STOCK *sb.*] An object of scorn.

a **1586** SIDNEY *Arcadia* III. (Sommer) 301 Clinias, finding himselfe the scorning-stocke of euery companie.

†**'scornless,** *a. Obs. rare*⁻¹. [f. SCORN *sb.* + -LESS.] Free from insult or contempt.

c **1400** *26 Pol. Poems* 27 Speke no good of frend ne foo, Let non skorneles fro ȝow wende.

†**'scornliche,** *adv. Obs. rare*⁻¹. [f. SCORN *sb.* + *-liche*: see -LY².] Scornfully.

c **1300** *Beket* 710 (Percy Soc.) 34 The Kyng bihuld him al anhoker, and scornliche somdel louȝ.

scorny ('skɔːnɪ), *a. vulgar*. [f. SCORN *sb.* + -Y¹.]

Todd (1818) quoted *Mirr. Mag.* but the earliest ed. reads *scoruy*, SCURVY.

Scornful, contemptuous.

1836 HALIBURTON *Clockm.* Ser. I. xii, And off she sot, looking as scorney as a London lady. **1867** G. MUSGRAVE *Nooks & Corners O. France* I. 334 The 'scorny' look I gave to these ridiculous lumps.

scorodite ('skɒrəʊdaɪt). *Min.* Also skorodite. [ad. G. *skorodit* (1818), f. Gr. σκόροδ-ον garlic: see -ITE¹ (so called from its odour when heated).] Hydrous phosphate of iron, found in pale-green or brown crystals and crusts.

1823 W. PHILLIPS *Min.* (ed. 3) 321 Skorodite. **1836** T. THOMSON *Min. Geol.*, etc. I. 475 Scorodite. **1857** DANA *Man. Min.* (1862) 249 Scorodite.

†**scorp,** *v. Sc. Obs. rare.* [Of obscure origin: cf. SCRIP *v.*²] *intr.* To mock, deride, scoff.

1535 STEWART *Cron. Scot.* I. 544 Thir ȝoung lordis sum scorpit with greit scorne, Sayand agane [etc.]. *a* **1572** KNOX *Hist. Ref.* 93 (Jam.) Thair was presentit to the Quein Regent ..a calfe having two heidis, whairat sche scorppit [1586, 1846 scripped, 1644, 1790 skipped], and said, 'It was bot a comoun thing'.

scorp (skɔːp), *sb. Mil. slang.* Abbrev. of SCORPION (sense 7); an inhabitant of Gibraltar. Also *Rock-scorp*.

1912 *Jock Scott, Midshipman: His Log* iv. 32 By 'scorps' he meant rock scorpions, the name bestowed on the inhabitants of Gibraltar. **1957** W. TUTE *Rock* I. 16 Millingham.. married a Rock Scorp. *Ibid.* 19 Perks and privileges for the ruling classes. Fifteen in a room for the poor-quality 'Scorps' whose Rock it was. **1973** *Publishers Weekly* 17 Sept. 59/3 Covering the rock's social strata, from the native 'scorps' to the British Governor.

‖**Scorpæna** (skɔː'piːnə). Also 8 scorpena. [L., ad. Gr. σκόρπαινα a kind of fish; app. irreg. fem. f. σκορπίος, SCORPION.

The fish named σκόρπαινα by the ancients was prob. so called from being prickly (cf. the cognate σκορπίς, σκορπίος, which are names of fishes expressly described as having spines). The application of *Scorpæna* as a mod. generic name is due to the resemblance of the word to It. *scorpina* (see SCORPENE).]

In early use, a name applied vaguely (like the vernacular synonyms *scorpion-fish, sea-scorpion*) to various prickly fishes, chiefly of the families *Scorpænidæ* and *Cottidæ*. Now only as the name of a genus (Linnæus 1758) of acanthopterygian fishes, originally of wide extent, but subsequently much restricted; the typical genus of the family *Scorpænidæ*.

1706 PHILLIPS (ed. Kersey), *Scorpæna*, or *Scorpides*, the lesser Scorpion-fish. **1752** J. HILL *Hist. Anim.* 269 The red Scorpæna, with numerous beards. **1772** *Cook's Voy.* (1790) I. 155 In all the coves of this bay we found plenty of cuttle-fish,..scorpenas, or rock-fish [etc.]. **1774** GOLDSM. *Nat. Hist.* (1824) III. 62 The Scorpæna or Father-lasher.

Hence **scor'pænid**, a fish of the family *Scorpænidæ*. **scor'pænoid**, *a.* of or pertaining to the *Scorpænidæ*; *sb.* a scorpænoid fish.

1842 J. RICHARDSON in *Ann. & Mag. Nat. Hist.* IX. 120 *Centropristes scorpenoides* (Cuv. & Val.), Scorpenoid Centropristes. **1862** T. GILL in *Proc. Acad. Nat. Sci. Philad.* 329 Scorpænoids. **1880** GÜNTHER *Stud. Fishes* 413 The habit of living on the bottom has also developed in many Scorpænoids separate pectoral rays, by means of which they move or feel. *Ibid.* 417 To complete the list of Scorpænoid genera, we have to mention *Tænianotus* [etc.]. **1885** *Riverside Nat. Hist.* (1888) III. 249 The latter [name]..is inapplicable to the Scorpænids, because they are entirely unlike the cod.

scorpene ('skɔːpiːn). Forms: 8 scorpen, 9– scorpene. [Anglicized form of SCORPÆNA; in the U.S. perhaps ad. the cognate Sp. *escorpina*, It. *scorpina*.] = SCORPÆNA; now only *U.S.* as a name for *Scorpæna guttata*.

1777 G. FORSTER *Voy. round World* I. 126 Scorpens, mullets, horse-mackrel, and many other sorts. **1884** GOODE, etc. *Nat. Hist. Aquatic Anim.* 263 Scorpene (*Scorpæna guttata*)..known by the names 'Scorpene', 'Scorpion', and 'Sculpin'.

scorper ('skɔːpə(r)). [A misspelling of *scauper*: see SCALPER[1].] **a.** *Wood-* and *Metal-work.* 'A gouging-tool for working in a depression, as in hollowing bowls, butter-ladles, etc. Also used in removing wood or metal from depressed portions of carvings or chasings' (Knight *Dict. Mech.* 1875). **b.** A jeweller's instrument for drilling holes and cutting away parts of the metal-work around settings to hold precious stones (*Cent. Dict.* 1891).

1843 HOLTZAPFFEL *Turning* I. 164 Small gouges, chisels, and scorpers of various forms and sizes [for working alabaster]. **1883** MOLLETT *Dict. Art & Archæol.*, *Scorpers*, in wood engraving, tools used for cutting away large spaces after outlining or engraving, so as to leave only the drawing in relief. **1884** F. J. BRITTEN *Watch & Clockm.* 230 Scorper, a kind of graver used for squaring the corners of sinks, easing watch bezels and other purposes.

†**scorpiac**, *a.* *Obs.*[−1] [a. late Gr. σκορπιακ-ός pertaining to a scorpion, f. σκορπίος SCORPION: see -AC.] Stinging like a scorpion; in quot. *fig.*

a **1670** HACKET *Abp. Williams* I. (1693) 82 To wound him first with Arrows of sharp-pointed Words, and then to Sting him with a Scorpiack censure.

scorpillyng: see under SCAPPLE *v.*

Scorpio ('skɔːpɪəʊ). *Astr.* and *Astrol.* [L., see SCORPION.]

1. A zodiacal constellation, the Scorpion. Also, the eighth sign of the zodiac, named from this; situated between Libra and Sagittarius; entered by the sun about 23 October.

c **1391** CHAUCER *Astrol.* I. §8 The names of the Twelve Signes, as Aries..Scorpio. **1398** TREVISA *Barth. De P.R.* III. x. (1495) 313 The sygne of Scorpio hath the hous of deth and of drede. *a* **1563** SACKVILLE *Induct. Mirr. Mag.* v, Scorpio dreading Sagittarius dart. *a* **1670** HACKET *Abp. Williams* I. (1693) 82 The two malignant Signs of the Zodiaque, *Sagitary* and *Scorpio*. **1741** *Poor Robin* C 3 b, Next *Scorpio* comes, an ugly Beast. **1899** R. H. ALLEN *Star-n.* 364 In southern latitudes Scorpio is magnificently seen in its entirety.

2. a. *attrib.* or as *adj.*, born under or ruled by the sign of Scorpio.

1894 E. KIRK *Influence of Zodiac upon Human Life* xviii. 156 When Scorpio people live on the higher plane, they are very superior individuals. **1901** M. MAYO *Our Fate & Zodiac* 104 The..astute Scorpio man is..clever in..taking advantage of the upward revolutions of the wheel. **1930** W. WILSON *Astrology* iii. 60 Scorpio people are often found devoting themselves to art. **1964** L. MACNEICE *Astrol.* iii. 95 Some modern Scorpio types excel at skin diving. **1970** 'D. HALLIDAY' *Dolly & Cookie Bird* iii. 23 He was Scorpio: I asked him.

b. A person born under the sign of Scorpio.

1968 T. WOLFE *Electric Kool-Aid Acid Test* i. 5 Black Maria, a Scorpio herself, rummages through the Zodiac. **1972** *Guardian* 15 Jan. 9/4 He and Rommel and Montgomery all shared the same birth date, November 17, and all were Scorpios. **1976** M. MILLAR *Ask for Me Tomorrow* xv. 122, I thought Scorpios were supposed to be creative.

Hence **'Scorpian** = SCORPIO 2 b.

1951 M. E. HONE *Mod. Text Bk. Astrol.* iv. 68 Just as this rulership brought energy and initiatory force to the Arien, it brings it to the Scorpian. **1980** R. RENDELL *Lake of Darkness* i. 7 Scorpians are magicians, astrologers, alchemists, surgeons, bondsmen and undertakers.

scorpioid ('skɔːpɪɔɪd), *a.* and *sb.* [ad. Gr. σκορπιοειδής, f. σκορπίο-ς SCORPION: see -OID.]

A. *adj.*

1. *Bot.* (See quot. 1875.)

1839 LINDLEY *Introd. Bot.* I. ii. (ed. 3) 160 The cyme of Monocotyledons..is *helicoid* or *scorpioid*, according as its peduncles are *homodromal* or *antidromal*. **1875** BENNETT & DYER *Sachs' Bot.* 159 *note*, The term scorpioid was introduced by H. P. De Candolle..to express a unilateral cyme the undeveloped portion of which is usually rolled up. .. Bravais amended De Candolle's definition of the scorpioid cyme by pointing out that the flowers are in two rows parallel to the pseud-axis. **1896** G. HENSLOW *Wild Flowers* 156 The flowers are arranged in scorpioid or curled racemes.

2. *Zool.* **a.** Resembling a scorpion; belonging to the scorpion family. **b.** Resembling the tail of a scorpion; 'cincinnal; coiled in a flat spiral' (*Cent. Dict.*).

1864 WEBSTER, *Scorpioid*, Scorpion-like.

B. *sb.*

1. *Bot.* (See quot.)

1855 OGILVIE *Suppl.*, *Scorpioid*, an inflorescence which is rolled up towards one side, in the manner of a crosier, unrolling as the flowers expand. **1866** in *Treas. Bot.*

2. *Zool.* A scorpion or scorpion-like animal.

1887 HEILPRIN *Distrib. Animals* 146 The discovery of a true scorpioid (Palæophoneus) in the Upper Silurian deposits of both Sweden and Scotland.

scorpioidal (skɔːpɪ'ɔɪdəl), *a.* *Bot.* [Formed as prec. + -AL[1].] = SCORPIOID *a.* I.

1835 J. S. HENSLOW *Bot.* I. iv. 85 If..one bud only is developed in the dichotomous cyme, and always on the same side of the axis, it assumes a peculiar character, termed 'scorpioidal'. **1857** A. GRAY *First Less. Bot.* (1866) Gloss., *Scorpioid* or *Scorpioidal*.

‖**scorpioides.** *Obs.* Also 7 *erron.* scorpoides. [mod.L. *scorpioīdes*, a. Gr. σκορπιοειδές, neut. of σκορπιοειδής: see SCORPIOID.] Scorpion grass.

1578 LYTE *Dodoens* I. xlii. 61 Scorpioides or Scorpions grasse..is a small, base or lowe herbe. **1669** EVELYN *Kal. Hort.*, *Apr.* (ed. 3) 15 Sow divers Annuals to have Flowers all Summer; as..Scorpoides, Medica, Holyhock [etc.]. **1706** PHILLIPS (ed. Kersey), *Scorpioides*, a kind of Pulse.

†**scorpiolocust.** *Obs.* *rare*[−1]. [ad. mod.L. *scorpiolocust-a*, f. L. *scorpi-us* (see SCORPION) + *locusta* LOCUST.] A locust resembling a scorpion (see Rev. ix. 3–10).

1561 DAUS tr. *Bullinger on Apoc.* xxxix. 256 Whome by the iust iudgement of God these Scorpiolocustes [orig. *scorpiolocustæ*] distroie with their poyson.

scorpion ('skɔːpɪən). Also 3 scorpiun, 4–5 scorpyo(u)n, scorpien, 4–6 scorpioun, scorpione, 5 scorpyone, (scarpyn, 6 scorpiowne, 7 scorpean). [a. OF. *scorpion*, *scorpiun* (also *escorpiun*; mod.F. *scorpion*) = Pr., Sp. *escorpion*, Pg. *escorpião*, It. *scorpione*:—L. *scorpiōnem* (*scorpio*), extended form of *scorpius* (whence It. *scorpio*), a. Gr. σκορπίος.

The word has been adopted into all the Teut. langs.: OHG. *scorpjo*, *scorpo*, MHG., MDu. *schorp(e*, MLG. *schorpie*; also, in forms showing later adoption from Fr. or Latin, mod.Ger. *skorpion*, MDu., mod.Du. *schorpioen*, MLG. *schorpion*, Sw., Da. *skorpion*.]

1. a. An arachnid of any of the genera (*Scorpio*, *Buthus*, *Androctonus*, etc.) forming the group *Scorpionidæ*, having a pair of large nippers and a general resemblance to a miniature lobster; they inhabit tropical and warm temperate countries in both hemispheres. The intense pain caused by the sting of the scorpion (situated at the point of the tail) is proverbial.

a **1225** [see b]. *a* **1300** *Cursor M.* 693 Þe scorpion for-bare is stang Fra bestes þar he lai amang. **1377** LANGL. *P. Pl.* B. XVIII. 153 For of alle venymes foulest is þe scorpioun. **1382** WYCLIF *Luke* xi. 12 Ethir if he schal axe an ey, whether he schal dresse to him a scorpioun? *c* **1475** *Pict. Voc.* in Wr.-Wülcker 766/4 *Hic scorpio*, a scarpyn. **1593** SHAKS. *2 Hen. VI*, III. ii. 86 But well fore-warning winde Did seeme to say, seeke not a Scorpions Nest, Nor set no footing on this vnkinde Shore. **1683** ROBINSON in *Ray's Corr.* (1848) 137–8 Since my coming to Montpellier I have seen several scorpions creeping on the walls... Animals stung by these scorpions fall generally into tremblings and convulsive motions. **1770** GOLDSM. *Des. Vill.* 352 Those poisonous fields with rank luxuriance crowned, Where the dark scorpion gathers death around. **1806** SHAW *Gen. Zool.* VI. 485 The common Italian Scorpion usually measures something more than an inch in length from the head to the setting on of the tail. *Ibid.* 486 The *Scorpio Afer* of Linnæus, or great African Scorpion. **1882** E. R. LANKESTER in *Linn. Soc. Jrnl.* XVI. *Zool.* 455 The beautiful citron-coloured Scorpion, *Androctonus funestus*. *Ibid.* 460 A large number of Italian Scorpions belonging to the species *Euscorpius italicus*, *E. carpathicus*, and *E. flavicaudus*. *Ibid.* 462 The *Androctonus occitanus* or yellow Scorpion of Southern France and Spain. **1902** —— in *Encycl. Brit.* XXV. 538/2 The desert Scorpion, *Buthus australis*.

b. in allusions to various fabled habits or properties of the animal.

The flesh of the scorpion was supposed to be a cure for its own sting (see also 1 e). The alleged fact, related by ancient writers, that a scorpion, when surrounded by a ring of fire, will commit suicide by stinging itself, is discredited by naturalists, though many persons in modern times have claimed to have observed it.

a **1225** *Ancr. R.* 206 Þe scorpiun is ones cunnes wurm þet haueð neb, ase me seið, sumdel iliche ase wummon, & is neddre bihinden, makeð feir semblaunt, & fikeð mid te heaued, & stingeð mid te teile. *c* **1386** CHAUCER *Merch. T.* 814 O thou fortune Instable, Lyk to the Scorpion, so deceyuable, That flaterest with thyn heed, whan thou wolt s[t]ynge. *a* **1625** FLETCHER & MASS. *Cust. Country* v. v, Women..rellish much of Scorpions, For both have stings, and both can hurt, and cure too. *a* **1711** KEN *Edmund* Poet. Wks. 1721 II. 137 The Scorpion sucks the Poison he convey'd, An antidote to his own Poison made. **1813** BYRON *Giaour* xvi, The Mind, that broods o'er guilty woes, Is like a Scorpion girt by fire. **1819** SHELLEY *Cenci* II. ii. 70 And we are left, as scorpions ringed with fire. What should we do but strike ourselves to death?

c. *transf.* and *fig.*

a **1225** *Ancr. R.* 206 Ich ne der nemen þeo unkundeliche kundles of þisse deouel scorpiun, attri iteiled. *c* **1386** CHAUCER *Manciple's T.* 167 Traitour quod he, with tonge of Scorpion Thou hast me broght to my confusion. **1500–20** DUNBAR *Poems* iv. 57 That scorpioun fell [*i.e.* Death] hes done infek Maister Johne Clerk, and James Afflek. *a* **1548** HALL *Chron.*, *Hen. V* 44 Some private Scorpion in your heartes..hath caused you to conspire my death and confusion. **1605** SHAKS. *Macb.* III. ii. 36 O, full of Scorpions is my Minde, deare Wife. **1719** YOUNG *Busiris* II. i, That thought has fixed a scorpion on my heart That stings to death. **1825** T. H. LISTER *Granby* xvii. (1836) 112 'That detrimental class, the Scorpions.' 'What do you mean?' 'Why, younger brothers.' **1924** R. CAMPBELL *Flaming Terrapin* iii. 42 But life, a scorpion of tenacious hold, Fastened upon their spirits.

d. *Her.* A representation of a scorpion as an armorial bearing (see quot. 1780).

1780 EDMONDSON *Her.* Gloss. s.v., It is..usually borne erect, or with its head strait upwards,..in which case it is, in blazon, called a *Scorpion*, without any addition..; but when it is borne with the head downwards, it is to be called, in blazon, a *Scorpion reversed*. **1906** VINYCOMB *Fict. & Symb. Creatures in Art* 122 The Scorpion..is generally borne erect.

†**e. oil of scorpions, scorpion's oil**: an oily substance formerly prepared from scorpions, used as an antidote against the sting of a scorpion, and for other medicinal purposes. *Obs.*

1594 NASHE *Unfort. Trav.* L 1, Ere the officers come to extend, Ile bestow an hundred pound on a doale of bread, which Ile cause to be kneaded with scorpions oyle, that will kill more than the plague. **1607** TOPSELL *Four-f. Beasts* 185 Wherunto he layed Garlicke, Rue, and oile of Scorpions. **1663** BOYLE *Usef. Exp. Nat. Philos.* I. ii. 48 The Oyl of Scorpions is not onely Antidotal against their Stings, but is witnessed..to be very useful to bring away the descending Stone of the Kidneys. **1741** *Compl. Fam.-Piece* I. i. 57 Take Oil of Scorpions, and Oil of Bees-wax, of each a like Quantity.

f. Applied to other animals resembling or popularly confounded with the scorpion: (*a*) to arachnids of the closely related groups *Pseudoscorpionidæ* (tailless or false scorpions, including the chelifers or book-scorpions) and *Pedipalpi* (including the genus *Thelyphonus*, known as whip-scorpions); (*b*) in the U.S., to tarantulas, centipedes, various lizards, etc. (*Cent. Dict.* 1891); †(*c*) see WATER-*scorpion*.

1709 [see *scorpion-lizard* in 8 c]. **1863** WOOD *Illustr. Nat. Hist.* III. 679 Book Scorpion, *Chelifer Wideri*.

2. *Astr.* The constellation and (now somewhat rarely) the zodiacal sign SCORPIO.

c **1384** CHAUCER *H. Fame* II. 948 Til that he sey the Scorpioun, Whiche that in heuen a sygne is yit. *c* **1400** *Treat. Astron.* 4 (MS. Bodl. Add. B. 17), The viij signe is Scorpio, he regneþ in octobre and is y cleped the signe of a Scorpion þ[t] is an Adder. **1593** G. HARVEY *New Letter* Wks. 1884 I. 278 Not much vnlike the progresse of the resplendent Sunne in the Scorpion. **1667** MILTON *P.L.* x. 328 Satan in likeness of an Angel bright Betwixt the Centaure and the Scorpion stearing His Zenith. **1754** HILL *Urania* s.v. *Scorpio*, The Scorpion is not a very large constellation, but, for its extent, it contains a considerable quantity of stars, and some of them very conspicuous. *Ibid.*, They call this..Cor Scorpionis, the Scorpion's Heart. **1785** W. HERSCHEL in *Phil. Trans.* LXXV. 256 In the body of the Scorpion is an opening. **1868** LOCKYER *Guillemin's Heavens* (ed. 3) 382 The bifurcation [of the Galaxy] continues through the Wolf, the Altar, the Scorpion, and Sagittarius. **1870** MRS. LOCKYER *Flammarion's Marv. Heavens* 81 The Scales and the Scorpion only formed one sign with the Latins before Augustus: the Scales were then the claws of the Scorpion. **1880** LONGF. *Poet's Cal.*, Oct., Then on the frigid Scorpion I ride.

3. Applied to certain fishes armed with spines: **a.** Used to render L. *scorpio*, *scorpius*, Gr. σκορπίος, in ancient writers. **b.** In Australia and America, the local name for certain species of *Scorpænidæ* (cf. SCORPÆNA, SCORPENE, and *scorpion fish*).

c **1520** ANDREW *Noble Lyfe* III. lxxxvi. in *Babees Bk.*, The Scorpion of the see is so named because whan he is taken in any mannys handes he pricketh him with his stinge of his tayle. **1608** TOPSELL *Serpents* 110 Catterpillers..are also a very good meate to diuers byrdes..& to a certaine Sea-fish called a Scorpion. *Ibid.* 223 The Scorpion of the water or of the Sea, whose discourse or history is to be found among the fishes. **1874** HILL in Tenison-Woods *Fish N.S. Wales* (1882) 49 The scorpion or Fortescue, as these fish are popularly termed by fishermen, have been known for a long time, and bear that name no doubt in memory of the pain they have hitherto inflicted. **1884** [see SCORPENE].

4. †**a.** A name for Aconite. **b.** The scorpion plant, *Genista scorpius*.

1601 HOLLAND *Pliny* XXVII. iii. II. 271 And for that the root [of Aconite] doth turne and crooke inward in manner of a Scorpions taile, there be that give it the name Scorpion. **1608** TOPSELL *Serpents* 231 The greene Scorpion which is bredde of Basill,..beeing beaten and pounded with the herbe Scorpion, and so made into pills, then dryed and put into a glasse, are very profitable to him that hath the Falling-sicknesse. **1840** PAXTON *Bot. Dict.*, Scorpion, see *Genista scorpius*.

5. a. In the figurative passage 1 Kings xii. 11 (and 2 Chron. x. 11), where chastisement 'with scorpions' is referred to as a symbol for severe oppression, the word has commonly been supposed to denote a kind of whip made of knotted cords, or armed with plummets of lead or steel spikes, so as to inflict excessive pain. Allusions to the passage are common, esp. (after Milton) in the phrase ***a whip*** or ***lash of scorpions***.

1382 WYCLIF *2 Chron.* x. 11 My fader beet ȝou with scourgis, I forsothe schal beten ȝou with scorpiouns [**1388** Y schal bete ȝou with scorpiouns, that is, hard knottid roopis]. **1390** GOWER *Conf.* III. 229 If he hem smot with roddis smale, With Scorpions thou schalt hem smyte. *a* **1632** T. TAYLOR *God's Judgem.* I. I. x. (1642) 26 They..chose rather to bee..scourged with Scorpions..than yeeld to deny their Maker. **1667** MILTON *P.L.* II. 701 Back to thy punishment, False fugitive, and to thy speed add wings, Least with a whip of Scorpions I pursue Thy lingring. **1788** V. KNOX *Winter Even.* (1790) I. xx. 180, I speak my thoughts freely, though I know the editors of newspapers have vengeance in their own hands, and are able to repel their assailants, with a lash of scorpions. **1816** BYRON *Siege of Corinth* xxi. 31 Scourge, with a whip of scorpions, those Whom vice and envy made my foes.

b. Hence used quasi-*Hist.* as the name of a supposed ancient instrument of torture. Also *Antiq.* as the name of a mediæval weapon (see quot. 1870).

1541 ELYOT *Image Gov.* xxxix. 98 His correction mought be no lasse than that he being al naked, shuld by his lybertines be fyrst of all whipped throughoute the citie of Rome with whyppes full of ruelles called Scorpions. **1817** SHELLEY *Rev. Islam* x. viii, He..bade the torturing wheel Be brought, and fire, and pincers, and the hook, And scorpions. **1870** BLACK tr. *Demmin's Weapons of War* 425 Scorpion or flail, with four chains without balls,..a Hussite weapon of the fifteenth century [figured].

6. (tr. Gr. σκορπίος, L. *scorpio, scorpius.*) An ancient military engine for hurling stones, darts, and other missiles, used chiefly in the defence of the walls of a town.

1382 WYCLIF *1 Mac.* vi. 51 He..ordeynyde..tourmentis for to cast stoons and darts, and scorpiouns for to sende arowis [**1388** scorpiens, **1535** COVERDALE scorpions to shute arowes; **1609** *Douay*]. **1584** HUDSON *Du Bartas' Judith* III. 112 Here croked coruies, fleeing bridges tal, Their scathfull scorpions that ruynes the wall. **1600** HOLLAND *Livy* XXIV. 533 They within shot closely against the enemies, some arrowes out of bowes, some quarrels out of scorpions and brakes. *a* **1693** *Urquhart's Rabelais* III. Prol., Balists, scorpions, and other such warlike engines. **1840** [see ONAGER 2]. **1879** FROUDE *Cæsar* xix. 325 The slings, the crossbows, the scorpions were all at hand and in order.

7. *Military slang.* A nickname for a civil inhabitant of Gibraltar. Also ***Rock-scorpion***.

1845 FORD *Handbk. Spain* I. 342 The houses..are fit only for..'scorpions', as those born on the Rock are called. **1889** H. M. FIELD *Gibraltar* 34 A choice variety of natives of Gibraltar, called 'Rock scorpions'.

8. *attrib.* and *Comb.*: **a.** simple attrib. (often *fig.*), as ***scorpion-kiss, -nest, -sting***; ***scorpion-like*** adj.

1961 R. GRAVES *More Poems* 33 Lady Morphia—Her *scorpion kiss and dark gyrating dreams. **1581** J. BELL *Haddon's answ. Osorius* 497 So much rayling in such *scorpionlike nipping & bitternesse. **1668** H. MORE *Div. Dial.* IV. xv. (1713) 320 Scorpion-like Locusts. **1813** BYRON *Corsair* II. iv, Dream they of this our preparation, doom'd To view with fire their *scorpion nest consumed? **1797** *The College* 2 Hardly could..Syd'nham's worth her *scorpion-sting assuage.

b. With sense 'stinging like a scorpion' (cf. sense 5), as ***scorpion curse, lash, whip***, etc.

1803 HEBER *Palestine* 111 Israel's sons by *scorpion curses driven. **1744** AKENSIDE *Pleas. Imag.* II. 513 His hand, Armed with a *scorpion lash. **1900** *Pilot* 23 June 526/2 But exactitude in the hands of second-rate scholars is a *scorpion-scourge. **1824** LADY BLESSINGTON *Jrnl.* May in E. Clay *Lady Blessington at Naples* (1979) 104 Byron..was..lashed into satire by the *scorpion whips of envy. **1865** RUSKIN *Sesame* i. §31 It [the nation] must discipline its passions, and direct them, or they will discipline it, one day, with scorpion whips.

c. Special combinations: †**scorpion-bow**, ? = sense 6; **scorpion-broom** = *scorpion plant* (b); **scorpion-bug** *U.S.*, the water-scorpion (*Cent. Dict.* 1891); **scorpion fish**, any spiny fish of the genus *Scorpæna* or family *Scorpænidæ*; also, an East Indian cat-fish (*Saccobranchus*); **scorpion-fly**, an insect of the family *Panorpidæ*, the slender abdomen of which is armed with forceps, and curls like the tail of a scorpion; **scorpion iris**, *Iris alata*, a native of Spain and Northern Africa; **scorpion-lizard**, some kind of North American lizard; **scorpion lobster**, a long-tailed decapod crustacean of the family *Thalassinidæ*; **scorpion oil** = *oil of scorpions*: see sense 1 e (*Cent. Dict.*); **scorpion orchid**, an orchid belonging to the genus *Arachnis*, esp. *A. flos-aeris*, native to Malaysia; = *scorpion-plant* (*a*); **scorpion plant**, (*a*) a Javanese orchid, *Arachnanthe moschifera* (*Renanthera arachnitis*), having creamy-white or lemon-coloured flowers, somewhat resembling a spider; (*b*) a plant of South-western Europe, *Genista scorpius*, also called *scorpion-broom*, or *-thorn*; **scorpion senna**, the *Coronilla Emerus*, a common plant of Southern Europe, with bright-yellow flowers; **scorpion-shell**, a gastropod of the Indian seas and Pacific, of the genus *Pteroceras*, having a development of long tubular spines from the outer lip of the aperture; **scorpion-spider**, a name given to various arachnidans (see quots.), now usually any arachnidan of the order *Pedipalpi*, a whip-scorpion; **scorpion's tail**, any plant of the genus *Scorpiurus*; **scorpion('s-thorn** = *scorpion plant* (b); **scorpion-wort**, (*a*) = SCORPION-GRASS; (*b*) *Ornithopus scorpioides*, native of Southern Europe.

1641 HINDE *J. Bruen* xxxviii. 118 Cyprian strikes them through, as with a *Scorpion bow. **1884** W. MILLER *Plant-n.* 199 *Genista scorpius*, *Scorpion Broom. Scorpion-plant. **1661** LOVELL *Hist. Anim. & Min.* 221 *Scorpion-fish... They are not the worst of fishes, especially if taken in the winter, yn stony places, & the pure Sea. **1863** WOOD *Illustr. Nat. Hist.* III. 247 Red Scorpion fish—*Scorpæna scrofa.* **1883** F. DAY *Indian Fish* (Fish. Exhib. Publ.) 36 In some fresh-water siluroids they [the eggs] are of a light pea-green, as in the scorpion fish, *Saccobranchus fossilis.* **1668** CHARLETON *Onomast.* 48 *Scorpio alatus*, the *Scorpion-Fly. **1869** G. GUYON in *Hardwicke's Sci. Gossip* 1 Jan. 23 The Scorpion-fly is quite harmless. **1900** *Field* 15 Dec. 936/1 The *Scorpion Iris (*I. alata*).—Bulbs of this lovely blue iris are now flowering in pots in a cool greenhouse. **1709** LAWSON *Voy. Carolina* 131 The *Scorpion-Lizard is no more like a Scorpion, than an Hedge-Hog; but they very commonly call him a Scorpion. He is of the Lizard Kind, but much bigger. **1858** BAIRD *Cycl. Nat. Sci.* s.v. *Macroura*, The *scorpion lobsters of India, *Thalassina*, which live a part of their lives on land. **1897** H. N. RIDLEY in *Jrnl. Straits Branch Roy. Asiatic Soc.* xxx. 68 *Bunga Kasturi. Renantha moschifera* Lindl. (*Orchideae*). 'Musk-flower.' The *scorpion orchid. **1937** M. COVARRUBIAS *Island of Bali* x. 336 Their garden is filled with golden flowers that grow side by side with the pandanus, the scorpion orchids, the.. pineapples. **1961** A. D. HAWKES *Orchids* 108 The multicolored flowers are generally produced in considerable numbers, and their strange form has given them the common name of 'Scorpion Orchid'. **1971** *Ceylon Observer Mag.* 19 Sept. 2/6 (Advt.), Epidendrums & Scorpion Orchids, several colours. **1866** *Treas. Bot.*, *Scorpion-plant, *Renanthera arachnitis*; also *Genista scorpius.* **1731** MILLER *Gard. Dict.*, *Emerus*, *Scorpion Sena. **1862** H. MARRYAT *Year in Sweden* II. 271 Among the ruins grows the scorpion senna. **1752** J. HILL *Hist. Anim.* 144 The *Scorpion-shell, commonly called the Spider-shell. **1859–62** SIR J. RICHARDSON, etc. *Mus. Nat. Hist.* (1868) II. 341 Genus Pterocera.—The Scorpion Shells, as they are called. **1802** tr. *Pallas' Trav.* I. 112, I had before observed the *Phalangium araneodes*, or *scorpion-spider. **1880** SILVER & Co. *S. Africa* (ed. 3) 179 The large and wonderfully swift scorpion-spiders [*Galeodes*] abound in the dry upland districts. **1884** SEDGWICK, etc. tr. *Claus' Text-bk. Zool.* I. 506 *Pedipalpi* (Scorpion-Spiders)... The Scorpion-spiders are allied both to the Spiders and the Scorpions. **1548** TURNER *Names of Herbes* (E.D.S.) 41 Heliotropium mai be called in englishe *Scorpiones tayle. **1835** PARTINGTON *Brit. Cycl. Nat. Hist.* I. 747/1 The *Scorpiurus* (scorpion's tail) of botanists. **1866** *Treas. Bot.* s.v. *Scorpiurus*, [The seed-pod] has a fancied resemblance to the tail of some reptile—whence its name, Scorpion's-tail. **1760** J. LEE *Introd. Bot.* App. 326 *Scorpion's Thorn, *Ulex.* **1578** *Scorpion-wort [see SCORPION GRASS]. **1611** COTGR., *Oreille de lievre*, Scorpionwort, or scorpiongrasse. **1725** BRADLEY *Fam. Dict.*, *Scorzonera*, or *Scorpion-wort*, a Plant that has Leaves a span long. **1852–6** WRIGHT *Dict.*, *Scorpion-wort*, the plant *Ornithopus scorpioides.*

scorpion grass. A plant of the genus *Myosotis*; the forget-me-not or mouse-ear. Also with qualifying words, denoting particular species or varieties.

Lyte and some other botanists assign the name to *Scorpiurus sulcatus* ('scorpion's tail'), 'with which various species of *Myosotis* are associated' (Britten & Holland).

1578 LYTE *Dodoens* I. xlii. 61 Bysides these two kindes of Scorpioides, there is yet twoo other small herbes whiche some do also name Scorpion grasse, or Scorpion worte. **1608** TOPSELL *Serpents* 254 To this end they doe prescribe Bay-berries, Scorpion-grasse [etc.]. **1690** RAY *Synopsis Meth. Stirpium* (1724) 229 Mouse-ear Scorpion-grass. *c* **1710** PETIVER *Cat. Ray's Eng. Herbal* Tab. xxix, Water Scorpion-grass, Field Scorpion-grass, Small Scorpion-grass. **1763** MILLER *Gardener's Dict.* (ed. 8) Index, Scorpion-grass, or Caterpillar, see Scorpiurus. **1833** *Proc. Berw. Nat. Club* I. No. 1. 29 *Myosotis sylvatica*—Wood Scorpion-grass. **1865** GOSSE *Land & Sea* (1874) 235 The early scorpion-grass or hill forget-me-not.

scorpionic (skɔːpɪˈɒnɪk), *a. rare.* [f. SCORPION + -IC.]

1. Pertaining to the scorpion.

a **1711** KEN *Edmund* Poet. Wks. 1721 II. 331 Which like Apocalyptick Locusts fierce, Their Scorpionick Poison did disperse. **1886** PROCTOR in *Sci. Amer.* 3 July 3/3 Below the Serpent Bearer we find the Scorpion (*Scorpio*), now fully risen, and showing truly scorpionic form.

2. *Astrol.* (With capital initial.) Of, pertaining to, or characterized by the sign of Scorpio.

1924 C. E. O. CARTER *Conc. Encycl. Psych. Astrol.* 145 Scorpionic afflictions often cause nasal obstructions, especially when the mutable element is prominent in the horoscope. **1972** *Mainichi Daily News* (Japan) 6 Nov. 12/1 Today's natives are not truly 'Scorpionic' in nature as each reflects unique qualities.

scorpionid (ˈskɔːpɪəʊnɪd), *a.* [f. mod.L. *Scorpionidæ* pl., f. L. *scorpiōn-em* SCORPION: see -ID.] Of or pertaining to the group *Scorpionidæ* of arachnidans, typified by the genus *Scorpio*.

1895 in *Funk's Stand. Dict.* **1902** *Nature* 25 Sept. 529/2 The facts do not prove the total independence of the scorpionid and limuloid series. *Ibid.*, The Silurian Scorpions simplify the existing Scorpionid type.

†**ˈscorpionist.** *Obs. rare*⁻¹. [f. SCORPION + -IST.] One born under the sign Scorpio.

1689 *Wonderful Predict. Nostredamus* 3 When the two Scorpionists [Jas. II and Louis XIV] conjoin'd shall be.

†**ˈscorpionly**, *a. Obs. rare*⁻¹. [f. SCORPION + -LY[1].] Scorpion-like.

1573 DAUS tr. *Bullinger on Apoc.* (ed. 2) 120b, Of their Scorpionly tayles, and of the fiue monethes I haue spoken before.

†**scorse**, *sb. Obs. rare*⁻¹. [f. SCORSE *v.*[1]] Barter, exchange.

1590 SPENSER *F.Q.* II. ix. 55 Yet liuely vigour rested in his mind, And recompenst him with a better scorse: Weake body well is chang'd for minds redoubled forse.

scorse (skɔːs), *v.*[1] *Obs.* exc. *dial.* Also 6 scorss, skose, skoase, 6–8 scorce, 6–7, 9 scose, 7 scoarse, scoorse, skorce, 7–8 scource, 8 scoss, *dial.* scoase (see also *Eng. Dial. Dict.*). [Early 16th c. *scose*, *scorse*, related to the synonymous COSS, CORSE *vbs.*

Prof. Skeat suggests that the vb. is a back-formation from SCORSER, and that this arose from *horse-scorser*, corrupt form of HORSE-CORSER.]

1. *trans.* To barter, exchange.

1509 BARCLAY *Shyp of Folys* (1874) I. 159 And for one god scosyth gladly twayne. **1548** FORREST *Pleas. Poesye* 481 Pryuate Commodye withe Commone wealthe to scorse: as Rentis to come downe from owterage so hye too Price indifferent to helpe manye bye. **1565** JEWEL *Replie Harding's Answ.* viii. §5. 382 These partes bicause they are ioined in one Mysterie, therfore oftentimes thei scorce names, the one enterchangeably with the other. **1590** SPENSER *F.Q.* III. ix. 16 But Paridell sore brused with the blow, Could not arise, the counterchaunge to scorse. **1598** T. BASTARD *Chrestoleros* VI. xxii. (1880) 76 He that will loue through water and through fire,.. Which will not scorse me for a better friend. **1612** DRAYTON *Poly-olb.* xii. 45 Their fortune will'd that after they should scorse Blowes with the big-boan'd Dane, exchanging force for force. **1618** AINSWORTH *Annot. Lev.* xxvi. 10 *Not alter* or, not scourse it, nor change it. **1623** MIDDLETON *More Dissemblers* v. i. 84, I know the barber will scourse it [a fiddle] away for some old cittern. **1706** PHILLIPS (ed. Kersey), To *Scoss* or *Scourse*, (old word) to change. **1853** W. D. COOPER *Sussex Gloss.* (ed. 2), *Scorse*, or *Scose*, to exchange.

2. *intr.* To make or effect a barter or exchange,

1589 WARNER *Alb. Eng.* VI. xxxi. 139 Pollitians knowe to cheapen, what to offer, when to skoase [*rime* cloase]. **1591** HARINGTON *Orl. Fur.* xx. lxxviii. (1634) 159 One was on foote the tother on a horse You thinke perhaps the hors-man vantage had No sure, no whit; he would have wished to skorce For why, at last to light he must be glad. **1600** HEYWOOD *1st Pt. Edw. IV*, III. i. (1613) F 1, *K. Ed...* Wilt thou take my courser for thy mare? *Ho...* If I were so mad to scorce, what boote wouldst thou giue me? **1614** B. JONSON *Barth. Fair* III. iv, Will you scourse with him? you are in Smithfield, you may fit your selfe with a fine easy-going street-nag. **1662** *Rump Songs* I. 209 Did'st thou not scourse, as if enchanted For Articles Sir Thomas granted?

Hence ˈ**scorsing** *vbl. sb.*

1509 BARCLAY *Ship of Fools* (1874) II. 141 Of folysshe exchanges scorsynges and permutacions. **1611** COTGR., *Compermutant*, changing, scoorsing, bartering, interchanging. *Ibid.*, *Courratage*, brokage; scoursing, horse-scoursing. **1674** JEAKE *Arith.* (1696) 479 Barter (vulgarly called Truck and Scosing) and the Concerns thereof..may be comprised under the 10 following Cases.

†**scorse**, *v.*[2] *Obs.* (? *nonce-wd.*) [f. It. *scorsa* a run, f. *scorrere*:—L. *excurrĕre*: see EXCUR.] *trans.* To chase.

1596 SPENSER *F.Q.* VI. ix. 3 Him..From the country back to priuate farmes he scorsed [*rimes* coursed, forsed].

†ˈ**scorser.** *Obs.* [f. SCORSE *v.*[1] + -ER[1].] One who exchanges or barters. See also HORSE-CORSER.

1531 ELYOT *Gov.* I. x, Virgile leaueth farre behynde hym all hakneymen, and skosers. **1567** JEWEL *Def. Apol.* VI. 738 Christe sommetime thruste sutche Buiers, Sellers, Brokers, & Scorsers out of the Temple. **1611** COTGR., *Compermutant*, a changer, scoorser [etc.]. **1617** [see HORSE-CORSER]. **1755** JOHNSON s.v. *Scourse*, A *horse scourser*.

scorsheatis: see SCROCHAT *Sc. Obs.*

scort, obs. form of SHORT.

scortation (skɔːˈteɪʃən). *rare.* [n. of action to L. *scortārī*: see next and -ATION.] Fornication.

1556 KNOX *Baptism* Wks. 1855 IV. 127 The Halie Gaist.. wald have restraynit and exceptit it, as he hath done scortatioun. **1651** BAXTER *Inf. Bapt.* 85 The sanctifying of the unbelieving Husband or Wife cannot be meant of making or continuing the Marriage lawfull, in opposition to Adultery (or scortation). **1658** ROWLAND tr. *Moufet's Theat. Ins.* 919, I see no reason why the modesty of the Bee and of the Drone, whereby they abandon publick scortation and venery, should debar them of the private use of copulation. **1794** tr. *Swedenborg's Delights Wisd. Conjugial Love* (1811) II. 312 It is a scortation more opposite to conjugial love than the common scortation, which is called simple adultery. **1885** L. OLIPHANT *Sympneumata* 113 Rapacity,..filth, and scortation.

† **scor'tator.** *Obs. rare*⁻¹. [L. *scortātor*, agent-n. f. *scortārī* to associate with harlots, f. *scort-um* a harlot.] (See quot. 1656.)

1615 T. ADAMS *Lycanthropy* 26 There be..luxurious scortators, and their infectious harlots. **1656** BLOUNT *Glossogr.*, *Scortator*, a whoremonger, a hunter of Harlots.

scortatory ('skɔːtətərɪ), *a. rare.* [f. prec.: see -ORY.] 'Pertaining to or consisting in, fornication or lewdness' (Webster, 1864).

1794 (*title*) tr. Swedenborg's Delights of Wisdom concerning Conjugial Love: after which follow the pleasures of Insanity concerning Scortatory Love. **1860** EMERSON *Cond. Life, Worship* Wks. (Bohn) II. 396 Here are..churches that proscribe intellect; scortatory religions. **1922** JOYCE *Ulysses* 199 Twenty years he dallied there between conjugal love and its chaste delights and scortatory love and its foul pleasures. **1942** DYLAN THOMAS *Let.* 30 Aug. (1966) 259, I hope..that the Monico made up..for the absence of one ventripotent scortatory Krut.

scortch, scorte, obs. ff. SCORCH, SHORT.

scortitsche: see SCROCHAT *Sc. Obs.*

† **'scory.** *Obs.* [Anglicized form of SCORIA.] (See quot.)

1607 TOPSELL *Four-f. Beasts* 182 The little scories or iron chips which flie off from the Smithes hotte iron while he beateth it.

scorza ('skɔːzə). *Min.* Also **skorza.** [Ger. (1800: see Chester *Dict. Min.*), said to be Wallachian.] An obsolete name for epidote, when found in the form of dark green sand.

1821 URE *Dict. Chem.*, *Scorza*, a variety of epidote. **1837** DANA *Syst. Min.* 293, **1868** WATTS *Dict. Chem.*, Skorza.

scorzalite ('skɔːzəlaɪt). *Min.* [f. the name of E. P. *Scorza* (b. 1899), Brazilian mineralogist + -ITE¹.] A basic phosphate of aluminium, ferrous iron, and magnesium, $(Fe^{2+},Mg)Al_2(PO_4)_2(OH)_2$, that forms an isomorphous series with lazulite and occurs in masses of brittle, blue, monoclinic crystals.

1947 PECORA & FAHEY in *Bull. Geol. Soc. Amer.* LVIII. 1217 The new minerals are named in honour of Dr. Evaristo Scorza and Dr. Antonio José Alves de Souza... Scorzalite is a massive, blue hydrous iron magnesium aluminum phosphate. **1949** *Amer. Mineralogist* XXXIV. 83 The Corrego Frio pegmatite, Minas Gerais, Brazil,..has yielded three new phosphate minerals since its discovery in 1942. Two of these new minerals, scorzalite and souzalite, are described in this paper. **1975** *Fortschritte der Mineral.* LII. Suppl. 288 Scorzalite from the Angarf-Sud pegmatite [in Morocco] is always observed intimately associated with muscovite.

† **scorzoner.** *Obs. rare.* [Anglicized form of SCORZONERA. Cf. F. *scorsonère* (also spelt *scorzonère*).] = SCORZONERA.

1597 GERARDE *Herbal* II. ccxlii. 599 In English we may call it Scorzoner after the Spanish name, or Vipers grasse. **1694** SALMON *Bate's Dispens.* (1713) 343/1 A Dyet of Veal and Chicken Broth, with Scorzoner and Sarsaparilla in it.

scorzonera (skɔːzəʊ'nɪərə). Also *rarely* 7 **scorsonera, skarsinarie, scozonera,** 8 **scorchanarrow, -enarrow.** [a. It. *scorzonera* (whence mod.L. *scorzonēra*) = F. *scorsonère, scorzonère*, Sp. *escorzonera*, Pg. *escorcioneira*; prob. f. It. *scorzone* some kind of venomous snake, Sp. *escorzon* (Cat. *escorçu*), some kind of toad or lizard deemed venomous. Cf. the following:

1580 J. FRAMPTON *Monardes' 2 Med. agst. Venom* 133 They call this herbe *Escuerçonera* because it doeth heale..the bytinges of this beast called *Escorçu* [printed *Estorçu*] in the Catalan tongue, and the same roote is like too the sayde beast.]

A plant of the modern genus (Tournefort, 1700) *Scorzonera*, esp. *S. Hispanica* or black salsify, much cultivated in Europe for its root which is used as a vegetable and somewhat resembles the parsnip. *S. Hispanica* was also formerly called *viper's-grass.* Also the root of this plant.

It was supposed to be good against the bites of vipers and other venomous creatures.

1629 PARKINSON *Parad.* 301 Wee call them in English Vipers grasse, or Scorsonera. **1666** OLDENBURG *Let. to Boyle* 15 Nov. *B.'s Wks.* (1744) V. 363 Colonel Blunt presented the company..with excellent scorzoneras, which he said might be propagated in England as much as parsnips. **1690** in *Thanes of Cawdor* (Spald. Club) 353, 2 drope of skarsinarie ..ane unce of Turkie persell. **1732** ARBUTHNOT *Rules of Diet* in *Aliments*, etc. I. 250 Scorzonera, demulcent in the Small Pox. **1738** *Ochtertyre House Bk.* (S.H.S. 1907) 142 Eggs bufft harrings and scorchanarrow. **1756** J. HILL *Brit. Herbal* 444 Tall, narrow-leaved Scorzonera. **1866** *Treas. Bot.* s.v., *Scorzonera hispanica*..is a native of Spain, but is cultivated in this country; and its root is sold in the markets as Scorzonera. **1882** *Garden* 11 Nov. 425/3 Salsafy and Scorzonera can be strongly recommended for culture. **1884** W. MILLER *Plant-n.* 122 Scorzonera, French, *Scorzonera picroides* (*Picridium vulgare*). Scorzonera, Garden, *Scorzonera hispanica.*

b. *attrib.*

1666 W. BOGHURST *Loimogr.* (1894) 76 Juniper berryes, *Scorzonera roots. **1731** *Gentl. Mag.* I. 91 Sow scorzonera salsfy, and slip skerrits of the last years growth. **1772** GRAVES *Spir. Quix.* (1820) II. 155 Mr. Selkirk asked him, what the virtues of that *Scorzonera-water were, which he observed he drank every day after dinner.

Scot (skɒt), *sb.*¹ Forms: 1 *pl.* **Scottas,** 3–6 **Scotte,** 4 **Skot, Skotte,** 6 **Skott,** (**Skote**), 7 **Scott,** 5– **Scot.** [OE. ***Scot**, pl. *Scottas*, ad. late L. *Scottus*; first in writers of *c* 400. Late Latin had a variant *Scōtus* (cf. med.Gr. Σκῶτος), which became the usual form in med.L. A third form, *Scŏtus*, may perh. be inferred from the ON. *Skotar* pl., though the examples of it in med. Latin verse are prob. mere mistakes.

The source of the late Latin word is obscure. There is no evidence that it represents the native name of any Gaelic-speaking people (the Irish *Scot*, an Irishman, pl. *Scuit*, appears to be a learned word from Latin), nor does it exist in Welsh, though Welshmen in writing Latin have from the earliest times used *Scoti* as the rendering of *Gwyddel* (Gaels). It may possibly be an adoption of a name bestowed at an early period by Britons or Gauls on a Gaelic people (cf. the Gaulish personal names *Scottos, Scottios*); Sir J. Rhŷs has suggested that it may have meant 'tattooed', cogn. w. Welsh *ysgwthr* a cutting, carving, or sculpturing; other conjectures have also been offered.

The OHG. *Scotto* (MHG., mod.G. *Schotte*), MDu. *Schotte, Schot* (mod.Du. *Schot*), agree with the Eng. form; adoptions from literary Latin appear in OF. *Escot*, Sp., Pg. *Escoto*, It. *Scoto.*]

1. a. *Hist.* One of an ancient Gaelic-speaking people, first known to history as inhabitants of Ireland, who in the 6th century A.D. settled in the north-west of Great Britain, and from whom the northern part of the island ultimately received its name.

Down to the reign of Alfred, *Scottas* was the ordinary word for Irishmen (as *Scotland* for Hibernia). In the next reign there were relations between the Anglo-Saxon kingdom and the kingdom of the Scots in North Britain, and from that time onward the name was no longer associated with Ireland except in historical statements.

O.E. Chron. an. 891, Þrie Scottas comon to Ælfrede cyninge, on anum bate butan ælcum ȝereþrum of Hibernia. *a* **900** *Bæda's Hist.* I. i. (1890) 28 Hibernia Scotta ealond. *c* **1205** LAY. 5575 Bruttes & Wailsce, Scottes & Densce. *c* **1386** CHAUCER *Man of Law's T.* 482 This Constable was no thyng lord of this place..But kepte it strongly many wyntres space, Vnder Alla, king of al Northhumbrelond,..Agayn the Scottes. **1387** TREVISA *Higden* (Rolls) I. 331 And þat londe [Hibernia] hatte Scotland also, for Scottes woned þere somtyme, or þey come into þe oþer Scotland, þat longede to Bretayne. *c* **1400** *Brut* lxxvi (1906) 76 Arthure turnede him aȝeyne þere þat he was, into þe place þat he hade lefte þe Scottes. **1570–6** LAMBARDE *Peramb. Kent* 2 These Scots (as them selues do write) were a people of Scythia, that came first into Spaine, then into Ireland, and from thence to the North part of Britaine. **1596** DALRYMPLE tr. *Leslie's Hist. Scot.* I. 1. 80 The ȝeir quhen the scottis cam in the Iles of Albion first, quhilkes we cal Hebrides now. **1606** WARNER *Alb. Eng.* XIV. lxxxiii. (1612) 346 Till the Picts, a People stout, Were by th' inuading Irish-Scots long thence debelled out. **1797** *Encycl. Brit.* (ed. 3) XIV. 560/1 When the Scots became masters of the low country. **1873** BURTON *Hist. Scot.* (ed. 2) I. 286 A chief among the Scots of Ulster, ..who lived in the middle of the third century. **1882** RHŶS *Celtic Brit.* v. 154 Now the Scots were Christians, while the Picts ruled over by Brude were still pagans. *Ibid.*, Columba, who was connected with the royal family of the Dalriad Scots, came over from Ireland in the year 563.

† **b.** *Comb.*, as *Scot-lede, -thede*, the people of the Scots. *Obs.*

c **1205** LAY. 20047 Þer liðen to-somne alle Scotleode. *Ibid.* 20417 Al Scot-þeode he ȝaf his ane þeine.

2. A native of Scotland, a Scotchman, a Scotsman. † *Irish Scot*: a Highlander.

From the 17th c. to the 19th c. chiefly *Hist.* exc. in jocular or rhetorical use. In Scotland, and more recently in England, in the 20th c. there has been an increasing tendency (orig. in newspaper writing) to the more extended use of the word. Cf. SCOTCH, SCOTCHMAN.

1338 R. BRUNNE *Chron.* (1810) 304 At Foukirke in Scotlond, Scottis escapid none. *a* **1352** MINOT *Poems* (ed. Hall) ii. 1 Skottes out of Berwik and of Abirdene. **1387** TREVISA *Higden* (Rolls) II. 73 Þe see þat departeþ Englische men and Scottes in þe est half. *c* **1475** *Harl. Contin. Higden* (Rolls) VIII. 520 The firste Edwarde..wan Scotlonde, magre the Scottes stronge. **1513** [? SKELTON] in Flügel *Neuengl. Lesebuch* (1895) 155 Of the out yles ye rough foted scottes we have well eased you of the bottes. *a* **1536** *Songs, Carols.* etc. (E.E.T.S.) 102 A litill balet..made at Mʳ. Shawes table by a Skote. **1536** A. BOORDE in Ellis *Orig. Lett.* Ser. III. II. 303 Shortly to conclude, trust yow no Skott, for they wyll yowse flatteryng wordes, and all is fal[s]hode. **1585** PILKINGTON *Expos. Nehemiah* iv. 13. 61 If any shoot ill fauouredly, we saie he Shooteth like a Scott. **1587** GOLDING *De Mornay* ii. 22 It is..one selfesame Sunne that maketh the Ethyopian blacke, and the Scotte yellowish. **1596** SHAKS. *1 Hen. IV*, I. iii. 212 Those same Noble Scottes That are your Prisoners. **1631** PORY in *Crt. & Times Chas. I* (1848) II. 125 The same Mackey, a Western or Irish Scot,..was, of all the Scots, most affected by the King of Sweden. **1639** *Hamilton Papers* (Camden) 78 For who knoethe, when your Maᵗⁱᵉ is neer the borders, what Scots may flocke to you, if I be gone. **1793** BURNS *Bruce's Addr.* i, Scots! wha hae wi' Wallace bled, Scots! wham Bruce has aften led. **1849** MACAULAY *Hist. Eng.* i. I. 66 In perseverance, in self-command, in forethought, in all the virtues which conduce to success in life, the Scots have never been surpassed. **1876** BANCROFT *Hist. U.S.* VI. xli. 281 Paul Jones, a Scot by birth, in the service of the United States.

Comb. **1643** [ANGIER] *Lanc. Vall. Achor* 18 We (Scot-like) knew not the meaning of a Pardon.

3. *dial.* (See quots.)

1787 MARSHALL *Rural Econ., Norf.* 387 *Scots*, Scotch cattle. **1886** *Field* 7 Aug. 217/3 Prime large oxen 4s. 6d. to 4s. 8d. ditto Scots &c. 4s. 8d. to 5s.

4. *slang.* (See quots.) Also as *adj.*

1812 J. H. VAUX *Flash Dict.*, *Scot*, a person of an irritable temper, who is easily put in a passion, which is often done by the company he is with, to create fun, such a one is declared to be a fine *Scot.* **1823** 'J. BEE' *Dict.* 155 *Scot*, a butcher's designation of a fractious man, the small Scots oxen coming to their doom with little resignation to fate; indeed, all animals try harder to retain life than man. **1859** *Hotten's Slang Dict.* 87 *Scot*, temper or passion; 'oh! what a scot he was in'. **1864** ELIZ. MURRAY *Ella Norman* II. 53, 'I am tired.'—'Yes and in a greater scot than I ever saw you. Why, we can raise you worse than Ma!' **1916** W. OWEN *Let.* 9 Dec. (1967) 417 Major Melville, a snotty, acid, scot, impatient, irritated wretch.

scot (skɒt), *sb.*² Also 3–4 **scoth,** 4 **scott,** 5–6 **scotte,** 6 **skot(t, skotte.** [Ultimately identical with OE. *sc(e)ot, ȝesc(e)ot* SHOT *sb.*; its formal relation to this is somewhat uncertain.

There can be little doubt that ME. *scot* is in part of Scandinavian origin, a. ON. *skot*; but in some instances it may represent the OF. *escot* (mod.F. *écot*), which is an adoption of the Teut. word; in some uses, again (esp. in ROME-SCOT) the OE. written form may have been preserved traditionally or revived from documents.]

1. A payment, contribution, 'reckoning'; esp. payment for entertainment; a or one's share of such payment; chiefly in the phrase *to pay* (*for*) (*one's*) *scot*: *lit.* and *fig.*

1297 R. GLOUC. (Rolls) 6001 Verst hii wolde ete & drinke ..& suþþe þe louerd of þe hous quelle..& suþþe brenne al is hous al uor hor scot ywis. **1340** *Ayenb.* 51 And þanne me hine [*sc.* the glutton] anhongeþ. Þis is þet scot: þet me ofte payþ. **1398** TREVISA *Barth. De P.R.* VI. xxiii. (1495) 213 After souper that is freely yeue it is not honest to compell a man to pay his scot. *c* **1430** *Pilgr. Lyf Manhode* III. xxii. (1869) 147 Þat is þilke þat biseecheth bred for þe loue of god, and wole in no place pay scotte for no thing þat she dispendeth. **1483** CAXTON *G. de la Tour* i iij b, God payeth yᵗ grete scot for he rendred to C. double. **1534** MORE *Comf. agst. Trib.* II. Wks. 1177/2 If so be..that they haue founde out so easye awaye to heauen, as to take no thought, but make mery,..and then lette Chrystes passion paye for all the scotte. *c* **1566** *Merie Tales of Skelton* in *S.'s Wks.* (1843) I. p. lviii, Ise bay for your skott to London. **1729** P. WALKDEN *Diary* 4 July (1866) 29, I asked him what I owed him;..I gave him half-a-crown, but he gave me 6d. back... So we are clear of all the scots that I know of. **1759** in *Catal. Archives All Souls' Coll.* (1877) 227 The scots have been very high. **1860** EMERSON *Cond. Life, Wealth* Wks. (Bohn) II. 346 No system of clientship suits them; but every man must pay his scot. **1870** A. STEINMETZ *Gaming Table* I. viii. 214 Some silly lad..allows himself to be..wheedled into paying their scot. **1879** PATTISON *Milton* iii. 36 He paid his scot by reciting from memory some of his youthful Latin verses. **1879** MISS JACKSON *Shropsh. Word-bk.*, *Scot*, an ale-house reckoning.

† **b.** *Comb.*, as *scot-penny.*

1319 in Gross *Gild Merch.* (1890) II. 13 Solvent denar' qui Scot peny vocatur. **1338** *Andover Gild Rolls* ibid. 335 Summa denariorum receptorum de scotpanes, sigepanes et hanspanes in domo inferiori xlii.*s.* v.*d.*

† **2.** A customary tax laid on, or a contribution paid by subjects according to their ability; a custom paid to the use of a sheriff or bailiff; a local or municipal tax. *Obs.*

1387 TREVISA *Higden* (Rolls) II. 97 Scot, a gaderynge in work of baylifes. **1432–50** tr. *Higden* ibid., Scot, that is the paymente of a certeyne money to the vtilite of the lorde. **1545** ELYOT *Dict.*, *Cloacarium*, scotte in a towne for clensynge of commune draughtes. **1646** J. BENBRIGGE *Usura Accom.* 15 So they may..at least be eased in their Scots and Taxes.

3. *spec.* A tax levied on the inhabitants of the marshes and levels of Kent and Sussex (see quots.).

1793 A. YOUNG *Agric. Sussex* 22 In Pevensey, and generally in all the levels, is raised a tax by the acre, called Scot, both general and particular. The general scot is applied for the purposes of paying water-bailiffs expenses. ..The particular scot is applied for the..looking after the streams and sewers. **1896** *Daily News* 1 June 4/6 This 'scot' is a special rate on the agriculturists of the marshes, and in some years has amounted to as much as 8s. in the £.

4. *scot and lot* (earlier *lot and scot*): a tax levied by a municipal corporation in proportionate shares upon its members for the defraying of municipal expenses. Phrase, *to pay* (a person *off*) *lot and scot* (fig.), to pay out thoroughly, to settle with. Also *shot and lot*: see SHOT *sb.*

1227 in Gross *Gild Merch.* (1890) II. 211 Si aliquis natiuus alicuius in prefato Burgo manserit,..et fuerit in prefata Gilda et Hansa et loth et Scoth cum eisdem Burgensibus [etc.]. **1320** *Rolls of Parlt.* I. 377/2 Quod cum illa villa de Pevenese..fuerit..in Lote & Scott cum illa villa de Hastinges. **1494** in *Eng. Gilds* (1870) 189, I shalbe redy at scotte and lotte, and all my duties truly pay and doo. **1537** in W. H. TURNER *Select. Rec. Oxford* 150 Robt. James..shall bere almaner of skotte and lotte. **1540** *Act 32 Hen. VIII*, c. 42 §6 The said barbours..shal beare and pay lot and scot..within the sayd citie. **1596** SHAKS. *1 Hen. IV*, v. iv. 115 Twas time to counterfet, or that hotte Termagant Scot, had paid me scot and lot too. **1640** *Jrnl. Ho. Commons* II. 14 The Election was free to every one that paid Scot and Lot. **1710** ADDISON *Whig Exam.* No. 5 ¶3 The freeholders of Great Britain, as well as those that pay scot and lot. **1822** GALT *Sir A. Wylie* xii. I. 92 Ye maun just gang your ways, for scot nor lot will I pay you, or the like o' you. **1835** *App. Munic. Corpor. Rep.* I. 5 The Juries are selected by the bailiffs from the inhabitants paying scot and lot. **1844** DICKENS *Mart. Chuz.* xxiv, I'll pay you off scot and lot by and bye. **1865** — *Mut. Fr.* I. xvi, She paid scot and she paid lot when she had money to pay. **1876** BROWNING *Pacchiarotto* xiii, This notable Club Pacchiarotto Had joined long since, paid scot and lot to, As free and accepted 'Bardotto'.

b. *attrib.*

1718 PRIOR *Protogenes & Apelles* 12 Protogenes, Historians note, Liv'd there, a Burgess Scot and Lot. **1809** MALKIN *Gil Blas* III. iv. ¶8 This is really too flattering, interrupted the scot and lot gentleman. **1831** *Lincoln Herald* 29 Apr., By Scot and Lot Voting. **1835** *App. Munic. Corpor. Rep.* II. 1059 (Seaford, Kent) The Commonalty are the scot and lot inhabitants. **1869** ROGERS *Hist. Gleanings* I. 67 The scot-and-lot voters. **1898** J. E. C. BODLEY *France* II. III. iii. 157 Scot-and-lot electors.

scot (skɒt), *sb.*[3] [Cf. Icel. *Skotti*, a nickname for 'a horse whose body and tail are of different colours' (Vigf.), *skott* a (fox's) tail; also SCUT *sb.*]

1. A name of a horse. Now *dial.* (Suffolk): see E.D.D.

c **1386** CHAUCER *Prol.* 616 This Reue sat vpon a ful good stot, That was al pomely grey, and highte Scot. *Ibid. Friar's T.* 245 Hayt Brok, hayt Scot, what spare ye for the stones?

†**2.** An old name for the hare. *Obs. rare*$^{-1}$. Cf. SCOTART, SCOTEWINE.

a **1325** *Names of Hare* in *Rel. Ant.* I. 133 The scot, the deubert [etc.].

scot (skɒt), *v.* See also SHOT *v.* [f. SCOT *sb.*[2]]

†**1.** *intr.* To participate, share (*with* a person).

a **1225** *Ancr. R.* 348 Ase ȝe schotteð mid him of his pine on eorðe, also ȝe schulen scotten mid him of his blisse ine heouene.

b. *Sc.* in phr. *to scot and lot*: see SCAT *v.*[2]

1531 *Burgh Rec. Edin.* (1871) II. 53 Because the saidis vnfremen nowthir scottis lottis, walkis nor wardis within our said fredome. **1583** J. BALFOUR *Practicks* (1754) 48 Gif ony wedow buy and sell within burgh with the nichtbouris, sche sall scot and lot with thame in taxatiounis and utheris helpis.

2. *trans.* To lay (a person or property) under contribution of 'scot'; to assess.

c **1750** in *Catal. Archives All Souls' Coll.* (1877) 226 List of owners of land scotted of Lydd Wall. **1774** E. JACOB *Faversham* 28 All which lands and tenements are geldable by the abbot, and scotted and lotted as well as ourselves, for the service of our lord the king. **1864** LOWER in *Sussex Archæol. Collect.* XVI. 253 As low lands drained at a public or common charge are still said to be 'scotted'.

Hence **'scotted** *ppl. a.*, **'scotting** *vbl. sb.*

1545 *Aberdeen Reg.* (Jam.), Thair scotting & lotting, with the furing of his guids furth of Aberdeen to Leyth. **1893** *Doncaster Chron.* 10 Nov. 1/5 That the sum of £500 be allowed from the estate in reduction of the engine rates on the scotted lands.

'scotale, 'scot-ale. *Obs.* exc. *Hist.* Also 2 scot(t)hale, (scotteshale), 4 scotal(l. [f. SCOT *sb.*[2] + -ALE.] An 'ale' or festival at which ale was drunk at the invitation of the lord of the manor or of a forester or other bailiff, for which ale a forced contribution was levied.

[**1155-8** in *Cal. Charter Rolls* (1906) II. 472 Quod omnes sint quieti de burdel..et de scotala..ita quod vicecomes meus..scotalam non faciat.] **1190** in Stubbs *Sel. Charters* (1895) 266 Quod omnes sint quieti de jeresgieve et de scottes-hale, ita quod si vicecomes noster vel aliquis alius baillivus scotthale faciat. **1217** *Charter of Forest* vii, Nullus forestarius vel bedellus de cetero faciat scotale, vel [etc.] **1235-52** *Rentalia Glastonbury* (Somerset Rec. Soc.) 108 Item, potabit iij scotallas. **1474-5** in Swayne *Sarum Churchw. Acc.* (1896) 17 Et in clauis emptis pro domo scotale hoc anno, vd. **1598** MANWOOD *Lawes Forest* xxi. §4 (1615) 203/2 A Scottall or Scot-ale is, where any officer of the Forest doth keepe an Alehouse..and by colour of his office doth cause men to come to his house, and there to spend their money, for feare of hauing his displeasure. **1660** SOMNER *Gavelkind* 29 It seems to be the same with what was afterwards called Scot-ale, whereof you may read in Matth. Paris, the Charter of the Forest, Bracton, the Mirroir, and elsewhere. **1874** STUBBS *Const. Hist.* xiii. (1897) I. 672 Next to this the 'scot-ale' seems to have been the most burdensome local custom. The nature of this exaction is very obscure. It was however levied by the sheriff for his own emolument, probably as a reward for his services in maintaining the peace.

†**'scotart.** *Obs. rare*$^{-1}$. [? f. SCUT *sb.* + *-art*, -ARD. Cf. SCOT *sb.*[3] 2.] An old name for the hare.

a **1325** *Names of Hare* in *Rel. Ant.* I. 133 The hare, the scotart, the bigge, the bouchart.

scotch (skɒtʃ), *sb.*[1] In 5 skoch, 8 skotch, *dial.* squotch. [Cognate with SCOTCH *v.*[1]]

1. An incision, cut, score or gash.

c **1450** *Two Cookery-bks.* 102 Kut him in þe bakke in two or þre places, but noȝt þorgh, And drawe him in þe sket [*Douce MS.* skoch] next the hede, as thou doest a rounde pike. **1526** *Grete Herball* cclxxiii. (1529) P iv b, In that countree the people make scotches or clyftes in the barke of this tre. **1565** COOPER *Thesaurus, Cicatricosa vitis*, a vine full of scotches and choppes. **1606** SHAKS. *Ant. & Cl.* IV. vii. 10 Wee'l beat 'em into Bench-holes, I haue yet Roome for six scotches more. **1625** N. CARPENTER *Geog. Del.* I. ii. (1635) 37 A round bowle..indented here and there with scotches. **1655** WALTON *Angler* xiii. (1661) 194 Then give him [the eel] three or four scotches with a knife. **1684** *Lond. Gaz.* No. 1895/4 A pretty big chubbed Man,..a Scotch in his Face. **1787** GROSE *Prov. Gloss., Skotch, or Squotch*, a notch, or cut. **1787** W. H. MARSHALL *Norfolk* (1795) II. 387 *Scotches*, scores, or notches. **1832** L. HUNT *Boileau's Battle of Bks.* 51 All arm them as they can: one gives a scotch With 'Love's Decree'; another, with the 'Watch'.

2. *spec.* A line scored or marked upon the ground, in the game of HOPSCOTCH. Also *Comb.* †**scotch-hoppers, -hob**, names for the game.

1677 *Poor Robin* To Rdr., The time when School-boys should play at Scotch-hoppers. **1693** LOCKE *Educ.* §76 (1699) 116 Dancing and Scotch-hoppers would be the same thing to them, were the Encouragements and Discouragements equal. *Ibid.* §129. **1823** E. MOOR *Suffolk Words, Scotch-hob.* **1890** WEDGWOOD in *N. & Q.* Ser. VII. X. 64 Taking care that the tile shall be driven clear over the scotch, or scored line.

†**3.** Phr. *out of all scotch and notch*, ? beyond all bounds or calculation. Cf. SCOTCH *v.*[1] 1 b. *Obs.*

1589 *Marprel., Hay any Work* A ij b, The pleasure which you haue done vnto me, is out of all scotche and notche. **1594** LYLY *Mother Bombie* II. iii, We gird them and flout them out of all scotch and notch, and they cannot see it. **1596** NASHE *Saffron Walden* 9 Thou wilt be as ready as any catchpoule, out of all scotch & notch to torment him.

scotch (skɒtʃ), *sb.*[2] Also 7 skatch, 9 skotch. [Belongs to SCOTCH *v.*[2]: of obscure origin; perh. cogn. w. SCOTE *v.*

If the 17th c. form *skatch* be correct, the word may be identical with SCATCH *sb.*, stilt.]

1. A block placed under a wheel, a cask, or the like, to prevent moving or slipping.

1639 HORN & ROB. *Gate Lang. Unl.* xlii. §458 Behind there is a skatch to stay the wagon in some steep descent. **1861** J. B. KEENE *Pract. Gauging* 40 They [*sc.* casks] are to be firmly fixed, by means of scotches placed underneath, in a horizontal position, bung upwards. **1859** F. A. GRIFFITHS *Artil. Man.* (1862) 115 Two shod handspikes, and two scotches. **1877** *Field Exerc. Infantry* 415 The wheels must be well secured with lashing rope and scotches. **1897** *Daily News* 11 Feb. 8/5 The scotches failed, and the boiler began to back down the hill.

b. *fig.*

1601 SIR W. CORNWALLIS *Ess.* II. xlv. (1631) 251 It is time so soon as our breathing hath set a scotch upon Time. **1861** RUFFINI *Dr. Antonio* x, The Baronet, who did not like so many scotches put to his plans. **1887** *S. Chesh. Gloss.* s.v., So we often speak metaphorically of 'putting a *scotch* on a person's wheel', i.e checking him; and to put a *scotch* on a project is to put difficulties in its way.

2. (See quot.)

1875 KNIGHT *Dict. Mech., Scotch*, a slotted bar which slips upon a rod or pipe, and forms a bearing for a shoulder or collar thereon, so as to support it while a section above is being attached or detached. Used in boring and tubing wells.

Scotch (skɒtʃ), *a.* and *sb.*[3] Also 7 Scot'sh. [Contracted var. of SCOTTISH.

The three forms of the adj., *Scotch, Scottish, Scots*, are still current, with some difference in use, which, however, is somewhat unsettled. Down to the middle of the 16th c. the only form used in southern English was *Scottish*; but in the dialect of Scotland (and in that of the north of England in the 14th and 15th c.) the form was *Scottis* (cf. *Inglis* = English), subsequently contracted to *Scots*. So far as our quotations show, the contraction of *Scottish* into *Scotch* is not recorded before 1570 (in the compound *Scotchman*), though the colloquial pronunciation which it represents may well be much older; instances of *Scotch cap, Scotch jig* occur in 1591–99, but the adj. did not become common in literature until the second half of the 17th c. From that time until the 19th c. *Scotch* has been the prevailing form in England, though *Scottish* has always been in use as a more formal synonym. In Scotland, the authors who wrote in dialect (down to Ramsay and Fergusson early in the 18th c.) used *Scots*, while those who anglicized adopted the form *Scottish*. But before the end of the 18th c. *Scotch* had been adopted into the northern vernacular; it is used regularly by Burns, and subsequently by Scott; still later, it appears even in official language in the title of the 'Scotch Education Office'. Since the mid 19th c. there has been in Scotland a growing tendency to discard this form altogether, *Scottish*, or less frequently *Scots*, being substituted. At the beginning of the 20th c., while in England *Scotch* was the ordinary colloquial word, the literary usage prefered *Scottish* in applications relating to the nation or the country at large or its institutions or characteristics. Thus it was usual to speak of 'Scottish literature', 'Scottish history', 'the Scottish character', 'a Scottish lawyer', 'the Scottish border'. On the other hand, it would have sounded affected to say 'a Scottish girl', 'a Scottish gardener.' Although 'the Scottish dialect' is now the usual designation, it is seldom that *Scottish* is used as a sb. instead of *Scotch*. Recent usage favours *Scots* in 'Scots law', and it is now almost universal in historical references to money, as 'a pound Scots'.

In the 20th c. the word *Scotch* has been falling into disuse in England as well as in Scotland, out of deference to the Scotsman's supposed dislike of it; except for certain fixed collocations, (such as 'Scotch mist', 'Scotch whisky') *Scottish* (less frequently *Scots*) is now the usual adjective, and to designate the inhabitants of Scotland the pl. sb. *Scots* is preferred (see Gowers/Fowler *Mod. Eng. Usage* (1965)).]

A. *adj.*

1. a. Of persons: Of, belonging to, or native to, Scotland.

1606 WARNER *Alb. Eng.* XIV. lxxxiv. (1612) 350 Ferquard did with the fatall Chaire, earst spoke-of, send his Sonne. That thereupon of Scotch-Kings Here the Title first begunne, And all Scotch-Crownings earst as his, on it were Else-where done. **1654** H. L'ESTRANGE *Chas. I* (1655) 166 The Scot'sh Revolters in the state I left them, were not like to meliorate nor to goe lesse in animosity. *c* **1655** MILTON *Sonn., Forcers of Conscience* 12 By shallow Edwards and Scotch what d'ye call. **1701** *Cowel's Interpr., Acre*, an old sort of Duel fought by single Combatants, English and Scotch, between the Frontiers of their Kingdom, with Sword and Lance. *a* **1704** T. BROWN *Laconics* Wks. 1711 IV. 15 An English Bull-dog, and a Scotch Presbyterian, are of a different Species from all the Bull-dogs and Presbyterians in the World. **1775** *Brit. Chronol.* II. an. 1717, 19 June, Several of the Scotch clergy, being convicted a second time, of not praying for king George by name, were silenced for three years. **1838** W. BELL *Dict. Law Scot.* Pref. 7 To which no Scotch lawyer of the present century can refer, without [etc.]. **1860** THACKERAY *Round. Papers, On some carp at Sans Souci*, That tipsy Scotch gentleman who used to come to the chambers sometimes. **1861** PEARSON *Early & Mid. Ages Eng.* xxvi. 313 His marriage with Maud, the aunt of the Scotch king. **1894** SIR J. ASTLEY *Fifty Yrs. Life* II. 201 He had no Scotch blood in him that I know of! **1943** *Sun* (Baltimore) 25 June 12/7 My father came from Invernesshire and certainly never restricted the use of Scotch to the whiskey. It is only in recent years that certain Anglo-American friends have made me feel guilty of committing a particularly bourgeois *faux pas* by using the word. We always looked on Scottish as rather affected, overly poetic. **1976** *Times* 11 May 15/3 Professor Trevor Roper..tries to irritate and provoke by using the word 'Scotch' knowing well that many decent Scots..have come to regard this as a demeaning adjective.

b. *Scotch cuddy, draper,* †*merchant*, etc.: a travelling draper or pedlar: see quots. and SCOTCHMAN[1] 1 a.

1706 PHILLIPS (ed. Kersey), *Pedler*, one that sells small Wares about the Streets; a Hawker; a Scotch or wand'ring Merchant. **1818** SCOTT *Rob Roy* xxii, [He] spoke of Jarvie as a petulant, conceited Scotch pedlar, with whom there was no dealing. **1894** *Northumb. Gloss., Manadge-man*, an itinerant vendor of goods on credit for household requirements. Sometimes called in Newcastle a 'Scotch draper'. **1901** G. DOUGLAS *Ho. Green Shutters* 96 The 'Scotch Cuddy' is so called because he is a beast of burden, and not from the nature of his wits. He is a travelling packman, who infests communities of working men, and disposes of his goods on the credit system, receiving payment in instalments. *Ibid.* 98 Sandy..had been a Scotch Cuddy in the Midlands. **1908** E. PARRY in *Daily Chron.* 9 June 4/7 A Scotch draper is a credit travelling draper, and I believe they originally came from Scotland.

c. In the names of military bodies consisting of Scotchmen.

Scotch Greys: sometimes used for the official form *Scots Greys* (see GREY *sb.* 8).

1756 *Act 29 Geo. II*, c. 17 §5 The Corps in the Service of ..the United Provinces, distinguished by the Name of The Scotch Brigade. **1817** J. SCOTT *Paris Revisit.* (ed. 4) 139 At this moment the Scotch Greys poured in upon the enemy as a flood. **1818** SCOTT *Hrt. Midl.* iii, The corps long maintained in the service of the States of Holland, and called the Scotch Dutch. **1853** STOCQUELER *Milit. Encycl., Scotch Brigade*, a brigade of Scotchmen, gentlemen and others, who served under the elector of Bavaria in the reign of James I, and subsequently under Gustavus Adolphus in the thirty years' war.

d. Characteristic of Scotland or its people.

1815 R. BELL *Conveyance of Land* Introd. 8 The statute acting (agreeably to Scotch ideas) as a charter of confirmation in favour of every subsequent purchaser. **1834** M. SCOTT *Cruise of Midge* viii, 'What ship is that?' This was answered Scotch fashion—'What felucca is that?' **1900** *St. James's Gaz.* 9 Apr. 3/1 What the sailors call 'Scotch seamanship', which is all stupidity and main strength. **1906** E. DYSON *Fact'ry 'Ands* xvi. 209 Well, he's touched me three times in a week, and I'm as Scotch as most people. **1912** J. N. MCILWRAITH *Diana of Quebec* iii. 49 'You would be the first to throw me a penny..?' 'A sixpence, truly, if he be not too Scotch,' said Nelson. **1932** *Amer. Speech* VII. 403 Mr. ——, if you weren't so Scotch we could have a good time here.

e. *Scotch cousin*: a distant relative (in allusion to the practice in Scotland of tracing kinship to remote degrees). Also, with similar connotation, *Scotch sister*.

1861 J. S. MILL *Repr. Govt.* xviii. 335 The most important offices would be thrown to Scotch cousins and adventurers. **1864** *Times* 10 Aug. (Hoppe), A Scotch cousinship of ten removes. **1866** MRS. GASKELL *Wives & Daughters* I. xix. 219 She called her a sister, but whether it was a Scotch sister, or a sister *à la mode de Bretagne*, would have puzzled most people. **1887** MARY CHOLMONDELEY *Danvers Jewels* i, I have no deserving nephew or Scotch cousin.

2. a. Of things: Of or pertaining to Scotland or its inhabitants (often denoting a particular variety or quality of the thing named, e.g. *Scotch ale, ballad, cambric, carpet, paling, reel, rite, salmon, snuff, whisky*, etc.).

1591, 1595 [see SCOTCH CAP]. **1599** SHAKS. *Much Ado* II. i. 77 The first suite is hot and hasty like a Scotch jigge (and full as fantastical). **1669** DIGBY *Closet Opened* 114 The excellent Scotch Ale is made thus. *a* **1700** B. E. *Dict. Cant. Crew* s.v. *Luggs*, A Scotch Proverb. **1733** *S. Carolina Gaz.* 7 Apr. 4/3 (Advt.), To be sold..cut Tobacco, Scotch Snuff, and Pigtail. **1738** *Gentl. Mag.* VIII. 296/2 The Scotch Settlement there [at Darien]. **1774** Scotch carpet [see WILTON[1]]. **1785** *Spanish Rivals* 7, I have stuck to my master like a Scotch plaid, in all weathers. **1785** BURNS *Scotch Drink* i, I sing the juice Scotch bear can make us. *Ibid.* ii, O thou, my Muse! guid, auld Scotch Drink! **1792** F. BURNEY *Jrnl.* May (1972) I. 153 Miss Cooper..gave me a relation of her having been..at Mrs. Broadhead's masquerade as *Jenny*, from the Scotch ballad. **1808** SCOTT in *Lockhart* (1837) I. i. 58 The Scotch law lectures were those of Mr. David Hume. **1820** *Trials for High Treason Scot.* (1825) I. 93 We are here to deal with Scotch law in a Scottish court. **1832** *Scoreby Farm Rep.* 5 in *Libr. Useful Knowl., Husb.* III, Scotch-Paling, neat light fence, peculiarly adapted for gardens, for securing single trees,..was introduced at Scoreby [Yorkshire], from Lanarkshire, by John Wood, Esq., M.P., a few years ago. **1835** DICKENS *Sk. Boz* (1837) 2nd Ser. 39 Mr. Thomas Potter ordered the waiter to bring two goes of his best Scotch whisky, with warm water and sugar. **1838** W. BELL *Dict. Law Scot.* 5 In Scotch law language, however, the term *absolute disposition* is generally used in relation to heritable property. **1839** URE *Dict. Arts* 263 The three-ply imperial carpet, called the Scotch, is coming very much into vogue. **1855** J. F. W. JOHNSTON *Chem. Common Life* xiv. I. 337 While malt liquors give our Scotch and Irish whiskies. **1858** SIMMONDS *Dict. Trade, Scotch-cambric*, a cotton fabric made in imitation of French cambric. **1861** PEARSON *Early & Mid. Ages Eng.* xxviii. 337 The transition of races that was rapidly going on in the Scotch Lowlands. **1883** *Grove's Dict. Mus.* III. 437 The impressions of his [Mendelssohn's] Scotch tour in 1829. **1891** S. M. WELCH *Home Hist.* 183 It was not uncommon to see a couple of portly old gentlemen meeting on the street offering their boxes of Maccaboy, Rappee or Scotch, each to the other. *Ibid.* 376 [In] the 'Scotch Reel',..each lad must needs have two lassies. **1893** T. HARDY *Let.* 6 Oct. in Hardy & Pinion *One Rare Fair Woman* (1972) 28 Lady J[eune]..played and sang at least a dozen Scotch ballads to me. **1953** *Word for Word* (Whitbread & Co.) 10/2 *Scotch ale*, a draught or bottled ale of the Burton type, brewed in Scotland. **1960** *Connoisseur's Handbk. Antique Collecting* 251/1 *Scotch carpets*, double-cloth or ply weavings for the floor, also known as Kidderminster or Ingrain. **1965** V. CANNING *Whip Hand* xii. 143 We had.. Scotch salmon with a cucumber salad. **1969** *Daily Tel.* 30 Apr. 29/7 New definitions of whisky.. are contained in the Finance Bill, published last night... 'Scotch whisky' is to mean whisky which has been distilled in Scotland. **1978** J. MANN *Sting of Death* iii. 25 Alex would probably be ordering.. gulls' eggs and Scotch salmon. **1980** R. LEWIS *Certain Blindness* iii. 80 Parton put a pint of Scotch Ale in front of him.

b. As the epithet of various weights and measures, etc. (differing from the English standard), used formerly in Scotland. ***Scotch acre***, 6,084 square yards; ***Scotch ell***, 37·0958 inches; ***Scotch mile***, see MILE *sb.*[1] 1: etc. Cf. SCOTS *a.* 16, SCOTTISH *a.*

1774 PENNANT *Tour Scot. in 1772*, 314 The half-Davoch .. consists of ninety-six Scotch acres of arable land.. with a competent quantity of mountain or grazing land. **1785** BURNS *Death & Dr. Hornbook* vii, Its stature seem'd lang Scotch ells twa. **1786** —— *Auld Farmer's Salut. Mare* x, But sax Scotch mile, thou try't their mettle. **1797** *Encycl. Brit.* (ed. 3) X. 718/1 The Scotch quart contains 210 inches. **1799** J. ROBERTSON *Agric. Perth* p. vi, Table Weights etc., 1 Scotch pint = 103·4 cubic inches... A Scotch acre commonly = 6084 square yards. N.B. If the difference of inches were narrowly attended to in making the Scotch chain, a Scotch acre would be equal to 6150·7 square yards. **1801** *Farmer's Mag.* Apr. 179 A good crop of hay, upon an English statute acre, will not exceed 240 Scotch stone. **1818** SCOTT *Rob Roy* xix, At the rate of twelve shillings (Scotch) per diem. **1843** LOUDON *Encycl. Agric.* Suppl. (1857) §8308 The following table exhibits the cost per Scotch acre of draining in this method.

c. With the names of various animals and birds.

Scotch dipper, duck, teal, local U.S. for the *Charitonetta* or *Bucephala albeola* (in Cent. Dict. 1891 and later Dicts.).

a **1700** B. E. *Dict. Cant. Crew*, *Scotch-hobby*, a little sorry, scrubbed, low Horse of that Country. **1726** D. EATON *Let.* 31 Dec. (1971) 87, I think the Scotch cattell were dearer than if they had been bought in our country [i.e. district]. I mean cattel of their size might have been bought in our markets for less mony. **1847** W. C. L. MARTIN *The Ox* 61/1 Black Scotch cattle. **1877** *Encycl. Brit.* VI. 515/2 The chief breeds of coursing greyhounds now in vogue are the Newmarket, the Lancashire, and the Scotch. **1885** SWAINSON *Prov. Names Birds* 28 [The sedge-warbler is called] Scotch nightingale (Roxburgh; Stirling). **1887** *Field* 18 June 845/3 Some people at Felling-on-Tyne.. were taken in by buying skinned cats for 'Scotch hares'. **1980** A. BELL *Sydney Smith* 117 Scotch sheep provided material for Sydney's only contribution to agricultural literature.

d. With the names of various insects, esp. butterflies and moths. (See quots.)

1832 J. RENNIE *Butterfl. & Moths* 13 The Scotch Ringlet (*Hipparchia Blandina*, Leach) appears in August. *Ibid.* 19 The Scotch Argus (*Polyommatus Artaxerxes*, Stephens) appears at the end of July. *Ibid.* 135 The Scotch Pug (*Eupithecia cognata*, Stephens)... Scarce. Fifeshire and Mid Lothian. **1869** NEWMAN *Brit. Moths* 68 The Scotch Amulet (*Dasydia obfuscata*). **1876** J. GIBSON in *Encycl. Brit.* IV. 595/1 Other species are extremely local, as the Scotch Argus (*Lycæna artaxerxes*), confined to a few Scottish hillsides. **1887** *Cassell's Encycl. Dict.*, *Scotch-sawfly*, the genus Lophyrus.

e. *Typogr.* The epithet of a variety of modern typefaces deriving from one sent from an Edinburgh foundry in 1837 to the printing firm of S. N. Dickinson in Boston, Massachusetts. So ***Scotch-cut*** adj.

1847 S. N. DICKINSON *Hand-bk. Specimen Printing Type* Pref., Our Scotch Faces were selected from the very extensive Foundry of Alexander Wilson and Sons of Edinburgh and also from an eminent letter cutter of that city. *Ibid.*, The symmetry of the Scotch cut figures. *a* **1863** *Specimens of Borders, Ornaments, Rules, Dashes, etc. from Dickinson Type Foundry* (Boston, U.S.) Back cover, A superior collection of the Scotch-cut letter, so highly appreciated by the trade. **1900** T. L. DE VINNE *Practice of Typogr.* vi. 212 As first made the Scotch-face was a small, neat, round letter, with long ascenders, and not noticeably condensed. **1922** D. B. UPDIKE *Printing Types* II. xx. 193 As produced by Wilson it is a very handsome and serviceable letter, and in it we have another English type-family—the Scotch modern face. **1951** S. JENNETT *Making of Bks.* xiv. 248 Bodoni is an excellent letter, but capable of great degeneration, and in Scotch Roman we see the degeneration commencing. **1966** H. WILLIAMSON *Methods Bk. Design* (ed. 2) viii. 99 The original Scotch faces were a vaguely defined class, and generalization about their letter-forms is impossible.

3. As the designation of the variety of northern English which is vernacular in Scotland. Hence of words, expressions, etc., belonging to this, and of works composed in it. Cf. SCOTS *a.* 2, SCOTTISH *a.*

1797 *Encycl. Brit.* (ed. 3) XIV. 560/1 *marg.*, Causes of the purity of the Scotch dialect of this ancient language. **1801** W. BEATTIE (*title*), Fruits of Time Parings, being a small collection of original poems, Scotch and English. **1828** P. CUNNINGHAM *N.S. Wales* (ed. 3) II. 239 Many spoke the Scotch dialect so broadly as almost to puzzle *me* to unravel it. **1829** SCOTT *Rob Roy* Introd., To secure the adherence of stout, able-bodied, and, as the Scotch phrase then went, *pretty* men. **1863** *Smith's Dict. Bible* III. 1649/2 Similar to the Scotch pronunciation of the initial H. **1878** *Encycl. Brit.* VIII. 398/2 So in early Scotch books we find *zellow, ze, yat, yem.*

4. a. Special collocations: **Scotch bait** (see quot.); **Scotch Baronial** *a.* = *Scottish Baronial* s.v. SCOTTISH *a.* 5; **Scotch Blackface**, a sheep belonging to the breed so called, developed in mountain and moorland regions of Scotland and northern England, and distinguished by black legs and muzzle and long wool; **Scotch boiler** [so called from its having been introduced in Scottish shipyards], a fire-tube boiler in which combustion takes place inside the shell; † **Scotch boot** = BOOT *sb.*[3] 3; **Scotch (†barley) broth**, a soup containing meat, vegetables and pearl barley; † **Scotch bum**, a kind of bustle; **Scotch catch** *Mus.* = *Scotch snap*; **Scotch chocolate, coffee** *slang* (see quots.); **Scotch collops** (see COLLOP[1] 2 c); **Scotch douche** [= F. *douche écossaise*] (see quot.); **Scotch egg**, a hard-boiled egg enclosed in sausage-meat; **Scotch face** *Printing* (see quot.); † **Scotch fall**, an article of dress; **Scotch fiddle** *slang*, the itch (see FIDDLE *sb.* 4 c); **Scotch fines**, a particular quality of rags used in paper-making; **Scotch furnace**, 'a simple form of ore-hearth used in smelting lead ores' (*Cent. Dict.* 1891); **Scotch hand, hearth** (see quots.); † **Scotch-land**, Scotland; **Scotch marriage** (see MARRIAGE 2); **Scotch mist**, (*a*) (see MIST *sb.*[1] 1 c), also allusively; (*b*) something insubstantial, unreal, freq. used sarcastically in a retort or rhetorical question to imply that someone has imagined or failed to comprehend something; (*c*) a drink of whisky served with a twist of lemon; hence **Scotch-misty** *a.*, characterized by Scotch mist; **Scotch pancake** = *drop-scone* s.v. SCONE 1; **Scotch pebble** (see PEBBLE *sb.* 2 c); **Scotch peg**, rhyming slang for 'leg'; **Scotch prize** *Naut.*, a capture by mistake; † **scotch rabbit**, ? a 'Welsh rabbit'; † **Scotch saddle**, a particular variety of saddle (cf. *Scotissh sadell*, SADDLE *sb.* 1 b), also *attrib.* or *adj.*; **Scotch scale** *Mus.* (see quot.); † **Scotch-sleeve**, ? a person wearing sleeves of 'Scotch cloth'; **Scotch snap** *Mus.* (see quot.); **Scotch spur** *Her.*, a bearing representing a prick spur; **Scotch stone** (see quot.); **Scotch terrier**, a small stocky terrier of the breed so called, usually black or brindle, with thick, shaggy fur, erect, pointed ears and tail, and a square, bearded muzzle; formerly, a terrier belonging to one of several other Scottish races, now treated as separate breeds (cf. TERRIER *sb.*[2]); **Scotch woodcock**: see WOODCOCK *sb.* 3 d; **Scotch yoke**, a mechanism by which a steady circular motion can be transformed into a linear simple harmonic motion, consisting of a crank bearing a peg which, as the crank revolves, slides in a straight slot constrained to move to and fro along a straight line in a plane at right angles to the plane of the slot. See also SCOTCH BONNET, CAP, CLOTH.

1785 GROSE *Dict. Vulgar T.*, **Scotch bait*, a halt and a resting on a stick, as practised by pedlars. **1880** J. J. STEVENSON *House Archit.* I. xiv. 360 The *Scotch 'Baronial' architecture, as it is called, resembles that of the Renaissance châteaux of France. **1931** E. SACKVILLE-WEST *Simpson* II. vii. 144 Salathiel held up a glass globe, inside which was a miniature Scotch-baronial castle in china. [**1888** J. & C. SCOTT *Blackfaced Sheep* i. 1 The origin of the Scotch blackfaced sheep is shrouded in mystery.] **1945** J. F. H. THOMAS *Sheep* ii. 30 It deserves the title *Scotch Blackface because in that country it is of paramount importance. **1903** H. DE B. PARSONS *Steam-Boilers* v. 97 (*caption*) *Scotch boiler, single-ended, with common combustion-chamber. **1966** *McGraw-Hill Encycl. Sci. & Technol.* VIII. 119/2 Later boilers are of the express or water-tube type, burning fuel oil, though Scotch boilers are still used in some cases and may burn either coal or fuel oil. **1697** COLLIER *Ess. Mor. Subj.* I. (1709) 123 They.. immediately.. got a sort of *Scotch-Boot to bend their Hams in. **1747** H. GLASSE *Art of Cookery* vi. 65 (*heading*) To make *Scotch barley broth. **1834** T. HOOD *Tylney Hall* I. xv. 175 We shall have an ounce of mutton swimming in a tureen of barley-water—I've heard of their Scotch broths. **1969** R. & D. DE SOLA *Dict. Cooking* 203/1 *Scotch broth*, rich soup made of beef or mutton and vegetables, thickened with barley. **1607** DEKKER & WEBSTER *Westw.-Hoe* II. ii, That French gowne, Scotch fals, *Scotch bum, and Italian head-tire you sent her. **1785** GROSE *Dict. Vulgar T.*, **Scotch chocolate*, brimstone and milk. **1864** *Hotten's Slang Dict.*, **Scotch coffee*, biscuits toasted and boiled in water. Sea. **1883** CLARK RUSSELL *Sailor's Lang.*, *Scotch coffee*, hot water flavoured with burnt biscuit. **1891** *Century Dict.*, **Scotch douche*, a douche of hot water, beginning at a temperature of 40°C., increased gradually to 45–50°C., and immediately followed by cold water; more generally, a succession of alternate hot and cold douches. **1809** M. E. RUNDELL *New Syst. Domestic Cookery* (new ed.) VIII. 207 **Scotch eggs*. Boil hard five pullet's eggs, and without removing the white, cover completely with a fine relishing forcemeat. *c* **1965** A. CHRISTIE *Autobiogr.* (1977) XI. iv. 525 He fed us entirely on.. 'Scotch eggs'; excessively indigestible. **1972** P. D. JAMES *Unsuitable Job* i. 19 Pushing a half pint of shandy and a Scotch egg across the counter. **1977** D. WILLIAMS *Treasure by Degrees* xv. 145 A lonely Scotch egg.. was the only visible justification for the plastic proclamation 'Snacks at the Bar'. **1891** *Century Dict.* s.v. *Serif*, in the *Scotch-face it [the serif] is curved like a bracket on the inner side. **1607** *Scotch fall [see *Scotch bum*]. **1675** EARL OF ROCHESTER *Tunbridge Wells* 120 And then more smartly to expound the Riddle Of all this Prattle, gives her a *Scotch Fiddle. **1880** J. DUNBAR *Pract. Papermaker* 23 *Scotch Fines. **1884** *Girl's Own Paper* Jan. 155/3 Little rolls of butter (made with the two little wooden bats known as *Scotch hands). **1881** RAYMOND *Mining Gloss.*, **Scotch hearth*, a low forge or furnace of cast-iron, with one tuyere, in which rich galena is treated by a sort of accelerated roasting and reaction process. **1654** GAYTON *Pleas. Notes* III. iv. 88 In *Scotch-land. **1768** GOLDSM. *Good-n. Man* v, *Landlady*... For certain, *Scotch marriages seldom turn out well. **1647** J. C[LEVELAND] *Char. of Lond.-Diurn.* 7 This is he, that hath put out one of the Kingdoms eyes, by clouding our Mother-University, and (if the *Scotch-mist further prevaile) will extinguish this other. **1662** *Gusman's Ephemeris* A 2 b, Since the first Scotch Mist in England 20 [years]. **1679** C. NESSE *Antichrist* 204 By sundry vials powr'd upon it, a Scotch mist is upon it. *a* **1700**- [see MIST *sb.*[1] 1 c]. **1943** HUNT & PRINGLE *Service Slang* 57 *Scotch mist*, sarcastic comment on your eyesight, inferring that you are seeing things. **1962** *New Statesman* 18 May 708/2 'Are yer married?' 'Course she is. What do yer think that is? Scotch mist?' Rube points to my wedding-ring. **1965** O. A. MENDELSOHN *Dict. Drink* 303 *Scotch mist*, cocktail of Scotch whisky and lemon peel. **1974** *Pacifist* Feb. 13/1 What are all these price-rises we are suffering now? Scotch mist? **1977** W. H. MANVILLE *Good-bye* iii. 27 You can start by ordering me a Teacher's Scotch Mist on the rocks. **1866** CARLYLE *Remin.* I. 210 A windless, *Scotch-misty, Saturday night. **1930** BENNION & STEWART *Cake Manufacture* xiv. 122 Soda scones, *Scotch pan cakes, and milk scones,.. can be baked on the hot plate. **1977** D. WILLIAMS *Treasure by Degrees* viii. 71 Tea.. could be quite a different matter. He recalled some truly outstanding Scotch pancakes. **1857** 'DUCANGE ANGLICUS' *Vulgar Tongue* 17 **Scotch peg*, leg. **1917** W. MUIR *Observat. Orderly* xiv. 225 If he had occasion to allude to his leg he would probably have called it 'Scotch peg'. **1818** 'A. BURTON' *Johnny Newcome* III. 170 'Tis but a *Scotch prize he has stolen! **1867** SMYTH *Sailors' Word-bk.*, *Scotch prize*, a mistake; worse than no prize, or one liable to hamper the captors with heavy law expenses. **1747** MRS. GLASSE *Cookery* ix. 97 To make a *Scotch-Rabbit. Toast a Piece of Bread.., butter it, cut a Slice of Cheese,.. toast it on both Sides, and lay it on the Bread. **1598** FLORIO, *Naso schiacciato*, a flat *Scotch-saddle nose. *c* **1800** BUSBY *Dict. Mus.* **Scotch-Scale*, a Scale differing from that of the other nations of Europe by its omission of the *fourth* and *seventh*; a peculiarity from which all the genuine Scottish melodies derive their national and distinguished character. **1705** HICKERINGILL *Priest-cr.* II. iii. 30 Poor Lawn-Sleeves (or *Scotch-Sleeves).. was so assaulted, as.. he had probably perished by their violence. **1883** J. M. WOOD in *Grove's Dict. Mus.* III. 437 *Scotch Snap or Catch is the name given to the reverse of the ordinary dotted note which has a short note after it—in the snap the short note comes first and is followed by the long one. **1688** HOLME *Armoury* III. vii. 304/1 *Scotch Spur. **1847** *Gloss. Heraldry* 293 The Scotch or prick-spur has a spike instead of a rowel. **1881** *Encycl. Brit.* XII. 135/1 Among hones of less importance.. may be noted.. Water of Ayr stone, *Scotch stone, or snake stone, used for tools and for polishing marble. **1810** *Sporting Mag.* XXXVI. 61/1 Portraits of a poodle and *Scotch terrier. **1847** H. D. RICHARDSON *Dogs* vii. 70 There are two varieties of the common Scotch Terrier. **1863** [see TERRIER *sb.*[2] 1]. **1880, 1889** [see *Aberdeen terrier* s.v. ABERDEEN 2]. **1927** E. C. ASH *Dogs* II. ii. 422 Two kinds of terriers are described—the rough-haired Scotch and the smooth-haired English. **1927** HAM & CRANE *Mechanics of Machinery* ii. 27 Figure 36 shows an application of the *Scotch yoke as it has occasionally been used on small engines and steam pumps. **1959** KARPLUS & SOROKA *Analog Methods* (ed. 2) viii. 242 Mechanical Harmonic Synthesizers... The sine and cosine components are almost invariably generated by Scotch yoke mechanisms. **1966** *McGraw-Hill Encycl. Sci. & Technol.* I. 377/2 The modification of the Scotch yoke shown in Fig. 25 can be used to generate a tangent function over a limited range of the argument.

b. In names of plants: **Scotch asphodel** (see ASPHODEL 2 d); **Scotch attorney**, a name given in Jamaica to various species of *Clusia* or woody vines which twine round the trunks of trees and destroy them (cf. SCOTCHMAN 1 d); **Scotch barley**, (*a*) a Scotch variety of barley; (*b*) 'a variety of pot-barley (BARLEY *sb.* 1 b), made by simply grinding off the husk' (Ogilvie *Suppl.* 1855); **Scotch bear, bigg**, bear (*sb.*[2]), and bigg, grown in Scotland; **Scotch broom**, 'an American designation of the common broom, *Cytisus scoparius*' (Cent. Dict. 1891); **Scotch cinquefoile, crocus, curlies** (see quots.); **Scotch elm**, the wych-elm, *Ulmus glabra*; **Scotch fir** (see FIR 1); **Scotch gale** = GALE *sb.*[1]; **Scotch geranium**, *Geranium Robertianum* (Britten & Holland 1886); **Scotch grass**, the *Panicum molle* of the West Indies (see quots.); **Scotch greys**, a variety of oats; **Scotch heath** or **heather** (see quot.); **Scotch kale** (see KALE 1 b); **Scotch laburnum** (see LABURNUM); **Scotch lilac** (see quot.); **Scotch lovage** = LOVAGE b; **Scotch mercury** (see MERCURY *sb.* 10 d); **Scotch parsley** = LOVAGE b; **Scotch pine** (see PINE *sb.*[2] 2); also *attrib.*; **Scotch primrose** (see PRIMROSE 2); **Scotch rose** (see quot. 1820); † **Scotch scurvy-grass**, the sea-side bindweed, *Convolvulus Soldanella*. See also SCOTCH THISTLE.

1796 WITHERING *Brit. Plants* (ed. 3) II. 358 Tofieldia palustris.. *Scotch Asphodel, Marsh Tofieldia. **1864** GRISEBACH *Flora W. Ind. Islands* 787 *Scotch attorney: *Clusia*. **1871** KINGSLEY *At Last* v, The Matapalo (or Scotch Attorney, as it is rudely called here). **1707** MORTIMER *Husb.* (1721) I. 131 In Lincolnshire they sow a sort of Barley that they call *Scotch Barley. **1825** LOUDON *Encycl. Agric.* §4689 Of pot-barley there are two sorts, pearl and Scotch; both are produced by grinding off the husk. **1839** URE *Dict. Arts* 87 The *Scotch beer or bigg, is the *hordeum vulgare hexasticon*. *Ibid.* 91 An inferior Scotch bigg. **1843** BAXTER *Brit. Phænog. Bot.* VI. 470 Sibbaldia procumbens. Procumbent Sibbaldia.

*Scotch Cinquefoil. **1882** *Garden* 28 Jan. 66/2 The Cloth of Silver or *Scotch Crocus is a large variety of the Italian Crocus biflorus. **1891** *Century Dict.*, **Scotch curlies*, a variety of kale, so called from its curled leaves. **1799** W. NICOL *Pract. Planter* i. 34 The *Scotch Elm may with propriety be reared for this purpose [*sc.* ship-building] on thin gravelly soils. **1838** J. C. LOUDON *Arboretum et Fruticetum Britannicum* III. 1399 The Scotch elm has not so upright a trunk as the English elm. **1840** BAXTER *Brit. Phænog. Bot.* V. 386 Ulmus montana. Mountain Elm. Scotch Elm. Wych Elm. **1969** T. H. EVERETT *Living Trees of World* xiv. 131/1 The Scotch elm or wych elm..forms a rather open, broad-headed specimen. **1696** PLUKENET *Almagestum* Wks. 1769 II. 297 The *Scotch Firr. **1897** BARING-GOULD *Bladys* xxii, The wind sang in a Scotch fir rooted in the red cliff overhead. **1795** *Statist. Acc. Scot.* XIV. 60 Near to the King's Well, in the same barony, is to be found what is called the *Scotch-gale, a species of the myrtle. **1756** P. BROWNE *Jamaica* (1789) 133 *Scotch Grass. This plant is cultivated and thrives very luxuriantly in all the low and marshy lands of Jamaica. **1839** *Penny Cycl.* XIII. 75/1 The Scotch grass grows with great luxuriance by the sides of the rivers [of Jamaica]. **1805** R. W. DICKSON *Pract. Agric.* I. 578 The blue oat..is suggested in Miller's Dictionary as the sort known to farmers under the title of **Scotch Greys.* **1891** *Century Dict.*, **Scotch heath* or *heather*, most properly, *Erica cinerea*..; also (U.S.), the common heather, *Celluna vulgaris.* **1840** PAXTON *Bot. Dict.*, **Scotch laburnum*, see *Cytisus alpinus.* **1759** MILLER *Gard. Dict.* (ed. 7) s.v. *Syringa*, One of these [varieties] has white Flowers, one blue, and the third has purple Flowers; the latter is commonly known by the Title of *Scotch Lilac, to distinguish it from the other. **1731** *Ibid.*, *Ligusticum; Scoticum*.. *Scotch Lovage. **1774** PENNANT *Tour Scot. in 1772*, 310 *Ligusticum scoticum*, *Scotch parsley, or the *shunis* of this island [Hebrides]. **1731** MILLER *Gard. Dict.* s.v. *Abies* 3/2 The *Scotch Pine of Pinaster, will grow on the North or East side. **1840** LOUDON tr. *Köllar's Treat. Insects* 363 The Scotch Pine Bark-Beetle. *Hylesinus* (*Hylurgus*) *piniperda*, Fabr. **1863** PRIOR *Plant-n.* 184 *Scotch-Primrose. **1731** MILLER *Gard. Dict.* s.v. *Rosa* 6, The strip'd *Scotch Rose... The sixth Sort is found wild in Scotland. **1820** J. SABINE in *Trans. Hort. Soc.* (1822) IV. 281 The Scotch Rose has been, and still is, sometimes called the Burnet Rose; it is the Rosa spinosissima of the English authors. **1892** C. M. YONGE *Old Woman's Outlook in Hampshire Village* 161 The little thorny Scotch roses..are creeping over the cottages. **1972** *Country Life* 23 Mar. 695/1 Possibly the toughest of the wild roses is ..the Scotch or Burnet Rose which flourishes in the sand dunes of Great Britain and Germany. **1787** LIGHTFOOT *Flora Scot.* I. 140 Convolvulus foliis reniformibus pedunculis unifloris..Sea Bindweed. *Scotch Scurvy-Grass.

B. *sb.* (Elliptical uses of the adj.)

1. a. *the Scotch* (pl.): The inhabitants of Scotland or their immediate descendants in other countries.

1743 M. W. MONTAGU *Let.* 16 Sept. (1966) II. 310 Several Scotch pass here often. **1781** J. RIPLEY *Sel. Orig. Lett.* 41 Let the words English and Scotch be entirely obliterated and lost in that more ancient and significant word Britons. **1818** SCOTT *Rob Roy* iv, The Scotch of that period were guilty of similar injustice to the English. **1825** LOUDON *Encycl. Agric.* §4718 The fine powder which is produced by husking the corn,..forms the sowens of the Scotch. **1861** PEARSON *Early & Mid. Ages Eng.* xxviii. 337 Meanwhile, the Scotch were divided by a quarrel as to who should lead the van. **1979** *Jrnl. R. Soc. Arts* Jan. 107/2 Since then I have had the greatest admiration for the education offered to, or seized by, the Scotch—Miss Murray's word and her grandfather's.

b. ***Scotch and English***: the English Border name for prisoner's base; cf. *French and English* (see FRENCH *sb.* 2 b).

1802 W. HUTTON *Hist. Roman Wall* 105 The children of this day, upon the English border keep up the remembrance [of former scenes] by a common play, called *Scotch and English*, or, *The Raid* (inroad). **1825** JAMIESON, *English and Scotch*, a common game among young people. **1869** MRS. SOMERVILLE *Personal Recoll.* (1872) i. 22 In our play-hours [at school in 1790] we amused ourselves..at 'Scotch and English', a game which represented a raid on the debatable land, or Border between Scotland and England, in which each party tried to rob the other of their playthings.

2. The Scotch language: see A. 3.

a **1700** B. E. *Dict. Cant. Crew*, *Sawny*, a Fool. *He's a meer sawny*, he is very soft, tho' (in Scotch) it is only for Alexander. **1818** SCOTT *Hrt. Midl.* iv, Which is to say, in plain Scotch, the gallows. **1824** —— *Redgauntlet* let. iii, I myself have since that time acquired Scotch in perfection, and many a Scotticism withal. **1878** *Encycl. Brit.* VIII. 400/2 The revival of [interest in] Lowland Scotch last century. **1896** ASHBY-STERRY *Tale of Thames* viii, I can read French as well as I can English, but it is impossible for me to comprehend Scotch.

3. a. Often *elliptically* (the sb. being contextually known), e.g. for *Scotch whisky*; also = a glass of Scotch whisky. Also formerly for *Scotch snuff*. Also = *Scotch ale* (in sense A. 2 a), *face* (A. 2 e)

1778 S. FOOTE *Cozeners* III. ii. 76, I have a box of Scotch in my pocket. **1823** J. BADCOCK *Dom. Amusem.* 100 The finely levigated snuff, known as 'Scotch'. **1886-96** MARSHALL *He Slumbered* ('Pomes,' 118) (Farmer) In the early evening watches he had started well on Scotches. **1893** H. CRACKANTHORPE *Wreckage* 125 Two bitters and a small Scotch. **1894** SIR J. ASTLEY *Fifty Yrs. Life* II. 124 And over a drop of Scotch and a cigar discuss the leading topics of the day. **1898** G. B. SHAW *Plays* II. *You never can tell* 307 *Waiter*..Scotch and syphon for you, sir? **1906** *Linotype Bull.* Oct.-Dec. 6/2 (*heading*) 8-Point Scotch. **1945** O. SIMON *Introd. Typogr.* iii. 12 The roman lower-case letters of Scotch and Baskerville..are wide and generous. **1962** S. CHAPLIN *Watchers & Watched* x. 199 The beer was as bitter as bile... 'Is there anythin' wrong?' 'Your Scotch doesn't taste too well.' **1964** S. JENNETT *Making of Books* (ed. 3) xiv. 251 Though Scotch is a portent, it is not itself as poor as its descendants became. **1966** H. WILLIAMSON *Methods Bk. Design* (ed. 2) viii. 99 The first Scotch to be cut for machine composition was produced by the Merganthaler Linotype Co. in 1902. **1976** *Observer* (Colour Suppl.) 1 Feb. 9/3 All Scotches are blended spirits: a mix of malt and grain whiskies. The ratio can vary between 2 to 3 and 3 to 2, and a bottle of Scotch can be a mixture of 30, 40 or even more whiskies. **1977** *Listener* 3 Mar. 275/1 You could order 'a pint of Scotch'—Scotch Ale, because it is the cheapest beer, is still the majority drink on Tyneside.

b. *ellipt.* for *Scotch peg* (see sense A. 4 a above).

1859 HOTTEN *Dict. Slang* 87 *Scotches*, the legs. **1962** R. COOK *Crust on its Uppers* ii. 30 Down to wearing my head in its proper place and not between my scotches like a sporran.

scotch (skɒtʃ), *v.*[1] Forms: 5 scocche, skocche, schoche, 5–6 skoche, 6 scotche, 6–7 skotch, 6– scotch. [Of obscure origin; identity with SCORCH *v.*[3] (first in 16th c.) is hardly possible.]

1. a. *trans.* To make an incision or incisions in; to cut, score, gash. ? *Obs.*

c **1412** HOCCLEVE *De Reg. Princ.* 3727 With his nayles cracched he his face, And scocched [*Roxb.* skocched] it with knyues, and to-rente. *c* **1450** *Two Cookery-bks.* 101 Schoche him [the fish] by þe hede in þe backe,..And skoche him in two or iij. peces in þe bak, but noȝt thorgh. **15..** *Scot. Field* 218 *Chetham Soc. Misc.* II, Our Englishmen full egerly attilde them to shott; Skochen the cruell Scottes with their kene arrowes. **1562** TURNER *Herbal* II. 46 b, If ye will haue the iuice, ye must scotche & pryck the rootes in many places. **1576** TURBERV. *Venerie* xliii. 131 When they haue well skotched it [the deer-skin] with their wood-kniues, that the houndes may the more easily teare off the fleshe. **1596** NASHE *Saffron Walden* Ep. Ded. C 3 b, I..will deliuer him to thee to be scotcht and carbonadoed. **1601** HOLLAND *Pliny* IV. v. I. 74 Thus many creekes doth scotch and cut Peloponnesus. **1651** T. BARKER *Art of Angling* (1653) 17 Wash the Eele cleane... Scotch it all along both the sides. **1675** HAN. WOOLLEY *Gentlew. Comp.* 129 Scotch with your knife the back of the Carp. **1747** MRS. GLASSE *Cookery* 33 When you have clear'd the Pig of both [skin and hair], scotch him down to the Bones.

absol. **1573** TUSSER *Husb.* (1878) 73 How euer ye scotch, saue pole and crotch.

†**b.** Phr. *to notch and scotch.* (? A term used in Tennis: cf. SCOTCH *sb.*[1] 3.) *Obs.*

1607 SHAKS. *Cor.* IV. v. 198 He scotcht him, and notcht him like a Carbinado. **1797** MME. D'ARBLAY *Lett.* Dec. (1891) IV. 49 They play all day at tennis, and learn with vast skill to notch and scotch and go one.

2. a. Theobald's generally accepted conjectural reading of *Macb.* III. ii. 13, 'We have scotch'd the snake, not kill'd it' (see SCORCH *v.*[3]), has become a stock quotation, in which the verb *scotch* is taken to mean: To inflict such hurt upon (something regarded as dangerous) that it is rendered harmless for the time.

1798 COOKE in *Ld. Auckland's Corr.* (1862) III. 393, I fear relaxation and too much clemency; but the snake must be killed not scotched. **1820** BYRON *Mar. Fal.* III. ii. 268 Would that the hour were come! We will not scotch, But kill. **1843** LE FEVRE *Life Trav. Phys.* II. II. viii. 279 The malaria is scotched, not killed, and the intermittent returns at some future period. **1879** MERIVALE *Early Ch. Hist.* ii. 86 It was by Augustine most of all that the Arian heresy was scotched, if not actually killed. **1894** BARING-GOULD *Deserts S. France* II. 115 From the time of St. Louis, the feudal power in France was scotched, though far from killed.

b. To crush, stamp upon, stamp out (something dangerous).

1825 *Q. Rev.* XXXII. 277 If we, in our own language, were to scotch the insidious forgetfulness, *we* might, perhaps, be accused of 'coarse and insulting abuse'; and shall therefore only cite the gentle remonstrance of Lord Byron. **1880** A. H. HUTH *Buckle* I. iii. 189 Attempting to scotch the pestiferous germs of heresy. **1908** *Expositor* Dec. 527 Fanaticism which constitutes a danger to mankind should be scotched.

c. To refute conclusively or stamp out (a rumour, report, etc.); to frustrate (a plan or hope); to quash, destroy, bring to nothing. (Perh. influenced by SCOTCH *v.*[2] 1 b.)

1926 in H. W. Fowler *Dict. Mod. Eng. Usage* 518/2 The contradiction of a rumour affecting any particular company ..is seldom entirely scotched by directorial statements. *Ibid.*, We hope the proposal for a Government news service for the Colonies is finally scotched by the debate. **1947** H. S. GLADWIN *Men out of Asia* xxvi. 270 The question has been raised as to whether they [*sc.* helmets] were not copies from late European models, but this idea was scotched by Captain Cook who found them in fashion in Hawaii. **1955** *Times* 27 July 13/1 He did so with sufficient force..to scotch once and for all any lingering doubts or rumours that the pound is to be devalued by stealth. **1966** *Listener* 2 June 792/2 The closing words of his book firmly scotch any hope we may have of evading the central question. **1976** *Australian* 30 June 1/7 The Prime Minister..is to meet the Russian Ambassador..next month to scotch reports of a serious rift in Soviet-Australian relations.

Hence **scotched** *ppl. a.*, cut, scarred; also in ***scotched collops***, an etymologizing perversion of *Scotch collops*; **'scotching** *vbl. sb.*

1559 FECKENHAM in Strype *Ann. Ref.* (1709) I. App. ix. 26 There was no scotchinge nor cuttinge of the Faces and Legs of the Crucifix and Image of Christ. **1625** LISLE *Du Bartas, Noe* 98 The Lombard left,..Unto the skotched [*balafrez*] Hunnes the divers furrowd marge Of Ister. **1708** W. KING *Art Cookery* 21 A Cook perhaps has mighty things profest, Then sent up but two Dishes nicely drest, What signifie Scotcht-Collops to a Feast.

scotch (skɒtʃ), *v.*[2] Also 8 skatch. [f. SCOTCH *sb.*[2]]

1. *trans.* To block or wedge (a wheel, log, gate, etc.) so as to keep from moving or slipping. Also with *up* (see quot. 1898). Also *fig.*

1642 FULLER *Holy & Prof. St.* II. xiii. §4 Hedges and counterhedges..serve for barracadoes, and will stick as bird-lime in the wings of the horse, and scotch the wheeling about of the foot. **1645** T. HILL *Olive Branch* (1648) 29 If now jealousies and misunderstandings should creep in, and scotch the wheel. **1663** DRYDEN *Wild Gallant* I. i. (1669) 2 Then will I first scotch the Wheeles of it, that it may not run. **1706** PHILLIPS (ed. Kersey) To *Skatch a Wheel.* **1713** M. HENRY *Conc. Meekness & Quietn. of Spirit* (1822) 141 Abigail prudently scotched the wheels of his passion. **1844** EMERSON *New Eng. Reformers* Wks. (Bohn) I. 259 Stop, dear nature, these incessant advances of thine; let us scotch these ever-rolling wheels. **1859** F. A. GRIFFITHS *Artil. Man.* (1862) 125, 2 has charge of the..skidding, scotches the wheels. **1866** *Cornh. Mag.* Sept. 323 It was..noticed that near most of the gates that would have had to be opened, a stone was lying, as if it had been used to 'scotch' it. **1887** *S. Chesh. Gloss.* s.v., To *scotch* a ladder is to 'foot' it, and thus prevent its slipping. **1895** LD. WATSON in *Law Times Rep.* LXXIII. 636/2 Hopper..insufficiently scotched the waggon which ran down the incline and killed the deceased. **1898** ANSTED *Dict. Sea Terms* s.v., To be *scotched up* is to be supported, as a boat may be when propped or 'scotched up' against a quay by timber shores or legs.

b. *fig.* To render inoperative, cripple the action of; to frustrate (a plan).

1876 L. STEPHEN *Eng. Th. 18th C.* I. 33 The name of Spinozism was of course dreaded by them [*sc.* the Deists]; they take care both to avoid the imputation, and to make it undeserved by carefully scotching their logic. **1895** in *Funk's Stand. Dict.* **1897** 'O. RHOSCOMYL' *White Rose Arno* 163, I scotched the project of retreat for this council, at any rate.

†**2.** *intr.* (Chiefly with negative.) To hesitate, scruple, boggle, or stick *at*; to hesitate *to do* something. Also, to haggle *with* a person *for* something. *Obs.* exc. *dial.*

1601 DENT *Pathw. Heaven* 74 For when [men] come to giuing vnto holy and necessarie vses, then they will sticke at a pennie, and scotch at a groat, and euery thing is too much. **1627** J. CARTER *Plain Expos.* 47 He will haue vs value our humilitie, loyaltie, and pliablenesse to the higher powers.. at so high a rate, as to scotch at no hardship, to giue them, or their assignes, iust content. *Ibid.* 81 God hath giuen the greater,..wherefore out of question, hee will not scotch with vs for the lesse. *a* **1825** FORBY *Voc. E. Anglia*, *Scotch v.* to spare; to refrain... So when we say 'I did not scotch to tell him my mind', we mean 'I did not at all mince the matter'. **1887** *S. Chesh. Gloss.*, *Scotch*, to hesitate, stick at. 'He scotches at nowt'.

3. *intr.* Of a horse: ? To boggle, shy.

1894 SIR J. ASTLEY *Fifty Yrs. Life* II. 216 Soon after he [*sc.* a racehorse] started he began to scotch, and was on the point of stopping to kick.

Hence **'scotching** *vbl. sb.* Also **'scotcher** *nonce-wd.*, an implement for scotching or blocking.

1800 MAR. EDGEWORTH *Parents' Assist.* (1856) 460, 'I call this thing my scotcher,' said Paul, 'because I always scotch the wheels with it.' **1859** F. A. GRIFFITHS *Artil. Man.* (1862) 110 This is called scotching, or chocking.

scotch, variant of SCUTCH *sb.* and *v.*

Scotch bonnet.

1. A Scotch cap (cf. BONNET *sb.* 1.)

1759 L. WOOD *Jrnl.* 27 June in *Essex Inst. Hist. Coll.* (1882) XIX. 70 It Came out in order this Day that no officer in yᵉ Rigement Should wear a Scotch bonet. *a* **1803** J. BEATTIE (*title*), To the Right Honourable Lady Charlotte Gordon, Dressed in a Tartan Scotch Bonnet, with plumes. **1840** DICKENS *Old C. Shop* xvii, Their Scotch bonnets, were ornamented with plumes of jet black feathers. **1876** A'BECKETT *Holiday in Scot. Highlands* 29 The sentry..in spite of wearing a Scotch bonnet, had evidently been born in the sister island.

2. *pl.* **a.** The fairy-ring mushroom, *Marasmius oreades.* **b.** The bonnet-pepper, *Capsicum tetragonum.*

1696 RAY *Synopsis Stirp. Brit.* (ed. 2) 13 Fungus lamellatus,..Scotch-bonnets. **1858** SIMMONDS *Dict. Trade*, *Scotch-bonnets*, a name for the champignon; also for a variety of capsicum. **1861** H. MACMILLAN *Footn. Page Nat.* 256 Every one is familiar with the common campignon or Scotch bonnets, which form those sour ringlets in the grassy meadows popularly called fairy rings. **1866** in *Treas. Bot.*

Scotch cap.

1. A man's head-dress made of thick firm woollen cloth, without a brim, and decorated with two tails or streamers.

One form is the GLENGARRY which is elongated, with a depression in the middle. Another is the BALMORAL, which is round and flat, the top projecting all round the head.

1591 SPENSER *M. Hubberd* 209 Vpon his head an old Scotch cap he wore. **1595** *Locrine* IV. ii. 20 *Stage-Direction*, Enter Strumbo with a pitchforke and a scotch-cap. **1889** CLARK RUSSELL *Marooned* (1890) 274 Nothing was wanting to him but his Scotch cap.

2. *U.S.* **a.** The wild black raspberry, *Rubus occidentalis.*

1891 in *Century Dict.*

b. The salmon-berry, *Rubus parviflorus.*

1902 in WEBSTER *Suppl.*

Scotch cart. Chiefly *S. Afr.* Also scotch cart. [Prob. f. SCOTCH *a.* + CART *sb.*; S. Afr. uses may represent derivation from Afrikaans *skotskar*, ad. G. *schuttkarren*, but this is unproved.] A light and strongly built two-wheeled cart, used chiefly for transporting rough materials such as gravel, manure, etc.

1845 *Cape of Good Hope Almanac* (Advt.), Best Scotch Carts and wheelbarrows made to order. **1850** *Mary Wedlake's Priced List Farming Implements* 33 (*heading*)

Scotch Carts. These very light carriages, so superior in point of draught to the old heavy dung carts used in most counties of England, are daily substituted for those ponderous machines. **1895** R. CHURCHILL *Men, Mines & Animals in S. Afr.* xiii. 210, I accordingly borrowed a Scotch cart (a light two-wheeled covered waggon) and a span of eight oxen, with which went also two 'salted' horses. **1938** D. FORBES *My Life in S. Afr.* vi. 87 He also fixed up a scotch cart to carry the alluvial ground to the stream. **1949** *Cape Argus Mag.* 14 May 2/6 At first a few skins were sent in from farms, then.. they began to arrive in sugar pockets,.. and finally by the Scotch-cart load. **1970** G. E. EVANS *Where Beards wag All* i. 31 A Scotch cart was popular round here. .. They'd carry about a ton. *Ibid.* 34 The extra spokes and felloes on a Scotch cart were probably needed on its home ground where a strong wheel was essential on a rougher terrain than is to be found in East Anglia. **1974** *Standard Encycl. S. Afr.* X. 571/1 The Scotch-cart, with or without springs, was always popular with farmers because it could be tilted backwards to enable its load to be discharged.

† **Scotch cloth.** *Obs.* A textile fabric resembling lawn, but cheaper; said to have been made of nettle fibre.

1675 GREW *Anat. Plants, Trunks* (1682) 139 Hemp, is nothing else but the Sap-Vessels of the Barque of the Plant so called. And Scotch-Cloath, is only the Housewifery of the same Parts of the Barque of Nettle. **1696** J. F. *Merch. Wareho. laid open* 37 Scotch Cloth.. is a sort of white Sleasie Soft-Cloth,.. and since Callico hath been dear, is much used for Linnens for Beds and for Window Curtains. *a* **1704** T. BROWN *Dial. Dead, Reas. Oaths* Wks. 1711 IV. 76 A Physician turn'd a Zealous Expounder of the Bible; or a Sworn Friend of Scotch-Cloth, reconciled to Lawn-Sleeves. **1738** *Gentl. Mag.* VIII. 147/1 A high Altar.. at which a brawny Priest officiated in a Habit of Scotch Cloth.

attrib. **1705** HICKERINGILL *Priest-cr.* (1721) I. 54 Because this is a Prying Age, and Scholarship and Craft is not now.. confin'd to a Cassock, or Scotch-cloth Sleeves.

scotcheon, obs. form of SCUTCHEON.

scotcher, variant of SCUTCHER.

'Scotchery. *nonce-wd.* [f. SCOTCH *a.* + -ERY.] Scotch characteristics.

1740 H. WALPOLE *Let. to Conway* 23 Apr., His solemn Scotchery is a little formidable.

Scotchgard ('skɒtʃgɑːd). A proprietary term in the U.S. for a series of organofluorine chemicals employed as waterproof grease- and stain-resistant finishes for textiles, suede, leather, etc.

1956 *Official Gaz.* (U.S. Patent Office) 1 May TM 7/1 Minnesota Mining and Manufacturing Company, St. Paul, Minn... *Scotchgard.* For chemical composition for application to various surfaces to repel grease and oil therefrom. First use Aug. 26, 1955. **1959** *Times* 12 Jan. 11/5 Scotch-Gard: Finish.. for use on wool, cotton, or synthetic fibres to improve oil, grease, and water stain-resistance. Durable for dry-cleaning. Shortly to be marketed. **1962** *N.Y. Times Mag.* 9 Sept. 106 (Advt.), Lightweight suede 'Gliders' [*sc.* shoes] Scotchgard treated to resist stains. **1969** A. J. HALL *Stand. Handbk. Textiles* (ed. 7) v. 334 One such fluoro-chemical is Scotchgard F.C. 208 and when this, together with.. water-repellent Velan, is dried into cotton fabric and followed by a curing.. at about 130°C. for 5 min., the fabric acquires a combined water and oil repellency which withstands repeated washing with soap.

Scotchify ('skɒtʃɪfaɪ), *v.* [f. SCOTCH *a.* + -(I)FY.] *trans.* To render or make Scotch. Hence **'Scotchified** *ppl. a.*; also **,Scotchifi'cation.**

1795 *Jemima* II. 94 That man.. who sometimes talks scotchified. **1817** J. EVANS *Excurs. Windsor*, etc. 487 The general character of the place [Ostend] was marked by the long windows and Scotchified gable ends of the houses. **1824** J. GILCHRIST *Etym. Interpr.* 272 Even the English are perceived to be Scotchified in their speech after a short residence in the North. **1832** *Fraser's Mag.* VI. 501 [It] is only a Scotchification of a well-known Spanish proverb. **1850** T. MᶜCRIE *Mem. Agnew* 211 They begged him not to 'Scotchify' their Sunday. **1891** *Daily News* 19 Jan. 5/6 The 'Scotchification of Essex'—we use the local expression... It is all owing to Scotch agriculturists taking a fancy for Essex farms.

Scotchiness ('skɒtʃɪnɪs). [f. SCOTCHY *a.* + -NESS.] The state or condition of being Scotchy.

1815 SOUTHEY *Lett.* (1856) II. 411 [Murray's letters have] a certain cast of Scotchiness about them. **1876** J. BROWN *Lett.* (1907) 247 Your mother would have rejoiced in Bogle—his sense, his homeliness,.. his Scotchiness.

scotchion, obs. form of SCUTCHEON.

Scotch-Irish, *a.* **a.** Belonging to that part of the population of northern Ireland which is descended from Scotch settlers. Also *absol.* in plural sense. So **Scotch-Irishman. b.** Of mixed Scots and Irish descent.

1744 W. MARSHE *Jrnl.* 21 June in *Coll. Mass. Hist. Soc.* (1801) 1st Ser. VII. 177 The inhabitants [of Lancaster, Pa.] are chiefly High-Dutch, Scotch-Irish, some few English families, and unbelieving Israelites. **1789** J. MORSE *Amer. Geogr.* 313 [The Irish of Pennsylvania] have sometimes been called Scotch-Irish, to denote their double descent. **1876** BANCROFT *Hist. U.S.* IV. iii. 333 But its convenient proximity to the border counties of Pennsylvania and Virginia had been observed by Scotch-Irish Presbyterians and other bold and industrious men. **1883** *Harper's Mag.* Feb. 421/2 The so-called Scotch-Irish are the descendants of the Englishmen and Lowland Scotch who began to move over to Ulster in 1611. **1897** *Outing* (U.S.) XXX. 136/2 Late in the afternoon we got into the Scotch-Irish part of the valley. **1903** J. FOX *Little Shepherd of Kingdom Come* x. 117 Broadcast, through the people, was the upright sturdiness of the Scotch-Irishman, without his narrowness and bigotry. **1916** J. WEBSTER *Dear Enemy* 187 That Scotch-Irish ancestry of mine. **1948** H. MACLENNAN *Precipice* (1949) i. 5 The Scotch and the Scotch-Irish who had flooded into Ontario. **1963** W. K. ROSE *Lett. Wyndham Lewis* 1. 1 An English girl of Scotch-Irish descent. **1980** G. M. FRASER *Mr. American* xvii. 312 Reason is the last thing you can look for in a Scotch-Irish Protestant. *Ibid.* xix. 361 The Scotch-Irish who saw their freedom threatened.

† **'Scotchism.** *Obs. rare*⁻¹. [f. SCOTCH *a.* + -ISM.] A Scotch peculiarity. (Cf. SCOTTICISM.)

1737 OZELL *Rabelais* III. 231 *note*, This is not a Scotch-ism but an Irish-ism.

Scotchlite ('skɒtʃlaɪt). The proprietary name of a light-reflecting material containing a layer of minute glass lenses.

1941 *Official Gaz.* (U.S. Patent Office) 6 May 29/2 Minnesota Mining & Manufacturing Company, St. Paul, Minn... *Scotchlite* for light reflecting material in sheet form. Claims use since Dec. 1, 1939. **1947** *Daily Progress* (Charlottesville, Va.) 28 Oct. 4/1 A Minnesota motorist.. conceived the idea of covering bicycle frames with Scotchlite, a material used on reflectorized highway signs. **1957** *Times Survey Brit. Aviation* Sept. 8/5 Scotchlite is a tough, plastic reflective film. **1964** *Times* 7 Feb. p. iv/1 (Advt.), Scotchlite reflective sheeting.. consists essentially of a white or coloured reflecting surface covered with minute, optically-perfect glass lenses. On top of the lot goes a clear plastic protective coating. **1970** *Trade Marks Jrnl.* 17 June 961/1 *Scotchlite*... Sign faces made of or incorporating plastics embedded with light reflective substances. Minnesota Mining and Manufacturing Company.., United States of America; manufacturers. **1972** *Police Rev.* 10 Nov. 1444/1 'Scotchlite' markings on Police vehicles.

Scotchman ('skɒtʃmən). Also 6 Scotcheman, 7 *Sc.* Scotsshman. [f. SCOTCH *a.* + MAN.]

1. a. A man of Scottish nationality.

Formerly, the usual English name; the prevalent form used by Scotch people was SCOTSMAN. SCOTSMAN is now the preferred form on both sides of the border (see small-type note s.v. SCOTCH *a.* and *sb.*³).

1570 LEVINS *Manip.* 21/3 Scotcheman, *Scotus.* **1597** P. LOWE *Chirurgerie* title, The Whole Covrse of Chirurgerie. .. Compiled by Peter Lowe Scotchman. **1632** MASSINGER *City Madam* II. ii, May the Great Fiend, booted & spurr'd With a Sithe at his girdle, as the Scotchman saies, Ride headlong down her throat. **1671** FRASER *Polichron.* (S.H.S.) 491 After the peace he went up to Pole with other Scotssh-men. **1706** PHILLIPS (ed. Kersey), *Scots* or *Scotch-men*, the People of Scotland, a part of Great Britain. **1763** JOHNSON in *Boswell* (1791) I. 231 The noblest prospect which a Scotch-man ever sees is the high-road that leads him to England! **1773** MACPHERSON *Ossian's Poems* (1806) I. *Dissert.* 37 A Scotchman, tolerably conversant in his own language, understands Irish composition. **1820** SCOTT *Monast.* Introd. Ep., 'Then,' said I, 'you are a native Scotchman..?' 'Not so, answered the monk; 'I am a Scotchman by extraction only.' **1821** LAMB *Elia* I. *Imperf. Sympathies*, I have been trying all my life to like Scotchmen and am obliged to desist from the experiment in despair. **1977** K. M. E. MURRAY *Caught in Web of Words* xi. 209 For a Scotchman James was certainly extraordinarily lacking in hard-headedness.

Comb. **1833** L. RITCHIE *Wand. by Loire* 26 Determining.. to be exceedingly prudent and Scotchman-like.

b. (Also *Flying Scotchman.*) A familiar name for the Scotch express (London to Edinburgh) on the Great Northern and on the London & North-Western Railway. Cf. IRISHMAN b (*b*) and SCOTSMAN b.

1873 J. BLACKWOOD *Let.* 6 Jan. in *Geo. Eliot Lett.* (1956) V. 365 'The Flying Scotchman', the stoker's name for the train that goes between London and Edinburgh in little more than 9 hours! **1874** R. C. RAPIER *Signals Railw.* 56 On arriving at King's Cross, the Flying Scotchman had not yet departed. [**1879** Flying Scotsman: see SCOTSMAN b.] **1881** REYNOLDS *Engine-driving Life* 59 The same express-men.. were proceeding down a bank.. at about 3 a.m. in summer with the 'Scotchman'. **1885** G. DOLBY *Dickens as I knew him* 33 A railway carriage which was being dragged along at the rate of fifty miles an hour by the 'Flying Scotchman'. **1892** *Strand Mag.* Feb. 195 This Scotch Express (significantly named 'The Flying Scotchman') is believed to be the fastest train in the world. **1913** D. H. LAWRENCE *Sons & Lovers* vii. 165 You should see the Flying Scotchman come through.

c. A travelling draper or pedlar: see SCOTCH *a.* 1 b. *dial.* (See examples in *Eng. Dial. Dict.*)

1719 T. MARCHANT *Jrnl.* 10 June in *Sussex Arch. Coll.* (1873) XXV. 184 In all 15s. 9d., to John Gracie, a Scotchman, for M. Balcombe. **1793** C. SMITH *Old Manor House* I. vi. 138, I had not enough money.. to buy my new cotton gown, when Alexander Macgill the Scotchman called here. **1851** MAYHEW *Lond. Labour* I. 381 Mother, here's the Tallyman, Mother, here's the Scotchman.

d. *Scotchman hugging a Creole*, a West Indian name for various species of *Clusia*.

1835 M. SCOTT *Tom Cringle* xiv, Do you see that Scotch-man hugging the Creole? **1889** *Boston* (Mass.) *Jrnl.* 25 May 6/6 One more queer tree is the wild fig, familiarly called 'Scotchman hugging a Creole'.

e. A New Zealand name for a smaller kind of the prickly bushy grass called 'Spaniard' (*Aciphylla colensoi*).

1895 W. S. ROBERTS *Southland in 1856*, 39 (Morris) As we neared the hills speargrass of the smaller kind, known as 'Scotchmen', abounded, and although not so strong and sharp-pointed as the 'Spaniard', would not have made a comfortable seat.

2. *Naut.* A piece of hide, wood, or iron, etc. placed over a rope to prevent its being chafed.

1841 R. H. DANA *Seaman's Man.*, *Scotchman*, a large batten placed over the turnings-in of rigging. **1850** R. G. CUMMING *Hunter's Life S. Afr.* (1902) 1/2 On the top of this are placed coarse Kaffir mats made of reeds, which act as a Scotchman (to use a seafaring phrase), to keep the waggon sail, which is of stout canvas, from chafing. *c* **1860** H. STUART *Seaman's Catech.* 83 A Scotchman should be made of leather,.. to allow the new skin to harden. **1882** NARES *Seamanship* (ed. 6) 68 How is the lower rigging protected from being cut by the futtock rigging? By lashing iron Scotchmen on the shrouds.

3. *S. African.* A florin. (See quot. 1879.)

1879 ATCHERLEY *Trip Boërland* 55 In dealing with the Kafirs, I frequently heard the term 'Scotchman' applied to a two-shilling piece: and upon enquiry was informed that an enterprising gentleman of that nationality having once passed a large number of florins to the Kafirs as half-crown pieces, the latter had ever since christened the florin 'Scotchman'. **1887** RIDER HAGGARD *Jess* x, Jantjé spat upon the 'Scotchman', as the natives in that part of Africa [Transvaal] call a two-shilling piece.

4. *U.S.* The 'Scotch duck', *Charitonetta* (or *Bucephala*) *albeola*.

1895 in *Funk's Stand. Dict.*

5. *colloq.* A Scotch fir.

1901 'LUCAS MALET' *Sir R. Calmady* VI. vii, 'What shall we do with it [a piece of land]?' 'Oh, plant,' she said. 'With the ubiquitous Scotchman?' 'It wouldn't carry any-thing else, except along the boundaries.'

Scotchness ('skɒtʃnɪs). [f. SCOTCH *a.* + -NESS.] Scotch quality or character.

1865 G. MACDONALD *A. Forbes* xxviii, Annie had a certain Scotchness in her which made her draw back from the offer. **1892** STEVENSON *Let. to J. M. Barrie* (1899) II. 247 My own Scotchness tends to intermittency.

Scotch tape. Also **scotch tape.** The proprietary name of a make of adhesive tape; also applied *loosely* to any adhesive tape. Hence **Scotch-tape** *v. trans.*, to affix or join with adhesive tape; **Scotch-taped** *ppl. a.*, affixed or made fast with adhesive tape.

[**1945** *Official Gaz.* (U.S. Patent Office) 16 Oct. 373/1 Minnesota Mining & Manufacturing Company, St. Paul, Minn... Scotch for pressure-sensitive adhesive tape. Claims use since January 1928.] **1947** R. LEE *Electronic Transformers & Circuits* ii. 28 Electrical grade scotch tape is widely used for anchoring leads. **1949** R. CHANDLER *Little Sister* ix. 54 To the lining of the toupee a piece of.. paper was fastened by Scotch tape. **1955** 'J. WYNDHAM' in 'E. Crispin' *Best SF* 81 There was a wire, scotch-taped to the upper side of the bag. **1957** V. NABOKOV *Pnin* iv. 99 Carrying his purchase, wrapped in brown paper and Scotch-taped, he entered a bookstore. **1961** WODEHOUSE *Ice in Bedroom* xxvi. 222 Her lips.. shall be sealed, if necessary with Scotch tape. **1961** J. H. GRIFFIN *Black like Me* 86 The whites frequently.. Scotch-tape these notices to the wall. **1969** K. AMIS *Green Man* i. 26 Coloured photographs.. Scotch-taped to the walls. **1976** *Observer* 24 Oct. 28 It [*sc.* Sellotape] still has 75 per cent of the market over here, though in America Scotch Tape has become the generic term. **1977** *Time* 31 Jan. 24/1 Carter wrote at least three more drafts, sometimes spreading the paragraphs out like pieces of a jigsaw puzzle and Scotch-taping them into a new arrangement.

'Scotch,woman. [f. SCOTCH *a.* + WOMAN; orig. two words.] A woman who is a native of Scotland or of Scotch descent.

1818 SCOTT *Hrt. Midl.* xxxiii, The neat, clean, quiet-looking little Scotchwoman, who now stood before her. **1827** —— *Chron. Canongate* v, Knowing her honesty,.. and, although a Scotchwoman, her cleanliness and excellent temper.

Scotchy, *sb. colloq.* [f. SCOTCH *a.* + -Y.] A nickname for a Scotchman.

1861 *Two Cosmos* II. 62 Will you come it now, Scotchy, and I don't mind if I forgive you if you can lick me? **1949** E. COXHEAD *Wind in West* ii. 59 Are you really such a prim little Scotchy that you don't see the difference between one chap and another?

Scotchy ('skɒtʃɪ), *a.* [f. SCOTCH *a.* + -Y.] Having the characteristics of what is Scotch.

1815 SOUTHEY *Lett.* (1856) II. 414 It is impossible that any compositions can be more booksellerish and more Scotchy. **1896** ASHBY-STERRY *Tale of Thames* viii, I don't read them all [*i.e.* Scott's novels]. Some of the very Scotchiest ones I *cannot* stand.

Comb. **1874** A. J. C. HARE *Story My Life* (1900) IV. xvii. 258 A great Scotchy-looking house.

† **scote,** *sb.*¹ *Obs.* [Cf. Du. *schoot* 'sheet' (i.e. rope), whence OF. *escoute* (mod.F. *écoute*).] ? A kind of cable.

1394 *Issue Roll*, Easter 17 Rich. II, 5 Sept. (Devon), [Five cables, weighing 5941 lbs... two] scotes [weighing 348 lbs.].

† **scote,** *sb.*² *Obs. rare.* [? a. MDu. *schote*, a definite quantity of some article.] = BEAT *sb.*³

1633–4 *N. Riding Rec.* III. 365 A labourer for stealing 7 scotes of hemp. *Ibid.*, A labourer presented for stealing 7 beates or scotes of hemp.

scote (skəʊt), *sb.*³ *dial.* [Of obscure origin: cf. Norw. *skota* pole, bar, forked stick; also OF. *escot* (mod.F. *écot*) stump.] (See quot. 1890.)

1839 *Herefordsh. Gloss.*, *Scote*, a dragstaff (Glouc.). **1890** *Glouc. Gloss.* 132 *Scote*, an ironshod staff attached to the axle of the hind wheel of a waggon to prevent it running back down hill.

scote (skəʊt), *v. Obs.* exc. *dial.* Also 7–8 scoat, 9 scort. [f. SCOTE *sb.*³ Cf. SCOTCH *v.*²] *trans.* To set a drag upon (the wheel of a wagon).

1642 R. HARRIS *Serm.* 45 This is that that scoat's the businesse in publike. **1678** PHILLIPS (ed. 4), To *Scout*, to put a Stone or peece of Wood under a Cart to stop it from going forward. **1890** *Glouc. Gloss.* 132 *Scort* or *Scote.*

scotei'nography. *nonce-wd.* [f. Gr. σκοτεινό-ς dark + -γραφία: see -GRAPHY.] Illegible writing.
1779 TWINING *Let.* 17 Sept., in *Parr's Wks.* (1828) VIII. 267, I thought myself a tolerable adept in this art of scoteinography, but I give you the wall.

†**scote'ography.** *Obs.* [irreg. f. Gr. σκότεο-ς gen. of σκότος darkness + -γραφία writing: see -GRAPHY.] (See quot.)
1803 J. GOUGH in *Nicholson's Jrnl.* VII. 53 Scoteography or the Art of Writing in the Dark.

scoter ('skəʊtə(r)). [Of obscure origin.] A duck of the genus *Œdemia*, esp. *Œdemia nigra*, a native of the Arctic regions and common in the seas of Northern Europe and America. Also ***scoter-duck***.
1674 RAY *Collect., Catal. Birds* 96 The Scoter: *Anas niger.* **1768** PENNANT *Brit. Zool.* (1776) II. 494 Scoter... This bird is allowed in the Romish church to be eaten in Lent. **1808–13** A. WILSON & BONAPARTE *Amer. Ornith.* (1831) III. 212 Scoter duck. **1845** *Zoologist* III. 1077 The scoter.. has occurred twice in winter at some water in Basing parish. **1870** GILLMORE tr. *Figuier's Reptiles & Birds* 239 The writers of the Middle Ages and the Renaissance.. had very vaguely described the Scoter Duck.

†'**scoterlope**, *v.* *Obs.* [Metathesis of SCOPPERLOIT *v.*, after LOPE *v.*] *intr.* ? To wander aimlessly.
1583 GOLDING *Calvin on Deut.* xix. 113 God mindeth to try our obedience, by restreining vs from.. scoterloping ouer the fieldes [orig. F. *de courir à travers champs*] to raught at euerie thing that we like off.

scotewache, obs. variant of SCOUTWATCH.

†**scotewine.** *Obs. rare*⁻¹. [Cf. SCOT *sb.*³ 2, SCOTART.] An alleged name for the hare.
a **1325** *Names of Hare* in *Rel. Ant.* I. 133 The scotewine, the skikart.

scot-free, *a.* Also *rarely* 6 scotchfree, 7 scotts-free. See also SHOT-FREE. [f. SCOT *sb.*² + FREE *a.* Cf. MDu. *schotvrî* (the mod.Du. *schotvrij* 'shot-proof' is independently formed), OSw. *skutfri-r.*] Free from payment of 'scot', tavern score, fine, etc.; exempt from injury, punishment, etc.; scatheless. Almost exclusively *predicative*; esp. in the phrase *to go scot free*.
In the mod. use of the expression, 'scot' is probably often interpreted as a mere intensive.
? **12..** *Charter of 1066* in Kemble *Cod. Diplom.* IV. 191 Scotfre and gauelfre, on schire and on hundrede. **1531** TINDALE *Expos. 1 John* (1537) 22 The poore synner shulde go Skot fre without oughte at all. **1546** *St. Papers Hen. VIII*, XI. 129 What damages their cuntrey and peple had suffred by this warre, and that Your Majestie went not all scott free. *a* **1548** HALL *Chron., Edw. IV*, 233 They payed no money, but were set scot free. **1567** MAPLET *Green Forest* 93 Daniell scaped scotchfree by Gods prouidence. **1579–80** NORTH *Plutarch, Tiberius & Caius* (1595) 878 Caius.. had charged the poore citizens with an annuall rent for the lands.. Liuius .. did please them by.. letting them haue the lands scotfree. **1622** MABBE tr. *Aleman's Guzman d'Alf.* II. 231 The first speaker scapes scot-free. **1665–6** WOOD *Life* (O.H.S.) II. 73 Oxford escaped scot fre of the plague. **1740** RICHARDSON *Pamela* (1824) I. 117 She should not, for all the trouble she has cost you, go away scot-free. **1792** WOLCOT (P. Pindar) *Odes of Condolence* Wks. 1794 III. 237 Scot-free the Poets drank and ate; They paid no taxes to the State! **1819** SCOTT *Ivanhoe* xii, Do as much for this fellow and thou shalt pass scot-free. **1858** R. S. SURTEES *Ask Mamma* xiv. 45 The sporting inhabitants thereof preferred the money-griping propensities of a certain Baronet.. to the scot-free sport with the frigid civilities of the noble Earl. **1875** STUBBS *Const. Hist.* xiv. I. 133 The people had not been heavily taxed, and the clergy had passed.. scot-free. **1877** BLACK *Green Past.* xiii, When some notorious offender has got off scot free.
¶**b.** ? Mis-used for: Without inflicting damage.
1652–66 in Gilbert *Contemp. Hist. Irel.* I. 25 [They] shooted at him with earnest leuell, and not scotts-free for presently he was tumbled to the earth deadly wounded.

‖**scotia** ('skəʊʃɪə). *Arch.* [L. *scotia* (Vitruvius), a. Gr. σκοτία, f. σκότος darkness (so called from the dark shadow within the cavity); cf. F. *scotie.*] A hollow moulding. = CASEMENT 1.
1563 SHUTE *Archit.* 11 The nethermost Trochilus or Scotia. **1664** EVELYN tr. *Freart's Archit.* 125 Our Workmen retain the antient Scotia.. but more vulgarly they call it the Casement. **1789** SMYTH tr. *Aldrich's Archit.* (1818) 90 Other particles of an order are hollow, the common name to which is scotia. *a* **1878** SIR G. SCOTT *Lect. Archit.* (1879) I. 152 In England another kind of base is frequent, in which a bead is substituted for the scotia.

†'**Scotian**, *a.* *nonce-wd.* [f. med.L. *Scōtia* Scotland + -AN.] Of or belonging to Scotland.
1803 LEYDEN *Scenes Infancy* I. 232 But long Their fame shall flourish in the Scotian song.

Scotic ('skɒtɪk), *a.* Also 8–9 Scottic. [ad. late L. *Scōticus, Scotticus*, f. *Scōt-us, Scott-us*: see SCOT *sb.*¹]
†**1.** Used as a designation for the Scottish dialect.
c **1645** HOWELL *Lett.* (1655) II. 74 The English speech.. hath.. divers subdialects.. but her chiefest is the Scotic, which took footing beyond Tweed about the last conquest.
2. Pertaining to the ancient Scots.
1796 MORSE *Amer. Geog.* II. 183 The uncorrupted native language of the Irish is the Gaedhloc, or Scottic. **1851** D. WILSON *Archæol. & Preh. Ann. Scot.* 470 Cairbre Riada, a celebrated Scottic warrior. *Ibid.* 479 The Scotic line of princes. **1873** *Contemp. Rev.* XXI. 253 Our method of colonization has failed with the children of the Scotic race. **1882–3** *Schaff's Encycl. Relig. Knowl.* II. 1232 Celestius, the companion of Pelagius, is supposed by some to have been of Scotic, i.e., Irish origin. **1902** MACBAIN in Skene *Highlanders Scot.* 400 Donald being likely a Scotic prince.

†'**Scotical**, *a.* *Obs. rare*⁻¹. [Formed as prec. + -ICAL.] Of or belonging to Scotland; Scottish.
a **1548** HALL *Chron., Hen. IV* (1550) 16b, Wherof the occasion shall bee to you declared accordyng to the Scotticall histories.

Scotican ('skɒtɪkən), *a.* [f. late L. *Scōtic-us* (see SCOTIC), after ANGLICAN.] Of or pertaining to the Scots ecclesiastically.
1635 [see ANGLICAN *a.* 1]. **1830** CHAMBERS *Jas. I*, II. ix. 257 Equalizing the Anglican and Scotican Churches. **1844** *Bp. Sage's Wks.* I. Mem. 23 They regarded the Scotican Church.. as schismatical.

Scoticè, -icism: see SCOTTICÈ, -ICISM.

Sco'tiety. *humorous nonce-wd.* [f. the name *Scōtus*, in imitation of scholastic terms.] The essential nature of John Duns Scotus.
1655 FULLER *Ch. Hist.* III. 97 The very Scotiety of Scotus belongeth to England as his Native Country.

Scotify: see SCOTTIFY.

†'**Scotism**¹. *Obs.*⁻⁰ [f. late L. *Scōt-us* SCOT + -ISM.] = SCOTTICISM.
1570 LEVINS *Manip.* 146 [Words that end in *isme*] be of three sortes... The second be taken of a countrey or language, as of.. Scotte, *Scotisme, Scotismus.*

Scotism² ('skəʊtɪz(ə)m). *Theol.* [ad. med.L. *Scōtismus*, f. *Scōt-us* (see SCOTIST) + -ISM.]
1. The teaching of Scotus or the Scotists.
a **1871** G. S. MORRIS tr. *Ueberweg's Hist. Philos.* (1872) I. 454 Scotism is.. like Thomism, one of the doctrines in which Scholasticism culminates. **1886** *Encycl. Brit.* XXI. 429/2 Herværus Natalis (*ob.* 1323) and Thomas Bradwardine (*ob.* 1349) were determined opponents of Scotism. **1900** *Month* July 50 This would go to show that Scotism, for which England had been celebrated in the middle ages, had already lost its hold on English Catholic thought.
2. *pl.* (*nonce-use*). Subtleties such as are characteristic of the Scotists.
1645 MILTON *Tetrach.* 28 These ages wherin Canons, and Scotisms, and Lumbard Laws, have dull'd, and almost obliterated the lively Sculpture of ancient reason.

Scotist ('skəʊtɪst), *sb.* and *a.* *Eccl.* [ad. med.L. *Scōtista*, f. *Scōtus*: see below.] **a.** *sb.* A follower or disciple of John Duns Scotus (known as 'The Subtle Doctor'), a scholastic philosopher and theologian of the 13th c., whose system in many respects was opposed to that of Thomas Aquinas. (See DUNCE.) **b.** *adj.* Belonging to the Scotists.
1530 [see DUNCE, etym. note]. **1562** tr. *Jewel's Apol.* 21 How happeneth it then that the Scotistes and the Thomistes do agree no better about merytes of conueniency, and merites of duety? **1661** tr. *Erasm. Life Colet* in *Colet's Serm.* 75 His Bishop.. was a superstitious and stubborn Scotist. **1709** POPE *Ess. Crit.* 244 Scotists and Thomists now in peace remain Amidst their kindred cobwebs in Duck-lane. **1884** *Catholic Dict.* (1897) 826/2 Decrees were passed requiring the Scotist doctrine to be taught in all the Franciscan schools. **1886** *Encycl. Brit.* XXI. 429 This primacy of the undetermined will.. was the central contention of Scotists against the Thomist doctrine.

†**Sco'tistical**, *a.*¹ *Obs.* [f. prec. + -ICAL.] Pertaining to or characteristic of the Scotists.
1600 tr. *Garzoni's Hosp. Incur. Fooles* A 4b, Betweene them and Folly there is a iust Logicall equipollence.. and a Scotisticall Identitie. **1716** M. DAVIES *Athen. Brit.* III. *Diss. Drama* 4 The Thomistical and Scotistical Schools and Preaching Orders of Dominicans, Franciscans [etc.].

†**Sco'tistical**, *a.*² *Obs.* [f. SCOT *sb.*¹ + -ISTICAL (see -ISTIC).] ? Favouring what is Scottish.
1650 A. B. *Mutat. Polemo* 14 Neither can they imagine whether these Scotisticall Pioneers will be Scots or no Scots.

†'**Scotistry.** *Obs. rare*⁻¹. [f. SCOTIST + -RY.] The habit of thought proper to a Scotist.
1651 FULLER *Abel Rediv., Colet* 105 His own Bishop, of whose Sophisticall Scotistry the Deane made no great account, and the Bishop as little of his Ciceronian Divinity.

†'**Scotize**, *v.* *Obs.* Also 6–7 scottize. [f. SCOT *sb.*¹ + -IZE.] *intr.* To imitate the Scots; to favour Scottish ways. Hence '**Scotizing** *ppl. a.*
1593 ABP. BANCROFT *Dangerous Positions* 41 *headline*, English Scottizing for Discipline. **1607** SIR J. HARINGTON *Nugæ Ant.* (1804) II. 25 His Majestie had long since understanding of his wryting against the genevising and scotising ministers. **1623** W. LISLE *Ælfric on O. & N. Test.* To Rdr. 13 An Englishman Scottizing once to our King was roundly reproued for it. **1659** GAUDEN *Tears Ch.* III. xix. 323 A Scotizing zeal. *a* **1662** HEYLIN *Laud* IV. (1668) 328 The English had Scotized in all their Practises. *Ibid.* v. 460 Thereby drawing on himself the general hatred not only of the Scots, but Scotizing English.

†'**Scotized**, *ppl. a.* *Obs.* [f. prec. + -ED¹.] Imbued with Scottish (ecclesiastical) principles.
1657 SANDERSON *Serm.* Pref. §24 The rigid Scotised, through-paced Presbyterian on the one side and the giddy Enthusiast on the other. **1711** G. HICKES *Two Treat. Chr. Priesth.* Pref. Disc. 220 The High-scotized Flyers.. among the Presbyterians.

Scotland Yard ('skɒtlənd jɑːd). The name of the head-quarters of the Metropolitan Police, situated from 1829 to 1890 in Great Scotland Yard, a short street off Whitehall in London; from then until 1967 in New Scotland Yard, on the Thames Embankment; and from 1967 in New Scotland Yard, Broadway, Westminster: used allusively to designate the detective department of the Metropolitan Police force. Also *attrib.*
1864 M. E. BRADDON *Henry Dunbar* II. xiv. 260, I have called again upon the Scotland-Yard people, and I gave them a minute description of the scene. *Ibid.* III. iv. 49 Not that anybody would try to thwart me,.. if they knew that I was detective officer Henry Carter, of Scotland Yard. **1864** [see BLUEBOTTLE 2]. **1881** *Punch* 9 July 6/2 As in all great crimes, they [*sc.* criminals] are too much for Scotland Yard and the Seldom-at-Home Secretary. **1907** [see REWARD *sb.*¹ 4d]. **1909** [see PHONE *v.* a]. **1926** E. WALLACE *Ringer* 1 Nobody knows, but Scotland Yard and—Henry Arthur Milton. **1939** T. S. ELIOT *Old Possum's Bk. Pract. Cats* 33 He's the bafflement of Scotland Yard, the Flying Squad's despair. **1962** J. MCCABE *Mr. Laurel & Mr. Hardy* i. 36 A backer for the troupe, a Scotland Yard detective. **1974** N. FREELING *Dressing of Diamond* 87 Just forget all the detective stories of bumbling Scotland Yard Inspectors.

†'**scotnail.** *north. Obs.* Forms: 4 scot-, 4–5 schot-, 5 shot-. [Cf. Du. *schotspijker* (f. *schot* ? partition + *spijker* nail).] Some kind of nail. Cf. SCOTSEM-NAIL.
1349–50 in *Bp. Hatfield's Surv.* (Surtees) 202 In spykings ferri, lednaylls, schotnaylls et bordnaylls empt. pro aula cooperienda ut supra, 3s. 10d. **1349–50** *Durh. Acc. Rolls* (Surtees) 550 Spykyng', et Scotnayls pro fonte infra Abbathiam. **1374** *Ibid.* 211 Et in spikyngs, schetnaill' [? *read* schotnaill'], stanbrod.. 42s. 5d. **1449–50** *Ibid.* 239, 200ma del spikyngez, 200ma del shotnaill. **1454** *Ibid.* 149 Item.. ij wayneclowtez cum spikyng et shotnayll.

Scot Nat (skɒt næt), *sb.* and *a.* Abbrev. of SCOTTISH NATIONALIST *a.* and *sb.* Cf. SCOTS NAT.
1970 [see NAT *sb.*⁴]. *a* **1974** R. CROSSMAN *Diaries* (1976) II. 550 He'd told me that the Scot. Nat. woman might win and the Tories would certainly lose their deposit. **1974** *Sunday Post* (Glasgow) 28 Apr. 5/5 Even by Willie Ross's standards, last weekend's attack on the Scot. Nats. was vitriolic. **1975** *Times* 8 Sept. 12/7 Both Tory and Labour politicians in Scotland.. will be tempted to enter into an auction with ScotNats over devolution.

Scoto-¹ ('skɒtəʊ, 'skəʊtəʊ), combining form of late L. *Scōtus* SCOT *sb.*¹, prefixed (with hyphen) to ethnic adjs. (rarely sbs.) either with the sense 'belonging to Scotland', as in ***Scoto-Britannic***, ***-Celtic***, ***-English***, ***-Gaelic***, ***-Gallic***, ***-Norwegian***, ***-Scandinavian*** adjs., ***Scoto-Norman*** sb., or with the sense 'partly Scottish and partly...', as in ***Scoto-Irish*** adj. **Scoto'phobia**², a morbid dread or dislike of the Scots or things Scottish; hence '**Scotophobe**.
1650 B. *Discolliminium* 45 The good man is in such a wofull Scoto-Britannick pickle. **1824** G. CHALMERS *Caledonia* III. III. vi. 253 This Scoto-Irish people. **1828–43** TYTLER *Hist. Scot.* (1864) I. 249 The Saxons and the Scoto-Normans. **1837** LOCKHART *Scott* II. 332 The clergy of the primitive Scoto-Celtic Church. **1846** C. INNES *Liber de Calchou* (Bannatyne Club) Pref. 30 The permanent incorporation of the Scoto-Saxon lowlands with the kingdom of Scotland proper. **1851** D. WILSON *Archæol. & Preh. Ann. Scot.* 490 The subsequent history of the Scoto-Norwegian kingdoms. *Ibid.* 522 Scoto-Scandinavian relics. **1858–61** RAMSAY *Remin.* vi. (1870) 245 Scoto-Gallic words were differently situated. **1867** BURTON *Hist. Scot.* I. vii. 261 The Scoto-Irish saints. **1876** SMILES *Sc. Natur.* viii. (ed. 4) 138 Their language is Gaelic, whereas that of the rest of the county [Banffs.] is Scoto-English. **1905** *Athenæum* 7 Oct. 466/1 Most purely Scoto-Gaelic words prefix the article. **1974** *Listener* 25 Apr. 520/3 There is undoubtedly a strong streak of Scotophobia in the English character. **1976** *Times Lit. Suppl.* 2 July 823/3 This 'never ending clan of Macs and Donalds upon Donalds', as one Scotophobe put it in the 1760s. **1980** B. LENMAN *Jacobite Risings in Britain* 289 A glance at the huge correspondence which Sir Everard organized so meticulously for Cumberland is very revealing about the origins of his royal master's sustained Scotophobia.

scoto-² ('skəʊtəʊ), comb. form repr. Gr. σκότος darkness, as in '**scotophase** *Biol.*, an artificially imposed period of darkness; an artificial night; '**scotophobia**¹ *Psychol.*, fear or dislike of the dark; hence **scoto'phobic** *a.* See also SCOTOSCOPE.
1971 *Nature* 6 Aug. 401/2 Bovines restrained inside environmentally controlled stalls (24 ± 3° C; 70 ± 7% relative humidity; 12 h photophase: 12 h scotophase per 24 h photocycle). **1975** *Ibid.* 25 Dec. 711/2 We considered whether the insects perceive the actual duration of photophases (or scotophases). **1938** *Brit. Jrnl. Psychol.* Apr. 372 Photo-phobia (in some animals) sufficiently strong to make them go always to D; the opposite trait, 'a-photo-phobia' or 'scoto-phobia' being present in an equal proportion of the animals. **1971** *New Scientist* 3 June 559/3 The scotophobic effect seems to be very specific for this structure.

scotograph (ˈskəʊtəgrɑːf, -æ-). [f. Gr. σκότο-ς darkness + -γραφος: see -GRAPH.] An instrument for writing in the dark, or without seeing.

1869 NUTTALL *Dict. Sci. Terms, Scotograph*, an instrument with which a blind person may write.

scotography (skəʊˈtɒgrəfɪ). *rare.* [f. Gr. σκότος darkness: see -GRAPHY.] The exhibition of the effect of the Röntgen rays; the production of a picture by means of such rays; = RADIOGRAPHY. Hence **scotoˈgraphic** *a.* = RADIOGRAPHIC *a.*

1896 SIR ALFRED WILLS in *Times* 10 Mar. 12/2 [The X rays] have very little in common with light. Would not 'scotography' be a better name for their work than 'photography'? **1896** *Westm. Gaz.* 18 Mar. 1/3 A correspondent who was present on Friday sends us some notes of that remarkable 'skotographic' séance.

‖**scotoma** (skəʊˈtəʊmə). *Path.* Pl. **scotomata** (skəʊˈtəʊmətə), **scotomas.** [late L. *scotōma*, a. Gr. σκότωμα dizziness, f. σκοτοῦν to darken, make dim-sighted, f. σκότος darkness.]

†**1.** Dizziness accompanied by dimness of sight; = SCOTOMY. *Obs.*

1543 TRAHERON *Vigo's Chirurg.* Interpr. s.v. *Scotomia*, Some go about, to make a foolysh difference of scotoma, and vertigo. **1822–29** *Good's Study Med.* (ed. 3) IV. 534 Hence Linnéus..has even made scotoma, or dizziness with blindness and a tendency to swoon, a distinct genus also.

2. An obscuration of part of the visual field, due to lesion of the retina or of the ophthalmic centres in the brain. Also *fig.*

1875 WALTON *Dis. Eye* 645 Without limitation of the visual field or scotomata,..direct vision may be much diminished in the region of the yellow spot. **1897** *Allbutt's Syst. Med.* III. 219 Central scotoma, or loss of vision in the central part of the field, is common [in diabetes]. **1943** *Horizon* Oct. 257 As with all neurotics, the confessions of Kierkegaard only contain a grain of the truth; the analytic scotoma constantly intervenes. **1957** F. B. WALSH *Clin. Neuro-Ophthalm.* (ed. 2) ix. 606/3 Retinal lesions are not rare in cases of Leber's optic atrophy. There may be complaint of chromatopsia and ring scotomas.

†**scotoˈmatical**, *a. Obs. rare.* [f. med.L. *scotōmatic-us* (f. *scotōma*: see prec.) + -AL[1].] Suffering from or under the influence of scotoma.

1656 BLOUNT *Glossogr.* **a 1691** BAXTER in *Reliq. B.* (1696) I. II. 199, I was then under great Weakness and Soporous or Scotomatical Ilness of my Head.

scotometer (skəʊˈtɒmɪtə(r)). *Ophthalm.* [f. SCOTO(MA + -METER.] An instrument for diagnosing and measuring scotomata.

1890 G. FERDINANDS in *Brit. Med. Jrnl.* 27 Sept. 741/1 Those who frequently meet with cases of toxic amblyopia.. must have found the small coloured squares used in detecting scotomata both an inadequate and inconvenient test... To obviate these disadvantages I have had made for me a little instrument..which I propose to call a scotometer. **1932** *Optician* LXXXIII. 397/1, I did not take the fields for white, relying on the evidence of the scotometer. **1961** S. VAN WIEN tr. *Huber's Eye Symptoms in Brain Tumors* i. 75 For a quick survey to determine the presence of a scotoma for color, the so-called scotometer is suitable.

Hence **scoˈtometry**, the use of a scotometer; **scotoˈmetric** *a.*

1921 *Proc. R. Soc. Med.* XIV. (Ophthalm. Sect.) 49 The purpose for which scotometry is of such importance is the determining of the increase of the blind spot in cases of suspected glaucoma. **1944** *Amer. Jrnl. Ophthalm.* XXVI. 349 (*heading*) The form and character of rod scotometry. **1955** *Jrnl. Neurol., Neurosurg. & Psychiatry* XVIII. 224/2 Scotometric studies suggested small infarctions in each infracalcarine striate cortex.

‖**scoˈtomia.** *Path.* [med.L., irreg. f. *scotōma*, after names of diseases in *-ia.*] = SCOTOMA I.

1543 TRAHERON *Vigo's Chirurg.* Interpr. s.v., *Scotomia*. They shoulde saye, Scotoma, and it is a disease, when [etc.]. **1728** CHAMBERS *Cycl., Scotomia*, or *Scotoma*, in medicine, a dizziness or swimming in the head. **1879** KHORY *Digest Med.* 13 There may be flashes of light or muscæ volitantes or scotomia.

scotomization (skəʊtəmaɪˈzeɪʃən). *Psychol.* [a. F. *scotomisation* (Pichon & Laforgue in R. Laforgue *Le Rêve et la Psychoanalyse* (1926) vii. 184), f. Gr. σκοτ-οῦν to darken, make dim-sighted: see -IZATION.] (See quot. 1927.) So **ˈscotomize** *v. trans.*; **ˈscotomized** *ppl. a.*

1927 R. LAFORGUE in *Internat. Jrnl. Psycho-Anal.* VIII. 473 In an earlier work I have defined scotomization (or the forming of mental 'blind spots') as a process of psychic depreciation, by means of which the individual attempts to deny everything which conflicts with his ego. *Ibid.* 477 If he scotomizes them [*sc.* such stimuli as do not belong to the field of consciousness],..they seek for gratification in narcissistic compensations, and force him to a compensatory activity whose scotomized sources are hidden from him. **1954** *Brit. Jrnl. Psychol.* XLV. 233 This criticism [of horrific test pictures] does not imply any scotomization of the capacity of the child..to conceive of the horrible. **1969** P. A. ROBINSON *Freudian Left* 145 The functionalists concluded from the mere fact that a culture existed that it..functioned harmoniously. They would thus 'scotomize' all of those psychoanalytic facts which drew attention to the terrible price we pay for civilization. **1977** A. SHERIDAN tr. *J. Lacan's Écrits* ii. 22 Freud seems suddenly to fail to recognize the existence of everything that the ego neglects, scotomizes, misconstrues in the sensations that make it react to reality.

†**ˈscotomy.** *Path. Obs.* [Anglicized form of SCOTOMIA.] = SCOTOMA I.

c 1400 *Lanfranc's Cirurg.* 118, & if þat he hadde scotomie, þat is to seie a maner sijknes, whanne þat þer semeþ as flien or oþere smale gnattis fleen tofore his yȝen. **a 1500** in James *West. MSS. Trin. Coll. Camb.* (1902) III. 494 Scotomye is such a sekenes of the Brayne that maketh a man to seme that he sethe flyes or blake thingis in þe eyre. **1533** ELYOT *Cast. Helthe* II. xxxiv. (1541) 50 In swellyng of the body and legges ..mygrimes, and scotomies, which is an imagination of darkenes. **1605** B. JONSON *Volpone* I. iv. (1607) C 2, How do's he, with the swimming of his head? *Mos.* O, Sir, tis past the Scotomy; he, now, Hath lost his feeling, and hath left to snort. **a 1640** MASSINGER, etc. *Old Law* III. ii, I ha got the Scotony [*sic*] in my head already, The whimzy: you all turne round, do not you dance gallants? **1710** T. FULLER *Pharmacop.* 222 We employ it [i.e. the Infusion] with happy Success in..Scotomy, &c.

scotophase: see SCOTO-[2].

scotophil (ˈskəʊtəʊfɪl), *a. Biol.* Also **skoto-, -phile.** [ad. G. *skotophil* (E. Bünning 1944, in *Flora* CXXXVIII. 95): see SCOTO-[2] and -PHIL, -PHILE.] Applied to that phase of the circadian cycle of a plant or animal during which light inhibits, or does not influence, reproductive activity; opp. *photophil, -phile* s.v. PHOTO- I.

1952, etc. [see *photophil* adj. s.v. PHOTO- I]. **1959** F. W. WENT in R. B. Withrow *Photoperiodism & Related Phenomena in Plants & Animals* VII. 554 The leaf angle.. is small in the scotophil and large in the photophil phase. **1960** *Cold Spring Harbor Symp. Quantitative Biol.* XXV. 257 In this part of the rhythm the endodiurnal system is in the scotophile state according to Bünning... The second scotophile phase is hardly weaker than the first one. **1971** *New Scientist* 29 July 254/2 The circadian rhythm [of house finches] was imagined to comprise two half cycles.., one of which was reckoned to be dark-requiring (scotophil). **1972** *Nature* 21 Apr. 407/1 The state..during which light has a promotive effect on flowering..and the state during which light is innocuous..could be respectively the photophil and skotophil phases of Bünning.

Hence **scotoˈphilic** *a.*, scotophile; **scoˈtophily**, the state of an organism in a scotophile phase.

1960 *Cold Spring Harbor Symp. Quantitative Biol.* XXV. 265/1 According to this view long and short day effects depend on whether the photoperiod of light break coincides with the 'scotophilic' phase during the second half-cycle. **1960** Scotophily [see *photophily* s.v. PHOTO- I]. **1976** *Sci. Amer.* Feb. 115/2 He proposed that the measurement of the length of the day or the night was accomplished by an endogenous, or built-in, daily rhythm that consisted of two half-cycles, one photophilic ('light-loving') and the other scotophilic ('dark-loving').

scotophobia: see SCOTO-[2]; **Scotophobia:** see SCOTO-[1].

scotophobin (skəʊtəʊˈfəʊbɪn). *Biochem.* [f. SCOTO-[2] + φόβ-ος fear + -IN[1]; cf. *scotophobia*[1] s.v. SCOTO-[2].] An oligopeptide isolated from the brains of rats which have been trained to avoid darkness, and which is claimed to induce dark avoidance in untrained rats and possibly also in animals of other species.

1970 G. UNGAR et al. in *Proc. Western Pharmacol. Soc.* XIII. 150 We propose to give the name 'scotophobin' to the new substance. **1971** *New Scientist* 3 June 559/3 The peptide, called scotophobin, contains only 15 amino acids. **1975** *Behavioral Biol.* XV. 470 Acceptance of these assumptions forces us to reject the hypothesis that 'fear of the dark' was encoded in scotophobin. **1976** F. WARNER *Killing Time* II. ix. 61 We could inject Scotophobin and induce a fear of the dark.

scotopic (skəʊˈtɒpɪk), *a. Physiol.* [f. SCOTO-[2] + -OPIA + -IC.] Of, pertaining to, or designating vision in dim light, believed to involve chiefly the rods of the retina. So **scoˈtopia**, the condition of scotopic eyes.

1915 J. H. PARSONS *Introd. Study Colour Vision* ii. 17 If the eye has been kept completely free from light for a considerable period it is said to be dark-adapted. I shall speak of vision under these circumstances as scotopia..and the dark-adapted eye as a scotopic eye. **1924** J. P. C. SOUTHALL tr. W. Nagel in *H. von Helmholtz's Treat. Physiol. Optics* II. 345 The so-called *Dämmerungssehen* (or twilight vision, scotopia), when the eye is dark-adapted and the light stimulus is weak. **1937** *Nature* 6 Mar. 409 It is generally accepted that visual purple plays an essential part in the process of scotopic vision. **1946** *Ibid.* 31 Aug. 303/2 S. Hecht also arrives at the conclusion that the absorption of the visual purple is less than 20 per cent, by comparing the scotopic luminosity curve with the absorption curve of visual purple. **1972** H. J. EYSENCK et al. *Encycl. Psychol.* III. 182/1 *Scotopia*, twilight vision... With twilight vision a person is insensitive to color and his peripheral vision is better for fine detail than his central vision, since there are no rods in the fovea. **1973** 'A. HALL' *Tango Briefing* xiv. 169 My eyes were adapting to scotopic vision, the torchlight growing brighter.

ˈscotoscope. *rare* [f. Gr. σκότο-ς darkness + -SCOPE.] An instrument which enables the user to see in the dark.

1664 PEPYS *Diary* 13 Aug., There comes also Mr. Reeve with a microscope and scotoscope..a curious curiosity it is to discover objects in a dark room with. **c 1670** COLLINS in Rigaud *Corr. Sci. Men* (1841) II. 291 The perfection of telescopes, microscopes, scotoscopes, and burning glasses. **1964** *Applied Optics* III. 671 The scotoscope can be arranged to give a color presentation; however, when this is done, it is at the expense of a fairly high percentage of the photons incident from the scene.

†**ˈScotry.** *Obs. rare*[−1]. [f. SCOT *sb.*[1] + -RY.] The Scots collectively.

c 1470 HARDING *Chron.* CCXL. (1812) 420 *note*, Betuene the see of the West occion, And the hilles of Scotlonde occident, The wilde Scotrie have their propre mancion.

Scots (skɒts), *a.* (*sb.*) Orig. *Sc.* and northern. Forms: 4 **Skot(t)is**, 4–6 **Scottis**, 5–7 **Scottes**, 6 **Skottes, Scotes, Scotis**, 6–8 **Scotts**, 7– **Scots.** [Orig. *Scottis*, northern var. of SCOTTISH. (Cf. *Inglis* ENGLISH.)

For the relation in use between this form and the two others, see SCOTCH *a.*]

1. Of or belonging to Scotland or its inhabitants, Scottish, Scotch.

a 1352 MINOT *Poems* (ed. Hall) i. 79 And þarfore many a Skottis brid With dole er dight þat þai most dwell. **1473** WARKW. *Chron.* (Camden) 2 The Scottes host. **1500–20** DUNBAR *Poems* lxxxvii. 40 Fair gem of joy, Mergreit of the I meyne: Gladethe thoue Queyne of Scottis regioun. **1513** DOUGLAS *Æneis* I. Prol. 103 This buik I dedicaite, Writing in the language of Scottis natioun. **1622** MALYNES *Anc. Law-Merch.* 80 Scots-coale, Wheat, Barley and all kind of graines in both Kingdomes. **1637** MONRO *Exped.* II. 23 The other Scots Officers of the Regiment. **1797** DR. BURNEY *Let. to Mme. D'Arblay* 28 Sept., A Scots lady. **1827** HALLAM *Const. Hist.* xvii. (1857) III. 337 The Scots parliament took care to bring on the crisis by the act of security in 1704. **1902** BUCHAN *Watcher by Threshold* 125 He thought Scots games inferior to southern sports.

b. Qualifying the name of a coin or a money of account (in contradistinction to *sterling*), as ***mark Scots, penny Scots, pound Scots, shilling Scots*** (see the sbs.). Also in names of weights and measures denoting a particular variation from the English standard, ***Scots acre, boll, mile, pint, stone, Troy weight*** (see the sbs.). Now *arch.* or *Hist.*

1520 *Charges conc. Dk. Albany* in G. Douglas *Wks.* (1874) I. Introd. 109 Fourty thousand pund of Scottis money. *Ibid.*, Bettir than ten thousand pundis Scottis. **1632** [see MILE *sb.*[1] 2]. **1641** in Cochran-Patrick *Rec. Coinage Scot.* (1876) I. Introd. 30 The king hes vpon the coinage of euerie Scots staine of siluer bulyion 64 li. **1697** in A. I. Ritchie *Churches of St. Baldred* (1880) 39 Whoever shall desire the great bell to be rung to any burial, must pay for the same ten shillings Scots. **1765** *Museum Rust.* IV. 455 From eleven to twelve pecks, Linlithgow measure, of Dutch or Riga seed, is generally sufficient for one Scots acre. **1775** *Brit. Chronol.* an. 1719 II. 51/2 An act for laying a duty of two pennies *Scots*..upon every pint of ale or beer that shall be vended or sold within the town of Inverness. **1791** BURNS *Tam o' Shanter* 7 We think na on the lang Scots miles..That lie between us and our hame. **c 1792** *Encycl. Brit.* (ed. 3) X. 718/1 It was enacted by..James VI that it [the pint] should contain 55 Scots Troy ounces of the clear water of Leith. **1801** *Farmer's Mag.* Jan. 72 In one instance, the produce is stated to be..92 Scots bolls per English statute acre. **1824** SCOTT *Redgauntlet* xx, What say ye to another pot? or shall we cry in a blithe Scots pint at once? **1838** W. BELL *Dict. Law Scot.* s.v. *Schools*, The salaries of the schoolmasters were to be fixed at from 300 to 400 merks Scots. *Ibid.* s.v., Sterling money is twelve times the value of the same denomination of Scots money. **1883** *American* VI. 270 A legacy by word of mouth is good to the extent of £100 Scots, or £8 6s. 8d. sterling.

c. With reference to law. Cf. SCOTTISH *a.* I e.

In this application recent literary usage favours the form *Scots* rather than *Scottish* or *Scotch*, but Scottish legal writers have apparently never followed this rule.

1766 BLACKSTONE *Comm.* II. iv. 57 These inferior feudatories..held what are called in the Scots law 'rere-fiefs'. **1773** (*title*) An Institute of the Law of Scotland..By Jon Erskine..Sometime Professor of Scots Law in the University of Edinburgh. **1820** *Trials for High Treason Scot.* (1825) I. 15 The old Scots law of treason was by no means well defined.

d. In the names of trees and plants. More commonly SCOTCH.

c 1710 CELIA FIENNES *Diary* (1888) 20 On yᵉ right side of yᵉ house is a large grove of firrs halfe scotts halfe norroway. **1728** BRADLEY *Dict. Bot.* II, *Scots Scurvy-Grass*, i.e. *Soldanella*. **1797** *Encycl. Brit.* (ed. 3) XIV. 761/2 The [*pinus*] *rubra*, commonly called the Scots fir, or pine. **1908** *Q. Jrnl. Forestry* Jan. 70 The whole enclosure was planted in the spring of 1905 with oak,..larch, and Scots pine.

†**e.** ***Scots goose***: the barnacle goose. (So Norfolk dial. *Scotch goose*: see *E.D.D.*)

1668 CHARLETON *Onomast.* 98 *Anser Bernicla*, the Barnacle, or Scots-goose.

2. Of language: **a.** The distinguishing epithet of the dialect of English spoken by the inhabitants of the Lowlands of Scotland. Also *absol.* as *sb.*, the Scottish dialect.

1542 *Sc. Acts Mary* (1814) II. 415/1 It salbe lefull to all oʳ souirane ladyis lieges to haif þe haly write baiᵗ þe new testament and þe auld in þe vulgar toung In Inglis or scottis of ane gude and trew translatioune. **1563** WINȜET *Cert. Tractates* Wks. (S.T.S.) I. 74 'By' in Scottis and in Inglis toung is nocht ane. **1596** DALRYMPLE tr. *Leslie's Hist. Scot.* II. 179 Translating the Æneids of Virgil in scotis; sa rycht ..that ilk scotis verse concordet with the latin. **1788** in *Shirrefs' Poems* (1790) p. xxvi, For Scots is neither flat nor lame:..When we had kings and courts at hame, They spake nae ither. **1818** SCOTT *Rob Roy* xxvii, Kilted loons that dinna ken the name o' a single herb or flower in braid Scots, let abee in the Latin tongue. **1839** HALLAM *Lit. Eur.* II. v. §77 It would be a great omission to neglect..the Scots and English ballads. **1861** *Two Cosmos* I. 294 To use a good old-fashioned Scots phrase. **1902** BUCHAN *Watcher by Threshold* 281 She speaks broad Scots.

b. Used quasi-*Hist.* for: Scottish Gaelic. *rare*[−1].

1831 SCOTT *Cast. Dang.* v, An antique language,.. being a species of Scots or Gaelic, which few would have comprehended.

3. Characteristic of or peculiar to Scotland or a Scotsman. Now *rare* or *Obs.*

1616 W. HAIG in J. Russell *Haigs* (1881) 163 That Scots kindness (ever ready to a friend, but oft inconsiderate). **1812** *Sporting Mag.* XXXIX. 17 Captain Barclay.. has reduced Crib from upwards of sixteen stone to the above weight, by Scots living.

4. *Mil.* **a.** In names of regiments in the British Army, as ***Scots Fusiliers, Scots Greys*** (see GREY *sb.* 8), ***Scots Guards.*** **b.** In names of bodies of mercenaries in foreign service, as ***Scots Brigade, Scots Dutch*** (see the equivalent forms under SCOTCH).

1637 MONRO *Exped.* II. 25 Which.. thereafter was still called the Scots Briggad commanded by Hepburne. **1646** *Sc. Acts Chas. I* (1870) VI. I. 597/2 Sr. Robert Murray Lieut: colonell to the Scotis Regiment of the guard in France. **1823** SCOTT *Quentin D.* vii. *note*, Such disputes between the Scots Guards, and the other constituted authorities of the ordinary military corps, often occurred. **1862** A. K. MURRAY *Scottish Regiments* 70 The Scots Fusilier Guards, with the Grenadiers and Coldstreams, were stationed in the chateau and grounds of Hougomont. **1867** BURTON *Hist. Scot.* III. xxvii. 108 The celebrated Scots Guard was established—it is said to have begun in the few who survived the slaughter at Verneuil. **1883** *Macmillan's Mag.* XLVII. 443 Twenty-five mounted infantry of the 2nd Battalion Royal Scots Fusiliers. **1893** STEVENSON *Catriona* xii. 132 Lieutenant-colonel in a regiment of the Scots-Dutch.

† **'scotsem-nail.** *Obs.* Also 4 scotsem, scotsum-, scotsom-, 5 scotseme-, scotesem-, schotsem-. [Presumably formed as SCOTNAIL; the middle syllable may be SEAM *sb.*, rivet.]

1336 in J. R. Boyle *Hedon* (1895) App. 17 In C. clavis de scotsem emptis.. iij d. **1371** *Fabric Rolls York Minster* (Surtees) 7 In 10.m. de Scotsomnail emptis pro celura. **1408** *Durham Acct. Roll* in *Eng. Hist. Rev.* XIV. 518, ccclx schotsemnaylle, c ad viiid; c clavis parvis [etc.]. **1434** *Fabric Rolls York Minster* (Surtees) 53 In xij.m de stone-brodes, in v.m Scotesemnailes, 5s. 5d. In vij.m DCCC Scotsemnailes, 9s. 2d.

Scots-Irish, *a.* **a.** = SCOTCH-IRISH *a.* Also as *sb.* **b.** = SCOTCH-IRISH *a.* b.

1972 *Listener* 21 Dec. 854/2 The hostility of the Catholic Irish and the Protestant Scots-Irish. *Ibid.* 854/3 The Protestant Scots-Irish community. **1973** *Guardian* 27 June 13/3 The USA has taken to calling itself 'Scots-Irish' rather than 'British'. **1973** 'D. SHANNON' *No Holiday for Crime* (1974) iv. 62 Once in a while my Scots-Irish wife uses a little ESP. **1980** —— *Felony File* i. 35 The feudal household his Scots-Irish girl had wished on him.

Scotsman ('skɒtsmən). Forms: 4 **Scottis man,** 5 **Scottys man, Scottes man, Scotesman,** 5–6 **Scottisman, Scottesman,** 6 **Scotisman,** 7 **Scotts man,** 7–8 **Scots-man,** 6– **Scotsman.** [f. SCOTS *a.* + MAN (orig. two words).]

a. = SCOTCHMAN.

c **1375** BARBOUR *Bruce* XI. 8 Quhen he herd schir Philip say, That Scottis men had set ane day To fecht [etc.]. *c* **1425** WYNTOUN *Cron.* IX. xxi. 401 Þar Scottismen fel gret tynsaille. *c* **1490** *Paston Lett.* III. 366, I conceyve also that the same Thomas is noysed in Norffolk for a Scotesman borne. **1515** *Minute of Council* in G. Douglas *Wks.* (1874) I. Introd. 61 My Lord Gouernour traistit nocht that ony Scotisman in the realme wald sek help at Inglismen in his doingis. **1548** W. PATTEN *Exped. Scot.* D viij b, But what saynte so euer he bee, he is sure no Scottes mans frend. **1565** STAPLETON tr. *Bede's Hist. Ch. Eng.* III. xxi. 97 These priestes were called Cedda, Adda, Betti, and Diuna, who was a scottes-man borne, the other thre english. **1637–50** ROW *Hist. Kirk* (Wodrow Soc.) 441 Books and Treatises published by Scotts men. **1780** *Mirror* No. 82 The Earl of Bute, who was both a Scotsman and a favourite. **1818** SCOTT *Hrt. Midl.* iv, Are not we, like them, Scotsmen and burghers of Edinburgh? **1902** GAIRDNER *Eng. Ch. 16th Cent.* xiii. 246 The Protector might.. have reckoned on the devotion of a little band of Scotsmen in a Scottish stronghold by the sea to assist him.

b. (Also ***Flying Scotsman.***) Now the more usual form of (*Flying*) *Scotchman*: see SCOTCHMAN 1 b.

One of British Rail's express trains from London to Edinburgh still bears this name, though the particular steam locomotive so named was withdrawn from service on 14 Jan. 1963.

1879 *G.N.R. Tourist-guide* 1 The splendid express known as the 'Flying Scotsman'. **1932** P. BLOOMFIELD *Imaginary Worlds* 34 Pretending.. that our O gauge railway round the nursery floor is really the line taken by the 'Flying Scotsman'. **1936** J. MASEFIELD *Let. from Pontus* 57 On the railway beside us the Scotsman went by. **1952** A. ANDERSON *Flying Scotsman* 3 Our train is the Flying Scotsman which has left King's Cross at 10 a.m. daily for over 90 years. **1962** C. H. ELLIS *Flying Scotsman* i. 11 The Special Scotch Express sooner or later became the 'Flying Scotch Express', which in turn was transformed into 'Flying Scotchman' and later still, probably when English people began to read Robert Louis Stevenson, into 'Flying Scotsman'. That eventually became the official title. **1974** *Times* 7 Dec. 3/2 The Flying Scotsman.. the majestic old LNER puffer... The Flying Scotsman.. is at present stabled steamless at Carnforth.

Hence **'Scotsmanship,** the nature or quality of a Scotsman.

1828 *Examiner* 56/2 If there is gallantry in Dudley, conceit in Ellenborough, Scotsmanship in Melville. **1894** R. WALLACE in *Life & Last Leaves* (1903) 485 'Proud' of his Scotsmanship, he might [etc.].

Scots Nat (skɒts næt). *colloq.* [f. SCOTS *a.* + NAT *sb.*[4]; cf. SCOT NAT *sb.* and *a.*] A member of the Scottish National Party (see SCOTTISH *a.* 5). Hence **Scots 'Nattery** (*nonce-wd.*) Scottish Nationalism.

1974 *Undercurrents* July–Aug. 3/2 The British did take the precaution.. of incorporating Rockall into the county of Inverness—which may or may not be a smart move depending on which way the Scots Nats jump. **1977** *Times* 23 June 16/1 The delectable MP for East Dumbartonshire, Margaret Bain.. a good Scots Nat and true. **1978** *Times* 21 Jan. 14/4 Successive waves of Scots Nattery going back to J. M. Bannerman.

'Scotswoman. [SCOTS *a.*] = SCOTCHWOMAN.

1820 SCOTT *Abbot* iii, 'The slothful hinds!' exclaimed Mary, thinking and feeling like a Scotswoman of the period. **1822** —— *Nigel* viii, The old Scotswoman.

Scott (skɒt). *Electr. Engin.* [The name of Charles F. *Scott* (1864–1944), U.S. electrical engineer, who devised the connection in 1894 (*Electrician* 6 Apr. 640).] ***Scott connection***: a way of connecting two single-phase transformers to convert a three-phase voltage to a two-phase one (or to two single-phase ones), or vice versa: on the three-phase side the mid-point of the main transformer is connected to one terminal of the second transformer; the remaining three terminals form the terminals for the three-phase supply; the two-phase supply is taken from the two pairs of terminals on the other side. So ***Scott-connected*** adj.

[**1911** BOHLE & ROBERTSON *Transformers* xi. 321 (*heading*) Scott's two-phase to three-phase connection.] **1926** J. L. BEAVER *Elem. Alternating Currents* ix. 200 The so-called 'Scott' connection is an arrangement of *two* single-phase transformers, whereby three-phase power may be obtained from a two-phase circuit or vice versa. **1935** MONSETH & ROBINSON *Relay Systems* x. 304 (*caption*) Scott-connected transformer differential protective scheme. **1947** R. LEE *Electronic Transformers & Circuits* viii. 214 When autotransformers are used on three-phase supply lines, they may be connected the same as two-winding transformers in star, delta, open-delta, or Scott connections. **1966** BROSAN & HAYDEN *Adv. Electr. Power & Machines* vi. 243 The Leblanc system was invented about five years after the Scott connexion when the latter had obtained a firm foothold in Britain and its use was therefore confined to the Continent. *Ibid.*, The general case of determining the regulation of a Scott-connected group is somewhat involved.

Scott(e, variant forms of SCOT.

scottall, scottel(l, obs. ff. SCOTALE, SCUTTLE.

Scottic, variant of SCOTIC.

‖**Scotticè, Scoticè** ('skɒtɪsi:), *adv.* [med.L. *Scotticē, Scōticē*, f. late L. *Scottic-us, Scōtic-us* Scottish.] In Scotch.

1818 SCOTT *Hrt. Midl.*, *note* L, *Lockman*, so called from the small quantity of meal (Scottice, *lock*) which he was entitled to take. **1861** *Two Cosmos* II. 129 An enormous pair of old worn-out shoes (Scottice, bauchles).

Scotticism, Scoticism ('skɒtɪsɪz(ə)m). [f. late L. *Scōtic-us* (*Scotticus*) + -ISM. The spelling with *tt* has prevailed owing to the analogy of *Scottish.*]

1. An idiom or mode of expression characteristic of Scots; esp. as used by a writer of English.

1717 DE FOE *Mem. Ch. Scot.* II. 137 This is a Scoticism in Speech. **1759** W. ROBERTSON *Hist. Scot.* VIII. Wks. 1851 II. 323 Many of those vicious forms of speech, which are denominated *Scotticisms*, have been introduced by them [lawyers] into the language. **1772** WESLEY *Jrnl.* 11 Dec. (1827) III. 470 The book is wrote with great accuracy of language, (allowing for a few Scotticisms). **1815** L. HUNT *Feast of Poets* Notes 62 His style in prose, setting aside it's Scotticisms, is very well where [etc.]. **1892** B. MATTHEWS *Americanisms & Briticisms* 16 The Scotticisms of the North Briton.

2. Scottish sympathies.

1807 G. CHALMERS *Caledonia* I. II. i. 230 His ardour of Scoticism hurries him headlong, from the paths of truth. **1862** LOWELL *Lett.* I. 361 He seems to me a remarkably good critic, where his Scoticism doesn't come in his way.

Scotticize ('skɒtɪsaɪz), *v.* [f. late L. *Scotticus* (*Scōticus*) Scottish, Scotch (see SCOTIC) + -IZE.]

1. *trans.* To imbue with Scottish ideas or characteristics.

1763 WILKES *N. Briton* No. 34 None but Scots or Jacobites or such English as are Scotticized, must expect favour or preferment under him. **1859** MASSON *Brit. Novelists* iii. 204 He [Scott] has Scotticized European literature.

2. To give a Scottish form to (a foreign word); to turn (a work) into Scottish dialect.

1874 SMALL *Douglas' Wks.* I. Pref. 165 He accordingly, in his version of Virgil, does not scruple to Scotticise a Latin word. **1901** LAW *N.T. in Scots* (S.T.S.) Introd. 15 A Scotticised transcript of it was added.. at the end of the volume.

Scottie ('skɒtɪ). Shortened f. *Scotch terrier* s.v. SCOTCH *a.* 4.

1907 F. T. BARTON *Terriers* xviii. 131 If a Scottie has not a sound jacket to keep out the mountain dew and rain, he ought not to take a leading place at any show. **1939** *Country Life* 11 Feb. p. xxi/2 (Advt.), For Sale.—Exceptionally strong Scottie puppies. **1945** A. CHRISTIE *Sparkling Cyanide* I. iv. 40 She came out one morning with a small black Scottie dog. **1957** R. MASON *World of Suzie Wong* II. ii. 124 Her dog.. was a Scottie with an absurd, sad, long face. **1971** 'L. EGAN' *Malicious Mischief* (1972) i. 4 Scotties are nice dogs. **1973** M. AMIS *Rachel Papers* 159 Glancing downwards, my rig, in its pink muff, looked unnatural, absurd, like an overdressed Scottie dog.

Scottified ('skɒtɪfaɪd), *ppl. a.* Also 7 **scotified.** [f. next + -ED[1].] Having Scottish characteristics.

1644 NEEDHAM *Case of Commonw.* 67 The ambition of a few scotified English. **1763** WILKES *N. Briton* No. 37 ¶4 The chaste and scrupulous integrity of the knot of Tories, Scottish members, and Scottified English. **1814** SCOTT in *Lockhart* (1839) III. 315, I think you will like it [*The Lord of the Isles*]: it is Scottified up to the teeth.

Scottify ('skɒtɪfaɪ), *v.* Also **Scotify.** [f. SCOTT(ISH) + -(I)FY.] *trans.* To render Scottish.

1869 F. J. FURNIVALL *Forewords Q. Eliz. Acad.* 17 The conclusion then forced on me was, that Adam Loutfut.. had copied the poem from an original, and scottified it as he copied. **1881** *Athenæum* 8 Jan. 55/3 The chap-books sold by Scotch pedlars at the annual Lammas Fair of Kirkwall [Orkney] played an important part in Scottifying the vernacular. **1902** G. G. SMITH *Spec. Mid. Scots* p. xxxv, It may be a 'Scotifying' of S[outhern] *those.*

Hence **,Scottifi'cation,** the process of 'Scottifying'; quasi-*concr.* a rendering into Scottish dialect.

1869 F. J. FURNIVALL *Forewords Q. Eliz. Acad.* 17 Which scottification I hope some day to print opposite Caxton's own text. **1894** A. J. BALFOUR in *Times* 23 July 3/2, I watch with satisfaction the gradual Scottification of England by this great golfing propaganda. **1900** *Westm. Gaz.* 11 May 2/2 Scotification is clearly Lord Rosebery's policy.

Scottish ('skɒtɪʃ), *a.* and *sb.* Forms: [1 Scyttisc, Scyttysc, Scittisc], 2 **Scottysc,** 3 **Scottisc,** 5 **Scottissh,** 6 **Scottys(s)he, Skottishe, Skottyshe,** 6–7 **Scottishe, Skottish,** 7–9 **Scotish,** 6– **Scottish.** [Late OE. (12th c.) *Scottisc*, a new formation on *Scotta* SCOT *sb.*[1] + *-isc*, -ISH[1], replacing the older *Scyttisc* with umlaut. Cf. MDu., Du. *schotsch*, LG. *schottsch*, G. *schottisch* (earlier *schöttisch*), ON. *skotzk-r.*] **A.** *adj.*

1. a. Of or belonging to Scotland or to the people of Scotland; esp. of persons: of Scotch nationality, birth, or descent. †***Scottish cap*** = SCOTCH CAP.

[*c* **900** tr. *Bæda's Hist.* III. xxi. (1890) 222 Se nyhsta wæs Scyttisces cynnes; þa oðre wæron Englisce.] *c* **1205** LAY. 20355 Patric þe ricche mon þat wes a Scottisc þein scone an his londen. *c* **1450** *Merlin* xiii. 197 For thei were but two scottissh myle fro the town. **1507** in *Songs, Carols*, etc. (E.E.T.S.) 154 Þer was gret plente of Skottishe samon. **1548** W. PATTEN *Exped. Scot.* L vij, The Skottish gouernor.. caused the erle Bothwel to be let out of prison. **1553** in *Roy. Engin. Jrnl.* 3 Mar. (1910) 174 Euery souldiour to have Jackes covered wth fustian & Skullis with Scotishe cappes. **1596** SHAKS. *1 Hen. IV*, I. iii. 259 Then once more to your Scottish Prisoners. Deliuer them vp without their ransome straight. **1618** J. TAYLOR (Water-P.) *Pennyless Pilgr.* E 4, The olde Prouerbe of a Scottish Miste was verified, in wetting mee to the skinne. **1637** MONRO *Exped.* I. 55 Here also our Scottish High-landmen are prayse-worthy. **179.** BURKE *Let. to W. Smith* Wks. IX. 407 A zealous Anglican or Scottish Church principle. **1827** SCOTT *Chron. Canongate* ii, A.. broken-down Scottish laird. **1876** BANCROFT *Hist. U.S.* II. xlii. 559 The settlement of the Scottish emigrants at Port Royal.

b. In the names of various trees and plants: cf. SCOTCH 4 b, SCOTS 1 d.

1855 MISS PRATT *Flower. Pl.* V. 279 *Scottish Asphodel. **1796** WITHERING *Brit. Plants* (ed. 3) II. 297 *Scottish lovage, or Sea Parsley. **1855** MISS PRATT *Flower. Pl.* IV. 232 *Scottish Primrose. **1597** GERARDE *Herbal* II. ccxciii. 690 *Soldanella*.. in English Sea Withwinde,.. of some ..*Scottish Scuruie grasse.

†**c.** (See quot.)

1623 J. TAYLOR (Water-P.) *Praise Hemp-seed* 7 Many a Gallant.. Hath got the Spanish pip,.. or the Scottish fleas, or English Pox, for al's but one disease.

d. *Mil.* ***Scottish Guard*** = *Scots Guard.* ***Scottish Rifles*** (see quot 1888).

1823 SCOTT *Quentin D.* v, With these followers, and a corresponding equipage, an Archer of the Scottish Guard was a person of quality and importance. **1888** LAWRENCE-ARCHER *Brit. Army* 240 The King's Own Scottish Borderers. *Ibid.* 246 The Cameronians... This peculiar old corps.. now forms the first battalion of the Scottish Rifles.

e. Used with reference to law. Cf. SCOTS *a.* 1 c.

1726 (*title*) Minor Practicks, or, a Treatise of the Scottish Law. Composed by.. Sir Thomas Hope.. Advocate to His Majesty King Charles I. **1826** SCOTT *Jrnl.* 9 June, The consequence of this will in time be, that the Scottish Supreme Court will be in effect situated in London. Then down fall—as national objects of respect and veneration—the Scottish Bench, the Scottish Bar, the Scottish Law herself. **1875** *Encycl. Brit.* II. 639/2 *Art and Part*, a term used in Scottish Law to denote the aiding or abetting [etc.].

†**2. Scottish earth** *Min.*, strontian. *Obs.*

1796 KIRWAN *Elem. Min.* (ed. 2) I. 13 Scottish, or Stronthian Earth.

†**3.** *transf.* Marked by Scottish characteristics.

1532 MORE *Confut. Barnes* VIII. Wks. 739/2 The rude rimelesse runninge of a scottishe ieste. **1610** MARCELLINE *Triumphs Jas. I* To France B 4 b, My life is innocent, my heart Christian, my tongue to Scottish, and he is too good and wise a King, to bee flattered by any. *c* **1620** A. HUME

Brit. Tongue I. vii. (1870) 18 The assumption is Scottish, and the conclusion false.

4. Applied to the language (see SCOTS *a.* 2).

1780 *Mirror* No. 83 The Scottish dialect is our ordinary suit; the English is used only on solemn occasions. **1818** SCOTT *Rob Roy* iv, This was the first time I had heard the Scottish accent. **1862** *Chamb. Encycl.* IV. 66/1 Gavin Douglas (died 1522), whose best work is a translation of Virgil's Æneid into Scottish verse.

5. *Comb.*, as ***Scottish-American, -hearted***, adjs.; **Scottish Baronial** *a.*, designating a style of architecture typical of the semi-fortified houses of the medieval Scottish nobility, and revived in the nineteenth century (cf. *Scotch Baronial* s.v. SCOTCH *a.* 4 a); **Scottish Blackface** = *Scotch Blackface* s.v. SCOTCH *a.* 4 a; **Scottish Chaucerians,** the distinguishing epithet applied to a number of fifteenth- and sixteenth-century Scottish poets influenced by and imitating the work of Geoffrey Chaucer; **Scottish-French,** French spoken by Scots; **Scottish-Irish** = SCOTCH-IRISH; **Scottish National Party,** a political party formed in 1934 by an amalgamation of the National Party of Scotland and the Scottish Party, which seeks autonomous government for Scotland (cf. SCOTTISH NATIONALIST *a.* and *sb.*); **Scottish terrier** = *Scotch terrier* s.v. SCOTCH *a.* 4 a.

1905 W. JAMES in *McClure's Mag.* May 3/1, I wish to pay my tribute to the memory of a *Scottish-American friend of mine who died five years ago. **1978** N. GOSLING *Paris 1900–14* 49 Debussy had picked the Scottish-American star Mary Garden. **1938** L. MACNEICE *I crossed Minch* vii. 98 Oban has many hotels in the *Scottish Baronial style. **1956** L. E. JONES *Edwardian Youth* iv. 87 The newly-built Scottish Baronial building which contains the Main Gateway [of Balliol College, Oxford]. **1979** R. LAIDLAW *Lion is Rampant* vi. 49 The house..was a massive structure, built..in the Scottish Baronial style. **1937** A. FRASER *Sheep Farming* ii. 22 Only a few years ago I was concerned with the export of *Scottish Blackface sheep to Palestine. **1974** *Times* 23 Feb. 14/2 Several farmers may turn out their Swaledale or Scottish Blackface, Herdwick or Lonk sheep onto one moor. **1902** G. GREGORY SMITH *Specimens of Middle Scots* p. xlv, To say this of the '*Scottish Chaucerians' is almost a platitude. **1927** E. P. HAMMOND *Eng. Verse between Chaucer & Surrey* p. xi, Rhythm in Chaucer and the English Chaucerians—Verse-Forms—The Scottish Chaucerians—Vocabulary. **1935** A. BAUGH *Hist. Eng. Lang.* vi. 192 The fifteenth century is sometimes known as the Imitative Period since so much of the poetry..was written in emulation of Chaucer... In the north the Scottish Chaucerians, particularly Henryson, Dunbar, Gavin Douglas, and Lindsay, produced significant work. **1937** *Oxf. Compan. Eng. Lit.* (ed. 2) 154/1 *Chaucerians, Scottish*, name given to a group of 15th cent. Scottish writers (of whom Dunbar and Henryson are the chief) who imitated Chaucer in some of their work. **1966** *Amer. N. & Q.* May 139/1 Robbins-Cutler now include..the so-called Scottish Chaucerians. **1823** SCOTT *Quentin D.* v, The well-known sound of the *Scottish-French was as familiar in the taverns near Plessis, as that of the Swiss-French in the modern *guinguettes* of Paris. **1818** —— *Hrt. Midl.* xviii, Walking hand in hand with the real noble *Scottish-hearted barons. **1876** BANCROFT *Hist. U.S.* IV. xviii. 443 Presbyterians of *Scottish-Irish descent. **1934** *Times* 26 Feb. 16/5 Resolutions were unanimously passed at a conference of the National Party of Scotland in Glasgow approving of a union with the Scottish Party, subject to that Party's agreement, the united parties to be called the *Scottish National Party. **1973** *Scotsman* 12 Jan. 9/2 Mr. Douglas Drysdale, a former vice-chairman of the Scottish National Party, has been appointed..for liaison among other nationalist bodies in Scotland. **1980** BUTLER & SLOMAN *Brit. Polit. Facts 1900–79* (ed. 5) ii. 162 Scottish National Party. The party was formed in 1928 as the National Party of Scotland. In 1933 it merged with a body called the Scottish Party (founded 1930) and the name was then changed to the Scottish National Party. **1837** T. BELL *Hist. Brit. Quadrupeds* 230 The other [terrier] is called the *Scottish or Wire-haired Terrier. **1894** R. B. LEE *Hist. & Descr. Mod. Dogs: Terriers* xi. 251 It was about the year 1874 that a newspaper controversy brought the Scottish terrier prominently before the public. **1956** D. CASPERSZ *Popular Scottish Terrier* i. 17 The Scottish Terrier descends directly from a race of small terriers of great antiquity.

B. *sb.* (absolute uses of the adj.)

1. The Scottish language.

1759 ROBERTSON *Hist. Scot.* Wks. 1851 II. 368 The letters were very early translated into Scottish. **1818** SCOTT *Rob Roy* xxxv, Nor was there the least tincture of that vulgarity, which we naturally attach to the Lowland Scottish. **1886** *Encycl. Brit.* XXI. 541/2 Bellenden also translated the first five books of Livy into Scottish.

2. *the Scottish* (with pl. sense): the Scots. *rare.*

1632 *Swed. Intelligencer* II. 13 The Scottish have hitherto had the honour and the danger, to be the first men that are put upon such a businesse. **1814** SCOT *Wav.* xviii, The large measure which the Scottish allowed of their land. **1831** —— *Cast. Dang.* xx, The necessary conditions were speedily agreed on, which put the Scottish in possession of this stronghold.

†**'Scottish,** *v. Obs. rare*$^{-1}$. In 7 Scotish. [f. the adj. (Cf. *to English.*)] *trans.* To render in the Scottish tongue.

1623 LISLE *Ælfric on O. & N. Test.* To Rdrs. c 4 b, At length I lighted on Virgil Scotished by the Reuerend Gawin Douglas.

†**'Scottishman.** *Obs.* [f. SCOTTISH *a.* + MAN.] = SCOTSMAN.

[**1387** TREVISA *Higden* (Rolls) VI. 389 Þe Scottyshe men.. took a carabum..and wente Þerynne.] **1523** SURREY in Ellis *Orig. Lett.* Ser. I. I. 215 Bothe with thies contreymen and Scottishmen. **1530** PALSGR. 268/1 Scottyssheman, *Escoyssoys.* **1548** W. PATTEN *Exped. Scot.* G vij, The Scottish-mens pykes wear as long or lenger then their staues. **1632** *Swed. Intelligencer* I. 86 One Scottish-man protested he had kill'd 18 men with his owne hand. **1748** SMOLLETT *Rod. Rand.* xlii. Contents (1760) II. 41 We are accosted by a priest, who proves to be a Scottishman. **1808** SCOTT in *Lockhart* I. i. 3 Every Scottishman has a pedigree. **1831** —— *Cast. Dang.* xix, It seems almost unnatural for Scottish-men and English to meet and part without a buffet.

'Scottish 'Nationalist, *a.* and *sb.* **A.** *adj.* Of or pertaining to the Scottish National Party (see SCOTTISH *a.* 5) or its programme. **B.** *sb.* A member of this party.

1936 'H. MACDIARMID' in *Lucky Poet* (1943) iii. 145 The long confused and inefficient Scottish Nationalist groping. **1953** E. SIMON *Past Masters* IV. 246 This Scottish Nationalist you've got there. **1968** *Daily Progress* (Charlottesville, Va.) 11 July C14/1 Winifred Ewing was a noted narker in Glasgow before she became the only Scottish Nationalist in the House of Commons. **1976** LD. HOME *Way Wind Blows* xv. 206 A Scottish Nationalist Party had grown up which had begun to advocate separation from England.

So **'Scottish 'Nationalism,** the political programme or ideals of the Scottish National Party.

1935 N. MITCHISON *We have been Warned* I. 73 'Don't you think..there's something in Scottish Nationalism?' 'Not while it's run by ladies and gentlemen.' **1953** E. SIMON *Past Masters* IV. 246 Scottish Nationalism, as I see it, is an absurdity.

Scottishness ('skɒtɪʃnɪs). [f. SCOTTISH *a.* + -NESS.] The quality of being Scottish.

1859 RAMSAY *Remin.* 154 It is the Scottishness that gives the zest. **1933** *Times Lit. Suppl.* 3 Aug. 523/1 Henryson was sage and serious. It was part of his Scottishness. **1956** N. PEVSNER *Englishness of Eng. Art* (rev. ed.) 125 It is easy to recognize Scottishness in the Scottish castle of the seventeenth century. **1976** *Listener* 19 Feb. 209/3 The BBC in Scotland should be asked..to abandon the excessive concern with Scottishness.

Scottishry ('skɒtɪʃrɪ). [f. SCOTTISH *a.* + -RY; cf. IRISHRY, WELSHRY, etc.] Scottish character or nationality; a Scottish trait, Scottishness.

1958 C. WATSON *Coffin, scarcely Used* iv. 44 'Ye hear tha' frae the wee booy!' he chortled... 'For heaven's sake, drop that phoney Scottishry, Rupert.' **1973** *Daily Tel.* 24 Nov. 11/1 The whole business of Highland Scottishry is so technical that an Englishman may find himself rebuked on a point of Gaelic or a question of optics. **1979** *Ibid.* 17 Aug. 14/3 Fake Scottishry of the kind which reduces the noble name of the last Lord of the Isles, Donald Dubh, to the almost indistinguishable name of the cartoon duck.

Scotty ('skɒtɪ), *sb. colloq.* [f. SCOT *sb.*[1] + -Y.] A nickname for a Scotchman.

Scotty ('skɒtɪ), *a.* [f. SCOT *sb.*[1] + -Y.]

a. Having the characteristic temperament of a Scot. **b.** (With small initial.) [Cf. SCOT *sb.*[1] 4.] Angry, 'cross'.

1892 STEVENSON *Let. to J. M. Barrie* (1899) II. 247 We are both Scots besides, and I suspect both rather Scotty Scots. **1901** *Blackw. Mag.* Feb. 220/2 It made me scotty with every one and every thing. **1896** E. TURNER *Little Larrikin* xvii. 191 I'm *blessed* if I know what I've done this time... Don't be scotty, Marcia. **1936** M. FRANKLIN *All that Swagger* xxxv. 334 Uncle William is as scotty as a French hen with her feathers the wrong way.

scotylle, scouce: see SCUTTLE, SCOUSE.

scoug, scouk: see SCUG, SKULK.

scoul, scould, obs. forms of SCOWL, SCOLD.

scoulding: see SCULDING *Orkney and Shetl.*

scoule, obs. form of SCOLD, SCULL.

scoulerite ('skuːlərɑɪt). *Min.* [Named after Dr. J. *Scouler.*] An impure variety of mesole; also, a pipe-stone from N. America, having a similar composition.

1840 R. D. THOMSON in *Lond. & Edin. Phil. Mag.* Ser. III. XVII. 408 My son..distinguished it [this mineral] by the name of Scoulerite, in honour of Dr. Scouler. **1843** J. E. PORTLOCK *Geol.* 215 The Scoulerite variety occurs, rarely, at Portrush in small spheres. **1850** ANSTED *Elem. Geol., Min.* etc. §422 Scoulerite, Pipestone.

scoulion, scoull(e, obs. ff. SCULLION, SCHOOL.

scoult, obs. form of SCOUT *sb.*[4]

scoulyon, scoum, obs. ff. SCULLION, SCUM.

scoumar, variant of SCUMMER, pirate.

scoumfit(e, -phit, etc.: see SCOMFIT.

scoundrel ('skaʊndrəl), *sb.* and *a.* Also 6 **skown-, skoundrell, scondrell,** 7 **skundrell, scoundril,** 8 **scoundrell.** [Of unknown origin.

Derivation from Sc. SCUNNER *sb.* and *v.* is inadmissible on phonological grounds; and although *scoundrel* is now vernacular in Scotland (pronounced ('skunrəl) or ('skundrəl)), all the early examples of the word are English. The phonetic character of the word suggests a Fr. origin; it might conceivably represent an AF. derivative of *escondre* to abscond, but the late date of its first occurrence is against this supposition.]

A. *sb.* 'A mean rascal, a low petty villain' (J.). Now usually with stronger sense: An audacious rascal, one destitute of all moral scruple.

1589 WARNER *Alb. Eng.* VI. xxxi. 137 Must I, thought I, giue aime to such a Skrub and such a Saint, That Skowndrell, and this Counterfeit. **1589** R. HARVEY *Pl. Perc.* 22 You see my quarter staffe, is it not a blesse begger, thinke you? A washing blow of this is as good as a Laundresse,.. and must needs dry beate a skoundrell, if it be artificially managed. **1594** LODGE *Wounds Civ. War* IV. G 3, *Clown.* Haue I master thou scondrell? I haue an Orator to my master. **1601** SHAKS. *Twel. N.* I. iii. 36 By this hand they are scoundrels and substractors that say so of him. **1605** CHAPMAN *All Fooles* v. i. I 3, Your Mother..a lustie stoute Woman, bore great Children, you were the verie skundrell of am all. **1623** BINGHAM *Xenophon* 119 If you take away my life, you shall put an honest man to death for a cowards and a scoundrels sake. **1711** SWIFT *Jrnl. to Stella* 17 Nov., I often advised the dissolution of that Parliament, although I did not think the scoundrels had so much courage. **1734** POPE *Ess. Man* IV. 212 If your ancient, but ignoble blood Has crept thro' scoundrels ever since the flood. **1775** JOHNSON in *Boswell* 7 Apr. (1791) I. 478 Patriotism is the last refuge of a scoundrel. **1834** SOUTHEY *Doctor* liii. (1862) 121 When a woman is married for the sake of her fortune, the chances are five hundred to one that she marries a villain, or at best a scoundrel. **1837** DICKENS *Pickw.* xxxi, 'They are great scoundrels,' said Mr. Pickwick. **1877** TENNYSON *Harold* IV. i, My father, Who shook the Norman scoundrels off the throne. **1879** FROUDE *Cæsar* xv. 224 He saw these high-born scoundrels coming home loaded with treasure. **1886** STEVENSON *Treasure Isl.* i, If you keep on drinking rum, the world will soon be quit of a very dirty scoundrel!

b. *attrib.* and *appositive.*

1837 CARLYLE *Fr. Rev.* II. I. ii, Of a Jourdan Coupe-tête, who has skulked thitherward..and will raise whole scoundrel-regiments. **1850** —— *Latter-d. Pamph.* II. 9 [Model Prisons.] The 'sympathy' of visitors..for his interesting scoundrel-subjects..was evidently no joy to this practical mind. Pity, yes:—but pity for the scoundrel-species? **1894** H. NISBET *Bush Girl's Rom.* 120 This scoundrel-fool Shafton had been the cause of his misfortunes.

B. *adj.* Now *rare.*

1. Of a person: That is a scoundrel; having the characteristics of a scoundrel; scoundrelly. Of a company: Composed of scoundrels.

1643 MILTON *Divorce* II. i. (1645) 33 We read, not that the scoundrel people, but the choicest, the wisest, the holiest of that nation have frequently us'd these lawes. *a* **1700** B. E. *Dict. Canting Crew, Scab,* a..Scoundril-Fellow. **1710** SWIFT *Jrnl. to Stella* 21 Dec., I met that beast Ferris,..and that scoundrel dog is as happy as an emperor. **1715** HEARNE *Collect.* (O.H.S.) V. 53 The Printer is that scoundrel Rascal Curle. **1727–46** THOMSON *Summer* 1638 The cruel wretch.. has squander'd vile, Upon his scoundrel train what might have cheered A drooping family of modest worth. **1807** CRABBE *Par. Reg.* III. 789 We'll vex those scoundrel-boys. **1833** L. RITCHIE *Wand. by Loire* 187 The scoundrel governor..was the Duke of Montpensier.

2. Pertaining to or characteristic of a scoundrel. Of conduct: Mean, unprincipled.

1681 HICKERINGILL *Dial. Philautus & Timoth.* iii. 5 Shouldest thou not in all justice and Conscience, instance something..that deserves..such scoundrel, Billings-gate Ribaldry..? *a* **1704** T. BROWN *Declam. in Def. Gaming* Wks. 1709 III. I. 134 What..is there more scoundrel? What more beastly, than a man depriv'd of his Manhood..by an Inundation of Claret? **1729** MANDEVILLE *Bees* II. 101 An Italian No-man of Scoundrel Extraction. **1731** MEDLEY *Kolben's Cape G. Hope* (1738) I. 227 He [*sc.* the Hottentot dog] makes such a Scoundrel-Figure, that all his good Qualities together, are hardly a Ballance for it. **1738** J. HILDROP *Let. Commandm.* (ed. 4) 17 Stealing we all know is the most pitiful, scoundrel Act of Injustice. **1748** THOMSON *Cast. Indol.* I. l, 'A penny savèd is a penny got'—Firm to this scoundrel maxim keepeth he. **1757** WARBURTON *Lett. to Hurd* xciii. (1809) 218 He..died..here in England; but of so scoundrel a temper, that he avoided ever coming into my sight. **1757** MRS. GRIFFITH *Lett. Henry & Frances* (1767) III. 84, I am shocked at the mean, scoundrel Behaviour of Mr. P——. **1850** THACKERAY *Pendennis* lviii, Her parents.. encouraged me, with all sorts of coarse artifices and scoundrel flatteries.

†**3.** Of a thing: Base, degraded in character or type. *Obs. rare.*

1700 ASTRY tr. *Saavedra's Royal Politician* II. 160 Trade was ruin'd by this troublesome, scoundrel Metal. **1727** A. HAMILTON *New Acc. E. Ind.* II. xxxviii. 75 Their Religion is also a Sort of scoundrel Mahometism.

Hence **'scoundrel** *v. trans.*, ? to treat as a scoundrel, to vilify. **'scoundreldom,** the world of scoundrels, scoundrels collectively; also = SCOUNDRELISM. †**'scoundrelish** *a.*, befitting a scoundrel. **'scoundrelry,** scoundrels collectively. **'scoundrelship,** the behaviour of a scoundrel, scoundrelism.

1701 W. NICOLSON *Let.* 9 May in Evelyn *Diary & Corr.* (1906) 721 This being one of the matters wherein I am scoundreled by the late reply of Dr. Wake. **1705** ROWE *Biter* I. i, I being in somewhat scoundrelish, or, as your Honour calls it, scurvy Terms with him my self. **1837** CARLYLE *Diamond Necklace* xvi, Let the eye of the mind..astound itself with the magnificent extent of Scoundreldom; the deep, I may say unfathomable, significance of Scoundrelism. **1856** *Chamb. Jrnl.* VI. 361, I was dirty and grim-looking enough to represent any amount of scoundrelship. **1859** SALA *Tw. round Clock* (1861) 415 It is astonishing to find how much foreign riff-raff and alien scoundrelry will turn up at a masquerade. **1864** *Reader* 23 Jan. 101/1 With such consummate scoundrelship in the foreground, one may be pretty sure..that there is no lack of incident. **1864** KINGSLEY *Rom. & Teut.* iii. 68 All greedy villains and adventurers, the scoundreldom of the whole world. **1876** FROUDE *Hist. Eng.* lxix. XII. 111 Either as an effect of looseness of life, or from inherent scoundreldom of temperament.

scoundrelism ('skaʊndrəlɪz(ə)m). [f. SCOUNDREL *sb.* + -ISM.] The character, conduct, or practices of a scoundrel; also, a piece of scoundrelism, a scoundrelly act or trait.

1611 COTGR., *Villaquerie*, villanie, roguerie, rascalitie, skowndrellisme. **1773** JOHNSON in Boswell *Tour Hebrides* (1785) 111 Why, Sir,..There is generally a scoundrelism about a low man. **1837** CARLYLE *Fr. Rev.* I. v. ix, Thus.. shall the Bastille be abolished from our Earth; and with it, Feudalism, Despotism; and one hopes, Scoundrelism generally. **1890** G. B. SHAW *Fabian Ess., Socialism* 194 Hungry mobs, nuclei of all the socialism and scoundrelism of the city. **1902** F. E. HULME *Proverb Lore* ii. 62 The epigrams [of John Davies] are, most of them, of a most offensive character... There are two hundred and ninety-two of these scoundrelisms.

scoundrelly ('skaʊndrəlɪ), *a.* [f. SCOUNDREL *sb.* + -LY[1].] Having the character of a scoundrel; of, belonging to, or characteristic of a scoundrel; characterized by scoundrelism.

1790 BURNS *Let.* 2 Mar., Mankind are by nature benevolent creatures, except in a few scoundrelly instances. **1816** SCOTT *Antiq.* vi, I have directed the constables to take up that old scoundrelly beggar, Edie Ochiltree, for spreading disaffection. **1826** COBBETT *Rur. Rides* (1885) II. 266, I read on till I got to the base and scoundrelly part of the address. **1847** THACKERAY in *Fraser's Mag.* Jan. 116/2 Tom Starlight, the poacher,..inveighing against the tyranny of a scoundrelly aristocracy. **1862** CARLYLE *Fredk. Gt.* VIII. iv. III. 18 Money back? 'I will none of His scoundrelly money'. **1885** *L'pool Daily Post* 9 Feb. 4/8 A scoundrelly pasha..opened the gates of the city and let the Mahdi in.

† **'scoundrelously**, *adv. rare*⁻¹. [f. SCOUNDREL + -OUS + -LY[2].] In a scoundrelly manner.

1681 HICKERINGILL *Dial. Philautus & Timoth.* xiii. 28 Thou handlest the matter..so scoundrelously, and so far below the Rules of all Logick and Morality.

scouner, obs. form of SCUNNER *v.*

scoup (skaʊp), *v.* Chiefly *Sc.* Forms: 5-6 scoupe, 6 skowp, 8 scowp, 7- scoup. [Of obscure origin; perh. cognate with the synonymous SCOPE *v.*[2]] *intr.* To bound, caper, skip. Of an animal: To go with leaps and bounds.

a **1425** *Cursor M.* 23569 (Trin.) Mony þingis may we do þat better were vndone þen so As for to scoupe [*Cott.* skip, *Fairf.* lepe, *Gött.* schope] & to ryn Whenne bettur tyme were to blyn. **1530** PALSGR. 699/2, I scoupe, as a lyon or a tygre dothe, whan he doth folowe his pray, *je vas par saultées.* I have sene a leoparde scoupe after a bucke. *a* **1585** MONTGOMERIE *Cherrie & Slae* 23 The hart, the hynd, the dae, the rae,.. War skowping all fra brae to brae, Amang the water broxe. **1721** RAMSAY *Elegy on Patie Birnie* vi, The corky cowp That to the Papists' country scowp, To lear' ha, ha's. **17..** —— *Addr. of Thanks* iii, Lads..scowp around like tups and bulls. **1739** A. NICOL *Nature without Art* 87 Your Head's sae fu' o canty Tales That scoups o'er many Muirs and Dales. **1756** *Pennecuik's Collect. Sc. Poems* 55 But dawt red-coats and let them scoup Free, for the fou of cutty-stoup. **1818** SCOTT *Hrt. Midl.* xxvi, 'Wha the deil are ye?' said the fat dame to poor Jeanie,..'scouping about a decent house at sic an hour in the morning?'

b. *Phrase.*

a **1802** *Ld. Thomas & Fair Annie* xv. in Child *Ballads* II. 70/1 The shame [*i.e.* the Devil] scoup in his company. **1824** SCOTT *Redgauntlet* Let. xi, Deil scowp wi' Red-gauntlet!

Hence **'scouping** *vbl. sb.* Also **'scouper**.

a **1572** KNOX *Hist. Ref.* IV. Wks. 1848 II. 416 Witnes the Lordschip of Abercorne,..and diverse utheris..gyffin in heritage to scouparis, dansaris, and dalliaris with damis. *a* **1585** POLWART *Flyting w. Montgomerie* 757 Land lowper, light skowper, ragged rowper like a raven. **1593** B. BARNES *Parthenophil & P.* Ode xi. in Arb. *Garner* V. 457 To see the frisking, and the scouping!

scoupe, obs. form of SCOOP.

scour (skaʊə(r)), *sb.*[1] Also 4 skour(e, skowr(e, scowr, 6 scoure. [See SCOUR *v.*[1]]

1. The action of moving rapidly or going in haste; a run or rush. †Adv. phr. *good scour* = with hasty movement, at a good pace (*obs.*).

a **1300** *K. Alis.* 4276 To his ost he farith, good skour. *c* **1796** J. BURNESS *Thrummy Cap* 31 Sae on they gaed at a gude scow'r. **1820** L. HUNT *Indicator* No. 16 (1822) I. 122 Robin..was a fine eager-looking dog, and seemed to have all his faculties ready for a scour.

† **2.** An onset or attack. *Obs.*

a **1400** *Rel. Pieces fr. Thornton MS.* 96 Thane schalle erthe for erthe suffire scharpe scowrrys [*v.r.* schouris]. **1575** *Gamm. Gurton* v. ii. 196 (Manly), *Hodge.* Was not wel blest, Gammer, to scape that scoure?

3. The rush of a driving wind.

1808 JAMIESON, *Skour* of wind. **1906** G. A. B. DEWAR *Faery Year* 65 The thrushes and blackbirds love the driving scour and the wind-rocked tree.

scour (skaʊə(r)), *sb.*[2] Also 8-9 scower. [f. SCOUR *v.*[2]]

1. An apparatus for washing auriferous soil. Cf. SCOUR *v.*[2] 11 d.

1619 ATKINSON in *Macfarlane's Geogr. Collect.* (S.H.S.) III. 30 In all these places following..natural gold is to be found out, & you shall alwayes find skilfull seekers and discoverers thereof..for to use the Trough or Skower; but not very perfit in the Buddle. **1824** G. CHALMERS *Caledonia* III. VI. viii. 733 The places where the gold mines were formerly wrought, at the gold scours, in the valley of the Elwan.

2. The action of a current or flow of water in clearing away mud or other deposit; in *Civil Engineering*, an artificial current or flow produced for this purpose; also, an engineering work constructed for the purpose of producing such a current. Also, the abrading or transporting action of a current of any other material.

17.. in Lediard *Life Marlborough* (1736) III. 438 The useless Refuse, took a cleansing Scour, Along the rapid Scheld's intrenched Shore. **1729** in Labelye *Result View Level Fens* (1745) 39 Experienced Mechanick-Practice in making Drains, Sluices, Banks, Scours, &c. **1736** BADESLADE *New Cut Canal* 5 Capt. Perry was making Sluices..to hold up Water to make a Scour, by the force of which he expected to drive the Sand to Sea and deepen that River. **1745** LABELYE *Result View Fens* 33 As to artificial Scours by means of Reservoirs, or relieving Basons or Sluices. **1878** HUXLEY *Physiogr.* 146 The scour of the ebb-tide co-operates with the rapid flow of the river to sweep away any sediment. **1890** *Engineer* LXVIII. 452 (Cent.) There is a low water depth of only about 4 ft., but this is to be increased by about 20 ft. by dredging and scour. **1904** *Jrnl. Geol.* XII. 575 With these destructional effects assigned to glacial agency, a novel possibility is at once suggested as to the part played in their persistent development by glacial scour, or coarse abrasion. **1909** *Daily News* 15 Dec. 9 A small piece of land at the far end of the reservoir..together with..15 manholes, one air valve, three scours in connection with the pipe line. **1933** SCHUCHERT & DUNBAR *Textbk. Geol.* (ed. 3) xix. 425 The ice and the scour of the last glaciers removed all weak materials. **1954** *Jrnl. Geol. Soc. Australia* I. 77 The wind scour is able to drive the sand into heaps which migrate slowly down wind. **1975** *Offshore* Sept. 49-17/1 Scour is probably the greatest menace to offshore structures and pipelines.

3. A place in a river where the bottom is scoured by the stream; a river-shallow with a gravel bottom.

1681 CHETHAM *Angler's Vade-m.* xli. §6 (1689) 310 In March they shoot into the Scours to spawn. **1787** BEST *Angling* (ed. 2) 30 Angle..for pearches, in scours. **1833** BOWLKER *Art of Angling* 82 The haunts of Roach, during spring, are on the shallows and scowers. **1872** TAUNT *Map of Thames* 21/2 Below are fine scours and deeps, affording good fishing.

4. *Sc.* A hearty drink (*of* a beverage); a 'swig'. Cf. SCOUR *v.*[2] 11 e.

1724 RAMSAY *Tea-t. Misc.* (1733) II. 167 If that her tippony chance to be sma' We'll tak a good scour o't, and ca't awa. **1728** —— *Robt., Richy, & Sandy* 132 We'll take a scour o't to put aff our pain.

5. A kind of diarrhœa in livestock. Also *pl.* (chiefly *U.S.*).

1764 *Museum Rust.* I. 450 It actually gives, or inclines them to a scower (and other disorders well known to the shepherds). *Ibid.* II. 9 A remedy for the white scour in sheep. **1802** WILLICH *Dom. Encycl.* IV. 60/2 The White Scour is an uncommon looseness, occasioned by feeding sheep on putrescent vegetables. **1848** *Rep. Comm. Patents 1847* (U.S.) 507 They say the disease called the 'scours' is the principal one to which sheep are liable. **1881** SHELDON *Diary Farming* 61/2 An effectual preventive of 'scour', a malady from which young calves, when reared away from their mothers, are constantly liable to suffer. **1950** [see BEESTINGS 1]. **1970** W. H. PARKER *Health & Dis. in Farm Animals* xvii. 226 In sheep the disease causes the same wasting but without the scour. **1973** M. CROWELL *Greener Pastures* 16 Rameses II [*sc.* a sheep] has lately been having scours, or loose-bowel trouble. **1975** *N.Z. Jrnl. Agric.* Sept. 3/1 The hens..also appear to have a green scour. **1981** 'E. PETERS' *St. Peter's Fair* i. 18 They're having trouble..with scour among the calves.

6. The detergent matter used in scouring wool.

1888 *Encycl. Brit.* XXIV. 657/1 The wool..was rinsed in a current of clean water to remove the 'scour'.

7. An act of scouring, cleansing, or polishing. *Mod. colloq.* Give the floor a good scour.

8. *Austral.* and *N.Z.* A building in which wool is scoured.

1925 L. G. D. ACLAND *Early Canterbury Runs* (1930) 1st Ser. vi. 123 The Creek Station..was leased to T. P. Bartrum from 1879 onwards, and he established a wool scour there. **1934** T. WOOD *Cobbers* xvi. 195 The scour was a long open shed on stilts, with sheep-pens leading into it and out of it.

9. *Comb.*: **scour-hole**, a hole made in mud or sand by the scour of the tide; **scour-way** (see quot.); †**scour-wort**, a name suggested for *Saponaria officinalis*.

1890 KIPLING *City Dreadf. Nt.* 24 She sank there, and the next tide made a *scour-hole on one side of her. **1895** *Funk's Stand. Dict.*, **Scourway*, Geol., a drainage-furrow caused by a strong current, as by a glacial river flowing over a gravel plain. **1548** TURNER *Names Herbes* (E.D.S.) 66 Radicula.. if we had it here, it myghte be called in english sopewurt or *skowrwurt.

scour (skaʊə(r)), *v.*[1] Forms: 4 scur(e, schoure, 4-7 skour(e, scoure, 5-8 scowr(e, 6-7 skowr(e, 7-8 scower, 6- scour. [Of obscure origin.

In some of the senses explained below there may have been coalescence of words of identical form but etymologically unconnected; it is difficult in some uses to distinguish between this verb and SCOUR *v.*[2], by association with which its sense-development has certainly been influenced. The relation to the cognate SCOUR *sb.*[1] is uncertain; from the early date of the latter, it is perh. more likely to be the source of the verb than a derivative of it, so that the sb. may be ad. ON. *skúr* storm, SHOWER *sb.*, and the vb. may correspond to Norw. *skura* to rush violently. In the originally military uses, the vb. may perh. be partly a back-formation from SCOURER.

The current view, that the verb is a. OF. *escourre* (:—L. *excurrĕre*, f. *ex-* out + *currĕre* to run) seems untenable, as the OF. word would normally have assumed in ME. the form *scurre* instead of *scoure*.]

1. a. *intr.* To move *about* hastily or energetically; *esp.* to range about in search of something, or in movements against a foe.

1297 R. GLOUC. (Rolls) 390 Corineus herwiþ harde smot & stured [MS. α scurede, β scured, γ scuryd] him aboute, & made is wey bi eiþer side & percede þe route. *c* **1470** HENRY *Wallace* IX. 180 Skour weyll about for scoukaris in the se. **1477** *Paston Lett.* III. 185 In plesurys new, your hert dooth score and raunge So hye and ferre. **1576** TURBERV. *Venerie* lxii. 176 Lette him carie them [the hounds] home vncoupled, that they may skoure at large and skommer. **1594** KYD *Cornelia* IV. i. 196 He that..fearles scowres in danger's coasts, T'enlarge his countries liberty. **1603** KNOLLES *Hist. Turks* (1621) 641 Barbarussa thus scouring alongst the coast of Italie,..strucke such an exceeding terrour into the mindes of the citizens [etc.]. **1615** HEYWOOD *Four Prentises* I. D 3 b, Sirra go you and scoure about the hill. **1647** TRAPP *Comm. Rev.* iv. 6 Furnished with six wings apiece..to scoure about for the peoples benefit. **1692** R. L'ESTRANGE *Fables* ccxxiv. 196 There was a Freak took an Ass in the Head, to Scoure abroad upon the Ramble. **1706** PHILLIPS (ed. Kersey), *To Scour about*, to ramble or run raking about. **1735** SOMERVILLE *Chase* III. 323 While these intrepid Bands..out-fly the Storm, And scowring round, make Men and Beasts their Prey. **1837** CARLYLE *Fr. Rev.* III. II. ii, Furnishers scour in gigs over all districts of France. **1865** A. SMITH *Summer in Skye* I. 152 How John Kelly shouted and objurgated, and how his dog scoured about! [driving cattle]. **1879** SALA in *Daily Tel.* 26 June, The City authorities scoured fruitlessly about in quest of a new site for a debtors prison.

b. To move rapidly, go in haste, run. Chiefly with advs., indicating the direction, etc.

13.. *K. Alis.* 3722 Lordynges, he saide, hit is nought to fleon! We buth the ost and the water bytwene... Hit is beter that we to heom schoure [*Bodl.* scoure], So longe so we may dure. *c* **1375** *Sc. Leg. Saints* xi. (*Symon & Judas*) 297 þai wysmen þan scouryt þam faste. **1512** *Helyas* in Thoms *Prose Rom.* (1858) III. 104 The swanne put him afore the shippe, the which he made to scoure upon the water in suche wise that they were anon ferre fro Lyleforte. **1590** SPENSER *F.Q.* I. ii. 20 The lady..from him fled away with all her powre: Who after her as hastily gan scowre. *a* **1600** *Floddan F.* iii. (1664) 23 The Scots anon they scoured in And plyed apace unto their prey. *a* **1630** *Tom Thumb* 410 in Hazl. *E.P.P.* II. 229 She took him up between her jaws, And scower'd up a tree. **1632** J. HAYWARD tr. *Biondi's Eromena* 39 The Galley scowred away a maine course. **1692** R. L'ESTRANGE *Fables* lxxxiii. 81 They..Scoure off themselves and leave Those that Trust them to pay the Reck'ning. **1707** J. STEVENS tr. *Quevedo's Com. Wks.* (1709) 139 He scour'd after me as hard as he could. **1719** DE FOE *Crusoe* II. (Globe) 566 Away he scowered, and left my Pilot..a compleat Victory. **1810** SOUTHEY *Kehama* XXIII. xi, Through the red sky terrific meteors scour. **1842** BORROW *Bible in Spain* viii. 51, I.. scoured on my way with more speed than before. **1851** CARLYLE *Sterling* II. iv, Sterling..took to daily riding in summer; scouring far and wide on a swift strong horse. **1865** LIVINGSTONE *Zambesi* viii. 181 Dogs turn tail and scour off in dismay.

†**c.** (Without adv.) To depart in haste, run away, decamp. (Chiefly *colloq.* or *slang.*) *Obs.*

a **1592** GREENE *Alcida* (1617) H 2, Wherevpon the mariners reioyced, hoising vp sailes, and thrusting into the maine, we scowred and returned home to the court. **1687** SEDLEY *Bellamira* Prol., Till all the Ladies and some Gallants scowre. **1688** SHADWELL *Sq. Alsatia, Expl. Cant, To Scamper, to rubb, to scowre*, to run away. **1688** LUTTRELL *Brief Rel.* I. 486 Some of them that lay most obnoxious are scowring; several of which are taken and secured making their escapes. **1697** VANBRUGH *Relapse* IV. iv. (*end*), No, no; fire over their Heads only to fright 'em; I'll warrant the Regiment scours when the Collonel's a Prisoner. **1753** FOOTE *Englishm. in Paris* I. Wks. 1799 I. 35 How the powder flew about, and the Monsieurs scour'd.

2. a. *trans.* To pass rapidly over or along (a tract of land or water); *esp.* to traverse in quest of something, or in order to capture or drive away a foe.

Cf. SCOUR *v.*[2] 8.

c **1380** WYCLIF *Sel. Wks.* II. 363 And þis lore shulden prestis lerne, and speciali hey prelatis, siþ þei shulden scure, [*v.r.* skoure] þe weie to þe oost þat comeþ aftir. **1456** SIR G. HAYE *Law of Arms* (S.T.S.) 230/11 Gif a Franche knycht.. had runnyn before Bordeaulx to scoure the contree and tak prisouneris. *a* **1513** FABYAN *Chron.* VI. cxciii. 196 This Edgar..vsed, in the somer tyme, to scowre the see with certeyne shyppes of warre. **1553** BRENDE *Q. Curtius* D viij, By that time such as were sent before to scowre the countrey, came in, and reported. **1568** GRAFTON *Chron.* II. 464 The king before he would take his voyage, sent the Erle of Huntyngdon to serche and scowre the Seas. *Ibid.* 833 The noble men..without any tariyng, scouryng the wayes as fast as their horses could runne. **1594** KYD *Cornelia* V. 79 Euen so our battails..Dyd scoure the plaines in pursuite of the foe. **1636** *3rd Rep. Hist. MSS. Comm.* 73/2 You..may spare part [of your fleet] to scour the Channel to the Land's End westward. **1667** MILTON *P.L.* 529 And Scouts each Coast light-armed scoure, Each quarter, to descrie the distant foe. **1776** JOHNSON *Let. to Boswell* 5 Mar., I know not but we may scour the country together, for I have a mind to see Oxford and Lichfield. **1807** G. CHALMERS *Caledonia* I. III. iii. 342 Their piratical countrymen..scoured those coasts, in quest of prey. **1837** CARLYLE *Fr. Rev.* I. v. v, Patrols..scour the streets, all that night. **1856** STANLEY *Sinai & P.* xi. (ed. 3) 390 The sloping hills..scoured by herds of gazelles. **1885** C. F. HOLDER *Marvels Anim. Life* 116 He went aloft, scoured the hold, examined the galley.

b. *fig.* To run over in the mind, with the eye, etc.

1882 'MARK TWAIN' *Prince & Pauper* xxv. 300 Scour and scan me to thy content. **1883** *Sunday Mag.* July 432/2, I stand here scouring the universe with my imagination. **1909** MAX BEERBOHM *Yet Again* 69 You scour the list vaguely, and order a pint of 273.

3. *spec.* in 17th-18th century slang (cf. SCOURER[1] 2). **a.** *intr.* To roam about at night uproariously, breaking windows, beating the watch, and molesting wayfarers.

1673 SHADWELL *Epsom Wells* II. i, You drink Burgundy perpetually and Scower as you call it. **1687** SEDLEY *Bellamira* III. i. Wks. 1778 II. 152, I went home drunk, and scour'd outragiously. **1712** STEELE *Spect.* No. 358 ¶1 There is no Inhabitant of any standing in Covent-Garden, but can tell you a hundred good Humours, where People have come off with little Blood-shed, and yet scowered all the witty Hours of the Night. **1717** PRIOR *Alma* III. 233 From Milksop He starts up Mohack:..So thro' the Street at Midnight scow'rs: Breaks Watch-men's Heads, and Chair-men's Glasses. **1756** *Gentl. Mag.* XXVI. 37 As bees for honey range from flow'r to flow'r, From house to house I see Mundungus scow'r!

b. *trans.* To ill-treat or 'maul' (the watch, wayfarers, etc.) while roistering in the streets.

1681 DRYDEN *Sp. Fryar* Prol. 39 Scowring the Watch grows out of fashion wit. **1687** SEDLEY *Bellamira* IV. i. Wks. 1778 II. 177 *Mer.* The house is beset: What's here, scourers? .. *Cun.* We'll scour 'em for a company of uncivil fellows, thus to disturb lovers at their innocent recreations. **1692** *Scarronides* II. 33 Our Watch they scowre, and greet with ill-blows. **1723** *Briton* No. 19 (1724) 83 They got drunk,.. scower'd the Watch, abused the Constable.

c. To roister through (the streets).

1691 *Comedy, Win her & Take Her* I. i. 2 We'le scour ev'ry street And kick all we meet. **1753** *Scots Mag.* Oct. 491/2 We scoured the street after our nocturnal revel.

scour (skaʊə(r)), *v.*[2] Forms: 3-4 **schur, skur,** 3-5 **scur(e,** 3-7 **skour(e,** 4-7 **skowre,** 4-8 **scowr(e, scoure,** 5-6 **score,** 5-7 **skore, scoore,** 6 **skower,** 5-9 **scower,** 9 *dial.* **scaur,** 4- **scour.** [Prob. a. MDu. or MLG. *schûren* (mod.Du. *schuren*, mod.LG. *schüren*), whence mod.G. *scheuern* and MSw., Sw. *skura*, Da. *skure*; Du. has also a vb. *schuieren* to brush, which is prob. a dialectal variant. The Du. and LG. word is prob. a. OF. *escurer* (mod.F. *écurer*) = Pr., Sp. *escurar*, It. *sgurare*, *scurare* (rare):—popular L. **excūrāre* (med.L. *escūrāre*, *scūrāre*) to polish, scour, f. *ex-* out + *cūrāre*, in class. Latin to take care of (f. *cura* care), in med.L. also to clean (so F. *curer*).

Direct adoption from OF. *escurer* is not likely, as the word should in that case have become *scure* in mod.Eng. (cf. *cure*, *pure*). The same objection applies to the hypothesis of adoption from monastic Latin, unless it be supposed that the word had been English for some centuries before the date of the first known examples. Possibly the word was brought in as a technical term by Flemish workmen.]

1. a. *trans.* To cleanse or polish (metal, earthenware, wood, etc.) by hard rubbing with some detergent substance. Sometimes with compl. adj., as *bright*, *clean*. Also const. *of*, *from* (rust, etc.).

?*a* **1366** CHAUCER *Rom. Rose* 540 Hir heer was as yelowe of hewe As any basin scoured newe. *c* **1440** *Alphabet of Tales* 223 Sho..wasshid dysshis & skowrid pottys. *c* **1450** *Merlin* xx. 313 Thei..scowred hauberkes and furbisshed swerdes and helmes. **1530** PALSGR. 707/1, I scoure vessel, I make it bright and cleane. **1576** GASCOIGNE *Steele Gl.* (Arb.) 78, I see you Peerce, my glasse was lately scowrde. **1598** HAKLUYT *Voy.* I. 62 They skowre them so bright that a man may behold his face in them. **1622** MABBE tr. *Aleman's Guzman d' Alf.* I. 132, I was..in my Masters Kitchen, scowring of the Panns and the Spits. **1697** DRYDEN *Æneid* VI. 1114 By dint of Sword his Crown he shall increase; And scour his Armour from the Rust of Peace. **1709** *Female Tatler* No. 4/3 When the Cook Maid's Sick, he'll..scowre down the Stairs. **1712** ARBUTHNOT *John Bull* III. vii, Grudging a quarter of a pound of Soap and Sand to scowre the Rooms. *c* **1714** ARBUTHNOT, etc. *Mem. Martinus Scriblerus* I. iii, The Truth was, the Maid..had scoured it as clean as her Andirons. **1836** THIRLWALL *Greece* xiv. II. 195 His slaves were scouring the vessels of gold and silver displayed on the sideboard. **1848** THACKERAY *Van. Fair* liv, [He] passed by the scared female who was scouring the steps. **1878** HUXLEY *Physiogr.* 193 The stone largely used for scouring paint is a lava of very porous texture.

b. *fig.* Also with *over*, *up* (cf. 'polish up'). Now *rare* or *Obs.*

a **1300** *Cursor M.* 25867 Els moght moght na clensing fire þi saul skur to make it schirre. *Ibid.* 28058 Þarfor ilkan i rede forloke þat þai..skir þam sua wit þair in-sight, þair conscience sua clene and bright, þat þai þar-in leue nakin thing þat ani nede haf o scuring. *c* **1375** *Sc. Leg. Saints* xviii. (*Egipciane*) 1219 þai..þat þame-self ofe syne wil scoure. *c* **1430** *Pilgr. Lyf Manhode* IV. xli. (1869) 195 She leueth no thing þat she ne correcteth and skowreth and forbisheth. *c* **1450** *Mirk's Festial* 93 Wherfor þys tyme of Lenton ys ordeynt only to scowre and to clanse your concyens of all maner roust and fulþe of synne. **1556** PARKER *Ps.* cxix. 140 Skord cleane full out thy word is seene: fine tride from drosse impure. **1594** HOOKER *Eccl. Pol.* IV. xii. §5 Some few ..who..are not so scowred of their former rust, as to forsake their auncient perswasion. **1608** DAY *Law Trickes* I. i, How the daw Scoures ore his rustie phrases! **1611** SPEED *Chron.* IX. xxiv. 871/2 [Q. Eliz. said] I haue been enforced this day to scowre vp my old Latine, that hath laine long in rusting. **1617** MORYSON *Itin.* I. 161, I will..scoure up that little Toscane language, which..shall be remaining unto me. **1639** FULLER *Holy War* I. v. (1640) 7 Heraclius..scoured bright an old holy-day with a new solemnitie. **1654** —— *Two Serm.* 58 Such who by Art and Education..have scoured over the dimme inscription of the Morall Law, that it appeared plaine unto them.

c. *absol.* or *intr.*

a **1450** *Knt. de la Tour* viii. (1906) 11 Score so long on this plate till ye haue hadde awey all the blacke spottis. **1591** SHAKS. *Two Gent.* III. i. 315 Item, she can wash and scoure. **1710** STEELE *Tatler* No. 248 ¶5 The Wench in the Kitchen sings and scours from Morning to Night. **1859** GEO. ELIOT *Adam Bede* xxxii, Listening to all manner o' gossip when they should be down on their knees a-scouring.

d. *trans.* (*hyperbolically*). To thrust (a sword, knife) in a person's body.

1613 HAYWARD *Will. I* 68 Encouraging one another..to scoure their swords in the entrailes of their enemies. **1818** SCOTT *Hrt. Midl.* xxx, Have ye a mind I should scour my knife between your ribs, as my mother says?

e. To clean the inside of (a gun) after firing.

1611 BEAUM. & FL. *Knt. Burn. Pestle* V. i, Let me see your peece neighbor Greene-goose, when was she shot in? *Greene.* And like you maister Captaine, I made a shot euen now, partly to scoure her, and partly for audacity. **1627** CAPT. SMITH *Seaman's Gram.* xiii. 61 Souldiers scowre your peeces. **1658** A. FOX tr. *Wurtz' Surg.* I. iii. 9 Even as Musquetieres are scouring their Musquets after much shooting.

†**f.** *slang.* To wear (fetters); to sit in (the stocks). *Obs.*

c **1450** *Mankind* 634 in *Macro Plays* 24 Me semyth ȝe haue scoryde a peyr of fetters. **1533** J. HEYWOOD *Pardoner & Frere* 602 Thou shalt not escape me, Tyll thou hast scouryd a pare of stokys. **1561** AWDELAY *Frat. Vacab.* (1869) 84 To skower the cramp-rings, to weare boltes or fetters. *a* **1700** B. E. *Dict. Cant. Crew*, *Scoure*, to wear.

g. *U.S.* Of a plough, to pass through the soil easily, without earth adhering to the mould-board; freq. in negative contexts. Also *fig.*, to succeed.

1871 *Northern Vindicator* (Estherville, Iowa) 6 May 3/1 The contemptible wretch who stole the collar to the saw at the steam mill a few weeks ago, has come to the conclusion that his meanness did not 'scour', as he anticipated, and hence he placed the collar under a board pile in town where it was discovered on Monday last. **1881** J. PERIAM *Amer. Encycl. Agric.* 742/2 In the average soil there [*sc.* in eastern U.S.] the cast-iron plow would scour perfectly. **1887** W. H. LAMON in *Washington Critic* 3 Sept. 3/1 He [*sc.* Lincoln] said to me on stand, immediately after the [Gettysburg] speech: 'Lamon, that speech won't scour. It is a flat failure, and the people are disappointed.' **1948** *Sat. Even. Post* 7 Feb. 109/1 Then his old moldboard plow wouldn't scour, and after we'd sharpened it he broke the beam.

2. a. *trans.* To remove grease or dirt from (cloth, wool, silk, etc.) by some detergent process.

1467-8 *Rolls of Parlt.* V. 630/1 The said Clothes..clene scowred, full dryed, and redy to the sale. *c* **1483** CAXTON *Dialogues* 34 *Rescourer vne robe*, Skowre agayn a goune. **1496** *Coventry Leet Bk.* 574 To scoure & fresche old bonettes. **1565** *Act 8 Eliz.* c. 11 §2 The same Cappe [shall] be first well scoured and closed upon the Banke. **1601** HOLLAND *Pliny* XIX. i. II. 5 There is a kind of Poppies much sought after for blaunching and bleaching of linnen cloths; for being skoured therewith, it is wonderfull how white and pure they will looke. **1626** BACON *Sylva* §362 In some Lakes the Water is so Nitrous, as if Foule Cloaths be put into it, it scoureth them of it selfe. **1683** WILDING in *Collect.* (O.H.S.) I. 257 For scouring my Coate 00 00 06. **1751** *Chambers' Cycl.* s.v. *Dying, Dying of thread* is begun by scouring it in a lye of good ashes. **1844** G. DODD *Textile Manuf.* iii. 107 When the cloth is woven, he sends it..to be 'scoured' and 'fulled'. **1888** *Encycl. Brit.* XXIV. 657/1 Stale urine was a favourite medium in which to scour wool.

b. *absol.* Also *fig.*

1624 QUARLES *Job Militant* Med. vi. 41 Teares, mingled with thy Blood can scower so, That Scarlet sinnes shall turne as white as Snow. **1626** BACON *Sylva* §362 Warme Water scoureth better than Cold.

3. a. To wash vigorously (the hands, face, teeth); to 'scrub'. Now only *jocular.*

1589 WARNER *Alb. Eng.* VI. xxx. (1612) 147 Vnto the Trough he hies, And skowres his coly fists and face. **1602** *How to chuse good Wife* III. iii. F 4, He had a pound of sope to scowre his face. **1675** HOBBES *Odyssey* (1677) 72 They.. gave him th' oyl to scour his skin withal. *a* **1704** *Compleat Servant-Maid* (ed. 7) 65 To wash the Face, to keep it smooth and to scower it clean. **1712** SWIFT *Midas* 71 British Midas' dirty Paws; Which..the Senate strove to scour. **1871** R. ELLIS *Catullus* xxxvii. 20 And teeth a native lotion hardly scours quite pure.

b. *transf.* To cleanse (the teeth) by chewing some substance. Also, †*to scour one's mouth on*, to abuse, vilify.

1598 FLORIO To Rdr. a viij, Let Aristophanes and his comedians make plaies, and scowre their mouthes on Socrates. **1781** C. JOHNSTON *Hist. J. Juniper* I. 83 To eat cold beef, and drink strong beer for breakfast, and to scour his teeth after it with a quid of tobacco.

4. To cleanse (a wound, ulcer, the entrails of an animal) by treating with some medicament.

c **1420** *Liber Cocorum* (1862) 9 Take, wasshe tho isues of swannes anon, And skoure tho guttus with salt ichon. **1547** BOORDE *Brev. Health* Pref. 4 That they clense and scoure the woundes from al corupcion. **1612** WOODALL *Surg. Mate* Wks. (1653) 31 This unguent serveth well to cleanse and scowre ulcers. **1747** MRS. GLASSE *Cookery* (1796) xviii. 290 Take your eel and scour it well with salt.

5. a. To clear out (a channel, ditch, drain, etc.) by removing dirt, weeds, etc. Also with *out*, †*up*.

1412-20 LYDG. *Chron. Troy* II. 754 The canel skoured was so clene. **1519** *Presentm. Juries* in *Surtees Misc.* (1890) 31 The grett Inquest..commandes all wattersewers..be dykid and scoried by Withesonday. **1523** FITZHERB. *Husb.* §123 Than scoure the olde dyche, and cast it vp newe. **1579** in W. H. Turner *Select. Rec. Oxford* (1880) 403 The..ryvers.. shalbe ryde and scowred. **1589** IVE *Pract. Fortif.* 3 It may haue the riuer turned into the ditch to skowre the ditch of any thing that may be cast into it. **1645** SYMONDS *Diary* (Camden) 231 A large ditch..lately scowred and cast vp. **1657** G. THORNLEY *Daphnis & Chloe* (1893) 79 He scowred the Fountains, that the Water might be clear and transparent. **1724** DE FOE *Mem. Cavalier* (1840) 52 Working hard to scour their moats. **1740** J. LEAFORD *Observ. S. Level Fens* 21 It is proposed..To scour out St. John's Eau, and lay the Earth on the Norfolk side. **1747** FRANKLIN *Lett.* Wks. (1887) II. 81, I first scoured up my ditches and drains, and took off all the weeds. **1785** BURKE *Sp. Nabob of Arcot's Debts* Wks. 1906 III. 232 These watercourses again call for a considerable expense to keep them properly scoured and duly levelled. **1844** H. STEPHENS *Bk. Farm* II. 433 The hedger now resumes his work of water-tabling and scouring ditches. **1886** *Act 49 & 50 Vic.* c. 49 §9 The Admiralty may..dredge scour and deepen the foreshore and bed of the sea within the said limits.

b. *to scour a hedge* (see quot. 1847).

1562 *Act 5 Eliz.* c. 13 §5 The Hayes, Fenses, Dykes or Hedges..shall from time to tyme be diked, scoured, repaired and kept lowe. **1847** HALLIWELL, *Scour.* (1) To scour a hedge, to deepen the ditch, and to breast up the hedge with the soil taken out. *North.*

6. a. To clear out or cleanse by flushing with water.

1587 FLEMING *Contn. Holinshed* III. 1547/1 So as by the space of foure daies there could be no water reteined within the pent, to scowre the mouth of the hauen. **1619** S. ATKINSON *Gold Mynes Scot.* (Bannatyne Club) 1 Sufficient water..for..scowring places..with which all sorts of earth are to be washed or scowred. **1642** FULLER *Holy & Prof. St.* IV. xix. 339 If his land accosteth the sea, he considereth.. what Keys are rusty with sands and shelves, and what are scoured with a free and open tide. **1839** *Civ. Engin. & Arch. Jrnl.* II. 86/1 The projection of this isle,..forcing the tide-wave southward, causes it to run northward, again, with great force, and scour out the Bay of Weymouth. **1847** LYELL *Princ. Geol.* xix. (ed. 7) 263 During other seasons of the year, the ocean makes reprisals, scouring out the channels.

b. with *away*: To form (a channel) by flushing.

c **1683** *Cowley's Voy.* in *Cook's Voy.* (1790) III. 846 There cannot be so great a lack of water, but must needs scowre a channell away at the ebbe deepe enough for shipping to goe in.

c. To clear or refresh (the throat) with liquor. *Sc.*

1787 W. TAYLOR *Scots Poems* 4 (E.D.D.) Upo' that hint I scour'd my rusty throat. **1801** W. BEATTIE *Fruits of Time Parings* (1873) 15 (ibid.) Lat's see a drappie o' yer beer, To scour my crap.

7. a. Of a medicine, or of one who administers it: To purge (an animal, a person, the body, etc.); to evacuate (the stomach or bowels). Also, to cleanse (worms, fish, etc.) by purging.

1375 BARBOUR *Bruce* III. 542 Thai eyt it with full gud will, That soucht [nane othir] salss thar-till Bot appetyt, that oft men takys; For weill scowryt war thar stomakys. **1577** B. GOOGE *Heresbach's Husb.* I. (1586) 35 b, At which tyme they are very good to skowre horses. **1594** KYD *Cornelia* III. ii. 71 Like to a Curre that Carrion hath deuour'd, And cannot rest, vntill his mawe be scour'd. **1610** HOLLAND *Camden's Brit.* I. 434 Ponds or Stewes..to feed Pikes and Tenches fat, and to scoure them from the strong and muddy fennish taste. **1653** WALTON *Angler* vi. 138 A Lob or Garden worm, which should be wel scowred, that is to say, [kept] seven or eight dayes in Moss before you fish with them. **1656** RIDGLEY *Pract. Physic* 87 Clysters in great quantity if you would scowre the guts. **1691** *Braggadocio* III. i. 35, I hate to have a puddle o' your Outlandish Nusance cloging my Stomach. *Top.* Puh.—a scouring Bottle of Pontack will scour it again, Mun. **1765** *Treat. Dom. Pigeons* 29 Pease, wheat, and barley are apt to scour your Pigeons too much. **1817** J. MAYER *Sportsman's Direct.* (ed. 2) 132 Scour them [*sc.* gentles] in sand, in a flannel bag. **1843** MRS. CARLYLE *Lett.* I. 210 [He] immediately proceeded to scour him with the most potent medicines. **1856** 'STONEHENGE' *Brit. Sports* I. v. ii. §3. 236/2 All these worms should be scoured, a process which consists in starving them, by placing them in damp moss. **1888** J. INGLIS *Tent Life in Tigerland* 72 This food..has a tendency to scour the animals.

b. *absol.* Of medicine or food: To act as a purge.

1597 GERARDE *Herbal* II. xlvi. 261 Pellitorie of the wall.. hath force to scoure. **1657** W. COLES *Adam in Eden* xx. 42 The ordinary great Celandine..scowreth and cleanseth effectually. **1884** *Farm & Home* 25 Oct. 275/2 Potatoes and middlings tend to scour.

c. *refl.* Chiefly of worms and fish: To become clean by purging.

1594 PLAT *Jewell-ho.* III. 12 These wormes did first scoure themselves, either in mosse, lome, or bran. **1661** LOVELL *Hist. Anim. & Min.*, *Isagoge* d 4 b, Pond-fish..are not so sweet as river fish, except they have been kept in rivers to scoure themselves. *Ibid.* d 6 b, Snailes..are best towards winter having scoured themselves. **1867** F. FRANCIS *Angling* iv. (1880) 104 Pike..spawn from early April to the end of May,..and, after a short rest,.. scour themselves in the streams or shallows.

d. *intr.* (for *refl.*) To be purged. Of worms, fishes, etc.: To be cleansed by purging. Of livestock: To have diarrhœa.

1592 *Repentance of Robert Greene* D 2, Al his paine was in his belly. And although he continually scowred, yet still his belly sweld. **1616** SURFL. & MARKHAM *Country Farm* IV. xvi. 514 The wormes..will not onely liue long therein, but also scoure and feed. **1681** CHETHAM *Angler's Vade-m.* iii. §16 (1689) 26 The Dew preserves them [*sc.* baits] and makes them scour and thrive. **1707** MORTIMER *Husb.* (1721) I. 242 If you turn Sheep into Wheat or Rye to feed, let it not be too rank..lest it make them Scowre. **1725** *Bradley's Fam. Dict.* s.v. *Bait*, A dead Man's Skull beaten to powder for the Worms to scour in. **1764** *Museum Rust.* II. 147 Those which had the lask, and scowered. **1909** *Daily News* 5 May 4 Young spring grass is about the worst food for calves, causing them to scour very badly.

8. a. *fig.* To rid, clear (a place, the sea, etc.) *of* or *from* an enemy or other undesirable occupants.

Closely associated with SCOUR *v.*[1] 2.

a **1300** *Cursor M.* 475 He..schurd [*Gött.* skourd, *Trin.* scoured] þat curt o þam sa clene, þat sithen þar sted was neuer sene. **1531** *Dial. on Laws Eng.* II. xlvii. [li.] 97 b, The lord of the narowe see is bounde..to scoure the see of pyrattes. **1603** DRAYTON *Bar. Wars* VI. lxiv, As..Some fleet-wing'd haggard..th'ayre of all her feath'red flocks doth skower. **1611** BEAUM. & FL. *Knt. Burn. Pestle* V. i, And like a sort of true-borne Scauingers, scoure me this famous Realme of enemies. *a* **1627** HAYWARD *Ann. Q. Eliz.* (Camden) 49 He was appointed to skowre the seas from unlawfull adventurers. **1698** FRYER *Acc. E. India & P.* 98 It is the Catwals Business with a Guard of near Two hundred Men, to scower the Streets..of idle Companions. *a* **1701** MAUNDRELL *Journ. Jerus.* 28 Feb. (1732) 4 Maintaining the ways in good repair, and scouring them from Arabs, and Robbers. **1716** B. CHURCH *Hist. Philip's War* (1865) I. 180 Church received a Commission..to Scoure the Woods of some of the lurking Enemy. **1786** W. THOMSON *Watson's Philip III*, VI. (1839) 317 This..contributed not a little to scour the sea from the pirates. **1826** SCOTT *Diary* in Lockhart *Life* (1839) IX. 17 He might have done well there could he have scoured his brains of politics. **1876** VOYLE & STEVENSON *Milit. Dict.* (ed. 3) s.v., *To scour the country* means to clear the country of the enemy for miles around.

b. *fig.* (of a devastating plague).

1607 J. DAVIES *Summa Totalis* (Grosart) 21/2 The Plague (which late our Mother-Citty scour'd And erst the Kingdome made halfe desolate!)

9. *fig.* To beat, scourge. Hence, to punish, treat severely.

c **1386** CHAUCER *Pars. T.* ¶596 He..broghte a yerde to scoure with the child. *c* **1400** *Rule St. Benet* 1536 þe nouices, whils þai er 3ing Aw to be scorid for swilk a thing. *c* **1425** LYDG. *Testament* Minor Poems (Percy Soc.) 255 Of the yeerde somtyme I stood in awe, To be scooryd that was al my dreede. *c* **1440** *Alphabet of Tales* 259 He tuke a wand and skowrid þaim bathe. *c* **1485** *Digby Myst.* (1882) III. 737 3a! thys hard balys on þi bottokkys xall byte!..cum vp, 3e horsons, and skore a-wey þe yche! *c* **1590** MARLOWE *Faustus* 977 Ile teach ye to impeach honest men: stand by, Ile scowre you for a goblet. [**1599** SHAKS. *Hen. V*, II. i. 60 If you grow fowle with me Pistoll, I will scoure you with my Rapier, as I may, in fayre tearmes.] **1662** PEPYS *Diary* 4 Feb., We shall scoure him for it. **1730** FIELDING *Author's Farce* I. viii, But I will pay the dog, I will scour him.

10. To sweep or rake (a place, position, a body of men, etc.) with gun-shot. Also, to command (a position, etc.) with one's guns.

1563 W. COTHE in *15th Rep. Hist. MSS. Comm.* App. II. 32 Our steple..on the which stoode iii fayre Demi-Colveryns to skowre the topp of the hills. **1578** T. N. tr. *Conq. W. India* 320 Cortes unshipped three peeces of ordinance to scoure the Cawsey, which was full of enemies. **1589** IVE *Pract. Fortif.* 11 That the artillerie which shoulde scoure the front of yᵗ one Bulwarke might lye couered in the other Bulwarke. *c* **1620** FLETCHER & MASS. *Double Marriage* II. i, How many saile of wel man'd ships before us,..Have we pursued and scowerd. **1630** R. JOHNSON *Kingd. & Commw.* 304 The South part..is well defended with Casemats, the better to scoure the Curtaine. **1704** *Lond. Gaz.* 4082/3 The Ditch is doubly Palisadoed, with very good Flanks within, to scour the Moat when they enter. **1706** PHILLIPS (ed. Kersey), To *Scour the length of a Line*, to rake a Line from end to end with the Shot, so that every Bullet which comes in at one end, sweeps all along to the other. **1781** SIMES *Milit. Guide* (ed. 3) 12 Small parties of light cavalry to scour the flanks. **1802** C. JAMES *Milit. Dict.* s.v. *Firing*, *Street Firing* is the method of firing adopted to defend or scour a street, lane, or narrow pass of any kind. **1876** BANCROFT *Hist. U.S.* V. xx. 567 He ordered up heavy artillery and scoured the woods with grape.

11. To remove, get rid of. Chiefly with advs., as *away*, *off*, *out*. **a.** To remove (rust, dirt, etc.) by cleansing or hard rubbing. Also *fig.*

c **1410** LYDG. *Life Our Lady* lxv. (? 1484) kj, He came for our sauacion To scoure aweye the rust of al our blame. *c* **1440** *Promp. Parv.* 450/2 Scowryn [*Winch. MS.* scoryn] a-wey ruste, *erugino, erubigino*. **1596** SHAKS. *1 Hen. IV*, III. ii. 137, I will..staine my fauours in a bloody Maske: Which washt away, shall scowre my shame with it. **1631** SANDERSON *Serm.* II. 15 The stains will not easily (if at all) be scoured off again. *a* **1674** CLARENDON *Hist. Reb.* XV. §31 He would often speak that there was much of good in the order of bishops, if the dross were scoured off. **1806** J. BERESFORD *Miseries Hum. Life* xi. No. 18 (ed. 3) I. 263 The face or hands..begrimed with that mysterious sort of filth, which, as soon as you have, with great difficulty, scoured it away, returns again and again. **1866** REDGRAVE *Cent. Painters* II. 605 Many a one whose qualifications consist only in the reckless impudence with which he dares to use the spirit or the alkali to scour off dirt and art together, places a half-washed portrait in the window, and dubs himself a restorer.

b. To drive (an enemy, etc.) *out of* the land.

1470 HENRY *Wallace* VII. 16 How thai suld tak on hand The rychtwys blud to scour out of Scotland. *a* **1600** *Floddan F.* viii. (1664) 73 The gray gooswing did work such greif, And did the Scots so skoure and skaile. **1603** KNOLLES *Hist. Turks* (1638) 287 After that Scanderbeg had thus..scoured the Turks out of euery corner of Epirus. **1605** SHAKS. *Macb.* v. iii. 56 What Rubarb, Cyme, or what Purgatiue drugge Would scowre these English hence? **1642** FULLER *Holy & Prof. St.* v. iii. 365 King Saul, who had formerly scoured Witches out of all Israel. **1655** —— *Ch. Hist.* III. 112 Fullers earth, a precious ware is daily scowred hence, though by law forbidden to be transported.

c. To discharge, evacuate, purge away (a humour, disease, excrement, etc.).

1577 B. GOOGE *Heresbach's Husb.* IV. (1586) 190b, It scowreth away the collections of a Plurisy beginning. **1620** FLETCHER *Chances* III. ii, Has given me a dam'd Glister,..Has almost scour'd my guts out. **1620** VENNER *Via Recta* vii. 157 It concocteth and scowreth downwards crude and phlegmaticke humors. **1657** W. COLES *Adam in Eden* ciii, The same stamped with Honey..consumeth and scowreth away the Ulcers of the Head. **1694** MOTTEUX *Rabelais* IV. xliii, They sow..but..Wind-flowers,..herbs that may make One break wind to the purpose, these scowre them off carefully. **1737** BRACKEN *Farriery Impr.* (1757) II. 84 There are Horses which put off, or scour off their Meat (as we say) very fast.

d. To remove or clear away by flushing with water.

c **1582** T. DIGGES in *Archæologia* XI. 227 Beache..vnder the Sowthern jawe of the haven mowth..by the force of the Master Sluce shall allway be scowred and remooued. **1596** HARINGTON *Metam. Ajax* 42 By turning a streame of water on the mickesons, he scowred away that in a weeke, that an hundred could scant haue done in a yeare. **1619** ATKINSON in *Macfarlane's Geogr. Collect.* (S.H.S.) III. 31 Their usual manner is, when they seek for Gold..to frame or make a long seuch or scowring place into which they bring the stream of water, to scowr away the light earth from the heavy sandy earth. **1849** LYELL *2nd Visit U.S.* (1850) II. 152 The tide enters far up each channel, scouring out mud and sand.

†**e.** To drink *off* (a health). *Obs. Sc.* (Cf. SCOUR *sb.*[2] 3.)

1718 RAMSAY *Christ's Kirk Gr.* III. xi, He..scour'd aff healths anew, Clean out that day.

†**scour**, *v.*[3] *Obs. rare.* [Aphetic f. *discour(e*, DISCOVER.] *trans.* To divulge, reveal, disclose.

1584 MUNDAY *Fidele & Fortunio* 12 in *Archiv Stud. neu. Spr.* CXXIII. 48 Heare you Maister Fortunio..Doo but scoure your minde to mee, and shut vp your greef: Either Ile finde you some ease, or you shalbe hangd for a theef.

†**'scourage**[1]. *Obs.* Forms: 5 scur-, 6 scurr-, scower-, scourage, scouradge. [f. SCOUR *v.*[1] + -AGE.] The act of scouting or skirmishing. Phr. *to make* or *keep scourage*.

1470 HARDYNG *Chron.* Pref. i To scarmyse als, and make sykyr scurage. **1520** in *Rutland Papers* (Camden) 43 It is ordred that Sir Griffythe Ryce, Sir William Bulmer, Sir Richard Tempest, with theyre cumpanyes, shall make scurrage that day for discoueryng the cuntrey for the kings suertie. **1557** LD. WARTON in Strype *Eccl. Mem.* (1721) III. II. 266 Our Men..upon their Retyre followed them with Scowerage towards Tividale. **1560** in J. Scott *Berwick-upon-Tweed* (1888) 448 Yf any soldiers of the garrison be appointed to keep scourage. **1579** DIGGES *Stratiot.* 108 He is to appoynt which bands of Horse shall go to the watch or scouradge.

'scourage[2]. *rare.* In 7 -idge. [f. SCOUR *v.*[2] + -AGE.] Material for scouring; 'refuse water after cleansing or scouring' (Ogilvie, 1882).

a **1603** T. CARTWRIGHT *Confut. Rhem. N.T.* (1618) Pref. 30 The sope, niter and scouridge, that the Iesuites are able eyther to beg, to borrow, to steale, or otherwise come by; are not able to cleanse the vulgar translation.

scoure, obs. form of SCORE *sb.* and *v.*

scoured (skaʊəd), *ppl. a.* [f. SCOUR *v.*[2] + -ED[1].]

1. Polished by rubbing; cleansed by scrubbing with a detergent. Also *fig.*

c **1450** *M.E. Med. Bk.* (Heinrich) 186 Droppe hyt in a clene scoured bacyn. **1535** COVERDALE *Ezek.* i. 7 They glistred, as it had bene fayre scoured metall. **1549** COVERDALE, etc. *Erasm. Par. Eph.* iv. 17–22 He cannot be sene, but onely with the scoured iyes of the soule. **1675** HAN. WOOLLEY *Gentlew. Comp.* 141 Set it a-boiling in a clean scoured skillet. **1705** tr. *Bosman's Guinea* 465, I saw seven white scoured Elephants Teeth. **1852** MRS. STOWE *Uncle Tom's C.* xviii, Dinah would contract such an immoderate attachment to her scoured tin, as to insist upon it that it shouldn't be used again for any possible purpose.

b. With *out*, of a glass: Cleaned out, emptied. *Sc.*

1805 J. NICOL *Poems* I. 158 (Jam.) An' ilka blade had fill'd his wame, Wi' monie scour'd-out glasses.

2. Of silk, wool, etc.: Treated with a detergent.

166. PETTY in Sprat *Hist. Roy. Soc.* (1667) 305 The same scowred Silk. **1716** GAY *Trivia* III. 270 The new-scower'd Manteau. *c* **1830** MRS. SHERWOOD *Houlston Tracts* III. No. 81. 6 She wore a scoured silk trimmed with gimp. **1868** J. TURNER *Woollen Manuf. Assist.* 56 To find weight of greasy wool required to produce a certain weight of scoured wool.

b. quasi-*sb.* = scoured wool.

1894 *Times* 14 Mar. 3/4 The Continent again purchased freely of scoureds. **1897** *Daily News* 19 Mar. 9/5 Good bodied and light dry scoureds maintain previous series' prices.

3. Purged; cleansed by purging.

1653 WALTON *Compl. Angler* xi. (1878) 87 At a well scowred lob-worm he [*sc.* the barbel] will bite as boldly as at any bait. **1873** G. C. DAVIES *Mount. & Mere* xiii. 106 A small well-scoured red worm will take them when nothing else will.

scourer[1] ('skaʊərə(r)). Forms: 5 skoverour, skowrrour, skouriour, scorer, -ar, 6 scurer, skourer, 6–8 scowrer, 8 scowerer, 5– scourer. See also SCURRIER. [In sense 1 orig. aphetic f. DISCOVERER (OF. *descouvreor*); afterwards confused with the agent-n. f. SCOUR *v.*[1] + -ER[1].]

†**1.** One sent out to reconnoitre; a scout or avant-courier; = DISCOVERER 2 and SCURRIER.

a **1400** *Morte Arth.* 3118 Than skyftes þes skouerours, and skippes one hyllis, Discoueres for skulkers that they no skathe lymppene. *c* **1470** HENRY *Wallace* III. 103 Send twa skowrrouris to wesy weyll the playne. *Ibid.* IV. 431 Set skouriouris furth the contre to aspye. *c* **1471** *Arriv. K. Edw. IV* (Camden) 28 The Kynge..sent afore hym his forrydars and scorars, on every syde hym. *c* **1500** *Melusine* xxx. 224 Thenne he loked on the ryght syde vpon a lytel mountaynne & sawe the grete batayll, and sawe the watche and the scourers al about the oost. **1534** MORE *Comf. agst. Trib.* II. Wks. 1181/2 Out was our scurer sent agayn,..to shew wher aboute yᵉ place was. **1553** BRENDE *Q. Curtius* H vij, By the spring of the day the scourers that he sent before to discover, returned to him wyth reporte that Darius was comming. **1565** COOPER *Thesaurus*, *Antecursor*, a fore runner,..a scourer. **1579** DIGGES *Stratiot.* 109 To give order that the Scowrers come not out of the fielde till the Trumpet sounde. **1826** HOR. SMITH *Tor Hill* (1838) I. 39 The scourers now took the lead, looking vigilantly around them.

2. In the 17th–18th c.: One who made a practice of roistering through the streets at night, beating the watch, breaking windows, etc.

1672 WYCHERLEY *Love in Wood* V. ii, No Burgundy man or drunken Scourer will reel my way. **1684** WOOD *Life* (O.H.S.) III. 120 Several lusty fellows..pull'd down some of the railes before Ball: Coll: and broke windowes in S. Giles and Magd. parishes. These they call 'Scourers'. **1691** SHADWELL (*title*) The Scowrers. **1712** STEELE *Spect.* No. 276 ¶3 [He] has been, he tells me, a Scowrer, a Scamperer, a Breaker of Windows. **1716** GAY *Trivia* III. 325 Who has not heard the Scowrer's Midnight Fame? **1849** MACAULAY *Hist. Eng.* xi. III. 58 In those days of highwaymen and scourers.

3. One who ranges over (land or sea).

1878 B. HARTE *Hoodlum Band* ii, Who but the Pirate Prodigy—the relentless Boy Scourer of Patagonian seas?

scourer[2] ('skaʊərə(r)). Also 5 scourour, 6 skourer, 6–8 scow(e)rer, 7 skowrer. [f. SCOUR *v.*[2] + -ER[1].] One who, or a thing which, scours.

1. a. One who polishes or cleanses by hard rubbing. Used esp. as the designation of certain servants in the Royal Household.

1576 in Nichols *Progr. Eliz.* (1823) II. 39 Ten services to the Porters and Skowrers of all sides. **1647** HAWARD *Crown Revenue* 32 Six Porters, and Scourers, Larges at Easter:—5.0.0. **1662** *Comenius' Janua Ling. Triling.* 103 The sword-cutler [maketh] swords, which the scourer furbisheth. **1669** E. CHAMBERLAYNE *Pres. St. Eng.* 317 Three Turn-broaches, each 18*l.* 5*s.* Two Scowrers, each 18*l.* 5*s.* **1767** S. PATERSON *Another Trav.* I. 209 So scowerers assist painting, and plaisterers mend statuary. **1840** THACKERAY *Catherine* ii, A small person..acted as scourer, kitchen-wench, and scullion. **1901** *Westm. Gaz.* 18 Apr. 12/2 The 'Kitchen Staff' comprised a chief cook.., two assistant cooks, four scourers, three kitchenmaids.

b. *fig.* (with *new*). One who furbishes afresh or renovates.

1554 T. MARTIN *Marr. Priests* ii. Bj, Oure menne (beinge but newe scourers of their olde heresie).

2. One who cleans wool, cloth, clothes, etc.

1574 *Life Abp. Parker* B vij b *marg.*, His Father was an honest poore man, a scourer or Calender of worsteddes of Norwich. **1688** *Lond. Gaz.* No. 2328/4 One Zechariah Pickford,..a Scowrer by Trade,..is lately gone away with a Cantoon grey cloth Bed. **1756** FOOTE *Engl. ret. fr. Paris* I. Wks. 1799 I. 102 Carry..his coat to a scowrer's. **1832** MARRYAT *N. Forster* xxxi, Bottlecock and Co., Dyers, Callenderers, and Scourers. **1886** *Lond. Gaz.* 5 Jan. 68/1 Dyer and Scourer—Robert Pullar, Perth.

3. One who cleans out drains, etc.

c **1515** Masser scourer [see MASSER[2]]. **1536** in *Gentl. Mag.* (1813) May 427 John Wylkynson of Busshopgate strete in London, scourer of synks. **1540** *MSS. Dk. Rutland* (Hist. MSS. Comm.) IV. 309 Maser scowrer. **1902** C. G. HARPER *Cambridge Road* 206 The main drains are scoured by 'scourers'.

4. An implement or contrivance for scouring or scrubbing.

1859 *Rep. Comm. Patents 1858* (U.S.) I. 378 Scourer G, blast spouts EF, and fan C, [are] combined and arranged relatively with each other. **1884** KNIGHT *Dict. Mech.* Suppl., *Scourer*, a form of grain cleaner in which the berry is subjected to a rubbing action to remove all extraneous matters. **1885** *Harper's Mag.* Jan. 276/2 Hides brought to the currying..are put under a 'scourer', a machine constructed of a number of diminutive wheels, which are made to move powerfully and swiftly over the yet damp hide.

†**5.** A wad or sponge for cleaning out the bore of a gun; a ramrod fitted with such a contrivance.

1467 *Maldon* (Essex) *Court Rolls* (Bundle 43, No. 14), I posnet, I scourour, et I ladell. **1591** *Garrard's Art Warre* 4 His scowrer must be trimmed on the end with a Lynnen cloth. **1611** COTGR., *Esqueuillon*, a Spunge, or Scourer for a peece of Ordnance. **1616** J. LANE *Contn. Sqr.'s T.* v. 249 With ladles, chargers, skowrers, carthridges. **1631** in Rymer *Fœdera* XIX. 315 For a new Musket with Mould, Worm and Scowrer. *ol.* xvs. vid. **1708** *Lond. Gaz.* No. 4455/4 Fine Triangle Worms.., experienc'd for drawing of Balls out of Pieces, with Scowerers and Washers to them. **1711** *Milit. & Sea Dict.* (ed. 4), *Rammer*, or *Scourer*, is a Rod belonging to all Fire-Arms..serving to thrust down the Powder and Ball.

6. A purgative agent, a cathartic.

1719 QUINCY *Compl. Disp.* 96 Spleenwort..has..been reckon'd..a Scowrer of the Spleen. **1840** BLAINE *Encycl. Rural Sports* §3113. 1002 The process of worm scouring is somewhat mechanical... Sound moss is the best scourer.

'scouress. *nonce-wd.* [-ESS.] A female scourer.

1648–60 HEXHAM, *Een Schuerster*, a Scouresse or a Woman scourer.

scourge (skɜːdʒ), *sb.* Forms: 3–5 schurge, 3–6 schourge, scurge, 3–7 skurge, 4 schorge, 4–5 skourge, scowrge, 4–6 skorge, scorge, 6 scourdge, squorge, 7 skurdge, scurdge, 4– scurge. [a. AF. *escorge*, *escurge*, related (the precise nature of the relationship is obscure) to OF. *escorgiee* (mod.F. *écourgée*) = It. *scuriada*, *scuriata* (earlier *scoriata*):—popular L. **excoriāta* scourge, lit. strip of hide, f. late L. *excoriāre* to strip off the hide, f. *ex-* EX- + *corium* hide.

Another view is that the sb. is a verbal noun from *escorgier* to scourge, and that this directly represents late L. *excoriāre* in the sense to skin by flogging (cf. HIDE *v.*). OF. had also a parallel form *corgie* sb., an English adoption of which appears to occur in the following example:

13.. *S.E. Legendary* (MS. Bodl. 779) in *Archiv Stud. neu. Spr.* LXXXII. 410/107 Wit stauis & wit courgis he let hem bete so faste.]

1. a. A whip, lash. Now only *rhetorical*, with reference to the torturing of human beings, or to ascetic discipline. Formerly *gen.*, e.g. in †*top and scourge* (see TOP *sb.*).

The use as applied to a whip for a top still survives *dial.*: see E.D.D.

a **1225** *Leg. Kath.* 1551, & beaten hire bare flesch & hire freoliche bodi mit cnottede schurgen. *a* **1300** *Cursor M.* 25542 Wit knotted skurges hard and lang. *c* **1330** *Arth. & Merl.* 8445 (Kölbing) He laid on wiþ schourge & bad hir go. *c* **1375** *Sc. Leg. Saints* xxxviii. (*Adrian*) 41 And bad his tormentouris son bring Skurgis of senonis felly mad. **1382** WYCLIF *John* ii. 15 And whanne he hadde maad as a scourge of smale coordis, he castide out alle of the temple. [So in most later versions.] *a* **1400–50** *Alexander* 1924 Laches me þis losengere..þat I may him skelp with a skorge. *c* **1430** LYDG. *Min. Poems* (Percy Soc.) 147 Oon knelith doun, requerith of the tothir, Pleyn remissioun of oold cursidnesse, Bete with a scorge, took it with meeknesse. *a* **1500** *St. Margaret* 196 in *Brome Bk.* 113 They bete hyre with scowrgys stronge. **1535** COVERDALE *Ps.* lxxxviii. 31, I wil vyset their offences with the rodde, and their synnes with scourges. **1567** *Gude & Godlie Ball.* 153 First I was betin lang, With scurgis scharp and strang. **1609** BIBLE (Douay) *3 Kings* xii. 11 My father bette you, with scourges, but I wil beate you with scorpions. **1644** SYMONDS *Diary* (Camden) 47 Escocheons with severall bearings alluding to the passion, of the scourge, whip &c. **1732** LEDIARD *Sethos* II. VII. 83 Scourges of cords..made the blood flow from every part. *a* **1793** G. WHITE *Poem* in *Selborne* (1854) 8 The happy schoolboy brings transported forth His long forgotten scourge, and giddy gig. **1842** TENNYSON *St. Sim. Styl.* 177 Mortify Your flesh, like me, with scourges and with thorns. **1871** R. ELLIS *Catullus* xxv. 11 The scourge's heavy branding.

†**b.** A blow with a whip. *Obs. rare*$^{-1}$.

1741 tr. *D'Argens' Chinese Lett.* xii. 74 The next Moment he called for Cords, to imitate the frowzy St. Dominic, who gave himself 300,000 Scourges every Week.

2. *fig.* and in figurative context; chiefly, a thing or person that is an instrument of divine chastisement.

the Scourge of God (= L. *flagellum Dei*): a title given by historians to Attila, the leader of the Huns in the 5th century.

1382 WYCLIF *Isa.* xxviii. 15 Scourge flowend [Vulg. *flagellum inundans*; **1611** the ouerflowing scourge]. *c* **1386** CHAUCER *Clerk's T.* 1157 He..suffreth vs as for oure exercise With sharpe scourges of Aduersitee fful ofte to be bete in sondry wise. **1387** TREVISA *Higden* (Rolls) V. 247, I am Athila, Goddes scourge [L. *Ego sum Attila flagellum Dei*]. *c* **1400** *26 Pol. Poems* 44 þat sellen soules for temperal getyng, þey maken skourges to here owe betyng. **1574** tr. *Marlorat's Apocalips* 32 The faithfull had neede of inuincible constancie and incredible pacience, that they may know them to be gods squorges, and the instrumentes of his wrath. **1611** CORYAT *Crudities* 162 Came that *Flagellum Dei* that scourge of God into Italy, Attila, King of the Hunnes. **1781** GIBBON *Decl. & F.* III. xxxiv. 368 If Attila equalled the hostile ravages of Tamerlane, either the Tartar or the Hun might deserve the epithet of the *Scourge of God*. **1819** SHELLEY *Cenci* III. i. 316 Mocking our poverty, and telling us Such was God's scourge for disobedient sons. **1925** D. H. LAWRENCE *Reflections on Death of Porcupine* 157 Attila, the Scourge of God, who helped to scourge the Roman world out of existence, was great with power.

3. a. A cause of (usually, widespread) calamity. Applied, e.g. to a cruel tyrant, a warrior, a war, a disease that destroys many lives. **b.** One who 'lashes' vice or folly.

Primarily identical with the figurative sense 2; but used without conscious reference to divine chastisement.

c **1535** LD. J. BUTLER in Ellis *Orig. Lett.* Ser. II. II. 48 OConnor that evyr hath bene the oonly scourge of the Englishe pale..is his right hand. **1560** DAUS tr. *Sleidane's Comm.* 410 b, Marques Albert ye scourge of priests. **1596** SPENSER *Sonn., Scanderbeg*, The scourge of Turkes, and plague of infidels, Thy acts, o Scanderbeg, this volume tels. **1603** FLORIO *Montaigne* I. xxvi. 89 Glory and curiositie are the scourges of our soules. **1607** SHAKS. *Cor.* II. iii. 97 You haue bin a scourge to her enemies. **1726–46** THOMSON *Summer* 1499 Raleigh, the scourge of Spain! **1727** TINDAL *Rapin's Hist. Eng.* IV. 275 Though this terrible Scourge [the plague] had fallen no less heavy on France, Philip was making great Preparations to renew the War. **1756** C. LUCAS *Ess. Waters* II. 60 The great Swift, that severe scourge of the vices and follies of his time. **1821–2** SHELLEY *Chas. I*, II. 301 And I speak it not As loving parliaments, which, as they have been..The scourges of the bleeding Church, I hate. **1879** WALLEY (*title*) The Four Bovine Scourges: pleuro-pneumonia, foot-and-mouth disease, cattle plague, tubercle (scrofula). **1882** 'OUIDA' *Maremma* I. 23 He had the same temper as of old made the tyrants of Padova and Verona..the scourges of their generation.

†**4.** [After L. *flagellum*.] An offshoot of a vine or other tree, a sucker. *Obs.*

1382 WYCLIF *Isa.* xvi. 8 The lordis of Ientiles hewen doun his scourges; vnto Iaser thei ful camen. *c* **1440** *Pallad. on Husb.* III. 113 The squorges hie & graffes from the folde,..for fruitful let hem not be tolde. **1578** LYTE *Dodoens* I. liv. 80 Beluedere..hath diuers small shutes or scourges.

5. *attrib.* and *Comb.*, as *scourge-procuring*, *-proof*, *-tormented* adjs.; **scourge-crop** [cf. SCOURGE *v.* 3], the result of a method of cultivation which impoverishes land; †**scourge-stick**, a whip used with a child's top (also *transf.*); †**scourge-top**, a whip-top.

1842 J. AITON *Dom. Econ.* (1857) 192 When a minister's incumbency is apparently drawing to a close, one *scourge crop after another is sometimes taken from a glebe. **1593** NASHE *Christ's T.* (1613) 137 Wherefore did our Sauiour thunder forth such a terrible woe against the causers of offence, or discontent, but that it was the most heynous *scourge-procuring transgression of all others? **1808** COLERIDGE *Lett.* (1895) II. 528 The ass's skin is almost *scourge-proof. *c* **1500** *World & Child* (Roxb. Club) A ij b, I can with my *scorge stycke My felowe vpon the heed hytte. **1585** HIGINS *Junius' Nomencl.* 297 *Flagellum*..: a scowrgesticke. **1662** J. T. *Grim, Collier of Croydon* 18, I am whipt up and down with the scourge-stick of Love. **1693** LOCKE *Educ.* §130 (1699) 243 But if they had a Top, the Scourge-stick, and Leather-strap should be left to their own making and fitting. **1627** W. HAWKINS *Apollo Shroving* Prol. 5 *Prol.*.. We play at our best game. *Lala.* What? Blow-point?.. *Prol.* No. Tomboy, no. Nor *scourge-top, nor Trusse, nor Leape-frog. **1888** *Longman's Mag.* XIII. 516 Scourge-tops, peg-tops and humming-tops were all patronised. **1900** SWINBURNE *Astræa Victrix* 66 We loosed not on these knaves Their *scourge-tormented slaves.

scourge (skɜːdʒ), *v.* Forms: 3, 6 scurge, (3 scruge), 3–4, 6 skurge, 4 schourge, (4–5 schorge), 4, 6 skourge, skurge, 4–7 scorge, 5 sc(h)owrge, skorge, chorge, shorge, 5–6 skowrge, squo(u)rge, 3– scourge. [a. OF. *escorgier*, either f. *escorge* SCOURGE *sb.* (which however occurs in AF. only), or directly repr. late L. *excoriāre* (see the sb.).]

1. *trans.* To beat with a scourge; to whip severely, flog. Now *rhetorical* (cf. SCOURGE *sb.* 1).

1297 R. GLOUC. (Rolls) 5304 Hii nome him an scourgede him & suþþe naked him bounde To a tre. *a* **1300** *Cursor M.* 16398 Iesus..to scruge he taght þem til. *Ibid.* 19356 For þan wit suepes þai þam suang, And scurged sare, þai let þam gang. **1382** WYCLIF *John* xix. 1 Therfore Pilat took thanne Jhesu and scourgide. *c* **1400** in *Hampole's Wks.* I. 203 Then Pilate comandede theyme þat he sulde be betyne & schorugede. **1447** BOKENHAM *Seyntys* I. 337 (Horstm.) The tormentours hyr shorgyd so cruelly That lyk as watyr in a ryuer So ran hyr blood owt plenteuously. *Ibid.* III. 283 And anone she chorgyd was so cruelly That uerrey pete it was to behold & se. **1508** KENNEDIE *Flyting w. Dunbar* 327 With ane hauthorne skurge thy self and dyng. **1530** PALSGR. 731/2, I squourge one with whyppys, *je fouette.* **1625** *Peebles Charters*, etc. (1872) 413 Item, to the man that scorgit Issobell Gray xiijs. 4d. **1642** MILTON *Apol. Smect.* Wks. 1851 III. 291 They scourg'd the confessors of the Gospell. **1725** DE FOE *Voy. round World* (1840) 87 Our people did scourge him severely from head to foot. *a* **1873** LYTTON *Pausanias* II. i, Let him pass,..he will get scourged if he is too late. **1903** A. SMELLIE *Men of Covenant* (1908) I. ix. 167 It was his habit to scourge and afflict himself.

b. With complementary adv. or phrase: To drive or force by or as by blows of a whip.

1667 MILTON *P.L.* IV. 914 Till the wrauth, Which thou incurr'st by flying..scourge that wisdom back to Hell Which taught thee yet no better. **1744** ARMSTRONG *Art Preserv. Health* II. 18 This vital fluid [*sc.* the blood]..scourg'd for ever round and round, Enrag'd with heat and toil, at last forgets Its balmy nature. **1812** LANDOR *Ct. Julian* v. ii, How bitter is the tear that fiery shame Scourges and tortures from the soldier's eye. **1870** BRYANT *Iliad* I. II. 47 If I Shall fail to..send thee forth, Howling,..Scourged from the council with a storm of blows.

c. In figurative context.

1591 SHAKS. *1 Hen. VI*, I. i. 4 Comets importing change of Times and States, Brandish your crystall Tresses in the Skie, And with them scourge the bad reuolting Stars. **1821–2** SHELLEY *Chas. I*, II. 218 For the waves never menace heaven until Scourged by the wind's invisible tyranny. **1887** *Times* 11 Aug. 13/3 The great masted ironclads throb and shake..and their great screws scourge the water behind them.

2. *fig.* To punish, chastise, correct (often said of God, with reference to Heb. xii. 6); to 'lash' with satire or invective; to afflict, torment; to devastate (a country) with war or pestilence.

1382 WYCLIF *Heb.* xii. 6 Forsoth he scourgith euery sone that he receyueth. **1387–8** T. USK *Test. Love* III. ix. 74 So that goddes hand, whiche that merciably me hath scorged, herafter in good plite from thence merciably me kepe and defende. **1530** PALSGR. 707/1 God hath scourged the lande of Italye very sore in our tyme. **1540** —— *Acolastus* v. iii. Z j b, To seke out Pelargus agayne, which scourgeth or tourmenteth hym selfe with vnreasonable .i. endlesse cares. **1570–6** LAMBARDE *Peramb. Kent* (1826) 225 This house, and the whole Ile was scourged thrice within the space of twenty yeeres and a little more by the Danes. **1607** DEKKER *Wh. Babylon* H 4, You shall with rods of iron scourge these treasons. **1799** *Monthly Rev.* XXX. 530 The wars that have scourged Europe since the treaty of Westphalia. **1835** LYTTON *Rienzi* I. iii, That is the way one patrician always scourges the insolence of another. **1876** T. HARDY *Ethelberta* xlviii, God has got me in his power at last, and is going to scourge me for my bad doings.

3. *Sc.* To exhaust the fertility of (land). Said of a crop; also of the agriculturist. Also *absol.*

1799 J. ROBERTSON *Agric. Perth* 166 Both crops scourge the ground. **1830** *Kyle Farm Rep.* 47 in *Lib. Usef. Knowl., Husb.* III, A tenant..was unable to make the necessary outlays on his farm, and forced to scourge as far as he could. **1842** J. AITON *Dom. Econ.* (1857) 55 He will find it to be his interest to scrouge every thing out of the land. **1888** J. HARRISON *Scot in Ulster* vii. 111 Flax..is a crop which scourges the ground.

4. *Comb.* †**scourgemutton** (lit. a scourger of sheep), one who is irrationally cruel.

1581 J. BELL *Haddon's Answ. Osor.* 181 b, This cruell scourgemotton [orig. *Orbilius*] weried throughly w^t whippyng poore Luther miserably,..doth now at the length hyde his rod. *Ibid.* 385 This cruell scourgemutton.

scourged (skɜːdʒd), *ppl. a.* [f. prec. + -ED^1.]

1. Beaten, flogged.

1543 TRAHERON *Vigo's Chirurg.* 232 Ye shall applye vpon the scourged place this cerote [following]. **1563–83** FOXE *A. & M.* 2062/1 In this societie of the scourged professors of Christ, was also one Iames Harris. **1693** S. HARVEY *Dryden's Juvenal* IX. (1697) 238 Let the Great Man, whom gaping Crowds attend, Fear a scourg'd Slave. **1713** YOUNG *Last Day* II. 242 Now tell the scourg'd Impostor he shall bleed! **1831** GEN. P. THOMPSON *Exerc.* (1842) I. 454 There will always be a difference of opinion on the amount of evil between the oppressor and the oppressed, between the scourger and the scourged. **1853** O. W. HOLMES *Poem Amer. Med. Assoc.* 47 The scourged racer.

trans. **1821** JOANNA BAILLIE *Metr. Leg., Wallace* liv. 5 While the scourged oak and shaken pine Aloft in brighten'd verdure shine.

2. Of land: Exhausted by improper cultivation.

1880 *New Virginians* I. 85 A sign of scourged land and disgraceful farming.

scourger (ˈskɜːdʒə(r)). Also 6 *Sc.* skurgeare, 7 *Sc.* scurger. [f. SCOURGE *v.* + -ER.]

1. One who scourges or flogs; † an official charged with the duty of whipping offenders.

1580 HOLLYBAND *Treas. Fr. Tong, Rabroveur de petits enfans*, a scourger, a rebuker of children by the way. **1612** R. SHELDON *Serm. St. Martin's* 23 The mercilesse scourgers whipped and tormented him. **1662** *Aberdeen Reg.* (1872) IV. 203 The tuo litle housses under the Gallowgait Port to be ane duelling hous to the said scurger dureing his service. **1828** P. CUNNINGHAM *N.S. Wales* (ed. 3) II. 321 Every district magistrate has..a scourger, to inflict corporal punishment. **1886** SPURGEON *Treas. Dav.* cxxix. 3 The scourgers tore the flesh as ploughmen furrow a field.

b. (See quot.)

1892 *Labour Commission* Gloss., *Scourger*, a cab-driver who treats his horse with undue severity.

2. *fig.* One who punishes or oppresses; one who 'lashes' with satire or invective.

1533 BELLENDEN *Livy* II. xv. (S.T.S.) I. 189 The pepill had na litill Indignacioun, þat þis marcius suld rise sa haistelie to be þare new fleschour and skurgeare. **1577–87** HOLINSHED *Chron.* III. 1242/2 Joseph de Chancie..was tresuror in the second yeere of the scourger of the Scots king Edward the first. **1812** BYRON *Ch. Har.* I. lii, The West must own the Scourger of the World. **1881** W. R. NICOLL *Incarn. Saviour* xxiii. 377 He was the scourger of Pharisees.

†**3.** = FLAGELLANT. *Obs.*

1537 *Orig. & Sprynge of Sectes* 22 Scourgers of the .I. secte. *Ibid.* 37 Scourgers of the .II. secte. **1728** TINDAL *Rapin's Hist. Eng.* VI. 467 The Sect of the Scourgers.

scourging (ˈskɜːdʒɪŋ), *vbl. sb.* [f. SCOURGE *v.* + -ING^1.] The action of the vb. SCOURGE.

1. Infliction of blows with a whip. Also *fig.*

a **1340** HAMPOLE *Psalter* xxxi. 13 Many ere þe scourgynges the swyngyns of synful: bot hopand in lord mercy sall vmgif. *c* **1425** *Processional Nuns Chester* (1899) 31 Ihu thy Crowne satt full soore and thy scowrgynge when thow bett wore. **1513** DOUGLAS *Æneis* VII. vi. 133 Thou may skurgeyngis and strakis in lugeings rais, And thow of frendis may mak mortale fays. **1563–83** FOXE *A. & M.* 2060/1 The scourging of Thomas Greene. *c* **1570** W. WAGER *The longer thou livest* 142 (Brandl), I am good at scourging of my Toppe. **1625** T. GODWIN *Moses & Aaron* v. (1641) 206 This beating or scourging was commanded, Deut. 25. 2, 3. where the number of stripes was limited, which the Iudge might not exceed. **1796** BURKE *Corr.* (1844) IV. 390 You remember with what indignation I heard of the scourging of the solider at Carrick. **1824** W. IRVING *T. Trav.* I. 257 In spite of all the scourgings I suffered at that school. **1893** *Athenæum* 30 Sept. 445/3 Those whom we have seen put to death certainly bore no traces of recent scourging.

b. As a part of religious discipline.

c **1386** CHAUCER *Pars. T.* 1055 Thanne is discipline eek in knokkynge of thy brest, in scourgynge with yerdes, in knelynges. *a* **1425** *Cursor M.* 23289 (Trin.) And for þei wolde no scourgyng þole for loue of heuen kyng þei shul be beten euer on on. *a* **1440** *Found. St. Bartholomew's* (E.E.T.S.) 41 Betwene oure squorgyng, ȝeue we thankyngys to God. **1665** J. SPENCER *Disc. Vulg. Proph.* 42 Severe disciplines of the body by excessive fastings and scourgings.

†**2.** *transf.* Correction. *Obs. rare.*

c **1374** CHAUCER *Compl. Mars* 42 And þus she norisseþe him in hir manere With no thinge but with skowrgynge of hir chere.

3. A picture of the scourging of Our Lord: = FLAGELLATION b.

1756–7 tr. *Keysler's Trav.* (1760) II. 350 Here is also the scourging of Christ, and the four seasons by Albani.

4. The action of impoverishing the soil by reckless methods of cultivation.

1842 J. AITON *Dom. Econ.* (1857) 192 Let the same rule hold in respect to an outgoing incumbent which restricts an outgoing tenant, and let that rule be—no scourging.

ˈ**scourging**, *ppl. a.* [f. SCOURGE *v.* + -ING^2.]

1. That chastises with a scourge. *lit.* and *fig.*

c **1586** C'TESS PEMBROKE *Ps.* LXXIII. ii, The scourging plagues, which on their neighbours fall, Torment not them. **1602** MARSTON *Antonio's Rev.* IV. iii, There is a thing call scourging Nemesis. **1600** C. EDMONDS *Observ. Cæsar's Comm.* VII. xv. 79 Our English nation caried a scourging hand in France. **1706** E. WARD *Hud. Rediv.* I. v. 20 Next, lay thy scourging Hand, good L..d Upon that High-Church Scribe, Ned Ward.

2. That impoverishes (ground under cultivation).

a **1799** SIR W. MURRAY in J. Robertson *Agric. Perth* 167 *note*, Perhaps lint..is not a very scourging crop. **1851** *Chamb. Jrnl.* 3 May 279/2 Exhausting the natural soil with a scourging succession of grain crops.

Scourian (ˈskʊrɪən, ˈskaʊrɪən), *a.* *Geol.* [f. *Scourie*, name of a crofting village on the west coast of Sutherland + -AN.] Of, pertaining to, or designating the earlier metamorphism undergone by the Lewisian rocks of the Pre-Cambrian in NW Scotland, the rocks formed by this metamorphism, and the structures to which they belong. Also *absol.*, these rocks and structures.

1950 SUTTON & WATSON in *Q. Jrnl. Geol. Soc.* CVI. 243 In the following pages the Lewisian is..regarded as belonging to two metamorphic complexes, the first, or Scourian, being older and the second, or Laxfordian, younger than the dolerite dykes. These names are taken from localities in Sutherland where the relations of the two complexes are particularly clearly displayed. **1959** *Nature* 5 Dec. 1793/1 Three samples came from the Outer Hebrides, three from the Laxfordian, and two from the Scourian. **1961** *Q. Jrnl. Geol. Soc.* CXVII. 241 The Scourian metamorphic rocks in the vicinity of Scourie are primarily hornblende- or pyroxene-bearing gneisses containing very little mica or potassium-feldspar. *Ibid.* 242 The Scourian metamorphism occurred at least 2460 m.y. ago. **1965** A. HOLMES *Princ. Physical Geol.* (ed. 2) xiii. 370 (*caption*) The peaks are of Torridonian Sandstone, resting unconformably on Lewisian Gneiss (Scourian division). **1969** BENNISON & WRIGHT *Geol. Hist. Brit. Isles* iii. 42 The trend of the Scourian is not known since no really large structures have been found associated with the granulites. **1979** *Nature* 22 Feb. 643/1 The ~2,400 Myr age for the emplacement of the Scourie dyke swarm indicates that the Scourian tectonic episode had ceased by the beginning of the Proterozoic.

scouridge, scourie: see SCOURAGE, SCAURIE.

scouring ('skaʊərɪŋ), *vbl. sb.*[1] [f. SCOUR *v.*[1] + -ING[1].] The action of advancing as a scout, of roving with hostile purpose, of moving swiftly about, of overrunning a country, etc.

c **1471** *Arriv. K. Edw. IV* (Camden) 3 By the scuringe of suche persons as for that cawse were, by his said rebells, sent afore into thos partes for to move them to be agains his highnes, the people were sore endwsed to be contrary to hym. **1607** SHAKS. *Timon* v. ii. 15 The Enemies Drumme is heard, and fearefull scouring Doth choake the ayre with dust. **1611** COTGR., *Escumement*,..a scowring of the seas. **1829** W. IRVING *Conq. Granada* I. xlii. 371 Journeying securely along the pleasant banks of the Xenil, so lately subject to the scourings of the Moors. **1872** SPENCER *Princ. Psychol.* II. 541 As the motions are superfluous bounds and scourings around.

attrib. **1781** SIMES *Milit. Guide* (ed. 3) 11 Scouring parties of light cavalry. **1905** *Daily Chron.* 1 June 4/2 It was in the course of these scouring operations that Admiral Rozhdestvensky was captured on board a destroyer.

'scouring, *vbl. sb.*[2] [f. SCOUR *v.*[2] + -ING[1].]

1. a. The action of polishing or cleaning by hard rubbing.

a **1300** [see SCOUR *v.*[2] 1 b]. **1398** TREVISA *Barth. De P.R.* XVI. i. (1495) 552 By frotynge and scourynge of grauel golde, bras and yren is made bryght. *c* **1440** *Promp. Parv.* 197/1 Glacynge, or scowrynge [*Winch. MS.* shoryng] of harneys, *pernitidacio, perlucidacio.* **1477–9** *Rec. St. Mary at Hill* 80 For scowryng of the Standardis candilstikkis, & the Rode loft. **1547** in E. B. Jupp *Carpenters' Co.* (1887) 387 Paid to the bedylls wyffe for skoryng of the vessell, iiij d. **1620** SANDERSON *Serm.* I. 140 Brass and copper and baser metals are kept bright with scowring. *c* **1714** ARBUTHNOT, etc. *Mem. M. Scribl.* I. iv, Thus..hath Heaven..afflicted me with the scouring of my Shield. **1862** MORRALL *Needle-making* 11 The next process is scouring.

b. *fig.*

1528 TINDALE *Obed. Chr. Man* 147 b, Those doctours.. nether thought or once dreamed..of any soch whisperinge or of pardons, or scouringe of purgatory as they have fayned.

2. The process of cleansing wool, cloth, etc.

1464 *Mann. & Househ. Exp.* (Roxb.) 251 Payd to the taylor, for makenge, lynynge, and scorynge of my masterys blake gown, iij.s. ix.d. **1467–8** *Rolls of Parlt.* V. 630/1 The seid brode sette Clothes, after all the said sufficiant and perfit werkmanship, scowring, full dryng. **1548** *Act 2 & 3 Edw. VI*, c. 26 White Ashes..are verie necessarie..for the ..dyinge and scowringe of wollen Clothe. **166.** PETTY in Sprat *Hist. Roy. Soc.* (1667) 304 Scowring and Washing of Stuffs to be dyed, is to be done with special Materials. **1713** *Guardian* No. 38 (1756) I. 163 It is the last time my black coat will bear scouring. **1879** *Cassell's Techn. Educ.* IV. 339/2 After the sorting, the first process is scouring, by which the wool is cleansed from the grease.

3. The action of cleaning out a ditch, a gun-bore, etc.; the clearing of a channel by flushing or by a natural flow of water. Also with *out*.

1458–9 *Durham Acc. Rolls* (Surtees) 411 In le scurryng unius fossati. **1479–80** in *Finchale Priory Charters* (Surtees) p. ccclxvii, Pro le scowryng fossatorum et factura sepium. **1497** *Naval Acc. Hen. VII* (1896) 234 Abought skowryng & clensyng of..the Kynges dokke. **1543** in *Lett. & Pap. Hen. VIII*, XVIII. II. 118 For skoryn of a water souer. **1571** *Act 13 Eliz.* c. 18 §8 The scowring, clensinge, repayring, and keping of the said Ryver of Lee. **1575** *Nottingham Rec.* IV. 159 Payd for skowryng of the guns to Thomas Lockesmeth ij s. **1662** PETTY *Taxes* 12 The cutting and scowring of rivers into navigable. **1780** [see HORSE *sb.* 24]. **1859** T. HUGHES (*title*) The Scouring of the White Horse. **1878** HUXLEY *Physiogr.* 147 There is sufficient scouring out of the mouth [of the river] to keep its channel open. **1898** *Jrnl. Sch. Geog.* (U.S.) Oct. 283 This scouring cuts the uplands into hills, but eventually they, too, are worn down.

4. a. The action of purging the bowels. †Also *concr.*, a purgative medicine.

1575 TURBERV. *Faulconrie* 234 If these receytes and skowrings yeelde no remedie then must you to the actual cauterie. **1614** MARKHAM *Cheap Husb.* I. i. 9 Let exercises and mashes of sweet Mault after, be his usual scowrings. **1682** *Lond. Gaz.* No. 1742/4 All sorts of Drugs for Purging, Scouring, and Sweating of Running-Horses or Hunters.

b. The state or fact of being purged; a looseness or flux of the bowels, diarrhœa; *esp.* as a disease in livestock (= SCOUR *sb.*[2] 2).

1597 GERARDE *Herbal* III. clix. 1378 Lungwoort.. stoppeth the bloudie flix, and other flixes and scouringes, either vpwards or downwards. **1615** CROOKE *Body of Man* 92 Hee ate a pound of Cherries, heereupon he fell into a scowring. **1753** *Chambers' Cycl.* Suppl. s.v. *Sheep*, It generally throws them into scowerings. **1787** 'G. GAMBADO' *Acad. Horsem.* (1809) 26 Horses full of grass are very subject to scourings. **1884** F. J. LLOYD *Sci. Agric.* 297 Diarrhœa. This is termed when applied to animals, 'scouring'.

†5. The action of clearing or ridding of undesirable occupants or the like. *Obs.*

1606 HOLLAND *Sueton.* 92 The skouringe or riddance of the worke-house prisons.

6. The action of beating, drubbing or chastising; also *fig.* Phr. ***to scape*** or ***escape a scouring.***

1426 LYDG. *De Guil. Pilgr.* 17000 Blyssed be the betynges and skowrynges that compellyn a chylde to declyne from his trespacys and his errours. **1588** *Marprel. Epist.* (Arb.) 44 With what a manly countenance you giue your brethren this scouring. **1600** HOLLAND *Livy* XXII. 457 In my former Consulship, I hardly escaped a scouring. **1663** DRYDEN *Wild Gallant* v. i. (1669) 70 What a scowering have I scapt to night. **1721** DE FOE *Mem. Cavalier* x. (1840) 187 Aylesbury escaped a scouring for that time. **1771** SMOLLETT *Humph. Cl.* 8 June (1815) 140 Certain it is, I have not 'scaped a scouring.

7. *concr.* Dirt or refuse removed by scouring.

1588 LAMBARDE *Eiren.* IV. iv. 475 If any person..haue cast the scouring of any ditch..into the high way. **1652** FRENCH *Yorksh. Spa* iii. 34 The Sulphur-Well in York-shire smells like the scowring of a Gun that is very fowl. **1771** SMOLLETT *Humph. Cl.* 28 Apr. (1815) 53 It is very far from being clear with me, that the patients in the pump-room don't swallow the scourings of the bathers. **1831** T. L. PEACOCK *Crotchet Castle* i, The Thames (not yet polluted by the tide, the scouring of cities, or even the minor defilement of the sandy streams of Surrey). **1857** KINGSLEY *Misc.* (1859) II. 371 And out of the scourings of that vast mass of chalk was our gravel-pit made.

†b. Dirt or scum naturally collected. *Obs.*

1591 SPENSER *Virg. Gnat* 229 The frogs, bred in the slimie scowring Of the moist moores.

c. *fig.* (esp. of persons: cf. OFF-SCOURING 2 b).

1721 *Lett. Mist's Jrnl.* (1722) I. 76 The Scum and Scouring of the People. **1838** DICKENS *O. Twist* xl, The associate of the scourings of the jail and hulks. **1853** H. REEVE in *Life & Corr.* (1898) I. 271 How far will the next 'Quarterly' support this strain? Unhappily Croker's influence still condemns us to several sheets of his scourings.

8. *Tanning.* (See quot.)

1797 *Encycl. Brit.* (ed. 3) XVIII. 307/1 (*Tanning*) After which they [the hides] are removed into another pit called a *scowering*, which consists of water strongly impregnated with vitriolic acid, or with [etc.].

9. *attrib.* and *Comb.*, as ***scouring cloth, -work***; also **scouring bit** (see quot.); †**scouring clay** or **earth**, fuller's earth; **scouring drops** (see quot. 1867); †**scouring house**, a room where plate, pewter, etc. is scoured; also *fig.*; **scouring machine, mill**, an apparatus for scouring cloth after weaving; **scouring paper**, emery-paper, glass-paper, or the like; **scouring powder**, an abrasive powder used for cleaning kitchenware, etc.; **scouring power** (see quot. 1855); †**scouring-rod** = *scouring-stick*; **scouring rush**, *Equisetum hyemale*; **scouring sand**, a kind of sand used for scouring; †**scouring-stick** = SCOURER[2] 5; also *transf.* (jocular); †**scouring-stocks**, a form of scouring-machine; **scouring-stone**, a stone used for cleaning paved floors; †**scouring woman**, a charwoman.

1860 *Eng. & Foreign Mining Gloss., Derbysh.* 43 **Scouring bit*, a bit attached to the ends of boring rods for the purpose of extracting the rubbish. **1660** MARVELL *Let.* 29 Nov., Wks. (Grosart) II. 26 To-morrow will be carryed up that [bill] against transporting Wooll,..Fullers Earth and all *Scowring clay. **1907** *Yesterday's Shopping* (1969) 120/3 *Scouring Cloth—yard 0/5½ Scouring or Paint Cloths—each 0/4. **1976** W. TREVOR *Children of Dynmouth* iii. 58 He reached for a scouring cloth on a line that stretched above the sink. **1808** *Times* 19 Jan. 1/3 Bayley's *Scouring Drops, for taking grease out of silk, woollen cloth, &c. **1867** BRANDE & COX *Dict. Sci.* etc., *Scouring Drops*, the essential oils of lemon and of bergamotte are sold under this name. **1661** PETTY in T. Birch *Hist. Roy. Soc.* (1756) I. 61 The best Wooburn earth resembleth Castle-soap not obscurely, that and all other *scowring earths consisting..of very fine sand, answering to the salt in soaps [etc.]. **1603** *Inv.* in Gage *Hengrave* (1822) 21 Y[e] chamber over y[e] *skoringe house. *Ibid.* 22 Y[e] scooring house. **1647** TRAPP *Comm. 2 Tim.* ii. 21 O happy be you that you be now in this scouring house: for shortly you shall be set upon the celestial shelf. **1851–4** *Tomlinson's Cycl. Usef. Arts* (1867) II. 938/1 This form of washer is called a **scouring-machine* in Yorkshire. **1882** *Encycl. Brit.* XIV. 387/2 Another machine now largely used by curriers is the scouring machine. **1969** A. J. HALL *Stand. Handbk. Textiles* (ed. 7) iii. 110 The construction and operation of scouring machines..are such as to disturb the wool as little as possible. **1799** G. SMITH *Laboratory* I. 399 They must before they are sent to the dye house, be well scowered in a *scowering mill. **1771** MRS. HAYWOOD *New Present* 252 To rub the stove and fire-irons with *scowring-paper. **1858** SIMMONDS *Dict. Trade, Scouring-Paper Maker*, a manufacturer of emery and glass papers for brightening metals, &c. **1949** D. SMITH *I capture Castle* v. 61 She.. scrubbed her hands until she got it [*sc.* dye] all off. She used our last grains of *scouring powder. **1975** N. FREELING *What are Bugles blowing For?* vi. 37 She tacked off to write 'scouring powder' on her shopping list. **1838** *Civil Eng. & Arch. Jrnl.* I. 338/1 He..expresses his complete disapproval of the *scouring power. **1855** OGILVIE *Suppl., Scouring-power*, the efficiency of a stream of water employed to carry away shingle, &c., from the mouth of a harbour, river, and the like, by flushing. **1697** DAMPIER *Voy.* I. 118 Lance-wood..is very hard, tough and heavy, therefore Privateers esteem it very much..to make..*Scowring-Rods for their Guns. **1845–50** MRS. LINCOLN *Lect. Bot.* 113 In the *scouring rush (*Equisetum*), the quantity of silex is such, that housekeepers find it an excellent substitute for sand, in scouring wood or metals. **1648** HEXHAM II, *Schuer-zandt*, *scouring-sand, or gravell. **1700** in *Phil. Trans.* XXV. 1539 Not unlike what we call white scowering Sand. **1577–87** HOLINSHED *Chron.* III. 1228/1 One of the gunners..was shot in the side with a piece of *scowring stick, left in one of the calivers. **1602** DEKKER *Satirom.* Wks. 1873 I. 229 Wher's the Sering thou carriest about thee? O have I found thee my scowring-sticke. **1625** MARKHAM *Souldiers Accid.* 3 Straight scowring stickes, headed at the one end with Rammers of horne, suitable to the bore of the Piece. **1687** A. LOVELL tr. *Thevenot's Trav.* I. 72 They..ram down a sizable Bullet with the Scowring-stick, which is all Iron. **1835** URE *Phil. Manuf.* 187 The helves of the fulling-mallets are placed in a position different from those of the *scouring-stocks. **1648** HEXHAM II, *Een schuer-steen*, a *Scouring stone. **1894** SPEIGHT *Nidderdale* 380 A small excavation from which in former times scouring-stones for the flagged floors of Ripley Castle were obtained. *c* **1610** MIDDLETON, etc. *Widow* II. i, I ha'..no child of mine own, But two I got once of a *scowring woman. **1620** FLETCHER *Chances* I. vi, To..consume my selfe in candles, And *scowring works, in Nurses Bells and Babies. **1806** A. HUNTER *Culina* (ed. 3) 154 [This soup] may be considered as an assistant to Archæus, when he has any scouring work to perform.

'scouring, *ppl. a.*[1] [f. SCOUR *v.*[1] + -ING[2].] That moves about with hostile purpose; *spec.* roistering through the streets.

1691 SHADWELL *Scowrers* v. iii. 51 They tell me you were disturb'd with Roysters, and scowreing Rogues. **1704** SWIFT *Mech. Operat. Spirit* ii, A set of roaring, scouring companions, overcharged with wine. **1716** GAY *Trivia* III. 314 If hapless you Should chance to wander with the scow'ring crew.

'scouring, *ppl. a.*[2] [f. SCOUR *v.*[2] + -ING[2].]

1. That cleanses; detergent.

1594 PLAT *Jewell-ho.* II. 31 Those scowring effectes, for the which it [*sc.* Fullers' earth] is diuerse wayes had in vse amongst vs. **1600** SURFLET *Country Farm* III. xxvii. 484 The wood being burned doth yeelde a sharpe smoke, and the ashes a verie scouring lee.

2. Purging, cathartic.

1597 GERARDE *Herbal* II. xvi. 199 Lampsana is of nature hot, and somewhat abstersiue or scowring. **1656** RIDGLEY *Pract. Physick* 11 Scowring things, as figs. **1743** *Lond. & Country Brewer* II. (ed. 2) 93 Barley..is scouring.

fig. **1617** HIERON *Wks.* II. 196 To see how that scowring potion of Reproofe would worke to his humiliation, before he would minister to him any Cordials. **1864** BUNYAN *Holy Life Beauty Chr.* 43 Repentance is the scouring grace, 'tis that which purges.

3. Of slag: Having an erosive action on the hearth of the furnace.

1880 WRIGHT in *Encycl. Brit.* XIII. 296/1 If the slag becomes more or less of a 'scouring' character. **1884** W. H. GREENWOOD *Steel & Iron* 110 Heavy burdens and a reduced temperature of the furnace are accompanied by a scouring slag or cinder, flowing as freely as water.

4. Of livestock: suffering from diarrhœa. Cf. SCOUR *sb.*[2] 5.

1752 T. BOULT *Vet. Recipe Bk.* in *Henry Bristow Ltd. Catal.* (1974) No. 206. 31 To cure a Scowering Cow. **1973** *Country Life* 8 Feb. 360/1 A scouring cow is a very highly stressed animal.

5. *U.S.* Of a plough: see SCOUR *v.*[2] 1 g.

1856 *Rep. Comm. Patents: Agric. 1855* (U.S. Dept. Agric.) 170 It was ploughed as near it as possible with a double-shovel scouring plough. **1943** C. CROW *Great Amer. Customer* 71 He bought old sawmill blades with which he made self scouring plows which cut through the soil as clean as a razor.

Hence **'scouringly** *adv.* (in quot. = cathartically).

1528 PAYNELL *Salerne's Regim.* (1541) 67 Muste prouoketh one to pysse, by reason y[t] the erthy partes scouryngly bitethe the bladder.

scourse, obs. variant of SCORSE *v.*[1]

'scoury, *a.*[1] *Sc.* Also 6 **skowry**, 9 **scoory**. Shabby, disreputable. Hence **'scouriness**.

1500–20 DUNBAR *Poems* xxxii. 15 The tod wes nowder lene nor skowry, He wes ane lusty reid haird lowry. **1792** A. WILSON *Poems & Lit. Prose* (1876) II. 27, I wha stand here, in this bare scoury coat Was ance a packman. **1814** *Saxon & Gael* III. 58 (Jam.) That little whippy maun be casting up our poortith and your scouriness. *a* **1894** J. SHAW in R. Wallace *Country Schoolmaster* (1899) 352 A 'scoory-looking blade', a broken-down looking tramp.

†**'scoury**, *a.*[2] *Obs. rare*[−1]. [? f. SCOUR *v.*[1] or [2] + -Y.] ? Scouring, bitter, sharp.

a **1774** FERGUSSON *Farmer's Ingle* Poems (1845) 39 May Scotia's summers aye look gay and green Her yellow hairsts frae scoury blasts decreed.

scouse (skaʊs). Also **scouce**. [Shortened from LOBSCOUSE.]

1. = LOBSCOUSE.

1840 R. H. DANA *Bef. Mast* v, The cook had just made for us a mess of hot 'scouse'. **1876** C. H. DAVIS *Polaris Exp.* vi. 163 A couple pounds of which we used last night making scouse. **1884** *Pall Mall Budget* 22 Aug. 13/2 Bear and walrus were boiled up with vegetables and made into scouce or soup.

2. Transferred uses. (Often with capital initial.) *slang.* **a.** A native or inhabitant of Liverpool.

1945 *Southern Daily Echo* 27 Dec. 4/3 He was stopped by his Lordship and asked to explain the meaning of three words—'oppo', 'Geordie' and 'scouse'. His interpretations were: 'oppo' slang for opposite number, friend or colleague, 'Geordie'—a native of Newcastle-upon-Tyne; 'scouse'—a native of Liverpool where they eat 'scouse' (stew). **1960** O. MANNING *Great Fortune* II. 148 'I'm a scouse,' he said. 'From the dregs of the Liverpool soup.' **1969** R. AIRTH *Snatch!* ix. 91 'Where's home?' 'Liverpool.' 'A scouse. Fancy that.' **1980** *Times* 20 June 11/6 A roly-poly, amiable

Liverpudlian, with the Scouse's seemingly god-given gift of being able to send up an overblown..occasion.

b. The dialect of English spoken in Liverpool. Also, the manner of pronunciation or accent typical to the 'scouse'.

1963 *Guardian* 3 June 10/5 This rock group suddenly made Liverpool fashionable in the entertainment world. After their fist two records it became necessary for people in the business in London to learn a few words of Scouse. **1966** 'L. LANE' *ABZ of Scouse* Introd., As a dialect—for it *is* a dialect and not just a regional accent—Scouse has many curious features. **1979** *Times* 20 Nov. 4 A touch of Scouse in the pronunciation will be entirely acceptable.

c. *attrib.* or as *adj.*

1960 *Spectator* 14 Oct. 565 A horrifyingly plausible spiv, even down to that awful 'scouse' accent. **1965** G. MELLY *Owning Up* vi. 67 Albert Kinder, a scouse promoter who intended to tie up jazz in the North. **1969** I. & P. OPIE *Children's Games* x. 276 'Film Stars' is the most popular guessing game in Britain... Other names: 'Initials', 'Pop Stars', 'TV Stars', and, in Liverpool, 'Filmy', a typical scouse apocope. **1973** *Guardian* 1 Aug. 1/8 Scouse House was the tongue-in-cheek name given to the Merseyside Development Office. **1976** *Observer* 8 Aug. 11 (Advt.), Ar Alf sez darrevry Scouse Big'ead's brood special fer d'Pool, like.

Scouser ('skaʊsə(r)). *slang.* [f. prec. + -ER[1].] = SCOUSE 2 a.

1959 *Times* 8 Dec. 13/6 Their [*sc.* Liverpool workers'] catarrhal speech would identify them as 'Scousers' wherever English is recognized. **1966** 'L. LANE' *ABZ of Scouse* 93 *Scouser*, an inhabitant of Merseyside, not necessarily a Liverpudlian. This book assumes a narrower definition, namely, a Merseysider who speaks Scouse. **1966** P. MOLONEY *Plea for Mersey* 22 A scouser lass known as R. Mury. **1973** *Guardian* 5 Mar. 8/2 Here was Ted Whitehead, born in Scotland Road and therefore a scouser of the scousers, with a real Liverpool play. **1976** *Liverpool Echo* 22 Nov. 6/6 It's pretty well established that where there's a ship there you'll find a Scouser.

†**scout**, *sb.*[1] *Obs.* exc. *dial.* Also 4 scowte. [a. ON. *skúte* (in Icel. 'cave formed by jutting rocks', Vigf.); cf. *skúta* to jut out, cogn. with *skióta* to SHOOT *v.*] A high overhanging rock.

13.. *Gaw. & Gr. Knt.* 2167 Þe skwez of þe scowtes skayued hym þoȝt. **1781** HUTTON *Tour to Caves* (ed. 2) 94 Gloss., *Scout*, an high rock. **1869** in *Lonsdale Gloss.*

scout, *sb.*[2] *Obs.* exc. *Sc.* Forms: 4 scoute, 5 skowte, scowte, 5, 9 *Sc.* scout, 9 *Sc.* scoot. [? cogn. w. SCOUT *v.*[2]] A term of contempt applied both to men and women.

c **1380** *Sir Ferumb.* 2285 Roland cryede an heȝ 'mountioye' wan he be-huld þay scoute. *c* **1425** *Seven Sag.* (P.) 2218 The godman..callyd hys wyf foule scout. *c* **1450** *Cov. Myst.* (Shaks. Soc.) 217 Come forthe, thou stotte! com forthe, thou scowte! *c* **1485** *Digby Myst.* (1882) I. 313 Avaunt, ye skowtys [*addressed to women*], I defye you euery-chone. **1822** GALT *Sir A. Wylie* I, 'Base scoot!' exclaimed Andrew,..'what puts such a thought into your head?' **1825** JAMIESON, *Scoot, Scout*, a term of the greatest contumely, applied to a woman; as equivalent to trull, or camp-trull. **1869** R. LEIGHTON *Scotch Words*, etc. 18 The learned, pious, yet unworthy skoot, Neglects his sacred trust to catch a troot!

scout (skaʊt), *sb.*[3] Forms: 5 scowte, 5–7 skowt, 5–8 scowt, 5, 9 scut, 6 skut, 6–8 scute, 7 scaut, schut, skeut, 7, 9 skute, 5, 8–9 schout, 9 scoot, 7– scout. [a. MDu. *schûte* (mod.Du. *schuit*: see SCHUIT) = ON. *skúta* (Sw. *skuta*, Da. *skude*). Cf. SHOUT *sb.*] A flat-bottomed boat; 'a Dutch vessel, galliot rigged, used in the river trade of Holland' (Smyth *Sailor's Word-bk.* 1867).

'A boat called *skoute*,' app. Flemish, is mentioned in *Close Roll 20 Edw. II* (Latin; 26 Sept. 1326).

1419 *Liber Albus* (Rolls) 239 Item, de qualibet scut descendente in dicta Ripa [*i.e.* Queen-Hythe], cum busca sive blado, capiendus est i denier. **1436** in *Exch. Rolls Scot.* IV. 679 Pro naulo barce vocate scowte. **1497** *Acc. Ld. High Treas. Scot.* I. 382 Item to ane scowt that baid apone the King, and landit his folk and hed thaim on burd. **1550** BALE *Image Both Ch.* xviii. B b vj, All they that occupye boates, wheries, and scutes, or sayle vpon the sea. **1582** STANYHURST *Æneis*, etc. (Arb.) 136 Where skut's forth launched. *a* **1609** ALEX. HUME *Day Estivall* 32 The Salmon out of cruifs and creils Up hailed into skowts. **1617** MORYSON *Itin.* I. iv. 42 We went in a skeut by water..one mile to Dockam. **1700** T. BROWN *Acc. Journ. Exon.* Wks. 1709 III. II. 101 Had I been travilling in a Dutch Scout, or a Gravesend Tilt-Boat, I could not have been treated with less Manners. **1769** *De Foe's Tour Gt. Brit.* (ed. 7) II. 157 Hoys, Bilanders and Schouts,..vessels peculiar to their inland and coasting Navigation. **1827** *Linc. & Lincolnsh. Cabinet* 18 The Witham..covered with..a portable kind of boats called *schouts*. **1893** STEVENSON *Catriona* xxii. 261 Ye can get a passage down the Maes in a sailing scoot.

attrib. **1493** *Halyburton's Ledger* (1867) 34 Item to the schout man ilk pip 4 g^s^. *Ibid.* 37 Item for schout hir, toyll, and pynor fe, 12 g^s^.

b. A vessel more or less similar used in warfare. Cf. SCOUT *sb.*[4] 5.

1703 *Lond. Gaz.* No. 3950/4 A Scout, of an unknown Name, taken by the Chester. **1799** CAPT. WINTHROP in *Naval Chron.* II. 343 Lieutenant Searle..commanded a schoot converted into a gun-boat.

scout (skaʊt), *sb.*[4] Forms: 6 scoult, skowlt, scowte, 6–7 scoute, skout, 7 scowt, skowt, 6– scout. [a. OF. *escoute* fem., action of listening, *concr.* listener, scout, vbl. noun from *escouter* to listen = Pr. *escoltar*, Sp. *escuchar*, Pg. *escutar*, It. *ascoltar*:—L. *auscultāre*.

The compound SCOUT-WATCH appears in our quots. much earlier than the simple word.]

1. The action of spying out or watching in order to gain information; chiefly in the phrases ***on*** or ***in*** **(*the*)** ***scout***, ***to the scout***. Also, an instance of this; a scouting or reconnoitring expedition. Also ***scout-round***.

1553 BRENDE *Q. Curtius* H vij, But those y^t^ discovered for the Percians, were but a .M. horsemen, whiche kepynge the scoute a farre of, semed to the Macedons to be a great army. **1587** FLEMING *Contn. Holinshed* III. 1980/2 The order of their march was this,..the light horsemen..tended to the skout a mile or two before. **1618** BOLTON *Florus* I. xvii. (1636) 50 None of these things hindered the Generall from sending his brother in scowt, to discover the pase. **1687** A. LOVELL tr. *Thevenot's Trav.* II. 199 There are Malabar Barks commonly upon the scout, especially in the evening, skulking behind some Points of Land. **1719** DE FOE *Crusoe* I. (Globe) 203, I set my self upon the Scout as often as possible. **1775** P. SCHUYLER in Sparks *Corr. Amer. Rev.* (1853) I. 29 Capt. Baker..without my leave, went upon a scout and..was shot. **1788** COWPER *Mrs. Throckmorton's Bulfinch* 34 A beast forth-sallied on the scout, Long-back'd, long-tail'd, with whisker'd snout. **1864** SIR T. SEATON *From Cadet to Colonel* xviii. 373, I thought it advisable to send Hodson on scout to Bilram. **1892** BIERCE *In the Midst of Life* 23 The commander asked him if in his scout he had learned anything of advantage to the expedition. **1906** 'MARK TWAIN' in *Harper's Mag.* Aug. 328/2 We are back at Fort Paxton once more, after a forty-day scout. **1975** P. DICKINSON *Lively Dead* xxii. 137 They'd enough reason to send a bloke to do a preliminary scout round. **1978** F. BRANSTON *Sergeant Ritchie's Conscience* i. 12 'Organized a scout-round for the weapon?' 'Only in the immediate area.' **1980** A. PRICE *Hour of Donkey* iv. 55 Wimpy's scout through the wood must..be..completed... Bastable contented himself with cautious peering round each blind bend.

2. a. *Mil.* One sent out ahead of the main force in order to reconnoitre the position and movements of the enemy. Hence occas. in wider sense: One sent out to obtain information.

1555 EDEN *Decades* (Arb.) 91 He fownde two scoutes of his ennemyes. **1591** SHAKS. *1 Hen. VI*, v. ii. 10 What tidings send our Scouts? **1644** SYMONDS *Diary* (Camden) 7 Some bodyes of theire horse and many of their scoutes appeared on the hill. **1667** MILTON *P.L.* VI. 529 Others from the dawning Hills Lookd round, and Scouts each Coast light-armed scoure, Each quarter, to descrie the distant foe. **1725** DE FOE *Voy. round World* (1840) 346 While they lay here.. expecting the return of their Scouts, they used what diligence they could in getting provisions. **1816** SCOTT *Antiq.* iii, Davy Wilson..was the very prince of scouts for searching blind alleys, cellars, and stalls, for rare volumes. **1837** W. IRVING *Capt. Bonneville* III. 53 The captain, therefore, continued to maintain the most vigilant precautions; throwing out scouts in the advance, and on every rising ground. **1869** BROWNING *Ring & Bk.* XII. 724 This foul-mouthed friar shall find His Noah's-dove that brought the olive back, Is turned into the other sooty scout, The raven. **1896** R. S. S. BADEN-POWELL *Matabele Campaign* iv, Without special training a man cannot have a thorough confidence in himself as a scout.

†**b.** *fig.* and in fig. context. *Obs.*

1598 SYLVESTER *Du Bartas* I. vi. 630 The Ears..The bodie's Scouts. **1613** PURCHAS *Pilgrimage* (1614) 889 In this sea we may see many Ilands which Nature hath seemed to set,..as skowts to espie, and as Garrisons to defend their soueraigne, Earth. **1633** G. HERBERT *Temple, Search* v, I sent a sigh to seek thee out,..Wing'd like an arrow: but my scout Returns in vain. **1659** W. CHAMBERLAYNE *Pharonnida* III. iv. (1820) II. 65 Had not the wise endeavours of her maid ..grief's pale scouts betrayed, By sly deceit.

c. *Boy Scout* (also with small initials): a member of an organization (first established in 1908 by Gen. Baden-Powell) consisting of boys who meet periodically to practise exercises and to undergo training in the duties belonging to a scout; now, a member of the Scout Association, or one of its associate, or parallel, organizations whose ideals of good citizenship and a healthy active life are promoted at regular meetings of scout groups in Great Britain, the British Commonwealth, the United States, and elsewhere throughout the world. Various specialized divisions of the movement are distinguished, as *cub scout*, *sea scout* s.v. SEA *sb.* 23 a, *Venture Scout* s.v. VENTURE *sb.*, etc.

The term 'Boy' has now been officially omitted from the title of the organization in the U.K., U.S., and elsewhere. *Girl Scout* has been the official name for the U.S. equivalent to the Girl Guide since 1912: see GUIDE *sb.* 2 d.

[**1908** R. S. S. BADEN-POWELL *Scouting for Boys* 3 We had an example of how useful Boy Scouts can be on active service, when a corps of boys was formed in the defence of Mafeking.] **1908** *Scout* 18 Apr. 1 Although the Boy Scouts have only been set going within the last two months, they are rapidly increasing all over the country. **1909** *Daily Mail* 6 Sept., The following message from the King was read at Lieutenant-General Baden-Powell's review of the Boy Scouts at the Crystal Palace on Saturday... 'The King is glad to know that the Boy Scouts are holding their first annual parade. Please assure the boys that [etc.]'. **1909** B. W. HENDERSON in *Times* 21 Sept., At Oxford we have seen the number of Boy Scouts rise from 30 to 300 in nine months, and there are no scouts, I believe, outside the organization. **1910** 'SCOUTMASTER' *Boy Scout* i. 1 General Sir Robert S. Baden-Powell, the founder of the Movement, recognised this when he first propounded his scheme for boy scouts... The Movement was started less than three years ago. **1924** 'A. D. SEDGWICK' *Little French Girl* I. v. 39 Alix heard of a Women's Institute, of Boy Scouts and Girl Guides. **1959** *Listener* 27 Aug. 304/1 There's something of the boy scout about M. Debré. **1978** *Broadcast* 27 Mar. 20/3 We wish that..people would stop calling us 'Boy' Scouts. Ten years ago we adopted the title, 'Scouts', in a process of updating our appeal to young people.

(*b*) *fig.* and *transf.*, freq. with reference to the honesty, preparedness, or supposed inexperience of a (Boy) Scout (see quots.).

1918 I. S. COBB *Glory of Coming* p. xiii, The Poilus called our soldiers 'Boy Scouts' and spoke of our effort as 'The Second Children's Crusade'. **1929** F. A. POTTLE *Stretchers* 60 The noncoms (who for weeks had been calling us 'Boy Scouts') hung a blue ribbon on the bulletin board. **1945** L. SHELLY *Jive Talk Dict.* 22 *Boy scout*, an immature male. **1962** *Amer. Speech* XXXVII. 267 *Boy scout*,..a traffic policeman who spends much of his time in helping motorists with flat tires, stalled cars, empty gas tanks, and so on. **1965** A. NICOL *Truly Married Woman* 84 Bandele had said, threateningly, that he had better not mention his name, but he could go and be a Boy Scout on his own. **1969** *Sunday Mirror* (Sydney) 13 Apr. 9/4 The accused officer has always been known as a 'boy scout'—a policeman who goes strictly by the book. **1977** J. I. M. STEWART *Madonna of Astrolabe* iii. 57 It was Mark's idea. Mark's absolutely the Boy Scout.

(*c*) *attrib.* and *Comb.*

1909 *Daily Chron.* 9 July 8/2 The youth of the three kingdoms of the boy scout movement. **1914** W. OWEN *Let.* 1 June (1967) 257 Certain of my Boy-Scout acquaintance. **1936** W. R. F. COLLIS *Silver Fleece* v. xvi. 266 Above all he hated..the 'boy scout' mentality, the modern tendency to march about in mobs, wearing coloured shirts, shouting, and beating up anybody who doesn't shout with you. **1950** 'E. CRISPIN' *Frequent Hearses* iv. 198 'What about the knife?' 'An oversized boy-scout affair..ground razor-sharp.' **1967** J. PORTER *Chinks in Curtain* v. 53 All right, chum, and what would you have done? Given the Boy Scout salute? **1978** S. BRILL *Teamsters* ii. 43 His father was a teetotaler, a boy-scout husband who came home every night.

(*d*) Hence ***Boy Scoutery***, ***Scoutism***, the activity or attitude of a Boy Scout; also *fig.*; ***Boy Scoutish*** adj., characteristic of a Boy Scout. (Freq. with pejorative connotations.)

1937 WYNDHAM LEWIS *Blasting & Bombardiering* v. ii. 234 He never got us under canvas it is true—we were not the most promising material for Ezra's boyscoutery. **1938** 'G. ORWELL' *Homage to Catalonia* iv. 49 We and they used to make daylight patrols there. It was not bad fun in a Boy Scoutish way. **1942** WYNDHAM LEWIS *Let.* (1963) 325 A curiously beastly case of boyscoutism, of arrested development or cretinism. **1962** L. DEIGHTON *Ipcress File* xiv. 84 Calling me 'boy-scoutish' which he knew would hit me where it hurt. **1963** J. VAIZEY *Educ. in Class Society* 6 These and other [travel and cultural] schemes..would.. tend to counterbalance people's enthusiasm for the Boy Scoutism of the Duke of Edinburgh's award. **1967** E. GRIERSON *Crime of One's Own* xi. 96 You must be mad... You've had that look about you ever since you started this boy-scoutery.

d. A bee searching for a new site for a swarm to settle or a new source of food.

1835 *Penny Cycl.* IV. 153/1 It is said that bees send out scouts before leaving the hive, to search for a convenient situation for their new abode. **1909** S. L. BENSUSAN *Children's Story of Bee* vii. 108 The scouts..might have been seen following their aërial roads to where the swarm was stationed. *Ibid.* 110 The last of the old queen's scouts had come bringing news of a hive—clean, sweet-scented and empty—in a garden across the valley. **1954** D. ILSE tr. *von Frisch's Dancing Bees* v. 28 While the main swarm hangs from a branch in quiet idleness, its 'scouts' are busily at work, searching in all directions to find a suitable abode.

e. One sent out by an organization (as a sports club, recording company, etc.) to look for suitably talented persons with a view to their employment by that organization; a talent scout.

1905 *Sporting Life* 2 Sept. 25/4 Padden..is the official scout of the St. Louis Club. **1926** WHITEMAN & MCBRIDE *Jazz* iii. 65 Vaudeville scouts approached us. Our pictures were in the papers. **1948** *Sporting Mirror* 19 Nov. 2/2 As chief scout for Derby County he will make sure that no young Midlander with real talent fails to get a chance to develop his soccer. **1952** A. LOMAX *Mister Jelly Roll* 291 'Fritz Pollard' introduced me to..Williams who was then a scout for the Paramount Recording Company. **1968** *Blues Unlimited* Sept. 15 They had their scouts out looking for anyone who could make records. **1976** E. DUNPHY *Only a Game?* iii. 92 He was being watched by Manchester City. Their scout left before the end.

f. An official of the A.A. or R.A.C. employed to assist motorists on the road. (No longer in use.)

1909 *Q. Rev.* Jan. 143 The scouts have, beyond doubt, done a great deal to check reckless driving. **1929** E. LINKLATER *Poet's Pub* xviii. 200 They passed a scout of the Automobile Association. 'You should have returned that A.A. man's salute.'

g. *slang.* A fellow, chap, person. Freq. in approbatory use, as ***good scout***, etc., and as an affectionate term of address.

1912 M. NICHOLSON *Hoosier Chron.* 129 Dad's a good old scout and he's pretty sure to do it. **1921** WODEHOUSE *Indiscretions of Archie* vii. 61 You'll never be lonely with Peter around. He's a great scout. Always merry and bright. **1922** J. A. DUNN *Man Trap* xii. 168 You didn't tell me your name, old scout. **1933** E. O'NEILL *Ah, Wilderness!* (1934) III. i. 96 Nat Miller's a good scout. **1934** A. WILSON *Such Darling Dodos* 198 She had only two roles with men—tomboy and good scout. **1953** 'N. BLAKE' *Dreadful Hollow* 112 'It's time I sent him a report.' 'Pop? No need, old scout.' **1965** 'J. LE CARRÉ' *Looking-Glass War* iv. 38 I've got nothing against old Adrian. He's a good scout.

3. A body of men sent out to gain information. Now only *U.S.*

1577–87 HOLINSHED *Chron.* III. 1198/2 The English scout, being thirtie good harquebutters, were set upon by the enemies. *a* **1619** BEAUM. & FL. *Knt. of Malta* IV. ii, *Mount.* What were those past by? *Roc.* Some scout of Souldiers, I think. **1716** B. CHURCH *Hist. Philip's War*

(1867) II. 57 He immediately sent away a Scout of 60 Men. **1775** L. BROWN in Sparks *Corr. Amer. Rev.* (1853) I. 462 Being informed..that two scouts, of fifty men each, were sent out often. **1798** I. ALLEN *Hist. Vermont* 92 He sent a scout of about 300, mostly Indians, to hunt at the mouth of Otter Creek. **1867** J. N. EDWARDS *Shelby & his Men* xxiii. 412 At Current river a scout of fifty were encountered. **1940** W. FAULKNER *Hamlet* II. i. 127 A scout of two or three would lurk about the Varner fence.

4. a. One who keeps watch upon the actions of another; a watchman. †Formerly often in opprobrious sense: A mean spy, a 'sneak': cf. SCOUT *sb.*[2] Also *spec.*: in oil-drilling operations, one employed by a company to keep watch on the activities of other companies; in *Sport*, one employed to observe and report on the performance of rival teams or clubs. Also, †a policeman.

1584 A. MUNDAY *Fidele & Fortunio* 465 in *Arch. Stud. neu. Spr.* CXXIII. 57 As close as I can, in this place I wil stand, Unseen vnto any, yet vewing of all: A prety scowte to take a knaue in a pit-fall. **1596** BACON *Max. & Use Com. Law* II. (1635) 4 These constables should keepe watch about the towne for the apprehension of rogues and vagabonds, and night-walkers, and eves-droppers, scouts, and such like. **1691** MOUNTFORT *Greenwich Park* v. ii. 54, I suppose the Spark was come, for one of her Scouts came and whisper'd her. **1748** SMOLLETT *Rod. Rand.* xv, For though I be a poor cobler's son I am no scout. **1789** [see HORNY *sb.* 2]. **1809** MALKIN *Gil Blas* IV. xi. ¶7 Lamela performed the office of a scout. **1821** P. EGAN *Life in London* II. iii. 231 Turning the corner of Old Bedlam, A scout laid me flat upon my face. **1838** DICKENS *O. Twist* III. xlvi. 213 They'll have him yet, for the scouts are out, and by to-morrow night there'll be a cry all through the country. **1883** *Century Mag.* July 327/2 The leading oil brokers of Bradford and Oil City employed scouts to watch it [the boring] after the hole had got down nearly to the depth where it was expected the oil-bearing sandstone would be reached. **1883** *Derrick's Handbk. Petroleum* (1898) I. 357 Scouts have squatted on the Reed and Brenneman lease..and are keeping a vigilant watch on the well; efforts to dislodge the scouts have proved unavailing. **1904** *Dialect Notes* II. 388 *Scout*,..a man sent to obtain information regarding a mystery. **1949** *Athletic Jrnl.* Oct. 20/1 The scout should familiarize himself long before the season starts with the types of defense that have been used by opponents in the past. **1973** C. CALLOW *Power from Sea* i. 14 The..oil industry employs men to keep tabs on the competition and has given them the euphemistic term of 'scouts'. **1976** M. MACHLIN *Pipeline* ii. 32 There had to be a scout on that plane.

b. *slang.* Used allusively for 'watch' = pocket timepiece.

1688 SHADWELL *Sq. Alsatia* II. i. 23 Sirrah. Here's a Scout: What's a Clock? what's a Clock, Sirrah? *a* **1700** B. E. *Dict. Cant. Crew, Scout*, a Watch. **1821** HAGGART *Life* (ed. 2) 28 Sporting an elegant dross-scout, drag, and chats... I succeeded in undubbing the stretch which slung the scout round her waist.

5. a. A type of war-vessel adapted for the purposes of reconnoitring. Cf. *scout-ship, vessel*; also SCOUT *sb.*[3] b, which may have been confused with this.

1706 *Lond. Gaz.* No. 4233/1 The Monk and Experiment Men of War,..put ashore near Cape de Gat a French Scout of 40 Guns. **1867** SMYTH *Sailor's Word-bk., Scouts*, small vessels of war for especial service. **1896** *Daily News* 20 Apr. 5/1 Many of our older scouts and commerce-protectors will show a higher rate of speed. **1902** *Westm. Gaz.* 24 Oct. 6/2 The Admiralty have accepted the tenders of [certain shipbuilding firms]..for the construction by each firm of one vessel described as a 'scout'. These scouts are a new departure in the Navy.

b. An airship or aeroplane used for reconnoitring; a lightly-armed fighter aeroplane. Also *attrib.*

1909 A. BERGET *Conquest of Air* II. vii. 260 Airships or aeroplanes? As 'combatants' or 'scouts'? **1914** *Daily Express* 31 Dec. 3/4 We have 'scouts' which can beat anything the enemy can bring against us. **1916** H. BARBER *Aeroplane Speaks* Pl. xi, The little Gnome-engined scout biplanes. **1928** E. BLUNDEN *Undertones of War* viii. 82 On account of the aforementioned ceremonial parade, with the gleaming bayonets and accoutrements not unnoticed by German flying Scouts, the town was shelled by heavy guns on the day that we departed. **1942** *R.A.F. Jrnl.* 2 May 1 Among the planes..is an approximately equal number of bombers, pursuit planes, and scouts. **1978** H. WOUK *War & Remembrance* xxx. 304 The air raid proved to be only some old-type scout bombers buzzing a battleship of the screen and then running away from the Zeroes into the light clouds.

6. †**a.** *Cricket.* = FIELDSMAN a. Also in *Baseball. Obs.* **b.** A boy who is employed to run after the balls at 'practice'. (Cf. SCOUT *v.*[1] 1 c.)

1824 MISS MITFORD *Village* Ser. I. 178 He was..nothing of a scout to John Simmons. **1837** DICKENS *Pickw.* vii, It fell upon the tip of the bat, and bounded far away over the heads of the scouts. **1851** LILLYWHITE *Guide to Cricketers* 54 Mr. Dark engages..to attend on the Marylebone Club..six boys as scouts. **1856** *Spirit of Times* 27 Dec. 276/3 One of these swiftly-delivered balls, when stopped by a skillful batsman, is sure to give the outmost scout employment. **1870** EMERSON *Misc. Papers, Plutarch* Wks. (Bohn) III. 347 They are like the baseball players, to whom the pitcher, the bat, the catcher, and the scout are equally important. **1898** J. A. GIBBS *Cotswold Village* xi. 241 So also one may say.. after the famous Gloucestershire hitter [*sc.* Grace] has made things merry for spectators and scouts alike. **1924** N. CARDUS *Days in Sun* 49 Supposing the fieldsmen were set.. with still a number of them idle on the off-side, with great gaps between the leg-side scouts.

7. In pigeon-shooting: An outlying marksman set to prevent the escape of wounded birds.

1859 'STONEHENGE' *Shot-gun* I. ii. 9 But if a bird, so hard hit by the shooter that, in the opinion of the referee, it would have fallen within bounds, is shot at by a scout, the shooter may be allowed another bird.

8. *attrib.* and *Comb.*, as ***scout boat***, †***canoe***, ***-craft***, ***hut***, ***knife***, ***-law***, †***-path***, ***patrol***, †***-shallop***, ***-ship***, ***vessel***; **scout bee** (sense 2 d); **scout car**, (*a*) *U.S.*, a police patrol car; (*b*) *Mil.*, a fast armoured vehicle used for reconnaissance and liaison; † **scout-ken** *slang* (see quot.); **Scout Law**, a code of conduct enjoined upon (Boy) Scouts; **Scout's honour**, the honour on which a (Boy) Scout promises to obey the Scout Law; freq. *transf.*, as an expression of one's good faith.

1924 A. M. STURGES *Pract. Beekeeping* 306/1 *Scout-bees. **1935** J. C. KENLY *Cities of Wax* xvi. 165 A scout-bee..had just brought in news to her hive that she had discovered a honey gold-mine. **1963** T. A. SEBEOK in J. A. Fishman *Readings Sociol. of Lang.* (1968) 23 [M. Lindauer] traces how the scout bees announce the location of suitable nesting places by means of the dance in the cluster. **1975** *Country Life* 20 Feb. 448/2 This swarm..was resting while scout bees looked for a suitable site. **1717** in *Statutes at Large S. Carolina* (1838) III. 24 For the *scout boat on Port Royal Island, a Captain and six private men. **1862** F. MOORE *Rebellion Record* V. II. 182 The scout-boats of Com. Montgomery notified him of the presence of the Federals. **1902** *Westm. Gaz.* 16 July 7/3 Designs and tenders..for ten scout boats. **1798** COL. BARROW in *Naval Chron.* (1799) I. 247, I sent out two *scout canoes. **1933** *Sun* (Baltimore) 5 May 11/2 *Scout car No. 7..answered fifty-five calls in the Pimlico section of the Northern district. *a* **1944** K. DOUGLAS *Alamein to Zem Zem* (1946) 40 A Daimler scout car, flying a red cross, was moving and halting,..collecting wounded. **1960** R. M. OGORKIEWICZ *Armour* xxxi. 434 A far more advanced Daimler scout car was also designed before the war, and the first built in December 1939. *Ibid.* 435 Originally the Daimler scout cars were intended for liaison within the tank regiments of the armoured divisions,..but after the 1940 campaign their use was extended, as was that of armoured cars. **1977** H. INNES *Big Footprints* I. ii. 47 More craters. A burned-out scout car, some lorries gaping holes, then we were clear of the battlefield. **1908** R. S. S. BADEN-POWELL *Scouting for Boys* 24 A scout's badge..is given him when he passes the tests in *scout-craft necessary to make him a scout. **1910** *Chambers's Jrnl.* Feb. 114/2 They are taught scout-craft, which includes the art of stalking wild creatures. **1937** *Sun* (Baltimore) 2 July 6/1 Thousands of Boy Scouts gathered in a giant arena tonight to watch a pageant of scoutcraft and history. **1977** N. ADAM *Triplehip Cracksman* v. 54 Using my entirely non-existent knowledge of scoutcraft, I snuck up it in the closing shadows. **1974** *Times* 10 Jan. 18/7 The *Scout huts in New Zealand. **1976** L. HENDERSON *Major Enquiry* ix. 54 He got bored with working in the scout hut. **1812** J. H. VAUX *Flash Dict.*, **Scout-ken*, a watch-house. **1937** E. GARNETT *Family from One End Street* v. 99 Hadn't he wanted a *scout knife as long as he could remember. **1977** J. PORTER *Who the Heck is Sylvia?* xvi. 150 The kid..clipped his scout knife back on his scout belt. **1908** R. S. S. BADEN-POWELL *Scouting for Boys* 49 The *Scout Law. **1922** *Encycl. Brit.* XXX. 487/2 The Scout Promise, to carry out, on his honour, as far as in him lies, the Scout Law, is the binding disciplinary force. **1931** E. WAUGH *Remote People* 134 A Somali boy presented himself for examination in scout law. **1972** P. BLACK *Biggest Aspidistra in World* I. vi. 51 An establishment striving..to do its best according to the Scout Law, continued to pervade the spirit of Children's Hour. **1750** in Temple & Sheldon *Hist. Northfield, Mass.* (1875) 378 About twelve or fifteen Indians Way-laid the *Scout-Path from Fort Dummer to Colerain. **1909** *Daily Chron.* 21 Aug. 5/4 To direct and help those who were forming *scout patrols all over the world. **1704** S. SEWALL *Diary* 1 Apr. (1879) II. 98 Read Brother's Letter about a *Scout-Shallop. **1694** LUTTRELL *Brief Rel.* III. 356 A *scout ship of theirs [the French] taken gives account that [etc.]. **1849** GROTE *Hist. Greece* II. lviii. (1862) V. 166 They awaited the return of the three scout-ships from Egesta. **1908** R. S. S. BADEN-POWELL *Scouting for Boys* 49 A *Scout's Honour is to be trusted. **1956** 'E. MCBAIN' *Cop Hater* (1958) xx. 168 'Provided it's not for publication.' 'Scout's honour,' Savage said. **1959** [see BROWNIE[1] 2]. **1974** A. ROSS *Bradford Business* 175 'I'll try my best, Charlie,' I said, 'scout's honour.' **1869** *Daily News* 13 July, The *scout vessels I have mentioned were necessary enough at first. **1902** *Westm. Gaz.* 17 July 4/1 Tenders had been asked for a new 'Scout' vessel.

scout (skaʊt), *sb.*[5] Forms: 6 scowt, 7 scoute, 7–9 skout, 9 (*dial.*) scoot, 8– scout. [Of obscure origin: connexion with COOT *sb.*[1] appears to be impossible.] A local name for various sea-birds native to Great Britain; as the Guillemot (*Alca troile*), the Razor-bill (*Alca torda*), and the Puffin (*Fratercula arctica*). ***green scoot***: a local name for the Green Cormorant (*Phalacrocorax Graculus*).

1596 DALRYMPLE tr. *Leslie's Hist. Scot.* I. 26 Ane certane kynd of fowle, in our mother toung named the Skout. **1635** BRERETON *Trav.* (Chetham Soc.) 98 Abundance of fowl breed here, solem-geese, storts, scoutes, and twenty several sorts of fowl. *a* **1672** WILLUGHBY *Ornith.* III. III. iv. (1676) 244 *marg.*, Alia avis est quam Scoti circa insulam Bassam, & Northumbrici circa Fernas insulas Skout vocant. **1710** SIBBALD *Hist. Fife & Kinross* 45 The Fowls which most frequent the Bass are..the Scout, the Scarts [etc.]. **1805** G. BARRY *Orkney Isl.* 305 The Guillemote..here the skout, remains with us all the winter. **1852** MACGILLIVRAY *Brit. Birds* V. 392 *Phalacrocorax Graculus.* The Green Cormorant... Green Scout. **1893–4** *Northumb. Gloss.*, *Scoot*, the guillemot, *Uria troile.* So-called near Spittal.

scout (skaʊt), *sb.*[6] [Of unknown origin: identity with SCOUT *sb.*[4] has been conjectured, but evidence is wanting.] At Oxford (also at Yale and Harvard): A college servant.

Until recently, a male servant; but in the first quot. the word seems to be applied to a woman (unless 'goody' is peculiarly used).

1708 HEARNE *Collect.* (O.H.S.) II. 117 One shilling to goody Earl a Scout y[t] belongs to Oriel Colledge. **1750** *Student* I. 55 My scout, indeed, is a very learned fellow. **1800** *Sporting Mag.* XV. 85 Waked at eight o'clock by the scout, to tell me the bell was going for prayers. *a* **1851** *Yale Lit. Mag.* XI. 282 (Hall *College Words*), We had to send for his factotum or scout, an old black fellow. **1888** MRS. H. WARD *R. Elsmere* 52 The scout who intrusively asked him every morning what he would have for breakfast. **1935** D. L. SAYERS *Gaudy Night* v. 91 'The scouts are all women of excellent character, so far as I know,' said the Bursar. **1972** *Oxford Times* 26 May 1/3 Miss Bootes, who has been a scout at St. Hilda's College for 25 years, was presented with the teapot on Wednesday.

scout (skaʊt), *v.*[1] Also 4–6 skowt, 6 scoute, skoute, 6–7 scowt, 7 skout. [f. SCOUT *sb.*[4]]

1. a. *intr.* To act as a scout, to play the spy; to travel about (in search of information).

13.. *E.E. Allit. P.* B. 483, & ho skyrmez vnder skwe & skowtez aboute, Tyl hit was nyȝe at þe naȝt & noe þen sechez. *a* **1575** GASCOIGNE *Posies, Dan Barth.* 108 Such was his hap..To watche and warde at euery time and tyde, Though foes were farre yet skowted he alwaye. **1590** SIR R. WILLIAMS *Brief Disc. War* 31 Besides, they must skoute, discouer, with all dueties that belongs vnto an Armie. **1601** SHAKS. *Twel. N.* III. iv. 193 Scout mee for him at the corner of the Orchard like a bum-Baylie. **1644** SYMONDS *Diary* (Camden) 7 We scouted beyond Cumner, and mett with some of them. **1756** WASHINGTON *Lett.* Writ. 1889 I. 257 If they are at greater distances, it is inconvenient for the soldiers to scout. **1826** SCOTT *Woodst.* x, It will be necessary that I scout abroad a little. **1855** MACAULAY *Hist. Eng.* xx. IV. 665 Keyes, who had been out scouting among his old comrades, arrived with news more ominous still. **1886** STEVENSON *Kidnapped* xx. 192 Keeping only one eye above the edge of our..shelter, [he] scouted all round the compass.

transf. **1704** SWIFT *Mech. Operat. Spir.* ii. Misc. (1711) 303 These are the Men who pretend to understand a Book, by scouting thro the Index.

b. To skulk, lie hid (as a spy) in concealment. *Obs.* exc. *dial.* (See E.D.D. *s.v.*)

1577 KENDALL *Flowers of Epigr.* 23 The little Conie loues to scoute, In Berries that are digged out. **1633** HART *Diet of Diseased* Introd. 3 Many of these supposed Physitians..lie skouting in corners of the famous Citie of London.

†**2.** = FIELD *v.* 5. *Obs.*

1786 *County Mag.* Nov. 171/3 One that can throw well, likewise scout, He for a long stroke must stand out. **1828** [implied in SCOUTING *vbl. sb.*[1] 2]. **1887** HAVERGAL *Hereford. Gloss.* s.v., In Herefordshire cricket fields, to scout out = to field out. **1908** *Daily Chron.* 14 Aug. 4/7 On many suburban cricket grounds, where the small boys of the neighbourhood gather to field (or scout, as they call it) for the members at the nets. **1928** *Observer* 1 July 29/4 An arrangement by which Tate is required to rest from his bowling by scouting at deep square leg.

†**3.** *trans.* With adv., ***to scout round***: to surround with a watch. Also in *passive*, to be followed *about* by spies. *Obs.*

1619 FLETCHER *Bonduca* v. ii, Take more men, And scout him round. **1671** WOOD *Life* (O.H.S.) II. 227, I must be a papist: and then, upon that account, I was scouted about.

4. To reconnoitre, to examine with a view to obtaining information.

1704 SWIFT *Batt. Bks.* Misc. (1711) 260 One surveys the Region round, while the t'other scouts the Plain. **1821** CLARE *Vill. Minstr.* II. 23 The fox is loth to 'gin a long patrole, And scouts the woods, content with meaner prey. **1871** *Daily News* 24 July, Bazaine has been condemned by every military authority in Europe for not scouting the ravine of Gorze. **1900** *Ibid.* 25 May 7/2 Major Karri Davies, with eight men of the Light Horse, were ordered to scout the country.

scout (skaʊt), *v.*[2] Forms: 7 scowt, skowt, 8– scout. [Of Scandinavian origin: cf. ON. *skúta*, *skúte* sb., a taunt, prob. f. root of *skióta* to SHOOT. Cf. ON. *skútyrði*, also *skotyrði*, abusive language.]

†**1.** *trans.* To mock at, deride. Also *absol. Obs.*

1605 MARSTON *Dutch Courtezan* Prol., As for some few, we know of purpose here To taxe and scowt. **1610** SHAKS. *Temp.* III. ii. 130 Flout 'em, and cout 'em: and skowt 'em, and flout 'em. **1691** WOOD *Life* (O.H.S.) III. 357 He scouted me and told of 'virtue' (for 'vertue') [i.e. that the former was bad spelling]. **1768** GOLDSM. *Goodn. Man* II, When he speaks upon his legs, by the Lord he's prodigious, he scouts them.

2. To reject with scorn (a proposition); to treat as absurd (an idea); to dismiss scornfully the pretensions of (a person, a work, etc.).

1710 PALMER *Proverbs* 102 They pass the rhodomontade till they're expos'd and scouted. **1711** HEARNE *Collect.* (O.H.S.) III. 133 Those who laugh at and scout it. **1782** MME. D'ARBLAY *Let.* 6 Apr. (1891) I. 426 The people..who have been fond of blood and family, have all scouted *title* when put in any competition with it. **1819** F. HAMILTON *Nepal* 315 All alliances with the chief,..are scouted by the purer inhabitants of the southern mountains. **1822** HAZLITT *Table-t.* Ser. II. x. (1869) 212 Many great philosophers have not only been scouted while they were living, but forgotten as soon as they were dead. **1849** DICKENS *Barn. Rudge* xxxix, His turned-up nose..scouted all things of earth with deep disdain. **1872** *Q. Rev.* Jan. 251 Simple and obvious remedies are scouted or neglected. **1883** MRS. R. RITCHIE *Bk. Sibyls* i. 47 The poem..was scouted at the time and violently attacked. **1884** TENNYSON *Becket* II. ii, I am glad that France hath scouted him at last. **1898** BODLEY *France* II. III. v. 247 The King..scouted the idea of his functions being reduced to those of an English monarch.

scout, scoutchin: see SCOOT *sb.*[1], SCUTCHEON.

scouted (ˈskaʊtɪd), *ppl. a.* [f. SCOUT *v.*[2] + -ED[2].] Scorned, flouted.
1810 *Naval Chron.* XXIII. 38 No public breakfasts cheer these scouted tars.

ˈ**scouter.** Also 7 **skooter, scowter.** [f. SCOUT *v.*[1] + -ER[2].]
†**1.** A scout or spy. *Obs.*
1642 in *10th Rep. Hist. MSS. Comm.* App. IV. 434 To Robert Addams..for goeing as a skooter to Coventry to hearken out how nere the soldiers were cominge. **1645** SYMONDS *Diary* (Camden) 193 The horse..were persued by a body of the enemyes horse and loose scowters. *c* **1776** in W. Irving *Washington* (1856) II. 606 A famous scouter and wood-hunter. **1827** J. F. COOPER *Prairie* xviii, But this is a scouter in his war-paint! **1867** J. N. EDWARDS *Shelby & his Men* xiv. 232 One of the truest scouters who ever fired a pistol.
2. An adult member of the (Boy) Scout movement. Cf. GUIDER s.v. GUIDE *sb.* 2 d.
1930 H. W. BENSON *Summer Camp* 27 [The Patrol Leader] must be taught..to decentralize... A Scouter or Rover will probably be required to show him how to set about this. **1948** *Lawton* (Okla.) *Constitution* 4 July 3/5 A large number of cubbers and scouters were present with their families. **1976** *Burnham-on-Sea Gaz.* 20 Apr., A strong committee should be established, to be responsible for fund-raising activities, leaving the various scouters to carry on their roles as cub-scout leaders.

‖**scouˈtette, scouttet.** *Obs. rare.* [MDu. *schoutet, schoutheet*: see SCHOUT.] = SCHOUT.
1534 *St. Papers Hen. VIII*, VII. 543 Yisterdaye I had the Scouttet and Lordes of this town at dynner with me. *Ibid.* 547 The Quene hath send owt hyr placarts of comandment to all drossarts, scoutettes, ballyys, and othyrs offyssers of the conttres abowth.

scouth (skaʊθ). *Sc.* Also 8–9 **scowth, skouth.** Opportunity, scope. Also, abundance, plenty.
Also in phrase *scouth and routh*: see *Eng. Dial. Dict.*
1591 R. BRUCE *Serm.* (1843) 387 There are Bands which circle & fetter him, that he hath no scouth or liberty to run out. **1728** RAMSAY *Robt., Richy, & Sandy* 10 He seeks the dowy glen That he may scowth to a' his mourning len. **1785** BURNS *To Rev. J. M'Math* x, They talk o' mercy, grace, and truth, For what?—to gie their malice skouth On some puir wight. **1815** FINLAYSON *Rhymes* 38 (E.D.D.) The sturdy tiller o' our plains, Whose work demands nae scowth o' brains.

scouting (ˈskaʊtɪŋ), *vbl. sb.*[1] [f. SCOUT *v.*[1] + -ING[1].] The action of the vb. SCOUT.
1. a. Spying, reconnoitring.
1644 SYMONDS *Diary* (Camden) 22 Some scowting beyond Banbury that evening; little or no hurt on neither side. **1754** in Temple & Sheldon *Hist. Northfield, Mass.* (1875) 285 However, if the scouting be faithfully performed, there will not, I apprehend, any considerable body of the enemy get within ye line aforesaid undiscovered. **1893** LELAND *Mem.* I. 30 Often I sat on a little cricket at his feet, and listened to tales of battles, scoutings, and starving.
attrib. **1756** R. ROGERS *Jrnl.* 28 Apr. (1765) 17 They discovered a scouting party of three or four hundred Indians. **1856** W. IRVING *Washington* III. 852 He had recently signalized himself in scouting-parties. **1895** A. C. HAMLIN in M. A. Jackson *Mem. Stonewall Jackson* (ed. 2) 548 A Federal scouting party could have come up the Hazel Grove road and seized him as a prisoner of war. **1941** B. SCHULBERG *What makes Sammy Run?* xi. 199 The other members of the Wall Street scouting party were punctual.
b. The exercises practised by 'boy scouts'. Also, the Scout movement itself.
1908 R. S. S. BADEN-POWELL *Scouting for Boys* 1 Instruction in scouting should be given as far as possible through practises, games, and competitions. **1966** *Listener* 20 Oct. 570/1 'Scouts go mod', the headline said—as if the cut of the new mushroom-coloured, tapering long trousers was the most important feature of the new pattern of Scouting. **1976** *Eastern Even. News* (Norwich) 9 Dec. 6/4 I'm sure there must be lots of men with souvenirs from their Scouting days. **1977** *Times* 27 June 16/8 Olave, Lady Baden-Powell..exemplified the potential of Scouting and Guiding for world peace.
c. The activity of a scout (SCOUT *sb.*[4] 2 e or 4 a).
1908 *Baseball Mag.* Nov. 1/1 There was the reconnoitering, scouting, feints, retreats, invasions, and then preparations made by all the ball-and-bat generals for the final big battle. **1961** J. S. SALAK *Dict. Amer. Sports* 382 *Scouting*, viewing an opposing team in action before playing them. **1968** *Blues Unlimited* Nov. 5 Joe Bihari..asked him to do some scouting for Modern Reds, as well as playing on further second dates.
†**2.** Fielding at cricket. *Obs.*
1815 *Suffolk Chron.* 2 Sept., The Needham players are remarkable for excellent scouting. **1828** *Sporting Mag.* XXIII. 38 Both were so completely knocked up, with alternately bowling and scouting, as to be nearly incapable of walking home. **1885** F. GALE *Life of Hon. Robert Grimston* vii. 77 Lords' forty years ago was practically a country ground... There were no nets, but ground boys did the scouting. **1908** W. E. W. COLLINS *Leaves from Old County Cricketer's Diary* xi. 191 Quite a young soldier..did most of the scouting in the far country.

†ˈ**scouting,** *vbl. sb.*[2] *Obs.* [f. SCOUT *v.*[2] + -ING[1].] A snubbing reproof, a scolding.
1794 MARIA J. HOLROYD *Lett.* (1896) 301, I gave Louisa a good scouting for indulging her moralizing turn.

scouting (ˈskaʊtɪŋ), *ppl. a.* [f. SCOUT *v.*[1] + -ING[2].] That scouts; watching, exploring, spying.
1663 *Brief Acc. Turks Late Exped.* 21 There followed into the Town a great Body of Tartars after these scouting Troupers. **1820** CLARE *Rural Life* (ed. 3) 31 The owls mope out, the scouting bats Begin their giddy round. **1907** *Standard* 19 Jan. 7/5 Scouting air vessels could follow night and day every movement of the armies.

†ˈ**scoutinger.** *Obs. rare*[−1]. [? f. SCOUTING *vbl. sb.* + -ER[1]; or f. SCOUT *sb.*[4] after *harbinger, messenger*, etc.] ? A military scout, a spy.
1642 *True Copy of Let. from Oxford* 7 A good scoutinger is worth a kingdome, being the very key of the worke, and for want of it, many rare opportunities are lost.

scoutmaster, scout-master (ˈskaʊtmɑːstə(r)). [f. SCOUT *sb.*[4] + MASTER *sb.*[1]]
1. a. A leader or captain of a band of scouts. Now usu. the officer who has charge of a 'troop' of (boy) scouts.
1579 DIGGES *Stratiot.* 99 The Scout maister oughte diligently to viewe and note rounde aboute the campe. **1590** SIR R. WILLIAMS *Brief Disc. War* 16 The General of the horsmen hath to serue him, his Lieftenant, Colonels, Captaines, and Scoutmasters. **1633** T. STAFFORD *Pac. Hib.* II. xxi. 235 Captaine Crofts the Scout-Master [was killed] with a shot in the backe. **1755** *Gentl. Mag.* XXV. 54 Parson Hudson, an able divine, was his scout-master, and Chillingworth his engineer. **1819** SCOTT *Ivanhoe* xxxv, The scout-master arrived after a brief delay. **1908** R. S. S. BADEN-POWELL *Scouting for Boys* 25 The badge is worn by scout masters on the left side of the hat or cap. **1910** *Chambers's Jrnl.* Feb. 117/2 Officers, called scout-masters, must be over eighteen. **1928** R. KNOX *Footsteps at Lock* v. 42 The scout-master, a man of some age and education. **1942** E. WAUGH *Put out More Flags* i. 14 His binoculars which she remembered vaguely having lent to the scout-master. **1977** S. BRETT *Star Trap* xi. 126 He's a scout-master and tends to be off camping..most weekends.
fig. **1644** SIR E. DERING *Prop. Sacr.* d iiij b, Archbishop Laud..takes the words which Heylin (his Scoutmaster) had found passable.
b. *scoutmaster general*: (Hist.) The chief of the intelligence department of the Parliamentary army.
1644 WHITELOCKE *Mem.* (1853) I. 321 Scoutmaster general Bedford came to the house with letters from the commissioners in the army, of the particulars of the battle at Newbury. **1647** SPRIGG *Anglia Rediv.* 326 (List of Officers), Major Watson, Scoutmaster Gen. to the Army. **1682** BUNYAN *Holy War* 289 Forasmuch as he [Mr. Prywell] was so naturally inclined to seek their good, and also to undermine their foes, they gave him a Commission of Scoutmaster-general. **1736** CARTE *Ormonde* II. 498 No body was more active in procuring these witnesses, than the Bishop of Meath, who had been Scoutmaster General to Oliver Cromwell's army.
¶**2.** Erroneously used for SCHOUT.
1652 EARL MONM. tr. *Bentivoglio's Hist. Relat.* 5 The Sheriffs [of the cities of Holland] together with the Scout-master [orig. *Sculteto*] deal in the administration of Justice both Civill and Criminall. **1690** *Moral Ess. Pres. Times* vii. 117 There is in every one of these parishes of Holland, one they call a Scout-Master, which is the chief Magistrate of it.
Hence ˈ**scoutmastering,** the occupation of a scoutmaster; ˈ**scoutmasterish,** ˈ**scoutmasterly** *adjs.*, resembling or characteristic of a scoutmaster.
1937 'G. ORWELL' *Road to Wigan Pier* x. 192 Shouted out of existence with a few scoutmasterish bellows of good-will. **1954** E. HYAMS *Stories & Cream* 9 The stout, genial Scoutmasterly fellow. **1957** L. DURRELL *Justine* II. 124 I've done quite a bit of scoutmastering. **1964** K. G. GRUBB *Layman looks at Church* v. 152 Any form of voluntary activity from local government to scout-mastering is in the same difficulty, namely that the pressures and claims of business make voluntary work impossible. **1979** K. BONFIGLIOLI *After You with Pistol* v. 21 He patted me on the shoulder in a scoutmasterly way.

†ˈ**scout-watch.** *Obs.* Forms: 4 **scowte-, skowtte-,** 4–6 **skowte-,** 4–7 **skoute-,** 5 **scote-,** (*erron.* **skoulk-**), 7 **skowt-,** 5–8 **scout(e-,** 4 **-wach,** 4–5 **wacche,** 5–6 **-wache, watche,** 6–8 **-watch.** [f. SCOUT *sb.*[4] + WATCH *sb.*]
1. A sentinel, spy; one that keeps guard.
13.. *E.E. Allit. P.* B. 838 In grete flokkez of folk, þay fallen to his ʒatez, As a scowte-wach scarred, so þe asscry rysed. *a* **1400** *Morte Arth.* 2468 Skayres thaire skottefers, and theire skowtte-waches. **1442** *Beckington's Jrnl.* (1828) 97 Whan they were approched nigh the same towne there comme upon theym the skoulk wache, and there a showte was made of St. George d'Angleterre. **1470–85** MALORY *Arthur* I. xiii, But the scoute watche by her hoost cryed lordes att armes for here be your enemyes at your hand. **1562** [? PILKINGTON] *Burn. Paules Ch.* (1563) B v, The word *Episcopus* is Greke, and signifies a Scoutwatche, an ouerloker or Spie. **1609** BIBLE (Douay) *2 Kings* xiii. 34 And the servant that was the scoutewatch, lifted up his eies, and looked: and behold much people came by a byway. **1706** PHILLIPS (ed. Kersey), *Scouts* or *Scout-Watches*, Sentinels that keep Guard in the advanced Posts.
2. The action of keeping watch and guard.
1464 *Mann. Househ. Exp.* (Roxb.) 161 Item, my mastyre payd the same day to ix. men that made scotewache on horse bakke, vj. s. viij. d. **1532** HERVET *Xenophon's Treat. Househ.* (1768) 75 It is best to kepe watches and scoutwatches both by nyght and by daye. **1556** J. HEYWOOD *Spider & F.* lxiv. 2 Being in scoutwatch: a spider spiyng me, In the head spiders name: wild me speedilie, To tell this to you all. **1616** J. LANE *Contn. Sqr.'s T.* v. 357 Make skowt-watch, inrodes, gett intelligence.
3. A body of men told off for the purposes of watching and keeping guard.
1523 LD. BERNERS *Froiss.* I. xvi. 17 If theyr Scoutwatche hard any noyse, or mouyng of people drawyng to the cite warde, than incontynent they shulde gyue them knowledge. **1611** SPEED *Hist. Gt. Brit.* IX. xix. §50. 723 Neither durst he for the Kings Scout-watch demand direction to Tamworth.

scouty-aulin (ˈskutɪˈɑlən). *dial. Sc.* Forms: 8 **scuti-allan,** 8–9 **scouti-aulin,** 9 **scoutiallin, scouty-, scootie-allan, scoute-, scouti-allen, scouty-aulin.** [app. f. **scouty*, **scooty* adj. (f. *scout* = SCOOT *v.*[1] 1) + *aulin, allan*, which is used separately as the name of the bird. Cf. the synonymous *dirty allan.*] The Arctic Gull or Skua (*Stercorarius crepidatus*, or *richardsoni*).
1701 BRAND *Descr. Orkn.* etc. (1703), There is a Fowl there called the Scutiallan, of a black colour, and as big as a Wild Duck. *a* **1795** G. LOW *Fauna Orcad.* (1813) 118 The Arctic Gull... Orc. Scouti-Aulin. **1852** MACGILLIVRAY *Brit. Birds* V. 492 *Lestris Richardsonii.* Richardson's Skua. .. Scoute-allen. **1896** NEWTON *Dict. Birds* 870 It [*Stercorarius crepidatus*] is..the Shooi of the Shetlands, and the Scouti-allen of the fishermen of Orkney and on the east coast of Scotland.

ˈ**scovan.** *Mining* (Cornw.). [Related to next.] = SCOVE *sb. scovan lode*: see quots.
1778 PRYCE *Min. Cornub.* 90 A Scovan Lode, is formed of a hard compact crystalline Stone, either of a brown or black hue, according to the colour of the Tin with which it is mixed. *Ibid.* 105 If it takes its course through a Scovan Lode, it mostly damages..the Scovan. **1814** W. PHILLIPS in *Trans. Geol. Soc.* II. 118 When tin ore is intimately mingled with quartz and chlorite, the vein is termed a scovan load. **1860** *Eng. & Foreign Mining Gloss., Cornw.* (ed. 2) 22 *Scovan lode*, a lode having no gossan on its back or near the surface.

scove. *Mining* (Cornw.). [Prob. from Celtic Cornish.] (See quots.)
1778 PRYCE *Min. Cornub.* 90 The Ore is often rich, ponderous, and solid in this Stone; and when it is worth one half for Metal, they call it Scove. **1808** POLWHELE *Cornish-Eng. Vocab.* 56/2 We say of a rich lode '*tis all skove; pure and clean.* **1880** D. C. DAVIES *Metallif. Min.* 420 *Scove* C[ornish], very pure tin that hardly needs dressing.

ˈ**scovel(l.** *Obs.* exc. *dial.* [a. early mod.F. *escouvelle* (Cotgr.), dim. of *escouve* (:—L. *scōpa*) broom. (The ordinary Fr. word for the baker's 'malkin' is *écouvillon*, OF. *escouvillon.*)] A baker's malkin.
1562 WITHALS *Dict.* 44 b/1 A scouell, dragge, or malkyn, wherewith the floore of the ouen is made cleane, *peniculus.* **1662** *Comenius' Janua Ling. Triling.* 84 But first he [*sc.* the baker] rakes the fire from it with a scovel (maukin, colerake). **1688** HOLME *Armoury* III. 317/1 Bakers Terms in their Art... A Scovel, a Maukin, an Oven sweep.

scovillite (ˈskəʊvɪlaɪt). *Min.* [f. the name of the *Scoville* ore-bed, Salisbury, Conn., U.S., its locality: see -ITE.] Hydrous phosphate of cerium, yttrium, and other rare metals; rhabdophanite.
1883 BRUSH & PENFIELD in *Amer. Jrnl. Sci.* Ser. III. XXV. 463. **1884** *Athenæum* 12 Apr. 479/1 The author [Mr. W. N. Hartley] shows that a new mineral, scovillite, described by Brush and Penfield..is but a variety of rhabdophane. **1892** [see *Rhabdophanite*: s.v. RHABDO-].

ˈ**scovin.** *Obs.* exc. *dial.* Also 7 **scoven.** [Altered form of SCOVEL.] = SCOVEL.
1657 C. BECK *Universal Char.* H 7, A malkin or scoven. **1884** *Upton-on-Severn Gloss., Scovin*, a cloth, mat, or old fishing-net, attached to a pole and used for cleaning out a baker's oven.

ˈ**scovy,** *a. dial.* Also **scovey, scawvy.** [Cf. SCAWE, SCAWED *a.*] Streaked, mottled, smeared.
1777 *Horæ Subsecivæ* 382 (E.D.D.) Scovy wool, wool of several colours, not duely mixt in scribling, but streaky... Scovy cloth, when the abb, or the woof is not all of the same colour,..and the cloth appears in streaks or lines. **1864** T. Q. COUCH *Wds. E. Cornw.* in *Jrnl. R. Inst. Cornw.* Mar., *Scovey*, spotted, mottled. **1892** SARAH HEWETT *Peasant Sp. Devon* 120 *Scawvy* = smeary. 'Go an' scrub thickee planche floor again; 'tez za scawvy I'm ashamed tu zee 'n.'

†**scow, skow,** *sb.*[1] *Sc. Obs.* [Possibly a. Du. *schouw* (see next) in an unrecorded sense; the HG. etymological equivalent, *schalte*, has in Bavarian dialects the sense 'wood for coopers, thin laths' (*Deutsches Wb.* s.v.).] *pl.* Strips of wood for wattle-work, barrel-staves, fixing thatch, etc.
1524–5 *Burgh Rec. Edin.* (1869) I. 221 Thai had maid expenssis vpoun the standand graith of the commoun mylnis in stra, scowis, rauchteris, lyme [etc.]. **1538** *Aberdeen Reg.* XVI. (Jam.), Girchtstingis & skowis. **1543** *Ibid.* XVIII. (ibid.), Tymmer skowis Suadene buirdis, guirdstingis and boddummis. **1614** *Shipping Lists of Dundee* in Wedderburne *Compt Buik* (S.H.S.) 246 The said bark laitlie arryved frome Melstrand contenand..auch thowsand barrellis of Skowie [? *read* Skowis] & ane hundreth pyp stalffis. **1705** *Sc. Acts Anne* (1824) XI. 293/2 Knaple, skows, hoops, dutch nets..shall be free of custome.

scow (skaʊ), *sb.*[2] *U.S., Scotland, Ireland.* Also **skow.** [a. Du. *schouw*, MDu. *schouwe, schoude* = LG. *schalde*, HG. dial. *schalte* punt-pole, boat propelled by a pole; related to OS. *scaldan* to push (a boat) from the shore. Cf. Gael. *sgoth.*]
1. a. A large flat-bottomed lighter or punt.
1780 JEFFERSON *Corr.* Wks. 1859 I. 254, I have empowered Colonel Carrington to have twelve boats, scows or batteaux, built. **1841** CARLYLE in Froude *Life in Lond.* I. 221 Three fishers too, whose rude Annan voices I heard busy in their skows in the Gallowbank Pool. **1848** BARTLETT *Dict. Amer., Scow*... On Lake Ontario they are sometimes rigged like a schooner or sloop, with a lee-board or sliding

keel, when they make tolerably fast sailers. **1862** W. H. RUSSELL in *Times* 4 Apr., By 2 o'clock..about 8,500 men were on their way to..Fortress Monroe. They were carried in 12 large river steamers, some of which tugged scows for horses and artillery. **1877** LD. HATHERLEY in *Law Rep., App. Cases* II. 842 The navigation [on the river Leven] appears to be carried on in what are called scows, large barges, I suppose we should call them. **1878** BRET HARTE *Hoodlum Band* 102 A long, low, sloop-rigged scow,..worked her way out of the mill-dam towards the Sound. **1880** *Antrim & Down Gloss., Skeow*, a large flat barge, used to receive the mud raised by a dredging machine. **1884** G. ALLEN *Strange Stories* 154 Captain Pierpoint arranged to take down a scow or flat-bottomed boat, laden with grain, from Milwaukee for the Erie Canal. **1909** *Times* 27 Jan. 6/5 For the water he would use skows (flat-bottomed boats) which would also be capable of progressing upon the ice.

b. *U.S.* A small flat-bottomed racing yacht.

1929 B. HECKSTALL-SMITH '*Britannia*' & *her Contemporaries* viii. 82 The result of these changes was that ten years after the Britannia was built the type of racing yacht had developed into a scow with a fin keel. **1932** *Sun* (Baltimore) 13 Aug. 18/7 Pitted against the High Tide was the Inland Laker type sailing scow Elusive. **1970** *Globe & Mail* (Toronto) 25 Sept. 30/1 The Australian tub, Gretel, hit the American scow, Intrepid. **1976** *Oxf. Compan. Ships & Sea* 762/2 *Scow*,..used in the U.S.A. today to describe a small flat-bottomed racing yacht fitted with bilge boards or retractable bilge keels.

c. *transf.* Applied to one of several containers or vehicles used for transporting loads (see quots.).

1942 *Amer. Speech* XVII. 104/2 *Scow*, truck with extraordinary capacity for a big load. **1961** F. H. BURGESS *Dict. Sailing* 180 *Scow*,..A shallow tray for hoisting small packages of cargo. **1971** M. TAK *Truck Talk* 136 *Scow*,..a low-sided trailer used for hauling pipe, steel, stone, gravel, scrap and similar cargo. **1973** *Amer. Speech 1969* XLIV. 208 *Scow*, low-sided truck or rig used for hauling pipe or steel. **1977** *New Yorker* 18 July 23/2 There is even, in a projected television series, a pilot of a spaceship (an interplanetary garbage scow) who is called Adam Quark.

2. Applied locally to a coracle.

1825–82 JAMIESON, *Skow*, a small boat made of willows, &c. covered with skins, Moray.

3. *attrib.* as *scow-crew*; *scow-shaped* adj.; **scow schooner, sloop** *U.S.* (see quot. 1885).

1775 J. ADAMS in *Fam. Lett.* (1876) 60 Father Smith prayed for our scow crew, I doubt not. **1885** *17th Ann. List. Merchant Vessels U.S.* p. xxx, Scows are built with flat bottoms and square bilges, but some of them have the ordinary schooner bow. They are fitted with one, two, and three masts, and are called *scow-sloop* or *scow schooner*, according to the rig they carry. **1913** J. LONDON *Valley of Moon* 269 At the foot of Castro street..the scow schooners, laden with sand and gravel, lay hauled to the shore in a long row. **1951** H. I. CHAPELLE *Amer. Small Sailing Craft* 334 A few scow schooners were built with round bilges, but they were comparatively rare. **1897** *Outing* (U.S.) XXIX. 547/1 A clumsy, scow-shaped cattle-boat. **1885** Scow sloop [see *scow schooner* above]. **1941** H. I. CHAPELLE *Boatbuilding* 28 The New Jersey oyster garvey, the Maine scow sloop, and the San Francisco scow schooner represent examples of the practical use of such hull forms. **1953** *Sunday Sun Mag.* (Baltimore) 18 Oct. 24/4 An oddity in the sloop rig was the scow sloop, once common at the head of the Chesapeake near Havre de Grace... The last in service..was abandoned about 1940.

scow (skaʊ), *v.*[1] [f. prec.] **a.** *intr.* To cross *over* (a river) by means of a scow. **b.** *trans.* (See quot. 1828–32.)

1749 W. DOUGLASS *Summary* I. 460 The ferry is about 80 rod, and..runs two or three knots, scowed over in about 9 minutes. **1751** J. MACSPARRAN *Diary* 1 Oct. in *Letter Book* (1899) 58 He and a Boy..were Scowing wood. **1828–32** WEBSTER, *Scow*, to transport in a scow. **1929** W. HEYLIGER *Builder of Dam* 39 From this point I will scow the supplies over to the job.

scow (skaʊ), *v.*[2] *Naut.* [Of obscure origin.] *trans.* in *to scow an anchor*: on a foul bottom, to bend the cable to the crown and stop it within the ring, so that in weighing the seizing may be broken and the anchor tripped. Hence **scowed** *ppl. a.*

1878 D. KEMP *Man. Yacht Sailing* 366 Scowing an Anchor. **1879** W. ROSSITER *Dict. Sci. Terms*, Scowed anchor.

scow (skaʊ), *v.*[3] *north. dial.* [Origin uncertain; prob. related to SCOWBANKER.] *intr.* To loiter, idle; to shirk work, play truant. Hence **'scowing** *vbl. sb.*

1901 F. E. TAYLOR *Folk-Speech of S. Lancs.* s.v. *Scow*, to idle about. **1905** in *Eng. Dial. Dict.* V. 265/2 Now then, you're always scowing. **1959** I. & P. OPIE *Lore & Lang. Schoolch.* xvii. 372 *Sagging*..is definitely the prevailing term [for playing truant] amongst delinquents in all parts of Liverpool. A student..adds 'scowing' as a Liverpudlian expression. **1966** F. SHAW et al. *Lern Yerself Scouse* 58, *I wuz scowing*, I was having an unofficial spell of leisure time.

'scowbanker. *slang* (? and *dial.*). Also 8 scou-, -bancker, 9 skow-, skull-. [Of obscure origin. Adm. Smyth (*Sailor's Word-book*, 1867) gives a word *scow-banker* with the explanation 'a manager of a scow'; but this is prob. a mistake.] A loafer (see quots.). Also, †one who engages in unfair business practices, a dishonest or unscrupulous trader.

1750 G. BEEKMAN *Let.* 4 Dec. in P. H. White *Beekman Mercantile Papers 1746–1799* (1956) I. 136 You may thank a Sett of People Called Scowbanckers..that Seed has Run so high this two years past. Our town is full of them and there is Scarce a Vessell Comes along the wharffe but there is Imediately a half a Dozen of Them aboard bidding against Each other. **1764** —— *Let.* 30 Nov. in *Ibid.* 478 Our Vandue houses are Crowded with Linens for Sale belonging to the Scoubankers who are Offering of it from house to house for Less then Prime Cost which hurts the merchant much. **1864** *Hotten's Slang Dict.* 233 *Skow-Banker*, a fellow who loiters about the premises of any one willing to support him without the necessity of working for his living; a rogue, a rascal. Common at Melbourne, Australia. **1866** A. MICHIE *Retrospects & Prospects* 9 (Morris) A skull-banker is a species of the genus loafer... He is a haunter of stations, and lives on the squatters,..affecting to seek work and determining not to find it. **1898** E. E. MORRIS *Austral English*, *Skull-banker*, or *Scowbanker*, a slang name in Australia for a loafer, a tramp.

Hence **'scowbank** *v. intr.*, to loaf; also *sb.* = SCOWBANKER. **'scowbanking** *ppl. a.*

1868 B. BRIERLEY *Fratchingtons* iii. 40 If skeawbankin' fro aleheause to aleheause isno' drinkin', what is? **1881** CLARK RUSSELL *Sailor's Sweeth.* I. ii. 44 A sprinkling of black-browed scowbanks from Mediterranean ports. **1888** *Sheffield Gloss.* Suppl., He's a scow-banking sort of fellow! **1901** F. E. TAYLOR *Folk Sp. S. Lanc.* (E.D.D.), He does nowt bu' skeaw-bank abeawt o day.

scowde, obs. form of SCOLD *v.*

scowder ('skaʊdə(r)), *sb. Sc.* Forms: 8 scowder, scouder, 9 scowdher, scouther. [f. the vb.]

1. Scorching, slight burning

a **1774** FERGUSSON *Election* Poems (1845) 40 Till, in a birn, beneath the crook Theyre sengit wi' a scowder, To death that day. **1793** T. SCOTT *Poems* 358 (E.D.D.) Love has gie'n his heart a scouder. **1816** SCOTT *Black Dwarf* vii, If things be otherwise than weel wi' Grace Armstrong, I se gie you a scouther, if there be a tar-barrel in the five parishes.

2. *Anglo-Irish.* (See quot.) *lit.* and *fig.*

1830–2 W. CARLETON *Traits Ir. Peas.* (1844) II. 131 'Franky,' they would say, 'is no finished priest in the larnin'; he's but a scowdher'. Now a scowdher is an oaten cake laid upon a pair of tongs placed over the..embers... In a few minutes the side first laid down is scorched: it is then turned, and the other side is also scorched.

scowder ('skaʊdə(r)), *v. Sc.* Forms: 6 skolder, skowder, 7 scouther, 8 scouder, 7– scowther, scowder. [Of obscure origin: with the 16th c. form *skolder* cf. the synonymous SCALDER *v.*]

a. *trans.* To scorch, burn slightly. **b.** *intr.* To undergo scorching. Hence **'scowdered** *ppl. a.*, scorched; also see quot. 1781. **'scowdering** *ppl. a.*, scorching; also (of cold, etc.) withering, blighting.

1508 DUNBAR *Flyting* 122 Fy! skolderit skyn, thow art bot skyre and skrumple. *Ibid.* 171. **1535** STEWART *Cron. Scot.* II. 534 His skowdrit skyn wes blak as ony ruke. **1606** BIRNIE *Kirk Buriall* (1833) 4 By scowdring their skins in the Sunne. **1672** *Pasquil on Stair Family* in *Bk. Scotish Pasquils* (1868) 183 On shoulder clap made her Mess James embrace, And lick the dreepings of his scouther'd face. *a* **1774** FERGUSSON *Farmer's Ingle* viii. Poems (1800) 134 For weel she trows,.. That kye hae tint their milk wi' evil eie, And corn been scowder'd on the glowin kill. **1776** C. KEITH *Farmer's Ha'* x, Gude scoudered bannocks. **1781** HUTTON *Tour to Caves* (ed. 2) Gloss., *Scowder'd*, over-heated with working. **1799** J. STRUTHERS *Poet. Wks.* (1850) II. 202 Cauld winter wi' his scowdering eye. **1831** MISS FERRIER *Destiny* I. xx, Your cook's not a good hare-dresser... After all, I believe it's only a little scowthered. **1856** G. HENDERSON *Pop. Rhymes Berwick* 54 We'll..send them [*sc.* witches] hame, To scouther forever in h——'s blue flame! **1875** STEVENSON *Lett.* (1899) I. 109 The snell an' scowtherin' norther blaw Frae blae Brunteelan'.

scower, obs. form of SCORE, SCOUR.

scowl (skaʊl), *sb.*[1] Also 6 scowle, 7 scoul. [f. SCOWL *v.*] A louring or malevolent look.

1500–20 DUNBAR *Poems* xxxiii. 123 The air was dirkit with the fowlis, That come..With skryking, skrymming and with scowlis, To tak him in the tyde. **1625** in Ellis *Orig. Lett.* Ser. I. III. 206, I suppose none but a Queene could have cast such a scowl. *a* **1764** R. LLOYD *Genius, Envy & Time* 9 Each letter'd, grave, pedantic dunce Wakes..And, being dull, looks wond'rous wise, With solemn phiz, and critic scowl. **1847** TENNYSON *Princess* VII. 114 By axe and eagle sat, With all their foreheads drawn in Roman scowls, ..The fierce triumvirs. **1860** ABP. THOMSON *Laws Th.* §27. 39 Natural signs, as a scream to express terror, a scowl for hatred. **1909** *Blackw. Mag.* Sept. 369/2 He was received with scowls and curses.

b. *transf.* Of clouds, the elements, etc.

1648 CRASHAW *Delights of Muses, Death Herrys*, A ruddy storme whose scoule Made Heavens radiant face looke foule. **1878** BROWNING *Poet's Croisic* Prol. 2 Sky—what a scowl of cloud.

†**scowl,** *sb.*[2] *U.S. Obs.* ? Corrupt f. SCOW.

1778 T. ANBUREY *Trav. America* (1789) II. lix. 278 We crossed the river in scowls, which are flat bottom boats, large enough to contain a waggon and horses. **1796** H. WANSEY *Jrnl.* 56 While our coachee, and all its passengers were passing this fine river in a scowl.

†**scowl,** *sb.*[3] *dial. Obs.* Forms: 6 skoole, skole, scowle, scoule, 8 scoil. [Cf. SCOWLES.] Rubbish, debris.

1538–9 in R. N. Worth *Cal. Tavistock Par. Rec.* (1887) 17 Itm for Carynge awaye of the Skoole there ij^{d}. *Ibid.* 18 Itm for Carynge oute of the Skole of the churche ij^{d} ob. **1561–2** *Ibid.* 26 Itm payd for Carying of Scowle that laye in the churche yarde ij^{s} viij^{d}. **1574–5** *Ibid.* 33 Itm paid for caryadge awaie of the scoule, iiij^{d}. **1777** *Horæ Subsecivæ* 380 (E.D.D.) *Scoil*, rubbish; the head of a quarry before the solid rock is reached.

scowl (skaʊl), *v.* Forms: 4 skoul, 5 schoul, 5–6 scowle, 6 skoule, 6–8 scoul, 6–7 scoule, 7– scowl. [Prob. of Scandinavian origin; cf. Da. *skule* of the same meaning.]

1. *intr.* To look with louring brows and a malignant or threatening expression; to look angry or sullen. Const. *at, on, upon.*

1340 HAMPOLE *Pr. Consc.* 2225 Devels sal..raumpe on hym, and skoul, and stare. *c* **1400** *Land Troy Book* 16158 Menelaus hadde grete envy Off that quene Pantasaly,..On hir that tyme ful foule he schouled And seyde: that [etc.]. *c* **1440** *Promp. Parv.* 450/1 Scowle, wythe eyne, *oboculo.* **1535** COVERDALE *Job* xvi. 9 Myne enemy skouleth vpon me with his eyes. **1573** TUSSER *Husb.* (1878) 21 A mistres that scowles. **1590** SPENSER *F.Q.* II. ii. 35 But with bent lowring browes, as she would threat, She scould, and frownd with froward countenaunce. **1593** SHAKS. *Rich. II*, V. ii. 28 Euen so, or with much more contempt, men's eyes Did scowle on Richard. **1702** YALDEN *Æsop at Crt.* viii. 33 Shall I [*sc.* Phoebus] the universe benight..Because you [*sc.* an owl] rail and scoul. **1803** JANE PORTER *Thaddeus* i, His brow scowled. **1828** SCOTT *F.M. Perth* xiii, Albany scowled, but was silent. **1856** EMERSON *Eng. Traits, Wealth* Wks. (Bohn) II. 71 Whether it were not possible to make a spinner that would not rebel, nor mutter, nor scowl, nor strike for wages? **1882** B. D. W. RAMSAY *Recoll. Mil. Serv.* I. vi. 119 We met many disbanded soldiers,..but beyond scowling at us they did us no harm.

b. To be exhibited or expressed frowningly or with a scowl. *poet.* or *rhetorical.*

1719 YOUNG *Busiris* I. i, A sullen gloom Scowls on his brow, and marks him thro' the dusk. **1812** CRABBE *Tales* xv. 296 Amazement scowl'd upon his clouded face. **1824** W. IRVING *T. Trav.* I. 89 A menace scowled upon the brow.

2. *transf.* and *fig.* Of inanimate things (sometimes personified): To assume a gloomy, forbidding, or threatening aspect.

1587 CHURCHYARD *Worthies of Wales* N 4, When.. Clowdes waxe cleere, that now doth lowre and skoule. **1622** MABBE tr. *Aleman's Guzman d' Alf.* I. 56 What squint-ey'd Starre hath scowl'd vpon me? **1695** BLACKMORE *Pr. Arth.* I. 312 The Day returns, the Heav'ns no longer scowl. **1783** COWPER *Task* III. 541 Not so when winter scowls. Assistant art Then acts in nature's office. **1846** KEBLE *Lyra Innoc.* (1873) 16 Fretting cares scowl far aloof. **1905** J. B. FIRTH *Highways of Derbyshire* 168 The edge..scowls down upon a bleak Staffordshire moorland.

3. *trans.* in *nonce-uses.* To send forth with a scowl; to express with a scowl.

1667 MILTON *P.L.* II. 491 As when..the dusky clouds.. o'respread Heavn's chearful face, the lowring Element Scowls ore the darkn'd lantskip Snow, or showre. **1757** GRAY *Bard* II. iii, Fell Thirst and Famine scowl A baleful smile upon their baffled Guest.

Hence **'scowling** *vbl. sb.* Also **'scowler.**

1575 *Gammer Gurton* I. i, There is howlynge and scowlyng, all cast in adumpe, With whewling and pewling. **1858** O. W. HOLMES *Aut. Breakf.-T.* viii. (1859) 188, I had rather meet three of the scowlers than one of the smilers.

scowld(e, scowle: see SCOLD, SCALE *sb.*[1]

†**scowled,** *a.* ? Striped.

c **1440** *Promp. Parv.* 450/1 Scowlyd, *radiatus.*

scowles, *sb. pl. dial.* [Of obscure origin: cf. SCOWL *sb.*[3]] (Also *scowl-holes.*) See quots. Hence **scowle** *v. intr.*, (of mine-workings) to cave in.

1835 *4th Rep. Dean Forest Comm.* 3 The excavations, provincially called Scowles, which exist in many parts of the Forest, have evidently been made for the purpose and in the course of getting out the ore. **1884** *N. & Q.* Ser. VI. X. 288 The word applied to the actual quarries is usually scowl-holes, Scowles having become a place-name in several localities. **1890** *Glouc. Gloss., Scowles*..A very common word here [*i.e.* Forest of Dean] for the sides of workings in coal or iron mines falling in. The miners say 'scowling in'.

'scowlful, *a. nonce-wd.* [f. SCOWL *sb.* + -FUL.] Full of or characterized by scowling.

1881 F. T. PALGRAVE *Vis. England* 278 The musket gripp'd; the brow firm set; a scowlful smile of joy.

scowling ('skaʊlɪŋ), *ppl. a.* [f. SCOWL *v.* + -ING[2].] That scowls; having a sullen or malignant expression of countenance.

1552 HULOET, Skowlyng of countenaunce, *superciliosus.* **1577** KENDALL *Flowers of Epigr.* 15 b, Then euery skowlyng scholemaster would read with harshie voyce Thy verse. *a* **1586** SIDNEY *Arcadia* II. (Sommer) 125 But Miso..came with skowling eyes to deliuer a slauering good morrow to the two Ladies. *c* **1618** MORYSON *Itin.* IV. (1903) 290 The Conversation of gentlemen is very Austere, full of scowling gravity. **1748** RICHARDSON *Clarissa* (1811) VIII. 158 Daughters, who surveyed her with scouling, frightened attention. **1852** MRS. STOWE *Uncle Tom's C.* xviii, Prue had a peculiar scowling expression of countenance. **1871** DIXON *Tower* III. viii. 75 A young man..with sickly face and scowling brow.

b. *transf.*

1513 DOUGLAS *Æneis* VII. xiii. 19 Or on the scharp craggy rochis hie,..Wyth hingand hewis and mony a skowland bra. **1583** T. WATSON *Poems* (Arb.) 114 What scowling cloudes haue ouercast the skie. **1727–46** THOMSON *Summer* 1124 In rueful gaze The cattle stand, and on the scowling heavens Cast a deploring eye. **1872** BLACKIE *Lays Highl.* 2 Wilt thou change the smiling Erin For the scowling Pictish skies?

Hence **'scowlingly** *adv.*, with a scowling face.

1755 in JOHNSON. **1838** *Fraser's Mag.* XVIII. 32 The.. beldame..scowlingly opened the door.

scowlke, scowmar: see SCULK, SCUMMER.

scowly ('skaʊlɪ), *a.* [f. SCOWL *sb.*[1] or *v.* + -Y[1].] Given to scowling; sullen, morose.

1951 H. GILES *Harbin's Ridge* 64 He did take to drinking mighty heavy, and he got to acting sully and scowly. **1970** *Daily Tel.* (Colour Suppl.) 28 Aug. 21 Her scowly freckled face lights up when she laughs.

scowmfet(e, scowner: see SCOMFIT, SCUNNER.

scowp(e, scowrge: see SCOOP, SCOURGE.

scowry, var. SCAURIE; obs. f. SCOURY.

scowse, var. SCUSE, aphetic f. *excuse* vb.

scowt(e, scowth: see SCOUT, SCOUTH.

scoyer, scoymes, -ous: see SQUIRE, SQUEAMOUS.

scoyr, obs. Sc. form of SCORE.

scr-. 1. While as a general rule an initial *sc-* or *sk-* in a mod.Eng. word indicates that the word is not of OE. origin (OE. *sc-* being normally represented, in dialects as well as in standard English, by *sh-*), it is doubtful whether the rule applies to the combination *scr-*. The modern representation of OE. *scr-* in dialects varies between (ʃr-), (ʃər-), (ʒr-), and (sr-), and there is some reason for supposing that in some localities it normally becomes (skr-). Several words of undoubted OE. descent (there being no corresponding form in Scandinavian) have in ME. or in mod.E. two parallel forms with (ʃr-) and (skr-) respectively: e.g. *shred, screed,* from OE. *scréade*; *shrew,* dial. *screw,* from OE. *scréawa*; ME. *screpe* and *schreape,* from OE. *screpan* to scrape. The same variation of the initial consonant appears in some other words, which have not been found in OE., but which have Teut. cognates: *scream,* ME. also *schreame*; *scram* and *shram* dial. to benumb, to paralyse (cf. OE. *scrimman* of similar meaning); *shrog* and *scrog* dial., a bush. As the combination (skr-), unlike the Midland (sr-), is consistent with the articulatory habits of standard English, some dialectal forms with this beginning have found their way into the literary language; in one instance (*screed, shred*) an OE. word with *scr-* survives in two parallel forms with differentiation of meaning. In view of these facts, it seems doubtful whether there is sufficient ground for the usual assumption of Scandinavian origin for words like *scrape,* which existed in OE. (*scrapian*) as well as in ON. (*skrapa*).

2. Many Eng. words beginning with *scr-* agree more or less closely in meaning with other words differing from them in form only by the absence of the initial *s*. Examples of such pairs are *crab* (apple), *scrab*; *crag* (neck), *scrag*; *cramble, scramble*; *cranch, scranch*; *cratch, scratch*; *crawl, scrawl* (v.[1]); *creak, screak*; *crimple, scrimple*; *cringe, scringe*; *croak, scroak* (dial.); *crump, scrump*; *crumple, scrumple*; *crunch, scrunch*; *crush, scrush* (dial). It does not appear that these coincidences are due to any one general cause (see the articles on the several words), but it is probable that the existence of many pairs of synonyms with *scr-* and *cr-* produced a tendency to change *cr-*, in words expressive of sounds or physical movements, into *scr-* so as to render the word echoic or phonetically symbolic; apparent examples are *scrawl* vb.[1], *scranch, scrunch, scringe, scroak*.

For other instances in dialects see Wright *Eng. Dial. Gram.* §323, where examples are also given of parallel forms with (sk, k) before a vowel or (w).

scraa, variant of SCRAW.

scrab (skræb), *sb.*[1] *Sc.* and *north.* Also 6 skrab. [Prob. of Scandinavian origin: cf. Sw. dial. *skrabba* of the same meaning, Sw. *scrabba* sea-scorpion.] The crab or wild apple = CRAB *sb.*[2] Also *attrib.*, as ***scrab-apple, scrab-tree.***

1467–8 *Durham Acc. Rolls* (Surtees) 92 Pro ij bus. de Scrabbez emp. pro verius inde fiend., xxij*d.* **1513** DOUGLAS *Æneis* VII. iii. 18 Braid trunschouris dyd thai fyll..Wyth wyld scrabbis and wther frutis large. **1528–9** *Durham Acc. Rolls* (Surtees) 163 Scrabstre medow. **1562** TURNER *Herbal* II. 47 Malus Sylvestris in Englyshe in the Southe countre, a Crab tre, in yͤ North countre a Scrabtre. **1587** *Wills & Inv. N.C.* (Surtees 1860) 157, iiij mells for brusing of skrabbes, 6ᵈ. **1595** DUNCAN *App. Etym.* (E.D.S.), *Vnedo, fructus arbutii,* a scrab-aple. **1894** *Northumbld. Gloss., Scrab-apple.*

†**scrab,** *sb.*[2] *Sc. Obs.* [Cf. SCRUB *sb.*] In plural, 'Stumps of heath or roots' (Jam.).

1768 ROSS *Helenore* I. 20 A hal half mile she had at least to gang, Thro' birns an' pits an' scrabs, and heather lang.

scrab (skræb), *v. Obs.* exc. *dial.* Also 5 skrab. [a. Du. *schrabben*: allied to SCRAPE *v.*]

1. *trans.* To scratch, claw. *lit.* and *fig.*

1481 CAXTON *Reynard* xxxix. (Arb.) 106 Reyner..stode aboue the wynde skrabbing and casting wyth his feet the duste [orig. *boven wijnds staen scrabben in dat slof*]. **1808** W. TAYLOR in *Monthly Mag.* XXVI. 111 The police of the metropolis is already curious..enough: without employing new ferrets to scrab the remaining pleasures out of their skulking-holes. **1823** MOOR *Suffolk Words* s.v., A dog scrabs a rabbit from its burrough. **1880** *Antrim & Down Gloss.* s.v., The cat near scrabbed his eyes out.

2. To snatch, grab.

1890 P. H. EMERSON *Wild Life on Tidal Water* xxiii. 100 When we see them Tom Taylors [i.e. Stormy Petrels] we scrab the nets in quick as we can.

Hence **scrabbed** *ppl. a.*, scratched; also in ***scrabbed eggs*** (see quot.). **'scrabbing** *vbl. sb.*

a **1825** FORBY *Voc. E. Anglia, Scrabbed-eggs,* a lenten dish, composed of eggs boiled hard, chopped and mixed, with a seasoning of butter, salt, and pepper. **1880** S. LAKEMAN *Kaffir-Land* 13 That small garden..was overrun with weeds and scarred with poultry scrabbings. **1890** *Daily News* 20 Nov. 5/1 Small heed was paid in those days to scrabbed face and bleeding hands.

scrabble ('skræb(ə)l), *sb.*[1] [f. SCRABBLE *v.*]

1. A scrawling character in writing, hence, a document composed of such characters. Also, a picture composed of or characterized by careless or hastily-executed line-work.

1842 P. F. TYTLER in Burgon *Mem.* xiv. (1859) 311 Peregrine's letters they could read, but the Duchess of Suffolk..defied them..with her fearful scrabbles. **1862** MISS YONGE *Countess Kate* i, With some peaked scrabbles and round whirls intended for smoke. **1867** SMYTH *Sailor's Word-bk., Scrabble,* a badly written log. **1881** RUSKIN in *19th Cent.* Oct. 517 Yesterday..came to me from the Fine Art Society, a series of twenty black and white scrabbles. **1908** *Athenæum* 11 Apr. 457/2 A composition of some grace, but much of it executed in a scrabble of lines which wants repose.

2. *U.S.* A scramble; a confused struggle, a 'free-for-all'.

1794 *Gazette of U.S.* 21 Feb. 3/2 The Frenchman..in a scrabble swore he would have another hem to his ruffle, and in the very scrabble lost his shirt. **1849** T. T. JOHNSON *Sights in Gold Region* 66 We often got caught by the waves, and had a grand scrabble to reach dry land. **1911** R. D. SAUNDERS *Colonel Todhunter of Missouri* 43 Whoever wins will win after the toughest scrabble you and me ever saw in Missouri politics.

3. The action or sound of scrabbling (SCRABBLE *v.* 2 a).

1894 T. B. ALDRICH *Two Bites at Cherry* 145 The next sound I heard was the scrabble of the animal's four paws as he landed on the gravelled pathway. **1946** D. C. PEATTIE *Road of Naturalist* i. 12, I could not hear her breathing, but I heard another sound... Someone else was trying, with a faint scrabble, to find his way out.

Scrabble ('skræb(ə)l), *sb.*[2] Also scrabble. **a.** The proprietary name of a game in which players use tiles displaying individual letters to form words on a special board.

1950 *Official Gaz.* (U.S. Patent Office) 10 Jan. 334/2 The Production and Marketing Corporation, Newtown, Conn. .. *Scrabble.* For Game including Board and Playing Pieces. Claims use since Dec. 1, 1948. **1953** *New Yorker* 30 May 17/2 We present for your edification the history of Scrabble, the biggest thing in games since Monopoly and maybe the biggest thing ever. *Ibid.* 18/1 It was as if everyone alive were suddenly clamoring to play Scrabble. **1954** *Trade Marks Jrnl.* 21 July 736/1 *Scrabble...* 'Board games.' *Production and Marketing Corporation* (a Corporation organised and existing under the laws of the State of Connecticut, United States of America; Merchants). **1957** T. GIRTIN in *Pick of Punch* 150/1 My suspicions were first aroused while I was losing to my wife at 'Scrabble'. **1959** C. SPRY *Favourite Flowers* iii. 25 For relaxation I sometimes play the spelling game of Scrabble and in consequence am wearing to ribbons the unwieldy volumes of the *Shorter Oxford English Dictionary.* **1962** A. SAMPSON *Anat. of Britain* xxvii. 450 He likes going home early,..and plays bridge or scrabble in the evenings. **1971** C. BONINGTON *Annapurna South Face* ix. 107 After the meal we played liar dice or Scrabble. **1978** J. MATSON *Dear Osborne* xxii. 151 Scrabble, Shove Ha'penny and Draughts indicate the levels of skills and activities.

b. *attrib.* and *Comb.*

1954 *Newsweek* 26 Apr. 57 To help Scrabble fans, crossword-puzzle addicts, and other persons troubled for a word ending in 'x', 'y', or 'z', a 'reverse' dictionary has been compiled at the University of Massachusetts. **1956** N. STREATFEILD *Judith* II. 117 Cynthia sprawled over the Scrabble board. **1960** *Sunday Express* 11 Sept. 6/6, I leave it to Oscar, the Scrabble-playing cat, to dredge up obscure words. **1967** *Sci. Amer.* Sept. 268/1 The Double-Crostic and games of the Scrabble type can be thought of as combinatorial play in which 26 elements (letters) are arranged into sets (words). **1977** B. GARFIELD *Recoil* x. 103 Anna made a word on the Scrabble board and watched him enter the score.

scrabble ('skræb(ə)l), *v.* Also 7 scrable. [a. Du. *schrabbelen* (in sense 2; for sense 1 cf. *schrabbelaar* 'bad writer, scrawler', Verdam), frequentative of *schrabben* SCRAB *v.*]

1. *intr.* To make marks at random; to write in rambling or scrawling characters; to scrawl, scribble.

1537 BIBLE (Matthew's) *1 Sam.* xxi. 13 And he..raued in their handes and scrabled on the dores of the gate. [So **1611.**] **1625** [cf. SCRABBLED *ppl. a.*]. *a* **1628** PRESTON *Serm. bef. His Majestie* (1630) 86 We reckon men mad..when they scrabble vpon the walls. **1854** MISS A. E. BAKER *Northampt. Gloss., Scrabble,* to write in an uncouth and unsightly manner; to make unmeaning marks, as boys often do with chalk on a wall or gate. *a* **1889** in Baring-Gould & Sheppard *Songs of West* (1905) 67 So with his finger dipp'd in blood, He scrabbled on the stones.

b. *trans.* To write or depict (something) in a scrawling manner; also, to scrawl upon (something).

1856 MISS YONGE *Daisy Chain* II. v. (1879) 386, I do scrabble down things that tease me by running in my head, when I want to clear my brains. **1857** H. MILLER *Sch. & Schm.* ii. 21 One of my first attempts at a work of art was to scrabble his initials with my fingers, in red paint, on the house-door. **1883** *Spectator* 5 May 557 Technically the painting is better..though the white ruff of the collie could be improved by being toned down, and not being scrabbled about so much. **1894** *Cornhill Mag.* June 635 The face of the cliff is..scrabbled all over with marks of men's hands making homes for themselves in the living rock.

2. *intr.* Of an animal: To scratch about hurriedly with the claws or paws; hence, of a person, to scratch or scrape about with the hands or feet.

1600 SURFLET *Country Farm* I. xv. 93 Cast out..fresh straw right ouer against the barne, where the pullen vse to scrabble. **1668** J. HOWE *Blessedn. Righteous* xiii. 240 Tis a low, Dunghil spirit; fit for nothing but to rake, and scrabble in the dirt. **1863** WOOD in *Intell. Observ.* IV. 22 The mole.. then scrabbled about until he came upon the rest of the worm. **1896** KIPLING *Seven Seas* 74 Gangs of the prying gull That shriek and scrabble on the river hatches. **1900** ELINOR GLYN *Vis. Elizabeth* (1906) 62 Upon which Victorine looked coy, and began scrabbling with her toes on the parquet.

b. *trans.* To make scratching movements with.

1890 W. H. POLLOCK in *Longm. Mag.* Aug. 406 The parrot ..scrabbled his beak on the edge of his food-can.

3. *intr.* Of a person: To scramble on hands and feet; to stumble or struggle along; *lit.* and *fig.*; also *occas.* of an animal. Now somewhat *rare.*

1638 *2nd Relat. Accidents Wydecombe* 23 Then presently the rest of the people scrabled forth the Church as well as they could. **1666** BUNYAN *Grace Abound.* §198, I did liken myself..unto..a child that was fallen into a mill-pit, who, though it could make some shift to scrabble and sprawl in the water, yet [etc.]. **1678** —— *Pilgr. Progr.* I. 167 Little-faith came to himself, and getting up made shift to scrabble on his way. **1738** *Universal Spectator* 11 Nov. 3/3 The Hog had scrabbled up Stairs, shook the Child out of its blankets, [and] kill'd it. **1742** WESLEY *Extr. Jrnl.* 1 Mar. (1749) 32 The boat..was driven down among the rocks: on one of which we made shift to scrabble up. **1774** J. ADAMS in *Fam. Lett.* (1876) 12 One member of the General Court, he said, as they came down stairs after their dissolution at Salem said to him, 'Though we are killed, we died scrabbling, did not we?' **1812** J. HENRY *Camp. agst. Quebec* 115 Scrabbling out of the cavity, without assistance. **1854** MISS A. E. BAKER *Northampt. Gloss.* s.v., I have hard work to get a living, but I hope I shall manage to scrabble on. **1894** BLACKMORE *Perlycross* xxxvi, A dozen or so of poor creatures,..too tipsy to battle with the wind,..wallowed upon sacks, and scrabbled under the stanchion-boards, where the gaiety [of the Fair] had been. **1900** F. T. BULLEN *Idylls of Sea* 184 The poor possessors of only a four-oared galley hope to rise to the dignity of a lugger, so that they may quit scrabbling along the shores.

4. *trans.* To scratch or rake (something) *up, off, out,* etc. hurriedly; to obtain by scratching or raking about.

1657 BUNYAN *Vindic. Gospel Truths* (1862) II. 203 How dost thou run about the bush, seeking to scrabble up an answer. **1658** F. OSBORNE *Trad. Mem. K. Jas.* 85 The King ..casting himselfe upon the heap scrabled out the quantity of 2 or 3 hundred poundes. **1808** *Sporting Mag.* XXXII. 82 The wool, with part of the skin scrabbled off. **1863** BARING-GOULD *Iceland* 121 The snow had been scrabbled up by the puffed hands in the death agony. **1899** F. T. BULLEN *Way Navy* 95 The trimmers must lie flat and scrabble the coal away as fast as it is pelted down. **1905** E. NESBIT *Amulet* i. in *Strand Mag.* May 587/2 It scrabbled a hasty hole in the sand.

5. *intr.* To struggle or scramble *for* (something).

1698 VANBRUGH *Prov. Wife* III. (1709) 32 That Phantome of Honour, which Men in every Age have so contemn'd, they have thrown it amongst the Women to scrabble for. **1861** C. C. ROBINSON *Dial. Leeds* 399 A generous juvenile 'scrammles' a handful 'o' peis', which are instantly 'scrabbled' for.

scrabbled ('skræb(ə)ld), *ppl. a.* [f. SCRABBLE *v.* + -ED[1].] Inscribed with scrawling characters, written in a scrawling style.

1625 JACKSON *Orig. Unbelief* xlvii. 425 [They] frame such compositions of sacred lines, as men in phrenzie..do out of scrabled walls or painted cloaths. **1857** H. MILLER *Sch. & Schm.* vii. 141 The blank spaces were occupied with deplorably scrabbled couplets. **1880** WEBB *Goethe's Faust* II. iv. 101 A scrabbled parchment, signed and sealed.

†**'scrabblement.** *Obs. rare*[−1]. [f. SCRABBLE *v.* + -MENT.] Writing of a rambling character like that of a madman.

a **1603** T. CARTWRIGHT *Confut. Rhem. N.T.* (1618) 219 Of the departed Saints Patronage, wee reade not, but in the scrablements of the Iesuites.

scrabbling ('skræblɪŋ), *vbl. sb.* [-ING[1].] The action of the vb. SCRABBLE; also, an instance of this.

1582 STANYHURST *Æneis* IV. (Arb.) 116 Al they the like poste haste dyd make, with scarboro scrabbling. **1631** BOLTON *Comf. Affl. Consc.* xiv. (1635) 74 Such..speeches are but as so many catches and scrabblings of a man over head in water. *a* **1650** P. FLETCHER *Father's Test.* (1670) 20 They were suddenly frighted by some noise (perhaps the scrabling of their cat or dog). **1958** *Washington Post* 31 Oct.

A 3/1 The kind of digging, scrabbling and clawing that accomplished the rescue of the 12 who were brought out alive early today. **1974** D. SEARS *Lark in Clear Air* v. 60 I'd never known anything other than hard times. Nor did rough scrabbling impose other than normal conditions on Brulé Township.

scrabe (skreɪb). *Sc.* and *north.* Also 7 **skrabe**, 9 scraib. [a. Da. *scrabe*, ad. Færöese *skrápur*: cf. next.] The Manx Shearwater, *Puffinus anglorum.*

1676 J. S. tr. *Debes' Descr. Færoe* ii. 144 The other eatable Sea Fowls are found in great quantities.., namely the Skrabe [etc.]. *Ibid.* 145 The Skrabe builds..under the Earth, scraping with its Beak and Claws,..whence it is called Skrabe. **1886** *Encycl. Brit.* XXI. 781 *note*, Scraib and Scraber are also used [for the Shearwater] in Scotland.

scraber (ˈskreɪbə(r)). *Sc.* [Of obscure origin; in Gaelic *sgrabair*. Cf. prec.] A name for the Black Guillemot, *Uria Grylle*, and the Manx Shearwater, *Puffinus anglorum.*

1698 M. MARTIN *Voy. St. Kilda* (1749) 30 The Scraber [the black Guillemot, *Uria Grylle*], so called in St. Kilda. **1768** PENNANT *Brit. Zool.* II. 412. **1852** MACGILLIVRAY *Brit. Birds* V. 441 *Puffinus Anglorum.* The Manx Shearwater... Scrabe. Scraber. **1857** F. O. MORRIS *Hist. Brit. Birds* VI. 33 Black Guillemot. Common Scraber.

†**scrabroun.** *Obs. rare*[−1]. [ad. corrupt form (see Diefenbach) of L. *crābrōn-em, crābro* hornet.]

1388 WYCLIF *Exod.* xxiii. 28 And Y schal sende out bifore scrabrouns [1382 stynggynge flies, Vulg. *crabrones*].

scrac(c)h, obs. forms of SCRATCH.

scrae (skre), *sb.*[1] *Sc.* Also **scray, skrae.** [? Subst. use of SCRAE *a.*]

1. A diminutive or skinny person.

1803 JAMIESON in Scott *Minstrelsy* III. 363 [To a crying child], Lie still, ye skrae. **1823** LOCKHART *Reg. Dalton* VII. ii. III. 119 Yon poor shaughlin' in-kneed bit scray of a thing! **1819** W. TENNANT *Papistry Storm'd* (1827) 136 Lean skraes o' men.

2. 'A shrivelled old shoe' (Jam.).

1721 KELLY *Sc. Prov.* 251 Mickle Sorrow comes to the Screa, e'er the Heat come to the Tea [= toe]. Spoken when one holds his Shoe to the Fire to warm his Foot.

scrae (skreɪ), *sb.*[2] *Orkney* and *Shetland.* [a. ON. *skreið* dried fish.] Dried fish. Also *scrae-fish.*

1806 P. NEILL *Tour Orkney & Shetl.* 78 The gables of the cottages here, were..hung round with hundreds of small coalfish,..strung upon spits, and exposed to dry, without salt. The fishes dried in this manner are called scrae-fish.

scrae (skre), *a. Sc.* Also **skrae.** [? a. LG. *schrae, schra, schrade*, etc. (see Grimm s.v. *schrade*) lean, dried up, shrivelled.] Thin, lean. Also *Comb.* **scrae-shanked** *a.*

1822 HOGG *Three Perils of Man* II. vii. 232 The skrae-shankit Laidlaws. **1898** L. E. HAMILTON *Mawkin of the Flow* xviii. 241 This skrae-shankit laddie.

scrae, var. SCREE *Sc.* and *north.*, debris of rock.

scrafis(c)h, -fissh, etc.: see SCRAYFISH.

scrag (skræg), *sb.*[1] Also 6 **skrag, skragge,** 8 **scraig, scragg.** [As the senses are those of the older CRAG *sb.*[2] (and *sb.*[3]), it is probable that this is an alteration of that word, due to some feeling of phonetic expressiveness.

The senses below are placed in the order of their first appearance in our quots.; the order of arrangement in CRAG *sb.*[3] is prob. in accordance with that of development.]

1. A lean person or animal. (In depreciatory use.) Cf. CRAG *sb.*[3] (which occurs only in Udall).

1542 UDALL *Erasm. Apoph.* 270, I feare..yonder same spare slendre skragges and pale salowe coloured whooresoonnes [orig. L. *graciles illos ac pallidos*]. **1582** STANYHURST *Æneis* III. (Arb.) 89 We beheld a windbeaten hard shrimp, With lanck wan visadge,..A meigre leane rake ..When the skrag had marcked [etc.]. *c* **1600** *Lust's Dom.* IV. v, You see I am but a scrag, my Lord; my legs are not of the biggest. **1602** DEKKER *Satirom.* L 4 b, Horace was a goodly Corpulent Gentleman, and not so leane a hollow-cheekt Scrag as thou art. **1608** TOPSELL *Serpents* 66 The elder sort of them are rough, hard, thinne and leane scragges,.. nothing but skinne and bone. *c* **1815** SCOTT in *Lockhart* (1837) III. 379 May be some bird had whispered Daisy [his charger] that I had been to see the grand reviews at Paris on a little scrag of a Cossack, while my own gallant trooper was left behind. **1845** S. JUDD *Margaret* II. v. (1881) 255 We are going to catch every scrag that comes this way from the Pest.

2. The lean and inferior end of a neck of mutton (or veal). Also (earlier) *scrag-end* (also used *transf.*). Cf. *crag-end*, CRAG *sb.*[2] 3.

a **1644** QUARLES *Virgin Widow* v. i, The Devill a bit of meat have I gotten these nine dayes, but once a leane scrag end of a Neck of Mutton. **1728** E. S[MITH] *Compl. Housew.* 29 To dress a Neck of Mutton. Take the best End..and cut it into Stakes..: Take the Scrag-End of the Mutton, break it in pieces [etc.]. **1747** MRS. GLASSE *Cookery* ii. 33 A Leg of Mutton..: Or a fine Neck, with the Scraig cut off. *Ibid.* 35 Shalot-Sauce for a Scraig of Mutton boiled. **1752** FIELDING *Amelia* v. ii, They sat down..to a scrag of mutton and broth. *a* **1754** —— *Fathers* III. i, I may not marry whom I please, but must have crammed down my throat some..scrag end of a woman of quality. **1769** MRS. RAFFALD *Eng. Housekpr.* (1778) 61 Cut a scrag-end of a neck of veal in pieces. *Ibid.* 63 Take a scrag of veal [etc.]. **1771** MRS. HAYWOOD *New Present* 32 Boil the scragg an hour before you put in the other end [of the neck]. **1820** LAMB *Elia* Ser. I. *Christ's Hosp.*, In lieu of..our scanty mutton scrags on Fridays..he had his hot plate of roasted veal. **1837** HOOD *Hymeneal Retrospect.* I. viii, That neck, not a swan could excel it in grace,.. Though now a grave 'kerchief you properly place, To conceal the scrag-end of your charms! **1848** THACKERAY *Bk. Snobs* xix, Lady MacScrew..serves up a scrag-of-mutton on silver. **1874** MRS. H. WOOD *Master of Greylands* xxxi, I could only get the scrag end this morning, aunt: the best end was sold.

3. The neck (of a sheep). Cf. CRAG *sb.*[2] 3.

1842 BISCHOFF *Woollen Manuf.* (1862) II. 384 The scrag or neck should be strong and masculine. **1869** *Daily News* 7 Aug., The judges thought the breed much improved, both in their scrags and general symmetry.

4. *slang.* The neck (of a human being).

[**1756**: ? Implied in SCRAG *v.* 1.] **1829** *Vidocq's Mem.* IV. 266, I adwise you to nose on your pals,..that'll be the best vay To save your scrag. **1847** C. BRONTË *Jane Eyre* xxxvii, I have your little pearl necklace at this moment fastened round my bronze scrag under my cravat. **1857** 'DUCANGE ANGLICUS' *Vulgar Tongue* 43 And you must sport..a yellow wipe tied loosily Round your scrag. **1887** HENLEY *Villon's Straight Tip* 27 Until the squeezer nips your scrag.

5. scrag-whale, a finner-whale of the sub-family *Agaphelinæ*, esp. *Agaphelus gibbosus*, common in the North Atlantic; so also † *scrag-tail whale.*

1701 C. WOLLEY *Jrnl. New York* (1860) 39 A Scrag-tail Whale. **1725** DUDLEY in *Phil. Trans.* XXXIII. 258 The Scrag Whale is near a-kin to the Fin-back, but, instead of a Fin upon his Back, the Ridge of the After-part of his Back is scragged with half a Dozen Knobs or Nuckles. **1835** O. MACY *Hist. Nantucket* I. ii. 28 A whale, of the kind called 'scragg', came into the harbor. **1850** GRAY *Catal. Mammalia Brit. Mus.* I. 18 *Balæna gibbosa.* The Scrag Whale.

scrag (skræg), *sb.*[2] Now chiefly *dial.* [Of obscure origin: cf. SHRAG, SCROG, SHROG *sbs.*]

1. A stump of a tree; also, a rough projection (on a pole, trunk, or stump of a tree, rock, etc.).

1567 TURBERV. *Epit.* etc. 99 b, The sielie Beast to scape the Dogs did iumpe vpon a roote. The rotten scrag it burst, from Cliffe to Seas he fell. **1574** R. SCOT *Hop Garden* 30 It is very necessarie that your Poales be streyght without scrags or knobbes. **1855** CARLYLE *Misc. Ess.* (1857) IV. 346 His wish was,..Only liberty to cut, of scrags and waste wood, what would suffice for his charring-purposes, in those wild forests. **1886** STEVENSON *Kidnapped* xviii. 174 It was a rough part, all hanging stone, and heather, and bit scrags of birchwood. **1890** *Glouc. Gloss.*, *Scrag*, a crooked, forked branch. **1894** BLACKMORE *Perlycross* xvi, He took the springy spar of ash..and getting a good purchase against a scrag of flint, brought the convexity of his pole to bear on the topmost jag of boulder.

2. Rough, rocky and barren ground.

1858 CARLYLE *Fredk. Gt.* VIII. v. II. 359 Friedrich Wilhelm found it scrag and quagmire; and left it what the Tourist sees. *Ibid.* IX. iii. II. 426 Fields grew green again, desolate scrubs and scrags yielding to grass and corn. *Ibid.* XVIII. x. V. 242 Nypern, with its bogs and scrags.

scrag (skræg), *sb.*[3] *slang. rare.* [f. SCRAG *v.*: see sense 1 b, quot. 1897.] In Rugby football, a rough tackle.

1903 WODEHOUSE *Tales of St. Austin's* 105 There's all the difference between a decent tackle and a bally scrag like the one that doubled Tony up.

scrag (skræg), *v.* Chiefly *slang.* [f. SCRAG *sb.*[1]]

1. a. *trans.* To hang (on the gallows).

1756 TOLDERVY *Hist. 2 Orphans* III. 111 Many an honester man than he..has been scragg'd... Scragg'd, said she, is being hung in chains. **1780** R. TOMLINSON *Slang Pastoral* 10 If he does, he'll to Tyburn..be dragg'd, And what kiddy's so rum as to get himself scragg'd. **1827** LYTTON *Pelham* lxxxiii, If he pikes, we shall all be scragged. **1842** BARHAM *Ingol. Leg.* Ser. II. *Dead Drummer*, So Justice was sure,..And the Sergeant, in spite of his 'Gammon', got 'scragg'd'.

b. To wring the neck of; also, to garotte.

1823 'JON BEE' *Dict. Turf* 213 Cock-feeders, when they twist the necks of their dungs, call it scragging them. **1883** W. E. NORRIS *No New Thing* xxv, 'Confound the fellow!' he exclaimed; 'I wish to heaven his mother had scragged him when he was a baby!' **1886** W. H. MALLOCK *Old Order Changes* I. 290 That I might send some minion to meet him and have him scragged on the road. **1897** *Encycl. Sport* I. 429/2 (Football), *Scrag*, (R.) to screw an opponent's neck under the arm in order to induce him to drop the ball.

c. To treat (someone) roughly, to manhandle.

1835 *Sessions Paper of Central Criminal Court* May 87 He did not take him by the collar and shake him—he did not collar him at all till after the blow was struck, nor push him at all—I did not hear Emerson say, 'You b——, I'll *scrag* you.' **1901** *Daily Colonist* (Victoria, B.C.) 31 Oct. 4/3 'What makes the crowd get up and yell?' inquired the fairy maid. 'They've scragged a man, they've scragged a man,' the woolly rooter said. **1938** [see KNOCKING-SHOP]. **1947** N. BALCHIN *Lord, I was Afraid* 52 Before he could say another word they scragged him. **1959** I. & P. OPIE *Lore & Lang. Schoolch.* x. 198 The term 'scragging' is recurrent everywhere, and seems in fact to be different from giving someone a 'beating up' or 'bashing'. One boy makes the distinction: 'To scrag is a more gentle way of having a kind of hurtful revenge. You pull his hair and take his tie off and that sort of thing.' **1969** —— *Children's Games* vii. 219 The first one to get off, gets scragged by the other lads. **1977** H. FAST *Immigrants* III. 193 Now they've scragged me, ruined me, destroyed me.

d. To kill, murder. *U.S.*

1930 D. RUNYON in *Collier's* 20 Dec. 13/4 John the Boss is a very fine character, and it is a terrible blow to many citizens when he is scragged. **1938** —— *Furthermore* iii. 51, I see by the papers where three Brooklyn citizens are scragged. **1950** *Reader's Digest* Nov. 57 If they aim at me they will overshoot or undershoot and scrag some scared civilian.

2. (Not *slang.*) To subject (a spring or suspension system) to scragging (see below). Also with *out*: to shorten the normal length of a spring by (a specified amount) by means of scragging.

Orig. in a different sense (see quot. 1909).

1909 WEBSTER, *Scrag*, Mech., to bend, as spring steel to test it. **1923** T. H. SANDERS *Laminated Springs* xi. 89 That spring would be subjected to probably another $3\frac{1}{2}$ ins. or even 4 ins. test to 'scrag out' the unwanted $\frac{1}{2}$ in. *Ibid.* xxxvii. 396 (*caption*) The finished spring being scragged. **1958** A. D. MERRIMAN *Dict. Metall.* 308/1 The spring is wound somewhat longer than the required length and then scragged by compressing it to closure several times. **1969** *Maxi Workshop Man.* (Brit. Leyland Motor Corp.) x. A7 After fitting a new displacer unit to the front or rear suspension, the system should be scragged by raising the fluid pressure, to above its normal pressure, for a short period. **1972** *Pract. Motorist* Oct. 87/2 If the displacer isn't scragged, it takes up a 'set' with the car's weight upon it —it becomes permanently compressed and the car assumes a list.

3. *Comb.*: **scrag-boy,** the hangman.

17.. in W. *Ireland 60 Years Ago* (1847) 88 De scrag-boy may yet be outwitted.

Hence **ˈscragging** *vbl. sb.*, in senses of the vb.; also *spec.* the process of extending a new spring beyond the desired normal length, and then compressing it, in order to improve its strength and set; an analogous process applied to a hydraulic suspension system in a motor vehicle; also *attrib.* in *scragging-post*, the gallows; **ˈscragger,** the hangman.

1812 J. H. VAUX *Flash Dict.*, *Scragging-post*, the gallows. **1834** H. AINSWORTH *Rookwood* v. i. 383, I wish I was as certain of my reward, as that Turpin will eventually figure at the scragging post. **1837** DICKENS *Pickwick* x, Never mind George Barnwell,..it's always been my opinion, mind you, that the young 'ooman deserved scragging a precious sight more than he did. **1897** P. WARUNG *Old Regime* 213 We're all a-stuffed in 'ere till the scragger comes along for you fellows. **1923** T. H. SANDERS *Laminated Springs* xi. 90 American practice invariably indulges in scragging machines of the 'bull-dozer' type. *Ibid.* xxxvii. 395 An illustration of 'scragging' as carried out in this country is shown by Fig. 201, which shows a 12-plate..spring undergoing its test. **1936** HORNER & SPRAGUE *Dict. Terms Mech. Engin.* (ed. 6) 486 *Scragging*, the process of testing carriage and locomotive springs by impulsive loading. **1949** A. HYND *We are Public Enemies* 79 The Ash Brothers had committed the scragging. **1959** 'M. INNES' *Hare sitting Up* II. iii. 61 We absolutely soaked them with our water jugs, and they gave us a wonderful scragging afterwards. **1969** *Maxi Workshop Man.* (Brit. Leyland Motor Corp.) x. A7 (*heading*) Displacer unit 'scragging'. **1977** R. B. ROSS *Handbk. Metal Treatments & Testing* 338 Scragging... The process is that the spring, when initially formed, is made longer than the design requirements. By applying the necessary compression load, the length of the spring is reduced and at the same time compressive stresses are applied to the surfaces of the spring.

†**scragged,** *a.*[1] *Obs.* Also 6 **skragged.** [? Alteration of CRAGGED. Cf. SCRAG *sb.*[2]] Rough and irregular in outline; of ground, rugged and barren. Also *fig.* Cf. CRAGGED *a.*[1]

1519 HORMAN *Vulg.* 177 Beste hylly grounde is nat that: the whiche is hye vpright, and skragged, but that the whiche is ful of wodde, herbes, and grasse. **1641** MILTON *Ch. Govt.* Concl. 53 The universities..fed with nothing but the scragged and thorny lectures of monkish and miserable sophistry. **1692** BENTLEY *Serm.* viii. §10 (1724) 331 Is there then any physical deformity in the Fabric of a Human Body; because our Imagination can strip it of its Muscles and Skin, and shew us the scragged and knotty Backbone? **1725** [see SCRAG *sb.*[1] 5].

scragged (skrægd), *a.*[2] Also 6 **skregged,** 7 **scregged.** [f. SCRAG *sb.*[1] + -ED[2].] Scraggy.

a **1591** H. SMITH *Serm.* (1592) 1030 Many of vs..after twenty or thirty yeares feeding, are as skregged and leane as we were before. **1607** T. TWINE *Patt. Paineful Advent.* viii. F, Her bodie of comely stature,..not scregged with leanenesse, nor vndecently corpulent. **1684** tr. *Bonet's Merc. Compit.* III. 100 That Noble Person..scragged, as it seems, of a cold and dry temper..was frequently taken with the Colick. **1702** VANBRUGH *False Friend* I, The Handsome, she's all Divinity..; The scragged lean pale Face, has a shape for Destruction. **1800** MRS. HERVEY *Mourtray Fam.* II. 45 That man with the scragged neck.

scraggled (ˈskræg(ə)ld), *ppl. a.* [Formed as next + -ED[1].] Drawn with rough and irregular strokes.

1858 *Sat. Rev.* 20 Nov. 507/1 The hazy and lazy impertinence which asked us to accept a blue blot for a man, and a scraggled scratch for a tree.

scraggling (ˈskræg(ə)lɪŋ), *ppl. a.* [As if f. **scraggle* vb. (f. SCRAG *sb.*[1] and *sb.*[2]) + -ING[2].]

†**1.** Scraggy, meagre. *Obs. rare*[−1].

1616 T. ADAMS *Sacrif. Thankfulness* 20 The Lords Sacrifice must be fatte and faire; not a leane, scraggling, starued Creature.

2. Straggling, irregular in outline or distribution.

a **1722** LISLE *Husb.* (1752) 79 They, by being weak, were forced to plough the ground scragling. **1766** MRS. S. PENNINGTON *Lett.* III. 169 Where scraggling sloes their ebon branches spread. **1854** MISS A. E. BAKER *Northampt. Gloss.*, *Scraggling*, irregular, scattered. Applied principally to a village where the houses are situated irregularly... Also applied to vegetation that grows wild and disorderly. **1870** HAWTHORNE *Eng. Note-bks.* I. 471 The remains [of Hastings Castle] being somewhat scanty and scraggling.

scraggly ('skrægh), *a.* [Formed as prec. + -Y.] Irregular or ragged in growth or form; scraggy. Chiefly *U.S.*

1869 MRS. STOWE *Oldtown Folks* xlii. 534 That's all we scraggly old people are good for. **1879** TOURGEE *Fool's Errand* vii. 26 He had a long scraggly beard. **1892** *Harper's Mag.* Dec. 115/1, I watched her struggling up the.. hillside, passing in and out of sight among the scraggly pines. **1946** C. MCCULLERS *Member of Wedding* II. 57 A street preacher ..was preaching on a corner to a group of warehouse coloured boys and scraggly children. **1959** T. GRIFFITH *Waist-High Culture* (1960) 172 We are like an animal that casts off its skins too quickly; no wonder we look scraggly. **1976** *National Observer* (U.S.) 13 Mar. 12/3 At least I'm not spread-eagled any more in my skivvies and scraggly black socks.

Comb. **1889** MARY E. WILKINS *Far-away Melody* (1890) 28 The walls.. had a scraggly-patterned paper on them.

scraggy ('skrægı), *a.*[1] [f. SCRAG *sb.*[1] + -Y.]

1. Of persons, animals, or their limbs: Lean, thin, bony. Chiefly in depreciatory use.

1611 COTGR., *Cadavreux*,..leane, skraggie, fleshlesse. *Ibid.*, *Rachais*, leane, carrion, scraggie. **1732** ARBUTHNOT *Diet* (1735) 290 A Body hard, dry, scraggy, hairy, warm.. with firm and rigid Muscles [etc.] are Signs of strong, rigid, and elastic Fibres. **1740** RICHARDSON *Pamela* (1824) I. 84 He is a giant of a man for stature;..large-boned and scraggy. **1781** JUSTAMOND *Priv. Life Lewis XV*, II. 133 Her sister, who was thin and scraggy. **1848** THACKERAY *Bk. Snobs* xviii, A bevy of dowagers, stout or scraggy. **1851** MRS. CARLYLE *Lett.* II. 143, I hope the summer will plump out my poor scraggy arms. **1871** L. STEPHEN *Playgr. Eur.* iv. 250 Our party started..in a long procession, mounted on scraggy ponies. **1898** W. WHITE *Jrnls.* 214 There were too many scraggy necks and shoulders.

b. *transf.* and *fig.* Meagre, thin, scanty.

1837 CARLYLE *Misc.* (1857) IV. 64 The scraggiest of prophetic discourses. **1881** *Spectator* 24 Dec. 1654 'Receive me, thy poor Christian..' is very poor and scraggy, when compared to the stately simplicity of..'Recevez-moi' [etc.]. **1897** GLADSTONE *Let.* 25 June, in *Daily News* 30 June 7/2, I thank you for the Newark paper, a contrast with the scraggy sheet which strove to live there in my time.

2. Of meat: Lean. *scraggy end* = scrag-end.

1725 *Bradley's Fam. Dict.* s.v. *Broth*, The scraggy End of a Neck of Mutton. **1871** M. COLLINS *Marq. & Merch.* I. ii. 65 He ate..scraggy chops.

Hence '**scraggily** *adv.*[1]; '**scragginess**[1].

1865 MISS BRADDON *Sir Jasper* i, That general scragginess which distinguishes the arrangements of a gentleman's servants when they are cast upon their own resources. **1867** CARLYLE *Remin.* II. 148, I recollect being thankful (scraggily thankful) for the day of small things. **1869** *Pall Mall Gaz.* 9 Sept. 12 Where..do all the scraggy, bad-fleshed beasts come from..and what is the cause of their scragginess?

scraggy ('skrægı), *a.*[2] [f. SCRAG *sb.*[2] + -Y.

In some applications difficult to distinguish from SCRAGGY *a.*[1]]

Rough, irregular or broken in outline or contour; esp. of rocks, rugged; of a stem or branch, knotted, full or projections; of trees, ragged, stunted or scanty in growth.

1574 R. SCOT *Hop Garden* (1578) 35 If your Poales be scraggye, so as you cannot stryp the stalkes from them. **1686** B. RANDOLPH *Pres. St. Morea* 6 The Walls are high, and their Foundations on scraggy Rocks. **1708** J. PHILIPS *Cider* I. 8 A scraggy Rock, whose Prominence Half overshades the Ocean. **1796** KIRWAN *Elem. Min.* (ed. 2) II. 276 [Black Cobalt ore] Its surface scraggy and botryoidal. **1815** MME. D'ARBLAY *Diary* (1876) IV. lxvi. 365 The walk was immensely long..through the scraggy and hilly streets. **1858** CARLYLE *Fredk. Gt.* IV. ix. II. 21 There is game abundant in the scraggy woodlands. **1859** R. F. BURTON *Centr. Afr.* in *Jrnl. Geog. Soc.* XXIX. 1 The plateaus produce..bush and scraggy thorn. **1886** RUSKIN *Præterita* I. 396 To use a broken scraggy touch for the tops of mountains.

Hence '**scraggily** *adv.*[2]; '**scragginess**[2].

1882 BLACKMORE *Christowell* ii, Within a landyard the lane is jumping scraggily, with ribs of solid rock. **1885** *Harper's Mag.* Jan. 274/1 With their scraggy edges looking the very climax of scragginess.

scraich, scraigh (skrex), *v. Sc.* [Echoic: cf. SCRAUGH, SKREIGH *vbs.*, parallel onomatopœias with different vowels.] *intr.* To utter a harsh cry. So **scraich, scraigh** *sb.*, a harsh cry. (See *Eng. Dial. Dict.* s.v. *Screigh.*)

1785 BURNS *Ep. to Lapraik* i, While..Paitricks scraichan loud at e'en..Inspire my Muse.

scraip, obs. Sc. form of SCRAPE *v.*

scrall, obs. form of SCRAWL, SCROLL.

scram (skræm), *sb.*[1] [Var. SCRAN *sb.*] = SCRAN *sb.* 2.

1831 S. LOVER *Legends & Stories Ireland* 96 Bad scram to you, you thick-headed vagabone. *Ibid.* Gloss. *Bad scram*, bad food. **1881** J. SARGISSON *Joe Scoap* 148 He cot a model eh what he thowt t'shap on't sud be, oot of a lump eh baykin-scram. *a* **1935** [see AID *sb.* 1 b]. **1936** F. CLUNE *Roaming round Darling* xxiv. 246 After unloading flour, spuds, tea, sugar —every kind of scram, we lobbed inside the house.

scram (skræm), *sb.*[2] *Nucl. Physics.* [f. SCRAM *v.*[3]] The rapid shutting down of a nuclear reactor, usu. in an emergency. Freq. *attrib.*

Both this word and SCRAM *v.*[3] are possibly derived from SCRAM *v.*[2]

1953 *Nucleonics* June 40/2 Momentary-contact types [of push button] used to operate..scram circuits. **1955** *Ibid.* Sept. 53/2 Scram is initiated if preset power level is exceeded by 20%. **1959** *New Scientist* 26 Mar. 696/3 The [*Nautilus* submarine] Mark I had a constant plague of 'scrams' from such slight causes as vibration from a crew member's walking through the reactor compartment. **1968** F. KERTESZ *Lang. Nuclear Sci.* (Oak Ridge Nat. Lab. TM 2367) 21 During the experiment that culminated on December 2, 1942 in the accomplishment of the first controlled nuclear chain reaction, a safety rod was held by a rope running through the pile and weighted on the opposite end. The young physicist in charge was told to watch the indicator; if it exceeded a certain value he was to cut the rope and scram. Since then the term *scram* is used to designate the emergency shutdown of a reactor. Today the urgency is lost and the word scram indicates simply a fast-shutdown operation. **1973** D. R. INGLIS *Nuclear Energy* iv. 117 Emergency shutdown or scram equipment must be very sure to function properly.

scram (skræm), *a. s.w. dial.* Also skram. [Cogn. w. SCRAM *v.*[1]] Abnormally small, insignificant-looking, puny. ***scram hand***, a withered hand (Elworthy, *West Som. Gloss.*); hence Comb. ***scram-handed*** adj.

1825 J. JENNINGS *Dial. W. Eng.* 69 *Skram* adj., awkward; stiff, as if benumbed. *Ibid.*, *Skram-handed* adj., having the fingers or joints of the hand in such a state that it can with difficulty be used; an imperfect hand. **1853** PULMAN *Rustic Sk.* (1871) Gloss., *Scram*, small, puny. 'What a scram cheeld!' **1872** HARDY *Greenwood Tree* v, There's sure to be some poor little scram reason for't. **1891** —— *Tess* xxix, I'd ha' knocked him down wi' the rolling-pin—a scram little feller like he!

scram (skræm), *v.*[1] *s.w. dial.* Also 9 **scramb, skram.** [var. of SHRAM *v.*; cf. OE. *scrimman* (once; ? str. vb.) to shrivel, shrink.] *pass.* To be paralysed; to be benumbed (with cold). Also *transf.* of a wheel. Hence '**scrammed** *ppl. a.*

[*c* **1400** *Beryn* 2381 A Crepill..with hondis al for-skramyd.] **1697** R. PIERCE *Bath Mem.* I. x. 235 He..being.. willing to play; but, not having a ready Use of his Lower Parts, could not, but was Scramm'd, drawn up altogether. **1825** J. JENNINGS *Dial. W. Eng.* 69 To *Skram* v. a., to benumb with cold. **1847** HALLIWELL, *Scrambed*, deprived of the use of some limb by a nervous contraction of the muscles. *Somerset.* **1876** HARDY *Ethelberta* xlii, On a frosty winter night he'll keep me there..till my arms be scrammed for want of motion. **1894** BEATRICE WHITBY *Mary Fenwick's Dau.* III. iii. 63 When the engine stops, her wheels get clogged up, and scrambed [with snow].

scram (skræm), *v.*[2] *slang* (orig. *U.S.*). [Prob. abbrev. of SCRAMBLE *v.*; but cf. G. *schramm* imp. sing. of *schrammen* to go, depart, run away.] *intr.* To depart quickly. Freq. *imp.*

1928 W. WINCHELL in *N.Y. Evening Graphic* 4 Oct. 23 His [*sc.* Jack Conway's] popular slang creations include ..'scram', meaning 'git out!' **1933** *Punch* 11 Jan. 29/3 Son, beat ut, d'ya get me?—Gwawn—S-C-R-R-A-M! **1937** D. L. SAYERS *Busman's Honeymoon* iv. 84 Well, I must scram. **1940** N. MITFORD *Pigeon Pie* iv. 75 She gave a sort of shriek ..and scrammed. **1947** D. M. DAVIN *Gorse blooms Pale* 172 You tell her to scram. **1952** J. CANNAN *Body in Beck* vii. 146 'Perhaps you would be good enough to withdraw.'.. Sebastian said, 'He means scram.' **1962** WODEHOUSE *Service with Smile* vii. 97 Go away, boy!' he boomed. 'You mean 'Scram!', don't you, chum?' said George, who liked to get these things right. **1973** A. HUNTER *Gently French* xi. 96 Kindly hook it... I just want you to scram.

scram (skræm), *v.*[3] *Nucl. Physics.* [Etym. unkn., but see note s.v. SCRAM *sb.*[2]] **a.** *trans.* To shut down (a nuclear reactor), usu. in an emergency.

1950 *Amer. Speech* XXV. 27 The point of neutron intensity at which the reactor is 'scrammed'—shut down, automatically or otherwise. **1953** *Nucleonics* Jan. 40/2 The operator is provided with a control console from which he can change the position of rods, switch into automatic control, and scram the reactor. **1959** *New Scientist* 26 Mar. 695/3 A highly sensitive system of eighty different control circuits was designed to anticipate any dangerous instability of the reactor and within a fraction of a second initiate an emergency shutdown, or in the jargon of the nuclear engineer, 'scram' the reactor. **1973** D. R. INGLIS *Nuclear Energy* iv. 95 The current can also be used, when it gets too strong, to trigger the emergency control rods and 'scram' or shut down the reactor. **1975** *Nature* 16 Oct. 526/1 At 1251, the operator decided to shut the reactor down by inserting the control rods into the core, thereby cutting off the chain reaction (in operator's parlance, he manually 'scrammed' the reactor).

b. *intr.* Of a nuclear reactor: to shut down, usu. in an emergency.

1957 *Nucleonics* Feb. 56/3 After a reactor scrams, the question immediately arises: What circuit caused the scram and what happened during shutdown? **1979** *New Scientist* 19 Apr. 174/1 At 2350 lb/sq. in, the reactor automatically 'scrammed' and seconds later the pressure began to drop.

Hence '**scramming** *vbl. sb.*

1958 *Nucleonics* May 64 The entire basis for scramming.. may well need to be re-examined for future power reactors.

scramasax ('skræməsæks). *Antiq.* Also **-saxe,** and in L. form **-saxus.** [a. OFrankish **scrâmasahs* (latinized: 'cum cultris validis, quos vulgus *scramasaxos* vocant', Gregory of Tours, 6th c.), f. **scrâmo* of uncertain meaning + *sahs*: see SAX *sb.*[1]] A large knife used by the Franks in hunting and in war; identified by antiquaries with a particular type of weapon found in Teutonic burial-mounds.

1862 *Proc. Soc. Antiq.* 4 Dec. 163 One of these weapons was the scramasaxus, or knife-shaped sword of the Anglo-Saxons, with one edge. *Ibid.*, Index, Scramasax from Little Hampton. **1870** BLACK tr. *Demmin's Weapons of War* 35 The long dagger or cutlass about twenty inches in length, called a scramasaxe. **1917** W. M. F. PETRIE *Tools & Weapons* v. 27 Examples from Mainz.., termed scramasax, are likewise equal-curved. **1923** C. FOX *Archaeol. Cambridge Region* vi. 301 To the period 950–1066 probably belongs a fine scramasax from Barrington..with damascened blade. **1936** *Antiquity* X. 374 Typological studies of Saxon scramasaxes and spear-heads. **1962** H. R. ELLIS DAVIDSON *Sword in Anglo-Saxon Eng.* 41 Mention may be made of the short dagger or dirk (*scramasax* or *handseax*). *Ibid.* 43 A scramasax from the Thames bears the twenty-eight characters of the runic alphabet. **1977** J. I. M. STEWART *Madonna of Astrolabe* xvii. 243 Although he possessed a mass of material of great archaeological interest and considerable value, the *scramasax* was his only major treasure.

scramble ('skræmb(ə)l), *sb.* [f. SCRAMBLE *v.*]

1. A struggle with others for something or a share of something; hence, an indecorous struggle, a confused or disorderly proceeding.

1674 *Essex Papers* (1892) I. 201 The Truth is, yᵉ Lands of Ireland have bin a meer scramble, & yᵉ least done by way of orderly distribution of them as perhaps hath ever been known. **1687** WOOD *Life* 5 Sept. (O.H.S.) III. 237 His majesty..seeing the people begin to scramble after the victualls..he stood still to see the beginning of the scramble. **1692** R. L'ESTRANGE *Fables* I. ccclxxv. 347 Somebody threw a Handful of Apples among them, that set them presently together by the Ears upon the Scramble. **1745** in *Priv. Lett. Ld. Malmesbury* (1870) I. 21 He declined making purchases in land, that by leaving what he had in money, the scramble might be made the easier among those that came after him. **1788** A. FALCONBRIDGE *Acc. Slave Trade* 33 Sometimes the mode of disposal [of slaves] is that of selling them by what is termed a scramble... The negroes were..placed together in a large yard,..the doors of the yard were suddenly thrown open, and in rushed a considerable number of purchasers ..[who] seized such of the negroes as they could..lay hold of. **1839** CARLYLE *Chartism* iii. (1858) 12 The arrangements of good and ill success in this perplexed scramble of a world. **1839** DK. WELLINGTON *Let.* 12 Nov. in *Croker Papers* (1884), It is probable that Lord Melbourne's Government ..will..give us a better chance of tranquility than a Government formed by a scramble of Tories! **1860** MISS YONGE *Stokesby Secr.* ii. (1880) 191 Lessons were always rather a scramble. **1870** LOWELL *Among my Bks.* Ser. II. (1873) 107 That scramble after undefined and indefinable rights which ends always in despotism. **1907** LD. CURZON *Frontiers* 8 But the scramble for new lands..will become less acute as there is less territory to be absorbed.

2. a. An act of scrambling or struggling progression; a scrambling journey.

1755 JOHNSON, *Scramble*... 2. Act of climbing by the help of the hands. **1851** MAYNE REID *Scalp Hunt.* xli, A scramble of five miles brought us to the eastern end of the valley. **1865** G. MACDONALD *Alex. Forbes* viii, The rats made one frantic scramble and were still. **1873** HALE *In His Name* i, Félicie liked nothing better than a brisk scramble to the top.

b. A motor-cycle race across rough and hilly ground.

1926 in H. Golding *Wonder Bk. of Motors* 177 Such races as the 'T.T.' and the various other Trials and 'Scrambles' organized by the larger clubs afford manufacturers an opportunity of submitting their machines..to..severe tests. **1935** *Encycl. Sports* 539/2 *Scramble*, form of motor-cycle trial in which the competitors..traverse a course marked out over moorland or heath... Among a certain section of motor cyclists scramble events are very popular. **1959** *New Statesman* 14 Nov. 658/1 About 50,000 people now turn out every week to watch the dozen or so scrambles organised throughout the country. **1969** *Daily Tel.* 25 Oct. 8/8 A scramble can best be described as a motorised form of a cross-country race over a short, rough course sometimes reserved for the purpose and often adjacent to a road-racing circuit. **1977** 'E. CRISPIN' *Glimpses of Moon* xi. 213 The motor-cycle scramble had arrived.

c. *Mil. slang.* A rapid or operational take-off by a group of aircraft. Cf. sense 4 of the vb.

1940 G. BARCLAY *Diary* 2 Sept. in *Fighter Pilot* (1976) 44, I came on the state after this scrap and we had three scrambles. [**1954** I. JONES *Tiger Squadron* xxii. 228 To Sailor's dismay, his scramble order had not been received quickly enough.] **1957** G. WALLACE *R.A.F. Biggin Hill* xi. 139 Three scrambles a day were common, often more. **1963** *Times* 11 June 7/1 The royal visitors watched a 'scramble' of four R.A.F. Vulcan bombers of the quick-reaction alert force. **1969** P. RICHEY *Fighter Pilot* p. xii, He wanted to publish it if I would finish it. I did so..in the evenings after a day spent instructing on fighters in Gloucestershire and, later, between 'scrambles' and fighter sweeps. **1976** *Derbyshire Times* (Peak ed.) 3 Sept. 24/4 Featured in the spectacular flying display will be a scramble (operational take-off) by a pair of Vulcan bombers.

d. *U.S. Football.* An impromptu movement by a quarterback to evade tacklers. Cf. sense 1 d of the vb.

1971 TARKENTON & YATES *Broken Patterns* 52 Naturally the scramble plays were the most spectacular. **1972** J. MOSEDALE *Football* vi. 89 A man who played as though he invented the scramble.

3. *Cookery.* A dish composed of hastily-mixed ingredients; an informal meal of such dishes. Cf. SCRAMBLING *ppl. a.* 1.

1893 YONGE & COLERIDGE *Strolling Players* xxii. 187 Selva's Irish hospitality could allow no one to depart in the rain, and her Irish happy-go-luckiness saw nothing to be ashamed of in a scramble. **1898** J. D. BRAYSHAW *Slum Silhouettes* 42 Some of the ladies of the district, deeming the short cut to a poor man's soul was through his vitals, invited them to a free 'muffin scramble'. **1938** E. WAUGH *Scoop* I. i. 18 The recipe for a dish named 'Waffle Scramble'. **1958** *Woman's Own* 17 Sept. 15/1 Halve the rolls... Fill with the tuna scramble.

4. *Comb.*, as **scramble net** *Naut.*, a heavy net down which persons may climb from a ship in an emergency; also in *gen.* use, the webbing of a child's climbing frame.

1944 *Amer. Speech* XIX. 106 The *scramble net* (a new term in this war; it is an oversize cargo net hung over the side in times of imminent peril as an aid to getting down to water level without breaking your back). **1948** A. BARON *From City from Plough* 134 Sailors pulled at cords and the wet scramble nets thumped over the sides. **1953** *Physical Educ. in Primary School* (Min. of Educ.) II. vi. 32 (*caption*) Infants using a scramble net which is supported on a fixed tubular metal frame. **1976** *Outdoor Living* (N.Z.) I. II. 49 (*caption*) Other attachments, such as a scramble net could be put on the frame as children outgrow the present equipment. **1979** 'G. BLACK' *Night Run from Java* xiii. 162 The patrol boat crew [was] going down the scramble net into the lifeboat.

scramble ('skræmb(ə)l), *v.* [Of obscure origin; first recorded late in the 16th c. Cf. dial. *scramb*, *scrame* 'to pull or take together with the hands' (Hutton *Tour to Caves*, ed. 2, 1781), also SCRAWM, SCAMBLE, and CRAMBLE *vbs.*]

1. a. *intr.* To raise oneself to an erect posture, to get through or into a place or position, by the struggling use of the hands and feet; hence, to make one's way by clambering, crawling, jumping, etc. over difficult ground or through obstructions. Cf. SCAMBLE *v.* 4.

a **1586** SIDNEY *Arcadia* II. (Sommer) 221 The cowardly wretch fell down, crying for succour, & (scrambling through the legs of them that were about him) gat to the throne. *Ibid.* III. 320 But Amphialus scrambled vp againe. **1614** J. TAYLOR (Water P.) *Water-worke* Ded., But if you will not assist me, I will attend the next hightide, & scramble vp into Pauls Church-yard. **1619** FLETCHER *M. Thomas* I. iii, *Dor*... I know she loves him. *Alice*. Yes, and will not lose him, Unless he leap into the Moon,..And then she'l scramble too. **1622** MABBE tr. *Aleman's Guzman d'Alf.* I. 132 My Master & my Mistrisse..scrambled (as well as they could) to bed [after a drinking-bout]. **1687** A. LOVELL tr. *Thevenot's Trav.* II. 67 We..then scrambled up a very high and steep hill. **1740** CIBBER *Apol.* (1756) I. 52 In this alarm our troops scrambled to arms. **1772** PENNANT *Tours in Scot.* (1774) 339 The height was taken by a little boy, who scrambled to the top. **1837** W. IRVING *Capt. Bonneville* II. 117 Sometimes they scrambled from rock to rock, up the bed of some mountain stream. **1842** TENNYSON *St. Simeon* 181, I hardly, with slow steps,..and much exceeding pain, Have scrambled past those pits of fire. **1855** BROWNING *Fra Lippo* 65 There was a ladder! Down I let myself, Hands and feet, scrambling somehow. **1877** OWEN *Desp. Wellington* p. xxvi, Lake's..over-confident attempts to scramble into Bhurtpore without proper appliances.

b. *transf.* and *fig.*

1670 G. H. *Hist. Cardinals* II. III. 180 Girolamo Farnese ..has made a shift, without any Foreign assistance, to scramble into several Honours. **1785** COWPER *Tiroc.* 125 Lisping our syllables, we scramble next, Through moral narrative, or sacred text. **1863** COWDEN CLARKE *Shaks. Char.* xvi. 411 He is a fellow who will scramble through the world with a light heart. **1879** MISS BRADDON *Vixen* i, He had only time to scramble through a hurried toilet. **1900** ELINOR GLYN *Vis. Elizabeth* (1906) 93, I had not even scrambled into my clothes when the clock struck five.

quasi-*refl.* (with *complement*). **1815** JANE AUSTEN *Emma* iii, A..boarding-school,..where girls might be sent to be out of the way, and scramble themselves into a little education.

c. *trans.* To collect or gather *up* hastily or in disorder; also, to cause (a crowd) to move in hurried confusion. Also (freq. with advbs.), to cause (something) to move in the direction or manner indicated without proper control; to deal with hastily or ill-advisedly.

1822 M. A. KELTY *Osmond* I. 214 She had scrambled the boy's nine-pins into a bag. **1833** T. HOOK *Love & Pride* xi, He hastily scrambled up the papers. **1853** LYTTON *My Novel* VIII. v, Juliet, scrambling up her hair, darted into the house. **1859** SALA *Gaslight & D.* xxix. 339 These poor wretches have been scrambling and scraping their passage-money together for months. **1869** *Punch* 3 July 270/2 One 'Lord Hamilton' who had been scrambling away his money, at a low public in Shadwell. **1898** *Westm. Gaz.* 9 Nov. 7/1 There is no earthly reason for rushing and scrambling the crowds into tight-fitting places. **1911** *Q. Rev.* July 218 Amendments hastily scrambled through committee in a House of Commons. **1931** *Times* 28 Feb. 4 The putter scrambled the ball in from a foot away. **1976** *Oadby & Wigston* (Leics.) *Advertiser* 26 Nov. 15/1 His shot hit the bar, and eventually Snee and his defence scrambled the ball free.

d. *intr. U.S. Football.* (See quot. 1976.)

1964 *Birmingham* (Alabama) *News* 26 Oct. 20/1 Campbell had to scramble to get off passes to Jimmy Martin, Scotty Long or Ronnie Baynes. **1968** *N.Y. Times* 13 Aug. 31 It was Tarkenton who engineered this monumental upheaval, mainly because he bewildered the Packers with his scrambling. **1976** *Webster's Sports Dict.* 373/2 *Scramble*,.. of a football quarterback, to run around behind the line of scrimmage dodging would-be tacklers after initial pass protection has broken down before passing or running.

2. a. *intr.* To strive or struggle with others for mastery; to contend with a crowd for a share of food, coin, wealth, etc. Cf. SCAMBLE *v.* 1.

c **1590** A. GORGES *Let. to R. Cecil* in P. F. Tytler *Life Raleigh* (1833) 132 At the first I was ready to break with laughing to see them two scramble and brawl like madmen. **1603** KNOLLES *Hist. Turks* (1621) 1289 Many of them, in scrambling for the money that was cast abroad,..having their hands and fingers cut off. **1637** MILTON *Lycidas* 116 Of other care they little reck'ning make, Then how to scramble at the shearers feast, And shove away the worthy bidden guest. **1692** RAY *Creation* II. (ed. 2) 56 Had we wanted this Member [*sc.* the hand] in our Bodies, we must have lived.. without any Artificial..Meats; but must have scrambled with the wild Beasts for Crabs and Nuts. **1696** BROOKHOUSE *Temple Opened* 33 The Servants of God were not left to scramble for their Livings. **1722** WOLLASTON *Relig. Nat.* ix. 205 When we are got out [into the world], and left to scramble for ourselves, how many hardships and tricks are put upon us. **1790** BURKE *Fr. Rev.* Wks. 1808 V. 77 Which exposed their sure inheritance to be scrambled for and torn to pieces by every wild litigious spirit. **1848** W. H. KELLY tr. *L. Blanc's Hist. Ten Y.* II. 549 Princes..were seen scrambling for lucre with footmen and prostitutes. **1862** LADY DUFF-GORDON in F. Galton *Vac. Tourists* (1864) 163 He..amused himself by making the little blackies scramble for halfpence in the pools left in the bed of the river.

b. *trans.* To contend or struggle with others for (a share of something distributed); hence, to seize rapaciously or unscrupulously.

1647 R. STAPYLTON *Juvenal* 5 A little basket now before the doore They set forth, to be scrambled by the poore. **1654** H. L'ESTRANGE *Chas. I* (1655) 126 His [the king's] revocation..of such things as had been depredated and scrambled away from the Crown in his Father's minority. **1656** OSBORN *Adv. Son* 27 The meanest; who have the impudence to scramble up any thing that suits to their advantage.

c. To scatter (money, etc.) to be scrambled for.

1851 MAYHEW *Lond. Labour* II. 563/2 And then they scrambles money between us. **1875** *New Q. Rev.* Oct. 202 A fairy princess,..who scrambles the diamonds to the crowd.

3. a. To cook (eggs) in the manner called 'scrambled'.

1864 in WEBSTER. **1903** *Munsey's Mag.* XXIX. 247 She scrambled eggs and bacon, and ate them.

b. *fig.* To jumble or muddle (something).

1927 G. ADE et al. *Let.* 4 Mar. (1973) 118 When you are in the native quarter [of Algiers] you can well imagine you are in the Old Testament which has been scrambled, stood on edge and saturated with all the disagreeable odors in the world. **1950** *Times Lit. Suppl.* 27 Jan. 55/4 The characters have been 'scrambled' so that none shall be recognizable. **1962** *Listener* 5 Apr. 603/1 The different arts are being run together and the borders of art and nature are being scrambled. **1977** *Time* 10 Jan. 43/1 Their landing permits had been deliberately scrambled by the Cuban government in league with the Nazis, who wanted the ship to sail from port to port searching for asylum.

c. To make (a telephone or radio signal of a voice) unintelligible by means of a scrambler (see SCRAMBLER 3 a); to render (a television transmission) usable only by a subscriber equipped with a suitable unscrambling device. Also *transf.* and *absol.*

1927 *Gen. Electr. Rev.* XXX. 84/2 A Hammond multiplex system may be used with seven intermediate carrier waves which are scrambled and sent out by a single transmitter and then unscrambled at the receiving station so that each controls one of the seven light beams. **1929** *Times* 9 Nov. 12/2 An improved means for ensuring the secrecy of radio-telephonic conversations by 'scrambling' the words of the message—that is, by changing high frequencies to low frequencies and *vice versa*, so that the conversation is completely unintelligible until the 'inverted' conversation has been retranslated. **1949** F. MACLEAN *Eastern Approaches* III. xii. 445 When we resumed our conversation [on the telephone], the Prime Minister was off on a new tack. 'Shall we scramble?' he said gaily. I replied that I thought I was scrambled. **1955** *Times* 4 June 6/6 All three work on the principle of a device attached to the subscriber's television set which 'scrambles' the programmes to be televised until a fee is paid to unscramble them. **1959** E. H. CLEMENTS *High Tension* v. 74, I was beginning to wonder..whether we ought to scramble the telephone. **1978** G. GREENE *Human Factor* II. iv. 89 There was the usual confusion: one of them pressing the right button too soon and then going back to normal transmission just when the other scrambled.

4. *Mil. slang.* **a.** *intr.* Of an aircraft (as a fighter plane, etc.) or crew: to effect a rapid take-off; to become airborne quickly. orig. *R.A.F.*

1940 G. BARCLAY *Diary* 2 Sept. in *Fighter Pilot* (1976) 44 The squadron scrambled and intercepted some Do215s and Me110s. **1941** [see ANGEL *v.* 2]. **1942** BRENNAN & HESSELYN *Spitfires over Malta* 15 The signal to scramble came at about eleven o'clock... We rushed to our aircraft and in less than two minutes were off the ground. **1944** *Daily Tel.* 15 May 5/3 Hardly were they past the carrier than two Corsairs 'scrambled' off the deck to 'intercept an enemy plane'. **1952** *Times* 22 Feb. 6/4 A red Very light was fired as a warning to the pilots to 'scramble', and exactly 80 seconds later the first fighter was in the air. **1962** R. W. CLARK *Rise of Boffins* ii. 53 Another great time-saver was the use of a code for passing instructions to the fighters, and such R.A.F. terms as 'scramble' (for take-off)..were invented during these experiments [on radar interception, 1936]. **1977** *R.A.F. News* 5–18 Jan. 1/1 A Wessex SAR helicopter of 22 Squadron's E flight was scrambling from Manston.

b. *trans.* To cause (an aircraft) to become airborne quickly.

1940 G. BARCLAY *Diary* 3 Sept. in *Fighter Pilot* (1976) 46 The squadron was off the ground which was the main thing, but they were scrambled too late to intercept. **1953** *Sun* (Baltimore) 18 Sept. 2/2 Col. Richard T. Hernlund.. showed reporters he could 'scramble' the interceptors and get them into the air almost instantly. **1971** *Daily Tel.* 20 July 8/7 The final decision to scramble fighters or launch nuclear missiles is..made by..highly trained officers. **1975** *Radio Times* 14 Aug. 38/1 A call to the coastguard and the nearest rescue helicopter can be scrambled within seconds. **1978** R. V. JONES *Most Secret War* xli. 383 It was clear that their technique was to 'scramble' their fighters on a raid warning and instruct them to orbit one of a number of visual and radio beacons. **1981** *Times* 9 June 6/8 The Iraqis..gave no indication whether Iraqi jet fighters had been scrambled in an attempt to shoot down the Israeli planes.

5. *Comb.*, as **scramble button**, a button which activates a scrambler (sense 3 a) when pressed.

1962 L. DEIGHTON *Ipcress File* xxx. 194 The wall phone rang... I saw Jay push the 'scramble' button.

scrambled ('skræmb(ə)ld), *ppl. a.* [f. SCRAMBLE *v.* + -ED[1].]

a. In the senses of the verb.

1609 ARMIN *Maid of More-Cl.* G j b, Ha, what scrambled ends heape vp confusedly? **1873** BLACK *Pr. Thule* xviii, The scrambled dinners in the small cabin. **1930** *Daily Express* 6 Sept. 4/6 A series of mixed or 'scrambled' wave lengths, the key to which would only be in the possession of individual subscribers to the television service. **1949** *Jrnl. R. Aeronaut. Soc.* LIII. 29/1 Subjected to the rapid change of temperature when simulating 'scrambled take-offs'. **1951** *Good Housek. Home Encycl.* 170/2 Pack..loosely rolled or 'scrambled' sheets of newspaper..over the surface. **1962** L. DEIGHTON *Ipcress File* xi. 70, I will want to use a phone in private—a scrambled line if possible. **1975** J. I. M. STEWART *Gaudy* xii. 218, I pictured Mogridge..in some high-powered but unobtrusive car—one equipped, no doubt, with telephonic devices enabling him to hold scrambled conversations with various quarters of the globe as he went along.

b. ***scrambled egg***(s), (*a*) a dish of eggs broken into the pan and fried with milk, butter, salt, and pepper. Cf. SCRABBED *ppl. a.*

1864 SALA in *Daily Tel.* 9 Feb., 'Here you,' he cried ..'bring me..some scrambled eggs'. **1897** M. L. HUGHES *Mediterr. Fever* v. 192 In the later stages eggs lightly poached or scrambled may safely be used.

(*b*) fig., the gold braid or insignia worn on an officer's dress uniform (esp. the cap); hence by metonymy, an officer. *slang* (chiefly *Forces*').

1943 C. H. WARD-JACKSON *It's Piece of Cake* 52 *Scrambled egg*,..an officer of the rank of Group Captain or above. *Ibid.* 53 *Scrambled eggs*, the gold braid or oak leaves on the peak of the dress service cap of an officer of the rank of Group Captain or above. **1946** J. BATTEN *Dirty Little Collier* iv. 32 Most collier men hate their 'scrambled egg' caps, and won't wear them at all. **1958** M. DICKENS *Man Overboard* iv. 60, I don't care about the scrambled egg, but it may be a bit tough at first, not being an officer. **1961** C. BROOKE-ROSE *Middlemen* i. 7 A blue-grey uniform with three rings round his wrist. Then four. Then a big broad one and scrambled eggs. **1968** J. LOCK *Lady Policeman* ix. 84 The car drivers.. don't know which one to obey..being intimidated by all that scrambled egg on their caps. **1973** R. DOUGALL *In & Out of Box* xiii. 157 An older pilot with some 'scrambled-egg' on his cap was produced. **1978** *Detroit Free Press* 5 Mar. (Parade Suppl.) 14A/4 (Advt.), Capture the soaring spirit of American history—proud cap has smart military styling with golden 'scrambled eggs' & braid trim hand-sewn on the visor.

'scramblement. *nonce-wd.* [f. SCRAMBLE *v.* + -MENT.] The action or an act of scrambling.

1747 MRS. DELANY *Life & Corr.* (1861) II. 481 After the dinner is over the common people are let in to carry off all that remains..; you may imagine what a notable scramblement it occasions.

scrambler ('skræmblə(r)). [f. SCRAMBLE *v.* + -ER[1].]

I. 1. One who scrambles. (Cf. SCAMBLER.)

1687 WOOD *Life* 5 Sept. (O.H.S.) III. 237 Dr. Derham.. was here noted for a scrambler, being in his scarlet, so notorious that they flung things in his face. **1716** ADDISON *Freeholder* No. 40 ¶1 All the little scramblers after fame fall upon him, publish every blot in his life [etc.]. **1806** W. TAYLOR in *Ann. Rev.* IV. 251 Nature..proportions the multiplication of the people to their comforts, and thus provides an everlasting supply of scramblers for subsistence. **1861** *Sat. Rev.* 7 Sept. 236 A scramble for sovereigns..would be sure to attract plenty of scramblers. **1871** L. STEPHEN *Playgr. Eur.* xiii. (1894) 337 The mountaineer..is not a mere scrambler. **1954** M. CONNOLLY *Power Tennis* 66 Many times I have seen a scrambler unnerve a much better player merely by returning her best placements. **1958** *Oxford Mail* 27 Aug. 4/9 Most of Britain's leading motor-cycle scramblers will be at Brill on October 5. **1961** *Times* 29 Apr. 3/2 Can it be that his consummate skill as a scrambler is beginning to weigh on him? **1967** *Time* 17 Mar. 55 He is known in the trade as a 'scrambler', who would just as soon run as throw, who can turn a potential 10-yd. loss into a 50-yd. gain. **1972** J. MOSEDALE *Football* vi. 86 Quarterbacks usually identified as scramblers got that reputation because they had to run after inept teammates failed to block for them.

II. That which scrambles. **2.** A plant, often a climbing one, depending on the support of others.

1902 L. H. BAILEY *Cycl. Amer. Hort.* IV. 1935/2 There are many useful climbers among the scramblers. **1953** *Brit. Commonwealth Forest Terminol.* (Empire Forestry Assoc.) I. 116 Scrambler. A plant which, owing to lack of rigidity in its stem, and absence of special climbing organs, uses other vegetation as its support. **1974** *Country Life* 21 Mar. 642/3 This large-flowered scrambler [*sc.* a Cretan Aristolochia] is probably not very hardy.

3. a. An electronic device used, esp. in telephony and radio, to make speech signals unintelligible, usu. by dividing the signal into distinct frequency ranges which are separately inverted and displaced in frequency.

1950 G. HACKFORTH-JONES *Worst Enemy* i. 24 This line, which linked me directly with the Rear-Admiral, was fitted with a device known as a 'scrambler' which was completely secure against listening in and it was therefore possible to speak freely and at length at all times. **1968** *New Scientist* 19 Dec. 657/3 A simple scrambler that will turn high speech frequencies into low speech frequencies and vice versa can be bought for about £100. **1973** 'I. DRUMMOND' *Jaws of Watchdog* ii. 31 The radio..had a scrambler, so that if the message was picked up accidentally it sounded like static. *a* **1974** R. CROSSMAN *Diaries* (1975) I. 41 Having made a big fuss about national security to George Wigg I have decided to be extremely careful in everything I do personally so I've had scramblers and big safes installed in London as well as here at Prescote. **1981** A. MELVILLE-ROSS *Tightrope* vi. 36

You can get me..the Minister's Private Secretary..on the scrambler.

fig. **1958** *Listener* 13 Nov. 791/3 Your work of art..has to suffer a further change as it goes through the scrambler of your reader's prejudices.

b. *attrib.*, as ***scrambler line, phone, system, telephone.***

1958 L. DURRELL *Balthazar* ii. 29 His work was invisibly dictated by a scrambler telephone. **1958** *Listener* 25 Sept. 462/2 It is a variant of the scrambler system which has been long in use for confidential telephonic communication. **1965** *Times* 16 Feb. 12/2 The 'scrambler' telephone can now be bought for £50 by individual companies. **1966** J. BINGHAM *Double Agent* xi. 162 He lifted the scrambler telephone... 'A scrambled phone is safe, but not entirely safe.' **1974** G. MARKSTEIN *Cooler* lxviii. 234 He..made a call on the scrambler line to London. **1975** 'M. SINCLAIR' *Long Time Sleeping* ix. 115 Pringle..switched on the scrambler phone and started writing. **1977** C. FORBES *Avalanche Express* II. xi. 118 Scholten took the call on his scrambler phone.

scrambling ('skræmblɪŋ), *vbl. sb.* [-ING[1].]

a. The action of the vb. SCRAMBLE; an instance of this.

1598 CHAPMAN *Achilles Shield* Ded., His [Virgil's] skirmishes are but meere scramblings of boyes to Homers. **1641** MILTON *Ch. Discipl.* I. 9 The Bishops, when they see him tottering, will leave him, and fall to scrambling, catch who may, hee a Patriarch-dome, and another what comes next hand. **1792** BARLOW *Constit. of 1791*, 13 Money.. creates a perpetual scrambling for power. **1819** BYRON *Juan* II. cvii, At last, with swimming, wading, scrambling, he Roll'd on the beach, half senseless. **1888** GARNETT *Emerson* ii. 86 An age was impending of selfish scrambling and shameless manœuvring. **1908** M. M. HARPER *Rambles in Galloway* vii. 109 We were amply repaid for all our scramblings and genuflexions by the extent and beauty of the prospect. **1930** *Engineering* 14 Nov. 626/1 The apparatus used for this scrambling, as it is called, is installed at the Central Telegraph Office. **1942** V. E. R. BLUNT *Use of Air Power* viii. 72 Wireless telegraphy and radio telephony..by 'scrambling' can now be made secret. **1955** 'N. SHUTE' *Requiem for Wren* 166 We were in the process of scrambling when the Jerries came over. **1959** *New Statesman* 14 Nov. 658/1 The simplest definition of scrambling is: the racing of motor bikes over rough ground. **1978** *Guardian Weekly* 24 Sept. 22/5 Scrambling, as distinct from fell walking and rock climbing, is a Cinderella of a sport.

b. *attrib.*, as ***scrambling club, -ground, -place***; **scrambling net** *Mil.* = *scramble net* s.v. SCRAMBLE *sb.* 4; also *transf.*

1961 *Guardian* 17 Mar. 3/3 Motor-cycle scrambling clubs. **1974** G. MOFFAT *Corpse Road* iv. 64 She belonged to a scrambling club, which means walking... It doesn't mean rock climbing. **1884** *Pall Mall Gaz.* 2 Feb. 1/1 The Soudan flung away to be the scrambling-ground of the piratical adventurers of the world. **1959** *New Scientist* 30 July 125/1 Home grown seeds are extracted from cones, sometimes collected by means of a 'scrambling net'..thrown over a tall tree. **1964** C. WILLOCK *Enormous Zoo* v. 75 The long-forgotten sensation of climbing down the scrambling net of a troop transport into a landing craft. **1973** A. ROSS *Dunfermline Affair* 36 The scrambling net which the *Hermione* put over her side. **1878** E. JENKINS *Haverholme* 49 He..protested against making the House of Commons a mere scrambling place for office.

scrambling ('skræmblɪŋ), *ppl. a.* [f. SCRAMBLE *v.* + -ING[2]. Cf. SCAMBLING *ppl. a.*]

1. Of persons: That scramble or contend one with another. Also applied to a meal at which the partakers help themselves to what they can get.

1607 BEAUMONT *Woman Hater* III. iv, Farewell my fellow Courtiers all, with whome, I haue of yore made many a scrambling meale In corners, behind Arasses, on staires. **1697** DRYDEN *Virg. Past.* VIII. 42 Scatter thy Nuts among the scrambling Boys. **1831** JANE PORTER *Sir E. Seaward's Narr.* III. 17 We enjoyed our scrambling meal infinitely more than we did our dinner yesterday. **1834** HT. MARTINEAU *Moral* II. 52 To be divided..among a scrambling multitude.

2. Irregular or rambling in form or habit. Of a plant: Of straggling or rambling growth.

1688 HOLME *Armoury* II. 86/2 Scrambling Trees are such as grow confusedly wide and spreading, and will not be kept in order. **1826** SCOTT *Woodstock* xxi, A huge old scrambling bed-room. **1830** LINDLEY *Nat. Syst. Bot.* 46 Shrubs, having sometimes a scrambling habit. **1851** *Florist* 228 Scrambling Roses, to be pegged down during their season of growth, do not make the kind of effect in beds that one could wish. **1863** PRIOR *Plant-n.* 200 Scrambling Rocket.

b. Of a person: Shambling, uncouth.

1765 COWPER *Lett.* 14 Sept., I am upon good terms with ..five families, besides two or three odd scrambling fellows like myself. **1821** SCOTT *Kenilw.* x, What should such an ill-favoured, scrambling urchin do at court?

3. Irregular, unmethodical.

1778 PR. FREDERICK in *Buccleuch MSS.* (Hist. MSS. Comm.) I. 417 There had been a scrambling fight between Admiral Biron and Monsieur Destin. **1780** *Newgate Cal.* V. 196 The ceremony was a business of so scrambling and shabby a nature, that she could as safely swear she was *not*, as that she *was* married. **1795** NELSON 29 July in Nicolas *Disp.* (1845) II. 64 The scrambling distant fire was a farce. **1829** CARLYLE *Misc.* (1857) II. 45 Their too purblind, scrambling controversies. **1878** STUBBS *Mediæval & Mod. Hist.* vii. 137 Peter [of Blois] seems to have led a scrambling sort of literary existence. **1893** G. TREGARTHEN *Austral. Commw.* 244 The scrambling, and inefficient administration of the law.

Hence '**scramblingly** *adv.*

1653 BLITHE *Eng. Improv. Impr.* (ed. 3) To Husbandman, Half or one third part of so much land as many of you Till, shall..yeeld you as much corn as all that great quantity scramblingly husbanded. **1923** D. H. LAWRENCE *Ladybird* 242 For some time..Alexander gingerly and scramblingly led the way. The slope of ice was steeper, and rounded, so that it was difficult to stand up. **1949** D. L. SAYERS tr. *Dante's Inferno* XXIV. 221, I..came Scramblingly up and sat down.

scrambly ('skræmblɪ), *a.* [f. SCRAMBLE *sb.* + -Y[1].] **1.** Of a person, limb, etc.: that scrambles, clambers, or claws. Also applied to an informal meal. Cf. SCRAMBLING *ppl. a.* 1.

In quot. 1900 applied to a jumble of people at a meal. **1900** R. PROCTOR *Dairy* 26 Mar. in V. Scholderer *Fifty Ess. 15th- & 16th-Cent. Bibliogr.* (1966) 34 A company of about 16... A most amusing scrambly supper in a room calculated to hold four at most. **1943** C. MCCULLERS in *Harper's Bazaar* Aug. 140/3 The hunchback reached in the box with his scrambly little fingers. **1977** *Time* 5 Dec. 49/1 Little scrambly front legs and big thumping back legs.

2. Characterized by scrambling or clambering over rough terrain; that necessitates such action.

1900 G. BELL *Let.* 28 Feb. (1927) I. v. 65 We had a very scrambly walk back. **1932** A. CHRISTIE *Peril at End House* ii. 34 There's a scrambly cliff path down to the sea.

scramjet ('skræmdʒɛt). *Aeronaut.* [f. the initial letters of *s*upersonic *c*ombustion + RAMJET.] A ramjet in which combustion takes place in a stream of gas moving at supersonic speed.

1966 *New Scientist* 19 May 429 (*caption*) Supersonic combustion ramjets ('scramjets') theoretically could extend flight speeds to at least Mach 14. **1972** D. G. SHEPHERD *Aerospace Propulsion* iv. 110 There is considerable interest in supersonic combustion as this is the key to the scramjet.

scran (skræn), *sb. slang* and *dial.* Also **skran.** [Of obscure origin; the coincidence with mod.Icel. *skran* rubbish, odds and ends (Björn Haldorson, 18th c.) is prob. accidental.]

†**1.** (See quot. 1725.) *Obs.*

1724 in *Bacchus & Venus, Collect. Canting Songs* (1737) N 2, E'er for the Scran he had tipt the Cole. **1725** *New Cant. Dict.*, *Scran*, a Reckoning at a Boozing-ken.

2. a. A collection of eatables; provisions for a slight repast or picnic; a portion of food carried by a labourer into the field for a meal. Also *spec.* in *Naut. slang*, food, rations. ***cold scran***, cold refreshment. **b.** Broken victuals; rarely, scraps of butchers' meat.

1808 JAMIESON s.v. *Skran*, 1. *Fine skran*, a phrase used by young people when they meet with any thing, especially what is edible, which they consider as a valuable acquisition, S. 2. The offals or refuse of human food, thrown to dogs, Loth. **1826–30** T. WILSON *Pitman's Pay* I. lxxxi. (1843) 14 Se weel she ettles what aw get..That nyen can say we.. want for owther claes or scran. **1851** MAYHEW *Lond. Labour* I. 418 Most of the lodging-house keepers buy the 'scran' (broken victuals) of the cadgers. **1857** 'DUCANGE ANGLICUS' *Vulgar Tongue, Scran*, food. Thieves. **1859** *Hotten's Slang Dict., Scran*, pieces of meat, broken victuals. **1887** *Kent Gloss., Scran*, a snack of food; the refreshment that labourers take with them into the fields. *a* **1892** MILLIKEN *'Arry Ballads* 3 But to cart you off sudden to Chawbaconshire and cold scran... I call it 'ard lines. **1916** 'TAFFRAIL' *Pincher Martin* i. 8 Them two's on watch now, but they'll be down at eight bells clamourin' for their scran like a lot o' wolves. *a* **1935** T. E. LAWRENCE *Mint* (1955) 135 'Scran up!' he called in his sailor's belling tone against my ear. **1974** *Sentinel* (Ottawa) X. II. 6/3 He's the chief cook on board, responsible for the preparation and serving of food—or 'scran', according to the hands—to 280 hungry mouths about three times a day.

3. Phrase. ***bad scran to*** —— ! = 'bad luck to'. Chiefly *Anglo-Irish.*

1841 LEVER *Charles O'Malley* lxxxv, Bad scram [*sic*] to me if I wouldn't marry you out of a face this blessed morning just as soon as I'd look at ye. **1867** KENNEDY *Banks Boro* xxv. 190 But bad scran to the note they'd give me back.

4. (From the verb.) The action of collecting broken victuals.

1864 *Hotten's Slang Dict.* (1865) s.v. *Scran*, Scranning or 'out on the scran', begging for broken victuals.

5. *Comb.*: **scran bag**, (*a*) a cadger's receptacle for broken victuals; (*b*) a soldier's haversack; (*c*) a receptacle for impounded articles negligently left lying about the deck by sailors; hence **scran-bag** *v.*, to impound (such articles); **scran-pock** *Sc.* (see quot.); **scran wallet** *Sc.* = *scran-bag* (*a*).

1855 [Burn] *Autobiog. Beggar-boy* 17 Your professional pickpocket looks down with contempt upon a knight of the *scranbag. **1864** *Hotten's Slang Dict.* 222 *Scran bag*, a soldier's Haversack. **1898** *Tit-Bits* 26 Mar. 493/3 The 'scran-bag' as the sailors term it, is the receptacle for all loose articles of clothing, &c., which are left about the ship by the men. **1903** L. YEXLEY in G. T. Wilson *Log of H.M.S. Phaeton* p. i, The Scran Bag. **1899** F. T. BULLEN *Way Navy* 20 We came to the cells, and, lo! the only prisoner was a 'bike', '*scran-bagged' and awaiting ransom by its owner. **1825** JAMIESON Suppl., **Skran-pock*. 1. A beggar's wallet.. Loth. 2. A bag meant for receiving the spoil or plunder of the dead who may have fallen in battle, when it is gathered by the women who follow the army. S.O. The term was thus explained, at the time of the trial of the Radicals at Falkirk, A. 1819. **1861** QUINN *Heather Lintie* (1863) 192 Regardless o' '*scran-wallat' watchers, Or vile nefarious beggar catchers.

scran (skræn), *v.* [f. SCRAN *sb.*]

1. *slang.* **a.** *trans.* To provide with 'scran' or food. **b.** *intr.* To collect scran or broken victuals.

c **1742** in Hone *Every-day Bk.* (1827) II. 527 Tickets to be had for three Megs a Carcass to scran their Pannum-Boxes. **1839** in 'Ducange Anglicus' *Vulgar Tongue* (1857) 33 *Scranning*, begging. [Peculiar to the Scotch.] **1859** *Hotten's Slang Dict., Scranning*, begging for broken victuals.

2. *Sc. trans.* and *intr.* (See quots.)

1825 JAMIESON, Suppl., To *Skran*, to make a promiscuous collection of things in whatever way, either by fair or by foul means, Edin. **1867** W. GREGOR *Banffsh. Gloss., Skran*, to gain; to gather; to catch; as, 'Fin we're at the Heilan fishan, we're eye skrannin' something'.

scranch (skrɔːnʃ), *sb. dial.* [f. SCRANCH *v.*] A 'scranching' noise or sound.

1881 T. E. BROWN *Fo'c's'le Yarns* 188 It [*sc.* the storm] come With a rip and a roar,..Rip-rip-rip—you know the scranch of it.

scranch (skrɔːnʃ), *v. Obs.* exc. *dial.* Also **scraunch.** [App. an onomatopœic formation, related to CRANCH *v.* (which is slightly later in our quots.); cf. *crunch, scrunch* vbs., and SCR- 2.

Mod.Du. and LG. have a vb. of similar form and sense: *schransen* to eat heartily, in 16th c. (Kilian) *schrantsen*, 'mandere, dentibus frangere', W. Flem. *schranzen* to crunch, chew noisily.]

1. *trans.* = CRUNCH *v.* 1.

1620 SHELTON *Quixote* II. xiii. 78 Sancho fell to, without inuitation, and champed his bits in the darke, as if he had scraunched knotted cordes. **1658** ROWLAND *Moufet's Theat. Ins.* 983 Locusts..have teeth..with which they easily eat ears of corn, and scranch them with a great noise. **1672** MARVELL *Reh. Transp.* I. 84 [He] epicurizes upon burning Coals, drinks healths in scalding Brimstone, scraunches the Glasses for his Desart. **1706** PHILLIPS (ed. Kersey), To *Scranch*, to crunch, crack, or break any hard thing between the Teeth. **1707** *Curios. in Husb. & Gard.* 72 We see the Swine scranching the Acorns. **1712** STEELE *Spect.* No. 431 ¶3, I then took a strange Hankering to Coals; I fell to scranching 'em. **1755** JOHNSON, To *Scranch*, To grind somewhat crackling between the teeth. The Scots retain it. **1785** [R. GRAVES] *Eugenius* I. vi. 35 Flora..scranching her apple. **1823** MOOR *Suffolk Words, Skranch*, the act of chewing or munching any thing that sounds short under the tooth, green apples, raw carrots, hard biscuits, &c. 'How 'a dew skransh em'. **1894** *Northumb. Gloss., Scranch, scrunch*, to grind with a crackling noise between the teeth.

2. = CRUNCH *v.* 2.

1845 JUDD *Margaret* I. xvii. (1874) 158 A troop of boys and girls..were coming up the hill, goring and scranching the crust [of the snow] with their iron corks. **1853** G. J. CAYLEY *Las Alforjas* I. 261 [It] broke, being scranched in my pocket, when I fell off pony-back.

Hence '**scranching** *vbl. sb.* and *ppl. a.*

1846 W. SANDYS [Jan Treenoodle] *Spec. Cornish Dial.* 38 (E.D.D.) Apples ripe for scranching. **1854** MISS A. E. BAKER *Northampt. Gloss.* s.v. *Scraunch*, A bow drawn in, an awkward, unskilful manner across a violin makes a scraunching noise.

scranky ('skræŋkɪ), *a. Sc.* and *north.* Also **sk-.** [Cf. Norw. *skrank* lean, large-boned figure (Ross); ? cogn. w. SHRINK *v.*] Lean, slender, scraggy.

17.. RAMSAY *Addr. Thanks* xiv, Ye lads of little rent, Wha ..did lament Your purses being skranky. **1826** J. WILSON *Noct. Ambr.* Wks. 1855 I. 289 The skranky ancle bespeaks skranky neck and bosom. **1835** M. SCOTT *Cruise Midge* xiv, It was a desolate-looking place..lumbered..with several skranky leathern-backed Spanish chairs. **1882** J. WALKER *Sc. Poems* 114 Poor devils, scranky as the kitchen tongs.

scrannel ('skrænəl), *a.* [Cf. Norw. *skran* lean, shrivelled.] **a.** Thin, meagre. Now chiefly as a reminiscence of Milton's use, usually with the sense: Harsh, unmelodious.

1637 MILTON *Lycidas* 124 Their lean and flashy songs Grate on their scrannel Pipes of wretched straw. **1667** H. MORE *Div. Dial.* II. xviii. (1713) 145 As lank and scrannel as a Calf that sucks his Dam through an hurdle. **1788** ANNA SEWARD *Lett.* (1811) II. 92 His voice has a scrannel tone. **1858** G. MACDONALD *Phantastes* xvii. 209 Voices like those of children in volume, but scrannel and harsh as those of decrepit age. **1862** SMILES *Engineers* III. 20 Time..which he spent in birdsnesting, making whistles out of reeds and scrannel straws [etc.]. **1868** BROWNING *Ring & Bk.* VI. 1000 Now from the stone lungs sighed the scrannel voice. **1889** *Antiquary* Nov. 196 It would have..made the scrannel list of honest men show thinner still in history. **1908** DOBSON *De Libris* 191 In this cash-cradled Age, We grate our scrannel Musick. **1927** E. F. BENSON *Lucia in London* ii. 60 It was strange..to hear..the foe of all modern music.. producing these scrannel staccato tinklings that had so often made her wince. **1934** [see MIMSEY *a.*]. **1951** AUDEN *Nones* (1952) 54 His scrannel music-making. **1976** *New Yorker* 1 Mar. 89/1 But the music Berlioz heard in St. Peter's was scrannel stuff, and it was years before he himself received the commissions to compose.

b. *Comb.*: **scrannel-piping**, the use of a 'scrannel pipe'.

1831 CARLYLE *Sartor Res.* III. x, A kind of infinite, unsufferable, Jew's-harping and scrannel-piping.

scranny ('skrænɪ), *a.*[1] Chiefly *dial.* [Cf. SCRANNEL.] Lean, thin. Of diet: Poor, meagre.

1820 CLARE *Rural Life* (ed. 2) 89 Want! thy confinement makes me scranny. **1820** SHELLEY *Œd. Tyr.* I. 268 *Rat*... Creeping thro' crevice, and chink, and cranny, With my snaky tail, and my sides so scranny. **1867** E. WAUGH *Owd Blanket* iii. 71 Hard work..an' poor scranny livin'.

scranny ('skrænɪ), *a.*[2] *dial.* Crazy, wild, 'silly'.

1858 BAILEY *Age* 178 The people must go scranny once a year. **1862** J. C. JEAFFRESON *Bk. Doctors* xxiii. 259 His niece's scranny lover. **1886** *S.W. Linc. Gloss.* s.v., Oh, dear! I'm well nigh scranny. The bairns are fit to drive one scranny.

scrap (skræp), *sb.*[1] Forms: 4–7 scrappe, 8 *Sc.* scrape, 6– scrap. [a. ON. *skrap* scraps, trifles

(Sw. *skrap*, Da. *skrab*), f. root of *skrapa* SCRAPE *v.*]

1. *pl.* The remains of a meal; fragments (of food); broken meat. *rare* in *sing.* Also *fig.*

1387 TREVISA *Higden* (Rolls) I. 15 ȝif I miȝte gadre somwhat of þe crommes þat falleþ of lordes bordes... And also ȝif I myȝt gadre eny scrappes of þe releef of þe twelf cupes. **1526** *Pilgr. Perf.* (W. de W. 1531) 151, I shall in generall, gather certayne scrappes & crommes that holy doctours hath left behynde them in wrytynge. *c* **1550** CHEKE *Matt* xv. 27 For yᵉ whelpes eat of yᵉ scrappes yᵗ fal from yeer Mʳˢ. table. **1588** SHAKS. *L.L.L.* v. i. 40 They haue beene at a great feast of Languages, and stolne the scraps. **1610** ROWLANDS *Martin Mark-all* E 3, *The muggill will tip you fat scraps and glorious bits*, the Beadle will well bumbast you. **1612** BACON *Ess.*, *Of Judicature* (Arb.) 456 Those that ingage Courts in quarrels of Iurisdiction,..for their own scrappes and aduantage. **1621** BURTON *Anat. Mel.* I. ii. IV. vi. 207 He drinks water, and liue's of wort leaues, pulse, like a hog, or scraps like a dog. **1690** LOCKE *Hum. Und.* Ep. to Rdr., He who has raised himself above the alms-basket, and not content to live lazily on scraps of begged opinions, sets his own thoughts on work to find and follow truth. **1718** POPE *Odyss.* XVII. 259 'Twas but for scraps he ask'd. **1768–74** TUCKER *Lt. Nat.* I. 239 Feeding them only with delusive expectations and stale scraps of enjoyment. **1810** CRABBE *Borough* xiii. Wks. 1834 III. 221 Scraping they lived but not a scrap they gave. **1856** MACAULAY *Johnson* Misc. Writ. 1860 II. 274 He appeased the rage of hunger with some scraps of broken meat. **1859** GEO. ELIOT *Adam Bede* xxi, He brought out of the pantry a dish of scraps [for a dog].

2. A remnant; a small detached piece; a piece very small by comparison with the whole; a fragmentary portion. Often with negative context = (not) the least piece. **a.** (*a*) Of material things.

1583 STUBBES *Anat. Abus.* II. 39 Neuer so little scraps or shreds or short ends of lace. **1682** BUNYAN *Holy War* (1905) 261 If Mansoul come to be mine, I shall not..consent that there should be the least scrap, shred, or dust of Diabolus left behind. **1726** SWIFT *Gulliver* III. ii, Like the scraps of paper fastened by school-boys at the end of the string that holds their kite. **1761** GRAY *Let. J. Brown* 24 Sept, Then I got a scrap of supper, and..walked home. **1819** SCOTT *Ivanhoe* xxxvi, As she passed through the crowd,..a scrap of paper was thrust into her hand. **1837** HT. MARTINEAU *Soc. Amer.* II. 27 Not a scrap of meat, or an ounce of biscuit, was left on board. **1878** BLACK *Green Past.* xxix, Without a scrap of jewellery either round her neck or on her hands.

(*b*) ***scrap of paper***: applied contemptuously to a document containing a treaty or pledge which one does not intend to honour.

The phrase is said to have been used by the German Chancellor, Bethmann-Hollweg (1856–1921), in connection with German violation of Belgian neutrality in August 1914 (cf. G. *ein Fetzen Papier*). Some later examples allude to this.

1840 *Chambers's Edin. Jrnl.* 11 Apr. 94/1 He no more dreamt of..honouring his scraps of paper..than of paying the national debt. **1914** E. GOSCHEN *Let.* 8 Aug. in *Coll. Diplomatic Documents rel. Outbreak Europ. War* (1915) 111 The Chancellor said that..just for a word—'neutrality',—just for a scrap of paper Great Britain was going to make war on a kindred nation. **1918** *Daily Mail Year Bk. 1919* 62/1 Those familiar with the 'scrap of paper' theory need hardly be told that the pledges given by the German Emperor.. were not observed. **1932** K. CAMPBELL *Sarah, Duchess of Marlborough* 83 James made it plainer every day..that, compared with his Church, the constitution of England and his own coronation oaths were mere scraps of paper. **1954** W. K. HANCOCK *Country & Calling* iv. 111 The British Empire, not so many years back, had professed itself to be at war with the doctrine that a treaty was only 'a scrap of paper'. **1974** M. GILBERT *Flash Point* vi. 50 The First World War was fought over a small thing. A scrap of paper. **1980** *Times* 3 July 17/2 The Treaty of Union..wasn't a sacrosanct document, but in empirically English fact, just a 'scrap of paper'.

b. Of immaterial things, conversation, literary compositions, etc.

1607 MARSTON *What you will* II. i, A horse, a horse, my kingdom for a horse, Looke the I speake play scrappes. **1693** LOCKE *Educ.* § 166. 209 Languages are to be learn'd only by reading, and talking, and not by scraps of Authors got by Heart. **1700** CONGREVE *Way of World* I. v, He is a Fool with a good Memory, and some few Scraps of other Folks Wit. **1711** STEELE *Spect.* No. 96 ¶2, I..was forced to get what Scraps of Learning I could by my own Industry. **1728** WODROW *Corr.* (1843) III. 359 My Lord Grange took up the debate,..in a very distinct discourse, which I cannot pretend to resume; it's but scrapes I can give. **1767** WESLEY *Jrnl.* 17 July, In my scraps of time..I read over that..poem. **1847** TENNYSON *Princess* II. 353 Follow'd then A classic lecture,..With scraps of thundrous Epic lilted out By violet-hooded Doctors. **1868** FREEMAN *Norm. Conq.* II. App. 613 There is not a scrap of evidence in support of it. **1879** MᶜCARTHY *Own Times* II. xxix. 400 He could turn to account every scrap of knowledge..which he happened to possess. **1888** BURGON *12 Gd. Men* I. i. 22 The following note..is almost the only scrap of his early private correspondence which has reached me.

c. A small picture, cutting, etc. to be put in a SCRAP-BOOK or used for ornamenting a screen, box, or the like.

1880 *N. & Q.* Ser. VI. II. 212/1 Having mounted many scraps of many kinds, including photos, I have found nothing so good as a..solution of gum arabic.

d. A small person. *colloq.*

1898 H. JAMES *Two Magics* 60 'Perhaps she likes it!' 'Likes *such* things—a scrap of an infant!' **1928** E. P. OPPENHEIM *Chron. Melhampton* v. 146, I wasn't here for long, and I was a scrap of a fellow those days. **1939** N. STREATFEILD *Luke* 109, I didn't know the poor little scrap could look so radiant. **1958** *Woman's Jrnl.* Mar. 77/2 'The woman?'.. 'They picked her up late last night. Poor little scrap.'

3. *pl.* **a.** The pieces of blubber, fish, etc. remaining after the oil has been extracted. Also *collect. sing.* **b.** (See quot. 1823.) *dial.*

Cf. the synonymous CRAP *sb.*¹ 3.

1631 E. PELHAM *Gods Power* 22 The Frittars or Graves of the Whale. *marg. note.* These be the Scraps of the Fat of the Whale, which are flung away after the Oyle is gotten out of it. **1823** MOOR *Suffolk Words*, *Scraps*,..the small pieces of fat pork remaining after the operation of boiling for the purpose of extracting the lard. **1839** T. BEALE *Sperm Whale* 187 The crisp membranous parts after the oil is extracted, and which are called by whalers 'scraps', serving for fuel. **1878** L. MADDOCKS *Menhaden Fish. Maine* 32 The article bears the same name when bought and sold as material for the superphosphate manufacturers, being called *green* or *dry* scrap, according to the moisture contained. **1879** G. B. GOODE *Catal. Anim. Resources U.S.* 187 Oil-factory scraps. Fish-scraps. **1898** F. T. BULLEN *Cruise Cachalot* iii. (1900) 18 The fires were fed with 'scrap'.

4. *Founding.* **a.** *pl.* Remnants of metal produced in cutting up or casting. **b.** = SCRAP-IRON.

a. 1790 KEIR in *Phil. Trans.* LXXX. 367 In cutting out the rolled plated metal into pieces of the required forms and sizes, there are many shreds, or scraps as they are called, unfit for any purpose but the recovery of the metals by separating them from each other. **1891** *Labour Commission Gloss.* s.v., When the bottom of a puddling furnace requires renewing, malleable scrap-iron is put in and burned up till the bottom is covered with a coating of silica. This operation is termed 'putting scraps on'.

b. 1846 GREENER *Gun* 136 'Twopenny' or 'Wednesbury skelp'..is made of an inferior scrap. **1890** W. J. GORDON *Foundry* 109 The pigs are to form the bath in which wrought iron and steel scrap is to be melted.

5. *attrib.* quasi-*adj.* Consisting of scraps.

1815 *Gentl. Mag.* LXXXV. II. 540/1 The scrap-knowledge of musick is immethodically made up of second-hand quotations. **1890** W. J. GORDON *Foundry* 14 Nine tons and more of mild scrap steel. **1902** *Daily Chron.* 4 Jan. 6/6 While two women..were digging for scrap coal into a disused railway embankment.

6. *attrib.* and *Comb.*, as ***scrap dealer***, ***dealing***, ***gatherer***, ***merchant***, ***-metal***; **scrap basket**, a waste-paper basket; **scrap-box**, a receptacle for scrap-iron; **scrap-cake**, (*a*) *dial.* (see quot. 1877); (*b*) the solidified residuum of tried-out fat; (*c*) refuse of fish, etc.; **scrap dinner**, a makeshift dinner; **scrap-furnace**, one for melting scrap-iron; **scrap-ground** = *scrapyard* below; **scrap-hopper**, a trough used in trying out blubber; **scrap man**, one whose business is the collection and sale of scrap-metal and its salvageable accessories; **scrap-monger**, one who deals in (literary) scraps; **scrap paper**, paper that may be repulped or used again; rough paper for casual jotting; **scrap-pie**, a pie consisting of scraps or remains of meals; **scrap pudding** (see quot.); **scrap screen** chiefly *Hist.*, a screen or divider (as in a nursery) decorated with scraps (sense 2 c); **scrapyard**, the site of a scrap-heap; *spec.* a place where disused motor vehicles, etc., are scrapped. Also SCRAP-BOOK, -HEAP, -IRON.

1872 C. M. YONGE *P's & Q's* ix. 94 If she put it in the *scrap basket, Persis herself might look in and see the writing. **1912** E. POUND *Let.* Dec. (1971) 13, I won't quarrel with you over what you see fit to put in the scrap basket. **1858** GREENER *Gunnery* 15 If they could return and see their handiwork consigned to the *scrap-box as old iron. **1877** *Holderness Gloss.*, *Scrap-keeaks, cakes made of dough mixed with scraps of fat or dripping. **1879** *U.S. Comm. Fish & Fisheries* V. 174 This cheese or scrap-cake is ground to different degrees of fineness. **1976** *Loughborough Monitor* 26 Nov., He had worked as a *scrap dealer while claiming supplementary benefit. **1977** *Belfast Tel.* 22 Feb. 4/1 (*caption*) For *scrap dealing..two heads better than one. **1776** in *Archives of Maryland* XI. 96 Will it be agreeable to the Governor and yourself to take a *Scrap Dinner with me tomorrow. **1824** MISS MITFORD *Village* Ser. I. 182 Mr. Sidney always came unseasonably... So sure as we had a scrap dinner, so sure came he. **1861** FAIRBAIRN *Iron* 89 Balling and *scrap furnaces. **1586** T. B. *La Primaud. Fr. Acad.* I. 136 Parasites and *scrap-gatherers at free-cost feasts. **1927** *Observer* 21 Aug. 19/2 Six years is about the maximum age of the cars taken for scrapping in America. Some reach the *scrap-ground much earlier. **1879** G. B. GOODE *Catal. Anim. Resources U.S.* 175 *Scrap-hopper. **1927** *Observer* 21 Aug. 19/2 The *scrap man's interest in these vehicles is purely that of a replacement part merchant. **1977** *Custom Car* Nov. 5/1 When it comes to fridge pumps, beware. The scrapman is out to con you. **1978** R. V. JONES *Most Secret War* i. 5 It certainly was tough, the future of my contemporaries encompassing everything from barrow boy to millionaire *scrapmerchant and trade union peer. **1941** *Proc. Prehist. Soc.* VII. 130 The Bronze Age pieces must be ..*scrap-metal. **1962** A. BATTERSBY *Guide to Stock Control* 3 The petty cash box resembles the scrap-metal example in reverse. **1786** WOLCOT (P. Pindar) *Ep. Boswell* 23 Thou, curious *scrapmonger, shalt live in song When Death hath still'd the rattle of thy tongue. **1885** *Encycl. Brit.* XVIII. 228/2 The materials for the commoner classes of work are old waste and scrap paper, repulped... For very delicate relief ornaments, a pulp of *scrap paper is prepared. **1960** M. SPARK *Bachelors* xi. 195 Marlene walked solemnly downstairs and demanded some scrap paper from the hall porter. **1969** C. IRVING *Fake!* (1970) iii. 39 He..made some preliminary sketches for several hours on scrap paper. **1829** CAROLINE BOWLES (Mrs. Southey) *Chapters on Churchyards* II. i. 23 Just as the 'young gentlemen' had risen from their Saturday's commons of *scrap-pie and stick-jaw. **1876** J. PAYN *Halves* xii, 'Scrap pie' and unattractive cutlets. **1886** *W. Somerset Word-bk.*, *Scrap pudding, a pudding made by mixing flour with the small pieces of meat left after the fat of a pig has been melted down to lard. **1873** *Young Englishwoman* Jan. 51/3 Lizzie would be glad if the Editor could give her any information as to making a *scrap screen. **1899** M. BEERBOHM *More* 173 They will make the scrap-screen their background. **1962** N. MARSH *Hand in Glove* v. 148 The room was masked from its entrance by an old-fashioned scrap screen. **1964** S. NOWELL-SMITH *Edwardian England* iv. 201 The dark, cosy Victorian nursery.. brightened by the varnished scrap-screen. **1963** *Times* 11 Jan. 10/3 (*heading*) Tow breaks on way to *scrapyard. **1978** T. ALLBEURY *Lantern Network* iv. 59 A scrapyard with big double gates.

scrap (skræp), *sb.*² *slang.* Also 8–9 scrapp.

†**1.** (See quots. 1725, 1809.) *Obs.*

1679–80 C. HATTON in *H. Corr.* (Camden) 217 The factious personns of his gange,..now mightily commiserat him, as if his accusation wase only to carry on yᵉ pretended Presbiterian plot; for in truth they are in great feare Sʳ Robᵗ. Payton shou'd bring them into yᵉ scrappe. **1725** *New Cant. Dict.*, *Scrap*, a Design, a purpos'd Villainy, a vile Intention; also a perpetrated Roguery: *He whiddles the whole Scrap*; He discovers all he knows. **1809** G. ANDREWES *Dict. Slang*, *Scrapp*, a villainous scheme.

2. a. A struggle, scrimmage, tussle; a boxing-match. Also *gen.*, a contest.

1846 *Swell's Night Guide* 75 By way of varying the slang, the mock combat turns into a right good scrap. **1874** [see SCRAP *v.*²]. **1885** G. DOLBY *Dickens* iv. 102 Papers, which he threw carelessly amongst a group of passengers to be scrambled for—producing an effect more resembling a 'scrap' in a game of football than the action of a lot of sober citizens. **1905** *Century Mag.* Aug. 485/1 A suggestion to match the two coxswains..for a 'feather-weight scrap'. **1916** [see BANDBOX c]. **1959** [see GO *sb.* 4 b]. **1973** *Times* 10 Dec. 9/5 In a final that provided a keen scrap rather than a match of high quality, they beat the Etonians. **1977** J. CLEARY *High Road to China* v. 158 My chaps..[are] itching for a scrap, y'know.

b. A contest of words; a row, quarrel, squabble; a heated discussion.

1890 BARRÈRE & LELAND *Dict. Slang* II. 210/1 Having a *scrap up* is having a quarrel, a row. **1900** *Dialect Notes* II. 57 *Scrap*,..a quarrel of words, sometimes good-natured. **1903** *N.Y. Tribune* 6 Sept. 2/2 In directing the proceedings..Mr. Hill was careful to sidetrack anything containing the germ of a 'scrap'. **1928** J. GALSWORTHY *Swan Song* II. xi. 199 It was his impression that they'd been having a scrap.

scrap (skræp), *v.*¹ *dial.* [var. of SCRAB *v.*] *intr.* (See quot. 1895.)

c **1475** *Cath. Angl.* 324/2 (MS. Addit.), To Scrappe as a hen dose, *ruspare.* **1895** *E. Angl. Gloss.*, *Scrap*, to scratch in the earth; as a dog or other animal having that propensity.

scrap (skræp), *v.*² *slang.* [f. SCRAP *sb.*²]

a. *intr.* To fight, box. Also, to scrimmage.

1874 *Hotten's Slang Dict.* 280 *Scrap*, to fight. Also used as a substantive. **1891** *Anthony's Photogr. Bull.* IV. 137 Look ..at the football picture opposite; note the two quarter backs, scrapping with each other in friendly combat.

b. *trans.* To box with (an opponent). Also *fig.*

1893 P. H. EMERSON *Signor Lippo* xvii. 83, I could put up my dooks, so I was backed to scrap a cove bigger nor me. **1936** L. C. DOUGLAS *White Banners* xvi. 335, I have given him until June first to scrap it out with himself.

c. *intr.* To quarrel, squabble; to engage in heated argument or angry dispute.

1895 W. C. GORE in *Inlander* Nov. 65 *Scrap*,..to quarrel. **1900** *Dialect Notes* II. 57 *Scrap*,..to quarrel, sometimes good-naturedly. **1923** *Daily Mail* 28 June 5 Are you going on scrapping over this garden fence for the rest of your lives? **1941** B. SCHULBERG *What makes Sammy Run?* vii. 120 The play..was one of those things about two red-blooded guys who are always scrapping and loving each other.

scrap (skræp), *v.*³ [f. SCRAP *sb.*¹]

1. *trans.* To break up into scrap-iron (machinery or ironwork which has become worn out or superseded); to consign to the scrap-heap. Also *fig.*

1902 *Daily Chron.* 27 Oct. 8/4 The Americans would 'scrap' it [*sc.* a machine] at once if they discovered that something better had got on the market. **1904** G. B. SHAW *Comm. Sense Municipal Trading* 41 Private enterprise..will not start a new system until it is forced to scrap the old one. **1906** *Morning Post* 6 July 6/6 A clause which will have to be 'scrapped'. **1908** *Sat. Rev.* 11 July 38/1 The policy of.. building fast small cruisers while scrapping numerous vessels of older type.

2. To make scrap or refuse of (menhaden or blubber).

1891 in *Century Dict.*

scrapable ('skreɪpəb(ə)l), *a.* [f. SCRAPE *v.* + -ABLE.] Capable of being scraped.

1840 CAROLINE FOX *Old Friends* (1882) 71 [A picture] which, upon examination, he found scrapable; he scraped, and developed a Coreggio.

'scrap-book. [f. SCRAP *sb.*¹]

a. A blank book in which pictures, newspaper cuttings, and the like are pasted for preservation. Hence occas. as the title of a printed book of miscellaneous contents.

1825 (*title*) The Scrap Book, or a selection of..anecdotes. **1854** THACKERAY *Leech's Pict.* (1869) 328 Great swollen scrap-books,..full of the comic prints of grandpapa's time. **1881** LANG *Library* 2 An assortment of broadsheet ballads and scrapbooks, bought in boyhood, was the nucleus of Scott's library.

b. *transf.* A loosely-constructed documentary review programme, normally covering a particular year or period, presented on radio by the B.B.C.

1933 *Radio Times* 8 Dec. 719/2 Scrapbook for 1913. *Ibid.* 740/2 This is no history book—just a scrapbook of cherished fragments. **1939** H. Nicolson *Diary* 3 Dec. (1967) 47 After the news there is a B.B.C. scrap-book for 1910. **1947** L. MacNeice *Dark Tower* 69 Features..have..a great diversity of form. Some of them are as loosely constructed as scrap-books. **1959** *Listener* 23 July 150/2 The programmes..were almost identical exercises in the well-proven genre of biographical scrap-book. **1972** P. Black *Biggest Aspidistra in World* i. v. 43 The famous Scrapbooks, in popularity and appreciation the most successful dramatised radio series ever produced in Britain..began in 1933... The title Scrapbook first appeared in *Radio Times* in 1932.

c. *attrib.*

1897 H. James *Spoils of Poynton* i. 5 Trumpery ornament and scrapbook art. **1934** C. Lambert *Music Ho!* i. 75 Diaghileff..was able to invest with a revolutionary glamour the scrapbook mentality which in his later years he exploited with so marked a success.

Hence **ˈscrap-book** *v.*, to place in a scrap-book; hence **ˈscrap-booking** *vbl. sb.*

1879 'Mark Twain' *Let.* 12 Nov. (1917) I. 369 Put the enclosed scraps in the drawer and I will scrap-book them. **1881** —— *Tramp abroad* xlvi, I scrap-booked these reports during several months. **1883** *North Star* 25 Oct. 3/2 We trust that our wage-earning readers especially will scrap-book these Letters, for after-study. *c* **1898** 'Mark Twain' *Autobiogr.* (1924) I. 139 He usually postponed the scrap-booking until Sunday.

scrape (skreɪp), *sb.*[1] [f. scrape *v.*]

I. Means, act, or result of scraping.

1. An instrument for scraping, a scraper. †a. A scraping tool held in the hand (*obs.*). b. *Eastern U.S.* 'A small dredge' (Funk's *Stand. Dict.*).

c **1440** *Pallad. on Husb.* iv. 607 Or brasen scrapis out of euery dalke Hem scrape [orig. *uncinis æreis tollendi sunt vermes ex ficu*]. **1688** Holme *Armoury* iii. xx. (Roxb.) 247/1 The Fourth is an Iron Scrape..set in a wooden handle, it is for the skullion to scrape and cleane the furnice hole.

2. An act of scraping. a. *gen.*

1483 *Cath. Angl.* 324/2 A Scrape (*MS. Addit.* to Scrappe) as a hen dose; *ruspare*. **1553** Ascham *Disc. Germ.* 27 b, And how soone *emig* [read *einig*] may be turned into *ewig*, not with scrape of knife, but with the least dash of a pen, so that it shall neuer be perceiued, a man that will proue, may easely see. **1611** Cotgr. *Gratture*, a scratch, a scrape.

b. *scrape of a pen* (Sc.): a hasty scribble, a small scrap of writing. Cf. scribe *sb.*, scrip *sb.*

1690 Earl of Melfort in Ellis *Orig. Lett.* Ser. ii. IV. 198 And in all this time we have not one scrape of a pen to free us from all these pains we suffer. **1814** Scott *Wav.* xlii, It ..wad cost but the scrape of the pen to make it out. **1830** Galt *Lawrie T.* ix. viii, Just give me a scrape of a pen to him to transfer the amount to your credit.

c. An awkward bow or salutation in which the foot is drawn backwards on the ground. Often coupled with *bow* or *leg*.

1628 Earle *Microcosm.*, *Scholler* (Arb.) 41 But his scrape is homely, and his nod worse. **1660** Wood *Life* (O.H.S.) I. 366 That they might make long legs and scrapes to them. **1721** Amherst *Terræ-Filius* No. 39 (1726) II. 50 A formal fellow..going to see an acquaintance of his..made a thousand scrapes and cringes. **1722** De Foe *Col. Jack* vi, I ..made him abundance of bows and scrapes. **1787** J. P. Andrews *Anecd.* (1790) 146 He drew from his purse a guinea, and with a scrape, made an uncouth offer of it. **1842** Lover *Handy Andy* i, To every one of these assurances.. Andy made a bow and a scrape. **1869** Blackmore *Lorna D.* xv, Uncle Reuben made his very best scrape and then walked up to the table.

d. A drawing of the bow over the violin.

c **1807** Jane Austen *Watsons* in *Minor Wks.* (1954) 327 No sound of a Ball but the first Scrape of one violin. **1831** Coleridge *Table-t.* 7 July, He can actually sell the tones of his fiddle at so much a scrape. **1847** Disraeli *Tancred* iv. xi, Baroni appeared..with his violin. He gave a scrape or two, and the audience became orderly.

e. *jocular*. A shave.

1859 *Hotten's Slang Dict.*, *Scrape*, low wit for a shave. **1879** G. Macdonald *Sir Gibbie* iv, I's jist gang ower to the barber's an' get a scrape.

f. *Fencing*. (See quots.)

1889 Pollock, etc. *Fencing* (Badm. Libr.) 52 The scrape. —If slang were allowed, this ought to be called the 'scrooge'; but there is no English word which precisely reproduces the French *froissé*. It is delivered in tierce when the adversary has his point too low, or his arm stretched out. *Ibid.*, Giving his sword a scrape which ought to unnerve his hand for the moment. **1897** *Encycl. Sport* I. 385/1 (Fencing), The *scrape* (this is the nearest English word for the French *froissé*) is made only in the high lines and mostly in the upper line (tierce).

g. A sound of scraping.

1886 Hall Caine *Son of Hagar* ii. xiv, The harsh scrape of Natt's clogs was on the gravel.

h. A dilatation of the cervix and curettage of the womb; *spec.* an induced abortion. *slang.*

1968 J. Hudson *Case of Need* iii. i. 172 The word got around..that she got a bad scrape. **1972** *Rochdale's Alternative Paper* No. 6. 10/2 The most common method [of abortion] in Britain for pregnancies of less than three months is D. & C. (better known to most women as a scrape). **1980** M. Drabble *Middle Ground* 62 She was having a D and C, a routine scrape.

3. One who 'scrapes' or uses excessive economy, a miser. *Obs.* exc. *dial.* (see *E.D.D.*).

1727 Bailey vol. II, *A Scrape*, as meer Scrape, a saving industrious Person.

4. a. A place scraped bare on a hillside. *dial.*

1781 Beckford *Th. upon Hunting* (1802) 258, I have known them lie in sheep's scrapes, on the sides of hills, and in small bushes. **1848** Barnes *Poems Rural Life* (ed. 2) Gloss., *Scrape*, a sheep-scrape; a bare place, where the turf has been scraped off by sheep's feet on a steep down-side. **1894** Patterson *Newfdld. Words* in *Trans. Amer. Folk-Lore Soc.* (E.D.D.), *Scrape*, a rough road down the face of a bank or steep hill, used specially in regard to such as are formed by sliding or hauling logs down.

b. A place where the soil has been scraped up.

1862 *Athenæum* 27 Sept. 391 The deer which..were addicted, at certain seasons, to dig up the land with their fore feet, in holes to the depth of..half a yard, contributed a new word to our language. These were called 'scrapes'. **1901** *Scotsman* 9 Apr. 7/4 Rabbit holes and scrapes at once appeared in shoals to the terror of the old golfers.

c. *Ornith.* A shallow pit in the ground excavated by a bird, usu. during a courtship display; also, the action of making such a pit.

1926 *Ibis* II. 7 All the scrapes noted were within about fifty or sixty yards from a nest. **1940** H. F. Witherby et al. *Handbk. Brit. Birds* IV. 385 In more advanced scrapes female with back to male will peck in bottom of scrape. **1942** E. A. Armstrong *Bird Display* ii. 27 An unmated female red-necked phalarope makes scrapes in the herbage, and from the first day of finding a mate this 'ceremony' often follows coition... Before laying, the female visits the various scrapes and lays an egg in one of them. **1961** [see *scrape ceremony* s.v. scrape *v.* 10 b]. **1967** B. Campbell *J. Hanzák's Pictorial Encycl. of Birds* 254/2 The nest is a shallow scrape lined with small stones or shells.

5. A layer (of butter) scraped thin; chiefly in ***bread and scrape*** (colloq.).

1848 C. Brontë *Jane Eyre* vii, A double ration of bread.. with the delicious addition of a thin scrape of butter. **1861** *London Rev.* 16 Feb. 170 Cutting the children's bread and scrape! **1873** Miss Broughton *Nancy* xlvii, Some people have their happiness thinly spread over their whole lives, like bread and scrape!

6. (See quot. 1879.)

1856 Olmsted *Slave States* 343 It [turpentine] is occasionally..scraped off, and barreled by itself. It is, therefore, known in market as 'scrape'. **1879** F. H. Butler in *Encycl. Brit.* IX. 711/1 The concreted turpentine obtained in the United States by making incisions in the trunk of a species of pine, *Pinnus australis*,..is commercially known as 'scrape'. **1884** C. S. Sargent *Rep. Forests N. Amer.* 517 The yield of the 'scrapes'..is estimated..at from 60 to 70 barrels of 280 pounds [of turpentine] each.

7. On a woodwind instrument, the part of the cane that is scraped to a narrow edge in the production of a reed. Also, the style of this scraping.

1954 *Grove's Dict. Mus.* (ed. 5) VI. 161/2 According to the quality of the cane from which it is made, and the character of its 'scrape', a reed [of an oboe] may be responsive or unyielding. **1961** Sprenkle & Ledet *Art of Oboe Playing* 95/2 The French scrape has a rather long tip. **1980** *Early Music* July 363/2 There are 3 basic scrapes..of which no. 1 is the most common.

II. 8. An embarrassing or awkward predicament or situation, usually one into which a person is brought by his own imprudence and thoughtlessness.

[Prob. from the notion of being 'scraped' in going through a narrow passage: see scrape *v.* 4 c, and the later sense 9.]

1709 Steele & Swift *Tatler* No. 71 ¶8 A Youngster in a Scrape, is a Word out of Date. **1714** Mrs. Manley *Adv. Rivella* 89 Cleander told Rivella what a Scrape they were brought into. **1740** tr. *De Mouhy's Fort. Country-Maid* (1741) I. 273, I congratulated myself on my Dexterity in getting out of the Scrape. **1755** Johnson, *Scrape*, difficulty; perplexity; distress. This is a low word. **1771** Franklin *Autobiog.* Wks. 1840 I. 11, I was generally the leader of the boys and sometimes led them into scrapes. **1818** Byron *Juan* i. xx, And let few opportunities escape Of getting her liege lord into a scrape. **1845** Disraeli *Sybil* ii. vii, Every scrape of the government was a step in the ladder to the great boroughmonger. **1861** Hughes *Tom Brown at Oxf.* v, Here one has only just to take care of oneself, and keep out of scrapes. **1867** Trollope *Chron. Barset* xlvi, If you don't take care, young man,..you will find yourself in a scrape with your Madalina. **1873** Black *Pr. Thule* iv, If anyone was in a scrape about money.

scrape (skreɪp), *sb.*[2] *dial.* [Of obscure origin; the ON. *skreppa* mousetrap has been compared, but connexion is very doubtful.] A trap for catching birds; = shrape *sb.*

1620 J. Wilkinson *Treat. Statutes* 124 Next you shall enquire if there be in euery parish..a crow net,..and it is not enough to haue one, but it must be vsed, & scrapes made in the winter to that purpose. **1668** Worlidge *Dict. Rust.*, A Shrape, or Scrape, a place baited with Chaff or Corn to entice Birds. **1706** Baynard *Cold Baths* II. 425 Catch'd like Sparrows in a Scrape of Chaff. **1877** E. Leigh *Cheshire Gloss.* 177 *Scrape*, seeds or corn laid on the snow, in order to get a raking shot at birds.

scrape (skreɪp), *v.* Pa. t. and pa. pple. **scraped** (skreɪpt). Also 6 *Sc.* **scraip(e, skraip** (pr. pple. **screpand, screpping,** 7 *rarely* pa. pple. **scrapen.** [ME. *scrape* (also shrape), perh. (see scr- 1) directly repr. OE. *scrapian* (see quot. under sense 4); perh. a. the corresponding ON. *skrapa* to scrape, erase, in Icel. to clatter (Sw. *skrapa*, Da. *skrabe* to scrape) = MDu., Du. *schrapen*:—OTeut. type **skrapōjan*, f. root **skrap-*, ablaut-var. of **skrep-* in OE. *screpan* (str.; ME. screpe wk.) to scrape.

Other cognates are Du., LG. *schrappen* to scrape (whence G. *schrappen, schrapfen*), MHG. *schrepfen* (mod.G. *schröpfen*) to scarify; the Du. *schrabben* scrab *v.* is prob. more remotely connected.

The Teut. root **skrep-*: *skrap-* may be a metathetic form of **skerp-*: *skarp-* (see sharp *a.*); cf. OE. *scearpian* to scarify.]

1. a. *trans.* To remove (an outer layer or something excrescent or adhering) by drawing across the surface the edge of some instrument held nearly perpendicularly. Chiefly with advs., *off, away, out,* or const. *from, off, out of.*

1382 Wyclif *Job* ii. 8 The whiche with a sherd scrapide [1388 schauyde] awei the quyture, sittende in the dunghil. **1387** Trevisa *Higden* (Rolls) VIII. 213 Þat men of þat lond ete þe flesche of her owne children, and meny screpede of þe pouder of an hil and ete it as it were mele. *c* **1440** *Pallad. on Husb.* iv. 608 Or brasen scrapis out of euery dalke Hem scrape. *c* **1440** *Promp. Parv.* 450/2 Scrapyn, or schavyn a-wey, *abrado*. **1526** *Pilgr. Perf.* (W. de W. 1531) 240 b, He scraped yᵉ stynkyng fylth & corrupcyon of her deed body. **1535** Coverdale *Lev.* xiv. 43 After yᵗ the stones are broken out, & the playster scraped of [etc.]. **1568** Grafton *Chron.* II. 16 Of this Robert reporteth Reynulph that he scraped from one Beame of his Church in Couentrie fiue hundreth marke, to fill the hande of king William. **1597** Shaks. *2 Hen. IV*, i. i. 205 He..doth enlarge his Rising, with the blood Of faire King Richard, scrap'd from Pomfret stones, Deriues from heauen, his Quarrell, and his Cause. **1613** Purchas *Pilgrimage* (1614) 550 With kniues in their hands, to scrape from their legs the bloud-leeches. **1686** N. Cox *Gentl. Recreat.* (ed. 3) v. 94 After your Groom has..scrapt off all the Sweat from your Horses. **1729** Swift *Direct. Serv.* i. Wks. 1751 XIV. 23 When you cut Bread for a Toast,..lay it on the Coals;..and, if you find it toasted quite through, scrape off the burnt Side, and serve it up. **1782** Cowper *Gilpin* 189 But let me scrape the dirt away That hangs upon your face. **1786** Chelsum *Hist. Engrav. Mezzotinto* 6 These parts are scraped away in a greater or less degree, as the lights are intended to be stronger or weaker. **1845** Budd *Dis. Liver* 191 Covered by a soft pulpy matter, which may be readily scraped away. **1855** Tennyson *Brook* 193, I scraped the lichen from it [the tombstone]. **1877** R. H. Hutton *Ess.* (ed. 2) I. 37 Like dry colours scraped off a picture.

†b. *spec.* To erase (writing, etc.) with a knife. Chiefly with advs. *out, away, off,* and const. *out of.*

The earliest recorded use; the older screpe *v.* occurs in the same sense. Sometimes (as in quot. 1563–83) the sense appears to be: To delete by crossing through with a pen.

1303 R. Brunne *Handl. Synne* 7044 And commaunded alle yn rape A-wey þat wrytyng for to skrape. ? **1384** Chaucer *Wordes unto Adam* 6 So ofte a daye I mot thy werk renewe, Hit to correcte and eek to rubbe and scrape, And al is through thy negligence and rape. *c* **1430** *Pilgr. Lyf Manhode* ii. xxi. (1869) 83 Which thing if it so were, riht so alle hise ordenaunces shulden be put out of the book, and defaced and scraped. ? *a* **1500** *Chester Pl.* (Shaks. Soc.) 190, I will skrape this awaie anon, Their as a virgine is wrytten on, I will wryte, a good woman. **1530** Palsgr. 707/1 Scrape out this lyne, it is falsely written. **1532** More *Confut. Tindale* Wks. 421/1 A..learned priest, that through out al the ghospels scraped out *diabolus* and wrote *Iesus Christus*. **1563–83** Foxe *A. & M.* 1591/2 Then he tooke his penne & said that he would scrape it out for my pleasure. **1577** Holinshed *Chron.* II. 1189/1 Bookes..beautified with Images, the heads wherof had bin scraped off. **1600** J. Hamilton *Facile Traictise* 152 Screpping out the wordis (*ful of grace*) and putting in..(*frelie beloouit*). *Ibid.* 276 Screpand out thir wordis, *Except* [etc.]. **1603** Shaks. *Meas. for M.* i. ii. 9 Thou conclud'st like the Sanctimonious Pirat, that went to sea with the ten Commandements, but scrap'd one out of the Table. **1688** Holme *Armoury* iii. xv. (Roxb.) 19/2 One end was sharpe to make the letters, the other end broad with an edge, to scrape what was amise, out againe.

transf. and *fig.* *c* **1350** *Will. Palerne* 448 Faire so his figure is festened in mi ȝout [*read* þout], þat wiþ no coyntise ne craft ne can y it out scrape. **1387** Trevisa tr. *Higden* (Rolls) IV. 431 Haue mynde of Moyses, hym was levere be scraped out of þe book of lyf. *a* **1548** Hall *Chron.*, *Edw. IV*, 203 His vnhappy predestinate chaunce coulde not by any pollicy be put by, nor by any instrument scraped away. *c* **1580** Sidney *Ps.* ix. xii, The poore in sprite Shall not be scrapt, from out of heav'nly score. **1598** Shaks. *Merry W.* iv. ii. 231 Yes, by all meanes: if it be but to scrape the figures out of your husbands braines.

2. a. To deprive of an outer layer or to free from excrescent or adhering matter by drawing the edge of some instrument over the surface; to abrade, clean, or render smooth, or to obtain scrapings from, by this process.

c **1430** *Two Cookery-bks.* 18 Take þe Mawes of Turbut, Haddok, or Codelyng, & pyke hem clene, & skrape hem, & Wasshem clene. **1530** Palsgr. 707/1, I scrape a parchement skynne to make it the better to write on. *Ibid.*, Scrape the knedynge troughe or you put in the meale. **1535** Coverdale *Lev.* xiv. 41 Then shall he command..the house to be scraped within rounde aboute. **1560** Daus tr. *Sleidane's Comm.* 43 And with a piece of glasse he skrapeth his fingers. **1592** Shaks. *Rom. & Jul.* i. v. 2 Where's Potpan, that he helpes not to take away? He shift a Trencher? he scrape a Trencher? **1631** Gouge *God's Arrows* i. §25 *Onicha*, a kind of spice very cleare, which being scraped giveth an extraordinary sweet savour. **1645** Milton *Colast.* 19 It may bee his trenchers were not scrap't. **1662** Faithorne *Art Graving* 48 After you have graved part of your work, it will be necessary to scrape it with a sharp edge of another Graver. **1678** Moxon *Mech. Exerc.*, *Joinery* 70 These hard woods are..more properly said to be Scraped than Plained. **1725** *Bradley's Family Dict.* s.v. *Horse-radish*, The Root..is scraped and used with Vinegar for Sauce to roast Beef, Mutton, &c. **1791** Boswell *Johnson* an. 1783 (1811) IV. 205 He..scraped the joints of his fingers with a pen-knife, till they were quite red and raw. **1848** Thackeray *Van. Fair* xli, The gravel walk and terrace had been scraped quite clean. **1860** Tyndall *Glac.* ii. xxii. 349 Ice at 32° may..be scraped with a knife with even greater facility than some kinds of chalk. **1880** *Standard* 12 Apr. 2/8 He at once seized him and discovered that he had a gold band bracelet,..worth about 5*l*... It had evidently been tested, for it was 'scraped' in more than one place. **1884** *Pall Mall Gaz.* 16 Oct. 2/2 An ironclad's..bottom is always foul when she cannot be periodically docked and scraped. **1891** *Labour Commission* Gloss., *Scraping*, cleaning the spars of a ship and parts of the hull with a small piece of sharp iron, steel, or glass.

b. To remove the dirt from the soles of (one's boots or shoes) by drawing them over a door-scraper.

1844 DICKENS *Mart. Chuz.* xliii, I'd scrape my shoes on the scraper of the door.

c. Used jocularly for: To shave.

1773 FERGUSSON *Poems* (1807) 280 Their barber bauld his whittle crooks And scrapes them for the races.

d. To inscribe or portray on stone by scraping away the surface.

1532 MORE *Confut. Tindale* Wks. 728/2 But if he feele it written there in dede as he saith he doth, then he feleth it scribled and scraped in his hert by the croked clouen clawes of the deuill. **1581** L. ALDERSEY in *Hakluyt's Voy.* (1589) 182 The outside of the [holy] sepulchre is very foule, by meanes that euery man scrapes his name and marke vpon it. **1848** THACKERAY *Van. Fair* xliv, The family arms were just new scraped in stone.

e. To produce (a mezzotint engraving) by scraping the prepared copper plate. Also *absol.*

1747 *Sculptura-Hist.-Techn.* 225 Mezzotinto, called Scraping or Burnishing on Copper. **1762–71** H. WALPOLE *Vertue's Anecd. Paint.* (1786) III. 239 Several prints were made from his works, and several plates he etched and scraped himself. **1892** *Pall Mall Gaz.* 18 Feb. 3/1 The painter has scraped a mezzotint from his picture.

f. To clean or empty *out* by scraping.

1894 'R. ANDOM' *We Three & Troddles* xxi. 198 When you have done with that jam you might let me have the pot to scrape out. **1919** E. SHACKLETON *South* xii. 237 As the cook and his 'mate' had the privilege of scraping out the saucepans, there was some anxiety to secure the job. **1925** *Morris Owner's Man.* 14 Thoroughly scrape out and oil cams until they work quite freely.

g. To draw (hair) tightly *back* from the forehead. Cf. SCRAPED *ppl. a.* 2 b.

1926 'O. DOUGLAS' *Proper Place* xxxi. 280, I couldn't have believed she had such pretty, soft hair for she wore it scraped back.

†**3. a.** Of a beast or bird: To remove (soil, etc.) by scratching with the feet or claws; to make (a hole) by scratching. Also *absol.* or *intr.* to scratch in the ground. *Obs.*

c **1430** *Sir Tryam.* 392 (Percy Soc.) Hys gode hownde.. scraped on hym bothe ryne and mosse, And fro hym nevyr wolde gone! *c* **1440** *Alphabet of Tales* 308 Sho [a wolf] began to skrape & grafe abowte þe rowte with hur naylis. *c* **1440** *Promp. Parv.* 450/2 Scrapyn, as hennys, *ruspor.* **1530** PALSGR. 707/1 Yonder dogge scrapeth to make a hole to hyde his dyner in. **1538** ELYOT *Dict.*, *Scalpturio*, to scrape as a Cocke dothe, or other fowles. ?*a* **1598** *D. Ferguson's Sc. Prov.* No. 327 (1785) 13 He is a proud tod that will not scrape his ain hole.

fig. **1662** STILLINGFL. *Orig. Sacræ* I. v. §5 Those Arabick traditions which that author scrapes as much for, as Æsops Cock did on the Dunghill. *Ibid.* III. ii. §4 Scraping and searching into the natures of things.

b. *trans.* with adv. or phrase. †*to scrape out, forth*: to dig out with the nails or claws. Also *fig.*

1530 PALSGR. 707/1 She loved nat her housbonde whyle he lyved, and now she wolde be gladde to scrape hym out of the yerthe with her nayles. **1549** *Compl. Scot.* To Rdr. 12 For ane hen that seikis hyr meyt in the mydding, may scraipe sa lang amang the fyltht, quhil sche scraip furtht sum ald knyfe that hes been tynt. **1845** GOSSE *Ocean* iv. (1849) 205 The females [turtles].. lay their eggs in holes [in the sand] which they scoop out with their fin-like feet. The work being accomplished, the sand is again scraped back over the eggs, and the surface made smooth as before.

†**4. a.** To scratch with the finger-nails or claws; also *intr.* Also, to caress (a dog, etc.) by scratching or clawing. *Obs.*

c **1000** *Sign Language* §67 in *Techmers Zeitschr.* II. (1885), ȝif þu æȝera beþurfe, þonne scrapa þu mid þinum fingre up on þinne wynstran þuman. *a* **1400–1450** *Bk. Curtasye* 87 in *Babees Bk.*, Yf þy nown dogge þou scrape or clawe, þat is holden a vyse emong men knawe. *c* **1440** *Promp. Parv.* 450/2 Scrapyn, a(s) bestys (*MS. S.* schrapen), *scalpo.* **1577** KENDALL *Flowers of Epigr.* 97 Thou likst ill men, ill men thee laude. So Mules of mules are scrapt and clawd. **1607** TOPSELL *Four-f. Beasts* 163 The little Dog, seeing his true maister returned home, ranne barking to the doore,.. fawning and scraping his Lord and maister also.

†**b.** Phr. *go scrape!* app. a form of contemptuous dismissal. *Obs.*

1611 COTGR., *Envoyer au grat*, to send a grazing; a Maister to put away his man; (and, perhaps from this phrase came our contemptuous, *Goe scrape*).

†**c.** To scratch, lacerate (with thorns). *Obs.*

c **1430** LYDG. *Min. Poems* (Percy Soc.) 113 The pryst demyd them devylles both, wyth them he wolde not mett; He sparyd nother hylle, nor holte, busche, gryne, nor grett; Lord! he was fowle scrapyd!

†**d.** To make a scratching noise with the fingernails on (a door), by way of an unobtrusive signal. In later use *intr.* with const. *at*. *Obs.*

Cf. SCRATCH *v.* 7.

c **1400** *Beryn* 481 ȝit trowid he no gyle, but went[e] nere to, And scrapid the dorr welplich, & wynyd with his mowith. **1718** *Free-thinker* No. 24. 173, I hope we shall never.. condescend to Scrape, instead of Knocking, at a Great Man's Door. **1829** LYTTON *Devereux* IV. vi, We came to the door of a second chamber, at which Fleuri scraped gently.

5. a. (*fig.* of sense 3.) 'To gather by great efforts, or penurious or trifling diligence' (J.); to amass, get possession of, collect, or bring together with difficulty. Now only with *together* or *up*.

[**1540** PALSGR. *Acolastus* II. i. H ij b, It shuld not greue me .. to scrape my lyuyng out of the harde stone walles, with my nayles.] **1549** COVERDALE, etc. *Erasm. Par. Ephes.* Prol., Whan was there more haftyng and craftyng to scrape money together.. than now. **1559** *Mirr. Mag.*, *Northumbld.* xvi, Who in my cause al that he could ey skrapte. **1588** *Munday's Banq. Daintie Conceits*, '*The Statelie pine*' v, The wealthy chuffe, that.. scrapes and scratches all the mucke he may. **1596** SPENSER *F.Q.* v. ii. 27 Thereafter all that mucky pelfe he tooke,.. The which her sire had scrap't by hooke and crooke. **1617** MORYSON *Itin.* III. 178 Busie.. in scraping up money for such idle expences. **1644** MILTON *Educ.* 2 We do amisse to spend seven or eight yeers meerly in scraping together so much miserable Latin, and Greek. **1654** JER. TAYLOR *Real Pres.* 142 But to make up this also he does *corradere* scrape together some things extrinsecal to the words of this authoritie. **1654** WHITLOCK *Zootomia* 278 The greatest, but not best part of men.. scrape up Wealth by Hooke, or by Crooke. **1655** FULLER *Ch. Hist.* x. i. 24 The Prelaticall party complained, that to swell a number, the non-conformists did not chuse, but scrape Subscribers. **1712** ADDISON *Spect.* No. 299 ¶2 By the Age of Five and twenty I had scraped together Four thousand two hundred Pounds Five Shillings, and a few odd Pence. **1805** H. K. WHITE *Let.* Apr. *Life & Rem.* (1850) 330 The poor Tallow-chandler, who.. at length scraped money enough to retire. **1841** D'ISRAELI *Amen. Lit.* (1867) 683 The fervent dean scraped together all his properties.. to endow it [a College]. **1888** BURGON *Lives 12 Gd. Men* II. x. 272 The first money he was able to scrape together by strict frugality. **1890** 'L. FALCONER' *Mlle. Ixe* iii. 80 They really must scrape some men together to balance all these heavy girls.

b. *to scrape (an) acquaintance*: to get on terms of acquaintance *with* by careful effort and insinuation; rarely with *up*. So †*to scrape kindred.*

'A low phrase. To curry favour, or insinuate into one's familiarity' (J.). Cf. †*to scratch acquaintance*, SCRATCH *v.* 1 e.

1600 ROWLANDS *Lett. Humours Blood* Epigr. xxxi, One newlie practiz'd in Astronomie.. Would scrape (forsooth) acquaintance of the skie, And by his arte, goe knocke at heauen dore. **1602** *How a Man may Chuse gd. Wife* F 1 b, O this acquaintance was well scrapte of me. **1641** C. BURGES *Serm.* 5 Nov. 58 Although God be gratiously indulgent, yet is he not inconsiderately prodigall of mercies to all that scrape acquaintance with him in their troubles. **1658** W. BURTON *Itin. Anton.* 157 Affecting relation to Troy, and scraping kindred thence. **1740** RICHARDSON *Pamela* (1824) I. lx. 402 Mrs. Harris scraped acquaintance with Mrs. Thomas. **1825** MRS. SHERWOOD *Yng. Forester* (Houlston Tr.) I. 5 He contrived to scrape acquaintance with certain smugglers. **1844** ALB. SMITH *Adv. Mr. Ledbury* lix, Two or three of the immates.. with whom Jack had already scraped up an acquaintance. **1880** L. OLIPHANT *Land of Gilead* i. 8 After establishing ourselves.. we went out to look about us, and scrape acquaintance with the people. **1904** F. WHISHAW *Lovers at Fault* v. 43 Her two dearest friends had contrived to scrape acquaintance without introduction.

c. *absol.* and *intr.* To hoard up penuriously; to save or economize; to gather together money, etc. with labour and difficulty. Now chiefly *dial.*

1552 LATIMER *Serm.*, *St. Andr. Day* (1562) 120 They intend to gette that money agayne which they haue layed out, and afterwarde to scrape for purchasyng. **1552** —— *1st Sund. Epiph.* (1584) 302 b, Euery manne scrapeth for hymselfe. *a* **1591** H. SMITH *Serm.* (1594) 109 Zacheus, which before hee had seene Christ, knew nothing but to scrape; but as soone as he had heard Christ, all his minde was set vpon giuing. **1592** *Nobody & Someb.* D 3, Let them grieue That scrape for wealth, I will the poore relieue. **1760** GOLDSM. *Cit. W.* lxv, She scraped and scraped at pleasure, till I was almost starved to death. **1835** *Court Mag.* VI. 74/2 How he got it [so much money], save by scrape—scraping, the Lord alone knows. **1881** *Century Mag.* Nov. 133 You do have a hard time, don't you?.. to slave and tug and scrape to get a house over your head.

d. In *fig.* phr. *to scrape* (*the bottom of*) *the barrel* (or *bucket*): to collect with difficulty something inferior; to obtain something (as by necessity) from a poor source. *slang* (orig. *U.S.*).

1942 *Time* 12 Jan. 57/1 The medical profession.. [is] closer to scraping the bottom of the bucket.. than any other occupation, trade or profession. **1955** *N.Y. Times Bk. Rev.* 30 Oct. 1/1 It was built in the spring of 1864, when the Confederacy was scraping the bottom of its barrel of men and resources. **1957** *Essays in Criticism* VII. 342, I was scraping the barrel for evidence. **1961** B. FERGUSSON *Watery Maze* viii. 203 The insistence of the Americans that the Casablanca assault should be much the strongest.. meant scraping the bottom of the barrel to find extra ships, craft and crews. **1970** *Times* 5 Nov. 14/4 Professor Barlow explains how necessary it is to 'scrape the barrel' for even the most minor scraps of information. **1981** *Times* 18 Aug. 1/3 We shall have to pay something. I hope to be able to scrape the barrel and come up with something.

6. Used disparagingly for: To play (a fiddle); occas. *to scrape catgut*; to play (a tune, etc.) on the fiddle. Cf. F. *râcler.* Chiefly *absol.*

1599 [see CATGUT 1]. **1607** DEKKER & WEBSTER *Westward Hoe!* v. i, They are but rozining, sir, and theile scrape themselues into your company presently. *Mono.* Plague a their Cats guts and their scraping. **1623** MASSINGER *Dk. of Milan* II. i, You shall scrape, and Ile sing, A scuruie Dittie to a scuruie tune. *a* **1672** WOOD *Life* (O.H.S.) I. 189 Like contry fidlers [to] scrape for our livings. **1764** *Oxf. Sausage* 37 Save where some Fiddler scrapes a drowsy Tune. **1779** V. KNOX *Ess.* lxxi. (1782) I. 310 It is.. necessary to do little else than scrape and pipe. **1840** R. H. DANA *Bef. Mast* xxvii, The musicians were still there.. scraping and twanging away. **1842** LEVER *J. Hinton* ix, While fiddles, French-horns, and dulcimers, scraped and blew their worst. **1848** DICKENS *Dombey* lviii, He.. was scraping consolation out of its deepest notes.

7. a. To rub harshly on (a surface) in passing along or over it, so as to cause abrasion or produce a grating noise; to draw (something) roughly over a surface.

1731 POPE *Ep. Burlington* 152 The chiming Clocks to dinner call; A hundred footsteps scrape the marble Hall. **1857** O. W. HOLMES *Autocrat* iii, Somebody happened to scrape the floor with his chair just then; which accidental sound.. broke the charm. **1871** DARWIN *Descent of Man* II. xiii. 61 Turkey-cocks scrape their wings against the ground, and some kinds of grouse thus produce a buzzing sound. **1897** *Encycl. Sport.* I. 473/1 (Golf) *Sclaff*, to scrape the surface of the ground with the sole of the club head before striking the ball.

b. *intr.* To graze *against* or *on.*

1774 GOLDSM. *Nat. Hist.* (1776) IV. 344 When the animal therefore is compelled to make a step forward, it scrapes on the back of the nails along the surface. **1853** KANE *Grinnell Exp.* xlvi. (1856) 423 Fangs of broken ice, which scraped against the beach as the tides rose and fell.

†**c.** *transf.* To pass very closely *along*. *Obs.*

1603 KNOLLES *Hist. Turkes* (1621) 750 Then scraping along the island Prochita.., he put into the bay of Puteoli.

d. To draw one's feet noisily over the floor. Hence †*trans.* to insult by doing this in a public assembly (*obs.*). Also *to scrape down*: to silence (a speaker) by making a noise with the feet.

1561 [see SCRAPING *vbl. sb.* 1 b]. **1773** JEBB in Disney *Mem.* J.'s Wks. 1787 I. 57 The young men were offended at him [Wilgress] for his behaviour as proctor, and therefore *scraped* him. When the sermon was over, the vice-chancellor called to the proctors, to take the names of all the gentlemen in one of the galleries. **1785** [see SCRAPING *vbl. sb.* 1 b]. **1832** *Tour through College* 25 (Hall *College Words*), They not unfrequently rose to open outrage or some personal molestation, as.. 'scraping him'. **1855** MACAULAY *Hist. Eng.* xxii. IV. 749 Another [orator] was coughed and scraped down.

8. a. *intr.* To make obeisance, to bow drawing the foot back, 'to make an awkward bow' (J.).

Often *to bow and scrape*, with contemptuous reference to over-ceremonious politeness or reverence.

1645 GIPPS *Serm.* 12 Who will scrape to a keeper for a piece of Venison, who may have free accesse to the master of the game to aske and have? **1646** J. WHITAKER *Uzziah* 24 Have you not known some in a low condition, to bow and scrape? **1761** CHURCHILL *Rosciad* 396 By turns transform'd into all kinds of shapes, Constant to none, Foote laughs, cries, struts, and scrapes. **1818** SCOTT *Hrt. Midl.* xxviii, He ducked with his head and shoulders, scraped with his more advanced hoof, and withdrew to his own domains. **1867** TROLLOPE *Chron. Barset* xxxv. I. 301 Bowing and scraping and rubbing his hands together.

†**b.** trans. *to scrape a leg*: to make a leg (see LEG *sb.* 4). *Obs.*

1602 [see LEG *sb.* 4]. **1672** H. MORE *Brief Reply* 328 Scraping many legs to him, and desiring him to tell his demands. *Ibid.*, And scraping many Legs, asked a largess of the Knight. **1681** D'URFEY *Progr. Honesty* v. 5 Sure he has some suit to beg, That thus he sneaks and scrapes a Leg.

9. a. *intr.* *to scrape along*: to manage or 'get along' with difficulty. *to scrape through*: to get through a trial, an examination, so as just to escape failure. Also with other advs. or advb. phrases in similar senses, as *to scrape by, home, in*, etc.

1884 W. CUDWORTH *Yorksh. Dial. & Character Sk.* 33 (E.D.D.) Boath him an' his father hed scraped along withaht wommanly help. **1905** VACHELL *The Hill* iii. 51 We must mug up our 'cons' well enough to scrape along without 'puns' and extra school. **1907** ELINOR GLYN *Three Weeks* i, He scraped through his 'Smalls' and his 'Mods'. **1927** *Observer* 18 Sept. 17/3 Mr. Blythe, who at the last election scraped home in Monaghan. **1951** *Sport* 6–12 Apr. 17/2 The Airmen just scraped through with a 3–2 win. **1958** *Times* 16 Dec. 4/4 (*heading*) Chigwell scrape home. **1958** [see MILLION 2 f]. **1966** *Listener* 1 Dec. 829/1 Osbert Lancaster.. depends on words rather than drawing, understandably since his drawing.. only just scrapes by. **1973** M. WOODHOUSE *Blue Bone* iv. 35 The family didn't get on with the Germans and they only just barely scraped by with the Communists. **1978** 'M. M. KAYE' *Far Pavilions* vii. 114 As long as he can shoot and ride, I suppose he'll scrape past.

b. *trans.* (causatively.) *to scrape* (a person) *through*: barely to enable him to get through.

1897 FLANDRAU *Harvard Episodes* 243 A futile effort to scrape Billy through an examination. **1902** *Westm. Gaz.* 7 July 7/2 The.. tests of fitness for promotion,.. for which officers cram up a little theoretical knowledge, just sufficient to scrape them through.

c. To acquire or obtain (something) with difficulty. *colloq.*

1963 *Guardian* 9 Aug. 7/1 He read English at Oxford. 'But I only scraped a third.' **1967** *Listener* 2 Mar. 283/1 The Congress Party, which has ruled the country since independence in 1947, has just managed to scrape a majority in the central parliament. **1980** *Early Music* Apr. 234/1 Nor does *castrato* appear in the index (though Farinelli scrapes a mention).

10. *Comb.* **a.** in contemptuous designations of persons, as †**scrape-all** (see quot.); †**scrape-good**, a miser, also *adj.* miserly; **scrape-gut**, a fiddler; †**scrape-pelf**, **-penny**, **-scall**, a miser; †**scrape-shoe**, ? an obsequious person, a toady. **b. scrape ceremony** *Ornith.*, a display by a bird, involving the excavation of a shallow pit in the ground and the pressing of the bird's breast into this, freq. performed during courtship; hence **scrape-ceremonial** *a.*; †**scrape-pan**, an instrument for scraping a salt-pan.

a **1700** B. E. *Dict. Cant. Crew*, **Scrape-all*, a Money-Scrivener; also a miserable Wretch, or griping Fellow. **1926** HUXLEY & MONTAGUE in *Ibis* II. 10 Nervous picking at grass .. may be seen during incubation, *scrape-ceremonies and before coition. **1949** *British Birds* XLII. 8 Both sexes indulge in the 'scrape' ceremony and in many of the actions characteristic of nest-building. **1961** D. A. BANNERMAN *Birds Brit. Isles* IX. 15 The main type of sexual behaviour preceding coition is the tail-display... At this stage the scrape-ceremony is very common, a typically male performance by which he lures the female to one scrape after another. *Ibid.* X. 247 Dotterel and red-necked phalarope.. share very similar *scrape-ceremonial and egg-laying behaviour. **1611** COTGR., *Caqueduc*, a niggard, micher, miser, *scrape-good. *a* **1693** *Urquhart's Rabelais* III. iv, None will there be..a Scrape-good wretch or churlish hard hearted refuser. **1837** LOCKHART *Scott* I. v. 152, I greatly doubt, sir, you were born for nae better than a *gangrel *scrape-gut.* **1746** T. LOWNDES *Brine Salt improved* 10 And then instantly, with the common iron *scrape-pan, stir the Brine very briskly in every part of the pan for about a minute. **1626** W. FENNER *Hid. Manna* (1652) 28 No covetous, nor drunkard, *scrape-pelfe, nor swearer,.. partaketh of it with you. **1584** LODGE *Alarum agst. Vsurers* 3b, Assuring him y[t] he is to think wel of his master *scrapepenie y[e] vsurer. **1755** [see SCRAPER 1]. **1602** *Withals Dict.* 80/1 Regarding nothing but the gaine, a Scraper, or *scrape-scall. **1607** *Puritan* I. iii. 12 Why, how now, we three? Puritanicall *Scrape-shoes, Flesh a good Fridayes! **1632** MASSINGER *City Madam* IV. i, Live scrape-shoo, and be thankfull.

scrapeage ('skreɪpɪdʒ). *rare*$^{-1}$. [f. SCRAPE *v.* + -AGE.] That which is scraped off.

1851 [see RAKEAGE].

scraped (skreɪpt), *ppl. a.* [f. SCRAPE *v.* + -ED^1.]

1. Deprived of the surface, or freed from excrescent or adherent matter, by scraping. Also, reduced to the condition of scrapings.

1597 A. M. tr. *Guillemeau's Fr. Chirurg.* 20b, They stoppe it with scraped linte. **1769** MRS. RAFFALD *Engl. Housekpr.* (1778) 21 Garnish it with..scraped horse-radish. **1853** WHYTE MELVILLE *Digby Grand* i, My companion escaped.. with no greater injury than a black eye and a scraped shin. **1897** W. ANDERSON *Lupus* 8 Applying caustic potash to the scraped area. **1897** *Allbutt's Syst. Med.* III. 543 Scraped raw beef, taken at first in very small quantities, has been well borne.

2. a. Collected together or amassed. Also ***scraped-up, together.***

1598 MARSTON *Sco. Villanie* H 4, His huge long scraped stock Of well penn'd playes. **1840** DICKENS *Old C. Shop* ii, And add a few scraped shillings every week to the money you can hardly count. **1897** MARY KINGSLEY *W. Africa* 387 By the aid of it..and a carefully scraped-up candle and a box of matches, the fire soon blazes. **1965** *Listener* 3 June 828/1 In June 1942 the hastily scraped together force called 23rd Indian Division, with which I was serving, was isolated from the rest of the world.

b. Designating women's hair that has been drawn back tightly from the forehead. Also ***scraped-back.*** Cf. SCRAPE *v.* 2g.

1970 'D. HALLIDAY' *Dolly & Cookie Bird* viii. 118 Her deep-set eyes smiling gratefully under the grey, scraped-back hair. **1977** *Times* 16 Sept. 7/8 Her scraped hair, self-effacing manner, and busy hands. **1978** I. MURDOCH *Sea* 156 Her scraped-back hair revealed her bulky rounded brow.

3. *Sc.* in ***well-scraped, ill-scraped,*** said of the tongue of a person as having or lacking refinement and courtesy of speech. Cf. FILED *ppl. a.*

1785 R. FORBES *Poems Buchan Dial.* 24 Thersites, Wha for's ill-scrappit tongue..got on his back Puss wi' the nine tails hung. **1818** SCOTT *Rob Roy* xxvii, It's ill-scraped tongues like yours, that make mischief atween neighbourhoods and nations. **1820** —— *Monast.* xxvi, Martin should keep a weel-scrapit tongue in his head. **1858**, **1884** Ill-scraped [see ILL- B.].

†**'scrapelet.** *Obs.* In 7 skraplet. [f. SCRAPE *sb.* + -LET.] A small scraping.

1615 LISLE *Du Bartas, Noe* Pref. 1 Conyes..do make many skraplets and profers on the ground before they dig earnestly for their neast or litter.

†**'scrapeling.** *Obs. rare*$^{-1}$. [f. SCRAPE *v.* + -LING.] A money-grubber, miser.

1629 GAULE *Distractions* 321 Is it you..old Pouch-penny? Methought, twas some such Scrapeling.

scraper ('skreɪpə(r)). [f. SCRAPE *v.* + -ER^1.]

I. One who scrapes.

1. a. One who 'scrapes together'; *esp.* one who strives meanly to make and save money, a money-grubber. Now *rare.*

1561 T. NORTON *Calvin's Inst.* III. 216 As about this present question he taketh in a maner al out of Augustines boke of repentance, which is foolishly botched of good & bad by som scraper together. **1619** HIERON *Wks.* I. 35 The rakers and scrapers of this world,..as though there were no God in heauen to make prouision for them, lay about them, leauing no vile vngodly oppressing courses vnassayed. **1633** G. HERBERT *Temple, Ch. Porch* xxvi, Never was scraper brave man. **1755** JOHNSON, *Scraper*, a miser; a man intent on getting money; a scrapepenny. **1882** BESANT *All Sorts* xlii, Everywhere there are scrapers and scatterers; the scrapers are few, and the scatterers are many.

†**b.** An unscrupulous plunderer. *Obs.*

1598 BARRET *Theor. Warres* I. ii. 11 Not in the spoile of apparel, robes, and trash, Least he be accounted an vnruly scraper, as too many now a dayes be. *a* **1604** HANMER *Chron. Irel.* (1809) 320 Hugh Tirell his fellow scraper, tooke from the poore Priests at Armagh, a great brasse panne.

2. a. One who scrapes (something specified or implied). ***mezzotint scraper***: see SCRAPE *v.* 2e.

1591 PERCIVALL *Sp. Dict.*, *Escarvador*, a scraper, *Scalptor.* **1762–71** H. WALPOLE *Vertue's Anecd. Paint.* (1786) III. 234 *note*, He was both painter and scraper in mezzotinto. **1788** LD. R. SEYMOUR in *Murray's Mag.* I. 484 A Carrot Scraper in St. James' Market, who sleeps in a little Kennel. **1839** URE *Dict. Arts* 943 After which it [parchment] is transferred to the *scraper.* This workman employs here an edge tool of the same shape as the fleshing-knife, but larger and sharper.

b. A derogatory term for a fiddler.

1611 CHAPMAN *May-day* IV. i, Strike vp, Scrapers. **1709** ADDISON *Tatler* No. 157 ¶16 Mr. Bickerstaff..summons all his Disciples, whether..Toasts, Smarts,..Musicians or Scrapers, to make their Appearance at the Playhouse. **1835** CARRICK, etc. *Laird of Logan* (1841) 140 'Year!' responded the astonished scraper of cat-gut. **1898** BESANT *Orange Girl* I. i, A common scraper on a crowd like a one-legged man with a Jack in the Green.

c. A contemptuous term for a barber.

1792 *New Year's Morning Edin.* 12 (E.D.D.) Gart the puir scraper tyne his feet. **1869** *Public Opinion* 19 June (Farmer), The beard and moustache, which the sailors in the Royal Navy will be permitted to wear, thereby doing away with the objection that blue-jackets have to the scraper.

3. A bird that 'scrapes' or scratches in the soil. Used *Ornith.* to render mod.L. *Rasores*, a former order of gallinaceous birds.

1615 CHAPMAN *Odyss.* XXIV. Epil., Yet this inestimable Pearle, wil all Our Dunghil Chanticleres, but obuious call; Each Moderne scraper, this Gem scratching by; His Oate preferring far. **1837** MACGILLIVRAY *Brit. Birds* I. 100 Order I. Rasores. Scrapers. **1894** *Month* Oct. 163 The old school of ornithologists divided them..into birds of prey, perchers, climbers, scrapers, waders, and swimmers.

II. An instrument for scraping with.

4. A scraping instrument held in the hand. **a.** *gen.* and in various technical applications: see quots.

1552 HULOET, Scraper or rubber, *scalprum.* Scrapynge knyffe, *scalprum.* **1751** CHAMBERS *Cycl.* s.v. *Bookbinding*, Manner of gilding books on the edges.—The book, being put in the press, between two boards, is scraped with a knife called a scraper. **1849** *Weale's Dict. Terms, Scraper*, a piece of iron used to take out the pulverized matter which remains in a hole when bored previous to blasting. **1852** MORFIT *Tanning & Currying* (1853) 203 Over which the skin..is laid with the hair side up; and he then scrapes the surface strongly from above downward, with the scraper. **1894** SIR J. ASTLEY *Fifty Yrs. Life* I. 14, I hated scraping ham—that was a job I did bar; for in the first place, it isn't easy, and the next, you are more likely to scrape your knuckles with the scraper than the ham. **1895** *Stores' Price List*, Artists' Scrapers. 2½ in. Steel Blade, Ebony Handle. *Ibid.*, Steel pipe bowl scraper.

b. (*a*) *Antiq.* Used to render the L. *strigil* (see STRIGIL). (*b*) 'An instrument with which to clean the tongue by scraping off the fur' (*Cent. Dict.* 1891). (*c*) An instrument for scraping off the sweat from horses.

(*a*) **1581** MULCASTER *Positions* xxxiv. (1887) 123 Then with certaine scrapers called Strigiles, they had all their filth scrapte of their bodies. **1756** C. SMART tr. *Hor., Sat.* II. vii. (1826) II. 165 Is that boy guilty, who by night pawns a stolen scraper for some grapes? **1904** BUDGE *3rd & 4th Egypt. Rooms Brit. Mus.* 43 Iron strigil, or skin-scraper.

(*b*) **1685** *Lond. Gaz.* No. 2040/4 A Gold Scraper for the Tongue. **1895** *Stores' Price List*, Tongue Scrapers (Tortoiseshell and Ivory).

(*c*) **1667** DK. NEWCASTLE *Method of Dressing Horses* 124 But, the Best of all is the Knife-[of-]Heat, which is the Scraper; for, when he is Hot, Scraping of Him gets all the Sweat..out of him. **1875** KNIGHT *Dict. Mech.* **1895** KIPLING *Maltese Cat* in *Pall Mall Gaz.* 26 June 2/2 [A polo pony] stiffening up to get all the tickle out of the big vulcanite scraper.

c. An instrument (of various forms) used for scraping off paint, tar, adhesive labels, etc. from wooden surfaces.

A common form in nautical use consists of a triangular plate of metal, with a handle inserted perpendicularly in the middle; another form has a curved blade between two handles.

1691 T. H[ALE] *Acc. New Invent.* 80 Cleaned with brushes, or Scrapers if barnicled. **1883** CLARK RUSSELL *Sailors' Lang.*, *Scraper*, a triangular iron instrument for scraping the deck.

d. *Engraving.* A three-sided tool used to remove burrs left by the graver, etching needle, or dry-point, or to obliterate lines. Also the similar instrument used in 'scraping' mezzotint.

1747 *Sculptura-Hist.-Techn.* 225 Take a Burnisher, or Scraper, and burnish that Part of the Plate. **1883** MOLLETT *Dict. Art & Archæol.*, *Scraper*, an engraver's tool for removing burrs.

e. An implement of varying construction used by primitive peoples for removing the hair from skins. Hence, in prehistoric archæology, applied to a particular type of flint implements (otherwise known as *thumb-flints*), from their conjectured use.

1865 LUBBOCK *Preh. Times* 71 The so-called 'scrapers'.. are oblong stones, rounded at one end, which is brought to a bevelled edge by a series of small blows. **1872** J. EVANS *Anc. Stone Implements* xiii. 268 One of the simple forms into which flakes are susceptible of being readily converted has, in consequence of its similarity in character to a stone implement in use among the Esquimaux for scraping skins and other purposes, received the name of a 'scraper', or, to use the term first, I believe, employed by the late Mons. E. Lartet, a *grattoir.* **1900** *Archæol. Æliana* XXII. 83 A 'thumbflint' or 'scraper' and also a large rough flint core were found by a tenant of one of the glebe farms.

f. More fully ***cabinet scraper.*** A thin rectangular piece of metal whose sharpened long edge is pushed over the surface of wood to smooth it.

1909 WELLS & HOOPER *Mod. Cabinet Work* v. 72 A carefully sharpened scraper frequently permits of about twelve resharpenings in all. **1924** H. G. PHILLIPS *Cabinetmaking* i. 14 A very fine shaving is taken off with the scraper, which leaves the surface ready to be glasspapered. **1970** *Canadian Antiques Collector* Jan. 27/2 The only satisfactory method is the use of a cabinet scraper. **1977** *Reader's Digest Bk. Do-it-Yourself Skills & Techniques* ii. 77/1 Cabinet scrapers give a satin-smooth finish to hardwood. *Ibid.*, If a scraper becomes hot and produces dust instead of shavings during use, it needs resharpening.

g. *Mus.* A simple percussion instrument.

1953 J. G. MOORE in *Dict. Jamaican Eng.* (1967) 396/1 The scraper, a corrugated stick across which is rubbed a plain stick [in pocomania and revivalist services]. **1956** M. STEARNS *Story of Jazz* (1957) v. 53 The typically African instruments, such as drums, gourd rattles, and scrapers. **1958** E. BORNEMAN in P. Gammond *Decca Bk. Jazz* xxi. 275 One of the many..indigenous African string instruments, hand drums, scrapers, shakers and gong-gong. **1961** A. BAINES *Musical Instruments through Ages* i. 27 Scrapers have survived into modern times, for instance in the folk music of Venezuela. **1976** D. MUNROW *Instr. Middle Ages & Renaissance* 32/2 Most of the instrumental types described are of very ancient origin indeed, drums, rattles, and scrapers being the commonest instruments of primitive man.

5. An appliance, usually consisting of a metal blade with a horizontal upper edge, fixed outside the door of a house for persons to scrape off upon it the dirt from the soles of their boots or shoes before entering.

1729 SWIFT *Direct. Serv.* iii. Wks. 1751 XIV. 47 Never clean your Shoes on the Scraper, but in the Entry,..by which..the Scraper will last the longer. **1833** J. BENNETT *Artificer's Lexicon* 366 Scrapers. Garden, hall, and door, from 1*s.* 6*d.* **1871** *Punch* 2 Dec. 235/2 Due observance of the scraper and the door-mat.

6. *Lithography.* (See quot. 1875.)

1825 J. NICHOLSON *Operat. Mechanic* 304 Behind the inking-cylinder K, a rubber, or scraper, is placed, to press very lightly against the cylinder, and to prevent the ink accumulating in rings round the cylinder. **1875** KNIGHT *Dict. Mech.*, *Scraper*, the board in a lithographic press whose edge is lowered on to the tympan-sheet, to bring the requisite pressure upon the paper.

7. a. A machine (or scoop) drawn by horses or oxen for excavating ditches, canals, etc., for levelling and making roads, or for raising and removing soil, dirt, weeds, etc. a short distance. In mod. use *spec.* an earth-mover, either self-propelled or towed, that works on the principle of a scoop.

1815 T. B. HAZARD *Nailer Tom's Diary* (1930) 442/2 Delivered C. R. Potter p[ai]r Scrapers and a Chain to hich horseis with. **1823** *New England Farmer* II. 9 The most expeditious, effectual, and economic mode of making a drain would undoubtedly be to use oxen, and a scraper or ox-shovel, as it is sometimes called. **1840** H. S. TANNER *Canals & Rail Roads U.S.* 259 *Scraper*, a machine drawn by horses or oxen, for excavating trenches, for canals, rail-roads, &c. **1884** *Longman's Mag.* Feb. 414 Subsequent snows are removed by means of a 'scraper', a kind of scoop upon wheels which is drawn over the ice by horses. **1886** *Encycl. Brit.* XX. 588/1 A horse scraping machine which delivers the mud at the side is also used, the blades of the scrapers being mounted obliquely. **1930** *Engineering* 7 Mar. 306/1 There are three of these scrapers in each warehouse, their function being to drag down the potash from the several heaps into the central longitudinal opening in the floor. **1939** C. W. TOWNE *Her Majesty Montana* 120 Abolishing the back-breaking labor of mucking, power driven scrapers and mechanical mucking machines are now usual. **1958** *Engineering* 14 Feb. 219 For outside work the three most important types of machine—all rubber tyred—are the self-propelled scrapers, mechanical shovels and the cranes. **1974** *Encycl. Brit. Micropædia* VIII. 996/2 The scraper is the dominant tool in highway construction.

b. An instrument for scraping dirt, mud, etc. from roads, etc. Also ***road-scraper.***

1831 LOUDON *Encycl. Agric.* (1857) §2464 The scraper may be described as a broad hoe, of treble the usual size and strength, used in cleaning roads or court-yards, and sometimes in cleaning grassy surfaces. *Ibid.* §3133 The Dutch hoe is a good road and lawn scraper. **1858** SIMMONDS *Dict. Trade, Scraper*,..a long hoe for cleansing roads of mud. **1909** *Daily News* 22 Dec. 6/1 There were some men out with scrapers, but..until late in the afternoon, pedestrians had to wade through..the..streets ankle deep in slush.

c. *U.S.* A small dredge for taking oysters, etc.

1881 E. INGERSOLL *Oyster-Industry* 247 *Scraper*, a small dredge. Chiefly spoken of with reference to scallops. **1887** G. B. GOODE, etc. *Fisheries U.S.* v. II. 571.

8. = PIG *sb.*^{1} 9.

1897 B. J. CREW *Practical Treat. Petroleum* xiv. 449 Under ordinary circumstances the scraper passes rapidly through the lines, cutting off all the sedimentary matter that has adhered to the pipes. **1959** *Petroleum Handbk.* (Shell Internat. Petroleum Co. Ltd.) (ed. 4) 330 A radioactive cartridge may be fitted to the scraper as a means of locating it, should the scraper become stuck in the line. **1976** M. MACHLIN *Pipeline* xlviii. 497 The oil itself, at seven miles an hour, took four and a half days to make the trip from Prudhoe to Valdez, pushing the scraper before it to separate it from the test water in the pipes.

III. Slang or jocular uses.

9. *Anglo-Irish.* Phrase: ***to take to one's scrapers***: to take to one's heels, decamp.

1792 S. BURDY *Life of Rev. Philip Skelton* 84 The militia men..took to their scrapers to save themselves. **1824** MACTAGGART *Gallovid. Encycl.* 47 She took to her 'scrapers', as the Irish phrase it. **1842** LOVER *Handy Andy* xxxvi, He took to his scrapers.

10. A cocked hat.

Perh. with allusion to the shape: see 4c.

1818 'A. BURTON' *Johnny Newcome* I. 24 And John in Uniform arrayed: Behold him! with his dirk and scraper, And new Coatee, as stiff as paper. **1828** MOIR *Mansie Wauch* xi. 95 He had a well-worn scraper on his head, peaked before and behind. **1867** SMYTH *Sailor's Word-bk.*, *Scraper*... Also, metaphorically, a cocked hat, whether shipped fore-and-aft or worn athwart-ships.

IV. 11. *attrib.* and *Comb.*, as in ***scraper-knife***; **scraper board** *Art* (see quot. 1972); also, a piece of this material; **scraper-box**, the frame holding the 'scraper' of a lithographic press; **scraper-mat**, a door-mat of wire or parallel strips of metal serving the purpose of a scraper; **scraper-plane** = *scraping-plane* (see SCRAPING *vbl. sb.* 3); **scraper ring**, a piston ring whose function is to scrape oil off the cylinder wall.

1895 E. J. WALL tr. *Fritz's Photo-Lithography* i. 25 A smooth white *scraper board made by Angerer and Göschl of Vienna, which has a very even film of chalk, and which takes the lines clean and vigorously, is especially suitable for pen and ink work. **1925** *Art & Publicity (Studio: Special Autumn No.)* (Advt., verso front cover), Scraper boards with plain, embossed, or tinted surface for drawing for reproduction of line or half-tone. **1945** J. C. TARR *Printing To-day* viii. 95 Line engravings are also made from scraper-board originals. This board is covered with a thick layer of china clay and size upon which indian ink can be drawn or brushed, and scratched away with a knife. **1972** P. CROY *Graphic Design & Reproduction Techniques* (ed. 2) 162 Scraper board technique is an interesting method of producing white-and-black drawings. Scraper board consists of a base card coated with white and black chalk layers. The surface layer is scratched..exposing the underneath layer. Scraper board can be bought with a white surface and a black under-layer. **1853** URE *Dict. Arts* II. 79 The..*scraper-box [in the lithographic press]. **1903** *Daily Mail* 3 Sept. 7/3 The bee-keeping beginner should provide himself with..a *scraper-knife, a comb foundation [etc.]. **1884** *Health Exhib. Catal.* 89/1 Metal *Scraper-Mats.. suitable for all gravel-walk entrances. **1895** *Stores' Price List*, Adjustable *scraper Planes... For scraping and finishing Veneers [etc.]. **1918** W. E. DOMMETT *Dict. Aircraft* 35 The lowest ring, when placed at the bottom of the skirt, is known as a '*Scraper Ring'. **1928** C. F. S. GAMBLE *Story North Sea Air Station* xiii. 216 In the early days considerable difficulty was experienced with these engines owing to the rapid deterioration of the scraper rings fitted on the piston heads. **1980** HAYNES & LEGG *Citroën CX Owners Workshop Man.* i. 29/1 The oil control ring is fitted to the bottom groove, the scraper ring to the middle groove, and the compression ring to the top groove.

'scrape-trencher. *Obs.* exc. *Hist.* [f. SCRAPE *v.* + TRENCHER.] A servant whose office was to scrape the trenchers after use. (In Oxford colleges the term was in regular use till the 18th c.)

1603 H. CROSSE *Vertues Commw.* (1878) 77 Euery slouenly seruingman, and greasie scrape-trencher will exceede the bounds of his calling. **1607** G. WILKINS *Miseries Enf. Marr.* I. A 2, But stay, here is a Scrape-trencher arriued. **1688** HOLME *Armoury* III. 199/1 The Common Servants to each Hall..are..the Porter, Scrape Trencher, Cook, and his under Servants. **1691** *Case of Exeter Coll.* 3 Ferdinand Smith, Scrape-trencher of the Colledge. **1772** FOOTE *Nabob* III. Wks. 1799 II. 318 Mr. Scrape-trencher, let's have no more of your jaw! **1862** GRANT *Capt. of Guard* i, A train of cut-throats, swashbucklers, and scrapetrenchers.

attrib. **1857** SIR F. PALGRAVE *Norm. & Eng.* II. 496 The King should present himself wholly disarmed, not having even a scrape-trencher blade or whittle-dagger.

'scrap-heap. [f. SCRAP *sb.*¹] A heap of SCRAP IRON; an accumulation of disused and broken-up ironwork for refounding. Hence *fig.* in phrases, as ***to cast on*** or ***consign to the scrap-heap***, to cast aside as worn out or superseded.

1838 *Civil Eng. & Arch. Jrnl.* I. 121/1 *note*, All its contemporary rivals [*sc.* locomotive engines] that have escaped the fate of the 'scrap heap' have been re-made. **1891** [see SCRAP IRON]. **1903** G. B. SHAW *Man & Superman* xxxi, This is the true joy of life..; the being thoroughly worn out before you are thrown on the scrap heap. **1937** V. BARTLETT *This is my Life* xv. 258, I don't know who bought that car in the end or how soon it reached the scrap heap. **1956** *Railway Mag.* Nov. 749/2 No. 6 was rescued from an inglorious demise on the scrap heap. **1967** G. F. FIENNES *I tried to run Railway* iv. 40 Engines long past their time for the scrap-heap were being kept going. **1972** *Times* 16 May 2/2 He felt he had been thrown onto the scrap heap after 20 years' service. **1977** *Times* 7 Oct. 15/6 A socialist determination to drive fewer people onto the scrap heap. **1980** A. CLARKE *Last Voyage* ix. 100 They didn't send me to the scrap-heap straight away. Gave me a little job.

Hence **'scrap-heap** *v. trans.*, to consign to the scrap-heap. So **'scrap-heaping** *vbl. sb.*

1905 *Daily News* 4 Dec. 6 The recent scrap-heaping of war vessels. **1907** *Westm. Gaz.* 4 Mar. 7/3 They cannot very well 'scrap-heap' the boats.

scrapi'ana, *pl. rare.* [quasi-L., f. SCRAP *sb.*¹ or SCRAPE *v.*: see ANA.] A collection of literary scraps or 'scrapings'.

1792 (*title*) Scrapeana. Fugitive Miscellany. **1811** MRS. JACKSON in *Sir G. Jackson's Diaries & Lett.* (1873) I. 256, I shall finish the last volume of scrapiana I began here. **1818** (*title*) Scrapiana: or elegant extracts of wit: being a complete collection of humorous pieces in prose and in verse. **1958** E. BLUNDEN *War Poets 1914–1918* 27 That denomination 'Eye-Witness', used in the first stage of the war to cover official scrapiana from the observation posts.

scrapie ('skreɪpɪ). Also †scrapy. [f. SCRAPE *v.* + -IE, -Y⁶.] A subacute, invariably fatal, disease of sheep and goats, characterized by degeneration of the central nervous system, leading to uncoordinated gait and itching.

1910 *Vet. Jrnl.* LXVI. 711 Shepherds and farmers..class more than one disease with totally different symptoms under the head of Scrapy. **1913** *Jrnl. Compar. Path. & Therapeut.* XXVI. 317 The term 'scrape' or 'scrapie' is a popular one which has been applied to a disease of sheep on the borders of England and Scotland. **1914** J. P. MCGOWAN *Investigation into Dis. of Sheep called 'Scrapie'* i. 11 The disease has existed in Britain since before the middle of the eighteenth century under such names as 'scrapie', 'scratchie', 'rubbers', 'rickets', 'goggles', 'shakings', 'shrew-croft', and 'cuddie-trot'. **1925** *Glasgow Herald* 22 Apr. 7 Scrapie has mainly been confined to a certain area of the country. **1952** I. E. NEWSOM *Sheep Dis.* iv. 120 Scrapie is a chronic neurosis of sheep and goats characterized by intense pruritus, progressive incoordination, weakness, paralysis and death. **1975** *Times* 25 Aug. 8/5 Scrapie, an incurable disease of the nervous system, has afflicted various breeds of sheep for many years. **1979** *Nature* 11 Jan. 127/1 Scrapie, a subacute neuromuscular disease of middle-aged sheep, has been attributed variously to an infection or to heredity. The clinical disorder follows progressive symmetrical decay of neurones in localised brain sites,..associated with a terminal axon dystrophy. **1981** *Brit. Vet. Jrnl.* CXXXVII. 108/2 Although scrapie is caused by a virus-like agent, the development of clinical disease depends on genetic factors.

scrapill, obs. form of SCRAPPLE *sb.*¹ and *v.*

scraping ('skreɪpɪŋ), *vbl. sb.* [-ING¹.]

1. a. The action of the verb SCRAPE in various senses. Also in *fig.* phr. ***scrapings of the barrel*** (see SCRAPE *v.* 5 d).

c **1440** *Promp. Parv.* 450/2 Scrapynge, or schawynge, *rasura, abrasio.* **1577** HOLINSHED *Chron.* II. 1189/1 The Abbot of saint Albons sent the boke so disfigured with scrapings & blotting out..vnto the king. **1612** DEKKER *If it be not good* D 3 b, Each one sweares (By Orpheus fiddle-case) they will tickle your eares If they can doo 't with scraping. **1641** MILTON *Ch. Govt.* Wks. 1851 III. 130 All your learned scraping in antiquity. **1818** SCOTT *Rob Roy* xv, They [the poultry] had siccan a skarting and scraping in the yard, that there's nae getting a bean or pea keepit for them. **1834** DICKENS *Sk. Boz, Steam Excursion*, Here the scraping [*i.e.* bowing] was renewed. **1842** BROWNING *Pied Piper* iv, Only a scraping of shoes on the mat. **1853** KANE *Grinnell Exp.* x. (1856) 72 The scraping of my pen over the paper. **1897** *Allbutt's Syst. Med.* IV. 430 It is better to treat each focus independently by scraping or by the excision of a wedge. **1959** *Listener* 22 Jan. 154/1, I think Bill Slim was a very great man, because he made do with practically the scrapings of the barrels.

b. The noise produced by drawing something roughly over a surface. †Also, the action of expressing disapproval of a speaker by shuffling the feet (see SCRAPE *v.* 7 d).

1561 T. HOBY tr. *Castiglione's Courtyer* I. K 2 b, Then was there hard a great scraping of fete in the floore. **1785** GROSE *Dict. Vulgar T., Scraping*, a mode of expressing dislike to a person or sermon, practised at Oxford by the students, in scraping their feet against the ground during the preachment. *a* **1801** G. WAKEFIELD *Mem.* (1804) I. 94 A comical incident..respecting that scraping of the Proctor, Mr. Wilgress, whilst preaching. **1894** HALL CAINE *Manxman* 436 There was the scraping of a chair behind the speaker. **1897** 'A. HOPE' *Phroso* xvii. (1905) 327 The scraping of men's limbs and the rasping of cloth on the rock.

2. *pl. concr.* That which is scraped off, up, or together. Rarely *sing.*

1511–12 *Acc. Ld. High Treas. Scot.* IV. 321 The scrapenis of certane giltin weschele. **1533** *Respublica* I. i. 97 The fliettance, the scrapinges,.. The skimmynges, the gubbins of booties and praies. **1575** GASCOIGNE *Posies, Flowers* 33 Catche, snatche, and scratche for scrapings and for crommes. **1607** TOPSELL *Four-f. Beasts* 391 The scraping of the inward parts of his own hooues beaten into powder and mingled with wine. **1678** *Phil. Trans.* XII. 1063 A fourth sort we have which we call Scrapings, that is a course sort of Salt..that cleaves to the tops of the sides of the Phats. **1730** SWIFT *Lady's Dressing Room* 40 The Bason takes whatever comes, The Scrapings from her Teeth and Gums. **1790** SPEECHLY *Cult. Vine* 33 The dust and scrapings from roads. **1835** DICKENS *Sk. Boz, The Streets, Morning*, An apprentice ..thinking of..the miseries of the milk and water, and thick bread and scrapings. **1899** *Allbutt's Syst. Med.* VIII. 704 The microscopic examination of scrapings reveals at once their [*sc.* certain diseases'] characteristic fungi.

fig. **1566** T. STAPLETON *Ret. Untr. Jewel* I. 32 The scrapinges of malice it selfe. **1860** TENNYSON *Sea Dreams* 77, I..trusted him with all, All my poor scrapings from a dozen years Of dust and deskwork.

3. *attrib.* and *Comb.*, as ***scraping-iron, -knife, machine, -plane, -tool***; **scraping-ground**, a place where deer scrape or rub the velvet off their antlers.

1877 HALLOCK *Sportsman's Gaz.* 89 (Cent.) The lordly bucks begin their nocturnal rambles over their favourite runways and *scraping-grounds. **1717** *Protestant Merc.* 16 Aug. 4 The Tree..scraped on the Bark, as if it had been done with a *Scraping-Iron or Addice. **1906** *Daily Chron.* 16 Feb. 6/6 The pressure of the scraping-iron used by the workman was sufficient to knock a huge hole in the vessel. **1382** WYCLIF *Jer.* xxxvi. 23 He kutte it with a *scraping knife of the scribe. **1662** *Comenius' Janua Ling. Triling.* 87 A Butcher..scalds swine all over first with hot water, and scrapes them with a scraping knife. **1852** MORFIT *Tanning & Currying* (1853) 166 For removing the hair, the scraping-knife alone must be used. **1886** *Scraping machine [see SCRAPER 7 a]. **1846** HOLTZAPFFEL *Turning* II. 483 This tool is called a *scraping plane, and is used for scraping the ivory keys of piano-fortes, and works inlaid with ivory, brass, and hardwoods. **1591** PERCIVALL *Sp. Dict.*, *Escoplo*, a *scraping toole, a plaine for a carpenter.

'scraping, *ppl. a.* [f. SCRAPE *v.* + -ING².]

1. That scrapes, in various senses of the verb SCRAPE.

1599 *1st Pt. Ret. Parnass.* Prol. 2 That scrapinge legg, that dopping curtisie. **1790** BURNS *Let. to Mrs. Dunlop* 8 Aug., A quality rather rare in compliments of these grinning, bowing, scraping times. **1824** SCOTT *Redgauntlet* ch. xix, The blind scraping scoundrel [a fiddler]. **1879** *Organ Voicing* 17 A scraping or chiffing noise is sometimes heard accompanying a note. **1890** H. G. DAKYNS *Xenophon* I. Introd. 121 *note*, Scraping courtiers and nodding satellites.

2. *esp.* Money-grubbing, miserly.

1593 SHAKS. *Rich. II*, v. iii. 69 He shall spend mine Honour, with his Shame; As thriftlesse Sonnes, their scraping Fathers Gold. *a* **1618** RALEIGH *Prerog. Parl.* 27 The Duke of Lancaster was as scraping as shee. **1732** FIELDING *Miser* III. iii, You are never mentioned but by the names of covetous, scraping, stingy. **1861** THORNBURY *Turner* (1862) I. 74 He had always been brought up to be saving and thrifty by the careful scraping old barber, his father.

Hence **'scrapingly** *adv.*, in a scraping manner.

1680 J. SHARP *Serm. on Eccl.* iii. 10, 26 That live scrapingly and uncharitably,..all their lives long.

scrap iron. [f. SCRAP *sb.*¹]

1. Iron which has already been cast or wrought and broken up or cast aside for re-casting or re-working; broken pieces and small articles of old and disused ironwork. Also *attrib.*

scrap wrought iron, scrap consisting of pieces of malleable iron, which when re-cast produces a superior iron.

1823 'JON BEE' *Dict. Turf* 214 Mere 'gatherers of scrap-iron'. **1839** *Civil Eng. & Arch. Jrnl.* II. 432/2 The bolts to be of the best scrap iron. **1862** *Times* 13 Aug. 4/2 In another ..process scrap wrought iron is melted in admixture with pig iron. **1891** *Labour Commission Gloss.* s.v., In Government yards, where they do not sell old boilers, &c. these are broken up and the pieces are placed in heaps (scrap heaps) and sold as old iron. Men employed at this are said to be on *scrap iron work*.

2. *fig.* An alcoholic drink of poor quality. *U.S. slang.*

1942 Z. N. HURSTON in *Amer. Mercury* July 85 Maybe a shot of scrap-iron or a reefer. **1958** *Washington Post* 1 Nov. 1/1 A trio of investigators warned the drinking public yesterday to beware of a new bootleg concoction, 'scrap iron', noted more for its voltage than vintage. **1970** C. MAJOR *Dict. Afro-Amer. Slang* 101 *Scrap iron*, bad liquor.

scraplet ('skræplɪt). Forms: 6 **scrappelet**, 9 **scraplet.** [f. SCRAP *sb.*¹ + -LET.] A small scrap.

1519 HORMAN *Vulg.* 160 Fet a voyder to haue awey this scrappelettis [*quisquilias*]. **1878** E. W. BENSON *Cathedral* viii. 123 He thinks his little scraplets will do more for him and his people than the 'History of the Jews'. **1891** A. JAMES *Diary* 7 May (1964) 203 We have a good scraplet of garden. **1972** *Time* 17 Apr. 63/1 He tests every anthology to see if some scraplet of Chandler's small output will turn up.

scrapling ('skræplɪŋ). [f. SCRAP *sb.*¹ + -LING.] A small scrap. (See E.D.D. s.v. *Scrappling.*)

1843 TENNYSON in *Mem.* (1897) I. 220 Don't be angry at this scrapling.

scrappage ('skræpɪdʒ). [f. SCRAP *sb.*¹ or *v.*³ + -AGE.] = SCRAPPING *vbl. sb.*²

1949 *Sun* (Baltimore) 24 Mar. 8/3 Scrappage of passenger cars in 1948 was approximately half of the normal scrappage rate. **1950** *Engineering* 6 Jan. 26/3 Internal stresses may lead to serious scrappage on account of cracking. **1960** *Economist* 22 Oct. 359/1 Apart from natural growth in the population, sales are wholly for replacement and are related to the rate of scrappage and obsolescence. **1972** *Guardian* 29 Mar. 14/2 He says that the scrappage rate for US cars is roughly stable at 40 per cent of the new registration increase. **1976** *Nature* 17 June 540/2 The causes are recognised engineering factors such as shaft seals, maintenance operations, permeation and eventual scrappage.

scrappe, obs. form of SCRAP.

†'scrapper¹. *Obs. rare*⁻¹. [f. SCRAP *sb.*¹ + -ER¹.] One who collects scrap-iron.

1648 in *Victoria Hist. Sussex* II. 245 Russell the scrapper for pickinge of soe much iron as made three tunne and 17 hundred at 3ʰ per tunne.

scrapper² ('skræpə(r)). *slang.* [f. SCRAP *v.*² + -ER¹.]

1. a. A pugilist.

1874 in *Hotten's Slang Dict.* 280. **1904** J. A. RIIS *Roosevelt* v. 104 He was a scrapper first, last, and all the time, with but little regard for whom he tackled, so long as he had him.

b. *transf.* in *gen.* use.

1976 *National Observer* (U.S.) 20 Nov. 13/4 On auction day, Harry Miner..said with his country twang, 'Vivien was a scrapper'. **1977** 'D. RAMSAY' *You can't call it Murder* ii. 124 'She was a real scrapper, Judy was.' O'Shea went on to give instances of her capacity for scrapping. **1979** *Dædalus* Summer 157 This is the Dewey..who had a long and honorable record as a scrapper for the rights of citizens of the democracy.

2. *N. Amer.* A fish that is hard to land once caught.

1959 *Moosehead Gaz.* (Dexter, Maine) Feb. 18/3 Tiny dry flies in drab patterns..brought the silvered scrappers with a rush. **1968** *Globe & Mail* (Toronto) 3 Feb. 40/1 The large-mouth is a right obliging and powerful scrapper. **1974** *Sunday* (Charleston, S. Carolina) 28 Apr. (Cartoon Suppl.) 8 (Advt.), This palm-size powerhouse has all the guts in the world to wear down any scrapper you're liable to hook.

scrappet ('skræpɪt). Also **scrappit.** [f. SCRAP *sb.*¹ + -ET¹.] A small quantity or amount, a little scrap.

1901 *Pilot* 19 Jan. 75/2 Scrappets of science such as can be read in penny weekly papers. **1901** L. MALET *Hist. Sir Richard Calmady* v. v. 415 There's selfishness now, if you like—to appropriate a virtue *en bloc*, not leaving a rag, not the veriest scrappit of it for anybody else! **1905** F. HARRISON in *Westm. Gaz.* 24 Feb. 6/3 Political interest is transferred to scrappets in halfpenny prints. **1941** E. R. EDDISON *Fish Dinner in Memison* xiii. 209 'A scrappet of ham: just half of that littlest slab,' she said. **1971** C. BONINGTON *Annapurna South Face* xv. 194 They warned me that they had very little food—just the odd scrappets that Dougal had taken up that morning.

scrappily (ˈskræpɪlɪ), *adv.* [f. SCRAPPY *a.*[1] + -LY[2].] In a scrappy manner.

1886 MAX MÜLLER in *Contemp. Rev.* June 779 Carlyle.. was still a raw, narrow-minded, scrappily educated Scotchman. **1909** *Athenæum* 28 Aug. 244/2 The attempt at final summary is rather a failure, being written scrappily.

scrappiness (ˈskræpɪnɪs). [f. SCRAPPY *a.*[1] + -NESS.] The state or condition of being scrappy.

1867 *Lond. Rev.* 17 Aug. 183 What shall we say of the local newspaper? its essence is scrappiness. **1881** *Athenæum* 25 June 840/3 The great fault of his selection [*sc.* Arnold's *Poetry of Byron*] is its scrappiness.

scrapping (ˈskræpɪŋ), *vbl. sb.*[1] *slang.* [f. SCRAP *v.*[2] + -ING[1].] Fighting; boxing. Also *attrib.* Also *transf.* in *gen.* use.

1891 *Pall Mall Gaz.* 28 May 7/3 Discussing the rival merits of a wrestling match, of a lottery, and of a scrapping match. **1897** HOWELLS *Landl. Lion's Head* 387, I got to scrapping with a man,..and he left his marks on me. **1902** *Blackw. Mag.* July 40/1 What do you want me for? Is it for a straight 'scrapping' with Boers? **1937** *Times Lit. Suppl.* 2 Jan. 4/3 One is apt to consider that the campaign ended, except for some hardly necessary 'scrapping', with the capture of Baghdad. **1977** [see SCRAPPER[2] 1 b].

ˈscrapping, *vbl. sb.*[2] [f. SCRAP *v.*[3] + -ING[1].] The action of 'sending to the scrap-heap'.

1905 *Daily Chron.* 23 May 4/4 The scrapping or sale of ships that ought to have been retained. **1907** *Morn. Post* 17 Jan. 2/3 The scrapping of ships.

scrapple (ˈskræp(ə)l), *sb.*[1] *dial.* Forms: 4 scrapill, scrapyll, 7 skrapple, 7–9 scraple, 9– scrapple. [f. SCRAPE *v.* + -EL. Cf. WFlem. *schrepel* in the same sense.] A tool used for scraping or raking up.

1354 in *Finchale Priory Charters* (Surtees) p. xxxvij, j scrapill, j securis. **1397** *Ibid.* p. cxviij, Item j por et j scrapyll. **1615** W. LAWSON *Country Housew. Gard.* (1626) 46 A skrapple of iron..For Nettles and ground-Iuy after a showre. **1825** JAMIESON, *Scraple*, 1. An instrument used for cleaning the Bake-board, Roxb. 2. One for cleaning a cow-house. **1875** W. DICKINSON *Cumbriana* 51 The girl came out with a small coal-rake, to which the old dame pointed, saying, 'Whè, that's what a scrapple may be!'

ˈscrapple, *sb.*[2] *U.S.* [dim. of SCRAP *sb.*[1]] An article of food made from scraps of pork, etc. stewed with meal and pressed into large cakes.

1855 *Rural New Yorker* 10 Feb. 47/3, I observe a call for a recipe for making 'Scrapple', and some other homely dishes. **1871** NAPHEYS *Prev. & Cure Dis.* I. ii. 59 The sausage and scrapple of New Jersey. **1881** *Harper's Mag.* Jan. 181 Milk, eggs, sausage, scrapple, vegetables, and poultry, all fresh from the farm. **1910** 'O. HENRY' *Whirligigs* x. 130, I never cared especially for feuds, believing them to be even more over-rated products of our country than grapefruit, scrapple, or honeymoons. **1942** H. W. VAN LOON *Van Loon's Lives* 632 Dante has become a taste that has to be acquired like a love for figs or scrapple. **1943** [see PONHAUS]. **1975** R. STOUT *Family Affair* (1976) ii. 20 A plate of slices of home-made scrapple.

ˈscrapple, *v. dial.* Also 6 skraple, 8 scraple. [f. SCRAPPLE *sb.*[1]] To scrape or use a 'scrapple'.

1504 *Nottingham Rec.* III. 321 For skraplyng of ij. trees. **1711** HEARNE *Collect.* (O.H.S.) III. 138 This pavem[t], after a little earth was scrapled away from its surface..was very fresh and faire. **1847** HALLIWELL, *Scrapple*, to grub about. *Oxon.* **1881** J. SARGISSON *Joe Scroap's Journ.* 48 (E.D.D.) They scrapplt up t'wet spots gayly weel.

scrappy (ˈskræpɪ), *a.*[1] [f. SCRAP *sb.*[1] + -Y.] Consisting of scraps; made up of odds and ends; disjointed, unconnected.

1837 HOWITT *Rur. Life* (1842) 474 If you take any of the volumes of the living poets [in Germany], you are amazed at ..the short and scrappy nature of their effusions. *a* **1849** POE *Marginalia* xliii. Wks. 1864 III. 509 The partial genius is flashy—scrappy. **1858–9** THACKERAY *Virgin.* lvi, It may be that..there is a dreadfully scrappy dinner, the evident remains of a party to which I *didn't* invite you. **1864** BROWNING *Youth & Art* 62 Each life's unfulfilled, you see; It hangs still, patchy and scrappy. **1888** FRITH *Autobiog.* III. vii. 156 This chapter..is intended to be desultory, disjointed,..scrappy, in fact. **1897** MARY KINGSLEY *W. Africa* 436 My classical knowledge is scrappy. **1930** *Daily Express* 6 Oct. 16/6 Both sides resumed their previous rough tactics, and the play became scrappy in consequence. **1976** *Milton Keynes Express* 28 May 54/3 Inter City were unlucky at the start of the second half and then play became scrappy and several unnecessary fouls were committed.

scrappy (ˈskræpɪ), *a.*[2] orig. *U.S.* [f. SCRAP *sb.*[2] or *v.*[2] + -Y[1].] Inclined to scrap or fight; aggressive, pugnacious, quarrelsome.

1895 W. C. GORE in *Inlander* Nov. 65 *Scrappy*,.. quarrelsome. **1935** F. SCOTT FITZGERALD *Let.* 11 May (1964) 264 It was fine seeing you but I was in a scrappy mood about Tom Wolfe. **1941** B. SCHULBERG *What makes Sammy Run?* v. 83 All the instinct for self-preservation of a scrappy kitten. **1977** *Rolling Stone* 7 Apr. 52/1 She was only five feet tall, but she was scrappy—her sister Rebecca Julian remembers her once beating up a bully to protect their little brother. **1977** *Time* 27 June 33/1 'This puts transatlantic air travel in the pocket of the workingman,' proclaimed Freddie Laker, the scrappy founder of Britain's Laker Airways.

scrapy (ˈskreɪpɪ), *a.* [f. SCRAPE *v.* + -Y.] Having or producing a harsh grating noise.

1890 'L. FALCONER' *Mlle. Ixe* ii. 47, I get tired of hearing her scrapy voice. **1890** *Working Men's Coll. Jrnl.* 101 A particularly loud and scrapy violin.

scrapyll, obs. form of SCRAPPLE *sb.*[1]

†**scrash,** *v. Obs. rare*[−1]. [Onomatopœic var. of CRASH *v.*] = CRASH *v.* 1.

1640 tr. *Verdere's Rom. of Rom.* III. iii. 8 Hee seized upon the Knights Shield with his teeth, and pulling it easily from him,..hee scrashed it into a thousand pieces whilst hee trampled it under his feet.

scrat, *sb.*[1] *Obs.* exc. *dial.* Forms: 5 skratt, scrat(t)e, scrette, 6 scrayte, skarth(t, (*erron.* karthe), scarcht, scratche, 6–7 skrat, 7–8, 9 (*dial.*) scrat, scart, scratch. See also SCARTH *sb.*[2] [Perh. repr. OE. *scratta (? miswritten *scritta*), app. (in spite of the difference of sense) corresp. to ON. *skratte* wizard, goblin, monster, mod.Icel. *skratti* devil (MSw. *skratte* goblin); cf. OHG. *scrato, skraz* (pl. *skrazzâ, skrezza*) satyr, wood-demon, MHG. *schrat(e, schraz, schraz,* goblin, elf; for many mod.Ger. derivatives see Grimm s.v. *schrat.*]

1. A hermaphrodite.

c **1000** ÆLFRIC *Gloss.* in Wr.-Wülcker 161/11 *Hermafroditus*, wæpenwifestre, *uel* scritta [? *read* scratta], *uel* bæddel. **14..** *Nom.* ibid. 695/2 *Hic et hec armifraudita*, a skratt. *c* **1475** *Pict. Voc.* ibid. 793/31 *Hec armifodrita*, a scrate. **1482** CAXTON *Trevisa's Higden* II. i. 73 Somtyme one of man-kynde is both man & woman & suche..in englyssh is called a scrette [1527 scratte]. **1552** HULOET, Scrayte whyche is both male and female. *a* **1578** LINDESAY (Pitscottie) *Chron. Scot.* I. xxxi. (S.T.S.) I. 145 Ane bairne borne quhilk had baitht the kyndis of maill and famell, callit in our langage karthe [*v.rr.* scarcht, scratche]. **1600** HOLLAND *Livy* XXXIX. 1036 An Hermaphrodite or Skrat. **1634** T. JOHNSON *Parey's Chirurg.* XXV. iv. (1678) 592 Hermaphrodites, or Scrats. **1691** RAY *N.C. Words*, A *Scrat*; an Hermaphrodite: used of Men, Beasts, and Sheep. **1878** *Cumberld. Gloss.*, *Scrat, scart, scratch*;..a female hermaphrodite sheep.

2. *dial.* (See quot.) Cf. SCRATCH *sb.*[2]

1855 ROBINSON *Whitby Gloss.*, *Scrat*, Satan, generally with the prefix—old, 'Aud Scrat'.

scrat, *sb.*[2] *Obs.* exc. *dial.* Also 6 scratte. [f. SCRAT *v.*]

1. An act of scratching, a mark resulting from scratching. Also, †a weal made by a whip.

1542 UDALL *Erasm. Apoph.* 84 b, The markes or scrattes of the stripes declared as plainly as if he had spoken it..how he had been handled. **1865** ATKINSON *Danby Gloss.*, *Scrat*, a scraping, or scratching together, with pains and toil.

2. A small portion or part of anything.

1593 G. HARVEY *Pierce's Super.* 172 The golden Asse, in the superabundance of his rich humours, promiseth many other golden mountaines; but hath neuer a scrat of siluer. **1877** *Holderness Gloss.*, *Scrat*, a trifle, or minimum of income... 'He's not woth a scrat'. **1896** LUMSDEN *Poems* 89 Sma' wheat was saun, an' maist o' that Was droun'd out to a waesome scrat Ere Mayday cam.

3. One who scrapes; a saving, miserly person.

a **1700** B. E. *Dict. Cant. Crew* s v. *Flay*, ..*He'll flay a Flint*, of a meer Scrat or Miser. **1866** MRS. LYNN LINTON *Lizzie Lorton* xvi. II. 77 Bella was an industrious, hard-working little body, generally called a 'lile scrat' by her neighbours.

scrat, *v. Obs.* exc. *dial.* Forms: 3–6 scratte, 4–6 skrat, 5 skratt, 6 scratt, 4– scrat. Also 6 SCART *v.* [Early ME. *scratte*, of difficult etymology.

The sense coincides with that of MSw. *kratta* to scratch (so also in mod.Sw. dial.; cf. Sw. *kratta* to rake) = OHG. *krazzôn* (G. *kratzen*):—OTeut. **krattôjan*, believed to be the source of It. *grattare*, Sp., Pg. *gratar*, F. *gratter* to scratch, GRATE *v.*[1] Possibly the ME. word may be an alteration (see SCR- 2) of an unrecorded **cratte* (either:—OE. **crattian* or adopted from Scandinavian), representing this Teut. verb. Another possibility is that the word may be a. OF. *esgrater*, f. *es-* (see ES-) + *grater, gratter* (see above).]

1. *intr.* To use the nails or claws for attack; to scratch (*at* a person).

a **1225** *Ancr. R.* 186 And nis þet child fulitowen þet schreþeð [*MS. T* scratteð] aȝean, & bit upon þe ȝerde? *c* **1500** *Smyth & Dame* 374 in Hazl. *E.E.P.* III. 215 All way fast gan she scrat At hym wyth all her myght. **1526** SKELTON *Magnyf.* 1314 A peryllous thynge, to cast a cat Vpon a naked man, and yf she scrat. **1790** MRS. WHEELER *Westmld. Dial.* (1821) 69 They braaid, skrat, an fout, like mad fowk.

2. *trans.* To lacerate, wound, or mark superficially by dragging the nails, claws, or anything pointed or prickly, over the skin or surface.

1340 HAMPOLE *Pr. C.* 7378 Ilk ane scratte other in þe face. *c* **1375** *Sc. Leg. Saints* xxxi. (*Eugenia*) 365 For-þi hyr face scho skratit þare, And of hyre hewid rugit þe hare. *c* **1440** *Alphabet of Tales* 515 And þan he come home all tobittyn and skrattyd with thornys and breers. **1530** PALSGR. 707/2 The catte hath scratte hym by the face. **1577** HELLOWES *Gueuara's Chron.* 197 Hee caused the brestes of the priests to be scrat with combs of yron in his presence. **1621** BURTON *Anat. Mel.* III. iii. II. i. 684 It is an ordinary thing for women in such cases, to scrat the faces, slit the noses of such as they suspect. **1797** BRIDGES *Hom. Trav.* I. 235 If they won't fight, their steps he traces, And..scrats their faces.

†**b.** *fig.* in *passive.* To be superficially marked.

1559 AYLMER *Harborowe* A 3 b, A little scratted with som shewe and apparance of learning.

c. with advs.: To pull *out*, scrape *off* with the claws or nails.

c **1500** *Robt. Deuyll* in Thoms *Prose Rom.* (1828) I. 9 He scratte out theyr eyen. **1589** NASHE *Martin's Months Mind* Ep. Ded., We shall reach them a rappe, as they will neuer clawe of, except they scratt off the skinne from the verie bones.

3. To rub lightly with the finger-nails, etc., to relieve itching or the like; = SCRATCH *v.* 2.

1542 UDALL *Erasm. Apoph.* 324 Scrattyng his hedde with one fynger. **1576** TURBERV. *Venerie* xlvii, Sometimes he would skrat his thyghes with his foote. **1598** HALL *Sat.* VI. i, And bite my nayles, and scrat my dullard head.

4. *intr.* Of a bird or animal: To rake in the ground with the claws. Also *transf.* of persons.

1556 J. HEYWOOD *Spider & F.* xv. 58 While ye were in that diche scrallyng, And scratting in the myre to saue your life. **1621** BURTON *Anat. Mel.* I. ii. III. xii. 156 Seeing a Crow scrat vpon the muck-hill, [he] returned in all hast. **1859** GEO. ELIOT *Adam Bede* i, If a man..scrats at his bit o' garden, and makes two potatoes grow i'stead o' one [etc.].

b. *trans.* with advs. To get *out*, *up*, by scratching.

a **1560** BECON *Fl. Godly Prayers* Pref., Wks. II. 176 The Iewes were compelled for very hunger..to scratte out the most filthy and stinking dounge,..and for very famine to eate it. **1864** MRS. H. WOOD *Trev. Hold* I. ii. 22 The hole was scratted out by the dog. **1886** *Chesh. Gloss.* s.v., Th' ens have been i' th' garden, and scratted up everythink.

5. *intr.* (fig. of 4). To struggle to make a living or to gain money: SCRATCH *v.* 5.

1579 W. A. *Spec. Rem. Lawless Love* cj (Roxb. Club), He ..scrapes and scrattes as though all were his owne, And hoordes it vp within his bagges to rust. **1587** *Mirr. Mag.*, *Wolsey* ii, Ambitious minde, a world of wealth would haue, So scrats and scrapes, for scorfe, and scoruy drosse. **1861** GEO. ELIOT *Silas M.* xiv, We may strive and scrat and fend, but its little we can do arter all.

Hence **ˈscratting** *vbl. sb.*, and *ppl. a.*

c **1375** *Cursor M.* 11823 (Fairf.), & wiþ skratting he toke þe skurf he barked ouer as a turfe. **1555** WATREMAN *Fardle Facions* II. viii. 179 Thei canne finde none ende of their scrattinge, but the more thei haue, the fellier gnaweth their longing. **1593** CHURCHYARD *Challenge* 1 The restles race, that mortall men doe runne, Seemes smooth to sight, yet full of scratting breers. **1602–3** in P. F. Tytler *Hist. Scot.* (1864) IV. 312, I hope you will bear with my molesting you too long with my scrattinge hand. **1667** LACY *Sauny the Scott* II. i. (1698), I take as Muckle Pleasure, Sir, in Scratten and Scrubben, as ye de in Tiplin and Mowing.

scratch (skrætʃ), *sb.*[1] [f. SCRATCH *v.*]

I. Result of scratching.

1. a. A slight tearing or incision of the skin produced by a sharp instrument. (Sometimes applied slightingly to a trifling flesh-wound.) Cf. SCRAT *sb.*[2]

a **1586** SIDNEY *Arcadia* I. (Sommer) 82 Al the Lion could do, was with his paw to teare of the mantle and sleeue of Zelmane, with a little scratch, rather then a wound. **1592** SHAKS. *Rom. & Jul.* III. i. 96 *Ben.* What art thou hurt? *Mer.* I, I, a scratch, a scratch, marry 'tis inough, Where is my Page? go Villaine fetch a Surgeon. **1613** BEAUM. & FL. *Philaster* v. i, *Leon.* Are all his wounds well? *Tra.* All, they were but scratches, but the losse of blood made him faint. **1672** WISEMAN *Wounds* I. x. 96 But if the bloud..be recent, it possibly happened from some scratch of your Terebra. **1719** DE FOE *Crusoe* II. (Globe) 394 The third had a little scratch in the shoulder. **1828** SCOTT *F.M. Perth* iii, Surely a few drops of blood from a scratch, and a few silly words from a foolish wench's lips, are not to part father and son. **1851** TENNYSON *Edwin Morris* 63, I would have hid her needle in my heart, To save her little finger from a scratch. **1889** CORBETT *Monk* i. 10 The young ensign passed through the four months of..fighting without a scratch.

b. *fig.*

1592 TIMME *Ten Eng. Lepers* vii. H 2 b, Rase it over but with a little scratch, and all the matter of love is gone. **1682** SIR T. BROWNE *Chr. Mor.* (1756) 94 Angred pride makes a noise, like Homerican Mars, at every scratch of offences. **1759** H. WALPOLE *Let. to Mann* 30 Nov., Our loss is a scratch, one lieutenant and thirty-nine men killed [etc.].

c. slang. ***no great scratch***: of no serious importance, of no great value.

1844 *Maj. Jones' Courtship* 136 (Bartlett), There are a good many Joneses in Georgia, and I know some myself that ain't no great scratches. **1864** *Hotten's Slang Dict.* s.v., 'No great scratch', of little worth.

2. a. *pl.* A disease of horses, in which the pastern appears as if scratched; = *cratches*, CRATCH *sb.*[2] 2.

1591 PERCIVALL *Sp. Dict.*, *Arestin*, the scratches in a horses pasterns, *Scabies in equorum suffragine.* **1650** B. *Discolliminium* 16 My Mare hath the Scratches on her hinder Heeles. **1754** BARTLET *Gentl. Farriery* xxxvii. (ed. 2) 305 Scratches in the heels have so much affinity with the grease..that [etc.]. **1881** *Scribner's Monthly* XXII. 644 The history of a galled shoulder or of an obstinate case of scratches.

fig. **1596** NASHE *Saffron Walden* 26 So hath hee.. vncessantly perswaded me to preserue my credit from iadish dying of the scratches.

b. The mange. Cf. CRATCH *sb.*[2] 1.

1828 *Sporting Mag.* XXIII. 26 The appearance of mange, or scratch as it is sometimes called, among my hounds.

3. A mark or furrow produced by the grinding contact of two substances; a shallow linear incision.

1662 FAITHORNE *Art Graving* 48 And if you perceive any scratches in your plate, rub them out with your burnisher. **1677** MOXON *Mech. Exerc.*, *Smithing* 15 The course File cuts deep and makes deep scratches in the work. **1816** J. SMITH *Panorama Sci. & Art* II. 818 The scratch made on the glass at the commencement, need scarcely be more than a point. **1863** DANA *Man. Geol.* 538 There are deep scratches or groovings in the rocky surface of the country across which the stones were carried. **1907** HODGES *Elem. Photogr.* 25 Any adherent grit will cause scratches.

4. a. A rough or irregular mark made by a pencil, paint-brush, etc.; hence, a slight sketch, a hasty scrawl.

1646 EVELYN *Diary* Apr., 400 leaves full of scratches of Indians. **1653** URQUHART *Rabelais* I. xxviii, Drawing scratches on the hearth with a stick burnt at the one end.

1752 MRS. DELANY *Life & Corr.* (1861) III. 124, I send you a little scratch not worthy to be called a sketch. **1785** COWPER *Let. to Newton* Wks. 1836 V. 153 Every scratch of his pen was accounted a treasure. **1811** BYRON *Let. to Dallas* Wks. 432 *note*, A scratch under *last*, to show where the joke lies. *a* **1871** DE MORGAN *Budget Parad.* (1872) 466 If any one should have the sense to leave out of his Greek the unmeaning scratches which they call accents. **1908** *Outlook* 14 Nov. 655/2 The scratch of a Minister's pen may be worth millions of dollars to some favoured person or some inside syndicate.

b. Money, esp. paper money. *slang* (orig. *U.S.*).

1914 JACKSON & HELLYER *Vocab. Criminal Slang* 74 *Scratch*,..paper currency... 'He's got a bundle of scratch'. **1916** *Lit. Digest* 19 Aug. 424/2 Money is given a score of names; the most used is 'kale', 'scratch', or 'dough'. **1931** *Writer's Digest* Oct. 29 Don't mess with that iron money; get the scratch. **1939** *New Yorker* 1 Apr. 19/2 She..also had plenty of scratch, being the bank president's daughter. **1941** J. SMILEY *Hash House Lingo* 47 *Scratch*, coins. **1955** POHL & KORNBLUTH *Space Merchants* xiv. 123 Here's some scratch, and shop when you get a chance. **1957** N. MARSH *Off with his Head* xii. 269, I wouldn't have done it only I wanted the scratch like hell. **1967** I. HAMILTON *Man with Brown Paper Face* vii. 102 Alfred Mays..had enough scratch to run two homes. **1972** D. ANTHONY *Blood on Harvest Moon* xiv. 118 She runs some kind of talent agency. Probably a tax write-off... She doesn't need the scratch. **1978** G. MCDONALD *Fletch's Fortune* xv. 106 As soon as Fletch got the story from each girl..he found himself..getting up the scratch to bus her home. **1980** *Private Eye* 6 June 7/1 This state-funded legal nonsense—which is..putting even more scratch into the bulging wallets of the lawyers.

5. *Sporting.* A line or mark drawn as an indication of a boundary or starting-point; †in *Cricket*, a 'crease' (*obs.*); in *Pugilism*, the line drawn across the ring, to which boxers are brought for an encounter. Hence in various phrases (often *fig.*), as ***to come up to (the) scratch***, up to the required standard; ***to bring to the scratch, to toe the scratch***, etc.

1778 COTTON in Nyren *Yng. Cricketer's Tutor* (1833) 67 Ye strikers..Stand firm to your scratch, let your bat be upright. **1821** *John Bull* 7 Jan. 29/3 He started a few seconds before the time and came up in speed to the scratch at the moment appointed. **1830–57** DE QUINCEY *Bentley* Wks. VII. 131 No prudent champion, however game, would have chosen to offer himself to the scratch for a second round. **1843** DICKENS *Let.* 17 June (1974) III. 513 Pray, as a Member of the Committee, come up to the Scratch. **1848** A. BRONTË *Tenant of Wildfell Hall* II. xi. 202 Your uncle and aunt have long been wanting us to go there, you know; but somehow, there's such a repulsion between the good lady and me, that I never could bring myself up to the scratch. **1861** C. M. YONGE *Young Step-Mother* xiii. 156 The Vicar ..was meditating a fresh one [*sc.* attempt], if..he could bring his churchwarden up to the scratch. **1881** *Sportsman's Year-bk.* 37 [Pigeon shooting rules.] 21. In Shooting Matches..The shooter is bound in his turn to appear at the scratch within five minutes when called upon. **1894** SIR J. ASTLEY *Fifty Yrs. Life* I. 41 Some eight or ten toed the scratch, and I won very easily. **1911** G. B. SHAW *Getting Married* 226 It's about the wedding... We cant get our man up to the scratch. Cecil has locked himself in his room and wont see or speak to any one. **1934** 'G. ORWELL' *Burmese Days* ix. 142 If they won't come up to scratch you can always get hold of the ringleaders and give them a good bambooing on the Q.T. **1953** D. GARNETT *Golden Echo* vi. 133 All Edward's friends were mobilised and came loyally up to scratch. **1960** C. DAY LEWIS *Buried Day* II. viii. 164 Those of us who had pretensions to brain Maurice brought up to scratch by loosing on them the full force of his personality. **1978** *Taxi* 16 Feb. 11/4 (Advt.), Cold weather can cause you a lot of problems if your cab's electrics aren't up to scratch.

b. The starting-point in a handicap of a competitor who receives no odds; sometimes *colloq.* used *ellipt.* for such a competitor. Also *fig.*; esp. in phr. ***from scratch***, from a position of no advantage, knowledge, influence, etc., from nothing.

1867 *Athlete for 1866*, 9 W. Collett, scratch 1. **1876** *Bicycle Jrnl.* 18 Aug. 7/1 Mr. Tom Sabin, of the Coventry Bicycle Club, has won, during last week, three races from scratch. **1886** *Field* 31 July 182/2 In the [lawn tennis] match between Messrs. G. Butler (owes 15) and E. A. Butler (scratch), the odd set again had to be resorted to. **1922** JOYCE *Ulysses* 454 A poor foreign immigrant who started scratch as a stowaway and is now trying to turn an honest penny. **1936** *Economist* 2 May 233/1 Nazi Germany, starting her rapid re-armament 'from scratch' in 1933, was fortunate enough to have a surplus capacity in all sections of her heavy industries. **1939** 'G. ORWELL' *Coming up for Air* II. v. 103 We'd no fishing tackle of any kind, not even a pin or a bit of string. We had to start from scratch. **1953** S. KAUFFMANN *Philanderer* v. 77 He took one look at her and thought: If I want that, I must begin all over again right from scratch. **1957** L. F. R. WILLIAMS *State of Israel* 53 Another branch of communications which has been built up from scratch to a degree of efficiency. **1962** *Guardian* 21 Mar. 2/5 The whole Treasury block could..have been rebuilt from scratch for the money. **1978** *Peace News* 25 Aug. 7/2 The daily routine was a crash programme of tuition provided by civilians, mainly Russian or other Slavic emigrés, in Russian from scratch to A-level standard, which was achieved in 10 months. **1979** *Fortune* 29 Jan. 77 NASA is not exactly starting from scratch out there in space; it is building on promising experiments done on prior space flights.

c. *Sporting.* A horse or other animal withdrawn from the list of entries for a race or other competition.

1938 *Mr.* Dec. 128/2 *Scratch*,..a horse withdrawn from a race. **1947** *Sun* (Baltimore) 20 Dec. 12/1 The overnight favorite..was a late scratch. **1960** WENTWORTH & FLEXNER *Dict. Amer. Slang* 450/2 *Scratch*,..a horse that has been withdrawn from a race after midnight of the night before the race. **1979** *Arizona Daily Star* 8 Apr. c2/3 We kept hoping there would be a scratch in the fast heat... I must have asked a hundred times if there were any scratches.

6. a. The sound produced by the friction of two more or less rough surfaces.

1787 MME. D'ARBLAY *Diary* 8 Nov., At the Royal doors there is always a particular kind of scratch used, instead of tapping. **1898** G. B. SHAW *Arms & Man* I. 8 There is a scratch, and the flame of a match is seen in the middle of the room.

b. A rough hiss heard from the loudspeaker (or horn) when a record is played and caused by the friction of the stylus in the groove.

1908 *Talking Machine News* I. 9/1 Scratch seems to be filtered out of the reproduction. **1926** *Punch* 2 June p. iii (Advt.), Columbia new process records. The only records without scratch. **1942** [see *ground noise* s.v. GROUND *sb.* 18]. **1949** G. A. BRIGGS *Sound Reproduction* xix. 117 Cutting out a slice of scratch also removes a slice of music or whatever is being reproduced. **1961** E. N. BRADLEY *Records & Gramophone Equipment* ii. 43 Possessors of old 78 r.p.m. records who play these on new lighweight equipment may find a quite distressing amount of scratch and surface noise.

7. *Salt making.* (See quot.) Also *attrib.*

Perhaps so called because *scratched* from the side of the pan. Possibly, however, it is a different word: cf. SCRATCHINGS.

1723 BROWN in *Phil. Trans.* XXXII. 354 Whilst the Brine is boyling, there precipitates a hard crusty Matter,..Part of it fixes on the Bottom of the Iron Pan so hard, as to be afterwards dug off; and this the Workmen call Scratch. **1753** *Chambers' Cycl.* Suppl., *Scratch*, in the language of the salt-workers of our country, the name of a calcarious earthy or stony substance, which separates from sea water in boiling it for salt. Scratch pans, in the English salt-works, a name given to certain leaden pans, which [etc.]. **1797** *Encycl. Brit.* (ed. 3) XVI. 627/1 At the four corners of the salt-pan, where the flame does not touch its bottom, are placed four small lead pans called scratch pans.

II. 8. a. An act of scratching.

1765 *Museum Rust.* III. 157, I pass a moderate-sized roller over the field, and then give it a slight scratch with a pair of light harrows. **1844** O. W. HOLMES *Verses for After-dinner* 28 No rubbing will kindle your Lucifer match, If the fiz does not follow the primitive scratch. **1861** HUGHES *Tom Brown at Oxf.* xxxvi, Lifting the back of his short hat off his head to make room for a scratch. **1899** *Daily News* 31 Mar. 4/7 The little finger is going to descend on the nearly bald pate and gently tickle it—the scratch of feigned wonderment or perplexity. **1932** H. C. WYLD *Universal Dict. Eng. Lang.* 1068/3 Dogs enjoy a good scratch.

b. A skirmish, a trivial fight.

1840 DE QUINCEY *Style* Wks. XI. 218 The philosopher should not have had it all his own way; there should have been a 'scratch' at least between us.

†III. 9. (See quot.) *Obs.*

1618 ATKINSON *Gold Mynes Scot.* (Bannatyne Club) 1 The iron raake or scratch to cull and devide the great stones.

IV. 10. Ellipt. for *scratch periwig* (see 12).

Possibly the etymological notion was 'a periwig that gives opportunity for scratching the head'.

1755 *Connoisseur* No. 77 ¶1 His long lank greasy hair may be exchanged in Middle-Row for a smart bag or a jemmy scratch. **1764** *Oxf. Sausage* 26 Quips, and Cranks, and wanton Wiles, That love to live within the one-curled Scratch. **1806** SURR *Winter in Lond.* II. 119 A stout short man, with a flaxen scratch. **1830** O. W. HOLMES *Treadmill Song* 30 Don't pull his hair, Because he wears a scratch. **1904** BARONESS VON HUTTEN *Pam* 285 Either his hair is beginning to grow, or he is wearing a craftily made scratch.

11. In Billiards and related games: **a.** a lucky stroke, a fluke ? *obs.*; **b.** a shot that incurs a penalty. Cf. SCRATCH *v.* 12.

a. **1850** M. PHELAN *Billards without Master* 12 It is amusing to observe the effect produced on some players by what is technically called a 'scratch', or fortuitous stroke. **1859** G. W. MATSELL *Vocabulum* 122/1 When a player wins a stroke or count by accident, without deserving it, he is said to have made a scratch. **1869** 'MARK TWAIN' *Innocents Abroad* xii. 116 We had played billiards..on an ancient table that made the balls..perform feats in the way of..almost impossible 'scratches'. **1907** *N. Amer. Rev.* Nov. 333, I saw nothing there in the way of science and art that was more wonderful than shots [in Billiards] which I had seen Texas Tom make..all calculated shots, and not a fluke or a scratch among them.

b. **1913** J. T. STODDARD *Science of Billiards* vii. 153 One ball is forfeited for a failure to hit any ball, or for pocketing the cue ball ('scratch'). **1974** *Rules of Game* 85/3 Scratches are also incurred during safety play on a ball frozen to a cushion, and when a player's cue ball jumps off the table. **1975** *Way to Play* 195/3 At his third scratch in succession, a player loses one point for the third scratch, plus 15 points for the three successive scratches.

V. 12. *attrib.* and *Comb.*

a. attributive uses of sense 5 b, as ***scratch boat, -car, -line, machine, -man, -player, -race, runner***.

1896 *Rudder* July 220/2 A table of time allowances has been figured out..using the 130-foot boat as '*scratch boat' (to use a foot-racing term). **1950** *Sun* (Baltimore) 18 Mar. 12/1 The Ticonderoga..was named the scratch boat. This means she is favored to finish first in the long race. **1908** *Westm. Gaz.* 21 Apr. 4/2 Two thousand two hundred and thirty-one yards separated the limit car from the *scratch car. **1897** *Encycl. Sport* I. 62/1 (Athletics) **Scratch line*, the mark from which the length of any race is measured. **1955** *Times* 22 Aug. 4/5 The race..resolved itself in the closing stages into an exciting tussle between Mr. Clifford, in the *scratch machine, and Mr. Peter Vanneck, in the longest handicap aircraft. **1877** *Bicycle Jrnl.* 7 Sept. 6/1 The ultimate result was a brilliant and well earned victory by the two *scratch men. **1888** *Athenæum* 16 June 760/3 The tone of brutality towards bad players which *scratch players always adopt. **1897** *Encycl. Sport* I. 473/1 (Golf) *Scratch player*, a good player, who receives neither handicap nor penalty. **1864** *Hotten's Slang Dict.*, **Scratch-race* (on the Turf), a race where any horse, aged, winner, or loser, can run with any weights. **1888** P. FURNIVALL *Phys. Training* 6 Next comes the knotty point as to whether the rider intends training for handicaps or scratch races. **1976** *Star* (Sheffield) 30 Nov., Bert Oliver (Kelty), British professional 110 metres champion, is the *scratch runner in the Skol Sprint 110 metres handicap on January 1 and January 3.

b. Special combinations (some of which may perh. be referred to the verb): **scratch-block**, a scribbling block (cf. sense 4); **scratch-card**, an instrument for polishing metals formed by fastening long lengths of steel wire upon a pad of leather or cloth; **scratch-carding**, the use of the *scratch-card*; **scratch-cat**, humorous epithet for a spiteful person; **scratch-coat** (? *U.S.*), a rough coating of plaster scratched before it is quite dry in order that the following coat may adhere properly; hence **scratch-coated** *a.*, treated with such a coating of plaster; ***scratch-coating*** vbl. sb.; **scratch-comma**, a diagonal stroke used by some early printers in place of the comma; **scratch-cradle**, a name for CATS-CRADLE; **scratch dial**, a set of marks found on the walls of old churches, usually considered to be an ancient form of sundial; **scratch-figure** *Typogr.* = *scratched figure*; **scratch filter** *Electr.*, a filter designed to reduce the audibility of scratches and hiss in sound reproduction; **scratch-finish** (see quot.); **scratch-grass**, a dial. name for *Galium Aparine*, *Cynosurus cristatus*, and, in U.S., *Polygonum sagittatum*; **scratch hardness**, the hardness of a metal or mineral as estimated by measuring the width of a scratch made on the material by a diamond point under a specified load; **scratch hit** *Baseball* (see quot. 1976); †**scratch-hoeing** (see quot.); **scratch hole**, a hole or trench scratched out of the ground; **scratch-knot**, a simple form of scratch-brush consisting of a single bunch of wire; **scratch-pan** (see sense 7); **scratch paper** *N. Amer.*, scribbling paper; **scratch-periwig** = *scratch-wig*; **scratch-plough** *v. trans.*, to plough very shallowly; **scratch-rattle** = SCRATCH-BACK 2; **scratch sheet** *U.S. Sporting*, a printed list of the entries in the day's races and their odds; also *transf.*; **scratch stock** (see quot. 1966); **scratch-weed**, *Galium Aparine*; **scratch-wig**, a small, short wig; **scratch-work**, (*a*) (see quot. 1710); (*b*) scratched lines on an engraving plate. Also SCRATCH-BRUSH.

1897 FLANDRAU *Harvard Episodes* 192 His note-books and *scratch block were lying open. **1839** *Scratch card [see SCRATCH-BRUSH]. **1839** F. A. GRIFFITHS *Artil. Man.* 3 The operation of *scratch-carding is..to commence. **1880** 'OUIDA' *Moths* I. 39 She was the most obstinate, humdrum, nasty old *scratch-cat in the County. **1891** *Century Dict.*, **Scratch-coat.* **1953** VAN DEN BRANDEN & KNOWLES *Plastering Skill & Practice* i. 5 Of the three coats, the first coat, or scratch coat, is a thin coat... The purpose of the scratch coat..is to..provide a good base for the plaster coats that will follow. **1823** J. F. COOPER *Pioneers* xi, The brown sides of the *scratch-coated walls. **1911** *Encycl. Brit.* XXI. 785/2 For the first coat a layer of well-haired coarse stuff.. is put on with the laying trowel. This is termed 'pricking up' in London, and in America '*scratch coating'. **1888** JACOBI *Printers' Voc.*, **Scratch comma*, a sign thus / used in old documents and reprints. It is now used as a shilling mark. **1892** LOUNSBURY *Stud. Chaucer* I. 342 The mark that goes under the name of a scratch-comma. **1822** NARES *Gloss.* s.v. *Cratch*, A childish game, corruptly called *scratch-cradle. **1914** *Proc. Somerset Archæol. Soc.* LIX. II. 26 The name *Scratch Dial has been given to this ancient form of sundial. **1938** *Times Lit. Suppl.* 15 Jan. 39/1 The woodwork follows —roofs, benches, pulpits; and then scratch-dials and aumbries, mural paintings and windows bring up the rear. **1960** J. BETJEMAN *Summoned by Bells* v. 49 Was that the reason why the pale grey slides Of tympana, scratch dials and Norfolk screens So pleased me at his lectures? **1967** C. A. VEARNCOMBE *Hist. of Church of St. Lawrence the Martyr* (Lydeard St. Lawrence, Somerset) 19 This doorway has a scratch dial on the east, 3 ft. 9 in. above the plinth. **1888** JACOBI *Printers' Voc.*, *Scratch figures. **1929** K. HENNEY *Princ. Radio* xvi. 289 Similar filters are used in phonograph reproduction to eliminate the needle noise. They are called *scratch filters and may tune somewhere between 3000 and 5000 cycles. **1935** NILSON & HORNUNG *Pract. Radio Commun.* viii. 349 It will be necessary to attenuate the high frequencies... This may be accomplished by introducing a series-resonant circuit similar to that used for scratch filters. **1977** *Rolling Stone* 5 May 80/2 Watch for this spec when you consider the usefulness of rumble and scratch filters on your next amp or receiver. **1891** *Century Dict.*, **Scratch-finish*, a finish for decorative objects of metal-work, in which a surface otherwise smooth is diversified by small curved scratches forming irregular scrolls over the whole field. **1846–50** A. WOOD *Class-bk. Bot.* 475 *Polygonum sagittatum.* *Scratchgrass. **1886** BRITTEN & HOLLAND *Plant-n.*, Scratch Grass. **1928** *Jrnl. Iron & Steel Inst.* CXVII. 893 Annealing these cold-rolled single crystals at 250°C..gave no measurable rise of *scratch hardness. **1962** R. WEBSTER *Gems* II. 488 For the gemmologist, scratch hardness, based on the standard minerals in Mohs's list, is the only practical basis for experiment. **1972** *Jrnl. Physics* D.V. 1293 Scratch hardness measurements reflect a greater degree of anisotropy in the properties of crystals than the corresponding indentation techniques. **1917** C. MATHEWSON *Second Base Sloan* 166 Four men faced Chase in the third, the first getting a *scratch hit. **1935** *Encycl. Sports* 63/1 *Scratch-hit*, a weak hit into the infield. **1943** *Amer. Speech* XVIII. 103 A 'single' in the third inning becomes a 'scratch hit' in the fourth. **1976** *Webster's Sport Dict.* 374/1 *Scratch hit*, a batted ball that enables a batter to reach base safely but that is neither an error nor a clean base hit. 1733 Tull *Horse-Hoeing Husb.* vii. 56 The Shallow Horse-Hoeing.. is but an Imitation of the Hand-Hoe,.. and may be properly called *Scratch-Hoeing. 1923 Kipling *Irish Guards in Great War* I. 6 The German trenches, which were rather in the nature of *scratch-holes. 1969 G. Coppard *With Machine Gun to Cambrai* xxi. 87 We lived a mean and improverished sort of existence in lousy scratch holes. 1905 Hasluck *Electro-plating*, Fig. 44 *Scratch-knot. 1899 B. Tarkington *Gentl. Indiana* xiii. 223 Sheets of blank *scratch-paper lay before them, and they relaxed not their knit brows. 1934 J. O'Hara *Appointment in Samarra* (1935) vii. 214 He wanted to work.., and he tried to the extent of getting out some scratch-paper and pencils. 1971 *Islander* (Victoria, B.C.) 12 Sept. 9/5 When I take down a recipe from someone it is usually on a piece of scratch paper. 1979 *Farmington* (New Mexico) *Daily Times* 27 May 6c/4 (Advt.), Newsprint roll end paper 20c. a pound.., or else we will cut scratch paper, any length & width desired for 35c a pound. 1771 Smollett *Humph. Clinker* 31 May, Our.. footman.. lost his *scratch periwig. 1926 D. H. Lawrence *Plumed Serpent* x. 170 The land was being *scratch-ploughed by a pair of oxen and a lump of pointed wood. 1870 Bartley *1 Square Mile E. London* 50 The abolition of Greenwich and other fairs having much damaged the sale of the *scratch-rattle toy, which was his speciality. 1939 *Sun* (Baltimore) 30 Nov. 24/6, I noticed that one of the girls was looking at a *scratch sheet. 1956 T. Betts *Across Board* 170 William Armstrong.. published the first scratch sheet that ever appeared on the newsstands of New York. The year was 1917. 1964 L. Hairston in J. H. Clarke *Harlem* 288, I.. took the resumé scratch-sheet.. background.. workin' experience.. and such particulars. 1973 *N.Y. Law Jrnl.* 8 May 4/4 The person who reads the *New York Times* or *Daily News* or even the scratch sheets. 1934 P. A. Wells *Design in Woodwork* iii. 28 Lines or bandings round a panel,.. can be pleasant.. if not overdone. These are grooved in with a *scratch stock, a simple tool made in the workshop. 1966 A. W. Lewis *Gloss. Woodworking Terms* 85 *Scratch stock*, tool for making small beads, mouldings, or grooves of inlays by scraping *along* the grain of the wood. 1976 F. E. Sherlock *Enjoying Home Carpentry & Woodwork* vii. 76 The scratch stock is very useful for the fine woodworker who wishes to inlay veneer lines. 1855 Miss Pratt *Flower, Pl.* III. 154 (Goose-grass or Cleavers)... Leaves, stems, and globular fruits are all bristly, and the latter often cling to the clothing,.. thus it is called..*Scratchweed. 1868 *Paxton's Bot. Dict.*, *Scratch-weed*. 1775 Mme. D'Arblay *Early Diary* 26 Mar., [Garrick] was himself in a most odious *scratch wig. 1889 Gretton *Memory's Harkback* 7 A good-humoured, easy-going veteran in a scratch wig. 1710 J. Harris *Lex. Techn.* II, **Scratch-work*, in Italian, *Sgrafitti*, was a way of Painting in Fresco, by preparing of a black Ground, on which was placed a white Plaster; and this White being taken off with an Iron Bodkin, the Black appears thro the Holes, and serves for Shadows. 1910 W. de la Mare *Three Mulla-Mulgars* i. 6 She is shown veiled on the rude pots of Assasimmon and in Mulgar scratch-work. 1977 *Times Lit. Suppl.* 14 Jan. 40/2 Reworked by Blake with scratchwork and blank ink... In this intermediate proof Blake has made these alterations through scratchwork and pen lines, in preparation for reworking the plate.

scratch (skrætʃ), *sb.*[2] *colloq.* (now chiefly *dial.*) [Alteration of scrat *sb.*[1], after scratch *v.*] A name for the devil, usually *Old Scratch*.

1740 *Christmas Entertainments* iv. (1883) 38 Old Scratch or Nicholas the Antient. 1756 Amory *Buncle* (1825) I. 303 Scratch was the name I had for the evil one. 1762 [see old *a.* 9]. 1858 Trollope *Three Clerks* xx, He'd have pitched me to Old Scratch.. if [etc.]. 1873 Will Carleton *Farm Ball.* 43 Do you mind my melon-patch—How you gobbled the whole batch,.. just to raise the scratch?

scratch (skrætʃ), *a.* [Orig. the sb. used attrib.]

1. Hastily sketched, roughly drawn.

1853 R. S. Surtees *Sponge's Sp. Tour* xx. 98 A scratch map he had made on a bit of paper.

2. a. Gathered together promiscuously, hastily assembled. *scratch vote, division, majority*: one which, owing to accident or stratagem, does not represent the actual state of opinion in a constituency or deliberative body (cf. *snap*, *snatch*). Of a game or match: impromptu, played by scratch teams. Freq. also of a meal.

1851 J. Pycroft *Cricket Field* x. 189 That is the time that some.. batsman, whose eminence is little seen amidst the loose hitting of a scratch match, comes.. to the wicket and makes a stand. 1851 *London at Table* i. 23 The butler.. giving directions to what the four-in-hand club used to call 'a scratch team' of servants. 1859 Jephson *Brittany* ix. 147 Our pack was what is called a 'scratch pack'. Every one contributed a dog or two. 1864 *Times* 17 Mar. (Hoppe), Compared with the Oxford men, those sent up by Cambridge on this occasion were little better than a scratch crew. 1872 Lever *Ld. Kilgobbin* lxiii, The company was what he irreverently called.. a scratch team. 1874 E. J. M. Collins *Frances* III. x. 234 Frances and Cecilia, coming down, found a hasty luncheon, and everybody busy at it... When this scratch luncheon was over, everybody went out. 1883 Sherer *At Home & in India* 119 A scratch troop of domestics.. secured all the glass doors. 1891 *Newcastle Daily Jrnl.* 9 Oct. 4/6 All he looks forward to is a scratch majority, obtained.. by keeping the whole question in the dark. 1900 *Edin. Rev.* Jan. 266 Scratch brigades.. hastily constituted with scratch staffs. 1903 [see cart *v.* 1 d]. 1923 J. Manchon *Le Slang* 258 *A scratch breakfast*, un déjeuner improvisé. 1942 *R.A.F. Jrnl.* 18 Apr. 10, I then commanded a scratch squadron of rather ropey machines. 1944 *Return to Attack* (Army Board, N.Z.) 15/2 Some of the men were keeping warm.. by playing scratch football. 1952 [see organize *v.* 2 d]. 1953 S. Kauffmann *Philanderer* vi. 103 They sat down to a scratch meal at about nine. 1973 'J. Patrick' *Glasgow Gang Observed* xviii. 146 Facilities for 'scratch' games of football. 1981 J. R. L. Anderson *Death in High Latitude* v. 85 If you don't mind a scratch meal I'd be delighted if you could stay to supper.

b. *absol.* A scratch crew.

1896 *Daily News* 26 Mar. 7/2 The eights paddled up steadily against the ebb, the scratch stopping short at Barnes with the Dark Blues going on. 1908 *Daily Chron.* 2 Apr. 6/5 It is not so easy to race away from a fresh scratch towards the end of a twelve minutes row.

scratch (skrætʃ), *v.* Forms: 5 scracch, scartch, 6 scratche, skratch(e, scarche, 6–7 scrach, 5– scratch. [App. produced by a confusion of the synonymous scrat, cratch *vbs.*

First in Caxton. The form *scartch, scarche*, which occurs once in Caxton and once in Du Wes, may possibly be a mere misprint, although metathesis of *ra* is not uncommon.]

1. a. *trans.* To wound superficially by dragging the claws or finger-nails over the skin. Also, in wider sense: To wound superficially with anything pointed and hard dragged over the skin or in contact with its moving surface, so as to produce a slight linear tearing or abrasion. (Cf. sense 3 f.)

1474 Caxton *Chesse* ii. i. (1883) 20 He scracchid hym in the visage. *c* 1489 —— *Sonnes of Aymon* xxii. 491 For she scartched her face and pulled her heres from her hede for grete sorow. 1530 Palsgr. 720/1 Se howe she hath scratched me by the face. *c* 1532 Du Wes *Introd. Fr.* ibid. 943 To scarche, *esgratigner*. *Ibid.* 945 To scratche, *esgratigner*. 1541 R. Copland *Galyen's Terap.* 2 D ij b, He hath scratched hymself in any party, as on the arme, and sodaynly is rysen a blyster or pustule. 1591 Shaks. *Two Gent.* i. ii, How way-ward is this foolish loue; That (like a testie Babe) will scratch the Nurse, And presently, all humbled kisse the Rod? 1638 Sir T. Herbert *Trav.* (ed. 2) 238 Who to expresse their zeale the better, burne and scratch their armes and breasts, cutting their flesh. 1766 Gray *Impromptus* 6 Bishop of Chester,.. If you scratch him will fester. 1870 Bryant *Iliad* I. v. 155 A golden buckle scratched her tender hand. 1872 Calverley *Fly Leaves* (1884) 57 But all too soon my kitten Became a full-sized cat, by which I've more than once been scratch'd and bitten. 1968 B. Evans *Dict. Quotations* 602/1 Scratch a Russian, and you will wound a Tartar. 1977 'D. Cory' *Bennett* ii. 64 Scratch a Spaniard, Hunter thought, and he oozes an offended formality instead of blood.

b. With adv.: To tear *out* (e.g. the eyes) or to drag *off* (a portion of the skin, a pimple, etc.) with the claws or nails.

1591 Shaks. *Two Gent.* iv. iv. 209, I vow, I should haue scratch'd out your vnseeing eyes. 1609 B. Jonson *Masque of Queens* Wks. 1616 I. 952, I scratch'd out the eyes of the Owle before. 1674 Brevint *Saul at Endor* 120 Thus when she killed one once and scratcht out the eie of another.

c. *absol.* or *intr.* To use the claws or nails as weapons of offence. Also occas. of inanimate things, to produce a scratch or superficial abrasion.

1589 *Pappe w. Hatchet* Lyly's Wks. 1902 III. 406 If a field may be pitcht we are readie: if they scratch wee will bring cattes. *a* 1629 Goffe *Courag. Turk* iii. iii. (1632) E 3, Enter some Truls both sides, they fight and scratch. 1839 Hood *Rural Felicity* 28 But, mercy on us, how nettles will sting, and how the long brambles do scratch. 1855 Macaulay *Hist. Eng.* xxi. IV. 666 It was better to die biting and scratching to the last than to be worried without resistance or revenge. 1885 *Sat. Rev.* 3 Jan., Children, especially when they grow to years of discretion, should not scratch.

†d. *fig.* To skirmish or fight without doing serious injury. *Obs.*

1596 Nashe *Saffron Walden* O 4, Euerie circumstance I cannot stand to reckon vp, as how wee came to take knowledge of one anothers being there, or what a stomacke I had to haue scratcht with him. 1625 in Rushw. *Hist. Coll.* (1659) I. 193 What is it for his Allies to scratch with the King of Spain, to take a Town to day, and lose it tomorrow.

2. a. *trans.* To rub or scrape lightly (a part of the body) with the finger-nails or claws (e.g. to relieve itching). So *to scratch one's head*, as a gesture indicating perplexity; also *fig.*

1530 Palsgr. 707/2 Come, scratche my backe, I pray the. 1590 Shaks. *Mids. N.* iv. i. 7 Scratch my head, Peaseblossome. 1617 Moryson *Itin.* iii. 83 In the morning when they turne them [their Hogges] forth, they scratch them with their fingers, as Barbers doe mens heads. 1645 Evelyn *Diary* 29 Sept., An antiq of a dog in stone scratching his eare. 1712 Steele *Spect.* No. 498 ¶3 The fellow thereupon surrendered his whip, scratch'd his head, and crept into the coach. 1822 Byron *Juan* vi. 100 He scratch'd his ear, the infallible resource To which embarrass'd people have recourse. 1961 J. Baker *Cottage by Springs* xvii. 100 The supervisors, who occasionally arrived in shining saloon cars, scratched their heads over the problem. 1963 *Observer* 24 Nov. 21/4 We wait for the report, read it, and then scratch our heads. 1969 *Listener* 13 Nov. 667/1 We thought we'd take this year off and scratch our head and see whether we can do something better. 1973 *Times* 26 July 33/1 The advent of the school holidays means that millions of children will soon be embarking on long car journeys to the seaside or the Continent and just as certainly many parents will be scratching their heads over the car sickness.

b. *intr.* for *refl.*

1590 Shaks. *Mids. N.* iv. i. 28 If my haire do but tickle me, I must scratch. 1698 Fryer *Acc. E. India & P.* 92 So stupid, that notwithstanding Chints, Fleas, and Muskeeto's, torment them every Minute [they] dare not presume to scratch where it itches. 1810 *Spirit Publ. Jrnls.* XIII. 71 My dogs itch and scratch with the mange.

c. *you scratch my back and I'll scratch yours* and varr. Cf. claw *v.* 5 b.

1704 E. Ward *All Men Mad* 18 Scratch me, says one, and I'll scratch thee. 1858 'A. Ward' *Let.* 27 Jan. in *Maine: Guide 'Down East'* (1937) iii. 363 You scratch my back and i will scratch your back. 1885 *Pall Mall Gaz.* 12 Jan. 1/2 The homely adage, 'Scratch my back and I'll scratch yours.' 1928 *Manch. Guardian Weekly* 10 Aug. 104/1 He goes on to spoil the effect by accusing Liberals of hypocrisy and being false to the principle of justice embodied in the phrase 'Scratch me and I'll scratch you'. 1937 'G. Orwell' *Road to Wigan Pier* ii. 33 In order that.. the Nancy poets may scratch one another's backs, coal has got to be forthcoming. 1954 M. Ewer *Heart Untouched* viii. 132 It's the advertisers getting extra publicity. It's everybody scratching everybody else's back. 1961 J. Heller *Catch-22* (1962) iv. 33 A little grease is what makes this world go round. One hand washes the other. Know what I mean? You scratch my back, I'll scratch yours. 1978 P. Hill *Enthusiast* v. 61 Local farmer, got 'is own slaughter 'ouse. 'Ee scratches my back, I scratch 'is, know what I mean?

3. a. *trans.* To make slight linear abrasions on (a surface of any kind). Also *fig.* Esp. in phr. *to scratch the surface* (*of*): to make only slight progress in understanding, taking effective action (on), etc.; not to penetrate very far (into). See also sense 3 f.

1669 Evelyn *Diary* 13 July, Observing that.. some idle persons began to scratch and iniure them [*viz.* marbles]. 1794 Sullivan *View Nat.* I. ix. 73 Marble is soft, and can be scratched with a knife. 1832 G. R. Porter *Porcelain & Glass* xvi. 324 These specimens were sufficiently hard to scratch rock-crystal. 1863 Dana *Man. Geol.* 676 The stones which have produced the furrowing are sometimes scratched themselves. 1915 *New Republic* 13 Feb. 41/1 With all his earnest intention Amherst merely scratches the surface of the immense field of American social endeavor. 1932 Wodehouse *Louder & Funnier* 269 But this has merely scratched the surface. 1936 L. Hellman *Days to Come* iii. 90 You haven't seen anything. They didn't scratch the surface here. 1969 *Listener* 13 Nov. 654/3 When it [*sc.* contraception] is attempted on a mass scale, as in India, it barely scratches the surface of the problem. 1971 D. Potter *Brit. Eliz. Stamps* xiii. 147 This simplified account can only scratch the surface of a story which is as intriguing and rewarding as the collecting of stamps themselves. 1977 *Time* 9 May 48/2 The industry.. has been on a hot sales streak since 1973, when energy consciousness-raising really began. And the market has barely been scratched.

absol. 1878 Huxley *Physiogr.* 134 The coarse sediment scratching along the bottom, helps to tear it up.

b. *hyperbolically.* To furrow (the soil) very lightly for the purpose of cultivation.

1697 Dryden *Virg. Georg.* iii. 797 The lab'ring Swain Scratch'd with a Rake, a Furrow for his Grain. 1733 Tull *Horse-Hoeing Husb.* vii. 62 Sarrition scratched and broke so small a part of the Earth's Surface. 1860 *Chamb. Encycl.* I. 82/1 The ground, in such cases, requires no further culture than treading in the seed by animals or slightly scratching the surface with bushes. 1878 Bosw. Smith *Carthage* 422 Its cultivators—if those who just scratch the surface of the earth may be so called.

c. To produce (marks) or portray (an object) by light incisions on a surface.

1644 Symonds *Diary* (Camden) 71 Another huge large stone, three pictures of men in armes scratcht upon the stone. 1741 Middleton *Cicero* II. viii. 235, I had scratched, as it were, out of the block, some faint resemblance of an image. 1872 Tennyson *Gareth & Lynette* 522 When both were children, and in lonely haunts Would scratch a ragged oval on the sand, And each at either dash from either end.

†d. *intr.* In the election of the Lord Mayor: To put a mark against the name of the candidate voted for. *Obs.*

1773 *Chron.* in *Ann. Reg.* 142/1 The number of aldermen who scratched for each being equal, it was decided.. by the casting voice of the present Lord-Mayor.

e. *trans.* To polish = scratch-brush *v.*

1856 G. Gore in *Orr's Circ. Sci., Pract. Chem.* 76 After being again washed in water, they are 'scratched' at the brush. 1877 G. B. Gee *Silversmith's Handbk.* x. 161 After either of the processes of whitening or plating, the work has to be scratched, unless required to be left a dead white.

f. *scratch a —— and find a ——* and varr.: suggesting the true or fundamental character of any particular group, nation, etc.

In some cases *scratch* is interpreted as meaning 'to wound superficially': see quots. under sense 1 a.

1823 J. Gallatin *Diary* 2 Jan. (1914) 229 Very true the saying is, 'Scratch the Russian and find the Tartar.' *c* 1863 J. R. Green *Let.* in *N. & Q.* (1965) Sept. 348 They say, if you scratch a Russian you always find the Tartar beneath. 1888 Mrs. Oliphant *Second Son* I. xiv. 242 I don't put any faith in Russians... 'Scratch a Russian and you'll come to the Tartar.' 1892 I. Zangwill *Children of Ghetto* III. ii. vi. 81 Scratch the Christian and you find the pagan—spoiled. 1924 G. B. Shaw *St. Joan* iv. 52 Scratch an Englishman, and find a Protestant. 1926 D. Parker *Enough Rope* 60 Scratch a lover, and find a foe. 1966 *Listener* 10 Feb. 217/3 Scratch a Muse and as often as not you find nothing you can fathom, not even a woman. 1973 *Freedom* 2 June 3/4 'Scratch a liberal and you find a fascist,' says Westall. What bloody nonsense is this? Did he invent the saying himself to fit his present convenience? And what do you get when you scratch a Tory, a Fabian, a Social Democrat, a Marxist-Leninist? 1977 C. McCullough *Thorn Birds* xvii. 445 Scratch Justine's surface and you find a rebel.

4. *intr.* Of a bird or animal: To remove earth, etc., with the claws. Also *trans.* with advs., *to scratch out*, to extricate or disinter with the claws; *to scratch up*, to heap up by scratching.

c 1520 Andrew *Noble Lyfe* in *Babees Bk.* (1868) 220 They put their bylles in the erthe sometyme so depe that they can nat gete it vp agayne & than they scratche theyr billes out agayn with theyr fete. 1617 Moryson *Itin.* i. 247, I found they [*sc.* jackals] had scratched up the earth almost to his body. 1867 Miss Broughton *Cometh Up* xxiv, We.. found the doomed chanticleer scratching and scraping peaceably on the dunghill.

5. *fig.* **a.** To struggle to make money, to 'scrape'. Also *trans.* to scrape up (money). Now *dial.* exc. *transf.*: *to scratch for oneself* (orig. *U.S.*), to fend for oneself; *to scratch* (*around*) *for* (something), to struggle for, to labour to achieve or find, to experience difficulty in acquiring, etc.

1509 BARCLAY *Ship of Fools* (1874) I. 43 If he can be a fals extorcyoner Fasynge and bostynge to scratche and to kepe He shall be made a comon costomer. *c* **1550** *Vertuous Scholehous* C 6, Thou doest scratche and rake so long at home. **1560** PILKINGTON *Expos. Aggeus* (1562) 66 Is it tyme for you that ye scrape and scratch together, all ye can laye youre handes on? **1850** H. C. WATSON *Camp-Fires of Revolution* 30 Then each one had to scratch for himself. **1856** A. CARY *Married* 304 Shaking off the other child, [she] told him to scratch for hisself a time, while she began to prepare the supper. **1900** *Pearson's Mag.* May 475/2 For this they put by ivery ha' penny they could scratch an' save. **1930** V. PALMER *Passage* I. viii. 65 He and Bob had to scratch for a living the best way they could. *Ibid.* 160 We'll have to scratch for another year or two to pay off the new boat. **1947** K. TENNANT *Lost Haven* ii. 42 How much better did it look when you went off with that.. moll, and left me and the kids to scratch for ourselves? **1953** T. A. G. HUNGERFORD *Riverslake* 202 If his mob gets in next election they'll whip up a nice old depression, just like they did the last time, and we'll all be scratching for jobs again. The only difference is that there'll be a million or so of these bludgers scratching with us. **1960** WENTWORTH & FLEXNER *Dict. Amer. Slang* 451/1 *Scratch for* (*something*)..*scratch around for* (*something*), to look for an object, to try to obtain something, esp. money or a much-wanted object; fig., to scratch in the same way a chicken does in searching for food. **1961** WEBSTER s.v., Turned out at an early age to scratch for themselves. **1962** A. MARSHALL *This is Grass* 202 Not that I read much. I've been too busy scratching for a crust. **1970** *Globe & Mail* (Toronto) 25 Sept. 3/5 They moved to hake and really did a job on that. Now, they're scratching for what's left of the hake. **1976** *Laurel* (Montana) *Outlook* 9 June 16/3 This leaves the city scratching for a means to financing garbage disposal. **1976** J. SNOW *Cricket Rebel* 104 Walters scratched around for 42 during which he was given a life by another blunder by Rowan. **1979** 'A. HAILEY' *Overload* III. x. 239, I scratched around for more details... Here are the exact dates of the convention and a preliminary program.

b. *intr.* with adv. To get *along*, *on*, *through* with difficulty.

1838 HALIBURTON *Clockm.* Ser. II. iv. 53, I think a body might have a chance to make out to scratch along to live here. **1867** MISS BROUGHTON *Cometh Up* xxix, I suppose we shall manage to scratch on pretty much as other people do. **1887** *Kentish Gloss.* s.v., 'Times is bad, but I just manage somehows to keep scratching along'. **1890** *Eng. Illustr. Mag.* Dec. 152 Charley..contrived to scratch through for the Edinburgh M.D.

c. *intr.* To depart in haste, to make off with all speed. Freq. const. *for*. *U.S. colloq.*

1847 J. S. ROBB *Streaks of Squatter Life* 109 I'm cussed if I hadn't to turn round, too, and scratch for the snag agin! **1875** 'MARK TWAIN' in *Atlantic Monthly* Mar. 285/2 The moment it splits at the top..I know I've got to scratch to starboard in a hurry. **1887** *Outing* (U.S.) May 120/1 As I fired the gun and the horses scratched away from the mark. **1904** S. E. WHITE *Blazed Trail Stories* i. 5 This little town will scratch fer th' tall timber..when the boys goes in to take her apart.

d. With *up*: to produce with difficulty, to scrape up.

1922 H. CRANE *Let.* 24 Dec. (1965) 110, I am growing bald trying to scratch up new ideas in housekeeping and personal hygiene. **1930** 'SAPPER' *Finger of Fate* 188 It was six o'clock before the police arrived, and by that time we had scratched up a bit of breakfast and were feeling better.

†**6. a.** *trans.* To seize rapaciously, as a bird with its claws; to get possession of by effort or with difficulty. *to scratch acquaintance* = 'to scrape acquaintance' (see SCRAPE *v.* 5 b). *Obs.*

1582 G. MARTIN *Manif. Corrupt. Script.* vi. 96 What a peeuish, malicious, & impudent corruption is this,..to seeke to scratch aduantage of the word Presbyter, & to make it signifie an Elder, not a Priest. *c* **1610** ROWLANDS *Terrible Batt.* 2 The great and good report which my beloued friend ..hath giuen of you, hath made me more then halfe in loue with you, which makes me thinke in some sort (as the rude and rusticke phrase is) to scratch acquaintance of you. **1658–9** LUDLOW in *Burton's Diary* (1828) III. 145 If we take the people's liberties from them, they will scratch them back again. **1680** C. NESSE *Ch. Hist.* 387 Satan, with all his savage sanhedrims, could not yet scratch Christs Apostles out of their mansions.

†**b.** intr. *to scratch for*, to struggle fiercely to obtain.

1581 J. BELL *Haddon's Answ. Osor.* 415 Such as will skratch for heaven by force [orig. *violentis illis, qui regnum Dei rapturi sunt*], must undertake no small travayles. **1618** FLETCHER *Loyal Subj.* IV. iii, And were I fit to be your wife ..Trust me I would scratch for ye but I would have ye.

7. a. trans. *to scratch out*: to erase (writing) with a penknife. Also (cf. 3 c), to delete by crossing through with a pen.

1711–12 SWIFT *Jrnl. to Stella* 25 Jan., I have often scratched out passages from papers and pamphlets sent me, ..because I thought them too severe. *a* **1720** SEWEL *Hist. Quakers* (1765) I. IV. 253 [He] did, with his knife, scratch out the letters. **1849** MACAULAY *Hist. Eng.* viii. II. 302 The butler refused to scratch Hough's name out of the buttery book.

b. To erase the name of (a person) from a list; hence †to expel from a club or society (*obs.*); to expunge from a list of candidates or competitors; *Sporting*, to withdraw (a horse or other animal) from the list of entries for a race or other competition.

1685 *Roxb. Ball.* (1888) V. 607 They kick'd me out of Goldsmiths'-Hall..; One cursed Tory scratch'd me! **1825** *Examiner* 762/1 All payments should be made on the quarterly night, or be scratched; if ladies got intoxicated, they would be scratched. **1851** MAYHEW *Lond. Labour* I. 343 Of course I got 'scratched' from the trade Society. **1852** DICKENS *Bleak Ho.* lxiii, 'Scratch you out of her will, I think you mean?' 'Of course I do. In short..I mean—*to*—Scratch me.' **1859** *Hotten's Slang Dict.* s.v., Tomboy was scratched for the Derby at 10 A.M. on Wednesday. **1885** *Truth* 28 May 854/2 If he is not to start, the sooner Lord Alington scratches him the better.

c. *U.S. Politics.* Of a voter: To erase the name of (one or more of the candidates) from the party ticket. Also *absol.*

1841 *Politician's Register for 1841* 3 Messrs. Ritner and Shulze, the Harrison Senatorial Electors, were scratched by a number of voters, and ran behind their colleagues. **1847** *Knickerbocker* Apr. 382 (Th.), He never scratched the regular ticket. **1880** *Scribner's Monthly* Oct. 909/1 They sometimes take the liberty of scratching a name, but they prefer, when the nominations are not too bad, to vote the regular ticket. **1888** BRYCE *Amer. Commw.* III. lxvi. II. 494 The number of candidates is often so great, and the knowledge which the average citizen has..of them so small, that many who would be glad to 'scratch' or 'paste' have really no data for doing so. **1890** C. L. NORTON *Polit. Americanisms* 100. **1904** *N.Y. Tribune* 8 Nov. 6 Vote the straight Republican ticket, without scratching. **1949** *Western Polit. Q.* Mar. 107 Thousands of voters scratched their ballots.

d. *intr.* for *refl.* To withdraw from a competition; *jocularly*, to withdraw one's acceptance of an invitation.

In Oxford University, formerly said of an undergraduate who after having entered for an examination, and perhaps having done all or part of the paper work, withdrew his name before undergoing the *viva voce*, with the intention of presenting himself for the examination at a later time.

1866 *Mysteries of Isis* 292 He was ploughed for 'Smalls' as you know; eventually he had 'scratched' at 'Mods', and on a second attempt had been again ploughed. **1878** *Athletic World* 5 Apr. 12/1 Middlesex scratched to Charing Cross [in a cup-tie]. **1897** *Punch* 6 Nov. 210/2 Wonder..how many people will scratch at the last moment.

†**8.** *intr.* To fish with a line with three or four hooks attached. *Obs.*

1659 T. BARKER *Angling* (ed. 2) 41 Nicholas Harridans.. hath killed many a dish of Barbells that way with scratching.

9. a. To drag the nails or claws over a surface so as to make a faint grating noise. Also, of a pen, to move over the paper with a slight noise.

1703 *Rules of Civility* 14 At the door of a Prince..it would be rude to knock; we are only to scratch. [Cf. quot. 1787 in SCRATCH *sb.*[1] 6.] **1909** *Daily News* 2 Oct. 4/6 He [a dog] scratched so persistently at the door, that they let him have his way.

¶**b.** The verb-stem (or the imperative) is sometimes used quasi-adv. to express the sound of scratching.

1848 MRS. GASKELL *Mary Barton* xxix, The pen went.. scratch, scratch over the paper. **1858** LYTTON *What will He do* I. i, Scratch across his back went one of those ingenious mechanical contrivances familiarly in vogue at fairs.

c. *trans.* To rub gratingly on a rough surface.

1875 F. T. BUCKLAND *Log-Bk.* 98 A match being scratched on a box for ignition. **1864** LOWELL *Fireside Trav.* 163 One may scratch a thought half a dozen times and get nothing at last but a faint sputter.

10. a. To scribble, write hurriedly or carelessly. Also with advs.

1806 SCOTT *Fam. Lett.* June (1894) I. ii. 47, I also scratched down another ballad the morning of the day of meeting. **1883** READE in *Harper's Mag.* June 98/1, I..left her to scratch him a receipt. **1889** LADY WATERFORD in Hare *Two Noble Lives* (1893) III. 461 The usual scene, Jenny singing and me scratching off letters for the second post.

b. To forge (banknotes or other papers). *U.S. slang.*

1859 G. W. MATSELL *Vocabulum* 77/2 *Scratch*, to write; to forge. **1926** *Flynn's Mag.* 6 Nov. 518/2 Well, scratch th' note an' we'll blow. **1935** N. ERSINE *Underworld & Prison Slang* 65 *Scratch*, *v.* to forge checks or other papers.

11. *intr.* Of horses: To contract the disease known as 'the scratches' in the hoofs.

1737 BRACKEN *Farriery Impr.* (1757) I. 345 They would grease and scratch sooner behind than before.

12. *U.S.* In billiards and related games: (*a*) *intr.* to make a stroke that incurs a penalty; *spec.* to hit the cue ball into a pocket; (*b*) *trans.* to hit (the cue ball) badly, incurring a penalty; *spec.* to hit (the cue ball) into a pocket. Cf. SCRATCH *sb.*[1] 11.

1909 in WEBSTER s.v. scratch *v.i.* **1959** N. MAILER *Advts. for Myself* (1961) 75 He shot poorly, hit the wrong ball and scratched. **1964** SULLIVAN & CRANE *Young Sportsman's Guide to Pocket Billiards* ix. 91 *Scratch*, a playing stroke in which the player forfeits his playing turn. Most often caused by 'scratching' a ball unintentionally into a pocket. **1974** *Rules of Game* 85/3 A player may scratch the cue ball into a pocket at the break shot or during continuous play. **1977** *New Yorker* 4 July 24/2 This kid asked me, 'Do you ever scratch?'.. I said, 'I ain't never scratched in my life.'.. Just then, I took this shot and the cue ball went right in the pocket. He said, 'Well, you've scratched now.'

13. *Comb.* (with object), as ***scratch-eye*** adj.; **scratch-my-back** = SCRATCH-BACK 2; **scratch-penny**, a money-grubber (cf. *scrape-penny*).

1681 COLVIL *Whigs Supplic.* (1751) 36 It turned to a *scratch-eye scuffle. **1887** *Mayor's Proclam. Oxf.* 19 Aug. (*St. Giles's Fair*), Any person..who may prove to have assaulted any..person,..by means of a squirt, *scratch-my-back. *c* **1817** HOGG *Tales & Sk.* V. 213 Are the military to starve, that a *scratchpenny may thrive?

'scratchable, *a. nonce-wd.* [-ABLE.] Capable of being scratched. (Cf. SCRATCH *v.* 3 b.)

1858 CARLYLE *Fredk. Gt.* XVIII. viii. (1872) VII. 236 [The] country..is now under poor plough-husbandry, arable or scratchable in all parts.

'scratch-back. [f. SCRATCH *v.* + BACK *sb.*[1]]

1. An instrument for scratching the back to allay itching, usually in the form of a small hand of ivory or metal fixed to a long handle; a back-scratcher.

1842 *Ainsworth's Mag.* I. 20 What is it but..a fan, lazy-tongs, parasol, or scratchback? **1864** *Chambers' Bk. of Days* II. 238/1 [Description]. **1880** GOLDW. SMITH *Cowper* vii. 107 It is almost as easy to get a personal memento of Priam or Nimrod as it is to get..a spinning wheel, a tinder box, or a scratch-back.

2. A toy formed on the principle of a rattle, producing a sound of tearing cloth when rubbed upon a person's back.

1858 LYTTON *What will He do* I. i, But to pay such a price for a scratch-back!—Prodigal! **1865** KNIGHT *Passages Work. Life* III. xii. 263 Greenwich Fair too has died out—its bonnettings and its scratch-backs.

scratch blue (skrætʃ bluː). [f. SCRATCH *v.* + BLUE *sb.*] Used *attrib.* and *absol.* to designate a decoration of incisions filled with blue pigment found on eighteenth-century stoneware or stoneware so decorated. Cf. *scratched blue.*

1924 RACKHAM & READ *Eng. Pottery* vi. 88 In the Liverpool museum there is a mug of 'scratch blue'. **1957** MANKOWITZ & HAGGAR *Conc. Encycl. Eng. Pott. & Porc.* 28/1 A salt-glazed mug with 'scratch blue' decoration is inscribed with..the date 1742. **1960** H. HAYWARD *Antique Coll.* 251/1 '*Scratch blue' ware*, a class of white salt-glazed stoneware decorated with..ornaments and inscriptions incised upon the wares in the unfired 'green state'. **1969** G. WILLS *Eng. Pott. & Porc.* 88 The incised wording was emphasised by dusting it, before firing and glazing, with powdered cobalt-blue; a type of decoration..known as 'scratch blue'. **1971** L. A. BOGER *Dict. World Pott. & Porc.* 308/2 It is thought that this scratch blue ware may also have been made at Liverpool and in other parts of England.

scratchboard ('skrætʃbɔəd). *Art.* Also **scratch board.** [f. SCRATCH *v.* + BOARD *sb.*] Cardboard specially treated and coated so that the surface can be scratched away to create drawings, etc.; a board of this type. Cf. *scraper board* s.v. SCRAPER 11.

1930 C. E. WALLACE *Commercial Art* iv. 119 *Scratchboard Drawing.*—Scratchboard is a cardboard with an enamel surface of special finish. Drawings are made on it with ink and are afterwards scratched with a knife to obtain lights and special effects. **1942** *School Arts* (U.S.) Mar. 229/1 Why not try some scratchboard in your commercial art classes?.. Scratchboard is a lightweight cardboard, coated on one side with a clay-like composition. **1948** H. MISSINGHAM *Student's Guide in Commercial Art* II. 57 Scratch boards are available in a great variety of surfaces and tones. The surface is coated with clay preparation and is drawn or scraped away where desired. **1964** TURNBULL & BAIRD *Graphics of Communication* xii. 223 Using a bristol board coated with chalk, an artist can produce a scratchboard drawing by covering an area with ink and then scratching the ink and chalk from the surface of the board. **1976** *National Observer* (U.S.) 24 Jan. 20/1 Scratchboard—clay-coated cardboard on which you draw and scratch away.

scratch-brush ('skrætʃbrʌʃ), *sb.* [f. SCRATCH *sb.* or *v.*] A brush of fine wire used in gilding, electroplating, etc. to polish or clean articles of metal.

1797 *Encycl. Brit.* (ed. 3) VII. 740/1 First, the gilded piece of metal is rubbed with a scratch brush (which is a brush composed of brass wire) till its surface is made smooth. **1839** F. A. GRIFFITHS *Artil. Man.* 3 The [gun] barrel..is to be well rubbed over with a steel scratch card or scratch brush, until the rust is..removed. **1873** SPON *Workshop Rec.* Ser. I. 174/2 For delicate objects, scratch-brushes are made of spun glass. **1877** G. B. GEE *Silversmith's Handbk.* x. 162 The beautiful frosted surfaces to be seen upon silver lockets..are all produced by means of the scratch-brush.

b. *attrib.* **scratch-brush lathe**, a lathe with a circular revolving scratch-brush.

1856 G. GORE in *Orr's Circ. Sci., Pract. Chem.* 48 'Scratch brush' lathes..for scouring and preparing the surfaces of metal articles to receive a deposit. **1877** G. B. GEE *Silversmith's Handbk.*, Fig. 40 Scratch-brush Lathe.

scratch-brush ('skrætʃbrʌʃ), *v.* [f. prec. sb.] *trans.* To polish by means of a scratch-brush.

1799 G. SMITH *Laboratory* I. 87 Take it out and scratch-brush it in clean water. **1884** F. J. BRITTEN *Watch & Clockm.* 135 The articles must be..rinsed in water and scoured with sand, or scratch-brushed.

Hence **'scratch-brusher**, a workman who operates a scratch-brush; **'scratch-brushing** *vbl. sb.*, the process in which a scratch-brush is used.

1839 F. A. GRIFFITHS *Artil. Man.* 3 The barrel will [then] be sufficiently corroded for the operation of scratch-brushing. **1885** *Brit. Alm. Comp.* 94 (Occupations) Scratch brusher.

'scratch-build, *v.* Also **scratchbuild, scratch build.** [f. SCRATCH *sb.*[1] + BUILD *v.*] *trans.* To build (a model) from scratch, using no specially prepared components. So **'scratch-building** *vbl. sb.*; **'scratch-built** *ppl. a.*

1961 C. J. FREEZER *Railway Modelling* x. 95 (*heading*) Scratch building. **1967** *Railway Modeller* '*Shows You How*'

Booklet No. 19 (*title-page*) Our cover photograph shows one of the finest scratchbuilt model railways in the world, Peter Denny's Buckingham Branch. *Ibid.*, Scratchbuilding is the craft of modelmaking from raw materials and basic components. **1974** *Times* 17 Apr. 14/2 Parren said he hoped to attract young members by encouraging the scratch building—that is, building to scale from scratch—of modern locomotives. **1975** G. SCARBOROUGH *Tank & AFV Modelling* (Airfix Magazine Guide No. 5) ii. 7/1 Conversion and scratch-built projects of most of the popular subjects. *Ibid.* 19/1 This leaves us with the basic hull to scratch-build.

scratched (skrætʃt), *ppl. a.* [-ED¹.]

1. a. In senses of the verb SCRATCH. ***scratched figure*** (Typogr.): A numeral figure with a slanting line drawn across it, used in printing examples of arithmetical operations involving cancelling. ***scratched blue*** = SCRATCH BLUE.

1562 A. BROOKE *Romeus & Juliet* 2422 With scratched face, and heare betorne. **1771** LUCKOMBE *Hist. Printing* 256 Scratched figures..were used here in that Species of Arithmetic which is called Division. **1871** *Amer. Encycl. Printing* (ed. Ringwalt), *Scratched Figures*..are frequently called canceled figures. **1883** L. M. SOLON *Art of Old Eng. Potter* vi. 79 Some..processes deserve special attention. The 'scratched blue' for instance enjoyed a successful run. **1890** *Anthony's Photogr. Bull.* III. 409, I purchased a small printing frame..and some scratched negatives from a local photographer. **1940** *Chambers's Techn. Dict.* 748/2 *Scratched blue*.., incised ornament on unbaked clay, sprinkled with cobalt glass, then fused in the kiln.

Prov. **1584** LYLY *Alex. & Camp.* IV. iv, Truth is never with out a scracht face. **1625** J. ROBINSON *Ess.* xxxiii. Wks. 1851 I. 142 Truth goes with a scratched face, less or more.

b. *Sporting.* Withdrawn (from a race, etc.).

1869 'WAT. BRADWOOD' *The O.V.H.* xix, The peccant owner of the scratched animal.

†**2.** *slang.* Drunk. *Obs.*

1622 J. TAYLOR (Water-P.) *Water Cormorant* B4b, For though hee be as drunke as any Rat, He hath but catcht a foxe... Or some say hee's bewitcht, or scratcht or blinde.

scratcher ('skrætʃə(r)). [f. SCRATCH *v.* + -ER¹.]

1. a. One who scratches, in various senses of the vb.

1557 EDGEWORTH *Serm.* Repert., Giuers of their owne shale be riche, scratchers of other mens be euer at beggers state. **1674** N. FAIRFAX *Bulk & Selv.* To Rdr., They must look for no better fare from a world of Bears and Scratchers, than [etc.]. **1736** AINSWORTH, *Scalptor*, a graver, a cutter in metal, a scratcher, an etcher. **1771** SMOLLETT *Humph. Cl.* 26 June (1815) 197 His master declared he was the best scratcher in the family. **1852** JERDAN *Autobiog.* I. xxiv. 203 We have a considerable proportion of very superficial scratchers of the soil, both among authors and critics.

b. *Ornith.* Used in *pl.* to render mod.L. *Rasores*, in Illiger's system (1811) an order of birds including the families *Gallinacei*, *Epollicati*, *Columbini*, *Crypturi* and *Inepti*. Cf. SCRAPER 3.

1831 *Montagu's Ornith. Dict.* (ed. Rennie), *Rasores* (Illiger), Scratchers, a family of birds who scratch their food from the earth. **1851** RICHARDSON *Geol.* (1855) 310, 4th Order.—Rasores (or Scratchers, fig. 213).

c. *U.S. Politics.* A voter who 'scratches', i.e. declines to support some of the candidates named on his party ticket. Cf. PASTER.

1880 *Scribner's Monthly* Feb. 621/2 Mr. Evarts will be obliged to look among the 'scratchers',..for the indorsement of..Civil Service Reform. **1883** *Atlantic Monthly* LII. 327 To whom a 'scratcher' or a 'bolter' is more hateful than the Beast.

d. In certain trades: A scratch-brusher.

1881 *Instr. Census Clerks* (1885) 96 Electro and other Plated Ware Manufacturer..Scratcher. **1884** *B'ham Daily Post* 24 Jan. 3/3 Chandelier-Trade.—Women Scratchers wanted.

e. orig. *U.S. Cant.* (See quots.)

1859 G. W. MATSELL *Vocabulum* 77/2 *Scratcher*, a forger; a copyist. **1894** *N. Amer. Rev.* Apr. 454 A professional forgery gang consists of: First, a capitalist or backer; second, the actual forger, who is known among his associates as the 'scratcher'. **1927** *Writer's Monthly* Nov. 387/2 Forgers, and floaters of bad money, checks or commercial paper, are 'scratchers', 'scratchmen' and 'shovers'. **1941** V. DAVIS *Phenomena in Crime* iv. 48 The actual forger, known by such names as 'the scratcher', 'the scribe', 'the penman', may consider himself extremely fortunate if his period of office exceeds two years.

2. An instrument used for scratching. **a.** A tool used in plastering to roughen the surface of the preliminary coating.

1812 P. NICHOLSON *Mech. Exerc.* 312 (Plastering) Scratcher, the instrument for scratching the plaster, as its name implies. **1873** SPON *Workshop Rec.* Ser. I. 121/2 After the coat is laid on, it is scored in diagonal directions with a scratcher.

†**b.** = SCRATCH-BACK 2.

1835 DICKENS *Sk. Boz, Greenwich Fair*, The noise of these various instruments,..the shouting, the 'scratchers', and the dancing, is perfectly bewildering.

c. *Comb.* (See quot. 1858.)

1858 SIMMONDS *Dict. Trade*, *Scratcher-up*, a bookbinder's tool. **1902** HASLUCK *Bookbinding* iv. 52 After lightly pasting the back of each book, a 'scratcher up' is drawn several times ..down the back.

d. A device put down an oil or gas well to clear the bore or create turbulence mechanically.

1877 J. F. CARLL *Oil Well Records & Levels* iv. 90 A 'scratcher' is a round brush..made of steel wire. When it is to be used the tubing is drawn from the well, a few barrels of benzine are poured in and the scratcher is..run down to the oil rock, where it is worked up and down..to scratch or scrub the walls of the well. **1974** D. K. SMITH in P. L. Moore et al. *Drilling Practices Manual* xvi. 426 Scratchers or wall cleaners. 1. Rotating... 2. Reciprocating. *Ibid.* 427 Install scratchers spaced according to location of permeable zones.

†**'scratchets**, *pl. Obs. rare.* [f. SCRATCH *sb.*¹ + -ET¹.] = *scratches*, SCRATCH *sb.*¹ 2 a.

1611 FLORIO, *Crepáccij*, the scratchets, or rats-tailes in a horse; some horsemen say they are little chaps or rifts about the coronet of the horses hoofe. **1683** SNAPE *Anat. Horse* I. ii. (1686) 3 Inflammations or breakings out, which we call *Grease in the heels* or *Scratchets*.

ˌscratchifi'cation. *jocular nonce-wd.* [f. SCRATCH *v.* + -(I)FICATION.] A spiteful attack.

1840 MISS EDGEWORTH *Let.* in H. Zimmern *Mem.* (1883) 206 Among the various scratchifications and scarifications in this volume, you may remark that there have been reiterated scratches at Mrs. and Miss Wilmot.

scratching ('skrætʃɪŋ), *sb. Obs.* exc. *dial.* Chiefly pl. Also 5 *pl.* **scrachenis.** [App. a corrupt form of the word which appears variously as CRATCHEN, CRACON, CRACKLING 3, CRAWKE; cf. also the synonymous CRITON (F. *cretons*), CROOTE (Wyclif).] **a.** The refuse of tallow remaining after refining. **b.** The residue of pork fat left after rendering lard: = CRACKLING 3 b.

c **1440** *Psalmi Penit.* ci. 3 (1894) 36 My bones beth drie and forsoke, As scrachenis [Vulg. *cremium*] that beth for-fryed. **16..** *More's note to Ray's N.C. Words*, *Greaves or Scratchings*, sebi reliquiæ. **1859** GEO. ELIOT *Adam Bede* xviii, She'd take a big cullender to strain her lard wi', and then wonder as the scratchins run through. **1867** F. FRANCIS *Angling* ii. (1880) 70 Scratching as they term greaves on the Trent. **1883** *Knowledge* 18 Aug. 99/1 'Scratchings'—a delicacy greatly relished by our British ploughboys, but rather too rich in pork fat. **1899** *Fishing Gaz.* 2 Dec. 455/1 Scratchings, or..the refuse of the tallow chandlers' boilings, is anything but a desirable substance to handle.

scratching ('skrætʃɪŋ), *vbl. sb.* [-ING¹.]

a. The action of the vb. SCRATCH in various senses.

1549 LATIMER *Ploughers* (Arb.) 24 For what shall I loke for amonge thornes but prickyng and scrachinge? **1606** SHAKS. *Tr. & Cr.* II. i. 30, I would thou didst itch from head to foot, and I had the scratching of thee. **1760-72** H. BROOKE *Fool of Qual.* (1809) IV. 37, I heard a scratching about my bed; I am sure it must be rats. **1817-8** COBBETT *Resid. U.S.* (1822) 60 In the broadcast method the after-culture must, of course, be confined to hoeing, or, as Tull calls it, scratching. **1860** TYNDALL *Glac.* I. xv. 100 We crossed the Grimsel pass, and traced the [glacier] scratchings to the very top of it. **1884** *Boston* (Mass.) *Jrnl.* 7 Oct. 1/8 There is always more or less scratching of names of the Electors, and a recount would be necessary to settle this point alone. **1899** *Allbutt's Syst. Med.* VIII. 490 Pruritic dermatoses in which rubbing and scratching are induced.

b. *attrib.* and *Comb.*, as ***scratching tool***; **scratching-board**, a board upon which are posted the names of those who have withdrawn from a competition; **scratching ground, -shed, shelter**, a part of a poultry-run reserved for the dust-bath; **scratching post**, a stake (or the like) against which animals rub themselves to allay itching.

1891 N. GOULD *Double Event* 118 Judging from the *scratching-board there would be good fields. **1901** *Westm. Gaz.* 26 Jan. 1/3 One of the Crick hens..wearied of her legitimate *scratching-grounds, and flew over the low wall that divided the holdings of the neighbours. **1890** J. MACDONALD *Light in Africa* iii. 37 Cattle got among their tent ropes, and they erected '*scratching posts' to keep them away from their camp. **1895** *Outing* (U.S.) XXVII. 47/1 We little dreamed that one of our nags would use the bow of our birch as a scratching post. **1968** *New York City* (Michelin) 73 Abercrombie and Fitch... One can find almost anything here, from a ten-cent fish hook to..a scratching post for your cat. **1902** L. WRIGHT in *Encycl. Brit.* XXXI. 881/2 In several cases it [the colony plan] has been abandoned for the system of houses and *scratching sheds. **1880** A. R. WALLACE *Isl. Life* vii. 111 The harder blocks would serve as *scratching and grinding tools.

scratching ('skrætʃɪŋ), *ppl. a.* [-ING².] That scratches, in various senses of the verb.

1577 KENDALL *Flowers of Epigr.*, *Trifles* 3 A Crowne of thorne with scratching pricks our Christ did willing weare. **1614** LATHAM *Falconry* (1633) 34 These kinde of scratching Hawks, that I did never love should come too neere my fingers. **1865** DICKENS *Mut. Fr.* I. ii, Like the legs of scratching poultry.

†**'scratchingly**, *adv. Obs. rare*⁻¹. [f. SCRATCHING *ppl. a.* + -LY².] In a scratching manner.

a **1586** SIDNEY *Arcadia* II. (Sommer) 122 b, Like a cat, when scratchingly she wheeles about after a mouse.

scratchless ('skrætʃlɪs), *a.* [f. SCRATCH *sb.*¹ + -LESS.] Without a scratch; without scratch (SCRATCH *sb.*¹ 6 b).

1829 P. EGAN *Boxiana* 2nd Ser. II. 750 But Jack came off quite scratchless. **1887** BROWNING *Parleyings, Apollo & Fates*, Not scratch-less but unscathed, he somehow eluded Each blow fortune dealt him. **1978** *Gramophone* June 31/2 After the war Sterling pursued improvements on a big scale and one recalls in particular what were called the Columbia 'scratchless' records.

scratch pad. Also scratch-pad, scratchpad. [f. SCRATCH *sb.*¹]

1. A scribbling block. Also *attrib.* and *fig. colloq.* (orig. and chiefly *U.S.*).

1895 *Montgomery Ward Catal.* Spring & Summer 111/2 Desk or Scratch Pads, made from white laid, smooth finish paper for pen or pencil. **1906** *Dial. Notes* III. 155 Can you let me have a nickel to get a scratch-pad? **1931** W. G. MCADOO *Crowded Years* xv. 220 He called it a 'scratch-pad draft'..that..was not to be taken as final. **1939** R. CHANDLER in *Dime Detect. Fict.* Aug. 48/1 The paper was from a scratch pad. It would have been very nice if it had had a message on it. **1960** *News Chron.* 4 Feb. 6/4 Desk and telephone and scratch-pad and paper-clips. **1966** *Listener* 9 June 838/3 A boy in bellbottoms lamented (or was it bragged?) he had a 'scratchpad memory'. **1970** 'W. HAGGARD' *Hardliners* iii. 26 She struck out a line from her scratch-pad and the editor watched her. **1978** W. F. BUCKLEY *Stained Glass* xix. 190 Blackford sat on the couch and made motions requesting a scratch pad.

2. *Computers.* A small, very fast memory for the temporary storage of data or for indirect addressing of the main memory; usu. *attrib.*

1965 *Proc. Conf. Amer. Federation Information Processing Societies* XXVII. I. 667/2 General-purpose commercial processors with scratchpad memories did not appear on the market until 1959. *Ibid.* 676/2 The magnetic core scratch-pad has an access limitation of one register per cycle. **1970** O. DOPPING *Computers & Data Processing* x. 135 The small, fast memory, which is well suited for data and instructions that are going to be used very often, is sometimes called a scratch pad memory. **1977** *Design Engin.* July 77/2 It incorporates a 2k × 8-bit mask-programmable read-only memory, a 64 × 8-bit scratchpad random-access memory, four 8-bit input/output ports and a binary timer. **1979** *Personal Computer World* Nov. 83/2 The user program runs in a stack whose pointer is extracted from TGTSTK (FOFA in the scratchpad RAM).

scratchy ('skrætʃɪ), *a.* Also 8 **scrachy.** [f. SCRATCH *sb.*¹ + -Y.]

†**1.** *Farriery.* Affected with the disease known as 'the scratches'; see SCRATCH *sb.*¹ 2. *Obs.*

1710 *Lond. Gaz.* No. 4788/4 Lost.., a..Mare.., her Legs very hairy and scrachy. **1800** *Med. Jrnl.* III. 294 Being well fed, or want of exercise, will frequently excite swellings, which are by no means connected with a scratchy heel.

2. Of work executed with the pen or brush: Composed of scratches, as opposed to bold, firm lines.

1827 HOOD *Progress of Art* ii, Some scratchy strokes.. Suffic'd for my design. **1866** MRS. CARLYLE *Lett.* III. 332 Such a scratchy, illegible hand. **1892** *Nation* 29 Dec. 502/2 The illustrations are..occasionally scratchy.

3. Of hair: Scanty, straggling.

1820 L. HUNT *Indicator* No. 46 (1822) I. 371 His mane is scratchy and lax.

4. a. Apt to scratch.

1866 COCKAYNE *Sax. Leechd.* III. 402 This interlineation .. has been written with a scratchy pen. **1874** SYMONDS *Sk. Italy & Greece* (1898) I. viii. 145 He swept the frescoes over with a scratchy broom.

b. Of sound: rough, grating. Of a sound-recording: characterized by scratch (SCRATCH *sb.*¹ 6 b).

1889 *Cent. Dict.* s.v., A scratchy noise. **1961** WEBSTER s.v., Scratchy tune came from the phonograph. **1961** L. HUGHES *Ask your Mama* 3 In the quarter of the negroes Where the doors are doors of paper Dust of dingy atoms Blows a scratchy sound. **1976** W. TREVOR *Children of Dynmouth* ii. 43 He told Stephen to sit on it, in a voice that wasn't as scratchy as usually it was. **1977** *Film & Television Technician* Jan. 5/2 He precariously wound up the oldest gramophone this side of the Urals so that we might hear a scratchy 78 recording of some Russian choir singing the Creed. **1978** *Oxford Times* (City ed.) 17 Feb. 19 The mono recordings are primitive and scratchy.

c. *fig.* Ill-tempered, peevish, catty.

1925 E. H. YOUNG *William* xxxii. 277 I'm no heroine. I'm a nasty, scratchy, impatient little beast. **1936** L. C. DOUGLAS *White Banners* viii. 180 But if she was going to write him any more scratchy letters..it might turn out badly. **1949** N. MARSH *Swing, Brother, Swing* ix. 214 We're both scratchy. I told her I thought the unfortunate Rivera was ghastly and she thinks I'm shaking my curls at Mr. Alleyn. **1958** *Spectator* 27 June 835/2 The small, scratchy, pert, unhappy son. **1971** P. PURSER *Holy Father's Navy* I. ii. 11 Irby..was a bit scratchy. She said, 'Why is it we can never go anywhere on time?' **1977** 'J. LE CARRÉ' *Honourable Schoolboy* i. 31 Nor did the dwarf's own..version meet with much success, which made him very scratchy.

5. *Sporting.* Of action: Ill-sustained, uneven, 'ragged'. Also *transf.*

1881 *Sportsman's Year-bk.* 100 Over a short course, where a fast, scratchy stroke often gets a bad boat home in front. **1894** *Field* 9 June 829/1 Galston's action was of a scratchy character, and Sempronius did not look at his best. **1908** *Daily Chron.* 2 Apr. 6/5 The Dark Blues did several starts, some of which were scratchy and some were good. **1933** J. B. PRIESTLEY *Wonder Hero* ii. 36 He had taken her away from her bed-sitting room and scratchy living, and had made her queen it in a fine service flat in Knightsbridge.

Hence **'scratchily** *adv.*

1927 *Daily Express* 27 May 13/2 Wethered,..reaching the turn rather scratchily in forty-two, stood one down. **1975** R. L. DUNCAN *Dragons at Gate* (1976) i. 27 Chamber music drifting scratchily from an old Victrola.

scrath (skraθ). *Sc.* [Metathesis of *scarth*, SCART *sb.*¹] = SCART *sb.*¹, SCARF *sb.*⁴

16.. in *Macfarlane's Geogr. Collect.* (S.H.S.) II. 133 The Scrath, the Badoch are two great black fowls. **1880** 'SHIRLEY' (J. Skelton) *Crookit Meg* xxi. 228 A large scrath with a look of insatiate gluttony stamped on its ugly face. **1893** *Blackwood's Mag.* Aug. 228 Some æons ago, the scrath and the phoca had the [Orcadian] islands pretty much to themselves.

'scrattle, *v. dial.* [Frequent. f. SCRAT *v.*]

1. *intr.* To keep on scratching; *trans.* to scrape *away* by quickly repeated movements.

1739 SHENSTONE *Let.* Wks. 1777 III. 5, I sat down, and wrote thus far: scrattle, scrattle, goes the pen. **1817** WILBRAHAM *Chesh. Gloss.*, *Scrattle*, to scratch, as fowls do. **1870** *Daily News* 16 Apr., 'The authoress..can toil through a long day 'scrattling' the snow away from frozen sheep.

2. (See quot. 1864.)

1817 H. L. PIOZZI *Let.* 4 Jan. in *Autobiogr. Mrs. Piozzi* (1861) II. 187 Coal carts scrattling up the hill often used to make me think—'Hinc ex audiri gemitus, et sæva sonare Verbera; tum stridor ferri, tractæque catenæ.' **1855** KINGSLEY *Westw. Ho!* xxx, Nobody..cared for nothing but scrattling up and down alongshore like to prawns in a pule. **1864** —— *Roman & Teuton* 175 With west-country-men, to scrattle still means to scramble or shuffle about.

Hence **'scrattling** *vbl. sb.* and *ppl. a.*, scraping, scratching.

1861 HUGHES *Tom Brown at Oxf.* iii, A bouncing and scrattling was heard on the stairs, and a white bull-dog rushed in. **1913** D. H. LAWRENCE *Sons and Lovers* iv. 75 In this flamin', scrattlin' place.

†**'scrattop.** *Obs. rare*⁻¹. [? For *scrat-up*, f. SCRAT *v.* + UP *adv.*] (A term of abuse.)

1593 NASHE *Strange Newes* G 3 b, Why thou arrant butter whore, thou cotqueane, & scrattop of scoldes, wilt thou neuer leaue afflicting a dead Carcasse.

scraugh (skrɑx), *sb. Sc.* [Belongs to SCRAUGH *v.*] A loud, hoarse cry.

1818 SCOTT *Br. Lamm.* xxiv, I blew sic points of war, that the scraugh of a clockin-hen was music to them. *a* **1826** MOIR in J. Wilson *Noctes Ambr.* Wks. 1855 I. 198 The old woman o'er the way To our cheer a scraugh gave back. **1893** *Northumbld. Gloss.* s.v., The scraugh of a heron.

scraugh (skrɑx), *v. Sc.* Also 9 scrauch. [Echoic: cf. SCRAIGH, SKREIGH *vbs.*] *intr.* To utter a loud hoarse cry.

1805 A. SCOTT *Poems* 15 (Jam.) Thus gaed they on wi' deavin din, A' scraughin, yelpin thro' ither. **1818** SCOTT *Hrt. Midl.* xviii, And if ye are deaf, what needs ye sit cockit up there, and keep folk scraughin' t'ye this gate? **1831** J. WILSON *Noct. Ambr.* Wks. 1856 III. 102 The unhappy somnambulists are scrauching.

Hence **'scraughing** *ppl. a.*, in quot. harsh guttural.

1849 R. CURZON *Monasteries Levant* IV. vi. 421 My knowledge of his scraughing language did not extend very far. **1897** F. MACKENZIE *Sprays N. Pine* xviii. 231, I carena though I never hear your scrauchin' voice again.

†**scraw,** *sb.*¹ *north. Obs.* Also 5 skraw. [a. ON. *skrá* a dry skin, a scroll.] A scroll or tag of parchment or leather.

c **1460** *Towneley Myst.* xxiii. 516 How felowse, se ye not yond skraw? It is writen yonder within a thraw. **1483** *Cath. Angl.* 325/2 A Scrawe..., *cedula*. *a* **1641** SPELMAN *Glossarium* (1664) 459 Pictatium est epistola brevis & modica; vel schedula de membrana excisa; vel illa particula corii, quæ soleæ repeciatæ insuta est... Anglicè A scraw, or a speck, or a clout of a shoo.

scraw (skrɔː), *sb.*² *dial.* (Anglo-Irish, Sc., Manx.) Also 8 scra, 9 scraa. [a. Irish and Gael. *sgrath*, pronounced (skrɑː).]

1. A turf used for covering the roof of a hovel beneath the thatch, or for burning.

1725 SWIFT *Drapier's Let.* vii. Wks. 1755 V. II. 152 That odious custom..of cutting scraws (as they call them) which is flaying off the green surface of the ground to cover their cabins, or make up their ditches. **1823** *Ann. Reg., Chron.* 37 Witness dug down, and on the rim of the ground got a scraw, under which he discovered a body stark naked. **1894** HALL CAINE *Manxman* I. iv. 19 Fixing her hazy eyes on the scraas under the thatch.

†**2.** A thin covering of grass-grown soil formed upon the surface of a bog. *Obs.*

1776 G. SEMPLE *Building in Water* 120 This Bog is generally covered over with a Scraw, or Scurff of mossy Grass. **1820** MAR. EDGEWORTH *Mem. R. L. Edgeworth* II. 316 A slight surface of peat heath or grass, called by the common people a shaking scraw.

3. *Comb.*, as ***scraw-spade***; †***scraw-built*** adj.

1789 D. DAVIDSON *Seasons, Spring* 42 Down frae the scraw-built shed the swallows pop. **1830** CARLETON *Traits* (1843) I. 294 A scraw-spade is an instrument resembling the letter T, with an iron plate at the lower end, considerably bent, and well adapted to the purpose for which it is intended [cutting sods].

†**scraw,** *sb.*³ *Obs.* Also 6 skralle. [? a. Du. *schraag* trestle.] A frame upon which textile fabrics are hung to dry.

c **1563** *Churchw. Acc. St. Dunstan, Canterbury* (MS.), Item solde [a] skralle for a Towell. **1791** HAMILTON *Berthollet's Dyeing* I. II. II. ii. 161 A kind of broad ladder.. called a scraw or scray, on which the fleece is drained. **1837** WHITTOCK *Bk. Trades* (1842) 192 In dyeing wool in the fleece, a kind of broad ladder with very close rounds, called by the Dyers of this country, a 'scraw' or 'scray' is used.

†**scraw,** *v. Obs. rare*⁻¹. [Echoic: cf. L. *screāre*.] *intr.* To clear the throat, to 'hawk'. Hence †**'scrawing** *vbl. sb.*

1656 RIDGLEY *Pract. Physick* 38 If it come forth by spitting alone, it proceeds from the gums; if by scrawing from the Throat [etc.].

scrawl (skrɔːl), *sb.*¹ Forms: 8 scrall, skrawl, skrale, 7- scrawl. [f. SCRAWL *v.*²]

1. Something scrawled; a hastily and badly written letter, a careless sketch.

1693 CONGREVE *Old Bach.* v. vii, There, read. (*Shows Letters.*) That.. That's a Scrawl of Quality. **1739** LADY M. W. MONTAGU *Let. to C'tess Pomfret* Jan. (1893) II. 37, I forget you are at Paris, and 'tis not polite to trouble you with such long scrawls as might perhaps be supportable at Monts. **1792** SCOTT *Let.* in Lockhart (1837) I. vii. 188 Taking the advantage..of my father's leaving this place, who will take charge of this scrawl, I sit down to answer your favour. **1840** THACKERAY *Paris Sk.-bk.* (1867) 52 A scrawl from his pencil brings an enormous price. **1882** B. D. W. RAMSAY *Recoll. Mil. Serv.* I. xi. 286 An hour or two had not elapsed before I received a scrawl in Sir Colin's own handwriting.

†**b.** *pl.* Scrawled or illegible characters. *Obs.*

1728 TICKELL *Horn-bk.* 34 So from the letters of our native tongue, Put in Greek scrawls, a mystery too is sprung. *a* **1767** HARTE *Vis. Death* 264 In sable scrawls I Nero's name perus'd. **1807** CRABBE *Par. Reg.* II. 290 Mark now in what confusion, stoop or stand, The crooked scrawls of many a clownish hand.

2. A careless, illegible style of handwriting.

1710 SWIFT *Jrnl. to Stella* 3 Nov., A bad scrawl is so snug. **1775** MME. D'ARBLAY *Early Diary, Let.* Nov. (1889) II. 90 Her hand-writing..was a..miserable scrawl. **1865** DICKENS *Mut. Fr.* I. xv, The scrawl of childish hands.

scrawl (skrɔːl), *sb.*² *dial.* [Perh. f. SCRAWL *v.*¹ But cf. OF. *escrouelle* river-shrimp.] (See quot. 1847.)

1847 HALLIWELL, *Scrawl*, the young of the dog-crab, or a poor sort of crab itself. *Linc.* **1861** TENNYSON *Sailor Boy* 12 And on thy ribs the limpet sticks, And in thy heart the scrawl shall play.

scrawl, *v.*¹ *Obs.* exc. *dial.* Forms: 4, 6-7 scrawle, 5-6 scraule, 6 scrale, skrall(e, skrawl, 6-7 scraul, scrall, 6-8, 9 (*dial.*) scrawl. [App. an altered form of CRAWL *v.*, perh. suggested by SPRAWL *v.* of cognate meaning.]

†**1.** *intr.* To spread the limbs abroad in a sprawling manner; to gesticulate. *Obs.*

c **1380** WYCLIF *Serm.* ccxxx. Sel. Wks. II. 204 And þis spirit cryinge, made him scrawle [*v.rr.* spraule, scraule], or, al to-teeryinge him, went oute from him. **1560** PHAER *Æneid* ix. A a 2, As he there did pendant skralle; He pluckt him back by foarce. **1582** STANYHURST *Æneis* II. (Arb.) 51 Hee freams, and skrawling to the skye brayes terribil hoyseth.

2. To move with a scrambling and shuffling motion. = CRAWL *v.*¹ I.

1530 TINDALE *Lev.* xi. 41 All that scrauleth vpon the erth. **1573-80** TUSSER *Husb.* (1878) 108 If gentils be scrauling, call magget the py. **1611** SPEED *Hist. Gt. Brit.* IX. xxiv. §84. 1155 Not so few as one hundred and twentie of knowne Iesuites and Seminaries scrawled like Frogs, thorow her faire soyle. **1677** COLES *Eng.-Lat. Dict.*, To scrall (stir); *motito*. **1719** D'URFEY *Pills* I. 127 He scrawling, she tugging, with hawling and lugging, Through Window at last he got in. **1851** *Cumberland Gloss.*, Scrawling. **1892** C. A. CLARKE *Tum Fowt Sketches* 40 (E.D.D.) T' poor pig what had just scrawled through t' bottom o' t' cart.

†**3.** *transf.* To teem. = CRAWL *v.*¹ 5. *Obs.*

1530 TINDALE *Exod.* viii. 3 And the ryuer shall scrale with frogges. **1643** LIGHTFOOT *Glean. Ex.* (1648) 14 The waters ..scrawle with frogges.

scrawl (skrɔːl), *v.*² Also 7 scraul, scrall. [Perh. a use of SCRAWL *v.*¹, the development of sense being suggested by the coincidence of the initial cons.-group with that of *scrabble*, *scribble*, *scroll*.]

1. *trans.* To write or draw in a sprawling, untidy manner.

1612 [implied in SCRAWLING *vbl. sb.*]. **1629** QUARLES *Argalus & Parth.* III. Wks. (Grosart) III. 274 To whom poore Vulcan..Scrall'd many a thank. **1748** LADY M. W. MONTAGU *Let. to C'tess Bute* 26 July (1893) II. 169, I enclose to you a rough draft of it [my garden] drawn (or more properly scrawled) by my own hand. **1781** COWPER *Truth* 156 Who, where'er he came, Scrawl'd upon glass miss Bridget's lovely name. **1879** MᶜCARTHY *Own Times* xxvii. II. 304 The war correspondent now scrawls his despatches as he sits in his saddle under the fire of the enemy. **1887** JESSOPP *Arcady* vii. 215 [The] accomplishment of scrawling their names at the bottom of a cheque.

b. To cover (a surface) with scrawling inscriptions or marks. Also with *over*.

1647 COWLEY *Mistr., Written in Juice Lemmon* ii, Like Hypocrites, which seem unspotted here; But when they sadly come to dye, And the last Fire their Truth must try, Scrauld ore like thee, and blotted they appear. **1771** SMOLLETT *Humph. Cl.* 13 July (1815) 237 The windows of all the inns are scrawled with doggrel rhimes. **1841** BORROW *Zincali* I. ix. I. 153 Many people carry papers about with them, scrawled with hieroglyphics. **1860** MOTLEY *Netherl.* I. i. 2 Letters..all to be scrawled over in the margin by the diligent old man. **1889** RIDER HAGGARD *Allan's Wife* 36 The western tempest was scrawled all over with lines of intolerable light.

2. *intr.* To scribble, to write carelessly or awkwardly. Also † *to scrawl it*.

1611 COTGR., *Griffonner*, to write fast, and ill; to scrible, to scrall it. [**1647**: ? *indirect passive*; see 1 b.] **1748** RICHARDSON *Clarissa* (1811) IV. 47, I have ordered Dorcas..to be always scrawling with a pen, lest inky fingers should give suspicion. **1842** TENNYSON *Day-dream* 142 The butler drank, the steward scrawl'd. **1878** BROWNING *Poets Croisic* 75 Splash and scrawl, Completed lay thy piece, swift penman Paul!

†**scraw'lation.** *Obs. rare*⁻¹. [f. SCRAWL *v.*¹ + -ATION.] ? Disorderly behaviour.

1774 TOPLADY *Let.* 11 Jan., Wks. (1853) 853 Perhaps it may conduce to render both your antagonist, and his antecedent scrawlation (forgive a homely Devonshire term), more conspicuous, than they might otherwise have been.

scrawled (skrɔːld), *ppl. a.* [f. SCRAWL *v.*² + -ED².] Scribbled, badly written. Also *transf.* and *fig.*

1848 THACKERAY *Van. Fair* lviii, Many other scrawled memoranda regarding the bygone frequenters of the house. **1895** MRS. H. WARD *Bessie Costrell* ii. 27 A wide plain travelled into the sunset, its level spaces cut by the scrawled elms and hedgerows of the nearer landscape. **1910** J. BUCHAN *Prester John* xxi. 351 There..was the body of Henriques, lying scrawled on the sand. **1939** DYLAN THOMAS *Map of Love* 4 This weak house to marrow-columned heaven, Is corner-cast, breath's rag, scrawled weed,..crow stalk, puffed, cut, and blown.

scrawler ('skrɔːlə(r)). [f. SCRAWL *v.*² + -ER¹.] One who writes carelessly.

1734 SWIFT *Let. to Miss Hoadly* 4 June, I will shew the paper to every female scrawler I meet, who will soon spread about the town, that your writing and spelling are ungenteel and unfashionable, more like a parson than a lady. **1831** TRELAWNY *Adv. Younger Son* I. ix. 65 The paltry, dirty scrawler [the captain's clerk].

scrawling ('skrɔːlɪŋ), *vbl. sb.* [f. SCRAWL *v.*² + -ING¹.] The action of SCRAWL *v.*²; scribbling, careless untidy writing.

1612 BRINSLEY *Lud. Lit.* xx. 230 Schollars now will be carefull to keepe their Greeke Testaments faire from blotting or scrauling. **1764** REID *Inquiry* iv. §2. 108 Is it not pity that the refinements of a civilized life, instead of supplying the defects of natural language, should root it out, and plant in its stead..the scrawling of insignificant characters? **1809** W. IRVING *Knickerb.* VI. viii. (1820) 424 The drop of ink which hangs trembling on his pen, which he may either dash upon the floor, or waste in idle scrawlings. **1848** DICKENS *Dombey* xxxvii, After much painful scrawling and erasing,..the old woman produced this document.

†**'scrawling,** *ppl. a.*¹ *Obs.* [f. SCRAWL *v.*¹ + -ING².] Crawling.

1561 DAUS tr. *Bullinger on Apoc.* (1573) 219 The duste brought forth the scralling lise. **1589** *Rare Tri. Love & Fortune* I. in *Five Old Plays* (Roxb. Club) 84 Brought up in blood, and cherish with scrauling snakes. **1637** G. DANIEL *Genius of this Isle* 285 Here Scrauling wretches, too, too bad to tell, Endure a Torment.

scrawling ('skrɔːlɪŋ), *ppl. a.*² [f. SCRAWL *v.*² + -ING².] That scrawls. Of handwriting: Careless, untidy, illegible.

1747 CARTE *Hist. Eng.* IV. 375 Parsons..could make a shift to write a scrawling hand. **1860** *All Year Round* No. 52. 33 He was continually shaking sand from a pepper-box over scrawling entries in marble-covered copy-books. **1886** G. ALLEN *Maimie's Sake* xvii, Written..in a loose, scrawling uneducated hand.

scrawly ('skrɔːlɪ), *a.* [f. SCRAWL *v.*² or *sb.*¹ + -Y.] Badly or untidily written; irregularly designed.

1833 MRS. STOWE in C. E. Stowe *Life* (1889) 70 The envelope was written in a scrawny, scrawly, gentleman's hand. **1859** G. WILSON *Life E. Forbes* iii. (1861) 76 Its statements are exceedingly brief, some in ink, many in pencil, all of them very scrawly. **1901** *Pall Mall Gaz.* 27 May 6/1 Three yellowish eggs with their unmistakable black, scrawly marks.

Hence **'scrawliness.**

1867 W. JAMES *Let.* 17 Sept. (1920) I. 103 Excuse the scrawliness of this too hurriedly written letter. **1903** F. W. H. MYERS *Human Pers.* II. 168 Before one can feel sure that the resemblance is in more than some formal scrawliness.

scrawm (skrɔːm), *v. dial.* [App. a phonetically symbolic formation after words beginning with *scr-*.] *trans.* To scratch.

In dialects also in other senses: To scramble, sprawl; to climb, clamber; to scribble, scrawl: see *Eng. Dial. Dict.*

1880 TENNYSON *North. Cobbler* iv, He scrawm'd an' scratted my faäce like a cat. **1886** *S.W. Linc. Gloss.*, *Scrawm*, to scratch, scrawl; as of a foot-rule packed up carelessly with tools,—'They're scrawming it all over'.

scrawny ('skrɔːnɪ), *a. orig. U.S.* [Variant of SCRANNY.] Lean, scraggy.

1833 [see SCRAWLY]. **1847** EMERSON *Poems, Alphonso* Wks. (Bohn) I. 408 Yon pale, scrawny fisher fools, Gaunt as bitterns in the pools. **1876** C. D. WARNER *Winter on Nile* ii. 35 What a lot of scrawny old women. **1883** W. H. BISHOP *Old Mexico* xxiii. 333 The..tough, fragrant, but scrawny, eucalyptus is much in use as a shade-tree. **1946** D. C. PEATTIE *Road of Naturalist* iv. 43 The one where my scrawny, bronchitic body would find itself was stone-cold, a dirty grey, so I would mentally adjourn to the other. **1977** J. F. FIXX *Compl. Bk. Running* vi. 80 Frank Shorter, who won an Olympic gold medal in the 1972 marathon, is 5 feet 10½ inches and weighs a scrawny 134. **1977** *New Yorker* 27 June 59/2 This beautiful beast that I, a scrawny little thing, am destroying.

Hence **'scrawniness,** scragginess.

1863 HAWTHORNE *Our Old Home* (1883) I. 390, I often found,..in the persons of such of my dear countrywomen as I now occasionally met, a certain meagreness, (Heaven forbid that I should call it scrawniness!)

scray¹ (skreɪ). In 9 scraye. [History obscure: cf. the synonymous Welsh *ysgràen*, *ysgràell*.] The common tern, *Sterna hirundo*.

1668 WILKINS *Real Char.* II. v. §4. 155 Sea-swallow, Scray. **1678** RAY *Willughby's Ornith.* 353 In other places of England they are called Scrays. **1813** MONTAGU *Ornith. Dict.* Suppl., Tern—Common... Rittock or Rippock, Spurre, Scraye. **1852** MACGILLIVRAY *Brit. Birds* V. 638.

scray². *dial.* [? Altered form of SPRAY.] A bush.

c **1650** *Robin Hood & Butcher* 14 in *Percy Folio MS.* I. 20 Robin he marcht in the greene forrest, vnder the greenwood scray. **1869** E. PEACOCK in *Once a Week* 27 Mar. 230 The thorn scray grows at the horn of the river.

scray[3]. *dial.* = SCRAW *sb.*[3]
1791 [see SCRAW *sb.*[3]].

†'**scrayfish.** *Obs.* Forms: 4 scrafisse, -fysse, -fisch, -fish, skrafysch, -fissh, schraf(f)ysch, 5 scra(y)fysche. [Corruptly ad. OF. *escrevisse* (mod.F. *écrevisse*): see CRAYFISH *sb.*] A crayfish.
1309-10 *Durham Acc. Rolls* (Surtees) 6 De lx de Scrafisse. **1333-4** *Ibid.* 20 In xxvij Skrafysch, playc' [etc.]. **1355-6** *Ibid.* 555 Et in 30 Skrafisshes empt. pro d'no Priore. 5*s.* 9*d.* **1397** in *Finchale Priory Charters* (Surtees) p. cxviii, Item vj scraffysch. **1483** *Cath. Angl.* 324/2 Scrayfysche (*MS. A* Scrafysche); *vbi* stokfysche.

†'**scrayfoot.** *dial. Obs.* [? f. SCRAY[3].] *attrib.* in *scrayfoot pot*, a pot with a tripod support.
1512 *Bury Wills* (Camden) 249 Bras potte called a scrayfote potte.

scraze (skreɪz), *v. dial.* [App. a blending of SCRATCH and GRAZE *vbs.*] *trans.* To scratch, graze (see E.D.D.). Hence **scraze** *sb.*, a scratch or graze.
1703 EVELYN *Mem.* (1857) III. 397 A defluxion which fell into one of my legs, caused by a slight scraze on my shin bone, falling on a stump as I was walking in Brompton Park. **1865** *East Kent Gazette* 7 Jan. 4/5, I found a small scraze of the right shin, which might have been caused by a fall.

†'**screable,** *a. Obs.*[—0] [f. L. *screā-re* to hawk, hem: see -ABLE.] See quot. and cf. EXCREABLE.
1656 BLOUNT *Glossogr.*, *Screable* (*screabilis*) that may be spitted out. **1721** in BAILEY. **1755** in JOHNSON.

screade, obs. form of SCREED.

screak (skri:k), *sb.* Now chiefly *dial.* For forms see the vb. [f. SCREAK *v.*]
1. A shrill cry; a shrill grating sound.
1513 DOUGLAS *Æneis* II. xii. 14 The ȝing childring, and frayit matrounis eik, Stude all on raw, with mony peteous screik. *Ibid.* IV. viii. 111 And oft with wild skrek the nycht oule, Heich on the ruif, allane, was hard ȝoule. **1614** H. A. *Scourge of Venus* (1876) 30 What may these scremes & dolefull scriks portend. *a* **1710** BP. BULL *Serm.* xx. (1713) III. 801 Others peep forth into the Light, as it were only to see it, and having, by a Skreek or two given Testimony to the Misery of this Life, presently die and vanish. **1727** *Philip Quarll* 87 His Landlady gave a Screek as if she had seen the Devil. **1768** PENNANT *Brit. Zool.* I. 223 Their note of anger or fear is very harsh, between a chatter and a skreek. **1799** SOUTHEY *Eng. Ecl.*, *Dancing Bear* 3, I would rather hear catcourtship Under my bed-room window in the night, Than this scraped catgut's screak. **1819** W. TENNANT *Papistry Storm'd* (1827) 34 And siccan hidyous yells and shrieks!—A' the warld soundit wi' their skrieks! **1894** *Tablet* 8 Sept. 362 The old flagellants..whipped themselves to the screak of the fife and the roll of the drum.
b. *in a screek*, ? crying out with pain.
1681 O. HEYWOOD *Diaries* (1885) IV. 81 Very sick, much pained, had been in a screek most part of the night.
2. A name for some species of SHRIKE.
1802 MONTAGU *Ornith.* s.v. *Shrike*, Murdering-bird. Skreek, or Skrike. Night-jar.
3. *screak of day*, daybreak (*dial.*: see E.D.D.). Cf. SKREIGH, SKRIKE, CREEK *sb.*[2], CREKING.
1768 *Ross Helenore* (1789) 51 Ilka morning by the screak o' day, They're set to wark. **1830** CARLETON *Traits* (1843) I. 60 That morning we were all up at the skriek of day.

screak (skri:k), *v.* Now chiefly *dial.* Forms: *α.* 5-6 screke, 6 skrek(e, screake, *Sc.* screik, 6-7 screeke, skreeke, 6-8 screek, scriek, 6-9 skreak, skreek, skriek, 7-8 screeck, 6- screak. *β.* 6 skrick(e, *pa. pple.* skrigd, 7 scrick(e, scrik. See also SKRIKE. [a. ON. *skrækja*, prob. echoic; cf. SCREECH, SHRIEK *vbs.* In dialects there are parallel forms with other vowels, symbolizing different varieties of sound, as *scraik*, *scrawk*, *scroke*.]
1. *intr.* To utter a shrill harsh cry; to screech or scream. Also with *out*.
? *a* **1500** *Chester Pl.* (Shaks. Soc.) II. 37 (*Passion*), Though he sore skricke, A buffitte shall bytte. **1567** DRANT *Horace*, *Ep.*, *A.P.* Biiij, They all would screeke vnto the skye and laughe at hym aloude. **1605** ARMIN *Foole upon F.* (1880) 14 The cracke made them all screeke out. **1609** HOLLAND *Amm. Marcell.* XIV. x. 25 Dreadfull spectres and fansies skreaking hideously round about him. *a* **1670** HACKET *Cent. Serm.* (1675) 588 The Impenitent shall howl, the Unjust skreek out. **1707** tr. *Wks. C'tess D'Anois* (1715) 374 She skreem'd, she skreek'd, she baul'd, she yaul'd. **1722** DE FOE *Plague* (1884) 78 Her Mother..scriekt out. **1787** *Minor* II. x. 98 The situation made the servant screak.
b. of certain animals.
1607 TOPSELL *Four-f. Beasts* 513 When mice cry and screeketh aboue their ordinary custome, it presageth an alteration and change of the Weather. **1614** H. A. *Scourge of Venus* (1876) 30 To heare the night-crowes scrik, and goblins play. **1863** KINGSLEY *Water-Bab.* 32 The very magpies and jays followed Tom up, screaking and screaming.
c. Of things such as an ungreased hinge or axle: To make a shrill grating sound. Cf. CREAK *v.*
1565 COOPER *Thesaurus* s.v. *Strideo*, *Tibia stridebat cantu*, screaked. **1609** BIBLE (Douay) *Amos* ii. 13 Behold I wil screak under you, as a wayne screaketh loden with hay [Vulg. *stridebo..stridet*]. **1676** HOBBES *Iliad* XVI. (1677) 247 The yoke screeks [XVI. 470 κρίκε δὲ ζυγόν]. **1715** tr. *Pancirollus' Rerum Mem.* I. IV. xvii. 222 They oil'd the Hinges of the Door, least they should screak and make a Noise. **1731** MILLER *Gard. Dict.* s.v. *Vitis*, Especially when the Screw is perceiv'd to be rough, or screaks in the Nut when the Trendle is turn'd. **1843** DICKENS *Christm. Carol* iv. 130 Stop till I shut the door of the shop. Ah! How it skreeks? **1904** *Westm. Gaz.* 14 July 2/3 The noise that the slate pencil can make in the hands of a child..can only be rendered by a word which is onomatopœic if not correct—'screak'.
2. *trans.* To cry *out* or utter with a screak.
1569 W. HUBBARD *Ceyx & Alc.* A vij, She screeketh out, why doest thou flie and leaue me alone. **1598** Q. ELIZ. *Plutarch* xiv. 19 Whan..old man had skrigd out, 'O worthi me whom nide to spike constrains.

†'**screaker.** *Obs.* In 6 skreker. [-ER[1].] One who screaks.
1549 CHALONER *Erasm. on Folly* I iij, But and if the skreker (the preacher I woulde haue saied) falleth out of his purpose.

'**screaking,** *vbl. sb.* [-ING[1].] The action of the verb SCREAK; utterance or emission of a shrill cry or grating sound.
1565 COOPER *Thesaurus* s.v. *Stridor*, To heare the screakyng or crashyng of a saw. **1597** MORLEY *Introd. Mus.* 7 So that vnder Gam vt the voice seemed as a kinde of humming, and aboue E la a kinde of constrained skricking. **1668** CULPEPPER & COLE *Barthol. Anat.* III. ix. 149 The noise of Water-streams, or the screekings of Grass-hoppers. **1722** DE FOE *Plague* (1754) 95 Terrible Shrieks and Skreekings of Women. **1728** MORGAN *Algiers* I. iv. 129 These Brutes, whose Language resembled the Screeking of Bats. **1816** SCOTT *Old Mort.* xiv, The screaking of a cracked fiddle. **1905** *Westm. Gaz.* 12 May 4/2 A silence broken only by the perpetual 'skreeking' of the katydids in the locust-trees.

'**screaking,** *ppl. a.* [-ING[2].] That screaks; that makes a shrill strident sound.
1565 COOPER *Thesaurus* s.v. *Aridus*, *Sonus aridus*, a shrill screkyng sounde. **1567** TURBERV. *Epit.* etc. 125, I would become a Cat To combat with the creeping Mouse and scratch the screeking Rat. **1615** ROWLANDS *Melancholie Knt.* 30 Your skreeking Parrot will distract my sence. **1686** PLOT *Staffordsh.* 384 Which joynt..moves not without a strong screaking pressure of the parts. **1825** HAZLITT *Spirit of Age* 88 With a harsh screaking voice.

screaky ('skri:kɪ), *a.* Also screeky, skreaky, skreeky, skrieky. [f. SCREAK *sb.* or *v.* + -Y.] Apt to screak.
1884 'MARK TWAIN' *Huck. Finn* xxvii. 272 A melodeum—a sick one..pretty skreeky and colicky. **1892** *Dial. Notes* (U.S.) v. 231 (Kentucky Words) *Skrieky*, creaky. **1893** R. BRIDGES *Humours of Court* III. ii. 2473 I'll shut him in the screeky cupboard. **1909** *Dialect Notes* III. 404 'My shoes are skreaky.' 'I hate skreaky doors.' *a* **1961** in WEBSTER, Bats..making their screaky sounds.

†'**screaling.** *Obs. rare.* [app. in some way related to Norw. *skræling*, Da. *skrælling* weakling, OIcel. *Skrǽlingjar* (pl.), the name given to certain American aborigines.] A dwarf, pygmy.
1594 BLUNDEVIL *Exercises* IV. (1597) 270, *Descr. of P. Plancius his Map*, This Countrey is inhabited of Dwarfes called in Latine *Pigmei*, being in height 4 foote as those be of Groynland, which are called Screlings [*printed* Serelings; *edd.* 1622, 1637 Sereelings]. **1613** W. H. in R. Anton *Moriomachia*, Their indifferent dealings Did proue them to meane Knights, not Gyants, nor Screalings.

scream (skri:m), *sb.* In 6 *Sc.* screym, skreyme, 7 schreeme, 8 skream. [f. SCREAM *v.*]
a. A shrill piercing cry, usually expressive of pain, alarm, or other sudden emotion.
1605 SHAKS. *Macb.* II. iii 61 And (as they say) lamentings heard i' th' Ayre; Strange Schreemes of Death. **1708** POPE *Ode on St. Cecilia's Day* 57 Dreadful gleams, Dismal screams. **1820** SHELLEY *Prometheus* I. 498 Oh, ye who shake hills with the scream of your mirth. **1842** APPERLEY *Life Sportsman* ii. 33 His scream, or view-halloo, is, indeed, wonderful. **1848** THACKERAY *Van. Fair* xxxix, She dropped them with a scream of terror. **1877** A. B. EDWARDS *Up Nile* xix. 563 It was a sharp, sudden scream, following a shot.
b. *transf.* Applied to the shrill cry of certain birds and beasts, and to any similar noise.
1513 DOUGLAS *Æneis* XII. v. 76 And sone the other fowlis heich in the sky Turnit agane, with mony screym [*ed.* 1710 skreyme] and cry, To chais and to assail thar aduersair. **1774** GOLDSM. *Nat. Hist.* (1776) V. 14 The scream of a peacock. **1810** SCOTT *Lady of L.* I. x, The eagles answer'd with their scream. **1849** ALB. SMITH *Pottleton Legacy* xvi. 138 The engine gave a shrill scream. **1855** TENNYSON *Maud* I. iii, Listening now to the tide.., Now to the scream of a madden'd beach dragg'd down by the wave.
c. A cause of laughter; a very amusing person or situation. *colloq.*
1888 *Boston Herald* 24 Jan. 5/1 It [*sc.* 'Bewitched'] is something more than a sketch, and a good deal less than a comedy, and its designation on the bill, 'farcical scream', perhaps conveys a good idea of its character. **1906** H. GREEN *At Actors' Boarding House* 209, I thought I'd die laughing at his making love..and me with a husband doing his bit back in Auburn. It was a perfect scream, wasn't it, Kate? **1915** *Home Chat* 9 Oct. 45/2 'He's married.'.. 'It's a fact. His bailiff told our chauffeur... Isn't it a scream?' **1919** [see PERFECT *a.* B. 5 f]. **1929** R. C. SHERRIFF *Journey's End* III. ii. 71 Oh, skipper, you *are* a scream—and no mistake! **1946** E. O'NEILL *Iceman Cometh* (1947) I. 68 Listen, it was a scream. **1974** *Guardian* 30 Jan. 11/1 Like the bearded lady, Lorna has curiosity value... 'Yes, isn't it a scream?' she says. **1977** J. FLEMING *Every Inch a Lady* III. iv. 131 They're good... That Tommy Raffles is a scream!
d. The giving of information or evidence, *spec.* against one's accomplices in crime. *slang.*
1925 E. WALLACE *Melody of Death* vii. 113 'Look here, George,..is it a scream?' 'A scream?' Mr. Wallis was puzzled innocence itself. 'Will you turn King's evidence?' said the other shortly.
e. An urgent message. *slang.*
1929 'SEAMARK' *Down River* i. 21 'Smuggling?' queried the surgeon. 'That's the line, sir. Had a scream from Headquarters about it only this morning.'
f. *Jazz.* The sound produced when a high note is played loudly on a wind instrument. Also *attrib.*
1933 *Metronome* Jan. 34 A scream is produced somewhat the same way as the rip, only in the rip the note is cut off shortly, but in the scream it is held. **1952** B. ULANOV *Hist. Jazz in Amer.* (1958) xxi. 275 The sustained scream notes. **1962** CHARTERS & KUNSTADT *Jazz: Hist. N.Y. Scene* xvi. 200 Each section answering the other in 'screams' (chords) was the feature of 'Tiger Rag'.

scream (skri:m), *v.* Forms: 2 scræme, 3 screame, 4-5 screme, skreme, 7 schreame, 8 skreem, skream, 7- scream. [Early ME. *scræmen*, *screamen*, *schreamen*, perh.:—OE. **scrǽman*. Cf. mod.WFris. *skrieme* to weep (for the sense-development cf. *weep*, *cry*):—OFris. **skrêma*. Early ME. *sc* may stand for either (sk) or (ʃ); see the rare parallel form SHREAM. In Shakspere's *schreame*, *schreeme* (see SCREAM *sb.*) *sch* probably stands for (sk), after the spelling of words of classical derivation.]
1. a. *intr.* To utter a shrill piercing cry, normally expressive of pain, alarm, mirth, or other sudden emotion. Also, to produce unpleasantly loud and shrill upper notes in singing. Also with *out*, *away*.
a **1200** *Twelfth Cent. Hom.* 128 þær is ece eadiȝnesse; þær eald ne graneð, ne child ne scræmeð. *c* **1230** *Hali Meid.* 37 þat wif..þat ihereð, hwen ha cumeð in, hire bearn screamen [*MS. Bodl.* schreamen]. *c* **1325** *Pol. Songs* (1839) 158 Heo biginnith to shryke ant scremeth anon. *c* **1400** *Laud Troy Bk.* 9998 A dredful dreme that lady dremed, That In hir sclepe sche cried & scremed. **1483** *Cath. Angl.* 325/2 To screme. **1634** BRERETON *Trav.* (Chetham Soc.) 6 Others elder..guided these little ones, and sung, screaming, and squeaking, and straining their voices. **1706** PHILLIPS (ed. Kersey), To *Scream* or *Scream out*, to cry out, especially as one that is scar'd or frighted. **1707** tr. *Wks. C'tess D'Anois* (1715) 374 She skreem'd, she skreek'd. **1775** JOHNSON *Tax. no Tyr.* 4 These antipatriotic prejudices are the abortions of Folly impregnated by Faction... They are born only to scream and perish. **1782** COWPER *Mutual Forbearance* 27 Yes, truly—one must scream and bawl—I tell you, you can't hear at all! **1821** SCOTT *Kenilw.* xxxiii, 'Nay, scream away if you like it,' said he, still holding her fast. **1825** DANNELEY *Encycl. Mus.*, To *Scream*, is to sing in so loud a manner that the tones of the voice cannot be appreciated. **1855** MACAULAY *Hist. Eng.* xix. IV. 311 She screamed for help.
b. Of certain birds and beasts: To emit their characteristic shrill cry.
c **1340** *Nominale* (Skeat) 747 *Putois garit.* Fulmarde scremyth. *c* **1400** *Destr. Troy* 910 A wonderfull noyse [the cry of the dragon] Skremyt vp to the skrow with a skryke ffelle. **1605** SHAKS. *Macb.* II. ii. 16, I heard the Owle schreame, and the Crickets cry. **1720** POPE *Iliad* XVII. 529 So flies a Vulture thro' the clam'rous Train Of Geese, that scream, and scatter round the Plain. **1757** GRAY *Bard* 38 The famish'd Eagle screams, and passes by. **1860** TYNDALL *Glac.* I. xi. 87 A marmot screamed near me. **1894** HALL CAINE *Manxman* 415 Under the cliffs, where the sea-birds scream.
c. Of an inanimate thing: To make a noise like a scream. *spec.* to travel swiftly with a screaming noise; also hyperbolically and *transf.*, of a person.
1784 COWPER *Task* IV. 478 The fiddle screams Plaintive and piteous. **1792** WOLCOT (P. Pindar) *Odes of Condolence* Wks. 1794 III. 233 Wild screams the trumpet's brazen note so clear. **1827** SCOTT *Chron. Canongate* iv, There it [the sign of an inn] hung, creaking, groaning, and screaming in every blast of wind. **1882** F. W. H. MYERS *Renewal of Youth* 138 Winds that screamed and storms that fled. **1886** CORBETT *Fall of Asgard* II. 159 The ships screamed and groaned,..as they ground together. **1943** HUNT & PRINGLE *Service Slang* 57 *Screaming downhill*, making a power dive in a fighter aircraft. **1954** *Amer. Speech* XXIX. 101 'It screams!'; i.e., it really moves. **1957** P. MOORE *Science & Fiction* 60 Airmen screaming towards the ground in a steep dive. **1975** E. HILLARY *Nothing Venture, Nothing Win* x. 155 We had discussed the..likelihood of no one getting to the South Col the next day and finally decided that Tenzing and I should scream up as a booster party to make sure that the Sherpas got there. **1976** *Wymondham & Attleborough Express* 10 Dec. 24/4 Alan Green..unleashed a full-blooded volley from just inside the area that screamed into the top of the net. **1976** A. WHITE *Long Silence* vii. 53 One of the fighters [*sc.* planes] screamed down to take a closer look. **1981** *Economist* 24 Jan. 97/2 A tenth of a second is about as long as a star falling into a black hole would be expected to 'scream'.
d. quasi-*trans.* with complementary adv. or phr.
1801 SCOTT *Let.* in *Lockhart* (1837) I. x. 334 Bugles indeed we have; but it is only to scream us out of bed at five in the morning. **1862** F. W. ROBINSON *Owen* IV. ix, If he stayed there by her side, she would scream the house down in a minute more.
e. To turn informer; to give evidence against one's accomplices. *slang.*
1925 E. WALLACE *Melody of Death* vii. 114, 'I don't want to hear any more about your conscience,' said the officer wearily. 'Do you scream or don't you?' 'I don't scream,' said Mr. Wallis emphatically. **1967** J. MORGAN *Involved* 114 He never got paid..and my information is he's ready to scream.
2. *fig.* **a.** To express oneself angrily, excitedly, etc., in speech or writing.

[**1775**: see 1.] **1880** G. A. Simcox in *Macm. Mag.* XLI. 401 The Bishop of Exeter 'screamed' at the idea of having to listen to the same speaker for two months. **1883** *Brit. Q. Rev.* Oct. 445 'The Times'—..it screamed, it bullied, it worked itself up into a perfect whirlwind of wrath. **1890** *Spectator* 7 June, We receive quite as many communications screaming at us for 'insufferable complaisance' towards Mr. Gladstone.

b. To cry out *for*.

1906 E. Dyson *Fact'ry 'Ands* viii. 95 Ther job's simply screamin' fer a statesman iv your sort. **1930** 'Sapper' *Finger of Fate* 147 With every nerve in his body screaming for the stuff [*sc.* whisky]. **1978** R. Ludlum *Holcroft Covenant* xi. 131 She did not walk; she glided—an extraordinary body screaming for observation as a prelude to invasion and satisfaction.

c. To communicate (something) strongly.

1957 [see beddable *a.*].

d. *to scream on* (someone), to insult in 'playing the dozens' (see play *v.* 16 e). *U.S. Blacks'*.

1970 H. E. Roberts *Third Ear* 12/1 *Screaming on*, telling someone off;..embarrassing someone publicly. **1974** H. L. Foster *Ribbin', Jivin', & Playin' Dozens* v. 198 Sometimes, 'loud mouthing' or 'loud talking', 'sounding', 'screaming on someone' or even 'bogarding' are synonyms for woofing.

3. *trans.* To utter with a scream. Also with *out*.

1710 Steele *Tatler* No. 15 ¶ 2 Clapping me on the Back and skreaming a Lullaby. **1823** Byron *Island* iv. xiii, The sea-birds..screaming high their harsh and hungry dirge. **1836** Dickens *Sk. Boz, Streets—Night*, Mrs. Macklin..has no sooner opened her little street-door, and screamed out 'Muffins!' with all her might, than [etc.]. **1866** C. M. Yonge *Dove in Eagle's Nest* I. ix. 189 'Peace, thou fool!' screamed the old lady. **1890** Doyle *White Company* xxxi, Screaming out the doggerel lines which had long been the watchword of the Jacquerie. **1976** B. Freemantle *November Man* x. 131 'The servants can't hear, Jocelyn,' she screamed.

screamer ('skriːmə(r)). [f. scream *v.* + -er[1].]

1. One who screams; one who sings in shrill piercing tones.

1712 Swift *Jrnl. to Stella* 15 Nov., She must have been tortured with the noise of the Grub Street screamers mentioning her husband's murder to her ears. **1818** Scott *Hrt. Midl.* xxvi, The screamer aforesaid, who added good features and bright eyes to the powers of her lungs. **1830** Cunningham *Brit. Painters* I. 208 An age which lavished its tens of thousands..on Italian screamers. **1851** Mayhew *Lond. Labour* I. 223/2 The ballad singers—or street screamers, as we calls 'em.

2. An animal that utters a cry like a scream.

1801 Southey *Thalaba* iii. xxxix, Forth from her shadowy haunt Flies the large-headed screamer of the night. **1818** Scott *Rob Roy* xxvii, These tiresome screamers of the morass [the lapwing and curlew]. **1892** W. H. Hudson *Naturalist in La Plata* i. 15 At night when camping out I have heard its [the aguará's] dismal screams, but the screamer was sought in vain.

3. *spec.* **a.** A name for the birds of the S. American family *Palamedeidæ*; esp. the kamichi or Horned Screamer, and *Chauna chavaria*, the Crested Screamer.

The name Crested Screamer is also given to the Seriema or Cariama (*Palamedea cristata* Linn., *Dicholophus cristatus* Illiger) of Brazil.

1773 Pennant *Genera of Birds* 43 *Palamedea* of Linnæus, *Anhima* and *Cariama* of Brisson... I call it Screamer, from the violent noise it makes. Only two species. **1785** Latham *Gen. Synopsis Birds* III. i. 18 Horned Scr[eamer]. *Palamedea cornuta* Lin. *Ibid.* 20 Crested Scr[eamer]. *Palamedea cristata* Lin. **1869–73** T. R. Jones *Cassell's Bk. Birds* IV. 91 The Brazilian Cariama, or Crested Screamer (*Dicholophus cristatus*). *Ibid.* 95 The Screamers (*Palamedeæ*) constitute a group of strange birds. *Ibid.* 96 The Aniuma or Horned Screamer (*Palamedea cornuta*) is characterised by a horn upon the brow. **1892** W. H. Hudson *Naturalist in La Plata* i. 20 The spur-winged crested screamer; a noble bird as large as a swan.

b. A local name for the swift.

1813 Montagu *Ornith. Dict.* Suppl. **1852** F. O. Morris *Brit. Birds* II. 75.

4. *slang.* **a.** A person, animal, or thing of exceptional size, attractiveness, etc.; a splendid specimen; e.g. a well-grown or beautiful female; a 'heavy swell'; a large fish; a large sum of money. *slang.*

1837 A. Greene *Glance at New York* (Bartlett 1860), The folks are all waiting to see the fast steamer..; Ah, here she is now; sir, ain't she a screamer? **1846** Mrs. Kirkland *West. Clearings* 44 'But she's a screamer of a girl,' persisted Master George; 'I'd rather have her than all the rest.' **1850** Smedley *Frank Fairleigh* xiii, Well, you are a screamer, and no mistake,..Be merciful towards the ladies. **1853** Whyte Melville *Digby Grand* xx, I am in for a 'screamer', and the bill for which I am arrested is only a ruse to prevent my leaving England. **1861** Hughes *Tom Brown at Oxf.* xxxvi, I ..lost one screamer just up the back ditch there. He must have been a four-pounder.

b. A composition of a startling or exaggerated character; e.g. a thrilling or funny story, a 'screaming' farce. Also, a person who tells exaggerated stories.

1831 *Louisville Public Advertiser* 17 Oct. 2/3 The principal character in this production, is, to use his own elegant language, a *screamer*. **1844** Dickens *Mart. Chuz.* xvi, A peculiar style of broad-side-essay called 'a screamer'. **1849** *Theatrical Programme* 4 June 16/1 At the Adelphi crowds muster nightly to see..Wright and Bedford in a 'screamer'. **1849** Alb. Smith *Pottleton Legacy* xxiii. 234 'Stranger,' said the man..'you are a screamer!' **1854** *Househ. Words* VIII. 77 Actors speak of such and such a farce being a 'screamer'. **1872** 'Mark Twain' (*title*) Screamers; a gathering of scraps of humour, delicious bits, and short stories. **1888** in *Echoes fr. Oxf. Mag.* (1890) 111 And I'll write you a regular screamer If you dare to come up in the Long.

c. An exclamation mark.

1895 in *Funk's Stand. Dict.* **1908** *Bohemian* XIV. 643/2 Few of us have forgotten..the origin of 'yellow' as descriptive of that class of journalism addicted to 'screamers'. **1927** *Amer. Speech* II. 239 Exclamation points may be 'screamers', 'astonishers', or 'shouts'. **1933** D. L. Sayers *Murder must Advertise* viii. 132 'Waste Nerve-Power!' Capital N, capital P, and screamer. Got that? **1960** *Guardian* 17 Sept. 12/6 Some newspapermen call the ! a screamer. **1972** *Ibid.* 18 Aug. 11/1, I once worked for an editor who cut out all the screamers—that's what you and I call exclamation marks.

d. A very powerful shot in a game.

1896 W. Park *Game of Golf* 269 Screamer, a very long stroke, so called from the whistling noise made by the ball. **1926** Wodehouse *Heart of Goof* i. 13 He stepped off the sixteenth, after hitting a screamer down the centre of the fairway. **1959** *Sunday Times* 9 Aug. 28 (Advt.), When you hit a screamer..you'll be glad you played Slazenger 279. **1963** V. Canning *Limbo Line* xvii. 227 Amadeo hit a screamer, dead straight and slightly left of the middle of the fairway. **1977** *Tennis World* Sept. 17/1 A 'heavy serve', one might think, means a fast serve. Wrong again. The term to denote velocity is 'big' or occasionally 'cannonball' or 'screamer'.

e. An informer, a tale-teller; a complainer.

1903 Farmer & Henley *Slang* VI. 126 *Screamer*,..a thief who, robbed by another thief, applies to the police. **1961** *John o' London's* 30 Nov. 610/3 An informer..is now more often referred to..as a *singer* or a *screamer*. **1968** *Telegraph* (Brisbane) 19 June 58/7 The man I was talking to said, 'Hang on a minute, I've got a screamer coming in.' When he came back I asked him what a screamer was. It turned out to be someone who complains about defects in a car he has bought.

f. In full *screamer headline*. A large headline.

1926 [see rap *v.*[1] 1 d]. **1945** L. Shelly *Jive Talk Dict.* 17/1 *Screamers*, newspaper headlines. **1975** *New Yorker* 4 Aug. 20/1 'Gifts flow profusely at 124 West 42nd St. and 625 Madison Ave' was the screamer on a flyer handed to us on Forty-second. **1979** J. Drummond *I saw him Die* ii. 24 The murder was on the front page. Screamer headline.

g. *Jazz.* A passage featuring loud high notes played on a wind instrument; such a note.

1940 *Swing* Nov. 28 It's another riff tune..plus (or minus) a screamer featuring the leader's horn. **1948** *Down Beat* 1 Dec. 13 *Minor* is a screamer but not without change of pace. **1958** K. Goodwin in P. Gammond *Decca Bk. of Jazz* xiii. 149 His ability to produce stratospheric screamers with apparent ease was utilized to add bite and drive to the brass sections.

h. A bomb that makes a screaming sound as it drops.

1942 'R. Crompton' *William carries On* ii. 42 Her reactions to 'screamers'. **1943** Hunt & Pringle *Service Slang* 57 *Screamer*, a whistling bomb, i.e. a bomb with a device attached to cause a screaming sound as it descends.

i. *the screamers* = *the screaming habdabs* s.v. habdabs.

1948 Partridge *Dict. Forces' Slang* 163 *Screamers, the*, an evident dislike of operational flying. **1952** M. Tripp *Faith is Windsock* i. 17 'Cut it out, you two,' said Bergen, 'you give me the screamers.'

j. *two-pot screamer*, one who easily shows the effects of alcohol. *Austral.*

1959 D. Hewett *Bobbin Up* 21 Look at Lou. She's a two pot screamer, always 'as been. **1972** J. de Hoog *Skid Row Dossier* 95 It says experienced and sober, ya bloody two-pot screamer.

screaming ('skriːmɪŋ), *vbl. sb.* [f. scream *v.* + -ing[1].] The action of the verb scream.

c **1400** *Destr. Troy* 10182 The skrew for þe skrykyng & skremyng of folke, Redoundet with dyn drede for to here. **1687** T. Brown *Saints in Uproar* Wks. 1730 I. 72 Such roaring and screaming, such swaggering and bouncing. **1768–74** Tucker *Lt. Nat.* (1834) II. 443 Nor may we pretend to faint away at the screamings of a country church, because we happen to have a fine ear..for music. **1892** Henley *Song of Sword* 9 A noise Of the screaming of eagles.

'screaming, *ppl. a.* [-ing[2].]

1. a. That screams; sounding shrilly.

1602 B. Jonson *Poetaster* To Rdr. 100 Like so many screaming grasse-hoppers. **1700** Dryden *Theodore & Honoria* 100 And from afar he heard a screaming sound, As of a Dame distress'd, who cry'd for Aid. **1781** Cowper *Hope* 353 The screaming nations, hov'ring in mid air, Loudly resent the stranger's freedom there. **1892** Bierce *In Midst of Life* 89 Storms of screaming grape, which..splintered the trees. **1896** A. E. Housman *Shropshire Lad* xxxv, Far the calling bugles hollo, High the screaming fife replies.

b. *screaming eagle* (U.S. slang) = *ruptured duck* (b).

1946 *Newsweek* 18 Mar. 34/1 'Ruptured duck': GI for the discharge button which ex-service men wear in their lapels, also, 'homecoming pigeon' and 'screaming eagle'. **1948** A. M. Taylor *Lang. World War II* 172 Ruptured Duck... Also nicknamed Screaming Eagle.

2. *transf.* and *fig.* **a.** Tending to excite screams of laughter; said esp. of a farce.

1854 'C. Bede' *Verdant Green* ii. x, It was a situation for a screaming farce. **1873** Hopkins *Making Worst of it* viii, The gorgeous and screaming new and original burlesque drama.

b. Violent or startling in effect; glaring, blatant, obvious.

1848 Thackeray *Van. Fair* xxi, '——!' burst out his father with a screaming oath. **1883** *Harper's Mag.* Apr. 700/2 When we..added these startling spots of colour..the effect was rather screaming. **1922** J. Hergesheimer *Bright Shawl* (1923) 205 The shawl..was malevolent, screaming in color. **1944** 'G. Orwell' *Coll. Essays, Journalism & Lett.* (1968) III. 168 The 'screaming' advertisement started some time in the nineteen-twenties. **1963** *Australasian Post* 14 Mar. 51/1 I'd be a screaming nong if I didn't recognise you as a creep. **1965** *Listener* 9 Dec. 941/1 None of..the anarchy of competing posters and screaming shop signs. **1968** *Globe & Mail Magazine* (Toronto) 13 Jan. 6/3 The commonly held stereotype of a homosexual is called, in gay jargon, a screaming queen. **1972** B. Rodgers *Queens' Vernacular* 177 *Screaming*, flagrantly homosexual. **1976** *National Observer* (U.S.) 25 Sept. 13/1 Such segregation was..a screaming mockery of the Bill of Rights. **1977** *New Yorker* 15 Aug. 22/1 The *News* and the *Post* ran screaming headlines. **1981** *Daily Tel.* 20 Feb. 17/1 Spring colours are bright pink and screaming green with khaki chino skirts for women and khaki chino trousers for men.

c. *slang.* First-rate, splendid.

1864 *Hotten's Slang Dict.*, *Screaming*, first rate, splendid. **1879** Miss Braddon *Cloven Foot* I. vi. 125 'Well', cried the manager, radiant, 'a screaming success. There's money in it.' **1883** E. Pennell-Elmhirst *Cream Leicestersh.* 314 The Belvoir have, again, had a screaming run, a brilliant day, and a grand finish. **1897** *Badminton Mag.* IV. 386 The Rioters had come out of the wood on a screaming scent.

d. *screaming habdabs*, etc.: see habdabs. *screaming meemies*, etc.: see meemies *sb. pl.*

3. Comb., as *screaming-scared* adj.

a **1963** C. S. Lewis *Poems* (1964) 106 My body awakes in bed Screaming-scared.

Hence **'screamingly** *adv.*; chiefly in the phr. 'screamingly funny' (cf. prec. 2 a).

1847 Kinglake *Eothen* 173 The joyous girls will suddenly, and screamingly, and all at once, explain to each other that [etc.]. **1879** Geo. Eliot in Cross *Life* (1885) III. 368 You would be screamingly amused by one. **1892** *Cornhill Mag.* Apr. 444 They are screamingly funny.

screamy ('skriːmɪ), *a. colloq.* [f. scream *sb.* or *v.* + -y.] Given to screaming; having a screaming voice or sound; *fig.* characterized by exaggerated or undignified expression of anger, complaint, or the like; violent or glaring in colour.

1882 *Spectator* 25 Feb. 265/1 The two thoroughly unworthy and screamy [sonnets] on Carlyle's *Reminiscences*, by Mr. Swinburne. **1885** *Truth* 11 June 927/1 Dining-rooms..fidgety with glitter, gilt, and screamy colouring. **1891** *Jrnl. of Educ.* 1 Nov. 572/2 We deprecate the 'screamy' temper in which so many of the aggrieved feel and write.

Hence **'screaminess.**

1884 Haweis *Mus. Life* 233 A word about violin strings... Thick strings will mellow the screaminess of a Stainer. **1891** *Spectator* 9 May 666/2 She impairs its effect for English readers by a certain screaminess of tone.

screane, obs. form of screen *v.*

†**scre'ation.** *Obs.*$^{-0}$ [f. L. *screāre* to hawk, hem: see -ation.] Hawking or spitting.

1658 Phillips, *Screation*, a spitting.

screbel, screble, obs. forms of scribble *v.*[1]

screch, obs. form of screech *v.*

†**screde**, *v. Obs. rare.* [dial. var. of *shrede*, shride *v.*] *trans.* To clothe, array.

a **1400** *Octouian* (W.) 1676 In armes that owghte the Sarsyns deede The Crysten knyghtes gonne hem screde.

scree (skriː), *sb.* Also 9 *erron.* scrae. [a. ON. *skriða* landslip (Sw., Da. *skred*), cogn. w. *skriða* to slide, glide (= OE. *scrīðan* to go, glide).

The existing form of the sing. is prob. a back-formation from the pl. *screes*, in which the medial ð is dropped as in 'clo'es' for *clothes*.]

A mass of detritus, forming a precipitous, stony slope upon a mountain-side. Also the material composing such a slope.

1781 J. Hutton *Tour to Caves* (ed. 2) Gloss. 96 *Skirl*, or *screes*, small stones or pebbles. **1813** Scott *Trierm.* iii. viii, Far on the sloping valley's course,..Shingle and Scrae, and Fell and Force, A dusky light arose. **1851** *Fraser's Mag.* XLIV. 137 The cliffs, and screes, and snowpatches looked uglier and steeper. **1905** Weyman *Starvecrow Farm* 209 And now the screes of Bow Fell, flecked with snow, were not more cold and hard than her face.

attrib. **1888** Davison in *Q. Jrnl. Geol. Soc.* XLIV. 232 The instability of scree-material being so great, the causes of its motion are consequently numerous.

screech (skriːtʃ), *sb.*[1] Forms: 6 skreeche, 7 scriech, screitch, skreech, 7–8 skriech, 8 schreetch, skreetch, 7– screech. [f. screech *v.* Cf. scritch *sb.*]

1. A loud shrill cry, usually one expressive of violent and uncontrollable pain or alarm.

1560 *Ovid's Narcissus* A ij b, Ecco..the dobbeler of skreeche [*rime* speche]. **1614** Sylvester *Bethulia's Rescue* ii. 238 Th' one insulting proud; Th' other in skriechés, and sad cryes, as loud, Deafned the shores. **1615** G. Sandys *Trav.* i. 11 A great lamentation, accompanied with grones and skreeches. **1628** Ld. Carleton in Ellis *Orig. Lett.* Ser. i. III. 259 But to returne to the screeches made att the fatall blow given. **1722** De Foe *Plague* (1884) 109 A Woman gave three frightful Skreetches. **1743** Appleton *Serm.* 93 Draw forth Teares, yea, to cause Schreetches and screamings out. *a* **1822** Shelley *Hate-song* 3 He sang a song which was more of a screech [*rime-word* ditch] 'Gainst a woman that was a brute. **1851** Hawthorne *Ho. Sev. Gables* xix. (1852) 230 Shouting to her at mouth-wide screech. **1864** C. Geikie *Life in Woods* vii. (1874) 128 Suddenly an unearthly sound broke from one side, a sort of screech.

†*fig.* **1671** Flavel *Fount. Life* xii. 35 Oh what a fearful scriech will thy Conscience give.

2. A name for various birds having a harsh discordant cry, e.g. the Barn-owl (*Strix flammea*), the Swift (*Cypselus apus*), the Missel-thrush (*Turdus viscivorus*), etc. Now only *dial.*

1637 G. Daniel *Genius of this Isle* 346 Where the owle And yelling Screitch, (full of portent and Fate) Late kept. **1802** Montagu *Ornith. Dict.*, Swift... Screech. **1822**

SHELLEY tr. *Goethe's Faust* ii. 67 Are the screech, the lapwing, and the jay, All awake as if 'twere day? **1852** F. O. MORRIS *Brit. Birds* II. 75 Swift... Black Martin. Screech.

3. *transf.* A harsh, squeaking sound made by some inanimate object.

1832 HT. MARTINEAU *Hill & Valley* iii. 46 He was completely roused by a creak and screech of the latticed window. **1863** HAWTHORNE *Our Old Home* II. 85 We could hear the galloping sweep of a railway train.. and its discordant screech.

4. *attrib.* and *Comb.* **a.** Simple attrib., with the sense 'screeching, loud and discordant'.

a **1830** COCKBURN *Mem.* (1856) 179 A wild-looking.. man with sandy hair, a screech voice, and staring eyes.

b. In dial. names of birds with reference to their characteristic cry (cf. sense 2), as **screech-bird, -thrush**, the Fieldfare (*Turdus pilaris*); **screech-cock, -drossle, -thrush**, the Missel-thrush (*Turdus viscivorus*); **screech-devil, -martin**, the Swift (*Cypselus apus*); **screech-hawk**, the Nightjar (*Caprimulgus Europæus*). See *Eng. Dial. Dict.*

1802 MONTAGU *Ornith. Dict.*, Swift... Screech Martin. **1839** MACGILLIVRAY *Brit. Birds* II. 114 *Turdus viscivorus*. The Missel Thrush... Screech Thrush.

¶**5.** Misused for SCREAK, SKREIGH, break of day.

1883 F. M. CRAWFORD *Dr. Claudius* iii, I am a very early bird: I get up at the screech of dawn.

screech (skriːtʃ), *sb.*[2] *slang.* [ult. ad. Sc. dial. *screigh* whisky.]

a. Whisky. **b.** Any strong alcoholic liquor, freq. one of inferior quality. **c.** *Newfoundland.* A specific rum, or a specific mixture of rums.

1902 FARMER & HENLEY *Slang* VI. 126/1 *Screech, subs.* (common), whiskey. **1944** T. H. WISDOM *Triumph over Tunisia* viii. 68 The famous and kindly *Peres Blanc* from the Monastery at near-by Thibar had supplied them with drink from the monks' own cellars, and the popular drink was one that had been aptly christened 'Screech' by '111'. **1945** W. H. PUGSLEY *Saints, Sinners & Ordinary Seamen* 231 [The rating] gets hold of some bootleg scotch—'high life', they call it on the West Coast, and 'screech' in Newfie—and then he's away to.. Cells or Detention. **1957** B. HUTCHISON *Canada: Tomorrow's Giant* 24 He is a little addicted to the Island's national drink called 'Screech'. **1958** *Maclean's Mag.* 27 Sept. 63/3 Screech is a mixture of rums now sold by the liquor board under a new label that displays.. the legend 'Newfoundland's Famous Screech'. **1959** *Manch. Guardian* 7 July 7/4 There has been some concern at the violence during fights ashore between servicemen following the drinking of a local concoction known in the service [the Navy] as 'Screech'. It is made of a local wine, 'Imbeet', mixed with Coca Cola. **1963** [see NEWFIE]. **1964** C. ROUGVIE *Medal from Pamplona* vi. 80 'Beer and screech.' 'Screech?' .. 'It's a term embracing all cheap Canadian wines.' **1973** *Daily Colonist* (Victoria, B.C.) 29 Aug. 2/2 The taste of beer must rank somewhere between buttermilk and Newfie Screech. **1979** *Globe & Mail* (Toronto) 17 Oct. 6/1 But allow us to explain. Screech, the hairy-chested Newfoundland libation, is based on Jamaican rum which arrives on the tight little island in 40-gallon, fire-charred oak barrels.

screech (skriːtʃ), *v.* Forms: 6 **skrech**, 7 **screch, skriech, scrietch**, 8 **skrietch, screetch**, 7– **screech**. [Echoic modification of SCRITCH *v.*]

1. *intr.* To utter a sharp, piercing cry, as of pain or alarm; to scream or call out with a shrill voice; also occas. used *transf.* of inanimate things.

1577 KENDALL *Flowers of Epigr.* 26 b, Thou weepest still, thou skrechest shrill, thou halest from head thyne heares. **1602** MARSTON *Antonio's Rev.* III. iii, Now croakes the toad and night crowes screech aloud. **1704** *Lond. Post* 28–30 June 2/1 The Nurse and 2 Maids who lay in a Room backwards, were heard to Skriech out a considerable time, in a most pitiful manner. **1792** WOLCOT (P. Pindar) *Odes of Condolence* Wks. 1794 III. 232 The fiddles screech with rapture one and all. **1853** KANE *Grinnell Exped.* xix. (1856) 146 Crowds of Auks and Ivory Gulls, screeching with execrable clamor. **1862** MRS. H. WOOD *Mrs. Hallib. Troub.* III. x, I screeched out all the more.. when I remembered the quarrel that had took place at dinner. **1888** HENLEY *Bk. Verses* 152 A draggled fishwife screeches at the gates. **1919** [see GRAB *v.* 3 b].

2. *trans.* To utter (a word or sentence) with a loud, shrill, piercing sound.

1844 DISRAELI *Coningsby* v. iv. 205 'Rigby', screeched a hoarse voice, 'don't you mind'. **1889** BARRIE *Window in Thrums* 149 Next minute she screeches, 'What, what, what?'

3. To cause to utter a shrill, squeaking noise. *rare.*

1862 LADY DUFF-GORDON in F. Galton *Vac. Tourists* (1864) 161 When I went into the hall, a Dutchman was screeching a concertina hideously. **1972** 'M. SINCLAIR' *Norslag* iv. 35 The ancient lift operative.. had been less than polite as he had screeched the gates open for him.

screecher (ˈskriːtʃə(r)). [f. SCREECH *v.* + -ER[1].]

1. One who screeches. *lit.* and *fig.*

1869 J. BURROUGHS *Wake-Robin* viii. (1895) 210 The fly-catchers.. are not properly songsters, but are classed by some writers as screechers. **1884** *St. James's Gaz.* 25 Jan. 6/2 They are as unpatriotic in their way as screechers about Bulgarian atrocities. **1908** *Academy* 11 July 27/2 These screechers are beginning to learn that hysterics are of little use where argument is concerned.

2. A dial. name for several birds having a harsh screaming cry; e.g. the Swift (*Cypselus apus*), the Gull-billed Tern (*Sterna anglica*), and the Missel-thrush (*Turdus viscivorus*).

1848 *Zoologist* VI. 2290 The common swift is in G[loucestershire] a 'screecher'. **1864** ATKINSON *Bird-n.*, Screecher... Gull-billed Tern. *Sterna Anglica.*

screeching (ˈskriːtʃɪŋ), *vbl. sb.* [f. SCREECH *v.* + -ING[1].] The action of the vb. SCREECH; shrill crying, howling.

1616 BRETON *Good & Badde, Vnquiet Woman* Wks. (Grosart) II. 12/2 Her voice is the skrieching of an owle. **1673** HICKERINGILL *Gregory F. Greybeard* 307 This rat-catcher owl.. with her howtings and scrietching she spoils the musick. **1753** MISS COLLIER *Art Torment.* Concl. (1811) 221 How have I seen a whole company made uneasy from the screeching of a cork between some person's fingers! **1777** W. DALRYMPLE *Trav. Sp. & Port.* cxxix, They make a most disagreeable screetching. **1828** SCOTT *F.M. Perth* vii, 'I prithee, peace', said Craigdallie, who was obviously tired of the tuneless screeching of the worthy deacon. **1871** O. W. HOLMES *Smiling Listener* 54 More banging, more screeching of fiddle and drum. **1976** *National Observer* (U.S.) 4 Dec. 15/2 A lot of this stuff is going to come to a screeching halt quickly, and we're not going to do the screeching.

screeching (ˈskriːtʃɪŋ), *ppl. a.* [f. SCREECH *v.* + -ING[2].] That screeches. Hence **ˈscreechingly** *adv.*

1816 SCOTT *Let.* in *Lockhart* (1839) V. 141 My old peacock, who chooses to.. sit below my bedroom window to keep me awake with his screeching lamentation. **1854** *N. Brit. Rev.* XXI. 217 Old ones cry out screechingly. **1886** W. J. TUCKER *E. Europe* 209 The screeching appeals which greeted the discovery of our misdemeanour.

ˈscreech-owl. Also 7 **skreech-**, 8 **scriech-**. [f. SCREECH *v.*; altered form of SCRITCH-OWL.]

1. a. A name for the Barn Owl (*Aluco flammeus* Fleming, *Strix* Linn.), from its discordant cry, supposed to be of evil omen.

1593 SHAKS. *2 Hen. VI*, I. iv. 21 The time when Screech-owles cry, and Bandogs howle. **1612** DEKKER *London Triumphing* B 1 b, Let Bats and Skreech-Owles murmure at bright Day. **1711** ADDISON *Spect.* No. 7 ¶2 A Screech-Owl at Midnight has alarmed a Family, more than a Band of Robbers. **1773** G. WHITE *Selborne, To Barrington* 8 July, From this screaming probably arose the common people's imaginary species of screech-owl, which they superstitiously think attends the windows of dying persons. **1837** CARLYLE *Fr. Rev.* III. VI. vi, Long-winded, unmelodious as the screech-owl's, sounds that prophetic voice. **1872** CALVERLEY *Fly Leaves* (1884) 5 And the screech-owl scares the peasant As he skirts some churchyard drear.

b. A small North American owl of the genus *Otus*, esp. *O. asio.*

1671 J. OGILBY *America* 147 The Birds both common and peculiar [to New England] are thus recited:.. The long-liv'd Raven, th' ominous Screech-Owl. **1812** A. WILSON *Amer. Ornithol.* V. 83 Red Owl.. is.. well known by its common name, the Little Screech Owl. **1884** *Cent. Mag.* Nov. 121 The screech-owl would shake and shiver in the depths of the wood. **1949** *Amer. Forests* Oct. 23/2 The weird call of the more or less familiar screech owl is probably the best known of all the owls. **1960** [see *jumby-bird*]. **1975** *Islander* (Victoria, B.C.) 2 Nov. 3/1 The screech owl is the one I hear and see most often.

2. *transf.* Applied to a bearer of evil tidings, or one who presages misfortune.

1606 SHAKS. *Tr. & Cr.* v. x. 16 Let him that will a screech-oule aye be call'd, Goe in to Troy, and say there, Hector's dead. **1819** SCOTT *Ivanhoe* xxx, 'Vile murderous hag!' replied Front-de-Bœuf; 'detestable screech-owl!' **1896** JANE BARLOW *Mrs. Martin's Comp.*, etc. 50 To be pitied for havin' to put up wid the ould screech-owl's foolish talk.

3. *attrib.*

1796 WOLCOT (P. Pindar) *Satire* Wks. 1812 III. 409 Of Screech-owl satire Pitt has shorn the wings. **1815** SCOTT *Guy M.* ii, The harsh and dissonant voice, and the screech-owl notes to which it was exalted when he was exhorted to pronounce more distinctly. **1837** CARLYLE *Fr. Rev.* III. VI. vi, Then, secondly, his rejected screech-owl Oration.

screechy (ˈskriːtʃɪ), *a.* [f. SCREECH *sb.*[1] + -Y[1].] Of a voice: Given to screech; loud, shrill, and discordant. Also *transf.*

a **1830** COCKBURN *Mem.* (1856) 154 His voice.. got sputtering and screechy when he became excited. **1865** *Pall Mall Gaz.* 24 Apr. 10 She has a moderate mezzo soprano, rather reedy and screechy in its upper notes. **1891** *Leeds Mercury* 8 Oct. 8/6 Vilification of the screechiest kind.

screed (skriːd), *sb.* Forms: 4 **screade**, 5 **screde**, 6 *Sc.* **skreid, screid**, 7 **skread**, 8–9 **skreed**, 7– **screed.** [Variant of SHRED *sb.*, repr. OE. *scrēade*; cf. SCR- I.]

I. 1. a. A fragment cut, torn, or broken from a main piece; in later use, a torn strip of some textile material. Also *collect. sing. Obs.* exc. *dial.*

c **1315** SHOREHAM I. 824 Þaȝ eny best devoured hyt,.. Ech screade ȝet al so longe hys godes body, Ase lest þe fourme of brede. *c* **1425** *Voc.* in Wr.-Wülcker 655/11 *Hoc presegmen*, screde. *a* **1460** *Pol. Poems* (Rolls) II. 252 Robes made of scredes. *a* **1510** DOUGLAS *Conscience* 7 Of his habite out cuttit thay ane skreid. **1560** ROLLAND *Seven Sages* 37 Scho raif hir clais all into screid. **1825** CROKER *Fairy Leg.* I. 162 He has been sometimes seen going about with hardly a skreed to cover him. **1894** CROCKETT *Raiders* (ed. 3) 208 By a screed o' her druggit goown tangled on a blackthorn.

b. A strip of land; a parcel of ground.

1615 BRATHWAIT *Strappado* 220 Thou Ahab, thou that by extortion gaines, Some Skreads of Land to better thy demains. **1644** SLINGSBY *Diary* (1836) 126 Northscales, a town in Wawne [Walney] Iseland w[ch] is a narrow screed of land lying before Fourness. **1793** SMEATON *Edystone L.* §337 The sea encroached upon these cliffs, by taking off parallel Screeds. **1843** *Lincolnsh. Topogr. Soc. Papers* 64 The triangular screed of land lying on the north side of the Cross-cliff hill, was the ancient Swine-grun of Lincoln. **1889** RAINE *Hist. Hemingborough* 165 There is a long screed or tongue of land called Bishop's Meadows.

c. An edging, a bordering strip; the border or frill of a woman's cap. *dial.*

1828 CARR *Craven Gloss.*, *Skreed*, a border or shred of cloth. **1849** C. BRONTË *Shirley* xxiii, The screed, or frill of the cap, stood a quarter of a yard broad round the face of the wearer. **1855** *Whitby Gloss.*, A *Screed*, a border or edge of paper, or other flat surface. 'A cap screed.'

2. *fig.* **a.** A long roll or list; a lengthy discourse or harangue; a gossiping letter or piece of writing.

a **1789** in Ross *Helenore* To Author p. vii, I here might gie a skreed of names. **1812** CHALMERS *Let.* in Hanna *Mem.* (1849) I. 293 Mr. Manson threatens a long screed of poetry on the subject. **1816** SCOTT *Fam. Let.* 28 Dec. (1894) I. 392 The lady would not be kept from Eildon Hills when there was any worthy.. to give her a screed of doctrine. **1884** *St. James's Gaz.* 31 Oct. 7/1 What Montaigne meant by his 'emprunts' was something altogether different from Mr. Tregellas's great screeds of cribbing. **1902** A. DOBSON *S. Richardson* v. 117 Richardson's reply is a screed of malevolence.

b. A piece, portion (of a literary work).

1829 SCOTT *Jrnl.* 12 June, After dinner I.. took a screed of my novel.

†**c.** A (drinking) bout. *Obs.*

1815 SCOTT *Guy M.* xxv, Naething confuses me unless it be a screed o'drink at an orra time. **1823** GALT *Entail* xxxii, Had he no deet amang hands in one o' his scrieds wi' the Lairds o' Kilpatrick, I'm sure I canna think what would hae come o' me and my first wife. **1828** J. WILSON *Noct. Ambr.* Wks. 1856 II. 59 A skreed in any room of his house clears my head for a month.

3. *Plastering.* **a.** An accurately levelled strip of plaster formed upon a wall or ceiling, as a guide in running a cornice or in obtaining a perfectly even surface in plastering; a strip of wood used for the same purpose. More generally in *Building*, a level strip of material formed or placed on any surface (e.g. a floor or a road) as a guide for the accurate finishing of it. Also, a levelled layer of material forming part of a floor or other horizontal surface.

1812 P. NICHOLSON *Mech. Exerc.* 308 Floating Skreeds differ from cornice skreeds in this, that the former is a strip of plaster, and the latter wooden rules for running the cornice. **1846** *Penny Cycl.* Suppl. II. 431/2 Ledges or margins of plaster, called screeds, are formed at the angles. **1855** REINNEL *Masons'* etc. *Assist.* 61 The work must be correctly plumbed up by means of flat-headed nails, and screeds for the guidance of the floating rule formed with Roman cement. **1937** S. C. B. STUBBS *Building Encycl.* IV. 1241/2 Screeding. A cement and sand floating on a floor, laid in preparation for a subsequent paving or on a wall for wall tiling, is known as a screeding. Often it is called simply a screed, because it is brought up level by the use of screeds. *Ibid.*, In the case of floors.. it is usual to use the batten itself as a screed without forming the floated strip alongside, and hence we find the battens often referred to as the screeds. **1952** D. NIELD *Building Constr. Illustr.* iii. 35 Cross reinforcement is laid over the beams and the whole covered with a layer of fine concrete (screed). **1956** DAVIES & PETTY *Building Elements* ix. 270 A screed of cement and sand is laid later to provide a smooth and level surface for whatever floor finish is to be used. **1961** *Times* 3 July (Archit. Suppl.) p. vii/3 Heating by electric wires embedded in the concrete screed is becoming quite common. **1974** W. E. KELSEY *Building Construction* v. 87 Although the term screed is applied to the whole final surface, it is also used to describe the narrow strips of wet cement used as a guide to the thickness of the top layer. **1978** *Cornish Guardian* 27 Apr. 33/6 (Advt.), Uneven floors made smooth with latex screed.

b. *Comb.*: ***screed board, rail, strip***; **screed-coat**, a coat of plaster made level with the screeds (*Cent. Dict.* 1891).

1949 A. G. GEESON *Gen. Building Repairs* (ed. 11) I. vi. 335 By moving the screed board with a slight tamping motion, the surface will be slightly roughened. **1968** *Gloss. Formwork Terms* (*B.S.I.*) 25 A tamper may be constructed so that it also acts as a screed board. *Ibid.* 22 *Screed rail*, a guide fixed at the perimeter of a concrete pour to act as a datum and support for a screed board. **1977** *Club Tennis* Mar. 13/3 The actual laying of the surface is done by screed strips and straight edge and the court is rolled and trowelled to a perfect level.

c. (See quot.)

1901 *J. Black's Carp. & Build.*, *Home Handicr.* 92 The concrete [for the floor should be].. thrown on.. and its upper surface brought perfectly level by passing a 'screed', or large wooden straight-edge, over it.

II. 4. *Sc.* [From the verb.] A rent, tear. Also *fig.* ? *Obs.*

a **1728** RAMSAY *Tit for Tat* iii, He had lent ane's Guts a Skreed, Wha had gi'en him a broken Head. **1786** BURNS *Holy Fair* iv, Ye, for my sake, hae gien the feck Of a' the ten comman's A screed some day.

5. *Sc.* A sound as of the tearing of cloth; hence, 'any loud, shrill sound' (Jam.).

a **1805** MACNEILL *Poems* (1844) 125 Fearfu' ye sang till some agreed The notes war true; Whan grown mair bauld, ye gae a screed That pleased nae few. **1805** J. NICOL *Poems* II. 12 (Jam.) Their cudgels brandish'd 'boon their heads, —Their horns emittin martial screeds.

screed (skriːd), *v. Obs.* exc. *dial.* Forms: 5 **screde**, 8 **skreed**, 8– **screed**. [Orig. a var. of SHRED *v.*, repr. OE. *scrēadian*; in later use f. SCREED *sb.*]

1. a. *trans.* To shred, tear, rip.

c **1430** *Two Cookery Bks.* 30 Take Apples, & pare hem, an smal screde hem in mossellys. **17..** *Fair Helen* xiii. in Child *Ballads* II. 212/2 And out he took a little pen-knife, And he screeded the winding-sheet.

b. *intr.* for *refl.*

1818 SCOTT *Rob Roy* xxxi, Had I been in ony o' your rotten French camlets now, or your drab-de-berries, it would hae screeded like an auld rag wi' sic a weight as mine.

2. *intr.* To produce a sound as of tearing cloth. Hence, of a musical instrument, to make a loud shrill sound.

a **1706** *Watson's Collect. Sc. Poems* I. 38 It made me Yelp, and Yeul, and Yell And Skirl and Skreed. **1756** *Pennecuik's Collect. Sc. Poems* 77 He gar'd his pipe, when he did play, Baith skirl and skreed. **1835** CARRICK, etc. *Laird of Logan* (1841) 77, I mind the verra tune that the fiddler played to us, as weel as if I heard the bow screeding o'er the strings the noo.

3. ***to screed off, away***: to give audible expression to, to relate or repeat (a matter) readily from memory.

a **1774** R. FERGUSSON *Poems* (1807) 239 Sing then, how, on the fourth of June, Our bells screed aff a loyal tune. **1839** BALLANTINE in *Whistle-Binkie* Ser. II. 5 There's nae Carritch question, nor auld Scottish sang, But the loun screeds ye aff in the true lowland twang.

4. *Building.* **a.** To level (a surface) by means of a screed; to apply (material) as a screed to a floor surface. (Cf. SCREED *sb.* 3 a.)

[**1825**: see SCREEDING *vbl. sb.*] **1898** F. W. MACEY *Specifications in Detail* 68 State if screeded in lime and hair mortar instead. **1944** E. LUCAS in R. Greenhalgh *Pract. Builder* ii. 104/2 The second coat must be screeded to bring the surface level. **1949** A. G. GEESON *Gen. Building Repairs* (ed. 11) I. vi. 333 The surface is finished by screeding it with a straightedge. **1970** *Daily Tel.* (Colour Suppl.) 5 June 35 Concrete can also be screeded to floors in old houses. *Ibid.* 39/2 How to screed a concrete floor.

b. With advbs.: ***screed in***, to finish off a surface around (an object, as a frame) by means of a screed; ***screed off***, to take *off* (excess material) from a surface by means of a screed.

1898 F. W. MACEY *Specifications in Detail* 63 Hair mortar in brickwork is only used for screeding in door and window frames. **1949** K. S. WOODS *Rural Crafts of England* IV. xi. 180 The plaster was laid on very evenly, and then 'screeded off' with a long straight-edge known as a 'screeding-rule'. **1950** *N.Z. Jrnl. Agric.* Jan. 58/3 The surplus mix [of concrete] being screeded off with a straight-edge.

screeder ('skriːdə(r)). [f. SCREED *v.* + -ER[1].] A person employed to lay floor screeds.

1976 *Derbyshire Times* (Peak ed.) 3 Sept. 11/7 (Advt.), Floor screeders and quarry tilers.—One or two reliable layers required. **1977** *Evening Post* (Nottingham) 24 Jan. 11/2 (Advt.), Floor Screeders required (male-female) for long term contract in Nottingham.

screeding ('skriːdɪŋ), *vbl. sb. Plastering.* [f. SCREED *sb.* + -ING[1].] The forming of the screeds. The action of SCREED *v.* 4. Also *concr.*, the material of a screed.

1825 J. NICHOLSON *Oper. Mech.* 617 When the screeding is finished, compo is prepared in larger quantities and..the workmen spread it..over the wall in the space left between each pair of screeds. **1898** F. W. MACEY *Specifications in Detail* 68 The mortar to be used in the screeding in of frames. **1936** *Archit. Rev.* LXXIX. 8 The floors are reinforced concrete slabs with two layers of cork separated by a layer of hard screeding. **1937** [see SCREED *sb.* 3 a]. **1956** DAVIES & PETTY *Building Elements* ix. 272 Screeding is carried out by the use of fine mix, generally one part of cement to three or four of sand.

screef (skriːf), *sb.* Also scrief, 9 skreef. [dial. var. of SCURF *sb.*[1], SCRUFF *sb.*[1]] **1.** *Sc.* and *Forestry.* A layer of vegetation on the surface of the ground.

1817 J. CHRISTIE *Instructions for Hunting* 39 Without a bit of screef aboon, But bare and naked craigs o' stane. **1866** W. GREGOR *Dialect of Banffshire* 163 There's a fine skreef o' girs on that shift. **1925** R. L. CASSIE *Gangrel Muse* 33 An' swack little feeties trip licht o' the screef, I' the reelin' an' furlin' o' fairies. **1934** *Forestry* VIII. 21 Where there is a skin of peat ..it is preferable to plant in a ploughed furrow, or in a screef with loosened soil. **1952** *Buchan Observer* 7 Oct., You may weel spier fa's to cast yer divots, gin sae be that ye ken o' a bittie o' gweed screef.

2. Special Comb.: **screef-mark**, an area from which surface vegetation has been cleared.

1950 R. JENKINS *So Gaily sings Lark* xxii. 203 With the spade the vegetation was scraped away, and in the black 'scrief-mark' as it was called an L notch was made, into which the tree was carefully inserted, the earth being firmed again by careful pressure of the heel.

screef (skriːf), *v. Sc.* and *Forestry.* Also scrief. [f. prec. Cf. SCURF *v.*, SCRUFF *v.*[1]] *trans.* To clear (surface vegetation) from the ground.

1926 *Trans. Buchan Field Club* XIII. 82 Small places had the turf skinned off or 'scriefed'. **1930** *Forestry* IV. 20 Screef the surface lightly with the flat end [of a mattock], and then loosen up the patch with the pick end. **1948** *Country Life* 8 Oct. 739/3 To screef is to clear the ground of surface vegetation (such as heather) with a mattock or comparable tool.

So '**screefing** *vbl. sb.*

1930 *Forestry* IV. 85 Short of removing the surface layers of the fire traces by 'screefing' or turning it in with the plough..it is usual to get rid of the surface vegetation by controlled burning. **1953** H. L. EDLIN *Forester's Handbk.* ix. 151 It is seldom necessary to remove weed growth completely, though screefing, or the paring away of surface vegetation with a mattock, may be practised where trees are very slow to get away..or where manure is applied. **1962** *Finnish Paper & Timber* XIII. 162 When the weight and efficiency of the tractor was increased and the screefing equipment made more manoeuvrable over rough going suitable machinery for the work had been found.

screel (skriːl), *sb. dial.*, *Sc.*, and *Barbados.* [f. next.] The cry of a bird, a child, etc.; the piercing note of a whistle.

1876 C. C. ROBINSON *Gloss. Mid-Yorks.* 117/2 *Screel* (skri·h'l), v. n. and sb., to cry, in a shrieking manner; gen. **1922** *Glasgow Herald* 8 Aug. 6 With nothing to mar your peace so serene Save the screel of the curlew or sunset's red sheen. **1953** G. LAMMING *In Castle of my Skin* v. 91 At the same hour every morning the whistle screel shot up like an alarm through the rumbling of cart wheels.

screel (skriːl), *v. dial.*, *Sc.*, *N. Ir.*, and *Barbados.* Also skreel. [Prob. imitative or ad. ME. *skrille* scream: see SKIRL *v.*[1]] *intr.* To screech, to scream, to utter a high-pitched or a discordant cry. Occas. used *transf.* of inanimate things. So '**screeling** *vbl. sb.*

1875 W. D. PARISH *Dict. Sussex Dial.* 106 *Skreel*, e[ast], to scream. **1889** M. PEACOCK *Taales fra Linkisheere* 103 What wi' yammerin' bairns, an' what wi' screälin' wimmin. **1934** *Punch* 14 Nov. 543 Though kelpies walk both bold and free And icy winds skreel off the sea. **1953** C. DAY LEWIS *Italian Visit* vi. 61 Again again again, the frogs are screeling Down by the lilypond. **1953** G. LAMMING *In Castle of my Skin* vi. 113 Mother..lashed me thoroughly. Bob heard the screeling, and came to our house listening. **1965** *Dundee Courier* 10 Apr. 8 Herring gulls skreeled.

screen (skriːn), *sb.*[1] Forms: (? 4 scren), 5–6 screne, 5–7 skrene, skreene, 6 scren, skreine, 7 skrein, 6–7 screene, 7 schreen(e, 8 skreyn, 7–9 skreen, 7– screen. Also 6–7 scrine, skrine. [Of difficult etymology. The sense corresponds with that of F. *écran*, OF. *escran* (1318 in Hatz.-Darm.), in glossaries also *escrin*, *escren* (Du Cange s. vv. *Antipirgium*, *Antypira*); Godefr. gives one instance of *escrime* fem. in the same sense. The ME. *skrene*, *skreene*, however, does not admit of being regarded as an adoption of any of these forms; though it may represent some AF. variant or derivative. The form has probably been influenced by confusion with *screne* = SCRINE, chest, coffer.

The OF. *escrin*, *escren* (? whence *escran*) is prob. a. OHG. *skirm*, *skerm* (mod.G. *schirm*) of the same meaning; the fem. *escrine* is presumably a derivative of the same word.]

1. A contrivance for warding off the heat of a fire or a draught of air. **a.** A piece of furniture consisting usually of an upright board or of a frame hung with leather, canvas, cloth, tapestry, or paper, or of two or more such boards or frames hinged together. Cf. FIRE-SCREEN.

The meaning of the word in quots. 1393–1403 is uncertain; it is not impossible that they ought to be placed under SCRINE, coffer. In quot. 1530 the meaning may be a fireguard.

1393 *Test. Ebor.* (Surtees) I. 194 Unum skreu [? *read* skren] ferreum. **1403** *Nottingham Rec.* II. 20, j. skrene, iijs. **14..** *Voc.* in Wr.-Wülcker 564/24 *Antipera*, a screne. *c* **1440** *Promp. Parv.* 450/2 Screne.., *ventifuga.* *c* **1460** *Bk. Curtasye* 462 in *Babees Bk.*, And fuel to chymné hym falle to gete, And screnes in clof to y-saue þo hete Fro þo lorde at mete when he is sett. **1530** PALSGR. 271/1 Skrene made of wycars to put bytwene the fyre, *escrain*, *estrane*. **1603** *Inv.* in Gage *Hengrave* (1822) 27 Itm, one great foulding skreene of seaven foulds. **1630** BP. HALL *Occas. Medit.* cxii. (1633) 282 This screene, that stands betwixt me and the fire, is like some good friend at the Court, which keepes me from the heate of the unjust displeasure of the great. **1711** *Hermit* 25 Aug. 2/1 Indian Skreens must be purchased to succeed Abraham and Isaac [on tapestry]. **1854** *Househ. Words* VIII. 58/2 Tables, chairs, pole-screens and cheval-screens. **1899** COWAN *Hist. Kiss* 230 There was a draught-screen just at the door.

b. A frame covered with paper or cloth, or a disk or plate of thin wood, cardboard, etc. (often decorated with painting or embroidery) with a handle by which a person may hold it between his face and the fire; a hand-screen. Also applied to a merely ornamental article of similar form and material.

1548 *MS. Harl.* 1409 lf. 61 Two litle Skrenes of silke to hold againste the fier. **1688** HOLME *Armoury* III. xvi. (Roxb.) 83/1 The first is nominated a screene, it is a thing made round of crisped paper, and set in an handle to hold before a Ladies face, when she sits neere the fire. **1712** STEELE *Spectator* No. 336 ¶2 [They] plague me..to cheapen Tea or buy a Skreen. **1852** DICKENS *Bleak Ho.* ii, Is it what you people call law-hand? she asks..toying with her screen.

c. A wooden seat or settle with a high back to keep away draughts.

1826 WILBRAHAM *Cheshire Gloss.* (ed. 2) 77 *Skreen*, a wooden settee or settle, with a very high back, sufficient to screen those who sit on it from the external air. **1879** in MISS JACKSON *Shropsh. Word-bk.* Suppl. 512.

d. A contrivance, originally in the form of a screen (sense 1 a), for affording an upright surface for display:

(*a*) of objects; e.g. for exhibition; a frame for photographs resembling a folding screen.

1859 R. HUNT *Guide Mus. Pract. Geol.* (ed. 2) 46 The screen on the eastern wall..exhibits the russet and bird's eye marble, in the base. **1888** *Lady* 25 Oct. 374/3 Some of the most delightful panel screens for photographs I ever set eyes on.

(*b*) Of images; e.g. a flat vertical surface prepared for the reception of images from a magic lantern or the like; *spec.* (i) a usu. large white surface for receiving the image from a film projector; (ii) a small fluorescent screen, esp. one in a television set (so ***little screen***) or in a VDU or monitor used with a computer; hence, the VDU or monitor itself; (iii) *transf.* (usually with definite article), moving pictures collectively; the cinema; the film world.

1810 *New Family Receipt-bk.* 257 To make Transparent Screens for the Exhibition of the Phantasmagoria. **1846** *Penny Cycl.* Suppl. II. 254/2 Magic lantern is a species of lucernal microscope, its object being to obtain an enlarged representation of figures, on a screen in a darkened room. **1881** [see ZOETROPE]. **1902** *Encycl. Brit.* XXVIII. 54/1 Screens which become fluorescent under the influence of the Röntgen rays are generally made of platino-cyanides. **1910** *Moving Picture World* 19 Feb. 249/1 People..like to see on the screen what they read about. **1915** *N. Y. Times* 15 Nov. 11/1 Unlike the legitimate stage, the screen does not have to wait for a dramatist to become inspired before it may present the topic of the hour. **1920** MRS. P. CAMPBELL *Let.* 20 Dec. in *B. Shaw & Mrs. Campbell* (1952) 215, I am much too aged for Eliza on the Screen! **1926** *Nature* 3 July 19/2 Every possessor of a 'televisor' will be in a position to see on his screen the performers in operas and plays as well as hearing them. **1928** E. WALLACE *Double* i. 11 'What is her name?' 'Mary Dane... Mary Dane—sounds like something off the screen, doesn't it?' **1932** *Ann. Reg. 1931* 48 Death robbed the screen of Lya de Putti, best remembered for her performance in 'Variety', and Tyrone Power, veteran character actor. **1943** K. TENNANT *Ride on Stranger* iv. 37 He's marvellous!.. Six feet tall and fair wavy hair. He ought to be on the screen. **1946** *B.B.C. Year Bk.* 20 A badly-produced programme may make you feel that the screen is small and cramped, but if the programme is good enough you will look at the screen not as a picture within a frame but as a view seen through a window. **1949** *Radio Times* 15 July 13/4 *Music from the movies.* Melodies from the screen in swingtime and symphony. **1956** R. M. LESTER *Towards Hereafter* v. 63 Personages very well known in the world of industry, politics, stage, screen and radio. **1961** I. MURDOCH *Severed Head* xxi. 179 Violence, except on the screen, is always pathetic, ludicrous and beastly. **1970** D. D. BENICE *Introd. Computers & Data Processing* vi. 123 There is a keyboard for entering data and commands and a light pen for indicating design changes by 'writing' on the screen. **1975** *Listener* 2 Jan. 23/1 The cumulative effect of watching the little screen for hours on end. **1976** A. DAVIS *Television: First Forty Years* 121 In the beginning, television had little or no time to devote to religion, for there were only two hours of transmissions on weekdays, and on Sundays the screen stayed blank. **1977** *Private Eye* 1 Apr. 10/3 It's all here at-a-glance—everything you want to see and know about the glamorous, dynamic world of the little screen. **1982** L. J. GOLDSTEIN *TRS-80 Model III Programming* ii. 43 The Model III screen contains 16 lines so you can display only 16 program statements at one time. **1984** J. HILTON *Choosing & using your Home Computer* 178/1 When the program is run, the first thing that will appear on the screen will be the PRINT statements starting at line 230. **1984** *Which Micro?* Dec. 2 (Advt.), Output is information from the computer to..a screen. **1985** *Daily Tel.* 8 July 11/8 The text is simply typed on screen. **1986** *Ibid.* 6 May 18/2 National Westminster Bank is planning to put screens displaying share prices and stock market information into a select number of branches.

(*c*) *Photogr.* More fully ***focusing screen.*** A flat piece of glass on which the image formed by a camera lens is focused prior to making the exposure.

1858 [see FOCUSING *vbl. sb.* 2]. **1879** *Cassell's Techn. Educ.* III. 1 (Photogr.) A screen of ground-glass. **1902** A. WATKINS *Photogr.* 19 With the lens full open you will probably notice the image on the screen is not quite so sharply defined at the extreme corners as it is in the centre. **1962** A. GÜNTHER *Microphotogr. in Libr.* 23 Focusing is rather critical, and a precision camera with focusing screen should therefore be used. **1977** J. HEDGECOE *Photographer's Handbk.* 14 Some photographers find focusing on a screen more difficult than focusing with an image-coinciding rangefinder.

e. *Mining.* (See quot.)

1883 GRESLEY *Gloss. Coal Mining, Screen*,..a cloth brattice or curtain hung across a road in a mine to direct the ventilation.

f. Any thin extended surface set up to intercept shot in gunnery trials.

1879 *Manual Artill. Exerc.* I. 17 The shot passes through two screens placed a certain distance apart. *Ibid.*, The velocity of the shot at the various screens [is] calculated from a comparison of the screen and time records. **1880** *Encycl. Brit.* XI. 300/1 The shot, after leaving the gun, cuts the wire of the first screen, and subsequently the wire of the second screen.

g. *Cricket.* An erection of canvas or wood placed behind the bowler, outside the playing area, to provide a white background and a shield from moving objects behind the bowler's arm. Cf. *sight-screen* s.v. SIGHT *sb.*[1] 17.

1894 N. GALE *Cricket Songs* 31 O Bowler... He sends you clean beyond the screen. **1908** W. E. W. COLLINS *Leaves Old Country Cricketer's Diary* ix. 153 To be sure the light—this was his account—was all wrong. Anyhow we moved the screen three times to accommodate him, and even so he was not altogether happy. **1977** J. LAKER *One-Day Cricket* 107, I eventually emerged from behind the screens.

h. *N. Amer.* and *Austral.* A frame covered with a fine netting of wire or the like, used in a window or a doorway to exclude insects.

1895 *Montgomery Ward & Co. Catal.* Spring & Summer 389/1 Adjustable Window Screen, so constructed as to form a perfect joint with the parting strip, so that it is not necessary to remove the screen in order to close the window. **1956** W. R. BIRD *Off-Trail in Nova Scotia* ii. 51 As Saturday was a warm day everyone along the road was busy, putting up screens. **1971** *Sunday Australian* 8 Aug. 8A/6 (Advt.), Insect screens and screen doors that are custom-made. **1977**

Detroit Free Press 11 Dec. 21-A 1, I opened the window, but I couldn't get the screen off and it was getting very hot.

2. a. *Arch.* A partition of wood or stone, pierced by one or more doors, dividing a room or building into two parts.

c **1460** *Bk. Curtasye* 28 in *Babees Bk.*, And sithen byfore the screne þou stonde In myddys þe halle. **1553** BALE tr. *Bp. Gardiners Serm.* Hj b, I am..compelled to take my wyfe Truthe to me, whan she commeth agayne at leynght peeping behynde the scrine. **1589** *Hay any Work for Cooper* 44 When he hadd gotten some fatte meat of O the fellowes table, would go to the skrine, and first wipe his mouth on the on[e] side and then O the other, because he wanted a napkin. **1596** SPENSER *F.Q.* v. x. 37 Streight th' other fled away, And ran into the Hall, where he did weene Him selfe to saue: but he there slew him at the skreene. **1684** BUNYAN *Pilgr.* II. 118 He always loved good talk, and often would get behind the Skreen to hear it. **1851** TURNER *Dom. Archit.* I. ii. 44 Behind the screen, or 'in the screens' as it was called was ..the Lavatory. **1875** STUBBS *Const. Hist.* I. xi. (1897) 380 The name [chancellor], derived probably from the *cancelli*, or skreen behind which the secretarial work of the royal household was carried on.

b. *Eccl.* (See CHANCEL-*screen*, ROOD-SCREEN.)

1643 EVELYN *Diary* 24 Dec., They greatly reverence the Crucifix over the skreene of the Quire. **1762–71** H. WALPOLE *Vertue's Anecd. Paint.* (1786) II. 265 He committed the same error at Winchester, thrusting a screen in the Roman or Grecian taste into the middle of that cathedral. **1826** SCOTT *Woodst.* i, Two fair screens of beautiful sculptured oak had been destroyed. **1908** F. BOND (*title*) Screens and Galleries in English Churches.

c. A wall thrown out in front of a building and masking the façade.

1842 R. BROWN *Dom. Arch.* 318 *Screen*, a row of columns with their continued entablature, erected along the top of a dwarf-wall, between which and the dwelling-house is a court, generally attached to palaces. **1886** C. E. PASCOE *Lond. of To-day* xxxi. (ed. 3) 283 The screen on the Whitehall side [of the Admiralty]. *Ibid.* xxxii. 295 Devonshire House, a large mansion with a screen in front, at the corner of St. James's Street.

d. *Mil.* = *screen-battery* (sense 9 below).

1876 VOYLE & STEVENSON *Milit. Dict.* (ed. 3) 35 Small openings are made in the screens corresponding with the embrasures of the batteries.

e. *Geol.* A roughly tabular body of older rock separating two intrusions.

1910 W. B. WRIGHT in *Summ. Progr. Geol. Surv. 1909* 33 About a quarter of a mile further inland, in the midst of the granophyre, a vertical screen of lava occurs... This screen varies much in thickness, being as little as 10 feet in one place, but reaching 300 feet in others... The granophyre on the outside of this screen is a distinct intrusion from that inside. **1942** M. P. BILLINGS *Structural Geol.* xv. 284 If the central block subsides several times.., a number of concentric ring-dikes will form. A remnant of the older country rock left between two ring-dikes is called a screen.

3. *transf.* **a.** Applied to any object, natural or artificial, that affords shelter from heat or wind.

Ramsay's application of the word to a scarf worn by a woman over the head has been echoed by later writers as if it were a dialectal specific sense.

1538 ELYOT *Dict.*, *Vmbella*, a lyttel shadow, also a skrine to kepe away the light of the sonne. **1642** FULLER *Holy & Prof. St.* III. vii. 167 A South-window in summer..needs the schreen of a curtain. **1724** RAMSAY *Tea-t. Misc.* (1733) I. 66 My mistris in her tartan screen. **1784** tr. *Beckford's Vathek* (1868) 31 When the sun began to break through the clouds they ordered a pavilion to be raised, as a screen from the intrusion of his beams. **1818** SCOTT *Hrt. Midl.* xxv, Her tartan screen served all the purposes of a riding-habit, and of an umbrella.

b. Something interposed so as to conceal from view. Also *fig.*

1605 SHAKS. *Macb.* v. vi. 1 Now neere enough: Your leauy Skreenes throw downe, And shew like those you are. *a* **1674** TRAHERNE *Chr. Ethics* (1675) 91 All Things are naked and open before his Eyes, and there be no Walls to exclude, or Skreens to hide..nor Distance to over come, but all Things equally neer and fair. *a* **1704** T. BROWN *On the Beauties* Wks. 1730 I. 44 Next, over all, must Phryne's skin be drawn ..Through which most lovely and unfaithful screen The various passions of the soul are seen. **1788** BURKE *Sp. agst. W. Hastings* Wks. XIII. 284 The screen, the veil spread before this transaction, is torn open by the very people themselves, who are the tools in it. **1818** SCOTT *Hrt. Midl.* xiv, The sun set beyond..the screen of western hills. **1851** GALLENGA *Italy* 23 He sought, it would be difficult to say whether a comfort or a screen in the observance of religious practices.

c. *Mil.* A small body of men detached to cover the movements of an army.

1892 HOME & PRATT *Précis Mod. Tactics* 81 The dispersion on a wide front which is necessary to obtain what is generally called the cavalry screen necessarily entails weakness. **1894** GALL *Mod. Tactics* (ed. 3) 175 Large bodies of infantry when there is a possibility of contact with the enemy will be covered by what is now called a screen of troops in extended order.

d. A line or belt of trees planted to give protection from the wind.

1644 EVELYN *Diary* 21 Mar., A pretty garden,..having at the entrance a skreene at an exceeding height, accurately cutt in topiary worke. **1791** W. GILPIN *Forest Scenery* II. 75 In a part of the skreen, which divides these grounds from the road, we have an opportunity of remarking the disagreeable effect of trees planted alternately. **1842** J. WILSON *Chr. North* (1857) I. 246 Screens of oak and sycamore trees. **1882** *Garden* 28 Jan. 65/1 All..screens of Privet, Beech, Holly, Yew, &c. to be kept thick must be cut annually.

e. *Meteorol.* A shelter that surrounds meteorological instruments and protects them from direct sunlight and precipitation, usu. painted white and louvred to provide indirect ventilation.

1881 W. MARRIOTT *Hints to Meteorol. Observers* 10 The screen should be placed over short grass in a freely exposed situation. **1902** *Encycl. Brit.* XXX. 699/1 Various forms of open lattice work and louvre screens have been devised and used.., in all of which the wind is supposed to blow freely through the screens, while the latter cut off the greater part of the direct sunshine. **1923** F. WILD *Shackleton's Last Voy.* i. 12 One large screen, containing hair hygrograph, standard thermometer and thermograph. **1975** J. SCOTT *Fun with Meteorol.* 36/1 Ideally the thermometer bulbs should be about 4 ft. above ground level and the screen should have a north opening door to eliminate direct sunlight when it is opened.

f. A windscreen of a motor vehicle; also formerly, (*a*) a secondary screen to shield the occupants of the back seat in an open car; (*b*) a screen of celluloid for protecting the sides of an open car.

1904 A. B. FILSON YOUNG *Complete Motorist* vii. 176 When a cover is used it should have a removable glass screen in front. **1912** *Motor Manual* (ed. 14) iii. 99 Most cars now have adjustable and detachable glass or celluloid windscreens as a protection against the weather, dust, etc; screens can also be made of wire gauze and waterproof material. **1925** *Morris Owner's Man.* p. xi (Advt.), There are ..rear screens and rear screens. **1955** *Times* 10 May 7/7 Perhaps the only fault from the driver's point of view is that his windscreen wiper is badly located and does not clean enough of the right-hand side of the screen. **1959** *Motor Manual* (ed. 36) vi. 186 Whatever the type of motor, it is usually combined with a suitable speed-reducing mechanism so that the wiper blades shall move reasonably slowly across the screen.

g. *U.S. Sports.* (See quots. 1961 and 1976.)

1939 *Sat. Even. Post* 7 Oct. 89/2 These are the components of a good passing game: the pitcher, receivers, and screen behind which the thrower can successfully operate. **1951** [see PICK *sb.*[3] 10]. **1961** J. S. SALAK *Dict. Amer. Sports* 383 *Screen* (basketball), term used to describe a maneuver of the offensive team in which one player, by moving in front of opponent, 'screens' or 'screens out' that opponent from his teammate. A screen generally is worked in an effort to free one of the offensive team members for a shot at the basket. *Ibid.* 384 *Screen* (handball), an assumed or retained position on the court which prevents the opponent from getting to, or playing the ball. **1967** B. STARR *Quarterbacking* 173 Screen passes are effective countermoves by the offense when the defense is applying heated pressure on the passer. **1975** *New Yorker* 7 Apr. 100/3 On offense, they zipped the ball around fast and moved with purpose, setting the picks and screens that their principal plays..called for until someone got open for a good shot. **1976** *Webster's Sports Dict.* 374/1 *Screen*, a maneuver in various sports by which an opponent is legally cut off from the play.

4. *fig.* **a.** A means of securing from attack, punishment, or censure. Also, anything which intervenes obstructingly.

1610 SHAKS. *Temp.* I. ii. 107 To haue no Schreene between this part he plaid, And him he plaid it for, he needes will be Absolute Millaine. **1625** BACON *Ess.*, *Envy* (Arb.) 514 There be so many Skreenes betweene him, and Envy. **1760** *Ann. Reg.* III. *Misc. Ess.* 213 A worthless rascal who has found out the art of deceiving under the screen of royal authority. **1817** JAS. MILL *Brit. India* II. v. viii. 651 He would not have scrupled to form for himself a screen out of his own ambiguity. **1877** NORTHCOTE *Rom. Catacombs* I. i. 24 They furnished a real and legal screen for the protection of the Christian Society. **1878** BROWNING *La Saisiaz* 56 There's no longer screen betwixt soul and soul's joy.

b. (*a*) See quot. 1710; (*b*) a chaperon. ? *nonce-uses.*

1710 STEELE *Tatler* No. 171 Advt., All false Buyers at Auctions being employ'd only to hide others, are from this Day forward to be known in Mr. Bickerstaff's Writings by the Word Screens. **1818** SCOTT *Rob Roy* xiv, I will bribe old Martha with a cup of tea to sit by me and be my screen.

5. a. An apparatus used in the sifting of grain, coal, etc. Cf. SCRY *sb.*

1573 TUSSER *Husb.* (1878) 37 A skuttle or skreine, to rid soile fro the corne. **1667** MERRET in *Phil. Trans.* II. 466 The Skreens are made with two partitions, to separate the dust from the Corn. *c* **1710** CELIA FIENNES *Diary* (1888) 101 A frame..made all of small wire just as I have seen fine Screens to screen Corne in. **1760** MILLES in *Phil. Trans.* LI. 538 The smaller coal is separated from the clay by a skreen, or grated shovel. **1805** DICKSON *Pract. Agric.* I. Pl. xiv, The corn passes through the skreen G into the hopper H. **1844** H. STEPHENS *Bk. Farm* I. 547 There is a portable screen or harp for riddling and depositing the stones. **1872** RAYMOND *Statist. Mines & Mining* 61 An improvement has been made ..by the substitution, at several mills, of coarse screens, with apertures one-quarter of an inch in diameter, instead of the one-eighth-inch screens heretofore in use.

b. An arrangement of bars at the end of an overflow pipe, to prevent the escape of fish from a pond.

1888 GOODE *Amer. Fishes* 57 They had..gone through the screen at the mouth of the pipe.

6. a. Applied to various portions of optical, electrical, and other instruments, serving to intercept light, heat, electricity, etc.

1819–23 BARLOW *Optics* in *Encycl. Metrop.* (1845) III. 474/2 A skreen of gauze, or gummed muslin posited vertically. **1878** *Encycl. Brit.* VIII. 29/1 What are called electrical screens, i.e. sheets of metal used to defend electrical instruments, &c., from external influences. **1893** SLOANE *Electr. Dict.*, *Screen*, Electric, a large plate or a hollow case or cage of conducting material connected with the earth, and used to protect any body placed within it from electrostatic influences. **1915** HAWKHEAD & DOWSETT *Handbk. Wireless Telegr.* (ed. 2) 263 Some valves are fitted with an additional screen of copper gauze covering the outside of the glass bulb... This screen protects the valve from heavy spark discharges in the neighbourhood. **1931** B. BROWN *Talking Pictures* v. 127 A special sound-porous screen is used when the speakers are placed directly behind the picture. Most of the sound screens used in this country are of the woven type and of loose construction. **1950** *High Voltage Cables* (British Insulated Callender's Cables Ltd.) (ed. 2) i. 4 The screen functions as an earth conductor in close contact with the insulation. **1978** A. M. PORTIS *Electromagnetic Fields* xiv. 544 We wish..to discuss the scattering by various kinds of apertures in a two dimensional dielectric screen.

b. *Radio.* An arrangement of parallel wires located between a transmitting aerial and the earth's surface, serving to reduce the loss of power from the aerial to the earth.

1922 R. KEEN *Direction & Position Finding by Wireless* i. 5 Experiments were being carried out in Germany..in connection with the screening of a vertical aerial... In other countries work..led to the complete wire screen or reflector. **1952** E. A. LAPORT *Radio Antenna Engin.* ii. 123 It is desirable to bring the ground wires to the surface a short distance from the radiator base so as to form a good ground screen above the soil near the antenna base where the electric field strengths are high. **1961** H. JASIK *Antenna Engin. Handbk.* xxiv. 16 If a screen is designed for both high and low bands in the VHF range, the over-all size should be determined by the lowest frequency.

c. *Electronics.* = *screen grid.*

1927 *Amateur Wireless* XI. 269/1 The presence of the outer grid between the inner grid and the plate or anode naturally acts to some extent as a screen, and since this is connected to H.T. which is effectively at earth potential, we have a capacitative screen between the two electrodes. **1933** *Jrnl. Franklin Inst.* CCXVI. 418 Close to this first grid, and coaxial with it and the cathode, is a second spiral used to screen the control grid from the fields of the plate and called therefore the 'screen grid' or simply the 'screen'. **1942** *Electronic Engin.* XIV. 639/3 This formula..gives less accurate results for pentodes and tetrodes unless the transconductance to the screen is taken into account. **1962** D. F. SHAW *Introd. Electronics* xi. 234 The defect in the tetrode characteristics..is eliminated by the insertion of a third grid, called the suppressor grid, between the anode and the screen.

7. *Printing.* **a.** A transparent plate, covered with two crossing sets of closely spaced parallel lines or with a uniform pattern of fine dots, behind which a photosensitive surface is exposed to obtain a half-tone image or as a step in forming the image carrier in a gravure process; also, in *Photogr.*, a patterned transparent plate or film that is combined with a negative during printing to give a textured appearance to the finished print.

1894 *Amer. Dict. Printing & Bookmaking* 465/2 Half-tone plates are made by passing the rays of light from a negative through a screen which is ruled or dotted. **1902** *Encycl. Brit.* XXIX. 411/1 This was finally accomplished by the insertion of a screen, in the camera, between the lens and the plate —the effect of which was to break up the whole surface of the negative into dots. **1940** [see *contact screen* s.v. CONTACT *sb.* 6]. **1946** H. WHETTON *Practical Printing & Binding* xxv. 299/2 When the tissue is dry it is ready for screening. The cross-lined screen used in photogravure differs from those used in the production of half-tones. **1967** KARCH & BUBER *Offset Processes* v. 158 Coarser screens, such as the 65-line screen, are used in newspapers printed by letterpress. **1977** J. HEDGECOE *Photographer's Handbk.* 255 The picture, below left, was made by sandwiching the screen with a 2¼ ins sq..negative so that the pattern appeared relatively small.

b. The fine gauze or mesh (orig. of silk: cf. SILK SCREEN *sb.*) used in screen printing.

1934 F. A. BAKER *Silk Screen Practice* xvii. 114 Doubtless most screen operators have had visions of the ideal screen shop. **1938** BIEGELEISEN & BUSENBARK *Silk Screen Printing Process* v. 105 Either organdy or silk may be used as the screen for film stencils. **1957** *Screen Printer & Display Producer* July 3/2 The mesh is coated with a solution to form the screen for the photographic stencil. **1967** V. STRAUSS *Printing Industry* vii. 521/1 After the screen is ready, it may either be proofed or be used for running without proofing.

8. An instance or the action of screening (see SCREEN *v.* 4).

1954 [see *screen test* (sense 9a)]. **1974** M. C. GERALD *Pharmacol.* iv. 77 In a general blind screen, a range of doses of the compound are injected into test animals..and gross behavioral observations are made with an eye toward detecting any activity. **1975** *Language for Life* (Dept. Educ. & Sci.) xvii. 263 The majority of children scoring low on the group intelligence test have already been the subjects of consultation between head teachers and psychologists; consequently this second screen is now regarded as serving no more than a 'mopping up' purpose.

9. *attrib.* and *Comb.* **a.** *gen.*, as ***screen-bulkhead***, †***-fan***, ***fence***, ***image***, ***-plantation***, ***-shape***, ***test***, ***-work***, (also *fig.*); †***screen-faced***, †***-like*** adjs.; **screen-battery** *Mil.* (see quot.); **screen-cell**, a part of a gaol where a prisoner may be kept under constant observation; **screen-chamber**, an enclosure containing a screen (sense 5); **screen-cloth**, (*a*) the material used to cover a screen; metal or plastic mesh, esp. for covering a window or door screen (Webster), or for sifting material; (*b*) *Mining*, a mat hung in an airway to promote ventilation; **screen current** *Electronics*, the current flowing in the screen grid of a valve; **screen-door**, a metallic or textile outer door of a pair, used for protection against insects or storms; also *Naut.*, for protection against explosions; **screen grid** *Electronics*, a grid placed between the control grid and the anode of a valve to reduce the capacitance between these electrodes; **screen-man**, a worker at the screen (sense 5), *spec.* in the

Coal-trade = SCREENER; **screen(-)memory**, *Psychol.*, a Freudian term, orig. tr. as 'concealing memory', for a childhood memory whose apparently indifferent content screens from consciousness some (usu. previous) significant emotional event; **screen-painting**, pictorial decoration of church screens; **screen (†forward) pass** *N. Amer. Football* (see quot. 1976); **screen-perch** (see quot.); **screen plate** *Photogr.*, an obsolete form of colour plate in which minute filters in primary colours are incorporated in the plate itself; freq. *attrib.*; **screen porch** *N. Amer.*, a veranda protected by a screen against insects; **screen print** *sb.*, (*a*) a picture or design produced by screen printing; (*b*) screen-printed fabric; **screen printer**, one who works at screen printing; **screen printing**, a printing process used esp. for pictorial matter in which the ink is transferred to the surface to be printed through a fine screen (sense 7 b) stretched in a frame, the non-printing parts of the screen having been rendered impervious; so **screen-print** *v. trans.*, to print (a surface or a design) in this way; **screen-printed** *ppl. a.*; **screen process**, the process of screen printing; freq. *attrib.*; **screen table** (see quot. 1794); **screen temperature** *Meteorol.*, the temperature as measured by a thermometer in a screen (sense 3 e); **screen-tower**, an elevated building containing a series of screens (sense 5); **screen voltage** *Electronics*, the voltage applied to the screen grid of a valve; **screen wall**, a wall that serves as a screen; so **screenwalling**; **screen-wash**, the cleaning of a windscreen automatically; also *attrib.*, of a substance added to water used in screenwashing; **screen-washer**, a device which washes a windscreen by directing a jet of water on to its exterior from below; **screen-wiper**, a windscreen wiper.

1876 VOYLE & STEVENSON *Milit. Dict.* (ed. 3) 35 A *screen battery is a parapet of earth running across the front of the batteries and thus forming a screen. **1797** *Encycl. Brit.* (ed. 3) XVII. 404/1 The beam abaft, which comes under the *screen bulkhead. **1892** *Pall Mall Gaz.* 24 Oct. 5/2 He was confined in a *screen cell. **1877** RAYMOND *Statist. Mines & Mining* 432 The screens are provided with latticed hoppers, which allows a current of air to flow freely up through the *screen-chambers. **1603** *Inv.* in Gage *Hengrave* (1822) 27 A *skreen cloth..of green kersey. **1889** *Pall Mall Gaz.* 22 Apr. 3/1 By the expenditure of a few shillings in hanging a mid wall of screencloth a plentiful supply of air could have been obtained. **1946** *Sun* (Baltimore) 7 Oct. 2/5 Sales of bronze and copper screen cloth were allowed on an adjustable prices basis. **1974** G. S. ORMSBY in P. L. Moore et al. *Drilling Practices Manual* vi. 152 The particle size a shale shaker can remove depends almost completely upon the size and the shape of the mesh openings in the screen cloth. **1936** E. D. MCARTHUR *Electronics & Electron Tubes* v. 72 In this region, the *screen-current characteristic is the exact opposite of the plate-current characteristic. **1962** D. F. SHAW *Introd. Electronics* xi. 232 The characteristics of a tetrode are more complex than those of a triode because of the additional variables of screen voltage and screen current. **1975** D. G. FINK *Electronics Engineer's Handbk.* xiv. 8 Multi-grid tubes require screen-grid modulation in conjunction with the control-grid modulation to achieve space-charge modulation and to minimize screen current. **1840** *Civil Engin. & Arch. Jrnl.* III. 84/1 Its effect is..unavoidably impaired by the interference of two pairs of *screen doors. **1889** I. M. RITTENHOUSE *Maud* (1939) vii. 225 And after he'd gone I stood staring and staring out of the screen-door at nothing. **1914** 'BARTIMEUS' *Naval Occasions* vi. 39 The screen-door..opened from the battery to the quarter-deck. **1933** E. O'NEILL *Ah, Wilderness!* (1934) I. 16 *Mrs. Miller.* That boy! (*She rushes to the screen door and out on the porch, calling*:) Tommy! You mind what your Pa told you! **1974** *News & Courier* (Charleston, S. Carolina) 19 Apr. (Wickes Lumber Advt. Suppl.) 6 Screen doors in many styles, sizes & finishes. **1977** *Gay News* 24 Mar. 13/4 Such matters as who should fix the screen door, or do the cooking ..seem to fall into place as if by prearrangement. **1979** *Sunset* Apr. 56/1 The Boulevard Cafe, with open-air lunch counter, fly fans, and a banging screen door to an indoor counter, has been serving highway customers the same way for over 32 years. **1601** MUNDAY *Downf. Robt. Earl Huntingdon* B 4 b, Is it thy part, thou *screenfac't snotty nose, To hinder him that gaue thee all thou hast? **1664** BUTLER *Hud.* II. iii. 367 Are sweating Lanthorns, or *Screen-fans, Made better there than th'are in France? **1856** MORTON *Cycl. Agric.* II. 817 Along the side [of the plantation] most exposed to the sea-breeze, erect a *screen fence composed of turf [etc.]. **1928** G. E. STERLING *Radio Man.* 167 The connection to the *screen grid is made to the regular grid connection on a standard socket. **1930** *Manch. Guardian* 20 Sept. 15/7 A remarkable constructors' set known as the 'Osram Music Magnet Four', comprising two screen-grid stages, detector, and low frequency stages. **1942** *Electronic Engin.* XV. 10/1 When used as a triode the suppressor and screen grids are connected to anode. **1974** HARVEY & BOHLMAN *Stereo F.M. Radio Handbk.* ii. 15 Carrier voltage is applied in push-pull via T_1 to the control grids of the two valves, whilst the modulating signal is supplied to the screen grids from T_2 which also provides push-pull drive. **1897** *Knowledge* 1 Sept. 217/2 Any mixture of indefinite light with the *screen image has the effect of so much fog. **1937** *Discovery* Feb. 45/1 For production of the screen image a high intensity automatic arc is being used. **1611** COTGR., *Araroye*, a round or *skreene-like ornament of feathers, worne by the West-Indian Sauages at their backes. **1851** GREENWELL *Coal-trade Terms Northumb. & Durh.* 48 *Skreenmen. **1891** *Labour Commission Gloss.*, *Screeners* or *Screenmen*, men at bank who shovel the coals over the flat of the screens into the wagons and clean them. **1924** J. RIVIERE tr. *Freud's Recollection, Repetition* in *Coll. Papers* II. xxxii. 368 In many cases I have had the impression that the familiar childhood-amnesia, which is theoretically so important to us, is entirely outweighed by the *screen-memories. **1940** *Chambers's Techn. Dict.* 749/1 *Screen memory*, early childhood impressions and ideas which break through into consciousness, but are distorted and condensed into something which is unrecognisable to the individual. **1957** L. DURRELL *Justine* I. 78 It is perhaps what the Freudians would call a screen-memory of incidents in her earliest youth. **1962** J. STRACHEY tr. *Freud's Screen Memories* in *Compl. Wks.* III. 320 A screen memory may be described as 'retrogressive' or as having 'pushed forward' according as the one chronological relation or the other holds between the screen and the thing screened off. **1967** KANZER & BLUM in B. B. Wolman *Psychoanal. Techniques* iv. 107 An examination of the painful episode as a nucleus (screen memory) with an infinity of ramifications, which involved the entire relationship of the patient with his father. **1906** G. E. FOX in *Victoria Hist. County Norfolk* II. 542 The *screen paintings at Barton Turf, Edingthorpe, Harpley, Potter Heigham, Houghton-le-Dale, Lessingham, Ranworth, and Walpole-St.-Peter, have all been assigned to the fifteenth century. **1937** A. G. LITTLE *Franciscan History & Legend in English Mediaeval Art* ii. 15 (*heading*) Screen Paintings... The painting of the lower panels of the rood and parclose screens of English churches with saints was confined almost entirely to the latter end of the 15th century. **1934** C. WALSH *Intercollegiate Football* 345/2, 1908–'*Screen' Forward Pass (no longer legal). **1955** E. POPE *Football's Greatest Coaches* xxviii. 326 Zuppke originated the system of pulling back guards to protect the passer, the screen pass. **1970** *Globe & Mail* (Toronto) 26 Sept. 39/1 Ernie Carnegie gave the Redmen the lead with an 80-yard touchdown from a screen pass. **1976** *Webster's Sports Dict.* 374/2 *Screen pass* or *screen football*, a short forward pass to a back in the flat in front of whom a wall of interference has been formed by linemen who have moved over after the snap. **1979** *Arizona Daily Star* 5 Aug. c 9/1 Sproul..found Ivery on a screen pass and Ivery weaved his way down the left sideline for the deciding touchdown. **1891** HARTING *Bibl. Accipitr.* 229 *Screen-perch, the form of perch used for hawks when kept in a room. **1965** P. WAYRE *Wind in Reels* x. 142 Trained birds of prey are often tied to a screen-perch in their mews at night, this is a padded perch from the underneath of which hangs a sheet of thick canvas or hessian well-weighted at the bottom to keep it taut. **1971** *Country Life* 8 Apr. 799/3 Hawks have to be set to roost on a screen perch which prevents them from bating off and entangling themselves. **1799** J. ROBERTSON *Agric. Perth* 420 Soften the rigour of winter, by sheltering the lower farms with *skreen-plantations. [**1898** *Sci. Trans. R. Dublin Soc.* VI. 134 The lined screen which can bring about this will only show its individual colours when placed under the microscope. It is then seen to consist of closely ruled adjacent lines in reddish-orange, yellowish-green, and blue tints. This screen, applied closely to the sensitive surface, analyses the image in the camera.] **1909** G. L. JOHNSON *Photogr. Optics & Colour Photogr.* v. 238 This *screen plate is covered with a panchromatic emulsion. **1930** O. WHEELER *Photogr. Printing Processes* xvii. 218 Screen-plate processes for the production of transparencies..are undoubtedly of great merit. **1970** M. J. SETHNA *Photography* 8 John Joly's 'screen-plate' method led to the 'autochrome' plates made in 1907 by the Lumière brothers. **1973** D. A. SPENCER *Focal Dict. Photogr. Technol.* 548 *Screen plate process*, additive colour process in which the image is both recorded and viewed through a mosaic or reseau of microscopically small colour filter elements. The emulsion is exposed through the mosaic and reversal processed to yield an additive colour transparency. **1962** M. E. MURIE *Two in Far North* I. iv. 36 Mother baked pies, many of them, and doughnuts. These were put out into the cache or the *screen porch and frozen. **1970** *New Yorker* 28 Feb. 48/2, I went around to the side and up on the screen porch, lifted the window to the library, and climbed in. **1979** *Arizona Daily Star* 5 Aug. (Advt. Section) 14/9 Screen porch, sun deck, 2 car garage, 3 car carport. **1938** BIEGELEISEN & BUSENBARK *Silk Screen Printing Process* viii. 184 If a photograph or wash drawing is to be reproduced, it is first sent to a photoengraver, who makes a '*screen print' from it. **1957** *Observer* 1 Dec. 11/5 Chinese 'Sampan' screen-prints of water, reeds and flowers made full-skirted dresses. **1973** *Country Life* 21 June 1808 The characteristic screen print..is an edition of 100 published by Christie's Contemporary Arts at £65 each. **1976** *Dumfries & Galloway Standard* 25 Dec. 11/4 (Advt.), Screen prints 120 cm. wide. Modern designs. Metre usually £1·60. Now 99p. **1952** *Archit. Rev.* CXI. 194 (*caption*) Curtains and chair-cover privately *screen-printed for Jane Drew. **1970** *Daily Tel.* (Colour Suppl.) 15 May 14 We made our real breakthrough when we screen-printed ceramic colours on to flat ware. **1957** *Screen Printer & Display Producer* July 4/2 The older type of *screen printed transfers, which have been available to potters for some ten years.., have become well established as a medium for high quality multi-colour relief decoration. **1969** *Sears Catal.* Spring/Summer 43 Long-sleeve screen-printed Sweatshirts. **1938** BIEGELEISEN & BUSENBARK *Silk Screen Printing Process* i. 12 The *screen printer may make prints which so closely resemble wood-block prints that only an expert can distinguish the difference. **1977** *Daily Times* (Lagos) 11 Jan. 22/5 (Advt.), Wanted. Experienced Screen-Printers. Apply..to Clem Advertising Productions. **1934** F. A. BAKER *Silk Screen Printing* iii. 21 (*heading*) Silk and other gauzes used in *screen printing. **1936** [see *hand block* s.v. HAND *sb.* 65]. **1958** *Observer* 17 Aug. 7/3 The firm of Taco use beautiful hand screen-printing of fruit and leaves on cotton ottoman, a process that takes twelve screens. (These days one has to say 'hand screening' because so much screen-printing is being done with the Swiss Buser automatic multicolor machine.) **1980** *Daily Tel.* 11 July 15/4 The exhibition confirms..that screen-printing has become a major medium for the living artist. **1930** B. ZAHN *Silk Screen Methods of Reproduction* 37 The specification for a paint for *screen process work. **1938** BIEGELEISEN & BUSENBARK *Silk Screen Printing Process* i. 7 Applicability of the screen process to the fine and applied arts has been recognized rather belatedly. **1967** KARCH & BUBER *Offset Processes* ii. 35 (*caption*) Screen process presses are often used for printing on glass bottles. **1970** *British Printer* July 69/1 Screen process had always been particularly versatile in handling a variety of surfaces and shapes which could not easily be printed by any of the three main printing processes. *Ibid.* 74/2 All screen-process inks contain inflammable solvents. **1888** *Lady* 25 Oct. 374/3 A smaller frame, *screen shape,..to hold six 'midget' photographs. **1794** T. SHERATON *Cabinet-Maker & Upholsterer's Drawing-Bk.* II. 395 *Of the *Screen-Table.* This table is intended for a lady to write or work at near the fire; the screen part behind securing her face from its injuries. **1971** *Country Life* 30 Sept. (Suppl.) 29 (Advt.), A rare Sheraton period mahogany screen table, 17″ wide. £245. **1913** *Rep. Brit. Assoc. Adv. Sci. 1912* 740 The explanation lies in the removal of air which has been chilled by radiation from the plant, and its replacement by air at '*screen-temperature'. **1972** *Daily Tel.* 1 Sept. 12/4 In Scotland the screen temperature fell to 32 degrees F (0 degrees C) at Tummel Bridge, Perthshire. **1954** *Cancer* VII. 1184/2 Large numbers of women could receive a *screen test for carcinoma of the cervix with minimal utilization of professional personnel. **1971** *Nature* 9 July 105/1 Observations suggest that it is possible to devise an *in vitro* 'screen' test for potentially carcinogenic substances. **1877** RAYMOND *Statist. Mines & Mining* 447 All [the ore] was elevated some seventy feet to the top of the *screen-tower. **1936** E. D. MCARTHUR *Electronics & Electron Tubes* v. 72 This..is fulfilled when the anode voltage becomes less positive than the *screen voltage. **1945** *Electronic Engin.* XVII. 332/1 To obtain best results the control grid and screen voltages must be correctly chosen. **1962** Screen voltage [see *screen current* above]. **1900** *Yorksh. Archæol. Jrnl.* XV. 303 The *screen-wall between the pillars of the nave. **1936** A. W. CLAPHAM *Romanesque Archit.* iii. 53 This eastern screen-wall..appears only in the Apulian school. **1971** *Country Life* 30 Sept. 819/3 To guard against possible intrusion a screen wall was raised. **1976** *West Lancashire Even. Gaz.* 13 Dec. 9/5 (Advt.), Very low-priced ..quality fencing, wood and concrete posts, sheds, timber, *screen-walling. **1970** *Times* 5 Mar. 16 Another new feature is the 'cyclic' wipers which give not only slow and fast speeds but..eight wipes in conjunction with the *screen-wash. **1976** *Scotsman* 24 Dec. 11/2 Sachets of screenwash additive are useful, however, not only in preventing washers from freezing in cold weather but in dissolving the road grime and grease that can smear or even scratch the windscreen. **1958** *Observer* 17 Aug. 15/7 The test car also had the simplest and most efficient *screen washer I have seen so far. **1962** [see ACCESSORY *sb.* 1]. **1977** *Lancashire Life* Mar. 118/4 It still has cloth seats, heated rear window and electric screenwashers. **1928** E. WALLACE *Double* iii. 32 With his *screen-wiper swinging madly, his mackintosh black with driving rain, Dick Staines came to Brighton. **1930** *Punch* 22 Jan. 92/3 Aggie must have something, a new mascot, a screen-wiper .., a new wing. **1970** *Railway Mag.* Oct. 558/1 With the aid of..efficient screen-wipers on the locomotive, there was no difficulty in sighting the signals. **1977** *Lancashire Life* Mar. 118/4 The screenwipers have not been re-set for right hand drive. **1648–58** HEXHAM s.v. *Voye*, The Top of some *schreene-worke. **1850** *Parker's Gloss. Archit.* (ed. 5) I. 416 The oldest piece of screen-work that has been noticed is at Compton church, Surrey. **1858** FROUDE *Hist. Eng.* II. 354 Unhappily, behind the screen-work of these poor saints, a whole Irish insurrection was blazing in madness and fury. **1904** GASQUET *Eng. Monastic Life* ii. 20 In some places, it is true, certain screenwork divisions appear to have been devised.

b. *spec.* with reference to the cinema or television screen, esp. in the *transf.* sense (see 1 d above), as ***screen actor***, ***actress***, ***adaptation***, ***beauty***, ***credit***, ***début***, ***fan***, ***fever***, ***kiss***, ***rights***, ***set***, ***star***, ***story***, ***version***, ***world***, ***worthiness***; ***screen-filling***, ***-struck*** [after *stage-struck*], ***-worthy*** adjs.; **screenplay**, the script from which a motion picture film is produced; formerly, the film itself; also *attrib.*; **screen test**, a filmed test of the performing abilities of a prospective film actor, or the film shot on such an occasion; hence **screen-test** *v. trans.*; **screen time**, the time allotted to or occupied by a film or television production; **screen writer**, a writer of film scripts; hence **screen-writing** *vbl. sb.* and *ppl. a.*

1915 *Film Fun* Dec. 1 The screen actor has the best of it in holiday season. **1977** *Times* 7 Oct. 11/4 Valentino..was actually a very good screen actor. **1916** *N.Y. Times* 8 May 7 It is rumored that never again is this clever screen actress to play such a rôle. **1939** A. HUXLEY *Let.* 18 Nov. (1969) 448, I am working at present on the screen adaptation of *Pride and Prejudice*. **1919** H. L. WILSON *Ma Pettengill* ii. 38 It is the face of one of our famous screen beauties. **1922** Screen credit [see CREDIT *sb.* 13 d]. **1977** R. LUDLUM *Chancellor MS.* vi. 78 They're willing to..remove your name from the screen credits..not the title, of course. **1915** *N.Y. Times* 22 Nov. 12 'The Martyrs of the Alamo', the Triangle picture in which Douglas Fairbanks made his screen début. **1923** T. LANE *What's Wrong with Movies?* vi. 100 The general run of screen fans want to do very little thinking when they go to the cinema. **1915** Screen fever [see *screen-struck* adj.]. *a* **1963** J. LUSBY in B. James *Austral. Short Stories* (1963) 231 The Eccentric's reel..concluded with a screen-filling close-up of the stolid face of an armourer. **1951** M. MCLUHAN *Mech. Bride* (1967) 101/2 Shirley Temple gets her first screen kiss in a picture you'll never forget. **1971** *Petticoat* 17 July 28/3 Peter..was signed up by Walt Disney to give Hayley Mills ..her first screen kiss. **1916** *N.Y. Times* 7 Feb. 9/3 (*heading*) Anna Held's debut in a screen play. **1925** *Ladies' Home Jrnl.* Jan. 37/3 Screen play by Walter Woods. **1938** A. HUXLEY *Let.* 18 Nov. (1969) 437 They have followed their usual procedure and handed my treatment over to several other people to make a screen-play out of. **1945** R. CHANDLER *Let.* 13 Oct. in *R. Chandler Speaking* (1966) 43 He has gone so long without writing—unless you count a couple of screenplay jobs. **1977** *Times Lit. Suppl.* 24 June 750/3 A screenplay..is subsumed in the completed movie. **1980** *Times* 22 Nov. 4/8 Mr Cimino has written his own screenplay. **1920** *Q. Rev.* July 185 The feverish haste exhibited at the present time to secure the screen-rights of classics in the world of fiction. **1974** *She* Jan. 83/1 Bought screen rights to *Boy Shoots Girl*... Now to find writer to do Treatment. **1948** 'T. CLAYMORE' *Nest of Vipers* x. 195

Listening critically, I felt that she needed a Hollywood screen set and a background of soft music for these speeches. **1914** R. Grau *Theatre Science* x. 211 So here we have the unique spectacle of an idolized screen star earning a prima donna's honorarium for stage appearances at night only. **1977** J. Aiken *Last Movement* ix. 167 Seeing a screen star for the first time in the flesh. **1914** R. Grau *Theatre Science* xii. 256 Thousands are impatiently awaiting the appearence of those publications which fictionize the screen stories. **1946** D. L. Sayers *Unpopular Opinions* 124 Wishing..that they too could live like the heroes and heroines of these witless million-dollar screen stories. **1915** *Film Fun* Dec. 1 Screen-struck. Everybody wants to get into motion pictures. It is an epidemic of screen fever. **1922** I. & H. Klumph *Screen Acting* xvi. 89 Then..she went back to her work of checking up on the scenes..and gave her screen test no more thought. **1933** *Sat. Even. Post* 17 June 14/1 Harry Rapf, one of the M-G-M executives, happened to see me dancing at the Winter Garden in New York City and asked me to make a screen test. **1952** M. McCarthy *Groves of Academe* (1953) iv. 57 The cold peroxided beauties who..were here while waiting for a screen-test. **1970** *Sunday Times* 26 Apr. 29/2 He screen-tested me... And I was offered one of the three star parts in the production. **1948** *Hansard Commons* 21 Jan. 219 Overseas producers..enjoy the same proportion of British screen time they have had in the past few years. **1973** *Listener* 20 Sept. 391/1 In a typical year, the BBC sells 11,000 hours of television screen-time abroad. **1978** *Broadcast* 29 May 10/1 The problem of screen-time for groups on the extreme political fringe. **1915** *N.Y. Times* 20 Sept. 9 The screen version of 'Peer Gynt' begins with the reindeer ride and ends with the rescue of Peer. **1933** *Radio Times* 14 Apr. 75/1 In *Cavalcade* (both stage and screen versions). **1981** *Listener* 1 Jan. 22/1 The screen version of *David Copperfield*..went way beyond the accepted running time of movies of that period. **1915** *Film Flashes* 11 Dec. 4 Are we to live only for ourselves, forgetting our brothers and sisters of the screen world? **1928** *Daily Express* 7 May 9/2 The production..has been booked by Provincial Cinematograph Theatres, a booking generally regarded throughout the world as the hall-mark of screen-worthiness. **1928** *Daily Tel.* 12 June 10 Rachel... Her brief meteoric career needed no fantastic embellishments to make her story screenworthy. **1980** *Times Lit. Suppl.* 23 May 582/2 Though the screen-play for *The Tin Drum* was 'revised and augmented' by Günter Grass, Volker Schlöndorff's success has relatively little to do with making phrases screenworthy. **1921** *Moving Picture Stories* 12 Aug. 26/3 A Robertson-Cole picture..written by..two well-known screen writers. **1958** *Times Lit. Suppl.* 15 Aug. p. xxviii/5 How many genuine screen-writers have achieved any success in this country? **1974** *Listener* 17 Jan. 68/1 My first opportunities as a screenwriter were..in this country, but my career..has been in Hollywood. **1941** B. Schulberg *What makes Sammy Run?* vi. 124 Have screen-writing job for you. **1973** [see pot-boiler 2a]. **1977** *Listener* 20 Oct. 498/1 In the 1930s, it was fairly easy to get a handle on the politics of the screenwriting community.

c. With reference to VDU screens, as ***screen display***; ***screen-based***, ***-oriented*** adjs.; **screen dump**, the process of causing what is displayed on a screen to be printed out; an occurrence of this, or the resulting print-out; **screen editor**, a program that enables one to edit what is displayed on a screen; so **screen editing**; **screen print**, a facility for producing a print-out of what is displayed on a VDU; (see also in sense 9a).

1978 *Business Systems & Equipment* Mar. 59/1 This small electronics company..has recently designed a *screen-based stand alone word processor with floppy disc storage and a daisy-wheel printer. **1985** *Marketing* 28 Feb. 43/1 It [*sc.* Telex]..provides a written record, which, unlike its screen based equivalents, can act as a long-term reminder to the recipient. **1982** *Computerworld* 11 Jan. 65 Features include two pages of *screen display, upper- and lowercase keyboard [etc.]. **1981** *Kilobaud Microcomput.* Apr. 174/3 Vendors of *screen dump programs. **1983** *Austral. Personal Computer* Apr. 55/3 Graphics output, using special dot symbol spokes, can cope with Lisa screen dumps, but they are not really as good as the dot matrix version. **1985** *Personal Computer World* Feb. 62/1 (Advt.), Screen dump rom available for £11.50. **1976** *Jap. Telecommunications Rev.* Jan. 37 CRT Character Display Equipment..performs a high level of *screen editing function. **1984** *DEC Professional* Dec. 83 We discussed full screen editing and split screen windows. **1979** *Software Pract. & Experience* Feb. 121 Building a screen editor as a front end to a line editor..permits one computer to edit another's files. **1982** C. P. Pfleeger *Machine Organiz.* vii. 165 A text editor can be either a line editor, a cursor editor, or a screen editor... To a screen editor, a file is a series of pages, each page being just as much material as will fit onto the screen of the display terminal. **1985** *Daily Tel.* 8 July 11/8 Most modern machines now have sufficiently good screen editors to permit an alternative and simpler approach which is ideal for documents up to one page long. **1979** *Rec. 12th Asilomar Conf. 1978* 437/1 *Screen-oriented editors differ from other editors in their use of high speed video terminals to display the contents of large sections of a file being edited. **1985** *Jrnl. Computers in Math. & Sci. Teaching* IV. II. 24 A microcomputer..for interactive, screen oriented, problem solving in reaction thermodynamics. **1981** *Micro* (U.S.) Sept. 27/1 The program described in this article is a *screen print utility for the Atari 400/800. **1983** *80 Microcomputing* Jan. 22/3 The current Genie has a 1·5K ROM..that adds a lowercase driver, a flashing repeating cursor, screen print, [etc.]. **1985** *Computerworld* 13 May 82/4 The product is said to support IBM Virtual Diskette file transfer software and transfer to disk storage, screen print and color or

screen (skriːn), *sb.*[2] *Cant.* ? *Obs.* [? Connected with screeve *sb.* and *v.*] A bank-note. Chiefly in *queer screen*, a forged bank-note.

1789 G. Parker *Life's Painter of Variegated Characters* xv. 153 *Rum screen*, a bank note. *Ibid.* 179 *Screen*, a bank note. **1795** H. Potter *New Dict. Cant & Flash Lang.* (ed. 2) 53 *Skreen*, a bank note. **1811** *Lexicon Balatronicum*, s.v. *Screen*, Queer screens; forged bank notes. **1812** J. H. Vaux *Flash Dict.*, *Queer screens*, forged Bank-notes. **1830** Lytton *P. Clifford* xxxi, Bill Fang..was stretched for smashing queer screens. **1864** *Hotten's Slang Dict.*, *Screen*, a bank note. *Queer Screen*, a forged bank note.

screen (skriːn), *v.* Forms: 5 screane, 7 screene, skreene, 7–9 skreen, 7– screen. [f. screen *sb.*[1]]

1. a. *trans.* To shelter or protect with or as with a screen, *from* heat, wind, light, missiles, or the like.

c **1632** *Poem* in *Athenæum* 27 Jan. (1883) 121/2 From whose inward light The Angells with their wings must skreene their sight. **1671** Milton *P.R.* iv. 30 Back'd with a ridge of hills That screen'd the fruits of the earth and seats of men From cold Septentrion blasts. **1728** Chambers *Cycl.* s.v. *Eye*, To screen his Eye, he will presently cover it therewith. **1784** Cowper *Task* iii. 440 He therefore timely warn'd himself supplies Her want of care, screening and keeping warm The plenteous bloom. **1823** W. Scoresby *Jrnl. Whale Fish.* 201 The adjoining mountains..skreened the ice near their bases, from the solar rays. **1879** Geikie *Geol.* in *Encycl. Brit.* X. 268/2 Being hard, they resist the action of the falling drops and screen the earth below them.

b. To shut off by something interposed. *rare.* Now only with *off*.

1700 Dryden *Sigism. & Guisc.* 211 The Curtains closely drawn, the Light to skreen. **1861** Tyndall *Fragm. Sci.* (1871) 384 You will perhaps try whether the magnetic power is not to be screened off.

c. *Electr.* To protect from external electric or magnetic fields; to cover (a wire or circuit) in order to prevent it from radiating electrical interference.

1922 *Wireless World* 1 July 416/1 The problem is to screen the receiving apparatus from the effects induced directly by the oscillator. **1931** *B.B.C. Year-bk. 1932* 422 It will..be advisable to screen the coils L_1, L_2, the tuning condenser K_1, and the secondary circuit, L_3, K_2. **1950** *Engineering* 3 Feb. 140/2 On wireless-carrying vehicles electrical equipment must be screened. **1960** *Practical Wireless* XXXVI. 393/1 The lead from the input socket is screened. **1971** L. T. Agger *Introd. Electr.* viii. 119 It is sometimes necessary..to screen a space from external electrostatic influence, as in protection against lightning of buildings containing explosives.

2. a. To hide from view as with a screen; to shelter from observation or recognition.

1686 Goad *Celest. Bodies* ii. iv. 196 Clouds..shall skreen the Sun from us. **1711–12** Swift *Jrnl. to Stella* 6 Jan., When he came out, Mr. Secretary..walked so near him that he quite screened me from him with his great periwig. **1784** Cowper *Task* i. 168 Our fav'rite elms, That screen the herdsman's solitary hut. **1818** Scott *Rob Roy* xxv, A small hedge, which imperfectly screened the alley in which I was walking. **1844** H. H. Wilson *Brit. India* iii. vii. III. 357 The Coorgs effectually screened themselves behind the bushes. **1893** *Hansard's Parl. Deb.* 30 Mar. 1500 To send vessels to sea whose lights are screened on different principles.

b. *Mil.* To employ a body of men to cover (an army's movements). Also *absol.* (Cf. screen *sb.*[1] 3c.)

1881 Bell tr. *C. von Schmidt's Instr. Training Cavalry* 173 In all these different cases the leading thought..must..be to see without being seen, reconnoitre and screen. **1884** Trench *Cavalry in Mod. War* 270 The duties to be performed by the division—*i.e.*..to screen the movements of one's own army, to unmask those of the enemy [etc.]. **1899** *Westm. Gaz.* 11 Dec. 1/3 The duty of reconnoitring the foe and screening the friend.

c. In immaterial senses.

1670 Cotton *Espernon* i. iv. 151 The artifice of his Enemies so skreen'd his merits from his Majesties observation, that he receiv'd very little thanks for his labour. **1692** Bentley *Boyle Lect.* i. 6 There are some Infidels among us, that..to avoid the odious name of Atheists, would shelter and skreen themselves under a new one of Deists. **1813** Shelley *Q. Mab* v. 27 Compelled by its deformity, to screen With flimsy veil of justice and of right, Its unattractive lineaments.

d. To surround (a nuclear reactor or other source of ionizing radiation) with a mass of material intended to absorb the radiation.

1915 Colwell & Russ *Radium, X Rays & Living Cell* vi. 160 If the radium applicator is screened by the interposition of ·5 mm. of lead..the results are different. **1931** G. E. Birkett *Radium Therapy* ii. 36 The radium in solution should be heavily screened to protect people working in adjacent rooms. **1946** *Ann. Reg. 1945* 354 The pile was not screened well enough to protect the personnel from the injurious effects of the intense radiation emitted by the unstable fission products.

e. *U.S. Sports.* To shield (a team-mate) from attack by opponents; to act as a shield against (opponents). Also *intr.* Cf. screen *sb.*[1] 3g.

1922 P. D. Haughton *How to watch & understand Football* 7 To stop the runner who is so thoroughly screened by interferers. **1951** *Sun* (Baltimore) 24 Dec. (B ed.) 13/2 Watch when they screen for a shooter [in Basketball]. **1961** [see screen *sb.*[1] 3g].

3. a. To shield or protect from hostility or impending danger; *esp.* to save (an offender) *from* punishment or exposure; to conceal (a person's offence).

c **1485** *Plumpton Corr.* (Camden) 58 If I shold therfore screane myself, & my frynds also, & not put me therfore to hurt. **1630** Bp. Hall *Occas. Medit.* cxii. (1633) 283 But how happy am I, if the interposition of my Saviour..may screene mee from the deserved wrath of..God. **1693** Locke *Educ.* §214 (1699) 376 He that Travels with them is to skreen them; get them out when they have run themselves into the Briars [etc.]. **1738** *Gentl. Mag.* VIII. 141/2 Were there any Hopes that he could ever be brought to skreen the most notorious Corruption, I dare say he would meet with the Approbation of this virtuous Society. **1780** *New Newgate Cal.* V. 206 All his artifices could not screen him from the justice of his country. **1817** Jas. Mill *Brit. India* II. v. ix. 696 Mr. Hastings had taken presents, and skreened himself by giving them up at last to the Company. **1824** W. Irving *T. Trav.* II. 244 Great exertions were made to screen him from justice, but in vain. **1850** Browning *Easter-D.* ix, No misery could screen The holders of the pearl of price From Caesar's envy. **1894** Sir J. Astley *Fifty Yrs. Life* II. 4, I more than once helped—or at any rate screened—a man who had taken a drop too much.

†**b.** *intr.* To interpose oneself as a protection.

1655 tr. *Com. Hist. Francion* v. 11, I..took no care to approach to his assistance, being unwilling to skreen betwixt him and the abuse.

4. a. *trans.* To sift by passing through a 'screen'.

1664 Evelyn *Kal. Hort.*, May 67 Mixing it [*sc.* earth] with ..very mellow Soil, screen'd and prepar'd some time before. **1693** Moxon *Mech. Exerc.* (1703) 251 A Skreen.. with which one Man will Skreen as much Lime..as two Men can with a Sieve. **1763** *Museum Rust.* (ed. 2) I. 79 If it is necessary to screen all the corn at this time, a small screen is fixed under the aperture of the second floor. **1815** J. Smith *Panorama Sci. & Art* I. 191 Sea-coal ashes, sifted or skreened through a sieve or skreen ⅛ an inch wide. **1847** *Act 10 & 11 Vict.* c. 89 §28 Every Person who..slacks, sifts or screens any Lime. **1901** *Daily Chron.* 11 July 7/6 Screening water through fine gauze was sometimes substituted for filtration.

†**b.** *fig. Obs.*

1657 Reeve *God's Plea* 249 How ought we to skreen and riddle our soules concerning the steyn of blood-shed.

c. To examine systematically in order to discover suitability for admission or acceptance; *spec.* (*a*) to examine (a person) for unwanted attributes or objects, esp. political disloyalty; (*b*) to test (chemicals) for their suitability for use as drugs.

1943 *Sun* (Baltimore) 14 May 1/3 These offices 'screen' a list of prospects for the employers. **1945** *Manch. Guardian* 18 July 8/1 The recruits had come forward from the disbanded Guardia del Popolo and from most various sources and all would be screened carefully. **1949** *Cancer Res.* IX. 625/1 More than 1,000 chemical agents have been screened against Sarcoma 37 *in vivo*. **1956** W. Graham *Sleeping Partner* x. 82 When you said you were bringing an assistant to Harwell, of course we had to have her screened. **1958** *Listener* 19 June 1015/2, I am within a few yards of the Customs desk... My wife had packed all the declared trinkets in one bag, and that is all he wants to see. He screens it in fifteen seconds flat. **1962** *Sunday Times* 14 Jan. 1/7 Every flight arriving from Europe was screened by medical and immigration officials for Pakistani immigrants. **1970** *New Scientist* 11 June 538/2 Drug companies are trying to weed out drug-takers from their staffs and to screen applicants so as to avoid taking on more. **1971** *Daily Tel.* 19 Apr. 15/7 Electronic equipment at airports to 'screen' passengers for weapons and so on. **1974** M. C. Gerald *Pharmacol.* iv. 77 Of the 15,000 compounds our government screened as substitute antimalarials, only two..were found to be superior to quinine. **1979** *Daily Tel.* 21 May 12/7 Mr Corliss describes only those events which were reported in reputable scientific journals, where all material is rigorously screened, and 'mis-identifications and hoaxes are kept to a minimum'.

d. To select or separate by means of a screening process.

1943 *Sun* (Baltimore) 10 Dec. 6/7 The Attorney General said he believed it was possible to screen loyal from disloyal Japanese. **1976** *National Observer* (U.S.) 5 June 8/3 The experiment involves 20 communities, screened from an original list of 250 where some citizen efforts at decision-making already have cropped up.

e. To examine (a person, esp. as one of a large group) for disease or defects other than as a response to a request for treatment.

1944 [implied in screening *vbl. sb.* 2c]. **1950** *Amer. Jrnl. Public Health* XL. 275/1 A population group in one city is screened for tuberculosis. A separate program is conducted ..to screen a population group for diabetes. **1970** *Observer* 12 Apr. 25/5 We could therefore soon be in a position to screen the whole population to see which recessive genes they carry. **1970** *Daily Tel.* 10 Oct. 8/4 Mass radiography is the easiest way for the man in the street to be screened.

f. To examine or search (data or an article) for any content of particular relevance or interest.

1956 A. H. Compton *Atomic Quest* 27 The committee had begun to function that soon afterwards was screening physics news for items of possible military importance. **1964** *Ann. N.Y. Acad. Sci.* CXV. 569 The system proposed.. allows the raw experimental data to be screened and digested directly by a small fast hybrid computer. **1977** *Jrnl. R. Soc. Arts* CXXV. 228/2 For the genetic resources material to be of any value to the breeder it must be evaluated or 'screened'.

g. screen out: to sift or separate; to exclude or eliminate by some screening process.

1943 *Sun* (Baltimore) 3 Aug. 11/1 The stalks are put through a mechanical disintegrator which reduces them to a juicy puree and screens out the toughest fibers. **1946** *Cancer Res.* VI. 490/1 In resorting to histologic and cytologic studies to screen out the inactive compounds we have made the assumption that damage induced by active compounds would become evident within 48 hours after injection. **1955** *Publ. Amer. Dial. Soc.* xxiv. 51 There is an increasing tendency to screen out all argot and slang in the presence of outsiders. **1967** M. Argyle *Psychol. Interpersonal Behaviour* x. 195 The method..releases extremely powerful emotional forces, and those not able to profit from them should be screened out. **1968** *International Herald Tribune* 3 Sept. 7/3 The FBI has improved its methods of screening out inaccurate reporting. **1971** *Sci. Amer.* Oct. 42/3 The detector was located underground to screen out relatively low-energy particles produced in the atmosphere. **1975** *New Yorker* 21 Apr. 54/2 The company's instructions to its managers do seem to indicate an employment policy favoring people of conventional outlook and screening out people who might harbor tendencies towards nonconformist intellectualizing. **1979** *Bull. Amer. Acad. Arts & Sci.* Feb. 17 The committee will not screen out applications.

5. In the Inns of Court: To post upon a screen or notice-board.

1870 *Echo* 10 Jan., An attempt was made by the Benchers to shame them into honesty by 'screening' or posting their names in the dining hall. **1895** *Daily News* 22 Oct. 5/3 The Treasurer of the Inner Temple.. has caused to be screened in the vestibule of the Hall an invitation [etc.].

6. *Printing.* To obtain an image of (a picture, type, etc.) through a screen (SCREEN *sb.*[1] 7).

1948 R. R. KARCH *Graphic Arts Procedures* ix. 247 Both type matter and illustrations are screened. **1952** R. W. & E. W. POLK *Practice of Printing* (rev. ed.) xxiv. 198 In display, sometimes a heading or a block of type is screened to create a desired effect. **1972** *Physics Bull.* Sept. 532/1 Continuous tone pictures are 'screened' to allow reproduction by normal printing methods.

7. To show (a picture) on a screen; to project on to a screen as with a magic lantern or film projector; to exhibit as a production for the cinema or television. Also *intr.*, to be (well or ill) suited for reproducing on a cinema or television screen.

1913 *Writer's Mag.* Nov. 188/2 Because you fail to sell your story, in spite of the fact that you see others of the same type screened, will not be proof that editors are prejudiced against you. **1915** *Durham County Advertiser* 18 June 8/7 'Tommy Atkins', a stirring patriotic picture.. will be screened at an early date. **1919** H. L. WILSON *Ma Pettengill* ii. 67 She'll screen well, and she's one of the few that can turn on the tears when she wants to. **1962** *Rep. Comm. Broadc. 1960* 66 Programmes of national appeal screened by all or most of the companies. **1973** *Guardian* 10 Apr. 1/6 A revised version of Granada Television's controversial documentary about Mr John Poulson.. will be screened on April 30. **1976** *National Observer* (U.S.) 18 Dec. 9/2 When the movie was screened, the key obscenity standard was whether a sex work was 'utterly without redeeming social value'.

8. *Comb.*: **screen-berth** (see quot.).

1867 SMYTH *Sailor's Word-bk.*, *Screen-berth*, pieces of canvas temporarily hung round a berth, for warmth and privacy.

screenage ('skriːnɪdʒ). [f. SCREEN *sb.*[1] + -AGE.] The material used as a screen for ionizing radiation; such screens collectively; the action or the efficiency of screening.

1929 S. CADE *Radium Treatment of Cancer* i. 5 The necrosis is in inverse proportion with the screenage. **1930** *Brit. Med. Jrnl.* 8 Feb. 234 The screenage, amounting to the equivalent of just over 1 mm. of platinum, consists of monel metal, brass, aluminium, and wood. **1933** WARD & DURDEN-SMITH *Recent Advances in Radium* vi. 67 The screenage for seeds most commonly used at the Radium Institute is 0·5 millimetre of gold. **1940** S. CADE *Malignant Dis. & Treatment by Radium* viii. 177 Screenage of eye applicators by substances of low or medium atomic weight, such as wax, rubber, and palladium, may.. still further reduce the incidence of eye complications. **1956** C. W. WILSON *Radium Therapy* (ed. 2) x. 239 When lead screenage is added to a radium source filtered by 0·5 mm. platinum so as completely to surround the source, the transmission curve is virtually a straight line up to 20 cm. thickness of lead.

screened (skriːnd), *ppl. a.* [f. SCREEN *v.* + -ED[1].]

1. a. Protected by a screen, sheltered. Also freq. with adverbs, as ***screened-in, -off***.

1696 WHISTON *Theory of Earth* IV. iv. 355 In the more retired and skreen'd Plains and Valleys. **1833** T. HOOK *Parson's Dau.* III. xi, A screened-off place was made up for the maids. **1872** BROWNING *Ring & Bk.* IX. 567 Midnight meetings in a screened alcove Must argue folly in a matron. **1946** J. O'HARA in *New Yorker* 6 July 18 Eben Townsend was sitting on the screened-in porch smoking his after-dinner cigar. **1968** R. M. PATTERSON *Finlay's River* i. 39 We slept that night on the floor in the screened-in veranda, very comfortable and protected against the rain and the mosquitoes. **1973** J. WAINWRIGHT *Pride of Pigs* 78 They led him.. to the ward, and pointed out the screened-off bed. **1978** P. NIESEWAND *Underground Connection* 1 The screened-off telephone switchboard. **1979** *Arizona Daily Star* 5 Aug. (Advt. Section) 18/3 Enjoy the breezes and mountain views from large screened-in Arizona room. **1981** P. MALLORY *Killing Matter* iii. 33 A broad screened-in porch where Holly Devereaux sat in a rattan chair.

b. *fig.* Concealed, hidden away.

1844 *Queen's Regul.* 123 The positive absence of Crime is the criterion of a well-established Discipline, not its screened existence.

c. *Meteorol.* Placed in or measured in a screen (see SCREEN *sb.*[1] 3 e).

1894 *Daily News* 3 Jan. 5/4 Thirteen degrees of frost in the heart of London is a record which is not often obtained from a screened glass. **1920** *Westm. Gaz.* 2 Dec. 6/4 At Greenwich, a minimum screened temperature of 27 deg. was registered.

2. a. Sifted by means of a screen.

1677 J. W[ORLIDGE] *Art Gard.* I. iii. 32 The Gravel Walkes ..which if made with a fine skreened red Gravel do very much adorn your Garden. **1807** A. YOUNG *Agric. Essex* II. 193 He now does them [*sc.* the drains] with picked and skreened stone. **1838** *Civil Engin. & Arch. Jrnl.* I. 341/2 A composition of 'screened' (otherwise almost uselessly small) coal, river mud, and tar. **1858** SIMMONDS *Dict. Trade*, *Screened-coal*, sifted or large coal; that from which the breeze or fine dust has been separated.

b. In the sense of SCREEN *v.* 4 c.

1957 *Economist* 26 Oct. 321/1 A drive for Party members among discreetly screened intellectuals, who responded 'sincerely' to the 'blooming-flowers' campaign by seeing, hearing and speaking no evil, is also under way; the first 25 recruits are proudly announced from the professorial staff of Tientsin university. **1962** L. DEIGHTON *Ipcress File* xv. 86 The screened personnel available to us. **1967** *Times Rev. Industry* July 89/3 The procedures of some 41 companies suggest that the higher the level of responsibility the less frequently a manager gains important external information from publications compared with other sources. But this may merely mean that information from publications is received in a screened form from other folk. **1979** J. GARDNER *Nostradamus Traitor* xlix. 242 The screened call came in from Washington.

3. Posted upon a screen. (See SCREEN *v.* 5.)

1897 *Westm. Gaz.* 12 May 4/3 Two are described in the screened list, as gentlemen.

4. a. *Electr.* Of a wire, circuit, or appliance; having a conducting cover or shield, intended to reduce the radiation or reception of interference.

1922 *Wireless World* 1 July 416/2 A design for a screened oscillator was prepared. **1926** S. O. PEARSON *Dict. Wireless Techn. Terms*, *Screened Aerial*, an aerial beneath which is spread a network of wires to act as a counterpoise. **1927** *Amateur Wireless* XI. 269/1 Following on these lines two practical forms of screened valve have been designed. *Ibid.* 269/3 The valve can then be built into a screened circuit,.. if a slot is cut in the external screen. **1933** *Practical Wireless* 4 Feb. 962/2 The ingenious screened wiring kit manufactured by Remax Radio is the very thing for temporary or permanent screening. **1936** *Ibid.* 16 May 232/2 (*heading*) Screened leads. **1943** *Gloss. Terms Electr. Engin.* (*B.S.I.*) 82 *Screened cable*, as used for electricity supply. A multicore cable in which the insulation of each conductor is separately enclosed in a conducting film in order to ensure a radial electric field surrounding the conductor, the films being in electrical connection with one another and with the metallic sheath of the cable and usually earthed. **1970** J. EARL *Tuners & Amplifiers* vi. 134 Screened cable must be used on these low-level inputs to avoid excessive hum coupling.

†**b.** *Electronics.* ***screened grid***: in a thermionic valve, a control grid having a screen grid around it. Usu. *attrib. Obs.*

1929 *Radio Times* 8 Nov. 409 (Advt.), You could not get a better 3-valve set than the Brown Screened Grid Receiver. **1930** *Manch. Guardian* 20 Sept. 15/7 Thanks to the screened-grid valve, the old monster multi-valve set is now practically a back number. **1943** C. L. BOLTZ *Basic Radio* x. 164 The pentode has ousted the screened-grid valve from radio circuits.

5. Projected on a screen; shown at the cinema or on television.

1917 C. N. BENNETT *Kinematography* ix. 160 (*heading*) Distortion of the screened image. *Ibid.*, [It] shows the normal proportions of the screened picture. **1966** *Listener* 24 Nov. 775/3 Selectivity in exposure, perception, attention, retention, etc., means that the effect of screened violence will not be constant and will vary from person to person.

6. *Printing.* Of an image or surface: obtained with the aid of a screen (SCREEN *sb.*[1] 7); bearing a pattern formed by a screen.

1946 H. WHETTON *Practical Printing & Binding* xxv. 299/2 Type or pictures have now to be printed upon the screened tissue. **1952** R. W. & E. W. POLK *Practice of Printing* (rev. ed.) xxxi. 232 (*caption*) Example of surprinting on 120-line screened background of varying densities. **1973** M. ASTRUA *Man. Colour Reproduction* I. 106 For the preparation of screened positives or negatives, a study has been made of suitable screens.

screener ('skriːnə(r)). [f. SCREEN *v.* + -ER[1].]

1. (See quot. 1816.)

1816 J. H. H. HOLMES *Coal Mines Durh. & Northumb.* 247 *Screeners*, men employed to screen the coals, which descend an iron screen into the wagon, and suffer the small coal or culm to pass through. **1892** *Daily News* 21 Mar. 6/2 The screeners.. who sift and load the coal at the pit bank.

2. In other senses of the verb (see quots.).

1913 *Dialect Notes* IV. 57 *Screener*, a person who 'screens' cranberries. **1951** *Sun* (Baltimore) 24 Dec. (B ed.) 13/2 Watch the defensive man as he hooks his arm around the screener and swings around [in Basketball]. **1967** D. FRANCIS *Blood Sport* iv. 48 'A screener,' he said. 'How come Teller found you?' **1977** *Lancet* 16 July 131/1 In 1974 McCarthy and Widmer calculated that screening by consultants of recommended elective surgical procedures could reduce the number of operations performed, with great savings in cost. Orthopædic, urological, and gynæcological surgical procedures were the ones most usually contested by a second opinion screener.

screenful ('skriːnfʊl). [See -FUL.] As much or as many as can be displayed at one time on the screen of a cinema or of a television set or VDU, or similar device.

1966 C. MACKENZIE *Paper Lives* viii. 116 Nigel was watching the last ten minutes of 'Deadwood Gulch' and a screenful of Indians. **1969** *Listener* 30 Jan. 133/2 *Sword of Swords*,.. in Mandarin with English and Chinese subtitles (a screenful). **1974** *Nature* 10 May 102/1 A page is a screenful of data; there are 24 rows on each page and each row has 40 characters. **1977** *Times* 30 Nov. 16/8 The Post Office's Viewdata project.. might be used to enable customers to dial up screenful of information.

screening ('skriːnɪŋ), *vbl. sb.* [-ING[1].] The action of the vb. SCREEN in various senses.

1. a. The action of sheltering or concealing with or as with a screen.

1788 BURKE *Sp. agst. W. Hastings* Wks. XIII. 246 It was done for the screening of his own guilt. **1893** *Hansard's Parl. Deb.* 30 Mar. 1500 The new Order in Council in reference to the screening of side lights in passenger vessels.

attrib. **1881** BELL tr. *C. von Schmidt's Instr. Training Cavalry* 231 Four squadrons being placed in 1st line for screening and reconnoitring purposes.

b. The action or practice of shielding from electric and magnetic fields, esp. by means of an enclosing cover of conducting or magnetic material. Freq. *attrib.*

1840 *Annals Electr., Magn., & Chem.* IV. 293 The screening might, in some way, be connected with an instantaneous current in the plate. *Ibid.*, A certain thickness of metal is.. required to produce the screening effect. **1891** *Electrician* 17 Apr. 722/1 Electrostatic screening is of fundamental significance throughout electric theory. **1922** *Wireless World* 1 July 416/1 Magnetic screening from a steady field can be accomplished by surrounding the apparatus by a heavy iron screen. **1929** *B.B.C. Year-bk. 1930* 339 A copper sheet shield may be fixed to the rear of the panel for screening purposes. **1951** *Good Housek. Home Encycl.* 232/2 Most modern refrigerators are provided with suitable screening arrangements to prevent interference with other electrical appliances. **1962** A. NISBETT *Technique Sound Studio* 241 Although it has no screening effect its thickness ensures that the physical separation of successive layers of the magnetic coating is sufficient to maintain printing at a low level. **1970** J. SHEPHERD et al. *Higher Electrical Engin.* (ed. 2) vii. 225 The object of shielding (or screening) is to prevent a magnetic field from existing at some particular point.

c. The action of an obstruction (such as a hill or a building) in attenuating or blocking broadcast signals.

1907 J. ERSKINE-MURRAY *Handbk. Wireless Telegr.* xvii. 231 That the bending of the lines and not their absence is, in part at least, the cause of this apparent screening, is rendered still more probable by the observation that though no signals could be received close to the land, in one instance, they could be obtained at a greater distance from the transmitter by moving the ship away from the land in a straight line. **1920** *Discovery* Apr. 116/1 Mountains.. close to a wireless station may produce serious screening in that direction. **1926** R. W. HUTCHINSON *Wireless* ix. 154 An aerial passing along a passage between the gable ends of two houses.. is not efficient owing to the screening effect of the houses. **1967** G. J. KING *Pract. Aerial Handbk.* iv. 102 There are invariably pockets of low signal field round the area, due to heavy screening etc. (depending on frequency), where lofty outside aerials are needed to secure the full advantage of the local transmitter.

d. *Physics.* The reduction of the electric field about an atomic nucleus by the space charge of the surrounding electrons. Also in *Comb.*, as **screening constant**, the difference between the atomic number of a nucleus and its effective charge, reduced by screening.

1922 A. D. UDDEN tr. *Bohr's Theory of Spectra* III. iv. 121 The effect of the presence of the electrons in inner groups upon the motion of the electrons in outer groups as a first approximation may be expected to consist in a simple screening of the nucleus. **1925** G. A. LINDSAY tr. *M. Siegbahn's Spectrosc. of X-Rays* vi. 163 These doublets may be roughly explained by the screening of the nuclear charge. *Ibid.* 166 The screening constants.. must depend in general on the quantum number, and on the magnitude and form of the orbit determined by it. **1965** PHILLIPS & WILLIAMS *Inorg. Chem.* I. ii. 54 The magnitude of the screening constant indicates the extent to which the full nuclear charge of an element is hidden from the electrons in a particular shell of the core. **1970** G. K. WOODGATE *Elem. Atomic Struct.* v. 82 The direct Coulomb interaction e^2/r_{12} raises the degeneracy in l because the amount of screening depends on the eccentricity of the orbit of the outer electron.

e. *Physics.* = SHIELDING *vbl. sb.* 2 b.

1922 F. E. SIMPSON *Radium Therapy* vi. 45 It is best to use rather simple and uniform screening until familiarity is obtained with the effects of radium on the tissues.

f. *Basketball.* Obstruction. See SCREEN *sb.*[1] 3 g.

1951 *Sun* (Baltimore) 24 Dec. (B ed.) 13/2 In the old American League, the ball changed hands if the referee called screening or blocking.

2. a. A sorting or sifting carried on by means of a 'screen'.

1725 *Bradley's Fam. Dict.*, *Skreyn*, an Instrument.. made of Lath for the Skreening of Earth, Sand, Gravel, &c. **1763** MILLS *Pract. Husb.* III. 128 This was then easily separated by proper screening, and the wheat proved so good, that the bakers bought it at the highest market price. **1877** RAYMOND *Statist. Mines & Mining* 451 Screening through fine screens is, at best, a very imperfect.. operation.

b. *pl.* Material which has passed through the operation of screening. *spec.*, an inferior grade of wheat or polished rice.

1730 WRIGLESWORTH *Jrnl. of the 'Lyell'* 23 Sept., This morning put out another Boat Load of our Screenings. **1824** 'A. SINGLETON' *Letters from South & West* 111 Their usual fare, is, a peck of corn in the ear a week, which they must break in their hand-mills; and the *grit*, or refuse, a Rice, like the western *screenings* of wheat. **1867** P. L. SIMMONDS *Commerc. Dict. Trade Products*, *Screenings*, a name in the United States for the inferior wheat that is removed by the screens and fans. **1885** *Law Times' Rep.* LII. 427/2 The footpaths.. should be made of good gravel or ballast, or fine stone screenings. **1901** *Yearbk. U.S. Dept. Agric. 1900* 135, 9,400 pounds of screenings, and 3,500 pounds of brewer's rice. **1906** *Chambers's Jrnl.* June 453/1 Tons of rock are.. crushed for screenings and ballast. **1923** A. BRUTTINI *Uses of Waste Materials* II. ii. 133 By the term screenings are understood the siftings of cereals and other grains. *Ibid.*, Screenings are.. made into dog biscuits.

c. Systematic examination of a large number of subjects, esp. for the detection of unwanted attributes or objects.

1944 *Sun* (Baltimore) 8 Jan. 1/1 The preliminary screening physical examination will be discontinued, except for individuals with obvious physical defects. **1946** *Cancer Res.* VI. 490/2 Compounds found in the first screening to possess potency in damaging or killing cells of sarcoma 37.. were subjected to further experimentation. **1958** *New Statesman* 6 Sept. 263/3 Some 3,000 Algerians, arrested immediately after the wave of terrorism, were brought there for screening. **1960** *Guardian* 11 Mar. 7/4 Dr. Glover.. advocates a psychiatric 'screening' of the entire child population in order to detect pathological tendencies to violence. **1964** HUEPER & CONWAY *Chem. Carcinogenesis & Cancers* v. 177 The highest priority for carcinogenic screening should be assigned to those chemicals with which large parts of the general population have contact. **1970** *Nature* 31 Oct. 416/1 Electrophoretic mass screening of blood proteins for new mutations..would be formidable. **1974** *Times* 27 Apr. 5/7 Herr Brandt..said he was generally satisfied with the screening of Federal employees... Herr Guillaume had been thoroughly screened, but not given the highest grade of security clearance. **1974** M. C. GERALD *Pharmacol.* iv. 77 There has been very exhaustive screening of soil samples from almost all parts of the world in an attempt to discover new antibiotics.

d. With *out*. Cf. SCREEN *v.* 4 g.

1943 *Sun* (Baltimore) 15 Mar. 5/6 The 'screening out' of school children who need medical attention.

3. The posting of an offender's name upon a screen or public notice-board.

1908 *Westm. Gaz.* 28 Mar. 7/1 The Benchers..have imposed the penalty of a reprimand and 'screening'.

4. The action of SCREEN *v.*[1] 8; *spec.*, a particular showing of a film.

1923 E. S. VAN ZILE *That Marvel—the Movie* 121 Mr. Harding..has suggested the screening of Wells's 'Outline of History'. *Ibid.* 198 The actual screening of the story was begun. **1928** H. CRANE *Let.* 5 Feb. (1965) 316 We have met some movie actors, attended some studio screenings, etc. **1954** *Recorder* 8 Jan. 1/2 The telegram..'solemnly protested' against the screening of a Mass. **1960** *Guardian* 25 Aug. 8/5, I was present ten days prior to its [*sc.* a film's] screenings at Karlovy-Vary. **1974** 'G. BLACK' *Golden Cockatrice* v. 81 The first screening was an old Disney short. **1977** *Times* 23 June 20/4 Many of the journalists who did attend the screenings revealed an uneasiness.

5. *Printing.* The process of exposing a photosensitive surface or forming an image through a screen (SCREEN *sb.*[1] 7).

1946 [see SCREEN *sb.*[1] 7]. **1967** KARCH & BUBER *Offset Processes* v. 168 A device..now permits direct screening of halftone copy that removes the screen dots and reduces the graininess from enlargements. **1973** M. ASTRUA *Manual of Colour Reproduction* I. 100 For printing continuous tone we have to resort to the optical device of 'screening', that is, to the conversion of the various densities of the image..into small dots.

6. *attrib.* and *Comb.*, as (sense 2 c) ***screening device, experiment, method, operation, procedure, process, programme, technique, test***; (sense 4) ***screening room***; **screening clinic**, a clinic at which medical screening is carried out.

1966 *Listener* 4 Aug. 151/1 Last year saw the growth of municipally run screening clinics. In Rotherham and Glasgow there were queues of citizens in the streets waiting to be X-rayed and have other simple examinations. **1977** *Spare Rib* Sept. 19/4 The aim of developing a well woman screening clinic. **1952** M. MCCARTHY *Groves of Academe* iv. 63 Despite a high tuition and other screening devices..something..had worked to give the college a peculiarly plebeian and subversive tone. **1971** J. ANDERSON in B. de Ferranti *Living with Computer* vii. 61 New screening experiments are under way at present. **1946** *Jrnl. Amer. Med. Assoc.* 1 June 377/2 [The smear test] can be carried out on a large scale as a screening method. **1950** *Hansard Commons* 7 Nov. 769 Mr Shepherd asked the Prime Minister what inquiries he has made into the efficiency of the screening methods of M.I.5. **1974** *Times* 19 Dec. 4/3 Downing Street refused to say how long the screening operation took. **1964** *Observer* 12 July 4/6 Mammography..is thought by some to be useful as a 'screening' procedure for women without symptoms to pick up breast cancer at a very early stage. **1949** *Cavalier Daily* (Univ. of Va.) 22 Oct. 4/2 Applicants could not get their visas approved by the Hungarian government without undergoing a screening process by the American Festival Committee. **1975** *Language for Life* (Dept. Educ. & Sci.) xiv. 215 The screening process might extend across the point of transfer. **1954** *Cancer* VII. 1183/2 A screening program to detect cancer of the cervix. **1974** M. TAYLOR tr. *Metz's Film Lang.* vi. 156 Inside the screening room. **1978** *Detroit Free Press* 16 Apr. 23 A/1, I absolutely refused to allow 'Rabbit Test' to be shown to anyone in a screening room. **1945** *Amer. Assoc. Adv. Sci. Res. Conf. Cancer* 318/2 Utilizing a number of 'screening' techniques to evaluate the place of a variety of compounds as to their ability to impair the metabolism of malignant cells. **1942** *Nation* 27 Apr. 41 Since Jan. 1 Selective Service has given only what is called a 'screening test'. The registrant strips, walks to and away from the doctor and if he has all his limbs and his eyesight and no immediately apparent organic defect, is passed. **1951** *Jrnl. Amer. Med. Assoc.* 11 Aug. 1401/1 The detection center serving..as a laboratory facility to which the physician can refer his patients for screening tests. **1969** *Times* 15 Mar. 7/8 A swift and reliable system is necessary to meet the ideal of offering every woman an annual screening test for signs of cervical cancer.

screening ('skri:nɪŋ), *ppl. a.* [f. SCREEN *v.* + -ING[2].] That screens; that hides or protects.

1817 HUGHSON *Walks through London* 395 The screening colonade of the latter will be taken down. **1861** GEO. ELIOT *Silas M.* I. ii, He felt hidden even from the heavens by the screening trees and hedge. **1936** *Practical Wireless* 16 May 232/2 Provided that the screening cans are connected to the earth terminal no interaction should be experienced between those components. **1942** *Electronic Engin.* XV. 284/3 Grid 3 is situated between two screening grids maintained at a positive potential of 100 volts. **1943** *Gloss. Terms Electr. Engin.* (*B.S.I.*) 58 *Line choking coil* (*screening reactor*), an inductor connected in series with electrical plant and serving to reduce the effects of high-frequency or steep-fronted surges by absorption or reflection. **1966** *McGraw-Hill Encycl. Sci. & Technol.* XII. 81/2 Military screening smokes.

screenless ('skri:nlɪs), *a.* [-LESS.] Having no screen; having had no screen used in its production; unprotected.

1921 *Blackw. Mag.* Sept. 348/2 In that screenless life friendship frankly condoled with weak nerves. **1976** *National Observer* (U.S.) 3 July 14/2 As the day progressed the screenless windows admitted less breeze and more heat and insects. **1980** *Times Lit. Suppl.* 12 Sept. 988/2 A scrupulously faithful facsimile of the lithograph edition, made by a new Screenless Printing Process.

'screeny, *a. nonce-wd.* [f. SCREEN *sb.* + -Y.] ? Resembling the kind of decoration usual on screens.

1820–2 PYNE *Wine & Walnuts* (1823) I. xx. 262 Reynolds ..observing that Wilson's pictures were screeny in effect. This was in allusion to the sudden effects of his lights on the shadows.

screeve (skri:v), *sb. Sc.* and *slang*. Also scrieve, scrive. [f. SCREEVE *v.*[2]]

a. A piece of writing; †**b.** *spec.* a banknote, = SCREEN *sb.*[2] (*obs.*); **c.** a begging letter (now the usual sense).

1788 W. BRODIE 10 Apr. in Roughead *Trial of Brodie* (1906) 154 Acquaint him I glimed the scrive I had of him. **1801** *Sporting Mag.* XIX. 88 Fearns asked, what he gave for the one-pound screeves? **1812** J. H. VAUX *Flash Dict.*, *Screeve*, a letter, or written paper. **1897** CROCKETT *Lad's Love* xxix, Juist gie me a screeve o' a note to that effect.

screeve (skri:v), *v.*[1] Now *dial.* Also 5 scryve, 9 screive. [Aphetic a. OF. *escreve-r* (usually said of wounds):—L. **excrepāre*: see ES- and CREVE.] *intr.* Of a wound: To open and discharge matter. In mod. dial., to ooze, exude moisture.

a **1450** *Le Morte Arth.* 382 His woundis scryved and stille he lay And in his bedde he swownyd thrye. **1882** *Lancs. Gloss.*, *Screeve*, to froth at the mouth as in a fit. **1886** *Cheshire Gloss.*, *Screeve*, to ooze out, to exude moisture. **1887** *S. Cheshire Gloss.* s.v., A sack of corn may screive; liquid manure in a pigsty is said to screive out. But the word is specially used of moisture exuding from a corpse.

Hence **'screeving** *vbl. sb.*

c **1400** *Lanfranc's Cirurg.* 121 In scryuyngis of þe brayn panne.

screeve (skri:v), *v.*[2] *slang.* Also scrieve. [Ultimately from L. *scrībĕre* to write; the proximate source is uncertain; possibly It. *scrivere*.

Cf. Sc. (Ayrshire) *scrieve*, 'to read or write quickly or continuously' (Jam.); but connexion of the slang word with this is very doubtful.]

1. *trans.* To write.

1851 MAYHEW *Lond. Labour* I. 246 Ah! once I could 'screeve a fakement' (write a petition).

2. *intr.* To draw pictures on the pavement with coloured chalks; to be a 'pavement artist'.

1851 MAYHEW *Lond. Labour* I. 415, I then took to screeving (writing on the stones). **1876** MRS. EWING *Jan of Windmill* xxxi. 302 A street-artist who was 'screeving', or drawing pictures on the pavement in coloured chalks. **1887** HENLEY *Villon's Straight Tip* 1 Suppose you screeve?

screeve (skri:v), *v.*[3] *dial.* [app. a. ON. *skrefa* to stride (Norw. *skreva*, Da. *skræve*, Sw. *skrefva* to open one's legs wide, straddle.] *pass.* Of horses: To have the legs split apart in running on ice.

18.. WHEELER *Fens* App. 12 (E.D.D.) *Screeve*, a term used to describe an accident which occasionally happened to horses in the fens when running over ice in winter their legs became parted and torn off at the joint. **1895** *Naturalist* 321 The poor horses..got on the ice in winter, and were screeved.

screever ('skri:və(r)). *slang.* Also 9 scriever. [f. SCREEVE *v.*[2] + -ER[1].]

1. A begging letter writer.

1851 MAYHEW *Lond. Labour* I. 313 'He writes a good hand', exclaimed one, as the screever wrote the petition.

2. A pavement artist.

1876 MRS. EWING *Jan of the Windmill* xxxv. 336 The horrors of his life as a screever. **1894** MARKS *Pen & Pencil Sk.* II. 100 The pavement-artist, or 'scriever', as he is called in the profession.

scremus, obs. Sc. form of SKIRMISH.

screpand, obs. Sc. pr. pple. of SCRAPE *v.*

†**screpe,** *v. Obs.* [OE. *screpan* str. v.: see SCRAPE *v.* Cf. SHREPE *v.*] *trans.* To scrape, scratch *out*, erase. In OE. also *intr.* to scratch.

c **725** *Corpus Gloss.* 1828 *Scalpio*, scriopu. *Ibid.* 1805 *Scarpinat*, scripið. *c* **975** *Rushw. Gosp.* Mark ix. 18 And fæmeð & gristbites mið toðum & screpes. [Mistranslates *arescit*.] *c* **1000** *Sax. Leechd.* II. 38 Screp þonne of þam fæte þat biþ swiðe god sealf þam men þe hæfð þicce bræwas. *a* **1225** *Ancr. R.* 344 Vor nis non so lutel þing of þeos þet þe deouel naueð embreued on his rolle. Auh schrift screapeð hit of, and makeð him uorte leosen muchel of his hwule. *c* **1230** *Hali Meid.* 33 Ha beoð iscrepte ut of liues writ in heuene.

screpping, obs. Sc. pr. pple. of SCRAPE *v.*

†**scresent,** var. of or error for CRESCENT *sb.* 3 b.

1486 *Bk. St. Albans, Her.* d vij b, Powderit with croslettys molettys Scresentis smale briddis or other difference.

†**screte,** *a. Obs. rare*[−1]. Supple, pliant.

c **1440** *Promp. Parv.* 450/2 Screte, or lethy [*Winch. MS.* Streyte, or lythy], *gracilis, lentus.*

screutore, obs. form of SCRUTOIRE.

screvelio, obs. form of SCRIVELLO.

screw (skru:), *sb.*[1] Forms: 5 scrwe, skrew(e, 6–7 skrue, skrew, 6–8 scrue, 7– screw. [Apparently, in spite of the difference of sense, a. OF. *escroue* fem., also *escro* masc. (mod.F. *écrou*) female screw, nut; not found in the other Rom. langs. The Teut. langs. have (though not recorded from their earliest periods) a word meaning 'screw' which may be related in some way to the OF. word: MLG., MDu., *schrûve* (mod.Du. irreg. *schroef*), late MHG. *schrûbe* (mod.G. *schraube*), Sw. *skrufva*, mod.Icel. *skrúfa*, Da. *skrue*. The North-eastern OF. *escruve*, a screw (misread *escrime*: the examples are placed by Godefr. under that word), is prob. from MDu.

The ultimate etymology of the Fr. word, and the nature of its relation, if any, to the Teut. words, remain obscure. Diez's suggestion that it represents the L. *scrobem*, ditch, is phonologically impossible. Baist, followed by Kluge, would refer both the Fr. and the Teut. words to the L. *scrōfa* sow (in med.L. also an engine for undermining walls), comparing the Sp. *puerca* sow, also (= *tuerca*) female screw; but this does not account for the Teut. forms. The supposition that the Fr. word is an adoption from the MLG. *schrûve* presents very great difficulties.]

I. The general name for that kind of mechanical appliance of which the operative portion is a helical groove or ridge (or two or more parallel helical grooves or ridges) cut either on the exterior surface of a cylinder (***male screw***) or on the interior surface of a cylindrical cavity (***female screw***). Hence applied to various other contrivances resembling this.

Ordinarily *screw* without defining word is taken to mean a male screw, which seems indeed to be the proper sense in Eng.; but there are occasional exceptions in speaking of instruments in which the female screw is the moving part of the combination.

A screw is called *right-handed* or *left-handed* according as the rotation necessary to carry the screw away from the operator is towards his right or his left.

1. A male screw (see above) with a correspondingly grooved or ridged socket in which it can revolve or which can revolve upon it; used for the purpose of converting a motion of rotation into a motion of translation bearing a fixed proportion to it.

a. As an apparatus for raising weights or applying pressure or strain.

For a supposed earlier instance see quot. 1393 under SCREEN *sb.* 1; *skreu* being prob. a misreading for *skren*, screen. Whether quot. 1497 belongs to this word is somewhat doubtful; the spelling *skrewe* would not be expected to occur so early if the Fr. etymology is correct.

1404 *Durham Acc. Rolls* (Surtees) 396 Item 1 rabitstoke cum 2 scrwes. **1497** *Naval Acc. Hen. VII* (1896) 95 Skrewe with her apperell. *Ibid.* 122 Lading gynnes ij. Skrewes j. Wilkyn rammes iij. **1599** T. M[OUFET] *Silkwormes* 35 Then those great coches which themselues did driue With bended scrues, like things that were aliue? Ingenious Germane, how didst thou conuey Thy Springs, thy Scrues, thy rowells, and thy flie? **1629** MASSINGER *Picture* IV. ii, He moues like the faery King, on scrues and wheeles Made by his Doctors recipes. **1683** MOXON *Mech. Exerc., Printing* xxv. 352 He puts them into the Standing Press..observing to set in every Pile..an equal number of Books, that each Pile may equally feel the force of the Screw. *a* **1711** KEN *Blandina* Poet. Wks. 1721 IV. 520 Then on the Rack the Saint they stretch, Her Limbs with Screws and Pulleys retch. **1768** TUCKER *Lt. Nat.* I. iii. 59 A curious engine compounded of wheels, screws and pulleys. **1825** J. NICHOLSON *Oper. Mech.* 14 The hollow screw, or the counterpart in which a screw operates, when in the form of a small movable piece, is called a nut, and the cavity is termed a female screw. **1861** F. CAMPIN *Hand-turning* v. 105 Double, triple, and quadruple screws, are those which have two, three, or four distinct threads upon them.

b. Considered as one of the mechanical powers; in mechanical theory treated as a modification of the inclined plane.

1570 J. DEE *Math. Pref.* c iij b, For, in many thinges, the Skrue worketh the feate, which, els, could not be performed. **1648** WILKINS *Math. Magic* I. ix. 56 The sixth and last Mechanick faculty, is the Screw, which is described to be a kind of wedge that is multiplyed, or continued by a helicall revolution about a Cylinder. **1764** J. FERGUSON *Lect.* iii. 43 The screw..cannot properly be called a simple machine, because it is never used without the application of a lever. **1825** J. NICHOLSON *Oper. Mech.* 14 The screw is applied to mechanical purposes chiefly to obtain great pressures in small distances. **1879** *Cassell's Techn. Educ.* I. 33/2 The efficiency of the screw is largely diminished by friction... This contrasts the screw with the lever, for in the latter the effect of friction is quite imperceptible.

c. Used for regulating or measuring longitudinal movement.

1612 WOODALL *Surg. Mate* (1639) 7 Of the Speculum oris with a screw. **1833** ARNOTT *Physics* II. 158 The coal..was moved up like the wick of a lamp, by its screw. **1840** *Civil Engin. & Arch. Jrnl.* III. 78/1 This movement may be also effected..by a screw and pinion. **1881** F. CAMPIN *Mech. Engin.* iv. 50 The lathe generally travels the tool rest by a screw called the 'leading screw'. **1883** *Encycl. Brit.* XVI. 244/2 The screws of micrometers are generally made with 50 or 100 threads to the inch.

d. With various qualifying words. ***bench screw***: a joiner's vice. ***double screw***: one with a pair of screws to carry the vice-cheek with a parallel motion. ***endless screw***: see ENDLESS *a.* 4 b. ***perpetual screw*** = prec. ***screw of Archimedes, water screw*** = ARCHIMEDEAN screw.

1574 EDEN in *Decades* Life 47/1 An engin..wherewith a man with the strength of onely one hande, by helpe of the instrument called Trispaston (which in our tongue some cal an endlesse Scrue), brought a Shyp..from the lande into the sea. **1641** Water screw [see COCHLEA]. **1648** WILKINS *Math. Magic* I. ix. 60 Another invention, commonly styled a perpetuall screw, which hath the motion of a wheel, and the force of a screw. **1655** MRQ. WORCESTER *Cent. Invent.* §54. 35 How to make a Water-scrue tite, and yet transparent. **1678** MOXON *Mech. Exerc.* iv. 60 The Bench-Screw..to Screw Boards in whiles the edges of them are Plaining or Shooting. *Ibid.* 61 Sometimes a double Screw is fixed to the side of the Bench. **1807** T. YOUNG *Nat. Philos.* I. 328 A single pipe wound spirally round a cylinder which revolves on an axis in an oblique situation, has been denominated the screw of Archimedes. **1821** R. TURNER *Arts & Sci.* 91 *note*, When the screw acts in a wheel, it is called a perpetual screw. **1848** L. HUNT *Jar of Honey* 187 The lower deck could be pumped by a single man, with the aid of a machine,..which we..name the screw of Archimedes.

e. ***the screws*** (rarely ***the screw***): an instrument of torture formerly in use, designed to compress the thumbs of a prisoner in order to extort a confession; the 'thumbikins'. Cf. THUMBSCREW.

1663 *Aron-bimn.* 32 The Bedlam, and the chain, the whip and the skrews, all the violences of a severe discipline. *a* **1715** BURNET *Own Time* xvi. (1900) II. 422 Little screws of steel were made use of, that screwed the thumbs... They put his thumbs in the screws; and drew them so hard, that [etc.]. **1788** COWPER *Negro's Compl.* 31 Your knotted scourges, Matches, blood-extorting screws. **1840** HOOD *Up the Rhine* 177 Crush the thumbs of the Jew With the vice and the screw, Till he tells where he buried his treasure. **1855** MACAULAY *Hist. Eng.* xiii. III. 259 Carstairs..hated prelacy with the hatred of a man whose thumbs were deeply marked by the screws of prelatists.

2. *fig.* **a.** A means of 'pressure' or coercion.

1648–9 *Eikon Bas.* xiv. 113 When Politicians most agitate desperate designs against all that is settled..in Religion, and Laws, which by such scrues are cunningly, yet forcibly wrested by secret steps..from their known rule and wonted practise. **1664** H. MORE *Myst. Iniq.* 50 There being sufficient Props and Engines, nay Screws and Pulleys, if you will, to raise mens Love and Devotion. **1796** G. WALPOLE in B. Edwards *Proc. Maroon Negroes* 19 All this will..prove to your lordship the impropriety of holding forth more harsh conditions..: Should there be any person so dull..as to think that another turn of the screw would be better, ask him this question. **1803** WELLINGTON in Gurw. *Desp.* (1837) I. 497 This chief ought..to be pressed upon this point..and all the screws, menaces, &c. might be brought to bear upon him. **1855** *Illustr. Lond. News* 28 July 126/2 His Lordship owned himself unable to resist the mild influences of the 'screw' [*sc.* of a deputation]. **1861** *Times* 22 Aug., The farmer..the tradesman..the passengers who travelled less frequently.., had all felt the screw before it touched the Railways. **1883** *Pall Mall Gaz.* 3 Nov. 3/1 If any body wants anything nowadays, he must put on the screw on the powers that be, and the only efficacious screw is that of agitation.

b. Phrases. ***to put on, apply, turn the screw*** or ***screws*** and similar phrases: (*a*) to apply moral pressure; also, used of other kinds of pressure, e.g. the pressure of competition; (*b*) to force the payment of a debt or loan; also *rarely*, to limit the giving of credit. Also, occas., used of blackmail.

1834 C. A. DAVIS *Lett. J. Downing* xiv. 96 And if they don't they put the screws on 'em. **1845** JUDD *Margaret* II. vii. (1874) 290 We didn't put on the screws half hard enough. The Insargents ought to have been hung. **1852** *Dow's Serm.* I. 302 (Bartlett 1859) Love strains the heart-strings of the human race, and not unfrequently puts the screws on so hard as to snap them asunder. **1859** BARTLETT *Dict. Amer.* s.v., *To put the screws on; to turn the screws*, to press, and figuratively to extort, to enforce payment in money transactions; to force a debtor, by any compulsory means, to pay. **1860** *All Year Round* 26 May 160 When there is work and plenty of it, the operatives turn the screw upon the masters. **1861** HUGHES *Tom Brown at Oxf.* x, These creditors..are sueing him in the..Court, thinking now's the time to put the screw on. **1882** E. O'DONOVAN *Merv Oasis* I. 317 The local authorities kept on the screw for their own private benefit. **1883** SIR H. COTTON in *Law Times Rep.* XLIX. 150/2 It cannot be said that he did it..for the purpose of putting the screw on the company, and forcing them to abandon a defence *bona fide* claimed by them. **1888** BRYCE *Amer. Commw.* II. xliii. 133 *note*, Occasionally the assessors of a country town take it into their heads to apply the screw. **1894** P. L. FORD *Honorable Peter Stirling* xli. 241 Then I can put the screws on him safely, you think? **1917** W. J. LOCKE *Red Planet* xxiii. 298 Gedge's nocturnal waylaying of him..was another unsuccessful attempt to tighten the screw. **1938** E. AMBLER *Cause for Alarm* xi. 170 Everything ..was prepared. It was only a question of waiting for Vagas to begin to turn the screw. **1977** *Navy News* Sept. 39/3 David Stracey kept the screws on, lunching with figures of three for 15 off ten overs. **1981** A. MORICE *Men in her Death* viii. 93 She worked out this scheme for a phoney kidnap, to put the screws on.

3. a. A metal pin or bolt (cylindrical or, more commonly, slightly tapering) with a spiral ridge upon its shank, used in joining articles of wood or metal, fastening fittings to wordwork, etc. (It is turned and driven in by means of a screwdriver or spanner.)

Blake's screw: see quot. 1879. ***wood screw***, a more definite name for the screw commonly used for woodwork.

1622 F. MARKHAM *Five Dec. War* I. ix. 35 See that the breech [of the gun] be strong and close, all the screwes and pinnes about it fast and sure. **1768** TUCKER *Lt. Nat.* II. I. ii. 22 And then I look upon the boards, the legs, the hinges, the screws, the glue..as one thing, which I call a table. **1794** W. FELTON *Carriages* (1801) I. 105 A nut headed screw, is a large, thick screw with a strong thread. **1816** J. SMITH *Panorama Sci. & Art* I. 39 A screw-plate is a cheap and handy instrument for making screws. **1841** *Penny Cycl.* XXI. 109/1 The blanks for wood-screws were formerly forged by the workmen who make nails. **1879** *Cassell's Techn. Educ.* III. 256/1 The outside planking is temporarily secured to the frames by fastenings, known as 'Blake's screws'... These screws consist of bolts with an eye formed on one end and a wood-screw cut on the other. **1885** J. B. LENO *Boot & Shoemaking* xvi. 131 Brass, and Iron Screws. These are usually employed in clump work.

b. ***a screw loose***: fig. something wrong in the condition of things; a dangerous weakness in some arrangement. Now usu. with reference to persons or their mental faculties, esp. in colloq. phr. ***to have a screw loose***: to be eccentric, insane, or mentally retarded. *slang.*

1810 *Sporting Mag.* XXXVI. 166 The others..had got a screw loose. **1821** *Ibid.* VII. 192 A screw, it seems, has been loose between Neat and the Champion of England. **1848** ALB. SMITH *Chr. Tadpole* xli, It was evident that there was a screw loose in the programme. **1833** E. FITZGERALD *Lett.* (1889) I. 21 In fact, a genius with a screw loose, as we used to say. **1844** DICKENS *Martin Chuz.* xiii, I see well enough there's a screw loose in your affairs. **1870** R. BROUGH *Marston Lynch* xii. 110 There may be some little screw loose between him and the..step-daughter. **1873** TROLLOPE *Eustace Diamonds* III. lxiii. 128 Something crooked about Lizzie,—a screw loose, as people say. *Ibid.* lxix. 215 Folks as would have a screw loose somewheres. **1883** V. STUART *Egypt* 314 Who will put his finger upon the loose screw? **1884** *St. Louis Post-Dispatch* 4 June 7/4, I really think this wonderful woman has a screw loose in her mental organization. **1928** [see NUT *sb.*[1] 7 c]. **1959** I. & P. OPIE *Lore & Lang. Schoolch.* x. 179 A person who is 'wanting in the upper storey'..has a screw loose. **1963** *Times* 1 Feb. 8/7 He asked Mr. Galbraith if when he came across a person who was 'limited intellectually' he normally referred to him as 'having a screw loose'. **1974** S. E. MORISON *European Discovery of America: Southern Voyages* xxx. 725 His idea of England's opening a traffic with China independent of Spain and Portugal was sound. But there was a screw loose somewhere in Cavendish. **1977** *Lancashire Life* Nov. 63/1 An endearing little chap with a screw loose.

c. Helical grooving or ridging.

1879 *Cassell's Techn. Educ.* I. 34/2 A bolt 12 inches long, and with 2 inches of screw on the end.

4. a. Each of the component parts of a screw-fastening or screw-joint.

1648 *Bury Wills* (Camden) 217, I give him alsoe my chaine of beads with scrues. **1684** R. H. *School of Recreation* (1696) 165 And lastly his Landen Hook, with a Screw at the end to screw it into the socket of a Pole. **1688** HOLME *Armoury* III. xv. (Roxb.) 22/2 The second..a long round Inke-horne, some haue only a screw at each end, one for Inke, the other to put in the pens. **1800** *Med. Jrnl.* IV. 181 The tube is divided into four parts, which are well joined by screws.

†**b.** ***needle and screw, screw and bodkin***: some kind of fastening for jewellery. *Obs.*

1605 in *Heriot's Mem.* (1822) App. VII. 202 Item, put to v great diamondis, v needles, and v scrues of gold. **1607** *Ibid.* 213 Item, made a screw and a bodkin for a jewell. *c* **1610** *Ibid.* 217 For gold, and making of a needle and a skrew for the King of Denmark's picture.

5. The worm or boring part of a gimlet; also, †the gimlet itself.

1577 HARRISON *England* I. viii. 19/1 in *Holinshed*, Which some doe liken..to a vice, skrew, or wide sleeue, bycause they are very small at the east end, and large at west... They resemble the slope course of the cutting part of a skrew or gimlet. **1633** G. HERBERT *Temple, Confession* x, No scrue, no piercer can Into a piece of timber work and winde, As Gods afflictions into man. **1812** P. NICHOLSON *Mech. Exerc.* 34 At the lower end [of the auger] is a worm or screw of a conic form, for entering the wood.

6. a. An instrument terminating in a 'worm' for screwing into something in order to pull it out; esp. a corkscrew; also, the 'worm' itself. Also *fig.*

screw or kettle = corkscrew (*i.e.* wine) or hot water (*i.e.* grog).

1657 W. MORICE *Coena quasi Κοινὴ* Dial. iii. 145 They must be strange Scrues and Wires that shall draw this conclusion from the Text. **1702** Bottle Screw [see BOTTLE *sb.*[1] 5]. **1768–74** TUCKER *Lt. Nat.* (1834) II. 461, I have stopped the bottle with a good cork; I can draw it out again with a screw. **1819** *Edin. Ann. Reg.* (1823) XII. App. 74 James Smith proved his making a worm or screw to the ramrod of the pistol. **1832** J. BARRINGTON *Sk.* III. iv. 44 He was the hardest-goer either at kettle or screw..of the whole grand-jury. **1835** W. H. MAXWELL *My Life* II. i. 7 Good eating, produced good drinking;..and the commander politely inquired whether I would be for 'screw or kettle'.

b. A gunner's instrument. *Obs.* exc. *Hist.*

? **1594** BARWICK *Disc. Weapons* 8 His scrues and wormes to serue all for his skowring sticke. **1611** COTGR., *Tirebourre*, a worme, or skrue; the Instrument wherewith a charged Cannon is vnladen. **1870** C. C. BLACK tr. *A. Demmin's Weapons of War* 499 Swiss cannon rammer..the end of which contains a wadding screw.

7. A screw-propeller (see PROPELLER 3).

hoisting screw, one adapted to be disconnected and lifted when not required for use.

[**1788** M. CUTLER in *Life*, etc. (1888) I. 408 We.. constructed a machine in the form of a screw with short blades, and placed it in the stern of the boat, which we turned with a crank. **1815** R. TREVITHICK in *Abridgm. Specif. Patents, Marine Propulsion* (1858) 62 A worm or screw..which revolves in a cylinder,..or without a cylinder, at the head, sides, or stern of a vessel.] **1838** *Civil. Engin. & Arch. Jrnl.* I. 385/1 The propeller or paddle..will be worked by a communicating shaft, acting upon a screw called the Archimedean screw, in the application or use of which the invention is grounded. **1839** *Ibid.* II. 442/2 The screw [of the *Archimedes*] consisted of one whole turn of a single thread, 7 feet in diameter, and 8 feet pitch. **1861** MURRAY *Shipbuilding* 131/1 The hoisting screw has been adopted generally for war-steamers. **1867** DICKENS *Lett.* (1880) II. 302 The passage here was delightful, and we had scarcely motion beyond that of the screw.

8. A ship driven by a screw-propeller.

(Ellipt. for *screw-steamer.*)

[**1844** *Proc. Inst. Civ. Engin.* III. 82 A diagram of the propeller used on board the 'Liverpool Screw'.] **1861** in M. Willson Disher *Cowells in Amer.* (1934) 330 Destroyed the line-of-battleship New York, on the stocks, besides scuttling the Merrimac, first-class screw, the German-town, sloop of war. **1867** DICKENS *Lett.* (1880) II. 310 These screws are tremendous ships for carrying on, and for rolling. **1876** A'BECKETT *Holiday in Scot. Highlands* 2 The 'Seven Stars' was a long three-masted screw. **1887** *Scribner's Mag.* I. 533/2 Many of the iron screws..are still in..service.

9. a. Something having a spiral course or form.

1649 G. DANIEL *Trinarch., Rich. II*, ccclxvi, This subtle Gin Thus open'd, & hee following the Scrue, Run in a Labirinth, without a Clew. **1682** *Phil. Collect.* XII. 151 They have a skrue or spiral Valve within them..; this skrue in both the *Intestina* winds about twenty turns. **1833** BREWSTER *Nat. Magic* x. 251 The German also exhibited his strength in twisting into a screw a flat piece of iron. **1857** GOSSE *Omphalos* 136 [Screw-pine.] A tree of this size makes a 'screw', or imperfect spire of leaves in about three years. **1869** BLACKMORE *Lorna D.* x, There was scarcely the screw of his tail to be seen.

b. = *screw-stone* (see 24).

1729 WOODWARD *Catal. Eng. Fossils* II. 102 A Mass of Stone, with several of these Screws... From the same Mine. *c* **1774** J. WALCOTT *Descr. Petrifactions* 41 Stones. Which represent the interior form of univalve shells; in which they were moulded when soft... From Fig. 48. to Fig. 54. inclusive are called by the quarry-men Screws. **1860** R. DAMON *Geol. Weymouth & Portl.* 76 The common 'screw', *Cerithium Portlandicum*, so characteristic of the roach [-bed], is almost entirely absent.

10. *slang.* **a.** (See quots.)

1795 POTTER *Dict. Cant* (ed. 2), *Screw*, a false key. **1811** *Lex. Balatron.*, *Screw*, a skeleton key... To stand on the screw signifies that a door is not bolted, but merely locked. **1812** J. H. VAUX *Flash Dict.*, To *screw* a place is to enter it by false keys; this game is called *the screw*. Any robbery effected by such means is termed *a screw*. **1896** *Westm. Gaz.* 29 May 2/1 So the next night I borrows a bunch of screws —them's skeleton keys—and an old jemmy.

b. A prison warder, a turnkey.

1812 P. EGAN *Boxiana* 1st Ser. I. 122 Where *flash* has been *pattered* in all that native purity of style, and richness of eloquence, which would have startled a *High Toby Gloque*, and put a *Jigger Screw* [*i.e.* a prison warder] upon the alert. **1821** —— *Life in Lond.* ii. (1869) 60 Washing the ivory with a prime screw. *Ibid.* xiv. 379 The officer..was compelled to put him under the screw. **1877** *Five Yrs. Penal Serv.* ii. 77 The slang name for all the officials is 'screws'. **1902** *Chambers's Jrnl.* June 367/1 Should there be a superfluity of 'screws' (warders) on the spot..your door is opened and the regulation bun..is handed in. **1933** [see *gold braid* s.v. GOLD[1] 10]. **1948** [see BENT *ppl. a.* 5 a]. **1970** G. F. NEWMAN *Sir, You Bastard* viii. 223 The lights never out, pervy screws watching every movement. **1977** *New Yorker* 24 Oct. 68/2 Men..call their keepers 'guards', 'officers',..'screws'.

II. Senses derived from SCREW *v.*

11. a. An act of screwing up; a turn of the screw.

1709 WODROW *Corr.* (1843) I. 84 So I term those that.. are followers of Mr McMillan, and some that are a screw higher than he. **1781** COWPER *Truth* 385 What is man?.. An instrument, whose chords upon the stretch, And strain'd to the last screw that he can bear, Yield only discord in his Maker's ear. **1796** EARL BALCARRES in B. Edwards *Proc. Maroon Negroes* 20, I am perfectly with you, that the pin ought not to receive another screw; but also clear that it ought not to be relaxed.

b. *Billiards.* A stroke by which a twist is given to the cue-ball by striking it below its centre; also, the twist resulting from this stroke, esp. in the phrase ***to put on screw***.

1849 H. TURNER *Billiards* (title-page), The Side Stroke —the Screw—and the Double. **1856** PARDON ('Capt. Crawley') *Billiards* (1859) 17 The Screw or Twist..is made by striking your ball very low, with a sort of jerk. **1866** —— *Billiard Bk.* iii. 38–9 The High Oblique Screw. The effect of the High Screw is to cause the ball to jump a little, and to twist back on reaching the Object-ball. *Ibid.* ix. 106 The Slow-screw is made with a decided twist, your ball struck low. **1873** BENNETT & 'CAVENDISH' *Billiards* 190 Balls thus struck are said to be played with screw.

c. *Cricket.* A twist imparted to the ball in its delivery. Also a ball to which a spin has been imparted at its delivery. Also in *Lawn Tennis.*

1840 *Bell's Life* 2 Aug. 2/2 Morewood joined Morrier, who at length received a 'Winchester screw', which shattered his timber. **1865** J. PYCROFT *Cricketana* ix. 169 Clarke could put on a decided screw..with a ball well pitched up. **1867** SELKIRK *Guide to Cricket Ground* 35 *Screw*, a twist put upon the ball by the bowler to make it vary in pace and direction after the pitch. **1868** *J. Lillywhite's Cricketers' Compan.* 62 Southerton's 'screws' were the main cause of Kent's discomfiture. **1891** W. G. GRACE in *Outdoor Games* 13 The next ball, very swift, with lots of screw on, is snicked into the slips. **1931** A. POWELL *Afternoon Men* III. xxiii. 203 She served under-handed screws that Pringle could not take.

d. *Rowing.* The action of swinging the body from one side to the other during the stroke. (Cf. SCREW *v.* 18 a.)

1875 W. B. WOODGATE *Oars & Sculls* viii. 64 For the fault which causes the screw may be his own, though unconnected with his swing.

12. *coarse slang.* **a.** A prostitute; a woman considered in sexual terms; a (good, bad, etc.) sexual partner (in this use, prob. *transf.* from sense b).

1725 *New Canting Dict.*, *A screw*, a Strumpet, a common Prostitute. **1937** Partridge *Dict. Slang* 738/1 *Screw*,..a woman *qua* sexual pleasure. **1942** Berrey & Van den Bark *Amer. Thes. Slang* §507/2 *Prostitute*,..screw. **1966** 'L. Lane' *ABZ of Scouse* 93 'A bloody good screw' might refer to an attractive girl. **1969** S. Coulter *Embassy* xi. 120, I like to figure you're my regular screw, see. A whole lot more exciting. **1976** M. Machlin *Pipeline* xlix. 507 As a matter of fact, he's not such a great screw, but at least he isn't a nag, the way *you* are.

b. An act of sexual intercourse, esp. of a hasty and casual nature. Also *fig.*

1929 F. Scott Fitzgerald *Let.* 9 Sept. (1963) 307 Here's a last flicker of the old cheap pride: the *Post* now pays the old whore $4000 a screw. **1937** Partridge *Dict. Slang* 738/1 *Screw*,..an act of copulation. **1967** A. Wilson *No laughing Matter* III. 387 He felt randy as hell but he hadn't even got the price of a quick screw. **1971** P. L. Cave *Chopper* ii. 12 Five or six Angel birds sat around over cold cups of coffee waiting for a fast ride or a quick screw. **1978** G. Greene *Human Factor* IV. ii. 209, I like a good screw as much as the next man, but it's not all that important, is it?

13. *slang.* A tonic, a 'pick-me-up'.

1877 *Five Yrs. Penal Serv.* iii. 232 He was in the habit of taking every morning a 'screw' in the shape of a little dose of bitters to correct the effects of the last evening's festivities.

14. a. The state of being twisted awry; a contortion (of the body or features).

1708 *Hickelty Pickelty* in Ashton *Soc. Life Q. Anne* I. 140 The nice Management of his Italian Snuff box, and the affected Screw of his Body, makes up a great Part of his Conversation. **1828** *Lights & Shades* I. 195 You are all in a screw: every limb is disjointed: you lisp and you smile. **1848** Dickens *Dombey* i, Running up to him with a kind of screw in her face and carriage, expressive of suppressed emotion.

b. ***the screws***: rheumatism (cf. screwmatic *a.* and *sb.*). *slang.*

1897 G. Bartram *People of Clopton* 51 In bed roarin' mad wi' the screws. **1970** G. E. Evans *Where Beards wag All* ix. 107 Now I know all about the east wind, and I can't move my left leg without having the *screws*. **1976** 'L. Black' *Healthy Way to Die* ii. 11 Any rheumatism? An occasional touch of the screws, she admitted.

15. A small portion (of a commodity) wrapped up in a twist or cornet of paper; esp. a penny packet (of tobacco); also, a wrapper of this kind.

1836 Dickens *Sk. Boz, Tuggses at Ramsgate*, The poisonous voice of envy distinctly asserted that he..retailed ..tobacco by the screw, and butter by the pat. **1839** 'J. Fume' *Paper on Tobacco* 114 A penny paper of tobacco is in London termed a screw. **1844** Dickens *Martin Chuz.* xxxvi, A knife, some butter, a screw of salt. **1848** Thackeray *Van. Fair* lvii, A halfpenny-worth of snuff in a cornet or 'screw' of paper. **1893** Miss F. M. Peard *Swing of Pendulum* i, Followed by children shyly inviting him to buy paper screws, containing each four or five strawberries.

16. One who forces down (prices) by haggling; a stingy, miserly person.

1835 Frith *Autobiog.* (1888) III. iii. 46 Aunt is just as great a screw as ever. **1848** Thackeray *Van. Fair* viii, They both agreed in calling him an old screw; which means a very stingy, avaricious person. **1893** C. G. Leland *Mem.* II. 211 He and his wife had the reputation of being fearful screws.

17. *U.S. College slang.* (See quot.)

1851 B. H. Hall *College Words* 265 In some American colleges, an..unnecessarily minute, and annoying examination of a student by an instructor is called a *screw*. The instructor is often designated by the same name. An imperfect recitation is sometimes thus denominated. *Ibid.*, Passing such an examination is often denominated *taking a screw*.

18. A look, stare, or gaze; esp. in phr. ***to have a screw at***: to look at. *slang* (orig. *Austral.*). Cf. screw *v.* 15.

1919 W. H. Downing *Digger Dialects* 44 *Screw* (vb. or n.), look. **1928** [see rumble *v.*[1] 6]. **1933** *Bulletin* (Sydney) 23 Aug. 12/2 (*caption*) *Election Canvasser*: 'Is your wife a Feminist?' *The Worm*: 'S-sh have a screw at me.' **1934** T. Wood *Cobbers* vi. 84 Have a screw at that bullick. *a* **1966** 'M. na Gopaleen' *Best of Myles* (1968) 57 And of a Sunda the Frenchmen do be walkin' around the gardens havin' a screw at the statues. **1969** *New Society* 13 Nov. 762/3 The skinhead contribution to their parents' beliefs is this characteristic rigour. 'If we see any hippies, you know, they give you the screw, you know. I don't like it,' says Bill, using 'screw' to mean 'stare'.

III. Senses of obscure origin.

19. A horse not perfectly sound; also *transf.*, a cow not perfectly healthy.

Perh. originally a race-horse that can be made to obtain a place by 'screwing' on the part of the jockey.

1821 *Sporting Mag.* VIII. 262 The farrier..pronounced her 'a most complete screw'. **1847** *Illustr. Lond. News* 2 Oct. 219/2 Mr Drinkald [won] the Chester Cup, with an old screw. **1859** Meredith *R. Feverel* xviii, 'Doctor', replied Sir Austin, 'if you had a pure-blood Arab barb would you cross him with a screw?' **1864** *Hotten's Slang Dict.* (1865), *Screw*, an unsound, or broken-down horse, that requires both whip and spur to get him along. **1891** *Law Times* XC. 395/1 Defendant bought the cow in question and a smaller one.. remarking that they were both screws. **1893** Chesney *Lesters* III. II. xxi. 12 Lionel was mounted on an obvious screw, but in good going condition.

20. *slang.* Salary, wages.

1858 D. Beveridge *Let.* in Ld. Beveridge *India called Them* (1947) ii. 26 Their delay in announcing an augmentation of screw. **1864** *Hotten's Slang Dict.*, *Screw*, salary or wages. **1884** Hunter & Whyte *My Ducats* xxviii. (1885) 453, I said it was in payment of my screw—my salary, I mean. **1894** Doyle *Sherlock Holmes* 58 The screw was a pound a week. **1917** A. Huxley *Let.* 8 Apr. (1969) 123, I go there next week—screw, they tell me, from £200 to £250. **1939** D. L. Sayers *In Teeth of Evidence* 91 Is he in a good way of business? Good screw, I mean? Comfortable, and all that? **1959** T. S. Eliot *Elder Statesman* III. 95 He's offered me the job With a jolly good screw, and some pickings in commissions. **1981** 'M. Innes' *Lord Mullion's Secret* ii. 20 Cyprian would have to be found... 'A niche with a good screw to it.'

IV. *attrib.* and *Comb.*

21. Simple attrib. **a.** with the meaning 'of or belonging to a screw', as ***screw-arbor***, ***-curve***, ***-head***, ***-hole***, ***motion***, ***-worm***.

1777 Ramsden *Descr. Engine* 1 A Circle of Brass being fixed on the *Screw Arbor. **1856** *Orr's Circ. Sci.*, *Mech. Philos.* 247 The drawing of a *screw-curve. **1688** Holme *Armoury* III. 436/1 A Key for a *Screw Head. **1835** Sir J. Ross *N.-W. Passage* iii. 52 The *screw holes in the flaunches. **1852** Seidel *Organ* 63 There is upon every key a *screw-worm and brass wire.

b. with the meaning, 'of or pertaining to a screw-propeller', as ***screw-blade***, ***-post***, ***-shafting***.

1844 *Proc. Instit. Civ. Engin.* III. 77 The *screw blades. **1882** Ogilvie, **Screw-post*, the inner stern-post through which the shaft of a screw propeller passes. **1886** *Pall Mall Gaz.* 5 Aug. 3/2 A warship..with all her armour in its place, her *screw-shafting and propeller fitted.

c. with the meaning 'fitted with, or driven by means of, a screw-propeller', as ***screw boat***, ***ship***, ***steamer***, ***steamship***, ***vessel***, also ***screw fleet***, a fleet of screw-vessels.

1848 Woodcroft *Steam Navig.* 91 The screw boat, the *Francis B. Ogden*. *Ibid.* 101 The first screw steamer, the *Ericsson*. **1850** E. P. Halsted *Screw-fleet of Navy* Introd. 4 These trials..caused their Lordships to lay the foundation of our present Screw Fleet, by ordering the construction of 'Screw ships'..to the extent of twenty-three vessels. *Ibid.* ii. 12 Screw-frigates. *Ibid.* 14 Screw-corvettes. **1852** J. Bourne *Screw Propeller* x. 216 H.M.S. 'Amphion', the first screw vessel constructed in this country. **1854** F. Moresby *Two Admirals* (1909) 158 The ability of the screw fleet to hold the Russian ships in check. **1861** Murray *Shipbuilding* 132/2 Results of Trials made in her Majesty's Screw-ships. **1886** *Encycl. Brit.* XXI. 825/2 Screw steamship propulsion.

d. Used in names of appliances operated by or working upon a screw, as ***screw-borer***, ***-brake***, ***candlestick***, ***-clamp***, ***-collar***, ***-elevator***, ***-feed***, ***gill***, ***lever***, ***lifting jack***, ***-pad***, ***-valve***, ***-ventilator***.

1766 *Complete Farmer* s.v. *Borer*, **Screw-borer*, an instrument..for searching or exploring the nature of any soil. **1871** Z. Colburn *Locomotive Engin.* xxv. 268/2 A *screw-brake is applied to the engine. **1688** Holme *Armoury* III. 315 *Screw Candlestick, with double sockets..; by the help of the Screws the sockets are raised or lowered according to pleasure. **1825** J. Nicholson *Oper. Mech.* 302 These gallies are attached to the four sides of the central axis of the prism by the *screw-clamps. **1854** Pereira *Lect. Polar. Light* 301 By means of a *screw-collar he managed to vary the distance between the first and second compound lens. **1884** Knight *Dict. Mech.* Suppl., **Screw Elevator*. **1874** Raymond *6th Rep. Mines* 512 In place of the *screw-feed..a new hydraulic feed has been tried with success. **1853** Ure *Dict. Arts* (ed. 4) I. 765 Thus constructed the '*screw gill' continues to be the most esteemed in principle. **1884** W. S. B. McLaren *Spinning* v. §65. 62 Screw gill boxes. **1801** *Encycl. Brit.* Suppl. II. 796/2 s.v. *Weaving*, The rollers..are cylinders, pressed together by a *screw lever. **1851** *Offic. Catal. Gt. Exhib.* 236 Improved *screw lifting jacks. **1813** J. Thomson *Lect. Inflam.* 257 Pressure is made with a *screw-pad over the extremity of the wounded artery. **1850** Fownes *Elem. Chem.* (ed. 3) 159 Furnished with a *screw-valve of peculiar construction.

22. Objective and obj. genitive, as ***screw-chasing***, ***-cutter***, ***-cutting***, ***-maker***, ***-making***, ***-manufacturer***, ***-slotting***; instrumental, as ***screw-driven***, ***-propelled***, ***-torn*** adjs.; parasynthetic, as ***screw-stoppered***, ***threaded*** adjs.

1888 *Lockwood's Dict. Mech. Engin.*, **Screw Chasing*, the cutting..of screw threads in the lathe by means of chasing tools. **1846** Holtzapffel *Turning* II. 605 The temporary *screw-cutter possesses the same interval or thread as before. **1909** *Daily Chron.* 2 Feb. 9/7 Wanted..Engineer. —Good general turner and screw cutter. **1832** Babbage *Econ. Manuf.* xi. 82 *Screw-cutting. **1846** Holtzapffel *Turning* II. 580 The screw-cutting lathe. **1955** *Times* 6 June 6/6 Experience has shown that paddle tugs are more efficient than *screw-driven tugs for work in confined basins. **1831** J. Holland *Manuf. Metal* I. 209 A Staffordshire *screw-maker. **1747** *Gen. Descr. Trades* 21 *Screw-making is also a Branch by itself. **1841** *Penny Cycl.* XXI. 109/1 In the infancy of screw-making the thread was formed with a file. **1853** Ure *Dict. Arts* (ed. 4) II. 588 The screw-making machine. **1848** Woodcroft *Steam Navig.* 101 The *New Jersey* was the first *screw-propelled vessel practically used in America. **1888** *Lockwood's Dict. Mech. Engin.*, **Screw Slotting*, the slotting of the grooves in the heads of cheese-headed and button-headed screws. **1891** *Daily News* 1 Dec. 7/4 Two tin gallon cans, *screw-stoppered, full of naphtha. **1907** Hodges *Elem. Photogr.* 29 Never..use screw-stoppered beer or other bottles. **1865** in *Abridgm. Specif. Patents, Nails* (1873) 291 *Screw-threaded bolts. **1897** Kipling *Capt. Cour.* vii. 143 The little schooner staggered ..in a rush of *screw-torn water, as a liner's stern vanished in the fog.

23. a. Similative, as in ***screw-twist***; ***screw-like***, ***-shaped*** adjs.; ***screw-wise*** adv.; also quasi-adj. with the meaning 'spiral', as in ***screw gut***, ***gutter***, ***motion***, ***stair***, ***stair-case***.

1681 Grew *Musæum* I. §v. i. 99 The *Skrew-Gut of the Raja..winds between parallel lines like a Screw or Stair-case. **1833** Loudon *Encycl. Archit.* §738 The water might be conducted more regularly from the apex to the base..by forming round it a *screw gutter. **1705** *Observ. Seed-Vessels Polypodium* in *Phil. Trans.* XXV. 1872 The *Screw-like parts of the Seed Vessel. **1883** *Encycl. Brit.* XV. 754/2 Screw-like or helical motion. **1882** Minchin *Unipl. Kinematics* 244 *Screw Motion of a Liquid. **1760** J. Lee *Introd. Bot.* I. xiii. (1776) 34 The Figure of the Filaments is either..Spiral, *Skrew-shaped, as in Hirtella [etc.]. **1867** N. Macleod *Starling* II. x. 116 He.. lived in a very small house, above his shop, which was reached by a *screw stair. **1786** Mackenzie *Lounger* No. 87 §6 A *screw stair-case. **1894** R. Bridges *Nero* II. III. ii. 1234 Very few Are what they show the world: there's a *screw-twist In every mind. **1687** A. Lovell tr. *Thevenot's Trav.* III. 46 Fasten to each of the two pieces that are to enter into one another, some Iron, Copper, or Silver wire, turned *Screw-wise.

b. Similative (quasi-*adj.*), as in ***screw-shell***, ***snail***, ***-turbo***, applied to various gasteropods with slender spiral shells.

1731 Medley *Kolben's Cape G. Hope* II. 212 There is a Sort of Water-Snails at the Cape, which the Europeans there call Screw-Snails. **1753** *Chambers' Cycl.* Suppl., *Turbo*, the Screw-Shell... 5. The screw-Turbo, with variegated lines and spots. **1819** Turton *Conchol. Dict.* 62 *Helix Terebra*. Screw Snail-shell. *Ibid.* 95 *Murex Gyrinus*. Screw Rock-shell. *Ibid.* 165 *Strombus*. Screw-shell. *Ibid.* 216 *Turbo Terebra*. Screw Turban. **1859–62** Sir J. Richardson, etc. *Mus. Nat. Hist.* (1868) II. 339 The family of Turret or Screw shells (*Turritellidæ*).

24. a. Special combinations: **screw-alley, -area** (see quots.); **screw auger**, an auger with a spiral shank; **screw axis** *Cryst.*, an axis such that a combination of rotation about it and translation along it constitutes a symmetry operation, but neither does so alone; **screw-barrel** *sb.*, (*a*) a fire-arm with a screwed barrel; (*b*) *Mech.* (see quot. 1888); **screw-barrel** *a.*, (*a*) of a fire-arm, having a screwed barrel (see screwed *ppl. a.* 5 b); (*b*) of a microscope, having a threaded barrel by means of which the microscope is focused; **screw battery**, a battery composed of screw-guns (see below); **screw-bell** (see quot.); **screw-blank**, the piece of metal upon which a thread or worm is to be cut to form a screw; **screw-block** *Basketry*, a device for holding stakes rigid during rectangular work; **screw board** (see quot.); **screw-bolt**, a bolt with a thread or worm at the end to be secured by means of a screw-nut; hence **screw-bolt** *v.*, *trans.*, to fasten with a screw-bolt; hence **screw-bolting** *vbl. sb.*, the use of screw-bolts; **screwbound** *a.*, (*a*) fastened or held by a screw or screws (sense 10 a in quot.); (*b*) (see quot. 1966); **screw-box**, †(*a*) = nut *sb.*[1] 11; (*b*) a tool for cutting the thread on a wooden screw; **screw bulb**, an electric light bulb having a threaded base enabling it to be screwed into a socket; **screw-cap** (see quot. 1875); also more generally, = *screw top*; hence **screw-capped** *a.*; **screw-chuck**, a variety of lathe-chuck (see quot.); **screw compressor** (see quot. 1967); **screw-coupling** (see quot.); **screw-cut** *a.*, fashioned as a screw, furnished with a screw-thread; **screw-die** = die *sb.*[1] 6 a; **screw dislocation** *Cryst.*, a form of crystal defect characterized by a unit distortion of the lattice in a particular direction such that the lattice planes perpendicular to that direction form continuous spiral sheets; **screw-dock** *U.S.*, a dock in which the cradle is raised by screws; **screw-dog**, a clamp adjustable by a screw, to hold timber while being sawn; **screw-dollar** *U.S.*, 'a medallion of which the obverse and reverse may be screwed together to form a box' (*Cent. Dict.* 1891); **screw-drill**, a drill with a spiral shank; **screw engine**, (*a*) a machine for raising water by means of a screw, a water-screw; (*b*) a steam-engine adapted to drive a screw-propeller; **screw-eye**, (*a*) a screw having a loop or eye for its head; (*b*) 'a long screw with a handle, used in theatres by stage carpenters in securing scenes' (*Cent. Dict.*); **screw-eyed** *a.*, having the eyes screwed up; **screw-fish** ? *U.S.*, 'fish packed under a screw press' (*Cent. Dict.*); **screw fly** *U.S.*, a blow-fly of the genus *Cochliomyia*, *C. hominivorax* or *C. macellaria*, which deposits eggs on animal carcasses or open wounds; **screw forging**, a screw-blank of forged iron; **screw-gear**, gear consisting of an endless screw and a toothed wheel; **screw-grip (action)**, see quot. and grip *sb.*[1] 5; **screw-gun**, see quot. 1877–81; **screw-hammer**, an adjustable spanner with a heavy, hammer-like head; **screw-hook**, (*a*) see quot. 1688; (*b*) see quot. 1875; (*c*) a small hook, usually of brass, with a screwed shank to screw into woodwork; **screw-jack** = Jack *sb.*[1] 10; **screw-joint**, (*a*) *Mech.*, a joint formed by screwing together the ends of piping, etc.; (*b*) *Anat.*, a joint in which there is a slight lateral sliding of one bone upon the other; **screw-key**, (*a*) = *screw-wrench*; (*b*) a key furnished with a thread or worm; **screw-line** *Bot.* (see quot.); **screw-lock**, one operated by turning a wormed key on a similarly wormed pin; **screw-machine**, (*a*) a machine operated by a screw; (*b*) a machine for making screws (Knight *Dict. Mech.* 1875); (*c*) see quot. 1884; **screw-man** *U.S. Hist.*, a worker who packed bales into cotton-ships;

screw-mandrel, a screw-cutting mandrel having on its spindle screws of various sizes and pitches; **screw medal** *U.S.* = *screw-dollar* (Cent. Dict.); **screw micrometer** (see MICROMETER 2); **screw mill**, a mill for driving screw-cutting machinery; **screw-moulding**, (*a*) the moulding of screws in sand for casting; (*b*) the forming of screws in metal collars, caps, etc. (*Cent. Dict.*); †**screw mouth**, an ill-shaped mouth; **screw-nail**, a screw or wood-screw (see sense 3); **screw nut** = NUT *sb.*[1] 11; †**screw pelican** *Dentistry* (see quot.); **screw pile**, a foundation pile with a screw at its lower end adapted for screwing instead of driving; hence **screw-pile, -piled** *adjs.*, built upon screw piles; **screw-plate**, a hardened steel plate for cutting the threads of small screws by means of a series of drilled and tapped holes of various diameters; **Screw Plot** *Hist.*, an imaginary plot to destroy the Queen and the Court on Thanksgiving Day, 1710, by the removal of some of the iron bolts from the timbers of the roof of St. Paul's in order to cause its fall; **screw-press**, a machine in which pressure is applied by means of a screw; **screw propeller** (see PROPELLER 3); **screw-pump**, an ARCHIMEDEAN screw; †**screw range**, ? a cooking range with screw adjustment for the grate; **screw-rasp**, a kind of file (see quot.); **screw rod**, a binding or connecting rod with a screw and nut at one or both ends (*Cent. Dict.*); †**screw-rope**, ? a rope for use with some form of screw-jack; **screw-rudder** (see quot.); **screw shackle (joint)**, a variety of coupling joint; **screw-shaft**, (*a*) a shaft having a screw-thread cut upon it; (*b*) see quot. 1869; **screw spanner** = *screw-wrench*; **screw-spike** (see quot.); **screw stock** = DIE *sb.*[1] 6a; **screw-stone**, a stone containing the hollow cast of an encrinite (= *pulley-stone*, PULLEY *sb.*[1] 5); **screw tail**, a dog's tail which is twisted or crooked; **screw-tap**, (*a*) a screw of hardened steel used for cutting an internal or female screw; (*b*) a draw-tap with a screw-down plug; **screw-thread**, the spiral ridge of a screw; also, one complete turn of its thread regarded as a portion of a unit of length of the axis of the screw; **screw tool**, a lathe-tool for cutting screws; **screw-tool cutter** (see quot.); **screw top**, a round cap or lid that can be screwed on to a bottle, jar, or the like; also *attrib.*; hence **screw-topped** *a.*; **screw-turn** (*dial.*), **-turner**, a screwdriver; †**screw-ways** *adv.*, in a spiral or twisted direction; **screw-well** (see quot.); **screw-wheel**, the toothed wheel associated with the endless screw in screw-gearing; **screw-wire**, a cable-twisted wire used to fasten the soles of boots to the uppers (*Cent. Dict.*); **screw-wise** *adv.*, after the manner of a screw, spirally; **screw worm**, (*a*) see quot. *a* 1892; (*b*) *U.S.*, the larva of a screw fly, which has spiny hairs encircling each segment; **screw-worm chuck** = *screw-chuck*; **screw worm fly** = *screw fly*; **screw-wrench**, a wrench or spanner adapted to fit over or grasp the heads of screw-bolts, nuts, etc., and turn them. Also SCREW-CUT, -CUTTER, -CUTTING, SCREWDRIVER, SCREW-PIN.

1866 *Chamb. Encycl.* VIII. 685/2 In screw-steamers,..a tunnel, known as the *screw-alley, has to be kept open for the shaft of the screw from the engine-room to the stern. **1888** *Lockwood's Dict. Mech. Engin.*, **Screw Area* in a propeller is the area of the circle described by the tips of the blades. **1825** J. NEAL *Bro. Jonathan* III. 149 They were at work..with broad axes and *screw augers. **1903** H. HILTON *Math. Crystallogr.* xvi. 146 The combination of a rotation about an axis and a translation parallel to it is called a screw about that axis; and if such a combination brings a figure U to self-coincidence the axis is called a *screw-axis of symmetry for U. **1937** W. L. BRAGG *Atomic Struct. Minerals* i. 13 It is the possibility of screw axes and glide planes, in addition to rotation axes and reflection planes, which gives rise to the large number of space-groups. **1974** *Nature* 11 Jan. 85/2 Dark-field observation could establish the presence of centres of symmetry, glide planes and screw axes, which could lead to the establishment of the space group. **1742** *Phil. Trans.* XLII. 173 A short *Screw-barrel Pistol. **1753** HANWAY *Trav.* (1762) I. III. xl. 179 Being ignorant also how to use the screw-barrels, he offered to return them. **1888** *Lockwood's Dict. Mech. Engin.*, *Screw Barrel*, a chain barrel having a continuous spiral groove cut around its periphery to receive the links edgeways. **1926** *Catal. Optical & Gen. Sci. Instrum. Optical Convention 1926* 287 Ivory screw-barrel microscope: by J. Wilson, with eight powers (unsigned, *circa* 1706). **1956** *Nature* 7 Jan. 8/1 Another contemporary scientist interested in optics was the Dutch microscopist Nicolaas Hartsoeker, born on March 26, 1656. He published in 1694 an 'Essai de Dioptrique' in which he illustrated his invention, the screw-barrel microscope, generally associated with the name of Wilson, who introduced it to England. **1877–81** VOYLE & STEVENSON *Milit. Dict.* Suppl. 26/2 The *screw battery did excellent service in the last Afghan war. **1881** RAYMOND *Mining Gloss.*, **Screw-bell*, a recovering tool in deep boring, ending below in a hollow screw-threaded cone. **1833** J. HOLLAND *Manuf. Metal* II. 147 The *screw-blank being exactly turned in the lathe to the thickness and length required. **1924** C. CRAMPTON *Cane Work* 34 *Oblong Cane Base*... This kind of base cannot be made without using a 'screw lock', which acts as a vice for holding the sticks or stakes in an upright position. The *screw block consists of two wooden blocks with thumbscrews for tightening purposes. **1959** D. WRIGHT *Baskets & Basketry* ii. 45 A *Rectangular Base* is made in a screw-block. **1887** *Archit. Publ. Soc. Dict.*, **Screw board*, or *Side board*, the vertical board at the side of a carpenter's bench pierced with holes.. which admit of pins for holding up the object to be planed [etc.]. **1793** SMEATON *Edystone L.* §42 The..fastening of the outside uprights to the solid, by means of Jag-bolts, or *screw-bolts. **1795** HERSCHEL in *Phil. Trans.* LXXXV. 376 Two loops..are *screw-bolted to the ends of them. **1869** SIR E. REED *Shipbuild.* xxi. 475 *Screw-bolting has been almost universally adopted in the French iron-clads. **1892** G. B. SHAW in *Pall Mall Gaz.* 22 Feb. 2/3 In order that they might secure the door on the outside and so retain my audience *screwbound to the last syllable of the vote of thanks. **1966** A. W. LEWIS *Gloss. Woodworking Terms* 85 Hinge is screwbound when the heads of the screws are not sunk correctly into their counter-sinking. **1677** MOXON *Mech. Exerc.* i. 5 The Nut or *Screw-Box hath also a Square Worm. **1846** HOLTZAPFFEL *Turning* II. 593 The instrument which is commonly employed for making long screws in the soft woods, namely, the screw box. **1960** *Practical Wireless* XXXVI. 302/2 A 500mA fuse..takes the form of 6V, 0·5A *screw bulb. **1875** KNIGHT *Dict. Mech.*, **Screw-cap*, 1. A cover to protect or conceal the head of a screw. 2. A cover for a fruit-jar. **1897** *Sears, Roebuck Catal.* 35/2 Ointment pots. Flint glass. Nickle screw cap. **1936** *Lancet* 3 May 1160/2 The United Glass Bottle Manufacturers, Ltd., have produced a double-shell metal cap for bottles and pots. This cap has all the advantages of the ordinary screw-cap. **1972** *Gloss. Electrotechnical, Power Terms* (*B.S.I.*) IV. iii. 17 *Screw cap*, cap..in the form of a screw thread. **1898** *York Glass Company* (*Ltd.*) *Price List* 3 Pomade Bottles..Metal *Screw Capped. **1964** M. HYNES *Med. Bacteriol.* (ed. 8) iv. 35 They are conveniently disposed for use in quantities of about 3 ml. in 1 oz. screw-capped bottles. **1895** *Mod. Steam Eng.* 87 The *screw-chuck..shows on its right side a flat circular surface, from the centre of which projects a large, coarse, conical screw for holding firmly any large piece of wooden work. **1958** *S. Afr. Mining & Engin. Jrnl.* LXIX. 243/1 The rotary *screw compressor is built on the principle of an invention made by Professor A. Lysholm of Stockholm. **1967** *Gloss. Terms Materials Handling* (*B.S.I.*) III. 17 *Screw or worm type compressor*, a rotary compressor having left hand and right hand worms in close engagement, which entrain the air or gas and eject it at a higher pressure. **1975** *Offshore Engineer* Dec. 57/1 Atlas Copco is to supply six ZR4 screw compressors and ancillary equipment to be built into two modules by the fabricating engineers. **1875** KNIGHT *Dict. Mech.*, **Screw-coupling*, (*a*) a device for joining the ends of two vertical rods or chains and giving them any desired degree of tension; (*b*) a screw-socket for uniting pipes or rods. **1794** *Rigging & Seamanship* X 2 b, Cylindrical pieces of wood or iron, *screw-cut at one end. **1846** HOLTZAPFFEL *Turning* II. 593 On cutting external screws, with *screw dies. [**1940** J. M. BURGERS in *Proc. Physical Soc.* LII. 25 Dislocation lines of this character will be said to be of the screw type.] **1948** *Rep. Conf. Strength of Solids, 1947* (Physical Soc.) 46 We may take the simpler case of a *screw dislocation (Burgers' second type), lying along the *x* axis. **1966** *McGraw-Hill Encycl. Sci. & Technol.* III. 585/1 Screw dislocations have been shown to be important for crystal growth from the vapor phase. **1978** P. W. ATKINS *Physical Chem.* xxviii. 931 The surface defect formed by a screw dislocation is a ledge, possibly with some kinks, where growth can occur. **1864** WEBSTER, **Screw-dock*. **1867** SMYTH *Sailor's Word-bk.*, *Gridiron*... The Americans also use for a similar purpose an apparatus called a screw-dock. **1869** RANKINE *Machine & Hand-tools* Pl. Q 16, 4 The carriages to support the ends of the timber are furnished with adjustable *screw-dogs. **1869** C. KNIGHT *Mechanician* 126 A *screw-drill..is advantageous for drilling long holes. **1767** J. FERGUSON *Lect.* Suppl. 22 Archimedes's *Screw-Engine for raising water. **1852** J. BOURNE *Screw Propeller* ix. 199 Screw engines are divisible into two great classes—geared screw engines and direct-acting screw engines. **1873** *Abridgm. Specif. Patents, Nails*, etc. 332 *Screw-eyes, adapted for holding stair rods [etc.]. **1810** *Splendid Follies* I. 158 The demure looking *screw-eyed cat. **1884** R. ALDRIDGE *Life on Ranch* 191 We were a good deal troubled ..by what is called '*screw fly'. **1945** J. J. MATHEWS *Talking to Moon* 20 Sometimes their hides were torn, thus inviting screw flies. **1818** E. WOOLLEY in *Abridgm. Specif. Patents, Nails*, etc. (1873) 19 The *screw forging is formed or shaped from round or cylindrical rod iron. **1875** KNIGHT *Dict. Mech.*, **Screw-gear*. **1908** *Westm. Gaz.* 14 May 4/2 The commutator is driven by screw-gear from the magneto driving shaft. **1897** *Encycl. Sport* I. 498/2 [Guns] The *Screw Grip Action... The barrels..are held down, first by the ordinary Purdey bolt system operated by a vertical shaft ..; this shaft carries upon it the 'screw grip'..working in a square-threaded screw cut in..the breech. **1877–81** VOYLE & STEVENSON *Milit. Dict.* Suppl. 26/1 To be added to the list of M.T. guns is the *screw gun, which takes in two, being fastened together by a screw, hence its name. **1896** H. G. WELLS *Wheels of Chance* iv. 24 Just then the *screw-hammer slipped off the nut. **1909** *Chambers's Jrnl.* Jan. 61/1 The inner screws are then driven into the board to be lifted by a screw-hammer to secure a firm purchase. **1975** R. A. SALAMAN *Dict. Tools* 530/2 This smith-made example was sometimes called a 'Screw Hammer' because the upper jaw of the Wrench was made in the form of a Hammer and could be used as such. **1688** HOLME *Armoury* III. xvi. (Roxb.) 87/1 Two *screw hookes (or Boate hookes with screws). **1875** KNIGHT *Dict. Mech.*, *Screw-hook* (Surgical), an instrument for withdrawing foreign bodies from the ear or nostrils. **1719** DE FOE *Crusoe* iv. (Globe) 54 In the Carpenter's Stores I found.. a great *Skrew-Jack. **1846** HOLTZAPFFEL *Turning* II. 680 Cast-iron water-pipes with *screw joints. **1882** *Syd. Soc. Lex.*, *Cochlearthrosis*... Screw joint. **1850** OGILVIE, *Screw wrench or key. **1852** SEIDEL *Organ* 28 The screw-key..is an invention of our own time. **1855** in *Abridgm. Specif. Patents, Locks* (1873) 134 A screw pin (being an exact counterpart of the key, which is a screw-key) is fitted to the lock plate. **1869** C. KNIGHT *Mechanician* 16 Screw keys.. have screwed ends, for the convenience of having a nut to prevent the key slipping back..while in use. **1900** B. D. JACKSON *Gloss. Bot. Terms*, **Screw-lines*, spirals in phyllotaxis. **1685** *Lond. Gaz.* No. 2037/4 A black-brown Gelding.., with a *Screw-lock on his near Foot before. **1841** *Penny Cycl.* XXI. 108/2 The ingenious *screw-machine which was invented by Mr. Hunter..consists of one convex screw which works in the interior of another convex screw. **1884** *Health Exhib. Catal.* 115/2 Standard Screw Machine for attaching the soles of boots and shoes with screws instead of rivets. **1885** J. B. LENO *Boot & Shoemaking* xxiii. 189. **1856** C. NORDHOFF *Merchant Vessel* iv. 38 A lighter-load of cotton came down, and with it, a stevedore and several gangs of the **screw men*, whose business it is to load cotton-ships. **1950** BLESH & JANIS *They all played Ragtime* ii. 39 The fellows who put bales in place were screwmen. **1680** MOXON *Mech. Exerc.* xi. 199 Another sort of Mandrel is called the *Screw-Mandrel. **1846** HOLTZAPFFEL *Turning* II. 612 The screw-mandrel or traversing mandrel. **1798** S. SHAW *Staffordsh.* I. 109/1 The brook..turned a corn mill, which was converted into a *screw mill..about 1766. **1707** *Wks. C'tess D'Anois* (1715) 374 She would not change her flat Nose and her *skrew Mouth for all Gratiosa's Beauty. **1660** FULLER *Mixt Comtempl.* xxxiv. 51 *Screw-nailes, which had holes prepared for their reception. **1831** J. HOLLAND *Manuf. Metal* I. 199 The wood screw, or, as it is sometimes called.., the screw nail. **1815** J. SMITH *Panorama Sci. & Art* I. 39 The pin by which the spirals of a *screw nut are formed, is called a tap. **1688** HOLME *Armoury* III. 435/1 A *Screw Pelican,..a kinde of pincers to draw out the..grinding teeth withall. **1840** *Civil Engin. & Arch. Jrnl.* III. 182/2 The foundation of the building is formed of seven *screw piles. **1893** KIPLING *Many Invent.* 6 Dowse was in charge of a *screw-pile Light called the Wurlee Light. **1840** *Civil Engin. & Arch. Jrnl.* III. 181/2 The *screw-piled pillars. **1677** MOXON *Mech. Exerc.* i. 7 The *Screw-plate is a plate of Steel..with several holes in it, each less than other. **1884** F. J. BRITTEN *Watch & Clockm.* 232 Screw a piece of steel of the desired size in an ordinary right-handed screw plate. **1722** A. BOYER *Hist. Q. Anne* 480 Which pretended *Screw-Plot, (as it was afterwards called) many of the Tories..were ready enough to charge upon the Whigs. **1688** HOLME *Armoury* III. 371/1 He beareth Gules, a Stationers, or Book-Binders *Screw-press, Or. **1864** BURTON *Scot Abr.* II. i. 23 *note*, The device on its title-page of the press-man at work on the screw-press of the day. **1839** *Screw propeller [see PROPELLER 3]. **1776** G. SEMPLE *Building in Water* 42 [The water] that soaked from the Bed of the River..we conveyed into the S.E. Corner for the *Screw-pump. **1798** *Times* 28 June 4/1 The very neat and excellent Household Furniture, Plate, China, a capital *Screw Range, a Copper, and other Effects. **1688** HOLME *Armoury* III. 388/1 A Flote, or *Screw-Rasp..is three Square, smooth on one side, and toothed like a Saw on the other two. **1497** *Naval Acc. Hen. VII* (1896) 118 Gynne rope with an hoke of iren..j, *Skrew rope. **1875** KNIGHT *Dict. Mech.*, **Screw-rudder*, an application of the screw to purposes of steering, instead of a rudder. **1882** W. J. CHRISTY *Joints* 102 *Screw Shackle Joint. This..is used by the carpenter with tie-rods. *Ibid.* 126 Coupling Joint... Amongst builders it usually takes the form of a hinge, union, screw shackle [etc.]. **1852** J. BOURNE *Screw Propeller* x. 216 The bearings of the *screw shaft are of cast iron. **1853** URE *Dict. Arts* (ed. 4) I. 787 These gills are supported and traversed by their extremities, taken into the threads of two screw shafts. **1869** C. KNIGHT *Mechanician* 386 The screw-shafts of a pair of engines properly include the crank-shaft, all the intermediate shafts, and the propeller-shaft. *Ibid.* 120 *Screw spanners..may be made to fit nuts and heads of several different diameters. **1875** KNIGHT *Dict. Mech.*, **Screw-spike*, a round spike having a shallow screw-thread cut on a portion of its stem. It is driven partly home and screwed the remaining distance. **1846** HOLTZAPFFEL *Turning* II. 605 These *screw stocks were found to cut very rapidly. **1729** WOODWARD *Catal. Eng. Fossils* II. 102 This is one of those Bodies that are call'd, tho' improperly, *Screw-Stones. From a Lead-Mine near Worksworth, in the Peak, Derbyshire. **1829** J. PHILLIPS *Geol. Yorksh.* 109 The screw-stones which are casts in the central hollow of crinoidal columns. **1894** R. B. LEE *Hist. & Descr. Mod. Dogs* (*Non-Sporting*) ix. 239 The *screw tails, which are so peculiar to the [bulldog] breed, are objected to by a few authorities as indicating excessive in-breeding. **1965** JOHNSON & GALIN *Compl. Bk. Dogs* (1968) vi. 255 If your dog has a screw or twisted tail..he may suffer from infection or sores under the skin. **1677** MOXON *Mech. Exerc.* ii. 31 The *screw-tap, that makes the Screw in the Nut. **1869** E. A. PARKES *Pract. Hygiene* (ed. 3) 14 Common taps do not answer, and the best screw taps..must be used. **1812** P. NICHOLSON *Mech. Exerc.* 353 *Screw Threads, the parts which are left standing between the spiral grooves of the screw. **1854** RONALDS & RICHARDSON *Chem. Technol.* (ed. 2) I. 271 The rocking motion of the bars is accomplished by what is vulgarly called a drunken screw-thread. **1817** SCHELLEN *Spectrum Anal.* §25. 88 In order to measure accurately the amount of motion the value of a screw-thread must be ascertained. **1812** P. NICHOLSON *Mech. Exerc.* 370 *Screw Tools are employed in cutting of screws of various sizes of threads. **1846** HOLTZAPFFEL *Turning* II. 591 The cutter [*sc.* tap] is then called a hob, or a *screw-tool cutter. **1895** *Montgomery Ward Catal.* Spring & Summer 195 Large size pocket flask with collapsion cup, cover *screw top. *Ibid.*, Screw top, satin engraved pocket flask. **1907** E. NESBIT *Enchanted Castle* xi. 314 A beer bottle with a screw top. **1937** G. GREENE *19 Stories* (1947) 59 There's a bottle in my pocket. Have a drink... It has a screw top. **1951** *Good Housek. Home Encycl.* 335/2 Boil the angelica..dry off..store in screw-top jars. **1963** *Times* 3 June 11/6 Make a French dressing with oil, tarragon-flavoured wine vinegar, dry mustard, salt and pepper and a pinch of castor sugar and pour into a *screw-topped container. **1972** Screw-topped [see *marble-stoppered* s.v. MARBLE *sb.* 8c]. **1831** J. HOLLAND *Manuf. Metal* I. 208 So that a *screw-turner will only operate upon the screws in one direction. **1705** DERHAM in *Phil. Trans.* XXV. 2140 Which not only separateth the fibres of the Iron..but also changeth their situation from Longways to *Skrew-ways. **1867** SMYTH *Sailor's Word-bk.*, **Screw-well*, a hollow trunk over the screw of a steamer, for allowing the propeller to be disconnected and lifted. **1825** J. NICHOLSON *Oper. Mech.* 428 The *screw-wheel to act in the worm. **1731** MEDLEY tr. *Kolben's Cape G. Hope* II. 126 The horns of the Hottentot hart..run up twisting, *screw-wise, to about half their length. **1884** *Leisure Hour* Feb. 84/2 The screw-pine..with long prickly leaves set screw-wise. **1879** *Investigation of Diseases of Swine* (U.S. Dept. Agric.) 208 Ticks, *screw-worm, and the large horse or cow fly have destroyed many animals. *a* **1892** G. H. KINGSLEY *Sport & Travel* v. (1900) 120 Wherever we stopped in the woods we could hear the queer creaking rasp of the big boring grub which they call the screw-worm. **1897** *Allbutt's Syst. Med.* IV. 704 To the larva of the latter [Sarcophaga Georgina] the term 'screw worm' has been applied. **1936** E. CALDWELL in *New Yorker* 22 Aug. 22/1 He hated weeds worse than he did boll weevils or screwworms. **1955** *Sci. Amer.* Oct. 50/3 The screwworm is a major pest of cattle in the U.S. Southeast. **1973** *Nature* 20 Apr. 494/1 The formidable task of re-eradicating the screw worm from the United States. **1908** V. L. KELLOGG *Amer. Insects* 344 A flesh-fly of serious importance is the terrible *screw-worm fly,..which lays its eggs on flesh.. and often in the nasal passages of domestic animals and human beings. **1955** *Sci. News Let.* 29 Jan. 78/1 The screwworm fly may be eradicated from Florida and controlled in Texas, where its maggots cause millions of dollars loss to livestock men each year. **1978** *Nature* 22 June 606/2 The well publicised eradication of the screw-worm fly from Florida. **1850** *Amer. Agriculturist* Sept. 285/2 *Adjustable *Screw Wrench.*—This is just about one of the most useful little farming tools ever purchased. **1858** SIMMONDS *Dict. Trade*, *Screw-wrench*, a turn-screw; a bed-wrench. **1866** *Chamb. Encycl.* VIII. 571/2 *Screw-wrench*, a tool used for grasping the flat sides of the heads of large screws.

b. In names of plants, as **screw-bean, -mezquit, -moss** (see quots.); **screw-palm, -pine**, any of the plants belonging to the N.O. *Pandanaceæ* (see quot. 1836); also *attrib.*; **screw-stem**, a plant of the N. American genus *Bartonia* (or *Centaurella*); **screw-tree** (see quot.).

1866 *Treas. Bot.* 930/1 *Prosopis pubescens*,..is the *Screw-bean or *Screw Mezquit of the Americans..and is so called from the screw-like form of its pods. **1869** C. C. PARRY in W. A. Bell *New Tracks N. Amer.* II. 289 In the river bottoms we meet with luxuriant growths of mezquit and 'screw-bean'. **1817** PURTON *Brit. Plants* II. 540 *Tortula.* *Screw-moss. **1867** J. HOGG *Microsc.* II. i. 309 The common or Wall Screw-moss. **1851** E. FORBES *Veg. World* i. in *Art Jrnl. Illustr. Catal.*, Hats, made of the leaves of *screw-palms. **1836** BUCKLAND *Geol. & Min.* (1837) I. 503 The Pandaneæ, or *Screw-Pines..abound in the Indian Archipelago... Their aspect is that of gigantic Pine apple plants having arborescent stems. **1861** BENTLEY *Man. Bot.* 687 Pandanaceæ.—The Screw-pine Order. **1873** DRURY *Usef. Plants India* 325 *Pandanus odoratissimus*... Fragrant Screw-pine. **1902** A. ALCOCK *Nat. in Indian Seas* 58 Scenery, which consists chiefly of slimy creeks and screw-pine swamps. **1846–50** A. WOOD *Class-bk. Bot.* 454 *Centaurella autumnalis*... *Screw-stem. **1756** P. BROWNE *Jamaica* 330 The *Screw Tree. [*Helicteres Jamaicensis*, Jacq.] This curious shrub is very frequent in the low gravelly hills.

screw (skruː), *sb.*[2] Also 7, 9 **scrow**. [Prob. of Fr. origin: cf. F. *escrouelle* (Cotgr.), now *écrouelle*, of the same meaning.] A small crustacean of either of the genera *Gammarus* and *Niphargus*; a river-shrimp.

1684 R. SIBBALD *Scotia Illustr.* II. VII. x. 34 Squilla, nostratibus the Scrow. **1808** JAMIESON, *Scrow*, the name given most commonly to the minute cancri observed in pools and springs,..also occasionally applied to some of the aquatic larvae of flies and beetles. **1834** J. WILSON *Let.* 27 June, in J. Hamilton *Mem.* v. (1859) 186 We found their interior crammed full of screws, or fresh-water shrimps. **1846** BROCKETT *N.C. Words* (ed. 3), *Scrows*, the small shrimp-like insect found in fresh-water pools. **1850** A. WHITE *List Specim. Crustacea Brit. Mus.* 52 *Gammarus fluviatilis.* The Freshwater Screw. **1857** —— *Brit. Crustacea* 182 *Gammara locusta*, Common Coast Screw. *Ibid.* 187 *Niphargus aquilex*... The Well Screw.

screw (skruː), *sb.*[3] *Orkney* and *Shetl.* Also **scroo, skroo, skrew** (see E.D.D.). [a. Norw. *skrue*, *skruv*, ON. *scrúf*.] A small stack (of corn, hay or straw).

1814 SHIRREFF *Agric. Shetld.* 155 Forty Linlithgow bolls are sometimes preserved in one of these piles, here called beaks or screws. **1897** SIR H. MAXWELL *Mem. Months* 46 The slender ricks, locally called 'screws'..shaped like pepper-castors.

screw (skruː), *v.* Forms: 7 **scrue, (screue), skrue, screwe, 7–8 skrew, 6– screw**. [f. SCREW *sb.*[1] Cf. Du. *schroeven*, G. *schrauben*, Icel. *skrúfa*, Sw. *skrufva*, Da. *skrue*.]

I. To attach with a screw or screws.

1. *trans.* To attach with an inserted screw or screws; hence *fig.*, to fix firmly. ***to screw down, up***: to close and secure with screws.

1611 SHAKS. *Cymb.* II. ii. 44 Why should I write this downe, thats riueted, Screw'd to my memorie. **1669** STURMY *Mariner's Mag.* II. xvi. 93 The best way to hold the Quadrant..is to skrew it with a Brass-Pin..to a Staff. **1669** in Willis & Clark *Cambridge* (1886) II. 559 The outward dores to have..locks to them well scrued on. **1768** TUCKER *Lt. Nat.* II. I. ii. 25 If while our backs are turned an unlucky boy screws a piece of deal upon one of the leaves [of a table]. **1762** *Gentl. Mag.* Jan. 43 The coffin being skrewed down before she came. **1792** in *Abridgm. Specif. Patents, Fire-arms* (1859) I. 33 The trigger has a spring screwed to the frame. **1815** J. SMITH *Panorama Sci. & Art* I. 30 A square piece of wood,..being firmly screwed to the under side of the board. **1862** MRS. H. WOOD *Mrs. Hallib.* II. vii. 183 Think of being screwed down in a coffin, and put into the cold ground. **1885** J. B. LENO *Boot & Shoemaking* xxiii. 189 The boot, instead of being nailed or riveted, is by this machine really screwed together. **1885** *Law Rep.* 15 *Q.B.D.* 359 A metal cap was put over the shaft and screwed to the bearer.

II. To press, strain, or force with or as with a screw.

2. a. To force, press, or strain, by or as by means of a screw; to compress or hold fast in or as in a vice. ***to screw up***: to tighten by turning a screw. †Also, to torture with 'the screws'.

1612 WOODALL *Surg. Mate* (1639) 7 This Speculum serveth to screw open the mouth..for conveying nourishment. **1620** *Swetnam Arrayned* IV. ii. I. 3, You haue spoke to mutch alreadie, you damn'd Rogue But weele reward..you for't. Skrew his iawes. **1677** MOXON *Mech. Exerc.* ii. 30 Screw the shank..in the Vice. **1680** *Ibid.* xii. 208 And screw your Work a little lightly up: Then..you may without more ado screw up your Work tight. **1820** KEATS *Hyperion* II. 25 Cœus, and Gyges..Were.. Dungeon'd..and all their limbs Lock'd up like veins of metal, crampt and screw'd. **1902** HASLUCK *Bookbinding* xi. 104 Screw the book into the press.

b. transf. ***to screw in, up***: to compress the waist of (a person) by tight-lacing.

1785 HOLCROFT *Tales of Castle* (ed. 2) I. 17 Ridiculous vanity made her bear..to be screwed up till she could scarcely breathe. **1815** JANE AUSTEN *Emma* iii, The mistress of a school—not of a seminary..where young ladies for enormous pay might be screwed out of health and into vanity. **1825** T. HOOK *Sayings* Ser. II. *Man of Many Fr.* (Colburn) 107 The eldest girl..was screwed in, and poked out, to look like a woman.

3. a. To stretch tight by turning a screw; *esp.* to increase the tension or pitch (of a musical string) by winding up the screws or keys. Chiefly with *up*. Often in figurative context.

1652 BENLOWES *Theoph.* III. xcviii, Love, to high Graces key skrues up low Natures Strings. **1656** EARL MONM. tr. *Boccalini's Advts. fr. Parnass.* I. xii. (1674) 15 They break the strings by scruing them up too high. **1679** DRYDEN *Troilus & Cr.* Pref. b 1 b, For what melody can be made on that Instrument all whose strings are screw'd up at first to their utmost stretch, and to the same sound? **1760** STERNE *Tr. Shandy* III. v, Being a lover of such kind of concord as arises from two such instruments being put in exact tune,—he would instantly have skrew'd up his to the same pitch. **1864** TENNYSON *Aylmer's F.* 469 Screw not the chord too sharply lest it snap.

transf. **1831** O. W. HOLMES *My Aunt* 30 They pinched her feet, they singed her hair, They screwed it up with pins.

absol. **1677** W. HUGHES *Man of Sin* II. xii. 216 Agatho screwed a Note above Ela when he Decreed,..that the Popes Decrees should be received as if S. Peters mouth had confirmed them.

b. *fig.* With object a person or his attributes.

1605 SHAKS. *Macb.* I. vii. 60 *Lady.* We faile? But screw your courage to the sticking place, And wee'le not fayle. **1615** CHAPMAN *Odyss.* IX. 438 [He] occasion gaue For me to vse my wits; which to their height, I striu'd to skrew vp. **1617** FLETCHER *Valentinian* II. i, All your arts..screw to th' highest; For my main piece is now a-doing. **1646** QUARLES *Judgem. & Mercy* I. Wks. (Grosart) I. 69/1 Let's skrue our pamper'd hearts a pitch beyond the reach of dull-browd sorrow. **1648** J. BEAUMONT *Psyche* XXI. clxx, The Voice, though scrued to appear Divine, seem'd something out of tune to Her. **1672–5** COMBER *Comp. Temple* Pref. (1702) 6 When we need Variety and Novel Expressions to skrew us up into a Devotion. *a* **1677** [see PEG *sb.*[1] 2 a]. **1823** *Examiner* 272/2 The first series of calculations by which the Bourbon government was screwed up to undertake this awful.. business. **1840** TENNYSON *Vis. Sin* IV. vii, Let me screw thee up a peg: Let me loose thy tongue with wine. **1868** M. PATTISON *Academ. Org.* v. 269 To screw up their exertions to an unnatural pitch. **1873** TRISTRAM *Moab* v. 92, I had some difficulty in screwing my courage..to open an abscess. **1886** STEVENSON *Dr. Jekyll* x, My love of life screwed to the topmost peg.

refl. **1841–44** EMERSON *Ess.* vii. *Prudence* Wks. (Bohn) I. 100 He..must screw himself up to resolution. **1858** S. BROOKS *Gord. Knot* xlvi. (1860) 348 Whether Earnshaw screwed himself up to assent to the terms that night, or [etc.]. **1868** C. ROSSETTI *Let.* in *Life Anne Gilchrist* (1887) 173, I am not certain that in any case I should have screwed myself up to accept it [*sc.* an invitation], as I am shy amongst strangers.

c. With immaterial object; *esp.* to stretch, strain, force the meaning of (words).

1628 PRYNNE *Censure Mr. Cozens* 32 Those Prayers were published..in the very infancy of Reformation,..therefore our Author may not racke and scrue them to our Aged and noone-tide seasons of the Gospell. **1640** HOWELL *Dodona's Gr.* 127 Matters being scrued up to this height. *a* **1658** CLEVELAND *Poems* (1659) 98 Since then the Heroes of the pen with mee Nere scrue the sense With difference, We all agree, agree. **1664** POWER *Exp. Philos.* I. 69 Let us screw our Enquiry a little further. **1698** CLARK *Scripture Justif.* Ep., I have not first taken up a Notion and then screwed and wrested Scripture to countenance and confirm it. **1807** JEFFERSON *Writ.* (1830) IV. 67 The British commissioners appear to have screwed every article [of a treaty] as far as it would bear. **1790** BURKE *Fr. Rev.* 213 Or, rigidly screwing up right into wrong, did they convert a legal claim into a vexatious extortion? **1802–12** BENTHAM *Ration. Judic. Evid.* (1827) IV. 215 This may be done..by jurisprudential construction, screwing up misdemeanours into felonies.

d. ***to screw up***: to raise (a payment, rent, etc.) to an exacting or extortionate figure.

1631 W. BRADFORD *Hist. Plymouth Plant.* (1896) 357 He scrued vp his poore old father in laws accounte to aboue 200[li] and brought it on y[e] generall accounte. **1654** *Nicholas Papers* (Camden) II. 126 He is now only bussy to scrue up his pension by Lord Percy,..and he hath gott an order to be this day paid two pounds. **1696** in *Home Papers* (Hist. MSS. Comm., 1902) 270 When wee got 2 secretaries the admission of Writers was scrued up to 800 merks. **1697** VANBRUGH *Æsop* IV. ii, I screw up their rents till they break and run away. **1725** SWIFT *Drapier's Let.* vii. Wks. 1824 VII. 40 The rents of Ireland,..have been of late so enormously raised and screwed up. **1838** LYTTON *Alice* I. vii, While some of my tenants appear to pay nominal rents..others are screwed up higher than any man's in the country. **1883** *Fortn. Rev.* Nov. 676 Screw up your rents as your neighbours are doing.

4. To operate or adjust (an instrument) by turning its screw.

1708 J. PHILIPS *Cider* II. 100 When the Press, by utmost Vigour screw'd, Has drain'd the pulpous Mass. **1795** *Phil. Trans.* LXXXV. 140 Whilst the instrument was screwing to its focus. **1803** *Med. Jrnl.* X. 158 The surgeon always screws the tourniquet till he suppresses the pulse in the lower part of the limb. **1837** BROWNING *Strafford* I. i, How that man taught Tyranny..To ply the scourge yet screw the gag so close That strangled agony bleeds mute to death. **1902** HASLUCK *Bookbinding* iv. 52 The standing press..is screwed down tightly.

5. To extort by pressure. **a.** To force or draw out (information, a secret, the truth, etc.) *from* a person by moral pressure; to draw *out* by close questioning; to force the admission of.

In quot. 1715 lit. to force *out* by applying the thumbscrew.

1622 MABBE tr. *Aleman's Guzman d'Alf.* II. 65 A certaine friend of his,..told him..that euery one might scrue what he would from me, and draw all those secrets from me. **1632** B. JONSON *Magn. Lady* I. vii, *Int.* Hee Will screw you out a Secret from a Statist—. *Com.* So easie, as some Cobler wormes a Dog. **1650** STAPYLTON *Strada's Low-C. Wars* v. 137 Was any of his Ministers of State so dull-brained,..to suffer these mysterious parts of Government to be scrued out of his mouth or hands? **1699** W. CLAGETT *17 Serm.* 370 The court by multiplying questions may screw out the truth at last. *a* **1715** BURNET *Own Time* xvi. (1900) II. 423 Upon what was screwed out of these two persons,..six or seven gentlemen of quality, were clapt up. **1794** SCOTT *Let.* 5 Sept. in *Lockhart*, He tried them on every side, and screwed out of them the evidence they were so anxious to conceal. **1818** —— *Rob Roy* xix, I screwed out of him these particulars.

b. To force or exact (money) *out of* or *from* (an unwilling giver, a miserly or necessitous person); to get (something) *out of* (a person) by pressure.

1693 *Humours Town* 95 What they can in any way screw out of the Necessitous. **1700** T. BROWN *Amusem.* 127 Finding not a Penny to be screw'd out of the Prig. **1718** OZELL tr. *Tournefort's Voy. Levant* I. 128 They made a thousand Scruples before they would let us see them [*sc.* Alum mines]; only to skrew a little Mony out of us. **1838** DICKENS *Nich. Nick.* viii, They held..that their business.. was to get as much from every boy as could by possibility be screwed out of him. **1878** SIMPSON *Sch. Shaks.* I. 51 Cecil, not being able to screw it out of the Queen, had to pledge his own credit. **1882** *Century Mag.* XXIV. 785 The rate of taxation is simply the maximum that can be screwed out of the people.

6. To put compulsion upon, to constrain, oppress. **a.** To oppress (a person, esp. a tenant) with exactions; also ***to screw down, to screw out of***, to deprive of or dispossess of by extortion.

1658 *Whole Duty Man* ix. (1687) 90 Landlords, who.. rack and skrew them beyond the worth of the thing. **1792** BURKE *Corr.* (1844) IV. 80 The system of laws which..had screwed the Roman Catholics out of their landed property. **1826** COBBETT *Rural Rides* (1885) II. 191 In order to see how the labourers are now screwed down, look at the following facts. **1838** *Lett. fr. Madras* (1843) 225 They are so screwed by taxes,..that they never have a farthing in hand. **1842** LOVER *Handy Andy* li, 'The lord' had been screwed out of a good sum of money by way of separate maintenance. **1848** THACKERAY *Van. Fair* xxxix, He quarrelled with his agents and screwed his tenants by letter.

b. To force (a seller) to lower his price, to 'beat down'.

1677 YARRANTON *Eng. Improv.* 178 The severe customs.. that some of the greatest Traders..use unto some of their own Trade, by scruing and pinching them in such things they sell them in their necessity. **1745** *De Foe's Eng. Tradesman* (1841) I. xix. 179 They should not stand and haggle and screw the shopkeeper down. **1851** MAYHEW *Lond. Labour* I. 294/2 They're fairish customers, but they often screw me. **1853** LYTTON *My Novel* XII. vii, Why I am not sure that it is already bought—that is, paid for... Spend-quick complains that Levy screws him.

c. To examine rigorously. *Obs.* exc. in *U.S.* college slang (see quot. 1851). Also *absol.*

1626 B. JONSON *Staple of N.* v. iii, And there hee sits like an old worme of the peace.., screwing, Examining, and committing the poore curres. **1639** N. N. tr. *Du Boscq's Compl. Woman* Pref., They examine all the conceits, they weigh all the words, they scrue all the syllables [orig. F. *ils espluchent toutes les syllabes*]. **1851** B. H. HALL *College Words* 265 *Screw*, to press with an excessive and unnecessarily minute examination. **1851** O. W. HOLMES *Song of 'Twenty-nine'* 10 At last the day is ended, The tutor screws no more.

d. *slang* (chiefly *N. Amer.*). To defraud (a person, esp. of money), to cheat; to deceive, to 'rook'; freq. as *pa. ppl.* in ***to be*** (or ***get***) ***screwed***.

1900 *Dialect Notes* II. 58 *Screwed*,..in phrase 'to get *screwed*'..deceived. **1936** J. STEINBECK *In Dubious Battle* vi. 94 'What you want to strike for?' ''Cause we're gettin' screwed..the company's store is takin' five per cent house-cut.' **1959** J. OSBORNE *Paul Slickey* I. v. 48 We want to screw, screw, screw the Income Tax Man. **1966** H. KEMELMAN *Saturday Rabbi went Hungry* xxxiii. 213 In the business dealings between Hirsh and Goralsky, it wasn't Goralsky that got screwed. It was the other way around. **1974** *Saturday Night* (Toronto) Feb. 12/3 Your chances of being screwed by a Canadian factory owner then were just as good as your chances of being screwed by an American factory owner now. **1979** *Tucson Mag.* Jan. 24/2 The Richard Nixon school of thought on public scandal, that being that it's all right to screw the people as long as you were given a large mandate in the previous election.

7. To produce, attain, or elicit with an effort. Also with *out*, *up*, or complementary phrase.

1679 ALSOP *Melius Inq.* II. v. 325 All that can possibly be screwed out of these instances of Paternal Authority is no more than this. **1814** *Sporting Mag.* XLIII. 47 One of our Place-mongers..To serve a Premier and betray the Nation At length screwed out a situation. *c* **1820** S. ROGERS *Italy*, *Bergamo* 54 Screwing a smile into his dinnerless face. *a* **1848** O. W. HOLMES *Nux Postc.* 33 It's a vastly pleasing prospect, when you're screwing out a laugh, That your very next year's income is diminished by a half. **1859** DARWIN *Life & Lett.* (1887) II. 106 If you could screw time to send me ever so brief an answer. **1869** J. GREENWOOD *Seven Curses Lond.* ix. 170 If I entrust my tailor with stuff for a suit, and it afterwards comes to my knowledge that he has 'screwed' an extra waistcoat out of it. **1874** HELPS *Soc. Pressure* ii. 32 Another inventor screws light out of coals. **1898** J. B. WOLLOCOMBE *Morn till Eve* ii. 15 Gillard..saw his opponent in front of him, doing his utmost to screw up a trot.

8. *intr.* To be parsimonious.

1849 THACKERAY *Let.* 10 Apr., I must screw and save in order to pay off the money. **1855** —— *Newcomes* xliv, Did you ever hear of me screwing? No, I spend my money like a man.

III. To turn a screw.

9. *trans.* To work (a screw or something fashioned as a screw) by turning.

1635 QUARLES *Embl.* I. Invoc., Rowze thee, my soul,.. Skrue up the heightned pegs Of thy Sublime Theorboe foure notes higher. **1640** HOWELL *Dodona's Gr.* 23 He resolvd to governe them by subalterne Ministers, who it seems scrud up the pinnes of power too high. **1648** WILKINS *Math. Magic* I. ix. 59 The chief inconvenience of this instrument is, that in a short space it will be screwed unto its full length. **1665** HOOKE *Microgr.* 13 That a pin be screw'd so firm and hard, that though it has a convenient head to it, yet it can by no means be unscrew'd by the fingers. **1680** MOXON *Mech. Exerc.* xii. 208 Screw your Pike wider or closer, according as the length of your Work requires. **1688** HOLME *Armoury* III. xxii. (Roxb.) 273/1 The Spanner..is put on the Nut heads and so to screw and unscrew them at pleasure. **1856** *Farmer's Mag.* Nov. 396 A series of posts driven or 'screwed' (with Mitchell's Archimedian screw) into the ground. **1869** C. KNIGHT *Mechanician* 122 The simplest mode..consists in screwing a hard steel screwed plate on to the piece to be made into a screw. **1879** *Cassell's Techn. Educ.* I. 34/2 Their nuts [may be] kept tight by the simple process of screwing a second nut down home on the top of the first.

10. a. To insert or fix one thing *in, into, on, to,* or *upon* another or two things *together* by a turning or twisting movement, one or both having the surface or part of it cut into a screw for the purpose.

1612 WOODALL *Surg. Mate,* Enema Fumosum (1639) G 2, Put the pipe prepared into the fundament..with the first short pipe screwed to it. *Ibid.* G 2 b, The stopple to be screwed upon the head thereof. **1687** A. LOVELL tr. *Thevenot's Trav.* II. 79 These trumpets are taken in two at the middle..; when they have a mind to sound, they skrew the two parts together. **1688** HOLME *Armoury* III. xv. (Roxb.) 22/1 A pockett Inkhorne with..the penner or top screwed on it. **1774** MACKENZIE *Maritime Surv.* 28 Screw the Ball firm in the Socket. **1849** MACAULAY *Hist. Eng.* xiii. III. 371 Mackay..ordered all his bayonets to be so formed that they might be screwed upon the barrel without stopping it up. **1883** F. CAMPIN *Details of Mach.* xi. 159 The bolt is screwed into some part of the cast-iron framework.

b. *fig.* †(*a*) To implant firmly (a notion) by means of gradual insinuation; to contrive to insert. Also *refl.* to insinuate oneself by degrees (into a person's favour, etc.). *Obs.* (*b*) colloq. ***to have one's head screwed on right*** or ***the right way***, and similar phrases, implying the ability to use one's brains to one's own advantage, or to 'know what one is about'. ***to screw one's head on tight***, to make an effort to prevent its being 'turned'.

1611 SPEED *Hist. Gt. Brit.* VII. xliv. (1632) 414 That opinion was skrewed deeper into their fearefull conceit by a cloud appearing. **1621** BURTON *Anat. Mel.* II. iii. II. 389 Others buy titles,..and by all meanes skrew themselues into ancient families. **1622** MABBE tr. *Aleman's Guzman d'Alf.* II. 339 Thus by little and little, I went scruing my selfe into his seruice, getting more ground still vpon him. **1634** SIR T. HERBERT *Trav.* 160 Howbeit a while after they got breath, and screwed into their good fauour and opinion King Cazell. **1642** FULLER *Holy & Prof. St.* I. ii. 5 Ill customs being not knockt, but insensibly scru'd into our Souls. **1674** *Govt. Tongue* ix. 157 No discourse can be administred, but..they [*sc.* Boasters] will..screw in here and there some intimations of what they did or said. **1667** DRYDEN & DK. NEWCASTLE *Sir M. Mar-all* II. ii, You would do well to screw yourself into her father's good opinion. **1680** C. NESSE *Church Hist.* 47 He trys his skill by an intrinsick engine, screwing himself into the minds of Israel. **1821** P. EGAN *Life in London* v. 278 A well-known dashing *Prig,* whose *Head* was considered to have been *screwed on* the right way. **1826** SCOTT *Prov. Antiq. Scot.* 194 He had screwed himself into the partial confidence of Laird Bour. **1855** BURN *Autobiog. Beggar-boy* (1859) 95 It was true I had a small quantity of brains, but the fact was, my head was not screwed on right to enable me to turn them to my advantage. **1897** M. CREIGHTON *Let.* Life & Lett. (1904) II. vii. 235, I feel it necessary to screw my head on tight and go my own way gently. **1900** *Daily News* 12 Dec. 7/5 Elizabeth has, to use a slang phrase, 'her head very well screwed on'.

c. *intr.* in passive sense. To be adapted for joining or taking apart by means of component screws.

1680 MOXON *Mech. Exerc.* xiv. 235 A Brass Coller with a Female Screw in it, to screw on the Mandrel. **1776** G. SEMPLE *Building in Water* 18 The Rods were in three Pieces ..which screwed together occasionally. **1791** GILPIN *Forest Scenery* II. 43 He carried with him a gun, which screwed into three parts, and which he could easily conceal in the lining of his coat. **1821** *John Bull* 18 June 215/1 The head [of the vessel] screws off at the middle of the neck. **1881** F. CAMPIN *Mech. Engin.* iv. 53 The face-plate which screws on the mandrils.

d. trans. *to screw out*: to take out (a screw) by turning; to unscrew. *rare.*

1611 SPEED *Hist. Gt. Brit.* IX. xviii. (1632) 904 Euill opinions once fastened in mens hearts, hardly can be screwed out againe. **1841** *Penny Cycl.* XXI. 109/1 An apparatus for screwing the patterns..out of the mould, so as to leave the impression of the thread uninjured.

11. *intr.* To penetrate as a screw; to penetrate with a winding course. In quots. *fig.*, to worm one's way.

1614 C. BROOKE *Ghost Rich. III*, xxxix, Proud of this Knowledge I scru'd into the state, And of that Nature got intelligence. **1627** P. FLETCHER *Locusts* II. xxviii, By flattery They [*sc.* the Jesuits] worme and scrue into their conscience. **1640** HOWELL *Dodona's Gr.* 80 They have a way to scrue into the most inmost Closets of Princes. **1642** D. ROGERS *Naaman* 447 To scrue and dive into the hearts of men by degrees.

IV. To move in a twisting direction.

12. a. *trans.* To twist round, esp. to twist with violence so as to alter the shape. ***to screw one's neck***: to kill by wringing the neck. ***to screw up***: to twist (e.g. a piece of paper) into a spiral form.

a **1711** KEN *Hymns Evang.* Poet. Wks. 1721 I. 173 The Pillars on which arch'd Heav'ns rely, Were on their sev'ral Bases screw'd awry. **1852** DICKENS *Bleak Ho.* viii, They all pinched me at once, and in a dreadfully expert way: screwing up such little pieces of my arms that I could hardly forbear crying out. **1869** 'WAT. BRADWOOD' *The O.V.H.* xxiv, Jack screwed his moustache,..in deep deliberation. **1872** *Routledge's Every Boy's Ann.* Dec. 46/1 I'll screw his neck. **1888** F. HUME *Madame Midas* I. ii, I wish you'd screw that bird's neck, Slivers; he's too clever by half.

b. To spoil, ruin; to pervert; to upset, disturb mentally. *U.S. colloq.*

1938 'E. QUEEN' *Four of Hearts* iv. 54 'For gossakes!' yelled Lew, jumping up. 'That screws everything!' **1955** W. GADDIS *Recognitions* I. v. 183 She got fed up with him screwing the Sunday roast, so she shot herself. **1968** *Win* 15 Oct. 4/1 Democracy has gotten screwed, not just in Chicago but long before that. **1976** *National Observer* (U.S.) 14 Aug. 1/2 Your parents' divorce can screw you all over. It did me. I was shocked.

c. *colloq.* (orig. and chiefly *U.S.*). ***to screw up***: (*a*) *intr.*, to blunder, make an error; (*b*) *trans.*, to make a mess of, spoil, ruin; to confuse, upset, disturb mentally.

This use may have originated as a euphemism for *to fuck up* (see FUCK *v.* 3) after sense 13 below.

1942 *Yank* 23 Dec. 19 You screw up on the drill field! You goof off at inspection. **1943** M. HART *Winged Victory* I. ix. 90 My father-in-law says the OPA is screwing everything up. **1946** *Amer. Jrnl. Sociol.* Mar. 419 The common obscene expression which has the meaning in some way or another to bungle a job or to make a bad choice... There are a few acceptable substitutes such as 'screw up'. **1951** J. D. SALINGER *Catcher in Rye* xix. 176 It really screws up my sex life something awful. **1955** W. GADDIS *Recognitions* I. v. 182 He's a drunk... He gets all screwed up with religion. **1967** *Melody Maker* 16 Dec. 8/6 Those people who are supposed to be propagating the Lord's word—they're screwing it all up. **1972** M. J. BOSSE *Incident at Naha* 83 Did I screw up by admitting that you knew about the package? **1978** J. IRVING *World according to Garp* xviii. 382 He said that women's lib had screwed up his wife so much that she divorced him. **1979** 'A. HAILEY' *Overload* I. i. 6 But you and your people really screwed up today! **1981** P. NIESEWAND *Word of Gentleman* xxvii. 188 Military men usually screw things up ..and the people are bloody glad to see the back of them.

13. *coarse slang.* **a.** *intr.* To copulate, have sexual intercourse (*with* a person). **b.** *trans.* Usu. of a man: to copulate with, have sexual intercourse with (someone).

1725 *New Canting Dict.*, *To Screw*, to copulate with a Woman. **1796** F. GROSE *Class. Dict. Vulgar Tongue* (ed. 3), *To screw*, to copulate. **1927** O. W. HOLMES *Let.* 1 July in *Holmes-Laski Lett.* (1953) II. v. 958 It is enough to mention his emulating a spider by screwing a woman while he killed her by biting and, put in as an extra, chewing her throat. **1937** J. T. FARRELL *Can all this Grandeur Perish* 147 Him.. picking up bums in public dance halls and screwing them in hallways and taxicabs. **1945** G. ENDORE *Methinks the Lady* vi. 120 She thinks just because she married a sailor she can screw the whole Navy. **1952** S. KAUFFMANN *Philanderer* (1953) iv. 66 The first thing we do is..to run a few signed stories in the book, instead of all that anonymous 'I-got-screwed' stuff. **1958** N. LEVINE *Canada made Me* 16 Those who cry the most saying goodbye, screw the first. **1963** T. PYNCHON *V.* i. 10 Santa's bag is filled with all your dreams come true: Nickel beers that sparkle like champagne, Barmaids who all love to screw. **1968** *Southerly* XXVIII. 38 'We have a free relationship,' Joe said. 'She's gone off to screw some old friend.' **1972** 'G. HARDING' *Skytrap* iii. 48 You've spent the afternoon screwing with *him*, haven't you? **1975** D. LODGE *Changing Places* i. 7 All women longed to be screwed by a god, it was the source of all religion.

c. In phr. ***to screw around*** (AROUND *adv.* 5 a): to be sexually promiscuous, to 'sleep around'; hence in weakened sense, to mess or fool about. orig. *U.S.*

1939 J. STEINBECK *Grapes of Wrath* ii. 14 Goin' all over the world drinkin' and raisin' hell and screwin' around. **1950** H. E. GOLDIN et al. *Dict. Amer. Underworld Lingo* 186/2 *Screw around*,..to clown and play the fool, paying scant attention to business. 'Don't you screw around when you're hustling (stealing) with me.' **1964** *New Statesman* 17 Apr. 610/3 He drinks.., screws around, lives in debt, cannot get his work published. **1972** D. S. VISCOTT *Making of Psychiatrist* iii. 43 Her husband is screwing around and she feels abandoned. **1974** *Times* 1 Apr. 6/8 All right—I am going to get him over because I am not going to screw around with this thing. **1978** R. LUDLUM *Holcroft Covenant* iv. 51 They're honest guys. They wouldn't screw around. **1981** T. HEALD *Murder at Moose Jaw* vi. 67 I've been sort of screwing around a little. .. I don't want to upset my husband, but a girl only has one life.

d. Used in imprecations and exclamations, as an equivalent to FUCK *v.* 2.

1949 A. MILLER *Death of Salesman* I. 61 'In the business world some of them think you're crazy.'.. 'Screw the business world!' **1960** R. DAHL *Kiss, Kiss* 298 'Don't shout. There might be keepers.' 'Screw the keepers!' he cried. **1962** 'E. McBAIN' *Like Love* vii. 102 'You sore?' 'Yes.' 'Screw you,' Kling said. **1979** 'A. HAILEY' *Overload* II. v. 129 She was drowned out by a chorus of, 'screw the profiteers!' and 'power belongs to the people!'

14. a. To twist awry, contort (the features, body, mouth); to twist (one's head, oneself) *round* in order to look at something.

1599 B. JONSON *Ev. Man out of Hum.* v. i, Screw your face a t'one side thus, & Protest. **1612** *Two Noble K.* v. i. 117 The aged Crampe Had screw'd his square foote round, The Gout had knit his fingers into knots. **1635-56** COWLEY *Davideis* III. 55 Sometimes a violent laughter scru'd his face. **1645** QUARLES *Solomon's Recant.* ii. *Solil.* ii. Wks. (Grosart) II. 174/2 What pleasure is't, to skrue An Antick face and grimme. **1673** DRYDEN *Marr. à la Mode* IV. iii, Oh how you'd..scrue your Face into a submissive Smile. *a* **1680** S. BUTLER *Characters* (1908) 134 He is always giving Aim to State Affairs, and believes by screwing of his Body he can make them shoot which Way he pleases. **1815** SCOTT *Guy M.* ii, Some grotesque habits of..screwing his visage while reciting his task, made poor Sampson the ridicule of all his school-companions. **1821** W. IRVING *Sk.-Bk.* I. 74 (Rip van Winkle) The self-important man..screwed down the corners of his mouth, and shook his head. **1837** DICKENS *Pickw.* ii, Screwing himself round to catch a glimpse in the glass of the waist buttons. **1881** FENN *Vicar's People* xlvi, Setting his teeth, and screwing his mahogany-brown face into a state of rigid determination. **1889** F. COWPER *Capt. of the Wight* 304 From where Ralph stood, by screwing his head a little he could just see the top of the masts.

fig. **1647** C. HARVEY *School of Heart* Poems (Grosart) 171 An heart..That's..screw'd aside with stubborne wilfulnesse, Is onely fit to be cast forth.

b. ***to screw up***: to contract the surrounding parts of (the mouth, eyes).

1743 FIELDING *Journey fr. this World* I. ii, But that female spirit screwing up her mouth, answered, she wondered at the curiosity of some people. **1852** DICKENS *Bleak Ho.* xvi, Jo screws up his mouth into a whistle. **1883** F. M. CRAWFORD *Dr. Claudius* ii, Mr. Barker screwed up his eyes and put out his jaw.

†**c.** To produce (a gesture) by contortions. *Obs.*

1635 QUARLES *Embl.* I. x. 41 See how their curved bodies wreathe, and skrue Such antick shapes as Proteus never knew. *Ibid.* IV. iii. 193 My antick knees can turne upon the hinges Of Complement, and skrue a thousand Cringes.

15. a. *trans.* To look at, watch (a person); *spec.*, to eye (a person) before a fight. **b.** *intr.* To look. *slang* (orig. *Austral.*).

1919 [see SCREW *sb.*[1] 18]. **1938** F. D. SHARPE *Sharpe of Flying Squad* 333 Screw..can also mean 'to look'. ('Screw over there', 'look over there'.) **1960** *Guardian* 29 Dec. 3/1 The accused..told them to stop 'screwing' him, which meant apparently to stop looking at him. **1964** *New Statesman* 10 Apr. 555/2 'No, no,' the Mods in the dance hall shouted 'screw..means to look you up and down.' **1978** P. MARSH et al. *Rules of Disorder* iv. 104 You get someone screwing you (staring) or just standing there all cocky like.

16. To propel by a spiral movement; to force or squeeze (one's body) by a tortuous movement *into, through,* etc. (a comparatively small space).

1635 SWAN *Spec. M.* vi. §2 (1643) 201 They [springs] do (as it were) scrue themselves up to the convenientest place of breaking out. **1669** STURMY *Mariner's Mag.* v. i. 2 A Silk thred [is] twisted and screwed through a small hole..and fastned with a small wooden pin. **1690** C. NESSE *Hist. & Myst. O. & N. Test.* I. 109 If the subtle serpent can but see a hole..he will easily screw in his whole body. **1719** D'URFEY *Pills* I. 127 He screw'd himself under the Bed. **1812** SCOTT *Fam. Lett.* 2 Sept. (1894) I. 257 We are all screwed into the former farmhouse. **1835** [see SCREWER]. **1872** BAGEHOT *Physics & Pol.* (1876) 42 They have screwed themselves into the uncomfortable corners of a complex life. **1868** PITT-RIVERS *Prim. Warfare* II. 125 [The boomerang] is caused to rise by virtue of its rotation, screwing itself up in the air.

17. *intr.* To wind spirally.

1823 J. BADCOCK *Dom. Amusem.* 55 They [*sc.* the shoots of the honeysuckle] coalesce for mutual support, the one screwing round the other to the right, the other to the left.

18. *Sporting.* **a.** intr. *Rowing.* (See quot. 1898.)

1875 W. B. WOODGATE *Oars & Sculls* viii. 68 Possibly.. each man [*sc.* of a pair of oarsmen] may screw to match the other instinctively. **1898** *Encycl. Sport* II. 297/2 (Rowing) *Screw*, to swing the body from one side to the other during the stroke, instead of swinging straight backward and forward. If the man swings toward his oar during the stroke he is said to screw 'into the boat'; if away from it 'out of the boat'.

b. trans. *Rugby Football.* To cause (the scrummage or one's opponents in a scrummage) to twist round by pushing in a body to the right or left. Also *absol.* (Said of either set of forwards composing a scrummage.)

1887 SHEARMAN *Athletics & Football* 311 One team.. cleverly 'screwing' the scrimmage and taking the ball out. **1889** H. VASSALL *Rugby Football* 32 It is no use trying to screw as long as your opponents have command of the ball. You must then..devote your energies to stopping your opponents from screwing you. **1897** *Encycl. Sport* I. 408/2 You must wheel to the side on which you can best screw off your adversaries, and then rush ahead with the ball. **1901** *Scotsman* 11 Mar. 4/8 The Englishmen screwed the first scrum in capital style.

c. *Games.* To impart a screw or twist to (the ball); to cause to swerve. Also *absol.*

1839 *Bentley's Miscell.* VI. 348 Cue in hand,..chalking, screwing, and pocketing..after a most extraordinary fashion. **1881** FORGAN *Golfer's Handbk.* 35 *Screw*, see *Draw* [i.e. to drive widely to the left hand]. **1887** SHEARMAN *Athletics & Football* 350 The back knows..when he should kick true, or when he should 'screw'.

d. *intr.* (for *refl.*) *Racing.* Of a horse: To force his way *through.* Also *trans.* Of a rider: To force (a horse) *over* (an obstacle); ***to screw in***, to force to the front at the finish of a race.

1840 Blaine *Encycl. Rural Sports* §1658. 470 Others [*sc.* horses] however screw through, that is, they actually push themselves through these hedges. **1842** Lever *J. Hinton* viii, I have been trying a new horse in the Park, screwing him over all the fences. **1856** H. H. Dixon *Post & Paddock* 48 Alfred Day..screwing in Vivandière half a head in front of Butler.

19. *intr.* Of Polar ice-floes: To ram together.

1901 [see screwing *vbl. sb.*]. **1909** *Westm. Gaz.* 4 Sept. 9/2 At the 88th degree the ice screwed badly.

20. To depart hastily, go away; to get *out*, push *off*. *slang* (orig. *U.S.*).

1896 Ade *Artie* iii. 26, 'Look here,' I says, 'you screw right away from here.' **1903** A. H. Lewis *Boss* ii. 18 'Screw out!' cried he... 'We don't want any of your talk!.. Put him out!' **1912** —— *Apaches of New York* iv. 84 As I don't want no part of it, I screws out. **1947** *Horizon* Sept. 205 Come on, let's screw out of here and find something. **1974** D. Richards *Coming of Winter* i. 23 Now if you don't screw off out of here, I'll use the phone.

V. In various uses from senses of the sb.

21. *trans.* To break into (a house, etc.) by means of a 'screw' or skeleton key. Also, more generally, to break into (a house, safe, etc.), to burgle.

1812 J. H. Vaux *Flash Dict.* Mem. 1819 II. 204 To screw a place is to enter it by false keys. **1879** *Macm. Mag.* XL. 503/1 We went and screwed (broke into) his place, and got thirty-two quid. **1896** A. Morrison *Child of Jago* xxiv. 236 He was..King of High Mobsmen... He did no vulgar thievery: he never screwed a chat, nor claimed a peter. **1938** F. D. Sharpe *Sharpe of Flying Squad* 333 *Screw*, to break open houses and safes. **1953** H. Clevely *Public Enemy* xxvii. 219 You want to go inside for screwin' that ware'ouse. **1958** [see bung *sb.*[4]]. **1973** 'J. Patrick' *Glasgow Gang Observed* x. 88 Yir a brave wee boay that'll screw three shoaps in the wan night.

22. To furnish with a helical groove or ridge; †to rifle (a firearm) (*obs.*); to furnish (a screw-blank, pin, cylinder, etc.) with a thread or worm; to cut a screw-thread *upon*.

1635 A. Rotsipen in *Abridgm. Specif. Patents, Fire-arms* (1859) I. 22 To rifle, cutt out, or screwe barrells as wyde or as clos or as deepe or as shallowe as shalbe required. **1680** R. H. *Milit. Discipl.* I. ii. 22 Carabins..whose Barrel..is screwed and rifled: that is to say, wrought and crevassed in the inside..in form of a Screw. **1833** J. Holland *Manuf. Metal* II. 145 The vice-pin intended to be screwed..is placed in the stock. **1869** C. Knight *Mechanician* 346 Screwed plugs..for screwing nuts to stated diameters. **1880** *Daily Tel.* 23 Dec., The breech part,..with the front end screwed for the purpose of uniting with the barrel.

absol. **1870** *Amateur Mech. Workshop* 46 It is of great importance when screwing..that the pin should be passed perpendicularly through the tool.

23. *intr.* To travel on the water by means of a screw-propeller; also *trans.* in ***to screw its way***.

1860 W. H. Russell *Diary India* I. vii. 94 We lay-to during the night, and now we are screwing up against the.. current. **1862** H. Marryat *Year in Sweden* I. 165 We screwed slowly along till we landed on the little jetty. **1898** *Westm. Gaz.* 1 Sept. 2/1 The boat rolled and screwed its way northward.

24. *trans.* To make a screw of (a horse), to 'crock'.

1890 'R. Boldrewood' *Col. Reformer* (1891) 102 Jedwood will see you far enough before he gives you another one in his place, if you screw him doing his work.

VI. 25. The verb-stem in comb. **a.** with advs., as **screw back** (see quot.); **screw-down** *a.*, adapted to be closed by screwing; **screw-in, -on** *adjs.*, that may be attached by screwing into or on to something else; also as *sb.*; **b.** with sbs., as **screw cannon** (also **screw-back cannon**) *Billiards*, a cannon made by striking the ball very low down and so causing it to recoil from the object ball; **screw kick, shot, stroke** (in various games: see quots.), one that causes the ball to swerve; **screw-smile** *nonce-wd.*, a forced smile.

Most of these admit of being regarded as combinations of screw *sb.*[1] II.

1884 W. Cook *Billiards* 12 **Screw Back*, the same rotary motion [as that described under *screw*] causing the ball to run backwards after striking another ball. **1866** Pardon *Billiard Bk.* xi. 125 Another very good stroke is the Wide *Screw Canon... This may be made with a slow twist.. from the baulk. **1873** Bennett & 'Cavendish' *Billiards* 325 A screw-back cannon may here be made by playing a three-quarter ball on the red, without side, No. 2 strength. **1862** *Catal. Internat. Exhib.* II. x. 54 Strong round-way *screw-down bib and stop cocks. **1889** Welch *Text Bk. Naval Archit.* xi. 124 Their upper ends are fitted with screw-down valves. **1924** G. L. Mallory *Let.* 12 Apr. in E. F. Norton *Fight for Everest: 1924* (1925) 215 Pukka wooden tables with three-ply wooden tops and *screw-in legs. **1966** P. O'Donnell *Sabre-Tooth* iii. 41 Thin steel shafts made from short screw-in sections. **1976** *Alyn & Deeside Observer* 10 Dec. 3/2 A player can cost his club almost £65 a season in boots alone! *Screw-ins [*i.e.* screw-in studs] cost about £17, rubbers about £14 and flats (training shoes) £7. **1887** Shearman *Athletics & Football* 349 The back may turn the ball with a *screw kick. **1928** A. L. Matthison *Stoving Finishes* 54 A *screw-on cap for instance, involving the operations of stamp, screw and knurling machine, is easily withstood by a high grade coating lacquer. **1935** 'G. Orwell' *Clergyman's Daughter* i. 13 The communion bell had had a screw-on clapper, which had come loose. **1967** [see O.D. s.v. O 5 d]. **1979** *Amat. Photographer* 10 Jan. 74/1 Buy enough storage bottles, with screw-on caps, to accommodate all the liquids you use. **1887** *Field* 5 Nov. 714/1 [Assoc. Football] The Harrow captain..putting in a low *screw shot. **1897** *Encycl. Sport* I. 252/2 [Croquet] The chop, *screw, or stop stroke. *Ibid.* 254/1 It resembles the screw shot in billiards. **1879** Meredith *Egoist* xiii, The well-known *screw-smile of duty upholding weariness worn to inanition.

screwable ('skru:əb(ə)l), *a.* [f. screw *v.* + -able.] Capable of being screwed.

18.. *Engineer* LXIX. 411 (Cent.) A screwable bracket.

screwage ('skru:ɪdʒ). *rare*$^{-1}$. [f. screw *sb.*[1] + -age.] The action or process of screwing.

1865 Carlyle *Fredk. Gt.* xx. vi. IX. 105 The Butes and Hardwickes working incessantly with such rare power of leverage and screwage in the interior parts.

screwball ('skru:bɔ:l), *sb.* and *a.* Chiefly *U.S.* Also **screw-ball, screw ball.** [f. screw *sb.*[1] + ball *sb.*[1]; for sense 2 cf. oddball.]

A. *sb.* **1.** †**a.** *Cricket.* A ball bowled with 'screw' or spin. *Obs.* **b.** *Baseball.* A ball pitched with reverse spin against the natural curve. Also *fig.* and *attrib.*

1866 'Capt. Crawley' *Cricket* 35 A 'screw' ball, which in slow bowling would describe the arc of a circle from the pitch to the wicket, becomes in fast bowling a sharp angle. *Ibid.* 36 The dotted line shows the direction of a slow screw ball *screwing* in from the leg. **1928** *N.Y. Times* 7 Oct. xi. 2/3 Haines is a large, healthy individual with..a 'screw ball' that ducks under many a well-meant swing with a hickory bludgeon. **1933** *Ibid.* 2 Aug. 20/1 Hubbell pitched his customary shrewd game for five innings then his deceptive screw ball lost its baffling influence. **1937** *Sun* (N.Y.) 1 June 24/3 'I thought Joe Robinson was mentioned [for the Supreme Court].' 'Yes, but it seems the President insists on screwball pitching.' **1949** *Sun* (Baltimore) 15 Oct. 12/5 Buxton, a 35-year-old screwball artist, was purchased from Oakland. **1960** *Time* 3 Oct. 47/2 Spahn started to perfect a screwball and a slider. **1971** L. Koppett *N.Y. Times Guide Spectator Sports* i. 15 Baseball men use the term screwball for either type of reverse curve, but the pitch is used primarily by left-handers.

2. a. An eccentric; a madman, a 'nut-case'; a fool. Freq. as a term of mild abuse. *slang.*

1933 P. Gallico in *Sat. Even. Post* 12 Aug. 56/3 McKabe was already heading for the door. He heard Billers say: 'Who is that screwball?' **1939** Wodehouse *Uncle Fred in Springtime* viii. 115 You are going to Blandings Castle now, no doubt, to inspect some well-connected screwball? **1944** H. S. Truman *Let.* 18 Aug. in M. Truman *Harry S. Truman* (1973) ix. 184 He should have been arrested as a screwball but wasn't. **1954** J. Steinbeck *Sweet Thursday* xxv. 163 He was a scientist, but whether brilliant or a screwball nobody ever knew. **1956** E. Pound tr. *Sophocles's Women of Trachis* 20 No use bothering with this screw-ball. **1956** W. H. Whyte *Organization Man* (1957) xviii. 239 To talk of the problem in terms of the lone genius or the screwball is to confuse the issue. **1978** S. Brill *Teamsters* v. 186 The word one got on Carey at Teamsters headquarters..was that he was a 'screwball', 'a weirdo', a 'strange guy', or..'a naïve kid'.

b. *spec.* Used, chiefly *attrib.* or as *adj.* (esp. as ***screwball comedy***) of a kind of fast-moving, irreverent comedy film produced in the U.S. in the 1930s, of which eccentric characters were the chief feature, or of persons, etc., connected with such films.

1938 *Collier's* 26 Feb. 58/3 Wellman was named 'Screw-ball Bill' six or seven years ago and has, beyond any doubt, lived up to his title. **1938** *N.Y. Times* 2 Sept. 21/2 Metro-Goldwyn-Mayer..has popped up with another of those screwball comedies—this one called 'Three Loves Has Nancy'. **1939** L. Jacobs *Rise of Amer. Film* 536 Among the women Carole Lombard is the most outstanding in her 'screw-ball' activity. **1959** *Times* 6 Apr. 3/4 The situation, that of girl thwarted at every turn in her moneyless search for somewhere to sleep, suggests a 1930s screwball comedy. **1974** S. H. Scheuer *Movie Bk.* 190 Perhaps James Whale's *Remember Last Night?* (1935) first brings together all of the elements of the classic screwball comedy—beautiful people with money to burn [etc.]... The pace and movement are pure screwball. *Ibid.*, [Cary] Grant developed the perfect screwball hero. **1978** *Time* 3 July 44/2 *Heaven Can Wait* is a light, screwball fantasy about a Los Angeles Rams quarterback (Beatty) who dies and comes back to life as an eccentric millionaire.

3. *slang.* Fast jazz improvisation or unrestrained 'swing'. Also *attrib.*

1936 *Delineator* Nov. 10/2 Barrel-house, gut-bucket, screw-ball, Dixieland..the cats are lickin' their chops, *they're* friskin' their whiskers. **1938** [see barrel-house 2]. **1947** R. P. Dodge in A. McCarthy *Jazzbook* 64 When inspiration leaves the player..he becomes what is known as a screw-ball player. I must say that I prefer the jump style to the screw-ball style.

B. *adj.* Eccentric; mad, crazy. Also *absol. slang.*

1936 *Metronome* Feb. 21/4 *Screw-ball*, crazy without knowing. **1938** E. Hemingway *Fifth Column* (1939) ii. i. 53, *I* think he is screwball. **1943** R. Chandler *Lady in Lake* (1944) xxxi. 167 That purple hat.., that messed-up make-up.., the jittery screwball manner. **1948** F. Brown *Murder can be Fun* (1951) iv. 51, I know it all sounds screwball, but here we go. **1958** S. Ellin *Eighth Circle* iii. i. 173 'It must have done you a lot of good.' 'If I get home in one piece from this screwball deal, I'll know it did.' **1976** *National Observer* (U.S.) 6 Mar. 11/3 You and I know that there is a correlation between the creative and the screwball. **1976** J. McClure *Rogue Eagle* ii. 34 The only whites..are two old guys who run the place—a couple of screwball recluses.

Hence as *v. intr.*, to pitch a screwball; also *transf.*, to travel like a screwball; **'screwballism,** (*a*) screwball behaviour, lunacy; (*b*) the screwball genre in films.

1942 Berrey & Van den Bark *Amer. Thes. Slang* §676/15 *Pitch a curve*,..put hooks on the ball, screwball. **1946** J. W. Day *Harvest Adventure* iv. 48 Partridges sky-rocketed and screwballed overhead and fled to safety. **1947** *Sun* (Baltimore) 9 Aug. 8/4 Jesse Flores was screwballing along with no signs of trouble. **1971** D. E. Westlake *I gave at the Office* 182 The dividing line between apocalyptic visions and screwballism is a very fine one indeed. **1974** S. H. Scheuer *Movie Bk.* 190 William Powell playing the servant to a whole wacky family in *My Man Godfrey*,..or Claudette Colbert smiling her way through *Midnight*,..immediately come to mind as high points of screwballism.

screwdriver ('skru:draɪvə(r)).

1. A tool for turning screws into or out of their places. It is shaped like a chisel, with a blunt end which fits into the nick in the head of the screw.

1779 in *Dict. Amer. Eng.* (1944) IV. 2045/1, 1 doz. draw rings, screw driver, and gimlet. **1812** P. Nicholson *Mech. Exerc.* 353 Screw Driver, a tool used to turn screws into their places. **1840** Thackeray *Catherine* vii, A screwdriver and a crowbar. **1842** Gwilt *Archit.* §2109 Some [bits]..are provided with a screw-driver for sinking small screws into wood.

Comb. **1893** *Dunglison's Dict. Med. Sci.* (ed. 21), *Screw-driver teeth*, peculiar teeth seen in young subjects of hereditary syphilis.

2. *punningly.* One who drives a 'screwy' horse.

1835 Apperley *Nimrod's Hunting Tours* 215 (Farmer) Mr. Charles Boultbee, the best screw driver in England.

3. A cocktail made of vodka and iced orange juice. orig. *U.S.*

1956 *House & Garden* Feb. 112/2 *Screwdriver.* This has become the most popular drink the West Coast has seen in years. Merely add 2 ounces of vodka to a tall glass of orange juice. Ideal for Sunday brunch. **1959** M. Dolinsky *There is no Silence* v. 79, I didn't have the *screwdriver* she wanted, but she settled for a bourbon and soda. **1967** F. Warner *Madrigals* 30 Draining down screwdrivers in topless Broadway. **1977** *Times* 10 Aug. 14/4 The men who dispense manhattans, grasshoppers and screwdrivers..by the shakerful.

Hence **'screwdrive** *v.* (nonce-wd.), *trans.*, to drive in as if with a screwdriver.

1894 Clark Russell *Good Ship Mohock* I. 105 He stared at me for some moments fixedly, as though he would screw-drive his gaze through my brain.

screwed (skru:d), *ppl. a.* [f. screw *v.* + -ed[1].]

1. Attached or fastened with inserted screws, or by means of component screws. Also ***screwed-down, screwed-on.***

1770 *Ann. Reg.* 19 The great superiority of the Russians may be attributed..to their charging with screwed bayonets. **1851** H. Melville *Moby Dick* II. ii. 3 You would have seen him..spread them before him on his screwed-down table. **1874** Ruskin *Fors Clav.* IV. xxxix. 53, I was stopped..by a sign over a large shop advising me to buy some 'screwed boots and shoes'. **1885** J. B. Leno *Boot & Shoem.* xxiii. 189 With a screwed boot..the fastening actually holds for its entire length in the leather. **1886** *Encycl. Brit.* XXI. 831/1 The principal disadvantage in the use of standard screwed soles is the great difficulty met with in removing..an old sole. **1965** D. Francis *Odds Against* iv. 48 He..added an inch to its length in the shape of a screwed-on photo electric light meter.

†**2.** Strained or forced with or as with a screw. Of wit: Strained to its highest pitch. *Obs. rare.*

1648 J. Beaumont *Psyche* xi. l, And rais'd her self to that transcendent pitch Of Monstrousness, which never any Fiend With Hell's most scrued wit before could reach.

3. Furnished with an adjustable screw.

1688 Holme *Armoury* iii. 398/1 A single Beak Pellican with a screw,..called a Screw'd tooth Forcer.

4. Twisted round or awry. **a.** Of the face: Contorted. Of (the surrounding parts of) the eyes: Contracted. Also with *up.*

1697 Vanbrugh *Relapse* (1708) Pref., As for the Saints (your thorough-pac'd ones I mean, with screw'd Faces and wry Mouths) I despair of them. **1710** Steele *Tatler* No. 257 ¶1 Notwithstanding..the Pliancy of the Matter in which the Images are wrought..he did not think it possible for it to be twisted and tortured into so many skrew'd Faces and wry Features. **1728** Swift in *Intelligencer* (1729) No. 8. 70 Thy screw'd-up Front, thy State grimace. **1785** Burns *Holy Fair* x, On this hand sits a chosen swatch, Wi' screw'd up, grace-proud faces. **1901** C. Holland *Mousmé* 15 [His] gravely screwed-up eyes.

†**b.** Winding, spiral. *Obs. rare*$^{-1}$.

1655 Mrq. Worcester *Cent. Invent.* §48 A scrued Ascent, instead of Stairs.

c. Twisted into a spiral form.

1855 Dickens *Dorrit* i. xix, He held the usual screwed bit of whity-brown paper in his hand, from which he ever and again unscrewed a spare pinch of snuff.

5. a. Having a helical groove or ridge on its surface. ***screwed plate*** = *screw-plate* (see screw *sb.*[1] 24). ***screwed work,*** the cutting of screws.

1655 Mrq. Worcester *Cent. Invent.* §71 (1663) 51 A Key perfectly square, with a Scrue turning within it..and no heavier then the triangle-scrued Key. **1716** Halley *Lights in Air* in *Phil. Trans.* XXIX. 421 Certain skrewed or striate Particles, adapted to the Pores they are to enter. **1819** Peckston *Gas-Lighting* 299 Service-pipes..are.. screwed at one end, and furnished with a screwed socket at the other. **1843** Holtzapffel *Turning* I. 72 [The wood of the apple-tree] is better adapted..for screwed work. **1869** C. Knight *Mechanician* 122 Screwed plates are..screw formers for rods, wire, small bolts [etc.]. **1883** F. Campin *Details of Mach.* xix. 224 The strength of a bolt or any description of screwed end must be determined from its diameter. **1907** H. A. Bethell *Mod. Guns* 9 The screwed breech of the gun is cut away to match.

b. Of a firearm: Furnished with a screwed barrel, i.e. one having a helically grooved bore.

1646 Evelyn *Diary* (1850) I. 240 (Geneva) Excellent screwed guns. **1657** *Burton's Diary* (1828) II. 485 The two persons being apprehended, they were found to have screwed pistols. **1678** *Lond. Gaz.* No. 1271/4 A Case of screw'd barril Pistols. **1680** R. H. *Milit. Discipl.* I. ii. 23 The King commands at present that in every Troop of his Guards be carried eight rifled or screwed Carabins.

6. Partly intoxicated; 'tight'.

1837 J. S. Coyne *Queer Subject* I. ii. 7 I've been drinking ..and I'm thinking, That I'm nearly screw'd outright. **1838** Barham *Ingol. Leg., Witches Frolic*, Alone it stood, while its fellows lay strew'd, Like a four-bottle man in a company screw'd, Not firm on his legs, but by no means subdued. **1859** Lang *Wand. India* 381 Intoxicated! not a bit of it! Screwed, nothing more! **1881** F. A. Paley in *Fraser's Mag.* Feb. 202 We read in Plato of Alcibiades coming to a party somewhat 'screwed'. **1891** Kipling *Light that Failed* xi, I swear I can see all right when I'm—when I'm moderately screwed.

7. *Comb.* **screwed-surfaced joint** *Anat.* = *screw-joint* b (see screw *sb.*[1] 24); **screwed-up**, (of a condition, situation, etc.) forced (to a certain pitch); excessively intricate; (now esp. with ref. to sense 12c of the vb.) confused, mixed up; (of a person) in trouble; muddled, upset, neurotic.

1875 W. Turner *Hum. Anat.* I. 68 An important modification of the ginglymus is the screwed-surfaced joint. **1907** M. A. von Arnim *Fräulein Schmidt & Mr. Anstruther* lxxiv. 372, I don't love you..it makes me tired just to think ..of the bother of it, of the perpetual screwed-up condition of mind and body to a pitch above the normal. **1924** F. Hopman tr. *Huizinga's Waning of Middle Ages* viii. 99 The whole genre of *Les Cent Nouvelles Nouvelles*..implies, no less than the screwed-up system of courtly love, an attempt to substitute for reality the dream of a happier life. **1943** *Yank* 26 Nov. 4/3 Oh, Lord, he thought, whatever I do, I'm a screwed-up sheep. **1967** L. Forrester *Girl called Fathom* xiii. 158 The Capitán is correct to call this 'a screwed up situation'. **1970** E. Pace *Saberlegs* xvi. 150 She has every right to be screwed up—or simply to be lonely. **1974** E. Brawley *Rap* (1975) II. xviii. 308, I grew up on army bases all over the world. I'm one of your typical screwed-up army brats, I guess. **1980** *Times* 22 Mar. 5/5 Modern society is obsessed with romanticizing ancient societies... This total fantasy about them being basically modern scientists is really screwed up.

screwer ('skruːə(r)). [f. screw *v.* + -er[1].]

1. One who or that which screws. Also with *up*.

1654 R. Whitlock *Zootomia* 484, I am, saith he, incredibly taken with Musick and Dancing..it seemeth a Screwer up of lower Passions (more than Pins). **1826** Cobbett *Rural Rides* (1885) II. 198 A cruel screwer down of the labourers. **1835** Ure *Philos. Manuf.* 214 The locks of flax are screwed into the holders by a boy called the screwer. **1842** Col. Hawker *Diary* (1893) II. 342, I left the carbine in charge of Jones, a very clever 'screwer together'. **1881** Greener *Gun* 285 The gun is sent to the screwer to have the trigger-plate let in and the breech pin fitted.

2. A burglar; a 'screwsman'. *Criminals' slang.*

1932 'S. Wood' *Shades of Prison House* p. ii, The smash-and-grab man, the afternoon screwer of poor men's houses, the whiz-man and the homosexual pervert end up—in gaol! **1947** [see bust *sb.*[3] d].

screwiness ('skruːɪnɪs). [f. screwy *a.* + -ness.] The state or condition of being screwy.

1872 *Daily News* 26 Aug., [The horses] are certainly on the confines of screwiness. **1886** Baring-Gould *Court Royal* I. vi. 96 A screwiness about money.

screwing ('skruːɪŋ), *vbl. sb.* [f. screw *v.* + -ing[1].] **a.** The action of the verb (in its various senses); also, an instance of this.

1673 *Remarques Humours Town* 54 A scruing up the courage of a friend to those fantastick heights. **1680** Bunyan *Mr. Badman* (1905) 115 Extortion is a screwing from men more than by the Law of God or men is right. **1738** Swift *Pol. Conversat.* Introd. 18 Every Turn of their Hands, every Screwing of their Bodies. **1812** [see screwsman]. **1825** T. Hook *Sayings* Ser. II. *Sutherl.* (Colburn) 27 The tall gentleman..played billiards with uncommon skill, and possessed all the delicate arts of chalking, and twisting, and screwing. **1840** Blaine *Encycl. Rural Sports* §1647. 468 For screwing and creeping, however, he beat every horse we ever rode. *Ibid.* §1658. 470 Screwing..is a method of getting through the thick hedges that cannot be got over. **1848** *Illustr. Lond. News* 22 Jan. 36/2 Cheapness, economy, or 'screwing' will be found at the bottom of most railway casualties. **1901** *Munsey's Mag.* XXV. 610/2 But if the vessel is caught in an 'ice screwing', the ramming together of giant floes, it will be crushed like an eggshell. **1903** *Daily Chron.* 21 July 11/1 Counsel explained that 'screwing' meant committing burglary. **1952** S. Kauffmann *Philanderer* (1953) xv. 248, I have eaten up my honour with random screwing. I have defiled myself. **1958** A. Wilson *Middle Age of Mrs. Eliot* 262 Married to an old man. You've never had a proper screwing. **1971** C. Fick *Danziger Transcript* 70, I fail to see how an ancient screwing can be of current interest.

b. *attrib.* and *Comb.* (in the sense 'cutting screw threads'), as ***screwing apparatus, -engine, -machine, table, tackle, tool, trade***; **screwing die, stock** = *screw die, stock* (see screw *sb.*[1] 24).

1850 Ogilvie, *Screwing-machine*, a highly important implement..for forming the screws of bolts and nuts by means of the machinery of the factory. **1861** F. Campin *Hand-Turning* 120 Dies very similar to the above are also used in a machine called a screwing-engine. **1869** Rankine *Machine & Hand-tools* Pl. R 1, Sets of screwing dies. *Ibid.*, This form of screwing stock..produces threads approximating in accuracy to those cut by the slide lathe. **1870** *Amateur Mech. Workshop* 47 The above [stock] forms the most usual screwing apparatus of the general mechanic. **1875** Knight *Dict. Mech.*, *Screwing-table*, a kind of screw-stock, used for forming threads of screw-bolts or wooden screws. **1890** *Daily News* 22 Sept. 2/6 Lifting and screwing tackle are in good demand. **1909** *Installation News* III. 58 Screwing tools.

screwing ('skruːɪŋ), *ppl. a.* [f. screw *v.* + -ing[2].] That screws (in the senses of the verb).

1707 in *Sewall's Diary* (1879) II. 39* The Governour, with his Son Paul..are very Screwing and Exacting upon the People. **1737** Swift *Let.* 30 Mar., Wks. 1841 II. 789 Your society has raised the rents..to four times the value of what they formerly paid; which is beyond all I have ever heard even among the most screwing landlords of this impoverished kingdom. **1889** *Daily News* 25 May 5/4 Screwing ice, maëlstroms, and impassable ice..stopped them. **1960** [see blag *sb.*]. **1966** L. Southworth *Felon in Disguise* v. 81 A geezer called Teagueman..does a bit of driving for the screwing mobs.

screwish ('skruːɪʃ), *a. rare.* [f. screw *sb.*[1] + -ish.] Of the nature of a screw.

1570 J. Dee *Math. Pref.* c iiij b, Archimedes, setting to his Skruish Engine, caused Hiero the king, by him self, at ease, to remoue her [*sc.* a ship]. **1829** *Sporting Mag.* XXIII. 285 How unlucky then that he chanced to have so screwish a set [of horses].

screwless ('skruːlɪs), *a.* [f. screw *sb.*[1] + -less.] Without a screw or screws.

1913 in Webster. **1962** L. S. Sasieni *Dispensing* i. 35 The 'Ilford' screwless mounting. **1976** *Golf International* 13–29 May 32/2 Most manufacturers change to what's termed the screwless face insert, for wooden clubs.

screwmatic (skruː'mætɪk), *a.* and *sb. colloq.* [A humorous perversion of rheumatic *a.* and *sb.*, after screw *sb.*[1] (see sense 13b).]

A. *adj.* = rheumatic *a.* 4b. *rare.*

1893 P. H. Emerson *On Eng. Lagoons* 50, I had the screwmatic fever three times.

B. *sb. pl.* = rheumatic *sb.* 1.

1895 P. H. Emerson *Birds, Beasts, & Fishes Norf. Broadland* 396 'Wiper's oil' is a reputed specific for 'screwmatics'. **1916** E. V. Lucas *Vermilion Box* 209 Wet, and rats,..and dirt and screwmaticks. **1974** P. Wright *Lang. Brit. Industry* iv. 44 Sometimes corruption has been helped by folk etymology, where the speaker supplies an imagined source for the word from what it seems to say; e.g. *screwmatics* (rheumatism).

screw-pin. [screw *sb.*[1]] A pin with a screw cut upon it: **a.** the screw of a vice; also *fig.*; **b.** an adjusting screw, finger screw; **c.** the pin which forms the foundation of a screw.

1614 T. Freeman *Rub & Gt. Cast* G 2, Since these three [*sc.* Chaucer, Lydgate and Gower] knew to turne perdy The Scru-pin of Phylosophy As well as they [*sc.* the Greeks and Romans]. **1631** in Rymer *Fœdera* XIX. 315 For a whole Worke, consisting of the Pan, the cover of the Pan, the Scutchion and the screw Pynn. *a* **1646** J. Gregory *Posthuma* (1650), *Terrestrial Globe* 265 It [the Quadrant] is..affixed to the Meridian with a little Screw-pin, to bee removed at pleasure. **1677** Moxon *Mech. Exerc.* i. 29 The Nut is turned about hard upon the Screw-pin. **1765** H. Timberlake *Mem.* 16, I pulled the trigger, which missing fire, broke off the upper chap and screw-pin. **1826** *Sporting Mag.* XVII. 175 A screw-pin, by which to regulate the main-springs of locks of every description of fire-arms. **1833** J. Holland *Manuf. Metal* II. 146 The screw-pin is some-times infirm, in consequence of its having but partially resisted the torsion. **1884** C. G. W. Lock *Workshop Receipts* Ser. III. 115/2 By means of a nut on the screw-pin they are pressed closely together.

screwsman ('skruːzmən). *slang.* [f. screw *sb.* + man *sb.*: after *cracksman*, etc.] A thief; a house-breaker, a burglar; also, a safe-breaker.

1812 J. H. Vaux *Flash Dict.* Mem. 1819 II. 204 *Screwsman*, a thief who goes out a screwing. **1879** [see dead *a.* A. 18b]. **1910** *Dundee Advertiser* 8 Jan. 7, I believe you are a 'screwsman'. Where's the jemmy and the 'twirls'? **1928** *Daily Express* 19 Sept. 1/5 When released he came to London, and was among those whom the police call 'screws men', who break into houses to steal articles easily sold. **1936** [see dragging *vbl. sb.*]. **1955** P. Wildeblood *Against Law* III. 137 Suppose there's some screwsman that the law's got an eye on. **1963** 'J. Prescot' *Case for Hearing* iii. 49 What does our imaginary screwsman do? He gets his hands on the keys..to take impressions. **1976** J. O'Connor *Eleventh Commandment* iv. 63, I took up my old profession of being a screwsman again.

'screw-up. *colloq.* (orig. *U.S.*). Also **screwup.** [f. vbl. phr. *to screw up*: see screw *v.* 12c.] A blunder, muddle, or mess; a state or situation of confusion or mental disturbance.

1960 Wentworth & Flexner *Dict. Amer. Slang* 453 *Screw-up*,..a chronic blunder. **1967** G. Legman *Fake Revolt* 23 The inability to *feel*, and the fear of touch, especially in sex... This is the key to the whole sexual screw-up of our time. **1971** Laver & Collins *Education of Tennis Player* v. 84 Bad courts were just one more factor in a general screw-up. **1975** *New Yorker* 19 May 24/2 Stewart Stern..tries to equate the American woman's supposed incapacity for love with the whole American screwup of recent years. **1977** C. McFadden *Serial* iv. 14/1 Everybody knew..that the rational mind was a screw-up.

screwy ('skruːɪ), *a.* [f. screw *sb.*[1] and *v.* + -y[1].]

1. Slightly 'screwed' or tipsy.

1820 T. Creevey in *C. Papers* (1904) I. 339, I..drank an extra bottle..: not that I was the least screwy, but [etc.]. **1855** Thackeray *Newcomes* xlvii, Blest if I did'nt nearly drive her into a wegetable cart. I was so uncommon scruey!

2. Of a person: Given to screwing, mean, stingy.

1851 Mayhew *Lond. Labour* I. 295/1 Mechanics are capital customers..; they're not so screwy. **1861** J. Pycroft *Agony Point* xliii. (1862) 367 Whereas before we never knew what we could afford..and I used to feel a very unpleasant 'screwy' sensation from one year's end to the other. **1876** Miss Braddon *J. Haggard's Dau.* xxx, He was so hard upon 'em, and that screwy, never a drop of milk or a fagot to give 'em. **1887** Blackmore *Springhaven* II. xx. 287 To a scrimpy and screwy man..such a position would have done a deal of harm.

3. Of a horse: That is 'a screw'; unsound.

1852 Smedley *L. Arundel* xxiii, It's like turning a screwy horse out to grass. **1899** Baring-Gould *Book of West* I. vii. 106 Two likely-looking hunters, perhaps a little screwy, were brought round.

4. Of a track: That winds about.

1891 Atkinson *Last of Giant Killers* 15 A jaggy, steep, screwy little trackway.

5. *slang* (orig. *U.S.*). Mad, crazy; eccentric; foolish; ridiculous.

1887 *Lantern* (New Orleans) 8 Oct. 3/3 Do, now, please to stop them notes which are so full of screwy talk. They make me tired. **1930** D. Runyon in *Collier's* 22 Mar. 54/2 'I am wondering how much you will take to hold still and let me shoot you, Jack?' 'Why,' Handsome Jack says, very much astonished, 'you must be screwy.' **1942** E. Waugh *Put out More Flags* iii. 163 They like the little pattering feet about the house—I know it sounds screwy but it's the truth. **1948** M. Allingham *More Work for Undertaker* xiii. 166 We feel our clients are screwy but not bloodstained. **1959** 'J. Bell' *Easy Prey* viii. 87, I think the whole idea is screwy... I can't see her risking her own life to save a murderess. **1966** R. H. Rimmer *Harrad Experiment* 42 Sheila was Tom's date and I had Tom's sister, Ruth, for a date. Sound screwy? **1978** J. Wainwright *Jury People* liv. 199 The prison psychiatrist.. can be told crap. He'll believe it... If anybody's screwy, it's *him*.

screwze, obs. form of scruze *v.*

†**scrib**[1]. *Obs.* [? var. of scrub.] ? A miser. (Quot. 1608 is obscure, and the text may be corrupt; with 'bonny scribs' cf. 'bonny scrubs' in scrub *sb.*[3])

1600 Breton *Pasquils Madcap* 16 If she haue playde the thrifty prowling scribbe, To purchase Grasse to greaze the Bullockes ribbe. **1608** Middleton *Mad World* III. iii, Why then set forward; and as you scorne..tweluepenny Pandarisme, and such base bribes, guard me from bonny Scribs, and bony Scribes [*ed.* 1640 *adds* and bony rags]. **1634** *Withal's Dict.* 575 *Promus magis quam condus.* He is none of these miserable scribs, but a liberall Gentleman.

†**scrib**[2]. *nonce-wd.* Abbreviation of scribble *sb.*

1795 Dr. Burney *Let. to Mme. D'Arblay* 7 May, It strikes three o'clock;..and I must send off my scrib.

scribable ('skraɪbəb(ə)l), *a. Obs.* exc. *arch.* Also 5 scryvable. [irreg. f. L. *scrībĕre* to write: see -able. The form *scryvable* represents a possible OF. **escrivable*.] Suitable for being written on.

14.. Lydg. *Ballad of deceitful Women* 44 Though al the erth..Were parchemyn smothe, whyte and scribable. *c* **1450** *M.E. Med. Bk.* (Heinrich) 182 Wyt leþer or in good [*v.r.* scribable] pauper. *Ibid.* 14 Scryuable. *a* **1500** *Arnolde's Chron.* (1502) 26 Paper scribabil the bale, vi. d'. **1889** Lowell *Lett.* (1894) II. 412 One filled every scribable corner of his foolscap.

scribacious (skraɪ'beɪʃəs), *a. rare.* Also incorrectly *-atious.* [f. L. *scrībĕre* to write + -acious.] Given to, or fond of, writing. Hence **scri'baciousness**, fondness for writing.

a **1677** Barrow *Pope's Suprem.* (1680) 165 We have some Letters of Popes (though not many; for Popes were then not very scribacious..). **1870** Emerson *Soc. & Solit., Books* Wks. (Bohn) III. 87 Cornelius Agrippa 'On the Vanity of Arts and Sciences' is a specimen of that scribatiousness which grew to be the habit of the gluttonous readers of his time.

scribal ('skraɪb(ə)l), *a.* [f. scribe *sb.* + -al[1].]

1. Of, pertaining to, or characteristic of a scribe or copyist, or his work.

1857 *Fraser's Mag.* LVI. 674 Jobares was an easily committed scribal corruption of Jomanes. **1868** R. Morris *O.E. Hom.* Pref. 6 The scribal blunders that it contains. **1893** Skeat in *Athenæum* 17 June 765/1 Scribal errors abound throughout [Chaucerian MSS.].

2. Of or pertaining to the Jewish scribes.

1863 *Smith's Dict. Bible* III. 1164/2 (*Scribes*) We must look back to what is known of the five pairs..of teachers who represented the scribal succession. **1896** *Expositor* Feb. 109 The saying..is diametrically opposed to the Scribal method of teaching.

†'**scribbet.** *Obs.* Also 7 scribet. [? f. scribe *v.* + -et[1].] A charcoal for drawing.

1673–4 Grew *Anat. Trunks* etc. (1675) 75 It [sallow] maketh an excellent Coal for Painters Scribets. **1725** *Bradley's Fam. Dict.* s.v. *Sallow*, Sallow-Coal is..the best of all for Painters Scribbets to design their Work with.

'**scribblage.** *nonce-wd.* [f. scribble *v.* + -age.] Scribblings, ephemeral writing.

1805 W. Taylor in *Monthly Mag.* XX. 39 The polemic scribblage of theology and politics.

scribblative ('skrɪblətɪv), *a. rare.* Also **scriblative.** [f. scribble *v.*[1] + -ative. Cf. *talkative.*] Pertaining to scribbling.

1829 Southey *Sir T. More* II. 48 All of which are.. denied by our professors of the arts babblative and scribblative. **1881** *Sat. Rev.* 26 Feb. 282/2 He did not see anything that hundreds and thousands of professors of the arts gaddative and scriblative have not seen before him.

'scribblatory, *a. nonce-wd.* [f. SCRIBBLE *v.*[1] + *-atory*: see -ORY.] Tending to cause scribbling.
1802–12 BENTHAM *Ration. Judic. Evid.* (1827) V. 246 The dilatory, scribblatory.. mode of the courts of equity.

scribble ('skrɪb(ə)l), *sb.* Also 7–8 **scrible.** [f. SCRIBBLE *v.*[1]]

1. Something hastily or carelessly written, esp. a depreciatory term for a letter (usually one's own); also, a worthless or trivial composition.
1577 SIDNEY *Lett.* Misc. Wks. (1829) 304 But I will leaue [that] till I may my selfe say it unto yow, and so, his speeches at my farewell, w[ch] I am afraide I was in the beginninge of these scribbles to longe in. **1592** UNTON *Corr.* (Roxb.) 397 Your honors pardon I crave for this my shorte and hastie scribbles. **1632** HIDE in *Randolph's Jealous Lovers* To Author, When they that write by guesse, Scatter their scribbles, and invade the presse. **1691** WOOD *Ath. Oxon.* II. 155 He made a shift to get a lively-hood by his mendicant scribbles. **1711** HEARNE *Collect.* (O.H.S.) III. 131 In the Margin.. are some scribbles. **1730** SWIFT in *Portland Papers* (Hist. MSS. Comm.) VI. 33 If a scribble comes out complaining of our hardships here, it is infallibly laid at my door. **1814** J. ADAMS *Wks.* (1856) X. 96 As you seem to have found some amusement in some of my scribbles, I beg your acceptance of another morsel. **1865** PRINCESS ALICE *Mem.* 14 Aug. (1884) 107, I have made little scribbles on the way.

2. Hurried or negligent and irregular writing; an example of this. Also, a number of irregular and unmeaning marks made with pen or pencil.
1709 STEELE & SWIFT *Tatler* No. 70 ¶7, I shall trouble you with no more Scribble. **1788** TWINING in *Select Papers T. Family* (1887) 185, I shall refer you for my thanks to the packet which you will receive, containing no less than five sheets of scribble. **1828** D'ISRAELI *Chas. I*, I. ii. 19 The hand-writing of Charles.. was elegant, and opposite to the slovenly scribble of his father. **1841** HAWTHORNE *Amer. Note-bks.* (1868) II. 21 Did you ever behold such a vile scribble as I write since I became a farmer? **1881** FITCH *Lect. Teach.* 192 The scribble of men who think good writing a thing for clerks and shopmen. **1896** *Amer. Annals Deaf* Feb. 70 The speed of writing, even at a scribble, hardly exceeds thirty words a minute.

†**b.** *transf.* A hurried manner of walking. *Obs.* (? *nonce-use.*)
1665 HOWARD *Committee* I. i, O are you come, Long look't for comes at last. What,—you have a slow set pace, As well as your hasty scribble sometimes.

3. *attrib.* and *Comb.*
1653 [F. PHILIPS] *Consid. Crt. Chancery* 24 Other Mungrel and Scrible dashed hands made out of the Roman and Italian. **1907** *Edin. Rev.* July 230 The conventional 'scribble' foliage has descended to oblivion with the drawing books of our fathers.

scribble ('skrɪb(ə)l), *v.*[1] Forms: 5 scribyl, 6 scribel, -il, -ul, screble, scrybel, skrible, 6–7 scryble, scrible, 6– scribble. [app. ad. late med.L. *scrībillāre* (cf. rare class. L. *conscrībillāre*), a diminutive formation on L. *scrībĕre* to write. Cf. G. *skribbeln*, *skribeln*, for which recent writers substitute *schreibeln*, f. *schreiben*; OHG. had *scribilôn* (? *î*), 'scriptitare'.]

1. *trans.* To write hastily or carelessly. **a.** To write in an irregular, slovenly, or illegible hand through haste or carelessness; also, to produce (marks, a drawing, etc.) or portray (an object) by rapid and irregular strokes like those of hurried writing. **b.** To write hurriedly or thoughtlessly, so that what is written is faulty in style or worthless in substance.
c **1465** *Plumpton Corr.* (Camden) 14 Scribled in hast with mine owne hand in default of other helpe. **1490** *Paston Lett.* III. 363 Scribyllyd in the moste haste, at.. Aucland. **1513** MORE *Rich. III*, Wks. 56 For al y[e] time.. could scant haue suffised vnto y[e] bare wryting alone, all had it bene but in paper & scribled forth in hast at aduenture. **1537** LAYTON in *Lett. Suppress. Monasteries* (Camden) 77 Scribullede this Satterday, an written with the hasty hand of your assurede servant. **1575** G. HARVEY *Letter-bk.* (Camden) 90 An answer to a.. vayne letter.. scribblid longe since. **1653** DOROTHY OSBORNE *Lett.* (1903) 15 This (if you can read it, for 'tis strangely scribbled) will be enough to answer yours. **1692** BENTLEY *Boyle Lect.* ii. 38 That the innumerable Members of a 'Human Body'.. were at first fortuitously scribbled, and by meer accident compacted into this beautifull, and noble, and most wonderfully usefull Frame. **1710–11** SWIFT *Jrnl. to Stella* 31 Jan., So I could not scribble my morning lines to MD. **1764** *Oxf. Sausage* 184, I scribble Verses? why you know, I left the Muses long ago. **1842** S. SHARPE *Egypt under Romans* iii. 66 Travellers.. have at all times been fond of carving or scribbling their names on the spot. **1884** *Publisher & Bookbuyer's Jrnl.* 15 Nov. 19/1 Writers who scribble bosh. **1899** M. CREIGHTON in *Life & Lett.* (1904) II. xii. 403, I must scribble a line to tell you how much I feel for you.
fig. **1532** MORE *Confut. Tindale* Wks. 728/2 But if he feele it written there in dede as he saith he doth, then he feleth it scribled and scraped in his hert by the croked clouen clawes of the deuill.

c. With various advs., as *away*, *down*, *out*. †Also *to scribble up*: to compile hastily.
1583 J. HAWKINS in *Archæologia* XXXIII. 193, I have breffiye.. scryblyd out a note of the joynnynge of thordynary and extraordynary together, which I send. **1596** H. CLAPHAM *Briefe Bible* II. 234, I haue for your vses, sodainly scribled vp this Breviarie of the Bible. **1619** HALES *Golden Rem.* II. (1673) 70 His sudden and unexpected departure hath made me scrible up this more rudely and concisely than I had intended. **1800** LAMB *Lett.* (1849) 113, I could not resist so facile and moderate demand, so scribbled out another, omitting sundry things. **1826** J. W. CROKER in *C. Papers* (1884) 20 Mar., I was easily induced to take up my pen.. and I scribbled away a reply. **1831** GREVILLE *Mem.* 31 July (1875) II. 174, I have scribbled down all I can recollect of a very loose conversation. **1901** *Athenæum* 31 Aug. 294/1 The liquid brush-work with which the light leaves of the oak were rapidly and easily scribbled down by the painter.

d. To cover with scribblings. Chiefly with *over*.
1540 PALSGR. *Acolastus* Ep. Ded. A iij b, They chuse moste commonly the very worste [words], and therewith scryble the bokes of theyr latyne auctours. *a* **1593** MARLOWE *Ovid's Elegies* II. v. 18 Not silent were thine eyes, the board with wine Was scribled, and thy fingers writ a line. **1593** SHAKS. *2 Hen. VI*, IV. ii. 88 Is not this a lamentable thing.. that Parchment being scribled ore, should vndoe a man. **1667** MILTON *P.L.* VIII. 83 How [they will] gird the Sphear With Centric and Eccentric scribl'd o'er, Cycle and Epicycle, Orb in Orb. **1702** ADDISON *Dial. Medals* III. Wks. 1766 III. 154 Having scribbled over both sides [of the medal], they are forced, as it were, to write upon the margin. **1717** BERKELEY *Tour in Italy* Wks. 1871 IV. 519 Most of these obelisks are scribbled over with hieroglyphics. **1852** THACKERAY *Esmond* I. iii, The page found my lord's sheet of paper scribbled over with dogs and horses. **1859** TENNYSON *Merlin & V.* 527 Thou read the book! And every margin scribbled, crost, and cramm'd With comment. **1882** B. D. W. RAMSAY *Recoll. Mil. Serv.* II. xiii. 26 The walls of every room are scribbled over with the names of visitors.
fig. **1651** HOBBES *Leviath.* II. xxx. 176 The Common-peoples minds.. scribbled over with the opinions of their Doctors.

2. *intr.* To write something hastily or carelessly, either as to handwriting or composition; to produce abundance of worthless writing. Also, to make random or irregular lines resembling careless writing.
1534 CRANMER *Let.* cxviii. Misc. Writ. (Parker Soc.) II. 291, I have.. made them to write their shepe mark, or some other mark, as they can.. scribble. **1601** Q. ELIZ. *Let. to Mountjoy* in *Moryson's Itin.* II. (1617) 151, I end, scribling in hast, Your loving Soveraigne. E. R. **1661** MARVELL *Let. to Mayor of Hull* 1 June, If I wanted my right hand yet I would scribble to you with my left, rather than neglect your business. **1721–2** BOLINGBROKE in *Swift's Lett.* (1766) II. 23 The expression is equivocal; a fault, which our language often betrays those, who scribble hastily, into. **1780** COWPER *Progr.* 318 Ye.. teach her.. To scribble as you scribbled at fifteen. **1782** MISS BURNEY *Cecilia* x. vi, Contenting himself with doing nothing but scribble and scribe. **1844** DICKENS *Mart. Chuz.* v, I have scribbled myself but have not yet published. **1880** *Print. Trades Jrnl.* XXX. 35 If a man scribbles for a Newspaper, or writes a magazine article. **1888** BURGON *12 Good Men* II. v. 36 He utilized a railway journey.. to get out his writing materials, and to scribble on a kind of swing-desk.

b. *to scribble on*: to go on or continue scribbling or writing carelessly.
1575 GASCOIGNE *Posies, Herbs* 141 My hasty hand forth-with doth scribble on apace. **1683** *Agathocles* 6 The harden'd Wretches sinn'd, and scribbled on.

c. quasi-*trans.* with complementary adv. or phrase.
a **1704** T. BROWN *Laconics* Wks. 1711 IV. 25 Stay but a while, and you'll find he'll scribble himself out of his little Reputation. **1734** POPE *Let. to Swift* 15 Sept., I have scribled the remainder of this page full. **1837** LYTTON *E. Maltrav.* I. xv, At our age we have passion, fancy, sentiment; we can't read them away, nor scribble them away.

†**3.** *Comb.* as **scribble-mania** = SCRIBBLEOMANIA; **scribble-paper** = *scribbling paper*; **scribble-wit**, a wit who scribbles (see quot.).
1672 WYCHERLEY *Love in Wood* II. i. 26 *Lyd.* But what is your Chamber-Wit or Scribble-Wit? *Dap.* He.. searches all the Records of Wit, to compile a breviate of them for the use of Players [etc.]. **1792** COLERIDGE *Let. to M. Evans* (1895) 35, I have never had the scribble-mania stronger on me. **1854** 'C. BEDE' *Verdant Green* II. ii, Having furnished the table with pens, ink, and scribble-paper.

scribble (skrɪb(ə)l), *v.*[2] Forms: 7–8 scrible, 7 scruble, 8– scribble. [Prob. from LG.; cf. the synonymous G. *schrubbeln*, *schrobbeln*, *schrobeln*, *schruppeln*, *schroppeln*, Sw. *skrabbla*; the vb. is a frequentative f. LG., Ger. *schrubben*, *schrobben*: see SCRUB *v.*] *trans.* To card or tease (wool) coarsely, to pass through a 'scribbler'.
1682 [implied in SCRIBBLER[2], SCRIBBLING *vbl. sb.*[2]]. **1687** *Rec. Cloth Manuf. New Mills* (S.H.S.) 142 That noe cloath.. be permitted to be woven, scribled or dressed by any of our servants. **1733** P. LINDSAY *Interest Scot.* 106 At Gallowshiels are made a few coarse Kerseys,.. and was their Wooll better scribled,.. they might serve in place of the lowest-pric'd York-shires. **1835** URE *Philos. Manuf.* 181 The wool having been scribbled in the ordinary way. **1884** W. S. B. M[c]LAREN *Spinning* (ed. 2) 53 All woollen yarns are carded or, to use another name, 'scribbled'.

scribbleable ('skrɪb(ə)ləb(ə)l), *a. nonce-wd.* [f. SCRIBBLE *v.*[1] + -ABLE.] Capable of being scribbled or written on.
1867 HOWELLS *Ital. Journ.* 83 Every scribbleable inch of its walls.

scribbled ('skrɪb(ə)ld), *ppl. a.*[1] [f. SCRIBBLE *v.*[1] + -ED[1].] Carelessly or hastily written or composed; also hastily or carelessly written on.
1548 W. THOMAS *Ital. Gram.* Epist. (1567), I knowe these fewe scribledde rules to bee muche imperfect. **1591** HORSEY *Trav.* (Hakluyt Soc.) 266, I.. haue forboren to incert.. som propper inferrences for explanacion of such names.. and terms, as you haue not been used to read, especially in so scribled a hand. **1595** SHAKS. *John* v. vii. 32, I am a scribled forme, drawne with a pen Vpon a Parchment, and against this fire Do I shrinke vp! **1621** ELSING *Debates Ho. Lords* (Camden) 52 Mr. Sergeaunt Crewe and Mr. Attourney perused the scrybled booke and perfected the same in the places marked by their noates taken therof. **1643** F. BELL in Mrs. Hope *Franciscan Martyrs Eng.* xiv. (ed. 3) 194 By chaunce they found in my pockett a little ragg of scribbled paper in Spanish. **1656** *Disc. Auxil. Beauty* 54 Ill scribled bills; which seem to be as so many charms or spells. **1909** P. C. SIMPSON *Life of Rainy* II. xxi. 183 It is a scribbled and unfinished draft.

Hence †'**scribbledly** *adv. rare.*
1681 H. MORE *Expos. Dan.* Pref. 7 It being writ.. so scribbledly as I may so say, and brokenly. **1685** —— *Illustr. Dan.* v. 55 The writing being writ more scribbledly on purpose.

scribbled, *ppl. a.*[2] [f. SCRIBBLE *v.*[2] + -ED[1].] Carded, or passed through a 'scribbler'.
1835 URE *Philos. Manuf.* 171 The scribbled wool is weighed.

scribbledehobble ('skrɪb(ə)ldɪˌhɒb(ə)l). James Joyce's nonce-formation on SCRIBBLE *sb.* or *v.*[1], prob. influenced by such a word as *hobbledehoy*, the etymology of which is obscure. Hence, the name given to one of Joyce's notebooks (see quot. 1961).
1922 JOYCE in T. E. Connoly *James Joyce's Scribbledehobble* (1961) 5 Scribbledehobble.. I'm feeling so funny all over the same. **1939** —— *Finnegans Wake* II. 275 That royal pair.. have discusst.. why lui lied to lei and hun tried to kill ham, scribbledehobbles, in whose veins runs a mixture of, are head bent and hard upon. **1961** *Times Lit. Suppl.* 20 Oct. 754/3 Of the fifty *Finnegans Wake* notebooks now in the Lockwood Memorial Library the *Scribbledehobble* book is the largest... It contains words, phrases, clichés, anecdotes, ideas, scraps of information and other memoranda. **1977** J. GARVIN in D. Ó Muirithe *Eng. Lang. in Ireland* 113 *Scribbledhobble* [sic], a note-book.. compiled by him [*sc.* Joyce] in 1923.. contain[s] simple phrases probably culled from his wife's conversations.

'**scribbledom.** *nonce-wd.* [f. SCRIBBLE *sb.* + -DOM.] The practice of 'scribbling'.
1887 MISS BETHAM-EDWARDS *Next of Kin Wanted* II. xvii. 221 Without any apprenticeship to the sublime art of scribbledom, she could write sweet, unalloyed, rustic English.

'**scribbleism.** *nonce-wd.* [f. SCRIBBLE *sb.* + -ISM.] Scribbling.
1801 COLERIDGE *Let. to Southey* (1895) 363 Other perseverants in the noble trade of scribbleism.

scribblement ('skrɪb(ə)lmənt). [f. SCRIBBLE *v.*[1] + -MENT.] Something scribbled; = SCRIBBLE *sb.* 1.
a **1608** DEE *Relat. Spir.* I. (1659) 175, I see lines and scribblements (as before) going athwart the lines. *c* **1662** F. KERBY in *O. Heywood's Diaries* (1883) III. 24 The intents of them who first set down these scribblements. **1784** COWPER *Let. to Unwin* 20 Oct., I am tired of this endless scribblement. Adieu! **1785** —— *To same* 22 Oct., The crabbed epigrams and scribblements of the minor poets. **1833** CARLYLE in *Froude* (1882) II. 382 In about a week hence.. I shall be done with this scribblement. **1887** T. A. TROLLOPE *What I remember* II. xvii. 349 The exhortation addressed to me.. was the writer's characteristic mode of exciting me to new scribblements.

ˌ**scribbleo'mania.** [f. SCRIBBLE *v.*[1] + -MANIA.] The craze or mania for scribbling.
1815 [see -MANIA]. **1877** M. PATTISON in *Fortn. Rev.* XXII. 660 Catherinot is a bye-word, the typical case of scribbleo-mania,—of the *insanabile scribendi cacoethes.*

scribbler[1] ('skrɪblə(r)). [f. SCRIBBLE *v.*[1] + -ER[1].]

1. One who scribbles or writes hastily or carelessly; hence 'a petty author; a writer without worth' (J.).
a **1553** UDALL *Roister D.* III. v. (Arb.) 58 Fare thou well scribler.. *Scriuener.* Fare ye well bibbler. **1610** BP. HALL *Agst. Brownists* ii. 5, I neuer yet could see any Scribler so vnlearned, as that he durst not charge his opposite with ignorance. **1682** DRYDEN *Religio Laici* Pref. 7 The first Presbyterian Scribler. **1727** A. HAMILTON *New Acc. E. Ind.* I. Ded., I have known some Scriblers, or Authors, dedicate their Works to great Men who they hardly knew any more of than their illustrious Names. **1778** MME. D'ARBLAY *Diary* Aug. (1891) I. 25 She talked.. very highly of a new novel called 'Evelina'; though without a shadow of suspicion as to the scribbler. **1825** MACAULAY *Ess., Milton* ¶46 Venal and licentious scribblers, with just sufficient talent to clothe the thoughts of a pander in the style of a bellman. **1880** L. STEPHEN *Pope* v. 124 The Dunciad was thus a declaration of war against the whole tribe of scribblers.
attrib. **1834** *Tait's Mag.* I. 727/1 Slave parasite and joker, With scribbler-satirist.

2. A scribbling-book or pad. Chiefly *N. Amer.*
1906 *Daily Colonist* (Victoria, B.C.) 11 Jan. 10/5 (Advt.), 1000 Scribblers and Exercise Books.. 2c each. **1913** *T. Eaton & Co. Semi-Ann. Sale Catal.* No. 36. 17/2 *School Outfit*.. 2 Exercise Books, 2 Scribblers, 1 Writing Pad, ruled. **1916** JOYCE *Portrait of Artist* (1969) iii. 105 Stephen, leaning back and drawing idly on his scribbler, listened to the talk about him. **1939** L. M. MONTGOMERY *Anne of Ingleside* xxxix. 309 We write each other letters in our scribblers and exchange them. **1964** L. EDEL *Diary of Alice James* p. v, She kept the record of her sickroom world in two closely-written scribblers. **1969** K. GILES *Death cracks Bottle* vi. 57 [He] had taken a page from his scribbler and written on it.

'**scribbler**[2]. [f. SCRIBBLE *v.*[2] + -ER[1].]

1. A person who scribbles wool, or who tends a scribbling-machine.
1682 *Rec. Cloth Manuf. New Mills* (S.H.S.) 16 To ingage 2 shear-men, 2 weavers and 2 scrublers. **1733** P. LINDSAY *Interest Scot.* 109 We have but few Scriblers who

understand the close mixing of Wooll on the Cards for Medleys. **1774** *Act 14 Geo. III*, c. 25 §1 If any Picker, Scribbler, Spinner or Weaver..shall not return all working Tools..delivered out. **1776** ADAM SMITH *W.N.* I. i. I. 14 The wool-comber.., the dyer, the scribbler [etc.].

2. A machine for scribbling (wool).

1805 J. LUCCOCK *Nat. Wool* 146 The chief point of attention in the scribbler is to break it [the staple] no further than the hookedness of the pile will admit of. **1884** W. S. B. McLAREN *Spinning* (ed. 2) 191 We now have the wool ready for the scribbler, or first carding machine.

attrib. **1825** J. NICHOLSON *Oper. Mech.* 391 The scribbler-engine has three distinct parts or cylinders in one frame.

'scribble-ˌscrabble, *adv.*, *sb.*, and *a. colloq.* [Reduplicated formation on SCRIBBLE *v.*]

†**A.** *adv.* In a scribbling manner. *Obs.*

1589 R. HARVEY *Pl. Perc.* (1590) 22 A Iewes letter scrible scrable ouer the Copurtenaunce of a mans countenance, will dash a body wickedly.

†**B.** *adj.* Covered with scribble. *Obs.*

1702 FARQUHAR *Twin-Rivals* v. iii, Uboo, here ish nothing but scribble scrabble Paper, I tink.

C. *sb.* †**1.** A scribbler. Also, ? a harum-scarum person. *Obs.*

1665 HOWARD *Committee* I. i, By your grave and high demeanor make yourself Appear a hole above Obadiah; lest your Mistriss Should take you for another scribble scrabble as he is. **1707** *Muses Mercury* I. 216 I'll be your Arbitrator, Quo' Scribble Scrabble; so he op'd The Oyster fat, and at a sup, He swallow'd down the Creature.

2. A scribble; hasty or careless writing.

1760 LADY M. W. MONTAGU *Let.* 12 Feb. (1967) III. 232, I see you laugh..at the vanity of my supposing any thing valuable in my scribble scrabbles. **1838** W. IRVING *Life & Lett.* (1866) III. 123 But enough of this scribble scrabble. **1839** *Ibid.* 145, I am running on into idle 'scribble scrabble' about a matter now passed away.

So **'scribble-scrabble** *v.*, *trans.*, to scribble.

1860 W. COLLINS *Wom. White* (1861) 255 The respectable lawyers who scribble-scrabble your deeds and your wills.

scribbling ('skrɪblɪŋ), *vbl. sb.*[1] [f. SCRIBBLE *v.*[1] + -ING[1].]

1. The action of the verb SCRIBBLE *v.*[1]

c **1532** LATIMER *Let. to Baynton* in Foxe *A. & M.* (1583) 1751/2, I had made an end of this scribling, and was beginning to write it agayne more truely and more distinctly, and to correcte it. **1536** BEERLEY in *Lett. Suppress. Monasteries* (Camden) 132 My lowly and myck scrybullyng unto your nobull grace at this tyme. **1709** POPE *Ess. Crit.* 595 When they promise to give scribbling o'er. **1820** BYRON *Blues* II. 9 What with learning, and teaching, and scribbling, and shining In science and art.

2. Something scribbled; a scrawl or scribble.

1705 HEARNE *Collect.* 11 Dec. (O.H.S.) I. 124 In this Book are a great many scribblings of William Smith. **1835** W. IRVING *Abbotsford* ¶2, I..had reason to think, from the interest he had taken in some of my earlier scribblings, that a visit from me would not be deemed an intrusion. **1856** STANLEY *Sinai & P.* i. (ed. 3) 58 Their likeness to the scribblings of casual travellers in halting-places. **1894** R. B. SHARPE *Birds Gt. Brit.* I. 47 There are distinct scribblings near the larger end [of the eggs], similar to those of a Yellow Bunting.

3. Short for *scribbling paper*.

1859 *Stationers' Hand-bk.* 64 Demy Scribling (scribling demy), a writing paper of a printing demy size.

4. *attrib.* as ***scribbling-block***, ***-book***, ***diary***, ***pad***, ***paper***; **scribbling itch**, tr. L. *Cacoethes scribendi*.

1908 *Outlook* 26 Sept. 397/1 With pencil and *scribbling-block in his hand. **1850** THACKERAY *Pendennis* xlii, He had taken the manuscript out of a long-neglected chest, containing..old Oxbridge *scribbling-books, his old surplice, and battered cap and gown. **1883** *Stationers' & Booksellers' Jrnl.* Advt. iii, Small *Scribbling Diary. **1787** WOLCOT (P. Pindar) *Ode upon Ode* Wks. 1812 I. 440 I'm much afraid of that same *scribbling-itch. **1905** A. DOBSON *De Libris* 149 But that some scribbling itch attacked Him in and out of season. **1938** N. MARSH *Artists in Crime* xiii. 189 Nigel had been left to write a very guarded story..on one of Troy's *scribbling-pads. **1967** C. DRUMMOND *Death at Furlong Post* i. 5 The Chairman looked doubtful; his Board appeared absorbed in their scribbling pads. **1803** *Gradus ad Cantabr.* 118 **Scribbling paper*, an inferior sort used by the mathematicians, and in the lecture room.

'scribbling, *vbl. sb.*[2] [f. SCRIBBLE *v.*[2] + -ING[1].] The action of SCRIBBLE *v.*[2]; the first process in the operation of carding wool.

1683 *Rec. Cloth Manuf. New Mills* (S.H.S.) 56 For piking scribling and oyll. 10s. **1835** URE *Philos. Manuf.* 165 Scribbling is merely a rude species of carding the oiled wool. **1879** *Cassell's Techn. Educ.* IV. 339/2 The various stages in the manufacture of woollen cloth, then, are:—..8. Oiling and teasing. 9. Scribbling by first carding-engine.

b. *attrib.* as ***scribbling-card***, ***-machine***, ***-mill***, etc.

1682 *Rec. Cloth Manuf. New Mills* (S.H.S.) 17 One dozen scrubleing cards. **1795** *Statist. Acc. Scot.* XV. 80 They have erected a teasing or scribling, and a carding machine. **1796** *Monthly Mag.* May 350/1 The scribbling mill at Holbeck, near Leeds, has been lately consumed by fire. **1805** J. LUCCOCK *Nat. Wool* 179 Kemps are commonly much coarser than the wool in which they are found, and often so intermingled with it as not to be separated even by the motion of the scribbling machine. **1857** *P.O. Directory Yorksh.* 1051 Scribbling Millers. **1876** W. CUDWORTH *Round abt. Bradford* 373 Extensive premises..containing willeying, moiting, scribbling, and condensing machinery. **1888** J. PATON in *Encycl. Brit.* XXIV. 659/1 Fig. 4—Diagram of Scribbling Card.

'scribbling, *ppl. a.* [f. SCRIBBLE *v.*[1] + -ING[2].]

1. Given to scribbling.

1595 *Hist. France* Ep. Ded. A 4, In this scribling age. **1641** HOWELL *Vote* ii, Scribling pamphletors who story stain With loose imperfect passages. **1765** GOLDSM. *New Simile* 2 Long had I sought in vain to find A likeness for the scribbling kind.

†**2.** Badly or carelessly written. *Obs. rare.*

1592 G. HARVEY *Four Lett.* Wks. (Grosart) I. 187 Is this Greene with the running Head, and the scribling Hand. **1621** SIR G. CALVERT in *Fortescue Papers* (Camden) 154 An yll favored piece of paper and a scribling hand.

Hence **'scribblingly** *adv.*, in a scribbling manner.

1653 in *Shropsh. Parish Documents* (1903) 246 What was disorderly and scribblingly set down on this side was taken out of a luse paper. *a* **1697** AUBREY *Lives* (1898) I. 10 These minutes which I have hastily and scriblingly here sett downe. **1860** in WORCESTER.

scribbly ('skrɪblɪ), *a.* [f. SCRIBBLE *sb.* + -Y.] Characterized by scribbling, resembling a scribble. **scribbly gum**, *Australian*, a variety of gum-tree (see quots.).

1883 F. M. BAILEY *Synopsis Queensland Flora* 174 (Morris) Scribbly or White-Gum... A tree, often large, with a white, smooth, deciduous bark, always marked by an insect in a scribbly manner. **1898** MORRIS *Austral Engl.* s.v. *Gum*, Scribbly Gum *Eucalyptus hæmastoma*, Smith. Scribbly Blue Gum *E. leucoxylon*, F. v. M. (South Australia).

scribe (skraɪb), *sb.*[1] Also 4–6 **scrybe**. [ad. L. *scriba* writer, amanuensis, secretary, f. *scrībĕre* to write. Cf. F. *scribe* (14th c. in Hatz.-Darm.), Sp., Pg. *escriba*, It. *scriba*.] A writer; one whose business is writing. In various specific or limited applications.

1. *Jewish Hist.* A member of the class of professional interpreters of the Law after the return from the Captivity; in the Gospels often coupled with the Pharisees as upholders of ceremonial tradition.

Used, after the Vulgate *scriba*, to render Gr. γραμματεύς in the New Testament. The corresponding Heb. word is *sōphēr*, active pple. of *sāphar* to write, to count, number. In Biblical Heb. the sb. had generally the sense 2 below; it was also used for a man of learning, a scholar, and as the designation of Ezra (Ezra vii, Neh. viii. 9, etc.) it comes near to the post-Biblical use.

1377 LANGL. *P. Pl.* B. xv. 383 And so may sarasenes be saued, scribes and iewes. **1382** WYCLIF *Matt.* vii. 29. [And in all later versions.] **1390** GOWER *Conf.* I. 14 And thus for Pompe and for beyete The Scribe and ek the Pharisee Of Moises upon the See In the chaiere on hyh ben set. **1532** MORE *Confut. Tindale* Wks. 510/2 These heretikes may properly bee called not onelye mercennaries,..but also verye Scribes and Pharisees... For these be false Scribes, that is to wit wryters, not wryting any true bokes of scripture, but fals gloses and contrary commentes vpon scripture. **1671** MILTON *P.R.* I. 261 What was writ Concerning the Messiah, to our Scribes Known partly. **1862** STANLEY *Jew. Ch.* (1877) I. xix. 365 The Religion.. was fully revealed.., not prophets were needed to declare it, but 'scribes' to expound and defend it.

2. *Anc. Hist.* A general designation for any public official (whether of high or low rank) concerned with writing or the keeping of accounts; a secretary, clerk.

The usual rendering of L. *scriba* and Gr. γραμματεύς, and of Heb. *sōphēr*: cf. the note under sense 1.

1382 WYCLIF *2 Kings* xviii. 18 Forsothe Eliachym,.. prouost of the hous, wente out to hem, and Sobna, scribe [1388 scryueyn], and Joache, the sone of Azaf, chauncelere. **1611** BIBLE *2 Kings* xxv. 19 The principall Scribe of the hoste [*marg.* Or, scribe of the captaine of the hoste], which mustered the people of the land. **1838** THIRLWALL *Greece* xxxii. IV. 230 Tisamenus, who..had filled the office of a public scribe. **1849** LAYARD *Nineveh* xiii. II. 76 The secretaries and scribes from the palace left their divans.

†**3.** Used as the official designation of various public functionaries performing secretarial duties.

1530 PALSGR. 268/1 Scrybe in a spyrituall court, *scribe*. Scrybe in a temporall court, *greffier*. **1533** *Acc. Ld. High Treas. Scot.* VI. 160 To Thome Cameroune, scribe to the futband v s. **1533** in *Sel. Pleas Crt. Admiralty* (1894) I. 93 The noble John Aborow Englysheman patron of the shypp Saynt Mighell... And allso the noble John Andreas allso Englysshman scrybe of the saide shipp consenting [etc.]. **1560** *Maitland Club Misc.* III. 225 Gevin vnder the Seill quhilk we wse..and the subscriptioun manuall of our scribe [of a kirk session]. **1562** *Burgh Rec. Edin.* (1875) III. 153 The council continewis Jhonne Young, writer, thair scribe, and ordanis him to serue [etc.]. **1581** LAMBARDE *Eiren.* IV. iv. (1588) 431 If any Ordinarie, or his scribe, or register have taken mo, or greater fees..then he ought to take. **1641** BAKER *Chron.*, *Hen. VIII* (1653) 396 Amongst other Officers of the Court [of Hen. VIII's divorce], Stephen Gardiner.. sate as chief scribe. The Court being set, the Judges commanded silence, whilst their Commission was read; which done, the Scribes commanded the Cryer to call the King. *a* **1707** S. PATRICK *Autobiog.* (1839) 13 And soon after made me the college scribe, which brought me in a great deal of money, many leases being to be renewed.

†**4. a.** One who writes at another's dictation; an amanuensis. *Obs.*

a **1513** FABYAN *Chron.* VI. clix. (1533) 88b, One of the foresayde two persones so condempned was scrybe to the pope. **1591** SHAKS. *Two Gent.* II. i. 146 That my master being scribe, To himselfe should write the Letter. **1598** B. JONSON *Ev. Man in H.* v. i. 323 These two gentlemen..very strongly supposing me to be your worships scribe, entreated me to procure them a warrant. **1838** LYTTON *Calderon* i. 64 This remarkable personage had risen from the situation of a confidential scribe to the Duke of Lerma.

b. *fig.*

a **1475** ASHBY *Dicta Philos.* 961 The first vertue is to kepe man is tong, For it is scribe of his discrecion, For what it wol say it writith at longe. **1860** FARRAR *Orig. Lang.* vii. 152 The senses themselves can tell us nothing except in so far as they are 'scribes of the soul'.

5. A copyist, transcriber of manuscripts; now esp. the writer of a particular MS. copy of a classical or mediæval work.

1535 JOYE *Apol. Tindale* (Arb.) 43, I tolde his scrybe, euen him that wrote and corrected the testament for him. **1611** BIBLE *Transl. Pref.* ¶6 The Grecians..had many of their seruants, ready scribes, to copie them [the books] out. *a* **1638** MEDE *Wks.* (1672) 878 If the Scrivener, whom I hired to write me out a fair Copy thereof, had not disappointed me, I could ere this have lent you a Copy, it may be, as good as the Authors; I believe somewhat more distinct, by such directions as I gave my Scribe. **1746** FRANCIS tr. *Horace, Art of Poetry* 481 We ne'er those Scribes with Mercy treat, Who, though advis'd, the same Mistakes repeat. **1850** SIR F. MADDEN *Wycliffite Bible* List of MSS. No. 65 Each scribe has peculiarities of orthography. **1861** PALEY *Æschylus* (ed. 2) *Supplices* 247 *note*, If the nominative had been found by a scribe in his copy, he was not very likely to have altered it. **1892** LOUNSBURY *Stud. Chaucer* I. 375 No one familiar with the work of the scribe will be disposed to pay too much respect to his authority.

6. a. A penman, one (more or less) skilled in penmanship. Now somewhat *arch.*

1588 SHAKS. *Tit. A.* II. iv. 4 Write downe thy mind, bewray thy meaning so, And if thy stumpes will let thee play the Scribe. **1705–6** PENN in *Pennsylv. Hist. Soc. Mem.* X. 111, I must rcommend him to your care, being a scribe and an accomptant. **1849** JAMES *Woodman* ii, I could make out plain court hand a great deal better when written by a good scribe. **1852** DICKENS *Bleak Ho.* liii, Mr. Bucket..is no great scribe; rather handling the pen like the pocket-staff he carries about with him.

†**b.** (See quot.) *Obs. rare.*

1696–1715 *Laws Maryland* ii. (1722) 3 One Master, One Usher, and One Writing-Master or Scribe to a School.

7. a. Used (more or less playfully) for: One who writes or is in the habit of writing; an author; the writer (of a letter, etc.).

1585 JAS. I *Ess. Poesie* (Arb.) 31 Your shameles rymes,.. ô Scrybes prophane [orig. *Profanes escriuains*]. **1712** ADDISON *Spect.* No. 475 ¶4, I have been engaged in this Subject by the following Letter, which comes to me from some notable young female Scribe. **1778** MME. D'ARBLAY *Diary* 20 July (1891) I. 16 As I am often writing..he commonly calls me the scribe. **1886** TUPPER *Autobiog.* 60 Some frivolous larks in the Waterford days, wherewith I need not say the present scribe had nothing to do. **1892** DU MAURIER *Peter Ibbetson* I. 7, I am but a poor scribe, ill versed in the craft of wielding words and phrases.

b. Applied to a political pamphleteer or journalist; chiefly with contemptuous notion, a party hack. (Coloured by sense 4.)

1826 COBBETT *Rur. Rides* (1885) II. 100 The impudent scribes would make us believe, that England was formerly nothing at all, till they [the Scotch] came to enlighten it. **1830** D'ISRAELI *Chas. I*, III. xiv. 303 Leighton seems to have been the first of our political scribes..who [etc.]. **1884** *St. James's Gaz.* 8 Feb. 3/1 So conscious are the scribes of the Government of the state of feeling in the country. **1885** *Liverpool Daily Post* 1 June 5/3 The youngest scribe of a Tory organ could manage national affairs much better.

c. *U.S.* A newspaper reporter.

1929 D. RUNYON in *Hearst's Internat.* July 58/1 Dave grabs the scribe..and is taking him out for an airing!.. Taking a newspaper guy..out for an airing is apt to cause talk. **1930** *Amer. Speech* VI. 120 *Scribe*,..reporter, writer: Judge Quashes Police Charges Against Scribe (here, a reporter). **1962** *John o' London's* 25 Jan. 82/3 A reporter is a *scribe* or *scribbler*.

†**8.** A cuttle-fish. (See quot.) *Obs.*

1655 MOUFFET & BENNET *Health's Improv.* xviii. 151 Cuttles, (called also..scribes for their incky humour).

9. *Comb.*, as **scribe palsy**, 'writers' cramp' (*Dunglison's Dict. Med. Sci.* 1876); **scribe-work** *nonce-wd.*, work for 'scribes' or clerks.

1829 W. IRVING *Life & Lett.* (1864) II. 415 There is likely to be but moderate scribe work in the legation.

scribe (skraɪb), *sb.*[2] [f. SCRIBE *v.* Cf. SCRIVE *sb.*[2]]

1. A tool for scribing (see SCRIBE *v.*) in *Carpentry*, *Building*, etc.

1812 P. NICHOLSON *Mech. Exerc.* 212 (Bricklaying) The Scribe is a spike or large nail ground to a sharp point, to mark the bricks on the face and back by the tapering edges of the mould, in order to cut them.

b. *attrib.* **scribe-awl** (see quot.); **scribe-mark**, a mark made with a scribing-iron on a log, etc.; a mark scored on stone as a guide for cutting.

1875 KNIGHT *Dict. Mech.*, *Scribe-awl*, an awl used for making lines to be followed in sawing or cutting out work. **1881** YOUNG *Every Man his own Mech.* §156 The following are the 'scribe marks' indicating the quality of Memel and Dantzic timber. **1883** NASMYTH *Autobiog.* xiv. 256 The delicate scribe marks by which the mason some 1900 years ago lined out his work on the blocks of stone he was about to chip. **1888** BURT *Stand. Timber Meas.* 278 Table of Scribe Marks of Cubic Contents on Log Timber.

2. *dial.* A written mark; a scrap of writing: usually ***scribe o' the pen***. (Cf. SCRAPE *sb.*[1] 2 b.)

1805 R. ANDERSON *Cumbld. Ball.*, *Ruth* iii, She..Ne'er yence sent the scribe of a pen. **1829** BROCKETT *N.C. Words* (ed. 2), *Scribe of a pen*, a letter. **1903** CROCKETT *Banner of Blue* viii. 88 Jeems Carlyle never wrote a scribe o' print, or hand-write either.

scribe (skraɪb), *v.* [Of obscure history; in sense 1 perh. aphetic for DESCRIBE *v.*; in sense 2 partly ad. L. *scrībĕre* to write, partly f. SCRIBE *sb.*[1] Cf. SCRIVE *v.*]

1. In technical uses. **a.** *trans.* Originally, in *Carpentry*, to mark the intended outline of (a piece of timber) with one point of a pair of compasses, moved parallel with the other point which is drawn along the edge of the piece to which the 'scribed' piece is to be fitted. Now in wider sense: To mark or score (wood, metal, bricks) with a pointed instrument (often regulated by a gauge or similar contrivance) in order to indicate the outline to which the piece is to be cut or shaped; to draw (a line, etc.) in this way.

Now done on other materials, and by means of a fine laser beam as well as pointed instruments.

1678 MOXON *Mech. Exerc.* VII. 112 To make these two peeces of Stuff joyn close together all the way, they Scribe it, (as they phrase it,) thus [a long explanation follows]. **1688** HOLME *Armoury* III. 101/2 *Scribe*, is the drawing of a line or stroak with the Compasses upon a piece of stuff that is straight, thereby to cut it so as it may join to an Irregular piece, whether bowed or cornered. **1811** *Self Instructor* 528 With your ivory point scribe them. **1878** MAYER *Sound* 154 With the separated points of a pair of spring dividers scribe around the edge of the templet. **1902** P. MARSHALL *Metal Tools* 18 The edge against which the required line is scribed. **1967** *Electronics* 6 Mar. 218 (Advt.), Their 4-sided diamond scriber often leaves rough, chipped lines when it scribes crystalline wafers for dicing. **1975** J. B. HARLEY *O.S. Maps* i. 11 A second sheet of plastic material..is placed in exact registration with the first, and is then used for plotting and scribing the contours. **1977** *Engin. Materials & Design* Aug. 30/1 Blank sheets of fired alumina ceramic are accurately located on the table and, working from a datum point, the laser scribes a grid matrix system of close and regularly spaced blind holes.

b. Hence, to shape the edge of (a piece of timber, metal, etc.) so that it will fit into the irregular edge of another piece or to an uneven surface. (See quot. 1842.)

1679 MOXON *Mech. Exerc.* VIII. 140 The Joysts are always scribed to project over..the Roundness or waynniness of the upper side of the Girder. **1812** P. NICHOLSON *Mech. Exerc.* 177 To Scribe one piece of Board or Stuff to another. *Ibid.*, Thus the skirting boards of a room should be scribed to the floor. **1830** HEDDERWICK *Mar. Archit.* 259 Make a mould for the foot of the stem with its cog or coak, scribing it so that it will fit very completely. **1837** WHITTOCK *Bk. Trades* (1842) 289 (*Gun-Maker*) Parts of the locks and springs are 'scribed' in to the butt of the gun-stock. **1842** GWILT *Encycl. Archit.* Gloss., *Scribing*, fitting the edge of a board to a surface not accurately plane, as the skirting of a room to a floor. In joinery, it is the fitting one piece to another, so that the fibres of them may be perpendicular to each other, the two edges being cut to an angle to join. **1844** H. STEPHENS *Bk. Farm* II. 69, 6 slots are then laid at due distances upon the heads, and the latter are scribed to the size of each slot, to regulate the mortises.

c. To draw (lines) on wood with a pointed tool.

1890 W. J. GORDON *Foundry* 59 A drawing-board..on which the lines are first chalked and then carved, or scribed.

d. To mark (timber, a cask, etc.) with a scribing-iron.

1859 [implied in SCRIBING *vbl. sb.* 2]. **1883** CLARK RUSSELL *Sailors' Lang.*, *Scribe*, to mark packages in bond with the number and weight. **1888** BURT *Stand. Timber Meas.* 75 The Raze Knife, for scribing the numbers and contents on the logs for identification.

e. To delineate with incised marks.

1896 KIPLING *Seven Seas, Story of Ung* 12 He..Pictured the mountainous mammoth..Out of the love that he bore them, scribing them clearly on bone.

2. a. *intr.* To act as a scribe, to write. **b.** *trans.* To write down. *rare* exc. *dial.*

1782 MISS BURNEY *Cecilia* x. vi, Contenting himself with doing nothing but scribble and scribe one day. **1787** J. CLARKE *Lakes* Introd. 26 *To scribe* is still to write. **1801** SOUTHEY in Robberd *Mem. W. Taylor* (1843) I. 378 As if the author of 'Joan of Arc' and of 'Thalaba' were made a great man by scribing for the Irish Chancellor of the Exchequer. **1838** *Fraser's Mag.* XVII. 322 A writer..scribing about Jeffery as if it was a living thing. **1882** STEVENSON *Fam. Stud., Pepys* (1888) 299 He desires that..gentleman,..to recall..the very line his own romantic self was scribing at the moment. **1894** CROCKETT *Raiders* (ed. 3) 364 Patrick Walker (he that scribes the stories of the sufferers and has had them printed).

scribed (skraɪbd), *ppl. a.* [f. SCRIBE *v.* + -ED[1].]

1. *Carpentry, Building*, etc. In sense 1 of the verb.

1882 W. J. CHRISTY *Joints* 61 [Mason's Joints] Scribed Joint.—This occurs where stone cornices and mouldings unite with corresponding ornamentations in cast iron. *Ibid.* 74 [Joiner's Joints.] Scribed Joint is formed by scribing. **1971** *Physics Bull.* July 405/2 Conventionally the individual units are separated from a block by scribing with a diamond wheel and then breaking the ceramic along the scribed line. **1977** *Engin. Materials & Design* Aug. 29/3 The new installation..will provide the electronics industry with a high speed service based on..the supply of scribed wafer from its own stock of ceramic materials.

2. *Her.* Of an escutcheon: Having its base formed by two undulating curves meeting at the apex.

1892 E. CASTLE *Engl. Book-plates* 128 The square-sided, eared, scribed or angular based escutcheon.

scribedom ('skraɪbdəm). [f. SCRIBE *sb.*[1] + -DOM.] The (Jewish) scribes as a body.

1863 *Smith's Dict. Bible* III. 1164/2 (*Scribes*) The spirit of Scribedom was growing.

scribel, obs. form of SCRIBBLE *v.*[1]

†**'scribelet.** *Obs. rare*[−1]. In 6 scriblet. [f. SCRIBE *sb.*[1] + -LET.] An insignificant scribe or writer.

1599 *Broughton's Let.* ii. 10 Your scriblets, forsooth, must countenance the Bible.

scriber ('skraɪbə(r)). [f. SCRIBE *v.* + -ER[1].]

1. A tool or appliance for scribing.

1834–6 P. BARLOW in *Encycl. Metrop.* (1845) VIII. 296/2 The chisels [of the mortising machine] are provided with small teeth..: these are called scribers. **1869** C. KNIGHT *Mechanician* 109 A scriber for marking diagrams on tables or plattens, is a piece of steel wire which [etc.]. **1875** *Carpentry & Join.* 58 With a steel scriber or sharp hard pencil trace each dovetail carefully on the end of the wood. **1908** *Remin. Stonemason* 104 The workman runs round the pattern with a sharp-pointed tool called a scriber. This scriber ploughs a minute furrow in the stone.

attrib. **1869** C. KNIGHT *Mechanician* 111 A scriber-block is an instrument consisting of two principal parts; these are the movable scriber, and the block to which the scriber is attached... Scriber-blocks are principally used to mark straight lines upon engine-work of all classes. **1902** P. MARSHALL *Metal Tools* 19 A little chalk rubbed over the surface of the metal will often enable the scriber lines to be more clearly seen.

2. (See quot. 1968.)

1968 'B. MATHER' *Springers* v. 52 A scriber is a circular piece of paper-thin copper which fits out of sight under the moving part of the [telephone] dial which has a tiny sharp point set in it. The pressure of the dialler's finger is sufficient to bring the point down on the copper... The resultant marks..can tell..what numbers have been called. **1978** J. BARNETT *Head of Force* xvi. 153 We installed scribers under the dials of public phones adjacent to suspect premises.

scribeship ('skraɪbʃɪp). *rare*[−2]. [f. SCRIBE *sb.*[1] + -SHIP.] The office or function of a scribe.

1624 BP. MOUNTAGUE *Gagg* To Rdr. 5 The Scribe was some puny-nouice in euery point of Scrib-ship. **1810** in *Spirit Publ. Jrnls.* XIV. 149 Myself his scribe, and all my scribeship then To note how many casks were gaug'd.

scribing ('skraɪbɪŋ), *vbl. sb.* [-ING[1].]

1. The action of the verb SCRIBE.

1710 J. HARRIS *Lex. Techn.* II, *Scribing*, when the Joyners would fit a piece of Board, &c. to an irregular Surface, or any other irregular Piece: they [etc.]. **1876** PAPWORTH in *Encycl. Brit.* IV. 494/1 This operation is called scribing, and the result of it is evidently to make the skirting fit down on the floor with the utmost precision. **1896** KIPLING *Seven Seas, Story of Ung* 50 Ung, a maker of pictures, fell to his scribing on bone. **1969** G. C. DICKINSON *Maps & Air Photographs* v. 75 Scribing..consists in producing a negative-type drawing by scraping away an opaque coating applied to glass or dimensionally stable plastic sheets. **1975** J. B. HARLEY *O.S. Maps* i. 14 The use of scribing instead of traditional drawing was an especially important development. **1977** *Engin. Materials & Design* Aug. 29/3 The first half of 1977 also saw the introduction by Laser Cutting Ltd of what is believed to be Europe's first facility specifically designed to provide a high quality service for ceramic scribing by laser.

2. *concr.* The identifying mark on a cask, etc.; *pl.* incised markings on stone, etc.; also, writings, scribblings.

1859 M'CLINTOCK *Voy. 'Fox' in Arctic Reg.* xiii. 242 The heading [of a cask] has been brought on board, but the 'scribing' upon it is very indistinct. **1895** *Nature* 28 Nov. 83 A number of mysterious rock-scribings. **1895** *Athenæum* 14 Dec. 839/1 Many of them [megalithic remains] are marked with scribings and other ornamentations. **1897** CROCKETT *Lad's Love* Ded. 9 But if you like my scribings not—well, pass; at least I was entirely happy when I wrote them.

3. *attrib.* In the names of various instruments or appliances for 'scribing', as ***scribing-block, gauge, -iron, plate, point, speed***, etc. (See quots.)

1863 F. CAMPIN *Mech. Engin.* 66 (Cent.) A *scribing-block, which consists of a piece of metal joined to a wooden block at one end, and having at the other a point; it is useful for making centres, and for similar purposes. **1902** P. MARSHALL *Metal Tools* 19 Sometimes..a scriber is used in conjunction with a scribing block or surface gauge. **1839** URE *Dict. Arts* 269 A *scribing cutter is made to traverse round, and cut the pieces [*sc.* for the heads of casks]. **1895** *Mod. Steam Eng.* 84 *Scribing gauge. **1858** SIMMONDS *Dict. Trade*, **Scribing-iron*, an iron-pointed instrument for marking casks and logs of timber. **1969** *R. & E. Coordinator* Apr. 9/2 A new glass-based *scribing plate for the generation of microphotography masters, precision printed circuits, and other applications requiring extremely clean, sharp lines. **1879** *Nature* 30 Oct. 623/1 It is necessary that one and the same *scribing point should describe the sum of the two motions. **1971** *Physics Bull.* Dec. 743/3 The *scribing speed is 360 in min^{-1}.

scribism ('skraɪbɪz(ə)m). [f. SCRIBE *sb.*[1] + -ISM.] The teaching and literature of the ancient Jewish scribes (SCRIBE *sb.*[1] 1); the qualities of the scribes.

1657 J. WATTS *Scribe, Pharisee*, etc. II. 203 As of all the other your Texts alleged against us, so of this, and the Scribism of the same. **1850** F. W. ROBERTSON *Serm.* Ser. III. v. (1857) 72 With our Evangelicalism, Tractarianism, Scribeisms, Pharisaisms, we have ceased to front the living fact. **1892** BRUCE *Apologetics* II. iv. 219 A risk which the subsequent career of scribism shows to have been far from imaginary.

†**scri'bistical**, *a. Obs. rare*[−1]. [f. SCRIBE *sb.*[1] + -ISTICAL.] Characteristic of or relating to the scribes (SCRIBE *sb.*[1] 1).

1600 W. WATSON *Decacordon* (1602) 61 Their Pharisaical holinesse and Scribisticall zeale and religion.

scriblative, variant of SCRIBBLATIVE *a.*

scrible, etc., obs. forms of SCRIBBLE, etc.

Scriblerian (skrɪ'blɪərɪən), *sb.* (and *a.*) [f. the name of Martinus *Scriblerus*, a character invented by members of the Scriblerus Club (see below); cf. SCRIBBLER[1] + -IAN.] A member of the Scriblerus Club formed *c* 1713 by Pope, Swift, Arbuthnot, and others, who produced the *Memoirs of Martinus Scriblerus* (publ. 1741) in order to ridicule lack of taste in learning. Also as *adj.*

1935 L. M. BEATTIE *John Arbuthnot* iv. 271 Swift's experience as a Scriblerian must have affected the turn given to numerous observations in *Gulliver*. *Ibid.* 276 In its humor for humor's sake it is typically Scriblerian. **1950** C. KERBY-MILLER *Mem. Martinus Scriblerus* 1 The activities which may be labeled Scriblerian spanned a period of almost three decades. *Ibid.* 31 The Scriblerians began collecting material of all sorts. **1969** P. KÖSTER in *Philol. Q.* Apr. 207 Although the subtlety of this satiric segment may have been *caviare* to all but the refined taste of Arbuthnot's fellow Scriblerians, the 'String of Epithets' could not be ignored by any but the grossest ear. **1977** —— in R. A. Wisbey *Computer in Literary & Linguistic Res.* IV. 133 Unfortunately.., there are no examples of Scriblerian collaboration in which the shares of Arbuthnot and Swift are already known.

scrick, scrief, varr. SKRIK, SCREEF.

†**scrick-shoe.** *Obs. rare*[−1]. [a. MDu. *schricschoe*, f. stem of *schricken* to stride + *schoe* SHOE *sb.* Cf. MHG. *schriteschuoch*, mod.G. *schlittschuh*, in the same sense.] A skate.

1659 HOOLE *Comenius' Vis. World* (1672) 275 Boyes exercise themselves in runing, either upon the Ice, in Scrick-shooes,..or in the open field.

scriddan ('skrɪdən). *Sc.* Also scridan. [a. Gael. *sgriodan*.] (See quot. 1820.)

1793 *Statist. Acc. Scot.* VI. 249 The farms which are bases to high mountains, as in Kintail, suffer great losses from what is called Scriddan, or 'mountain torrent'... The farm of Auchuirn..was, in 1745, rendered uninhabitable..by an awful Scriddan. **1820** *Glenfergus* I. 203 (Jam.) When the rain falling on the side of a hill, tears the surface, and precipitates a large quantity of stones and gravel into the plain below, we call it a scridan. **1820** *Marmaiden o' Clyde* I. in Whitelaw *Bk. Sc. Ballads* (1857) 93/2 There's no ae burn in braid Clydesdale But wimples at my will, Nor a scridden broun that but my leave Comes tumbling doun the hill.

†**scride**, *v. Sc. Obs.* [? Echoic: cf. SCREED *v.*] *intr.* To make a shrill sound. Hence **scriding** *vbl. sb.*

c **1690** in *Roxb. Ball.* (1888) VI. 608 What? shall my Viol silent be, or leave her wonted Scriding?

scrie, scrieh: see SCRY, SKREIGH.

scrieve (skriːv), *v.*[1] *Sc.* Also **screeve, skrieve, screive, scrive.** [app. a. ON. *skrefa* to stride.] *intr.* To move or glide along swiftly. (See also *Eng. Dial. Dict.* and Jam.)

1785 BURNS *Halloween* xxiv, She thro' the whins, an' by the cairn, An' owre the hill gaed scrievin. —— *Sc. Drink* v, But oil'd by thee, The wheels o' life gae down-hill, scrievin, Wi' rattlin glee. **1822** HOGG *Perils of Man* I. 54 Scrieving o'er law and dale. **1896** CROCKETT *Grey Man* i. 3 A screed of muirburn screeving across the hills.

scrieve (skriːv), *v.*[2] *Shipbuilding.* [Dialectal var. SCRIVE *v.* (*Eng. Dial. Dict.*); cf. SCREEVE *v.*[2]] = SCRIVE *v.* 2. Freq. in *Comb.* as **scrieve-board** = SCRIVE-BOARD.

1898 T. H. WATSON *Naval Archit.* vi. 54 The Scrieve Board is a platform of well-seasoned deals... Sometimes both sides of the ship are scrieved in. **1901** T. WALTON *Steel Ships* vii. 180 He then transfers from the mould loft floor to the scrieve board the midship section of the vessel... He also scrieves in all decks, stringers, keelsons, and floors. **1921** *Flight* XIII. 214/1 Many engineers and aircraft builders do not realise to what fine limits naval architects have to work when scrieving out the lines. **1951** *Engineering* 15 June 730/1 Beside this striking exhibit is the scrieve board corresponding to it, showing all the details of the construction. **1957** [see LOFTSMAN].

scrieve, var. SCREEVE *sb.*

scrift(e, obs. forms of SHRIFT.

scriggle ('skrɪg(ə)l), *sb.* Chiefly *dial.* [f. SCRIGGLE *v.*] A wriggle; also, a scrawly piece of writing.

1832 J. WILSON *Noct. Ambr.* in *Blackw. Mag.* Apr. 697 Unproductive of so much as the scriggle of a single tadpole. **1895** *E. Angl. Gloss.*, *Scriggle*, a quick motion caused by tickling, a wriggle. **1905** *Daily Chron.* 18 Sept. 4/5 The last scriggle I had from him came on Friday night.

scriggle ('skrɪg(ə)l), *v.* Chiefly *dial.*: see Eng. Dial. Dict. Also **sk-**. [Phonetically symbolic: cf. SCRUGGLE *v.*] *intr.* To wriggle or struggle.

1806 BLOOMFIELD *Wild Flowers, Horkey* 169 They skriggl'd and began to scold, But laughing got the master. **1830** W. TAYLOR *Hist. Surv. Germ. Poetry* II. 359 How brisk [the fish] play And swarm, and scriggle everywhere! **1895** *E. Angl. Gloss.*, *Skriggle*, to wriggle or struggle away.

Hence **'scriggler**, a wriggling creature; **'scriggling** *ppl. a.*, that 'scriggles'; **'scriggly** *a.*, wriggly, scrawly.

1823 E. Moor *Suffolk Words* 355 A skrigglen eel. **1854** Miss Baker *Northampt. Gloss.* II. 207 A person who writes a light, scratchy, irregular hand, is said to write a *scriggling* hand. **1888** Fenn *Dick o' Fens* 232 The scriggly legs of a beetle. **1895** A. Patterson *Man & Nature on Broads* 51 Into it [the eel-set] the scrigglers swim. **1905** *Daily Chron.* 16 Nov. 4/6 L. F. Austin's scriggly manuscript.

†**scright.** *Obs.* In 4 **skrythe** (*but rimed with* -nyghte). [f. skrike *v.*] A shout, cry.

13.. *St. Cristofer* 315 in Horstm. *Altengl. Leg.* (1881) 459 Whene þat it was abowte mydnyghte, Byȝonde þe water he herde a skrythe, Full lowde one heghte he herde it cry.

scriit, variant of scrite, writing.

scrike, scriker, scriking: see skrike *sb.* and *v.*

scrim (skrɪm). [Of obscure origin.]

1. A kind of thin canvas used for lining in upholstery, and for other purposes. Also *attrib.* Now freq. made of muslin, sacking, or similar material. Also in *Mil.* use.

1792 *Statist. Acc. Scot.* VI. 514 A few yard-wides called Scrims. **1875** Knight *Dict. Mech.*, *Scrims*, thin canvas glued on the inside of a panel to keep it from cracking or breaking. **1881** *Carter & Co.'s Pract. Gardener* 75 It is a good plan to have coarse scrim canvas strained over the ventilators. **1881** T. Moore in *Encycl. Brit.* XII. 220/2 They should have attached to them scrim cloth (a sort of thin canvas), which admits light pretty freely, yet is sufficient to ward off ordinary frosts. **1885** *N.Y. Weekly Sun* 13 May 6/7 White goods, scrim curtains and table damasks have a fairly liberal outlet. **1895** *Daily News* 2 Feb. 2/6 The recent briskness in scrims has shown no sign of falling off. **1936** R. Hyde *Passport to Hell* xiii. 199 The huge spoil-dumps were camouflaged with green boughs and scrim. **1942** H. A. Maddox *Dict. Stationery* (ed. 2) 97 Scrim. The coarse textured net fabric used for attaching to the glued backs of cheap cased-in books. **1947** D. M. Davin *Gorse blooms Pale* 179 A man sat screened by scrim on the latrine. **1961** *Wall St. Jrnl.* 24 Jan. 1/4 Most of the testing..involves use of knitted paper in such unglamorous jobs as backing, or 'scrim', for more costly synthetic fibers. **1964** *Weekly News* (Auckland) 29 Apr. 41/2 Later there will be shrubs that have been wrenched and their roots balled up in scrim. **1970** *New Society* 5 Mar. 386/1 One technique, SRM (scrim-reinforced material), uses heat to laminate a scrim of random-laid fibres to wadding; the heat reactivates the bonding glue.

2. A piece of scrim used as a window-covering; *spec.* a thin, gauze-like, curtain material. Usu. as ***window scrim.***

1915 E. G. Pilling *Anzac Memory* (1933) 119 Look out of the broken, scrim-covered window across fields white with snow. **1969** Widdowson & Halpert in Halpert & Story *Christmas Mumming in Newfoundland* 149 Some would put on what they used to call muslin, you know. Muslin or scrim, window scrim.., you know, like you'd have for a curtain; you could see out through it. **1970** G. F. Newman *Sir, you Bastard* ii. 61 Outside on the balcony was a small piece of window scrim.

3. a. *Theatr.* and *Cinemat.* Gauze cloth used for screens or for filtering theatrical lighting; a screen of this material. orig. and chiefly *U.S.*

1928 A. E. Krows *Equipment for Stage Production* vii. 90 The foliage..is painted on a canvas drop..and, after being cut away, is mounted..to a curtain made of a coarse netting called scrim. **1937** F. Napier *Curtains for Stage Settings* vi. 101 The space below the aperture can be filled in with brown paper, decorated with panels outlined in paint or chalk, but it must be pasted on to butter muslin or scrim to make it more durable. **1939** N. Coward *Play Parade* II. p. x, *Scrim*, American term for a Gauze Cloth. **1950** *People* (Austral.) 15 Mar. 46/1 She was told she would be seated behind a 'scrim' (stage jargon for a gauze screen). **1957** V. J.-R. Kehoe *Techn. Film & T.V. Make-Up* i. 17 A spotlight to add highlight to the cheekbone, with a scrim over the light to soften the beam. **1975** *New Yorker* 26 May 90/2 The Prince and the Lilac Fairy get into a boat that remains motionless as a scrim painted with leaves and branches moves sideways across the stage. **1977** *Time* 27 June 45/1 The vast (5,000 sq. ft.) shuffle area is a stage, with theatrical lighting, scrims and backdrops rising as high as 85 ft.

b. *fig.* A veil or screen; something that conceals what is happening.

a **1963** S. Plath *Crossing Water* (1971) 37 The salt Scrim of a sea breeze. **1970** H. & F. Schreider *Exploring Amazon* vii. 154 The city of Manaus shimmered through the great scrim of rain like a stage setting from the pageant of its own lost glory. **1972** *Publishers' Weekly* 12 June 16/1 France and the French did more than serve as a scrim for vagabonding Americans. **1977** *Time* 6 June 10/2 The full story of Podgorny's dismissal may remain forever behind the scrim that veils the Kremlin's backstage dramas.

†**'scrimer.** *Obs. rare*$^{-1}$. In 7 scrimure. [aphetic var. of escrimer.] A fencer.

1602 Shaks. *Ham.* iv. vii. 101 (Qo.^{2}) The Scrimures of their nation He swore had neither motion, guard nor eye, If you opposd them.

†**'scrimish,** *sb. Obs.* Forms: 6 **skrimishe, skrymisshe, scrimishe, scresmys, screamishe.** [f. scrimish *v.* Cf. the later form scrimmage *sb.*]

1. = skirmish *sb.*

1557 Machyn *Diary* (Camden) 144 The xvij day of July was a scresmys at Margyson be-twyn the Englysmen and Frenchemen. **1562** Montgomery in *Archæologia* XLVII. 224 As the auncient and faulmous Romainges..who exercised theire souldiors to the screamishe, to marche in battaile [etc.]. *Ibid.* 226 To be instructed yn martiall fealtes ..whithe the marche, scrimishe, and order of battaile.

2. An alarm, an outcry. *rare.* Cf. scrimmage 2.

1505 in *10th Rep. Hist. MSS. Comm.* App. v. 391 Every man that answerith not the crye or skrimishe at every of the town gattes..with his feansabull weapon, to paie and forfayte xii.*d.*

†**'scrimish,** *v. Obs.* In 6 **skrymysshe, skryssmys.** [variant (after OF. *escremiss-*) of skirmish *v.* (a. OF. *eskermiss-*), q.v. for the full history. Cf. the later form scrimmage *v.*] *intr.* To skirmish.

1523 Ld. Berners *Froiss.* I. xviii. 9 b, And some of the oste mounted on good horses, and rode forth to skrymysshe with theym. **1554** Machyn *Diary* (Camden) 60 Ther the qweyns men and [Wyatt's] men dyd skryssmys.

scrimmage ('skrɪmɪdʒ), **scrummage** ('skrʌmɪdʒ), *sb.* Forms: α. 5 **scrymmage,** 6 **scrymage,** 7 **scrimage,** 7, 9 **skrimmage,** 8 **skrimage,** 8–9 **scrimmage;** β. 9 **skrummage, scrummage.** [Altered form of scrimish *sb.*, the ending being associated with **-age** *suffix*. Cf. the parallel *skirmage*, obs. var. of skirmish *sb.*

This is now used primarily as a sporting term. The older *i*-form is common in all senses, and has become predominant in American Football, whilst the *u*-form is preferred in Rugby Football.]

†**1.** = skirmish *sb.* Also, a fencing bout. *Obs.*

c **1470** Henry *Wallace* iii. 359 Ane Inglisman, on the gait, saw he play At the scrymmagis a bukler on his hand. *Ibid.* ix. 458 Then Longaweill, that ay was full sawage, With Wallace past, as ane to that scrymmage. **1549** *MSS. Dk. Rutland* (Hist. MSS. Comm.) IV. 356 To ij Duchemen that were hurt in the scrymage at Dunbar, xs. **1567** Drant *Horace, Ep.* i. xviii. F v, The Oste deuydes their bargies, and the water scrymage then..in foishe guyse is playde by youthely men. **1643** *Par. Reg. St. Mary's Beverley* 30 June, O'r great scrimage in Beverley & god gave us the victory.

†**2.** An outcry, alarm; = scrimish *sb.* 2. *Obs.*

1632 *Acts Durham High Comm. Crt.* (Surtees) 30 Shee heard her mistris..make a great skrimmage or outcry.

3. a. *colloq.* A noisy contention or tussle; also, a confused struggle between persons, often with exchange of blows; a free-fight scuffle. Also *fig.* (freq. after sense 4).

α. **1780** Johnson *Lett.* 6 June, Mrs. Vesey protests that I do not love them since that skrimage. **1826** J. F. Cooper *Mohicans* xx, That we shall have what you may call a brisk push of it, is probable; and it may happen, a brush, a skrimmage. **1844** *Catholic Weekly Instr.* 127 The wild exultant cry so frequently heard in an Irish scrimmidge. **1884** *Manch. Exam.* 15 Nov. 5/2 There was generally a chance of a scrimmage with the police when these mounted processions took their outing. **1897** Mary Kingsley *W. Africa* 138 Fearful scrimmage heard going on all the time on the deck below. **1900** H. A. Jones *Mrs. Dane's Defence* i. 17 Have you made a mess of your life?.. I wonder how many poor women have been sacrificed in the—scrimmage? **1930** E. M. Brent-Dyer *Chalet Girls in Camp* vi. 93 After something like a scrimmage they got the thing right. **1957** L. Durrell *Justine* iii. 185 The whole portentous scrimmage of sex. **1979** *This England* Winter 28/2 The doors of St. Paul's revolve like Marks and Spencer's onto the scrimmage round its book-stalls.

β. **1823** E. Moor *Suffolk Words* 356 *Skrummage*, a battle, a fray; probably skirmish. **1830** Marryat *King's Own* xxvi, In two scrummages only two men were killed out of hundreds. **1833** —— *P. Simple* xiii, 'Was there a fight?' 'Not much of a fight—only a bit of a skrummage—three crowner's inquests, no more.' **1905** *Daily Chron.* 15 July 6/3 [The] entrance arrangements, which necessitated a scrummage lasting from five to fifteen minutes to those who were ticket-holders. **1959** A. Sillitoe *Loneliness of Long-Distance Runner* 23 Mam had forgotten to buy me one in the scrummage of shopping.

b. *dial.* A confused, noisy proceeding. (Cf. *Eng. Dial. Dict.* and scrimmage *v.* 2.)

1855 Kingsley *Westw. Ho!* xxx, If everybody's caranting about to once, each after his own man, nobody'll find nothing in such a scrimmage as that.

4. a. *Rugby Football.* Originally, a confused struggle in which the players on either side endeavor to force their opponents and the ball towards the opposite goal; now, an ordered formation in which the two sets of forwards pack themselves together with their heads down and endeavour by pushing to work their opponents off the ball and break away with it or heel it out. Phr. ***to carry the scrimmage***, to gain ground in a scrimmage. ***to hold the scrimmage***, to prevent one's opponents from gaining ground.

α. **1864** *Field* 10 Dec. 403/2 After several severe scrimmages in the School goal, a run-in was obtained. **1887** Shearman *Athletics & Football* 311 The first and essential requisite to a forward team is that it should be able to 'hold', if not always to 'carry the scrimmage'.

β. **1857** Hughes *Tom Brown* i. v, Then the two sides close and you can see nothing for minutes but a swaying crowd of boys, at one point violently agitated. That is where the ball is... This is what we call a scrummage, gentlemen. **1867** *Routledge's Handbk. Football* 47 A Scrummage commences —i.e. the holder puts the ball down on the ground, and all who have closed round on their respective sides begin kicking at the ball. **1889** H. Vassall *Rugby Football* 32 A team must contain enough honest workers to be able to hold the scrummage. **1892** *Outdoor Games* 548 A maul, or tight scrummage. *Ibid.* 549 A loose scrummage may be described as half way between a maul and a dribble.

b. A tussle for the ball among players (in various games).

1883 F. M. Crawford *Mr. Isaacs* viii, [Polo] Twice the ball was sent over the line..by long sweeping blows from Isaacs, who ever hovered on the edge of the scrimmage. **1889** *Field* 12 Jan. 61/3 [Hockey] Lucas putting the ball through out of a scrummage in front of goal off the goal-keeper. *Ibid.* 89/1, [Association] A scrimmage in the mouth of the goal appeared likely to result in a further point.

c. *Amer. Football.* (*a*) A sequence of play which is started when two lines of opposing players are ranked parallel to the goal-lines, and a centre holds the ball between the teams before handing or passing it to one of his backs (†see also quot. 1883); ***line of scrimmage, scrimmage line***: the (imaginary) line separating two teams at the beginning of such a play.

1880 *Harvard Advocate* 8 Oct. 18/2 With such a number of rushers to enter in the scrimmages..it was found almost impossible for either side to make a goal or a touch-down. **1883** *Foot-Ball Rules* (Amer. Intercollegiate Assoc.) 6 A *scrimmage* takes place when the holder of the ball puts it down on the ground and puts it in play by kicking it or snapping it back. **1896** Camp & Deland *Football* xiv. 412 The man who puts the ball in play in a scrimmage, and the opponent opposite him cannot pick up the ball until it has touched some third man. **1899** W. Camp in *Football* (Badm. Libr.) 287 (American Football) Someone upon his side.. must place the ball on the ground at that spot for a 'scrimmage', as it is termed. **1909** *Crimson-White* (Univ. of Alabama) 18 Nov. 4/2 It finds half a dozen Alabama players bunched at the end of the scrimmage line. **1910** W. Camp *Bk. Foot-Ball* ii. 26 The American scrimmage, while coming directly from the English play, bears now no similarity to it. Instead of an indiscriminate kicking struggle we have the snap-back and quarter-back play. The snap-back snaps the ball back with his hands; the quarter seizes it and passes it to any man for whom the ball is destined in the plan of play or he may himself run with it. **1929** G. Bickley *Handbk. Athletics* 105 The offensive team must have *seven* men on the line of scrimmage or be penalized. **1941** *Daily Progress* (Charlottesville, Va.) 14 Jan. 11 A player can elect to run back a punt from scrimmage if the ball is caught in the end zone. **1960** P. W. Bryant *Building Championship Football Team* 49 The defensive ends line up in a four-point stance as close to the line of scrimmage as they can get. **1972** J. Mosedale *Football* i. 6 On an early play from scrimmage, he spilled Thorpe for a loss. **1981** *NCAA Football Rules & Interpretations* FR-30 The neutral zone is the space between the two lines of scrimmage and is established when the ball is ready for play.

(*b*) A session in which an offensive squad practises plays against a defensive squad.

1916 *Mobile* (Alabama) *Register* 6 Oct. 12/3 Long practices with a hard scrimmage each evening..was the schedule all week. **1929** G. Bickley *Handbk. Athletics* 95 'Block somebody!' should be heard on the football field every time a play is run in practice scrimmage. **1954** N. Stone *Coach Tommy of Crimson Tide* 17 After two weeks of work on fundamentals and a few basic plays, the first scrimmage was held. **1968** *Birmingham* (Alabama) *News* 7 Sept. 14/1 Jordan planned a Saturday afternoon scrimmage with freshmen running the SMU offense and defense.

'scrimmage, 'scrummage, *v.* [f. the sb.]

1. *intr.* 'To skirmish, quarrel; to scramble; to argue' (*Eng. Dial. Dict.*).

a **1825** Forby *Voc. E. Anglia*, *Scrimmage, Scrummage* v., to skirmish, &c.

2. To bustle about.

1833 T. Hook *Love & Pride* vi, You keep here, sir, while I go skrimmiging about the premises. **1883** Pennell-Elmhirst *Cream Leicestersh.* 255 Without a scent, hounds scrimmaged hither and thither with the cubs in the low dense gorse. **1887** Hare *Story Life* (1900) VI. 59 She scrimmaged at the fire, and raked out all she possibly could.

3. a. *Rugby Football.* To put (the ball) in a scrummage as a means of re-starting the game when and where it has been temporarily stopped, as for some breach of the rules; also, to propel or take along in a scrimmage.

1881 *Sportsman's Year-bk.* 165 The ball is scrummaged where the act of off-side was committed. **1887** *Field* 19 Nov. 790/1 The ball had been dead a short way outside, and when scrummaged off was removed out of danger. **1892** *Outdoor Games* 540 If it [*sc.* the ball] is scrummaged over [the goal-line], the chances are ten to one that the defending side avert disaster by means of a touch-down.

b. *Amer. Football.* To engage in a scrimmage; *spec.* to practise plays with squads of offensive and defensive players (see sense 4 c (*b*) of the sb.).

1910 *Crimson-White* (Univ. of Alabama) 6 Oct. 1/3 Then the two teams lined up and scrimmaged for quite a time. **1934** *Birmingham* (Alabama) *Age-Herald* 15 Sept. 12/7 For the third consecutive practice day, the Vanderbilt Commodores scrimmaged Monday. **1965** *Tuscaloosa* (Alabama) *News* 9 Sept. 13/6 The Bulldogs scrimmaged Wednesday.

'scrimmager, 'scrummager. [f. scrimmage *v.* + -er^1.] One who takes part in a scrimmage.

1881 *Sportsman's Year-bk.* 263 [Hockey] A somewhat heavier stick best suits the scrimmager. **1889** H. Vassall *Rugby Football* 28 But as every [forward] player..has to go into scrummages whether he likes it or not, he can at least learn not to spoil the play of the genuine scrummagers.

fig. **1903** *Q. Rev.* Apr. 534 It is the fashion to decry those hardy scrimmagers whose battle-pieces occupy so much of the old reviews.

'scrimmaging, 'scrummaging, *vbl. sb.* [f. scrimmage *v.* + -ing^1.]

a. The action of the vb.

1887 Shearman *Athletics & Football* 304 It became necessary to choose some for their scrimmaging, and others for their dribbling and following up. **1889** *Field* 26 Jan. 123/1 A lot of fast scrummaging was indulged in. **1895** W. C. Gore in *Inlander* Nov. 66 *Scrummaging*, ..a term used in the old style of foot-ball to indicate a series of efforts at goal without material results. **1955** *Times* 3 Aug. 3/7 They were beaten by nine points to six by superior scrummaging, prodigious kicking, and keen tackling. **1978** *Rugby World*

Apr. 44/3 The selectors..dropped Faulkner and Quinnell, reducing the efficiency of the scrummaging.

b. *attrib.*

1887 *Field* 19 Nov. 790/1 The forwards are a capital set in the open, but lack scrummaging power. **1887** SHEARMAN *Athletics & Football* 305 The loose scrimmaging system.

'scrimmaging, *ppl. a.* [f. SCRIMMAGE *v.* + -ING².] That scrimmages; bustling, fussy.

1853 R. S. SURTEES *Sponge's Sp. Tour* xiv. (1893) 75 Mrs. Jawleyford..was a very scrimmaging, rough-and-ready sort of woman. *Ibid.* lii. 293 Their management [pack of hounds] was only of the scrimmaging order.

scrimmy ('skrɪmɪ), *int.* [Orig. unknown.] A child's exclamation of astonishment (preceded by *my* or *oh*).

1896 E. TURNER *Little Larrikin* xxv. 315 It's a pound to start with. My scrimmy, you never saw such a lot as were after it! **1914** D. H. LAWRENCE *Prussian Officer & Other Stories* 221 Those old geese, oh, scrimmy, they didn't know where to turn.

scrimp (skrɪmp), *a.* and *adv.* [This and the related SCRIMP *v.* first appear in the 18th c. The origin is obscure; cognate forms are Sw., Da. *skrumpen* shrivelled, MHG. *schrimpfen* (Mid.Ger. *schrimpen* str. vb.) to contract, *trans.* to wrinkle up (the nose), G. *schrumpfen* to shrivel; also SHRIMP *sb.*, in ME. a diminutive creature. More remotely allied are OE. *scrimman* to be paralysed, SCRAM *a.*]

A. *adj.* Scant, scanty, meagre.

1718 WODROW *Corr.* (1843) II. 380 They say the young man is none of the greatest abilities, and the people are not so much for him, and his call scrimp; and it's alleged this aversion comes from the Presbytery. **1725** RAMSAY *Gentle Sheph.* III. iv, He gangs about sornan frae Place to Place, As scrimp of Manners as of Sense and Grace. **1733** W. CRAWFORD *Infidelity* (1836) 59 Our own soul..is..too scrimp an image to give us either a full or clear representation of him. **1812** SIR J. SINCLAIR *Syst. Husb. Scot.* I. 15 The accommodations necessary for preparing the grain for market ought never to be too scrimp. **1854** MISS KEDDIE *Phemie Millar* I. ii. 24 Mrs. Millar in a scrimp dark green woollen dress. **1876** SMILES *Sc. Natur.* xviii. 386 Edward, though poor and scrimp of means, has always enjoyed a happy home. **1897** *Westm. Gaz.* 9 Nov. 1/3 Their scrimp management of the most lucrative investment in the world.

†**B.** *adv.* Scarcely, barely. *Obs.*

1824 MISS FERRIER *Inher.* xl, Not that he's come so far as to need it—for it's but scrimp six miles. **1834** M. SCOTT *Cruise Midge* xi. (1863) 189 And I can scrimp deny that same.

scrimp (skrɪmp), *v.* Also *Sc.* skrimp. [See SCRIMP *a.*]

1. *trans.* To keep on short allowance; esp. with regard to food.

a **1774** FERGUSSON *Poems* (1807) 254 At Hallow-fair, whare browsters rare..dinna scrimp ye o' a skair O' kebbucks frae their pantries. **1818** SCOTT *Hrt. Midl.* xxxix, I trust you winna skrimp yoursell for what is needfu' for your health. **1886** TENNYSON *Locksley Hall After* 221 There the Master scrimps his haggard sempstress of her daily bread.

2. To cut short in amount; to be sparing of.

1834 *Tait's Mag.* I. 726/2 Pensions and sinecures were now defensible By wisdom's rules; and who could think of scrimping 'em. **1875** TENNYSON *Q. Mary* III. iii, Do not scrimp your phrase, But stretch it wider.

3. *intr.* To economize, to be niggardly.

1848 LOWELL *Biglow P.* Ser. I. viii. Poems 1890 II. 131 While we are saving and scrimping at the spigot, the government is drawing off at the bung. **1909** *New York Observer* 2 Sept. 313/2 The result of overwork in frequent but fruitless endeavors to scrimp on household expenses.

Hence **'scrimping** *vbl. sb.* and *ppl. a.*

1855 MRS. WHITCHER *Widow Bedott P.* xxvii. (1883) 123 Bethiar Nobles..knows..how every lady in town carries on her kitchenary consarns, how scrimpin' they live, and all that. **1893** LELAND *Mem.* I. 290 This wretched scrimping prevailed through the whole business.

scrimp (skrɪmp), *sb.* [f. the vb.] **a.** The act or process of scrimping; shortage, meagre allowance; economy, niggardliness.

1864 R. M. BALLANTYNE *Let.* 29 Jan. in E. Quayle *Ballantyne the Brave* (1967) viii. 169 I'm sorry to hear about the scrimp with cash. Use the money I sent you. **1933** [see DOOR-STEP b]. **1970** G. F. NEWMAN *Sir, you Bastard* viii. 243 An existence without scrimp or worry.

b. Something constrained or crabbed (in quot., of handwriting). *rare.*

1939 V. WOOLF *Let.* 14 Apr. (1980) VI. 326 You're the only one of my friends who will take the trouble to read such a scrimp of a hand.

scrimped (skrɪmpt), *ppl. a.* Also 8 *Sc.* scrimpit, -et. [f. SCRIMP *v.* + -ED¹.] Stinted, contracted, narrow.

1725 RAMSAY *Gentle Sheph.* I. i, A Mind that's scrimpit never wants some Care. **1786** BURNS *Ep. to J. S.* iii, That auld, capricious carlin, Nature, To mak amends for scrimpet stature, She's turn'd you off a human-creature On her first plan. **1889** *Daily Tel.* 22 Apr. 2 The 4th West Surrey had the new haversack, the cover of which is too scrimped.

scrimpiness ('skrɪmpɪnɪs). [f. SCRIMPY *a.*¹ + -NESS.] 'Scrimpy' quality, meagreness.

1858 SURTEES *Ask Mamma* li, Monsieur, rising in the gig, showing the scrimpiness of his coat.

†**'scrimple**, *v. Obs. rare.* [Cf. CRIMPLE *v.*; also SCRUMPLE *v.* and G. *schrumpeln, schrumpfeln.*] *trans.* To shrivel with fierce heat, to scorch. Also, to crumple, crinkle. Hence †**'scrimpled** *ppl. a.*

1535 STEWART *Cron. Scot.* (Rolls) III. 396 The Scottis hirdis..Of scrymplit ledder mony closbow maid. *a* **1572** KNOX *Hist. Ref.* Wks. 1846 I. 17 A trane of powder was.. sett a fyre, quhilk gave to the blessed martyre of God a glaise, skrimpled his left hand, and that syd of his face.

scrimply ('skrɪmplɪ), *adv.* [f. SCRIMP *a.* + -LY².]

1. In a niggardly, parsimonious manner.

1724 RAMSAY *Health* 364 Nor scrimply save from what's to merit due. *a* **1728** —— *Miser & Minos* 6 He..scrimply fed on Crumbs and Water. **1864** J. BROWN *Jeems* 5 Nature ..had finished off the rest of Jeems somewhat scrimply, as if she had run out of means.

2. Barely, scarcely.

1786 BURNS *Vision* I. xi, Down flow'd her robe, a tartan sheen, Till half a leg was scrimply seen. **1873** *Contemp. Rev.* XXI. 432 It is a cheap and easy course, but scrimply honest.

scrimpy ('skrɪmpɪ), *a.*¹ [f. SCRIMP *a.* + -Y.] Of meagre dimensions, scanty.

1855 ROBINSON *Whitby Gloss.*, *Scrimpy.* **1866** MRS. GASKELL *Wives & Dau.* xiii, A..jacket over her scrimpy and short white petticoat. **1883** *Mag. of Art* Aug. 402/1 A hall and staircase less abjectly 'scrimpy' than those usually met with.

scrimpy, *a.*² [f. SCRIMP *v.* + -Y¹.] Of persons: inclined to scrimp or economize; mean, niggardly.

1918 J. SULLY *My Life & Friends* i. 9 In those days wedded folk had not begun to be scrimpy in the duty of bringing children into the world. **1919** 'K. MANSFIELD' *Let.* 28 Oct. (1951) 356, I wish the printers would not be so scrimpy, cutting the noses off the words. **1979** *Amat. Photographer* Feb. 88/1 If there's a good picture don't ever be scrimpy with film.

scrimshank ('skrɪmʃæŋk), *v. slang* (orig. and chiefly *Mil.*). Also skr-. [Of obscure origin.]

a. *intr.* To shirk duty. Hence **'scrimshanking** *vbl. sb.* and *ppl. a.*; also **'scrimshank** *sb.*, (*a*) an act of 'scrimshanking'; = *scrimshanker*; **'scrimshanker**, a shirker.

1890 BARRÈRE & LELAND *Slang* Scrimshank *v.*, Scrimshanker. **1893** KIPLING *Many Invent.* 135 If Mulvaney stops skrimshanking..I lay your lives will be trouble to you. **1902** *Blackw. Mag.* Jan. 2/2 A skrimshanking Tommy. **1903** *Pilot* 17 Oct. 378/1 We all know that you are due for a long skrim-shank next month. **1913** *Chambers's Jrnl.* Jan. 40/1 There's nothing to be had here but a couple of nigger skrim-shankers. **1915** *Blackw. Mag.* Jan. 66/1 It means that he is trying to get his discharge. Bring him along: I'll soon find out whether he is skrim-shanking or not. **1926** T. E. LAWRENCE *Seven Pillars* (1935) IV. xliv. 254, I was furious with..Gasim, a gap-toothed, grumbling fellow, skrimshank in all our marches, bad-tempered, suspicious, brutal. **1929** R. GRAVES *Good-bye to All That* xv. 203 The Actor said he was skrim-shanking and didn't want the battle. This was unfair. The Surrey-man looked properly sick. **1932** Skrimshanker [see PASSENGER 6]. **1937** P. BOTTOME *Mortal Storm* viii. 98 One must not do their duties for them, or pet them into skrim-shanking. **1945** E. WAUGH *Brideshead Revisited* 299 Brigade expects us to clean up the house for them. I should have thought some of those half-shaven scrim-shankers I see lounging round Headquarters might have saved us the trouble. **1960** *Universe* 30 Dec. 3/3 This quietly-spoken Irishman can be very firm with scrimshankers. **1966** *Listener* 28 July 127/3 Scrimshanking, when it's a question of getting a job finished. **1975** I. MURDOCH *Word Child* 147, I was just telling Hilary we saw him skrimshanking yesterday. **1978** *Verbatim* May 1/2 It exposes the shirking *scrimshank*, who presumably preserves his legs from unnecessary exertion.

scrimshaw ('skrɪmʃɔː), *sb. Naut.* [Of obscure origin; the surname *Scrimshaw*, if not actually the source, may have influenced the form of the word. Cf. prec.] A general name (also ***scrimshaw work***) for the handicrafts practised by sailors by way of pastime during long whaling and other voyages, and for the products of these, as small manufactured articles, carvings on bone, ivory, or shells, and the like. Also **'scrimshaw** *v.*, *trans.* to decorate or produce as scrimshaw work; *absol.* to employ oneself in scrimshaw work; **'scrimshander, -shandy** = SCRIMSHAW *sb.*; **'scrimshoner**, one who practises scrimshaw work.

1825–6 in *Amer. Neptune* (1952) XII. 104 All hands employed scrimshonting. **1850** N. KINGSLEY *Diary* 15 Dec. (1914) 161 There is plenty of time to tinker or read or do any kind of 'Scrimshonging' any-one feels disposed to do. **1851** H. MELVILLE *Moby Dick* I. 14, I found a number of young seamen..examining..divers specimens of scrimshander. *Ibid.* II. 128 Other like skrimshander articles. *Ibid.* II. xv. 128 The skrimshandering business. **1864** *Hotten's Slang Dict.*, *Scrimshaw*, anything made by sailors for themselves in their leisure hours at sea is called Scrimshaw-work. **1883** CLARK RUSSELL *Sailors' Lang.*, *Scrimshandy*, an Americanism signifying the objects in ivory or bone carved by whalemen during their long voyages. **1883** *Fisheries Exhib. Catal.* 198 Collection illustrating the games, amusements, literature, art-work of the fishermen; musical instruments, carvings ('scrimshandy'), &c. *Ibid.* 207 Walrus tusks scrim-shawed, and frame made of walrus ivory. **1887** GOODE, etc. *Fisheries of U.S.* v. II. 231 Scrimshawing is.. the art..of manufacturing useful and ornamental articles at sea. **1898** F. T. BULLEN *Cruise of 'Cachalot'* viii. 83 The great jaw-pans were sawn off, and placed at the disposal of anybody who wanted pieces of bone for 'scrimshaw', or carved work. *Ibid.* xxi. 258 Such pieces as were useful to the 'scrimshoners' for ornamenting their nicknacks. **1906** B. LUBBOCK *Jack Derringer* 171 Specimens of skrimshander, rare shells and Japanese nitchkies in cabinets. **1933** J. MASEFIELD *Bird of Dawning* 201 Narwhal's horns on which the scrimshaw worker was cutting crude designs of rope, sennits, ladies, hearts, arrows and clipper-ships. **1948** *Atlantic Monthly* Jan. 108/1 The Whaling Museum.. displays a shelf of skrimshandering tools made by hand on the whaleship *Awashonks.* **1972** *Times* 16 Sept. 10/1 'Scrimshaw' stoppers, worked by sailors on whalebone.

scrin (skrɪn). *dial. Mining.* Also 9 **skrin, scrinn.** [Cf. MDu. *schrinde, schrunde* (Kilian) = OHG. *scrunta* (mod.G. *schrunde*) fissure, crack, OHG. *scrintan* (MHG., MDu. *schrinden*) to crack.] (See quot. 1881.)

1747 HOOSON *Miner's Dict.* D 4, In Scrins they are usually made by Choaking in long Stones between the two Sides. **1829** *Glover's Hist. Derby* I. 65 Small (lead) veins, usually called *strings*, or *scrins*, often extend from the rake. **1836** R. FURNESS *Astrologer* I. Wks. (1858) 135 In shaft, and scrinn, broad-rake, flatt, pipe, and vein, His mode of timbering shew'd all others mean. **1881** RAYMOND *Mining Gloss.*, *Scrin*, or *Skrin*, Derb., a small subordinate vein.

scrinch (skrɪntʃ), *v. U.S.* [Cf. SCRINGE *v.*] *intr.* To sit closely, to squeeze together.

1869 MRS. WHITNEY *We Girls* vi, Nor have to scrinch all up..for fear she'd touch us.

†**scrine.** *Obs.* Forms: α. 3, 5–6 scryne, 6 scrine, scrynne, skryne, 6–7 skrine; β. 5 screne, 6 screene. [a. OF. *escrin* (mod.F. *écrin* jewel-case):—L. *scrinium* box for books and papers, writing-desk, whence OE. *scrín* SHRINE *sb.* Cf. MDu., Du. *schrijn* (MDu. also *schrein, schreen*, whence possibly the β forms above).] A box for the safe-keeping of valuables; *spec.* a chest in which the relics of saints are preserved, a SHRINE.

a **1300** *Leg. Rood* (1871) 46 Þe quene of seluer and [of] gold an riche scryne wroȝte. **14..** *Voc.* in Wr.-Wülcker 610/35 *Scrinium, vas vel locus ubi libri vel thesauri servantur*, a screne. *c* **1450** *Mirk's Festial* 180 He com to þe chyrch and to þe scryne of Saynt Wenefryd. *a* **1553** UDALL *Royster D.* IV. vii. (Arb.) 73, I haue seene your head with it full many a tyme, Couered as safe as it had bene with a skrine. **1556** *Chron. Grey Friars* (Camden) 94 Item the vth day of Januarij [1555] was sent Edwardes day and thene was sett up the scrynne at Westmyster. **1570** LEVINS *Manip.* 69/31 A screene, *scrinium.* **1591** G. FLETCHER *Russe Commw.* vi. 17 b, In the great Church..is erected a stage whereon standeth a scrine that beareth vpon it the Imperiall cappe and robe of very riche stuffe. **1648** HEXHAM II, *Een Schrijne*, a Skrine, or a Coffin.

b. *fig.*

1542 UDALL *Erasm. Apoph.* 145 b, The mynde or solle of manne is..housed or hidden within the tabernacle or skryne of the bodye.

†**'scrinerary.** *Obs. rare*⁻¹. [ad. It. *scrinerario*, erron. form of *scriniario.*] = SCRINIARY.

1670 G. H. tr. *Hist. Cardinals* I. III. 85 The Chancellor.. had under him twelve Scrineraries, and one Proto-Scrinerary.

scringe (skrɪndʒ), *sb.* [Belongs to SCRINGE *v.*²] A kind of seine net. Also ***scringe net.***

1851 *Act 14 & 15 Vict.* c. 26 §6 It shall not be lawful for any Person to use for the Purpose of taking Herrings..any Sweep, Circle, Ring Net, or Scringe Net, or any Net prohibited by the said..Acts. **1895** 'J. BICKERDYKE' *Sea Fishing* 282 There are broadly speaking, three descriptions of seine nets: (1) the common or deep-water seine, (2) the tuck seine, and (3) the ground seine, foot seine, or scringe.

scringe, *v.*¹ *Obs.* exc. *dial.* Also 9 (*dial.*) skreenge, skringe. [Altered form of CRINGE: see SCR-.]

1. *trans.* To screw up (one's face); to shrug (the back or shoulders) from cold.

1608 ARMIN *Nest Ninn.* (1880) 51 This morrall motion gaue the world such a buffet, that she skrindge [? *read* skringed] her face as though she were pincht home. **1823** E. MOOR *Suffolk Words* 355 *Skringe*, screw, shrink; in this sense, sheep clipped in cold weather are said to skringe their backs up.

2. To squeeze violently.

1790 MRS. ANN WHEELER *Westmorld. Dial.* iii. 73 Tom.. fel a top on him an skreengd him terrably. **1854** MISS BAKER *Northampt. Gloss.*, *Skringe.*

3. *intr.* To flinch, cower.

a **1825** FORBY *Voc. E. Anglia*, *Scringe*,..to cringe; to shrink as it were from fear of chastisement. **1861** LOWELL *Biglow P.* Ser. II. i. Poems 1890 II. 230 That makes Európean tyrans scringe in all their gilded pel'ces. **1897** BARTRAM *People of Clopton* vii. 192 Ye needn't scringe, Exeter, tain't so baad as all that.

scringe (skrɪndʒ), *v.*² *dial.* Also screenge, skreenge. [Prob. a use of the dialectal *skreenge* 'to scourge, flog' (Jam.).] *intr.* To fish with a scringe net. Also *trans.* Hence **'scringing** *vbl. sb.* and *ppl. a.* Also **'scringer.**

1825 JAMIESON, *Skreengin.* 2. A mode of fishing with small nets during the night, without the aid of torches, on the coast of Argyleshire. This mode of fishing is simply *scourging* the water. **1898** MACMANUS *Bend of Road* 208 Her bate wasn't to be foun', nor yet her like again, an' screenge all Irelan' with a herrin' net. **1901** *Scotsman* 4 Mar. 10/1 It is a fashion for yacht owners to say that scringing, if carried on by their crews, is not carried on by their consent. *Ibid.*, On the calm summer nights scringing crews will travel long distances. *Ibid.*, Professional scringers are in no sense sportsmen.

'scriniary. [ad. late L. *scrīniārius*, f. *scrīnium*: see SCRINE.] A keeper of the archives.

1866 STUBBS *Lett.* (1904) 104 The Archbishop of Treves was Ludolf, and a Ludolf was scriniary in 978, and may have been the same person.

scrip (skrɪp), *sb.*¹ *arch.* Forms: 3–7 **scrippe**, 4–5 **scripe, skrippe**, 4–6 **skrip**, 5 **scryp(e, skryppe**, 5–6 **skryp, scryppe**, 3– **scrip**. [Prob. a. OF. *escrep(p)e* wallet, purse, bag for alms (later *escerpe, escharpe*, mod.F. *écharpe* scarf). Cf. SHRIP.

ON. had *skreppa* (Sw. *skräppa*, Da. *skreppe*) in the same sense, but it is doubtful whether the word is native or from OF. The OF. word is commonly supposed to be of Teut. origin; cf. the MHG. gloss 'scherbe, *pera*' (Graff.). The commonly cited OE. *scripp* has no existence; the supposed instance is a scribal or editorial mistake for *scip* (ship).]

A small bag, wallet, or satchel, *esp.* one carried by a pilgrim, a shepherd, or a beggar.

In ME. frequently coupled with BOURDON² (= staff); cf. OF. *escrepe et bordon.*

a **1300** *K. Horn* 1093 Horn tok burdon and scrippe. *a* **1300** *Cursor M.* 11425 Þair scrippes..þam failed neuer o drinc ne fode. **1393** LANGL. *P. Pl.* C. VIII. 180 Ich seyh neuere palmere with pyk ne with scrippe [*v.r.* shrippe] Asken after hym. *c* **1400** *Rom. Rose* 7405 She had a burdoun al of Thefte And a scrippe of Fainte Distresse. **1483** CAXTON *Gold. Leg.* 262/3 [He] clad hym with thabyte of a pylgryme ..a scryppe on his sholder and a pylgryms staff in his right honde. **1524** in G. Oliver *Historic Coll.* (1841) App. 15 A staffe and scryppe of Seynt James. **1572–3** in Nichols *Progr. Eliz.* (1823) I. 324 A scrippe of mother-of-perle,..hanging at three little cheines of golde. **1610** FLETCHER *Faithf. Sheph.* I. i, Every Shepherds Boy Puts on his lusty green, with gaudy hook, And hanging scrip of finest Cordevan. **1648** HERRICK *Hesper., Captiv'd Bee* 23 He laid his little scrip Of hony 'fore her Ladiship. **1661** MORGAN *Sph. Gentry* II. viii. 104 Argent a Cheveron between three Palmers scrips Sable. **1766** GOLDSM. *Hermit* vii, A scrip with herbs and fruits supplied. **1840** DICKENS *Barn. Rudge* xlv, He wore, hanging with a long strap round his neck, a kind of scrip or wallet, in which to carry food. **1870** MORRIS *Earthly Par.* I. II. 458 A staff he bore, but nowise was he bent With scrip or wallet.

allusively. **1587** GREENE *Penelopes Web* D 1, Fallen from a Crowne to a Cottage, and from a Scepter almost to a Scrip.

Comb. **1530** PALSGR. 799 Scryppe wyse, lyke or in maner of a scryppe.

†**scrip**, *sb.*² *Sc. Obs.* [f. SCRIP *v.*²] A scornful grimace.

1470 HENRY *Wallace* VI. 143 Ane maid a scrip, and tyt at his lang suorde.

scrip (skrɪp), *sb.*³ [App. an alteration of SCRAP *sb.* and SCRAPE *sb.*, with weakened vowel expressive of smallness; prob. influenced by association with SCRIPT *sb.* See E.D.D.]

1. A small piece or scrap (of paper, usually with writing upon it; rarely, of other things). *Obs.* exc. *dial.*

1617 HIERON *Wks.* II. 92 There is not the least scrip of the bill kept in hand for any second demand, when once the bond is cancelled. **1676** C. HATTON in *Hatton Corr.* (1878) 134, I punish myself yᵗ I may revenge myself on you for yʳ little scripps of paper. **1681** E. MURPHY *State Irel.* §16 He would not save the least scrip of his goods. **1691** LOCKE *Consid. Lower. Interest* (1692) 25 That cannot be till scrips of Paper can be made current Coin. **1704** J. PITTS *Relig. Mohammetans* v. 33 They'll not suffer a scrip of clean Paper to lie on the Ground. **1754** SHEBBEARE *Matrimony* (1766) I. 243 Of such strange Importance can Love make a Scrip of Paper, and a few black Lines. **1809** W. IRVING *Knickerb.* To Public (1849) 27 And here have I..collected, collated, and arranged them, scrip and scrap. **1922** J. BUCHAN *Huntingtower* i. 21 *The Compleat Angler* seemed to fit his mood... Decidedly it was the right scrip for his pilgrimage.

2. *scrip* (*of a pen*): a small scrap of writing. Cf. SCRAPE *sb.*¹ 2 b, SCRIBE *sb.*² 2. *Obs.* exc. *dial.*

1710 R. WARD *Life H. More* Pref., It was the Expression of a very great Person, That not a Scrip of the Doctor's should be lost. **1775** JEFFERSON *Let.* Writ. 1892 I. 489, I never had received the scrip of a pen from any mortal breathing. **1779** J. ADAMS in *Fam. Lett.* (1876) 357 For God's sake never reproach me again with not writing or with writing scrips. **1874** *N. & Q.* Ser. v. I. 66, I sent you a 'scrip' at once, to thank you for the parcel, and now write more fully. **1909** *Westm. Gaz.* 13 Apr. 2/3 When I write to you, I often sigh To see so poor a scrip.

3. *U.S.* [Prob. influenced by SCRIP *sb.*⁴]

a. Fractional paper currency.

1889 MACOUN *List Canadian Plants*, The price of the list is 50 cents per copy. Scrip preferred to postage stamps.

b. A certificate of indebtedness issued as currency or in lieu of money.

1790 P. FRENEAU *Poems* (1795) 430 In Scrip (not Scripture) he was fond to plod, Scrip was his prayer-book, scrip his word of God: Scrip was his joy, and scrip his dear delight. **1831** *Deb. Congress U.S.* 4 Jan. 405/1 The bill.. proposed an exchange of scrip for land. **1898** *Kissimmee* (Florida) *Valley Gaz.* 18 Feb. 3/5 It is suggested that scrip be issued for the amount. **1943** S. MENEFEE *Assignment: U.S.A.* III. ix. 211 The workers are no longer paid in 'scrip' usable only in the company stores.

c. = *land scrip* s.v. LAND *sb.* 12.

1837 in *Laws of Republic of Texas* (1838) I. 266 It shall be the duty of the commissioner of the general land office..to cause so much of the vacant lands of the republic to be surveyed and sectionized..as will be sufficient to satisfy all claims against the government for scrip sold, soldiers' claims, and head rights. **1884** *Congress. Rec.* 10 June 4994/2 [The lumbermen] have long been in the habit of getting it [*sc.* pineland] under different forms of scrip, under the soldiers' additional scrip, under the Sioux half-breed scrip, [etc.]. **1935** [see *land shark* s.v. LAND *sb.*¹ 12]. **1978** *Washington Post* 8 Apr. E2/4 The scrip bears a face value up to $200... Buyers are permitted to accumulate as much scrip as they wish, but may only use it in exchange for 15 percent or $1,000, whichever is less, of the commission on a house transaction.

scrip (skrɪp), *sb.*⁴ [Short for SUBSCRIPTION.]

1. a. (Short for †*subscription receipt.*) Originally, a receipt for a portion of a loan subscribed. Now, in strict commercial use, a provisional document entitling the holder to a share or number of shares in a joint-stock undertaking, and exchangeable for a more formal certificate when the necessary payments have been completed; often *collect. sing.* Hence, in loose or popular language, applied to share certificates in general.

1762 T. MORTIMER *Ev. Man own Broker* (ed. 5) iv. 174 The receipts for the 3 per Cent. Annuities, are called by the Brokers, Scrip, and Light-Horse... In the month of March ..just after the second payment, a person may buy a receipt for 500*l.* Scrip. for 25*l.* **1796** GROSE *Dict. Vulgar T.* (ed. 3) s.v., Scrip is also a Change Alley phrase for the last loan or subscription. What does scrip go at for the next rescounters? what does scrip sell for delivered at the next day of settling? **1820** G. G. CAREY *Guide Publ. Funds* 10 When the loan is in progress..the separate parts..are called Scrip. **1828–32** WEBSTER s.v., A certificate of stock subscribed to a bank or other company, or of a share of other joint property, is called in America a scrip. **1833** THACKERAY in *National Standard* 18 May, The eighths, halves, and quarters, scrip, options, and shares. **1848** *Rev. Statutes Wisconsin* (1858) 40 No scrip, certificate, or other evidence of state debt. **1850** CARLYLE *Latter-d. Pamph.* vii. 4 You find a dying railway, you say to it, Live, blossom anew with scrip. **1855** TENNYSON *Brook* 4 Lucky rhymes to him were scrip and share. **1865** *Shareholders' Guard.* 8 Nov. 847/2 'Scrip'..is applied to the stocks given in exchange for a loan, as Reduced Scrip, Consol Scrip, &c. **1888** F. HUME *Mme. Midas* I. ii, The small table before him was covered with scrip. **1901** *Rules Stock Exch.* 141 In case the payment of an instalment on Foreign or other Scrip falls on a Settling-day.

b. *attrib.*

1798 *Chron.* in *Ann. Reg.* 33/1 Robert Reaves the stock broker who was..found guilty..of forging scrip-receipts. **1839** DE LA BECHE *Rept. Geol. Cornw.* etc. 565 The number of shares has amounted to 10,000 or more in the scrip mines. **1841** THACKERAY *Gt. Hoggarty Diam.* xi, The shares were scrip shares, making the dividend payable to the bearer. **1850** CARLYLE *Latter-d. Pamph.* vii. 3 Mounted on some figure of a Locomotive, garnished with Scrip-rolls proper. **1869** REDFIELD *Law Railways* (ed. 4) I. 7 They have no right to decline accepting such scripholder, as a shareholder. **1881** *Chicago Times* 4 June, The directors of the Atlanta and West Point railroad have decided to issue a scrip dividend of 100 per cent. interest. **1882** OGILVIE, *Scrip-company*, a company having shares which pass by delivery, without the formalities of register or transfer. **1901** *Rules Stock Exch.* 129 Every bond or scrip share is to be considered perfect, unless it be much torn or damaged.

c. Special combination: **scrip issue** *Econ.*, the issue of additional shares free of charge to shareholders in proportion to the shares already held; an instance of this.

[**1951** M. S. RIX *Investment Arithmetic* xiv. 141 If a company..issues to the shareholders further..ordinary capital.., it will announce the issue of a capital (or scrip) bonus of one new share of 10s. for three existing 10s. shares held.] **1955** *Times* 2 May 20/6 The scrip issue of a corresponding number of fully paid Ordinary shares of 5s. each. **1964** *Financial Times* 31 Jan. 16/1 Guinness Mahon is to better its dividend forcast, aided by..a scrip issue.

2. *Bookselling.* (Short for *subscription price.*) A trade price 25% below the published price.

So called because this was originally the price at which books were sold by the publisher to the booksellers who 'subscribed' them, i.e. agreed before publication to take a certain number of copies. Later, however, 'scrip' became the most unfavourable trade terms that were given, the ordinary trade rate being known as 'sale price'.

1884 *Bookseller* 6 Nov. 1173/1 To enter the books at scrip. **1897** *Publishers' Circular* 3 July 8/2 Those dealers who refuse to come into the arrangement..should be supplied at no better terms than scrip.

scrip (skrɪp), *sb.*⁵ *slang.* Also 'scrip. [Shortened form of PRESCRIPTION.] = SCRIPT *sb.*³

1966 O. NORTON *School of Liars* iv. 72, I wasn't to worry if I found his tablets in the bathroom, because Chris had given him a 'scrip for some more and he had had it filled on the way up. **1967** M. GLATT et al. *Drug Scene* ii. 22 In this country..he can find drugs. Say he is not due to pick up a 'scrip' (prescription) for two hours..he can usually find someone. **1973** *Guardian* 25 Apr. 16/6 Failures of execution while we [*sc.* the Labour Party] were in government... Teeth, specs, scrips. **1975** J. F. BURKE *Death Trick* (1976) ii. 29 The little cloisonné pillbox..contained some uppies for which she had no scrip. **1977** *Times* 19 Sept. 17/6 Is there not a sickness in Whitehall which needs curing by Dr Owen before he gives us a scrip for our local [Rhodesian] consumption?

†**scrip**, *v.*¹ *Obs. rare.* In 5 **skryp.** [f. SCRIP *sb.*¹] *refl.* To provide oneself with a scrip.

1426 LYDG. *De Guil. Pilgr.* 6515 Whan they hem skryppen euerychon.

†**scrip**, *v.*² *Sc. Obs.* Also 6 **skrip(e**, 7 **scirp.** [Cf. SCORP *v.*] **a.** *trans.* To mock, deride. **b.** *intr.* To scoff, jeer.

c **1450** HOLLAND *Howlat* 67 Sum skripe me with scorne. **1500–20** DUNBAR *Fenȝeit Freir* 97 The ja him skrippit with a skryke. *a* **1572** KNOX *Hist. Ref.* Wks. 1846 I. 119 The Cardinall scripped and said, 'It is but the Island flote'. **1651** CALDERWOOD *Hist. Kirk* (1843) II. 278 When Lethington had viewed the Apologie, he scripped and said, '*Homines obscuri*'. **1658** R. BAILLIE *Lett. & Jrnls.* (1841) III. 362 They scirp at all we can doe or say for peace.

†**'scriple**, *sb. Obs.* Also 4 **scripil(le, scripul**, 5 **scrypull**, 6 **scripple.** [ad. L. *scrīpulum*, var. of *scrūpulus, -um* SCRUPLE, esp. in the sense of 'small weight'.] = SCRUPLE *sb.*¹ and ².

c **1380** WYCLIF *Sel. Wks.* II. 201 Þus seien seintis, þat him wantiþ not scripul of privy felowship, þat leeveþ to blame an open synne. **1382** —— *Exod.* xxx. 13 A sicle, that is, a nounce, hath twenti half scripilles. *Ibid. 1 Sam.* xxv. 31 This shal not be to thee..into scripil of herte [Vulg. *in scrupulum cordis*]. *c* **1440** *Pallad. on Husb.* II. 418 Putte theryn A scriple of foyl, and half a scriple of fyn Saffron. *c* **1450** *Mirk's Festial* 18 This holy apostoll preuet so oure fay, þat he lafte no scrypull yn no parte þeryn. **1540** J. HEYWOOD *Four PP.* 614 Here is a syrapus de Bizansys A lyttell thynge is ynough of thys For euen the weyght of one scrippull Shall make you stronge as a crippull.

†**'scriple**, *a. Obs. rare.* In 5 **scrypyll.** [Origin obscure, but cf. SCRUPLENESS.] Scrupulous.

a **1500** MEDWALL *Nature* I. 1281 (Brandl) Yf he vary agayne Of scrypyll ymagynacyon.

scripless ('skrɪplɪs), *a.* [SCRIP *sb.*¹] Without scrip or wallet. (With allusion to Matt. x. 10.)

1850 J. HAMILTON *Mem. Lady Colquhoun* vi. 234 Then it was that on the adherents of the new and scripless Institution was poured out that spirit of joyful contribution. **1867** R. PALMER *Life P. Howard* 3 As purseless, scripless and shoeless as the seventy-two disciples of Christ.

scripophily (skrɪ'pɒfɪlɪ). [Arbitrarily f. SCRIP *sb.*⁴ + -O + -PHILY (see -PHILOUS).] The collection of old bond and share certificates as a pursuit. Also, articles of this nature considered *collect.* Hence **'scripophile**, one who practises scripophily.

1978 *Times* 9 May 25/1 The winner of our competition to find a name for the hobby of collecting old bonds and share certificates is Arthur Howell of Brighton. He suggested 'scripophily', a word effectively half-English and half-Greek, combining scrip (a provisional certificate as for shares, share certificates, [etc.]..) with *philein* (to love). *Ibid.* 25/5 Commander Ross..plans to start a scripophiles' club. **1978** *Daily Tel.* 18 Nov. 25/1 The first ever auction of old bond and share certificates will be held at Stanley Gibbons next Friday. 'Scripophily' is the name of the new fascination. **1979** *National Times* (Austral.) 14 July 45/1 The Wall Street Journal in a front-page article predicted a bright and sound investment future for scripophiles. **1980** *Daily Tel.* 8 Dec. 7/1 (Advt.), Thursday 11 December 2 pm Scripophily & Paper Money. Illus. Catalogue 75p by post.

scrippage ('skrɪpɪdʒ). [f. SCRIP *sb.*¹ + -AGE.] In Shakspere's phr. ***scrip and scrippage***, modelled on ***bag and baggage***; rarely used independently.

1600 SHAKS. *A.Y.L.* III. ii. 171 Come Shepheard, let vs make an honorable retreit, though not with bagge and baggage, yet with scrip and scrippage. **1812** SCOTT *Fam. Lett.* 20 Sept. (1894) I. viii. 259, I wrote to Morritt that I would make a raid on him with bag and baggage, scrip and scrippage about Monday. **1855** *Chamb. Jrnl.* IV. 218, I.. found I should be knocked entirely to pieces by the graze and jam of the boxes and scrippage, as the tide of carrier-ponies crushed past me.

†**'scripper.** *Cant. Obs.* (See quot.)

1591 GREENE *Not. Discov. Cosenage* (1592) C 2, In high Lawe The theefe is called a High lawier. He that setteth the Watch, a Scripper. **1608** DEKKER *Belman of Lond.* (ed. 2) G 4 b.

'scrip-scrap. *colloq.* [reduplication of SCRAP *sb.*] Miscellaneous scraps; odds and ends.

[**1804** J. COLLINS (*title*) Scripscrapologia.] **1894** *Leisure Hour* Feb. 266 [Heading of a collection of snippets.] Scrip-scrap.

script (skrɪpt), *sb.*¹ Also 5 **skript.** [In ME. an etymological spelling of SCRITE (so OF. *escript* for *escrit*:—L. *scrīptum*); later, ad. L. *script-um*, neut. pa. pple. of *scrībĕre* to write, used subst.]

1. Something written; a piece of writing. Now *rare.* † *script of mart*: see MART *sb.*⁵

c **1374** [see SCRITE]. *c* **1400** *St. Alexius* (Laud 108) 409 In his hond he fond a skript [*Vernon MS.* skrit; *rime* as tyd]. **1600** HOLLAND *Livy* XLII. 1129 He delivered unto them a script to this effect as followeth. **1624** FLETCHER *Wife for Month* I. ii, Do you see this Sonnet, This loving Script? do you know from whence it came too? **1665** J. ELIOT *Commun. Ch.* Pref., A few copies of this small script are printed. **1690** EVELYN *Let.* Aug. in *Pepys' Diary* (1879) VI. 168 This hasty script is to acquaint you that [etc.]. **1722** *Hearne's Collect.* (O.H.S.) VII. 315 He delivered to me a Parchment Script.. the words of which Script here follow. **1781** W. POLLARD *Let. to Dr. Parr* 25 Feb. in *P.'s Wks.* (1828) VIII. 383, I once more repeat, that any script of paper assuring me of your welfare will give me the greatest satisfaction. **1879** E. ARNOLD *Lt. Asia* VIII. ad fin., Forgive this feeble script, which doth thee wrong, Measuring with little wit thy lofty Love. **1900** *Contemp. Rev.* Mar. 374 The green banner with its script of gold.

fig. **1891** *Harper's Mag.* Mar. 534/2 A beardless face, full of the script of years.

2. a. Handwriting, the characters used in hand-writing (as distinguished from print). Also *attrib.*, as in ***script hand, letter.***

1860 S. S. HALDEMAN *Analyt. Orthogr.* iii. 25 Script and printing are essentially different. **1865** M. PATTISON *Ess.* (1889) I. 86 The press in each country..reproduced exactly the script-hand of each country. **1885** 'S. Luska' *As it was written* 184 The writing is German Script. **1887** (*title*) Script Letters for Perforating and Sewing. **1899** Hutton in *Life of H. Calderwood* (1900) 288 It was written in full on a sheet of ship paper in his own clear script.

b. *Typogr.* (In full ***script type***.) A kind of type devised to imitate the appearance of handwriting.

1838 Timperley *Printers' Man.* 63 Script Type. Script was in former times called Cursive. **1841** W. Savage *Dict. Printing* 751 Since 1820 the English letter founders have produced a variety of beautiful Scripts of different sizes. **1846** *Wood & Sharwood's Spec. Bk. Type*, Great Primer Script, cast on a common Square Body.

c. Used *attrib.* of systems of shorthand which resemble longhand in general appearance and in the movements of the hand that are required.

1888 (*title*) Science Victorious!.. Published by the Script Phonography Co. of Scotland. *Ibid.* 7 Shorthand constructed on the Script or one-slope principle. **1907** *Daily Chron.* 16 July 6/6 The shorthand was Mr. Malone's script system.

d. A style of handwriting resembling typography, both in the shape of the characters and in their not being joined together. In full ***script-writing***; cf. *print-script* s.v. Print *sb.* 16 a. (Freq. used in the teaching of young children.)

1920 C. W. Kimmins in *Child Study* Dec. 18 These norms for cursive writing were obtained from London children with the same words and under the same conditions as those for script-writing. **1937** R. Tanner *Lettering for Children* 9 A.. more profitable method is.. to use the infants' school script to form a simple running italic hand. **1948** H. K. F. Gull *From Two to Seven Plus* v. 146 It is not necessary to discuss the relative values of script and cursive writing, for to-day script is almost universal in the infant school. **1955** P. Rudland (*title*) From scribble to script. **1959** J. C. Gagg *Beginning Three R's* xii. 83 Both the 'Marion Richardson' script and 'Italic' are found in infant schools also, in unjoined forms. **1966** D. E. M. Gardner *Experiment & Tradition in Primary Schools* iv. 156 This scale shows specimens of children's writing in script and also in cursive hand.

3. A kind of writing, a system of alphabetical or other written characters.

1883 Sayce *Fresh Lt. fr. Anc. Monum.* i. 15 The inscriptions of Nineveh turned out to be written in the same language and form of cuneiform script. **1883** I. Taylor *Alphabet* I. 268 Thus both scripts were probably employed concurrently for a considerable period. **1899** *Athenæum* 26 Aug. 277/2 A.. knowledge of Japanese, especially of its complicated scripts. **1909** *Expositor* May 437 Recent excavation has carried the history of the use of the Babylonian script in Palestine a little further.

4. *Law.* 'The original or principal instrument, where there are part and counterpart'. Cf. *rescript*.

1856 Bouvier *Amer. Law Dict.* (ed. 6) s.v. *Part*, Covenants were formerly made in a script and rescript, or part and counterpart.

5. a. In theatrical parlance, short for manuscript. (Written *'script*.)

1897 *Westm. Gaz.* 13 May 10/1 Hearing of the success of the play from a friend, Macready wrote asking to see the 'script. **1900** *Ibid.* 22 Mar. 10/1 Mrs. Campbell has had the 'script of 'Tess' on her hands for quite a while.

b. The typescript of a cinema or television film; the text of a broadcast announcement, talk, play, or other material.

1931 P. Dixon *Radio Writing* i. 5 It is a curious craft—writing for radio. There is little glory.., for.. network regulations forbid mentioning the name of the author of a script. **1931** *Writer* May 170/1 It is also noted for the guidance of competitors that entries should take the form of a rough shooting script. **1942** *Punch* 11 Feb. 112/1 Time was I loved it not, the mystic microphone. In some confined and subterranean crypt, Cooped with its faceless visage and my script, I did my stuff. **1952** A. Huxley *Let.* 22 Mar. (1969) 643, I am just about to start work on the script of a film on Gandhi. **1962** A. Nisbett *Technique Sound Studio* ii. 34 (*caption*) Microphone Position. Showing a good position for speech, with head well up (and not too close). Script also held up and to side of microphone. **1976** *Encounter* June 54/2 In his preface to the scripts, however.. he dissociated himself from these films. **1980** S. Brett *Dead Side of Mike* vi. 60 He had read his [radio] script... He didn't find it particularly funny... Charles had made a brief journey into television comedy. He hadn't found much of that script very funny either.

fig. **1954** *Sun* (Baltimore) 15 May 26/1 Another 'near perfect' murder with a script paralleling Baltimore's Grammer case. **1968** *Wall St. Jrnl.* (Eastern ed.) 28 Feb. 13 It's easy to think of a dozen different scripts for events of the next few weeks.

c. *transf.* in *Soc. Psychol.* The social role or behaviour appropriate to particular situations, esp. of a sexual nature, that an individual absorbs through his culture and association with others.

1968 Simon & Gagnon in *Etc.* June 175 All human sexual experience is scripted behavior. Without the proper elements of a script that defines the situation, names the actors, and plots the behavior, little is likely to happen... The scripts we bring to such [interpersonal] encounters are most typically non-sexual. **1973** —— *Sexual Conduct* (1974) i. 19 The term *script* might properly be invoked to describe virtually all human behavior in the sense that there is very little that can in a full measure be called spontaneous. **1979** Luria & Rose *Psychol. Human Sexuality* iv. 111 Boys learn a different script from girls.

6. An examinee's written answer paper or papers.

1923 P. B. Ballard *New Examiner* i. 27 The man who sets an examination paper will 'knock it off' in an hour or two, but the man who reads the scripts will have to toil over them for days. **1936** C. Burt in Hartog & Rhodes *Marks of Examiners* 294 The assumption that those correlations are due solely to the common influence of the true value of the scripts. **1961** J. P. Tuck in *Gen. Cert. Educ.* 8 In each case scripts which had already been marked we re-allotted to other examiners. **1978** H. Carpenter *Inklings* iii. iii. 136 He has written it on the back of old examination scripts.

7. *attrib.* and *Comb.*, as (sense 5) ***script conference, editor*** (also ***-edit*** vb. trans.), ***-reader, supervisor, unit, -writer, -writing***; **script †clerk, girl** orig. *Cinemat.*, an assistant to the film director, who takes details of scenes filmed and performs other administrative functions; also in *Broadcasting*.

1927 *Current Hist.* Apr. 63/2 With scenarios in hand the script clerk (always a woman, because of the feminine aptitude for detail) takes down in shorthand everything that occurs. **1950** 'E. Crispin' *Frequent Hearses* iv. 35 It's a role which gets more and more etiolated.. as one script conference follows another. **1977** M. Babson *Murder, Murder, Little Star* vi. 42 Turning back into the script conference, his voice rose. **1968** *Punch* 13 Nov. 684/2 I'm script-editing a marvellous new television serial. **1959** W. S. Sharps *Dict. Cinematogr.* 127/2 *Script editor*,.. the person responsible in a film production organization for finding, selecting and adapting suitable script material. **1974** *Radio Times* 14 Mar. 33/4 A comedy series.. Script editor John Chapman. **1928** *Sat. Even. Post* 3 Mar. 5/3 It was Miss Donovan, the script girl, a friend of many years. **1951** R. Benchley *My Ten Years in Quandary* 82 A girl, known as the 'script-girl', holds the book of the picture and is supposed to check up. **1980** L. St. Clair *Obsessions* v. 110 The.. script girl.. dashed into Mimeo with a stack of scripts. **1956** *B.B.C. Handbk.* 1957 78 A number of specialist script-readers and adapters. **1957** M. Kennedy *Heroes of Clone* ii. i. 14 She's supposed to be the Script Supervisor's secretary but she really runs the whole Department. **1965** *B.B.C. Handbk.* 203 All television scripts should be submitted to: Script Supervisor, Television, BBC Television Centre. **1956** *Ibid.* 1957 78 A Script Unit which deals with the 200–300 scripts and texts submitted every month. **1966** *Writing for B.B.C.* iv. 13 Scripts are handled centrally by a Script Unit, consisting of a script editor and a number of assistants. **1915** C. J. Caine *How to write Photoplays* 105 A script writer should make it a point to see that wherever a leader is broken into a scene it is not only absolutely necessary, but also somewhat of a help to the artistic value of the scenario. **1939** L. Jacobs *Rise of Amer. Film* xvii. 327 The best scenarists in the industry were.. the long-experienced motion picture script writers. **1948** E. Waugh *Loved One* 4 Sir Francis, in prime middle-age, was then the only knight in Hollywood, the doyen of English society, chief script-writer in Megalopolitan Pictures and President of the Cricket Club. **1964** M. McLuhan *Understanding Media* ii. xxx. 299 The resonating dimension of radio is unheeded by the script writers. **1972** *Guardian* 9 Feb. 12/3 The whole team, including directors, studio managers, script writers, cameramen. **1980** G. Greene *Doctor Fischer of Geneva* xvi. 123, I wrote it myself. Not the script writer or the director. It came to me suddenly.. on the set. **1945** 'G. Orwell' in *New Saxon Pamphlets* iii. 38 Films that are all wrong from the bureaucratic point of view will always have a tendency to appear. So also with painting, photography, script-writing, reportage. **1972** *Guardian* 24 June 9/4 Script writing is full of communication tricks; the walk to the door, the slow turn, then: 'Oh, and by the way——'.

†script, *sb.*² *Obs.* [Var. of scrip *sb.*⁴] = scrip *sb.*⁴ 1.

1768 Tucker *Lt. Nat.* II. iii. 374 The Bank of England give no interest upon their notes, whereas the Bank of the Universe improve what we have lying there to immense advantage, far beyond what could be made in Script by any Jew or clerk in the secretary office let into secrets.

script (skrɪpt), *sb.*³ *slang* (orig. *U.S.*). Shortened form of prescription 2, esp. one for narcotic drugs. Cf. scrip *sb.*⁵

1951 *Even. Sun* (Baltimore) 27 Mar. 4/1 He [*sc.* a drug-addict] may have found he could acquire prescriptions, or *'script'* from a doctor who had his price. **1953** W. Burroughs *Junkie* iii. 40, I got a codeine script from an old doctor by putting down a story about migraine headaches. **1972** J. Brown *Chancer* ii. 33 You're just like a bloody junkie I know. Gets his script at mid-day every day, then works his fixes out. **1980** J. Winchester *Solitary Man* xiv. 136 He completed the script and handed it across the desk.

script (skrɪpt), *v.* [f. script *sb.*¹] *trans.* To adapt (a story, novel, etc.) for broadcasting or filming; to write the script for (a broadcast or film). Also *absol.* and *fig.* Hence **'scripting** *vbl. sb.*

1935 in A. P. Herbert *What a Word!* ii. 58 The original story has been scripted by L. du Garde Peach. **1940** *Writer's Jrnl.* Oct. 8/1 Charles Martin is again scripting for radio. **1958** *Oxf. Mag.* 6 Mar. 354 There are two bit parts.. which have been scripted with far more thought than parts of that size usually receive. **1959** *Observer* 22 Mar. 22/7 Cunning scripting, polished production and team-work added up to snug fireside entertainment. **1960** K. Amis *New Maps of Hell* (1961) iii. 67 A British writer who has since scripted two rather.. horrific science-fiction films. **1974** J. Wainwright *Hard Hit* 17 It must be hell scripting a book like that for the screen. **1977** O. Schell *China* (1978) i. 22 And then, as if scripted by my own thoughts, a European woman walks through this flow of Chinese faces. **1980** *Times Lit. Suppl.* 26 Sept. 1062/2 Garbo's talking version [of *Anna Karenina*].. was rather grandly scripted by Clemence Dane, Salka Viertel and S. N. Behrman.

scripted ('skrɪptɪd), *a.* *Cinemat.* and *Broadcasting.* [f. script *sb.*¹ or *v.* + -ed.] Furnished with script; read or spoken from a prepared script as opp. extempore; adapted (esp. for film from a novel or play). Also *fig.*

1949 *Richmond* (Va.) *Times-Dispatch* 26 Jan. 13/2 The current vehicle is so well scripted, so solidly performed and so neatly combined with documentary elements,.. that the audience has the impression of belonging to the police force. **1953** *Ann. Reg.* 1952 iv. 449 Previously an unscripted defamatory broadcast was treated as slander whilst a scripted one was libel. **1962** A. Nisbett *Technique Sound Studio* 252 It may be a matter of supplying sufficient 'pointers' in scripted speech. **1975** *Language for Life* (Dept. Educ. & Sci.) x. 157 Some teachers will have nothing to do with the scripted play.

scripter ('skrɪptə(r)). orig. *U.S.* [f. as prec. + -er¹.] A script-writer.

1940 *Amer. Speech* XV. 205/1 *Scripter*, a film writer. **1941** *Time* 7 July 66/3 Another cinema scripter.. appeared on the set. **1945** *Sat. Rev. Lit.* (U.S.) 14 Apr. 31/1 No question but that the expert scripter, dialogician, and screen playwright is the future king of Hollywood. **1960** *News Chron.* 23 Sept. 10/4 We must be grateful to the dialogue scripter. **1968** *Punch* 14 Aug. 221/1 At present I am a scripter of strip-tease shows.

scription ('skrɪpʃən). [ad. L. *scriptiōn-em*, f. *scrībĕre* to write. Cf. OF. *escripsion, escricion.*]

†1. A writing; a document; an inscription. *Obs.*

1597 A. M. tr. *Guillemeau's Fr. Chirurg.* 5 b, To imploye their time in the readinge of my scriptsons [*sic*] and writinges. **1607** Bp. J. King *Serm. 5 Nov.* 34 Let the scription of those tables bee. *Non nobis domine* [etc.]. **1693** Dryden *Ded. 3rd Misc.*, I care not much if I give this handle to our bad illiterate Poetasters, for the defence of their Scriptions, as they call them.

2. The action of writing. *rare.*

1802–12 Bentham *Ration. Judic. Evid.* (1827) I. 279 Recordation, registration, scription. **1973** *Screen* Spring/Summer 122 There exist.. two types of reference to the idea of language in general cinema theory which lead to two conceptions that I shall distinguish as those of a 'cinema of speech', mode of natural expression, and of a 'cinema of writing', activity of scription, production, transformation, analysis.

3. Handwriting; a kind of handwriting. *rare.*

1846 Maskell *Mon. Rit.* II. p. xxxiv, The vellum is rough, and the scription careless. **1849** Rock *Ch. of Fathers* I. 18 *note*, This Anglo-Saxon MS. is of the early part of the ninth century, and a fac-simile of its scription is given by Hickes. *Ibid.* I. iii. 275 Britain taught Ireland a peculiar style of scription.

†scripti'tation. *Obs.* *rare*⁻¹. [ad. L. **scriptitātiōn-em*, n. of action f. *scriptitāre*, frequent. of *scrībĕre* to write.] Continual writing.

1653 R. Baillie *Dissuas. Vind.* (1655) 38 The Brownists, whose contrary scriptitations had divulged all their divisions.

scriptitious (skrɪp'tɪʃəs), *a.* *rare.* [f. L. *script-*, ppl. stem of *scrībĕre* to write + -itious.] Committed to writing. Hence **scrip'titiously** *adv.*

1802–12 Bentham *Ration. Judic. Evid.* (1827) I. 55 Scriptitious or scriptitiously delivered depositional testimony.

scriptless ('skrɪptlɪs), *a.* [f. script *sb.*¹ + -less.] Of a film, broadcast, etc.: without a script (sense 5); unscripted, extempore.

1962 *Punch* 4 July 30/2 Almost every major scriptless programme put out by sound radio and TV. **1968** *Guardian* 22 Sept. 8/4 The film was, we are told, scriptless; the actors made up the dialogue as they went along. **1973** *Listener* 22 Mar. 393/3 The dialogue seemed largely scriptless.

†scriptoir, -our. *Obs.* [Aphetic a. OF. *escriptoire*, ad. L. *scriptōrium*: see scriptorium and cf. scrutoire.] A pen-case.

1474 Caxton *Chesse* iii. iii. (1883) 93 And that is signefied by the scriptoire and the penne. **1513** Douglas *Æneis* xii. Prol. 305, I hynt a scriptour and my pen furth tuike, Syne thus begouth of Virgill the twelt buike.

scriptor¹ ('skrɪptə(r)). *rare.* Also 6 -our. [a. L. *scriptor*, agent-n. f. *scrībĕre* to write. Cf. OF. *escriptor, scripteur.*] A writer, a scribe.

1535 Stewart *Cron. Scot.* (Rolls) I. 306 Tacitus, The Roman scriptour. **1847** Ld. Lindsay *Chr. Art* I. p. clxxiii, No art was allowed there except that of the scriptor.

scriptor². *Obs.* exc. *Hist.* Also 8 -ure, -ore. [? Etymologizing refashioning of *scritoire*, scrutoire.] A writing-desk, escritoire.

1683 J. Locke *Let.* 26 Aug. (1976) II. 602, I think you were best lock my book of accounts up in my scriptor when you go out of town. **1716** in J. O. Payne *Engl. Cath.* (1889) 84 Several of the goods were very good, and particularly a scriptore. **1724** *Let. to W. Woods* Swift's Wks. (1824) VII. 76 Every monied man, instead of a scriptore, or an iron chest,.. must have a warehouse. **1732** in W. Macgill *Old. Ross-sh.* (1909) 137 A Scripture [escritoire]. **1752** *Ibid.* 140 Old wainscot Scriptore. **1955** R. Fastnedge *Eng. Furniture Styles* iii. 87 Small walnut and marquetry fall-front writing cabinets.. continued to enjoy popularity... These pieces.. were then [*c* 1700] called 'scriptors', or 'scrutoirs'. **1965** *Listener* 22 Apr. 604/1, I would like to take as the focal object a charming and famous scriptor or writing desk from Ham House.

scriptorial (skrɪp'tɔərɪəl), *a.* [f. late L. *scriptōrius* scriptory + -al¹.] Relating to or used for writing. Hence **scrip'torially** *adv.*, in a scriptorial manner, in writing.

1831 CARLYLE in Froude *Life* (1882) II. 156, I must not take all your encomiums about my scriptorial genius. **1859** *Macm. Mag.* 31 Graphic or scriptorial materials. **1933** *Trans. Philol. Soc.* 73 So much of the scriptorial work appears to have been done in later O.E. times. **1970** B. M. H. STRANG *Hist. Eng.* iii. 162 Westminster, already a great ecclesiastical centre with important scriptorial resources. **1974** V. NABOKOV *Look at Harlequins* (1975) I. iv. 19 This is corroborated scriptorially.

†**scrip'torian**, *a. Obs.* [Formed as prec. + -AN.] = SCRIPTORY *a.*

1656 BLOUNT *Glossogr.*, *Scriptorian*, of, belonging, or serving to writing.

‖**scriptorium** (skrɪp'tɔərɪəm). Pl. scriptoria, -iums. [med.L. f. L. *script-*, *scrībĕre* to write: see -ORIUM.] A writing-room; *spec.* the room in a religious house set apart for the copying of manuscripts.

1774 T. WEST *Antiq. Furness* Expl. Ground Plan, H, the chapter-house, over which were the library and scriptorium. **1828** H. ANGELO *Remin.* (1830) I. 66 The attics or scriptoriums of the poets of the last age. **1874** GREEN *Short Hist.* iii. §1 (1882) 113 Writing-rooms or scriptoria, where the chief works of Latin literature..were copied and illuminated. **1907** *Times, Lit. Suppl.* 18 Jan. 17/1 Drowsy intelligences and numbed fingers in a draughty scriptorium, will easily account for deviations.

scriptory ('skrɪptərɪ), *a.* and *sb. rare.* [ad. L. *scriptōri-us*, f. *script-*, *scrībĕre* to write: see -ORY.]

A. *adj.* **1.** Pertaining to or used in writing.

a **1682** SIR T. BROWNE *Misc. Tracts* i. (1683) 82 Reeds, Vallatory, Sagittary, Scriptory, and others. **1827** CARLYLE *Germ. Rom.* III. 21 Let the English reader fancy a Burton writing, not an *Anatomy of Melancholy*, but a foreign romance, through the scriptory organs of a Jeremy Bentham. **1905** *Daily Chron.* 31 Jan. 4/3 There is a tendency nowadays to unify the scriptory characters of all languages.

2. Expressed in writing, written.

1704 SWIFT *Tale of Tub* ii. 67 Of Wills, *duo sunt genera*, Nuncupatory and Scriptory. **1805** EUGENIA DE ACTON *Nuns of Desert* II. 133 Selwyn..was assured that Aurora had no intercourse, either verbally or scriptory, with any one.

B. *sb.* A writing-room, scriptorium.

a **1483** *Liber Niger* in *Househ. Ord.* (1790) 35 These clerks to have dynners & soupers to theyre scriptory. **1844** PALEY *Church Restorers* 14 It was the favourite scriptory of the writer.

scriptour: see SCRIPTOR[1], SCRIPTURE.

†**'scriptule.** *Obs.* [ad. L. *scriptulum*, var. spelling of *scrīpulum* = *scrūpulus* SCRUPLE.] The weight called a scruple.

1601 HOLLAND *Pliny* XXXIII. iii. II. 463 A scriptule of gold was taxed and valued at twentie sesterces.

scriptural ('skrɪptjʊərəl), *a.* [ad. mod.L. *scriptūrāl-is*, f. L. *scriptūra* SCRIPTURE.]

1. Based upon, derived from, or depending upon Holy Scripture.

1641 J. JACKSON *True Evang. T.* I. 53 A method..very Scripturall, and Authentick. **1725** WATTS *Logic* III. iv. (1736) 333 The Importance of any scriptural Doctrine or Duty. **1832** J. J. BLUNT *Sk. Reform. Eng.* v. 95 An eager appetite for Scriptural knowledge was excited among the people. **1858** HAWTHORNE *Fr. & It. Note-bks.* (1871) II. 219 Immense engravings of Gothic or scriptural scenes. **1881** STUBBS *Med. & Mod. Hist.* xii. (1886) 288 The translation of the Bible and Scriptural formulæ of prayer.

2. Of or pertaining to writing.

1802–12 BENTHAM *Ration. Judic. Evid.* (1827) III. 28 Cases of scriptural forgery [draw] upon the arts of the engraver, the paper-maker [etc.]. **1841** D'ISRAELI *Amen. Lit.* (1867) 73 The day arrived that even barons were incited to scriptural attempts.

scripturalism ('skrɪptjʊərəlɪz(ə)m). [f. prec. + -ISM.] Close adherence to or dependence upon the letter of Holy Scripture.

1858 J. MARTINEAU *Stud. Chr.* 33 In every branch..of the Genevan Reformation..a rigorous Scripturalism prevails. **1899** DOWDEN in *Contemp. Rev.* July 24 The spirit of the Reformation..lost some of its more liberal temper in a narrow Scripturalism.

So **'scripturalist**, †? one well versed in Holy Scripture; an advocate of scripturalism.

1725 DE FOE *Tour Gt. Brit.* II. iii. 20 King Charles II ridiculing the warm Disputes among some Critical Scripturallists..concerning the visible Church. **1857** GLADSTONE *Glean.* (1879) VI. 84 Those Scripturalists of the present day, who conceive that the measure..aims at the vindication of Bible freedom against the tyranny of the church.

scripturality (skrɪptjʊə'rælɪtɪ). [f. SCRIPTURAL + -ITY.] The quality or condition of being scriptural or based upon Holy Scripture.

1831 *Fraser's Mag.* III. 487 We give them credit for scripturality of creed. **1842** G. S. FABER *Prov. Lett.* (1844) II. 62 If we reject unscripturalities, we must, would we be consistent, reject Scripturalities also. **1904** J. GIBSON *Waldenses* 11 The boldness and scripturality of the preaching.

scripturalize ('skrɪptjʊərəlaɪz), *v. rare.* [f. SCRIPTURAL + -IZE.] *trans.* To render scriptural.

1858 F. W. FABER *Spir. Confer.* 382 This I must heighten, modify and scripturalize a little.

scripturally ('skrɪptjʊərəlɪ), *adv.* [f. SCRIPTURAL + -LY[2].] In accordance with the Scriptures; by means of Scripture.

1679 PENN *Addr. Prot.* II. iii. Wks. 1782 IV. 80, I shall briefly say something of what is *not* faith, before I speak of that which appears to me to be truly and scripturally such. **1833** J. H. NEWMAN *Arians* i. §4 (1876) 112 A scripturally-worded creed. **1977** YARNOLD & CHADWICK *Truth & Authority* 12 It is by reference to the scripturally formed 'common faith' of the community that the individual tests his own belief, rather than by an appeal to the words of the Bible as to an ultimate authority.

scripturalness ('skrɪptjʊərəlnɪs). [f. as prec. + -NESS.] = SCRIPTURALITY.

1874 MORLEY *Compromise* i. (1888) 35 Firm persuasion of the greater scripturalness of episcopacy. **1881** *Brit. Q. Rev.* Jan. 42 Not upon the scripturalness or the rationality of her creed, but upon its ecclesiastical authority.

†**scriptu'rarian.** *Obs.* [f. mod.L. *scriptūrārius* (see next) + -AN.] One who makes Holy Scripture the sole authority for religious belief.

A form *scripturarius* (? after *textuarius*) occurs in mod.L.; the printed reading in quot. 1718 may be due to the author.

1678 *Lively Oracles* vi. §1. 165 Protestants..being call'd by them [Romanists] in contemt the Evangelical men, and Scripturarians. **1718** PRIDEAUX *O. & N. Test. Connected* II. v. (1719) 265 From hence they had the name of Karraites, which is as much as to say *Scriptu[r]arians.*

†**'scripturary.** *Obs.* [ad. mod.L. *scriptūrārius*, f. *scriptūra* SCRIPTURE: see -ARY.] = prec.

1659 THORNDIKE *Epil. Trag. Ch. Eng.* I. xxvi. 190 But, there is another sort of Jews called Scripturaries,..which admit nothing but the leter of the Scriptures.

scripture ('skrɪptjʊə(r)), *sb.* Forms: 4–6 scriptur, scrypture, 5 scryptour, skreptour, skrypt(o)ur, 5–7 scriptour, 6 scriptuir, scriptor, scryptor, skrypture, skripture, scriture, 4– scripture. [ad. L. *scriptūra* writing, f. *script-*, *scrībĕre* to write: see -URE. Cf. OF. *escriture*, also written *escripture* (mod.F. *écriture*), Sp., Pg. *escritura*, It. *scrittura*.]

1. (Usually with capital initial.) **a.** The sacred writings of the Old or New Testament, or (more usually) of both together; Holy Writ; the Bible. Often with *holy* prefixed.

α. ***Scripture*** (without demonstrative).

a **1300** *Cursor M.* 327 For-þi es godd, als sais scripture. *c* **1400** *Rom. Rose* 6452 And this ageyns holy scripture. **1447** BOKENHAM *Seyntys* Prol. 60 (Horstm.) And to thys manyfold of nature Exaunplys accordyth weel scrypture. *c* **1485** *Digby Plays, Mary Magd.* 1522 And on þe sonday, he gan rest take, as skryptur declaryth pleyn. *c* **1511** *1st Eng. Bk. Amer.* (Arb.) Introd. 31 They haue theyr scrypture in ye Greekes speche. **1565** STAPLETON tr. *Staphylus' Apol.* 167 He acknowledgeth the bookes off the Machabees for Scripture. **1596** SHAKS. *Merch. V.* I. iii. 99 Marke you this Bassanio, The diuell can cite Scripture for his purpose. **1638** CHILLINGWORTH *Relig. Prot.* I. ii. 54 Scripture is as perfect a rule of Faith as a writing can be. **1746** HERVEY *Medit.* (1818) 53 Every page of scripture will sanctify thy passion. **1849** MACAULAY *Hist. Eng.* i. I. 82 The extreme Puritan.. employed, on every occasion, the imagery and style of Scripture. **1852** MANNING *Grounds of Faith* ii. 28 Holy Scripture is Holy Scripture only in the right sense of Holy Scripture. **1888** *Encycl. Brit.* XXIII. 264 The revelation of God in nature is presupposed by that in Scripture.

β. ***the*** **(*Holy*)** ***Scripture***. Now *rare*.

a **1300** *Cursor M.* 22168 Queþer þat he be crist or nai, þat þai of here þe scriptur sai. *a* **1450** *Knt. de la Tour* lxxxii. (1906) 105 Ensaumple is of Sarra, whom the scripture hathe in gret Recommendation. **1676** GLANVILL *Ess. Philos. & Relig.* v. 24 That there is a God; or, That the Scripture is his Word. **1741** JOHNSON *Morin* in *Gentl. Mag.* XI. 377/2 After his Return [from Mass] he read the Holy Scripture, dined at eleven [etc.]. **1831** SCOTT *Ct. Robt.* xxviii, I have.. renounced what the Scripture calls the pride of life.

γ. pl. ***the*** **(*Holy*)** ***Scriptures***. († In early use also without article.)

1382 WYCLIF *John* v. 39 Seke ȝe scripturis. **1526** TINDALE *1 Cor.* xv. 4 Accordynge to the scriptures [**1382** WYCLIF vp the scripturis, **1388** after scripturis]. *c* **1560** A. SCOTT *Poems* (E.E.T.S.) i. 171 Caus everye stait to þair vocatioun go, Scolastick men þe scriptouris to descrywe, And maiestratis to vse þe swerd also. **1651** HOBBES *Leviath.* III. xxxiii. 206 The Scriptures are not made Laws, by the Universall Church. **1704** NELSON *Fest. & Fasts* xviii. (1739) 229 The Perfection and Perspicuity of the holy Scriptures. **1782** PRIESTLEY *Nat. & Rev. Relig.* I. Pref. 35, I would teach the knowledge of the scriptures only. **1831** SCOTT *Ct. Robt.* i, But while many of the converts were turning meekly towards their new creed, some..were limiting the Scriptures by their own devices. **1871** E. F. BURR *Ad Fidem* i. 7 The Scriptures, illuminators of mankind.

b. A particular passage or text of the Bible. Now *rare* (after biblical use).

1382 WYCLIF *Mark* xii. 10 Wher ȝe han not rad this scripture [so all later versions], The stoon the which [etc.]. **1565** ALLEN *Defence Purg.* xvii. 283 For which we haue broughte diuerse scriptures, all construed by most learned fathers for that sense. **1607** R. WILKINSON *Serm. Whitehall* 1 This whole chapter is a scripture written for women. **1818** SCOTT *Hrt. Midl.* xxvii, I have marked a scripture..that will be useful to us baith. **1845** KITTO *Cycl. Bibl. Lit.* s.v. *Scribes*, At the close of this striking Scripture our Lord thus describes these men. **1864** TENNYSON *Aylmer's F.* 44 Worse than had he heard his priest Preach an inverted scripture, sons of men Daughters of God.

c. Something as surely true as Holy Scripture; = GOSPEL *sb.* 4.

1573 G. HARVEY *Common-pl. Bk.* (Camden) 10 Marri not so, that I can strait wai take it for scripture what soeuer he hath giun his wurd for.

d. *sing.* or *pl.* Sacred writings or records.

1581 MARBECK *Bk. of Notes* 257 A Councell..decreed.. that no Scripture be read in the Church, but Canonicall. **1764** GIBBON *Misc. Wks.* (1814) IV. 358 His [Homer's] works and those of his successors were the scriptures of the nation. **1841** ELPHINSTONE *Hist. India* I. v. 225 The system ..professes to be founded on the authority of the Vêdas, and appeals for proofs to texts from those Scriptures. **1854** THOREAU *Walden* (1884) 116 Most men do not know that any nation but the Hebrews have had a scripture.

e. *fig.* and *allusively*.

1742 YOUNG *Nt. Th.* IX. 644 'Tis elder Scripture, writ by God's own hand; Scripture authentic! uncorrupt by man. **1774** BURKE *Sp. Amer. Tax.* Wks. II. 369 Here, Sir, is a canonical book of ministerial scripture; the general epistle to the Americans. **1839–48** BAILEY *Festus* 281 *Festus.* What are ye orbs? The words of God—the Scriptures of the skies? **1908** W. RALEIGH in *S. Lee's Shaks. Tr. & Cr.* Introd. 16 This scripture [Guido's *History of Troy*] was divulged in England, for the benefit of the men of Shakespeare's time, in two principal versions.

f. The study of the Bible and the Christian religion as a school subject; a scripture lesson.

1927 M. DE LA ROCHE *Jalna* xiv. 165 When the time came for questions and examinations in Scripture, Finch.. usually stood at the foot of the class. **1931** 'G. TREVOR' *Murder at School* ii. 32 Ellington had to rush away to take a class in scripture. **1963** BARNARD & LAUWERYS *Handbk. Brit. Educ. Terms* 162 *Religious Instruction/Education*... Other terms are 'Religious knowledge', 'Divinity', and 'Scripture'. **1968** G. MITCHELL *Three Quick & Five Dead* i. 24 'Edward teaches history and something he calls R.K.' 'Religious Knowledge,' said Laura. 'They used to call it Scripture in my young days.' **1977** D. KOSSOFF *You have a Minute, Lord?* 45, I went to a trade school,..where poetry was not offered..and 'Scripture' was unknown.

2. The action or art of writing; handwriting, penmanship. Also *concr.* written characters. Now *rare*.

1432–50 tr. *Higden* (Rolls) II. 255 Somme men have chaungede the names for feirenesse of scripture. **1426–7** in *Cal. Proc. Chanc. Q. Eliz.* I. (1827) Introd. 21 Symkyn hathe had the hole scripture rased of a chartre undre the seal of armez of my lord of York. **1471** RIPLEY *Comp. Alch.* Recapit. i. in Ashm. (1652) 186 By Fygures, and by Colors, and by Scrypture playne. **1535** COVERDALE *Ezra* iv. 7 The scripture of yᵉ letter was wrytten in the Syrians speach. **1847** DISRAELI *Tancred* II. xii, The handwriting was of that form of scripture which attracts; refined yet energetic; full of character. **1875** RUSKIN *Fors Clav.* lviii. 295 The wooden blocks of Germany abolished the art of scripture.

3. An inscription or superscription; a motto, legend, or posy. Also, in generalized use, inscribed words. *Obs.* exc. *arch.*

13.. *E.E. Allit. P.* B. 1546 When hit þe scrypture hade scraped wyth a strof penne. *c* **1374** CHAUCER *Troylus* III. 1369 Sone after this they speke of sondry thinges, As fil to purpos of this aventure, And pleyinge entrechaungeden hir ringes, Of which I can nought tellen no scripture. **1420** HEN. V *Let.* in Rymer *Fœdera* (1709) IX. 907/2 As touching the Scripture of the Seeles, us seemeth that this word Regent may be owte wel ynogh. *c* **1440** *Gesta Rom.* xxxii. 123 (Add. MS.), On the balle was this scripture written, he that shall pleye with me [etc.]. **1447** BOKENHAM *Seyntys* x. 234 (Horstm.) In hys hand holdyng a scrypture, Wych wrytyn was wyᵗ lettrys of gold. **1463** *Bury Wills* (Camden) 40 My owune seel of silvir, therin a egle with scripture. **1533** J. COKE in Ellis *Orig. Lett.* Ser. II. II. 44 With a scripture over her head, saiyng that Love was lighter then a fether. **1540** *Test. Ebor.* (Surtees) VI. 98 For my grave a picture of latten ..with scriptur about it and the iiij evangelistes. **1556** *Chron. Grey Friars* (Camden) 90 The xviij. day of the same monyth [July 1554] stode a man on the pyllery..with a paper and a scryptor on hys hed, that was consentynge there-to. *a* **1600** *Flodden F.* IV. (1664) 32 A certain scrall, whose scripture said, Jack of Norfolk be not too bold. **1771** *Antiq. Sarisb.* 199 Three fair basons,..with a Scripture, Orate pro anima Will. Normanton. **1900** HOPE in *Yorks. Archæol. Jrnl.* XV. 296 A scroll with this scripture ..*Benedicite fontes Domino.*

4. a. A written record or composition; *pl.* writings. *Obs.* exc. *arch.*

Sometimes with more or less allusion to sense 1; cf. 1 d, 1 e.

1382 WYCLIF *Isa.* xxxviii. 9 The scripture of Ezechie, king of Juda. *c* **1386** CHAUCER *Knt.'s T.* 1186 And over his heed ther shynen two figures Of sterres, that been cleped in scriptures, That oon Puella, that other Rubeus. *a* **1400–50** *Alexander* 2119 (Ashmole) Scamandra þe silre flode þe scriptour it callis. *c* **1450** LOVELICH *Merlin* 5799 So now we knowen be that scripture of these aventures. **1611** SHAKS. *Cymb.* III. iv. 83 What is heere, The Scriptures of the Loyall Leonatus, All turn'd to Heresie? **1755** SMOLLETT *Quix.* (1803) II. 239, I am not so well read in the scriptures of errantry as your worship. **1845** TRENCH *Huls. Lect.* I. 15 Through a Scripture alone, that is, through a written record, could any great epoch..transmit itself unimpaired to the after world. **1876** SWINBURNE *Erechtheus* 517, I had made no question of thine eyes or heart, Nor spared to read the scriptures in them writ, Wert thou my son.

†**b.** In generalized use: Written composition.

1390 GOWER *Conf.* II. 89 Thei that writen the scripture Of Grek, Arabe, and of Caldee. *c* **1430** LYDG. *Min. Poems* (Percy Soc.) 5 But for to tellyng alle the circumstaunces.. Conveyed be scripture with fulle grete excellense; Alle to declare, I have noone eloquence. **1430–40** —— *Bochas* I. xv. (1494) e iij, And as poetis recorde by scripture He callyd was the faire adonydes. **1534** LD. BERNERS *Gold. Bk. M. Aurel.* (1546) C iiij, There haue bene many famous and renoumed by scripture and lerning. **1595** *Locrine* I. ii. 34, I will dite an aliquant loue-pistle to her, and then she hearing the grand verbositie of my scripture, will loue me presently.

†**c.** ***in scripture***: in writing; on record. *Obs.*

c **1374** CHAUCER *Boeth.* I. pr. iv. (1868) 17, I haue put it in scripture and remembraunce. *c* **1470** HARDING *Chron.*

LXXIII. xix, The Secretorye shulde put it in scrypture. **1535** COVERDALE *Ecclus.* xliv. 5 They..brought forth the pleasaunt songes in scripture. **1571** CAMPION *Hist. Irel.* II. vii. (1633) 99 It shall never bee chronicled, nor remaine in scripture,..that Ireland was lost by my negligence. **1609** BIBLE (Douay) *1 Macc.* xii. 21 It is found in Scripture of the Spartians, and the Jewes that they are bretheren.

5. *attrib.* and *Comb.* **a.** Simple attributive, with the sense 'of or pertaining to Holy Scripture', as in ***Scripture-lesson, light, mine, sword***; 'recorded in Holy Scripture', as in ***Scripture account, history, miracle, saint, story***.

1718 ATTERBURY *Serm.* (1734) I. 195 The *Scripture Accounts of these things are short. **1693** J. EDWARDS *Author. O. & N. Test.* I. 305 Mr. Selden..avers that the most impious Customs among the Gentiles had their Original from *Scripture-History. **1821** SCOTT *Kenilw.* iii, Scenes taken from Scripture history. **1867** W. L. COLLINS *Public Schools* 56 There is a *Scripture or Greek Testament lesson at 4. **1627** SANDERSON *Serm.* (1681) I. 262 By reason of the darkness of their understandings, and the want of *Scripture-light. **1781** COWPER *Hope* 298 That cannot bear the blaze of scripture light. **1781** —— *Retirem.* 698 Strong judgment lab'ring in the *scripture mine. **1751** J. BROWN *Ess. on Shaftesbury's Charac.* 284 This seems to be the true light, in which the evidence arising from the *scripture-miracles ought to be placed. **1671** WOODHEAD *St. Teresa* I. Pref. 12 The Prayers of the greatest and most illuminated *Scripture-Saints are rather frequent. **1711** STEELE *Spect.* No. 142 ¶2 The Tapestry Hangings, with the great and venerable Simplicity of the *Scripture Stories, had [etc.]. **1736** *Gentl. Mag.* VII. 345/1 The World assails thee with ambition, wield Thy *scripture-sword.

b. attrib., passing into adj., with the senses 'used in or adopted from Holy Scripture', as in ***Scripture expression, language, name, phrase,*** †***speaking, style, word***; 'derived from, prescribed by, or conformable to Holy Scripture, scriptural', as in ***Scripture church, doctrine, notion, proof, rule, view, warrant***.

1720-1 *Lett. fr. Mist's Jrnl.* (1722) II. 94 One might justly have expected, that their Opposition to the *Scripture Church should have been clearly demonstrated, from the Writings of the New Testament. **1712** S. CLARKE (*title*) The *Scripture Doctrine of the Trinity. **1658** SIR T. BROWNE *Hydriot.* i. 2 Collectible from *Scripture-expression. **1791** BOSWELL *Johnson* an. 1773, 3 Apr., A scripture expression may be used, like a highly classical phrase, to produce an instantaneous strong impression. **1745** J. MASON *Self-Knowl.* I. iii. (1853) 33 A good and a bad Principle, (called in *Scripture-Language the Flesh and the Spirit). **1713** STEELE *Guardian* No. 132/4 When thou art converted, thou must take to thee a *Scripture-Name. **1861** MRS. STOWE *Pearl Orr's Isl.* iv. 24 Miss Jones..called her twins Tiglath-Pileser and Shalmaneser—Scriptur' names both, but I never liked 'em. **1659** PEARSON *Creed* 353 For in this particular the *Scripture-notion of priority excludeth an antecedent, but inferreth not a consequent. **1649** MILTON *Eikon.* i. 10 The lip-work of every Prelatical Liturgist, clapt together, and quilted out of *Scripture phrase. **1827** [APPERLEY] *Turf* (1852) 125 The Scripture phrase..is now every day being verified, the race not being to the swift. **1594** HOOKER *Eccl. Pol.* II. vii. §9 *Scripture-proofe..in strength & value exceedeth all. **1672** *Disc. Conc. Evang. Love* 68 The sentence of Natural Reason, or *Scripture-Rule. **1834** *Tracts for Times* No. 22. 7 To try this Athanasian Creed by Scripture rules. **1617** HIERON *Wks.* (1620) II. 369 The last clause, 'Thou wilt not despise', is to be obserued also, as being such which, in *Scripture-speaking, betokeneth more then is expressed. **1686** [HICKES] *Spec. B. Virg.* 30 S. Ignatius.. mentions her by the name of plain Mary in the *Scripture-stile. **1791** *Fash. World* 216 From a *scripture view of what real religion is. **1834** *Tracts for Times* No. 24 (*title*) The Scripture View of the Apostolic Commission. **1818** SCOTT *Rob Roy* xix, The bits o' stane idols were broken in pieces by *Scripture warrant. **1626** BACON *Sylva* §948 There are vsed also *Scripture-Words. **1851** PUSEY *Let. Bp. London* (ed. 3) 127/1 That wide-opened Hand, trickling (in Scripture-words) with 'the Blood of God'.

c. Objective and objective-genitive, as in ***Scripture knowledge, quoter, scorning*** (adj.), ***searcher***; adverbial, as in ***Scripture diviner, learned*** adj. (hence ***-learnedness***), ***-read*** adj.

1826 W. E. ANDREWS *Exam. Fox's Cal. Prot. Saints* 253 His list of heterogeneous fanatics and *scripture-diviners. **1661** BOYLE *Style of Script.* (1675) 140 Every new degree of *Scripture-knowledge. **1579** W. WILKINSON *Confut. Fam. Love* A ij b, Vnto which..holy annoynting no conceited *Scripturelearned or Doctour of the letter..hath in these days attained. **1607** T. ROGERS *39 Art.* vi. (1625) 28 In whose bookes nothing is more frequent then the tearming of Gods reuerend ministers, and preachers, Scripture-learned. **1608** H. CLAPHAM *Errour Right Hand* 49 Leaue your *Scripture-learnednesse, and submit your selfe to the spirit of Loue. **1828** P. CUNNINGHAM *N.S. Wales* (ed. 3) II. 268 [In women-convict ships] there was not a single *Scripture-quoter, such as we find in men-ships. **1888** DOUGHTY *Arab. Des.* I. 144 Great *scripture-read scholars. **1593** NASHE *Christ's T.* 58 Bold blasphemies and *Scripture-scorning ironies against God. **1844** LD. LEIGH *Walks in Country* 129 The humble *scripture-searcher prays for grace.

d. Special combinations: **Scripture Janus** *nonce-wd.*, one who quotes Holy Scripture 'both ways'; †**Scripture-proof** *a.*, secured by Holy Scripture; **Scripture reader,** (*a*) a reader of the Scriptures; so ***Scripture-reading***; (*b*) one who is employed to read the Bible to the uneducated poor in their own houses (*Obs.* exc. *Hist.*); **Scripture-wort,** letter-lichen.

1715 PITTIS *Life Radcliffe* 53, I cannot be induc'd to love a *Scripture-Janus, such as is the Arch-Bishop of Glascow. **1641** SANDERSON *Serm.* (1681) II. 5 When their doctrines were found not to be *Scripture-proof. **1647** TRAPP *Comm. 1 Cor.* ii. (1656) 663 Our whole preaching must be Scripture-proof, or it will burn, and none be the better for it. **1625** GODWYN *Moses & Aaron* I. ix. 43 They had their name..*Karaim*,..or *Scripture readers, because they adhered to Scripture alone. ?**1854** MRS. GASKELL *Lett.* (1966) 274 'Scripture readers' are men, sent & paid by a London society to any clergyman who applies for them to help him to read the bible in his parish. **1862** H. MAYHEW *London Labour* Extra vol. (ed. 2) p. xxii, It is the special duty of the Scripture readers to visit from house to house. **1882** OGILVIE, *Scripture-reader*, one employed to read the Bible in private houses among the poor and ignorant. **1849** STOVEL *Canne's Necess.* 55 These *scripture-reading believers in the Lord. **1856** *Scripture-wort [see *letter-lichen*, LETTER *sb.*[1] 9]. **1866** in *Treas. Bot.*

†**'scripture,** *v. Obs.* [f. SCRIPTURE *sb.*] *trans.* To write, place on record.

c **1470** HARDING *Chron.* CXLII. xv, At Newerke died, at Worcester sepultured, In chronicles, as is playnly scryptured. *Ibid.* CXLVII. ii, As some menne wrote the right lyne to depryue, Through great falshed made it to bee scriptured.

†**'scriptured,** *a. Obs.* Also 6 scryptured. [f. SCRIPTURE *sb.* + -ED[2].]

1. Learned or versed in the Scriptures; well acquainted with Holy Scripture.

1532 MORE *Confut. Tindale* Wks. 391/2 Me semeth it is.. of such a scriptured manne not very scripturelye spoken. **1533** —— *Answ. Poysoned Bk.* Wks. 1093/1 Whither he bee scryptured or not, he hath a very bare barain wytte when he can wene y[t] this argument were aught.

2. Warranted by Holy Scripture.

1606 BIRNIE *Kirk-Buriall* (1833) E 2 b, Although there be nothing more plentifully scriptured nor buriall exemples.

3. Covered with writing.

1856 D. G. ROSSETTI *Burden of Nineveh* xx, Those scriptured flanks it cannot see. **1899** T. S. MOORE *Vine-dresser* 35 When I read from the scriptured scroll Those ancient words I prize.

scriptureless ('skrɪptjʊəlɪs), *a.* [-LESS.] Not according to or founded upon the Scriptures.

1563 DAVIDSON *Answ. to Kennedy* in *Wodrow Soc. Misc.* I. 238 He callis thaim factious men, because thay will not subscrive to Scriptureles Councels. **1606** BIRNIE *Kirk-Buriall* (1833) B 3, Buriall is ordinarilie traduced as a scripturelesse thing. **1885** A. BLACKBURN in *Homiletic Rev.* July 57 There is a godless spiritualism, a Christless Unitarianism, and a Scriptureless 'new theology'.

†**'scripturely,** *a. Obs.* [f. SCRIPTURE *sb.* + -LY[1].] Scriptural.

1549 OLDE *Erasm. Par. Eph.* Prol. 2 In scripturely fastyng, in ghospellike prayer. **1597** J. PAYNE *Royal Exch.* 45 The which scripturely speche S. Paul vseth thus.

†**'scripturely,** *adv. Obs.* [-LY[2].] Scripturally.

1532 [see SCRIPTURED *ppl. a.*[1]].

scripturian (skrɪp'tjʊərɪən), *sb.* and *a. rare.* Also 7 -ean. [f. SCRIPTURE *sb.* + -IAN.]

A. *sb.* A biblical scholar; a scripturist.

1599 CHAPMAN *Hum. Days Mirth* G 3 b, *Flo.* Cursed be he that maketh debate twixt man & wife. *Lem.* O rare scripturian! you haue sealed vp my lips. *a* **1612** HARINGTON *Epigr.* (1633) IV. lxxxiii, Great Scriptureans.., That cite Saint Paul at every bench and boord.

B. *adj.* = SCRIPTURARIAN *a.*

1826 *Examiner* 35/2 An Irish Priest..had called him a Bible-reading vagabond, a Scripturian rapscallion, &c. merely because he refused to part with his Bible.

scripturiency (skrɪp'tjʊərɪənsɪ). [f. SCRIPTURIENT: see -ENCY.] A mania for writing.

1652 URQUHART *Jewel* Wks. (1834) 262 Though scripturiency be a fault in feeble pens. **1685** *Reflect. on Baxter* 1 The Disease of Scripturiency in R. B. taken notice of. **1717** *Entertainer* No. 3. 18 This Bladder of Scripturiency.

scripturient (skrɪp'tjʊərɪənt), *a.* and *sb.* [ad. L. *sripturient-*, pres. pple. of late L. *scriptūrīre* to desire to write, f. L. *script-*, *scrīběre* to write.]

A. *adj.* Having a desire for writing or authorship. Now *rare.*

1643 *Copy of Two Lett.* 5 This I know, that a Scripturient Engine, may finde matter enough for exercise in Gerson, Bucerus..and other moderne Authors, which yet lye unanswered. **1710** R. WARD *Life H. More* 151 He labour'd under the Scripturient Disease. *a* **1711** KEN *Lett.* Wks. (1838) 84 There is a remarkable scripturient person, who keeps correspondence with your adversaries here. **1872** G. M. HOPKINS *Let.* 4 Jan. in *Further Lett.* (1938) 88, I was then scripturient and quickening towards letter-heat.

B. *sb.* One who has a passion for writing.

1659 HEYLIN *Examen Hist.* II. Pref., Most of our late Scripturients affecting rather to be doing, then to be punctuall and exact in what they doe.

†**'scripturing,** *vbl. sb. Obs.* [f. SCRIPTURE *sb.* + -ING[1].] Reading or discussing of the Scriptures.

1588 J. UDALL *Diotrephes* (Arb.) 7 As for these controuersies and this Scripturing, I neuer trouble my selfe with it.

scripturism ('skrɪptjʊərɪz(ə)m). [f. SCRIPTURE *sb.* + -ISM.]

1. Reliance upon the Scriptures alone; devotion to Scripture.

1864 GLADSTONE in Morley *Life* v. x. (1903) II. 165 This rude shock to the mere scripturism which has too much prevailed. **1889** T. K. CHEYNE *Orig. Psalter* v. (1891) 202 The Song of the Sun was provided with a new conclusion more in harmony with the intense Scripturism of the post-Exile period.

2. A Scripture phrase or expression.

1884 J. W. HALES *Notes & Ess. on Shaks.* 181 There are several 'scripturisms' in Hamlet.

scripturist ('skrɪptjʊərɪst). [f. SCRIPTURE *sb.* + -IST.]

1. One who is versed in the Scriptures.

1661 BOYLE *Style of Script.* (1675) 140 To engage us to grow ready Scripturists. **1713** NELSON *Life Bull* 509 He was also esteemed a very good Grecian and a great Scripturist. **1792** W. NEWCOME *Eng. Biblical Transl.* 6 Wiclif was not only a good divine and scripturist, but well skilled in the civil, canon, and English law. **1878** C. STANFORD *Symb. Christ* ii. 38 The Puritan fathers, those devout Scripturists, delighted to say that they found in Scripture a hundred and eight of His names.

2. One who bases his religious belief or opinions upon Scripture alone.

1624 GODWYN *Moses & Aaron* (1641) 47 The Sadduces were termed..*Karaim*, Biblers, or Scripturists. **1737** WATERLAND *Rev. Doctr. Eucharist* Introd. 9 It must argue great Conceitedness..for a Man to expect to be heard, or attended to, as a Scripturist, or a Textuary, in opposition to the Christian World.

†**'scripulous,** *a. Obs. rare.* Also 5 screpulus, 6 scripulus. By-form of SCRUPULOUS: cf. SCRIPLE *sb.*

1464 *Coventry Leet Bk.* 328 For-somoche as the mater dependyng betwix Joh. Abery & Will. Bedon on that oon partie and Will. Huet on the other..ys screpulus & doubtefull. **1549** *Compl. Scot.* 165 Sum scripulus preistis, hefand there consciens subiect to traditions. **1601** YARINGTON *Two Lament. Trag.* I. iii. in Bullen *O. Pl.* IV., Peace, conscience, peace, thou art too scripulous. *Ibid.* IV. vi, It cannot out Unlesse your love will be so scripulous That it will over-throwe your selfe and me.

scris, variant pl. form of SCRITE.

scritch (skrɪtʃ), *sb. arch.* Also 6 skrych, 6-7 scrich, skrich, 7 skritch. [See the vb.] A screech, shriek, loud cry.

1513 MORE in *Hall's Chron. Rich. III* (1550) 4 b, With pitefull scriches she repleneshyd the hole mancion. **1599** HAKLUYT *Voy.* I. 560 Monstrous skritches are heard round about this mountaine. **1635** J. HAYWARD tr. *Biondi's Banish'd Virg.* 190 Gave she not her selfe over to scritches and cries. **1797** COLERIDGE *Christabel* I. xvii, Perhaps it is the owlet's scritch. **1833** TENNYSON '*My life is full*' 20 Sudden scritches of the jay. *a* **1963** S. PLATH in *Atlantic Monthly* (1968) Sept. 59/1, I hear..water sloshing, the scritch of a comb in frizzled hair.

†*Comb.* **1582** STANYHURST *Æneis* IV. (Arb.) 120 Up to the sky staring, with belling skrichcrye she roareth.

scritch (skrɪtʃ), *v. arch.* Forms: 3, 6-7 scrich, 4 skriche, 6 skritche, 6-7 skrich, 6- scritch. [Onomatopœic: cf. SKRIKE, SHRIEK *vbs.*] *intr.* To utter a loud cry, screech, shriek.

a **1250** *Owl & N.* 223 (Jesus MS.) þu scrichest & yollest to þine fere, þat hit is gryslich to ihere. **13..** *Seuyn Sag.* (W.) 1290 Loude he gan to crie and skriche [*rime* diche]. **1566** PAINTER *Pal. Pleas.* I. 45 She cried out, and all her maides skriched with her. *a* **1586** SIDNEY *Arcadia* v. (1598) 441 Then would she imagine..she heard the cries of hellish ghosts, then would she skritch out for succour. **1632** J. HAYWARD tr. *Biondi's Eromena* 99 With a shril voice he suddenly scritch'd out. **1652** GAULE *Magastrom.* 181 The pyes chattering about the house, the owles scritching. **1840** BROWNING *Sordello* II. 458 Only let..the hungry curlew chance to scritch Or serpent hiss it, rustling through the rift, However loud, however low. **1944** W. DE LA MARE *Coll. Rhymes & Verses* 70 Down to the shore skipped Lallerie, His parrot on his thumb, And the twain they scritched in mockery. **1957** H. NICOLSON *Journey to Java* v. 88 The evening breeze stirs the tree above us and we hear the keel birds scritching.

Hence **'scritching** *vbl. sb.* and *ppl. a.*

1592 NASHE *Strange Newes* F 1, Like a scritching night-owle. **1603** KNOLLES *Hist. Turks* (1621) 314 Then began their sorrowes afresh, with pitious scriching and teares. **1626** BACON *Sylva* §700 Squeaking or skriching Noise. *Ibid.* §713 Feare causeth Palenesse;..Starting; and Skritching. **1648** GAGE *West Ind.* 155 This is a very rude sport, and full of scriechíng and hideous noise. **1888** DOUGHTY *Arab. Des.* I. 305 We heard scritching owls somewhere in the still night.

'scritch-owl. *arch.* exc. *Southern U.S.* Forms: see SCRITCH *sb.* [f. SCRITCH *sb.* + OWL.] = SCREECH-OWL.

1530 PALSGR. 268/1 Scrytche houle a byrde. *Ibid.* 271/1 Skrytche heule. **1590** SHAKS. *Mids. N.* v. 383 Whil'st the scritch-owle, scritching loud, Puts the wretch that lies in woe, In remembrance of a shroud. **1609** B. JONSON *Masque of Queens* Wks. 1616 I. 951 The Scrich-owles egges, and the feathers blacke,..I haue been getting. **1697** COLLIER *Ess. Mor. Subj.* II. (1709) 24 The Warbling of Cats and Scritch-Owls. **1813** COLERIDGE *Remorse* IV. iii. 6 The scritch-owl only wakes. **1944** *Publ. Amer. Dial. Soc.* II. 49 *Scritch-owl*, screech-owl. **1960** V. WILLIAMS *Walk Egypt* 269 Mary Morning cried, 'I seen something sliding.' 'A rat. A scritch-owl.'

transf. and *fig.* **1594** *Contention* II. (1843) 151 Bring forth that fatall scrichowle to our house, That nothing sung to vs but bloud and death. **1641** J. JACKSON *True Evang. T.* III. 187 What is poore, and silly man alone, but a very scrich-owle, and satyre.

attrib. **1790** COLERIDGE *Music*, 'Tis thou who pour'st the scritch-owl note.

'scritch-scratch. [Reduplicated formation on SCRATCH.] Continual scratching. Hence **scritch-scratching** *vbl. sb.*

1842 *Blackw. Mag.* LI. 320 One could not work; he never could whilst men were making such a scritch-scratch with their pens. **1881** ETHEL COXON *Basil Plant* I. 67 Do leave that confounded scritch-scratching alone this afternoon.

1977 *Time* 14 Feb. 33/2 At any hour of the day or night one can hear the scritch-scratch of individual snow shovels.

†**scrite.** *Obs.* Also 3-4 scrit, 4 scritte, skryt(e, scriit, skrite, *pl.* scris, 4-5 scryt(e, 5 skrit. [Aphetic a. OF. *escrit*: see ESCRIPT.] A writing, written document.

1297 R. GLOUC. (Rolls) 7682 Let it write clene ynou & þat scrit dude iwis In þe tresorie at westmunstre þere it ȝut is. *a* 1300 *Cursor M.* 17634 þai..raght him for to rede þat scritte. 1303 R. BRUNNE *Handl. Synne* 7002 To Seynt Ihon he wrote a skryte. 13.. *Sir Beues* 1240 (A.) Al in solas and in delit þow most him bere þis ilche scriit! *c* 1320 *Sir Tristr.* 1944 Swiche cas him was bi falle As we finde in scrite. *c* 1330 R. BRUNNE *Chron. Wace* (Rolls) 8071 We fynde writen in our scrytes Of swylk manere of spyrites. 1338 —— *Chron.* (1810) 224 þe chartres and þe scris. 13.. *K. Alis.* 2936 (Bodl. MS.), þat ich habbe by a skryt ȝou seide Oiþer ȝee shullen ben sore ennoyed. *c* 1374 CHAUCER *Troylus* II. 1130 She..seyde scryt [*v.rr.* scrit, script] ne bille, For loue of god ..Ne bryng me noon. *a* 1400 in *Eng. Gilds* (1870) 357 Treweleche a-countes ȝelde to godemen of þe town twyȝes by þe ȝere, by skore oþer by scryt. *a* 1400 *St. Alexius* (Vernon) 409 In his hand he heold a skrit. *c* 1450 *St. Cuthbert* (Surtees) 6520 þis semys agayn saint bede scrite.

†**scrithe,** *v. Obs.* Forms: 1 scríðan, 3 scriþen, 4 skrith, skrythe, 5 scrith(e, scryth(e; *pa. t.* 1 scráð, 3 scrað, scroð; *pa. pple.* 1 scriden, scriðen, 3 iscriðen, 5 scrithen, -in, -yn. [A Common Teut. str. vb.: OE. *scríðan* = OS. *scrîðan, scrîdan*, OHG. *scrîtan* (MHG. *scrîten*, G. *schreiten*), ON. *skríða*:—OTeut. **skrîþan*, **skrîdan*.]

1. *intr.* To go, pass; in OE. also, to glide, creep; to wander.

Beowulf 163 Hwyder helrunan hwyrftum scriþað. *c* 1205 LAY. 4109 þa iherde Stater..mid muchele Scot ferde he scrað to þisse londe. *Ibid.* 10809 Whar beo ȝe mine Scottes scriðeð me biside. *a* 1352 MINOT *Poems* (ed. Hall) v. 68 þe schipmen of Ingland sailed ful swith þat none of þe Normandes fro þam might skrith.

2. In immaterial sense.

a 1000 *Guthlac* 942 (Gr.) Daȝas forð scridun. *c* 1340 HAMPOLE *Pr. Treat.* (1866) 2 *note* 3, þer skrythes into my mynde delyciost swetnes. 1434 MISYN *Mending of Life* xi. 126 In þi swetnes scryth in-to me.

b. To fall or lapse (*into* sin).

1434 MISYN *Mending of Life* i. 107 Truly a man I saw of qwhome þai sayd þat fyftene ȝere his body [he] chastisyd with meruelus scharpnes and afterward skrithyn into synne with his seruandis wife. 1435 —— *Fire of Love* II. i. 70 Ȝit many after penans has fallin fro innocence eftsoynes scrythand to ydilnes. 1483 *Cath. Angl.* 326/1 To be Scrythen (Scrythin *A.*), *illabi*.

3. *intr.* and *refl.* To urge, entreat.

c 1250 *Gen. & Ex.* 1055 He..scroð him wel, And bead hem hom to is ostel To herbergen wið him ðat niȝt. *Ibid.* 1834 Iacob was wo ðat he is for-soc, And scroð him so ðat sum he ðor tok. *Ibid.* 2023 Often ȝhe ðrette, often ȝhe scroð, Oc al it was him o-like loð.

Hence †**scrithing** *ppl. a.*, passing away, wandering, erring.

1435 MISYN *Fire of Love* I. xxii. 49 Criste truly had no scrithyng þoghtis. *Ibid.* II. ix. 92 As if maners or riches or fayrnes frenschyp be had with yll maners, riches scriþinge, fayrnes wastyd.

†'**scrithel,** *a. Obs.*$^{-0}$ In 5 scrythylle. [repr. OE. **scriðol* (found in *wídscriðol* far-wandering, roving), f. root *scrið-* (see prec.).] Fleeting.

1483 *Cath. Angl.* 326/1 Scrythylle, *labilis*.

scritoire, scritore, obs. ff. SCRUTOIRE.

†**scritory.** *Obs.* Anglicization of ESCRITOIRE.

1687 MIEGE *Gr. Fr. Dict.* II, Scritory, a great sort of Cabinet with Drawers, and the conveniency of a Table to write upon, *bureau*. 1706 PHILLIPS (ed. Kersey), *Scrutoir*, or *Scritory*.

scrittoir, scriture: see SCRUTOIRE, SCRIPTURE.

†**scrivan.** *Obs.* Anglicized form of next.

In the examples relating to India it may be a. Pg. *escrivão*.

1511 *Guylforde's Pilgr.* (Camden) 16 There scryuan euer wrytyng our names man by man as we entred in the presens of the sayd Lordes. 1632 LITHGOW *Trav.* x. 460 [He] commanded the Scriuan to draw vp a Warrant. 1698 FRYER *Acc. E. India & P.* 112 Few of their Great Men or Merchants can read, but keep a Scrivan of the Gentues. 1711 C. LOCKYER *Acc. Trade in India* 153 Scrivans at the fort. Scrivans and boatmen at Canton.

attrib. 1632 LITHGOW *Trav.* x. 450, I was brought forth before these foure Caualliers,..and the Scriuan-table set, with pen and paper to write my confession.

‖**scri'vano.** *Obs.* Also 7 scriuana, skrivano, 8 *pl.* scrivani. [It. = F. *écrivain* (see SCRIVEIN). Cf. prec. and ESCRIVAN.] A professional writer; a notary; one who keeps accounts; a clerk, etc.

1581 J. BELL *Haddon's Answ. Osorius* 403 There must a Bull be desired at the length I suppose, or some scrow of Release from the Popes Scrivanoes. 1596 NASHE *Saffron Walden* O 2, If there were euer a paltrie Scriuano, betwixt a Lawiers Clark & a Poet, or smattering pert Boy [etc.]. *c* 1605 E. SCOT in Purchas *Pilgrims* (1625) I. III. 169 He bad me I should shew his Scriuana those Captaines. 1626 SHIRLEY *Brothers* IV. i, You do not know the quirks of a Scrivano, A dash undoes a Family. 1782 *Ann. Reg.* II. 14 The scrivani, or commissaries, who have the department of warrants, arrests, and police, are allowed no pay.

†**scrive,** *sb.*[1] *Obs.* A shriek, a noise.

c 1400 *Destr. Troy* 9511 The shippes on a shene frye shot þai belyue, That the low vp lightly launchit aboute; And all chrickenede with the scriue þurgh the styrn ost.

scrive (skraɪv), *sb.*[2] [f. SCRIVE *v.* 2.] = SCRIBE *sb.*[2]

1839 CHATTO *Wood Engraving* 2 'To scrive'..signifies, in our own language, to cut numerals or other characters on timber with a tool called a scrive.

scrive (skraɪv), *v.* Also 4 skr-. [Formation somewhat uncertain; perh. aphetic for DESCRIVE.]

†1. a. *trans.* To describe. b. *intr.* To write. *Obs.*

13.. *Ipotis* 399 (Vernon MS.) in Horstm. *Altengl. Leg.* (1881) 345 Glotenye, I wol now skriue, Is among monkunne ful ryue. *c* 1430 *Hymns Virgin* (1895) 58 How mankinde dooþ bigynne is wondir for to scryue so. *a* 1529 SKELTON *Agst. Garnesche* iv. 91 It semyth nat thy pyllyd pate Agenst a poyet lawreat To take vpon the for to scryue. 1530 PALSGR. 707/2, I scryve a thyng, I discrybe the maner of it, *je descris*.

2. *trans.* = SCRIBE *v.*

1829 BROCKETT *N.C. Gloss.* (ed. 2), *Skrive*, to mark or scratch wood or metal. 1839 [see SCRIVE *sb.*[2]]. 1874 THEARLE *Naval Archit.* 143 When the lines of the sections or frames are accurately drawn, they are scratched or 'scrived' in by a sharp-pointed tool.

scrive, obs. (north.) form of SHRIVE *v.*

scrive-board ('skraɪvbɔəd). *Shipbuilding.* [f. SCRIVE *v.*] A large drawing-board made of planks, on which the lines of a vessel are scribed.

1869 SIR E. REED *Shipbuild.* xx. 429 The name commonly given to these boards by the workmen is the scrive or scriving boards. 1890 W. J. GORDON *Foundry* 59 When the lines are passed as accurate, moulds or skeleton outlines of them are taken, and thus they get transferred to the 'scrive-boards', from which the shipwrights work.

†**scrivein, -eyn.** *Obs.* Also 4 -ayn, scryvane, -ein, -eyne, screweyny, 4-5 scry-, 5 skry-, skreveyn. [Aphetic a. OF. *escrivain, -ein*, etc. (mod.F. *écrivain*): see ESCRIVAIN.]

= SCRIVENER 1.

a 1300 *E.E. Psalter* xliv. [xlv.] 2 My tunge is penne of þe scriuayn swiflich wrytand. 1340 *Ayenb.* 44 þise scriueyns þet sseweþ guode lettre ate ginnynge and efterward makeþ wycked. *c* 1374 CHAUCER *To Scriv.* 1 Adam scryveyne if euer it þee byfalle Boece or Troylus for to wryten nuwe. 1389 *Eng. Gilds* 119 Yis gylde schal hawe..to screweynys. *Ibid.*, And if ony of hem for-sake hys office,..eyther screweyny [schal payn] a qwarter of wax. *c* 1400 tr. *Secreta Secret.*, *Gov. Lordsh.* 106 Al-so it fallys þat þou chese of wyse men & of Skreueyns, sweche þat hauyn perfeccion of enournede eloquence, & of sotyll record; And right as þe Skryueyn ys enterpretour of þy wyl [etc.]. 1430-40 LYDG. *Bochas* II. xv. (1494) hj b, Of a scryueyn Bochas maketh mencion.

‖**scrivello** (skrɪ'vɛləʊ). Also 8 screvelio, (9 crevelle). Pl. -oes, -os. [repr. Pg. *escrevelho*, ?var. of *escaravelho* pin, peg. Cf. F. *escarbeille*, *-belle*, *-balle*.] An elephant's tusk weighing less than 20lb.

1735 S. ATKINS *Voy. Guinea* 181 The screvelios are small, from 15 to 4 lbs. weight. 1757 *List of Cargoes* in Beatson *Nav. & Mil. Mem.* (1790) II. 187, 14 scrivellos. 1819 *Rees' Cycl.*, Crevelles. 1864 R. F. BURTON *Dahome* 41 The horn is a small scrivello with a large oblong hole near the point. 1891 *Times* 24 Oct. 4/5 Billiard ball pieces and cut descriptions few sold. Ball scrivelloes dearer.

scriven ('skrɪv(ə)n), *v.* [Back-formation f. SCRIVENER.] *trans.* and *intr.* (with *advs.*) To write as a scrivener does.

a 1685 LD. GUILFORD in North *Life* (1742) 311 Here's a Mortgage scrivened up to ten Skins of Parchment; and the King's Attorney General is content with six lines. 1839 MRS. GORE *Courtier* iii, The attorney's clerks..were scrivening away in Mr. Heneage's justice-room.

scrivener ('skrɪv(ə)nə(r)). Forms: 4 scriveyner, 4-6 skrivener, 5 skri-, scryvenere, skerevener, 5-6 scry-, skryvener, 6 skryvynar, scryvenar, -our, skrevener, 7 scrivender, scrivenor, scrivner, 5- scrivener. [f. SCRIVEIN + -ER[1].

The form *escrivener* occurs in 1415 (*York Myst.* ed. 1885, Introd. p. xxvi).]

1. A professional penman; a scribe, copyist; a clerk, secretary, amanuensis.

c 1375 in *Trans. Shropsh. Archæol. Soc.* Ser. III. (1901) I. 121 Reinaldus le scrivueyner. *c* 1402 LYDG. *Compl. Bl. Knt.* 194 But even-lyk as doth a skrivenere That can no more what that he shall wryte, But as his maister besyde doth endyte. 1455 in E. B. Jupp *Carpenters' Co.* (1887) 10 Item payd to the skerevener for the dyvyce of the ordinaunce and for þe wrytyn in pabir iij^s iiij^d. 1530-1 *Act 22 Hen. VIII*, c. 13 No person or persones straungers, beyng a comon baker, bruer, surgeon or scryvenour shalbe enterpret or expounded hande craftesmen. *a* 1548 HALL *Chron.*, *Hen. VII* 46 Richard Scelton a tayler and Jhon Asteley a Skrevener. 1602 ROWLANDS *Greenes Ghost* 18 This fellow came into a Scriueners shop to haue a letter written to his wiues mother. *a* 1619 FOTHERBY *Atheom.* II. i. §3 (1622) 176 The Scriuener of Nature [said of Aristotle by Suidas]. *a* 1680 BUTLER *Rem.* (1759) I. 210 Scriveners take more Pains to learn the Slight Of making Knots, than all the Hands they write. 1829 SOUTHEY *Sir T. More* II. 91 A very little suffices for the stock in trade, upon which the scribes and scriveners of literature, who take upon themselves to direct the public, set up. 1899 *Allbutt's Syst. Med.* VIII. 19 Thereupon the scrivener throws the burden of pen-prehension upon other muscles.

transf. 1607 TOURNEUR *Rev. Trag.* I. iii, Thou hast beene Scriuener to much knauery then. 1806 WOLCOT (P. Pindar) *Tristia* Wks. 1812 V. 339 Sir, let fools say, what fools think fit Trust to that upright Scrivener, call'd Time.

attrib. 1483 *Rolls of Parlt.* VI. 256/2 The third to teche to Write, and all suche thyng as belonged to Scrivener Craft.

b. *scrivener's cramp, palsy*, writer's cramp.

1855 DUNGLISON *Med. Lex.*, *Scrivener's cramp*. 1877 *Encycl. Brit.* VI. 543/2 The disease known as Writer's Cramp, or Scrivener's Palsy.

†c. An author. *Obs.*

a 1660 *Contemp. Hist. Irel.* (Ir. Archæol. Soc.) III. 90 All the politicke scriuners that euer handled such a subjecte.

d. 'A writing-master' (Halliwell, 1847).

2. A notary.

1477-9 *Rec. St. Mary at Hill* 83 Item, to—masse, Scryvenere, for ouerseyng the olde endentures of the same howse. 1577 HELLOWES tr. *Guevara's Fam. Epist.* 83 As God made you a Knight, if he had made you a Scriuener, you would haue bene more handsome to colour Cordouan skinnes, then to haue written processe. 1596 SHAKS. *Tam. Shr.* IV. iv. 59 My Boy shall fetch the Scriuener presentlie. 1622 MALYNES *Anc. Law-Merchant* 100 The Bills were tendered with a Scriuener according to their agreement. 1656 H. PHILLIPS *Purch. Patt.* (1676) 3 Some skilful Lawyer, and knowing Scrivener. 1706 PHILLIPS (ed. Kersey), *Scrivener*, one that draws up and engrosses Writings or Deeds, as Bonds, Bills, Leases, Releases, &c. 1712 E. COOKE *Voy. S. Sea* 85 Notaries, Scriveners, and Clerks of the Court of Justice. 1806-7 J. BERESFORD *Miseries Hum. Life* XXI. (1826) 296 Why what the plague? where is this scoundrel of a scrivener? what if I should die before be comes!

attrib. 1757 MRS. GRIFFITH *Henry & Frances* (1766) IV. 44 Vulgar Phrases, and scrivener Id[i]oms.

3. One who 'received money to place out at interest, and who supplied those who wanted to raise money on security' (Tomlins). Also *money scrivener*. *Obs.* exc. *Hist.*

1607 DEKKER & WEBSTER *Northward Hoe!* II. D 2 b, Here was a scriuener but euen now, to put my father in minde of a bond, that wilbe forfit this night. 1625 BACON *Ess.*, *Of Riches* (Arb.) 237 The Scriueners and Broakers doe valew vnsound Men. 1637 *Prynne Docum.* (Camden) 77 To make inquiry into the breach of the statute, that noe scrivener shoull take above 5^s brokadge in the £. 1677 YARRANTON *Eng. Improv.* 8 Let a Gentleman..come to a Money Scrivener, and desire Four thousand pounds to be lent him on all his Land. *a* 1700 DRYDEN tr. *Hor. Epodes* ii. 5 How happy in his low Degree, Who leads a quiet Country Life, Discharg'd of Business, void of Strife, And from the griping Scrivener free? 1704-84 [see MONEY *sb.* 8]. 1706 ESTCOURT *Fair Example* III. i. 28 *Sir Ch.* Sir, I am oblig'd to you, you shall have my Note. *Fan.* No, but I won't, I am no Scrivener, Sir; there's a Bill payable at sight. 1818 CRUISE *Digest* (ed. 2) II. 207 T. Gibson and Co. being scriveners, and having large sums of money of other peoples' in their hands, had lent Mr. Stiles [etc.].

Hence '**scrivenership** *rare*$^{-0}$.

1611 COTGR., *Escrivainerie*, Scriuenership.

scrivenery ('skrɪv(ə)nərɪ). Also 9 (Dicts.) scrivenry. [f. SCRIVENER: cf. -ERY, -RY.]

1. The occupation of a scrivener; writing, as of a copyist or clerk.

1847 LE FANU *T. O'Brien* 257 He pursued his scrivenery with industrious taciturnity. 1891 *Law Times* XCII. 99/1 The books are beautiful specimens of scrivenery, and from cover to cover may be searched without finding a blot.

attrib. 1887 *Whitaker's Almanack*, Law Offices, etc., Scrivenery Department.

2. A room in which scriveners work.

1897 *Times* 26 Feb. 3/6 Mr. Spedding's Biography.. disclosed..that Bacon and his brother Anthony kept a scrivenery financed by Essex. 1898 *Proc. Soc. Antiq.* 20 Jan. 39 Nineteen lines of beautiful script, possibly written in the scrivenery attached to the court.

scrivening ('skrɪv(ə)nɪŋ), *vbl. sb.* [f. SCRIVEN *v.* + -ING[1].]

1. Writing, esp. of a mechanical or arduous kind.

1809 MAR. EDGEWORTH *Ennui* xxi. (1893) 237 He.. would, after two or three hours' hard scrivening,..permit me to yawn, and stretch, and pity myself, and curse the useless repetitions of lawyers. 1883 STEVENSON *Silverado Sq.* 221 When I had done my scrivening, Hanson strolled out.

b. *attrib.*

1828 *Craven Gloss.*, *Scrivenin time*, time appropriated to writing. 1856 R. A. VAUGHAN *Mystics* VI. i. (1860) I. 141 Had I that same scrivening art at my service, I should write me a book setting forth what I..observed. 1896 CROCKETT *Grey Man* xi. 79 Two sheets of clean scrivening paper.

2. *money scrivening*: the business of a money scrivener. *Hist.*

1885 *Weekly Notes* 68/1 They did a considerable business in money scrivening, receiving money from clients both for specific and general investment.

'**scrivening,** *ppl. a.* [Formed as prec. + -ING[2].] Following the occupation of a scrivener.

a 1754 FIELDING *Fathers* Prol., Now Slipslop enters..tho' this scriv'ning vagrant Salted my virtue, which was ever flagrant. 1814 MAR. EDGEWORTH *Patronage* xxiii. (1893) I. 364 When he was a scrivening nobody in his garret.

†'**scrivenliche,** *adv. Obs. rare*$^{-1}$. [f. SCRIVEN + -LY[2].] In the manner of a scrivener.

c 1374 CHAUCER *Troylus* II. 1206 (MS. Harl. 3943) Ne scryvenlich [*v.rr.* scryuenyssh, scriuenisshli(che, etc.] or craftly þow it write.

†'**scriver.** *Obs.* [? f. SCRIVE + -ER[1]. Cf. SCREEVER.] = SCRIVENER.

1689 *Lond. Gaz.* No. 2479/4 Huntley Bigg, Scriver, near the New Exchange. *c* 1700 in *Law's Memor.* (1818) 199 *note*, Another that was scriver to a troop, who was sitting in a chamber himself,..the house fell and smoored him.

ˈscriving, *vbl. sb.* [-ING[1].] The action of SCRIVE *v.*; *attrib.* in **scriving-board** = SCRIVE-BOARD; **scriving-iron** = *scribing-iron*.

1847 HALLIWELL, *Scriving-iron*, an instrument used for numbering trees for sale. **1869** [see SCRIVE-BOARD].

scrob, obs. form of SCRUB *v.*

scrobe (skrəʊb). [ad. L. *scrob-is* trench.]

†**1.** A trench. *Obs. rare*[−1].

1686 GOAD *Celest. Bodies* I. vi. 17 Enjoining to dig their scrobes, for the Planting of Trees at the Full Moon.

2. *Ent.* (See quot.)

1891 *Century Dict.*, *Scrobe*,..(*a.*) A groove in the side of the rostrum in which the scape or basal joint of the antenna is received, in the weevils or curculios. (*b.*) A groove on the outer side of the mandible, more fully called mandibular scrobe. **1895** *Funk's Stand. Dict.*

†**ˈscrobicle.** *Obs. rare*[−0]. = SCROBICULE.

1721 BAILEY, *Scrobicle*, a little Ditch.

scrobicular (skrəʊˈbɪkjʊlə(r)), *a.* [f. mod.L. *scrobicula* or late L. *scrobiculus* SCROBICULE + -AR.] Pertaining to or surrounded by scrobicules.

1888 ROLLESTON & JACKSON *Anim. Life* 558 In *Palaeoechinidae*... The larger tubercles are surrounded by a smooth area—the scrobicula—and this by a ring of smaller scrobicular tubercles which bear correspondingly small spines. **1900** *Lankester's Treat. Zool.* III. 287 Generally surrounded by a circle of granules called the 'scrobicular circle'.

scrobiculate (skrəʊˈbɪkjʊlət), *a. Bot.* and *Zool.* [Formed as prec. + -ATE[2].] Having many small depressions; furrowed or pitted; *Ent.* foveate.

1806 TURTON tr. *Linn. Syst. Nat.* VII. Expl. Terms, *Scrobiculate.* **1882-4** COOKE *Brit. Fresh-w. Algæ* I. 77 Zygospore globose or broadly elliptic, dark olive, scrobiculate, formed in the canal of conjugation.

So **scroˈbiculated** *a.*

1860 R. FOWLER *Med. Voc.* **1881** WATSON in *Linn. Soc. Jrnl.* XV. 269 Rounded, almost scrobiculated varix.

scrobicule (ˈskrəʊbɪkjuːl). *Biol.* [ad. mod.L. *scrobicula* or late L. *scrobiculus*, dim. of *scrobs* (see SCROBE).] A small pit or depression; *spec.* the smooth area around the tubercles of a sea-urchin.

1880 C. R. MARKHAM *Peruv. Bark* 39 It would appear that at one period of growth these little pits or scrobicules are wanting, but when the plant is in full vigour they are markedly prominent. **1900** *Lankester's Treat. Zool.* III. 287 Around the base of each primary tubercle is a smooth, level surface called the 'scrobicule'.

scrobiculous (skrəʊˈbɪkjʊləs), *a. Bot.* [f. mod.L. *scrobiculōs-us*, f. *scrobiculus* or *scrobicula*: see prec. and -OUS.] = SCROBICULATE.

1889 WAGSTAFFE *Mayne's Med. Voc.* (ed. 6), *Scrobiculous* Bot., applied the same as *Scrobiculate.*

†**scrochat.** *Sc. Obs.* Forms (*pl.*): 5 **scro(s)chatis, scorzat(t)is, schrozatis**, 5-6 **scorchet(t)is**, 6 **schorchattis, scorcheatis, -sheatis, scrottiszarttis, scrotchertis, schoiretts, schorters(s, schortschettis**, 7 **scortitsche.** [Of obscure origin.] A kind of sweetmeat.

1448 *Aberdeen Reg.* (1844) I. 17 A propyne to our souerane lord..xij half pundis of scorchetis. **1496** *Halyburton's Ledger* (1867) 15 Item 12 li scrozattis, cost 5s. **1552-3** *Burgh Rec. Edin.* (1871) II. 276 Item, on the sacrament day gevin to the Bischop of Ross that bure the sacrament, in wyne and scrottiszarttis that extendit to xvj[s] viij[d]. **1581-2** *Aberd. Acc.* in *Spalding Club Miscell.* V. 54 Item, payt to Alex. Cullen vyff for vyn and schoiretts. **1583-4** *Ibid.* 55 Schorterss. *Ibid.* 56 Schortschettis. **1647-8** *Ibid.* 110, 10 pond scortitsche and confectionis.

scrod (skrɒd). *U.S.* Also **scrode, schrod.** [Possibly a. Du. †*schrood*, MDu. *schrode* piece cut off = OE. *scréade* SHRED *sb.* The variant ESCROD is difficult to explain.

Some U.S. dictionaries have a verb *scrod*, 'to shred, to prepare for cooking by tearing in small pieces,' which they assign as the source of this word.]

A young cod weighing less than three pounds, *esp.* one that is split and fried or boiled. Also used of young forms of other fishes, esp. the haddock, or a fillet cut from one of these fishes.

1841 *Spirit of Times* 16 Oct. 396/2 Supplied with a few ship biscuit [*sic*], a dried scrod, a bottle of good swizzle [etc.]. *a* **1873** MRS. SPOFFORD in *Casquet Lit.* IV. 9/2, I.. made the nicest little supper ready—scrod, as brown outside and as white inside as a cocoa-nut is, and cold turkey [etc.]. **1894** *Outing* (U.S.) XXIII. 404/2 Eighteen hundred-weight of scrod. **1949** *Chicago Tribune* 25 Feb. II. 4/6 As served in famous Boston restaurants, scrod is simply a tail piece of filleted haddock or cod dipped in oil, then bread crumbs and boiled in a moderate oven. **1949** O. NASH *Versus* 54, I lunch and sup on schrod and soup. **1971** M. SMITH *Gypsy in Amber* (1975) viii. 60 She slid a fish knife down the flaccid spine of the scrod. **1978** J. CARROLL *Mortal Friends* III. iv. 303 'The scrod, please,' Brady said when the waiter arrived. **1979** *United States 1980/81* (Penguin Travel Guides) 84 Boston is justly famous for its seafood, especially the ubiquitous scrod, which is actually young cod—or is it grown-up cod cut into fillets?

scroddled (ˈskrɒd(ə)ld), *a.* [Of obscure origin; cf. LG. *schrodel* scrap.] (See quot.)

1884 KNIGHT *Dict. Mech.* Suppl., *Scroddled Ware.* (*Ceramics.*) Ceramic ware, made by taking scraps and pieces of differently colored clays, such as are left over in making vases and plaques, and laying them together, joined but not intermixed, so as to produce a marbled or mottled effect.

scroddy (ˈskrɒdɪ), *a.* [Orig. unknown.] Mean, paltry. (In contemptuous use of amount or condition.) (Appar. restricted to D. H. Lawrence.)

c **1909** D. H. LAWRENCE *Collier's Friday Night* (1934) III. 63 Now, Beat! (*Offering the grapes.*).. Go on—have some!.. What a scroddy few! Here, have some more. **1912** —— in *Nation* 16 Mar. 982/1 Tha gets 'appen a scroddy twenty-two shillin'. **1912** —— *Let.* Oct. (1932) 69 Tell Bunny we don't believe his last scroddy letter was meant for us.

scrodgill (ˈskrɒdgɪl), *sb.* ? *U.S.* [Cf. SCROUGER.] = *pull-devil* (see PULL- 2). Hence **ˈscrodgill** *v. trans.*, to take or catch with a 'scrodgill'.

1891 in *Century Dict.*

†**scrof**, *a. Obs.* [? f. *scrof*, SCRUFF *sb.*[1]] Rough.

13.. *E.E. Allit. P.* B. 1546 When hit þe scrypture hade scraped with a scrof [*MS.* strof] penne.

scrofe, obs. form of SCRUFF, SCURF.

†**ˈscroffles**, *sb. pl. Obs.* Also 5 **scurffyls, skorphillys**, 5-6 **scrofulus, scruphules**, 5-7 **scrophules**, 6 **scrofules.** [a. OF. *scrophules*, ad. L. *scrōfulæ*: see SCROFULA.] Scrofulous swellings.

[*c* **1000** *Sax. Leechd.* III. 62 Cyrneles & scrofelles.] *a* **1400-50** *Stockh. Med. MS.* 141 It desolwyth skorphillys. *c* **1400** *Lanfranc's Cirurg.* 19 (Addit. MS.) þe þridde entencioun is to remevyn þat þat ys to myche as scurffyls [Ashm. MS. scrofulus] of þe hed & þe nekke. **1483** CAXTON *Gold. Leg.* 243/4 A poure woman that had a sone whyche was gretely tormented with scrophules. **1541** COPLAND tr. *Guydon's Quest. Chirurg.* S j b, Propre for scrophules and kyrnelles. **1576** BAKER *Jewell of Health* (1597) 144 b, Instill two or three droppes into the eare of the pacient, on that syde where Scroffles be. **1684** tr. *Bonet's Merc. Compit.* XVI. 573 A certain Woman had the Scroffles all over her Neck.

scrofula (ˈskrɒfjʊlə). Also 5-9 **scrophula**, 6 **skurfula**, 7-8 **schrophula**; *pl.* 5-7 **scrophule**, 7 **scrofulæ.** [In early use pl. after late L. *scrōfulæ* swelling of the glands, dim. of *scrōfa* breeding sow (supposed to be subject to the disease: cf. the use of Gr. χοιράδες, pl. of χοιράς like a hog's back). Later in sing. form after med.L. *scrofula*, *scrophula* (also *schrof-, scrufula*).

From L. pl. are: F. *scrofules* (see SCROFFLES), G. *skrofeln*, Sw. *skrofler*; also F. *écrouelles* (:—pop. L. **scrofellas*: see ESCROELES, CREWELS); from L. sing., It. *scrofola*, Sp. *escrófula*; also from pop. L. type OE. *scrofell.* See also SCURFLE.]

A constitutional disease characterized mainly by chronic enlargement and degeneration of the lymphatic glands. Also called KING'S EVIL and STRUMA.

α. plural. c **1400** *Lanfranc's Cirurg.* 207 Also blood is medlid wiþ greet fleume & malancolie, & engendriþ glandulas & Scrophulas... Also greet fleume is medlid with malancoli, & þerof comeþ glandula & Scrophule. **1527** ANDREW *Brunswyke's Distyll. Waters* D iij, The sam withdryveth Scrofulas wher so ever they be on the body. *a* **1625** LODGE *Poore Mans Talentt* (1881) 13 For the Scrophulæ or Kinges euill. **1670** *Phil. Trans.* V. 2080 Most inhabitants of which are troubled with the Scrofulæ or Kings Evil. **1694** SALMON *Bate's Dispens.* (1713) 411/1 An absolute Cure for all kinds of Struma's or Schrophula's whatsoever.

β. sing. **1791** BOSWELL *Johnson* an. 1712, Young Johnson had the misfortune to be much afflicted with the scrophula, or King's-evil. **1843** GRAVES *Syst. Clin. Med.* xx. 248 Scrofula has a tendency to attack every tissue in the body. **1897** *Allbutt's Syst. Med.* IV. 597 Thus in the sixties and the seventies it was as common to see persons marked by the scars of scrofula as it still was to see the ravages of small-pox.

scrofulide (ˈskrɒfjʊlɪd). *Path.* [a. F. *scrofulide* (Hardy), f. *scrofule* SCROFULA.] A scrofulous or strumous skin-disease.

1864 W. T. FOX *Classif. Skin Dis.* 20 Scrofulides. **1899** *Allbutt's Syst. Med.* VII. 470 The sudden retrocession of an extensive eruption of phlegmonous scrofulides.

scrofulism (ˈskrɒfjʊlɪz(ə)m). [f. SCROFULA + -ISM.] A scrofulous diathesis.

1893 *Dunglison's Dict. Med. Sci.* (ed. 21). **1894** GOULD *Illustr. Dict. Med.*

scrofulitic (skrɒfjʊˈlɪtɪk), *a.* [irreg. f. SCROFULA + *-itic*, after *rachitic*, etc.] Scrofulous.

1866 *Morn. Star* 13 Nov., The Margate Infirmary is for scrofuletic patients. She was in no way scrofuletic [*sic*]. **1882** O'DONOVAN *Merv Oasis* II. 387 Fifty per cent. of the population..had..scrofulitic and scorbutic ailments.

scrofulo- (ˈskrɒfjʊləʊ), used as combining form of SCROFULA, forming adjs. with the sense 'characterized by scrofula and ...'.

1878 A. M'L. HAMILTON *Nervous Dis.* 59 The children.. were generally scrofulous or scrofulorachitic. **1899** *Allbutt's Syst. Med.* VIII. 473 The chronic scrofulo-tuberculous gummata..can hardly be mistaken.

‖**scrofuloderma** (ˌskrɒfjʊləʊˈdɜːmə). Pl. **-dermata** (-ˈdɜːmətə). Also anglicized **ˈscrofuloderm.** [mod.L., f. SCROFULO- + DERMA.] A skin-lesion considered to be of scrofulous origin. So **ˌscrofuloˈdermia** [see -IA[1]], the condition of being affected with scrofulodermata.

1857 W. J. E. WILSON *Dis. Skin* (ed. 4) 321 Scrofuloderma. **1888** J. N. HYDE *Dis. Skin* (ed. 2) 492 The Small Pustular Scrofuloderm. **1899** *Allbutt's Syst. Med.* VIII. 795 Scrofulodermia may appear in the same class of subjects as lupus.

Hence **ˌscrofuloˈdermic** *a.*

1899 *Allbutt's Syst. Med.* VIII. 801 The second variety of scrofulodermic lesion appears as an ulceration limited to the neighbourhood of the natural apertures.

†**ˈscrofulose**, *a. Obs. rare*[−1]. In 8 **scroph-.** [ad. mod.L. *scrofulōs-us*, f. SCROFULA: see -OSE.] = SCROFULOUS.

1753 R. RUSSELL *Diss. Sea Water* 70 Cancerous, scrophulose, and scorbutic Humours.

‖**scrofulosis** (skrɒfjʊˈləʊsɪs). *Path.* [mod.L., f. SCROFULA + -OSIS.] Scrofula without tubercle; 'scrofulous diathesis' (*Syd. Soc. Lex.*).

1860 R. FOWLER *Med. Voc.*, *Scrophulosis*, the condition of being scrofulous. **1876** tr. *Wagner's Gen. Pathol.* 457 Scrofulosis is a disease especially of childhood and youth.

scrofulous (ˈskrɒfjʊləs), *a.* Also 7-9 **scrophulous.** [f. SCROFULA + -OUS. Cf. F. *scrofuleux.*]

1. Caused by, or of the nature of scrofula.

1612 WOODALL *Surg. Mate* (1639) 395 A body having *Struma*, or scrupulous [*sic*] tumours. **1732** ARBUTHNOT *Aliments, Rules of Diet* 386 The English Consumptions, generally speaking, proceed from a Scrophulous Disposition. **1856** MACAULAY *Biog.* 78 (*Johnson*), He had inherited from his ancestors a scrofulous taint.

fig. **1784** COWPER *Task* IV. 582 Excess, the scrofulous and itchy plague That seizes first the opulent [etc.].

2. Affected with, or suffering from, scrofula.

1708 SWIFT *Abol. Chr.* Wks. 1755 II. I. 86 What would become of the race of men in the next age, if we had nothing to trust to beside the scrophulous consumptive productions furnished by our men of wit and pleasure? **1855** MACAULAY *Hist. Eng.* xiv. III. 479 Charles once handled a scrofulous Quaker, and made him a healthy man and a sound Churchman in a moment.

3. *transf.* Having the appearance of being affected with scrofula.

1837 P. KEITH *Bot. Lex.* 79 The punctured leaf assumes a wrinkled, reddish, and scrofulous appearance.

4. *fig.* Of literature, etc.: Morally corrupt.

1842 BROWNING *Solil. Span. Cloister* viii, Or, my scrofulous French novel On grey paper with blunt type! **1866** THORNBURY *Greatheart* III. 328 Eight or ten numbers of the most scrofulous of the French novels. **1889** *Ch. Times* 28 June 593/2 Holywell-street was re-named 'Booksellers'-row' because of its scrofulous reputation.

Hence **ˈscrofulously** *adv.*, **ˈscrofulousness.**

1727 BAILEY vol. II, *Scrofulousness.* **1847-54** WEBSTER, *Scrofulously.* **1894** GOULD *Illustr. Dict. Med.*, *Scrofulousness.*

scrog (skrɒg), *sb.* Chiefly *Sc.* and *north.* Forms: 4 **skrogg**, 5 **scroge**, 7 **skrog**, 6- **scrog(g.** [App. related to SCRAG *sb.*[2]; cf. SHROG.]

1. A stunted bush; usually *pl.*, brushwood, underwood.

a **1400** *Morte Arth.* 1641 Discoueres now sekerly skrogges and other, That no skathelle in the skroggez skorne vs hereaftyre. **1483** *Cath. Angl.* 326/1 A Scroge; *vbi* A buske. **1513** DOUGLAS *Æneis* IX. Prol. 37 Full litill it wald delite To write of scroggis, broym, haddir, or rammale. **1615** W. LAWSON *Country Housew. Gard.* (1626) 32 What an infinite number of bushes, shrubs, and skrogs of hazels, thornes, and other profitable wood. **1719** RAMSAY *3rd Answ. to Hamilton* 18 Yet sometimes leave the Riggs and Bog, Your Howms, and Braes and shady Scrog. **1820** *Blackw. Mag.* VI. 568, I have gathered nuts from the scrogs of Tynron. **1893** STEVENSON *Catriona* xi, In a bit scrog of a wood by east of Silvermills.

b. *Her.* A branch of a tree: a blazon sometimes used by Scottish heralds.

1780 EDMONDSON *Her.* Gloss., *Scrogs*, the term used by the Scots in blazoning a small branch of a tree. **1828-40** BERRY *Encycl. Herald.* II, *Scrogie*, or *Scroggie*, az. a chev. or, betw. two scrogs, or starved branches, in chief, and a man's heart in base, ar. **1868** CUSSANS *Heraldry* vi. (1893) 104 Amongst Scotch Heralds a Branch is termed a Scrog.

2. a. The blackthorn. **b.** The crab-apple tree.

1691 RAY *N.C. Words* 61 Scrogs; Blackthorn. **1853** [see 3].

3. *attrib.*, as **scrog-apple, -branch, -bush, -tree.**

1853 G. JOHNSTON *Bot. E. Bord.* 79 Pyrus Malus.. Crab-apple: Scrogs or *Scrog-apple. **1824** SCOTT *St. Ronan's* xxxvi, 'Scrogie Touchwood, if you please,' said the senior; 'the *scrog branch first, for it must become rotten ere it become touchwood.' **1596** DALRYMPLE tr. *Leslie's Hist. Scot.* I. 288 The kingis body is layd on a horse, and twa myles frome the castell castne in a *scrogg buss. **1824** SCOTT *St. Ronan's* xviii, He got a handsome piece of parchment, blazoned with a white lion for Mowbray, to be borne quarterly, with three stunted or scrog-bushes for Scrogie, and became thenceforth Mr. Scrogie Mowbray. **1887** R. M. CALDER in *Minstrelsy of Merse* (1893) 259 The *scrogg tree in the meadow.

scrog (skrɒg), *v. dial.* [f. SCROG *sb.*] *trans.* To cut with a hook.

1847 *Jrnl. R. Agric. Soc.* VIII. II. 282 Beans are either pulled by women or cut with a hook, 'scrogged'. **1893** in Cozens-Hardy *Broad Norfolk* 84 *Scrog*, to cut field beans with a sickle or hook.

scrogged (skrɒgd), *ppl. a.* [f. SCROG *sb.* + -ED[2].] Stunted, dwarfed.

1814 W. NICHOLSON *Poet. Wks.* (1897) 149 The auld scrogged hawthorn, where aft we had met. **1878** in Miller & Skertchly *Fenland* iv. 130 *Scrogged*, twisted, stunted.

scroggin ('skrɒgɪn). *Austral.* and *N.Z.* [Etym. unknown.] A nourishing snack of raisins, chocolate, nuts, etc., eaten esp. by travellers.

1949 H. WADMAN *Life Sentence* 58 We've still got the scroggin with us, if we get hungry on the way down. **1966** G. W. TURNER *Eng. Lang. in Austral. & N.Z.* vii. 161 A tramper..keeps going on *scroggin*, a mixture of raisins, sultanas, chocolate, boiled lollies and anything sustaining and easily carried. **1970** *Courier-Mail* (Brisbane) 10 Dec. 23/3 Scroggin, is a mixture of peanuts, almonds, mixed fruit and chocolate well-mulched together to form a high protein and calorie meal. **1971** *N.Z. Listener* 19 Apr. 56/5 It was hard yakka, nothing but a plate of burgoo and a handful of scroggin since sparrow-chirp.

scroggy ('skrɒgɪ), *a.* Chiefly *Sc.* and *north.* Also 5 scrogghy, (scourgy), 6 skroggy, 8 scrogy, 8–9 scroggie. [f. SCROG *sb.* + -Y[1].] Abounding in stunted bushes or underwood. Also, of trees: Stunted.

c **1440** *Gesta Rom.* viii. 19 (Harl. MS.) And þe wey toward þe Cite was stony, þorny, and scroggy. *Ibid.* 20 This stony & scourgy wey. *c* **1470** HENRY *Wallace* v. 131 At the mur syde, in till a scrogghy slaid. **1513** DOUGLAS *Æneis* VIII. vi. 84 Quhair now standis the goldin Capitoll, Vmquhyll of wyld buskis rouch skroggy knoll. **1728** RAMSAY *Robt., Richy, & Sandy* 11 The clinty craigs and scrogy briers. **1788** BURNS *My Hoggie* 8 We heard nought but the roaring linn, Amang the braes sae scroggie. **1843** HARDY in *Proc. Berw. Nat. Club* II. xi. 66 A sprinkling of scroggy birches.

scrolar ('skrəʊlə(r)), *a. Math.* [f. SCROLL *sb.* + -AR.] Pertaining to a 'scroll'.

1869 CAYLEY *Math. Papers* (1893) VI. 334 If there be on a surface a right line which is such that the tangent plane is different at different points of the line, the line is said to be scrolar.

scroll (skrəʊl), *sb.* Forms: 5–8 scrowle, 6 scrolle, schrole, skrole, scrall, 6–7 scroule, 6–8 scrole, 7 scroul, scrowll, skroule, 7–9 scrowl, 8 scrawl, 6– scroll. Also ESCROLL. [In 15th c. *scrowle*, altered form of the earlier SCROW.

Possibly due to assimilation to *rowle*, ROLL *sb.* The form would be abnormal as an adoption of OF. *escro(u)ele*, dim. of *escro(u)e* ESCROW, SCROW.]

1. a. A roll of paper or parchment, usually one with writing upon it.

14.. *Nom.* in Wr.-Wülcker 682/26 *Hec sidula*, a scrowle. *a* **1513** FABYAN *Chron.* VII. (1533) 152 b, He therfore redde the scrowle of resignacyon him selfe, in maner and fourme as foloweth. **1526** TINDALE *Rev.* vi. 14 And heven vanysshed awaye as a scroll when hitt is rolled togedder. **1588** SHAKS. *Tit. A.* IV. ii. 18 What's heere? a scrole, & written round about? *c* **1590** MARLOWE *Faustus* 562, I, of necessitie, for here's the scrowle, Wherein thou hast giuen thy soule to Lucifer. *a* **1648** LD. HERBERT *Hen. VIII* (1683) 456 Thus bowing his head to look upon a scroul lapt about his finger, he made a pause. **1704** SWIFT *Tale of Tub* ii. Wks. 1751 I. 58 An old Parchment Scrowl was tagged on according to Art in the Form of a Codicil annexed. **1742** W. COLLINS *Ode, Manners* 76 Let some retreating Cynic find Those oft-turn'd scrolls I leave behind. **1820** SHELLEY *Witch Atl.* xix, Other scrolls whose writings did unbind The inmost lore of Love. **1868** TENNYSON *Lucretius* 12 He past To turn and ponder those three hundred scrolls Left by the Teacher, whom he held divine. **1879** FROUDE *Cæsar* xxvi. 460 A stranger thrust a scroll into his hand, and begged him to read it on the spot.

b. *fig.*

1649 JER. TAYLOR *Gt. Exemp.* III. Disc. xv. 34 God was pleased to shew the scrowles of his eternall counsels. **1817** SHELLEY *Rev. Islam* II. 765 And now, to me The moonlight ..Interpreted those scrolls of mortal mystery. **1891** F. THOMPSON *Sister-Songs* (1895) 32 Summoned by some presaging scroll of fate.

c. *transf.*

1656 COWLEY *Pindar. Odes, Isa.* xxxiv. iii, The wide-stretcht Scrowl of Heaven. **1862** TYNDALL *Mountaineer.* iii. 26 As the day sinks, scrolls of pearly clouds draw themselves around the mountain crests. **1886** STEVENSON *Kidnapped* 12, I saw a scroll of smoke go mounting.

d. A roll or bundle of any material.

1852 DICKENS *Bleak Ho.* xxix, Chesney Wold is shut up, carpets are rolled into great scrolls in corners of comfortless rooms. **1856** KANE *Arct. Expl.* II. xvii. 177, I took Sir John Franklin's portrait..and cased it in an India-rubber scroll.

e. ***Scroll of the Law***: in Judaism, a scroll containing the Torah or Pentateuch; = SEFER TORAH. Also *absol.*

1887 *Jewish Rec.* 11 Mar. 6/1 The Ark, containing only two very small scrolls of the law, was simply a deal cupboard. **1907** I. ZANGWILL *Ghetto Comedies* 395 There was an Ark with scrolls of the Law in the room. **1949** *Spectator* 4 Nov. 595/2 The Ark was opened and the Scrolls of the Law revealed. **1976** C. BERMANT *Coming Home* I. v. 63 Sacred Scrolls of the Law..prayer-shawls, and an entire kosher field kitchen..followed us south. **1978** H. KEMELMAN *Thursday Rabbi walked Out* (1979) xii. 73 In the morning services..we read from the Scroll.

2. a. A piece of writing, *esp.* a letter.

1534 STARKEY *Let. to Cromwell* in *England* (1878) p. ix, Syr, the grete gentylnes of you so manyfestely schowyd toward me,..gyuyth me yet a lytyl more boldnes to trowbul you wyth the redyng of thys scrole. **1606** SHAKS. *Ant. & Cl.* III. viii. 5 Do not exceede The Prescript of this Scroule. **1723** WODROW *Corr.* (1843) III. 101 Forgive me this long scroll, which is not my ordinary, and give my wife's and my humble duty to your lady and family. **1808** SCOTT *Marmion* v. xxi, And that between them then there went Some scroll of courteous compliment.

b. A list, roll, or schedule (of names). Also *fig.*

1546 *Supplic. Poore Commons* (E.E.T.S.) 78 A scrowle, wherin wer written the names of the parishes wherof he was parson. **1556** in Burnet *Hist. Ref.* (1681) II. II. II. xxviii. 302 To whose hands..any of the said Accompts, Books, Scroles, Instruments, or other Writings..did or is come. **1590** SHAKS. *Mids. N.* I. ii. 16 Now good Peter Quince, call forth your Actors by the scrowle. **1621** BP. HALL *Heaven upon Earth* §7 Neither can it suffice for peace, to haue crossed the old scrole of our sinnes, if we preuent not the future. **1667** MILTON *P.L.* XII. 336 Such follow him, as shall be registerd Part good, part bad, of bad the longer scrowle. **1820** HAZLITT *Lect. Dram. Lit.* 1 Men whom fame has eternised in her long and lasting scroll. **1903** MORLEY *Gladstone* v. v. (1905) I. 718 He was..to add another to the long scroll of tragedies in the house of Austria.

c. A draft or copy (of a letter). ? *Sc.* ? *Obs.*

1790 [see *scroll-copy* in 6 c]. **1855** BREWSTER *Newton* II. xxvi. 382 He wrote scrolls of almost every letter he composed. **1889** STEVENSON *Master of Ballantrae* 165 The best will be to reproduce a letter of my own..of which (according to an excellent habitude) I have preserved the scroll.

3. a. A strip or ribbon-shaped slip of paper with a legend inscribed; a graphic or plastic representation of this.

a **1600** *Flodden F.* iv. (1664) 32 A certain scrall, whose scripture said, Jack of Norfolk be not too bold. **1644** SYMONDS *Diary* (Camden) 17 This motto is in divers severall scrowlls: 'Mercy and Grace'. **1751** HURD *Poet. Imit.* 148 Painters continuing, for a long time, to put written scrolls in the mouths of their figures; and contriving, by this expedient, to make them tell their business to the spectator.

b. *Her.* The ribbon-like appendage to a coat of arms, on which the motto is inscribed; = ESCROLL 2. Also, *transf.* the words inscribed upon the scroll.

1610 GUILLIM *Heraldry* VI. vi. (1611) 265 Three or foure words which are set in some Scrole or Compartement, placed usually at the foot of the escocheon. **1828–40** BERRY *Encycl. Herald.* I, *Scroll*, part of the outward ornaments of the shield, achievement or escocheon of arms in which the motto is inscribed. **1859** TENNYSON *Vivien* 326 A knightly shield..; the scroll 'I follow fame'.

c. App. used for: A streamer, narrow flag.

1808 SCOTT *Marmion* IV. xxviii, A thousand streamers flaunted fair..Scroll, pennon, pensil, bandrol there O'er the pavilions flew.

4. An ornament resembling a scroll of paper partly unrolled.

a. A convoluted or spiral ornament; *spec.* the volute of the Ionic and Corinthian capitals. **b.** *Shipbuilding.* A curved piece of timber bolted to the knee of the head. **c.** The curved head of instruments of the violin kind, in which the tuning-pins are set. **d.** *U.S.* A flourish (or sometimes a circle) added to a person's signature to represent a seal, and having the same value.

a. **1611** COTGR., *Vrilles*, hooke-like edges or ends of leaues (called by some of our workemen Scrolls, and) sticking out in the upper parts of pillers, and of other peeces of Architecture. **1655** EVELYN *Diary* 2 Mar., A most rich achat cup..having a figure of Cleopatra at the scroll. **1663** GERBIER *Counsel* 88 For scrowles to the said windowes, six shillings a piece. **1704** J. HARRIS *Lex. Techn.* I, *Scrowles*, or *Volutes.* **1762–71** H. WALPOLE *Vertue's Anecd. Paint.* I. (1786) 285 The capitals are gilt and painted with ugly scrolls and compartments, in the taste of that reign. **1823** P. NICHOLSON *Pract. Build.* 200 The Scroll is the termination of the hand-rail of a geometrical stair, in the form of a spiral. **1884** W. C. SMITH *Kildrostan* 43 Dark slabs carved with the great Cross-sword, And..the galley, with scrolls all round.

b. **1797** *Encycl. Brit.* (ed. 3) XVII. 394/2 The upper part [of the upper cheek] may run in a serpentine as high as where the shoulder of the figure is supposed to come, at which place it may be turned off with a scroll. The distance from the scroll to the heel of the figure is called the hair-bracket. **1898** ANSTED *Dict. Sea Terms*, *Scroll* or *scroll-head.*

c. **1836** DUBOURG *Violin* i. (1878) 8 The Scroll, that crowning charm of the fiddle's form. **1875** G. HART *Violin* 288 He calmly set himself to open the parcel containing his dissected 'Strad', when..he failed to find its scroll.

d. **1856** BOUVIER *Amer. Law Dict.* (ed. 6) II. 500 *Scroll*, a mark which is to supply the place of a seal, made with a pen or other instrument on a writing. In some of the states this has all the efficacy of a seal. **1871** *Amer. Encycl. Printing* (ed. Ringwalt), Scroll is also used for the flourish made at the end of a signature, representing a seal.

5. a. Applied variously in technical use to scroll-shaped or spiral parts, figures, etc. (see quots.).

1868 [see *scroll-wheel* in 6 c]. **1875** KNIGHT *Dict. Mech.*, *Scroll*, (*Hydraulic Engineering.*) A spiral or converging adjutage around a turbine or other reaction water-wheel, designed to equalize the rate of flow of water at all parts around the circumference of the wheel, by decreasing the capacity of the chute in its circuit. **1891** *Century Dict.*, *Scroll*, the mantling or lambrequin of a tilting-helmet. (Rare.) *Ibid.*, *Scroll*, in *anat.*, a turbinate bone.

b. *Geom.* A skew ruled surface.

1862 CAYLEY *Math. Papers* (1892) V. 90 The skew surface of the third order, or 'cubic scroll'..may be considered [etc.].

c. *Physical Geogr.* A crescent-shaped strip of land formed of material deposited on the inside of a river meander. Cf. *point bar* (*b*) s.v. POINT *sb.*[1] D. 14.

1902 W. M. DAVIS in *Bull. Mus. Compar. Zööl. Harvard* XXXVIII. 300 The flood plain must be scoured out for a certain stretch..around the concave banks and along the up-valley side of every lobe; while a scroll of new flood plain ..is added around the end and on the down-valley side of the lobe. **1939** A. K. LOBECK *Geomorphol.* vii. 223 The following observable characteristics of mature streams may be taken to indicate that a graded profile has been established..: (*a*) Flood plain, with natural levees; (*b*) meanders, with abandoned meander scrolls, cutoffs, and oxbow lakes; [etc.]. **1960** *Geogr. Bull.* XIV. 92 The abandoned meander scars and oxbows have radii of 1 to 2 miles, a size fully equal to the meander loops and scrolls of the lower course of the modern Horton River. **1975** R. V. RUHE *Geomorphol.* iv. 72/2 Fresh meander scars, abandoned channels, and flood-plain scrolls are in a channel belt one to two miles wide along the present channel.

6. *attrib.* and *Comb.* **a.** Simple attrib., with the sense: Consisting of, having the form of, or decorated with scrolls, scrolled; as ***scroll back, bracket, -case, foot, -handle, -keystone, -leg, -moulding, -work***; ***scroll-leaved, -patterned, -shaped*** adjs.; ***scroll-wise*** adv.

1958 S. SPENDER *Engaged in Writing* 13 The guests..in their *scroll-back chairs. **1969** J. GLOAG *Short Dict. Furnit.* 590 *Scroll back*, upholsterer's term for a single chair with the back curved at the top to form a scroll. **1976** *Cumberland News* 3 Dec. 29/3 (Advt.), Three piece..scroll back suite. **1936** *Burlington Mag.* July 25/1 A baluster finial, supported by three beaded *scroll-brackets. **1976** *Southern Even. Echo* (Southampton) 18 Nov. 28/4 As well as scroll brackets, the canopies can also be supported by Georgian-style columns. **1896** *Daily News* 5 Mar. 7/4 A clock by Vulliamy, in *scroll case. **1935** *Burlington Mag.* July 36/1 The same *scroll-feet curved inwards and enriched with a row of silver pearls. **1960** H. HAYWARD *Antique Coll.* 251/2 Designs for chairs with scroll feet were included in the third edition of Chippendale's *Director.* **1977** FLEMING & HONOUR *Penguin Dict. Decorative Arts* 715/2 *Scroll foot*, the foot especially of a mid-c 18 English chair-leg in the form of a tight scroll. **1878** NESBITT *Catal. Glass Vessels S. Kens. Mus.* 128 Vase..with two *scroll handles. **1813** *Gentl. Mag.* LXXXIII. I. 38/1 To this arch a *scroll key-stone, and to the postern ditto plain key-stones. **1876** G. M. HOPKINS *Wreck of Deutschland* xxi, in *Poems* (1967) 58 In thy sight Storm flakes were *scroll-leaved flowers. **1850** *Parker's Gloss. Archit.*, *Roll-moulding...* It is sometimes called the *scroll moulding, from its resemblance to a scroll of paper or parchment with the edge overlapping. **1866** GEO. ELIOT *F. Holt* xlv, As if she had to work out her deliverance from bondage by finishing a *scroll-patterned border. **1896** *Daily News* 5 Mar. 7/4 A large Louis XV. ormolu cartel clock,..in a *scroll-shaped case. **1851** H. MELVILLE *Moby Dick* II. xliv. 298 To the whale, his tail is the sole means of propulsion. *Scroll-wise coiled forwards beneath the body, and then rapidly sprung backwards. **1857** GOSSE *Omphalos* vii. 129 Young leaves..coiled up scroll-wise at their tips. **1739** GRAY *Let. to West* 22 May, Sugar-loaves and minced-pies of yew; *scrawl-work of box, and little squirting jets-d'eau. **1840** *Civ. Engin. & Arch. Jrnl.* III. 2/1 The three doors will be of oak, relieved by the quaint and beautiful ramified iron scroll-work so characteristic of this style of architecture.

b. objective; as ***scroll-cutter, -cutting, -filer***; instrumental; as ***scroll-cut*** adj.

1837 *Civ. Engin & Arch. Jrnl.* I. 75/1 Separated by *scroll-cut standards. **1892** *Daily Chron.* 28 Apr. 8/1 Gun Engraving. Wanted at once good *scroll cutter. **1873** RICHARDS *Operator's Handbk.* 125 For *scroll cutting, slitting, and with narrow blades generally, the matter of teeth has not such importance. **1881** *Instr. Census Clerks* (1885) 91 Whitesmith...*Scroll Filer.

c. Special combinations: **scroll-bone** (see quot.); † **scroll chair**, a chair with a carved scroll ornament; **scroll-chuck**, a lathe-chuck with a spiral arrangement for operating the jaws; **scroll-copy** *Sc.*, a rough draft or copy; **scroll-creeper** *Arch.* (see quot.); **scroll-drum** *Mech.*, a drum of tapering form; **scroll-finis**, a scroll containing the word 'finis'; **scroll-gall** *Bot.*, a malformation consisting in the curling over of a leaf caused by an insect; **scroll-gear** (see quot.); **scroll-guard**, (see quot. 1824); **scroll-head** = sense 5 b; **scroll-iron, -lathe** (see quots.); **scroll painting**, a painting on a scroll, of a style widely used in the East (esp. Japan); the practice of painting on scrolls; **scroll picture**, a picture on a scroll (see *scroll painting*); **scroll salt** (see quot. 1977); **scroll-saw**, a saw for cutting scrolls; so *scroll-sawing*; **scroll-wheel**, a wheel actuated by scroll-gear.

1891 *Century Dict.*, **Scroll-bone...* The principal scroll-bones are the ethmoturbinals, maxilloturbinals, and sphenoturbinals. **1614** in *Archæologia* XLII. 354 One highe Chaire with a longe cushin, two *scrowle chaires, two highe stooles. **1875** KNIGHT *Dict. Mech.*, **Scroll-chuck.* **1790** SCOTT *Let.* in *Lockhart* (1837) I. vi. 172, I send you the *scroll copy of an essay on the origin of the feudal system. **1829** —— *Rob Roy* Postscr., These were taken from scroll copies in the possession of his Grace the present Duke. **1825** FOSBROKE *Encycl. Antiq.* I. 90* Crockets,..by professionalists termed "*scroll creepers". **1875** MARTIN *Winding Mach.* 42 It would..be advisable..to give up all idea of using *scroll drums like those used in England and in Germany. **1856** MRS. BROWNING *Aur. Leigh* III. 957 That fair *scroll-finis of a wicked book. **1895** OLIVER tr. *Kerner's Nat. Hist. Plants* II. 530 *Scroll-galls are caused by gall-mites, leaf-lice [etc.]. **1875** KNIGHT *Dict. Mech.*, **Scroll-gear*, a gear-wheel of spiral or snail form. **1820** COL. HAWKER *Diary* (1893) I. 194 The keeper..hooked the gun by the *scroll guard and brought it up. **1824** —— *Instr. Yng. Sportsmen* (ed. 3) 54 *Scroll-guard*, an extra bow, continued from the guard [which defends the triggers], to steady the hand. **1867** SMYTH *Sailor's Word-bk.*, **Scroll-head.* **1871** Z. COLBURN *Locomotive Engin.* xxxii. 303/1 *Scroll-irons. **1886** *Lockwood's Dict. Mech. Engin.*, *Scroll Irons*, small brackets attached to the underside of railway wagons, to which the ends of the bearing springs are attached. **1884** KNIGHT *Dict. Mech.* Suppl., **Scroll Lathe*, one adapted to turn spiral and scroll work, such as balusters, table and piano legs. **1911**, etc. *Scroll painting [see MAKIMONO]. **1936** *Burlington Mag.* Oct. 161/1 One of the most characteristic forms of Japanese pictorial art of the medieval periods, is that of treating a subject in long scroll-paintings. **1970** *Oxf. Compan. Art* 1225/1 Scroll painting with Buddhist themes was introduced to Japan from China in the 8th c. **1977** J. VAN DE WETERING *Japanese Corpse* (1978) ix. 95 He has some very famous scroll paintings. **1899** KIPLING *From Sea to Sea* I. xi. 300 The *tokonama*..held one *scroll-picture of bats wheeling in the twilight. **1923** S. MERWIN *Silk* (1924) 177 The larger scroll pictures were the last to appear from the bale. **1630** in W. Prideaux *Mem. Goldsmiths' Company*

(1896) I. 150 Complaint by Margaret Unwin.. against Mr. Dickinson.. for selling her a *scroll salt untouched. **1949** N. M. PENZER in *Apollo Ann.* 48/1 (*heading*) Scroll salts. *Ibid.* 48/2 So far as known examples indicate, the scroll-salt in England lasted from about 1630–1690. **1977** FLEMING & HONOUR *Penguin Dict. Decorative Arts* 715/2 *Scroll salt*, a salt-cellar of silver or pottery surmounted by three little scrolled arms. **1851** C. CIST *Sk. Cincinnati in 1851* 206 In the first story are located.. the machinery for a *scroll saw.. and the apparatus by which the veneering is done. **1875** KNIGHT *Dict. Mech.* Suppl., *Scroll saw*... The band-saw is a scroll-saw, and operates continuously. **1888** *Amer. Jrnl. Psychol.* I. 473 On the outside of the door is tacked up a circle cut from thin wood with a scroll saw. **1874** *Spon's Dict. Engin.* VIII. 3093 This class of sawing is usually termed sweep or *scroll sawing for the heavier class of work, and fret sawing for the lighter or ornamental kinds. **1868** J. TURNER *Woollen Manuf. Assist.* 18 To find revolutions of rim for 1 of scroll... Divide the product of the driven (1st sh. roller wheel, 1st short wheel, 1st *scroll wheel and scroll) by the product of the drivers.

scroll (skrəʊl), *v.* Also 7 scrool. [f. SCROLL *sb.*]

1. *trans.* To write down in a scroll (SCROLL *sb.* 1, 3). *rare.*

1606 WARNER *Alb. Eng.* XIV. lxxxix. 361 And from his mouth was scroold this Mott: So I do euery day. **1630** DRUMM. OF HAWTH. *Flowres of Sion* 43 But thou in thy great Archieues scrolled hast In parts and whole, what euer yet hath past. **1852** C. W. H[OSKINS] *Talpa* 8 The motto which might be scrolled up over so many a splendid door-way.

2. †**a.** To draft, make a rough copy of. *Obs.* **b.** ? *Sc.* To engross. Also *absol.*

a. **1730** T. BOSTON *Acc. My Life* (1908) 305, I had brought up the Account of My Life as scrolled in shorthand characters to the day of my beginning it. **1818** SCOTT *Hrt. Midl.* viii, I'll scroll the disposition in nae time.

b. **1814** SCOTT *Wav.* xlii, He wald scroll for a plack the sheet, or she kenn'd what it was to want.

3. *intr.* for *refl.* To roll or curl up. Also *fig.*

1868 M. C. LEA *Photogr.* 428 (Cent.) When gum mucilage is used, the addition of a very little glycerine will make it hold better, and diminish its tendency to separate or scroll. **1958** R. MACAULAY *Lett. to Sister* (1964) 265 The new high altar.. is very splendid... Gold leaves scrolling round the pillars. **1976** *National Observer* (U.S.) 9 Oct. 25/4 My life.. had a tendency to spread, to scroll and festoon like the frame of a baroque mirror.

4. *intr.* (See quot.)

1962 A. NISBETT *Technique Sound Studio* viii. 149 An 'overlap' is made by starting to record each new disc half a minute or more before the old one is due to run out; the extent of the overlap is indicated by 'scrolling' (i.e. by momentarily increasing the cutter's rate of travel towards the centre of the disc).

Hence **'scrolling** *vbl. sb.*; *ppl. a.*, forming or decorated with scrolls.

1731 T. BOSTON *Acc. My Life* (1908) 332 With some difficulty I carried the scrolling of my letter some length. **1936** *Burlington Mag.* Jan. 40/1 Inlaid with mother-o'-pearl with a scrolling design. **1979** *Times* 24 Nov. 4/6 The body of the piece is richly encrusted with scrolling ormolu.

scrollage ('skrəʊlɪdʒ). [f. SCROLL *sb.* + -AGE.] Decoration in the manner of a scroll.

1847 WINSTON *Glass* I. 65 Flowing tendril-like scrollages.

scrolled (skrəʊld), *ppl. a.* [f. SCROLL *sb.* or *v.* + -ED.]

1. In the form of, or decorated with, scrolls.

1603 *Inv.* in Gage *Hengrave* (1822) 26 Itm, two scrowled cheyers. **1863** GEO. ELIOT *Romola* v, Trim doors, with conspicuous scrolled hinges. **1887** HISSEY *Holiday on Road* 27 The scrolled plaster-work between the oaken beams.

b. *transf.* Curled.

1863 SALA *Last Crusader* 208 The haughty angelica, the scrolled acanthus. **1876** GEO. ELIOT *Dan. Der.* i, An envoy with a scrolled mustache.

2. Inscribed with mottoes.

1875 HENLEY *Bk. Verses* (1888) 69 The silken shrouds with spells are manned, The hull is magically scrolled.

3. *Anat.* (See quot.)

1891 *Century Dict.*, *Scrolled*, in *anat.*, turbinated as a bone; scroll-like.

scrollery ('skrəʊlərɪ). [f. SCROLL *sb.* + -ERY.] Scroll-work.

1892 L. F. DAY *Nat. Ornament* xi. 194 One is inclined to ask what the little Love.. is doing amongst the scrollery. **1901** E. L. ARNOLD *Lepidus* 196 A fine sweep of tesselated pavement, not quite perfect,.. but still wonderful enough in its green and white scrollery, its vines and doves.

scrolloping ('skrɒləpɪŋ), *ppl. a.* [Fanciful portmanteau formation by Virginia Woolf, prob. combining SCROLL *sb.*, LOLLOP *v.*, etc.] Characterized by or possessing heavy, florid, ornament. Also *transf.* and as *pres. ppl.*, proceeding in involutions, rambling.

1923 V. WOOLF *Diary* 7 Feb. (1978) I. 232 Like Vita she detests the scrolloping honours of the great, calls her family dull and stupid. **1927** —— *New Dress* in *Forum* (N.Y.) May 706 Just for a second.., there looked at her, framed in the scrolloping mahogany, a gray-white.. charming girl. *Ibid.* 707 The scrolloping looking-glass. **1928** —— *Orlando* ii. 96 He tore, in one rending, the scrolloping emblazoned scroll. *Ibid.* v. 208 Cucumbers 'came scrolloping across the grass to his feet'. **1931** —— *Waves* 308 Then I scoff at the floridity and absurdity of some scrolloping tomb.

scrolly ('skrəʊlɪ), *a.* [f. SCROLL *sb.* + -Y.] Scrolled, scroll-like.

1845 FORD *Handbk. Spain* I. 373 It is difficult to distinguish.. the modern Arabic character from the scrolly ornaments. **1883** *Harper's Mag.* Mar. 538/2 Who were now buying the scrolly chiffoniers?

scronch (skrɒntʃ). Also schronch, scrunch. [Orig. uncertain; perh. var. SCRUNCH *sb.*] Among American Blacks, a kind of slow dance (see quot. 1970).

1926 C. VAN VECHTEN *Nigger Heaven* 286 *Scronch*, a dance. **1935** Z. N. HURSTON *Mules & Men* (1970) I. x. 224 Jim Presley's melody crying like repentance as four or five couples took the floor. Doing the slow drag, doing the schronch. **1970** C. MAJOR *Dict. Afro-Amer. Slang* 101 *Scrunch*, (1900's–30's) a slow, dragged-out dance. **1974** *Black World* Aug. 22/1 In Polk County,.. place where the blues are born, place where they dance the scronch and the belly-rub.

scrone, obs. Sc. form of SCORN *sb.*

scroo, scrooby: see SCREW *sb.*³, SCRUBY.

scrooch (skruːtʃ), *v. dial.* and *colloq.* (orig. and chiefly *U.S.*). Also scrouch. [Dialectal var. of SCROUGE *v.*, perh. reinforced (in later uses) by CROUCH *v.*¹; see also SCRINCH *v.*, SCRINGE *v.*¹ and SCRUNCH *v.*] **1.** *intr.* = SCROUGE *v.* 1 b, c; to crouch or bend. Freq. with *down*. Also *fig.*

1844 'J. SLICK' *High Life N.Y.* II. xxix. 196 When she did kinder start up, it was jest to scrouch a leetle closer to me than she was afore. **1869** [see CUT *v.* 21 d]. **1884** 'MARK TWAIN' *Huck. Finn* ii. 8 We scrouched down and laid still. **1922** JOYCE *Ulysses* 734 Scrooching down on me like that all the time with his big hipbones. **1948** A. LOMAX in A. Dundes *Mother Wit* (1973) 475/2 Natchez scrooched up on the step. **1955** *Time* 14 Nov. 116/2 The focus scrooches down pretty quickly on the kind of hot grits that generally go with the greens Hollywood loves best. **1956** B. CLEARY *Fifteen* i. 31 He was.. tall enough so a medium-sized girl could.. not feel she had to scrooch down when she walked beside him.

2. *trans.* = SCROUGE *v.* 1 d.

1929 [implied in SCROOCHED *ppl. a.*]. **1958** C. MCCULLERS *Square Root of Wonderful* II. 90 When I hear the words agony or labor, it makes me scrooch up my behind.

Hence **scrooched** *ppl. a.*; **'scrooching** *vbl. sb.*; **'scroochy** *a.*, characterized by scrooching, cowering.

1844 'J. SLICK' *High Life N.Y.* II. 229 The white figger at t'other eend the entry was.. lookin kinder scroochy. **1885** H. JACKSON *Zeph* ii. 71 Sittin' all scrouched into a heap. **1929** W. FAULKNER *Sartoris* IV. 282 He right dar now, watchin' dis lantern wid his eyes scrooched up. **1941** B. A. WILLIAMS *Strange Woman* vii. 521 Will accused him of scrooching down to make the hole seem deeper than it was. **1957** E. EAGER *Magic by Lake* vii. 158 He marched to his appointed jar (which happened to be the one in which Katharine sat scrooched).

scroo(d)ge, var. forms of SCROUGE *v.*

scroof(fe, scrool, obs. ff. SCRUFF, SCROLL *v.*

Scrooge (skruːdʒ). Also scrooge. The name of the curmudgeonly employer in Dickens' *A Christmas Carol* (1843), used allusively to designate a miserly, tight-fisted person or killjoy. Hence **Scrooge-like** *a.*

1940 *N. & Q.* CLXXIX. 87/2 Old Scrooge, for a killjoy who grudges other people the pleasures that he cannot enjoy himself, and Mr. Micawber.. are both frequent types, but more definitely literary. **1953** *Sun* (Baltimore) 14 Dec. 1/6 Britons, who have been looking forward to their gayest Christmas since before the war, suddenly face the threat that a railway strike will paralyze the nation on the eve of the holiday week. A Labor party paper called union leaders who ordered the strike 'scrooges'. **1960** *Guardian* 18 Nov. 10/6 People.. were heard to wonder why this nonsense had to go on... But these were a minority of Scrooges. **1976** *Monitor* (McAllen, Texas) 10 Oct. 1B/7 Jim 'Catfish' Hunter, baseball's foremost 'money' pitcher, turned in a Scrooge-like performance Saturday. **1980** *Times* 5 Dec. 5/8 Scrooges who wish to prove their repentance this Christmas should send out for woodcock, the most expensive delicacy.

scroop (skruːp), *sb.*¹ [Echoic; cf. SCROOP *v.*]

a. A harsh, strident, or scraping noise.

a **1859** *Household Words* XXX. 139 This man could mimic every word and scroop and shout that might be supposed proper to such a scene [the pulling of teeth]. **1868** MISS BRADDON *Trail of Serpent* VI. iv, The door opened with a scroop. **1892** *Chamb. Jrnl.* 12 Nov. 734/2 There is always a scroop of chairs moving on the stone floor.

b. The rustling sound and crisp feel associated especially with silk but capable of being imparted also to other fabrics by special treatment.

1892 G. H. HURST *Silk Dyeing* i. 9 Dilute mineral acids have no appreciable action on silk, but they have the property of imparting to it a peculiar 'scroop' or crackle. **1921** C. SALTER tr. *Ganswindt's Dyeing Silk* 32 The so-called 'scroop' of silk.. is only observed in scoured silk that has been treated with weak acids. **1954** *Economist* 24 Apr. 291/1 Non-cellulose synthetics may be too hot in summer.. and.. it is difficult to give them such qualities as 'scroop', the trade name for the rustle that women like. **1961** BLACKSHAW & BRIGHTMAN *Dict. Dyeing & Textile Printing* 154 Scroop... This property can be imparted to textile materials other than silk by, for example, soap in conjunction with an organic acid. **1974** *Encycl. Brit. Micropædia* IX. 208/2 Scroop.. is not a natural property of the fibre [*sc.* silk] but is developed by processing treatments, and does not indicate quality.

scroop, *sb.*² *rare*⁻¹. ? Perh. a mistake for SCRUFF.

1850 E. BRONTE *Wuthering Heights* iii, I took my dingy volume by the scroop, and hurled it into the dog-kennel.

scroop (skruːp), *v.* [Echoic.

Cf. *skruke*, 'the noise made by a chair being drawn along a brick floor' (Cozens-Hardy, *Broad Norfolk*, 1893).]

intr. To make a strident, grating, or scraping sound; to grate, creak, squeak.

1787 GROSE *Prov. Gloss.* s.v., The jack scroops. **1826** COBBETT *Rur. Rides* (1885) II. 194 It is boundless joy to me, to contemplate this infernal system [of paper-money] in its hour of wreck: swag here; crack there: scroop this way: souse that way. **1849** ALB. SMITH *Pottleton Legacy* xxxiv. 401 She heard the shutters of the dairy scroop on their hinges. **1886** J. ASHBY-STERRY *Lazy Minstrel* 110 The iron gate scrooped on its hinges.

Hence **'scrooping** *vbl. sb.*

1849 ALB. SMITH *Pottleton Legacy* xxxiv. 410 Without any of the scrooping or vibrating that usually accompanies a pull-up. **1884** MISS BRADDON *Ishmael* II. 232 Opening the doors as cautiously as a practised burglar, lest the porter or his wife should be awakened by the scrooping of a bolt.

†**scrophe.** *Obs. rare.* [ad. med.L. *scropha* in the originals.] App. a measure of land.

The addition 'or diches' is prob. due to a mistaken guess at the meaning.

c **1450** *Godstow Reg.* 279 To Petir of Esserugge, half j. acre of mede in Roweneye,.. with iij. scrophis of the seid half acre liyng to them. *Ibid.* 290, ij. yerdes of mede in Farnhull .. with iiij. scrophis or diches. *Ibid.* 292, ij. Rodis and iiij. scrophis of mede [L. *scrophas prati*] in Farnehulle.

‖**scrophularia** (skrɒfjʊ'lɛərɪə). *Bot.* Also 7–8 scrof-, 7 schroph-. [mod.L. (sc. *herba*), f. med.L. *scrophula* SCROFULA: see -ARY.] A genus of monopetalous plants (the fig-worts), typical of the N.O. *Scrophulariaceæ*; a plant of this genus.

[**1527** ANDREW *Brunswyke's Distyll. Waters* B iv, Scrofularia in latyn. The best parte & tyme of his dystyllacyon is the rote wasshed, and the leues stroped fro the stalkes and so togyder dystylled.] **1663** BOYLE *Usef. Exp. Nat. Philos.* II. v. viii. 192 Our Chymist told me he had made such *Prima entia* of Scrophularia. **1741** *Compl. Fam.-Piece* II. iii. 385 You have besides the scarlet Lichnis,.. Spanish Scrophularia [*printed* Scorphularia], Larkspur.

Hence **scrophulari'aceous** *a.*, belonging to the N.O. *Scrophulariaceæ*; **scrophu'lariad**, a plant of this order.

1846 SMART Suppl., *Scrophulariaceous*. **1866** *Treas. Bot.* 126/2 *Bartsia*, unpretending annuals, belonging to Scrophulariads. **1884** *Athenæum* 20 Sept. 375/2 The classification of the labiates, the scrophulariads, the Leguminosæ [etc.].

scrophularin ('skrɒfjʊlərɪn). *Chem.* [f. SCROPHULAR-IA + -IN¹.] A bitter substance obtained from *Scrophularia nodosa* (knotted figwort).

1868 WATTS *Dict. Chem.* V. 209 *Scrophularia nodosa* contains a bitter substance called by Walz α-scrophularin... *Sc. aquatica* contains a bitter substance β-scrophularin.

scrophularineous (ˌskrɒfjʊlə'rɪnɪəs), *a.* [f. mod.L. *Scrophularineæ* + -OUS.] Of or pertaining to the *Scrophularineæ* (or *Scrophulariaceæ*).

1845 G. DON in *Encycl. Metrop.* VI. 108* Scrophularineous Plants. **1882** G. ALLEN in *Cornhill Mag.* Jan. 32 The scrophularineous family, to which the snapdragon belongs.

†**scrophulary.** *Obs.* Also 5 scropholarie, 6 scrophularye. Anglicized form of SCROPHULARIA (cf. F. *scrofulaire*).

c **1400** *Lanfranc's Cirurg.* 269 Ouþir take scropholarie þe rynde þerof & grinde it wiþ grese, & make þerof an emplastre. **1578** LYTE *Dodoens* I. xxxi. 44 The roote.. euerlasting, putting forth yearely new springs, as also doth the rootes of the other two Scrophularies. **1725** *Bradley's Fam. Dict.* I. s.v. *Cancer*, Tisans composed of Maiden-Hair, Ceterach, great Scrophulary or Knot-grass.

scrophules: variant of SCROFFLES *pl.*

†**'scroppit**, *a. Sc. Obs. rare.* 'Mean, scraping, niggardly' (Jam.).

? *a* **1550** *Peder Coffeis* 10 in *Lyndesay's Min. Poems* (1871) 588 Thay are declarit in sevin pairtis; Ane (scroppit cofe) quhen he begynnis, Sornand all and sindry airtis, For to by hennis reid-wod he rynnis.

scroschatis: see SCROCHAT *Sc. Obs.*

scrotal ('skrəʊtəl), *a.* [ad. mod.L. *scrōtālis*, f. SCROTUM.] Of or pertaining to the scrotum.

1800 *Med. Jrnl.* III. 331 A. B... had many years been subject to a large scrotal hernia. **1899** *Allbutt's Syst. Med.* VIII. 808 Sinuous raised infiltration of the scrotal skin.

†**'scrotcher.** *Obs. rare*⁻¹. ? = CROCHE *sb.*²

1611 COTGR. s.v. *Semé*, *Teste de cerf bien semée*, a Stags head which hath all it spillers, rochers, and scrotchers on both sides.

scrotchertis: see SCROCHAT *Sc. Obs.*

scrotiform ('skrəʊtɪfɔːm). *Bot.* and *Biol.* [f. SCROTUM + -(I)FORM.] Pouch-shaped.

1775 J. JENKINSON *Brit. Plants* 256 *Scrotiform*, in the form of the *Scrotum*. **1856** HENSLOW *Dict. Bot. Terms*, *Scrotiform*. **1866** *Treas. Bot.*

scrotocele (ˈskrəʊtəʊsiːl). *Path.* [f. *scroto-* combining form of SCROTUM + CELE.] A scrotal hernia.

1693 tr. *Blancard's Phys. Dict.* (ed. 2), *Scrotocele*, a Rupture of the *Scrotum.* **1858** MAYNE *Expos. Lex.* **1898** *Syd. Soc. Lex.*

scroto-femoral (ˌskrəʊtəʊˈfɛmərəl), *a. Path.* [formed as prec. + FEMORAL.] Pertaining to the parts about the scrotum and the thigh.

1899 *Allbutt's Syst. Med.* VIII. 510 The popliteal hollow, the groins, the scroto-femoral flexures.

scrottiszarttis: see SCROCHAT *Sc. Obs.*

‖**scrotum** (ˈskrəʊtəm). *Anat.* [L. *scrōtum.*]

a. The pouch-like tegument enclosing the testicles.

1597 A. M. tr. *Guillemeau's Fr. Chirurg.* 21/2 The Scrotum, which we call the bagg wherin the testicles are contayned. **1690** R. DAVIES *Jrnl.* (Camden) 114 He was shot through the scrotum, and thereby forced to retire. **1772** D. LYSONS *Pract. Ess.* 66 His neck, abdomen, scrotum, legs, and all parts of his body were greatly tumified. **1878** BRYANT *Pract. Surgery* I. 46 Where much cellular tissue exists, oedema will rapidly show itself, as in the eyelids or scrotum.

b. *Comb.*, as *scrotum-tightening* adj. (now with allusion to Joyce's use).

1922 JOYCE *Ulysses* 7 Isn't the sea what Algy calls it: a grey sweet mother? The snotgreen sea. The scrotum-tightening sea. *Epi oinopa ponton.* **1935** E. E. CUMMINGS *Let.* 3 Oct. (1969) 145 & jump you out right inwardly at the Isful.. quote scrotumtightening unquote omnivorously eternal thalassa pelagas or Ocean. **1976** *Listener* 22 July 80/1 The English do not like the sea unless it happens to be blue and smooth and warm... No scrotum-tightening sea, to borrow James Joyce's heroic adjective.

scrouch, var. SCROOCH.

scrouge (skruːdʒ, skraʊdʒ), *sb. colloq.* or *vulgar.* Also **scrowge.** [f. SCROUGE *v.*]

1. A crush, squeeze, or crowd.

1839 C. CLARK *J. Noakes* cxxiii, Agin these shows, oh, what a scrowge! **1887** C. KEENE *Let. in Life* xii. (1892) 383, I went to the Academy 'Swarry' last night—the usual scrouge.

2. *U.S.* (See quot.)

1851 B. H. HALL *College Words, Scrouge*, an exaction. A very long lesson, or any hard and unpleasant task, is usually among students denominated a *scrouge.*

scrouge (skruːdʒ, skraʊdʒ), *v. colloq.* or *vulgar.* Now chiefly *U.S.* Also 8–9 **skrowdge**, 9 **scroodge, scrooge, scroudge, scrowge, skrouge.** [App. an onomatopœic alteration of SCRUZE.]

1. a. *trans.* To incommode by pressing against (a person); to encroach on (a person's) space in sitting or standing; to crowd. Also, to push or squeeze (a thing). Also *fig.*

1755 JOHNSON s.v. *Scruze*, This word..is still preserved, at least in its corruption, *to scrouge*, in the London jargon. **1756** TOLDERVY *Hist. 2 Orphans* III. 198, I assure you, that I am not used to be skrowdged by any man, not even my husband; therefore, pray sit farther from me. **1811** *Ora & Juliet* III. 131, I hope, Miss, I don't scrouge you? **1830** *Constellation* (N.Y.) 11 Sept. 2/5 The room was so completely crowded, that one could not have scrouged the little end of nothing, sharpened, between them. **1840** DICKENS *Old C. Shop* xxxix, Kit had hit a man on the head with a handkerchief of apples for 'scrowdging' his parent with unnecessary violence. **1868** F. J. FURNIVALL *Babees Book* p. xxxvi, By Harrison's time, A.D. 1577, rich men's sons had not only pressed into the Universities, but were scrooging poor men's sons out of the endowments meant only for the poor. **1888** E. EGGLESTON *Graysons* xxxiii. 348 You know what *I* am—a good, stiddy-going, hard-working farmer, shore to get my sheer of what's to be had in the world without scrouging anybody else. **1896** *Westm. Gaz.* 24 July 7/2 A barrister applied at Westminster Police-court to-day for a summons against a solicitor's clerk, alleged to have 'scrooged' applicant when..he tried to obtain a seat at the *Drummond Castle* inquiry the other day. **1944** L. E. SMITH *Strange Fruit* xxix. 362 There'll be lynchings as long as white folks and black folks scrouge each other—everybody scrambling for the same penny.

b. *intr.* Also *fig.*

1798 *Aurora* (Philadelphia) 13 Dec. 2/1 Upstairs I scrouged to the front. **1821** EGAN *Life in London* viii. (1870) 194 Who's that that scroudges?—you shan't shove my wife. **1873** *Punch* 14 June 247/1 He, like the rest, scrooged and elbowed and leaned forward to see. **1908** K. GRAHAME *Wind in Willows* i. 2 So he scraped and scratched and scrabbled and scrooged, and then he scrooged again and scrabbled and scratched and scraped, working busily with his little paws. **1949** H. HORNSBY *Lonesome Valley* xxviii. 377 He was in the top of a tree that scrouged against the sky, and they were cutting the tree down and he was falling with the tree.

c. To draw oneself into a compact shape. Cf. SCROOCH *v.* 1.

1905 *Dialect Notes* III. 64 There I was, all scrooged up in a corner. *a* **1930** 'H. STONE' in Murdoch & Drake-Brockman *Austral. Short Stories* (1951) 118 Derned if this ben't an errand... Don't see how I be a-goin' to scrooge through, 'tall, 'tall. **1937** S. V. BENÉT in *Atlantic Monthly* Dec. 685/2 So he sort of scrooged back in a corner and waited his chance. **1948** 'LA MERI' *Spanish Dancing* x. 144 Since there was seldom a sidewalk, one scrooged against their chalky walls to allow the old victoria carriages to pass. **1979** G. SWARTHOUT *Skeletons* 230, I scrooged down in my chair, laid my head back, stretched out my legs.

d. *trans.* To draw tight; to squeeze or screw *up* (the eyes, etc.). Cf. SCROOCH *v.* 2.

1909 R. A. WASON *Happy Hawkins* 162 The old man looked at me with his little shiny eyes all scrouged up.

2. *U.S.* (See quot.)

1851 B. H. HALL *College Words, Scrouge*,..said of an instructor who imposes difficult tasks on his pupils.

Hence **'scrouging** *vbl. sb.*

1843 B. R. HALL *New Purchase* II. 59 (Bartlett 1860) After hard scrouging each way some hundred yards, we came together and held a council. **1894** HALL CAINE *Manxman* IV. xvi. 263 Such pushing and scrooging, you never seen the like.

'scrouger. [f. SCROUGE *v.* + -ER¹.]

1. *U.S.* Anything exceptional in size, capacity, etc.; a 'bouncer'.

1822 *Amer. Beacon* (Norfolk, Va.) 6 Sept. 4/1 The bargemen..are divided into classes, such as Tuscaloosa Roarers, Alabama Screamers, Cahawba Scrougers, and the like gentle names. **1837** *Davy Crockett's Almanack Wild Sports 1838* I. IV. 13 He found me a real scrouger. I brake three of his ribs. **1847** ROBB *Squatter Life* (Bartlett 1860), The gals among them warn't any of your pigeon critters,..but real scrougers; any of 'em could lick a bar easy. **1852** HALIBURTON *Traits Amer. Humour* xxi. (1866) 119 A drum, and a regular scrouger at that.

2. A fishing-line fitted with several hooks used for illegal fishing (= SCRODGILL).

1897 KIPLING *Capt. Cour.* viii. 157 A man..had been convicted of using a tackle with five or six hooks—a 'scrowger' they call it—on the Shoals.

scrounge (skraʊndʒ), *v.*¹ *colloq.* (orig. *dial.*). Also **scrunge.** [Prob. altered f. dialectal *scringe* to pry about (see *Eng. Dial. Dict.*); the word gained general currency through its widespread use amongst servicemen in the war of 1914–18.]

1. *intr.* To sponge *on* or live at the expense of others. Also with *off.*

1909 WEBSTER, Scrunge. **1922** *Glasgow Herald* 1 May 6, I did not see anything in front of me except scrounging on my own people. **1950** G. GREENE *Third Man* ii. 20, I badly need another drink, but I can't keep on scrounging on a stranger. Could you change me a pound..into Austrian money? **1978** R. WESTALL *Devil on Road* xiii. 97, I could go and scrounge off the parents for the rest of the vac.

2. a. *intr.* To seek to obtain by irregular means, as by stealth or begging; to hunt about or rummage (*for* something).

1909 J. R. WARE *Passing Eng.* 217/2 *Scrunging* (Country Boys'), stealing unripe apples and pears—probably from the noise made in masticating. **1915** W. H. L. WATSON *Adv. Despatch Rider* v. 58 George and I..'scrounged' for eggs and bread. **1918** G. GOODCHILD *Behind Barrage* vi. 94 You may scrounge for rations, kit, pay, or leave. Signallers.. usually scrounge for wire. Scrounging for wire is legitimized by the War Office. **1930** BROPHY & PARTRIDGE *Songs & Slang 1914–18* 160 *To scrounge about*, to go seeking an opportunity of stealing. **1961** 'E. MCBAIN' *'Til Death* xiii. 153 Facing the world outside the police department, scrounging for a job when I'm no longer a boy. **1973** M. & G. GORDON *Informant* xliv. 165 Scrounging around in her case for a freshly laundered slip, she cast curious glances at Chris.

b. *trans.* To appropriate; to acquire by irregular means, by stealth, or by begging; to 'pinch', to 'cadge'.

1917 A. G. LEE *Let.* 24 Nov. in *No Parachute* (1968) viii. 172 Now to scrounge the watch from its casing! **1919** [see BUCKSHEE *sb.* and *a.*]. **1923** G. H. MCKNIGHT *Eng. Words & their Background* 67 British supplies were scrounged. **1939** *Star* 2 Dec. 4/1 The Southern Railway gave a staggering figure for the specially dimmed bulbs which had been stolen (I beg pardon, scrounged) from their carriages in the first weeks of the war. **1945** *Sun* (Baltimore) 14 Dec. 6/5 Food, cigarettes, chocolate, clothing, flour and canned meat which the supply team has 'scrounged' from excess military stores. **1958** *Times Lit. Suppl.* 10 Oct. 573/3 The crude overtures of Moondoggie and the other Huck Finn louts who scrounge a lazy summer from any foolish young woman whose parents can provide them with a meal. **1976** *National Observer* (U.S.) 31 Jan., Some of these [newspapers] I picked up free in the press room; others I scrounged at the lower-lobby newsstand.

Hence **scrounge** *sb.*, the action of scrounging; **scrounged** *ppl. a.*; **'scrounger**, one who scrounges; **'scrounging** *vbl. sb.* and *ppl. a.*

1909 WEBSTER, Scrunger. **1918** E. S. FARROW *Dict. Mil. Terms, Scrounger*, a slang term for a soldier with plenty of resource in getting what he wants. **1919** tr. *A. L. Vischer's Barbed Wire Dis.* 44 The complaints about 'scrounging', which are nothing but outbreaks of loss of moral judgment. **1927** *Daily Express* 17 Aug. 3 (*heading*) Suffolks on the scrounge. Village trek for recruits. **1941** *New Statesman* 29 Mar. 316/2 'Scrounged' cups, plates, cutlery and even food. **1946** *Sun* (Baltimore) 23 Oct. 4/3 There is a blunt reminder that 'pilfering' by a native is indistinguishable from 'scrounging' by an American soldier, and that 'chiseling' and resale of Post Exchange supplies is not an act peculiar to Filipinos. **1950** *Landfall* Mar. 127, I drained my fifth warm bottle-full ages ago and have been on the scrounge ever since. **1956** L. GODFREY in *Pick of Today's Short Stories* 94 'Besides,' added Trouncer..'it's a good scrounge.' **1956** A. L. ROWSE *Early Churchills* viii. 151 The King, who sank back into the more consoling, if hardly less scrounging, arms of the Duchess of Portsmouth and Nell Gwynn. **1959** *Times Lit. Suppl.* 26 June 382/4 A curious collection of notes assembled under the title 'Autolycism', after Autolycus, an Athenian of scrounging habits. **1968** *Science* 3 May 522 He was a talented scrounger who in the early stages of the development of the cyclotron was able to find an available 85-ton magnet. **1974** *Listener* 7 Nov. 593/3 Reading an old, scrounged *Daily Mirror.* **1978** P. MARSH et al. *Rules of Disorder* ii. 31 You learn to scrounge. Anybody's a good scrounger around here. **1981** 'J. GASH' *Vatican Rip* i. 7 I'm an antique dealer... I was on the scrounge and feeling very sorry for myself.

scrounge (skraʊndʒ), *v.*² *U.S. colloq.* [Cf. SCROUGE *v.*, but perh. related to dialectal *scringe*, *scrunge* to rub with force (*Eng. Dial. Dict.*: see prec.).] *trans.* To move with a rubbing or squeezing action.

1939 J. STEINBECK *Grapes of Wrath* x. 123 Ma chuckled lightly and scrounged the clothes in and out of the bucket. **1954** —— *Sweet Thursday* xxii. 139 You keep an old lemon rind, and every time you wash your hands you scrounge your fingernails around in it.

scrow (skrəʊ), *sb.* Also 3–6 **scrowe**, 5 **skraw**, ?**skrew**, 5–7 **skrow**, 6 **schrowe**, 6–7 **skro.** [Aphetic a. AF. *escrowe* (see ESCROW).]

†**1.** = SCROLL *sb.* 1. *Obs.*

a **1225** *Ancr. R.* 282 ȝif þu hauest knif oðer cloð, mete oðer drunch, scrowe oðer quaer, holi monne uroure. **13..** *Coer de L.* 3395 Looke every mannys name thou wryte, Upon a scrowe off parchemyn. **1382** WYCLIF *Matt.* xxiii. 5 Filateries, that ben smale scrowis. *c* **1400** *Brut* ccxxxi. 313 And whan they had þus swore, þey token her scrowes that þe othes were comprehendid in, to the Notaries. *c* **1450** *M.E. Med. Bk.* (Heinrich) 99 Wryte þis charme on a skrowe. **1550–1** *Rec. St. Mary at Hill* 392 Paid for a scrow to syng on ij d. **1596** DALRYMPLE tr. *Leslie's Hist. Scot.* II. 397 Tha offir to the Quene a scrow of requeist conteining sum poyntes of thair schisme, inuentiounis, and deuyses. **1615** *Irish Act Jas. I*, c. 9 (1621) 444 Yet neuerthelesse all estreates of such fines..shall..be orderly charged and deliuered by scrowes into the office of the pype in the court of Exchequer.

†**b.** *pl.* Writings. *Obs.*

1508 KENNEDIE *Flyting w. Dunbar* 26 Dirtin Dumbar, quhome on blawes thow thy boist? Pretendand the to wryte sic skaldit skrowis. *a* **1513** FABYAN *Chron.* VII. 624 Knowynge that yᵉ sayd Baylly vsed to bere scrowys and prophecye aboute hym, shewyng to his company that he was an enchanter and of ylle disposicion. *a* **1585** MONTGOMERIE *Flyting* 112 Thy scrows obscure are borowed fra some buike. **1646** *Stirling Burgh Rec.* (1887) I. 190 The haill actis and scrowis that ar not buikit..in the counsall book.

†**2.** The expanse of heaven, the sky. *Obs.*

c **1400** *Destr. Troy* 910 As þe welkyn shold walt, a wonderfull noyse Skremyt vp to the skrow with a skryke ffelle.

†**3.** A note, memorandum. *Obs.*

1424 *Paston Lett.* I. 18 This scrowe is mad only for the informacion of the worthy and worshipfull lordes the arbitrores. *c* **1538** R. COWLEY in Ellis *Orig. Lett.* Ser. II. II. 94 There coulde be founde no maner roll, boke, or scrowe of the Kinges Revenues.

†**b.** A list, inventory, schedule. *Obs.*

a **1545** in *Archæologia* XXXIV. 38 Two prepositores in euery forme, whiche doth giue in a schrowe the absentes names at any lecture. **1596** DALRYMPLE tr. *Leslie's Hist. Scot.* II. 196 Heirefter how lang king Frances lyuet, he labouret to put the scotis in the skrow of his maist faythful seruandes.

†**c.** *clerk of the scrow* = *rotulorum clericus*, Clerk of the Register. *Obs.*

1596 DALRYMPLE tr. *Leslie's Hist. Scot.* II. 435 James Makgil quha clark is called of the lytle scrow.

4. *pl.* or *collect. sing.* Strips or clippings of hide or leather used for making glue.

1339–40 *Sacrist Rolls Ely* (1907) II. 99 Item in iiij buss. de strowes [*read* scrowes] empt. pro cole [*i.e.* glue] inde faciend. **1811** *Dues on Goods* in *Thom's Hist. Aberd.* II. 54 Scrows of ox and cow, or other hides, per ton, 0. 4. 0. **1879** *Encycl. Brit.* X. 133/1 So prepared the 'scrows' or glue pieces, as they are termed, may be kept a long time without undergoing change.

scrow (skraʊ), *a. dial.* [? cogn. w. SHREW.] (See quots.)

1674 RAY *S. & E.C. Words* 77 *Skrow*: surly, dogged, used most adverbially, as to look skrow [*printed* shrow], i.e. to look sowrly. **1859** HUGHES *Scouring W. Horse* vii. 182 Owld Tovey at this did look main scrow. **1883** *Hampsh. Gloss.*, *Scrow*, (1) Cross. (2) Angry, scowling. (3) Dark, threatening, as weather, 'A scrow night'.

scrow, variant of SCREW *sb.*²

scrowl (skraʊl). A thin incrustation, calcareous or silicious, upon the wall of a lode.

1778 W. PRYCE *Min. Cornub.* 99 What they call a Scrowl of the true Lode in the Cross-Gossan. **1884** R. HUNT *Brit. Mining* 912.

†**scroyle** (skrɔɪl). *Obs.* Also 7 **scroile.** [Of obscure origin.

The conjecture that it is a. OF. *escroele*, scrofulous sore, is not quite satisfactory as to form, and the assumed development of sense, though plausible, has no evidence.]

A scoundrel, wretch.

1595 SHAKS. *K. John* II. i. 373 By heauen! these scroyles of Angiers flout you, kings. **1601** B. JONSON *Poetaster* IV. iii. 35, I cry mercy (my good scroile) was't thou? [Cf. *ante* 20 By thy leaue, my neat scoundrell.] **1622** J. TAYLOR (Water-P.) *Water-cormorant* E 3, Then vpon Sabbath dayes the scroyle beginnes With most vnhallowed hands, to weed vp sinnes. **1794** I. WILLIAMS *Crying Epist.* 20 P—t was presuming when a young beginner: S—d—y's a Scroyle—A—d—n's a luckless winner! **1821** SCOTT *Kenilw.* xix, 'Hang him, foul scroyle, let him pass,' said the mercer.

scrub (skrʌb), *sb.*¹ Also 6 **schrub.** [var. of SHRUB: see SCR- 1.]

I. 1. A low stunted tree. Cf. SHRUB.

1398 TREVISA *Barth. De P.R.* XVII. xxv. (Tollem. MS.), In euery scrub [orig. *in omni frutice*], where þe reynebowe schineþ strayte þeron, þe same swetnesse of smel is all þe while, þat þe bowe schineþ þere. **1597** *Regul. Manor of Scawby, Lincs.* (MS.), That none shall take or carrye away any common ffurrs, being common rootes or scrubbes. **1868** HUNTLEY *Gloss. Cotswold Dial.*, *Scrub*, shrub.

2. *collect.* **a.** Stunted trees or shrubs, brushwood; also, a tract of country overgrown with 'scrub'. Also, in Austral. and N.Z. usage, any tract of heavily wooded country, whether bearing small or large bushes or trees.

1805 P. G. King in *Hist. Records Australia* (1915) 1st Ser. V. 586 *A Scrub*—consists of Shrubs of low growth, Soil of a bad quality with small Iron gravelly Stones, in general Rocky Scrub and Brush may..be called the Underwood of the Forest, but it is not infrequent on the Sea Coast for Scrubs to be void of trees. **1809** A. Henry *Trav.* 281 At four o'clock in the afternoon, we reached a little scrub, or bushy tract, on which we encamped. **1833** Sturt *S. Australia* I. i. 21 We encamped about noon in some scrub. **1841** *N.Z. Jrnl.* II. xlviii. 285 Every part is covered with vegetation, fern, scrub, copse and forest. **1860** J. McD. Stuart *Jrnl.* 9 Apr. (1864) 153 At four miles arrived on the top, through a very thick scrub of mulga. **1873** *Gentl. Mag.* Jan. 60 There are few trees, but plenty of scrub and bushes. **1885** H. Finch-Hatton *Advance Australia!* 152 Upon one occasion a traveller was riding quickly round the corner of a scrub, when he came suddenly on to a camp of wild Blacks. **1911** E. M. Clowes *On Wallaby* i. 5 These [prisoners] were packed off next day in boats, and let loose in the dense scrub where St. Kilda and Prahan now stand. **1947** K. Tennant *Lost Haven* vii. 105 She had been leading the children in botany expeditions through the scrub. **1966** 'J. Hackston' *Father clears Out* 16 Chester tried to cannon off the road and pocket us in the scrub. **1977** *Weekly Times* (Melbourne) 19 Jan. 34/1 In silence the two men rode towards the river but, turning left into the scrub before the bridge, they skirted the town.

b. *transf.* and *fig.*

1860 C. Kingsley *Miscell.* I. 295 The Elizabethan poets dwindled down into a barren scrub of Vaughans and Cowleys, etc. **1885** Rider Haggard *K. Solomon's Mines* vii, He felt his chin, on which the accumulated scrub of a ten day's beard was flourishing.

c. ***the Scrubs***: ellipt. for Wormwood Scrubs Prison in Greater London. Also *erron.* **Scrubbs.**

The element *Scrubs* in the place-name is app. identical with scrub *sb.*[1] (see *Conc. Oxf. Dict. Eng. Place-Names* (1936) 510/1).

1923 in J. Manchon *Le Slang.* **1930** G. Baker *Soul of Skunk* II. ii. 161 At the end of my first temporal month, I gibed at the Scrubbs... The broadest of my prison grins must have been that which I bestowed upon the Scrubbs' librarian. **1941** G. Greene *When Greek meets Greek* in *19 Stories* (1947) 171 Before his first stay at the Scrubs he had held a number of positions. **1966** A. Prior *Operators* vi. 64 He had..taken his medicine, which had turned out to be three years in the Scrubs. **1976** M. Maguire *Scratchproof* iv. 58 'Catherine put him in the Scrubbs for twelve months,' Gibson continued. 'It was in all the papers, you must have read about it.'

3. spec. ***mallee scrub*** (*Eucalyptus oleosa*) and ***horizontal scrub*** (*Anodopetalum biglandulosum*), native trees of Australasia, common in thickets and undergrowth. ***tea-scrub***: see tea-tree.

1857 Howitt *Tallangetta* xii. II. 2 This Mallee scrub.. consists of a dense wood of a dwarf species of gum-tree. **1909** G. Smith *Nat. Tasmania* 117 The most formidable constituent of this underscrub is the..Horizontal Scrub.

II. 4. a. A breed of cattle distinguished by their small size. Now in extended sense (*N. Amer.*): an animal of inferior breed or pedigree; a beast of poor physique or performance. †**b.** A dwarf; a person of mean presence.

a. 1555 *Act 2–3 Phil. & Mary* c. 3 §1 Persons..have layde theyr Landes..to feeding of Sheepe, Oxen, Runtes, Schrubbes, Steeres & Heckfers, and suche other lyke Cattell. **1581** Lambarde *Eiren.* IV. iv. 449 Oxen, rontes, steeres, scrubs, heifares, or kine. **1812** *Columbia Centinel* 31 Oct. 2/3 May the usefulness of our Institution be acknowledged;—its *speed* drive *scrubs* from the *course.* **1858** C. L. Flint *Milch Cows* 28 We meet with good milkers of all forms, from the round close-built Devon to the coarsest-boned scrub. **1884** *Harper's Mag.* July 297/2 The latter receives most of the 'through Texans', the old cows, and the 'scrubs' and 'culls' from the better lots. **1888** *Harper's Mag.* Jan. 325/1 The colonel's horse—an old 'scrub' he had borrowed—'bucked'. **1901** *Daily Colonist* (Victoria, B.C.) 26 Oct. 8/2 Mr. Wilson, manager of the Toronto Poultry farm, says he can not get enough [chickens] of superior quality, and many others say the same. No one wants 'scrubs', the days of which are numbered. **1934** J. M. Cain *Postman always rings Twice* xiv. 157 All the really fine pumas come from Nicaragua. These California..things are just scrubs compared to them. **1936** M. Mitchell *Gone with Wind* xxx. 509 They knew thoroughbred horses from scrubs. **1972** Fredrickson & East *Silence of North* vii. 52 We had a dog team of sorts, two scrubs that weren't worth much but could pull a load of traps and other gear on a homemade toboggan.

b. 1611 Cotgr., *Vn manche d'estrille*, a dwarfe, elfe, dandiprat, low scrub.

5. *transf.* **a.** A mean insignificant fellow, a person of little account or poor appearance.

1589 Warner *Alb. Eng.* VI. xxxi. 137 Must I, thought I, giue aime to such a Skrub and such a Saint, That Skowndrell, and this Counterfeit. **1657** Trapp *Comm. Ps.* lxii. 4 Neither is there ever a better of these glavering companions, dissembling scrubs. **1749** Fielding *Tom Jones* VIII. iv, He is an arrant scrub, I assure you. **1876** T. Hardy *Ethelberta* xlvii. II. 256 Any poor scrubs in our place must be fools not to think the match a very rare and astonishing honour, as far as the position goes.

b. *slang.* A disreputable woman; a prostitute, tart.

1900 *Dialect Notes* II. 58 *Scrub*,..a disreputable woman who frequents the streets. **1964** *New Statesman* 10 Apr. 555/2 A 'scrub' is a Rocker girl; that is, someone not fond of washing, according to the Mods, and a bit of a tart.

c. *U.S. Sport.* (*a*) A player belonging to a second or weaker team (freq. in *pl.*); a team composed of such players. Also *fig.* Cf. scrub *a.* 4.

1892 *College Index* (Agric. & Mech. Coll. Alabama) Nov. 23 Arranged similarly, but with darker stockings, stand the inimitable 'scrubs', and although their name is rather depreciatory, they themselves are not to be scoffed at. **1903** *N.Y. Even. Post* 28 Oct. 9/5 The halfback tries his mettle against the scrubs. **1920** W. Camp *Football without Coach* 62 Do not let the absence of a scrub disturb you in the least. Many a team is better off without a second eleven. **1956** B. Holiday *Lady sings Blues* (1973) xxi. 173, I wouldn't have known the first team from the scrubs, but Ehrlich told me the prosecutor and the judge were the best they had. **1961** J. S. Salak *Dict. Amer. Sports* 385 *Scrub*, a player of the second, or weaker, team; one not good enough to be on the first team.

(*b*) (See quot. 1910.)

1892 *Dialect Notes* I. 214 'Scrub' in New England is that form of base ball played when there are too few players to have opposing sides. **1896** W. A. White *Real Issue* 66 Just before school was called Piggy Pennington was playing 'scrub'. **1910** *Dialect Notes* III. 447 *Scrub*, a game of baseball played by a half dozen or more persons (when there are not enough to 'choose up' for two nines), in which the players move up as a batter is retired. **1917** C. Mathewson *Second Base Sloan* 126 At the end of a week or so they were playing 'scrub' every noon hour.

III. *attrib.* and *Comb.*

6. *attrib.* and *Comb.*: (sense 2), as ***scrub bull, bush, -cattle, fire, horse, jungle, -land; scrub-covered*** adj.; (sense 1), as ***scrub-tree***; **scrub-cutter** *Austral.* and *N.Z.*, (*a*) a machine for cutting scrub; (*b*) one who cuts scrub; hence **scrub-cutting** *vbl. sb.*; **scrub-dashing** *vbl. sb. Austral.* (see quot. 1941); **scrub-itch**, a skin-disease peculiar to the jungles of New Guinea; **scrub-rider** *Austral.*, one who rides in search of cattle that have escaped into the scrub; **scrub tick**, either of two small, brown, hard-bodied ticks found in Australia, *Hæmaphysalis bispinosa* or *Ixodes holocyclus*, the bush tick; **scrub typhus**, an acute rickettsial fever transmitted to man by mites normally parasitic upon small rodents; cf. ***mite(-borne) typhus*** s.v. mite[1] 3.

1908 A. Gunn *We of Never-Never* xviii. 238 Tales of *scrub-bulls, maddened cow-mothers. **1946** A. Marshall in Murdoch & Drake-Brockman *Austral. Short Stories* (1951) 317 He was an old scrub bull,..who roamed the timbered hills beyond the Murray. **1954** [see centre *sb.* 11 h]. **1977** *Listener* (N.Z.) 15 Jan. 34/3 Jeremy Delacy, the 'scrub bull', eccentric conservationist station-owner who has parted company with the local 'establishment'. **1897** D. McK. Wright *Old Station Days* 11 Cobwebs..jewelled the *scrub-bushes o'er. **1959** *Tararua* (N.Z.) XIII. 45 One curious term is *scrub bush.* So far as I can make out it is applicable to the individual plants which go to make up tall scrub. At any rate a tall plant of teatree may be called a *scrub bush.* **1870** A. L. Gordon *Bush Ballads* 14 'Twas merry 'mid the blackwoods, when we spied the station roofs, To wheel the wild *scrub cattle at the yard. **1900** W. S. Churchill in *Morning Post* 19 Mar. 5/7 The proper left of this position rests on the rocky *scrub-covered hill of Hlangwani. **1980** S. Wilson *Dealer's War* I. ii. 26 Grey scrub-covered hills. **1886** R. Stout *Notes Progress N.Z.* 28 The following..are manufactured in the colony—viz., ploughs, chaff-cutters..disc-harrows..*scrub-cutters. *a* **1930** H. Stone in *Austral. Short Stories* (1951) 115 But them scrub-cutters... They do need constant watchin. **1937** J. West *Sheep Kings* ix. 87 He purchased a new block of bush land, and employed another gang of men to break it in—timber-men and scrub-cutters and post-splitters. **1965** M. Shadbolt *Among Cinders* xxii. 210 Probably the place had been built by scrub-cutters. **1911** 'Kiwi' *On Swag* iii. 7 We were on a job of *scrub cutting. **1968** *Wanganui* (N.Z.) *Chron.* 15 Nov. 10/5 (Advt.), Scrub-cutting contract for 120 acres. **1977** C. McCullough *Thorn Birds* vi. 117 The grass had lasted just long enough eked out by scrub-cutting from the more juicy trees. **1941** Baker *Dict. Austral. Slang* 64 **Scrub-dashing*, riding through bush or scrub, esp. after strayed cattle or brumbies. **1946** F. D. Davison *Dusty* xv. 166 Fred had offered Tom work; odd jobs around the homestead..while Fred did the scrub-dashing. **1944** *Living off Land* vii. 148 Slower-burning *scrub fires..call for strategy. **1965** S. T. Ollivier *Petticoat Farm* i. 1 Harry stood at the roadside and watched the white pumice dust.. hanging in the air like smoke from a scrub fire on a fine day. **1823** J. F. Cooper *Pioneers* xvii, The rider of *scrub-horses. **1893** D. Ferguson *Bush Life in Australia & N.Z.* 301 The scrub confused and handicapped [the thoroughbred] whilst Selina was a scrub horse. **1909** K. Mackay *Across Papua* 125 We were now in the region of leeches and *scrub-itch. **1910** *Blackw. Mag.* Jan. 113/1, I saw my first tiger in a *scrub-jungle two miles from the Nepal frontier. **1934** 'G. Orwell' *Burmese Days* iv. 69 It was scrub jungle at first, with dense stunted bushes. **1953** D. A. Bannerman *Birds Brit. Isles* I. 256 The buntings spread over the plains of India, chiefly affecting cultivation and scrub-jungle. **1779** W. McKendry *Jrnl.* 4 Oct. in *Proc. Mass. Hist. Soc.* (1886) 2nd Ser. III. 472 Came over *skrub land this day. **1852** Mundy *Antipodes* (1857) 15 Innumerable tracks for equestrians across the stunted scrub-land. **1955** H. Klein *Winged Courier* xiv. 90 All around her lay scrubland, marsh and swamp. **1955** J. Thomas *No Banners* xxiii. 230 The road and the lane make a kind of elongated 'V', with the two arms separated by this scrub-land. **1976** K. Royce *Bustillo* iv. 47 Across the scrubland, the market was preparing its stalls. **1977** 'J. le Carré' *Hon. Schoolboy* xvii. 404 The perfect tarmac road ran..over the flat scrubland. **1881** A. C. Grant *Bush-Life in Queensland* (1882) xv. 150 A favourite plan amongst the bold *scrub-riders. **1891** *Queenslander* 3 Jan. 36/3 The *scrub tick is a small animal with eight legs when mature, flat, brown in colour. **1936** *Discovery* Oct. 306/2 If the camp is in the scrub..scrub ticks have to be faced. **1965** *Austral. Encycl.* VIII. 499/1 In the genus *Haemaphysalis* are ..two introduced species: a scrub tick..originally from India, and a dog tick. **1749** Lady Luxborough *Lett. to Shenstone* (1775) 163, I ordered a crooked row of *scrub trees to be fallen. **1888** Lighthall *Yng. Seigneur* 153 A hamlet of thirty or forty cabins crowded together among some scrub trees in the midst of a stony moor. **1929** W. Fletcher et al. in *Trans. R. Soc. Trop. Med. & Hygiene* XXIII. 61 The K. form has a patchy distribution, and its virus, like the virus of the tsutsugamushi disease, has its home in circumscribed areas of untilled open country, particularly in land which after being cleared of jungle has been allowed to grow up in weeds and scrub... Because cases of the K. form have their origin in such places, we propose that this kind of tropical typhus should be called *scrub-typhus. *Ibid.*, The epidemiology of this rural, or scrub-typhus, is very similar to that of the sporadic typhus-like disease of India which Megaw attributes to the bites of ticks. **1961** R. D. Baker *Essent. Path.* ix. 241 During World War II tsutsugamushi disease, scrub typhus, was prevalent among our troops in the Far East, and many fatalities occurred. **1978** *Jrnl. R. Soc. Med.* LXXI. 507 Scrub typhus is a febrile illness, endemic in much of the roughly triangular area bounded by Japan, Pakistan and Australia.

b. In names of animals and birds; as **scrub-bird**, a bird of the Australian family *Atrichiidæ*; see also *noisy scrub bird* s.v. noisy *a.* 1 b; **scrub-fowl, -hen**, a grey and brown mound-building bird, *Megapodius freycinet*, found in coastal areas of northern Australia; **scrub jay** *U.S.*, a blue jay with no white markings, *Aphelocoma cœrulescens*, found only in parts of Florida; **scrub-robin**, any bird of the genus *Drymodes*, Gould; **scrub-tit, -wren**, small birds of the order *Sericornis*, Gould (Morris, *Austral Eng.*); **scrub-turkey**, a large mound-building bird, *Alectura lathami*, found in Australian forests and having a red head and brown body; **scrub wallaby**, one of several wallabies belonging to the genus *Macropus* and living in woodland; **scrub wren**, a small Australian bird belonging to the genus *Sericornis.*

1869 J. Gould *Birds of Australia* Suppl. Pl. 26 *Atrichia rufescens.* Rufescent *Scrub-bird. **1908** *Scrub fowl [see dead-alive *a.*]. **1943** C. Barrett *Austral. Animal Bk.* xvii. 151 The scrub-fowl burrows into the mass to deposit each egg. **1864** J. Rogers *New Rush* II. 33 The monster *Scrub-hen, waddling past, Affrights. **1938** M. K. Rawlings *Yearling* xxiv. 302 *Scrub jays flew across the road. Their solid blue feathered coats..were prettier than the bluebirds'. **1947** R. T. Peterson *Field Guide to Birds* (ed. 2) 159 Florida, or Scrub, Jay... Look for this crestless Jay only in the stretches of 'scrub' in Florida. **1976** *Southern Evening Echo* (Southampton) 15 Nov. (Advt. Suppl.) 4/2 Scrub jays..feed their brothers and sisters. **1848** J. Gould *Birds of Australia* III. Pl. 10 *Drymodes Brunneopygia*, Gould, *Scrub Robin. **1872** C. H. Eden *Queensland* 124 The *scrub turkey (*Talegalla Lathami*)..much resembles the English hen turkey, though but little larger than a fowl. **1885** Scrub-turkey [see chucky-chucky]. **1940** F. D. Davison *Woman at Mill* 86 The scrub turkey had her home, her nesting mounds of leaf and forest debris. **1967** *Courier Mail* (Brisbane) 26 June 8 Normal mounding activity by feverishly active scrub turkeys in South-Eastern Queensland begins late in June, ending the following March. **1896, 1926** *Scrub wallaby [see *brush-wallaby* s.v. brush *sb.*[1] 4]. **1947** K. Tennant *Lost Haven* xii. 199 The marks of a scrub wallaby fossicking the high-tide drift. **1970** W. D. L. Ride *Guide Native Mammals Austral.* 46 Scrub wallaby..inhabiting woodland, forest edges, and coastal scrub. **1901** A. J. Campbell *Nests & Eggs Austral. Birds* I. 249 This smart *Scrub Wren possesses chiefly a western distribution. **1943** C. Barrett *Austral. Animal Bk.* xxxii. 278 The Australian scrub-wrens..are fussy, plain-coloured little birds, which spend most of their time on or near the ground, keeping to the undergrowth. **1965** *Austral. Encycl.* VIII. 48/2 Most of the scrub-wrens build domed nests of soft bark and fibre in thick vegetation.

c. In names of Australasian and American trees and plants; as **scrub oak**, (*a*) one of several North American dwarf oaks; (*b*) *Casuarina cunninghamii*; **scrub palmetto**, a small, slow-growing palm of the genus Sabal; **scrub pine**, any of several Australasian and American trees, *spec.* one of several North American dwarf pines, esp. *Pinus virginiana*, or its wood; **scrub vine** (see quots.). Also **scrubwood** (see quots.).

1766 J. Bartram *Jrnl.* 13 Jan. in *Trans. Amer. Philos. Soc.* (1944) XXXIII. 42/1 We came to Round-Lake,..almost surrounded with palmetto, pine, and *scrub-oak. **1805** Pike *Sources Mississ.* (1810) 40 Found some scrub oak. **1884** E. P. Roe in *Harper's Mag.* Feb. 457/1 An envious scrub-oak tore it off. **1918** W. Cather *My Antonia* II. xiv. 272 The dogwoods and scrub-oaks began to turn up the silvery underside of their leaves. **1947** V. H. Cahalane *Mammals N. Amer.* 365 One pair of these pockets can carry as many as twenty-seven scrub-oak acorns. **1964** R. Murphy *Pond* i. 9 The second-growth pine woods, had gone back to brush, green-brier, scrub oak. **1938** M. K. Rawlings *Yearling* iv. 40 Pushing through the low..*scrub palmettos..was less laborious. **1968** Mrs. L. B. Johnson *White House Diary* 23 Nov. (1970) 740 The landscape was low and flat, clotted with scrub palmettos. **1791** P. Fidler *Jrnl.* 30 Oct. in *Publ. Champlain Soc.* (1934) XXI. 517 A high point of Rocks & *scrub pine. **1818** [see New Jersey]. **1832** [see *grey pine* s.v. grey, gray *a.* 8]. **1872** Coues *N. Amer. Birds* 103 In sparse low woodland, cedar thickets and old fields grown up to scrub-pines. **1884** Sargent *Forests N. Amer.* 199 *Pinus clausus* Vasey... Sand Pine. Scrub Pine. Spruce Pine. **1898** Morris *Austral Eng.* s.v. *Pine*, Scrub Pine, *Frenela endlicheri.* **1949** *Sat. Even. Post* 9 Apr. 162/3 In front of the fireplace was a coarse-haired bearskin, scarred with burns from the snapping embers of scrub pine and cotton wood. **1976** M. & G. Gordon *Ordeal* (1977) xi. 71 They walked slowly through a forest of scrub pine. **1866** *Intell. Observ.* No. 52. 242 The *scrub-vine, a species of cassytha. **1898** Morris *Austral Eng.* s.v. *Bauera*, A shrub, *Bauera rubioides* ..the Scrub Vine, or Native Rose. **1874** *Treas. Bot.* Suppl. s.v. *Commidendron*, *C. rugosum* is called the *Scrub Wood and Gum Shrub. **1875** MELLISS *St. Helena* 284 *Aster glutinosus* ... The indigenous plant called 'Scrubwood' is a native of the low, outer zone of the Island.

scrub (skrʌb), *sb.*[2] Also scrubb. [f. SCRUB *v.*]

1. a. The action or an act of scrubbing. Also *spec.* with *up*: see SCRUB *v.*[1] 3 d; freq. *attrib.*

1621 J. TAYLOR (Water-P.) *Praise Beggery* D 1 b, Then (after a scrub or a shrug) you must conceiue he meetes with a Lawyer, and fitting his phrase to his language, hee assaults him thus, and ioynes issue. **1900** *Daily News* 14 Aug. 5/1 Afterwards the Carlton goes over to the Junior Carlton, the senior club requiring a scrub up. *a* **1902** S. BUTLER *Way of All Flesh* (1903) lxxii. 331 Ellen had given it another scrub from top to bottom. **1937** *Archit. Rev.* LXXXI. 52 (*caption*) A detail in one of the surgeon's 'scrub-up' lobbies, looking through an observatory window into an operating theatre. **1953** K. TENNANT *Joyful Condemned* xxxix. 383 Rene eyed May's house possessively. 'First thing..this gets a good scrub.' **1964** G. L. COHEN *What's Wrong with Hospitals?* vii. 125 The surgeon..spared me five minutes between a thyroidectomy and his next scrub-up. **1973** *Daily Tel.* 27 July 3/5 The theatre suite, consisting of the operating room, the anaesthetic room, the scrub-up room and the doctors' rest room.

b. Movement of part of a tyre over the road surface while in contact with it.

1936 *Proc. Inst. Automobile Engineers* XXX. 733 Features in independent springing..tending to prevent 'scrub' when the suspension is functioning. **1959** *Manch. Guardian* 27 July 2/3 Braking and acceleration also cause scrub. **1973** *Country Life* 11 Oct. 1077/3 Hard cornering produces front-tyre scrub, but the back wheels stay firmly on the road.

c. *slang.* A cancellation or abandonment, *spec.* of a flying mission. Cf. SCRUB *v.*[1] 4 a.

1952 M. TRIPP *Faith is Windsock* i. 14 We are marking time at the moment, three scrubs in a row. **1958** *N.Y. Times Mag.* 16 Mar. 10/2 The backstage crew is made up of engineers and technicians who work themselves to a frazzle during the long countdown..which may end not in a firing but in a series of 'holds' or a 'scrub'—cancellation. **1962** V. GRISSOM in *Into Orbit* 125, I was prepared for the scrub, and it was not long in coming.

2. A broom or brush with short hard bristles. Also *spec.* in *Glass-painting*, a brush used to scrape out lights in a coat of paint. Cf. SCRUB *v.*[1] 5 b.

1687 MIÈGE *Gt. Fr. Dict.* 11, Scrub, or old Broom, *un vieux Balais*... She has but a Scrub to sweep the Room withall. **1829** *Yng. Lady's Bk.* 466 The brushes used [for painting on velvet] are called scrubs. **1882** *Worc. Exhib. Catal.* iii. 57 Brushes for slippers, deck and paint scrubs. **1896** H. HOLIDAY *Stained Glass as Art* I. 23 The lights are taken out..with a hoghair brush with the hairs cut short, called a scrub. **1902** E. R. SUFFLING *Treatise on Art of Glass Painting* v. 89 Hog-hair fitches are converted into what glass painters call 'scrubs'... Scrubs are made in a variety of shapes—skew, round, flat, square, pointed. **1972** R. & G. METCALF *Making Stained Glass* 134 Employing some of the longer-haired scrubs to stipple the edges of the remaining matt.

3. One who scrubs; a hard-worked servant, a drudge. Perhaps with some reference to *sb.*[1] 5.

[**1707** FARQUHAR *Beaux' Stratagem* Dram. Pers., *Scrub*, Servant to Mr. Sullen.] **1709** [E. WARD] *Rambling Fuddle-Caps* 10 [The cook-wench says] Altho' I'm a Scrub that is doom'd to a Kitchin. **1776** BURNEY *Hist. Mus.* I. 304 He [Pan as described by Lucian] was a kind of *Scrub*, a drudge, fit for *all work*. **1888** *Poor Nellie* 447 A young girl of fifteen—a kitchen scrub he had never seen before.

4. The third grade in the quality of the heads of teasels; cf. KING, MIDDLING, QUEEN.

1766 *Museum Rust.* VI. 2 Another, or third sort, are such of the largest, or those which grew on the middle stem, as are damaged by the mildew, wet, or other accident... These therefore are thrown to a third sort, and denominated scrubs. **1813** [see QUEEN *sb.* 9 a].

5. *attrib.* **scrub-grass** (see quots.).

1814 BRACKENRIDGE *Views Louisiana* 206 Through all these islands, and on the Missouri bottoms, there are great quantities of rushes, commonly called *scrub grass. **1898** *Syd. Soc. Lex.*, *Scrub-grass*, a syn. for *Scouring rush* [*Equisetum hyemale*].

†**scrub**, *sb.*[3] *Obs.* [? f. SCRUB *v.*: cf. SCRUBBADO.] The itch.

1709 O. DYKES *Eng. Prov.*, *Union Prov.* (ed. 2) 7 We English are as much afflicted with the Scurvy, as they are with the Scrub. **1719** D'URFEY *Pills* V. 311 The Pox, the Mulligrubs, the Bonny Scrubs.

scrub (skrʌb), *a.* [attrib. use of SCRUB *sb.*[1]]

1. Mean, insignificant, contemptible.

1710–11 SWIFT *Jrnl. to Stella* 13 Jan., Upon Steele's leaving off, there were two or three scrub Tatlers came out, and one of them holds on still. **1743** H. WALPOLE *Let. to Mann* 3 Oct., How dismal,..how scrub does this town look. **1813** SCOTT 9 Jan. in *Lockhart* III. i. 36 Charlotte is with me just now at this little scrub habitation. **1840** J. P. KENNEDY *Quodlibet* 158 If he..makes a little fortune, we can call him a..Scrub Aristocrat. **1881** *Harper's Mag.* June 88/2 Her little scrub-class in the Sunday-school. **1901** M. E. RYAN *That Girl Montana* ix. 125 There are always a lot of scrub whites ready to take advantage of war signals.

†**2.** ? = Bob (tail). *Obs.*

1711 *Lond. Gaz.* No. 4888/4 A large scrub Tail, dapple grey.

3. Chiefly *U.S.* **a.** Of vegetation: low-growing, stunted.

Not clearly distinguishable from *Combs.* s.v. SCRUB *sb.*[1] 6 a.

1749 [see *scrub-tree* s.v. SCRUB *sb.*[1] 6 a]. **1779** W. MCKENDRY *Jrnl.* 29 Aug. in *Proc. Mass. Hist. Soc.* 2nd Ser. III. 465 Their breastwork was made of pine Logs cover[d] with green skrub bushes. **1816** U. BROWN *Jrnl.* 9 June in *Maryland Hist. Mag.* (1915) X. 266 Pines of a scruby kind, Jack Oaks and other Scrub wood. **1872** *Rep. Vermont Board Agric.* I. 78 Men are as choice of a little scrub apple tree.. as they would be were it classed among the favorite varieties of the day. **1904** G. STRATTON-PORTER *Freckles* ix. 196 There was a swarm of wild bees settled on a scrub-thorn only a few yards away. **1975** A. BERGMAN *Hollywood & Le Vine* (1976) viii. 104 A residential street that ended in sand and scrub bush.

b. Of livestock: of inferior breed or physique.

1744 W. ELLIS *Mod. Husbandman* Apr. xviii. 118 A petty Dealer,..keeping a scrub Horse, for carrying Fish about the Country. **1839** *Jrnl. Indiana Ho. Representatives* 8 Jan. 232 The half-blooded calves of the improved Durhams will sell, at weaning, for $20, while those of our scrub breed will only bring 3. **1868** *Rep. Iowa State Agric. Soc. 1867* 130 The general idea pervades the minds of our farmers that a larger ..animal of blooded stock can be produced by the same amount of feed, than can be made with the same feed fed to scrub stock. *Ibid.*, Our stock is scrub. **1930** C. ADDISON in *Hansard Commons* 30 Oct. 269 Imported Irish stock is of an enormously higher standard than it was a few years ago. That is due to the fact that they have eliminated the 'scrub' bull. **1948** *Minneapolis Morn. Tribune* 28 Sept. 11/5 She couldn't resist givin' him a Home, even though she had to admit that he was a very *ugly* lookin' scrub cat. **1973** B. BROADFOOT *Ten Lost Years* i. 7, I slept in the barn with about six of the sorriest looking scrub horses you have ever seen. Broom tails.

4. a. (Cf. SCRUB *sb.*[1] 5 c and SCRATCH *sb.*[1]) **scrub-crew, -nine** (see quot. 1891); **scrub-race, -game**, an impromptu race or game between competitors who have not trained beforehand; also *fig.*

1891 *Century Dict.* s.v. *Scrub*, *Scrub-crew*, *nine*, etc. in contests or games, a crew, nine, or the like, the members of which have not trained beforehand. **1868** *N.Y. Herald* 11 Aug. 9/4 A club..presenting on the field the appearance of a 'scrub nine'. **1791** *Address of Lad who carries Connecticut Courant* (broadside), Did not our pious father S—n Run a scrub race with Mr. Chairman? **1804** *Fredericktown* (Maryland) *Herald* 10 Mar. 3/3 His antagonists seem sanguine enough for any bet, that he is either to be distanced, or will make but a scrub race for the amusement of the Gentlemen of the turf. **1807–8** W. IRVING *Salmag.* (1824) 283 To start in a scrub-race for honour and renown. **1878** *N. Amer. Rev.* CXXVII. 14 The scrub-race of American politics. **1894** *Outing* XXIV. 145/1 In a scrub race the helmsman cracks on until the lee gunwale is almost on a level with the water. **1947** C. PRICE *Trails I Rode* 190 He had put in most of his life travelling around the country with some kind of an old scrub race horse.

b. Hence in general sporting use. Of a team or player: not first-class, not of regular standing; of a game: played by scrub or scratch teams. Also *fig.*

1867 *Ball Player's Chron.* 7 Nov. 1/1 A scrub match was arranged with seven of the Star nine and two others against ten in the field. **1892** J. L. FORD *Dr. Dodd's School* i. 5 The school eleven..were playing a practice game of football with a scrub eleven enrolled for the occasion. **1920** W. CAMP *Football without Coach* 63 You will have your regular center playing against a scrub center. **1947** *Chicago Tribune* 29 Jan. 29/2 Perhaps football could be cleaned up if it had more scrub teams. **1951** *Daily Progress* (Charlottesville, Va.) 19 Mar. 1/3 The Chinese have employed in the past second-rate troops in the front line. Behind them are superior troops ready to take advantage of any breakthrough made by the scrub team.

scrub (skrʌb), *v.*[1] Forms: 3–4 scrobbe, 6–7 skrub, 6– scrub. [Of obscure history: adopted from or corresp. to MLG., MDu. *schrobben*, *schrubben* (whence G. *schrubben*, *schruppen*, Sw. *skrubba*, Da. *skrubbe*), perh. related to SCRAPE; cf. GRUB *v.*

The existence of the variant SHRUB *v.* suggests the possibility that there may have been an OE. **scrobbian* or **scrybban*. In the mod. sense 3 the word may perh. have been re-imported from Du. as a nautical term: cf. *swab*.]

†**1.** *trans.* To curry-comb (a horse). *Obs.*

13.. *K. Alis.* 4310 The knave greytheth the hors, and scrobbeth [*Laud MS.* þe knaues graiþen her hors, & shrubben].

†**2.** To scratch, rub (a part of one's body). Also *intr.* for *refl.* *Obs.*

1596 NASHE *Saffron Walden* O 2 b, He put his hand in his pocket but to scrub his arme a little that itcht. **1598** MARSTON *Sco. Villanie* II. vi. E 8, Capro reads, sweares, scrubs, and sweares againe, Now by my soule an admirable straine. **1643** LIGHTFOOT *Glean. Exod.* 17 He is glad to get a potsheard to skrub himselfe. **1725** *Bradley's Fam. Dict.* s.v. *Vives*, With a Clout fastned to a Stick scrub the Place four or five Mornings, until the inflam'd Part becomes soft and ripe.

3. a. To clean (esp. a floor, wood, etc.) by rubbing with a hard brush and water. Also *fig.*

c **1595** MAYNARDE *Drake's Voy.* (Hakluyt Soc.) 13 If part of our companie had been sent thither upon our first arrival at Rio de la Hacha, doubtles we had done much goode, but now they [the Spaniards] had scrube [? *read* scrubd] it very bare. **1697** DAMPIER *Voy.* I. 52 We careen'd Capt. Wright's Bark and scrubb'd the Sugar-prize and got 2 Guns out of the Wrecks. **1709** W. KING *Art of Love* VIII. 1104 You'll scrub the rooms, or make the bed. **1828** SCOTT *F.M. Perth* Introd., I hastened to the spot, and found the well-meaning traveller scrubbing the floor like a housemaid. **1896** A. AUSTIN *England's Darling* I. ii, These poor arms you fold about you now Oft scrub the settle, scour the pans, and knead The homely dough.

b. *transf.* To rub with something bristly.

1844 THACKERAY *Arabella* in *Colburn's New Monthly* II. 170 He has a kind word for both, and scrubs the little girl's fresh cheek with his bristly beard.

c. *absol.* or *intr.*

1870 J. P. SMITH *Widow Goldsmith's Daughter* xxvi. 416 She began to clean the boots..while she whistled a jig and scrubbed for dear life. **1895** 'G. MORTIMER' *Like Stars that Fall* ii. 22, I must scrub and clean for you the rest of my life.

d. *intr.* for *refl.* To wash (usually with a brush) and disinfect the hands and forearms prior to performing or assisting at a surgical operation. Usu. with *up*.

1900 GOULD & WARREN *Internat. Text-bk. Surg.* I. xi. 283 While scrubbing, it is best to keep the hands and arms immersed in hot water, and particular attention should be given to the finger-nails. **1919** E. W. H. GROVES *Surg. Operations* i. 10 The sister scrubs up, covers herself in sterile gown, cap, gloves, and mask. **1944** *Brit. Jrnl. Surgery* XXXII. 25/2 The insertion was carried out by a member of the theatre staff who had 'scrubbed up' and donned the usual cap, mask, gown, and gloves. **1966** I. JEFFERIES *House-Surgeon* x. 185, I scrubbed, with Bernard alongside me asking questions about operative technique. **1976** *Lancet* 25 Dec. 1402/2 His asepsis was extraordinary. When he had spent the requisite ten minutes scrubbing up, he would dip his hands routinely into three successive bowls containing fluids of different colours.

e. *intr.* Of a horse-rider: to rub the arms and legs urgently upon a horse's neck and flanks to urge the horse to move faster.

1958 J. HISLOP *From Start to Finish* viii. 68 If you are riding a long-striding horse, you will find that you must scrub more slowly than on a short-striding horse. **1961** F. C. AVIS *Sportsman's Gloss.* 236/2 *Scrub*, of a jockey, to move the arms and legs, particularly as the end of a race is approaching. **1977** *Horse & Hound* 14 Jan. 21/1 By now the field was spreadeagled and scrubbing to keep in touch with the hounds.

4. a. *trans.* To cancel, scrap, call off; to eliminate, erase; to reject, dismiss. Also with *out*. *colloq.*

The current widespread use was reinforced by the popularity of the expression amongst servicemen in the war of 1939–45 (see quot. 1945).

1828 W. SCOTT *Jrnl.* 22 Mar. (1941) 212 If I were alone, I could scrub it [*sc.* a visit to London], but there is no doing that with Anne. **1943** H. E. BATES *There's Something in Air* 77 He was worked up to a very high state of tension..when Control informed him that the whole show would be scrubbed. **1944** *Yank* 30 June 8 At 1400 hours there was a briefing; at 1500 the mission was scrubbed. **1945** *Spectator* 25 May 478/1 The author can possibly justify the inclusion of the term 'scrub', meaning 'to cancel', in a collection of R.A.F. slang. The expression is in common use in the Royal Navy and has been for many generations. It derives from the days when all signals and orders were written on a slate. When the signals were cancelled or orders executed, the words on the slate were 'scrubbed out' or, equally correctly 'washed out'. **1953** *Sun* (Baltimore) 4 May 2/2 What do you mean that my mission is scrubbed? It's my mission and no one scrubs my mission but me. **1958** 'J. BROGAN' *Cummings Report* xix. 202 He might have told the operator to scrub it from the record. **1962** *Listener* 8 Feb. 247/2 At the end of the war some people realized that the best thing to do would be to scrub it [*sc.* the national debt] out. **1965** J. PORTER *Dover Three* xiii. 148 She doesn't sound the type of woman we're looking for. Scrub her! **1974** 'P. B. YUILL' *Bornless Keeper* ii. 17, I suggest scrubbing that thing on the Kent miners, can't see any foreign sales there. **1980** *News & Observer* (Raleigh, N. Carolina) 28 Oct. 10/1 Metropolitan Opera House musicians voted Monday to accept a new contract with the opera company, ending—at least temporarily—a strike that forced the Met. to scrub the 1980 season.

b. *intr.* To manage with difficulty, to 'scrape' *along*. Also with *on*. *colloq.*

1831 M. EDGEWORTH *Let.* 29 Mar. (1971) 507 He..has run through two large fortunes and is now scrubbing on upon a few thousands. **1889** W. DAVIDSON *Stories N.Z. Life* ii. 48 Dennis O'Brien had scrubbed along for many years, a miserable kind of existence, saving and hoarding, and living on the 'smell of an oil rag'. **1901** MERWIN & WEBSTER *Calumet 'K'* xi. 202 The rest of the road had to scrub along as best it could. **1905** G. BELL *Let.* 17 Apr. (1927) I. x. 212, I hope in a week or so I shall begin to scrub along.

c. *trans.* To reprimand severely; to punish *Mil. slang* (chiefly *Naut.*).

1911 [see MATELOT 1]. **1916** 'TAFFRAIL' *Pincher Martin* v. 76, I..jolly nearly got badly scrubbed for exceeding my duty and abducting the General. **1949** J. R. COLE *It was so Late* 62 That was my first station after they scrubbed me.

d. *intr.* Const. *round*. To dispense with, ignore; to drop (a subject). (See also quot. 1943.) *slang* (orig. *Mil.*). Cf. sense 4 a above.

1943 HUNT & PRINGLE *Service Slang* 58 *Scrub round*, to wash off the slate, to agree to forget, to let bygones be bygones. **1948** PARTRIDGE *Dict. Forces' Slang* 163 One declines an invitation to a party with 'Thanks very much, but you'll have to scrub round me, I'm Duty Boy to-morrow'. **1962** J. WAIN *Strike Father Dead* v. 222 'I just said I didn't want to break the contract we had at present,' I said. 'I felt it was no good trying to scrub round it.' **1964** T. WHITE tr. *P. Leulliette's St. Michael & Dragon* 189, I was required to do no less than fifteen days' cells. Reason: disobedience. Luckily, the captain had a sense of humour and finally scrubbed round it.

5. a. *techn.* To treat (a material, esp. a gas or vapour) so as to remove impurities, usu. by bringing it into contact with a liquid; to wash *out* or remove (impurities) in such a way.

1885 C. G. W. LOCK *Workshop Receipts* Ser. IV. 5/1 The particular arrangement of the interior of the scrubber adopted here, is that patented by Henry Green of Preston, and used in the gasworks there for scrubbing gas. **1931** HOFFERT & CLAXTON *Motor Benzole* viii. 211 In this type of washer, the gas is scrubbed by the oil in the form of a fine spray in six or more superimposed sections or chambers, through which the gas ascends in turn. **1941** *Thorpe's Dict. Appl. Chem.* (ed. 4) V. 461/1 The [coal] gas is cooled by passage through condensers before scrubbing out the ammonia. **1961** G. CLAXTON *Benzoles* viii. 213 The greater proportion of the benzole is scrubbed out of the gas by means of wash oil. **1972** *Sci. Amer.* Oct. 26/1 Cooled and scrubbed with water to remove dust, the clean gas could be burned itself to provide the desired clean heat. **1974** *Daily*

Tel. 22 Feb. 7/6 The diver inside the suit operates at ordinary surface pressures, and breathes oxygen which is continuously scrubbed and recirculated. **1979** *Sci. Amer.* Oct. 74/2 Consideration is being given to adding nitrogen-removing devices to the procedures that now 'scrub' sulfur dioxide..from stack gases.

b. *Glass-painting.* To scrape away (paint) or to scrape *out* (lights) with a scrub. Cf. SCRUB *sb.*² 2.

1897 L. F. DAY *Windows* vi. 65 The practice in the sixteenth century was mainly, by a process of scrubbing lights out of matted or washed tints of brown, to get very considerable modelling. **1910** *Encycl. Brit.* XII. 106/2 The modelling was got by scrubbing away the paint with a dry hog-hair brush.

6. In *Comb.*, as ***scrub-broom, -girl, -man, pail, -water, -woman***; (sense 3 d) ***scrub nurse, room.***

1675 V. ALSOP *Anti-Sozzo* iii. §2. 223 He brings nothing New, his Rayling faculty, like an old *Skrub-broom, being worn to the Stumps. **1839** MRS. KIRKLAND in Griswold *Prose Writers Amer.* (1847) 464 Fetch the broom, Betsey! and the scrub-broom, Betsey! **1905** *Cleveland* (Ohio) *Plain Dealer* 24 Jan. 3 Once a soldier in the army of the great white czar, now a *scrubman in one of the large department stores. **1927** *Amer. Speech* II. 312/2 The '*scrub nurse' is she who handles the instruments and works within the sterile field, differing from the 'dirty nurse' who may touch only contaminated or unsterilized things. **1958** F. G. SLAUGHTER *Daybreak* I. vii. 54 He stepped out of the hard white cone of the operating lights in response to a scrub nurse's signal. **1972** M. CRICHTON *Terminal Man* II. i. 57 Two scrub nurses were working in the cavernous gray-tiled space. They were setting out sterile tables and drapes. **1927** *Amer. Speech* II. 312/1 In the Operating Room one finds '*scrub rooms' where the surgeon and his assistants literally scrub their arms and hands with brushes and green soap. **1977** D. BENNETT *Jigsaw Man* 13 The surgeon..strode briskly to the scrub-room... The scrub-nurse removed his mask and gloves. **1935** Z. N. HURSTON *Mules & Men* 336 It is put in *scrub water to scrub the house. **1975** *New Yorker* 28 July 31/2 He catches her scent of gray scrubwater as she passes. **1873** *N.Y. Herald* 16 Sept. 8/5 We have a specimen of this watch-dog policy in the case of a poor *scrub woman. **1895** *Forum* (N.Y.) Jan. 556 A majority of the mothers work out as washerwomen or scrubwomen. **1942** E. PAUL *Narrow St.* i. 2 Eugénie, a pale, brown-eyed scrubwoman not yet forty. **1973** E. MCGIRR *Bardel's Murder* i. 6 A scrubwoman did what was necessary in the cleaning line. **1980** G. M. FRASER *Mr American* xxii. 428 There's one way of treating a suffragette who's a scrub-woman..and another of treating a peer's daughter.

†**scrub,** *v.*² *Obs.* Also skrub. [? f. SCRUB *sb.*¹ (sense 5).] *intr.* To go in mean attire.

a **1591** H. SMITH *Serm. Wedd. Garmt.* 18 Therfore when we may goe in our maisters attire, shall wee scrubbe like beggars patched in our rags? **1597** BP. HALL *Sat.* I. iii. 7 Now souping in side robes of Royalty, That earst did skrub in lowsie brokery.

scrubbable ('skrʌbəb(ə)l), *a.* [f. SCRUB *v.*¹ + -ABLE.] That may be scrubbed without damage or injury; capable of being cleaned by scrubbing.

1923 *Daily Mail* 29 May 10 Matone's 'scrubbable' matt finish is fadeless. **1960** *House & Garden* Oct. 150/3 Wallpaper..guaranteed scrubbable for seven years. **1976** *Woman's Day* (U.S.) Nov. 123/2 Vinyl wall covering is scrubbable.

†**scru'bbado.** *Obs.* Also 7 scrubadoe, 7–8 scrubado. [f. SCRUB *sb.*³ + -ADO: cf. SCABBADO.] The itch.

1651 BIGGS *New Disp.* 112 He was still troubled with his guest, the scrubadoe. **1709** *Female Tatler* No. 6/4 A new Nostrum for the Scrubbado. **1729** FIELDING *Author's Farce* III. Air xii, Were I laid on Scotland's Coast, And in my Arms embrac'd my dear, Let Scrubado do its most, I would know no Grief or Fear.

†**'scrubbed,** *a. Obs.* [f. SCRUB *sb.*¹ + -ED².]

1. Stunted, dwarfed.

1596 SHAKS. *Merch. V.* v. i. 163 Now by this hand I gaue it to a youth, A kinde of boy, a little scrubbed boy No higher then thy selfe, the Iudges Clearke. **1607** J. NORDEN *Surv. Dial.* v. 237 They suffer their sheepe and cattell to bruize them [Furze bushes] when they are young, and so they grow to scrubbed and low tufts, seldome to that perfection that they might. **1723** T. TAYLOR in *Portland Papers* (Hist. MSS. Comm.) VI. 87 The first wood..consisting all of oaks, but very scrubbed ones. **1835** W. IRVING *Tour Prairies* xvii, Straggling forests of the kind of low scrubbed trees already mentioned.

2. Squalid, insignificant. *rare*⁻¹.

1688 BUNYAN *Heavenly Footman* (1724) 72 Consider, therefore, that as bad as thou have got thither; thither went scrubbed, beggarly Lazarus, &c.

scrubbed (skrʌbd), *ppl. a.* [f. SCRUB *v.*¹ + -ED¹.] Cleaned by scrubbing. Also *fig.*

1870 J. P. SMITH *Widow Goldsmith's Daughter* ii. 19 Chandos and Christabel were presentable children: both..were kept scrubbed and combed, and 'cleaned up' within an inch of their lives. **1905** E. M. ALBANESI *Brown Eyes of Mary* xvi. 213 The sight of the old kitchen, with its scrubbed boards and red tiles. **1958** *Listener* 18 Dec. 1050/2 'People Today' gave us a fresh, scrubbed and shiny picture of Hawick.

scrubber¹ ('skrʌbə(r)). [f. SCRUB *v.*¹ + -ER¹.]

1. One who, or something which scrubs.

1839 MRS. KIRKLAND in Griswold *Prose Writers Amer.* (1847) 464 Her floor is scoured every night, after all are in bed but the unlucky scrubber, Betsey, the maid of all work. *a* **1864** GESNER *Coal, Petrol.* etc. (1865) 166 Steam at forty lbs. is an excellent scrubber.

2. An instrument for scrubbing. **a.** A scrubbing-brush. (In mod. Dicts.) **b.** An apparatus for cleansing coal-gas from impurities. More widely, any apparatus or installation for scrubbing (SCRUB *v.*¹ 5).

1853 S. HUGHES *Gas-works* 42 The scrubber or breeze condenser is used for the same purpose. **1876** *Engineering* 16 June 514/2 It was yet an open question which were the better, washers or scrubbers. **1948** *Petroleum Handbk.* (ed. 3) xvi. 231 The crude product is then neutralized in a caustic scrubber and fractionated to remove light gases. **1974** L. DEIGHTON *Spy Story* xv. 154 The CO_2 scrubber that cleans the air in an atomic submarine before recirculating it. **1975** *N.Y. Times* 14 Apr. 49/2 The air standards..require utilities..to install costly pollution-control systems called scrubbers to clean emissions from coal with a high sulphur content. **1977** *Lancet* 9 July 76/2 The gas containing benzene was..passed through a wet scrubber, and channelled into an activated-charcoal absorber unit, where benzene was recovered and recycled.

scrubber² ('skrʌbə(r)). [f. SCRUB *sb.*¹ + -ER¹.]

1. *Austral.* and *N.Z.* **a.** A person or animal that lives in the scrub.

1859 H. KINGSLEY *G. Hamlyn* xxix, The captain was getting in the 'scrubbers'—cattle which had been left..to run wild in the mountains. **1869** in *Occas. Papers Univ. Sydney Austral. Lang. Res. Centre* (1980) No. 17. 55 'Were there any scrubbers—croppies—out here thin?'.. 'Four-murra [= very] wicked fellows!' **1890** 'R. BOLDREWOOD' *Col. Reformer* (1891) 411 Don't you stick at home all your life, like a mallee scrubber. **1897** D. MCK. WRIGHT in Chapman & Bennett *Anthol. N.Z. Verse* (1956) 42 New fences climb the warm brown spurs to guard the scrubber ewes. **1966** *Sunday Mail Mag.* (Brisbane) 9 Oct. 4/2 At the start of every cattle movement the 'scrubbers' (delinquent cattle) are noted, and are disciplined fast. **1978** O. WHITE *Silent Reach* v. 54 Scrubber bulls have been turned into stud paddocks.

b. *fig.* An ill-bred or degenerate animal; an ill-favoured, despicable person.

1876 D. KENNEDY *Colonial Travel* xviii. 249 We four adventurers..each..mounted on the shaggiest of small 'scrubbers', with a pannikin and a coil of rope dangling..at his saddle-bow. **1941** BAKER *Dict. Austral. Slang* 64 *Scrubbers*, cattle or horses that have run wild in the scrub and have deteriorated in condition. (2) Any weedy or unpleasant person. **1966** —— *Austral. Lang.* (ed. 2) iii. 66 *Scrubber*, a poor-looking, ill-bred horse. **1966** G. W. TURNER *Eng. Lang. Austral. & N.Z.* iii. 54 *Scrubbers*, 'cattle that have run wild and deteriorated in condition', suggested figurative uses. It may mean *urchin*: I remember as a child hearing the phrase 'dirty little scrubber', and, not knowing the bush sense of the word, thinking it illogical.

c. The grey kangaroo, *Macropus giganteus.*

1968 K. WEATHERLY *Roo Shooter* 137 Scrubber is the name that shooters give to the grey kangaroo. **1977** J. L. HARPER *Population Biol. Plants* xiii. 422 The grey kangaroo or scrubber..and..the red kangaroo..are regarded as pests by some sheep farmers.

2. *slang.* [Perh. properly related to SCRUBBER¹.] A prostitute, a tart (see also quot. 1965); an untidy, slatternly girl or woman.

1959 *Encounter* May 30 'The scrubbers': very young girls who follow jazz bands round the country. **1962** R. COOK *Crust on its Uppers* ii. 29 This aged scrubber, Mrs. Marengo ..she was so old, forty. **1965** G. MELLY *Owning Up* xiv. 172 The word 'scrubber' has cropped up quite frequently in this story, and perhaps the time has come to attempt a precise definition of what it means, or rather meant, for I understand that in the beat world it has become debased and now means a prostitute. In our day this was not the case. A scrubber was a girl who slept with a jazzman but for her own satisfaction as much as his. **1968** J. MITCHELL *Undiscovered Country* I. 134 'She's only a scrubber.' 'A what?' 'It's the new word for "short-term sexual partner".' **1970** G. GREER *Female Eunuch* 264 The most recent case in which contempt for menial labour has devised a new term of abuse for women is the usage of *scrubber* for a girl of easy virtue. **1973** B. MATHER *Snowline* viii. 95 'She looked a scrubber. That means—' 'A mare that runs wild in the scrub country, copulating indiscriminately with stray stallions. Derivation Australian, but also applied to women of similar propensities in other parts of English-speaking world.' **1974** H. J. PARKER *View from Boys* 213 *Scrubber*, used instead of 'tart' which has a non-derogatory meaning. 'A right scrubber' is a girl who's rough-looking, whore-like.

'scrubbery. [f. SCRUB *v.*¹ + -ERY.] Drudgery.

1834 BECKFORD *Italy* I. 31, I escaped the ennui of this endless scrubbery. **1884** MRS. F. MILLER *Ht. Martineau* 108 Brains tell in the mean and dirty scrubbery of life as well as in pleasanter things.

scrubbily ('skrʌbɪlɪ), *adv. rare.* [f. SCRUBBY *a.*¹ + -LY².] In a mean or paltry manner; shabbily.

1891 G. GISSING *New Grub Street* I. vi. 142 'By-the-by, how has *The Study* been in the habit of treating you?' 'Scrubbily.' 'I'll make an opportunity of talking about your books to Fadge.'

scrubbing ('skrʌbɪŋ), *vbl. sb.* [-ING¹.] The action of SCRUB *v.*¹, in various senses.

†**1.** Scratching. *Obs.*

1622 MABBE tr. *Aleman's Guzman d'Alf.* I. 119 The cattell went grazing on the humane Pasture of my miserable corps; I awaked with their nibbling, fell a scrubbing, and [etc.]. **1667** [see SCRATTING *vbl. sb.*, under SCRAT *v.*]

2. a. Rubbing with a hard brush and water; *transf.* rubbing with something bristly.

1681 [see SCRUBBING-BRUSH]. **1693** DRYDEN *Juvenal* VI. (1697) 141 To shun the scrubbing of a bearded Kiss. **1749** BERKELEY *Word to Wise* Wks. III. 445 A little washing, scrubbing, and rubbing, bestowed on their persons and houses.

b. *Surg.* The action of SCRUB *v.*¹ 3 d. Also with *up.*

1898 WHARTON & CURTIS *Pract. of Surg.* viii. 156 This scrubbing should be employed for several minutes; the hands are then rinsed to remove the soap, and are soaked for two minutes in a 1 to 1000 bichloride of mercury solution. **1910** H. A. HAUBOLD *Preparatory & After Treatm. in Operative Cases* vi. 127 The object of the scrubbing is not to destroy the bacteria, but to remove them. **1937** 'J. BELL' *Murder in Hospital* vi. 109 The 'scrubbing up' process occupied about ten minutes. **1969** B. WEIL *Dossier IX* xviii. 142 The space between the sides of the theatre and the walls had been fitted out for scrubbing up with washbasins. **1976** J. ARCHER *Not Penny More, not Penny Less* xii. 140 'Jean-Pierre, you scrub up as instructed.'.. Jean-Pierre appeared from the scrubbing-up room. **1978** ROAF & HOOKINSON *Basic Surg. Care* ix. 141 All preparation must be made beforehand to ensure that it is unnecessary to touch any unsterile surface once scrubbing is complete.

†**3.** A beating, a drubbing. *Obs.*

1813 SIR R. WILSON *Priv. Diary* II. 485 Three thousand French horse..have given Scheubler a severe scrubbing.

4. The action of SCRUB *v.*¹ 5; removal of impurities from a material (usu. a gas or vapour).

1896 B. REDWOOD *Treat. Petroleum* II. 424 The scrubbing process consists in passing the gas through a series of coke towers in which it is exposed to streams of oil and water, the volatile hydrocarbons being removed by the oil, and the ammonia by the water. **1921** W. H. FULWEILER in A. Rogers *Industr. Chem.* (ed. 3) xx. 499 The gas is forced to pass in contact and bubble through the scrubbing liquid by a series of partitions arranged across the flow of gas. **1959** *Engineering* 23 Jan. 99/3, I am insufficiently informed of the details of gas scrubbing practice to say whether the systems at present in use are satisfactory. **1976** *Offshore Engineer* Apr. 61/1 There is continuous scrubbing of the air (many other subs have manual bleed-in and scrubbing) with direct readouts of O^2 and CO^2 levels as well as silica gel drying agents to remove moisture. **1976** *Physics Bull.* Apr. 160/2 A reduction of η to about zero or even slightly negative can be achieved by ion 'scrubbing' of the vacuum chamber surfaces in a high pressure argon glow discharge.

5. = SCRUB *sb.*² 1 b.

1936 *Proc. Inst. Automobile Engineers* XXX. 739 Tyre wear due to lateral reaction, where location is high, offsets that which occurs in independently sprung cars due to 'scrubbing' when cornering. **1959** *Manch. Guardian* 27 July 2/3 Wear is the result of relative movement between tyre and road—'scrubbing' in other words. **1979** *Truck & Bus Transportation* Sept. 72/1 A third axle was placed between the front and rear axles to act as a turning pivot for the whole trailer. The result—no more scrubbing.

6. *Comb.*, as ***scrubbing-board.***

1889 H. S. EDWARDS in *Century* XXXVIII. 84/1 Her great black, muscular arms drooped towards the scrubbing-board that reclined in the tub. **1969** E. H. PINTO *Treen* 155 It is believed that ribbed wooden scrubbing boards..originated in Scandinavia and the manufacture spread to other countries during the 19th century.

†**'scrubbing,** *ppl. a.*¹ *Obs.* [f. SCRUB *v.*² + -ING².] Squalid, beggarly.

1603 DEKKER *Wonderf. Yr.* Dj, Hungry Coffin-sellers, scrubbing Bearers, and nastie Graue-makers. **1622** MASSINGER *Virg. Mart.* III. iii, Nor do I care From what a lauish hand your money flies, So you giue none away, feed beggers... And to the scrubbing poore.

scrubbing, *ppl. a.*² [f. SCRUB *v.*¹ + -ING².] That scrubs (a floor, wood, etc.).

1868 M. H. SMITH *Sunshine & Shadow in N.Y.* 362 The crowd is composed of the millionaire and the hod-carrier.. madame flashing jewels, and the scrubbing-woman who cleans paint and washes linen. **1936** M. DE LA ROCHE *Whiteoak Harvest* xvi. 198 Two scrubbing women were sent to prepare the house for Sarah.

scrubbing-brush ('skrʌbɪŋbrʌʃ). Also 7 scrubing-brush. [f. SCRUBBING *vbl. sb.*] A brush with hard bristles for scrubbing purposes.

1681 GREW *Musæum* II. §i. iv. 204 The outward Skin being taken off, the Fruit looks and feels like a round Scrubing-Brush. **1712** ARBUTHNOT *John Bull* III. i. 7 She never would lay aside the Use of Brooms and scrubbing Brushes. **1893** BARING-GOULD *Cheap Jack Zita* xxxiii, A woman over her soapsuds and scrubbing-brush.

†**'scrubbish,** *a. Obs. rare.* [f. SCRUB *a.* + -ISH¹.] Like a 'scrub', contemptible.

1798 *Sporting Mag.* XI. 43 The Dutch, truckling, scrubbish.

scrubble ('skrʌb(ə)l), *v.* [App. var. SCRABBLE *v.*] = SCRABBLE *v.*

c **1854** MRS. GASKELL *Lett.* (1966) 274 It will..cost *two guineas*,..and so I must scrubble up money for that. **1920** D. H. LAWRENCE *Lost Girl* vi. 105 Country..now scrubbled all over with mining villages. **1927** J. ELDER *Thomasina Toddy* i. 11 The blanket..comes up and scrubbles on your face, all rough and horrid. **1957** H. NICOLSON *Let.* 26 Dec. (1968) 342 They played *God Save the Queen*, and all the old English boys scrubbled up on their crutches.

scrubby ('skrʌbɪ), *a.*¹ [f. SCRUB *sb.*¹ + -Y.]

1. Stunted, under-developed.

1591 HARINGTON *Orl. Fur.* XIII. xxxiv. 98 A short thicke planke stood on a scrubby post That seru'd them for a boord to drinke and eat. **1727** SWIFT *Baucis & Phil.* 177 The other Tree was griev'd, Grew scrubby, dy'd a-top, was stunted. **1794** W. PEARCE *Agric. Berks* 55 Woods... The scrubby stuff is..burnt into charcoal. **1860** WRAXALL *Life in Sea* ii. 30 The ground is..covered with scrubby lichens.

2. Covered with scrub or brushwood. Also, consisting of or in the form of scrub.

1676 PETTY *Polit. Anat. Irel.*, etc. (1691) 115 About two Millions of Rocky, Boggy, and Scrubby Pasture, commonly call'd Unprofitable. **1835** T. BATMAN in *K. Cornwallis's New World* (1859) I. 373 The country, however, proved too scrubby to enable the dogs to have a fair run. **1901** M. FRANKLIN *My Brilliant Career* iii. 14 The school was situated on a wild scrubby hill. **1936** D. MCCOWAN *Animals Canad. Rockies* xvi. 144 It finally reached a haven in the scrubby thicket. **1957** M. SPARK *Comforters* ix. 233 He saw the bits of paper come to rest, some on the scrubby ground, some among the deep marsh weeds. **1971** *Sci. Amer.* Sept. 130/1 It takes less energy to support a pound of biomass in a mature tropical rain forest than it does in the grassy or scrubby forest stages that precede maturity. **1979** D. KYLE *Green River High* vi. 82 We were edging on to scrubby land, patches of low, tangling heather.

3. Insignificant, shabby, paltry, of poor appearance.

1754 J. SACKVILLE *Let.* 4 Sept. in *16th Rep. R. Comm. Hist. Manuscripts: Rep. MSS. Mrs. Stopford-Sackville* I. 40 in *Parl. Papers 1904* (Cd. 1892) 1 He still continues to persecute me, and acts in regard to me in a most scrubby manner. **1782** MISS BURNEY *Cecilia* v. xii, To be treated like a little scrubby apprentice? **1860** MRS. CARLYLE *Lett.* III. 35, I am so sorry to put you off with such a scrubby letter. **1894** MRS. F. ELLIOT *Roman Gossip* i. 22 They were but a very scrubby mixture of the lowest peasants. **1913** [see HONEST *a.* 4 d]. **1967** *Southerly* XXVII. 75 It would work out, as it always did, under a cover of scrubby banality. **1975** *New Yorker* 5 May 18/3 (Advt.), A great deal of talent has been badly used, though James Caan has some good scenes as scrubby, anxious Billy Rose.

scrubby (ˈskrʌbɪ), *a.*^{2} [f. SCRUB *v.*^{1} + -Y.] Rough, bristly.

1856 LEVER *Martins of Cro' M.* xl. 411 'Well, I should like to see her', drawled out Merl, as he smoothed down his scrubby mustachios.

†**ˈscrubly**, *adv. Obs. rare*$^{-1}$. [f. SCRUB *a.* + -LY^2.] Meanly, shabbily.

1732 LD. TYRAWLY in *Buccleuch MSS.* (Hist. MSS. Comm.) I. 383 This room few of my predecessors made use of..; and..such of them as did furnish it, did it very scrubly.

†**ˈscruby**. *north. Obs.* Also 6 scrubby, 6, 9 scrubie, 7 scrobie, scrooby. [Perh. a metathetic alteration of SCORBUTE or its source.] Scurvy. Also 16th c. *scruby ill. Comb.* **scruby-grass**, scurvy-grass.

1551 TURNER *Herbal* I vj, The scuerbuch whyche is called in the North cuntre the scruby ell [**1568** the scrubby ill, or the crepel ill]. **1597** GERARDE *Herbal* II. lxxxii. 325 In English it is called Spoonewort, Scrubie grass, and Scuruie grasse. **1655** LAMONT *Diary* (Maitland Cl.) 87 This year, Mr. Jhone Duncan..died of the Scrobie. **1676** Row *Contn. Blair's Autobiog.* App. (1848) 593 Scruby, gout, and gravel. **1691** RAY *N.C. Words* 61 *Scrooby-grass*.

†**scrud**, *v. Obs. rare*$^{-1}$. [Of obscure origin: cf. SCRUB *v.*] (See quot.)

1483 *Cath. Angl.* 326/1 To Scrud (Scrvde *A*); *ubi* to rub.

scrue, obs. form of SCREW *sb.*^{1} and *v.*

scruff (skrʌf), *sb.*^{1} Forms: 1, 7–9 scruf, 5 scrofe, 6 scruffe, *Sc.* skrufe, skruif(e, skruiff, scruef, 6–8 scroof, 7 scroofe, scrooffe, 7– scruff. [Metathetic var. of SCURF *sb.*^{1}]

†**1. a.** A scabby or scaly condition of the skin; = SCURF *sb.*^{1} 1. *Obs.*

[*c* **1000** *Sax. Leechd.* I. 316 Wið scruf, & wið sceb.] **14..** *Metr. Voc.* in Wr.-Wülcker 626, *Glabra*, scrofe or scalle.

†**b.** A scab. *Obs. rare*$^{-1}$.

1710 *Lond. Gaz.* No. 4716/4 Stoln.., a black Gelding.., with a large Wart or Scruff over his near Eye.

2. = SCURF *sb.*^{1} 2.

1526 *Grete Herball* clx. (1529) K ij b, Agaynst the scruffe of the heed and habundaunce of lyce. **1678** HOBBES *Decam.* x. 124 Jumbling them together make them rub off their scruf from one another. **1843** R. J. GRAVES *Syst. Med.* xxvii. 339 Where there was a copious detachment of scruf.

3. A thin crust or coating. Cf. SCURF *sb.*^{1} 4.

1591 BRUCE *Serm.* T 2 b, The outwarde scroofe, suppose it appeareth to be whole, where the inward is festered, auaileth nothing, bot maketh it to vndercoate again. **1695** *Sc. Acts Will. III* (1822) IX. 452/2 Pulling up..Bent Juniper and broom bushes which did loose and break the surface and scrooffe of the saids hills.

4. a. Applied to what is worthless or contemptible; refuse, litter; †*spec.* base money; also used (like 'dross', 'muck') as a contemptuous term for money.

1559 in Knox *Hist. Ref.* II. Wks. 1846 I. 403 They spair not planelie to brek doun and convert the guid and stark money..into this thair corruptit skruiff and baggage of Hard-heidis and Non Suntis. *c* **1560** A. SCOTT *Poems* (S.T.S.) i. 65 Thai brocht þair bastardis, wᵗ þe skrufe thai skraip To blande þair blude wᵗ barrownis be ambitioun. **1656** BLOUNT *Glossogr.*, *Scruff*, is a kinde of fuel, which poor people..gather up at ebbing water, in the bottom of the Thames about London, and consists of Coal, little sticks of Wood, Cockle-shells, and the like. **1768** *Woman of Honor* II. 103 The..dirty current..carrying away with it the little trifling straw, scruff, and bubbles on its surface.

†**b.** (See quot.) *Obs.*

1673 *Cal. Treas. Bks.* (1909) IV. 404 As to the importation of whale fins, commonly called scruffe, which you conceive ought to pay as whalebone, you are to state a case.

c. A scruffy person, an oaf, a layabout; a contemptible or inferior person, someone of no breeding. Also *collect.*, scum, riff-raff.

1836 W. CARLETON *Traits & Stories of Irish Peasantry* (ed. 4) II. 342 Oh, you scruff of the earth. **1896** G. F. NORTHALL *Warwickshire Word-Book* 203 *Scruff*, a wastrel, raffish rogue. **1905** J. WRIGHT *Eng. Dial. Dict.* V. 290/1 The village is well enough but for the scruff that comes in. **1958** *People* 4 May 12/4 'A nice class of fellow, too,' he said. 'Not one of the scruff.' **1960** D. STOREY *This Sporting Life* I. v. 116 Every scruff in town's crept in. I don't like it. **1968** J. LOCK *Lady Policeman* iii. 22 The 'scruff' might merely be an arty or beat type being deliberately scruffy and the very young face might belong to a grown woman. **1973** 'H. CARMICHAEL' *Too Late for Tears* x. 121 Nature gives some of us the wrong heredity... So you're a scruff and John Piper's a gentleman. **1977** *Listener* 20 Jan. 72/2 Writing books or theatre plays is the only proper pursuit for a literary lady or gent, and..people who write for the new forms are money-grubbing scruffs who have sold their souls to the ghastly mass media.

5. *Comb.*: **scruff-stone**, ? rubble.

1869 BLACKMORE *Lorna D.* ii, Old Cop..had jammed the double gates in under the scruff-stone archway.

scruff (skrʌf), *sb.*^{2} Also *dial.* scruft. [Corrupt form of SCUFF *sb.*^{2}, assimilated to prec.] The nape of the neck.

1790 GROSE *Prov. Gloss.* (ed. 2), *Scruff*, the nape of the neck. North. **1834** MARRYAT *P. Simple* xxix, He would have fallen overboard, if I hadn't caught him by the scruff of the neck. **1892** J. K. JEROME in *Idler* June 498 We adopted a more pressing method, and coaxed the dog out by the scruff of his neck.

transf. **1869** BLACKMORE *Lorna D.* xxix, 'John Fry, you big villain!' I cried, with John hanging up in the air by the scruff of his neck-cloth.

scruff (skrʌf), *v.*^{1} Also 8 scruiff. [f. SCRUFF *sb.*^{1}]

1. a. *trans.* To touch slightly, graze (see Jam. and E.D.D.); also *fig.* to treat superficially, slur *over*. orig. *Sc.* and *north.*

Examples in *Sc.* use with various spellings (as *screef, scrief, scriff*, etc.) may be found in *S.N.D.* s.v. *scruif, n., v.*

1658 [implied in SCRUFFER below]. **1707** *Min. Ayr Presbyt.* (MS.), He doth often change his text, and doth not raise many heads and doth not prosecute such as he names, but scruffs them. **1713** *Humble Plead. Good old-way* 92 Many scandalous practises of Presbyterian ministers in some places, tho flagrant and notour, little heeded, and, when complained of, scruiffed over with private accomodations. **1720** E. ERSKINE *Wks.* (1871) I. 91 Many there are who scruff over the duty in a superficial manner. **1862** *St. Andrews Gaz.* 3 Oct. 3/3 The boy was sleeping on the cart and fell down, and..his head was a little 'scruffed' on the wheel. **1876** C. CLOUGH ROBINSON *Gloss. Dial. Mid-Yorks.* 118/2 One will be told to get a besom and *scruff* the snow off the doorstone. **1896** P. A. GRAHAM *Red Scaur* 347, I felt it scruff his chafts. **1920** C. SANDBURG *Smoke & Steel* 25 Wearing leather shoes scruffed with fire.

b. in *Golf*, to graze (the turf) when striking the ball. Also *absol.* or *intr.*

1857 H. B. FARNIE *Golfer's Man.* (1947) 74 *Scruff*, slightly razing the grass in striking. **1926** *Amer. Speech* I. 633/1 *Scruff*, to graze the grass with the club in striking.

c. in *Painting*, to stroke (oil colour) lightly over a rough surface.

1950 [implied in SCRUFFING *vbl. sb.* below]. **1970** *Oxf. Compan. Art* 1055/1 A scumble must..be applied irregularly—dragged or scruffed—in such a way that small areas of the under colour show through.

2. [As a back-formation from SCRUFFY *a.*] *to* ***scruff oneself up***: to make oneself scruffy.

1970 G. LORD *Marshmallow Pie* ii. 19 Scruff yourself up a bit over the weekend. You know, sweat a bit and that. **1970** *Guardian* 6 Apr. 9/4 The hardest thing..was to make those girls look really scruffy... You don't *look* like a plumber's wife, we kept saying... She didn't scruff herself up enough ..for what the part demanded.

Hence **ˈscruffer**; **ˈscruffing** *vbl. sb.*

1658 in J. Campbell *Balmerino* (1899) 410 Calling him [the minister] a betrayer of sowles, a scruffer of Scriptures. **1950** *Chambers's Encycl.* X. 310/2 The 'scruffing' trick: the brush laden with dry (light) paint is rapidly dragged over a darker tone. **1961** M. LEVY *Studio Dict. of Art Terms* 100 *Scruffing*, an application of paint which skims the surface of a painting area, but does not take in the depressions of the panel or canvas texture.

scruff (skrʌf), *v.*^{2} [f. SCRUFF *sb.*^{2}]

a. *trans.* To seize (a person) by the nape of the neck.

1885 H. FINCH-HATTON *Advance Australia!* 100, I once had a narrow escape of being 'scruffed' by an alligator.

b. To seize and hold (a calf) while it is being branded or castrated. *Austral.*

1881 A. C. GRANT *Bush-Life in Queensland* I. xvi. 228 The smaller calves are scruffed. **1909** *Chambers's Jrnl.* Dec. 810/2 After the calves are separated from their mothers.. the former are one by one 'scruffed'—that is, seized by a couple of men and held down while knife and branding-iron are applied. **1931** F. D. DAVISON *Man-Shy* (1934) v. 71 It was the red heifer's turn... 'Get the ropes. She's too big to scruff,' he said.

c. To push roughly; manhandle. *rare.*

1926 J. BLACK *You can't Win* ix. 121 After they got done scruffing me around, two of them took me by each arm. **1941** BAKER *Dict. Austral. Slang* 64 *Scruff, to*, to attack, manhandle a person.

scruffo (ˈskrʌfəʊ). *slang.* = SCRUFF *sb.*^{1} 4 c.

1959 C. MACINNES *Absolute Beginners* 183 One of the scruffos turned and looked at his choice companions. **1976** *Tel.* (Brisbane) 10 June 40/1 They are not scruffoes, layabouts, or dole cheats.

scruffy (ˈskrʌfɪ), *a.* [f. SCRUFF *sb.*^{1} + -Y.]

a. Scaly, covered with scurf.

1660 HOWELL *Parly of Beasts* 76 The Serpent goes to Fenell when he would..cast off his old scruffy skin to wear a new one. **1841** LEVER *C. O'Malley* xxx, Every man, woman, and child has a brown, scruffy, turf-like face. **1885** *U.S. Cons. Report* No. lviii. 150 (Cent.) The sheep [in South Africa] becomes scruffy and emaciated.

b. Shabby, mean, dirty; slovenly, messy, untidy. Also *Comb.*, as ***scruffy-looking*** adj.

1871 'MARK TWAIN' *Screamers* ii. 16 When he'd got the blues, and feel kind o' scruffy, aggravated, and disgusted.. he would curl up..and go to sleep. **1925** FRASER & GIBBONS *Soldier & Sailor Words* 253 *Scruffy*, dirty: slovenly: untidy in appearance. **1931** *Star* 8 May 6/3 Anyone who has travelled through lottery countries and seen the hundreds of scruffy ticket-shops in the cities. **1935** *Punch* 5 June 656/1 'Mine,' said the scruffy-looking chap who had started by borrowing a match, 'is a tragedy of jealousy.' **1940** BLUNDEN *Poems 1930–40* 204 While I leisured it so, from the verge of the street Those scruffy old weeds in a flash had me beat. **1951** AUDEN *Nones* (1952) 29 A rather scruffy-looking god Descends in a machine. **1958** *Times Lit. Suppl.* 16 May 274/1 Always late, crumpled and scruffy, perpetually in debt, hourly expecting the sack, Greare takes refuge..in Mittyesque fantasies. **1967** A. N. SHERWIN-WHITE *Racial Prejudice in Imperial Rome* I. 4 It is because they..live..in a scruffy fashion, following the impulses and necessities of beasts. **1974** N. FREELING *Dressing of Diamond* 122 His chin was badly shaved: it gave him a dirty look, and sort of scruffy.

Hence **ˈscruffily** *adv.*; **ˈscruffiness**.

1974 *Times* 5 Oct. 13 That general 'scruffiness' could easily be rectified. **1977** *Listener* 4 Aug. 145/2 Making herself look scruffily bizarre is a time-consuming business.

scruge, obs. form of SCOURGE *v.*

†**ˈscruggle**, *v. Obs.*$^{-0}$ [Cf. STRUGGLE, SCRIGGLE *vbs.*] *intr.* To contend, struggle.

1530 PALSGR. 707/2, I scruggell with one to gette from hym, or by cause I wyll nat obey his correction.

scruish, scruitore: see SCREWISH, SCRUTOIRE.

scrum (skrʌm), *sb.* [Abbreviated form of SCRUMMAGE.]

1. = SCRIMMAGE *sb.* 4. Also *ellipt.* for *scrum-half.*

1888 *Pall Mall G.* 22 May 11/2 The Englishmen are particularly weak behind the 'scrum'. **1921** [see FLY *sb.*^{2} 1 e]. **1930** R. CAMPBELL *Poems* 11 See the fat nouns like porky forwards sprawl Into a scrum that never heels the ball. **1978** *Church Times* 23 Mar. 7/3 He pictured that duty as being like a forward's in a rugger scrum; he must put his head down and shove blindly.

Comb. **1896** *Allbutt's Syst. Med.* I. 652 The impetigo or scrum-pox of Rugby football players..seems to be traced to chafing by jerseys infested with pyogenetic cocci.

2. *transf.* A confused, noisy throng (at a social function or the like).

1950 J. CANNAN *Murder Included* ii. 23, I kept wondering where *you* were..in that awful scrum. **1959** P. MOYES *Dead Men don't Ski* I. 11 The handsome, fair-haired young man emerged from the scrum at the bar. **1965** P. O'DONNELL *Modesty Blaise* iii. 32 She looked towards the manœuvring scrum at the bar. **1976** *Eastern Daily Press* (Norwich) 19 Nov. 1/4 Cindy, as the new Miss World likes to be called, was surrounded by the traditional scrum of over 100 press photographers. **1979** *Globe & Mail* (Toronto) 4 May 9/5 But he warned reporters after the second scrum yesterday, 'We're going to have to stop having these impromptu press conferences.'

3. *Comb.*, as **scrum-cap**, a cap worn to protect the head in a scrum; **scrum-half**, the half-back who puts the ball into the scrum; also, by extension, the scrum-half's position in a team.

1917 *Harrods General Catal.* 449/4 *Scrum Caps.* All Crochet Work, 3/3 each; all netting, 2/0 each; and Padded Ear Caps, 2/6. **1933** C. DAY LEWIS *Magnetic Mountain* in *Coll. Poems* (1935) 118 But will it suffice To wear a scrum-cap against falling skies? **1976** *Field* 18 Nov. 986/2 The headgear is authentic—more sensible than the top-hats once worn, less so than the scrum-caps which some favour now. **1906** GALLAGHER & STEAD *Compl. Rugby Footballer* v. 69 Wallace played in every position except that of scrum half. **1922** *Somerset County Herald* 11 Feb. 4/3 As scrum-half [he] manfully overcame his disadvantage in weight. **1951** *Sport* 30 Mar.–5 Apr. 6/3 Another surprise 'cap' is that of Ike Proctor at scrum-half. **1978** *Rugby World* Apr. 3/2 The most exciting confrontation that day will be the scrum-half battle between Gareth Edwards and Jérôme Gallion.

scrum (skrʌm), *v.* [f. the sb.] *intr.* To jostle, crowd.

1925 A. S. M. HUTCHINSON *One Increasing Purpose* I. xxv. 153 The trouble with me is..feeding and frivoling at night and weekends where the masters live and where we scrum at shows. **1938** P. LAWLOR *House of Templemore* ix. 98 Young calves 'scrumming' to dip their heads in the long troughs of milk. **1939** G. GREENE *Confidential Agent* I. i. 3 A rugger team was returning home and they scrummed boisterously for their glasses. **1948** C. DAY LEWIS *Otterbury Incident* iv. 49 Everyone was scrumming around behind him.

scrum (skrʌm), *a.* School and College slang abbrev. of SCRUMPTIOUS *a.* ? *Obs.*

1895 W. C. GORE in *Inlander* Nov. 65 *Scrum*, prob. from scrumptious, with which it is synonymous. **1913** J. VAIZEY *College Girl* xviii. 250 'Good cakes?' 'Scrum!'

scrumble (ˈskrʌmb(ə)l), *v.*^{1} *rare.* [Perh. a blend of SCRAPE *v.* or SCRATCH *v.* + CRUMBLE *v.*] *trans.* To scrape or scratch *out of* or *from* (something).

The two examples perhaps represent independent nonce-formations.

1906 W. B. YEATS *King's Threshold* in *Poems, 1899–1905* 223 I'll scrumble the ermine out of his skin! **1975** P. LIVELY *Going Back* iv. 43 We scrumble the soft innards from the loaf and hold it high above us and now it snows bread upon the snow.

scrumble (ˈskrʌmb(ə)l), *v.*^{2} [App. alteration of SCUMBLE *v.*] *trans.* To produce a smeary or grainy effect on (paint). Hence **ˈscrumbled** *ppl. a.*

1921 *Spectator* 9 Apr. 454/2 The paint has been scrumbled, i.e. if you look into it, it does not present a flat surface, it shows variations something like the grain of wood. **1937** *Sunday Times* 17 Jan. 30/3 Dining room designed in the Tudor style with scrumbled walls and beamed ceilings. **1959** *Spectator* 8 May 652/2 In his later large decorations..the light colours, the scrumbled paint and the botanist's eye meet in something very far from mythology on one hand, and neurosis on the other.

scrummage, variant of SCRIMMAGE *sb.*

scrummy ('skrʌmɪ), *a. colloq.* [f. SCRUM(PTIOUS *a.* + -Y[1].] Excellent, fine, 'smashing'; enjoyable, delicious.

1915 MRS. H. WARD *Eltham House* i. 14 You've got to change and rest..before dinner!.. You've got to put on a scrummy frock too! **1918** GALSWORTHY *Five Tales* 122 He's promised to take mother and me to the theatre and supper afterwards. Won't it be scrummy! **1923** 'R. CROMPTON' *William Again* viii. 147 The cakes had been scrummy. **1928** —— *William—the Good* viii. 220 'Does it [*sc.* the trap-door] go out on to the roof?' called the Outlaws... 'Yes, it does. It's scrummy. Right on the edge of the roof.' **1960** *News Chron.* 8 July 8/5 Out spring the five white tubers of a corpse's hand. Scrummy! **1977** *Harper's & Queen* Nov. 52/2 Scrummy French food in cosy surroundings.

scrump (skrʌmp), *sb. dial.* [Cf. SCRIMP *a.* and *v.*] Anything withered or dried up. *spec.*, a withered or stunted apple.

1840 LADY C. BURY *Hist. Flirt* xxiii, You two old scrumps, suppose you sit an hour in the pump-room. *a* **1887** JEFFERIES *Field & Hedgerow* (1892) 193 A mouse is baked in the oven to a 'scrump', then pounded to powder. **1887** PARISH & SHAW *Dict. Kentish Dial.* 138 *Scrump*, a stunted, badly-grown apple. **1896** G. F. NORTHALL *Warwickshire Word-Bk.* 203 *Scrumps*, sb. pl. Apples.

scrump (skrʌmp), *v. dial.* or *slang.* [f. the sb.] *trans.* To steal (apples), esp. from orchards. Also *transf.* and *absol.*

1866 R. HALLAM *Wadsley Jack* iv. 17 Dick Greasy..ax'd me if I'd mak' one to goa a scrumpim', that is, fetchin' apples off sumboddy's trees. **1931** 'G. ORWELL' *Hop-Picking* in *Coll. Essays* (1968) I. 71 *Scrump, to*, to steal. **1945** B. NAUGHTON in C. Madge *Pilot Papers* I. 101 They'd come scrumping..in Woolworths, or over at the market, or from the street stalls. **1951** A. BARON *Rosie Hogarth* III. i. 137 Scrumping apples, remember?.. God didn't put 'em on that tree for Mr. Moggeridge. **1966** M. TORRIE *Heavy as Lead* xiv. 169 His lordship was going scrumping... You know. Kids scrump apples, Sir G. scrumped rock garden plants. **1972** K. BONFIGLIOLI *Don't point that Thing at Me* i. 3 English policemen..dare not even spank the bottoms of little boys caught scrumping apples nowadays.

Hence **scrumped** *ppl. a.*; **'scrumper**, one who scrumps; **'scrumping** *vbl. sb.*

1946 *Scrutiny* XIII. 293 There is to be, after all, no development in Fant's moral powers: only, as it were, a schoolboy scrumping of all the redeeming fruits of experience. **1957** *Times* 20 Aug. 5/1 Scrumping is an offence which perhaps no one in this court-room has not committed. **1969** M. WIGGIN *Cottage Idyll* ii. 26 One scoundrel sent me a..message to the effect that he would like his cherished scrumping stick back. **1973** D. ORGILL *Jasius Pursuit* i. 9 If the police had to jail every hippy fruit-scrumper, the prisons would soon be overcrowded. **1976** A. HILL *Summer's End* vii. 98 Scrumped apples always taste better than bought ones. **1981** *Daily Tel.* 3 Mar. 3/1 (*heading*) Rector used stick on girl scrumper.

†**'scrumple**, *sb. Obs. rare*[−1]. [var. form of CRUMPLE; see SCR- 2.] A wrinkle, crease.

1508 DUNBAR *Flyting* 122 Fy! skolderit skyn, thow art bot skyre and skrumple.

'scrumple, *v.* [f. the sb.] *trans.* To crush, fold, wrinkle. Also freq. with *up*.

c **1575** *Balfour's Practicks* (1754) 188 Ane chartour, sasine, or uther evident, being be chance brint, singit be the fire, scrumpillit, or the seil thairof meltit and brokin. **1894** MOSS *Cheadle* 172 Her rough hair was scrumpled into a chenille net. **1939** A. RANSOME *Secret Water* xxii. 261 She jumped up, grabbed the message, scrumpled it up and poked it into the stove. **1954** M. PROCTER *Hell is a City* I. ii. 23 It [*sc.* money in notes] came out of my bag all scrumpled up anyhow, just as I'd stuffed it in. **1961** R. M. DASHWOOD *Provincial Daughter* 83, I discover shirt scrumpled up in polythene bag at bottom of wardrobe. **1971** G. EWART *Gavin Ewart Show* I. 25 His secretary has a habit of scrumpling the top copies.

Hence **'scrumpled** *ppl. a.*

1813 E. WEETON *Jrnl.* Dec. (1969) II. 115 She thrust something into my hand... It felt like a small parcel of scrumpled paper. **1902** *Longman's Mag.* Sept. 441 A scrumpled face. **1947** A. RANSOME *Great Northern?* xvii. 210 He pulled the scrumpled up paper out of his knapsack and spread it out again.

scrumptious ('skrʌmpʃəs), *a. colloq.* or *vulgar.* [Prob. identical with the dial. *scrumptious* 'mean, stingy, close-fisted', related to *scrimption* small quantity, f. SCRIMP *v.* The transition to sense 1 below is not impossible; for the development of sense 2 cf. NICE *a.*]

1. Fastidious, hard to please. ? *U.S.* only.

1845 JUDD *Margaret* II. vii. (1874) 291, I don't mean to be scrumptious about it, Judge; but I do want to be a man, if I ..haven't so much eddication as the rest.

2. a. *U.S.* Stylish, handsome. **b.** Used as a vague epithet of enthusiastic praise: First rate, 'glorious'. Now esp. of food: delicious. So **'scrumptiousness**, the state or condition of being scrumptious.

1836 HALIBURTON *Clockm.* Ser. I. xxiii, A little tidy scrumptious looking slay. **1865** MEREDITH *R. Fleming* xxxi, Hang me, if ever I see such a scrumptious lot. **1881** *Punch* 30 July 47/2 There is a certain exquisite scrumptiousness and goloptiousness about Real Turtle. **1894** SOMERVILLE & 'ROSS' *Real Charlotte* II. xxxii. 247 The cake was scrumptious. **1901** F. HUME *Golden Wang-ho* iv, 'I shan't show it [the picture] to anyone til it's done..; then you'll say it is scrumptious'. **1922** JOYCE *Ulysses* 740 You will always think of the lovely teas we had together scrumptious currant scones and raspberry wafers I adore. **1930** *Magnet* 25 Jan. 6/2 'It's lovely butterscotch—scrumptious!' **1976** A. L. ROWSE *Cornishman Abroad* 14 The scrumptious meal she cooked, Cornish duck and Californian avocado stuffed with shrimp, our own cream from the farm with the delicious sweet.

scrumptiously ('skrʌmpʃəslɪ), *adv.* [-LY[2].] In a scrumptious manner, excellently, deliciously.

1844 A. S. STEPHENS *High Life in N.Y.* I. xvi. 237 The frocks answered just as well to make bonnets out on, arter she'd dashed out in 'em once or twice, and the sleeves and waist cut up scrumptiously for ruffles and furbelows. **1927** *Observer* 1 May 8 He shows us 'Life' and 'High Life' simultaneously, so scrumptiously and yet with O such a touch of wanton wistful weariness! **1976** *New Yorker* 17 May 167/1 It is all scrumptiously pretty.

scrumpy ('skrʌmpɪ). *dial.* or *colloq.* [f. SCRUMP *sb.* + -Y[6].] Rough cider, made from small or unselected apples. Also *attrib.* in ***scrumpy cider***.

1904 in *Eng. Dial. Dict.* s.v., These apples are of no good but to make scrumpy of. **1932** [see NOBBLE *v.* 3]. **1962** G. COMPTON *Too Many Murderers* xii. 87 Scrumpy was only eightpence a pint. **1973** C. BONINGTON *Next Horizon* viii. 114 A brisk five-minute walk took you to the Coronation Tap, where you could down a pint of scrumpy cider and eat home-made pies. **1977** *Times Lit. Suppl.* 4 Mar. 242/4 Another [pub] sold evil-smelling 'scrumpy', producing its own extensive Saturday-night network of vomit.

scrunch (skrʌntʃ), *sb.* [f. SCRUNCH *v.*]

1. The noise made by scrunching.

1857 DUFFERIN *Lett. High Lat.* 219 Leaning forward in expectation of the *scrunch* I knew must come. **1892** 'VERNON LEE' in *Contemp. Rev.* May 670 Its snow was becoming less crisp (before you might have almost heard its scrunch).

2. An act of scrunching.

1854 THACKERAY *Newcomes* I. 297, I brought my heel well down on his little varnished toe and gave it a scrunch.

scrunch (skrʌntʃ), *v.* [Cf. CRUNCH *v.* and SCR- 2.]

1. *trans.* To bite with a crushing noise, = CRUNCH *v.* 1.

1825 JENNINGS *Obs. Dial W. Eng.* 66 A person may be said to scrunch an apple or a biscuit, if in eating it he made a noise. **1838** SOUTHEY *Doctor* cxliv. (1848) 366 This horse would eat oysters with great delight, scrunching them shells and all between his teeth.

2. a. To crush, tread crushingly upon; also, to squeeze into small compass; = CRUNCH *v.* 2.

1861 SALA *Dutch Pictures* viii. 111 An old lady..scrunches the boots of her opposite neighbours. **1880** *Print. Trades Jrnl.* xxx. 33 Paper as everyone knows, burns well when scrunched up. **1895** SYMONDS in *Life* I. iii. 71, I scrunched the muddy gravel, beneath the boughs of budding trees.

b. *refl.* To squeeze oneself into compact shape. Cf. SCRINCH, SCRINGE *vbs.*

1844 KINGLAKE *Eöthen* (1845) 265 Now belaying, and now letting go—now scrunching himself down into mere ballast. **1851** MAYHEW *Lond. Labour* II. 566/1 The first night I slept out..I..scruntched [*sic*] myself into a doorway, and the policeman passed by..without seeing me.

c. *U.S. intr.* for *refl.* To squeeze oneself into a compact shape; to huddle *up*, *together*; to cower or crouch *down*.

1884 'MARK TWAIN' *Huck. Finn* i. 4 Miss Watson would say,..'Dont scrunch up like that, Huckleberry—set [*sic*] up straight.' **1939** J. STEINBECK *Grapes of Wrath* ii. 11 'Scrunch down on the running board till we get around the bend,' he said. **1951** T. CAPOTE *Grass Harp* ii. 63 We scrunched together to make a place for Riley. **1972** D. DELMAN *Sudden Death* ii. 48 Wally knew something bad was about to happen to him; you could tell from the way he scrunched up, as a man will, sometimes, when a punch is telegraphed. **1974** K. MILLETT *Flying* (1975) IV. 394 In the North Terminal I scrunch into a bench and wait for Nell. **1978** J. IRVING *World according to Garp* xv. 311 He let her lean against him, though she was slightly taller..and in order to rest her head against him, she had to scrunch down.

3. *intr.* To produce a sound of being crushed.

1844 W. BARNES *Dorset Poems, Lydlinch Bells* 6 When vrozen grass, as white's a sheet, Did scrunchy sharp below our veet. **1851** MAYHEW *Lond. Labour* I. 403/1, I could hear the stones scrunch under his feet.

Hence **'scrunching** *vbl. sb.* and *ppl. adj.*

1869 S. R. HOLE *Bk. about Roses* 263 That yellow-bellied abomination, the grub which produces the saw-fly, in this month attacks the Rose... The process of 'scrunching' is disagreeable, but it *must* be done. **1897** MARY KINGSLEY *W. Africa* 189 But after some alarming scrunching sounds, and creaks from the canoe, we were shot ignominiously out down river. **1927** A. CLARKE *Son of Learning* I. 9 The sloppiness of custard, the sourness of green apple, With crunching, munching, scrunching.

scrunch, var. SCRONCH.

scrunched, *ppl. a.* (and *pa. pple.*) [f. SCRUNCH *v.*]

a. Crushed, crunched, squeezed, squashed. Also freq. with *up*.

1835-7 DICKENS *Sk. Boz, Last Cab-driver*, He had compromised with the parents of three scrunched children, and just 'worked out' his fine for knocking down an old lady. **1910** C. E. MONTAGUE *Hind let Loose* xi. 219 Some ebb.. would leave..the foreshore only littered with..tobacco-ashes, used matches, scrunched-up envelopes. **1963** C. D. SIMAK *They walked like Men* iii. 13 Balls of scrunched-up copy paper tossed onto the floor. **1974** T. P. WHITNEY tr. *Solzhenitsyn's Gulag Archipelago* I. II. i. 504 All that was left in that scrunched-up wad the engine room of the law had spewed out into the prisoner transport was a greed for life, and no understanding whatever.

b. Hunched, huddled, cowering. Usu. with *up*; occas. with *back*, *down*, etc. Chiefly *U.S.*

a **1902** S. BUTLER *Way of All Flesh* (1903) lv. 253 He looks that worrited and scrunched up at times. **1905** *N.Y. Sunday World* 11 June (Mag. Section) 8/2 You sit there with your shoulders scrunched up, giving an imitation of Reginald Vanderbilt driving his coach. **1931** *Virginia* (Louisiana) *Q. Rev.* Jan. 106 The twins lay upon the spare bed... 'Look at dis'n all scrunched up.' **1962** W. FAULKNER *Reivers* vii. 158 Otis was scrunched back against the wall. **1966** N. S. HAYNER *New Patterns in Old Mexico* ix. 167 One of the men approached the padre with his back scrunched up. **1976** *National Observer* (U.S.) 12 June 22/3 The wolves stayed where they were, scrunched motionless against the far wall. **1977** *Rolling Stone* 7 Apr. 58/1 That night Carl Sagan and I sat scrunched down in a sofa in his Pasadena apartment.

scrunchy ('skrʌntʃɪ), *a.* [f. SCRUNCH *v.* + -Y[1].] That scrunches; that emits a crisp, crunching sound when crushed.

? **1905** *Eng. Dial. Dict.* Suppl. 168/2 *Scrunchy*, of frozen grass: emitting a crisp, crunching sound when trodden on. **1907** W. DE MORGAN *Alice-for-Short* xxvi. 274 Of course you may have scrunchy toast if you like. **1927** *Daily Express* 6 Dec. 11 The delicious, scrunchy crispness of 'Ovaltine' Rusks. **1937** *John o' London's Weekly* 29 Jan. 722/2 The minor roads are paved with scrunchy white shells. **1974** *Country Life* 13 June 1580/3 The vegetable..runs to flower without first making the desired, juicy, yummy, scrunchy, foliage.

scrunt (skrʌnt). *Sc.* Anything stunted or worn out, esp. the stump of a tree.

1535 STEWART *Cron. Scot.* (Rolls) III. 115 And no redres that ȝe will mak thairfoir, Nocht worth ane scrunt of all that to restoir. **1894** CROCKETT *Raiders* vii. 75 In the midst of the bit scrunts of birks and..thorns.

scrunty ('skrʌntɪ), *a.* orig. *Sc.* and *north. dial.* [f. SCRUNT.] Stunted, shrivelled, stumpy.

1811 A. SCOTT *Poems* 59 [A bird] wha, on his native scrunty thorn, 'Mang birds o' song bude hail the morn. **1849** in C. Brontë *Shirley* vii. 148 Then whudder awa' thou bitter biting blast, And sough through the scrunty tree. **1868** W. SHELLEY *Wayside Flowers* 55 He'd been sae scrimpit o' his corn His scrunty banes stood brent in sight. **1947** A. MCCORMICK *Galloway* 219 The scrunty aul' buddy has nae smeff. **1951** AUDEN *Nones* (1952) 54 A scrunty beggar With one glass eye and one hickory leg. **1963** S. PLATH *Bell Jar* i. 10 A short, scrunty fellow detached himself and came into the bar with us.

scrupilous(e, obs. forms of SCRUPULOUS.

scruple ('skruːp(ə)l), *sb.*[1] Also 6–7 scrupul, 6–8 scrupule; and see SCRIPLE, SCRIPTULE. [ad. L. *scrūpulus*, more freq. *scrūpulum* (also *scrīpulum*, *scrīplum*, *scrīptulum*, *scrīptlum*, whence SCRIPLE, SCRIPTULE), commonly regarded as identical with *scrūpulus* SCRUPLE *sb.*[2], the sense 'small weight or measure' being supposed to be developed from the etymological sense 'small pebble'.

The assumed sense-development presents no difficulty, but the relation between the forms with *ū* and those with *ī* has not been satisfactorily explained, and some scholars dispute the identity of the word.

Cf. F. *scrupule* (15th c.), Sp. *escrúpulo*, Pg. *escrupolo*, It. *scrupolo, scrittolo* (:—L. *scriptulum*), G. *skrupel*.]

A small unit of weight or measurement.

1. A unit of weight = 20 grains, $\frac{1}{3}$ drachm, $\frac{1}{24}$ oz. Apothecaries' weight. Denoted by the character ℈.

[1382-: see SCRIPLE.] **1564-78** BULLEYN *Dial. agst. Pest.* (1888) 42 Take Theriaca..ij Scruples..; bole Amoniacke, prepared, half a Scruple. **1590** BARROUGH *Physick* (1596) A viij b, A Scruple is twentie barley cornes. **1632** MASSINGER *Emperor East* IV. iv, With some few scruples of sassa-fras and Guacum. **1710** P. BLAIR *Misc. Observ.* (1718) 63 It weighed betwixt a Scruple and half a Dram. **1843** T. WATSON *Lect. Physic* I. xxxix. 700 It consists of the iodide of mercury, mixed with lard, in the proportion of two scruples to the ounce.

attrib. **1879** *St. George's Hosp. Rep.* IX. 647 He was ordered scruple doses of salicylate of ammonia.

¶**b.** Alleged values of doubtful authority.

1656 BLOUNT *Glossogr.*, *Scruple* (*scriptulum*), is of Troy weight seven grains and an half. **1688** HOLME *Armoury* III. 339/1 A scruple is 14 graines. **1728** CHAMBERS *Cycl.* s.v., Among Goldsmiths, the Scruple is 24 Grains.

2. One-sixtieth of a degree; a minute of arc.

first, second, third scruple, the first, second, third power of one-sixtieth. Cf. MINUTE *sb.*[1], etymological note.

1610 HOLLAND *Camden's Brit.* I. 205 The latitude fiftie degrees, and fortie scruples or minutes. *Ibid.* 474 Two and fiftie degrees and fortie scrupuls from the Aequator. **1655** FULLER *Hist. Camb.* 16 Northampton lying within twenty nine scruples of the same degree of longitude with Oxford. **1709-29** V. MANDEY *Syst. Math., Arith.* 75 A Degree is subdivided into Minutes, or First Scruples, 60′. A First Scruple, into Seconds, 60″. Seconds, into Thirds, and so on.

†**b.** *Astr.* in special collocations (see quots.).

In some Dicts. *scruple* is said to be synonymous with DIGIT 4, but this seems to be an erroneous inference from statements like that in quot. 1728.

1633 H. GELLIBRAND *App. Longitude* in T. James *Voy.* R2, The middle motion of the ⊙ Center... The Prosthaphæresis of the Center add... The Proportional Scruples.—l. **1658** GADBURY *Doctr. Nativities* II. 229 Then ..take out the Scruples of proportion, and reserve them until anon. **1728** CHAMBERS *Cycl.* s.v., Scruples eclipsed are that Part of the Moon's Diameter which enters the Shadow, expressed in the same Measure wherein the apparent

Diameter of the Moon is expressed. See *Digit. Ibid.*, *Scruples* of Immersion, or Incidence, are an Arch of the Moon's Orbit, which her Centre describes from the Beginning of the Eclipse, to the Time when its Centre falls into the Shadow... *Scruples* of Emersion, are an Arch of the Moon's Orbit, which her Centre describes in the Time from the first Emersion of the Moon's Limb, to the End of the Eclipse.

†3. As a unit of time. **a.** ***scruple of an hour***: the sixtieth part of an hour, a minute: more fully ***first scruple***, the successive smaller fractions of the sexagesimal scale being called ***second scruple*** (= our 'second'), ***third, fourth, fifth,*** etc. ***scruple***. **b.** Similarly, the day of 24 hours was divided sexagesimally into ***first, second,*** etc. ***scruples***, the 'first scruple' being = 24 minutes. **c.** In Rabbinical chronology, the 1080th part of an hour, equal to 1-18th of a minute (= late Heb. *ḥeleq*; the attribution of this measure to the Arabs is a mistake). *Obs.*

a. **1603** HEYDON *Def. Judic. Astrol.* iv. 143, I haue a plumbe watche..and this, with one motion giueth me so perfectly, both the minute and second scruple of time, that hauing obserued [etc.]. **1631** QUARLES *Samson* Med. xxi. 128 How can it be expected, we have power To hold out Seige, one scruple of an hower. **1640–72** WILKINS *Disc. New Planet* II. (1684) 124 If a Man, leaping up in a Ship, may abide in the Air one second scruple of an hour. *c* **1653** T. WHALLEY in *Ussher's Lett.* (1686) 603 [A computation expressed in sexagesimals of an hour is referred to as being] in hourly scruples.

b. **1709–29** V. MANDEY *Syst. Math., Arith.* 77 Astronomically, a Day is divided as an Integer, into first Scruples 60′. A Prime or first Scruple into 60″, and so on.

c. **1728** CHAMBERS *Cycl.* s.v., The Chaldee Scrupule is 1/1080 Part of an Hour; called, by the Hebrews, Helakim. These Scruples are much used by the Jews, Arabs, and other Eastern People. **1788** MARSDEN in *Phil. Trans.* LXXVIII. 419 The lunar month..according to the computation of the Arabian Astronomers, consists of 29 days, 12 hours, and 792 scruples or parts in 1080.

†4. A Roman land-measure of ten feet square, being the 24th part of an *uncia* and 288th of a *jugerum*. *Obs.*

1674 JEAKE *Arith.* (1696) 114 A Scruple of an Arpent is 1/48 of an Arpent or 10 Feet Square every way.

5. One-twelfth of an inch; a line. Also, one-tenth of a geometrical inch. (*Cent. Dict.*)

1802 H. MARTIN *Helen of Glenross* III, This to me, who never leave one scruple of an inch of my paper unadorned by my literary genius.

6. *fig.* A very small quantity or amount; a very small part or portion.

1574 HELLOWES *Gueuara's Fam. Ep.* (1577) 77 There is no loue in this worlde so perfecte, as that whiche holdeth no scruple of interest. **1603** SHAKS. *Meas. for M.* I. i. 38 Nature neuer lends The smallest scruple of her excellence But [etc.]. **1644** MILTON *Areop.* (Arb.) 54 Look into Italy and Spain, whether those places be one scruple the better. *a* **1680** BUTLER *Rem.* (1759) I. 111 Each Word and Syllable brought to the Scale, And valu'd to a Scruple in the Sale. **1830** GALT *Lawrie T.* II. i, In the choice of a second wife, one scruple of prudence is worth a pound of passion.

scruple ('skru:p(ə)l), *sb.*[2] Also 6 scrupule, (scrupple, scropple). [ad. F. *scrupule* (14th c.), ad. L. *scrūpulus*, lit. a pebble (recorded only in late L.), fig. a cause of uneasiness, scruple, dim. of *scrūpus* rough or hard pebble, used fig. by Cicero for a cause of uneasiness or anxiety.

Cf. F. *scrupule* (14th c.), Sp. *escrúpulo*, Pg. *escrupulo*, It. *scrupolo*, G. *skrupel*.]

1. A thought or circumstance that troubles the mind or conscience; a doubt, uncertainty or hesitation in regard to right and wrong, duty, propriety, etc.; esp. one which is regarded as over-refined or over-nice, or which causes a person to hesitate where others would be bolder to act. Often, ***scruple of conscience***.

1526 *Pilgr. Perf.* (W. de W. 1531) 63 b, He wyll..lette the ..symple persone from the performynge of his dutyes.., by the reason of..feares and scruples. *c* **1534** MORE *Wks.* 1435/1 Though men..say it is no consience but a foolish scruple. *a* **1548** HALL *Chron., Hen. VIII* 179 The kyng of England..was in a great scruple of his conscience and not quiet in his mynde. **1602** SHAKS. *Ham.* IV. iv. 40 (2nd Qo.) Some crauen scruple Of thinking too precisely on th'euent. **1660** JER. TAYLOR *Duct. Dubit.* I. vi. Rule 1, A Scruple is a great trouble of mind proceeding from a little motive. **1692** R. L'ESTRANGE *Fables* xli. 43 Upon the nicest Scruples of Honour. **1759** FRANKLIN *Ess.* Wks. 1840 III. 389 The assembly did not, however, start any scruple on this head. **1788** GIBBON *Decl. & F.* xlix. V. 90 The scruples of reason, or piety, were silenced by the strong evidence of visions and miracles. **1854** FABER *Growth in Holiness* xvii. (1872) 317 A scruple is..a vain fear of sin where there is no reasonable ground for suspecting sin. **1868** E. EDWARDS *Ralegh* I. ii. 34 They had to deal with enemies who were troubled with few scruples.

b. in generalized sense. (Sometimes = scrupulosity.)

1547–8 *Ordre of Commvnion* 7 To the satisfaccion of his mynde, and auoydyng of all scruple and doubtfulnes. **1660** JER. TAYLOR *Duct. Dubit.* I. vi. Rule 2 §1 This is a right course in the matter of scruple; *proceed to action*. **1689** EVELYN *Diary* 21 Feb., The Abp. of Canterbury and some of the rest, on scruple of conscience..enter'd their Protests and hung off. **1788** GIBBON *Decl. & F.* xlix. V. 90 At first, the experiment was made with caution and scruple. **1848** BARONESS BUNSEN in Hare *Life* (1879) II. iii. 114 He expresses much concern and scruple about the trouble he occasions. **1872** BLACKMORE *Maid of Sker* vi, Just as I had made up my mind to lift up the latch, and to walk in freely, as I would have done in most other houses, but stood on scruple with Evan Thomas.

c. Phr. ***without scruple***.

1526 TINDALE *Acts* x. 29 Therfore cam I unto you with outen scruple [*orig.* ἀναντιρρήτως]. **1598** SHAKS. *Merry W.* v. v. 157. **1788** GIBBON *Decl. & F.* xlix. V. 98 The Jewish king, who had broken without scruple the brazen serpent. **1849** MACAULAY *Hist. Eng.* ii. I. 186 Attacked by the civil power, they without scruple repelled force by force.

d. Phr. ***to have scruples***; ***to have little, no scruple***, etc. Const. *about* (a matter), *in* (doing something).

1719 DE FOE *Crusoe* I. 340, I had some little Scruple in my Mind about Religion, which insensibly drew me back. **1736** *Gentl. Mag.* VI. 709/2 That the Quakers can have no Scruple of Conscience in paying Tythes. **1828** MACAULAY *Ess., Hallam's Const. Hist.* (1897) 80 A man without truth or humanity may have some strange scruples about a trifle. **1850** J. W. CROKER in *C. Papers* 14 June (1884) I. i. 18 If you have the slightest [objection], pray have no scruple in leaving my curiosity ungratified. **1865** KINGSLEY *Herew.* viii, [They] had little scruple in applying to a witch.

e. ***to make scruple*** (also ***a, no,*** etc. ***scruple***): to entertain or raise a scruple or doubt; to hesitate, be reluctant, esp. on conscientious grounds. Const. infin.; also with *of* (*at, in*) = to stick at, hesitate to do or allow, etc. ? *Obs.* (Cf. F. *faire scrupule*, with similar constructions.)

1589 NASHE *Pasquill & Marf.* B j, They presume to make a shrewde scruple of their obedience. **1591** SAVILE *Tacitus, Hist.* I. lxxxix. 51 Making a scruple that the holy shields called Ancilia were as yet not layed up againe. **1603** B. JONSON *Sejanus* IV. v. (1605) I 4 b, *Lac.* But is that true, it 'tis prohibited To sacrifice vnto him? *Ter.* Some such thing Cæsar makes scruple of, but forbids it not. **1605** BACON *Adv. Learn.* II. xxiii. §36 Cæsar..made no scruple to professe that hee had rather bee first in a village, then second at Rome. **1639** N. N. tr. *Du Bosq's Compl. Woman* I. 57 The superstitious make more scruple of a little sinne then of a great. **1669–70** MARVELL *Corr.* cxxxii. Wks. (Grosart) II. 298 One of those who thinke it the greatest point of wisdome to make the most scruples. **1722** DE FOE *Moll Flanders* (1840) 210, I made no scruple at taking these goods. **1845** FORD *Handbk. Spain* I. 14 Small scruple is made by the authorities in opening private letters.

†2. A doubt or uncertainty as to a matter of fact or allegation; an intellectual difficulty, perplexity, or objection. ***beyond a scruple***, beyond doubt or cavil. *Obs.*

The phrase 'scruple of suspition' (quot. 1534) perh. contains an etymologizing reference to SCRUPLE *sb.*[1] 6. Cf. 'un seul scrupule de doubte', 16th c. in Littré.

1534 MORE in Ellis *Orig. Lett.* Ser. I. II. 49 In eny parte of all which my dealing, whither eny other man may peradventure put eny dowt, or move eny scruple of suspition. **1568** GRAFTON *Chron.* II. 644 For auoyding of which scruple and ambiguity: Edmund Erle of Marche.. made his tytle and righteous clayme. **1597** MORLEY *Introd. Mus.* 16 In the Table there is no difficultie..yet, to take away all scruple, I will shew you the vse of it. **1662** STILLINGFL. *Orig. Sacræ* I. v. §2 The only scruple is whether it was used in their sacred accounts or no. *a* **1718** PENN *Innocency with open Face* Wks. 1726 I. 267, I hope my Innocency will appear beyond a Scruple. **1725** DE FOE *Voy. round World* (1840) 22 Our captain..raised several scruples about the latitude which we should keep in such a voyage. **1741** HARRIS *Three Treat.* III. I. (1765) 140 A Subject, where one's own Interest appeared concerned so nearly would well justify every Scruple, and even the severest Inquiry.

†b. Disbelief or doubt *of*. ***to have*** or ***make scruple of***: to hesitate to believe or admit. Also rarely with *how* and clause. *Obs.*

1597 SHAKS. *2 Hen. IV*, I. ii. 149 But how I should bee your Patient, to follow your prescriptions, the wise may make some dram of a scruple, or indeede, a scruple it selfe. **1611** —— *Cymb.* v. v. 182 Whereat, I wretch Made scruple of his praise. *a* **1628** PRESTON *New Covt.* (1634) 116 When there is no scruple in our hearts of Gods love towards us. **1662** EVELYN *Chalcogr.* 12 That Letters, and consequently Sculpture, was long before the Flood, we make no scruple of. **1666–7** MARVELL *Corr.* lxix. Wks. (Grosart) II. 210 If you find any thing perplext in it, I shall..resolve any scruple that you may have of its exposition. **1672** VILLIERS (Dk. Buckhm.) *Rehearsal* I. (Arb.) 33 If you make the least scruple of the efficacie of these my Rules, do but come to the Play-house, and you shall judge of 'em by the effects.

†c. ***without scruple***: without doubt or question, doubtless. (Used to qualify an assertion.) *Obs.*

1612 SELDEN *Illustr. Drayton's Poly-olb.* xi. 189 As is, without scruple, apparant in the date of the synod. **1690** CHILD *Disc. Trade* (1698) 49 The same house to be sold.. would have yielded without scruple 1000 or 1200 l.

¶d. A suspicion *of* (something). *rare*[−1].

1597 SIR R. CECIL in Ellis *Orig. Lett.* Ser. I. III. 42 Wherein that you may see the poore unfortunate Secretarie will leave no scruple in you of lack of industry, to yeald you all satisfaction..I have thought good to [etc.].

†e. A quibble, fine distinction. *Obs.*

1709 FELTON *Diss. Classics* (1718) 43 If there is any Thing else Commentators concern themselves about, it is Property of Expression, or rather some Verbal Niceties, and Grammatical Scruples.

3. *Comb.*, as †***scruple-drawer*** (applied to a confessor), ***-monger***; ***scruple-selling*** ppl. a.

a **1704** T. BROWN *Laconics* Wks. 1711 IV. 19 The late Ordinary of Newgate, Mr. Smith, who was one of the most famous *Scruple-drawers of his Time. **1675** WALTON *Hooker* in Wordsw. *Eccl. Biog.* (1818) IV. 223 There were also many of these *Scruplemongers that pretended a tenderness of conscience, refusing to take an oath before a lawful magistrate. *a* **1704** T. BROWN *Reas. Oaths* Wks. 1711 IV. 91 b, Printed by one of those Godly Wholesale Dealers in Scandal, those *Scruple-selling Vermin of the Poultry.

scruple ('skru:p(ə)l), *v.* Also 7 scrupule, scroople. [f. the sb. Cf. OF. (15th c.) *scrupuler* 'examiner scrupuleusement' (Godefroy).]

1. *trans.* To have or make scruples about; to demur to, take exception to, question the propriety or expediency of (something done or to be done); to hesitate or stick at (doing something). ? *Obs.*

1627 W. SCLATER *Exp. 2 Thess.* (1629) 175 Was euer a Papist knowne to scruple this sinne? Not to extenuate it as veniall? **1692** LOCKE *3rd Let. Toleration* iii. Wks. 1714 II. 347 Perhaps it is because he scruples the Cross in Baptism. **1721** DE FOE *Mem. Cavalier* (1840) 302 Let no man scruple my honourable mention of this noble enemy. **1748** CHESTERF. *Lett.* II. cxlv. 18 He scrupled no means to obtain his ends. **1837** HALLAM *Lit. Europe* III. iii. §86 *note*, It seems reasonable not to scruple the use of a word so convenient.

†2. To doubt, question, hesitate to believe (a fact, allegation, etc.); to question the truth, goodness, or genuineness of. *Obs.*

1640 D. CAWDREY *Three Serm.* (1641) 13 The Truth of this Grant may well be scrupled. **1660** tr. *Amyraldus' Treat. conc. Relig.* III. viii. 474 The Doctrine of a Third [Person] ought not to be scrupul'd. **1752** J. GILL *Trinity* iv. 75 Though the Father's Deity is not scrupled, or called in question. **1787** R. TYLER *Contrast* III, Though I don't scruple your veracity, I have some reasons for believing you were there. **1846** W. H. MILL *Five Serm.* (1848) 142 The charge of ignorance of the Gospel is often made against those who scruple statements resembling..this.

†b. with obj. a sentence introduced by *that* or *whether*. *Obs.*

1642 *Collect. Rights & Priv. Parlt.* 9 They at the first scrupuled, whether or no they might take up armes for their own defence against that cruell arrest. **1651** BIGGS *New Disp.* ¶275 It is not to be scrupled that the omnipotent and wise Creator saw and judged all things that he had made to be good. **1665** MANLEY *Grotius' Low C. Warres* 7 They were of invincible spirits to undergo all manner of..dangers, whereby it was scrupled by the rest of the World, Whether they were more greedy or Honour or Wealth?

†3. *causative.* To excite scruples in (a person), to cause to feel scruples. *Obs.*

1638 CHILLINGW. *Relig. Prot.* I. vi. §72. 380 But all of them..fear the event of such a tryall [of their religion] that they may be scrupled and staggered and disquieted by it. **1657** J. WATTS *Scribe*, etc. III. 72 The dangerous tentations of the Devil, wherewith he and his instruments..do mainly assault the mindes, and scruple the consciences,..of the weaker amongst us. **1689** *Col. Rec. Pennsylv.* I. 255 If he had anything that scrupled him in matter of Law.

4. *intr.* To entertain or raise scruples; to hesitate, demur, †doubt. Chiefly ***to scruple at*** (also in indirect passive). Now *rare*.

1639 SALTMARSHE *Pract. Policy* 120 When you are to be engaged in imploiment, and your abilities are doubted and questioned, and therefore you are scrupeld at. **1686** tr. *Chardin's Trav. Persia* 63 Although M. de Nointel scrupl'd at first, yet he consented at length. **1708** *Misc. Curiosa* III. 407 Whilst I was scrupling at this Relation, they brought me Gallasius his Commentary upon Exodus. **1824** SOUTHEY *Sir T. More* (1831) I. 26 The sovereigns..who scrupled at no means for securing themselves on the throne. **1861** BUCKLE *Civiliz.* (1873) II. viii. 481 His love for the Church was a passion and he scrupled at nothing which could advance its interests.

b. quasi-*refl.* with complement: To allow one's scruples to drive one *out of*.

1786 J. NEWTON in J. Bull *Mem. W. Bull* (1864) 163 Mr. R. of Birmingham has indeed had some sceptical qualms about his situation in the Church, and some thoughts of seceding or dissenting from us... I shall be sorry if he scruples himself out of a sphere of usefulness.

5. *Const.* inf.: To hesitate or be reluctant (*to do* something), esp. on conscientious grounds, or out of regard for what is fit and proper. (The current use.)

1660 F. BROOKE tr. *Le Blanc's Trav.* 357 Fathers not scrupling to make their own children victims. **1667** MILTON *P.L.* IX. 997 He scrupl'd not to eat Against his better knowledge. **1687** A. LOVELL tr. *Thevenot's Trav.* II. 119 The Muletors scrupuled to let us have Mules to Ride on. **1761** HUME *Hist. Eng.* II. xxxv. 279 The lords for some time scrupled to pass this clause. **1864** BRYCE *Holy Rom. Emp.* x. (1875) 164 The Pope did not scruple to preach a crusade against the Emperor himself. **1871** R. ELLIS tr. *Catullus* p. xix, Nor have I scrupled to forsake the ancient quantity in proper names.

Hence '**scrupled** *ppl. a.*, questioned, made an object of scruple. '**scrupling** *vbl. sb.* and *ppl. a.*

1641 *Vindic. Smectymnuus* 36 Unable to give solid satisfaction to a scrupling conscience. **1665** WITHER *Lord's Prayer* 127 Therefore the scrupling at this conditional Petition is causless. **1670** BAXTER *Cure Ch. Div.* 381 Let all Rulers multiply unnecessary scrupled impositions in their own dominions. **1696** WHISTON *Theory of Earth* II. 151 One of the most scrupled and exceptionable Points of his Narration, that of the Universal Deluge. **1818** scrupling [see RAP *v.*[1] 3 c]. **1827** HALLAM *Const. Hist.* (1876) III. xv. 173 The bill of comprehension proposed to parliament went no farther than to leave a few scrupled ceremonies at discretion. **1894** *Athenæum* 24 Nov. 708/3 [He] scorned the constraint which prevents a scrupling dullard from describing what he never saw.

'**scrupleless**, *a. rare*[−1]. [f. SCRUPLE *sb.* + -LESS.] Having no scruples, unscrupulous.

1823 SCOTT *Peveril* xliv, Your Grace's swordsmen have had ill-luck of late; and it is hard, since you always choose the best hands, and such scrupleless knaves too.

† **'scrupleness.** *Obs. rare.* Also 5 scrupulenes, 6 scrupulnes. [irreg. f. SCRUPLE *sb.* + -NESS.] Scrupulousness.

1489 CAXTON *Faytes of Armes* IV. i. 230 To take awaye all scrupulenes. **1549** *Compl. Scot.* xix. 165, I exort ȝou.. to put al cerimonial scrupulnes furtht of ȝour hartis. **1573–80** TUSSER *Husb.* (1878) 69 (*heading*) Against fantasticall scruplenes. **1647** HEXHAM I, Scruplenesse of conscience.

scrupler ('skru:plə(r)). [f. SCRUPLE *v.* + -ER[1].] One who scruples, one who has scruples.

Applied *spec.* to the Scots divines who objected to take the Abjuration Oath in 1712.

1631 BP. HALL *Rem. Wks.* (1660) 295 Away then with those nice scruplers. **1650** J. DURY *Just Re-proposals* 20 To satisfie scruplers, all their scruples must be first known. **1712** T. BOSTON *Acc. Life* (1908) 191 There the lawfulness of the Oath of Abjuration was debated *pro* and *con*, .. betwixt the scruplers and the clear brethren. **1843** *Wodrow's Corr.* II. 401 Warden.. refused to swear the Abjuration Oath, even after the change of its form in 1719, which induced the greater number of scruplers to take it.

'scruplesome, *a.* *rare*[−1]. [f. SCRUPLE *sb.* + -SOME.] Inclined to be scrupulous.

c **1800** MAR. EDGEWORTH *Let.* in Emily Lawless *Mem.* (1904) 95 It was raining very hard, and Pat in his yellow waistcoat, which you know he is scruplesome about wetting.

† **scrupose,** *a.* *Obs.* [ad. L. *scrūpōsus*, f. *scrūpus* rough or sharp stone: see -OSE.] Rough, jagged.

1753 *Chambers' Cycl.* Suppl. s.v. *Corallina*, The feathered, scrupose coralline.

scrupulant ('skru:pju:lənt). *Eccl.* [f. L. *scrupulus* + -ANT[1].] One who is over-scrupulous in confessing his sins; one who suffers from scrupulosity of conscience.

1938 'H. KINGSMILL' *English Genius* 199 George Fox was not what the Catholic Church calls a scrupulant. **1961** J. B. SHEERIN *Sacrament of Freedom* x. 133 The scrupulous person.. breaks contact with reality when it comes to the matter of sin. In some cases, a scrupulant is sane about sin in general and has a blind spot only in regard to one particular type of sin. **1961** *Theol. Stud.* June 232 When dealing with a scrupulant.. persuade him.. of the pathological element in his personality.

† **'scrupular,** *a.* *Obs. rare.* [ad. L. *scrūpulār-is* (*scrīp-*), f. *scrūpul-um* SCRUPLE *sb.*[1]] Of or amounting to a scruple in weight.

1656 BLOUNT *Glossogr.*, *Scrupular*, of or belonging to a scruple, small. **1771** RAPER in *Phil. Trans.* LXI. 492 The latter coins of this scrupular standard are like the Denarii of the age in which they were struck.

scrupule, obs. f. SCRUPLE *sbs.* and *v.*

scrupulist ('skru:pjʊlɪst). [f. L. *scrūpul-us* SCRUPLE *sb.*[2] + -IST.] One who has scruples or raises difficulties.

1681 R. L'ESTRANGE *Casuist Uncas'd* 5 The Rebells assaulting of their Sovereign.. might have given your Scrupulists as hard thoughts of the Faction that did it. **1711** SHAFTESB. *Charac.* Misc. II. iii. (1737) III. 109 These are the Scepticks or Scrupulists, against whom there is such a Clamour rais'd. **1863** *Times* 14 Oct. 8/4 Foolish scrupulists, who in a matter of life and honour would not use their only weapons of defence because carved with objectionable figures.

† **'scrupulize,** *v.* *Obs.* [formed as prec. + -IZE.] **a.** *trans.* To scruple at. **b.** *intr.* To make scruples.

1625 BP. MOUNTAGU *App. Cæsar* 244 If in this, why not in other Articles that eyther are or may be so scrupulized..? **1642** FEATLY *Vertumnus* 126, I admire that any man hath so long scrupulized to the losse of himselfe and fortunes. **1678** R. L'ESTRANGE *Seneca's Mor.* I. xii. (1696) 49 Whensoever my duty calls me, 'tis my part to attend, without Scrupulizing upon Forms, or Difficulties.

scrupulosity (skru:pju:'lɒsɪtɪ). [a. F. *scrupulosité* (14th c. in Littré) or ad. L. *scrūpulōsitāt-em*, f. *scrūpulōs-us* SCRUPULOUS: see -ITY.]

1. The state or quality of being scrupulous (see the adj.).

1526 *Pilgr. Perf.* (W. de W. 1531) 66 Our lorde for his tender mercy preserue all those that entendeth this holy iourney of perfeccyon from.. scrupulosite and pusillanimite of spiryte. **1654** EVELYN *Diary* 12 July, Thence we went to New College, where the Chapel was in its ancient garb, notwithstanding the scrupulositie of the times. **1690** STILLINGFL. *Serm.* xxxv. Wks. I. 558 Avoid a needless Scrupulosity of Conscience, as a thing which keeps our Minds always uneasie. **1759** JOHNSON *Rasselas* xxvi, Age looks with anger on the temerity of youth, and youth with contempt on the scrupulosity of age. **1849** MACAULAY *Hist. Eng.* ii. I. 273 It would have been thought strange scrupulosity in him to quit his post, because his advice as to matters not strictly within his own department was not taken by his master. **1879** GEO. ELIOT *Theo. Such* 5 When I was a lad I danced a hornpipe with arduous scrupulosity.

b. An instance of this; †a scruple.

a **1562** G. CAVENDISH *Wolsey* (1893) 123 It was a certeyn scrupulositie that prykked my concyence. *a* **1600** HOOKER *Eccl. Pol.* VI. iv. §7 Or else.. we fall into timorous scrupulosities. **1831** LAMB *Recoll. Royal Academ.* in *Mrs. Leicester's School*, etc. (1886) 309 For the thousand tints—the grains—which in life diversify the nose, the chin, the cheek.. he cared nothing at all about them. He left such scrupulosities to opticians and anatomists. **1879** FARRAR *St. Paul* I. 264 It shows that Peter had already abandoned Rabbinic scrupulosities.

†**2.** *Astr.* [After SCRUPLE *sb.*[1] 3.] Minute determination (of time). *Obs.*

1633 H. GELLIBRAND *App. Longitude* in T. James *Voy.* R 3, The scrupulosity of time is vnknowne, and therefore we cannot argue the) true place from thence.

scrupulous ('skru:pjʊləs), *a.* Also 6 scrupilous(e, scrupulouse, scrupulus. Cf. SCRIPULOUS. [ad. F. *scrupuleux* (16th c., *scrupuleusement* 14th c.), or ad. L. *scrūpulōs-us*, f. *scrūpul-us*: see SCRUPLE *sb.*[2] and -OUS.]

1. Troubled with doubts or scruples of conscience; over-nice or meticulous in matters of right and wrong. Also (of things, actions, etc.), characterized by such scruples.

1450–1530 *Myrr. our Ladye* 52 Yt is good in suche case to be gouernyd by the consayle of a dyscrete gostly father leste the dome of hys owne conscyence be other to scrupulous or to recheles. **1513** MORE *Rich. III*, Wks. 58/1 Of spirituall men thei toke such as had wit,.. & had no scrupilouse consience. **1528** HENRY VIII in R. Hall *Life Fisher* F.'s Wks. (E.E.T.S.) II. 61 Whiche thinge.. ingendred such a scrupilous doubt in me, that my mind was incontinently accombred, vexed, and disquyeted. **1593** SHAKS. *3 Hen. VI*, IV. vii. 61 *Rich.* Why Brother, wherefore stand you on nice points?.. *Hast.* Away with scrupulous Wit, now Armes must rule. **1594** HOOKER *Eccl. Pol.* IV. xi. §5 Abusing their libertie and freedom to the offence of their weake brethren which were scrupulous. **1667** in *Cath. Rec. Soc. Miscell.* III. 64 And yet, though he spent so much time in examining his consciens, he was not the least scrupulous nor long at Confession. **1765** BLACKSTONE *Comm.* I. vi. 226 Whatever doubts might be formerly raised by weak and scrupulous minds about the existence of such an original contract. **1835** I. TAYLOR *Spir. Despot.* iii. 108 The common people superstitious, fanatical, scrupulous, licentious. **1907** A. C. BENSON *Altar Fire* 134 The religion recommended was a religion of scrupulous saints and self-torturing ascetics.

†**b.** Prone to hesitate or doubt; distrustful; cautious or meticulous in acting, deciding, etc. Also (of actions, etc.), characterized by doubt or distrust; (of objections) cavilling. *Obs.*

1559 W. CUNINGHAM *Cosmogr. Glasse* 46 It is truely said, that knowledge hath no enemie but ignoraunce. There are .. no small number of Lactantius sort, not scrupulous enemies onely, but also Physicians, of whom [etc.]. **1560** DAUS tr. *Sleidane's Comm.* Pref. 2b, Thucydides was so desyrous of the verity, and so doubt full and scrupulous in wryting of his story. **1611** CORYAT *Crudities* 67 The Italians are so curious and scrupulous in many of their cities.. that they will admit no stranger within the wals.. except he bringeth a bill of health from the last citie he came from. **1614** RALEIGH *Hist. World* II. xxiii. §4. 574 But in filling vp the blankes of old Histories, we neede not be so scrupulous. *a* **1681** WHARTON *Apotelesma* Wks. (1683) 44 Nor any one [*sc.* art or science] that can truly say, it is free from every scrupulous exception. **1695** WOODWARD *Nat. Hist. Earth* Acc. Observ. 8, I have been the more scrupulous and wary, in regard the Inferences drawn from these Observations are of some importance.

†**c.** with *const.*: Loth or reluctant, through scruples, *to* (do something); doubtful or suspicious *of* (a person or thing); chary *of* or *in* (doing something); anxious or fearful *about*. *Obs.*

1608 D. T[UVILL] *Ess. Pol. & Mor.* 125 Hee was no way scrupulous to circumvent, and kill, *insontes sicuti sontes*. **1643** SIR T. BROWNE *Relig. Med.* I. §3. 4 And therefore I am not scrupulous to converse and live with them. *c* **1645** HOWELL *Lett.* (1650) II. 32 The Father is scrupulous of the Son, the Son of the Sisters, and all three of me, to whose award they referr'd the business three severall times. **1658** SIR T. BROWNE *Hydriot.* i. 5 The Jews.. as they raised noble Monuments and Mausolæums for their own Nation, so they were not scrupulous in erecting some for others. **1662** STILLINGFL. *Orig. Sacræ* II. ix. §21. 320 The primitive Christians were very scrupulous of calling the Emperours *Dominus*. **1754** RICHARDSON *Grandison* IV. xxi. 161 She often directed herself to me in Italian. I do not talk it well: But.. I was not scrupulous to answer in it. **1785** PHILLIPS *Treat. Inland Nav.* 33 Those.. whom I have consulted on the subject, where I was scrupulous of my knowledge. **1845** S. JUDD *Margaret* II. viii. (1871) 284 Don't you stir out of the house; I am scrupulous about what might happen.

d. *absol.* (*the scrupulous* = scrupulous persons.)

1625 B. JONSON *Staple of N.* III. ii. 118 'Tis the house of fame, Sir, Where both the curious, and the negligent, The scrupulous, and carelesse;.. all doe meet. **1690** LOCKE *Hum. Und.* III. vi. §12 There are some Birds.. whose Bloud is cold as Fishes, and their Flesh in taste so near akin, that the Scrupulous are allow'd them on Fish-days.

†**2.** Of a thing: Causing or raising scruples; liable to give offence; meriting scruple or cavil, dubious, doubtful. *to make it scrupulous*: to scruple, hesitate (*to do* something). *Obs.*

a **1548** HALL *Chron., Hen. VII* 57 The scrupulous stynges of domesticall sedicion. **1574** HELLOWES *Guevara's Fam. Epist.* (1577) 66 If your warre had ben vpon Ierusalem, it were to be holden for iust, but for that it is vpon Marsillius, alway we hold it for scrupulous. **1593** *Tell-trothe's New Yeare's Gift* 3 And it being my hap to enquire first from whence hee came, hee made it not scrupulous to certifie his comming from hell. **1622** BACON *Holy War* Misc. Wks. (1629) 117 As the Cause of a Warre ought to be Iust; So the Iustice of that Cause ought to be Euident; Not Obscure, not Scrupulous. **1685** BUNYAN *Quest. Seventh-day Sabbath* ii. 16 This yet seems to me more scrupulous, because that the punishment due to the breach of the Seventh-day Sabbath was hid from men to the time of Moses.

†**b.** Of the nature of a mere scruple. *Obs.*

1605 in *10th Rep. Hist. MSS. Comm.* App. v. 372 Let not any man mervaylle of the manyfould downefalles into synne, or think it a thing scrupulous.

3. Careful to follow the dictates of conscience; giving heed to the scruples of conscience so as to avoid doing what is wrong; strict in matters of right and wrong.

A use of sense 1 developed chiefly in contexts with a negative expressed or implied.

1545 ELYOT *Dict.* s.v. *Religiosus*, *In testimonio religiosi*, scrupulouse in bearynge wytnesse. **1849** MACAULAY *Hist. Eng.* ii. I. 210 His more scrupulous brother ceased to appear in the royal chapel. **1863** MRS. GASKELL *Sylvia's Lovers* iii, Yet, though scrupulous in most things, it did not go against the consciences of these good brothers to purchase smuggled articles.

b. With inf.: Careful (to do something) in obedience to one's conscience.

1729 BUTLER *Serm.* Wks. 1874 II. 50 We should be religiously scrupulous and exact to say nothing.. but what is true.

4. Of actions, etc.: Rigidly directed by the dictates of conscience; characterized by a strict and minute regard for what is right.

1756 BURKE *Tracts Popery Laws* Wks. IX. 338 This point is carried to so scrupulous a severity, that chamber practice, and even private conveyancing.. are prohibited to them under the severest penalties. **1779** *Mirror* No. 37 While he gave to business the most scrupulous attention. **1855** MACAULAY *Hist. Eng.* xiii. III. 248 William saw that he must not think of paying to the laws of Scotland that scrupulous respect which he had wisely and righteously paid to the laws of England. **1876** MISS BRADDON *J. Haggard's Dau.* I. 9 A scrupulous honesty recommended him even to careful housekeepers.

5. Minutely exact or careful (in non-moral matters); strictly attentive even to the smallest details; characterized by punctilious exactness.

1638 JUNIUS *Paint. Ancients* 77 Examining.. every little moment of Art with such infatigable though scrupulous care. **1711** ADDISON *Spect.* No. 160 ¶4 Where we would make some Amends for our want of Force and Spirit, by a scrupulous Nicety and Exactness in our Compositions. **1779** JOHNSON *L.P.*, *Cowley* (1805) I. 44 Thus all the power of description is destroyed by a scrupulous enumeration. **1837** DICKENS *Pickwick* ii, Great men are seldom over scrupulous in the arrangement of their attire. **1862** MILLER *Elem. Chem.*, *Org.* (ed. 2) 11 Scrupulous attention to the purity of the matter submitted to analysis is of course of primary importance. **1881** WESTCOTT & HORT *Grk. N.T.* Introd. §11 A scrupulous jealousy as to their text. **1863** GEO. ELIOT *Romola* v, Shelves, on which books.. were arranged in scrupulous order. **1886** *Manch. Exam.* 14 Jan. 5/4 The various performances were gone through with scrupulous exactitude.

†**6.** Wrought or produced with minute care and exactness. *Obs.*

1634 RAINBOW *Labour* (1635) 34 If seelings be an ornament, what are scrupulous carvings?

scrupulously ('skru:pjʊləslɪ), *adv.* [-LY[2].] In a scrupulous manner; with scruple, doubt, or cautiousness; with conscientious strictness; with minute care or punctilious exactness.

1533 ELYOT *Cast. Helthe* (1541) 51 Most diligently, and as I mought say, most scrupulously to be obserued. **1696** TRYON *Misc.* ii. 33 'Tis well known how Scrupulously the Pythagoreans.. abstained from Flesh. **1712** ADDISON *Spect.* No. 291 ¶9 Works.. which are scrupulously exact and conformable to all the Rules of correct Writing. **1847** C. BRONTE *Jane Eyre* xxviii, An elderly woman, somewhat rough-looking, but scrupulously clean. **1880** L. STEPHEN *Pope* ii. 56 In all this, by Pope's own showing, Addison seems to have been scrupulously fair.

scrupulousness ('skru:pjʊləsnɪs). [-NESS.] The quality of being scrupulous (see the adj.).

1526 *Pilgr. Perf.* (W. de W. 1531) 82 Spirituall.. diseases: ..as glotony, lechery, and scrupulousnes. **1577–87** HOLINSHED *Chron.* III. 872/2 To the end that none should haue anie scrupulousnesse of conscience in so dooing. **1689** W. A. *Herbert's Acc. Exam.* 55 Such was Sir Edward's great scrupulousness, and tenderness, where the Life of Man was concern'd. **1742** RICHARDSON *Pamela* IV. 13 If a precise or unnecessary Scrupulousness be avoided. **1863** A. BLOMFIELD *Mem. Bp. Blomfield* II. x. 208 Nothing could exceed his scrupulousness, about running into debt. **1877** M. ARNOLD *Last Ess. Church* 35 Religion is a matter where scrupulousness has been far too active.

scruse, variant of SCRUZE, to squeeze.

scrutable ('skru:təb(ə)l), *a.* [As if ad. L. **scrūtābilis*, f. *scrūtārī*: see SCRUTATOR. Cf. It. *scrutabile*.] That can be understood by scrutiny. Chiefly in implied contrast with *inscrutable*.

c **1600** *Distr. Emperor* I. i. in Bullen *Old Pl.* (1884) III. 176 If the thoughts of men were scrutable To man and mongst men. **1718** HICKES & NELSON *J. Kettlewell* II. xlviii. 153 Magnifying the Providence of God, which is by Mortals Scrutable. **1856** MRS. BROWNING *Aur. Leigh* IV. 320 Cognisant Of the less scrutable majesties. **1878** *Life G. Combe* I. ii. 23 Nobody conceived the cause of these phenomena to be scrutable.

scrutate (skru:'teɪt), *v. rare.* [f. L. *scrūtāt-*, ppl. stem of *scrūtārī*: see SCRUTATOR.] *trans.* To search out; to investigate.

1882 BERESFORD-HOPE *Brandreths* II. xxix, Scrutating all a sovereign yearns to learn.

scrutation (skru:'teɪʃən). [ad. L. *scrūtātiōn-em*, n. of action f. *scrūtārī*: see next.] Minute search or examination.

1593 NORDEN *Spec. Brit., M'sex* I. 37 After long scrutation and inquisition, this well was found and performed the cure. **1638** T. WHITAKER *Blood of Grape* 20 For though we be very curious in our scrutation [etc.].

scrutator (skruːˈteɪtə(r)). [a. L. *scrūtātor*, agent-n. f. *scrūtārī* to examine, scrutinize, app. f. *scrūta* pl., 'old or broken stuff, trash, frippery, trumpery' (L. & Sh.); the etymological sense of the vb. is supposed to be 'to search even to the rags' (*ibid.*).]

1. One who examines or investigates.

1593 NORDEN *Spec. Brit., M'sex* I. 10 Master Camden, a singuler scrutator of antiquities. **1676** HALE *Contempl.* I. 452 The very disquisition concerning any one part of the Brain, the Eye, the Nerves, the Blood hath perplexed the most exact Scrutators. **1822** *Q. Rev.* XXVIII. 188 He threw down the gauntlet of defiance to the learned scrutators into the hidden mysteries of hieroglyphical lore. **1879** MEREDITH *Egoist* xlii, She would have declared herself innocent before the scrutator.

2. *spec.* One whose office it is to examine or investigate closely, *esp.* one who acts as an examiner of votes at an election, etc.; a scrutineer.

1618 HALES *Let. fr. Synod of Dort* Golden Rem. II. (1673) 2 The manner of election was by Scrutiny... The Scrutators were two of the Seculars,..these calculated the voices and pronounced the election. **1734-5** *Act 8 Geo. II*, c. 6 §4 The justices of the peace..shall be scrutators of the ballot. **1908** *Athenæum* 16 May 609/3 Messrs. M. S. Giuseppi and W. A. Littledale were appointed scrutators of the ballot.

b. As the title of a university official. (See quots.) Now only *Hist.*

1580 GRINDAL *Let. to Burleigh* in Strype *Life* (1710) 251 The said Mr. Barrow..alledgeth another [university] Statute, made by Grace,..concerning the Scrutators. **1665** J. BUCK in Peacock *Stat. Cambridge* App. B, p. lv, The Scrutators also doe..give over their office by delivery of their keys to the V. Ch. **1793** *Acc. Proc. Camb. agst. W. Frend* 195 The statutes which relate to the duty of scrutators and moderators on passing graces. **1831** SIR W. HAMILTON *Discuss.* (1852) 412 *note*, In Oxford..the two Proctors.. were necessarily chosen, one from the Northern, the other from the Southern men; also the two Scrutators, anciently distinct (?) from the Proctors. **1835** in Willis & Clark *Cambridge* (1886) III. 117 The Vicechancellor, Proctors, and Scrutators examine the votes received. **1841** PEACOCK *Stat. Cambridge* 25 The two scrutators were elected by the non-regents of each congregation, to collect the votes, and announce the decisions of their house, in the same manner as was done by the two proctors in the house of regents.

scrutatory (ˈskruːtətərɪ), *a.* [f. L. *scrūtāt-*, *scrūtārī*: see SCRUTATOR and -ORY.] Searching, examining.

1893 *Temple Bar* XCVIII. 151 Loripont dropped a scrutatory glance.

†**scrute**, *v.* *Obs. rare*$^{-1}$. [ad. L. *scrūtārī*: see SCRUTATOR.] *trans.* To scrutinize.

1536 *Primer Eng. & Lat.* 121 My synne and inequite why doste thou scrute so.

scrutener, -enous, -y: see SCRUTINEER *sb.*, etc.

‖**scrutin** (skrytɛ̃). [Fr., vote.] In Fr. combinations, referring to contrasting electoral systems: **scrutin d'arrondissement** (darɔ̃dismɑ̃) [lit., electoral district vote], a system of voting in France by which votes are cast for a single representative of an electoral district; **scrutin de liste** (list) = *list vote* s.v. LIST *sb.*^{6} d.

1851 *Ann. Reg. 1850* I. 230/2 According to Article 30, the election is effected in the department and by *Scrutin de liste.* **1911** J. H. HUMPHREYS *Proportional Representation* viii. 172 List systems of proportional representation are based upon the block vote or *scrutin de liste.* **1921** J. BRYCE *Mod. Democracies* I. xx. 270 Three times this method was dropped and replaced by the *Scrutin d'arrondissement* (the scheme of one-membered constituencies). Now the *Scrutin de liste* has returned once more. **1954** [see *list vote* s.v. LIST *sb.*^{6} d]. **1960** MACRIDIS & BROWN *De Gaulle Republic* xiii. 236 The cabinet decided to adopt the *scrutin d'arrondissement* with *ballottage.*

scrutinant (ˈskruːtɪnənt), *a.* *rare.* [a. F. *scrutinant*, pr. pple. of *scrutiner* to scrutinize, f. *scrutin* SCRUTINY.] Occupied in scrutinizing.

1876 RUSKIN *Fors Clav.* lxxii. 378 Live here in my Venetian palace..scrutinant of dome, cloud and cockle-shell.

†**ˈscrutinate**, *v.* *Obs. rare.* [f. F. *scrutin-er* (see prec.) + -ATE^{3}.] *trans.* = SCRUTINIZE.

a **1734** NORTH *Life Ld. Kpr. Guilford* (1742) 43 The Court ..scrutinated all Points of Form.

†**ˈscrutinator.** *Obs.* [quasi-Latin agent-noun f. SCRUTINE *v.*] = SCRUTINEER *sb.*

1691 W. B. *Hist. Roman Conclave* v. 15 These Votes..are set upon a File..by one of the Scrutinators.

†**ˈscrutine**, *v.* *Obs.* [a. F. *scrutine-r*, f. *scrutin* SCRUTINY.] *intr.* To make an investigation or examination. Hence †**ˈscrutining** *vbl. sb.*

1592 GREENE *Upst. Courtier* H2b, They..departed to scrutine of the matter by inquirie amongst themselues. **1657** W. MORICE *Coena quasi Κοινή* v. 62 Free admission to the Sacrament..without any scrutining or proof of their real holiness.

scrutineer (skruːtɪˈnɪə(r)), *sb.* Forms: α. 6 scrutener, 7-8 scrutiner; β. 7- scrutineer. [f. SCRUTINY + -ER^{2}, -EER^{1}.]

1. One whose duty it is to scrutinize or examine; esp. one who acts as an examiner of votes at an election, etc. Also, *spec.* in *Motor Racing* and *Motor-Boat Racing*, an official who inspects a car or boat in order to ensure that it complies with the regulations.

1557 *Order of Hospitalls* B vij b, That there be..elected.. ij Scruteners to gather in the Legacies. **1617** COLLINS *Def. Bp. Ely* I. iv. 182 Else what neede the Canon either the Fathers consent, or the scrutiner to begin with *placet vobis?* **1682** LUTTRELL *Brief Rel.* (1857) I. 229 The scrutineers of the poll relating to the lord mayor have mett severall times. **1773** *Gentl. Mag.* XLIII. 102 The balloting began at eleven o'clock in the forenoon, and ended at Six, when the scrutineers reported to the Directors. **1811** SHELLEY *St. Irvyne* iii. Pr. Wks. (1888) I. 152 He gazed on the mysterious scrutineer who stood before him. **1894** *Proc. Incorp. Assoc. Munic. Engin.* XX. 3 The Scrutineers report the result of the voting as follows. **1932** S. C. H. DAVIS *Motor Racing* xxii. 270 Caracciola's Mercédès was rejected by the scrutineers. **1963** *Times* 4 June 14/7 The scrutineers' protest was upheld and both cars ruled ineligible. **1968** *Guardian* 19 Mar. 9/3 In the windy entrance lobby..there is a photograph of Mr Novotny... There is also a lady of the militia... Once past these two scrutineers you cross a yard..., and enter the works proper. **1972** [see next]. **1976** *Church Times* 16 July 6/5 A passport to immortality consisting of 'Cranford', 'Cousin Phillis' and 'Wives and Daughters' is convincing enough in all conscience for the most demanding of literary scrutineers.

2. (With capital initial.) A contributor to *Scrutiny*, a literary journal edited by F. R. Leavis (see LEAVISIAN *sb.* and *a.*), and others, between 1932 and 1953; a follower of Leavis. *rare.*

1958 J. RAYMOND in *Times Lit. Suppl.* 15 Aug. p. xxxii/1 The difficulty of writing on a general theme like this is to decide at the beginning just what we are attempting to discuss... The Situation (desperate of course) of the Contemporary Writer? The Collapse of the Essay?.. Scrutineers All—and After? **1978** J. MARCUS in *Ibid.* 12 May 528/5 The Scrutineers have taught generations of British students that Virginia Woolf was a snob.

scrutineer (skruːtɪˈnɪə(r)), *v.* [f. prec.] *trans.* In *Motor Racing* and *Motor-Boat Racing*: to inspect (a car or boat) in order to ensure that it complies with the regulations. Hence **scrutiˈneering** *vbl. sb.*

1930 E. WAUGH *Vile Bodies* x. 175 Changed the whole engine over after they'd been scrutineered. Anyone else would have been disqualified. **1932** S. C. H. DAVIS *Motor Racing* xxii. 270 That..served to emphasize..the weakness of scrutineering on the day before the race. **1971** *Sunday Express* (Johannesburg) 28 Mar. 7/1 The scrutineering area for checking whether cars comply with regulations. **1971** *E. Afr. Standard* (Nairobi) 13 Apr. 1/3 The margin on the road was four points, but the gap was narrowed when the two Datsuns went to scrutineering. **1972** C. MUDIE *Motor Boats & Boating* 150 Other boats will begin to arrive with tall tales of fantastic practice performances and all will build up to scrutineering the day before the race. Each boat has to present itself to a team of scrutineers who will check the hull and machinery. *Ibid.*, (*caption*) The scrutineering team check each boat before an important race.

†**ˈscrutinist.** *Obs. rare.* [f. SCRUTIN-Y + -IST.] ? A curious investigator.

1669 WORLIDGE *Syst. Agric.* 207 They [certain ploughs] are of no great Advantage to the..Husbandman, onely invented to satisfie the minds of some scrutinists.

scrutinization (ˌskruːtɪnaɪˈzeɪʃən). [f. SCRUTINIZE *v.* + -ATION.] The action of scrutinizing.

1922 *Autocar* 10 Nov. (Advt. Suppl.) p. lxxxv, Our unique methods of scrutinisation and the introduction of every detailed improvement. **1976** *Kybernetes* V. 36/1 If a particular scrutinization fails a logico-grammatical test, then its rejection requires the reformulation of a Postulated Hypothesis.

scrutinize (ˈskruːtɪnaɪz), *v.* [f. SCRUTIN-Y + -IZE.]

1. *trans.* To subject to scrutiny; to examine methodically and with close attention.

1671 SALMON *Syn. Med.* Introd. 6 We have with much labour scrutinized the best Authors, &c. **1764** REID *Inquiry* vi. §6 Des Cartes gave a noble example of turning our attention inward and scrutinizing our sensations. **1800** MRS. HERVEY *Mourtray Fam.* I. 295 She began..to scrutinize her heart, with an uncommon degree of severity. **1876** MISS BRADDON *J. Haggard's Dau.* I. 75 Mr. Pentreath scrutinised his son through his spectacles, perhaps to make sure that he was sober. **1881** FROUDE *Short Stud.* IV. II. iv. 215 The closer all such documents are scrutinised the more clear becomes the nature of their origin.

b. *spec.* with reference to votes. (Cf. SCRUTINY 2 c.)

1750 H. WALPOLE *Let. to Mann* 25 Feb., The Westminster election, which is still scrutinising, produced us a parliamentary event this week.

†**2.** *intr.* To make scrutiny. Const. *into.* *Obs.*

1699 LUTTRELL *Brief Rel.* (1857) IV. 256 The bank is now scrutinizing upon whom the choice of the new directors is fallen. **1742** *Lond. & Country Brew.* I. (ed. 4) 17 The latest and best Doctors have so far scrutinised into the prime Cause of our British Malady the Scurvy as to affirm [etc.]. **1743** in *Etoniana* (1865) 69 After prayers and sacrament they began to vote... Thus they continued scrutinising and walking about. **1788** *Trifler* No. 9. 114 They will have a better opportunity of scrutinizing into the minutest circumstances.

Hence **ˈscrutinizing** *vbl. sb.* and *ppl. a.*; **ˈscrutinizingly** *adv.*

1782 MISS BURNEY *Cecilia* I. iv, With the scrutinizing observation of a man on the point of making a bargain. **1810** BENTHAM *Packing* (1821) 172 Thus it is that to any scrutinizing eye the secret, had there been any, would have been betrayed. **1828** *Blackw. Mag.* XXIV. 49 We look rather more scrutinizingly into its expression. **1883** ANNIE S. SWAN *Aldersyde* I. ii. (ed. 2) 34 Her restless black eyes wandered scrutinizingly over the face and figure of her comely young kinswoman.

scrutinizer (ˈskruːtɪnaɪzə(r)). [f. SCRUTINIZE *v.* + -ER^{1}.] One who scrutinizes.

1728 MORGAN *Algiers* II. iii. 250 Marmol, to whom I refer every curious Scrutinizer, relates this whole story very differently. **1839** J. W. CROKER in *C. Papers* 14 Mar., The eye is a cold and jealous scrutiniser of those that are opposite to us. **1863** COWDEN CLARKE *Shaks. Char.* xvi. 401 The scrutiniser into her course of conduct will allow that she is at once grave, sedate, witty, social, humorous, cheerful.

scrutinous (ˈskruːtɪnəs), *a.* Now *rare.* Also 6 scrutinus, 7 scrutenous. [ad. F. †*scrutineux* (1512 in Godefr.), f. *scrutin* SCRUTINY: see -OUS.] Closely examining; searching.

1599 NASHE *Lenten Stuffe* 21 How impetrable hee was in mollyfying the adamantinest tiranny of mankinde..those that be scrutinus to pry into, let them [etc.]. **1618** M. BARET *Vineyard Horsem.* I. Ded. to King 9 Although my Artlesse pen hath not made it so delightfull as to reuiue the dead senses of all scrutenous braines, which no Tullies Eloquence as yet could euer perswade. **1745** ELIZA HEYWOOD *Female Spect.* No. 3 (1748) I. 159 They cannot be too scrutinous into the principles of the persons entrusted with the direction of them. **1822-29** *Good's Study Med.* (ed. 3) V. 695 Dr. Gordon, after a scrutinous examination, has added his testimony to the same fact. **1891** *Blackw. Mag.* CL. 815/2 Don't let us be too searching and scrutinous.

scrutinously (ˈskruːtɪnəslɪ), *adv.* [f. SCRUTINOUS *a.* + -LY^{2}.] In a scrutinous manner.

1649 MARBURY *Habakkuk* i. 3 (1650) 21 To look into his brethren; I do not say so scrutinously as the Hypocrite in the Gospel, who [etc.]. **1654-66** EARL ORRERY *Parthen.* (1676) 364, I was begging Ventidius to enquire scrutinously who the Parthian was. **1751** ELIZA HEYWOOD *Betsy Thoughtless* II. 130 Having scrutinously examined all within reach of his view. **1813** W. TAYLOR in *Monthly Mag.* XXXV. 216 The more scrutinously the book of Genesis is analysed, the more evident it becomes that [etc.].

scrutiny (ˈskruːtɪnɪ), *sb.* Also 5 scrutyny, 6 scruteny, -enie, 6-7 scrutinie. [ad. late L. *scrūtinium*, f. *scrūtārī*: see SCRUTATOR. Cf. OF. *scrutinie*, *scrutine*, mod.F. *scrutin*, Sp., Pg. *escrutinio*, It. *squittino*, *scrutinio*, *scruttino*.]

1. a. The formal taking of individual votes, as a method of electing to an office or dignity, or of deciding some question proposed to a deliberative assembly; an instance of this procedure.

Now chiefly in *Canon Law*. In English municipal and university procedure, 'scrutiny' was commonly resorted to only when the result of show of hands or acclamation was not accepted, so that in some examples it is doubtful whether the word partakes more of this sense or of sense 2 c. In Oxford University, the Latin formula *Fiat scrutinium*, 'let a scrutiny be made', is still employed, but the English word is rarely if ever used with reference to present practice.

c **1450** in Aungier *Syon* (1840) 288 The thre formes of eleccion schal be declared..That is to say, the wey of the holy-goste, the wey of scrutyny, and the wey of compromys. **1555** EDEN *Decades* (Arb.) 123 After many scrutinies they elected one Iohn Quicedus. **1573** G. HARVEY *Letter-bk.* (Camden) 46 Whereuppon he and M. Jackson went strait wais up to the table to cal for our voices in 'scrutinie'. **1600** HOLLAND *Livy* x. 360 The people went to a scrutinie and began to giue their voices. **1620** *Cheque Bk. Chapel Royal* (Camden) 9 By a scruteny he was ellected. **1623** WOTTON *Lett.* (1907) II. 275 We have at last a new Pope, after many scrutinies. **1670** G. H. *Hist. Cardinals* III. II. 285 The Election of the Pope is usually in three manners, the first by Scrutiny, the second by Access, and the third by Adoration. **1705** HEARNE *Collect.* (O.H.S.) I. 62 The Proctors went to a Scrutiny. **1708** *Lond. Gaz.* No. 4493/3 Upon a Scrutiny the following Persons were declared to be duly elected Directors. **1897** *Catholic Dict.* (ed. 5) 311 *Election...* In canon law, the act of choosing a fit person for a vacant post. .. The actual choice may be made in one of three ways: by inspiration.., by scrutiny, or by compromise.

†**b.** A vote in one's favour, a suffrage. *Obs.*

1523 SKELTON *Garl. Laurel* 781 Of all gentylwomen he hath the scruteny, In Fames court reportynge the same.

c. (See quot.)

1728 CHAMBERS *Cycl.* s.v., Scrutiny is also used, in the Canon Law, for a Ticket, or little Paper Billet, wherein, at Elections, the Electors write their Notes privately, so as it may not be known for whom they vote.

2. Investigation, critical inquiry; an instance of this. Formerly often (now *rarely*) const. *into*, † *of.*

1604 DRAYTON *Moses* I. 6 At three monthes a scrutinie was held, And serchers then sent euery where about. **1604** R. CAWDREY *Table Alph.*, *Scrutinie*, diligent Search, inquiry. **1641** J. JACKSON *True Evang. T.* III. 190 Let us..stretch the scrutiny to that Angelicall birth-Caroll of our blessed Lord. **1671** MILTON *P.R.* IV. 515, I thought thee worth my nearer view And narrower Scrutiny. **1680** EVELYN *Diary* 30 Oct., An accurate scrutinie of all my actions past. *a* **1701** MAUNDRELL *Journ. Jerus.* (1721) 38 Making..an exact scrutiny into this antiquity. **1786** BURKE *Art. agst. W. Hastings* Wks. 1842 II. 186 To threaten him with scrutinies into his conduct. **1855** MACAULAY *Hist. Eng.* xviii. IV. 176 The closest scrutiny will detect little that is not deserving of approbation. **1856** RUSKIN *Mod. Paint.* III. IV. xvi. §16 Whatever may first lead us to the scrutiny of natural objects, that scrutiny never fails of its reward. **1876** MOZLEY *Univ. Serm.* ii. 35 He is safe from his own scrutiny.

b. *Eccl.* (See quot. 1897.)

1728 in CHAMBERS *Cycl.* **1897** *Catholic Dict.* (ed. 5) 832/1 *Scrutiny* (*scrutinium*). An examination of those who were about to receive baptism... The days appointed for the different scrutinies varied in different places... In the Roman Church, under Pope Siricius, there were apparently three scrutinies only; at a later date, seven.

c. An official examination of the votes cast at an election, in order to eliminate any votes that are invalid, and to rectify or confirm the numbers stated in the return. (Cf. 1 a.)

1728 CHAMBERS *Cycl.* s.v., Among us, Scrutiny is chiefly used for a strict Perusal, and Examination of the several Votes hastily taken at an Election. **1750** H. WALPOLE *Let. to Mann* 31 Jan., The Westminster election is still hanging in scrutiny; the Duke of Bedford paid the election, which he owns to have cost seven thousand pounds; and Lord Gower pays the scrutiny, which will be at least as much. **1838** W. BELL *Dict. Law Scot.* 887 It is frequently necessary to subject the votes of both parties to a scrutiny. **1875** *Encycl. Brit.* III. 290/1 It has been found possible to render voting perfectly secret and to provide for a scrutiny.

†**d.** *Winchester School.* 'An examination of the seven seniors and seven juniors in College, on the subject of their personal comfort, etc.' (R. G. K. Wrench, *Winchester Word-Book*, 1891).

In the original Latin statutes the section relating to this subject is headed 'De Scrutiniis seu Capitulis ter in Anno in Collegio Celebrandis'.

3. In recent use: The action of looking searchingly at something; a searching gaze.

1796 MME. D'ARBLAY *Camilla* III. 183 The celebrated Mrs. Berlinton still appeared not to undergo a scrutiny. **1818** SCOTT *Hrt. Midl.* xi, He adjusted his hat fiercely, turned round, and came forward, as if to meet and defy scrutiny. **1853** C. BRONTE *Villette* vi, I observed him throwing a glance of scrutiny over all the passengers. **1863** GEO. ELIOT *Romola* i, One [man] was stooping slightly, and looking downward with the scrutiny of curiosity. **1865** DICKENS *Mut. Fr.* III. ix, It was natural that John Harmon should have his own secret reasons for a careful scrutiny of her countenance. **1909** *Blackw. Mag.* Sept. 402/1 A brief scrutiny informed him that she was neither in the ball-room nor the supper-room.

†'**scrutiny**, *v.* *Obs.*$^{-0}$ [f. SCRUTINY *sb.*] *trans.* = SCRUTINIZE.

1755 in JOHNSON.

scruto ('skru:təʊ). *Theatre.* [Of obscure origin.] A spring trap-door, made of strips of wood or whalebone, flush with the floor of the stage. Also *attrib.*

1853 *Punch* XXIV. 128/2 The working of various mysterious engines of machinery called 'sloats' and 'scruto-pieces'. **1859** *Ibid.* XXXVI. 58/2 Gorgeous transformations, on which..scruto-work, gas-battens, and all the resources of 'sink and fly', have been lavished. **1861** *Ibid.* XL. 14/1 A land of..scruto-work and profiling, And shivering *coryphées*.

scrutoire (skru:'tɔə(r), -'twɑ:(r)). Forms: α. 7–8 scritoire, -ore, 7 'scritore, 8 scrittoir. β. 7–9 scrutoir(e, -ore, 8 'scrutore, scrutor, screutore, scruitore. [Aphetic ad. F. *escritoire*: see ESCRITOIRE, which appears later in our quots. The change from *i* into *u* in *scrutoire*, *escrutoire* (18th c.) is unexplained.] = ESCRITOIRE.

α. **1678** *Trial of Coleman* 41 bis, Then I came to his own Study where his 'Scritore was. **1682** OLDHAM *Imit. 3rd Sat. Juv.* Poems & Transl. (1684) 198 One gives a fine Scritore or Cabinet. **1715** NELSON *Addr. Pers. Qual.* p. xi, He searched his Scrittoir for something further to give me. **1718** PRIOR *Solomon* Pref. ¶14, I had locked up these Papers in my Scritoire. **1752** HUME *Ess. & Treat.* (1777) I. 372 Bank-stock, or India-bonds..are not idle, even when in his scritoire.

β. **1665** SIR T. HERBERT *Trav.* (1677) 44 There they sell.. Scrutores or Cabinets of Mother of Pearl. **1698** in *MSS. Ho. Lords* N.S. (1905) III. 345 He had several trunks and a scrutoir in the ship. **1750** H. WALPOLE *Let. to Mann* 22 Dec., A person who had stolen sixty guineas out of his scrutoire. **1823** DE QUINCEY *Dice* Wks. 1859 XI. 293 There was still preserved in the house a scrutoire fixed in the wall. *a* **1844** F. HOWES *Horace, Sat.* I. i. (end), But hold!—You'll think I've pillaged the scrutoir Of blear Crispinus. **1853** J. G. M. RAMSEY *Annals of Tennessee* 132 These issues of the North-Carolina Treasury..are still found in great abundance in the scrutoires and chests of the old families. **1978** W. M. SPACKMAN *Armful of Warm Girl* 33 And he himself unpacked..a manila folder of assorted private relics, which he stowed one by one in the upstairs scrutoire.

attrib. **1737** HOPPUS *Salmon's Country Build. Estim.* (ed. 2) 110 Cabinet Locks..and Scruitore Locks.

scrutty ('skrʌtɪ), *a. rare.* [Origin unknown.] Dirty, dusty, scruffy.

1914 M. BEERBOHM *Let.* 27 Apr. (1964) 234 The Arnold Bennetts—very dusty and scrutty but nice—alighted from a motor-car here yesterday. **1970** T. HUGHES *Crow* 68 He tried hating the sea But instantly felt like a scrutty dry rabbit dropping on the windy cliff.

scruyde, obs. form of SHROUD *v.*

scruze (skru:z), *v.* Now *dial.* Also 7–8 scruse, (7 screwze). [? Suggested by SCREW and SQUEEZE *vbs.*] *trans.* To squeeze.

1590 SPENSER *F.Q.* II. xi. 46 Having scruzd out of his carrion corse The lothfull life. *Ibid.* II. xii. 56 Whose sappy liquor, that with fulnesse sweld, Into her cup she scruzd with daintie breach Of her fine fingers. **1611** SPEED *Hist. Gt. Brit.* IX. vii. (1623) 530 Those huge sums, which he had scruzed out of Stephen. **1624** BP. HALL *True Peace-Maker* Wks. (1625) 542 The oppressing Gentleman, that..scruzes his Tenants to death. **1664** *Court & Kitchin Eliz. Cromwell* 114 Scruze into it the juice of two or three lemons. **1683** MOXON *Mech. Exerc., Printing* 186 The whole Stick of Letters..are screwzed together. **1706** PHILLIPS (ed. Kersey), To *Scruse*, to crowd, to press or thrust hard.

scrwe, obs. form of SCREW *sb.*[1]

†**scry**, *sb.*[1] *Obs.* Forms: 4–6 scry(e, 5–6 skry(e, 6 scrie, skrie. [Aphetic form of ASCRY or ESCRY: cf. SCRY *v.* In many places it is impossible to tell whether we should read *ascry(e* in one word, or *a scrye* in two: see quotations below.]

1. Crying out, shout, exclamation, clamour.

Quot. *a* 1450 was misunderstood by Skinner (*Etymologicon*, 1671), who interpreted 'scrye of foules' to mean a flock of wild fowl. The error was repeated by Blount 1674, and appears in many dictionaries.

1419 *Ordin. War.* xii. in *Black Bk. Admir.* (Rolls) I. 462 For unlawefull scryes..that none escrie the whiche is called mount. **1440** J. SHIRLEY *Dethe K. James* (1818) 16 With the which the ladis, and all the wemen, mayd a sorowfull skrye. *a* **1450** *Fysshynge w. Angle* (1883) 5 The blastes of hornys and the scrye of foulis. **1470** HENRY *Wallace* IV. 671 The scry sone rais, the bald Loran was dede. **1513** DOUGLAS *Æneis* VIII. xi. 33 Thayr was also engravyt all at rycht The syluer ganer, flyghterand wyth lowd skry. **1553** BRENDE *Q. Curtius* 41 b, Towardes that parte where the skrye was heard. **1581** STYWARD *Mart. Discipl.* I. 54 Euerie one to help other to arme and diligentlie to resort to the place of seruice, at scrie or larum vpon paine. **1616** *Barbour's Bruce* XIX. 564 The noyis weill soyn raiss and the skry. **1819** W. TENNANT *Papistry Storm'd* (1827) 137 Wi' skirl, and skry, and rallion-shout, Stood thick and far the rabble-rout.

2. An attack; a reconnoitre.

1523 LD. BERNERS *Froiss.* I. xviii. 24 Euery nyght the Englisshe oste made good and sure watche, for they doubted makyng of skryes. **1568** GRAFTON *Chron.* II. 249 To make a skrye in the Scottes hoste. **1577–87** HOLINSHED *Chron.* III. 813/1 On a daie the Frenchmen made a skrie toward the English campe.

scry (skraɪ), *sb.*[2] *Obs.* exc. *dial.* (see E.D.D.). Also 7 scrie, 9 scree. [App. related to SCREEN *sb.* 5.] A kind of sieve.

c **1615** BOYS *Wks.* (1629) 347 Winnowed corne is..made cleane by the fanne and scrie, for the masters owne vse: so though our enemie sift vs, his scrying is but our trying. *Ibid.* 428 He must be like the scry, keeping the good seed but casting away the dust and vnprofitable darnell. **1892** *Auction. Catal. Kent Farm Sale*, Manure scry.

scry (skraɪ), *sb.*[3] [f. SCRY *v.*[2]] Something 'scried' in a crystal.

1898 A. LANG *Making of Relig.* v. 95 The 'scries' which came right were sometimes those of which the 'agent', or person scried for, was consciously thinking.

†**scry**, *v.*[1] *Obs.* [Aphetic form of DESCRY *v.*[2]] *trans.* To describe.

a **1400** *Sir Degrev.* 1859, I knewe never mane so wys, That couth telle the servise, Ne scrye the metys of prys Was servyd in that sale. *c* **1440** *Bone Flor.* 333 That men myght mewse on many a yere, Or he hyt scryed wyth stevyn. **1568** T. HOWELL *Arb. Amitie* (1879) 69, I neede no scribe to scrie my care, in restlesse rigour spreade.

scry (skraɪ), *v.*[2] Also 6 skrie. [Aphetic f. DESCRY *v.*[1]]

1. *trans.* To descry, see, perceive. *Obs.* exc. *dial.*

1555 PHAER *Æneid* III. (1558) G iv, Whom Phebus token trees & starres of heauen, hath taught to skrie. **1570** DEE *Math. Pref.* a iv, Landmarkes from the sea..well hable to be skried. *c* **1595** CAPT. WYATT *R. Dudley's Voy. W. Ind.* (Hakl. Soc.) 57 Our Generall..was the first that scryed a sayle. *a* **1734** NORTH *Examen* I. iii. ¶43 (1740) 147 The most that any close Inspection can scry out of, it is that a Party was found that would oppose the Exclusion Bill. **1807** STAGG *Poems* 41 Forth frae the bit they scry'd it furst, Agean the demon springs. **1855** *Whitby Gloss.* s.v. *Scried*, 'I scried it lang afore I com at it'.

absol. **1589** R. ROBINSON *Gold. Mirror* (Chetham) 8 As I ken'd him farre, as eyes could scry.

2. *intr.* To see images in pieces of crystal, water, etc. which reveal the future or secrets of the past or present; to act as a crystal-gazer.

Revived in the 19th c as a technical term: cf. SCRYER.

1528 W. STAPLETON *Confess.* (P.R.O.), His said boye did scrye unto him, which said spirytt I had after myself. And for a tryall..he caused his servaunt to goo hyde a certeyn money in the gardeyn, and I shewed for the same and oone Jakeson scryed unto me, but we could not accomplisshe our purpose. **1894** A. LANG *Cock Lane & Common-sense* 223 Thus the conditions under which the scryer can scry, are, as yet unascertained. **1897** —— *Dreams & Ghosts* iii. 61 In using the ball she..succeeded in seeing..persons..familiar to people for whom she 'scried', but totally strange to herself.

Hence '**scrying** *vbl. sb.*, crystal-gazing.

a **1608** DEE *Relat. Spir.* II. (1659) 4, I thereupon appointed with myself to bring the Childe to the place, and to offer him, and present him to the service of Seeing and Skrying from God. **1894** A. LANG *Cock Lane & Common-Sense* 212 The practice of 'scrying', 'peeping', or 'crystal-gazing' has been revived in recent years. **1902** F. PODMORE *Mod. Spiritualism* IV. vi. II. 297 The substances commonly used for scrying—crystal, glass, water,..etc.

scry, *v.*[3] *Obs.* exc. *dial.* (see E.D.D.). Also 9 scree. [f. SCRY *sb.*[2]] *trans.* To sift (corn, etc.). In quot. *fig.* Hence '**scrying** *vbl. sb.*

c **1615** BOYS *Wks.* (1629) 428 He must scry the Sermons of the Prophets and try the spirits, examining all things, and then holding that which is good. *Ibid.*, Scrying [see SCRY *sb.*[2]].

scry (skraɪ), *v.*[4] *Sc.* and *north.* Also 8 skry. [Aphetic form of ASCRY, ESCRY, a. OF. *escrier* to cry out.] *trans.* To proclaim (a sale, etc.).

1710 RUDDIMAN *Gloss.* to *Douglas' Æneis* s.v., To skry a Fair, i.e. to proclaim it. **1871** W. ALEXANDER *Johnny Gibb* xi. (1881) 70 If Samie Pikeshule had a roup to scry.

scryer ('skraɪə(r)). Also 6 scrier, 6, 7, 9 skryer. [f. SCRY *v.* + -ER[1].] One who 'scries'; a crystal-gazer.

1549 in *Narr. Reform.* (Camden) 334 Thomas Malfrey.. and a woman..are scryers of the glasse. **1555** EDEN *Decades* (Arb.) 319 The scrier which decerneth the veine of the myne goth before the workemen. *a* **1608** DEE *Relat. Spir.* I. (1659) 91 He..willed me to use John my Boy as my Skryer. **1691** WOOD *Ath. Oxon.* I. 244 Kelley was several times..false to Dee, yet he mostly performed the office of Skryer. **1889** *Proc. Soc. Psych. Research* XIV. 495 Dee's..scryer or seer, Kelly. **1900** *Edin. Rev.* Jan. 36 The profession of skryer, crystal-gazer, or speculator.

scrymppys, obs. pl. of SHRIMP *sb.*

†**scu.** *Obs.* Also 4 *pl.* skwez. [? repr. OE. *scuwa*, *scúa* shadow; the *sc* for the normal *sh* may be due to the influence of the corresponding ON. *skugge*: see SCUG *sb.*] **a.** A shadow. **b.** A screen.

13.. *Gaw. & Gr. Knt.* 2167 þe skwez of þe scowtes skayued hym þoȝt. *c* **1440** *Promp. Parv.* 450/2 Scu, spere in a howse, *idem quod* screne, *scrineum*, *ventifuga*.

scua, obs. form of SKUA.

†'**scuage.** *Obs.* [Aphetic form of ESCUAGE.] = ESCUAGE 2, SCUTAGE.

c **1450** *Godstow Reg.* 206 þat þe foresayde Abbesse & couente..be free & quiet of scuage & sute of here myllys. *c* **1460** *Osney Reg.* 48 Be lose and quite fro scuage, tallage, & all oþer seculer exaccions.

scuba ('skju:bə, 'sku:bə). Also **SCUBA**. [f. the initials of *s*elf *c*ontained *u*nderwater *b*reathing *a*pparatus.] Self-contained apparatus designed to enable a swimmer to breathe while under the water. Also (rarely) *collect.* and *ellipt.* for *scuba-diving* vbl. sb. Freq. *attrib.* and *Comb.*, esp. in **scuba-dive** *v. intr.*, to swim under water using such apparatus; so **scuba-diver**, **scuba-diving** *vbl. sb.* and *ppl. a.*

1952 HAHN & LAMBERTSEN *On using Self Contained Underwater Breathing Apparatus* (U.S. Nat. Acad. Sci.) 1 Within the last 3–5 years we have witnessed..a rapid increase in the numbers of self contained underwater breathing apparatus (SCUBA) in use... SCUBA are now in relatively large scale use by spearfishermen and sports swimmers. **1957** *Time* 25 Feb. 49/1 Most types of scuba are of the open-circuit design which supply air on demand, and discharge exhaled air into the water. **1962** (*title*) The new science of skin and scuba diving. **1963** G. L. PICKARD *Descriptive Physical Oceanogr.* v. 57 In clear ocean water the superior penetration of blue and green light is evident.. when SCUBA diving. **1963** *Today's Health* June 18/2 The scubacide victim is the person who tries to become a scuba diver in one fatal lesson (self-taught). **1966** T. PYNCHON *Crying of Lot 49* ii. 31 It [*sc.* a housing development] was to be laced by canals with private landings for power boats, a floating social hall,..all for the entertainment of Scuba enthusiasts. **1973** P. O'DONNELL *Silver Mistress* v. 82 Under the hull..two scuba-suited figures clung to magnetic limpets clamped to the steel plates. **1975** *New Yorker* 26 May 17 (Advt.), Swimming, scuba and long beautiful beaches. **1977** *Ibid.* 4 July 83/1 In 'The Deep'..Nick Nolte plays a scuba-diving hero called David. **1980** *Nature* 4 Sept. 12/1 Scuba dive over the lost road of Atlantis.

Hence as *vb.*; also '**scubaing** *vbl. sb.* (in quot. spelt *scubering*).

1973 B. MATHER *Snowline* xix. 234 Some of the boys are keen on scubering, water-skiing and fishing. **1977** *Rolling Stone* 16 June 74/5 (Advt.), Hike, swim, scuba, snorkel, sail.

†**scubard.** *Obs. rare*$^{-1}$. [a. OF. (*en*) *escobart.*] *in scubardis*: secretly, in private.

a **1300** *Cursor M.* 26936 Sum men in scubardis til oþer men telles þair folis, and sais amang riot ron 'All men wat wel þat i ha don'.

scuchen, -in, -(i)on, obs. ff. SCUTCHEON *sb.*[1]

scud (skʌd), *sb.*[1] Also 7 scudde, 8 scudd. [f. SCUD *v.*; in some uses perh. onomatopœic.]

1. a. The action of scudding; hurried movement.

1609 B. JONSON *Case Altered* IV. iv, O how she skudded, O sweet scud, how she tripped, O delicate trip and goe. *a* **1700** B. E. *Dict. Cant. Crew*, *Scud*, the Course or motion of the Clouds, in Fleeting. **1853** HERSCHEL *Pop. Lect. Sci.* i. §54 (1873) 42 The scud of the clouds before the wind. **1880** MEREDITH *Tragic Com.* xviii. (1892) 241 At times he came flashing through the scud of her thoughts.

b. A certain figure in skating.

1892 *Gentlew. Bk. Sports* I. 145 The hand-in-hand figures, such as the Mercury, the Q scud, the half-double scud [etc.].

2. a. Light clouds driven rapidly before the wind.

1669 DRYDEN & DAVENANT *Tempest* I. i, The Scud comes against the Wind, 'twill blow hard. **1762** FALCONER *Shipwr.* II. 128 The black'ning ocean curls; the winds arise; And the dark scud in swift succession flies. **1814** SCOTT *Ld. of Isles* I. xiii, The darkening scud comes on. **1885** H. O. FORBES *Nat. Wand. E. Archip.* 209 Peaks..along whose flanks the clouds rolled upwards in white humps and scuds.

b. A driving shower (of rain or snow).

1687 A. LOVELL tr. *Thevenot's Trav.* II. 187 With every change [of wind] we had a scud of Wind and Rain. *a* **1722**

Lisle *Husb.* (1752) 3 After such a scudd of rain cool cloudy weather ensues. **1825** Cobbett *Rur. Rides* 207, I had but one little scud during the day; just enough for St. Swithin to swear by. **1879** *Gd. Words* Jan. 48 The rain blowing in drizzling scuds.

c. A sudden gust of wind.

1694 Motteux *Rabelais* v. xviii. (1737) 76 Some Gusts, or Scuds of Wind..arose. **1863** 'C. Bede' *Tour in Tartan-land* 293, I beheld my wife..borne in a wild scud immediately in front of the three-abreast horses. **1893** 'Q.' (Quiller-Couch) *Delect. Duchy* 193 A sullen pond, over which the wind drove in scuds.

d. Ocean foam or spray driven by the wind; also *transf.* of ice or snow.

1850 B. Taylor *Eldorado* xxi. I. 143 Bailing out the scud thrown over the gunwale by every surge. **1894** N. Brooks *Tales of Maine Coast* 218 The air was drenched with spume and flying scud.

transf. **1884** Howells *Silas Lapham* (1891) I. 63 She..was..shielding her face from the scud of ice flung from the mare's heels. **1969** N. W. Parsons *Upon Sagebrush Harp* xv. 85 Usually, at dawn the wind died and a knee-high scud sharp as glass would skitter sullenly along the surface of the hard-packed snow.

e. *attrib.* Also *Comb.*, as **scud-like** *a.*

1860 *Merc. Marine Mag.* VII. 342 Light scud clouds driving across heavy masses show wind and rain. **1866** G. M. Hopkins *Jrnls. & Papers* (1959) 138 A 'dirty' looking kind of clouds, scud-like, rising. **1897** *Daily News* 4 Mar. 7/1 The boat disappeared in a yeast of scud rain and spindrift.

3. *School slang.* A swift runner.

1857 Hughes *Tom Brown* i. v, You ain't a bad scud, not by no means. *Ibid.* i. vii, Unless you're a first-rate scud.

scud (skʌd), *sb.*[2]

†**1.** Dirt, refuse. *Obs.*

1641 Best *Farm. Bks.* (Surtees) 95 For now the scudde and scumme passed away, and the dyke was as cleare and fresh att the last as att the first.

2. *Coal-mining.* (See quot. 1883.)

1829 *Glover's Hist. Derby* I. 59 Scud or ming coal. **1883** Gresley *Gloss. Coal-mining*, *Scud*, iron pyrites embedded in coal seams. *Ibid.*, *Scud* (Leicester), very thin layers of soft matter, such as clay, sooty coal, &c.

3. *Tanning.* Dirt, lime, fat, and fragments of hair which must be removed from a hide. Cf. scud *v.*[3] 2.

1885 A. Watt *Art of Leather Manufacture* xxvi. 324 The 'scud' is removed by working the pelt upon the beam with the blunt knife. **1969** T. C. Thorstensen *Pract. Leather Technol.* vi. 96 The hair-destruction system may result in uneven swelling and in the formation of scud (surface dirt) on the hides. *Ibid.* 98 The strong oxidizing action of the chlorine dioxide and chlorine results in the bleaching of the hair, and there is no dark scud left on the hide.

scud (skʌd), *sb.*[3] *dial.* [Belongs to scud *v.*[4]] A wisp of twisted straw, used for stopping a drain.

1843 *Jrnl. R. Agric. Soc.* IV. i. 26 We fill up either with haulm.., or ling,..or a scud of straw, or turf. **1847** *Ibid.* VIII. ii. 279 The materials..are 'haulm' (stubble), straw, 'scuds' (twisted straw), ling, or bushes.

scud (skʌd), *v.*[1] Also 6 scudde, skude, squdde, 6–7 scudd, 6–8 skud, 7 scude. *Pa. t.* 7 scud; *Pa. pple.* 6 scudde. [Of obscure etymology.

First recorded in the 16th c., but prob. much older in colloquial use. The initial *sc* shows that the word cannot descend from OE.: if not formed onomatopœically or by phonetic symbolism, it was presumably adopted either from Scandinavian or from LG. or Du. Formally, a possible origin would be MLG., MDu. *schudden* to shake (:—OS. *scuddian*), whence Sw. *skudda*, Da. *skudde*; but the sense seems not sufficiently near. The ON. *skunda*, to hasten, agrees in sense but not in form. It has been usual to refer the word to Da. *skyde* (with long vowel) to shoot (= ON. *skióta*), *skud* shot (= ON. *skot*), but the Da. change of *t* into *d* is a late development, and is not represented in Eng. words of Anglo-Danish origin. It may be noted that several dialects have a synonymous *scut* vb., of which *scud* may be an altered form. As the earliest instance of *scud* refers to the movement of a hare, and this has always been a prominent application of the vb., it seems possible that it may be connected with *scut* sb., the tail of a hare, sometimes applied to the animal itself.]

1. a. *intr.* To run or move briskly or hurriedly; to dart nimbly from place to place.

1532 More *Confut. Tindale* Wks. 721/2 Tindall hath, as ye haue hearde, scudded in & out lyke an hare yͭ had .xx. brace of greyhoundes after her. **1553** *Respublica* 1632, I have trodde & scudde tyll my winde is almost paste. **1567** Drant *Horace, Epist.* i. i. B viij, Sumtymes I skude abowt the towne in ciuyll matters drounde. **1602** Marston *Ant. & Mel.* iv. H 1, My sinewes tremble, and my panting heart Scuds round about my bosome to goe out. **1613–16** W. Browne *Brit. Past.* i. ii. 25 The Trout within the weeds did scud. **1707** *Curios. in Husb. & Gard.* 344 Animals..bounding over the Hills, and skudding along the Plains. **1812** Byron *Childe Har.* i. lxx, Some Richmond-hill ascend, some scud to Ware. **1822** Lady Granville *Lett.* 10 Mar. (1894) I. 223, I never saw him so slim and active, and he scuds into dinner [etc.]. **1830** Tennyson *'How' & 'Why'* 30 The black owl scuds down the mellow twilight. **1866** J. H. Newman *Gerontius* iv. 30 They scud away as cowards from the fight. **1894** Mrs. Ritchie *Chapters fr. Mem.* ix. 131 He stood looking at us fixedly,..and the train scudded off.

b. In the imperative: Be off! Make haste!

1602 Middleton *Blurt* iv. i. 68 Nay, scud:..begone and mum. **1649** Dk. Newcastle *Country Capt.* iii. 51 Scud and bringe wine you varletts. *c* **1854** Thackeray *Wolves & Lamb* i. Wks. 1869 XXII. 353 There's the outer bell. Scud, you vagabond!

2. To sail or move swiftly on the water. Now chiefly (and in technical nautical use exclusively), to run before a gale with little or no sail.

1582 Stanyhurst *Æneid* iii. (Arb.) 85 Italye see yoonder: thither with nauye be squdding. *a* **1592** Greene *Opharion* (1599) 39 (*Song of Arion*) Seated vpon the crooked Dolphins back, Scudding amidst the purple coloured waues:.. Neptune..Threw forth such stormes as [etc.]. **1600** Holland *Livy* xxxvii. 951 Pausistratus..skudded amaine with his ship to the entrance of the haven. **1669** Sturmy *Mariner's Mag.* i. ii. 17 She scuds before the Sea very well. **1697** Dryden *Æneid* v. 1086 They scud before the Wind. *a* **1704** T. Brown *Walk round Lond., Thames* Wks. 1709 III. iii. 60 The next [person] that we met was a jolly Parson, skudding from Lambeth-House in a Skuller. **1769** Falconer *Dict. Marine* (1780) s.v. *Scudding*, A ship either scuds with a sail extended on her foremast, or, if the storm is excessive, without any sail, which..is called scudding under *bare poles.* **1845** Darwin *Voy. Nat.* vi. 109 Having fairly scudded before the gale, we arrived by the middle of the day at the Sauce posta. **1884** Lady Brassey in *Good Words* Mar. 163/1 There was too much wind to scud.

3. Of clouds, foam, etc.: To be driven by the wind.

1699 Garth *Dispens.* v. 93 The rising Mists skud o're the dewy Lawns. **1793** Coleridge *Songs of Pixies* ii, When..scuds the cloud before the gale. **1833** Tennyson *Dream of Fair Wom.* 39 Crisp foam-flakes scud along the level sand, Torn from the fringe of spray. **1853** C. Bronte *Villette* xxxviii, They [the hours] passed like drift cloud—like the rack scudding before a storm.

4. *trans.* To pass, travel, or sail quickly over.

1632 Lithgow *Trav.* x. 424 Then scud I France, and cross'd the Pyrheneise. *c* **1750** Shenstone *Ruined Abbey* 197 His less'ning flock In snowy groups diffusive scud the vale. **1802** Scott *Cadyow Castle* xiii, The startled red-deer scuds the plain.

transf. **1895** Meredith *Amazing Marr.* I. iv. 41 Immense was the range of vision scudding the peaks.

5. *dial.* **a.** To throw (a flat stone) so as to make it skim the surface of a body of water. **b.** To shoot or discharge (a load of herrings) into the hold of a vessel.

See *Eng. Dial. Dict.*, and cf. *scudding-pole, -stone* (scudding *vbl. sb.*[1] b).

1874 Holdsworth *Deep-sea Fishing* 110 'Scudding the fish', as it is termed, enables them to be easily shaken out of the net, whence they fall on the deck and then through temporary openings into the well or hold.

6. *Sc.* To slap, beat, strike, spank; to beat down.

1814 W. Nicholson *Tales in Verse & Miscellaneous Poems* 123 And farmers, keen to cut the crap, Lest win's should scud it. **1866** J. Smith *Merry Bridal* (ed. 2) 23 Lassie, when I get ye I'll scud ye till I'm sair. **1925** *United Free Church Mission Record* Dec. 569/2 The risen wind scudded my cheek—wet, stinging, and with the bite of the sea. **1976** *Scotsman* 24 Dec. (Weekend Suppl.) 1/1 Any more cracks and I'll scud yer hint end for ye.

scud, *v.*[2] *Sc.* ? *Obs.* [Of obscure origin: cf. scuds *sb. pl.*] *trans.* 'To quaff, to drink liberally' (Jamieson, 1808).

a **1728** Ramsay *Monk & Miller's W.* 3 You wha laughing scud brown Ale, Leave Jinks a wee, and hear a Tale.

scud (skʌd), *v.*[3] [? f. scud *sb.*[2]]

1. *dial.* (See quot.)

1788 W. H. Marshall *Yorksh.* II. 350 *Scud*, to clean or scrape with a 'spittle' [i.e. a small spade].

2. *Tanning.* To remove remaining hairs, dirt, etc., from (skins or hides) with a hand-knife.

1880 *Times* 27 Sept. 12/6 The cost of unhairing, fleshing, and scudding all kinds of skins appears to have been reduced. **1883** R. Haldane *Workshop Receipts* Ser. ii. 372/2 The..remaining hairs, and other dirt, can now be very readily scudded out.

scud (skʌd), *v.*[4] *dial.* [Belongs to scud *sb.*[3]] *trans.* To make straw into 'scuds'.

1803 Young *Annals Agric.* XL. 332 (E.D.S.) Straw twisted together (provincially called skudded) is used [in covering drains]. **1843** *Jrnl. R. Agric. Soc.* IV. i. 40 The system of shallow parallel drains filled with wood and straw, or straw only, twisted or 'scudded', is universally adopted.

scuddaler ('skʌdələ(r)). *Shetl.* Also scudler, skudler. [Of obscure origin: Hibbert's explanation (quot. 1822) is untenable.] The leader of a band of maskers.

1821 Scott *Pirate* ii, It augured well of the expedition if Mordaunt could be prevailed upon to undertake the office of skudler, or leader of the band. **1822** Hibbert *Shetl. Isles* 560 The whole are under the controul of a director, named a scudler. [*Footnote*, An ancient Shetland name given to the pilot of a Scuda or twelve-oared boat.] **1888** Mrs. Saxby *Lads of Lunda* 211 Who disguise their persons, and under the guidance of a Scuddaler, do pass from house to house entertaining the folks.

scudder ('skʌdə(r)). [f. scud *v.*[1] + -er[1].] One who or that which scuds.

In recent Dicts.

scuddick ('skʌdɪk). *slang* and *dial.* Also **scuddock, scuttick, skiddi(c)k, skuddick;** (see E.D.D. and skerrick). An extremely small coin or amount. Also, something very small.

1823 'Jon Bee' *Dict. Turf*, *Scuddick* is used negatively; 'not a scuddick'—not any brads, not a whinn, empty clies. **1831** *Election Sp. Newport* (I.W.) 20 Apr. (E.D.D.), I won't pay one scuttick towards the taxes. **1840** E. Howard *Jack Ashore* xlvii, So I..offers the chaps their wages in advance—true-blue Jacks—wouldn't take a scuddick—so up anchor and off. **1863** Robson *Bards of Tyne* 303 To hear fine Sinclair tune his pipes Is hardly worth a scuddock. **1901** 'Zack' *Tales of Dunstable Weir* 248 Poor little skiddick! Shall I go for the doctor?

scudding ('skʌdɪŋ), *vbl. sb.*[1] [f. scud *v.*[1] + -ing[1].] The action of the verb in various senses.

1583 Golding *Calv. on Deut.* xxiv. 140 There is scudding from aultar to aultar. **1769** Falconer *Dict. Marine* ii. (1780), *Treou*, a square-sail, used in scudding. *c* **1850** *Rudim. Navig.* (Weale) 81 Scudding will tend to carry the ship beyond its influence.

b. *Comb.*: **scudding-pole**, 'a pole erected for the purpose of shooting herrings conveniently into the hold' (E.D.D.); **scudding-stone**, a thin stone that can be made to skim the surface of a body of water.

1874 Holdsworth *Deep-Sea Fishing* 110 The 'scudding-pole'..is fixed fore and aft between the mitch-board and the mast. **1897** Ld. E. W. Hamilton *Outlaws of Marches* xv. 166 While her great bobble of a lad's aye flinging scuddin'-stanes in Keeldar's Pool.

scudding ('skʌdɪŋ), *vbl. sb.*[2] *Tanning.* [f. scud *v.*[3] + -ing[1].] The action of the vb. scud[3]. Also *attrib.*

1882 Paton in *Encycl. Brit.* XIV. 384/1 This is partly accomplished by going over the hide on the beam with a scudding knife. *Ibid.* 389/2 The general sequence of unhairing..scudding, washing, and treating with the bran drench is the same as in the case of other skins.

scudding ('skʌdɪŋ), *ppl. a.* [f. scud *v.*[1] + -ing[2].] That scuds, in senses of the vb.

1545 Ascham *Toxoph.* ii. (Arb.) 126 That shafte whiche one yeare for a man is to lyghte and scuddinge, for the same selfe man the next yeare may chaunce be to heuy and hobblynge. **1762** Falconer *Shipwreck* iii. 35 What regions now the scudding ship surround. **1849** Helps *Friends in C.* ii. iv. (1851) II. 6 Strange images are sought out in the scudding clouds.

†**'scuddle**, *v.*[1] *Sc. Obs.* In 6 scudle. [? Back-formation from scudler.] **a.** *trans.* To wash (dishes). **b.** *intr.* 'To act as a kitchen-drudge' (Jam. 1828–81).

1581 *Satir. Poems Reform.* xliv. 194 The fyre to big, and scudle dischis clene.

scuddle ('skʌd(ə)l), *v.*[2] Now *dial.* [Frequentative f. scud *v.*[1]] *intr.* To run away hastily, to scuttle. 'A low word' (Johnson, 1755).

1577 Grange *Golden Aphrod.* G iv, The Goddesses..skuddelyng and sekyng to defende themselues. **1661** R. Burney *Κέρδιστον Δῶρον* 77 Lucifer might scuddle away as a subordinate sinner. **1706** Phillips (ed. Kersey), To *scud*, or *Scuddle away*, to scamper or run away all of a sudden. **1766** [Anstey] *Bath Guide* xiii. 45 How the Misses did huddle, and scuddle, and run. **1886** A. D. Willock *Rosetty Ends* (1887) 38 They gathered themsel's up an' scuddled awa into the hoose.

scuddy ('skʌdɪ), *a.*[1] and *sb.* *Sc.*

A. *adj.* Naked. Also *scuddy-naked*.

1829 J. Wilson *Noct. Ambr.* Wks. 1855 II. 267 Some skuddy-naked, some clothed in duds. **1831** *Ibid.* III. 286 Strip a kintra lass..perfectly skuddy. **1906** N. Munro in *Blackw. Mag.* Jan. 79/1 Scuddy little dolls.

B. *sb.* A naked child. Also, an unfledged bird.

1815 W. Finlayson *Simple Sc. Rhymes* 92 (E.D.D.) Wad ye hae them to rin like scuddies Without a rag? **1865** Janet Hamilton *Poems, Ess. & Sk.* (1870) 67 The mavis nest O' naked scuddies fu'.

'scuddy, *a.*[2] [f. scud *sb.*[2] + -y.] Turbid, full of sediment.

1797 *Encycl. Brit.* (ed. 3) XVIII. 872/2 It sometimes happens that wines scuddy and stubborn will not fall with one or even two forcings. **1872** Thudichum & Dupré *Treat. on Wine* xx. 633 The wines are spoiled during fermentation, become acidified, scuddy. **1964** R. Braddon *Year Angry Rabbit* xi. 94 Jacks..at once flung himself gratefully into a chair, spilling half his cold, scuddy tea into his lap as he did so.

scude, obs. form of scud *v.*

†**'scudler**. *Sc. Obs.* Also 5 scudler, 6 scudlar, skuddiller. [App. a. early OF. **escudeler* (later *escuelier*), f. **escudele* (later *escuele*, mod.F. *écuelle*) dish. Cf. squiller.] A scullion.

c **1470** Henry *Wallace* v. 1027 In the kyching scudleris lang tyme had beyne. **1536** Bellenden *Cron. Scot.* (1821) I. 179 He commandit al scudlaris..to be exilit within ane certane day. **1595** Duncan *App. Etym.* (E.D.S.), *Lixa*, a scullion, or scudler; *calo.* **1596** Dalrymple tr. *Leslie's Hist. Scot.* I. 196 The skuddilleris and kitchine boyes, and a few suddartis..invade the Ennimies. **1638** *New Litany* in *Bk. Sc. Pasquils* (1868) 57 From horsruber, scudler, scold and hagge, Tinker, treulerd, slouene and sluit.

scudler, variant of scuddaler.

‖**scudo** ('skudəʊ). Pl. scudi ('skudi), 8 *erron.* scudis. [It. = OF. *escu* (mod.F. *écu*), Sp., Pg. *escudo* shield, hence used as the name of a coin bearing a shield:—L. *scūtum* shield.] A silver coin and money of account formerly current in various Italian states, usually worth about 4 shillings.

In some states a gold scudo of the same value was also used, and occasionally the name was given to gold coins of much higher value.

1644 Evelyn *Diary* 29 Nov., I am told the gardener is annually allowed 2000 scudi for the keeping it. **1766** *Ann. Reg.* 121 She found means by her industry to save a sum of 6000 scudis. **1848** Thackeray *Van. Fair* lxiv, Everybody who had a balance of above five hundred scudi was invited to the balls which this prince of merchants gave.

scuds, *sb. pl. Sc.* [? f. SCUD *v.*[2]] Ale, beer.

1711 RAMSAY *On Maggy Johnstoun* iv, We guzl'd Scuds. **1806** J. COCK *Simple Strains* (1810) I. 104 I'll strive to smooth your thrawart fate Wi' whisky and gude scuds.

†**scuet.** *Obs. rare*$^{-1}$. [Of obscure origin: possibly an error for *scuer* skewer.] ? = SKEWER.

1634 SIR T. HERBERT *Trav.* 150 In some Buzzars they haue Camell or Mutton cut in mammocks or small bits put vpon scuets and carbonaded.

scufe. *Sc.* Also scoof, scuff. [Cf. ON. *skúfa* to shove, push.] (See quot.)

1825–80 JAMIESON, *Scoof, Scufe*, a sort of battledoor made of wood, used for striking the ball at Tennis, in order to save the palm of the hand from the severity of the stroke, Teviotdale. *Ibid., Scufe, Scuff*, a bat used by boys for playing at hand-ball, Roxb.

scuff (skʌf), *sb.*[1] Also skuff. [? f. SCUFF *v.*]

1. *Sc.* A slight glancing blow; a 'brush' with the hand. ***to get upon the skuff***, to get to scuffling.

1824 MACTAGGART *Gallovid. Encycl.* s.v., The scuff is the wind, as it were; the scuff of a cannon ball, blows a man to pieces. **1825** JAMIESON, Suppl., *Scuff*. 1. The act of grazing, or touching lightly. 2. A stroke, apparently a slight one, Banffs. **1839** MOIR *Mansie Wauch* xxiii. 292 After giving his breeches-knees a skuff with his loof, to dad off the stoure. **1854** H. MILLER *Sch. & Schm.* (1858) 337 We got upon the skuff after you left us. **1899** J. STRANG *Lass of Lennox* xv, 'She was a dacent woman Lucky'... 'She was a' that', says he, gie'in' his een a bit scuff wi' the back o' his haun'.

b. *transf.* A gust or puff of wind or rain.

1895 CROCKETT *Men of Moss-Hags* xlviii, It was a dark, gloomy day, with.. scuffs of grey showers scudding among the hilltops.

2. a. The noise made by the 'scuffing' of feet: see SCUFF *v.* 2b.

1899 B. M. DIX *Hugh Gwyeth* xvi, They rode a long space in silence, save for the soft scuff of the horses now and again as they came upon a stretch of sandy road.

b. A mark made by scraping or rubbing.

1954 J. STEINBECK *Sweet Thursday* v. 35 Brown calf shoes.., scuff on the right toe. **1976** B. LECOMBER *Dead Weight* i. 11 A thousand scuffs and scratches in the shabby wood and leather.

3. A rowdy crowd, rabble; also, one of such a crowd. Cf. SCURF *sb.*[1] 4.

1856 J. BALLANTINE *Poems* 67 On Queen's birth-days, thy squibs and pluffs Slappit in face o' drucken scuffs. **1879** *Macm. Mag.* XL. 501/1 This got a scuff (crowd) round us.

4. A type of slipper or sandal without a back. Chiefly *U.S.*

1909 in *Cent. Dict. Suppl.* **1938** *Sears, Roebuck Catal.* Fall/Winter 324/3 Adorable Slip-on 'Scuffs'. No trouble at all to slip in or out of these cunning, snug 'scuffs'. **1945** *Creative Footwear* Apr. 106/2 (Advt.), Shearling scuff, leather sole. **1953** S. RANSOME *Drag Dark* xiv. 140 In the snow in her stocking feet, her red scuffs lost behind her. **1968** J. IRONSIDE *Fashion Alphabet* 135 *Mule*, loose slipper with front vamp only, no back. Also called a 'scuff'. **1974** *Spartanburg* (S. Carolina) *Herald* 18 Apr. (Kmart Advt. Suppl.) 1 Soft-stepping flowered cotton terry cloth scuffs, molded rubber sole.

scuff (skʌf), *sb.*[2] Forms: *α. dial.* 8–9 skuft, 9 skufft, scuft. *β.* 9 scuf, scuff. [Of obscure origin: cf. the variant forms SCRUFF *sb.*[2], CUFF *sb.*[4]

It is usually assumed that the form *scuft* is the original, and that the word is ad. ON. *skopt* (poet.) hair = Goth. *skuft*. But there is little affinity of sense with the ON. word. The NFris. *skuft*, 'back of the neck of a horse', sometimes cited as cognate, seems to be = Du. *schoft* shoulder.]

The nape of the neck (only in references to seizing by the 'scuff (of the neck)'.

α. **1787** GROSE *Provinc. Gloss.*, *Skuft* (of the neck), the cuff or back of the neck. **1818** WILBRAHAM *Chesh. Gloss.*, *Skufft*, the back part of the neck. **1878** HARTLEY *Clock Alm.* 31 (E.D.D.) He seized Dawdles by th' scuft o' th' neck.

β. **1823** in *Spirit Publ. Jrnls.* 129 The champion caught the scampering coppersmith by the 'scuff of the neck'. *a* **1846** LANDOR *Imag. Conv.* Wks. 1853 II. 91/1 Take them by the scuf, and out with 'em. **1864** M. EYRE *Lady's Walk S. France* xiii. (1865) 159, I caught him [a dog] by the scuff of his neck.

scuff (skʌf), *v.* Also 6 scuffe, 7, 9 skuff. [Of uncertain and possibly mixed origin; perh. connected with SCRUFF, SCURF *vbs.*; possibly in part of onomatopœic origin (cf. quot. 1825 in SCUFF *sb.*[1] 2, and the Sc. dial. phrase 'to go scuff', to fly past with a whizzing noise). With sense 4 cf. CUFF *v.*; with sense 3b cf. SCUFFLE, SHUFFLE *vbs.*]

†**1.** *trans.* ? To evade, shirk (duty). Cf. SCRUFF *v. Sc. Obs.*

1595 DUNCAN *App. Etym.* (E.D.S.), *Eludo*, to scuffe, to shift off.

2. a. To touch lightly in passing; to strike with a slight glancing blow; to brush against (an object); to wipe off (something) with such a blow or stroke.

1824 MACTAGGART *Gallovid. Encycl.*, *Scuff*, to touch, to graze. **1826** G. BEATTIE *John o' Arnha* (ed. 5) 63 [The bird] Now soar'd aloft, now scuff'd the ground. **1832–53** A. CRAWFORD in *Whistle-binkie* III. 84 The sun clam up.. And frae his e'ebrows scuff'd the mornin' dew. **1867** GREGOR *Banffsh. Gloss.*, *Scuff*, to wipe very lightly; as, 'Scuff the stew aff o' yir sheen'.

b. To scrape (the ground, boards, etc.) with the feet; to wear off by treading.

1897 BEATTY *Secretar* xlviii, To whilk speech, after I had skuffed the boards with my feet,.. I made answer. **1905** TREVES *Other Side of Lantern* II. xvii. 115 A common of worn earth from which a million feet have scuffed whatever living thing has grown upon it.

3. a. *intr.* To walk (through dew, dust, snow, etc.) so as to brush it aside or throw it up; hence *trans.*, to throw *up* (dust by this manner of walking).

1768 ROSS *Helenore, Rock & wee pickle Tow* xvii, With a pair of rough rullions to scuff thro' the dew. **1893** *Wiltsh. Gloss.* s.v., To 'scuff up' the dust.. by dragging a foot along the road. **1900** *Academy* 28 Apr. 363/1 How pleasant it is to scuff along amidst the clattering leaves!

b. To shuffle with the feet.

1847 HALLIWELL, *Scuff*, to shuffle in walking. *West.* **1890** *Glouc. Gloss.* **1896** *Warwicksh. Gloss.* **1902** *Blackw. Mag.* Jan. 41/1, I vainly tried to scuff over the boards with my leather-soled shoes in the same noisy fashion as the men whose hobnailed boots scraped and banged against the wood.

4. *trans.* To buffet (a person).

1841 *Blackw. Mag.* L. 482/1 By these [persons].. this man of medicine is huffed and scuffed about. **1845** *Round Preacher* ii. 40 The gentleman.. scuffed and kicked him. **1875** J. BALLANTINE *Gaberlunzie's Wallet* (ed. 3) Gloss. (E.D.D.), Scuffs his ear.

5. *intr.* for *pass.* **a.** To become marked, worn, or damaged by rubbing or scraping.

1934 WEBSTER, s.v., Soft bindings scuff easily. **1978** *Radio Times* 18–24 Mar. 80 (Advt.), For kids who play rough, shoes that won't scuff.

b. Of a metal part: to undergo scuffing (SCUFFING *vbl. sb.* 3).

1959 *Engineering* 23 Jan. 117/3 The untreated mild steel rings scuffed shortly after being put under test. **1970** H. J. WATSON *Mod. Gear Production* xvi. 283 The peaks [of helical gears] were prone to scuff or pit in service largely owing to the high local loading on the restricted areas.

6. *Comb.*, as **scuff-resistant** adj., resistant to scuffing; hence **scuff resistance**.

1967 *Times Rev. Industry* May 84/3 The growing demand for higher gloss and better scuff and product resistance has led to the development of synthetic resin based types [of varnish]. **1959** *Spectator* 21 Aug. 219 (Advt.), Everything from scuff-resistant flooring and unbreakable gramophone records to transparent polyethylene wrapping. **1978** *Radio Times* 18–24 Mar. 80 (Advt.), A shoe that's an astonishing 30 to 40 times more scuff-resistant than normal leather.

†**scuffe.** *Obs. rare*$^{-1}$. (See quot.)

1599 HAKLUYT *Voy.* II. I. 169 Other seruingmen there were with the sayd Bassas, with red attire on their heads, much like French hoods,.. with scuffes or plates of mettall, like vnto the chape of an ancient arming sword, standing on their foreheads like other Janisaries.

scuffed (skʌft), *pa. pple.* and *ppl. a.* [f. SCUFF *v.* + -ED[1].]

a. Of clothing, etc.: Worn, shabby. *Sc., Anglo-Irish*, and *U.S.*

1819 TENNANT *Papistry Storm'd* (1827) 90 And scapularies scuff'd and shent.. Lay hither-thither on the bent. **1839** CARLETON *Fardorougha* (ed. 2) 62 Differing very little in his dress from an absolute squireen, save in the fact of his Caroline hat being rather scuffed. **1879** *New York Tribune* 12 Dec. (Cent.), How to restore scuffed gloves.

b. Of shoes, a floor, etc.: worn or marked by rubbing, scraping, or treading. Also with *up*.

1927 *Scribner's Mag.* Apr. 381/2 It wasn't a large room but everything in it, from the scuffed leather slippers to the stout .. easy chairs, proclaimed a man who knew how to put himself at ease. **1973** R. THOMAS *If you can't be Good* (1974) xii. 99 The beat-up desks.. and the scuffed-up floor. **1975** J. GORES *Hammett* (1976) vii. 51 The hardwood floor waxed but well-scuffed, ready for dancers. **1978** *Morecambe Guardian* 14 Mar. 17/3 Generally speaking there are two categories of small boy.. the studious, eyes-down-in-a-book type and the outdoor scuffed shoes clothes-in-a-mess variety.

c. *Engin.* Of a metal part: worn by scuffing.

1934 *Jrnl. R. Aeronaut. Soc.* XXXVIII. 310 Cases have come to one's notice where engines have suffered from troubles in the form of scored, or, as our friends in America term it, 'scuffed' pistons. **1941** [see SCUFFING *vbl. sb.* 3].

scuffer[1] ('skʌfə(r)). *dial.* or *slang* (chiefly *north.* and *Sc.*). Also scufter. [Origin obscure; perh. f. SCUFF *sb.*[2] or *v.*] A policeman.

1860 HOTTEN *Dict. Slang* (ed. 2) 209 *Scufter*, a policeman. **1886** A. G. MURDOCH *Scotch Readings* 1st Ser. (ed. 2) 78 The policeman.. was familiar [to].. him as.. 'the Scufter'. **1959** I. & P. OPIE *Lore & Lang. Schoolch.* xvii. 369 In Penrith children still commonly use the old northern name 'Scufty' or 'Scufter', a term which had been thought to be obsolete. **1961** PARTRIDGE *Dict. Slang* Suppl. 1263/1 *Scuffer*, a policeman: Liverpool: C. 20. Ex. dial. *scuff*, to strike... Cf. *scufter*. **1966** P. MOLONEY *Plea for Mersey* 45 Scuffer! Scuffer! on the beat, With thy elephantine feet, You can't see the way to go Cos yer 'at comes down too low. **1967** J. WAINWRIGHT *Talent for Murder* 17 Are you from the slops, sonny?.. The scuffers. The jacks. Are you from the coppers, sonny? **1970** T. LEWIS *Jack's Return Home* 49 What do you think I should do? Go to the scuffers? **1978** *Daily Mail* 25 Jan. 12/2 The strange language of a group who call themselves 'bogeys', 'bobbies' or 'scuffers'. They are, of course, regional variations describing policemen.

scuffer[2] ('skʌfə(r)). *N. Amer.* [f. SCUFF *sb.*[1] or *v.* + -ER[1].] = SCUFF *sb.*[1] 4 (see also quot. 1939).

1911 *Daily Colonist* (Victoria, B.C.) 5 Apr. 7/1 (Advt.), Correct spring styles in America's best footwear.. Broadwalk Scuffers for children. **1935** *Amer. Speech* X. 9/2 *Scuffers* and *ghillies* are words of the fashion page. **1939** M. P. PICKEN *Lang. of Fashion* 130/3 Scuffer.. child's sandal-like play shoe, light-weight and flexible with sturdy sole. Also used for sportswear by adults.

scuffing, *vbl. sb.* [f. SCUFF *v.* + -ING[1].]

1. The action of brushing against or scraping: see SCUFF *v.*

1883 STALLYBRASS tr. *Grimm's Teut. Myth.* III. 967 A man.. hears at midnight a scuffing of shoes. **1895** *Century Mag.* Aug. 571/1 There was a scuffing of many feet on the beach below.

2. (See quot. 1928.)

1928 HOLT & COOKE in *Bur. Standards Jrnl. Res.* I. 25 A considerable part of tread wear may be caused by the slipping of portions of the tread over the road surface in changing from the normal to the deflected condition and vice versa. This might be termed a scuffing action. **1955** W. H. CROUSE *Automotive Chassis & Body* vi. 157 High-speed operation causes much more rapid tire wear because of the high temperature and greater amount of scuffing and rapid flexing to which the tires are subjected.

3. *Engin.* The roughening of a metal surface designed to rub against another when the lubrication is inadequate to prevent local fusion and tearing of the two surfaces.

1941 *Engineering* 11 Apr. 286/1 Should a local breakdown of the lubricating-oil film occur, the two surfaces may momentarily become fused. With the reciprocating movement of the parts, a shearing action takes place,.. causing disruption of the surfaces. An example of this effect, which is known as piston-ring 'scuffing', is seen in Fig. 1, which shows the surface of a scuffed piston ring. **1950** *Engineering* 17 Mar. 310/1 Failure of a gear lubricant to prevent the teeth from making metallic contact may result in destruction of the tooth surfaces by 'scuffing', 'seizing', or 'welding': all different degrees of welding. **1961** *New Scientist* 26 Jan. 218/3 'Scuffing' of valve gear cams and the tappets that run against them occurred. **1966** G. W. MICHALEC *Precision Gearing* viii. 354 Scoring and scuffing are associated with welding (or seizing) and plastic deformation.

scuffle ('skʌf(ə)l), *sb.*[1] Also 7 skuffle. [f. SCUFFLE *v.*[1]]

1. A scrambling fight; an encounter with much hustling and random exchange of blows; a tussle.

Comb. *scuffle-royal* (nonce-wd.) after *battle-royal*.

1606 SHAKS. *Ant. & Cl.* I. i. 7 His Captaines heart, Which in the scuffles of great Fights hath burst The Buckles on his brest. *c* **1645** HOWELL *Lett.* (1650) I. II. xix. 32 Ther was a scuffle lately here 'twixt the Duke of Navers and the Cardinal of Guise, who.. meeting the last week.. from words they fell to Blows. **1670** BAXTER *Cure Ch.-div.* (ed. 3) Pref. II. §7 B4, I tell you again that a battel or a foot-ball skuffle will not settle the discomposed and divided Churches. **1725** DE FOE *New Voy.* (1840) 354 There had been a scuffle among them in which one of their canoes had been overset. **1760–72** H. BROOKE *Fool of Qual.* (1809) II. 17 A scramble, boys, a scramble! Hereupon a scuffle-royal instantly ensued. **1818–19** BYRON *Don Juan* II. xcii, Just like a black eye in a recent scuffle. **1876** FREEMAN *Norm. Conq.* IV. xviii. 107 The victor in this struggle, a scuffle rather than a battle, again took possession of the Earldom. **1891** 'J. S. WINTER' *Lumley* ii, A friendly scuffle between a fox-terrier pup and a fine black cat.

b. *transf.* and *fig.* Now *rare*. Formerly often, † a heated controversy.

1641 MILTON *Ch. Discipl.* II. 69 Such poore drifts to make a Nationall Warre of a Surplice Brabble, a Tippet-scuffle. **1662** H. MORE *Antid. Ath.* I. ix. §2 (1712) 26 All those changes and varieties we see in the World are but the result of an Eternal Scuffle of coordinate Causes. **1664** [see SCAMBLE *sb.*[2]]. **1675** BAXTER *Cath. Theol.* I. I. 22 And here the Thomists and Scotists have another skuffle, Whether [etc.]. **1731** T. BOSTON *Mem.* vii. (1899) 111 With the student above referred to I had had some scuffles on the Arminian points. **1770** BURKE *Pres. Discont.* 74 They were not afraid .. that their resolution to stand or fall together should, by placemen, be interpreted into a scuffle for places.

2. The action of scuffling; confused utterance (of speech); shuffling (of feet).

1899 B. CAPES *Lady of Darkness* 260 His wry jaw and crippled scuffle of speech. **1905** TREVES *Other Side of Lantern* IV. viii. (1906) 290 The scuffle of naked feet upon the stones makes little more sound than the rustle of a snake.

scuffle ('skʌf(ə)l), *sb.*[2] [a. Du. *schoffel* weeding-hoe.]

1. = SCUFFLER[2].

1798 J. MIDDLETON *Agric. M'sex.* v. 96 Every farmer of arable land should possess himself of a scuffle... This implement is used in the same manner as a harrow: its feet cut up the weeds, and, altogether, it pulverizes the soil. **1805** R. SOMERVILLE *Agric. Surv. E. Lothian* 69 The Horse-hoe or Scuffle.. is used more or less in all drill crops. **1856** 'STONEHENGE' *Brit. Rural Sports* I. I. v. §1. 49 Another very considerable proportion was left in rough fallow, undisturbed by the scuffle.

2. A gardener's thrust-hoe. *local* and *U.S.*

1797 S. DEANE *Newengland Farmer* (ed. 2) 95/2 *Dutch Hoe*, sometimes called a *Scuffle*; an iron instrument, with a sharp steeled edge, nearly in the shape of the letter D. **1825** J. LORAIN *Nature & Reason harmonized in Practice of Husbandry* 191 The scuffle (or D hoe as it is sometimes called) will destroy weeds growing on a level surface. **1841** HARTSHORNE *Salop. Antiq.* 558 *Scuffle*, a hoe, chiefly used in gardens for cutting up weeds. **1848** LOWELL *Biglow Papers* Ser. I. iii, Where so much is to do in the beds, he were a sorry gardener who should wage a whole day's war with an iron scuffle on those ill weeds that make the garden-walks of life unsightly. **1879** MISS JACKSON *Shropsh. Word-bk.*, *Scuffle*, a garden implement used for cutting off weeds at the roots, —generally known as a Dutch hoe.

scuffle ('skʌf(ə)l), *v.*[1] Also 6 skufle, 7 skuffle. [A frequentative formation on a base perh. of

Scandinavian origin: cf. Sw. *skuff* a push, *skuffa* to push, f. Teut. root **skuf-* (*skub*): see SHOVE, SHUFFLE *vbs.*

The Eng. SCUFF *v.* (which is later in our quots.) can hardly be directly connected; cf. however sense 5 below with SCUFF *v.* 3 b.]

1. a. *intr.* To struggle confusedly *together* or *with* another or others; to fight at close quarters in a disorderly manner, with pulling, pushing, and random delivery of blows; to tussle.

1590 R. HARVEY *Pl. Perc.* 6 Shall we haue neighbors children, lie skufling in the kennel together by the eares like bride well birds? **1600** HOLLAND *Livy* II. 75 He..rushed amongst the thickest of the Veientians, and skuffled with many of them together. **1612** DRAYTON *Poly-olb.* XII. 196, I ..haue seene in former dayes The best Knights of the world, and scuffled in some frayes. **1622** BEAUM. & FL. *Philaster* v. i, Weele skuffle [1st ed. 1620 *reads* shuffle] hard before he perish. **1743** N. APPLETON *Serm.* 21 They scuffle, and oftentimes quarrel as Children. **1849** ALB. SMITH *Pottleton Leg.* ix. 64 The field-mice..scuffled amongst the corn. **1852** MRS. STOWE *Uncle Tom's C.* xxxix, Only groans and people scuffling and rolling round on the garret-floor half the night!

b. *transf.* and *fig.* Now *rare*; in the 17th c. often with the sense: †To contend vigorously or resolutely.

1601 HOLLAND *Pliny* XXXVI. xv. II. 585 When the great men of the citie, Cæsar and Pompey, were skuffling together by the eares, hee knew well how to fish in a troubled water. **1639** N. N. tr. *Du Bosq's Compl. Woman* I. 7 Here I must needs scuffle with two great errors. *a* **1668** LASSELS *Voy. Italy* (1670) I. 99 [Genoa] is so well fortified on the other side ..that they could scuffle notably in their own defence. **1678** R. L'ESTRANGE *Seneca's Mor.*, *Ep.* xxviii. (1696) 614 Both at Sea and Land we Tug and Scuffle for Dominion and Wealth. **1796** BURKE *Regic. Peace* Wks. VIII. 181 Even when their perverse and litigious nature sets them to equivocate, scuffle, and fight about the terms of their written obligations. **1841** CATLIN *N. Amer. Ind.* (1844) II. lviii. 249 To scuffle for a few years upon the plains with the wild tribes,..for the flesh and the skins of the last of the buffaloes.

2. a. *trans.* To put *on*, *out*, *up*, etc. in a scrambling or confused manner.

1579 TOMSON *Calvin's Serm. Tim.* 63/1 There should be a..discipline [in the Church], to the end that matters might not be huddeled and scuffled vppe together confusedly, and without order. **1839** *Lett. fr. Madras* (1843) 285, I had to rise and scuffle all my things out into the other half of the building..in a heavy rain. **1844** ALB. SMITH *Adv. Mr. Ledbury* xxxi. (1886) 96 Scuffling on his dressing-gown, [he] advanced towards them. **1863** J. G. WOOD in *Intell. Observ.* IV. 22 [The mole] passing the worm underneath his body from his fore to his hind feet in a very peculiar manner, scuffling it, as it were, backwards and forwards.

b. To obtain, collect, raise (money). Also with *up* and *intr.* (const. *up on*). *slang* (chiefly *U.S.*).

1946 MEZZROW & WOLFE *Really Blues* (1957) 378 *Scuffle up*, raise, collect, get together. **1956** B. HOLIDAY *Lady sings Blues* (1973) vii. 66, I stayed around Philly a couple of days before I could scuffle up enough to get back to New York on the bus. **1965** 'MALCOLM X' *Autobiogr.* (1966) xvi. 389 Trying to scuffle up on some bread. **1973** *Brit. Jrnl. Sociol.* XXIV. 203 It is surely of immense sociological significance that when a Ras-Tafarian 'scuffles' a fare (he might beg, borrow or steal it), he seeks to migrate not to Ethiopia, as we would expect, but to Britain or the United States.

3. a. *intr.* To struggle *through*, *on*, *along*; hence, to go hurriedly and superficially (*through* or *over* some operation).

1784 COWPER *Tiroc.* 340 The rude will scuffle through with ease enough, Great schools suit best the sturdy and the rough. **1844** H. STEPHENS *Book of Farm* II. 218 They are usually scuffled over in the morning with the currycomb. **1844** THACKERAY in *Punch* VII. 83/2 Scuffling through our blessed meals, that we may be early on the road. **1885** RUNCIMAN *Skippers & Sh.* 235 You go to school and scuffle on the best way you can.

b. To survive with difficulty, to make a bare living by uncongenial or degrading means. *slang* (chiefly *U.S.*).

1939 W. HOBSON *Amer. Jazz Music* (1940) 173 At the bottom of the economic pile are those musicians who have nothing which could accurately be called a job but are taking whatever one-night stand happens along; this is called 'scuffling'. **1956** S. LONGSTREET *Real Jazz Old & New* xviii. 147 *Scuffle* is to get by. **1956** M. STEARNS *Story of Jazz* (1957) xvii. 212 The Basie band was scuffling. 'It was a cracker town but a happy time,' Basie recalls. **1961** RIGNEY & SMITH *Real Bohemia* p. xvi, *Scuffle*, to live by one's wits, not by a gig. **1972** T. KOCHMAN *Rappin' & stylin' Out* 164 'Scuffling' in the idiom means barely making it from day to day, generally by engaging in nonprestigious..activities such as begging, collecting and returning pop bottles for the deposit, working at odd jobs for minimum wages, etc.

4. To go in hurried confusion; to move with much effort and fuss; also *trans.* (causatively).

1838 *Lett. fr. Madras* xx. (1843) 204 The bearers, Peons, and people whom I had scuffled half out of their lives to get ready in time. **1840** THACKERAY *George Cruikshank* (1869) 298 The outward rush of heroes,..scuffling at the door, is in the best style of the grotesque. **1886** RUSKIN *Præterita* I. 412 Drive the populace headlong past it as fast as they can scuffle.

5. To move with a shuffling gait; also, to shuffle (with the feet).

1825 T. HOOK *Sayings* Ser. II. *Passion & Princ.* vi, The man..scuffling slipshod along the sanded floor. **1896** 'IAN MACLAREN' *Brier Bush* 219 Is't true Elspeth scuffled wi' her feet at the laist head [of the sermon] and gar'd him close?

6. *Comb.*: **scuffle-shoe** *nonce-wd.*, a person of 'slipshod' habits.

1895 MEREDITH *Amazing Marr.* xxxv, So scathing was Gower's tone of irate professor to shirky scholar—or it might be put, German professor to English scuffle-shoe.

Hence **'scuffling** *vbl. sb.* and *ppl. a.* Also **'scufflingly** *adv.*

1599 NASHE *Lenten Stuffe* 43 This scuffling or bopeepe in the darke they had a while without weame or bracke. **1610** HOLLAND *Camden's Brit.* II. 134, I may passe over with silence the skuffling skirmishes which hapned euery daie. **1622** FLETCHER *Prophetess* IV. v, Your scurvie scuffling trade. **1709** *Brit. Apollo* II. *Supernum. No.* 2. 3/2 They had a scuffling for it. **1796** SOUTHEY *Lett. fr. Spain* (1799) 351 A noise like scuffling of feet. **1868** MISS BRADDON *Dead-Sea Fruit* i, The wrestling, and scuffling, and striving, and struggling of modern commerce. **1886** KIPLING *Departm. Ditties*, etc. (1899) 91 My Son, if a maiden deny thee and scufflingly bid thee give o'er. **1894** —— *Jungle Bk.* 51 The monkeys..would..fight and cry in scuffling crowds.

scuffle ('skʌf(ə)l), *v.*^{2} [f. SCUFFLE *sb.*^{2} Cf. Du. *schoffelen.*] *trans.* To scarify or stir the surface (of land) with a thrust-hoe or horse-hoe; to hoe (a crop), cup up (weeds), turn in (seed) by means of a scuffle or scuffler.

1766 *Complete Farmer* s.v. *Walk* 7 Z 3/1 If they [*sc.* walks] are scuffled over with a Dutch hoe in dry weather, and raked smooth, it will destroy the moss and weeds. **1805** DICKSON *Pract. Agric.* I. Pl. x, The seed is by this implement scuffled in. **1807** T. RUDGE *Agric. Glouc.* (1813) 110 The land is immediately 'scuffled' or torn to pieces with the scuffler. **1863** *Intell. Observ.* IV. 199 A labourer..scuffling turnips.

Hence **'scuffling** *vbl. sb.* (also *attrib.*).

1802 W. AMOS *Drill Husb.* 243 Mellow land..requires no other preparation than scuffling, harrowing &c. **1844** H. STEPHENS *Book of Farm* III. 959 The [mould-board] plough ..is convertible into a scuffling or cleaning plough, or horse-hoe. *Ibid.*, A second mortise is punched in each wing-bar to receive the scuffling coulters.

'scuffle-hunter. *Naut. slang.* (See quots.)

1796 COLQUHOUN *Police Metrop.* (ed. 3) 54 The prevailing practice of discharging and delivering the cargoes of ships by a class of aquatic labourers, known by the name of lumpers and scufflehunters. *Ibid.* 66 Those (who are distinguished by the nick-name of *Scuffle-hunters*) prowl about the wharfs.., under pretence of asking employment: but their chief object is to pillage and plunder whatever comes in their way. **1840** MARRYAT *Poor Jack* xviii, We've.. the Scuffle Hunters, and the River Pirates.

scuffler^{1} ('skʌflə(r)). Also 7 **scufler.** [f. SCUFFLE *v.*^{1} + -ER^{1}.] One who scuffles.

1633 MARMION *Fine Comp.* III. iv. F 2 b, *Fid.* Ile belabour you the next time I meet you. *Cap.* What Scufler, dost thou thinke ile faile my friends? No Hector I scorne it. **1642** *Tom Nash his Ghost* (title-p.), To the three scurvy Fellowes of the upstart Family of the Snufflers, Rufflers and Shufflers; the thrice Treble-troublesome Scufflers in the Church and State. **1961** F. G. CASSIDY *Jamaica Talk* x. 215 A *scuffler* is a thief. **1965** H. WILLIAMSON *Hustler* vi. 169 He said he was a hustler, but he really wasn't nothin' but a goddamn scuffler.

scuffler^{2} ('skʌflə(r)). [f. SCUFFLE *v.*^{2} + -ER^{1}.] An agricultural implement for scarifying and stirring the surface of the ground, esp. between the rows of crops; a horse-hoe.

1797 BILLINGSLEY *Agric. Somerset* (ed. 2) 278 I verily think, that his [J. Cooke's] instruments called the scuffler, and scarifier, are the best contrivances I ever beheld, for the pulverization of the soil, and the destruction of weeds. **1891** *Times* 5 Oct. 3/2 The best remedies for the pest..being nitrate of soda..and the use of scufflers, or of horse-hoes.

b. Each of the scuffling coulters of a scuffler.

1844 H. STEPHENS *Book of Farm* III. 959 In returning it to the double mould-board state, it is only necessary to remove the scufflers and the feathered share.

scuffy ('skʌfɪ), *a. Sc.* [f. SCUFF *v.* + -Y]. = SCUFFED *a.* Also *fig.*

1858 M. PORTEOUS *Real 'Souter Johnny'* 32 Some scuffy chiels to mak a boddle On thy sweet muse hae daured to saddle..Brain brats that ye wad scorn to cuddle Or think were thine. **1895** W. C. FRASER *Whaups of Durley* xiii. 189 He wears black claes, awfu' scuffy.

scuft, dial. variant of SCUFF *sb.*^{2}

scufter, var. SCUFFER^{1}.

scufting ('skʌftɪŋ). (See quots.)

1688 HOLME *Armoury* III. 85/2 Bran or Scufting, the Husk of the Corn. **1881** *Leic. Gloss.* s.v. *Meal*, The various qualities of meal are distinguished into—1. Bran. 2. Shorts. 3. Scuftings, pollards, or shorts-and-sharps.

scug (skʌg), *sb.*^{1} *Sc.* and *north.* Forms: 5–7 (9) scoug, 6 skug, (skowg, skugg, 7 skough, scugg, scugge), 9 sco(o)g, skoug, 6– scug. [a. ON. *skugge* wk. masc., shadow (Sw. *skugga* fem., Norw. *skugge*, Da. *skygge*) = OE. *scu(w)a*, OHG. *scuwo* shade, Goth. *skuggwa* mirror :—OTeut. **skuwon-*.]

1. Originally, shadow; the shade or shelter afforded by a rock, bush or the like; hence, a shelter. ***to take scug***: to take shelter.

1513 DOUGLAS *Æneis* VI. iv. 8 And skuggis dym of a full dern wod schaw. *Ibid.* 74 As Jupiter,..With erdis scug hydis the hevynis all. *Ibid.* VII. Prol. 47 Thik drumly scuggis dirknit so the hevyne. **1596** DALRYMPLE tr. *Leslie's Hist. Scot.* (1888) I. 30 In the scoug of the craig and castell is a verie quyet hauining place. *Ibid.* II. 321 Hume with sum of his cumpaniounis slipis quyetlie in the skug [orig. *ad umbracula*], and thair he rested and hid him selfe. **1823** GALT *Entail* xxi, Instead o' gallanting awa under the scog and cloud o' night. **1825** BROCKETT *N.C. Gloss.*, *Skug*, a sheltered place. **1890** 'H. HALIBURTON' *In Scottish Fields* 33 Hastening through the rain to rustic scoogs or the shelter of friendly cottages.

b. *fig.* Cloak, pretence, outward show.

1456 SIR G. HAYE *Law Arms* (S.T.S.) 281 How thai suld be punyst that beris otheris armes wrangwisly, in entencioun to do mys under scoug of thame covertly. *a* **1578** LINDESAY (Pitscottie) *Chron. Scot.* (S.T.S.) II. 282 That the said lord micht have sic ane skug of him [*sc.* a counterfeit bishop] to the eies of the peopill that be him he micht obteine the proffeit of the said benefice. **1606** BIRNIE *Kirk-Buriall* xix. (1833) F 3, Under skough of the conscience scruple. **1688** A. SHIELDS *Notes & Heads* (1709) 17 (Jam.) Some did boast of their pretended performances, and so make them a scugg to hide their knavery with. **1871** W. ALEXANDER *Johnny Gibb* (1873) 215 But brawly kent I that a' this was but a scoug to keep some ither thing oot o' sicht.

scug (skʌg), *sb.*^{2} *dial.* A squirrel.

1718 J. FOX *Wanderer* 73 He first chid me, then depriv'd me of my poor skug. **1804** CHARLOTTE SMITH *Conversat.*, etc. I. 123 Scug does not very willingly expose himself in the open day far from his trees.

scug (skʌg), *sb.*^{3} *School slang.* Also **skug.** (See quot. 1881.) Also in extended use. Also *attrib.* Hence **'scuggish, 'scuggy** *adjs.*

1825 C. M. WESTMACOTT *Eng. Spy* I. 82 Come fill the bowl with Bishop up, Clods, Fags, and Skugs, and Muttons. *Note*, Scug or Skug, a lower boy in the school, relating to sluggish. **1847** MRS. GORE *Castles in Air* xix, Whereas, to lay by ten thousand a-year out of eighteen, till his best days are gone by, makes what, at Eton, we used to call, a scug of him at once. **1881** *Everyday Life in Public Sch.* 312, *Scug*, Et[on]. Har[row]. Negatively, a boy who is not distinguished in person, in games, or social qualities. Positively, a boy of untidy, dirty, or ill-mannered habits; one whose sense of propriety is not fully developed. **1911** R. NEVILL *Floreat Etona* iii. 98 Once it began to be considered 'scuggish', the fate of Eton pugilism was sealed. **1916** E. F. BENSON *David Blaize* v. 101 These are all college houses, in-boarders, and rather scuggy compared to out-boarders. *Ibid.* viii. 143 You were such a scug, you see, that you didn't do those things when it was scuggish not to. **1922** S. LESLIE *Oppidan* iv. 48 A *Tug* was something between a *scug* and a hireling chorister. *Ibid.* v. 57 The sad sight of a *Pop* wearing a *scug*-cap. **1928** *Observer* 15 Apr. 29/4 A band of what I can only describe as 'Scugs' in bowler hats. **1940** E. F. BENSON *Final Edition* ii. 27 Mr. Luxmore..wrote to a friend in withering disdain of him and his official purple as a Monsignor, declaring that he was just the same 'sharp insignificant little scug as he had been at Eton'. **1962** J. P. CARSTAIRS *Pardon my Gun* ii. 28 He was a bit of a scug but what the hell. **1980** D. MARLOWE *Rich Boy from Chicago* xxi. 314 Many refused to talk..dismissing Lambert as a 'scug', a loathsome queer.

scug (skʌg), *v. Sc.* and *north.* Forms: 6, 8–9 scug, 6, 9 scoug, 9 sco(o)g, skug. [f. SCUG *sb.*^{1}]

1. *trans.* To shade, shelter, screen, protect.

1513 DOUGLAS *Æneis* VII. ii. 24 Joyfull and blyth thai entir in the flude, That derne about scuggit wyth bewis stude. *Ibid.* VIII. vi. 90. *a* **1774** FERGUSSON *Song*, '*My ain kind Deary, O!*' 7 At thornie dike and birken tree, We'll daff, and ne'er be weary, O! They'll scug ill een fra you and me. **1822** GALT *Sir A. Wylie* II. ii. 21 I'll gang..mysel, and muddle about the root o' this affair till I get at it... Naebody in this country-side kens me; I'll be scoggit wi' my ain hamely manner. **1825** BROCKETT *N.C. Gloss.*, *Skug*, to hide, to screen. **1898** C. SPENCE *From Braes of Carse* 29 He has hives o' bees..Weel scouged wi' shrubs..Frae ony blast the wind can blaw.

absol. **1818** *Edin. Mag.* Sept. 154/1 He hadnae call'd on the Halie Name That scugs in the evil hour.

2. *refl.* and *intr.* To take cover or shelter, to hide.

1819 W. TENNANT *Papistry Storm'd* (1827) 187 Within their sacrify'd abodes Scougin' themsel' frae stanes and clods. **1823** W. JAMESON *Mem. & Lett.* (1845) 94, I went to His holy table and felt like one in the pelting of a storm, scugging under Immanuel.

3. *trans.* To take shelter from (the elements).

1812 W. GLASS *Caledonian Parnassus* (1814) 20 Beneath the ivy-twining bow'r, Where aft I've scoug'd the simmer show'r. **1886** 'H. HALIBURTON' *Horace* (1900) 43 Wind and snaw, Are far abune oor fit, But while we scoog them, let them blaw.

scuggery ('skʌgərɪ). *north. dial.* [f. SCUG *sb.*^{1} + -ERY.] Concealment, secrecy.

a **1568** *Henryson's Two Mice* xiv. (Bannatyne MS.), In skugry ay, throw rankest girss and corne, And wondir sly, full preuely cwth thay creip. **1788** W. H. MARSHALL *Yorksh.* II. 350 In *scuggery*, in secrecy; hid, as from creditors.

†**'scuggy,** *a. Sc. Obs. rare*$^{-1}$. In 6 **skogy.** [f. SCUG *sb.*^{1} + -Y.] Shady, gloomy.

1513 DOUGLAS *Æneis* VII. x. 54 Quham the sydis of a thik wode of tre Closis full derne wyth skogy bewis hie.

scuil(l, obs. forms of SCHOOL.

scul, obs. form of SCHOOL, SKULL.

sculc, sculcare, obs. ff. SKULK, SKULKER.

sculch (skʌlʃ). *dial.* and *U.S.* Also **sculsh, scultch, skultch.** [var. of CULCH.] = CULCH 1, 2.

1847 HALLIWELL, *Sculsh*, rubbish. **1865** W. WHITE *Eastern Engl.* II. 236 Here from time to time the men throw into the river what they call 'skultch', which an outsider would call rubbish... Of such stuff as this a comfortable bed [for oyster spawn] is made. **1891** M. COLE *Cy Ross* 38 They dumped the tunnel full of big rock an' sculch.

sculck, obs. form of SKULK.

†**sculd.** *Obs. rare*$^{-1}$. [Connected with ON. *skilja* to divide.] A parting.

a **1300** *Cursor M.* 15541 Þis ilk night sal be a sculd [*Gött.* a skaile, *Fairf.* parting, *Trin.* a scateryng] betuix you and me.

†**'sculding, 'scoulding.** *Obs. Orkney* and *Shetl.* [a. Norw. *skulding* accusation.] (See quot.)

1576 in *Oppress. Orkney & Zetld.* (1859) 49 The Laird.. chargit ten houshaldis for scoulding. **1576** *Ibid.* 51 Thair is ane branche of this law of Granderie, callit Sculding, that is to say, ane brute or sclander of thift, pykrie, or sic uther crymes, rasit by the deid of ane single persoun [etc.].

sculduddery (skʌl'dʌdərɪ). *Sc.* and *U.S.* Also 8 sculdudry, 8–9 **sculduddry,** 9 **skulduddery**; cf. also SKULDUGGERY. [Of obscure origin.]

1. 'A term, now used in a ludicrous manner, to denote those causes that come under the judgment of an ecclesiastical court, which respect some breach of chastity' (Jam.).

Jamieson's words imply that the word was originally in serious use, but of this there seems to be no evidence.

1713 CENTLIVRE *Wonder* III. iii. Wks. 1760 III. 42 But I'm seer ther's na sike honest People here, or there wou'd na be so muckle Sculdudrie [*note* Fornication]. **1714** RAMSAY *On J. Cowper* 5 There's none..Could sa'r sculdudry out like John. *c* **1730** BURT *Lett. N. Scot.* (1818) I. 190 If any one be brought before a presbytery &c., to be questioned for sculduddery, *i.e.* fornication or adultery. **1818** SCOTT *Hrt. Midl.* xvi, [They] can find out naething but a wee bit skulduddery for the benefit o' the Kirk-treasurer.

2. Obscenity.

1821 GALT *Legatees* ix. Let. xxxii. 271 All the sculduddery of the business might have been well spared from the eye of the public. **1824** SCOTT *Redgauntlet* Let. xi, Speaking blasphemy and sculduddry.

3. *attrib.* passing into *adj.* **a.** Concerned with 'sculduddery' as a punishable offence. **b.** Of literature or conversation: Obscene.

1756 A. PENNECUIK *Coll. Sc. Poems* 136 Sculdudry-fowk may now sing dool, And steep their graith in a cald pool. *a* **1779** D. GRAHAM *Misc. Writ.* (1883) II. 135 They did na like sculdudery wark, but said na meikle against it. **1824** SCOTT *Redgauntlet* Let. xi, The rental-book..was lying beside him; and a book of sculduddry sangs was put betwixt the leaves.

scule, obs. form of SCHOOL.

sculk, -er, -ing: see SKULK, -ER, -ING.

scull (skʌl), *sb.*^{1} Also 4–5 skulle, 7 scul, 5 sculle, 4–9 skull. [Of obscure origin.

Some would identify it with SKULL bowl, goblet, supposing that the name refers to the hollowed form of the blade; but this seems very improbable.]

1. A kind of oar. **a.** An oar used to propel a boat by working it from side to side over the stern of the boat, reversing the blade at each turn. Also in *Comb.*, as **scull-hole** = *sculling-hole* s.v. SCULLING *vbl. sb.* b. **b.** An oar, shorter and lighter than a 'rowing' oar, so that a pair can be operated at once by one person, who sits midway between the sides of the boat.

1345–6 in Nicolas *Hist. Royal Navy* (1847) II. 477 [For four large and long oars called] skulles [4*s.* 8*d.*]. **1486** *Naval Acc. Hen. VII* (1896) 13, ij sculles..for the bote of the said ship. **1495** *Ibid.* 193 After skullys..j. *a* **1500** *Piers of Fullham* 275 in Hazl. *E.P.P.* II. 12 And for to rowe in a barge with a skulle Avayleth not but the flud be at full. **1530** PALSGR. 268/2 Scull to rowe with, *auiron.* **1674** PETTY *Disc. R. Soc.* 56 Suppose a Paralellipipedon-Boat or Vessel, of breadth fit for a pair of Skulls..and of length sufficient for 9 such Skulls or Oars. **1843** G. LITTLE *Life on Ocean* 63 The crew got the bight of the rope fore and aft the boat, leading it from the stern over the scull-hole. **1856** KANE *Arct. Expl.* II. xxix. 287 We moved on in deep silence, with a single scull astern. **1869** DICKENS *Mut. Fr.* I. i, The girl rowed, pulling a pair of sculls very easily. **1875** W. B. WOODGATE *Oars & Sculls* xv. 118 On a sliding seat the sculls, like oars, should be a trifle longer inboard. **1973** W. ELMER *Terminol. Fishing* iv. 125 Many of the smallest boats are not fitted with rowlocks or tholes, but have a notch in the transom for sculling (*sculling-notch* or *scull-hole*).

†**2.** A boat propelled with a scull or a pair of sculls; a sculling-boat. *Obs.*

1611 COTGR., *Napelette*, a small skiffe, scull, or cocke-boat. **1661** PEPYS *Diary* 3 Dec., Thence by water..being carried by him in oares that the other day rowed in a scull faster than my oares to the Towre.

†**3.** One who sculls; a sculler. *Obs. rare.*

1663 BUTLER *Hud.* I. iii. 89 He loves, but dares not make the motion;..Like..rowing Skull, he's fain to love, Look one way and a nother move. **1719** D'URFEY *Pills* (1872) III. 5 Where Sculls did once row, Men walk to and fro.

4. *pl.* A sculling race.

1878 *Athletic World* 5 Apr. 8/2 The following races have been fixed..Lowe Senior Sculls, July 22;.. Handicap Sculls, Aug. 21.

5. An act of sculling.

1886 TUPPER *Autobiog.* 59 The gallop with Mr. Murrell's harriers, or the quick scull to Iffley. **1897** MRS. RAYNER *Type-writer Girl* xvii. 176 To ask me to fill in a journal with the day's events is like asking a galley-slave to take a scull in a pleasure-boat after his toil is over.

†**scull,** *sb.*^{2} *Obs.* Also 6–7 skul, 7 scul. [? Shortened from SCULLION.] A scullion. Also Comb. *scull-boy.*

1566 DRANT *Horace, Sat.* II. iii. G 4 b, Foulers, fishers, sculls, podingwrightes, the trulls of Tuscus streate. **1598** tr. *G. de la Perriere's Mirr. Policie* D d, The Romane law.. ordained that honest Romane wiues should be exempt from ..playing the skuls in the kitchen. **1643** VICARS *Looking Glass* 35 God most wisely..makes them..to be but as it were, the very drudges and scull-boyes of his Church. **1743** A. BUSH in Howell *St. Trials* (1813) XVII. 1196 He was a little scull that used to go of errands.

scull (skʌl), *sb.*^{3} A name given locally to various species of gulls.

1813 MONTAGU *Ornith. Dict.* Suppl., Gull-Arctic. Larus Parasiticus... Provincial. Scull. **1852** MACGILLIVRAY *Brit. Birds* V. 492 *Lestris Richardsonii.* Richardson's Skua... Scull. **1885** SWAINSON *Prov. Names Birds* 210 Common Skua (*Stercorarius catarrhactes*)... Scull.

scull (skʌl), *v.* Also 7–9 **skull.** [f. SCULL *sb.*^{1}]

1. a. *intr.* or *absol.* To proceed by means of a boat propelled with a scull or a pair of sculls; to use a scull or a pair of sculls in propelling a boat. Also ***to scull it,*** and with complement denoting the position of the sculler.

1624 [impled in SCULLING *vbl. sb.*] **1679** V. ALSOP *Melius Inquir.* 159 Others have nothing to do but skull away with the Tide when it comes in. **1834** M. SCOTT *Cruise Midge* ii, As we sculled along in the clear creek. **1851** MAYNE REID *Rifle Rangers* ii, I had steamed it down the Mississippi, and sculled it up the Orinoco. **1892** FURNIVALL *Hoccleve's Minor P.* Forew. 47 *note*, When he peeld to scull bow down-stream.

b. *transf.* Of a fish: To propel itself. Of the tail: To act as a propeller.

1850 SCORESBY *Cheever's Whalem. Adv.* (1858) viii, He has two curious fins to scull with. **1894** *Outing* (U.S.) XXIV. 59/1 A long greenish form with fins that wavered slowly, and a tail that sculled with just sufficient power to keep its owner in his hiding-place.

c. *trans.* To make (a particular stroke) in sculling.

1875 W. B. WOODGATE *Oars & Sculls* xv. 116 It is possible to scull a much longer stroke than can be rowed.

2. a. *trans.* To propel (a boat) by means of a scull or a pair of sculls. Also *refl.* of a fish, etc., to propel itself as by a scull or sculls.

1665 HOOKE *Microgr.* 186 [Serving] for the finns and tail, for the Oars and Ruder of this little creature [*sc.* a water-insect], wherewith it was able..to move himself any whither, and to skull and steer himself as he pleas'd. **1773** *Hist. Brit. Dom. N. Amer.* II. ii. §12. 217 He [the whale] sculls himself in the water with a large horizontal tail. **1798** S. WILCOCKE in *Naval Chron.* (1799) II. 63 They [*sc.* the boats] are sculled instead of being rowed. **1865** DICKENS *Mut. Fr.* I. i, Another boat..dropped alongside. 'In luck again, Gaffer?' said a man..who sculled her.

b. *intr.* Of a boat: To admit of being sculled (well, easily, etc.).

1891 *Century Dict.* s.v., The boat sculls well.

3. *trans.* To convey (a person) by water in a sculling-boat or by sculling.

1827 GLADSTONE in Morley *Life* (1903) I. I. ii. 43 Sculled Hallam to Surly after 6. **1883** 'OUIDA' *Wanda* I. 246 He went home sculling himself across the lake. **1903** MORLEY *Gladstone* I. I. ii. 40 The more sinewy Gladstone used to scull him up to the Shallows.

4. *intr.* To skate without lifting the feet from the ice.

1895 in *Funk's Stand. Dict.* **1938** [implied in SCULLING *vbl. sb.* a]. **1976** *Webster's Sports Dict.* 376/1 *Scull or skull*,..to propel oneself forward or backward by alternately moving the heels or the toes apart and together changing from an outer edge on the outward movement to an inner edge on the inward movement.

5. a. ***to scull about,*** to lie about; *spec.* of objects left on the deck of a ship instead of being put away. *colloq.*

1917 'TAFFRAIL' *Sub* v. 136 You went round..with a large bag. In this you placed all..articles..found 'sculling' about. **1938** C. MORGAN *Flashing Stream* III. 263 Don't leave it [*sc.* a key] sculling about. **1943** C. S. FORESTER *Ship* 12, I want those mess-traps brought back... Don't leave them sculling about on the decks.

b. ***to scull around*** (or ***about***), to move about aimlessly; also *fig. colloq.*

1921 *Daily Colonist* (Victoria, B.C.) 20 Mar. 19/7 My opposite number..has one or two questions pertaining to his own branch sculling around in his mind. **1935** M. EGAN *Dominant Sex* I. 12 *Angela.* Where have you been these ages? *Alec.* Oh, sculling round the country on business. **1950** [see NUMBER *sb.* 5 c]. **1961** B. FERGUSSON *Watery Maze* vi. 151 While these ideas were sculling around Whitehall, there arrived from Moscow..M. Molotov. **1981** 'J. Ross' *Dark Blue & Dangerous* xxiii. 137 What with Wiffen and one or two others who were there sculling about, the picture is a little confusing.

scull: see SKULL.

scull(e, obs. ff. SCHOOL.

sculduggery, see SKULDUGGERY.

scullen, obs. form of SCULLION.

sculler ('skʌlə(r)), *sb.* Also 6 scullar, skoller, -oer, 7 skullar, 7–8 **skuller.** [f. SCULL *v.* + -ER^1.]

1. One who propels a boat by means of a scull or a pair of sculls; one skilled in the management of a sculling-boat.

1530 PALSGR. 268/2 Scullar, *batellier.* **1563** FOXE *A. & M.* (1596) 1081/2 He went ouer unto Westminster bridge with a Sculler, where he entred into a Whirry that went to London. **1660** PEPYS *Diary* 2 Nov., I was told the Queen was a-coming; so I got a sculler for sixpence to carry me thither and back again. **1751** SMOLLETT *Per. Pic.* lxx, Ply for employment like scullers at Hungerford stairs. **1755** JOHNSON, *Sculler*, one that rows a cockboat. **1875** W. B. WOODGATE *Oars & Sculls* xv. 116 If anything, a sculler can reach his hands an inch or two farther forward than the oarsman.

2. A boat propelled by sculling; a sculling-boat; also, rarely † ***a pair of scullers.***

double-sculler, a sculling-boat to seat two scullers.

1567 HARMAN *Caveat* xi. (1869) 54 He went to the water syde and toke a Skoller [ed. 1573 skolloer], and was sette ouer the Water into Saincte Georges feldes. **1585** HIGINS *Junius' Nomencl.* 220/2 *Linter*, a wherry or sculler. *a* **1640** W. FENNER *Sacrif. Faithfull* (1648) 211 A man cannot row upon the maine ocean in a paire of Scullers. **1697** DRYDEN *Virg. Georg.* IV. 735 Her Soul already was consign'd to Fate, And shiv'ring in the leaky Sculler sate. **1760** *Brit. Chron.* 23 Jan. 79 On Sunday evening a skuller, with twelve people in it, struck on a hawser..and overset. **1861** DICKENS *Gt. Expect.* liv, Early as it was, there were plenty of scullers going here and there that morning, and plenty of barges. **1902** *Working Men's Coll. Jrnl.* VII. 366 Our skipper told us our boat drew too much water..and persuaded us to hire a double-sculler.

†**3.** A sculling oar. *Obs. rare*$^{-1}$.

1766 *Maldon* (Essex) *Borough Deeds* (Bundle 79. no. 14), [Gideon Whetstone, mariner] saw him sink and try'd with his sculler to feel for him but could not reach him.

†**4.** *attrib.* and *Comb.*, as **sculler-boat,** a sculling-boat; **sculler-man,** one who plies a sculling-boat for hire. *Obs.*

1663 PEPYS *Diary* 1 May, Going thither..I met a boy in a sculler-boat. **1815** *Ann. Reg., Chron.* 109 The other captain and the scullerman were saved. **1822–29** *Good's Study Med.* (ed. 3) V. 598 With us it [Nigrescent leprosy] is chiefly found among soldiers, sailors, sculler-men, stage-coachmen [etc.].

†**'sculler,** *v. Obs. rare*$^{-1}$. [f. SCULLER *sb.*] = SCULL *v.* 3.

1681 HICKERINGILL *Black Non-Conf.* Introd., Wks. 1716 II. 4 What they paid for being Sculler'd back again, is not in the Book of Rates..for Charon's Boat is always empty of Passengers back again.

scullery ('skʌlərɪ). Forms: α. 4 squilleryе, 5–6 squillery, 6 -erie, squyllary, squylery, suyllarye; β. 5 skulery, 6 skullary, scullary, -arie, -erie, 6–7 skullery, 7 -erie, 5– scullery. [a. OF. *escuelerie*, f. *escuelier* SQUILLER.]

1. The department of a household concerned with the care of the plates, dishes, and kitchen utensils. Also the room or rooms in which the work of this department is carried on. *Obs.* exc. *Hist.*

α. [**1330** *Rolls of Parlt.* II. 33/1 Johan de la Squillerye.] **1445** in *Turner's Dom. Arch.* (1859) III. I. 78 To make in all hast possible..a new halle with a squillery, saucery, and surveyng place. *a* **1548** HALL *Chron., Hen. VII* 10 b, He had been a turne broche and executed such vile offices in the kynges kytchyn & suyllarye for a space. **1576** in Nichols *Progr. Eliz.* (1823) II. 43, 1 Sergiant and Clerk of the Squillery.

β. *c* **1440** Scullery [see SAUCERY]. **1481–90** *Howard Househ. Bks.* (Roxb.) 179 [Given] to the kinges cookes white x.s. And to the skulery iij.s. iiij.d. **1520** [see SAUCERY]. **1555** LATIMER *Let.* in Foxe *A. & M.* (1570) III. 1911/2 And as for suffrage,..I have leaser haue the suffrage of iacke of the skullery. **1583** in Nichols *Progr. Eliz.* (1823) II. 402 The kitchin, with bylinge-house, scullery, pastry, and larders. **1634** W. WOOD *New Eng. Prosp.* II. vi. 67 Some of their scullerie having dressed these homely cates, presents it to his guests. *a* **1656** BP. HALL *Rem. Wks.* (1660) 258 Holding it unbeseeming that the businesses of the scullery should be done in our parlour. **1708** CHAMBERLAYNE *Pres. St. Gt. Brit.* (1710) 537 Her Majesty's Household Officers [etc.]. Scullery.

†**b.** ***silver scullery***: the department concerned with the care of the silver utensils. *Obs.*

1686 *Lond. Gaz.* No. 2149/4 Whoever shall give notice thereof unto any Officer of the King's Silver Scullery, shall have two Guinea's Reward. **1725** *Ibid.* No. 6364/1 The Officers of the Board of Greencloth, or Silver Scullery.

†**c.** Kitchen refuse. *Obs.*

1659 GAUDEN *Tears Ch.* II. xxxiii. 258 Besides the black pots, among which these doves [*sc.* ministers of the Church] must lie, I mean the soot and scullery of vulgar insolency.. and fanatick contempt.

2. In modern use: A small room attached to a kitchen, in which the washing of dishes and other dirty work is done; a back kitchen.

1753 MISS COLLIER *Art Torment.* I. i. (1811) 36 In the wash-house or the scullery, performing the most laborious offices. **1869** E. A. PARKES *Pract. Hygiene* (ed. 3) 332 Attached to the wards are attendants' rooms, scullery [etc.]. **1882** MISS BRADDON *Mt. Royal* II. x. 229 Everything must have a name, even the slate that roofs your scullery.

3. *attrib.* and *Comb.*, as ***scullery board, boy, maid, man, work.***

1519 HORMAN *Vulg.* 156 Wasshe all the grecy dysshes.. and set them clene vpon the *squylery bourde. **1675** HAN. WOOLLEY *Gentlew. Comp.* 217 [Directions] To *Scullery-Maids in great Houses. **1595** in *Sussex Archæol Collect.* VII. 210 The *Scullerye man and his Office.

sculling ('skʌlɪŋ), *vbl. sb.* [f. SCULL *v.* + -ING^1.]

a. The action of the verb.

1624 CAPT. SMITH *Virginia* VI. 225 Being with skulling and bayling the water tired. **1820** SCORESBY *Arctic Reg.* I. 466 As a boat is forced along, with a single oar, by the operation of skulling. **1875** W. B. WOODGATE *Oars & Sculls* xv. 118 Recovery is a matter of greater ease in sculling than in rowing. *Ibid.*, Double sculling is faster than pair-oar rowing. **1938** D. CUMMINGS *Figure Skating as Hobby* iii. 19 You can try sculling. Feet together, put your weight on the inside of both your skates..bend your knees, push down, move your feet apart, straighten slightly and bring them together again. **1973** R. S. OGILVIE *Basic Ice Skating Skills* II. 49 This progression across the ice by moving both feet in and out is known as *sculling*. Sculling..can be done forward as well as backward. *Ibid.* 175 *Sculling*,.. a method of two-footed progression forward or backward by an in-and-out movement of the feet.

b. *attrib.* and *Comb.*, as ***sculling-boat***, ***outrigger***, ***race***; **sculling boy**, one who sculls a wherry for hire; **sculling-crutch** (see quot.); **sculling eight**, **four**, a sculling-boat propelled by eight or four pairs of sculls respectively; **sculling float**, a flat-bottomed sculling-boat; **sculling-hole**, a hole for a sculling oar; **sculling motion**, **stroke**, that resembling the motion or stroke of a sculling oar; **sculling-notch**, **sculling score** = *sculling-hole*; **sculling oar**, an oar used in sculling over the stern of a boat.

1856 'STONEHENGE' *Brit. Rural Sports* I. I. ix. 76/2 It has a deck like the outrigger *skulling-boats used on the Thames. **1673** R. HEAD *Canting Acad.* 125 The *Skulling-boy [? a public house bearing this sign] lying just over the Gate. **1898** *Encycl. Sport* II. 168/2 (Punt shooting) **Sculling-crutch*, the spur on the starboard side of the punt in which the fowler 'sculls' with his oar. **1885** *Sculling eight [see *sculling four*]. **1874** J. W. LONG *Amer. Wild-fowl* xxii. 230 They may also be approached.. in the *sculling-float. **1885** FURNIVALL in *N. & Q.* Ser. VI. XI. 324/1 The first '*sculling four'.. was put on the Thames, at my suggestion.. in 1883; and.. the first '*sculling eight' was brought out.. in January, 1885. **1892** —— *Hoccleve's Minor P.* Forew. 47 *note*, How different it was yesterday, in our narrow sculling-four! **1874** J. W. LONG *Amer. Wild-fowl* iv. 91 The *sculling-hole.. is placed six inches to larboard of centre of stern. **1933** BAMFIELD & PALMER *Art of Sailing* ix. 76 Have a *sculling notch cut in the stern, shod with a strip of brass. **1973** Sculling-notch [see SCULL *sb.*[1] 1 a]. **1833** J. RENNIE *Alph. Angling* 51 It [the tail of fish] acts very much like the *sculling oar of a boat. **1946** F. B. COOKE *Cruising Hints* (ed. 6) xxvii. 244 Every yacht's dinghy should have a *sculling score in the transom. **1960** —— *Yachting with Economy* xxi. 146 When leaving the yacht to get the kedge, place the warp in the sculling score.

scullion ('skʌljən). Forms: α. 6 squylyon; β. 5 sculȝon, scwlione, *Sc.* skulȝeoun, 6–7 scullian, skullion, -an, scullen, 6 scolion, (-yon, scoulion, -yon, skolyon, scullyon, schoolyone, scullyan, 7 skullen), 6– scullion. [Perh. an alteration of F. *souillon* scullion, due to assimilation to SCULLERY.] A domestic servant of the lowest rank in a household who performed the menial offices of the kitchen; hence, a person of the lowest order, esp. as an abusive epithet. Now only *arch.*

α. *a* **1533** LD. BERNERS *Huon* xxxvii. 118 Squylyons of yᵉ kechyn.

β. **1483** *Cath. Angl.* 326/1 A Sculȝon (Scwlione *A.*), *calcula*, *lixa*. **1515** BARCLAY *Egloges* iii. 17 Me thought the scullians like fendes of their lookes Came forth with whittels. **1531** ELYOT *Gov.* (1580) 151 The Jewes.. made of the Gabaonites, being theyr confederates, their scullyons, and drudges. **1579** LOUTH in *Narr. Reform.* (Camden) 50 There Cooke in that hyghe court was dressed lyke a schoolyone. **1597** SHAKS. *2 Hen. IV*, II. i. 65 Away you Scullion, you Rampallian, you Fustillirian. **1602** —— *Ham.* II. ii. 616. **1610** HOLLAND *Camden's Brit.* I. 542 Haveloke.. having beene first a skullen in the King's Kitchin. **1768** GOLDSM. *Good-n. Man.* I. i, Ay, it's the way with them all, from the scullion to the privy-councillor. **1872** TENNYSON *Gareth & Lynette* 151 Among the scullions and the kitchen-knaves.

b. *attrib.*, as ***scullion-boy***, ***-clout***, ***-maid***, ***-work***.

1624 BP. MOUNTAGU *Gagg* Pref. 18 And those Tararag-males, the Decretall Epistles of the Popes *scullen-boyes making. *c* **1500** *Rowlis Cursing* 121 in Laing *Anc. Poet. Scot.*, With *skulȝeoun clowttis and dressing knyvis. *c* **1684** *Roxb. Ball.* (1889) VI. 267 Would I have been a *scullian-maid, or a servant of a low degree. **1632** SHERWOOD, A *scullion wench, *Souillonne*. **1658** A. FOX *Wurtz' Surg.* 342 Such a one, which is forced to do all manner of *skullion work? **1700** C. NESSE *Antid. Armin.* (1827) 8 If it be but skullion-work to brighten vessels.

c. quasi-*adj.* Base, mean.

1658 [cf. *scullion work* above]. **1824** BYRON *Deformed Transf.* I. i. 128 The forester Hunts not the wretched coney, but the boar.., leaving paltry game to petty burghers, who leave once a year Their walls, to fill their household caldrons with Such scullion prey. **1870** EMERSON *Soc. & Sol.*, *Courage* Wks. (Bohn) III. 114 We must have a scope as large as Nature's to deal with beast-like men, detect what scullion function is assigned them.

scullionish ('skʌljənɪʃ), *a.* *rare*⁻¹. [f. SCULLION + -ISH.] Befitting a scullion.

1850 B. TAYLOR *Eldorado* xix. (1862) 195 The most ludicrous combination of scullionish and poetical ideas it was ever my lot to hear.

scullionize ('skʌljənaɪz), *v.* *rare*⁻¹. [f. SCULLION + -IZE.] *intr.* To perform the office of scullion.

1853 KANE *Grinnell Exp.* xxxiv. (1856) 309 He has scullionized at the 'Trois Frères', and played *chêf* to a London club-house.

† **'scullionly**, *a.* *Obs.* *rare.* [f. SCULLION + -LY[1].] Pertaining to or used by a scullion.

In the quot. from Milton (Wks. 1738 I. 304), given by Todd and some later Dicts., the correct reading is 'cullionly'.

1623 tr. *Favine's Theat. Hon.* IX. i. 342 This Doue beheld her selfe as dead and entranced,.. among the Scullionly potts, spits, and dripping pans, of Indian.. Infidels.

† **'scullionry.** *Obs.*⁻⁰ [f. SCULLION + -RY.] (See quot.)

1611 COTGR., *Marmitonnage*, Scullionrie, or th' Office of a Scullion. *Ibid.*, *Souillonnerie*, scullionerie, drudgerie.

scullionship ('skʌljənʃɪp). [f. SCULLION + -SHIP.] The business of or period of employment as a scullion. Also as a mock title.

1622 MABBE tr. *Aleman's Guzman d'Alf.* I. 150 If.. I had not before indured some stormes of Aduersity, neuer in that faire weather of my Scullion-ship [orig. Sp. *sollastria*], should I haue knowne how to Sayle in my putting forth from the Kitchen. **1707** *Wks. C'tess D'Anois* (1715) 434 What would your Skullionship have with the King, I pray now?

‖ **scu'llogue.** *Obs.* [Irish *sgológ*: cf. SCALLAG, SCOLOC.] An Irish farm labourer.

1665 R. HEAD *Eng. Rogue* I. (1666) 5 The [Irish] Rebels.. met with my Mother, attended by two Scullogues, her menial servants. **1681** T. DINELEY in *Jrnl. Kilkenny Archæol. Soc.* (1858) I. 176 The scullogues, in digging for turfe, find large whole trees of oake, elme and firr. **1690** MACKENZIE *Siege London-Derry* 1/1 For his Army here could not bear it, to see themselves out-rivall'd by a Crew of Scullogues in their Prince's Favour.

† **sculp**, *sb.*[1] *Obs.* [f. SCULP *v.*[1]]

1. An engraving or wood-cut used as an illustration in a book.

1696 EVELYN *Let. to Place* 17 Aug., I do not say the Holland Sculps are ill perform'd; but [etc.]. **1706** PHILLIPS (ed. Kersey), *Sculp*, a Cut, Print, or Engraved Picture; as *A Book full of fine Sculps.*

2. A piece of sculpture.

c **1845** J. MORRIS in Pollen *Life & Lett.* (1896) 23 Two sculps in the marble tell the same tale. **1883** *Daily News* 18 Jan. 5/7 Perhaps no statue, except the unfortunates in Trafalgar-square, and the melancholy meeting of 'sculps' in Parliament-square, was more sharply criticised at the time of its erection.

sculp (skʌlp), *sb.*[2] *N. Amer. dial.* [f. SCULP *v.*[2]]

a. In early or *arch.* use, a human scalp. **b.** The skin of a seal with the blubber attached.

1743 J. ISHAM *Observations on Hudsons Bay* (1949) 93 They make an offering, putting a painted Stick up, some with a cross hanging a hatchet,.. or Ice Chissel, or what Else they have on the top, with the sculp of their Enemies, when they go to Warr. **1758** in *Essex Inst. Hist. Coll.* (1881) XVIII. 180 They obtained fifty-two Sculps and two Prisoners. **1804** LEWIS & CLARK *Orig. Jrnls. Lewis & Clark Exped.* (1905) VII. 64 They took the 65 of the Mahars sculps and had them hung on Small poles. **1840** JUKES *Excurs. Newfoundld.* (1842) I. 273 The [seal-]skin in this state is called the 'pelt', and sometimes the 'sculp'. **1845** W. G. SIMMS *Wigwam & Cabin* 1st Ser. 53 A pretty fellow.. at his time of life to be looking after sculps of women and children. **1895** *Outing* (U.S.) XXVII. 23/2 The 'sculp' of the dog hood sometimes weighs six hundredweight. **1904** W. CHURCHILL *Crossing* vi. 61 You damned Dutchmen.. I wish the devils had every one of your fat sculps. **1921** J. BUCHAN *Path of King* xii. 242 Maybe the Indians have got his sculp.

sculp (skʌlp), *v.*[1] [f. L. *sculp-ĕre* to carve.]

† **1.** *trans.* To carve or engrave (upon something).

c **1535** DU WES *Introd. Fr.* in *Palsgr.* 947 To grave or sculpe, *grauer*. **1638** SANDYS *Paraphr. Job* xix. 26 Oh.. that the tenor of my just complaint Were sculpt with steele on Rocks of Adamant! **1673** BLOUNT *World of Errors* A 2, A pompous Frontispiece, wherein are sculped our two famous Universities. *a* **1695** WOOD *City of Oxford* (O.H.S.) III. 170 Out of whose mouth on a scroule is this sculped: *Sancta Trinitas* [etc.].

† **2.** To cut *out* with a graving tool. *Obs.*

1683 MOXON *Mech. Exerc.*, *Printing* xiii. §4 [He] digs or Sculps out the Steel between the.. Marks.. on the Face of the Punch.

3. To sculpture. Now chiefly *colloq.* or *jocular.*

1784 *Sel. Fables* Life Æsop 8 The Athenians.. erected a noble statue.. sculped by the famous Lysippus. **1887** STEVENSON *Lett.* 21 Nov., St. Gaudens the sculptor sculping me.

b. *intr.* or *absol.*

1889 W. E. NORRIS *Miss Shafto* (1890) 36, I wouldn't for the world deny that you can sculp or sculpt, or whatever the proper word is. **1893** KIPLING *Many Invent.* 26 Men who write, and paint, and sculp.

Hence **'sculping** *vbl. sb.*

1683 MOXON *Mech. Exerc.*, *Printing* xiii. §4 The Letter-Cutter does not expect to perform this Digging or Sculping at one single Operation.

sculp (skʌlp), *v.*[2] *N. Amer. dial.* [Cf. SCALP *v.*]

a. *trans.* To scalp (a person) (now *arch.*); to skin (a seal).

1758 in *Essex Inst. Hist. Coll.* (1881) XVIII. 109 Taring his Nails out by ye Roots, Sculping alive and such like torments, they wou'd shout and yell. **1759** in *Ibid.* (1882) XIX. 188 [He] retook one of ye Prisoners and killed and sculpt one of ye Indians. **1834** W. A. CARRUTHERS *Kentuckian in New York* I. 24 But as to shootin and sculpin Injins, that's a thing there is no bones made about. **1840** JUKES *Excurs. Newfoundld.* (1842) I. 274 They skin, or, as they call it, 'sculp' them with a broad clasp-knife, called a sculping-knife. **1845** W. G. SIMMS *Wigwam & Cabin* 1st Ser. 44 They'll be sculped, every human of them, in their beds. *Ibid.* 51 We heard of murders and sculpings on every side. **1883** *Fisheries Exhib. Catal.* (ed. 4) 175 Drawings exhibiting Sealers.. Sculping young Seal. **1884** SWEET & KNOX *On Mexican Mustang through Texas* xviii. 246 I'm a scout from the Far West, whar.. the coyote sleeps in the deserted wigwams of the skulpt Indian. **1921** J. BUCHAN *Path of King* xii. 243 The Shawnees cotched me and Jim... They'd ha' sculped us if it hadn't been for Jim.

b. *fig.* To strip (a person) of all his possessions.

1904 W. CHURCHILL *Crossing* vi. 61 We've all been burned out and sculped up river.

sculpin ('skʌlpɪn), *sb.* Also 8 scolping, sculpion, 9 skulpin, sculpen, sculping. [? Corruption of SCORPENE.]

1. A name for various small worthless fish having a spiny appearance: **a.** A fish of the genus *Callionymus*, e.g. *C. draco*; **b.** A fish of the genus *Cottus*, e.g. *C. virginianus*; **c.** *Hemitripterus hispidus* or *americanus*; **d.** *Scorpæna guttata* (see SCORPENE); also † ***sculpin fish.***

1672 W. HUGHES *Amer. Physit.* 7 A Sculpin Fish.. called by us in those parts, the Sea Hedge-Hog. **1712** E. COOKE *Voy. S. Sea* 342 The Sea Porcupine, or a sort of Sculpion. **1767** tr. *Cranz' Greenland* I. 95 The Ulkes, *scorpius marinus*, which we call Toadfish, or in Newfoundland Scolping. **1778** COOK *Voy. Pacific* IV. v. (1784) II. 379 We caught a few sculpins about the ship. *a* **1849** HAWTHORNE *Twice-told T.*, *Village Uncle*, The very air was fishy, being perfumed with dead sculpins, hardheads, and dogfish. **1860** O. W. HOLMES *Prof. Breakf.-t.* i, Now the Sculpin (*Cottus Virginianus*) is a little water-beast which pretends to consider itself a fish. **1884** GOODE, etc. *Nat. Hist. Aquatic Anim.* 258 'Deep-water Sculpin'... This fish, *Hemitripterus hispidus* or *H. americanus*, attains the length of two feet, and is conspicuous by reason of its russet-orange or brick-red colors [etc.]. **1890** E. GOSSE *Life of P. H. Gosse* 114 The large, richly coloured sculpen (Cottus), so common in the clear water round the wharves of Carbonear.

2. *transf.* A mean, worthless person or animal.

1833 MARRYAT *P. Simple* ii, What are you gaping at, you young sculping? **1836** HALIBURTON *Clockm.* Ser. I. xxvii, Go along, you old sculpin [a horse], and turn out your toes. **1877** SARAH O. JEWETT *Deephaven* (1893) 105 Ye see the miser'ble sculpin thought I'd never stop to open the goods.

'sculpin ('skʌlpɪn), *a.* *U.S.* [f. prec.] Worthless, despicable.

1864 LOWELL *Fireside Trav.* 126 Existence on such sculpin terms,.. What is it all but dross to me.

sculpt (skʌlpt), *v.* [ad. F. *sculpter*, f. L. *sculpt-*, ppl. stem of *sculpĕre*; but apprehended as a back-formation from SCULPTOR.]

1. *trans.* To sculpture; *absol.*, to practise the art of sculpture. Hence **'sculpting** *vbl. sb.* and *ppl. a.*

1864 *Reader* 5 Mar. 300/1 Galileo.. says: As to what sculptors argue, that Nature moulds men but does not paint them, I reply that she makes them not less by painting than sculpture, because she both sculpts and colours. **1876** BESANT & RICE *Gold. Butterfly* xxi, It isn't enough to go to shops and buy pictures. We must go in for sculpting too. **1883** KATH. S. MACQUOID *Her Sailor Love* v. i. II. 135 A well-known sculptor.. had been commissioned by the squire of Trant to sculpt his wife. **1884** *Pall Mall G.* 14 Oct. 2/2 Mr. Watts's well-known principle is.. that the sculptor should paint and the painter should sculpt. **1886** O. LODGE in *Liverpool Univ. Coll. Mag.* Mar. 138 The statues we sculpt.. the less said about them the better. **1894** SIR E. SULLIVAN *Woman* 105 A sculptor advised a young sculpting friend to lose no time in completing the bust of the deceased husband whenever it was ordered by the inconsolable widow. **1928** *Daily Express* 16 June 4/5 He sculpts in almost every material. **1931** *Sun* (*Baltimore*) 13 Mar. 12/7 Somebody proposed that instead of being depicted as astride a horse (steed, charger) this general be sculpted as a figure seated in a motor car. **1966** J. RICHARDSON *George IV* 332 The statue (known as the Copper Horse) had been sculpted by Westmacott. **1977** *Times* 5 Sept. 5/7 My uncle, my mother's brother, draws beautifully and sculpts.

2. *transf.* To shape, form, mould.

1967 *Times Rev. Industry* Apr. 86/3 Numerical control of machine tools is obtainable in a number of forms, from the simple point-to-point positioning system, through straight-line machining systems, to the complex continuous path systems which can sculpt any shape capable of being expressed numerically. **1972** *Sci. Amer.* Mar. 45/1 (Advt.), High-level signal lights, neatly sculpted into the rear deck of the car.

† **sculp'tated**, *a.* *Obs.* *rare*⁻¹. [irreg. f. F. *sculpter* (see prec.) + -ATE[3] + -ED[1].] Sculptured.

1653 R. SANDERS *Physiogn.* 243 The ears very round, plain, and not sculptated.

sculpted ('skʌlptɪd), *ppl. a.* [f. SCULPT *v.* + -ED[1].] = SCULPTURED *ppl. a.* Also *fig.*

1961 in WEBSTER. **1976** *Listener* 22 Apr. 510/1 The dialogue was full of sculpted pauses, a gain for poetry but a loss for credibility. **1978** P. PORTER *Cost of Seriousness* 17 Seeing grief in formal state Upon a sculpted angel group. **1978** A. & G. RITCHIE *Anc. Monuments Orkney* 5 The landscape is typical of that produced by Old Red Sandstone, predominantly gentle and rounded, but rising to spectacularly sculpted cliffs along the west and north coasts.

† **'sculpter.** *Obs.* *rare.* Also 7 sculptor. [As if ad. L. type **sculptrum*, f. *sculpĕre* to engrave.] Some kind of graving tool.

1680 MOXON *Mech. Exerc.* xiii. 225 The Tool, which is commonly a Graver, or sometimes a Sculptor, fit to such Moldings as are to be made on the Mettal. *Ibid.*, Afterwards with Sculptors, Round or Flat, or great or small, they work their intended Moldings. **1683** —— *Printing* xiii. §3 He uses the Knife-backt Sculpter. *Ibid.* §4 With.. proper shaped and Pointed Sculptors and Gravers, [he] digs or Sculps out the Steel.

† **'sculptile**, *a.* and *sb.* *Obs.* Also 7 sculptill. [a. L. *sculptilis*, f. *sculpt-*, ppl. stem of *sculpĕre* to carve, sculpture.]

A. *adj.* Sculptured, graven. Also *fig.*

1621 *Gude & Godlie B.* App. 237 Let be thy sculptill honouris vaine. **1646–58** SIR T. BROWNE *Pseud. Ep.* V. ix. (ed. 4) 300 The commandment against sculptile Images. **1679** RYCAUT *State Grk. Ch.* 322 All carved Images they abhor, and Anathematize the adorers of Sculptile Representations. **1816** SINGER *Hist. Cards* 135 Adopting a lighter and more regular character, but still using sculptile or sculpto-fusile types.

B. *sb. pl.* Graven images [= L. *sculptilia*, Vulg.].

a **1340** HAMPOLE *Psalter* lxxvii. 64 þere sculptils þai lout, noght god. **1382** WYCLIF *Micah* i. 7 Alle sculptilis, or grauen ymagis. **1609** BIBLE (Douay) *Ps.* xcvi. 7 Let them al be confounded that adore sculptils.

† **'sculpto-'fusile,** *a. Obs.* [f. *sculpto-* taken as comb. form of L. *sculptus* engraved + FUSILE *a.* The word in Meerman's Latin is *sculptofūsus* (*fūsus* pa. pple. of *fundĕre* to cast).]

(See quot.)

1816 SINGER *Hist. Cards* 167 Meerman..was an advocate for sculpto-fusile types, or types of which the body was cast and the letter engraved.

sculptor ('skʌlptə(r)). [a. L. *sculptor*, agent-n. f. *sculpĕre* to carve, engrave, sculpture. Cf. F. *sculpteur*, Sp. *escultore*, Pg. *esculptor*, It. *scultore*.]

1. One who practises the art of sculpture; chiefly, an artist who produces works of statuary in stone (esp. marble) or bronze.

1634 SIR T. HERBERT *Trav.* 59 A Pegasus: an inuention of the Sculptor, to express his workemanship. **1656** BLOUNT *Glossogr.*, *Sculptor*, a graver or carver. **1680** MORDEN *Geog. Rect.*, *Modena* (1685) 209 Here are many Sculptors both for Ivory and Wood. **1718** LADY M. W. MONTAGUE *Lett.* II. liii. 78 His sculptors could have made no other figure so proper for that purpose as this statue. **1841** W. SPALDING *Italy* II. 231 Jacopo della Quercia, a sculptor whose works are now to be sought in Siena, Lucca, and Bologna. **1893** *Academy* 13 May 413/1 The fronts of the mansion were decorated with statues by skilled sculptors.

† **2.** An engraver. *Obs.*

1641 EVELYN *Diary* 24 May, He brought over Wenceslaus Hollar, the sculptor. **1658** SIR T. BROWNE *Gard. Cyrus* ii. 42 Sculptors in their strongest shadows, after this order doe draw their double Haches.

3. *Astr.* (See quot.)

1852 HIND *Astron. Vocab.* 52 *Sculptor*, an abbreviation for *Apparatus Sculptoris*, one of the southern constellations introduced by Lacaille.

sculptress ('skʌlptrɪs). Also 7 **sculpteress.** [f. SCULPTOR + -ESS.] A female sculptor.

1662 EVELYN *Chalcogr.* Table & Contents, Propertia de Rossi (a sculpteress) 52. *Ibid.* iv. 52 The glory of the Sex, Propertia de Rossi a Florentine Sculptress. **1825** COLERIDGE *Let. to J. Gillman* (1895) 743 The ci-devant sculptress with all her kaleidoscopic freaks and symmetries! **1889** ALGER *Englishm. in Fr. Rev.* 251 Mrs. Damer, the amateur sculptress.

sculptural ('skʌlptjʊərəl), *a.* [f. SCULPTURE *sb.* + -AL[1].]

1. Of or pertaining to sculpture.

1819 SHELLEY *Lett.* Prose Wks. (1888) II. 287 The moulding of the face modelled with sculptural exactness. **1849** RUSKIN *Sev. Lamps.* v. §8. 144 Sculptural sketching exactly correspondent to a painter's light execution of a background. **1864** BURTON *Scot Abr.* I. v. 319 There will naturally be associated with it those relics of sculptural ribaldry,..to be found in the decorations of old ecclesiastical buildings.

b. *transf.*

1898 *Allbutt's Syst. Med.* V. 59 The wall of the cavity presents none of that sculptural detail which [etc.].

2. Having the qualities of a piece of sculpture.

1849 PATMORE in *Quaritch's Rough List* Nov. (1899) 123 The poems seem to me to be too sculptural. **1880** 'OUIDA' *Moths* II. 362 She is faultlessly made, face and form... It is like sculpture... What I said—she is sculptural.

sculpturally ('skʌlptjʊərəlɪ), *adv.* [f. SCULPTURAL + -LY[2].]

1. By means of sculpture.

1825 *Examiner* 290/2 The sculpturally translated beauties of Painting. **1859** RUSKIN *Two Paths* v. 222 The quaint beauty and character of many natural objects..is sculpturally expressible in iron only.

2. In accordance with the canons of sculptural art.

1880 'OUIDA' *Moths* II. 269 Those slender beautiful white arms, that Paris said were sculpturally faultless. **1890** *Harper's Mag.* Jan. 222/1 All are sculpturally muscled.

sculpturation (skʌlptjʊə'reɪʃən). [f. SCULPTURE *v.* + -ATION.] A marking resembling sculpture.

1866 R. TATE *Brit. Mollusks* iv. 218 Its minute size and its sculpturations serve to distinguish it.

sculpture ('skʌptjʊə(r)), *sb.* Also 6 **sculture.** [ad. L. *sculptūra*, f. *sculpĕre* to carve, engrave, sculpture. Cf. F. *sculpture* (15–16th c.; an older synonym was *sculpeüre*, f. *sculper* to 'sculp'), Sp. *escultura*, Pg. *esculptura*, It. *scultura* (whence the 16th c. Eng. form *sculture*).]

1. Originally, the process or art of carving or engraving a hard material so as to produce designs or figures in relief, in intaglio, or in the round. In modern use, that branch of fine art which is concerned with the production of figures in the round or in relief, either by carving, by fashioning some plastic substance, or by making a mould for casting in metal; the practice of this art.

Now chiefly used with reference to work in stone (esp. marble) or bronze (similar work in wood, ivory, etc. being spoken of as *carving*), and to the production of figures of considerable size. Thus to apply the term, e.g. to die-sinking or to stone-carving on a small scale would now be regarded as a transferred use.

1390 GOWER *Conf.* II. 83 Zenzis fond ferst the pourtreture, And Promotheüs the Sculpture. **1563** SHUTE *Archit.* A ij, And hauing the sayde trikes and deuises aswell of sculture & painting as also of Architecture. **1570** DEE *Math. Pref.* d iij b, Though I mencion not Sculpture, in my Table of Artes Mathematicall. **1763** J. BROWN *Poetry & Mus.* xxxv. 76 The Excellence of Sculpture is the Effect of repeated Experience, which refers itself to the Works of Nature, as to its Archetype. **1817** SHELLEY *Rev. Islam* I. 573 Nor in painting's light, or mightier verse, Or sculpture's marble language. **1873** SYMONDS *Grk. Poets* x. 320 Sculpture is the language of the body, music the language of the soul.

b. †The operation of cutting or engraving (*obs.*); the operation of sculpturing.

1661 LOVELL *Hist. Anim. & Min.* Isagoge e 8 b, All may have Sculpture by the powder of smiris, except the adamant. **1860** RUSKIN *Mod. Paint.* V. IX. vi. §20. 262 The dog.. watches the progress of the sculpture with a grave interest.

c. Kind or quality of sculptured work.

1653 MARVELL *Corr.* Wks. (Grosart) II. 4 And I shall hope to set nothing upon his spirit but what may be of a good sculpture.

2. *concr.* **a.** The product of the sculptor's art; that which is sculptured (†or engraved); sculptured figures in general.

1390 GOWER *Conf.* III. 167 And of what Ston his sepulture Thei sholden make, and what sculpture He wolde ordeine therupon. **1638** SIR R. COTTON *Tower Rec.* 23 For money is not meerely to bee esteemed in respect of the sculpture or figure. **1750** GRAY *Elegy* 79 Some frail memorial still erected nigh, With uncouth rhimes and shapeless sculpture deck'd. **1815** J. SMITH *Panorama Sci. & Art* II. 763 When sculpture is represented, as it is always supposed to be white marble or stone, the engraving should be light and smooth.

fig. **1645** MILTON *Tetrach.* 28 These ages wherin Canons, and Scotisms, and Lumbard Laws, have dull'd and almost obliterated the lively Sculpture of ancient reason.

b. In particularized sense: A work of sculpture; a sculptured (†or engraved) figure or design.

1616 BULLOKAR *Eng. Expos.*, *Sculpture*, a caruing, a grauing. **1667** MILTON *P.L.* I. 716 Cornice or Freeze, with bossy Sculptures grav'n. **1756–7** tr. *Keysler's Trav.* (1760) II. 66 A pretty church..remarkable for its exquisite marble sculptures. **1847** TENNYSON *Princess* v. 54 Like some sweet sculpture draped from head to foot, And push'd by rude hands from its pedestal. **1870** LUBBOCK *Orig. Civiliz.* ii. (1875) 53 In some places of Western Europe, rock sculptures have been discovered.

fig. **1658** GURNALL *Chr. in Arm.* II. verse 14 III. i. 207 Righteousness..is a sculpture, the Spirit ingraves on none, but the children of God. **1678** CUDWORTH *Intell. Syst.* I. v. §47. 675 The Divine art and wisdom..would..everywhere impress the sculptures and signatures of itself.

†**3.** A picture or illustration printed from an engraved plate or block; an engraving; engravings collectively. *Obs.*

1654 OGILBY *Wks. Virg.* title-p., Translated, adorn'd with Sculpture and illustrated with Annotations. **1670** —— *Africa* title-p., Adorn'd with peculiar Maps, and proper Sculptures. **1691** T. H[ALE] *Acc. New Invent.* Introd. 13 An admirable Draught or Sculpture of this Ship..in four large sheets of Dutch Paper, will shortly be published. **1779–81** JOHNSON *L.P.*, *Dryden* Wks. 1816 IX. 324 Settle..had published his play with sculptures and a preface of defiance.

4. *Nat. Hist.* Marking of the skin, shell, or surface of any animal or plant resembling that produced by a carving tool.

1826 KIRBY & SP. *Entomol.* III. xxxiv. 397 The sculpture of the integument of insects is often very remarkable. **1833** LYELL *Princ. Geol.* III. 277 In a few the claws are visible, and the sculpture, and even some degree of local colouring are preserved. **1859** DARWIN *Orig. Spec.* v. (1873) 116 But in some of these plants the seeds also differ in shape and sculpture. **1894** *Geol. Mag.* Oct. 434 In its sculpture *Ammonites Bainii*..somewhat resembles the present species.

5. *attrib.* and *Comb.*, as ***sculpture-gallery***; ***sculpture-like*** adj.

1834 MRS. HEMANS *Scenes & Hymns of Life, Water-lily* 237 Thou sculpture-like and stately River-Queen! **1856** W. HUGHES *Treas. Geog.* 250/2 The glyptothek, or sculpture-gallery [of Munich].

sculpture ('skʌlptjʊə(r)), *v.* [f. SCULPTURE *sb.*]

1. *trans.* To represent in sculpture, to carve (a design or figure) from the solid.

1645 EVELYN *Diary* June, The altar is cover'd with a canopy of ophit, on which is sculptur'd the storie of the Bible. **1852** T. PARKER *Ten Serm. Relig.* ii. (1863) 36 As they who sculptured loveliness in stone two thousand years ago. **1875** MCILWRAITH *Guide Wigtownshire* 33 A square stone, on which dials have been carefully sculptured.

b. *transf.* and *fig.*

1817 SHELLEY *Rev. Islam* IX. 3746 That record shall remain..And fame, in human hope which sculptured was, Survive the perished scrolls of unenduring brass. **1835** *Penny Cycl.* IV. 154/1 The wax-workers..do not possess the power of sculpturing the cells. **1852** T. PARKER *Ten Serm. Relig.* ii. (1863) 36 All the manly excellence that we slowly meditate and slowly sculpture into life. **1860** TYNDALL *Glac.* I. vi. 42 The edges..are soon sculptured off by the action of the sun.

2. To decorate with sculpture. Also *passive* (*Nat. Hist.*), to bear marks resembling sculpture.

1645 EVELYN *Diary* 25 Jan., The very bell, cover of a book, sprinkler &c. were all of the rock, incomparably sculptur'd with the holy story in deepe Levati. **1737** POPE *Imit. Hor., Ep.* II. ii. 264 Gold, Silver, Iv'ry, Vases sculptur'd high. **1835** J. DUNCAN *Beetles* (Nat. Lib.) 155 The thorax is sculptured with numerous excavated dots.

sculptured ('skʌlptjʊəd), *ppl. a.* [f. SCULPTURE *v.* + -ED[1].]

1. Produced or represented by sculpture. Also, covered or adorned with sculpture.

c **1710** T. PARNELL *Night-piece on Death* 41 Whose pillars swell with sculptured stones. **1807** WORDSW. *White Doe* vii. 347 Sculptured Forms of Warriors brave. **1894** J. T. FOWLER *Adamnan* Introd. 61 The sculptured crosses and round tower.

2. *Nat. Hist.* Having a conformation or markings similar to those produced by sculpture.

Often in specific names, rendering L. *sculptus* or *insculptus*.

1819 TURTON *Conchol. Dict.* 221 *Turbo insculptus.* Sculptured Turban. **1853** T. BELL *Brit. Stalk-eyed Crustacea* 263 Sculptured Shrimp.

3. Shaped in a manner resembling sculpture.

1966 J. S. COX *Illustr. Dict. Hairdressing & Wigmaking* 132/2 *Sculptured curl*, a firmly and smoothly formed curl showing the comb-teeth lines. *Sculptured hair style*, a hairdress with hard, firm, definite lines in its constituent parts; not fussy, light or tapered. **1970** *Which?* Sept. 268/1 Now, however, you will also find twists, loop-pile and sculptured pile—a pattern formed by mixing loops of different heights or looped and cut pile. **1974** *Times Lit. Suppl.* 24 May 544/3 The second president of General Motors invented the scheme of elaboration and development, bright colours, sculptured lines and rising prices. **1974** *Times-Picayune* (New Orleans) 15 Aug. v. 6/1 The bride..wore a peau de soie gown styled with a sculptured yoke of re-embroidered lace and a cameo neckline.

'sculpturer. *rare.* [f. SCULPTURE *v.* + -ER[1].] One who sculptures; †a sculptor.

1732 LE BLON in Hogarth *Anal. Beauty* (1753) Pref. 13 The sculpturers, the architects, &c., began to apply it to their several arts.

Comb. **1835** *Penny Cycl.* IV. 154/1 The cells are made by the sculpturer-bees, who are smaller than the wax-workers.

sculpturesque (skʌlptjʊə'rɛsk), *a.* [f. SCULPTURE *sb.* + -ESQUE.] Like sculpture, having the qualities of sculpture.

1835 PARTINGTON *Brit. Cycl. Arts* I. 10/2 A more sculpturesque effect. **1876** GEO. ELIOT *Dan. Der.* xiii, Her face [was] rather emaciated, so that its sculpturesque beauty was the more pronounced.

absol. **1873** PATER *Renaissance* viii. 197 His insight into the typical unity and repose of the sculpturesque. **1883** SYMONDS *Ital. Byways* v. 83 The sublime of sculpturesque in crag structure is here.

Hence **sculptu'resquely** *adv.*

1883 *Athenæum* 10 Mar. 319/1 On our right..appears Joseph, in red and yellow garments, which are sculpturesquely disposed.

sculpturing ('skʌlptjʊərɪŋ), *vbl. sb.* [f. SCULPTURE *v.* + -ING[1].]

1. The action of SCULPTURE *v.*; *concr.*, a sculptured marking.

1842 H. MILLER *O.R. Sandst.* iv. (ed. 2) 108 The sculpturings seem intended evidently for effect. **1879** LE CONTE *Elem. Geol.* I. ii. 11 Thus land-surfaces everywhere, especially in mountain-regions, are cut away by a process of sculpturing. **1888** ROLLESTON & JACKSON *Anim. Life* 501 The chitinoid cuticle..is more or less marked by hexagonal areæ and by various sculpturings (dots, pits, lines, &c.).

2. *Bot.* The structural ornamentation of the surface of a pollen grain or spore.

1943 G. ERDTMAN *Introd. Pollen Analysis* v. 43 The outer surface of the exine may sometimes be provided with some sculpturing or ornamentation. The ornamentations of sculptured pollen grains are exceedingly varied. **1967** M. E. HALE *Biol. Lichens* ii. 37 The spores are unornamented, although exospore sculpturing is reported in *Tholurna.* **1970** *Watsonia* VIII. 4 The sculpturing of the perispore of *D[ryopteris] assimilis* differs from that of *D. dilatata* and *D. carthusiana* in density and shape and size of projections.

† **'sculpturist.** *Obs. rare.* [f. SCULPTURE *sb.* + -IST.] A sculptor.

1689 E. HOWARD *Caroloiades* A 2 b, The skillfull Sculpturist, out of some rough Mass of Stone, polisheth and forms his several figures.

† **'sculptury.** *Obs. rare*[−0]. [Alteration of SCULPTURE, after words in *-ury.*] Sculpture.

1623 COCKERAM I, *Sculpturie*, a caruing or grauing. **1647** HEXHAM I, Sculptury, *Graveringe ofte snijdinge.*

sculsh, variant of SCULCH.

‖ **scult,** *sb. Obs.* [LG. *schulte.*] = SCHOUT.

1548 HALL *Chron., Hen. VII* (1550) 17 [They] sent to hym ..the Scult called Peter Longoll.

† **scult,** *v. Obs.* ? = SKULK *v.*

1622 PRESTON *Godly Man's Inq.* i. 6 For shame Adam skulted in the groue of Paradise. *a* **1652** BROME *Eng. Moor* v. i. (1659) 74 The man Scults closs i' th' house here.

scum (skʌm), *sb.* Forms: 3, 5 scume, 4 skume, 4–6 scome, 5–7 scumme, 6 scumme, skomme, scoomme, 6–7 skumme, 7 skom(e, 7–8 skum, scumm, 5– scum. [Identical with MLG. *schûm* masc. (MSw., Sw., Norw., Da. *skum*), MDu. *schuum* masc., neut., *schûme*, fem. (Du. *schuim* neut.), OHG. *scûm* masc. (MHG. *schûm*, mod.G. *schaum*):—OTeut. **skūmo-*, f. Teut. and Indogermanic root **skeu-* to cover. The Teut. word was adopted in Rom. as OF. *escume* (mod.F. *écume*), Pr., Sp., Pg. *escuma*, It. *schiuma*. For the shortening of the vowel (which, as the spelling *scome* shows, had taken place already in the 14th c.), cf. *thumb*, *plum*.

The proximate source is uncertain. The word cannot represent an OE. **scúm*, which would have given an initial *sh*. The locality of the early quots. does not favour adoption from Scandinavian, and the word is not found in ON., the mod. Scandinavian form being prob. from LG. The mod. Eng. form cannot well come from the OF., though that may have been the source of the ME. *scume*, assuming that the *u* represents the sound (y:). Possibly the form adopted from OF. may have been replaced by one imported from MDu. or MLG. as a term of brewing or some other industry.]

†**1.** Foam, froth; *pl.* bubbles. *Obs.*

In the first quot. the identity and meaning of the word are doubtful.

a **1250** *Prov. Ælfred* 334 in *O.E. Misc.* 122 For hit seyþ in þe loþ as scumes forteoþ. **1340** *Ayenb.* 32 Ase deþ þe tavernyers þet velleþ þe mesure mid scome. *c* **1374** CHAUCER *Boeth.* IV. met. vii. 39 And the bristlede boor markede with scomes [L. *spumis notavit*] the shuldres of Hercules. **1398** TREVISA *Barth. De P. R.* XIX. xi. (1495) 871 Also white matere is gendryd of thynnynge and spredynge of ayre as it faryth in skume. **1490** CAXTON *Eneydos* xv. 53 Gnawyng his bytte garnysshed wyth botones of golde, alle charged wyth the scume of the horse. **1534** LD. BERNERS *Gold. Bk. M. Aurel.* (1546) K k, They haue growen as a hole piece, and sodeynly wasted as a skumme. **1598** SYLVESTER *Du Bartas* I. v. 336 Those small white Fish to Venus consecrated, Though without Venus' ayd they be created Of th' Ocean scum. **1694** tr. *Marten's Voy. Spitzbergen* in *Acc. Sev. Late Voy.* II. 29 The following Wave raiseth it again, with much curled and foaming Scum.

fig. **1637** RUTHERFORD *Lett.* (1664) 169 The scum & froth of my letters I father upon my own unbeleeving heart. **1642** FULLER *Holy & Prof. St.* V. xvi. 421 Though malice boyled hot in their hearts, yet no scumme ran over in their mouthes.

2. †**a.** Dross which rises to the surface in the purifying of a metal; refuse, slag. *Obs.*

1526 *Grete Herball* clx. (1529) K iij, One or two vnces of lytargy or scomme of syluer. **1604** E. G[RIMSTONE] *D'Acosta's Hist. Indies* IV. ix. 233 There was great store of these poore mettalls, whereof they made no great account, but were reiected..as the skumme of the good mettall. **1811** W. J. HOOKER *Iceland* (1813) II. 201 No. 1 [a specimen of lava] resembles externally the scum of iron.

b. A film or layer of floating matter formed upon the surface of a liquid in a state of fermentation, ebullition, etc.; hence, a film formed upon stagnant, foul water, etc. More generally, any undesirable surface layer or deposit, usu. but not necessarily on a liquid.

c **1440** *Promp. Parv.* 449/2 Scome, or scum of fletynge, *spuma*. **1530** PALSGR. 268/2 Scumme of a potte, *escume*. **1555** EDEN *Decades* (Arb.) 321 Floting aboue the water lyke a scoomme. **1661** J. CHILDREY *Brit. Baconica* 122 Whereon floweth a thick skum of liquid Bitumen. **1707** MORTIMER *Husb.* (1721) I. 283 Put it [the finest honey] up warm into Pots by it self;..two or three days time work up a Scum of course Wax, Dross, and other stuff. **1748** *Anson's Voy.* I. v. 63 After it [water] has been in the cask a day or two it begins to purge itself,..and is soon covered over with a green scum. **1820** SHELLEY *Sensit. Pl.* III. 70 Spawn, weeds, and filth, a leprous scum, Made the running rivulet thick and dumb. **1851** CARPENTER *Man. Phys.* (ed. 2) 18 The green scum, which floats upon ponds, ditches, &c., and which consists of the cells of a minute Cryptogamic Plant. **1857** *G. Bird's Urin. Deposits* (ed. 5) 380 When saccharine urine is left in a warm place, a scum soon forms on its surface. **1940** *Chambers's Techn. Dict.* 750/1 *Scum*,..a surface formation of lime crystals appearing on new cement work. **1941** *Thorpe's Dict. Appl. Chem.* (ed. 4) V. 573/1 Silica scum is sometimes found on the top of tank-melted glass if the melting temperature is not very high. **1967** E. CHAMBERS *Photolitho-Offset* xiv. 211 The albumen image..may look clear and free from ink when the grain is full of scum, which will readily ink-up on the press run with the soft machine ink.

c. *fig.*

1648 JENKYN *Blind Guide* i. 12 Scum and scurrility making up his whole book. **1819** SHELLEY *Peter Bell 3rd* IV. xvi. 3 A leaden-witted thief—just huddled Out of the dross and scum of nature. **1875** FARRAR *Silence & Voices* iii. 63 Her literature became a seething scum of cynicism and abomination.

d. *coarse slang* (chiefly *U.S.*). Semen.

1967 *Wentworth & Flexner Dict. Amer. Slang* Suppl. 703/1 *Scum* (taboo),..semen... *Scumbag* (taboo),..a condom. **1972** R. A. WILSON *Playboy's Bk. of Forbidden Words* 257 *Scum*, the semen.

3. *transf.* **a.** Applied to persons: The offscourings of humanity; the lowest class of the population of a place or country.

1586 MARLOWE *1st Pt. Tamburl.* III. iii, These are the cruell pirates of Argeire, That damned traine, the scum of Affrica. **1610** B. RICH *Descr. Irel.* 37 The Kerne of Ireland are next in request, the very drosse and scum of the Countrey. **1712** ARBUTHNOT *John Bull* III. vi. 25 Scoundrels! Dogs! the Scum of the Earth! **1768–74** TUCKER *Lt. Nat.* (1834) II. 56 Many of the scum of our people have been employed in protecting us against foreign enemies. **1889** R. BUCHANAN *Heir of Linne* i, Away, ye scum o' Egypt and o' Scotland.

†**b.** In particularized sense: An assemblage or body of 'scum'. *Obs.*

1594 SHAKS. *Rich. III*, V. iii. 317 A scum of Brittaines, and base Lackey Pezants. *a* **1618** RALEIGH *Apol.* 28, I know.. what a Scumme of men you have. **1622** BACON *Hen. VII*, 235 As for the Seueritie vsed vpon those which were taken in Kent, it was but vpon a Scumme of People. **1819–22** SHELLEY *Chas. I*, ii. 234 Unleash the sword and fire, that in their thirst They may lick up that scum of schismatics. **1829** SCOTT *Anne of G.* xxxiv, I was lately Charles of Burgundy, called the Bold—now am I twice beaten by a scum of German peasants.

†**c.** Applied to an individual: A worthless wretch. *Obs.*

1598 SHAKS. *Merry W.* I. i. 168 Froth, and scum thou liest. **1607** DEKKER & WEBSTER *Northw. Hoe* V. H 3 b, Out you base scums, come you to disgrace mee in my wedding shooes? **1818** SCOTT *Hrt. Midl.* lii, Knockdunder answered, 'that the soul of such a scum had been long the tefil's property'.

4. *attrib.* and *Comb.*, as ***scum-gatherer***; ***scum-like*** adv.; **scum-board**, †**-pan** = SCUMMER *sb.*[1]; **scum-soap**, a lathering soap [? orig. G. *schaumseife*]; **scumspittle** *nonce-wd.*, ? scummy or frothy spittle.

1898 *Daily News* 10 Feb. 6/4 Much fat floats on the surface, and is cleared off with *scum-boards. **1586** T. B. *La Primaud. Fr. Acad.* I. 649 After that sollicitors were suffered in the middest of them all, to be, as it were, the *skum-gatherers of suits. **1821** BYRON *Juan* III. c, That trash of such sort not alone evades Contempt, but from the bathos' vast abyss Floats *scumlike uppermost. **1648** HEXHAM II, *Een Schuym-pan*, a Scummer, or a *Scumme-pan. **1852** J. J. SEIDEL *Organ* 145 A mixture of fine olive-oil and *scum-soap. **1922** JOYCE *Ulysses* 446 The bulldog growls,..a gobbet of pig's knuckle between his molars through which rabid *scumspittle dribbles.

scum (skʌm), *v.* Forms: 4–5 **scume**, 4–6 **scome**, 4, 6–8 **skum**, 5 **scom**, 5–6 **scomme**, **skom**, 5–7 **scumme**, **skumme**, 6 **scoum**, **skume**, 7 **scumm**, 5– **scum**. [f. the sb. Cf. OHG. *scûmen* (MHG. *schûmen*, mod.G. *schäumen*), MLG., MDu. *schûmen* (mod. Du. *schuimen*), Da. *skumme*, Norw. *skuma*, Sw. *skumma*; also OF. *escumer* (mod.F. *écumer*) and SKIM *v.*]

†**1.** *trans.* To clear (the surface of a liquid) of impurities or floating matter; to SKIM. Also, to remove as scum, to skim *off*. *Obs.*

1398 TREVISA *Barth. De P. R.* XIX. lx. (1495) 897 The pigmentaries other the leche skumyth awaye the fylthe warely wyth a fether. *c* **1400** *Lanfranc's Cirurg.* 242 Take þe white of an ey & scume it, & loke þat þere falle no filþe þeron. *c* **1440** *Promp. Parv.* 450/1 Scummyn lycurys, *despumo*. **1509** WATSON *Ship of Fools* lvii. (1517) O j b, This foole settynge his pottes to the fire is so lunatyke that he taketh no hede to scumme them. **1590** SPENSER *F.Q.* II. vii. 36 Some scumd the drosse that from the metall came; Some stird the molten owre with ladles great. **1607** TOPSELL *Four-f. Beasts* 650 That which swimmeth aboue in the manner of fat, they scum it off with their handes, and put it away in a vessell of Tinne. **1662** *Comenius' Janua Ling. Triling.* 82 The next day after she [*sc.* the milkmaid] skums the cream which swims on the top. **1748** *Phil. Trans.* XLV. 551 As it is dissolving in Water, I have scummed off from some Lumps of it a dark-purple bituminous Substance. **1817** KITCHINER *Cook's Oracle* (1818) 59 The oftener it is scummed, and the cleaner the top of the water is kept, the cleaner will be the meat.

b. *transf.* and *fig.*

1592 NASHE *P. Penilesse* 19 b, Thou hast skumd ouer the schoole men, and of the froth of their folly, made a dish of diuinitie Brewesse, which the dogges will not eate. **1675** PLUME *Life Hacket* 37 Till the heats which boyl in the blouds of youth were well scum'd off, if not quite boyl'd away. **1796** COLERIDGE *Watchman* ii. 38 We shall select from each speech whatever lines contain a fact or argument not before urged in the debate, scummed and clarified in the following manner.

†**2.** To scour (the sea or land). Cf. F. *écumer la mer*. *Obs.*

c **1420** *Brut* 385 And for to speke moore of the Erle of the Marche, þat þe King hadde sette to scom þe see and the Coostez of Engelonde for enymys. **1470–85** MALORY *Arthur* I. xiii. 52 Soo by Merlyns aduys ther were sente fore rydars to skumme the Countreye. **1670** MILTON *Hist. Eng.* II. Wks. 1851 V. 89 Without certain seat, they liv'd by scumming those Seas and shoars as Pyrats. **1690** I. MATHER *Vind. N. Eng.* 44 in *Andros Tracts* (1869) II. 62 Are not at least Four of the 12, Inhabitants of other Towns? Must they Scumm Water-Town and Cambridge also to pack a Charles-Town Jury?

†**3.** To pass lightly over, 'skim' (a surface). *Obs.*

1513 DOUGLAS *Æneis* IV. v. 149 Lyke a foull that.. Fleis by the watir, scummand the fludis law.

†**b.** *fig.* To study superficially, 'skim'. Also *intr.* (Const. *upon.*) *Obs.*

1625 BP. MOUNTAGU *App. Cæsar* 248 You understand not the state of Limbus Patrum, nor the depth of the Question, but scumme upon the surface, and gibberish you cannot tell for what. **1664** EVELYN tr. *Freart's Archit.* Pref. 1 There was no need to have scumm'd them [*sc.* those books] thus superficially over.

†**c.** *absol.* ? To skim the air. *Obs.*

1513 DOUGLAS *Æneis* XIII. ii. 120 Lyke as quhen that the gredy gled on hycht Scummand vp in the ayr oft turnis his flycht. **1585** JAS. I *Ess. Poesie* (Arb.) 44 Thus whill she vsde to scum the skyes about, At last she chanced to sore out ower the see Calld *Mare Rubrum*.

†**4.** *to scum together*: to collect as scum. *Obs.*

1570–6 LAMBARDE *Peramb. Kent* (1826) 431, I had almost forgotten to tell you here, of that adoe which Thomas Fawconbridge..made at London with a handfull of rakehelles which he had scummed together in this our shire.

5. *intr.* †**a.** To rise to the surface as scum. *Obs.*

1481 CAXTON *Myrr.* II. xxiii. 115 The erthe whiche is in the bottom of thise valeyes [of the sea] scumeth for the hete of the sonne vpward. **1525** LD. BERNERS *Froiss.* II. xlix. 170 Golde and syluer was no more spared then thoughe it had rayned out of the clowdes, or scomed out of yᵉ see.

†**b.** To foam (at the mouth). *Obs.*

c **1380** *Sir Ferumbr.* 3888 Wan Agolafre haþ herd hym speke, For angre þat he ne drast him wreke, A skuntede [*read* skumede] als a bore. **1485** CAXTON *Chas. Gt.* 156 Galafre.. began to scumme at the mouth.

c. To throw up foul matter as a scum; to become covered with a scum.

1661 [implied in SCUMMING *vbl. sb.* 1 b]. **1769** MRS. RAFFALD *Eng. Housekpr.* (1778) 342 Stir them twice a day at least, or they will scum over. **1839–52** BAILEY *Festus* 53 Belike you think your lives will dribble out As brooks in summer dry up. Let us see! Try: dike them up: they stagnate—thicken—scum. **1873** SPON *Workshop Rec.* Ser. I. 373/2 The mass scums very much.

scum-: see SCOM-.

scumbag (ˈskʌmbæg). *coarse slang* (chiefly *U.S.*). Also **scum bag**. [f. SCUM *sb.* + BAG *sb.*]

1. A condom.

1967 [see SCUM *sb.* 2 d]. **1968–70** *Current Slang* (Univ. S. Dakota) III–IV. 106 *Scum bag*, a condom. **1974** *Time Out* 6 Dec. 21/1 Young blades carried their sheaths or condoms or ..'scumbags' in their wallets.

2. A base, despicable person. Also as a term of vulgar abuse.

1971 *Courier-Mail* (Brisbane) 23 Dec. 5/2 Another called him a 'scumbag' and said he should have been killed. **1973** E. BULLINS *Theme is Blackness* 80 [Ann] No, you can't think that about me! [Peter] Why can't I, scumbag? **1976** G. V. HIGGINS *Judgement of Deke Hunter* iv. 29, I had three scumbags that went to trial. **1977** *Zigzag* Apr. 34/2 What little scumbag would say something like that?

ˈscumber, *sb.* *Obs.* exc. *dial.* Also 7 **skommer**, **skomber**, 7, 9 (*dial.*) **skummer**. [f. SCUMBER *v.*] The dung of a dog or fox. Hence *dial.*, filth, dirt.

1647 HEXHAM I, Skummer or filth, *Schuym ofte ruyligheyt*. **1655** MENNES & J. SMITH *Mus. Delic.* (1656) 4 For here [Epsom] old Ops her upper face Is..safroniz'd with mortall scumber. **1671** PHILLIPS (ed. 3), *Scumber*, (a Term in Hunting) the dung of a Fox. **1688** HOLME *Armoury* II. vii. 133/2 Terms..proper for the Ordure..of several Beasts... An Hound,..and all sorts of the Dog kind, its called, Skommer, or Skomber. **1825** J. JENNINGS *Dial. W. Eng.* 69 *Skummer*, a foulness made with a dirty liquid, or with soft dirt.

ˈscumber, *v.* *Obs.* exc. *dial.* Forms: 4–5 **scombre**, 6 **skammer**, **skom(m)er**, 6–8 **scummer**, 7 **scumer**, 7–8 **scumber**, 7–9 (9 *dial.*) **skummer**. [App. aphetic a. OF. *descombrer* (mod.F. *décombrer*) to relieve of a load. Cf. DISCUMBER *v.*, of equivalent formation.]

1. *intr.* Of a dog or fox: To evacuate the fæces. Also *jocularly* of a person.

c **1400** *Master of Game* xx. (MS. Digby 182), Also y will teche þe childe to leede þe houndes to scombre twyse on þe daye. **1508** DUNBAR *Flyting* 113 Bettir thow ganis to leid ane doig to skomer..than with thy maister pingill. **1576** TURBERV. *Venerie* 176 Lette him carie them home vncoupled, that they may skoure at large and skommer. **1611** COTGR. s.v. *Chien*, *Tandis que le chien chie le loup s'en va*: Prov. While the dog scummers the wolfe scuds away. **1656** *Choyce Drollery* 37 Beware of fire when you scumber.

fig. **1611** J. DAVIES *Commend. Verses to Coryat's Crudities* 49 And for a Monument to After-coommers Their Picture shall continue (though Time scummers Vpon th' Effigie).

2. *trans.* To void (ordure); *fig.* to produce (something foul). Also *dial.* (see quot. 1825).

1596 NASHE *Saffron Walden* V 2, Where he and his Brother..scummerd out betwixt them an Epistle to the Readers against all Poets and Writers. **1694** MOTTEUX *Rabelais* IV. lii, For four or five Days I hardly scumber'd one poor butt of Sir-reverence. **1819** KEATS *Let. to Haydon* 3 Oct., I have not seen the portentous Book which was skummer'd at you just as I left town. **1825** J. JENNINGS *Dial. W. Eng.* 69 To *Skummer*, to foul with a dirty liquid, or to daub with soft dirt.

Hence †**ˈscumbering** *vbl. sb.*, the excrement of a dog or fox.

1611 FLORIO, *Schinchimurra*,..a skummering of a dog. **1817** J. MAYER *Sportsman's Direct.* (ed. 2) 203 You may know if it is a good scenting day, by the smoke and strong scent of their scummerings.

scumble (ˈskʌmb(ə)l), *sb.* [f. SCUMBLE *v.*] A thin coat (of colour) put on by scumbling; a softened effect produced by scumbling (see SCUMBLE *v.* 1 and 2).

1834 T. H. LISTER *Anne Grey* iii, [The uncertainty as to] whether your drawing is..to be brought suddenly to a sharp edge, or a scumble, by the entrance of a visitor. **1859** GULLICK & TIMBS *Painting* 230 After a time the scumble partially sinks into the colour over which it is laid. **1862** THORNBURY *Turner* I. 77 It is carefully and thinly painted with thin scumbles of semi-opaque colour. **1880** MUCKLEY *Handbk. Painters* 75 When the tint forming the scumble is nicely calculated, no doubt a more delicate and transparent grey will be the result, than when produced by solid painting.

transf. **1884** *Harper's Mag.* Sept. 528/2 A golden scumble of October haze.

scumble (ˈskʌmb(ə)l), *v.* [? Frequentative f. SCUM *v.*; cf. quot. s.v. SCUMMING *ppl. a.*]

1. a. *trans.* In *Oil Painting*. To soften or render less brilliant (the colours in a portion of a picture) by overlaying with a thin coat of opaque or semi-opaque colour; to spread or 'drive' (a colour) thinly over a portion of a picture in order to soften hard lines or blend the tints; to produce (an effect) by this process.

1798 *Trans. Soc. Arts* XVI. 280 The artist then painted the lights with pure white..where the light was brightest..; and, where the demi-tints were afterwards to be, scumbling it thinner by degrees. **1830** CUNNINGHAM *Brit. Painters* I.

234 Over that is scumbled thinly and smooth a warmer tint. **1866** REDGRAVE *Cent. Painters* II. 112 The hills and distant bay are scumbled into a mighty haze. **1872** C. KING *Sierra Nevada* x. 212 I'll scumble in a sunset effect. **1882** P. G. HAMERTON *Graphic Arts* xxi. 232 If ground colours are to be scumbled over they ought not to be full of strong and deep brush-marks.

b. *absol.*

1868 TYRWHITT *Handbk. Pict. Art* II. v. 336 *note*, To scumble is to use partly opaque colours and white, in the same way [as in glazing]. **1870** *Pall Mall Gaz.* 2 Nov. 11 M. Legros has in no single place permitted himself to scumble or retouch.

2. In *Pencil, Chalk,* or *Monochrome Drawing.* (See quots.)

1815 [implied in SCUMBLING *vbl. sb.* below]. **1854** FAIRHOLT *Dict. Terms Art, Scumbling*..is produced by lightly rubbing the blunt point of the chalk over the surface, or spreading the harder lines by the aid of the stump.

3. *transf.* of natural effects.

1905 J. H. McCARTHY *Dryad* 92 More frequent clouds now scumbled the sky. **1974** V. NABOKOV *Look at Harlequins* (1975) VI. i. 227 The summer tan..would scumble, I knew, the liver spots on my temples.

Hence **'scumbled** *ppl. a.*, **'scumbling** *vbl. sb.*

1815 R. BROWN *Princ. Pract. Perspective* 76 *Scumbling* is giving a kind of rough shadow to trees, grass, gravel-walks, &c. in a drawing when it is nearly finished. It is performed with a brush having some dark colour in it, and nearly dry. **1816** SIR J. REYNOLDS *Char. Painters of Italy* 113 A..description of the effect of glazing or scumbling, such as was practised by Titian. **1849** [see DRIVE *v.* 12]. **1859** GULLICK & TIMBS *Painting* 229 Scumbling..is used to modify certain portions of a picture which may require to be rendered cooler, greyer, and less definite. **1862** THORNBURY *Turner* II. 198 His light tints, the result of pearly scumblings, make his light pictures as luminous as his water-colour drawings. **1868** TYRWHITT *Handbk. Pict. Art* II. v. 354 This system of covering the canvas with scumbled shade first and painting on the lights seems the best for a beginner. **1877** 'OUIDA' *Puck* xxv, Fancying they have got 'atmosphere' in dabs of grey and yellow, and..'sunset' in scumbled lakes and ochres. **1967** *Listener* 12 Jan. 48/3 A verb 'to scumble', which means to blur and soften the outlines. A great deal of our national life seems to me to be scumbled. **1977** *Times* 19 Nov. 9/2 The confusion of the times..the scumbling of boundary lines.

scumless ('skʌmlɪs), *a.* [f. SCUM *sb.* + -LESS.] Lacking or forming no scum.

1881 TYNDALL *Ess. Floating Matter of Air* 151 In one of them [i.e. the tubes] the infusion was scumless throughout.

scummed (skʌmd), *ppl. a.* [f. SCUM *v.* + -ED[1].]

1. Skimmed, deprived of any matter floating upon the surface.

c **1425** tr. *Arderne's Surgery* 40 If þou haue noȝt redy þe forseid tapsimell, be þe same done wiþ scomed hony. **1681** CHETHAM *Angler's Vade-m.* xlii. §1 (1689) 315 Take scummed milk which hath stood so long that no more cream will rise from it. **1703** T. N. *City & C. Purchaser* 207 You may temper your Lime and Sand with scum'd Milk. **1833** J. RENNIE *Alph. Angling* 67 The scummed fat of a pot wherein fresh meat has been boiled.

2. Covered with foulness or scum.

1909 *Blackw. Mag.* Feb. 221/2 An old Arab reservoir from whose scummed and stagnant waters the third class passengers push to fill their water bottles.

†'scummer, *sb. Obs.* Forms: 4 scummar, schumour, scomeoure, skumo(u)r, scomor, 4–6 scommer, skumer, 4–5, 7 scomer, 5 scowmar, scomur(e, scomour, scomowre, scommyr, schomore, scummour, scummowre, scwmure, skumoure, 5–6 skomer, 6 scommar, skomor, skwmmer, 6–7 skommer, skummer, 7 scumur, 8 scumer, 6–9 scummer. [f. SCUM *v.* + -ER[1]; in sense 1 after OF. *escumoir* (mod.F. *écumoire*), in sense 2 after *escumeor* (mod.F. *écumeur*) respectively instrumental noun and agent-noun to *escumer* to skim, f. *escume*: see SCUM *sb.*]

1. A shallow ladle or sieve for removing scum or floating matter from the surface of a liquid.

1326 *Durham Acc. Rolls* (Surtees) 15 In..uno schumour pro coquina, 12*d.* **1399** *Fabric Rolls York Minster* (Surtees) 18, j scomor cum j podyngiren. **1487** *Paston Lett.* III. 466 A ladill and a scomer of laton. **1582** HESTER *Secr. Phiorav.* III. xxxiii. 48 Thereon will come a thinne skime, the whiche ye shall gather together with a Scummer. **1644** NYE *Gunnery* I. (1647) 16 Be you ready, as scum shall rise, to take it away with a scummer. **1727** *Bradley's Fam. Dict.* s.v. *Conserve*, You must suffer your Scummer or Spattle to drain. **1825** J. NICHOLSON *Oper. Mech.* 360 Another large iron ladle pierced like a scummer.

2. One who scours the sea; a rover, pirate. [So F. *écumeur de la mer.*]

1375 BARBOUR *Bruce* XIV. 375 Ane scummar [*MS. E* scowmar] of the se. **1398** TREVISA *Barth. De P.R.* XV. civ. (1495) 526 The men of Norwey..ben stronge skumoures and see theues. **1585** T. WASHINGTON tr. *Nicholay's Voy.* IV. xv. 130 Pirates, Coursaries, and Skummers of the sea.

3. One who gathers scum. Also *fig.*

1602 *Narcissus* (1893) 440 That same youthe's the scummer of all skorne. **1653** URQUHART *Rabelais* II. xxx, Pope Boniface VIII. a scummer of pots.

†'scummer, *v. Obs. rare.* [f. SCUMMER *sb.*]

1. *intr.* To make a predatory raid.

1633 *Swed. Intelligencer* IV. 121 Having again thus scummerd over the frontiers of Paderborn, he passes the river Weser.

2. *trans.* To scour, furbish up.

1679 V. ALSOP *Melius Inq.* Introd. 33 If some of the old superstitious Ceremonies (when well scraped and wiped) were left for decency,..why were not the rest scummer'd up, that the Worship might be more decent?

scummer, variant of SCUMBER.

†'scummerfare. *Obs. rare.* [f. SCUMMER *sb.* (sense 2) + FARE *sb.*] Piracy.

1358 in S. P. H. Statham *Dover Charters* (1902) 86 Que bona et quanta cepissent per Skomerfare, tempore quo dictus Custos optinuerit ballivam suam. **1390** GOWER *Conf.* III. 321 Out of a barge faste by, Which hidd was ther on Scomerfare, Men sterten out.

scumming ('skʌmɪŋ), *vbl. sb.* [f. SCUM *v.* + -ING[1].]

1. a. The action of removing scum from the surface of a liquid. Also *fig.*

1611 COTGR., *Escumement*,..a scumming, or skimming. **1704** SWIFT *Batt. Bks.* Misc. (1711) 220 There is a Brain that will endure but one Scumming:..Wit, without Knowledg, being a sort of Cream. **1832–53** *Whistle-binkie* III. 37 There is naething abroad like our hearty aitmeal, Nor guid sheep-head-kail, for nae outlandish woman Has the gumption to ken that they need sic a scummin'.

attrib. **1683** PETTUS *Fleta Min.* I. 333 Put the Salt-Petre gently..in it, and turn it about with the scumming Spoon.

†b. The action or process of forming or throwing up a scum. *Obs.*

1661 RABISHA *Cookery Dissected* 40 Set it over the fire, watch the boyling and scumming thereof; then [etc.].

2. *concr.* in *sing.* and *pl.* The matter removed in the form of scum from the surface of a liquid. †Also, the matter rising to the surface as scum.

1530 PALSGR. 268/1 Scomyng of a pot, *escume de pot.* **1567** GOLDING *Ovid's Met.* VII. 368 And where the fire had from the pan the scumming cast..the ground did springlike florish there. *c* **1720** W. GIBSON *Farrier's Dispens.* iii. (1734) 133 Most Apothecaries make this Syrup with the brownest Sugar, and reserve the Scummings for Clysters. **1841** *Mangnall's Questions* 415 From the scummings of the sugar when boiling an inferior kind of spirit is made.

'scumming, *ppl. a.* [-ING[2].] That scums. (In quot. app. = *scumbling.*)

1818 *Sporting Mag.* II. 89 This most eminent artist has lately adopted..a sort of scumming, smearing, slubbering way of sketching.

scummy ('skʌmɪ), *a.* [f. SCUM *sb.* + -Y.]

1. Having the nature or appearance of scum.

1577 tr. *Bullinger's Decades* (1592) 297 The skummie froathe is not mixed with the oyle. *a* **1618** SYLVESTER *Job Triumphant* IV. xli, Hee makes the deep sea like a pot to boyl, A pot of Oyntment (casting scummy Soyl). **1818** KEATS *Endym.* III. 330 To breathe away as 'twere all scummy slime From off a crystal pool. **1839–52** BAILEY *Festus* 44 This fair earth..'Tis but the particoloured, scummy, dross Of the original element wherefrom The fiery worlds were framed. **1936** A. RANSOME *Pigeon Post* xxix. 312 'What'll it look like when we see it again?'..'All scummy on the top... The pure gold'll be underneath.' **1967** E. CHAMBERS *Photolitho-Offset* xiv. 215 Under-exposure produces a weak, soft stencil, so that the image thickens-up in development and results in stencil breakdown and a scummy plate. **1979** K. M. PEYTON *Marion's Angels* ii. 29 At high-water springs the river came right up over the saltings..and sent scummy fingers up the garden path.

fig. *a* **1586** SIDNEY *Arcadia* IV. (1598) 414 These were the skummy remnant of those rebels. **1690** C. NESSE *Hist. & Myst. O. & N. Test.* I. 140 The strength of his faith dashes down all the scummy bubbles of carnal reasonings.

2. Abounding in scum. Also *fig.*

1593 NASHE *Christ's T.* 83 London, thou art..the Sea that sucks in all the scummy chanels of the Realme. **1727** BAILEY vol. II, Scummy, frothy, dreggy, &c. as a boiling Pot.

3. *transf.* and *fig.* Filthy, dirty; despicable, disreputable. Also *Comb.* orig. and chiefly *U.S. colloq.*

1932 [see PIG *sb.*[1] 5]. **1952** B. MALAMUD *Natural* 67, I don't like the scummy tricks you play on people. **1973** E. BULLINS *Theme is Blackness* 78 Hey, you white scummy-lookin' bourgeois bitch, take me to dinner? **1977** R. E. HARRINGTON *Quintain* xvii. 202 Meeting scummy little men at..squalid Parisian restaurants. **1979** *Maledicta* III. 133 The scummy millionaire Marxist profs I know don't spend one *red* penny of their own: Let the workers & peasants pay!

scunage, variant of SKEVINAGE *Obs.*

scunch (skʌnʃ). *Arch. Obs.* exc. *dial.* Also 7 scunche, 9 sconce. [Shortened from SCUNCHEON. Cf. SQUINCH.] = SCUNCHEON.

1611 COTGR., *Escoinson*, a Scunche; the backe part of the iaumbe of a window. **1899** DICKINSON & PREVOST *Cumbld. Gloss., Scunch, Sconce, Scunchen*, the stone or brick reveal of a door or window.

scuncheon ('skʌnʃən). *Arch.* Forms: 4 scochon, 5 sqwynchun, sconchon, scouchon, skonchon(e, skochyn, skownsiom, sconcheon, 8 skimshion, 9 scuncheon, (scontion, scuntion, scunchen). [a. OF. *escoinson*, also written *escochon*, *escouchon* (mod.F. *écoinson*), app. f. *es-* EX- + *coin* angle. Cf. the later form SCOINSON.] The bevelled inner edge of the side or jamb of a window, door, etc.

In the earlier quots. the sense is uncertain. Godefr. gives for *escoinson* a sense 'piece of stone or wood projecting inside a building, to support a beam, etc.'

1435 *Contract Fotheringhay Ch.* (1841) 27 The said Stepill ..shall be chaungid and turnyd in viij panes, and at every Scouchon a boutrasse fynysht with finial. **1450** in *Hist. Dunelm. Script. tres* App. 325 Pro factura..j sol skownsiom. **1473** *Churchw. Acc. St. Mich. Cornhill*, For sconcheons and a felet for the same pewes. **1487–8** *Durham Acc. Rolls* (Surtees) 651 Et sol. Will. Mayson pro dolacione..36 skonchones ad 3d., 9s.; 17 jawmys ad 4d., 5s. 8d. **1490** in Rogers *Agric. & Prices* III. 559/4, 4 skochyns [for library window @]/8. **1789** in Macgill *Old Ross-sh.* (1909) 195, I mean to build a house..to be built of what is called solid mud except the corners, door, and window skimshions, Lintols and soles [etc.]. **1833** LOUDON *Encycl. Archit.* §929 Soffits, Ingoings, Scuncheon Linings, &c... The scuncheons (the beveled parts, splays, or elbows, of the inside of a window opening, where the shutters are placed) of the two parlour windows are to have framed linings to correspond with the shutters. **1844** H. STEPHENS *Book of Farm* §60 I. 144 The corners of its [*sc.* the door's] scuncheon should be rounded off. *Ibid.* §214 I. 200 Scontions of all voids [*i.e.* spaces for doors and windows] are..measured over and above the rubble-work. *Ibid.* §2847 III. 1007 When the dyke has a scuncheon for its end, a large boulder ..should be chosen as the foundation-stone. **1885** *Blacklaws Quarry Price List*, Scuntions, 20 in. by 11 in. by 7 in. each 7d.

†b. *attrib.* in *scuncheon anglers*, *scuncheon-crest*, of obscure meaning.

1372 *Ely Sacrist Roll* in Willis *Arch. Nomencl.* 38 In 8 scochoncrestes magnis empt'. 8s. pro pet. 12d. **1429–30** in Willis & Clark *Cambridge* (1886) II. 445 Pro xvij ped' et di de sqwynchuncrest v[s]. **1443** *Ibid.* I. 386, xij coynes iiij skouchons-anglers and viij Square Anglers to the..legement table.

scunfest, obs. f. pa. pple. of SCOMFISH *v. dial.*

scunge (skʌndʒ), *sb. colloq.* (orig. *Sc.*). Also **skunge.** [Origin unknown: cf. next.] **a.** A sly or vicious person. **b.** A scrounger or sponger. **c.** As a vague term of abuse.

1824 J. MACTAGGART *Scottish Gallovidian Encycl.* 424 *Scun*, plan, draft. A scunge, a sly fellow; a maid seducer. **1900** in *Sc. Nat. Dict.* (1971) VIII. 104/1 A scunge has a crappin' for a'corns. **1912** G. CUNNINGHAM *Verse Maistly in Doric* 184 Jock, ye scunge! Come oot the dresser. **1948** *Football Times* 11 Sept., 'You great big skunge', meaning that you were always on the 'mootch'. **1967** *Comment* (N.Z.) June 14/1 He obviously thought I must be a bit of a scunge asking political questions. **1976** R. BARNARD *Death on High C's* iv. 44 'Big joke, scunge,' said Gaylene, giving him the sort of shove that would have sent a lesser man through the wall.

scunge (skʌndʒ), *v. colloq.* (orig. and chiefly *Sc.*). Also **scundge, scunje,** etc. [Origin unknown: cf. prec. and SCROUNGE *v.*[1]] *intr.* To prowl around looking for food, etc.; to scrounge, to sponge. So **'scunging** *ppl. a.*

1843 J. B. PRATT *Life & Death Jamie Fleeman* (ed. 9) iv. 32 Hame wi you, ye scunging tyke, hame! **1844** W. CROSS *Disruption* xxxi. 341 Neither will ye scunge after the gentry like McQuirkie. **1905** *Eng. Dial. Dict.* V. 299/2 *Scunge*, to slink about; to fawn like a dog for food. **1964** X. HERBERT *Larger than Life* 243 Senile wrecks..coveting and scundging and bickering. **1966** *Huntly Express* 30 Sept. 2 It's maybe been a scunjin' dog.

‖scungille (skun'dʒille). Pl. scungilli. [ad. It. dial. *scunciglio* conch, seashell, prob. alteration of It. *conchiglia* seashell, shellfish.] A mollusc or conch, esp. the meat of a mollusc eaten as a delicacy.

1953 A. BONI *Talisman Italian Cookbk.* 65 Scungilli Marinara... ½ pound of scungilli (pulp of conch)... Boil scungilli about 15 minutes and drain. **1963** T. PYNCHON *V.* iii. 62 He tended each seashell on his submarine scungille farm. **1972** *Village Voice* (N.Y.) 1 June 75/1 (Advt.), Italian-American fish specialties. Shrimp, calamari, scungilli, mussels, [etc.]. **1980** D. E. WESTLAKE *Castle in Air* i. 12 Stuffing scungilli and spaghetti into her mouth.

scungy ('skʌndʒɪ), *a.* Chiefly *Austral.* Also scungey. [f. SCUNGE *v.* + -Y[1].] Mean, dirty, disreputable. Also *Comb.*

1966 BAKER *Austral. Lang.* (ed. 2) x. 215 *Scungey*, dirty, untidy, disreputable. **1969** *Coast to Coast 1967–8* 86 Y' hate me, don'tya? Don'tya? Don'tya, eh? Answer me, y' scungy bitch. Answer me! **1970** *Telegraph* (Brisbane) 10 Mar. 8/5 Nowadays people..talk about 'that scungy place, Bondi'. It's the truth, but it hurts. **1978** *Courier-Mail* (Brisbane) 19 May 5/5 Sometimes you see scungy-looking grapes that are worth a lot of money. **1980** R. ANSELL *To fight Wild* 56 The dressing on her leg was getting very scungy but I wasn't game to touch it until the bone had had time to begin setting.

scunk, obs. form of SKUNK.

scunner ('skʌnə(r)), *sb.* orig. *Sc.* and *north.* Forms: 7, 9 skunner, 8 skonner, 8–9 sconner, 5–6, 8– scunner. [f. SCUNNER *v.*]

1. Orig., a loathing disgust; now freq. in a milder sense: a grudge, repugnance, dislike esp. in the phrase ***to take a scunner at, against,*** or ***to.***

a **1500–20** DUNBAR *Poems* xxvii. 34 In harte he tuke ȝit sic ane scunner. **1697** W. CLELAND *Poems* 106 (Jam.) We might have miss'd a beastly blunner, Had we not spewed out our skunner Against this Test. **1755** R. FORBES *Ajax*, etc. 29 It was enough to gi' a warsh-stamack'd body a scunner. **1827** SCOTT *Surg. Dau.* ii, I thought she seemed to gie a scunner at the eggs and bacon that Nurse Simson spoke about to her. **1881** R. G. WHITE *Words & Uses* (ed. 3) 252 Cultivated and well-meaning people sometimes take a scunner against some particular word or phrase. **1900** R. J. MUIR *Mystery Muncraig* ii. 21 He had never told his weakness to his brother, having had a 'scunner' against doing so. **1911** F. E. CRICHTON *Soundless Tide* ii. 20 He tuk some soort of a scunner til her, an' now he's just left her sittin'. **1927** J. BUCHAN *Witch Wood* i. 21 You'll give our young brother a scunner of the place. **1935** L. KERR *Woman of Glenshiels* xiii. 207 It fair gies ye the scunner the way they all grumble. **1957** V. PALMER *Seedtime* ii. 15 He remembered he had taken a scunner against McCoy when he had flown down to her wedding. **1964** *Scotsman* 12 Nov. 5 Many of them have taken a scunner at religion because they took a scunner at it at school. **1974** P. De Vries *Glory of Hummingbird* ix. 123 He had taken a scunner to me... What had soured him on me..had been Jake's replacing him with me. **1977** L. Meynell *Hooky gets Wooden Spoon* xiii. 152 Thirty per cent of the calls..originated in personal spite, someone had taken a scunner against the next-door neighbours.

2. *Sc. dial.* **a.** Of persons: a nuisance, a pest, a good-for-nothing.

1796 J. Lauderdale *Poems* 91 Some poor waff detested scunner. **1899** *Shetland News* 11 Feb. 7/3 Yon black pairts is whaur som' o' da scunners o' boys is been makkin' slides. **1926** W. Queen *We're a' Coortin* III. i. 69 Ye wee, bowly-leggit scunner ye. **1940** *Horizon* II Nov. 243 He was aye sittin' in ma road. A fair scunner! **1958** *Banffshire Jrnl.* 1 Apr. 7/1 A fraisie, meally-mou'd twa-faced scunner o' a lad.

b. Of things: a nuisance, a hardship, a plague, a vexatious matter.

1865 J. Horne *Poems* 24 Faigs, borrowed money is a sconner. **1917** A. S. Neill *Dominie Dismissed* xi. 138 'Bairns is just a scunner,' said Sarah. 'Ye'll hae to stop yer typewriter or ye'll waken them.' **1926** W. Queen *We're a' Coortin* I. i. 10 It's a richt scunner walkin' up that long avenue tae the big hoose. **1947** H. W. Pryde *1st Bk. McFlannels* i. 4 Ah thocht the room floor was bad, but this is a fair scunner.

scunner ('skʌnə(r)), *v. Sc.* and *north.* Forms: *α.* 4, 7, 9 **skunner**, 4–5 **skoner**, 5 **scowner**, **skowner**, **scouner**, 8 **sconner**, 7 **scunder**, 7– **scunner**; *β.* 6 **skynner**, **skinner**. [Of obscure origin.

The sense naturally suggests connexion with SHUN *v.*, but there is no variant with *sh-*, and no cognate verb in Scandinavian. The suffix is app. the frequentative -ER^{5}. But cf. the earlier synonym SCURN *v.*]

1. *intr.* †**a.** To shrink back with fear, to flinch. **b.** To be affected with violent disgust, to feel sick.

1375 Barbour *Bruce* v. 201 (Edin. MS.) Bot thai war skownrand vounder sair Sa fer in Scotland for to fair. *Ibid.* XVII. 651 Bot thai..skunnyrrit [*v.r.* scounryt] tharfor nakyn thing, Bot went stoutly till assalyng. *c* **1425** Wyntoun *Cron.* II. xvi. 1451 Syne faynt of kynde al women was, And mekil skonerande for to se blude. *a* **1578** Lindesay (Pitscottie) *Chron. Scot.* (S.T.S.) I. 47 The rest of the Douglassis skynnrit [*v.r.* skinnerat], thinking the marieage to be wnlesum. **1635** T. Jackson *Creed* VIII. xxx. 354 The Jew..perhaps would not so much as have scunnered at the Altar, if our Saviour had beene offered upon it, specially in the Temple. *c* **1643** R. Baillie in *Sc. Metr. Psalter* (1864) 36/2 Seducers in this land have drawne on their followers to scunder at and reject our whole psalmes in meeter. *a* **1728** Ramsay *Fable* xix. 8 Their sickly stamacks scunner'd at the prey. **1786** Burns *To James Smith* xxii, And yill an' whisky gie to Cairds, Until they sconner. **1826** J. Wilson *Noct. Ambr.* Wks. 1855 I. 121 It's no features, though they're bad aneuch in general, but the expression that makes me skunner. **1894** Crockett *Stickit Minister* 121 When he preached on the Sabbath he gied the fowk no gospel to ca' gospel, but he did mak them scunner with the Law.

2. *trans.* To disgust, sicken.

1871 W. Alexander *Johnny Gibb* (1873) 216 It was aye 'oor Patie's this', an' 'oor Patie's that', till it wud 'a scunner't a tyke. **1901** G. Douglas *Ho. Green Shutters* 282 It always scunnered me, for I aye liked things tidy.

Hence '**scunnering** *ppl. a.*, sickening.

1820 *Blackw. Mag.* Aug. 513 When it's fairly on lowe, its thick and steaming scent wad smother the scunnering smell o' an acre o' corses.

‖**scuola** ('skwola). Pl. scuole. [It., = school.] In Venice, any of the buildings in which the medieval religious confraternities or guilds used to meet, a guild-hall; also *Hist.*, one of these guilds.

1851 J. Ruskin *Stones of Venice* I. 340 It is the most curious in conception of all the pictures in the Scuola. **1888** *Encycl. Brit.* XXIV. 155/1 Much of the splendour of Venice ..was due to the wealth and religious zeal of the various trade guilds or confraternities, called *scuole* by the Venetians. **1902** R. Fry *Let.* 14 Oct. (1972) I. 198 Jacopo Bellini is known to have painted a large number of decorative pieces for the Venetian *Scuole* and these are, I believe, part of one of these series. **1936** A. B. Greene *Sunshine & Dust* xxiii. 397 In the Scuola, some wood-carvings of the life of St. Roche are worth study. **1961** L. Mumford *City in History* Note to plate 21, The architectural quality..is repeated..in the..scuola or guild hall. **1962** *Listener* 13 Sept. 386/2 The crucifix still exists.. in the Church of S. Giovanni Evangelista in Venice; it was originally made for the *scuola* of that church, to house..a fragment of the True Cross. **1965** H. Honour *Compan. Guide to Venice* iv. 53 The members of one *scuola* visited prisoners and paid for the last rites of those who were executed. **1974** *Country Life* 25 Apr. 978/1 Most of the *Scuole* of Venice were..suppressed by the Napoleonic régime... Though teaching formed part of their function, the main aims of the *Scuole* were charitable.

scup (skʌp), *sb.*^{1} *U.S.* [a. Du. *schop.*] A swing.

1848 Bartlett *Dict. Amer.*, Scup... A New York word. **1849** Miss Warner *Wide Wide World* xi, A scup! maybe you don't know it by that name [said Mr. Van Brunt]; some.. folks call it a swing.

scup (skʌp), *sb.*^{2} *U.S.* [Shortened a. Narragansett *mishcup* 'thick-scaled', f. *mishe* large + *cuppi* scale.] The fish *Pagrus argyrops*; = PAUGIE.

1848 Bartlett *Dict. Amer.*, *Scup.* **1873** S. Powel in *Rep. U.S. Fish Commission* 1871–2, 74 The scup are known to be schooling, wandering fish of the high seas, and come from the Gulf Stream and from the Florida Cape.

scup (skʌp), *v. U.S.* [a. Du. *schoppen*, cf. *schop*, SCUP *sb.*^{1}] (See quot.)

1848 Bartlett *Dict. Amer.*, *To Scup*..to swing. Common in New York.

scuppaug ('skʌpɔːg). *U.S.* [Shortened a. Narragansett *mishcuppâuog*, pl. of *mishcup*: see SCUP *sb.*^{2}] = SCUP *sb.*^{2}

1873 T. Gill *Catal. Fishes East N. Amer.* 27 *Stenotomus argyrops* (Linn.) Gill.—Scup; scuppaug; porgy (New York). **1884** Goode, etc. *Nat. Hist. Aquatic Anim.* 386 The Scup.. is often known in New England as the 'Scuppaug'.

scupper ('skʌpə(r)), *sb.* Forms: 5 **skopor**, **skopper**, 6 **scopper**, 7 **scuper**, **scopeboard** (*erron.*), 7–8 **scoper**, **skupper**, 6– **scupper**. [Of disputed etymology.

Some regard it as an agent-n. f. SCOOP *v.* (sense 1); others as an adoption of an AF. derivative of OF. *escopir* to spit. Cf. G. *speigat* scupper, f. *speien* to spit.]

1. a. *Naut.* Chiefly *pl.* An opening in a ship's side on a level with the deck to allow water to run away.

1485, 1497 [see *scupper-nail*, *-leather*, in 2]. **1592** Wyrley *Armorie, Ld. Chandos* 34 Voiding scoppers voided out their bloud. **1622** Drayton *Poly-olb.* xviii. 418 The whilst those mightie Ships out of their scuppers pour'd Their trayterous cluttred gore. **1669–79** T. B[ateman] *Asia* lf. 48 With girdlines from the said cradle to her ports or Scopeboards. **1748** *Anson's Voy.* III. iv. 443 We made a great quantity of water through our hawse-holes, ports and scuppers. **1834** Marryat *P. Simple* xxxv, Every scupper of her running blood and water. **1883** Stevenson *Treas. Isl.* III. xiii, The Hispaniola was rolling scuppers under in the ocean swell.

†**b.** Used for: A pump. ? *nonce-use.*

1610 Holland *Camden's Brit.* To Rdr. 2 Whereas coniectures are certain detections of things vnknowne..I have alwaies thought that they were to be accounted among the skuppers [orig. *inter autlias*] wherewith Time worketh and draweth Veritie out of Democritus his deepe dungeon.

c. *fig. coarse slang.* A depreciatory term for a woman, *esp.* a prostitute.

1935 A. J. Pollock *Underworld Speaks* 102/2 *Scupper*, a prostitute. **1970** G. Greer *Female Eunuch* 265 More familiar terms in current usage refer to women as receptacles for refuse,..as *tramp*, *scow*, *scupper.* **1972** F. Warner *Lying Figures* IV. 40 *Sapph* You were always firm... *Laz* Your limbs and trunk were in angles of contingency. *Sapph* I was your scupper.

2. *attrib.* and *Comb.*, as **scupper-hole**, **-hose**, **-leather**, **-nail**, **-shoot** (see quots.).

c **1590** E. Wright in *Hakluyt's Voy.* (1599) II. II. 163 Euery *scupper-hole, and other place where it [*sc.* rain] ranne downe. **1702** *Milit. & Sea Dict.* (1711), *Skuppers*, or *Skupper-Holes* are the Holes close to all the Decks, through the Ship's sides, through which the Water runs out of the Ship from the Decks. **1903** H. Clifford *Free Lance* x. 82 Her scupper-holes spouting. **1769** Falconer *Dict. Marine* (1780) s.v., The scuppers of the lower deck of a ship of war are usually furnished with a leathern pipe, called the *scupper-hoase, which hangs downward from the mouth or opening of the scuppers. The intent of this is to prevent the water from entering, when the ship inclines under a weight of sail. **1497** *Naval Acc. Hen. VII* (1896) 298 *Skopperlethers & Skoppernayles. **1702** *Milit. & Sea Dict.* II. (1711), *Skupper-Leathers* are the round Leathers nail'd over the Skupper-Holes,..which keep out the Sea-Water from coming in, and yet let any Water run out from the Deck. **1485** *Cely Papers* (Camden) 180 For ij^{c} *skopor nayll vj^{d}. **1702** *Milit. & Sea Dict.* II. (1711), *Skupper-Nails*, are little short Nails, with broad Heads, made on purpose to nail on the Skupper Leathers. *c* **1850** *Rudim. Navig.* (Weale) 135 *Scupper nails.* **1867** Smyth *Sailor's Word-bk.*, **Scupper-shoots*, metal or wooden tubes which carry the water from the decks of frigates to the sea-level.

scupper ('skʌpə(r)), *v.* [perh. f. prec. sb., but the connexion of meaning is not clear.]

a. *trans.* To surprise and massacre. *Mil. slang.*

1885 *Pall Mall Gaz.* 2 Apr. 3/2 The fierce warriors who 'scupper' Tommy Atkins within the lines of Suakin. **1885** *St. James's Gaz.* 31 Mar. 4/1 Being quietly chopped to pieces in their beds, or 'scuppered', as some grim wits have termed it. **1896** Kipling *Seven Seas* 98 We preach in advance of the Army, We skirmish ahead of the Church, With never a gunboat to help us When we're scuppered and left in the lurch. **1896** *Daily News* 19 May 8/1 It was pretty much like a 'scuppering' surprise in the Eastern Soudan. **1902** *Blackw. Mag.* Mar. 333 It's a great relief to find that advance squadron hasn't been scuppered.

b. *colloq.* To defeat, ruin, destroy, put an end to.

a **1918** [see KNOCK *v.* 14 a]. **1948** [see DITCH *v.*^{1} 6 c]. **1957** *Economist* 19 Oct. 235/1 The suspicion is still alive that there would have been secret rejoicing in Whitehall if the French Assembly had scuppered the common market. **1957** L. Durrell *Justine* III. 155 You can help us scupper them, old man. **1962** *Times* 2 Mar. 4/2 Underwood followed up his kick ahead and, when scuppered, found Rogers, as ever, there for a try at the post. **1974** *Times* 7 Feb. 14/8 If the Government wants to welsh on its promise, it will have to scupper Mr Money's Bill. **1981** W. Winward *Ball Bearing Run* iv. 51 'We're scuppered,' said Fallon... It was a crushing blow.

scuppernong. ('skʌpənɒŋ). *U.S.* [The name of a river in North Carolina.] **a.** A cultivated grape-vine belonging to the variety of the southern muscadine, *Vitis rotundifolia*, so called, originally found in the region of the Scuppernong River; also, the fruit of a vine of this kind. Also *attrib.*

1811 *Raleigh* (N. Carolina) *Star* 7 Mar. 40/2 Doctor James Mease..having seen Mr. Blount's account of the Scuppernong Grape..has requested of us to procure for him some specimens of the vine. **1829** *Free Press* (Tarboro, N. Carolina) 27 Feb. 3/3 Among them the Scuppernong, a native of North Carolina, growing in a swamp. **1857** *Harper's Mag.* May 746/1 The dwellings in the Piny Woods ..almost always have..a trellis supporting an extensive scuppernong grape-vine. **1868** *Rep. U.S. Commissioner Agric.* (1869) 215 The Scuppernong grape does best in low lands. **1901** C. T. Mohr *Plant Life of Alabama* 136 The scuppernong grape yields its crops year after year with regular abundance. **1938** M. K. Rawlings *Yearling* ix. 74 The Scuppernong grapevine, a gift from his mother's kin in Carolina, was in bloom for the first time. **1944** *Clarke County Democrat* (Grove Hill, Alabama) 14 Dec. 1/5 The deer became entangled in a growth of scuppernong vines. **1949** B. A. Botkin *Treas. S. Folklore* II. i. 146 The poetic fable of the origin of the purple scuppernong grape in the seedling that sprouted on the edge of the pool stained with her blood from the silver arrow. **1972** J. Hewitt *N.Y. Times Cook Bk.* 308/1 Scuppernong Nectar South Carolina 12 pounds scuppernong grapes 1 cup white vinegar [etc.].

b. Wine made from the scuppernong grape. In full, **scuppernong wine**.

1825 *Catawba Jrnl.* (Charlotte, N. Carolina) 2 Aug. 3/1 The editor..having had a taste of the Scuppernong wine from North-Carolina, extols it in the highest terms. **1846** *Spirit of Times* 25 Apr. 97/1 A keg of 'Scuppernong' is on its way to us, having been shipped from Wilmington, N.C. **1854** Longf. *Catawba Wine* ii, It is not a song Of the Scuppernong From warm Carolinian valleys. **1862** 'E. Kirke' *Among Pines* xvii. 280 [He] brought forth a box of Havanas, and a decanter of Scuppernong. **1887** *Century Mag.* XXXIV. 335/2 Then she..begged Mrs. Colonel Ledbeter to give her her recipe for making the scuppernong wine she had heard so much praised. **1936** M. Mitchell *Gone with Wind* xxxviii. 685 It never occurred to him that a decent woman would drink anything stronger than scuppernong wine.

'**scuppet**, *sb. Obs.* exc. *dial.* Forms: 5–6 **scopett**, 6 **scopytt**, **skuppat**, 8 **scoopet**, **skippet**, 9 **scuppett**, **skoppit**, 6, 9 **scuppet**. [App. f. *scope* SCOOP *sb.*^{1} (sense 2) + -ET^{1} (possibly an AF. formation on the Eng. sb.).] A spade used for trenching and in making ditches; also, a similar instrument used for turning hops while drying.

1485 *Naval Acc. Hen. VII* (1896) 40 Shovilles shodde.. xxiiij, Scopettes..xij. **1573** Tusser *Husb.* (1878) 17/19 Sharpe cutting spade, for the deuiding of mow, With skuppat and skauel, that marsh men alow. **1764** *Museum Rust.* II. 194 Help the water out of the ruts with scoops or skippets. **1843** *Jrnl. R. Agric. Soc.* IV. II. 582 In this marsh I limed 120 rods of bank during the summer with unslacked lime, and in the winter it might have been moved with a barn scuppet. **1892** *Auction Catal. Farm Sale* (Kent), Hop scuppet.

'**scuppet**, *v. Obs.* exc. *dial.* Also 7 **scoppet**. [f. prec.] *trans.* To shovel (*out*, *away*). Also *fig.*

1599 Nashe *Lenten Stuffe* 28 Our mitred Archpatriarch.. scuppets not his benificence into their mouthes with such freshwater facility as M. Ascham..would imply. *a* **1656** Bp. Hall *Rem. Wks.* (1660) 77 Vain man, can he possibly hope to scoppet it out so fast as it fills. **1837** E. Fitzgerald *Lett.* (1889) I. 37, I take a spade, and scuppet away the snow from the footpaths.

scuppled ('skʌp(ə)ld), *a. nonce-wd.* [Cf. SCUFFLE *v.*^{2}] Grooved, furrowed.

1873 G. M. Hopkins *Jrnls. & Papers* (1959) 235, I saw big smooth flinty waves, carved and scuppled in shallow grooves.

scur (skɜː(r)). [Origin unknown.] A small horn found in polled cattle and sheep or their cross-bred offspring, not rooted in the skull but loosely attached by the skin. Hence **scurred** *a.*, having scurs.

1882 *Nat. Live Stock Jrnl.* (Chicago) Oct. 460/1 A heifer with only 'scurs', as the modified horns sometimes found in Polled cattle and in cross-bred offspring of Polled and horned breeds, are called in Scotland. **1902** W. Bateson *Mendel's Princ. Heredity: A Defence* 6 The offspring of the Polled Angus cow and the Shorthorn bull is almost invariably polled or with very small loose 'scurs'. **1919** J. Biggar *Galloway Cattle* 7 The Galloway increased the total of polled stock in the county, and knocked out the 'scurs' or abortive horns very considerably. **1960** *Farmer & Stockbreeder* 23 Feb. 81/1 Not every heterozygous bull showed scurs. *Ibid.* 22 Mar. 81/1 Some had small loose horns, some just had scurs. **1963** *Guardian* 3 Dec. 6 Only about half the ewes carry thin spiky horns, the others being polled or 'scurred'.

scur, variant of SKIRR *v.*; obs. f. SHOWER.

scurage, **scurby**: see SCOURAGE^{1}, SCURVY *sb.*

scurdge, obs. form of SCOURGE *sb.*

'**scurdy**. *Sc.* ? *Obs.* A kind of rock, whinstone.

1789 J. Williams *Min. Kingd.* I. 71 Basaltine rocks are.. called skurdy in the north of Scotland. **1866** Mitchell *Hist. Montrose* ii. 19 The town was built of trap rock or scurdy.. with free stone dressings.

scure, obs. form of SKEWER.

scurell(e, **scurer**, obs. ff. SQUIRREL, SCOURER^{1}.

scurf (skɜːf), *sb.*^{1} Forms: 4–5 **scorf**, 4, 7 **skurf**, 5–7 **scurfe**, 6 **scorfe**, **skorfe**, **skurffe**, 6–7 **scurff(e**, **skurfe**, 1, 3, 6– **scurf**. See also SCUFF *sb.*^{1}, SHROFF^{1}. [Late OE. *scurf* ? masc., a later form, prob. due to Scandinavian influence (cf. OSw. *skorver*, acc. *skorff*, *skurff*, mod.Sw. *skorv*, Da. *skurv*, mod.Icel. *skurfur* pl.) of OE. *sceorf* (also *scruf*: see SCRUFF *sb.*[1]), corresp. to MLG., LG. *schorf*, MDu. *schorf(t*, *schurf(t*, Du. *schurft* fem., OHG. *scorf* (MHG., mod.G. *schorf* masc.) :—OTeut. **skurbo-*, **skurfo-*, prob. from the root represented in OE. *sceorfan* str. vb., to gnaw, *scearfian* to cut into shreds (= OHG. *scarbôn*).]

† **1.** A morbid condition of the skin, esp. of the head, characterized by the separation of branny scales, without inflammation. *Obs.*

c **1000** *Sax. Leechd.* I. 316 Wið scruf [*v.r.* scurf] & wið sceb. *a* **1300** *Cursor M.* 11823 Wit þe crache him tok þe scurf, þe fester thrild his bodi thurgh. **1398** TREVISA *Barth. De. P.R.* VII. iii. (1495) 223 Ofte thyse scales cleue to the rotes of the heere, vnnethe suche skalles other scorf is heelyd. *c* **1450** *St. Cuthbert* (Surtees) 4140 All þe bolnyng went away, And þe scurfe with in a day. **1526** SKELTON *Magnif.* 1958, I am lowsy and vnlykynge and full of scurffe. **1570** LEVINS *Manip.* 190/37 Scurfe, itch, *prurigo*. **1607** TOPSELL *Four-f. Beasts* 681 They which drink or eat sow milk fal into scurffes and Leprosies. **1661** LOVELL *Hist. Anim. & Min.* 25 The gall helpeth the leprosy and scurfe.

† **b.** A similar condition in animals. *Obs.*

c **1440** *Pallad. on Husb.* VI. 138 And ouer yeer they wol been in good poynte Withouten scorf or scalle in cors or ioynte. **1523** FITZHERB. *Husb.* §116 There is a disease amonge horses that is called the scabbe, and it is a skorfe in dyuers places of his body. **1607** TOPSELL *Four-f. Beasts* 28 The vrine with the owne dung,..taketh away the scurffe of Oxen.

2. The scales or small laminæ of epidermis that are continually being detached from the skin; esp. such scales detached in abnormally large quantity as a consequence of disease, or forming accumulations at the roots of the hair or elsewhere. †Formerly also, a single scale or lamina of this kind.

a **1000** *Bede's Eccl. Hist.* V. ii. (MS. B.), Se..swa micle hreofle & scurf [*v.rr.* scyrf, sceorfe; L. *furfures*] on his heafde hæfde, ðæt him næfre æniȝ feax on ufan ðam heafde acenned beon meahte. *c* **1440** *Promp. Parv.* 451/1 Scurf, of scabbys, *squama, squamula*. **1483** CAXTON *Gold. Leg.* 326/1 Of kyrnellys & botches of his face & of scurffys there ranne grete plenty of blood. **1540** PALSGR. *Acolastus* Prol. Biij b, By whiche their so doing, they clawe of their owne skabbe, i. their new gathered skurfe, therby makynge their skynne rawe agayne. **1579** LANGHAM *Gard. Health* (1633) 7 The flowers sodden in lée, and the head washed therwith taketh away the skurfe..thereof. **1786** J. HUNTER *Treat. Vener. Dis.* VI. ii. (1810) 473 It broke out after in venereal scurfs, upon the skin. **1815** ELPHINSTONE *Acc. Caubul* (1842) I. 341 The bather is scrubbed by the men of the bath till every particle of dirt or scurf is cleared off his skin. **1870** SWINBURNE *Ess. & Stud.* (1875) 270 His bones foul with leprous scurf and green corruption of the grave.

b. *transf.* in *Bot.* Minute scales found on the leaves of certain plants.

1839 LINDLEY *Introd. Bot.* (ed. 3) 63. **1857** A. GRAY *First Less. Bot.* (1866) Gloss.

3. Any incrustation upon the surface of a body; rust, †a scab (*obs.*); a saline or sulphurous deposit, mould, or the like. Now *rare*.

c **1440** *Promp. Parv.* 451/1 Scurfe, of metel, *scorium*. **1538** ELYOT *Dict.*, *Crusta*,..the scurfe of a scabbe or wounde [? *read* (with ed. 1548) the scurfe or scabbe of a wounde]. **1581** STAFFORD *Exam. Compl.* ii. (1876) 59 Then there is no rust nor scurfe that diminisheth the goodnes or wasteth the substaunce of Gold. **1624** CAPT. SMITH, etc. *Virginia* III. 58 The waters..had left a tinctured spangled skurfe, that made many bare places seeme as guilded. **1665** HOOKE *Microgr.* 135 Growing Trees..that have been long expos'd to the Air and Rain, will be all over cover'd with a greenish scurff. **1667** MILTON *P.L.* I. 672 There stood a Hill not far whose griesly top Belch'd fire and rowling smoak; the rest entire Shon with a glossie scurff, undoubted sign That in his womb was hid metallic Ore, The work of Sulphur. **1752** *Phil. Trans.* XLVII. 410 The bottom of the great crater, which was before an indurated scurf of bitumen and sulphur, is now full of large rents or openings. **1842** TENNYSON *Vision of Sun* v. 5 By shards and scurf of salt, and scum of dross.

b. *fig.*

?**1533** LATIMER *Let. to Morice* in Foxe *A. & M.* (1583) 1741/2, I neuer denyed Pilgrimage. And yet I haue sayed that much scurffe must be pared away ere euer it can be wel done, superstition, idolatry, [etc.] **1642** D. ROGERS *Naaman* 30 Job was an holy man, yet such naturall scurffe the Lord saw to lurke in his spirit that he was faine..at last to wring this speech from him. **1697** DRYDEN *Æneid* VI. 1011 Then are they happy, when by length of time The Scurf is worn away, of each committed Crime. **1854** EMERSON *Lett. & Soc. Aims, Poet. & Imag.* Wks. (Bohn) III. 153 'Tis boyish in Swedenborg to cumber himself with the dead scurf of Hebrew antiquity.

c. *spec.* A deposit of coke on the inner surface of a gas retort.

1884 C. G. W. LOCK *Workshop Rec.* Ser. III. 81/2 Pieces of the hard coke obtained as scurf in gas retorts are sometimes employed.

† **4.** A thin layer of turf. *Obs.*

1708 *Phil. Trans.* XXVI. 59 The first is by cutting of the Scurf of the Ground, making up the Turf so cut in heaps, and when the Sun has dryed these Heaps, they are then set on Fire. *a* **1726** KING in *Nat. Hist. Irel.* 106 Now that swerd or scurf of the earth, that consists of the roots of grass, being lifted up and made fuzzy by the water in winter..is dried in the spring.

5. a. The 'scum' of the population. *rare.*

1688 in Ellis *Orig. Lett.* Ser. II. IV. 143 Some of the scurf and meaner part run in to them, as they would to see a show. **1870** LONGF. *Dante's Inferno* XV. 111 Thou hadst seen there, If thou hadst had a hankering for such scurf [*di tal tigna*], That one, who by the Servant of the Servants From Arno was transferred to Bacchiglione.

b. *slang.* A contemptible person, esp. a miser, skinflint. Also *spec.*, an employer who pays less than the usual rate of wages; a labourer who accepts less than the usual rate; also *attrib.*

1851 MAYHEW *Lond. Labour* II. 208 The inferior paying class..are..known among their work-people as 'scurfs'. *Ibid.* 236 Let me now speak of the Scurf labourers. *Ibid.*, A scavager, working for a scurf master, gave me the following account. **1854** *Househ. Words* VIII. 75 A low person is a snob, a sweep, and a scurf. **1889** A. T. PASK *Eyes Thames* 39 The crowd of loafers on the quay. These are the 'scurfs' or 'ufflers' who hang about for any odd jobs.

scurf (skɜːf), *sb.*[2] Also 5 scurffe, 7 scurfe, 7–8 skurff, 8 scurff; 7 *pl.* scurves. [Possibly identical with SCURF *sb.*[1]

The fuller form *salmon-scurf*, though not found in our quots. before the 19th c., may be the original; for *scurf* in the sense of something inferior of its kind, cf. SCURF *sb.*[1] 5 and SCRUFF *sb.*[1]]

The Sea-trout, *Salmo eriox* or *S. trutta*.

1483 *Cath. Angl.* 326/2 A scurffe, *quidam piscis*. **1557** TURNER in *Gesner's Hist. Anim.* IV. (1558) 1296 *Accepi eundem in alijs Britanniæ prouincijs uocari* a Gray trout, & *in alijs* a Skurf. **1655** MOUFET & BENNET *Health's Improv.* (1746) 283 There are two sorts of them [Bull-trouts], Red Trouts..and Gray Trouts or Skurffs. **1740** R. BROOKES *Art of Angling* 26 The Scurf..or Salmon-Peale..differs in shape from a Salmon in not having a forked Tail. **1861** *Act 24 & 25 Vict.* c. 109 §4 All migratory Fish of the Genus Salmon, whether known by the Names herein-after mentioned, that is to say, Salmon..Bull Trout, Whitling, Scurf,..or by any other local Name. **1865** COUCH *Brit. Fishes* IV. 200 The Scurf, Bull Trout.

scurf (skɜːf), *v.* [f. SCURF *sb.*[1]]

† **1.** *trans.* To cover with a scurf or incrustation. *Obs. rare.*

[**1599**: Implied in SCURFING *vbl. sb.*] *a* **1658** LOVELACE *To E.R.* 36 So..Scurf'd all ore with its unseemly crust. The Diamond, from 'midst the humbler stones, Sparkling, shoots forth the price of Nations. **1699** T. BOSTON *Art Manfishing* (1899) 30 Many this way, by having the wound scurfed over, are rather killed than cured.

2. *intr.* To rise *up* in the form of scurf.

1862 THORNBURY *Turner* II. 168 The pure gold runs here and there to schist, the dross now and then is scurfing up upon the surface.

3. *trans.* To remove by scraping; to chip off (hard deposits) from the surface of a boiler or retort.

1839 *Civ. Engin. & Arch. Jrnl.* II. 361/2 Scurfing castings,..1*s.* 0*d.* **1879** J. PATON in *Encycl. Brit.* X. 92 A carbonaceous deposit forms on the sides of the retorts, which requires to be periodically removed by 'scurfing' with chisels.

scurfed (skɜːft), *a.* [f. SCURF *v.* + -ED[1].] Covered with scurf.

1646 *Full Relat. Fountain Halberstadt* 11 A Boy of Egeln, which had a scurffed head.

scurfer ('skɜːfə(r)). [f. SCURF *v.* 3 + -ER[1].] An operative who removes incrustations of dirt from boilers, metal plates, etc.

1881 *Instructions to Census Clerks* (1885) 36 Scurfer (Ships). **1921** *Dict. Occup. Terms* (1927) §699 *Scurfer, retort scurfer* (gas works);..chips off deposited gas carbon from sides of retorts when it gets too thick. *Ibid.* §952 *Boiler cleaner, boiler scaler, boiler scraper, boiler scurfer,..scurfer boy*..; removes 'scale' (incrusted deposit) from inner surface of boilers and from boiler tubes.

scurffyls, variant of SCROFFLES *pl. Obs.*

scurfily ('skɜːfɪlɪ), *adv.* [f. SCURFY *a.* + -LY[2].] In a manner resembling scurf; like scurf.

1870 HOOKER *Stud. Flora* 174 *Viburnum Lantana*, Scurfily pubescent.

scurfiness ('skɜːfɪnɪs). Also 6 scorffynesse. [f. SCURFY *a.* + -NESS.] The condition of being scurfy or covered with scurf.

a **1529** SKELTON *Dk. Albany* 140 In lousy lothsumnesse And scabbed scorffynesse. **1657** W. COLES *Adam in Eden* ciij, The same stamped with Honey..consumeth and scoureth away..all scurfinesse of the Head and Face. **1799** UNDERWOOD *Dis. Childhood* (ed. 4) II. 20 Some infants early contract a scurfiness on the head.

b. *Bot.* (See quot. 1900.)

1857 A. GRAY *First Less. Bot.* (1866) Gloss., Scurfiness. **1900** B. D. JACKSON *Gloss. Bot. Terms*, *Scurf*..*Scurfiness*, the appearance produced by membranous scales.

scurfing ('skɜːfɪŋ), *vbl. sb.* [f. SCURF *v.* + -ING[1].]

† **1.** The formation of scurf. *Obs. rare*$^{-1}$.

1599 A. M. tr. *Gabelhouer's Bk. Physicke* 359/1 [A prescription] for all manner of scurfinge of the externalle skinne.

2. An incrustation formed in boilers or retorts.

1884 C. G. W. LOCK *Workshop Rec.* Ser. III. 104/2 Get new carbons, made out of gas-retort 'scurfing', as it is called.

scurfy ('skɜːfɪ), *a.* [f. SCURF *sb.*[1] + -Y.]

1. Covered with scurf; suffering from cutaneous disease. Also, of the nature of scurf.

1483 *Cath. Angl.* 326/2 Scurfy, *vbi* scabbyde. **1692** *Lond. Gaz.* No. 2803/4 A bright bay Mare,..with..scurffy Heels before. **1758** J. S. *Le Dran's Observ. Surg.* (1771) Dict. Cc 2, *Lepra*, a dry Scab that makes the Skin scurfy. **1804** *Med. Jrnl.* XII. 404 By persevering in the use of these remedies, ..the white scurfy scales intirely disappeared. **1899** *Allbutt's Syst. Med.* VIII. 513 A head which has been scurfy for many years becomes sore and eczematous.

2. *transf.* Covered as with scurf incrusted; resembling scurf.

1731 *Phil. Trans.* XXXVII. 201 Those Diamonds that lay more superficially, and exposed to the Air and Sun were more scurfy, and by Consequence lost more by polishing than the other. **1849** W. H. HARVEY *Sea-Side Bk.* 232 Very similar to the barnacle is the animal of the *Balanus*, whose shells cover, in scurfy patches, the surface of exposed rocks.

b. *spec.* in *Bot.* (See quots.)

1796 WITHERING *Brit. Plants* (ed. 3) I. 79 Scurfy (*squarrosus*) applied to a cup in compound flowers, the scales of which are bent outwards at the ends, so as to give the whole a ragged appearance. **1871** W. A. LEIGHTON *Lichen-Flora* 9 Thallus crustaceous, squamose, scurfy, powdery [etc.].

† **3.** Of turf: Forming a thin crust. *Obs. rare*$^{-1}$.

1710 *Phil. Trans.* XXVII. 297 A Scurfy Heath Turf will at last grow on the Top of it.

scurge, obs. form of SCOURGE *sb.* and *v.*

scuril, scuring, obs. ff. SCURRIL *a.*, SCOURING.

scurling, variant of SKIRLING.

† **scurn**, *sb. Obs. rare*$^{-1}$. [f. SCURN *v.*]

Hesitation, bashfulness.

a **1300** *Cursor M.* 8963 Sco lift hir skirt wit-vten scurn, And bar-fote wode sco þat burn.

† **scurn**, *v. Obs.* Forms: 3 skur(r)n, 4 skurne, scurn(e. Cf. SHURN. [Of obscure origin; perh. cognate with ON. *skirra-sk* (see SCARE *v.*). Cf. SCUNNER *v.*] *intr.* To shrink, flinch, take fright.

a **1300** *Cursor M.* 19446 He sagh him croised þat ilk turn þat he for staning suld not skurn. *Ibid.* 20960 Noght he skurnd wit hir stang, Bot on his hand þer scho was fest, He schok and in þe fir hir kest. *c* **1325** *Metr. Hom.* 24 Quen sun and mon sal thusgat turn, Than sal the sinful sar scurn. *c* **1330** R. BRUNNE *Chron. Wace* (Rolls) 120 And menne besoght me..To turne it bot in light[e] ryme. þai sayd, if I in strange it turne, To here it, manyon suld skurne.

† **scurr.** *Obs. rare*$^{-1}$. [ad. L. *scurra* buffoon.] A buffoon or jester.

1596 DALRYMPLE tr. *Leslie's Hist. Scot.* I. 121 Bardis, scurris,..wt sik sort of persouns, lat skurge. **1823** MACTAGGART *Gallov. Encycl.*, *Scurr*, a low blackguard.

scurr, variant of SKIRR *v. dial.*

scurrage, variant of SCOURAGE[1] *Obs.*

scurrick, variant of SKERRICK.

† '**scurrier.** *Obs.* Forms: α. 5 scurrour, 6 scurrer, skurrer, skyrrer; β. 6 scurreour, -iour, -ior, -yer, scurier, 6–7 scurrier. [App. aphetic a. OF. *descouvreor* DISCOVERER; cf. the Sc. forms *discurrour, discuriour* (14–16th c.), and the 14th c. *skouerour* s.v. SCOURER[1]. The coincidence of sense with *currour*, COURIER *sb.* 2, has probably influenced the form. The It. *scorridore* (agent-n. f. *scorrere* to run out: cf. EXCUR *v.*) has the same meaning, but there is no equivalent OF. **escoureor*.] One sent out to reconnoitre; a scout, avant-courier.

c **1470** HENRY *Wallace* VII. 796 Apon the moss a scurrour sone fand he. **1525** LD. BERNERS *Froiss.* (1812) II. xxxiii. 99 He sente forthe scurrers to aduyse the dealynge of their ennemyes. **1536** BELLENDEN *Cron. Scot.* (1821) I. 94 Claudius,..send his scurriouris to spy the nature of the cuntre. *c* **1540** tr. *Pol. Verg. Eng. Hist.* (Camden) 21 John Fastolf..had intelligence of his comming, by meane of scurryers. *a* **1548** HALL *Chron.*, *Hen. VIII* 119 Then the Dukes skyrrers made profer afore the toune, out of the whiche issued a great compagnie of horsemen and skyrmished with the Dukes horsemen. **1607** B. BARNES *Divils Charter* II. i. C 4 b, Our scurriers, Are now return'd. *fig.* **1537** *St. Papers Hen. VIII*, II. 491, I wolde not haue the Deputye, representing the Kinges person, be a comen skurrer for every lyght mater; but, whan he shulde begynne a warre, begynne it upon a juste goode grounde, and [etc.].

'**scurrifunge**, *v.* ? *dial.* Also scurry-. [A word of jocular formation, used in various senses with little or no discoverable connexion.] **a.** ? *trans.* To scrub, scour. **b.** *intr.* (See quot. 1777.) **c.** ? To wriggle about.

1777 *Horæ Subsecivæ* (MS.) in *Eng. Dial. Dict.*, s.v. Scurrifunge, to lash tightly; coïre. **1789** COWPER *Let. to Lady Hesketh* 6 June, Half a dozen tooth brushes... Two of the brushes abovesaid must be for inside scurryfunging, viz. they must be hooked. **1894** *Punch* 1 Sept. 102/1 So he scurryfunged around with his stomach on the ground,.. And he spied 'a stag of ten'.

scurrile, scurril ('skʌrɪl), *a.* Now somewhat *arch.* Forms: 6–7 scurrill, skurrill, 7 skurrile, scuril, 6– scurrile, scurril. [a. F. *scurrile*, †*scurrille* (14th c.), or ad. L. *scurrīlis*, f. *scurra* buffoon.] = SCURRILOUS.

1567 DRANT *Horace, A.P.* B 1, If I, or you the taunting grace can iudge from scurrill gere. **1586** A. DAY *Eng. Secretary* I. (1595) 4 That it containe not base, filthy or scurrile matter. **1606** SHAKS. *Tr. & Cr.* I. iii. 148 With him Patroclus..Breakes scurrill Iests. **1644** MILTON *Areop.* (Arb.) 43 It had bin plainly partiall..to correct him for grave Cicero, and not for scurrill Plautus. **1701** ROWE *Amb. Step-Moth.* II. ii. (1720) 30 With scurrile Taunts and blackest Infamy They load my Name. **1838–43** ARNOLD *Hist. Rome* II. xxxvii. 479 Scurril songs, and gestures, and clapping of hands, were the only answer returned to him.

1854 TRENCH *Synon.* xxxiv. 141 Which would attract many ..whom scurrile buffoonery would only revolt and repel. **1883** R. W. DIXON *Mano* II. v. 83 All which full oft she turned to scurril jest.

¶App. misused for: Rough, rugged, 'unfriendly'.

1632 LITHGOW *Trav.* VI. 262 Wee came to the most scurrile and timorous Discent of the whole passage. *Ibid.* IX. 423 Wee Coasted the scurrile and Rockey face of Norway.

†**'scurrilely,** *adv. Obs.* In quots. scurril(l)y. [f. SCURRILE *a.* + -LY².] In a scurrile manner.

1647 HEXHAM I, Scurrilly, *Als een rabaut.* **a 1707** S. WILLARD *Body Div.* (1726) 903/1 [In praying] we may do nothing rashly, nothing scurrily, or unbecomingly.

scurrility (skə'rɪlɪtɪ). Forms: α. 6 scurrilite, -illitie, skurrillity, 6–7 scur(r)ilitie, scurrillity, 7– scurrility; β. 6–7 squirilitie, 6 squirrilitie, 7 -ility. [a. F. *scurrilité* (15th c.), or ad. L. *scurrīlitās*, f. *scurrīlis*: see SCURRILE *a.* and -ITY.] The quality of being scurrilous; buffoon-like jocularity; coarseness or indecency of language, esp. in invective and jesting.

α. **1508** DUNBAR *Flyting* 58 Scarth fra scorpione, scaldit in scurrilitie. **1526** *Pilgr. Perf.* (W. de W. 1531) 90 b, Scurrilite or spekynge of fylthy wordes. **1588** SHAKS. *L.L.L.* v. i. 4 Your reasons at dinner haue beene..pleasant without scurrillity. **1654** GATAKER *Disc. Apol.* 3, I list not to contend with him in scurrilitie and bad language. **1759** SYMMER in Ellis *Orig. Lett.* Ser. II. IV. 414 The hawkers..every day have some new piece of scurrility against him, to bawl about the streets. **1849** MACAULAY *Hist. Eng.* v. I. 650 He was, as usual, interrupted in his defence by ribaldry and scurrility from the judgment seat. **1874** GREEN *Short Hist.* vii. §1. 346 The Sacrament of the Mass..was attacked with a scurrility and profaneness, which passes belief.

β. **a 1566** R. EDWARDS *Damon & Pithias* (1908) Bj b, I came not yet to be the Kinges foole, Or to fill his eares with seruile squirilitie. **1577** STANYHURST *Descr. Irel.* ii. 6 b in *Holinshed*, The heathen misliked in an orature squirilitie. **1607** DEKKER & WEBSTER *Westw. Hoe* II. i. B 4 b, So long as your mirth bee voyde of all Squirrility.

b. Something scurrilous.

1589 PUTTENHAM *Eng. Poesie* I. xxxi. (Arb.) 76 Such among the Greekes were called Pantomimi, with vs Buffons, altogether applying their wits to Scurrillities & other ridiculous matters. **1733** POPE *Dunc.* II. 299 *note*, Concanen ..was author of several dull and dead scurrilities in the British and London Journals. **1830** D'ISRAELI *Chas. I*, III. xi. 244 Who could have imagined that the writers of these scurrilities were scholars.

†**c.** Buffoon-like behaviour. *Obs.*

1614 J. NORDEN *Labyrinth Mans Life* L 4, Heroicke acts, that make men honorable, Are only sweet and most inestimable; The rest are false, found mere scurrilitie, By which some loose, both fame and dignitie. **1624** HEYWOOD *Gunaik.* I. 24 We may as well say, Cats, Goates and Apes, are by chance given to voracitie, lust, and squirilitie.

Hence †**scu'rrilitiship** *nonce-wd.*, ? the state of persons who indulge in scurrility.

1592 NASHE *Strange Newes* G 2 b, Maister Bird shall.. meeter it mischieuously in maintenance of their scurrilitiship and ruditie.

scurrilize ('skʌrɪlaɪz), *v. rare.* [f. SCURRILE *a.* + -IZE.] *trans.* †**a.** To attack with scurrility, speak scurrilously of. **b.** To make scurrilous.

1609 [W. BARLOW] *Answ. Nameless Cath.* 157 What is this vncircumcised Iesuite, that hee should, in so base tearmes, scurrilize so great a King? **1884** SYMONDS *Shaks. Predec.* i. 5 All inducements to degrade or scurrilise the theatre.. ended in [etc.].

scurrilous ('skʌrɪləs), *a.* Also 6 skurulous, 7 scurulous, scurrillous. [f. SCURRILE *a.* + -OUS.] 'Using such language as only the licence of a buffoon can warrant' (J.); characterized by coarseness or indecency of language, esp. in jesting and invective; coarsely opprobrious or jocular.

1576 GASCOIGNE *Needles Eye* Wks. 1910 II. 419 What shall we thinke of skurulous, deceyptfull, byting, slanderous ..wordes? **1597** HOOKER *Eccl. Pol.* v. Ded. §7 The scurrilous and more then Satyricall immodestie of Martinisme. **1611** SHAKS. *Wint. T.* IV. iv. 215 Forewarne him, that he vse no scurrilous words in's tunes. **1651** HOBBES *Leviath.* II. xxi. 110 Sometimes a scurrilous Jester, as Hyperbolus. **1716** ADDISON *Freeholder* No. 23 ¶1 They are grown scurrilous upon the Royal family. **1828** MACAULAY *Ess., Hallam* (1851) I. 56 They might be violent in innovation and scurrilous in controversy. **1874** GREEN *Short Hist.* vii. §2. 359 The old scurrilous ballads were heard again in the streets.

Hence **'scurrilously** *adv.*, in a scurrilous manner; †after the manner of a buffoon. Also **'scurrilousness.**

1597 BEARD *God's Judgem.* II. xxxvi. (1631) 431 Such as shamed not as soone as they had glutted their..heads with wine, to fall scurrilously a dauncing. **1666** PEPYS *Diary* 17 Oct., Heard the Duke discourse, which he did mighty scurrilously, of the French. **1727** BAILEY vol. II, *Scurrilousness*, scandalous Language, saucy Drollery, Buffoonry. **1789** W. BELSHAM *Ess.* (1799) II. 369 He has been..scurrilously reviled as the genuine successor and counterpart of..Hugh Peters.

scurrio(u)r, scurrour: see SCURRIER.

scurry ('skʌrɪ), *sb.* [f. SCURRY *v.*]

1. The act of scurrying; a hurried movement, a rush; hurry, haste, bustle. ***hurry and scurry***: cf. HURRY-SCURRY *sb.*

1823 E. MOOR *Suffolk Words* 356 *Skurry*, haste, impetuosity. **1830** W. IRVING *Life & Lett.* (1864) II. 437 It was such a treat after the hurry and scurry, and heartless bustle of London. **1865** TROLLOPE *Belton Est.* xix. 218 Belinda would usually come down in a scurry as she heard her mother's bell. **1873** G. C. DAVIES *Mount. & Mere* v. 34 Unsuspecting gulls..took to wing with a tremendous scurry. **1910** *Q. Rev.* Jan. 181 Far away from the scurry and the scramble..of London life.

2. *Sporting.* A short quick run or race on horseback.

1824 W. TAYLOR in *Monthly Mag.* LVII. 407 They travelled for adventures to the courts Of princes,—where at tournaments and skurries, Fame could be earn'd. **1829** *Sporting Mag.* XXIV. 51 A very fast scurry with Lord Lonsdale the day before I left. **1885** *Field* 17 Jan. 63/3 To wind up, a Flat Scurry, at catch weights, usually gave good sport. *Ibid.* 21 Feb. 219/3 Although only a few fields separate the two coverts,..more than one coat changed colour during the short scurry. **1898** *Daily News* 6 Sept. 4/7 There are still at Doncaster too many of the five furlong scurries.

b. A run (made by an animal).

1865 *Daily Tel.* 4 Mar., She [the hare] steals the help of a scurry up the ditch-bottom. **1874** S. BEAUCHAMP *Grantley* I. xiii. 247 [The dog] has his scurry..night and morning.

3. A fluttering assemblage (e.g. of birds, snow, foam) moving or driven rapidly through the air. †Also, a confused tangle of material.

1839 THACKERAY in *Corsair* 26 Oct. *Stray Papers* (1901) 177 Ladies at work at a frame in the midst of a great skurry and labyrinth of worsted balls, making slipper-tops [etc.]. **1858** B. TAYLOR *Northern Travel* xxvi. 267 The birds circled overhead, or dropped like thick scurries of snow-flakes on the water. **1868** HUNTLEY *Gloss. Cotswold Dial.*, *Skurry*, a flock in confused flight. **1873** LOWELL *Lett.* (1894) II. 123 That flight of baby angels caught up and whirled along in the wake of Gabriel like a skurry of autumn birds. **1880** BLACKMORE *May Anerley* I. xviii. 312 A scurry of foam flew like pellets from the rampart.

scurry ('skʌrɪ), *v.* Also skurry. [In sense 1, app. a back-formation from SCURRIER. In the current sense perh. taken from HURRY-SCURRY, a reduplication of HURRY *v.*]

†**1.** *intr.* ? To ride out as a 'scurrier'. *Obs.*

1580 NORTH *Plutarch, Annibal* (1595) 1135 Then he commaunded the horsemen of the Numidians to scurrie to the trenches of the Romanes, to intise him to come to battell.

2. To go rapidly, move hurriedly. Often with advbs., as *off*, *away*.

1810 SOUTHEY *Kehama* v. xiii, The wind..opens the clouds; Scatter'd before the gale, They skurry through the sky. **1839** THACKERAY *Major Gahagan* v, The ladies.. skurried out of the apartment. **1872** BLACK *Adv. Phaeton* xvi. 219 They scurry away like rabbits when they see her coming. **1894** MRS. ANNE RITCHIE *Chapters from Mem.* ii. 14 Remembered events come cheerfully scurrying up one after another.

b. ***hurry and scurry***: cf. HURRY-SCURRY *v.*

1857 TROLLOPE *Barchester T.* xix. (1858) 145 Charlotte hurried and skurried about the room hither and thither, doing or pretending to do many things. **1889** J. K. JEROME *Idle Thoughts* 140 How petty seems the work on which they are hurrying and skurrying.

3. *trans.* To cause to go hastily or move rapidly.

1850 THACKERAY *Lett.* 26 Feb., Off we set,..skurrying the policemen off the road. **1853** F. W. NEWMAN *Odes of Horace* I. xv, When the traitor-swain with ships of Ida Scurried o'er the wave his hostess Helen. **1892** GARLAND *Little Norsk* iv. 32 The wind..scurried the snow south or east.

Hence **'scurrying** *vbl. sb.* and *ppl. a.*

1862 THORNBURY *Turner* I. 75 A view of flustered and scurrying fishing-boats in a gale of wind. **1869** 'WAT. BRADWOOD' *The O.V.H.* xix, A hurrying, scurrying crowd of horses. **1878** TENNYSON *Q. Mary* III. v, The scurrying of a rat, Affrighted me. **1883** ROLLINS *New Eng. Bygones* 93 The scurrying drops came thicker and thicker. **1885** *Harper's Mag.* Feb. 398/2 There was a sound of skurrying steps.

†**scurryvaig.** *Sc. Obs.* [? ad. L. *scurra vagus* wandering buffoon.] A vagabond.

1513 DOUGLAS *Æneis* VIII. Prol. 68 Swingeouris and scurrevagis [*v.r.* skuryvagis], swankeis and swanis. **1819** *St. Patrick* III. 305 (Jam.) Ye may hide the vile scurrievaig.

S-curve, -curved: see S I. 2 c.

†**scur'vetical,** *a. Obs. rare*⁻¹. [Irreg. f. SCURVY.] Good against the scurvy, scorbutic.

1663 in Myddelton *Chirk Castle Acc.* (1908) 165 Paid for a pint of scurveticall water, 2s. 6d.

†**'scurvical,** *a. Obs. rare*⁻¹. [f. SCURVY *sb.* + -ICAL.] = SCURVIED.

1728 *Brice's Weekly Jrnl.* 8 Mar. 3 Offensive Breath, often occasioned by..Scurvical Gums.

scurvied ('skɜːvɪd), *a.* [f. SCURVY *sb.* + -ED².] Affected with scurvy.

1856 KANE *Arctic Expl.* II. v. 65 The scurvied sick of Rensselaer. *Ibid.* vii. 83 Able to empty a slop-bucket or rub a scurvied leg.

scurvily ('skɜːvɪlɪ), *adv.* Now *arch.* [f. SCURVY *a.* + -LY².] In a scurvy manner.

a. Shabbily, meanly; sorrily, unsatisfactorily.

1599 B. JONSON *Cynthia's Rev.* v. iii. Wks. 1616 I. 243 His hat was carried skiruily. **1671** CLARENDON *Dialogues* Tracts (1727) 306 We are scurvily used, but that is because we are scurvy fellows, and deserve no better. **1707** *Reflex. upon Ridicule* 236 Her Fondness for a Spark of hers was scurvily interpreted. **1710** SWIFT *Jrnl. to Stella* 12 Dec., And, passing an evening scurvily enough, [I] did not come home till eight. **1827** SCOTT *Surg. Dau.* iv, I will lay no bets about Miss Grey,..I think I should act very scurvily, if I were to make her the subject of any idle debate betwixt you and me. **1873** BROWNING *Red Cott. Nt.-cap* 111 The young pair quitted Paris to reside At London: which repaid the compliment But scurvily.

†**b.** Sourly, rudely. *Obs.*

1607 MIDDLETON *Fam. Love* IV. i. (1608) E 4 b, Speak pittifully, looke scuruily, and dissemble cunningly. **1647** J. BERKENHEAD *On Happy Collect. Fletcher's Wks.* 90 Such boyst'rous Trifles Thy Muse would not brooke, Save when she'd show how scurvily they looke.

†**'scurviness.** *Obs.* [f. SCURVY *a.* + -NESS.] The quality or condition of being 'scurvy'.

1548 ELYOT *Dict.*, *Psorothalmia*, a scuruinesse of the browes with an ytche. **1596** MASCALL *Govt. Horses* 138 The scratches is a long scuruines right behind the legge. **1607** TOPSELL *Four-f. Beasts* 83 Leprosies, botches, and scuruinesse of the skinne. **1648** HEXHAM II, *Schorftheydt*, *ofte Schorftigheydt*, Scurvynesse, Scabbinesse, or Manginesse. **1727** BAILEY vol. II, *Scurviness*, Badness, Naughtiness, Sorriness.

scurvy ('skɜːvɪ), *sb.* Forms: α. 6 skurvie, 6–7 scurvie, 7 skirvye, 7–8 scurvey, 6– scurvy; β. 6 scurby, skyrby, scorbie, 7 scorby. [Subst. use of SCURVY *a.* (cf. *scurvy disease* under sense 1 of the adj.); the specific sense was determined by the use of the word to render the like-sounding F. *scorbut*, MLG. *schorbûk*, etc. (see SCORBUTE), and the β. forms above proceed from assimilation of the native to the foreign word. See also SCRUBY.]

1. a. A disease characterized by general debility of the body, extreme tenderness of the gums, foul breath, subcutaneous eruptions and pains in the limbs, induced by exposure and by a too liberal diet of salted foods; SCORBUTUS. Now recognized as due to insufficient ascorbic acid (vitamin C) in the diet.

Formerly used more vaguely, including what is now distinguished as PURPURA.

α. **c 1565** R. BAKER in *Hakluyt's Voy.* (1589) 151 Our legs now..swolne euery ioint withall With this disease, which, by your leaue, the Scuruie men doe call. **c 1603** HEYWOOD & ROWLEY *Fortune by Land & Sea* III. i. (1655) 21 They'l find work enough about home to keep us from the scurvey. **1620** J. MASON *New-found-land* in *Mem.* (1887) 149 A great roote grows in fresh water ponds that is good against the skiruye. **1712** E. COOKE *Voy. S. Sea* 35 About 30 more had the Scurvy. **1742** *Lond. & Country Brewer* I. (ed. 4) 17 Our British Malady the Scurvy. **1840** R. H. DANA *Bef. Mast* xxxv. 133 The scurvy had begun to show itself on board. **1898** *Allbutt's Syst. Med.* V. 586 Scurvy is a general apyretic and non-contagious disorder. **1966** DUNLOP & ALSTEAD *Textbk. Med. Treatment* (ed. 10) 390 Scurvy is a nutritional disease which results from prolonged subsistence on diets practically devoid of fresh fruits and vegetables. **1968** PASSMORE & ROBSON *Compan. Med. Stud.* I. v. 10/1 Five major diseases: scurvy, beriberi, pellagra, keratomalacia and rickets, arise as a result of a dietary lack of one of the vitamins.

β. **1586** A. H. tr. *Guillemeau's Treat. Eyes* title-p., A worthy treatise of the eyes &c. together with a profitable treatise of the scorbie. **1597** GERARDE *Herbal* I. xii. 195 The disease..which we in England call the Scuruie, and Scurby, and vpon the seas the Skyrby. *Ibid.* II. lxxxii. 325 Which excellent plant, Cæsars soldiers..found to preuaile.. against that plague and hurtfull disease..called *Scorbutum*; in English the Scuruie, and Skyrbie.

†**b.** *pl.* Attacks of this disease. *Obs.*

1592 NASHE *P. Penilesse* Wks. 1904 I. 171 Hee lyes in brine, in Balist, and is lamentable sicke of the scuruies. **1628** WITHER *Brit. Rememb.* I. 400 Sloath-bred Scurvies. **1732** ARBUTHNOT *Rules of Diet* in *Aliments*, etc. 257 A temperate Sea-Salt, very useful in Scurvies. **1764** FOOTE *Mayor of G.* I. Wks. 1799 I. 162 Your scurvies, and gouts.

†**2.** A disease of cattle. Cf. SCURF *sb.*¹ 2.

1604 E. G[RIMSTONE] *D'Acosta's Hist. Indies* VI. xv. 465 If the mangie or the scurvie which they call carache take any beast they were presently commaunded to bury it quicke, lest it should infect others.

3. *attrib.* and *Comb.*, as ***scurvy-rickets***, ***-spot***; †***scurvy-ale***, medicated ale intended as an antidote to scurvy (cf. *scurvy-grass ale*); †***scurvy-weed***, ***-wort*** = SCURVY-GRASS.

1618 J. TAYLOR (Water-P.) *Pennyless Pilgr.* C 2, We had a sort of Ale, called *Scuruy Ale. **1897** *Allbutt's Syst. Med.* III. 18 In infants I have known *scurvy-rickets mistaken for rheumatism. **1856** KANE *Arct. Expl.* I. xiv. 163 The *scurvy-spots that mottled our faces. **1568** TURNER *Herbal* I. (ed. 2) 90, I could neuer learne anye name of it, but *Scurby wede, or *Scurby wurt.

scurvy ('skɜːvɪ), *a.* Forms: 6 skurvy, scurvye, skurvie, skyrvye, 6–7 scurvie, 7 scirvy, skirvie, scurvey, 6– scurvy. [f. SCURF *sb.*¹ (with regular change of *f* into *v*) + -Y. Cf. the later SCURFY *a.*; also Sw. *skorfvig*, LG. *schorfig*, Du. *schurftig*.]

†**1.** Covered with scurf; suffering from, or of the nature of, skin disease; scurfy, scabby. *Obs.*

scurvy disease: *spec.* = SCURVY *sb.*

1515 BARCLAY *Egloges* iii. (1570) B vj b, Iugglers and pipers, and scuruy wayfarers. **a 1529** SKELTON *E. Rummyng* 140 A sorte of foule drabbes All scuruy with scabbes. **1535** COVERDALE *Lev.* xxi. 20 Whether he be blynde,..or is gleyd, or is skyrvye or scaulde. **1577** FRAMPTON *Joyful News* II. (1596) 38 Shee was healed of her skuruie disease very well. **1580** HOLLYBAND *Treas. Fr. Tong*, *Le mal Saint-Mein*, the Scuruie disease. **1597** GERARDE *Herbal* I. xl. 60 The bran of Wheate..rubbed vpon them that be scuruie and mangie, easeth the partie very much. **1610** MARKHAM *Masterp.* II. lxxviii. 351 This medicine is well approued to cure..Moully heeles, or any other sciruy scalls whatsoeuer. **1642** D. ROGERS *Naaman* 439 Contrary to the scurvy and unsightly flesh of a leper. **1758** J. S. *Le Dran's Observ. Surg.* (1771) Dict. Cc7 *Psoriasis*, a Scurvy Scabbiness in the Body.

b. *transf.* Of vegetable growths: Resembling scurf, scurfy.

1763 MILLS *Pract. Husb.* IV. 319 The situation..should communicate to the vines a moisture which is neither bitter nor salt; for either of these will vitiate the taste of the wine, and give a scurvy rough coat to every plant that grows on such land. **1837** P. KEITH *Bot. Lex.* 42 A ring of scurvy and diseased matter.

2. *fig.* Sorry, worthless, contemptible. Said both of persons and things. Cf. SCABBED *a.* 2. Also of treatment, etc.: Shabby, discourteous. Now somewhat *arch.*

1579 NORTHBROOKE *Dicing* 64b, Looke that thou flee and eschewe this scabbed and scuruie company of Dauncers. **1587** *Mirr. Mag., Wolsey* ii, Ambitious minde, a world of wealth would haue, So scrats and scrapes, for scorfe, and scoruy drosse. **1592** KYD *Sp. Trag.* III. v. 1411 Ist not a scuruie iest that a man should iest himselfe to death? **1604** SHAKS. *Oth.* IV. ii. 140 The Moore's abus'd by some most villanous Knaue, Some base notorious Knaue, some scuruy Fellow. **1632** LITHGOW *Trav.* III. 107 He reporteth..that the scuruy Ile of Manne, is so abundant in Oates, Barley, and Wheate, that it supplieth the defects of Scotland. **1710** SWIFT *Jrnl. to Stella* 19 Nov., Steele and I sat among some scurvy company over a bowl of punch. **1710–11** *Ibid.* 9 Jan., We only had a scurvy dinner at an alehouse. **1751** SMOLLETT *Per. Pic.* (1779) II. lxv. 217 The music of a scurvy organ and a few other instruments. **1823** SCOTT *Peveril* xliv, Take your hand from my cloak, my Lord Duke,..I have a scurvy touch of old puritanical humour about me. I abide not the imposition of hands. **1876** BLACKIE *Songs of Relig.* 113 The bare brae seems clad in mockery, With one thin belt of lean, and scurvy trees. **1902** BRENAN *House of Percy* II. ii. 83 Scant preferment and scurvy friendship..the Earl received.

†**b.** quasi-*adv.*

1623 WEBSTER *Duchess Malfi* III. ii, How scurvy prowd he would looke when the treasury was full!

'scurvy-grass. *Bot.* Forms: see SCURVY *sb.*; also SCRUBY-*grass.*

1. A cruciferous plant, *Cochlearia officinalis*, believed to possess anti-scorbutic properties.

a **1597** GERARDE *Herbal* II. lxxxii. 323 Round leafed Scuruie grasse is a low or base herbe. **1611** MIDDLETON & DEKKER *Roaring Girl* F2b, Would any husband suspect that a woman crying, Buy any scurui-grasse, should bring loue letters amongst her herbes to his wife. **1741** *Compl. Fam.-Piece* I. iv. 247 Take..of Scurvygrass half a Bushel. **1767** *Byron's Voy. round World* 47 We carried off a great quantity of cocoa nuts, scurvy-grass, and other vegetables, for the use of the sick. **1856** KANE *Arct. Expl.* I. xxi. 269 Peterson brought me quite a handful of scurvy-grass (*C. fenestrata*). **1872** H. MACMILLAN *True Vine* vii, The saxifrage and the scurvy-grass give a faint tinge of verdure to the snow-white sterility of the arctic lichens.

β. **1622** R. BANISTER 113 *Dis. Eyes* N5b, Scorby-grasse, water-cresses, brooke-lime.

†**b.** *spirit of scurvy-grass*: a volatile oil distilled from the plant. *Obs.*

1676 GREW *Anat. Plants, Lect.* ii. (1682) 242 Spirit of Scurvy-grass maketh no Luctation with any Acid. **1694** SALMON *Bate's Dispens.* (1713) 184/2 If it be made with Spirit of Scurvy-grass [etc.].

†**2.** *sea* or *Scottish scurvy-grass*: the sea bindweed, *Convolvulus soldanella.*

1597 GERARDE *Herbal* II. ccxciii. 690 *Soldanella*..in English Sea Withwinde,..of some Sea Folefoote, and Scottish Scuruie grasse. **1676** T. GLOVER *Virginia* in *Phil. Trans.* XI. 629 *Soldanella* or Sea-Scurvygrass.

†**3.** = *scurvy-grass ale* (see 4). *Obs.*

1664 ETHEREDGE *Love in Tub* I. ii 5 And but this morning the Chandler refus'd to score a quart of Scurvy-grass. **1708** J. CHAMBERLAYNE *St. Gt. Britain* I. III. vii. (1743) 188 There are sold in London..many sorts of ales, very different, as Cock, Steponey,..Betony, Scurvy grass, &c.

4. *attrib.* and *Comb.*, as †**scurvy-grass ale**, ale medicated with scurvy-grass; similarly †*scurvy-grass drink*; †**scurvy-grass medicine**, a medicine containing scurvy-grass as the chief ingredient.

1661 in W. M. Myddelton *Chirk Castle Acc.* (1908) 152 Pd for a qrte of *scurvigrasse ale and plaine ale 8d. **1679** J. LOCKE in Ld. King *Life* 135 There are also several sorts of compounded ales, as cock-ale,..scurvy grass-ale, college-ale, &c. **1658–9** WOOD *Life* (O.H.S.) I. 273 *Scurvy-grass drink began to be frequently drunk in the mornings as physic-drinke. **1609** T. COCKS *Diary* (1901) 77/5 Paide for longe pepper graynes, cloves, mace, and saffron for my *skurvye-grasse medicine, vj d.

scurzonera, obs. rare form of SCORZONERA.

†**scu'sation.** *Obs.* Also 5 **skeusacion, skew(y)sasyon, skosacion, skwsacion, -cyon.** Aphetic form of EXCUSATION.

c **1430** *Freemasonry* 112 (Halliw.) And to that semble he most nede gon, But he have a resenabul skwsacyon. *c* **1440** *Alphabet of Tales* 52 When sho cuthe gett no skosacion to helpe hur with, bod at sho trewid vereli[e] to dye, sho shrafe hur vnto þe preste [etc.]. **1477** *Paston Lett.* III. 215 He seydyt [*sic*] but for a skwsacion.

†**scuse,** *sb. Obs.* Also 6 **skuse,** 7 **schuce.** Aphetic form of EXCUSE *sb.*

1523 LD. BERNERS *Froissart* I. ccclxiii. 52 So the knight coude make no scuse. *a* **1553** UDALL *Roister D.* v. ii, Better (they say) a badde scuse, than none. **1592** GREENE *Disput.* 8 Tis as hard to find a Hare without a Muse, as a woman without a scuse. *a* **1634** CHAPMAN *Alphonsus* III. (1654) 35 If all be well with us, that schuce shall serve.

scuse (skju:z), *v.* Also 6 **scowse, skewse, skuse,** 9– **'scuse.** Aphetic form of EXCUSE *v.* Now chiefly in representations of colloq. speech, esp. in form 'scuse.

1491 CAXTON *Vitas Patr.* (W. de W. 1495) II. 186 They that had done it scused them. **1532** MORE *Confut. Tindale* Wks. 577/2 To skewse hym and keepe hym from beatynge. **1556** *Chron. Grey Friars* (Camden) 70 He wolde have gevyne moch to a be scowsyd. **1594** R. C[AREW] *Tasso* (1881) 110 Ile you to Captaine skuse. *c* **1611** CHAPMAN *Iliad* XXIV. 250 Would to heauen, that all the abiect blood, In all your veines, had Hector scusde. **1830** GALT *Lawrie T.* III. ix. (1849) 114 The gentleman will 'scuse me'. **1864** DICKENS *Our Mutual Friend* (1865) I. 231 'Scuse me, Lawyer Lightwood, it's a part of the truth. **1887** T. E. BROWN *Doctor* 22 'Scuse me, your honour. **1902** [see EXCUSE *v.* 6b]. **1922** JOYCE *Ulysses* 418 All poppycock, you'll scuse me saying. **1971** G. SIMS *Dead Hand* I. iv. 46 Scuse fingers.

scut (skʌt), *sb.*[1] Also 6–7 **scutte,** 6–8 **skut(t,** (9 **scud).** [Of obscure origin: prob. allied to SCUT *a.*

Connexion with ON. *skut-r* stern of a vessel (Norw. *skut* either end of a boat), or with mod.Icel. (*tóu-*) *skott* (fox's) tail, has often been assumed, but appears unlikely.]

1. a. A short erect tail, esp. that of a hare, rabbit, or deer. (Quot. 1530 may belong to sense 2, which is recorded earlier.)

1530 PALSGR. 268/2 Scutte. **1576** TURBERV. *Venerie* 243 The tayle of an Hare and Conney is called their Skut. **1598** SHAKS. *Merry W.* v. v. 20 My Doe, with the blacke Scut? **1601** HOLLAND *Pliny* XI. I. 352 Those that be long shagged and rugged, have very little and short skuts, as Beares. **1646** SIR T. BROWNE *Pseud. Ep.* VI. x. 329 How the Indian Hare came to have a long tayle, whereas that part in others attains no higher then a scut? **1770** G. WHITE *Selborne, To Pennant* Mar. (1789) 79 It's scut [the moose's] seemed to be about an inch long. **1868** CUSSANS *Her.* (1893) 89 The tail of a Fox is called the Brush;..of a Hare or Rabbit (heraldically termed *Coney*), the Scut. **1869** BLACKMORE *Lorna D.* xix, The goat ..rushed at him..his little scut cocked like a gun-hammer.

†**b.** (See quot.) *Obs.*

1601 HOLLAND *Pliny* XXXII. v. II. 434 If the husband take a frogg and spit her..alength upon a reed, so as it goe in at the skut or nature [*printed* mature] behind and come foorth againe at the mouth.

2. †**a.** A hare. *Obs.*

c **1440** *Promp. Parv.* 451/1 Scut, hare. **1523** SKELTON *Garl. Laurel* 632 Masid as a marche hare, he ran lyke a scut.

b. *Hunting.* The hare as the object of the chase. Also *fig.*

1809 MALKIN *Gil Blas* VIII. ix. (Rtldg.) 296 The minister was ready to burst with laughing, to see me so eager after the scut. **1826** *Sporting Mag.* XVII. 378 This day being devoted to the scut, we accompanied Mr. Lyster. **1877** *Coursing Cal. 1876* 21 Handling her hare in grand style, never left the scut until she killed. *Ibid.* 78 Keeping well to the scut, she never gave her opponent a chance. **1921** GALSWORTHY *To Let* III. xi. 310 He sat there a long time dreaming his career, faithful to the scut of his possessive instinct.

Hence **'scutted** *a.* (only in *Comb.*)

1634 W. WOOD *New Eng. Prosp.* II. xv. 89 An English Mare..stumbled into one of these traps;..the Indians.. seeing such a long scutted Deere, praunce in their Merritotter [etc.].

†**scut,** *sb.*[2] *Obs. rare.* [Perh. a. early mod.Du. *schut, schutte* embankment.] ? An embankment.

1561 *Nottingham Rec.* IV. 124 Tellyng of the skutte and other worke about the Bryges.

†**scut,** *a.* and *sb.*[3] *Obs.*$^{-0}$ [Of obscure origin: perh. related in some way to SHORT *a.*, SKIRT *sb.*]

a. *adj.* Short. **b.** *sb.* A short garment.

c **1440** *Promp. Parv.* 451/1 Scut, or schort, *curtus, brevis. Ibid.*, Scut, garment, *nepticula.*

scut (skʌt), *sb.*[4] *dial.* or *slang.* Also **scutt, skut.** [? Var. of SCOUT *sb.*[2]] A term of contempt for a person.

1873 TROLLOPE *Harry Heathcote* (1874) vi. 146, I thought you was ringing trees for that young scut at Gangoil? **1895** M. E. FRANCIS *Frieze & Fustian* 63 I'll pinnance ye, ye little scut! **1901** *Longman's Mag.* Sept. 405 Moran, ye scut! don't be skirmishin'. **1916** J. B. COOPER *Coo-oo-ee* viii. 95 The likes of them skuts to find fault with my cookin'—'deed it's more than O'Callaghan himself would dare do. **1929** W. DEEPING *Roper's Row* ix. 96 He always was a precocious little scut. **1936** M. FRANKLIN *All that Swagger* xxvii. 254 You speak like a low-down scut. **1970** L. SANDERS *Anderson Tapes* xii. 41 You bloody scut! Forget it! **1978** 'M. M. KAYE' *Far Pavilions* lxiii. 863 You'd think those scutts could have given us a bit more notice... It's a shabby lot they are.

scut (skʌt), *sb.*[5] *U.S. colloq.* [Origin unknown: cf. prec.] Tedious menial work. Freq. *attrib.* in *scut work.*

1960 WENTWORTH & FLEXNER *Dict. Amer. Slang* 454/1 *Scud, scut,*..hard, boring, or tedious tasks; minor details that are unrewarding and time-consuming. **1972** *Newsweek* 10 Jan. 37/2 Huber inflicted a fair amount of scut work on the boy—washing dishes, fetching books and journals from the library. **1976** *National Observer* (U.S.) 20 Mar. 14/2, I did all the scutwork: paid the bills, ran the houses, drove the children. **1978** L. PRYOR *Viper* (1979) iii. 40 The servants.. were..brought from Iran and Turkey to do the scut work. **1978** *Maledicta* II. 69 *Scut*, menial medical procedures that must be carried out, usually relegated to the least senior member of the medical team.

†**scut,** *v. Obs.* [? f. SCUT *a.*] *trans.* To dock, cut short.

1530 PALSGR. 707/2, I scutte, *je docque.*

scut, variant of SCOUT *sb.*[3]

scutable, obs. form of SKEW-TABLE.

scutage ('skju:tɪdʒ). *Obs.* exc. *Hist.* Also 5 **scutagie.** [ad. med.L. *scūtāgium*, f. *scūtum* shield, after OF. *escuage*: see ESCUAGE.] A tax levied on knight's fees; chiefly in restricted sense, such a tax paid in lieu of military service.

c **1460** *Oseney Reg.* 123 þe foresaide [canons] schall aquite towarde Richard ffiȝt Odone and his heyres (þat is to say, ij. s. iiij. d., how that euer þe scutage goo, weþer it be more or lasse). *a* **1513** FABYAN *Chron.* VII. (1811) 345 A taske callyd the scutage. **1583** FOXE *A. & M.* (ed. 4) 276/1 The king more and more incensed against hym,..called him to a counte of..scutagies, gifts, presents, scapes of prisoners. **1766** BLACKSTONE *Comm.* II. v. 74 We find in our antient histories, that,..when our kings went to war, they levied scutages on their tenants..to defray their expenses, and to hire troops. **1874** STUBBS *Const. Hist.* I. xii. 454 The term *scutage*, now first employed, indicates that the assessment of the knights' fees was coming into use. **1884** TENNYSON *Becket* I. i, It seem'd to me but just The Church should pay her scutage like the lords.

scutal ('skju:təl), *a.* [ad. mod.L. *scūtālis*, f. L. *scūtum* shield: see SCUTUM.]

1. *Zool.* Of the nature of or pertaining to a scutum.

1857 GOSSE *Omphalos* 218 On each of the scutal valves in this individual I can count about 260 growth-lines.

2. In etymological sense: Of or pertaining to a (heraldic) shield. ***extra-scutal*** adj., of a heraldic device, placed outside the shield.

1868 CUSSANS *Her.* ii. 43 A good example of these scutal monstrosities. **1900** PIXLEY *Hist. Baronetage* v. 244 Some Baronets add the badge as an extra-scutal appendage to their arms.

†**'scutarde**[1]. *Obs. rare.* = SCOTART.

a **1400** *Med. Rec.* in *Rel. Ant.* I. 52 Tak a scutarde als hale als he es taken, and bryn him in a newe potte al to powder.

†**'scutarde**[2]. *Sc. Obs.* [? f. *scute*, SCOUT *v.* + -ARD.] ? One who pours out.

1508 DUNBAR *Tua Mariit Wemen* 92 Ane skabbit skarth, ane scorpioun, ane scutarde behinde.

scutate ('skju:teɪt), *a.* [ad. L. *scūtātus* provided with a shield, f. *scūtum* shield: see SCUTUM.]

1. *Zool.* Covered with scuta or large flat scales.

1826 KIRBY & SP. *Entomol.* IV. xlvi. 274 Scutate (*Scutata*). Covered with large flat scales. **1858** W. CLARK *Van der Hoeven's Zool.* II. 265 *Hydrophes.* Head scutate, small.

2. *Bot.* Buckler-shaped.

1836 LOUDON *Encycl. Plants* 925 Root scutate. *Ibid.* Gloss., *Scutate*, formed like an ancient round buckler. **1837** P. KEITH *Bot. Lex.* s.v. *Algæ*, Where a root exists it is merely a fibrous or scutate base.

Hence **scu'tated** *a.* = SCUTATE *a.* 1.

1802 SHAW *Gen. Zool.* III. 221 Scutated lizard, *Lacerta Scutata. Ibid.* 518 Scutated Snake, *Coluber Scutatus.* **1839** *Penny Cycl.* XIII. 445 Head scutated.

scutation (skju:'teɪʃən). *Zool.* [f. SCUTATE *a.*: see -ATION.] Arrangement of scuta.

1852 *Zoologist* X. 3402 The integument of the naked part of the foot [presenting] its well-marked scutation. **1881** OWEN in *Nature* XXIII. 402 The horny scutation of lizards.

scutch (skʌtʃ), *sb.*[1] Now chiefly *dial.* [f. SCUTCH *v.*] A stroke with a stick or whip.

1611 COTGR., *Fessée*, a scutch on the breech, a lash on the buttocks. *Ibid.*, *Singlet*, a scutch,..or ierke with a rod, &c.

scutch (skʌtʃ), *sb.*[2] Also 8 **skutch,** 9 **scotch.** [a. OF. *escouche* (15th c.; mod.F. *écouche*).

The remarkable correspondence of the OF. word with the mod.Norw. synonym *skoka* suggests that it may be of Scandinavian origin. By Hatz.-Darm., however, it is regarded as f. **escoucher, escousser* to scutch, thrash, and this is identified with *escousser* to shake:—pop.L. **excussāre* (cf. EXCUSS *v.*).]

1. = SCUTCHER.

c **1791** *Encycl. Brit.* (ed. 3) VII. 291/2 Common flax; which from the skutch proceeds to the heckle. **1836** L. HEBERT *Engin. & Mech. Encycl.* I. 510 Arms to which are attached scotches revolving within a cylindrical casing. **1845** *Encycl. Metropol.* VIII. 702/2 An instrument somewhat resembling a curry-comb, and called a hand-scutch. **1891** *Century Dict.* s.v. *Scutcher*, The fluted rollers *b, b'*, which seize it and present it to the scutches or beaters, *c.*

2. 'One of the pieces of wood which in a thrashing mill beats out the grain' (Jam.). Cf. SCUTCHER.

1805 R. SOMERVILLE *Agric. E. Lothian* 77 The purpose of separating the grain from the straw might be accomplished ..by skutches acting upon the sheaves by their velocity, and beating out the grain.

scutch (skʌtʃ), *sb.*[3] *dial.* [Var. of SQUITCH, altered form of QUITCH *sb.*[1]]

1. = QUITCH *sb.*[1] Chiefly in Comb. ***scutch-grass*** in the same sense.

1685 *Phil. Trans.* XV. 957 It has turned the Bog into a green sod, with a very fine scutch grass on it. **1763** *Museum Rust.* I. lxx. 307 It is only fit for wet, or bog lands, growing from every joint, like the scutch, or couch grass. **1785** TRUSLER *Mod. Times* II. 105 What he could not lay down properly, he suffered nature to lay down for him with scutch grass, thistles and docks. *a* **1889** 'CUTHBERT BEDE' (Webster 1897), The smoke of the burning scutch.

2. a. *dial.* Rubbish (see *Eng. Dial. Dict.*). **b.** *Glue-making.* (See quot.)

1883 R. HALDANE *Workshop Rec.* Ser. II. 301/2 The matter left in the pans after boiling is termed 'scutch'.

scutch (skʌtʃ), *v.*[1] Now chiefly *dial.* Also 8–9 **skutch.** [Of somewhat uncertain etymology.

Commonly assumed to be a transferred use of SCUTCH *v.*[2], which, though later in our quots., must from its etymology have existed at least from the 15th c. This is not impossible (cf. *thrash*), but more probably the present verb is an independent onomatopœic formation: cf. *scotch* vb.]

trans. To strike with a stick or whip, to slash, switch. Also *intr.* to strike *at.*

1611 COTGR., *Singler,*..also, to switch,.. scutch, or scourge with a rod. **1643** Z. BOYD *Battle Newburn* (1853) 12 The Scots them scutcht both upon back and shoulder. **1652** BROME *City Wit* I. i. A6, What Scold hath scutch'd thy skonce? **1746** J. COLLIER (Tim Bobbin) *Misc. Wks.* (1775) 57 Shou'd they naw be..scutcht with' seme Rod wi'ther Clarks? **1829** J. HUNTER *Hallamsh. Gloss., Scutch,* to strike with a thin switch, which is often done to snakes by cruel boys. **1867** BRIERLEY *Daisy Nook Sk.* 53 He skutcht at him wi' his whip. **1886** C. SCOTT *Sheep-farming* 204 The master should always give his orders in an even, calm voice, devoid of passion, so that the dog cannot tell from his tone whether he is to be scutched or not.

scutch (skʌtʃ), *v.*[2] Also **skutch.** [a. OF. **escoucher, escousser*: see SCUTCH *sb.*[2]]

1. *trans.* To dress (fibrous material, flax, hemp, cotton, silk, wool) by beating.

1733 [see SCUTCHING *vbl. sb.*[2]]. **1763** in *Scottish Forfeited Estates Papers* (S.H.S. 1909) 225 A person skilled in raising, breaking, scutching and heckling of lint. **1812** SCOTT *Fam. Lett.* 23 Jan. (1894) I. 242 A heckle is the many-toothed implement with which hemp is broken and scutched. **1844** G. DODD *Textile Manuf.* v. 159 When the heads of flax are ready for working, they are 'scutched' out at the ends. **1880** O. CRAWFURD *Portugal, Old & New* 194 Some portion of the flax..is broken and skutched by hand. **1884** *Spectator* 26 Apr. 548 Wool must be scutched to be worn.

absol. **1808** *Ann. Reg., Charac.* 101 To try whether any improvement can be made in the mode of skutching. **1839** URE *Dict. Arts* 345 Indeed, each machine not only beats, scutches, but blows.

2. *Tanning.* (See quot.)

1688 HOLME *Armoury* III. 86/1 Scutching the Bark is, cleansing it from Moss, and the rough crusty outward Bark.

3. To strike the grain from (ears of corn). Cf. SCUTCHER[2] 2.

1844 H. STEPHENS *Bk. Farm* II. 271 The feeder-in supplies the mill in small quantities with the stick, so as the roughs may have time to be thoroughly scutched by the drum.

4. *Comb.*: **scutch-mill, -rake** (see quot. 1858).

1852 *Act 15 & 16 Vict.* c. 34 For the Erection of Buildings suitable to Scutch Mills for Flax in Ireland. **1858** SIMMONDS *Dict. Trade, Scutch-mill,* a mill for preparing flax. *Scutch-rake,* a flax dresser's implement.

Hence **scutched** *ppl. a.*

1853 URE *Dict. Arts* (ed. 4) I. 785 A holder, containing a strick of scutched flax.

†**scutcha'nele** *v. Obs.* [f. *scutchanele,* obs. f. COCHINEAL.] *trans.* To colour with cochineal.

1596 NASHE *Saffron Walden* I 1 b, To haue scutchaneled and painted his pickerdeuant.

scutchenel, obs. form of COCHINEAL.

scutcheon ('skʌtʃən), *sb.*[1] Forms: 4 **scochoun,** 4–5 **scochon,** 5 **skochonne,** 6 **scocheon(e, scotchion, -yon, skotcheon,** 7 **scotcheon;** 4–5 **skochen,** 5–6 **scochen,** 6 **schochen;** 5 **scoochion,** 6 **schoocheon, skoochion;** 5 **scotchyne,** 5–6 **skochyn;** (5 **scogion, scogen, skecon, squechon**); 5 **scouchon,** 6 **scoucheon, scou(t)chin, skouchin;** 5 **scuchon,** 6 **schuchion, scuchen, -in, -ion, skuchin, skuttchin,** 6–7 **scutchin, -ion,** 7 **schucheon, scutshion, skutchin,** 6– **scutcheon.** Sometimes written *'scutcheon.* [Aphetic variant of ESCUTCHEON.]

1. = ESCUTCH-EON 1. Formerly often †*scutcheon of arms.*

a **1366** CHAUCER *Rom. Rose* 893 With losenges and scochouns. *c* **1380** WYCLIF *Wks.* (1880) 99 For as scottis token þe skochen of armes of seynt george & here-bi traieden englischemen, so [etc.]. **1395** *E.E. Wills* (1882) 4 Tapites of sute,..ypouthered with chapes and scochons, in the corners, of myn Auncestres armes. **1459** *Paston Lett.* I. 477 Item, j. ball of coper gilt, embrauded rechely with j. skogen hongyng therbi. *c* **1470** *Rauf Coilȝear* 684 Greit Squechonis on hicht, Anamalit and weill dicht. **1486** *Bk. St. Albans, Her.* b iv, Fesy target is whan a scogion or an engislet is made in the myddull of the cootarmure. *Ibid.* e iii b, It shall be shewyt in thys scoochon next folowyng. **1529** MORE *Suppl. Soulys* Wks. 335/2 Setting vp oure skouchins & cote armours on yᵉ wall. **1527** in Gage *Hengrave* (1822) 47 For xiij skuttchens with armes. **1540** WRIOTHESLEY *Chron.* (Camden) I. 112 Which were all rychlie hanged with schuchions and targattes and banners. **1548** ELYOT *Dict., Scutulum,* a littell shielde or scouchin. **1555** EDEN *Decades* (Arb.) 342 The scuchen of armes gyuen to Colon by Don Ferdinando. **1578** LYTE *Dodoens* IV. xxviii. 485 The leaues be smal and tender (triangled like a scuchion). **1588** SHAKS. *L.L.L.* v. ii. 567 My Scutcheon plaine declares that I am Alisander. **1601** LYLY *Love's Metam.* I. i, I will hang my Skutchin on this tree in honour of Ceres. **1602** DEKKER *Satirom.* B 1 b, They [*sc.* flowers] sticke like the scutchions of madame chastity, on the sable ground. **1611** CORYAT *Crudities* 318 Betwixt two golden scutchins ouer the dore. **1646** SIR T. BROWNE *Pseud. Ep.* v. i. 233 In the Crest and Scucheon of many Noble families. **1682** BUNYAN *Holy War* (1905) 218 His Scutcheon was the three burning Thunder-Bolts. ?**1718** POPE *Let. to Dk. Buckhm.* Lett. (1737) 199 A vast arch'd window beautifully darken'd with divers scutcheons of painted glass. **1808** SCOTT *Marm.* I. xii, And on the gibbet-tree reversed His foeman's scutcheon tied. **1820** KEATS *St. Agnes* xxiv, A shielded scutcheon blush'd with blood of queens and kings.

b. *fig.* = ESCUTCHEON 1 b.

c **1440** *Gesta Rom.* liv. 236 (Harl. MS.) God haviþe iij. scochens, scil. [the] powere, the whiche is the scochon of the fadir; he hathe wisdome, þe which is þe scochon of the sone [etc.]. **1683** *Apol. Prot. France* iv. 18 Had not Heresie,.. been so great a blot in her Scotcheon. **1780** BURKE *Sp. Œcon. Reform.* Wks. III. 246 Carefully avoiding a sort of blot in their scutcheon, which they think would degrade them for ever. **1838** *J. M. Wilson's Tales Borders* IV. 151 You have blotted..the proudest scutcheon of England. **1843** LYTTON *Last Bar.* IV. v, A scutcheon as stainless as the best.

c. *transf.*

a **1678** MARVELL *Clorinda & D.* 3, I have a grassy Scutcheon spy'd, Where Flora blazons all her Pride.

†**d.** Used for: A shield. *Obs.*

1600 HOLLAND *Livy* v. 215 Here are the fires of Vesta, here be the scutcheons come downe from heaven.

2. A hatchment. = ESCUTCHEON 2.

1711 in Macgill *Old Ross-sh.* (1909) 152 Ane accompt off the Laird of Balnagowns ffuneral charges... Wm. Kerr painter in Nairne for Scutchins. **1739** H. WALPOLE *Let. to R. West* 21 Apr. *Priv. Corr.* (1820) I. 19 The burial..was a most vile thing... No plumes,..led horses, scutcheons, or open chariots. **1781** COWPER *Hope* 265 The busy heralds hang the sable scene With mournful 'scutcheons. **1814** BYRON *Lara* I. iii, A hundred scutcheons deck with gloomy grace The Laras' last and longest dwelling place. **1814** SCOTT *Ld. of Isles* II. xxviii, It..Rends Honour's scutcheon from thy hearse. **1850** THACKERAY *Kickleburys* (1851) 7 When Sir Thomas Kicklebury died..who does not remember the scutcheon with the coronet..that flamed over No. 36?

†**3.** A badge. *Obs.*

1442 *Coventry Leet Bk.* 200 Sub Condicione quod habeant vnum Trumpet, prout infra fit mencio etc. & les skecons sub securitate inventa habebunt etc. **1530** PALSGR. 267/2 Scochen a badge, *escuisson.* **1594** G. ELLIS in *Buccleuch MSS.* (Hist. MSS. Comm.) 25 He is upon a journey, messenger like, with a skuchin on his breast. **1598** GRENEWEY *Tacitus, Germanie* vi. 270 For a skutchion of their superstition, they carry the pictures of wilde Boares.

4. Anything shaped like an escutcheon. †**a.** A brooch. *Obs.*

1483 *Cath. Angl.* 326/1 A scuchon, *monile,* & cetera, vbi a bruche.

†**b.** *Arch.* (See quots.)

1565 COOPER *Thesaurus, Tholos,*..a scochen in the middes of a timber vaute where the postes reste. **1656** BLOUNT *Glossogr., Thole,* a knot in the midst of a timber vault, where the ends of the posts meet, called a Scutchin.

c. *Horticulture.* A piece of bark cut more or less in the form of a shield, and bearing a bud, for grafting between the wood and the bark of a stock. = ESCUTCHEON 3 d and SHIELD *sb.*

[After F. *en écusson* (16th c. in Littré).]

1572 MASCALL *Plant. & Graff.* v. 34 The fourth maner to graffe..is to graffe in the scutchion. *Ibid.* 35 With the pointe of a sharpe knyfe softly raise the sayd shield or scutchion, round about, with the oylet in the middest. **1658** EVELYN *Fr. Gard.* (1675) 63 After your scutcheon has put forth its first sap, you may prune it at top. **1706** LONDON & WISE *Retir'd Gard.* I. 162 The Figure of a Scutcheon ought to resemble that of a V, when 'tis taken off from the Stock with its young Shoot. **1759** MILLS tr. *Duhamel's Husb.* I. ii. (1762) 4 The tree might be grafted by a scutcheon.

†**d.** The plate of a gun-lock. *Obs.*

1631 in Rymer *Fœdera* XIX. 315 For a whole Worke, consisting of the Pan, the cover of the Pan, the Scutchion, and the screw Pynn. **1783** JUSTAMOND tr. *Raynal's Hist. Indies* IV. 82 Placentia..at present..supplies fourteen thousand four hundred [fire-locks], with the scutcheons of their locks.

e. A key-hole plate, a name-plate, etc. = ESCUTCHEON 3 c.

1706 PHILLIPS (ed. Kersey), *Scutchion,*..a small Plate of Iron or Brass to be set before a Lock. **1794** W. FELTON *Carriages* (1801) I. 162 The Keyhole is covered with a double Scutcheon. **1842** FRANCIS *Dict. Arts,* etc., *Scutcheon,* ..an ornament put round a key hole, door handle, knob of a door, or other similar object. **1851** TURNER *Dom. Archit.* II. i. 10 The scutcheons of locks are frequently ornamented. **1875** KNIGHT *Dict. Mech.* 2078 *Scutcheon,* a name plate on a coffin, pocket-knife, or other object.

f. *Zool.* A large scale or bony plate, a scute.

1846 *Amer. Jrnl. Sci.* Ser. II. I. 368 The head and anterior part of the body [of this fossil fish] are covered with large osseous plates of scutcheons. *Ibid.* 369 The central lateral scutcheon plates. **1851** MANTELL *Petrifactions* v. §ii. 448 The teeth, spines, or fin-rays, tubercles and scutcheons, vertebrae,..are the only parts preserved in a fossil state.

5. *attrib.* and *Comb.*, as (sense 1) ***scutcheon fashion***; (sense 4 b) ***scutcheon-graft*** sb. and vb., ***-grafting***; (sense 4 d) ***scutcheon lock***; also ***scutcheon-like*** adj., ***scutcheonwise*** adv.

1614 SELDEN *Titles Hon.* 353 The Baron is made by giuing him a square Ensigne, or Banner, but the Banneret, by an Ensigne in *Scutchion fashion. **1706** LONDON & WISE *Retir'd Gard.* I. 169 Make use of the Slit or the *Scutcheon-Graft. **1727** *Bradley's Fam. Dict.* s.v. *Grafting,* Let them be *Scutcheon-grafted. **1706** LONDON & WISE *Retir'd Gard.* I. 159 In *Scutcheon-grafting we cut the Body of the Stock to Four Inches. **1600** SURFLET *Country Farm* III. xvii. 454 The *scutcheon like graft. **1851** MANTELL *Petrifactions* v. §2. 439 [*Blochius longirostris*] has..scutcheon-like scales. **1850** CHUBB *Locks & Keys* 9 There is one adaptation of the principle of this lock, designed as a '*scutcheon lock'. **1693** EVELYN *De La Quint. Compl. Gard.* I. 10 The most common and best Method of Graffing, is either cleftwise, or *Scutcheonwise.

'scutcheon, *sb.*[2] *Arch.* (*Hist.*) Modernized form of ME. *scochon, scouchon,* etc.: see SCUNCHEON.

1850 *Parker's Gloss. Archit.* (ed. 5) I. 417 *Scutcheon,*..an old name for the angles of buildings or parts of buildings, such as window-jambs, &c., but apparently for those only which are more obtuse than right angles.

†**'scutcheon,** *v. Obs.* (? *nonce-wd.*) [f. SCUTCHEON *sb.*[1]] *trans.* To trick *out* on a scutcheon.

1596 NASHE *Saffron Walden* Q 4 b, To approue his Heraldrie [he] scutchend out the honorable Armes of the smoakie Societie.

scutcheoned ('skʌtʃənd), *ppl. a.* [f. SCUTCHEON *sb.*[1] + -ED[1].]

1. Furnished or decorated with scutcheons.

1813 SCOTT *Trierm.* III. xv, The scutcheon'd emblems which it bore, Had suffer'd no decay. **1863** WHITTIER *Countess* 148 Far off her lover sleeps as still Within his scutcheoned tomb.

2. *Zool.* Bearing scutcheons or scutes.

1846 *Amer. Jrnl. Sci.* Ser. II. I. 371 This is so far as we know, not only the first instance of finding scutcheoned fishes in this country, but also [etc.].

scutcheonless ('skʌtʃənlɪs), *a.* [f. SCUTCHEON *sb.*[1] + -LESS.] Having no scutcheon.

1692 E. WALKER tr. *Epictetus' Enchir.* xxx, No honour.. shall I have, But 'Scoch'onless descend into the Grave.

†**'scutcheonry.** *Obs. rare.* [f. SCUTCHEON *sb.*[1] + -RY.] Emblazoned figures collectively.

1827 POLLOCK *Course T.* x. (1860) 280 Reading the fiery scutcheonry that blazed On high, upon the great celestial bow.

†**'scutcher**[1]. *Obs.* [f. SCUTCH *v.*[1] + -ER[1].] A stick, a whip.

1611 COTGR., *Verge,*..a whisker, switch, or scutcher, to ride with. *Ibid.* s.v. *Singlant.*

'scutcher[2] ('skʌtʃə(r)). Also **scotcher, skutcher.** [f. SCUTCH *v.*[2] Cf. OF. **escouchoir,* in 15th c. *escoussour* flail.]

1. An implement or apparatus for scutching.

Variously applied to: A hand tool for scutching flax or hemp, a scutch-blade; one of a number of projections on a revolving drum or axle in a scutching-machine; a machine (of various kinds) for scutching flax, silk, cotton, etc.

1766 *Compl. Farmer* s.v. *Hemp* A 3/1 The workman.. strikes it with the sharpened edge of a long, flat, and strait piece of wood, commonly called a swingle hand, or scutcher. **1771** *Encycl. Brit.* II. 604/2 A lint-mill with horizontal scutchers upon a perpendicular axle. **1825** J. NICHOLSON *Oper. Mech.* 379 A scotcher, revolving rapidly upon its axis, strikes the cotton with its two edges. **1856** *Farmer's Mag.* Nov. 379 It is grasped at the proper moment by the holding apparatus of the second pair of the scutchers. **1875** KNIGHT *Dict. Mech.* 2079 *Scutcher*..a beating-engine, in which floss and refuse silk..is brought to a downy condition.

attrib. **1839** URE *Dict. Arts* 347, GH and MN are the two scutcher frames.

2. The part of a thrashing machine which strikes off the grain.

1797 *Encycl. Brit.* (ed. 3) XVIII. 507/1 While the scutchers strike off the grain from the straw as it passes through. **1844** H. STEPHENS *Bk. Farm* II. 285 The essential parts of the thrashing apparatus, the feeding-rollers and the beater or scutcher. **1861** SMILES *Engineers* II. 110 Mr. Oxley is said to have afterwards tried the plan of stripping the corn from the straw by means of a scutcher.

3. A person employed in scutching.

1847 NICHOLLS in *Jrnl. R. Agric. Soc.* VIII. II. 457 Having a slit..into which the scutcher slips the flax. **1891** S. WEBB in *Econ. Jrnl.* I. 641 Average Earnings per Week in 1885 of Scutchers.

†**'scutchery.** *Obs.* Knavery. (Chiefly in Nashe.)

1594 NASHE *Unfort. Trav.* C, Yet left I not here, but committed a little more scutcherie. **1594** —— *Terrors of Nt.* E iij b, Now that he [Senior Sathan] is thoroughly steeled in his scutcherie he playes aboue boord boldly. **1595** [J. DANDO & H. RUNT] *Maroccus Ext.* (Percy Soc.) 15 His private scutcherie wounds not the commonwealth farther than that his whoore shall haue a house rent free.

†**'scutchin.** *Obs.* ? Corruption of CUTCH[1], catechu.

1818 *Art Bookbinding* 78 Add half a pint of the spirits of wine, and one pennyworth of yellow scutchin.

scutchin, -el, obs. ff. SCUTCHEON, COCHINEAL.

'scutching, *vbl. sb.*[1] [f. SCUTCH *v.*[1] + -ING[1].] The action of SCUTCH *v.*[1]

1611 COTGR., *Singlement,*..a whisking, lashing, ierking, scutching. **1641** R. BAILLIE *Lett. & Jrnls.* (Bannatyne Cl.) I. 326 Discourse falling in concerning the Deputie's scutching of a gentleman with a rod. **1641** HINDE *J. Bruen* xi. 36 Not to be fierce and furious..in immoderate..scutching and lashing. **1962** H. G. GREEN *Time to pass Over* xii. 142 I'll damn well have to give you a scutching for this.

scutching ('skʌtʃɪŋ), *vbl. sb.*[2] [f. SCUTCH *v.*[2]]

1. The action of SCUTCH *v.*[2]; the process of beating flax stalks to get rid of the straw and prepare the fibre for hackling; the similar operation applied to hemp, cotton, silk, etc.

1733 P. LINDSAY *Interest Scot.* 159 There must be at every Mill, besides the Boys that attend the breaking and scutching of the Mill, at least, two or three skilful Flax-dressers. **1766** *Compl. Farmer* s.v. *Hemp* A 3/1 After the hemp has been broken, it undergoes a second operation, which is commonly termed swingling or scutching. **1836** L. HEBERT *Engin. & Mech. Encycl.* I. 539 The hand methods of breaking and scotching of flax. **1844** G. DODD *Textile Manuf.* i. 26 This process called 'scutching', or 'batting' or 'blowing'—is effected in various ways:—The cotton is laid [etc.]. **1851-4** *Tomlinson's Cycl. Usef. Arts* (1867) I. s.v. *Hemp*, The after processes of scutching and heckling [*sc.* hemp and flax] are likewise similar. **1875** [see BLOWING *vbl. sb.*[1] 1 b]. **1902** [see DROPPING *vbl. sb.* 5 b]. **1931** S. A. G. CALDWELL *Preparation & Spinning of Flax Fibre* I. i. 15 The old method of scutching by hand has now given place to mill scutching. **1937** W. E. MORTON *Introd. Study of Spinning* I. iv. 84 It is the essential purpose of scutching to remove only the boon and the bark. **1973** *Times* 7 May 11/5 One particularly alarming process, scutching, was always done by hand, and I am surprised that a whole generation of Ulstermen have any fingers uncrushed, for to scutch you feed a hank of flax under the karate-chop action of a wooden propeller!

concr. **1887** JAMIESON Suppl., *Scutchings, Scutchins*, refuse lint or flax that remains after the process of scutching; waste tow.

2. *attrib.*, as ***scutching apparatus, arm, barrel, blade, board, machine, mill, season***; **scutching knife**, a tanner's tool (cf. SCUTCH *v.*[2] 2); **scutching shaft**, in a cotton mill, the revolving shaft which carries the first beater; **scutching-stock**, the support on which the flax or hemp is placed in a scutching machine; **scutching-sword**, a scutch-blade; **scutching tow**, the refuse of flax after scutching.

1812 SIR J. SINCLAIR *Syst. Husb. Scot.* II. App. 48 The wheels and *scutching apparatus. **1839** URE *Dict. Arts* 346 This last fan is suppressed in many blowing machines, as the *scutching arms supply a sufficient stream of air. *Ibid.*, In the figure we see the feed-cloth, the *scutching barrel, the squirrel suction [etc.]. **1973** L. RUSSELL *Everyday Life Colonial Canada* ix. 111 A *scutching blade, a wooden tool shaped like a butcher's knife. **1854** DELAMER *Flax & Hemp* 66 The *écouche-pied*, or *scutching-board. **1688** HOLME *Armoury* III. 350/2 Instruments belonging to the Tanners Trade; the first is a *scutching Knife. **1969** E. H. PINTO *Treen* 301 Old Irish, Scottish and English scutching knives are usually plain and straight bladed. **1837** *Penny Cycl.* VIII. 95/1 The *scutching machine is used to open the locks of cotton and separate its fibres. **1839** Scutching machine [see *blowing-machine* s.v. BLOWING *vbl. sb.*[1] 5]. **1901** T. THORNLEY *Cotton Spinning* I. iii. 75 The rollers..are seldom used on any scutching machines. **1847** *Jrnl. R. Agric. Soc.* VIII. 457 The growers, after having steeped their flax at home, send it to some *scutching-mill to be dressed. **1851-4** *Tomlinson's Dict. Usef. Arts* (1867) I. 452/2 The *scutching-shaft, makes 2,000 turns per minute. **1771** *Encycl. Brit.* II. 604/2 This sloping stroke is got by raising the *scutching-stock some inches higher than the centre of the axle. **1875** KNIGHT *Dict. Mech.* 2079 Scutching is performed with the *scutching sword *a* held in the right hand. **1853** URE *Dict. Arts* (ed. 4) I. 789 The yield was 187 lbs. of flax; and of *scutching tow, 12 lbs. 6½ oz. fine.

scutchion, obs. form of SCUTCHEON.

scute (skjuːt), *sb.*[1] Also 7 **sceute, skute.** [ad. L. *scūtum* shield, whence OF. *escut, escu* (F. *écu*).]

1. An English name for the French coin called *écu*: see ÉCU, ESCU. *Obs.* exc. *Hist.*

c **1400** *Three Kings of Cologne* 100 As men clepe in þis contrey gold of biȝende þe see Scutys, Motouns or floryns. **1420** *Treaty of Troyes* in Rymer *Fœdera* (1709) IX. 916 The forsayd Katerine shall take and haue Douer in our Roiaulme of Englond..to the Somme of forty Mill. Scutes be Yere; of the whiche Tweyne algates shall be worth a Noble Englyssh. *c* **1483** CAXTON *Dialogues* 17 Scutes of the kyng [F. *escutz du roy*], Ryallis nobles of englond. *c* **1522** SKELTON *Why Nat to Courte* 167 With scutes and crownes of gold I drede we are bought and solde. **1549-50** EDW. VI *Jrnl.* Rem. (Roxb.) 251 The French to pay 200,000 scutes within three days after the delivery of Boullein. **1606** G. W[OODCOCKE] *Lives Emperors* in *Hist. Justine* L l 4, The King of England demanded of the Emperor interest for fiue hundred thousand skutes which he had borrowed. **1611** SPEED *Hist. Gr. Brit.* IX. xv. (1623) 812 Forty thousand sceutes, that is, two to a Noble. **1671** H. M. tr. *Erasm. Colloq.* 80 Peter bought a maids kiss for a scute [orig. *scutato emit*].

¶ **b.** Used as a (? jocular) name for an English coin; ? a crown. *Obs.*

1472 SIR J. PASTON *Let.* 8 Jan. in *P. Lett.* III. 33, I beseche yow to remember my brother to doo hys deveyr thatt I maye have agayn my stuffe,..how so evyr he doo, thoghe I scholde gyffe xx[ti] Scutes by hys advyse to my Lady Brandon. **1472** —— *Let.* 22 Nov. *Ibid.* 64, I thynke verrely to come to gyff him xx scutys.

c. Used vaguely for a coin of small value.

1594 NASHE *Christ's T.* To Rdr. *ij b, Therein I imitate rich men who hauing gathered store of white single money together, conuert a number of those small little scutes into great peeces of gold, such as double Pistols and Portugues. **1596** —— *Saffron-Walden* Q 1, The diuell a scute had he to pay the reckoning. **1605** CHAPMAN *All Fools* v. i. H 4 b, And from a paire of Gloues of halfe a crowne To twenty crownes: will to a very scute Smell out the price. **1834** SIR H. TAYLOR *Artevelde* I. I. iii, Five hundred marks—I'll bate you not a scute.

† **2.** An escutcheon. *Obs.*

1575 GASCOIGNE *Posies, Flowers* 51 He..bare the selfe same armes that I dyd quarter in my scute.

3. A disk, small piece. Now only *dial.*, a small patch of leather on the sole of a boot or shoe; also, a metal heel- or toe-plate. (See *Eng. Dial. Dict.*)

In the first quot. prob. merely *transf.* from sense 1.

1635 T. HEYWOOD *Hierarchie* IX. 574 Round scutes of horne, and pieces of old leather. **1775** ASH, *Scute*,..a small piece of leather set on a shoe.

4. *Zool.* A large scale or bony plate, forming part of the integument of certain animals, as the tortoise, armadillo, echinoderms, various fishes, etc.

1848 OWEN in *Times* 14 Nov. 8/6 Without scales, scutes, or other conspicuous modifications of hard and naked cuticle. **1870** GILLMORE tr. *Figuier's Reptiles & Birds* i. 10 The stiff epidermal scutes crossing the under surface of the body. **1873** MIVART *Elem. Anat.* 278 The 'scales' of Fishes should rather be termed 'scutes'. **1887** *Encycl. Brit.* XXII. 107/2 A scute is a hardening of the outermost portion of the dermis, with an investment from the deepest layer of the epidermis.

scute (skjuːt), *sb.*[2] *Zool.* [f. SCUTE(LLAR *a.*]

The name of any of a group of closely linked X-linked genes in *Drosophila* which act to reduce the number of scutellar bristles; also, a phenotype produced by these genes.

1923 BRIDGES & MORGAN *Third-Chromosome Group Mutant Characters Drosophila Melanogaster* 160 Scute arose in the line selected for increased number of scutellar bristles. **1923** *Anat. Rec.* XXVI. 397 In three of these species the closely linked [*sc.* to yellow] character 'scute' or 'scutellar' is also known. **1940** *Genetics* XXV. 566 The great phenotypic similarity of the three scutes in question is an expression of the extreme similarity of their gene arrangements. **1974** GOODENOUGH & LEVINE *Genetics* xi. 500 The *Basc* chromosome..carries the *Bar* eye gene *B*.., the *apricot* eye color gene *apr*, and a double inversion involving the *scute* (*sc*) region of the chromosome.

scute, obs. form of SCOUT *sb.*[3]

scutel (ˈskjuːtəl). [ad. mod.L. *scūtellum.*]

1. *Ent.* = SCUTELLUM 2.

1806 TURTON tr. *Linn. Syst. Nat.* VII. Expl. Terms, *Scutel*, the portion of the back of an insect which is situated between the thorax and abdomen. **1862** T. W. HARRIS *Insects Injur. Veget.* (ed. 3) 23 The wings of beetles are covered and concealed by a pair of horny cases or shells, meeting in a straight line on the top of the back, and usually having a little triangular or semicircular piece, called the scutel, wedged between their bases. **1875** *De Saussure's Synopsis Amer. Wasps* 160 Scutel flat. Post-scutel arcuate on its posterior border.

2. *Bot.* = SCUTELLUM 1.

1819 *Pantologia.* **1900** B. D. JACKSON *Gloss. Bot. Terms.*

scutel(l, obs. forms of SCUTTLE *sb.*[1]

‖ **scutella** (skjuːˈtɛlə). Pl. **scutellæ.** [mod.L.; originally a use of L. *scutella* platter, but mistaken for a dim. of L. *scūtum* shield, and hence altered in application.] = SCUTELLUM in various senses.

1771 *Encycl. Brit.* II. 224/2 They [*sc.* snakes] have a number of scuta, or hard crusts, on the belly; and scutellæ, or scales, on the tail. **1837** P. KEITH *Bot. Lex.* s.v. *Scutella*, The little shields or cups found on the thalli of the Lichens, are by botanists designated scutellæ. **1859** DARWIN *Orig. Spec.* i. (1878) 16 The number of scutellæ on the toes.

scutellar (skjuːˈtɛlə(r)), *a.* *Ent.* [f. SCUTELLUM + -AR.] Of or pertaining to a scutellum.

1826 KIRBY & SP. *Entomol.* III. xxxv. 561 Another nervure..appears to diverge upwards from the scutellar angle to the Intermediate Area.

scutellarin (skjuːˈtɛlərɪn). *Chem.* [f. mod.L. *Scutellaria* (f. *scutella* dish) + -IN.] (See quot.)

1883 MARTINDALE *Extra Pharmacop.* 240 Scutellarin... The dried extract of *Scutellaria lateriflora*—mad-dog skull-cap..given as a nervous stimulant.

scutellate (ˈskjuːtɪleɪt), *a.* [ad. mod.L. *scutellātus*, orig. f. L. *scutella* platter, but apprehended as f. SCUTELLUM: see -ATE. Cf. SCUTULATE.]

1. *Bot.* (See quots.)

1785 MARTYN *Rousseau's Bot.* xxxii. 497 The sections of the genus [Lichens] are,..2. Scutellate, or such as have little shields, or roundish receptacles with a rim. **1821** W. P. C. BARTON *Flora N. Amer.* I. 79 Calix scutellate as in the whole genus. **1857** A. GRAY *First Less. Bot.* (1866) Gloss., *Scutellate*..saucer-shaped or platter-shaped. **1887** W. PHILLIPS *Brit. Discomyc.* 284 Cup superficial,..sessile, scutellate. *Ibid.* Gloss., *Scutellate*, formed like a dish or saucer, orbicular and nearly flat.

2. *Zool.* **a.** *Ent.* Of an insect: 'Having a visible scutellum'.

1826 KIRBY & SP. *Entomol.* IV. 332.

b. *Ornith.* Of the feet of birds: Covered with scutella.

1872 COUES *Key N. Amer. Birds* 46 A tarsus so furnished is said to be scutellate, before or behind, or both. **1893** NEWTON *Dict. Birds* 511 The *podotheca* or covering of the tarsus, which is scutellate behind as well as in front.

c. Of certain structures: Shaped like a platter.

1849-52 *Todd's Cycl. Anat.* IV. 4/2 Amœba enclosed in an urceolate or scutellate shell. **1856-8** W. CLARK *Van der Hoeven's Zool.* I. 48 *Arcella*, Ehrenb. Lorica scutellate, globose, or hemispherical.

scutellated (ˈskjuːtɪleɪtɪd), *ppl. a.* [f. prec. + -ED[1].] = prec.

1729 WOODWARD *Catal. For. Fossils* II. 28 It seems to be part of the scutellated Bone of a Sturgeon. **1872** COUES *Key N. Amer. Birds* 11 Thrushes with booted tarsi, and thrushes with scutellated tarsi.

scutellation (skjuːtɪˈleɪʃən). *Zool.* [f. SCUTELLATE *a.*: see -ATION.] **a.** Scutellate formation (of the feet of birds). **b.** Arrangement of scutes or scales (in lizards, serpents, etc.).

1872 COUES *Key N. Amer. Birds* 47 The Crus, when bare below, may present scutellation. **1882** GÜNTHER in *Encycl. Brit.* XIV. 733/2 Scutellation similar to that of the skinks. **1887** —— *Ibid.* XXII. 195/2 The Venomous Colubrine snakes which combine with the possession of a perfect poison apparatus the scutellation and general appearance of the typical non-poisonous snakes.

scutelliform (skjuːˈtɛlɪfɔːm), *a.* [f. SCUTELLUM + -FORM.] Having the form of a scutellum.

1826 KIRBY & SP. *Entomol.* III. xxxv. 538 In many of the species here quoted the prothorax is producted posteriorly into a long scutelliform horizontal horn. **1830** LINDLEY *Nat. Syst. Bot.* 212 The cuculli were also observable, but still very small and green, nearly scutelliform. **1882** *Encycl. Brit.* XIV. 554/1 The disciform apothecia..present various shapes.., (*a*) peltate..(*b*) *lecanorine*, or scutelliform.

scutellum (skjuːˈtɛləm). Pl. **scutella.** [mod.L.; app. in origin a supposed correction of *scutella* (see SCUTELLA), due to the notion that this was a dim. of L. *scūtum* shield; the applications are based on the rendering 'little shield'.

The correct L. dim. of *scūtum* was *scūtulum*, which some mod. scientific writers have adopted as a basis for derivatives, using, e.g., SCUTULATE instead of *scutellate*.]

1. *Bot.* **a.** (See quots.)

1760 LEE *Introd. Bot.* III. xxii. (1765) 227 *Scutellum*, a small Buckler, which is a concave orbiculate Fructification, the Margin of which is elevated on every Side. **1793** MARTYN *Lang. Bot.*, *Scutellum*... An orbicular concave fructification (in some Lichens). **1866** in *Treas. Bot.*

b. An anterior cotyledon in certain grasses.

1832 LINDLEY *Introd. Bot.* I. ii. 191 In wheat there is a second small cotyledon on the outside of the embryo, inserted a little lower down than the scutelliform cotyledon. This last is called scutellum by Gærtner, who considered it of the nature of vitellus. **1880** BESSEY *Bot.* 451 The first leaf of the young plant (the cotyledon or scutellum). **1882** VINES tr. *Sach's Bot.* 620 In Grasses, however, the whole of the plumule projects from the seed, the scutellum only remaining behind in it.

c. (See quot.)

1900 B. D. JACKSON *Gloss. Bot. Terms*, *Scutellum*..the conical cap of the endosperm in Cycadeae.

2. *Zool.* **a.** *Ent.* The third of the four sclerites composing any segment of the tergum of an insect; usually, the mesoscutellum.

1819 SAMOUELLE *Entomol. Compend.* 266 Two stripes near the scutellum. **1896** tr. *Boas' Zool.* 259 A triangular median portion of the mesothorax (scutellum) remains uncovered.

b. *Ornith.* One of the horny plates which cover the feet of certain birds.

1840 MACGILLIVRAY *Man. Brit. Ornith.* I. 64 Toes short, feathered, all with two scutella at the end. **1884** COUES *Key N. Amer. Birds* (ed. 2) 249 *Mimus*... Tarsal scutella always distinct.

scutibranchiate (ˌskjuːtɪˈbræŋkɪət), *a.* and *sb.* [f. mod.L. *Scūtibranchiāta* neut. pl., f. *scūt-um* shield + *branchiæ* gills: see -ATE[2].]

a. *adj.* Pertaining to the *Scutibranchiata*, a group of gasteropods comprising the sea-ears and limpets. **b.** *sb.* A member of this group.

1836 *Todd's Cycl. Anat.* II. 391/1 With the exception of the Scutibranchiate..orders, the heart is single. **1883** *Science* II. 22/1 It treats of..scutibranchiate limpets.

Also, in the same senses, **scutiˈbranchian** *a.* and *sb.*; **scutibranch** (ˈskjuːtɪbræŋk) *a.* and *sb.*

1839 *Penny Cycl.* XIV. 322/1 The third class, Gastropods, are divided into the following orders and suborders:—.. Scutibranchians.

† **ˈscutifer.** *Obs.* Also 5 **skotifer, skottefer.** [a. med.L. *scūtifer*, f. L. *scūtum* shield + *-fer, ferre* to carry.] A shield-bearer; one who bears his master's shield.

a **1400** *Morte Arth.* 2468 Skayres thaire skottefers, and theire skowtte-waches. *Ibid.* 3034 Skotiferis. *c* **1450** *Brut* 540 Scutifers of þe Kynges house. *c* **1450** HOLLAND *Howlat* 691 Scutiferis and sqwyeris, and bachilleris blyth.

scutiferous (skjuːˈtɪfərəs), *a.* [f. med.L. *scūtifer* (see prec.) + -OUS. Cf. -FEROUS.]

1. 'That bears a Buckler or Shield' (Blount *Glossogr.* 1656).

2. *Zool.* = SCUTIGEROUS (*Cent. Dict.* 1891).

scutiform (ˈskjuːtɪfɔːm), *a.* Chiefly *Anat.* [ad. mod.L. *scūtiformis*, f. *scūt-um* shield + *forma*: see -FORM.] Shield-shaped.

1656 BLOUNT *Glossogr.*, *Scutiform*, fashioned like a Scutcheon or Shield. **1696** PHILLIPS (ed. 5) *Scutiform Gristle*, the first, the broadest and the biggest of the two Gristles of the Larynx, resembling a Buckler. **1826** KIRBY & SP. *Entomol.* IV. xlvi. 330 A single joint of the hand is dilated into a broad scutiform plate. **1822-34** *Good's Study Med.* (ed. 4) I. 382 Two flat plates, composing the thyroid or scutiform cartilage. **1882** VINES tr. *Sachs' Bot.* 447 The two upper give rise to the first leaf (cotyledon), which, on account of its peculiar form, is known as the 'scutiform leaf'.

So † **ˈscutiˌformal** *a.*

1694 W. COWPER *Myotomia Ref.* 82 The Thyroidal or Scutiformal Cartilage.

‖ **scutiger** (ˈskjuːtɪdʒə(r)). [Late L. *scūtiger* shield-bearing, f. *scūt-um* shield + *-ger, gerĕre* to carry; in med.L. used subst. for 'esquire'.]

1. *jocular nonce-use.* A squire.

1839 SYD. SMITH *Ballot* Wks. 1859 II. 306/2 All set upon the unhappy scutiger; and the squire, unused to be pointed at,..is driven to the brink of suicide.

2. *Zool.* A centipede of the genus *Scutigera*; any member of the family *Scutigeridæ*.

1842 BRANDE *Dict. Sci.* etc., *Scutigers, Scutigera*, the name of a genus of unequal-legged Chilopodous Myriapods, which frequent houses..in the South of Europe.

scutigeral (skjuːˈtɪdʒərəl), *a. nonce-wd.* [f. SCUTIGER + -AL[1].] Pertaining to a squire.
1819 SYD. SMITH *Game Laws* Wks. 1859 I. 259/2 After many years of scutigeral folly—loaded prisons—nightly battles—poachers tempted—and families ruined, these principles will finally prevail.

scutigerous (skjuːˈtɪdʒərəs), *a. Zool.* [f. med.L. *scūtiger* (see SCUTIGER) + -OUS.] Provided with a scute or with scuta (*Cent. Dict.* 1891).

scutiped (ˈskjuːtɪpɛd). *Ornith.* [f. L. *scūt-um* shield + *ped-em, pēs* foot.] (See quot.)
1842 BRANDE *Dict. Sci.* etc., *Scutipeds*, the name given by Scopoli to one of the divisions of his binary system of ornithology, including those birds which have the anterior part of the legs covered with segments of unequal horny rings terminating on each side in a groove.

scutle, obs. form of SCUTTLE *sb.*[1], *sb.*[4], and *v.*[1]

scutshion, scutte: see SCUTCHEON, SCUT *sb.*[1]

scutt, var. SCUT *sb.*[4]

scuttel(l, obs. form of SCUTTLE.

scutter (ˈskʌtə(r)), *sb.* Chiefly *dial.* [f. SCUTTER *v.*[2]] An act of 'scuttering'; a hasty, scrambling, noisy rush.
1826 J. WILSON *Noct. Ambr.* Wks. 1855 I. 238 Ilka half-hour there was a toutin o' horns lang tin anes, I'm sure, frae the scutter o' broken-winded soun. **1847** E. BRONTE *Wuthering Heights* xiii. (1850) 127 The dog's endeavour to avoid him was unsuccessful; as I guessed by a scutter down stairs, and a prolonged piteous yelping. **1935** E. POUND *Let.* 23 May (1971) 274 The turn of the wave and the scutter of receding pebbles. **1961** H. R. F. KEATING *Rush on Ultimate* i. 9 Clearly visible from their moderate height the violent scutter of human activity—figures running up and down on the beach in short sharp bursts. **1980** *Times* 16 Jan. 14/8 The Anglo-Egyptian treaty was settled up in 1936 in a sort of scutter.

†ˈ**scutter**, *v.*[1] *Obs. rare*[−1]. App. a var. of SQUITTER *v.*, *intr.* to have diarrhœa.
1565 *K. Daryus* (Brandl) 1140 Nay then I wil geue you no bread and butter. Here, take some, it will make thee to scutter.

scutter (ˈskʌtə(r)), *v.*[2] orig. *colloq.* and *dial.* [? Alteration of SCUTTLE *v.* with substitution of suffix -ER[5].] *intr.* To go hastily with much fuss and bustle, as from excitement or timidity. Also *fig.*
1781 in *Mrs. Delany's Corr.* Ser. II. (1862) III. 44 She staid abt 24 hours, then scutter'd away to Badminton. **1862** MRS. H. WOOD *Mrs. Hallib.* xxvii, The men..scuttered down the stairs. **1892** KIPLING *Life's Handicap* 160 A whirling dust-devil would scutter across the plain for a couple of miles. **1892** JANE BARLOW *Irish Idylls* iv. 102 She scuttered off towards her dwelling. **1916** A. BENNETT *Lion's Share* xvii. 128 Miss Ingate scuttered to Audrey. 'Well,' she whispered. 'Here I am.' **1920** WODEHOUSE *Jill the Reckless* (1922) xxi. 313 All these people... Scuttering about and thinking they know all there is to know. **1934** E. POUND *ABC of Reading* II. 99 Inferior passages where he..has..scuttered over less interesting matter. **1947** A. RANSOME *Great Northern?* vi. 82 A family of baby water-hens scuttered across. **1948** L. MACNEICE *Holes in Sky* 38 A pebble Scutters from under the wheel. **1972** R. ADAMS *Watership Down* viii. 28 They watched him..shake a shower of drops out of his fur and scutter into the alder bushes.
Hence ˈ**scuttering** *vbl. sb.* (also *attrib.*).
1848 W. E. FORSTER in T. W. Reid *Life* (1888) I. 232 We heard cannon firing and a mighty scuttering among the guards. **1888** FENN *Dick o' the Fens* xxvi. 364 Noises in the fen..mingled with the quacking of the ducks and the scuttering of the drakes. *Ibid.* 367 The scuttering noise made by a duck dabbling its bill in the ooze.

scuttle (ˈskʌt(ə)l), *sb.*[1] Forms: 1, 4 scutel, 4–5 scutell, 5 scutelle (scutylle, scwtylle, scotel(l, scotill, -ylle, scotle, schewtell, scuttyl, skuttel, skuttyl), 6 skottell, (scutle) 6–7 scuttell, 6–9 skuttle, 6– scuttle. [OE. *scutel* in sense 1, prob. pronounced with (sk), ad. L. *scutella* dish, platter; the word appears in other Teut. langs.: ON. *skutill*, MDu., Du. *schotel*, MLG. *schötel*, OHG. *scuȥȥila* (MHG., G. *schüssel*).
The development of sense 2 is somewhat strange, but there seems no reason to doubt the identity of the word.]
†**1.** A dish, trencher, platter. *Obs.*
c **1050** *Ags. Voc.* in Wr.-Wülcker 280/22 *Catinus*, scutel. **14..** *Pict. Voc.* ibid. 770/21 Nomina pertinencia coquine... *Hec scutella*, a scotylle. **1701** *Cowel's Interpr.* (ed. Kennett), *Scutella*,..sax. Scutel, Scuttle, any thing of a flat and broad shape, like a Shield, especially a Plate or Dish, as [*read* a] shallow wooden Bowl or Platter is still call'd a Scuttle.
2. a. A basket for sifting or winnowing corn; hence, a large shovel to cast grain in winnowing, a casting-shovel. Now only *dial.*
1366–7 in *Finchale Priory Charters* (Surtees) p. lxxij, Et in pane equorum, cum ferrura..scutels sive pal', cribris [etc.]. **1411–12** *Durh. Acc. Rolls* (Surtees) 139 In j vanga, j shouill, j scotill, j boll empt. *xd. ob.* **1427–8** *Ibid.* 142 In ij scotill empt., 6d. **14..** *Nom.* in Wr.-Wülcker 726/7 *Hoc ventilabrum*, a scotylle. **1573** TUSSER *Husb.* (1878) 37 A skuttle or skreine, to rid soile fro the corne. **1681** WORLIDGE *Dict. Rust.* (ed. 3) s.v. *Skepe*, A *Skepe*, or *Scuttle*; a flat and broad Basket made to winnow corn withal. **1701** *Cowel's Interpr.* (ed. Kennett) s.v. *Scutella*, In Kent the broader Shovel with which they turn Malt or Corn, is call'd the Skuttle. **1819** W. & H. RAINBIRD *Agric. Suffolk* (1849) 299 (E.D.D.) *Scuttle*, the large casting shovel used in barns for moving threshed corn,..and especially for casting it from side to side of a barn the whole length of a dressing place that the light grains may fall short.
b. A large open basket wide at the mouth and narrow at the bottom, usually of wickerwork, used for carrying corn, earth, vegetables, etc.
1404 *Durham Acc. Rolls* (Surtees) 398 Item in orreo..1 berlepe novum, 2 scotlys, 4 wedhokys. **1415–16** *Ibid.* 225 Pro 2 sceteles virgeis pro cova. *c* **1440** *Alphabet of Tales* 184 And he..garte þaim..make skuttels & lepis of wandis evyn vnto evyn. **1541** in J. H. Glover *Kingsthorpiana* (1883) 81 Ther be bones of dede persones dygged up wt conyes whiche would fylle a scutle. **1560** *Nottingham Rec.* (1889) IV. 124 For a skottell to serue ye tyllar, iij d. **1570** *Wills & Inv. N.C.* (Surtees) I. 318 In the Larder Howse, buttertubbes scuttles and other stuff. **1601** HOLLAND *Pliny* XXXIII. iv. II. 467 The earth and stones..they are faine to carie from under their feet in scuttles and baskets, upon their shoulders. **1635** QUARLES *Embl.* III. viii. 158 Alas! and what's a man? A scuttle full of dust. **1655** TERRY *Voy. E. India* ix. 203, I have observed them to lay down scuttles or broad open wicker Basketts upon the ground. **1759** *Phil. Trans.* LI. 283, I had the mortification..to see all the tiles and a chimney shoot off from the house, as if shot out of a skuttle. **1814** T. HAYNES *Treat. Strawberry*, etc. (ed. 2) 40 After which, afford a good dressing with..manure..; which will most easily be performed by taking it out of scuttles or wheelbarrows on each side the bed.
c. = COAL-SCUTTLE 1.
1849 ALB. SMITH *Pottleton Leg.* vii. 46 Fourteen skuttles of coals. **1909** *Blackw. Mag.* Dec. 774/1 A brass scuttle stood by the fireplace.
d. *Comb.*, as *scuttle-carrier, -maker*; **scuttle-mouth** (see quot.).
1611 COTGR., *Hotteur*, a Basket-carrier, or *Scuttle-carrier. **1483** *Cath. Angl.* 327/1 A *Scutelle (Scutylle *A.*) maker, *scutellarius*. **1610–11** in *N. Riding Rec. Soc.* (1884) I. 208 [They] present..John Welbanck.., brewer, and Geo. Murrey.., scuttle maker..as vagrants and sturdy rogues. **1851** MAYHEW *Lond. Labour* I. 75/1 The very large shelly oysters..were introduced from the Sussex coast... The costermongers distinguished them by the name of '*scuttle-mouths'.
3. The part of a motor vehicle which connects the bonnet with the body. Also *attrib.*
1914 *Chambers's Jrnl.* Mar. 206/1 The scuttle-dash protects his body and chest from the wind. **1922** *Autocar* 10 Nov. 973 The coachwork, which now tapers from bonnet to scuttle in an unbroken sweep. **1925** *Morris Owner's Man.* 71 Under the butterfly nut at the back of the bonnet hinge (on top of the scuttle). **1963** *Times* 4 June 7/7 Above 65–70 m.p.h...., road noise was high and there was some scuttle shake. **1970** *Motoring Which?* July 109/2 Front wing to scuttle seams cracking, driver's seat had cut through carpet. **1973** 'A. HALL' *Tango Briefing* vii. 94 A hole appeared in the scuttle three inches forward of the windscreen. **1980** *Daily Tel.* 5 Mar. 12/6 Even on some of the worst French road surfaces there was hardly any sign of scuttle shake.

scuttle (ˈskʌt(ə)l), *sb.*[2] Forms: 5 skottelle, 7 scottel, scutle, 7–8 skuttle, 6– scuttle. [Of obscure origin; identical with F. *écoutille* hatchway, in 16th c. *escoutille*, = Sp. *escotilla*, Pg. *escotilha*; the sense 'scuttle' is expressed by the derivatives F. *écoutillon*, Sp. *escotillon*, Pg. *escotilhão*.
The Eng. word is commonly believed to be adopted from the Fr., and this from the Sp.; but the relation between the three, and the ultimate etymology, remain uncertain. According to a quotation given by Jal, the Fr. word formerly meant the hatch or trap-door covering the hatchway; if this was the original sense, the word might be a derivative of Du. or LG. *schutten* to shut; cf. Eng. *shuttle* (of a dam).]
1. *Naut.* A square or rectangular hole or opening in a ship's deck smaller than a hatchway, furnished with a movable cover or lid, used as a means of communication between deck and deck; also a similar hole in the deck or side of a ship for purposes of lighting, ventilation, etc.
1497 *Naval Acc. Hen. VII* (1896) 323 A chayne of yron for the skottelles of the haches. *c* **1595** CAPT. WYATT *R. Dudley's Voy. W. Ind.* (Hakluyt) 20 Wee have had in a watch in the night a fish flie into a little scuttle of a cabbin, noe bigger then the hande of a man. **1622** *Recov. of the 'Exchange' fr. Pirates* D 3, He had ropes, and iron hookes to make fast the scottels, gratings, and cabbines. **1644** MANWAYRING *Sea-man's Dict.*, A *Scuttle* is a square hole..cut through any Hatch or any part of the Deck to goe downe by..: also for vent for the Ordnance, there are small scuttles with grateings..: Also all the little windowes and holes which are cut-out aloft in the Captaines, or Masters cabbins, are called Scuttles. **1673** *Lond. Gaz.* No. 754/1 Some hurt in his face, received when he was making a Sally out of the Scuttle, to drive the Dutch from the Deck. **1726** SHELVOCKE *Voy. round World* 51 Two small skuttles to give light into the great cabbin. **1833** M. SCOTT *Tom Cringle* xv. (1842) 355 A room ..lighted by a long scuttle, or skylight, in the deck above. **1874** THEARLE *Naval Archit.* 223 *Scuttles*..are openings by which to obtain access to certain compartments when necessary,..scuttles in some cases are covered with *cap* and in others with *flush* covers. In the former they..are termed *cap scuttles*, and in the latter..*flush scuttles*. **1899** F. T. BULLEN *Log Sea-waif* 186 The second mate..was hanging over the open scuttle, absorbed in watching the game.
b. A hole cut or bored through any part of a ship, esp. for salving the cargo. Cf. SCUTTLE *v.*[2] 2.
1780 *Phil. Trans.* LXX. 102 Several scuttles or holes in the ship's side were made..to facilitate the discharge of the ..cargo.
c. The lid of a scuttle-hole or hatchway.
1688 CLAYTON in *Phil. Trans.* XVII. 784 We hoised out a Boat, and took one of the Scuttles that cover'd one of the Hatches of the Ship. **1697** DAMPIER *Voy.* I. 474 We..took up..a small Hatch, or Scuttle rather, belonging to some Bark. **1769–80** FALCONER *Dict. Marine* II, *Ecoutille qui s'emboîte*, a hatchway with a scuttle which covers its border. **1908** PAASCH *From Keel to Truck* 118 *Scuttle*,..the term is also given to the framing and the thick piece of glass (Bull's-eye) by which the aperture is closed.
2. An opening in the roof, floor, wall, etc. of a building closed with a shutter or lid; a trap-door; also the shutter of such an opening. Now only *U.S.*
1707 MORTIMER *Husb.* (1721) I. 148 For the Hole in the Door, have a small Scuttle to shut down when you go in. **1737** [implied in *scuttle hinge*, see 4 below]. **1828–32** WEBSTER, *Scuttle*, a square hole in the roof of a house, with a lid. **1877** WHITTIER *Witch of Wenham* II. xvi, She forced the oaken scuttle back; A whisper reached her ear: 'Slide down the roof to me' it said. **1902** R. STURGIS *Dict. Archit.* III. 524 Occasionally smaller skylights are in the form of glazed scuttles arranged to be opened for access to the roof.
†**3.** (See quot.) Cf. SHUTTLE.
1705 *Act 4 & 5 Anne* c. 8 [21], Owners..of..Mills, upon any..rivers..shall constantly keep open One Scuttle or small Hatch of a Foot Square in the Waste Hatch or Water course..for the Salmon to pass and repass freely.
4. *Comb.*: **scuttle-cask** = SCUTTLE-BUTT a.; **scuttle-hatch**, a lid or covering of a scuttle; **scuttle hinge**, a hinge for a scuttle or trap-door; **scuttle-hole** = sense 1.
1803 *Naval Chron.* X. 183 Water from the *scuttle-cask on the quarter-deck. **1627** CAPT. SMITH *Seaman's Gram.* ii. 7 A *scuttle-hatch is a little hatch doth couer a little square hole we call the Scuttle. **1737** HOPPUS *Salmon's Country Build. Estim.* (ed. 2) 107 *Scuttle Hinges..are sold by the Dozen. **1684** I. MATHER *Rem. Prov.* 5 The *scuttle-hole of the quarter-deck. **1828** P. CUNNINGHAM *N.S. Wales* (ed. 3) II. 212 Scuttle-holes, to open and shut for the admission of air, are cut along the ship's sides.

†ˈ**scuttle**, *sb.*[3] *Naut. Obs.* Also 6 **skutele**. [Of obscure origin; not easily to be connected with either of the preceding sbs.] A platform at the head of a lower mast; a 'top'.
1597 BEARD *Theatre God's Judgem.* I. ii. (1631) 4 Their carefull watchfulnesse..ought to serue them for sails, cables, ankrs, masts, and skuttles, whereby to gouerne and direct the Vessel. **1611** COTGR., *Hune*, the scuttle of the mast of a ship. **1653** URQUHART *Rabelais* II. xxviii. 181 Let down this white wine of Anjou, from the scuttle [orig. *la Hune*] of the mast of the ship. **1671** H. M. *Erasm. Colloq.* 172 On the top of the main mast stood one of the Marriners, in the skuttle [orig. *in galea*]..looking about him, if he could see any land. **1763** *Brit. Mag.* IV. 592 This mast..has at its extremity a scuttle like that of the masts of a ship.

scuttle (ˈskʌt(ə)l), *sb.*[4] Forms: 6 scottell, scuttel(l, 8 scutle, skuttle, 7– scuttle. [Altered form of CUTTLE *sb.*[1]] = CUTTLE *sb.*[1] Also *scuttle fish.*
1530 PALSGR. 268 Scottell a fysshe, *seiche*... Scuttell fysshe, *saiche*. **1644** DIGBY *Nat. Bodies* xxxvi. §11. 315 The scuttle fish, when he is in straights of being taken..casteth out a blackenesse that is within him. **1712** ADDISON *Spect.* No. 476 ¶4 Our Disputants put me in mind of the Skuttle Fish, that when he is unable to extricate himself, blackens all the Water about him, till he becomes invisible. **1876** GOODE *Fish. Bermudas* 10 The 'Scuttle', a large Octopus.
b. *attrib.* **scuttle-bone, shell** = CUTTLE-BONE.
1530 PALSGR. 268 Scottell bone,..Scuttell bone, *os de saiche*. **1703** DAMPIER *Voy.* III. I. 114 We began to see some Scutle-bones floating on the Water. *Ibid.* 130 We saw.. abundance of Scuttle-shells swimming on the Sea.

scuttle (ˈskʌt(ə)l), *sb.*[5] Also 8 skuttle. [f. SCUTTLE *v.*[1]] The action or an act of scuttling.
1. a. A short hurried run.
1623 WEBSTER *D'chess Malfi* III. ii, Pluto the god of riches, When he's sent (by Iupiter)..goes limping,..but when he's sent One the diuells arrand, he rides poast, and comes in by scuttles. **1712** ADDISON *Spect.* No. 323 ¶7 From Twelve to One. Shut my self up in my Chamber, practised Lady Betty Modely's Skuttle. **1755** JOHNSON, *Scuttle*... 3. (From *scud.*) A quick pace; a short run; a pace of affected precipitation. **1967** O. WYND *Walk Softly, Men Praying* iv. 49, I stopped a scuttle back to his den with yet another request.
b. *Political slang.* (See SCUTTLE *v.*[1] 1 b.)
Probably now with an admixture of SCUTTLE *v.*[2] 1 b.
1884 *Pall Mall Gaz.* 30 Dec. 5/1 In other words, scuttle, if adopted as a ministerial policy, may lead to the evacuation of Downing-street, for the evacuation of Egypt is quite impossible for at least a year yet. **1892** C. RHODES in *Daily Tel.* (1901) 12 Oct. 9/7, I was horrified..to read a speech of Mr. Gladstone's evidently foreshadowing a scuttle if he came in. **1906** *Daily News* 16 June 6/4 The word scuttle.. in the Jingo Press, where the 'policy of scuttle' is used whenever we give up something to a small Power. **1954** *Economist* 7 Aug. 428 Mr. Attlee has always been particularly offended by Tory charges of 'scuttle' during his years in office. **1967** *Daily Express* 17 Feb. 2/2 The speed-up of the scuttle is inadvertently revealed in the Defence White Paper. **1969** *Guardian* 31 July 8/1 President Nixon has ruled out both a military solution and a 'scuttle'.
2. In Manchester: A street faction-fight between bands of young people.
1864 in G. Milner *Odds & Ends* (1875) I. 43 When the boys of one street take offence at boys of another street, they often fall to fighting in a body. This is called a 'scuttle'.

scuttle (ˈskʌt(ə)l), *v.*[1] Also (? 5 scottle), 7 scutle, 8 skuttle. [? Altered form of SCUDDLE *v.*[2]
It is doubtful whether the 15th c. *scottle* belongs to this word, the sense being somewhat obscure.]
1. *intr.* To run with quick, hurried steps. Chiefly with *away, off*.
a **1450** [implied in SCUTTLING *vbl. sb.*[1]]. **1657** THORNLEY *Daphnis & Chloe* (1893) 21 Then she told him all that had happened; how she scutled up to Dorco; how [etc.]. **1681** OTWAY *Soldier's Fortune* I. (1683) 4 So away he scuttled with as great joy as if he had found the Philosophers stone. **1739** H. WALPOLE *Let. to R. West* 20 July, We scuttle up-stairs in

great confusion. **1785** Grose *Dict. Vulgar T.*, *Scuttle off*, to run away. **1814** Scott *Wav.* lxv, With the first dawn of day, old Janet was scuttling about the house to wake the Baron. **1858** R. S. Surtees *Ask Mamma* xxi. 74 Causing the conceited hares to scuttle away for the..hills. **1871** J. R. Green *Lett.* iii. (1901) 278 The bit of ground..which everybody scuttles over by train. **1882** Besant *Revolt of Man* xiv, In a moment the house was empty. It is not too much to say that the Duchess scuttled.

b. *transf.* in *Political slang.* To withdraw in a precipitate and undignified manner from the occupation or control of a country. Cf. scuttle *sb.*[5] 1 b.

App. first used in 1883 with reference to the suggested abandonment of England of its control in Egypt. Still not uncommon in journalistic use.

1883 Ld. R. Churchill *Sp.* 18 Dec. (1889) I. 79 Now—so says Mr. Gladstone at the Guildhall—we, the Liberal Government..are going to scuttle out of this pandemonium as soon as we can. **1884** *Pall Mall Gaz.* 4 July 1/2 Even if we were going to scuttle next year from Egypt.

2. In Manchester: To take part in a 'scuttle' or street-fight. See scuttle *sb.*[5] 2.

1890 *Daily News* 14 Aug. 5/1 Five men, or rather lads, were in the dock [at the Manchester City Sessions] charged with 'scuttling'... The prisoners, arming themselves with belts and clasp knives, made their way through the Manchester streets stunning or stabbing, without provocation, every one who came in their way.

scuttle ('skʌt(ə)l), *v.*[2] [f. scuttle *sb.*[2]]

1. a. *trans.* To cut or bore a hole or holes in the sides or bottom of (a vessel, boat, etc. for the purpose of sinking her). Hence, by extension: to sink (one's own vessel) deliberately; to submerge; to destroy or smash (a car, aeroplane, etc.). Also *refl.*, of a vessel.

1642 in R. H. Hore *Hist. Wexford* (1900) I. 300 He went ..on board and scuttled and set fire to the ships. **1779** J. Ramsay *Let.* 23 Nov. in *Parl. Papers 1910* (Cd. 5038) XXXV. 675 Captain Wilkinson is particularly celebrated for having said..he wished that all the English sugar islands were skuttled (sunk). **1790** Beatson *Nav. & Mil. Mem.* I. 91 Orders had been given to scuttle each ship for sinking,.. and they had all a large square plug ready to pull out when the signal..was given. **1821** Byron *Juan* iii. xli, He was the mildest manner'd man That ever scuttled ship or cut a throat. **1877** Froude *Short Stud.* Ser. iv. 106 The vessel.. had been scuttled. **1939** *Times* 16 Dec. 7/3 The German steamer Adolf Leonhart (2,989 tons) was scuttled by her crew in the South Atlantic when she was intercepted by a British warship. *Ibid.* 18 Dec. 8/1 The Admiral Graf Spee the German 'pocket battleship' which was cornered by British warships, scuttled herself outside Montevideo harbour last night. **1941** *Collier's* 20 Dec. 50/1 Bruce, in a heavy sedan, had come banging out of his driveway to a collision. No one was hurt, but the flivver was scuttled. **1942** *R.A.F. Jrnl.* 13 June 10 The enemy would reveal herself by firing her guns or scuttling herself. **1955** *Times* 1 June 2/7 His Black Sea fleet had been scuttled and the war was confined to a narrowing circle round Sebastopol.

b. *fig.* (esp. in political contexts).

1888 *Ch. Times* 3 Feb. 89 A few of them once had a fine Protestant appearance, but they have been scuttled by three recent discoveries. **1940** *Star* 15 May 3/2 A favourite way of settling an argument is to exclaim, 'You go and scuttle yourself!' **1942** *Capital* 20 Jan. 1/3 The ill-concealed Axis maneuver, apparently part of a..scheme to scuttle the [Rio de] Janeiro conference. **1955** *Times* 16 May 5/1 'Now they scuttle us,' said Mr. Oatley, 'by slapping controls on what can be considered the cornerstone of every household—a domestic cooker.' **1965** Mrs L. B. Johnson *White House Diary* 21 Oct. (1970) 329 The day..began with bad news. The Rent Subsidy Bill had been scuttled without opportunity to work on it. **1976** *National Observer* (U.S.) 24 Apr. 18/3 Earlier this month the White House, in apparent agreement, scuttled a legislative proposal to deregulate cable TV. **1977** *Time* 7 Nov. 21/3 His effort to pay off a campaign promise to maritime unions by fixing the percentage of imported oil that must be carried in U.S. ships was scuttled.

2. a. To cut a hole in (the deck of a vessel), esp. for the purpose of salving the cargo (see quot. 1867).

1789 A. Duncan *Mariner's Chron.* (1805) IV. 37 It was thought necessary to scuttle the deck close aft, which.. would enable them to get up and throw overboard some of the provisions and stores. **1816** 'Quiz' *Grand Master* i. 21 The decks are scuttl'd, and we lay Far in the hollow of the sea. **1867** Smyth *Sailor's Word-bk.*, To *scuttle*, to cut or bore holes through part of a ship when she is stranded or overset, ..in order to save any part of her contents.

b. *transf.*

a **1797** C. Macklin in *Europ. Mag.* (1801) XL. 16/1 Sir, I remember the time when the price of admission here [at Sadler's Wells] was but threepence, except a few places scuttled off at the sides of the stage at sixpence.

3. Pugilistic slang. *to scuttle* (a person's) *nob*: to break (his) head.

1834 F. S. Mahony *Reliques F. Prout* in *Fraser's Mag.* Dec. 671/1 I'll..scuttle your nob with my fist. **1842** Barham *Ingol. Leg.*, *Dead Drummer*, What!..desart..and then rob! And go scuttling a poor little Drummer-boy's nob.

scuttle-butt, scuttlebutt ('skʌt(ə)lbʌt). [See scuttled *ppl. a.*] **a.** *Naut.* A cask of drinking-water on board ship; a drinking-fountain. Also *fig.*

1805 J. J. Moore *Midshipman's or Brit. Mariner's Vocab.*, *Scuttle-butt*, or cask, is a cask having a square piece sawn out of its bilge and lashed upon the deck. It is used to contain the fresh water for daily use. **1832** E. C. Wines *Two Years & Half in Navy* I. iii. 45 At sea the marines in succession all do duty as sentries in the following places;—one at the cabin door, one at the scuttle-butt, one at the brig. **1840** R. H. Dana *Bef. Mast* xxxii. 123 Going to the scuttle-butt for a drink of water. **1844** J. F. Cooper *Afloat & Ashore* II. xi. 178 People never can tell so much of other person's affairs, without bailing out most of their ideas from their own scuttle-butts. **1846** Young *Naut. Dict.*, *Scuttled-butt* or (as it is generally abbreviated) *Scuttle-butt*, a cask with a square hole cut in its bilge, kept on deck to hold water for ready use. **1920** *U.S.S. Oklahoma Sea-Bag* 25 July 2/1 The Scuttle Butt has justified its existence as a source of prognostic rumor. The water is freezing cold—the Scuttle Butt is iced. .. Come down and get a drink of cold water. **1972** F. van W. Mason *Roads to Liberty* 104 Katie, on her way to draw water from the scuttlebutt, saw a flying fish.

b. *slang* (orig. *U.S. Naut.*). Rumour, idle gossip, unfounded report.

1901 *Smoking Lamp* June 55/2 (*title of miscellany column*) Scuttle butt. **1933** *Leatherneck* July 18/1 We will endeavor to convey all of the scandal, scuttle-butt, dope and dopes to you through the.. Editor. **1943** *Sun* (Baltimore) 20 Sept. 11/7 Also a cause for betting was the ultimate destination. In navy slang 'scuttlebutt' was rife and had the ship bound everywhere from China to Murmansk. **1950** 'D. Divine' *King of Fassarai* iv. 20 I'd got the scuttle-butt about that from the Marine Corps boys. **1966** K. Giles *Big Greed* 76 He'd heard a rumour that the Frog drank..but he dismissed it as a scuttlebutt. **1977** *Time* 11 Apr. 17/1 Rawlings Co. now makes the official major league baseball after a 101-year Spalding reign, and the scuttle-butt is that Rawlings is turning out a rabbit ball. **1980** *Rydge's* (Sydney) Jan. 23/1 They are privy to vast amounts of corporate intelligence (and scuttlebutt) that runs daily around the Rialto.

c. *attrib.*, as **scuttle-butt gossip**, (*a*) one who exchanges gossip at a scuttle-butt; (*b*) the gossip exchanged there; **scuttle-butt yarn**, a yarn originating from talk around a scuttle-butt.

1901 *Smoking Lamp* May 18/1 (*title*) Scuttle butt gossip. **1918** R. W. Kauffman *Our Navy at Work* xiii. 198 It's wilder than anything the scuttle-butt gossips could make up! *Ibid.* 199 Ships are full of..rumours..which originate in talk exchanged around the skuttle-butt, or drinking barrel, so that all wild stories are branded as 'scuttle-butt yarns'. **1923** *Our Navy* 1 May 15/2 While these rumors are branded as of the 'scuttle butt' variety they persist as rumors. **1930** P. Buranelli *Maggie of Suicide Fleet* ii. 57 There are stories and rumors, scuttle-butt gossip.

Hence '**scuttlebutt** *v. intr.*, to gossip, to spread unfounded stories.

1945 H. I. Phillips *Private Purkey's Private Peace* xi. 62 There were many who felt..Oscar was just scuttle-butting.

scuttled ('skʌt(ə)ld), *ppl. a. Naut.* [f. scuttle *v.*[2] + -ed[1].] Having a hole cut in it. *scuttled butt* = scuttle-butt a.; so *scuttled cask*, *puncheon*.

1743 Bulkeley & Cummins *Voy. S. Seas* 160 We sent ashore in a scuttled Puncheon some wearing apparel [etc.]. **1777** G. Forster *Voy. round World* I. 86 A centry was placed at the scuttled-cask, and a regular allowance of water was daily served out. **1840** R. H. Dana *Bef. Mast* iii, Filling the 'scuttled butt' with fresh water. **1846** Young *Naut. Dict.*, *Scuttled-butt* or (as it is generally abbreviated) *Scuttle-butt*, a cask with a square hole cut in its bilge, kept on deck to hold water for ready use.

scuttleful ('skʌt(ə)lfʊl). [f. scuttle *sb.*[1] + -ful.] As much as will fill a scuttle.

c **1440** *Alphabet of Tales* 109 He tuke a skuttylfull of corn. **1600** Surflet *Country Farm* ii. xli. 253 You must first put horse dung..a scuttle full to euerie border. **1897** Watts-Dunton *Aylwin* v. i, I thought the gift as entirely gratuitous, *mon cher*, as giving a scuttle-ful of coals to Newcastle.

scuttler[1] ('skʌtlə(r)). [f. scuttle *v.*[1] + -er[1].]

1. a. *Political slang.* One who advocates a policy of 'scuttle' (see scuttle *sb.*[5] 1 b).

1884 *Pall Mall G.* 1 Dec., Thus the scuttlers..will be restrained from saying a word about scuttling.

b. *U.S.* A local name for the lizard *Cnemidophorus sexlineatus* (Cent. Dict. 1891).

1886 *Trans. Amer. Philol. Assoc.* XVII. 46 Scuttler or streakfield (striped lizard).

2. In Manchester: One who takes part in a 'scuttle' or street-fight. See scuttle *sb.*[5] 2.

In the first quot. app. used for: A street urchin, 'gamin'. If the word is identical with that current in Manchester, the writer seems to have misapprehended its meaning.

1867 C. G. Gordon *Let.* (*Manchester*) 21 Sept. in *Lett. to Sister* (1888) 23 The poor scuttlers here, male and female, fill me with sorrow. They wear wooden clogs,..and make such a noise. [Also in later letters dated from other places, 1882–3, *ibid.* pp. 253, 271, 300, 302; sometimes glossed 'boy' by the editor.] **1887** *Daily News* 7 Feb. 6/2 A gang of 'scuttlers' who parade the streets [of Manchester] at night and assault passengers with belts and frequently with knives.

scuttler[2] ('skʌt(ə)lə(r)). [f. scuttle *v.*[2] + -er[1].] One who scuttles a ship; esp. with the design of 'losing' her and claiming the insurance-money.

1869 *Daily News* 11 Dec., The over-insured..as well as the scuttler, should be..punished severely. **1884** *Manch. Exam.* 9 Aug. 5/1 Supposing the scuttlers..had not bungled in the business, the ship would have been among the missing.

scuttling ('skʌt(ə)lɪŋ), *vbl. sb.*[1] [f. scuttle *v.*[1] + -ing[1].] The action of scuttle *v.*[1]

a **1450** *Mankind* in *Macro Plays* 4 *Nought.* 3ys, Mary, I prey yow, for I loue not þis rewelynge [*sc.* of dancing]... Go to! for I haue hade a praty scottlynge. *Mercy.* Nay, brother, I wyll not daunce. **1873** 'Cuthbert Bede' *Little Mr. Bouncer* 147 The scuttling of rabbits in and out of their holes. **1884** [see scuttler[1] 1 a]. **1890** [see scuttle *v.*[1] 2]. **1894** Hall Caine *Manxman* iv. xiv. 256 It was the scuttling of the feet of the towns-people as they ran to meet the procession.

scuttling ('skʌt(ə)lɪŋ), *vbl. sb.*[2] [f. scuttle *v.*[2] + -ing[1].] The action of scuttle *v.*[2]

1622 Sir R. Hawkins *Voy. S. Sea* xvii. 40 Great care is to be had also..in Hooping or Scutling of Caske. **1748** *Anson's Voy.* ii. xiii. 269 The other ships..were prepared for scuttling. **1877** Gladstone *Glean.* IV. xx. 350 It does not at once appear how the Canal could be secured against the furtive scuttling of ships.

scuttling ('skʌt(ə)lɪŋ), *ppl. a.* [f. scuttle *v.*[1] + -ing[2].] That scuttles; characterized by scuttling.

1895 C. R. B. Barrett *Surrey* vii. 171 A stray water-hen made a flapping, scuttling progress across the pool. **1900** *Longm. Mag.* Apr. 541 A couple of skulking scuttling spies. **1904** *Ibid.* Dec. 122 The patter of scuttling sheep could be heard on the soft turf.

scuttock ('skʌtək). *local.* [Perh. a dim. of scout *sb.*[6]: see -ock.] The common guillemot.

1813 Montagu *Ornith. Dict.* Suppl., Guillemot, Foolish, Uria Troile... Provincial... Skuttock [1831, 545 Scuttock].

scutty ('skʌtɪ). [? f. scut *sb.*[1] + -y.] A name applied locally to the wren (see quots.).

1885 Swainson *Prov. Names Birds* 35 Wren (*Troglodytes parvulus*)... From its short bob-tail it has the name of.. Scutty (Sussex). **1899** *Pall Mall Mag.* Nov. 355 The wren ..is commonly known [in Ireland] by the name of 'Scutty' ..on account of its short, upright tail.

scuttyl, obs. form of scuttle *sb.*[1]

scutulate ('skju:tjʊlət), *a.* Also *erron.* scutilate. [ad. mod.L. *scūtulāt-us*, f. L. *scūtulum* dim. of *scūtum* shield.] = scutellate. Also '**scutulated** *a.*

1827 R. Jameson tr. *Cuvier's Theory of Earth* (ed. 5) 310 Two-thirds of the leg, and the whole length of the toes, are scutulate. **1848** Hepburn in *Proc. Berw. Nat. Club* II. 276 Tarsus short,..scutulate in front. **1885** C. F. Holder *Marv. Animal Life* 127 [Other species] are the..spotted, scutulated, coral-colored, and the black-tail rattlesnakes.

scutule ('skju:tjʊl). [ad. L. *scūtulum* (in sense 1 through It.), f. *scūtum* shield.]

†**1.** ? An escutcheon-shaped marking. *rare*[−1].

1592 R. D. *Hypnerotomachia* 48 Because the circumduct and compassing coulers, meeting together in the selfe same smoothe and cleane stones, did yeeld a reflection, no part being faultie, eyther of the square checkers or scutuls and Trigons [orig. *scutuli, trigoni, quadrati*].

2. *Zool.* A small scute or dermal plate.

1841 *Penny Cycl.* XIX. 469/2 Rhinoceros... One-horned; ..scutules of the skin angled at the margin.

‖**scutulum** ('skju:tjʊləm). Pl. scutula. [mod.L. use of L. *scūtulum*, dim. of *scūtum* shield.]

a. *Path.* A shield-shaped crust or disc developed in the skin-disease favus.

1888 J. N. Hyde *Dis. Skin* (ed. 2) 598 The inferior surface of this disk or scutulum rests upon the scalp. **1899** *Allbutt's Syst. Med.* VIII. 862 The characteristic lesion [of favus] is a small yellow-coloured disc or scutulum. *Ibid.* 863 In old scabs the scutula are lost.

b. *Zool.* A scutellum.

1902 in *Webster's Suppl.*

‖**scutum** ('skju:təm). Pl. scuta ('skju:tə). [mod.L. use of L. *scūtum* shield, f. Indogermanic root **sku-* (:**skeu-*) to cover, whence sky *sb.*

The L. *scūtum* denoted specifically the large oblong shield, in contradistinction to the *clipeus* or buckler.

In mod. anatomical Latin the word was formerly used as a name for the knee-cap and for the thyroid cartilage.]

1. *Bot.* 'The broad dilated stigma in some asclepiads' (*Treas. Bot.* 1866).

1832 Lindley *Introd. Bot.* i. ii. 122 The circular space in the middle of the top of the orbiculus is the *scutum*.

2. *Ent.* The second segment of each of the three divisions of the tergum in insects.

The scuta respectively of the pronotum, mesonotum, and metanotum are called proscutum, mesoscutum, and metascutum. The term *scutum* alone sometimes = *mesoscutum*.

1830 MacLeay in *Zool. Jrnl.* V. 169 The *scutum*, whether the collar be apparent or not, is therefore the second piece of the mesothorax. **1833** F. Walker in *Entomol. Mag.* I. 26 A yellow line extends along the suture [of *Decatoma biguttata*], between the scutum and the parapsides of the mesothorax.

3. *Zool.* A shield-like dermal plate; a scute.

1771 [see scutella]. **1870** H. A. Nicholson *Man. Zool.* lxiv. (1875) 482 [The true Lizards and the Monitors] are chiefly separated by the..fact that the abdomen and head are covered with ordinary scales, and not with large 'scuta'. *Ibid.* Gloss., *Scuta*, applied to any shield-like plates; especially to those which are developed in the integument of many reptiles.

scutylle, obs. form of scuttle *sb.*[1]

scuwe, scwe: see skew.

scuzzy ('skʌzɪ), *a. N. Amer. colloq.* [Perh. blend of scummy *a.* + fuzzy *a.*] Dirty, grimy; murky. So **scuz(z)** *sb.*, a dirty, messy person.

1968 *Sunday Sun* (Baltimore) 3 Nov. D1/5, I..did 'Midnight Cowboy' where I'm *Ratso Rizzo*, a complete scuzz. **1969** *Publ. Amer. Dial. Soc.* li. 16 *Scuzzy*, *groady*, *skoady*, and *grungy* should probably be listed also under 'Blends'... *Scuzzy*, for example, seems to imply *fuzzy* and *scummy*: 'Your teeth are scuzzy.' **1972** J. Wambaugh *Blue Knight* vi. 78 One white, bearded scuz in a dirty buckskin vest and yellow headband. **1974** A. Fowles *Pastime* vii. 63

The scuzzy, grey, February days, neither cold nor clear. **1976** *Daily Colonist* (Victoria, B.C.) 14 Apr. 5/4 Perhaps Mr. Vander Kalm has good intentions about evicting scuzzy malingerers from the dole.

scwle, scwylle, rare obs. ff. SCHOOL *sb.*[1]

scwtylle, scwyer, obs. ff. SCUTTLE, SQUIRE.

†**'scybal.** *Obs. rare.* Also 5 **squibal.** [a. F. *scybale*, ad. med.L. *scybalum.*] = SCYBALUM.

c **1425** tr. *Arderne's Surg.* 76 Water alon & salt boiled togidre and ȝette in by a clistrye bringeþ out squiballez. *Ibid.* 78 Þis [clistery] bryngeþ out hard squiballez of what euery cause þai be withholden. **1694** MOTTEUX *Rabelais* IV. lxvii, Sir-reverence, Ordure,.. Scybal or Syparathe.

scybalous ('sɪbələs), *a. Path.* [f. med.L. *scybalum* + -OUS.] Of or pertaining to, or of the nature of, scybala.

1799 *Med. Jrnl.* I. 349 These stools, small in quantity, having a scybalous appearance, and constantly mixed with blood. **1897** *Allbutt's Syst. Med.* III. 735 Scybalous masses may frequently give rise to diarrhœa.

‖**scybalum** ('sɪbələm). *Path.* Usually pl. scybala. [med.L. *scybalum*, a. Gr. σκύβαλον.] One of a collection of round masses of constipated fæces formed in the bowels in certain diseases.

1684 tr. *Blancard's Phys. Dict.*, *Scybala*, are Sheeps, or Goats, &c. Buttons, or Excrement. **1808** *Med. Jrnl.* XIX. 308 One scanty stool without scybala. **1889** MATTHEWS *Dis. Women* xiv. (ed. 4) 98 A Scybalum is a rounded or oval mass of fæces.

scye (saɪ). *Tailors' term.* [A use of a Sc. and Ulster dialect word (written also *sey, sci, si, sie, sy* in glossaries) meaning 'the opening of a gown, etc., into which the sleeve is inserted; the part of the dress between the armpit and the chest' (E.D.D.); of obscure etymology.] The opening in a coat into which a sleeve is inserted.

[**1825** JAMIESON *Suppl.* s.v. *Sey*, The sey of a gown or shift is the opening through which the arm passes.] **1830** DAVEY *Syst. Cutting* 7 Measure the distance from the top of the back to the bottom of the back scye. **1899** WHITEING *No. 5 John-St.* xviii, What's wrong with the Scye? **1909** *Daily News* 22 Oct. 12/1 There is.. a very clean fit about the scye, and an excellent shoulder.

scyelite ('saɪəlaɪt). *Min.* [f. the name of Loch *Scye* in Caithness + -LITE.] A combination of mica with hornblende-picrite.

1885 JUDD in *Q. Jrnl. Geol. Soc.* XLI. 401 The Scyelite (altered Mica-Hornblende-Picrite) of Caithness.

scyle, scylful, obs. ff. SKILL, SKILFUL.

scylence, -ens, obs. forms of SILENCE.

Scylla ('sɪlə). [L.; a. Gr. Σκύλλα.] A rock upon the Italian side of the Straits of Messina facing CHARYBDIS (q.v. for the proverbial use); also personified as a dangerous sea-monster.

c **1520** ANDREW *Noble Lyfe* III. lxxii, Scilla is a monster in the see betwene Italye & Sicill, it is great ennemye vnto man. ? *a* **1547** ? SURREY in *Tottel's Misc.* (Arb.) 241 Seas.. Which we [*read* me] haue tossed sore: From Sicilla [*read* Scilla] to Caribdis cliues. *c* **1580** W. SPELMAN *Dialoge* (1896) 3, I fell from Silla into Caribdes, from euyll to woors. **1596** SHAKS. *Merch. V.* III. v. 19. *c* **1620** T. ROBINSON *Mary Magd.* 607 Or as yᵉ iawes of Scyllas barkinge hounds, That aye for greedinesse of booties raue. **1651** *Reg. Comm. Gen. Assembly* (1909) 244 Our former Warnings.. hes stiered a steadie course betwixt the Shylla of Malignants and Charibdis of Sectaries. **1703** KELSEY *Serm.* 290 The Scylla's and Charibdis's which have swallowed up many Mortals. **1865** H. KINGSLEY *Hillyars & Burtons* iii, Alas, the poor father in avoiding Charybdis had run against Scylla.

scylling, scyment, obs. ff. SHILLING, CEMENT.

scymetar, -er, scymitar, -er: see SCIMITAR.

scymme, obs. form of SKIM.

scymmer: see SCUMMER *sb.*, SKIMMER *sb.*

scyn, scyne, obs. ff. SKIN *sb.*, SHINE *v.*

scyon, scyoure: see SCION, SYRE.

‖**scypha** ('saɪfə). *Bot.* [mod.L. *scypha*, a. Gr. σκύφη, var. of σκύφ-ος drinking cup.] = SCYPHUS.

1832 LINDLEY *Introd. Bot.* I. iii. 205 *Scypha*, is a cup-like dilatation of the Podetium, bearing shields on its margin. **1856** HENSLOW *Dict. Bot. Terms*, *Scypha*, *Scyphus*. **1900** B. D. JACKSON *Gloss. Bot. Terms*, *Scypha* or *Scyphus*.

scypher, obs. form of CIPHER *v.*

scyphi- ('saɪfɪ), combining form of L. *scyphus* cup (see SCYPHUS), used in scientific terms, chiefly *Bot.* and *Zool.* (Properly, this form should be used only for compounds with Latin words, and SCYPHO- for those with Greek words; but this rule has often been neglected.) **scyphiferous** (saɪ'fɪfərəs) *a.* [-FEROUS] *Bot.*, bearing a scyphus; = SCYPHOPHOROUS. **'scyphiform** (-fɔːm) *a.* [-FORM], (*a*) *Bot.*, resembling a scyphus in shape; (*b*) *Zool.*, 'boat-shaped, scaphoid' (*Cent. Dict.*). **scy'phiphorous** (-fərəs) *a. Bot.* = SCYPHOPHOROUS, SCYPHIFEROUS. ‖**scy'phistoma** *Zool.* = SCYPHOSTOMA. Hence **scy'phistomoid** *a.*, of or belonging to a scyphistoma (in quot. *absol.*); **scy'phistomous** *a.* (*Cent. Dict.*).

1871 W. A. LEIGHTON *Lichen-Flora* 57 Podetia from disk of laciniæ,.. *scyphiferous. *Ibid.* 2 Apothecia biatorine on *scyphiform or simple podetia. **1879** *Ibid.* (ed. 3) 521 *Scyphiphorous. **1870** H. A. NICHOLSON *Man. Zool.* (1875) 122 The **Scyphistoma* assumes the aspect of a pile of saucers, arranged one upon another with their concave surfaces upward. **1902** G. H. FOWLER in *Encycl. Brit.* XXVII. 131 The non-sexual *scyphistomoid (corresponding to the hydroid) alternating with the medusoid.

scypho- ('saɪfəʊ, saɪ'fɒ), representing Gr. σκυφο-, combining form of σκύφος cup (see SCYPHUS), chiefly in scientific terms: cf. SCYPHI-. **scy'phogeny** (-dʒɪnɪ) [-GENY], *Bot.*, production of ascidia. **'scyphomancy** (-,mænsɪ) [-MANCY], divination by means of a cup. ‖**,scyphome'dusa** [mod.L.], *Zool.*, a group of Hydrozoa. Hence **scyphome'dusan, -me'dusoid** *adjs.* (Cent. Dict.). **'scyphophore** (-fɔə(r)) [ad. mod.L. *scyphophor-us*], *Zool.*, a member of the *Scyphophori*, an order of physostomous fishes (*Cent. Dict.*). **scy'phophorous** (-fərəs) *a.* [-PHOROUS], *Bot.* = SCYPHIFEROUS. **scyphopolyp** (-'pɒlɪp) [POLYP], a cup-shaped polyp; also *attrib.* **scy'phostoma** [Gr. στόμα mouth], *Zool.*, a non-sexual hydroid form of the Hydrozoan Acraspeda (also called SCYPHISTOMA).

1900 B. D. JACKSON *Gloss. Bot. Terms*, **Scyphogeny*. **1855** SMEDLEY *Occult Sci.* 293 The existence of a kind of *scyphomancy, or divination with a cup, is supposed to be alluded to. **1881** E. R. LANKESTER in *Encycl. Brit.* XII. 553/1 And now the ancestry took two distinct lines, which have given rise respectively to the two great groups into which the *Hydrozoa* are divisble—**Scyphomedusæ* and the *Hydromedusæ*. **1871** W. A. LEIGHTON *Lichen-Flora* 64 Nigrescent and albo-guttate at the base, *scyphophorous, scyphi proliferous. **1882** tr. *Haeckel* in *Challenger Rep., Zool.* IV. II. p. xiii, The Acraspedæ [originate] from *Scyphopolyps by terminal gemmation. *Ibid.* p. xiv, Developed from the Scyphopolyp nurse. **1878** BELL *Gegenbaur's Comp. Anat.* 98 The *Scyphostoma seems to be more highly organised than most of the Hydroid-Polyps. **1888** ROLLESTON & JACKSON *Anim. Life* 787 *note*, Haeckel believes that the Tesseroniæ possess a Scyphostoma stage.

scyphose ('saɪfəʊs), *a. Bot.* [f. SCYPH-US + -OSE.] Having a scyphus or scyphi.

1879 W. A. LEIGHTON *Lichen-Flora* (ed. 3) 521 *Scyphose*, bearing thalline cups as in *Cladonia*.

scyphozoan (,saɪfəʊ'zəʊən), *sb.* and *a.* [f. mod.L. class name *Scyphozoa* (A. Goette 1898, in *Zeitschr. f. Wiss. Zool.* LXIII. 292), f. SCYPHO- + *-zoa* (see ZOON).] A jellyfish belonging to the class Scyphozoa; of or pertaining to an animal of this kind.

[**1892** J. A. THOMSON *Outlines Zool.* x. 137 (*caption*) Contrast between a Hydrozoon and a Scyphozoon medusoid.] **1915** SHIPLEY & MACBRIDE *Zool.* (ed. 3) iii. 75 The construction of the Scyphozoan organ is quite different. *Ibid.* 78 The original Scyphozoan was probably an organism like a polyp. **1938** R. BUCHSBAUM *Anim. without Backbones* viii. 95 *Aurelia* is one of the commonest of the scyphozoan jellyfish. **1967** P. A. MEGLITSCH *Invertebrate Zool.* vi. 148/1 Stauromedusae are the most unusual scyphozoans.

‖**scyphulus** ('saɪfjʊləs). *Bot.* [mod.L. *scyphulus*, dim. of SCYPHUS.] (See quot. 1856.)

1856 HENSLOW *Dict. Bot. Terms*, *Scyphulus*, the cup-like appendage from which the seta of Hepaticæ arises. Used also synonymously with Scypha.

‖**scyphus** ('saɪfəs). *Bot.* Pl. scyphi ('saɪfaɪ). [mod.L. use of L. *scyphus*, ad. Gr. σκύφος a large drinking vessel without a foot.] **a.** A name given by Haller to the corona of certain plants when forming a cup or funnel-shaped appendage. **b.** A dilatation of the podetium in lichens bearing shields on its margin. Cf. SCYPHA.

1777 ROBSON *Brit. Flora* 23 A scyphus is a fructification in the form of a cup, in some species of Archil. **1832** LINDLEY *Introd. Bot.* I. ii. 121 The most common form of appendage is the *corona*,.. forming sometimes an undivided cup, as in Narcissus, when it becomes the *scyphus* of Haller. **1866** *Treas. Bot.*, *Scyphus*. **1871** W. A. LEIGHTON *Lichen-Flora* 63 Scyphi denticulate at the margins. *Ibid.* 64 Dilated upwards into a scyphus.

scyrle, obs. form of SHRILL *a.*

scyrmyssh, obs. form of SKIRMISH *v.*

scyrrhosity, obs. form of SCIRRHOSITY.

scyrt, obs. form of SHORT *v.*

scyrtte, obs. form of SKIRT *sb.*

scysme, obs. form of SCHISM.

†**'scytal(e.** *Obs.* Also 6 **scitale**, 7 **scytal(l, scythale.** [ad. L. *scytalē* (med.L. *scitalus*), a. Gr. σκυτάλη, app. a use of σκυτάλη staff: see next.

Owing to a misreading of σκυτάλην for μυγάλην in Columella VI. xvii (ed. Stephanus 1543), the word was frequently supposed to have the sense of shrew-mouse.

In mod. zoological Latin *scytalē* is used as the name of a genus of snakes (the type of the order *Scytalidæ*), and also as the specific name of a coral-snake (*Tortrix scytale*).]

A serpent mentioned by ancient writers, described as resembling a round staff of uniform thickness. Also, a figure of this as a heraldic bearing.

1572 BOSSEWELL *Armorie* II. 62 O beareth Argente, on a Pale Vert, a Scitale, proper. This serpente is so called, because he shinethe with suche diuersitie of speckles vpon his backe, that all that looke thereon haue wonder, and likinge to see him. **1608** TOPSELL *Serpents* 232 This Scytall is very full of markes or spots vppon the back so variable and delectable, that it possesseth the beholders with admiration. **1613** PURCHAS *Pilgrimage* VI. i. 467 The Scythale is admirable in her varied jacket. **1677** GILPIN *Demonol.* (1867) 421 No otherwise doth he keep them at a gazing admiration of worldly pomp,.. than the serpent Scytale doth with passengers, whom she stays, by amazing them with her beautiful colours, till she have stung them. **1770** J. & W. LANGHORNE *Plutarch, M. Crassus* III. 465 His army resembled the serpents called *Scytalae*.

‖**scytale** ('sɪtəliː). *Antiq.* Also 6 in Latin form **scytala.** [Gr. σκυτάλη staff, also *spec.*: see below.] A method of secret writing practised by the Spartans, consisting in writing the message on a strip of parchment wound spirally round a cylindrical or tapering staff, so that it became illegible when the parchment was unrolled, and could be read only by the use of a staff of precisely the right form and size. Hence, a secret dispatch conveyed by this method.

1580 NORTH *Plutarch, Lysander* (1595) 487 To him selfe they sent immediately that which they call Scytala... The Scytala is in this sort. When the Ephori doe send a Generall, or an Admirall to the warres, they cause two litle round staues to be made [etc.]... These two litle staues they call Scytales. *Ibid.*, This litle scrowle of parchment also is called as the rowle of wodde, Scytala. **1640** G. WATTS tr. *Bacon's Adv. Learn.* VI. 268 A Spartan letter sent once in a Scytale or round cypher'd staffe. **1838** THIRLWALL *Greece* xxxvii. V. 17 A scytalé would at all times be sufficient to procure whatever they wished.

scyte, obs. f. SITE *sb.*[1], SHEET *sb.*

Scyth (sɪθ). *Obs.* exc. *Hist.* Forms: 4 **Sithe (Schyte, Schite,** 5 **Scite, Shite, Scytte),** 7 **Scythe,** 9 **Scyth.** [ad. L. *Scytha*, Gr. Σκύθης.]

a. A Scythian.

1387 TREVISA *Higden* (Rolls) II. 257 Of Egipcians in þe souþ, and of Sithes [MS. *a* Schytes; Caxton, Shites] in the norþ. **1480** CAXTON *Descr. Scot.* (1520) 1/1 Scottes ben called as it were scyttes for they came out of Scicia. **1557** NORTH *Gueuara's Diall. Pr.* (1619) 707/1 The Greekes the Romaines,.. the Scythes were alwayes temperat in eating and drinking. **1596** SPENSER *State Irel.* Wks. (Globe) 632/2 The old English also which there remayneth have gotten up theyr cryes Scythian-like... And herein also lyeth open an other manifest proof that the Irish be Scythes or Scotts. **1871** P. SMITH *Anc. Hist. East* xxiii. §12 (1881) 473 The *Sacæ* of Greek writers on Persian affairs are simply Asiatic Scyths. **1914** D. G. HOGARTH *Ancient East* iii. 122 The predatory Scyth.. probably lacked skill to inscribe them. **1950** [see CIMMERIAN]. **1964** *Listener* 6 Feb. 238/2 So we came to the plain and the Scyths. **1973** R. L. FOX *Alexander* iv. 75 The barbarian Scyths and Thracians.

b. = SCYTHIAN *sb.* 1 b. *rare.*

1972 B. THOMSON *Premature Revolution* I. vii. 130 The 'Scyths' revived the old Slavophile faith in the Russian peasantry, as a bastion of spiritual values in an age of materialism... Usually the 'Scyths' were concerned with purely Russian questions, but Blok's poem *The Scyths* (*Skify*, 1918) reveals a chauvinistic and aggressive side to the movement.

scythe (saɪð), *sb.* Forms: α. 1 **siȝdi, siðe,** 3–6 **syþe,** 4–7 **sith,** 5 **cithe, (sythy),** 5–6 **cythe,** 6 **syith,** 6–7 **syth, sieth,** 7 **siethe, seith, sight, syeth,** 3–9 **sythe,** 4–9 **sithe;** β. 5 **seth,** 7 **saith;** γ. 7 **scith, scithe,** 7– **scythe.** [OE. *siðe* masc., earlier **siȝði* (written *siȝdi* in Epinal Gl.) = LG. *seged, seid, sicht*, ON. *sigð-r* (mod.Icel. *sigð* fem., Norw. *sigd, sigde, sidde* masc.):—OTeut. **segiþjo-z*, f. root **seg-* to cut, whence the synonymous OS. *segisna* (MLG., MDu. *seisene*, Du. *zeisen, zeis*), OHG. *segansa* (MHG. *segense, seinse*, G. *sense*).

The etymologically correct spelling *sithe* was preferred by Johnson, but his authority has not prevailed against the currency of the spelling with *sc*, due to erroneous association with L. *scindere* to cut. Cf. *scissors*.]

1. An agricultural implement for mowing grass or other crops, having a long thin curving blade fastened at an angle with the handle and wielded with both hands with a long sweeping stroke.

α. *c* **725** *Corpus Gloss.* 834 *Falcis*: wudubil, siðe, riftras. *c* **825** *Epinal Gloss.* 62 *Falces*, uudubil, sigdi, riftr. *c* **1000** ÆLFRIC *Hom.* II. 162 Befeoll an siðe of ðam snæde into anum deopan seaðe. **13..** *Coer de L.* 6788 They slowen Sarezynes al soo swythe, As gres fallyth fro the sythe. **1382** WYCLIF *Isa.* ii. 4 Thei shul bete togidere their swerdes in to shares and ther speres in to sithes. **1404** *Durham Acc. Rolls* (Surtees) 396 Item.. 1 fot ax, 1 cithe, 1 hamer. **1523** FITZHERB. *Husb.* §23 Take hede that thy mower mow clene and holde downe the hynder hand of his sith. **1580–3** GREENE *Mamillia* I. 12 The grasse looketh better being vncut, then that which withereth with the sieth. **1612** DRAYTON *Poly-olb.* xvi. 48 Thou sawest great-burthen'd Ships through these thy valleys pass, Where now the sharp-edg'd Sithe sheeres vp the spyring grasse. **1632** MILTON *L'Allegro* 66 And the Mower whets his sithe. **1766** *Ann. Reg.*

62 Samples of home-made sithes. **1822** T. Taylor *Apuleius* vi. 120 There, likewise, were sithes, and all the instruments of harvest. **1828–32** Webster, *Sythe.*

β. **14..** *Nom.* in Wr.-Wülcker 728/40 *Hec falx*, a sykyl, or a seth. **1625** *Althorp MS.* p. lxi, To Gibson one daie waiting on my lo. of Southampton in the parke with the saith yor lop bid him call for 00 01 00.

γ. **1602** J. Bruen in Hinde *Life* (1641) 147 My son.. took up a scith to see how he could mow, and the scith entered in at his stocking. **1716–8** Lady M. W. Montague *Lett.* I. xxxviii. 151 He was.. followed by.. several reapers.. with scythes in their hands, seeming to mow. **1863** Macdonald *D. Elginbrod* I. x. (1871) 47 The day arrived when the sickle must be put into the barley, soon to be followed by the scythe in the oats. **1875** J. Wilson in *Encycl. Brit.* I. 362/1 The common scythe.. is very extensively used for reaping grain in all parts of the kingdom.

2. *transf.* and *fig.*, esp. as the attribute of Time or Death.

1387–8 T. Usk *Test. Love* I. Prol. 99 Sithen al the grettest clerkes.. with their sharpe sythes of conning al mowen and mad therof grete rekes and noble. **1506** *Kal. Sheph.* (Sommer) 90 They fyght and cose on eche other wonder with the sythe of deuyls dredabyll. *c* **1600** Shaks. *Sonn.* xii, And nothing gainst Times sieth can make defence Saue [etc.]. **1659** Pecke *Parnassi Puerp.* 112 Time devours Things; His Sithe our Legs will hit. *a* **1711** Ken *Hymnotheo* Poet. Wks. 1721 III. 185 See how Death preys on humane Race; Out with his Scythe the Tyrant goes, Great Multitudes at once he mows. **1809** Byron *Bards & Rev.* 632 Whet not your scythe, suppressors of our vice! Reforming saints! **1854** Brewster *More Worlds* i. 16 The swarm of human life.. has never been perceptibly reduced by the scythe of famine, of pestilence, or of war. **1883** O. W. Holmes *Loving-cup Song* 29 Old Time his rusty scythe may whet.

3. A weapon having a long curving blade resembling a reaping hook. *Obs.* exc. *Hist.* with reference to scythed chariots (see SCYTHED *a.*).

α. *a* **1300** *Havelok* 2553 Hand-ax, syþe, gisarm, or spere. *a* **1400–50** *Alexander* 3058 For-þi þe chariots in þe chace choppid þaim to deth, þe cartis þat I carpid of with þe kene sithis [*v.r.* sythez]. *c* **1500** *Melusine* 302 But the geaunt stert vp lyghtly, in grete yre, & as geffray passed by, he smote hys hors behynd with hys sythe of fyn stele. **1610** Holland *Camden's Brit.* I. 30 They use axeltrees armed at both ends with hookes and sithes.

4. *attrib.* and *Comb.*: **a.** Simple attrib., as ***scythe-blade, -handle, -smith, -stick, -stroke*** (also *fig.*), ***-sweep, -work; scythe-like*** adj.

a **1400–50** *Alexander* 3023 Chariotis.. sett apire side full of *sythe-bladis, Kene keruand as knyfes. **1829** Scott *Rob Roy* Introd. 2nd half, He supplied the want of guns and swords with scythe-blades set straight upon their handles. **1707** Mortimer *Husb.* (1721) II. 51 It is also good for Rake and *Scythe-handles. *c* **1835** *Encycl. Metrop.* (1845) XXIII. 464/2 Giving the edge of the fin a *scythe-like shape. **1633** J. Clarke *Two-fold Praxis* 24 In the street next above, bee shoesmiths, *sythesmiths, bladesmiths, cutlers. **1890** Amphlett *Hist. Clent* 119 Philip Cix, also a scythesmith. **1831** Loudon *Encycl. Agric.* (1857) §7799 *Scythe-sticks and stones for sharpening scythes, hay-knives. **1913** D. H. Lawrence *Mowers* in *Smart Set* Nov. 12 There's four men mowing down by the river; I can hear the sound of the *scythe strokes, four Sharp breaths swishing. **1940** W. S. Churchill *Into Battle* (1941) 216 This armoured scythe-stroke almost reached Dunkirk—almost but not quite. **1856** Allingham *Mowers* 7 A *scythe-sweep, and a scythe-sweep, We mow the grass together. **1598** Sylvester *Du Bartas* II. ii. III. *Colonies* 713 Their flowry Fleece Affords us *Sithe-work yearly twice or thrice. **1904** Edith Rickert *Reaper* 183 He was stiff with scythe-work.

b. objective, as ***scythe-grinder, -maker, whetting; scythe-bearing*** adj.

1633 Drumm. of Hawth. *Poems* (1656) 165 The old Lucadian *Syth-bearing Sire.. for thee feeles flames of sweet desire. **1619** *Canterb. Marr. Licences* (MS.), Robert Brooke of Goudhurst, *sightgrinder. *Ibid.*, Edward Male of Goudhurst, *sightmaker. **1833** J. Holland *Manuf. Metal* II. 55 Hay and straw knives are manufactured by the scythe-makers. **1857** FitzGerald *Let. to Cowell* 27 June, One wakes to the tune of the Mower's *Scythe-whetting.

c. similative, as † ***scythe-billed, -shaped,*** † ***-tusked*** adjs.

1668 Charleton *Onomast.* 103 *Falcinellus*.. the *Scyth-bill'd Heron. **1815** S. Brookes *Introd. Conchol.* 80 The animal of *Anomia tridentata* has two flat arms somewhat *scythe-shaped. **1612** *Two Noble K.* I. i. 79 Most dreaded Amazonian, that hast slain The *scythe-tusk'd boar.

d. instrumental, as ***scythe-armed*** adj.

1811 Scott *Don Roderick* II. xxv, The scythe-arm'd Giant turn'd his fatal glass. **1838** Thirlwall *Greece* xxxiii. IV. 304 Scythe-armed chariots.

5. Special combinations, as † **scythe-bill**, a suggested name (after mod.L. *Falcinellus*) for the Glossy Ibis; **scythe-chariot** *Hist.* = *scythed chariot* (see SCYTHED *a.*); **scythe-cradle**, a framework of wood fastened to a scythe for carrying the mowings clean into the swath; **scythe-hook, -sickle**, a reaping-hook with a smooth cutting blade as contrasted with one in which the edge is cut into teeth; † **scythe-land** (see quot.); † **scythe-sand** (see quot.); **scythe-snathe, -sned** *dial.*, the curved handle to which the blade of the scythe is attached; **scythe-stone**, a whetstone for scythes; also in *Comb.*

1678 Ray *Willughby's Ornith.* 295 The Falcinellus of Gesner and Aldrovand, which we may English, The *Sithe-Bill. **1695** J. Edwards *Author. O. & N. Test.* III. 215 With these *sithe-chariots they mowed men down. **1695** Kennett *Par. Antiq.* s.v. *Carecta*, In Kent a *Sithe-cradle, or rack of wood fastened to a sithe for carrying the mow'd barley clean into the swath. **1884** *Century Mag.* Jan. 447/1 Grain was reaped with sickles, though '*scythe-cradles' were not unknown. **1844** H. Stephens *Bk. Farm* III. 1079 The smooth-edged sickle, or *scythe-hook. **1597** Skene *De Verb. Sign.* s.v. *Husbandland*, Hvsbandland conteinis commonly 6. aikers of sok & *syith land: That is of sik land as may be tilled with ane pleuch, or may be mawed with ane syith. **1686** Plot *Staffordsh.* 154 An excellent sand to whet their Sithes, whence it has the denomination of *Sithe-Sand. **1844** H. Stephens *Bk. Farm* III. 1055 The *scythe sickle is so called, because of its being provided with a cutting edge. **1845** S. Judd *Margaret* II. i. (1871) 184 His bare head pillowed on a *scythe-snath. **1907** 'J. Halsham' *Lonewood Corner* xix. 212 Ne'er he nor his father afore him ever bought a *scythe-sned. **1688** *Lond. Gaz.* No. 2413/4 Who hath formerly been an Apprentice to a *Scythe-Stone Cutter near Darby. **1879** Rutley *Study of Rocks* xiv. 278 The Rotherham stone is worked for building purposes and for grindstones, and that at Hart Hill for scythe-stones.

scythe (saɪð), *v.* [f. SCYTHE *sb.*]

† **1.** *intr.* To use a scythe. *Obs.* $rare^{-1}$.

1573–80 Baret *Alv.* M 541 He that sietheth with a bill, or he that vseth a sieth or hooke, a mower, *falcarius.* [After Elyot's (and Cooper's) rendering of *Falcarius*: 'He that fighteth with a bill'.]

2. a. *trans.* To cut or mow with a scythe.

1597 Shaks. *Lover's Compl.* 12 Time had not sithed all that youth begun. **1892** Henley *Song of Sword* 9 Where the tall grain is ripe Thrust in your sickles:.. Scything and binding The full sheaves of sovranty.

b. *fig.* To cut down swiftly and drastically.

1970 *Daily Tel.* 12 Mar. 22/3 Net attributable profits are scythed from £602,000 to £210,000.

3. *intr.* To move with a sweeping motion as of one mowing with a scythe.

1897 Kipling *Capt. Courageous* v. 111 The foresail scythed back and forth against the blue sky. **1946** J. W. Day *Harvest Adventure* vii. 107 'Pleu-eu! Pleu-eu! Pleu!' and whimbrel went scything off low across the water, putting up a mixed lot of sandpipers. **1955** E. Pound *Classic Anthol.* II. 94 Feckless Huns town'd in Tsiao, seized Huo, lacking provisions, Scythed into Hao up to its border. **1966** Gillman & Haston *Eiger Direct* v. 107 John scythed up on his skis and stopped in a spray of snow. **1978** *Antiques & Art Monitor* 28 Oct. 23/3 High-rise aerial perspectives of a motorway scything through a city.

scythed (saɪðd), *ppl. a.* [f. SCYTHE *sb.* and *v.* + -ED.]

1. Furnished with a scythe; esp. *Hist.* (= Gr. δρεπανηφόρος, L. *falcatus*) of war-chariots provided with scythes fastened to a revolving shaft projecting from the axle-trees; attributed by classical writers to the Persians and the Britons.

a **1400–50** *Alexander* 3821 For with his florantis olifants him folowed a thousand, Of sithid chariotis. **1618** Bolton *Florus* (1636) 120 Three hundred thousand foot, and not a lesse number of Horse, and of seithed Chariots. **1750** Warton *Verses, Montaubon* 19 Galgacus' scythed, iron car. **1816** Scott *Bl. Dwarf* vi, Let Destiny drive forth her scythed car through the.. trembling mass of humanity. **1922** Joyce *Ulysses* 649 Humanely his driver waited till he (or she) had ended, patient in his scythed car.

2. Cut down with a scythe.

1865 Swinburne *Poems & Ball.* Ser. I. 209 *Before Parting*, And yet who knows what end the scythèd wheat Makes of its foolish poppies' mouths of red?

3. *fig.* Swept over as though by a scythe.

1952 Dylan Thomas *Coll. Poems* 172 Who knows the rocketing-wind will blow The bones out of the hills, And the scythed boulders bleed.

scytheless (ˈsaɪðlɪs), *a.* [f. SCYTHE *sb.* + -LESS.] Without a scythe.

1817 Coleridge *Limbo* 5 Scytheless Time with branny hands. **1857** Ruskin *Pol. Econ. Art* ii. (1868) 98, I tell you, Time is scytheless and toothless; it is we who [etc.].

scytheman (ˈsaɪðmən). Also 8–9 **scythesman.** [f. SCYTHE *sb.* + MAN *sb.*[1]]

1. One who uses a scythe.

1577 Peacham *Gard. Eloq.* P ij b, Reapers cutting downe Corne in euery fielde, Sithmen labouryng harde. **1605** *1st Pt. Jeronimo* III. ii, As sithmen trim the long haird Ruffian fields, So fast they fall. **1797** Coleridge in J. Cottle *Early Recoll.* (1837) I. 215 When the scythes-man o'er his sheaf Caroll'd in the yellow vale. **1844** H. Stephens *Bk. Farm* III. 1050 The scytheman requires a person to follow him and carefully gather the corn he has mown into sheaves in bands. **1894** Crockett *Raiders* 297 Three kinds of sand he brought me to see, but not being a scytheman I could not tell the difference.

b. A member of an irregular body of troops, armed with a scythe as a weapon.

1849 Macaulay *Hist. Eng.* vi. II. 23 Another said that he should be glad to know how the Devonshire trainbands, who had fled in confusion before Monmouth's scythemen, would have faced the household troops of Lewis. **1889** Doyle *Micah Clarke* 138 See that your scythesmen line the quickset hedge upon the right.

2. *fig.* Applied to Time and to Death.

1818 Scott *Rob Roy* x, 'The old scythe-man has moved so rapidly,' I answered, 'that I could not count his strides.' **1844** W. H. Maxwell *Scotland* xxxix. (1855) 305 Time, that villanous old scytheman. **1909** *Daily News* 1 Apr. 4 The stroke of the dread scythesman.

scyther (ˈsaɪðə(r)). [f. SCYTHE *v.* + -ER[1].] A mower; *esp.* with allusion to Time. Cf. SCYTHEMAN.

1863 Macdonald *D. Elginbrod* I. x. (1871) 47 David.. was the best scyther in the whole country side. **1901** Meredith *Reading of Life* 2 And unto the pallid Scyther Either points us.

† **ˈScythiac**, *a. Obs.* [See -AC.] = SCYTHIAN.

1794 Sullivan *View Nat.* II. 280 There is a strong similarity between the Hebrew and the Scythiac languages.

Scythian (ˈsɪθɪən; now freq. ˈsɪðɪən), *a.* and *sb.* Also 6–7 **Sythian.** [f. L. *Scythia*, a. Gr. Σκυθία (f. Σκύθης SCYTH) + -AN.]

A. *adj.*

1. Pertaining to Scythia, an ancient region extending over a large part of European and Asiatic Russia, or to the nomadic people by whom it was inhabited.

1567 Golding *Ovid's Met.* xv. 312 Hypanis That springeth in the Scythian hilles. **1587–90** Marlowe *1st Pt. Tamburl.* I. i. 44 Tamburlaine, that sturdie Scythian thiefe. **1596** Spenser *State Irel.* Wks. (Globe) 630/1 For though it [Nomadism] be an old Scythian use, yet it is very behoofull in that countrey of Ireland. *a* **1625** Beaum. & Fl. *Four Plays in One, Tri. Death* vi, What Scythian snow so white? what crystal chaster? **1776** Mickle tr. *Camoens' Lusiad* Introd. 14 The irruptions of northern or Scythian barbarians. **1882** Ruskin *Bible of Amiens* iii. 100 The northern kingdoms are moated from the Scythian desert by the Vistula.

transf. **1814** Scott *Wav.* xviii, All the domestic accommodations of milk, poultry, butter, &c., were out of the question in this Scythian camp.

2. Special collocations: **Scythian antelope** = SAIGA; **Scythian disease** [for the reason for the name, cf. Herodotus I. cv], atrophy of the male organs of generation, accompanied by loss of masculine attributes (*Syd. Soc. Lex.* 1898); **Scythian insanity**, the mental perversion occurring in the Scythian disease, manifested in the assumption of female dress and habits (*ibid.*); † **Scythian lamb**, = BAROMETZ; **Scythian stone**, some mineral.

1608 Topsell *Serpents* 147 The gall of this beast [*sc.* the Dart] mixed with the Sythian Stone, yealdeth a very good Eye-salue. **1659** R. Lovell *Herbal* 524 Scythian Lamb *Agnus Scyth.* **1781** Pennant *Quadrupeds* I. 86 Scythian Antelope. **1800** Shaw *Gen. Zool.* II. 339 The Saiga or Scythian Antelope, is an inhabitant.. of all the deserts from the Danube and the Dnieper to the river Irtish.

† **3.** *Philol.* Used as a designation for the Ural-Altaic family of languages. *Obs.*

1885 Whitney *Philol.* in *Encycl. Brit.* XVIII. 779/1 Ural-Altaic (Scythian, Turanian) Family.

B. *sb.*

1. a. A person belonging to the race by which Scythia was inhabited; = SCYTH.

1543 Becon *Invect. agst. Swearing, Cert. Laws* Wks. 1560 I. 223 b, The law among the Scythyans was yt, if [etc.]. **1590** Marlowe *2nd Pt. Tamburl.* III. v, Raile not proud Scythian. **1596** *Edward III*, II. i. 72 That it may rayse drops in a Tarters eye, And make a flyntheart Sythian pytifull. **1781** Gibbon *Decl. & F.* xxvi. (1787) II. 563 *note*, In speaking of all, or any, of the northern shepherds of Europe, or Asia, I indifferently use the appellations of *Scythians*, or *Tartars*. **1883** Morfill *Slavonic Lit.* ii. 38, I shall not discuss the question here as to whether the Scythians were a Mongolian or Indo-European race.

b. *Russ. Lit.* An advocate of Scythism (sense c).

1923 *Contemp. Rev.* Aug. 193 There is an immense wealth of pride in these *Scythians*, they heartily and sincerely despise the West. **1970** M. Ginsburg tr. *Zamyatin's Soviet Heretic* 22 Ivanov-Razumnik.. leader of the Scythians, a literary group that included Blok and Bely. **1974** Moore & Parry *Twentieth-Cent. Russ. Lit.* ii. 18 He was now briefly one of the Scythians, who confronted the new social events with fervor and a sense of exultation.

2. The language of Scythia.

1668 Wilkins *Real Char.* I. i. §3. 3 The European Tartar, or Scythian, from which some conceive our Irish to have had its original. **1870** [see BABYLONIAN *sb.* 2]. **1894** [see MEDIC *sb.*[2]]. **1939** L. H. Gray *Foundations of Lang.* xiii. 425 Hesychios.. cites words.. from many non-Classical languages, such as.. Scythian. **1972** W. B. Lockwood *Panorama Indo-Europ. Lang.* xii. 235 The exiguous records of the Median language are of the same character as those of Scythian and Sarmatian.

3. Comb. *Scythian-like* adj. and adv.

1596 Spenser *State Irel.* Wks. (Globe) 632/2 The old English also which there remayneth have gotten up theyr cryes Scythian-like, as the Geraldins Croum-abowe. *Ibid.* 633/1, I thought this manner of lewd crying and howling not impertinent to be noted as uncivill and Scythian-like.

Scythianism: see SCYTHISM c.

Scythic (ˈsɪθɪk), *a.* [ad. L. *Scythicus*, a. Gr. Σκυθικός, f. Σκύθ-ης SCYTH.] Scythian.

1623 Lisle *Ælfric on O. & N. Test.* Pref. 5 But we shall hence, some to the thirsty Moore, To swift Oront of Creet, to Scythicke shore. **1634** Sir T. Herbert *Trav.* (1638) 20 The Arimaspi.. not seldome from their Scythic holes attempting the conquest of Mammon inclos'd in the Rhyphean hills. **1802** Pinkerton *Mod. Geog., Turkey in Asia* II. 15 The original population of these regions consisted chiefly of Scythic nations. **1871** P. Smith *Anc. Hist. East* xxiii. §12 (1881) 473 *note*, The Scythic element in the population of Western Asia.

† **ˈScythical**, *a. Obs.* [Formed as prec. + -AL[1].] Befitting the Scythians, barbarous.

1559 Morwyng *Evonym.* Pref. A ij b, There is also.. a heauenlye water.. whiche boothe Democritus and Mercury Trimegistus knewe: callinge it sometimes a deuine water, sometimes a Scythicall liquor. **1602** F. Hering *Anat.* 20 Such Schythicall.. torturing and massacring of Men.

scything ('saɪðɪŋ), *ppl. a.* [f. SCYTHE *v.* + -ING².] That cuts like a scythe; having the sweeping action of a scythe. Also *fig.*

1822 'B. CORNWALL' *Flood of Thessaly* I. 448 Fierce as the North In March, when scything blasts strip all the bones. **1960** E. HAMILTON *Great Teresa* i. 37 The black, scything wings of swifts dipping and swerving. **1963** *Times* 17 May 5/4 Smith's scything forehand stroke. **1978** *Daily Tel.* 18 Feb. 1 Some victims were killed by collapsing masonry and scything debris.

scything ('saɪðɪŋ), *vbl. sb.* [f. SCYTHE *v.* + -ING¹.] The action of the verb; the result of this, scythed grass, etc. Also *fig.*

1969 *Gloss. Landscape Work (B.S.I.)* v. 21 *Scything*, 1. The cutting of grass with a scythe. 2. Now usually the cutting of long grass, or other vegetation, either with a scythe or by a machine with reciprocating blades. **1969** M. POOLE in R. Blythe *Akenfield* xii. 196 Back she arrived later when I was lying on the scythings. **1978** *Maledicta* II. 232 In order to give you a taste of the 'vilest venom' of scholarly verbal aggression mentioned in our first issue..I wish to share with you excerpts from Zizi Quirk's scything of *Maledicta*.

Scythism ('sɪθɪz(ə)m, 'sɪðɪz(ə)m). [ad. late Gr. Σκυθισμός, f. Σκύθης SCYTH: see -ISM.]

†**a.** The type of paganism to which the religion of the Scythians belonged. *Obs.* **b.** (See quot. 1793.) *Obs.*

1609 BIBLE (Douay) *Gen.* Contin. Ch. 48 The second mother of al Sectes beginning after the floud..was Scythisme. **1793** HELY tr. *O'Flaherty's Ogygia* Pref. 59 The Scythians are looked upon to be the most ancient people. *Ibid.* 70 Where-fore that interval of time..between the deluge and the Babylonian monarchy..is denominated a scythesm, as Epiphanius affirms. **1816** G. S. FABER *Orig. Pagan Idol.* I. 86 From their supposed founders..we may call the one Scythism, and the other Ionism.

c. *Russ. Lit.* A movement among Russian men of letters soon after the Revolution of 1917 which favoured the peasant values of Asiatic Russia as against Western European civilization. Also **'Scythianism**.

The term is a rendering of Russ. *skifstvo*.

1921 D. H. LAWRENCE *Sea & Sardinia* v. 164, I am glad that Russia flies back into savage Russianism, Scythism, savagely self-pivoting. **1923** *Contemp. Rev.* Aug. 193 National Bolshevism is of much more recent growth than either Bolshevism or Scythianism. **1926** *Encycl. Brit.* III. 1070/1 Moscow became the scene of a struggle between what may be called 'Europeanism' and what is known there as 'Scythism'. Scythism, which achieved the miracle of rallying to the Bolshevik standard the Russian reactionaries who were most violently opposed to it, inculcates scorn and hatred of western civilization, and aims at nothing less than Asia's vengeance on Europe. **1958** E. H. CARR *Socialism in One Country* I. ii. 60 After the publication of Blok's poem the name 'Scythism' (Skifstvo) came to be applied, not to a literary movement, but to a tendency which inspired many writers in the first years of the revolution. **1963** G. STRUVE in Hayward & Labedz *Lit. & Revol. in Soviet Russia* 4 R. Ivanov-Razumnik..the main ideologist, in the early days of the Revolution, of the so-called 'Scythianism'. **1972** B. THOMSON *Premature Revol.* I. vii. 130 The peasant poets were..more sympathetic to the Social-Revolutionaries than to the Bolsheviks... Under the guidance of Ivanov-Razumnik they formed a movement, called *Scythianism* ('*Skifstvo*').

'Scythized, *a. rare.* [f. L. *Scyth-a* SCYTH + -IZE + -ED¹.] Assimilated to the Scythians.

1861 W. L. BEVAN *Student's Man. Anc. Geog.* I. iii. §7 (1864) 35 The inhabitants of this district were partly Scythized Greeks, but mainly Scythians.

Scytho- ('saɪθəʊ), combining form of L. *Scytha*, *Scythēs* SCYTH; prefixed (with hyphen) to ethnic sbs. or adjs. with the sense 'partly Scythian and partly...', as in ***Scytho-Aryan, -Greek, -Median***.

1844 W. D. COOLEY *Larcher's Notes on Herod.* IV. cv. II. 57 The Scytho-Greeks. **1871** P. SMITH *Anc. Hist. East* xxiii. §10 (1881) 472 *note*, Which is sometimes expressed by calling them Scytho-Aryans. *Ibid.* §12. 473 The Persian and Scytho-Median columns [of the Achæmenid inscriptions].

'Sdeath (zdɛθ), *int. Obs.* exc. *arch.* A euphemistic abbreviation of *God's death* (see GOD *sb.* 14 a) used in oaths and asseverations.

1606 *Sir G. Goosecappe* I. ii, S'death they put not all their virtues in their smockes..as our Ladies doe. **1607** SHAKS. *Cor.* I. i. 221 Sdeath. **1616** B. JONSON *Ev. Man in Hum.* II. i, 'Sdeath, he mads me. **1697** CIBBER *Woman's Wit* III. 31 S'Death, Sir, is that a Question to ask a Dying Man? **1735** POPE *Prol. Sat.* 61 'Sdeath I'll print it. **1821** SCOTT *Kenilw.* xl, 'Sdeath? to think on it is distraction! **1869** BROWNING *Ring & Bk.* XI. 1279 'Sdeath! Here's a coil raised.

†**sdeign**, *sb. Obs. rare.* In 6 sdeigne, sdaine. [ad. It. *sdegno*, f. *sdegnare*: see next.] Disdain.

1594 SPENSER *Amoretti* v, Scorn of base things, & sdeigne of foule dishonor. **1596** —— *F.Q.* v. v. 51 So she departed, full of griefe and sdaine.

†**sdeign**, *v. Obs.* Also 6 s'dain, sdaine, sdayn, s'deigne, 7 sdain, sdein. [ad. It. *sdegnare*, aphetic var. of *disdegnare* to DISDAIN. Sometimes used as an English shortening of *disdain*.]

1. *trans.* = DISDAIN *v.* in various senses.

1590 SPENSER *F.Q.* III. i. 40 They sdeigned such lasciuious disport. *Ibid.* 55. **1591** —— *M. Hubberd* 679 As if he.. sdeign'd the low degree. **1596** —— *F.Q.* v. v. 44 Yet durst she not disclose her fancies wound,..for doubt of being sdayned. **1596** FITZ-GEFFREY *Sir F. Drake* xxv. B 5, Sdaine nott that our harsh plaints should beate your eares. **1599** H. BUTTES *Dyets Drie Dinner* Aa3, Come welcome Guest: s'deigne not..this shot-free entertainement. **1614** DRUMM. OF HAWTH. *Tears Death Mœliades* A3b, The Shepheards left their Flocks with downe-cast Eyes, Sdaining to looke vp to the angrie Skies. **1667** MILTON *P.L.* IV. 50 Lifted up so high I sdeind subjection.

2. *intr.* = DISDAIN *v.* 3.

1590 MARLOWE *Edw. II*, v. ii. H4b, Why yongling, s'dainst thou so of Mortimer?

†**'sdeignful**, *a. Obs.* Also 6 sdainfull, 8 'sdeignfull. [f. SDEIGN *sb.* + -FUL.] Disdainful.

1596 SPENSER *F.Q.* v. ii. 33 In sdeignfull wize he drew vnto him neare. **1598** TOFTE *Alba* (1880) 22 A Sdainfull thought through Hatred doth arise. **1600** FAIRFAX *Tasso* VII. xlii. 125 The Prince (whose lookes his sdainfull anger show). *Ibid.* XX. cxxviii. 389 She shrikes, and twines away her sdeignfull eies. **1748** SHENSTONE *Schoolmistress* xxix. in Dodsley *Poems* I. 259 As he who now with 'sdeignfull fury thrill'd Surveys mine work; and levels many a sneer.

†**'Sdeynes**, *int. Obs.* Shortened form of *God's deynes*, *God's dines*: see DINES.

1616 B. JONSON *Ev. Man in Hum.* II. i, 'Sdeynes, I know not what I should say to him, i' the whole world. [**1601** *reads* Faith...] *Ibid.* II. ii, 'Sdeynes, and I swallow this, Ile nere draw my sword..againe. [**1601** *reads* S'blood and I...]

†**'Sdiggers**, *int.* = *God's diggers* (see GOD *sb.* 14).

1687 A. LOVELL tr. *Bergerac's Com. Hist.* 25 S'diggers.

‖**'sdrucciola**, *a. Obs. rare.* [It. *sdrucciola* (sc. *rima*), fem. of *sdrucciolo*), lit. 'slippery', whence Sp. *esdrújulo*, used similarly with reference to versification.] Epithet of that kind of rhyme in which the words ending the lines are accented on the antepenultimate; trisyllabic (rhyme).

English writers on verse have sometimes used *sdrucciolo*, or the phrase *versi sdruccioli*, as a foreign technical term, esp. in referring to Italian poetry.

a **1586** SIDNEY *Apol. Poetry* (Arb.) 71 Lastly, euen the very ryme it selfe, the Italian cannot put in the last silable, by the French named the Masculine ryme, but still in the next to the last, which the French call the Female; or the next before that, which the Italians terme *Sdrucciola*. The example..of the *Sdrucciola* [is] *Femina, Semina*. **1605** CHAPMAN *All Fools* II. i. 176 In any Rime Masculine, Feminine, Or Sdruciolla [*printed* Sdrnciolla].

†**se**, *pron.* (*def. art.*) *OE.* and early *ME.*: see THE.

‖**se** (se), *sb. Chinese Mus.* Also **che, she, tche.** [a. Chinese *sè*.] A twenty-five-stringed plucked musical instrument, somewhat similar to the zither.

This ancient instrument was already widely used during the Spring and Warring States period (770–476 B.C.). The number of strings was not fixed in ancient times. In quot. 1955, wrongly described as a lute.

1874 C. ENGEL *Catal. Mus. Instruments in S. Kensington Mus.* 53 The ancient stringed instruments, the *kin* and *chê*, were of the dulcimer kind. *Ibid.* 182 *Tche*. Wood, mounted with bone. Sixteen thin brass wires. The movable bridges belonging to the instrument are wanting. **1884** J. A. VAN AALST *Chinese Mus.* 62 The Sê..is said to have been invented by P'ao Hsi.., and to have had originally 50 strings... But the sê now in use has 25 strings..elevated on a movable bridge. **1908** A. C. MOULE in *Jrnl. N. China Branch R. Asiatic Soc.* XXXIX. 108 Shê (Che)... A horizontal psaltery, curved above and flat below... There are twenty-five silk strings..stretched along the body. **1955** A. FANG in E. Pound *Classic Anthol.* p. xi, Of the two kinds of lute, the *k' in* has seven strings and the *se* twenty-five. **1977** KWANG-CHIH CHANG *Archaeol. Anc. China* (ed. 2) ix. 402 Remains of wooden bases for the musical instrument *se* have been collected from the tombs.

se, obs. form of SAY *sb.*³

1567 *Wills & Inv. N.C.* (Surtees 1835) I. 267, xxix milk bowells & skeles, one stand, one se, ij kyrnes.

se, obs. form of SO *adv.*, SEE *sb.* and *v.*, SHE.

se-, *prefix*, occurring only in Latin derivatives, represents the L. *sē-*, identical with the OLatin *sē* (also *sēd*) prep. and adv., without, apart. With prepositional force the L. *sē-* occurs in one or two adjs., as *sēcūrus* secure (from **sē cūrā* without care); with advb. force (= apart) it is chiefly found in verbs, of which the following (as also their derivatives) have come into English in adapted forms: *sēcēdere, sēcernĕre, sēclūdere, sēdūcĕre, sēgregāre, sēparāre*. The form *sēd-* occurs in *sēditio* sedition (lit. 'going apart').

The L. *sē, sēd* is believed to be related to the pronoun *sē*, oneself. It is disputed whether the *d* of *sēd* is an ablative sign or represents a particle *-de*.

sea (siː), *sb.* Forms: 1 sǽ, (2 seo), 2–3 sæ, 2–6 se, see, 4 (*Ayenb.*) ze, (seo, sse), 4–5 cee, 4–6 *Sc.* sey, 6 *Sc.* seye, sie, 2– sea. *Pl.* 1 sǽs, sǽas, sǽ, 4 sen, 4–5 sees, 4–6 (chiefly *Sc.*) seis, 6 seaes, sease, (saezes), seeis, *Sc.* seyis, seyes, 6– seas. [Common Teut.: OE. *sǽ* str. masc. and fem. corresponds to OFris. *sê* masc., OS. *sêo, sêu*, dat. *sêwa* masc. (MLG. *sê*, MDu. *see* masc. and fem., Du. *zee* fem.), OHG. *sêo, sê*, dat. *sêwe* masc., sea, lake, pond (MHG. *sê* masc. and fem., sea, lake, mod.G. *see* masc., lake, *see* fem., sea), ON. *sǽ-r, sjá-r, sjó-r* masc. (Sw. *sjö*, Da. *sø*), Goth. *saiw-s* masc., sea, also marsh:—OTeut. **saiwi-z*.

The word has no certain affinities, and it is doubtful whether the *w* represents a pre-Teut. *w* or (by Verner's Law) a pre-Teut *qᵘ* (or *kw*). On the assumption of a guttural root, and of the priority of the sense 'marsh' (occurring in Gothic) it has been suggested that the word may be cogn. w. OHG. *gisig* (*gisic, gezik*), found in glosses as a collective for ponds or marshes (*stagna, paludes*), and with the OHG. *sîgan* to flow down, sink, OE. *sīgan* to descend: see SYE *v.*]

I. The simple word.

1. a. The continuous body of salt water that covers the greater part of the earth's surface. Often *poet.* with epithet as *broad, deep* (see DEEP *a.* 1), †*large, salt* (see SALT *a.*¹ 1), †*side, wide, wild*, etc.

Since Early Middle English always with prefixed article, exc. in phrases with preps. (see esp. 1 c and 10–17).

Beowulf 2394 Ofer sæ side. *c* **1205** LAY. 30496 On þare sæ brade. *c* **1275** *Moral Ode* 82 in *O.E. Misc.* 61 He makede fysses in þe sea. *c* **1385** CHAUCER *L.G.W.* 2163 In an yle, amid the wilde see. *c* **1386** —— *Knt.'s T.* 1098 Fletynge in the large see. *c* **1400** *Destr. Troy* 1982 Blouen to þe brode se. *c* **1430** *Syr Gener.* 6553 Toward the cee he rode a pase. **1593** SHAKS. *Rich. II*, II. i. 46 This precious stone, set in the siluer sea. **1647** H. MORE *Philos. Devot.* 32 As the thankfull Rivers pay What they borrowed of the Sea. **1779** COWPER *Olney Hymns* III. xv. 3 God moves in a mysterious way, His wonders to perform; He plants his footsteps in the sea, And rides upon the storm. **1807** WORDSW. *Sonn. to Liberty* I. xii, Two Voices are there; one is of the sea, One of the mountains; each a mighty Voice. **1842** TENNYSON *Farewell* 1 Flow down, cold rivulet, to the sea.

b. For *ocean sea, sea ocean, sea of ocean*, see OCEAN *sb.* 1. Also ***the great sea (of ocean)***.

c **1290** *St. Michael* 632 in *S. Eng. Leg.* I. 317 The gret se of occean. *Ibid.* 654 þe eorþe amidde þe grete se ase a luyte bal is round. **1500–20** DUNBAR *Poems* lxvi. 67 Our all the grit se occeane. **1513** DOUGLAS *Æneis* IV. ix. 14 Neir by the end of the gret occiane see, Thar as the son..gois doun.

c. Often coupled with *land*, to express the idea of the whole surface of the earth; similarly † ***sea and earth, sea and sand***. Also with preps., as ***by land and sea, on sea or land***, etc.

c **1000** *Ags. Gosp.* Matt. xxiii. 15 Ðe befarað sæ & eorþan þæt ʒe don anne elþeodine. **1338** R. BRUNNE *Chron.* (1810) 281 At his wille to be, bi se & bi land. **1340** *Ayenb.* 37 Of zuichen þer byeþ uele maneres ine londe and ine ze. *a* **1352** MINOT *Poems* (ed. Hall) iii. 1 God þat schope both se and sand. *c* **1366** CHAUCER *A.B.C.* 50 Neither in erthe nor in see. *c* **1386** —— *Man of Law's Prol.* 127 Ye seken lond and see for yowre wynnynges. *a* **1400** *Pistill of Susan* 254 Was neuer more sorweful segge bi see nor bi sand. **1475** *Bk. Noblesse* (Roxb.) 8 Batailes bothe by lond and see. **1530** LYNDESAY *Test. Papyngo* 756 Quhat thow hes hard, be landis, or be seis, Off ws Kirkmen. **1805** WORDSW. *Eleg. Stanzas, Peele Castle* 15 The light that never was, on sea or land. **1849** MACAULAY *Hist. Eng.* iii. I. 300 Cimon and Lysander, Pompey and Agrippa, had fought battles by sea as well as by land.

d. *pl.* Different parts or tracts of the ocean. (Often merely *poet.* or *rhetorical*, like *waters*.)

c **825** *Vesp. Psalter* xxiii. 2 He ofer sæas [Vulg. *super maria*] ʒesteaðelade hie. *c* **1000** ÆLFRIC *Gen.* i. 10 And God ʒeciʒde þa drignisse eorðan and þæra wætera ʒegaderunga he het sæs [Vulg. *maria*]. *c* **1430** LYDG. *Lyke the Audience* 44 in *Pol. Rel. & L. Poems* (1903) 49 Shipmen..that haue experience In troubly seis. **1550** BP. DAY in Ellis *Orig. Lett.* Ser. III. III. 303 No lesse vnpleasaunt..than it is to the merchaunte to sayle againe in those seeis wherin he hathe suffered shipwrack before. **1600** *Will* in *Yorks. Archæol. Jrnl.* (1902) XVII. 121 In the name of Gode, the maker of heven and yerth, the saezes and all that therin ys. **1605** SHAKS. *Macb.* II. ii. 62 This my Hand will rather The multitudinous Seas incarnadine. **1820** KEATS *Ode to Nightingale* vii, Magic casements, opening on the foam Of perilous seas. **1871** R. ELLIS *Catullus* iv. 18 To carry thence a master o'er the surly seas.

e. In a more or less pregnant use, with reference to naval operations, the shipping trade, the profession or employment of a sailor, life on shipboard, etc. ***to keep the sea***: to prevent the enemy from occupying it, to keep it clear for one's own ships and traffic.

1338 R. BRUNNE *Chron.* (1810) 161 Bernard of Bayoun, þat was kepand þe se [orig. *ke la mer gardait*]. *c* **1386** CHAUCER *Prol.* 276 He wolde the see were kept for any thing Bitwixe Middelburgh and Orewelle. **1414** *26 Pol. Poems* xiii. 108 Whanne ʒe han made pes wiþynne,..Strengþe ʒoure marche, and kepe þe see. **15..** '*Doun by ane Rever*' 41 in *Dunbar's Poems* (1893) II. 306 Gif thow beis ane marchand man, And wynnis thy living be the see. **1556** *Chron. Grey Friars* (Camden) 18 Thys yere the lorde Talbot..was made ..amyralle of the see. **1625** BACON *Ess., Greatness Kingd.* (Arb.) 489 To be Master of the Sea, is an Abridgement of a Monarchy. *Ibid.* 491 The Command of the Seas. *a* **1674** CLARENDON *Hist. Reb.* XI. §64 Who did not think that the fleet could have been so soon ready for sea. **1707** FREIND *Peterborow's Cond. Sp.* 178 Without the assistance of the sea, the best dispositions in Italy are useless. **1745** *Life Bampfylde-Moore Carew* 9 His Friends..put him on board a Man of War, but neither the Sea, nor any settled Employ agreeing with his wandering Inclinations, he soon forsook the King's Service. **1776** ADAM SMITH *W.N.* II. v. I. 447 The antient Egyptians had a superstitious antipathy to the sea. **1849** MACAULAY *Hist. Eng.* iii. I. 302 As soon as he came back from sea he was made Colonel of a regiment of foot. **1889** *Sat. Rev.* 16 Mar. 304/1 We are afraid that few Englishmen at present claim the sovereignty of the seas for their country.

f. Proverbs, proverbial phrases, and similitudes.

1591 SHAKS. *Two Gent.* IV. iii. 33 A heart As full of sorrowes, as the Sea of sands. **1601** —— *Twel. N.* II. iv. 103 As hungry as the Sea. **1637–1894** [see DEVIL *sb.* 22 b]. **1614** T. GENTLEMAN *England's Way to win Wealth* 45 *marg.*, The Sailors Prouerbe: The Sea and the Gallowes refuse none.

g. high sea. (Now usually *pl.*) The deep or open sea; the main sea or main. *spec.* in *Law* (*sing.* and *pl.*): (*a*) The main sea; the sea as far as it is regarded as being within the jurisdiction of the courts of admiralty; (*b*) The area of the sea not within the territorial jurisdiction of any nation, but the free highway of all nations.

Cf. F. *haute mer*, L. *altum* (*mare*), and the OE. compound *héahsæ* quoted below.

[*a* **1000** *Boeth. Metr.* xi. 3 Se is eac wealdend woruldȝesceafta heofones & eorðan & heahsæ.] *c* **1300** *Havelok* 719 And sone did he leyn in [a ship] an ore, And drou him to þe heye se. *a* **1400–50** *Alexander* 61 He saȝe þam in þe hiȝe see sailand to-gedire. **1490** CAXTON *Eneydos* vi. 27 Whan they were well on the waye oute of the lande, in the hye see. *c* **1532** LD. BERNERS *Huon* xlvi. 155 They..came in to the hye see and had wynde at wyll. **1765** BLACKSTONE *Comm.* I. Introd. iv. 107 The main or high seas are part of the realm of England. **1836** W. IRVING *Astoria* III. xvii. 226 They had heard of the frigate Phœbe and the Isaac Todd being on the high seas. **1888** BRYCE *Amer. Commw.* I. 580 Piracies and felonies committed on the high seas.

2. a. A part of the general body of salt water, having certain land-limits or washing a particular coast, and having a proper name, as *the Red, Black, Irish, Adriatic Sea.* †*the great sea*: the Mediterranean. *the Severn Sea* (arch.): the Bristol Channel. †Formerly sometimes in pl., as *the Red, Irish, Indian Seas*; cf. NARROW SEAS.

c **825** *Vesp. Psalter* cxxxv. 13 Se todaelde ðone readan sae. *c* **1290** *St. Michael* 636 in *S. Eng. Leg.* I. 317 Ech oþur se among us here, ne beo heo so gret non, Nis bote a lime of þulke se. **1382** WYCLIF *Numb.* xxxiv. 6 The west plage forsothe shal begynne fro the greet see. [So **1611** and **1884** (*Revised*)] **1390** GOWER *Conf.* I. 362 To passe over the grete See To werre and sle the Sarazin. **1500–20** DUNBAR *Poems* viii. 13 To the Turk sey all land did his name dreid. **1533** BELLENDEN *Cron. Scot.* I. (1541) A i, Pharo..quhais son..wes drownit..wᵗ all his army in yᵉ reid seis. **1563** SACKVILLE *Induct. Mirr. Mag.* v, The Beare, that in the Iryshe seas had dipt His griesly feete. **1577–87** HOLINSHED *Chron.* I. 167/1 The Danes..comming into the Seuerne sea. **1614** T. GENTLEMAN *England's Way to win Wealth* 20 When as they [*sc.* herrings] come into Yermouth Seas yearely about S. Luke, and sometimes before. **1634** SIR T. HERBERT *Trav.* 43 The River Indus, which their ingulfes herselfe into the Indian Seas. **1635** SWAN *Spec. Mundi* vi. §2 (1643) 187 The sea, is a part of the ocean, to which we Cannot come but through some strait. **1641** EVELYN *Diary* 28 Sept., We sailed over a sea call'd the Plaet, which is an exceeding dangerous water. **1886** *Encycl. Brit.* XXI. 578/2 Any part of the ocean marked off from the general mass of water may be called a sea. In geography the name is loosely applied: for instance, the Arabian Sea is an open bay, Hudson's Bay is an enclosed sea.

b. *the four seas*: the seas bounding Great Britain on the four sides. Phr. *within the four seas* = in Great Britain.

a **1325** *MS. Rawl. B.* 520 lf. 30 þe chef lordes..þat beȝ of plener age ant bi þinne þe four sen ant out of prisone. *a* **1400–50** *Alexander* 4406 þe soile ne þe foure sees suffice ȝowe nouthire. **1642, 1886** [see FOUR *a.* 1].

c. *Astr.* [tr. L. *mare* (see MARE⁴).] The name of 'seas' is still given to those darker portions of the moon's surface which were formerly supposed to be covered with water.

1667 R. HOOKE *Micrographia* I. lx. 245 Those mountains, which are by Hevelius call'd the Apennine Mountains, and some other, which seem to border on the Seas of the Moon. **1698** C. HUYGENS *Celestial Worlds Discover'd* II. 130 Those vast countries which appear darker than the other, commonly taken for and call'd by the name seas, are discover'd with a good long telescope, to be full of little round cavities. **1833** J. F. W. HERSCHEL *Treat. Astron.* vi. 229 What is, moreover, extremely singular in the geology of the moon is, that although nothing having the character of seas can be traced, (for the dusky spots which are commonly called seas, when closely examined, present appearances incompatible with the supposition of deep water,) yet there are large regions perfectly level, and apparently of a decided alluvial character. **1873** PROCTOR *Moon* 383 Index to the Map of the Moon. Table I. Grey Plains, usually called Seas. **1907** G. P. SERVISS *Moon* iii. 146 This..does not invalidate what I have said about the lunar 'seas', or plains, darkening near sunset more rapidly than we should expect them to do, as a simple result of the low angle at which the sunlight strikes them. **1949** *Jrnl. Brit. Interplanetary Soc.* VIII. 185 The origin of the characteristic features of the lunar surface, craters, mountain ranges and 'seas', is far from being understood. **1974** *Times* 17 Apr. 16/3 It seems that the maria and the basins of the lunar 'seas' are of volcanic origin.

3. A large lake or landlocked sheet of water, whether salt or fresh. *Obs.* exc. in *inland sea* and in proper names, as the Sea of Galilee, the Dead Sea, the Caspian Sea, the Sea of Aral.

c **893** K. ÆLFRED *Oros.* I. i. §9 þeah sume men secgen þæt [the Nile] þær wyrcð micelne sæ [*vastissimo lacu exundare*]. *c* **1000** *Ags. Gosp.* John vi. 1 Æfter þyson for se hælend ofer þa galileiscan sæ, seo is tiberiadis. *a* **1225** *Ancr. R.* 230 And te swin anonriht urnen & adreinten ham suluen iðer see. *c* **1250** —— [see DEAD SEA]. **1375** BARBOUR *Bruce* xv. 275 A myle wes betuix the seis. **1590** [see INLAND B. 1]. **1665** SIR T. HERBERT *Trav.* (1677) 186 This [the Caspian], as other Seas, is a gathering together of perpetual Waters nourished with Springs. **1876** *Encycl. Brit.* V. 176/1 The Caspian Sea ..is the largest of those salt lakes or closed inland seas which may be considered as 'survivals' of former oceanic areas.

4. The volume of water in the sea considered in regard to the ebb and flow of the tide. †*full sea*, high tide (also *fig.*) †*the sea was in*, it was high water.

c **1000** *Sax. Leechd.* III. 176 þonne þu wyte þæt sæ si ful. *c* **1205** LAY. 22019 Whænne þa sævledeð. *Ibid.* 22025 þenne þa sæ falleð in. **1390** GOWER *Conf.* I. 35 The See now ebbeth, now it floweth. *c* **1391** CHAUCER *Astrol.* II. §46 In which place of the firmament the mone being, maketh fulle see. **1470** HENRY *Wallace* x. 419 The sey was in, at thai stoppyt and stud; On loud he cryt and bad thaim tak the flud. *a* **1500** *Brut* (Lamb. MS.) 583 Remembres how ye drowned at full see. **1536** in *Sel. Pleas Crt. Admiralty* (1894) I. 58 Goyng from the porte of London at a full see with a full wynde. **1621** BURTON *Anat. Mel.* Democr. to Rdr. 27 A Satyrrical Roman in his time thought all vice, folly, and madness were at a full sea. **1677** W. HUBBARD *Narrative* (1865) I. 181 But it was now full Sea with Philip his Affairs. **1805** FORSYTH *Beauties Scot.* III. 512 During spring tides these sluices are opened, and at full sea they are shut.

5. a. With an epithet indicating the roughness or smoothness of the waves, the presence or absence of swell, etc. Hence without qualification = a heavy swell, rough water.

c **888** K. ÆLFRED *Boeth.* xiv. §1 Ful oft we faȝeniað smyltre sæ. *c* **1205** LAY. 12005 þe sæ wes wunder ane wod and ladliche iwraððed. **1390** GOWER *Conf.* I. 282, I wode as doth the wylde Se. **1555** TOWRSON in *Hakluyt's Voy.* (1589) 103 We..found the entrance very ill, by reason that the sea goeth so high. **1641** EVELYN *Diary* 27 Sept., We..sailed again with a contrary and impetuous wind, and a terrible sea. *c* **1743** WOODROOFE in *Hanway's Trav.* (1762) I. IV. lix. 275 When there is any sea, the breakers are visible. **1745** P. THOMAS *Jrnl. Anson's Voy.* 114 We found a large underrolling Sea. **1769–80** FALCONER *Dict. Marine* s.v., A long sea implies an uniform and steady motion of long and extensive waves; on the contrary, a short sea is when they run irregularly, broken, and interrupted, so as frequently to burst over a vessel's side or quarter. **1834** MARRYAT *P. Simple* xxviii, We were now past Devil's Point, and the sea was very heavy. **1837** T. HOOK *Jack Brag* xx, It was pitch-dark, a good deal of sea on. **1840** LONGF. *Wreck of Hesperus* xi, Some ship in distress, that cannot live In such an angry sea! **1865** *Daily Tel.* 8 Dec. 5/6 During the passage..they had continued fine weather, and no sea.

b. The direction of the waves or swell.

1769–80 FALCONER *Dict. Marine, Sea*..is..applied by sailors..to their [waves'] particular progress or direction. Thus they say,..the sea sets to the southward. Hence a ship is said to head the sea, when her course is opposed to the setting or direction of the surges. *Ibid.* II, *Franchir la lame*, to head the sea; to sail against the setting of the sea.

c. A large heavy wave.

1582 STANYHURST *Æneis* I. (Arb.) 21 Theire ships too larboord doo nod, seas monsterus haunt theym. **1632** LITHGOW *Trav.* III. 93 Two huge broken Seas, which twice couered the..boat. **1769–80** FALCONER *Dict. Marine, Sea*..is..applied by sailors, to a single wave... Thus they say, a heavy sea broke over our quarter, or we shipped a heavy sea. **1861** LADY DUFF-GORDON in F. Galton *Vac. Tourists* (1864) 121 A sea struck us on the weather side. **1892** W. PIKE *Barren Ground N. Canada* 26 The heavy fresh-water seas broke with great violence on the weather shore.

d. Roughness of the sea brought about by wind blowing at the time.

1927 G. BRADFORD *Gloss. Sea Terms* 152/1 The waves prevailing at any time are spoken of collectively as the sea, but they must be due to the wind then blowing. **1970** J. VERHOOGEN et al. *Earth* vii. 341/1 In the presence of the generating wind, waves have steep, sharp, asymmetric crests, and broad troughs, and the whole water surface is irregularly choppy. This condition is known as sea. **1977** *Offshore Engineer* July 35/1 In August 1975, the LWC began by using graphical methods to produce sea-swell forecast charts, combining 'sea', or wind-driven waves and 'swell', which is persistent wave movement continuing after the wind has dropped.

6. *salt* or *bitter sea*: sea-water. *poet.*

1602 MARSTON *Antonio's Rev.* IV. ii. G 3 b, They'l..eat like salt sea in his siddowe ribs. **1697** DRYDEN *Virg. Georg.* IV. 622 His finny Flocks about their Shepherd play, And rowling round him, spirt the bitter Sea. **1840** LONGF. *Wreck of Hesperus* xxi, The salt sea was frozen on her breast.

7. *fig.* With reference to metaphorical sailing, drowning, waves, etc.; also, a copious or overwhelming quantity or mass (*of* something). See also 4.

a **1200** *Vices & Virtues* 45 On ðessere michele sea of ðare bitere woreld. **1574** HIGINS *Mirr. Mag.* I. Induct. v, Sithe those on whom, for Fortunes giftes we stare, Ofte sooniste sinke in greatest seas of care. *a* **1586** SIDNEY *Apol. Poetrie* (Arb.) 59 A whole Sea of examples woulde present themselues. **1602** SHAKS. *Ham.* III. i. 59 To take Armes against a Sea of troubles. **1613** —— *Hen. VIII*, III. ii. 360, I haue ventur'd..This many Summers in a Sea of Glory, But farre beyond my depth. **1632** MASSINGER *Emp. East* III. ii, The peoples ioy In seas of acclamations flow in, To wait on yours. **1667** MILTON *P.L.* x. 718 In a troubl'd Sea of passion tost. **1692** T. WATSON *Body Divin.* 365 Men will for a drop of Pleasure drink a Sea of Wrath. **1816** SCOTT *Antiq.* i, The elder traveller..plunged, nothing loath, into a sea of discussion concerning urns, vases [etc.]. **1822** LAMB *Elia* Ser. II. *Conf. Drunkard*, To waste whole seas of time upon those who pay it back in little inconsiderable drops of grudging applause. **1872** BAGEHOT *Physics & Pol.* (1876) 220 A complex sea of forces and passions trouble men in life and in action.

8. *transf.* **a.** A large level tract (*of* some material substance or aggregate of objects).

1585 T. WASHINGTON tr. *Nicholay's Voy.* IV. x, In al this sandy sea, is found no water. **1644** EVELYN *Diary* 2 Nov., We could perceive nothing but a sea of thick cloudes. **1654** *Ibid.* 22 July, After dinner,..we passed over the goodly plaine, or rather sea of carpet. **1667** MILTON *P.L.* III. 440 So on this windie Sea of Land, the Fiend Walk'd up and down alone. **1770** LANGHORNE *Plutarch* (1851) II. 598/2 The billows of an immense sea of sand surrounding the whole army. **1849** MACAULAY *Hist. Eng.* x. II. 655 All the space as far as Charing Cross was one sea of heads. **1862** MISS BRADDON *Lady Audley* xxxvii, His uncle's wife, in a criminal dock, hemmed in on every side by a sea of eager faces. **1869** TOZER *Highl. Turkey* I. 340 The open country extends in a sea of green vegetation.

b. Hyperbolically, a great quantity of liquid, esp. (in figurative context) of blood. So, allusively, *Red Sea* (see 2), with reference to blood or wine.

1598 CHAPMAN *Hero & Leander* iii. 323 And all this while the red sea of her blood Ebd with Leander. **1646** QUARLES *Sheph. Oracles* vii. 83 Oyl-steep'd Anchovis, landed from his brine, Came freely swimming in red seas of wine. **1756** BURKE *Nat. Soc.* Wks. I. 77 These wars, which have spilled such seas of blood. **1821** SCOTT *Kenilw.* i, We will have one of Friar Bacon's pupils..to conjure them [such troublesome thoughts] away..—Or, what say you to laying them in a glorious red sea of claret, my noble guest? **1864** LOWELL *Fireside Trav.* 239 The ghost of a creed..may be laid, after all, only in a Red Sea of blood.

c. *Physics.* A (physical or mathematical) space filled with particles of a certain kind, *esp.* one in which only the particles near the boundary or surface are significant.

1955 [see FERMI 1]. **1965** PHILLIPS & WILLIAMS *Inorg. Chem.* I. vi. 207 Because there are electron energy levels lying only very little above the surface of the calm Fermi sea, electrons can take up energy at normal temperatures in a metal and so make a contribution to the specific heat. **1972** *Sci. Amer.* Apr. 26/3 Once an atom has lost an electron it becomes a positive ion that finds itself in a deep electrostatic potential well created by the surrounding sea of negative electrons. **1979** *Ibid.* Sept. 76/3 These events are explained by interactions involving a 'sea' of quarks and anti-quarks that have a virtual existence in the vicinity of a proton.

9. *Antiq.* The great brazen laver in the Jewish Temple. [Literally from Heb.]

1382 WYCLIF *1 Kings* vii. 23 He made forsothe the ȝoten see. *c* **1450** *Mirour Saluacioun* (Roxb.) 47 Thilk see of brasse Whilk in the entree of the Temple of Jerusalem sette was. **1899** SAYCE *Early Israel* vi. 251 In the court of the temple was a 'sea' or 'deep', like that which was made by Solomon.

II. Phrases.

10. at sea. a. Out on the sea, on ship-board; (sailing, trafficking, fighting, etc.) on the sea; in employment as a sailor. Also †*at the seas.*

a **1300** *Cursor M.* 13284, At see sant Iohn and Iam he fand. **1585** T. WASHINGTON tr. *Nicholay's Voy.* I. v. 4 Wee discouered at the Seas [Fr. *en plaine mer*] two Foystes. **1596** SHAKS. *Merch. V.* I. i. 177 Thou knowst that all my fortunes are at sea. **1601** HOLLAND *Pliny* XXXIV. v. II. 491 The beakeheads..which were taken from them in a conflict at sea. **1672** C. MANNERS in *12th Rep. Hist. MSS. Comm.* App. v. 24 The Duke is at sea allready, to draw by his example others to the fleete. *a* **1687** SIR W. PETTY *Polit. Arith.* iii. (1690) 55 To persuade the World how considerable the King of France was..at Sea. **1793** [see AT *prep.* 5]. **1836** MARRYAT *Midsh. Easy* XIX, I have not been long at sea, and, of course, cannot know much about these things.

b. *fig.* In a state of mind resembling the condition of a ship which is out of sight of land and has lost her bearings; in a state of uncertainty or perplexity, at a loss. Also *all at sea.*

1768 BLACKSTONE *Comm.* III. xxvii. 440 If a court of equity were still at sea, and floated upon the occasional opinion which the judge who happened to preside might entertain of conscience in every particular case. **1818** CRUISE *Digest* (ed. 2) I. 486 If there were not the same rules of property in all courts, all things would be as it were at sea; and under the greatest uncertainty. **1855** DICKENS *Dorrit* II. ix, Mrs. Tickit ..was so plainly at sea on this part of the case..that Clennam was much disposed to regard the appearance as a dream. **1893** SELOUS *Trav. S.E. Africa* 219, I was rather surprised to find that he seemed all at sea, and had no one ready to go with me.

c. *worse things happen at sea* and varr.: a consolatory catch-phrase.

1829 P. EGAN *Boxiana* 2nd Ser. II. 346 The Fancy were too game to complain..., contenting themselves with the old saying, 'that worse accidents occur at sea!' **1869** C. H. SPURGEON *John Ploughman's Talk* v. 41 To be poor is not always pleasant, but worse things than that happen at sea. **1948** 'N. SHUTE' *No Highway* xii. 297 Oh well, worse things happen at sea. I expect we shall get over it. **1978** M. KENYON *Deep Pocket* viii. 97 Worse things 'ave 'appened at sea, he told himself, if 'e shoots..you'll 'ardly feel a thing.

11. beyond (the) sea or seas. Out of the country, in foreign parts, abroad. Cf. BEYOND B. 1. For *beyond-sea* as adj. see BEYOND D.

c **900** tr. *Bæda's Hist.* v. xix. (1890) 458 Mid þy he þa ȝena wæs beȝeondan sæ wuniende. *a* **1122** *O.E. Chron.* an. 1041 (MS. C.) Fram beȝeondan sæ. *c* **1205** LAY. 29149 Sum fleh bi-ȝeonden sæ in to Bruttaine. **1340** *Ayenb.* 165 Ine þe londe be-yende þe ze. **1485** *Rec. St. Mary at Hill* 28 A standyng bed, corven with estrich borde of beyond see makyng. **1536** in *Sel. Pleas Crt. Admiralty* (1894) I. 56 All my goods whersoever they may be found as well on this syde the see as beyende the see. **1555** *Burgh Rec. Edin.* (1871) II. 227 Sindry schippis cumin furth of Burdeaux, Scherand, and vtheris places beyond sey. **1590** J. SMYTH in *Lett. Lit. Men* (Camden) 58 When her Majestie called me from beeyond the seas. **1640** MAY *Hist. Parl.* I. ii. 23 The Reformed Churches beyond the Seas. **1710** SWIFT *Jrnl. to Stella* 26 Oct., He is a very ingenious man, and a great scholar, and has been beyond sea. **1879** MISS BRADDON *Cloven Foot* xxxii, The husband, or lover, may have been out of the way—beyond seas, perhaps.

12. by sea. †**a.** Close to the sea, at the sea-side. (Now *by the sea*). **b.** By way of the sea, on or over the sea (as a mode of transit or conveyance). **c.** In the region of the sea, at sea. (See also sense 1 c.)

c **1205** LAY. 1485 Heo forð fusden toward sele Brutun þer he bi sæ wonede. **1375** BARBOUR *Bruce* XIII. 615 Send the Kyng by se Till Balmeburch in his awne cuntre. *c* **1470** HENRY *Wallace* IX. 1131 Few fled with him, and gat away be see. **1625** BACON *Ess., Greatness Kingd.* (Arb.) 489 We see the great Effects of Battailes by Sea. **1719** DE FOE *Crusoe* I.

(Globe) 6 One of my Companions being going by Sea to London. *Ibid.* 293, I had been very unfortunate by Sea. [**1836** LONGF. (*title*) The Castle by the Sea.] **1891** LD. HOBHOUSE in *Law Times Rep.* LXV. 562/2 From the Melbourne factory they carried butterine by sea to Sydney.

† **13. by long sea.** Short for *by long sea passage*: see LONG *a.*[1] 18. Also *by the long seas.*

1645 EVELYN *Diary* Aug., I made a collection of divers curiosities..which I sent for England by long sea. **1694** LUTTRELL *Brief Rel.* (1857) III. 290 Two dispatches are sent to our fleet at Cadiz, one by way of the Groyn, the other by long sea. **1721** STRYPE *Eccl. Mem.* II. iii. II. 265 To pass into Ireland, either by the long Seas, or by Bristow.

14. on or **upon the sea.** (In early use *on* or *upon sea.*) **a.** On the sea's surface, afloat, at sea, on shipboard. In OE. also = in the sea. **b.** Of a dwelling, etc.: At the sea's edge, on the sea-coast.

c **900** tr. *Bæda's Hist.* I. xiii. (1890) 48 We..oððe sticode beoð oððe on sæ adruncene. *a* **1000** *Colloq. Ælfric* in Wr-Wülcker 94 For hwi ne fixast þu on sæ. *O.E. Chron.* an. 877, þa mette hie micel yst on sæ. *c* **1200** ORMIN 13296 þatt iss to farenn uppo sæ, To fisskenn affterr fisskess. *c* **1330** R. BRUNNE *Chron. Wace* (Rolls) 9795 Colgrim had a broþer on þe se. **1389** *Eng. Gilds* (1870) 48 þorow losse on þe se. *a* **1400–50** *Alexander* 83 For he him-self is on þe se with siche a somme armed. *c* **1489** CAXTON *Sonnes of Aymon* xiv. 327, I fled in to Spayn to Alaffre vpon the see. **1560** in *Sel. Pleas Crt. Admiralty* (1897) II. 25 The marrynors..in eny ship or vessel laboring and travayling upon the seas. **1568** GRAFTON *Chron.* II. 711 The Bastard..made sayle with all haste, and roued on the Sea, as before he was accustomed. **1832** TENNYSON *Pal. of Art* 97 In a clear-wall'd city on the sea. **1860** W. WHITING *Hymn*, '*Eternal Father, strong to save*' 6 O hear us when we cry to Thee For those in peril on the sea.

15. over (the) sea. a. Of motion: Across the sea, to the other side of the sea. **b.** Of position: On the other side of the sea; abroad. Cf. OVER-SEA *a.* and *adv.*, OVER-SEAS *adv.*

O.E. Chron. an. 894 (end) Ond þæt wæs ymb twelf monað þæs þe hie ær hider ofer sæ comon. *c* **1205** LAY. 3502 Ouer sea icomen, hauene sone anomen. **1338** R. BRUNNE *Chron.* (1810) 25 He..ferde ouer the see, & conquerd Normundie. **1377** LANGL. *P. Pl.* B. XIII. 392 If I sent ouer see my seruauntz to Bruges. **1458** *Cal. Anc. Rec. Dublin* (1889) 300 Ther marchandys, the wyche they takyth ovre the se. **1583–1886** [see OVER-SEAS *adv.*]. **1616–1895** [see OVERSEA *adv.*]. **1845** BROWNING *Time's Revenges* 1 I've a Friend, over the sea.

16. a. to sea (also †*to the sea*). Out on the water, on a voyage, or on ship-board. *to go to sea*, to go aboard ship, go on a voyage; to enter upon, or follow, the profession of a sailor; †also with ellipsis of the verb. *to put, put off, put out, to sea*: see PUT *v.*[1] 7, 8, 46 n, 48 j. *to stand out to sea*: see STAND *v.*

c **900** tr. *Bæda's Hist.* I. xiii. (1890) 48 Us drifað þa ellreordan to sæ. *c* **1205** LAY. 19368 To þere sa heo wenden. *c* **1275** *Ibid.* 11968 Hii seileden [down the Thames] forte hii to see come. *c* **1375** *Sc. Leg. Saints* xviii. (*Egipciane*) 474 Til I percase a-pone a day saw men of luby & egipe hast þame to sey, for to schype. **1488** *Paston Lett.* III. 344 All suche capeteyns as wente to the see in Lente..makythe them redy to goo to the see ageyn as schortely as they can. **1584** COGAN *Haven Health* ccxvii. 216 Wherefore if any be desirous to vomit, let them rather go to the Sea. **1591–5** SPENSER *Colin Clout* 209 Let him to sea. **1677** YARRANTON *Eng. Improv.* 41, I waited upon the Lord Clarendon and some other Gentlemen to Sea. **1686** tr. *Chardin's Trav. Persia* 53 The Ottoman Fleet..putting to sea from Constantinople, Landed in Candy. **1726** SHELVOCKE *Voy. round World* 61 He knew I was not allowed an ounce of fresh provisions to sea with me. **1849** MACAULAY *Hist. Eng.* v. I. 550 On the afternoon of the second of May he stood out to sea before a favourable breeze.

b. In the Naut. proverbial phr. *he that would go to sea for pleasure, would go to hell for a pastime* and varr.

1899 A. J. BOYD *Shellback* viii. 110 Shentlemens vot goes to sea for pleasure vould go to hell for pastime. **1910** D. W. BONE *Brassbounder* xxvi. 289 He gave a half-laugh, and muttered the old formula about 'the man who would go to sea for pleasure, going to hell for a pastime!' **1924** R. CLEMENTS *Gipsy of Horn* iii. 50 'He who would go to sea for pleasure would go to hell for a pastime' is an attempt at heavy satire. **1933** M. LOWRY *Ultramarine* i. 50 Well, a man who'd go to sea for fun'd go to hell for a pastime.

17. to take the sea (also †*to take sea, the seas*, ME. *to nim the sea*). To go on board ship, embark; to start on a sea-voyage, launch forth, put out to sea (said also of the ship). Cf. F. *prendre la mer.*

c **1205** LAY. 1281 Bi Ruscikadan heo nomen þa sæ. *Ibid.* 4966 þer he þa sæ nom. *c* **1400** *Laud Troy Bk.* 4099 And Achilles toke the see With his vitayles and his naue. *c* **1489** CAXTON *Sonnes of Aymon* xxiv. 530 Reynawde dyde doo hale vp saylle, & toke the see. **1542** UDALL *Erasm. Apoph.* 287 The maryners,..beeyng lothe to take yᵉ seaes, Pompeius hymself first of al entreed into the shippe. *a* **1604** HANMER *Chron. Irel.* (1809) 366 For want of skill they could not take the seas, but were tossed with winde and weather, along the Coast. **1641** EARL MONM. tr. *Biondi's Civil Warres* IV. 68 The 27. of April he tooke sea at Dover. **1867** SWINBURNE *Ess. & Stud.* (1875) 119 The first hymn of Orpheus as Argo takes the sea. **1890** S. LANE-POOLE *Barbary Corsairs* vii. 83 He..was able to take the sea with a fleet of eighty-four vessels. **1903** *Daily Chron.* 30 July 3/1 All the ships..are able to touch 24 knots, but their lines and the way they take the sea is cause of common complaint.

III. Attributive uses and combinations.

18. Simple attributive: **a.** Of or belonging to the sea or a sea, as *sea-arm, -basin, -bed, †-bore, brim, -brink, †-flash, harbour, -haven, -marge, -pull, -romp, -spray, -surge, -swell, -swill, -tide, -wave.*

1637 HEYWOOD *Descr. Royall Ship* (1638) 28 The Great Colosse..who bestrid The spacious Rhodian *Sea-arme. **1865** W. G. PALGRAVE *Arabia* II. 203 Between the islands runs a narrow sea-arm. **1884** GEIKIE *Phys. Geog.* xiv. (1886) 123 Most of the great *sea-basins. **1937** *Discovery* Sept. 279/2 The *sea-bed gave out a bluish light. **1975** *Offshore* Sept. 49–04/1 Other firms in this business include Heerema, with three special ships designed to drill seabed holes up to 1,200 ft in 700 ft of water. *c* **1325** *Metr. Hom.* (Small) 135 That betes thaim wit dede and word Als *se bare betes on schip bord. **1621** G. SANDYS *Ovid's Met.* IX. (1626) 225 With blood the *sea-brimme blusht. **1879** F. W. ROBINSON *Coward Consc.* I. iii, A country full of life and animation even to its sea-brim. *a* **1300** *Horn* 151 (Camb. MS.), Bi þe *se brinke No water þe na drinke. *c* **1820** S. ROGERS *Italy* (1839) 84 On the sea-brink, another train they met. **1634** SIR T. HERBERT *Trav.* 7 Sometimes the surges or *Sea-flashes doe rebound top-gallant height. **1648** HEXHAM II, *Een Zee-haven*, A *Sea-haven, or a *Sea-harbor. **1843** CARLYLE *Past & Pr.* v. 89 No monstrous pitchy City, and Seahaven of the world! **1610** SHAKS. *Temp.* IV. i. 69 Thy *Sea-marge stirrile. **1923** H. BELLOC *Sonnets & Verse* 159 The rank sea-marge. **1976** *New Yorker* 8 Mar. 122/3 The bird has been watched on the sea-marge of Jamaica Bay. **1896** KIPLING *Seven Seas* 68 The *sea-pull drew them side by side, gunnel to gunnel laid. **1876** G. M. HOPKINS *Wr. Deutschland* xvii, in *Poems* (1967) 57 They..rolled With the *sea-romp over the wreck. **1812** SIR J. SINCLAIR *Syst. Husb. Scot.* I. 47 Withering mentions a thorny shrub..which stands the *sea-spray. **1912** E. POUND *Ripostes* 25 Known on my keel many a care's hold, And dire *sea-surge. **1930** —— *XXX Cantos* vii. 25 Ear, ear for the sea-surge. **1880** W. WHITMAN *Daybks. & Notebks.* (1978) III. 628 A little *sea-swell on the water. **1927** H. CRANE *Let.* 12 Sept. (1965) 306 The movement of the verse..of the 'Ave Maria', with its sea-swell crescendo. **1601** HOLLAND *Pliny* v. i. I. 90 It..is not only overflowed by the *sea tides. **1727–46** THOMSON *Summer* 1600 The loud *sea-wave. **1860** TYNDALL *Glac.* I. xxv. 185 The sea-waves ..sometimes reach the shore before the wind which produces them. **1878** G. M. HOPKINS *Poems* (1967) 74 Till a lifebelt and God's will Lend him a lift from the *sea-swill.

b. That is an attribute or quality of the sea, as *sea-beat, -blink, -calm, -murmur, -music, -roughness, -shine, -smell, -sound, -voice, -wash.*

a **1953** DYLAN THOMAS *Quite Early One Morning* (1954) 16 Sea captains..going down into a..cabin of sleep, rocked to the *sea-beat of their ears. **1850** B. TAYLOR *Eldorado* xxxiii, Far away to the right I saw the *sea-blink along the edges of the sky. **1821** *Sea-calm [see *sea-roughness* below]. **1818** SHELLEY *Eugan. Hills* 347 A dell..Which the wild *sea-murmur fills. **1819** —— *Prometh.* III. iii. 27 And thou, Ione, shalt chant fragments of *sea-music. **1821** LAMB *Elia, Witches* (end), The billows gradually subsiding, fell from a *sea-roughness to a sea-calm, and thence to a river motion. **1867** AUGUSTA WILSON *Vashti* xiv, The greenish *sea-shine breaking through the dense foliage. **1880** SWINBURNE *Studies in Song* 179 Streak on streak of glimmering seashine crosses All the land. **1833** TENNYSON *Rosalind* ii, Fresh as the early *seasmell blown Through vineyards from an inland bay. **1961** *Sea-sound [see HIGHVELD]. **1974** *BP Shield Internat.* Oct. 18/2 All sea-sounds were eclipsed by the noise of the drilling operation. **1859** TENNYSON *Guinevere* 245 And strong man-breasted things stood from the sea, And sent a deep *sea-voice thro' all the land. **1930** T. S. ELIOT *Ash Wednesday* 20 The lost lilac and the lost sea voices. **1955** C. TOMLINSON *Necklace* 9 The sea-voice Tearing the silence from the silence. **1930** W. DE LA MARE *On Edge* 297 With the *sea-wash in her ears. **1965** E. RICHARDSON *Living Island* 123 There is no sigh of wind and scarcely a whisper of seawash.

c. Consisting of sea, as *sea-approach, -frontier, †-limit, -path, pool, †-tract, -valley.*

1913 J. MASEFIELD *Mainsail Haul* (ed. 2) 139 The defences to the *sea-approach were powerful. **1940** E. COLSTON SHEPHERD *Britain's Air Power* 9 The more usual work of these [coastal reconnaissance] aircraft is that of continuous patrol over all the sea approaches to Germany. **1905** *Westm. Gaz.* 15 Aug. 3/1 The *sea-frontier of England. **1577** DEE *Memor. Navig.* 59 All, within the *Sea-limits of our Brytish Royallty. **1653** MILTON *Ps.* viii. 22 Fowl of the Heavens, and Fish that through the wet *Sea-paths in shoals do slide. **1596** SPENSER *State Irel.* 2, I heard it often wished also..that all that land were a *Sea poole. **1883** *Fisheries Exhib. Catal.* p. lxxxvii, A Seapool arranged as a grotto. **1600** R. JOHNSON *Kingd. & Commw.* 169 So huge a *sea-tract full of hauens. **1857** EMERSON *Poems* 81 *Sea-valleys and the deep of skies Furnished several supplies.

d. (Phenomena) occurring at sea, as *sea-cloud, dew, -dusk, -gust, -meteor, -storm, -sunset, †-tempest*; also designating actions or events which take place at sea, as *sea-burial, -death, -rescue.*

1838 POE *Narr. A. G. Pym of Nantucket* vii. 74 The mate ..ordered the men to..allow it [*sc.* the body] the usual rites of *sea-burial. **1811** SCOTT *Don Roderick* xxxvi, That *sea-cloud, in size like human hand. **1922** JOYCE *Ulysses* 51 *Seadeath, mildest of all deaths known to man. **1888** F. COWPER *Captain of Wight* (1889) 306 The *sea-dew glittered on spar and mast and straining sail. **1916** JOYCE *Portrait of Artist as Young Man* (1969) v. 226 Swallows flying through the *seadusk over the flowing waters. **1970** T. HUGHES *Crow* 31 The curlew trawled in seadusk through a chime of wineglasses. *c* **1866** G. M. HOPKINS *Poems* (1930) 138 She listened how the *sea-gust shook. **1874** *Trans. Highland Soc.* 245 Great loss and much misery is often caused by these destructive 'sea-gusts'. *a* **1818** M. G. LEWIS *Jrnl. W. Ind.* (1834) 39 The above-mentioned floating lights are a kind of *sea-meteors. **1959** *Listener* 6 Aug. 217/3 A British *sea-rescue plane. **1976** *Morecambe Guardian* 7 Dec. 25/6 A dramatic sea rescue during the early hours of July 5. **1610** SHAKS. *Temp.* I. ii. 177 And now I pray you Sir,..your reason For raysing this *Sea-Storme? **1839–52** BAILEY *Festus* 428 Nor that it now sinks Like a *sea-sunset. **1871** TENNYSON *Last Tourn.* 505 A low sea-sunset glorying round her hair. *c* **1400** *Sc. Trojan War* II. 1011 And sene þat so þe *see-tempestes Lownyt not, nor yhet toke restes.

e. (*a*) Deposited by or in the sea, as *sea-clay, †-gravel, -mud, -ooze, -slob, †-slub, -slutch, -stone, †-turf, -warp*; (*b*) formed by the sea, as *†sea-concretion*; (*c*) proceeding from the sea, as *sea-blast, fog, fret, -gale, haze, -mist*, etc.

1798 SOUTHEY *Henry the Hermit* 25 And underneath a rock that shelter'd him From the *sea-blast, he built his hermitage. **1531** *Lett. & Pap. Hen. VIII*, V. 183 Longe cartes caryng of see turff and *see clay from the floo marke. **1695** J. EDWARDS *Author. O. & N. Test.* III. 282 Others would persuade us that it [Stone-henge] is a *sea-concretion. **1796** H. HUNTER tr. *St.-Pierre's Stud. Nat.* (1799) I. 171 Long belts of land and *sea-fogs, which accompany the melting of all ices. **1834** J. J. AUDUBON *Ornith. Biogr.* II. 201 The sea-fog began to approach the land so swiftly, that..we judged it prudent to return to our vessel. **1893** KIPLING in *Pall Mall Budget* 14 Dec. 1950/2 West you'll turn and south again beyond the sea-fog's rim. **1972** *Gloss. Aeronaut. & Astronaut. Terms (B.S.I.)* xv. 6 *Sea fog*, fog formed at sea, usually by condensation of moisture in the lower layers of a warm air current passing over a relatively cold sea surface. **1842** C. RIDLEY *Let.* Feb. in *Cecilia* (1958) vii. 86 This evening everything was thawing but I imagine it was only what they call a *sea fret. **1846** BROCKETT *N.C. Words* (ed. 3), *Sea-fret*, a wet mist, or haze proceeding from the sea inland. **1882** W. B. SCOTT *Poet's Harvest Home* 33 But still she stared across the bar Through blinding locks and blind seafret. **1963** *Times* 13 June 4/6 Those who came yesterday out of the heat in the surrounding country were surprised to find Brighton enveloped in a sea fret, which..reduced visibility to a furlong or two. **1821** SCOTT *Pirate* i, A garden..produced such vegetables as..the *sea-gale would permit to grow. *c* **1440** *Jacob's Well* 304 þin herte is lyche þe *see-grauel & sande, þat sokyth in, & drynketh in, all waterys, and ȝit þe see is neuere full. **1864** TENNYSON *Enoch Arden* 673 Till anon drawn thro' either chasm,..Roll'd a *sea-haze and whelm'd the world in gray. **1893** KIPLING in *Pall Mall Budget* 14 Dec. 1947/2 The *Northern Light* drove into the bay and the *sea-mist drove with her. **1974** L. DEIGHTON *Spy Story* i. 11 A flurry of sea mist that rolled in upon us. **1726** LEONI *Alberti's Archit.* II. 125/2 If their holes were stopt up with *Sea-mud, or ashes, it wou'd destroy them. **1669** WORLIDGE *Syst. Agric.* (1681) 68 All manner of *Sea-Owse, Owsie-mud, or Sea-weeds,.. are very good for the bettering of Land. **1823** E. MOOR *Suffolk Words*, **Sea-roke*, a fog or mist suddenly approaching from the direction of the sea. **1869** *Zoologist* Ser. II. IV. 1943 A gray sea-roke drifting in across the sand-dunes. **1883** *Chamb. Jrnl.* 20 It was no easy matter to distinguish between salt *seascud and driving rain. **1776** M. MURRAY in *A. Young's Tour Irel.* (1780) I. 279 Part [manured] with *sea-slob and lime mixed. **1610** W. FOLKINGHAM *Art of Survey* I. x. 30 They vse both Orewood, Sea-sand, and *Sea-slubbe for soylings. **1795** J. HOLT *Agric. Lanc.* 126 *Sea slutch, from the Ribble and Wyre, is in some places adjacent, made use of as a substitute for marle. **1860** TENNYSON *Sea Dreams* 52 A full tide Rose with ground-swell, which, on the foremost rocks Touching, upjetted in spirts of wild *sea-smoke. **1918** D. H. LAWRENCE *New Poems* 27 Sad he sits on the white *sea-stone. **1922** JOYCE *Ulysses* 291 From his girdle hung a row of sea-stones. **1936** *Geogr. Jrnl.* LXXXVIII. 105 Bib Nambas..are very Melanesian,..with a frequent pigmoid strain, often with white seastones through their noses. **1531** *Sea turf [see *sea-clay* above]. **1705** ADDISON *Italy, Pesaro* etc. 142 Expos'd to the Winds and Salt *Sea-Vapours. **1839** *Civ. Engin. & Arch. Jrnl.* II. 450/1 By introducing fascine jetty work, which greatly accelerated the deposit of the *sea warp.

f. Situated in or by the sea, as *sea-cape, -cave, †-city, crag, -down, -dune, -flat, garden, -grove, -hall, -home, -marsh, pen, -point, -quag, -scar, -terrace, -track, -wold, -wood.*

a **1876** M. COLLINS *Th. in Garden* (1880) II. 251 *Seacapes divine which the merry winds whiten. **1805** SCOTT *Last Minstrel* VI. xxiii, But the *sea-caves rung, and the wild winds sung, The dirge of the lovely Rosabelle. **1849** M. ARNOLD *Forsaken Merman* 61 Come back to the kind sea-caves! **1917** D. H. LAWRENCE *Look! We have come Through!* 26 They dwelt in a huge, hoarse sea-cave. **1979** *Amer. Poetry Rev.* Mar.–Apr. 45/2 Three craft..negotiate intricate sharp turns and arcs through..narrow canals into sea-caves. **1600** J. PORY tr. *Leo's Africa* I. 29 All the *sea-cities and inland-cities of Barbarie. **1595** DUNCAN *App. Etym.* (E.D.S.), *Scopulus*,..a *sea-craig. **1865** SWINBURNE *Chastelard* I. ii. 30 Between the *sea-downs and the sea. **1885** TENNYSON *Flight* xxiii, We shall light upon..Some lodge within the waste *sea-dunes, and hear the waters roar. **1823** COBBETT *Rur. Rides* (1885) I. 275 The wheat on..the *sea-flats at Havant. **1881** W. D. HAY *Three Hundred Years Hence* vii. 135 With..*sea-garden food, life in these deep-down Harbours is by no means unenjoyable. **1947** I. L. IDRIESS *Isles of Despair* xxxvii. 246 The sea gardens of the lagoons. **1977** *Times* 14 May 12/7 Snorkelling among the magnificent sea gardens which eddy among the rocks. **1830** TENNYSON *Merman* ii, Then we would wander away..To the pale-green *sea-groves. *Ibid.*, I would fill the *sea-halls with a voice of power. *a* **1746** HOLDSWORTH *On Virg.* (1768) 400 There could be no fleet lying there, no *sea-marshes, no lines drawn across them to intercept communication. **1835** J. J. AUDUBON *Ornith. Biogr.* III. 241 The Long-billed Curlew spends the day in the sea-marshes. **1982** 'J. GASH' *Firefly Gadroon* vi. 65 The sea marshes show between the long runs of banks and dykes. **1976** *Daily Colonist* (Victoria, B.C.) 3 Oct. 32/3 They [*sc.* salmon fry] were transferred to *sea pens on barges..and continued rapid growth in salt water. **1736** *Gentl. Mag.* VII. 357/2 To be built on the *sea-point of the same Island. **1882** STEVENSON *New Arab. Nts.* II. ii. 15 The Graden Floe and the other *sea quags that fortified the shore against invaders. **1535** STEWART *Cron. Scot.* II. 415 Ane fair castell standand on the *se skar. **1868** LD. LYTTON *Chron. & Char., Siege Constant.*, The solemn obelisks And sombre cypress stripe with blackest shade *Sea terraces. **1884** GEIKIE *Phys. Geog.* xxiii. (1886) 217 Fig. 40 View of an old sea-terrace or raised beach, with sea-worn caves on its inner margin. **1890** KIPLING *Gipsy Trail* in *Poems 1886–1929* (1929) III. 284 Out on a clean sea-track. **1949** E. MUIR *Coll. Poems* (1960) 164 The smooth sea-tracks that open and close again. **1830** TENNYSON *Mermaid* iii, We would run to and fro, and hide and seek, On the broad *sea-wolds in the crimson shells. **1902** BUCHAN *Watcher by*

Threshold 113 A *sea-wood of alders slipping from the hill's skirts to the water's edge.

g. Occasionally = 'at the sea-side', as ***sea-place, -quarters, -sojourn, †-watering-place.***

1824 Coleridge *Let. to H. F. Cary* (1895) 733 Both Mrs. G. and myself have returned much benefited by our sea-sojourn. **1833** T. Hook *Parson's Dau.* II. xiv, 'Where's St. Leonard's?' 'Oh, the sea watering-place, close to Hastings'. *Ibid.* III. iii, The proposition of her removal to some sea-watering place. **1861** Mrs. Carlyle *Lett.* III. 81 East Cliff ..would be perfect as sea-quarters if it weren't for the noise. **1877** P'cess Alice *Mem.* 25 July (1884) 356 The nicest sea-place I have been as yet.

h. Pertaining to the sea as a sphere of warlike operations, as ***sea army, battle, campaign, conquest, dominion, empire,*** etc.

1600 E. Blount tr. *Conestaggio* 181 The arriuall of his *sea-armie. **1835** *Partington's Brit. Cycl. Arts* s.v. *Signals*, The movements of a sea-army having a necessary dependence on the wind, they cannot [etc.]. **1598** Hakluyt *Voy.* I. 12 In the yeere 1156..there was a *Sea-battell fought. **1940** N. Last *Diary* 9 Apr. in *Nella Last's War* (1981) 47, I kept..wondering if our sailors were winning in the reported sea battle. **1678** Marvell *Growth Popery* Wks. 1875 IV. 264 This fatal conclusion of all our *Sea-champaynes. **1627** May *Lucan* III. Argt., Brutus maintaines The siege, and Cæsars first *Sea-conquest gaines. **1652** Needham tr. *Selden's Mare Cl.* 58 The *Sea-Dominion of the Lydians. **1696** B. Kennett *Rom. Antiq.* II. I. iv. (1717) 46 The *Naumachiæ*, or Places for the Shows of *Sea-Engagements. **1712** Addison *Spect.* No. 299 ¶2 Such an one commanded in such a Sea Engagement. **1910** *Nation* 22 Jan. 671/2 They controlled a *Sea-empire over the Aegean. **1577** Dee *Memor. Navig.* 59 Our *Sea-forces preuayling. **1669** R. Montagu in *Buccleuch MSS.* (Hist. MSS. Comm.) I. 444 Four *sea regiments of three thousand men a-piece. **1682** C. Irvine *Hist. Sc. Nomencl.* Ded. *iv, By your careful Conduct, you made Britain triumph over her most powerful *Sea-Rival. **1577** Dee *Memor. Navig.* 21 Appropriat to her peculiar Iurisdiction and *Sea Royallty. *Ibid.* 5 That expert and hardy Crue of some Thousands of *Sea soldiers wold be to this Realme a Treasor incomparable. **1708** J. Chamberlayne *St. Gt. Brit.* I. II. ii. (1710) 53 He can soon Man the same with the best Sea-Soldiers in the whole World. **1615** *Trade's Incr.* 33 This goodly engine of our *sea-state. *a* **1649** Drumm. of Hawth. *Jas. IV*, Wks. (1711) 64 A *sea-victory obtained by Sir Andrew Wood. **1727** Arbuthnot *Tables Anc. Coins*, etc. 241 This *Sea War cost the Carthaginians five hundred Quinquiremes.

i. Sea-going, as sea-boat, ***sea-coble, -ship.*** Also in fanciful terms descriptive of various kinds of sea-going vessels, as ***sea-car, -castle, -coffin, †-kennel, -terrier, †wasp.***

1851 C. L. Smith tr. *Tasso* XVII. liv, Over the self-same paths which the *sea-car Had traced in coming, backward hence it goes. **1655** Marq. Worcester *Cent. Invent.* §16 How to make a *Sea-castle or Fortification Cannon-proof. **1841** Ld. J. Manners *England's Trust* 18 On furthest ocean's heaving breast meanwhile Ride the sea-castles of our merchant-isle. **1878** Tennyson *Revenge* iv, Till the Spaniard came in sight, With his huge sea-castles heaving upon the weather bow. **1505** *Berwick Reg.* in *Var. Collect.* (Hist. MSS. Comm.) I. 9 That all the *see cowbells commynge frome the se shall lande upon this syde of the water of Twede. **1565** [see coble[1] 2]. **1899** *Pall Mall Mag.* Feb. 230 Many coasters were called *Sea-coffins after Mr. Plimsoll..denounced the ship-owner as the rapacious destroyer of his species. **1676** Wycherley *Pl. Dealer* III. i, You shou'd be ty'd up again, in your *Sea-kennel, call'd a Ship. **1535** Coverdale *1 Kings* x. 22 The kynges *Seeshippe yᵗ sayled vpon the See with yᵉ shippe of Hiram. **1838** Longf. *Beowulf* 20 He bade him a sea-ship..prepare. **1865** E. Burritt *Walk to Land's End* 275 The Fowey seamen made a remarkable reputation in their day with their little *sea-terriers. **1666** Dryden *Ann. Mirab.* cliii, She seems a *sea-wasp flying on the waves.

j. Pertaining to life at sea; used or worn at sea; as ***sea-biscuit, -boot*** (also in Naut. slang phr. ***a face like a sea-boot***, a dejected or wry expression; hence ***sea-booted*** adj.), ***-bread, cap, †-cates, -clothes, coat, †compass, -rig, -stock,*** etc. Also, characteristic of life at sea or of seamen, nautical, as ***sea-bow, -gibberish, -hornpipe, -language, manners,*** etc.

1680–90 Temple *Ess. Health & Long Life* Wks. 1731 I. 283 A Spoonful of Powder of *Sea-bisquet. **1851** H. Melville *Whale* ix, A low rumbling of heavy *sea-boots among the benches. **1916** 'Taffrail' *Pincher Martin* viii. 150 Wot's up wi' yer? You've got a face on yer like a sea-boot. **1946** *Nature* 14 Sept. 386/2 Land Army hose, sea-boot stockings,..and jungle-green pullovers also came under the scheme. **1971** G. M. Brown *Fishermen with Ploughs* 47 His sea boots filled, and Willag said no more. **1897** Kipling *Capt. Cour.* v. 107 With his *sea-booted feet cocked up on the table. **1933** L. Luard *All Hands* 44 The decks..were alive with jovial sea-booted men. **1748** Smollett *Rod. Rand.* (1812) I. 11 My uncle after two or three *sea-bows expressed himself in this manner. **1834** A. Underwood *Jrnl.* Dec. in *Southwestern Hist. Q.* (1928) Oct. 131, I in company with two of my fellow passengers started taking with us some *sea bread water &c. determined to camp out that night. **1876** Davis *Polaris Exp.* xi. 261 A hash made of dried salmon and *sea-bread. **1601** Shaks. *Twel. N.* III. iv. 364 Now you haue no *sea-cap on your head. **1688** Jane Barker *Poet. Recreat.* I. 92 The best of *Sea-Cates we wish for thy Diet. *c* **1578** Frobisher in *Proc. Rec. Comm.* (1833) 562 At Bristo, wher his carde and his *se-clothes dyd ly to pawne. **1933** W. de la Mare *Fleeting* 45 His stiffening sea-clothes grey with salt. **1687** *Lond. Gaz.* No. 2290/4 A black Negro..having a *Sea-Coat lin'd with white Bays. **1570** J. Dee *Math. Pref.* a iv b, Certaine Landmarkes..well hable to be skried, in what point of the *Seacumpase they appeare. **1712** J. James tr. *Le Blond's Gardening* 81 This Instrument is generally furnished with the Sea Compass. **1867** Smyth *Sailor's Word-bk.*, *Sea-pie*,..a favourite *sea-dish in rough weather. **1889** *Century Dict.*, *Furling-line*, a line wound spirally about a sail and its yard in furling. Also called **sea-gasket*. **1608** Sylvester *Du Bartas* II. iv. III. *Schisme* 929 Strike, strike our saile (the Master cryes) amain,..but hee cryes in vain; For, in his face the blasts so bluster ay, That his *Sea-gibb'rish is straight born away. **1602** Shaks. *Ham.* v. ii. 13 Vp from my Cabin My *sea-gowne scarft about me in the darke. **1699** Dampier *Voy.* II. I. 91 My Guide carried my Sea-gown, which was my covering in the night. **1745** *Life Bamfylde-Moore Carew* 58 He..furnishes himself with a tattered *Sea-Habit. **1687** *Lond. Gaz.* No. 2256/4 With a *Sea Hankerchief about his Neck. **1855** Dickens *Dorrit* I. vi, The doctor was amazingly shabby, in a torn and darned rough-weather *sea-jacket [etc.]. **1798** O'Keeffe *Wild Oats* I. i, *John.* You know, on our quitting harbour—. *Sir Geo.* Damn your *sea-jaw, you marvellous dolphin, give the contents of your log-book in plain English. **1884** Sir F. S. Roberts in *19th Cent.* June 1069 *Sea-kits should be issued gratis [to the army] as required. **1728** Chambers *Cycl.*, *Offing*, in the *Sea-language, that part of the Sea a good distance from Shore. **1928** L. P. Smith *Words & Idioms* 20 The sea-languages of the world. **1838** *Civ. Engin. & Arch. Jrnl.* I. 358/1 A *sea lead is charged at its heavy end with a small iron tube. **1740** Johnson *Life Drake* Wks. 1816 XII. 99 Bred from his earliest years to the labour and hardships of a *sea life. **1853** Kane *Grinnell Exp.* v. (1856) 35 The recurring noonday, the meridian starting-point of sea-life. **1829** Marryat *F. Mildmay* iv, My *sea manners were not congenial to the drawing-room. **1668** *Lond. Gaz.* No. 262/4 A *sea Neckcloth about his neck. **1659** Torriano, *Avaria*, a *sea-phrase, viz. a..distribution of the losse made, when [etc.]. **1778** Miss Burney *Evelina* (1791) II. xxxvii. 248, I suppose it to be some sea-phrase. **1886** Stevenson *Kidnapped* x, Then there came a single call on the *sea-pipe, and that was the signal. **1840** R. H. Dana *Two Years before Mast* 4, I made my appearance on board at twelve o'clock, in full *sea-rig. *c* **1611** Chapman *Iliad.* II. 538 King Agamemnon, on these men, did well-built ships bestow To passe the gulfie purple sea, that did no *sea rites know. **1884** 'H. Collingwood' *Under Meteor Flag* 172 He made an elaborate *sea-scrape with his right foot. **1857** Dufferin *Lett. High Lat.* (ed. 3) 400 [We] were nearly run into ourselves by a clumsy merchantman, whom we had the relief of being able to abuse in..the most racy *sea-slang. **1748** *Anson's Voy.* I. ix. 91 Some place..where ships might refresh and supply themselves with the necessary *sea-stock for their voyage. **1840** F. D. Bennett *Whaling Voy.* II. 349 This fruit..is very eligible for sea-stock. **1892** C. H. Fretwell *Anc. Mariner* 38, I..purchased my sea-stock of warm clothing, intending to join on the following day. **1659** Rushw. *Hist. Coll.* 415 All manner of Tackle, *Sea-stores, and Ammunition. **1834** Marryat *P. Simple* viii, We were ordered to the dock-yard to draw sea-stores. **1603** Dekker *1st Pt. Honest Wh.* I. ii. *Stage-dir.*, Enter Fustigo in some fantastic *sea-suit. **1710** Pope *Let. to H.C.* (1735) I. 105, I agree with you in your Censure of the Use of *Sea-Terms in Mr. Dryden's Virgil. **1898** Ansted (*title*), A Dictionary of Sea Terms. **1747** Mrs. Glasse *Cookery* xi. 125 To make *Sea Venison.

k. Applied to pay received or 'due for actual service in a duly-commissioned ship' (Smyth *Sailor's Word-bk.* 1867).

in sea-pay, *† at sea-wages*: (of a sailor) in actual service on the sea; (of a ship) in commission.

1490 *Act 7 Hen. VII*, c. 1 §2 If the Captain be at Sea-wages, he [shall] shew the departing..of the said Soldier..to the Admiral of the Navy. **1667** Pepys *Diary* 29 Aug., My Lord Crewe and his friends take it very ill of me that my Lord Sandwich's sea-fee should be retrenched. **1758** *M.P.'s Let. on R.N.* 6 When such Ships shall have been eighteen Months in Sea-pay, the Wages of the first twelve Months shall be paid. **1889** *N. & Q.* 7th Ser. VII. 81/2 The fleet then left by Pepys in sea-pay comprised 76 vessels, and the men numbered 12,040.

l. Applied to works of art or literature, narratives, etc., representing the sea or life at sea, as ***sea-eclogue, -sonnet, -story, -subject, -tale, -yarn,*** etc. So also ***sea-painter, -poet.***

1712 (*title*) Nereids: or *Sea-Eclogues. **1909** *Q. Rev.* July 140 Joseph Autran the *sea-poet of Marseilles. **1659** *Lady Alimony* III. iii. F 4, Let us have a *Sea-sonnet before we launch forth in our Adventure-Frigot. **1855** (*title*) *Sea Stories: tales of discovery, adventure, and escapes. **1885** *Academy* 21 Nov. 338/3 Mr. Russell undoubtedly 'struck oil' with his earlier sea-stories. **1850** Marg. F. Ossoli *Wom. in 19th Cent.* (1862) 267 Painters of *sea-subjects. **1888** F. M. Crawford *With Immortals* II. 129, I used to..listen to the *sea-tales of the sailors. **1890** 'R. Boldrewood' *Col. Reformer* (1891) 157 Spinning *sea-yarns all night.

m. Applied to nautical maps and charts, as ***†sea-chart, -map, -plat,*** etc. Also sea-book, -card 1.

c **1635** N. Boteler *Dial. Sea Services* (1685) 266 This *Sea-cart is also called a Plot. **1745** Pococke *Descr. East* II. I. 210 The modern sea carts make it [Cyprus] only one hundred and thirty-five [miles] in length. **1669** Sturmy *Mariner's Mag.* IV. iii. 157 By the true *Sea-chart you are arrived at G. **1883** *Encycl. Brit.* XV. 520/2 By 1601 Mercator's projection was in use for all sea charts. **1632** Sherwood, A sea-card, or *Sea-map, *Carte marine, Hydrographie.* **1839** *Penny Cycl.* XIV. 405/1 There are two kinds of terrestrial maps—geographic or land maps, and hydrographic or sea maps. **1697** Dampier *Voy.* I. 416 The Drafts or *Sea-plats being first consulted, it was [etc.].

n. By sea; also, pertaining to navigation or maritime or naval affairs; as ***sea-business, -carriage, †-concernment, -crossing, -passage, -passenger, -route, -trade, -trader, -trading, -traffic, -transport, †-wandering,*** etc. Also sea-voyaging.

1625 K. Long tr. *Barclay's Argenis* IV. xv. 289 The hurly-burly of such as were unskilfull in *sea-business, was like to bring no lesse danger than the storms violence. **1712** M. Henry *Daily Commun. with God* (1866) 45 Whatever your employment be, in country-business, city-business, or sea-business,..go about them in the fear of God. **1766** Smollett *Trav.* I. xx. 315 This wine is of a strong body,..and improves by *sea-carriage. **1868** Rogers *Pol. Econ.* iii. (1876) 20 The relative values of food, clothing, metals, and sea-carriage remain the same. *a* **1687** Petty *Pol. Arith.* I. (1691) 27 Wherefore he whom this latter Party doth affectionately own to be their Head, cannot probably be wronged in his *Sea-concernments by the other. **1615** *Trade's Incr.* 2 A man may runne a course this way [by fishing] to enrich himselfe..more easily..then any other *sea-course can persuade vs to. **1619** Hieron *Wks.* I. 643 It is an allusion to a sea-course: When he the admirall hangs out a lanterne, and all that come behind steere to that. **1936** *British Birds* XXIX. 367 They undertake a 1,200 mile *sea-crossing from Greenland to Ireland. **1962** H. R. Loyn *Anglo-Saxon England* i. 24 A sea-crossing is perilous to tribal institutions. *a* **1586** *Sea-discipline [see land-service]. **1666** Marvell *Corr.* lviii. Wks. (Grosart) II. 197 The *sea-news is not good from severall places. **1634** Sir T. Herbert *Trav.* 2 The description of our *Sea passage. **1873** M. Arnold *Lit. & Dogma* (1876) 181 Because a man has frequently to make sea-passages, he is not gifted with an immunity from sea-sickness. **1592** Greene *2nd Pt. Conny-catching* Wks. (Grosart) X. 89 Syrens, who sitting with their watching eies vpon the rockes to allure *Sea-passengers to their extreame preiudice. **1858** Timbs *Curiosities of Sci.* Ser. I. 184 Ocean highways: how *sea-routes have been shortened. **1886** C. E. Pascoe *Lond. Today* xliii. (ed. 3) 372 In communication with the Continent by the shortest sea route. **1664** Exton *Maritime Dicæol.* I. iii. 14 Other things..done—either on or at the sea, concerning *Sea-trade. **1899** C. J. Cutcliffe Hyne *Further Adv. Capt. Kettle* i. 4 Kettle had come across many types of *sea-trader in his time. **1921** *Nineteenth Cent.* July 150 She failed..to become a great *sea-trading nation. **1885** J. F. Payne in *Encycl. Brit.* XIX. 166/2 Two insular outbreaks [of plague]..both thought to be cases of importation by *sea-traffic. **1847** Webster, **Sea-traveling*, traveling by sea voyages. **1599** Nashe *Lenten Stuffe* 50 Like..Vlysses (well knowne vnto them by his prolixious *seawandering).

o. In designations of persons, as living or exercising their functions at sea, as ***sea-boy, -carpenter, -commander, -fellow, -friend, -robber,*** etc.; †also occas. quasi-*adj.*, that is a sailor, nautical, as ***sea-lover, -philosopher, -reader.***

1597 Shaks. *2 Hen. IV*, III. i. 27 Canst thou (O partiall Sleepe) giue thy Repose To the wet *Sea-Boy, in an houre so rude. **1860** Gen. P. Thompson *Audi Alt.* cxii. III. 38 A Hull sea-boy went to see his master when his time was out. **1753** *Chambers' Cycl.* Suppl., *Scarfed*, in the *sea carpenter's language, is the same as pierced, or fastened or joined in. **1718** Blackmore *Alfred* III. (1723) 87 Rigid *Sea-Chiefs and turbulent of Mind. **1672** Wiseman *Wounds* II. App., To Rdr., My design was to help the *Sea-Chirurgions. **1659** Rushw. *Hist. Coll.* I. 4 One of the last *Sea-Commanders then living bred under Queen Elizabeth. **1909** E. Pound *Personae* 37 As Glaucus tasting the grass that made him *sea-fellow with the other gods. **1918** D. H. Lawrence *New Poems* 27, I wish a wild sea-fellow would come down the glittering shingle. **1661** J. D[avies] *Civil Warres* 326 Coll. Popham one of their *Sea-Generalls. **1666** Evelyn *Diary* 2 Dec., Van Tromp, the Sea Generall. **1669** Sturmy *Mariner's Mag.* v. xiii. 85 Hand-Granadoes [are]..made by *Sea-Gunners upon a Mould made with Twine. **1758** J. Blake *Plan Mar. Syst.* 42 To *sea-lads under 18 not more than 22s. 6d. per month. *c* **1688** Pepys *Mem. R.N.* in Moorhouse *Pepys* (1909) 253 For ascertaining the duty of a *sea-lieutenant, and for examining persons pretending to that office. **1723** *Pres. St. Russia* II. 341 The same happened to another Sea-Lieutenant Michucow. **1797** *Sporting Mag.* X. 322 A *sea-looby that did not know how to reckon. **1695** Congreve *Love for Love* IV. xii, What, has my *sea-lover lost his anchor of hope then? **1600** Abp. Abbot *Expos. Jonah* viii. 169 These *sea-people in like sort might well thinke of the Lord, and yet not leaue their idolatry. **1748** Smollett *Rod. Rand.* xxxii. (1760) I. 248, I was much pleased and edified with the maxims of this *sea-philosopher. **1726** Shelvocke *Voy. round World* Pref. 4, I do not here pretend to give my *Sea-Reader a compleat system of the Navigation on the coasts of Chili, Peru, &c. **1513** Douglas *Æneis* VII. vii. 48 Ȝone fals *see rewir will leif in sturt. **1595** Duncan *App. Etym.* (E.D.S.), *Pyrata*, a sea-rewar, a pyrate. **1568** Grafton *Chron.* II. 435 When the Erle..had not founde one Pirate or *Sea robber, he [etc.]. **1870** Morris *Earthly Par.* III. IV. 305 On the mast Hung the sea-robbers' fair shields, lip to lip.

p. In appellations of mythological or other imaginary beings supposed to inhabit the sea, as ***sea-cattle, -deity, -giant, -girl, -goblin, -idol,*** etc.

1710 W. King *Heathen Gods & Heroes* l. (1722) 179 He [Proteus] is said to ride in a Chariot drawn by *Sea-Cattle, a sort of Horses with two Legs, and Tails like Fishes. **1613** Purchas *Pilgrimage* (1614) 677 Neptune with his ruder *Sea-Deities. **1888** F. M. Crawford *With Immortals* (1890) 294 The match between gods and *sea-giants for souls of sailors. **1917** T. S. Eliot *Prufrock* 16 *Sea-girls wreathed with seaweed red and brown. **1923** E. P. Mathers tr. *J. C. Mardrus's Bk. of Thousand Nights & One Night* VII. 80 Suddenly they saw twelve sea girls..come up out of the water and dance a round upon the sand. **1939** Dylan Thomas *Map of Love* 5 The sea-girls' lineaments Glint in the staved and siren-printed caverns. **1823** Scott *Ess. Romance* (1874) 97 Begot betwixt a monster and a *sea-goblin. **1855** Kingsley *Heroes, Argon.* v. 161 In that cave lives Scylla, the *sea-hag. **1671** Milton *Samson* 13 This day a solemn Feast the people hold To Dagon thir *Sea-Idol. **1604** *Meeting of Gallants at Ordinarie* 22 Riding upon a *Sea-mare. **1589** Greene *Menaphon* (Arb.) 52 How oft haue I descending Titan seene His burning locks couch in the *Sea-queenes lap. **1590** Spenser *F.Q.* II. xii. 24 The horrible *Sea-satyre, that doth shew His fearefull face in time of greatest storme.

q. That lives in the sea, or is found in the sea, esp. as opposed to a similar thing found or living on land, or in fresh water.

1601 Holland *Pliny* XXII. xxii. II. 128 Others affirme, that Alimon is a sea-wort, of a salt and brackish tast. **1611** Speed *Theat. Gt. Brit.* xl. (1614) 79/2 Sea-winkles, cockles and other sea-fish. **1767** tr. *Cranz' Greenland* I. 60 Of the Land and Sea Vegetables. **1848** Owen in *Times* 14 Nov. 9/1 The Sea Saurians of the Secondary periods of geology. **1859** Ld. Lytton *Wanderer* (ed. 2) 329 My coat..Salt as a sea-sponge. **1867** Brande & Cox *Dict. Sci.* s.v. *Sea-serpent*, Mesozoic sea-reptiles (*Ichthyosaurus, Plesiosaurus*). **1888** L.

A. Smith *Music of Waters* 341 The herring fishery in the Isle of Man is the staple industry of the place—the Manx sea-harvest it is called. **1916** Joyce *Portrait of Artist as Young Man* (1969) iv. 171 The sea harvest of shells and tangle. **1922** —— *Ulysses* 38 Signatures of all things I am here to read, seaspawn and seawrack. **1922** *Ibid.* 289 Golden ingots, silvery fishes,..purple seagems and playful insects. **1979** *Dallas* (Texas) *Times Herald* 30 May 8-E/1 Fans of the delicacy [*sc.* seaweed] believe that the term 'sea vegetables' would..enhance the image of native dishes.

19. Objective, as † ***sea-binding***, ***-convulsing***, † ***drying***, ***-framing***, ***-loving***, † ***-shouldering***, etc., adjs. Also ***sea-rider***, † ***-wright*** sbs.

1616 W. Browne *Brit. Past.* I. iv, O ye *sea-binding cleeves! *Ibid.* II. i. 10 By thickets which aray'd The high *Sea-bounding hill, so neare she went [etc.]. **1861** S. Brooks *Silver Cord* xvii, The basin in which stood..the *sea-compelling Poseidon. **1821** Shelley *Hellas* 474 The *sea-convulsing fight. **1605** Sylvester *Du Bartas* II. iii. IV. *Captaines* 294 Let faint Women shake At their Drad God, at their *Sea-drying Lord. **1601** R. Chester *Love's Mart.* (1878) 78 The flowing Riuer Thamasis is nam'd, Whose *Sea-ensuing Tide can neare be tam'd. **1860** Tennyson *Sea Dreams* 33 They..Ran in and out the long *sea-framing caves. **1862** Wood *Illustr. Nat. Hist.* II. 700 The Dunlin.. is the commonest of the *sea-loving Sandpipers. **1939** W. B. Yeats *Last Poems* 29 That *sea-rider Oisin led by the nose Through three enchanted islands. **1590** Spenser *F.Q.* II. xii. 23 Spring-headed *Hydraes* and *sea-shouldring Whales. **1616** W. Browne *Brit. Past.* II. i. 26 Bearded Goates, that on the clouded head Of any *sea-suruaying Mountaine fed. *c* **1586** C'tess Pembroke *Ps.* xcv. ii, The sea is his, and he the *sea-wright was.

20. Similative, as ***sea-cold*** (hence ***sea-coldly*** adv.), ***-colour***, ***-blue***, ***-deep***, ***-grey***, ***-shot***, ***-smiling***, ***-wide*** adjs. Cf. SEA-GREEN.

1850 Tennyson *In Mem.* xc[i], Or underneath the barren bush Flits by the *sea-blue bird of March. **1921** W. de la Mare *Veil* 78 In *sea-cold Lyonesse. **1931** A. Huxley *Cicadas* 57, I reach for grapes, but from an inward vine Pluck sea-cold nipples, still bedewed with brine. **1955** E. Bowen *World of Love* vi. 105 'You mean, you were late at the sea?' 'Not at all,' said Antonia *sea-coldly. **1610** Holland *Camden's Brit.* I. 233 Three springs of hote water, of a blewish or *sea colour. **1896** Housman *Shropshire Lad* xiv, *Sea-deep, till doomsday morning, Lie lost my heart and soul. **1906** *Academy* 6 Jan. 14/1 Our ancient *sea-grey town. **1970** T. Hughes *Crow* 34 Seeing sea-grey mash a mountain of itself. **1874** G. M. Hopkins *Jrnls. & Papers* (1959) 248 The *sea-shot blue-and-green woollen gown our Lady wears. **1922** Joyce *Ulysses* 277 Charming, *seasmiling and unanswering Lydia on Lidwell smiled. **1756** Dyer *Fleece* IV. 220 Those [lakes] a *sea-wide surface spread.

21. Instrumental, as † ***sea-partition***; ***sea-bathed***, ***-blown***, ***-bounded***, † ***-broke***, † ***-circled***, ***-deserted***, ***-divided***, ***-driven***, ***encircled***, ***-fed***, ***-lulled***, ***-scented***, ***-strewn***, ***-sucked***, ***-tossed***, † ***wrecked*** adjs.

1640 Sandys *Christ's Passion* I. 80 *Sea-bath'd Hesperus, who brings Night on. **1857** J. G. Whittier in *National Era* 22 Oct. 170/5 So to us who walk in summer through the cool and *sea-blown town. **1945** J. Betjeman *New Bats in Old Belfries* 27 Whose fantastic mausoleum Sings its own seablown Te Deum. **1610** Niccols *Winter night's Vision, Mirr. Mag.* 573 Our *sea-bounded Britanie. **1649** G. Daniel *Trinarch., Hen. V*, clx, As a brave Vessell, *Sea-broke, lyes to Hull. **1594** Nashe *Unfort. Trav.* Wks. (Grosart) V. 20 Their *sea-circled Ilands. **1820** Shelley *Witch* iv, The *sea-deserted sand. **1649** G. Daniel *Trinarch., Hen. V* lxxviii, *Sea-Devided France. **1581** W. S. *Compend. or Briefe Exam.* 8 b, Towards what Coastes yee be *Sea dryuen. **1730–46** Thomson *Autumn* 926 Round the *sea-encircled globe. **1597** Drayton *Heroic. Ep.* 44 b, This *Sea-inuirond Ile. **1922** Joyce *Ulysses* 238 A sailorman, rustbearded,..eyes her. A long and *seafed silent rut. **1735** Somerville *Chase* III. 431 All now is plain, Plain as the strand *sea-lav'd. **1847** J. R. Lowell *Poet. Wks.* (1912) 121 Fair Beatrice's spirit wandering now In some *sea-lulled Hesperides. **1921** W. de la Mare *Veil* 85 The mild noon air of Spring again Lapped shimmering in that sea-lulled lane. **1597** J. Payne *Royal Exch.* 3 Neyther *sea particion nor distans of plase can be anye lawfull excuse to be..silent. **1592** in Sir J. Picton *L'pool Munic. Rec.* (1883) I. 70 *Sea rounded groundes. **1845** Browning *Meeting at Nt.* ii, Warm *sea-scented beach. **1648** Herrick *Hesper.* 85 (*Welcome to Sack*), Far more welcome then the happy soile, The *Sea-scourg'd Merchant, after all his toile, Salutes with tears of joy. **1744** Young *Nt. Th.* VII. 32 He whom *Sea-sever'd Realms obey. **1892** W. B. Yeats *Countess Kathleen* 125 When fades the *sea-strewn rose of day. **1934** T. S. Eliot *Rock* ii. 56 Many left their bodies to the kites of Syria Or sea-strewn along the routes. **1934** Dylan Thomas *18 Poems* 33 Half of the fellow father as he doubles His *sea-sucked Adam in the hollow hulk. **1966** *New Statesman* 11 Feb. 196/1, I used To think of the soul As round and smooth Like a sea-sucked pebble. **1725** Pope *Odyss.* IV. 827 *Sea-surrounded realms. **1610** Shaks. *Temp.* II. i. 251 She that from whom We all were *sea-swallow'd. **1616** W. Browne *Brit. Past.* II. i. 3 Into as fayre a Baye As euer Merchant wisht might be the rode Wherein to ease his *sea-torne Vessels lode. **1608** Shaks. *Per.* III. Gower 60 Vpon whose Decke The *seas tost Pericles appeares to speake. **1594** Lodge & Greene *Looking-gl.* (1598) F 2, You returne thus *sea-wrackt as I see.

22. Locative, as ***sea-based***, ***-bred***, ***-built***, † ***-lost***, ***-packed***, ***-potent***, ***-setting*** adjs.; also ***sea-setting*** sb.

1839–48 Bailey *Festus* 67/1 Like *seabased icebergs. **1695** Congreve *Love for L.* Dram. Pers., Ben, Sir Sampson's younger Son, half home-bred, and half *sea-bred. **1666** Dryden *Ann. Mirab.* lvii, The *sea-built forts in dreadful order move. **1624** Quarles *Sion's Elegies* II. xi. D 1 b, As a *Sea-lost Rouer, Shee roames, but can no land of peace discouer. **1891** *Century Dict.*, **Sea-packed*, packed at sea or during a voyage, as fish to be sold on arrival in port. **1743** Francis tr. *Hor., Odes* III. xxviii. 9 The *Sea-potent King, And Nereids. **1685** Dryden *Albion & Alb.* III. i, *Sea-racing Dolphins are train'd for our Motion. **1655** Marq. Worcester *Cent. Invent.* Index 2 A *Sea-sailing Fort. **1839–48** Bailey *Festus* xix. 211 My soul sank within me like a star *Sea-setting. **1865** A. Smith *Summer in Skye* I. 200 [The] wan sea-setting of the moon. **1789** E. Darwin *Bot. Gard.* I. 15 *Sea-wilder'd crews the mountain-stars admire.

23. a. Special combinations: **sea-affairs**, nautical or naval affairs, or things occurring at sea; † **sea-agate**, ? an agate with green wave-like markings; **sea-air** *attrib.*, pertaining to or involving both the sea and the air; **sea-anchor**, (*a*) (see quot. 1769); (*b*) = *drift anchor* (see DRIFT *sb.* 19 c); † **sea-artist**, a master of the art of navigation; **sea-bag** *U.S.*, a seaman's travelling bag or trunk; also *transf.*, a heavy artillery shell; **sea bed**, † (*a*) a bed for use on board ship (*obs.*); (*b*) the floor of the sea; **sea-beggar** *Hist.* [= F. *gueux de mer*], a seaman of the small fleet organized by William of Orange in 1572 to combat the Spaniards; **sea-blacking** *jocular*, the effect of sea-air in darkening the skin; **sea-blessing** *Naut. slang* = *sailor's blessing* s.v. SAILOR 5 c; **sea-bloom**, **-blossom**, a flower or blossom of marine vegetation; **sea-bow**, a phenomenon similar to the rainbow, formed by the action of light on sea-spray; † **sea-brace**, a piece of timber used to strengthen a framework against the stress of the waves; **sea-breach**, (*a*) a breaker; (*b*) an irruption of the sea; **sea-break** = prec. (*b*); **sea-brief** (see quot. 1875); **sea-bud**, a bud of marine vegetation, also *attrib.*; **Sea Cadet**, a member of the Sea Cadet Association (see quot. 1976), a voluntary youth organization which seeks to foster and develop for public benefit a sea cadet corps and to provide sea training and promote education in maritime affairs; **sea-cap** (see quot.); † **sea-carriage**, a gun-carriage for a ship's gun; **sea-change**, a change wrought by the sea; now freq. *transf.* with or without allusion to Shakespeare's use (quot. 1610), an alteration or metamorphosis, a radical change; **sea chest**, (*a*) a seaman's chest or box for his own clothing, etc.; (*b*) (see quot. 1909); **sea-clam**, **-clamp**, 'a clam, clamp, or forceps closed by a weight, for use with deep-sea sounding-lines' (*Cent. Dict.* 1891); **sea-cloth**, (*a*) a painted cloth spread over the stage and moved so as to represent waves; (*b*) cloth used for making sailors' clothing; **sea clutter** = *sea return(s)* below; **sea-cobble**, a pebble rounded by the action of the sea, used for paving and building; † **sea-common** (see quot.); **sea-cook**, a cook on board ship; esp. in ***son of a sea-cook*** used as a term of abuse; **sea-corpse** *poet.*, the corpse of a person drowned at sea; **sea-crust**, the incrustation formed on an iron ship during a sea-voyage; **sea-daddy** [cf. Du. *zeevader*], an old sailor who befriends and instructs a midshipman; **sea-dingle** (now only *arch.*), an abyss or deep in the sea; † **sea-distemper** = SEA-SICKNESS; **sea-door**, a means of access (to a country) from the sea; † **sea-drags**, **-dust** (see quots.); **Sea Dyak**: see DYAK; **sea-edge**, the brink of the sea; also *spec.* 'the boundary between the icy regions of the "north water" and the unfrozen portions of the Arctic Sea' (Smyth *Sailor's Word-bk.* 1867); **sea-farm**, 'an area of sea-bottom devoted to the cultivation of molluscs; an oyster-farm' (*Funk's Stand. Dict.* 1895); also **sea-farmer**; **sea-farming** *vbl. sb.*, mariculture; also as *ppl. a.*; **sea-fencible**, an old coastguard; **sea-fever**, longing or desire for the sea or sailing on it; **sea-fire**, phosphorescence at sea; **sea-flier**, one of the longipennine natatorial sea-birds, as gulls, etc.; **sea-fort**, a fort on the coast; **sea-gauge**, (*a*) (see quot.); (*b*) 'the depth that a vessel sinks in the water' (Webster 1828–32); **sea-gipsy**, one of a roving tribe of fishermen of Malayan type living all their life on the sea, in the Malay Archipelago; **sea-glass**, † (*a*) isinglass; (*b*) (see quot. 1895); † **sea-grave** = *sea-reeve*; **sea-grocer**, 'a sobriquet for the purser' (Smyth *Sailor's Word-bk.*); **sea-guard**, a guarding or protecting by sea; † **sea-gulf**, a whirlpool; † **sea-head**, ? a sea-wall or bank; **sea-horizon**, the line where sky and sea seem to meet: in *Navigation*, 'the small circle which bounds the portion of the surface visible to a spectator in the open sea' (Harbord *Gloss. Navig.* 1863); **sea-ice** (see quot. 1835), also simply, the ice of the sea, frozen sea-water; **sea ivory**, ivory from the tusks and horns of marine mammalia (see also sense 23 f below); **sea-jockey** *N. Amer.*, a nimble sailor; the sailor of a small craft; occas. *derog.* (cf. JOCKEY 5 b); **sea-keeping**, of a ship, hovercraft, etc.: the endurance of (rough) conditions at sea; **sea-kindly** *a.*, (of a ship) easy to handle at sea; hence *sea-kindliness*; **sea-lake**, a land-locked portion of the sea, a lagoon; **sea-lane**, a route at sea for shipping; **sea-league**, three nautical miles; **sea-ledger**, ledger tackle (see LEDGER *sb.* 8) used in sea-fishing; **sea-letter** = *sea-brief*; **sea-lift** *N. Amer.*, a large-scale transportation of troops, supplies, etc., by sea (cf. AIRLIFT 2); hence as *v. trans.*, to transport by sea; **sea-loch** *Sc.*, an inlet of the sea; **sea-lock**, a lock at the marine extremity of a ship canal; **sea-log**, an official record of a ship's voyage (see also quot. 1867); **sea-longing**, a yearning for the sea, sea-fever; **sea-lord**, a naval lord (of the Admiralty); **sea-mail**, mail conveyed by sea; a service for conveying letters, parcels, etc., by sea (not an official term); so as *v. trans.* (*rare*), to send by sea; cf. AIRMAIL; **sea marker**, a device which can be dropped from an aircraft to produce a distinctive patch on water below it; † **sea-master**, a sailing-master; **sea-mile**, a geographical or nautical mile (see MILE *sb.*[1] 3); **sea-mine** (see MINE *sb.* 3); **sea-mount**, a large natural elevation rising abruptly from the ocean floor, usu. entirely underwater; an underwater mountain; **sea-mountain**, (*a*) a high wave; (*b*) a mountain covered or partly covered by the sea; **sea-net**, a net used in sea-fishing; † **sea-office**, an office on board ship; **sea-pass** (see quot.); **Sea People(s)** = *Peoples of the Sea* s.v. PEOPLE *sb.* 1 c; **sea-peril** = *sea-risk*; **sea-preacher**, ? = SEA-LAWYER; **sea-price** *Naut. colloq.*, an inflated price; **sea-pup** *jocular*, a 'young sea-dog', a child of a sailor or fisherman; **sea-purple** = PURPLE *sb.* 3, also the dye derived from it; **sea-rainbow** = *sea-bow*; **sea-rake**, a rake used for collecting shell-fish, etc., a clam-rake; † **sea-rat**, a pirate; **sea-rate**, **reach** (see quots.); **sea-reeve**, an officer who took care of the maritime rights of the lord of the manor, and watched the shore and collected wrecks; **sea return(s)**, unwanted radar images due to reflection from a rough sea; **sea-risk**, 'liability to losses by perils of the sea' (Smyth *Sailor's Word-bk.*); **sea-road** *rare*, a route by sea; **sea-run** *a.*, 'having returned to the sea after spawning, as an anadromous fish' (*Cassell's Suppl.* 1902); **sea-runner**, ? = *sea-flier*; **sea-running** *a.*, 'anadromous; entering rivers to spawn and returning to the sea' (*Cassell's Suppl.*); † **sea-ruttier** = RUTTIER; **sea scout**, a member of the (Boy) Scout movement engaged in activities pertaining to the sea and seamanship; **sea-scurvy**, the form of scurvy incident of life on ship-board; **sea seiche**, a seiche ocurring in the open sea; **sea-sergeant** (see quot. 1867); **sea-shoal**, (*a*) a shoal of fish in the sea; (*b*) a shoal or bank in the sea; † **sea-shoe** (in *phrase*: see quot.); **Sea Sled** (see quot. 1948) (a proprietary name in the U.S.); **sea-slope**, a slope facing the sea; **sea-sorrow** *arch.*, a catastrophe or cause of trouble at sea; **sea-speed**, the ordinary speed of a vessel when at sea, as distinguished from *full speed*; **sea-stack** = STACK *sb.* 7; **sea-state**, the degree of turbulence at sea, esp. as measured according to a scale of average wave height; **sea-stick**, a herring cured at sea; **sea-stroke**, the stroke of a heavy wave; **sea-tan**, tan produced by exposure to sea-air; **sea-tath** (see TATH 3); **sea-time**, (*a*) time spent at sea in service; (*b*) the way of reckoning time at sea; (*c*) the duration of a journey at sea; **sea-toss** *colloq.*, 'a toss overboard into the sea' (*Cent. Dict.*); **sea-train**, (*a*) a ship used for the transportation of railway cars; (*b*) a group of ships carrying supplies or equipment; **sea-transom**, 'that which is bolted to the counter-timbers, above the upper, at the height of the port-sills' (Smyth *Sailor's Word-bk.*); **sea-trap**, a trap in the sea for catching fish, etc.; † **sea-trod** *a.*, sea-faring; **sea-turn**, (*a*) a gale or breeze (usually accompanied by mist, etc.) from the sea; (*b*) 'a tack into the offing' (Smyth *Sailor's Word-bk.*); **sea-valve**, 'any one of several valves in the bottom or side of a steamship communicating with the sea below the water-line' (*Cent. Dict.*); † **sea-wake**, the duty of watching the sea; † **sea-warth**, the sea-shore; † **sea-watch**, (*a*) a chronometer; (*b*) (see quot. 1769); **sea-wax** = MALTHA 2; **sea-wise** *a.*, versed in the ways of the sea; also *absol.* as *sb.*; **sea-wit**, a naval jester or wit; also, nautical wit or facetiousness; **sea-woman**, (*a*) a mermaid; (*b*) a female sailor; a woman working at sea; **sea-work**, a work or construction in the sea, also naval work or work on a ship or in service; † **sea-**

yoke, a combination of pulleys and ropes for working the helm in stormy weather.

1633 T. Stafford *Pac. Hib.* III. vi. (1821) 546 Conversant in *Sea-affaires. **1726** Swift *Gulliver* III. i. 2 Having experienced my knowledge in sea-affairs to be at least equal to his, he would enter into any engagement to follow my advice. **1798** O'Keeffe *Wild Oats* I. i, Since you've..retired to live in quiet, on your estate, and had done with all sea affairs. **1939** J. Masefield *Live & Kicking Ned* 29 He told me something of sea-affairs. *a* **1593** Marlowe *Hero & Leander* I. 138 The wals were of discoloured Iasper stone, Wherein was Proteus carued, and o'rehead, A liuelie vine of greene *sea agget spread. **1945** L. E. O. Charlton *Roy. Air Force* 266 A strong Japanese battle fleet..delivered an attack ..reminiscent of the *sea-air battles of Midway and the Coral Sea. **1959** H. Barnes *Oceanogr. & Marine Biol.* iii. 106 Information about temperature and salinity conditions and their variation enables deductions to be made about physical processes taking place in the sea-air interface. **1769** Falconer *Dict. Marine* II, *Ancre du Large*, the *sea anchor, or that which lies towards the offing. **1877** J. Dixon in *Daily News* 19 Oct. 6/4 She also had a floating bag, or sea anchor, to keep her head to windward. **1669** Sturmy *Mariner's Mag.* IV. i. 138 Such young Sea-faring Men, as are desirous to be *Sea-Artists or Navigators. **1918** M. Denig *Let.* July in K. Cowing *Dear Folks at Home* (1919) 250 A few big '*sea-bags' had hit near by. **1919** *Sea-Bag* 9 Feb. 3 Down in the bottom of a sea bag you may find the suit that a German Sub would have fired at if we had been lucky enough to really see a Fritz. **1926** J. W. Thomason *Fix Bayonets!* 148 If Brother Boche had kept flingin' them seabags around here, he'd a-hurt somebody. **1958** J. Kerouac *On Road* II. ii. 187 He grabbed his seabag and threw things into that. **1977** *N.Y. Rev. Bks.* 23 June 6/2 How easy it would have been at that point, one thinks, for the Marine Corps to have packed up its sea bags and departed. **1637** in *Archives of Maryland* (1887) IV. 76 The Inventary of the goods & chattells of mr John Baxter... I. rugg & an old *sea-bed. **1722** Defoe *Moll Flanders* 381 My Governess..came down herself..bringing me in the first Place, a Sea Bed, as they call it, and all its Furniture. **1774** N. Cresswell *Jrnl.* 8 Apr. (1925) 9 Bought a Sea Bed; paid Captn. Parry my passage. **1838** *Penny Cycl.* XI. 142/2 So as to stain the whole sea-bed for 1000 feet or yards in depth. **1845** M. Russell in *Encycl. Metrop.* XIII. 603/1 Repulsed by the *Sea-beggars, he [the Count de Bossu] endeavoured to seek a refuge in Dort. **1922** P. S. Allen *Let.* 30 Mar. (1939) xvi. 183 We are now on our way to Rotterdam..to attend..the 350th anniversary of the recapture of Brill by the 'Sea-beggars' from the Spaniards on 1 April 1572. **1963** *Times* 22 Feb. 17/3 He spoke for an hour to a packed audience of intent undergraduates and history dons about..the 'invasion' of the Netherlands by Prince William of Orange's sea beggars. **1840** R. H. Dana *Bef. Mast* xxx, It was surprising to see how much soap and fresh water did for the complexions of many of us; how much of what we supposed to be tan and *sea-blacking we got rid of. **1883** W. C. Russell *Round Galley Fire* 109 The *sea-blessings showered out by the cook as he chases his dishes and pans and burns his fingers. **1912** W. I. Downie *Reminisc. Blackwall Midshipman* ii. 19 Sea blessings galore descended on my unfortunate head. **1933** S. Bradford *Shell-Backs & Beachcombers* viii. 181 The mate..gave me his sea-blessing for having recommended such a man to him. **1819** Shelley *Ode W. Wind* 39 The *sea-blooms and the oozy woods which wear The sapless foliage of the ocean. **1865** Swinburne *Chastelard* I. ii. 38 Some *sea-blossom stripped to the sun and burned At naked ebb. **1728** Chambers *Cycl.* s.v. *Rainbow*, The Marine or *Sea-Bow is a Phænomenon sometimes observ'd in a much agitated Sea. **1776** G. Semple *Building in Water* 131 You may also extend the..Sills..toward the Sea, and thereon fix your five *Sea-braces. *c* **1610** Beaum. & Fl. *Philaster* v. iii, Let me stand the shock of this mad *sea-breach, Which I'le either turne, or perish with it. **1697** Collier *Ess. Mor. Subj.* II. (1709) 14 You might as good attempt to..stop a Sea-breach by proving the Water gets nothing by overflowing. **1884** *Chamb. Jrnl.* 3 May 275/1 The whole coast also suffers much from sea-breaches. *a* **1688** J. Wallace *Descr. Orkn.* (1693) 19 How great is the power of the *Sea-break may appear from this, that..there are by the violence of the sea & winds, large stones thrown up..a great way above the rock. **1566** *Reg. Privy Council Scot.* I. 481 The lettres of marque, or *sey brevis of the Kingis of Denmark, Swaden, or ony uther foreign Prince. **1755** Magens *Insurances* II. 460 All kind of Ships and Vessels..shall be only obliged to shew unto the Officers acting in the Ports of the said States,..their Passport commonly called a Sea-Brief. **1875** Bedford *Sailor's Pocket Bk.* vi. (ed. 2) 224 The Sea-letter, or Sea-brief,..is the document which entitles the Master to sail under the Flag..of the Nation to which he belongs; and it also specifies the nature and quantity of the cargo [etc.]. **1817** Shelley *Pr. Athanase* II. iv. 11 The grass in the warm sun did start and move, And *sea-buds burst under the waves serene. **1830** Tennyson *Mermaid* ii, My starry sea-bud crown. **1976** *Times* 13 May 5/8 The Navy League, formed 81 years ago to press for more naval power for Britain, announced yesterday that it is changing its name to the *Sea Cadet Association. **1977** *Navy News* June 32/5 Members are grateful to the Leicester Unit, Sea Cadet Corps, for the use of their H.Q. for branch meetings. **1867** Smyth *Sailor's Word-bk.*, *Sea-cap, the white drift or breaks of a wave. *White horses* of trades. **1669** Sturmy *Mariner's Mag.* IV. xii. 64 *Sea-Carriages are made..as the Block-maker that makes them hath Rules for. **1610** Shaks. *Temp.* I. ii. 400 Nothing of him that doth fade, But doth suffer a *Sea-change Into something rich, & strange. **1917** E. Pound *Lustra* 193 Full many a fathomed sea-change in the eyes That sought with him the salt sea victories. **1923** J. M. Murry *Pencillings* 164 The characters which have suffered this sea-change, 'of whose bones are coral made', are the only unpleasant characters we remember. **1948** A. C. Baugh *Lit. Hist. England* II. IX. 173 An interesting paper suggesting that romance is transplanted epic, which has undergone a kind of sea-change in the passage. **1974** R. Helms *Tolkien's World* ii. 32 Even before *The Hobbit* was published he was at work on its sequel, a work in which Middle-earth has undergone a wondrous sea change. **1976** *Listener* 8 Apr. 450/3 The Messianic vision..has undergone some strange sea-changes outside Judaism. **1977** 'E. Crispin' *Glimpses of Moon* vii. 117 He..could, moreover.. bring about a sea-change in the image of even the most bumbling police officers going about their duties, so that they emerged as prodigies of intelligence, zeal and kindness. **1669** Sturmy *Mariner's Mag.* v. xiii. 86 Like a *Sea Chest. **1883** Stevenson *Treas. Isl.* i, His sea-chest following behind him in a hand-barrow. **1909** *Cent. Dict.* Suppl., *Sea-chest*, in ship-building, a short open pipe extending from the outside plating to the interior just inside the inner bottom, the inner end of which is closed by a sea-valve placed in a position accessible from the interior of the vessel. **1942** G. C. Manning *Man. Ship Construction* (1943) iii. 76 Sea valves must be so placed as to be easily worked from the engine-room platforms. When they make connection with the sea through the double bottom or otherwise so that they would require a long neck if fastened directly to the shell they are attached to sea chests which are secured on the inside of the shell plating. **1972** L. M. Harris *Introd. Deepwater Floating Drilling Operations* 248 All sea chest strainers were removed. The sea valves were opened and examined. The sea chests were thoroughly examined. **1883** Stevenson *Treas. Isl.* VI. xxxi. 263 'He was a seaman,' said George Merry, who..was examining the rags of clothing. 'Leastways, this is good *sea-cloth.' **1890** 'Biff' Hall *Turnover Club* xviii. 172 The wings are removed, and what is technically known as a 'sea cloth' takes their place. **1891** *Century Dict.*, *Sea-cloth*, *Theat.* **1901** *Referee* 4 Aug. 3 (Cass. Suppl.) The quicksand in 'Wrestler Joe' was crudely represented by a black 'sea-cloth'. **1905** 'Q' *Shining Ferry* III. xviii. 218 A bustious, big fellow, with a round hat like a missionary's, and all the rest of him in sea-cloth. **1946** *Sea clutter [see clutter *sb.* 2c]. **1970** P. Clissold *Radar in Small Craft* ii. 26 Sea clutter is not likely to be of any consequence beyond three or four miles, but at short range it can obscure stronger targets. **1810** *Hull Improv. Act* 36 Paved with such good and substantial *sea-cobbles. **1584** in *3rd Rep. Hist. MSS. Comm.* 5/1 All fishermen may fish in and upon *sea-commons, that is, all such places in rivers, creeks, or bays as are covered by the water at high tide. **1706** E. Ward *Wooden World Diss.* (1708) 82 A *Sea-Cook has been an able Fellow in the last War. **1806** J. Davis *Post-Captain* v. 27 'A precious husband!' exclaimed captain Brilliant... 'A son of a sea-cook! If he was to fall overboard, I would not heave him a rope.' *c* **1825** Choyce *Log Jack Tar* (1891) 30 [They] struck the landlord, and called him an out-landish son of a sea-cook in his own house. **1865** H. Kingsley *Hillyars & B.* lv, If he got any more cheek from him, or any other..post and rail son of a sea-cook. **1922** Joyce *Ulysses* 624 Boisterously trolling, like a veritable son of a seacook. **1977** A. Hunter *Gently Instrumental* iv. 59 You're a right son of a seacook, aren't you? **1878** G. M. Hopkins *Poems* (1967) 74 They say who saw one *sea-corpse cold He was all of lovely manly mould. **1896** Kipling *Seven Seas*, *Coastwise Lights* 21 Go, get you gone up-Channel with the *sea-crust on your plates. **1899** 'Martello Tower' *At School & at Sea* 80 'Mas'r Tower', said my *sea-daddy to me one quiet evening, 'I was wantin' to say a word to you, sir.' *a* **1240** *Sea dingle [see dingle *sb.*]. *c* **1931** Auden in M. Roberts *New Signatures* (1932) 30 Doom is dark and deeper than any sea-dingle. *a* **1641** Finett *For. Ambass.* (1656) 153 Giving to the Queen some time of refreshing after her *Sea-distempers, before he would see her. **1745** *Life Bampfylde-Moore Carew* 22 So violently were Bampfylde and his Friend afflicted with the Sea-Distemper. **1861** Lowell *Pickens-and-Stealin's Rebell.* Wks. 1890 V. 83 The seceding States, every one of which had a *sea-door open to the invasion of an enemy. **1884** Joaquin Miller *Memorie & Rime* (N.Y.) 120 Portland sits at the sea-door [of Oregon]. **1706** Phillips (ed. Kersey), **Sea-Drags*,..any thing that hangs over the Ship in the Sea; as Shirts, Gowns, &c. or the Boat when it is towed. **1879** Geikie in *Encycl. Brit.* X. 266/1 The dust or sand of dried lakes or river-beds is sometimes borne away into the upper regions of the atmosphere,..it may descend again to the surface, in the form of 'red-fog', '*sea-dust', or 'sirocco-dust'. **1820** Scoresby *Acc. Arctic Reg.* I. 102 The Seven Icebergs are each, on an average, about a mile in length, and perhaps near 200 feet in height at the *sea-edge. **1910** N. Munro in *Blackw. Mag.* Aug. 231 The drystone dykes that marked them rose from the sea-edge dripping. **1968** E. S. Iversen *Farming Edge of Sea* ii. 31 The most important group of animals to *sea farmers are mollusks (clams, oysters, and mussels), crustaceans (shrimps, crabs, and lobsters), and fishes. **1962** *New Scientist* 18 Oct. 129 Sir Alister Hardy, of Oxford, the leading prophet of *sea-farming. **1972** *Aquaculture* I. 232 Seafarming is feasible and it can be carried out with profit. **1975** *Times* 24 Apr. 3/2 By next year the group of sea-farmers expect to have 1,250,000 Pacific oysters..ready for the market. A company, Western Aquaculture, is one of the sea-farming organizations. **1803** Sir J. Moore in *Tait's Mag.* (1834) I. 333/2 The Volunteers, *Sea-Fencibles, and all, were turned out. **1902** J. Masefield (*title of poem*) *Sea-fever. **1931** *Daily Express* 23 Sept. 9/4 Men with the sea-fever on them pottered about among the debris of the docks. **1980** P. Moyes *Angel Death* i. 9 The much smaller island.. has been infected by the current sea-fever to the point of constructing a small yacht basin. **1814** Scott *Ld. of Isles* Note ix, The phenomenon called by sailors *Sea-fire. **1903** Kipling *Five Nations* 74 Flying-fish about our bows, Flying sea-fires in our wake. **1947** K. Tennant *Lost Haven* ii. 30 About her the impersonal sea-fire broke and the strange lights vibrated and shone. **1869–73** T. R. Jones *Bk. Birds* IV. 175 The *Sea-fliers (*Longipennes*). *Ibid.* 219 The Oar-footed Sea-fliers (*Steganopodes*). **1879** Sir C. Nugent in *Encycl. Brit.* IX. 450/1 Fig., Plan of *Sea Fort, with continuous Iron wall. **1751** *Phil. Trans.* XLVII. 213 Upon the passage, I made several trials, with the bucket *sea-gage. **1817** Moore *Lalla Rookh*, *Fire-worshippers*, That Eastern Ocean, where the *sea-gipsies, who live for ever on the water, enjoy a perpetual summer in wandering from isle to isle. **1848** *Simmonds' Col. Mag.* Jan. 49 The sea-gipsies skimming over the waters in prahus filled with their wives and children. **1747** Cooke in *Hanway's Trav.* (1762) I. IV. lviii. 266 We observed a great quantity of *sea-glass [*note* Commonly called isinglass, of which lanthorns are made]. **1895** *Outing* (U.S.) XXVII. 240/1 Our object in visiting the reefs was to look through the sea-glasses, which consist of funnels of wood about a yard long, with a piece of glass at the lower end. **1583** in *N. Riding Rec.* (1894) I. 250 [They] have had *seagroves [? *read* sea-graves] chosen..from tyme to tyme for the presenntynge of all such wreckes and Regall fishes. **1876** Bancroft *Hist. U.S.* III. v. 366 It was Grenville who introduced a more than Spanish *sea-guard of British America. **1902** *Times* 15 Aug. 5/3 The [naval] review of this week may also be regarded as a kind of national stock-taking of the Empire's sea-guard. **1571** Golding *Calvin on Ps.* xlii. 8 By y[e] name of (depth) he sheweth that y[e] temptacions, wherwith he was assaulted might bee compared too *seagulfes. *a* **1593** Marlowe *Dido* v. (1594) F4b, I hope that that which loue forbids me doe, The Rockes and Sea-gulfes will performe at large, And thou shalt perish in the billowes waies. **1531** *Lett. & Pap. Hen. VIII*, V. 181 Chawlke for making of a *see hedd be the West Bray gate, which was brokyn by the great rage of the see. **1821** Shelley *Hellas* 632 The Sirocco..drove his flock of thunder-clouds Over the *sea-horizon. **1878** Tyndall *Fragm. Sci.* (1879) I. x. 306 A luminous sheet which grazes the sea-horizon. **1835** Sir J. Ross *Narr. 2nd Voy.* Explan. Terms p. xv, **Sea ice*, ice within which there is a separation from the land. **1909** *Edin. Rev.* Oct. 484 Travelling over the sea-ice. **1851** H. Melville *Moby Dick* I. xvi. 111 Those thews ran not through base blocks of land wood, but deftly travelled through sheaves of *sea-ivory. **1883** *Fisheries Exhib. Catal.* (ed. 4) 78 Sea Ivories, Horns, Bone, &c. manufactured and rough. **1968** G. Jones *Hist. Vikings* I. i. 23 Southwards..went skins and furs, amber, sea-ivory, and slaves. **1847** H. Melville *Omoo* xvi. 58 Jermin, *sea-jockey that he was, sometimes stood in the fore-chains. **1897** *Outing* Dec. 234/1 Aboard one of these well-balanced and swift little vessels the sea jockey's art can easily be acquired. **1971** D. Conover *One Man's Island* 67 The sea jockeys have taken over the waterways... Outboard cruiser owners—sea jockeys, as we call them. **1963** *Times* 2 Mar. 8/4 Their employment in certain roles will depend largely on their *sea-keeping qualities. **1972** C. Mudie *Motor Boats & Boating* 144 Maximum speeds have crept up from some forty knots to eighty knots in ten years and seakeeping has improved out of all recognition with rough water speeds nearly doubled. **1897** F. T. Bullen *Cruise of 'Cachalot'* 133 But for the build and *sea-kindliness of the *Cachalot*, she could not have come out of that horrible cauldron again. **1936** C. Winchester *Shipping Wonders of World* I. 690/3 The Livonia..proved her 'sea-kindliness' by crossing the Atlantic in the worst of weather. **1976** *Yachting World* Oct. 110/2 Of course, the boat doesn't usually match true wind speed in open sea conditions, but it does exhibit truly phenomenal sea-kindliness with the hydrofoils set in moderate and heavy conditions. **1876** *Whitby Gloss.*, **Sea-kindly*. **1958** J. L. Kent *Ships in Rough Water* xi. 157 A seakindly ship is one which rides the seas in rough weather without shipping green water and with little spray blown inboard. **1981** *Times* 2 Feb. 22 There is a possibility of building hulls which can achieve speeds in excess of 30 knots on a waterline length of only 75 metres. These..should be extremely sea-kindly. **1827** Montgomery *Pelican Island* II. (1828) 30 A *sea-lake shone amidst the fossil isle. **1890** 'R. Boldrewood' *Col. Reformer* (1891) 161 The slumbering sea-lake. **1878** Tennyson *Revenge* v, And the little Revenge ran on thro' the long *sea-lane between. **1948** *British Birds* XLI. Suppl. 1 After some months on its sea-lanes one could not but feel that the true answer to any one question could only be known if it were possible to cover the whole area in a matter of a few days. **1978** J. A. Michener *Chesapeake* 346 Can we keep the sea lanes open? **1903** Kipling *Five Nations* 23 They forced the sea a *sea-league back. **1887** 'J. Bickerdyke' *Angling in Salt Water* 24 The *Sea Leger..is a very useful piece of tackle for catching flat fish. **1755** Magens *Insurances* II. 501 The Ships and Vessels belonging to the Subjects of the other Ally must be furnished with *Sea-Letters, or Passports, expressing the Name, Property and Bulk of the Ship [etc.]. **1848** Arnould *Law Marine Insur.* II. iii. (1866) II. 577 In New York..a difference has been held to exist between a passport and a sea-letter, the latter term being confined to a mere certificate of ownership. **1956** *Sun* (Baltimore) 19 Dec. 2/1 The General Eltinge will sail..tomorrow with the first of 5,500 Hungarian refugees to head toward the United States by sea... The *sealift complements commercial air services and the airlift inaugurated by United States military planes. **1967** *Economist* 4 Mar. 802/2 [The United States] has the air-lift and sea-lift capacity to be on hand whenever a power vacuum develops. **1972** S. Burnford *One Woman's Arctic* i. 15 It had been brought in by the annual sea-lift the year before. **1974** *Greenville* (S. Carolina) *News* 23 Apr. 14/3 The Middle East fighting proved, he says, our capacity to airlift and sealift needed munitions and equipment over long distances. **1980** *N.Y. News* 11 May 14/2 Officials put at 30,598 the total number of Cubans sealifted to freedom across the Florida strait. *c* **1645** in Macfarlane *Geogr. Collect.* (S.H.S.) II. 522 Ther is a *sealoch cumeth in betwixt both the countreys of Morrour and Knodeart. **1817** Coleridge *Biog. Lit.* xx. (1907) II. 84 Would any but a poet ..have brought all the different marks and circumstances of a sea-loch before the mind, as the actions of a living and acting power? **1934** Sea loch [see fiard, fjard]. **1975** J. G. Evans *Environment Early Man Brit. Isles* iii. 67 The various long bays of south-west Ireland, some of which, like the sea lochs of western Scotland, have been glacially deepened as well. **1839** *Civ. Engin. & Arch. Jrnl.* II. 11/1 The difficulties experienced in building the *sea lock at the eastern end of the [Caledonian] canal. **1959** *Times* 8 Dec. 13/6 Down at the sea-locks..the tugs would be worrying like strange small sea animals. **1853** D. G. Rossetti *Let.* 16 Apr. (1965) I. 131 Your '*sea-log' gave me the greatest pleasure. **1867** Smyth *Sailor's Word-bk.*, *Sea-log*, that part of the log-book relating to whatever happens while the ship is at sea. **1955** J. R. R. Tolkien *Return of King* 149 Deep in the hearts of all my kindred lies the *sea-longing. *a* **1973** —— *Silmarillion* (1977) xxiii. 244 The sea-longing woke in his heart. **1817** Canning in *Parl. Deb.* 322 The Admiralty ought to be constituted partly of lay and partly of *sea lords. **1872** *Daily News* 19 Jan., The First Sea Lord had charge of all ships in commission. **1907** *Who's Who* s.v. *Fisher*, Fisher, Admiral Sir John Arbuthnot,..2nd Sea Lord of Admiralty, 1902–3. **1951** R. Macaulay *Let.* 12 Aug. in *Lett. to Friend* (1961) 173, I think I shall airmail this [letter]... But I really will *seamail the next. **1971** *New Society* 14 Jan. 47/1 This [order coupon] gives inland and overseas rates (airmail and seamail). **1933** *Gloss. Aeronaut. Terms* (*B.S.I.*) 64 **Sea marker*, a device dropped from an aircraft on to water, providing a distinguishable patch for determining the drift-angle. **1944** 'N. Shute' *Pastoral* iii. 43 He began a chat with the Equipment Officer about sea-markers that did not mark. **1582** J. Dee *Priv. Diary* (Camden) 17 The same day cam M[r] Clement the *seamaster. **1796** Hutton *Math. & Phil. Dict.* I. 530 *Geographical Mile*, which is the *sea-mile or minute. **1871** Proctor *Lt. Sci.* 224 At the rate of three or four hundred sea-miles an hour. **1941** *Bull. Geol. Soc. Amer.* LII. 338 A number of remarkable submarine mountains, termed '*seamount' by the United States Board on Geographic Names, rise sharply to heights of 1 to more than 2 miles above the gulf floor. **1959** *New Scientist* 1 Jan. 14/1 The few Pacific seamounts whose summits do form islands are mostly coral atolls. **1962** [see GUYOT]. **1977** *Dædalus* Summer 118 Both noticed that the magnetic field over some seamounts could be explained only if the seamount was reversely magnetized. **1694** tr. *Marten's Voy. Spitzbergen* in *Acc. Sev. Late Voy.* II. 30 The Ships do not feel these smaller Waves but only the great ones, that are called *Sea-Mountains. **1774** Goldsm. *Nat. Hist.* (1824) III. 70 That extensive flat [the sand-banks off Cape Breton] seems to be no other than the broad top of a sea mountain,..surrounded with a deeper sea. **1851** *Act 14 & 15 Vict.* c. 26 §6 It shall not be lawful for any Person to use for the Purpose of taking Herrings any Drag Net, or *Sea Net mounted for trawling. **1669** Dryden & Davenant *Temp.* III. iii, This [the boatswain's whistle]..is a Badge of my *Sea-Office. **1864** Webster, **Sea-pass*, a document carried by neutral merchant vessels, in time of war, to show their nationality. **1928** C. Dawson *Age of Gods* xv. 358 It is extremely improbable that the *Sea Peoples actually penetrated into the Hittite homelands. **1957** *Antiquity & Survival* II. 145/1 Sisera stood at the head of the Canaanite coalition, and perhaps belonged to the Sea People who invaded Palestine in the 12th century B.C. and gained control of the sea-coast. **1978** N. K. Sandars *Sea Peoples* iv. 83 Wild northerners.. took ship to arrive on the borders of Egypt as those mysterious 'Sea Peoples' who so terrified Rameses III. **1811** E. H. East *Cases K.B.* (1812) XIV. 465 The ship..was run foul of by another vessel in a gale of wind, and from that and other *sea perils received so much damage as to be obliged to put into Warberg Roads. **1867** Smyth *Sailor's Word-bk.*, *Sea-peril*, synonymous with *sea-risk*. **1855** Hawthorne *Eng. Note-bks.* (1883) I. 566 The poor old fellow..seems to have been a mischief-maker,—what they call a *sea-preacher,—promoting discontent and grumbling. **1910** D. W. Bone *Brassbounder* 64 'Good ol' "*sea price",' said Martin. 'Many an 'appy 'ome, an' garden wit' a flagstaff, is built o' "sea price".' **1924** R. Clements *Gipsy of Horn* iv. 71 Sea-price is often a figure which a Maltee Jew would hesitate to ask. **1972** N. Ayland *Schooner Captain* xv. 134 All the bread he would let them have was a two pound loaf, for which he charged sea price. **1897** Watts-Dunton *Aylwin* II. iii, Associating with fisher-boys and all the shoeless, hatless '*sea-pups' of the sands. **1861** Paley *Æschylus* (ed. 2) *Agamem.* 921 *note*, Garments of the precious *sea-purple. *Ibid.* 933 *note*, The shores of Laconia..produced the sea-purple (*Murex trunculus*) little inferior to the Tyrian. **1753** *Chambers' Cycl.* Suppl. s.v. *Iris*, *Iris marina*, the **Sea Rainbow*. This elegant appearance is generally seen after a violent storm. **1902** R. W. Chambers *Maids of Paradise* x. 176 Dragging a *sea-rake over the ground [*sc.* the sand] behind her. **1634** Massinger *Very Woman* v. i, I'll make.. you the Neptunes of the Sea, you shall No more be *Sea-rats. **1867** Smyth *Sailor's Word-bk.*, **Sea-rate*, the going of a chronometer as established on board, instead of that supplied from the shore [etc.]. *Ibid.*, **Sea-reach*, the straight course or reach of a winding river which stretches out to sea-ward. **1855** Ogilvie *Suppl.*, *Sea-reeve. **1945** E. W. Cowan *Sea-Return Effects & their Elimination in AN/APS-6* (M.I.T. Radiation Lab. Rep. No. 707) 1 An airplane flying very close to the sea may be hidden by *sea return. **1959** *Listener* 12 Feb. 277/1 It is almost impossible to pick up that iceberg with the radar equipment, because of what we call 'sea return' or 'sea clutter'. **1966** D. Taylor *Introd. Radar & Radar Techniques* iii. 40 The actual performance obtained with this form of A.S.V. equipment depended on aircraft height, state of sea (because of sea returns), operator's experience, etc. **1727** Arbuthnot *Tables Anc. Coins*, etc. 273 He charged himself with all the *Sea-risque of such Vessels as carried Corn to Rome in the Winter time. **1884** *G.W.R. Time Tables* July 82 The Company will not be responsible for Sea risks of any kind. **1893** *Columbus* (Ohio) *Dispatch* 9 Nov., If fish disappeared from the *sea-roads and fiords. **1906** *Outlook* 19 May 677/1 We hold the great sea-roads to the East. **1907** T. C. Middleton *Geogr. Knowl. Discov. Amer.* 25 The Vivaldi brothers of Genoa..in 1291 essayed a sea-road to India. **1885** *Science* 22 May 424 The group [of Salvelini] includes fontinalis, known in the *searun condition as immaculatus. **1896** Jordan & Evermann *Fishes N. & Mid. Amer.* 492 Sea-run specimens are nearly uniform silvery. **1872** Coues *Key N. Amer. Birds* 324 Petrels..are oceanic birds..; excepting the *sea-runners, none of them dive. **1599** Nashe *Lenten Stuffe* 10 My Tables are not yet one quarter emptied of my notes out of their Table, which..is, as it were a *Sea Rutter diligently kept amongst them from age to age. **1911** R. S. S. Baden-Powell *Sea Scouting for Boys* 8 *Sea Scouts are of two kinds, viz. (1) Coastguard Scouts; (2) Seamen Scouts. **1912** C. Beresford in W. Baden-Powell *Sea Scouting & Seamanship for Boys* p. vi, The Sea Scouts were formed as an auxiliary to..the Boy Scouts. The object of the Sea Scouts is to teach lads at or near the sea seamanship, navigation, pilotage, knotting and splicing, how to handle boats under oars and sail, [etc.]. **1950** *Oxf. Jun. Encycl.* IX. 87/1 The boy who is fond of the sea can become a Sea Scout. .. There are Sea Scout Troops on rivers and inland waterways as well as on the sea. **1977** *Listener* 24 Mar. 382/3, I was a sea scout and sailed and rowed boats. **1748** *Anson's Voy.* II. i. 110 Languishing..for the land and its vegetable productions, (an inclination constantly attending every stage of the *sea-scurvy). **1835–6** *Todd's Cycl. Anat.* I. 423/2 In sea-scurvy..a similar state occurs. **1925** J. Proudman in *Monthly Notices R. Astron. Soc.* (*Geophysical Suppl.*) I. 247 By '*sea-seiches' we mean those oscillations of fairly definite period but of irregular amplitude and phase which are frequently observed on the sea coast. **1967** *Oceanogr. & Marine Biol.* V. 42 These modes have been called sea seiches ..and are basically similar to the transient oscillations or seiches set up by wind and atmospheric pressure in closed basins. **1744** *Gen. Even. Post* No. 1670 On Saturday the 14th Day of July next will be held the Anniversary Meeting of the Society of *Sea-Serjeants. **1867** Smyth *Sailor's Word-bk.*, *Sea-sergeants*, a society of gentlemen, belonging to the four maritime counties of South Wales... It was a secret association of early date, revived in 1726, and dissolved about 1765. **1738** [G. Smith] *Cur. Relat.* II. v. 8 There are a great many *Sea Shoals floating about the Sea, between which the Fishermen in still Weather look out for Whales. **1903** Morley *Gladstone* IV. vii. (1905) I. 346 Like quicksands or sea-shoals. **1769–80** Falconer *Dict. Marine* II, *Avoir le pied marin*, to wear *sea-shoes; or to walk firm in a ship like a sailor. **1916** *Rudder* Apr. 175 One noticeable thing about the *sea sled..is the absence of bow-wave. **1948** R. de Kerchove *Internat. Maritime Dict.* 639/2 *Sea sled*, a type of construction adopted for small craft of high speed in which the ordinary V bottom is inverted in order to collect a layer of air under the bows of the boat. **1957** *Official Gaz.* (U.S. Patent Office) TM-10/2 Norman A. McDonald, Skokie, Ill. Filed Jan. 24, 1957. Sea Sled..For Boats. First used Mar. 15, 1953. **1838** *Civ. Engin. & Arch. Jrnl.* I. 136/2 The Plymouth Breakwater..has a *sea-slope of about one in five. **1883** *Fortn. Rev.* Feb. 277 The sea-slope of the mountains. **1610** Shaks. *Temp.* I. ii. 170 Sit still, and heare the last of our *sea-sorrow. **1887** W. H. White *Mod. War Ships* 94 The '*sea-speeds' of all war-ships are always estimated on different assumptions. **1908** *Westm. Gaz.* 27 Apr. 10/2 The sea-speed aimed at in the contract will be about 16½ knots. **1899** *Geogr. Jrnl.* Mar. 288 The isolated rock-masses and *sea-stacks, which we are enabled to trace by means of the soundings. **1973** C. Bonington *Next Horizon* xxi. 292 A sea-stack on the north coast of Scotland. [**1963** *Meteorol. Gloss.* (Met. Office) (ed. 4) 222 The degree of sea disturbance is reported in a 'state of sea' code in which the scale number increases from 0 to 9 according to the average wave height.] **1967** *Jane's Surface Skimmer Systems 1967–68* 85/1 The journey has been covered successfully in *Sea States 2–4, with wave heights up to 5 ft 0 in (1·5 m). **1977** *Offshore Engineer* Apr. 74/1 The calculator multiplies measured value of the load by a factor determined by sea-state, and compares result with safe-load for the particular crane luff angle specified in manufacturer's table. *a* **1618** *Rates Marchandizes* M 4 b, Herrings, Shotten, vnpacked, or *Sea-sticks y[e] Last, cont. 18 barrels, iiij l. **1641** S. Smith *Herring Buss Trade* 7 The sea-sticks are all the Fishing season as they come from the sea..repact on shore. **1813** *Q. Rev.* IX. 291 All the Herrings caught and packed to be bought by Government at 25/ a barrel of sea-sticks. **1856** Emerson *Eng. Traits, Voy. to Eng.* 33 Chances of squall, collision, *sea-stroke, piracy, cold, and thunder. **1902** R. W. Chambers *Maids of Paradise* x. 176 She was a lithe creature ..with the *sea-tan on throat and knee. **1663** Pepys *Diary* 7 Jan., Commanders did never heretofore receive any pay for the rigging time, but only for *Seatime. **1793** Rennell in *Phil. Trans.* LXXXIII. 193, I have, through-out, reckoned according to sea time; that is, the day commences at noon. **1899** Mahan in *Eng. Hist. Rev.* July 483 The date of this Opinion is misleading to-day, because it uses the now obsolete sea-time. **1930** *Times* 26 Mar. 17/4 Her sea-time beat the Bremen's best..by eighteen minutes. **1933** J. Masefield *Bird of Dawning* 16, I wished to get sea-time, sir, so as to be able to pass for master. **1977** *Navy News* Aug. 22 (Advt.), Service includes normal roster sea-time in Leander and Type 12 frigates and small ships. **1847** H. Melville *Omoo* xxiv. 92 'Give him a *sea-toss!' 'Overboard with him!' **1933** *Nat. Geogr. Mag.* May 581/1 Freight-car contents are transferred here into the holds of liners, and recently a terminal was established which places loaded cars themselves within huge vessels called '*seatrains'. **1942** W. S. Churchill *Second World War* (1951) IV. I. xxii. 349 These equipments will sail for Suez..in two sea-trains taken from the Havana sugar traffic, doing 15 and 13 knots respectively. **1947** *Sun* (Baltimore) 14 July 7/3 The ships which..should be started this year..are..two for Alaskan trade specifically, two sea trains and two 'mystery'. **1876** Smiles *Sc. Natur.* xiv. 280 He usually visited his *sea-traps once a month. **1624** Chapman *Homer's Hymn to Apollo* 684 The Light himselfe..made the *Sea-trod ship [ποντοπόρος νηῦς] ariue them nere The Grapefull Crissa. **1627** Capt. Smith *Seaman's Gram.* x. 46 All the night it [the breeze] is from the shore which is called a Turnado, or a *Sea-turne. **1792** Belknap *Hist. New Hampsh.* III. 23 Sometimes the extreme heat of several days, produces, in the maritime parts, a sea turn, and in the inland parts, a whirlwind. **1883** Howells *Woman's Reason* I. 97 A dull chilly morning when the sea-turn was beginning to break in a thin, chilly rain. **1895** Kipling *Day's Work* (1898) 81 A *sea-valve that communicated directly with the water outside. **1915** Chesterton *Poems* 16 On them the sea-valves cluster and the grey sea-forests curl. **1201** *Rot. Chart.* (1837) 89/1 Quieta de schiris et hundredis..de *sewake, castelwerke, taillagio, cornagio, et de omni thelonio. *c* **888** K. Ælfred *Boeth.* xxxii. §3 Be *sæwaroðe. *c* **1450** *Mirk's Festial* 7 As he walket on þe see-warth, he segh a drownet man cast vp on þe watyr. **1767** *Ann. Reg.* X. I. 141/1 Two time-pieces or *sea-watches. **1769–80** Falconer *Dict. Marine* II. s.v. *Bordee*, *Faire la grande Bordee*, to set a watch of half the ship's crew, when in any dangerous road, usually called the sea-watch. **1807** T. Thomson *Chem.* (ed. 3) II. 455 *Sea wax, or maltha, is a solid substance found on the Baikal lake in Siberia. **1855** in *Ogilvie's Suppl.* **1934** *Sun* (Baltimore) 17 Sept. 12/1 The *sea-wise reason that in a strong breeze and an attendant unruly sea that elongated prow will come down and pound against the chop or plunge into a heavy swell. **1966** T. H. Raddall *Hangman's Beach* I. ii. 29 The sea-wise folk of Halifax awaited word from Europe. **1695** Congreve *Love for Love* III. vi, I swear Mr. Benjamin is the verriest Wag in nature; an absolute *Sea-wit. **1706** E. Ward *Wooden World Diss.* (1708) 98 He and his Brother Jacks lie pelting each other with Sea-Wit. **1728** ? Arbuthnot *A.'s Misc. Wks.* (1751) II. 164 In this Instance his absolute Sea-Wit seems to come somewhat short of the Mark. **1609** E. Grimston *Hist. Netherl.* 116 A *Sea-woman swimming in the Zuyderzee. **1901** *Westm. Gaz.* 22 Aug. 2/3 The green weed shone as silken as a sea-woman's hair. **1939** *Sun* (Baltimore) 1 July 20/2 Twenty-three seawomen sailed into Baltimore harbor yesterday afternoon aboard the ship William J. Stanford. **1963** *Punch* 21 Aug. 288/3 The endless queue of frustrated seawomen. **1528** *Lett. & Pap. Hen. VIII*, IV. II. 2228 The ordinary reparations of the town sluices, *see works [etc.]. **1567** Golding *Ovid's Met.* XIII. 1079, I Was given too seawoorkes, and in them mee only did apply. **1855** Kingsley *Westw. Ho!* xxix, He never saw sea-work to my remembrance. Never saw a shot fired by sea, except ours at Smerwick. **1897** *River & Coast* 29 May 12/2 Mr. Gibson well-known in connection with sea-work, including bridges, screw-pile piers, jetties, &c. **1704** J. Harris *Lex. Techn.* I, **Sea-Yoke*.

b. In the names of marine mammalia, as † **sea-boar**, some kind of large cetacean; **sea-canary**, a sailor's name for the white whale or beluga, *Delphinapterus leucas*, of the dolphin family (see quot.); **sea-goose**, 'a dolphin, so called from the shape of the snout' (*Cent. Dict.* 1891); **sea-leopard**, a name for various seals of the antarctic and southern seas, esp. of the genus *Ogmorhinus* (formerly *Stenorhynchus*); **sea-monk**, 'the monk-seal' (*Cent. Dict.*); † **sea-monoceros** = SEA-UNICORN 1; **sea-morse**, the morse or walrus, also *attrib.*; **sea-pellock** *dial.*, the porpoise (*E.D.D.*); **sea-pig**, applied to the porpoise, the dolphin, the dugong, etc. (see also PIG *sb.*[1] 4); **sea-seal**, the seal; † **sea-veal** = SEA-CALF.

1634 T. Johnson tr. *Parey's Chirurg.* XXV. xxi. 1005 The effigies of a *Sea-Bore. Olaus Magnus writes that this monster was taken at Thyle. **1879** E. P. Wright *Anim. Life* 130 When under water, they [dolphins] emit a peculiar whistling sound,..and on this account the seamen often call them *sea-canaries. **1664** Hubert *Catal. Rarities* (1665) 14 A *Sea-Leopard. **1825** Weddell *Voy. S. Pole* 22 Having seen some sea-leopards on shore, I sent the second mate to take them... This creature resembles the quadruped of the same name in being spotted. **1891** Flower & Lydekker *Introd. Mammals* 605 One species, *Ogmorhinus leptonyx*, the Sea-Leopard, widely distributed in the Antarctic and southern temperate seas. **1672** Josselyn *New-Eng. Rarities* 32 Sea Vnicorn or *Sea Mononeros. **1631** J. Rous *Diary* (Camden) 64 A *Sea-morce as big as an oxe. **1642** *Rates Merchandizes* 48 Sea morse teeth the pound 00. 05. 00. **1858** Simmonds *Dict. Trade*, *Sea-morse-teeth*, a name for the canines or tusks of the hippopotamus. **1826** *Sea-pig [see PIG *sb.*[1] 4]. **1879** E. P. Wright *Anim. Life* 130 [Dolphins] are sometimes also called 'sea-pigs'. **1398** Trevisa *Barth. De P.R.* XVIII. lxxii. (1495) 840 The skynne of the *see Sele. **1851** *Zoologist* IX. 3298 The common sea-seal or elephant is very numerous on our coast [California]. **1576** Fleming tr. *Caius' Eng. Dogs* (1880) 19 The sea Calfe,..other more largely name a *Sea Vele.

c. In names of birds: **sea-brant**, (*a*) *U.S.*, the white-winged scoter, *Œdemia deglandi*; (*b*) 'the brant- or brent-goose' (*Cent. Dict.* 1891); **sea-bumblebee** = *sea-dove* (ibid.); **sea-coot**, †(*a*) the cormorant; (*b*) the guillemot (see COOT *sb.*[1] 1); (*c*) a scoter of the genus *Œdemia* (Cent. Dict.); (*d*) the American coot (see COOT *sb.*[1] 2); **sea-coulter**, the puffin, *Fratercula arctica*; **sea-dotterel**, the turnstone, *Strepsilas interpres*; also a local name for the ring-plover; **sea-dove**, the little auk, *Mergulus alle*; **sea-drake**, a cormorant or sea-crow; also *U.S.*, the male eider-duck; **sea-goose** *U.S.*, a phalarope (see quot.); **sea-kittie**, a dial. name for the kittiwake, also for any sea-gull; **sea-magpie** = SEA-PIE[1]; † **sea-moit** [F. *mouette*], a sea-gull; † **sea-peacock**, the Balearic or Crowned Crane; **sea-piet, -pilot** = SEA-PIE[1]; **sea-plover**, a local name for *Squatarola helvetica*; **sea-quail** *U.S.*, the sea-dotterel or turnstone; **sea-skimmer**, a skimmer, a bird of the genus *Rhynchops*; **sea-titling**, the rock-pipit; † **sea turtle-dove** = SEA-TURTLE[1]; **sea-whaup** *Sc.*, a species of sea-gull; **sea-widgeon**, (*a*) 'the pintail duck'; (*b*) 'the scaup-duck' (*Funk's Stand. Dict.*); **sea-woodcock**, (*a*) some West Indian bird; (*b*) applied *dial.* to various birds, e.g. the bar-tailed godwit, *Limosa lapponica*, the oyster-catcher or SEA-PIE, and the little grebe, *Trachybaptes fluviatilis*.

1888 Trumbull *Names & Portr. Birds* 99 *Sea Brant. **1575** Turberv. *Faulconrie* 137 The flesh of the Bitter and *Sea Coote is good. **1684** Sibbald *Scotia Illustr.* II. III. vii. 22 *Avis Marina* *Sea-Coulter *dicta*. *a* **1672** Willughby *Ornith.* (1676) 231 *Morinellus marinus*... The Turnstone or *Sea-Dotterel. **1805** G. Barry *Orkney Isl.* 300 The Turnstone or Sea Dotterel (*charadrius morinellus* Lin. Syst.). **1826** J. F. Stephens in *Shaw's Gen. Zool.* XIII. I. 34 (*Mergulus melanoleucos*)... *Sea-dove. **1855** Kingsley *Westw. Ho!* xxvii, Or if I was a say-dove, to fly unto the shoor. **1632** Sherwood, *Sea-drake, sea-raven, or sea-cormorant, *diable de mer*. **1861** [see SEA-DUCK 1]. **1861** Coues in *Proc. Philad. Acad.* 229 The [*Phalaropus*] *fulicarius* and *hyperboreus* are both known by the..inappropriate, though curious name of '*Sea-geese'. **1885** Swainson *Prov. Names Birds* 206 Kittiwake (*Rissa tridactyla*)... *Sea kittie (Norfolk; Suffolk). **1805** *Sporting Mag.* XXV. 226 *Sea-magpye. **1681** Grew *Musæum* I. §iv. iv. 77 The Egg of the *Sea-Moit. **1774** Goldsm. *Nat. Hist.* (1824) II. 362 Some have described them [the Balearic cranes] by the name of the *Sea Peacock. **1710** Sibbald *Fife & Kinross* 46 *Hæmotopus Bellonii*, the *Sea-Piot. **1880** Black *White Wings* xx, There is no screaming sea-pyot to give warning. **1891** *Century Dict.*, **Sea-pilot*. **1682** A. Mudie *Pres. St. Scot.* i. 12 *Sea-plover, Pewits, Woodcoks [etc.]. **1888** Trumbull *Names & Portr. Birds* 186 *Sea Quail. **1839** *Penny Cycl.* XIII. 333/1 Brisson placed in his twenty-third order..the Gulls,.. Terns, *Sea-skimmer or *Rhyncopsalia*. **1872** Latham *Dict.*, **Sea-titling*. *a* **1672** Willughby *Ornith.* (1676) 245 *Columba Groenlandica dicta*. The Greenland-Dove or *Sea-Turtle-Dove. **1822** H. Ainslie *Pilgr. Land of Burns* 208 The *sea whaups cry As they rise frae the whitening roar. **1624** Capt. Smith *Gen. Hist.* v. 171 Coots and Red-shankes, *Sea-wigions, Gray-bitterns [etc.]. **1666** J. Davies *Hist. Caribby Isles* 106 There is another kind of Becunes, by some called *Sea-Wood-Cocks from the figure of the Beak. *a* **1682** Sir T. Browne *Norf. Fishes* Wks. 1835 IV. 329 A *scolopax* or sea woodcock of Rondeletius. **1887** A. C. Smith *Birds Wilts.* 423 In consequence of their great length of beak, they [*sc.* the bar-tailed godwits] are often called 'Sea Woodcocks'.

d. In the names of fishes, jelly-fishes, molluscs, shells, etc., as **sea-acorn** (see ACORN 4), also *sea-acorn shell*; **sea-anemone** (see ANEMONE 2); **sea-angel**, the angel-fish; **sea-arrow**, (*a*) a mollusc of the genus *Ommastrephes*; (*b*) a member of the *Sagittidæ*; **sea-attorney**, 'the ordinary brown and rapacious shark' (Smyth *Sailor's Word-bk.* 1867); **sea-barrel**, an ascidian of the class *Tunicata*; **sea-barrow**, the egg-case of the skate; **sea-basket**, a basket-fish or gorgon's head; †**sea-beard**, a sertularian coral (see quot.); **sea-biscuit** = *sand dollar* s.v. SAND *sb.*^{2} 10 b; †**sea-bleb** = SEA-BLUBBER 2; †**sea-blewling** [cf. G. *bläuling* pilchard], some bluish fish; **sea-blub** = SEA-BLUBBER 2; **sea-bread**, = *sea-cracker*; **sea-bristle**, a sertularian polyp, *Plumularia setosa*; **sea-bug**, †(*a*) a triton shell; (*b*) (see quot. 1884); **sea-bun**, the heart-urchin; **sea butterfly**, a mollusc of the sub-class *Pteropoda*; †**sea-button**, a sea-urchin (cf. *button-fish* s.v. BUTTON *sb.* 12); **sea-cactus**, a holothurian of the family *Thyonidæ*; **sea-cap**, 'a basket-shaped sponge which sometimes attains great size, found in Florida' (*Cent. Dict.*); †**sea-capon** (see quot.); **sea-carnation**, a kind of sea-anemone; **sea-caterpillar**, (*a*) a marine worm of the genus *Polynoë*; (*b*) a chiton shell; **sea-catfish**, a name for various marine siluroid fishes; **sea-centipede**, (*a*) a large marine errant annelid; (*b*) an isopod of the family *Idoteidæ*; †**sea-chameleon**, the BLEAK; **sea-chestnut**, a sea-urchin; †**sea-chough**, ? = SEA-CROW; †**sea-chub** (see quot.); **sea-clam** one of several species of clam found on the Atlantic coast of North America, esp. the surf clam, *Spisula solidissima*; cf. HEN-CLAM; **sea-clerk**, the calamary; **sea-cockroach**, a crustacean of the genus *Remipes*; †**sea-coralline**, a coralline or coral; **sea-corn** *U.S.*, the string of egg-capsules of the whelk; **sea-cracker** (see quot.); **sea-crawfish, -crayfish**, †(*a*) (see CRAYFISH *sb.* 2); (*b*) a crustacean of the genus *Palinurus* (= CRAYFISH *sb.* 3 b); **sea-cross**, a jelly-fish; †**sea-cup**, a polyp (see quot.); **sea-cut**, the cuttlefish or calamary; †**sea-cypress**, a sertularian polyp; **sea-dace**, the sea-perch or bass; **sea-danger**, a jelly-fish; †**sea-dart** (see quots. and DART *sb.* 5); **sea-date, sea date-shell** (see quots. and *date-shell* s.v. DATE *sb.*^{1} 4); †**sea dog-fish**, the SEA-FOX or SEA-APE; †**sea-emperor**, a swordfish; †**sea-fig**, a polyp (see quot.); **sea-finger** (see quots.); **sea-fir**, a sertularian polyp or coral; **sea-flea**, the sand-flea or sand-hopper; †**sea-forty-legs** = *sea-centipede*; **sea-frog** = ANGLER 2; †**sea-galliwasp**, a Jamaican name for *Elops saurus*; †**sea-gar**, a crustacean (see quot.); **sea-gherkin**, one of several small holothurians, akin to the sea-cucumber; **sea-ginger** (see quot.); †**sea-grasshopper**, a squill or mantis-shrimp; **sea-gudgeon** (see GUDGEON *sb.*^{1} 1 b); **sea-hag**, the hag-fish; **sea-hair**, a sertularian polyp; †**sea-hare-fish**, the SEA-HARE (*Aplysia*); †**sea hog-louse**, a sea-slater; **sea-honey-comb** (see *sea-corn* above); **sea-insect**, †(*a*) a coral-polyp (or '-insect'); (*b*) a crustacean; **sea-jelly**, a jellyfish; †**sea-kite**, a kind of flying-fish; †**sea-lampern** = *sea-lamprey* (*a*); **sea-lamprey**, †(*a*) = REMORA 1; (*b*) a marine lamprey, *Petromyzon marinus*; **sea-leech**, a marine annelid of the genus *Pontobdella*; **sea-lemon**, (*a*) a nudibranchiate gastropod of the family *Dorididæ*; (*b*) *Austral.*, 'a holothurian of the genus *Cuvieria*; sea-orange' (*Funk's Stand. Dict.*); **sea-lily**, a crinoid; †**sea-liver** (see quots.); **sea-locust** *arch.* [L. *locusta*], a lobster; **sea long-worm**, a nemertean worm of the family *Lineidæ* and genus *Lineus*; **sea mantis**, the mantis-shrimp; **sea-marigold**, a kind of sea-anemone; **sea-mat**, a polyzoan of the family *Flustridæ* and genus *Flustra*; **sea-mat acorn-shell** (see quot.); **sea-melon**, a holothurian of the family *Pentactidæ*; **sea-minnow**, †(*a*) the anchovy; (*b*) *dial.* (see quot.); **sea-moth**, a small fish of the family Pegasidæ, found in Indo-Pacific waters and having bony plates covering the body and enlarged pectoral fins; †**sea-mulberry**, a variety of coral (see quot.); †**sea-mushroom**, a sea-anemone; †**sea-nail** = *sea-finger* (above); †**sea-navel** (see quot.); **sea-necklace** (see *sea-corn* above); **sea-needle**, the gar-fish, *Belone vulgaris* (cf. NEEDLE-FISH); **sea-orange**, a large holothurian (*Lophothuria fabricii*) of a globose shape and orange-coloured; **sea-orb**, a swell, globe, or orb-fish; **sea-pad**, a star-fish; **sea-palm**, a crinoid (see quot.); **sea-panther**, †(*a*) ? a houndfish or shark; (*b*) 'a South African fish, *Agriopus torvus*, of a brown color with black spots' (*Cent. Dict.*); **sea-parson**, the stargazer; **sea-peach** (see quot.); **sea-pear**, an ascidian or sea-squirt of the genus *Boltenia*; †**sea-pelican** = *sea-dart*; †**sea-pencil**, the razor-shell or spout-fish; **sea-perch** (see PERCH *sb.*^{1} 2); **sea-pert**, the OPAH; **sea-pill-ball**, an isopod crustacean (*Sphæroma*), a globe-slater; **sea-pincushion**, (*a*) = *sea-barrow*; (*b*) 'a kind of starfish of the genus *Goniaster*' (Smyth *Sailor's Word-bk.*); †**sea-pipe**, ? a 'pipe-worm'; **sea-poacher**, the armed bull-head or pogge; **sea-porcupine**, the porcupine-fish, *Diodon hystrix*; **sea-potato** *local U.S.*, an ascidian, as *Boltenia reniformis* or *Ascidia mollis* (Cent. Dict.); †**sea-poult**, ? a sea-hen; †**sea-priest** (cf. *sea-parson*); **sea-pudding**, †(*a*) an *Actinia* or sea-anemone; (*b*) a large sea-cucumber; **sea-qualm**, a jelly-fish or cuttle-fish; **sea-quince** = *sea-orange*; †**sea-roach**, the cunner; **sea-roll**, 'a holothurian' (*Cent. Dict.*); **sea-rose**, (*a*) = *sea-corn*; (*b*) 'a sea-anemone, *Urticina nodosa*, found on Newfoundland, etc.' (*Cent. Dict.*); **sea-ruff** = RUFF *sb.*^{1} 1; **sea-ruffle** = *sea-corn*; **sea-sac**, any ascidian of the class *Tunicata*; **sea-salmon**, a pollack, also the spotted weakfish and the white sea-bass (*Funk's Stand. Dict.*); **sea-scallop**, 'the great northern scallop' (ibid.); **sea-scurf**, a polyzoan of the genus *Lepralia*; †**sea-shears**, ? = *sea-woodlouse*; †**sea-shilling** [Du. *zeeschelling*], a sea-urchin; **sea-shrub**, an alcyonarian polyp of the family *Gorgonidæ*, a sea-fan; **sea-silkworm**, a bivalve mollusc of the genus *Pinna*; **sea-slater**, a small isopod crustacean, *Ligia oceanica*; **sea-sleeve**, a cuttle-fish or calamary; †**sea-snapple** (see quot.); **sea-sow** *dial.*, the ballan wrasse; †**sea sparrow**, ? the plaice; †**sea sparrow-hawk**, the lizard- or snake-fish, *Synodus fœtens*; **sea-squirt**, any ascidian or tunicate, also *attrib.*; †**sea-star-flower**, a sea-anemone; **sea-stickle, -stickleback**, the (marine) fifteen-spined stickleback, *Gasterosteus spinachia* or *Spinachia vulgaris*; †**sea-stickling**, ? = the *glaucus* of Pliny; †**sea-stranger** *Sc.*, the adder-pike, *Trachinus vipera*; **sea-strawberry**, 'a kind of polyp, *Alcyonium rubiforme*' (Cent. Dict.); **sea-sucker**, a sucker, a fish of the family *Cyclopteridæ*; †**sea-sun**, a kind of starfish; **sea-sunflower**, a sea-anemone; **sea-surgeon**, 'a surgeon-fish' (*Cent. Dict.*); **sea-tamarisk**, a sertularian polyp; **sea-tench**, 'the black sea-bream, *Cantharus lineatus*' (Cent. Dict.); **sea-thorn** (see quot.); **sea tiger** = BARRACUDA; †**sea-tod** *Sc.*, the ballan wrasse, *Labrus maculatus*; †**sea-torchthistle**, a variety of sea-anemone; **sea-umbrella**, 'a pennatulaceous polyp of the genus *Umbellularia*' (Cent. Dict.); **sea-vampire**, 'a devil-fish or manto' (ibid.); **sea-washball**, a local name for the egg-case of the whelk; **sea wasp**, a poisonous jellyfish belonging to the order Cubomedusæ, found in Indo-Pacific waters; **sea-weasel**, 'an old name of the lamprey' (Smyth *Sailor's Word-bk.*); **sea-weever**, the greater weever (*Trachinus draco*); **sea-whip** = SEA-FAN; **sea-wife**, a kind of wrasse, *Acantholabrus yarrelli*; **sea wood-borer**, a wood-shrimp, *Chelura terebrans*; **sea-wood-louse**, (*a*) a sea-slater; (*b*) a chiton or coat-of-mail shell, so called from resembling the above; **sea-wreath**, a sertularian polyp.

1755 *Gentl. Mag.* XXV. 33 *Sea Acorns, *Balani.* **1879** E. P. WRIGHT *Anim. Life* 531 The Sea Acorn Shells. **1742** H. BAKER *Microsc.* II. v. 99 The *Sea-Mushroom*.., some Naturalists have called it the **Sea-Anemone.* **1855, 1881** [see ANEMONE 2]. **1891** *Century Dict.*, **Sea-angel.* **1896** tr. *Boas' Text-bk. Zool.* 384 There are Sharks (*Squatina*, the Sea-angel), which are somewhat flattened. **1851** WOODWARD *Mollusca* 73 The sailors call them '*sea-arrows' or 'flying squids' from their habit of leaping out of the water. **1854** A. ADAMS, etc. *Man. Nat. Hist.* 142 Sea-Arrows (*Sagittidæ*). **1849** H. MELVILLE *Mardi* I. 55 There is the ordinary Brown Shark, or *sea-attorney, so called by sailors. **1854** *Putnam's Mag.* Apr. 362/2 The dippers dip carefully, lest they get a stroke from the ray..or a rip from his cousin the 'sea-attorney'. **1876** tr. *Haeckel's Hist. Creat.* II. 150 Sea-sacs, Tunicata, Sea-squirts, *Sea-barrels. **1860** WORCESTER (cites *Gentl. Mag.*), *Sea-barrow. **1865** T. R. JONES *Anim. Creation* 65 The *Sea-baskets (*Gorgonocephalus*). **1755** J. ELLIS *Corallines* 15 Lobster's horn Coralline, or *Sea-beard. **1949** G. E. & N. MACGINITIE *Nat. Hist. Marine Anim.* xxvi. 236 The sand dollars, *sea biscuits, or cake urchins.. resemble very much flattened sea urchins. **1972** *Islander* (Victoria, B.C.) 12 Mar. 16/4 White people call them [*sc.* sea-urchins] sea-biscuits or sand-dollars. **1700** C. LEIGH *Nat. Hist. Lancs.*, etc. I. 133 We have frequently cast upon the sea-shore the *Sea-Blebs, the whole substance of which seems to be nothing but a perfect Gelly. **1668** CHARLETON *Onomast.* 135 *Glaucus Bellonii*... Idem forte, quem piscatores nostri *Sea-Blewling vocant. **1885** *Riverside Nat. Hist.* (1888) I. 89 Those called the Discophora, 'sea-nettles', '*sea-blubs', or jelly-fishes. **1888** *Sea-bread [see *sea-cracker* below]. **1755** J. ELLIS *Corallines* 19 *Sea-Bristles. **1843** *Zoologist* I. 209 Sea-bristles (*Plumularia setacea*). **1602** DOLMAN *La Primaud. Fr. Acad.* (1618) III. 783 The Triton (otherwise called the *sea Bug). **1884** GOODE, etc. *Nat. Hist. Aquatic Anim.* 701 These [Chiton] shells have been called by different names,..such as..'Sea-bug', and 'Sea-caterpillar'. **1882** *Cassell's Nat. Hist.* VI. 270 *Spatangus* (Heart-urchin or *Sea-bun). [**1883** *Science* I. 508/1 The winged..mollusks..known to the Neapolitan fishermen as *farfalle di mare*, or sea-butterflies.] **1909** SHACKLETON *Heart Antarctic* II. 266 A few *sea-butterflies (*Pteropods*) of large size and red colour. **1932** BORRADAILE & POTTS *Invertebrata* 494 The Pteropoda (sea butterflies)..are modified for pelagic life. **1972** M. S. GARDINER *Biol. Invertebrates* v. 161/1 Planktonic 'pteropods'..or 'sea butterflies'. **1668** CHARLETON *Onomast.* 183 *Echinus Minimus*..the *Sea-Button. **1854** A. ADAMS, etc. *Man. Nat. Hist.* 330 *Sea-Cactuses (*Thyonidæ*). **1620** VENNER *Via Recta* iv. 75 The Sole,..For whitenes [etc.]..far excelleth all other Sea fish, and therefore may well be termed the *Sea Capon. **1672** JOSSELYN *New-Eng. Rarities* 30 Soles, or Tonguefish, or Sea Capon, or Sea Partridge. **1767** J. ELLIS in *Phil. Trans.* LVII. 436 The *Actinia dianthus* or *Sea carnation. *a* **1843** SOUTHEY *Comm.-Pl. Bk.* (1851) IV. 401 Herrings [feed] on an insect called the *sea caterpillar. **1869** W. S. DALLAS tr. *F. Müller's Facts for Darwin* 111 The Sea Caterpillars (Polynoë) at first possess only a few body-segments. **1884** Sea-caterpillar [see *sea-bug* above]. **1882** JORDAN & GILBERT *Synopsis Fishes N. Amer.* 110 *Arius felis*... *Sea Cat-fish. *Ibid.* 111 *Ælurichthys marinus*... Sea Cat-fish. **1858** BAIRD *Cycl. Nat. Sci.* s.v. *Aunelida*, To this order [*Dorsibranchiata*] belong the *sea centipedes or *Nereidæ*. *Ibid.* s.v. *Isopoda*, The sea centipedes, *Idotea*. **1661** LOVELL *Hist. Anim. & Min.* 187 They are called *Sea Chameleons also. **1672** JOSSELYN *New-Eng. Rarities* 24 Sea Bleak or Bley, or Sea Camelion. **1666** *Sea-chestnut [see SEA-EGG 1]. **1672** JOSSELYN *New-Eng. Rarities* 24 *Sea Chough. **1668** CHARLETON *Onomast.* 151 *Capito*..the *Sea-Chub, or Pollard. **1765** J. BARTRAM *Jrnl.* 29 July in *Trans. Amer. Philos. Soc.* (1942) XXXIII. 16/2 There is many clam shels of different sises..ye very same with our *sea clams. **1782** [see HARD-SHELLED *a.* 1]. **1864** Sea-clam [see HEN *sb.* 6]. **1935** J. C. LINCOLN *Cape Cod Yesterdays* 49 Along the outer bar, almost two miles from shore..were the large 'sea clams'. **1960** J. J. ROWLANDS *Spindrift* 83 Sea clams are from four to six inches long and about four inches wide. **1623** COCKERAM III, *Calæmarie*, a fish called the *Sea Clarke, hauing as it were a knife and a pen. **1896** tr. *Boas' Text-bk. Zool.* 323 The Sea-clerk (*Loligo vulgaris*). **1792** M. RIDDELL *Voy. Madeira* 77 The *oniscus physodes*, or **sea-cockroach*, is about two inches long; it has fourteen feet without nippers. **1753** CHAMBERS *Cycl.* Suppl. s.v. *Corallina*, The small, fir-like, *sea-coralline. **1885** *Riverside Nat. Hist.* (1888) I. 333 Presenting an appearance well-described by the name '*sea-corn' applied to them by the New England fishermen. **1891** *Century Dict.*, *Sea-corn*. .. Also *sea-ear*, *sea-ruffle*, *sea-honeycomb*, *sea-necklace*, etc. **1888** HEILPRIN *Anim. Life Sea-shore* v. 115 The 'sea-bread' or '*sea-crackers', rounded yellowish masses..are also skeletal parts of sponges. **1601** HOLLAND *Pliny* XXXII. xi. II. 451 The *sea Craifish Cammarus. **1694** tr. *Marten's Voy. Spitzbergen* in *Acc. Sev. Late Voy.* II. 113 The sea Crawfish without a Tail, or Sea Spider. **1856** *Engl. Cycl., Nat. Hist.* IV. 174 The *Palinuri* or Sea-Crawfish, as they are popularly called, have the body nearly cylindrical. **1850** MISS PRATT *Comm. Things of Sea-side* v. 326 Our common species [of jelly-fish] are termed Sea-blubbers, Sea-dangers, Falling stars, or *Sea-crosses. **1755** J. ELLIS *Corallines* 87 *Alcyonium, seu Cyathus marinus.* *Sea Cup. **1601** HOLLAND *Pliny* IX. xv. I. 244 Good store of *Sea-cuts or Calamaries. **1755** J. ELLIS *Corallines* 7 *Sea-Cypress. *a* **1776** —— *Zoophytes* (1786) 38 *Sertularia cupressina.* Sea Cypress. **1668** CHARLETON *Onomast.* 143 *Apua*..the Spirling, Smy, or *Sea-Dace. **1863** WOOD *Illustr. Nat. Hist.* III. 231 The.. Basse, or Sea-Dace, or Sea-Perch. **1850** *Sea-danger [see *sea-cross* above]. **1664** HUBERT *Catal. Rarities* (1665) 17 A long narrow fish called the Sea-Pelican for the form of its head, also it is called the *Sea-Dart. **1797** HOLCROFT *Stolberg's Trav.* III. lxv. (ed. 2) 23 A kind of sea insect.. called..*Sea-date. **1858** BAIRD *Cycl. Nat. Sci.* s.v. *Lithodomus*, It [the bivalve *L. lithophagus*].. is generally known by the name of the 'sea date shell'. **1611** COTGR., *Peis espase*, the sea Fox, or *sea Dog-fish. **1672** JOSSELYN *New-Eng. Rarities* 25 *Sea Emperour or Sword Fish. **1755** J. ELLIS *Corallines* 82 *Alcyonium pulmonis instar lobatum*... *Sea Fig. **1748** *Veg. Renatus of Distemp. Horses* 42 Those small Shell Fishes they call Sea-nails or *Sea-fingers. **1876** SMILES *Sc. Natur.* xvi. 329 'Dead-men's paps, sea-fingers, etc.' (*Alcyonium digitatum*). **1633** JOHNSON *Gerarde's Herbal* III. clxv. 1574 *Abies marina Belgica*, Clus. Clusius his *Sea Firr. **1755** J. ELLIS *Corallines* 4 *Corallina marina Abietis forma*... Sea-Fir. *a* **1776** —— *Zoophytes* (1786) 36 *Sertularia abietina*, Sea Fir Coralline. **1870** NICHOLSON *Man. Zool.* vii. (1875) 90 The Sea-firs (*Sertularida*). **1658** ROWLAND tr. *Moufet's Theat. Ins.* 1127 The *Sea-fleas are larger... It shewes a wonderful deal of agility when men strive to catch it. **1750** G. HUGHES *Barbados* 259 The *Sea-Forty-Legs. **1601** HOLLAND *Pliny* XXXII. v. II. 434 The decoction of *sea-frogs sodden in wine and vinegre. **1854** BADHAM *Halieut.* 251 A sea-frog as prepared by the Neapolitan boatmen for a show. **1713** RAY *Syn. Pisc.* 159 *Saurus maximus non maculatus*; The Sean fish or *Sea Galley Wasp. **1674** —— *Catal. Fishes* 105 Shell-Fish. Crustaceous. Long Oyster, *Sea-gar, Red Crab: *Locusta marina.* **1841** E. FORBES *Brit. Starfishes* 229 The animals to which we have applied the name of *Sea-Girkins. **1884** GOODE, etc. *Nat. Hist. Aquatic Anim.* 841 The so-called Finger Coral or *Sea Ginger (*Millepora alcicornis*), the latter common name having reference to the smarting sensation which it imparts to the skin, on handling. **1668** CHARLETON *Onomast.* 175 *Squillæ*..*Mantis*..the *Sea-Grashopper. **1665** *Sea-gudgeon [see SEA-COB^2]. **1864** W. S. SYMONDS *Old Bones* (ed. 2) 122 The Sea Gudgeon, or common goby of the aquavivarium. **1881** *Encycl. Brit.* XII. 645/1 The skeleton of the Cyclostomata (or Marsipobranchii) (lampreys and *sea-hags). **1755** J. ELLIS *Corallines* 8 *Corallus muscosa denticulata procumbens* [etc.]. *Sea-Hair. *a* **1776** —— *Zoophytes* (1786) 39 *Sertularia operculata.* Sea-Hair Coralline. **1607** TOPSELL *Four-f. Beasts* 27 Against the venom of a *sea-Hare-fish. **1702** PETIVER *Gazophyl.* i. Tab. 1 *Asellus marinus, e nigro luteoque striatus.* *Sea-Hog-louse. **1664** HUBERT *Catal. Rarities* (1665) 27 A *Sea insect called the Sea Shears. **1755** J. ELLIS *Corallines* 73 On which different species of Sea Insects build their calcarious Nests. **1860** WRAXALL *Life in Sea* iii. 68 The hopping sea-insects and molluscs. *a* **1682** SIR T. BROWNE *Norf. Fishes* Wks. 1835

IV. 333 Squalders, or *sea-jellies. **1683–4** ROBINSON in *Phil. Trans.* XXIX. 478 The *Urtica Marina* (called Sea Gelly or Blubber). **1864** BROWNING *Death in Desert* 152, I seemed left alone Like a sea-jelly weak on Patmos strand. **1601** HOLLAND *Pliny* IX. xxvi. I. 249 The *sea Kite. **1672** JOSSELYN *New-Eng. Rarities* 27 Sea Kite or Flying Swallow. **1613** M. RIDLEY *Magn. Bodies* Pref. Magn. 3 The *sea-Lampron or Remora, that is thought to stay a ship under saile. **1616** BULLOKAR *Eng. Exp.*, **Sealamprie*, a fish called by some Remora. *c* **1617** MIDDLETON *Witch* I. ii. 209 A remora? what's that? *Hec.* A little suckstone; Some call it a sea-lamprey, a small fish. **1879** E. P. WRIGHT *Anim. Life* 467 The Sea Lamprey (*Petromyzon marinus*) is widely dispersed in the seas of Europe, North America, and West Africa. *a* **1682** SIR T. BROWNE *Norf. Fishes* Wks. 1835 IV. 334 *Hirudines marini*, or *sea-leeches. **1750** G. HUGHES *Barbados* 258 The Sea-Leech. The common People call this the Sea, or the Black-pudding. However, I shall call it, the Sea-leech. **1839** *Penny Cycl.* XIII. 382/2 The sea-leech is distinctly mentioned by Belon, Rondelet, [etc.]. *c* **1790** *Encycl. Brit.* (ed. 3) VI. 91/2 The argo, or lemon doris,.. called about Brighthelmstone the *sea-lemon. **1858** BAIRD *Cycl. Nat. Sci.*, *Doris*, the Sea Lemons. **1890** DOYLE *Capt. 'Pole-Star'* 13 Numerous small medusæ and sea-lemons. **1876** tr. *Haeckel's Hist. Creat.* II. 166 *Sea Lilies. Crinoida. **1611** COTGR., *Foye marin*, the *sea Liuer; a kind of Breame-like fish, that is but seldome seene. **1672** JOSSELYN *New-Eng. Rarities* 27 *Sea Locusts. **1853** KINGSLEY *Hypatia* x, The strange crabs and sea-locusts which crawled up and down the face of the masonry. **1813** BINGLEY *Anim. Biog.* (ed. 4) III. 405 The *sea long-worm. **1835** KIRBY *Hab. & Inst. Anim.* II. 58 The Stomapods.. are called *Sea Mantises. *a* **1776** J. ELLIS *Zoophytes* (1786) 7 *Actinia Calendula.* *Sea Marigold. **1802** BINGLEY *Anim. Biog.* (1805) III. 541 The Sea Marigold. *a* **1776** J. ELLIS *Zoophytes* (1786) 10 *Flustra.* The *Sea Matt. *Ibid.* 11 *Flustra truncata.* Square-top'd Sea Matt. **1863** WOOD *Illustr. Nat. Hist.* III. 449 *Flustra denticulata* (Toothed Sea Mat). **1819** TURTON *Conchol. Dict.* 76 *Lepas Alcyonii.* *Sea-mat Acorn-shell. **1854** A. ADAMS, etc. *Man. Nat. Hist.* 330 *Sea-Melons (*Pentactidæ*). **1672** JOSSELYN *New-Eng. Rarities* 23 Anchova or *Sea Minnow. **1894** *Northumbld. Gloss.*, *Sea-minnow*, the young of the coal-fish, *Merlangus carbonarius.* **1905** D. S. JORDAN *Guide to Study of Fishes* II. xiii. 239 These '*sea-moths' are fantastic little fishes. **1947** K. H. BARNARD *Pict. Guide S. Afr. Fishes* III. 76 The Dragon-fish or sea-moth.. is also encased in bony plates like the sea-horses... It derives its name of sea-moth from its habit of skimming over the surface of the water. **1978** *Nature* 26 Oct. 693/1 The sea moths are a small family (Pegasidae) of marine fishes found only in the Indian and Western Pacific oceans, from East Africa to Hawaii. **1752** WATSON in *Phil. Trans.* XLVII. 465 The soft lithophyton, usually call'd the *sea-mulberry. **1742** H. BAKER *Microsc.* II. v. 98 The *Sea-Mushroom, or Anemone: ..a little Animal found frequently on the Coasts of Normandy. **1678** PHILLIPS (ed. 4), **Sea-navel*, a turbinated and small shell-fish like a Navel. **1603** HOLLAND *Plutarch's Mor.* 200 Certaine fishes called the *Sea-needles [Gr. βελόνη]. **1769** PENNANT *Brit. Zool.* III. 274 This fish [the sea pike] is known by the name of the Sea Needle. **1753** *Sea orange [see ORANGE *sb.*[1] 4]. *c* **1800** MISS KNIGHT *Autobiog.* II. 256 Sea-oranges and Sea-lemons I have seen. **1861** HULME tr. *Moquin-Tandon* III. ii. 91 The Alcyonium Lyncurium of Lamouroux, commonly called the Sea-quince or Sea-Orange. **1774** GOLDSM. *Nat. Hist.* (1776) VI. 291 The *Sea Orb, which is almost round, has a mouth like a frog... Also called the Sea Porcupine. **1558** RONDELET *Gesner's Hist. Anim.* IV. 1106 *Eliota Anglus interpretatur* a Sterrefyshe. *Ego ab erudito quodam Anglo audiui nominari* a *Seepadde. **1661** [see PAD *sb.*[1] 2]. **1773** JOHNSON (ed. 4), *Sea-pad*, the star-fish. **1896** tr. *Boas' Text-bk. Zool.* 130 *Sea Palms (*Pentacrinus*) are large animals with ten arms, which may divide repeatedly. **1668** CHARLETON *Onomast.* 128 *Pardalus Marinus*.. the *sea-Panther. **1681** GREW *Musæum* I. §v. i. 91 The Spoted Houndfish or Sea-Panther. **1898** E. P. EVANS *Evol. Ethics* v. 184 On account of this sanctimonious look it [the fish called stargazer] is also known as the '*sea parson'. **1885** *Riverside Nat. Hist.* (1888) III. 57 The fishermen call some of the species of the genus *Cynthia* by the rather appropriate name '*sea peach'. *Ibid.*, 'The.. genus ..*Boltenia*.. embraces the '*sea pears' of the fishermen's terminology. **1664** *Sea-Pelican [see *sea-dart*]. **1755** *Gentl. Mag.* XXV. 82 The *Sea Pencil, or Watering Spout, is the most remarkable shell of this tribe. **1601** HOLLAND *Pliny* XXXII. xi. II. 452 The *sea Perches. **1857** PERLEY *Hand-bk. N. Brunswick* 25 The cunner, or sea-perch. **1882** TENISON-WOODS *Fishes N.S. Wales* 33 The Rock Cod [*Serranus*]... These are commonly called 'sea-perches'. **1880–4** F. DAY *Brit. Fishes* I. 119 *Lampris luna*... Opah, King-fish, *sea-pert. **1850** A. WHITE *List Spec. Crustacea Brit. Mus.* 75 *Sphæroma serratum.* Serrated *Sea Pill-ball. **1860** WORCESTER (cites *Gentl. Mag.*), *Sea-pincushion, the egg of the skate. **1755** *Gentl. Mag.* XXV. 32 *Sea Pipes, *Tubuli Marini.* **1808** NEILL in *Mem. Wernerian Nat. Hist. Soc.* (1811) I. 534 *Cottus cataphractus*.. *Sea-Poacher. **1836** W. YARRELL *Hist. Brit. Fishes* I. 70 The Armed Bullhead, Pogge. Lyrie, Sea-poacher, Pluck, Noble. **1905** D. S. JORDAN *Guide to Study of Fishes* II. xxv. 449 The sea-poachers or alligator-fishes, *Agonidæ*, are sculpins enclosed in a coat of mail. **1681** GREW *Musæum* I. §v. ii. 107 The *Sea-Porcupine, *Histrix Piscis.* **1858** BAIRD *Cycl. Nat. Sci.* s.v. *Diodontidæ*, The sea porcupine.., *Diodon hystrix*, is nearly spherical in shape. **1658** SIR T. BROWNE *Gard. Cyrus* iii. 53 The handsome Rhombusses of the *Sea-poult, or Werrell. **1672** JOSSELYN *New-Eng. Rarities* 29 Priest Fish or *Sea Priest. **1750** *Sea pudding [see *sea-leech* above]. **1756** P. BROWNE *Jamaica* (1789) 387 The Sea-Pudding. This insect ..is soft and glutinous, of a cylindric form, short, and furnished with a great number of small flabby *tentaculæ.* **1861** *Sea-quince [see *sea-orange* above]. **1694** tr. *Marten's Voy. Spitzbergen* in *Acc. Sev. Late Voy.* II. 168 Called *Sea-qualms by the Seamen, as if they were a thick Scum of the sea coagulated together. **1802** BINGLEY *Anim. Biog.* (1805) II. 373 The Sea-qualm (a kind of Cuttle fish). **1668** CHARLETON *Onomast.* 140 *Erythrynus*.. the *Sea-Roach. **1722** DIAPER tr. *Oppian's Halieut.* I. 135 Sea-Roach in ruddy Shoals frequent the Land. **1850** MISS PRATT *Comm. Things of Sea-side* v. 282 This mass of eggs is called on the coast bladder-chain,.. *sea-rose,.. or wash-ball. **1896** tr. *Boas' Text-bk. Zool.* 118 The *Actiniaria* (Sea-anemones, Sea-roses). **1668** CHARLETON *Onomast.* 140 The *Sea-Rough. **1672** JOSSELYN *New-Eng. Rarities* 27 Sea Ruff and Reeves. **1773** in JOHNSON (ed. 4) [and in later Dicts.]. **1876** tr. *Haeckel's Hist. Creat.* II. 150 *Sea-sacs. Tunicata. Sea-barrels. **1884** GOODE, etc. *Nat. Hist. Aquatic Anim.* 230 In the Gulf of Saint Lawrence they [*sc.* Pollock] are known as '*Sea Salmon'. **1881** *Cassell's Nat. Hist.* V. 279 The *Sea-scurfs. **1664** HUBERT *Catal. Rarities* (1665) 27 A Sea insect called the *Sea Shears: It hath many scales like a wood louse, two long hornes, and a forked tayle. **1713** PETIVER *Aquat. Anim. Amboinæ* Tab. iii, *Echinus planus*.. *Sea-Shilling. **1681** GREW *Musæum* II. §v. i. 242 *Sea-Shrubs. **1755** J. ELLIS *Corallines* 56 Next in Order to the Corallines, may be ranked the *Frutices coralloides*, or Sea-shrubs. **1870** NICHOLSON *Man. Zool.* xiv. (1875) 145 The *Gorgonidæ*, or 'Sea-shrubs'. **1822–29** *Good's Study Med.* (ed. 3) V. 291 Reaumur denominates the pinna the *sea-silk-worm. **1850** A. WHITE *List Specim. Crustacea Brit. Mus.* 71 *Ligia oceanica.* Great *Sea Slater. **1867** SMYTH *Sailor's Word-bk.*, **Sea-sleeve*, a name of the flosk or squid, *Loligo vulgaris.* **1658** PHILLIPS **Seasnapple*, a kind of Shell-fish, called in Latin *Cochlea Veneris*, i. *Venus* shell. **1838** JOHNSTON in *Proc. Berw. Nat. Club* I. vi. 172 *Labrus maculatus*... Ballan Wrasse... *Sea Sow. **1672** JOSSELYN *New-Eng. Rarities* 27 Plaice or *Sea Sparrow. **1743** CATESBY *Nat. Hist. Carolina*, etc. (1754) II. 2 The *Sea Sparrow-Hawk.. is a slender long Fish. **1850** MISS PRATT *Comm. Things of Sea-side* iii. 182 One of those strange looking things, commonly called *sea-squirts (*Ascidiæ*). **1880** [see APPENDICULARIAN]. **1767** J. ELLIS in *Phil. Trans.* LVII. 436 The Actinia aster, or *Sea star flower. **1896** tr. *Boas' Text-bk. Zool.* 390 The *Sea-Stickle (*Spinachia vulgaris*) is exclusively marine. **1880** GÜNTHER *Stud. Fishes* 506 The *Sea-Stickleback (*Gasterosteus spinachia*) is likewise a nest builder. **1896** tr. *Boas' Text-bk. Zool.* 377 *note*, The male Sea Stickleback (*Spinachia vulgaris*). **1668** CHARLETON *Onomast.* 123 *Glaucus*.. the *Sea-Stichling [*sic*]. **1710** SIBBALD *Fife & Kinross* 53 *Draco sive Araneus minor*; I take it to be the same our Fishers call the Otter-pike or *Sea-stranger. **1750** G. HUGHES *Barbados* 259 The *Sea-Sucker. **1883** *Fisheries Exhib. Catal.* 161 One form of sea-sucker (*Lepidogaster*) affixes its eggs to the inside of a dead shell. **1731** MEDLEY *Kolben's Cape G. Hope* II. 210 There is a sort of shell-fish at the Cape, which the Europeans there call *Sea-suns. **1773** COOK *Voy.* (1790) I. 323 Sea-suns and sea-stars, are small round shell-fish, and receive their denominations from the great variety of prickles, which shoot from them like rays of light. **1767** J. ELLIS in *Phil. Trans.* LVII. 436 The *Actinia helianthus* or *Sea-sun-flower. **1755** —— *Corallines* 4 *Corallina vesiculata sparsim et alternatim ramosa* [etc.].. *Sea-Tamarisk. *a* **1776** —— *Zoophytes* (1786) 36 *Sertularia tamarisca.* Sea-Tamarisk Coralline. **1602** CAREW *Cornwall* II. 127 They beare.. a *sea-tenche nayante proper. **1778** *Eng. Gazetteer* (ed. 2) s.v. *Holyhead*, Sea-tenches,.. and plenty of other fish. **1891** *Century Dict.*, *Pustule of the sea*, a sailor's name of sessile barnacles or acorn-shells. Also called **sea-thorns.* [**1924** L. L. MOWBRAY in J. O. La Gorce *Bk. Fishes* 143 Well deserving its nickname of 'The Tiger of the Sea', the carnivorous Barracuda.. darts at its prey on sight.] **1937** M. N. KAPLAN *Big Game Anglers' Paradise* IV. 180 Although ichthyologists gave the great barracuda the euphonious name *Sphyraena barracuda*, in common parlance it bears the *nom-de-guerre*, '*Sea-tiger'. **1963** Sea tiger [see PICUDA]. **1710** SIBBALD *Fife & Kinross* 53 *Turdi alia species*; It is called by our Fishers, the *Sea-Tod or Kingervie. *a* **1776** J. ELLIS *Zoophytes* (1786) 2 *Actinia Cereus.* *Sea Torch-thistle. **1755** —— *Corallines* 84 *Alcyonium, seu Vesicaria marina*... *Sea Wash-balls. **1910** A. G. MAYER *Medusæ of World* III. 504 The flexible part of the tentacles are [*sic*] armed with nematocysts, the stinging power of which is so great that the name '*Sea Wasp' is commonly given to these medusæ. **1966** J. H. BARNES in W. J. Rees *Cnidaria & their Evolution* 332 The origin of such stings was not known, but.. it must have been a sea wasp. **1977** C. MCCULLOUGH *Thorn Birds* xiii. 301 We're too far south here for sea wasps. **1902** H. H. LITTLEJOHN in *Encycl. Brit.* XXX. 609/1 *Trachinus draco* or *sea-weever. **1775** J. ELLIS in *Phil. Trans.* LXVI. 1 Those [Zoophytes].. called ..*Gorgoniæ*; and known in English by the names of sea-fans, sea-feathers, and *sea-whips. **1836** YARRELL *Brit. Fishes* I. 284 The *Sea Wife. *Labrus vetula* [**1841** (ed. 2) I. 339 *Acantholabrus Yarrellii*, Cuv. et Valenc.]. **1850** A. WHITE *List Spec. Crustacea Brit. Mus.* 56 *Chelura terebrans.* *Sea Wood-Borer. **1858** BAIRD *Cycl. Nat. Sci.*, *Chitonidæ*,.. *Sea Wood-lice. *Ibid.* s.v. *Isopoda*, The sea wood lice, *Asellidæ.* **1863** WOOD *Illustr. Nat. Hist.* III. 631 The Great sea-Slater, or Sea-woodlouse. **1860** *Sea-wreath [see SEA-BELL 2]. **1865** T. R. JONES *Anim. Creation* 35 The Sea-wreaths (*Sertulariæ*) are known to every sea-side visitor.

e. In names of seaweeds: **sea-apron**, the genus *Laminaria* (Cent. Dict. 1891); **sea-bamboo** *S. Afr.*, a large kelp, *Ecklonia maxima*; = SEA-TRUMPET 3; **sea-belt**, *Laminaria saccharina* (in Turner perh. *Zostera marina*); **sea-bottle**, the bladder-wrack; also applied to the pod or vesicle of some American fuci; **sea-catgut** = *sea-lace*; **sea-chitterling**, 'common name for the plant otherwise called *Enterophytum*' (Mayne *Expos. Lex.* 1858); †**sea-cluster, -colander** (see quots.); **sea-furbelow**, the *Laminaria bulbosa*; **sea-girdle**, *Laminaria digitata*; also = *sea-belt*; †**sea grass-wrack**, the seaweed *Zostera*; **sea-hanger**, *Laminaria bulbosa*; **sea-lace**, *Chorda filum*; **sea-lentil**, the gulf-weed; †**sea-lung-wort**, the seaweed *Ulva lactuca* or SEA-LETTUCE; **sea-membrane**, dulse, *Rhodymenia palmata* (Cassell's Encycl. Dict. 1887); **sea-network** (see NETWORK *sb.* 3); **sea-ore** (see ORE *sb.*[5]); **sea-points** = *sea-lace*; †**sea-ragged-staff**, ?the *Ascophyllum nodosum*; **sea-staff** = *sea-girdle*; **sea-tang, -tangle** (see TANG *sb.*[3], TANGLE *sb.*[1]); **sea-tape** (see quot.); **sea-thong**, one of several chord-like seaweeds, as *Chorda filum*, *Himanthalia lorea*, etc.; **sea-thread** (see quots.); **sea-turnip**, a seaweed of the genus *Nereocystis*, having a turnip-shaped protuberance of the stem; **sea-wand**, *Laminaria digitata* = TANGLE *sb.*[1] 2; **sea-whip, -whip-cord, -whiplash** = *sea-thong*; **sea-whistle**, *Ascophyllum nodosum.* See also SEA-OAK, SEAWARE, SEAWEED, SEAWRACK, etc.

1798 S. H. WILCOCKE tr. *Stavorinus' Voy. East Indies* I. I. i. 25 On the 10th of November, we saw for the first time trumpets, or *sea-bamboo, floating on the ocean. **1822** W. BURCHELL *Trav. Interior S. Afr.* I. ii. 28 The Dutch call this plant *Zee bambos* (sea-bamboo), and boys after cutting its stem to a convenient length when dry, sometimes amuse themselves in blowing it as a horn or trumpet. **1946** L. G. GREEN *So Few are Free* viii. 116 The place is called Bamboes Bay, because the sea bamboo is piled high on the beach after heavy gales. **1973** *Stand. Encycl. S. Afr.* IX. 562/2 The largest kelp of Southern Africa is the sea-trumpet or sea-bamboo.. which commonly reaches lengths of over 6 metres. **1548** TURNER *Names of Herbes* (E.D.S.) 27 Cingulum is named in greeke Zoster,.. & is like a gyrdel, wherefore it maye be named in englishe, fysshers gyrdle or sea gyrdel, or *sea belte. **1841** *Penny Cycl.* XXI. 156/1 *Laminaria saccharina*, or the sugar sea-belt. **1825** JENNINGS *Dial. W. Eng.* 66 Many of the species of the sea-wrack, or *fucus*, are called **sea-bottles*, in consequence of the stalks having round or oval vesicles or pods in them. **1859** J. M. JONES *Nat. in Bermuda* 176 That very curious marine plant, commonly designated the 'sea bottle'... These 'sea bottles' are transparent, and shaped like a small balloon. **1833** *Penny Cycl.* I. 322/2 The Chorda filum, or *sea cat-gut, of Orkney. **1777** LIGHTFOOT *Flora Scot.* II. 968 Gut Laver or *Sea Chitterling. **1728** BRADLEY *Dict. Bot.* II, *Sea-cluster, *Uva marina.* **1866** *Treas. Bot.*, **Sea-colander*, the American name in the North-eastern States of *Agarum Turneri.* **1808–30** *Edinb. Encycl.* X. 20/2 *Fucus bulbosus*.. sometimes called *sea furbelows. **1860** TENNYSON *Sea Dreams* 257 The dimpled flounce of the sea-furbelow. **1548** *Sea-girdle [see *sea-belt* above]. *c* **1550** LLOYD *Treas. Health* (*c* 1560) X 7, Take of dragons bloud, seagyrdel [etc.]. **1845** GOSSE *Ocean* i. (1849) 34 The sea-weed usually called in England the Sea-girdle... (*Laminaria digitata*). **1796** WITHERING *Brit. Pl.* (ed. 3) II. 497 *Zostera*... *Sea Grass-wrack. **1633** JOHNSON *Gerarde's Herbal* III. clxiv. 1569 The diuided one they may call *Sea Hangers. **1666** *Sea-lace [see *sea-point* below]. **1877** BRYANT *Sella* 136 The dulse with crimson leaves, and streaming far, Sea-thong and sea-lace. **1633** JOHNSON *Gerarde's Herbal* App. xxii. 1615 *Lenticula marina angustifolia.* Narrow leaued *Sea Lentill. **1597** GERARDE *Herbal* III. clix. 1377 *Lichen Marinus.* *Sea Lungwort, or Oister greene. **1657** W. COLES *Adam in Eden* cvi. **1666** MERRETT *Pinax* 40 *Fucus marinus rotundus*, *Sea points or laces. **1633** JOHNSON *Gerarde's Herbal* III. clxiv. 1569 M[r]. Thomas Hickes being in our companie did fitly name it *Sea ragged Staffe. *Ibid.* 1570 *Fucus spongiosus nodosus.* Sea ragged Staffe. **1865** MRS. L. L. CLARKE *Seaweeds* vi. 116 *Laminaria Digitata.* Sea-girdles, Tangle, *Sea-staff, Sea-wand, Cows'-tails. **1861** BENTLEY *Man. Bot.* 720 *Laminaria saccharina* is called **Sea-tape* in China, where it is used for food and other purposes. **1633** JOHNSON *Gerarde's Herbal* III. clxiv. 1568 *Quercus marina secunda.* *Sea Thongs. **1845** GOSSE *Ocean* i. (1849) 43 The common Sea-thong (*Himanthalia lorea*). **1843** *Zoologist* I. 209 The knotted *sea-thread (*Laomedea geniculata*). **1878** B. HARTE *Man on Beach* 39 The long, snaky, undulating stems of the *sea turnip. **1841** *Penny Cycl.* XXI. 156 *Laminaria digitata*, or *sea-wand. **1858** K. H. DIGBY *Children's Bower* II. 67 These sea-laces or *sea-whips. **1833** HOOKER *Brit. Flora* II. I. 275 *Chordaria flagelliformis*, Ag. (common *Sea-Whipcord). *Ibid.* 276 *Chorda Filum*, Lamour. (common *Sea Whip-lash). **1808–30** *Edinb. Encycl.* X. 19/1 Boys amuse themselves by cutting them [the fronds] transversely near the end, and making whistles of them; hence the name **sea-whistles* sometimes bestowed on the plant [*Fucus nodosus*].

f. In names of plants growing on the sea-shore: **sea arrow-grass**, a marsh plant, *Triglochin maritima*, with fleshy grass-like leaves and spikes of green flowers; **sea-ash**, *Xanthoxylon Clava-Herculis* or *carolinianum*; **sea-aster** = *sea-starwort*; †**sea ay-green** = *sea-houseleek*; **sea-beard**, a marine plant, *Cladophora* (*Conferva*) *rupestris*; **sea-beet**, (*a*) a variety of the common beet, *Beta vulgaris*, often called *Beta maritima*; (*b*) = *sea-lavender* b; **sea-bent**, *Psamma* or *Ammophila arenaria* (see BENT *sb.*[1] 1); **sea-berry**, †(*a*) some South American plant; (*b*) *Austral.*, applied to the genera *Haloragis* and *Rhagodia*; **sea-bindweed**, *Convolvulus soldanella*; **sea-blite**, *Suæda fruticosa*; **sea-buckthorn**, *Hippophaë rhamnoides*; **sea-bugloss** = *sea-lungwort*; **sea-burdock**, the small burdock or burweed, *Xanthium strumarium*; **sea campion**, *Silene maritima*; **sea-catchfly** = prec.; **sea-chickweed** = *sea-sandwort*; **sea cock's-foot-grass**, *Spartina stricta*; **sea coco, coco-nut** (see COCO 6); **sea-cole, -colewort**, (*a*) = SEA-KALE; †(*b*) = *sea-bindweed*; **sea convolvulus** = SEA-BELL 1, *sea-bindweed*; **sea-cushion** = SEA-PINK a; **sea cypress** (see quot.); **sea-daffodil**, the bulbous plant *Pancratium maritimum*, also the allied Peruvian plant *Hymenocallis* (*Ismene*) *calathina*; †**sea-dock**, *Acanthus mollis*; †**sea dog's grass**, a maritime variety of couch-grass; **sea-fennel**, samphire; **sea-gilliflower** = SEA-PINK a; **sea-goosefoot** = *sea-blite*; **sea-gromwell**, the sea-bugloss (*Cassell's Encycl. Dict.* 1887); **sea hard-grass**, one of various maritime species of hard-grass; **sea-heath**, a 'heath' of the genus *Frankenia*; **sea hog's-fennel** (see quot.); **sea-houseleek**, the aloe; †**sea-hull** = SEA-HOLLY; **sea-hulver** = SEA-HOLLY (see HULVER), also *attrib.*; **sea ivory**, a pale greyish lichen, *Ramalina siliquosa*, growing in flattened branches on sea-shore rocks; see also sense 23 a; †**sea-ivy**, ? = prec.; **sea-kemp** *Sc.* = *sea-plantain*; **sea-laurel**, the seaside laurel; **sea-lavender**, †(*a*) ? some species of *Heliotropium*; (*b*) *Statice Limonium* (see LAVENDER *sb.*[2] 1 b); **sea lungwort**, the oyster-plant, *Mertensia maritima*; **sea matgrass, matweed**, *Psamma arenaria*; †**sea-mugwort** = *sea-wormwood*; **sea myrtle** = *groundsel-tree* s.v. GROUNDSEL *sb.*[1] 2; †**sea-narcissus** = *sea-daffodil*; †**sea-navel, -navelwort**, some plant resembling the genus *Cotyledon*; **sea-onion** (see ONION *sb.* 2 c); **sea-orach**, *Atriplex littoralis*; **sea ox-eye**, the seaside ox-eye (see OX-EYE 3 e); **sea-parsley** (see quot.); †**sea-pennywort** = *sea-navelwort*; **sea-plantain**, *Plantago maritima*; **sea-poppy** (see POPPY *sb.* 3); †**sea pot-herb** = *sea-orach*; **sea-purslane** (see PURSLANE 2); **sea-purslane tree** (see quot.); **sea-radish**, a variety of the wild radish, sometimes regarded as a species (*Raphanus maritimus*); **sea-ragwort**, a common cultivated foliage-plant, *Senecio Cineraria* (or *Cineraria maritima*); **sea-reed, reed-grass** = *sea-bent*; **sea-rocket** (see ROCKET *sb.*[2] 3); **sea-rosemary**, (*a*) = *sea-blite*; (*b*) = *sea-lavender* b (Cent. Dict.); **sea sand-reed** (see quot.); **sea-sandwort**, a variety of sandwort, *Honkenya* (*Arenaria*) *peploides*, growing in the sand of the coasts of Europe and N. America; †**sea spike-grass**, thrift; **sea-spleenwort**, a fern, *Asplenium marinum*, growing on the rocky coasts of Western Europe; **sea-spurge**, a maritime spurge, *Euphorbia Paralias*; **sea spurrey, spurrey sandwort** (see quots.); **sea-starwort**, *Aster Tripolium*; **sea-stock** (also ***great sea stock***), *Matthiola sinuata*; †**sea stock-gillyflower** = prec.; **sea sulphur-weed, -wort**, *Peucedanum officinale*; **sea-thrift** = SEA-PINK a; †**sea trifoly**, *Astragalus Glaux*; †**sea wartwort**, a variety of spurge, *Euphorbia Peplis*; **sea-wheat, -wheatgrass**, the wheatgrass *Triticum junceum*, growing on the sandy seashore; **sea-withwind**, *Convolvulus Soldanella*; †**sea-wormwood**, *Artemisia maritima*.

1770 J. HILL *Herbarium Britannicum* II. 215 (*heading*) *Sea Arrow Grass. **1851** C. A. JOHNS *Flowers of Field* II. 245 Sea Arrow-grass... Salt marshes, common. **1975** J. G. EVANS *Environment Early Man Brit. Isles* ii. 37 A number of species..today confined to coastal or estuarine situations, such as sea arrow grass..and sea thrift. **1884** SARGENT *Rep. Forests N. Amer.* 30 *Sea Ash. **1812** CRABBE *Tales* x. I. 196 *note*, The *Sea-aster, the dullest of that numerous and hardy genus. **1925** G. BONNIER *Brit. Flora* 96 Sea Aster. Salt marshes: July–Sept. **1960** *Oxf. Bk. Wild Flowers* 136/2 Sea Aster..is common in salt-marshes and on cliffs and rocks round the coasts. **1551** TURNER *Herbal* I. B vj, Some haue called it semper viuum marinum, that is *sea aigrene. **1777** ROBSON *Brit. Flora* 317 *Conferva rupestris*... *Sea-beard. *c* **1710** PETIVER *Catal. Ray's Eng. Herbal* Tab. 8 *Sea Beet. **1838** G. DON in *Encycl. Metrop.* (1845) XXV. 28/2 *Statice limonium*, the Sea Beet, or Sea Lavender. **1866** *Treas. Bot.* s.v. *Beta*, The Sea Beet, *Beta maritima*, a perennial,..grows wild on the sea coast in various parts of Britain. **1551** TURNER *Herbal* II. 144 Sparta..is a kind of *sea bente or sea rishe. **1899** *Cumbld. Gloss.*, *Sea bent*, the sea-side grasses—*Psamma arenaria*, or *Ammophila arundinacea*, growing on the Bent hills at Maryport. *c* **1711** PETIVER *Gazophyl.* vi. 60 Brasil *Sea-berry... Its leaves very green, juicy, and thick like Purslain. **1884** W. MILLER *Plant-n.* 123 Sea-berry, of Australia, the genera *Haloragis* and *Rhagodia*. **1597** *Sea-bindweed [see SEA-BELL 1]. **1786** *Gentl. Mag.* LVI. I. 35 *Convolvulus Soldanella*, Sea Bindweed. **1762** W. HUDSON *Flora Anglica* 92 *Chenopodium*... *maritimum*... *Anglis*, *Sea Blite or white Glasswort. **1855** MISS PRATT *Flower. Pl.* IV. 267 *Suæda* (Sea-Blite). **1866** *Treas. Bot.* s.v. *Schoberia*, *S. fruticosa*, the Shrubby Sea-blite, abundant on the muddy coast of Norfolk,..locally known by the name of Sea Rosemary. **1731** MILLER *Gard. Dict.*, *Rhamnoides*, the *Sea Buckthorn. **1905** RIDER HAGGARD *Gardener's Year* Sept. 323 Four or five years ago I planted some hundreds of Sea-buckthorn upon the face of my cliff. **1884** W. MILLER *Plant-n.* 123 *Sea Bugloss, *Pulmonaria* (*Mertensia*) *maritima*. **1845–50** MRS. LINCOLN *Lect. Bot.* App. 186/2 *Xanthium*.. *strumarium* (cockle-burr, *sea-burdock). **1597** GERARDE *Herbal* II. cxxi. 382 *Lychnis marina Anglica*. English *Sea Campion. *Ibid.*, The sea rose campion. **1762** W. HUDSON *Flora Anglica* 164 *Silene*.. *amoena*... *Anglis*, Sea Campion. **1864** BRADY in *Intell. Observ.* V. 27 The *Sea Catchfly (*Silene maritima*). **1786** *Gentl. Mag.* LVI. I. 35 Arenaria Peploides, *Sea Chickweed, remarkable for the depth and length to which it runs its roots. **1837** BAXTER *Brit. Phænog. Bot.* III. 203 *Spartina stricta*. Twin-spiked Cord-grass. Smooth Sea-grass. *Sea Cock's-footgrass. **1795** tr. *Thunberg's Trav.* IV. 183 A Borassus or *Sea-Cocoa, brought from the Maldive islands. **1850** F. MASON *Nat. Product. Burmah* 168 *Sea cocoanut. **1548** TURNER *Names of Herbes* (E.D.S.) 20 Brassica syluestris groweth in Douer cliffes... It may be named in english *sea cole. **1578** LYTE *Dodoens* III. liv. 394 Of Soldanella or Sea Cawle. **1858** MAYNE *Expos. Lex.*, *Sea cole*, a common name for the *Crambe maritima*, or sea-kale. **1700** C. LEIGH *Nat. Hist. Lancs.*, etc. I. 93 *Sea-colewort. **1725**, **1794** [see COLEWORT 2 b]. **1796** WITHERING *Brit. Pl.* (ed. 3) II. 240 Scottish Scurvy Grass. Sea Colewort. Sea Bindweed. **1921** 'K. MANSFIELD' *Let.* 8 Aug. (1977) 227 Bathing dresses hanging over verandas, and sandshoes on window sills, and little pink '*sea' convolvulus. **1629** PARKINSON *Parad.* 317 *Caryophyllus Marinus*. Thrift, or *Sea Cushion. **1855** MISS PRATT *Flower. Pl.* II. 305 *Tamarix Anglica*..is in England commonly called *Sea Cypress. **1597** GERARDE *Herbal* I. lxxxv. 135 The sea Onion of Valentia, or rather the *sea Daffodill, hath many long and fat leaues. **1629** PARKINSON *Parad.* 98 *Narcissus Marinus Africanus, sive Exoticus Lobelii*. The Sea Daffodil of Africa. **1866** *Treas. Bot.* s.v. *Ismene*, The name of Sea Daffodil is given to *I. calathina*. **1387** *Sinon. Barthol.* (Anecd. Oxon.) 13/1 *Branca ursina, herbaest*, an. *scehock [? *read* scedock]. *c* **1450** *Alphita* (Anecd. Oxon.) 25 *Branca ursina*..sedokke. **1597** GERARDE *Herbal* Suppl., Sedocke [ed. 1636 Sea Docke] is the brank vrsine. **1758** BORLASE *Nat. Hist. Cornw.* 235 The bloody sea-dock, *Lapathum marinum sanguineum*. **1597** GERARDE *Herbal* I. xviii. 23 *Gramen Caninum marinum* *Sea Dogs grasse. **1731** MILLER *Gard. Dict.*, *Crithmum*;..Smaller Samphire, or *Sea-Fennel. **1629** PARKINSON *Parad.* 318 The greater or Leuant Thrift, or *Sea Gilloflower. **1806** *Gazetteer Scot.* (ed. 2) 403 The root of sea-gilliflower, *statice armeria*. **1856** A. GRAY *Man. Bot.* (1860) 366 *Chenopodina*... *Sea Goosefoot. **1843** BAXTER *Brit. Phænog. Bot.* VI. 476 *Rottbollia incurvata*... *Sea Hard-grass. *c* **1710** PETIVER *Cat. Ray's Eng. Herbal* Tab. 10 *Sea heath. **1762** W. HUDSON *Flora Anglica* 120 *Frankenia*..*lævis*.., smooth Sea Heath. **1855** MISS PRATT *Flower. Pl.* III. 55 *Peucedanum officinale* (*Sea Hog's-fennel, or Sulphur-weed). **1597** GERARDE *Herbal* II. cxxxiv. 410 The same effect *Sea Housleeke works as well as thees. **1608** TOPSELL *Serpents* 45 The Sea-thistle called *Eryngium marinum*, which some call *Sea-hull, or Huluer. **1548** TURNER *Names of Herbes* (E.D.S.) 36 Eryngium is named in englishe *sea Hulver or sea Holly. *a* **1592** GREENE *Mamillia* II. Wks. (Grosart) II. 288 Resembling the sea huluer leafe. **1966** *Oxf. Bk. Flowerless Plants* p. viii/1 '*Sea Ivory'..grows abundantly wherever there are rocks exposed at high-water mark. **1588** GREENE *Pandosto* (1607) C 4 b, To see if perchance the sheepe was browzing on the *Sea Iuie. **1889** *Century Dict.* s.v. *Kemp*, *Sea-kemp*, *Plantago maritima*, the sea-plantain. **1820** T. GREEN *Univ. Herbal* II. 875 *Sea Laurel. *Phyllanthus*. **1696** PLUKENET *Almagestum* Wks. 1769 II. 182 Heliotropium Gnaphaloides litoreum fruticescens Americanum, *Sea-Lavender Barbadensibus dictum. **1865** GOSSE *Land & Sea* (1874) 31 Enormous tufts of the common thrift or Sea-lavender. **1597** GERARDE *Herbal* III. clix. 1377 *Sea Lungwoort or Oister greene. **1797** J. E. SMITH *Eng. Bot.* VI. 368 (*heading*) Sea lungwort. **1960** Sea lungwort [see *oyster-plant* s.v. OYSTER 7 d]. **1840** PAXTON *Bot. Dict.*, *Sea matgrass, *Psamma arenaria*. **1843** BAXTER *Brit. Phænog. Bot.* VI. 408 *Ammophila Arundinacea*. *Sea Mat-weed. **1548** TURNER *Names of Herbes* (E.D.S.) 16 Arthemisia is of three sortes, the fyrst is the herbe that I cal *sea Mugworte. **1883** G. O. SHIELDS *Rustlings in Rockies* xxi. 195 Within the space of this five acres may be found..sea myrtle, grape vine and ivy of several varieties. **1938** M. K. RAWLINGS *Yearling* xxiii. 279 The October blooming of dog-fennel and *sea-myrtle had turned to a feathery fluff. **1664** EVELYN *Kal. Hort., May* (1679) 17 Flowers in Prime, or yet lasting,..Peonies,..*Sea-Narcissus [etc.]. **1597** GERARDE *Herbal* II. cxliv. 426 The *sea Nauell is of a diureticke qualitie. **1728** BRADLEY *Dict. Bot.* II. s.v. *Pennywort*, *Sea-Pennywort* is the *Sea-Navel*. **1597** GERARDE *Herbal* II. cxliv. 426 *Sea Nauel woort prouoketh vrine. [**1398** TREVISA *Barth. De P.R.* XVII. xliii. (1495) 628 Cepe caninum..is founde by the see syde therfore Plato callyth it Sepe marina as it were a see oyneon.] **1526** *Grete Herball* ccccxiii. (1529) Y iv, A squyll or *see onyon. **1548**, etc. [see ONION *sb.* 2 c]. **1845–50** MRS. LINCOLN *Lect. Bot.* 151 The genus *Atriplex*, (*sea-orache). **1856** A. GRAY *Man. Bot.* (1860) 213 *Borrichia*... *Sea Ox-eye. **1843** BAXTER *Brit. Phænog. Bot.* VI. 472 *Ligusticum scoticum*. Scotch Lovage. Scotch Parsley. *Sea Parsley. **1597** GERARDE *Herbal* II. cxliv. 425 Of *Sea Pennywoort. *Ibid.* xciv. 343 The *sea Plantaine hath small and narrow leaues. **1562** TURNER *Herbal* II. 77 It may be named in Englishe horned poppy or *see poppy, or yelow poppy. **1706** J. STEVENS *Span. Dict.*, *Salgada*, the Plant call'd *Sea-pot-herb. **1548** TURNER *Names of Herbes* (E.D.S.) 25 Cepaea Plinij groweth by the sea syde, and because it is very lyke Purcellayne, it maye be called in englishe *sea Purcellayne. **1578** [see PURSLANE 2]. **1786** ABERCROMBIE *Gard. Assist.* Arrangem. 26 *Atriplex Halimus*, *sea-purslane tree. **1847** BABINGTON *Brit. Bot.* (ed. 2) 32 *Raphanus maritimus*,..*Sea Radish. **1741** *Compl. Fam.-Piece* II. iii. 374 Buphthalmums, Sea Holly, *Sea Ragwort. **1852** G. W. JOHNSON *Gard. Dict.*, *Cineraria maritima* (sea Ragwort). **1575** LANEHAM *Let.* Pref. (1871) 160 Mercurius that playit on ane *sey reid. **1717** PARNELL *Homer's Battle Frogs & Mice* II. 77 Tap'ring Sea-Reeds for the polish'd Spear. **1861** S. THOMSON *Wild Flowers* III. (ed. 4) 213 The sea-reed, or *Ammophila arundinacea*, deserves our attention. **1777** *Sea reed-grass [see REED-GRASS 1]. **1866** *Sea rosemary [see *sea-blite* above]. **1856** A. GRAY *Man. Bot.* (1860) 548 *Calamagrostis arenaria* (*Sea Sand-Reed). **1850** MISS PRATT *Comm. Things of Sea-side* i. 35 The *sea sandwort (*Arenaria peploides*)..is very common. **1882** THOMSON in *Proc. Berw. Nat. Club* IX. III. 449 The Sea Sandwort (*Honkeneja peploides*). **1597** GERARDE *Herbal* I. xvi. 17 *Sea Spike grasse hath many small leaues. **1850** MISS PRATT *Comm. Things of Sea-side* i. 88 The *sea spleenwort (*Asplenium marinum*). **1859** J. C. ATKINSON *Walks & Talks* (1892) 337 A habitat of the sea-spleenwort. **1597** GERARDE *Herbal* II. cxxxii. 401 The first kinde of *Sea Spurge riseth foorth of the sands. **1855** MISS PRATT *Flower. Pl.* V. 9 *Euphorbia Paralias* (Sea Spurge). **1762** W. HUDSON *Flora Anglica* 169 *Arenaria*..*marina*... Sea Spurrey. **1853** MISS PRATT *Wild Fl.* II. 95 Sea Spurrey Sandwort, *Arenaria marina*. **1597** GERARDE *Herbal* II. lxxxviii. 334 *Tripolium*,.. is called..in English *Sea Star-wort. **1861** S. THOMSON *Wild Flowers* III. (ed. 4) 248 The sea-star-wort, or Michaelmas daisy. **1849** M. ARNOLD *Forsaken Merman* 69 The sandy down Where the *sea-stocks bloom. **1862** ANSTED *Channel Isl.* II. viii. 177 The purple flowers of the great sea stock (*Matthiola sinuata*). **1597** GERARDE *Herbal* II. cxv. 374 The *Sea Stocke Gilloflower hath a small wooddie roote very threddie. **1850** MISS PRATT *Comm. Things of Sea-side* i. 67 The *Sea Sulphur-weed (*Peucedanum officinale*) is a much more rare plant of the salt marsh. **1807** SMITH & SOWERBY *Eng. Bot.* XXV. 1767 *Peucedanum officinale*. *Sea Sulphur-wort. **1706** LONDON & WISE *Retir'd Gard'ner* I. 311 *Sea-Thrift, [is vivacious] by its Tufts. **1862** ANSTED *Channel Isl.* I. v. 112 A flower of the sea-thrift. **1548** TURNER *Names of Herbes* (E.D.S.) 40 Glaux..may be called in englishe *sea Trifoly. **1601** R. CHESTER *Love's Mart.* (1878) 82 Blessed thistle and Sea Trifoly. **1548** TURNER *Names of Herbes* (E.D.S.) 60 Peplis..may be called in english *sea wartwurt. **1597** GERARDE *Herbal* II. cxxxii. 407. **1839** MARY HOWITT *Marien's Pilgr.* VIII. xi, Where only the dry *sea-wheat grew. **1796** WITHERING *Brit. Plants* (ed. 3) II. 173 *Triticum*... *Sea Wheatgrass. **1597** GERARDE *Herbal* II. ccxciii. 690 Soldanella..in English *Sea With-winde. **1548** TURNER *Names of Herbes* (E.D.S.) 8 *Sea wormwod is hote in the seconde degree and dry in the fyrste, frenche wormwod is weaker then Sea wormwod is. **1747** WESLEY *Prim. Physick* (1762) 117 The Tops of Sea Wormwood. **1855** *New Cycl. Bot.* II. 461 *Artemisia maritima*. Sea Wormwood.

sea (siː), *v. nonce-wd.* [f. SEA *sb.*] *intr.* To go *along* as a part of the sea.

1839 BAILEY *Festus* xxi, To ride upon the broad-backed billow, Seaing along and plunging on his precipitous path.

sea, obs. form of SAY *sb.*[1]; SO.

ˈsea-adder. [ADDER[2].]

†**1.** A sea-serpent. *Obs.*

1601 HOLLAND *Pliny* VI. xxiii. 132 About these Islands [in the Persian Gulf] they might see sea-adders and serpents so monstrous great, that [etc.].

2. The Pipe-fish.

a **1672** WILLUGHBY *Hist. Pisc.* (1686) 160 Acui Aristotelis congener pisciculus, pueris Cornubiensibus *Sea-Adder*.. dictus. **1752** J. HILL *Hist. Anim.* 202 *Syngnathus*... The people of Yorkshire call it the Sea-worm; but it is more generally known in England by its Cornish name of the Sea-adder. **1896** tr. *Boas' Text-bk. Zool.* 391 The Sea-adder family (*Syngnathidæ*).

3. The sea-stickleback, *Spinachia vulgaris*.

1836 YARRELL *Brit. Fishes* I. 87 The Fifteen-spined Stickle-back. Great sea adder, Cornwall.

sea air. The air above or in the neighbourhood of the sea; air containing saline or gaseous matter derived from sea-water.

1685 BOYLE *Enq. Notion Nat.* vii. 318 Most persons, the first time they go to sea,..are, by the unwonted agitations, ..(assisted perhaps by the sea-air..) cast into that disease.. called the sea-sickness. **1707** SLOANE *Jamaica* I. 2 Joseph Acosta ascribes it [this sickness] to the Sea-Air. **1795** COLERIDGE *Refl. Place Retirem.* 67 And myrtles fearless of the mild sea-air. **1833** T. HOOK *Parson's Dau.* III. v, The advice of her physicians to try the effect of sea-air and sea-bathing. **1897** WATTS-DUNTON *Aylwin* II. iii, The English lady..has gone to live at Carnarvon to get the sea air.

sea-angler. [ANGLER[1].]

1. The Fishing Frog, = ANGLER[1] 2.

1653 WALTON *Angler* i. 22 For this reason some have called this fish the Sea-Angler. **1906** *Daily Chron.* 13 July 6/7 A 'sea-angler' has just been brought into Yarmouth.

2. An angler who fishes in the sea.

1893 *Fishing Gaz.* 11 Feb. 101/1 The British Sea-anglers' Society.

So **sea-angling** *vbl. sb.*, angling in the sea.

1833 J. RENNIE *Alph. Angling* 58 River, canal, pond, lake, and sea-angling. **1893** *Fishing Gaz.* 11 Feb. 101/1 At different sea angling resorts.

sea-animal. [ANIMAL *sb.*]

1. An animal or creature living in the sea.

1745 tr. *Egede's Descr. Greenland* 65 Of the Greenland Sea Animals, and Sea Fowl and Fishes. **1753** *Chambers' Cycl.* Suppl., *Hippocampus*,..a small sea animal caught in the Mediterranean. **1854** DICKENS *Hard T.* II. viii, Mr. Bounderby..sighed like a huge sea-animal. **1855** KINGSLEY *Glaucus* (1878) 91 One of the rarest of British sea-animals.

2. *transf.* Applied to a sailor.

1706 E. WARD *Wooden World Diss.* (1708) 107 Take this plain blunt Sea-Animal,..and you'll find him of more intrinsick Value to the Nation, than the most fluttering Beau in it.

ˈsea-ape. [APE *sb.*]

1. The sea-fox (*Alopias vulpes*). See APE *sb.* 5.

1607 TOPSELL *Four-f. Beasts* 5 The Dolphin recouereth by eating a sea-ape. **1769–1861** [see APE *sb.* 5].

†**2. a.** ? The manatee. **b.** The Northern manatee: see MANATEE 2. *Obs.* Also *attrib.*

1755 tr. *Pontoppidan's Nat. Hist. Norway* II. 191 These Mer-men, or, as we may rather call them Sea-apes. **1781** PENNANT *Quadrupeds* II. 544 Sea Ape Manati. Mr. Steller saw on the coast of America another very singular animal which he calls a Sea Ape: it was five feet long: the head like a dog's: [etc.].

3. 'The sea-otter; so called from its gambols' (*Cent. Dict.* 1891).

a **1891** H. PARTRIDGE (Cent.), When holding a fore-paw over their eyes in order to look about them with more distinctness, they are called sea-apes.

4. The Northern Chimæra (*C. monstrosa*).

1862 COUCH *Brit. Fishes* I. 145 Arctic Chimæra... Sea Ape.

ˈsea-apple. [APPLE *sb.*]

†**1.** The sea-urchin. *Obs.*

1666 [see SEA-EGG 1]. **1752** J. HILL *Hist. Anim.* 199 The roundish Centronia, with crooked..spines, the Sea apple.

2. The sea-coconut (see COCO 6).

1864 GRISEBACH *Flora W. Ind. Islands* 787 Sea-apple: *Manicaria Plukenetii*.

sea-bank. [BANK *sb.*[1]]

1. †**a.** The sea-coast or sea-shore; = BANK *sb.*[1] 9.

c **1350** [see BANK *sb.*[1] 9]. *c* **1450** *St. Cuthbert* (Surtees) 5173 To þe see bank þe cors þai bring. **1604** SHAKS. *Oth.* IV. i. 138, I was the other day talking on the Sea-banke with certaine Venetians. **1794** MRS. RADCLIFFE *Myst. Udolpho* xvi, My music leads to lofty groves, That wild upon the sea-bank wave.

b. A dune or sand-hill.

1848 CLOUGH *Amours de Voy.* 89 The cypress-spires.. Ever more growing,.. Over the low sea-banks, of the fatal Ilian city. **1865** SWINBURNE *Chastelard* I. ii. 31 The next [star], that saw not love, saw me Between the sea-banks and the sea.

c. A sand-bank; = BANK *sb.*[1] 5.

1828 FLEMING *Brit. Anim.* 191 This fish [the cod].. is eagerly sought after on those sea-banks which it frequents.

d. *attrib.*

a **1593** MARLOWE *Ovid's Eleg.* I. i. 34 Elegian Muse.. Girt my shine browe with Sea-banke Mirtle praise [*read* sprays].

2. An embankment built for protection against the sea, a sea-wall.

1647 HEXHAM I, The Sea-bankes, *De Zee-dijcken.* **1655** MARQ. WORCESTER *Cent. Invent.* §96 A way to make a Sea-bank so firm.. that a stream can have no power over it. **1733** *Act 6 Geo. II*, c. 37 §5 If any Person.. shall unlawfully and maliciously break down.. any Sea Bank. **1839** *Civ. Engin. & Arch. Jrnl.* II. 450/1 A Sea Bank constructed.. for the purpose of enclosing a quantity of sea marsh land.

attrib. **1852** WIGGINS *Embanking* 64 The execution of sea-bank work.

So **sea-banking**, the building of sea-banks.

1852 WIGGINS *Embanking* 2 Sea-banking, or sea-walling, has hitherto formed but a small portion of the practice of Engineers.

[**sea-bar**, 'the sea-swallow or tern' (in mod. Dicts.), comes from a misprinted entry in Ainsworth *Eng.-Lat. Dict.* (1736) which should read '*Sea-bat*, hirundo piscis' (i.e. the flying-fish).]

'sea-bass. [BASS *sb.*[1] Cf. Du. *zeebaars.*] A name for various fishes. **a.** *U.S.* A marine food fish of the family Serranidæ; cf. JEW-FISH. **b.** *U.S.* A sciænoid fish, *Cynoscion nobilis* of California (white sea-bass). **c.** *U.S.* The black sea-bass, *Centropristis striatus*, found along the Atlantic coast of North America. **d.** *U.S.* The sturgeon, *Acipenser transmontanus*, of the Pacific coast (*Cent. Dict.*). **e.** = BASS *sb.*[1] 2; LOUP *sb.*[4]

1765 [see BLACK FISH 1]. **1775** A. BURNABY *Trav.* 70 Fish are in the greatest plenty.., particularly.. sea-bass. **1849** H. W. HERBERT *Forester's Fish & Fishing U.S.* 242 The Striped Sea Bass. Rock Fish, Bar Fish. *Ibid.* 264 The Sea Bass. Black Sea Bass. **1884** GOODE, etc. *Nat. Hist. Aquatic Anim.* 378 *Cynoscion nobile.* This species is everywhere known as the 'Sea Bass' ('Sea-Trout'), sometimes as 'White Sea Bass', to distinguish it from the Black Sea Bass or Jew-fish. *Ibid.* 407 The Sea bass, *Serranus atrarius.* **1885** *Riverside Nat. Hist.* (1888) III. 215 In the Carolinas, Florida, and the Gulf, we meet with the names 'bass' and its variations, 'spotted-bass', 'red-bass', 'sea-bass'. *Ibid.* 223 The common sea-bass of the north, *Centropristis furvus.* **1888** [see BLACK FISH 1]. **1900** F. NORRIS *Blix* 129 There were.. sheaves of fishing-rods, from the four-ounce wisp of the brook-trout up to the rigid eighteen-ounce lance of the king-salmon and sea-bass. **1961** E. S. HERALD *Living Fishes of World* 177/2 The giant sea basses, sometimes called jewfishes,.. are the largest American serranids. *Ibid.* 192/1 The genus *Cynoscion* includes.. the California white seabass, *C. nobilis.* **1966**, **1969** [see LOUP *sb.*[4]]. **1973** J. GRIGSON *Fish Cookery* 104 To walk into a fishmonger's and see a tray of sea bass is a beautiful sight.

'sea-bat. [BAT *sb.*[1]]

1. A flying-fish, esp. the flying gurnard, *Dactylopterus volitans.*

1611 FLORIO, *Accola*, a sea Swallow or a Sea Bat. **1665** SIR T. HERBERT *Trav.* (1677) 39 The French call it *Aronder dumer* [sic], the Swallow of the Sea; others a Sea Bat, or Rere-mouse of the Sea. *a* **1672** WILLUGHBY *Hist. Pisc.* (1686) App. 24 Sea Batt. Belgis. An ex Acaraunis? **1884** GOODE, etc. *Nat. Hist. Aquatic Anim.* 255 The Sea-bat or Flying Gurnard.

2. The fish *Malthe vespertilio.*

1756 P. BROWNE *Jamaica* (1789) 457 The Sea-Bat. This curious fish.. by the expansion of its side-fins and its small ventrals, represents a bat in some measure. **1758** EDWARDS *Glean. Nat. Hist.* 156 The Sea-bat appeared to me.. all over of a dark brown or dusky colour. **1884** GOODE, etc. *Nat. Hist. Aquatic Anim.* 173 The Sea Bat, *Malthe vespertilio.*

3. A fish of the genus *Platax.*

1880 GÜNTHER *Fishes* 448 There are probably not more than seven species of 'Sea-bats' [*Platax*], if so many, and they all belong to the Indian Ocean and Western Pacific, where they are very common.

'sea-bath. [BATH *sb.*[1]] A bath or bathe in the sea. Also a place for sea-bathing.

1785 PHILLIPS *Treat. Inland Nav.* 43 Wivenhoe.. is at present a very pretty, clean town... There is a good sea-bath. **1833** *Cycl. Pract. Med.* I. 249/1 The cold shower-bath.. is found to suit better at this hour than the sea-bath. **1878** *Masque of Poets* 199 In sea-baths sheltered from the prowling shark He cooled his fever.

'sea-bathe, *v.* [Back-formation from next.] *intr.* (in quot. 1872 quasi-*trans.* with complement). To bathe in the sea. Hence **'sea-bathing** *ppl. a.*

1792 LADY TEMPLETOWN *Let.* 11 June in A. E. Newdigate-Newdegate *Cheverels* (1898) vii. 104 Eliza is sea-bathing at Ramsgate. **1872** RUSKIN *Fors Clav.* xix, The dirty population of Venice.. gets itself dragged by a screaming kettle to Lido next morning, to sea-bathe itself into a capacity for more tobacco. *a* **1930** D. H. LAWRENCE *Last Poems* (1932) 156 These all-but-naked sea-bathing city people. **1951** N. M. GUNN *Well at World's End* xviii. 141 We did nothing but sun-bathe and sea-bathe.

sea-bathing. Bathing in the sea.

1749 S. RICHARDSON *Let.* ? Nov.–Dec. (1964) 133 The sea-bathing I have not tried. **1753** R. RUSSELL *Diss. Sea Water* 142 He entered upon a Course of Sea Water,.. joining, as usual, the Sea Bathing towards the End of the Cure. **1771** SMOLLETT *Humph. Cl.* 26 June (1815) 207 To Scarborough; where I propose to brace up my fibres by sea-bathing. **1824** LAETITIA M. HAWKINS *Annaline* II. 115, I daresay [she] will not be restored even by sea-bathing. **1875** MCILWRAITH *Guide Wigtownsh.* 71 There is here excellent sea-bathing.

attrib. **1781** J. HARE *Let.* 13 Feb. in *15th Rep. R. Comm. Hist. MSS.* (1897) App. VI. 457 We are to go in about six weeks' time to some sea-bathing place. **1797** *Margate Guide* 63 The Sea Bathing Infirmary at West-brook. **1803** (*title*) A Guide to all the Watering and Sea-Bathing Places.

sea beach. [BEACH *sb.*] = BEACH *sb.* 3.

1742 *Rep. Comm. Houses Assembly S.-Carolina Exped. against St. Augustine* 21 He encamped that Night at Lacenela (the first Palmeta Hut on the Sea-Beach). **1775** ASH, *Seabeach*, the seashore. **1797** MRS. RADCLIFFE *Italian* ix, He left the palace and strolled down to the sea-beach. **1840** LONGF. *Wreck of Hesperus* 77 At daybreak, on the bleak sea-beach, A fisherman stood aghast. **1877** RUSKIN *St. Mark's Rest* I. i. 5 The place by the sea-beach in Palestine, where Dorcas worked for the poor.

attrib. **1864** BROWNING *Death in Desert* 153 To tell dry sea-beach gazers how I fared When there was mid-sea.

'sea-bean.

†**1.** A small stone or pebble (see quot. 1607).

1607 TOPSELL *Four-f. Beasts* 143 There is a little blacke stone in Nilus about the bignesse of a Beane... Such as these I saw at Lyons in France, which they called Sea-beanes, and they prescribed them to be hanged about a Nurses necke to encrease her milke. **1847** HALLIWELL, *Sea-beans*, small black pebbles. *Devon.*

2. A name given to the seeds of the tropical leguminous plant *Entada scandens*, carried by sea to the British coasts, and often made into trinkets.

1696 SLOANE *Catal. Plant. Jamaica* 70 Phaseolus maritimus rotundifolius, flore purpureo [etc.]... The Sea bean. **1867** SMYTH *Sailor's Word-bk.*

3. A small univalve shell of the family *Triviidæ*; also the operculum of any shell of the family *Turbinidæ*. Both are often used for charms, trinkets, etc.

1885 LADY BRASSEY *The Trades* 335 Dealers.. were constantly.. bringing all sorts of shells,.. sea-beans or bay-beans, and other marine curiosities. **1891** *Century Dict.*

'sea-bear. [BEAR *sb.*[1]]

†**1.** The sea-urchin. *Obs.*

1611 COTGR., *Oursin*, the sea Beare. **1668** WILKINS *Real Char.* II. v. §2. 128. **1694** MOTTEUX *Rabelais* IV. lx, Sea-Bears.

2. The ursine or fur-seal, *Callorhinus ursinus*, of the North Pacific. Also applied to the various smaller otaries (species of *Arctocephalus*) of the southern seas, as distinguished from the larger hair-seals, called SEA-LIONS. See also BEAR *sb.*[1] 5.

1771 PENNANT *Synopsis Quadrupeds* 344 Ursine Seal. There are three marine animals, which.. seem divided between the N.E. of Asia, and N.W. of America... These are.. the Sea Lion and the Sea Bear, and the Manati. **1847** [see BEAR *sb.*[1] 5]. **1880** H. W. ELLIOTT *Rep. Seal Isl. Alaska* (1884) 109 The eared-seal, or sea-bear (*Otaria ursina*).

3. A polar bear. *rare.*

1829 J. RICHARDSON *Fauna Bor.-Amer.* I. 30 *Ursus Maritimus*, Polar or Sea Bear. **1876** DAVIS *Polaris Exp.* xxi. 552 What is called the Sea-bear (*Ursus Maritimus*).

'sea-beast. A beast living in the sea.

c **1450** *St. Cuthbert* (Surtees) 1644 Se bestys serued him at hande. **1667** MILTON *P.L.* I. 200 That Sea-beast Leviathan. **1849** M. ARNOLD *Forsaken Merman* 39 Where the sea-beasts rang'd all round Feed in the ooze of their pasture-ground.

transf. **1695** CONGREVE *Love for L.* I. iv, If he be but as great a Sea-Beast, as she is a Land-Monster, we shall have a most Amphibious Breed.

'sea-beat, *a.* [BEAT *ppl. a.*] = next.

1579 SPENSER *Sheph. Cal.* Feb. 34 That, once sea-beate, will to sea againe. **1600** FAIRFAX *Tasso* XVI. lxxi, Wandering lonely on the sea-beat strand. **1725** POPE *Odyss.* IX. 196 Along the sea-beat shore Satiate we slept. **1883** STEVENSON *Silverado Sq.* (1886) 24 That gray country, with its rainy, sea-beat archipelago.

'sea-beaten, *a.* [BEATEN *ppl. a.*]

1. Of a ship, a sailor, etc.: Tossed about or beaten by the waves of the sea. Now *rare* or *Obs.*

1562 A. BROOKE *Romeus & Iuliet* 808 God graunt no daungers rocke.. wracke thy sea beaten barke. **1587** TURBERV. *Trag. Tales* Ded. A ij b, Following herein sea-beaten soldiers, and miserable mariners. **1606** BP. HALL *Heaven upon Earth* Ded., Ships.. both extremely Sea-beaten, and at last wracked. **1801** MRS. ROBINSON *Sylphid* III. 142 (Jod.) The sea-beaten sailor.

2. Of a shore, rock, etc.: Lashed by the sea.

1793 COWPER *A Tale* ('*In Scotland's realm*') 19 Sea-beaten rocks and naked shores, Could yield them no retreat. **1868** STEVENSON *Let.* July in *Scribner's Mag.* (1899) XXV. 31/1, I am utterly sick of this gray, grim, sea-beaten hole. **1883** *Longman's Mag.* Oct. 632 Quiet bays and sea-beaten cliffs.

'sea-beaver.

†**1.** = HIPPOCAMPUS 2. *Obs.*

1755 tr. *Pontoppidan's Nat. Hist. Norway* II. 51 The Sea-Beaver is another and larger Insect, peculiar to the sea... Called in the Mediterranean Hippocampus.

2. The sea-otter.

1759 DUMARESQUE in *Phil. Trans.* LI. 488 Many of them go thither, to catch sea-beavers. **1764** GRIEVE tr. *Krasheninnikoff's Kamtschatka* 130 The sea beavers [*Lutra marina*] have not the least resemblance to the other beavers.

sea-beef.

†**1.** Pickled beef used on shipboard. *Obs.*

1594 NASHE *Christ's T.* To Rdr.**, A prouerbe.. as stale as sea-biefe. **1606** DEKKER *Newes fr. Hell* Wks. (Grosart) II. 112 Though such kind of Theeuerie bee more stale then Sea-beefe.

2. The flesh of a porpoise or whale. Also locally applied to various food-fishes (*jocularly* to herring).

1672 JOSSELYN *New-Eng. Rarities* 27 Ling, Sea Beef. [Cf. quot. 1661 s.v. BEEF *sb.* 2 a.] **1850** SCORESBY *Cheever's Whalem. Adv.* vi. (1858) 77 The porpoise.. is harpooned.. and its carcass eaten by the name of 'sea beef'.

Seabees ('siːbiːz), *sb. pl.* Also with small initial. [f. representation of initial letters of *construction battalion* + pl. *-s.*] **a.** (Members of) the Construction Battalions formed as a volunteer branch of the Civil Engineer Corps of the U.S. Navy.

1942 *Army & Navy Jrnl.* 21 Mar. 790/2 'Seabees' is the new name chosen to designate the new Naval Construction Regiments... With the name an insignia has been adopted —a flying bee, fighting mad. On its head it sports a sailor hat. In its fore hand or leg it clutches a spitting 'Tommy Gun'; in its amidship hand, a wrench, and in its aft hand, a carpenter's hammer. **1945** D. DEMPSEY in *Best One-Act Plays of 1944* 21 I'm in the Seabees, which means I'm in the Navy. **1950** 'D. DIVINE' *King of Fassarai* xi. 90 'The Seabees are starting in here—' he placed his pencil on the chart. **1960** S. W. ROSKILL *War at Sea* III. I. 339 The 'Seabees' also proved themselves first-class fighting troops when the need arose. **1980** G. V. HIGGINS *Kennedy for Defense* xix. 174 Some cops were in the Seabees, lotta cops was in the Army.

b. *attrib.* or as *adj.* (Sometimes in *sing.* form.)

1942 *Sun* (Baltimore) 17 Nov. 13/3 Brief ceremonies attended by naval officers marked the placing in operation of the third 'seabees' center constructed in Virginia. **1977** *Hongkong Standard* 12 Apr. 8/4 Of the 1,400 navy men here, more than 800 are seabee construction workers who will leave when the facility is completed. **1981** G. V. HIGGINS *Rat on Fire* v. 35 You were running that Seabees reunion.

sea-bell.

1. A species of bindweed, *Convolvulus Soldanella.*

1597 GERARDE *Herbal* II. ccxciii. 690 Sea Withwinde, Sea Bindweed, Sea bels, Sea Coale, and of some Sea Folefoote, and Scottish Scuruie grasse. **1866** *Treas. Bot.*

2. A zoophyte of the genus CAMPANULARIA.

1860 tr. *Hartwig's Sea & Wonders* 278 The delicate feathery forms of the sea-wreaths, sea-feathers, and sea-bells (sertulariæ, plumulariæ, and campanulariæ).

'sea-bird. A bird frequenting the sea, or the land near the sea. Also *attrib.*

1589 RIDER *Bibl. Scholast.* 1704 A Seabirde great and ravenous, *charadrius.* **1662** J. DAVIES tr. *Mandelslo's Trav.* 259 We.. saw infinite multitudes of little Sea-birds. **1766** SMOLLETT *Trav.* I. xix. 301 All sea-birds are allowed by the church of Rome to be eaten on meagre days, as a kind of fish. **1865** TENNYSON *Captain* 71 The lonely seabird crosses With one waft of the wing. **1898** KEARTON *Wild Life at Home* 100 The Orkney and Shetland Islands are rich in sea-bird life.

'sea-bladder.

†**1.** The bladder-wrack. Cf. next 1. *Obs.*

1681 GREW *Musæum* II. §v. ii. 250 The Roped Sea-Bladder.. is also wrought with fibrous Veins, as the former.

2. The Portuguese man-of-war.

1860 WRAXALL *Life in Sea* x. 243 The Physaliæ, or Sea-bladders.

seable, obs. form of SEEABLE.

'sea-blubber. Also 7 -blobber. [BLUBBER *sb.*[1]]

†**1.** The bladder-wrack. Cf. prec. 1. *Obs.*

1681 GREW *Musæum* II. §v. ii. 250 Sea-Blobber. *Vesicaria marina...* 'Tis a Cluster of small roundish Bladders.. of a light brown colour.

2. A jelly-fish. See BLUBBER *sb.*[1] 3.

1683–4 ROBINSON in *Phil. Trans.* XXIX. 478 The *Urtica Marina* (called Sea Gelly or Blubber, tho' it be an Animal). **1769** *Ann. Reg.* I. 189/1 Boat-loads of what the sailors called sea-blubbers. **1845** GOSSE *Ocean* iii. (1849) 151 These *Medusæ*, or Sea-blubbers, as they are familiarly called, form a considerable portion of the Whale's food.

seaboard ('siːbɔəd), *sb.* and *a.* Forms: see SEA *sb.* and BOARD *sb.* Also 9 -bord. [f. SEA *sb.* + BOARD *sb.*]

A. *sb.*

†**1.** The plank to cover up the port-hole. *Obs.*

c **1400** *Beryn* 3001 Why close they the port with the see bord?

†**2.** With prepositions *a, at, on, to seaboard*, on or to the seaward side (of a ship, etc.). *Obs.*

a **1490** BOTONER *Itin.* (1778) 110 Et insula de Ushand jacet in le seebord anglice south et north. **1525** LD. BERNERS *Froiss.* II. cl. 165 Yᵉ wynde was so streynable on see borde, that they coude nat departe thence. **1535** STEWART *Cron. Scot.* I. 297 [He] With mony schip to se burd passit syne. *c* **1566** in *Hakluyt's Voy.* (1589) 390 There lay two rocks two miles to sea boord of vs. **1581** J. BELL *Haddon's Answ. Osorius* 70 To preserve their course the better at Seaboorde. **1582** LICHEFIELD tr. *Castanheda's Conq. E. Ind.* I. v. 13 Our men discried three Ilands a Seaboard. **1602** MANSEL *True Rep. Service* 1 My selfe being neerest that coast, Captaine Iones next vnto me, and the Dutch men of warre a Seaboord, and to the westward of him. *c* **1625** J. TAYLOR (Water-P.) *Braue Sea-fight* Wks. 1630 III. 40/2 The Enemie making all the sayle he could to Sea-boord of the English. *c* **1635** CAPT. N. BOTELER *Dial. Sea Services* (1685) 281

When a Ship..hath another Ship on her other side to Seaward, or (as the phrase is) to Sea-board.

†**3.** *by* (*be*) *seaboard*: by sea. *on seaboard*: at sea, on board ship. *Obs.*

1535 STEWART *Chron. Scot.* I. 369 Out of Denmark be se burd mony myle, Ane greit armie in Albione wes send. **1549** *Compl. Scot.* xi. 91 Nocht alanerly be gryt multitude of men of veyr, and ane grit nauen of schipis be seey burde, bot [etc.]. **1581** J. BELL *Haddon's Answ. Osorius* 420 Whenas beyng on Seaborde he was in daunger to be drowned. **1597** J. PAYNE *Royal Exch.* 32 In all my tyme on Seaboorde..I have knowen nombers that were on another disposition.

4. The line where land and sea meet, the coastline; the sea-shore or the land near the sea, esp. considered with reference to its extent or configuration.

1788 F. ASBURY *Jrnl.* 10 July (1821) II. 36 The Gnats are almost as troublesome here, as the moschetoes in the lowlands of the sea-board. **1825** J. NEAL *Bro. Jonathan* I. 78 Certain alarming movements on the sea-board. **1840** CARLYLE *Heroes* i. (1841) 26 On the seabord of this wild land [Iceland] is a rim of grassy country, where cattle can subsist. **1860** H. MILLER *My Schools* xiii. 143/1 The population of extensive Islands and seaboards of the country. **1867** FREEMAN *Norm. Conq.* (ed. 3) I. ii. 25 These kingdoms have a large sea-board. **1887** J. BALL *Nat. in S. Amer.* 124 The sea-board is nearly a straight line running from north to south.

Comb. **1897** MARY KINGSLEY *W. Africa* xxii. 316 The seaboard-dwelling Tschwis.

B. *adj.* Bordering on or adjoining the sea. *rare.*

1590 SPENSER *F.Q.* III. iii. 47 There shall a Lyon from the sea-bord wood Of Neustria come roring. **1828–32** WEBSTER, *Sea-bord, Sea-bordering*, bordering on the sea or ocean. **1888** J. SHALLOW *Templars' Trials* 8 The Hospitallers, whose property was largely sea-board, left Cyprus for Rhodes. **1909** *Daily Chron.* 18 Aug. 4/4 The French seaboard hotels.

Hence **ˈsea-boarder**, an inhabitant of the seaboard.

1611 SPEED *Hist. Gt. Brit.* v. vii. §3. 38 The Kentish [men] and Seaborders being full of humanity, and little differing from the French ciuility.

ˈsea-boat. [BOAT *sb.*]

1. a. A boat for the sea. **b.** A vessel considered in reference to her behaviour at sea. **c.** *spec.* A small, manœuvrable craft sent out from a larger vessel, as in cases of emergency at sea.

Beowulf 633 þa ic on holm ȝestah, sæ-bat ȝesæt mid minra secȝa ȝedriht. **1725** DE FOE *Voy. round World* (1840) 199 Our brigantine..an excellent sea-boat. **1727** ARBUTHNOT *Tables Anc. Coins*, etc. 241 The Roman Shipwrecks were occasion'd undoubtedly by their Ships being bad Sea-boats, and [etc.]. **1769** FALCONER *Dict. Marine* (1780), *Sea-Boat*, a vessel that bears the sea firmly, without labouring heavily. **1793** SMEATON *Edystone L.* §92 Any good sea-boat, may make her course good to Fowey. **1856** RUSKIN *Harbours of England* 1 One object there is still, which I never pass without the renewed wonder of childhood; and that is the bow of a Boat... The blunt head of a common bluff undecked sea-boat. **1892** R. C. LESLIE *Sea-Boat* 4 The building of a bluff-bowed, flat-floored sea-boat, is a much greater test of a boat-builder's skill than the construction of any form of longer and sharper craft. **1909** *Man. Seamanship* (Admiralty) II. viii. 142 Never call away a 'lifeboat' at sea except for the purpose of saving life; on all other occasions call away the 'sea boat'. **1914** 'BARTIMEUS' *Naval Occasions* xx. 179 The seaboat's crew had gone through an undress rehearsal of 'Man overboard!' **1963** H. C. DE MIERRE *Long Voyage* ix. 148 Port and starboard sea-boats had been put in the water. **1972** C. MUDIE *Motor Boats & Boating* 76 Over twelve feet in length..the types of boat begin to diverge from the general purpose dinghy..into seaboats for family use and for fishing.

attrib. **1888** R. EDMONDSTON & SAXBY *Home of Naturalist* 31 He always had unbounded faith in the sea-boat qualities of a Shetland sixaerin.

2. A name for a *Chiton* or coat-of-mail shell.

1884 GOODE, etc. *Nat. Hist. Aquatic Anim.* 701 These shells have been called by different names,..such as 'Woodlouse', 'Sea-boat',..'Sea-bug', and 'Sea-caterpillar'.

ˈsea-book.

†**1.** A sea-log (see SEA *sb.* 23 a). *Obs.*

a **1642** SIR W. MONSON *Naval Tracts* III. (1704) 336/1 The Captain may require a Copy of the Sea Book from the Purser.

2. (See quot. 1883). *Obs.* exc. *Hist.*

1726 SHELVOCKE *Voy. round World* 34 All arms, sea-books and instruments..is plunder. **1883** *Encycl. Brit.* XV. 519/2 When the loxodromic maps came into existence, handbooks with sailing directions were written to accompany them, hence the titles 'sailing directions', 'sea-books',..or cartas da marear.

3. A book representing life at sea, etc. (SEA *sb.* 18 l).

1894 CLARK RUSSELL in *My First Book* 30 It is the first sea book I ever wrote.

sea-border. The land bordering on the sea.

1686 *Charter of Romney-Marsh* title-p., Very useful..for all Lords of Towns, and other Landholders within Romney-Marsh,..and all other Marshes, Fenns, and Sea-Borders. **1880** SWINBURNE *Studies in Song* 180 These alone in all the wild sea-borders Fear no blast of days and nights that die.

†**sea-borderer.** *Obs. rare.* One who inhabits the land adjacent to the sea.

a **1593** MARLOWE *Hero & Leander* I. 3 On Hellespont..In view and opposit two citties stood, Seaborderers [earliest eds. (1598–1613) Seaborders], disioin'd by Neptunes might: The one Abydos, the other Sestos hight. **1599** NASHE *Lenten Stuffe* 46 Their heauenly hoods..decreede, that for they were either of them seaborderers and drowned in the sea, stil to the sea they must belong. **1670** COTTON *Espernon* III. ix. 442 A barbarous and inhumane people (as generally Sea-borderers are).

ˈsea-ˌbordering, *a. rare.* Bordering on the sea.

1597 BEARD *Theatre God's Judgem.* (1612) 533 Amongst sea-bordering Cities,..Tire in former ages was most famous. **1612** DRAYTON *Poly-olb.* XVII. 358 Tow'rds those Sea-bordring shores of ours. **1626** SIR D. DIGGS *Sp.* in Rushw. *Hist. Coll.* (1659) I. 302 All the Sea-bordering parts of this Kingdom. **1852** ANSTED *Phys. Geog.* in *Man. Geog. Sci.* I. 259 Those rich sea-bordering clays, whose fertility is such as to induce men to risk disease in swampy climates.

ˈsea-born, *a.* Born in or of the sea. **a.** Of persons, etc., chiefly mythological, esp. of Venus.

a **1593** MARLOWE *Dido* III. i. 763 Seaborne Nymphes shall swarme about thy ships. *a* **1645** WALLER *To my Lord Admiral* 55 Like Neptune and his Sea-borne Neece. *a* **1664** KATH. PHILIPS *To Lucasia* Poems (1667) 147 Eyes so sweet as these, No power that is Sea-born can displease. **1726** POPE *Odyss.* XVII. 160 Learn what I heard the sea-born Seer relate, Whose eye can pierce the dark recess of fate. **1871** R. ELLIS *Catullus* lxiv. 17 Sea-born Nymphs.

b. Produced by or having its origin in the sea.

1646 QUARLES *Sheph. Oracles* vii. 83 The Sea-born Sturgeon, and the broad-side Bream. **1764** GOLDSM. *Trav.* 121 Sea-born gales their gelid wings expand To winnow fragrance round the smiling land. **1808** SCOTT *Marm.* II. xvi, If on a rock..Saint Cuthbert sits, and toils to frame The sea-born beads that bear his name. **1868** *Rep. U.S. Commissioner Agric.* (1869) 402 During all the unknown.. geological ages in which these mountains of sea-born rocks have been slowly growing.

c. Of an island, etc. rising from the sea.

1726 POPE *Odyss.* XIX. 197 Ninety cities crown the seaborn Isle. **1817** BYRON *Beppo* x, That sea-born city [Venice] was in all her glory.

ˈsea-borne, *a.* [BORNE *ppl. a.*]

1. Conveyed by sea. (Said usually of articles of commerce.)

1823 *Edin. Rev.* XXXVIII. 236/1 Very few buildings have ..been erected of sea-borne stone. **1844** H. STEPHENS *Bk. Farm* III. 996 The best sea-borne English lime. **1850** HT. MARTINEAU *Hist. Peace* IV. xi. (1877) III. 79 A reduction of duties on sea-borne coal. **1864** BURTON *Scot Abr.* II. ii. 152 To the sea-borne traveller it is the most conspicuous stronghold along the sea-coast. **1910** *Spectator* 11 June 920/1 Germany would never run the risk of invading France by a sea-borne expedition.

2. Of a ship, etc.: Carried or floating on the sea. See also quot. 1867.

1840 *Evid. Hull Docks Comm.* 44 A dock of sufficient depth for sea-borne vessels. **1857** GOSSE *Omphalos* ii. 51 The impressions..would have been totally obliterated, if the trees had been sea-borne and shore-rolled, as pretended. **1867** SMYTH *Sailor's Word-bk.*, *Sea-borne*, arrived from a voyage: said of freighted ships also afloat.

3. *ellipt.* quasi-*sb.* Sea-borne coal. Used *attrib.*

1892 *Pall Mall Gaz.* 12 Feb. 5/1 The number of men on strike this morning is 7,500, many of the 'seaborne' men having left work since yesterday morning.

sea-bottom. The bottom or lowest depth of the sea; a tract of ground covered by a sea.

a **1400–50** *Alexander* 5532 How he miȝt seke doun sounde in-to þe see bothom. **1582** STANYHURST *Æneis* III. (Arb.) 93 Alpheüs..Vnder seabottoms this passadge ferreted. **1876** PAGE *Adv. Text-bk. Geol.* iii. 50 The heterogeneous deposit of a former sea-bottom. **1885** CHILD *Ballads* II. 50/1 A mermaid, from the sea-bottom, cries out to him.

ˈsea-bound, *a.*[1] [BOUND *ppl. a.*[2]] Bound or confined by the sea.

Cf. *sea-bounded* adj. (SEA *sb.* 21), with which this is often confused.

1636 G. SANDYS *Paraphr. Ps.* ii. 2 Subject all Nations to thy Throne, And make the Sea-bound Earth thine owne. **1828–32** WEBSTER, *Sea-bound, Sea-bounded*, bounded by the sea. **1902** *Westm. Gaz.* 3 June 3/2 The sea-bound lands. **1910** *Blackw. Mag.* Aug. 264/2 He lived..in a sea-bound solitude.

ˈsea-bound, *a.*[2] [BOUND *ppl. a.*[1]] Bound for or on the way to the sea.

1839–52 BAILEY *Festus* (ed. 5) 80 The sea-bound river. **1895** *Funk's Stand. Dict.* s.v., A sea-bound voyage. **1899** *Westm. Gaz.* 1. Aug. 4/3 To catch their sea-bound train.

ˈsea-bream.

1. A name applied to several sparoid fishes, esp. *Pagellus centrodontus.*

1530 PALSGR. 269/1 See breame a fysshe. **1613** R. HARCOURT *Voy. Guiana* 30 Of Sea-fish, there is Sea-breame, Mullet, Sole [etc.]. **1620** SHELTON *Quix.* II. xi. 64 Thou saydst she had eyes of Pearles, and such eyes are rather the eies of a Sea-Breame then a faire Dames. **1672** JOSSELYN *New-Eng. Rarities* 95 Sea Bream, which are plentifully taken upon the Sea Coasts, their Eyes are accounted rare Meat, whereupon the proverbial comparison, It is worth a Sea Breams Eye. **1752** J. HILL *Hist. Anim.* 253 The reddish Sparus.., The Sea-bream. **1840** *Cuvier's Anim. Kingd.* 297 Sparidæ (the Sea-bream Family). **1896** *Roy. Nat. Hist.* (ed. Lydekker) V. 347 The black sea-bream (*Cantharus lineatus*) of the British seas.

2. Applied to the coryphænoid genus *Brama.*

1710 SIBBALD *Fife & Kinross* 53 *Brama Marina nostras*, the Sea-Bream. **1891** *Century Dict.*

ˈsea-breeze. [BREEZE *sb.*[2]]

1. A breeze blowing from the sea.

1697 DAMPIER *Voy.* I. 348 Taking the advantage of the Land breezes by nyht, and the Sea breezes by day. **1743** BULKELEY & CUMMINS *Voy. S. Seas* 160 A Sea-Breeze came in, and blow'd so hard that we were obliged to weigh. **1769** W. STORK *Descr. East-Florida* (ed. 3) 25 The sea-breezes keep it in constant agitation. **1825** J. NEAL *Bro. Jonathan* I. 359 Before a strong sea-breeze. **1873** B. HARTE *Fiddletown* 28 The chill sea-breeze made him shiver. **1888** LOWELL *Hearts-ease & Rue* 130 Where sea-breeze and sunshine meet.

2. 'Also, a cool sea-drink' (Smyth *Sailor's Word-bk.* 1867).

Hence **sea-breezed** *a.*, having sea-breezes, or blown on by sea-breezes; **sea-breeziness**, the condition of being breezy or having sea-breezes. *fig.*

1760 BP. HILDESLEY in W. Hanbury *Charit. Found. Ch.-Langton* (1767) 114 Plants or trees..suitable to this seabreez'd island [Man] and its sandy gravelly soil. **1837** [see BREEZINESS]. **1903** *Daily Chron.* 25 Sept. 3/4 There is a seabreeziness about it [the book].

Seabright (ˈsiːbraɪt). Also with small initial. The name of a small town on the coast of New Jersey, used *attrib.* and *absol.* to designate a variety of flat-keeled fishing-boat from the region, esp. adapted for landing on beaches in heavy seas.

1911 *Rudder* XXV. 83 (*caption*) Jersey Coast fishermen getting one of their power Seabright skiffs off and on the beach. **1930** G. PINCHOT *To South Seas* i. 7 The bronze and mahogany launch was replaced by a Seabright dory twenty-two feet long by seven feet wide. *Ibid.* xii. 237 In the Seabright again I put it on the floor. **1971** P. J. GUTHORN *Sea Bright Skiff* v. 74 The Sea Bright skiff rum boats were progressively, but never completely, replaced by boats of V-bottom design.

ˈsea-bull. [BULL *sb.*[1]]

†**1.** The male of the sea-cow or seal. *Obs.*

a **1400–50** *Alexander* 3846 Of Seeles & of see-Bules a swyth grete nounbre. *Ibid.* 4098 A cowdrife breste [? *read* beste], Of sembalaunce as a see-bule. *c* **1520** ANDREW *Noble Life* III. xxxviii, Focas is a see bulle, & is very stronge & dangerous. **1688** HOLME *Armoury* II. 216/1 He beareth Argent, a sea Bulls-head couped, Sable.

2. The male of the sea-cow or hippopotamus.

1863 W. C. BALDWIN *Afr. Hunting* iii. 88 A large sea-bull lying asleep close inland behind some reeds.

seabylle, seac, obs. ff. SEEABLE, SICK.

sea-cabbage.

1. a. = SEA-KALE. **b.** *dial.* (See quot. 1904.)

1731 MILLER *Gard. Dict.*, *Crambe.* Sea-Cabbage. **1855** MISS PRATT *Flower. Pl.* I. 140 *Brassica oleracea* (Sea Cabbage). **1904** *Eng. Dial. Dict.*, *Sea Cabbage*, the great mullein, *Verbascum thapsus.*

†**2.** The sea-otter's cabbage. *Obs.*

1764 GRIEVE tr. *Krasheninnikoff's Kamtschatka* 131 They have three different ways of catching them: 1st. By nets placed among the sea cabbage [note *Fucus marinus*], whither the beavers retire in the night time.

sea-cale, variant of SEA-KALE.

ˈsea-calf. [CALF[1].] A common name for the seal, esp. the common seal, *Phoca vitulina.* [So med.L. *vitulus marinus*, F. *veau marin*, G. *seekalb.*]

1387 TREVISA *Higden* (Rolls) II. 13 þere beeþ ofte i-take dolphyns, and see calues [orig. *vituli marini*], and baleynes. **1558** GESNER *Hist. Anim.* IV. 831 Angli etiam nominant a Sea caulfe: uel Seele. **1563** HYLL *Art Garden.* (1593) 26 Some also hang..the skinne of the Sea-Calfe in the middle of the garden..as a proouved defence to it against tempestes. **1668** H. MORE *Div. Dial.* II. i. (1713) 89 The playing of two Sea-Calves before a Storm. **1880** *Standard* 20 May 3 The 'sea calves' of the North Atlantic are solely 'hair seals'.

attrib. c **1440** tr. *Pallad. on Husb.* I. 961 A seecalf skyn.

b. *allusively.*

1755 J. SHEBBEARE *Lydia* (1769) II. 67 You grow pert, madam, since you have caught your sea-calf. **1883** STEVENSON *Treas. Isl.* viii, 'Why what a precious old sea-calf I am!' he said.

ˈsea-captain. The captain or commander of a ship; usually applied to the captain of a merchant vessel.

1612 WEBSTER *White Devil* II. i. 380 To what scorn'd purpose else should we make choice Of him for a sea captaine? **1708** *Proclam.* 20 May in *Lond. Gaz.* No. 4440/1 In case any Sea-Captain, Inferior Commission or Warrant Sea-Officers belonging to any Ship of War..be absent. **1897** WATTS-DUNTON *Aylwin* II. xiii, The widow of a sea captain.

†**ˈsea-card.** *Obs.* [CARD *sb.*[2]]

1. A chart of the sea (see CARD *sb.*[2] 3 b and CHART *sb.*[1] 1 b). *Obs.*

1571 DIGGES *Pantom.* I. xxxv. L iij, You shall make a sea carde wherin you may by the former rules place Coastes, Harboroughes, Rockes, Sandes [etc.]. **1745** POCOCKE *Descr. East* II. II. 148 The whole, according to the sea-cards, being the bay of Contessa.

2. The card of the mariner's compass (see CARD *sb.*[2] 4).

1555 [see CARD *sb.*[2] 4]. **1618** FLETCHER *Chances* I. xi, We are all like sea-Cards, All our endeavours and our motions,.. still point at beauty. **1666** PEPYS *Diary* 22 Sept., A little gold frame for one of my sea-cards.

transf. **1710** SHAFTESB. *Adv. Author* I. iii. 53 Thus much for..those Rules of Art, those Philosophical Sea-Cards by which the adventuring Genius's of the times were won't to steer their Courses, and govern their impetuous Muse.

ˈsea-cat. [Cf. F. *chat de mer*, 'the smallest kind of dog-fish' (Cotgr.).]

1. A name for various fishes. **a.** The wolf-fish, *Anarrhichas lupus.* **b.** The great weever,

Trachinus draco. **c.** A shark, *Scyllium catulus.* **d.** *Chimæra monstrosa.* **e.** Any sea-catfish, as *Ælurichthys marinus.*

1601 HOLLAND *Pliny* XXXII. ix. II. 445 The fish named the Sea-cat or Weazill. **1710** SIBBALD *Fife & Kinross* 51 *Lupus Marinus Shonfeldii & Nostras*; our Fishers call it the Sea-Cat, or Cat-fish. *a* **1779** D. GRAHAM *Buck-Haven* Writ. (1883) II. 220 Spout-fish, sea-cats, sea-dogs. **1860** WRAXALL *Life in Sea* v. 108 The Spotted Shark, or Sea Cat (*Scyllium catulus*, Cuvier). **1884** GOODE, etc. *Nat. Hist. Aquatic Anim.* 628 The Gaff-topsail Catfish..is known [in various places] as the 'Sea Cat'. **1885** *Riverside Nat. Hist.* (1888) III. 72 *Chimæra monstrosa*,..sea-cat, sea-rat, etc. of fishermen.

2. † **a.** [Du. *zeekat.*] A squid or cuttlefish. *Obs.*

1601 HOLLAND *Pliny* XXXII. ii. II. 428 The foresaid writer Trebius Niger reporteth, That the sea-cats or Cuttle fishes ..wil flie out of the sea [etc.].

b. *S. Afr.* One of several species of octopus, esp. *Octopus vulgaris.*

1785 G. FORSTER tr. *Sparrman's Voy. Cape of Good Hope* I. ii. 26 The *sepia loligo*, and the *sepia octopodia*,..are known to our sailors by the name of black-fish and sea-cats. **1882** *Cape Q. Rev.* Oct. 36 Even the sea cat responded to the hook. **1913** W. W. THOMPSON *Sea Fisheries Cape Colony* ii. 51 The octopus or sea-cat..appears to find a more congenial habitat on the rocky stretches of sea-board. **1957** S. SCHOEMAN *Strike!* iii. 38 If seacat is used, a baby octopus put on whole will be most acceptable.

† **3.** The SEA-HARE. *Obs.*

1758 *Phil. Trans.* L. 586 Some call them..sea-cats.

† **4.** The sea-bear or common fur-seal. *Obs.*

1764 GRIEVE tr. *Krasheninnikoff's Kamtschatka* 123 The sea cat is about half the size of the sea lion; in form resembling the seal. **1772–84** *Cook's Voy.* (1790) V. 1668 Sea-cats..have long hairs standing out on each side of their mouths like those of a cat.

5. *Mil.* (In form **Seacat** or **Sea Cat.**) The name of a short-range, ship-to-air, guided missile (system).

1959 *Times* 5 Feb. 7/3 By early next year a considerable number of Britain's warships will be equipped with surface-to-air missiles, and these weapons..will almost certainly include the Short SX-A5 which was named the Seacat by the Admiralty and the Ministry of Supply yesterday. **1969** B. B. SCHOFIELD in P. Kemp *Hist. Royal Navy* xxvii. 294/1 In April 1958 a contract was awarded for the development of a close-range ship-to-air guided weapon to replace the 40-mm Bofors A/A guns in H.M. ships... This was achieved by the production of the Seacat missile. **1977** *Navy News* June 6 The 2,500 ton warship is armed with an automatic rapid fire 4·5 in. gun, Sea Cat and Exocet missile systems, and she operates a Wasp helicopter.

seace, obs. form of CEASE, SEISE.

'sea-cliff. A cliff on the seashore.

In Geology sometimes applied to rocks which are now inland, but were on the shores of ancient seas.

c **888** K. ÆLFRED *Boeth.* vii. §4 Swa fela welena swa þara sondcorna bið be þisum sæclifum. *c* **1205** LAY. 18638 He is mid sea cliuen [*c* **1275** see cluues] faste biclused. **1610** HOLLAND *Camden's Brit.* I. 634 Compassed with a triple ditch..cast in forme of a bowe, the string whereof is the sea-cliffe. **1769** *Atwick Inclosure Act* 5 The said allotments.. shall lie contiguous to the sea-cliff. **1830** LYELL *Princ. Geol.* II. vi. (1835) II. 28 An ancient sea-cliff is to be seen, now inland. **1876** PAGE *Adv. Text-bk. Geol.* iii. 50 Waves wearing away the sea-cliffs.

sea-coal ('siːkəʊl). [COAL *sb.*[1]]

† **1.** In Old English: Jet. *Obs.*

In early times jet was chiefly found washed ashore by the sea.

c **1050** *Voc.* in Wr.-Wülcker 416/2 Gagates, sæcol.

2. a. A name for mineral coal ('coal' in the ordinary modern sense) as distinguished from charcoal. Now only *Hist.*

Commonly explained as meaning 'coal brought by sea'. But *carbo maris* occurs in the *Newminster Cartulary* (Northumberland) *c* 1236 (see quot. in COAL *sb.*[1] 5 a); and in 1306 a Glamorganshire document (*Inquis. Post Mortem*, Ioan. de Clare, 35 Edw. I) speaks of 'unus puteus in quo fodiuntur *carbones maris*'. Unless we suppose that the documents were written by Londoners, or (what is very unlikely) that the London term had been adopted in the coal-producing regions themselves, these early examples appear to point to some different explanation. Possibly in early times the chief source of coal supply may have been the beds exposed by marine denudation on the coasts of Northumberland and South Wales. Cf. quot. *a* 1552. The name of Seacoal lane, London (*Secollane*), occurs 1339 in Riley *Mem. Lond.* 207.

c **1253** [see COAL *sb.*[1] 5 a]. **1282** [see *seacoal-pit* in 3]. **1371** in *York Minster Fabric Rolls* (Surtees) 9 Et in ij schaldres de secole emptis pro eodem, 10*s*. **1429** *Rolls of Parlt.* IV. 359/2 Under wodde..seecole, and in oþer manere. *a* **1552** LELAND *Itin.* (1769) VIII. 19 The vaynes of the se-coles by sometyme upon clives of the se, as round about Coket Island. **1635** [GLAPTHORNE] *Lady Mother* I. ii. in Bullen *Old Pl.* (1883) II. 112 The wholesome smell of seacole. **1645–52** BOATE *Ireland's Nat. Hist.* (1860) 101 The inhabitants.. want wood for firing (being therefore constrained to make shift with turf, or sea-coal, where they are not too far from the sea). **1663** DUDLEY (*title*) Metallum Martis: or Iron made with Pit-coale, Sea-coale, &c. **1673** SHADWELL *Epsom Wells* I. Wks. 1720 II. 194 You'll never leave that place of sin and sea-coal. **1769** *De Foe's Tour Gt. Brit.* (ed. 7) II. 151 The City of London, and Parts adjacent, as also all the South of England, are supplied with Coals, called therefore Sea-coal, from Newcastle upon Tyne, and from the Coast of Durham and Northumberland. **1818** SCOTT *Rob Roy* x, The rusty grate, seldom gladdened by either sea-coal or fagots.

b. *U.S. rare.* 'Soft coal as distinguished from anthracite' (*Funk's Stand. Dict.* 1895).

3. *attrib.*, as ***sea-coal ashes, fire,*** †***-meter,*** †***pit,*** †***prong, soot***; **sea-coal room**, a room with a sea-coal fire.

1699 EVELYN *Kal. Hort.* May (ed. 9) 64 Sift a little Lime discreetly with it, or rather *Sea-coal Ashes. **1597** SHAKS. *2 Hen. IV*, II. i. 95 Sitting..by a *sea-cole fire. **1817** BYRON *Beppo* xlviii, I like a seacoal fire, when not too dear. **1668** *Act for Preventing Fires*, etc. 6 The *Seacole-meters. **1282** *Dean Forest Survey*, Item una trenchea incipiens apud *Secole puttes. **1629** *Leather* 7 Our Sea-coale Pits being able ..to furnish the whole Iland. **1664** BUTLER *Hud.* II. iii. 1063 Whachum his *Sea-coal-Prong threw by, And basely turn'd his back to flie. **1719** D'URFEY *Pills* V. 84 We'll sit close and snug in a *Sea-coal Room. **1707** MORTIMER *Husb.* (1721) I. 121 Soot is very good for Corn and Grass, but *Sea-coal Soot is the best by much.

sea-coal, obs. f. *sea-cole* (see SEA *sb.* 23 f).

sea-coast.

1. The land adjacent to the sea; = COAST *sb.* 4.

13.. *Coer de L.* 4782 Kyng Richard and Phelyp, with her hoost; Wente foorth be the see-coost. *a* **1451** FORTESCUE *Wks.* (1869) 551 The coost of France is no longer by the narow see coost than from Calyce in Pycardy unto Seynt Malous in Bretany. **1590** SPENSER *F.Q.* II. x. 6 Those white rocks..Which all along the Southerne sea-coast lay, Threatning vnheedie wrecke. **1614** RALEIGH *Hist. World* III. vii. §5. 83 All the Sea-coast..[was] exposed to the waste of an enemie too farre ouer-matching him. **1790** BEATSON *Nav. & Mil. Mem.* II. 164 To defend the sea-coasts of his own dominions. **1831** SIR J. SINCLAIR *Corr.* II. 336 Prussia ..has a considerable range of sea-coast. **1876** A. S. MURRAY *Mythol.* iii. (1877) 38 The Sirens are strictly personifications, not of the sea, but of the dangers of the sea-coast to sailors.

2. *attrib.* or *adj.*

1622 MALYNES *Anc. Law-Merch.* 146 The Sea-coast Townes of France. **1719** DE FOE *Crusoe* I. (Globe) 103 So that I fancy'd now I had my Country House, and my Sea-Coast-House. **1866** *Treas. Bot.* s.v. *Lavatera, L. arborea*.. being a common plant in sea-coast cottage gardens.

Hence †**sea-coaster**, a wrecker; †**sea-coasting** *a.*, situated on the sea-coast.

c **1550** in *Trans. Roy. Hist. Soc.* (1902) XVI. 83 [To assist ship-owners against pillage by the] sea-coasters. **1610** HEALEY *St. Aug. Citie of God* XVIII. ii. 657 But their opinion that make Aegialia to be a sea-coasting citty is better.

'sea-cob[1]. [COB *sb.*[3]] A sea-gull.

1530 PALSGR. 268/2 Seecobbe a byrde, *mavue de mer.* **1544** TURNER *Avium Præcip.* D 8b, *De Gavia*..a se cob or see-gell. **1638** MAYNE *Lucian* (1664) 68 Feel the tongue and point of the hook with your fingers..and take you the boldnesse to be caught, and like a Sea-cob swallow the whole bait. **1725** BAILEY *Erasm. Colloq.* 285 Wherever I find an hungry Sea-cob, I throw him out a Bait. **1880** BARING-GOULD *Mehalah* I. ix. 176 What have these boys of their own?.. They have nothing, no more than the sea-cobs.

'sea-cob[2]. [COB *sb.*[1]] A fish (see COB *sb.*[1] 3).

1655 MOUFET & BENNET *Health's Improv.* (1746) 274 Two Sea-Gudgeons, called Paganelli,..which our western Fisher-men call by the Name of Sea-cobs.

'sea-cock. [COCK *sb.*[1]]

† **1.** A kind of crab. *Obs.*

1668 WILKINS *Real Char.* II. v. §2. 128 Sea cock. [Margin, *Cancer Heracleoticus.*]

2. A local name applied to various birds, (*a*) in quot. 1684 perh. the foolish or common guillemot, *Uria troile*; (*b*) the grey plover, *Squatarola helvetica*; (*c*) in Caithness 'the puffin, *Fratercula arctica*' (Eng. Dial. Dict.).

1684 SIBBALD *Scotia Illustr.* II. III. vii. 22 Avis Marina Sea-Cock *dicta.* **1885** SWAINSON *Prov. Names Birds* 181 Grey plover..Sea cock (Waterford).

3. A name for species of gurnard (see quots.). [So F. *coq de mer*, G. *seehahn*, Du. *zeehaan.*]

1704 tr. *Nieuhof's Voy. Brasil* Churchill's Collect. II. 348 The Sea-Cock is a Fish of a very odd shape, more like a Sea-Monster than a Fish. **1858** SIMMONDS *Dict. Trade, Sea-cock*, a species of gurnard (*Trigla cuculus* and *T. hirax*) much sought after by Russian epicures. **1881** *Cassell's Nat. Hist.* III. 96 The Sapphirine Gurnard... In some European languages the..crowing noises which these fishes produce have gained for them the name of Sea Cocks.

4. *jocularly.* A bold sailor or sea-rover.

1865 KINGSLEY *Herew.* iv, Such a gay young sea-cock does not come hither for naught. **1886** CORBETT *Fall of Asgard* II. 2 They cried to one another how no young sea-cock ever crowed with truer ring.

5. In a marine steam-engine (see quot. 1858).

1855 FRANKE *Beil's Technol. Dict.* II. 451 Sea-cock of a sea steam-engine (a cock placed on the pipe which goes from the boiler into the sea, through the side of the vessel). **1858** R. MURRAY *Marine Engines* (ed. 3) 29 It is better in the case of large engines to have two injection cocks fitted between the sea and each condenser,—one, the sea cock, close to the side of the vessel. **1895** *Times* 18 Mar. 7/4 The sea-cock was left open, and late at night the men on board were surprised to find the vessel gradually filling with water.

sea-conny. Also **seacunny, sea-cunny, seconny, seacony, sea-connie, secunnie.** [App. a perversion (after SEA *sb.* and perh. CON *v.*[2]) of Pers. *sukkānī*, f. Arab. *sukkān* rudder. The word appears in 16th c. Pg. as *socões* (pl.), and in English in 1805 as *soucan* (Yule).] A steersman or quartermaster in a ship manned by lascars.

1800 *Asiatic Ann. Reg.* III. 21/1 A Frenchman.. concerted a plan with a Spaniard and four of the seacunnies, for murdering the officers and seizing the ship. **1801** in A. Duncan *Marin. Chron.* (1804) II. 355 Leaving Captain Porter, who, with six Manilla seconnies, remained on board the wreck. *Ibid.* 356 This seconny afterwards went back to the wreck. **1801** *Naval Chron.* VI. 427 The Lascars..killed two of the..Seaconnies. **1806** *Ibid.* XV. 471 Had on board as helmsmen (*vulgo* seaconies) natives of Luconia. **1810** M. GRAHAM *Jrnl. Residence India* (1812) 85 The gunners and quarter-masters..are Indian-Portuguese; they are called *secunnies.* **1832** MARRYAT *N. Forster* xli, The crews are composed of..a small proportion of Portuguese sea-cunnies. **1888** CLARK RUSSELL *Death Ship* III. 172 When they have the Devil for a sea-cunny they will hit their port. **1929** D. J. MUNRO *Roaring Forties* xxxii. 160 With a crash and lurch that sent the secunnie (helmsman), at the wheel flying over the top of it the ship struck.

† **'sea-,cornet.** *Obs.* [CORNET *sb.*[1]]

1. A kind of shell-fish.

1601 HOLLAND *Pliny* IX. xxxviii. I. 259 The sea cornet Buccinum. **1666** J. DAVIES *Hist. Caribby Isles* 122 There are also seen in the Caribbies two sorts of those great Shells called Sea-Cornets, which are turned at the end like a Screw.

2. A cornet (musical instrument) used at sea.

1653 H. COGAN tr. *Pinto's Voy.* lviii, Throughout this Fleet they played on so many barbarous and ill accorded instruments, as Bels, Cymbals, Drums, and Sea-cornets.

'sea-cow. [COW *sb.*[1]]

1. The MANATEE; also applied to other sirenians, as the dugong. Often applied to the now extinct sirenian, ***Rhytina stelleri***, called ***Arctic, northern,*** or ***Steller's sea-cow.***

1613 R. HARCOURT *Voy. Guiana* 30 There is also a Sea-fish ..the Indians call it *Coiumero*, and the Spaniards *Manati*, but we call it the Sea-cow. **1769** E. BANCROFT *Guiana* 186 This is the Manatee, or Sea-Cow, called by the French Lamentin. **1859–62** SIR J. RICHARDSON, etc. *Mus. Nat. Hist.* (1868) I. 206 The Mexican Sea-cow (*Manatus latirostris*), a very large species, upwards of fifteen feet in length. **1883** FLOWER in *Encycl. Brit.* XV. 374/1 The *Rhytina* or Northern Sea-Cow was..limited to a single island in the extreme north of the Pacific Ocean.

2. The Morse or Walrus. Also *attrib.* ? *Obs.*

1668 CHARLETON *Onomast.* 169 *Walrus*..the Mors, or Sea-Cow. **1782** CAPT. COFFIN in *J. Adams' Wks.* (1851) III. 330 The sea-cow fishery was..carried on to great advantage. **1819** *Act 59 Geo. III*, c. 52 Tab. A., Sea Cow, Sea Horse, or Sea Morse Teeth, the cwt. 3. 4. 0. **1837** T. BELL *Brit. Quadrup.* 285 Walrus. Morse, Sea-cow, Sea-horse.

† **3.** [tr. Gr. βοῦς.] A kind of ray. *Obs.*

1722 J. JONES *Oppian's Halieut.* 227 βοῦς..the Sea-Cow or Broad-Ray.

4. [S. African Du. *zeekoe.*] The hippopotamus.

1731 MEDLEY *Kolben's Cape G. Hope* II. 129 There is seen in the large rivers about the Cape a very large animal call'd the Sea-Cow. **1863** W. C. BALDWIN *Afr. Hunting* i. 15 Nine or ten crocodiles..gorged with sea-cow, and fast asleep.

b. *attrib.* or *adj.*, as ***sea-cow sjambok, -whip,*** etc.

1850 R. G. CUMMING *Hunter's Life S. Afr.* (1902) 93/2 An equally persuasive sea-cow jambok. **1908** RIDER HAGGARD *Ghost Kings* viii. 102 We have sea-cow whips here.

5. A fisherman's name in the west of England for *Holothuria nigra.*

1884 *Proc. Zool. Soc.* 563.

'sea-crab. [CRAB *sb.*[1]]

1. A marine crab, as distinguished from a river- or land-crab.

1601 HOLLAND *Pliny* XXXII. x. II. 449 The ashes of the Sea-crab and Scolopendre both. **1756** P. BROWNE *Jamaica* (1789) 421 The common Sea-Crab or *Sherigo*. This species is very common in all the harbours of Jamaica. **1860** WRAXALL *Life in Sea* vi. 142 The Portunus, or real Sea-crab.

† **b.** In allusions. *Obs.*

1604 *Fr. Hubburd's Tales* in *Middleton's Wks.* (Bullen) VIII. 95 One amongst them..likened me to a sea-crab, because I went all of one side. **1636** FEATLY *Clavis Myst.* ix. 116 In which there is no more true controversie in point of law, than head in a sea-crab.

† **2. a.** Applied jocularly to a boatman. *Obs.*

1609 DEKKER *Gull's Horn-bk.* vii. Wks. (Grosart) II. 252 No, your Oares are your onely Sea-crabs, boord them, and take heed you neuer go twice together with one paire.

† **b.** *slang.* A sailor. *Obs.*

1785 in GROSE *Dict. Vulgar T.*

† **3.** A CRAB (*sb.*[1] 7) used at sea. *Obs.*

1689 *Patent Office* No. 262 A new Invencion or Sea-Crabbe for working in the Sea for Fishing and taking vp of Shipps.

'sea-craft.

1. Maritime skill, skill in navigation. Often written *seacraft.*

1727 ARBUTHNOT *Tables Anc. Coins*, etc. 221 Alexander.. to shew how little he considered the Sea-craft of the Persians,..employed none of that Country in his Fleet. **1865** W. G. PALGRAVE *Arabia* II. 246 Its population were pre-eminent in sea craft and traffic.

2. *Ship-building.* (See quot.)

1867 SMYTH *Sailor's Word-bk., Sea-crafts*,..a term for the scarphed strakes otherwise called *clamps.*

3. Sea-going craft; sea-vessels considered collectively.

1919 *Q. Rev.* Jan. 184 Vessels, whether sea-craft or air-craft. **1928** *Daily Express* 18 Jan. 1 Our oldest craft, seacraft.

'sea-crafty, *a. rare.* Skilled in seafaring matters. (Rendering OE. *laȝucræftiȝ* in Beowulf.)

1838 LONGF. *Beowulf's Exped. to Heort* 41 The warrior showed, Sea-crafty man! The landmarks, And first went forth. **1892** BROOKE *Early Eng. Lit.* x. 232 Beowulf and his sea-crafty men. **1955** J. R. R. TOLKIEN *Return of King* v. ix. 153 Sea-crafty men of the Ethir gazing southward spoke of a change coming with a fresh wind from the sea.

'sea-crow. [CROW *sb.*[1] Cf. Welsh *morfran.*]

1. A local name for various birds: (*a*) the cormorant, *Phalacrocorax carbo*; (*b*) the pewitgull, *Larus ridibundus*; (*c*) the chough, *Pyrrhocorax graculus*; (*d*) the razor-billed auk, *Alca torda*; (*e*) the common skua, *Stercorarius catarrhactes*; (*f*) the jackdaw; (*g*) the American coot, *Fulica americana*, and the black skimmer, *Rhynchops nigra*.

1579 T. STEVENS in *Hakluyt's Voy.* (1599) II. II. 100 But sometimes his other enemy, the sea-crow, catcheth him [a fish] before he falleth. **1668** CHARLETON *Onomast.* 95 *Graculus Palmipes*..the Cowt, or Sea-Crow. **1813** MONTAGU *Ornith. Dict.* Suppl., *Auk*, Razor-billed. Provincial... Sea-crow. **1897** 'ALLEN RAINE' *Welsh Singer* viii. 68 On the ledge of rock the jackdaws, or the 'little sea-crows', as they were called on the coast, had built their untidy nest of twigs.

†**2.** Used to translate Gr. κορακῖνος, a black river-fish. *Obs.*

1722 DIAPER tr. *Oppian's Halieut.* I. 213 Here Sea-Crows dwell, nam'd from their dusky Hue.

3. A local name for the sapphirine gurnard, *Trigla hirundo*.

1880–4 F. DAY *Brit. Fishes* I. 61.

sea cucumber. †**a.** [transl. of L. *cucumis*.] Some shell-fish. *Obs.* **b.** [= F. *concombre de mer*]. The common name for any holothurian, sometimes restricted to the *Psolidæ*.

1601 HOLLAND *Pliny* XXXII. xi. II. 451. **1841** E. FORBES *Brit. Starfishes* 209 The Sea-Cucumbers are the most typical of the Holothuriadæ. *Ibid.* 221 The Glassy Sea-Cucumber is a most beautiful and delicate animal, being almost transparent and of an opaline hue. **1879** E. P. WRIGHT *Anim. Life* 572 The body in the Sea Cucumbers is mostly cylindrical, and covered with a coriaceous skin.

sead, obs. f. SAD *a.*, SAID *ppl. a.*

sea-daisy.

†**1.** Some kind of sea-anemone. *Obs.*

*a***1776** J. ELLIS *Zoophytes* (1786) 2 *Actinia Bellis*, Sea Daisie.

2. = SEA-PINK a.

1838 SCROPE *Art Deer-stalk.* 388 The highest hills..are scattered over with the sea daisy and other plants. **1876** SMILES *Sc. Natur.* i, There..grew..the beautiful sea daisy.

'sea-,devil.

1. A devil supposed to inhabit the sea.

*c***1594** CAPT. WYATT *R. Dudley's Voy. W. Ind.* (Hakl.) 14, I thinke wee weare haunted with some divelish witches, or at least with some sea divells. *a***1711** KEN *Edmund* Poet. Wks. 1721 II. 23 The Sea-Devil, Dagon. **1891** KIPLING *Light that Failed* viii. (1900) 132 Sea-devils and sea-angels, and the soul half drowned between them.

2. A name for various ugly fish, as the fishing-frog, various large rays, etc. Cf. DEVIL-FISH.

1634 T. JOHNSON tr. *Parey's Chirurg.* XXV. xxi. 1004 The effigies of a Sea Devill. **1666** J. DAVIES *Hist. Caribby Isles* 105 There is sometimes taken by the Fishers a Monster which is ranked among the kinds of Sea-Devils,..what got it the name of Sea-Devil is, that above the eyes there are two little black horns..like those of a Ram. *a***1672** WILLUGHBY *Hist. Pisc.* (1686) 85 *Rana piscatrix.* The Toad-fish or Frog-fish, or Sea-Divel. **1842** in *Mem. Amer. Acad.* (1846) II. 516 *Cephaloptera vampyrus*, Sea-Devil. **1848** *Zoologist* VI. 1976 Angel Fish, *Squatina angelus.* This strange fish..is frequently called a 'monk' and still more commonly a 'sea-devil'. **1881** *Cassell's Nat. Hist.* V. 44 The Ox Ray or Sea-devil, *Dicerobatis giornæ.* **1882** JORDAN & GILBERT *Synopsis Fishes N. Amer.* 52 *Manta birostris*... Sea Devil; Devil Fish.

3. *fig.* Any formidable engine of submarine warfare.

1878 *N. Amer. Rev.* CXXVII. 230 One of these stealthy and effective sea-devils [torpedoes]. **1902** *Daily Chron.* 14 Oct. 5/2 The two British submarines..go out almost daily for the purpose of familiarising officers and seamen with the mechanism of these 'modern sea-devils'.

'sea-dike. [Cf. Du. *zeedijk*.]

1. An embankment against the sea, a sea-wall.

14.. *Pict. Voc.* in Wr.-Wülcker 797/40 *Hoc fossatum*, a sedyke. **1878** MILLER & SKERTCHLY *Fenland* i. 8 The old seadykes—like those along the coast of East-Holland in Lincolnshire.

2. *attrib.*

1395 in *East Anglian* (1871) IV. 79 [The iiij part of one labour in] Sedyksylver. *Ibid.* 92 [Of xxv labours by custom called] Sediksylver. **1567** DRANT *Hor. Epist.* I. xv. Evj, When I cum to seadyke syde [Lat. *ad mare cum veni*]. **1799** A. YOUNG *Agric. Lincs.* 272 The Old Sea-dike bank.

Hence **'sea-diked** *a.*

1851 S. WARREN *Lily & Bee* 22 In busy sea-dyked Holland.

'sea-dog. [Cf. Du. *zeehond*, G. *seehund*.]

1. The common or harbour seal, *Calocephalus vitulinus*; 'also (in California), one of the eared seals, *Zalophus californianus*' (Cent. Dict. 1891).

1598 W. PHILLIP tr. *Linschoten's Voy.* 415/2 Wee found great store of Sea wolues, which wee call Sea dogges. **1743** BULKELEY & CUMMINS *Voy. S. Seas* 132 A large Seal or Sea-Dog. **1808** SCOTT *Marm.* II. ii, The sea-dog..His round black head..Rear'd o'er the foaming spray. **1879** G. B. GOODE *Catal. Anim. Resources U.S.* 5 *Zalophus Gillespiei*... The Sea Dog. Pacific Coast.

2. A dog-fish or small shark. ? *Obs.*

1601 HOLLAND *Pliny* IX. xxxv. I. 255 If they [*sc.* mother-of-pearl shell-fish] be in the deepe, accompanied lightly they are with curst Sea-dogs [orig. *marinis canibus*]. **1613** PURCHAS *Pilgrimage* 401 In which [place] are many fishes called Sea-dogges. They which are weary of this world.. cast in themselues here to be deuoured of these fishes. **1725** POPE *Odyss.* XII. 118 The Sea-dog and the Dolphin are her food. **1802** PINKERTON *Mod. Geog., Europe* I. 11 The chief fisheries [of the Mediterranean] are those of the tunny, of the sword fish, and of the sea dog, a species of shark.

3. *Her.* (See quot. 1780.)

[**1758** J. KENNEDY *Curios. Wilton Ho.* 50 A Figure recumbent, leaning on a Sea-Dog, and representing the River Meander.] **1780** EDMONDSON *Heraldry* II. Gloss., *Sea-dogs*, are drawn in shape like the talbot, but with a tail like that of the beaver; a scalloped fin continued down the back, from the head to the tail; the whole body, legs, and tail, scaled, and the feet webbed. **1871** BURKE *Peerage* s.v. *Stourton*, Supporters.—Two sea-dogs, sa., scaled and finned, erm.

4. A privateer or pirate, esp. of the time of Queen Elizabeth I.

1659 PELL *Impr. Sea* Proem B 3, They hunt the Pirat.. and sometimes they find..a Dunkirk Hare, squatted down very closely..and then is there brave gain, when our Sea-dogs follow after her. **1788** JEFFERSON *Writ.* (1859) II. 387 A regard to the safety and liberty of our seamen..forbids us to give such prices for those in captivity as will draw on our vessels peculiarly the pursuit of those sea-dogs. **1877** DOWDEN *Stud. Lit.* (1889) 1 The galleons of the Spanish Armada were pulled down by the sea-dogs of Drake.

5. A sailor, usually one long used to the sea, chiefly with the epithet *old*.

1823 J. F. COOPER *Pilot* II. xi. 187 Ahead, heave ahead, sea-dogs! **1840** R. H. DANA *Bef. Mast* xxiii, The carpenter ..was an old sea-dog. **1855** KINGSLEY *Westw. Ho!* iii, Sniffing the keen salt air like a young sea-dog. **1887** BESANT *World went* xxix, Other Captains..are no whit behind the most old-fashioned sea-dog in courage.

6. A luminous appearance near the horizon, regarded by mariners as a prognostic of bad weather.

1825–80 JAMIESON, *Dog, Sea-dog*, a name given by mariners to a meteor seen, immediately above the horizon [see DOG *sb.*[1] 10]. *Ibid.*, The term, although used as synon. with *Weather-gaw*, properly denotes a luminous appearance of a different kind. For while the weather-gaw seems a detached section of a rainbow, the dog has no variety of colours, but is of a dusky white. **1867** SMYTH *Sailor's Word-bk.*, *Sea-dogg*, the meteor called also *stubb*.

7. *dial.* A rough wave in the mouth of a river.

1863 R. F. BURTON *Wand. W. Africa* I. 1 White sea-dogs coursed and worried one another over Father Mersey's breadth of mud. **1877** *N.W. Linc. Gloss.*, *Sea-dogs, Sea-hosses*, rough waves in the Humber and Trent.

Hence **'sea-doggery**, behaviour or practice characteristic of a sea-dog or sea-dogs (sense 5); sailors collectively.

1928 *Daily Express* 9 Oct. 3/3 A little grey Dover full of small, sturdy ships..and a general air—assisted by a strong smell of oil, pea soup and roasting mutton—of waggish sea doggery. **1961** *John o' London's* 20 July 111/3 A background of adventure and sea-doggery.

'sea-,dragon. [DRAGON[1].]

1. Various fishes, as the weever; the bullhead; a dragonet (*Callionymus*); a flying sea-horse, *Pegasus draco*; also a kind of pipe-fish (see quot. 1898).

1551 TURNER *Herbal* I. Avb, Wormwood..is good against..the bytinge of a shrewe, and the sea dragon. **1601** HOLLAND *Pliny* XXXII. v. II. 434 Since I haue named the sea-dragon [orig. *draco marinus*], this would be noted, That himselfe outwardly applied, is a remedie [etc.]. **1674** T. P., etc. *Eng. & Fr. Cook* 412 Potage of Vives or Sea-dragons. *Ibid.*, Take out your Sea-Dragons, and put them with Ragoust [etc.]. **1752** J. HILL *Hist. Anim.* 272 The Cottus with the second back fin white. The Sea-dragon. **1835** J. F. SOUTH in *Encycl. Metrop.* (1845) XXIII. 165/1 *Pegasus Draco*, Lin.; Sea Dragon. **1898** MORRIS *Austral Engl.*, *Sea-Dragon*, any Australian fish of any one of the three species of the genus *Phyllopteryx*, family *Syngnathiaæ*.

2. A mythical marine monster resembling a dragon.

1749 *Gentl. Mag.* XIX. 506 It [a creature resembling a winged alligator, said to have been lately captured in a mackerel-net] is said..to have been described by naturalists under the name of the Sea-Dragon. **1884** *Pall Mall Gaz.* 11 Sept. 2/1 When a junk is fully laden and on the eve of sailing, the crew commend themselves to the sea-dragon in a frightfully noisy religious service.

¶**3.** Misused to render F. *draconcule*, guinea-worm.

1775 *Phil. Trans.* LXV. 211 Those..enemies to man, the tape, the hair worm, and the sea dragon.

4. A popular name for any large marine saurian.

1896 H. WOODWARD *Guide Fossil Reptiles Brit. Mus.* 52 Most of the 'Sea-Dragons'..were obtained from the Lias of Street,..Lyme Regis [etc.].

seadrome ('siːdrəʊm). [f. SEA *sb.* + -DROME, after AERODROME.] A floating aerodrome, an offshore airport; *spec.* (in early use) one of a series of constructions on or at which a (sea) plane could alight (for refuelling) during a journey.

The *seadrome* exists solely as a concept. None has yet been built.

1923 *Daily Mail* 17 July 10 The feature of the project is that there should be eight 'seadromes'..moored permanently on the Altantic air route. **1936** J. GRIERSON *High Failure* xiv. 293 A series of floating platforms (colloquially called 'sea-dromes') on which planes could alight, spaced at intervals of 5–600 miles across the Atlantic. **1947** *Jrnl. R. Aeronaut. Soc.* LI. 143/2 If alighting places for flying boats were more easy to provide than aerodromes, could Mr. Lipscomb offer any reason why they..suffered from lack of 'sea-dromes', whereas there were plenty of very costly aerodromes for landplanes? **1948** *Trinidad Guardian* 18 June 2/1 (*heading*) Seadrome site inspected. **1969** *Daily Tel.* 4 Sept. 24/2 The seadrome scheme for Foulness plans a floating airport complex measuring five million square yards. **1970** *New Scientist* 22 Jan. 156/1 The two firms of engineers..are already discussing their plans for a 'Seadrome' with one of the Thames estuary development companies.

'sea-duck.

1. Any duck of the sub-family *Fuligulinæ*, as the common scoter, *Œdemia nigra*, and the eider-duck.

1753 *Chambers' Cycl.* Suppl., *Shoveler*,..the name of a species of sea-duck. **1861** COUES in *Proc. Philad. Acad.* 239 *Somateria mollissima*... Eider Duck. 'Sea-duck.' *Ibid.* 240 They are..known as 'Sea-ducks', the males being.. distinguished as 'Sea-drakes'. **1867** T. R. JONES *Nat. Hist. Birds* 506 The Tufted Sea-duck (*Fuligula cristata*).

2. A fish, the 'Bombay duck'.

1883 *Fisheries Exhib. Catal.* 351 Twelve Tins of Sardines ..and two of Sea-Duck in oil.

seadule, obs. form of SCHEDULE.

'sea-,eagle.

1. An eagle of the genus *Haliaëtus*, esp. the White-tailed Eagle, *H. albicilla* (see EAGLE *sb.* 6a). Also a name for the frigate-bird and the skua-gull.

1668 CHARLETON *Onomast.* 62 Haliætus, Aquila marina, the Sea-Eagle. **1710** SIBBALD *Fife & Kinross* 46 *Cataractes*, some call it the Sea-Eagle. **1805** G. BARRY *Orkney Isl.* 313 The Sea Eagle (*falco ossefragus*, Lin. Syst.) is often seen. **1817** SHELLEY *Laon* VII. xv, The sea-eagle looked a fiend, who bore Thy mangled limbs for food! *a***1843** J. F. SOUTH in *Encycl. Metrop.* (1845) XXV. 408/2 The Frigate Bird, Man-of-War Bird, Sea Eagle, and Halcyon, by all of which names it [*Tachypetes Aquilus*] is known to sailors, is commonly found between the tropics. **1848** MAUNDER *Treas. Nat. Hist.* 599, *Sea-eagle*, the Erne: also the name sometimes given to the Osprey. **1875–84** LAYARD & SHARPE *Birds S. Africa* 46 *Haliaetus vocifer.* African Sea-Eagle.

2. The eagle-ray (see EAGLE 6b).

1722 J. JONES *Oppian's Halieut.* 227 'Αετὸς..the Sea-Eagle, a kind of Ray. **1740** R. BROOKES *Art of Angling* II. lxvii. 188 The Sea-Eagle..has a Head almost like that of a Toad. **1836** YARRELL *Brit. Fishes* II. 591. **1847** [see EAGLE *sb.* 6b].

'sea-ear. [EAR *sb.*[1]]

1. A univalve mollusc of the genus *Haliotis*; an ormer or ear-shell.

1681 GREW *Musæum* I. §vi. i. 139 [Of Shells] The Sea-Ear. *Auris marina.* It hath its Name from its Figure. **1755** *Gentl. Mag.* XXV. 32 Univalves... Sea Ears, *Planæ.* These are very flat, resembling a man's-ear. **1772–84** *Cook's Voy.* (1790) IV. 1326 Muscles and sea-ears supply the place of other fish. **1883** N. OKOSHI *Fisheries Japan* (Fish. Exhib. Catal.) 16 The shells of sea-ear are now exported to Europe for the manufacture of buttons and other purposes.

†**2.** A plant [tr. L. *auris marina*]. *Obs. rare*[−1].

1668 WILKINS *Real Char.* II. iv. §3. 71 Herbs considered according to their leaves... Sea-ear. [marg. *Auris marina.*]

3. = *sea corn* (see quot. 1891, s.v. SEA *sb.* 23d).

'sea-eel. A salt-water eel, a conger.

*c***1050** *Voc.* in Wr.-Wülcker 447/36 *Murenula*, sæ͡æl. **1585** JAS. VI *Ess. Poesie*, Sonn. viii. (Arb.) 16 As whailes so huge, and Sea eylis rare, that be Myle longs, in crawling cruikis of sixtie pace. **1704** tr. *Nieuhof's Voy. Brasil* Churchill's Collect. III. 347 There is another kind of Sea-Eels, or rather Water-Serpents in the Indies, of about three foot long [etc.]. **1761** *Ann. Reg.* I. 189 A sea eel, 6 feet long..weighing 30lb. was lately taken..at Whitstable. **1886** SHELDON tr. *Flaubert's Salammbô* i. 15 On her neck she wore a collection of luminous gems which imitated in their medley the scales of a sea-eel.

'sea-egg.

1. An ECHINUS or sea-urchin.

1666 J. DAVIES *Hist. Caribby Isles* 126 There is found..a production of the Sea, called Sea-egges, or Sea-Apples... These Egges should rather be called Sea-Urchins or Sea-Chestnuts. **1758** BORLASE *Nat. Hist. Cornw.* 278 The round and flat sea-egg. **1885** C. F. HOLDER *Marvels Anim. Life* 84 Sea-eggs (black echini, with long needle-like spines).

2. A kind of medic, *Medicago Echinus*.

1884 W. MILLER *Plant-n.*, Sea-egg, *Medicago Echinus.*

sea-elephant. The elephant seal, *Macrorhinus elephantinus* or *proboscideus*. Formerly applied to the morse or walrus.

1601 HOLLAND *Pliny* IX. v. I. 236 There were sea-Elephants and Rams, with teeth standing out. **1634** T. JOHNSON tr. *Parey's Chirurg.* XXV. xxi. 1005 The Sea Elephant is bigger than the land Elephant, as Hector Boëtius writes in his description of Scotland. **1755** tr. *Pontoppidan's Nat. Hist. Norway* II. 157 Their two large teeth or tusks.. are as good as ivory for any kind of turn'd work; and therefore this creature [the walrus] is called by some the Sea-Elephant. **1798** [see ELEPHANT 6]. **1875** KIDDER *Nat. Hist. Kerguelen Isl.* 39 In former years the Kerguelen group of islands was noted as a favorite breeding-place for the sea-elephant (*Macrorhinus leoninus*, L.).

attrib. **1828** P. CUNNINGHAM *N.S. Wales* (ed. 3) II. 103 A considerable portion of sea-elephant oil is also procured at Macquarie Island. **1883** *Fisheries Exhib. Catal.* 201 Sea Elephant oil, crude and bleached.

sea-face. The face or side (of a cliff, etc.) exposed to the sea.

1889 *Played On* iii. 7 A bluff headland..on its sea-face presenting a sheer cliff of some two hundred feet. **1900** *Edin. Rev.* July 34 The Admiral's care now was to disarm the sea-face of the city fortifications.

attrib. **1897** *Westm. Gaz.* 9 Feb. 2/1 One of the most beautiful sea-face roads in the world.

'sea-fan. [FAN *sb.*[1]] An alcyonarian polyp of the sub-order *Gorgoniacea*, esp. *Rhipidogorgia* (*Gorgonia*) *flabellum*.

1633 JOHNSON *Gerarde's Herbal* App. xxiv. 1617 *Frutex marinus reticulatus*. Sea Fan. **1664** POWER *Exp. Philos.* I. 5 The Common Fly: her wings look like a Sea-fan with black thick ribs or fibers dispers'd and branch'd through them. **1755** J. ELLIS *Corallines* 67 *Keratophyton flabelliforme*.. Warted Sea-fan. **1902** G. C. BOURNE in *Encycl. Brit.* XXV. 456/2 The most familiar example [of the Axifera] is the pink sea-fan, *Gorgonia Cavolinii*.

attrib. **1789** E. DARWIN *Bot. Gard.* I. (1791) 121 Her [the [mermaid's] shell-wrack gardens, and her sea-fan bowers.

'sea-fardinger. *arch.* [? Alteration of Du. *zeevaarder* SEAFARER, after *passenger*.] A seafarer.

a **1550** SIR R. GRENVILLE in Tregellas *Cornish Worthies* (1884) II. (*title of poem*) Another, of Sea Fardingers, describing Euill Fortune. **1867** SMYTH *Sailor's Word-bk.*, *Sea-fardinger*, an archaic expression for a sea-faring man. **1889** 'Q.' (Quiller-Couch) *Splendid Spur* xix. 307 'Yo-heave ho!' like the salted seafardingers upstairs. Push, push!

'sea-fare. [FARE *sb.*[1]]

1. a. Food obtained from the sea. **b.** Fare or food on board ship.

1597 MIDDLETON *Wisd. Sol.* xix. 19 Her sea-fare now is land-fare of content;.. The fishes are her food, and they are sent Vnto drie land. **1850** B. TAYLOR *Eldorado* vi, The fresh milk, butter, and excellent beef of the country, were real luxuries after our sea-fare.

2. Travel by sea, a sea-voyage. *Obs.* exc. *dial.*

1601 WHEELER *Treat. Comm.* 20 These men.. linked and bound themselues together in Companie for the exercise of Merchandise and sea-fare, trading in Cloth, Kersies [etc.]. **1620** MARKHAM *Farew. Husb.* (1625) 137 These [kinds of Pulse] in cases of Sea-fare and War-fare ought principally to be eschewed & shunned.

seafarer ('siːfɛərə(r)). [f. SEA *sb.* + FARER. Cf. G. *seefahrer*, Du. *zeevaarder*.] A traveller by sea, esp. one whose life is spent in voyaging, a sailor.

1513 DOUGLAS *Æneis* v. xiii. 30 From the eft schip wprais anone the wind, And followit fast the se fararis behind. **1608** SHAKS. *Per.* III. i. 41 Yet for the loue Of this poore Infant, this fresh new sea-farer, I would it [the flaw] would be quiet. **1654** VILVAIN *Enchir. Epigr.* III. lxxi. 73 The 7 famous Sailers or Seafarers, who gav a girdle to the Geographic Globe. **1725** POPE *Odyss.* VIII. 180 A wand'ring merchant he frequents the main, Some mean sea-farer in pursuit of gain. **1876** BANCROFT *Hist. U.S.* I. ii. 27 Stephen Gomez, an able Portuguese seafarer.

transf. **1841** BROWNING *Pippa Passes* III, *1st Girl.* There goes a swallow to Venice—the stout seafarer! **1887** MORRIS *Odyss.* XI. 11 The sails of our seafarer were filled with the wind all day.

seafaring ('siːfɛərɪŋ), *sb.* [f. SEA *sb.* + FARING *vbl. sb.*] Travelling by sea; the business or calling of a sailor.

1592 WARNER *Alb. Eng.* Prose Addit. 190 After long and wearie Sea-faring. **1628** LE GRYS tr. *Barclay's Argenis* II. 108 My Countrey.. is Rhegium; my profession, sea-faring. **1712** STEELE *Spect.* No. 486 ¶4 She is the Wife of a Sailor, and the kept Mistress of a Man of Quality; she dwells with the latter during the Sea-faring of the former. **1879** BUTCHER & LANG *Odyss.* 172 All day long her sails were stretched in her seafaring.

b. *attrib.* quasi-*adj.* Of or pertaining to travelling, living or working at sea.

1601 R. JOHNSON *Kingd. & Commw.* (1603) 40 The skilfull prowesse and seafaring dexteritie of the English. **1745** *Life Bampfylde-Moore Carew* 22 An Insight into the Seafaring Life. **1867** FREEMAN *Norm. Conq.* I. ii. (1877) 56 The old sea-faring spirit seems to have died out.

'sea,faring, *a.* [f. SEA *sb.* + FARING *ppl. a.*]

1. Of persons: Travelling on the sea; following the sea as a calling, gaining a livelihood at sea. †Also *absol.* in pl. sense.

c **1200** *Trin. Coll. Hom.* 161 Ðan þe safarinde men seð þe sasterre, hie wuten sone wuderward hie sullen weie holden. **1405** *York Bidding Prayer* in *Lay-Folks Mass Bk.* 65 ȝe sal pray.. for al land tilland and for al see farand.. and for the fruyt that es on erthe. **1566** *Act 8 Eliz.* c. 13 §1 Beyng as beakons and markes of auncient tyme accustomed for Seafaryng men. **1590** SHAKS. *Com. Err.* I. i. 81. **1691** T. H[ALE] *Acc. New Invent.* p. lxx, Some Sea-faring People, inhabitants by the Thames-side in Wapping. **1744** BERKELEY *Siris* §117 To sailors and all seafaring persons. **1819** *Edin. Ann. Reg.* (1823) XII. App. 85 James Lincoln, a seafaring man at Sunderland, knew the prisoner Eden for twenty years. **1868** MISS BRADDON *Run to Earth* I. i. 2 The two men.. belonged to the seafaring community.

b. *transf.* Applied to a bird.

1880 SWINBURNE *Studies in Song* 86 Seafaring birds.

†**2.** Of a plant: Growing by the sea. *Obs. rare*$^{-1}$.

1670 W. SIMPSON *Hydrol. Ess.* 69 A marine salt.. works it self into the texture of those sea-faring plants.

'sea-,feather. [Cf. G. *seefeder*, *meerfeder*.] A coral or polyp of the family *Pennatulidæ*.

1624 CAPT. J. SMITH *Gen. Hist.* v. 171 *marg.*, The Sea feather. [Described in text.] **1633** JOHNSON *Gerarde's Herbal* App. xxiii. 1616 *Myriophyllum marinum*. The Sea Feather. **1750** G. HUGHES *Barbados* 288 The Sea Feathers. These seldom grow, on the Shores of this Island, above two Feet and an half high. **1896** tr. *Boas' Text-bk. Zool.* 115 Sea-feathers (genus *Pennatula* and others).

'sea-fern.

1. Any alcyonarian polyp or coral resembling a fern. Also *attrib.*

1688 HOLME *Armoury* II. 98/1 English Sea-Fern.. with brownish marks on the back, like land Fern. **1855** KINGSLEY *Glaucus* (1878) 86 The sea-fern tribe of branching polypidoms.

2. A fern, the sea-spleenwort.

1855 *New Cycl. Bot.* II. 601 *Asplenium marinum*. Sea Fern.

'sea-fight. A naval battle, a fight or engagement between ships at sea.

1600 E. BLOUNT tr. *Conestaggio* 292 Behold the issue of the sea fight. **1601** SHAKS. *Twel. N.* III. iii. 26. **1625** BACON *Ess.*, *Greatness Kingd.* (Arb.) 489 There be many Examples, where Sea-Fights haue beene Finall to the warre. **1690** EVELYN *Diary* 7 Mar., He concluded there would shortly be no other method of sea-fight. *c* **1700** in Walpole *Vertue's Anecd. Paint.* (1765) III. 59 Mr. William Vandevelde, senior, late painter of sea-fights to their majesties king Charles II. and king James dyed 1693. **1842** W. C. TAYLOR *Anc. Hist.* ix. §5 (ed. 3) 241 The naval engagement between the Corcyrians and Corinthians (B.C. 650) is the first sea-fight recorded in history. **1858** LONGF. *My Lost Youth* v, I remember the sea-fight far away, How it thundered o'er the tide!

'sea-fish, *sb.* [Cf. ON. *sǽfiskr*.] A fish of the sea as distinguished from a fresh-water fish.

a **900** CYNEWULF *Crist* 987 (Gr.) þonne on fyrbaðe swelað sæfiscas sundes ȝetwæfde. *c* **1205** LAY. 22550 Fulle sixti scipen.. ifulled.. mid gode sæ fisce [*c* **1275** see visce]. **1387** TREVISA *Higden* (Rolls) I. 335 Grete plente of samon, of lampreys, of eles, and of oþer see fisch. **1526** in *Househ. Ord.* (1790) 143 The King's purveyor of see-fish shall see that such provisions of see-fish.. bee good and of the best. **1634-5** BRERETON *Trav.* (Chetham Soc.) 76 Sea-fish upon the coast of Lanckashire perished in the storm fifty cart-load together. **1797** *Encycl. Brit.* (ed. 3) XIII. 537/1 This sea-fish [the oyster] occupies [etc.]. **1845** GOSSE *Ocean* ii. (1849) 80 Large pools for the preservation of sea-fishes. **1868** *Act 31 & 32 Vict.* c. 45 §5 The Term 'Sea-Fish' does not include Salmon.. but save as aforesaid, includes every Description both of Fish and of Shell-Fish which is found in the Seas to which this Act applies.

'sea-fish, *v. rare.* [Back-formation from SEA-FISHING.] *intr.* To practise sea-fishing.

1894 'J. BICKERDYKE' in *Blackw. Mag.* Sept. 428/2 Since I first commenced to seafish one of the greatest improvements.. is in connection with the rod.

'sea-,fisher.

1. One who fishes in the sea. †Also the fishing frog or angler. *Obs.*

1601 HOLLAND *Pliny* IX. xlii. I. 261 The fish called the sea Frog, (and of others, the sea Fisher) is as craftie everie whit as the other. **1893** *Fishing Gaz.* 6/3 An Amateur Sea Fisher's Club. **1898** 'J. BICKERDYKE' (*title*) Practical letters to young sea fishers.

†**2.** An officer of the royal household. *Obs.* Cf. quot. 1526 s.v. SEA-FISH *sb.*

1455 in *Househ. Ord.* (1790) *21 Th' Office of the Catery. .. William Hampton, See-Fyssher. **1526** *Ibid.* 143 Sea-Fisher.

So **sea-fisherman**, one who fishes in the sea.

1865 J. C. WILCOCKS (*title*) The Sea-Fisherman.. comprising the chief methods of Hook and Line Fishing in the British and other Seas.

'seafishery. The business or occupation, etc. of catching fish in the sea (see FISHERY 1). Also *pl. attrib.*, as in ***Sea Fisheries Act***.

1865 L. YOUNG *Sea-Fishing* v. 185 History of Sea-fisheries. **1868** *Act 31 & 32 Vict.* c. 45 §2 This Act may be cited as The Sea Fisheries Act, 1868.

'sea-,fishing, *vbl. sb.* [FISHING *vbl. sb.*[1]] Fishing in the sea.

1745 ELLIS *Mod. Husbandman* VI. II. 66 Sea-fishing is the .. healthiest Fishing of all others. **1833** J. RENNIE *Alph. Angling* 135 In sea-fishing.. your line ought to be sixty fathoms in length. **1890** F. G. AFLALO (*title*) Sea-Fishing on the English Coast.

'sea-float, *a. rare*$^{-1}$. [f. SEA *sb.* ? + (A)FLOAT *a.*] ? Afloat on the sea.

1880 G. MACDONALD *Diary Old Soul* Jan. 13 Boisterous wave-crest never shall o'erwhelm Thy sea-float bark.

'sea-flood. *Obs.* exc. *arch.* The sea, the tide.

c **893** K. ÆLFRED *Oros.* II. vii. 90 An sæflod com. *c* **1205** LAY. 2630 He lætte bi sæ flode ȝearkien scipen gode. *a* **1275** *Prov. Alfred* 146 in *O.E. Misc.* 111 Stronge it his to roȝen aȝen þe se flod. *c* **1440** *Alphabet of Tales* 521 þe se-flude vmlappid bothe hym & þe cow & þe calfe, & drownyd þaim. **1867** MORRIS *Jason* v. 91 The yellow sands the sea-flood's hem.

'sea-floor. 1. The floor of the sea.

1855 KINGSLEY *Glaucus* (1878) 60 The variety of its rocks, aspects, and sea-floors. **1922** [see OUTWANDER *v.*]. **1946** *Proc. Prehist. Soc.* XII. 24 The seal must have sunk in deep water and come to rest on the sea-floor. **1967** *Oceanogr. & Marine Biol.* V. 317 Two principal dispersal mechanisms affect shelf benthos; these are, (1) shallow seafloor connections and, (2) surface currents. **1981** *London Mag.* July 9 A door slams, a heavy wave, a door, the sea-floor shudders.

2. sea-floor spreading *Geol.*, (the hypothesis of) the formation of fresh areas of oceanic crust, occurring through the upwelling of magma at mid-ocean ridges and its subsequent outward movement on either side.

1961 R. S. DIETZ in *Nature* 3 June 854/1 [The concept proposed here, which can be termed the 'spreading sea-floor theory', is largely intuitive, having been derived through an attempt to interpret sea-floor bathymetry.] *Ibid.* 856/2 Sea floor spreading obviates this difficulty: continents never move through the sima. **1971** *Nature* 1 Jan. 9/2 The whole of geophysics has been transformed within a few years by the discovery of seafloor spreading. **1977** A. HALLAM *Planet Earth* 42/3 If its magnetic signature allowed an age to be assigned to each piece of ocean floor, it was possible to calculate a velocity for sea-floor spreading.

'sea-flower. A flower growing in or by the sea. Also, an actinia or sea-anemone. Also *attrib.*

1805 FORSYTH *Beaut. Scot.* II. 366 [The sea-anemones'] lively colours.. equal anything recited by natural historians of the sea-flowers of other climates. **1817** MOORE *Lalla Rookh, Fire-Worshippers* (near end), Fair as the sea-flower close to thee growing. **1819** SHELLEY *Prometh. Unb.* III. ii. 47 Nereids.. With.. starry sea-flower crowns. **1830** TENNYSON *Merman* ii, Dressing their hair with the white sea-flower. **1850** DANA *Geol.* i. 10 The waters abound in.. the variously coloured actinias or sea-flowers.

'sea-foam.

1. Foam of the sea.

a **1300** *Cursor M.* 14409 Moyses.. led þaim thoru þe see fame. **14..** *Sir Beuis* (MS. C.) 502 Til þay come to þe se fome. *c* **1460** *Emare* 805 When she was fled ouur þe see fome, The nobulle kyng dwelled at home, Wyth fulle heuy chere. **1611** COTGR. s.v. *Escumier*, Venus.. is fained to haue beene bred of the sea-foame. **1808** SCOTT *Marm.* II. i, The merry seamen laugh'd to see Their gallant ship so lustily Furrow the green sea-foam. **1865** SWINBURNE *Chastelard* I. ii. 31 Between the sea-foam and the sea.

b. *attrib.*

1611 COTGR., s.v. *Sel*, *Escume de sel*, Sea-foame salt.

†**2.** = SEA-FROTH 3. *Obs.*

1725 [see SEA-FORTH 3]. **1852** E. A. ANDREWS *Lat.-Eng. Lex.* s.v. *Alcyoneum*, Alcyoneum medicamen.. Sea-foam, a good remedy for white specks in the eyes.

3. [tr. Ger. *meerschaum*] = MEERSCHAUM.

1837 DANA *Syst. Min.* 256 Sea Foam; called also Meerschaum, and Magnesite.

'seafood. *orig.* and chiefly *U.S.* Food obtained from the sea; fish, crustacea, etc., used as food. Freq. *attrib.*

1836 *Knickerbocker* VIII. 423 She said that she had come to Screamy Point to get 'sea-food'. **1906** *N.Y. Even. Post* 10 Mar. 5 Up State residents are among the best customers of the sea food, fruit and produce dealers. **1927** *Weekly Dispatch* 1 May 1/2 The correct name of the Poydras levee [at New Orleans] is the Carnavon levee, so named by the Carnavon family in England, who built it in 1870 to protect the plantation and seafood packing plant they then owned. **1935** A. BAUGH *Hist. Eng. Lang.* xi. 462 A writer in the London *Daily Mail* recently complained that an Englishman would find 'positively incomprehensible' the American words.. *sea-food*,.. and *hired-girl*. **1944** T. BARBOUR *That Vanishing Eden* 166, I was dining with some friends at a popular seafood restaurant in Miami. **1953** J. HILTON *Time & Time Again* I. 6 'I hope you like sea-food.' .. 'Sea-food?.. Fish, that is? Oh yes, I do, indeed.' (.. True enough, though this 'sea-food' set Charles thinking that he also enjoyed 'land-food'.) **1965** H. GOLD *Man who was not with It* III. xxv. 234 Grack's contact man cooked in a diner on the seafood coast of Baltimore. **1978** K. HUDSON *Jargon of Professions* iii. 82 Twenty or thirty years ago.. fish was upgraded to seafood.

'sea-fowl. [Cf. OE. *Sǽfuȝol* occurring as a proper name in *O.E. Chron.* an. 560.] A sea-bird.

1340-70 *Alisaunder* 811 þan fetches hee a seafoule faire of his wynges. **1620** J. MASON *New-found-land* in *Mem.* (1887) 151 The sea fowles are gulles, sea pigeons [etc.]. **1767** tr. *Cranz' Greenland* I. 79 The sea-fowls have all alike webbed feet like a goose. *Ibid.* 82 The second class of sea-fowl. **1870** YEATS *Nat. Hist. Comm.* I. ix. (1872) 92 Innumerable sea-fowl skim the surf or sweep the sky.

attrib. **1898** KEARTON *Wild Life at Home* 103 The famous Noup of Noss is a perfect sea-fowl paradise.

'sea-fox. [tr. L. *vulpēs marīna* (Pliny).] The Thrasher-shark, *Alopias vulpes*, also called SEA-APE, etc. Also † ***sea fox hound***.

1591 SYLVESTER *Du Bartas* I. v. 287 The.. subtle Sea-Fox. **1668** CHARLETON *Onomast.* 128 *Vulpecula Marina*.. the Sea Fox Hound. *a* **1672** WILLUGHBY *Hist. Pisc.* (1686) 54 *Vulpes marina Rondelet*.. The Sea Fox or Ape. **1836** YARRELL *Brit. Fishes* II. 379 The Fox Shark. Sea-fox. Thresher.

sea-front.

1. That portion or side of a building, etc. which faces the sea.

1879 SIR C. NUGENT in *Encycl. Brit.* IX. 450/2 These forts .. are protected with shields or walls of iron upon their sea-fronts. **1881** FREEMAN *Venice* 142 We can trace out the long line of the sea-front of the palace which became a city.

2. The land on the side of a town, etc. facing the sea.

1879 SIR C. NUGENT in *Encycl. Brit.* IX. 450/1 Upon the sea fronts the works consist.. of isolated forts. **1886** C. E. PASCOE *Lond. of To-day* xix. (ed. 3) 188 A short distance from the sea-front.

sea-frontage. An extent of sea-front.

1897 D. BUTLER *Ch. & Par. Abernethy* i. 17 *note*, The western side has a sea-frontage of 1500 feet long.

'sea-froth.

†**1.** Seaweed. *Obs. rare.* (In quots. tr. L. *alga*.)

c **1440** *Pallad. on Husb.* IV. 329 Other, so doluen, kesteth seefroth yn. *Ibid.* 335 Oildregges ek is good, outher see-froth. *Ibid.* 621 Sefroth the ferthe is go To honge vp.

2. The froth or foam of the sea; sea-foam.

1582 STANYHURST *Æneis* I. (Arb.) 22 Neptun.. glyds on the seafroth, with wheales of gould wagon. **1825** J. NEAL *Bro. Jonathan* I. 272 A little white foam, like sea froth. **1895** W. B. YEATS *Poems* (1899) 235 Wool whiter than sea froth.

attrib. **1643** A. ROSS *Mel Helic.* 86 Fair Venus With her sea-froth countenance.

†3. (See quot.) *Obs. rare*$^{-0}$. Cf. SEA-FOAM 2.
1725 *Bradley's Fam. Dict.*, *Sea-Froth* or *Foam*; in Latin *Alcyonium*, in all appearance a sort of Spungy Plant found in the Sea..; some..take it to be the Scum of the Sea, which has been hardned by the Sun Beames.

4. Meerschaum (cf. SEA-FOAM 3).
1801 T. THOMSON *Min.* in *Encycl. Brit.* (ed. 3) *Suppl.* II. 217/1 Myrsen—Seafroth. **1856** *Eng. Cycl.*, *Nat. Hist.* IV. 731.

'sea-gate[1]. [GATE *sb.*[2]]
†1. Distance or journey by sea. *Obs. rare*$^{-1}$.
1576 in *Oppress. Orkney & Zetld.* (1859) 59 Fra the Yle of Brassay to Swounburgh, quhilk is twentie myles of seagait.

2. A long rolling swell; also, the condition in which two vessels are when thrown aboard one another by such a swell.
1583 *Fenton's Voy.* (MS. Cott. Otho E viii. 185), With the force of the winde and the Seagate our cable br[oke]. **1628** *World Encompassed by Drake* 50 The sea-gate being at that present very great. *c* **1635** CAPT. N. BOTELER *Dial. Sea Services* (1685) 142 Two Ships by lying aboard one another in a Sea-Gate (that is a Billow, or wave). **1704** J. HARRIS *Lex. Techn.* I, *Sea-Gate*, when two Ships are aboard one another by means of a Wave or Billow: The Sea-men say, They lie aboard one another in a Sea-Gate. **1867** SMYTH *Sailor's Word-bk.*, *Sea-gate* or *gait*.

†3. ? An inlet of the sea. *Obs.*
1598 SYLVESTER *Du Bartas* II. i. III. *Furies* 134 But, since his sin, the wofull wretch findes none..Beast, mountain, valley, sea-gate shore or haven, But bears his Death's doom openly ingraven.

'sea-gate[2]. [GATE *sb.*[1]]
1. A gate towards, or giving access to, the sea; or a convenient approach to the sea.
1861 J. M. NEALE *Notes Dalmatia* 115 The sea-gate..is Roman. **1869** TOZER *Highl. Turkey* I. 238 Over the sea-gate of the city stands the Lion of St. Mark.

2. A place of access to the sea.
1883 F. G. HEATH in *Century Mag.* Dec. 165/1 Plymouth, the great sea-gate of sunny Devon. **1896** *Daily News* 30 Dec. 6/2 Delagoa Bay, the seagate of Secheleland.

3. One of a pair of supplementary or outer gates opening outwards, placed sometimes at the entrance of an exposed dock or tidal basin, as a safeguard against a heavy sea.
1875 in KNIGHT *Dict. Mech.*

seage, obs. form of SIEGE *sb.*

'sea-girt, *a.* Girt or surrounded by the sea. (Sometimes said of a peninsula or of a place that has the sea almost completely surrounding it.)
1621 G. SANDYS *Ovid's Met.* I. (1632) 12 Sea-girt Tenedos. **1670** MILTON *Brutus* 9 in *Hist. Brit.*, In th' Ocean wide Beyond the Realm of Gaul, a Land there lies, Sea-girt it lies. **1797** D. SIMPSON *Plea Relig.* (1808) 170 The little sea-girt empire of the Knights of Malta. **1812** BYRON *Ch. Har.* II. xxviii, The joys and sorrows sailors find, Coop'd in their winged sea-girt citadel. **1818** SHELLEY *Rosal. & Helen* 1050 A green and sea-girt promontory. **1856** STANLEY *Sinai & P.* vi. (ed. 3) 262 That sea-girt city [Cæsarea]. **1897** 'A. HOPE' *Phroso* i, Round sea-girt rocks.

'sea-god. A god of the sea, a marine deity.
1565 COOPER *Thesaurus* s.v. *Deus*, *Cærulei dij*, Sea gods. **1602** CAMPION *Hymn in Praise of Neptune* 8 Euery Sea-god paies a Iem..To decke great Neptunes Diadem. **1840** THIRLWALL *Greece* liv. VII. 52 Here he again sacrificed to the sea-god, whose proper realm he had now entered. **1900** A. NUTT *Fairy Mythol. Shakes.* 31 Mongan, son of the Irish sea-god Manannan mac Lir. **1950** 'D. DIVINE' *King of Fassarai* xiii. 100 To-day the fish had been wary and the sea god not kind. **1978** R. MITCHISON *Life in Scotland* iii. 60 The islanders of north Lewis sacrificed to a sea god at Hallowtide.

So **'sea-,goddess**, a goddess of the sea.
1710 W. KING *Heathen Gods & Heroes* (1722) Index, *Ino*, a Sea-Goddess. **1835** THIRLWALL *Greece* v. I. 157 The son of a sea-goddess.

'sea-going, *sb.* Going or travelling by sea.
1848 DICKENS *Dombey* lxii, Released from sea-going, after that first long voyage with his young bride.
attrib. **1860** *All Year Round* No. 66. 380 Sea-going togs, and other requirements. **1895** *Pop. Sci. Monthly* July 401 The first seagoing chronometer..was made by him.

'sea-going, *a.*
1. a. Going on the sea, applied to a vessel which makes distant journeys as opposed to a coasting, harbour, or river vessel.
1829 MARRYAT *F. Mildmay* x, I should be sent out..in some sea-going ship. **1909** *19th Cent.* Dec. 1009 The personnel of the sea-going fleet.
in fig. context. **1848** DICKENS *Dombey* iv, The shop itself..seemed almost to become a snug, sea-going, ship-shape concern, wanting only good sea-room.

b. Capable of being used or suitable for use on a sea-going vessel; carried or conducted by sea.
1895 [see SEA-GOING *sb.*]. **1928** C. DAWSON *Age of Gods* viii. 182 The sea-going trade of the Ægean world. **1962** *Listener* 29 Mar. 540/1 Land-base missiles and sea-going missiles.

2. Going to the sea, esp. of a fish, catadromous.
1842 *Proc. Berw. Nat. Club* II. No. x. 4 Several of the different fry of the sea-going fish. **1888** GOODE *Amer. Fishes* 16 The sea-going rivers of Germany.

3. Travelling by sea, seafaring.
1855 KINGSLEY *Heroes*, *Argon.* v. 166 Alcinous the rich sea-going king. **1887** B. V. HEAD *Hist. Numorum* Introd. 37 Subsequently the Greeks..became a sea-going people.

'sea-grape. [GRAPE *sb.*[1]]
1. The glassworts, *Salicornia herbacea* and *Salsola Kali.*
1578 LYTE tr. *Dodoens* I. lxxviii. 116 *Salicornia*..in English Sea grape. **1839** BAXTER *Brit. Phænog. Bot.* IV. 307 *Salicornia herbacea*... Sea-grass... Sea-grape. **1855** MISS PRATT *Flower. Pl.* IV. 288 *Salsola Kali* (Prickly Saltwort)..is in country places often called Sea-grape.

†2. The plant *Ephedra distachya. Obs.*
1597 GERARDE *Herbal* II. cccclxiii. 958 Sea Grape is not vnlike to Horse taile. **1611** COTGR., *Raisin de mer*, sea Grape. **1728** BRADLEY *Dict. Bot.* II. s.v. *Polygonum*, Ephedra sive Anabasis, Climbing Knot-Grass or Sea-Grape. *Ibid.*, *Polygonum bacciferum*, sive Uva marina major, The great Sea-Grape.

†3. A fish mentioned by Pliny. *Obs. rare.*
1601 HOLLAND *Pliny* XXXII. x. II. 450 Likewise the fish called the Sea-grape [L. *uva*] putrefied in wine, doe infuse this vertue into the foresaid wine.

4. In W. Indies, the grape-tree or seaside grape, *Coccoloba uvifera.*
1806 T. MOORE '*I stole along the flowery bank*' i, Many a bending sea-grape drank The sprinkle of the feathery oar. **1884** SARGENT *Rep. Forests N. Amer.* 118 *Coccoloba uvifera*. .. Sea Grape.

5. *pl.* The clustered egg-cases of the cuttle-fish and other cephalopods.
1835-6 *Todd's Cycl. Anat.* I. 560/2 The eggs of the Cuttle-fish..resemble in this state a bunch of grapes, as the name 'sea-grapes'..implies. **1850** MISS PRATT *Comm. Things of Sea-side* iii. 233 That singular cluster..commonly called by the fishermen Sea-grapes, is a group of the eggs of the common cuttle-fish.

6. The gulf-weed, which has large bladders in clusters resembling grapes.
1825 LONGF. *Sea Diver* iv, They rested by the coral throne,..Where the pale sea-grape had o'ergrown The glorious dwellings made for them. **1850** MISS PRATT *Comm. Things of Sea-side* ii. 111 The Sea-grape is an olive-green weed, with..berries about as large as a pea.

'sea-grass. [Cf. G. *seegras*, *meergras*.]
1. A grass which grows by the sea. Also one of various grass-like plants: (*a*) = SEA-PINK a; (*b*) one of the glassworts, *Salicornia herbacea*; (*c*) the grass *Spartina stricta*.
1578 LYTE *Dodoens* IV. l. 509 Sea grasse... Some call it in Englishe our Ladies quishion. **1629** PARKINSON *Parad.* 318 In English, Thrift, Sea grasse, and our Ladies Cushion. **1791** W. GILPIN *Forest Scenery* II. 158 Its banks..are covered, like the other mud-lands of this country, with sea-grass, which gives them the air of meadows when the tide retires. **1837** BAXTER *Brit. Phænog. Bot.* III. 203 *Spartina stricta*. Twin-spiked Cord-grass. Smooth Sea-grass. Sea Cock's-foot-grass. **1839** [see SEA-GRAPE 1].

2. One of various plants and seaweeds growing in the sea: (*a*) a pondweed, *Ruppia maritima*; (*b*) the eel-grass or grass-wrack, *Zostera marina*; also, the dried stems of this plant, used in ropes, chair-seats, etc.; (*c*) the gulf-weed; (*d*) the *Enteromorpha compressa.*
1591 PERCIVALL *Sp. Dict.*, *Ova*, reeke, sea grasse, ducke weede, *Vlua, alga, lens palustris*. **1605** B. JONSON *Masque of Blackness*, Oceanus..was gyrlonded with *Alga*, or sea-grasse. **1762** W. HUDSON *Flora Anglica* 63 *Ruppia maritima*. .. Sea-grass. **1857-8** LONGF. *M. Standish* IV. 12 Welcome, O wind of the East..Blowing o'er fields of dulse, and measureless meadows of sea-grass. **1883** E. P. RAMSAY *Food Fishes N.S. Wales* (Fish. Exhib. Catal.) 48 The food of the Dugong consists of sea-grasses, chiefly a species of *Zostera*. **1900** *Jrnl. Soc. Arts* 12 Jan. 170/1 Sea grass is a long thin grass that grows on the protected flats of the Lower St. Lawrence River. *Ibid.* (*heading*) Canadian sea grass for upholstering. **1911** [see *porch chair* s.v. PORCH 8]. **1933** P. T. TUCKER *Riding High Country* ii. 31 His las' rope was sea grass. **1979** *Dictionaries* I. 64 Sea grass is..a derived product with a local name.

3. A variety of cirrus cloud.
1887 ABERCROMBY *Weather* 98.

4. *attrib.*
1864 SALA in *Daily Tel.* 2 Aug., Ligatures of seagrass twine—which cut like razors. **1895** *Outing* (U.S.) XXVI. 356/1 Off speeds the bass with an hundred foot pennon of sea-grass line trailing from his bloody jaws. **1911** *Daily Colonist* (Victoria, B.C.) 11 Apr. 7/1 (Advt.), Special sale of sea grass chairs. **1967** *Southerly* XXVII. 152 Immemorial deck-chairs and seagrass tables.

'sea-green, *a.* and *sb.* [Cf. F. *vert de mer.*]
A. *adj.* 1. Pale bluish-green.
1603 *Inv.* in Gage *Hengrave* (1822) 36 Saddles covered wth sea grene clothe. **1666** DRYDEN *Ann. Mirab.* xxi, Lawson..Whom sea-green Sirens from the rocks lament. **1809** SHAW *Gen. Zool.* VII. 388 Sea-green Roller, with..wings varied with blue, sea-green, and black. **1811** *Ibid.* VIII. 152 Sea-green Bee-Eater, with yellow throat. **1823** BYRON *Island* III. ii, Their sea-green isle. **1878** NEWCOMB *Pop. Astron.* III. iv. 354 [Uranus] has a decided sea-green color.

2. In phr. ***sea-green incorruptible***, applied to Robespierre by Carlyle (see quot. 1837) and now commonly used allusively (often followed by some other word) to designate a person of rigid honesty or uncompromising idealism. Also in extended use and *absol.*, impervious to moral corruption.
1837 CARLYLE *Fr. Rev.* II. IV. iv, O seagreen Incorruptible, thou shalt see! **1931** *Economist* 7 Mar. 492/1 Although Mr. Hu Han-min at Manking may be a 'sea-green incorruptible' of as pure a dye as Robespierre, the local representatives of the Party in the country districts are often oppressors of the poor. **1936** H. G. WELLS *Anat. Frustration* ix. 94 His [*sc.* Philip Snowden's] early appearance as the 'sea green incorruptible' of the British Labour revolution. **1958** *Spectator* 1 Aug. 157/1 Utopia is to be attained only by sea-green incorruptibility. **1960** C. P. SNOW *Affair* xl. 372 'I shall have to,' Skeffington replied, obdurate and sea-green. **1976** *Listener* 5 Aug. 143/3 He is, for all that, a man of sea-green integrity. **1977** *New Society* 17 Feb. 328/1 A former Chief Constable from the north west..a man of cast-iron integrity from a religious background and..a sea-green incorruptible.

B. *sb.*
1. A sea-green colour.
1598 CHAPMAN *Hero & Leander* IV. 73 With a pure Sea greene She did so queintly shadow euery lim. **1662** MERRETT tr. *Neri's Art of Glass* xx, Between a Sea-green and a skie-colour. **1848** THACKERAY *Van. Fair* ix, She..appeared..in draggled sea-green, or slatternly sky-blue.

†2. Houseleek. Cf. AY-GREEN, SENGREEN. *Obs.*
Perh. orig. a misprint: see the first quot.
1601 HOLLAND *Pliny* XVIII. xvii. I. 575 The hearb Housleek or Sea-greene [*Errata, read* Sengreene]. **1696** PHILLIPS (ed. 5), *Scolopender*,..a certain Medicine Herb,..such as Sea-green [etc.]. **1755** JOHNSON, *Seagreen*, saxifrage. A plant.

3. A collector's name for a moth, the *Hadena thalassina.*
1832 J. RENNIE *Butterfl. & Moths* 67.

4. *pl.* (*Sc.*) (See quot.)
1765-8 ERSKINE *Inst. Law Scot.* II. vi. §17 Sea-greens..*i.e.* grounds in some measure gained from the sea, but which still continue to be overflowed in spring-tides.

seagrim, obs. variant of SEGGRUM.

'sea-ground.
†1. The bottom of the sea (cf. GROUND *sb.* 1 a).
Beowulf 564 Sægrunde neah. *c* **1220** *Bestiary* 517 in *O.E. Misc.* 16 Ðis fis wuneð wið ðe se grund. *a* **1300** *Cursor M.* 20952 A dai and of a night to stound He [Paul] was stad atte see ground. *c* **1450** *St. Cuthbert* (Surtees) 640 The ankir...To þe se gronde doune slypp. **1611** SPEED *Hist. Gt. Brit.* IX. xii. 34 The ship..sunke sodainely to the Sea-ground.

2. *pl.* ? Land covered at high tide by the sea.
1826 BARNEWALL & CRESSWELL *K.B. Rep.* IV. 486 The messuage,..sea-grounds, oyster-layings [etc.]. *Ibid.* 491 The words *sea-grounds*, by themselves, would have been sufficient to pass the right of soil in the shore.

'sea-gull. Also 6 seegell. 1. = GULL *sb.*[1]
1542 *Rutland MSS.* (1905) IV. 324 For bringing seygwlles and other fowlles, vs. **1544** [see SEA-COB[1]]. **1576** FLEMING *Panopl. Epist.* 401 The counterfect philosopher..sheweth himself like unto a sea Gull among a sort of faire swannes. **1659** PELL *Impr. Sea* 236 A *Fezerallo*, is a black-coloured bird, but somewhat less than a Sea-Gull. **1766** GRAY *Kingsgate* 7 Here sea-gulls scream, and cormorants rejoice. **1837** DICKENS *Pickw.* xx, To watch the flight of a seagull. **1888** F. HUME *Mme. Midas* I. Prol., Flocks of white seagulls..were constantly circling round.
transf. and *fig.* **1599** NASHE *Lenten Stuffe* 60 That greedy seagull ignorance is apt to deuoure any thing. **1642** MILTON *Apol. Smect.* Wks. 1851 III. 276 Now trust me not, Readers, if I be not already weary of pluming and footing this Seagull, so open he lies to strokes.

2. A casual, non-Union, dock labourer. *N.Z. slang.*
c **1926** 'MIXER' *Transport Workers' Songbk.* 46 What a study! Let us paint it As the sea-gulls fly about, While the stringer birds are anxious For the meeting to come out. **1943** *2 N.Z.E.F. Times* 20 Sept. 5 As a result of a survey of non-Union labour on the wharves..500 out of 800 'sea-gulls' were interviewed at the Auckland District Man-power Office. **1959** G. SLATTER *Gun in my Hand* xvii. 225 Ended up as a sea-gull on the Wellington wharves loading up the Home boats. **1966** G. W. TURNER *Eng. Lang. Austral. & N.Z.* vii. 150 The watersiders have their own special language, but the only term I know from experience is *seagull*, the casual non-union labourer who picks up a job during busy times on the waterfront.

‖**seah** ('siːə). *Hebrew Antiq.* [Heb. *sᵉāh*, in the Eng. Bible translated 'measure' (e.g. Gen. xviii. 6, 2 Kings vii. 1), as is also the Græcized form σάτον in the New Testament (e.g. Matt. xiii. 33).] A Hebrew dry measure, equal (according to Rabbinical statements) to six times the cab (CAB *sb.*[1]) and to one-third of the ephah.
1705 ARBUTHNOT *Tab. Grec.*, etc. *Coins* 14, 15. **1737** WHISTON *Josephus*, *Antiq.* IX. iv. §4 Two seahs of barley should be sold in the market for a shekel, and a seah of fine flour should be sold for a shekel [*2 Kings* vii. 1]. *Ibid.* §5 A seah is equal to an Italian modius and a half.

sea-hare. [Cf. G. *see-*, *meerhase*, Du. *zeehaas*, in both senses.]
1. A mollusc, *Aplysia depilans* (and other species), having an oval body with four tentacles.
A rendering of the *lepus marinus* of Pliny, whose account is the source of most of the older English references. The designation is thought to be due to the resemblance of the two skinny lobes of the animal to the ears of a hare. Pliny's notion that the animal is venomous has no foundation.
1593 G. HARVEY *Pierces Super.* Wks. (Grosart) II. 251 Good against the empoisonment of the sea-hare. **1626** BACON *Sylva* §983 It hath beene anciently receiued, that the Sea-Hare hath an Antipathy with the Lungs, (if it commeth neare the Body,) and erodeth them. **1759** tr. *M. Adanson's Voy. Senegal* 208 Several soft fishes, as sea hares, cuttle fish, and polypus. **1854** H. MILLER *Sch. & Schm.* (1858) 65 The cuttle-fish and the sea-hare.

2. The Lump-fish: see LUMP *sb.*[2] *rare.*
1896 tr. *Boas' Text-bk. Zool.* 390.

'sea-hawk. [HAWK *sb.*[1]]
†1. Some kind of fish. a. ? The eagle-ray or sea-eagle. b. A flying fish. *Obs. rare.*

a. **1655** MOUFET & BENNET *Health's Improv.* (1746) 243 The Sea-Hawk is of hard Flesh and slow Digestion, as Galen avoucheth. **1661** LOVELL *Hist. Anim. & Min.* 235 Sea Hauke hath a very moist and soft flesh.

b. **1722** DIAPER tr. *Oppian's Halieut.* I. 714 Sea-Hawks [*orig.* ἴρηξ], the Swallow, and the wanton Sleve Their native Streams for airy Pastime leave.

2. One of various gull-like birds, as one of the skuas, and the frigate-bird.

1852 MACGILLIVRAY *Brit. Birds* V. 496 (Skua) The Sea-Hawk follows the frightened bird in all its motions. **1860** G. BENNETT *Gatherings Naturalist Austral.* 80 The Frigate-bird (*Tachypetes aquila*)..is also known by the name of Sea Hawk, or Man-of-war Bird.

sea-hedgehog.

1. An echinus or sea-urchin.

1602 CAREW *Cornwall* I. 32 The Sea-hedge-hogge,..is enclosed in a round shell,..garded by an vtter skinne full of prickles, as the land Vrchin. *a* **1682** SIR T. BROWNE *Norf. Fishes* Wks. 1835 IV. 333 *Echinus Echinometrites* sea hedgehog, whose neat shells are common on the shore.

attrib. **1845** GOSSE *Ocean* iv. (1849) 259 Fragments of coral, sea-hedgehog shells, and their broken off prickles.

2. The globe-fish or other diodont fish; so called from having erectile spines.

c **1711** PETIVER *Gazophyl.* vi. 60 Sea Porcupine... This thorny Fish, is a sort of Sea Hedge-hog. **1879** GÜNTHER in *Encycl. Brit.* X. 685/1 *Globe-fish* or *Sea-Hedgehog*.

'sea-hen.

1. A name for the piper-gurnard, *Trigla lyra*, and the lump-fish, *Cyclopterus lumpus*.

[Cf. G. *seehahn* (= 'sea-cock'), applied to both fishes.]

1611 COTGR., *Poullarde*, the Sea-henne; a fish. **1684** SIBBALD *Scotia Illustr.* II. II. 24 *Lyra, quibusdam* the Crowner, *aliis ex nostratibus* the Sea-Hen. **1892** H. A. MACPHERSON *Vertebr. Fauna of Lakeland* 480 The fishermen of the English Solway generally apply the title of 'Sea hen' to this species [*Cyclopterus lumpus*].

2. A local name for the common guillemot, *Uria troile*, and the great skua, *Stercorarius catarrhactes*.

a **1672** WILLUGHBY *Ornith.* III. III. iv. (1676) 244 *Northumbris & Dunelmensibus*, a Guillemot or Sea-hen. **1852** MACGILLIVRAY *Brit. Birds* V. 318 *Uria Troile.* Foolish Guillemot... Sea-hen. **1879** KUMLIEN *Contrib. Nat. Hist. Arctic Amer.* 94 *Buphagus skua*... 'Sea-hen' of whalemen.

‖**'sea-herr.** *Obs.* [? Du. *zeeheer*, f. *zee* SEA + *heer* lord.] One who has dominion over the seas.

1615 *Trade's Incr.* 7 Our neighbours the now *Sea-herrs*, the Nation..whose troubles begot their liberty [the Dutch].

'sea-hog. [HOG *sb.*¹; cf. G. *meerschwein*.]

1. A popular name for the porpoise. ? *Now rare.*

1580 HOLLYBAND *Treas. Fr. Tong*, *Marsouin*, a sea hog. **1686** J. DUNTON *Lett. fr. New-Eng.* (1867) 32 A vast number of Fishes called Sea-hogs, or Porpoises. **1760** *Ann. Reg.* 97 A porpus, or sea-hog,..came up the river as far as London-bridge. **1896** tr. *Boas' Text-bk. Zool.* 524 The Sea-hog or Porpoise (*Phocæna communis*).

†**2.** = HOG-FISH 3. *Obs.*

1668 [see HOG-FISH 3].

'sea-holly. The plant ERYNGO.

1548 TURNER *Names of Herbes* (E.D.S.) 36 Eryngium is named in englishe sea Hulver or sea Holly. **1642** *Rates Merchandizes* 48 Sea-holly rootes. **1741** *Compl. Fam.-Piece* II. iii. 374 Buphthalmums, Sea Holly, Sea Ragwort. **1882** *Garden* 15 Apr. 249/1 The ordinary Sea Hollies.

'sea-holm¹. *rare*⁻⁰. [HOLM¹.] 'A small uninhabited island' (J.); hence in later Dicts.

'sea-holm². [HOLM².] = SEA-HOLLY.

c **1550** LLOYD *Treas. Health* (*c* 1560) N v b, The herbe and rote of seaholme sodden and dronke with wyne. **1612** DRAYTON *Poly-olb.* I. 125 The Seaholme heere, that spreadeth all our shore,..Whose roote th' Eringo is. **1728** BRADLEY *Dict. Bot.* II, *Sea-Holm*, or *Hulver*, in Latin, Aquifolium. **1850** MISS PRATT *Comm. Things of Sea-side* i. 18 [*Eryngium maritimum*] is known on the several parts of our coast by a variety of names, as the sea hulver, sea holly, and sea holme.

attrib. **1602** CAREW *Cornwall* I. 19 The Seaholme roote.

'sea-horse. [Cf. G. *seepferd*, *seeross*.]

1. The walrus. [Cf. *horse-whale*, HORSE *sb.* 28 b.]

c **1475** *Pict. Voc.* in Wr-Wülcker 765/2 [*Nomina piscium marinorum*] *Hoc rosina*, a sehors. **1585** JAS. I *Ess. Poesie* (Arb.) 16 Daulphins, Seahorse, Selchs with oxin ee, And Merswynis, Pertrikis als of fishes race. **1613** PURCHAS *Pilgrimage* (1614) 748 *note*, Some call the Morse a Sea horse. *a* **1682** SIR T. BROWNE *Of Greenland* Wks. 1835 IV. 375 The stomachs of sea horses or morses. **1877** W. JONES *Finger-ring* 148 A ring made of a sea-horse's tooth.

¶ By extension apparently applied to the narwhal.

1674 tr. *Martiniere's Voy.* 115 The Horn of this Sea-horse, was full ten foot long,..wreathed..tapering.

2. A fabulous horse-like marine animal.

As represented in heraldry (and formerly in pageants) it has the fore-parts of a horse and the tail of a fish, like the steeds (*equi bipedes*, Verg. *Georg.* IV. 389) drawing the chariots of Neptune and Proteus as depicted in ancient paintings.

1587 FLEMING *Contn. Holinshed* III. 1340/1 Before the which [*sc.* the mint] there was a huge and monstrous sea-horsse of twentie foot high. **1648** HERRICK *Hesper., His Cavalier*, That dares bestride The active sea-horse, and.. Through that huge field of waters ride. *a* **1700** EVELYN *Diary* 27 Feb. 1644, In the third is Neptune sounding his trumpet, his charriot drawne by sea-horses. **1761** *Ann. Reg.* 238 The fishmongers pageants consisted of..two mairmaids and two Sea-horses. **1780** EDMONDSON *Heraldry* II. Gloss., *Sea-Horse*, the upper part is formed like the horse, with webbed feet, and the hinder part ends in a fish's tail. **1874** BLACK *Pr. Thule* 9 The black sea-horse that had been seen in Loch Suainabhal. **1885** *Encycl. Brit.* XIX. 559/1 s.v. *Poseidon*, Sometimes he was represented riding a bull, a horse, or a sea-horse.

3. a. = HIPPOCAMPUS 2.

1589 RIDER *Bibl. Scholast.* 1723 A sea horse, *hippocampa*. **1721** BRADLEY *Philos. Acc. Wks. Nat.* 69, Fig. 111. The Shell-Fish call'd the Sea-Horse, found upon the Coast of Italy. **1862** ANSTED *Channel Isl.* II. ix. 213 The curious little sea horse (*hippocampus brevirostris*).

b. The acanthopterygian fish *Agriopus torvus* (*Cent. Dict.*). ***flying*** or ***winged sea-horse***: a fish of the order or sub-order *Pegasidæ*.

1854 A. ADAMS, etc. *Man. Nat. Hist.* 83 The *Pegasi*, or Flying Sea-Horses. *Ibid.* 94 Winged Sea-Horses (*Pegasidæ*).

†**4.** The hippopotamus. *Obs.*

1600 J. PORY tr. *Leo's Africa* Introd. 30 The teeth of sea-horses: which creatures are commonly found in the riuers of Nilus, Niger, &c. **1678** DRYDEN *All for Love* I. I Sea-Horses floundring in the slimy mud. **1700** C. LEIGH *Nat. Hist. Lanc.* etc. I. 183 A young Hippopotamus or Sea-Horse. **1759** tr. *M. Adanson's Voy. Senegal* 133 The hippoptami [*sic*] or sea horses, are common.

5. A large white-crested wave; cf. *white horse*, HORSE *sb.* 24 b.

1877 *N.W. Linc. Gloss.*, *Sea-dogs, Sea-hosses*, rough waves in the Humber and Trent. **1886** A. PEMBER *Slipping away* i, Alice's eyes are fixed on the white sea-horses.

6. *attrib.* (senses 1 and 4), as ***sea-horse fat, hide, leather, oil, skin, tooth***.

1764 *Ann. Reg.* II. 12 The whale and the *sea horse fat they also boil with roots. **1601** HOLLAND *Pliny* VI. xxix. I. 144 There may a man have plentie of the *Sea-horse hides. *a* **1682** SIR T. BROWNE *Comm.-pl. Bks.* Wks. 1835 IV. 396 A girdle of *sea-horse leather. **1820** SCORESBY *Acc. Arctic Reg.* I. 507 On this adventure, 22 tons of *Sea-horse oil..were obtained. **1626** BACON *Sylva* §964 Rings of *Sea-Horse Teeth. **1858** SIMMONDS *Dict. Trade*, *Sea-horse tooth*, a name given to the teeth of the walrus, and of the hippopotamus, which yield ivory.

'sea-hound. [tr. L. *canis marinus* (Pliny).

Cf. G. *seehund*, Du. *zeehond*; also HOUND *sb.* 5, HOUND-FISH 1.]

1. A dog-fish.

13.. *K. Alis.* 5653 (Bodl. MS.), And a maner folk þer is yfounde þat men hem clepeþ Cee hounde. *c* **1330** R. BRUNNE *Chron. Wace* (Rolls) 3781 'Marebellow' [Fr. *marine bélue*] ys þe se hound. **1601** CHESTER *Lover's Mart.* (1878) 100 Here swimmes..The Sea-horse, Sea-hound, and the wide-mouth'd Plaice. **1669** J. DAVIES tr. *Olearius' Voy. Ambass.* IV. 133 In this place we saw a great number of Dog-fishes, or Sea-hounds. **1831** KEIGHTLEY *Mythol. Ital. & Gr.* I. xix. 247 She [Scylla]..catches the dolphins, sea-hounds, and other large animals of the sea which swim by.

2. Used *allusively*.

1905 MEREDITH *October Twenty-first* in *Outlook* 21 Oct. 533 [Nelson] Her sea-hound and her mortal stroke.

seaide, obs. 1st and 3rd ind. pa. t. of SAY *v.*¹

†**'seaish**, *a. Obs. rare.* [f. SEA *sb.* + -ISH.] Of or pertaining to the sea, marine.

1530 PALSGR. 323/2 Seeysshe, belongyng to the see, *marin*. **1579** W. A. *Remedy Agst. Love* F iij, Whose syns dooth more then seaish sands abound. **1586** WARNER *Alb. Eng.* I. iv. (1612) 13 How the Gods of Sun and Seas, offended, do require Each month a Virgin, to appease a Seaish Monsters ire. **1610** R. TOFTE *Hon. Acad.* 59 But what more wavering did you ever find Then Seaish waves, what more faire or unkind?

'sea-island, *a.* and *sb.* **A.** *adj.* The designation of a fine variety of cotton, *Gossypium barbadense*, distinguished by long silky fibres, grown on the islands off the coast of Georgia and South Carolina, now also acclimatized in other countries. Also *absol.*

1803 J. DAVIS *Travels in U.S.A.* 78 Of cotton there are two kinds; the sea-island and the island. The first is the most valuable. **1807** *Salmagundi* 15 Oct. 327 The lady of a Southern planter will..trail a bale of sea-island cotton at her heels. **1834** MCCULLOCH *Dict. Comm.* (ed. 2) 436 s.v. *Cotton*, The best of the first [*sc.* long stapled cotton] is the sea-island cotton, or that brought from the shores of Georgia. **1839** URE *Dict. Arts* 344 Having a breadth varying from $\frac{1}{800}$ of an inch in the strongest Smyrna or candle-wick cotton of the Levant, to $\frac{1}{2500}$ of an inch in the finest Sea-island. **1858** HOMANS *Cycl. Comm.* 438/1 The sea-island plant yields about 125 or 130 pounds of clean ginned cotton per acre. **1934** *Nat. Geogr. Mag.* Feb. 260/2 At Hampton Point and Retreat the first sea-island cotton was grown from seeds introduced from the island of Anguilla, in the West Indies. **1970** *Observer* 15 Mar. 48/6 (Advt.), Shirts and pyjamas made to measure, sea island poplins..pure silk. **1977** P. MOYES *To kill Coconut* xiii. 180 Sea Island isn't grown only in the Caribbean.

B. *sb.* An offshore mooring station where oil tankers can discharge their cargo and from which the oil can be pumped ashore.

1975 *Offshore Engineer* Sept. 17 (*caption*) When linked to the 'sea islands' already installed, it will be more than 1 km long. **1979** F. FORSYTH *Devil's Alternative* ix. 218 They berthed at 'sea islands', networks of pipes on stilts, well out to sea, from which their oil could be pumped ashore.

seak, obs. form of SICK.

'sea-kale. Forms: 7 sea-keele, 8–9 -cale, 8– sea-kale. [f. SEA + KALE *sb.*; cf. the southern form *sea-cole*, SEA *sb.* 23 f.]

1. A cruciferous plant, *Crambe maritima*, found wild on the shores of western Europe, and often cultivated for its young shoots.

1699 EVELYN *Acetaria* 16 Our Sea-keele (the ancient *Crambe*) and growing on our Coast [is] very delicate. **1732** ARBUTHNOT *Rules of Diet* in *Aliments*, etc. I. 257 Sea-Cole or Cale. **1795** *Times* 30 Apr. 1/4 Sea-Kale, a new Culinary Vegetable. **1847** BARHAM *Ingol. Leg.* Ser. III. *Wedding-day* (end), Every complexion less pale than sea-kale!

2. sea-kale beet, white beet, so called from its resemblance in colour.

1882 *Garden* 21 Jan. 50/1 White or Seakale Beet.

seake, obs. form of SACK *sb.*³ (wine), SICK.

'sea-king.

1. One of the piratical Scandinavian chiefs, who in the ninth and succeeding centuries ravaged the coasts of Europe. [After ON. *sækonungr*: cf. OE. *sǽcyning* (Beowulf).]

1819 LINGARD *Hist. Eng.* I. v. 253 The two sea-kings.. returned to Denmark. **1840** CARLYLE *Heroes* i. (1841) 52 Hrolf, or Rollo Duke of Normandy, the wild Sea-king. **1862** BURTON *Bk. Hunter* IV. 380 The races descended from ancient sea-kings. **1863** TENNYSON *Welcome to Alexandra* I Sea-kings daughter from over the sea.

2. Applied to the god of the sea.

1582 STANYHURST *Æneis* I. (Arb.) 21 Thee sea king Neptun. **1888** J. PAYN *Prince of Blood* XXV. (1892) 201 Like mermen in attendance upon the sea-king.

seal (siːl), *sb.*¹ Forms: *α.* 1 seolh, 4 ? selȝ; *Sc.* 5 selghe, 5–6 selcht, 5–7 selche, 5–8 selch, 6 saylch, selk, 9 sealgh. *β.* (1 siol-, seol-), 3–6 sele, 4–7 seel, 5 sel, ceel, cele, zele, seylle, 5–6 seele, seyle, sealle, 5–7 seale, 6 seall, seayle, seayll, 7 siele, seil, sayle, 7– seal. See also SOILE. [OE. *siol-*, *seol-*, declensional form of *seolh* (whence the *α* forms above, which are mainly Scottish) = OHG. *selah*, MLG. *sêl*, MDu. *seel*, *sael* (*-hont*), *zele*, ON. *sel-r* (Sw. *sjel*, *säl*, Da. *sæl*):—OTeut. *selho-z*.]

1. A member of the family *Phocidæ*, sub-order *Pinnipedia*, of aquatic carnivorous mammals, with limbs developed into flippers and adapted for swimming, and having an elongated body covered with thick fur or bristles and terminated by a short tail; *spec.* the Common Seal, *Phoca vitulina*, an inhabitant of all waters of the temperate and frigid zones. Also applied (chiefly with defining word: see 2) to amphibious mammals of other families closely resembling the Common Seal in appearance.

α. *c* **1000** *Sax. Leechd.* III. 34 Ðas onsænde seolh ofer sæs hrygc. **1383** *Durham Acc. Rolls* (Surtees) 434 Coopertus cum pelle de sely [? = selȝ]. *c* **1425** WYNTOUN *Cron.* III. i. 48 Þe carl was fat as any selche [*v.r.* selghe]. **1502** *Acc. Ld. High Treas. Scot.* II. 342 Item to ane man brocht ane quyk selch fra Pittinweme to Faukland to the King, xiiij s. **1549** *Compl. Scot.* vi. 60 The selcht, quhilk sum men callis the see volue. **1596** DALRYMPLE tr. *Leslie's Hist. Scot.* I. 57 Sey calues or saylches. **1789** D. DAVIDSON *Seasons* 17 Gib's now gane for the Western seas, Whare selchs an' pellucks whamble. **1821** SCOTT *Pirate* v, What the devil mean you by..levelling your gun at folk's heads as you would at a sealgh's?

β. *c* **893** K. ÆLFRED *Oros.* I. i. 18 On þæm sciprapum, þe beoð of hwæles hyde ȝeworht, & of seoles. *c* **1050** *Voc.* in Wr.-Wülcker 408/37 *Focus*, seol. *c* **1300** *Havelok* 755 He tok þe sele. **1409** *Durham Acc. Rolls* (Surtees) 53 In di. ceel de Tes, 4s. **1416** *Ibid.* 54 In 3 quarters unius zele et plays de Tese, 8s. 6d. *c* **1460** J. RUSSELL *Bk. Nurture* 823 in *Babees Bk.*, The baly of þe fresche samon, els purpose, or seele. *c* **1552** LELAND *Itin.* (1769) VII. 119 Seles when they cast theyr Calves they cum to Lond. **1579** HAKE *Newes out of Powles* iv. (1872) D iij, Straunge kindes of fysh at second course... As Porpesse, Seale and Salmond good. **1667** MILTON *P.L.* XI. 831 An Iland salt and bare, The haunt of Seales and Orcs. **1743** BULKELEY & CUMMINS *Voy. S. Seas* 159 To carry a Line to haul some of the Seal aboard. **1815** SCOTT *Ld. of Isles* IV. x, Staffa..Where..the shy seal had quiet home.

2. With defining word, e.g. *eared*, *elephant*, *fur*, *hair*, *harp*, *hooded*, *leonine*, *leporine*, *monk*, *pied*, *ribbon*, *ringed*, *rough*, *ursine seal*, etc. (see these words); also **bottle-nosed seal**, *Phoca leonina*; **crab-eating seal**, *Labodon carcinophaga*; **floe**, **small-ringed seal** = SPOTTED *seal*; **great seal**, *Phoca barbata* (Pennant); **Greenland**, **heart seal** = HARP *seal*; **marbled seal**, *Calocephalus discolor*.

1781 PENNANT *Quadrupeds* II. 525 Hooded Seal. *Ibid.*, Harp Seal... Our Fishers call this the Harp or Heart Seal. *Ibid.* 531 Bottle-nose Seal. **1841** *Penny Cycl.* XXI. 160/2 In the eye of the Greenland Seal..the cornea was thin and yielding. **1842** C. H. SMITH *Introd. Mammalia* 258 *Stenorhincus Leptonyx*, or Small Nailed Seal, from the South Seas. **1879** E. P. WRIGHT *Anim. Life* 124 The Grey Seal (*Halichoerus grypus*) is met with around the north and west coasts of Scotland. **1886** *Encycl. Brit.* XXI. 581/1 The small ringed seal or 'floe-rat' of the sealers (*Phoca hispida*). *Ibid.* 582/2 The floe or spotted seal.

3. Short for SEALSKIN.

1886 BECK *Draper's Dict.*, *Seal* (fur). This valuable fur is sought annually on the shores of Spitzbergen. **1886** *Leeds Mercury* 29 Dec. 4/4 An active demand for seals and plushes.

4. *attrib.* and *Comb.*: **a.** simple attributive, as ***seal-blubber, -bone, leather, -oil***; in sense 3, ***seal-coat.***

1873 *Routledge's Young Gentl. Mag.* Jan. 115/2 Such luxuries as *seal-blubber. **1616** *Shetland Witch Trial* in Dalyell *Darker Superst. Scot.* (1834) 384 The '*selch bone' with which Barbara stirred her milk to divine the product. **1901** *Munsey's Mag.* XXV. 351/1 The desire of a woman for a *seal coat. **1882** J. PATON in *Encycl. Brit.* XIV. 388/1 *Seal leather is generally finished on the grain side as 'levant' seal with a large coarse grain. **1732** in *Calendar State Papers, Amer. & W. Indies* (1939) 227 Value of *seal oil made last winter, £2478 10s. **1839** URE *Dict. Arts* 248, ⅛ of a gallon of good seal oil, weighs 6010 gr. **1973** L. RUSSELL *Everday Life Colonial Canada* xii. 155 Until the 1860s, seal oil was an important lamp fuel in the eastern colonies, and was also used in food and as a lubricant.

b. 'Connected with the catching of a seal', as ***seal-club, -lance, -pike, -ship, -shot, -trap.***

1820 SCORESBY *Acc. Arctic Reg.* I. 512 A blow with a '*seal-club'..on the nose, immediately stuns it. **1895** KIPLING *2nd Jungle Bk.* 161 Kotuko looked over the deer-sinew fastenings of his harpoon and his *seal-lance. **1908** *Daily Chron.* 29 Apr. 5/5 Both the Walrus and the Panther were among the oldest of the fleet of *seal-ships. **1842** *Seal-shot [see SEALING *vbl. sb.*[2] b]. **1876** C. H. DAVIS *Polaris Exped.* viii. 219 Hans set some *seal-traps, without success.

c. similative, as ***seal-brown, -like*** adjs.

1874 CARR *Judith Gwynne* vii, The boy shambled over in a seal-like manner. **1881** [see FAWN *sb.*[1] 3]. **1884** *Western Daily Press* 28 Nov. 7/4 Entire costumes are made of this attractive fabric..in colour a lovely seal-brown. **1963** B. VESEY-FITZGERALD *Cat Owner's Encycl.* 36 The body should be a solid colour of rich dark seal-brown shading.

d. objective, as ***seal-fisher, -fishery, -hunt, -hunter, -spearing.***

1820 SCORESBY *Acc. Arctic Reg.* I. 513 The *seal-fishers have to pursue them over the ice. **1785** J. KNOX *View Brit. Emp.* I. 351 The greatest *seal fishery is on the coast of Labrador. **1886** *Encycl. Brit.* XXI. 582/2 On the western shore of the White Sea the *seal-hunt is less productive than on the eastern. **1781** PENNANT *Quadrupeds* II. 524 Our Newfoundland *Seal-hunters. **1895** KIPLING *2nd Jungle Bk.* 172 The men used to sing it after *seal-spearing.

5. Special combinations: **seal calf**, the young of the seal; **seal-cloth** (see quot.); †**seal-fish** = sense 1; **seal-fur**, the skin of the Hair-seal (*Otaria*) used as a material for garments; **seal-grain**, a preparation of seal leather used in ornamental work; **seal-hole**, a hole in ice kept open by seals coming to it for air and getting out of the water through it; **seal-plush**, a fabric made to imitate seal-skin; **seal rookery** = ROOKERY 2 b; **seal-vat**, part of the apparatus used in the production of seal-oil.

c **1450** *St. Cuthbert* (Surtees) 566 Þer com a *cele calf and it toke. **1881** WARDLE *Handbk. Wild Silks India* 37 The manufacture, first accomplished in 1880 in England, of the fabric known as '*Seal cloth', which consists of a Tusser silk plush woven into a cotton back. *c* **1420** *Durham Acc. Rolls* (Surtees) 57 In j *Selfysh empt. per Celerarium, 3s. 4d. **1661** J. CHILDREY *Brit. Baconica* 160 Certain rocks, about which the Seal-fishes meet together. **1894** 'J. S. WINTER' *Red Coats* 121 The pitmen could afford to buy costly *seal-fur coats for their spouses. **1906** *Westm. Gaz.* 5 Dec. 10/2 A new series of white *seal-grain tablet calendars. **1895** KIPLING *2nd Jungle Bk.* 169 The new *seal-holes are not two days' distant. **1974** R. ADAMS *Shardik* iii. 22 He crouched and watched, vigilant as an Eskimo at a seal-hole. **1896** *Westm. Gaz.* 24 Sept. 3/2 An abomination of former times, a fabric known as '*seal plush'. **1901** *Daily Colonist* (Victoria, B.C.) 9 Oct. 8/3 That the contention..that the seal herds in the Behring Sea are decreasing is not being borne out by fact, is shown by recent advices from the *seal rookeries in the Pribyloffs. **1974** G. JENKINS *Bridge of Magpies* iii. 46 Possession [Island] was as inviting as a seal rookery—and as smelly. **1853** S. G. ARCHIBALD in Ure *Dict. Arts* II. 590 The *seal-vat consists of what are termed the crib and pan.

seal (siːl), *sb.*[2] Forms: 3–5 sel, seel, 3, 5 ceel, 3–6 sele, 3–4, 6 seile, 3, 5–6 seil, 4 sehel, cel, ceale, 4–5 sell, cele, seeal, 4–6 seele, seell, sealle, selle, 4–7 seale, 5 seaul, sill, 5–6 seyl, 5–7 seill, 5, 7 seall, 6 ceall, seyalle, *Sc.* sayll, 3– seal. [a. OF. *seel* (mod.F. *sceau*) = Pr. *selh-s*, Sp. *sello* (also in learned form *sigilo*), Pg. *sello* (also *sigillo*), It. *suggello* (also *sigillo*):—L. *sigillum* (in classical Latin only in plural), small picture, engraved figure, seal, dim. of *signum*: see SIGN *sb.*

The Latin word was at various periods adopted into several Teut. langs.: Goth. *siglō* neut., MHG. *sigel* masc. (mod.G. *siegel* neut.), MLG., MDu. *segel* (LG. *segel*, Du. *zegel* neut.), Sw. *sigill* neut., Da. *segl*, Icel. *sigli* neut. A compound form of the same meaning occurs in OE. *insegel* (see INSEIL *sb.*) = OHG. *insigili*. The OE. *siȝ(e)l* brooch (cf. OHG. *sigilla* 'lunula'), *siȝ(e)le* neut., necklace (= ON. *sigli*) are, in spite of the difference of sense, prob. connected with some early Teut. adopted form of L. *sigillum*.]

1. a. A device (e.g. a heraldic or emblematic design, a letter, word, or sentence) impressed on a piece of wax or other plastic material adhering or attached by cords or parchment slips to a document as evidence of authenticity or attestation; also, the piece of wax, etc. bearing this impressed device.

In modern (legal) practice the seal is often represented by a coloured wafer following the signature of each of the parties.

Leaden seals were used by the Popes, the Eastern Emperors, and certain other high dignitaries.

1258 *Charter of Hen. III* (Bodl. MS.) in *Phil. Soc. Trans.* 1880–1, 174* We senden ȝew þis writ open, sened wiþ vre seel. *c* **1290** *Beket* 627 in *S. Eng. Leg.* I. 124 Þe oþere bischopus al-so On þis chartre heore seles sette. *c* **1386** CHAUCER *Pardoner's Prol.* 9 And thanne my bulles shewe I alle and some Our lige lordes seel on my patente. **1428** *E.E. Wills* (1882) 79 On this my present testament I haue put my seal. **1497** *Certificate* in *Surtees Misc.* (1890) 51 In witnes herof,..we have put our seaulx. **1500–20** DUNBAR *Poems* xliii. 40 With expeditioun And full conditioun, Thair seilis ar to pendit. **1596** SHAKS. *Merch. V.* IV. i. 139 Till thou canst raile the seale from off my bond Thou but offend'st thy Lungs to speake so loud. **1644** EVELYN *Diary* 21 Apr., The University is..divided now..into that of four nations,.. who have each their respective protectors, severall officers, Treasurers, Consuls, Seales. **1728** CHAMBERS *Cycl.* s.v. *Bull*, Golden Bull..on the backside of it there are several knots of black and yellow silk; to which hangs a bull, or seal of gold. **1819–22** SHELLEY *Chas. I*, ii. 196 Let there be No seal on it, except my kingly word And honour as I am a gentleman. **1845** S. AUSTIN *Ranke's Hist. Ref.* v. ii. III. 49 As a proof, he subjoined Friedemann's letter and seal.

b. *fig.* A token or symbol of a covenant; something that authenticates or confirms; a final addition which completes and secures.

In allusion to 1 Cor. ix. 2, some of the Evangelical divines of the 19th c. were accustomed to speak of a preacher or a pastor as having 'many seals to his ministry' (i.e. persons converted through his preaching). The expression was often quoted derisively as an example of sectarian jargon.

c **1230** [see SEAL *v.*[1] 2]. **1526** TINDALE *1 Cor.* ix. 2 For the seale off myne Apostleshippe are ye in the lorde. **1590** SHAKS. *Mids. N.* III. ii. 144 O let me kisse This Princesse of pure white, this seale of blisse. **1594** NASHE *Unfort. Trav.* Wks. 1904 II. 325 To sweare and forsweare, and commit Iulian-like violence on the highest seales of religion. **1615** BEDWELL *Moham. Impost.* III. § 105 Iohn..was the last of the Prophets, & the seale of them all. **1667** MILTON *P.L.* IX. 1043 There they thir fill of Love and Loves disport Took largely, of thir mutual guilt the Seale, The solace of thir sin. **1775** SHERIDAN *Rivals* v. i, The solemn engagement..puts the seal of duty to an act of love. **1853** CONYBEARE *Church Parties, Ess. Eccl. & Social* (1855) 92 *note*, A preacher is said in this [the Recordite] phraseology to be 'owned' when he makes many converts, and his converts are called his 'seals'. **1863** MACLAREN in *Macm. Mag.* Feb. 277 Let no one undervalue this source of information: it gives the seal to all experimental knowledge.

c. Phrases. (*a*) † *to set to* (*one's*) *seal* [*to* is here adv., not prep.]: to affix one's seal; *fig.* to avouch one's conviction *that* (obs.). ***to set one's seal***: to affix one's seal *to* a document; *fig.* to express one's assent *to*. (*b*) ***under*** (***one's***) ***seal***: in a document attested by one's seal.

(*a*) *a* **1300** *Cursor M.* 6889 And ilk waand þat þai þere bare He sperd wit-in þer santuare, And wrat þe nam, and sett to sele, þat man suld oþer nan bitele. *c* **1400** *Brut* II. 560 Which appoyntement truly to be kept þe kyng and the said Ambassatoures sette-to þaire seales. *c* **1450** *Mirk's Festial* 41 And for Thomas wold not sette to hys sele of þe curset lawe ..he was dampned as a traytour. **1534** TINDALE *John* iii. 33 He that hath receaved hys testimonye hath set to his seale that God is true. [*So* **1611**; *Revised Version* **1881** hath set his seal to this, that God is true.] **1659** H. MORE *Immort. Soul* II. i. (1713) 58 To this Truth Mr. Hobbs sets his seal with all willingness imaginable, or rather eagerness.

(*b*) **1451** *Rolls of Parlt.* V. 215/1 Without the assent and wille of the said [4 persons named] by writing under their seales. **1536** *Cal. Anc. Rec. Dublin* (1889) 497 Under owre setye selle. **1613** SHAKS. *Hen. VIII*, II. iv. 222 By particular consent [I] proceeded Vnder your hands and Seales.

d. †***farthing seal***, ? = QUARTER *seal*. ***fisher's*** or ***fisherman's seal*** (see FISHER[1] 7). † ***secret, secre seal, seal manual***: see those adjs. † ***seal of*** (or ***at***) ***arms***, the impression of a signet engraved with the heraldic bearing of the owner.

1399 *Rolls of Parlt.* III. 437/2 Null Drap..ne soleit ensealez estre de nul Seal appelle le Ferthyng Seal. *a* **1400–50** *Alexander* 2802 To þe þat salutis I send þe sele of myn armes. **1478** in W. G. D. Fletcher *Shropsh. Grants of Arms* (1909) 12 In wyttnesse wherof I the said King of Armes to these presentes have sette my seall of armes and signed wt my hand. **1596** NASHE *Saffron-Walden* Wks. 1905 III. 68 A little epitomizd *Bradfords Meditations*, no broader volum'd than a Seale at Armes or a blacke melancholy veluet patch. **1623** *St. Papers, Col.* 1622–4, 203 The Company's seal-at-arms is so great, they can make no use thereof, having none but hard wax.

†**e.** A letter or other document bearing a seal; a promissory note. Also, a promise attested by one's seal. *Obs.*

c **1380** WYCLIF *Wks.* (1880) 66 Ȝe to spende at rome many ȝeris & daies, to paie for selis or bullis, to plede for benefices. *c* **1470** HENRY *Wallace* x. 606, I am so boundyn with wytnes to be leill, For all Ingland I wald nocht fals my seill. **1632** MASSINGER *Maid of Hon.* v. ii, I have a seale, or two to witnesse, yet..I'll never sue you.

†**f.** A stamp, usually in lead, fastened to a piece of material as a guarantee of quality or quantity.

1480 in *Cely Papers* (1900) 55 He schawll fynd clossyd in hys lettyr the sayll of ij sarpelers wholl. **1518** *Coventry Leet-bk.* 657 Then to sett vpon hit the Olyvaunt in lede, and of the Bak of the seall the lengh of the Cloth.

†**g.** A baker's stamped mark on bread. *Obs.*

a **1400** *Old Vsages Winchester* in *Eng. Gilds* (1870) 355 And þat eueryche bakere habbe hys seal y-knowe vpon hys loff.

h. The impression of one's signet placed upon an article as evidence of a claim to possession; *fig.* a mark of ownership.

1782 MISS BURNEY *Cecilia* x. v, [He] informed her she might put her seal upon whatever she meant hereafter to claim. **1821** SHELLEY *Hellas* 703 Her citizens, imperial spirits, Rule the present from the past, On all this world of men inherits Their seal is set. **1848** DICKENS *Dombey* xlvii, The haughty and indignant passions that now claimed her for their own, and set their seal upon her brow.

i. *transf.* An impressed mark serving as visible evidence of something.

1592 GREENE *Upst. Courtier* Wks. (Grosart) XI. 253 A fat knaue with a foggie face, wherein a cup of old sack hath set a seale. **1593** LODGE *William Longbeard* A 4 b, The good woman..espieng the seales of his shame shadowed in his blushing browes, tooke hold of his gowne sleeue, praieng him to staie a little while. **1603** SHAKS. *Meas. for M.* IV. i. 6 But my kisses bring againe, bring againe, Seales of loue, but seal'd in vaine, seal'd in vaine. **1620** *Westward for Smelts* (Percy Soc.) 45 Thou hast the seales on thy face, which those creatures (called whores) doe give. **1770** LANGHORNE *Plutarch* (1879) I. 66/2 His [Lycurgus'] tomb was struck with lightning; a seal of divinity which no other man..has had, except Euripides. **1849** RUSKIN *Sev. Lamps* v. § 1. 136 Sea sands are made beautiful by their bearing the seal of the motion of the waters.

j. An impression left by the foot of an animal in soft ground or mud, esp. that of the otter.

1686 BLOME *Gentl. Recr.* II. 100 The Mark or Seal of an Otter. **1735** SOMERVILLE *Chase* IV. 397 Ah on that yielding Sag-bed, see, once more His Seal I view. **1875** G. C. DAVIES *Rambles Sch. Field-club* xxxvi. 271 One man had been down to the river side, to see if he could discover the 'seal', or track of an otter.

2. a. A piece of wax or some other plastic or adhesive substance (originally, and still frequently, one bearing the impression of a signet: cf. sense 1), fixed on a folded letter or document, or on a closed door or receptacle of any kind, in such a way that an opening cannot be effected without breaking it.

†*flying seal*: see FLYING *ppl. a.* 3 c.

a **1272** *Luue Ron* 194 in *O.E. Misc.* 99 Þis rym mayde ich þe sende open and wiþ-vte sel. *a* **1300** *Cursor M.* 16907 Þai did þair seles þar-apon, ar þai þeþen went. **13..** *K. Alis.* 6666 (Bodl. MS.), He braak þe seal & þe lettre seie. **1382** WYCLIF *Rev.* v. 1 And I siȝe in the riȝthalf of the sittinge vpon the troone, a book..seelid with seuen seelis. **1591** SHAKS. *Two Gent.* III. i. 139 What Letter is this same?.. Ile be so bold to breake the seale for once. **1710** SWIFT *Jrnl. to Stella* 10 Nov., I forgot to leave a gap in the last line but one for the seal, like a puppy. **1859** TENNYSON *Elaine* 1264 But Arthur spied the letter in her hand, Stoopt, took, brake seal, and read it. **1861** PALEY *Æschylus, Agamem.* 592 *note* (ed. 2) 370, διαφθείρειν σημαντήρια is to spoil or tamper with the seals affixed to the doors and store-houses in the absence of the lord.

b. *fig.* That which 'seals a person's lips', an obligation to silence, a vow of secrecy; esp. ***the seal of confession*** or ***the confessional.*** Also (often with allusion to the 'seven seals' of Rev. v. and vi.), that which prevents the understanding of Holy Scripture or some other book.

a **1300** *Cursor M.* 27444 Or for it es als vnder sel O scrift him sceud al to consail. **1526** *Pilgr. Perf.* (W. de W. 1531) 301 Put blessed lorde the seale and locke of scylence to my mouth. **1632** MASSINGER *Emp. East* III. ii, What now I must deliuer Vnder the deepest seale of secrecy. **1692** R. L'ESTRANGE *Fables* xxi. 23 A Thing that's done in Hugger-mugger, under a Seal of Secrecy and Concealment. **1781** COWPER *Conversation* 544 They..wanting him to loose the sacred seal, Found him as prompt as their desire was true To spread the new-born glories in their view. **1831** LOVER *Leg. & Stor. Irel.* Ser. I. 73 ''Twas under the seal of confession', said I, 'that you disclosed the deadly secret, and under that seal my lips must have been for ever closed.' **1897** 'A. HOPE' *Phroso* vii. (1905) 126 The secret was out through Constantine's fault, not hers, and the seal was removed from her lips.

c. ***Hermes' seal, Hermetic seal*** (see HERMES 3 a, HERMETIC *a.* 2 b).

1569 J. SANDFORD tr. *Agrippa's Van. Artes* 158 b, The foolish misteries..of the seale of Hermes,..& of infinite like trifles.

d. ***seal of relics*** [med.L. *sigillum altaris*], a stone cemented above the aperture in which relics are placed at the consecration of an altar. (The use in quot. 1843 is prob. an error.)

1843 *Ecclesiologist* Sept. III. 6 A stone Altar may be provided two ways. Either make it a plain solid mass of masonry, the slab (technically called *seal* or *table*) of black granite or marble.., or [etc.]. **1897** *Catholic Dict.* (ed. 5) 238/1 The consecration endures till the altar-stone is broken or the seal of relics broken.

3. a. An engraved stamp of metal or other hard material used to make an impression upon wax, etc. affixed as a 'seal' (in sense 1 or 2). Cf. SIGNET.

a **1300** *Cursor M.* 557 Als prient of seel in wax es thrist, Þer in he has his licam fest. *c* **1380** WYCLIF *Sel. Wks.* III. 103 As þe tendre wex makeþ no preynte in þe seel, bot þe seel makeþ a preynt in tendere wex. **1463** *Bury Wills* (Camden) 15 A dowbill seel with two prentys. **1518** *Coventry Leet-bk.* 657 The sealles [for marking cloth] to be put in a Cofre with ij keys. **1591** LAMBARDE *Archeion* (1635) 56 And then, thus have you the Chancellor furnished with the Seale of Grace, and Seale of Common Iustice. **1600** J. PORY tr. *Leo's Africa* III. 160 Neere vnto the mint stande the gold-smiths shops, whose Consul or gouernour keepes the seale and stamps of the coine. **1770** LANGHORNE *Plutarch* (1851) I. 454/1 This seal he always wore and constantly sealed his letters with it. **1864** BOUTELL *Her. Hist. & Pop.* xxiv. 398 In taking these impressions, two dies or matrices..were employed; these were severally called the Seal and Counter-Seal. **1879** A. S. MURRAY in *Encycl. Brit.* X. 137/2 The favourite shapes [of gems] in Assyria were the cylinder pierced lengthways, and sometimes fitted with a swivel so as to be used as a seal [etc.].

fig. *c* **1386** CHAUCER *Wife's Prol.* 604 Gat tothed I was and that bicam me weel, I hadde the prente of seint Venus seel [*Cambr. MS.* seynt peterys sel]. **1670** DRYDEN *Tempest* IV. 53 He has a melting heart, and soft to all the Seals Of kindness; I will undertake for his compassion.

b. As a mark or sign of office. Chiefly ***the seals***, as the symbol of the position of Lord Chancellor or of Secretary of State.

c **1480** HENRYSON *Mor. Fab.* (S.T.S.) 1699 Syne cummis Uer quhen winter is away, The Secretar of Somer with his Seill. **1667** CHAS. II in Ellis *Orig. Lett.* Ser. II. IV. 316 As my purpose was also to say something to you concerning my taking the Seals from the Chancellor. **1710** LUTTRELL *Brief Rel.* (1857) VI. 571 A patent is passing the seales to create the marques of Kent a duke. **1775** *Brit. Chronol.* I. 3 Apr. 1704, The earl of Nottingham not being satisfied with the Queen's measures, resigned the seals as secretary of state. **1849** MACAULAY *Hist. Eng.* iv. I. 447 Sunderland.. was suffered to retain his seals. **1870** STANHOPE *Hist. Eng. 1701–13*, i. 6 The King sent to him the Earl of Jersey, with a peremptory order to return the Seals.

†**c.** The keeper of the seal of a court. (Cf. 4 b.)

1658 FANSHAW *Pract. Exch. Crt.* 102 The Seale of the Court. Is the Officer that keepeth the Seale of the Court all terme time under every Chanceller.

d. A device or inscription engraved on a seal.

1609 BIBLE (Douay) *Ecclus.* xlv. 14 A crowne of gold upon his miter graven with a seale of holines. **1610** HOLLAND *Camden's Brit.* I. (1637) 244 He used the Helme of a ship for a seale in his ring. **1818** BYRON *Juan* I. cxcviii, The seal a sunflower; '*Elle vous suit partout.*' **1851** TENNYSON *E. Morris* 105 She sent a note, the seal an *Elle vous suit*.

e. ***under the cold seal***: see quot.

1832 *M. Bacon's Abridgm. Law* (ed. 7) IV. 610 *marg. note*, Sometimes new magistrates are added under the cold seal, as it is termed; that is, their names are indorsed on the old commission, and the seal is pro formâ, applied again to the same wax.

f. A trinket, containing either an engraved stone for sealing letters, or a flat stone or piece of coloured glass in imitation of this, formerly often worn as an ornamental appendage to a watch-guard. Hence applied in plural to the bunch of trinkets of this and other shapes worn in this manner.

1837 DICKENS *Pickwick* x, A gold watch-chain, and seals, depended from his fob. **1848** THACKERAY *Bk. Snobs* xxxiv, A large plethoric man, with a bunch of seals in a large bow-windowed light waistcoat... His seals jingle as he walks.

†**g.** ***burning seal*** (Sc.): an iron for branding casks. *Obs.*

1692 in *Extracts Rec. Convent. Burghs Scot.* (1880) IV. 153 Each royall burrow that makes casks for export they are to keep ane burning sale,..and befor they be loadned the maker of the saids casks is..to call the visitor appoynted by the said toune whoe is to try the samen, and if sufficient to put the publict sale vpon them.

4. a. Great Seal. The seal (in sense 3) used for the authentication of documents of the highest importance issued in the name of the sovereign or (in a republic) of the highest executive authority; also, the impression of this on wax. Formerly also BROAD SEAL.

When England, Scotland, and Ireland were separate kingdoms, each had its own Great Seal, the custodian of which was normally the Lord High Chancellor; in England the Lord Keeper (of the Great Seal) was formerly sometimes a different person from the Chancellor, but under Q. Elizabeth the offices were united. Since the Union England and Scotland have only one Great Seal, of which the Chancellor has the custody; Ireland on the contrary has its own Great Seal, in the hands of the Irish Lord Chancellor. The Great Seal of the United States is kept by the Secretary of State.

c **1400** MAUNDEV. (1839) viii. 82, I hadde Lettres of the Soudan, with his grete Seel; and comounly other Men have but his Signett. **1432** *Rolls of Parlt.* IV. 418/2 Lettres Patentes of proteccion under his grete Seall. **1473** *Paston Lett.* III. 99 Item, the Kynge hathe sent ffor hys Great Seall. **1613** SHAKS. *Hen. VIII*, III. ii. 347 For your stubborne answer About the giuing backe the Greate Seale to vs, The King shall know it, and (no doubt) shal thanke you. **1685** BAXTER *Paraphr. N.T.* Mark xiv. 22 As the King maketh a piece of Wax to become his Great Seal, by which he conveyeth Land, Liberty and Life. **1726** SWIFT *Gulliver* I. iii, The Man Mountain shall not depart from our Dominions without our Licence under our great Seal. **1886** J. H. MIDDLETON in *Encycl. Brit.* XXI. 587/2 The great seal of the Commonwealth is a marvel of ugliness.

†**b.** *ellipt.* The custodian of the Great Seal, the Lord High Chancellor or Lord Keeper. *Obs.*

1621 ELSING *Debates Ho. Lords* (Camden) 15 Shall the Greate Seale come to the barr? First sende to him and heare his answere, before he be sent for to come to the barr. **1641** in *Fasti Aberd.* (Spalding Cl.) 153 And his majestie wills and declaires, that thir presentis sall be a sufficient warrand..to the great seill and to his majestie's heigh chancellar for appending of the said seill, without passing of any uther seills or registeris.

†**5. a.** An assembly for the purpose of witnessing the affixing of the Great Seal to documents; a sealing by the Chancellor or the Commissioners having the custody of the Great Seal. **b.** The place at which documents are sealed by the Chancellor. *Obs.*

[After F. *sceau*, 'l'action de sceller, le temps et le lieu où l'on scelle' (Littré).]

a. 1660 PEPYS *Diary* 20 Aug., Here I staid, and saw my Lord Chancellor come into his Great Hall, where wonderful how much company there was to expect him at a Seale. **1686** EVELYN *Diary* 5 May, There being a Seale it was fear'd that we should be requir'd to passe a doquett dispensing with Dr. Obadiah Walker. **1705** LUTTRELL *Brief Rel.* (1857) V. 602 This day the lord keeper held a public seal in the Middle Temple hall.

b. 1672 *Essex Papers* (1890) I. 43 By a Clause there I am forbid to intermedle in y[e] passing of any Charters to Corporacions, w[ch] for y[e] present stops that of Dundalke, for w[ch] I had granted a Warr[t], and it now stays at y[e] Seale til I can receive some directions from y[r] Lo[p].

†**6.** = BUTTON 2 c. *Obs.*

1611 COTGR. s.v. *Bosse*, The first putting out of a deeres head formerly cast; which our wood-men call, if it bee a red deeres, the burle, or seale.

7. *techn.* (transferred use of 2.) **a.** = *dip-pipe* (DIP *sb.* 11). **b.** The quantity of water or tar left in the dip-pipe for preventing the escape of gas. **c.** A small quantity of water left in a trap to prevent the escape of foul air from a sewer or drain. **d.** *gen.* Any means of preventing the passage of gas or liquid into or out of something, esp. at a place where two surfaces meet.

1853 S. HUGHES *Gas-works* 197 When the whole of the gas-holder was out of the water and hanging in air (with the exception of the water seal). **1875** KNIGHT *Dict. Mech.*, *Seal* 2. (Gas-works) a water-trap joint, as in gas-works, where the gas is drawn or forced beneath a plate, whose lower edge is beneath the level of the water in the tar-well. **1877** W. RICHARDS *Manuf. Coal Gas* 172 In estimating the capacity of a tank and its corresponding holder, due allowance must be made for the height of the dip or seal. *Ibid.* 210 An argument raised against telescopic gasholders is the liability of the water forming the lute, or seal, to freeze. *a* **1884** KNIGHT *Dict. Mech.* Suppl., *Seal*, an automatic valve closing a pipe. **1884** WARING in *Century Mag.* Dec. 263/1 The depth of seal is the distance from the surface of the water in the bowl to the top of the intake. **1889** —— *Sewerage* 282 This trap lost one inch of its seal in five trials out of ten. **1938** J. STRONG *Mod. Physical Lab. Practice* iv. 152 A method of making a vacuum-tight seal between metal and porcelain. **1970** K. BALL *Fiat 600, 600D Autobook* x. 118/2 The seal..is compressed on the forward stroke to prevent leakage past the plunger. **1974** *Encycl. Brit. Macropædia* XIII. 857/2 Metal-can closures operate by..vacuum seals (which rely on atmospheric pressure on the lid).

8. *attrib.* and *Comb.*: **a.** objective, as †***seal-cutter***, ***-cutting***, ***-engraver***, ***-engraving***, ***-keeper*** (also *fig.*).

1624 FLETCHER *Rule a Wife* IV. i, Brick me into that wall there for a chimney peece, And say I was one oth Cæsars, done by a *seale-cutter. **1847** LINDSAY *Chr. Art* I. p. ccix. *note*, A complete classification should include artists in wood-carving, in *cisellatura* or goldsmiths' work, in medal-casting, gem and *seal-cutting. **1786** J. WEDGWOOD *Let.* 24 June (1965) 295 The material..is..nearly as hard as agate. .. It will bear to be cut..at the *seal-engraver's lathe. **1842** FRANCIS *Dict. Arts*, etc., Seal engraver's lathe. **1948** D. DIRINGER *Alphabet* 73 From E.M.I. (thirtieth century B.C.) onwards, *seal-engraving was practised. **1560** DAUS tr. *Sleidane's Comm.* 119 *Seale keepers [orig. *sigilliferi*], Notaries, and such other lyke. **1848** THACKERAY *Van. Fair* xv, Why should he not declare him-self..seal-keeper of that young woman's conscience?

b. Special combinations: **seal-bag**, the case in which the official seals were formerly kept (*Cent. Dict.* 1891); **seal-cup**, in gas-works, the receptacle for tar or water in a seal or dip-pipe: **seal-cylinder** = CYLINDER *sb.* 4 a; †**seal-day** (*Guernsey*), a date fixed for the meeting of a State Council at which official papers received the seal; **seal-flower**, the plant *Dicentra spectabilis* (Miller *Plant-n.* 1884); **seal-lock**, a lock fitted with a 'seal' (often a small square of glass) which must be broken before the lock can be opened; **seal-master**, an official whose duty was to affix a seal to textile fabrics as a guarantee of the standard of excellence, etc.; †**seal-office** = sense 5 b, also *allusively*; **seal-pipe**, in gas-works, = *dip-pipe*; **seal-press**, a machine for embossing a device upon paper or other soft material (Knight *Dict. Mech.* 1875); **seal-ring**, a finger ring bearing a seal (cf. SIGNET *sb.* 1); **seal-stamp** = *seal-press*; **seal-stone**, a precious stone bearing an engraved device; **seal-top** *a.*, (of a spoon) having the handle finished with a seal (also ellipt. as *sb.*); †**seal-wax** = SEALING WAX; †**seal-work**, ornamentation resembling that of a seal; **seal-wort**, (*a*) *Sagina procumbens*; (*b*) = SOLOMON'S SEAL (*Polygonatum*).

1872 W. C. HOLMES & CO. *Manag. Gas Works* 108 Care should be taken to keep the *seal-cups of telescopic gas-holders..free from ice. **1874** KNIGHT *Dict. Mech.* s.v. *Dip-pipe*, The seal-cup is charged with tar. **1871** P. SMITH *Anc. Hist. East* xvi. §10 (1881) 339 fig., *Seal-cylinder on metal axis. **1682** WARBURTON *Hist. Guernsey* (1822) 93 At the next *seal-day..it may be sealed. **1871** *Patent* No. 1440 *Chronol. Index* 325 *Seal-lock manufacturer. **1905** *Rec. Cloth Manuf. New Mills* (S.H.S.) Introd. 75 No cloth could be sold unless it was sealed by the official *seal-master. *c* **1614** BEAUM. & FL. *Wit at Sev. Weap.* I. i, Here's first my hand, now't goes to the *Seale Office. [*Kisses her*.]. **1819** TAUNTON *Rep Cases Comm. Pleas* VII. 182 Until which hour, by the rule of Court, the seal-office ought not to be shut. **1875** KNIGHT *Dict. Mech.*, **Seal-pipe* (Gas), a pipe whose inlet or exit is beneath the surface of the water in a hydraulic main to prevent reflux of gas. **1608** MIDDLETON *Five Gallants* II. iii, My grandfather's *seal-ring. **1866** J. AYRE *Treas. Bible Knowl.* (1870) 804/2 According to Jewish writers the Hebrew women used seal rings. **1851** MAYNE REID *Scalp Hunters* xxvi, The brass *seal-stamp of the merchant's clerk. **1774** HILL *Theophr. Hist. Stones* 42 Hence the Word *Seal Stone, σφραγὶς or σφραγίδιον, became with them a common Word for what we call Gem. **1900** E. CLODD *Story of Alphabet* iii. 51 Seal-stones engraved with signs which are.. designed to convey information about their owners. **1898** *Daily News* 11 July 10/5 A 16th century *seal-top spoon. **1905** *Circle* May 35/1 An Elizabethan spoon, mark St. Catherine's wheel, £50; a 'seal-top', of the same reign, engraved L.C.F.M., £48. *c* **1714** ARBUTHNOT, etc. *Mem. M. Scribl.* I. xiv. (1741) 51 He saw his Monkey exceedingly busy in picking the *Seal-wax by little bits from a Letter. **1768** STERNE *Sent. Journ.* (1778) I. 146 (*The Letter*), La Fleur.. fetch'd sand and seal-wax. **1648** HERRICK *Hesper.*, *Temple* 63 A thin Subtile, and ductile Codlin's skin; Which o're the board is smoothly spred, With little *Seale-work Damasked. **1837** BAXTER *Brit. Phænog. Bot.* III. 199 *Sagina procumbens* ..*Seal-wort. **1863** PRIOR *Plant-n.*, Seal-wort,..the Solomon's seal.

seal, *sb.*[3] *Obs.* exc. *dial.* Also 5 **sele,** 6 **seale,** *Sc.* **seill.** [f. SEAL *v.*[2]] = SALE *sb.*[3] Also *attrib.*

c **1440** *Promp. Parv.* 452/1 Sele, horsys harneys, *arquillus*. **1530** PALSGR. 269/1 Seale horse harnesse. **1597** in *Spalding Club Misc.* (1841) I. 179 Scho tuik tua oxin, and band in on seill. **1844** H. STEPHENS *Bk. Farm* I. 135 Cattle are bound to the stake in various ways. One way is with an iron chain, commonly called a binder or seal. *Ibid.* 136 The seal-stake is placed in an inclined position to allow its top to be fastened to the wall.

seal, *sb.*[4] *Obs.* exc. *dial.* Also 6, 8–9 **sale,** 7 **seale,** 9 *Sc.* **sealh.** [See SALLOW *sb.*]

1. A willow. In Spenser: Willow twigs.

1579 SPENSER *Sheph. Cal.*, Dec. 81 Who to entrappe the fish in winding sale Was better seene, or hurtful beastes to hont? *Ibid. Gloss.*, *Sale* or *Salow*, a kind of woodde like Wyllow. **1682** *Quarter Sess. Rec.* 11 July in *N. Riding Rec. Soc.* VII. 57 For cutting and carrying away twenty seales. **1795** *Trans. Soc. Arts* XIII. 157 Seals, Black Cherry Trees, Balm of Gilead Trees. **1882** J. LUCAS *Stud. Nidderdale* 116 In Sykes Moss, most of the buried trees are sealhs, oaks, and birches.

2. A plantation of willow trees.

1794 DONALDSON *Agric. Northampt.* 34 The forest underwood, through the whole sale, or part which is cut, does not in general bring above 4*l*.

seal, *sb.*[5] *Obs.* exc. *dial.* Also 9 (*dial.*) **sale.** [Perh. repr. OE. *sæl*, *sęle* house.] (See quot. 1756.)

1756 C. LUCAS *Ess. Waters* II. 35 The houses in which the salt works are carried on..are also called Seals. **1882** MRS. CHAMBERLAIN *W. Worc. Gloss.*, *Sales*, or *Seals*, salt-works. (Droitwich.)

seal (siːl), *v.*[1] Forms: 3, 5–7 **seale,** 3 **seil,** 3–6 **sele,** 4–6 **seele,** 6 **seel,** (4 **ceel,** 4–5 **cele**), 5 *Sc.* **seyll, sell,** 6 *Sc.* **seil(l,** 6 **seall,** 5– **seal.** [a. OF. *seeler, seieler* (mod.F. *sceller*), f. *seel, seiel*: see SEAL *sb.*[2]]

I. To attest by a seal.

1. a. *trans.* To place a seal upon (a document) as evidence of genuineness, or as a mark of authoritative ratification or approval.

In legal use often coupled with *sign* or *deliver*; now chiefly in the full phrase 'signed, sealed, and delivered', indicating the complete execution of a deed.

1338 R. BRUNNE *Chron.* (1810) 29 Of him haf þei chartre seled with his seale. *a* **1400** *Old Usages Winchester* in *Eng. Gilds* (1870) 359 Myd wham men seleþ þe chartres of ffeffement of þe town. **1477** EARL RIVERS (Caxton) *Dictes* 11 Whan thou shalt commaunde eny lettres to thy klerke to be made, signe nor seale them not til thou haue ouer-seen thaim. **1592** WEST *1st Pt. Symbol.* §104 To do, suffer & make seale & deliuer al such assurances..as shal be deuised.. by the said R. **1596** SHAKS. *Merch. V.* I. iii. 146 Goe with me to a Notarie, seale me there Your single bond. **1653** EVELYN *Diary* 21 Jan., I went to London and there seal'd some of the writings of my purchase of Sayes Court. **1700** J. TYRRELL *Hist. Eng.* II. 763 The King's Charter which was formerly Sealed with Wax,..was now Sealed with Gold. **1719** DE FOE *Crusoe* II. (Globe) 465 They only desired one general Writing under my Hand for the whole, which I caused to be drawn up and sign'd and seal'd to them. **1818** CRUISE *Digest* (ed. 2) IV. 138 The deed was sealed and delivered, but no livery of seisin was given. **1855** MACAULAY *Hist. Eng.* xx. IV. 427 The Privy Council..ordered the Charter to be sealed.

absol. *c* **1470** HENRY *Wallace* x. 1148 The Bruce and he completyt furth thar bandis; Syn that samyn nycht thai sellyt with thar handis. **1596** DALRYMPLE tr. *Leslie's Hist. Scot.* II. 337 Thir to confirme, the King ilk ane seilis, and euerie ane than seilit, conforme to the Queines pleisure. **1685** EVELYN *Diary* 24 Dec., Attended by three of the Clearks of the Signet, we met and seal'd. **1692** R. L'ESTRANGE *Fables* IX. 9 Wherefore Friendships, Charities, and Kindnesses, should be well Weigh'd and Examin'd,.. before we Sign and Seal. **1818** SCOTT *Rob Roy* ix, How does Farmer Rutledge?..I hope you found him able to sign, seal, and deliver? **1825** T. HOOK *Sayings* Ser. II. *Sutherl.* (Colburn) 65 To-morrow, Sutherland, we will sign and seal.

b. *fig.* To authenticate or attest solemnly by some act compared to the affixing of a seal.

a **1600** *Satir. Poems Reform.* xix. 68 This commoun weil he luifit sa tenderlie,..His lufe to it he schew maist faithfullie, And with his blude he seillit it up at last. **1593** SHAKS. *3 Hen. VI*, V. vii. 29 The duty that I owe vnto your Maiesty, I Seale vpon the lips of this sweet Babe. **1655** SIR E. NICHOLAS in *N. Papers* (Camden) II. 275 Hee is resolued to credit nothing contrary to y[e] relation hee hath receiued, which though y[e] informer should seale with ten thousand sacraments will one day to his shame appeare notoriously false. **1761** GRAY *Williams* 6 The first in blood his infant honour seal'd.

c. To conclude, ratify, render binding (an agreement, etc.) by affixing the seals of the parties to the instrument. Also *fig.*, to ratify or clinch (a bargain) by some ceremonial act.

c **1470** HENRY *Wallace* VIII. 1567 Thai seyllyt the pes with out langar delay. **1560** DAUS tr. *Sleidane's Comm.* 105 Hereof were obligations made and sealed in the later ende of November. **1589** GREENE *Menaphon* (Arb.) 89 They plighted faith and troth, and Carmela..sealed it with a kisse. **1617** MORYSON *Itin.* III. 88 When they sell houses or lands, they bring a tun of beere or vessell of wine into the streete, and seale the bargaine by drinking with their neighbours. **1719** YOUNG *Busiris* III. i, Before the rising sun my lord arrives, To seal our vows. **1807** Crabbe *Par. Reg.* III. 968 Brides..and bridegrooms..By love or law compell'd their vows to seal. **1836** Thirlwall *Greece* xiii. II. 164 Peace was concluded, and sealed by a marriage.

d. To grant (a charter, etc.) under one's seal; †*fig.* to give (testimony, a promise, etc.) in an authoritative manner or with solemn pledges of good faith.

a **1625** Fletcher *Custom of Country* v. i, My hospitable word..Did I not Seale still to thee? **1628** Coke *On Litt.* §534 And as to the disseisee who sealed the same Deed, this shall enure but by way of confirmation. **1641** Hinde *J. Bruen* xxxi. 97 The University in his youth, and the countrey in his riper age, may, and will seale him a worthy testimony for a Gentleman. **1660** Pepys *Diary* 17 Mar., This day..I did seal my will to her [my wife], whereby I did give her all that I have in the world.

e. To impose (an obligation, a penalty) *on* a person in a binding manner.

1622 Massinger & Dekker *Virg. Mart.* v. ii, Who for the same cause in my presence seald His holy anger on his daughters hearts. **1633** Ford *Broken H.* III. iv, You have seal'd ioy close to my soule. **1870** C. J. Vaughan *Earnest Words* 110 A man who can speak thus..seems..to have sealed upon himself that which God never meant him for—a life of hardness and a death of despair!

f. *fig.* Of a thing or act: To attest or ratify as a seal does; to be a 'seal' of.

1648 Herrick *Hesper., Panegerick* 128 No Planke from Hallowed Altar..do's seale A curse to Thee or Thine. **1654** Z. Coke *Logick* 178 Extream Unction is a Sacrament: therefore, it sealeth spiritual graces. **1720** Pope *Iliad* xvii. 246 Then with his sable Brow he gave the Nod, That seals his Word. **1888** Lane *Illust. Notes Eng. Ch. Hist.* II. xxviii. 233 Those whose profession of Christianity had been sealed by the Sacrament of Holy Baptism.

g. To decide irrevocably (the fate of a person or thing); to complete and place beyond dispute or reversal (a victory, defeat, etc.).

1810 Shelley *Marg. Nicholson Fragm.* 9 Fate, envious Fate, has sealed my wayward destiny. **1817** —— *Revolt of Islam* iv. xxv, Why pause the victor swords to seal his overthrow? **1834** Pringle *Afr. Sk.* v. 197 A gun was levelled,..to seal the fate of this brave and generous officer. **1837** Disraeli *Venetia* III. vii, Tomorrow would seal his triumph. **1867** Smiles *Huguenots Eng.* v. (1880) 82 The massacre of Saint Bartholomew..sealed the fate of Mary Stuart.

2. a. To mark by a seal as reserved for a particular destination. Chiefly *fig.*, esp. in certain uses of New Testament origin: To designate, set apart, assign *to* another person or bind *together*, by an inviolable token or pledge.

a **1225** *St. Marher.* 4 He hit wat ful wel þe haueð iseilet to him me seolf. *c* **1230** *Hali Meid.* (MS. Bodl.) 14/128 Ant tu ..þet art iloten to him with meiðhades merke, ne brec þu nawt þet seil þet seileð inc to gederes. *c* **1374** Chaucer *Troylus* IV. 293 Syn ye Cryseyde and me han fully brought In-to your grace and boþe our hertes seled, How may ye suffre allas it be repeled? **1526** Tindale *Rev.* vii. 3 [The angel] cryed..saying: hurt not the erth..tyll I have sealed [*Wycl.* 1382 til we signe, 1388 til we marken] the seruauntes of oure god in their foreheddes. **1596** Spenser *State Irel.* Wks. (Globe) 646, I doe not blame the christening of them, for to be sealed with the marke of the Lambe..I hold it a good and gracious woorke. **1630** Shirley *Grateful Serv.* III. i, Hath some wound, Or other dire mis-fortune, seal'd him for The grave. **1827** Pollok *Course T.* x, Have not all my money, all my love, Been sealed and stamped with signature of heaven? **1865** Seeley *Ecce Homo* iv. (ed. 8) 32 God, who had sealed that [Abraham's] family for himself.

b. In allusions to Rev. vii. 5–8.

In the original passage the verb is not really construed with *of*, as in the imitative use.

[**1535** Coverdale *Rev.* vii. 5–8 Of the trybe of Iuda were sealed xij. M... Of the trybe of Beniamin were sealed xij. thousande. (Similarly **1611.**)] *a* **1637** B. Jonson *Underwoods* lxv. (*title*) An Epistle, answering to one that asked to be Sealed of the Tribe of Ben. **1906** *Macm. Mag.* Apr. 441 He was a king among us [*sc.* fishermen],—if two long seasons.. may entitle the writer of this modest tribute to account himself sealed of the tribe.

c. Among the Mormons, to set apart (a woman) by a solemn ceremony *to* a man as one of his 'spiritual wives'.

1857 J. Hyde *Mormonism* 84 (Bartlett 1860) People, according to Mormon technology, are married for time, but sealed for eternity.

3. To impress a seal upon (weights or measures) to indicate that their correctness has been tested by municipal or other lawful authority. Also, to place an official stamp on (merchandise, e.g. pieces of cloth) to certify that it is of standard measure or quality.

1467 *Coventry Leet-bk.* 334 The mesuris to be delyueryd by the comyn seriant to delyuer hem selyd with-owt money-takyng therfor. **1518** *Ibid.* 657 A Sealer to be ordeyned & sworne to stryke the Cloth & seale hit & wrete hit & fynde leed & to haue a peny for his labor. **1615** Brathwait *Strappado* 6 Those Who are appointed by their charge to know, Whether thy pots be sealed yea or no. **1862** Sala *Seven Sons* III. 4, I wonder they did not ask to see..the cat-o'-nine-tails, sealed with the seal of the visiting justice.

†**4. a.** *intr.* (Cf. 1 *absol.*) To set one's seal (*to* a document). Also *spec.* to set one's seal to or execute a promissory note; to become security *for* a person. Also *to seal under*. *Obs.*

1523 Ld. Berners *Froiss.* I. ccxiii. 263 At the request of the kyng of Englande, the frenche kyng..confyrmed and sealed to the gyfte of syr John Chandos, he to possede and to haue the same landes, as his true heritage for euer. **1596** Shaks. *Merch. V.* I. ii. 89 He borrowed a boxe of the eare of the Englishman, and swore he would pay him againe when he was able: I thinke the Frenchman became his suretie, and seald vnder for another. *Ibid.* I. iii. 172 Yes Shylocke, I will seal vnto this bond. **1632** Massinger *City Madam* I. ii, At the Academie of valour... Where they are taught the ways, Though they refuse to seal for a Duellist, How to decline a challenge. **1633** Marmion *Fine Comp.* III. iv. F 1 b, Hee is either trudging now vnto a broaker, Or to invite some new heire to a breakefast, To seale for the commodity.

†**b.** *fig.* To assent, lend one's support or authority *to* a statement or proposal. *Obs.*

1579 W. Wilkinson *Confut. Fam. Love* 10 It is sufficient ..that if they lauish out any vntruth, that I be pardoned for not sealyng vnto it. **1607** Chapman *Bussy D'Ambois* III. i. 34 *Gui.* I seale to that. **1665** Needham *Med. Medicinae* 353 And pray you, who is ignorant of this truth? Not an old woman in all the Town but will seal to it. **1683** Luttrell *Brief Rel.* (1857) I. 282, 85 were for sealing to the regulation required by his majestie, and 103 against it.

†**c.** *fig.* ? To make peace. *Obs.*

1596 Nashe *Saffron Walden* N 2, I haue not yet seald and shakt hands with him for making two such false Prophets of Saturne & Iupiter.

II. To fasten with or as with a seal.

5. a. *trans.* To fasten (a folded letter or other document) with melted wax or some other plastic material and impress a seal upon this, so that opening is impossible unless the seal is broken.

a **1225** *Ancr. R.* 388 Ase a king þet..sende his sondesmen biforen..mid lettres isealed. [*Cf. below*: ase lettres iopened.] *a* **1400** *Arthur* 272 þis lettre was celyd fast, Y-take the Messagerez on hast. *c* **1450** *Merlin* xxxi. 619 He drough oute the letter of kynge Rion that was seled with x seles roiall. **1560** Daus tr. *Sleidane's Comm.* 105 b, They wryte an aunswere to the Emperour..and delivered the same sealed to the intercessours. **1616** R. Cocks *Diary* (Hakl. Soc.) I. 113, I sealed up my packet letters for England. **1710** Swift *Jrnl. to Stella* 10 Nov., I will seal my letter early. *c* **1808** Porter *Russia & Swed.* (1813) I. ii. 14 [Nelson] desired Colonel Stewart to send some one below for a light, that he might seal his despatch. **1841** Thackeray *Gt. Hoggarty Diamond* iii, This letter, sealed with his lordship's own crown.

b. Said of the signet itself.

1848 Thackeray *Van. Fair* xxxv, The very seal that sealed it had been robbed from George's dead body as it lay on the field of battle.

c. To stamp the wax fastening (a letter) *with* something substituted for a seal.

1718 *Free-thinker* No. 108. 24 In breaking open the Second Letter, I observed it was sealed with a Thimble.

d. To fasten up (a letter, a parcel) with sealing-wax, a wafer, gum, or the like.

1818 Scott *Hrt. Midl.* xxviii, She sealed her letters carefully, and put them into the post-office with her own hand. **1848** Thackeray *Van. Fair* liii, This letter, sealed with a wafer, was despatched by one of the messengers.

6. a. To place a seal upon the opening of (a door, a chest, etc.) for security. Also with *up*.

a **1300** *Cursor M.* 17348 þai..did to sper þe dors fast, Locked bath wit-vte and in And seild wit þair seiles tuin. **1398** Trevisa *Barth. De P.R.* I. 8 And notwythstondynge that his sepulcre or graue was seelyd and syned & kept with knightes yet the thyrde day he rose in his humanite. **1592** Shaks. *Rom. & Jul.* v. ii. 11 The Searchers of the Towne.. Seal'd vp the doores, and would not let vs forth. **1865** Dickens *Mut. Fr.* I. viii, Then Mrs. Boffin and me seal up his box..and..I come down here in search of a lawyer to advise. **1891** C. Roberts *Adrift America* 56 When the train is composed mainly of empty cars, the doors are often open, and never sealed... But when they are full the little end doors are usually bolted, and the side doors sealed with a little leaden button or tag. It is an indictable offence to break these.

b. In figurative phrases, esp. ***to seal*** (a person's) ***lips***, to bind or constrain to silence or secrecy; ***to seal*** (a person's) ***eyes*** or ***ears***, to render blind or deaf, also to restrain from looking or listening. Also with *up*.

In *to seal the eyes*, this verb is not always distinguishable from the figurative use of seel *v.*

1633 Marmion *Fine Comp.* II. ii. E 4 b, I would seale my eares, Deafe as the sea, to shiprack't marriners. **1700** Dryden *Sigism. & Guisc.* 214 Sleep did his office soon, and sealed his sight. **1782** Miss Burney *Cecilia* I. viii, I make it quite a principle to seal up my lips the moment I perceive him. **1814** Byron *Lara* II. xxii, And seal'd is now each lip that could have told. **1864** Browning *J. Lee's Wife* IV. iii, Seal my sense up for your sake? **1888** *Sat. Rev.* 4 Feb. 140/1 The two Ruthvens' mouths were thus sealed for ever.

7. a. To place in a receptacle secured by a seal.

c **1420** *Brut* 355 þay waged batayle & cast doun her glowes; & þanne þey were take vp and seled, and the day & þe place of batayle assygned at Couyntre. **1530** Palsgr. 708/2, I have sent him all his writynges sealed in a bagge. *a* **1547** in J. R. Boyle *Hedon* (1875) App. 81 Thover plus of money..shalbe bagged and seallyde with xij[th] sealis.

b. *Chess.* ***to seal a move.*** Of a player in a match or tournament: To place in a sealed envelope a statement of the move he intends to make when the game is resumed after an adjournment.

1891 *Daily News* 16 Jan. 2/4 [This] move was sealed by Mr. Gunsberg at the adjournment. It is worthy of note that so far Mr. Steinitz has not sealed a move.

8. a. To close (a vessel, an aperture, etc.) securely by placing a coating of wax, cement, or lead, over the orifice, or, in wider sense, by any kind of fastening that must be broken before access can be obtained. ***to seal hermetically***: see the adv.

1661 in T. Birch *Hist. Roy. Soc.* (1756) I. 54 The spirit of wine must be the highest rectified. It will do better in a bolt-head sealed up hermetically. **1683** K. Digby *Chymical Secrets* 32 Then Seal it Hermetically. **1853** S. Hughes *Gas-works* 195 The cylinder..may be described as a cylinder inverted over a cistern of water, both the inlet and outlet pipes having their orifices above the surface of the water, so that the gas is hermetically sealed up within the holder, and can only escape through the outlet-pipe. **1877** W. Richards *Manuf. Coal Gas* 210 No ill effects are experienced—at least, so long as the holder remains sealed.

b. *Surg.* To close up (a wound) with a covering that is not to be removed until healing has taken place.

1862 *Med. Times & Gaz.* 6 Dec. 601/2 July 1.—The ulcer was sealed. 4th.—Unsealed, and found to be diminished in circumference half-an-inch; re-sealed. **1863** *Lancet* 8 Aug. 177/2. **1879** *St. George's Hosp. Rep.* IX. 659 Another method of practice handed down from very ancient times.. is to seal up the wound.

c. To render (a surface of wood, etc.) impervious by the application of a special coating.

1940 H. T. Davey *Wood Finishing* xvii. 202 When dealing with inlays it is best to seal them with shellac before attempting to spray. **1958** *Listener* 18 Dec. 1055/2 If you still want a glossy finish, you must seal the hard-board first, and the easiest way of doing that is to apply a thin coat of plastic emulsion paint. **1977** *Reader's Digest Bk. Do-It-Yourself Skills & Techniques* iv. 140/3 Some porous timbers may require two light coats, but do not apply any more than is needed to seal the surface.

d. To prevent access to and egress from (an area or space); to close (entrances) for this purpose. Usu. with *off*.

1931 *Industr. & Engin. Chem.* (Analytical Ed.) 15 Oct. 349/2 The tube is immersed in liquid air, and when the gasoline is frozen, the area *B* is sealed off. **1946** A. Vagts *Landing Operations* IV. lix. 775 The Germans..concluded that they must try to seal off the Cotentin at its base. **1948** *Sci. News* VII. 44 For the moment, treated areas are being 'sealed' by the total removal of all bush within a two-miles belt, and a watch is being kept to see what happens to the small remaining fly population. **1974** 'M. Innes' *Mysterious Commission* xi. 99 This cellarage had..been boarded over and sealed off from the studio. **1981** E. Clark *Send in Lions* v. 53 The search..began immediately. Air and sea ports were sealed.

9. a. To fasten *on* or *down* with wax or cement.

1665 Hooke *Microgr.* 38 When I have thus filled it, I can very easily in the..flame of a Lamp seal and joyn on the head of it. **1739** Lady M. W. Montagu *Let. to C'tess Pomfret* 10 Oct. (1893) II. 47 A gnat had saluted one of my eyes so roughly that it was for two days absolutely sealed down. **1769** Bancroft *Guiana* 219 The glass is then to be filled with rum, and the cork sealed down, to prevent its exhalation.

b. *fig.* To fasten, fix immoveably.

a **1661** Fuller *Worthies, M'sex* (1662) II. 189 Otherwise the hot Sun arising, sealeth (to use the Husbandmans Phrase) the Mildew upon the Straw. **1849** M. Arnold *Forsaken Merman* 82 But, ah, she gave me never a look, For her eyes were sealed to the holy book.

c. *intr.* To apply wax, etc. in fastening.

1894 Bottone *Electr. Instr.* 191 He then immediately seals all round the cork..with good red sealing wax.

10. *Building. trans.* To secure in position in a wall by means of mortar, cement, etc. [So F. *sceller*.]

1662 J. Davies tr. *Olearius' Voy. Ambass.* 242 Thence we were brought to the Kitchin... The great Cauldrons were all set in a row, and seal'd within the Wall.

11. *transf.* To enclose, shut *up* within impenetrable barriers. Also, to confine so as to prevent access or egress, and with *off*.

1667 Milton *P.L.* v. 966 If from this houre Within these hallowd limits thou appeer, Back to th' infernal pit I drag thee chaind, And Seale thee so, as henceforth not to scorne The facil gates of hell too slightly barrd. **1850** Tennyson *In Mem.* lv, Shall men..Who loved, who suffer'd countless ills, Who battled for the True, the Just, Be blown about the desert dust, Or seal'd within the iron hills? **1853** Kane *Grinnell Exp.* xxi. (1856) 162 In case we should lose our vessels or become sealed up in permanent ice. **1926** R. W. Lawson tr. *Hevesy & Paneth's Man. Radioactivity* i. 2 If we seal off 1·3138 gm. $RACl_2$..in an evacuated tube. **1940** W. Faulkner *Hamlet* II. i. 140 We sealed it up in a asbestos matchbox. **1946** A. Vagts *Landing Operations* IV. lix. 774 The choice facing Rundstedt and Rommel was between an attempt to throw the Allies back into the sea.., or sealing them off in the Cotentin.

†**III. 12. a.** *trans.* To impress (a mark) *upon*. **b.** *intr.* To make marks like those on a seal. *Obs.*

a. *a* **1225** *St. Marher.* 5 He haueð his merke on me iseilet. *a* **1585** Montgomerie *Flyting* 100 The castell ȝee weir well seiled on ȝour shoulder.

b. 1567 Maplet *Gr. Forest* 20 b, That which is grauen or by any wyse sealed vppon.

seal (siːl), *v.*[2] *dial.* [Specific use of OE. *sǽlan* to bind with a rope, f. *sál* rope (= OS. *sêl*, Du. *zeel*, OHG. *sâl*, mod.G. *seil*, ON. *seil*). Cf. Sw. *sela* to harness.] *trans.* 'To bind or fasten (cattle) in their stalls' (E.D.D.).

1633 in *J. Webster's Displ. Witchcraft* (1677) 348 His Father bad him go and fetch home two Kine to seal. **1729** P. Walkden *Diary* (1866) 61 Seeing her like for calving before morning, we brought her up and sealed her. *a* **1843** Southey *Comm.-pl. Bk.* (1851) IV. 552 As the wife of E. Fearnley was sealing up the cows [etc.].

seal (siːl), *v.*[3] [f. seal *sb.*[1]] *intr.* To hunt for seals.

1828 P. Cunningham *N.S. Wales* (ed. 3) II. 66 Now we have four vessels constantly whaling; six sealing. **1891** *Times* 27 Jan. 7/1 The claims of the Victoria sealers for compensation in consequence of their not being permitted to seal in the Behring sea.

sealable ('siːləb(ə)l), *a. rare.* [f. SEAL *v.*[1] + -ABLE.] That can be or requires to be sealed. Also, †suitable for use in sealing.

1477 *Rolls of Parlt.* VI. 190/2 That in the Citee of London.., such Clothes sealeable, be sealed with Leede as it hath be accustumed. **1656** BLOUNT *Glossogr., Sigillative*, sealable. **1979** *Nature* 19 Apr. p. xiv/2 The processing of liquids in sealable glass containers.

sealant ('siːlənt). [f. SEAL *v.*[1] + -ANT[1].] A substance designed to seal a surface or container against the passage of a gas or liquid; a material used to fill up cracks.

1945 *Materials & Methods* XXII. 1750 (*caption*) A bronze flame thrower part which required pressure tightness and chemical resistance on the part of the sealant. **1954** *Wall St. Jrnl.* 13 July 8/2 Goodrich tires have a further sealant—an extra layer of butyl in a gummy form which flows into and seals a puncture after the puncturing object is removed. **1966** T. PYNCHON *Crying of Lot 49* ii. 26 Barbed wire again gave way to the familiar parade of.. sealant makers, bottled gas works,.. and whatever. **1971** *Good Motoring* Sept. 4/2 The Beetle, a 'standard' model which has done about 100,000 miles on the road, was fitted with.. a magneto and sealant round doors and body. **1978** S. S. PENG *Coal Mine Ground Control* xii. 417 Mine sealant sprayed in a thin coating on the roof and rib not only strengthens.. but also seals the surface from the wet-dry cycles of the ventilated air.

sealapack, var. SILLAPAK.

'sea-lark. [LARK *sb.*[1] Cf. mod.L. *alauda marina*, F. *alouette de mer*, G. *seelerche, meerlerche.*]

1. A local name for various small birds frequenting the sea-shore, as (*a*) the ringed plover, *Ægialitis hiaticula*; (*b*) various sandpipers, as the dunlin, *Tringa alpina*, and the sanderling, *Calidris arenaria*; (*c*) the turnstone, *Strepsilas interpres*; (*d*) the sea-titling or rock-pipit, *Anthus obscurus*.

1602 CAREW *Cornwall* I. 35 Amongst the first sort, we reckon the Dip-chicke.. Coots, Sanderlings, Sea-larkes [etc.]. *a* **1672** WILLUGHBY *Ornith.* (1676) 230 *Charadrius sive Hiaticula*. The Sea-Lark. **1774** GOLDSM. *Nat. Hist.* (1824) II. 376 With bills very short—the Lapwing,.. the Turnstone, and the Sea-lark. **1893** NEWTON *Dict. Birds* 512 Sand-Lark and Sea-Lark are likewise names often given to some of the smaller members of the *Limicolæ*.

†**2.** The smooth blenny, *Pholis lævis*. *Obs.*

1694 MOTTEUX *Rabelais* IV. iii, A Sea-Lark.. is a Fish.. with cartilaginous Wings.. by the means of which, I have seen them fly about three Fathom above Water. **1740** R. BROOKES *Art Angling* II. xix. 124 The Sea-Lark or Bulcard.

'sea-law. A law relating to the duties and rights of persons on the seas. Chiefly in *plural*, applied by writers of the 16th and succeeding centuries to certain mediæval collections of customary laws relating to maritime affairs, esp. the Laws of Wisby, relating to the North Sea and the Baltic, and the Laws of Oléron, relating to the Atlantic.

1613 W. WELWOD (*title*) An Abridgement of all Sea-Lawes. **1664** EXTON *Maritime Dicæologie* I. iii. 13 Dionysius ascribeth the first making of Sea-laws to the Phenicians. **1909** W. ASHBURNER (*title*) The Rhodian Sea-Law.

sea-lawyer.

1. A shark, the tiger-shark. Also the grey or mangrove snapper.

1811 *Lex Balatron., Sea Lawyer*, a shark. **1876** GOODE *Catal. Fishes Bermudas* 54 *Lutjanus Caxis*... Gray Snapper... Its extreme cunning.. has gained it the soubriquet of 'Sea Lawyer'.

2. An argumentative sailor (see quot. 1867).

1829 W. N. GLASCOCK *Sailors & Saints* I. ii. 31 What tack are we on now?—got hold of a sea-lawyer it seems. **1848** C. C. CLIFFORD *Aristoph. Frogs* 37 But now they are sea-lawyers every one, And when you bid them pull, they do demur. **1867** SMYTH *Sailor's Word-bk., Sea-lawyer*, an idle litigious 'long-shorer, more given to question orders than to obey them. One of the pests of the navy as well as of the mercantile marine. **1873** [see *pleasure-navy* s.v. PLEASURE *sb.* 6 a]. **1953** DYLAN THOMAS *Under Milk Wood* (1954) 4 Alfred Pomeroy Jones, sealawyer, born in Mumbles. **1967** A. DUBUS *Lieutenant* iii. 78 Forget about this sea lawyer business and face your Goddamn punishment like a man.

sealchie, -kie ('siːlxɪ, 'siːlkɪ). *Orkney* and *Shetland*. Forms: 6 selchie, 8– selkie, 9 selky, selchy, sealkie, sealchie, saelkie, silkey, 9– silkie, silky. [dim. form of *sealgh* SEAL *sb.*[1]] = SEAL *sb.*[1] Also, in folklore, a creature or spirit having the appearance of a seal; *spec.* one able to assume human form.

c **1550** MONRO *Descr. Hebrides* (1774) 29 Ane ile callit Ellan Askerin,.. guid for fishing and slaughter of selchies. **1744** PRESTON *Zetland* in *Phil. Trans.* XLIII. 61 There are many Otters, which they call Tikes; and Seals, which they call Selkies. **1822** SCOTT *Pirate* xxviii, Our kinswoman has got a pretty seal, too—Here, sealchie, my man. **1852** in *Proc. Soc. Antiquaries Scotl.* I. 88, I am a man, upo' the lan' An' I am a Silkie in the sea. **1856** E. EDMONDSTON *Sk. & Tales Shetland Islands* vii. 80 The seal.. retired to the neighbourhood.. where a mermaid had her abode. The latter.. asked if she could help him. *Selkie* imagined she might, but only by regaining for him.. the covering of which he had been so ruthlessly bereft. **1888** MRS. SAXBY *Lads of Lunda* 90 Gibbie is no a sealkie, nae mair is Gibbie a cal-loo. **1899** J. SPENCE *Shetland Folk-lore* 24 In old times there was an aversion to and superstitious dread of killing a *selkie* lest it should be a metamorphic Finn. **1933** J. BUCHAN *Prince of Captivity* 28 He has heard the silkies singing at dawn on farther islets than St. Kilda. **1976** K. BRIGGS *Dict. Fairies* 354 In Orkney.. the great seal, the grey seal, the crested seal and others, are called 'the selkie folk' because it is believed that their natural form is human, that they live in an underwater world.. and put on seal-skins and the appearance of seals to enable them to pass through the waters from one region of air to another.

sealed (siːld), *ppl. a.* [f. SEAL *v.*[1] + -ED[1].]

1. a. Bearing the impression of a signet in wax (or other material), as evidence or guarantee of authenticity.

a **1225** *Leg. Kath.* 407, & sende iseelede writes wið his ahne kinering. *c* **1386** CHAUCER *Man of Law's T.* 736 Lo, heere the lettres seled of this thing. *c* **1511** *1st Eng. Bk. Amer.* (Arb.) Introd. 32/1 Also certefye yow with our lettres sealed. **1602** SHAKS. *Ham.* I. i. 87 A Seal'd Compact, Well ratified by Law, and Heraldrie. **1654** SIR E. NICHOLAS in *N. Papers* (Camden) II. 263 Wee have had much talke in Paris upon a project of sealed paper, wherein all contracts and legall busines should be written. **1905** *Daily Chron.* 29 June 2/2 Spanish 'sealed' bonds.. were better at the close.

b. Of weights and measures: Stamped with a mark affixed by a duly appointed officer as a guarantee of accuracy.

1522 *Coventry Leet-bk.* 683 Ordained that all bruers & Typlers order them-selffe to sell ther ale with Sealyd Mesures soche as byn ordenyd. **1573** TUSSER *Husb.* (1878) 38 Beame, scales, with the weights, that be sealed and true.

c. *fig.*

a **1619** FOTHERBY *Atheom.* II. xi. §4 (1622) 318 A sealed and infallible truth. **1637** RUTHERFORD *Lett.* (1664) 111 Concluded & sealed Salvation may goe through & be ended. **1664** H. MORE *Myst. Iniq.* II. II. vi. 373 Those true Members and marked or sealed Souldiers of Christ. *Ibid.*, The 144 thousand sealed Servants of God.

†**d.** ***sealed earth*** [med.L. *terra sigillata*, Gr. σφραγίς, σφραγῖτις]: a medicinal earth found in the Island of Lemnos, believed to possess antitoxic properties, sold by apothecaries in cubical blocks bearing a stamp, formerly an impression of the head of Artemis. Also any earth resembling this, in appearance or properties. *Obs.*

1526 *Grete Herball* ccccxliv. (1529) Z v, Sealed erthe is of grete vertue to staunche. **1693** *Phil. Trans.* XVII. 932 Our Author takes notice of Nine sorts of sealed Earths, which he hath observed to be sold by the Drugists of London, under the Title of *Terra Sigillata*. **1762** tr. *Busching's Syst. Geog.* V. 415 The principal of these are its good clay and sealed earth, as also its silver.

†**e.** ***sealed porter***: a porter having the sealed licence of one of the companies of porters. *Obs.*

1625 B. JONSON *Staple of N.* v. iii, I know he was a Porter, And a seal'd Porter for he bore the badge On brest I am sure.

f. *Nat. Hist.* In specific names: Bearing a mark resembling a seal.

1803 SHAW *Gen. Zool.* IV. 474 Sealed Sparus, *Sparus Sigillatus*.. marked on each side by a longitudinal paler stripe and a yellow-red ellipse behind each eye.

g. sealed book: any of the printed copies of the authentic Book of Common Prayer of 1662 certified under the Great Seal and deposited as a standard in Cathedrals and Collegiate Churches. (To be distinguished from the Annexed Book, which is the MS. copy of the Book of Common Prayer annexed to the official copy of the Act of Uniformity of 1662 preserved in the House of Lords.)

1710 NICHOLLS (*title*) A Comment on the Book of Common Prayer... The text of the whole being compared and amended according to the sealed Books. **1849** STEPHENS (*title*) The Book of Common Prayer... The text taken from the Sealed Book for the Chancery and collated with the Sealed Books for the King's Bench [etc.].

h. sealed pattern: in British military and naval use, a pattern (e.g. of a weapon or other article of equipment) accepted by the War Office or the Admiralty.

1850 [see *bull's wool, bullswool* s.v. BULL *sb.*[1] 11]. **1902** *Words of Eyewitness* 233 A useful lot, thinks Colonel Jones, but somewhat of an anxiety to his sealed-pattern soldier's mind.

i. ***Sealed Knot***, the name of an organization which re-enacts battles of the English Civil War for pleasure and charitable purposes.

The name is taken from a secret Royalist organization of the mid-seventeenth-century dedicated to the Restoration of the Stuart line.

1971 *Certificate of Incorporation* No. 1014700, I hereby certify that *The Sealed Knot* Limited is this day incorporated under the Companies Acts 1948 to 1967 and that the Company is limited. Given under my hand at London the 17th June 1971. **1976** A. PRICE *War Game* I. iii. 71 There are a number of these Civil War groups—the Sealed Knot was the first one. **1978** R. WESTALL *Devil on Road* ii. 7 I'd heard about the Sealed Knot. Guys.. poncing around in Cavalier gear, losing the Civil War all over again.

2. a. Fastened with a seal; closed in such a manner that access (to the contents) is impossible without breaking the fastening. ***sealed orders***: written directions given to the commander of a vessel concerning the destination of a voyage, which are not to be opened until the vessel has left port. ***sealed verdict***: a verdict delivered in a sealed packet in the absence of a judge. Also of a railway train or carriage: closed to entry or exit, or admitting restricted movement, during its journey (with allusion to Lenin's passage from Finland to Russia in 1917 in a train 'sealed' to prevent contact with German citizens).

a **1400–50** *Alexander* 5100 þan sendis scho to him sandismen with selid lettris. *c* **1450** *Mirour Saluacioun* (Roxb.) 2 And eke yᵉ seled welle [*Song Sol.* iv. 12].. and Balaam sterre. **1611** BIBLE *Transl. Pref.* 4 That person mentioned by Esay, to whom when a sealed booke was deliuered [etc.]. **1615** R. COCKS *Diary* (Hakl. Soc.) I. 89 He thought that Capt. Speck would be content to let hym carry our sealed letters. **1857** MILLER *Elem. Chem., Org.* (1862) 176 Berthelot found that by exposing the alcohol and the acid in sealed tubes for some hours [etc.]. **1872** LOWELL *Dante* Wks. 1890 IV. 237 Most men make the voyage of life as if they carried sealed orders which they were not to open till they were fairly in mid-ocean. **1894** FISKE *Holiday Stories* (1900) 38 Judge Gedney says that you can bring in a sealed verdict without waiting for him. **1949** *Radio Times* 15 July 3/1 We took a sealed train to Avonmouth, a crowded troopship out into the Atlantic. **1975** M. PEARSON *Sealed Train* vi. 90 The sealed carriage and its baggage wagon were.. drawn backward toward Switzerland. *Ibid.* 94 As the Sealed Train steamed north, the Kaiser's troops were striving.. to check the new Allied offensive. **1979** O. SELA *Petrograd Consignment* 159 Zinoviev.. has suggested that they travel through Germany in a sealed carriage, without stops.

b. *fig.* or in fig. context; also with ***up***. ***a sealed book***: often used predicatively of something involved in obscurity, or beyond a person's capacity to understand.

[**1611** BIBLE *Isaiah* xxix. 11 And the vision of all is become vnto you, as the wordes of a booke that is sealed.] **1814** LAMB *Let.* 29 Aug. (1888) 278 My left arm reposes on the *Excursion*. I feel what it would be in quiet. It is now a sealed book. **1818** BYRON *Juan* I. xlviii, This, too, was a seal'd book to little Juan. **1840** CARLYLE *Heroes* iii. (1841) 173 Nature with her truth remains to the bad, to the selfish and the pusillanimous, forever a sealed book. **1841** BORROW *Zincali* II. xi. III. 107 It is no longer a sealed language. **1881** O'SHAUGHNESSY *Songs of a Worker* 171 O bearer with sealed lips of all the lore Man yearns to know. **1884** W. JAMES in *Mind* IX. 201 No impression penetrates to the sealed-up sensibility. **1943** C. DAY LEWIS *Word over All* 17 Or a heightening At most of the sealed-up hour wherein we awaited What?

c. (See sense 2 c of the vb.)

1856 B. G. FERRIS *Mormons at Home* 114 (Bartlett 1860) The extra wives of the Mormons are called by some of them 'spirituals', by others sealed ones.

d. ***sealed-off***: closed so that neither access nor egress is possible.

1926 R. W. LAWSON tr. *Hevesy & Paneth's Man. Radioactivity* ii. 19 A wider evacuated tube with sealed-off ends and thick walls. **1938** *New Statesman* 19 Feb. 277/2 One is left wondering whether the town hall has sealed-off rooms, and whether the chief officials enter by different doors. **1963** B. FOZARD *Instrumentation Nucl. Reactors* iv. 42 For beta-particle measurements sealed-off tubes with thin end-windows can be used. **1978** R. LUDLUM *Holcroft Covenant* iii. 40 Are you telling me that two people got off that plane, walked through sealed-off corridors into the sealed-off, guarded customs area, and *vanished*?

e. ***sealed room*** = ***locked room*** s.v. LOCKED *ppl. a.* e. Also *absol.* in related use. (Freq. used in detective novels.)

1939 'M. INNES' *Stop Press* II. v. 286 Mr. Eliot's was distinctly not a mystery of the sealed-room type. **1944** J. D. CARR *Till Death do us Part* v. 52 If we have any clue to these sealed-room affairs, my guess is that there's the clue. **1971** A. MORICE *Death of Gay Dog* xii. 135 One victim and five suspects, all together in a sealed room, as the saying goes.

f. ***sealed-beam***: applied (usu. *attrib.*) to a motor-vehicle headlamp in which light source, reflector, and lens form a sealed, self-contained unit.

1939 *Daily Progress* (Charlottesville, Va.) 19 Aug. 4/1 The result of three years of cooperative effort by engineers.., the invention is described in a special story to The New York Times as a "sealed beam", which at once provides greatly increased range and breadth of light with stronger intensity through its high, or "country", beam and reduction of glare with increased illumination of the right side of the road with its low or "traffic" beam. **1954** [see PREFOCUSED *ppl. a.*]. **1965** *Economist* 23 Oct. p. x/1, Lucas did not adopt sealed-beam headlights.. until well after the Americans. **1972** 'S. ABBEY' *Bk. of Marina* xi. 97 Sealed-beam units form, in effect, large bulbs, each with either one or two filaments, an integral reflector and a front lens.

g. ***sealed source***: a pellet of radioactive material in a sealed capsule, used in radiotherapy and radiography.

1962 *B.S.I. News* Mar. 17/2 Radiography sealed-sources—pellets of radioactive material contained in sealed capsules. **1971** *New Scientist* 1 Apr. 26/2 The US market is estimated to be worth over $80 million a year with some ..$20 million on basic radioisotopes and sealed sources.

h. Of a road: surfaced with tar macadam, etc. Cf. TAR-SEALED *ppl. a.* Chiefly *Austral.* and *N.Z.*

1938 *Ann. Rep. Dept. Main Roads New South Wales 1937* 4 Generally, for country roads in New South Wales the sealed gravelled pavement has proved to be quite adequate. **1966** *Weekly News* (N.Z.) 5 Dec. 47/6 It was good to be back on the sealed highway. **1969** *Northern Territory News* (Darwin) *Focus '69* 11 (Advt.), Contractors for bitumen sealed surfaces across the Territory. **1977** *Weekly Times* (Melbourne) 19 Jan. 63/7 (Advt.), Situated on sealed road handy Frankston and Dandenong. **1979** B. L. C. JOHNSON *Pakistan* xii. 184/1 Roads of a high standard (sealed).. now total 27,152 km.

sea legs, *pl. jocular.* [Cf. F. *avoir le pied marin.*] In phrases, ***to have*** or ***get one's sea legs on***, ***to find one's sea legs***, to have or acquire the power of walking steadily on the deck of a ship. Also *fig.*

1712 W. ROGERS *Voy. round World* 8 They had..got their Sea-Legs. **1840** R. H. DANA *Bef. Mast* ii, In addition to all this, I had not got my 'sea legs on'. **1895** LLOYD GEORGE *Let.* 27 Mar. (1973) 83, I have got my sea legs in the House. They now listen to me with deference. **1898** BARING-GOULD *Old Eng. Home* xii. 286, I have been..a seaman for fifteen years, and have never yet found my sea-legs. **1977** *Rolling Stone* 7 Apr. 78/3 *Sailin'*, then, is a solid album by a promising singer/songwriter who is still finding her sea legs.

Hence **sea-legged** *a.*

1913 W. DE LA MARE *Peacock Pie* 109 Here is a sea-legged sailor. **1946** DYLAN THOMAS *Deaths & Entrances* 55 Goodbye to the man on the sea-legged deck.

sealer ('si:lə(r)), *sb.*[1] Forms: 4 seeler, 4, 6 seler, 5– sealer. [f. SEAL *v.*[1] + -ER[1].]

1. One who affixes a seal to a document.

1382 WYCLIF *2 Esdras* x. 1 Seler forsothe weren Neemias, Athersata [etc.]. **1485** *Rolls of Parlt.* VI. 337/2 The Sealer in the Chauncery. **1580** HOLLYBAND *Treas. Fr. Tong, Chauffecires*, sealers of patentes. **1708** *Lond. Gaz.* No. 4467/4 Complaint hath been made..that the Sealer to the Great Seal has demanded extraordinary Fees for his Attendance in the Country. **1819** TAUNTON *Rep. Cases Comm. Pleas* VII. 182 The sealer of writs is not guilty of a contempt in refusing to seal a writ on St. Luke's day. **1833** *Act 3 & 4 Will. IV*, c. 84 §2 As the Offices..of Chaff Wax and Sealer..become vacant..the Duties of such several Offices shall be performed by the said Purse-bearer.

2. †**a.** One who attaches the official mark or seal to leather or other material as evidence of quality, etc. *Obs.* **b.** An Inspector of weights and measures.

1467–8 *Rolls of Parlt.* V. 630/1 That all the seid Clothes.. be sealed by the Kyngs Awnager or Sealer. **1511–2** *Act 3 Hen. VIII*, c. 6 §1 The Alnager or Seler..shall put to every Wollen cloth..the Kynges Seales of leed. **1592** GREENE *Upst. Courtier* E ivb, Whereas your backes of al other shoulde bee best tanned, you bring them so full of horne to the market, that did you not grease the sealers of Leaden hall thoroughly in the fiste, they should neuer be sealed. **1835** *App. Munic. Corpor. Rep.* I. 431 (Barnstaple) The Sealers of Weights and Measures are appointed by the mayor and capital burgesses; they are paid by the fees charged for sealing. *Ibid.* II. 1095 (Axbridge) The office of the Ale Tasters and Leather Sealers has been long obsolete. **1858** *Rev. Statutes Wisconsin* 176 One sealer of weights and measures; and one overseer of highways.

†**3.** *fig.* One who gathers up and closes the efforts or labours of others. *Obs. rare*[−1].

1615 T. BEDWELL *Moham. Impost.* III. §106 Iohn was the sealer vp of the sayings of the Prophets.

†**4.** *slang.* (See quots.)

1688 SHADWELL *Sq. Alsatia* I. i. 7 Cheatly who has drawn in so many young Heirs, and undone so many Sealers. *Ibid. Expl. Cant, Sealer*, one that gives Bonds and Judgments for Goods and Money. **1785** GROSE *Dict. Vulgar T.*, *Sealer* or *Squeeze Wax*, one ready to give bond and judgment for goods or money.

5. One who or that which seals (SEAL *v.*[1] 8).

1881 *Instructions to Census Clerks* (1885) 58 Blacking Manufacture: Liquid:..Sealer. **1921** *Dict. Occup. Terms* (1927) §159 *Sealer, ink bottle*; seals filled bottles of ink with sealing wax or with paper seals. **1928** *Daily Express* 6 July 5/5 The machine seals the lids of special cans... Mr. A. Appleyard..and Mr. Hirst..have tested this British hand sealer scientifically. **1940** H. T. DAVEY *Wood Finishing* xvii. 199 The object of a sealer is to block the pores of the wood so as to stop the succeeding coats of lacquer sinking in. **1958** *Listener* 4 Sept. 359/2 Mix yourself some sanding sealer from starch and cellulose lacquer. **1971** *Home Preserv. Fruit & Veg.* (Min. Agric.) (ed. 13) 63 The can sealer must be cleaned thoroughly after use. **1977** *Reader's Digest Bk. Do-It-Yourself Skills & Techniques* iv. 140/2 Apply a light coat of the sealer by brush or cloth direct to the unfilled timber, working it well in.

6. *Canad.* A glass jar designed to preserve fruit, vegetables, etc.

1932 N. M. JAMIESON *Cattle in Stall* 12 Just take in a great half-gallon sealer and get it filled—for about half a dollar! **1959** *Weekend Mag.* (Montreal) 15 Aug. 39/2, I went into the fruit cellar, turned on the light and was actually picking up two quart sealers of icicle pickles. **1970** *Canad. Antiques Collector* July–Aug. 23/2 The demand for these preserving jars dwindled with the beginning of the cheap production of glass 'sealers' and the discovery of the method of canning in tins.

sealer ('si:lə(r)), *sb.*[2] [f. SEAL *v.*[3] + -ER[1].]

1. A vessel engaged in the sealing trade.

1820 W. SCORESBY *Acc. Arctic Reg.* I. 508 Many vessels equipped only as sealers, proceed annually into the Greenland Sea. **1904** *Times* 15 Aug. 4/3 The sealer Teresa is at Dutch Harbour..seized for using fire-arms..before.. season.

2. One who hunts the seal.

1770 G. CARTWRIGHT *Jrnl.* 31 Dec. (1792) I. 76 After breakfast we set off homewards, being accompanied by two of the sealers. **1825** J. F. COOPER *Lionel Lincoln* II. vi. 138 The sealers of New-England have been able to discover Terra Australis. **1842** BONNYCASTLE *Newfoundld.* II. 167 To pay the sealers, or the same men as cod-fishers, regular wages, would at present be impracticable. **1880** H. W. ELLIOTT *Rep. Seal Isl. Alaska* (1884) 164 The sealers on St. Paul..just as the season opens, invariably prophesy a bad year for seals.

sealery ('si:ləri). *rare.* [f. SEAL *sb.*[1] + -ERY.] The occupation of hunting the seal.

1895 KIPLING *2nd Jungle Bk.* 146 Coming back north.. for the musk-ox hunting and the regular winter sealery.

'**sealess**, *a. rare.* [f. SEA *sb.* + -LESS.] Having no sea, without sea.

1867 H. MACMILLAN *Bible Teach.* xv. (1870) 303 The greatest happiness of the sealess heaven.

sea-lettuce. The seaweeds *Ulva lactuca* and *U. latissima.*

1668 WILKINS *Real Char.* II. iv. §3. 71 Sea-lettice. **1732** [see LAVER *sb.*[1] 2]. **1753** *Chambers' Cycl.* Suppl., *Lactuca marina*, sea lettuce, in botany, a name used by some authors for the *lichen marinus*, commonly called oister green. **1875** *Encycl. Brit.* II. 218/2 [He] recommends the growth of sea-lettuce (*Ulva latissima*) in tanks, as suitable both for oxygenating the water and for food for the fishes.

sea-level.

1. The mean level of the surface of the sea, the mean level between high and low tide.

1806 *Gazetteer Scot.* (ed. 2) 550 The altitude of which is 1498½ feet above the sea level. **1869** E. A. PARKES *Pract. Hygiene* (ed. 3) 444 The height of the barometer at sea-level. **1894** *Nature* 26 July 293/2 The correction of the individual readings of the barometer to the sea-level.

2. A level or flat surface of the sea.

1873 M. COLLINS *Miranda* I. 168 She sat and worked, and looked across the vast sea-levels.

sealgh, sealie: see SEAL *sb.*[1], SEELY.

'**sea-light.** [LIGHT *sb.*]

†**1.** Phosphorescence seen at sea. *Obs. rare.*

1755 tr. *Pontoppidan's Nat. Hist. Norway* I. 5 A sea-light or a luminous appearance in the water, called by the Norwegians, Moor-Ild.

2. A beacon, lighthouse, or harbour-light to guide ships at sea.

1691–2 STILLINGFL. *Serm.* xxx. Wks. I. 487 It helps them to see their Folly, and like a Sea-light to a sinking Ship in a dark Night, makes those who are aboard, to behold their Misery, without helping them out of it. **1846** *Penny Cycl.* Suppl. II. 527/2 Sea-lights are commonly divided into two principal classes. **1867** MANNING *Eng. & Christendom* 164 They who destroy sea-lights are enemies of the human race.

'**sea-like**, *a.* and *adv.* [f. SEA *sb.* + -LIKE.]

A. *adj.* Resembling the sea.

1594 T. B. *La Primaud. Fr. Acad.* II. Ep. Ded., The tempestuous..waues of this sea-like worlde. **1610** HOLLAND *Camden's Brit.* I. 20 *Rapidus Garumna*, that is, the strong sealike and swift Garumna. **1776** MICKLE tr. *Camoens' Lusiad* VII. 285 Declining southward many a land they lave, And widely swelling roll the sea-like wave. **1878** H. M. STANLEY *Dark Cont.* I. xv. 403 The sea-like expanse of the Victoria Lake.

B. *adv.* After the manner of the sea.

1606 SHAKS. *Ant. & Cl.* III. xiii. 171 Our seuer'd Nauie too Haue knit againe, and Fleete, threatning most Sea-like. **1864** TENNYSON *Specimen tr. Iliad* 1 So Hector said, and sea-like roar'd his host.

'**sea-line.** [LINE *sb.*[2]]

1. The coast-line or sea-board.

a **1687** PETTY *Pol. Arith.* iv. (1690) 78 The Sea-line of England, Scotland, and Ireland, and the adjacent Islands, is about Three thousand Eight hundred Miles. **1884** W. C. SMITH *Kildrostan* I. i. 21 Oaks along the low sea-line Are greenly feathered with fern and moss.

2. The horizon, the line where sea and sky seem to meet.

1880 W. WATSON *Prince's Quest* (1892) 58 When the sealine grew O'erhazed with visible heat. **1888** STEVENSON *Across the Plains*, etc. (1892) 193 The sea-line rough as a wood with sails.

fig. *a* **1881** ROSSETTI *House of Life* x, May know The very sky and sea-line of her soul.

3. A line used at sea; (*a*) a sounding line; (*b*) a long line used in sea-fishing in deep water.

1828 *Blackw. Mag.* XXIV. 896 These passages are not cited with so vain a purpose as that of furnishing a sea-line for measuring the 'soundless deeps' of Jeremy Taylor. **1836** YARRELL *Brit. Fishes* II. 145 One mode is by deep sea-lines, called bulters, on the Cornish coast.

sealing ('si:lɪŋ), *vbl. sb.*[1] [f. SEAL *v.*[1] + -ING[1].]

1. a. The action of affixing a seal or stamp to a document as a ratification, or to a manufactured article as evidence of genuineness, measure, or quality.

1338 R. BRUNNE *Chron.* (1810) 300 For he had grantid þer to þe Chartre forto sele, & after þat selyng alle suld þei come þe barons & þe kyng, & tak of þam hard dome. **1463** *Bury Wills* (Camden) 26 Sum thrifty man..to be at the selyng. **1662** *Act 14 Chas. II*, c. 5 §2 The said Warden..shall have ..Power and Authority..to make Seales from time to time for the sealing of the same [Worsted-] Stuffs. **1818** CRUISE *Digest* (ed. 2) IV. 234 Testified by a writing under their hands and seals, attested by two or more witnesses; the attestation extending only to the sealing and delivery of the deed.

†**b.** *fig. Obs.*

1546 BALE *Eng. Votaries* I. (1560) 28b, Vowes, othes, oblygations and sealynges to the Beastes holy seruice. **1555** in Strype *Eccl. Mem.* (1721) III. App. xliii. 121 That God of his free mercy wil give us the ful sealing of his..grace.

2. a. The action of closing or fastening with a seal.

c **1375** *Sc. Leg. Saints* vii. (*Jacobus Minor*) 786 Bot Ihesus, quhene he rase fra dede,..al vnsterynge þe stekyne of þe presone & þe selynge, owte of þe can me ta. **1669** R. MONTAGU in *Buccleuch MSS.* (Hist. MSS. Comm.) I. 438 St. Alban's seemed mightily dissatisfied with this sealing up of the goods. **1884** tr. *Gaboriau's Little Old Man* v, The commissary of police was finishing the sealing-up of the cupboards in the bedroom.

b. *Surg.* The close bandaging of wounds, etc.; also the bandage.

1862 *Med. Times & Gaz.* 6 Dec. 601/2 Treatment of ulcers..by 'Sealing'. *Ibid.*, It was necessary to remove the sealing. **1863** *Lancet* 1 Aug. 148/1 The Sealing of Ulcers.

†**3.** = SEAL *sb.*[2] 1 j. *Obs. rare*[−1].

1591 COCKAINE *Treat. Hunting* D 2b, Your huntsman early in the morning..must goe to the water; and seeke for the new swaging of an Otter, and in the mud or grauell finde out the sealing of his foote.

4. a. The action of making an impression upon wax or other soft material by means of a signet.

1674 N. FAIRFAX *Bulk & Selv.* 176 Little otherwise Gods working or knowing differs from ours, as sealing or printing does from limning and drawing.

b. The impression made by such an act.

1904 *Q. Rev.* Oct. 392 Those monstrous shapes..appear in great variety on gem sealings. **1905** A. J. EVANS in *Ann. Brit. Sch. Athens* XI. 12 Among the fragmentary clay sealings..were several of religious import.

5. *Building*, etc. **a.** (See quot. and SEAL *v.*[1] 10.)

1728 CHAMBERS *Cycl.*, *Sealing*, in Architecture, the fixing a Piece of Wood or Iron in a Wall, with Plaister, Mortar, Cement, Lead, or other solid Bindings. **1823** P. NICHOLSON *Pract. Builder* 592.

b. The action or process of rendering impervious; also *concr.*, material used for this.

1955 C. JASPER *Handbk. Decorating & Painting* ii. 51 Sealing. The best form of treatment..for making the plaster suitable to receive oil paint, is to apply..alkali resisting primer. **1960** *McGraw-Hill Encycl. Sci. & Technol.* XIV. 532/2 Sealing..prevents penetration of or redissolution in subsequent finish coats. **1962** *Which? Car Suppl.* Oct. 139/2 The rubber sealing round the ventilating panes was not effective.

6. Among the Mormons: the ceremony of taking a 'spiritual' wife.

1856 B. G FERRIS *Mormons at Home* 114 (Bartlett 1860) These left-hand marriages are called sealings.

7. *attrib.* and *Comb.*, as †**sealing money**, a fee paid at the signing of a lease; **sealing-thread**, ? a thread or string laid upon, or covered with, wax before making an impression with the signet; **sealing-water**, water standing in the trap of a drain which prevents the escape of foul air from a sewer.

1599 in Fowler *Hist. C.C.C.* (O.H.S.) 350 Sometimes is noted how much beside the fine the tenants gave for *sealing mony. **1591** FLORIO *2nd Fruites* 89 Giue me some wax, some *sealing thrid, my dust box, & my seale. **1884** WARING in *Century Mag.* Dec. 260/2 The current thus produced is to carry the *sealing-water with it.

sealing ('si:lɪŋ), *vbl. sb.*[2] [f. SEAL *v.*[3] + -ING[1].] The hunting of the seal.

1839 *Southern Lit. Messenger* V. 3/1 In a few years [they] made Stonington famed for sealing. **1848** MAUNDER *Treas. Nat. Hist.* 805 *Sealing*, the operation of taking seals and curing their skins. **1870** *Daily News* 18 Apr., Sealing was exceptionally early this season.

attrib. **1786** G. CARTWRIGHT *Jrnl.* (1792) III. 237 All the sealing-posts now exhibit a very different appearance from what they originally did. **1842** JUKES *Excurs. Newfoundld.* I. 277 Captain Furneaux..killed two with his sealing-gun loaded with seal shot. **1858** GREENER *Gunnery* Advt. 2 W. G. will undertake contracts for quantities of arms..such as.. rifles or sealing guns. *Ibid.* 3 Sealing rifles. **1860** *Merc. Marine Mag.* VII. 4 Coasting, sealing, or fishing vessels. **1911** *Daily Colonist* (Victoria, B.C.) 26 Apr. 14/2 The United States expressed a willingness to compensate the owners of the sealing fleet for the loss of the industry. **1933** J. BUCHAN *Prince of Captivity* I. iii. 91 A sealing sloop had crawled up the coast as soon as spring opened the shore waters. **1977** *Time* 10 Oct. 62/1 Before he was out of his teens he had..shipped on a sealing expedition to the Bering Sea.

sealing ('si:lɪŋ), *ppl. a.* [f. SEAL *v.*[1] + -ING[2].] The seals. Usually *fig.*

c **1450** *Mirour Saluacioun* (Roxb.) 2 To make seling prove of the forsaid sothfastnes. **1682** FLAVELL *Fear* 102 The sealing graces are in you, the sealing spirit is ready..the sealing promises belong to you. **1856** RUSKIN *Mod. Paint.* III. IV. xiv. §40 It embodies in a few syllables the sealing difference between the Greek and the mediæval.

'**sealing-wax.** [f. SEALING *vbl. sb.*[1]] **a.** In early use, beeswax or a composition containing this, in later use a composition consisting of shellac, rosin, and turpentine, prepared for the purpose of receiving the impression of seals. Also *attrib.*

The modern 'sealing-wax' resembles wax in its fusibility and its plasticity when softened by heat, but its superior hardness when solidified renders it more capable of receiving a sharp and durable impression. It is usually coloured scarlet with vermilion, but black sealing wax is used for mourning, and green, blue, etc. for reasons of ornament.

13.. *Test. Christi* 143 in *Minor Poems fr. Vernon MS.* 647 þe selyng-wax was deore abouȝt,..And tempred al wiþ vermiloun Of my rede blod þat ran doun. **1580–1** *Act 23 Eliz.* c. 8 §3 Wares wrought with Waxe, as..Staff-Torches, Red Waxe or Sealing Waxe. **1694** *Phil. Trans.* XVIII. 194, I covered the Cork with Sealing-wax. **1712** tr. *Pomet's Hist. Drugs* I. 204 Black sealing Wax is..colour'd with Smoak Black. **1849** NOAD *Electricity* (ed. 3) 28 Mr. Woodward strongly recommends the covering the glass pillars..with sealing-wax varnish. **1894** BOTTONE *Electr. Instr.* 191 The top of the cork must also be well coated with sealing wax.

b. Used *attrib.*, esp. as **sealing-wax red**, to designate a bright red colour, vermilion.

1907 *Yesterday's Shopping* (1969) 156/2 These Colours Kept in Stock..Sealing wax red..Sky..Stone. **1912** MRS. P. CAMPBELL *Let.* Aug. in *B. Shaw & Mrs. Campbell* (1952) 35 The scullery maids..with their bloody nails and sealing-wax lips make my hair stand on end. **1930** [see *post-office red* s.v. POST OFFICE 3]. **1930** A. P. HERBERT *Water Gipsies* xxv. 380 Her lips were the hot sealing-wax lips which she knew he hated. **1939** *Burlington Mag.* Oct. 162/2 About 1550 the famous 'sealing-wax red' first appears on Turkish pottery. **1957** [see ISNIK].

'sea-lion.

†**1.** A kind of lobster or crab (see LION *sb.* 8).

1601 HOLLAND *Pliny* XXXII. xi. II. 452 Sea Lions, which haue cleies or armes in manner of Crabfishes, but in other respects resembling Locusts.

2. A fabulous animal. In *Her.* (see quot. 1780).

1661 TATHAM in Heath *Grocer's Comp.* (1869) 478 In the Reare.. are placed two Sea Lyons riding on the surface of the water, and on their backs two Trytons playing on retorted Pipes or Hornes antique, agreeable with the Musick of Neptune. **1780** EDMONDSON *Heraldry* II. Gloss., *Sea-lion.* The upper part is formed like that of a lion, and the lower part like the tail of a fish... Sometimes they are drawn erect, and on their tails; and then they are blazoned as follows: *Sea-lions erect on their tails.*

3. One of several large eared seals: **a.** (*a*) the largest otary of the North Pacific, *Otaria* (*Eumetopias*) *stelleri*, Steller's or the Northern sea-lion; (*b*) the Southern or Patagonian sea-lion, *Otaria jubata*; (*c*) the *Zalophus lobatus* of Australian seas, also the distinct species *Z. californianus* of the North Pacific.

1697 DAMPIER *Voy.* I. 90 The Sea Lion is a large creature about 12 or 14 foot long. **1748** *Anson's Voy.* II. i. 124 A sailor .. employed in skinning a young sea-lion. **187.** *Cassell's Nat. Hist.* II. 226 White-necked Otary, or Australian Sea-Lion [*Otaria albicollis*]. *Ibid.*, The Patagonian Sea Lion, or Cook's Otary [*Otaria jubata*]. **1880** H. W. ELLIOTT *Rep. Seal Isl. Alaska* (1884) 84 The northern sea-lion, *Eumetopias Stelleri.*

b. *transf.* [tr. G. *seelöwe.*] In full, ***Operation Sea-lion***, the code name for the German plan to invade the United Kingdom after the fall of France in the war of 1939–45. (Announced by Hitler in July 1940 and cancelled in October of that year.)

1949 W. S. CHURCHILL *Their Finest Hour* xiv. 261 Our excellent Intelligence confirmed that the operation 'Sea Lion' had been definitely ordered by Hitler. **1951** F. H. HINSLEY *Hitler's Strategy* iv. 83 In his [*sc.* Hitler's] mind 'Sea Lion' was never more than a colossal bluff. *Ibid.* x. 191 The final cancellation of operation 'Sea Lion'.. was less important for itself than as an indication of the state of mind to which Hitler had already been reduced. **1978** D. KYLE *Black Camelot* xi. 178 Heydrich.. must have obtained Raeder's copy after Sea Lion was cancelled.

Hence †**sea-lioness**, a female sea-lion. *Obs. rare.*

1750 PARSONS in *Phil. Trans.* XLVII. 111 But, if a shewman gives out, that his animal is a sea-lioness, he will easily report any other absurdity. **1771** tr. *Pernety's Voy. Malouine Isl.* (1773) 186 M. Guyot brought.. five sea-lionesses.

sea-lizard.

†**1.** Some kind of fish. *Obs. rare*$^{-1}$. [tr. L. *lacertus.*]

1601 HOLLAND *Pliny* XXXII. xi. II. 452.

2. A gasteropod of the genus *Glaucus.*

1860 G. BENNETT *Gatherings Nat. Austral.* 44 Fig. 3. The Sea Lizard (*Glaucus hexapterygius*).

3. An extinct saurian of the sea.

1859 DARWIN *Orig. Spec.* xiii. 379 The extinct gigantic sea-lizards.

sealless ('si:llɪs), *a. rare.* [f. SEAL *sb.*^{2} + -LESS.] Not bearing a seal; not possessing a seal.

1644 PRYNNE & WALKER *Fiennes's Trial* 5 The datelesse, namelesse,.. seallesse Proclamation. **1895** RASHDALL *Universities* I. 327 *note*, The Faculty of Theology continued sealless.

'sea-louse. [= L. *pediculus marīnus* (Pliny).]

1. A parasitic isopod crustacean of *Cymothoa* and allied genera; a fish-louse.

1601 HOLLAND *Pliny* XXXII. viii. II. 442 Those creepers or insects which be called sea-lice. *a* **1682** SIR T. BROWNE *Norf. Fishes* Wks. 1835 IV. 328 The gills of these fish we found beset with a kind of sea-louse. **1756** P. BROWNE *Jamaica* (1789) 393 Corephium... The Sea-Louse. This creature.. is often found sticking, like the Limpite, to the rocks. **1858** BAIRD *Cycl. Nat. Sci.* s.v. *Isopoda*, The genus *Cymothoa*.. is called the sea louse by fishermen on the coast.

2. The Molucca crab, *Limulus moluccensis.*

1681 GREW *Musæum* I. §vii. iii. 177 The Sharp-Tail'd Sea-Louse. *Pediculus marinus cauda acuta.* **1805** G. BARRY *Orkney Isl.* 310 In winter they [*sc.* Stares].. feed on what are called the sea-lice, or *cancer pulex* of Linnæus.

†**3.** A cowry. *Obs.*

1815 BURROW *Elem. Conchol.* 199 *Cypræa Pediculus* Sea Louse.

seal point. [f. SEAL *sb.*^{1} + POINT *sb.*^{1} A. 26 c.] One of the dark brown markings on the buff fur of one type of Siamese cat; also, a Siamese cat with markings of this colour. Hence **seal-pointed** *a.*

1934 P. WADE *Siamese Cat* xv. 101 Even the best Blue Pointed cannot.. equal in beauty our Seal Pointed cats. *Ibid.* 102 Let us concentrate on breeding perfect Siamese with deep seal points. **1939** I. M. MELLEN *Pract. Cat Bk.* i. 35 The adult body color of the Siamese is pale fawn.. and the seal brown, almost black ears, muzzle, tail and feet are called collectively 'points', the color described being known as seal point. *Ibid.* 39 (*heading*) Qualities of a good seal point Siamese. **1958** *Listener* 18 Sept. 410/2 The first Siamese to become a champion arrived in 1896. He was a seal point. **1966** 'K. A. SADDLER' *Gilt Edge* vi. 91 A seal point Siamese cat sneaked in. **1980** A. SCHOLEFIELD *Berlin Blind* iii. 106 He .. saw a cat. It was a beautiful sealpoint Siamese.

sealskin ('si:lskɪn), *sb.* and *a.* Forms: see SEAL *sb.*^{1}; formerly also **seal's skin.** [f. SEAL *sb.*^{1} + SKIN *sb.*] **A.** *sb.*

1. a. The skin of any of the Fur Seals, prepared for use as a garment, for the covering of a box, etc.

1325–6 *Ely Sacrist Rolls* (1907) II. 55 In selisskymys empt. ad easdem [campanas]. **1398** in J. R. Boyle *Hedon* (1875) App. 107 Et soluti pro iiij. sele skynnes pro cooperturis, vij.d. **1511–12** *Acc. Ld. High Treas. Scot.* IV. 201 The dichteyne of ane selk skyne. **1549** *Compl. Scot.* vi. 60 Tentis.. of selcht skynnis. **1594** NASHE *Unfort. Trav.* Wks. 1904 II. 316 His breast and his belly with seale skins they grated ouer. **1610** *Althorp MS.* in Simpkinson *Washingtons* (1860) App. 6, 3 hampers for the plate covered with sayle skinnes. **1631–2** *Aberd. Acc.* in *Spalding Club Miscell.* V. 149 For a trunk coverit with selches skyn. **1752** *Rec. Elgin* (1903) I. 464 Ilk dozen selch or salt watter otter skins ditto 1s. **1776** ADAM SMITH *W.N.* I. xi. I. 292 The price of raw hides is a good deal lower at present than it was a few years ago; owing probably to the taking off the duty upon seal skins. **1886** ASHBY-STERRY *Lazy Minstrel* 45 A dainty young damsel is Pearl, Beclad in the softest of seal skin.

b. Applied to textile fabrics imitating the appearance of sealskin.

1860 S. JUBB *Shoddy-trade* 53 Sealskins—These are a cloth made of mohair and other bright-haired materials. **1882** CAULFEILD & SAWARD *Dict. Needlework* 442 *Sealskin Cloth.* The yarn used for this kind of cloth is the finest kind of Mohair. *Ibid.* 450 *Silk Sealskin*, is a very beautiful patent textile, composed of Tussar Silk, and made in imitation of Sealskin Fur.

2. A garment made of sealskin.

1858 QUEEN VICTORIA *Let.* 27 Feb. in R. Fulford *Dearest Child* (1964) 62, I am so glad you find the sealskin comfortable; it is a nice warm thing. **1873** *Spectator* 8 Feb. 167 Ladies who pride themselves on their 'seal-skins', and who enjoy the comfort of them.

B. *adj.* Made of sealskin.

1769 FALCONER *Dict. Marine* (1780) L 1, The Indian's seal-skin jacket. **1837** LOCKHART *Scott* (1839) VII. 187 A pleasant sight it was to see the gallant old gentleman in his seal-skin cap and short green jacket. **1880** H. W. ELLIOTT *Rep. Seal Isl. Alaska* (1884) 80 Seal-skin sacques.

Hence **'sealskinned** *a.*

1599 NASHE *Lenten Stuffe* 66 His seale-skind riueld lippes.

sea-lungs. [tr. L. *pulmo marinus*, Gr. πλεύμων θαλάσσιος, said to be so called from the alternate contraction and expansion, as if breathing.

Cf. Sp. *pulmon marino*, 'a bright Froth in the Sea that shines' (Stevens. 1706).]

An acaleph of the CTENOPHORA.

1640 WATS *Bacon's Adv. Learn.* IV. iii. 215 Which [light] is likewise seen in the fervent froath of the Sea which they call the Sea-longs [orig. *Pulmonem marinum*]. **1653** R. G. tr. *Bacon's Hist. Winds* 234 Sea water violently stirred up with Oars, will give a light, & seem to burn, which kind of burning or light the Spaniards call the Sea-lungs. *c* **1675** SIR T. BROWNE *Misc. Tracts* (1684) 197 That passage of Pythæas mentioned by Strabo, that all the air beyond Thule is thick, condensed and gellied, looking just like Sea Lungs. [Strabo πλεύμονι θαλασσίῳ ἐοικός.] **1752** J. HILL *Hist. Anim.* 89 The Sea Lungs. This is a very singular and odd animal; it seems a mere lump, of a whitish semi-pellucid jelly. *a* **1776** J. ELLIS *Zoophytes* (1786) 175 *Alcyonium Pulmonaria.* Sea Lungs.

Sealyham ('si:lɪəm). [The name of *Sealy Ham* (House) near Haverfordwest, the home of the Edwardes family which developed the breed in the 19th cent.] A small stocky white terrier, sometimes with markings of other colours, distinguished by a thick, rough coat, drooping ears, a small, erect tail, and a square, bearded muzzle. Also *attrib.*

1894 R. B. LEE *Hist. & Descr. Mod. Dogs: Terriers* xvi. 386 There is a strain of terrier much talked about of late known as the Sealy Ham. **1907** [see *Jack Russell* (*terrier*) s.v. JACK *sb.*^{1} 38]. **1917** W. J. LOCKE *Red Planet* xix. 250 You remember Jingo, the Sealyham. **1924** [see CAIRN 2]. **1930** R. H. MOTTRAM *Europa's Beast* x. 241 The Sealyham.. merely slept. **1954** M. K. WILSON tr. *Lorenz's Man meets Dog* viii. 79 A Sealyham's love of fun, and his fidelity to his master can prove a real moral support to a melancholy type of person. **1966** J. BETJEMAN *High & Low* 12 Where's Kathleen Stokes with her Sealyhams? **1979** R. RENDELL *Means of Evil* 153 He emerged from the front door with two Sealyhams on a lead.

seam (si:m), *sb.*^{1} Forms: 1 **seam**, 4–5 **sem**, 4–6 **seme**, (4 **seem**), 4–6, 8 **seyme**, (6 **seym**), 6–7 **seame**, 5– **seam.** [Com. Teut.: OE. *séam* masc. = OFris. *sâm*, MDu. *sôm* (Du. *zoom*), OHG. *soum* hem (MHG., mod.G. *saum*), ON. *saum-r* seam (Sw. *söm*, Da. *søm*):—OTeut. **saumo-z*, f. **sau-* ablaut-variant of *su-* (cf. L. *suĕre* to sew), by-form of Indogermanic **syu-* in OE. *siwian* to SEW, Skr. *syūman* seam.]

I. Suture, junction.

1. a. The junction made by sewing together the edges of two pieces or widths of cloth, leather, etc.; the ridge or the furrow in the surface which indicates the course of such a junction; sometimes (cf. SEAMY *a.*) the protuding edges of the joined pieces on the wrong side of the cloth.

c **1000** ÆLFRIC *Hom.* II. 254 And heoldon his tunecan untoslitene, forðan ðe heo wæs eal buton seame. **1382** WYCLIF *John* xix. 23 Forsothe the coote was with out seem, and aboue wouun bi al. *c* **1400** *Laud Troy Bk.* 11174 A man may se to sow a sem In the furthest of the chirche A-boute mydnyght. *c* **1430** LYDG. *Min. Poems* (Percy Soc.) 201 Hire crowpe doth the semys shrede, Whan they so streyght lasyd been. **1577** HARRISON *England* II. vii. in *Holinshed*, Then must the long seames of our hose be set by a plumb-line. **1617** MORYSON *Itin.* III. 169 They weare short cloakes.. with one small lace to cover the seames. **1630** DRAYTON *Muses Eliz.* viii. 75 And euery Seame the Nimphs shall sew With th' smallest of the Spinners Clue. **1723** *Lond. Gaz.* No. 6150/3 A white great Coat,.. with two Gussits in the Shoulder-Seam. **1842** [see FELL *v.* 6]. **1843** HOOD *Song of Shirt* iii, Seam, and gusset, and band. **1885** J. B. LENO *Boot & Shoemaking* ix. 76 The Oxonian or Oxford Shoe.. was formerly closed with a flat seam.

†**b.** *Surg.* The joining of the edges of a wound by sewing. *Obs.*

1541 R. COPLAND *Guydon's Quest. Chirurg.* Liij b, Demaunde, Howe many and what maners are there of seames: Answere, Thre, that is a seam incarnatyfe... The other seame sowyng hyght restrayntyfe of blode... The thyrde is called the seame of conseruatyfe.. made.. to mayntayne the lyppes tyll the wounde be closed. **1541** —— *Galyen's Terap.* 2 Gij b, All the great vlceres ought to be conioyned, eyther by seames or by byndyng.

c. An embellished seaming used in joining costly fabrics; an ornamental strip of material inserted in or laid over a seam; also, material for this purpose.

c **1394** *P. Pl. Crede* 552 Þei ben y-sewed wiþ whiȝt silk & semes full queynte, Y-stongen wiþ stiches þat stareþ as siluer. **1496–7** *Rec. St. Mary at Hill* 33 A ffyne Corporas.. with semys of gold. *a* **1548** HALL *Chron., Hen. VIII*, 208 b, The semes of the same wer covered with brode wrethes, of goldsmithes worke. **1687** WOOD *Life* 3 Sept. (O.H.S.) III. 230 The king.. with an old French course hat on edged with a little seem of lace. **1833** T. HOOK *Parson's Dau.* II. vi, A small.. 'page' to aunt Eleanor.. who in that character.. wore red seams down his pantaloons.

d. *fig.* Also in colloq. phrases, as ***to burst*** (***fall apart***, etc.) ***at the seams.***

c **1386** CHAUCER *Pars. T.* ⁋42 Chidynge and reproche.. vnsowen the semes of freendshipe in mannes herte. **1589** *Pappe w. Hatchet* Lyly's Wks. 1902 III. 412 Hee runnes ouer his fooleries with a knaues gallop, ripping vp the souterlie seames of his Epistle. **1608** SHAKS. *Per.* II. i. 156 *Sec. Fish*[*erman*]... T'was wee that made vp this Garment [a coat of armour] through the rough seames of the Waters. **1693** ADDISON *Ess. Virg. Georgics* Wks. 1721 I. 250 Precepts .. should be so finely wrought together in the same piece, that no coarse seam may discover where they join. **1768–74** TUCKER *Lt. Nat.* (1834) II. 124 One or two of Horace's purple rags, botched together with coarse seams of abuse, will gain prodigious applause. **1962** ROSS & SINGER *Guilty Party* in *Plays of Year* XXIV. 74 You were bursting at the seams a little. Can we ease the strain for you? **1965** J. VON STERNBERG *Fun in Chinese Laundry* (1966) ii. 43 In a few instances when I thought that I would come apart at the seams.. I managed to make the director listen. **1969** 'V. PACKER' *Don't rely on Gemini* (1970) xv. 131 He had begun to fall apart at the seams—to imagine.. that the stars.. were conspiring against him. **1977** *Times* 30 Apr. 9/6 My marriage.. came apart at the seams.

†**e.** *transf.* An intervening strip. *Obs.*

1678 MARVELL *Growth Popery* 44 There is yet a Seam of Land between the French and us [the Dutch].

f. *Cricket.* The raised band of stitching around the centre of a ball. Cf. *seam bowler*, sense 10 below.

1888 STEEL & LYTTELTON *Cricket* iii. 119 The ball is usually, by a slow bowler, grasped firmly with all the fingers resting on the seam, as this gives more purchase and resistance for the fingers to operate. **1906** F. R. SPOFFORTH in Beldam & Fry *Great Bowlers & Fielders* 10 It is almost impossible to swerve unless the seam of the ball is up and down. **1948** C. SLY *How to bowl them Out* x. 75 The ball.. resembles the planet Saturn in that it has a ring or projecting ridge round its waist.. known as the seam. **1972** R. ILLINGWORTH *Young Cricketer* iii. 50 Grip the ball with the seam upright... Angle the seam to fine leg and not to third man.

g. ***French seam*** (Needlework), a double-stitched seam that is folded and sewn to resemble a plain seam on the right side.

1903 *Home Fashions* 12 Sept. 18/3 The sleeve is joined by French seam. **1964** *McCall's Sewing* 276/1 After cutting the panels, join them with tiny French seams.

†**2.** *Anat.* The line of junction of two bones forming an immovable joint, esp. in the skull; a suture. *Obs.*

c **1050** *Voc.* in Wr.-Wülcker 379 *Cerebrum*, seam þære heafodpannan. *c* **1400** *Lanfranc's Cirurg.* 108 Þe semis þat ben of þe brayn panne. **1552** UDALL tr. *Geminus' Anat.* Bvij b, The places where the bones do close together maye be called the seames. **1612** WOODALL *Surg. Mate* Wks. (1653) 91 If the offence of the *Pericranium* be in the suture or seam it is more dangerous [etc.]. **1653** [see LAMBDOIDAL *a.* 1]. **1668** CULPEPPER & COLE *Barthol. Anat.* I. xxii. 55 It hath a line.. which divides it into a right and left part, and is called a suture or seam.

3. An interstice formed by the abutting edges of planks; a narrow crevice between the edges and ends of the planks or plates of a ship. Chiefly *pl.*

c **1000** ÆLFRIC *Hom.* I. 20 Wyrc þe nu ænne arc,.. ȝehref hit eall, and ȝeclæm ealle þa seamas mid tyrwan. **1497** *Naval Acc. Hen. VII* (1896) 294 Payed for.. here & Scye.. layed in the Semys of the seid Ship. *a* **1618** [see CAULK *v.* 1]. **1666** DRYDEN *Ann. Mirab.* cxlvii, With boiling pitch, another near at hand,.. the seams instops. **1748** *Anson's Voy.* I. viii. 78 The ship.. let in the water at every seam. **1790** COWPER *On Rec. Mother's Picture* 103 Sails ript, seams op'ning wide, and compass lost. **1844** HOOD *Haunted House* II. xxv, The floor was redolent of mould and must, The fungus in the rotten seams had quicken'd. **1886** *Encycl. Brit.* XXI. 820/1 When the planks are fastened, the seams or the intervals between the edges of the strakes are filled with oakum.

4. A line, groove, furrow or the like formed by the abutting edges of two parts of a thing; an indentation or mark resembling this. **a.** on a surface of rock, stone, etc.

c **1330** R. BRUNNE *Chron. Wace* (Rolls) 13976 Þe blod ran þer as water stremes In chynes, in creuesses, & in semes. **13..** *E.E. Allit. P.* B. 555 As þe beryl bornyst byhouez be clene, þat is sounde on vche a syde & no sem habes. **1687** A. LOVELL tr. *Thevenot's Trav.* I. 134 That which at first seemed to be seams or joynings of the Stones, are only veins in the Rock. **1851** MAYNE REID *Scalp Hunt.* xli. 314 Shaggy pines hung top downwards, clinging in their [*sc.* rocks'] seams. **1874** SYMONDS *Sk. Italy & Greece* (1898) I. xi. 212 The seams between the layers of bricks..yield no point of vantage to the penknife. **1876** PAGE *Advd. Text-bk. Geol.* v. 91 The line that marks this separation between two strata is the seam or line of bedding.

b. on the face or body: †A long incised wound; †the parting (of the hair); a scar (of a healed wound); a deep wrinkle.

c **1400** *Laud Troy Bk.* 5631 In his front he him smot, The blod start out fot hot, He set on him a foule seme. **1585** HIGINS *Junius' Nomencl.* 24 *Discrimen capillorum*,..the seame of the head or parting of the haire. **1681** DRYDEN *Abs. & Achit.* 72 [They] looking backward..Saw seams of wounds,..In contemplation of whose ugly scars They cursed the memory of civil wars. **1765** GOLDSM. *Double Transf.* 86 In vain she tries her paste and creams, To smooth her skin or hide its seams. **1800** *Med. Jrnl.* III. 263 Those irregular marks, or seams, found after other applications, are not to be met with after the turpentine. **1817** SHELLEY *Rev. Islam* XII. x, The seams Of his rent heart..a creed Had seared with blistering ice. **1840** DICKENS *Barn. Rudge* i, A deep gash, now healed into an ugly seam. **1875** BUCKLAND *Log-Bk.* 59 No seams are preceptible in the features.

c. *Nat. Hist.* (*a*) *Bot.* (see quot. 1796); (*b*) *Conchol.* (see quot. 1816).

1577 B. GOOGE *Heresbach's Husb.* II. 94 b, Wallnuttes.. are set in the ground..the seame downeward, about the beginning of March. **1796** WITHERING *Brit. Plants* (ed. 3) I. 79 *Seam*, the line formed by the union of the valves of a seed-vessel. *Ibid.* 226 Berry not unlike a capsule,..coat very thin, opening by various seams. **1816** T. BROWN *Elem. Conchol.* 163 *Seam*, the line formed by the union of the valves.

†**d.** *Farriery* = *false quarter*: see FALSE *a.* 7 a.

1610 MARKHAM *Masterp.* II. lxx. 334 A False Quarter is a rift or open back seame..in..the hoofe. **1682** *Lond. Gaz.* No. 1712/4 Stolen.., two Gray Geldings, one..with Seams in his Heel. **1759** T. WALLIS *Farrier's Dict.*, *Seams*, or Seyms, in horses, are certain clefts in their quarters.

e. *Agric.* A furrow, (seed) drill.

1799 J. ROBERTSON *Agric. Perth* 153 The grassfield is ploughed before winter; it is harrowed thereafter, when the grass begins to shoot up in the seams. **1893** *Surrey Gloss.* s.v., You've no call to drill it, you've got a capital seam... I don't care for no seam, so long as I can bury the seed.

f. *dial.* (See quot.)

1870 H. STEVENSON *Birds Norf.* II. 311 The rest of the ground, from which the turf is cut, consists of alternate ridges or 'seams' of peat, and wide trenches.

g. *nonce-use.* Applied to a streak of lightning.

1860 TYNDALL *Glac.* I. v. 41 The seams of lightning which ran through the heavens.

5. *Geol.* A thin layer or stratum separating two strata of greater magnitude.

1592 *Sc. Acts Jas. VI* (1814) III. 556/2 Quhensoeuir ony myne or seme of mettaill wes found be ony of the leigis of this realme. **1684** *Phil. Trans.* XVII. 741 The Seam or Vein of Copper-Ore. *a* **1728** WOODWARD *Nat. Hist. Fossils* I. (1729) I. 166, I observ'd a Termination of a Seam, as they call it in the North, or a Stratum of Coal, where it divided into several thin Plates. **1794** KIRWAN *Elem. Min.* (ed. 2) I. 381 The seams are of a darker colour. **1815** BAKEWELL *Introd. Geol.* 179 Numerous beds or seams of coal occur in one coal field. **1851** MANTELL *Petrifactions* iii. §5. 304 The Kentish-rag is seen in nearly horizontal layers, separated by thin seams of loose sand.

6. a. A joint used in uniting the edges of sheet metal either by folding and pressing them together or by joining them with solder; also, the line produced by this process. ***false seam***: see quot. 1881.

1825 J. NICHOLSON *Oper. Mech.* 634 The method of joining by seams..consists in simply bending the approximate edges of the lead up and over each other, and then dressing them down close to the flat. **1855** FRANKE *Beil's Technol. Dict.* II. 451 Seam of a musket barrel (the jagged line produced by welding), *die Schweissnath. Soudure.* **1881** F. CAMPIN *Mech. Engin.* ii. 32 When the casting is quite cool the false seams formed at the junctions of the mould are chipped off. **1882** W. J. CHRISTY *Joints* 203 When the plumber forms pipes of large diameter out of sheet lead the seam is soldered.

b. *Metallurgy.* A superficial linear defect on worked metal usu. caused by closure of a blow hole.

c **1840** B. LEGGE *Guide to Iron Trade* 36 Having sems [*sic*] in a longitudinal direction. **1923** GLAZEBROOK *Dict. Appl. Physics* V. 362/2 These surfaces become oxidised both during cooling of the ingot and during reheating for forging or rolling, and give rise to rokes or seams. **1924** GREAVES & WRIGHTON *Pract. Microsc. Metallogr.* ix. 78 Seams show a similar microscopical appearance to rokes and are caused in rolling billets or bars by one portion of the metal folding over another. **1967** A. K. OSBORNE *Encycl. Iron & Steel Industry* (ed. 2) 373/2 Seams may also be caused by rippled surfaces or by recurrent teeming laps.

7. *Knitting.* [transferred use of 1.] A line of purled stitches (see PURL *v.*[1] 4) down the leg of a stocking, simulating the appearance of a joining. Also short for *seam-stitch.*

a **1825** FORBY *Voc. E. Anglia* s.v. *Purle*, The seams of stockings..are purled. **1849** ESTHER COPLEY *Compr. Knitting-bk.* 12 In stocking knitting, the 1st method [of reducing the number of stitches] is employed when a narrowing is required just before what is called the 'seam'. **1882** CAULFEILD & SAWARD *Dict. Needlework* 286/1 *Seam*, a name given to Purl Knitting, but usually indicating the one Purled Stitch down the leg of a stocking that forms the seam.

8. (See quot.)

1867 *Ure's Dict. Arts* II. 286 Such also are the rags known technically as 'seams'; being the clippings which fall from woollen rags under the scissors of the sorters.

II. 9. [Cf. ON. *saumar* pl.; also OE. *séamere* tailor.] Sewing, needlework; also in phr. †***work of seam.*** ***white seam***, plain needlework. *Obs.* exc. *dial.*

a **1400** *Octouian* 1865 Y dwellede yn Jerusalem With kyng and quene, And taught her maydenys werk of sem. **1581** *Nicol Burne's Disput.* 189 b, From threid, seyme, and neidil, To danse at the feidil. **1594** LYLY *Mother Bombie* I. iii, It is you that goe about to match your girle with my boy, shee beeing more fit for seames than for marriage. **1738** in *Fasti Aberd.* (1854) 447 The want of an accomplished gentlewoman for teaching white and coloured seam. *c* **1786** BURNS *Answ. to Ep. Tailor* ii, Gae mind your seam, ye prick-the-louse! **1818** MISS FERRIER *Marriage* xiv, With..a large work-bag well stuffed with white-seam, she took her place. **1837** CARLYLE *Fr. Rev.* III. II. v. 123 Citoyennes who bring their seam with them, or their knitting-needles. **1882** *Harper's Mag.* June 117 He asked her to put down her seam, and come for a walk.

III. 10. Comb.: **seam allowance**, the amount of material in sewing which is calculated to be taken in by a seam; †**seam-biter** *Sc.* (jocular), a tailor; **seam-blast** (see quot.); †**seam-bone**, each of the bones connected by the lambdoidal suture; **seam bowler** *Cricket*, a medium or fast bowler who uses the seam to make the ball deviate in the air or off the pitch during delivery; hence **seam-bowling; seam hammer, joint** (see quots.); **seam-lace** (Webster, 1864) = *seaming lace* (see SEAMING *vbl. sb.*); **seam-presser**, (*a*) (see quot.); (*b*) a tailor's goose for pressing seams (Knight *Dict. Mech.* 1875); †**seam-rend** *v.* [back-formation from *seam-rent* adj.] *trans.*, to tear apart at the seams; †**seamrent** *sb. rare*$^{-0}$ (see quot. 1755); **seam-rent** *a.*, rent or torn apart at the seams, *lit.* and *fig.*; (of a person) having torn garments; **seamrept, -ripped** *pa. pple.* and *ppl. a.*, ripped or torn apart at the seams; **seam-rip** (see quot.); **seam-roller**, (*a*) (see quot.); (*b*) = *seam presser* (*a*) (Ogilvie, 1882); **seam rubber, set** (see quots.); **seam-squirrel** *U.S. slang* (chiefly *Mil.*), a louse; **seam-stitch** (see 7 above) = *purl-stitch* (PURL *sb.*[1] 5); **seam welding**, a form of resistance welding in which a linear weld is obtained by means of rolling disc-shaped electrodes which produce a line of overlapping welds (see also quot. 1964); so **seam-weld** *v. trans.*; also **seam weld** *sb.*; **seam welder**, a machine for **seam welding.**

1949 I. R. DUNCAN *Compl. Sewing Book* xv. 301 Plain seams may be used for every type of garment... The amount of *seam allowance depends upon the material; generally from ⅜ to ½ an inch is required. **1964** *McCall's Sewing* 277/1 Press fold formed along edge of seam allowance. **1977** R. RICHARDSON *Discovering Patchwork* 63/2 Window templates made of clear plastic with a shaded area round the edge... The shaded area is the seam allowance. **1500-20** DUNBAR *Poems* xxvii. 10 The tailȝeour, baith with speir and scheild, Convoyit wes vnto the feild, With mony lymmar loun, Off *seme byttaris. **1860** WORCESTER (citing *Hale*), **Seam-blast*, a blast made by filling with powder the seams or crevices made by a previous drill-blast. **1576** BAKER *Jewell of Health* 170 b, Take the hinder *seame bones of dead men named Sutura lamdoides) those put into calcyning. **1948** J. ARLOTT *How to watch Cricket* iii. 14 The term '*seam-bowler' is almost identical [with 'pace bowler'] since it refers to those bowlers who use the seam to swing, or cut the ball. **1978** R. V. JONES *Most Secret War* xliv. 414, I had previously not believed such tales as the swinging of cricket balls by seam bowlers. **1956** R. ALSTON *Test Commentary* 136 Johnson persisted in a *seam-bowling attack. **1976** DEXTER & MAKINS *Testkill* 174 The steady England pressure which was now resting on the excellent seam bowling of Kirkstead. **1875** KNIGHT *Dict. Mech.*, **Seam-hammer* (Coppersmithing), a creasing hammer for flattening seams and joints. **1882** W. J. CHRISTY *Joints* 202 [Plumbers' Joints.] *Seam Joint is a mode of uniting the edges of sheets of metal by means of a seam. **1843** RANSOME *Implem. Agric.* 96 The *seam presser is, in fact, an abstract of a drill-roller, consisting of but two cylinders of cast iron, which, following the plough in the furrows, press and roll down the newly turned up earth. **1647** WARD *Simple Cobler* 76, I have here and there taken a few finish stitches..; but I cannot now well pull them out, unlesse I should *seame-rend all. **1755** JOHNSON, **Seamrent*, a separation of any thing where it is joined, a breach of the stitches. **1548** UDALL, etc. *Erasm. Par. Luke* iv. 31–7 Workes forbidden [on the Sabbath] as..to botche vp theyr garment beeyng broken or *seamerent. **1599** B. JONSON *Ev. Man out of Hum.* II. vi, I wonder at you..that you can consort your selues with such poore seame-rent fellowes. **1605** ROWLANDS *Hell's Broke Loose* 39 Our seame-rent Souldiers are exceeding bare. **1622** MASSINGER & DEKKER *Virg. Mart.* III. iii, All my hopes are seame-rent, and go wetshod. **1866** [R. HALLAM] *Wadsley Jack* ix (E.D.D.), One on 'em fell on me... I wor compleately seam-rent. **1886** *Cheshire Gloss.*, *Seam-rent*, said of a shoe when the upper leather begins to part from the sole. **1625** J. WODROEPHE *Marrow Fr. Tongue* 128 My shirt is all broken, rent, and *seamerept. **1891** *Labour Commission Gloss.*, **Seam Rip*, the ripping or tearing of the seams or joints of a boiler, caused by a too sudden expansion or contraction, &c. **1570** FOXE *A. & M.* (ed. 2) 363 b/2 Which coate of Christian vnitie, abeit of long time it had bene now *seameript before..: yet notwithstanding in some peece it held together in some meane agreement [etc.]. **1621** QUARLES *Argalus & P.* (1678) 93 His seam-ript Garments. **1887** *S. Chesh. Gloss.*, *Shem-ripped.* **1875** KNIGHT *Dict. Mech.*, **Seam-roller*, a burnisher, or rubber, for flattening down the edges of leather where two thicknesses are sewn together. *Ibid.*, **Seam-rubber.* **1885** J. B. LENO *Boot & Shoemaking* xxv. 202 Seam Rubber..for pressing seams in order that they may be made to lie flat. **1841** HARTSHORNE *Salop. Ant.*, **Seam Set*, a grooved wooden instrument used by shoemakers, for smoothing the seams of boots and shoes. **1843** HOLTZAPFFEL *Turning* I. 387 The seam-set for closing the seams [of thin metals]. *Ibid.* 393 The lap-joint..is set down flat with a seam-set. **1899** J. R. SKINNER *Hist. Fourth Illinois Volunteers* 129 When it was first rumored that the old confederate *seam squirrel had invaded our quarters, a small panic seized many. **1929** L. THOMAS *Woodfill of Regulars* 240 The rest of the boys..stopped chasin' seam-squirrels in their undershirts. *a* **1956** C. J. POST *Little War of Private Post* (1960) 255 There is the gray-back, or seam-squirrel, from the days of our Civil War. **1825** JAMIESON, *Pearl*, the *seam-stitch in a knitted stocking. **1920** *Whitaker's Electr. Engineer's Pocket-bk.* (ed. 4) 646 On light work, about 3 ft. of *seam weld can be made per min. **1980** L. M. GOWD *Princ. Welding Technol.* xi. 164 After the first weld has been made,..the current must be raised to maintain the size of the welds. Accepting this limitation, satisfactory continuous seam welds can be made. **1921** *Seam welder [see *seam welding* below]. **1959** NEUMANN & BOCKHOFF *Welding of Plastics* vii. 126 In using high-frequency seam welders, the breakdown strength of the plastic must be considered. **1976** *Western Mail* (Cardiff) 27 Nov. 6/5 Spot-welders, seam-welders and projection welding machines up to 20 KVA are also among the factory's equipment. **1917** OBERG & JONES *Machinery's Encycl.* VI. 496/2 By the *seam-welding process, two sheets of wrought iron or steel are welded together along the edge by a continuous lap-weld... Plates can be successfully seam-welded at a rate of about one foot per minute. **1921** *Automobile Engineer* XI. 108/1 Seam welding..can be adopted with advantage when a tight joint is required.., a seam welder differing from a spot welder mainly in that roller electrodes are used instead of the pointed electrodes. **1964** WORDINGHAM & REBOUL *Dict. Plastics* 158 *Seam welding*, with thermo-plastic materials, the method of forming a welded seam, either by the use of welding rollers ..for continuous welding, or by jig welding. **1975** BRAM & DOWNS *Manuf. Technol.* ii. 62 Seam welding is similar to spot welding, the difference being that the spots overlap each other, making a continuous weld seam.

seam (siːm), *sb.*[2] Forms: 1 **séam**, *Northumb.* **séom**, 3 *Ormin* **sæm**, 3–6 **seme**, 4–7 **seem**, 4 **sem**, 5 **ceme**, (*w. dial.*) **zeme**, 6 **seym(e**, **seayme**, (**sheme**), 6–7 **seame**, 9 *w. dial*, **zame**, **zeam**, 6– **seam.** [OE. *séam* masc., OHG., MHG. *soum* (G. *saum*), a W.Ger. adoption of med.L. *sauma*, *salma*, *sagma* load (a. Gr. σάγμα packsaddle, f. σαγ-, σάττειν to pack, load), whence It. *salma*, *soma* burden, Pr. *sauma* beast of burden, F. *somme* burden, Sp. *salma*, *jalma* tonnage (of a ship).]

1. A pack-horse load. *Obs.* exc. *dial.* In early use also *gen.*, †a load, burden.

c **950** *Lindisf. Gosp.* Luke xi. 46 Soð he cuoeð & iuh æs wisestum wæ forðon ȝie semað menn mid seamum [*c* **975** *Rushw.* seomum] ðaðe ȝebeara ne maȝon. *c* **1000** ÆLFRIC *Gram.* ix. (Z.) 59, *Honus* seam oððe byrðen. *c* **1200** ORMIN 3718, & asse..hafeþþ mikell afell To berenn upp well mikell sæm. *c* **1250** *Owl & Night.* 775 An hors is strengur þan a mon Ac..berþ on rugge grete semes. *c* **1250** *Gen. & Ex.* 1368 Ðor he leide hise semes [of camels] dun. *Ibid.* 2373 And .x. asses wið semes fest. *c* **1350** *Will. Palerne* 2554 Sum seluer for our semes in þe Cite to gete. **1860** *Eng. & For. Mining Gloss.* (ed. 2) *Cornwall terms*, *Seam*, a horse-load.

b. The amount of a horse-load; often identified with a definite quantity, varying according to the commodity and locality.

The 'seam' of glass is said to be 120 lbs. (in the 14th c. it was 100 lbs.); of grain, 8 bushels; of sand, 6–8 pecks; of apples, 9 pecks.

1318 *Durham Acc. Rolls* (Surtees) 373 Item de vitro j seme et di., prec. 10s. *a* **1325** *MS. Rawl. B. 520* lf. 43 Þe sem of glas contenez of .xx. ston, ant eueri ston of .v. pond. **1339-40** *Ely Sacr. Rolls* II. 90 In j sem ferri empt...xxiijs. **1377** LANGL. *P. Pl.* B. IV. 38 For, wot god, þei wolde do more for a dozeine chickenes..or for a seem of otes. *c* **1440** *Promp. Parv.* 65/2 Ceme, or quarter of corne, *quarterium*. *Ibid.* 452/1 Seem. **1459** *Yatton Chruchw. Acc.* (Somerset Rec. Soc.) 100, xxx zeme of bordys, xij[d] the zeme, and iij zeme of plangys xij[d] the zeme. **1531-2** *Durham Househ. Bk.* (Surtees) 113 Pro cariago j seayme salmonum, 10d. **1536** *MS. Acc. St. John's Hosp., Canterb.*, Payd for iij seymis of lyme to ye chymney. **1545** *Ludlow Churchw. Acc.* (Camden) 23 Item, for a sheme of wood at the makynge of the pascalle ..ij d. **1674** JEAKE *Arith.* (1696) 80 Glass, by the same Ordinance containeth 1 Seam, 24 Stones, 1 Stone 5 Pounds. **1675** *Phil. Trans.* X. 294 [Cornwall.] These useful Sands.. are fetched..on Horse-back; one Horse carrying about 13 or 14 gallons... Each seime (or hors-load) with the carriage comes to about 8d or 9d. **1679** BLOUNT *Anc. Tenures* 52 A Seam or Horseload of Oats, which in some places is accounted Eight Bushels, in others perhaps more properly, but four. **1705** *Lond. Gaz.* No. 4108/3 The Cargo.. containing 751 Seams of Barilla. **1813** T. RUDGE *Agric. Glouc.* 224 From ten to eleven 'seam', of nine pecks each, of juicy fruit, are generally sufficient for a hogshead of 100 gallons wine measure [of cider]. **1887** *Kentish Gloss.* s.v., A sack of eight bushels is now called a seam, because that quantity forms a horse-load.

c. Phrase. † ***sack and seam***: pack-horse traffic.

1631, **1829** [see SACK *sb.*[1] 1 e].

2. A cart-load; esp. a definite amount of 3 cwt. (of hay or manure) or 2 cwt. of straw. *w. dial.*

1726 *Brice's Weekly Jrnl.* 5 Aug. 4 Several paved Courts, wherein are made a Thousand Seams of Dung every Year. **1856** J. C. MORTON *Cycl. Agric.* II. 1126 *Seam* (Devons.), of dung, 3 cwts. **1880** *Cornwall Gloss., East Cornw., Seam,* or *Zeam,* a load of hay, manure, &c. It means with us no definite quantity, but a cart-load, waggon load, &c. **1888** 'Q' (Quiller-Couch) *Troy Town* xi, I wants you to..go to beach for ore-weed..an' carry so many seams as you can.

seam (siːm), *sb.*[3] Forms: 2–3 seime, 3 seim, 4–5 saym, (5 sayme, 5 sem), 5–6 seme, 6–7 saime, same, 6, 9 *Sc.* seyme, 7 seame, 8–9 *dial.* and *Sc.* saim, 7– seam. [a. OF. *saim* (also *saime* fem.), later *sain*, mod.Fr. only in *saindoux* lard; a Com. Rom. word, = Pr. *sagin-s, saïns*, Catal. *sagin, sagi*, Sp. *sain*, It. *saime*:—popular L. **sagimen*, related to classical L. *sagīna* fattening, fatness.]

†**1.** Fat, grease. *Obs.*

c **1200** *Eadwine's Canterb. Ps.* lxii. 6 Swæ swa mid seime & mid fetnesse ȝefelled beoð sawul min. *a* **1225** *Ancr. R.* 412 Ȝe ne schulen eten vleschs ne seim buten ine muchele secnesse. **13..** *E.E. Allit. P.* C. 275 Þer [*sc.* in the whale's belly] in saym & in sorȝe þat sauoured as helle, þer was bylded his bour. *c* **1483** CAXTON *Dialogues* 46/18 He coryeth his hydes with sayme of heryngs. **1513** DOUGLAS *Æneis* VII. xi. 61 And sum polyst scharp speyr heydis of steyll, To mak thaim brycht wyth fat cresche or same. **1541** R. COPLAND *Guydon's Quest. Chirurg.* Hiiij b, Mezentereon..is coucred..with glandynous grease, and is commonly called seame. **1595** *Balliol Coll. Acc.* (*MS.*), Item, for sem for the plumpe..and to Owen for mending of it, xviijd. **1606** SHAKS. *Tr. & Cr.* II. iii. 195 Shall the proud Lord, That bastes his arrogance with his owne seame... Shall he be worshipt. **1613** J. MAY *Est. Clothing* v. 27 They will not scoure the same cloth cleane, but leaue a bad substance of oyle and seame in it. **1634** T. JOHNSON tr. *Parey's Wks.* III. vii. 91 And there is another kind of fat, which is called *Sevum*, seame [orig. L. *sepum*],.. that is much dryer. **1651** J. C. *Poems* 1 A person of so rare a frame, Her bodie might be lin'd with' same. **1691** RAY *Collect. Words* 131 *Saime*, which we pronounce sometimes Seame. It signifies not only Goose-grease, but in general any kind of Grease or Sewet or Oil, wherewith out Clothiers anoint..their Wool. **1697** DRYDEN *Æneid* VII. 867 Part scour the rusty Sheilds with Seam.

2. Hogs' lard.

1530 PALSGR. 269/1 Seme for to frye with, *seyn de povrceau.* **1558** WARDE tr. *Alexis' Secr.* (1568) 40 Take.. halfe an unce of..Hogges grease or seyme. **1606** *Churchw. Acc. Pittington*, etc. (Surtees) 287 For a pound of swine's seame to the belles, iiij d. **1788** W. MARSHALL *Yorksh.* II. 349 *Saim*, hogs-lard. **1894** LATTO *Tammas Bodkin* vi, The ancient dames were..discussin' the efficacy o' hartshorn an' swine's seam as a cure for the rheumatics.

seam, *sb.*[4] *Sc.* and *north.* Also 5 seme, seyme, 9 (*Orkn. and Shetl.*) same. [Corresponds to ON. *saum-r* nail (Sw. *söm*, Da. *søm*), perh. identical with *saum-r* SEAM *sb.*[1]

The form represents the OE. *séam* SEAM *sb.*[1]; the sense is prob. due to the influence of the ON. formal equivalent.]

A kind of nail or rivet for fastening the overlapping edges of a clinker-built boat, the end of the nail being clinched on a rove (ROVE *sb.*[2], ROOVE *sb.*). Also *seam-nail* (*Northumb. Gloss.*, 1894).

Usually associated with *rove*, its counterpart.

1406 *Durham Acc. Rolls* (Surtees) 606 Item in exp. Ricardi Couhird..pro seme et Rufe, 2s. **1474–5** *Ibid.* 645 Cum seme, rove, clavis ferr. et lign., pice, et bitumine [for repairing a ferry-boat]. *c* **1425** *Noah's Ark* 26 in *Non-Cycle Mystery Plays* 20 Bid him go make a ship... All things I him fulfill, Pitch, tar, seam and rowe. **1494** *Acc. Ld. High Treas. Scot.* I. 253 Item, for thre stane and tua pund of seyme and rufe to the cokbate. *Ibid.* 254 Seme and ruyf. **1892** [see ROOVE *sb.*].

†**seam**, *v.*[1] *Obs.* In 1 sýman, séman, 2–5 seme. [OE. (**sieman*), *séman*, *sýman*:—WGer. **saumjan*, f. **saumo-z* SEAM *sb.*[2]] *trans.* To put a burden on, load, weigh down; also *intr.*, to weigh heavily.

c **950** *Lindisf. Gosp.* Luke xi. 46 Ðe semað menn mið seamum, ðaðe ȝebeara ne maȝon. *c* **1000** ÆLFRIC *Gen.* xliv. 13 (Gr.) And hiȝ..symdon hyra assan and cyrdon eft to þære birig. *c* **1200** *Trin. Coll. Hom.* 93 Ðe asse þe ure helende uppe set ben þo forsinegede..and sinne hem is loð to leten ..for hem þincheð þat godes hese heuieliche semeð. *c* **1250** *Gen. & Ex.* 1365 Ten kameles semeð [? *read* semed] forð he nam. *c* **1315** SHOREHAM *Poems* 82 Þo þat me oppone hys swete body þe heuye crouche semde. *c* **1450** *Mirk's Festial* 211 A man þat was..takyn wyt enmyes,..and was semot wyth yerns also mony as he myȝt bere.

seam (siːm), *v.*[2] [f. SEAM *sb.*[1]]

1. a. *trans.* To sew the seam or seams of; to fasten or join *on, together, up* with a seam or seams.

1582 STANYHURST *Æneis* IV. (Arb.) 100 There too watrye Iuno, the chaplayne Seams vp thee bedmatch. **1599** DEKKER *Shoem. Holiday* I. i, Here take this pair of shoes, cut out by Hodge, Stiched by my fellow Firk, seamed by myself. **1794** *Rigging & Seamanship* I. 93 All linings are seamed on. **1862** MRS. H. WOOD *Mrs. Hallib.* I. xviii, Some made the gloves; that is, seamed the fingers together and put in the thumbs.

absol. **1905** MABEL BARNES-GRUNDY *Vacill. Hazel* xix, I was seaming with black cotton.

†**b.** To furnish or ornament with an inserted seam; also, of a material, to serve as a seam for.

1590 GREENE *Mourn. Garm.* (1616) 11 His coat was greene, With welts of white, seamde betweene. **1604** *Meeting of Gallants* B2b, There was not so much Veluet stirring, as would haue..seamde a Lieftenants Buffe-doublet. *a* **1625** BEAUM. & FL. *Four Plays in One, Tri. Time* i, She shew'd me gowns and head-tires, imbroider'd wastcoats, smocks seam'd thorow with cut-works. **1740** SOMERVILLE *Hobbinol* I. 218 This Pair of Gloves, by curious Virgin Hands Embroider'd, seam'd with Silk, and fring'd with Gold.

c. *intr.* To sew. *dial.*

1833 HT. MARTINEAU *Berkeley the Banker* I. v. 104 The widow immediately went on seaming. **1886** *Cheshire Gloss.*, *Seam*, to sew a seam.

d. *Knitting. trans.* and *intr.* To form a seam-stitch; to make a seam or seam-stitch in (a piece of knitting).

1842 MISS F. LAMBERT *Hand-bk. Needlewk.* xvii. 303 [Knitting.] To *seam*, to knit a stitch with the cotton before the needle. **1886** BYNNER *A. Surriage* xiii. 142 She seamed and narrowed another entire round.

2. *trans.* To mark (a surface) with lines or indentations; to furrow. **a.** Said of a river, chasm, line of railway, etc. as marking the face of the earth.

1596 SPENSER *State Irel.* Wks. (Globe) 616/2 And sure it is yet a most beautifull and sweet countrey..seamed throughout with many goodly rivers. **1796** KIRWAN *Elem. Min.* (ed. 2) II. 242 The prisms [of Rock Crystal] are generally seamed perpendicularly to their axis. **1815** SCOTT *Ld. of Isles* III. xvi, The griesly gulfs and slaty rifts Which seam its shiver'd head. **1854** O. W. HOLMES *New Eden* 2 Scarce could the parting ocean close, Seamed by the Mayflower's cleaving bow, When [etc.]. **1863** KINGLAKE *Crimea* (1877) I. i. 1 The little rivers which seamed the ground. **1878** HOOKER & BALL *Marocco* viii. 179 The great mountain chain that rose steeply before us, seamed with snow that..lay in hollows..forming long vertical streaks. **1878** M. MACCOLL *3 Yrs. of Eastern Q.* x. (ed. 3) 241 Plains seamed by railways.

b. Said of a scar, wound, etc.; also of care or the passions as marking the face.

1695 BLACKMORE *Pr. Arth.* v. 147 Scars of Honour seam'd his manly Face. **1725** POPE *Odyss.* IV. 335 Seam'd o'er with wounds, which his own sabre gave. **1749** FIELDING *Tom Jones* I. viii, It would be much better for them, if their faces had been seamed with the small-pox. **1825** SCOTT *Betrothed* xxvii, A veteran whose face had been seamed with many a scar. **1859** TENNYSON *Elaine* 258 Seam'd with an ancient swordcut on the cheek. **1864** —— *Aylmer's F.* 814 Her.. meagre face Seam'd with the shallow cares of fifty years. **1865** DICKENS *Mut. Friend* III. x, His face..seamed with jealousy and anger.

c. *intr.* To become fissured; to crack.

1880 L. WALLACE *Ben-Hur* 400 Their lips began to parch and seam.

3. *trans.* To join (sheets of lead or metal) by means of a seam (see SEAM *sb.*[1] 6).

1703 T. N. *City & C. Purchaser* 194 The Sheets of Lead ..which are seam'd in the Platform. **1712** J. JAMES tr. *Le Blond's Gardening* 211 The Sheets of Lead..should be seamed one to another with Solder. **1795** HERSCHEL in *Phil. Trans.* LXXXV. 366 Seaming bars, setting tools, and claw-screws,..were made..to confine and stretch the parts as they were seamed together.

4. To furnish with a seam or thin stratum (of ore).

1899 E. J. CHAPMAN *Drama of Two Lives* 6 The rocky core Of those lone mountains, rent and old, Is seam'd and vein'd with glittering ore.

5. *Cricket.* **a.** *intr.* Of a pitch: to aid a seam bowler; of a ball: to swing during delivery on account of the seam.

1960 E. W. SWANTON *West Indies Revisited* 118 According to the players, the pitch was still 'seaming' a bit. **1974** *Reading Evening Post* 3 Sept. 14/7 Both opening bowlers made the ball seam considerably and Fletcher was next to go. **1976** *Liverpool Echo* 23 Nov. 18/7 The pitches out there have been known to seam.

b. *trans.* Of a bowler: to cause (a ball) to seam.

1963 T. BAILEY *Improve Your Cricket* ii. 81 At medium pace it is possible to seam the ball..and naturally to vary pace, length and angle of flight. **1976** J. SNOW *Cricket Rebel* 21 Thomson..and..Pountain..taking seven of the first eight wickets between them on a damp wicket which helped them seam the ball about.

†**seam**, *v.*[3] *Obs.* [f. SEAM *sb.*[3]] *trans.* To dress (wool) with grease.

1511–2 *Act 3 Hen. VIII*, c. 6 §1 Not excedyng in weight after the rate of xij pounde Wolle seymed above oon quarter of a pound for the waste. **1592** NASHE *P. Penilesse* A4b, Barrelling vp the droppings of her nose, in steede of oyle to saime wool withall.

'**sea-maid.** *poet.* = MERMAID 1. Also, a goddess or nymph of the sea.

1590 SHAKS. *Mids. N.* II. i. 154 And certaine starres shot madly from their Spheares, To heare the Sea maids musicke. **1603** —— *Meas. for M.* III. ii. 115 Some report, a Sea-maid spawn'd him. **1609** *Ev. Woman in Hum.* I. i. in Bullen *O. Pl.* IV, They call them Sea-maides or Mermaides, singing sweetelye. **1633** P. FLETCHER *Piscatory Ecl.* ii. 21 You fisher-boyes and sea-maids dainty crue Farewell. **1725** POPE *Odyss.* IV. 599 But the bright sea-maid's gentle power implor'd, With nectar'd drops the sick'ning sense restor'd. **1789** COWPER *Queen's Vis. London* 70 So, ancient poets say, serene The sea-maid rides the waves. **1818** MILMAN *Samor* I. 127 Rocks, where basks At summer noon the Sea-maid. **1859** LD. LYTTON *Wanderer* 28 We caught the gleam of sea-maids' hair.

So **sea-maiden.**

1893 D. O'DONOGHUE *Brendaniana* 89 The wonderful sea-maiden whom Brendan restored to life. **1898** N. MUNRO *J. Splendid* vii. 68 Stories..of fairies, wizards, water-horse, and sea-maiden.

'**sea-mall.** Also seamel(l. = SEAMEW.

The form *seamell* is perh. spurious, invented as a conjectural emendation of *scamels* in Shaks. *Temp.* II. ii. 176.

a **1672** WILLUGHBY *Ornith.* (1676) 262 *Larus cinereus minor.* The common Sea-Mall. **1752** J. HILL *Hist. Anim.* 448 The lesser Gull, or Sea-mall... The deep, grey, Sea-mall. **1778** STEVENS *Shaks. Temp.* II. ii. 176 Wks. I. 63 *note*, Theobald had very reasonably proposed to read sea-malls, or sea-mells. **1894** NEWTON *Dict. Birds, Sea-mall, -mel*, or *-mew* have been used indifferently for Gulls.

seaman ('siːmən). Pl. **-men.** [f. SEA *sb.* + MAN. Cf. Du. *zeeman*, G. *seemann*, ON. *sjómað-r*.]

1. a. *gen.* One whose occupation or business is on the sea; a sailor as opposed to a landsman. Now only *poet.* or *rhetorical.* Also, with qualifying word: One skilled in navigation. **b.** *spec.* A sailor below the rank of officer.

leading, able, ordinary seaman, the three grades (beginning with the highest) of seamen in the Royal Navy. ***merchant seaman***, a seaman in the merchant service.

Beowulf 329 Garas stodon, sæmanna searo samod ætgædere. *c* **1205** LAY. 1165 Brutus hit herde siggen þurh his sæ-monnen [*c* **1275** see mannen]. **1436** *Libel Eng. Policy* in *Pol. Poems* (Rolls) II. 166 That gode see-menne wold no more deferre, But bete theme home. *c* **1470** HENRY *Wallace* IX. 40 Semen he feyt, and gaiff thaim gudlye wage. **1540** *Act 32 Hen. VIII*, c. 14 The nauy..is..the maintenaunce of many masters mariners and seamen. **1595** SHAKS. *John* III. i. 92 But (on this day) let Sea-men feare no wracke. **1667** MILTON *P.L.* I. 205 Him..The Pilot..Deeming some Island, oft, as Sea-men tell,..Moors by his side. **1702** *Proclam.* 1 June in *Lond. Gaz.* No. 3815/2 To..Able Seamen, Ordinary Seamen, Two Eighth Parts. **1745** *De Foe's Eng. Tradesman* (1841) I. xxv. 248 Our seamen are.. esteemed the best sailors in the world. **1852** TENNYSON *Ode Dk. Wellington* 83 Mighty Seaman, this is he Was great by land as thou by sea. **1854** *Act. 17 & 18 Vict.* c. 104 §2 [Merchant Shipping Act.] 'Seaman' shall include every Person (except Masters, Pilots, and Apprentices..) employed or engaged in any Capacity on board any Ship. **1867** SMYTH *Sailor's Word-bk.* s.v., The able seaman is the seafaring man who knows all the duties of common seamanship... His rating is A.B... The ordinary seaman is less qualified. **1884** *Encycl. Brit.* XVII. 291 The personnel of the British navy is composed of two different bodies of men, the seamen and the marines, each of which has its appropriate officers. *Ibid.* 295/1 The crew of a ship of war consists of leading seamen, able seamen, ordinary seamen, engine-room artificers [etc.].

†**c.** ***seamen's beer***: see quot. *Obs.*

1795 SIR J. DALRYMPLE *Let. to Admiralty* 2 There are four kinds of beer in Britain: Strong Beer, Porter, Table Beer, or what is called Seamen's Beer, and Small Beer.

d. *attrib.* and *Comb.*: †**seaman card** = SEA-CARD; **seamancraft**, seamanship; **seaman-gunner** (see quot. 1867).

1636 W. STRODE *Floating Isl.* III. iii, No other rarities these many Ages But Powder, Printing, *Seaman Card, and Watches. **1871** BLACKIE *Four Phases Mor.* i. 21 In the navigation of which no *seamancraft could avail against miserable shipwreck. **1867** SMYTH *Sailor's Word-bk.*, **Seamen-gunners*, men who have been trained in a gunnery ship, and thereby become qualified to instruct others in that duty.

†**2.** = MERMAN 1. *Obs.*

1569 FENTON *Secret Wond. Nature* 53 Conradus Gesner writeth that there was seene at Rome in the great riuer, a sea man, or monster of the sea. **1610** HOLLAND *Camden's Brit.* I. 466 Plinie hath reported of..the seaman caught in the streights of Gibraltar. **1753** *Chambers' Cycl.* Suppl. s.v. *Siren*, The Philosophical Transactions also contain an account of a sea-man seen in the American seas.

seamanite ('siːmənaɪt). *Min.* [See quot. 1930 and -ITE[1].]

A rare hydrated phosphate and borate of manganese, $Mn_3^{2+}(OH)_2[B(OH)_4][PO_4]$, occurring as transparent, yellow, orthorhombic crystals.

1930 E. H. KRAUS et al. in *Amer. Mineralogist* XV. 220 In recognition of Professor [A. E.] Seaman's long and influential service as Professor of Geology and Mineralogy at the Michigan College of Mining and Technology, and his valuable contributions to the geology and mineralogy of the Upper Peninsula of Michigan, the authors propose the name of seamanite for this new mineral. **1971** *Ibid.* LVI. 1531 Seamanite is certainly a candidate for one of the most exotic of mineral structures. The Mn-O octahedral arrangement is one of the most peculiar and unexpected on record.

seamanlike ('siːmənlaɪk), *a.* and *adv.* [f. SEAMAN + -LIKE.] **a.** *adj.* Characteristic of or befitting a (good) seaman. **b.** *adv.* In a seamanlike manner.

1796 T. TWINING *Trav. Amer.* (1894) 2 But everything on board was seamanlike and neat. **1821** SCOTT *Pirate* xxx, Master Triptolemus Yellowley will tell you how seamanlike I piloted him to the little haven. **1881** *Times* 30 June 11/5 In the opinion of the Court the vessel was not navigated by the master with proper and seamanlike care.

seamanly ('siːmənlɪ), *a.* and *adv.* [f. SEAMAN + -LY.] = prec.

1798 SOUTHEY *Lett.* (1856) I. 51, I believe, had you been there, you would have rapped out some most seamanly oaths. **1885** CLARK RUSSELL *Strange Voy.* III. xiii. 238 But for the seamanly foresight of Nipper in anchoring a line to warp along with we shouldn't have been able to stir the raft from the ship's side. **1905** *Speaker* 11 Nov. 126/1 Their desires, apart from the desire to do their difficult work seamanly, are centred in seal-steaks and bear-soup.

seamanship ('siːmənʃɪp). [f. SEAMAN + -SHIP.] The art or practice of managing a ship at sea; the skill of a good seaman.

1766 SMOLLETT *Trav.* I. xiv. 241 The first captain..who knows as little of seamanship as I do of Arabic. **1855** MACAULAY *Hist. Eng.* xviii. IV. 236 They maintained the conflict with their usual courage and with more than their usual seamanship. **1886** *Encycl. Brit.* XXI. 589/1 Seamanship is the art of sailing, manœuvring, and preserving a ship or a boat in all positions and under all reasonable circumstances.

'sea-mark.

1. The boundary or limit of the flow of the sea. *lit.* and *fig.* †*full sea mark*, the limit of high tide.

1485 MALORY *Arthur* v. v. 168 And so weltryng and walowynge they rolled doune the hylle tyl they came to the see marke. **1572** in *9th Rep. Hist. MSS. Comm.* App. I. 277/2 This yere the kaiye on southesyde..was builded by the towne vnder full seamarcke. **1637** RUTHERFORD *Lett.* clxxiii. (1862) I. 406 As the houses of sand within the sea-mark, which the children of men are building. **1731** T. BOSTON *Mem.* (1899) 72 And here, I think, was the full sea-mark of my perplexing circumstances aforesaid. **1758** BORLASE *Nat. Hist. Cornw.* 51 A few violent repeated storms should..raise those sands above full Sea-mark. **1818** SHELLEY *Rev. Islam* I. xvi, On the bare strand Upon the sea-mark a small boat did wait. **1851** MRS. BROWNING *Casa Guidi Wind.* 18 We must look to it to excel as ye And bear our age as far, unlimited By the last sea-mark!

2. a. A conspicuous object distinguishable at sea which serves to guide or warn sailors in navigation.

1566 *Act 8 Eliz.* c. 13 That the foresayd Mayster Wardens ..of the Trinytie Howse..shall..set up suche and so many Beakons and Signes of the Sea..for Sea Markes. **1590** SPENSER *F.Q.* II. x. 6 The venturous Mariner..For safeties sake that same his sea-marke made, And namd it Albion. **1617** MORYSON *Itin.* I. 119 Upon the top of this Mountaine was a Tower,..upon which a light was hung for a sea-marke. **1778** *Eng. Gazetteer* (ed. 2) s.v. *Stoke*, The steeple is a sea-mark to ships that pass the mouth of the Orwell. **1843** ARNOLD *Hist. Rome* III. 284 Two solitary pillars still remain, and serve as a seamark to guide ships into the great harbour. **1877** TENNYSON *Harold* II. i, If I caught them, they should hang Cliff-gibbeted for sea-marks.

attrib. **1885** RUSKIN *Pleas. Eng.* 88 The sea-mark isle, Heligoland.

b. *fig.* and in fig. context, now esp. with allusion to Shakes. *Oth.* v. ii. 271.

1589 *Pasquil's Return* A iij b, I desire not to cast it out as a block..for any to stumble at,..but as a Sea-marke to discouer the quicksands of newe Religions. **1607** SHAKS. *Cor.* v. iii. 74 Like a great Sea-marke standing euery flaw, And sauing those that eye thee. **1693** O. HEYWOOD *Best Entail* vi. Wks. 1826 IV. 473 Wicked parents are set before you as sea-marks, to avoid, not as landmarks, to guide you. **1739** CIBBER *Apol.* (1756) II. 43 A Sea-mark of danger to future managers in their theatrical course of government. **1932** *Proc. Brit. Acad.* XVII. 57 He [*sc.* Virgil] fixed for the imagination of the Roman race..the limit of its aspiration and achievement, the very sea-mark of its utmost sail. **1955** *Times* 11 May 11/4 Often they even marked, though not the very butt and seamark of his utmost sail, at least his objective for the time being.

'sea-maw. Now *dial.* Forms: 5 semawe, -mow, 6 -maw, 7- sea-maw. [MAW *sb.*³] = SEAMEW.

c **1425** *Voc.* in Wr.-Wülcker 641/1 *Hec fuliga*, semawe. *c* **1440** *Promp. Parv.* 452/2 Semow, bryd, *aspergo*. *c* **1450** [see MAW *sb.*³]. *a* **1490** [see MOW *sb.*³]. **1544** TURNER *Avium Præcip.* D 7, De Folica..Anglicè a white semaw with a black cop. **1605** DRAYTON *Man in Moon* 183 The greedie Sea-maw fishing for the fry. **1818** SCOTT *Hrt. Midl.* xliv, Like sea-maws and clack-geese before a storm.

Sc. Proverb. **1721** KELLY *Sc. Prov.* 118 Give your own Sea Maws your own Fish Guts. If you have any Superfluities give them to your poor Relations. **1816** SCOTT *Antiq.* xv, Ye ken my gudeman likes to ride the expresses himsell—we maun gie our ain fish-guts to our ain sea-maws. **1895** P. H. HUNTER *James Inwick* xix, Na, na, we'll keep oor ain fish guts for oor ain sea maws!

seame, obs. Sc. form of SEEM *v.*

seamed (siːmd), *ppl. a.*¹ [f. SEAM *v.*² + -ED¹.] In the senses of the verb.

1656 L. THETFORD *Markham's Perf. Horseman* 122 A rough, grosse seamed Hoof, shewes an age or over-heating. **1864** WHITTIER *Poems, What the Birds said* 25 O'er dusky faces, seamed and old..We saw your star-dropt flag uncoil. **1871** L. STEPHEN *Playgr. Eur.* iv. (1894) 101 The seamed and distorted rocks. **1885** MISSES BRIETZCKE & ROOPER *Needlewk. & Knitting* II. 99 Purl knitting is also called seamed knitting.

'seamed, *ppl. a.*² *rare*⁻⁰. [? erron. inferred from *enseamed*: see ENSEAM *v.*¹ I.] (See quot.)

1864 *Chamb. Encycl.* s.v. *Falconry*, When in good condition, she [a hawk] is enseamed; when out of condition, seamed. Hence in later Dicts.

seamer ('siːmə(r)). [f. SEAM *v.*² + -ER¹. (OE. had *seámere* tailor, f. *seám* SEAM *sb.*¹)]

1. a. (See quot. 1843.) **b.** A seaming-machine.

1843 *Penny Cycl.* XXVII. 181/1 There are three classes of operatives engaged [in the stocking-trade]: the 'winders'..; the 'stockingers'; and the 'seamers', who make the stockings out of the pieces thus produced... The 'seamers' are women. **1872** T. COOPER *Life* 141 He had also to pay so much per dozen to the female 'seamer' of the hose. **1884** [see *seaming-machine*, SEAMING *vbl. sb.*].

2. *Cricket.* A seam bowler; also, a delivery by a seam bowler.

1952 *Observer* 25 May 10/1 R. Smith, with his medium-paced 'seamers'—to use a modern and not too unmeaning term—and Bailey..began almost to persuade us that their names might be G. Lohmann and S. F. Barnes. **1955** *Times* 5 July 4/1 Silk was probably right in thinking that his seamers would get more out of it than his spinners. **1963** *Times* 13 June 3/1 It indicated that the intention of both captains was to rely entirely upon their seamers, which they duly did. **1976** DEXTER & MAKINS *Testkill* 140 With the new ball due well before lunch he sensibly switched to Flinders' leg-spin and Lytton's seamers.

seamew ('siːmjuː). Forms: 5–6 se(e)mewe, 6–7 sea mewe, (7 sea mue), 6– seamew. [f. SEA *sb.* + MEW *sb.*¹] The common gull, *Larus canus.*

c **1430** LYDG. *Min. Poems* (Percy Soc.) 202 The semewe with his fetherys whyte. **1480** CAXTON *Ovid's Met.* XI. xxi, They ben called Alcyones or see mewes. **1555** EDEN *Decades* (Arb.) 184 Seemewes, gulles. **1667** MILTON *P.L.* XI. 831 An Iland salt and bare, The haunt of Seales and Orcs, and Sea-mews clang. **1725** POPE *Odyss.* v. 86 The chough, the sea-mew, the loquacious crow. **1812** BYRON *Ch. Har.* I. Song. i, The breakers roar, And shrieks the wild sea-mew. **1890** R. BOLDREWOOD *Col. Reformer* (1891) 149 The yacht, sweeping like a seamew over the..billow.

seamfree ('siːmfriː), *a.* (and *sb.*) [f. SEAM *sb.*¹ + FREE *a.*] Of stockings: = SEAMLESS *a.* Also *absol.* as *sb.*

1959 *Manch. Guardian* 27 July 4/2 Plaza..have a seamfree called 'Riviera' which wears well. **1960** *Sunday Express* 14 Feb. 14/4 The percentage of seam-free stockings sold today is steadily rising. **1976** *Leicester Trader* 24 Nov. 2/4 There are several styles [of stockings] to choose from at Plants including Wolsey Monte Carlo seamfree 15 denier at 59p a pair.

†**'seaming,** *sb. Obs.* A variety of apple.

1664 EVELYN *Kal. Hort.*, *Aug.* 72 The Seaming Apple.

seaming ('siːmɪŋ), *vbl. sb.* [f. SEAM *v.*² + -ING¹.]

a. The action of SEAM *v.*²; also *concr.*, a seam or seams.

c **1450** *Mirour Saluacioun* 3205 Hire sons cote inconsutyle with out semyng. **1541** R. COPLAND *Guydon's Quest. Chirurg.* L ij b, Questyons vpon the Anathomy of seamynge or stytchynge. **1631** T. POWELL *Tom of All Trades* 47 Let them [i.e. your daughters] learne plaine workes of all kind, so they take heed of too open seaming. **1795** HERSCHEL in *Phil. Trans.* LXXXV. 365 A kind of seaming, well known to those who make iron funnels for stoves. **1880** *Plain Hints* 55 For those who are called upon to do seaming and felling, these [pieces of calico] will be divided, so as to form two pieces. **1884** KNIGHT *Dict. Mech.* Suppl., *Seaming*, the marginal line which surrounds a seine, and to which the meshes are seized.

b. *attrib.* and *Comb.*, as ***seaming bar, machine, mallet, stitch, twine***; **seaming lace**, lace used for insertion in or for covering and ornamenting seams; **seaming plough**, one for drawing seed-drills.

1795 *Seaming bar [see SEAM *v.*² 3]. **1616** B. JONSON *Devil an Ass* II. v. 9 That weares such petticoates, and lace to her smocks, Broad *seaming laces (as I see 'hem hang there). **1858** SIMMONDS *Dict. Trade*, *Seaming-lace*, a coach-maker's lace, used to cover seams and edges. **1865** MRS. BURY PALLISER *Hist. Lace* 300 *note*, 'Seaming' lace and spacing lace appear to have been generally used at this period [Jas. I] to unite the breadths of linen, instead of a seam sewed. We find them employed for cupboard cloths,..shirts, &c. through-out the accounts of King James and Prince Charles. **1847** *Rep. Comm. Patents 1846* (U.S.) 214 My improved *seaming machine for turning down and forming a seam of the flange surrounding the bottoms of the buckets. **1875** KNIGHT *Dict. Mech.*, *Seaming-machine*, a machine for forming the joints at the edges of sheet-metal plates. **1884** *Ibid.* Suppl., *Seaming Machine.* The Royer & Lincoln seamer..trims woven goods neatly and evenly; and joins the margin of cloth outside the seam. **1703** T. N. *City & C. Purchaser* 193 So much of the Sheet as lies over the Cavity is set down into it with the *Seaming-mallet. **1842** LANCE *Cottage Farmer* 16 There may be a *seaming plough pass over the land,..to draw the drills; the seed may then be cast thinly. **1880** *Plain Hints* 16 The shape of the *seaming-stitch is quite different to hemming. **1794** *Rigging & Seamanship* I. 92 The seams..are..stitched up..with double *seaming twine.

seamless ('siːmlɪs), *a.* Also 5 semlesse, semeles. [f. SEAM *sb.*¹ + -LESS.] **1.** Without a seam; of a garment, woven without a seam. Now *esp.* of tubing and women's stockings or tights.

The word was used very freely by 17th c. divines in such phrases as ***Christ's seamless coat, garment, vest***, etc. with reference to John xix. 23, as typifying unity in the Church.

1483 *Cath. Angl.* 329/1 Semlesse (*MS. A.* Semeles), *inconsutilis*. **1624** DONNE *Wks.* (1839) V. 265 Christ..suffered his flesh to be torn, but not his seamless garment. **1876** *Encycl. Brit.* IV. 218/2 Solid or seamless brass tubes.. are made by drawing down short thick cast cylinders of brass till they reach the desired gauge or thinness. **1880** *Times* 21 Sept. 4/4 The one novelty..in the exhibition is a small case of absolutely seamless boots. **1901** *Westm. Gaz.* 5 Feb. 8/1 An ingenious system of building extremely light, seamless boats. **1904** GOODCHILD & TWENEY *Technol. & Sci. Dict.* 146/1 The [cycle] frame is generally formed of thin seamless steel tubing. **1921** *Daily Colonist* (Victoria, B.C.) 4 Oct. 5/1 Seamless (fashioned without seams). The women's hose knit to fit without a seam. **1959** *Observer* 22 Mar. 3/8 The seamless stocking, or 'circular' as the trade calls it, has always been made, but used to be thought of as an inferior thing. **1968** *Economist* 9 Nov. 94/1 Tubes is commissioning a new seamless tube mill, where profits ought to start this autumn. **1969** A. J. HALL *Stand. Handbk. Textiles* (ed. 7) iii. 154 The seamless hose are knitted on circular machines.

Comb. *a* **1661** FULLER *Worthies*, *York-Sh.* (1662) III. 208 Wearing seamless-woven-coats.

2. *fig. spec.* as ***seamless web***, orig. with reference to the concept of history as an integral whole (see quot. 1898).

1862 E. DICKINSON *Poems* (1955) I. 246 As if some Caravan of Sound Had parted Rank, Then knit, and swept —In Seamless Company. **1898** POLLOCK & MAITLAND *Hist. Eng. Law bef. Edw. I* (ed. 2) I. I. i. 1 Such is the unity of all history that any one who endeavours to tell a piece of it must feel that his first sentence tears a seamless web. **1929** *Oxf. Poetry* 12 A small patch of light on the seamless blank. **1952** AUDEN *Nones* 39 The three wise Maries come Sossing through seamless waters. **1964** [see INTEGRALISM]. **1976** T. EAGLETON *Crit. & Ideology* iii. 94 *The Prelude* is *formally* fissured by its ideological contradictions, unable to rise to the seamless impersonal epic it would wish itself to be. **1977** *Time* 10 Oct. 10/3 'Many of us find it intellectually difficult', he said, 'to penetrate the seamless web of the Japanese politico-economic system.'

Hence **'seamlessly** *adv.*

1906 SAINTSBURY *Hist. Eng. Prosody* I. 367 The whole web is woven seamlessly and without break.

seamlet ('siːmlɪt). [f. SEAM *sb.*¹ + -LET.] A small seam or stratum.

1891 J. C. ATKINSON *Moorland Parish* 395 The bed of laminated clay, with intercalated seamlets of very fine sand.

'sea-monk.

†**1.** The monk-fish. *Obs.*

1611 FLORIO, *Mónaco*..a fish called a Sea-munke. **1666** J. DAVIES *Hist. Caribby Isl.* I. xvii. 101 There is another kind of Porposes which..from the resemblance there is between their heads and the frocks of Friers, some call them Monks-heads, and Sea-Monks [orig. F. *Moines de Mer*].

2. 'The monk seal' (*Cent. Dict.* 1891).

sea monkey. 1. A heraldic animal which is part monkey, part fish.

1909 A. C. FOX-DAVIES *Compl. Guide Heraldry* xiii. 230 It may be as well to allude to the asserted heraldic existence of the sea-monkey, though I am not aware of any instance in which it is borne.

2. A brine shrimp, *Artemia salina*, often used as food for fish in aquaria.

1973 *Sunday Mail* (Brisbane) 3 June 6/2 'Sea monkeys'.. are currently booming in the United States. They come as a parcel of eggs that look like dried crystal. But..after the eggs are dropped into water they grow into what looks like sea shrimp. **1976** 'D. HALLIDAY' *Dolly & Nanny Bird* ii. 29 'They're Sea Monkeys.'.. 'Brine shrimps... Fish eat them.'

sea-monster. A monster of the sea.

1. A huge fish, cetacean, or the like.

c **1586** C'TESS PEMBROKE *Ps.* CIV. xi, Sea-monsters there, their plaies and pastymes show. **1611** BIBLE *Lam.* iv. 3 Euen the sea-monsters [*marg.* or, sea calues] draw out the breast. **1762** *Ann. Reg.* 103 A sea-monster was cast ashore..near Leith. It is supposed to be of the shark kind. **1860** WRAXALL *Life in Sea* ii. 27 This sea-monster [*Rhytina Stelleri*]..had a black skin an inch thick.

2. A fabulous marine animal of terrifying proportions and shape.

1596 SHAKS. *Merch. V.* III. ii. 57 When he did redeeme The virgine tribute, paied by howling Troy To the Sea-monster. **1599** B. JONSON *Cynthia's Rev.* IV. i, Like a sea-monster, that were to ravish Andromeda from the rocke. **1667** MILTON *P.L.* I. 462 Dagon his Name, Sea Monster, upward Man And downward Fish. **1917** E. POUND *Lustra* 86 The sea-monster Bulges the squarish bronzes. **1952** C. DAY LEWIS tr. *Virgil's Aeneid* III. 65 Below, she is a weird sea-monster With dolphin's tail and a belly of wolverine sort.

3. *jocular.*

1761 COLMAN *Jealous Wife* III. i, He is a perfect Sea-Monster, and always looks and talks as if he was upon Deck.

sea-moss.

1. A kind of seaweed; = CORALLINE *sb.*¹ I.

1548 TURNER *Names of Herbs* (E.D.S.) 21 Bryon thalassion named in latin Muscus marinus is of two sortes. .. The one kynde is called Vsnea marina, & it may be called in english sea mosse, it groweth aboute stones and shelles in the sea. **1579** LANGHAM *Gard. Health* (1633) 594 Sea mosse is good to be laid to hot tumors. **1612** DRAYTON *Poly-olb.* xviii. 761 From Shepey, sea-moss some [bring], to cool his boiling blood. *c* **1711** PETIVER *Gazophyl.* vi. 58 Soft-feathered Cape Coralline... This elegant Sea Moss is not brittle like the Shop Coralline. **1877** BRYANT *Sella* 177 Thou shalt sleep Thy weariness away on downy banks Of sea-moss.

2. = CARRAGEEN.

1891 in *Century Dict.*

3. = *sea-mat* (SEA *sb.* 23 d).

1885 *Encycl. Brit.* XIX. 429/1.

seamost ('siːməʊst), *a. rare.* [f. SEA *sb.* + -MOST.] Situated nearest the sea.

1626 *Sir F. Drake Revived* (1628) 47 He sent the Lyon, to the seamost Island of the Catiuaas, to discry the truth of the report. *a* **1851** MOIR *Poet. Wks.* (1852) II. 26 Thy seamost town, Yclept in Saxon Chronicles Eske-mouthe.

'sea-mouse. [Cf. L. *mūs marīnus* (Pliny), some shell-fish.]

1. A marine dorsibranchiate annelid of the family *Aphroditidæ*, esp. *Aphrodite aculeata.*

c **1520** L. ANDREWE *Noble Life* III. lvii. in *Babees Bk.*, Mus marinus, the see mouse, gothe out of the water, &..laith her egges in..the erthe. **1580–3** GREENE *Mamillia* I. Wks. (Grosart) II. 98 The Lyon cooleth his stomacke with eating the Seamouse. **1664** HUBERT *Catal. Rarities* (1665) 16 A Sea Mouse, so called from the forme of his head and beard; this fish..but for his finnes..is something like a Serpent in colour, and is about a foot long. **1752** J. HILL *Hist. Anim.* 90 The subcylindric variegated Aphrodita. The Sea Mouse. **1854** H. MILLER *Sch. & Schm.* (1858) 64 The brilliant metallic plumage of the sea-mouse (*Aphrodita*), steeped as in the dyes of the rainbow, excited our admiration. **1863** WOOD *Illustr. Nat. Hist.* III. 706 The Sea-mouse, as the creature is called from its hairy coat. **1894** HALL CAINE *Manxman* III. vii. 141 The sea-mouse shining like fire.

2. [? For **sea-mose*; cf. *titmouse*.] A local name for the dunlin and other small shore-birds.

1885 SWAINSON *Prov. Names Birds* 194 Dunlin (*Tringa alphina*)... Sea mouse (Lancashire; Dumfries). *Ibid.* 203 Little Tern (*Sterna minuta*). Sparling (West Lancashire). Where the eggs and young are called 'sea mice'. **1894** *Northumb. Gloss.*, *Sea-mice*, the small waders; the sanderling,..the stints,..the dotterils.

seamster, sempster ('siːmstə(r), 'sɛm(p)stə(r)). *arch.* Forms: α. 1 **sǽmestre, séamystre, sémestre**, 1–2 **séamestre**, 4 **semstere**, 4–7 **semster**, 5–7 **semester**, 6 **seamester**, (*Sc.* **semestair, -are, semistar**, 6–7 *Sc.* **semister**), 7– **seamster**; β. 6 **shempster**, 7 **seampster**, 6– **sempster**. [OE. *séamestre*, fem. formation corresponding to *séamere* tailor: see SEAMER and -STER.] One who sews; one whose occupation is sewing, esp. the making and mending of garments; a tailor, seamstress.

Originally a designation of a woman, but in OE. already applicable to a man. Now only applied to one of the male sex, *seamstress* being commonly used for a female sewer.

α. *c* **995** in Kemble *Cod. Diplom.* VI. 131 Ane crencestræn, and ane semestran. *c* **1000** ÆLFRIC *Gram.* xxx. (Z.) 190/6 *Sartum* (of ðam is *sartor* seamystre, *sartrix* heo). *a* **1100** *Ags. Voc.* in Wr.-Wülcker 312 *Sartrix*, seamestre. **1379** *Poll-tax W. Riding* in *Yorks. Archæol. Jrnl.* VI. 327 Margareta filia dicte Matilde, *Semstere*. *c* **1400** *Destr. Troy* 1585 Sadlers, souters, semsteris fyn. **1479** *Nottingham Rec.* II. 300 Cecily ..semster. **1527** *Acc. Ld. High Treas. Scot.* V. 314 Item, to Jonet Dowglas, semestair of the Kingis lynnyng claithis, xxv li. **1573** TUSSER *Husb.* (1878) 176 Good semsters be sowing of fine pretie knackes. **1601** F. GODWIN *Bps. of Eng.* 372 This woman was commended to him for a very cunning seamster. **1630** BRATHWAIT *Eng. Gentlem.* (1641) 255 A gentleman is a man of himselfe, without the addition of either Taylor, Millener, seamster or haberdasher. **1857** KINGSLEY *Two Y. Ago* I. x. 159 Tom was a good seamster, as all travellers should be. **1858** CARLYLE *Fredk. Gt.* x. iii. II. 611 He told me, 'The Duke of Strelitz was an excellent seamster'; fit to be Tailor to Your Majesty in a manner. **1890** S. J. DUNCAN *Soc. Departure* 213 He was squatting on the floor of a room..with two or three fellow seamsters.

β. **1550** BALE *Eng. Votaries* II. E iij, A yong wench ther, which was a very connyng shempster. **1599** BRETON *Will of Wit*, etc. (Grosart) 59/1 If hee bee a good taylor, shee is a good sempster. **1659** HEYLIN *Certamen Epist.* 331 They might have put up all their gettings into a Sempsters Thimble, and not filled it neither. **1719** D'URFEY *Pills* IV. 102 Sempsters, Tire-women. **1765** STERNE *Tr. Shandy* II. v, [Corporal Trim] attending my uncle Toby..as a valet, groom, barber, cook, sempster, and nurse. **1836** N. H. NICOLAS *Walton's Angler* Life 2 *note*, Izaak Walton followed the trade of a sempster or haberdasher.

†**b.** *attrib.*

1571 *Wills & Inv. N.C.* (Surtees 1835) 362, vj clowtes of fyne semster nedles. **1599** *Return fr. Parnass.* I. i. 372 He.. bringes out signiour Barbarisme in a case of nightcapps,.. like a blocke in a seamster-shopp.

Hence **'sempstering** *vbl. sb. rare*, the occupation of a seamster. Also *attrib.*

1822 LAMB *Elia* Ser. I. *Compl. Decay of Beggars*, Expiating their fallen condition upon the three-foot eminence of some sempstering shop-board. **1874** HARDY *Far fr. Mad. Crowd* xli, She's been picking up a living at seampstering.

seamstress, sempstress ('siːmstrɪs, 'sɛm(p)strɪs). Forms: α. 7 **semstress(e, seamestress**, 8 **seemstress**, 9 **semstress**, 7– **seamstress**; β. (7 **sempstresse, sempstriss**), 7– **sempstress**. [f. SEAMSTER, SEMPSTER + -ESS.] A woman who seams or sews; a needlewoman whose occupation is plain sewing as distinguished from dress or mantle-making, decorative embroidery, etc.

α. **1644** HOWELL *Twelve Treat.* (1661) 47 A great masse of money and plate was brought into the Guild-hall, the Semstresse brought in her silver Thimble,..the Cook his Spoons. **1665** PEPYS *Diary* 8 Apr., To the Old Exchange, and there, of my pretty seamstress, bought four bands. **1711** STEELE *Spect.* No. 182 ¶3 An Irish Fellow, who dresses very fine..and is the Admiration of Seamstresses who are under Age in Town. **1872** *Daily News* 24 July, The wrongs and hardships of the seamstress and the milliner have been set forth in thrilling poetry.

β. *a* **1613** OVERBURY *Charact., Maquerela* Wks. (1856) 100 Shee can easily turne a sempstresse into a waiting gentlewoman. **1659–60** PEPYS *Diary* 2 Feb, I..went to Mrs. Johnson, my Lord's sempstress. **1726** SWIFT *Gulliver* I. vi, Two hundred sempstresses were employed to make me shirts, and linen for my bed and table. **1758** JOHNSON *Idler* No. 33 ¶23 My sempstress..has lost the measure. **1871** *Daily News* 6 Nov., Among the prisoners..were two women —a sempstress..and a servant.

Hence **'seamstressing** *nonce-wd.*, the action of working as a seamstress. **'seamstress-ship**, the position, work, or skill of a seamstress.

1816 SCOTT *Antiq.* xvi, The little apartment was.. ornamented too by such relics of her youthful arts of sempstress-ship as Mrs. Hadoway had retained. *a* **1854** CAROLINE B. SOUTHEY *Poet. Wks.* (1867) 94 And near at hand [sat] The maiden sister friend..At her coarse sempstresship. **1873** MRS. WHITNEY *Other Girls* vii, Dull work in the great ware-rooms, or now and then all days' seamstressing in families.

†**'seamstressy.** *Obs. rare*$^{-1}$. [f. SEAMSTRESS + -SY.] The occupation or work of a seamstress.

1760 STERNE *Tr. Shandy* III. xlii, As an appendage to seamstressy, the thread-paper might be of some consequence to my mother.

†**'seamstry, 'sempstry.** *Obs.* [f. SEAMSTER + -Y.] The occupation or employment of a seamster or seamstress. Also *attrib.* in *seamstry-work*.

α. **1598** FLORIO, *Dietro punto*, a back-stitch in seamstrie worke. *c* **1630** *Trag. Rich. II* (1870) 38 Tis strange to take her from her semsterye. **1688** HOLME *Armoury* III. 97/2 Seamstry work follows next in order to that of a Taylor.

β. **1631** T. POWELL *Tom of All Trades* (1876) 173 She may learne what belongs to her improvement, for Sempstrie. **1695** A. DE LA PRYME *Diary* Mar. (Surtees) 53 The Quakers ..now were fine cloathes, and learns all sorts of sempstry and behavour. **1760–72** H. BROOKE *Fool of Qual.* (1809) I. 127 My wife had lately requested her to look out for some sempstry-work among the neighbours.

†**'seamy,** *a.*[1] *Obs. rare*$^{-1}$. In 6 **seymy**. [f. SEAM *sb.*[3] + -Y.] Greasy.

a **1529** SKELTON *Agst. Garnesche* iii. 169 Thou gresly gargone glaymy, Thou swety slouen seymy.

seamy ('siːmɪ), *a.*[2] [f. SEAM *sb.*[1] + -Y.]

1. Having a seam or suture; characterized by seams. **seamy side**, lit. the under side of a garment, etc. on which the rough edges of the seams are visible; *fig.* [after Shaks.] the worst, most degraded or the roughest side (of life, character, etc.).

1604 SHAKS. *Oth.* IV. ii. 146 Some such Squire he was That turn'd your wit, the seamy-side without, And made you to suspect me with the Moore. **1837** MRS. CAROLINE NORTON *Let.* 4 Nov. in Smiles *Publisher & Friends* (1891) II. 415, I begin to think it would be pleasanter to follow a marching regiment than to see the seamy side of this intellectual trade. **1859** *Sat. Rev.* 2 Apr. 403/1 He appreciated to a considerable extent, what we may perhaps venture to call the seamy side of human affairs. **1865** CARLYLE *Fredk. Gt.* x. ii. III. 223 The splendid and the sordid, the seamy side and the smooth, of Life at Cirey. **1882** L. STEPHEN *Swift* viii. 185 The righteous hatred of brutality and oppression which is but the seamy side of a generous sympathy. **1899** H. A. DOBSON *Paladin of Philanthropy* vi. 146 The knowledge of the seamy side of letters.

2. Of the nature of or resembling a seam or seams; marked with a seam.

1776 MICKLE tr. *Camoens' Lusiad* IV. 75 His crimson seamy scars reveal The sure-aim'd vengeance of the Lusian steel. **1786** BURNS *Addr. to Edinb.* v, Like some bold Vet'ran ..mark'd with many a seamy scar. **1857** GEO. ELIOT *Scenes Cler. Life, Amos Barton* ii, A one-eyed woman, with a scarred and seamy face. **1874** S. LANIER *Corn* 127 To where ..Yon old deserted Georgian hill Bares to the sun his piteous aged crest And seamy breast.

Comb. **1840** CARLYLE *Heroes* v. (1841) 289 The rough seamy-faced, rawboned College Servitor.

Hence **'seaminess.**

1875 BESANT & RICE *With Harp & Crown* ix, A gleam of light upon his face, which brought out the more forcibly the seaminess with which his passions were furrowing it. **1898** G. WYNDHAM *Poems of Shaks.* Introd. 60 Jonson's.. virulence..spared neither the seaminess of an opposite's apparel nor the defects in his personal appearance.

sean, alternative form of SEINE.

sean, obs. f. SCENE; variant of SENE *Obs.*, synod.

seanachie, variant form of SENNACHIE.

Seanad Eireann ('ʃænəd 'ɛərən). [Ir. *Seanad Éireann* the senate of Ireland.] The upper house of the parliament of the Republic of Ireland. Freq. *ellipt.* as **Seanad**.

1922 [see OIREACHTAS 2]. **1923** W. B. YEATS in *Senate Speeches* (1961) 36, I hope I have the leave of the Seanad to use a different form of words. **1937** *Bunreacht na hÉireann* (*Constitution of Ireland*) 48 Article 18. 1 Seanad Eireann shall be composed of sixty members, of whom eleven shall be nominated members and forty-nine shall be elected members. **1962** M. AMELLER *Parliaments* I. ii. 10 While the method of appointment of members of the Second Chamber is not altogether in keeping with ordinary democratic principles, that is offset by the fact that the powers of the Seanad are considerably curtailed. **1974** *Encycl. Brit. Macropædia* IX. 886/2 There are..60 members of the Seanad... The Seanad may delay..bills passed by the Dáil.

‖**séance** ('seɪɒns, ‖seɑ̃s). [Fr. *séance* a sitting, f. OF. *seoir* (:—L. *sedēre*) to sit.]

1. *gen.* A sitting of a deliberative or administrative body (esp. of a learned society), or of a number of persons assembled for discussion, or instruction by a lecturer, or the like. Also *séance royale*, a royal audience. *Loosely* (chiefly *U.S.*), a meeting or discussion.

1789 A. YOUNG *Jrnl.* 20 June in *Trav. France* (1792) I. 115 A message from the King.., that he should meet them on Monday; and, under pretence of preparing the hall for the seance royale, the French guards were placed..to prevent any of the deputies entering the room. **1803** LAMB *Let. to Manning* Wks. 1876 II. 216 Your séances and conversaziones, which I have a shrewd suspicion must be something dull. **1884** *Kendal Mercury* 3 Oct. 5/3 The British Association..should be a..secret conclave, and every one attending its seances for reportorial purposes deserves to have his ears cropped. **1922** JOYCE *Ulysses* 644 Come, he counselled, to close the *séance*. **1934** E. POUND *Eleven New Cantos* xxxiv. 16 At the Seance Royale last Thursday he had talked of His death in defence of the country. **1962** W. SCHIRRA in *Into Orbit* 32 We would lock ourselves up in our office at Langley until we had a solution that satisfied us all... We called a session like this a 'seance'. **1977** *Time* 17 Jan. 41/1 For an hour most nights, he conducts a long-distance séance (at $3 a minute) with..his Australian proconsul, from the..desk in his study.

2. *spec.* A meeting for the investigation or exhibition of spiritualistic phenomena.

1845 WARBURTON *Cresc. & Cross* I. xv. 153 The hour was so late that no other boys were to be found; and so the seance broke up. **1860** *All Year Round* No. 66. 373 The spirits rapped out their dismissal, and the séance was at an end. **1881** FROUDE *Short Stud.* Ser. IV. (1883) 225 The disciple who has been at a spiritualist's séance. **1902** F. PODMORE *Mod. Spiritualism* I. ii. I. 41 The development of the Poltergeist performance into the phenomena of the séance-room.

3. a. A 'sitting' for medical treatment.

1875 H. C. WOOD *Therap.* (1879) 37 The electrical séances should be tri-weekly, each lasting about fifteen minutes, and they should be persevered in for months. **1887** D. MAGUIRE *Art Massage* (1888) 101 After the third massage séance, the patient ceased having these mishaps during several hours.

b. A 'sitting' for a portrait.

1877 DISRAELI *Let.* 14 Apr. (1929) viii. 117 Now I am going to the Palace for my 3rd Seance [to Von Angeli]. **1919** R. FRY *Let.* 21 Oct. (1972) II. 460 All wanted me to draw their portraits so that every evening in the café I had to have a *séance*.

seane, variant of SENE *Obs.* synod.

'sea-,nettle. The popular name of certain radiate marine animals of the class *Acalephæ*, having the property of stinging when touched. †Formerly applied also to the sea-anemone.

1601 HOLLAND *Pliny* XXXII. x. II. 449 The Sea-nettle (a fish so called). **1747** *Gentl. Mag.* 121 Among which he reckons..the sea-star and sea-nettle. **1835** KIRBY *Hab. & Inst. Anim.* I. vi. 197 These belong to what are vulgarly called the jelly-fish or sea-nettles. **1862** ANSTED *Channel Isl.* II. ix. (ed. 2) 239 Acalephæ, or Sea Nettles.

seangreen, obs. form of SENGREEN *Obs.*

seannachie, variant form of SENNACHIE.

seant, obs. form of SEEING *ppl. a.*

'sea-nymph.

1. *Myth.* A nymph (NYMPH *sb.* 1) supposed to inhabit the sea; a Nereid.

1565 GOLDING *Ovid's Met.* I. 353 The Seanymphes wondred under waves the townes and groves to see. **1601** [see NEREIDES]. **1610** SHAKS. *Temp.* I. ii. 402 Sea-Nimphs hourly ring his knell. **1710** W. KING *Heathen Gods & Heroes* xxxix. (1722) 166 The Sea Nymphs were in great Numbers call'd Nereides. **1815** SCOTT *Ld. of Isles* III. xxviii, Hark! hears he not the sea-nymph speak Her anger in that thrilling shriek! **1871** PALGRAVE *Lyr. Poems* 49 O Italy, mother of nations Like her own fair sea-nymph's brood, Who turn and rend their mother.

2. An antarctic petrel, *Procellaria nereis*.

1875 J. H. KIDDER *Nat. Hist. Kerguelen Isl.* I. 31.

'sea-oak. [tr. mod.L. *quercus marina*.] The seaweed *Fucus vesiculosus*, and other seaweeds of similar appearance; bladder-wrack.

1597 GERARDE *Herbal* II. clix. 1378 *Quercus marinus.* Sea Oke, or Wrake. **1598** SYLVESTER *Du Bartas* II. I. i. *Eden* 598 There lives the Sea-Oak [orig. *le chesne marin*] in a little shell. **1657** W. COLES *Adam in Eden* cvi, Sea Oke or Wrake. **1700** C. LEIGH *Nat. Hist. Lanc.*, etc. I. 92 In some of the Alga's or Sea-Oaks I have observ'd various Capsulæ impleted with a pellucid Gelly. **1796** [see TANG *sb.*[3]]. **1822–29** *Good's Study Med.* (ed. 3) III. 358 The bibulous marine plants which..have been applied to the strumous tumours in the form of epithems, as sea-wrack (*fucus vesiculosus*), sea-tang (*alga marina*), and sea-oak (*quercus marina*).

b. *attrib.*: **sea-oak coralline, sertularia**, the polyp *Sertularia pumila*.

1754 J. ELLIS in *Phil. Trans.* XLVIII. 632 This species I have call'd the sea-oak coralline, from its being most frequently found..adhering to the largest species of the *quercus marinus*. **1802** BINGLEY *Anim. Biog.* (1813) III. 482 The Sea Oak Sertularia. **1882** *Cassell's Nat. Hist.* VI. 290 The Sea Oak Coralline is a common example.

sea-officer. Now somewhat *rare* (very common in 17–18th c.). A naval officer.

1669 R. MONTAGU in *Buccleuch MSS.* (Hist. MSS. Comm.) I. 456 Out of these [gentlemen] the King intends always to choose his sea officers. **1708** *Proclam.* 20 May in *Lond. Gaz.* No. 4440/1 In case any..Warrant Sea-Officers belonging to any Ship of War..be absent. **1833** T. HOOK *Parson's Dau.* I. vii, Saying which..the gallant sea-officer quitted the Parsonage. **1860** GEN. P. THOMPSON *Audi Alt.* III. 129 The first of England's living sea-officers.

sea-otter. 1. a. A marine otter of the shores of the North Pacific, *Enhydris marina* or *lutris*.

1664 HUBERT *Catal. Rarities* (1665) 14 A Sea-Otter. **1710** SIBBALD *Fife & Kinross* 49 Lutra Marina, the Sea-Otter,.. differeth from the Land-Otter, for it is bigger, and the Pile of its Furr is rougher. **1772–84** *Cook's Voy.* (1790) V. 1738 Sea-otters are amphibious. **1818** SCOTT *Rob Roy* xxxiv, A large leathern pouch,..made of the skin of the sea otter. **1836** W. IRVING *Astoria* I. 174 Numbers of canoes soon came off, bringing sea-otter skins to sell. **1879** *Cassell's Techn. Educ.* I. 74/1 The fur of the sea-otter is thick, soft, and woolly.

b. sea-otter's cabbage, the large seaweed *Nereocystis Lütkeana* of the North Pacific, the fronds of which are a favourite resort of sea-otters.

1866 *Treas. Bot.*

2. The thick dark fur of *Enhydra lutris*.

1813 A. HENRY *Jrnl.* 19 Nov. in E. Coues *New Light Early Hist. Greater Northwest* (1897) II. 753 His son had a robe of two sea otters, for which he demanded 48 beavers. **1915** *Chambers's Jrnl.* Jan. 48/2 Of sea-otter, too, perhaps one of the loveliest furs of all, the supply is failing. **1956** J. G. LINKS *Bk. Fur* III. 139 A sea otter collar to his coat was to the great industrialist of the last century what a private stratocruiser is to his successor.

ˈsea-owl.
1. The lump-fish, *Cyclopterus lumpus*.
1601 [see LUMP *sb.*[2] 1]. *a* **1672** [see COCK-PADDLE]. **1836** YARRELL *Brit. Fishes* II. 270.
2. The puffin.
1842 BONNYCASTLE *Newfoundld.* II. 234 The puffin (*alca arctica*) which may be called the sea-owl, from its extraordinary head and wise look.

† sea-ox. *Obs.*
1. The hippopotamus. Cf. SEA-COW.
1600 J. PORY tr. *Leo's Africa* IX. 335 The creatures therein [in the Nile] contained are exceeding strange, as namely sea-horses, sea-oxen, crocodiles [etc.]. *Ibid.* 344 The sea-oxe being couered with an exceeding hard skinne is shaped in all respects like vnto the land-oxe; saue that in bignes it exceedeth not a calfe of sixe moneths olde. **1607** TOPSELL *Four-f. Beasts* 328 Some Græcians call him sometimes a Sea-horsse, and sometimes a Sea-oxe. **1660** F. BROOKE tr. *Le Blanc's Trav.* 202 A hundred Elephants, caparison'd with the skins of Sea-oxen. *Ibid.*, This *Besigu* beares a bow and quiver, a short sword, and a coat of Sea-oxe. **1791** SMELLIE tr. *Buffon* (ed. 3) VI. 278.
2. The walrus or morse.
1613 PURCHAS *Pilgrimage* 626 Neere to New-found-land in 47 deg. is great killing of the Morse or Sea-oxe.

sea-parrot.
1. The puffin.
1664 HUBERT *Catal. Rarities* (1665) 9 A Sea-Parret or Coppernose of Greenland. **1694–1865** [see PARROT *sb.* 3 a].
2. One of several fishes (see PARROT-FISH).
1666 J. DAVIES *Hist. Caribby Isl.* 98 There are also in these Parts certain Fishes scaled like a Carp, but as to colour are as green as a Parrot, whence they are by some called Sea-Parrots. **1706, 1883** [see PARROT *sb.* 3 b].

sea-pen. [PEN *sb.*[2]] A polyp of the genus *Pennatula* or family *Pennatulidæ*.
1763 J. ELLIS in *Phil. Trans.* LIII. 420 This Animal was well known to the ancients by the name of the Sea-Pen. **1768** SOLANDER *Let. to J. Ellis* in *Ann. Reg.* (1769) XII. 188/2 We can hardly buy a plate of shrimps [at Rio de Janeiro], without finding a dozen of your *Pennatula reniformis*, or kidney shaped sea pen, among them. **1840** F. D. BENNETT *Whaling Voy.* II. 102 The sandy beach of the bay is strewn with..sponges, sea-pens [etc.]. **1879** E. P. WRIGHT *Anim. Life* 591 fig., The sea pen (*Pteroides spinosus*). **1883** C. F. HOLDER in *Harper's Mag.* Jan. 184/2 The sea-pens are remarkable for their phosphorescence.

sea-pheasant.
1. The turbot.
1633 [see PHEASANT 2 b]. **1672** JOSSELYN *New-Eng. Rarities* 26 Hallibut or Sea Pheasant. **1737** in W. Walker *Bards Bon-Accord* (1887) 161 Turbot, far requested for his white And mellow flesh, sea-pheasant often named.
2. The pintail duck, *Dafila acuta*; also the longtailed duck, *Harelda glacialis*.
a **1672** WILLUGHBY *Ornith.* (1676) 289 *Anas caudacuta*... Sea Pheasant: The Cracker. **1674, 1837** [see PHEASANT 2 b]. **1842** BONNYCASTLE *Newfoundld.* II. 236 The pintail duck.. from its plumage and the shape of its tail is called the sea pheasant. **1845** ELIZA ACTON *Mod. Cookery* (ed. 2) 285 To roast the pintail, or sea-pheasant. **1893** in Cozens-Hardy *Broad Norf.* 47 *Sea-Phaysant*..Longtailed Duck.

sea-pie[1]. [PIE *sb.*[1]] A common name for the oyster-catcher, *Hæmatopus ostralegus*. Also used in *Her.* as an armorial bearing (see quot. 1780).
1552 *Acc. P'cess Eliz.* 40 in *Camden Misc.* (1853) II, Paid in rewarde..to Mr. Levetts servauntes for bringing of sea-pies, x. s. *c* **1557** S. BURROUGH in *Hakluyt's Voy.* (1599) I. 279 In this place we found plenty of young foule, as Gulles, Seapies, and others. **1615** MARKHAM *Pleas. Princ.* viii. (1635) 37 The Sea-pie is a great devourer of all sorts of Fish. **1747** MALLET *Amyntor & Theod.* Wks. 1759 I. 127 The Sea-Py ceas'd At once to warble. **1772–84** *Cook's Voy.* (1790) IV. 1323 Among the rocks are found black sea pies, with red bills. **1780** EDMONDSON *Heraldry* II. Gloss., *Sea-pie*, a water-fowl, of a dark brown colour, with a red head, and the neck and wings white. **1862** KINGSLEY *Water Bab.* iv. 140 The sea-pies with their red bills and legs, flew to and fro from shore to shore. **1873** BLACK *Pr. Thule* ix. 141 Not even a gull or a sea-pye crossed the..moorland.
transf. **1607** DEKKER & WEBSTER *Northw. Hoe* I. B 2 b, Now blew-bottle? what flutter you for[,] Sea-pye? *Servingman.* Not to catch fish, sir.

sea-pie[2]. [PIE *sb.*[2]] A dish of meat and vegetables, etc. boiled together, with a crust of paste, or 'in layers between crusts, the number of which denominate it a two or three decker' (Smyth *Sailor's Word-bk.* 1867).
1751 *Affect. Narr. of Wager* 66 They shot several wild Fowl, some of which they roasted, putting the rest into what we call a Sea Pye. **1827** SCOTT *Surg. Dau.* vi, Lobscous, sea-pie, and other delicacies of a naval description. **1886** CUNLIFFE *Rochdale Gloss.*, *Sea-pie*, a pie of potatoes and flesh baked in a pan over the fire. **1897** MARY KINGSLEY *W. Africa* 227 Using it also in the preparation of a sort of sea-pie they [the natives] make with meat and fish.
transf. **1847** THACKERAY in *Fraser's Mag.* Jan. 123 Pictorially, *The Drawing-Room Scrap-Book* is a sea-pie, made up of scraps that have been served at many tables before.

ˈsea-piece. [PIECE *sb.* 17 b.] A picture representing a scene at sea.
1656 EVELYN *Diary* 10 July, A piece representing Sir F. Drake's action in the year 1580, an excellent sea-piece. **1681** GREW *Musæum* IV. §iii. 378 A Sea-Piece, consisting wholly in Inlay'd-work, of several Colours, in Stone. **1712** ADDISON *Spect.* No. 489 ¶4 Great Painters..very often employ their Pencils upon Sea-Pieces. **1797** HOLCROFT tr. *Stolberg's Trav.* (ed. 2) II. lxii. 420 He has painted a moonlight sea piece. **1892** BRIGHTON *Sir P. Wallis* 228 Two sea-pieces by Musin occupy a considerable space.

sea-pigeon.
1. A name given (locally) to various birds, as the rock-dove, *Columba livia*, the black guillemot, *Uria grylle*, the grey kittiwake, *Larus canus*.
1620 J. MASON *New-found-land* in *Mem.* (1887) 151 The sea fowles are gulles, sea pigeons. **1664** HUBERT *Catal. Rarities* (1665) 9 A Sea-Pidgeon of Green-land. **1767** tr. *Cranz' Greenland* I. 84 The sea-pidgeon..is like the willock in almost every thing, except its being less. **1819** STEPHENS in *Shaw's Gen. Zool.* XI. 23 Sea pigeon. (*Columba littoralis.*) *Ibid.* 24 It occurs in abundance in New Guinea and Java; by the natives of the latter, it is distinguished by the name of the Sea Pigeon. **1861** COUES in *Proc. Philad. Acad.* 256 They [Black Guillemots] are universally known to the natives and fishermen [of Labrador] as 'Sea-pigeons'. **1870** GILLMORE tr. *Figuier's Reptiles & Birds* 285 The Grey Kittiwake (*Larus canus*) is often called the Sea Pigeon. **1885** SWAINSON *Prov. Names Birds* 168 Rock Dove (*Columba livia*)... Sea pigeon (Ireland).
2. *U.S.* A large green sea-slug.
1885 C. F. HOLDER *Marvels Anim. Life* 169 One of the sea-slugs, a great green creature, commonly known on the [Florida] reef as the sea-pigeon.

sea-pike[1]. [PIKE *sb.*[4]] One of various fishes, as (*a*) a gar-fish, esp. *Belone vulgaris*; (*b*) any fish of the family *Sphyrænidæ*, esp. the genus *Sphyræna*; (*c*) the hake, *Merlucius vulgaris*; (*d*) a fish of the family *Centropomidæ*, of tropical America, esp. *Centropomus undecimalis* (Cent. Dict. 1891).
1601 HOLLAND *Pliny* XXXII. ii. II. 427 The sea pike Lupus. **1611** COTGR., *Peis escome*, the sea Pike, or Spit-fish. **1668** CHARLETON *Onomast.* 136 *Sphyræna*..*Lucius Marinus*, the Sea-Pike, or Spitt-Fish. **1769** PENNANT *Brit. Zool.* III. 274 The common sea pike, or sea needle, sometimes grows to the length of three feet, or more. **1840** *Cuvier's Anim. Kingd.* 294 *Sphyræna*, the Sea Pike, which has been confounded with the *Esox* or True Pike. **1860** BARTLETT *Dict. Amer.* (ed. 3), *Bill-fish*, (*Belone truncata*) a small sea-fish... Also called Sea-pike. **1880–84** F. DAY *Brit. Fishes* I. 301 *Merluccius vulgaris*... The hake,..or sea-pike. **1898** MORRIS *Austral Engl.*, *Sea-Pike*, a fish of New South Wales, *Lanioperca mordax* Günth., of the family *Sphyrænidæ*.

sea-pike[2]. [PIKE *sb.*[5]] A trident.
1870 BRYANT *Iliad* XV. II. 109 He bore A sea-pike two and twenty cubits long.

sea-pine.
1. See PINE *sb.*[2] 2.
1753 *Chambers' Cycl.* Suppl. s.v. *Pine*, 5. The wild sea-pine... 6. The Idæan sea-pine. **1845** BROWNING *Englishm. in Italy* 191 The flat sea-pine crouches.
2. A dark-coloured seaweed. ? *Obs.*
1762 W. HUDSON *Flora Anglica* 470 *Fucus*..*incurvus*.., black Fucus, or Sea Pine. **1777** ROBSON *Brit. Flora* 310 *Fucus incurvus*... Black Wrack. Sea Pine.

sea-pink. [PINK *sb.*[4]] **a.** The plant Thrift, *Armeria maritima*. †**b.** *Cerastium repens*.
1731 MILLER *Gard. Dict.*, *Statice*; Thrift or Sea Pink. **1759**, etc. [see PINK *sb.*[4] 1 b]. **1850** ALLINGHAM *Poems, Before Breakf.* ii, Now the cliff spreads its cheerful adorning Of matted sea-pink under foot. **1897** 'ALLEN RAINE' *Welsh Singer* viii. 68 Flinging himself on the sea-pinks.

seaplane (ˈsiːpleɪn). [f. SEA *sb.* + PLANE *sb.*[5]] An aeroplane designed to be able to operate from water; *spec.* one with floats, in contrast to a flying boat.
1913 [see HYDROPLANE *sb.* 3]. **1914** *Daily Express* 2 Nov. 5/2 The old cruiser Hermes..had been recently used as a seaplane-carrying ship. **1921** *Daily Colonist* (Victoria, B.C.) 5 Oct. 12/3 Seaplane stations have been established by the Air Board of Canada. **1938** *Sun* (Baltimore) 21 July 1/8 Hooked together—the seaplane Mercury above and the flying boat Maia below—the two planes rose from the river Shannon this evening. **1954** P. K. KEMP *Fleet Air Arm* 87 Three cross-Channel steamers were taken up to be transformed into seaplane carriers. **1973** [see REFUEL *v.* 2].

sea-plant. [PLANT *sb.*[1]] A plant growing in the sea or in salt-water, a marine or maritime plant.
1681 GREW *Musæum* II. §v. i. 247 These, and other Sea-Plants hereafter describ'd. **1764** *Ann. Reg.* II. 10 A sea-plant which they boil in seal's fat. **1860** WRAXALL *Life in Sea* viii. 184 They [sea-hares] inhabit the rocks on the coast, and crawl about on the sea-plants.

sea-poose, variant of SEA-PURSE (sense 4).

sea-pork. **a.** 'The flesh of young whales in the western isles of Scotland' (Smyth *Sailor's Word-bk.* 1867). **b.** *Local U.S.* (see quot.).
1885 *Riverside Nat. Hist.* (1888) III. 58 *Amaræcium*, a genus [of compound ascidians] common on our coasts, forms large colonies... The general color is much like that of boiled salt pork,..and the fishermen..call them sea-pork.

seaport (ˈsiːpɔət). [PORT *sb.*[1]] A harbour or port on the sea-coast; a town or city on such a harbour. = PORT *sb.*[1] 1 and 2.
1596 DALRYMPLE tr. *Leslie's Hist. Scot.* I. 12 It hes thir tounes Kircoubrie, Wigtoune, and the quhyt Case, al the thrie gude seyportes. **1712** E. COOKE *Voy. S. Sea* 388 We shall pass by the Sea-Ports, having mention'd them in the precedent Chapter. **1735** BERKELEY *Querist* §266 Wks. 1871 III. 378 The sea-ports of Galway, Limerick, Cork. **1849** MACAULAY *Hist. Eng.* iii. I. 335 Bristol, then the first English seaport. **1874** GREEN *Short Hist.* iv. §3 (1882) 184 The great merchant city..sank..into a petty seaport.
b. *attrib.*, esp. in ***seaport town*** (cf. PORT-TOWN 2).
1705 *Proclam.* 18 Jan. in *Lond. Gaz.* No. 4090/1 Until they Arrive at some Sea Port-Town. **1838** DICKENS *Nich. Nick.* xxii, Portsmouth is a seaport town. **1909** *Edin. Rev.* Oct. 391 Apollo meets the Seaman at a seaport tavern.

sea-pouce, variant of SEA-PURSE (sense 4).

sea-power.
1. A nation or state having international power or influence on sea. Cf. POWER *sb.*[1] 6 b.
1849 GROTE *Greece* II. xxxix. V. 67 The conversion of Athens from a land-power into a sea-power. **1890** MAHAN *Infl. Sea-power Hist.* 225 Before that war [of the Spanish succession] England was one of the sea powers; after it she was *the* sea power, without any second. **1906** W. M. RAMSAY in *Expositor* Apr. 365 Tarsus..became a harbour and a sea power.
2. The strength and efficiency of a nation (or of nations generally) for maritime warfare.
The currency of the term in its more abstract use is due to Captain A. T. Mahan's book, *Influence of Sea-power on History* (1890). In a letter of 19 Feb. 1897, printed in E. Marston, *After Work* (1904) 257, Capt. Mahan states that the combination was deliberately adopted by him 'in order to compel attention'.
1883 SIR J. R. SEELEY *Expansion Eng.* 89 Commerce..was swept out of the Mediterranean by the besom of the Turkish sea-power. **1885** *Encycl. Brit.* XVIII. 574/1 Themistocles.. the founder of the Attic sea-power. **1902** SIR C. BRIDGE in *Encycl. Brit.* XXXII. 493/1 In the first and greatest of the contests waged by the nations of the East against Europe—the Persian wars—sea-power was the governing factor.

seapoy, seapt, obs. forms of SEPOY, SEPT *sb.*

sea-purse. Also (in sense 4) sea-pouce, -puss, -poose.
1. A zoophyte of the genus ALCYONIUM. ? *Obs.*
1806 TURTON *Linn. Syst. Nat.* IV. 653 *Alcyonium Bursa*.. Sea Purse.
2. The horny egg-case of a skate, ray, or shark; a mermaid's purse.
1856 *Eng. Cycl., Nat. Hist.* IV. 530 The young [of Skates] are deposited..in their horny cases... These..are sometimes called sea-purses. **1891** C. L. MORGAN *Anim. Life & Intell.* 220 Each is also protected by a horny case with pointed corners—the so called sea-purse of seaside visitors.
3. A siphonaceous alga, *Codium bursa*, which resembles a sponge.
1853 *Eng. Cycl., Nat. Hist.* I. 115 *Codium*, the Sea-Purse, is a hollow, sub-globose, dark green plant, composed [etc.].
4. *U.S., Atlantic coast.* [ad. the Algonquian language Munsee (Delaware) *sepoûs*, brook, small river: see Mathews *Dict. Americanisms* (1951).] A swirl of the undertow or a double undertow formed by two waves meeting at an angle, making a small whirlpool on the surface of the water, dangerous to bathers.
1842 W. P. HAWES *Sporting Scenes* I. 102, I kept watch of him—when I came to a sea poose—I went in and to the east of it. **1891** *Century Dict.*, *Sea-purse*,..2. A swirl of the undertow [etc.]... Also called *sea-pouce* and *sea-puss*. **1896** *Athletic Sports, Surf & Surf bathing* (1898) 247 As the word is ignored by Webster, I shall invent my own spelling and write it 'sea-poose'. This term is loosely used in different parts of the coast. **1904** *N.Y. Tribune* 29 May II. 7/1 McDonald was a good swimmer, but, getting caught in a sea puss, was shot out to the deep sea with great velocity. **1932** *Sun* (Baltimore) 5 Sept. 6/3 The sea-purse swooped in and picked up a girl bather, who was suddenly seen to whirl about on the surface of the water like a cork.

seapy, obs. form of SEPOY.

sea-quake, seaquake. [after EARTHQUAKE.] A convulsion or sudden agitation of the sea from a submarine eruption or earthquake.
1680 C. NESSE *Church Hist.* 333 This σεισμὸς..is usually understood of an earth-quake, but here 'tis a sea-quake. **1774** GOLDSM. *Nat. Hist.* (1824) I. 53 A violent agitation, or heaving, of the sea... This agitation..may be called, for the sake of perspicuity, a seaquake; and this also is produced by volcanoes. **1827** *Blackw. Mag.* XXI. 273 The phenomenon called a mare moto or seaquake, was heaving the waters of the harbour. **1889** HICKSON *Nat. N. Celebes* iii. 45 This was accompanied by a terrible seaquake.

seaquarium (siːˈkwɛərɪəm). Pl. seaˈquaria. [f. SEA *sb.* + A)QUARIUM.] An aquarium for large marine animals.
1955 *Travel* Dec. 54/2 On the other side of the Sunshine State, at Miami Beach, a new $2,000,000 Seaquarium features giant fishbowls of what is probably the largest collection of tropical marine life in the world. **1959** *Listener* 30 July 186/1 A diver feeding dolphins in the Miami Seaquarium, Florida. **1962** *New Scientist* 15 Mar. 607/2 The great natural aquaria (or seaquaria or oceanaria) in Florida and California. **1969** *Daily Tel.* 24 Apr. 16/3 The seaquarium's Manatee tank is only five feet deep. **1978** *New York* 3 Apr. 74 Come bask in the warmth of exotic..Sonesta Beach Hotel & Tennis Club... Room with private balcony. Admission to the Seaquarium and Crandon Park Zoo. **1982** *Times* 21 Jan. 4/5 The three Clacton whales were kept in Iceland in a 'seaquarium'.

sear (sɪə(r)), *sb.*[1] Forms: 6 serre, 6–7 seare, 7 saer, 9 sere, scear, sear. [Of obscure history.
Commonly regarded as a. OF. *serre* grasp, something that grasps or holds fast, f. *serrer* to grasp, hold fast, press close, repr. late L. *serāre* to bar, bolt, f. L. *sera* bar for a door. The

Fr. word, however, has app. not been found with this specific meaning; in the sense 'foot of a bird of prey' (SERE *sb.*[1]) it is still current, and in OF. it also meant a lock or bolt.]

1. A portion of a gun-lock which engages with the notches of the tumbler in order to keep the hammer at full or half cock, and which is released (at full cock) by pressure upon the trigger.

1596 LAMBARDE *Peramb. Kent* (ed. 2) 452 Euen as a pistole that is ready charged and bent, will flie off by and by, if a man do but touch the Seare. **1622** F. MARKHAM *Bk. War* I. ix. 35 Let the Cocks and Trickers be nimble to goe and come; for as concerning Seares, they are vtterly out of date. **1688** HOLME *Armoury* III. xviii. (Roxb.) 135/1 The seuerall parts of a Fire lock.. The saer or dog. **1802** *Trans. Soc. Arts* XX. 246 Further motion being prevented by a notch in the small sear. **1864** WHEELWRIGHT *Spring Lapl.* 200 It [a gun-lock] seemed to be altogether destitute of a scear, but with a famous mainspring. **1898** *Proc. Soc. Antiq.* 17 Mar. 109 The cock is caught by the nose of the sear projecting from the lock-plate. **1903** SIR M. G. GERARD *Leaves fr. Diaries* x. 367 The bent of the sear had broken—the piece being at half-cock.

b. *tickle* or *light of the sear* (fig.): easily made to 'go off', readily yielding to any impulse (cf. quot. 1596 above). So † *to go glib upon the sear*.

?**1560** *Dial. Comen Secretarye & Jelowsye* 7 She that is fayre, lusty, and yonge,.. Thynke ye her tayle is not lyght of the seare. **1583** H. HOWARD *Defensative* H iv, Discouering the moods and humours of the vulgar sort,.. to be so loose and tickle of the seare, as there wanted nothing but a leader, of great courage and deepe wisedome to begin the game. **1600** BRETON *Pasquil's Fooles-cap* B 2, An idle Mate, Whose tongue goes all too glibbe vpon the seare. **1602** SHAKS. *Ham.* II. ii. 337 The Clowne shall make those laugh whose lungs are tickled [*read* tickle] a th' sere.

2. *Comb.*, as **sear-nose**, the end of the sear which engages with the notches in the tumbler; **sear-pin**, **-pivot**, the bolt upon which the sear turns; **sear-spring**, a spring which keeps the sear in position, also, in some gun-locks a spring which throws the hammer back to half-cock after a discharge (also *attrib.* in ***sear-spring cramp***, ***-pin***).

1859 *Musketry Instr.* 16 The arm of the sear is that part on which the trigger acts to raise the *sear-nose out of the full bent of tumbler. **1853** URE *Dict. Arts* II. 251 The *sear-pin. **1892** GREENER *Breech-loader* 16 Tumbler and *scear pivots. **1688** HOLME *Armoury* III. xviii. (Roxb.) 135/1 The *saer spring or feather spring. **1831** DARWIN in *Life & Lett.* (1887) I. 211 Two sere-springs, four nipples or plugs. **1844** *Queen's Regul. Army* 96 *note*, One *Sear-Spring Cramp, for Arms with back-action Locks. **1892** GREENER *Breech-loader* 15 The bridle and *scear-spring pins.

sear (sɪə(r)), *sb.*[2] Also 6 **seare**. [f. SEAR *v.*] A mark or impression produced by searing. Also *fig.*

1874 O'SHAUGHNESSY *Music & Moonlight* 122 Her dear wan life is dearer to me keeping The sear upon its whiteness of her fall. **1875** MANNING *Internal Mission Holy Ghost* viii. 216 If you had ever been burnt, there would remain the sear of the burn as long as you live.

sear (sɪə(r)), *v.* Forms: 4–6, 9 **sere**, 5–8 **seer**, (6 **cear**), 6–7 **seare**, 6– **sear**. [OE. *séarian* = OHG. *(ar-)sôrên*:—OTeut. type **saurǽjan*, f. **sauro-*, OE. *séar* dry, SERE *a.*]

1. *intr.* To dry up, to wither away; to become sere. Now *rare*.

?*c* **890** in Cockayne *Shrine* 168/22 Grenu [leaf] weaxað.. hy eft onginnað searian. *c* **1430** LYDG. *Reson & Sens.* 2736 Ful of trees.. whose fressh beaute and grenesse.. Nouther Sere, nor wexen olde. **1496** *Dives & Pauper* (W. de W.) I. xxviii. 66/2 Whan other herbes sere and drye up. **1530** PALSGR. 709/2 This tree wyll seere within a yere or twayne. **1878** *Scribner's Monthly Mag.* XVI. 332/2 As the autumn seared and browned and grayed at last into winter. **1901** A. AUSTIN *Royal Homecoming* x, What Nature feels when Autumn stacks and seres, Or Yule-gusts blow.

2. *trans.* To cause to wither, to blight.

1412–20 LYDG. *Chron. Troy* I. 1655 Eke ȝonge trees to sere, rote and rinde, And afterward make hem, agein kynde, With lusty braunchis blosme and budde newe. *c* **1550** CHEKE *Matt.* xxi. 19 And yᵉ fig tree was seered bi and bi. **1561** HOLLYBUSH *Hom. Apoth.* 25 b, The same heate dryeth or seereth the stomake. **1784** COWPER *Task* III. 30 When summer sears the plains. **1815** SHELLEY *Alastor* 249 His scattered hair Sered by the autumn of strange suffering Sung dirges in the wind. **1876** SWINBURNE *Erechtheus* 1459 If no fire of sun or star untimely sear the tender grain. **1896** A. AUSTIN *England's Darling* III. i, How often have I crushed their [reeds'] crackling stems, Sered by the wind and manacled in ice.

†**b.** *to sear up*: to subject to a process which causes withering, to dry up from the roots. *Obs.*

1430–40 LYDG. *Bochas* VIII. xv. (1494) D iij b, The frutles trees vp seryd to the rote. **1589** HAKLUYT *Voy.* 97 They cut the branches euery eueníng, because they are seared vp in the day by the heate of the Sunne.

3. To burn or char (animal tissues) by the application of a hot iron; to cauterize (a wound, the stump of an amputated limb, etc.) in order to destroy virus or prevent the flow of blood.

1530 PALSGR. 709/2, I sere with a hoote yron, as a smyth or cyrurgien dothe. **1555** W. WATREMAN *Fardle Facions* I. vi. 107 If [it ware] a wenche, they [Amazons] streighte ceared yᵉ pappes, that thei might not growe to hindre them in the warres. **1634** CANNE *Necess. Separ.* (1849) 145 A chirurgeon trieth all gentle means before lancing, searing, or cutting off. **1778** JOHNSON in *Boswell* 20 Apr., It is a sad thing for a man .. to bleed to death, because he has not fortitude enough to sear the wound, or even to stitch it up. **1831** YOUATT *Horse* 227 Preventing bleeding by searing the vessels with a hot iron. **1865** *Jrnl. R. Agric. Soc.* Ser. II. I. II. 252, I prefer searing at about eight or ten weeks as a.. more humane process than drawing... I have never lost a lamb from searing.

b. *fig.* Chiefly after 1 Tim. iv. 2, to render (the conscience) incapable of feeling.

1582 N.T. (Rhem.) *1 Tim.* iv. 2 Having their conscience seared [**1611** seared with a hote iron]. **1633** FORD *'Tis Pity* v. I. 2, Thy Conscience youth is sear'd. *a* **1674** TRAHERNE *Chr. Ethics* (1675) 190 They are obdurate and seared, that cannot discern and feel the wound which they inflict on themselves, who grieve and offend their Creator. **1772** MACKENZIE *Man World* I. iii, To give firmness to sensibility .. without searing its feelings where they led to virtue. **1816** BYRON *Fare thee well* xv, Sear'd in heart, and lone, and blighted, More than this I scarce can die. **1851** ROBERTSON *Serm.* Ser. IV. xv. (1863) 116 Christianity does not sear the human heart; it softens it. **1868** FREEMAN *Norm. Conq.* (1876) II. viii. 130 A long career of ambition, craft, and despotic rule never utterly seared his conscience. **1879** SPENCER *Data of Ethics* xiv. §93. 245 The destructive activities carried on against external enemies sear it [sympathy].

c. *to sear up*: to close (a wound, vein, etc.) by actual cautery. Also *fig.*

1600 W. WATSON *Decacordon* (1602) 41 [The Jesuits] haue bespattered with a most dangerous Gangrene, the whole bodie misticall of Christ (which vnlesse it be seared vp with hot irons here in England, wil neuer come at Rome to be soundly cured). **1629** B. JONSON *New Inn* II. i, The rogue deserues.. To be crop'd with his owne Scizzers.. And ha' the stumps sear'd vp with his owne searing candle. **1697** COLLIER *Ess. Mor. Subj.* II. 145 The Vein of Rhetorick was seared up. **1768–74** TUCKER *Lt. Nat.* (1834) I. 644 Then for the worm of conscience,.. they have seared up his mouth with a hot iron that he cannot bite. **1839** HALLAM *Lit. Eur.* III. iv. §79 The political system of Hobbes, like his moral system,.. sears up the heart.

†**d.** To brand, stigmatize. Also *fig. Obs.*

c **1520** SKELTON *Magnyf.* 360 And boyes to the pylery gan me plucke,.. And some bade sere hym with a marke. **1601** SHAKS. *All's Well* II. i. 176 A divulged shame Traduc'd by odious ballads: my maidens name Seard otherwise. **1611** —— *Wint. T.* II. i. 73 Calumnie will seare Vertue it selfe. **1638** *Brief Relat.* 21 Now the Executioner being come, to seare him and cut of his eares, Mr. Prynne spake these words to him [etc.]. **1644** MILTON *Divorce* I. i. (ed. 2) 7 Not to suffer the ordinance of his goodnes and favour, through any error to be ser'd and stigmatiz'd upon his servants to their misery and thraldome.

4. In wider sense: To burn, scorch; †to put *out* (one's eyes) by burning. Also *fig.* ? *Obs.*

1590 SPENSER *F.Q.* I. xi. 26 The scorching flame sore swinged all his face, And through his armour all his bodie seard. **1593** NASHE *Christ's T.* Wks. 1904 II. 136 To the intent that.. he might with the bright reflection of his [the sun's] beamy radiation seare out his eyes. *c* **1610** BEAUM. & FL. *Philaster* II, All the Court shall hoot thee through the Court Fling rotten Oranges, make ribald Rimes, And sear thy name with Candles upon walls. **1650** FULLER *Pisgah* III. xiii. 349 Tophet.. where children were offered to Moloch, searing them to death with his burning imbracements. **1652** GATAKER *Antinom.* 8 Poor souls for fear of searing their lips, dare not put the cup to their mouths. **1725** POPE *Odyss.* v. 307 A lofty wood Whose leafless summits to the skies aspire, Scorch'd by the sun, or sear'd by heav'nly fire. **1810** SCOTT *Lady of L.* III. x, For as the flames this symbol sear, His home, the refuge of his fear, A kindred fate shall know.

sear, variant of SERE *a.*; obs. Sc. f. SORE.

sear(e cloth: see CERE-CLOTH.

sea-raven.

1. The cormorant.

[A transl. of L. *corvus marinus*: see etymol. note s.v. CORMORANT.]

1611 COTGR., *Corbeau d'eau*, a Cormorant. *Corbeau de mer*, the same; or, the sea-Rauen. **1774** GOLDSM. *Nat. Hist.* (1776) VI. 102 When the great sea-raven, as Jacobson informs us, comes to take away their young, the puffins boldly oppose him.

2. †**a.** A fish mentioned by Pliny. *Obs.* **b.** A large North American fish, *Hemitripterus americanus*, also called deep-water sculpin.

1601 HOLLAND *Pliny* XXXII. xi. II. 451 [List of fishes.] The Sea-Raven Corvus. **1672** JOSSELYN *New-Eng. Rarities* 29 Sea Raven. **1836** J. RICHARDSON *Fauna Bor.-Amer.* III. 50 *Hemitripterus Americanus*... The Sea-raven.. inhabits the cod-banks on the coast of New York, Nova Scotia, and the Gulf of St. Lawrence. **1888** GOODE *Amer. Fishes* 302 The Sea-raven is decidedly palatable.

†**c.** A large African fish. *Obs. rare*[−1].

1797 *Encycl. Brit.* (ed. 3) XVI. 15/2 *Sea Raven*, or *corvo marino*, of Kongo in Africa,.. is about six feet long, and big in proportion.

searce (sɜːs), *sb.* ? *Obs.* Forms: [? 4 **sace**], 5 **saarce**, **sars**, **sarsse**, **sarche**, 5–7 **sarce**, 6 **cearse**, 6–8 **serce**, **searse**, 7 **sarse**, **serse**, 7–8 **sierce**, 7–9 **search**, 5–9 **searce**. [ME. *saarce*, a. (with unexplained insertion of *r*) OF. *saas* (mod.F. *sas*) = Pr. *sedas*, Sp. *cedazo*, It. *staccio* (Neapolitan *setaccio*):—pop.L. **sætāceus* (*pannus*), lit. (cloth) made of bristles, f. L. *sæta* bristle.] A sieve or strainer. (In the first quot. the word may be AF.)

[**1329–30** *Durham Acc. Rolls* (Surtees) 17, I sace, 4*d.*] *c* **1440** *Promp. Parv.* 441/2 Saarce, instrument. **1459** *Inv. Sir J. Fastolf's Goods* in *Paston Lett.* I. 490 Item,.. j. sars of brasse. Item,.. j. sarche of tre. **1546** LANGLEY tr. *Pol. Verg. de Invent.* III. i. 65 Siues and sarces of heare. **1578** BANISTER *Hist. Man* I. 10 The couer.. Galen likeneth to a searse, as though it were full of holes. **1594** *Good Huswife's Handmaide* 52 When it [the flour] is baken, it will be full of clods, and therefore ye must searse it through a search. **1624** QUARLES *Job Militant* med. iv. 17 My Mem'ry's like a Searce of Lawne (alas) It Keepes things grosse, and lets the purer passe. **1669** STURMY *Mariner's Mag.* v. xii. 66 Sift it through a fine Sieve, or a Search. **1674** RAY *Coll. Words, Prepar. Tin* 122 The fine [tin] is lewed in a fine sierce. **1719** DE FOE *Crusoe* I. (Globe) 124 My next Difficulty was to make a Sieve, or Search, to dress my Meal. **1780** MACKENZIE *Mirror* No. 93 ¶9 His brain, poor man! was like a gauze searce, it admitted nothing of any magnitude. **1839** URE *Dict. Arts* 262 Adding the fish-glue dissolved in a great deal of water, and passed through a searce [*printed* searee]. **1844** N. PATERSON *Manse Garden* 147 Put all the earth through a search or riddle, of which the wires are one inch apart.

fig. **1603** FLORIO *Montaigne* II. xii. (1632) 296 Yet will our selfe overweening sift his divinitie through our searce. **1655** FULLER *Ch. Hist.* VI. 279 Whereas other Orders of Monks and Fryers were after their first institution sifted (as I may say) thorough many other searches. **1662** GURNALL *Chr. in Arm.* III. verse 18. I. xvii. 330 His Mediation is the fine searse through which our prayers are boulted.

b. *Comb.*, as † ***searce-net***; † ***searce-wise*** adv.

1526 *Grete Herball* ccccxxxv. (1529) Z iij, Take veray small powdre therof and passe it through a sarcenet. **1601** HOLLAND *Pliny* XI. xxiv. I. 323 The long yarne in her web wrought serce-wise.

searce (sɜːs), *v.* ? *Obs.* Forms: 5 **saarce**, **sarge**, **serge**, (**sayeres** ?), 5–6 **sarse**, 5–7 **sarce**, 6 **searsse**, **cerse**, **cearce**, **serche**, 6–7 **serse**, **seirce**, 6–8 **sierse**, 7–8 **sierce**, 5–9 **searce**, 6–9 **searse**, **search** (see also E.D.D.). [f. SEARCE *sb.*; cf. F. *sasser*.] *trans.* To sift through a searce.

c **1400** *Lanfranc's Cirurg.* 183 Grynde all þese & sarce hem. *c* **1430** *Two Cookery-bks.* 20 Take Appelys an sethe hem, an Serge [*Ashmole MS.* Sarge] hem þorwe a Sefe in-to a potte. *c* **1440** *Pallad. on Husb.* XI. 414 Bete al this smal, and sarce hit smothe at al. *c* **1440** *Promp. Parv.* 441/2 Saarcyn, *colo*. **1543** TRAHERON *Vigo's Chirurg.* II. ii. 15 Take of the cromes of breade well cerced a pounde. **1545** RAYNOLD *Byrth Mankynde* 84 Strewe vpon it yᵉ powder.. beaten very smal & searched through sylke. **1575** TURBERV. *Faulconrie* 301 Beate it into pouder and serce it through a fine cloth. **1675** HAN. WOOLLEY *Gentlew. Comp.* 118 Grate a penny loaf, and seirce it through a Cullender. **1719** DE FOE *Crusoe* I. (Globe) 124 Fine thin Canvas, or Stuff, to search the Meal through. **1741** *Compl. Fam.-Piece* I. ii. 187 Searce some fine Sugar over them. **1747** MRS. GLASSE *Cookery* 141 Take two Pounds of Flour, a Pound of Sugar finely search'd, mix them together. **1799** G. SMITH *Laboratory* I. 8 Be very careful.. that.. all these ingredients be well mixed together and searsed through a fine sieve.

b. *transf.* and *fig.*

c **1535** NISBET *N.T.*, *Rom.* Prol. (S.T.S.) III. 315 The mare grundly it is searssit, the preciouser thingis ar founde in it. **1591** SYLVESTER *Du Bartas* I. iii. 147 The dry Earth, having these waters (first) Through the wide sieve of her void entrails sierst. **1623** WEBSTER *Devil's Law-Case* II. i. C 4 b, You haue Potecaries.. will put foure or fiue coxcombs into a sieue..; theyle searse them through like Ginny Pepper. **1644** DIGBY *Nat. Soul* v. §3. 395 When we haue sifted and searsed the essence of any notion whatsoeuer. **1831** SCOTT *Ct. Robt.* x, His eye was of that piercing kind which seems designed to search and winnow the frivolous from the edifying part of human discussion.

Hence **searced** *ppl. a.*, **ˈsearcing** *vbl. sb.*

1544 PHAER *Regim. Lyfe* (1546) Cc iv b, Than take pouder of stauisacre serced and myngle all togyther. **1599** B. JONSON *Cynthia's Rev.* v. iv, Tut, it is the sorting,.. and the searcing, and the decocting, that makes the fumigation, and the suffumigation. **1662** MERRETT tr. *Neri's Art of Glass* v. 14 Good and well sersed Tarso. **1688** HOLME *Armoury* III. 337/2 The Searce, or Searcer.. is a fine Sieve with a Leather cover.. to keep the Dant.. that nothing be lost of it in the Searceing. **1707** SLOANE *Jamaica* I. Introd. 18 The searc'd and dry Farina is spread in the Sun to dry further.

searcer (ˈsɜːsə(r)). Also 6 **serchar**, 6–7 **sercer**, 7 **searser**, 8–9 **searcher**. [f. SEARCE *v.* + -ER[1]. With sense 1 cf. OF. *sas(s)oire* sieve (Godefroy); with sense 2 cf. F. *sasseur*.]

1. A searce or sieve.

1545 RAYNOLD *Byrth Mankynde* 121 All these beate together and serche them through a serchar. **1577** B. GOOGE *Heresbach's Husb.* I. 11 b, Siues, Sercers, Boulting tubbes. **1639** T. DE GRAY *Compl. Horsem.* 266 Searce it through a fine searcer. **1676** *Phil. Trans.* XI. 754 The Author hath often observ'd, that having in the morning put an Egg near these Searsers [indigo-sifters], it hath been found in the evening all blew within. **1688** [see SEARCED *ppl. a.*]. **1883** R. HALDANE *Workshop Rec.* Ser. II. 446/1 The pulp is.. passed through a 'searcher', to remove the tough skin and pips.

2. One who searces or sifts. *rare*[−0].

1611 COTGR., *Sasseur*, a sifter, searcer, boulter of corne, &c. **1755** JOHNSON, *Searcer*, he who searces.

search (sɜːtʃ), *sb.* Forms: 4–6 **serche**, 5 **serge**, 5–6 **searche**, 5–7 **serch**, 6 **sertche**, **serse**, 6– **search**. [a. AF. *serche* (Rolls of Parlt. 1314–5, 1353), OF. *cerche* (mod.F. *cherche*), vbl. sb., f. *cerchier*: see SEARCH *v.* In some uses prob. an Eng. formation on the verb.]

1. a. The action or an act of searching; examination or scrutiny for the purpose of finding a person or thing. Const. *after*, *for*, †*of* (the object sought). †Also, investigation of a question; effort to ascertain something.

c **1400** *Destr. Troy.* 524 The woman.. shewid forth her ernd.. In sauyng hir seluen and serche of his wille. *c* **1450** *Cov. Myst.* (1841) 292 Thurwe alle Galyle a serge to make, Yf Ihesu be enteryd ȝour pepyl among. *c* **1460** FORTESCUE *Abs. & Lim. Mon.* xiv. (1885) 142 This serche which we nowe haue made.. hath be a digression ffrom the mater in wich we labour. **1530** PALSGR. 269/1 Sertche enquyre, *enqueste*. **1565** ALLEN *Def. Purg.* I. vi. 61 b, Let vs entre into the searche of the meaning of these two textes, withe suche plainesse and sinceritye that [etc.]. **1570** LEVINS *Manip.*

82/20 A Serse, *scrutinium*. **1608** SHAKS. *Per.* III. Prol. 16 By many a dearne and painefull pearch Of Perycles the carefull search,.. Is made with all due diligence. *c* **1610** *Women Saints* 43 When after earnest serch none could be founde, whome they iudged worthie of her. **1681–6** J. SCOTT *Chr. Life* (1747) III. 127 [Ministers] who by their..diligent Search of Scripture, were..to qualify themselves to teach [etc.]. **1697** DRYDEN *Virg. Past.* I. 38 Nor did my search of liberty begin, Till my black hairs were chang'd upon my chin. **1744** AKENSIDE *Pleas. Imag.* II. 29 Where studious ease consumes the silent hour In shadowy searches and unfruitful care. **1746** FRANCIS tr. *Horace, Epist.* I. i. 16 Farewel to Verses, for the Search of Truth And moral Decency hath fill'd my Breast. **1829** SCOTT *Rob Roy* Introd. 2nd half, Robin Oig absconded, and escaped all search. **1860** TYNDALL *Glac.* II. xxvii. 390, I..resolved to devote another year to a search among the chief glaciers. **1875** JOWETT *Plato* (ed. 2) IV. 352 The whole of our discussion from the very beginning has been a search after knowledge. **1888** J. A. H. MURRAY *N.E.D.* Pref. 16 Those who..have been always ready to undertake searches in connexion with groups of words at which the Editor and his staff were actually working.

quasi-*personified*. **1675** OTWAY *Alcibiades* II. i, Beyond what Search can see or Fancy track.

b. Phrases. *in search of* (= F. *en cherche de*): In quest of; in order to find; also, *predicatively*, occupied in searching for. *to make (a) search* (see MAKE *v.*[1] 59a): to search (*for* some lost, concealed, or desired object).

1455 *Cal. Anc. Rec. Dublin* (1889) 287 That they make serch withyn har qarterys. **1555** EDEN *Decades* (Arb.) 77 To make diligent searche and inquisition what maner of people inhabited the land. **1595** SHAKS. *John* II. i. 428 If zealous loue should go in search of vertue, Where should he finde it purer then in Blanch? **1610** —— *Temp.* II. i. 323 Lead off this ground and let's make further search For my poore sonne. **1644** EVELYN *Diary* 5 Nov., I received instructions how to behave in towne, with directions to masters and bookes to take in search of the antiquities, churches, collections, &c. **1716–8** LADY M. W. MONTAGU *Lett.* I. xxiii. 70, I might run into Turkey in search of liberty. **1809** HAN. MORE (*title*) Coelebs in Search of a Wife. **1849** MACAULAY *Hist. Eng.* ii. I. 234 Search was made; and Godfrey's corpse was found in a field near London. **1879** LUBBOCK *Sci. Lect.* iii. 71 Some species..ascend bushes in search of aphides. *Mod.* I am at present in search of a house.

†**c.** Object of search. *Obs.* (? *nonce-use.*)

1806 H. SIDDONS *Maid, Wife, & Widow* I. 244 Content is the end, the search of all mankind.

†**d.** In wider sense: Examination (with regard to quality, conduct, etc.). *Obs.*

1523 *Act 14 & 15 Hen. VIII*, c. 2 Euery such stranger, occupieng any mistery or handy craft..shalbe under the serche and reformacion of the wardens. **1613** J. MAY *Decl. Estate Clothing* iv. 17 The Law hath effectually prouided for the search in all points, that in euerie place where cloth is made and sold, two, foure, six, or eight shall bee appointed for the search thereof, that it be according to law.

2. *spec.* **a.** An examination of a ship's cargo, etc. for the purpose of enforcing customs duties.

1462 *Paston Lett.* II. 107 The seyd Chapman is of no reputacion,..and be colour of hise office of supervisor of the searche shal gretly hurte the port. **1686** tr. *Chardin's Trav. Persia* 62 The saique, which is a sort of Turkish Vessel that takes the Commander aboard, is not expos'd to the search of the Customers. **1700** LAW *Counc. Trade* (1781) 260 By multiplying of oaths, searches, dangers and difficulties. **1891** OLVER & O'REILLY *Imperial Tariff* 82 Such search, so far as passengers' baggage is concerned, need in future only be made by the officers when requested to do so by the police.

b. An examination of a register or of documents in public custody, for the discovery of information which is believed to be contained therein.

1465 *Paston Lett.* II. 243 John Salatt hathe made a serge in the regestre..aftre the wylles and testements. **1554** in *Shropsh. Parish Documents* (1903) 54 For the serche of the Regestre at lychefylde vi[s] viii[d]. **1836** *Act 6 & 7 Will. IV*, c. 86 §37 For every general Search of the said Indexes shall be paid the Sum of Twenty Shillings.

†**c.** Self-examination of conscience, mental introspection. *Obs.*

1526 *Pilgr. Perf.* (W. de W. 1531) 234 The exercyse..is called a meditacyon, as longe as it is with any inquisicyon, serche, or difficulty of y[e] mynde. **1659** A. HAY *Diary* (S.H.S.) 50, I..then retired myself to my preparatioun and weeklie search, and had a very comfortable allowance in some meditations. *a* **1673** SWINNOCK in Spurgeon *Treas. Dav.* Ps. iv. 4 The most successful searches have been made in the night season.

d. *right of search*: the right, recognized by the law of nations, by which a duly commissioned ship of war of a belligerent state is empowered, outside neutral waters, to stop and examine a merchant vessel for contraband; also *occas.* in wider sense (cf. quot. 1817). *visit and search*: see VISIT *sb.*

1798 *Deb. Congress U.S.* 12 June (1851) 1907 Gentlemen appeared to confound the right of search with the right of capture. **1817** BROUGHAM in *Parl. Deb.* 9 July 1800 The only means of ultimate success consisted, in his opinion, in the adoption of some arrangement among the greater powers of Europe, which should establish a mutual right of search [of slave vessels]. **1879** MCCARTHY *Own Times* II. 345 The plenipotentiaries before separating came to an agreement on the subject of the right of search, and the rules generally of maritime war.

†**3.** Range to which search extends. *Obs.*

1610 B. JONSON *Masques, Pr. Henries Barriers* 89 Beyond the paths and searches of the sunne Let him tempt fate. **1792** S. ROGERS *Pleas. Mem.* I. 361 That eye so finely wrought, Beyond the search of sense.

4. Searching effect (of cold or wind). Cf. SEARCH *v.* 9.

1609 DEKKER *Raven's Almanack* Wks. (Grosart) IV. 196 By which meanes the spring to some people..proue [*sic*] as fatall and as busie in priuie Searches as the fall of the Leafe. **1902** *Blackw. Mag.* Nov. 591/2 Outside there was the drip of the thatch eaves, the old search and pity of the wind, but they heard not these.

5. *concr.* applied to persons: †**a.** A searcher, examiner; *spec.* in a Bridgetin convent, the official title of the sisters (at Sion House four in number) who were under the Prioress entrusted with the supervision of the behaviour of the nuns. *Obs.*

Cf. the similar use of SEARCHER 2c.

c **1450** in Aungier *Hist. Syon* (1840) 251 In the chaptyr noon schal..speke..but the president, the chantour, the serches, and they that confesse her owen defautes. **1450–1530** *Myrr. our Ladye* 154 Yet she muste aske forgyuenesse afterwarde and the soueranye and serches that haue cure of the relygyon oughte to se that she be sadly correcte. **1652** J. WRIGHT tr. *Camus' Nat. Paradox* IX. 215 The Shee-Inquisitors came first thither to doe their Office. .. There was not one of the three Searches, but judged this good Office as feasable as reasonable.

†**b.** A search-party. *Obs.*

1604 SHAKS. *Oth.* I. i. 159 That you shall surely find him Lead to the Sagitary the raised Search.

6. *attrib.* and *Comb.*, as *search area, -making, -party, plane, team*; **search coil** *Electr.* = *exploring coil* s.v. EXPLORING *vbl. sb.*; †**search-day**, ? an occasion of an official visitation; †**search-house**, the building or room in which goods are searched by the custom-house officers; **search-parade**, a periodical gathering of convicts in a prison for purposes of examination of their clothing for the detection of unlawful possessions; **search-room**, the room in the Public Record Office provided for members of the public who wish to search documents there preserved; **search-sheet** (see quot.); **search-warrant**, a warrant authorizing the searching of the dwelling of a person suspected of crime.

1973 H. NIELSEN *Severed Key* i. 13 Word of the airline crash had spread rapidly... Only the hardiest of the amateur sailors would be able to reach the *search area. **1977** *New Yorker* 27 June 62/3 The search area could not be reduced much below forty thousand square miles. **1897** *Electrician* 30 July 439/2 You travel along the line of the main, carefully tracking the cable with the *search coil, and listening intently at the telephone receiver. **1933** [see *fluxmeter, flux meter* s.v. FLUX *sb.* 13]. **1953** R. J. C. ATKINSON *Field Archaeol.* (ed. 2) i. 39 The soil is usually removed in a series of shallow layers, and the surface of each layer can be swept with the search-coil. **1547** in E. B. Jupp *Carpenters' Co.* (1887) 386 Item payd for oure dynner on the *serche day of oure lands, vj[s] iij[d]. *c* **1530** in Ellis *Orig. Lett.* Ser. II. II. 39 All our cariage was had home to the *serch house, where all my Master's apparail and the gentlemens, with the rest of the servaunts were serched to th' uttermost. **1495** *Cov. Leet-bk.* 568 And that þe shirrifs wekely make serch..vppon þe peyn to lese Cs. at euery tyme they be founde laches in *serch-makyng. **1903** [NEVILLE] *Penal Serv.* v. 43 The *search parade and the 'rub down' four times a day constitutes a sort of drill. **1884** *Graphic* 23 Aug. 202/1 A *search party was sent back, and presently they espied a pool of blood in the footpath. **1978** J. IRVING *World according to Garp* ii. 30 She quickly organized a search party among the healthier and more mobile patients. **1981** A. MORICE *Men in her Death* viii. 91 I'll be on my way. Robin will be sending out search parties if I'm not home soon. **1966** M. WOODHOUSE *Tree Frog* xxvi. 195 They would send out a *search plane as soon as it got light. **1978** R. LUDLUM *Holcroft Covenant* xxx. 348 A capsized craft fitting the description of the small boat was sighted by low-flying coastal search planes. **1897** *Dict. Nat. Biog.* LI. 211 The Record Office, where he ultimately became superintendent of the *search room. **1902** *Encycl. Brit.* XXX. 132/1 The deeds are indexed according to properties—each property having a separate number and folio called a '*search sheet', on which all deeds affecting it are referred to. **1976** L. SANDERS *Hamlet Warning* xxvii. 239 Organize your men into *search teams for the sectors they hold. **1739** W. STEPHENS *Jrnl.* 26 Mar. in *Colonial Rec. Georgia* (1906) IV. 306 It was thought proper to send out several Officers with a *search Warrant. **1752** FIELDING *Amelia* I. III. xi. 269, I believe I should have applied to a Magistrate for a Search-warrant for that Picture. **1818** SCOTT *Rob Roy* xiv, If there was to be a search-warrant granted, he thought the siller wad be fund some gate near to St. James's Palace. **1879** FARRAR *St. Paul* (1883) 130 The brethren who remained had either eluded his search-warrant, or been rescued from his power.

search (sɜːtʃ), *v.* Forms: *α.* 4–6 serch(e, cerche, 5 sorche, 5–6 sarche, searche, 6 sarych, scarche, sertche, seyrch, *Sc.* scearche, seirch(e, 7 cherch, 6– search; *β.* 5 serge, scerge, seerge, cerge; *γ.* 5–6 sers, 6 seirs, searse, *Sc.* searce, seirce, serce, serss, cers, cerse, cerss. [a. OF. *cerchier* (mod.F. *chercher*), corresp. to Pr. *cercar*, It. *cercare* to seek, Sp., Pg. *cercar* to surround:—late L. *circāre* to go round, f. L. *circus* circle.]

I. To explore, examine thoroughly.

1. *trans.* To go about (a country or place) in order to find, or to ascertain the presence or absence of, some person or thing; to explore in quest of some object.

α. *c* **1330** *King of Tars* 929 Thou scholdest come with-oute bost, And serche uche cuntray. *c* **1400** MAUNDEV. (1839) xxxi. 315, I..have..cerched manye fulle straunge places. **1480** CAXTON *Chron. Eng.* ccxxx. q3b, They wente and serched and skymmed the see. *a* **1548** HALL *Chron., Hen. IV*, 28b, When the erle had searched all the coaste of Fraunce, and had founde not one pirate or sea robber. **1611** BIBLE *Num.* xiii. 2 Send thou men, that they may search the lande of Canaan. **1697** DRYDEN *Virg. Georg.* IV. 170 The Guardian of the Bees, For Slips of Pines, may search the Mountain Trees. **1871** R. ELLIS *Catullus* xlvii. 7 Shall.. they, my jolly comrades, Search the streets on a quest of invitation?

β. *c* **1440** *Promp. Parv.* 453/2 Seergyn, or serchyn, *scrutor, lustro, perlustro.*

γ. *a* **1500** *Droichis Part of Play* 162 in *Dunbar's Poems* (1893) 320 Gar sers baith Louthiane and Fyf And vale to me a mekle wyf. **1513** DOUGLAS *Æneis* II. xi. 118 To toune agane I sped with all my mycht..Wilfull all aventuris new-lingis to assay, And for to serce Troy, every streit, and way.

2. To look through, examine internally (a building, an apartment, a receptacle of any kind) in quest of some object concealed or lost.

1387 TREVISA *Higden* (Rolls) IV. 443 Houses were besiliche y-serched ȝif out myȝt be y-founde. **1471** CAXTON *Recuyell* (Sommer) 51 He serchid all the palais of kyng lichaon, and maad thepiriens to sease his richesses. **1535** COVERDALE *1 Kings* xx. 6 Tomorow aboute this tyme wil I sende my seruauntes vnto the, y[t] they maye serch thyne house. **1598** SHAKS. *Merry W.* IV. ii. 167 Helpe to search my house this one time: if I find not what I seeke, shew no colour for my extremity. *a* **1656** BP. HALL *Rem. Wks.* (1660) 47 They..will search every Coach for you with Torches. **1819** SHELLEY *Cenci* IV. iv. 31 Even now they search the tower, and find the body. **1843** POE *Purloined Letter*, When G— detailed to us his mode of searching the premises.

3. a. To examine (a person) by handling, removal of garments, and the like, to ascertain whether any article (usually, something stolen or contraband) is concealed in his clothing.

1426 LYDG. *De Guil. Pilgr.* 2770 And also that ye wel provyde To cerche hem wel on euery syde, Thys synful folk, with pakkys large. **1474** CAXTON *Chesse* II. v. (1883) 62 The Iayler serchid her that she shold bere no mete ne drynke to her moder. **1646** EVELYN *Diary* Apr., The officers search'd us thoroughly for prohibited goods. **1687** LOVELL tr. *Thevenot's Trav.* 266 But not before we and our Goods had been searched at the Custome-house. **1843** POE *Purloined Letter*, He has been twice waylaid..and his person rigorously searched under my own inspection. **1891** OLVER & O'REILLY *Imperial Tariff* 82 A power is given to officers of the Board to search persons suspected of concealing prohibited goods about their persons.

†**b.** In wider sense: (see quot.). *Obs.*

1692 WOOD *Life* 20 Aug. (O.H.S.) III. 399 The maid was search'd and found to be with child.

c. *search me*: used (chiefly *imp.* in response to a question) to imply that the speaker has no knowledge of some fact or no idea what course to take. *colloq.* (orig. *N. Amer.*).

1901 MERWIN & WEBSTER *Calumet 'K'* iii. 37 'Search me,' said Denis. 'They've tied us up for these two weeks.' **1907** F. H. BURNETT *Shuttle* xxvi. 262 If this ain't the limit! You may search *me*! **1916** 'B. M. BOWER' *Phantom Herd* xi. 191 What ails that darned thing?.. You can search me. **1920** 'SAPPER' *Bull-Dog Drummond* ii. 60 'Why did he send his confidential secretary..to Belfast?' 'Search me,' said Hugh. **1930** E. WAUGH *Vile Bodies* i. 9 Word of eighteen letters meaning carnivorous mammal. Search me if I know how they do think of these things. **1949** G. DAVENPORT *Family Fortunes* III. i. 189 'How could the road be washed out—I went over it yesterday morning and it hasn't rained since!' 'Search me.' **1959** J. THURBER *Years with Ross* iv. 61 Faced with these formidable questions, any of his intimates.. might easily murmur..'God Knows' or 'Search me'. **1965** D. FRANCIS *For Kicks* viii. 110 'Where did he go for the summer?' I asked... 'Search me.' **1980** B. BAINBRIDGE *Winter Garden* xiii. 102 'But where am I going?' asked Ashburner... 'Search me,' said Bernard. 'It's supposed to be a surprise.'

4. To peruse, look through, examine (writings, records) in order to discover whether certain things are contained there.

α. **1387** TREVISA *Higden* (Rolls) I. 41 Ivlius Cesar..lokede and serchede stories and bookes of his ȝeres of doynge and dedes. **1526** TINDALE *N.T.* John v. 39 Searche the scriptures, for in them ye thynke ye have eternal lyfe. **1664** EXTON *Marit. Dicaeol.* Ded. a iij b, Having some time since in those sad and distracted times, bestowed some labour in searching and perusing..the Records. **1769** BURKE *Late St. Nat.* Wks. II. 52, I have been at the trouble to search the Journals in the period between the two last wars. **1963** in H. W. Baade *Jurimetrics* 13 Western Reserve University established a Center..which has been engaged..in the investigation of methods of searching literature by electronic machines.

γ. **1563** WINȜET tr. *Vincent. Lirin.* iii. Wks. (S.T.S.) II. 20 Than sall he do diligence to inquire and serce the sentences of our forefatheris conferrit amang thame selfis.

5. a. With immaterial object: To investigate, make oneself thoroughly acquainted with; to examine rigorously (one's own heart, thoughts, etc.); to examine, penetrate the secrets of (another's mind or thoughts). Also with *out.*

The phrase *search and sift*, common in the 16–17th c., perhaps indicates confusion with SEARCE *v.*

c **1386** CHAUCER *Melib.* §38 The sciences and the Iuggementz of oure lord god almyghty been ful depe, ther may no man comprehende ne serchen hem suffisantly. *c* **1400** *Sege Jerus.* (E.E.T.S.) 339 Þe cite haþ [vs] sent to serche ȝour wille, To here þe cause of ȝour comyng, [& what] ȝe coueyte wolde. **1535** COVERDALE *Ps.* cxxxix. 1 O Lorde, thou searchest me out, and knowest me. **1579** HAKE *Newes out of Powles* To Rdr. (1872) A iv. b, To searche and syfte owte the..deceytes that the lewde sorte of this people..doe vse to gette money with. **1591** SHAKS. *1 Hen. VI*, III. iii. 12 Search out thy wit for secret pollicies, And we will make thee famous through the World. **1663** BP. NICHOLSON *Catechism* 58 For hee will try, sift, search all things, and without flattery or favour proceed according to every mans works. **1697** DRYDEN *Virg. Georg.* III. 690 Receits abound; but searching all thy Store, The best is still at hand, to launch the Sore: And cut the Head. **1820** SHELLEY *Prometh. Unb.*

III. iii. 34 And we will search,.. For hidden thoughts,.. Our unexhausted spirits. **1842** MANNING *Serm.* xx. (1848) I. 295 We feel as if we saw the tokens of His presence.. coming and going in an awful way, as if to gaze upon us, and search out our very thoughts.

b. Of an impersonal agency: To test, reveal the nature of.

1586 A. DAY *Eng. Secretary* II. (1625) 2 The wit is searched by the outward quality or condition of a man. *a* **1616** BEAUM. & FL. *Custom Country* II. i, Prosperity does search a Gentleman's temper, More than his adverse fortune. **1818** SHELLEY *Rosalind* 257 For scorn whose arrows search the heart, From many a stranger's eye would dart.

6. To look scrutinizingly at.

1811 SIR A. BOSWELL *Clan-Alpin's Vow* II. 33 Fierce Malcolm watched the passing scene, And searched them through with glances keen. **1861** O. W. HOLMES *Agnes* II. 85 He searched her features through and through. **1867** AUGUSTA WILSON *Vashti* xxxi, While he drank, his eyes searched her face, and lingered admiringly on her beautiful hand.

†**7.** *to search up*: to dig up (the soil). *Obs.*

c **1400** *Destr. Troy.* 1534 Sone he raght vpon rowme, rid vp þe dykis Serchit vp the soile þere þe Citie was.

†**8.** To probe (a wound). *Obs.*

a **1400–50** *Alexander* 3132 To serche þaire saluys & þar saris with surgens noble. *c* **1450** *Merlin* xxxii. 664 And the wounded lete hem be ledde to townes, and serched theire sores. **1588** SHAKS. *Tit. A.* II. iii. 262 Now to the bottome dost thou search my wound. *a* **1625** FLETCHER *Valentinian* I. iii, You search the sore too deep. *a* **1631** DONNE *Poems* (1633) 150 So.. nice in searching wounds the Surgeon is. **1687** MIEGE *Gt. Fr. Dict.* II. s.v., To search a Wound, *sonder une Plaie.*

9. Of wind, cold, fire-arms, etc.: To penetrate, reach the weak places of.

1412–20 LYDG. *Chron. Troy* II. 7271 For Achilles, sturdy as a wal, Gan cerche scheltrouns & her rengis brake. *c* **1586** C'TESS PEMBROKE *Ps.* CIX. viii, Oile through flesh doth search the hidden bone. **1594** NASHE *Unfort. Trav.* Wks. 1904 II. 315 They basted him with a mixture of Aqua fortis, [etc.].. which.. searcht him to the marrowe. **1642** D. ROGERS *Naaman* 36 But now perhaps being searcht to the quicke [etc.]. **1822** BYRON *Werner* I. i. 723 The ice-wind.. Searching the shivering vassal through his rags. **1829** NAPIER *Penins. War* IX. ii. II. 394 The guns of the first corps .. were enabled.. to search the whole of the British line to the left.

†**10.** To examine in order to ascertain the character or dispositions of. *Obs. rare.*

1476 *Order of Council* in *York Myst.* Introd. 37, iiij of the most connynge.. to serche here, and examen all þe plaiers and plaies and pagentes. **1617** MORYSON *Itin.* I. 56 These [men of warre] used to send out in lesser boates some bodies of men, to search the Barkes, whether they be friends or not.

II. 11. a. To look for or seek diligently, to try to find. Now only with *out* exc. (*rarely*) *poet.*

α. **1338** R. BRUNNE *Chron.* (1810) 334 Sir Eymer had no drede, he serchid þam alle oute. *c* **1440** CAPGRAVE *Life St. Kath.* IV. 202 He sente oute letteris on-to euery Iustice To serche the cristene, to hange hem and to drawe. **1471** CAXTON *Recuyell* (Sommer) 36 We shall followe the and goo wyth the and serche our auentures in other landes. *Ibid.* 219 Perseus gaf hym [the monster] many woundes, serchyng his herte. And at laste he fonde hit. *c* **1500** *Melusine* 330 And thenne geffray cerched the keyes so longe tyl he fonde them. **1562** A. BROOKE *Romeus & Iuliet* 164 Yong damsels thether flocke, of bachelers a rowte, Not so much for the banquets sake, as bewties to searche out. **1608** *Acc. Exch., King's Rem.* 533/11 Item for Cherching moles in lyttle parke ijs. vj d. **1611** SHAKS. *Cymb.* V. v. 11 He hath bin search'd among the dead & liuing; But no trace of him. **1726** SWIFT *Gulliver* II. vi, These [Bishops] were searched and sought out through the whole Nation.. among such of the Priesthood as were [etc.]. **1820** SHELLEY *Hymn Merc.* xciv, Whilst they [the Fates] search out dooms, They sit apart and feed on honeycombs. **1842** TENNYSON *Daydream* L'Envoi iii, My fancy, ranging thro' and thro', To search a meaning for the song. **1887** *Weekly Times* 25 Feb. 8/1 His primary object is to search out the truth.

β. *c* **1440** CAPGRAVE *Life St. Kath.* 1803 It is but foly to spende ony labour Swiche preuy thingis for to serge and seeke. **1464** *Paston Lett.* II. 159 If it schuld be scergyd in the regester it wold take a fortenyght werk.

γ. *c* **1440** *York Myst.* xxxii. 275, I schall sers hym my selffe sen þou has hym solde. **1516–17** *Acc. Ld. High Treas. Scot.* V. 98 To Eicht, messinger, to ryd agane to Coldinghame, Duns, and Laudar, to cers and sek George Howme with souerties undir payne of hornyng. *a* **1586** *Satir. Poems Reform.* xxxvii. 59 It is bot slychtis ȝe haue seirsit, To cloik þe crafte quhairto ȝe ar Inclynd.

†**b.** To seek to discover. Chiefly with indirect question as object. Also with *out. Obs.*

α. *c* **1450** in Aungier *Syon* (1840) 257 If any.. besyly and curyously serche what other sustres or brethren speke betwene themselfe. **1538** STARKEY *England* I. i. 25 Fyrst therfor.. we wyl serche out, as nere as we can, what ys the veray and true commyn wele. **1571** DIGGES *Pantom.* Z j, Octaedrons side giuen, to searche his superficiall and solide contente. *Ibid.* Cc j b, Octaedrons side giuen, to searche out all his conteyned bodies, sides, diameters and axes. **1614** B. JONSON *Barth. Fair* Induct., Any State-decipherer,.. so solemnly ridiculous, as to search out, who was meant by the Ginger-bread-woman, who by the Hobby-horse-man [etc.]. **1644** MILTON *Educ.* 1 To search what many modern Ianua's and Didactics more then ever I shall read, have projected, my inclination leads me not.

β. **1513** DOUGLAS *Æneis* I. vi. 5 To sers and knaw To quhat kin coistis he with the wind was blaw. **1544** *Aberd. Reg.* (1844) I. 199 Item, the consell ordanis the maisteris of artilzery to pas with the mayster of kirkwark, and serss quhar ony irn may be gottin pertening the kyrk.

III. Absolute and intransitive uses.

[The difference between the sense of branch I and that of branch II vanishes when the vb. is used *absol.*]

12. To make a search. Const. *after, for, into.*

c **1330** R. BRUNNE *Chron. Wace* (Rolls) 13679 Þey serched ouer al vp & doun Til þey seye his gonfanoun. *c* **1450** *Merlin* xxiii. 423 Bot euer Grisandols serched thourgh the forestes, oon hour foreward, another bakke. **1535** COVERDALE *Job* viii. 8 Enquere of them that haue bene before the, search diligently amonge thy forefathers. **1654** EVELYN *Diary* 9 July, Advising the Students to search after true wisdome. **1702** ADDISON *Medals* i, He never thinks of the beauty of the thought or language, but is for searching into what he calls the Erudition of the Author. **1703** POPE *Thebais* 8 Cadmus searching round the spacious sea. **1774** GOLDSM. *Nat. Hist.* (1776) VI. 101 At the latter end of March.. come over a troop of their spies or harbingers, that stay two or three days, as it were to view and search out for their former situations. **1822** SHELLEY tr. *Calderon's Mag. Prodig.* i. 57 Search even as thou wilt, But thou shalt never find what I can hide. **1837** CARLYLE *Fr. Rev.* I. VII. iv, To see so many Judiths.. rushing out to search into the root of the matter!

†**13.** To devise means (*to do* something). *Obs.*

1338 R. BRUNNE *Chron.* (1810) 268 Now gos Turbeuile, & serchis day bi day, To do þe kyng a gile. *c* **1400** *Destr. Troy* 11193 Antenor & Eneas, with þaire avne sons, Serchid by hom-seluyn in sauyng hor lyues. *a* **1533** LD. BERNERS *Huon* lxvi. 229 He saw wel his brother serched all that he coude to fall at debate with hym. **1567** *Gude & Godlie Ball.* 100 Thair counsell is to seirche and to Inquyre, The Innocent with wrang for till accuse.

IV. 14. In special combs. with other vbs. forming verbal and substantival phrases (freq. used *attrib.*), as ***search and destroy*** (orig. *U.S.*), designating an uncompromising military strategy effected by the advance of troops through a given territory (first employed in the war in Vietnam); also *ellipt.*; ***search and rescue*** (orig. *U.S.*), designating a (chiefly *Mil.*) land or sea rescue service.

1966 *Economist* 22 Oct. 369/3 This is a different use of men from the highly mobile 'search and destroy' operations in which the American forces have been engaged up to now. **1970** [see *Green Beret* s.v. GREEN *a.* 13]. **1973** D. LEES *Rape of Quiet Town* iv. 57 Sarrat's unit conducted search-and-destroy missions. **1977** 'E. MCBAIN' *Long Time no See* xiii. 222, I was out there on a search-and-destroy. **1944** *Yank* 2 June 3/2 At last somebody thought of the Siberian Huskies assigned to a nearby Army search and rescue outfit. **1950** *Jrnl. R. United Service Inst.* XCV. 158 (*heading*) 'Search and rescue' radio watch. **1972** *Gloss. Aeronaut. & Astronaut. Terms* (*B.S.I.*) XIII. 3 *Search and rescue*, a service provided to notify the appropriate organizations of aircraft in need of search-and-rescue aid and to assist such organizations. **1977** *R.A.F. News* 11–24 May 9 (Advt.), Winching a capsized yachts-man to safety on board a Royal Air Force search-and-rescue Wessex.

search, variant of SEARCE *sb.* and *v.*

searchable ('sɜːtʃəb(ə)l), *a.* [f. SEARCH *v.* + -ABLE.] Capable of being searched.

1558 BP. WATSON *Sev. Sacram.* viii. 45 Otherwyse the maner of it is not searcheable. **1588** J. HARVEY *Disc. Probl.* 76 Fore-knowledge of future things and euents, inquirable by legitimate skill, or otherwise searchable by assured experience. **1683** SALMON *Doron Med.* III. 647 This and such like specificks are not searchable whilst in their body. **1827–44** WILLIS *Starlight* 8 The faded West looks deep, as if its blue Were searchable.

Hence **'searchableness**, 'the state of being searchable' (Webster, 1847, and in recent Dicts.).

†**'searchant**, *a.* and *vbl. sb. nonce-wd.* [f. SEARCH *v.* + -ANT, after *rampant*, etc.] **a.** *adj.* As a mock-heraldic term: Searching. **b.** *vbl. sb.* Used for rime (after Fr. gerunds).

1614 B. JONSON *Barth. Fair* Induct., A ciuill Cutpurse searchant. **1683** *Robin Consc.* in *Songs Lond. Prentices* (Percy Soc.) 79 A merchant Was so affrighted when I came, That presently he blush'd for shame, His countenance did show the same in searchant.

searcher ('sɜːtʃə(r)). Forms: α. 4–6 serchere, 4–7 sercher, 5 sercho(w)re, 5–6 serch(e)our, 6 sercheor(e, 5- searcher; β. 5 seergiour; also (with *i* for *j*) seriowre, cer(e)iowre, ceriore; γ. 6 sersour, *Sc.* searcer, seircear. [a. AF. *cerchour* (Rolls of Parlt.), OF. *cerchere, cercheor* (cf. mod.F. *chercheur*), f. *cerchier* SEARCH *v.*; (2) f. SEARCH *v.* + -ER[1]. The two formations, coincident in sense and in their modern phonetic development, do not admit of being distinguished.]

1. a. One who searches, in various senses of the verb; one who explores or investigates, or who endeavours to find something. Const. as the verb. Also ***searcher-out.***

α. **1382** WYCLIF *Jer.* xxx. 17 For cast awei thei clepeden thee Sion; this is she that hadde not aȝeen serchere [Vulg. *quæ non habebat requirentem*]. **1398** TREVISA *Barth. De P.R.* XVIII. xxix. (1495) 790 Sextius was a moost dylygente sercher of medycyn. **14..** *Voc.* in Wr.-Wülcker 608/7 *Rimatorium*, a serchour. **1553** BALE *Vocac.* 5, I haue bene in parell of the sea.., in parell of curiouse searchers. **1572** J. JONES *Bathes Ayde* I. 8b, The Phisicyon is a viewer and sercher out of Nature. **1576** FLEMING *Panopl. Epist.* 283 They dig the ground like greedie metal mongers, and insatiable searchers for siluer. **1620** SHELTON *Quix.* II. l. 332 Cid Hamete, the most punctuall Searcher of the very moats of this true History. **1726** LEONI tr. *Alberti's Archit.* I. 23/2 Pamphilus, an excellent Searcher into Antiquity. **1841** MYERS *Cath. Th.* III. § 10. 34 An honest earnest searcher of the Scriptures. **1884** CHURCH *Bacon* i. 20 He was not one of the high-minded and proud searchers after knowledge and truth, like Descartes.

β. *c* **1440** *Promp. Parv.* 67/1 Cereiowre (*v.rr.* ceriore, ceriowre), *scrutator, perscrutator. Ibid.* 453/2 Seriowre, or serchowre.

γ. **1562** WINȜET *Cert. Tractates* Wks. (S.T.S.) I. 24 Curius seircearis of the hie mysteriis of God.

b. ***searcher of (men's) hearts***: applied to God (chiefly with allusion to Rom. viii. 27, etc.).

1535 COVERDALE *Wisd.* i. 6 God is a witnesse of his reynes, a true searcher out of his hert. **1562** EDEN *Let.* 1 Aug. in Arb. *1st Eng. Bks.* Pref. 43/1 The only searcher of mens hartes, the eternall god. **1631** GOUGE *God's Arrows* I. § 32. 51 Before God the searcher of hearts. **1870** DICKENS *E. Drood* x, What may be in your heart when you give him your hand, can only be known to the Searcher of all hearts.

2. One whose office is to search. †**a.** An official appointed by a guild or company to resist the violation of its customs and laws, and to prevent the production of work below a certain standard of excellence. *Obs.*

1419 *Engl. Misc.* (Surtees) 14 It was accorded and assented be bathe the partys that the sercheours of the masons and of the wryghtes of this cite of York suld ga and see what were ryght for ayther party. **1516** *Nottingham Rec.* III. 345 The Sercheres of the Fysheres.. they suffer corupe fyshe and noght to be sold in the market. **1592** in *Vicary's Anat.* (1888) App. xv. 274 Imprimis, that y[e] Serchers and Maisters of the saide arte or science [that of Barber-Surgeons] be chosen euerye yeare. **1681** *Lond. Gaz.* No. 1655/3 The humble Address of the Master, Wardens, Searchers, Assistants, Freeholders, and Freemen of the Corporation of Cutlers in Hallamshire.

b. An officer of the custom-house appointed to search ships, baggage, or goods for dutiable or contraband articles.

α. **1422** *Rolls of Parlt.* IV. 176/1 Poisours, Sercheours, and all suche other Officers. **1494** *Act 11 Hen. VII*, c. 13 The Oath.. taken before the Customer or Searcher of the same Port. **1526** *Sc. Acts Jas. V* (1814) II. 306/1 Archibald douglace provest of Edinburgh to be serchor principale at þe port of leith. **1559** *Act 1 Eliz.* c. 11 § 7 Any.. searcher,.. or other officer, parteynyng to the subsidie, custome, or custome house. **1652** EVELYN *Diary* 3 June, I receiv'd a letter from Coll. Morley to ye Magistrates and Searchers at Rie, to assist my wife at her landing. *a* **1715** BURNET *Own Time* III. (1724) I. 475 And then some searchers were sent from the Custom House to look for some forbidden goods. **1840** R. ELLIS *Brit. Tariff for 1841*, 276 Landing Surveyor .. Searcher [etc.]. **1891** OLVER & O'REILLY *Imperial Tariff* 267 Goods.. may be received back into warehouse.. on receipt of a certificate of short shipment from the searcher.

β. **1461** *Paston Lett.* I. 78 The best takyng of schepynge is at Yernemuthe er Kyrley.. I schall haf favour he now wyt ther seergiours.

γ. **1598** in *Extracts Rec. Convent. Burghs Scot.* (1870) I. 75 Reformation to be put to the sersouris vpliftand ane extraordinar dewtie of x s. of ilk chalder of salt passing furth of this realme.

†**c.** One appointed to observe and report on any offences against discipline or good order in a religious house, a community, body of workmen, etc.

α. *c* **1490** CAXTON *Rule St. Benet* 132/19 And the serchers of the relygyon owe to see warely about þat they be occupyed in lecture therof sonday and other. **1538** ELYOT *Dict.*, *Circuitores*, the serchers of watches. **1604** E. G[RIMSTONE] *D'Acosta's Hist. Indies* VI. xv. 465 They had searchers to examine if they did employ themselves in these workes, and to punish the negligent. *c* **1620** BOYD *Zion's Flowers* (1855) App. 41 Searchers appointed.., to go through the town to see who Bann or Swear. **1845** *Coll. Biog. Soc. Jesus* 159 The Searcher, according to his commission, examined him.

γ. **1596** DALRYMPLE tr. *Leslie's Hist. Scot.* I. 218 He appoynted that the names of the offenders.. sulde, be the searceris, elected, and to that office chosen, (be) writne vpe and secreitlie endyted in the kingis bukes.

†**d.** As the designation of various municipal or government officials; e.g. a sanitary inspector; an inspector of markets; an examiner of certain articles of manufacture that were not allowed to be sold unless certified by him as of standard quality, etc. *Obs.*

1500 in *Extracts Rec. Convent. Burghs Scot.* (1870) I. 505 That thair be serchouris chosin within ilk burch,.. to serche and seik the personis brekeris of the saidis actis of parliament. **1514** *Cov. Leet-bk.* 639 þat ne weuer delyuer eny cloth.. tyll the serchers haue seen it whedir it be laufully wrought or no. **1518** *Ibid.* 663 [Ordained] that [four men named].. schal-be serchers of the Brode-well & the comen broke from the Hillmyll vnto seint Johyns at euery faute they ffynde the Offender to pay xij d. **1613** J. MAY *Decl. Estate Clothing* iv. 18 The best search made by the searchers in any place, is but to cast the Clothes into skales to see if they be weight or no. **1738** *Act 11 Geo. II*, c. 28 § 3 Which said Searchers shall and may have full Power.. to enter into and inspect all such Mills, Shops, Warehouses [etc.] of Makers, Merchants or Dealers in Narrow Cloth. **1835** *App. Munic. Corpor. Rep.* III. 1675 (Pontefract), 2 Searchers of the Corn-market.

†**e.** A person appointed to view dead bodies and to make report upon the cause of death. *Obs.*

1592 SHAKS. *Rom. & Jul.* V. ii. 8 The Searchers of the Towne Suspecting that we both were in a house Where the infectious pestilence did raigne. **1607** MIDDLETON *Mich. T.* IV. i, Then will I.. make an ende [*i.e.* pretend to die]... I haue indented with a couple of searchers, who.. shall fray them out a'th Chamber with report of sicknesse, and so la, I start vp, and recouer agen. **1616** R. C. *Times' Whistle* (1871) 121 Knowe, in my rage I have slaine a man this day, And knowe not where his body to conveigh And hide it from the searchers inquisition. **1625–6** in *Brit. Mag.* (1833) IV. 147 Itm paid for 2 redd wands for the searchers in the sycknes tyme 00 00 04. **1662** J. GRAUNT *Observ. Bills Mortality* 11 When any one dies.. the Searchers.. (who are antient Matrons, sworn to their Office) repair to the place where the dead Corps lies, and.. examine by what Disease or Casualty the Corps died. **1759** *Coll. Bills of Mortality* Pref. 7 Every parish appoints a searcher, whose business it is to examine the corpse, and to report the distemper.

f. An official appointed to search the clothing and person of any one arrested and detained by the police.

1726 SWIFT *Gulliver* I. v, I kept..a Pair of Spectacles in a private Pocket, which..had escaped the Emperor's Searchers. **1858** SIMMONDS *Dict. Trade*, Searcher,..a woman who examines female prisoners at a police station. **1863** *Times* 10 Aug. 9/6 The female searcher at the Kennington-lane police-station. **1890** M. WILLIAMS *Leaves of a Life* II. iv. 38 The searchers next came upon her handkerchief.

g. (See quot.)

1886 *Law Times* LXXXI. 152/1 Official searchers should be appointed whose duty it should be to search the register of charges.

3. An instrument used in making a search.

a. *Surg.* A probe or sound.

1597 A. M. tr. *Guillemeau's Fr. Chirurg.* 12/3 Try the thicknes of the bone with a little privette or searcher. **1831-40** LISTON *Elem. Surg.* II. (ed. 2) 650 After almost every operation for stone..a searcher is useful to ascertain whether or not all [fragments] have been removed.

b. *Farriery.* (See quot.)

1855 FRANKE *Beil's Technol. Dict.* II. 452 Searcher, of farriers (an instrument for examining the horse's hoof). **1873** *Weale's Dict. Terms* (ed. 4).

†**c.** (See quot.) *Obs. rare*$^{-1}$.

1775 FALCK *Day's Diving Vessel* 25 Also a marine searcher (of my own contrivance) being an iron, somewhat like a sounding lead, but with a sharp ragged spike.

†**d.** An instrument for testing the soundness of cannon after discharge; = GUN-SEARCHER. *Obs.*

1706 *Albany Fort Jrnl.* 1 July in G. Williams *Hudson's Bay Miscellany* (1975) 72/2 State of stores... 1 pair searchers for great guns. **1800** *Naval Chron.* IV. 54 Muzzle the searcher, and ram it home in the gun. **1859** F. A. GRIFFITHS *Artil. Man.* (1862) 55 They are..examined with a searcher after each round.

e. In microscopical work: An objective of low power used to obtain a general view of the object.

1870 ROYSTON-PIGOTT in *Q. Jrnl. Microsc. Sci.* X. 393 The Aplanatic Searcher is intended to improve the penetration [etc.]. **1898** P. MANSON *Trop. Dis.* xxxi. 451 An inch objective being used in the first instance as a searcher. **1899** CAGNEY tr. *Jaksch's Clin. Diagn.* (ed. 4) 436 The eye-pieces of extremely low power are called 'searchers'.

4. †**a.** *gen.* Something that searches or penetrates.

1694 SALMON *Bate's Dispens.* (1713) 381/1 A Glass of Infusion of Sassafras in Wine,..is a Searcher which immediately penetrates the whole Body. **1742** *Lond. & Country Brewer* I. (ed. 4) 61 But, to sweeten a Barrel, Kilderkin, Firkin, or Pin in the great Brewhouses, they put them over the Copper-hole for a Night together, that the Steam of the boiling Water or Wort may penetrate into the Wood; this Way is such a furious Searcher, that, unless the Cask is new hooped just before, it will be apt to fall in Pieces.

b. A penetrating or embarrassing question. *colloq.*

1923 J. MANCHON *Le Slang* 260 *Searcher*,..une question (ou un problème) embarrassante. **1951** N. M. GUNN *Well at World's End* xi. 81 He..asked me some questions, and searchers they were.

Hence †**'searcheress**, a female searcher; **'searchership**, the office of a searcher.

1582 STANYHURST *Æneis* IV. (Arb.) 117 Of theese drirye dolours eeke thow Queene Iuno the searchresse [L. *curarum conscia Iuno*]. **1462** *Paston Lett.* III. 97 Wherfor I beseke youre maistirshipp..that it lyke you to desyre the nomynacion of on of the officez, eythyr of the countroller or serchorship of Jernemuth, for a servaunt of yowrez. **1895** *Harper's Mag.* Apr. 718/2 The positions they fill are the 'judgeship', the 'searchership', the 'spankership' [etc.].

†**'searchery.** *Sc. Law. Obs.* Also 6 **sercheorie, searchearie, sercherie.** [f. SEARCHER *sb.* + -Y³; see -ERY.] That which is characteristic of the duty or office of a SEARCHER (sense 2). ***letters of searchery***: documents authorizing the prosecution of a search or examination.

1566 *Reg. Privy Council Scot.* I. 481 Certane allegeit lettres of sercheorie and utheris favourabill writtingis. **1634** *Reg. Mag. Sig. Scot.* (1897) 8/2 Officium inquisitionis lie searchearie bonorum inhibitorum ibidem. **1705** *Sc. Acts Aune* (1824) XI. 256/1 The office of searcherie of all prohibited and uncustomed goods comeing to or going from the said Burgh of Ely or port thereof.

searchful ('sɜːtʃfʊl), *a.* [f. SEARCH *sb.* + -FUL.] Full of anxious attention; diligent in search.

1594 CAREW *Huarte's Exam. Wits* iv. 48 The creature foresightfull, searchfull, apt for many matters..whome we call by the name of Man. **1607** BRETON *Murmurer* (Grosart) 10/2 Can the labourer, the foote bee wounded? but the body of the State will feele it, the head be carefull, the eye searchfull, and the hand bee painfull in the cure of it? **1893** D. O'DONOGHUE *Brendaniana* 11 A youth hostful, searchfull, lithe, He was a help to the men of Erin.

searching ('sɜːtʃɪŋ), *vbl. sb.* [-ING¹.] The action of the verb SEARCH in its various senses.

c **1400** *Destr. Troy* 9206 Hit semith me vnsertain, all serchyng of wayes Ys stokyn vp full stithly, shuld streche to my hele! **1501** *Reg. Privy Seal Scot.* I. 88/1 A Letter..of serching and sichtyng of skinnys.. with[in] the burgh of Hadingtoun. ?**1639** in Pettus *Fodinæ Reg.* (1670) 71 The searching in any Ship, Cellar, Warehouse, etc. **1750** tr. *Leonardus' Mirr. Stones* 155 It is sought for by mariners when they have no light, and from this searching it took the name of topaz. **1842** BISCHOFF *Woollen Manuf.* II. 23 [The] laws applying to the stamping, stretching, and searching of woollen cloth in the West Riding of Yorkshire. **1877** *Encycl. Brit.* VI. 322 A very difficult question rose in the American civil war with regard to the searching of mail bags.

¶**b.** Used for: Necessity of searching.

1527 *Prymer* Title, This prymer of Salysbury vse is set out a long without ony serchyng.

c. ***searching of heart***: inward self-scrutiny.

The reading of the Heb. text is uncertain, but the phrase has become proverbial in English.

1611 BIBLE *Judg.* v. 16 For the diuisions of Reuben, there were great searchings of heart. **1885** *Manch. Exam.* 11 June 4/7 The deserters should not be left solely to the searchings of their own hearts.

d. *attrib.* and *Comb.*, as ***searching-house***; **searching-candle** = CANDLE *sb.* 4 b; †**searching-instrument**, †**-iron**, †**-probe** (in quot. *fig.*), †**-tool** *Surg.*, a probe.

1672 WISEMAN *Wounds* I. viii. 66 The *searching Candle or Probe. **1858** *Chamb. Jrnl.* 17 July 34/1, I accompanied her upon her way, in custody, to the *searching-house [at the custom-house]. I did not see her searched, but [etc.]. **1591** PERCIVALL *Sp. Dict.*, *Tienta*, a *searching instrument, *Specillum*. **1597** A. M. tr. *Guillemeau's Fr. Chirurg.* 6/4 Your finger is the best *searchinge iron. **1658** A. FOX tr. *Wurtz' Surg.* I. vi. 22 Is it not enough, that one [Surgeon] with his searching iron shew his judgement and cruelty. **1770** LANGHORNE *Plutarch* (1879) I. 220/2 The *searching-probe of free advice. **1591** PERCIVALL *Bibl. Hisp.*, *Calador*, a *searching toole, *Specillum*.

searching ('sɜːtʃɪŋ), *ppl. a.* [f. SEARCH *v.* + -ING².] That searches, in various senses of the verb.

1. Of observation or examination: Minute, rigorous. Of a look: Penetrating, keenly observant.

c **1580** SIDNEY *Ps.* XVII. iii, Where silent Night might seeme all faultes to hide, Then was I, by thy searching insight tride. **1593** SHAKS. *Rich. II*, III. ii. 37 The searching Eye of Heauen. **1627** ABP. ABBOT in Rushw. *Hist. Coll.* (1659) I. 438 King James..had..a searching Wit of his own to discover his Servants, whom he put in trust, whether they took any sinister courses, or no. **1837** DICKENS *Pickw.* ii, He felt quite calm under his searching glance. **1861** BUCKLE *Civiliz.* (1873) III. iii. 184 A spirit of inquiry was abroad, so general and so searching that no country could entirely escape from its action. **1878** BOSW. SMITH *Carthage* 295 By a searching inquisition every free-born citizen..had been swept into the ranks. **1884** F. TEMPLE *Relat. Relig. & Sci.* vii. (1885) 215 St. Paul's evidence..cannot now be put to the test of searching questions.

b. Of an impersonal agency (e.g. of liquids, wind, rain, etc., or of bodily diseases): That finds out weak points, keen, sharp, 'piercing'. Also *fig.*

1593 SHAKS. *2 Hen. VI*, III. ii. 311 Bitter searching termes. **1597** —— *2 Hen. IV*, II. iv. 30 That's a maruellous searching Wine. **1602** MARSTON *Antonio's Rev.* IV. ii, These vinegar tart spirits are too pearcing, Too searching in the unglewd joynts of shaken wits. **1634** WOOD *New Engl. Prosp.* I. ii. (1865), The searching sharpnes of that purer Climate,.. caused death and sicknesse. **1746** HERVEY *Medit.* (1818) 147 Ere long, the searching beams will open these silken folds, and draw them into a graceful expansion. **1790** BURKE *Regic. Peace* iv. Wks. IX. 72 Even the Negroes in the West Indies, know nothing of so searching, so penetrating, so heart-breaking a slavery. **1851** CARLYLE *Sterling* xii, The rain was so searching, that she could not stay there long. **1873** MISS BROUGHTON *Nancy* i, The searching wind blows in dry and biting. **1898** *Allbutt's Syst. Med.* V. 85 The residual phlegm dislodged by the searching cough is exceedingly offensive.

2. Engaged in or given to searching.

1626 D'EWES in Ellis *Orig. Lett.* Ser. I. III. 216, I dare say he meant it plainlie, yet searching braines might picke much from it. **1710** NORRIS *Chr. Prud.* iv. 153 The searching Bee wanders from Flower to Flower. **1841** HELPS *Ess.*, *On Pract. Wisd.* (1842) 4 Many persons are considered speculative merely because they are of a searching nature.

searchingly ('sɜːtʃɪŋlɪ), *adv.* [f. SEARCHING *ppl. a.* + -LY².] In a searching manner.

1574 J. JONES *Nat. Beg. Growing & Living Th.* 48 Such as with all diligence, care, and coste studiously day and night serchingly Saile through the Occian Seas of Naturall Science. **1593** NASHE *Christ's T.* 38 b, Though I deale more searchingly then common Soule-Surgions accustome. **1837** *New Monthly Mag.* LI. 245 Mathews looked searchingly about. **1908** E. G. SIHLER *Testim. Animæ* i. 1 His book deals with many incidental questions warmly and searchingly.

searchingness ('sɜːtʃɪŋnɪs). [f. SEARCHING *ppl. a.* + -NESS.] Searching quality or nature.

1685 *Reflect. on Baxter* 2, I thought he had studied that Sacred Writing with that Care and Searchingness, that [etc.]. **1803** W. TAYLOR in *Ann. Rev.* I. 400 Passages of great feeling, animation, and searchingness. **1875** GREG *Misc. Ess.* iii. (1882) 71 Two Courts of Justice, after investigations of unequalled searchingness and duration had [etc.].

†**'searchless,** *a. Obs.* [f. SEARCH *sb.* + -LESS.] Inscrutable, impenetrable, resisting investigation.

1605 DRAYTON *Man in Moon* 383 Her searchlesse Judgement. **1706** WATTS *Horæ Lyr.* I. 55 Great God, how searchless are thy ways! **1818** SHELLEY *Rev. Islam* x. xlvi, He might man's deep and searchless heart display. **1834** *Tait's Mag.* I. 301 In searchless heaps of stifling dust We have buried the hearts of the wise and just.

'search-light. [f. SEARCH *sb.* + LIGHT *sb.*]

1. An electric arc-lamp fitted with a reflector and suspended in a frame so that it may throw a beam of light in any desired direction; used in naval defence and for signalling purposes, etc. Also, the beam of light thrown by such a lamp.

1883 *Pall Mall Gaz.* 2 Oct. 16/1 These Dynamos can be supplied..for arc, search-light, or incandescent lamps. **1884** *Ibid.* 18 Sept. 8/1 An admiral..reported..that no search lights..could enable him to prevent a torpedo boat steaming within 400 yards of his flagship. **1902** *L.C.C. Bye-law* in *Encycl. Brit.* XXV. 97/1 No person shall exhibit any searchlight so as to be visible from any street and to cause danger to the traffic therein. **1919** KIPLING in *Hutchinson's Story Mag.* July 12 And the crazy skies are lit By the searchlights of the Pit. **1929** S. LESLIE *Anglo-Catholic* xvi. 225 He pointed..to the Northern sky, across which dropped a silver ribbon of attenuated search-light. **1943** L. B. LYON *Evening in Stepney* 12 Across and across it move The search-lights, reckoning hate on a hidden clock.

fig. **1892** MRS. CROSSE *Red-letter Days* II. 195 Kinglake in his history reveals, with the searchlight of a detective, the secret chronicles of the 'Brethren of the Élysée'. **1904** S. G. TALLENTYRE *Life Voltaire* II. xl. 234 Each..turned on some miscarriage of civil justice the searchlight of truth.

Hence as *v. trans.*, to illuminate with a searchlight; also *fig.*

1914 W. DE MORGAN *When Ghost meets Ghost* I. xxix. 344 That officer..was searchlighting areas for want of something to do. **1966** *Prison Service Jrnl.* VI. 21/2 We find our own failings..are searchlighted.

seare, obs. form of CERE *v.*, SERE *sb.*¹ and *a.*

seared (sɪəd), *ppl. a.* [f. SEAR *v.* + -ED¹.]

1. Dried up, parched, withered.

1538 ELYOT *Dict.*, *Ramale*, a seryd or deed bowghe. **1599** THYNNE *Animadv.* (1875) 48 Of freshe coolor..whiche hathe no sered nor withered cooloor in his leafes. **1791** COWPER *Iliad* XIII. 687 Part [of the weapon] within his disk remain'd Like a seer'd stake. **1844** DICKENS *Mart. Chuz.* ii, The seared leaves only flew the faster for all this. **1886** W. J. TUCKER *E. Europe* 298 We reached the outskirts of the village, surrounded by rich pasture-lands and dense copses of thicket, now seared and bare.

2. Cauterized. Also *fig.*, of the conscience, heart, etc., rendered incapable of feeling.

1684 J. SHARP *Disc. Conscience* 7 If..we..talk of..a Tender Conscience or a Seared Conscience or the like. **1862** CALVERLEY *Verses & Transl.* (1894) 53 Seared is, of course my heart—but unsubdued Is, and shall be, my appetite for food. **1903** A. SMELLIE *Men of Covenant* vi. 90 Perhaps even this man, seared as his conscience was, felt a tremor of awe.

seared, obs. form of CERED *ppl. a.*

†**'searedness.** *Obs.* [f. SEARED *ppl. a.* + -NESS.] The condition of being seared.

1620 BP. HALL *Hon. Marr. Clergy* III. ii. 261 Hee wonders at my extreme prodigalitie of credit, and seardnesse of conscience, in citing an Epistle so conuicted. **1705** WALL *Inf. Bapt.* II. (1720) 329 That Socinian Doctrin seems to have infected all its Disciples..with such a Degree of Searedness, that [etc.]. **1782** J. BROWN *Nat. & Revealed Relig.* III. i. 228 Judicial blindness of mind, hardness of heart, searedness of conscience.

searfe, obs. form of SERVE *v.*

searge, variant of CIERGE, SERGE.

seargeant, obs. form of SERGEANT.

'sea-rim. [OE. *sǽrima*: see RIM *sb.*¹]

†**1.** The sea-shore. *Obs. rare.*

O.E. Chron. an. 897, þær mycel yfel ȝedydon, æȝðer ge on Defenum ge wel hwær be ðæm sæ riman. *Ibid.* an. 994 (Laud MS.) Be ðam sæ riman on East Seaxum. *c* **1205** LAY. 6216 We habbeoð isoht bi þisse sæ rime a lond..þe us were liðe þe we mihten on libben. *Ibid.* 10485 þa a þan ilke time verden bi sæ rime vtlaȝen to iwiten fulle sixti scipen.

2. The sea horizon.

a **1881** LANIER *Hymns of Marshes*, *Sunrise* 145 The wave-serrate sea-rim sinks unjarring. **1896** KIPLING *Seven Seas*, *Coastwise Lt.* 12 The lover from the sea-rim drawn—his love in English lanes. **1899** F. T. BULLEN *Way Navy* 28 Mast-head semaphores..to be read and answered by ships whose hulls are below the sea-rim.

searing ('sɪərɪŋ), *vbl. sb.* [-ING¹.] The action of SEAR *v.*; scorching, cauterizing; *concr.* a result of searing, a seared portion of something. Also *fig.*

1395 *Cartul. Abb. de Whiteby* (Surtees) II. 601 Pro seryng unius equi et cura alterius. **1552** HULOET, Blastynge or Searynge, as of corne. **1562** *Act 5 Eliz.* c. 14 §12 Persons that shall so offende..shall have..losse of Eares, slytting and searing of Nose. **1682** NORRIS *Hierocles* 82 As Physicians heel Malign Ulcers by Scarifyings and Searings. **1720** WELTON *Suffer. Son of God* II. xix. 525 When a Man neglects to pare off the first Searings of His Heart, He gradually goes on to Harden in his Obstinacy. **1858** W. ARNOT *Laws fr. Heav.* Ser. II. xli. 329 There must be a rude, hearty blow, for there is a hard searing to be penetrated.

b. *Comb.*: **searing-iron**, an iron used for cauterizing, branding, etc.

1541 [see IRON *sb.*¹ 4 b]. **1574** tr. *Marlorat's Apocalips* 2 They..yell oute as if they were burned with a searingyron. **1626** T. H[AWKINS] *Caussin's Holy Crt.* 131 Theyr phrensy would haue no other remedyes, but the searing-Iron, and fyre. **1683** tr. *Eusebius' Hist. Ch.* VIII. xiii. (1709) 170 His Eyes also (altho' he could not then see) were burnt out with Searing-irons. **1896** *Daily News* 11 Sept. 7/6 Mr. G. said his client denied using a searing iron to the mare's tail.

fig. **1646** J. HALL *Horæ Vac.* 36 Such a wonderfull Nature hath the word, that..it is as well a searing Iron, as a two edged sword. *a* **1649** DRUMM. OF HAWTH. *Hist. Jas. V*, Wks. (1711) 101 Since the Roman church had received..a deadly wound,..she was constrained to use a searing iron.

searing ('sɪərɪŋ), *ppl. a.* [f. SEAR *v.* + -ING².]

1. That withers or becomes parched.

1665 BRATHWAIT *Comment Two Tales* (1901) 49 You compare a Woman's Love..to barren Land,..thirsty and seering. **1849** J. HAMILTON *Life Lady Colquhoun* vii. 282

Instead of the roughening lake and the searing forest, God had showed her 'the pure river, clear as crystal' [etc.].

2. That scorches; burning, scarifying.

1818 KEATS *Endym.* III. 260 Will he touch me with his searing hand, And leave a black memorial on the sand? **1897** ANNE PAGE *Afternoon Ride* 60 The searing sunshine and hot winds of Africa.

fig. *a* **1860** S. MILLER in *Mem.* (1883) 89 Let us also fear lest it turn out a searing ordeal. **1899** CORNFORD *R. L. Stevenson* 163 The captain, with his searing memory of his child.

searing, searment: see CERING, CEREMENT.

searlesite ('sɜːlzaɪt). *Min.* [f. the name of John W. *Searles*, who put down the well in California from which the first specimen came: see -ITE[1].] A hydrated borosilicate of sodium, $NaBSi_2O_6.H_2O$, occurring as white monoclinic crystals.

1914 LARSEN & HICKS in *Jrnl. Washington Acad. Sci.* IV. 397 The mineral for which the name searlesite is proposed was found in samples from the deep well in Searles Lake, San Bernardino County, California. **1950** *Amer. Mineralogist* XXXV. 1017 In the stratum of trona 10 feet thick that is reached by the shaft at a depth of 1500 feet, subhedral crystals of searlesite up to 7 inches long, 4 inches wide, and one inch thick are not uncommon. **1974** *Mineral. Abstr.* XXV. 303/1 The phyllosilicate searlesite, $Na_2B_2(OH)_4Si_4O_{10}$, has been made from mixtures of Na_2O, B_2O_3, SiO_2 and excess H_2O heated under steam pressure at 250°C for up to 8 days.

sea-robin. [ROBIN[1].]

1. *U.S.* A gurnard or trigloid fish, esp. of the genus *Prionotus*.

1814 S. L. MITCHILL *Fishes N.Y.* 430 Gurnard, or Sea Robin, *Trigla lineata.* **1844** LINSLEY *Fishes Connecticut* in *Amer. Jrnl. Sci.* XLVII. 59 Prionotus strigatus, Cuv., Sea Robin, Grunter. **1884** GOODE, etc. *Nat. Hist. Aquatic Anim.* 255 The Sea-robin or Gurnard family..is represented on our Atlantic coast by several species. The most striking of them all is the Sea-bat or Flying Gurnard, *Dactylopterus volitans. Ibid.* 256 The web-fingered Sea-robin, *Prionotus palmipes.*

2. A local name for: **a.** *U.S.* The red-breasted merganser, *Mergus serrator* (Cent. Dict. 1891). **b.** The spotted fly-catcher, *Muscicapa grisola* (Cumberld. Gloss. 1899).

'sea-rod. [ROD *sb.*[1]]

1. A pennatulaceous polyp of the family *Virgulariidæ*. Cf. SEA-RUSH 2.

1750 G. HUGHES *Barbados* 288 The Incrusted Sea-Rods. **1877** H. A. NICHOLSON in *Encycl. Brit.* VI. 385/1 The 'Sea-pens' and 'Sea-rods' are compound *Alcyonaria*.

2. A fishing-rod used for sea-fishing (ROD *sb.* 5).

1902 'J. BICKERDYKE' in *Encycl. Brit.* XXXII. 487/1 Very excellent sea-rods have..been designed by anglers and tackle makers.

'sea-room. Space at sea free from obstruction in which a ship can be manœuvred easily. Esp. in phr. ***to have sea-room***, also ***to give*** or ***take sea-room***.

Also, (of a naval commander) † *to give* (the enemy) *sea-room*: to take flight.

a **1554** SIR H. WILLOUGHBY in *Hakluyt's Voy.* (1589) 269 Then perceiuing it to be a lee shoare, we gat vs into the sea, to the end to haue sea roome. **1579–80** NORTH *Plutarch, Philop.* (1595) 399 This ouerthrow made his enemies despise him vtterly, perswading themselues he was fled for altogether, & had giuen them sea rome. **1608** SHAKS. *Per.* III. i. 45 But Sea-roome, and the brine and cloudy billow Kisse the Moone, I care not. *a* **1613** OVERBURY *A Wife*, etc. (1638) 158 Give him Sea-roome in never so small a vessell. **1627** MAY *Lucan* III. (1631) 580 When so little Sea-roome did divide Both fleetes. **1698** CAPT. LANGFORD in *Phil. Trans.* XX. 410 So with the North Wind they may run away to the South, to get them-selves Sea-room. **1748** *Anson's Voy.* I. x. 104 We had sufficient sea-room. **1884** SELBORNE in *Law Rep. 9 App. Cases* 348 The danger in the gulf is greater, because there is less sea-room there.

fig. **1603** HOLLAND *Plutarch's Mor.* 198 If a word be issued out of the mouth, as out of her haven, and have gotten sea-roome,..away she goes. **1754** RICHARDSON *Grandison* VII. xliii. 215 Leave her sea-room, leave her land-room, and let her have time to consider, and she will be a Bride. **1842** H. WARE in *Longfellow's Life* (1891) I. 449 You want more sea-room for so grand an idea.

sea-rover. [ROVER[2].]

1. A pirate, = ROVER[2] 1. (Now often apprehended as meaning one who 'roves' over the sea: see ROVER[1] 3.)

1579–80 NORTH *Plutarch, Lucullus* (1595) 541 Besides what the Pyrates and sea-rouers had hidden. **1670** MILTON *Hist. Eng.* I. Wks. 1851 III. 10 A certain Iland long before dispeopl'd and left waste by Sea-Roavers. **1786** *St. Papers* in *Ann. Reg.* 280/1 They shall cause all such pirates and sea-rovers..to be brought to condign punishment. **1872** YEATS *Growth Comm.* 50 The Greeks like sea-rovers generally were first induced to build ships for the sake of plunder, rather than of commerce.

2. 'A ship or vessel that is employed in cruizing for plunder' (Webster, 1828–32).

Hence **sea-roving** *vbl. sb.* and *ppl. a.*

1840 CARLYLE *Heroes* i. (1841) 52 Nor was it altogether nothing, even that wild sea-roving and battling, through so many generations. **1847** WEBSTER, *Sea-roving, a.* wandering on the ocean. **1855** KINGSLEY *Heroes, Argon.* v. (1856) 134 Those crafty sea-roving Phæaces. **1900** W. WATT *Aberd. & Banff* i. 19 Thorfinn..went sea-roving like all his kindred.

searse, -er, obs. forms of SEARCE, SEARCER.

Sears-Roebuck (sɪəz 'rəʊbʌk), *a. U.S. slang.* Also **Sears and Roebuck**. The name of the American merchandising firm of *Sears, Roebuck* and Co., used allusively of an inexperienced, 'green', or amateurish person, or of something cheap or of little value.

1917 R. LORD *Captain Boyd's Battery, A.E.F.* (1919) ii. 23 Two tents of Shavetails (i.e. Reverse Officers, Ninety-Day Wonders, Sears & Roebuck Specials,..etc.) have been attached to us for instruction purposes. **1930** *Our Army* Jan. 4 He's a regular Sears-Roebuck product; three months of training, three tons of dignity and three ounces of horse sense. **1932** *Amer. Speech* VII. 270 *Sears-Roebuck driller*, an inexperienced and incapable driller. **1942** BERREY & VAN DEN BARK *Amer. Thes. Slang* §21/14 Cheap; paltry... *Sears-Roebuck.* **1971** M. TAK *Truck Talk* 137 *Sears-Roebuck license*, the license said to be held by an inferior driver.

searsucker, variant of SEERSUCKER.

sea-rush. [RUSH *sb.*[1]]

1. A species of *Juncus* (see RUSH *sb.*[1] 4 a). Also † ***sea-rush grass***.

1562 TURNER *Herbal* II. 144 b, Sparta..is a kind of sea bente or sea rishe. **1597** GERARDE *Herbal* I. xxiii. 30 The flowers of this Sea Rush grasse are faire and beautifull. **1600** J. PORY tr. *Leo's Africa* III. 160 They make them certaine socks of sea-rushes. **1712–13** HEARNE *Collect.* (O.H.S.) IV. 69 Our Saviour himself was to be crown'd with a Crown of Thorns made of y[e] same sea Rushes. **1725** *Bradley's Fam. Dict., Sea-Rush, Sea-Rush-Grass*, or *Spanish Trefoil*, a Plant whose Seed is very small, and black. **1796** WITHERING *Brit. Pl.* (ed. 3) II. 346 *Juncus acutus*,..Pricking large Sea-rush. Sand Hills on the sea coast of Merionethshire. Ray. **1882** 'OUIDA' *Maremma* I. 116 The pungent sea-rush grew in long lines along the shore.

2. = SEA-ROD 1.

1850 MISS PRATT *Comm. Things of Sea-side* iv. 262 The *Virgularia*, which the fishermen call Sea-rush. **1855** KINGSLEY *Glaucus* (1878) 37 Sea-rush (*Virgularia mirabilis*), a spine a foot long, with hundreds of rosy flowerets arranged in half-rings round it from end to end.

searve, seas, obs. ff. SERVE, CEASE.

'sea-salt, *sb.* Common salt obtained by the evaporation of sea-water. See SALT *sb.*[1] 1.

1601 HOLLAND *Pliny* XXXI. vii. II. 416 After which they esteemed most, all the sea salts. **1685** BOYLE *Salubr. Air* 86 A little sea-salt dissolv'd in a few spoonfulls of fair water. **1766** SMOLLETT *Trav.* I. xxiv. 358 The atmosphere being.. impregnated with sea-salt. **1836–41** BRANDE *Chem.* 362 Sea-salt, or chloride of sodium. **1883** STEVENSON *Treas. Isl.* iv, There was an old boat-cloak, whitened with sea-salt.

Hence **'sea-salted** *a.*, impregnated or seasoned with sea-salt.

1925 V. WOOLF *Mrs. Dalloway* 70 The brisk sea-salted air of their intimacy. *a* **1941** —— *Captain's Death Bed* (1950) 31 This gnarled and sea-salted man was no smug clergyman underneath.

'sea-salt, *a. rare.* [SALT *a.*[1]] Salt like the sea; impregnated with or containing sea-salt.

1588 SHAKS. *Tit. A.* III. ii. 20 That all the teares that thy poore eyes let fall May..Drowne the lamenting foole, in Sea salt teares. **1596** R. L[INCHE] *Diella* (1877) 78 In Sea-salt teares hee long hath liu'd. **1897** WATTS-DUNTON *Aylwin* XIV. iv, I was kissing Winnie's sea-salt lips.

sea-sand. Forms: see SEA *sb.* and SAND *sb.*[2]; also 5 see-sownde.

1. Sand of the sea or of the sea-shore.

c **1220** *Bestiary* 504 A neilond ðat sete one ðe se sond. *c* **1420** *Sir Amadace* (Camden) xlvii, The messingerus welke bi the see sonde. *c* **1450** *Mirk's Festial* 206 þen saw he a chylde syttyng on þe see-sownde. **1610** HOLLAND *Camden's Brit.* I. 184 A certaine kind of fruitfull Sea-sand. **1664** EVELYN *Kal. Hort., Apr.* (1699) 53 Sea-sand mingled with the Mould..contributes to the flourishing of this rare Exotick. **1798** COLERIDGE *Anc. Mar.* IV. i, Thou art long, and lank, and brown, As is the ribb'd sea-sand. **1845** GOSSE *Ocean* vi. (1849) 275 It is remarkable to see this graceful palm rising from the very sea-sand.

† **b.** *pl.* Grains of sea-sand. *Obs.*

1656 EARL MONM. tr. *Boccalini's Advts. fr. Parnass.* I. lxxvii. 158 [They] do for number equal the stars of heaven, or the sea-sands.

2. *pl.* Tracts of sea-sand; = SAND *sb.*[2] 3 a.

c **1420** *Anturs of Arth.* 268 He shal lighte ful lowe on þe se sondes. **1626** BACON *Sylva* §572 The Sea-Sands seldome beare Plants. **1644** VICARS *God in Mount* 160 The way thither is on the Sea-sands. **1838** LYTTON *Alice* I. iii, The rude steps that wound down the cliff to the smooth sea-sands.

sea-scape, seascape ('siːskeɪp). [Formed in imitation of LANDSCAPE *sb.*; see also SCAPE *sb.*[3]]

1. A picture of the sea, a sea-piece; sea-pieces collectively.

1799 *Hull Advertiser* 5 Jan. 2/4 One of the most eminent marine painters has painted sea-skips. **1876** *Macm. Mag.* Mar. 461 It is in these respects that the seascape with figures ..gains. **1893** *Times* 29 Apr. 13/2 For sea-scape we have.. one by a new painter.

2. A picturesque view or prospect of the sea.

1806 *Guide Watering Places* 190 A fine sea-scape from a terrace in the garden. **1883** LD. R. GOWER *Remin.* II. xxix. 313 The view from Europa Point [Gibraltar] is the finest seascape imaginable.

3. *attrib.*

1884 HUNTER & WHYTE *My Ducats* xi, I think you have met Floyd, the seascape painter. **1906** *Daily Chron.* 13 Mar. 3/4 Realistic seascape painting.

Hence **'sea,scapist**, a painter of sea-scapes.

1884 *Guardian* 28 May 802/2 The Dutch sea-scapist, Mr. Mesdag. **1900** *Daily News* 16 Oct. 6/6 Stanfield and Cooke, ..who painted not quite as the seascapists do now.

sea scorpion. † **a.** = SCORPION 3 a. *Obs.* **b.** Any fish of the *Scorpænidæ*, a scorpion-fish. **c.** A sculpin, a cottoid fish, *Cottus scorpius*.

1601 HOLLAND *Pliny* XXXII. vii. II. 438 The reddish sea scorpions. **1681** GREW *Musæum* I. §v. ii. 106. **1755** tr. *Pontoppidan's Nat. Hist. Norway* II. 160 The Ulk or Marulk, the Sea-Scorpion, called by the Ichthyologians Scorpius Marinus, because its bite is poisonous. **1758** G. EDWARDS *Glean. Nat. Hist.* Pl. 284 The Sea Scorpion. **1859–62** SIR J. RICHARDSON, etc. *Mus. Nat. Hist.* (1868) II. 122 The Sea-scorpion or Sutor (*Acanthocottus scorpius*). **1896** tr. *Boas' Text-bk. Zool.* 390 The Sea Scorpion (*Cottus scorpius*), with a large head, naked skin, spines on the head.

seasde, obs. pa. t. and Sc. pa. pple. of SEIZE *v.*

sease, obs. form of CEASE *v.*, SEISE, SEIZE.

seasen, obs. form of SEASON *v.*

'sea-,serpent.

1. a. Any ophidian inhabiting the sea; esp. any of the venomous snakes of the order *Hydrophidæ*, inhabiting the tropical Indo-Pacific Ocean.

1671 *Phil. Trans.* VI. 3093 There are Serpents in Ceylon, which they call Sea-Serpents, 8, 9, or 10 Ells long; (I suppose he speaks of Dutch measure). **1674** JOSSELYN *Two Voy. New-Eng.* 23 They told me..of a Sea-Serpent or Snake, that lay quoiled up like a Cable upon a Rock at Cape-Ann. **1859–62** SIR J. RICHARDSON, etc. *Mus. Nat. Hist.* (1868) II. 49 The Sea or Pelagic Serpents (*Hydrina*) are not very numerous in species.

b. ***the*** (***great***) ***sea-serpent***: a sea-monster of serpentine form and great length, frequently reported to have been seen at sea.

For conjectures as to the origin of the belief in the sea-serpent, see *Encycl. Brit.* (1886) XXI. 608–9.

1774 GOLDSM. *Nat. Hist.* (1776) VI. 193 To believe all that has been said of the sea-serpent, or the Kraken, would be credulity. **1820** BIGELOW in *Amer. Jrnl. Sci.* II. 147–164.

fig. **1885** *Western Daily Press* 6 Jan. 3/2 The affair, in short, has turned out to be the liveliest political 'sea serpent' seen for some time.

2. Applied to various fishes. † **a.** A kind of eel or muræna found in the Mediterranean. † **b.** = ELLOPS 2. **c.** The king of the herrings, *Regalecus glesne*.

1646 SIR T. BROWNE *Pseud. Ep.* III. xxiv. 169 Many there be which make out their nominations, as the Hedg-hog, Sea-serpents, and others. **1661** LOVELL *Hist. Anim. & Min.* Isagoge a 6 b, The Linge,..tunie,..sea-serpent, conger [etc.]. **1740** R. BROOKES *Art of Angling* II. lxxix. 201 The Sea-Serpent..is commonly about five Foot long..is taken very frequently in the Mediterranean. **1752** J. HILL *Hist. Anim.* 237 The cylindrick Muræna, with the tail naked and acute. The Sea-serpent... It is frequent in the Mediterranean. **1774** [see ELLOPS 2]. **1851** A. WHITE *List Brit. Fish Brit. Mus.* 40 Regalecus Glesne. King of the Herrings... Sea Serpent.

3. = SEA-SNAKE 4.

1891 in *Century Dict.*

4. (See quot.)

1831 SCOTT *Ct. Robt.* ii, Others navigated the Mediterranean in their sea-serpents, as they termed their piratical vessels.

Hence **sea-serpentism** *nonce-wd.*

1877 OWEN in *Q. Jrnl. Geol. Soc.* XXXIII. 699 The advocate for the sea-serpentism of the extinct Mosasauroids determines the pterygoids to be the palatines.

,sea-'service.

1. Service at sea; the condition or function of serving in the navy; naval service, as opposed to land-service. Also, service or employment (of a person, ship, etc.) on the high seas, as distinguished from shore or harbour duty.

1610 HOLLAND *Camden's Brit.* I. 811 The first Cohort.. was in pay for sea service. **1659** RUSHW. *Hist. Coll.* I. 429 [He] did..prepare and set out to Sea, a Royal Fleet for Sea-service. **1726** SHELVOCKE *Voy. round World* Pref. 25 A defection amongst my Officers (I mean those chiefly design'd for the Sea-Service..). **1858** GREENER *Gunnery* 118 The 13-inch mortars used for sea-service in the attack on Sweaborg. **1867** SMYTH *Sailor's Word-bk., Sea-going*, fit for sea-service abroad. **1909** *19th Cent.* Dec. 1011 The number of officers and men voted for sea service is much greater.

2. A service rendered at sea, or in naval warfare.

1654 GAYTON *Pleas. Notes* 67 Doe but recount..what honour a Ship hath..for some singular Sea-service.

'sea-shell. a. A marine shell, the shell of any salt-water mollusc.

a **900** *O.E. Martyrol.* 14 Jan. 18 Understregd mid sæscellum & mid scearpum stanum. **1707** MORTIMER *Husb.* 84 Sea-shells of any sort are a very great improver of Land. **1805** SOUTHEY *Madoc* II. ix. 192 Whose thunders, ever and anon, Commingling with the sea-shell's spiral roar Closed the full harmony. **1858** O. W. HOLMES *Mare Rubrum* 28 Like emptied sea-shells on the sand.

attrib. **1871** MRS. STOWE *Pink & White Tyranny* i. 4 He saw this distant vision of airy gauzes, of pearly whiteness, of sea-shell pink. **1901** F. HUME *Golden Wang-ho* i, Complexion of the most delicate sea-shell pink.

b. Material consisting of sea-shells.

1837 P. KEITH *Bot. Lex.* 251 Mineral manures are silica, lime, alumina, under the modifications of sand, clay,..marl, sea-shell, gypsum.

sea-shore. The coast of the sea, or the land lying adjacent to the sea; also, in more restricted sense, the ground actually washed by the sea at high tides (usually, covered with sand or shingle).

In *Law* commonly taken to denote the ground between the ordinary high and low water-marks. See Erskine *Inst. Law Scot.*, 1765–8, II. vi. §17.

1526 TINDALE *Heb.* xi. 12 So many in multitude..as the sonde of the see shore which is innumerable. **1529** *Reg. Mag. Sig. Scot.* (1883) 160/1 Salmonum piscariam super le seyschoire subtus villam de Inverbervy. **1610** HOLLAND *Camden's Brit.* I. 210 It hath a descent even to the very Sea shore. **1735** JOHNSON *Lobo's Abyssinia, Voy.* i. 7 Finding themselves too much crouded in their own Country, [they] had extended themselves to the Sea-shore. **1831** SCOTT *Ct. Robt.* v, He hastens to his bark on the sea-shore. **1843** RUSKIN *Mod. Paint.* I. II. I. vii. §5 The broad wild sea-shore, with its bright breakers, and free winds.

attrib. **1850** MISS PRATT *Comm. Things Sea-side* i. 81 The flower of the sea-shore medick. **1852** WIGGINS *Embanking* 78 One of these was sea-shore land.

seasible, obs. form of SEIZABLE.

'sea-sick, *a.*

1. a. Suffering from sea-sickness. Chiefly *predicative*.

*a***1566** R. EDWARDS *Damon & Pithias* (1908) B ij b, I am euen yet so Seasicke that I faynt as I go. **1611** SHAKS. *Wint. T.* v. ii. 128 The Shepherds Daughter..who began to be much Sea-sick. **1701** FARQUHAR *Sir H. Wildair* IV. i, Look ye, Captain, I shall be Sea-Sick presently. **1819** BYRON *Juan* II. xix, Here the ship gave a lurch, and he grew sea-sick. **1836** MISS MAITLAND *Lett. fr. Madras* (1843) 8 Towards evening, like all other sea-sick people, I grow very brisk. **1883** F. M. CRAWFORD *Dr. Claudius* vii. 109 [He] would.. make his rounds to see that every one was all right and nobody sea-sick.

fig. *a***1627** MIDDLETON *Wom. beware Wom.* II. ii, Her tender modesty is sea-sick a little.

b. ***sea-sick medicine, pill, tablet,*** a preparation taken to counter sea-sickness.

1925 E. H. YOUNG *William* iii. 29 Mother's going to give us some sea-sick medicine before we start. **1951** N. MITFORD *Blessing* II. xii. 268 The stewardess..stood over her with a bottle of sea-sick tablets. **1959** 'M. M. KAYE' *House of Shade* iii. 38 He..had made her take several seasick pills. **1969** G. M. BROWN *Orkney Tapestry* i. 17 In Scrabster they sip brandy or swallow sea-sick tablets. **1972** W. ELLIS *Knife Edge* ii. 20 Seasick pills. We must get some before we set off.

†**2.** Tired or weary of travelling by sea. *Obs.*

1592 SHAKS. *Rom. & Jul.* v. iii. 118 Come vnsauory guide, Thou desperate Pilot, now at once run on The dashing Rocks, thy Sea-sicke wearie Barke.

3. *nonce-use* [after *home-sick*]. Longing for the sea.

1826 MISS MITFORD *Village* Ser. II. 112 She..pined for the water, and was,..in a new sense of the word, sea-sick.

sea-sickness. Nausea and vomiting induced by the motion of a ship at sea.

1625 PURCHAS *Pilgrims* III. 926 *marg.*, Sea sicknesse whence. **1633** T. STAFFORD *Pac. Hib.* II. xxvii. 266 When his sea-sicknesse was past, he lodged in the Earles house. **1785** *Liberal Amer.* I. 141 Should I be attacked with the sea-sickness, I shall be unfit for..any thing. **1819** BYRON *Juan* II. xiii, The best of remedies is a beef-steak Against sea-sickness. **1844** DICKENS *Mart. Chuz.* xv, Martin was too far gone in the lassitude of sea-sickness.

fig. **1706** E. WARD *Wooden World Diss.* (1708) 8 This Pride of his, is the only Sea-sickness that he's plagu'd with.

attrib. **1865** BP. WILBERFORCE *Let.* in A. J. Wilberforce *Life* (1882) III. vi. 159 All was ready for my start to Cannes, down even to the sea-sickness powders. **1955** E. BLISHEN *Roaring Boys* III. 151 His sea-sickness pills he carried in a little phial. **1973** H. NIELSEN *Severed Key* i. 12 Find the seasickness pills in the first aid kit in the forward locker.

sea-side, seaside (ˌsiːˈsaɪd, ˈsiːˌsaɪd).

1. a. The margin or brink of the sea: chiefly with prepositions, as ***by*** or ***at the sea-side,*** also †***on*** or †***upon,*** and ***to the sea-side.*** Now *rare* or *Obs.*

*c***1205** LAY. 25661 Bi þere sæ side þet londe he weste wide. *c***1375** *Sc. Leg. Saints* iii. (*Andrew*) 25 þane þe angel can hym say, þat he to þe sey-syd sulde fare. *c***1400** MAUNDEV. (Roxb.) v. 15 At Tyre euen apon þe see side men may fynd many rubies. **1512** *Act 4 Hen. VIII*, c. 1 §2 All the inhabitantes.. to bee at the See side with such instrumentes as they have. **1533** CROMWELL *Let.* 6 Dec. in Merriman *Life & Lett.* (1902) I. 368 Your said ferme lieth nygh the see syde. **1617** MORYSON *Itin.* I. 148 Towards the West it lies open to the most pleasant Valy of Arno, which Valy continueth as far as Pisa and to the sea-side. **1619** in Foster *Eng. Factories India* (1906) 71 Promising the 12th following to meete and confer with Captain Bonner upon the shoare neere the sea syde. **1726** SHELVOCKE *Voy. round World* 55 Among the rocks by the sea-side you find what is commonly called the sea-egg. **1818** SCOTT *Hrt. Midl.* l, Jeanie..had walked down to the sea-side.

†**b.** *plural. Obs.*

1387–8 T. USK *Test. Love* III. i. (Skeat) l. 45 On the see-sydes, in the more Britayne,..the best [*sc.* pearls] ben engendred. **1600** SURFLET *Country Farm* II. xlix. 315 Rosemarie..groweth in any aire, but best by the sea sides.

†**c.** Formerly sometimes ***the sea's side.*** *Obs.*

*c***1400** *Cursor M.* 21049 (Edinb.) Of grauel bi þe seis side. **1530** TINDALE *Deut.* i. 7 Vnto the sees syde in the londe of Canaan. **1543** GRAFTON *Contn. Harding* 99 Those that dwel by the seas syde.

2. Now chiefly: The sea-coast as resorted to for health or pleasure.

1782 W. COWPER *Let.* Nov. (1904) II. 20 Mr. Bull..is gone to the seaside with Mrs. Wilberforce, and will be absent six weeks. **1797** ABERNETHY *Surg. & Physiol. Ess.* III. 112 As he had an opportunity of going to the sea-side, I encouraged him to do so. **1833** T. HOOK *Parson's Dau.* III. v, Thence to proceed to such town at the sea-side as she might suggest or the physicians recommend. **1859** HELPS *Friends in C.* Ser. II. (1877) I. i. 53 A family in the middle class of life going to the seaside. **1893** J. A. HODGES *Elem. Photogr.* (1907) 109 Exposed for sale in the shops at the sea-side.

3. The side towards or facing the sea.

1867 J. MACGREGOR *Rob Roy on Baltic* xii. 149 After returning from a delightful excursion on the sea side of the town. **1869** TOZER *Highl. Turkey* I. 317 On the sea-side of it rose the Mount Rumia.

4. *attrib.* or quasi-*adj.* Belonging to, situated or taking place at the sea-side. Freq. in ***seaside café, holiday, resort, villa.***

1781 W. COWPER *Let.* 26 Sept. (1904) I. 358 The modern passion for seaside entertainments. **1784** —— *Task* VI. 245 As countless as the sea-side sands. **1810** CRABBE *Borough* ix. 2 We amuse Ourselves..with sea-side walks and views. **1861** MRS. CARLYLE *Lett.* III. 86 Ramsgate, one of the most accessible sea-side places. **1868** BROWNING *Ring & Bk.* IX. 373 The Pope, we know, is Neapolitan And relishes a sea-side simile. **1873** *Young Englishwoman* June 281/1 The collars can be procured..of chemists at seaside resorts. **1909** *Sat. Even. Post* 5 June 17/2 As soon as the theaters or 'hall-shows', as the circus men call them, close, the summer-garden or seaside parks open. **1939** F. THOMPSON *Lark Rise* ii. 36 Children..went to parties and for sea-side holidays. **1967** N. FREELING *Strike out where not Applicable* 39 A messy, ugly building..that..had climbed beyond modest seaside-café beginnings. **1973** 'B. MATHER' *Snowline* xix. 228 Looking like a seaside landlady who has just caught her daughter in bed with the star lodger. **1974** *Listener* 3 Jan. 27/1 The opera..went on, with success, at the seaside resort. **1976** P. R. WHITE *Planning for Public Transport* vii. 141 The traditional seaside excursion demand has fallen, most weekend leisure trips now being made by car. **1981** 'W. HAGGARD' *Money Men* xi. 117 Dame Molly has rented a seaside villa.

b. In names of plants, etc. (often rendering L. *maritimus*), as ***sea-side alder, balsam, convolvulus, fiorin, oat,*** etc.; †***sea-side beech,*** a species of *Cinchona*; ***seaside finch*** *U.S.*, a small sparrow, *Ammospiza maritima*, found on the Atlantic coast of North America; ***seaside grape*** = SEA-GRAPE 4; ***seaside laurel*** (see the sb.); ***seaside sparrow*** = *seaside finch* above.

1884 SARGENT *Rep. Forests N. Amer.* 162 *Alnus maritima.* *Seaside Alder. **1756** P. BROWNE *Jamaica* (1789) 347 Croton 2... The small *Sea-side Balsam... Croton 4... The Sea-side Balsam. **1852** G. W. JOHNSON *Cottage Gard. Dict.*, Sea-side Balsam, *Croton eleut[h]eria.* **1777** W. WRIGHT in *Phil. Trans.* LXVII. 504 The *Sea-side Beech..rises only to twenty feet. **1855** MISS PRATT *Flower. Pl.* IV. 21 *Calystegia Soldanella* (*Sea-side Convolvulus). **1811** A. WILSON *Amer. Ornithol.* IV. 68 *Sea-side Finch..derives its whole subsistence from the sea. **1872** E. COUES *Key to N. Amer. Birds* 137 Sea-side Finch. Olive-gray, obscurely streaked on the back and crown. **1852** WIGGINS *Embanking* 104 The *agrostis maritima* or *sea-side fiorin. **1696** PLUKENET *Almagestum* Wks. 1769 II. 394 *Sea-side Grape. **1756, 1792** Sea-side grape [see GRAPE *sb.*[1] 3 b]. **1837** J. L. WILLIAMS *Territory of Florida* 37 The seaside grape..and custard apples are frequently found in the hummocks. **1929** R. HUGHES *High Wind in Jamaica* i. 16 The lane, or drive, was gorgeous: for the first few hundred yards it was entirely hedged with 'seaside grapes'. **1978** T. J. WRIGHT in V. H. Heywood *Flowering Plants of World* 78/2 The purple berries of the West Indian seaside grape..are eaten. **1822** LOUDON *Encycl. Gard.* (1824) Index, Uniola, *sea-side oat.. H[ardy] peren[nial] N. Amer. of easy culture. **1886** *Code Nomencl. & Check-list N. Amer. Birds* (Amer. Ornithologists' Union) 269 *Seaside Sparrow..Salt marshes of the Atlantic coast. **1937** T. G. PEARSON in Grosvenor & Wetmore *Bk. Birds* II. 272/2 The northern seaside sparrow inhabits..the vicinity of the ocean beaches. **1978** C. HARRISON *Field Guide Nests, Eggs & Nestlings N. Amer. Birds* 394 Seaside Sparrow.. breeds on salt marshes.

c. Special Combs., as ***seaside (picture-) postcard,*** a postcard of a type commonly sold at the sea-side, *spec.* one depicting a caricature of lewd or vulgar humour; ***seaside rock (candy),*** rock-candy in the form of a cylindrical stick, usu. with a cross-section displaying the name of a resort in coloured lettering, commonly sold at the seaside.

1955 M. ALLINGHAM *Beckoning Lady* ii. 22 They looked like a seaside picture-postcard..wedged in the tub cart together, with the donkey in front. **1957** R. HOGGART *Uses of Literacy* I. ii. 31 The fifty-year-old formality of seaside postcards: most of the year 'decent' working-class people would hardly approve of them, but on holiday they are likely to 'let up a bit' and send a few to friends—cards showing fat mothers-in-law and fat policemen, weedy little men with huge-bottomed wives, ubiquitous bottles of beer and chamber-pots. **1979** J. WAINWRIGHT *Duty Elsewhere* xv. 45 The exaggerated bawdiness of seaside postcards. **1963** *Listener* 3 Jan. 40/2 Seaside rock and candy-floss. **1968** W. GARNER *Deep, Deep Freeze* vii. 96 Carnality ran through her like the letters through seaside rock candy. **1978** R. HILL *Pinch of Snuff* xxv. 262 He left them in a three-cornered trap ..with a four-letter word burned on the lawn. Perhaps like sea-side rock it went all the way through.

'seasider. [f. SEA-SIDE + -ER[2].] A frequenter of the seaside. (In quot. 1976 used as the nickname of an Association football team.)

1870 *Amer. Naturalist* III. 230 The Savannah Sparrow, though only occasionally found breeding so far south as Massachusetts, is evidently a sea-sider. **1892** *Pall Mall Gaz.* 23 June 1/3 The average lady seasider in this country frugally wears out her summer finery by the 'sad sea waves'. **1976** *West Lancs. Evening Gaz.* 15 Dec. 1. 18/7 Alan Ball comes to Blackpool tomorrow to talk terms with the Seasiders when he will be offered some of the most attractive terms ever offered by Blackpool.

seasin, obs. form of SEISIN.

seasing, obs. form of SEISIN, SEIZING.

seasir, variant of SEISER, *Law. Obs.*

'sea-slug.

1. = TREPANG.

1779 FORREST *Voy. N. Guinea* 373 They lay at anchor, fishing for swallo, or sea slug, in seven or eight fathom water. **1884** *Pall Mall Gaz.* 'Extra' 24 July 20/2 This so-called 'Bêche de Mer' is a sea-slug, found among the Polynesian islands and in the Pacific seas generally.

2. Any marine gasteropod of the order *Opisthobranchiata* (see quot. 1879).

1845 GOSSE *Ocean* iii. (1849) 133 Its [a whale's] support is derived from creatures of very small bulk..such as shrimps, sea slugs, sea blubbers, and animalcules still smaller. **1855** KINGSLEY *Glaucus* (1878) 130 The Cucumaria is a low radiate animal—the sea-slug is a far higher mollusc. **1879** E. P. WRIGHT *Anim. Life* 550 The molluscs of this order [*Opisthobranchiata*] may be termed sea-slugs, since the shell, when it exists, is usually small and thin, and wholly or partially concealed by the animal.

seasment, obs. form of SESSMENT.

'sea-snail.

1. A name for various marine gasteropods.

*c***1000** ÆLFRIC *Gloss.* in Wr.-Wülcker 122/24 *Chelio, testudo, uel marina gugalia,* sæsnæl, *uel* pinewinclan. *c***1050** *Suppl. Ælfric's Gloss.* Ibid. 181/8 *Conche, uel cochlee,* scille, *uel* sæsnæglas. **1538** ELYOT *Dict.*, *Chelydros*, a see snayle. **1607** TOPSELL *Four-f. Beasts* 77 Take the blood of a sea-snaile, and for want thereof a common snaile. **1774** GOLDSM. *Nat. Hist.* (1824) III. 116 Of all sea snails, that which is most frequently seen swimming upon the surface..is the Nautilus. **1820** SCORESBY *Acc. Arctic Reg.* I. 543 *Clio helicina.* Sea-snail. **1860** G. BENNETT *Gatherings Naturalist Austral.* 41, I caught a *Janthina fragilis*, or Violet Sea Snail. **1865** MRS. L. L. CLARKE *Sea-weeds* i. 23 Bright yellow Nerits, the commonest sea-snail of our coast.

attrib. **1681** GREW *Musæum* I. §v. iv. 121 A Sea-Snail shell. **1850** MISS PRATT *Comm. Things of Sea-side* iii. 221 There is a shell lying about most of our beaches and sandy shores,.. called the Sea Snail-shell.

2. A fish of the family *Liparididæ*, esp. the *Liparis vulgaris*, or unctuous sucker.

*a***1672** WILLUGHBY *Hist. Pisc.* (1686) Tab. H 6, Liparis nostras. Sea Snail Dunelmensibus. **1769** PENNANT *Brit. Zool.* III. 105 The sea snail takes its name from the soft and unctuous texture of its body resembling that of the land snail. **1881** *Cassell's Nat. Hist.* V. 97 The Sea Snail..is often known as the Unctuous Lump-sucker.

sea-snake.

1. = SEA-SERPENT 1 b.

1755 tr. *Pontoppidan's Nat. Hist. Norway* II. 195 The Soe Ormen, the Sea-Snake, Serpens Marinus Magnus..is a wonderful and terrible Sea-monster. **1805** SCOTT *Last Minstrel* VI. xxii, Of that Sea-Snake, tremendous curl'd Whose monstrous circle girds the world. **1817** BYRON *Manfred* I. i. 79 Where the wind is a stranger, And the sea-snake hath life. **1830** TENNYSON *Mermaid* 23 That great sea-snake under the sea.

2. = SEA-SERPENT 1 a.

1827 BUCKINGHAM *Trav. Mesopot.* I. 446 *note*, Dampier met with sea-snakes about four feet long, four fingers broad, flat tail, and spotted with yellow, on the coast of New Holland. **1860** G. BENNETT *Gatherings Naturalist Austral.* 278 Two Sea-Snakes, caught on the coasts of Australia, are both venomous. One is the *Platurus laticaudatus*, of a bluish colour with black rings,..and the other is the *Pelamis bicolor*. **1887** GÜNTHER in *Encycl. Brit.* XXII. 197/2 Of Sea Snakes (*Hydrophidæ*) some fifty species are known.

3. A chain of salps. Cf. SEA-SERPENT 4.

1863 WOOD *Illustr. Nat. Hist.* III. 442 Sailors often call these chains of Salpæ by the name of Sea Snakes.

sea-snipe.

1. A local name for several of the sandpipers, as the dunlin, and the knot.

1767 tr. *Cranz' Greenland* I. 85 The least bird is a sea-snipe. **1862** WOOD *Illustr. Nat. Hist.* II. 700 The Dunlin is known under a variety of names, such as the Stint, the Ox-bird, the Sea-snipe, and the Purre. **1885** SWAINSON *Prov. Names Birds* 195 Knot (*Tringa canutus*)... Sea snipe (Dublin).

2. †**a.** A kind of gar-fish. *Obs.* **b.** The trumpet-fish or snipe-fish, *Centriscus scolopax*, so called from its long tubular snout.

1826–7 J. F. SOUTH in *Encycl. Metrop.* (1845) XVIII. 624/2 There are three varieties of it [*Esox Belone*], one of which, found in North America, is called the Sea Snipe. **1836** YARRELL *Brit. Fishes* I. 302 The Trumpet-fish. Sea-snipe... *Centriscus scolopax.* **1859–62** SIR J. RICHARDSON, etc. *Mus. Nat. Hist.* (1868) II. 132.

season (ˈsiːz(ə)n), *sb.* Forms: 4–5 seson(e, -un(e, -oun(e, -owne, -yn(e, ceson(e, -un, -oun(e, 5–6 *Sc.* sessoun, 6 *Sc.* sessone, sesone, -oun; 4 seysyne, 4–5 seyson(e, -oun, 5 seison; 6 *Sc.* saison, sasoun, -one; 4–5 seasun, 5 seasone, (seosynne), 5–6 ceason, 6 *Sc.* seasoun, 4– season. [ME. *seson*, a. OF. *seson, seison* (mod.F. *saison*) = Pr. *sazó-s*, Catal. *sahó*, Sp. *sazon*, Pg. *sazão*, It. dial. *sason*:—L. *satiōn-em* act of sowing (in vulgar Lat. time of sowing, seed-time), n. of action f. *sa-* root of *serĕre* to sow.

Not connected with the synonymous It. *stagione*, which represents L. *statiōn-em* STATION.]

I. A period of the year.

1. a. Any one of the periods, longer or shorter, into which the year is naturally divided by the earth's changing position in regard to the sun, and which are marked by varying length of day and night, by particular conditions of weather, temperature, etc. More specifically, each of the four equal periods—Spring, Summer, Autumn, Winter—into which the year is divided by the passage of the sun from equinox to solstice and from solstice to equinox; also, each of the two periods—the rainy and the dry—into which the year is divided in tropical climates.

Often with defining word prefixed, as *summer, winter, May, Lent season* (see the different words).

1340–70 *Alex. & Dind.* 929 But whan þe daies dimme ben hit doþ hem to mourne, For siht of þe sesoun þat semus vnbliþe. *c* **1350** *Will. Palerne* 29 þe sauor of þe swete sesoun & song of þe briddes. *c* **1386** CHAUCER *Prol.* 347 After the sondry sesons of the yeer, So chaunged he his mete and his soper. *c* **1400** tr. *Secreta Secret., Gov. Lordsh.* 72 Off þe ffoure seysouns of þe ȝere. **1548** LATIMER *Ploughers* (Arb.) 19 Fyrste for their labour of all ceasons of the yere. For there is no tyme of the yere, in whiche the ploughman hath not some speciall worke to do. **1671** MILTON *P.R.* II. 72 In such a season born when scarce a Shed Could be obtain'd to shelter him or me From the bleak air. **1719** DE FOE *Crusoe* I. 122 The rainy Season, and the dry Season, began now to appear regular to me. **1727** SWIFT *Gulliver* III. iv, All the Fruits of the Earth shall come to Maturity at whatever Season we think fit to chuse. **1822** *Trans. Hort. Soc.* (1826) VI. 115 Directions for forcing Onions to produce bulbs in clusters, at an early season. **1845–7** LONGF. *Evangeline* I. ii. 1 Now had the season returned, when the nights grow colder and longer. **1864** TENNYSON *Enoch Arden* 624 The sunny and rainy seasons came and went Year after year. **1866** MRS. GASKELL *Wives & Dau.* xlii, The autumn drifted away through all its seasons.

b. In personification and art-representation.

a **1700** EVELYN *Diary* 22 Oct. 1644, The 4 Seasons in white marble. **1821** SHELLEY *Adonais* xviii, Fresh leaves and flowers deck the dead Seasons' bier.

c. A day or period of the year marked by some special festivity, as Christmas and New Year.

1791 BURNS *Let. to Cunningham* 23 Jan., Many happy returns of the season to you, my dear friend! **1821** LAMB *Elia* I. *All Fool's Day*, The compliments of the season to my worthy masters, and a merry first of April to us all!

d. In reckoning time or age: A year, twelve-month. (Cf. *summer*.)

1827 ROBERTS *Voy. Centr. Amer.* 43 A child of about five years or 'seasons' old. **1833** TENNYSON *Two Voices* 82 Will thirty seasons render plain Those lonely lights that still remain, Just breaking over land and main?

2. A period or time of year mentioned with reference to the conditions of weather, etc. that characterize it in a particular year.

13.. *E.E. Allit. P.* A. 39, I entred in þat erber grene, In augoste in a hyȝ seysoun, Quen corne is coruen wyth crokez kene. *c* **1450** HOLLAND *Howlat* 7 So soft was the sessoun our Souerane dovne sent..., That all was amyable owr the air and the erd. **1526** TINDALE *Acts* xiv. 17 Gevynge vs rayne from heven and frutfull ceasons. **1663** EVELYN *Diary* 16 July, A most extraordinary wet and cold season. **1676** LADY CHAWORTH in *12th Rep. Hist. MSS. Comm.* App. v. 34 The season continues so seveere I cannot get away my ill cold nor goe out of the house. **1812** G. CHALMERS *Dom. Econ. Gt. Brit.* 298 The corn act..appeared..to have completely failed..owing to..the unfavourable seasons. **1855** TENNYSON *Maud* II. v. viii, The lily and rose That blow by night, when the season is good. **1871** SCHELE DE VERE *Americanisms* 540 *Season* is, in the South, often misused for 'weather'. 'This is a good *season* for planting' does not mean, this is the proper time, but, this is favorable weather for planting tobacco.

3. a. The time of year assigned to some particular operation of agriculture.

13.. *K. Alis.* 61 (Bodl. MS.), By ham [*sc.* the planets] men han þe seysyne To londe, to watre to corne to wyne. **13..** *E.E. Allit. P.* B. 523 Se-sounez schal yow neuer sese of sede ne of heruest. **1393** LANGL. *P. Pl.* C. VII. 112 (MS. F.) In cesoun of heruest-tyme. *c* **1400** *Destr. Troy* 178 And alse sede in þe season sowe it on þe erthe. **1664** EVELYN *Kal. Hort., Feb.* (1679) 10 Now is your Season for Circumposition by Tubs or Baskets of Earth. **1796** C. MARSHALL *Gardening* v. (1813) 63 The season for committing seeds to the ground should be early as the nature of the plant to be cultivated will bear.

b. *local.* (See quots.)

1778 [W. H. MARSHALL] *Minutes Agric.* 20 Oct. 1775 *note*, Season..signifies (here, at least) the state of the soil at seed-time. Thus, if at seed-time the soil be clean, in high tilth, and neither too wet nor too dry, the Farmer is said to have got a good season—or a fine season. If it be cloddy, a rough season. **1875** PARISH *Sussex Dial.* 101 *Season*, ground in good condition. **1876** *Surrey Gloss.* s.v., 'To make a good season' is to get the land in good condition for sowing.

4. The time of year when a plant flourishes, when it blooms or bears fruit, etc. (See also 15 b.)

a **1300** *Cursor M.* 22881 Ilkin frut in his sesun. *c* **1386** CHAUCER *Frankl. T.* 306 Appollo, god and gouernour Of euery plaunte, herbe, tree and flour, That yeuest, after thy declinacion, To ech of hem his tyme and his seson. *c* **1400** MAUNDEV. (1839) v. 49 Also in that Contree..Men fynden longe Apples to selle, in hire cesoun. **1535** COVERDALE *Ps.* i. 3 Like a tre..yᵗ bringeth forth his frute in due season. **1637** MILTON *Lycidas* 7, I come to pluck your Berries harsh and crude... Bitter constraint, and sad occasion dear, Compels me to disturb your season due. **1747–96** MRS. GLASSE *Cookery* xii. 184 Half a pint of green peas, when it is the season for them. **1883** R. W. DIXON *Mano* II. vi. 85 Grass and leaves may flourish all the year, But corn and fruit one season only own.

5. The time of year when an animal is in heat, pairs, breeds, migrates, is killed for food or hunted, etc. (Also ***pairing, breeding, close,*** etc. ***season***.) † ***of (the) season*** = in season (see 15 b).

c **1400** *Master of Game* (MS. Digby 182) iii, þere [*sc.* the bucks'] seson dureth fro þe moneth of May into þe mydle of Septembre. **1486** *Bk. St. Albans* e v, The seson of the fox [is] fro the Natiuyte Tyll the annunciacion of owre lady fre. *c* **1490** *Plumpton Corr.* (Camden) 86, I..desire and pray you to caus a bucke of season to be taken. **1576** TURBERV. *Venerie* lxxix. 240 The seasons of all Chaces. **1598** SHAKS. *Merry W.* III. iii. 169, I warrant you Bucke, And of the season too. **1603** —— *Meas. for M.* II. ii. 85 Euen for our kitchins We kill the fowle of season. **1697** DRYDEN *Virg. Georg.* III. 101 Six Seasons use; but then release the Cow, Unfit for Love, and for the lab'ring Plough. **1711** STEELE *Spect.* No. 78 ¶5 The Day was fix'd for the Entertainment, which was in Venison Season. **1737** BRACKEN *Farriery Impr.* (1757) II. Index 14 Not to leap many Mares in a Season. **1760–72** H. BROOKE *Fool of Qual.* (1809) III. 123 My neighbours were not as birds of the season; they neither despised nor forsook me because of my poverty. **1842** TENNYSON *Audley Court* 32 Then touch'd upon the game, how scarce it was This season. **1844** H. STEPHENS *Bk. Farm* III. 1112 Its effect upon the skin may also interfere with the coming of the season upon the ewe. **1857** HUGHES *Tom Brown* I. iii, Others went after butterflies and birds'-eggs in their seasons.

attrib. *c* **1400** *Master of Game* (MS. Digby 182) iv, þei [*sc.* Roebucks] renneth wele and longer þan dothe a grete hert in þe hye seson tyme.

6. *fig.* Time of ripeness or maturity. Cf. 15 c.

1508 DUNBAR *Tua Mariit Wemen* 289 Bot leit the sueit ay the sour to gud sesone bring. *a* **1639** CAREW *To A.L.* 79 O then be wise, and whilst your season Affords you days for sport, do reason. **1648** *Eikon Bas.* iv. 18 Whose..impatience was such, that they would not staie the ripening and season of Counsels, or fair production of Acts, in the order, gravitie, and deliberateness befitting a Parliament; but [etc.].

†7. A term or session of a court, university, or the like. Phr. ***to keep*** or ***hold season***. *Obs.*

? *a* **1400** *Arthur* 137 Arthour wolde of honour Hold a fest at Estour..; And sende Messanger To kynges ferre & neer ..To come to þis Dyner... They come þyder in gode aray, And kept þeire Ceson At the Castell Carlyon. *c* **1435** *Torr. Portugal* 2157 Sir Torent dwellid thare Fourty days in moche care, Season for to hold. **1669** EVELYN *Diary* 13 July, Which the Vice-Chancellor promis'd to do the next season. **1825** WARDROP in *M. Baillie's Wks.* I. Life 9 He there attended the Greek and Latin classes during the first two seasons; in the third season he became a diligent mathematician.

8. A period of time astronomically fixed or recurring. †Also, a period or phase of an eclipse.

1535 COVERDALE *Gen.* i. 14 That they maye be vnto tokens, seasons, dayes, and yeares. **1666** ROOK in *Phil. Trans.* I. 389 Those Seasons of the Eclipse, when there is the suddenest Alteration in the Apparences. **1671** MILTON *P.R.* III. 187 He in whose hand all times and seasons roul. **1820** KEATS *Hyperion* I. 293 The sacred seasons might not be disturb'd. Therefore the operations of the dawn Stay'd in their birth. **1871** R. ELLIS *Catullus* lxvi. 4 How in seasons due vanishes orb upon orb.

9. The portion of a year regularly devoted to a particular business, sport, or amusement, or when the greatest activity prevails therein. Often with defining word, as the *fishing, hunting, publishing, racing, theatrical, holiday season*. The period when such pursuits are inactive is called the *dead, dull,* or *off season*; see also SILLY *season*.

1687 LOVELL tr. *Thevenot's Trav.* I. 100 When I was at Chio, I could not have that Diversion, for then it was not the Season. **1718** *Free-thinker* No. 68. 86 Publick Business, and Publick Diversions, have the same Season. **1740** CIBBER *Apol.* (1756) I. 144 He bound himself to give them two plays every season. **1798** FORESTER in *Paget Papers* (1896) I. 115 We have this day had the best run of the Season. **1820** W. SCORESBY *Acc. Arctic Reg.* I. 248 In the season of 1684, fourteen of their ships were wrecked. **1856** H. H. DIXON ('The Druid') *Post & Paddock* 303 That gentleman bought Hermit and rode him for nine seasons. **1878** *Athletic World* 5 Apr. 7/2 Pickwick Bicycle Club. The season will be commenced by a run to..Edmonton on Saturday. **1891** E. KINGLAKE *Australian* 87 The 'season' in Australia—by which is indicated the dance-giving period—is winter and early spring.

10. The period of the year during which a particular place is most frequented for business, fashion, or amusement; esp. the time (now May to July) when the fashionable world is assembled in London. ***dead season***, the period when 'society' has departed from a place of resort.

1705 J. TAYLOR *Journ. Edinb.* (1903) 68 Most of the Gentry of the North of England and Scotland resort hither [to Scarborough] in the Season of the year, but we hapned to be something of the latest. **1709** STEELE *Tatler* No. 50 ¶7 Until the Company was gone, and Season over. **1760** H. WALPOLE *Let. to Mann* 20 Jan., You cannot figure a duller season: the weather bitter, no party, little money [etc.]. **1766** [ANSTEY] *Bath Guide* x. 6 What Numbers one sees, who, for that very Reason Come to make such a Figure at Bath ev'ry Season! **1789** *Triumphs Fortitude* I. 10 Be happy in all the enjoyments this dead season can afford. **1836** MARRYAT *Japhet* xxi, The season was now over, and everybody of consequence quitted the metropolis. **1870** H. SMART *Race for Wife* ii, She gave up her season in London.

11. *transf.* (from 2). †**a.** A spell of (bad or inclement) weather.

1605 SHAKS. *Lear* III. iv. 32 How shall your House-lesse heads..defend you From seasons such as these? **1667** MILTON *P.L.* x. 1063 And teach us further by what means to shun Th' inclement Seasons, Rain, Ice, Hail and Snow, Which now the Skie with various Face begins To shew us in this Mountain.

b. *spec.* The 'rains' or spells of wet weather in tropical countries. In the southern U.S., 'a shower of rain or period of damp weather suitable for setting out tobacco and other plants'.

1707 SLOANE *Jamaica* I. Introd. 15 After Seasons, i.e. three or four or more days rain, all manner of provisions, Maize, Guinea-corn, Pease, Potatos &c. are planted. **1766** STORK *Acc. E. Florida* 63 It often happens in the West-Indies, as it did last year, that when the ground is prepared, and the cane planted, the rains, or seasons as they are called, fail. **1873** *Routledge's Young Gentl. Mag.* July 478/2 The seasons were only just over, and all tropical nature was fresh.

II. *gen.* A time, period, occasion.

12. a. A particular time or period during which something happens, or which is defined by some characteristic feature or circumstance. See also NIGHT-SEASON, *mean season* (MEAN *a.*² 2).

a **1300** *Cursor M.* 3509 God was þe werld in þat sesun And mikel it bar o benisun. *Ibid.* 5419 Quils þam lasted þat sesun dere. *c* **1400** *Destr. Troy* 1442 A Sesyn of sorow þat þere suet after. *c* **1450** in Aungier *Syon* (1840) 268 Euery persone that ..hath there the rewle of the religion atte leste for that ceson. **1497** *Naval Acc. Hen. VII* (1896) 234 Duryng the season that the seid ship lay in the Dokke. **1568** GRAFTON *Chron.* II. 650 During this season the Queene was greatly encouraged with the victory, obteyned late at Wakefelde. **1665** BOYLE *Occas. Medit., Disc.* IV. iv. (1848) 69 When we greedily pursue after Honour, and Pleasure, of which this Life is not the proper Season. **1777** BURKE *Let. to Sheriffs of Bristol* Wks. 1842 I. 215 Calamity is unhappily the usual season of reflection. **1833** MACAULAY *Ess., War Success. Sp.* ¶5 His annual revenue..in the season of his greatest power. **1871** FREEMAN *Norm. Conq.* (1876) IV. xviii. 278 They may have been well pleased to accept a season of peace even at the hands of the stranger.

b. ***for a season***: for an indefinite period, for some time, for a while. Similarly, ***for a long, short,*** etc. ***season***. Also adverbially, without *for*.

1465 *Pol. Rel. & L. Poems* (1903) 1/17 Than stode y stille a litile Seson. **1481** *Coventry Leet-bk.* 500 There hath long season depended variance & contraeuersie betwixt you. **1526** TINDALE *Luke* iv. 13 He departed from hym for a season. *a* **1533** LD. BERNERS *Huon* lxxxv. 267 Than Oberon stode styll a season. **1668** CULPEPER & COLE *Barthol. Anat.* I. ix. 21 That it might further the Stomachs Concoction, and make the meats abide therein, a convenient season. **1790** COWPER *Iliad* XIX. 169 Or if it please thee, though impatient, wait, Short season. **1851** CARLYLE *J. Sterling* i, This most.. beautiful human soul; who walked with me for a season in this world. **1871** FREEMAN *Norm. Conq.* (1876) IV. xvii. 70 He was constrained for a season to leave the successors of Leofric and Siward in possession of [etc.].

13. a. (Without the idea of duration.) A time at which, or occasion when, something happens. ***at, †in this*** (or ***that***) ***season***, at this time; on this occasion; also adverbially without ***in. at, †in, on a season***, at a certain time. ***at all seasons***, at all times, always. ***at seasons***, on different or recurring occasions, from time to time. Also, ***fit, due, proper, just season***: cf. sense 14. Now *rare*.

13.. *Seuyn Sages* 3939 He says soth in this sesowne. **1340–70** *Alisaunder* 339 On a season isett assembled they boþe. *a* **1400–50** *Alexander* 881 Sone eftir in a seson, ..Come driuand fra Darius..Heraudis on heȝe hors. *c* **1400** *Ywaine & Gaw.* 903 Thus was syr Ywayne sted that seswne. *a* **1440** *York Myst.* xxvi. 42 We seke for youre socoure þis sesoune. **1470–85** MALORY *Arthur* XXI. xii. 858 So at a seson of the nyght they al wente to theyr beddes. **1497** BP. ALCOCK *Mons Perfect.* D iij, And many seasons of yᵉ daye sore wept in remembraunce of yᵉ same. **1519** *Interl. Four Elem.* (Percy Soc.) 31 Other thynges mo I have in store, That I coude tel therof, but now no more Tyll another season. **1526** TINDALE *Acts* xx. 18 After what maner I have bene wyth you at all ceasons. **1611** *R. Johnson's Kingd. & Commw.* 119 He may come to her house,..Court her in all places, and at all seasons. **1628** HOBBES tr. *Thucydides* (1822) 23 These things were done for you in a season when men going to fight against their enemies neglect all respects but of victory. **1686** tr. *Chardin's Coronat. Solyman* 122 He knew the proper season to shew the violence of his Revenge. **1692** R. L'ESTRANGE *Fables* ccxv. 187 There are Many Cases, and Many Seasons, wherein Men must either Bend or Break. **1711** STEELE *Spect.* No. 78 ¶5 You well know it is of great Consequence to clear Titles, and it is of Importance that it be done in the proper Season. **1827** SCOTT *Highl. Widow* ii, When Hamish..absented himself from her cottage at such season, and for such length of time as he chose. **1837** CARLYLE *Fr. Rev.* I. IV. iv, Pike and helm lie provided for thee in due season. **1850** TENNYSON *In Mem.* cxi. 8 The churl in spirit..Will let his coltish nature break At seasons thro' the gilded pale.

†b. Sometimes substituted for *time* in collocations proper to that word: as ***afore seasons*** = AFORETIME; ***in old season***, of old. *Obs.*

1463 in *Eng. Hist. Rev.* Apr. (1905) 301 He as yit stondeth destitute of cxj li. which he afore seisons hath..receyued yerely at þe fest of Estre. **1530** PALSGR. 143 *Avtemps jadis*, afore-season. **1582** STANYHURST *Æneis* I. (Arb.) 17, I that in old season..whistled My rural sonnet.

c. (***a man***, etc.) ***for all seasons***: (one) ready for any situation or contingency, adaptable to any circumstance.

Orig. used with reference to Sir Thomas More (1478–1535); cf. ERASMUS *Encomium Moriae* (1509) Pref., *omnium horarum hominem*.

1520 R. WHITTINTON *Vulgaria* fol. 14ʳ And as tyme requireth, [Thomas More is] a man of merueylous myrth & pastymes: and somtyme of sad grauite: as who say a man for all seasons. **1960** R. BOLT (*title*) A man for all seasons. **1968** *Listener* 26 Dec. 842/3 If there can really be no simple account of Mr Powell's general political position save that he is a man for all seasons, the same is true of his position on immigration. **1972** A. PRICE *Col. Butler's Wolf* xii. 131 She's a nice sort of girl... A girl for all seasons. **1973** *Listener* 29 Nov. 745/1 He [*sc.* John Kennedy] was a man for all seasons, a man for all people. **1976** M. BIRMINGHAM *Heat of Sun* viii. 114 The vulture..a bird for all seasons, I decided, ready to match one's every mood. **1981** M. WARNER *Joan of Arc* xiii. 263 Joan, a heroine for all seasons.

14. The right, proper, due or appointed time; a fit or favourable occasion, an opportunity. (Cf. 15 a.) Const. †*to*, *for*, *to* with inf.

a **1300** *Cursor M.* 29366 Als suith as he mai sesun se, And wend to rome at soilled be. **13..** *K. Alis.* 5251 The kyng of-sent erles and barouns, For to sopere it was seysouns. **1388** WYCLIF *Eccles.* viii. 6 Tyme and cesoun is to ech werk. *c* **1440** *Generydes* 271 So went she fourth hyr seosynne to endure. **1470–85** MALORY *Arthur* XIX. vi. 781 Thenne whan season was, they wente vnto their chambres. **1484** CAXTON *Æsop* VI. vii, Alle thynges which ben done & made in theyr tyme & season ben wel made. **1513** BRADSHAW *St. Werburge* I. 2793 A sensuall prynce..Taryed the season to fynde her solytary. **1642** D. ROGERS *Naaman* 29 Telling him..it was no season for him to take upon him imperiously. **1671** MILTON *P.R.* IV. 146 When my season comes to sit On David's Throne. **1790** J. BRUCE *Trav. Source of Nile* I. 78, I had sat up a great part of the night waiting a season for observation, but it was very cloudy. **1851** TENNYSON *To the Queen* 30 And statesmen at her council met Who knew the seasons when to take Occasion by the hand.

III. Phrases with prep.

15. in season. a. At the right and proper time, opportunely. Also (? chiefly *U.S.*), at the proper time or in good time *for* or *to do* something. *to be in season*, to be seasonable or opportune.

c **1330** R. BRUNNE *Chron. Wace* (Rolls) 2542 Þre ȝer after was he kyng, In ful sesyne made hys endyng. **1414** *Deed is Working* 79 in *26 Pol. Poems* 58 To chastyse fooles is ay in seson. **1484** CAXTON *Æsop* VI. vii, Therfore hit appiereth wel that the thynges whiche ben made in season ben wel made and done by reason. **1611** BIBLE *Isa.* l. 4 That I should know how to speake a worde in season [**1535** COVERDALE in due season] to him that is wearie. **1639** FULLER *Holy War* V. v. (1640) 236 After six moneths siege they surrendered the citie to their own honour, and shame of other Christians who sent them no succour in season. **1649** DAVENANT *Love & Hon.* V. i. 78, *Alt.* Good morrow, cavaliers. *Vas.* 'Twill be an houre yet before that greeting Be in season. **1760–72** H. BROOKE *Fool of Qual.* (1809) I. 168 [He] had just cleared one eye, in season, to remark where his enemy entered. **1844** DICKENS *Mart. Chuz.* xii, The two young men desired to get back again in good season. **1858** SEARES *Athan.* II. iii. 195 They arrive in season for the meeting. **1872** HOWELLS *Wedd. Journ.* (1892) 312 Mr. March has to be home by a certain day; and we shall just get back in season. **1906** W. WALKER *Calvin* v. 108 News of this intention reached him in season to effect his escape.

b. Of game, etc.: At the time for hunting, catching, etc. *to be in season*: (of a plant or animal) to flourish, be in its finest condition, be in the best state for eating; also, (of an animal) to be in heat. Similarly, *to come in* or *into season*.

1375 BARBOUR *Bruce* VII. 497 Than the deir war in sesoun. **1473** *Rolls of Parlt.* VI. 93/1 Oon Hert, to be taken in season ..and 11 Bukkes in season. **1558** *Act 1 Eliz.* c. 17 §1 Any Samons or Trowtes, not being in season. **1576** TURBERV. *Venerie* lxxix. 240 Conies are al wayes in season, either yong or old: but their skinnes are in best season from Alhallontide vnto Shrouetide. **1661** LOVELL *Hist. Anim. & Min.* 220 Salmon..come in season, and goe out with the Buck. **1665** BOYLE *Occas. Refl.*, *Disc.* IV. iv. (1848) 68 If the same Fruit were let alone till it were fully Ripe, and in Season. **1688** HOLME *Armoury* II. 135/1 The Hart or Stagg..is in Season ..from Midsummer until Holy-Rood Day. **1709** ADDISON *Tatler* No. 148 ⁋7 To eat every Thing before it comes in Season. **1772** FOOTE *Nabob* II. (1778) 31 Have you any pinks or carnations in bloom? *Crocus.* They are not in season, your honour. **1807** COL. HAWKER *Diary* (1893) I. 6 A very fine trout..he proved..to be very well in season. **1834** MEDWIN *Angler in Wales* I. 176 He is in high season, as proved by the crimson of his fins. **1865** *Reader* No. 154. 646/3 The fish being in perfect season from October to June. **1903** F. SIMPSON *Bk. Cat* iii. 38 Cats come in season about every three weeks during the spring and summer.

†**c.** *fig.* Flourishing, at one's best. *Obs.*

c **1400** *Rom. Rose* 4981 As longe as Youthe is in sesoun, They dwellen in oon mansioun. **1625** BACON *Ess.*, *Goodness* (Arb.) 205 Such Men, in other mens Calamities, are, as it were, in season.

d. Of a place of resort, etc.: (To be) fashionable, in a state of activity. Cf. sense 10.

1718 LADY M. W. MONTAGU *Let. to Lady Rich* 10 Oct., The fair of St. Lawrence is now in season. **1868** EARL OF WILTON *Sports Engl.* 68 From the first day of grouse to the last day of pheasants, London is never in season.

e. Of timber: Seasoned.

1627 CAPT. SMITH *Seaman's Gram.* I. 2 The masts and yards are chained together in some great water to keepe them from rotting, and in season.

16. out of season. a. Unseasonably, inopportunely; *predicatively*, unseasonable, inopportune.

1377 LANGL. *P. Pl.* B. XIII. 351 And as wel in lente as oute of lente, alle tymes ylyche, Suche werkes with hem were neuere oute of sesoun. **1548** UDALL *Erasm. Par.*, *Mark* i. 29–31 He loueth those that cal vpon him, cal they neuer so importunatly, and out of season. **1649** DAVENANT *Love & Hon.* IV. iv. 37 Although the rack be somewhat out Of season with my old bones. **1667** MILTON *P.L.* V. 850 So spake the fervent Angel, but his zeale None seconded, as out of season judg'd. **1718** *Free-thinker* No. 27. 190 True Wit and Good Sense..can be spoiled only by making use of them Improperly, or out of Season. **1864** 'HOLME LEE' *Silver Age* II. 239 Be consoled—you will have your joys, though they come rather out of season. **1868** TENNYSON *Lucretius* 267 Howbeit I know thou surely must be mine Or soon or late, yet out of season, thus I woo thee roughly.

b. Not in season; not at the time for hunting, catching, eating, etc. Also *fig.*

1500–20 DUNBAR *Poems* lix. 18 Off ane vod fuill far owt off seasoun, He wantis nocht bot a rowndit heid. **1683** ROBINSON in *Ray's Corr.* (1848) 132 We..could not meet with the Macreuse [the scoter], it being now out of season. **1781** H. NEWDIGATE *Let.* 15 Oct. in A. E. Newdigate-Newdegate *Cheverels* (1898) iii. 46 A Hamper of good things,..Pears & Pines in perfection, *Rouleaux* never out of season. **1847** A. BRONTË *Agnes Grey* xviii. 282, I pretended to want to save it [*sc.* a hare]..as it was so glaringly out of season. **1960** *Mrs. Beeton's Bk. Househ. Managem.* vii. 93 When a fruit is out of season in one part of the globe it is usually in season in another.

c. Not in fashion; not in its period of fashion.

1847 TENNYSON *Princess* Prol. 179 The hard-grain'd Muses of the cube and square Were out of season. **1891** FREEMAN *Sk. Fr. Trav.* 180 He will prefer Clermont out of season to Clermont in the season.

17. *in season and out of season*: at all times, without regard to what is considered opportune.

1526 TINDALE *2 Tim.* iv. 2 Be fervent, be it in season or out of season [εὐκαίρως ἀκαίρως]. **1841** HELPS *Ess.*, *Trans. Business* (1842) 93 He will be repeating his folly in season, and out of season, until at last it has a hearing.

†**18. *by season***: at the right time, in time. *Sc.*

1600 in Pitcairn *Crim. Trials Scot.* II. 180 This deponar desyrit Maister Alexander to dischone with him, be ressoun his awin culd nocht be sasone be preparit.

†**IV. 19.** [f. the vb.] Seasoning, relish, flavour.

c **1480** HENRYSON *Test. Cress.* 421 With Saipheron sals of ane gude sessoun. **1599** B. JONSON *Cynthia's Rev.* V. i. 16 Bearing no season, much lesse salt of goodnesse. **1599** SHAKS. *Much Ado* IV. i. 144 The wide sea Hath..salt too little, which may season giue To her foule tainted flesh. **1605** —— *Macb.* III. iv. 141 You lacke the season of all Natures, sleepe. *a* **1635** NAUNTON *Fragm. Reg.* (Arb.) 44 He had a large proportion of gifts and endowments, but too much of the season of envy. **1664** MARVELL *Corr.* Wks. (Grosart) II. 122 Those his Friends who formerly made his adversity more tolerable, and do now give the truest season and sweetness to his better fortune.

V. 20. Short for *season-ticket* (see 21).

1896 *Daily News* 29 Dec. 7/4 Asked for his ticket, he replied that he had left his season at home. **1901** *Westm. Gaz.* 2 Apr. 9/1 The company..is about to issue third-class seasons.

VI. 21. *Comb.*, as ***season-cracked***, ***-measured*** adjs.; **season-check** *U.S.* (see quot. 1905); **season cracking**, the occurrence of longitudinal cracks in cold-worked brass or bronze; so **season crack** *sb.* and *v. intr.*; **season ticket**, a ticket which admits the holder to travel on a boat or on a line of railway, to enter an exhibition, etc., an unlimited number of times during a season or specified period, at a reduced rate of payment; hence ***season-ticket holder***.

1887 J. KIRKLAND *Zury* 32 Ye see that *season-check in the butt-end [of a black-walnut log]. **1905** *Bull. Bureau of Forestry* (U.S. Dept. Agric.) No. 61. 33 *Check*, a longitudinal crack in timber caused by too rapid seasoning. .. Syn.: season check. **1909** WEBSTER, *Season cracks. **1915** *Trans. Amer. Inst. Metals* VIII. 322 It was found that all those cartridge cases which had season cracked had primers on. **1957** R. A. HIGGINS *Engin. Metall.* I. v. 87 A controlled low-temperature anneal..applied to hard-drawn 70/30 brass tube will effectively reduce its tendency to 'season-crack'..without reducing strength or hardness. *Ibid.* II. xiv. 292 Residual..stresses in cold-worked alloys often manifest themselves during service in the form of 'season cracks'. **1938** M. K. RAWLINGS *Yearling* xxvi. 347, I got a old dug-out right above here, is mighty sorry and *season-cracked, but hit'd carry you acrost the creek. **1910** *Brass World* VI. 269/1 One of the most annoying things that happens to brass while in use is its *season cracking. **1923** GLAZEBROOK *Dict. Appl. Physics* V. 410/2 The essential condition for 'season cracking' is the presence in the finished article of internal stresses of considerable magnitude. **1967** A. H. COTTRELL *Introd. Metall.* xxiii. 467 The season cracking of α-brass in ammoniacal environments may be due to local dezincification along the grain boundaries. **1827** J. H. NEWMAN *Lyra Apost.* xliii. (1836) 48 In childhood, when with eager eyes The *season-measured year I viewed. **1820** *Columbian Centinel* (Boston, Mass.) 2 Dec. 1/1 For sale, a Boston Theatre *Season Ticket, at a fair price. **1835** DICKENS *Sk. Boz*, *River*, The regular passengers, who have season-tickets, go below to breakfast. **1869** W. JAMES *Coll. Ess. & Rev.* (1920) 1 People who are comfortably in possession of a season-ticket over the Stygian ferry. **1953** C. DAY LEWIS *Italian Visit* i. 14 The season tickets that rattle us back and forth in a groove from Centre to circumference. **1862** J. SIMMONDS *Railway Travellers Handy Bk.* 48 We may here remind *season-ticket holders to renew their privilege. **1886** *Encycl. Brit.* XX. 228/2 The proportions of passengers, independent of season-ticket holders, were as follows.

season ('siːz(ə)n), *v.* Forms: 4 seasen, 4–5 ses(o)un, 4–6 seson, 5 seeson, sesyn, cesyn, -un, -on, 6 seasyn, (sayson, seacon), *Sc.* saison, sasoun, cessoune, 4– season. [a. OF. *saisonner* (cf. mod.F. *assaisonner*), f. *saison* SEASON *sb.*

Sense 1 is a development from the primary sense in OF., to ripen, to render (fruit) palatable by the influence of the seasons (cf. sense 4, which in Eng. appears much later).]

1. *trans.* To render (a dish) more palatable by the addition of some savoury ingredient.

13.. *Gaw. & Gr. Knt.* 889 Seggez hym serued semly innoȝe, Wyth sere sewes & sete, sesounde of þe best. *c* **1375** *Sc. Leg. Saints* Prol. 110 As salt sesonis all, þe hartiss at one crist will cale. *c* **1420** *Liber Cocorum* 9 Seson hit with sugur. *c* **1440** *Promp. Parv.* 67/1 Cesyn (*P.* cesun) or welle aray mete or drynke, *tempero.* **1530** PALSGR. 707/2, I season meate as a coke dothe, *je saysonne la viande.* *c* **1550** LYNDESAY *Tragedie* 357 Ane cunyng Cuke, quhilk best can cessone caill. **1661** LOVELL *Hist. Anim. & Min.* Isagoge c 5 If seasoned with salt, and spices, it [meat] is yet dryer. **1769** E. BANCROFT *Guiana* 324 All season their food with a great quantity of spices. **1806** A. HUNTER *Culina* (ed. 3) 68 Take three or four beef steaks cut thick, and season them with pepper, salt, and onion shred fine. **1867** PARKMAN *Jesuits N. Amer.* xxv. (1875) 366 Maize, pounded and boiled, and seasoned..with morsels of smoked fish.

b. *fig.* To mix, intersperse, or imbue with something that imparts relish; to adapt or accommodate *to* a particular taste.

1520 NISBET *N.T.*, *Col.* iv. 6 Youre word be sesonnit in salt euirmare in grace. **1592** SHAKS. *Rom. & Jul.* II. iii. 72 How much salt water throwne away in wast, To season Loue that of it doth not tast. **1596** KEMYS *Relat. 2nd Voy. Guiana* E 2 b, Pardon it..if..my speech, which is altogether vnsauourie, season it selfe with some of the leauen of your own discourse. **1667** MILTON *P.L.* x. 609 Till I [*sc.* Sin] in Man residing through the Race, His thoughts, his looks, words, actions all infect, And season him thy [*sc.* Death's] last and sweetest prey. **1675** W. OKELEY *Eben-ezer* Pref. A j, Every Narrator is under a strong Temptation to Season his Discourse to the Gusto of the time. **1699** DRYDEN *To John Driden* 60 You season still with sports your serious hours. **1711** ADDISON *Spect.* No. 166 ⁋6 Writers..who employ their Parts in propagating Immorality, and seasoning vicious Sentiments with Wit and Humour. **1822** SHELLEY *Faust* ii. 10 To..climb those rocks..Is the true sport that seasons such a path.

ironically. **1615** G. SANDYS *Trav.* 121 He had a hundred blowes on the feet to season his pastimes.

†**c.** *to season with the same liquor*: *fig.*, to imbue or endow with the same qualities. *Obs.*

1648 SYMMONS *Vind. K. Chas.* 36 Truly we do imagine that our subtile and suspected Brethren..would fain season us with the same liquor, which infecteth them.

†**d.** To qualify by a beneficial admixture; to moderate, alleviate, temper. *Obs.*

1594 SHAKS. *Rich. III*, III. vii. 149 To reproue you for this suit of yours, So season'd with your faithful loue to me. **1602** —— *Ham.* I. ii. 191 Season your admiration for a while With an attent eare.

†**2.** *transf.* To imbue with a taste or scent. *Obs.*

1559 MORWYNG *Evonym.* 270 They do al season the urin with their smel. *a* **1591** H. SMITH *Serm.* (1601) 538 What licour our vessels bee seasoned with at the first, they will taste of the same euer after.

†**b.** To imbue (a person, his mind) *with* opinions, ideas, etc.; in later use only in good sense (cf. 1 b).

1617 MORYSON *Itin.* II. 48 They who had his eare, might easily season him with good or ill opinion of his servants or strangers. **1709** STEELE & ADDISON *Tatler* No. 111 ⁋3 [Shakspere] seems to have had his Mind thoroughly seasoned with Religion. **1791** BOSWELL *Johnson* an. 1754, 6 Mar., Garrick, who I can attest from my own knowledge had his mind seasoned with pious reverence.

†**c.** *intr.* To savour *of*. *Obs.*

1618 FLETCHER *Chances* I. ix, Lose not your labour and your time together, It seasons of a fool, son, time is pretious.

†**3.** *trans.* To embalm. Also *fig.* *Obs.*

c **1440** *Alphabet of Tales* 458, & on þe morn when þai wold hafe opynd hym & sesond hym with spycis at he myght hafe bene curid, he rase vpp & was whikk. **1601** SHAKS. *Twel. N.* I. i. 30 She will..water once a day her Chamber round With eye-offending brine: all this to season A brothers dead loue, which she would keep fresh And lasting, in her sad remembrance. **1638** JUNIUS *Paint. Ancients* 171 He hath seene true dead bodies brought in the banquet, after they had been seasoned a good while and dried up.

4. To bring to maturity, ripen; to render fit for use by prolonged exposure to atmospheric influences, or by gradual subjection to conditions of the kind to be undergone in actual working; often, to dry and harden (timber) by long keeping.

1545 [see SEASONED 3]. **1555** EDEN *Decades* (Arb.) 99 They browght with them Cinamome and gynger: but not very good, bycause they were not there fully seasoned with the heate of the soone. **1617** MORYSON *Itin.* III. 74 The houses very seldome keepe out raine, the timbers being not well seasoned. **1686** PLOT *Staffordsh.* 161 They also heat their furnace for a weeks time with charcoal without blowing it, which they call seasoning it. **1725** DE FOE *Voy. round World* (1840) 71 Casks..which their coopers assisted us to trim, season, and fit up. **1858** O. W. HOLMES *Aut. Breakf.-T.* v. 53 Knowledge and timber shouldn't be much used till they are seasoned.

b. *intr.* for *refl.* To become seasoned.

1679 MOXON *Mech. Exerc.* ix. 155 They generally Rough-plain their Boards..that they may set them by to season. **1881** *Cassell's Fam. Mag.* VII. 511 An artificial method.. which has the effect of ageing the wood in a few hours, as well as if it had been kept seasoning for years.

c. *trans.* To fortify (a person) by habit against conditions that might otherwise be deleterious; to acclimatize.

1601 MOUNTJOY *Let.* in Moryson *Itin.* II. (1617) 108 They will come over well cloathed against the Winter and may have time to rest, and to be seasoned, till Christmas. **1760** GOLDSM. *Cit. W.* cxix, Many of them died, because they were not used to live in a gaol, but for my part it was nothing to me, for I was seasoned. **1812** BYRON *Ch. Har.* II. lxix. In war well season'd, and with labours tann'd. **1896** A. E. HOUSMAN *Shropshire Lad* lxii, And easy, smiling, seasoned sound, Sate the king when healths went round.

†**d.** To prepare or fit (a person); also, to discipline, train. *Obs.*

1602 SHAKS. *Ham.* III. iii. 84 Am I then reueng'd, To take him in the purging of his Soule When he is fit and season'd for his passage? **1612** BRINSLEY *Lud. Lit.* xxii. 253 How schollars may be seasoned and trained vp in Gods true Religion and in grace. **1644** MILTON *Educ.* 4 And withall to season them, and win them early to the love of vertue and true labour. **1658** CLEVELAND *Rustick Rampant* 16 The

Kentishmen, seasoned by this Priest or Prophet of the Idol, are easily tempted by the Essexians.

†**e.** To bring into a healthy condition. Also, to disinfect. *Obs.*

1601 HOLLAND *Pliny* XXIII. i. II. 148 As touching grapes preserved in earthen pots, they refresh and season the mouth which was out of tast. **1722** DE FOE *Plague* (1756) 281 Those people..did take particular Directions for what they called Seasoning of their Houses and abundance of costly things were consumed..which..not only seasoned those houses..but filled the air with very grateful smells.

†**f.** To temper (metal). *Obs. rare.*

1730 SAVERY *Magnet. Observ.* in *Phil. Trans.* XXXVI. 307 Steel cannot be seasoned too hard for Retension. *Ibid.* 328 With this little Bar naked I touched a small Dial-Needle made of Steel... I seasoned it very hard, and cleansed it well.

†**5.** Of a bird or beast of prey: To 'flesh' (its claws); hence *intr.* to seize *upon*. *Obs.*

It is possible that Palsgrave may have been thinking of *season* = SEISIN *v.*

1530 PALSGR. 707/2, I season upon a thynge, as a hauke dothe, *je assaysonne*. She saysonned upon the fesante at the first flyght. **1540** —— *Acolastus* II. iii. I iij b, This pray is worthy for our clawes .i. this is one as mete for vs to season vpon, as it is mete for any lyon..to season his pawes vpon his pray.

†**6.** To manure (land). *Obs.*

1563 HYLL *Art Garden.* (1593) 10 So that the same [dung] be scattered like seedes on the ground, wherby to season ground the better. **1589** PUTTENHAM *Eng. Poesie* III. xxv. (Arb.) 309 Or as the good gardiner seasons his soyle by sundrie sorts of compost.

†**7.** To impregnate, to copulate with. *Obs. rare.*

[**1511-38**: see SEASONING *vbl. sb.* 1 a.] **1555** EDEN *Decades* (Arb.) 383 When the male hath once seasoned the female he neuer after toucheth her. **1601** HOLLAND *Pliny* VIII. xlv. I. 224 This prince..would not suffer the Buls to come unto the Kine and season them, before they were both foure yeares old.

seasonable ('siːz(ə)nəb(ə)l), *a.* [f. SEASON *v.* and *sb.* + -ABLE.]

1. a. Occurring at the right season, opportune.

c **1412** HOCCLEVE *De Reg. Princ.* 578 For-þi ne lakke þou not age at al; Whan youþe is past, is age sesonable. **1455** *Paston Lett.* I. 349, I have written unto Yelverton, the justice, that he wol, at some sesonable tyme, common with Sir Thomas Tudenham. *c* **1586** C'TESS PEMBROKE *Ps.* CIV. xi, [All creatures] in seasonable tyde Their hungry eyes on thee their feeder throw. **1631** GOUGE *God's Arrows* Ded. (v), Are not these times seasonable..for such a Subject as is here handled? **1655** FULLER *Ch. Hist.* IV. i. 130 Here it will be seasonable to give in a List of Wicliffes Opinions. **1719** DE FOE *Crusoe* I. 294, His Caution was so seasonable, and his Advice so good, that [etc.]. **1869** J. MARTINEAU *Ess.* II. 94 This is a very seasonable book.

b. Of weather, etc.: Suitable to the time of year.

1380 WYCLIF *Sel. Wks.* III. 416 Heven lokes lesse to fruyt of þo erthe, monnes strength is lesse, here lyve is shortere, þo tyme is lesse sesounable, and charite withdrawen. **14..** *Tundale's Vis.*, etc. (1843) 155 Tho sesonabuldst wedur with-owton leyse That euer mon sawe dryvun tyl a nende. **1520** NISBET *Epist. O.T.* xxi. (S.T.S.) III. 284 As the flour of rosis in the dais of sesonnabile somer. *a* **1603** BACON *Maxims Com. Law* Ep. Ded. 6 It is your Majesties reigne that hath beene as a goodly seasonable spring weather to the advancing of all excellent arts of peace. **1793** SMEATON *Edystone L.* §261 Though the weather was not favourable for delivering their cargoes, yet it being seasonable, I determined they should keep out. **1819** KEATS *Ode to Nightingale* v, Each sweet Wherewith the seasonable month endows The grass, the thicket, and the fruit-tree wild. **1843** DICKENS *Christm. Carol* 10 His thread-bare clothes darned up and brushed, to look seasonable.

†**c.** Enduring but for a season, temporary. *Obs.*

1549 LATIMER *1st Serm. bef. Edw. VI* (Arb.) 38 Not a seasonable fayeth, which shall laste but a whyle, but a fayeth, whiche is continuynge in God.

†**d.** 'In season', said of game at the time when proper to be hunted and killed. *Obs. rare*$^{-1}$.

1596 HARINGTON *Metam. Ajax* 32 Doth not the keeper.. shew you his femishing, that thereby you may iudge if he be a seasonable deare?

e. Belonging to one's season or prime.

1883 R. W. DIXON *Mano* I. viii. 20 Thou poppy,..Why hangest thou down ere ripeness be begun, Ere yet be come thy seasonable hour?

†**2.** Capable of serving as seasoning; tasty, savoury. *Obs. rare*$^{-1}$.

c **1420** *Liber Cocorum* (1862) 28 Take brede..And drawȝhe hit þorowghe a clothe by kynde, With venegur gode and sesounabulle.

†**3.** Well seasoned, matured. *Obs. rare.*

1531-2 *Act 23 Hen. VIII*, c. 4 §2 Coupers..shall make the same vessels..of good and seasonable wodde.

¶**4.** *erron.* used for SEASONAL *a.* 2.

1923 *Glasgow Herald* 20 Mar. 9 Persons engaged in seasonable trades in which the duration of seasonable employment is too short to enable them to qualify for benefit. [**1980** *Listener* 10 Jan. 51/3 Will the BBC please note that the word they want is 'seasonable', not 'seasonal'. One has seasonable items like mince pies and carols; 'seasonal' is applied to rainfall and fluctuations in car sales, i.e., things that happen with the changing seasons.]

seasonableness ('siːz(ə)nəb(ə)lnɪs). [f. prec. + -NESS.] The quality of being seasonable; aptitude to time or circumstance; fitness of occurrence.

1546 LANGLEY tr. *Pol. Verg. de Invent.* I. iii. 5 The fruictfull rankeness of the soyle and seasonableness of the Aire. **1623** MARKHAM *Country Contentm.* I. xi. (1631) 76 The seasonablenesse, or vnseasonablenesse of the weather. **1740** WARBURTON *Vind. Pope's Ess. Man* vi. 108 The Seasonableness of this Reproof will appear evident enough to those who know, that [etc.]. **1831** MACKINTOSH *Hist. Eng.* II. 83 Frion, a discarded secretary of Henry, who, from the seasonableness of his defection, may be suspected at all times to have been more a spy on Perkin than a traitor to Henry. **1878** SEELEY *Stein* II. 535 The previous agitation lost at once its suitableness and seasonableness at the same time that all its objects were fully attained.

seasonably ('siːz(ə)nəblɪ), *adv.* [f. SEASONABLE *a.* + -LY^{2}.] **1.** In a fitting time; at the right moment; in due season.

1387-8 T. USK *Test. Love* II. vi. (Skeat) 67 Pardy, shine the sonne neuer so bright, and it bringe forth no hete, ne sesonably the herbes out-bringe of the earthe,..ye wolde wonder and dispreyse that sonne. **1575-85** ABP. SANDYS *Serm.* ii. 43 The prince will be but a steward hereof, seasonably to lay it out for publike vse. *a* **1671** LD. FAIRFAX *Mem.* (1699) 55 When I was almost senseless, my Surgeon came seasonably, and bound up the wound, and stopt the bleeding. **1711** HEARNE *Collect.* (O.H.S.) III. 246 This Sermon was very seasonably deliver'd. **1817** SOUTHEY *Wat Tyler* I. i, The sun would shine as cheerly, The rains of heaven as seasonably fall, Though neither of these royal pests existed. **1885** *Manch. Exam.* 28 Sept. 5/3 A controversy which has broken out seasonably in the columns of a London contemporary.

¶**2.** *erron.* used for SEASONALLY *adv.*

1928 *Britain's Industr. Future* (Liberal Industr. Inquiry) IV. xxvii. §7. 388 The hours worked in all the jobs concerned (omitting those in which hours varied weekly or seasonably).

†'**seasonage.** *Obs.* [f. SEASON *v.* + -AGE.] The action of seasoning; that which serves to season.

a **1716** SOUTH *Serm.* (1744) VIII. 408 The light; which is that, that gives a seasonage to all other fruitions, that..gives opportunity to the enjoyment of all the other senses. *Ibid.* IX. 152 Charity is the grand seasonage of every christian duty.

seasonal ('siːz(ə)nəl), *a.* and *sb.* [f. SEASON *sb.* + -AL^{1}.] **A.** *adj.*

1. Pertaining to or characteristic of the seasons of the year, or some one of them.

seasonal dimorphism, a variation in the appearance of different broods of the same insect according to the time of year at which they are produced.

1838 MUDIE *Phys. Man.* ii. 58 The call of the partridge —the seasonal song of the nightingale. **1844** H. STEPHENS *Bk. Farm* I. 291 The daily and seasonal motions of the earth. **1887** ABERCROMBY *Weather* 51 Changes which are due to.. the season of the year..we shall call..seasonal variations of the general character. **1888** ROLLESTON & JACKSON *Anim. Life* 238 The individuals of broods appearing at different times of the year often differ from one another in a marked manner. In this case the phrase seasonal dimorphism is employed. **1894** COIT in *Forum* (U.S.) May 285 The regular seasonal lack of work is no dire calamity.

b. *transf.* Pertaining to the seasons or periods of human life.

1843 J. MARTINEAU *Chr. Life* (1867) 3 The seasonal changes of character, of which I now speak. **1866** ALGER *Solit. Nat. & Man* II. 46 So shall we hereafter retrace in our successive sorrows the seasonal stages of our growth.

2. Of certain trades: Dependent on the seasons. Of workers, servants: Employed or engaged only during a particular season.

1904 *Daily News* 30 Dec. 6/2 The problem of the casual and seasonal worker. **1909** *Times* 13 Feb. 4/3 Hotel servants were not of the best class; they were seasonal. **1909** *Englishwoman* Apr. 225 Some trades are seasonal: there is a great rush of work to be done at one season and comparatively little at another.

3. Periodical, recurrent at more or less regular intervals.

1880 JEVONS *Methods Soc. Ref.* (1883) 313 The seasonal fluctuations of a small paper currency. **1893** SOLOMON in *Class. Rev.* Feb. 11/1 These regularly recurrent diseases.. are, I believe, called by the doctors 'seasonal'. **1899** *Allbutt's Syst. Med.* VIII. 557 In some patients the relapses have a certain seasonal periodicity.

B. *sb.* A periodical issued at certain seasons of the year.

1895 (*title*) The Evergreen: a Northern Seasonal. **1897** *Pall Mall Gaz.* 24 Nov. 11/3 Mr. Scott has decided to issue his 'Book Sales' as a seasonal instead of as an annual.

seasonality (siːz(ə)'nælɪtɪ). orig. *U.S.* [f. SEASONAL *a.* + -ITY.] **1.** The condition of being dependent on the seasons or other temporal cycle; the state of recurring at regular intervals.

1934 in WEBSTER. **1936** *S.P.E. Tract* XLV. 191 University professors and other persons of literary or academic reputation have been responsible for such coinages as ..*seasonality*. **1959** *Economist* 18 Apr. 218/2 The common seasonality of the tourist trade, horticulture and fishing makes these occupations awkward neighbours for year-round industrial enterprise. **1971** *Nature* 5 Feb. 406/2 The relatively sharp seasonality of fruiting and leaf formation would have effectively restricted exclusive arboreal feeding for an animal as large as a chimpanzee. **1976** J. S. FLEMMING *Inflation* xi. 109 Moreover baskets including foodstuffs will display seasonality which one would probably not want to reflect in the adjusted payments.

2. The degree to which a climate has distinct seasons.

1968 R. W. FAIRBRIDGE *Encycl. Geomorphol.* 721/2 No consideration has been given to seasonality of climate. **1972** *Sci. Amer.* June 64/1 A sharp reduction in coral diversity that began in late Eocene times and lasted throughout the Oligocene epoch seems to reflect a continued increase in seasonality of climate and a substantial lowering of mean temperatures.

seasonally ('siːz(ə)nəlɪ), *adv.* [f. SEASONAL *a.* + -LY^{2}.] **1.** At a certain time of year, at some seasons.

1834 MUDIE *Feathered Tribes Brit. Isl.* (1841) I. 22 One species is often found, at least seasonally, upon those grounds. **1887** *Athenæum* 12 Feb. 227/2 The fact of the moth being seasonally dimorphic was likely to introduce disturbing elements into the experiments.

2. According to the season.

1937 DAVIES & YODER *Business Statistics* v. 239 In January ..the unadjusted index was 88 and in February it was 91. This was a rise, but not so much as would be seasonally expected, as is shown by adjusted figures for the same months, which are 91 and 89. **1942** CROXTON & COWDEN *Appl. Gen. Statistics* xviii. 524 There will be an enormous drop in the seasonally adjusted data between December and January. **1971** *Daily Tel.* 17 Dec. 15 Seasonally adjusted.. the figures show an increase in borrowing by industry of about £50 million over the previous quarter. **1974** *Nature* 1 Feb. 269/2 Both parameters depend on the mesospheric circulation, whose main features at a particular latitude vary seasonally. **1982** *Guardian* 15 Apr. 14/2 The seasonally adjusted level of unemployment..remained at 11·8 per cent.

seasoned ('siːz(ə)nd), *ppl. a.* [f. SEASON *v.* + -ED^{1}.]

†**1.** Seasonable, opportune, suitable. *Obs. rare.*

c **1440** *Promp. Parv.* 67/2 Cesonyd, yn tyme.., *tempestus, tempestivus.* **1634** HEYWOOD *Maidenhead lost* III. F 4, It shall goe hard with mine affaires But Ile find season'd houres to visit them.

2. Flavoured, spiced.

c **1440** *Promp. Parv.* 454/1 Seasonyd, as mete, *temperatus.* **1709** ADDISON *Tatler* No. 148 ¶3, I have seen a young Lady swallow all the Instigations of high Soups, seasoned Sauces, and forced Meats.

b. *fig.*

1660 F. BROOKE tr. *Le Blanc's Trav.* 270 The company by this means had but a bad seasoned supper. **1742** YOUNG *Nt. Th.* VIII. 837 Joys season'd high, and tasting strong of guilt. **1864** KIRK *Chas. the Bold* I. iv. 217 Serving as a text for the highly seasoned discourses of the itinerant friars.

3. Fitted for use, matured, brought to a state of perfection. Of timber: Dried and hardened by keeping.

1545 ASCHAM *Toxoph.* II. (1904) 84 A stele muste be well seasoned for Castinge, and it must be made as the grayne lieth, & as it groweth or els it wyl neuer flye clene. **1633** G. HERBERT *Temple, Vertue* 14 Onely a sweet and vertuous soul Like seasoned timber, never gives. **1711** W. SUTHERLAND *Shipbuild. Assist.* 163 Season'd Plank or Timber; such as is thoroughly dry, and will not be apt to shrink. **1860** TYNDALL *Glac.* II. xxii. 346 Two pieces of seasoned box-wood. **1881** C. A. EDWARDS *Organs* 40 Well seasoned wood is sapless.

b. *fig.* and in figurative context.

1583 STUBBES *Anat. Abus.* I. D j b, These be well seasoned reasons, and substantiall asseuerations in deed. **1607** SHAKS. *Cor.* III. iii. 64 We charge you, that you haue contriu'd to take From Rome all season'd Office. **1881** BESANT & RICE *Chapl. Fleet* I. xii, I, who am now as seasoned as a port-wine cask.

c. Of persons or animals: Fortified by habit; acclimatized; familiarized with a certain mode of life or occupation; †trained, disciplined.

a **1643** CARTWRIGHT *Siedge* I. iv, I would not Venture my self with a stale Virgin, or A season'd Widow for a Kingdom. **1690** *Lond. Gaz.* No. 2526/4 Pair of Black season'd Stone-horses for a Coach. **1703** MARLBOROUGH *Lett & Disp.* (1845) I. 169 The difficulty..of replacing a seasoned regiment in this country. **1793** SMEATON *Edystone L.* §294 New hands.. would act with more courage, by having seasoned men amongst them. **1821** SCOTT *Kenilw.* ii, The wine had made some impression even on the seasoned brain of mine host. **1869** 'WAT. BRADWOOD' *The O.V.H.* xviii, The welter race, contested mainly by seasoned hunters, had less refusals. **1884** *Nonconf. & Indep.* 4 Sept. 865/1 A flying column of 4000 seasoned troops.

†**4.** Of soil: Manured. *Obs.*

1604 E. G[RIMSTONE] *D'Acosta's Hist. Indies* IV. i. 204 The rough and barren earth is as a substance and nutriment for mettalls; and that which is fertile and better seasoned [Sp. *de mas sazon*] a nourishment for plants.

†**5.** Embalmed. Also *fig. Obs.*

1644 MILTON *Areop.* (Arb.) 35 We should be wary therefore..how we spill that season'd life of man preserv'd and stor'd up in Books. **1673** CAVE *Prim. Chr.* III. ii. 274 The seasoned and embalm'd bones and heads of Martyrs.

†'**seasonedness.** *Obs.*$^{-1}$ [f. prec. + -NESS.] The state or quality of being (well) seasoned.

1679 MOXON *Mech. Exerc.* ix. 158 The well-seasonedness of the Boards.

seasoner ('siːz(ə)nə(r)). [f. SEASON *v.* + -ER^{1}.] One who, or something which seasons.

†**1.** One who seasons viands. *Obs.*

1598 FLORIO, *Conditore*, a seasoner, a cooke, a temprer, a comfiter. **1638** PENKETHMAN *Artach.* A j b, Yet behold The Seasoner heating, or with Bavin-fires Preparing th' oven as the Case requires. **1647** HEXHAM I, A seasoner, *Een sausse ofte confituer bereyder.*

2. Something that serves to season. *rare.*

1693 J. BEAUMONT *Burnet's Th. Earth* I. 63 Salt is..a good Seasoner. **1802** T. THOMSON *Chem.* II. 316 Muriat of Soda ..has been..in common use as a seasoner of food from the earliest ages.

fig. **1620** FORD *Linea Vitæ* (1843) 66 His actions are the seasoners of his speeches, as his profession is of his actions.

sea-song. A song such as is sung by sailors. Also *fig.*

1659 *Lady Alimony* III. iii. F 4, *Stage-dir.*, The Sea-Song [*follows*]. **1823** (*title*), [C.] Dibdin's Original Sea-Songs. **1859** LD. LYTTON *Wanderer, Thoughts at Sunset* ii, With a sea-song in mine ears Of the bronzen buccaniers. **1883**

STEVENSON *Treas. Isl.* i, Then breaking out into that old sea-song that he sang so often afterwards. **1944** BLUNDEN *Shells by Stream* 31 The wind may sing his sea-song later In your review as he will in mine.

seasoning ('siːz(ə)nɪŋ), *vbl. sb.* [-ING¹.]

1. The action of the verb SEASON.

†**a.** The act or time of impregnation. *Obs.*

1511 *MS. Acc. St. John's Hosp., Canterb.*, Payd for sesnyng of iij sowys jd. ob. **1538** ELYOT *Dict.*, *Admissura*, the acte or tyme whan beastes doth their kinde in generation. Seasoning. **1601** HOLLAND *Pliny* XVI. xxv. I. 471 This time, our rusticall peasants call the Seasoning, when as Nature.. is in the rut and furious rage of love.

b. The imparting of a flavour to a dish.

1601 R. JOHNSON *Kingd. & Commw.* (1603) 136 The nobility is very gallant,.. spending more then their reuenues in diet and apparell, and the seasoning of their meates. **1732** ARBUTHNOT *Aliments, Rules of Diet* 260 Vegetables used in Seasoning, as Thyme, Savory. **1790** BURKE *Fr. Rev.* Wks. 1808 V. 261 To stimulate their cannibal appetites by variety and seasoning.

c. The maturing of wood by drying, etc.; †also, tempering, hardening (of metals).

1641 BEST *Farm. Bks.* (Surtees) 112 Firre-deales are accounted better for bordeninge with then oake that hath not had time for seasoninge. **1730** SAVERY *Magnet. Observ.* in *Phil. Trans.* XXXVI. 330, I imagine it must be owing to some.. Difference in seasoning, it being almost impossible to make both Ends equally hard. **1859** BURTON in *Jrnl. Geog. Soc.* XXIX. 136 The rafters also are favourite places for small articles that require seasoning.

d. The process by which a person becomes hardened or inured to a strange climate, acclimatization.

1807 *Salmagundi* 16 May 198 Strangers always.. undergo a *seasoning* as europeans do in the West-Indies. **1812** BRACKENRIDGE *Views Louisiana* (1814) 111 It is a prevailing notion, that to be sick the first summer, is what every settler must expect... In some parts of the territory.. this seasoning is severely paid. *a* **1859** MACAULAY *Hist. Eng.* xxix. V. 229 This was merely the seasoning which people who passed from one country to another must expect. **1897** *Daily News* 30 Mar. 6/5 Anglo-Saxons who have had no tropical seasoning.

e. Hence, an attack, more or less severe, of ague or some kindred disease suffered by those who take up their abode for the first time in a tropical district.

1670 D. DENTON *Descr. New York* (1845) 18 The Climate hath such an affinity with that of England, that.. the name of seasoning.. hath never there been known. **1774** WESLEY *Wks.* (1872) XI. 67 About a fourth part more [of the slaves] die at the different islands, in what is called the seasoning. **1822–29** *Good's Study Med.* (ed. 3) II. 176 Its more common name, however, in the present day.. is yellow fever; and when the attack upon new comers is slight, *seasoning*.

fig. **1641** HINDE *J. Bruen* xxxi. 99 His desires and endeavours, for the seasoning of others, both persons and families, with the salt of true religion. **1910** *Q. Rev.* Jan. 223 The best of things are the better for liberal seasonings of laughter.

†**f.** Training, discipline. *Obs.*

1649 JER. TAYLOR *Gt. Exemp.* I. Disc. i. 38 It concerns the Parents care, in order to a vertuous and vitious life of the childe, to secure its first seasonings.

g. The process whereby a transported slave becomes inured to the conditions of slavery. *Obs.* exc. *Hist.*

1771 A. BENEZIT *Some Hist. Acct. Guinea* xiii. 130 At a moderate computation of the slaves who are purchased by our African merchants in a year, near thirty thousand die upon the voyage and in the seasoning. **1786** T. CLARKSON *Ess. Slavery & Commerce Human Species* III. iv. 139 This seasoning is said to expire, when the two first years of their servitude are completed; It is the time which an African must take to be so accustomed to the colony, as to be able to endure the common labour of a plantation, and to be put into the *gang*. **1804** R. BISSET *Defence of Slave Trade* 88 Instead of *thirty-three* in the hundred dying, as asserted by the author of the 'Concise Statement', *not three* in the hundred die of the seasoning. **1977** *Time* 7 Feb. 59/3 The passage took longer, with 'seasoning' camps at the beginning, usually on an island off the African coast.

h. The application of one of various finishes to leather after tanning.

1897 C. T. DAVIS *Manuf. Leather* (ed. 2) 358 A seasoning mixture is applied to the surface after tanning and before coloring. **1974** *Encycl. Brit. Macropædia* X. 763/2 In unpigmented seasoning [of leather], a simple glazing finish or seasoning may contain egg albumin, water, and gylcerin.

2. *concr.* Something added to a dish which gives it a distinctive or appetizing flavour.

1580 HOLLYBAND *Treas. Fr. Tong*, *Assaissonnement*, a seasoning. **1693** LOCKE *Educ.* §14. 13 Our Palates like the Seasoning and Cookery they are set to. **1769** MRS. RAFFALD *Eng. Housekpr.* (1778) 47 Rub them well with your seasoning. **1837** DICKENS *Pickw.* xxxi, Nice seasonin' for sassages, is trousers' buttons, Ma'am. **1861** HULME tr. *Moquin-Tandon* II. III. 175 It is necessary to prepare them [snails] with strong seasonings—as with plenty of ham, anchovies [etc.].

fig. **1819** SCOTT *Ivanhoe* iii, His favourite clown.. whose jests.. served for a sort of seasoning to his evening meal.

3. *attrib.* and *Comb.*: †**seasoning disease**, †**distemper**, †**fever** = sense 1 e; **seasoning room**, a store-room where tobacco is kept until matured.

1802 *Engl. Encycl.* IX. 293/1 All *seasoning diseases are of the inflammatory kind. **1701** WOLLEY *Jrnl. in New York* (1860) 25 It does not welcome its Guests and Strangers with the *seasoning distempers of Fevers and Fluxes. **1814** W. BROWN *Pist. Propag. Chr.* (1823) I. 627 He was attacked by the *seasoning fever. **1890** *Pall Mall Gaz.* 5 Aug. 2/1, I.. followed the tobacco from its arrival in the bale, through the *seasoning room, to the wetting and sorting tubs.

seasoning ('siːz(ə)nɪŋ), *ppl. a.* [f. SEASON *v.* + -ING².] That seasons, that adds a flavour or relish.

1562 J. HEYWOOD *Prov. & Epigr.* (1867) 183 No seasonyng lyckour, can season it well. **1697** DRYDEN *Virg. Georg.* III. 615 Sparingly they steep [cheese] With seas'ning Salt, and stor'd, for Winter keep. **1760** WOOLMAN *Jrnl.* vii. Wks. (1775) 125 The Lord.. was pleased to favour us with the Seasoning Virtue of Truth.

'seasonless, *a.* [f. SEASON *sb.* + -LESS.]

†**1.** Lacking flavour, tasteless, insipid. *Obs. rare*⁻¹.

1595 MARKHAM *Trag. Sir R. Grinuile* Ded. to Earl Southampton, And when the stubborne stroke of my harsh song Shall seasonlesse glide through almightie eares, Vouchsafe to sweet it with thy blessed tong.

2. Having or knowing no change of season.

1816 BYRON *Darkness* 71 The world was void,.. Seasonless, herbless,.. lifeless. **1895** A. AUSTIN in *Blackw. Mag.* Apr. 519 Then over the seasonless sea he [the cuckoo] came.

seasour, obs. form of SEIZURE.

sea spider.

1. A name for various marine spider-like creatures. **a.** A spider-crab or maioid.

1666 J. DAVIES *Hist. Caribby Isles* 120 The Sea-Spider is by some conceiv'd to be a kind of Crab. **1694** tr. *Marten's Voy. Spitzbergen* in *Acc. Sev. Late Voy.* (1694) II. 113 The Sea Crawfish without a Tail, or Sea Spider. **1752** WATSON in *Phil. Trans.* XLVII. 465 We observe a great variety in the operations of nature: the crab, the cuttle-fish, and the sea spider. **1863** WOOD *Illustr. Nat. Hist.* III. 559 On account of this great length of limb and small size of body, these crabs [*Leptopodia*] are often called Sea Spiders.

b. A marine arthropod of the group *Pycnogonida*, a pycnogonid.

1855 KINGSLEY *Glaucus* (1878) 80 A little black sea-spider, a Nymphon, who has this peculiarity, that possessing no body at all to speak of, he carries his needful stomach in long branches, packed inside his legs. **1909** SHACKLETON *Heart of Antarctic* II. 266 Here we first got the long-legged sea-spiders (*Pycnogonida*).

c. An octopus or other member of the family *Octopodidæ*.

1858 BAIRD *Cycl. Nat. Sci.*, *Octopodidæ*, Sea Spiders... The common sea spider, *O[ctopus] tuberculatus*. **1859–62** SIR J. RICHARDSON, etc. *Mus. Nat. Hist.* (1868) II. 311.

†**2.** A fish, = QUAVIVER, SEA-DRAGON 1. *Obs.*⁻¹

1672 JOSSELYN *New Eng. Rarities* 25 Sea Dragon or Sea Spider, Quaviver.

sea-spout.

†**1.** A sea-anemone. *Obs. rare.*

1731 MEDLEY *Kolben's Cape G. Hope* II. 212 The Sea-Spout is a very strange production of nature. It looks like a spunge or lump of moss, and sticks to the sea-rocks so fast that no beating of either winds or waves can move it. **1772–84** *Cook's Voy.* (1790) I. 323 The Sea-spout.. is of a green colour, emits water, and within is like a tough piece of flesh.

2. (See quot.)

1867 SMYTH *Sailor's Word-bk.*, *Sea-spout*, the jetting of sea-water over the adjacent lands, when forced through a perforation in a rocky shore; both its egress and ingress are attended with a rumbling noise, and the spray is often injurious to the surrounding vegetation.

†**sea-spring.** *Obs.*⁻¹ A spring-tide.

1627 HAKEWILL *Apol.* II. i. §1. 65 The high Seasprings of the yeare are alwayes neere unto the two Æquinoctialls and Solstices.

seasse, obs. form of CEASE, SEISE.

sea-star.

†**1.** A star which guides mariners at sea. *Obs.*

Chiefly repr. med.L. *stella maris*, a title given to the Virgin Mary, from the erroneous belief that it expressed the etymological meaning of the Heb. name Miriam, Mary.

c **1050** *Pseudo-Matth.* (Assmann) 8 Nu is hyre nama ȝereht.. sæsteorra. *c* **1200** ORMIN 2132 Forr hire name tacneþþ uss Sæsteorrne onn Ennglissh spæche, & ȝho beoþ æfre, & wass, & iss Sæsteorrne inn haliȝ bisne. *c* **1200** *Trin. Coll. Hom.* 141, 161. **1808** *Vesper Bk.* 112/2 Sea-star by which we sail, And gate of heav'nly rest! **1817** MOORE *Lalla Rookh, Fire-Worshippers* (near end), With nought but the sea-star to light up her tomb.

2. A starfish. [Gr. ἀστήρ, L. *stella* (*marina*).]

1569 FENTON *Secret Wond. Nature* 50 b, A kind of fishe called *Stella*, or Sea starre, bycause it hath the figure of a painted starre. **1594** NASHE *Unfort. Trav.* C 2, The fishes called Sea-starres, that burne one another by excessiue heate. **1658** SIR T. BROWNE *Gard. Cyrus* v. 72 Why amongst Sea-starres nature chiefly delighteth in five points? **1772–84** *Cook's Voy.* (1790) I. 323 Sea-suns and sea-stars, are small round shell-fish, and receive their denominations from the great variety of prickles, which shoot from them like rays of light. **1856** R. KNOX tr. *Edwards' Man. Zool.* §382 The sea stars, the holothuria.., and the sea-urchins, are types of this class [*Echinodermata*]. **1891** F. THOMPSON *Sister-Songs* (1895) 16 And her feet Were most sweet, Tinged like sea-stars, rosied brown.

sea-strand. *Obs.* exc. *arch.* = SEA-SHORE.

c **1000** ÆLFRIC *Hom.* (Thorpe) I. 68/29 Beraþ.. þa stanas to sæ-strande. *c* **1205** LAY. 9235 At Port-chæstre heo comen alond & stepen up a sæ strond [*c* **1275** þat see strond]. *c* **1303** in *Pol. Songs* (Camden) 188 Betere hem were at home in huere londe, Then for te seche Flemmysshe by the see stronde. **14..** *Beues* 515 (MS. C), They arevyd at þe see stronde. **1548** HALL *Chron., Hen. VI* (1550) 28 He.. came to the sea stronde at Douer. **1849** J. A. CARLYLE tr. *Dante's Inf.* xxx. 361 Hecuba.. on the sea-strand forlorn. **1865** SWINBURNE *Chastelard* I. ii. 31 Between the sea-strand and the sea. **1882** CHILD *Ballads* I. 112/2 They come to a sea-strand or other water.

sea-stream. [= OS. *sêo-strôm.*]

†**1.** An ocean current: *poet.* the sea. *Obs.*

a **1000** *Andreas* 749 (Gr.) Salte sæstreamas. *c* **1205** LAY. 326 He iwende sorhful ouer sea streames into Griclonde. *a* **1225** *St. Marher.* 9/34 þu steorest te sea stream þ hit fleden ne mot fir þan þu markedest.

2. (See quot.)

1820 SCORESBY *Acc. Arctic Reg.* I. 228 A stream is an oblong collection of drift or bay-ice, the pieces of which are continuous. It is called a sea-stream, when it is exposed on one side to the ocean, and affords shelter from the sea, to whatever is within it. **1867** in SMYTH *Sailor's Word-bk.*

seasur(e, obs. forms of SEIZURE.

sea-swallow.

1. = FLYING FISH. [After L. *hirundo* (Pliny).]

1598 FLORIO, *Accola*, a sea swallow, or a sea reare-mouse. **1601** HOLLAND *Pliny* IX. xxvi. I. 249 The sea Swallow flieth: and it resembleth in all points the bird so called. **1611** COTGR., *Arondelle de mer*, the flying fish called the sea Bat, or sea Swallow. **1664** HUBERT *Catal. Rarities* (1665) 19 A great flying-fish or Sea Swallow. **1740** R. BROOKES *Art of Angling* II. liii. 171 The Flying-Fish or Sea-Swallow.. is very common between the Tropicks. **1844** LINSLEY *Fishes Connecticut* in *Amer. Jrnl. Sci.* XLVII. 59 Dactylopterus volitans, Cuv., Sea Swallow, Long Island Sound.

2. a. A name for any one of the terns (from their general resemblance to swallows). **b.** The stormy petrel, *Procellaria pelagica*. **c.** An edible swiftlet of the genus *Collocalia*, found in south-east Asia.

1647 HEXHAM I. App., A Sea-swallow, *Een Zee-swaluwe.* **1668** CHARLETON *Onomast.* 90 *Hirundo Marina*, the Sea-Swallow. *a* **1672** WILLUGHBY *Ornith.* (1676) 269 *Larus Piscator* Aldrov... The lesser Sea-Swallow. **1734** ALBIN *Birds* II. Pl. 88 The greater Sea Swallow. **1831** M. RUSSELL *Anc. & Mod. Egypt.* xi. §3 (1832) 484 The *Sterna Nilotica*, or Egyptian sea-swallow. **1852** MACGILLIVRAY *Brit. Birds* V. 460 *Thalassidroma pelagica.* The Common Storm-Petrel... Sea Swallow. **1887** HALL CAINE *Deemster* vii, The sea swallow shot over him too, with its low mournful cry. **1902** *Encycl. Brit.* XXVI. 310/2 Animals of economic value [in Borneo] are the sea-swallows, whose edible nests are prized as the best in the archipelago.

3. The trepang or bêche-de-mer.

[= Du. *zeezwaluw*; but the second element represents the Malay name *swālā*.]

1802 *Naval Chron.* VIII. 380 Sea swallow (called beach de mar by the Portuguese, and trepong by the Malays).

sea-swine.

1. A porpoise. *Obs.* exc. *dial.*

1398 TREVISA *Barth. De P.R.* XIII. xxvi. (Bodl. MS.), Isidre.. spekeþ of þe see swyne þat is comynlich icleped suillus. *a* **1450** *Mirk's Festial* 2 The iij. day þe seeswyne and þe cloppys of þe see schull stond on þe see and make roryng noyse so hyddous. **1509** WATSON *Ship of Fools* lxx. (1517) Q vi, Loke that thou be well ware of the yre of the see swyne the whyche wyll folowe thy shyppe. **1671** RAY in *Phil. Trans.* VII. 2279 Most nations calling this fish *Porcus Marinus*, or the Sea-swine. **1884** *Leisure Hour* June 374/2 The porpoise.. was found on the table of the queen. The Saxons called it sea-swine.

2. *Sc.* (See quot. 1880–4.)

1803 *Sibbald's Fife & Kinross* 128 *note*, Several of them [Wrasses] are occasionally caught in the Firth of Forth, and are called by our fishers by the general name of Sea Swine. **1880–4** F. DAY *Brit. Fishes* I. 255 *Labrus lineatus*... Ballan-wrasse, sea-swine, Moray Firth, owing to its making a squeaking noise like a pig.

seat (siːt), *sb.* Forms: 2 *Kent.* sate, 2–3 sæte, 3–5 seete, 3–6 sete, sette, 4–5 seet, *Sc.* set, 5–6 *Sc.* seit(t, (5 *Sc.* seytte, 6 *Sc.* saitt, sate), 5–7 seate, *Sc.* sait, 6– seat. [a. ON. *sǽti* = OHG. *gasâzi* (MHG. *gesæze*, mod.G. *gesäss*), MDu. *gesaete*, *gesete* (mod.Du. *gezeet*):—OTeut. **(ga)sǣtjo-m*, f. **sǣt-* ablaut-var. of **set-*: see SIT. *v.*

The same grade of the root is represented in OE. *sǽt* (= ON. *sát*) str. fem., ambush, which occurs only in two obscure passages, and did not survive into ME.]

I. Action or manner of sitting.

†**1. a.** *gen.* The action of sitting. Also an assembly at a banquet. *Obs.*

c **1200** ORMIN 11059 He turrnde waterr inntill win.. Att an bridaless sæte. *a* **1300** *Cursor M.* 28471, I haue halden quen i was sett langsum setes at my mete. *Ibid.* 29085. *a* **1300** *E.E. Psalter* cxxxviii. 2 þou knew mi seete and mi risinge. *a* **1400** *Octavian* 1002 He fonde the boordys covyrde alle, And redy to go to mete; The maydyn.. In a kyrtulle there sche stode, And bowne sche was to sete. *c* **1400** *Rule of St. Benet* 32 Sain Benet.. sais þat vnait sete es il to þe saule. *c* **1420** *Chron. Vilod.* 2747 þis bysone mone full wery of sete he was And ryȝt gret lust he hadde to slepe.

b. *concr.* A setting or 'clutch' (of eggs). ? *dial.*

1892 *Wild & Tame* 33 A merchant in Norfolk had a seat of Duck's eggs hatched off.

2. Manner of sitting (on horseback). (Chiefly with qualifying adj.) Also *predicatively*, one who has a (good, etc.) seat, a (good, etc.) horseman.

1577 B. GOOGE *Heresbach's Husb.* III. (1586) 115 b, The ridgebone ouer the shoulders being something hie, giues the horseman a better seate. **1667** DK. NEWCASTLE *Meth. Dressing Horses* 205 The Seat is so much.. as it is the only thing that makes a Horse go Perfectly. **1693** LOCKE *Educ.* §186. 237 It conduces to give a Man a firm and graceful Seat on Horseback. **1787** 'G. GAMBADO' *Acad. Horsem.* (1809) 48 [Virgil] tells us the exact seat of a Roman dragoon. **1819** SCOTT *Ivanhoe* viii, Touch the Hospitaller's shield; he has the least sure seat, he is your cheapest bargain. **1840**

horseman. **1883** Miss F. M. Peard *Contradictions* II. 278 Miss Molyneux would never have fallen..for there wasn't a better seat in the county. **1891** N. Gould *Double Event* 295 He has a fine seat on a horse.

3. a. The sitting of a court or the like. Now *Sc.*

1635 *Maldon* (Essex) *Borough deeds* (Bundle 80. no. 2), The freeholders within the burrough summoned to appere att the forrest seate or sitinge at Chelmesford. **1638** *Ibid.* (Bundle 80. no. 3), xs. paid to Mr. Hamound for his charges att the justice seate. **1889** H. Johnston *Chron. Glenbuckie* iii. 35 We had had a long seat in the Boar's Head hearing reports frae the delegates.

†b. A sitting body, court of justice. ***justice seat***: see justice *sb.* 12. *Obs.*

1560 Daus tr. *Sleidane's Comm.* 150 Of the counsell, for that it is the hyghe judicial seate of the churche [*ecclesiæ supremum tribunal*]. **1604** E. G[rimstone] *D'Acosta's Hist. Indies* vi. xxv. 486 There were divers seates and iurisdictions, with their Counsellors and Iudges of the Court.

c. *Sc.* (More fully ***seat of session***.) The Court of Session, the supreme Civil Court of Scotland; esp. in ***lords of the seat***.

1500–20 Dunbar *Poems* xiii. 41 Sum sanis the Sait, and sum thame cursis. **1532** *Acc. Ld. High Treas. Scot.* VI. 59 To charge him to compere before the lordis of the sait to ansuer [etc.]. **1545** *Reg. Privy Council Scot.* I. 5 Becaus of the fere of the pest that is laytlie risyn in the toun of Edinburcht, the seite of Sessioun may nocht surelie remaine thairin. **1574** *Ibid.* II. 378 For the administratioun of justice upon offendouris,..in the north partis..far distant frome the ordinar sait of justice. **1818** Scott *Hrt. Midl.* iv, 'Is he a lord of state, or a lord of seat?'... 'A lord of seat—a lord of session.—I fash mysell little wi' lords o' state.'

d. *Sc.* The court of kirk-session. ? *Obs.*

1568 *Reg. St. Andrews Kirk Session* (1889) I. 313 The quhilk day Andro Alexander is admonisched be the Superintendent and Seat.

†4. 'Stool', evacuation of the bowels. (Cf. siege *sb.* 3 b.) *Obs.*

1697 *Phil. Trans.* XIX. 367 The Juice of the leaves of Betonica, in Spring, will not Work by Vomit and Seat as well as the Roots.

5. The 'set' or 'sit' (of a garment). ? *Obs.*

1824 Miss Ferrier *Inher.* xxi, And only look at my ruff!.. Colonel Delmour has spoil'd the seat of it.

II. Place or thing to sit upon.

6. a. The place on which a person is sitting, or is accustomed to sit; a place to seat one person at a table, in a public building, conveyance, etc.

c **1205** Lay. 30841 Þat folc hafden alle iȝeten and arisen from heore seten. *a* **1300** *Cursor M.* 15282 Quen þis super was all don, Iesus ras of his sette [*other texts* sete; *rime* lete]. *c* **1380** Wyclif *Sel. Wks.* II. 62 And þei loven first seetis at soperis. **1470–85** Malory *Arthur* x. vii. 424 Kynge Arthur ..maade hym knyght of the table round and his seate was where the good Knyghtes sir Marhaus seate was. **1567** *Gude & Godlie Ball.* 102 Full slyddrie is the sait that thay on sit. **1575** Gascoigne *Posies, Flowers* (1907) 91 Me thought I was a loft, and yet my seate full sure: Thy heart dyd seeme to me a rock which ever might endure. **1600** *Weakest goeth to Wall* G 2, Sexton, I haue sought thee in euery seate in the Church. **1697** Dryden *Virg. Georg.* iv. 496 Starting at once from their green Seats, they rise; Fear in their Heart, Amazement in their Eyes. **1716** Lady M. W. Montagu *Let. to C'tess of Mar* 14 Sept., She ordered me a seat at her right hand. *a* **1763** W. King *Polit. & Lit. Anecd.* (1819) 244 He went every Sunday to St. James's church, and used to sit in Mr. Salt's seat. **1832** Tennyson *Œnone* 21 Till the mountain shade Sloped downward to her seat from the upper cliff. **1873** O. W. Holmes *Addr. Opening Fifth Avenue Theatre* 99 See where the hurrying crowd..Streams to the numbered seat each paste-board fits. **1908** R. Bagot *A. Cuthbert* iii. 22 Then she stalked out of the church. Fortunately we were in the free seats, near the door.

transf. and *fig.* **1399** Langl. *Rich. Redeles* iii. 49 Thanne cometh..Anoþer proud partriche..And sesith on hir sete [*MS. alteration of* cete] with hir softe plumes, And houeth þe eyren. **1590** Shaks. *Mids. N.* ii. ii. 81 When thou wak'st, let loue forbid Sleepe his seate on thy eye-lid. **1741–2** Gray *Agrippina* 51 If bright ambition from her craggy seat Display the radiant prize. **1784** Cowper *Tiroc.* 432 For Providence..In spite of all the wrigglers into place, Still keeps a seat or two for worth and grace.

b. Hence, the use of, or right to use, a seat (in a church, theatre, conveyance, etc.). Cf. sitting.

1520 *Churchw. Acc. St. Giles, Reading* 9 Recd or Thoms Gyles for his wifes sete iiijd. *c* **1618** Moryson *Itin.* iv. (1903) 149 A Countesse..litle or nothing respected..in the Church, where she could hardly gett a seate. **1815** tr. *Paris Chit-Chat* (1816) III. 176 To-day it is discussed how much should be exacted for seats on the day when Monseigneur comes to confirm. **1844** O. W. Holmes *Lines Berksh. Jubilee* 51 We'll give you at least..a seat on the grass, And the best of old—water—at nothing a glass. **1879** J. Kerr *Ess. Castism & Sectism* 79 She paid a pound out of her own pockets for a seat in the church.

c. A right to sit as a member, or the position of being a member, of a deliberative or administrative body, *esp.* of Parliament or other legislative assembly; a place (whether occupied or temporarily vacant) in the membership of the House of Commons, Congress, or the like.

Sometimes qualified by the designation of that one of the contending parties to which the holder of the (Parliamentary) seat belongs: e.g. 'The polls for three Liberal and three Conservative seats will be declared to-morrow'.

1774 Burke *Sp. Amer. Tax.* Wks. II. 399 In the year sixty-five..not having the honour of a seat in this house. **1787** J. Jay in Sparks *Corr. Amer. Rev.* (1853) IV. 153 Members who will find it convenient to make their seats subservient to partial and personal purposes. **1798** Tyrwhitt in *Paget Papers* (1896) I. 138 All those who purchased Seats are selling as well as they can. **1818** Scott *Hrt. Midl.* li, He was generally respected by those of his own profession, as well as by the laity who had seats in the Assembly. **1849** Macaulay *Hist. Eng.* iv. I. 453 Jeffreys..very soon after the death of Charles, obtained a seat in the cabinet. **1885** *Manch. Exam.* 10 July 5/4 A seat on the Committee will compel them to hear..the first principles of economical science. **1885** *Encycl. Brit.* XVIII. 309/2 By the English Reform Act of 1867..twenty-six seats were taken from boroughs... Seven other English boroughs were disfranchised by the Scottish Reform Act of 1868, these seats being given to Scotland.

d. *U.S.* A place in the membership of the New York Stock Exchange.

1820 *Constitution N.Y. Stock & Exchange Board* in E. C. Stedman *N.Y. Stock Exchange* (1905) iv. 68 If two-thirds of the members present are for reinstating him, he shall again be entitled to his seat at the Board. **1882** J. D. McCabe *N.Y. by Sunlight & Gaslight* xxi. 337 A seat in the Board costs about $6000, and is the absolute personal property of its owner. **1948** *Time* 14 June 90/2 All who buy and sell on the floor must own Stock Exchange seats, which are currently worth about $65,000 apiece (1929 price: $625,000). **1972** *Times* 16 May (Wall Street Suppl.) p. viii/5 Among the brokers the numbers of 'seats' on the exchange remained unchanged at 1,366 (as it has done since December 1953).

7. a. Something adapted or used for sitting upon, as a chair, stool, sofa, etc. Also *spec.* a bench to seat one or more persons; a horizontal board or chair-like structure in a boat, coach, train, aeroplane, etc.; †a sedan chair.

c **1375** *Cursor M.* 14734 (Fairf.) Þaire setis [*Cott.* setles, *Trin.* seges] þer þai in con sete he kest ham doun vnder þaire fete. *c* **1440** *Pallad. on Husb.* i. 1094 Anend the setis [of a bath] sette hit so withoute The fourneys. **1584** *Churchw. Acc. S. Andrew's, Canterb.* (MS.), For a borde to make seates in the belfry & braggett's, vj. **1588** Hickock tr. *Frederick's Voy.* 40 b, The noble men neuer goe on foote, but are caried by men in a seat. **1667** Milton *P.L.* v. 392 Rais'd of grassie terf Thir Table was, and mossie seats had round. **1784** Cowper *Task* v. 162 But in order due Convivial table and commodious seat..were there. **1810** E. Weeton *Let.* 28 Dec. (1969) I. 318 Perhaps when Mr. and Mrs. P. go to Preston..I may get a seat with them..if they go in the chaise. **1818** Shelley *Rosalind* 106 They came To a stone seat beside a spring. **1875** Jowett *Plato* (ed. 2) III. 700 A light chariot without a seat. **1879** *Encycl. Brit.* IX. 848/1 [The Romans'] chairs, couches, and seats were of similar shape to those of the Greeks. **1976** *Daily Mirror* 16 July 9/6 The bosses are taking up too many first-class seats on main line commuter services. **1977** C. Forbes *Avalanche Express* vi. 68 Harry Wargrave occupied his normal seat..the gangway seat [in the aircraft].

b. In narrower sense: That part (of a chair, saddle, etc.) upon which its occupant sits. Also *spec.* of a lavatory.

1778 Miss Burney *Evelina* (1791) II. 251 Miss Mirvan and I jumped involuntarily upon the seats of our chairs. **1809** Malkin *Gil Blas* iv. xi. ¶5 Chairs without any seats. **1875** Knight *Dict. Mech.*, *Seat*, the broad part of a saddle on which the rider sits; also, the top piece on a gig saddle. **1879** *Encycl. Brit.* IX. 850/1 The seats, backs, and ends are stuffed and upholstered with rich materials. **1907** *Yesterday's Shopping* (1969) 518/2 Seat Covers..for use on 'w.c.'s'. **1938** E. Bowen *Death of Heart* i. iv. 81 Portia..re-wound the gramophone on the shut seat, and Stravinsky filled the bathroom. **1979** M. Hastings *Bomber Command* vi. 155 The Elsan toilet which most crews had used with acute caution since a 50 Squadron gunner left most of the skin of his backside attached to the frozen seat one icy night over Germany.

8. a. Contextually applied to the chair set apart for the holder of some position of authority or dignity, the throne of a king or a bishop, or the like, the throne of God or of an angel. Hence *fig.* the authority or dignity symbolized by sitting in a particular chair or throne. ***regal*** or ***royal seat*** (arch.), † ***seat-royal***, a royal throne.

a **1200** *Vices & Virtues* 105 *Iusticia et iudicium preparatio sedis eius*,..Rihtwisnesse and dom, hi makieð godes sate. *c* **1200** Ormin 11959 Þe deofell brohhte Jesu Crist Wiþþutenn o þe temmple Upponn an sæte uppo þe rof,.. Forr þær wass greȝȝþedd sæte o lofft Till þa þatt sholldenn spellenn. **1390** Gower *Conf.* II. 155 King of Crete He hadde be; bot of his sete He was put doun. *c* **1400** *Gamelyn* 855 Gamelyn sette him doun in the Iustices seet. *a* **1533** Ld. Berners *Huon* xlii. 141 Thou art not worthy to sytt in a sete royall. **1533** Bellenden *Livy* iii. xxii. (1903) II. 36 He callit þe consullis to raise ane new contentioun to þare seittis. **1593** Shaks. *3 Hen. VI*, i. i. 26 This is the Pallace of the fearefull King, And this the Regall Seat: possesse it Yorke. **1617** Purchas *Pilgrimage* (ed. 3) 595 The King comes forth in open audience, sitting in his Seat-royall. **1659** Hammond *On Ps.* xx. 6 Paraphr. 116 As if by his own right hand from heaven, his holy seat of mansion, he should reach out deliverance to him. **1667** Milton *P.L.* vi. 27 On to the sacred hill They led him high applauded, and present Before the seat supreme. **1676** Dryden *Aurengz.* v. i, I, for myself, th' Imperial Seat will gain. **1746** Francis tr. *Horace, Epist.* i. vi. 80 A third..Can give or take the Honours of the State, The Consul's Fasces, and the Prætor's Seat. **1820** Shelley *Witch of Atlas* 634 The king would dress an ape up in his crown And robes, and seat him on his glorious seat.

b. *spec.* The throne *of* a particular kingdom.

1599 Shaks. *Hen. V*, i. i. 88 Of his true Titles to some certaine Dukedomes, And generally, to the Crowne and Seat of France. *Ibid.* i. i. 269 We neuer valew'd this poore seate of England. **1896** A. Austin *England's Darling* i. i, And in the seat of Mercia Ceowulf rules.

† c. ***Apostolic seat*** [F. *Siège apostolique*], ***Holy seat*** [F. *Saint-Siège*], ***Peter's seat***: the papal chair, its occupant or his office. (Cf. see *sb.*) *Obs.*

1560 Daus tr. *Sleidane's Comm.* 16 b, He that hathe the Seate and faith of Peter, was ever taken for his successour. **1563** Winȝet tr. *Vincent. Lirin.* viii. Wks. (S.T.S.) II. 25 Pape Steuin.., Prælat of the Apostolik Sait [*apostolicæ sedis antistes*]. **1588** Parke tr. *Mendoza's Hist. China* 405 The authoritie where with they do it, is not knowen,..the seat apostolicke did neuer giue it them. **1673–4** Clarendon *Relig. & Policy* (1811) I. 202 The reserving of the first-fruits of all vacant benefices to the holy seat.

†d. As the title of an order of angels; = throne. (Used to render L. *sedes*.) *Obs.*

1398 Trevisa *Barth. De P.R.* ii. x. (1495) 37 The thyrde Ordre is the ordre of Thrones... Ysidore & therfore Denys calle theym þt hyghest setes [*sedes altissimæ*] for they ben hye as it were by auctoryte of god ordened for to deme... Sadde setes [*Sedes compactæ*] for they ben couenable & conuenyently Joyned towchynge the Joynture & conuenyentes of domes of god. **1577** tr. *Bullinger's Decades* iv. ix. 737/2 Truely the Apostle sayth, Whether seates, (thrones) whether lordships, whether principalities, whether powers.

9. a. The sitting part of the body; the posteriors. Also jocularly, ***seat of honour*** (and nonce-variations).

1607 Topsell *Four-f. Beasts* 189 A plaister thereof.. cureth also all tumours in the priuy parts, and in the seate. **1727** Gay *Fables* xxiii. 80 They stick with pins my bleeding seat. **1782** Cowper *Gilpin* 84 The snorting beast began to trot, Which gall'd him in his seat. **1785** R. Cumberland *Observer* No. 24 ¶12 With one kick, pretty forcibly bestowed upon the seat of dishonour. **1792** Wolcot *Pair of Lyric Ep.* 18 Behold him seiz'd, his seat of honour bare; The bamboo sounds—alas! no voice of Fame. **1796** Burke *Regic. Peace* iii. (1892) 148 The Turk..gave him two or three lusty kicks on the seat of honour. **1809** Malkin *Gil Blas* v. i. ¶3 My seat of vengeance was firked most unmercifully. **1820** Combe *Syntax, Wife* ii. 289 While with his spade the conq'ror plied, Stroke after stroke, the seat of shame, Which blushing Muses never name. **1835** Hood *Dead Robbery* iii, The stiff 'un that he thought to meet Starts sudden up, like Jacky-in-a-box, Upon his seat! **1878** *Athletic World* 10 May 66/2 A well-ventilated [bicycle-]saddle is the best preventative for those blisters which favour the seat of honour.

b. That part (of a garment, esp. of a pair of trousers) which covers the posteriors.

1835 Marryat *Jac. Faithf.* ii, I had a pair of trowsers with no seat to them. *a* **1849** Hawthorne *Twice-told T., Village Uncle*, Another [fellow] has planted the tarry seat of his trousers on a heap of salt.

10. The 'form' of a hare. Now *dial.*

[Cf. Gr. ἡ καθέδρα τοῦ λαγῶ Xen. *Cyneg.* iv. §4]

1735 Somerville *Chase* ii. 25 So the wise Hares Oft quit their Seats, lest some more curious Eye Shou'd mark their Haunts. **1856** 'Stonehenge' *Brit. Sports* i. ii. vi. 139 The Form of the Hare, or as it is sometimes called, her seat. **1962** *Sunday Express* 1 Apr. 21/5 These lairs [of hares] are usually called 'forms',..though in..Kent, the cosier word 'seats' is preferred. **1972** Evans & Thomson *Leaping Hare* iv. 52 They'll dig a little hole so they can cover, so they're level with the top of the land... A *seat* we call it.

11. *Boot-trade.* An engagement to work at making boots of a specified kind. Const. *of*.

1791 J. Lackington *Mem.* xvii. 114, I could not bear the idea of returning to the leather-branch; I therefore attempted and obtained a seat of Stuff in Bristol. *Ibid.* xviii. 118, I left my seat of work at Bristol, and returned..to Taunton. **1896** *Daily News* 2 Mar. 10/6 Boot trade. Wanted, a Seat of Woman's Work.

III. Residence, abode, situation. [Cf. L. *sedes*.]

12. Applied *spec.* (after L. *sedes*) to: The abiding place or resting place (of departed souls); a position in this place. Now *arch.* or *poet.*

c **1275** *Sinners Beware* 52 in *O.E. Misc.* 73 Wikede beoþ þe sete [*sc.* Hell] And the wurmes eke þat doþ þe saule teone. *a* **1300** *Cursor M.* 25448 Reu me lauerd..and wiss me waies þare þare santes has þair seli sete. **1390** Gower *Conf.* III. 36 Thanne he preide Unto the Patriarch and seide: Send Lazar doun fro thilke Sete, And do that he his finger wete In water. *c* **1440** *Alphabet of Tales* 416 Behold! I se hevyn oppyn & a seatt ordand for me. **1561** Daus *Bullinger on Apoc.* (1573) 218 b, The soules passing out of the body before the end and last iudgement go right into the blessed seates. **1593** Shaks. *Rich. II*, v. v. 112 Mount, mount my soule, thy seate is vp on high. **1707–45** Watts *Hymn*, '*How bright these glorious Spirits*', How came they to the happy Seats of everlasting Day? **1832** Tennyson *Œnone* 129 Gods, who have attain'd Rest in a happy place and quiet seats Above the thunder.

13. a. (Cf. 8.) A city in which a throne, court, government is established or set up; a capital.

c **1400** *Destr. Troy* 1630 Priam..a pales gert make Within the Cite full Solempne of a sete riall. **1585** T. Washington tr. *Nicholay's Voy.* ii. xiii. 49 Mehemet..resoluing to keep there the seat of his empire. **1595** T. Bedingfield tr. *Machiavelli's Florent. Hist.* i Rome, the antient Emperiall seate. **1678** Wanley *Wond. Lit. World* v. i. 467/2 Constantinople was taken by Mahomet, and made the chief Seat of the Turkish Empire. **1719** De Foe *Crusoe* ii. (Globe) 541 Peking, the Royal Seat of the Chinese Emperor. **1836** Thirlwall *Greece* xii. 85 This [Miletus] was the seat chosen by Neleus himself. **1851** Dixon *W. Penn* i. (1872) 4 His seat of government was far away from the coast.

b. (Cf. 8 c.) = see *sb.* Now only ***seat of a bishop***.

1387 Trevisa *Higden* (Rolls) II. 77 Þe chief moderchirche of al Wales, and þe chief sete [*Caxton* see]. *c* **1475** *Harl. Contin. Higden* (Rolls) VIII. 436 Maister John Barnette, bischop of Worcester, was translate to the seete of Bathe. *a* **1552** Leland *Itin.* IV. 16 The which was at that tyme nother of his Inheritaunce nor Purchace, but as a thing taken of the Sete of Wiccestre in Farme. **1582** *Reg. Privy Council Scot.* III. 474 The cheptoure of the seitt of Glasgow. **1888** Bryce *Amer. Commw.* II. lii. 296 In England a city is usually taken to be a place which is or has been the seat of a bishop.

14. a. The thing (esp. the organ or part of the body) in which a particular power, faculty, function or quality 'resides'; the locality of a disease, sensation, or the like.

1390 Gower *Conf.* III. 100 The dreie Colre..his propre sete [L. *domus*] Hath in the galle, wher he duelleth. **1398**

TREVISA *Barth. De P.R.* v. ii. (1495) 102 The heede is pryncypall place and seete of wyttes. **1676** GREW *Musæum, Anat. Stomach & Guts* vi. 26 The said Three Ventricles.. are the Seat of Tast. **1753** R. RUSSELL *Diss. Sea Water* 182 The Patient..complained only of those Parts, which were the late Seat of the Disease. **1777** PRIESTLY *Matt. & Spir.* I. iv. (1782) 47 We formed a judgment concerning the necessary seat of thought. **1842** J. H. NEWMAN *Par. Serm.* VI. vii. 98 The heart may be considered as the seat of life. **1843** R. J. GRAVES *Syst. Clin. Med.* xxviii. 363 Mercurial ostitis of the head is a very common form of disease: its more usual seats are the frontal and parietal bones. **1860** TYNDALL *Glac.* I. xxvii. 196 The air itself between the eye and the distant pines being the seat of the colour. **1862** H. SPENCER *First Princ.* II. v. §57 (1875) 185 The string is the seat of a tension generated by the motion of the ball. **1874** CARPENTER *Ment. Phys.* I. ii. §61 (1879) 63 The Sensorial centres whose seat is in the head. **1892** W. R. GOWERS *Man. Dis. Nerv. Syst.* I. 333 The lesions of chronic myelitis resemble those of acute myelitis in seat and distribution.

b. Similarly, of the soul or its parts.

1579 HAKE *Newes out of Powles* iv. (1872) D iij b, The stomack ouerchardgde..Doth make the minde and inwarde man vnfit for reasons seate. **1716–17** BENTLEY *Serm.* xi. 383 [His heart is] the Seat of selfishness. **1751** JORTIN *Serm.* I. iii. (1771) 57 A mind tormented with furious passions, the seat of hopes which are disappointed. **1847** R. W. HAMILTON *Rewards & Punishm.* viii. (1853) 365 Sin has its seat in the soul. **1850** MCCOSH *Div. Govt.* III. i. (1874) 309 We regard the will as the seat of all virtue and vice.

15. a. A place where something takes place, or where some particular condition of things prevails. *seat of war* [= L. *sedes belli*]: the region in which warfare is going on.

c **1560** A. SCOTT *Poems* xxxv. 4 Alwayis to fle iniquite And sait of syn and schame. **1565** COOPER *Thesaurus* s.v., *Sedes luxuriæ*. Cic. The seate or habitation of riot and sensualitie. **1593** SHAKS. *Rich. II*, IV. i. 140 In this Seat of Peace. **1662** STILLINGFL. *Orig. Sacræ* II. i. §2. 110 Those parts which were furthest remote from the seat of those grand transactions. **1673** TEMPLE *Observ. United Prov.* i. 44 The other retires into Holland, and makes that the seat of the War. *a* **1687** PETTY *Pol. Arith.* i. (1690) 9 A plain open Country..where the seat of War may be both Winter and Summer. **1736** BUTLER *Anal.* II. vii. 259 Foretelling, at what Time Rome or Babylon or Greece..should be the most conspicuous Seat of..Tyranny and Dissoluteness. **1803** WELLINGTON in Gurw. *Desp.* (1837) I. 432 Forage, for which every large body of troops must depend upon the country which is to be the seat of its operations. **1810** CRABBE *Borough* xii. 303 And who shall say where guided? to what seats Of starving villany? of thieves and cheats? **1876** A. J. EVANS *Through Bosnia* iii. 87 Many Croats and Slovenes..were..leaving for the seat of war. **1878** HUXLEY *Physiogr.* xvii. 278 The region which has been the seat of these changes.

b. A city or locality in which (a branch of trade, learning, etc.) is established.

1585 T. WASHINGTON tr. *Nicholay's Voy.* II. xiii. 49 Galata, being the seate of trade of the Geneuoises. **1610** HOLLAND *Camden's Brit.* I. 488 Cambridge..was a seat of learning about the time of King Henry the First. **1788** PRIESTLEY *Lect. Hist.* v. xxxvi. 264 So little attention was given to matters of science in Europe, their former seat. **1849** MACAULAY *Hist. Eng.* v. I. 585 Taunton..was a celebrated seat of the woollen manufacture. **1865** DIRCKS *Life Marq. Worc.* i. 1 Blackfriars was..the seat of fashion. **1868** FREEMAN *Norm. Conq.* (1876) II. vii. 153 It was in those days the chief seat of the Irish slave-trade.

16. a. A place of habitation or settlement (of a tribe, people, etc.). Also *transf.* (of birds).

1535 STEWART *Cron. Scot.* II. 217 Baith Scot and Pecht.. war baneist all out of tha boundis, And Saxonis sone in thair saittis set doun. *c* **1611** CHAPMAN *Iliad* xv. Comment., We often see with a clap of thunder doves or other fowles driven headlong from their seates. **1614** RALEIGH *Hist. World* IV. vii. §iii. 301 These Gaules were the race of those, that issued out of their Countrie, to seeke new seates in that great expedition. *a* **1674** CLARENDON *Hist. Reb.* xi. §146 The seat of the old Irish..was the province of Ulster. **1697** DRYDEN *Virg. Georg.* I. 327 Betwixt the midst [the torrid zone] and these [the frigid zones], the Gods assign'd Two habitable Seats for Humane Kind. **1762** HUME *Hist. Eng.* I. i. 2 The convenience of feeding their Cattle was even a sufficient motive for removing their seats. **1835** THIRLWALL *Greece* v. I. 149 Corinth, one of the principal seats of the Minyan race. **1853** J. H. NEWMAN *Hist. Sk.* (1873) II. i. 13 Central Europe was not at that time the seat of civilized nations.

†**b.** ***seat and soil*** [= L. *sedes ac solum* (Livy)]: a region of habitation. *Obs.*

a **1400–50** *Wars Alex.* 1749 All þe gracious godis..þat sauys sete & soile & sustaynes þe erth. **1614** RALEIGH *Hist. World* I. iii. §3. 38 [Certain places are said in Scripture to resemble Paradise:] being compared to a seat and soyle of farre exceeding excellencie. *Ibid.* §5. 40 Or if the soile and seate had not remained, then would not Moses, who wrote of Paradise about 850 years after the floud, haue described it so particularly.

c. = COUNTRY-SEAT.

1607 NORDEN *Surv. Dial.* III. 85 Let Princes haue their Palaces, and great men, their pleasant seates. **1610** HOLLAND *Camden's Brit.* I. 481 Rising-castle..the seat in times past of the Albineys. **1796** PEGGE *Anonym.* (1809) 325 Houses, better than farm-houses, but not sumptuous enough to be called seats or capital mansions. **1812** CRABBE *Tales* iii. 56 And guests politely call'd his house a seat. **1847** TENNYSON *Princess* Prol. 98 And here we lit on..lady friends From neighbour seats. **1859** W. COLLINS *Q. of Hearts* i, No gentleman's seat is within an easy drive of us.

†**17.** Local or geographical position or situation. ***seat of living***: habitat (of an animal). *Obs.*

1607 TOPSELL *Four-f. Beasts* 660 We shall manifest, that either the colour or seate of liuing, cannot agree with the *Strepsiceros*. **1614** RALEIGH *Hist. World* I. iii. §i. 33 The Lord God planted a garden, Eastward, in Eden... Of this seate and place of Paradise, all ages haue held dispute. **1663** BUTLER *Hud.* I. i. 173 He knew the Seat of Paradise, Could tell in what Degree it lies. **1695** WOODWARD *Nat. Hist. Earth* I. 36 But the Sea..left these Shells there as marks of its ancient bounds and seat.

18. Position (of ground, a city, habitation) as regards surroundings, climate, etc.; situation, site; hence, the position of a person or living thing with regard to habitation or situation.

1549 RUSSELL in Froude *Hist. Eng.* (1882) IV. 435 They found the rebels strongly encamped, as well by the seat of the ground as by the entrenching of the same. *a* **1566** R. EDWARDS *Damon & Pithias* (1908) C ij b, But mee thinkes, this is a pleasant Citie, The Seate is good, and yet not stronge. **1574** R. SCOT. *Hop Garden* (1578) 9 The Hoppe that lykes not..his seate, his grounde,..or the manner of his setting &c. commeth vp..small in stalke. **1591** FLORIO *2nd Fruites* 29 You are lodged then in a verie good seate [*In buon sito*]. **1605** SHAKS. *Macb.* I. vi. 1 This Castle hath a pleasant seat. **1615** G. SANDYS *Trav.* 6 Although the seate of the Towne be excessive hot, yet it is happily qualified by a North-East gale. **1625** B. JONSON *Staple of N.* III. Intermeane, In Siluer-streete, the Region of money, a good seat for a Vsurer. **1625** BACON *Ess., Building* (Arb.) 547 Hee that builds a faire House, upon an ill Seat, committeth Himselfe to Prison. **1673** TEMPLE *Observ. United Prov.* i. 44 Holland..was strong by its nature and seat among the Waters that encompass and divide it. **1693** DRYDEN *Persius* vi. 1 Has Winter caus'd thee, friend, to change thy seat, And seek in Sabine air a warm retreat? *a* **1701** SEDLEY *4th Bk. Virg. Georg.* Wks. 1778 I. 26 First, for your Bees a seat and station chuse Shelter'd from winds.

†**19. a.** A definite place (on a surface, in a body or organ, in a series). *Obs.*

1574 H. BAKER *Well-spring Sci.* (1617) 2 [In Numeration] a place is called a seat or roome that a figure standeth in. **1576** FLEMING tr. *Caius' Dogs* (1880) 2 Of these three sortes ..so meane I to entreate, that the first in the first place, the last in the last roome, and the myddle sort in the middle seate, be handled. **1578** BANISTER *Hist. Man* I. 9 That Seame ..rising from the hollowes of the temples, pearseth, through the middle seates of the eyes. **1653** LD. BROUNCKER tr. *Des Cartes' Compend. Mus.* 40 Unlesse all the Tones of these be removed by a Fourth or Fifth, from their proper Seat. **1676** in Willis & Clark *Cambridge* (1886) II. 521 The Seates or places where the same Bookes are to be putt..shall have the name of the said S[r] Thomas Sclater putt upon them. **1726** LEONI *Alberti's Archit.* I. 39 b, If..Buildings obstruct your Sight from discovering and fixing upon the exact Seat of every Angle. **1775** T. SHERIDAN *Art of Reading* 38 For many Contiguous letters [of the alphabet] as they now lie are performed in such different seats and with such different exertions of the organs.

†**b.** = LOCUS 2. *Obs.* (? *nonce-use.*)

1628 T. SPENCER *Logick* 14 Aristotle assigneth ten places, or seates of arguments, in the fourth Chapter of his Categories.

†**20.** A term of the game of Post and Pair. *Obs.*

1680 COTTON *Compl. Gamester* xxii. (ed. 2) 106 You must first stake at Post, then at Pair; after this deal two Cards apiece, then stake at the Seat.

IV. Basis, foundation, support.

†**21. a.** A place prepared for something to be erected or set up upon it; a building site. *Obs.*

1615 MARKHAM *County Contentm.* I. i. 14 Against the side of this hill would be cut or digged diuers large and broad seats one aboue an other,..which seats would bee..boorded ..on the sides..and also close boorded aloft,..the number of these seats would bee according to the number of your Hounds. *a* **1627** HAYWARD *Edw. VI* (1630) 85 A Church by Strand-bridge, and two Bishops houses, were pulled downe to make a seat for his new building. **1662** GERBIER *Principles* 14 But as for a Seate on Moorish Grounds.., in effect 'tis to Build perpetually.

†**b.** *transf.* in *Perspective.* (See quot.)

1815 R. BROWN *Princ. Pract. Perspective* 3 *Seat* is the space that an object would occupy on the ground plane.

22. That part of a thing upon which it rests or appears to rest, usually the broadest part; the base.

1661 N. N. *Drayning Fenns* 7 Banks..9 foot high and 60 foot wide at seat or bottom. **1681** GREW *Musæum* I. §vi. i. 139 The first..is the Edible Button Fish. These have very great Prickles, with Seats or Bases proportionable. **1828** P. NICHOLSON *Masonry* 37 A horizontal section of a wall, through the base-line, is called the seat of the wall. **1830** HEDDERWICK *Mar. Archit.* 118 *Seat*, the bottom part of a timber; the seat of the floors is that part which rests on the keel. *c* **1850** *Rudim. Navig.* (Weale) 114 The eddy which the ship draws after her at her seat or line of flotation. **1855** FRANKE *Beil's Technol. Dict.* II. 452 Seat of wooden bellows (the lower or fixed chest or box), *der Unterkasten, Gîte.*

b. The position of a horseshoe with respect to the hoof. Cf. SEATED *ppl. a.* 7.

1851 H. STEPHENS *Bk. Farm* (ed. 2) I. 338/1 The transparent shoe, showing the usual seat given to the shoe upon the forefoot.

23. *Mech.* A part or surface upon which the base of something rests.

1805 *Shipwright's Vade-m.* 129 *Seat*, the scarph or part trimmed out for a chock, &c. to fay to. **1844** H. STEPHENS *Bk. Farm* I. 414 The beam being received into the seats formed on..the palms [of a plough]. **1858** R. MURRAY *Marine Engines* (ed. 3) 71 It more frequently happens that the valve fits its seat so badly as to allow of the escape of steam. **1875** T. SEATON *Fret Cutting* 103 Carvers leave a level place called a seat, where this extra thickness is required, and glue on a piece. **1875** KNIGHT *Dict. Mech.*, *Seat*, that part of the bore of a chambered piece of ordnance at which the shell rests when rammed home. **1884** F. J. BRITTEN *Watch & Clockm.* 129 A hole is drilled so much less in size than the jewel as to allow of a firm seat for it. **1886** *Encycl. Brit.* XX. 583/1 To obtain the requisite convexity by rounding the formation surface or seat of the road.

b. The surface on which the head of a poppet-valve rests when the valve is closed.

1841 Valve-seat [see VALVE *sb.*[1] 8 a]. **1916**, etc. [see GRIND *v*[1] 5 b]. **1936** E. A. PHILLIPSON *Steam Locomotive Design* x. 353 The springs provided to assist the valves to return to their seats are located in the steam spaces. **1963** R. F. WEBB *Motorists' Dict.* 220 It is essential that the valve is accurately ground to match the seat so as to form an effective gas seal. **1970** K. BALL *Fiat 600, 600D Autobk.* i. 13 Refacing of the valve head seating area must be done on a special universal grinder enabling the angle of the seat to be accurately set.

24. *Mining.* **a.** The floor of a mine. **b.** The stratum (of clay, rock, etc.) upon which coal lies.

1860 *Eng. & Foreign Mining Gloss.* (ed. 2) 43 [Derbyshire terms.] *Seat*, or *Sole*, the floor or bottom of the mine. **1867** SMYTHE *Coal* 25 The floor, thill, or seat.., of the coal is an underclay.

25. *Shoemaking.* A piece of leather pegged or sewn to the boot as a foundation for the heel.

1882 *Worc. Exhib. Catal.* iii. 30 The nails..spread as they go in so as to nail the heel closely round the seat of the boot. **1895** *Hasluck's Boot Making* vii. 107 If a pegged seat is wanted, it must be arranged for before the boot is lasted, as it is necessary to skive the stiffener much thinner..than is wanted for a sewn seat.

†**26.** Used to render L. *sedes* in technical senses. **a.** *Anat.* ***seat of the heart***: see quots. 1398. ***seat of the skull***: app. the cheek-bone. **b.** *Surg.* [after Gr. βέλεος ἕδρη, Hipp.] See quot. 1634. *Obs.*

1398 TREVISA *Barth. De P.R.* v. xxxvi. (1495) 149 And the herte hath in the brede therof two grystlewe bones, whyche ben callyd the setes therof. *Ibid.* v. lix. 175 In the mydyll of the herte of a beest is a grystyll bone sette in the brede therof and that is callyd the seet and subtylte of the herte. **1552** UDALL tr. *Geminus' Anat.* B vij b/2 The seate of ye scull, whych we call the stonny seate [orig. *sedes calvariæ, quam lapidosam dicimus*]. *Ibid.*, Thys seate together wyth hys felowe on the other syde, we call the cheake bones. **1634** T. JOHNSON tr. *Parey's Chirurg.* x. i. 337 Hippocrates..in his Booke..seemes to have made 4. or 5. kinds of fractures of the Scull... The 4. is named Sedes, or a seat. *Ibid.* 338 Seate, when the marke of the weapon remaines imprinted in the wound, that the wound is of no more length, nor bredth than the weapon fell upon.

V. 27. Phrases. **a.** ***to hold, keep a*** or ***one's seat***: to remain seated, to keep from falling; also, to retain one's position as a Member of Parliament. Similarly, ***to lose one's seat***.

c **1400** *Destr. Troy* 7409 Than Achilles..Al to hurlet the helme of þe high prinse; But hym seluyn was safe, & his seate helde. **1599** SHAKS. *Hen. V*, I. i. 36 Nor neuer Hidra-headed Wilfulnesse So soone did loose his Seat. **1602** —— *Ham.* I. v. 96 While memory holds a seate In this distracted Globe. **1605** —— *Macb.* III. iv. 54 Sit worthy Friends:..Pray you keepe Seat. **1745** *Life Bamfylde-Moore Carew* 66 The Quack being no longer able to keep his Seat [on horseback] falls headlong. **1847** TENNYSON *Princess* v. 485 Part [of the riders] reel'd but kept their seats. **1881** GLADSTONE *Sp. at Leeds* 7 Oct. in *Times* 8 Oct. 6/3, I never was called upon.. to exercise an option between Leeds and Mid Lothian. My seat for both was lost by my acceptance of office.

b. † ***to make one's seat*** (obs.), ***to take a seat***: to sit down. ***to take one's seat***: to take the sitting-place assigned to one; to assume one's official position, to be formally admitted to Parliament or Congress.

c **1400** *Rule of St. Benet* 1791 Of þam þat er not redi þair To say þe grace & take þer sete. *c* **1425** *Cursor M.* 8291 (Trin.) On a bowȝe he [*sc.* an angel] made his sete Of þat tre þat was so swete. **1593** SHAKS. *3 Hen. VI*, III. iii. 10 On the ground, Where I must take like Seat vnto my fortune. **1789** COWPER *Queen's Vis. London* 2 When long sequester'd from his throne George took his seat again. **1802** MAR. EDGEWORTH *Moral T.* (1816) I. 222 The..judge having taken his seat. **1817** SHELLEY *Rev. Islam* II. 997 Ere this power can make In human hearts its calm and holy seat. **1818** CRUISE *Digest* (ed. 2) III. 238 A writ of summons was issued to him, and he took his seat accordingly. **1847** C. BRONTË *J. Eyre* xxxiv, I took a seat: St. John stood near me. **1855** MACAULAY *Hist. Eng.* xii. III. 203 About two hundred and fifty members took their seats. **1865** H. PHILLIPS *Amer. Paper Curr.* II. 49 [He] took his seat in congress as one of the delegates from Pennsylvania.

c. ***to take a*** or ***the back seat***, orig. *U.S.*, *fig.* to take up the least prominent position, to occupy a subordinate place.

1868 in *Farmer's Slang Dict.* s.v. *Back Seat*, [Andrew Johnson's famous saying in 1868 that in the work of Reconstruction traitors should take back seats.] **1888** BRYCE *Amer. Commw.* II. xlvi. 195 A leader came to care for his influence within his State chiefly as a means of gaining strength in the wider national field... The State, therefore, had, to use the transatlantic phrase, 'to take the back seat.'

d. ***the seat of one's pants***: see PANTS *sb. pl.* 1 e.

e. ***to be on seat***: to be present in one's office. *W. Afr. pidgin.*

1971 J. SPENCER *Eng. Lang. W. Afr.* 29 A very useful one which might be recommended to English-speaking communities elsewhere is the expression (to be) *on seat*, as in a sentence such as 'The Deputy Secretary is back on seat today'; meaning he is in the office, or generally available, as opposed to being absent. **1976** *Listener* 17 June 773/1 If you ask his servant where the district commissioner has gone, the servant tells you he is at the office with the impressive phrase: 'Master's on seat.'

VI. Combinations.

28. General relations: **a.** simple attrib., as ***seat-back, -cover, cushion, frame, lug, pillar, rail, reservation, row, stitch***; objective, as ***seat borer, maker, owner***.

1872 'MARK TWAIN' *Roughing It* iii. 30 The conductor bent all the *seat-backs down. **1976** M. BIRMINGHAM *Heat of Sun* ii. 21, I..turned my head, half expecting to be able to see over the seat-back. **1875** *Guide High Wycombe* 56 [Chair-] *seat-borer. **1881** C. C. HARRISON *Woman's Handiwork* III. 193 A *seat-cover of slate-green plush. **1970** *Washington Post* 30 Sept. B13/4 (Advt.), Morris Katz & Sons

Car Radio & Seatcover Center, Inc. **1860** G. A. Spottiswoode *Vac. Tour* 82 We suddenly saw *seat-cushions, books, and plaids neatly lifted out by the wind. **1881** Young *Every Man his Own Mech.* §781 The front and back of the *seat-frame are connected by short rails. **1875** *Guide High Wycombe* 56 [Chair-] *seat-maker. **1898** *Cycling* 34 The *seat pillar [of a bicycle] should never project more than two inches from the *seat lug. **1891** *Century Dict.*, **Seat-rail*,..one of the horizontal members of the frame which forms or supports the seat, as in a chair or sofa. **1973** W. McCarthy *Detail* iii. 181 He checked in for his *seat reservation. **1837** Carlyle *Fr. Rev.* II. vi. iii, The Thirty *seat-rows of that famed Slope are again full. **1895** *Hasluck's Boot Making* ii. 47 One way to sew them [*sc.* upper and sole] together again is by loop-stiching... The *seat-stitch is another way.

29. Special comb.: **seat-arch**, an arched recess in a wall having a flat place to serve as a seat; **seat-back**, a piece of tapestry, leather or other material for covering the back of a seat (*Cent. Dict.* 1891); **seat belt**, a safety belt for a person in a moving conveyance, *spec.* one worn in an aircraft, esp. at take-off or landing, or one worn in a motor vehicle as a protection in an accident or in an emergency stop; also *fig.*; hence **seat-belted** *a.*, wearing a seat belt; **seat-board**, (*a*) (see quot. 1884); (*b*) = *seat-tree*; (*c*) a board suspended from scaffolding to serve as a seat for a workman; (*d*) a board forming a seat in a vehicle; **seat-bone** *Anat.*, the innominate bone or hip-bone; more strictly the ISCHIUM; **seat-box** (see quot.); **seat-breaker**, a shoemaker's tool (see quot.); **seat-clay** = next (*Cent. Dict.*); **seat-earth**, one of the various names applied to the bed underlying a coal-seam; **seat-file**, a shoemaker's file for smoothing the 'seat' of a boot; **seat-holder**, (*a*) one who occupies a particular seat; (*b*) one who rents or owns a seat or sitting (esp. in a church, theatre, etc.); **seat-house** *dial.*, a dwelling-house, 'the manor on an estate' (Jam.); **seat-iron**, a shoemaker's tool (see quot.); **seat-mate** *N. Amer.*, one who shares the same seat with another; **seat-mile**, a statistical unit denoting one mile travelled by one passenger, *spec.* in travel by air; **seat-mongering**, trading in parliamentary seats; **seat-owner**, one who owns a 'pocket-borough' or a county seat; **seat-pack**, a parachute carried in a pack worn over the posterior; **seat-piece** *Shoemaking* = sense 25 (above); **seat-rent**, the amount paid for a sitting in a church; **seat-seller**, one who sells parliamentary seats; hence *seat-selling*; **seat-sock**, a sock for the heel of a boot or shoe; **seat-stone** = *seat-earth*; **seat-transom** *Naut.* (see quot.); **seat-tree**, the seat of a hand-loom; **seat wheel** (see quot. 1895); **seat-worm**, a threadworm, *Oxyuris vermicularis*, infesting the fundament.

1703 T. N. *City & C. Purchaser* 224 A pair of Stone-peers with *Seat-arches. **1932** *Luftfahrt* (Illustrierte technische Wörterbücher XVII) 128/3 *Seat belt. **1933** *Aeroplane* 27 Dec. 1101/2 'Please fix seat-belts.' (Note! not *safety* belts.) **1959** *B.S.I. News* Apr. 18/2 Arising from the interest now being displayed in seat belts for motorists, a new technical committee of the B.S.I. recently held its first meeting, at which it was decided that a British Standard for these articles would serve a useful purpose. **1966** T. Pynchon *Crying of Lot 49* vi. 150 You're chicken, she told herself, snapping her seat belt... She drove savagely along the freeway. **1970** C. Hampton *Philanthropist* iii. 32 He..came and sat next to me on the sofa, and I thought this is it, fasten your seat belts. **1977** B. Freemantle *Charlie Muffin* xix. 192 They had cleared the airport and the seat-belt sign had been turned off. **1967** J. Redgate *Killing Season* (1968) i. xv. 65 The redhead sat, *seat-belted, talking. **1873** J. H. Beadle *Undevel. West* iii. 70 The wagon made fearful lurches, and our *seatboard rattled over it in every direction. **1884** F. J. Britten *Watch & Clockm.* 233 Seat Board..in a long case clock [is] the shelf that supports the movement. **1891** H. Johnston *Kilmallie* I. i. 6 When the laddie's legs had grown almost sufficiently to warrant his elevation to the 'seat-board'. **1901** *J. Black's Carp. & Build., Scaffolding* 68 The crack in the side of the stack was successfully repaired by the men working from seat boards suspended from the platform above. **1662** *Comenius' Janua Ling. Triling.* 48 The *seat-bone under the loins is called the flank-bone. **1855** Ramsbotham *Obst. Med. & Surg.* 4 The os ischium, os sedentarium, or seat-bone. **1801** Felton *Carriages* (ed. 2) I. 149 The *seat-box, a box made to slide under the seat... It is..convenient to carry linen, &c. **1895** *Hasluck's Boot Making* viii. 130 To make up the seat after the seat has been nicely pared up, damp the leather and use the *seat breaker, rubbing it evenly round the seat. **1877** Huxley *Physiogr.* 236 Each bed of coal is supported by a layer of shale known as under-clay or *seat-earth. **1891** in W. Andrews *Bygone Northamptonshire* 194 The implements of [the shoemaker's] craft,..the awl, clincher.., hammer, *seat-file. **1825** Hone *Everyday Bk.* I. 1184 A large space, which..greatly to the discomfiture of the lower *seat-holders, was nearly occupied by spectators. **1842** Card. Wiseman *Ess.* (1853) I. 378 The English seat-holder surrounded by all the luxury of worsted-worked cushions [etc.]. **1483** in *Finchale Priory* (Surtees) 96 And the sayd S[r] Georg sall repare..the forsayd messuag' that is to say on *seyt house of v rowmys on berne of v rowmys. **1885** J. B. Leno *Boot & Shoemaking* xvii. 137 The *Seat Iron. This once popular piece of kit has been partially superseded by the seat wheel; but many of the best workmen still employ it to set the seat..before using the seat wheel. **1859** *Ladies' Repository* Nov. 645/1 She will tickle the neck of her *seat-mate with a bit of grass. **1885** *New York Times* 26 Dec., The mother, tho' wholly unaware of her seat-mate's identity, did her utmost to protect him. **1968** *Globe & Mail* (Toronto) 17 Feb. 7/1 A television interview by my hon. friend's seatmate. **1976** L. Sanders *Hamlet Warning* (1977) xv. 124 On the night flight to Lisbon ..his seatmate was a German auto parts specialist. **1953** *Wall St. Jrnl.* 24 Mar. 22/2 Mr. Cole predicted the combined airlines would have an annual capacity of 1,470,000,000 *seat miles..by June of next year. **1961** P. W. Brooks *Mod. Airliner* i. 26 The most important non-stop stage lengths have been achieved—notably London–New York, 3,500 seat-miles. **1977** *Guernsey Weekly Press* 21 July 1/4 The 'plane is claimed to be economical with a fuel consumption per seat-mile lower than that of any other modern commercial transport aircraft. **1813** *Examiner* 12 Apr. 237/1 My Lord Castlereagh's *seat-mongering. **1818** Cobbett *Pol. Reg.* XXXIII. 355 On the absolute sway of the great *seat owners over King, Ministers, and People. **1930** O. H. Kneen *Everyman's Bk. of Flying* xii. 217 For use in airplanes, the **seat pack* is generally used. **1946** W. F. Burbidge *From Balloon to Bomber* iii. 45 The 'seat pack' forms a cushion during the plane journey. **1885** J. B. Leno *Boot & Shoemaking* viii. 55 *Seat pieces for common work may be cut from almost any scraps of leather. **1865** *Ch. Times* 11 Mar. 76/4 The incumbent raised the *seat-rents to prevent the parishioners taking seats. **1821** Cobbett *Rural Rides* (1853) 14 Their blue arms and lips, would have made any heart ache, but that of a *seat-seller or a loan-jobber. **1817** —— *Pol. Reg.* XXXII. 14, I did not believe that there could be any such thing as *seat-selling. **1895** *Hasluck's Boot Making* viii. 145 Gent's boots or shoes will only want a *seat-sock. **1878** Green *Coal* i. 28 *Seat-stones vary very much in their composition, the generality of them are clays. **1805** *Shipwright's Vade-m.* 129 **Seat transom*, that transom which is fayed and bolted to the counter-timbers, next above the deck transom, at the height of the port sills. **1790** A. Wilson *Poems & Lit. Prose* (1876) II. 242 '*Groans fr. Loom*', Go,..live o'er a *seat-tree—on nought! **1885** *Seat wheel [see *seat iron* above]. **1895** *Hasluck's Boot Making* viii. 130 Run the seat-wheel evenly round [the edge of the seat], so that it leaves..one straight line of regular indentations. **1893** R. H. Harte *Local Therap.* 158 Lime-water is used with advantage as an injection to destroy *Seat-worms.

seat (siːt), *v.* [f. SEAT *sb.*]

1. a. *trans.* To place on a seat or seats; to cause to sit down.

1613 Shaks. *Hen. VIII*, i. iv. 31 So now y'are fairely seated. **1662** J. Davies tr. *Olearius' Voy. Ambass.* 298 Their Poets and Historians are great frequenters of these places... These are seated in a high Chair, in the midst. **1669** Evelyn *Diary* 15 July, This ended, we were..seated by the Vice-Chancellor amongst the Doctors on his right hand. **1672** Wiseman *Wounds* ii. 91 Seat him [*sc.* the patient] so as it may be for your conveniency. **1725** *Lond. Gaz.* No. 6382/4 The Great Master..seated the Proxy down in the Stall. **1805** T. Lindley *Voy. Brazil* 150 The old man seated me. **1847** C. Bronte *Jane Eyre* xxiii, He seated me and himself. **1859** Geo. Eliot *Adam Bede* xlv, Dinah raised her gently from her knees, and seated her on the pallet again.

fig. **1776** Toplady *Hymn*, '*Holy Ghost, dispel our Sadness*', Seat us with Thy saints in glory. **1859** Tennyson *Merlin & V.* 727 Because of that high pleasure which I had To seat you sole upon my pedestal Of worship.

b. *refl.* To take one's seat, sit down. Const. *at*, *in*, *upon*, etc.

1589 Greene *Menaphon* (Arb.) 37 Ist fit an Eagle seate him with a Flie? **1622** Mabbe tr. *Aleman's Guzman d'Alf.* ii. 100 To seate him-selfe sure in the Saddle. **1765** J. Brown *Chr. Jrnl.* 204 Yonder fly has seated himself upon the surface of a rough stone. **1779** *Mirror* No. 9 We went at an early hour, and seated ourselves in the middle of the pit. **1818** Scott *Hrt. Midl.* xx, 'Wha was it?'..said Effie, seating herself upright. **1833** T. Hook *Parson's Dan.* ii. xiv. Lady Catherine good-naturedly seated herself at the piano-forté. **1864** Lowell *Fireside Trav.* 245, I saw the landlady..seat herself amply before a row of baskets.

†**c.** *intr.* for *refl.* To sit down; also (of animals) to lie down. Of a hare: To sit in its form.

1596 Spenser *F.Q.* vi. ix. 4 The folds, where sheepe at night doe seat. **1609** W. M. *Man in Moon* (Percy Soc.) 7 Long had they not seated, but one knocked at the gate. **1610** Guillim *Heraldry* iii. xiv. (1660) 166 You shall say that a Hare Seateth or Formeth. **1686** Blome *Gentl. Recr.* ii. 76 A Hare Seateth or Formeth, a Coney sitteth. **1760–72** H. Brooke *Fool of Qual.* (1809) IV. 146 There, seating,..I will now tell you, my uncle, says he.

d. *trans.* To cause or enable to sit *in* or *on* a throne, chair of state or office, or other seat of authority or dignity. Hence, to establish (a person) in a position of authority or dignity. Formerly without const., †to enthrone (a king).

1593 Shaks. *3 Hen. VI*, i. i. 22 Before I see thee seated in that Throne, Which now the House of Lancaster vsurpes, I vow by Heauen, these eyes shall neuer close. **1600** E. Blount tr. *Conestaggio* 101 They doubted not to seate a King, at their pleasures. **1606** G. W[oodcocke] *Hist. Justine* ii. x. 13 Xerxes being thus mutually seated in the kingdome. **1667** Milton *P.L.* i. 720 To inshrine Belus or Serapis thir Gods, or seat Thir Kings. **1670** Cotton *Espernon* i. i. 22 By that means [she] seated her self absolute Mistress of that Court. **1715** Pope *Iliad* I. *Ess. Homer* 2 There is also in Mankind a Spirit of Envy or Opposition which makes them uneasy to see others of the same Species seated far above them in a sort of Perfection. *a* **1763** W. King *Polit. & Lit. Anecd.* (1819) 185 He [Burnet] was a better pastor than any man who is now seated on the bishops' bench. **1831** Scott *Ct. Robt.* xxiv, I could ill have kept my seat in the high place where Heaven has been pleased to seat me. **1847** Tennyson *Princess* iii. 143, I find you here but in the second place, Some say the third..We will seat you highest.

e. To put into a seat in a deliberative assembly.

1797 Burke *Let. Affairs Ireland* Wks. IX. 457 The new representative was at that time seated and installed by force and violence. **1818** Cruise *Digest* (ed. 2) III. 165 He was summoned to parliament..and was seated in the place of the ancient Barons of Berkeley. **1845** Disraeli *Sybil* iv. vii, Many of whom he has succeeded in seating in the parliament of his country. **1866** *Pall Mall Gaz.* No. 378. 1341/1 Mr. Kinglake has been seated for Bridgewater.

f. To find seats for; to accommodate with seats or sitting room; to assign seats to. Of a building, room, etc.: To afford sitting accommodation for.

1828–32 Webster, *Seat*,..to place in a church; to assign seats to. In New England..it is customary to seat families for a year or longer time; that is, assign and appropriate seats to their use. **1856** Merivale *Rom. Emp.* xli. (1871) V. 67 The first object..was to seat the greatest number of the people possible. **1887** *Pall Mall Gaz.* 9 Sept. 2/2 Each theatre should be registered and advertised as capable of seating a specified number.

2. *Passive.* To be sitting, to be in a sitting posture.

1608 Shaks. *Per.* ii. iv. 7 When he was seated in A Chariot of an inestimable value. **1703** Tate *Hymn*, '*While Shepherds watched*', While Shepherds watched their flocks by night All seated on the ground. **1791** Cowper *Yardley Oak* 139 Seated here On thy distorted root. **1848** Thackeray *Van. Fair* xxiv, Osborne from his chair regarded Dobbin seated blank and silent opposite to him. **1875** W. S. Hayward *Love agst. World* i, Three young men are seated at breakfast.

3. a. *trans.* To place as a resident in a district or country; to settle or establish (a people, a body of colonists, etc.) in a particular locality. Now *rare.*

1589 Warner *Alb. Eng.* Prose Addit. 161 Seated wee must bee, and here wee would be. **1599** Shaks. *Hen. V*, i. ii. 62 Charles the Great Subdu'd the Saxons, and did seat the French Beyond the Riuer Sala. **1612** in Capt. Smith *Map Virginia* ii. 96 M[r] West hauing seated his men at the Falles, presently returned... The President..followed him to the falles: where he found this company so inconsiderately seated, in a place not only subiect to the rivers invndation, but [etc.]. **1639** Fuller *Holy War* ii. xxvi. (1640) 77 The Carmelites..were first seated at Newenden in Kent. **1719** De Foe *Crusoe* i. (Globe) 197 Providence, which so happily had seated me at the Brasils, as a Planter. **1776** Gibbon *Decl. & F.* x. (1782) I. 295 In the age of the Antonines, the Goths were still seated in Prussia. **1797** Washington *Let.* Writ. 1892 XIII. 406 If..they could have been first seated as tenants. **1910** Hirth in *Encycl. Brit.* VI. 191/1 Whether the Chinese were seated in their later homes from time immemorial,..or whether [etc.].

†**b.** *refl.* To take up a permanent abode, to settle (in a place). *Obs.*

1601 R. Johnson *Kingd. & Commw.* (1603) 112 Whose tenants to injoy the liberties granted to Nepolitans, did forsake their owne..to seate themselves there. **1639** Fuller *Holy War* v. v. (1640) 236 They wonne the Island of Rhodes from the Turks..and there seated themselves. **1755** *Acts Assembly Pennsylv.* (1762) II. 54 Many Persons residing in this Province have seated themselves on certain large Tracts of Land, neither having Property therein, or paying Rent for the same. **1797** *Encycl. Brit.* (ed. 3) X. 693/1 At length, in 1638, the Dutch seated themselves here [Mauritius].

†**c.** *intr.* for *refl.* To settle down permanently, to establish a residence, to fix or take up abode. *Obs.*

1622 *Relat. Eng. Plant. Plymouth, New Eng.* 4 Some of our people..desired..to travaile by Land into the Countrey,.. to see whether it might be fit for vs to seate in or no. **1623** Bingham *Xenophon's Anab.* iii. ii. 48 If he perceiued, we prepared our selues to seat here. **1697** in W. S. Perry *Hist. Coll. Amer. Col. Ch.* I. 44 Abundance of People were desirous to seat there. **1709** J. Lawson *New Voy. Carolina* 141 [This] would doubtless be a great prejudice to the Planters that should seat there.

transf. **1612** T. Taylor *Comm. Titus* ii. 3 The knowledge of God seateth not in their hearts. **1655** Vaughan *Silex Scint.* i. 126 Thy root sucks but diseases; worms there seat And claim it for their meat.

d. *passive.* To have one's 'seat' or mansion in a specified place.

1683 Evelyn *Diary* 13 Oct., A..gentleman, seated neere Worcester, and very curious in gardening. *a* **1845** Barham *Ingol. Leg.* Ser. iii. *Blasphemer's Warning* (init.), In Kent we are told There was seated of old, A handsome young gentleman. **1859** *Symonds' Diary* (Camden) 75 *note*, Although the grandfather of Sir Richard became seated in Cornwall by his marriage with a coheiress of Trethurffe.

4. *trans.* With a thing as object: To place in a 'seat' or situation. (*Rare* exc. *passive* as in 5.)

a. To set or secure in its proper place; to fix in proper position on a base or support. Now only *Techn.* Also *intr.* for *refl.* to lie, rest *upon*, and with other consts.

1605 B. Jonson *Volpone* ii. i, In youth it perpetually preserues, in age restores the complexion; seat's your teeth, did they dance like Virginall iacks, firme as a wall. [Cf. 1667 s.v. SEATED *ppl. a.* 1.] **1662** R. Mathew *Unl. Alch.* 153 Clap into thy Furnace an iron Kettle, and let the bottom thereof seat upon the iron Barr. **1688** Holme *Armoury* iii. 89/2 Seat the Shooe, fit it to the Foot [of a horse]. **1872** *Spon's Dict. Engin.* v. 1804 The slotted head of the common wood screw is frequently split when much force is required to seat it or to remove it. **1916** Hirshfeld & Ulbricht *Steam Power* xi. 207 The valves are all double-seated.., that is, they seat at both ends. **1963** C. R. Cowell et al. *Inlays, Crowns, & Bridges* iv. 41 This must be done quickly otherwise the cement will begin to set and the restoration will not seat accurately. **1972** L. M. Harris *Introd. Deepwater Floating Drilling Operations* ix. 93 As the well-head seats on the previously set permanent guide structure and foundation-pile housing, it is latched and rigidly attached to the housing.

b. To locate or establish *in* a specified place.

1603 Knolles *Hist. Turks* (1638) 143 He himselfe made choice of the city Neapolis..to seat his regall Palace in. **1650** Bulwer *Anthropomet.* xi. (1653) 183 Neither would she have seated the mouth in so eminent, open, and conspicuous a place. *c* **1750** Shenstone *Elegy* i. 30 In thy youthful soul Love's gentle tyrant seats his awful throne.

†**c.** To found (a city). *Obs. rare.*

1612 HEYWOOD *Apol. for Actors* I. 23 Thebes, seated by Cadmus. *a* **1657** W. BRADFORD *Plymouth Plantation* (1856) 368 Their neigbours of yᵉ Massachusets..had some years after seated a towne (called Hingam) on their lands.

5. In *passive*, to have its seat, be situated.

a. Of a country, town, house, etc.: To be situated in a certain position; to have a certain kind of situation (e.g. as regards salubrity or pleasantness).

1577 B. GOOGE *Heresbach's Husb.* IV. (1586) 172 Euery house is not so seated, as it hath errable ground about it. **1593** SHAKS. *Lucr.* 1144 Some darke deepe desert seated from the way, That knowes not parching heat, nor freezing cold, Will wee find out. **1615** BRATHWAIT *Strappado* 83 A pleasant Vale seated belowe Some steepy Mount. **1631** WEEVER *Anc. Funeral Mon.* 284 The Mannor of Shurland seated Eastward from hence. **1633** HEYWOOD *Eng. Trav.* III. F 3 b, [The house] 'tis well seated, Rough-cast without, but brauely lined within. **1655** MARQ. WORCESTER *Cent. Invent.* § 100 To..furnish Cities with water though never so high seated. **1700** DRYDEN *Sigism. & Guisc.* 221 The Garden, seated on the level Floor. **1707** MORTIMER *Husb.* (1721) I. 93 Lands seated on Marle are usually very rich. **1857** *Zoologist* XV. 5618 The house was seated in a pretty garden. **1872** YEATS *Growth Comm.* 52 Seated on the confines of Europe and Asia, it [Byzantium] links the two shores of the Bosphorus. **1877** HUXLEY *Physiogr.* 213 London..is seated on clay.

b. Hence of a person with reference to his dwelling. Also *fig.*

1596 SHAKS. *Merch. V.* I. ii. 8 They are as sicke that surfet with too much, as they that starue with nothing; it is no smal happinesse therefore to be seated in the meane. **1598** HAKLUYT *Voy.* I. 65 When we came vnto Bathy..we were seated a good league distant from his tabernacles. **1601** B. JONSON *Poetaster* II. i. (*init.*), You are most delicately seated here, full of sweet delight and blandishment! an excellent ayre! **1624** WOTTON *Elem. Archit.* I. 5 By no meanes to build too nere a great Neighbour, which were in truth to bee as vnfortunately seated on the earth, as Mercurie is in the Heauens. **1803** WELLINGTON *To Lieut.-Gen. Stuart* in Gurw. *Desp.* (1835) II. 73 It appears..that we shall have a war immediately, or a protracted negotiation with Scindiah and the Rajah of Berar, seated upon the Nizam's frontier.

†**c.** Of a material object: To have a certain place (e.g. in the body, in a building). *Obs.*

c **1580** SIDNEY *Ps.* (1823) XXII. ix, Whose hart..Doth melt away, though it be inmost seated. **1632** G. HERBERT *Priest to Temple* xiii. (1830) 35 A poor man's box conveniently seated, to receive the charity of well-minded people. **1728** CHAMBERS *Cycl.* s.v. *Eye*, In Birds, and some other Creatures, the Eyes are so seated, as to take in near a whole Sphere.

d. Of a seed or fruit (with transferred notion of sense 2): To be fixed *on* something, or in a particular place.

1857 T. MOORE *Handbk. Brit. Ferns* (ed. 3) 8 The part of the vein on which the sorus is seated is called the *receptacle*. **1882–4** COOKE *Brit. Fresh-w. Algæ* I. 175 Dwarf males seated upon or about the oogonia.

e. Of an immaterial thing, a quality, feeling, etc.: To have its seat or abode in a certain place.

1602 SHAKS. *Ham.* III. iv. 55 See what a grace was seated on his Brow. **1622** FLETCHER *Sea Voy.* I. iii, The greatest plagues that humane nature suffers, Are seated here, wildnesse, and wants innumerable. **1691** HARTCLIFFE *Virtues* 263 Their Inclinations, which are seated in the Heart. **1748** MELMOTH *Fitzosborne Lett.* lii. (1749) II. 61 The latter [*i.e* generosity] is seated in the mind. **1820** HAZLITT *Lect. Dram. Lit.* 8 We there see..the same thoughts passing through the mind and seated on the lips.

f. Of a disease: To have its seat *in* a certain part of the body. Also *to be deeply seated*: lit. to be situated far below the surface; hence (often *fig.*) to be firmly established in the system, to be beyond the reach of superficial remedies.

a **1619** FOTHERBY *Atheom.* I. xiii. § 3 (1622) 140 His plague was seated into his bowells. **1647** N. WARD *Simp. Cobler* 6 Fiery diseases, seated in the spirit, embroile the whole frame of the body. **1843** R. J. GRAVES *Syst. Clin. Med.* xxvi. 330 Spongy chancres..were seated on the inner lamella of the prepuce. **1871** SMILES *Charac.* vii. 212 *note*, The disease had become too deeply seated for recovery. **1893** W. R. GOWERS *Man. Dis. Nerv. Syst.* (ed. 2) IV. 333 [Miliary tubercles are] seated in the pia mater.

†**6.** *trans.* To 'plant' with inhabitants, people, settle (a country). *Obs.* (App. *N. Amer.*)

1684 in *Pennsylv. Arch.* I. 85 Vpon Lands not Seated before in ye Dukes Time. **1776** C. CARROLL *Jrnl. Vis. Canada* in B. Mayer *Mem.* (1845) 78 The country on each side of the St. Lawrence is level, rich, and thickly seated; indeed, so thickly seated, that the houses form almost one continued row. **1784** WASHINGTON *Writ.* 1891 X. 366 To see these lands seated by particular societies.

7. To fix a seat on (a chair); to repair (trousers, a chair) by renewing or mending the seat.

1762 FOOTE *Orators* II. (1780) 46 As I was sitting cross-legged on my shop-board, new seating a cloth pair of breeches. **1828–32** WEBSTER, *Seat*,..to repair by making a seat new; as, to seat a garment. **1886** *Pall Mall Gaz.* 15 Apr. 14/1 Then the chair is handed over to the women to be 'seated'.

8. a. To furnish (a building, a room, etc.) with seats.

1818 SCOTT *Rob Roy* xx, A portion of which was seated with pews, and used as a church. **1870** F. R. WILSON *Ch. Lindisf.* 69 The nave is now seated with two rows of low-backed benches. **1899** *Eclectic Mag.* Feb. 201 A..carriage which was seated for fifteen.

b. (See quot.) Cf. 1 f.

1828–32 WEBSTER, *Seat*,..to appropriate the pews in, to particular families; as, to seat a church.

seatage ('si:tɪdʒ). [f. SEAT *v.* + -AGE.] Seating accommodation.

1889 *Daily News* 19 July 2/2 More than half the total seatage.

Seatainer ('si:teɪnə(r)). *Austral.* Also **seatainer**. [f. SEA *sb.* + CON)TAINER.] A container for the transportation of freight by sea.

1964 *Economist* 25 July 361/1 (Advt.), Carriage of all cargo in 'Seatainers'. **1965** S. J. BAKER *Ampol Bk. Australiana* (ed. 2) 112 World's first ship designed solely to carry 'seatainers'—large aluminium containers of uniform size inside which up to 17 tons of cargo may be packed. **1969** *Jane's Freight Containers 1968–69* 332/1 A new 'Seatainer' terminal will soon be brought into operation. **1974** *Australian* 12 Aug. 12/8 (*heading*) Seatainer important facility to Melbourne.

seated ('si:tɪd), *ppl. a.* [f. SEAT *sb.* and *v.* + -ED.]

1. Fixed in position. *Obs.* or *arch.*

1605 SHAKS. *Macb.* I. iii. 136 Whose horrid Image doth vnfixe my Heire, And make my seated Heart knock at my Ribbes. **1667** MILTON *P.L.* VI. 644 From thir foundations loosning to and fro They pluckt the seated Hills with all thir load, Rocks, Waters, Woods.

†**2.** With adverb: (Well) situated; (well) provided with a 'seat' or mansion. *Obs.*

1621 in Kempe *Losely MSS.* (1836) 456 Bruxells..being a well seated and well watered towne as evʳ I sawe. **1663** GERBIER *Counsel* b 5 Your..well seated Pallace with a wood at its back. **1720** DE FOE *Capt. Singleton* (1906) 278 Mr. Knox was so well seated, and could not be supposed to leave such an estate.

3. Sitting down; in a sitting posture or condition. *the Seated Lady*, the constellation Cassiopeia.

1818 SCOTT *Rob Roy* xx, The seated part of the congregation. **1870** *Murray's Handbk. Essex*, etc. 206 Seated figures of the Apostles serve as pinnacles of the buttresses. **1886** PROCTOR in *Sci. Amer.* 3 July 3/3 Low down, between north and north-east, we find the Seated Lady (*Cassiopeia*).

4. Of a room, etc.: Provided with seats.

1829 BENTHAM *Justice & Cod. Petit., Abr. Petit Justice* 37 The appeal goes..from the four-seated court in Westminster Hall to the House of Lords.

5. Provided with a seat, as a chair, pair of trousers, etc. Only in parasynthetic formations, as *double-, hard-, two-seated*, etc.

1841 J. T. HEWLETT *Parish Clerk* II. 163 Several hard-seated wooden chairs. **1898** *Cycling* 21 Cycling knicker-bockers should all be double-seated outside. **1903** *Westm. Gaz.* 25 Sept. 8/2 Two-seated vehicles.

6. *U.S.* (See quot.) *Obs.* exc. *Hist.*

1877 W. H. BURROUGHS *On Taxation* 208 In Pennsylvania, prior to 1844, seated lands, that is, lands occupied by residence, or cultivation, could not be sold for taxes.

7. Of a horseshoe: hollowed out so that the bearing surface rests on the wall of the hoof.

1831 W. YOUATT *Horse* xvii. 311 (*heading*) The concave-seated shoe. **1908** *Animal Managem.* (War Office) 227 Seating is the hollowing out of the bearing surface, opposed to the sole, so that a seated shoe bears on the wall alone.

seater ('si:tə(r)). [f. SEAT *sb.* and *v.* + -ER.]

†**1.** *N. Amer.* ? One who apportions the sittings in a meeting-house. *Obs. rare.*

1713 S. SEWALL *Diary* 4 May (1879) II. 381 Mr. Pemberton declares a Necessity of adding to the number of the Seaters. *Ibid.* 10 June II. 389 Mr. Pemberton..would not have me resign my Seaters place now.

2. As second element, designating a vehicle or article of furniture having a specified seating capacity, as *two-* (*three-*, etc.) *seater*.

1906 *Daily Chron.* 15 Nov. 3/6 Two-cylinder, two-seater car. **1916** H. BARBER *Aeroplane Speaks* Pl. xvi, The familiar biplanes with 80 h.p. Gnomes, and 5-seater with 100 h.p. Anzani. **1923** GALSWORTHY *Captures* 217 Hubert Marsland ..had occasion to stay the progress of his two-seater about ten miles from London for a minor repair. **1941** J. D. CARR *Case of Constant Suicides* iii. 44 A..five-seater car was drawn up before the tourist-office. **1966** 'A. HALL' *9th Directive* xx. 184 It was a massive black Lincoln sedan; a seven-seater executive-style transport. **1978** R. V. JONES *Most Secret War* iv. 39 It seemed that, if we developed the detector to the operational stage, it would have to be mounted in single seater fighters.

seater, var. SAETER, SETTER.

†**seath.** *Obs.* Also 7 **seth** (9 **seeth**). [OE. *séað* masc. = OFris. *sâth* (NFris. *soath, suad, suas*, EFris. *sôth, sôd*, WFris. *saed*), LG. *sood* draw-well, MHG. *sôt*:—OTeut. **saupo-z*.] A pit, hole, well, or pool.

c **950** *Lindisf. Gosp.* Mark xii. 1 Wingeard gesette monn & ymb-salde haȝa & dalf seað [L. *lacum*]. *c* **1205** LAY. 841 Heo nomen þær þær & wel hit biburiede inne deope seaðen. **1656** SMITH & WEBB *Vale-Royal* I. 66 A Seth or pit of that Brine. **1877** E. LEIGH *Cheshire Gloss.*, *Seath* or *Seeth*, an old word, found in some legal documents, for a brine-pit.

seath, var. SAITHE; obs. f. SEETHE *v.*

'**sea-thief.** [Cf. G. *seedieb.*] A pirate, a sea-rover.

c **1050** *Voc.* in Wr.-Wülcker 347/26 *Archipiratta*, heah sæðeof. **1387** TREVISA *Higden* (Rolls) I. 173 Sclaounia..haþ wylde men and see þeues. *Ibid.* VI. 415 þe see þeves of Danes. **1576** CURTEYS *Two Serm.* C j b, Th'one be Sea theeues suche as lye in the straights and corners of the Sea, & take other mens goods from them by force. **1627** DRAYTON *Elegies, Lady Aston's Dep.* 50 Or if some proling Rouer shall but dare, To seize the ship.., Let the fell fishes of the Maine appeare, And tell those Sea-thiefes, that [etc.]. **1891** E. PEACOCK *N. Brendon* I. 59 The sea-thieves were taken by surprise.

transf. **1591** SYLVESTER *Du Bartas* I. v. 340 Those small white Fish..Combine themselves, that their joynt strength doth hold Against the greediest of the Sea-theeves' sallies.

seathin, obs. form of SHITTIM.

'**sea-thistle.**

1. The sea-holly, *Eryngium maritimum*.

In quot. *c* 1265 perh. the water-caltrops (CALTROP 3).

c **1265** [see CALTROP 3]. **1608** TOPSELL *Serpents* 45 The Sea-thistle called *Eryngium marinum*, which some call Sea-hull, or Huluer. **1626** BACON *Sylva* § 568 *Eryngium*, (Sea-Thistle). **1805** FORSYTH *Beauties Scot.* II. 365 The coast..produces scurvy-grass, colewort, and sea-thistle. **1979** *Bull. Yorks. Dial. Soc.* Summer 7 The only kind of flowers were the dark blue sea thistle with very strong prickly leaves but no smell.

†**2.** The echinus or sea-urchin. *Obs.*⁻¹

1661 LOVELL *Hist. Anim. & Min.* 230 They are so full of prickles, that they cannot be held, therefore some call them the Sea Thistles.

†**3.** In full *sea-thistle weed*: ? gulf-weed. *Obs.*

1703 DAMPIER *Voy.* III. I. 14 We..saw Flying-fish, and a great deal of Sea-Thistle Weed floating. **1727** DORRINGTON *Philip Quarll* (1754) 66 We saw some Flying-fish, and a great deal of Sea-thistle swimming.

seating ('si:tɪŋ), *vbl. sb.* [f. SEAT *sb.* and *v.* + -ING¹.]

†**1.** The action of providing with a residence, or of settling in a country; quasi-*concr.* opportunity for settling, footing. Also (*N. Amer.*) colonization, settlement (of a country). *Obs.*

1596 SPENSER *State Irel.* Wks. (Globe) 666 Also doe I greatly mislike the lord Deputyes seating at Dublin. **1603** KNOLLES *Hist. Turks* (1638) 153 Promising also to giue them aid for the seating of them there [in Achaia and Bœotia]. **1611** SPEED *Hist. Gt. Brit.* V. vii. § 9 There are reported to haue come into Ireland..& finding no seating there to haue entered into Britaine. **1624** WOTTON *Elem. Archit.* 6 In the seating of our selues..Builders should bee as circumspect as Wooers. **1699** *Phil. Trans.* XXI. 441 At the first Seating of Maryland there were several Nations of Indians in the Country.

2. The action of providing with seats; the manner in which a building, etc. is seated; *concr.* the seats with which a building, etc. is provided.

1880 *Daily News* 7 Oct. 2/5 The seating of the church is but little altered. **1895** *Ibid.* 11 Dec. 5/3 Additional seating has been provided.

3. Material for upholstering the seats of chairs, etc.

1790 *Pennsylvania Packet* 11 Dec. 1/2 A very choice Parcel of Hair Seatings, of various widths and patterns. **1833** J. BENNETT *Artificer's Lexicon* 366 Seating. Horse-hair for sofas, chairs, &c. **1858** SIMMONDS *Dict. Trade*, *Seating*, horse-hair fabric, American leather, or other materials, made for covering the cushions of chairs, couches, &c. **1909** *Athenæum* 20 Mar. 340/1 Chair-seating..most of this seating is now done with split canes instead of rushes.

4. *Mech.* A fitted support for a part of a structure or machine, usually *pl.* or *collect. sing.*

1844 *Civil Eng. & Arch. Jrnl.* VII. 191/1 An arrangement like that of the plunger pump, which permitted both valves to be fixed in seatings. **1868** FAIRLEY *Gloss. Coal-Mining Bristol*, etc. 29 *Seating*, the place in the pumps where the clack is seated. **1889** HASLUCK *Model Eng. Handybk.* (1900) 71 The seatings for the lugs of the cylinder.

5. a. That part of a structure, etc. which rests on some other part. *Ship-building* (see quot. 1805: and cf. SEAT *sb.* 22).

1805 *Shipwright's Vade-mecum* 129 *Seating*, that part of the floor which fays on the deadwood; and of a transom which fays against the post. **1838** *Civil Eng. & Arch. Jrnl.* I. 178/2 The wedges were then struck, and the weight of the ribs thrown upon their seatings and head joints. **1889** in Anglin *Design of Structures* (1891) 488 All girders shall have seatings of the best hair felt, graduated in lengths so as to insure the pressure being on the centre of bearing when the greatest load is on the girder.

b. The raised outer part of a horseshoe which rests on the wall of the hoof; also, the hollowing out of a horseshoe so that the outer part rests on the wall of the hoof.

1831 W. YOUATT *Horse* xvii. 319 A strip of felt or leather is sometimes placed between the seating of the shoe and the crust. **1908** *Animal Managem.* (War Office) 228 The object of seating is to take pressure off the sole.

6. Of garments: the process of going out of shape at the seat.

1960 *Sunday Express* 11 Sept. 15/4 *Never* wear a slick, straight skirt without a tight-fitting slip beneath... That way there'll be no 'seating'. **1974** LIPPMAN & ERSKINE *Dressmaking made Simple* iii. 53 Linings are essential in straight skirts to prevent seating.

7. *attrib.* **a.** (of sense 4), as *seating block, -face, plate.*

1838 *Civ. Engin. & Arch. Jrnl.* I. 178/1 The masonry at each end [of the bridge] was ready to receive the cast-iron seating plates of the wood arch. **1884** *Health Exhib. Catal.* 55/1 Boiler Seating Blocks. **1925** *Morris Owner's Man.* 77 These two photographs show a valve before..and after grinding-in. Note the different appearance of their seating faces.

b. (In the sense of providing seats or sitting room for), as *seating accommodation, capacity, plan.*

1887 *Pall Mall Gaz.* 9 Sept. 2/2 In no case should the seating capacity [of a theatre] ever be exceeded. **1907** H. WYNDHAM *Flare of Footlights* i, The seating accommodation [of the theatre] embodied every new device for the comfort of its occupants that ingenuity could suggest. **1929** 'E. QUEEN' *Roman Hat Mystery* xxii. 303 We had already borrowed a seating-plan. **1949** M. MEAD *Male & Female* 406 Men holding the highest titles from each village were combined in a formal seating-plan. **1974** O. MANNING *Rain Forest* I. vi. 75 Millman, seating-plan in hand, put Murodi at Lady Urquhart's right and Ogden on her left.

seatless ('siːtlɪs), *a.* [f. SEAT *sb.* + -LESS.] Having no seat or seats (in any sense of the sb.).

1807 J. BARLOW *Columb.* II. 229 What a world their seatless nations led! **1826** *The Ass* 1 Apr. 1 A sleeveless coat and seatless breeches. **1859** *All Year Round* No. 30. 78 The third-class carriages..were..seatless and unsheltered cattle-trucks. **1871** *Pall Mall Gaz.* 19 Jan., Three seatless chairs.

Seato ('siːtəʊ, sɪ'eɪtəʊ). Also **S.E.A.T.O.**, **SEATO**. [Acronym f. the initial letters of *S*outh *E*ast *A*sia *T*reaty *O*rganization (after N.A.T.O.), set up in 1954.] A military alliance, lasting from 1954 to 1977, of Australia, New Zealand, France, Pakistan, the Philippines, Thailand, the United Kingdom, and the United States.

Pakistan withdrew from the alliance in 1972.

1954 *N.Y. Times* 23 July 16/1 Preparations are under way to call an international conference in August or September ..to devise a SEATO for the East to match NATO in the West. **1955** *Times* 31 May 6/7 The programme proposes the strengthening of the links of friendship with France, and membership of the S.E.A.T.O. pact. **1957** *Observer* 6 Oct. 10/6 Pakistan has openly shown that she would expect Seato to assist her in the event of an attack from India. **1966** 'A. HALL' *9th Directive* i. 14 We have the SEATO headquarters here... Bangkok is a key city in the South-east Asian complex. **1970** *Ann. Reg. 1969* 149 The fourteenth Seato Council met in Bangkok on 20–21 May. **1977** *Times* 30 June 6/4 The South-East Asian Treaty (Seato) Organization.. will fade into history tomorrow [*sc.* 30 June]..when the flags of its six remaining members, the United States, Britain, the Philippines, Thailand, Australia and New Zealand, are lowered from the organization's deserted headquarters in Bangkok for the last time.

'sea-toad.

1. A name given to several fishes, as **a.** The fishing-frog or angler, *Lophius piscatorius*. **b.** *U.S.* The sculpin. **c.** 'The toadfish, *Batrachus tau*' (Cent. Dict. 1891).

1558 RONDELET *Gesner's Hist. Anim.* IV. 961 Seetode *id est rubetam marinam Anglicè.* c **1640** J. SMYTH *Hund. Berkeley* (1885) 319 An haddocke, a Roucote, the sea tad. **1700** C. LEIGH *Nat. Hist. Lanc.*, etc. I. 186 The *Rana Piscatrix* or Sea-Toad found frequently in the River Wire in Lancashire. **1884** GOODE, etc. *Nat. Hist. Aquatic Anim.* 258 On our Atlantic coast are found several species of this family [Cottidæ], generally known by the name 'Sculpin', and also by such titles as..'Sea-toad', and 'Pig-fish'.

†**2.** ? Some kind of starfish. *Obs.*⁻¹

1710 SIBBALD *Fife & Kinross* 84 *Stella Marina squamosa*; the Fishers call it the Sea-Toad, for that in colour it resembles a Toad.

3. The great spider-crab (see quot.).

1857 A. WHITE *Brit. Crustacea* 22 The *Hyas*... Mr. Gordon says that the fishermen there [*sc.* Moray Firth] call it 'sea-tead', that is sea-toad.

4. ? *nonce-use.* A turtle.

1754 GARRICK *Prol. to J. Brown's 'Barbarossa'*, He eat a great Sea-Toad! It came from Indies—'twas as big as me, He call'd it Belly-patch and Capapee.

seaton, obs. form of SETON.

Seatonian (siː'təʊnɪən), *a.* [f. the name of the Eng. divine Thomas *Seaton* (1684–1741), the founder of the prize + -IAN.] ***Seatonian prize***: a prize awarded (since 1750) for religious poetry at the University of Cambridge. Also *ellipt.* (in quot., a poem to be submitted for this).

[**1773** (*title*) Musæ Seatonianæ. A complete collection of the Cambridge prize poems, from their first institution..to the present time.] **1795** A. W. TROLLOPE (*title*) The destruction of Babylon, a Seatonian prize poem. **1864** A. J. MUNBY *Diary* 27 Sept. in D. Hudson *Munby* (1972) 203 Finished my first Seatonian; hurriedly, and with brain throbbing. **1908** H. PENTIN *Judith* iv. 68 In the year 1865 'Judith' was the subject set for the Seatonian Prize Poem at Cambridge. **1961** *Listener* 31 Aug. 323/3 Very occasionally in the blank-verse wastes of the Seatonian prize-poems one comes across a single line..that adumbrates the future author of *A Song to David*. **1972** *Cambr. Univ. Reporter* 6 Dec. 391 The Examiners for the Seatonian Prize for the best English Poem on a sacred subject give notice that the subject for the year 1973 is '*Apocalypse*'.

sea-tortoise. A marine tortoise or turtle. Also Comb. *sea-tortoise-shell*.

[**1398** TREVISA *Barth De P.R.* XVIII. cviii. (1495) 850 The see Tortuca etyth all thynge and his mouth is stronger than any other beestes mouth.] **1601** HOLLAND *Pliny* XI. xxxvii. I. 339 The sea-Tortoise hath neither tongue nor teeth. **1681** GREW *Musæum* III. §i. i. 260 The spaces betwixt which [rows], are cancellated much after the manner of the Sea-Tortoiseshell. **1698** FRYER *Acc. E. Ind. & P.* 122 A Sea-Tortoise was brought to the Fort, in length Six Feet. **1750** G. EDWARDS *Nat. Hist. Birds* IV. 206 The Sea-Tortoise is commonly call'd by our Sea-Captains Turtle. **1881** FREEMAN in W. R. W. Stephens *Life & Lett.* (1895) II. 237 A terrapin is..a small turtle or sea-tortoise.

'sea-town. Now *rare.* (Common in 17th c.) A town situated on or near the sea, a sea-port town.

1578 J. STOCKWOOD *Serm. 24 Aug.* 36 Cesarea was a Sea-town, not far from the Mount Carmel. **1622** BACON *Hen. VII*, 61 A maritime Prouince, full of Sea-townes, and Hauens. **1796** BURKE *Regic. Peace* Wks. VIII. 373 These two islands, with their extensive, and every where vulnerable coast, should be considered as a garrisoned sea-town. **1905** *Westm. Gaz.* 30 Jan. 2/3 The darkening roofs of the sea-town.

†**sea-tree.** *Obs.*

1. A huge polyp [L. *arbor marina*].

1601 HOLLAND *Pliny* XXXII. xi. II. 451 [The 'greatest monsters' of the sea are] The Sea-Trees, Whirlepooles [etc.]. **1611** FLORIO, *Albero*,..a monstrous sea-fish, called the Sea-tree.

2. Some tree-like seaweed.

1601 HOLLAND *Pliny* XIII. xxv. I. 402 The branches and leaves of the sea trees, so long as they were under water looked greene, but when they be taken forth, presently dried with the heat of the Sunne. **1666** J. DAVIES *Hist. Caribby Isles* 127 Sea-Trees... Certain Trees which are immediately glaz'd with a salt-peter, which renders them extremely white. Some conceive them to be a kind of Coral. **1755** tr. *Pontoppidan's Nat. Hist. Norway* I. 152 The ocean here produces various species of large vegetables, which are known by the name of sea-trees. **1758** *Phil. Trans.* L. 634 This pivot..forms something like the knot of the sea-tree. **1823–4** in *Encycl. Metrop.* (1845) XV. 298/2 The sea-tree lines many parts of the coast [of St. Bartholomew], has its leaves platted together, and looks as if it was completely glazed.

'sea-trout.

1. The *Salmo trutta*, = SALMON-TROUT 1; also the bull or grey trout, *S. eriox*.

1745 tr. *Egede's Descr. Greenland* 91 Small Salmon or Sea-Trout of different Kinds and Sizes. **1769–76** PENNANT *Brit. Zool.* III. 259. **1875** F. FRANCIS in *Encycl. Brit.* II. 41/1 Next to the salmon ranks in value for sport the sea-trout. Of these there are two kinds: 1st, The salmon-trout (*Salmo trutta*); and 2d, The bull or grey trout (*Salmo eriox*).

2. In U.S. and Australia applied to other fishes.

1859–62 SIR J. RICHARDSON, etc. *Mus. Nat. Hist.* (1868) II. 126 The Sea-trouts of Australian seas belong to the genus *Arripis*. **1884** GOODE, etc. *Nat. Hist. Aquatic Anim.* 267 (*Hexagrammus decagrammus*..)... From San Francisco southward, the names 'Rock Trout' and 'Sea Trout' are common. *Ibid.* 362 With the other members of the genus [the Squeteague] is spoken of under the name 'Sea Trout'. **1891** *Century Dict.*, *Sea trout*, 1. Any catadromous trout or char, as the common brook-trout of the United States, *Salvelinus fontinalis*.

3. *attrib.*

1875 F. FRANCIS in *Encycl. Brit.* II. 41/1 A day's sea-trout fishing. **1904** GALLICHAN *Fishing & Shooting in Spain* 28, I was soon trying to lure him with a sea-trout fly.

sea-trumpet.

†**1.** A trumpet-shell or triton-shell. *Obs.*

1668 CHARLETON *Onomast.* 177 Cancellus in Buccino degens, the bigger Souldier-Crab dwelling in the Sea-Trumpet.

2. A kind of trumpet used at sea.

1776 BURNEY *Hist. Mus.* I. 522 The *Concha, Tromba Marina*, or Sea-Trumpet.

3. A very large seaweed, *Ecklonia buccinalis*.

So called from the use of the hollow upper part of the stem when dried, as used as a trumpet at the Cape of Good Hope.

1829 LOUDON *Encycl. Plants* (1836) 945 L[aminaria] buccinalis furnishes the singular vegetable production called the sea-trumpet. **1866** *Treas. Bot.* s.v. **1882** J. SMITH *Dict. Pop. Names Plants* 419 Trumpet, Sea (*Ecklonia buccinalis*) a strong-growing seaweed of the Laminaria section of Algæ.

seatsman ('siːtsmən).

†**1.** A shoemaker. *Obs. rare.* Cf. SEAT *sb.*

1719 D'URFEY *Pills* V. 241 The Character of a Seat's-man; written by one of the Craft.

2. One who makes the seats of clogs.

1881 *Instr. Census Clerks* (1885) 76 Patten, Clog Maker.. Clog Clasper. Clog Seatsman.

seattica, obs. form of SCIATICA.

†**'seat-town.** *Obs.*

1. A town used as the head-quarters of an army.

1591 SAVILE *Tacitus, Hist.* III. xxxii. 133 It was chosen.. for the seate-towne of the warre [L. *belli sedes*]. **1610** HOLLAND *Camden's Brit.* I. 237 Robert Bishop of Constance ..chose it for the Seat-towne of the whole warre.

2. A capital town, = SEAT *sb.* 13.

1601 HOLLAND *Pliny* VI. xxvii. I. 138 The auncient royall pallace and seat towne of the Persian K[ings].

sea-turtle¹. The black guillemot.

1678 RAY *Willughby's Ornith.* 326 The Greenland-Dove or Sea-Turtle: Columba Groenlandica dicta. **1752** J. HILL *Hist. Anim.* 446 The Colymbus with webbed feet, and three toes to each. The Sea-turtle. **1896** NEWTON *Dict. Birds* s.v. *Turtle*, Greenland Turtle and Sea-Turtle are sailors' names for the Black Guillemot.

sea-turtle². A marine turtle belonging to the families Cheloniidæ or Dermochelyidæ.

1612 W. STRACHEY *Trav. Virginia* (1849) 195/1 A sea turtle, tuwcuppewk. **1764** *Ann. Reg.* 92 Lately taken..on the Devonshire coast..a sea-turtle, about seven feet long. **1860** GOSSE *Rom. Nat. Hist.* (1861) 357 Two pairs of paddles, very much like those of a sea-turtle. **1888** H. C. BUMPUS in J. S. Kingsley *Riverside Nat. Hist.* III. 444 Sea-turtles are of considerable value as food. **1958** J. CAREW *Black Midas* iii. 35 Mendoza had trapped a sea turtle and four men had to lift it into his donkey cart.

seatwell, obs. form of SETWALL.

seau (səʊ). *Ceramics.* Also *erron.* †sceau. Pl. seaux. [Fr., lit. 'bucket'.] A vessel in the shape of a pail or bucket used for cooling wine, etc. (freq. forming part of dinner services of the eighteenth century).

1784 H. WALPOLE *Descr. Strawberry-Hill* 82 A sceau for liquors, of Seve. **1851** *Illustr. Catal. Gt. Exhib.* III. 710/1 Porcelain Inkstands, Seaux, Card Trays. **1869** C. SCHREIBER *Jrnl.* (1911) I. 37 Some Bleu du Roy vases, small,..a pair of sceaux of the same colour. *Ibid.* 53 Picked up..a marked St. Claud sceau at Bencoux's. **1875** E. METEYARD *Wedgwood Handbk.* Gloss. 409 Seaux formed a part of all costly dinners and dessert services, particularly if intended for foreign countries... A choice pair of seaux in sea-green jasper is in the Marjoribanks Collection. **1974** SAVAGE & NEWMAN *Illustr. Dict. Ceramics* 259 *Seau à bouteille*,..a bucket-shaped receptacle for holding ice to chill a single bottle of wine.

seau, seaul: see SEW, pottage; SEAL *sb.*²

sea-unicorn.

1. The Narwhal.

1646 SIR T. BROWNE *Pseud. Ep.* III. xxiii. 167 The Sea-Unicornes,..are of that strength and bignesse, as able to penetrate the ribs of ships. *a* **1711** KEN *Edmund* Poet. Wks. 1721 II. 30 The Angel a Sea-Unicorn espy'd. **1853** KANE *Grinnell Exp.* xxxvii. (1856) 340 That monodontal process which gives them their name of sea-unicorn.

attrib. **1858** SIMMONDS *Dict. Trade*, *Sea-unicorn Tooth*, a name for the spiral horn or tusk of the narwhal.

2. = SEA-BAT 3.

1830 J. F. SOUTH in *Encycl. Metrop.* (1845) XXI. 722 Near the openings of the nostrils is a little, hard, horny appendage, terminating in a tubercle, and hence the fish [*Malthe vespertilio*] has sometimes been called the Sea Unicorn.

'sea-,urchin.

1. An animal of the genus *Echinus* (see ECHINUS 1) or the order *Echinoidea*.

1591 SYLVESTER *Du Bartas* I. v. 382 What stile can worthily declare (O! Galley-Fish,..and Sea-Urchin) your dexterity In Sailor's Art. **1681** GREW *Musæum* I. §vi. i. 139 The round Sea-Urchin or Button-Fish. *Echinus orbicularis*. *Ibid.*, The Great Oval Sea-Urchin. *Echinometra Aristotelis*. **1704** PETIVER *Gazophyl.* iv. 36 Mr. James Cuninghame found this elegant Sea Urchin on the Coast of China. **1896** tr. *Boas' Text-bk. Zool.* 134 In some Sea-urchins the body is almost spherical.

¶**2.** Humorously applied to a young sailor.

1824 W. IRVING *T. Trav.* (1850) 414 The domineering spirit of this boisterous sea-urchin at length grew quite intolerable.

seave (siːv). *north.* Forms: 5, 9 seve, 5 seyfe, 5, 9 seive, 8 seave, 8–9 sieve, 6– seave, 9 seeave (see also Eng. Dial. Dict.). [a. ON. *sef* (Sw. *säf*, Da. *siv*).] A rush; also, a rushlight.

14.. *Nominale* in Wr.-Wülcker 712/9 *Hic papirus*, a seue [*printed* sene]. c **1450** *St. Cuthbert* (Camden) 470 He began þe seiues graythe, And made a fournays for þe bell. **1483** *Cath. Angl.* 327/2 A Seyfe, *iunccus*. **1594** in *Trans. Cumb. & Westm. Archæol. Soc.* (1903) III. 152 None..shall mowe or sheare any seaves between Tailbothe and Sleddaile. **1684** MERITON *Yorksh. Dial.* 72 Then strike a Fire, and leet a Seave I Reed. **1777** *Wallingfen Inclos. Act* 21 Seaves, reeds, whinns, or sods.

b. *attrib.*, as † *seave-busk* (= bush), *-candle*, *-light*; **seave-cap**, the black-headed bunting.

1483 *Cath. Angl.* 327/2 A *Seyfebuske, *iunccetum*. **1703** THORESBY *Let. to Ray* Philos. Lett. (1718) 336 *Seaves*, pill'd Rushes, of which they make *Seav Candles. **1864** ATKINSON *Prov. Names Birds*, *Seave-cap..Black-headed Bunting *Emberiza Schœniclus*.

seave, seaven, obs. ff. SIEVE *sb.*, SEVEN.

seaver, obs. form of SEVER.

sea-view.

1. A picture representing a scene at sea, a 'sea-scape'.

1781 REYNOLDS *Journ. Flanders & Holl.* Wks. 1797 II. 80 The picture..appears to be a sea-view. **1817** LADY MORGAN *France* v. (1818) II. 37 Altering the position of the pictures ..and adding to their number the sea-views of Vernet.

2. A view or prospect of the sea, or at sea.

1790 J. WOODFORDE *Diary* 10 May (1927) III. 188 My Brother and Wife..very highly pleased with Yarmouth and the Sea View. **1844** A. W. KINGLAKE *Eothen* iv. 63 The reality of that very sea-view, which had bounded the sight of the Greeks. **1864** A. McKAY *Hist. Kilmarnock* (1880) 289 A fine sea-view from the hills of Dundonald. **1872** CALVERLEY *Fly Leaves* (1903) 32 Those 'Lodgings with an ample sea-view', Which were..'To Let'. **1897** 'A. HOPE' *Phroso* ii. (1905) 25 About half-way up,..and commanding a splendid sea-view, stood an old grey battlemented house.

sea-voyage. A voyage by sea.

1609 FIELD *Woman a Weathercock* I. (1612) C 2, Captain, what think'st thou of such a woman in a long Sea Voyage? *a* **1649** DRUMM. OF HAWTH. *Poems* (1656) 204 Life a Sea-voyage is, Death is the Haven. **1726** SWIFT *Gulliver* II. iv, Having been long used to sea voyages, those motions, although sometimes very violent, did not much discompose me. **1875** JOWETT *Plato* (ed. 2) I. 224 [He] appeared to have newly arrived from a sea-voyage.

So **sea-voyager**, one who goes on a sea-voyage; **sea-voyaging**, going on a sea-voyage.

1622 DRAYTON *Poly-olb.* xix. Argt. 10 Our Brittish braue Sea-voyagers. **1856** EMERSON *Eng. Traits, Voy. to Eng.* Wks. (Bohn) II. 12 'There are many advantages', says Saadi, 'in sea-voyaging, but security is not one of them'. **1906** *Westm. Gaz.* 10 Apr. 10/1 Captain Alexander Simpson, who has just completed two million miles of sea-voyaging.

seavy ('siːvɪ), *a. north.* [f. SEAVE + -Y.] Containing 'seaves' or rushes, overgrown with rushes; also, composed of rushes.

1684 MERITON *Yorksh. Dial.* 41 Our Land is..full of strang whickens, Cat whins, and Seavy Furs. **1691** RAY *N.C. Words*, s.v. *Seaves.* Seavy ground, such as is overgrown with Rushes. **1851** *Cumbld. Gloss., Seevy-cap*, a cap made of rushes. **1892** M. C. F. MORRIS *Yorksh. Folk-Talk* 156 'Seavy flats' are merely the level pastures which.. grow an abundance of seaves or seves, the common soft rush.

seaw, var. SEW *v.*, to drain; obs. f. SHOW.

sea-wall.

1. A wall or embankment to prevent the encroachment of the sea, or to form a breakwater, etc.

In OE. a cliff by the sea.

Beowulf 1924 Hiȝelac..wunade..sæwealle neah. *c* **1440** *Jacob's Well* 6 þe more þe watyr in þe se is styred wyth þe wynde, þe more it flowyth, & brekyth out, ouer þe se-wallys in-to dyuerse placys. **1565** COOPER *Thesaurus, Agger*,..a water-banke: a sea wall. **1707** MORTIMER *Husb.* (1721) I. 29 The..making of Drains, Sea-walls [etc.]. **1862** ANSTED *Channel Isl.* I. iii. 52 The inroads of the sea..have been checked, wherever necessary, by a sea wall.

b. *N. Amer.* 'An embankment of stones thrown up by the waves on a shore' (*Cent. Dict.* 1891).

1896 *Trans. Roy. Soc. Canada* II. ii. 210 Sea-wall, a gravel or boulder ridge thrown up by the waves.

2. The sea as a wall or barrier of defence. Cf. *sea-walled. rare.*

1879 GEO. ELIOT *Theo. Such* xviii. 327 Many of us have thought that our sea-wall is a specially divine arrangement.

So **sea-walled** *a.*, surrounded or protected by the sea as a wall of defence; **sea-waller**, one who builds sea-walls; **sea-walling**, the building or repairing of sea-walls.

1593 SHAKS. *Rich. II*, III. iv. 43 When our Sea-walled Garden, the whole Land, Is full of Weedes. **1790** *Trans. Soc. Arts*, etc. VIII. 92 A contract was entered into with two companies of sea-wallers,..for the erection of a new wall. **1794** *Ibid.* XII. 115 One of the chief uses to which Chestnut is applied..is sea-walling, or embankments against the sea. **1852** WIGGINS *Embanking* 2 Having been for many years connected much with sea-walling, both in building and repairing.

‖**seawan(e, seawant** ('siːweɪn, -wɒnt). *Amer. Ind.* Also 9 **se(e)wan, zeband.** [Narragansett *seawohn* scattered, loose (in opposition to the strung beads, called *peag*).] Wampum.

1701 C. WOLLEY *Jrnl. New York* (1860) 32 Their Money is called Wampam and Sea-want. **1834** *Mem. Hist. Soc. Pennsylv.* III. 131 Their money consists of beads..these they called zeband. **1851** SCHOOLCRAFT *Indian Tribes* I. 85 Four grains of sewan made a penny. **1870** *Putnam's Mag.* VI. 525 Indian Shell Money generally, the true generic name of which was seawan in the Algonquin language.

seaward ('siːwəd), *adv.* (and quasi-*sb.*) and *a.* See also SEAWARDS. [f. SEA *sb.* + -WARD.]

A. In adverbial phrases and as adverb.

1. Phrases. **a.** *to (the) seaward*: towards the sea; in the direction of the sea; in the direction of the open sea, away from the land. *to the seaward of*: to or at a place nearer the sea (or, at sea, farther from the land) than.

[In the early examples *to* and *ward* form a compound prep. governing the interposed sb. In later use *seaward* seems to be apprehended as an absolute use of the adj.]

α. with article. **1387-8** T. USK *Test. Love* III. v. (Skeat) I. 75 Waters to the see-ward ever ben they drawing. *c* **1440** LOVELICH *Seint Graal* II. 86 Thanne Nasciens his weye gan to take, and faste to the Seward gan he schake. **1535** COVERDALE *Ezek.* xxxix. 11 Where..men go from the east to the see warde. *c* **1582** T. DIGGES in *Archæologia* XI. 225 To the Seawarde this Baye shall allway be defended and garded with a massye banke of beache. **1640** tr. *Verdere's Rom. of Rom.* III. xxxix. 174 [He] wheeled about with his forces to the Seaward. **1698** T. FROGER *Voy.* 142 We discovered a ship two leagues off to the Sea-ward. **1748** *Anson's Voy.* II. v. 177 Mr. Brett..did really discover her..steering off to the seaward. **1852** KINGSLEY *Andromeda* 27 The flame shone far to the seaward.

β. without article. **1540** in *Sel. Pleas Crt. Admiralty* (1894) I. 92 The maryners..imediately wente to see ward withowte ancre or cable. **1567** GOLDING *Ovid's Met.* VI. 508 The River ..to Seaward runnes a pace Through Phrygie. **1624** CAPT. SMITH *Virginia* VI. 216 Three Iles, seene farre to Sea-ward. **1683** CHALKHILL *Thealma & Cl.* 138 The Eagle..Soaring aloft to seaward took her flight. **1810** SCOTT *Lady of L.* III. ix, The billow..That far to seawards finds his source. **1890** DOYLE *White Company* xvii, The wrack had thickened to seaward, and the coast was but a blurred line.

b. In mod. use, *from (the) seaward*: from the direction in which the sea lies.

1719 DE FOE *Crusoe* II. (Globe) 404 It blew a terrible Storm of Wind that Evening from the Seaward. **1855** KINGSLEY *Westw. Ho!* xx, A point where she [the ship] could not be seen from the seaward. **1856** GROTE *Greece* II. xcii. XII. 128 The defenders were powerfully aided from seaward by the Persian ships with their numerous crews. **1882** DE WINDT *Equator* 128 On the approach from seaward Cadiz..presents more the appearance of a Moorish town than a European city.

2. *adv.* Towards the sea or the open sea (away from the land).

1610 HOLLAND *Camden's Brit.* I. 318 Couched betweene a high cliffe sea-ward and as high an hill land-ward. **1725** POPE *Odyss.* IV. 681 The rock rush'd sea-ward. **1849** M. ARNOLD *Forsaken Merman* 128 When sweet airs come seaward From heaths starr'd with broom. **1877** HUXLEY *Physiogr.* 126 The total quantity of matter..carried seaward is something enormous. **1883** KAY in *Law Rep. 11 Q.B. Div.* 500 Helpsford Scar..is further seaward than the place where this accident occurred.

b. *Comb.*

1857 DUFFERIN *Lett. High Lat.* (ed. 3) 395 The seaward-facing crag. **1860** TENNYSON *Sea Dreams* 16 Now seaward-bound for health they gain'd the coast. **1864** —— *Enoch Arden* 559 In a seaward-gazing mountain-gorge They built ..a hut. **1888** STEVENSON *Across the Plains*, etc. (1892) 193 A strange sight it is to see (of an afternoon) the heights of Pulteney blackened by seaward-looking fishers, as when a city crowds to a review.

B. *adj.*

†**1.** Fresh from the sea. *Obs. rare*$^{-1}$.

c **1450** J. RUSSELL *Bk. Nurture* 642 in *Babees Bk.* 161 White heryinge in a dische, if hit be seaward & fresshe.

2. Going out to sea, going to seaward or in seawardly direction.

a **1621** DONNE *To Sir H. W. going Ambass. Venice* 14 After those loving papers which friends send With glad griefe, to your Sea-ward steps, farewel. **1795** SOUTHEY *Joan of Arc* VIII. 603 Marking the playful tenants of the stream..stem the sea-ward tide. **1830** H. N. COLERIDGE *Grk. Poets* (1834) 376 And he Anchises' famous son embark'd Captive Æneas in the seaward ship. **1904** EDITH RICKERT *Reaper* 188 He turned along the seaward road.

3. Directed or looking towards the sea; facing the sea, or the open sea; situated on the side or portion (of a thing) which is nearest the sea.

1725 POPE *Odyss.* IV. 1034 The sea-ward prow invites the tardy gales. ? **1803** COLERIDGE *Recoll. Love* ii, I lay On seaward Quantock's heathy hills. **1820** SCORESBY *Acc. Arctic Reg.* I. 104 Various heaps of broken ice denoted recent shoots of the seaward edge [of the glacier]. **1852** TENNYSON *Ode Wellington* 173 Your cannons moulder on the seaward wall. **1875** *Encycl. Brit.* I. 110/2 The seaward sides of the mountain ranges. **1902** *Act 2 Edw. VII*, c. 24 §7 (2) Two hundred yards from the seaward extremities of the work.

b. Of a wind: Blowing from the sea.

1810 *Naval Chron.* XXIII. 123 Sheltered from seaward winds. **1905** BEDE CAMM *Voy. of 'Pax'* 10 The large black sails were filled with a seaward breeze.

seawardly ('siːwədlɪ), *a.* and *adv.* [f. prec. + -LY.] **A.** *adj.* Habituated to looking seaward.

1849 G. CUPPLES *Green Hand* xi. (1856) 97 The keen gray seawardly eye, under the peak of the naval cap, kept changing and twinkling. **1890** CLARK RUSSELL *Ocean Trag.* I. v. 104 Dry, tough, burnt, seawardly chaps. **1890** —— *My Shipm. Louise* I. xiv. 296 His keen seawardly eye took in everything in a breath.

B. *adv.* Towards the sea. *rare.*

1902 *19th Cent.* Feb. 176 We see roof-ridge and telegraph-wire packed with seawardly attentive birds.

seawards ('siːwədz), *adv.* [f. SEA *sb.* + -WARDS.] = SEAWARD *adv.* In early use *to (the) seawards.*

1517 TORKINGTON *Pilgr.* (1884) 19 To the se wardes ys the Stopull of Craggs. **1585** T. WASHINGTON tr. *Nicholay's Voy.* I. xi. 13 Leauing the coast..we bare roome to seawards. **1621** in Foster *Eng. Factories Ind.* (1906) 241 All our Shipps ..stood off to seawards for that night. **1858** *Sat. Rev.* 20 Nov. 501/2 Near either shore [of the Atlantic] and seawards down to a depth of about two thousand feet, the composition of the sea-bottom varies greatly. **1902** BUCHAN *Watcher by Threshold* 114 He turned eagerly seawards.

'**sea-ware.** Also 8 **-were**, 8-9 **-waur(e.** [OE. *sǽwár*, f. *sǽ* SEA + *wár* 'alga': see WARE *sb.*[2]] Seaweed; esp. coarse, large seaweed thrown up on the shore by the sea, and used as manure, etc.

c **1000** ÆLFRIC *Voc.* in Wr.-Wülcker 135/21 *Alga*, sæwaur. *c* **1662** in G. Barry *Orkney Isl.* (1805) 452 Where they and the cows do eat together sea-ware. **1725** T. THOMAS in *Portland Papers* (Hist. MSS. Comm.) VI. 112 It is lately much improved by a manure of the sea-weed called the sea-were, which grows on the sea rocks, and is thence torn off by the waves and thrown upon the shore. **1763** *Museum Rust.* I. 29 [In Kent] sea-waure or sea-wracks, or sea-weeds, are reckoned a very good manure. **1856** EMERSON *Eng. Traits* xviii. 299 Multitudes lived miserably by shell-fish and sea-ware. **1899** *Folk-Lore* Sept. 278 She was taking home a load of sea-ware in a cart.

'**sea-washed,** *a.* **a.** Washed by the sea; exposed to the 'wash' of the sea.

1762-9 FALCONER *Shipwr.* III. 769 And those yet breathing on the sea-wash'd ground. **1830** SCOTT *Auchindrane* II. i, Our mighty Earl forsakes his sea-wash'd castle. **1890** 'R. BOLDREWOOD' *Col. Reformer* (1891) 113 The moon-lighted, sea-washed verandah.

b. *sea-washed turf*, a dense turf found in coastal regions of northern England.

1931 R. BEALE *Bk. Lawn* vi. 56 Turf can roughly be divided into three categories—Cumberland, Sea-washed or Marsh; Down, Heath or Moorland; and Meadow Turf. **1954** A. G. L. HELLYER *Encycl. Garden Work* 137/1 Sea-washed turf or Cumberland turf..owes its fineness to the fact that it is washed by salt water at high tides. **1962** I. GREENFIELD *Turf Culture* ii. 73 One [variety of creeping bent]..is a common constituent of the sea-washed turf used for bowling greens. **1977** *Lancs. Life* Nov. 82/4 Lancashire's only herd of wintering wild Bewick swans from Siberia..crop the sea-washed turf.

'**sea-water.**

1. The water of the sea, or water taken from the sea.

c **1000** *Sax. Leechd.* (Rolls) II. 28 Celeþonian seaw & sæwæter. *c* **1175** *Lamb. Hom.* 159 þe tere þet mon wepð for his aȝen sunne is alse salt water, and þer fore hit is inemned see water. *c* **1450** *Mirk's Festial* 167 Wyth his hond wyth a lytyll schell he toke of þe see-watyr and powret into þat put. **1601** HOLLAND *Pliny* XXXI. vii. II. 416 The salt made of sea-water. **1610** SHAKS. *Temp.* I. ii. 462 Sea water shalt thou drinke. **1657** W. COLES *Adam in Eden* xlvi. 90 On the Essex and Kentish shores, as far as the brackish Sea-water commeth. **1771** SMOLLETT *Humph. Cl.* 8 Aug. (1815) 282 Being drenched with sea-water. **1850** TENNYSON *In Mem.* xix. 6 The salt sea-water passes by. **1888** F. HUME *Mme. Midas* I. Prol., A rough blue suit of clothes, all torn and stained by sea-water.

b. *pl.*

1697 POTTER *Antiq. Greece* II. iv. (1715) 222 If the Sea-waters could be procur'd, they were preferr'd before all others. **1860** WRAXALL *Life in Sea* xv. 308 The iridescence of the sea-waters is most generally produced by living light-bearers.

c. *attrib.* and *Comb.*

1588 SHAKS. *L.L.L.* I. ii. 86 Tell me precisely of what complexion? *Boy.* Of the sea-water Greene sir. **1596** *Will* in *Longman's Mag.* Apr. (1905) 534 My see-water colored green cloke.

†**2.** A precious stone, the AQUAMARINE I. *Obs.*

[**1598**: cf. AQUAMARINE I.] **1617** MORYSON *Itin.* I. 235 Round stones called *Cornioli*, of yellow colour and others of white, called the Sea-water of India.

'**seaway, sea-way.**

1. a. A way over the sea; the sea as a means of communication; the open sea. Also (*nonce-use*) a channel made for the sea.

a **1000** *Ags. Ps.* viii. 8 (Thorpe) Fleoȝende fuȝlas, and sæfiscas, þa farað ȝeond þa sæ-weȝas. [Vulg. *qui perambulant semitas maris.*] *c* **1425** *Eng. Conq. Irel.* xxxiii. 80 From thens thay wentten to lysmore,..robbeden & prayeden, & by the see wey senten many grete prayes to Watyrford. **1856** KANE *Arct. Expl.* I. xxiv. 323 We passed beyond the protection of the straits into the open seaway. **1890** 'R. BOLDREWOOD' *Col. Reformer* (1891) 432 The graceful craft, leaning to the ..south wind, swept forth towards the sea-way. **1891** J. WINSOR *Columbus* App. 641 Sebastian Münster, in his maps ..makes a clear seaway to the Moluccas somewhere in the latitude of the Strait of Belle Isle.

b. An artificial or natural channel connecting two tracts of sea.

1866 *Daily Tel.* 11 Jan. 5/4 Xerxes cut a sea-way through Mount Athos. **1977** A. HALLAM *Planet Earth* 222/1 Towards the close of the period the old seaway of Tethys was progressively eliminated as the African plate moved northwards to impinge upon the Asian plate.

c. An inland waterway with passage to the sea, esp. one capable of accommodating large ocean-going vessels. *N. Amer.* (chiefly in phr. *St. Lawrence Seaway*).

1921 A. M. EVANS in *Chicago Daily Tribune* 4 Aug. 21/7 Coastwise trade between Chicago and Atlantic ports.. stands second only to the foreign commerce possibilities offered by the St. Lawrence seaway project. **1933** *Sun* (Baltimore) 23 June 3/1 (*heading*) Lakes-to-the-Gulf seaway dedicated... The joining of the Great Lakes with the Gulf of Mexico..by a $102,000,000 inland waterway was completed officially today. **1941** F. D. ROOSEVELT in *Great Lakes-St. Lawrence Basin: Hearings* (1942) I. 2, I recommend authorization of construction of the St. Lawrence seaway and power project, pursuant to the agreement of March 19, 1941, with Canada, as an integral part of the joint defense of the North American continent. **1959** *Times* 27 June 6/5 The royal yacht Britannia..entered the 2,300-mile St. Lawrence Seaway to mark the ceremonial opening of that great engineering project. **1968** *Encycl. Brit.* XIX. 910/2 The broader concept of the 'seaway', and one which is in general usage, includes the entire system of lakes, locks, canals, and rivers which have converted over 6,600 mi. (10,621 km.) of mainland Great Lakes shore line of the United States and Canada into another seacoast. **1976** *Leader-Post* (Regina, Saskatchewan) 24 June 1. 1/2 An oil spill that stretched 15 miles along the St. Lawrence Seaway.

2. 'The progress of a ship through the waves' (Smyth *Sailor's Word-bk.* 1867).

1787 BURNS *Addr. to Unco Guid* iv, Wi' wind and tide fair i' your tail, Right on ye scud your sea-way.

3. A rough sea. Usually *in a sea-way* (said of a ship).

1840 *Civ. Engin. & Arch. Jrnl.* III. 181/2 The effects of a sea-way upon the Eddystone or Bell Rock. *c* **1860** H. STUART *Seaman's Catech.* 62 Weights at the extremities cause a ship to be uneasy in a sea-way. **1867** SMYTH *Sailor's Word-bk.*, *Sea-way*,..said when a vessel is in an open place where the sea is rolling heavily. **1883** STEVENSON *Treas. Isl.* xxiii, The coracle..was a very safe boat.., both buoyant and clever in a seaway.

4. *attrib.*

1867 SMYTH *Sailor's Word-bk., Sea-way measurer*, a kind of self-registering log invented by Smeaton. [The term is not used in Smeaton's paper, *Phil. Trans.* XLVIII. (1754) 532.] **1907** *Daily Chron.* 6 Dec. 6/4 The Nantucket Lightship, warning seaway travellers of a deadly shoal.

sea-weary, *a. rare.* Weary or fatigued by, with, or of the sea.

a **1000** *Andreas* 862 (Gr.) Us sæweriȝe slæp ofereode. *c* **1205** LAY. 4619 We beoh sæ-werie men. **1901** TRENCH *Deirdre Wed* 101 Sea-weary, yes, but human still, and whole,—A circumnavigator of the soul.

seaweed ('siːwiːd). [f. SEA *sb.* + WEED *sb.*]

1. *collect.* Any marine plants of the class *Algæ* (see ALGA).

1577 B. GOOGE *Heresbach's Husb.* II. (1586) 56 b, Wrap it in seaweede. **1591** PERCIVALL *Sp. Dict., Alga marina*, reeks or sea weede, *Alga.* **1667** MILTON *P.L.* VII. 404 Part single or with mate Graze the Sea weed thir pasture. **1734** POPE *Ess. Man* iv. 292 Mark by what wretched steps their glory grows, From dirt and sea-weed as proud Venice rose. **1762** MILLS *Syst. Pract. Husb.* I. 91 A fresh manure of sea-weed being laid on each year that barley is sown. **1855** DICKENS *Dorrit* xx, Funeral garlands of sea-weed twisted about them by the late tide. **1906** OLIVE MALVERY *Soul Market* xvii. 268 Mattresses of American leather stuffed with sea-weed.

2. A particular marine alga.

a **1700** EVELYN *Diary* July 1645, Ashes made of a sea-weede brought out of Syria. **1756-7** tr. *Keysler's Trav.* (1760) IV. 195 He shewed some sea-weeds inclosed in crystal. **1837-42** HAWTHORNE *Twice-t. Tales, Foot-pr. on Sea-shore* 4 A sea-weed, with an immense brown leaf. **1894** H. DRUMMOND *Ascent of Man* 414 Whole classes in the plant world—the sea-weeds for instance—have no roots at all.

3. *attrib.* and *Comb.*, as ***seaweed belt, collector, -green*** sb. and adj., ***limpet, poultice***; ***seaweed-covered*** adj.; **seaweed-fern**, the hart's tongue, *Scolopendrium vulgare*; **seaweed-marquetry** (see quot. 1975).

1884 GEIKIE *Phys. Geog.* xiv. (1886) 120 The *sea-weed belt which fringes the land has an average breadth of about a mile. **1865** MRS. L. L. CLARKE *Seaweeds* ii. 42 A useful hand-book for the *seaweed collector. **1900** *Jrnl. Sch. Geog.* (U.S.) Jan. 28 *Seaweed-covered rocks. **1865** *Hardwicke's Sci. Gossip* 1 Aug. 190 The *Seaweed-fern. **1937** *Burlington Mag.* Oct. p. xxiii/1 A wine-ewer of translucent *seaweed green jade. **1965** [see KAWA-KAWA[1] 2]. **1976** J. WILSON *Let's Pretend* i. 7 The bunches of seaweed green ribbon. **1979** *Guardian* 28 Feb. 13/2 The skirt is a seaweed green verging on khaki. **1858** H. & A. ADAMS *Recent Mollusca* I. 467 The '*Sea-weed Limpet' is readily distinguished from the Rock Limpet. **1935** *Burlington Mag.* May 233/2 King William's writing-table in *seaweed marquetry, with his cypher. **1967** G. SIMS *Last Best Friend* xiv. 120 The carpet was a spinach-green Gobelin and there were Cromwellian chairs and a seaweed marquetry desk. **1975** *Oxf. Compan. Decorative Arts* 699/1 *Seaweed marquetry*, marquetry patterns composed of very fine elements resembling seaweed or endive leaves. **185.** MAYNE *Expos. Lex.*, *Cataplasma Fuci*, the *sea-weed poultice for scrofula [etc.].

Hence **'seaweeded** *a.*, covered with seaweed; **'seaweeding** *vbl. sb.*, the action of collecting seaweed; **'seaweedy** *a.*, covered with seaweed; characteristic of seaweed.

1832 FR. A. KEMBLE *Let.* in *Rec. Girlhood* (1878) III. 178 Those..sea-weedy shores. **1845** HIRST *Poems* 162 Half hidden in drifted sand, Sea-weeded, mossy, black with age, are bones. **1865** MRS. L. L. CLARKE *Seaweeds* i. 17 The preparations for a seaweeding. **1866** *Intell. Observ.* No. 53. 335 The sea-weedy smell.

sea-willow.

†**1.** The sea-buckthorn. *Obs. rare*$^{-1}$.

1548 TURNER *Names of Herbes* (E.D.S.) 41 Halimus..may be called in englishe sea wyllowe or prickwylowe because it hath the leaues of a wylowe and prickes lyke a thorne.

b. The papyrus or paper-reed, BIBLUS.

1807 ROBINSON *Archæol. Græca* IV. xv. 416 The ancient Greeks..preferred cables of rushes or sea-willow. [*Odyss.* XXI. 391 ὅπλον νεὸς ἀμφιελίσσης βύβλινον.]

2. A gorgoniaceous polyp.

1755 J. ELLIS *Corallines* 68 Sea-willow. *a* **1776** —— *Zoophytes* (1786) 89 *Gorgonia anceps.* Sea-Willow Gorgon.

sea-wind. A wind from the sea; a sea-breeze.

1604 E. G[RIMSTONE] tr. *D'Acosta's Hist. Indies* III. viii. 142 The land windes blow from mid-night to the sunne rising, and the sea windes vntill sunne setting. **1808** SCOTT *Marm.* II. xxxi, Then shall these vaults, so strong and deep, Burst open to the sea-winds' sweep. **1842** TENNYSON *Morte d'Arthur* 48 Over them the sea-wind sang Shrill, chill, with flakes of foam. **1873** SYMONDS *Grk. Poets* v. 128 Fruits such as only the southern sun and sea-wind can mature.

sea-wing.

1. *poet. nonce-use.* Means of 'flight' by sea.

1606 SHAKS. *Ant. & Cl.* III. x. 20 The Noble ruine of her Magicke, Anthony, Claps on his Sea-wing, and (like a doting Mallard) Leauing the Fight in heighth, flyes after her.

2. A wing-shell.

1681 GREW *Musæum* I. §vi. ii. 141 The Sea-Wing. *Pinna.* Each Valve is very like in shape to the Wing of a large Fowl, from whence I name it. **1813** BINGLEY *Anim. Biog.* (ed. 4) III. 459 The sea-wing.

sea-wolf.

†**1.** A fabulous amphibious beast of prey. *Obs.*

1297 R. GLOUC. (Rolls) 2812 Ac after hom þer ssal arise a worm of germanye & þe se wolf him ssal bringe vp. *a* **1587** GREENE *Card of Fancie* (1593) E iv, The Lyon salueth his sicknesse by eating the Sea Woolfe. **1607** TOPSELL *Four-f. Beasts* 749 The sea-wolfe of the ancient writers..is..a Foure-footed Beast that liueth both on sea and land, satisfying his hunger on the most part vpon fishes.

2. A voracious sea-fish; esp. the bass, *Labrax lupus*, and the wolf-fish, *Anarhichas lupus*.

1390 GOWER *Conf.* II. 265 Sche tok therafter the bouele Of the Seewolf. **1632** SHERWOOD, A base, or sea-wolfe, *bar.* **1694** MOTTEUX *Rabelais* IV. xix, I'll maul thee worse than any Sea-Wolf. **1784** ANDRÉ in *Phil. Trans.* LXXIV. 274 The teeth of the *Anarrichas Lupus*, or Sea-wolf. **1879** E. P. WRIGHT *Anim. Life* 433 The genus Anarrhichas, one native species of which, the Sea Wolf, grows to a length of seven feet (*A. lupus*).

†**3.** A seal; a sea-elephant or sea-lion. *Obs.*

1549 *Compl. Scot.* vi. 60 The sycond is the selcht, quhilk sum men callis the see volue. **1598** W. PHILLIP tr. *Linschoten's Voy.* 170/2 We saw..many Sea-wolues [orig. *zeewoluen*], which they hold for certain signes of the cape *de Bona Speranza.* **1698** T. FROGER *Voy.* 67 A great many Sea-wolves lying asleep on their backs, upon the surface of the water. **1725** POPE *Odyss.* xv. 517 The future food Of fierce sea-wolves [φώκησι], and monsters of the flood. **1771** tr. *Pernety's Voy. Malouine Isl.* (1773) 187 There are several kinds of sea wolves and lions. **1839** R. HAMILTON *Amphib. Carnivora* 208 *note*, The Proboscis Seal or Elephant Seal..is also..the Sea-Wolf of Pernetty.

4. quasi-*arch.* A pirate, sea-robber. Also in recent use, a privateer vessel.

1849-50 ALISON *Hist. Europe* VIII. liii. §22. 418 Their enemies were talking about sea wolves and maritime skill. **1860** LONGF. *Wayside Inn* I. *K. Olaf* XIX. vii, Sullenly answered Ulf, The old sea-wolf. **1867** SMYTH *Sailor's Word-bk.*, *Sea-wolves*, a name for privateers. **1884** *Pall Mall G.* 18 Sept. 5/2 Against fast sea-wolves of the *Alabama* type, we are tolerably secure.

sea-worm.

1. Any marine annelid.

1681 GREW *Musæum* I. §vii. iii. 178 Not being naturally Tubulous, but made so by a sort of Sea-Wormes. **1769-76** PENNANT *Brit. Zool.* III. 62 Porpesses..often descend to the bottom in search of sand eels and sea worms. **1800** *Hull Advertiser* 31 May 2/2 Ships which have made long voyages ..are subject to the sea worm. **1888** E. CLODD *Story Creation* iv. 30 Traces of marine organisms survive in the trails and borings of sea-worms.

†**2.** The pipe-fish. *Obs.*

1752 [see SEA-ADDER 2].

†**3.** A sea-serpent. *Obs. rare.*

1799 T. HOLCROFT *Mem.* (1816) III. 227 Finding this leviathan [the Kraken] so familiar to their belief, I next inquired if they had heard or knew any thing of the sea-snake, by some called the sea-worm.

'sea-worn, *a.* Worn or abraded by the sea; also worn out or wearied by a life on the sea.

1612 DRAYTON *Poly-olb.* ii. 218 That on the Sea-worne shore See at the Southerne Iles the Tides at tilt to runne. **1828** COLERIDGE *Gard. Boccaccio* 35 In the sea-worn caves. **1822** 'B. CORNWALL' *Sforza* ii, A sea-worn captain who Had sailed all 'round the world brought it for me. **1871** KINGSLEY *At Last* xi, The old sea-worn mountain wall.

seaworthiness ('siː,wɜːðɪnɪs). [-NESS.] The condition of being seaworthy.

1813 ELDON in Dow *Appeals Ho. Lords* (1814) I. 347 Want of sea-worthiness was sufficiently proved. **1823** W. SCORESBY *Jrnl. Whale Fish.* p. xvi, Every known principle calculated for producing strength, accommodation, sea-worthiness, and fast sailing..was adopted. **1876** T. ROBINSON *Job* iv. 28 Storms prove the ship's seaworthiness.

seaworthy ('siː,wɜːðɪ), *a.* [f. SEA *sb.* + WORTHY *a.*] Of a ship: In a fit condition to undergo a voyage, and to encounter stormy weather.

1807 ELLENBOROUGH in J. Campbell *Cases Nisi Prius* (1818) I. 2 The hull of the ship in this case was sufficient and sea-worthy. **1823** BYRON *Juan* X. iv, My slight, trim, But still sea-worthy, skiff. **1856** GROTE *Greece* II. xcv. XII. 376 Four hundred triremes in a seaworthy condition. **1864** TENNYSON *Enoch Arden* 657 The vessel scarce sea-worthy. **1902** W. GOW in *Encycl. Brit.* XXIX. 528/2 In a voyage policy it is an implied warranty that at the commencement of the voyage the ship shall be seaworthy for the particular venture insured.

sea-wrack. Forms: see WRACK.

1. *pl.* Property cast ashore by the sea. *Obs.*

1548 *Reg. Mag. Sig. Scot.* 61/1 Terras de Terbert, cum manerio, molendino et *lie sey-wrakis* earundem.

2. a. *collect.* Seaweed, esp. any of the large coarse kinds cast up on the shore, as *Fucus*, *Laminaria*, etc. Sometimes applied *spec.* to *Zostera marina*.

1551 TURNER *Herbal* I. K iv, Alga..is commonly called in englyshe see wrak. **1654** in *N. Riding Rec.* V. 161 [Indicted for unjustly taking 10 horse load of sea-wreck]. **1759** MARTIN *Nat. Hist.* II. *Yorksh.* 298 They gather up the Sea-wreck and lay it in Heaps. **1831** CARLYLE *Sart. Res.* I. ii, Wherein the toughest pearl-diver may dive to his utmost depth, and return not only with sea-wreck but with true orients. **1906** MRS. F. CAMPBELL *Dearlove* 29 A litter of brown sea-wrack.

b. A particular kind of seaweed.

1611 COTGR., *Spariée*, a sea-wrecke. *Ibid.*, *Varech*, a sea-wracke, or wrecke. **1658** SIR T. BROWNE *Gard. Cyrus* iii, The Spongy leaves of some Sea-wracks..are over-wrought with Net-work. **1681** GREW *Musæum* II. §v. ii. 248 The Bearded Sea-Wrack. *Fucus capillaris tinctorius.* **1846** LINDLEY *Veget. Kingd.* 145 *Zosteraceæ.*—Sea wracks. **1852** TH. ROSS tr. *Humboldt's Trav.* I. i. 33 To rank it provisionally among the sea-wracks.

c. *attrib.* **sea-wrack grass**, *Zostera marina*.

1829 LOUDON *Encycl. Plants* 8 *Zostera.* Sea Wrackgrass. **1840** PAXTON *Bot. Dict.* **1861** BENTLEY *Man. Bot.* 691 *Zosteraceæ*, the Sea-wrack Order.

seax, seayle, seayll: see SAX *sb.*[1], SEAL *sb.*[1]

seaze, obs. form of SEIZE *v.*, SESS *v.*

seazement, obs. variant of SESSMENT.

seazen, obs. form of SEISIN.

seazir, variant of SEISER.

seazning, obs. form of SEISINING.

†**se'bacean**, *a. Anat. Obs. rare*$^{-0}$. [f. L. *sēbāceus* SEBACEOUS + -AN.] (See quot.)

1656 BLOUNT *Glossogr.*, *Sebacean*, made of tallow or sewet.

sebaceous (sɪ'beɪʃəs), *a.* Also 9 **sebacious**. [f. L. *sēbāce-us*, f. *sēb-um* tallow: see -ACEOUS.]

1. Pertaining to, of the nature of, or resembling tallow or fat; oily, greasy.

1783 *Phil. Trans.* LXXIII. 240 The sebaceous substance generally called Spermaceti. **1838** *Penny Cycl.* XI. 52 *Gallinæ*..Body sebaceous, muscular, delicate. **1859** R. F. BURTON *Centr. Afr.* in *Jrnl. Geog. Soc.* XXIX. 85 The sebaceous odour of the skin amongst all these races is overpowering. **1894** A. MORRISON *Mean Streets* 176 His face was a sebaceous trickle of long features.

†**b.** ***sebaceous acid*** = SEBACIC *acid*. *Obs.*

c **1789** *Encycl. Brit.* (ed. 3) IV. 593/2 The metal [lead] is precipitated by sebaceous acid from the nitrous, in white needle-like crystals, easily soluble in water.

2. *Physiol.* **a.** Having the nature or characteristics of SEBUM; as ***sebaceous humour, secretion***, etc.

1747 tr. *Astruc's Fevers* 104 But why this sebaceous humour should be augmented in this case,..I will not undertake to answer at present. **1878** GAMGEE tr. *Hermann's Hum. Phys.* 158 The sebaceous secretion is closely allied to ..milk. **1899** *Allbutt's Syst. Med.* VI. 100 A dirty yellowish fluid containing..a large quantity of solid sebaceous material.

b. Connected with the secretion of sebum; as ***sebaceous crypt, duct, follicle, gland***, etc.

1728 CHAMBERS *Cycl.* s.v. *Gland*, Sebaceous glands. **1831** R. KNOX *Cloquet's Anat.* 309 It [axilla] is filled with sebaceous follicles which furnish an excretion, having a strong smell, and more or less coloured. *a* **1843** J. F. SOUTH in *Encycl. Metrop.* (1845) VII. 186/2 In many animals there are cavities or sacs of some size, upon the sides of which the sebaceous ducts open. **1870** H. A. NICHOLSON *Man. Zool.* lxxvii. (1875) 615 In all the Deer there is a sebaceous gland, called the 'lachrymal sinus', or 'larmier', which is placed beneath each eye, and secretes a strongly-smelling waxy substance. **1876** *Van Beneden's Anim. Parasites* 134 Another interesting acarus, which is developed in man in the sebaceous crypts of the nostrils.

3. *Path.* Of a cyst, tumour: Formed upon a sebaceous gland.

1872 BRYANT *Pract. Surg.* lx. 652 The external labia may also be the seat of sebaceous tumours. **1876** DUHRING *Dis. Skin* 124 Sebaceous cyst appears as a..roundish, more or less prominent tumor having its seat in the skin.

4. *Bot.* (See quots.)

1899 HEINIG *Gloss. Bot. Terms*, *Sebaceous*, containing or secreting oily or fatty matter. **1900** B. D. JACKSON *Gloss. Bot. Terms*, *Sebaceous*, like lumps of tallow. [So mod.L. *sebaceus* in Henslow *Gloss. Bot. Terms*, 1856.]

sebacic (sɪ'bæsɪk), *a. Chem.* [f. L. *sēbāc-eus* SEBACEOUS + -IC.] ***sebacic acid***: an acid obtained by the distillation of oleic acid. (Cf. SEBIC.)

1790 KERR tr. *Lavoisier's Elem. Chem.* 286 To obtain the sebacic acid, let some suet be melted [etc.]. **1836** [see SEBIC]. **1882** *Encycl. Brit.* XIV. 50/2 His [Kerner's] investigations on the influence of sebacic acid on animal organisms.

sebacin (sɪ'beɪsɪn). [formed as prec. + -IN[1].]

1. *Chem.* A hydrocarbon obtained by the dry distillation of calcium sebate with an excess of calcium carbonate.

1857 MILLER *Elem. Chem., Org.* 380. **1898** *Syd. Soc. Lex.*

2. *Bot.* (See quot.)

1898 *Syd. Soc. Lex.*, *Sebacin*, a fatty substance contained in the fruit of *Myristica sebifera*.

†**se'bacine.** *Phys. Obs. rare.* [? formed as prec. + -INE[5].] = SEBUM.

a **1843** J. F. SOUTH in *Encycl. Metrop.* (1845) VII. 186/2 The sebacine in weakly unhealthy persons is often secreted in large quantities.

sebacious, variant of SEBACEOUS.

Sebago (sɪ'beɪgəʊ). The name of a lake in Maine, U.S.A.; used *attrib.* in ***Sebago salmon*** or ***trout***, *Salmo sebago*, a variety of non-migratory salmon, native to lakes of eastern North America; see SCHOODIC.

1873 C. HALLOCK *Fishing Tourist* i. 31 The Sebago Trout ..is a monster trout. **1884** *Century Mag.* Apr. 905/1 The land-locked salmon called..the 'Sebago salmon'..is.. distinguishable from the sea-going salmon. **1884** GOODE, etc. *Nat. Hist. Aquatic Anim.* 470 The..'Fresh-water' Salmon, known..in different parts of Maine as 'Schoodic Trout', 'Sebago Trout'.

Se-baptism (,siː'bæptɪz(ə)m). *Eccl. Hist.* [f. L. *sē* oneself + BAPTISM, after the phrase *sē baptizāre* to baptize oneself.] The action of baptizing oneself.

1646 R. BAILLIE *Anabaptism* (1647) 173 Divinity admits not of Se baptisme, and permits not the baptized to be agents. **1881** H. M. DEXTER *Story J. Smyth* 34 Those who charged him with Se-baptism.

Se-baptist (,siː'bæptɪst). *Eccl. Hist.* [f. L. *sē* + BAPTIST: see prec.] One who baptizes himself; a name given to an offshoot of the Brownist sect, in the seventeenth century, from the action of their leader John Smith.

1610 R. BERNARD (*title*) Plaine evidences:..directed against..Mr. Smith the Se-baptist. **1732** NEAL *Hist. Puritans* (1754) I. 437 Mr. Smith..being at a loss for a proper administrator of the ordinance of baptism..plunged himself, and then performed the ceremony upon others, which gained him the name of a Se-Baptist.

So †**Se-bap'tistic** *a.*, pertaining to Se-baptists.

1610 R. BERNARD *Plain Evid.* 20 This hath he lost againe by his se-baptisticke way till he be chosen againe.

sebastan, obs. variant of SEBESTEN.

Sebastianism (sɪbæstɪ'ɑːnɪz(ə)m). Chiefly *Hist.* [f. the name of Dom *Sebastian* (1554–78), King of Portugal + -ISM; cf. Portuguese *Sebastianismo.*] (See quot. 1980.) Also **Sebasti'anist** (also *attrib.* or as *adj.*), ‖**-a**, an adherent or supporter of Sebastianism.

1881 R. F. BURTON *Camoens* I. 363 The 'Sebastianistas', as they were called, looked forward to a manner of Messiah. *Ibid.*, The Braganza House used the Sebastianist legend to strengthen Portuguese nationality. **1907** R. B.

CUNNINGHAME GRAHAM in G. C. Graham *Santa Teresa* p. vii, The few Sebastianists who, it is said, lingered in Portugal almost down to the present century. **1911** *Encycl. Brit.* XXIV. 566/2 'Sebastianism' became a religion. **1944** S. PUTNAM tr. *E. da Cunha's Rebellion in Backlands* ii. 112 The political mysticism of Sebastianism. Extinct in Portugal, it persists unimpaired today..in our [Brazilian] northern back-country. **1974** *Encycl. Brit. Micropædia* IX. 14/1 Sebastianistas believed that the King had not died during the battle. **1976** H. V. LIVERMORE *New Hist. Portugal* 165 The national rumour of Sebastianism had now taken firm root. **1980** *Times Lit. Suppl.* 4 July 764/2 Sebastianism takes its name from the myth current during the period of Spanish rule, that Portugal's King Sebastian, in fact killed in Morocco, would one day return to lead the nation to greatness and glory.

sebastine (sɪˈbæstɪn). Also -in. An explosive composed of nitroglycerine, charcoal, and saltpetre.

1884 KNIGHT *Dict. Mech.* Suppl., *Sebastine*... Patented in Sweden in 1872. **1889** CUNDILL *Dict. Explosives* 60 Sebastine. **1890** EISSLER *Mod. Explosives* 39 Sebastin. **1892** *Daily News* 24 June 5/2 A hundred and twenty cartridges charged with the compound were packed in a handbag, with a packet of 'sebastine' in the middle, and with mining gunpowder to fill all the intervening spaces.

‖**Sebat** (ˈsiːbæt), **Shebat** (ˈʃiːbæt). [Heb. *sh'bat.*] The eleventh month of the Jewish ecclesiastical year and fifth of the civil year.

1535 COVERDALE *Zech.* i. 7 Vpon the xxiiij. daye of the xj. moneth (which is the moneth Sebat [so 1611; 1885 *Revised* Shebat]). **1876** *Encycl. Brit.* IV. 678/2 Table VI.—Hebrew Months... Sebat.

sebate (ˈsiːbət). *Chem.* Also 8 sebat. [f. L. *sēb-um* tallow + -ATE[1]; in F. *sébate.*] A combination of sebacic acid with a base.

1794 G. ADAMS *Nat. & Exp. Philos.* (Amer. ed.) I. App. 547 Sebats of the alkaline earths and of alkalies. **1802** PYE *New Chem. Nomencl.* 33 Sebates. **1898** *Syd. Soc. Lex.*

Sebei (səˈbeɪ). Also Sabei, Sapei, Savei. [Native name.] A people inhabiting parts of eastern Uganda and western Kenya; a member of this people; also, their Nilo-Hamitic language. Also *attrib.* or as *adj.*

1902 H. JOHNSTON *Uganda Protectorate* II. xix. 868 The Sabei men also hang to their locks of hair and to their ear-lobes rather striking ornaments. *Ibid.*, The dwellings of the Sabei are like those of the Masaba Bantu tribes. **1935** THOMAS & SCOTT *Uganda* v. 86 Half-Hamitic languages are spoken by the Teso..and by the Sebei. **1953** TROWELL & WACHSMANN *Tribal Crafts of Uganda* i. 50 The Sebei are members of another branch of the Nilo-Hamites, being very closely related to the Suk-Nandi group in Kenya. *Ibid.* 51 Both Karamaja and Sebei fit their gourds with leather thongs for carrying. **1963** M. DE K. HEMPHILL in Oliver & Mathew *Hist. E. Afr.* I. xi. 419 The Sapei were moving to the west, and the Kony to the north. **1967** W. GOLDSCHMIDT *Sebei Law* p. vii, The first and outstanding debt is owed to the Sebei themselves, the officials, the informants, and the many citizens who helped to shape my image of Sebei customs. **1968** P. LADEFOGED et al. *Lang. in Uganda* II. 81 Kupsabiny, the language spoken by the Sebei, has some likeness to its neighbour, Suk (or Pokot), but is otherwise distinct from any other members of the group. **1973** *Sci. Amer.* July 77/1 Brideprice is the largest single outlay of goods that an ordinary Sebei makes in his lifetime. **1976** *Drum* (E. Afr. ed.) Nov. 18/2 All the Kenya tribes of the Luo, Masai, Kisii, Baluhya, Turkana, Sebei, Teso, Suk, Pokot, Nandi, Marakwet, Samburu, and Elgeyo are my grand-children. **1977** Savei [see SAPINY].

sebesten (sɪˈbɛstən). *Bot.* Also 7 sebastan, 8 sebest, (sebesta), 9 sebestin, sebestan. [a. Arab. *sabastān*, a. Persian *sapistān.*

Said to have been originally *seg-pistān*, lit. 'dog's teats'. The word is found in several European langs.: F. *sébeste*, Sp. *sebesten, sebasta*, Pg. *sebeste, -a*, It. *sebesten.*]

The plum-like fruit of a tree of the genus *Cordia* (formerly *Sebestena*); a preparation of this used as a medicine. Also the tree itself. Also *attrib.*

c **1400** *Lanfranc's Cirurg.* 74 Take a potel of water & of barly clensid .iiij.ʒ., juiube, sebesten ana. ʒ.ss. [etc.]. **1543** TRAHERON *Vigo's Chirurg.* Interpr., Sebesten bene frutes lyke prunes [etc.] *c* **1550** LLOYD *Treas. Health* (*c* 1560) R v b, Reasons, myrabolans, Sebesten sede. *Ibid.* Y iv, Take of violettes, sebesten, of Borage floures [etc.]. **1601** HOLLAND *Pliny* XVII. x. I. 511 The fruit Sebesten [L. *myxas*, F. *sebesten*] and the Servises may be graffed and planted both upon the same kind of stocke. **1698** FRYER *Acc. E. India & P.* 294 Pears, Prunellaes, Sebastans. **1725** *Bradley's Fam. Dict.* s.v. *Syrup for Asthmas*, Having boiled all for half an Hour more, put in the stoned Dates chopt with the Jujubes, Sebests and Raisins of the Sun. **1728** CHAMBERS *Cycl.* s.v. *Sebesten*, The Syrians make a kind of glue or birdlime, of the sebestens, called birdlime of Alexandria. **1828** *Lancet* 14 June 326/1 In diseases affecting the mucous membranes.. cardamom, licorice, and sebestin (fruits of *cordia myxa*) are used. **1858** BAIRD *Cycl. Nat. Sci.* s.v. *Cordiaceæ*, *Cordia Myxa*..is known as the Sebesten plum, and used formerly to be employed in disorders of the chest and urinary organs. **1866** *Treas. Bot.*, *Sebestans*, or *Sebestens*, the name under which the dried fruits of Cordia Myxa and C. latifolia have long been used as a medicine in India.

sebic (ˈsiːbɪk), *a. Chem.* [f. L. *sēb-um* tallow + -IC.] = SEBACIC.

1836 BRANDE *Chem.* 1186 *note*, Thenard's sebacic or sebic acid. **1898** in *Syd. Soc. Lex.*

sebiferous (sɪˈbɪfərəs), *a. Anat.* and *Bot.* [f. SEB-UM + -IFEROUS.] (See quots.)

1858 MAYNE *Expos. Lex.*, *Sebiferus*, bearing fat or grease, as the fruits of the *Myristica sebifera* and of the *Croton sebiferum*: sebiferous. **1898** *Syd. Soc. Lex.*, *Sebiferous*, fat-bearing, sebum-bearing. **1900** B. D. JACKSON *Gloss. Bot. Terms*, *Sebiferous*,..bearing vegetable wax or tallow.

sebific (sɪˈbɪfɪk), *a.* [f. SEB-UM + -IFIC.] Producing fat or a fatty substance.

1880 *Libr. Univ. Knowl.* (N.Y.) IX. 122 There exudes from the tip of the body a frothy mucous matter... This is the sebific fluid..secreted by the sebific or cement gland.

Sebilian (sɪˈbɪlɪən), *a.* (and *sb.*) *Archæol.* [ad. F. *Sébilien* (E. Vignard 1923, in *Bull. de l'Institut Franç. d'Archéol. Orientale* XXII. 3), f. the name of *Sebil*, a village in Upper Egypt: see -IAN.] Of or pertaining to an Upper Palæolithic and Mesolithic culture of Upper Egypt; also *ellipt.* as *sb.*

1932 *Antiquity* VI. 193 In the Nile Valley some rather peculiar industries, probably allied to the Aurignacian, are called Sébilian. **1936** L. S. B. LEAKEY *Stone Age Afr.* x. 193 In North Africa at Sebil, the Early Sebilian gradually evolves by way of a Middle Sebilian into a true Microlithic stage known as the Upper Sebilian. **1952** V. G. CHILDE *New Light Most Anc. East* iii. 32 The stage intermediate between the food-gathering culture of Sebilian hunters and the settled agriculture of the oldest sedentary inhabitants of Egypt. **1969** COLES & HIGGS *Archaeol. Early Man* II. xiii. 196 The later stages of the Sebilian material contain microlithic forms, and one associated with aurochs, buffalo and shell middens. Suggested dates for the Sebilian industries range from c. 16,000 to 11,000 B.P. **1976** *Sci. Amer.* Aug. 34/1 A fourth industry, the Sebilian..is found at Kom Ombo.

se'billa. *Obs. rare*[−1]. [Altered (? quasi-Sp.) form of F. *sébile* (†*sébille*, Cotgr.), wooden bowl.]

a. A wooden bowl used in the mechanical assay of ores. **b.** (See quot. 1875.)

1839 URE *Dict. Arts* 826 These kinds of assays [*sc.* mechanical]..are performed by a hand-washing, in a small trough of an oblong shape, called a *sebilla*. **1875** KNIGHT *Dict. Mech.*, *Sebilla*, a wooden bowl, to hold the sand and water used in sawing or grinding marble [etc.].

sebiparous (sɪˈbɪpərəs), *a.* [f. SEB-UM + -(I)PAROUS.] Producing sebum.

1855 DUNGLISON *Med. Lex.*, Sebaceous or Sebiparous Glands. **1876** DUHRING *Dis. Skin* 31 The sebaceous or sebiparous glands are always situated in the corium.

sebk(h)a, varr. SABKHA.

'seblet. *dial.* Also 9 siblet (see *E.D.D.*). [Metathesis of *sedlib*, SEEDLIP.] A basket in which seed is carried in sowing broadcast; see SEEDLIP. ***seblet cake***: see quot. 1855.

1633-4 *Althorp MS.* in Simpkinson *Washingtons* (1860) App. 64 For a seblet to sowe corne 00 01 00. **1852** BEARN in *Jrnl. R. Agric. Soc.* XIII. I. 101 The drill takes the place of the seblet. **1855** *Leisure Hour* 751 The seblet-cake was a seed-cake with which it was once the custom to regale the workmen when all the wheat for the season had been sown.

sebolith (ˈsɛbəlɪθ). *Path.* [f. L. *sēb-um* (see SEBUM) + -(O)LITH.] 'A calculus formed in a sebaceous gland' (*Syd. Soc. Lex.* 1898).

seborrhœa (sɛbəˈriːə). *Path.* Also (chiefly *U.S.*) seborrhea. [f. *sebo-* used as combining form of SEBUM + Gr. ῥοία flow, flux.] An excessive discharge from the sebaceous glands forming a greasy or scaly coating upon the skin.

1876 DUHRING *Dis. Skin* 48 Sebaceous crusts, as those of seborrhoea, are light yellow, dirty yellow, or blackish in color. **1899** *Allbutt's Syst. Med.* VIII. 759 The name seborrhœa..is not a satisfactory one. **1940** BECKER & OBERMAYER *Mod. Dermatol. & Syphilol.* v. 56/2 It is advisable to assume that seborrhea and the diseases to which it predisposes, namely acne vulgaris, seborrheic dermatitis and rosacea, do not appear before puberty. **1973** *Nature* 8 June 350/1 In Parkinsonism the associated seborrhoea is induced by excessive secretion of a pituitary sebotrophic hormone. **1978** J. KILMARTIN tr. *R. Aron-Brunetière's Beauty & Medicine* ii. 22 Even people with fairly mild seborrhea or acne are self-conscious about it.

Hence **sebo'rrhœic** (also **-rrheic**) *a.*, of the nature of, or pertaining to, seborrhœa.

1893 CROCKER *Dis. Skin* (ed. 2) 696 Seborrhœic Dermatitis. *Ibid.* 355 The last-named wishes to revert to the old term of seborrhœic wart. **1899** *Allbutt's Syst. Med.* VIII. 904 The diplococcus of seborrhœic eczema. **1955** *Sci. News Let.* 12 Feb. 104/3 The scientists have reported using the glands in cases of..seborrheic dermatitis. **1971** [see *liver spot* s.v. LIVER *sb.*[1] 7]. **1977** *Lancet* 27 Aug. 440/2 One troublesome feature.., the seborrhœic scalp rash, responds excellently to application of a tar shampoo.

sebotrophic (sɛbəʊˈtrəʊfɪk), *a. Physiol.* Also -tropic (-ˈtrəʊpɪk, -ˈtrɒpɪk). [f. SEB(UM + -O + -TROPHIC, -TROPIC.] Tending to stimulate sebaceous activity.

1957 LORINCZ & LANCASTER in *Science* 19 July 124/1 Methods of preparation and assay of a crude extract of anterior pituitary glands of hogs showing tropic effects on sebaceous, preputial, and Harderian glands in the rat are described. These effects can be called sebotropic because the ectodermal glands affected produce secretions rich in lipids. **1968** EBLING & ROOK in A. Rook et al. *Textbk. Dermatol.* II. xlv. 1335/2 Biological tests for sebotrophic activity..were carried out..on the preputial gland. **1973** [see SEBORRHŒA].

sebow, variant of SYBOW.

‖**sebum** (ˈsiːbəm). *Phys.* [mod.L. use of L. *sēbum* (also *sēvum*) suet, grease.] The fatty secretion which lubricates the hair and the skin.

[**1706** PHILLIPS (ed. Kersey), *Sevum*, or *Sebum*, Sewet, Tallow. **1728** CHAMBERS *Cycl.* s.v. *Glandula*, *Glandulæ Sebaceæ*..separate a greasy Matter, like *Sebum*, or Tallow. **1845** TODD & BOWMAN *Phys. Anat.* I. 83 The softer kinds of fat were denominated by the older anatomists *pinguedo*, *lard*; and the more solid, *sebum* or *sevum*, suet, tallow.] **1876** DUHRING *Dis. Skin* 33 The sebaceous glands secrete a fatty product known as sebum or sebaceous matter. **1887** AFFLECK in *Encycl. Brit.* XXII. 121/1 The sebum frequently accumulates in the sebaceous ducts, giving rise to the minute black points..to which the term comedones is applied. **1899** *Allbutt's Syst. Med.* VIII. 666 The secretion of sebum is diminished.

sebundy (sɪˈbʌndɪ). Also 8 sibbandy, -endy, sybundee, 8–9 sebundee, sib(b)undy, 9 sib(b)undi, sib(b)andi, seebundee, -y, shi-, sirbandi, sibondi. [Urdū *sibandī.*] A class of irregular soldiers in the Indian army chiefly employed in police and revenue duties and on local government service; also a member of this class.

1782 BURKE *Nabob of Arcot's Debts* App. IV. Wks. 1792 II. 536 One considerable charge upon the nabob's country was for extraordinary sibbendies, sepoys, and horsemen, who appeared to us to be an unnecessary incumbrance on the revenue. **1784** *Report* in Carmichael *Vizagapatam* 209 Sibbandy & Pike [= *pâik*] peons for the forts and hilly countries. **1803** WELLINGTON in Gurw. *Desp.* (1837) II. 171 In times of war the sebundy of the country are hired and paid. *a* **1821** R. LINDSAY *Anecd. Ind. Life* (1840) 19 *note*, Here I found him in the command of a regiment of Sebundees, or native militia. **1823** SIR J. MALCOLM *Central India* I. 326 In all these services Ameer Khan and his followers were employed as Sebundy, or local militia. **1858** J. B. NORTON *Topics* 168 An addition to the armed sebundies of Vizagapatam was necessary to this end, and it was proposed to locate a body of this force..in the very considerable town of Jeypoor.

attrib. **1803** WELLINGTON in Gurw. *Desp.* (1837) II. 169 It would be best to authorize the collectors to raise sebundy troops for these services.

sec (sɛk), *a.* [Fr.] Of champagne and other wines: = DRY *a.* 8. Also *fig.* Cf. *extra sec* s.v. EXTRA *adv.* a.

1863 T. G. SHAW *Wine, Vine & Cellar* xviii. 334 It is evident that the word 'sack' cannot be understood to have denoted sec (dry). **1891**, etc. [see EXTRA *adv.* a]. **1899** *Judge* (N.Y.) XVI. 419/2 Berton 'sec' Champagne. **1931** *Morning Post* 10 Aug. 4/3 The Bayreuth Festival... Wagner sec. **1960** WODEHOUSE *Jeeves in Offing* xvi. 165, I was in my room, having shed the moistened outer crust and substituted something a bit more *sec* in pale flannel.

sec, obs. form of SACK *sb.*[1], SICK *a.*

sec., abbreviation of SECANT, SECOND, SECRETARY, SECTION, etc.

1641 in *Nicholas Pap.* (1886) 8 Mr. Sec. Vane. **1878** *Athletic World* 5 Apr. 3/1 The Mile..was..won..in the fair time of 4 min. 40 3-5th sec. **1881** *Sportsman's Year-bk.* 125 A very fine race... Time, 1 min. 16⅗ secs. **1869** *Bradshaw's Railway Man.* XXI. 48 *Officers.*—Gen. Man., James Smithells; Sec., Archibald Gibson. **1953** WODEHOUSE *Performing Flea* 130 One of those tall, statuesque, frozen-faced secs who took his dictation in an aloof, revolted sort of way. **1956** A. WILSON *Anglo-Saxon Attitudes* II. ii. 319 'I'm afraid I can't stop now. I'm late for an appointment.' 'It won't take a sec,' said Vin. *a* **1960** E. M. FORSTER *Maurice* (1971) vi. 37 Wait a sec, and I'll come too. **1962** A. LURIE *Love & Friendship* x. 199, I wonder if you could hold the baby for me, Missus Turner, please, just for a sec. **1979** M. BOYCE *I was There!* 14/2 The Rugby Club's General Committee Banned 'Sine Die' their ticket Sec, my Uncle Will.

secability (sɛkəˈbɪlɪtɪ). *rare*[−1]. [ad. late L. *secābilitās*, f. *secābilis*: see next and -ITY.] Capability of being cut.

1842 T. GRAHAM *Elem. Chem.* I. iii. 119 It is possible that it [matter] may not be indefinitely divisible; that there may be a limit to the successive division or secability of its parts.

†**secable**, *a. Obs. rare*[−1]. [ad. late L. *secābilis*, f. L. *secāre* to cut: see -ABLE.] Capable of being cut.

1642 E. WIRLEY *Prisoners Rep.* A 4 b, 'T was a thicke wall built with soft freestone, and therefore the more secable.

‖**Secale** (sɪˈkeɪliː). *Bot.* [L. *secāle* rye.] A genus of grasses, represented by the common rye.

In *Pharmacy*, formerly used for *secale cornutum*, ergot.

1584 COGAN *Haven Health* v. (1612) 26 Secale commonly called Rie, a Graine much vsed in Bread. **1785** MARTYN *Rousseau's Bot.* xiii. (1794) 143 Secale or Rie has two flowers included in the same calyx.

‖**secament.** *Obs.*[−0] [ad. L. *secāmentum* (only pl., carved work), f. *secāre* to cut: see -MENT.] (See quot.)

1656 BLOUNT *Glossogr.*, *Secament*, that which is cut or shread from a Log or Block, as chips, and such like.

secancy (ˈsɛkənsɪ). [f. SECANT: see -CY.] The property or fact of being secant.

1857 C. DAVIES & W. G. PECK *Math. Dict.* s.v. *Secant*, If a secant line be revolved about one of the points of secancy until the other point of secancy coincides with it the secant becomes a tangent.

‖**'secans.** *Obs.* Pl. se'cantes. [L. form of next.] = SECANT *sb.*

The mod.L. *secans* in this use was introduced by Thomas Finck *Geom. Rotundi*, Basle 1583, pp. 73, 76.

1599 E. WRIGHT *Err. Navig.* D 1, The Secans of the latitude of each poynt. *Ibid.*, The Secantes answerable to the latitudes of each point or parellel.

secant ('si:kənt), *a.* and *sb.* [a. L. *secant-em*, pres. pple. of *secāre* to cut. Cf. F. *sécant* adj., *sécante* sb., Sp., Pg., It. *secante*.]

A. *adj. Geom.* Of a line or surface in relation to another line or surface; Cutting, intersecting.

1593 BLUNDEVIL *Exerc.* II. (1597) 57 b, They call the line Secant the Hipothenuse. **1864** WEBSTER, *Secant plane*, a plane cutting a surface or solid. **1866** PROCTOR *Handbk. Stars* 16 By increasing the true length in the proportion of the whole length of the secant line.. to that part of it which lies between the point of projection and the division-point in P.A.

B. *sb.* (Ellipt. for *secant line*.) **a.** *Trig.* One of the three fundamental trigonometrical functions (cf. TANGENT, SINE): *orig.* The length of a straight line drawn from the centre of a circular arc through one end of the arc, and terminated by the tangent or line touching the arc at the other end; in mod. use, the ratio of this line to the radius, or (equivalently, as a function of an angle), the ratio of the hypotenuse of a right-angled triangle to that of one side, the given angle (or, if obtuse, its supplement) being that contained between them. Abbrev. *sec.* See SECANS.

1593 BLUNDEVIL *Exerc.* II. (1597) 104 The Table of Secants. **1681** COLVIL *Whigs Supplic.* (1751) 23 In which scheme if ye draw some lines, Ye may have secants, tangents, signs. **1752** *Phil. Trans.* XLVII. 443 We have.. to find.. the secant of the spherical hypothenuse. **1811** HUTTON *Course Math.* III. 55 The secant of an arc. **1868** LOCKYER *Elem. Astron.* §516. 243 The secant of *A* (written *sec. A*).

b. *Geom.* A line that cuts another; esp. a straight line that cuts a curve in two or more parts.

1684 *Elem. Geom.* 24 From the Center D, draw the Secant DC. **1728** CHAMBERS *Cycl.* s.v., The Line AM.. is a Secant of the Circle AED. **1798** HUTTON *Course Math.* I. 304 The Angle formed, Without a Circle, by two Secants, is Measured by Half the Difference of the Intercepted Arcs. **1881** CASEY *Sequel to Euclid* 92 If from any point two tangents be drawn to a circle, the points of contact and the points of intersection of any secant from the same point form a harmonic system of points. **1887** J. H. SMITH *Geometr. Conic Sect.* 18 Hence a secant to the parabola cuts the curve in two points only.

secar, obs. form of SAKER[2].

1699 ROBERTS *Voy. Levant* 36 Jacomores Castle.. fortified with 20 Secar Iron Guns.

secateurs (sɛkə'tɜ:z, 'sɛkətɜ:z, formerly ‖sekatœrz), *sb. pl.* Also **sécateurs.** [ad. F. *sécateur*, as if ad. L. **secātor* (bad form for *sector*), agent-n. f. *secāre* to cut.] A kind of pruning shears with crossed blades. *rare* in *sing.*

1881 *Encycl. Brit.* XII. 234/1 For pruning purposes a variety of instruments have been invented, under the names of sécateurs, pruning-shears, pruning-scissors, &c. **1901** *Gardener* 12 Jan. 1052/2 In certain positions it is difficult to sever a shoot with the knife without steadying it with the other hand; the sécateurs steady and cut at the same time. **1909** *Daily Chron.* 13 Mar. 7/6 All dead stems should be removed with a sharp knife or secateur. **1924** H. H. THOMAS *Compl. Amateur Gardener* vii. 67 The pruning outfit should consist of.. a hone or sharpening stone,.. and sécateurs. **1937** *Carter's Blue Bk. Gardening 1937* 365 (Advt.), The amazing manner in which this Secateur quickly and cleanly cuts off the thickest of branches, very soon becomes a fascination to the user. **1967** E. MAVOR *Redoubt* x. 172 She dressed her enormous bulk in.. a baize gardening apron with capacious pockets for her bass and secateurs. **1968** R. H. W. BROWN *Gardening Complete* ii. 27 The tools which the gardener must have for a start are two spades, a fork, a rake, three hoes, a trowel, a dibber, a pair of secateurs, [etc.]. **1977** P. THROWER *Every Day Gardening* i. 16/1 (*caption*) If the garden includes numerous trees, shrubs and fruit trees a pair of long-handled secateurs is especially useful.

†**se'cation.** *Obs.* [Badly f. L. *secāre* to cut + -ATION.] (See quot. 1656.)

1656 BLOUNT *Glossogr.*, *Secation*, a cutting, sawing, parting, or dividing. **1657** J. WATTS *Scribe, Pharisee*, etc. I. 21 The best Physician comes seldom, and very hardly, to searing, or secation of a Member from the body.

secatour, variant of SECUTOR *Obs.*, executor.

secau, obs. form of SICCA[1].

†**'seccatored,** *ppl. a. Obs. rare*$^{-1}$. [f. It. *seccatore* a bore.] Bored.

1763 EARL MARCH *Let. to Selwyn* 1 July in Jesse *Selwyn & Contemp.* (1843) I. 247 Williams suspects you begin to be a little *seccatored*.

secchell, obs. form of SATCHEL *sb.*

Secchi ('sɛki). Also secchi. [The name of Angelo *Secchi* (1818–78), Italian astronomer.] *Secchi('s) disc*: a type of opaque white disc which is used in determining the transparency of water; the disc, maintained in a horizontal attitude, is allowed to sink and the depth at which it ceases to be visible from the surface is recorded.

Secchi and Cialdi first described the use of discs of this kind in 1865 (*Compt. Rend.* LXI. 101).

1913 *Science* 14 Nov. 703/1 The inland lakes of Wisconsin are not very transparent; the transparency, as shown by Secchi's disk, varying from less than 1 m. to about 7 m. **1931** *Trans. Wisconsin Acad.* XXVI. 337 The transparency as determined by the Secchi disc shows some correlation with the amount of organisms present in the water. *Ibid.* 419 Transparency.. is measured by the visibility of Secchi's disc. **1963** G. L. PICKARD *Descriptive Physical Oceanogr.* iii. 23 The colour of sea-water can be judged most conveniently against the white Secchi disc.. as it is lowered to determine the transparency of the water. **1975** *New Yorker* 12 May 80/3 They threw a secchi disc into the ocean to measure turbidity.

‖**secco** ('sekko), *a.* and *sb.* [It. *secco*:—L. *siccus* dry.] **A.** *adj.* in *Music.* (See quots.)

1876 STAINER & BARRETT *Dict. Mus. Terms*, *Sec* (Fr.), *Secco* (It.), dry, unadorned, plain, as *recitativo secco*, plain recitative, that is, without band accompaniments. **1883** GROVE *Dict. Mus.* III. 454/2 *Secco Recitative*, accurately *Recitativo Secco*—that is 'dry'... The simplest form of Declamatory Music, unrelieved either by Melody or Rhythm, and accompanied only by a Thoroughbass.

B. *sb.* **1.** In *Painting*, ellipt. for It. *fresco secco*, 'dry fresco', a process of painting on dry plaster with colours mixed with water.

1852 ROCK *Ch. of Fathers* III. I. 194 *note*, It is painted in secco, over the western side of the great arch. **1854** FAIRHOLT *Dict. Terms Art*, *Secco* (Ital.), fresco painting 'in secco' is that kind which absorbs the colours into the plaster, and gives them a dry, sunken appearance.

2. In *Music*, ellipt. for 'secco recitative'.

1960 *Times* 2 July 12/2 There are three tenor recitatives accompanied by piano in a modern equivalent of the old *secco*. **1969** *Daily Tel.* 18 Jan. 17/5 The beloved melody contains no fewer than 18 appoggiaturas actually written out by Mozart (he never does in seccos).

seccoon, variant of SECONDE *Fencing*.

seccotine ('sɛkəʊti:n), *sb.* [App. suggested by It. *secco* dry. Cf. -INE.] The maker's name for a composition serving as a strong adhesive. Hence **'seccotine** *v. trans.*, to cement with seccotine.

1894 *Trade Marks Jrnl.* 19 Dec. 1040 Seccotine. **1903** GROSS & COLE *Mod. Microscopy* (ed. 3) 220 Seccotine or some other liquid glue may be used with advantage. **1903** *Daily News* 23 May 8/4 These spots are sometimes made of velvet seccotined to the material that they adorn.

seccutur, variant of SECUTOR *Obs.*, executor.

sece, obs. form of CEASE.

secede (sɪ'si:d), *v.* [ad. L. *sēcēdĕre* to withdraw, f. *sē-* (see SE-) + *cēdĕre* to go.]

1. *intr.* †**a.** To go away from one's companions, go into retirement (*obs.*). **b.** *nonce-use.* Of a thing: To retire, withdraw to a distance. (A Latinism.)

1702 MATHER *Magn. Christi* III. Introd. (1852) 240 A strange work of God upon the spirits of men that were no ways acquainted with one another inspiring them, as one man, to secede into a wilderness, they knew not where. **1856** RUSKIN *Mod. Paint.* IV. v. xix. §31 The great mountains secede into supremacy through rosy depths of burning air.

2. a. To withdraw formally from an alliance, an association, a federal union, a political or religious organization.

The most prominent applications of the verb are to the action of a minority of a religious body, and to that of a state forming part of a federal union.

1755 JOHNSON, *To secede*, to withdraw from fellowship in any affair. **1777** BURKE *Let. to Rockingham* Wks. IX. 170 He is of opinion, that if you adhere to your resolution of seceding, you ought not to appear on the first day of the meeting. **1797** *Encycl. Brit.* (ed. 3) XVII. 226/2 Accordingly the ejected ministers declared in their protest that they were laid under the disagreeable necessity of seceding, not from the principles and constitution of the church of Scotland,.. but from the present church-courts. **1825** JEFFERSON *Autobiog.* Wks. 1859 I. 13 Possibly their colonies might secede from the Union. **1846** J. MACFARLANE *Late Secess. Ch. Scot.* 124 It were grievous misconception to suppose that all who seceded did so on the substantial merits of the question at issue. **1845** S. HINDS in *Encycl. Metrop.* X. 764/1 He who is convinced that his Church is essentially in error is bound to secede. **1848** THACKERAY *Van. Fair* xlvi, A member of the house from which old Sedley had seceded was very glad to make use of Mr. Clapp's services. **1876** E. MELLOR *Priesth.* viii. 391 The numerous clergy.. who have seceded to Rome. **1883** H. B. LEECH in *Contemp. Rev.* XLIII. 267 The law.. suggests a distrust of the State which secedes from a confederacy without justifiable excuse.

b. *rarely* in wider sense: To withdraw from taking part (in conversation).

1856 MISS MULOCK *J. Halifax* xii, The conversation fell to the three younger persons—I may say the two—for I also seceded, and left John master of the field.

3. *trans.* To withdraw (a component territory) from a federal union or the like; to detach or cede (a piece of land). *rare.*

1946 W. FAULKNER *Portable Faulkner* 739 A plot to secede the whole Mississippi Valley from the United States and join it to Spain. **1963** A. SMITH *Throw out Two Hands* xv. 156 Many people feel it was wrong.. for any park to secede part of itself for any reason.

Hence **se'ceded** *ppl. a.*

1894 *Daily News* 25 Apr. 4/7 Even in Birmingham multitudes of seceded Liberals are tired of serving the Tory party.

seceder (sɪ'si:də(r)). [f. SECEDE *v.* + -ER[1].]

1. One who secedes.

1755 JOHNSON, *Seceder*, one who discovers his disapprobation of any proceedings by withdrawing himself. **1787** SIR J. HAWKINS *Johnson* 425 *note*, I was the only seceder from this society. **1808** *Med. Jrnl.* XIX. 323, I had reason at this time to consider myself the first seceder from the established practice. **1844** H. H. WILSON *Brit. India* I. i. I. 101 Athough seceders in some respects from the orthodox religion of the Hindus, the Sikhs retain so many essential articles of the Brahmanical faith that [etc.]. **1851** W. E. SCUDAMORE (*title*) Letters to a Seceder from the Church of England to the Communion of Rome. **1861** *Sat. Rev.* 7 Dec. 570 He says that the Northern Americans would have been stigmatized as cowards if they had let the seceders go in peace.

2. *spec.* A member of the Secession Church.

1758 A. GELLATLY *Some Observ.* To Rdr. 2 *note*, As they made a Secession from the established Church, they are termed Seceders. **1771** SMOLLETT *Humph. Cl.* II. 8 Aug., There is a sect of fanaticks, who have separated themselves from the established kirk, under the name of Seceders. **1835** [T. JACKSON] *Man. Sects & Heresies* 112 *Seceders*, a numerous sect of Presbyterians in Scotland, who have withdrawn from the communion of the Established Church. .. The Seceders were formerly subdivided into Burghers and Anti-burghers..; but in 1829 the two bodies were re-joined under the name of the United Secession Church.

b. *attrib.*

1833 J. S. SANDS *Poems* 51 (E.D.D.) He raised a kirk himsel' alane Just on the great Seceder plan. **1834** *Tait's Mag.* I. 16/1 The Seceder meeting-house. **1854** H. MILLER *Sch. & Schm.* (1858) 544 Which I had overheard in my cousin the Seceder minister's house.

seceding (sɪ'si:dɪŋ), *ppl. a.* [f. SECEDE *v.* + -ING[2].] That secedes; *occas.* †belonging to the Secession Church.

1757 SMOLLETT *Hist. Eng.* (1760) XI. 54 The seceding members had again resumed their seats in the house of commons. **1758** A. GELLATLY *Some Observ.* To Rdr. 2 The seceding (or associate) Ministers thought [etc.]. **1868** G. DUFF *Polit. Surv.* (1868) 121 Reconstruction is readmission of the seceding States to political communion. **1886** GLADSTONE in Morley *Life* IX. vii. (1903) III. 322 Will the seceding colleagues come if they are asked?

secentismo, secentist, varr. SEICENTISMO, SEICENTIST.

secern (sɪ'sɜ:n), *v.* Also 7 secerne. [ad. L. *sēcernĕre*, f. *sē-* aside (see SE-) + *cernĕre* to separate, distinguish, secrete. In its physiological application (sense 2) the Latin word renders Gr. ἀποκρίνειν.]

1. *trans.* To separate; now only, to separate in thought; to place in a separate category, distinguish, discriminate.

1656 BLOUNT *Glossogr.*, *Secerne*, to divide, to lay or separate one from another, to sever, to chuse from among others. *Bac.* **1657** W. MORICE *Coena quasi Κοινὴ* iii. 148 A local and bodily secerning our selves from evil men. *a* **1734** NORTH *Exam.* I. iii. §92 (1740) 187 An Herculean Labour which.. few or none will undertake, and yet fewer be able throughout to secern the true from the false. **1836–7** SIR W. HAMILTON *Metaph.* xxvii. (1870) II. 156 Averroes secerns a sense of titillation and a sense of hunger and thirst. **1855** BAILEY *Mystic* 102 Whereby the good from ill they might secern. **1905** *Sat. Rev.* 15 Apr. 483 He knows that mimes cannot be utterly secerned from their life of mimicry.

2. *Phys.* To separate from the blood; to SECRETE. Now *rare.*

1657 W. MORICE *Coena quasi Κοινὴ* Pref. 18 Humors which .. being secerned and gathering head [etc.]. **1779** C. CRUTWELL *Adv. to Lying-in Women* 6 Milk.. being secerned. **1822–29** *Good's Study Med.* (ed. 3) II. 165 An unusual proportion of bile is secerned. **1849–52** *Todd's Cycl. Anat.* IV. 1114/1 The secretion of the gland.. is simply secerned from the circulating current for a time.

absol. **1626** BACON *Sylva* §680 Their Flesh doth assimilate more finely, and secerneth more subtilly.

secerned (sɪ'sɜ:nd), *ppl. a.* [f. SECERN *v.* + -ED[1].] Secreted.

1722 QUINCY *Lex. Phys.-Med.* (ed. 2) 17 The secerned Particles for Nourishment and Accretion. **1728** CHAMBERS *Cycl.* s.v. *Animal Secretion*, Diversities of secerned Fluids. **1822–29** *Good's Study Med.* (ed. 3) V. 262 Proving that most of the secerned materials are not formally existent in the blood.

secernent (sɪ'sɜ:nənt), *a.* and *sb.* [ad. L. *sēcernentem*, pres. pple. of *sēcernĕre*: see SECERN *v.*]

A. *adj.* That secretes.

1822–29 *Good's Study Med.* (ed. 3) V. 261 Peculiar ferments, conveyed by the blood to the secernent organ. **1835–6** *Todd's Cycl. Anat.* I. 65/2 The activity of the nutritive, secernent, and absorbent processes.

B. *sb. Phys.* **a.** A secreting organ.

1808 *Ann. Reg.* 115 The secernents of its cutis exude a sweet, saccharine, nutritive gum. **1822–29** *Good's Study Med.* (ed. 3) V. 261 Whence, indeed, the name of Secernents or Secretories, which mean nothing more than separating powers. **1844** HOBLYN *Dict. Med.*, *Secernents.*

†**b.** Something which promotes secretion. *Obs.*$^{-0}$

In Webster 1828, with reference to Darwin; see the following quot.:

[**1796** E. DARWIN *Zoon.* II. 694 Those things which increase the irritative motions, which constitute secretion, are termed secernentia.]

secerning (sɪˈsɜːnɪŋ), *ppl. a.* [f. SECERN *v.* + -ING[2].] = SECERNENT *a.*

a **1721** KEILL *Anim. Œcon.* (1738) 104 The Secretions are formed in the Blood, before they arrive at their secerning Glands. **1804** T. TROTTER *Ess. Drunkenness* iv. §11. 134 All secreted fluids partake of the vices of the secerning organ. *a* **1843** J. F. SOUTH in *Encycl. Metrop.* (1845) VII. 259/1 Of the Secerning Glands or True Glands.

secernment (sɪˈsɜːnmənt). [f. SECERN *v.* + -MENT.]

1. *Phys.* The action of secerning or secreting.

1822–29 *Good's Study Med.* (ed. 3) II. 310 The globules are produced while it lies on the surface of the sore, usually .. in about fifteen minutes after its secernment. **1835** KIRBY *Hab. & Inst. Anim.* II. xviii. 268 The means .. for rejecting from the body the residuum after the secernment .. of the finer life-supporting products.

2. Separation.

1894 *Yellow Bk.* I. 72 With the universal use of cosmetics and the consequent secernment of soul and surface.

secesh (sɪˈsɛʃ), *sb.* and *a.* *U.S. Hist. colloq.* [Shortened from SECESSION.] **A.** *sb.* **a.** A secessionist. Also secessionists collectively.

1862 O. W. HOLMES *Old Vol. of Life* (1891) 36 'There are two wounded Secesh', said my companion. **1879** TOURGEE *Fool's Errand* vi. 25, I was one of the original 'Secesh',—one of the immortal thirteen that voted for it in this county.

b. Secession.

1863 TROLLOPE in *Good Words* Dec. 858/2, I won't talk secesh to you out here in the cold. **1868** GREEN *Lett.* II. (1901) 203 A Limehouse grocer proclaims his secesh from Newton.

B. *adj.* = SECESSIONIST *a.*

1861 *Ohio Statesman* 6 Nov. in *A. E. Lee's Hist. Columbus* II. 102 The following distinguished secesh prisoners have been sent. **1862** 'ARTEMUS WARD' *His Bk.* (1865) 145 He axed what was my principles? 'Secesh!' I ansered. **1871** SIR S. NORTHCOTE in *Life* (1890) II. 38 The whole town [Richmond, Va.] is still 'Secesh' to the heart's core.

secesher (sɪˈsɛʃə(r)). *colloq. U.S.* [f. SECESH + -ER[1].] A secessionist.

1861 O. W. HOLMES *Sweet Little Man* 47 While the wind scatters the chaffy seceshers. **1861** LOWELL *Biglow P.* Ser. II. i. Poems 1890 II. 239 Knowin' t' much might spile a boy for bein' a Secesher.

†**seˈcess.** *Obs.* [ad. L. *sēcessus* (*u* stem), f. *sēcēdĕre*: see SECEDE *v.*] Withdrawing; retirement. Also a secession, revolt from allegiance.

1563 FOXE *A. & M.* (1596) 789/2 This sickenes tooke him after supper, with the which he vehemently contending, required secesse into a hye chamber. **1647** H. MORE *Song of Soul* 8/1 Silent Secesse, wast Solitude Deep searching thoughts often renew'd. **1663** HEATH *Flagellum* Pref. (1672) 2 For there have been more Revolts, Defections, and Secesses made in Europe, than for many Centuries before. **1675** A. HUYBERTS *Corner-Stone* 18 This contrivance was made .. merely for fear lest these should make a Secess to Mount Aventine, and set up for a popular Rebellion .. against the Senate of the Colledge.

secession (sɪˈsɛʃən). [ad. L. *sēcessiōn-em*, n. of action f. *sēcēdĕre*: see SECEDE *v.* Cf. F. *sécession* (17th c. in Hatz.-Darm.), Sp. *secesion*, It. *secessione*.]

†**1. a.** The action or an act of going away from one's accustomed neighbourhood, or of retiring from public view; the condition of living remote from one's former home, or retired from public view; retirement. *Obs.*

1604 F. HERING *Mod. Defence* Bj, Secession and departing the city hath beene a meane to preserue many [from the Plague]. **1645** BP. HALL *Peace-maker* viii. 64 The cels and cloysters of retired Votaries, whose very secession proclaimes their contempt of sinfull seculars. **1648** —— *Select Th.* Pref., To make use of my late Secession for the production of divers .. Tractates. **1659** PEARSON *Creed* (1839) 302 The unspotted soul of our Jesus was really and actually separated from his body, that his flesh was bereft of natural life by the secession of that soul. **1689** *Andros Tracts* II. 152 They [the Puritan founders of New England] resolved on a peaceable secession into a corner of the World. **1760** STERNE *Tr. Shandy* IV. xv, No desire—or fear—or doubt that troubles the air, .. that the imagination may not pass over without offence in that sweet secession. **1803** BEDDOES *Hygëia* x. 31 During this secession he lived under the same roof with an insane patient. **1847** YEOWELL *Anc. Brit. Ch.* x. 106 The secession of many eminent men from the island.

†**b.** Of a material thing: Departure, removal to a distance; separation. *Obs.*

1633 T. ADAMS *Exp. 2 Peter* v. 19 Natural darkness; .. necessarily following upon the secession or absence of the sun. **1646** SIR T. BROWNE *Pseud. Ep.* II. ii. 57 The accession of bodyes upon, or secession thereof, from its surface. **1797** CRUIKSHANK in *Phil. Trans.* LXXXVII. 213 The secession of the amnion from the chorion.

†**c.** (See quot.) *Obs.*

1706 PHILLIPS (ed. Kersey), *Secession of a Parliament*, the Adjournment or breaking-up of it.

2. a. *Rom. Hist.* Used to render L. *secessio* (*plebis*), the temporary migration of the plebeians to a place outside the city, in order to compel the patricians to grant redress of their grievances.

1533 BELLENDEN *Livy* II. xxiv. (S.T.S.) I. 231 At þat tyme war acceppit be þame may wikkit & soroufful lawis þan evir war acceppit be secessioun of pepill to þe sacrate montane. *a* **1760** W. DUNCAN *Cicero's Sel. Orat.* xiv. (1841) 298 At first, Caesar, you thought it only a secession, not a war. **1878** BOSW. SMITH *Carthage* 63 Nor need we relate .. how these same Plebeians, .. by .. their secessions to the sacred mount first obtained inviolable magistrates of their own.

†**b.** A desertion, repudiation of allegiance. *Obs.*

1601 BP. W. BARLOW *Serm. Paules Crosse* 23 They .. who with Shebah, .. will make a secession from their prince.

3. a. The action of seceding or formally withdrawing from an alliance, a federation, a political or religious organization, or the like. Hence, a body of seceders.

War of Secession: the American Civil War (1861–5), which arose out of the attempt of eleven of the Southern States to secede from the United States of North America.

1660 R. COKE *Power & Subj.* 222 The Sesession [*sic*] of the Church, King, and Kingdom of England, from the Papacy. **1670** in Somers *Tracts* I. 12 This Secession of Members did very much facilitate the Entry into, and Continuance of the War. **1697** S. SEWALL *Diary* 20 Sept. (1878) I. 460 That Mr. Cotton should make an orderly secession from the Church. **1777** BURKE *Let. to Rockingham* Wks. IX. 171 If the Secession were to be general, such an attendance, followed by such an act, would have force. **1825** MACAULAY *Ess., Milton* (1851) I. 21 After so many deaths, secessions and expulsions. **1845** *Encycl. Metrop.* X. 764/1 The Church of England .. would be naturally perpetuated as it now is, and every secession from it would be as truly a Schism. **1848** MRS. JAMESON *Sacr. & Leg. Art* (1850) 115 The secession of the Protestant Church. **1861** LOWELL *E Pluribus Unum* Pr. Wks. 1890 V. 53 Rebellion smells no sweeter because it is called Secession. **1861** *Times* 23 May, The term 'secession' is objected to, .. because 'secession', like 'federation', expresses an absolute equality and correlation of rights which .. the Northern States are not prepared to concede. **1872** YEATS *Growth Comm.* 355 If the private interest of any town could be better served by severance from the league there was no spirit to prevent a secession. **1879** *Encycl. Brit.* X. 469/2 (*Germany*), Several communities as well as individuals declared their secession from the Roman Church. **1885** M. PATTISON *Mem.* 235, I have spoken of the sudden lull which fell upon Oxford .. the moment the secessions to Rome were announced. **1888** A. JOHNSTON in *Encycl. Brit.* XXIII. 772/2 Some assurance of united action must have been obtained, for South Carolina ventured into secession.

b. *spec.* The separation from the Established Church of Scotland, initiated in 1733 by the Rev. Ebenezer Erskine and other ministers; the religious body (more fully ***the Secession Church***) which originated from this separation.

1733 E. ERSKINE, etc. *Protest* in A. Thomson *Hist. Secession Ch.* (1848) 72 Therefore we do .. protest that we are obliged to make a secession from them [the prevailing party in this Established Church], and that we can have no ministerial communion with them, till [etc.]. **1782** J. BROWN *Addr. Students of Div.* p. xviii, I look upon the Secession as indeed the Cause of God. **1860** J. CAIRNS *Mem. J. Brown* i. 3 That form of Scottish dissent, called the Secession .. had taken its rise in 1733.

c. *rarely* in wider sense: Withdrawal (from a share in conversation, etc.).

1843 LYTTON *Last of Barons* I. vi, Perfectly unconscious of the secession of his other listeners.

d. Also with capital initial. [tr. G. *Sezession.*] A radical movement in art that began in Vienna and was contemporaneous with, and related to, art nouveau; the style of this movement. Freq. with *the.* Cf. SEZESSIONSTIL, SECESSIONIST b (quot. 1901).

[**1890** *Art Jrnl.* July 221/1 The important secession which .. followed upon the recent retirement of M. Meissonier from all connection with the great annual exhibition of Paris. **1894** *Mag. of Art* XVII. 416/1 The secession of Munich is only one of the effects of the painter's shyness of regulation.] **1896** *Amer. Architect & Building News* 8 Feb. 63/1 'Secession' is a *nom de guerre* of the 'Verein Bildener Kuenstler Muenchens (A.V.)'. *a* **1935** F. PONSONBY *Recollections of Three Reigns* (1951) ix. 123 Inside it was composed of every style of mural decoration, but predominantly what was called 'art nouveau' or 'secession'. **1972** T. WALTERS *Art Nouveau* 6 The Secessionists .. were determined to carefully build up a whole revolutionary way of life in which every object .. whether a lavatory seat or an underground station, was designed to meet the ideals of the Secession.

†**4.** (See quots.) *Obs.*

1657 TOMLINSON *Renou's Disp.* I. xiv. 28 A Medicament is called Cathartick, or purging, because by some way it draws noxious humours out of our bodies, as by vomiting, or secession. **1724** BAILEY (ed. 2), *Secession* (among Physicians), the going off [1742 (ed. 10) of a Disease] by Secretion.

5. *attrib.* and *Comb.*: **a.** in sense 3 b, as in ***Secession church, movement, principles, synod***; **b.** with reference to the attempted secession from the United States (1861–5), as in ***secession-sympathizer***; **Secession War** = *War of Secession* (see 3).

1803 W. TAYLOR *J. Brown's Lett. on Toleration* Pref. 19 Evils which he saw coming on the Secession Churches. **1835** [T. JACKSON] *Man. Sects & Heresies* 113 In 1829 the two bodies were re-joined under the name of the United Secession Church. **1861** WHITTIER in *Life* (1893) 136 In so doing I seem to take sides with the secession-sympathisers of the North. **1867** *Chamb. Encycl.* IX. 645/2 It is not necessary to describe minutely the gradual extension of the 'Secession movement'. **1883** *Encycl. Brit.* XV. 132/2 This departure .. from Secession principles. *Ibid.*, Negotiations for union between the Burghers and Antiburghers resulted, in 1820, in the formation of the United Secession Synod. **1899** *Daily News* 19 Oct. 6/4 Colonel Henderson .. has long since made an exhaustive and minute study of the Secession War.

c. In sense 3 d, as ***Secession exhibition, school, style*** [tr. G. *Sezessionstil*].

1911 R. FRY *Let.* 13 Apr. (1972) I. 345, I thought that the Grafton might be used for a general secession exhibition of all non-academy art of any importance. **1949** *New Yorker* 5 Feb. 78/2 De Chirico .. declares that the École de Paris .. was really founded on the Munich Secession School. **1973** *Times* 18 Dec. (Hungary Today Suppl.) p. i/3 The *Vigszinhaz* .. is in the turn of the century *Secession* style, the Vienna version of *art nouveau.*

6. *attrib.* (quasi-*adj.*) in the senses: **a.** Belonging to the Secession Church; **b.** Favouring the cause of secession (from the United States), secessionist. (With capital S.)

1838 A. THOMSON *Hist. Secession Ch.* 171 The name among Secession authors which .. is best known in purely literary circles is that of Dr. Jamieson. **1863** BRIGHT *Sp. Amer.* 26 Mar. 127 Not Union planters only, but Secession planters began to bring in the produce.

secessional (sɪˈsɛʃənəl), *a.* [f. prec. + -AL[1].]

1. Of or pertaining to secession.

1884 *Manch. Exam.* 8 Apr. 5/1 If .. any whiff of secessional sentiment has blown upon him, he must have been restored to his better purpose.

2. *Sc.* Pertaining to the Secession Church. *Obs.*

1838 *United Secession Mag.* Feb. 103 Secessional Intelligence. **1844** J. MACFARLANE *Mem. J. Campbell* iii. 69 These [interests of Gospel truth] are insured in Secessional testimonies.

secessionism (sɪˈsɛʃənɪz(ə)m). [f. SECESSION + -ISM.] **a.** *U.S. Hist.* The principles of those in favour of secession. **b.** *Scottish Ch. Hist.* The principles and doctrine of the Secession Church.

1898 E. MARTYN *Neal Dow* xxxiv. in *New York Voice* 5 May 6/5 Lincoln .. found himself in possession of a bankrupt government, confronted by an arrogant secessionism. **1899** *Q. Rev.* July 177 Carlyle represented the 'dour' secessionism of the Border peasantry. **1904** R. SMALL *Hist. U.P. Congreg.* I. 328 Such were the workings of disrupted Secessionism at Alyth.

secessionist (sɪˈsɛʃənɪst), *sb.* (and *a.*) [f. SECESSION + -IST.] One who favours secession; one who joins in a secession. **a.** *spec.* in *U.S. Hist.* One in favour of the attempt of the Southern States to withdraw from the Union.

1860 BARTLETT *Dict. Amer.* (ed. 3), *Secessionists*, the party in the South which would dissolve the Union, or go out of it immediately, without the coöperation of other States. Another party, calling themselves 'coöperationists', would only dissolve it when other States had joined them. **1861** LOWELL *E Pluribus Unum* Pr. Wks. 1890 V. 52 The list of grievances put forward by the secessionists is a sham and a pretence. **1892** *Nation* (N.Y.) 14 July 32/2 The secessionists made war, not only on the Union, but on the progress of the age.

b. *gen.*

1881 G. J. HOLYOAKE in *Daily News* 26 Oct. 6/4 The Irish Secessionists. **1901** *Daily Chron.* 1 July 3/5 Their [*i.e.* Austrian painters] work suggests that as Secessionists, they have felt the necessity of doing something as no one has done it before. **1902** *Scotsman* 3 Jan. 6/2 Other 'secessionists' ['blackleg' workmen] managed to reach their homes safely, but only under strong police escort.

c. *attrib.* and *adj.*

1861 *Morn. Chron.* 3 Aug., The plough lying abandoned, as it was left by the secessionist owner. **1894** *Mag. of Art* XVII. 379 Salon of the Champ de Mars .. the secessionist Salon. **1898** MCCARTHY *Gladstone's Life* 239 Disraeli accepted the support of the secessionist Liberals. **1954** B. & R. NORTH tr. *M. Duverger's Pol. Parties* II. i. 294 If a party is clearly in a minority in the country as a whole but in a majority in certain districts its attitude becomes autonomist or even secessionist. **1962** *Daily Tel.* 9 Feb. 19/1 Mr. Gizenga, arrested and accused of 'secessionist activities'. **1978** *Detroit Free Press* 2 Apr. 16c/3, I learned of the secessionist movement in the Upper Peninsula.

†**seˈcessive,** *a. Obs.* [as if ad. L. **sēcessīvus*, f. *sēcēdĕre*: see SECEDE *v.*] Retired, private.

1653 URQUHART *Rabelais* I. xl, Like dung-chewers and excrementitious eaters, they are cast into the privies and secessive places, that is the Covents and Abbeys. *Ibid.* III. viii, Conserved and put in store as in a Secessive Repository, and Sacred Warehouse.

sech(e: see SEEK, SIEGE, SIGH, SITCH, SUCH.

sechell, secher, sechino, secir, obs. ff. SATCHEL, SEEKER, SEQUIN, SICKER.

Sechuana, var. SETSWANA.

seck, *a.*: see RENT-SECK.

seck(e, obs. forms of SACK *sb.*[1], *sb.*[3], SICK *a.*

secke, obs. pa. t. of SUCK *v.*

seckel (ˈsɛkəl). Also Seckle. [See quot. 1817.] A kind of pear. Also ***Seckel pear***.

1817 W. COXE *View Cultiv. Fruit Trees Amer.* 189 Seckle Pear... So called from Mr. Seckle of Philadelphia, the proprietor of the original tree. **1845** DOWNING *Fruits Amer.* 416 The Seckel pear. **1860** HOGG *Fruit Man.* 211 (Pears) Seckle (New York Red-cheek; Shakespear; Sicker).—Fruit small, obovate. Skin yellowish-brown [etc.].

secker, obs. form of SICKER *a.*

secket, dial. variant of SIKET (runnel).

seckle, var. SECKEL; and of SICKLE *a. Obs.*

secko ('sɛkəʊ). *Austral. slang.* [Shortened form of SEX *sb.* + -O².] A sexual pervert; a sex offender.

1949 R. PARK *Poor Man's Orange* v. 38 'Just look at that dirty ole secko, will you?' he said disgustedly. **1969** W. DICK *Naked Prodigal* i. 13 You look like you'd be the sorta bloke who'd take little kids down a lane and give 'em two bob, yuh bloody secko. **1974** *Bulletin* (Sydney) 6 Apr. 45/2 'I noticed Australians use a lot of diminutives, like Chrissie, pressie and journo.' 'In jails sex offenders are called seckos,' I told him.

secktur, variant of SECUTOR *Obs.*, executor.

†'**secky**, *a. Obs.* [? Corruption of *seggy*, SEDGY *a.*] ? Sedgy.

1610 W. FOLKINGHAM *Art of Survey* I. x. 28 They soile their sandy layers (both blacke and red) being seckie, tough and wet, with lime.

†'**secle.** *Obs.* Also 7 sæcle. [ad. (prob. independently by several writers) L. *sēclum, sæculum* age: see SECULAR *a.* For the forms obtained through Fr., see SIECLE.] A century, an age.

c **1532** DU WES *Introd. Fr.* in *Palsgr.* 1079 The Romayns [were wont to reken] by lustres.. and by indicions..: a secle is an hundred yere, and sometyme taken for a mannes lyfe. **1644** HAMMOND *Pract. Catech.* I. ii. (1646) 10 'Tis wont to be said that three generations make one sæcle, or hundred yeares. **1772** [T. NUGENT] tr. *Hist. Fr. Gerund* I. 352 To the argent season succeeded the secle hight ferruginous. **1846** KEIGHTLEY *Notes Virg., Bucol.* iv. Observ., The augural books of the Tuscans said that there were successive secles or ages assigned to states and empires.

secler(e, obs. forms of SECULAR.

secli, variant of SICKLE *v.*¹ *Obs.*

seclude (sɪ'kluːd), *v.* Also 6 secluid. [ad. L. *sēclūdĕre*, f. *sē-* (see SE-) + *claudĕre* to shut. Cf. OF. *seclorre*.

Now almost restricted to sense 2, which is close to the primary etymological meaning, though narrower than the use of *secludere* in Latin. Formerly often used loosely as a synonym of *exclude*: see 3, 4, 5 below.]

†**1.** *trans.* To shut off, obstruct the access to (a thing). Const. *from. Obs.*

1451 CAPGRAVE *Life St. Gilbert* 127 The last two dayes was his drynk secluded fro him, so closed wer his pipes. *a* **1548** HALL *Chron., Hen. VI*, 87 The sure nutriment of their liuyng was from them secluded.

2. †**a.** To shut up apart, to enclose or confine so as to prevent access or influence from without. Const. *from.* Also, to enclose or confine (a material thing) in a separate place. *Obs.* (merged in 2 b.)

1597 A. M. tr. *Guillemeau's Fr. Chirurg.* 32 b/2 To drawe therout all humors which are therin secluded. **1599** —— tr. *Gabelhouer's Bk. Physicke* 23/1 Take also a Peacock, seclud him in the decreasing of the Moon, on some clean Chamber, and collect the dung.. therof. *a* **1700** EVELYN *Diary* 19 Aug. 1641, The women were secluded from the men, being seated above in galleries. **1728–46** THOMSON *Spring* 1132 Let eastern tyrants from the light of heaven Seclude their bosom slaves.

b. In wider sense: To remove or guard from public view; to withdraw from opportunities of social intercourse. Often *refl.*, to live in retirement or solitude. Chiefly const. *from.*

1628 FORD *Lover's Mel.* II. ii, We are secluded From all good people. **1686** J. SCOTT *Chr. Life* II. vii. Wks. 1718 I. 416 He is secluded by the infinite sacredness of his own Majesty from all immediate converse and intercourse with us. **1726** SWIFT *Gulliver* II. vii, Great Allowances should be given to a King who lives wholly secluded from the rest of the World. **1748** MELMOTH *Fitzosborne Lett.* liv. (1749) II. 68 Virtue.. must either.. seclude herself in cells and desarts, or [etc.]. **1751** JOHNSON *Rambler* No. 159 ¶1 The studious part of mankind, whose education necessarily secludes them in their earlier years from mingled converse. **1788** GIBBON *Decl. & F.* xli. IV. 202 It was enviously secluded from the public view. **1781** V. KNOX *Liberal Educ.* iii. 35 He.. will suffer worse consequences from it, than if he had not been secluded from boys at a boyish age. *a* **1834** LAMB *Let. to Southey* in *Mrs. Leicester's Sch.*, etc. (1885) 338 It is an error more particularly incident to persons of the correctest principles and habits, to seclude themselves from the rest of mankind, as from another species, and form into knots and clubs. **1851** HAWTHORNE *Ho. Sev. Gables* xiv, Miss Hepzibah, by secluding herself from society, has lost all true relation with it. **1855** PRESCOTT *Philip II*, II. ii. I. 158 Shut up in his carriage, he seemed desirous to seclude himself from the gaze of his.. subjects. **1910** EMILY J. PUTNAM in *Contemp. Rev.* May 556 Under these conditions, it was apparently not necessary to seclude a wife; at any rate, the Roman matron of all periods enjoyed personal freedom.

c. To shut off or screen *from* some external influence.

1601 HOLLAND *Pliny* VI. xvii. I. 124 The region of the Attaci.. secluded from all noisome wind and aire. **1870** LOWELL *Among my Bks.* Ser. I. (1873) 170 Investigations and habits of thought that secluded them from baser attractions.

†**3.** To shut or keep out *from* a place, society, etc.; to deny entrance to. Sometimes with double object, To forbid (a person) to enter (a place, etc.).

1498 in J. Bulloch *Pynours* (1887) 57 And quha brekis this Statut.. salbe secludit and forboden the tone thai being conuikit thairintill. **1538** BALE *God's Promises* (1908) A ij, Man must nedes be lost, And cleane secluded, from the faythfull chosen sorte, In the heauens aboue. **1558** FORREST *Grysilde the Second* 85 So was goode Grysilde secluded the Courte. **1565** STAPLETON tr. *Bede's Hist. Ch. Eng.* 188 Vtterly to seclude from your presence and face.. the habit.. and figure of his countinaunce. **1680** *Spirit of Popery* Pref. 2 The Doctrines,.. for which the Jesuits are Secluded both Kingdoms by Capital Laws. **1680** *Papists bloody Oath of Secrecy* 4 Till the days of our Grand-Fathers, when in England the Pope and his Clergy were secluded.

†**b.** To debar *from* a privilege, advantage, dignity, succession, etc.; to prevent *from* doing something. Also const. *inf. Obs.*

a **1533** FRITH *Disput. Purgat.* To Chr. Rdr. A iij b, You haue bene of longe continuaunce secluded from the scriptures. **1549** COVERDALE, etc. *Erasm. Par. Heb.* iii. 7–13 Leste he.. dooe grieuouslye punyshe them, and seclude them from the rest and quietnes promised. **1556** ROBINSON tr. *More's Utopia* II. (ed. 2) 116 b, *marg.*, Irreligious people secluded [*text has* excluded] from all honours. **1557** *Order of Hospitalls* H 7, Upon every fault found, your staffes shall be taken from you, and [you] to be secluded for ever more for serving in those romes. **1560** DAUS tr. *Sleidane's Comm.* 137 b, And by that occasion usurped the Dukedome of Millan, secludyng Valentine [orig. *exclusa Valentina*]. **1574** in *10th Rep. Hist. MSS. Comm.* App. v. 333 Wives were alwaies secluded and barred to demande any intrest in their said thirde of the said fermes. **1613** SIR T. SMYTHE in *Buccleuch MSS.* (Hist. MSS. Comm.) I. 132 We now know what they endeavour, to seclude us from trading in those parts. **1628** COKE *On Litt.* 99 b, The heire cannot take anything.. when the ancestor himself is secluded. **1656** G. COLLIER *Answ. 15 Quest.* 5, I shall prove they ought to be secluded [from communion]. **1681** *Let. to Person of Honour conc. D. of M.'s Mother* 12 An apprehension of being otherwise Secluded from his Right over that kingdom. *a* **1722** FOUNTAINHALL *Decis.* (1759) I. 5 If the buyer.. must immediately offer it back, so soon as he knows the vitiosity, else will be secluded both from the *redhibitoria* and *quanti minoris.* **1775** JOHNSON *Tax. no Tyr.* 26 They are more secluded from easy recourse to national judicature.

†**c.** To regard as having no share (in something). Const. *from. Obs.*

1581 W. CHARKE in *Conf.* IV. (1584) D d iiij b, The ende why works are secluded from iustification doeth proue for me. **1586** A. DAY *Eng. Secretary* II. (1625) 57 Confessing that if any waies I haue erred vnto you, as I will not vtterly seclude my selfe from any errour, it was but.. by ignorance. *a* **1676** HALE *Prim. Orig. Man.* I. iii. (1677) 71 Almighty God, whom he totally secludes from the concerns of the World.

†**d.** With noun of action as obj.: To prohibit, preclude. *Obs.*

1566 SECURIS *Detection* B iij b, The.. sauegard of many a sick man.. shall be hyndred and secluded. **1578** *Reg. Privy Council Scot.* II. 681 That nane of his Hienes liegis.. mak ony bargayne, blok, or conditioun.. secluding the ressaving of ony of the Kingis lauchfull money in payment. **1579** RICE *Invective agst. Vices* C iij, Thou wilt perchaunce saie, that I am to harde to reprehende that thyng, that maie for an honest recreation bee frequented, where as the companie is sober,.. secludyng blasphemie, riot, dronkenship, and such like excesse. **1664** EVELYN *Kal. Hort., Nov.* (1679) 29 Enclose your tender Plants.. in your Conservatory, secluding all entrance of cold.

†**4.** To exclude from consideration, leave out of account. *Obs.*

a **1533** FRITH *Disput. Purgat.* Prol. A viij b, Imagininge that two men dispute this matter by naturall reason and phylosophye, secludynge Chryste and all scrypture. **1584** R. SCOT *Discov. Witchcr.* VIII. ii. (1886) 127 Onelie God and man knoweth the heart of man and therefore.. the divell must be secluded. **1607** TOPSELL *Four-f. Beasts* 435, I vtterly seclude al their opinions, which translate this word Arabian wolues, for the Hæbrew notes cannot admit such a version or exposition. **1620** E. BLOUNT *Horæ Subs.* 123, I doe not by this seclude society, and conuersation: for such a solitary, & vnsociable disposition, I hold to be worse then this Gadder. **1620** T. GRANGER *Div. Logike* 159 [This] Secludeth ambiguous, equiuocall, or doubtfull significations. **1656** JEANES *Mixt. Schol. Div.* 82 Alwayes provided, you abstract, and seclude that, which implieth imperfection. **1672** WALLIS in Rigaud *Corr. Sci. Men* (1841) II. 531 What I said.. was only to seclude that consideration from what was then in hand. **1682** H. MORE *Annot. Glanvill's Lux O.* 69 For such, says he, is God in the rest of his Attributes, if you seclude his Goodness. **1725** WATTS *Logic* I. ii. § 2 If we seclude space out of our consideration.

†**b.** The pr. pple. used absol. as quasi-*prep.*: Excepting, apart from. *Obs.*

1624 F. WHITE *Repl. Fisher* 414 Secluding the authoritie of the Roman Church, there is [etc.]. **1637** C. DOW *Answ. to H. Burton* 168 That we come to know the scriptures by the testimony of the church, and that secluding that, wee cannot .. bee perswaded that they are the word of God. **1638** in Spalding *Troub. Chas. I* (Bannatyne Club) I. 58 We condemn no Episcopall Government, secludeing the personall abuse therof. *a* **1677** BARROW *Serm.* iii. Wks. 1687 I. 27 But, secluding a regard to the Precepts of Religion, there can hardly be [etc.]. **1706** W. JONES *Palm. Math.* 129 If all the Negative Products made of the Roots taken by 2's, 3's, 4's, &c. (Secluding their Signs) are equal to all the Affirmative ones. **1728** tr. *Newton's Treat. Syst. World* 22 A body revolved in our air.. would (secluding the resistance of the air) compleat a revolution in 1 h. 24'. 27".

†**5.** To banish, expel *from* a country; to put out of an office or out of membership of a society. (Cf. EXCLUDE *v.* II.) *Obs.*

1572 WHITGIFT *Answ. Admonition* 40 God.. prescribeth no generall rule of secluding them from theyr ministerie, if they falling, afterwarde repent. **1632** LITHGOW *Trav.* I. 7, I choosed.. to seclude my selfe from my soyle. *a* **1734** NORTH *Life Ld. Keeper North* (1742) Pref. 3 He served his Country in diverse Parliaments, and was misled to sit in that of Forty, till he was secluded.

†**b.** To banish, put away (a thought, etc.). *Obs.*

1549 COVERDALE, etc. *Erasm. Par. Rom.* xv. 14–19 That all heauines and dissencion secluded, it maye please hym to fulfyll you with all ioye and concorde.

†**c.** To expunge from a record. *Obs.*

1550 BALE *Eng. Votaries* I. Ep. Ded., Secludynge theyr names from the lambes boke of lyfe.

d. *Textual criticism.* To exclude as spurious [= mod.L. *secludere*].

1893 A. PLATT in *Classical Rev.* Feb. 31/2 And why should this be secluded, when o 225–256 are retained, though the editors agree with Nitzsch in condemning them?

6. To separate, keep apart. †**a.** To separate as a barrier; to intervene so as to shut off (e.g. a portion of an army from the main body). *Obs.*

1610 HOLLAND *Camden's Brit.* I. 113 The Britwales or Welchmen.. were secluded from the English Saxons by a Ditch or Trench which King Offa cast. **1623** BINGHAM *Xenophon* 63 They were driuen to a necessitie, either by force to dislodge the enemy from the place and cut him off, or else to be secluded from the rest of the army. **1632** LITHGOW *Trav.* I. 22 Discending Mount Synais from La Croix Southward, which secludeth Sauoy. *a* **1652** J. SMITH *Sel. Disc.* VI. xiii. (1821) 299 Things.. that were cast into periods of time secluded one from another by vast intervals. *a* **1678** MARVELL *Loyal Scot* 93 Nothing but clergy could us two seclude, No Scotch was ever like a bishop's feud.

†**b.** To separate in thought, to consider apart *from. Obs.*

1655 FULLER *Ch. Hist.* VIII. 42 Take Queen Mary in her self abstracted from her Opinions, and by her self, secluded from her bloody councellours, and her Memory will justly come under Commendation.

c. To select and separate; to set aside for use.

1771 GOLDSM. *Hist. Eng.* I. 7 No plunder taken in war was used by the captor until the Druids determined what part they should seclude for themselves. **1876** GLADSTONE *Glean.* II. 333 This transitory literature.. requires immense sifting and purgation, like other coarse raw material, in order to reduce the gross to the nett, to seclude, and to express, the metal from the ore.

secluded (sɪ'kluːdɪd), *ppl. a.* [f. prec. + -ED¹.]

1. In senses of the vb., *esp.*: Shut up or withdrawn from view; †(of a privilege) withheld from the multitude; †(of a member of parliament) expelled, excluded.

1604 E. G[RIMSTONE] *D'Acosta's Hist. Indies* v. xi. 358 So the Divell hath his sacrifices,.. his secluded and fained holinesse, with a thousand sortes of false prophets. **1649** PRYNNE (*title*) A Vindication of the Imprisoned and Secluded Members of the House of Commons From the Aspersions cast upon them. **1660** *Trial Regic.* 86, I was one of the Secluded Members. *a* **1674** CLARENDON *Hist. Reb.* XVI. § 132 He made no scruple to declare, that in justice the secluded members ought to be admitted. **1790** BURKE *Fr. Rev.* Wks. V. 86 If she were communicating some privilege, or laying open some secluded benefit. **1842** J. PEDDIE *Exp. Jonah* vii. 119 Consider the secluded condition of Eastern monarchs. **1848** THACKERAY *Van. Fair* xvii, His secluded wife ever smiling and cheerful.

2. Of a place or dwelling: Remote or screened from observation or access; withdrawn from society; seldom visited on account of distance or difficulty of approach; sequestered, retired.

1798 WORDSW. *Poems Imag.* xxvi. *Tintern Abb.* 6 Once again Do I behold these steep and lofty cliffs, That on a wild secluded scene impress Thoughts of more deep seclusion. **1842** J. WILSON *Chr. North* (1857) I. 254 Is not the secluded scene felt to be most beautiful? **1849** MACAULAY *Hist. Eng.* v. I. 538 In that secluded province his father had bought a small estate. **1862** BURTON *Bk. Hunter* IV. 378 A secluded hollow near the small tarn called Lochcolissor. **1908** [Miss FOWLER] *Betw. Trent & Ancholme* 40 Over-hanging a secluded garden.

Hence **se'cludedly** *adv.*, **se'cludedness.**

1835 *New Monthly Mag.* XLIII. 455 A bower of the most approved secludedness and beauty. **1837** LOCKHART *Scott* I. v. 164 Both living secludedly, they had scarcely seen each other for many years.

secluding (sɪ'kluːdɪŋ), *ppl. a.* [f. SECLUDE *v.* + -ING².] That secludes.

a **1851** MOIR *Lines in Park of Kelburn* i. Poet. Wks. 1852 I. 194 The green secluding hills, that hem it round. **1857** J. HAMILTON *Less. fr. Gt. Biog.* 189 With no barrier round Him except His own secluding sanctity.

secluse (sɪ'kluːz), *a.* Now *rare.* [ad. L. *sēclūsus*, pa. pple. of *sēclūdĕre* SECLUDE *v.* Cf. OF. *seclus*, Sp. *secluso.*] Secluded; withdrawn from view or from society. †Also *absol.* in plural sense.

1597 BP. HALL *Sat.* II. ii. 4 Whom better fit some cotes of sad secluse. **1603** HARSNET *Decl. Pop. Impost.* iii. 11 Places ..for their situation, beeing remote and secluse from ordinary accesse. **1668** S. PATRICK *Pilgrim* xv. 111, I cannot see by what merit the Secluse do assume to themselves the title of Religious more than others. **1675** E. W[ILSON] *Spadacrene Dunelm.* 70 Penetrating by its tenuity of parts the most secret and secluse parts of our Bodies. **1858** *Sat. Rev.* 28 Aug. 203/2 His [W. S. Landor's] has always been a secluse, estranged existence. **1861** R. GARNETT in *Macm. Mag.* IV. 248 Who, secluse, a serious priest of Pallas, Daily, nightly, patient accumulatest Lore on lore.

Hence †**se'cluseness**, secludedness, seclusion.

1847 in WEBSTER. **1860** in WORCESTER (citing MORE).

seclusion (sɪˈkluːʒən). [ad. med.L. *seclusionem* (Diefenb.), f. L. *sēclūs-*, *sēclūdĕre*: see SECLUDE *v.*]

1. The action of secluding; †exclusion (*obs.*).

1623 COCKERAM I, *Seclusion*, a shutting apart. **1664** OWEN *Vind. Animad. Fiat Lux* xviii. 450 Nor can I gather that.. you suffered..for your..love to Monarchy: Seeing some of you would have been contented with its everlasting Seclusion. *c* **1680** *Let.* in Somers *Tracts* (1748) I. 131, I think it both unreasonable and unjust, for any Subject of England to attempt his Seclusion from the Crown. **1808** in *Encycl. Brit.* (1885) XIX. 748/2 Recognizing the importance of attempting reformation by the seclusion, employment, and religious instruction of prisoners.

attrib. **1895** *Law Times* 13 July 258 An inmate was subjected to the discipline of a 'seclusion cell'.

2. The condition or state of being secluded; an instance of this. ***in seclusion***, apart from society.

1784 COWPER *Task* III. 675 Oh, blest seclusion from a jarring world, Which he, thus occupied, enjoys! **1794** MRS. RADCLIFFE *Myst. Udolpho* xxx, Several days passed with Emily in total seclusion. **1856** STANLEY *Sinai & P.* i. (ed. 3) 96 The elevation and seclusion of some of its edifices, perched high among almost inaccessible rocks. **1872** J. G. MURPHY *Comm., Levit.* xii. Introd., The period of seclusion after child-bearing. **1886** RUSKIN *Præterita* I. 427 Brought up..in severe seclusion.

3. A place or abode in which one is secluded.

1791 MRS. RADCLIFFE *Rom. Forest* iv, La Motte had now passed above a month in this seclusion. **1829** I. TAYLOR *Enthus.* viii. 196 There was certainly as much piety without as within these seclusions—and much more learning. **1859** HAWTHORNE *Marb. Faun* viii, A seclusion, but seldom a solitude; for..all who breathe Roman air, find free admission. **1884** SINNETT *Esoteric Buddhism* ix. 148 They have sometimes been isolated in separate seclusions.

seclusionist (sɪˈkluːʒənɪst). [f. SECLUSION + -IST.] One who advocates seclusion; applied, e.g. to the supporters of monasticism, and (*Hist.*) to a Chinese or a Japanese who is adverse to the admission of foreigners to his country.

1839 I. TAYLOR *Ancient Chr.* I. iv. 521 The Jewish seclusionists well understood..that a community of goods was impracticable. **1886** *Atlantic Monthly* Nov. 604 If the progressionists had not seized the reins of government [in Korea], the seclusionists would soon have had everything their own way. **1887** *Fortn. Rev.* May 677 Now [in Japan] ..it would probably be difficult to find so much as one genuine seclusionist. *Ibid.*, The head of the seclusionist party.

seclusive (sɪˈkluːsɪv), *a.* [As if ad. L. **sēclūsivus*, f. *sēclūs-*, *sēclūdĕre*: see SECLUDE *v.*]

1. Serving or tending to seclude; disposed to seclude oneself, affecting seclusion.

a **1834** COLERIDGE (Worcester 1860). **1834** I. TAYLOR *Sat. Even.* 274 Religion or the devotional part of it is..by its necessary condition seclusive. **1890** F. BARRETT *Between Life & Death* I. ii. 29 Her ways were odd and seclusive. **1894** J. T. FOWLER *Adamnan* Introd. 38 On the top a palisade and quick hedge for seclusive enclosure. **1903** *Daily Chron.* 2 Feb. 4/6 The Royal Society electing him to their seclusive membership.

2. *Sc. Law.* Exclusive *of*.

1855 *Deed* in *Law Rep.*, 9 App. Cases 304 In liferent for her liferent alimentary use of the annual proceeds thereof allenarly, and seclusive of the jus mariti of [her husband].

Hence **seˈclusively** *adv.*, **seˈclusiveness**.

1822 *Examiner* 347/2 [The picture] Landscape with fall of water, &c. is poetical seclusiveness. **1883** W. JOLLY *Life J. Duncan* xxxix. 466 The enclosing hills seemed to shut out the cottage more seclusively from the world. **1885** J. M. LUDLOW in *Homil. Rev.* Apr. 282 What we may call their [Jewish Rabbins] seclusiveness of thought.

†**seˈclusory.** *Obs.*$^{-0}$ [ad. L. *sēclūsōrium*, f. *sēclūdĕre*: see SECLUDE *v.* and -ORY.] (See quot.)

1656 BLOUNT *Glossogr.*, *Seclusory*, a place where any thing is shut up a part from other; a Coop.

sec-mod (sɛk mɒd). Colloq. abbrev. of *secondary modern* s.v. SECONDARY *a.* 5 f.

1968 *Listener* 28 Mar. 421/2 The wretched life-style on offer to most sec-mod school-leavers. **1973** *Times* 31 May 10/7 Black and white kids, in their sec-mod school uniform.

seco- (ˈsɛkəʊ). *Chem.* [f. L. *sec-āre* to cut + -O.] A formative element used in naming derivatives, esp. of steroids, in which fission of a ring has occurred (see quot. 1951). Hence also as quasi-*adj.*

1951 R. S. CAHN et al. in *Jrnl. Chem. Soc.* 3535 Ring fission, with addition of a hydrogen atom at each terminal group thus created, shall be indicated by the prefix *seco*, the original steroid numbering being retained. **1959** L. F. & M. FIESER *Steroids* iv. 156 This was identified as the 2,3-secodicarboxylic acid..by saponification, oxidation to the 7-ketone, and Wolff-Kishner reduction to the known 2,3-secocholestane-2,3-dicarboxylic acid. **1961** I. E. BUSH *Chromatogr. Steroids* ii. 102 The opening of rings to form seco-dicarboxylic acids. *Ibid.* vi. 342 The C_{19} triols..are oxidized to the D-seco-16,17-dialdehydes. **1977** *Lancet* 16 Apr. 841/1 The physiological regulation of secretion of this *seco*-steroid by the kidney.

secobarbital (sɛkəʊˈbɑːbɪtəl). *Pharm.* Chiefly *U.S.* [f. SECO(NDARY *a.* + BARBITAL.] = QUINALBARBITONE.

1952 *Analytical Chem.* XXIV. 1605/1 Considerable differences in the [optical density] ratios at various wave lengths are found with these barbiturates. For example, at 270 mμ butylallylonal has the highest ratio, +0·81, followed by secobarbital +0·69. **1962** *New Scientist* 22 Feb. 426/1 Some results obtained with secobarbital..and other drugs are also mentioned. **1974** M. C. GERALD *Pharmacol.* xi. 205 Short-acting barbiturates such as..secobarbital ('red devils'). **1976** *Billings* (Montana) *Gaz.* 11 July 9-A/1 In order on DAWN's list of drugs most frequently recorded in crisis situations..were heroin, marijuana, aspirin, LSD, secobarbital (..known as 'red devils').

secodont (ˈsɛkəʊdɒnt), *a. Zool.* [f. L. *sec-āre* to cut + Gr. ὀδοντ-, ὀδούς tooth.] Of a tooth: adapted or suited for cutting. Of an animal: having such teeth.

1891 FLOWER & LYDEKKER *Introd. Mammals* 32 Trituberculism differentiating into a secodont and a bunodont series, according as to whether the dentition becomes of a cutting or a crushing type. **1968** R. ZANGERL tr. *Peyer's Compar. Odontol.* 244 Both upper and lower carnassials [in modern carnivores] are secodont; that is, they have sharp cutting edges that run parallel to the edge of the jaw.

secohm (ˈsɛkəʊm). *Electr. Obs.* exc. *Hist.* [f. SEC(OND *sb.*[1] + OHM[2].] A name proposed for a unit of inductance.

1887 AYRTON & PERRY in *Nature* 9 June 131/2 Hence we are driven to suggesting a temporary name for the unit, and as the first three letters in 'second' are common to the name in English, French, German, Italian, &c., and ohm is also common, we venture to suggest 'secohm' as a provisional name. **1948** *Atlantic Monthly* May 613/2 The motion to adopt 'henry' as the name of this unit..was seconded by.. Professor Ayrton, who had himself, a few years ago, proposed the word 'sec-ohm' as being a proper name for the unit of induction. **1963** JERRARD & MCNEILL *Dict. Sci. Units* 127 The secohm was equal to the product of one legal ohm and one second and its magnitude was about the same as a henry.

secomoure, obs. form of SYCAMORE.

Seconal (ˈsɛkənæl, -əl). *Pharm.* Also **seconal.** [f. SECON(DARY *a.* + AL(LYL.] A proprietary term for SECOBARBITAL. Also, a tablet of this.

1935 *Official Gaz.* (U.S. Patent Office) 23 July 727/2 Eli Lilly and Company, Indianapolis... *Seconal.* For products of secondary amyl allyl barbituric acid and the sodium salts thereof..useful as hypnotics. Claims use since Apr. 11, 1935. **1937** *Jrnl. Amer. Pharmaceut. Assoc.* XXVI. 1248 It was concluded that 'Seconal' had a shorter duration of action and that its minimal anesthetic dose and minimal lethal dose were smaller than those of 'Sodium Amytal'. **1938** *Trade Marks Jrnl.* 23 Feb. 218/1 Seconal. **1950** E. HEMINGWAY *Across River & into Trees* ii. 11 He was also anxious to lie down and take a seconal. **1958** 'A. BRIDGE' *Portuguese Escape* xiii. 217 She swallowed some Seconal with a gulp of water. **1959** N. MAILER *Advts. for Myself* (1961) 214 Drugging myself into sleep with an overload of seconal. **1965** G. MARX *Let.* 12 Oct. (1967) 68 At 8 we take two Seconals, three aspirin and a shot of LSD. **1973** M. AMIS *Rachel Papers* 176 'What did you give him?' 'Half a Mandie, a Seconal—I can't remember—and two Mogadon, I think.'

second (ˈsɛkənd), *sb.*[1] Forms: 4, 6 seconde, 6– second. [a. F. *seconde*, ad. med.L. *secunda*, fem. of L. *secundus* SECOND *a.*, used ellipt. for *secunda minuta*, lit. 'second minute', i.e. the result of the second operation of sexagesimal division; the result of the first such operation (now called 'minute' simply) being the 'first' or 'prime minute' or 'prime' (see PRIME *sb.*[2] 2).

The med.L. *secunda* is also represented by G. *sekunde*, Du. *secunde* fem. (whence Sw. *sekund* masc., Da. *sekund*). Med.L. had a neut. *secundum* (cf. *minūtum* a minute), whence Sp., Pg. *segundo*, It. *secondo*.]

1. *Geom.* (*Astr.*, *Geog.*, etc.) A sixtieth part of a minute, $\frac{1}{3600}$th part of a degree. See MINUTE *sb.*[1] 2, DEGREE *sb.* 9.

c **1391** CHAUCER *Astrol.* I. §8 Thise degrees of signes ben euerich of hem considered of 60 Mynutes, & euery Minute of 60 secondes. **1599** E. WRIGHT *Err. Navig.* D 2, Let the meridian (diuided into degrees, minutes, seconds, &c.) roule vpon a streight line. **1713** J. WARD *Young Mathem. Guide* (ed. 2) 350 Every Circle is suppos'd to be divided into 360.. Degrees; every Degree is sub-divided into 60 Parts call'd Minutes; and every Minute into 60 Seconds, &c. **1870** PROCTOR *Other Worlds* vii. 171 The star Alpha Centauri.. exhibits..an annual parallax of one second.

2. a. In measurement of time: The sixtieth part of a minute, $\frac{1}{3600}$th of an hour. Now one of the base units of the International System of Units, and scientifically defined in terms of the frequency of a spectral transition of an isotope of cæsium (see quot. 1968).

1588 A. KING tr. *Canisius' Catech.* g viij, Ye cowrse of ye sone, quhilk sence hes bene obserueit to be accompleseit in 365 dayes 5 houris 10 min: and 16 Secondis. **1695** CONGREVE *Love for Love* III. ix, At Ten a Clock, punctually at Ten. *Sir Samp.* To a Minute, to a Second; thou shalt set thy Watch, and the Bridegroom shall observe it's Motions. **1762** [W. YOUNG] *Treat. Weights & Meas.* 24 The pendulum which vibrates seconds at London, has been commonly esteemed 39,2 English inches. **1883** R. S. BALL in *Encycl. Brit.* XV. 668 [In the C.G.S. system] the unit of length is the *centimetre*, the unit of mass is the *gramme*, and the unit of time is the *second*. **1955** *Sci. Amer.* Mar. 52/2 Accordingly the International Committee is to define the second as: 1/31,556,925·975 of the tropical year 1900. **1968** *Nature* 16 Nov. 651/1 The basic unit of time in the International System of Units, formerly identical with the astronomical second of ephemeris time, is now based on a natural periodicity of the caesium atom and is defined in the following terms: 'the second is the duration of 9 192 631 770 periods of the radiation corresponding to the transition between the two hyperfine levels of the ground state of the caesium-133 atom'. **1975** *Oxf. Compan. Sports & Games* 975/1 This reduced the previous world records by half a second, the biggest single advance in the history of the events.

b. Used vaguely for an extremely short time, an 'instant'.

1825 SCOTT *Betrothed* iv, A momentum of speed which increased with every second. **1897** *Daily News* 14 June 5/7 There was a second's panic in the crowd. **1906** CHARL. MANSFIELD *Girl & Gods* xii, Do you mind if I slip away for just two seconds and take off this frock?

3. *attrib.* and *Comb.*, as **second-foot**, a unit of the rate of flow of water, equal to one cubic foot per second; **second- (seconds-) hand**, a hand or pointer of a timepiece indicating seconds; **second- (seconds-) mark** *Math.*, the character ″, denoting a second or seconds (either of angle or of time); **second- (seconds-) pendulum**, a pendulum of a timepiece vibrating seconds; **second pivot** (see quot.); † **second- (seconds-) watch**, a timepiece indicating seconds.

1898 *U.S. Dept. Agric. Yearbk. 1897* 640 Where water is abundant, the duty has been known to be as low as 50 acres ..to the *second-foot. **1914** RIES & WATSON *Engin. Geol.* v. 250 The height of the black lines illustrates the relative quantity of water expressed in cubic feet per second, or second feet, occurring throughout the year. **1928** *Manch. Guardian Weekly* 31 Aug. 178/3 The assumption is that the main river, suitably fortified with levees, can carry rather less than 2,000,000 cubic feet of water per second (or 2,000,000 second feet as it is briefly described). **1759** PRINGLE in *Phil. Trans.* LI. 250 Upon looking at a watch, which had a *second-hand,..he stopped me when I had counted 13 seconds. *c* **1850** *Rudim. Nav.* (Weale) 41 Your watch..should be furnished with a seconds-hand. **1888** LD. GRIMTHORPE in *Encycl. Brit.* XXIV. 398/1 In the chronograph watch there is, in addition to the centre seconds-hand, an independent seconds-hand which, when not in operation, stands at zero. **1888** JACOBI *Printers' Voc.*, **Seconds mark.* **1763** MURDOCH in *Phil. Trans.* LIV. 31 A *second-pendulum at the equator would be 39·154 inches long. **1837** WHEWELL *Hist. Induct. Sci.* (1857) II. 221 Determining the length of the seconds' pendulum in different latitudes. **1884** F. J. BRITTEN *Watch & Clockm. Handbk.* 233 [The] *Seconds Pivot..[is] the prolongation of the fourth wheel arbor to which the seconds hand of a watch is fixed. **1754** SMEATON in *Phil. Trans.* XLVIII. 537 A third observed, by a *seconds-watch, the time taken up in running these 357 feet. **1763** SHORT *ibid.* LIII. 329 Each observer had a Second-watch in his hand.

second (ˈsɛkənd), *a.* and *sb.*[2] Forms: 3–7 secund(e, 4–5 secounde, 4, 6 seconde, 4–6 secound, 5 secownde, seycond, 6 *Sc.* secunnd, sycond, 4– second. [a. F. *second* = Pr. *segon*, Sp., Pg. *segundo*, It. *secondo*, ad. L. *secundus* following (hence favourable, prosperous, primarily of a breeze), next, second, f. root of *sequī* to follow.

OE. had no proper ordinal for the number two (like G. *zweite*, Du. *tweede*, F. *deuxième*), the sense being expressed by *ōðer* (see OTHER *a.*); this being ambiguous, the Fr. word found early acceptance.]

A. *adj.*

1. a. Coming next after the first according to any contextually understood principle of enumeration (e.g. in order of time, position, rank, quality, conventional or arbitrarily adopted sequence): the ordinal corresponding to the cardinal two.

(*a*) with sb. expressed; also *predicatively*.

1297 R. GLOUC. (Rolls) 5724 In þe secunde ȝere þat he verst bissop was. **1303** R. BRUNNE *Handl. Synne* I. 9787 The secunde sacrament, y vndyrstonde, Ys graunted of þe bysshop honde. *c* **1386** CHAUCER *Sec. Nun's T.* 139 Euery secounde or þridde day sche faste. *c* **1440** *Jacob's Well* 46 Here brekyst þou þe secunde tyme þe x. comaundementes. **1507** *Acc. Ld. High Treas. Scot.* III. 290 The secund day of Maii. **1549** *Compl. Scot., Epist. Q. Grace* 6 Numa pompilius, the sycond kyng of rome. **1588** SHAKS. *L.L.L.* I. ii. 183 The first and second cause will not serue my turne. *a* **1674** CLARENDON *Hist. Reb.* XI. §151 The Convertine, a ship of the second rank. **1700** DRYDEN *Sigism. & Guisc.* 35 Youth, Health, and Ease, and most an amorous Mind, To second Nuptials had her Thoughts inclin'd. **1872** FITZGERALD *Omar* (ed. 3) lv, You know, my Friends, with what a brave Carouse I made a Second Marriage in my house. **1884** LD. BRABOURNE *Lett. Jane Austen* I. v. 87 Jane's picture of a clergyman is generally that of a second son who enters the profession in order to hold a family living.

(*b*) with ellipsis of sb. understood from the context.

a **1300** *X Commandm.* 25 in *E.E.P.* (1862) 16 Þe secunde [commandment] so is þis, sundai wel þat ȝe holde. **1387** TREVISA *Higden* (Rolls) II. 23 In Bretayn, beeþ many wondres... Þe firste is at Pectoun... Þe secounde is at Stonhenge by sides Salisbury. *c* **1470** HENRY *Wallace* VII. 111 The fyrst writtyng was gross letteris of bras, The second gold, the thrid was siluir scheyne. **1636** HEYWOOD *Challenge Beauty* IV. Wks. 1874 V. 50 If you Would add a second to this curtesie. **1748** RICHARDSON *Clarissa* IV. 201, I liked her at first sight, and better at second. **1814** CARY *Dante, Inf.* XVIII. 38 Ah! how they made them bound at the first stripe! None for the second waited, nor the third. **1858** *Chamb. Jrnl.* 20 Nov. 334/1 In the first of which objects, by the way, they have succeeded much better than in the second.

b. ***the second***: appended to a personal name to designate the second bearer of the name in a succession of persons (chiefly sovereigns, or persons jocularly likened to sovereigns). Also (now *rarely*) used to designate one resembling the person to whom the name belongs (cf. 4 below).

c **1386** CHAUCER *Man of Law's T.* 261 O Sowdanesse, roote of iniquitee, Virago, thou Semyrame the secounde. **1535** STEWART *Cron. Scot.* III. 4 Henrie the second rang into his steid, The emprice sone. **1558** W. FORREST (*title*) Grisild the Second. [Meaning Kath. of Aragon.] **1735** JOHNSON *Lobo's Abyssinia, Descr.* i. 44 In the Reign of King John the Second. **1886** C. E. PASCOE *London of To-day* xviii. (ed. 3) 165 'Dick' Tattersall, or Richard the Second, the grandson of the founder. **1891** SMILES *Publisher & Friends* I. 29 John Murray the Second—the 'Anak of Publishers', according to Lord Byron.

c. *Gram.* In ***second person***: see PERSON *sb.* 8. Also in ***second declension***, ***conjugation***, and in names of tenses, as ***second aorist***, ***future***, ***perfect***, where the reference is to a conventional order of enumeration adopted by grammarians.

By modern grammarians this method of designation has been almost entirely abandoned as regards tenses, and to a great extent as regards declensions and conjugations, descriptive terms being substituted for numerical.

1530 PALSGR. *Introd.* 31 Of the seconde conjugation. *c* **1532** DU WES *Introd. Fr.* in *Palsgr.* 1011 The Seconde Future. I shuld knele. **1580** HOLLYBAND *Treas. Fr. Tong*, Thirdly, the second perfect, *j'ay aimé*, I haue loued. *a* **1637** B. JONSON *Eng. Gram.* xiv. (1640) 60 The second Declension formeth the Plurall from the Singular, by putting to *n. Ibid.* xviii. 63 The second Conjugation. **1875** T. K. ARNOLD *Henry's First Lat. Bk.* 14 Verbs whose infinitive ends in *ēre*, are of the second conjugation.

d. *absol.* The person or thing that has been mentioned in the second place. So in *Heraldry* (see quot. 1868).

1572 BOSSEWELL *Armorie* 114b, He beareth Argent, a fesse Gules, betwene three Eaglettes Sable, membred and beaked of the second. **1868** CUSSANS *Her.* xi. (1893) 158 A tincture must never be mentioned twice in the same Blazon: should it occur again, it must be expressed as of the first (or field), of the second, of the last, &c., as the case may be.

2. a. Next in rank, quality, importance, or degree of any attribute, *to* (a person or thing regarded as first). Hence, in negative and limiting contexts, Inferior (*to none*, *only to* ...). [Cf. L. *nulli secundus*.]

c **1374** CHAUCER *Troylus* v. 836 Troylus was neuere vn-to no wight As in his tyme in no degre secounde. **1590** SHAKS. *Com. Err.* v. i. 7 Of very reuerent reputation sir,.. Second to none that liues heere in the Citie. **1593** —— *2 Hen. VI*, I. ii. 43 Nay Elinor, then must I chide outright, Presumptuous Dame, ill-nurter'd Elianor, Art thou not second Woman in the Realme? **1667** MILTON *P.L.* III. 409 Regardless of the Bliss wherein hee sat Second to thee, offerd himself to die For mans offence. **1754** GRAY *Poesy* 95 Nor second He, that rode sublime Upon the seraph-wings of Extasy, The secrets of th' Abyss to spy. **1821** CANNING *Sp.* 2 Apr. (1828) IV. 306 Among the names he had missed one, now no more, never second in the zeal of his resistance. **1860** TENNENT *Story Guns* (1864) 233 In the search for improvement failures have a value second only to success. **1861** GEO. ELIOT *Let.* 17 May (1954) III. 414, I doing little else but feel eminently uncomfortable, for which.. I have a faculty 'second to none'. **1872** YEATS *Growth Comm.* 49 Miletus was scarcely second to Tyre in luxury and wealth. **1961** J. HELLER *Catch-22* (1962) xi. 112 He would stand second to none in his devotion to country.

b. With following superlative: Having only one superior in the specified attribute. Cf. SECOND-BEST.

1533 *Test. Ebor.* (Surtees) VI. 41 My secunde gretest braspotte. **1880**, etc. Second last [see LAST *a.* 1 b]. **1910** W. M. RAINE *Bucky O'Connor* (1920) xx. 226 I'll agree to the second dearest in the world. **1959** J. KIRKUP tr. *S. de Beauvoir's Memoirs of Dutiful Daughter* II. 116 She was.. the second eldest daughter. **1977** *Word 1972* XXVIII. 104 The second-youngest of the fluent speakers. **1979** *Nature* 15 Feb. 561/2 *Secernosaurus* is the second most primitive hadrosaur known.

c. In designations of office, denoting the lower of two, or the next to the highest of several persons holding the same office; e.g. ***second captain***, ***lieutenant*** (see quots.), ***second lord*** (of the Admiralty, etc.), ***second master***, ***mistress*** (in a school), ***second mate*** (also in naut. slang phrases referring to measures of liquor), ***officer*** (in a merchant ship).

The Fr. expression *en second* (quot. 1702) occurs sometimes in Eng. official use in the 18th c.; 'officers en second' are mentioned, e.g. in the *London Gazette* 1716–20. Cf. SECOND *v.*[2]

1702 *Milit. Dict.* (1704), *Second Captain*, or *Lieutenant en Second*, one whose Company has been broke, and he is joyn'd to another, to act and serve under the Captain or Lieutenant of it... There are also Second Captains and Lieutenants of the First Creation, that is, who were never so in the other Companies... Second Lieutenants are much us'd among the Foot in France. **1709** *Lond. Gaz.* No. 4543/2 The second Lieutenant, and Mr. Lawrence,.. were shot through the Body. **1797** *Encycl. Brit.* (ed. 3) X. 36/1 *Second Lieutenant in the Artillery*, is the same as an ensign in an infantry regiment,.. and must assist the first lieutenant in the detail of the company's duty. **1843** J. F. COOPER *Ned Myers* II. ii. 61 Putting a second-mate's nip of brandy into my glass. **1853** 'C. BEDE' *Adv. Mr. Verdant Green* i. 6 The second master.. 'licked a feller' for a false quantity. **1866** *School Life at Winchester Coll.* xiv. 177 The *Roll* which was published every November, giving a list of the entire establishment of the College, commencing with the Warden, Head master, (Informator,) Second master, (Hostiarius,) the ten fellows, three chaplains; the under masters [etc.]. **1923** L. MAGNUS *Jubilee Bk. Girls' Public Day School Trust* iv. 58 Her retirement coincided with that of her Second Mistress, Mrs. Withiel. **1933** P. A. EADDY *Hull Down* 99 He pulls a pint bottle out of the case, and drawing the cork pulls out a good Second Mate's four fingers. **1952** V. NOAKE *Hist. Alice Ottley School Worcester* xiii. 140 Miss Spurling's successor.. was Miss Hilda M. Roden, second mistress of the Stamford High School, Stamford, Lincs. **1967** S. WATERS *Indentures Indorsed* xxxv. 232 A couple of second mate's pegs was usually enough to set us all singing. **1976** C. DEXTER *Last seen Wearing* xxx. 211 School masters, even experienced second masters, aren't all that highly recompensed.

d. *Mil.* ***second in command***: holding a position only subordinate to the chief commander of an army or one of its subdivisions. Often *absol.* (quasi-*sb.*).

1776 W. HOWE *Let.* 7 June in *9th Rep. R. Comm. Hist. MSS.* App. III. (rev. ed.) 35 in *Parl. Papers 1910* (Cd. 5038) XXXV. 675 The seniority of his rank.. would have placed him second in command in Canada had he not been previously employed to the southward. **1837** CARLYLE *Fr. Rev.* II. IV. iii, Poor Commandant Gouvion, watching at the Tuileries, second in National command, sees several things hard to interpret. **1882** *Manch. Guard.* 6 Sept. 5 Baker Pasha will be appointed second in command and 'adjoint' of the Turkish Commander in-Chief. **1939** C. S. FORESTER *Captain Hornblower, R.N.* xvi. 173 On his first commission his second-in-command had taken advantages of lapses on his part. **1982** *Observer* 16 Apr. 14/6 His second-in-command is a Sierra Leonean major.

e. *Mus.* Used to distinguish the next to the highest part in a piece of concerted music. Hence of a voice or instrument: Rendering such a part.

1724 *Short Explic. For. Wds. in Mus. Bks.*, *Violino Secondo*, the Second Violin. **1746** TANSUR *New Mus. Gram.* 131 If you would set a Second Treble, or Cantus, Medius, or Counter, to any Piece of Musick that was before in Two Parts, to make Three Parts; let it begin from the Bass on some different Cord from the Tenor [etc.]. **1769** Second voice [see CONTRALTO 2]. **1836** HICKSON *Singing Master* I. Pref. 4 The second parts will always be sung with most effect by boys between the ages of twelve and fourteen. **1885** W. S. GILBERT *Mikado* I. 15 Assuming the disguise of a Second Trombone, I joined the band in which you found me.

3. Having the degree of quality, fineness, etc. next to the best; of the second grade or class. Now only *Comm.* in certain customary uses.

In some applications there is also the notion of being produced by a second operation, after the best has been already obtained.

c **1440** *Pallad. on Husb.* XII. 482 And aftir oil secounde Is maad, that on a sadder mylle is grounde. **1577** B. GOOGE *Heresbach's Husb.* IV. (1586) 184 The fragments of the Coame.. heated and strained againe, doe make a seconde Hony. **1618** in *Archæologia* XLIV. 411 Item for second bread 2 0 0. **1638** PENKETHMAN *Artach.* D 4, When the second wheate (which is the Red being in meale) is sold for iiii l. the Quarter in the market. **1799** in *Spirit Publ. Jrnls.* III. 14 My coat.. made of good second cloth. **1842** BISCHOFF *Woollen Manuf.* II. 124 We used to have a certain description of cloth for livery purposes, called second cloth, made of English wool. **1856** *Jrnl. R. Agric. Soc.* XVII. II. 483 Each cow gives about 1 lb. per week of 'second butter', fetching 2*d.* per lb. less than the best. **1860** NEWLANDS *Carp. & Joiner's Assist.* Gloss., *Second Bricks*, bricks of a quality next to the finest mail stocks or cutters.

4. a. Other, another; additional to that which has already existed, taken place, been mentioned, etc. Often qualifying a proper name, to designate one who equals or closely resembles the bearer of the name.

c **1375** *Sc. Leg. Saints* xxvi. (*Nycholas*) 1068 He tuk þe secund coupe in hand, & one þe altare fore offerand It set. **1500–20** DUNBAR *Poems* vii. 17 Welcum in were the secund Iulius, The prince of knightheyd, and flour of cheualry. **1558** W. FORREST *Grisild the Second* (Roxb.) 30 A famous kynge [Hen. VII].. Called (in his tyme) the Seconde Salomon. **1589** GREENE *Menaphon* (Arb.) 62 And therewith her eyes distilled such abundance of teares, as.. made her seeme a more than second Niobe. *c* **1600** SHAKS. *Sonn.* lix, If their bee nothing new, but that which is, Hath beene before, how are our braines beguild, Which laboring for inuention beare amisse The second burthen of a former child? **1784** *Rolliad* viii. (1795) 49 Vansittart, thou, A second Hastings, if the Fates allow. **1805** SCOTT *Let.* in *Lockhart* (1837) II. ii. 59 Could any one bear the story of a second city being taken by a wooden horse? **1850** SIR F. MADDEN *Wycliffite Bible* List of MSS. No. 28, The Ms... has been corrected throughout by a second, but nearly contemporary scribe.

b. *Proverb*: ***habit*** (or ***usage***) ***is second nature***. Hence (without allusion to the proverb) ***to be*** (***come as***, etc.) ***second nature*** (***to*** one): to be as if natural or instinctive. Occas. in ellipt. constructions without a vb.

The L. form, *consuetudo est altera* (or *secunda*) *natura*, is found in St. Augustine and Macrobius, and approximately in Cicero (see Lewis & Short s.v. *Natura*); the notion occurs in Aristotle (e.g. *Probl.* IV. xxvi, *Eth. N.* VII. x) and other Greek writers.

1390 GOWER *Conf.* III. 23 For in Phisique this I finde, Usage is the seconde kinde. **1662** J. DAVIES tr. *Olearius' Voy. Ambass.* 89 That habit being as it were converted into a second nature. *a* **1729** J. ROGERS *Nineteen Serm.* xii. (1735) 254 Habits which.. are become a kind of second Nature to him. **1821** SCOTT *Kenilw.* xxxii, Those to whom long practice has rendered them [*sc.* frivolous fopperies] a second nature. **1910** S. E. WHITE in *Sunset* Apr. 421/1 Bob.. rolled over twice with the rapid, vigorous twist second-nature to a seasoned half-back. **1944** *Sun* (Baltimore) 28 Nov. 8/2 Civilian air defense comes as second nature to them. **1954** T. S. ELIOT *Confidential Clerk* III. 96, I do feel more at ease when I'm behind a desk: It's second nature. **1967** SINGHA & MASSEY *Indian Dances* xviii. 159 They become second nature to her when she is dancing.

c. ***second self***: a friend who agrees absolutely with one's tastes and opinions, or for whose welfare one cares as much as for one's own.

After L. *alter idem*, Gr. ἄλλος αὐτός and ἕτερος αὐτός (Arist. *Eth. N.* IX).

1586 T. B. *La Primaud. Fr. Acad.* (1594) I. 141 The mightie and inviolable bond of friendship, as of a second-selfe did constraine him to lend his eare to his friend. **1665** BRATHWAIT *Comment Two Tales* (1901) 93, I will offer to your choice two things, wherein please your self, and you shall please me who am your second self. **1778** MISS BURNEY *Evelina* xxvi, As to Miss Mirvan, she is my second self, and neither hopes nor fears but as I do. **1851** LYTTON *Not so bad* I. i. 6 Ha, Softhead! my Pylades—my second self!

transf. *c* **1600** SHAKS. *Sonn.* lxxiii. 8 Blacke night.. Deaths second selfe that seals vp all in rest.

†**5.** 'Helpful, lending assistance' (Schmidt). *Obs.*

1611 SHAKS. *Wint. T.* II. iii. 27 Nay rather (good my Lords) be second to me.

6. a. quasi-*adv.* Secondly, in the second place (*rare*); as the second in succession. Also, †for the second time.

1382 WYCLIF *Gen.* xxvii. 36 The riȝtis of my fyrst geting biforn he took a wey, and now secounde he hath vnder rauyshide my benysoun. **1536** CRANMER in Ellis *Orig. Lett.* Ser. III. III. 25 Seconde,.. I shewed the people that this thynge ought no thynge to move theym, for it was [etc.]. **1842** WHITEHEAD *R. Savage* (1845) II. vii. 271, I was confounded first, and incensed second. *a* **1859** DE QUINCEY *Posth. Wks.* (1891) I. 55 First, it was not to be too complete; second, even for this incompleteness it was not to be concentrated within a short time. *Mod.* Mr. A. opened the debate. Mr. B. spoke second.

b. ellipt. for *second class* (in travelling by rail, etc.).

1912 R. BROOKE *Let.* Jan. (1968) 334 The maids of the Ordinary Rich go second, with you and the normal me. **1937** W. H. SAUMAREZ SMITH *Let.* 10 July in *Young Man's Country* (1977) ii. 80 As I'm not getting Travel Allowance for this trip, I'd decided to travel 2nd. *a* **1976** A. CHRISTIE *Autobiogr.* (1977) VI. i. 289 Ladies travelling alone would never have travelled third class... Even ladies' maids always travelled second.

7. Combinations.

a. In syntactical combs. of a permanent nature or with special meaning (many of which are also used *attrib.* or as *adj.*, and are then written with hyphen), as *second cause*, *childhood*, *coming*, *course*, *cousin*, *death*, †*deliverance*, *empire*, *fiddle*, *fluxion*, *generation*, *house*, *intention*, *inversion*, *language*, *movable*, *notion*, *opinion*, *order*, *power*, *reading*, *secretary*, *sex*, *slip*, *story*, *string*, *subject*, *table*, *thought*(*s*, *vote*, *water*, *wind*, *year* (see these words); **second Adam**, **man** *Theol.*, titles given to Christ with ref. to 1 Cor. xv. 45, 47; **second advent** *Theol.*, the expected Second Coming of Christ as Judge (see ADVENT 2), hence **second adventist** = PREMILLENARIAN *sb.*; **second ballot**, a deciding ballot taken between the candidate who won a previous ballot without securing an absolute majority and the candidate with the next highest number of votes; also *attrib.* of an electoral system using this; **second banana** *slang* (orig. *U.S.*), a supporting comedian (cf. *top banana* s.v. TOP *sb.*[1] 34); **second base** (see BASE *sb.*[1] 15c); **second birth**, (*a*) *Theol.* = REGENERATION 2; †(*b*) = SECUNDINE 1; †(*c*) the entrance upon a new life after death; **second blessing** orig. *U.S.*, an experience of God's grace subsequent to conversion, believed by some Christian groups to be the means of receiving the power to live a sanctified life; **second bottom**, (*a*) *U.S.*, the first terrace above the normal flood plain of a stream; (*b*) *Austral.*, a second stratum of gold-bearing material found by sinking below the bottom (BOTTOM *sb.* 4c); **second breakfast**, a light meal taken late in the morning or early in the afternoon; **second business** (see quot.); **second car**, an additional family car; **second chamber**, in a legislature consisting of two chambers, the one which has chiefly the function of revising the measures prepared and passed by other; also *attrib.*; **second channel** *Radio* = IMAGE *sb.* 9; usu. *attrib.*; **second chop** (see CHOP *sb.*[5] 4); **second cut** *a.*, (*a*) (see quot. 1846); (*b*) *Austral.* and *N.Z.*, (the mark of) a blow made to remove badly-cut fleece; a piece of short or inferior wool produced by this; †**second day**, in Quaker usage, Monday; **second-degree** *Med.*, used to designate burns that are sufficiently severe to cause blistering but not permanent scarring (see quot. 1972); see also DEGREE *sb.* 6d; **second division** *Civil Service*, the lower grade of government clerks, admitted by a competitive examination of more limited range than that prescribed for the higher division; **second feature**, the supporting feature in a cinema programme; also *fig.* and *attrib.*; **second finger**, the finger next to the forefinger, the middle finger; **second floor**, the floor or storey of a building next but one above the ground-floor; also *attrib.*; **second front**, in the war of 1939–45, a front in Nazi-occupied Europe in addition to the Russian sector of fighting; also *fig.* and *attrib.*; **second fronting** *Philol.* [tr. G. *zweite Aufhellung* (K. Luick *Historische Grammatik der englischen Sprache* (1914) 164)], a sound-change in varieties of Old English by which the vowels *æ* (produced by an earlier fronting) and *a* became *e* and *æ* respectively; **second gear**, the gear next above the lowest or bottom gear on a motor vehicle or bicycle; **second girl** *U.S.*, an under-housemaid; **second greaser** *Naut. slang*, a second mate; †**second ground** *Paint.*, the middle distance (see MIDDLE *a.* 6); **second growth**, (*a*) a crop of vegetation replacing one previously destroyed; also *attrib.*; (*b*) the second category of growths (see GROWTH[1] 1 d) or qualities into which wines are divided; also *attrib.*; **second guard**, an additional guard on a sword hilt; **second head** *Venery* (see quots. and cf. HEAD *sb.*[1] 6 b); also *allusively*; **second home**, a second dwelling-place owned or supported in addition to the principal home; a home from home; also *fig.* and *attrib.*; hence **second homer**, the owner of a second home; **second horse** (see quot. 1827); also *attrib.*; †**second infancy**, second childhood (see CHILDHOOD 4); †**second inquest** *Law*, a petty jury; **Second Isaiah** = *Deutero-Isaiah* s.v. DEUTERO-; **second line** *Mil.* (see quot. 1876); also *attrib.*; also *gen.*: any second row or series; freq. *attrib.* or as *adj.*, esp. designating persons or things that rank second in ability, value, etc.; hence **second-liner**, **-lining** *vbl. sb.*; **second man**: see *second Adam* above; **secondman**, an assistant driver on a diesel or electric train, replacing the fireman on a steam train; **second messenger** *Physiol.*, a substance whose release within a cell is promoted by a hormone or 'first messenger', and which brings about a response by the cell; †**second minute** (see MINUTE *sb.*[1] and cf. PRIME *sb.*[2] and etymological note to *sb.*[1] above); **second moment** *Math.* (see quot.); **second mortgage**, a supplementary or puisne mortgage; †**second (motion) shaft** = LAYSHAFT; †**second mourning**, a style of dress allowed by etiquette to be worn when strict mourning is discarded; also *attrib.*; †**second nobles**, the lower nobility or gentry; **second person (of the Trinity)** *Theol.*, the Son (see PERSON *sb.* 7); **second price**, a charge lower than the highest for seats in a playhouse; **second ranker**, a member of the second rank, a second-liner; **second row** *Rugby Football*, the middle row of a team's pack; also *attrib.*; hence **second rower** *Austral.*, a second-row forward; **second scent** (*nonce-use*, after SECOND SIGHT: cf. quot.); **second seer**, one who practises SECOND SIGHT; **second service**, the Communion Service of the Church of England, as following Morning Prayer; (see also quot. 1844); **second shaft**: see *second* (*motion*) *shaft* above; **second sound** *Physics*, a form of longitudinal wave which has many properties in common with sound and is observed in superfluid helium (see quots. and cf. SOUND *sb.*[3]); **second speed** = *second gear*; †**second stature**, ? medium height; †**second stop** *Cricket* = *long-stop* s.v. LONG *a.*[1] A. 18 d; **second-stor(e)y man** *N. Amer. Criminals' slang*, a cat-burglar; **second strike**, a second, retaliatory attack conducted with weapons designed to withstand an initial nuclear attack or first strike; freq. *attrib.*; **second table**, the servants' table at a meal; also *spec.* the senior of two servants' tables; **second tap** *Engin.* (see quot. 1888); **second thigh**, the part of the rear leg of a quadruped that corresponds to the human calf; **Second War**, short for *Second World War*; **Second World** [after THIRD WORLD], (*a*) (following the outlook of the Chinese leadership) the developed countries apart from the two 'superpowers'; (*b*) (poss. reflecting the orig. implication of the term *Third World*) the Communist bloc; **Second World War**, the war which began with the German invasion of Poland on 1 Sept. 1939 and ultimately involved the majority of the nations of the world; hostilities ceased in Europe on 7 May 1945 and in the Far East on 12 Sept. 1945. Also SECOND BEST, SECOND-CLASS, SECOND HAND, SECOND-RATE, SECOND SIGHT.

1587 BIBLE (Genevan) *1 Cor.* xv. 45 (*marginal gloss*), To wit, with the Spirit of God, which descendeth from Christ the *second Adam, into us. **1655** J. TAYLOR *Unum Necessarium* vi. 362 Receiving more by the second Adam than we did lose by the first. **1667** MILTON *Paradise Lost* x. 383 The Tempter set Our second Adam in the Wilderness, To shew him all Earths Kingdomes and thir Glory. **1739** C. WESLEY *Hymn, 'Hark how all the Welkin rings'* ix, Second Adam from above, Reinstate us in thy Love. **1736** *Gentl. Mag* VI. 347/2 But all,..who hope And love his *second advent, will receive The same reward. **1910** *Rep. R. Comm. Electoral Syst.* 3 in *Parl. Papers* (Cd. 5163) XXVI. 295 The *Second Ballot.—A candidate, to be returned at the first election must receive an absolute majority of the valid votes cast. If no candidate obtains such a majority, a second election is held, at which (in the most usual form of the system) only the two candidates compete who received most votes at the first election. **1932** *News Chron.* 15 Mar. 9/1 The electorate, at the second ballot, were left to choose between Hindenburg, Marx and Thaelmann. **1954** B. & R. NORTH tr. *M. Duverger's Pol. Parties* II. i. 239 There were variations of procedure in the simple-majority second-ballot system. **1976** Second ballot [see PREFERENTIAL *a.* c]. **1953** *N.Y. Times* 24 May II. 11/2 In television and radio, Mr. Carney has played *second banana to many star comedy performers. **1974** *Ibid.* 28 Dec. 26/1 He [*sc.* Jack Benny] was often the butt of his second bananas, who devastated him with their barbs. **1977** *Time* 13 June 42/2 Their Yank allies, doubtless because they had second-banana roles in the original production 33 years ago, have dim, brief lives on the screen. **1513** BRADSHAW *St. Werburge* I. 2935 By the *seconde byrthe..we haue regeneracyon. **1545** RAYNALD *Byrth Mankynde* 39 And then secondlye, [issueth] the foresayd after birth: & therefore it may be iustly called ye second byrth or secondyne. **1643** DIGBY *Observ. Relig. Med.* 102 Assoone as Death hath played the Midwife to our second birth, our Soule shall then [etc.]. **1749** C. WESLEY *Hymn, 'Father, Son and Holy Ghost, In Solemn Power'* i, Plunge Her by a Second Birth Into the Depths of God. **1891** B. CARRADINE *Sanctification* ii. 14 My soul was reaching out.. for..what is properly called the **second* blessing. *Ibid.* iv. 33 This definition and explanation of entire sanctification, or the second blessing. **1940** *Amer. Sociol. Rev.* Oct. 741 The Pentecostal groups..believe further in the gift of tongues as an additional evidence of God's grace, awakened..by the 'second blessing'. **1977** *Christian* IV. 204 The call to Community has something of the aura of the conversion experience, or perhaps even more of the so called 'second blessing'. **1787** J. MATHEWS *Jrnl.* 23 Aug. in S. P. Hildreth *Pioneer Hist.* (1848) vii. 184 Went to view the Indian works, which are about a mile from the fort. They extend for about half a mile on the *second bottom. **1788** *Massachusetts Spy* 19 June 3/2 Next to these are what is called second bottoms, which are elevated plains, and gentle risings of the richest uplands. **1855** R. CALDWELL *Gold Era of Victoria* x. 116 As regards the question of 'second bottoms', which has excited considerable discussion,.. all such attempts must..end in disappointment and loss to those engaged in them. **1863** J. C. PATERSON *Gold Fields of Victoria 1862* vii. 80 There is no known reason why there should not be a second bottom on Bendigo Flat. **1905** CHAMBERLIN & SALISBURY *Geol.* iii. 195 (*caption*) Diagram illustrating a distinct terrace and a 'second bottom'.., which may be regarded as a low terrace. **1924** *Prof. Papers U.S. Geol. Survey* No. 126. 14/1 Bluffs 30 to 50 feet in height separate the flats of the gravel-covered terraces from the second bottoms. **1775** J. WOODFORDE *Diary* 2 Jan. (1924) I. 144 We stayed at Whitney and made a *second breakfast, we treated the maid at Whitney. **1802** M. NUGENT *Jrnl.* 15 Jan. (1907) ii. 72 Had fruit for the children at 10; then second breakfast a little after 11.—Dined at 3. **1967** O. HESKY *Time for Treason* xi. 83 Barzilai ..was regretting that he hadn't utilised this period..by having a 'second breakfast', a habit dear to the stomachs of those raised in certain parts of Europe. **1823** *Ann. Reg.* 214* By the phrase *second business is meant that sort of business in which the lead is given to the counsel who are not yet arrived at the dignity of a silk gown. **1966** *Guardian* 16 May 5/3 We had been trying to choose an inexpensive '*second car' for my wife. **1981** L. STEPHAN *Murder or Not* xi. 87 The Subaru was a second car, used by Mr Cook to commute to his job. **1828** J. S. MILL in *Westm. Rev.* Apr. 282 In whichever way selected, this *second chamber would have been..inveterately hostile to nearly every necessary reform. **1861** —— *Repr. Govt.* xiii. 231, I set little value on any check which a Second Chamber can apply to a democracy otherwise unchecked. **1932** C. L. BOLTZ *Everyman's Wireless* xv. 309 If the tuning circuit..is not sufficiently selective it is possible to receive..a signal whose frequency differs from that of the oscillator by the fixed intermediate frequency, but in the opposite direction... Such interference..is sometimes called '*second channel' interference. **1940, 1962** [see IMAGE *sb.* 9]. **1975** G. N. PATCHETT *Radio Servicing* III. ii. 11 It is essential to remove the second channel station before it reaches the frequency-changer or mixer. **1846** HOLTZAPFFEL *Turning* 820 Double cut files..are thus respectively named by the Lancashire.. makers:—1. Rough. 2. Middle-cut. 3. Bastard. 4. *Second-cut. 5. Smooth. 6. Superfine. **1882** ARMSTRONG & CAMPBELL *Austral. Sheep Husbandry* xiv. 168 In shearing the first side of the sheep, each blow should be continued round until the back-bone is passed; this avoids the second cut caused by the blow up the back which should not be allowed, as the 'cutting through' which results considerably depreciates the value of the wool. **1897** D. MCK. WRIGHT *Station Ballads* 34 Mighty lot of wool you've lost! Second cuts? Well, that ain't my fault, you've his wrinkled hide to thank. **1900, 1929** [see FRIBBY *a.* (*sb.*)]. **1950** *N.Z. Jrnl. Agric.* Oct. 311 An efficient shearer will not make many 'second cuts', but the presence of them among the fleeces in a bale will antagonize the wool buyer. **1691** G. FOX *Jrnl.* (1911) II. 367 For the yearly *second days Meeting in London. **1705** S. SEWALL *Jrnl.* 7 Dec. in *Mass. Hist. Soc. Coll.* (1879) VI. 147, I refer'd them to second-day Morning Dec[r] 10. to meet at the Secretary's Office. [**1807** MORRIS & KENDRICK *Edin. Med. Dict.* s.v. *Burn*, Burns are attended with a degree of inflammation, greater or less, according to the violence of the injury; and, according to the different appearances they put on, they may be divided into four different classes, 1. When the burnt part is affected only with a sense of heat and inflammation; 2. When it is also accompanied with intense pain and vesication; 3. When the integuments are converted into an eschar; and, 4. When all the soft parts are scorched to the very bone.] **1930** PACK & DAVIS *Burns* iv. 20 *Second Degree. Degree two is one of vesication. **1972** MILLER & KEANE *Encycl. & Dict. Med. & Nursing* 155/1 First-degree burns damage the epidermis; second-degree burns damage both epidermis and dermis; third-degree burns damage the epidermis, dermis and subcutaneous tissue. **1897** *Westm. Gaz.* 27 July 3/2 The large body of *Second Division clerks. **1927** *Melody Maker* May 515/1 It was quite an ordinary film. I should have only booked it as a *second feature, and then only if there was nothing else available. **1959** C. MACINNES *Absolute Beginners* 61 'You're a romantic!' she said. 'A second feature Romeo!' **1970** J. HANSEN *Fadeout* vi. 49 He..would sit up half the night..enchanted by the tired wisecracks..in forgotten RKO second features of the thirties. **1860** *Man. Artillery Exercises* (Army) 241 The cock resting against the knuckle-joint of the first finger; this and the *second finger only resting on the small of the stock. **1932** *News Chron.* 15 Mar. 8/6 Making the tips of his first and little fingers touch; then bringing the second finger smoothly under the arch thus formed. **1821** COLERIDGE *Let. to Allsop* 20 Oct. *Lett.* etc. (1858) 137 A house to the *second-floor window of which I had been gazing. **1840** THACKERAY *Shabby-genteel Story* vii, Suddenly the second-floor window went clattering up, and Fitch's pale head was thrust out. **1941** W. S. CHURCHILL *Let.* 4 Sept. in *Second World War* (1950) III. xxv. 407 There is no chance..of a *second front being formed in the Balkans without the help of Turkey. **1942** *New Statesman* 3 Jan. 3/2 The key to victory is to open..that 'second front in continental Europe' for which Stalin has publicly called. **1944** M. LASKI *Love on Supertax* ii. 24 He said he'd..make sure there were enough helpers handing out the Second Front leaflets. **1946** *Life* 11 Mar. 63/1 The Russians facetiously called Spam 'the second front'. **1961** E. WAUGH *Unconditional Surrender* I. i. 21 A scarred brick wall, on which..a zealous, arthritic communist had emblazoned the words, *Second Front Now*. **1963** A. HOWARD in Sissons & French *Age of Austerity* 30 The conservatives were waging what turned out to be a decisive second front. **1939** *PMLA* LIV. 19 The *second raising and fronting of West Germanic *a*, which changed *dæg* to *deg* and *dagas* to *dægas*, must..have occurred, not during the fifth century, but during the eighth and early ninth. **1959** A. CAMPBELL *Old Eng. Gram.* v. 64 Second fronting is not a general Merc[ian] change, for it is practically absent in *Ru.*[1], and ME sources show that it was limited to a small part of the vast Midland area. **1972** E. J. DOBSON *Eng. Text of Ancrene Riwle* p. lxxvi, The normal Mercian *ĕ* produced by indirect *i*-mutation followed by second fronting. **1902** *Second gear [see GEAR *sb.* 7 b]. **1976** T. HEALD *Let Sleeping Dogs Die* iii. 62 He.. kept the car at fifteen miles an hour in second gear. **1872** HOWELLS *Wedd. Journ.* (1892) 32 The human wave is beginning to sprinkle the pavement with cooks and *second-girls. **1888** *Second greaser [see GREASER 1 b]. **1916** F. W. WALLACE *Shack Locker* 145 The second greaser paused and added 'I didn't stop, sir.' **1934** C. MOORE *Twilight of Jibs & Topsails* xiv. 227 It started in the mate's watch, and I was in that of the—called in nautical parlance—'second greaser', meaning, of course, the second mate. **1801** FUSELI *Lect. on Art* i. (1848) 354 The series of figures on the *second or middle ground being described as placed above those on the foreground. [**1824** A. HENDERSON *Hist. Anc. & Mod. Wines* II. ii. 155 Among the secondary growths, those of Cramant, Avise, Oger, and Menil, are the most deserving of mention.] **1829** J. F. COOPER *Wept of Wish-ton-wish* I. ii. 26 Much of the surface of this opening..was now concealed by bushes of what is termed the *second growth. **1863** BATES *Nat. Amazon* iv. (1864) 94 Tracts of second-growth woods. **1879** TOURGEE *Fool's Errand* xliv. 327 With all her fearlessness as a horse-woman, she did not quite relish the idea of his bursting away through the low-branching second-growth to follow the pack. **1883** C. REDDING *Hist. Mod. Wines* v. 110 The best wines are from the *noirien* grape, and the best of the first growths fetch sixty-six francs, and of the second growths forty-four francs. **1920** [see GROWTH[1] 1 d]. **1980** P. ABLEMAN *Shoestring's Finest Hour* ii. 31 An admirable roast beef en croute..cheered down by a second-growth Pomerol of an excellent year. **1869** BOUTELL *Arms & Armour* 173 Finally, there is the *second guard (*seconde garde*), between the two extremities of the rings of the *pas-d'âne*. **1774** GOLDSM. *Nat. Hist.* (1824) I. xlv. 378 The old stags usually shed their horns first..; those of the *second head, (namely, such as are between five and six years old) shed their horns about the middle..of March. **1805** SCOTT *Guy M.* xxxviii, The buck of the second-head, for a buck of the first-head he was not, had hitherto been slapping his boots with his switch whip. **1883** QUEEN VICTORIA *Let.* 12 Dec. in R. Fulford *Beloved Mama* (1981) 153 Italy seems to be a *second home. I expect you will settle there some day. **1915** F. HARDY *Let.* 17 July in R. Gittings *Older Hardy* (1978) xiii. 167 A second home for the people I like, and who have been good to me. **1937** W. H. SAUMAREZ SMITH *Let.* 10 July in *Young Man's Country* (1977) ii. 79 The Saturday Club, which, since his wife's departure for England, is practically a second home to him. **1959** M. GILBERT *Blood & Judgement* xiii. 142 He was away from home a lot and..she began to think he'd set up a second home of his own somewhere. **1970** 'E. LATHEN' *Pick up Sticks* x. 85 All this second-home building helps. **1980** *Times* 1 Aug. 13/7 Roll on the revolution when..we shall be entitled to substantial state pensions, preferential housing and second homes. **1976** *Local Council Rev.* Summer 48 Bit by bit, house by house, the indigenous population is replaced by commuters or *second-homers. The village becomes a suburb in the fields. **1827** 'NIMROD' *Chace* (1852) 18 The '*second-horse man'..rides the second horse, which is to carry his master with the hounds after his having had one..chace on the first. **1860** WHYTE MELVILLE *Mkt. Harb.* 125 The second-horse men, notwithstanding their numbers, appeared to be all cut from the same pattern. **1599** MASSINGER, etc. *Old Law* I. i, Are there not.. Churchmen that even the *second infancy Hath silenc'd? **1681** *Addr. Grand Jury Chester* in *Lond. Gaz.* No. 1657/4 We Your Majesties most Loyal Subjects of the *second Inquest of the same County, at the same Assize, heartily and chearfully say Amen, and joyn with the Grand Jury in this Address. **1881** T. K. CHEYNE *Prophecies of Isaiah* II. 201 The present essay..relates exclusively to the last twenty-seven chapters: not as if chaps. i.–xxxix. constituted 'the First Isaiah', and chaps. xl.–lxvi. 'the *Second'. **1881** —— in *Encycl. Brit.* XIII. 380/2 The honied rhetoric of him whom we are accustomed to call the Second Isaiah. **1888** M. ROSENTHAL *Isaiah & Unity of his Prophecy* II. 57 Canon Cheyne..breaks up the so-called second Isaiah into several personages and various authorship... He thinks that second Isaiah was originally much shorter. **1977** G. W. H. LAMPE *God as Spirit* i. 31 It was now, in his own time, and not in some remote future, that Second Isaiah believed that the herald was coming. **1797** *Encycl. Brit.* (ed. 3) XVIII. 738/1

The first line ought to consist of 20 battalions, with . . 16 battalions in the *second line. **1876** VOYLE & STEVENSON *Milit. Dict.* 231 An army, when drawn up for battle, should be formed in three distinct lines; the first line to commence the battle, the second, to support it, and to fill up the gaps; the third . . as a reserve. **1904** *Westm. Gaz.* 17 May 9/1 The main body of the investing force will be composed of fortress and second-line troops. **1912** C. MACKENZIE *Carnival* (ed. 5) iv. 43 Lilli Vergoe, a second-line girl in the Corps de Ballet of the Orient Palace of Varieties. **1939** RUSSELL & SMITH in Ramsey & Smith *Jazzmen* 27 The funerals and parades always had a 'second line' which consisted of the kids who danced along behind. **1955** SHAPIRO & HENTOFF *Hear Me Talkin' to Ya* iii. 39, I was a 'second-line' kid. That meant I'd follow the big bands down the streets, and . . carry their cases while they played. **1969** *Daily Tel.* 6 Mar. 2 Numerous bright features also developed in the so-called second-line issues [of stock]. **1972** *Jazz & Blues* Sept. 10/1 The second line beat is the funky, calypso-like 2/4 cadence struck up by the bass drummer in a New Orleans funeral parade. **1975** *Cricketer* May 17/3 The Robins were still operating with their second-line bowlers. **1980** J. MELVILLE *Chrysanthemum Chain* 142 Those guys [*sc.* politicians] on your list are essentially second-line. **1958** C. WILFORD in P. Gammond *Decca Bk. of Jazz* ii. 40 The improvisations of master executants . . preserved on record, for ready imitation by a host of *second-liners. **1972** *Jazz & Blues* Sept. 10/1 These 'second liners' wave handkerchiefs and umbrellas and . . break into a dipping, funky-butt step—half shimmy, half strut—that is known as '*second lining'. **1981** *Times* 24 Apr. 18/2 Other companies reporting provided some good rises, particularly among second-liners. **1382** WYCLIF *1 Cor.* xv. 47 The firste man of erthe, ertheli; the *secunde man of heuene, heuenli. **1848** R. I. WILBERFORCE *Doctr. Incarnation* x. (1852) 233 Joined by supernatural union to that Second Man, the new Adam, Who is God's son by nature. [**1963** *Railway Gaz.* 15 Mar. 289 If such a method of operation can be agreed the many problems of providing a second man when moving locomotives light over running lines, terminal movements, and tripping will be simplified.] **1964** *Locomotive Jrnl.* LXXVII. 205/2 Scores of Trainmen (Drivers, Firemen/2nd Men, and Guards) in the Sheffield Area have their normal diagrammed turns tampered with in an effort by the B.R.B. to scratch a few complete crews together. **1977** *Modern Railways* Dec. 461/1, 12 years' haggling from which the one significant gain was agreement to phase out the secondmen in freight and shunting locomotive cabs by attrition. **1965** E. W. SUTHERLAND et al. in *Rec. Progress Hormone Res.* XXI. 640 The hormone (the first messenger) interacts with a component of the cell membrane to initiate increased accumulation of a mediator (the *second messenger), which then acts upon components of the effector cell. **1968** *Circulation* XXXVII. 300/1 Although cyclic AMP stands as the only well-established second messenger to date, data supporting such a role for cyclic GMP have been obtained. **1979** *Sci. Amer.* Sept. 127/1 The methylxanthine drugs, such as caffeine and theophylline, are thought to exert their effects by acting through the second-messenger system. **1641** WILKINS *Math. Magick* II. v. 184 In an hower a man will need at least 360 respirations, betwixt every one of which there shall be 10 *second minutes. **1694** *Phil. Trans.* XVIII. 67 A Temporaneous progressive motion of the parts of the Air at the rate of 276 Paces in a second Minute of time. *a* **1879** W. K. CLIFFORD *Elem. Dynamic* IV. (1887) 15 If the density of an area is proportional to the distance from a line in its plane, being reckoned positive on one side of the line and negative on the other, . . the mass-centre of the area . . is called the pole of the line in regard to the area; and the moment of it in regard to the line is called the *second moment of the uniform area in regard to the line, or of the line in regard to the uniform area. **1959** M. SHADBOLT *New Zealanders* 13 Finally, in desperation, he took out a *second mortgage on the farm to pay Mother's fare to New Zealand. **1974** *Guardian* 23 Jan. 11/6 Taking out a crippling second mortgage on their own house. **1977** M. ALLEN *Spence in Petal Park* xii. 56 One of the lines he offered was loans secured by a second mortgage. **1902** A. C. HARMSWORTH *Motors & Motor-Driving* x. 202 Immediately above this shaft is a *second shaft arranged parallel to it. **1904** A. B. F. YOUNG *Compl. Motorist* (ed. 2) iv. 116 On the top speed the drive is direct, the second motion shaft then lying idle. *Ibid.* 132 With their well-cut and thoroughly hardened gear-teeth the second shaft runs noiselessly. **1912** *Motor Manual* (ed. 14) v. 165 The two shafts in the gearbox are called respectively the first motion shaft and the second motion shaft. **1693** *Lond. Gaz.* No. 2843/4 A dark Grey *Second-Mourning Surtoot-Coat. **1712** TICKELL *Spect.* No. 410 ¶ 1 She was dressed . . in an agreeable Second-Mourning. *a* **1814** *Sailor's Ret.* I. iv. in *New Brit. Theatre* II. 322 Enter Lady Growl and Lucy Delves, in conversation—Lucy in second mourning. **1625** BACON *Ess., Of Empire* (Arb.) 301 Kings haue to deale with . . their Nobles; their *Second-Nobles or Gentlemen [etc.]. *c* **1380** ? WYCLIF *Wks.* (1880) 362 To þe *secunde persone in trinyte . . awnsweriþ þe state of þe clergy. **1513** BRADSHAW *St. Werburge* I. 837 A lorde Ihesu, the seconde persone in trynyte. **1821** BYRON *Let.* 4 Jan., It is then for the gallery and *second-price boxes. **1959** *Times* 20 Oct. 19/3 Substantial two-way business in industrial shares partly reflected switching out of low-yield shares into higher yielding *second rankers. **1977** *Belfast Tel.* 17 Jan. 4/1 A new account opened on an indecisive note with leaders keeping largely to Friday's levels. Among second-rankers Campari, 37p, Rotaprint, 24p. **1892** A. BUDD in F. Marshall *Football: Rugby Union Game* ix. 124 Having obtained it [*sc.* the ball], the practice is to deposit it behind the first or *second row of forwards. **1918** V. H. CARTWRIGHT in J. E. Raphael *Mod. Rugby Football* ix. 133 The two second row men . . should be the strongest forwards on the side. **1960** E. S. & W. J. HIGHAM *High Speed Rugby* iv. 186 The 3-2-3 formation requires two second-row forwards with very strong backs. **1969** *Australian* 24 May 36/7 Owen Butler and Dick Millard, the two towering NSW Country *second rowers, are specialist lineout jumpers. **1817** MOORE *Lalla Rookh, Fire-Worshippers* III. 45 That keen, *second-scent of death, By which the vulture snuffs his food In the still warm and living breath. **1826** *Examiner* 193/2 After reverting to the past, our *second-seer makes bold to conjecture the future. **1654** H. L'ESTRANGE *Chas. I* (1655) 200 While the *second-service was reading at the Communion Table . . it was disturbed by a Psalme begun. **1657** SPARROW *Rationale* 239 In the meanwhile that part of the Service which she [*sc.* the Church] uses may perhaps more fitly be called the Second Service then the Communion. **1844** J. C. ROBERTSON *How shall we conform to Liturgy of Church of England?* (ed. 2) xii. 168 That part of the communion-office which is appointed to be used when there is no administration of the sacrament, and which . . I shall, according to the custom of the seventeenth century, speak of as the 'Second Service'. **1920** M. WEBB *House in Dormer Forest* v. 56 On Sundays Solomon went once to church. Once a month he attended 'the second service'. **1964** C. MACKENZIE *Life & Times* III. 33 Glorified morning prayer would have to be endured before the bisected so called second service was reached. **1944** F. LEIB tr. E. Lifshitz in *Jrnl. Physics* (Moscow) VIII. 111/1 We look for the velocity v_s . . in the 'first' and '*second' sound waves. **1944** J. SMORODINSKY tr. V. Peshkov in *Ibid.* 381/1 There must be in this liquid [*sc.* helium] two kinds of periodic motions: the ordinary sound . . and the so-called 'second sound'. **1964** *New Scientist* 18 June 744/2 Second sound . . is not really sound at all, but a heat wave that combines two potentially useful properties of sound and heat. **1975** *Nature* 2 Oct. 359/3 M. B. Robin . . has . . detected the heat pulse from a non-radiative transition by means of the 'second sound' pulse propagated in super-fluid helium and recorded by a superconducting lead bolometer. [**1902** A. C. HARMSWORTH *Motors & Motor-Driving* x. 205 To obtain the second of the three speeds provided.] **1912** *Motor Manual* (ed. 14) iii. 74 *Second speed position. **1925** *Morris Owner's Manual* 10 When it has gained some headway, change into second speed. **1970** K. BALL *Fiat 600, 600D Autobook* vi. 57/1 Remove the second-speed driving gear, ballbearing and shaft retaining plate and slide out the reverse shaft and gear. **1632** LITHGOW *Trav.* VI. 296 The people . . are commonly all of the *second Stature. **1773** in H. T. Waghorn *Cricket Scores* (1899) 97 Lear (*2nd stop). **1847** W. DENISON *Cricketer's Companion* p. xv, The whole of this enormous quantity of 'byes' would seem to have been the result of inferior men having been appointed to the 'second or long-stop' situation. **1886** T. F. BYRNES *Professional Criminals of Amer.* 182 Pickpocket, burglar and *second-story man. **1916** [see *porch-climber* s.v. PORCH 8]. **1965** 'MALCOLM X' *Autobiogr.* 46 Hustlers . . sold 'reefers', or had just come out of prison, or were 'second-story men'. **1978** J. CARROLL *Mortal Friends* II. iii. 169 You're nothing but a pack of second-story workers, milkbottle robbers, and doormat theives! **1960** *Manch. Guardian* 27 July 16/3 Rockefeller's plea for 'all the money it takes' to ensure the United States 'the deterrent capability of a massive and superior *second strike'. **1960** *Ibid.* 12 Sept. 9/1 We would need superior reconnaissance and target acquisition systems... These would need to be supported by a secure second-strike capability to reduce the risk of being outflanked. **1963** *Listener* 31 Jan. 194/1 The Soviet Union almost certainly has a 'second strike' capacity too. **1976** LD. HOME *Way Wind Blows* x. 152 As a second-strike weapon it [*sc.* the Polaris submarine] was a real deterrent. **1814** JANE AUSTEN *Mansfield Park* I. x. 220 She was quite shocked when I asked her whether wine was allowed at the *second table. **1857** C. M. YONGE *Dynevor Terrace* I. xiv. 227 Their servants gave them-selves airs . . especially the butler, who played the guitar, and insisted on a second table. *a* **1911** D. G. PHILLIPS *Susan Lenox* (1917) II. xiii. 311 A man . . can go on up and up. But not for girls. Nothing doing but charity and pity and the second table and the back door. **1953** G. E. & K. R. FUSSELL *English Countrywoman* v. 133 The new cook expected to dine in the housekeeper's room, at a second table set up there. **1888** *Lockwood's Dict. Mech. Engin.* 309 **Second tap*, a tap intermediate in size between a taper and a plug tap. **1964** S. CRAWFORD *Basic Engin. Processes* i. 24 If the hole being tapped is an open or through hole the second tap is quite suitable for finishing the thread. **1893** M. H. HAYES *Points of Horse* iv. 40 The hock is extended, for the most part, by muscles which form the rear-most portion of the gaskin ('*second thigh'). **1933** L. E. NAYLOR *Mod. Fox Terrier* vi. 62 The worst possible form of hind-quarters consists of a short second-thigh and a straight stifle. **1972** *Country Life* 10 Feb. 332/1 He [*sc.* a foxhound] was first-rate in every requisite of the chase, remarkable for his muscular back and loins, buttocks and second thighs. **1964** M. MCLUHAN *Under-standing Media* xxxiii. 353 Multi-nationalisms had long deprived Europe of its economic unity. The Common Market came to it only with the *Second War. **1975** P. FUSSELL *Great War & Mod. Memory* vii. 247 The same principle of literary selection . . is visible in a poem of the Second War by Herbert Corby. **1974** *Times* 13 Apr. 5/7 Mr Teng announced that the 'socialist camp' no longer existed, and that the planet was divided into the First World, consisting of the two superpowers, the *Second World, consisting of the other developed countries, and the Third World, which included the developing countries. **1974** *Economist* 18 May 66/1 The conventional image of recent years has been of a first world of developed market economies, a second world of 'socialist' states, and the 'third world' of the developing nations. **1975** *Time* 8 Sept. (Canada ed.) 20/2 The 'Second World' of the Socialist countries will make a show of complete support. **1978** *Church Times* 25 Aug. 4/2 The scene was dominated by the post-war tension between the First and Second Worlds. **1979** *Dædalus* Spring 124 In this approach, Europe would be seen as playing the role of what Chinese diplomacy likes to refer to as 'the second world'. **1980** *Sci. Amer.* Sept. 107/2 The already industrialized countries of the capitalist and communist blocs (respectively the 'first world' and 'second world'). [**1930** H. G. WELLS *Autocracy of Mr. Parham* 257 (*heading*) Book the Fourth: The Second World War.] **1942** *Polit. Sci. Q.* Sept. 321 The economic developments associated with the *second World War have restored to American railroads a volume of traffic comparable to that which they handled before the great depression. **1949** *Radio Times* 15 July 35/1 Professor W. K. Hancock . . describes the plan for the series of Civil Histories of the United Kingdom during the Second World War. **1978** J. N. WARD *Following Plough* i. 17 My generation of theological students had to come to some sense of certainty about our vocation with minds much occupied by the imminence of the Second World War.

b. Chiefly with ppl. adjs. and with quasi-advb. sense, as † ***second brewed***, ***described***, † ***found***, ***-ranking***, ***recited***. Also in verbs formed on syntactical combs., as **second-colour** *v.* (*House painting*), *trans.* to cover with a second coat of paint.

1721 N. AMHERST *Terræ Fil.* No. 48. 257 Trap's *second-brew'd balderdash runs thus [etc.]. **1812** P. NICHOLSON *Mech. Exerc.* 316 When the priming is quite dry . . mix white lead, and a very small portion of red with linseed oil, . . and *second colour your work. *Ibid.* 317 This coat is technically called by painters second colouring old work. **1825** J. NICHOLSON *Oper. Mech.* 436 The sliding movement . . in the *second-described machinery. **1594** BLUNDEVIL *Exerc.* II. (1636) 109 Subtract the Arch of that Quotient . . and you shall have the *second found number. **1966** N. NICOLSON in H. Nicolson *Diaries & Lett.* (1966) 29 In 1927 he joined the Embassy in Berlin as its *second-ranking official. **18**

1. Elliptical uses of the adj. passing into quasi-sb. (mostly admitting of plural). **a.** ***second in blood***, † ***second of kin*** (Sc. Law): one related in the second degree of consanguinity.

1567 *Sc. Acts Jas. VI* (1814) III. 26/1 Item, Our Souerane Lord . . declaris, that secundis in degreis of consanguinitie, and affinitie . . may lauchfullie marie. **1582** *Reg. Privy Council Scot.* III. 481 Alexander Rutherfurd, alsua his sister sone, Alexander Chalmer, second and thriddis of kin to him. **1754** ERSKINE *Princ. Sc. Law* (1809) 66 By seconds in blood, are meant first cousins.

b. *Gram.* Used ellipt. for *second person* (only before *singular* or *plural*).

1530 PALSGR. *Introd.* 33 The seconde plurell endeth ever in EZ. **1841** LATHAM *Eng. Lang.* IV. xix. (1850) 298 The second singular of the preterite tense.

c. A place in the second class in an examination; one who takes such a place. Also, the competitor who comes next to the winner in a contest.

1852 BRISTED *Five Yrs. Eng. Univ.* (ed. 2) 283 To take even a good Second in Classics, one must [etc.]. **1892** SHEARMAN in *Eng. Illustr. Mag.* Mar. 445 This [the silver O.U.A.C. medal], and this alone, the winners and seconds receive for their place in the Oxford Sports. **1907** 'BARBARA BURKE' *Barbara goes to Oxford* 43 Miss Jones has a first-class and Miss Smith a second.

d. ***second of exchange*** (see EXCHANGE *sb.* 5, and cf. FIRST *a.* 7 b).

e. Chiefly *Baseball.* Used *ellipt.* for *second base* (see sense A. 7 a. above).

1861 *Sunday Mercury* (N.Y.) 20 Oct. 5/5 'Dicky' safely reached the second. **1900** ADE *Fables in Slang* 34 She believed that she could get away with any Topic that was batted up to her and then slam it over to Second in time to head off the Runner. **1976** *Billings* (Montana) *Gaz.* 6 July 1-c/5 Miquel Rodriquez was hurt while sliding into second on a wild pitch. **1977** *New Yorker* 19 Sept. 40/1 When he had fielded the soft-ball and his daughter was racing from first to second, he couldn't think what else to do.

f. Phr. ***to deal seconds*** (see quot. 1951). *U.S.*

1951 *Amer. Speech* XXVI. 101/1 *Seconds, to deal*, to deal cards other than the top card on the deck. It is practically impossible to detect this if the dealer is clever enough. **1978** M. PUZO *Fools Die* xviii. 194 Not a top-notch mechanic but one who could easily deal seconds. That is, Cully could keep the top card for himself and deal the second card from the top.

2. a. One next to another (considered as the first in a series) in rank, quality, etc. Also, †a second instance, a match *to* something.

1594 DRAYTON *Idea* 839 And see if Time (if he would strive to prove) Can shew a Second to so pure a Love. **1849** MACAULAY *Hist. Eng.* iii. I. 354 That City, being then not only without equal in the country, but without second, had . . exercised almost as great an influence on the politics of England as [etc.].

b. = *second in command.* (See A. 2 d.)

1604 SHAKS. *Oth.* II. iii. 144 And 'tis great pitty that the Noble Moore Should hazard such a place, as his owne Second With one of an ingraft Infirmitie. **1800** LD. KEITH in *Paget Papers* (1896) I. 257 From my late second [Lord Nelson] I derived no advantage. **1954** W. FAULKNER *Fable* 240 Company commanders and battalion seconds stained with the filth of front lines.

†**c.** *Printing.* A pressman's assistant. *Obs.*

1683 MOXON *Mech. Exerc., Printing* 319 The one [Pressman] they distinguish by the name of First, the other his Second, these call one another Companions: The First is he that has wrought longest at that Press.

d. = *second gear* (see sense A. 7 a above).

1907 M. PEMBERTON *Amateur Motorist* vi. 45, I got the 'second' in that time with a clash as of subterranean wheels. **1925** A. HUXLEY *Along Road* I. 19 The Citroën went into second and remained there; slowly we puffed up the long ascent. **1940** R. STOUT in *Mystery Book* 400 The roadster whirred by in second. **1973** M. WOODHOUSE *Blue Bone* xii. 140, I slipped the transmission up into second and poured on the power.

e. *Mountaineering.* The second climber of a team.

1907 G. D. ABRAHAM *Compl. Mountaineer* v. 67 A difficult overhanging pitch refused to yield to ordinary tactics; so I mounted on my second's shoulders. **1920** G. W. YOUNG *Mountain Craft* v. 230 The leader or last man will not, by the nature of the case, require the support of a good second. **1951** E. COXHEAD *One Green Bottle* i. 27 I'd planned to lead in rubbers. Seeing that my second's a beginner, and to be quite on the safe side. **1976** G. MOFFAT *Over Sea to Death* v. 53 She placed her slings, clipped in her rope and, watching it fall, caught her second's eye.

f. The second in command of a six or patrol in the Scouting and Guiding movement.

1917 R. E. PHILIPPS *Patrol System & Lett. to Patrol Leader* ii. 14 The Second is a boy selected by the Patrol Leader to be his assistant. **1949** W. HILLCOURT *Baden-Powell's Aids to Scoutmastership* I. 41 In this council it is often found convenient to admit the Seconds (Assistant Patrol Leaders) also as members. **1958** R. HAZLEWOOD *Scoutmaster's Guide from A to Z* 213 Originally called a 'corporal' the Second (No. 2 in the Patrol) is the P.L.'s assistant. **1969** *Policy, Organisation & Rules of Girl Guides Assoc.* (rev. ed.) 42 The Patrol is the group for work and play. It consists of not more than eight girls, including the Patrol Leader and Second.

†**3.** *pl.* = SECUNDINE. *Obs.*

1562 TURNER *Herbal* II. (1568) 163 The seed of it [gelovers]..dryveth doune floures, secondes, and the byrthe. **1657** W. COLES *Adam in Eden* ii. 5 The Root..is good for Women in Child-bed, to purge their Seconds and Termes.

4. *Mus.* **a.** A term for the interval represented by $\frac{9}{8}$; a tone two diatonic degrees above or below any given tone; the interval between any tone and a tone two diatonic degrees distant from it; the harmonic combination of two such tones.

1597 MORLEY *Introd. Mus.* 71 All such as doe not make concord as a second, a fourth, a seuenth. *a* **1620** CAMPION *Counterpoint* Wks. (1909) 199 If the Base descends or falls, a second, third or fourth. **1730** *Treat. Harmony* 15 The Second or Ninth of the key. **1788** CAVALLO in *Phil. Trans.* LXXVIII. 238 The second minor. **1873** W. A. BARRETT *Chorister's Guide* 94 The whole of the successive notes or intervals making a scale are seconds, the tones being called major and the semitones minor seconds.

b. The next to the highest part in a piece of concerted music. Hence, a voice suitable to such a part.

a **1774** GOLDSM. *Surv. Exp. Philos.* (1776) II. 159 So that we see how injudiciously the performers on glasses manage, who play firsts, seconds, and sometimes a base altogether upon an instrument, whose only excellence depends, not on its strength, but its simplicity of tone. **1840** J. T. G. HEWLETT *P. Priggins* iii, [I] passed two or three pleasant hours standing over a pianoforte and a very fine girl, to whom I was well contented to sing second. **1905** J. HEYWOOD *Music in Churches* 14 Some ladies persist in singing in thirds below the melody... This, I believe, is.. called 'putting in a second'.

5. *pl. Comm.* A quality (of bricks, flour, etc.) second and inferior to the best. Also *fig.*

c **1600** SHAKS. *Sonn.* cxxv, And take thou my oblacion, poore but free, Which is not mixt with seconds, knows no art. **1700** *Acts Assembly Pennsylv.* (1762) I. 11 If any Person ..offer to Sale any Trash or Seconds, rotten or frost bitten Tobacco, or such [etc.]. **1812** P. NICHOLSON *Mech. Exerc.* 225 The finest kind of marls [bricks] called firsts... The next best called seconds. **1823** J. BADCOCK *Dom. Amusem.* 30 A weakness which is occasioned by the millers' grinding their corn too much, particularly white samples, nearly the whole whereof is brought to market as seconds and thirds. **1858** SKYRING *Builders' Prices* 93 For seconds glass, up to 1 foot 7, deduct 1*d.* **1903** *Daily Chron.* 21 Apr. 2/6 Cork Butter.—Firsts, 86s; seconds, 80s; thirds, 78s. **1908** *Sears, Roebuck Catal.* 349/2 We could sell seconds for less money than any of our competitors if we dealt in that class of merchandise. **1942** E. PAUL *Narrow St.* iii. 20 This friend was able to sequester from the large department-store stock 'seconds' which had no detectable imperfections. **1952** [see IMPERFECT *sb.* 3]. **1972** *Accountant* 17 Aug. 195/2 Garages could fit 'seconds' without being spotted, or even swop old tyres. **1976** E. WARD *Hanged Man* ii. 9 They listened to the patter act of a Manchester huckster selling tea-set seconds.

†**6.** One-half. (On the analogy of *third*, *fourth*, etc.) *Obs. rare.*

1594 BLUNDEVIL *Exerc.* I. vii. (1636) 20 The Numerator is alwayes set above, and the Denominator beneath, having a little line drawne betwixt them thus $\frac{1}{2}$ which signifieth one second or one halfe. **1660** J. MOORE *Arith.* 5 As if the unite be conceived to be divided into two parts, the parts are called seconds or halves.

7. In systems of fractional numeration (or of weights or measures) having a constant modulus: The subdivision next but one below the unit, and next below the 'prime'; the lower subdivisions being usually called 'thirds', 'fourths', etc.

Cf. SECOND *sb.*[1], which is a special case of the sense here defined, but is treated separately because it was taken from med.L. or Rom.; the uses below may be most conveniently regarded as applications of the Eng. ordinal numeral suggested by SECOND *sb.*[1]

†**a.** *Scottish Troy Weight.* The 576th part ($1 \div 24^2$) of a grain. *Obs.*

1604 [see PRIME *sb.*[2]].

†**b.** (*a*) *Arith.* The quantity ·01 or $\frac{1}{100}$. (*b*) *Surveying.* The 100th part of a perch, = 1·98 inches.

1619 LYTE *Art of Tens* 14 Euerie vnite of a prime being diuided into ten parts, are called seconds. **1658** PHILLIPS, A *Second* in surveying, is the tenth part of a prime, and contains one inch, and 49 of 50 parts of an inch. **1766** HUTTON *School Master's Guide* 55 The 1st, 2d, 3d, 4th, &c. places of decimals, counting from the left-hand towards the right, are denominated the places of primes, seconds, thirds, and fourths, &c. respectively. **1794** CUNN *Doctr. Fractions* 61 Primes, or Tenth Parts. Seconds, or Hundredth Parts. Thirds, or Thousandth Parts.

c. *Duodecimals.* The twelfth part of a 'prime' or inch.

Formerly (if quot. 1703 be correct), the 144th part of an inch, the 12th being called a 'prime'.

1703 T. N. *City & C. Purchaser* 123 Inches by (12th) Parts, produce Seconds, or 12th Parts of the 12th Part of an Inch. **1714** CUNN *Doctr. Fractions* 119 To multiply any Integers, Primes, Seconds, &c. by a Multiple of 12 Integers; first Multiply by 12 [etc.]. **1842** GWILT *Archit.* §868 Feet and inches are marked with their initial letters, but twelfths or seconds by a double accent, thus 2″.

8. *pl.* A second helping of food at a meal; occas. the second or sweet course. *colloq.*

1792 D. O'CONNELL *Let.* 14 Sept. (1972) I. 4 We get very small portions at dinner; most of the lads..get what they call *seconds*, that is, a second portion every day. **1918** L. E. RUGGLES *Navy Explained* 124 When there is not enough of the first issue of rations the mess cook is requested to go to the galley and get 'seconds'. **1942** *Yank* 28 Oct. 8 We were more delighted than we can say to get a hamburger in a foreign land and went for seconds. **1960** 'R. EAST' *Kingston Black* xiv. 139 Kitty had served tinned fruit and farm cream for seconds. **1974** P. GZOWSKI *Bk. about this Country* 59/1 This dish has been served to hundreds of people over the years and requests for seconds (or even thirds) are usual. **1981** A. PRICE *Soldier no More* 121 Lexy scraped the frying pan... Would you like seconds, David darling?

II. 9. One who or something which renders aid or support to another. †**a.** *gen.*

1590 SIR R. WILLIAMS *Brief Disc. War* 23 When those that giue the first charge begin to retire or wax colde, the great Officers command their seconds to the assaults. **1610** SHAKS. *Temp.* III. iii. 105 Ile be thy Second. **1626** MIDDLETON *Women beware Women* II. ii. 295 We wish no better seconds in society Than your discourses, madam. **1632** LITHGOW *Trav.* VIII. 355 But the gold was my best second,..[and] was my continuall vade Mecum. **1650** FULLER *Pisgah* I. iii. 7 Glasses are but the seconds, which succeed on the Cupboard, when Plate the principall is otherwise disposed of. **1711–12** SWIFT *Jrnl. to Stella* 15 Mar., People will not understand: I am a very good second, but I care not to begin a recommendation, unless it be for an intimate friend. **1740** RICHARDSON *Pamela* (1824) I. lii. 382 She is very happy in Mrs. Jervis, who is an excellent second to her admirable lady.

b. *spec.* One who acts as representative of a principal in a duel, carrying the challenge, arranging locality and loading weapons. Similarly in a pugilistic contest.

1613 WEBSTER *Devil's Law-Case* II. i, *Erc.* Shall's haue no Seconds? *Con.* None, for feare of preuention. *Erc.* The length of our weapons? *Con.* Weele fit them by the way. **1632** *Star Chamb. Cases* (1886) 113 Indeed his second J. S. was acquitted, for that it appeared he knew not of the combatt before he came there. **1712** SWIFT *Jrnl. to Stella* 12 Dec., Colonel Hamilton, who was second to the Duke of Hamilton, is tried to-day. **1743** J. BROUGHTON in P. Egan *Boxiana* (1818) I. 51 In every main battle, no person whatever shall be upon the stage, except the principals and their seconds. **1814** SCOTT *Chivalry* (1874) 25 It was usual to have more seconds even to the number of five or six. **1841** *Fistiana* 63 That each man shall be attended to the ring by a second and a bottle-holder, the former provided with a sponge, and the latter with a bottle of water. **1852** THACKERAY *Esmond* I. xiv, 'There was no need for more seconds than one,' said the Colonel, 'and the Captain or Lord Warwick might easily withdraw.' **1897** *Encycl. Sport* I. 139/2 (Boxing) *Seconds*, men, generally professional boxers, appointed to attend on the contestants in the intervals between the rounds.

†**c.** Assistance, aid, support. Also pl. in the same sense. *Obs. rare.*

1603 B. JONSON *Sejanus* II. ii, This second (from his Mother) will vrge Our late dissigne, and spur on Cæsars rage. *a* **1609** SIR F. VERE *Comm.* (1657) 12, I gave them no second till I might perceive those within had spent their ready powder in their furnitures. *Ibid.* 18 An officer with two hundred souldiers..came to their seconds. **1640** tr. *Verdere's Rom. of Rom.* I. xix. 82 This blow so affrighted the enemy, that they had certainly retired to their trenches, if the Cariffe of Africca..had not..come into their second.

second ('sɛkənd), *v.*[1] [a. F. *second-er* (OF. *segonder*), †to come after (*obs.*), to favour (= Pr. *segondar*, Sp., Pg. *segundar*, It. *secondare*), ad. L. *secundāre* to direct favourably, favour, further, f. *secund-us* following, favourable: see SECOND *a.* In some uses partly an independent Eng. formation on the adj.]

1. a. *trans.* To support, back up, assist, encourage (a person, his actions, aims, etc.).

a **1586** SIDNEY *Arcadia* III. (Sommer) 246 Shall I (said she) second his boldnesse so farre, as to reade his presumptuous letters? **1601** SHAKS. *Jul. C.* III. i. 29 Where is Metellus Cimber, let him go, And presently preferre his suite to Cæsar. *Bru.* He is addrest: presse neere, and second him. **1650** BULWER *Anthropomet.* 148 He seconds that which he ought to withstand. **1719** SWIFT *To Young Clergym.* Wks. 1755 II. II. 9 If in company you offer something for a jest, and no-body seconds you in your own laughter. **1844** DISRAELI *Coningsby* III. v, His family had imbibed all his views, and seconded them. **1847** PRESCOTT *Peru* (1850) II. 201 So eagerly did he press forward the work, and so well was he seconded by the multitude of labourers at his command. **1875** STUBBS *Const. Hist.* II. xvi. 486 His efforts were seconded by a somewhat subservient parliament.

†**b.** To act as a second or assistant to (a leader).

1588 ALLEN *Admon.* 15 So jelous be all tyrants and vsurpers, of their state, and so lothe they are to be seconded by any other then of their owne creation. **1590** SIR R. WILLIAMS *Brief Disc. War* 16 What other Officers ought to second their great Officers.

†**c.** To follow, attend, accompany. In *pass.*, to be accompanied (*with*). *Obs.*

1600 SURFLET *Country Farm* VII. xxv. 847 The horsemen appointed to waite vpon the companie, must alwaies second and keepe by the sides of the dogs. **1601** B. JONSON *Poetaster* III. iv. Wks. 1616 I. 308 See, here's Horace, and old Trebativs, the great lawier, in his companie; let's auoid him now: He is too well seconded. **1632** LITHGOW *Trav.* IX. 381 The Bashaw went.., seconded with twelue followers.

d. To sing second to (a singer, song).

1586 BRYSKETT *Past. Aeglogue* 13 in Spenser *Astrophel*, With sobs and sighes I second will thy song. **1883** J. HAWTHORNE *Dust* I. 175 Lancaster would second Marion's soprano with his baritone.

e. *Mountaineering.* To act as a second (SECOND *sb.*[2] 2 e) to (the leader of a climb) or on (a climb). Also *absol.*

1951 E. COXHEAD *One Green Bottle* ii. 49 He wants someone to second him up the north wall. **1968** P. CREW *Encycl. Dict. Mountaineering* 106/1 To second a climb is to do a climb as the second man on the rope. **1972** D. HASTON *In High Places* i. 8 It's not hard to see why leading [on a rock climb] is that much more exciting than seconding.

2. *esp.* To support, back up (a combatant, a body of troops) in attack or defence. Also, to act as second to (a pugilist).

1588 WILLOUGHBY in *Defeat Sp. Armada* (Navy Rec. Soc.) II. 32 Those that are taken here cry out upon the Duke of Parma, that they are betrayed by him, because they were not seconded according to their expectation. **1590** SIR R. WILLIAMS *Brief Disc. War* 22 He deuides his troupes to second one the other, according to the widenes of the breach. **1607** SHAKS. *Cor.* V. vi. 57 Let him feele your Sword, Which we will second. *c* **1611** CHAPMAN *Iliad* XI. 306 Hector ..rusht with clamor on the king, right soundly seconded With troupes of Troians. **1645** SYMONDS *Diary* (Camden) 258 A party of Arcall horse charged the persuers, and were seconded by part of Prince Maurice's life guard. **1799** HT. LEE *Canterb. T.*, *Trav. T.* (ed. 2) I. 22 A young cavalier.. seconded him with so much spirit, that one of the villains was presently stretched upon the spot. **1821** *John Bull* 5 Mar. 89/3 The Black was seconded by Richmond and Paddington Jones. *c* **1850** *Arab. Nts.* (Rtldg.) 470 Being seconded by his slaves, who all promised to be faithful, he attacked the negro. **1884** *Manch. Exam.* 13 Aug. 5/1 Griffiths..is said to have seconded Henry, and to have interfered to prevent the fight being stopped.

†**b.** To reinforce with additional numbers.

a **1609** SIR F. VERE *Comm.* (1657) 5 In the mean time the enemie seconded their troops of shot with to the number of four or five hundred.

†**c.** To take the place of, succeed (a combatant who is *hors de combat*). *Obs.*

1593 SHAKS. *2 Hen. VI*, IV. ix. 35 But now is Cade driuen back, his men dispierc'd, And now is Yorke in Armes, to second him. **1597** —— *2 Hen. IV*, IV. ii. 45, 46 And though wee here fall downe, Wee haue Supplyes, to second our Attempt: If they mis-carry, theirs shall second them. **1614** RALEIGH *Hist. World* II. v. iii. §17. 542 Being ouer-pressed on either side, they had a safe retrait vnto their foot; and one troupe seconding another by course, returned to charge.

†**d.** *absol.* and *intr.* To render aid; to side *with*. *Obs. rare.*

a **1609** SIR F. VERE *Comm.* (1657) 11 A signall of drums, at which the first four troops should go to the assault; and another signall to the other four troops to second, if need required. **1654** FULLER *Comm. Ruth* 45 The mother, because her sonne is flesh of her flesh,..pleades it is right, that he should side and second with her.

3. a. To support (a speaker, a proposition) in a debate or conference by speaking in the same sense; *spec.* to rise to support (a mover or motion) as a necessary preliminary to further discussion or to the adoption of the motion.

1597 BACON *Ess.*, *Ceremonies* (Arb.) 28 It is a good precept generally in seconding another: yet to adde somewhat of ones owne. **1647** CLARENDON *Hist. Reb.* II. §75 This method was..diverted by other propositions, which being seconded took much time without pointing to any conclusion. **1685** EVELYN *Diary* 22 May, Mr. Seymour made a bold speech against many Elections..but no one seconded him. **1692** R. L'ESTRANGE *Fables* xxvii. 26 The Motion was Seconded and Debated. **1782** MISS BURNEY *Cecilia* VII. v, Mrs. Charlton.. instantly seconded the proposal. **1817** *Parl. Deb.* 23 The noble lords who moved and seconded the address. **1837** THIRLWALL *Greece* IV. xxxiv. 331 Cheirisophus seconded this proposal, and they immediately proceeded to the election.

absol. **1802** G. ROSE *Diaries* (1860) I. 496 Lord Lowther had been applied to to move the address... Lord Nelson was to second.

†**b.** To support, back (a statement, opinion, a person *in* his opinion); to confirm, corroborate (a report). *Obs.*

1596 LAMBARDE *Peramb. Kent* (ed. 2) 113 In which opinion, I am the more willing to dwell, bicause..I finde myselfe verie learnedly seconded by master Camden. **1605** B. JONSON *Volpone* II. i, I heard, last night, a most strange thing reported By some of my Lords followers, and I long To heare, how't will be seconded! **1607** SHAKS. *Cor.* IV. vi. 62 The Slaues report is seconded. *a* **1677** BARROW *Serm.* Wks. 1716 II. 97 Whose affirmation..I intend to second with particular instances. **1699** BENTLEY *Phal.* 278 Plato himself relates it as a Paradox; and no body that came after him, would second him in't. **1741** RICHARDSON *Pamela* (1785) III. xxxiii. 293 The Countess..ran on in my Praise.. and Lady Davers seconded her.

4. To further, assist the effect of, reinforce (a thing, activity, etc.). (With subject either a person or thing.)

a **1586** SIDNEY *Arcadia* III. (Sommer) 317 Nowe seconding their terrible blowes with cunning labouring the horses. **1639** DU VERGER tr. *Camus' Admir. Events* 127 Her froward husband..replyed with sharpe words seconded with such heavy blowes. **1665** TEMPLE *Lett.* Wks. 1731 II. 4 The Vigour of his Body does not second that of his Mind. **1759** JOHNSON *Rasselas* xlii, Seconding every fall of rain with a due proportion of sunshine. **1858** STANLEY *Arnold* I. v. 203 Deeds must second words when needful.

†**5. a.** (With little or nothing of the idea of furthering or assisting.) To follow up or accompany *with* (or *by*) some second thing. In *pass.*, to be followed, succeeded, or accompanied. *Obs.*

1609 TUVILL *Vade-mecum* (1629) 139 The Wise Physition doth neuer minister a Potion..but hee seconds it with something that is more pleasing and Delicious to the taste. **1631** WEEVER *Anc. Funeral Mon.* 54 This Proclamation was seconded by another, to the same purpose. *a* **1716** SOUTH *Serm.* (1744) XI. 220 After the overflowing of sin upon the whole earth, God in his justice seconds it with a deluge of waters. **1759–74** TOPLADY *Hymn*, '*I saw and lo!*', So sung the Saints. Th' Angelic train Second the anthem with a loud Amen.

†**b.** To add a second to; to follow or succeed as a second. *Obs.*

1655 EARL NORWICH in *Nicholas Papers* (Camden) II. 304, I would haue agayne seconded my last to him after the receipt of his in answer to my former, but y[t] I feard [etc.]. **1781** BENTHAM *Corr.* Wks. 1843 X. 110 To-day, at dinner, I had the favour of yours of the 29th, as to my not seconding my last letter sooner.

†**c.** To repeat (an action, esp. a blow). *Obs.*

1610 HEALEY *St. Aug. Citie of God* v. vi. 204 Natures powre is such that a woman hauing once conceiued cannot second any conception vntil she bee deliuered of the first. **1648** GAGE *West Ind.* 102 He struck off two of the Fryers fingers, and had undoubtedly seconded another blow..had not the Indians interposed themselves. **1667** MILTON *P.L.* x. 335 Hee..saw his guileful act By Eve, though all unweeting, seconded Upon her Husband. **1684** BUNYAN *Pilgr.* II. 110 Then Mr Great-heart seconded his blow, and smit the head of the Giant from his shoulders. **1737** [S. BERINGTON] *G. de Lucca's Mem.* (1738) 32 Before he could second his Shot, I gave him..a Stroke with my Broad Sword. **1831** SCOTT *Ct. Robt.* xxxiii, The Count was in the act of again seconding his blow.

†**6.** To match with a second instance. *Obs.*

1600 W. WATSON *Decacordon* (1602) 276 Our soueraigne Queene Elizabeth..is knowne to be in her owne high towring princely wisedome of as high a pitch..: in reach not to be seconded of any of these [kings and princes]. **1601** HOLLAND *Pliny* VII. xxv. I. 168 He left such a president behind him, as I forbid all men to match or second it. **1612** DRAYTON *Poly-olb.* xi. 256 Next Sebert them succeeds Scarce seconded againe for sanctimonious deeds. **1632** LITHGOW *Trav.* VIII. 369 [Fez] may rather second Grand Caire, than subioyne it selfe to Constantinople.

†**7.** To come second to (in quality). *Obs. rare*$^{-1}$.

1601 DOLMAN *La Primaud. Fr. Acad.* III. lxxxiii. (1618) 825 The white [dogs] are best... The browne doth second them [orig. *les secondent*].

Hence **ˈseconding** *vbl. sb.*

1613 CHAPMAN *Rev. Bussy D'Ambois* III. iii. 23 Nay we shall lay on hands of too much strength To need your secondings. **1837** CARLYLE *Fr. Rev.* I. II. v, Which indeed, with such seconding as he had, one may reckon heroic.

second (sɪˈkɒnd), *v.*[2] *orig. Mil.* [f. F. *second* in the phrase *en second*: see SECOND *a.* 2 c.] *trans.* To remove (an officer) temporarily from his regiment or corps, for employment on the staff, or in some other extra-regimental appointment. Also *transf.* of employees in other occupations and employments. Hence **seˈconded,** *ppl. a.*

1802 C. JAMES *Milit. Dict.* s.v., *Capitaine en Second..* *Lieutenant en Second..*are officers whose companies have been reduced, but who do duty in others, and are destined to fill up the first vacancies. We have borrowed the expression and say, *To be seconded.* When an officer is *seconded,* he remains upon full pay, his rank goes on, and he may purchase the next vacant step, without being obliged to memorial in a manner that a half-pay officer must. **1833** *Westm. Rev.* Apr. 308 How to cut down an army of 300,000 men to one of 100,000, with the least subsequent expense of half-pay, is a problem that ought to be solved..; and the solution would be found in the obsolete practice of *second*-ing (or as the proper pronunciation in a mess-room is, *segoond*-ing). **1869** *Times* 15 Apr. 9/3 As this officer was placed on the seconded list of the Royal Artillery..he will have to wait for a vacancy to occur. **1875** COLLEY in *Encycl. Brit.* II. 576/1 Officers holding certain appointments are 'seconded'—that is, their place in the regiment is filled up, and they become supernumerary, their names being shown in italics in the *Army List*; but they still belong to the regiment, and rise in it in due course. **1897** *Q. Rev.* July 242 The officers in question had been..'seconded' for service in the forces of the Chartered Company. **1920** *Westm. Gaz.* 22 May 10/1 It was finally agreed that Lord Moulton should be seconded to the service of the Corporation and of the dye industry for..one year. **1928** *Times* 21 July 13/3 They established an elaborate organization, under an important Minister, and manned by specially seconded Civil servants of high standing. **1955** *Times* 23 June 13/4 Mr. Mayne was seconded for special frontier duties, in the course of which he made many acquaintances and friends among the Pathans. **1977** *News of World* 17 Apr. 1/1 The Commission consisted of the chairman, deputy chairman, and 30 seconded civil servants.

†**secondar,** *a. Sc. Obs.* In 5–6 secundar(e. [ad. L. *secundārius* SECONDARY *a.*: see -AR[2]. Cf. SECONDARLY *adv.*]

Of second quality; of the second rank with respect to size; = SECONDARY *a.*

1474 *Acc. Ld. High Treas. Scot.* I. 26 Item iij quarteris of secundare vellus to the lynyng of the sammyn sleiffis. **1482** in *Charters*, etc. *Edinb.* (1871) 169 Of ilk grete schip xiii s iiii d. The secundare x s. The mydlest vi s. viii d. **1529** *Burgh Rec. Edinb.* (1871) II. 6 [Thai] sall sell thar best corne..for vj d the pek, and the secundar for v d the pek. **1566** in Hay Fleming *Mary Q. of Scots* (1897) 499 Sax pound of secundar threid in divers sortis.

secondarily (ˈsɛkəndərɪlɪ), *adv.* [f. SECONDARY *a.* + -LY[2].]

†**1.** In the second order in time or temporal sequence; for the (or a) second time; also, as the (or a) second action, event, etc. *Obs.*

c **1475** *Partenay* 512 Raymonde swere agayn secundarilie, That neuer no day forsworne wolde he be. **1477** SIR J. PASTON in *P. Lett.* III. 187 Snaylwell, by my grauntefadres will ones, and by my fadris will sceconderely [*sic*], is entaylyd to the issyw of my fadres body. *a* **1513** FABYAN *Chron.* v. lxxxviii. 65 [Vortimerus] gaue vnto theym a great Batayll vpon the Ryuer of Darwent... And secundaryly he faught with theym vpon y[e] Foorde called Epifoorde. **1527** ANDREW *Brunswyke's Distyll. Waters* M ij b, Dystylle them secondarely in a newe glasse in balneo marie. **1578** LYTE tr. *Dodoens* II. lxxxv. 263 The Rosemary floureth twise a yeare, once in the spring time of the yeare, and secondarily in August. **1609** BIBLE (Douay) *Ps.* lxvii. Comm., Other Apostles of divers tribes sent first to the Jewes, secondarily to the Gentiles.

†**2.** Secondly; in the second order or place (in an argument, discourse, or the like). (Very common in the 16th c.) *Obs.*

1523 [COVERDALE] *Old God* (1534) Lj, Secundaryly I fynde the saide ceremonies on euery syde sundry & vnlike among theym selues. **1534** in W. H. Turner *Select. Rec. Oxford* (1880) 128 And secondaryly, if such lycence..were suffered it should be the occasions of many frays, of much robory and bribery. **1599** SHAKS. *Much Ado* v. i. 221 They haue committed false report,..secondarily they are slanders,.. thirdly, they haue verified vniust things, and to conclude they are lying knaues. **1604** N. BOWND *Storeh. Comfort* iii. 26 Secondarily, if wee should neglect to pray for them. **1647** HEXHAM I, Secondarily or secondly, *Ten tweeden.*

3. As a secondary consequence, indirectly; through an intermediate agency or train of events.

1637 GILLESPIE *Eng. Pop. Cerem.* III. viii. 196 Whereupon secondarily and accidentally will follow their falling away from their Ecclesiasticall office and function. **1647** H. MORE *Song of Soul* II. III. i. 21 She sees more clear Then we that see but secondarily. **1678** CUDWORTH *Intell. Syst.* 732 Our Knowledge here is not After Singular Bodies, and Secundarily or Derivatively From them; but in order of Nature, Before them, and Proleptical to them. **1690** STILLINGFL. *Serm.* xxvii. Wks. I. 441 Those who had the Apostolical Office committed to them, (whether Primarily by Christ himself, or Secondarily by the Apostles, as Timothy and Titus and others) had great need of this Apostolical Spirit. **1748** HARTLEY *Observ. Man* I. iii. §3. 371 An Action that is not automatic primarily or secondarily. **1803** BEDDOES *Hygëia* IX. 11 It would be more exact to consider him as nervous because he has been gouty. He is only secondarily nervous. **1884** BOWER & SCOTT *De Bary's Phaner.* 459 The large medullary rays have originated secondarily from the primary ones.

4. (The chief modern sense.) With reference to other than temporal order: In the second place, second in order of importance, not first of all; subordinately.

1525 FITZHERB. *Husb.* §163 Wherfore thou must fyrst loue god principally, and thy neyghbour secondarely. **1621** DONNE *Serm.* xv. (1640) 151 Thereupon doe the Fathers.. take that place of Ezekiel..to be primarily intended of the last resurrection, and but secundarily of the Jews restitution. **1690** C. NESSE *Hist. & Myst. O. & N.T.* I. 51 The godly seed of the woman shall secondarily partake of this triumph. **1813** LEACH *Parl. Deb.* 15 Feb. in *Examiner* 22 Feb. 116/2 An office which was primarily judicial and secondarily political. **1899** J. F. HURST in *Amer. Jrnl. Theol.* Oct. 680 The first Prayer Book [of 1549] was based primarily, on the old Latin service-books, and secondarily on Archbishop Hermann's Consultation.

secondariness (ˈsɛkəndərɪnɪs). [f. SECONDARY *a.* + -NESS.] The quality of being secondary or subordinate.

1678 NORRIS *Misc., Let. Love & Mus.* (1687) 448 That then which is peculiar and discriminative must be taken from the Primaryness and Secondaryness of the Perception. **1878** EMERSON *Misc. Papers, Fort. Repub.* Wks. (Bohn) III. 397 The secondariness and aping of foreign and English life. **1883** *Century Mag.* XXVII. 70 Full of a girl's sweet sense of secondariness to the object of her love.

†**secondarly,** *adv. Obs. rare.* [f. SECONDAR *a.* + -LY[2].] = SECONDARILY.

1543 GRAFTON *Contn. Hardyng* 127 Neuerthelesse, this is not like to be true by diuers reasons. Fyrst, that [etc.].. Secondarely that [etc.]. **1560** *Maitland Club Misc.* III. 223 The greatnes of his offens first to God and to his Kirk Secundarlie towardes me dois merite no less. **1567** GOLDING *Ovid's Met.* VIII. 654 Render thou agen Thy twice given life, by bearing first, and secondarly when I caught this firebrand from the flame. **1771** *Antiq. Sarisb.* III. 33 God visibly and secundarly interferes in doing justice to the innocent.

secondary (ˈsɛkəndərɪ), *a.* and *sb.* Also 4–5 secondarye, secoundarie, secundari, -arye, 4–7 secundarie, 4–8 secundary, 5–7 secondari(e. [ad. L. *secundāri-us* of the second class or quality, f. *secund-us*: see SECOND *a.* and -ARY[1]. Cf. F. *secondaire* (1372 in Hatz.-Darm.), Pr. *secundari*, Sp., Pg. *secundario*, It. *secondario*.]

A. *adj.*

1. a. Belonging to the second class in respect of dignity or importance; entitled to consideration only in the second place. Also, and usually, in less precise sense: Not in the first class; not chief or principal; of minor importance, subordinate.

1386 *Almanak of Year* 1 Ther es difference bitwyx þe principal howce and þe secundary howce. ? *a* **1396** [? W. HYLTON] *Angels' Song* in Horstm. *R. Rolle* I. 178 For þe souereyn & þe essencial Ioye es in [þe] lufe of god.., and [þe] secundarie es in communynge & behaldynge of aungels. *c* **1425** *Orolog. Sapient.* iv. in *Anglia* X. 354/27 Siche oþere exercises..schulbe..demyd as secundarye and lesse worth. **1526** *Pilgr. Perf.* (W. de W. 1531) 151 Theyr outwarde labour is not theyr principall entent, but it is onely the secondary entent of theyr charite. **1532** MORE *Confut. Tindale* Wks. 492/2 Therfore these causes be but diuined and gessed at, and seme but very secundary. **1632** in *10th Rep. Hist. MSS. Comm.* App. v. 478 Your request in that particular was accompanied with some secundarie respectes not then made knowne unto us. **1735** J. PRICE *Stone Br. Thames* 15 Things..purely Ornimental, are no more than of secondary Consideration. **1742** YOUNG *Nt. Th.* VIII. 1171 Those secondary goods that smile on earth, He, loving in proportion, loves in peace. **1796** MORSE *Amer. Geog.* II. 6 Secondary powers are those of Turkey, Spain, Holland. **1801** ELIZ. HELME *St. Marg. Cave* (ed. 2) IV. 233 And is there no secondary motive for that wish, Isabel? **1838** GUEST *Eng. Rhythms* I. iv. I. 78 When the word contains two or more syllables there *may* be a second accent; this, of course, must be subordinate to the first, and is commonly called the *secondary accent.* **1866** GEO. ELIOT *F. Holt* xxxvi, Something that made the threat..only a secondary alarm. **1899** HEINIG *Gloss. Bot. Terms*, *Secondary*, subordinate. *Secondary axes*, those proceeding from the main axis. **1908** R. BAGOT *A. Cuthbert* ii. 12 Besides, the religious difficulty was only a secondary, a very secondary matter.

†**b.** Second best; of the second grade of quality.

1428 *E.E. Wills* (1882) 82 My Russet Candelstykes, and I paire Candelstekes secundaries next þoo. **1508** in *Ripon Ch. Acts* 330 My secondarie gowne. **1564** *Wills & Inv. N.C.* (Surtees 1835) 225 His best dublatt xij[d]..a secondari dublatt viij[d] a nother payre of hose viij[d]..one old dublatt iiij[d]. **1580** BLUNDEVIL *Cur. Horses Dis.* clxxxviii. 77 Take of ..Mirrh secondarie two pound [etc.]. **1601** HOLLAND *Pliny* XXXIII. viii. II. 477 They put secundarie Vermillion in an earthen pot.

c. Of a lower kind; entitled in a lower degree to the appellation. ***secondary wife***: †(*a*) a concubine; (*b*) a socially or legally recognized inferior wife in some societies; similarly ***secondary consort***. Also ***secondary marriage***, (*a*) concubinage; (*b*) marriage to a secondary wife (sense (*b*)); similarly ***secondary union***.

1382 WYCLIF *Gen.* xxv. 6 To the sonys forsothe of the secondarye wyues [Vulg. *concubinarum*] he ȝaue ȝiftis. *Ibid.* *Gen.* xxii. 24, *Judges* viii. 31, *Song Sol.* vi. 7. **1782** J. BROWN *Compend. View Nat. & Rev. Relig.* I. i. 24 Servants in families ought to be considered as secondary children, and have due instruction [etc.]. **1788** GIBBON *Decl. & F.* xliv. IV. 382 From the age of Augustus to the tenth century, the use of this secondary marriage [*i.e.* concubinage] prevailed both in the West and East. **1847** A. STRICKLAND *Lives Queens of England* X. ii. 328 He likewise obliged the princess to receive at her court, and to countenance the duke of Monmouth's mistress, or secondary wife, Lady Harriet Wentworth. **1924** D. HOSIE *Two Gentl. China* (ed. 2) ix. 91 The ladies of the household..often wield a power that must be reckoned with, if they are fond of intrigue, like a certain secondary wife of an official of our acquaintance. **1931** W. F. SANDS *Undiplomatic Mem.* 69 From kitchenmaid she was raised to the first rank of secondary consorts..and in due course became the mother of the monarch's third son. **1950** *Jrnl. R. Anthrop. Inst.* LXXX. 101/2 In view of the difficulty of establishing the exact nature of the forms of 'secondary marriage', 'the doctrine of presumption of marriage now applies to the Chinese'. *Ibid.* 103/1 A..significant shift of a class of women from the status of kept mistresses to that of secondary wives. **1950** I. SCHAPERA in A. Radcliffe-Brown *Afr. Systems Kinship* 149 A 'secondary union'..is merely an extension of an existing marriage. Its essential character is that, for the purposes of child-bearing, one of the original parties..is replaced by another person of the same sex, who is regarded as a bodily substitute, and not as an independent spouse. **1970** J. M. MESKILL in M. Freedman *Family & Kinship in China* 148 In the Wu-feng Lin genealogy.. secondary wives..are recorded as well as main wives.

†**d.** Of an official: Second in rank or status. Of a judge: Not chief or principal; = PUISNE *a.* 1 b.

c **1450** in Aungier *Syon* (1840) 337 The secundary preste schal sense the fyrste, and the principal senser of the lay brethern schal sense the seyd secundary preste thre castys. **1450** *Rolls of Parlt.* V. 196/2 Gilbert Maltoft, secondary Baron of oure Eschequier. **1599** in T. Stafford *Pac. Hib.* I. i. (1633) 7 If the said Iustice, or assistant, and secondary Iustice, shall depart [etc.]. **1607** in *Verney Papers* (1853) 96 With him as secondarie men in charge, was one maister Philip Giffard. **1630** WESTCOTE *View Devonsh.* (1845) 431 Sir John Whiddon..was also secondary Justice of the King's Bench.

e. Of persons: Second-rate. *rare.*

1827 HARE *Guesses* II. (1873) 349 Secondary men, men of talents, may be mixt up like an apothecary's prescription. **1829** LANDOR *Imag. Conv., Emp. China & Tsing-Ti* Wks. 1853 II. 148/1 He will never have a minister who is not taken from the ranks; never a man of genius, never an honest man; but secondary and plausible. **1836** —— *Pericles & Aspasia, Asp. to Anaxag.* ibid. 426/2 No writer of florid prose ever was more than a secondary poet.

f. Subsidiary, auxiliary; that is used only in the second resort, or that serves to assist something else.

1751 LABELYE *Westm. Bridge* 22 Every Arch..is double, the first..built with great Blocks of Portland Stone,..over which there is another Arch..bonded in with the under semicircular Arch... By means of these secondary Arches.. every Arch of Westminster Bridge is able to stand by itself. **1802** BINGLEY *Anim. Biog.* (1805) II. 232 Parrots..never climb nor creep without fastening by the bill; with this they begin, and they use their feet only as secondary instruments of motion. **1812** J. HENRY *Camp. agst. Quebec* 31 Our secondary guide and myself, thinking that we could manage the water slipped into our canoe. **1861** PALEY *Æschylus* (ed. 2), *Supplices* 916 *note*, A secondary chorus of attendants was actually present. **1874** LAWSON *Dis. Eye* 135 To be cut through with a small secondary knife. **1902** SIR G. S. CLARKE in *Encycl. Brit.* XXVII. 124/1 Secondary bases, or coaling stations,..are sources of maritime strength in proportion [etc.].

g. Used to designate punishments other than capital.

1831 *Edin. Rev.* Sept. 185 *note*, The difficulty of secondary punishments is much increased by observing that there is not a form of punishment which is not liable to some objections.

h. *secondary evidence* (Law): (see quots. 1921, 1976).

1810 in E. H. East *Rep. Cases King's Bench* VIII. 289 The fact of its loss being proved, so as to let in the secondary evidence of its contents; that matter was sufficiently established by parol. **1885** *Law. Rep. Chanc. Div.* XXIX. 290 A probate was not even secondary evidence of a lost will until the statute 20 & 21 Vict. **1921** S. L. PHIPSON *Law of Evidence* (ed. 6) i. 7 The term *secondary evidence*, on the other hand, is by common usage confined to documents; it deals only with the means of proving their *contents*; and it is in general admissible whenever the absence of the primary source has been satisfactorily explained. **1976** *Halsbury's Laws of England* (ed. 4) XVII. 9 In the unavoidable absence of the best or primary evidence of documents, the court will accept secondary evidence. This is evidence which suggests, on the face of it, that other and better evidence exists.

i. ***secondary association*** (Cytology): (see quot. 1931).

1931 W. J. C. LAWRENCE in *Cytologia* II. 353 It is now possible to demonstrate the occurrence of two different types of chromosome association in polyploids. We may define these two modes of association as follows: Primary association 1) arises from prophase pairing and 2) determines segregation. Secondary association 1) is a post-synaptic phenomenon and 2) does not affect segregation. It is a differential approximation of the bivalents in the equatorial plane. **1959** [see MULTIVALENT *sb.*].

†**2. a.** Having or entitled to the second place in an enumeration. *Obs. rare.*

a **1425** tr. *Arderne's Treat. Fistula*, etc. 58 [Enumerates three kinds of hæmorrhoids. Of which] þe secundary [i.e. the second hardest to cure] is rixis. **1432–50** tr. *Higden* (Rolls) III. 273 He pullede owte his eien for iij causes. The firste cause was for [etc.]... The cause secondary was for he myȝhte not beholde women withowte concupiscence. The thrydde cause was [etc.].

†**b.** quasi-*adv.* In the second place (in an enumeration, argument, etc.); secondly. *Obs.*

Perh. suggested by med.L. *secundāriē* adv., similarly used.

1455 *Rolls of Parlt.* V. 300/2 First to Goddes pleasure, secundarie for your owne suerte..and for the third to the universall wele..of this lond. *c* **1532** DU WES *Introd. Fr.* in *Palsgr.* 928 Secondary, *secondement.* **1538** STARKEY *England* II. ii. §14. 195 We myght bryng thys ij thyngys to effecte—that ys to say, to haue the cyuyle law of the Romaynys to be the commyn law here of Englond with vs; and, secondary that [etc.].

3. a. Belonging to the second order in a series related by successive derivation, causation, or dependence; derived from, based on, or dependent on something else which is primary; not original, derivative.

secondary cause: a proximate or instrumental cause, a cause produced by a primary or first cause. (Also used in sense 1.)

1398 TREVISA *Barth. De P.R.* IV. i. (1495) 76 Heete Colde Drye and Moyste ben callyd the fyrste qualitees... They ben also callyd the pryncipal qualytees, for of theym come all the secundarye effectes. **1567** ALLEN *Def. Priesthood* 15 Wrought by the principal cause, and yet by the office and ministery of some secondary cause appointed..for the same vse. **1583** STUBBES *Anat. Abus.* II. 59 We giue unto God the cheefest stroke..all other creatures being but the instrumentall, or secundarie causes. *c* **1645** HOWELL *Lett.* (1655) II. lxi. 86 So many mother languages,..besides secondary tongues and dialects, which exceed the number of their mothers. **1646** SIR T. BROWNE *Pseud. Ep.* V. xxi. 268 In this secondary and symbolicall sense it may be also understood. *a* **1676** HALE *Prim. Orig. Man.* (1677) 26 The secondary origination of Mankind, or the production of the Individuals by generation. **1738** *Gentl. Mag.* VIII. 62/1 Neither do I remember that I have seen much of it [*sc.* generosity] in any Moral Treatise, being perhaps but superficially handled, under the Notion of a secondary and derivative Virtue. **1777** PRIESTLEY *Matt. & Spir.* (1782) I. xii. 146 All secondary causes necessarily lead us to a primary one. **1788** GIBBON *Decl. & F.* xlix. V. 94 Of these pictures, the far greater part, the transcripts of a human pencil, could only pretend to a secondary likeness. **1790** *Phil. Trans. R. Soc.* LXXX. 247 (*heading*) Secondary triangles, subdivided into two sets, for the improvement of the maps of the country, and the plan of the City of London. **1830** LYELL *Princ. Geol.* I. 76 Convinced of the undeviating uniformity of secondary causes,..he determines the probability of accounts transmitted to him of former occurrences. **1877** *Smith & Wace's Dict. Chr. Biog.* I. 449/2 The literature upon Cerinthus is summed up in the following primary and secondary authorities. **1908** BREED & HOSMER *Princ. & Pract. Surveying* II. i. 5 From the sides of the primary triangles as bases a secondary system of triangles is laid out, the sides being shorter than those of the primary system. **1975** J. B. HARLEY *O.S. Maps* i. 7 This primary network is broken down successively into a secondary triangulation (giving a continuous network of stations between 8 km and 12 km apart), a tertiary triangulation (with a density of control points 4 to 7 km apart), and other lower orders of control.

b. Having only a derived authority; acting under the direction of another, subordinate. Cf. 1 d.

1667 MILTON *P.L.* V. 854 That we were formd then saist thou? and the work Of secondarie hands, by task transferd From Father to his Son? **1869** TOZER *Highl. Turkey* I. 256 It is doubtful whether the people, with their strong personal feeling towards their Gospodar, will be satisfied with applying to a secondary agency.

c. *Philos.* (*a*) Applied to those qualities or affections of bodies that were supposed to be derived from the four 'primary' qualities recognized by Aristotle, hot, cold, wet, dry. *Obs.* exc. *Hist.* (*b*) Applied to those properties or qualities of matter (such as colour, smell, taste, etc.) which are by Locke and others distinguished from 'primary' qualities as not existing (like the latter) in the bodies themselves independently of perception, but depending upon the action of the primary qualities on the percipient. Cf. PRIMARY *a.* 6 b.

(*a*) **1656** STANLEY *Hist. Philos.* VI. *Doctr. Aristotle* II. xiii. (1687) 380/1 Besides these principal affections there are others secondary, chiefly competent to homogeneous bodies, some passive, some active.

(*b*) **1666** BOYLE *Orig. Forms & Qual.* 43 There are simpler and more Primitive affections of Matter, from which these Secondary Qualities, if I may so call them, do depend. **1700** LOCKE *Hum. Und.* II. viii. §10 (ed. 4) 61 Such Qualities, which, in truth are nothing in the Objects themselves, but Powers to produce various Sensations in us by their primary Qualities, i.e. by the Bulk Figure, Texture, and Motion of their insensible parts, as Colours, Sounds, Tasts, &c. These I call secondary Qualities. **1856** FERRIER *Inst. Metaph.* 146 Among the secondary qualities [of matter] are classed heat and cold, colour and sound, taste and odour.

d. *Astr.* †***secondary movable***: any of the 'movables' except the primum mobile (*obs.*). ***secondary planet***: a satellite which revolves round a primary planet (PLANET *sb.*[1] 2). ***secondary system***: a subordinate system (composed of a primary planet and its satellites) within the solar system.

1664 POWER *Exp. Philos.* Pref. 4 The Secondary Planets of Saturn and Jupiter. **1690** Secondary movable [see MOVABLE *sb.* 1]. **1786–7** BONNYCASTLE *Astron.* iii. 39 Ten others, called secondary planets, or satellites, which regard their primaries as the centers of their motions. **1868** LOCKYER *Guillemin's Heavens* (ed. 3) 237 The secondary systems of which that [viz. the Solar] system itself is composed. **1868** —— *Elem. Astron.* §16 (1879) 88 The Moon..is one of the satellites, or secondary bodies.

e. ***secondary circle***: *Geom.* and *Astr.*, a great circle passing through the poles of another great circle perpendicular to its plane; see also *sb.* 3. ***secondary caustic*** *Math.* (see quot. 1857).

1704 J. HARRIS *Lex. Techn.* I, Secondary Circles. **1857** CAYLEY *Math. Papers* (1889) II. 339 The secondary caustic or orthogonal trajectory of the refracted rays, i.e. a curve having the caustic for its evolute.

f. ***secondary bow*** or ***rainbow***: a rainbow formed by rays twice internally reflected by the rain-drops; usually, an outer and fainter bow parallel with the primary bow.

1793 STURGES in *Phil. Trans.* LXXXIII. 1 In this shower two primary rainbows appeared,..with a secondary bow to each. **1859** PARKINSON *Optics* (1866) 236 The Secondary Rainbow. The space above the primary rainbow..seems darker than the rest; beyond this space appears a broader but fainter rainbow the colours of which are in reverse order to those in the primary. **1883** R. H. SCOTT *Elem. Meteorol.* 200 The secondary bow, presenting the prismatic colours in the reverse order to that just described.

g. *Cryst.* Of crystalline forms: Derivative, not primitive.

1805–17 R. JAMESON *Char. Min.* (ed. 3) 174 The manner in which secondary crystals may increase in magnitude, and still preserve their form. **1823** H. J. BROOKE *Introd. Crystallogr.* 69 The edge *c d*, of the secondary plane, being parallel to the diagonal *a b*, of the primary form. **1836–41** BRANDE *Chem.* (ed. 5) 122 The secondary forms are supposed to arise from decrements of particles taking place on different edges and angles of the primitive forms.

h. *Electr.* (i) Of a current: Induced. Hence of apparatus, etc.: Pertaining to an induced current. With reference to any device utilizing electromagnetic induction, esp. a transformer: of, pertaining to, or carrying the output electrical power.

1832 *Phil. Mag.* XI. 300 Although the principal current in A be continued, still the secondary current in B is not found to accompany it, for it ceases after the first moment. **1843** R. J. GRAVES *Syst. Clin. Med.* xxxi. 423, I applied the secondary electric current to the parts affected. **1847** *Patent Jrnl.* 16 Oct. 476/1 Upon the primary circuit being completed through the primary coils, a secondary circuit is induced through the secondary coils, but in an opposite direction. *c* **1865** J. WYLDE in *Circ. Sci.* I. 253/2 The secondary wire, is that in which a current is induced by its proximity to the primary one. **1881** S. P. THOMPSON *Elem. Lessons Electr. & Magn.* 365 Causing the inductive action in the secondary circuit at 'make' to be comparatively feeble. **1931** *B.B.C. Year-bk.* (1932) 436/2 The output of the secondary winding of the output transformer. **1947** R. LEE *Electronic Transformers & Circuits* iii. 58 Single-phase full-wave rectifiers with two anodes have higher secondary volt-amperes for a given primary v-a rating than a filament transformer. **1962** *Newnes Conc. Encycl. Electr. Engin.* 810/2 The induced secondary voltage E_s lags ϕ by 90° and the secondary current I_s lags behind E_s by an angle which depends upon the impedance of the secondary circuit. **1969** J. J. SPARKES *Transistor Switching* vi. 146 They are called secondary circuits to contrast them with the input circuits.

(ii) Of a cell or battery: in which the chemical reaction that generates the current is reversible and which therefore can store electrical energy supplied to it.

1872 *Jrnl. Chem. Soc.* XXV. 589 The author has investigated what proportion of the energy is lost whilst the secondary battery receives its charge. **1881** *Electrician* 3 Sept. 249/2 No one is inclined to underrate the claims of M. Planté in connection with this form of secondary battery. **1902** J. A. FLEMING in *Encycl. Brit.* XXVIII. 74/1 In connection with the generator, it is almost the invariable custom to put down a secondary battery, to enable the supply to be given after the engine has stopped. **1922** GLAZEBROOK *Dict. Appl. Physics* II. 72/2 There is no essential electro-chemical difference between the secondary cell and the primary cell when either is used as a generator of electrical energy. **1962** *Newnes Conc. Encycl. Electr. Engin.* 9/1 Also known as the storage cell or secondary cell, the accumulator is reversible, i.e. it can, after discharging, be brought back to a full state of charge by passing a reverse current through it. **1979** *Nature* 22 Mar. 335/2 (*caption*) Schematic for repeating cell in a forced ionisation secondary battery using a bipolar ion exchange membrane.

i. *Chem.* (i) Applied to compounds regarded as being derived from ammonia (†or water) by replacement of two hydrogen atoms by organic radicals (cf. PRIMARY *a.* 6 f (i)); also extended to analogous derivatives of other elements, esp. phosphorus. [The sense is due to Gerhardt & Chiozza, who used F. *secondaire* (*Compt. Rend.* (1853) XXXVII. 88).]

1854 *Q. Jrnl. Chem. Soc.* VI. 195 To convert the preceding compounds [*sc* . primary amides] into secondary amides, or amides representing a molecule of ammonia in which 2 atoms of hydrogen are replaced by the negative radicals, we heat these primary amides with an equivalent quantity of chloride of benzoyl, of cumyl, sulphophenyl, &c. **1888, 1889** [see PRIMARY *a.* 6 f (i)]. **1932** I. D. GARARD *Introd. Org. Chem.* xi. 154 Dimethylamine is a typical secondary amine. **1962, 1965** [see PRIMARY *a.* 6 f (i)]. **1974** *Encycl. Brit. Macropædia* XIII. 697/1 The reaction of amines with nitrous acid is an old and important reaction... From secondary amines, nitrosamines precipitate as non-basic, yellowish oils.

(ii) Applied to organic compounds other than amines, etc. (see prec. sense) in which the characteristic functional group is located on a saturated carbon atom which is itself bonded to two other carbon atoms. [Applied orig. to alcohols by H. Kolbe, who used G. *secundär* (*Ann. der Chem. und Pharm.* (1864) CXXXII. 102).]

1864 *Chem. News* 26 Nov. 260/1 By a secondary alcohol the author [*sc.* Kolbe] means a body in which two of the typical hydrogen atoms in a typical alcohol are substituted by two atoms of some other alcohol radicals. **1876** *Phil. Mag.* II. 162 To so-called normal butylic alcohol is generally assigned the structural formula $CH_2(C_3H_7)OH$; to secondary butylic alcohol the formula $CH(CH_3)(C_2H_5)OH$; [etc.]. **1876** *Encycl. Brit.* V. 562/2 The isomeric alcohols of the present series can thus be conveniently classified... 1 Primary alcohols... 2 Secondary alcohols... 3 Tertiary alcohols. **1900** PERKIN & KIPPING *Org. Chem.* vi. 107 Tertiary alcohols are, as a rule, more difficult to obtain than the primary or secondary compounds. **1932** I. D. GARARD *Introd. Org. Chem.* iii. 34 Secondary butyl alcohol..is made from butylene..just as isopropyl alcohol is made from propylene. **1972** R. A. JACKSON *Mechanism* v. 88 In general, primary compounds undergo S_N2 substitution more readily than do secondary compounds, and S_N2 reactions on tertiary compounds go with great difficulty if at all.

(iii) Applied to a saturated carbon atom which is bonded to two other carbon atoms; also, bonded to or involving such an atom. Of an ion or free radical: having (respectively) the electric charge or the unpaired electron located on a secondary carbon atom.

1903 A. J. WALKER tr. *Holleman's Text-bk. Org. Chem.* I. 46 If it [*sc.* a carbon atom] is linked to two carbon atoms it is named secondary; if to three, tertiary; if to four, quaternary. **1926** H. G. RULE tr. *J. Schmidt's Text-bk. Org. Chem.* 70 If two, three or all four valencies are linked to carbon, the atom under consideration is termed secondary, tertiary or quaternary respectively. **1950** E. R. ALEXANDER *Princ. Ionic Org. Reactions* iii. 42 We find..that a primary or secondary carbonium ion extracts a hydrogen atom with a pair of electrons from an alkane so as to form a secondary or tertiary carbonium ion. **1972** [see PRIMARY *a.* 6 f (iii)]. **1972** NORMAN & WADDINGTON *Mod. Org. Chem.* vi. 82 The order of stability of carbonium ions is tertiary > secondary > primary.

j. *Meteorology.* Said of a subsidiary depression taking place on the border of a primary cyclone. Cf. B. 10.

1876 R. H. SCOTT *Weather Charts* 76 It is not often, however, that we find the secondary depressions so clearly marked as in fig. 15.

k. Applied to bodily characteristics which are peculiar to one sex but are not essential to reproduction; sometimes the sexual ducts and organs are also included. Cf. PRIMARY *a.* 6 h.

1780 J. HUNTER in *Phil. Trans. R. Soc.* LXX. 529 It is my intention at present to extend my inquiry on this subject no farther than as to what relates to that resemblance which one sex bears to that of another in those distinguishing properties which I term secondary... There is often a change of the secondary properties of one sex into another. *Ibid.* 530 The male..loses that resemblance which he before bore to the female in various secondary properties, exclusive of what relates to the organs of generation. *Ibid.* 531 A change of those secondary characters. **1859** C. DARWIN *Orig. Species* v. 156, I think it will be admitted..that secondary sexual characters are very variable. **1871**, etc. [see PRIMARY *a.* 6 h]. **1926** H. M. KYLE *Biol. Fishes* xii. 290 It is amongst the freshwater Teleosts..that the secondary sexual characters are most developed... Usually it is the pectoral fins that are longer in the male. **1977** STEEN & PRICE *Human Sex & Sexuality* iv. 59 Androgens, of which testosterone is the principle one, control the development of secondary sex characteristics (distribution of hair, quality of voice, skeletal form, sebaceous gland activity).

l. *Geol.* Of a mineral: that is not an original constituent of the rock; formed by the alteration or replacement of primary constituents of the rock.

1886 [see PRIMARY *a.* 6 i]. **1897** G. P. MERRILL *Treat. Rocks* III. iii. 249 Those dikes containing so large a proportion of secondary epidote as to be of a dull greenish hue are almost invariably more enduring than the granites. **1931** A. JOHANNSEN *Descr. Petrogr. Igneous Rocks* I. ii. 28 Secondary minerals may be introduced by the addition of material such as boron, fluorine, etc., to form tourmaline, topaz, fluorite, etc. **1974** FLINT & SKINNER *Physical Geol.* vi. 94/2 Water combines with the remaining aluminum silicate radical to create the clay mineral kaolinite... The resulting kaolinite we call a secondary mineral, because it was not present in the original rock.

m. ***secondary shaft*** = LAYSHAFT.

1888 [see LAYSHAFT]. **1902** A. C. HARMSWORTH et al. *Motors* x. 205 Causing the secondary shaft..to be rotated. **1926** H. T. RUTTER *Mod. Motors* II. vii. 261 Parallel to the gear-shaft in the gear box is another shaft, which is called the 'lay' shaft, 'secondary', or countershaft.

n. ***secondary spectrum***: a fringe of colours bordering an image formed by a lens corrected for two wavelengths and due to the non-coincidence of the foci of other wavelengths.

1893 W. E. BAXTER tr. *H. van Heurck's Microscope* 370 The final upper lens, which is also a triplet, is used to destroy the secondary spectrum. **1932** HARDY & PERRIN *Princ. Optics* vi. 115 This residual chromatism gives rise to a fringe of color surrounding the image of an extended object, which is known as the secondary spectrum. **1978** R. KINGSLAKE *Lens Design Fund.* iv. 75 The fact that achromatizing a lens for two colors fails to unite the other colors is known as secondary spectrum; it should not be confused with the secondary chromatic aberration.

o. *Physics* and *Astr.* Of, pertaining to, or designating radiation that has been produced by the interaction of other (primary) radiation with matter. Of cosmic rays: produced in the earth's atmosphere by the impact of primary rays.

1898 *Sci. Abstr.* I. 128 The secondary rays emitted by the metal..pass some centimetres through the air. **1921** J. SCOTT-TAGGART *Thermionic Tubes* i. 11 Under some conditions the electron bombardment liberates a number of secondary electrons attached to the atoms of the plate. **1938** [see PRIMARY *a.* 6k]. **1944** *Electronic Engin.* XVI. 372/1 In order to avoid or minimise secondary emission it is necessary that grid structures shall be maintained reasonably cool during the operating life of a valve. **1959** [see PRIMARY *a.* 6k]. **1964** M. GOWING *Britain & Atomic Energy 1939–1945* i. 39 When the uranium oxide was bombarded with fast neutrons the initial fission did not propagate itself because the secondary neutrons lost energy. **1974** *Encycl. Brit. Macropædia* V. 200/1 Secondary cosmic rays consist mainly of subatomic particles that are short-lived..; they cannot have come far and are thus known to have been produced within the atmosphere.

p. ***secondary poverty***: effective poverty due to waste, inefficiency, or some other drain on resources, rather than to insufficiency of means.

1901 B. S. ROWNTREE *Poverty* p. viii, Families whose total earnings would be sufficient for merely physical efficiency were it not that some portion of it is absorbed by other expenditure... Poverty falling under this head is described as 'secondary' poverty. **1909** M. F. DAVIES *Life in Eng. Village* xii. 146 These people..appear to have a struggle to keep going, and their incomes do not probably exceed the limit of secondary poverty. **1970** M. REIN in P. Townsend *Concept of Poverty* ii. 60 If the diet is to..avoid building into its definition a confusion between primary and secondary poverty, then the standards of economy must be relaxed and a more realistic assumption of human error accepted.

q. Designating action taken by workers on strike to prevent other firms from doing business with the strikers' employers; *esp.* applied to a boycott or the picketing of the premises of firms not otherwise involved in the dispute. orig. *U.S.*

1909 *Pacific Reporter* XCVIII. 1083/1 This is the argument commonly advanced to establish the illegality of what has been called..a 'secondary' rather than a 'primary' boycott. **1916** L. WOLMAN *Boycott in Amer. Trade Unions* i. 142 The secondary boycott is distinctly different in effect from the simple strike; since..it inflicts injury upon an innocent third party. **1938** *Atlantic Reporter* CXCV. 379/2 The Legislature..never contemplated..'secondary picketing'. *Ibid.* 378/1 Secondary picketing is illegal. **1942** *Yale Law Jrnl.* May 1209 Secondary picketing against the employer's vendee, is the only effective means of publicizing the facts of a labor contest. **1979** *Daily Tel.* 13 Jan. 1/2 The Freight Transport Association said secondary picketing had been reduced in some areas, but expressed concern about the position in [the] Midlands where the dispute was unofficial. **1980** *Illustr. London News* Mar. 19/1 The Law Lords referred to their judgment in the case of McShane v Express Newspapers, in which they had decided that secondary blacking on the part of journalists, on the instruction of their union, fell within the immunity granted under section 13 of the 1974 Act.

r. Designating an earthquake S wave (see S 6).

1919, etc. [see PRIMARY *a.* 4h].

s. ***secondary industry***: industry that converts the materials provided by primary industry (see PRIMARY *a.* 6n) into commodities and products for the consumer.

1930 *Economist* 19 July 107/2 The design behind the former movement is clearly to enable nascent secondary industries to compete in the home market. **1944** [see LIGHT *a.*[1] 4c]. **1950** *N.Z. Jrnl. Agric.* Aug. 127/3 The tending of land, livestock, and crops has figured so prominently in the lives of New Zealanders—and will continue to do so despite the growth of secondary industries. **1977** D. M. SMITH *Human Geogr.* viii. 232 The mineral or crop may be exported in its raw state for processing in Europe or North America, thus depriving the producing country of a possible basis for building up secondary industry.

t. ***secondary air***: air supplied to a combustion zone where combustion with primary air is occurring.

1931 *Engineering* 9 Jan. 40/2 Complete combustion to CO_2 takes place at the end of the chamber, when an enveloping stream of secondary air meets the first stream. **1951** COHEN & ROGERS *Gas Turbine Theory* vii. 195 If devices are used to increase the turbulence and so distribute the secondary air more uniformly throughout the burning gases, the combustion efficiency will be improved but at the expense of increased pressure loss.

u. Of radar: relying on signals transmitted automatically by aircraft in response to signals reaching it from the radar.

1945 R. WATSON-WATT in *Nature* 15 Sept. 323 Radar in war fell into three convenient categories, each of which has come to stay in the peace... Secondary radar requires that small measure of co-operation which is involved in the fitting and switching on of an otherwise automatic responder. **1961** *Engineering* 6 Jan. 1/2 What secondary radar does for the controller on the ground is to give him identification of aircraft as they come within range. **1967** *New Scientist* 19 Oct. 151/2 Air traffic control is increasingly making use of secondary radar.

v. ***secondary structure*** (*Biochem.*), the three-dimensional form that the chain of a polynucleotide or polypeptide molecule assumes as a result of non-covalent bonds between neighbouring amino-acid residues.

1952 [see PRIMARY *a.* 6v]. **1960** *Nature* 8 Oct. 99/2 Ribonucleic acid is a single-stranded molecule the secondary structure of which arises from intramolecular interactions. **1974** [see PRIMARY *a.* 6v]. **1977** D. E. METZLER *Biochemistry* ii. 102/2 The value of β is always positive but that of τ can be negative, the secondary structure (Watson-Crick helix) being fully formed but with left-handed superhelical turns present.

4. a. Belonging to the second order in a series of subdivisions or ramifications. Chiefly *Bot.*

1796 WITHERING *Brit. Pl.* (ed. 3) III. 780 Fructifications near the rib of the 2dary wings. **1861** R. BENTLEY *Man. Bot.* 122 Adventitious or Secondary Root.—This name is applied to all roots which are not produced by the direct elongation of the radicle of the embryo. *Ibid.* 193 When the floral axis is thus branched, it is better to speak of the main axis as the primary axis.., its divisions as the secondary axes.., and their divisions as the tertiary axes. **1880** C. E. BESSEY *Botany* 147 Where the secondary leaves (leaflets) grow from an extremely short axis. **1883** HUXLEY *Pract. Biol.* xii. 157 Each of the hairs..is..seen to be covered over its whole surface with innumerable very fine secondary hairs; these are shortest near the base of the primary hair. **1973** H. C. BOLD *Morphol. Plants* (ed. 3) xxx. 570/2 Branches of the radicle are secondary roots; all other roots are adventitious.

b. Belonging to the second stage in a process of compounding or combination; consisting of two primary elements. ***secondary colours***: see COLOUR *sb.* 2.

1807 T. THOMSON *Chem.* (ed. 3) II. 467 By the term Secondary Compound is meant a combination of salifiable bases or primary compounds with each other. *Ibid.*, The secondary compounds..may be arranged under the five following classes. **1831** BREWSTER *Optics* vii. 69 Any mixtures or combinations of any of them [*sc.* primary colours] are called secondary colours. **1879** *Cassell's Techn. Educ.* I. 178/1 The primary or simple, and the secondary or mixed colours.

c. ***secondary road***: a road of a class lower than that of a main road; a minor road.

1903 in *Parl. Papers 1904* XXIV. 279 (Cd. 1793) p. vi, Roads of this class are known in different parts of the country as Secondary Roads, Contribution or Contributory Roads, 'Grant in aid' Roads, &c. **1929** A. HUXLEY *Let.* 1 Dec. (1969) 321 Even the secondary roads were tolerable. **1938** E. AMBLER *Cause for Alarm* xiv. 228 The only roads we'll have to worry about are..secondary roads. **1959** T. S. ELIOT *Elder Statesman* III. 88 It was late at night. A secondary road. I ran over an old man lying in the road. **1974** J. THOMSON *Long Revenge* iv. 45 He turned off into the network of secondary roads.

5. With reference to temporal sequence: Pertaining to a second period or condition of things; adventitious, not primitive. Chiefly in certain modern scientific and technical uses: see below.

†**a.** *gen.*

1471 RIPLEY *Comp. Alch.* Rec. in Ashm. *Theat. Chem. Brit.* (1652) 188 The Altytude of thy Bodys hyde..In every of thy Materyalls dystroyyng the fyrst qualyte: And secundary qualytes more gloryose repare in them anon.

b. *Geol.* In early use, applied (with some notion of sense 3) to partially crystalline rocks, often containing the remains of life on the earth. Now, Belonging to the second division of stratified rocks; of or pertaining to the strata between the Palæozoic or Primary, and the Tertiary; = MESOZOIC.

1813 SIR H. DAVY *Agric. Chem.* (1814) 192 Rocks are generally divided by geologists into two grand divisions, distinguished by the names of primary and secondary... The secondary rocks, or strata, consist only partly of crystalline matter; contain fragments of other rocks or strata; often abound in the remains of vegetables and marine animals; and sometimes contain the remains of land animals. **1818** W. PHILLIPS *Outl. Min. & Geol.* (ed. 3) 86 Rocks which include organic remains, must have been formed after the shells they contain; and therefore not being considered primitive, they are by some termed secondary rocks; whence the term used by geologists of primary and secondary formations. **1833** LYELL *Princ. Geol.* III. 324 By 'secondary', we mean those stratified rocks older than the tertiary, which contain distinct organic remains. **1882** GEIKIE *Text-bk. Geol.* VI. III. i. 759 The Mesozoic or Secondary series.

c. *Biol.* Belonging to or directly derived from the second stage of development or growth.

1857 HENFREY *Bot.* §659 The walls of almost all cells soon exhibit a departure from the original simple condition, arising from the formation of new lamellæ,..all over, or over particular parts of the inside of the primary membrane. These are distinguished as secondary layers. **1860** GOSSE *Hist. Brit. Sea-Anemones* Introd. 19, I have found a small round aperture in each primary and secondary septum. **1880** BESSEY *Bot.* 408 These new cells are developed on the one hand into tracheides, which compose the secondary wood, and on the other into parenchyma and fibrous tissue, composing the secondary cortex.

d. *Surg.*, etc. Performed or occurring after a definite time or occurrence. ***secondary amputation***: amputation performed after suppuration has set in. ***secondary hæmorrhage***: hæmorrhage occurring several days after a wound or operation.

1837 R. LISTON *Pract. Surg.* 325 Secondary hæmorrhage will sometimes follow when reaction has been established. **1850** OGILVIE, *Secondary amputation.* **1889** MACCORMAC *Surg. Operat.* II. 140 Secondary or consecutive operations are those performed after the acute inflammatory symptoms have subsided and suppuration has been fully established. **1891** MOULLIN *Surg.* 1371 Amputation..may be primary (within twenty-four hours); intermediary (before suppuration); or secondary (after suppuration).

e. *Path.* Characteristic of or pertaining to the second stage or period of a disease, esp. of syphilis.

1722 QUINCY *Lex. Phys.-Med.* (ed. 2), *Secundary Fever*, is that which arises after a Crisis, or the Discharge of some morbid Matter, as after the Declension of the Small-Pox, or Measles. **1786** J. HUNTER *Venereal Dis.* (1810) 431 To ascertain whether her secondary ulcers were infectious. **1799** BEDDOES in *Med. Jrnl.* I. 101 The symptoms were what are called secondary, and the disease in its most rooted and obstinate state. **1899** *Allbutt's Syst. Med.* VII. 677 True epilepsy may occur in the so-called 'secondary' stage of syphilis.

f. ***secondary education*** or ***instruction***: that between the primary or elementary education and the higher or university education; ***secondary school***, one in which such education is given; also ***secondary modern school***: a secondary school of a kind established by the Education Act of 1944, offering a general education to children not selected for grammar or technical schools (cf. *central school* s.v. CENTRAL *a.* 4 and *modern school* s.v. MODERN *a.* 2e); also (in colloq. use) *ellipt.* as ***secondary modern*** (freq. *attrib.*).

1809 R. L. EDGEWORTH *Ess. on Professional Educ.* i. 41 In the secondary schools for boys of nine or ten.., the principles of general grammar should be explained. **1835** *Southern Lit. Messenger* I. 275 Others classify them into 1st *primary* schools..2nd *secondary* schools, for the rudiments of Arithmetic, Geography, English Grammar, and further progress in reading and writing. **1861** M. ARNOLD *Pop. Educ. France* Introd. 39 The public secondary schools of France. **1863** —— in *Macm. Mag.* VIII. 355/1 The Royal Commissioners have thought themselves precluded..from making a thorough inquiry into the system of secondary instruction on the Continent. **1876** J. GRANT *Burgh. Sch. Scot.* II. ii. 128 Schools in which elementary and secondary instruction were formerly given. **1882** M. ARNOLD *Irish Ess.* 130 Schools giving secondary education, as it is called—that fuller and higher instruction which comes after elementary instruction. **1892** in *Parl. Papers* IX. 373 This Act may be cited as the Secondary School Teachers Registration Act, 1892. **1902** *Encycl. Brit.* XXVII. 663/2 The school which seeks to retain its pupil to the age of sixteen or seventeen, and to prepare him to enter a skilled trade or one of the minor professions, is a secondary or intermediate school. **1926** W. H. HADOW et al. *Rep. Consult. Comm. Educ. Adolescent* (Board of Educ.) 266 The expression 'secondary school' was borrowed from the French '*école secondaire*', which was used apparently for the first time in the *Rapport et projet de décret sur l'organisation générale de l'instruction publique*, submitted to the Legislative Assembly by Condorcet in April, 1792. **1937** *Burlington Mag.* Sept. 107/2 No student..can possibly acquire more than a secondary-school smattering in the subject. **1943** C. NORWOOD et al. *Curriculum & Examinations in Secondary Schools* (Board of Educ.) I. iii. 15 At the age of 11+, or earlier in some cases, a child would pass into one of the three types of secondary education which we have postulated, secondary Grammar School, secondary Technical School, secondary Modern School. **1955** *Punch* 30 Mar. 404/2 'The thing that makes me nervous,' I said tentatively, 'is if they fail their 11-plus and land up in a Secondary Modern.' **1956** H. LOUKES *Secondary Modern* i. 45 They are not to be regarded, these secondary modern children, as a backward group. **1961** M. KELLY *Spoilt Kill* II. 103 He taught maths in a secondary modern somewhere down south. **1976** *Yorkshire Evening Press* 9 Dec. 13/6 Derwent Secondary Modern School, York, was entered and £6.50 stolen. **1976** *Evening Post* (Nottingham) 14 Dec. 6/2 His early education finished at 14 when he left the Player Secondary School. **1982** *Guardian* 26 Apr. 3/2 Critics say it is a back door way of re-introducing grammar and secondary modern schools.

g. Archæol. ***secondary burial*** or ***interment***: a burial of human remains in a site used for burial at an earlier time (see also quot. 1960); ***Secondary Neolithic***: (of or pertaining to) that part of the Neolithic period in Britain marked by the fusion of native Mesolithic cultural elements with those of immigrant European agricultural peoples.

1865 J. LUBBOCK *Pre-Historic Times* iv. 110 It appears reasonable to conclude that these interments belong to the ante-metallic period; especially when..we find several secondary interments, plainly belonging to a later age. **1877** W. GREENWELL *Brit. Barrows* 13 These secondary interments have been made either by placing the body on the surface of an existing barrow..or by making an excavation into it. Secondary burials occur in all parts of a barrow. **1954** S. PIGGOTT *Neolithic Cultures* i. 15 These Secondary Neolithic cultures, as I have called them, were to form the basis of the ensuing British Bronze Age. **1960** K. M. KENYON *Archæol. in Holy Land* iv. 86 The burials as we find them were secondary. That is to say, the bones were only placed in their present position after the flesh had largely decayed. **1963** E. S. Wood *Collins Field Guide Archaeol.* I. iv. 60 The secondary Neolithic is now appearing more complicated than it looked a few years ago. **1963** H. N. Savory in Foster & Alcock *Culture & Environment* iii. 26 It is therefore no longer necessary to envisage a narrow horizon on which Primary and Secondary Neolithic and 'Beaker' elements can scarcely be disentangled. **1977** Kwang-chih Chang *Archaeol. Anc. China* (ed. 3) viii. 406 Three ways to dispose of the dead were distinguished..: cremation and ash urns; interment of the dorsal and stretched type; and probably secondary burials.

h. ***secondary succession*** (Ecol.): (see quot. 1905).

1905 F. E. Clements *Research Methods in Ecol.* iv. 247 Generally speaking, all successions on denuded soils are secondary... The great majority of secondary successions owe their origin to floods, animals, or the activities of man, and they agree in occurring upon decomposed soils of medium water-content. **1932** Fuller & Conard tr. *Braun-Blanquet's Plant Social.* xi. 279 Fires are always followed.. by a secondary succession, which tends anew towards the climax. **1973** P. A. Colinvaux *Introd. Ecol.* vi. 77 Secondary succession is best understood by considering what happens to a farm when it is abandoned.

i. ***secondary hardening*** (Metallurgy): a further hardening which occurs in some previously hardened steels when they are tempered; so ***secondary hardness***.

1915 Edwards & Kikkawa in *Jrnl. Iron & Steel Inst.* XCII. 12 The temperature at which this secondary hardening begins is progressively raised with increasing percentages of tungsten. *Ibid.*, As regards the temperature at which the maximum secondary hardness is obtained.. for the steel with no tungsten this is 494°. **1937** *Discovery* May 155/2 The tempering of high speed steel is primarily undertaken to give maximum secondary hardness. **1949** P. C. Carman *Chem. Constitution & Properties of Engin. Materials* v. 192 On tempering, the hardness decreases slightly between 300° and 500°C., and then secondary hardening takes place between 500° and 600°C. **1967** A. H. Cottrell *Introd. Metall.* xxv. 517 The steel is tempered at 650°C to produce secondary hardening by precipitation of alloy carbides.

j. *Psychol.* In various phrases. ***secondary conditioned reflex***: a reflex transferred from the original stimulus to one associated with it; similarly ***secondary conditioned stimulus***; ***secondary conditioning***: conditioning in which the response is transferred to a subsequent, associated stimulus; similarly ***secondary reinforcement***, ***reinforcer***, ***reward***.

1927 G. V. Anrep tr. *Pavlov's Conditioned Reflexes* iii. 34 The appearance of a black square in the dog's line of vision is now used as yet a further stimulus, which is to be given the character of a secondary conditioned stimulus. **1938** B. F. Skinner *Behav. Organisms* ix. 245, I am inclined to doubt the reality of secondary conditioning of a respondent in general. **1940** Hilgard & Marquis *Conditioning & Learning* iii. 63 Secondary rewards such as approval, money, prestige and so forth. **1944** B. Malinowski *Sci. Theory of Culture* xii. 138 The secondary reinforcement becomes attached to the instrumental performance as a whole, and to all its component parts. **1957** E. R. Hilgard *Introd. Psychol.* (ed. 2) x. 242/1 A feature of secondary reinforcement that is very important for human social behavior is its wide application. *Ibid.*, There is also experimental evidence in support of the principle that secondary reinforcers have wide generality. **1976** *Howard Jrnl.* XV. I. 12 The relics of past experiences, surviving through the mechanism of secondary reinforcement. **1977** R. A. Rescorla in Davis & Hurwitz *Operant-Pavlovian Interactions* vi. 155 No increase in response rate was produced by this supposed secondary reinforcer.

k. ***secondary recovery***, the recovery of oil by means of special techniques from reservoirs which have been substantially depleted; freq. *attrib.*

1940 P. D. Torrey in E. DeGolyer *Elements Petroleum Industry* xiii. 289 The two most commonly employed secondary recovery methods are water-flooding and gas-repressuring. **1945** L. M. Fanning *Our Oil Resources* iv. 96 In most instances secondary-recovery operations are more costly than primary operations. **1971** I. G. Gass et al. *Understanding Earth* xxiii. 330/2 Oil is obtained at this site by a technique of secondary recovery which involves the injection of water under pressure. **1973** C. J. May in Hobson & Pohl *Mod. Petroleum Technol.* (ed. 4) v. 174 Of perhaps more general interest is the application of secondary recovery methods to reservoirs which have been largely depleted by natural forces.

6. Connected with what is second in local position. **a.** ***secondary feather***, ***quill***: a feather growing from the second joint of a bird's wing. ***secondary wing***: one of the hind wings of an insect.

1768 Pennant *Brit. Zool.* (1776) II. 437 The tips of the secondary feathers white. **1802** Montagu *Ornith. Dict.* Expl. Techn. Terms, Secondary quill-feathers. **1826** Kirby & Sp. *Entomol.* III. 39 The secondary wings are sometimes smaller than the primary. **1837** *Penny Cycl.* VII. 367/2 The greater wing-coverts and secondary quills are greenish-black.

b. ***secondary constriction*** (Cytology): a chromosomal constriction not associated with the centromere.

1932 C. D. Darlington *Recent Adv. Cytol.* ii. 34 There are also found in many chromosomes 'secondary' constrictions which have no relationship with any present spindle attachment. **1957** C. P. Swanson *Cytol. & Cytogenetics* v. 131 The secondary constrictions seen in somatic metaphase chromosomes generally arise as the result of nucleolar formation. **1975** [see satellite *sb.* 9].

B. *sb.* [elliptical use of adj. Freq. in *pl.*]

1. a. *gen.* One who acts in subordination to another; a delegate or deputy; also a thing which comes second or subordinate in importance. Now *rare*.

1595 Shaks. *John* v. ii. 80, I am too high-borne to be proportied To be a secondary at controll. **1603** —— *Meas. for M.* I. i. 47 Old Escalus Though first in question, is thy secondary. Take thy Commission. **1635** Brathwait *Arcad. Princ.* II. 56 Causing Epimonos, her Secondary, to advance himselfe before her, shee willed him to returne the manner of his recovery. **1771** Goldsm. *Hist. Eng.* IV. 346 From being secondaries in the quarrel at length becoming principals. **1841** Emerson *Meth. Nature* (1844) 20 A certain admirable wisdom, preferable to all other advantages, and whereof all others are only secondaries and indemnities. **1858** J. Martineau *Stud. Chr.* 202 They are not principals, ..but only secondaries to the Editor, in the commission of this error.

b. A cathedral dignitary of second rank.

1436 *E.E. Wills* (1882) 105 To euery secundary & clerc of the chirch iiij[d]. **1616** *Cheque Bk. Chapel Royal* (Camden) 8 John Greene a secondary of the church of Exon. **1778** Warton *Hist. Eng. Poetry* II. 242 In the following stanza, where he [Barclay] wishes to take on board the eight secondaries, or minor canons, of his college. **1852** Hook *Ch. Dict.* (1871) 707 Secondaries is a general name for the inferior members of cathedrals, as vicars choral, &c.

c. An officer of the corporation of the City of London. †Also, an official in certain government offices and law courts: see quot. 1607.

1461 *Rolls of Parlt.* V. 467/2 Secundarie in the Office of oure prive Seall. *a* **1600** in H. Hall *Soc. Eliz. Age* (1886) 178 The Secondary of the Court for rettorne of 2 wrytts 4[s]. **1603** Stow *Surv. Lond.* 538 The Shiriffes of London, in the yeare 1471, were appointed..to haue..6 Clarkes, to wit, a Secondary, a Clarke of the Papers, and 4 other Clarkes. **1607** Cowel *Interpr.*, *Secundarie* (secundarius) is the name of an Officer next vnto the chiefe Officer: as the Secundarie of the fine Office: the Secundarie of the Counter,..Secundarie of the office of the priuie seale, *anno* I. *Ed.* 4. *cap.* I. Secundaries of the Pipe two: Secundarie to the Remembrancers two, which be Officers in the Exchequer. *Camden*. pag. 113. **1642** C. Vernon *Consid. Exch.* 45 Which is not to be allowed of upon Record in the Pipe, by the first Secondary there, untill [etc.]. **1682** *Lond. Gaz.* No. 1738/4 [He] appointed the Common-Serjeant, the Town-Clerk, the two Secondaries, and the four Attorneys of the Mayors Court,..to take the Poll. **1698** Luttrell *Brief Rel.* (1857) IV. 345 Mr. Aston, secondary to the master of the Kings bench office,..is dead. **1766** Entick *London* IV. 47 The secondary, whose office is to return writs, mark warrants, impannel juries for the courts both above and below, and also for the sessions. **1828** Archbold *Forms & Entries* (ed. 2) Pref. 6 For the Rules of the Common Pleas, I am indebted to Mr. Griffiths and Mr. Hewlett, Secondaries of that court. **1858** Simmonds *Dict. Trade*, *Secondaries' Court*, a small-debt court in the city of London. **1892** *Standard* 6 Feb. 3/6 Mr. Roderick, the Secondary [of the City of London],.. kept watch over the proceedings throughout the poll.

2. Short for *secondary planet* (see A. 3 d).

a **1721** [see primary *sb.* 2]. **1788** *Encycl. Brit.* (ed. 3) II. 494/1 The action of the primary planets upon their secondaries. **1852** Hind *Astron. Vocab.* 46 The moon is a secondary to the earth.

3. Short for *secondary circle*: see A. 3 e.

1715 tr. *Gregory's Astron.* (1726) I. 220 These Hour Circles are the same in Position, with the Circles of Declination;..because they are Secondaries to the Equator. **1786–7** Bonnycastle *Astron.* 434 Secondary circles of the sphere, are those circles which pass through the poles of some great circle: thus the meridian and hour circles are secondaries to the equinoctial, &c. **1889** J. Casey *Spherical Trig.* i. 4 A great circle passing through the poles of another circle (great or small) is called a secondary to that circle.

4. Short for *secondary colour*: see A. 4 b.

1854 Fairholt *Dict. Terms Art* s.v. *Secondary Colours*, The same result ensues when two secondaries are mixed in equal strength; thus Olive results from the union of green and violet.

5. *Path.* in *pl.* Secondary symptoms (of syphilis).

1843 R. J. Graves *Syst. Clin. Med.* xxix. 393 Some of these patients..have been pronounced to labour under secondaries. **1898** J. Hutchinson in *Arch. Surg.* IX. 361 After the first and second [infection] definite secondaries followed.

6. *Geol.* The secondary series of rocks, or any of the secondary formations.

In recent Dicts.

7. a. *Ornith.* Short for *secondary feather*.

1768 Pennant *Brit. Zool.* (1776) II. 420 All the other wing feathers, except the secondaries, are dusky. **1815** Stephens in *Shaw's Gen. Zool.* IX. I. 5 Coverts and secondaries green. **1872** Coues *Key N. Amer. Birds* 36 The Secondaries..are those remiges that are seated on the forearm.

b. *Ent.* Short for *secondary wing*.

1826 Kirby & Sp. *Entomol.* IV. 336 Secondary (*Secundariæ*), the posterior wings are so denominated if the superior wings, when at rest, are not placed upon them.

†**8.** *Philos.* Short for *secondary quality*. *Obs.*

1656 Stanley *Hist. Philos.* v. *Doctr. Plato* iv. (1687) 182/1 Intellection likewise must be two-fold, one of Primaries, the other of Secondaries.

9. *Electr.* Short for *secondary coil* or *wire*. Also, a secondary circuit, current, etc.

1837 M. Faraday in *Ann. Electr., Magnetism, & Chem.* I. 199 Why do secondaries almost annihilate the terminal effects of primitives? **1869** *Eng. Mech.* 17 Dec. 335/2 The secondary is wound..in vertical layers insulated by discs of sheet ebonite. **1891** *Nature* 25 June 187/2 The discharge tube in these experiments is made to form the secondary of what is essentially an induction coil. **1896** [see primary *sb.* 5]. **1923** E. W. Marchant *Radio Telegr. & Teleph.* v. 67 If the ratio of transformation is made too great, the primary circuit may be tuned for quite a different wave-length from the secondary. **1947** R. Lee *Electronic Transformers & Circuits* i. 5 The right-hand winding is connnected to a load and is called the secondary. **1967** [see primary *sb.* 5].

10. *Meteorology.* Short for *secondary depression*.

1887 Abercromby *Weather* 312 A secondary which would develop thunder in summer in Great Britain would only produce heavy rain in winter.

11. *Physics* and *Astr.* A secondary ray or particle, esp. a secondary cosmic ray.

1921 *Proc. Nat. Acad. Sci.* VII. 17 Practically no secondaries have a velocity of more than 5 volts, even when the exciting primary electrons have velocities of 300 volts. **1932, 1942** [see primary *sb.* 8]. **1964** *Cambr. Rev.* 24 Oct. 48/2 A shower of secondaries of total energy $\geqslant \epsilon$. **1975** D. G. Fink *Electronics Engineers' Handbk.* vi. 113 The yield.. drops at higher energies, since high-energy electrons penetrate deeper in the material and the secondaries generated there are unable to reach the material surface with enough energy to be emitted.

12. *Gram.* = adjunct *sb.* 5 b.

[**1914**: see adjunct *sb.* 5 b.] **1924** Jespersen *Philos. Gram.* xviii. 252 (*heading*) Secondaries and tertiaries. **1928** —— *Internat. Lang.* II. 97 The definite article is a secondary and therefore uninflected in number or gender. **1940** —— *S.P.E. Tract* LIV. 157 We thus distinguish between clause primaries, clause secondaries, and clause tertiaries. **1959** M. Schlauch *Eng. Lang. in Mod. Times* viii. 221 In this system a leading term..is a primary; its direct modifier (e.g. an adjective) is a secondary.

13. *Path.* An additional tumour arising from cells carried to the site from the initial tumour.

1952 Raven & Hancock *Cancer in Gen. Practice* xxii. 153 No treatment is effective except in the case of prostatic, and occasionally breast, secondaries which may respond to androgens or oestrogens. **1969** Bethell & Burg tr. *Solzhenitsyn's Cancer Ward* II. ii. 12 She could not come to terms with the possibility that radioactive gold might exist somewhere while her son's secondaries were penetrating his groin. **1977** *Proc. R. Soc. Med.* LXX. 199/2 Patients with hypercalcaemia and breast cancer usually have widespread osteolytic bone secondaries.

14. *U.S. Football.* The defensive backfield.

[**1912** *Collier's* 23 Nov. 11/2 He hears people about him rattling away about 'Minnesota shifts', 'secondary defense', and so on.] **1955** *Sports Illustr.* 12 Sept. 31/2 Four of them are ready to leap back into the secondary as line-backers. **1972** J. Mosedale *Football* ii. 18 Dutch is like a rabbit in a brush heap when he gets into the secondary. **1980** *Washington Star* 13 Aug. 65 The Redskins are confident their secondary is in fine shape without White... 'We're going to be fine in the secondary,' Beathard said. 'To hell with him.'

15. Short for *secondary school* or *secondary modern school*. *colloq.*

1962 L. Davidson *Rose of Tibet* 7 'Where does he teach?' 'He used to at the Edith Road Girls' Secondary in Fulham.' **1975** 'J. Bell' *Victim* xiv. 148 The passenger was a girl of twelve from a local comprehensive. Which led back to a London secondary in a northern suburb.

second best, second-best, *a.*

1. Next in quality to the first.

1439 *E.E. Wills* (1882) 114 To Watkyn Asshwell my secunde best furre and gowne. **1616** Shaks. *Will* in Knight *Life* (1843) 534 Item, I giue unto my wife my second best bed, with the furniture. **1837** Lockhart *Scott* I. iii. 95, I gather from Mr. Irving that these lines were considered as the second best set of those produced on the occasion. **1871** *Punch* 19 Aug. 67/1 Inviting your second best acquaintances to your second dance or dinner.

2. *absol.* (quasi-*sb.*) Something inferior to the best. †***to have the second best***: to get the worst of it (cf. 3).

1708 Sir W. Robinson in *3rd Rep. Dep. Kpr. Irel.* 37 Some people [are] of opinion that my lord is like to have but y[e] second best. **1881** *Illustr. Lond. News* 17 Jan. 65/2 Most people must be contented with second bests in this world.

3. quasi-*adv.* In phrase ***to come off second best***, to be defeated in a contest (see come *v.* 61 f).

1777 Abigail Adams in *Fam. Lett.* (1876) 319, I am glad to hear of fighting, even though we come off second-best. **1870** Miss Bridgman *R. Lynne* I. iv. 49 That lady was.. coming off second-best in the encounter.

second class, *sb. phr.* [Cf. second-class *a.*]

The second of a ranked series of classes in which things are grouped; esp. of university degrees, railway carriages, and mail.

1810 *Oxf. Univ. Calendar* 57 The second class is subdivided into two parts, according to the different degrees of merit. **1844** *Punch* VII. 258/2 In travelling by the second class, you will..be choked with dust and ashes from the engine. **1852** [see class *sb.* 5]. **1863** *Statutes at Large U.S.A.* XII. 705 The second class embraces all mailable matter exclusively in print, and regularly issued at stated periods. **1883** *U.S. Official Postal Guide* Jan. 733 'Nixes' is a term used..to denote matter of domestic origin, chiefly of the first and second class, which is unmailable. **1931** H. Crane *Let.* 20 June (1965) 373 The post (for books, etc. 2nd class) is apt to be very slow to Mexico.

second-class, *a.*

1. Of or belonging to the class (in any sense of the word) next to the first. Also *absol.* a place in the second class (in an examination); also a second-class railway ticket or compartment.

1837–8 *Civ. Engin. & Arch. Jrnl.* I. 324/1 A Birmingham first class coach weighs 3 tons 17 cwt. 2 qrs... I have not weighed our second class open carriages. **1839** *Bradshaw's Rly. Time Tables* 10th Mo. 25th, Birm'ham to L'pool, Gentlemen riding in their own Carriages charged Second Class Fares. *Ibid.*, L'pool to Manch., On Sundays—Second Class Train, 7 Morning. **1846** [see first-class B. 1]. **1861**

Chamb. Jrnl. 23 Mar. 177/2, I ride in second-class carriages, because the fare is cheaper than that of the first-class. **1863** A. H. CLOUGH *Poems* (ed. 2) 300 Punctual they met, a second-class he took. **1888** KIPLING *Wee Willie Winkie* (1907) 205 There was only one Second-class on the train. **1899** *Statesm. Year-bk.* 1123 The Sudan has been divided into.. three second-class districts. **1901** KIPLING *Kim* vii. 166 Father Victor.. put him into an empty second-class next to Colonel Creighton's first. **1956** *Times* 4 June 10/7 In 1875 one of the railway companies abolished 'second class', and called it 'third'.

b. *second-class matter* (U.S.): postal matter consisting of periodicals sent from the office of publication; now replaced by ***second-class mail*** (not restricted to the U.S.): mail sent at the lower of two rates; so ***second-class letter***, etc.

1873 *U.S. Postal Laws* II. viii. 176 Postage on second-class matter must be prepaid *in money*. **1883** *Sci. American* 6 Jan. (title) Entered at the Post Office of New York, N.Y. as Second Class Matter. **1968** *Times* 19 Mar. 2/1 Principal recommendations are: a two-tier system providing a first class letter service.. and a slower second class service. *Ibid.* 9/1 The proposal for a first and second class mail service is a confession of failure. **1972** R. HILL *Fairly Dangerous Thing* I. i. 11 A confirmation had been sent off the previous day, second-class mail. **1976** *Cumberland & Westmorland Herald* 4 Dec. 9/6 A second-class letter posted after the last collection on a Friday night would not be dealt with until the following Monday. **1981** G. HAMMOND *Revenge Game* xiv. 155 Put a second-class stamp on it and it may *never* get there.

c. ***second-class road***: a road of a second class; a B-road (see B 2 (ii)).

1906 *Min. Evidence R. Comm. Motor Cars* 191/2 in *Parl. Papers* (Cd. 3081) XLVIII. 89 The roads within the country used for heavy traffic may be divided into three classes: first-class roads,.. second-class roads, which require strengthening only, [etc.]. **1914** in *5th Ann. Rep. Road Board* 77 in *Parl. Papers 1914–16* XXXV. 127 The roads are to be divided into three classes—1. First Class; 2. Second Class; 3. All other roads. **1922** *Michelin Guide Gt. Brit.* (ed. 6) (Atlas) 31 Second-class roads are designated 'B' with its [*sic*] number. **1975** 'G. BLACK' *Big Wind for Summer* ii. 29, I drove.. into a second-class road that became acutely third class.

d. ***second-class citizen***: a person assigned to an inferior class of citizenship; one deprived of normal civic and legal rights; also in extended and *fig.* uses. Hence ***second-class citizenship***. orig *U.S.*

1942 *Time* 6 July 16/3 Finerty.. argued that destitute 'second-class citizens' like Waller were barred from serving on Virginia juries. **1948** G. ORWELL *Let.* 4 Jan. in *Coll. Ess.* (1968) IV. 401 Zilliacus wrote in demanding what amounts to Fascist legislation and creation of 2nd-class citizens. **1951** I. SHAW *Troubled Air* xv. 217 Cohen.. can't get into an hotel. He tells Levy, '..we're second-class citizens in this country.' **1958** J. K. GALBRAITH *Affluent Soc.* ix. 107 We relegate one important class of production to a second-class citizenship. **1965** *Austral. Encycl.* I. 322/1 These people [*sc.* convicts] were second-class citizens, well versed in the routines of unorthodox speech. **1972** D. LESSING *Golden Notebook* (ed. 2) p. viii, Women are second-class citizens, as they are saying energetically and competently in many countries. **1974** *Listener* 17 Jan. 95/3 To show what the graphic artist (a second-class citizen in the art world) is capable of. **1975** S. LAUDER *Killing Time on Corvo* xvii. 160 Brazil.. offered more opportunities to an educated girl than the restrictions, the second-class citizenship, of old-fashioned Portugal.

2. quasi-*adv.* By a second-class conveyance.

1863 MRS. GASKELL *Let.* 1 June (1966) 702 We shall have.. to return—I was going to say 2nd class. **1877** TROLLOPE *Amer. Senator* II. xxv. 268 Why could she not go by herself, second class, like any other young woman? **1906** UPWARD *Eben. Lobb* 206 Seymour says he came second-class,.. and he had absolutely no luggage. **1974** *Times* 22 Oct. 14/4 I'll pay rail fares, of course. Second class. I always travel second class.

‖**seconde** (səgɔ̃d). *Fencing.* Forms: 7 secunde, 8 second, 9 **seconde**. See also SEGOON. [Fr.: fem. of *second* SECOND *a.*]

†**1.** The half of a sword nearest the point. *Obs.*

1688 HOLME *Armoury* III. xix. (Roxb.) 159/2 The Secunde, is from the midle of the weapon to the point, which being the weakest part is only used to thrust or cut.

2. The second of the eight parries recognized in sword-play.

1707 SIR W. HOPE *New Meth. Fencing* 56 When a Man presents his Sword.. the Sword-Hand may have as many different Positions, as there are Degrees in a Circle,.. but.. the Masters of Old, were satisfied to reduce them to Four.., called, Prime, Seconde, Tierce, and Quarte... Seconde, or the Second Position.. is performed by holding the Sword, with the Thumb quite downward [etc.]. **1710** S. PALMER *Moral Ess.* 203 [A study] of more satisfaction and use.. than Tierce and Cart, Primé and Secònd, Dancing and Dress. **1807** ROLAND *Fencing* 53 You will acquire a more firm parade, as well as a much easier mode of delivering your riposte in seconde. **1889** POLLOCK, etc. *Fencing* 44 Eight [simple parries] are recognised; two for each line. They are called:—Prime, Seconde, Tierce [etc.]. *Ibid.* 47 To parry seconde, bring foil to seconde position.

secondee (sɪkɒn'diː). [f. SECOND *v.*² + -EE¹.] A person temporarily transferred to a new unit, department, etc.

1980 *Old Lady of Threadneedle St.* 16 June 56/2 As a Bank secondee I found no difficulty in being accepted in the Treasury. **1981** *Times* 10 Mar. 2/5 He was described as a 'secondee' or trainee in the Prime Minister's press office. **1982** *Ann. Rep. Nat. Westminster Bank 1981* 23 Feb. 15/1 Following their period of secondment, the Bank will benefit on their return from the wide experience that has been gained by the secondees.

seconder ('sɛkəndə(r)). Also 9 *Sc.* (in sense 2) secondar. [f. SECOND *a.* and *v.* + -ER¹.]

I. [from the adj.]

1. One who comes second, or in the second rank. Now only *local*, a second hand on a farm.

In quot. 1898 used to represent Anglo-Latin *secundarius*, SECONDARY *sb.* 1 b.

1598 BARRET *Theor. Warres* III. i. 35 To retire.. and charge againe, giuing place to his next fellow, or seconder. **1883** *Goole* (Yorksh.) *Weekly Times* 31 Aug. 5/2 (Advt.) Wanted, a Farm Servant, as seconder. **1898** A. F. LEACH *Beverley Act Bk.* I. Introd. 72 The Seconders (*secundarii*), clerks of the second form at Exeter [Cathedral]. *Ibid.*, In June, 1529, all the Seconders complained that [etc.].

2. A student of the second grade in social rank at St. Andrews University. *Obs.* exc. *Hist.*

1684 A. SKEINE *Let.* in *Scot. Antiq.* (1897) XI. 20 If he be a seconder his expence will be as folous. **1807** GRIERSON *St. Andrews* 160 Seconders and Terners are the only distinctions now in use. **1827** FERRIE in *Evid. Comm. Univ. Scot.* (1837) III. (St. Andrews) 35 The Primars are the sons of Noblemen; the Secondars are what they call Gentlemen Commoners in England. **1907** LANG *Hist. Scot.* IV. xvi. 406 All the winners are armigerous, so probably they were Secondars, as a rule.

II. [from the vb.]

3. a. One who supports (what is proposed by another); one who furthers the designs of another.

1623 CHAWORTH in Kempe *Losely MSS.* (1836) 477 The Parlement cumd, and in yᵉ first weeke yᵉ proposition being a breach wᵗʰ Spaine,.. &c. and the Prince yᵉ seconder of all Buckingham could propound. **1827** LYTTON *Falkland* I. 66, I find in myself a powerful seconder to my uncle's wishes. **1891** J. WINSOR *Columbus* viii. 175 Perez is said to have found a seconder in Luis de Santangel.

b. *spec.* One who seconds a motion.

1678 MARVELL *Growth Popery* 52 He Interrupted him and the Seconder of that Motion. **1780** BURKE *On Durat. Parlt.* Sp. (1816) II. 173, I do not tell the respectable mover and seconder.. that [etc.]. **1828** BROUGHAM in *Hansard's Parl. Deb.* XVIII. 49 His hon. and learned friend, the seconder, as well as the hon. mover of the Address. **1863** H. COX *Instit.* I. ix. 139 In the House of Lords, a question may be proposed without a seconder. **1890** A. G. BELL in *Proc. 12th Conv. Instructors of Deaf* 330, I would like to add my mite to the seconder of this resolution.

c. One who seconds a nomination or candidature introduced by a proposer.

1864 DICKENS *Lett.* (1880) II. 219 Will you write your name in the candidates' book as his seconder?

second-guess (ˌsɛkənd'gɛs, 'sɛkəndgɛs), *v. colloq.* (orig. and chiefly *N. Amer.*). [Prob. back-formation from next.]

1. *trans.* To anticipate the action of (a person), to out-guess; to predict or foresee (an event), to apprehend (simultaneously or beforehand) by guess-work.

1941 *Broadcasting* 22 Dec. 11/2 *Do not* try to second-guess or master-mind our military officials. Leave this for established military analysts and experts, who are experienced enough to await the facts before drawing conclusions. **1942** BERREY & VAN DEN BARK *Amer. Thes. Slang* §646/2 Predict the outcome [of a sporting event].., *second-guess. Ibid.* §733/7 'Dope the races.' (To figure out or prophesy probable results from past performances &c.).., *second-guess.* **1963** 'R. L. PIKE' *Mute Witness* viii. 137 Desperate people get panicky, and I never try to second-guess panicky people. **1974** *Globe & Mail* (Toronto) 22 Oct. 7/5 Any attempt to second-guess the economics of the situation to the end of the decade and beyond is a hazardous and probably futile task. **1976** *Publishers Weekly* 29 Mar. 49/2 Just when you think you've second-guessed [the author] WS, he turns the tables on you. **1980** *Sci. Amer.* Feb. 68/3 A mechanism by which his world-class backgammon program will develop a profile of an opponent's over-all playing style so that it can second-guess his moves and play accordingly.

2. To subject (a person or his action, esp. a decision) to criticism after the result of the action is known; to judge, question, or reconsider by hindsight. Also *refl.* and *absol.* or *intr.*

1946 [implied in *second-guessing* vbl. sb. below]. **1950** *Sun* (Baltimore) 27 Jan. 2/8 Second-guessing the conduct of Pacific war, Admiral Frederick C. Sherman points.. to a whole series of lost chances. **1951** *Ibid.* 28 Sept. (B ed.) 17/7 We lost 11 in a row and I still get nightmares thinking about some of those games. I'm still second guessing myself on some of them. **1955** *Galaxy Sci. Fiction* Apr. 86/2 They say that a century or so ago.. there were only about five billion [people]. But anyone can second-guess that. **1965** H. WAUGH *End of Party* x. 72 'They should have called the police,' Avery growled... Fellows said with a shrug. 'It's always easy to second-guess.' **1974** M. HOYT *Thirty Miles for Ice Cream* x. 126 We second-guessed that the spot where I went through [the ice] had been sheltered. **1978** J. KRANTZ *Scruples* viii. 223 Even Billy's New York lawyers approved, because Josh Hillman was an exceedingly brilliant lawyer... He protected Billy's interests without trying to second-guess their own, far more informed, decisions. **1980** *Daily Tel.* 4 Jan. 3/3 He had pointed out the defect [in the manufacture of a car] to Sir Michael, who had replied in a cavalier manner, saying it was not his job to 'second-guess' his designers.

Hence ˌ**second-'guessing** *vbl. sb.* (usu. in sense 2).

1946 *Richmond* (Va.) *Times-Dispatch* 26 Dec. 12/1 Pate, in naming Jake Kramer and Ted Schroeder as the entire United States Davis Cup team,.. left himself wide-open to what could be the greatest second-guessing attack of many years. **1963** *Life* 9 Aug. 44/3 The besetting sin of the theater is second-guessing, trying to anticipate what the public wants and what will be commercially sound. **1981** *Washington Post* 25 Feb. E 7/3 As Dennie walked back to the jocks' room, the Instructor couldn't resist a bit of second-guessing. 'I told you to stay on the rail,' he said.

second-guesser (ˌsɛkənd'gɛsə(r)). *colloq.* (orig. and chiefly *U.S.*). Also as two words. [f. SECOND *a.* + GUESSER, poss. in slang sense 'umpire (in baseball)', the orig. meaning being 'one who acts as if he is a second umpire': cf. also prec.]

a. In *Baseball*, a spectator who criticizes the playing of a team or the decisions of the umpire, usu. with the benefit of hindsight; hence *gen.*, one who criticizes (the actions or decisions of) another person after the event. **b.** One who predicts the result of a horse-race. *rare.*

1937 *Sporting News Record Bk.* 65 [*Guesser*, an umpire.] *Ibid.* 66 *Secondguesser*, one who is continually criticizing moves of players and manager. **1939** *New Yorker* 13 May 80/2 He may not be quite the wonder horse the flushed and eager second-guessers insist he is. **1941** B. SCHULBERG *What makes Sammy Run?* xi. 192 After *Deadline* the second-guessers were saying I could only make mellers [*sc.* melodramas]. **1942** BERREY & VAN DEN BARK *Amer. Thes. Slang* §637/3 *Second guesser*, a 'fan' who criticizes the umpire. **1950** R. CHANDLER *Let.* 9 Oct. (1966) 80, I suppose these primping second-guessers who call themselves critics think he shouldn't have written the book at all. **1953** BERREY & VAN DEN BARK *Amer. Thes. Slang* (1954) §671/5 *Second guesser*, a fan ready with advice on how the game should be played—after it is over. *Ibid.* §730/7 *Second guesser*, the pest who always knew what horse would win—after it was won. **1972** R. K. SMITH *Ransom* IV. 154 You're a professional second guesser, Stuart. Why didn't you speak up when we were discussing the question? **1978** *Times* 18 Apr. 16/5 President Johnson recognized the value of opposition and even appointed George Ball as his in-house second-guesser.

second hand, second-hand. [Cf. HAND *sb.* 10 c., F. *de seconde main*, and FIRST HAND.]

A. *phrase.* (*second hand.*)

†**1.** In subst. use: The second in a series of persons through whose hands something passes; an intermediary, middleman. *Obs.*

1654–66 EARL ORRERY *Parthen.* (1676) 492 His absence.. made him but from second hands, and confusedly learn it. **1681–6** J. SCOTT *Chr. Life* (1747) III. 49 He doth not mediate with him by a second-hand, or at a distance, but in his own Person. **1727** A. HAMILTON *New Acc. E. Ind.* I. Pref. 14 Those Reports came.. to him by Second or Third Hands.

2. In advb. phrases. **a.** ***at second hand*** (†also ***at the*** or ***a second hand, on the second hand***): (to buy, receive, learn, etc.) from another than the maker, or original vendor (of goods), or the primary source (of information, etc.). In the 18th c. also (? after Fr.) ***to hear from second hand.***

In the first quot. *as* may be a mistake for *at*; but perh. *second hand* may mean 'second purchaser'.

1474 *Coventry Leet Bk.* 401 Also the sise ys that no maner of man nor woman schall not stalle nor Regrate no markett.. wher thorough the markett shuld be the Wers and the pore Comons gretely hurte to by as the ijᵈᵉ honde. **1588** NASHE *Anat. Absurditie* Wks. 1904 I. 20 Whose thredde-bare knowledge beeing bought at the second hand, is spotted.. and defaced through translaters rigorous rude dealing. **1589** *Hay any Work* 44 The substance of the tale is true. I told you that I had it at the second hand. **1613** *Bodl. Day-bk.* (MS.) lf. 18 A note of such Books as were bought at London of Jhon Edwards at second hand. **1634** PEACHAM *Gentl. Exerc.* 62 So that I may say the eye receives the forme of the object at a second hand, as it were from the medium. **1654** SIR E. NICHOLAS in *N. Papers* (Camden) II. 2 You have done wisely to decline the correspondence of Sir Marm. Langdale at a second hand, thro' the consul's conveyance. **1665** *Surv. Affaires Netherlands* 132 Cathay, where they are forced to take their Rye, Hemp,.. and Musk, on the second hand of the Chinois. **1680** DODWELL *On Sanchoniathon* (1691) 12 He quoted him by memory, and at the Second hand. **1749** FIELDING *Tom Jones* III. v, For, to say the truth, there is no kind of flattery so irresistible as this at second-hand. **1753** WASHINGTON *Jrnl.* Writ. 1889 I. 481, I have heard from second-hand, that they intend to make no allowance for the fish we left there. **1833** MARRYAT *P. Simple* iii, 'Well, we don't want one of your father's sermons at second-hand,' replied the midshipman.

†**b.** ***at the second hand***: by a secondary operation. *Obs.*

1545 RAYNALD *Byrth Mankynde* 23 The meat & drinck which we dayly do eate, by dygestion, fyrst of yᵉ stomack, the fyne iuyce, therof is seperatyd from yᵉ drosse & grosser part, & then after at yᵉ second hand, the foresaid iuyce.. attract.. in to the lyuer.., there transmutid in to blud.

†**c.** ***by second hand***: through an intermediary, through another person as agent. *Obs.*

1721 SWIFT *South Sea* 70 When Stock is high, they come between, Making by second-hand their Offers.

†**d.** ***of second hand*** = SECOND-HAND *a.* 1. [a Gallicism].

1708 SHAFTESB. *Let. Enthusiasm* vi. 67 There is a sort of Enthusiasm of second hand.

B. *adj.* (*second-hand.*) [The phrase used attrib.] Obtained at second hand.

1. Not original or obtained from the original source; plagiarized or borrowed; imitative, derivative.

1654 WHITLOCK *Zootomia* 143 If a man cloath his discourse in a Language that is not second hand English, or but one degree above.. Caterwauling, why he is affected. **1738** SWIFT *Pol. Conversat.* Introd. 46 The Waiting-Woman, who, if she hath been bred to read Romances, may have some small subaltern or second-hand Politeness. **1779** SHERIDAN *Critic* I. i, Are you not called..a mock Mæcenas to second-hand authors? **1790** BURKE *Fr. Rev.* Wks. V. 397 You hold up, to chastise them, the second-hand authority of a king, who is only the instrument of destroying, without any power of protecting either the people or his own person. **1868** E. EDWARDS *Ralegh* I. x. 163 Even of this second-hand knowledge there was very little. **1904** FARRER *Gardens of Asia* 13 Second-hand impressions are as worthless as second-hand morality.

2. a. Not new, having been previously used or worn by another, as ***second-hand clothes, books,*** etc.

1673 WYCHERLEY *Gentl. Dancing-Master* v. 94, I will have no little, dirty, second-hand Charriot new forbish'd, but a large, sociable, well painted Coach. **1698** CROWNE *Caligula* I. 4 Second-hand cloaths he may as proudly wear. **1771** SMOLLETT *Humph. Cl.* 18 July (1815) 251 The traitor.. dazzled her with his second-hand finery. **1833** *Act 3 & 4 Will. IV*, c. 46 §82 All persons so dealing in second-hand articles without being first duly licensed. **1862** *(title)* The Library Circular of New and Second-Hand Books. **1892** ZANGWILL *Childr. Ghetto* I. 74 But a second-hand son-in-law of 22 is superior to many brand-new ones.

¶**b.** Said jocularly of food, with various notions.

1694 MOTTEUX *Rabelais* IV. lxvii, The Cupboard wherein second-hand-meat is kept [the bowels]. **1853** R. S. SURTEES *Sponge's Sp. Tour* xlvii. (1893) 250 The cook sent him a most moderate dinner, smoked soup, second-hand fish, scraggy cutlets, and sour pudding. **1862** MAYHEW *Lond. Labour* IV. 408/2 Miss Betsey would..enjoy whatever poultry or meat had not been touched; but anything that had been cut, anything 'second-hand', that dainty and haughty young lady would instruct her sister Kitty to give to the poor beggars. **1885** *Pall Mall Gaz.* 8 Sept. 12/1 What is technically called a 'second-hand joint', that is one that has had all its choice parts sliced off.

c. *absol.* or quasi-*sb.* A second-hand book.

1905 *Westm. Gaz.* 21 Oct. 18/2 If a book..doesn't get a good sale within the first two months, it is no good as a second-hand. **1966** J. B. PRIESTLEY *Salt is Leaving* i. 6 He might be going off to some auction sale—y'know, to buy some more secondhands.

3. ***second-hand bookseller, clothier,*** etc.: one dealing in second-hand goods. So ***second-hand bookselling, bookstall, shop, store,*** etc.

1656 HEYLIN *Surv. France* 148 They call it their Library; for my part, I should have thought it to have been the warehouse of some second hand Bookseller. **1795** J.-B. LECHEVALIER *Let.* in W. B. Stevens *Jrnl.* 24 Sept. (1965) III. 306 The old Plates, Plaisters, Sermons, Pieces of Iron, Brass and Copper that you purchased lately in that second hand Shop. **1862** *Library Circular* July 158 Advt., Messrs. Tinsley Brothers,..Wholesale, Retail, and Second-hand Booksellers. **1875** L. TROUBRIDGE *Life amongst Troubridges* (1966) 115 Here there were all sorts of things..old iron stalls, second-hand book stalls. **1886** C. E. PASCOE *Lond. of To-day* xxxix. (ed. 3) 330 The head of the second-hand bookselling trade of London. **1904** *Dialect Notes* II. 421 You can get most anything at the second-hand store. **1942** *Tee Emm* (Air Ministry) II. (recto rear cover), They may even end up on a second-hand bookstall. **1981** *Country Life* 16 July 205/1 A book very well worth looking out for in second-hand shops.

fig. **1902** *Daily Chron.* 3 Jan. 3/3 The modern second-hand dealers in popular criticism.

4. quasi-*adv.* = at second hand.

1849 ROBERTSON *Serm.* Ser. I. x. (1855) 181 Maxims learned second-hand by rote and not by heart. **1910** S. COOK in *Expositor* Aug. 115 Babylonian culture could continue to reach Canaan secondhand.

Hence **second'handness**; also (*rare*) **second-'handiness**, appearance of being second-hand.

a **1849** H. COLERIDGE *Ess.* (1851) II. 120 The staleness of their method and the second-handiness of their costume. **1886** FARRAR *Hist. Interpr.* 225 Four serious drawbacks of overhaste, second-handness, vehement prejudice and incessant vacillation.

second-'handed, *a.* Now chiefly *dial.* = SECOND-HAND *a.*

1682 in *Flemings in Oxford* (O.H.S.) II. let. ccxlvii, For a second handed gown, 14*s.* 6*d.* **1708** *Brit. Apollo* No. 51. 3/1 We..you implore, To send no more, A Second-handed Query. **1784** COWPER *Let. to Unwin* Wks. 1836 V. 87 My descriptions are all from nature: not one of them second-handed. **1842** J. AITON *Dom. Econ.* (1857) 73 He sets about purchasing a houseful of trash—second-handed chairs [etc.].

second-'handedness. [f. SECOND-HANDED *a.* + -NESS.] The quality or condition of being second-hand or hackneyed; secondhandness.

1905 G. B. SHAW *Let. c* Aug. (1972) II. 551, I have striven hard to open English eyes to the emptiness of Shakespeare's philosophy, to the superficiality and second-handedness of his morality. **1920** R. MACAULAY *Potterism* II. iii. 90 Once you are tied up with a party, you can only avoid second-handedness, taking over views ready made. **1929** A. N. WHITEHEAD *Aims Educ.* iv. 79 The second-handedness of the learned world is the secret of its mediocrity.

second-'hander. *colloq.* Also **secondhander.** [f. SECOND-HAND *a.* + -ER[1].] **a.** A second-hand commodity. **b.** A second-hand shop.

1896 'MARK TWAIN' in *Harper's Mag.* Aug. 350/2, I..see him buy a red flannel shirt and some old ragged clothes... I seen our other pal lay in *his* stock of old rusty second-handers. **1969** *Daily Tel.* (Colour Suppl.) 12 Dec. 27/4, I went to the secondhander and got some little nylon dresses, and bows for her hair. **1977** *Drive* Mar.-Apr. 40/3 Beware these secondhanders—they were made for fleet-buyers only.

secondine, obs. form of SECUNDINE.

seconding ('sɛkəndɪŋ), *ppl. a. rare*⁻¹. [f. SECOND *v.*[1] + -ING[2].] That acts as a second or supporter.

1748 RICHARDSON *Clarissa* VII. xlix. 191 Curse upon my contriving genius! Curse upon my intriguing head, and upon my seconding heart!

secondly ('sɛkəndlɪ), *adv.* [f. SECOND *a.* + -LY[2].]

†**1.** For a second time. *Obs.*

1382 WYCLIF *Lev.* xiii. 58 He shal wasshe secoundlich [Vulg. *secundo*] tho thinges that ben pure. **1608** in *Rep. MSS. in var. Coll.* (Hist. MSS. Comm. 1901) I. 287 But these malicious persons, not satisfied, waylaid your petitioner, and there and then secondly assaulted and wounded your petitioner. **1762–71** H. WALPOLE *Vertue's Anecd. Paint.* (1786) II. 201 She was secondly married to James Levingston Earl of Newburgh.

2. In the second place; as the second in serial order. Chiefly in the enumeration of heads or topics in a discourse.

c **1374** CHAUCER *Troylus* II. 1741 Secundelich þer yet deuyneth noon Vp-on yow two. *c* **1425** LYDG. *Assembly of Gods* 106 Furst, to begynne, thys Eolus hath [etc.]... Secundly,..Ofte of myn entent hath he made me mys. *c* **1450** HOLLAND *Howlat* 352 Syne in a feild of siluer secoundlie he beris Ane Egill ardent of air. **1535** COVERDALE *2 Kings* xvi. 19 Secondly, whom shulde I serue? *a* **1610** HEALEY *Epictetus* (1636) 51 Man, consider first the nature of the thing that thou intendest, and secondly thine owne nature. **1692** R. L'ESTRANGE *Fables* ccxiv. 185 We are Taught here Principally, Two Things; First,..And yet 2ly. How Prone we are to Indulge our Own Errors [etc.]. **1712** PRIDEAUX *Direct. Ch.-wardens* (ed. 4) 12, 1st, For absenting from Church. 2dly, For not abiding there till..Sermon be ended. **1863** LYELL *Antiq. Man* 36 Secondly, if the mud pierced through had been thrown down by the river in ancient channels, it would have been stratified.

†**3.** In the second place in order of importance, secondarily. Also (*nonce-use*), in an inferior manner. *Obs. rare.*

1526 *Grete Herball* cli. (1529) Ivb, Epithimium..hath vertue pryncypally to purge melancolyke humours, and secondely flewme. **1532** MORE *Confut. Tindale* Wks. 407/1 Tyndall handeleth his thyrde sygnificacion very secondly, and fareth as one that woulde fayne walke in the darke.

4. quasi-*sb.* The word *secondly* used in making subdivisions of a subject.

1759 [see FIRSTLY 3]. **1874** 'MAX ADELER' *Out of Hurly-Burly* vii. 87 The clergyman paused just as he was entering upon consideration of 'secondly'. **1898** J. A. ADAMS in *Advance* (Chicago) 28 Apr. 578/1 Jesus was not given to firstlies and secondlies.

secondment[1] ('sɛkəndmənt, sɪ'kɒndmənt). *rare.* [f. SECOND *v.*[1] + -MENT.] The action of seconding.

1837 W. E. FORSTER in T. W. Reid *Life* (1888) I. 93 Sir Robert Harvey proposed the Marquis of Douro... John Robberds, Nurse; with Dr. Evans's most violent secondment.

se'condment[2]. The action of SECOND *v.*[2] Also *transf.*; freq. in phr. ***on secondment.***

1897 *Q. Rev.* July 242 The practice of secondment seems to us as objectionable as the word is ungrammatical. **1955** *Times* 25 July 7/5 It should be possible for oversea universities to defray such losses..if they wish to attract teachers on secondment. **1964** M. GOWING *Britain & Atomic Energy 1939–1945* x. 288 Ways would have to be found of overcoming the staffing difficulty by various kinds of secondment. **1966** C. SWEENEY *Scurrying Bush* i. 14 From East Africa..I went to the Sudan on secondment to the Sudan Government. **1976** *Milton Keynes Express* 30 July 33/3 (Advt.), An experienced teacher required..to cover the secondment of the permanent teacher. **1982** *Guardian* 20 Apr. 1/4 Sir Michael was on secondment from Chloride, for which they received an undisclosed payment from BL.

secondness ('sɛkəndnɪs). [f. SECOND *a.* + -NESS.] The quality or fact of being second; *spec.*, in the philosophy of C. S. Peirce (see PEIRCE), the category of fact or reaction that gives to the category of idea or quality ('firstness') its actual existence or form.

c **1890** C. S. PEIRCE *Coll. Papers* (1931) I. §358. 184 When the second suffers some change from the action of the first, and is dependent upon it, the secondness is more genuine. **1903** —— *Ibid.* §24. 7, I think we have here a mode of being of one thing which consists in how a second object is. I call that Secondness. **1934** *Mind* XLIII. 490 Secondness comprises the actual facts of the world—the *hic et nunc* of things. **1966** F. J. COPLESTON *Hist. Philos.* VIII. xiv. 312 The meaning of an intellectual concept can be explicated in terms of the ideas of necessary relations between ideas of secondness and ideas of firstness, between..ideas of volition or action and ideas of perception. *Ibid.* 322 From one point of view secondness can be called 'fact', while from another .. it is existence or actuality. **1979** *Trans. Philol. Soc.* 177 The affixation of *me* will in El[amitic] terms have turned the '2nd' which *II-um* represents into '2nd-ness' for the mere purpose of rendering meaningful the addition to it of the locatival affix *ma*, 'in secondness' amounting in effect to an adverbial 'secondly'.

secondo (sə'kɒndəʊ). *Mus.* [It., = second.] In a pianoforte duet, the lower part; the pianist who plays this part.

1792 J. A. K. COLIZZI *Three Duets for Two Performers on Harpsichord or Piano Forté* 2 Secondo. **1883** GROVE *Dict. Mus.* III. 30/2 In pianoforte duets..*Secondo* or 2 *do* is put over that [*sc.* the part] for the 'bass' [player]. **1954, 1965** [see PRIMO *sb.* 1]. **1976** *Gramophone* Jan. 1218/1 The technical level of accomplishment, particularly on the part of the *secondo* player, is not all it should be.

second-rate, *a.* and *sb.* [See RATE *sb.*[1] 9, 9 b.]

A. *adj.* Of the second 'rate' (said of ships). Hence, Of the second class in point of quality or excellence; usually in vaguer (depreciative) sense. Not first-rate, of only moderate quality.

1669 SIR G. DOWNING in *St. Papers Dom.* 1668–9 (1894), 286 A second-rate ship. **1748** LADY M. W. MONTAGU *Let. to C'tess. Bute* 10 May (1893) II. 164 Any of the second-rate theatres in London. **1815** SCOTT *Guy M.* ii, The Laird himself was one of those second-rate sort of persons, that are to be found frequently in rural situations. **1875** RUSKIN *Lect. Art* i. 20 The severe exclusion of all second-rate, superfluous, or even attractively varied examples.

B. *sb.*

1. *Naut.* A war-vessel of the second rate (see RATE *sb.*[1] 9).

1679 *Lond. Gaz.* No. 1442/4 There are now two Second-rates upon the Stocks. **1748** SMOLLETT *Rod. Rand.* xxvii. (1760) I. 211 This he had procured by his interest at the Navy-Office; as also another [warrant] for himself, by virtue of which he was removed into a second rate.

2. *transf.* A person or thing of inferior class.

1799 *Monthly Rev.* XXX. 95 We still think that she [a lady novelist] ranks, with a degree of respect, as a 'second-rate'. **1804** SOUTHEY in Robberds *Mem. W. Taylor* I. 518 With reference to these poets, I place Dryden at the head of the second-rates. **1894** *Westm. Gaz.* 10 Oct. 2/3 We look upon him [Sardou] as a second-rate who might have been almost first-rate had he been sincere.

Hence **second-rateness,** (less frequently **second-ratedness**), the quality of being second-rate; **second-rater,** one who or something which is second-rate.

1826 HOOD *Backing the Favourite* 33 The second-raters seemed then a safer hit. **1865** MRS. WHITNEY *Gayworthys* II. 26 She forgot the old feeling of failure and of second-rateness, she found herself of consequence. **1891** G. H. KINGSLEY *Sp. & Trav.* (1900) 463 Some have to be contented with the second-ratedness of a swirly hole, as against the profundity of Lake Superior. **1905** G. B. SHAW *Irrational Knot* p. xiii, This consoles us for the undeniable secondrateness of the people we do know. **1916** E. POUND *Lett.* (1971) 87 Virgil is a second-rater, a Tennysonianized version of Homer. **1945** R. KNOX *God & Atom* vi. 84 We tacitly acknowledged in ourselves a kind of moral second-rateness which served as an excuse for low standards. **1955** Second-rater [see BEACHED *ppl. a.* 3]. **1976** *Times Lit. Suppl.* 17 Dec. 1576/4 The second-rateness of Douglas (but to be second-rate is to be next to first-rate). **1977** *Times Lit. Suppl.* 22 Apr. 481/2 His adamant opposition to American participation in Hitler's war damned him conclusively, for me, as a mean-minded second-rater or worse.

second sight.

1. a. A supposed power by which occurrences in the future or things at a distance are perceived as though they were actually present.

1616 *Maitland Club Misc.* II. 189 Be the secund sicht grantit to her..She saw Robert Stewart..and certane utheris with towis about thair craigis. *a* **1700** EVELYN *Diary* 16 Sept. 1685, There was something said of the second sight happening to some persons, especially Scotch. **1763** *Pastoral Cordial* 11 Their Faith and firm Belief In Second Sight, and Mother Shipton. **1827** SCOTT *Highl. Widow* v, These are Highland visions, Captain Campbell, as unsatisfactory and vain as those of the second sight. **1875** A. LANG in *Encycl. Brit.* II. 204/1 Persons possessing the Celtic *taishitaraugh*, or gift of second-sight.

b. *transf.* and *fig.*

1711 *Country-Man's Let. to Curat* 29 But the High-Church Doctors were not then Blessed with the second sight, as they have been of late. **1860** EMERSON *Cond. Life* viii. 178 When the second-sight of the mind is opened, now one colour or form or gesture, and now another, has a pungency [etc.].

2. The image or vision produced by the faculty of 'second sight'.

1763 'THEOPHILUS INSULANUS' *Second Sight* 35 From many cogent proofs, I am induced to think, that the Second Sight is not seen by the organ of the eye. *Ibid.* Index 187 Grant, Mr. James, his relation of a young man that saw the Second Sight.

3. *Natural Magic.* (See quot. 1883.)

1859 L. WRAXALL tr. *Robert-Houdin's Mem.* II. i. 4 Chance led me straight to the invention of *second sight.* **1883** *Cassell's Bk. Sports* 923 Clairvoyance, or Second Sight, when applied to conjurers' tricks and private entertainments, is the art of telling the name and description of articles by a person whose eyes are blindfolded. **1902** G. FAUR in *Encycl. Brit.* XXX. 427/2 In recent years the mystery known as 'Second Sight' has been vastly improved.

4. *attrib.*

1700 DR. HICKES *Let.* in *Pepys' Mem.* (1870) 696, I asked this question, to know whether..these Second Sight folks were Seers or Visionists.

Hence **second-sighted** *a.*, having the gift of second sight; †**second-sightedness**, the quality of possessing second sight; **second-sighter**, one who practises the power of second sight.

a **1694** in *Aubrey's Misc.* (1696) 154 These Events, which Second-sighted Men discover, or fore-tell. **1708** CHAMBERLAYNE *St. Gt. Brit.* II. I. ii. (1743) 322 This quality of second-sightedness is not rare. **1820** SHELLEY *Maria Gisb.* 137 She replies, Veiling in awe her second-sighted eyes. **1875** A. LANG in *Encycl. Brit.* II. 204/2 The *inyanga*, or second-sighted man. **1897** MARY KINGSLEY *W. Africa* xx. 460 You cannot see your own bush-soul, unless you are an Ebumtup, a sort of second-sighter.

secos, var. SEKOS.

secound(e, obs. forms of SECOND.

†**secourgeon, -ion.** *Obs. rare.* [a. F. *secourgeon* (in Estienne, orig. of this passage), var. of *escourgeon* (Cotgr. *scourgeon*, Walloon *socoran*).] = AMELCORN, an inferior variety of wheat.

1600 SURFLET *Country Farm* v. xx. 710 You may make meale likewise of other corne then of wheate, as of barley, rie, meslin, secourgeon. *Ibid.* 714 Breade made of Secourgion. **1688** HOLME *Armoury* II. 56/2 Secourgion is a lean, wrinkled and starved Corn, something like unto Barley.

†**secourse,** *sb. Obs. rare.* Also 7 secours. [a. F. *secours* (OF. *secorse, -ce, socorse* in Godef.) SUCCOUR *sb.*] Succour, aid, help, assistance.

1597 A. M. tr. *Guillemeau's Fr. Chirurg.* 54 b/2 Notwithstandinge all the secourse we coulde doe them, yet they dyed suddaynlye. **1610** in *Buccleuch MSS.* (*Hist. MSS. Comm.*) I. 89 To make use of such number of his subjects..for the secours of the Princes of Germany. **1632** LITHGOW *Trav.* x. 471 Our mercifull King..gaue secourse to thousands of your ship-wracked people for many moneths.

‖**secousse** (sə'kuːs). *Massage.* [a. F. *secousse* (15th c. in Hatz.-Darm.), vbl. sb. of †*secourre* (now *secouer*) to agitate, f. L. *succuss-, succutĕre*, f. *sub* under, below + *quatĕre* to shake.] **a.** (See quot.)

1887 D. MAGUIRE *Art Massage* iii. (ed. 4) 52 Secousses. These are agitated movements quickly executed and with sudden jerks.

b. *gen.* in Fr. sense. *poet. rare.*

1945 AUDEN *Coll. Poetry* 130 Blows a wind that whispers ..Of hopes that will not survive the *secousse* of this spring Of blood and flames.

secoutour, variant of SECUTOR *Obs.*, executor.

†**se'cre,** *a.* and *sb. Obs.* Also 4–5 secree. [a. OF. *secré*, var. of *secret*: see SECRET *a.* and *sb.*]

A. *adj.* = SECRET *a.* in various senses.

1. Not allowed to be revealed, hidden, occult.

c **1386** CHAUCER *Can. Yeom. Prol. & T.* 90 But I wol nat auowe that I seye And therfore keepe it secree I yow preye. *c* **1400** tr. *Secreta Secret., Gov. Lordsh.* 84 And þay gyf hym þe prys of alle science, secre and heuenly. *c* **1407** LYDG. *Reason & Sens.* 1675 This god is also messagere..For to report in special The secre thingis of the hevene. **1430–40** —— *Bochas* VIII. xxiv. (1554) 192/2 A ful precious stone,.. Powder of which will discure anone, If it be drunke (though it be secree) Of maydenhed the broken chastitee.

2. *secre seal.* **a.** A private seal of attestation affixed to a document; also *fig.* **b.** A seal fixed upon a closed letter or document.

1362 LANGL. *P. Pl.* A. III. 141 Heo may as muche do In a Moneþ ones, As ȝoure secre seal [1377 B. III. 145, 1393 C. IV. 183 secret seel] In Seuen score dayes. *Ibid.* VIII. 25 Bote vndur his secre seal [1377 B. VII. 23 secret seel; **1393** C. x. 27 secre seel] Treuþe sende a lettre. **1393** *Ibid.* C. x. 138 The whiche arn lunatik lollares..For vnder godes secre seel here synnes ben ykeuered.

3. Of a person: Reserved or reticent in conduct or conversation; close, discreet.

c **1385** CHAUCER *L.G.W.* 1528 And he was wis, hardy, secre, and ryche. **1412–20** LYDG. *Chron. Troy* I. 2001 Sche kepte hir cloos and wonderly secree, þat by hir chere no man myȝt see What þat sche ment.

b. Characterized by reserve or secrecy. Phrase, *in secre wyse.*

c **1374** CHAUCER *Troylus* I. 744 In his counseyl tellinge That toucheth love that oughte be secree; For of him-self it wolde y-nough out-springe. *a* **1386** —— *Doctor's T.* 143 This Iuge vn-to this cherl his tale hath toold In secree wise. **1440** in *Wars Eng. in France* (1864) II. 307 Sende me worde, yn the most secre wyse.

4. Intimate, privy. *rare*⁻¹.

1501 DOUGLAS *Pal. Hon.* I. xi, Sine nixt hir raid..Twelf damisellis..Quhilks semit of her counsell maist secre.

5. Of a place: Remote, retired, secluded. Also *rarely* of time, spent in seclusion.

c **1374** CHAUCER *Boeth.* I. pr. iv. 31 Thilke thinges that I hadde lerned of thee among my secree restingwhyles [L. *inter secreta otia*]. **1426** LYDG. *De Guil. Pilgr.* 4056, I am callyd Dame Penaunce. The cheff wardeyn..Off thylke yle most secre; The wych..Ys yhyd with-Inne a man. *c* **1550** ROLLAND *Crt. Venus* i. 652 In hir chalmer quhilk ay was most secre.

6. quasi-*adv.* Secretly; without witnesses.

c **1386** CHAUCER *Frankl. T.* 381 To noon oother creature.. Of this matere he dorste no word seyn. Vnder his brest he baar it moore secree Than euere dide Pamphilus for Galathee. *c* **1440** *Pallad. on Husb.* I. 541 So it be doon secre that no man se.

B. *sb.*

1. Something that is kept hidden or secret.

a. Something hidden from human understanding or knowledge; a divine or natural mystery.

c **1386** CHAUCER *Can. Yeom. T.* 894 For this science, and this konnyng, quod he, Is of the secree of the secretes pardee. *c* **1407** LYDG. *Reason & Sens.* 4879 Ful of mystery and secres And many vnkouth prevites. *c* **1430** *Pilgr. Lyf Manhode* I. lxxviii. (1869) 46 And þere weren shewed þee alle þe secrees of Nature. *c* **1450** LOVELICH *Grail* xvii. 57 He is a fool that don wele as I have do, To knowen the Secrees of his Saviour.

b. A private or secret matter; = SECRET *sb.* 3.

c **1386** CHAUCER *Monk's T.* 31 But to hise wyues toolde he his secree. *c* **1400** *Rom. Rose* 5260 For tweyn in nombre is bet than three In every counsel and secree. **1489** *Barbour's Bruce* (Edin. MS.) IV. 577 And couth rycht weill secreis conceil.

2. A prayer in the Mass recited by the priest in a low voice; = SECRET *sb.* 2.

1297 R. GLOUC. (Rolls) 12044 As he stod at is masse.. Biuore þe weued in is bedes, at þe secre riȝt, Com sir gui de mountfort..& villiche him slou. *c* **1375** *Sc. Leg. Saints* xxxix. (*Cosme & Damyane*) I Of haly messe in þe secre syndry sanctis set we se. *a* **1400** *Minor Poems fr. Vernon MS.* xlvii. 541 þen he biginnes his secre; Adoun þenne knele ȝe.

3. Secrecy. *in secree*, in private, secretly.

1390 GOWER *Conf.* I. 62 He seith in open, fy! to Sinne, And in secre ther is no vice Of which that he nis a Norrice. *c* **1470** HENRY *Wallace* IV. 403 Wallace with hyr in secre maid him glaid.

secrecy ('siːkrəsɪ). Forms: α. 5 secretee, 6 secretie, -ye; β. 6–7 secrecie (6 secricie,), secresie, 6–9 secresy, 6– secrecy. [In 15–16th c. *secretee, -tie*, app. f. SECRE *a.* or SECRET *a.* + -TY or -Y. Cf. med.L. *secretia* a royal treasury. Late in the 16th c. altered to *secrecie*, app. after words like *primacy*.]

1. The quality of being secret or of not revealing secrets; the action, practice, or habit of keeping things secret.

α. **1423** JAS. I *Kingis Q.* xcvii, Stude at the dure fair-calling hir vschere, That coude his office doon In connyng wise, And secretee, hir thrifty chamberere.

β. **1596** SHAKS. I *Hen. IV*, II. iii. 112 Constant you are, But yet a woman: and for secrecie, No Lady closer. **1597** MORLEY *Introd. Mus.* 116 If you conceale this I must thinke that..you begin to suspect my secrecy. **1616** BACON *Adv. to Villiers* Wks. 1872 VI. 41 And that the servants attending the clerks of the council be also bound to secrecy. **1617** MORYSON *Itin.* II. 50 By reason of his singular secrecy in keeping his purposes unknowne. *a* **1721** SHEFFIELD (Dk. Buckhm.) *Wks.* (1753) II. 167 For who could expect secrecy in such a slave of Cleopatra. **1778** MISS BURNEY *Evelina* (1791) II. xxiv. 150, I have Intreated Mrs. Selwyn to observe the strictest secrecy. **1819** SCOTT *Let.* in *Lockhart* (1837) IV. viii. 232 An intelligent friend on whose style of expression, prudence, and secrecy his Grace could put perfect reliance. **1855** MACAULAY *Hist. Eng.* xv. III. 532 He arranged his plan with characteristic prudence, firmness, and secresy. **1876** MOZLEY *Univ. Serm.* iv. (1877) 88 We appear to know a great deal of one another, and yet, if we reflect, what a vast system of secrecy the moral world is.

2. a. The condition or fact of being secret or concealed. *in secrecy*: secretly.

α. **1563** *Mirr. Mag., Ld. Hastings* xc, Your polytyke secretes gard with trusty loyaltye So shall they lurk in most assured secretye. **1581** HANMER *Jesuites Banner* D 3, His sacrificing Priestes hearing confession were woonte to reueale unto him, all that in secretie was deliuered vnto them.

β. **1575** GASCOIGNE *Glasse Govt.* IV. iv. Wks. 1910 II. 65, & because in all thinges Secresie is a great furderaunce, it shalbe best that we draw our selves apart unto one of your houses. **1590** MARLOWE *Edw. II*, II. i, A friend of mine told me in secrecie, That hees repeald and sent for backe againe. **1613** SHAKS. *Hen. VIII*, III. ii. 403 The Lady Anne, Whom the King hath in secrecie long married, This day was view'd in open, as his Queene. **1651** HOBBES *Leviath.* II. xix. 96 Nor is there any place,..wherein an Assemblie can receive Counsell with secrecie. **1756** BURKE *Vind. Nat. Soc.* Wks. 1842 I. 14 On his return to court, he was obliged to enter Rome with all the secresy of a criminal. **1819** MACINTOSH *Parl. Suffrage* Wks. 1846 III. 227 The first objection to this proposal is, that the Ballot would not produce secrecy. **1881** FENN *Vicar's People* xlvi, [He] removed his tobacco quid, and stuffed the dirty-brown, wet morsel into the secrecy of his trousers pocket.

†**b.** Retirement, seclusion. *Obs.*

1607 TOPSELL *Four-f. Beasts* 37 The males giue great honor to the females great with young, during the time of their secrecie. **1608** —— *Serpents* 15 There is a question, whether when they be in this secrecie or drouzines, they awake not to eate. **1667** MILTON *P.L.* VIII. 427 Thou in thy secresie although alone, Best with thy self accompanied, seek'st not Social communication.

3. a. quasi-*concr.* Something which is or has been kept secret; a secret; the secret nature or condition of something. Often *collect. sing.* or *plural*, secret matters, mysteries. *Obs.* or *arch.*

α. *c* **1450** LYDG. *Secrees* 38 The which book..Whylom compyled by Arystotilees, Which in sapience of Secretees hath the name. **1517** TUNSTALL in Ellis *Orig. Lett.* Ser. I. I. 134 Besids al other maters contenyd in our Lettres..oon is in them untowchyd by cause I wold not make my clerke privey to the secretie theroff.

β. **1573** TUSSER *Husb.* (1878) 17 To answere stranger ciuilie, but shew him not thy secresie. **1594** *Willobie's Avisa* xliv. (Grosart) 40 H. W...pyneth a while in secret griefe, at length..bewrayeth the secresy of his disease vnto his familiar friend W. S. **1598** YONG *Diana* 308 A famous Shepherd..to whose skill and knowledge, it seemed, nature it selfe with all her secrecies was subject. **1602** SHAKS. *Ham.* II. ii. 305 So shall my anticipation preuent your discouery of your secricie to the King and Queene. *a* **1617** P. BAYNE *On Eph.* (1658) Contents, The doctrine of our salvation is a hidden secrecy. **1633** FORD *Broken H.* II. iii, I'me not inquisitiue of secrecies without an inuitation. **1645** MILTON *Tetrach.* 44 Leaving secrecies to conscience. **1660** *Charac. Italy* 85 In the Secresies and Operations of Medecine none could excel Fracastorius [etc.]. **1665** BRATHWAIT *Comment. Two Tales* (1901) 20 He solemnly swears his Host to keep counsel in a secrecy of such high consequence. **1893** F. THOMPSON *Poems* 50, I in their delicate fellowship was one —Drew the bolt of Nature's secrecies.

†**b.** The secret parts (of a person). *Obs. rare*⁻¹.

c **1675** *Roxb. Ball.* (1890) VII. 59 A shirt out of his Cloak-bag presently plucked he, And put it on the woman to cover her secresie.

†**4.** The condition of being entrusted with a person's secrets; intimate acquaintance, confidence.

1577 HANMER *Anc. Eccl. Hist.* 165 Euen he who was of his secretie [1619 secrecy] and companion at meate. **1590** GREENE *Orl. Fur.* (1599) 18 But, Madame, marke a while, and you shall see, Your Father shake him off from secrecie. **1591–5** SPENSER *Colin Clout* 698 By creeping close into his secrecie. **1671** H. M. tr. *Erasm. Colloq.* Life A 2, He.. betook himself to a Monastery of regular Cannons, where for some years he had the secresie of Guilelmus Hermannus of Buda, a very studious and diligent youth.

5. Special Comb.: **secrecy system**, a system for ensuring the secrecy of transmitted speech by scrambling it at the transmitter.

1940 [see PRIVACY I b]. **1949** [see *communication theory* s.v. COMMUNICATION 12].

†**secrely,** *adv. Obs.* Also 4–5 secreely, sekerly, sekyrly. [f. SECRE *a.* + -LY².] Secretly.

c **1386** CHAUCER *Clerk's T.* 707 This Markys writen hath.. A lettre..And secreely [*v.rr.* secrely, secretely, secretly] he to Boloigne it sente. **1426** LYDG. *De Guil. Pilgr.* 5782 The grete Tresour wych verrayly Ys shet with-Inne secrely, Pore folkys for to fede. *c* **1440** *Generydes* 359 Whanne ye maye fynd good leyser and spase, That sekerly ye may speke with the kyng. *Ibid.* 3786 And in like wise cast your harnes vppon, Secrely, that no man yow Aspye.

†'**secrement.** *Obs. rare*⁻¹. [As if ad. L. **sēcrēmentum*, f. *sēcrē-*, *secernĕre* to secrete. Cf. *excrement*.] Secretion.

1664 POWER *Exp. Philos.* I. 29 Cuckow-Spitt.—That it is the sole exudation and Secrement of Plants, I cannot believe.

†**secreness.** *Obs.* Also 4 secreenesse, secrenes(se. [f. SECRE *a.* + -NESS.] Secretness.

c **1386** CHAUCER *Man of Law's T.* 675 O Messager, fulfild of dronkenesse..thou biwreyest alle secreenesse [*v.rr.* secre-, sekere-, siker-, sekurnesse]. *c* **1403** LYDG. *Temple of Glas* 295, & mirrour eke was she Of secrenes, of trouth, of faythfulnes. **1450** *Impeachm. Dk. Suffolk* in *Paston Lett.* I. 103 Beyng of your grete Privey Councell, and..knowyng the secrenesse [*Rolls of Parlt.* V. 178 secretenesse] thereof.

†**secrest,** *v. Obs. rare*⁻¹. [ad. Sp. *secrestar* = med.L. *secrestāre*, metathetic form of *sequestrāre*.] *trans.* To sequestrate (goods).

1588 PARKE tr. *Mendoza's Hist. China* 259 Hee did Iudge the Captaines to perpetuall prison..and did secrest all their goods [orig. *y secrestado todos sus bienes*].

secrestan, obs. form of SACRISTAN.

secret ('siːkrɪt), *a.* and *sb.* Also 4 secrette, 5–6 secrete, (5 sekret), 6 secreet, secrett, (seycrette, seacreate), *Sc.* secreit, sacreit, 6–7 secreate, 7 seacret, (secrit). [a. F. *secret* adj. and sb. (OF. also *secré*: see SECRE *a.* and *sb.*), ad. L. *sēcrētus* adj. (neut. *sēcrētum* used subst., a secret), orig. pa. pple. of *sēcernĕre* to separate, divide off: see SECERN *v.* Cf. Pr. *secret*, Sp. *secreto*, Pg. *secreto, segredo*, It. *secreto, segredo* (all used as adj. and sb.).]

A. *adj.*

1. Kept from knowledge or observation; hidden, concealed. **a.** Predicatively (esp. in *to keep secret*): Kept from public knowledge, or from the knowledge of persons specified; not allowed to be known, or only by selected persons.

1399 LANGL. *Rich. Redeles* Prol. 61 Lete ȝoure conceill corette it [*sc.* this treatise]..ffor ȝit it is secrette. **1474** [see 2]. **1481** in *E.E. Gilds* 317 Ye shal not dyscouer þᵉ counsell of þᵉ bretherynhod or of þᵉ crafte, þᵗ ye have knowlych of, þᵗ shold be sekret wᵗyn ouer-selfe. **1485** CAXTON *Paris & V.* (1868) 3 Parys kept his love secret. **1560** DAUS tr. *Sleidane's Comm.* 72, I kept nothing secret from your Ambassadours. **1600** E. BLOUNT tr. *Conestaggio* 47 The Renegados..kept his death secret. **1799** SICKELMORE *Agnes & Leonora* II. 164 It was as much to their interest as my own to keep the affair secret. **1831** SCOTT *Ct. Robt.* xxvii, The task in which he was engaged was to be kept most strictly secret. **1879** 'EDNA LYALL' *Won by Waiting* xxx, Bertha's flight must be kept secret.

b. Of a place: Removed from the resort of men; retired, remote, lonely, secluded, solitary; hence, affording privacy or seclusion. Also *rarely* of time. Chiefly *arch.*

1500–20 DUNBAR *Poems* lxxv. 1 In secreit place this hyndir nycht, I hard [etc.]. *a* **1586** SIDNEY *Apol. Poetrie* (Arb.) 32 To..plant goodnesse euen in the secretest cabinet of our soules. **1603** SHAKS. *Meas. for M.* IV. iii. 91 Put them in secret holds. **1604** DRAYTON *Moyses* I. 12 Softly she [i.e. Pharaoh's daughter] walkes downe to the secret flood,..In the coole streames to check the pampred blood. **1667** MILTON *P.L.* I. 6 Sing, Heav'nly Muse, that on the secret top Of Oreb, or of Sinai, didst inspire That shepherd. **1697** DRYDEN *Virg. Georg.* III. 662 Let not Sleep my closing Eyes invade In open Plains, or in the secret Shade. **1773** COWPER *Shrubbery* 19 They seek, like me, the secret shade. **1820** SHELLEY *Skylark* 44 Soothing her love-laden Soul in secret hour. **1830** TENNYSON *Poet* 10 With echoing feet he threaded The secretest walks of fame. **1858** HAWTHORNE *Fr. & Ital. Note-bks.* (1871) II. 31 Powers took us into a room apart—apparently the secretest room he had—and showed us some tools..of his own..invention. **1900** G. C. BRODRICK *Mem. & Impr.* 203 To exchange opinions..no longer through whispers in the secret chambers, but through open talk in drawing-rooms and even ball-rooms.

†**c.** Of a person, etc.: Secluded from observation. Chiefly *predicative*. *Obs.*

1528 GARDINER in Pocock *Rec. Ref.* I. xlvii. 90 Being compelled for want of apparel to keep ourselves secret one whole day. **1588** GREENE *Pandosto* (1607) B 1, Franion being secret in his chamber, began to meditate with himselfe in these termes. **1593** SHAKS. 2 *Hen. VI*, IV. iv. 48 In this Citty will I stay, And liue alone as secret as I may. **1607** TOPSELL *Four-f. Beasts* 206 When they are secret and alone by themselues, they will practise leaping, dancing, and other strange feats. **1667** MILTON *P.L.* VI. 522 So all ere day-spring, under conscious Night Secret they finish'd.

d. Of actions, negotiations, agreements, etc.: Done or entered into with the intention of being concealed; clandestine. †Also *rarely* of movements: Stealthy.

1548 HALL *Chron., Edw. IV* (1550) 13 b, He caused hym by secrete iourneys in the nyght to be conueyed to Middelham Castell in Yorkeshire. **1563** *Mirr. Mag., Ld. Hastings* lxxxix, So can god reape vp secrete mischiefs wrought, To the confusyon of the workers thought. **1611** BIBLE *Ps.* lxiv. 2 Hide me from the secret counsel of the wicked. **1635** W. AUSTIN *Medit.* 103 Secret therefore, must Abstinence be. **1642** D. ROGERS *Naaman* 428 Shall I make conscience of smaller, secreter offences, and shall I not much more abhor the grosser. *a* **1700** EVELYN *Diary* 14 Oct. 1670, The Treasurer, who put into my hands those secret pieces and transactions concerning the Dutch war. **1705** SHAFTESB. *Let. to Le Clerc* 8–13 Feb. in *N. & Q.* Ser. I. (1851) III. 98/1 [Lord Shaftesbury] entrusted him [Locke] with his secretest negotiations. **1710** STEELE *Tatler* No. 138 ¶1 Secret Kindnesses done to Mankind are as beautiful as secret Injuries are detestable. **1760–72** H. BROOKE *Fool of Qual.* (1809) III. 89, I heard secret treadings and mutterings. **1799** PAGET in *P. Papers* (1896) I. 152, I am led to think that there are Secret Articles in the Treaty of Campo Formio that are Monstrous. **1819** SHELLEY *Cenci* III. i. 320, I wasted The sum in secret riot. **1848** THACKERAY *Van. Fair* xv, Rebecca..owned there was a secret attachment. **1903** MORLEY *Gladstone* I. VI. vii. 366 All the highest abstract arguments were against secret voting.

e. Of doctrines, ceremonies, language, signs, methods of procedure, remedies, and the like: Kept from the knowledge of the uninitiated.

1526 *Pilgr. Perf.* (W. de W. 1531) 2 What so euer secrete doctryne of perfeccyon you take or lerne of this poore treatyse. **1809** G. ROLAND *Art Fencing* (1823) 142, I am frequently asked..Whether there are not certain secret thrusts, which Professors reserve for themselves. *Ibid.* 143 Others..have pretended to sell them secret passes, applicable on all occasions. **1825** SCOTT *Betrothed* ii, They ..were initiated into their order by secret and mystic solemnities.

f. Of feelings, passions, thoughts: Not openly avowed or expressed; concealed, disguised; also, in stronger sense, known only to the subject, inward, inmost. Hence said of the heart, soul, etc.

1500–20 DUNBAR *Poems* lxxxiv. 40 Go follow thame, quha will inconstance leir; Secreit invy [etc.]. **1548** UDALL, etc. *Erasm. Par. John* i. 47–9 Jesus yet declaring..how he knew the thoughts of men, were they neuer so secret. **1593** SHAKS. *Lucr.* 1065 Nor shall he smile at thee in secret thought. **1601** —— *Twel. N.* I. iv. 14, I haue vnclasp'd To thee the booke euen of my secret soule. **1659** HAMMOND *On Ps.* xvii. 3 Paraphr. 85 The searcher of the secretest thoughts. **1721** DE FOE *Mem. Cavalier* (1840) 135, I had a secret joy at the news. **1742** GRAY *Eton* 67 Or Jealousy with rankling tooth, That inly gnaws the secret heart. **1818** SHELLEY *Julian* 341 My secret groans must be unheard by thee. **1825** SCOTT *Talism.* vii, Holding them in his secret soul little better than the Saracens. **1862** H. SPENCER *First Princ.* I. i. § 5 (1875) 19 That the theological party regard Science with so much secret alarm. **1865** DICKENS *Mut. Fr.* I. ii, You will all of you execrate Lady Tippins in your secret hearts.

†**g.** Abstruse, recondite; beyond ordinary apprehension or beyond unaided human intelligence. Of a person or thing: Pertaining to or dealing with mystical or occult matters. *Obs.*

1535 COVERDALE *Ps.* l. 6 Thou..hast shewed me secrete wyszdome. **1582** N. LICHEFIELD tr *Castanheda's Conq. E. Ind.* I. xxix. 72 b, The Pilots (being not as yet acquainted with the secret signification of a spowte)..thought the same to bee a signe of faire weather. **1605** SHAKS. *Macb.* IV. i. 48 How now you secret, black, & midnight Hags? What is't you do? **1610** —— *Temp.* I. ii. 77, I..to my State grew stranger, being transported And rapt in secret studies. **1655** STANLEY *Hist. Philos.* II. iv. (1687) 66/2 Pericles..could easily reduce the exercise of his mind from secret abstrusive things to publick popular causes. **1656** EARL MONM. tr. *Boccalini's Advts. fr. Parnass.* II. lxxx. 361 Menante..is very diligent in prying into the very secretest passages of Pernassus. **1727** DE FOE *Syst. Magic* I. i. (1840) 3 They took it for granted that those seers dealt in all secret matters. **1775** HARRIS *Philos. Arrangem.* Wks. (1841) 325 Such, too, are those more secret operations of bodies, whether magnetic or electric.

h. Of a committee, conclave, etc.: Conducted with secrecy; that keeps its deliberations unknown to the public. Also ***secret session*** (orig. *U.S.*), a meeting of a legislative or deliberative body, conducted in secret.

1667 MILTON *P.L.* I. 795 The great Seraphic Lords and Cherubim In close recess and secret conclave sat. **1849** MACAULAY *Hist. Eng.* vi. II. 66 He early suggested to the King the expediency of appointing a secret committee of Roman Catholics. **1872** W. BAGEHOT *Eng. Const.* (ed. 2) p. xlvii, This objection might be easily avoided by requiring that the discussion upon treaties in Parliament like that discussion in the American Senate should be 'in secret session', and that no report should be published of it. **1916** H. H. ASQUITH in *Hansard Commons* 27 Nov. 37, I think it would be premature to consider this question till it has been decided whether a Secret Session should be held. **1940** W. S. CHURCHILL *Secret Session Speeches* (1946) 17 The reason why I asked the House to go into Secret Session was not because I had anything particularly secret or momentous to say. **1946** G. B. SHAW *Geneva* (ed. 2) 4 All threatening news was mentioned only in secret sessions of parliament, hidden under heavy penalties.

i. Hidden from sight; not discernible or visible; unseen (chiefly *poet.*). Also ***secret dovetail*** (Joinery): (see quot. 1972).

1559 *Mirr. Mag., Ld. Clifford* 5 Nought so secrete but at length is spied. **1577** KENDALL *Flowers of Epigr.* 6 b, So by the subtile secret baite the selie beast is taen. **1593** SHAKS. 2 *Hen. VI*, III. i. 174 Those that care and keepe your Royall Person From Treasons secret Knife. **1697** DRYDEN *Virg. Past.* IV. 145 Ye Boys, who pluck the Flow'rs,..Beware the secret Snake that shoots a Sting. **1764** GOLDSM. *Trav.* 433 With secret course, which no loud storms annoy, Glides the smooth current of domestic joy. **1781** COWPER *Charity* 369 Some [rills]..down the sloping hills, Winding a secret or an open course. **1817** SHELLEY *Rev. Islam* X. xix. 4395 The men ..Drew forth their secret steel, and stabbed each ardent youth. **1882** W. J. CHRISTY *Joints* 168 Mitred Dovetail Joint... It is also designated secret dovetail. **1963** F. HILTON *Adv. Carpentry & Joinery* x. 180/2 Two members are jointed using a secret dovetail and the third stub-tenoned, with the surfaces mitred. **1972** *Gloss. Terms Timber (B.S.I.)* 52 *Secret dovetail*, a dovetailed angle in which dovetails are used but do not show on the face of either member.

j. ***secret parts***, †***members***: the external organs of sex.

1577 KENDALL *Flowers of Epigr.* 23 The Stockdoues secrete parts make lumpishe, dull, and dedde: Shunne hym to eate. **1602** SHAKS. *Ham.* II. ii. 239 *Guil.* Faith, her priuates, we. *Ham.* In the secret parts of Fortune? **1644** *Reg. Privy Council Scot.* Ser. II. VIII. 101 They causit thair officers..search our bodies and secreitt memberis for witch-markis. **1664** HUBERT *Catal. Rarities* (1665) 12 A Nest of a Bird made like the secret parts of a man.

k. Of a door, chamber drawer, passage, or mechanical contrivance: Designed to escape observation or detection. ***secret ink***: 'invisible' or 'sympathetic' ink.

Hence ***secret springer***, one who makes secret springs.

1591 SHAKS. 1 *Hen. VI*, I. iv. 10 The English..Went through a secret Grate of Iron Barres, In yonder Tower, to ouer-peere the Citie. **1737** HOPPUS *Salmon's Country Build. Estim.* (ed. 2) 110 Secret Pad-Locks. **1794** MRS. RADCLIFFE *Myst. Udolpho* liv, Pointing out to her a secret drawer. **1807** CRABBE *Birth of Flattery* 35 But by a secret spring the wall would move. **1848** THACKERAY *Van. Fair* lxvii, Put away in what they call the secret drawers of the desk. **1852** —— *Esmond* III. xii, As characters written with secret ink come out with the application of fire. **1849** MACAULAY *Hist. Eng.* v. I. 667 Secret passages were made from dwelling to dwelling. **1858** SIMMONDS *Dict. Trade*, *Secret-springer*, one who puts in watch-springs. **1888** MRS. H. WARD *R. Elsmere* xlvi, A young 'secret springer', to use the mysterious terms of the trade [*sc.* watch-making].

†**l.** Of a sound: Little audible. *Obs. rare.*

1670 W. CLARKE *Nitre* 28 Being fired in the open air, it [gunpowder] maketh but a flash, and a more secret noise.

m. Of an agent: That works in secret. Of a person: That is secretly (what is expressed by the sb.).

1600 SHAKS. *A.Y.L.* I. i. 150 A secret and villanous contriuer against mee his naturall brother. **1667** MILTON *P.L.* IV. 7 [O that] our first Parents had bin warnd The coming of thir secret foe. **1700** DRYDEN *Pal. & Arc.* II. 560 There saw I how the secret Fellon wrought. **1700** —— *Sigism. & Guisc.* 46 Resolv'd..to be..A seeming Widow, and a secret Bride. **1726** SWIFT *Gulliver* I. v, Others, who were my secret Enemies, could not forbear some Expressions, which by a side-wind reflected on me.

n. quasi-*adv.* Apart; secretly, in secret. Also *Comb.* with adjs., as ***secret-breathed***, ***-dimpling***, ***-smiling***, ***-stimulating***, ***-tripping***.

1539 in W. A. J. Archbold *Somerset Relig. Houses* (1892) 81 He went to hys chambre, were he callyd me secrett un to hym. **1590** SHAKS. *Com. Err.* III. ii. 15 Be secret false: what need she be acquainted? *a* **1605** MONTGOMERIE *Misc. Poems* xxxiv. 28 Secreit to meit. **1724** EUSDEN *Ovid's Amours* II. v. 12 The secret-tripping Dame. **1726** POPE *Odyss.* XIX. 1 [Ulysses] Consulting secret with the blue-ey'd Maid. **1742** YOUNG *Nt. Th.* VII. 410 Nor is thy Life, O Virtue! less in Debt To Praise, thy secret-stimulating Friend. **1780** S. J. PRATT *Emma Corbett* (ed. 4) III. 156 The secret-breathed prayer. **1820** KEATS *Isabel* xliii, She had devised How she might secret to the forest hie. **1925** BLUNDEN *Eng. Poems* 83 Black was the secret-dimpling stream. **1928** —— *Retreat* 33 Thus the bright-templed rhyme Before the secret-smiling author came.

†**o.** ***in secret wise***, secretly. (Cf. SECRE *a.* 3 b.)

1563 *Homilies* II. xvii. *Rogation Wk.* I. 232 Only I woulde wyshe your affection inflamed in secrete wyse within your selfe. **1568** GRAFTON *Chron.* II. 198 The Scottes..in secret wise came downe into the marches of Yorkshire.

p. ***secret life***: a private life of a nature concealed from the common observer; *spec.* one consisting of covert sexual dealings.

1880 (*title*) My secret life. **1927** E. M. FORSTER *Aspects of Novel* v. 113 Happiness and misery exist in the secret life, which each of us lives privately. **1928** GALSWORTHY *Swan Song* III. vii. 272 A secret life and Lippinghall! Long, long might that conjunction be deferred! **1973** L. COOPER *Tea on Sunday* xxvii. 207 Did you know that Holdsworth has a secret life?.. Lisa..saw him just going out of the bar with a glamour girl. **1976** C. BERMANT *Coming Home* I. vii. 107 My secret life was now revealed to my parents.

2. a. Of a person: †Reserved or reticent in conduct or conversation (*obs.*); not given to indiscreet talking or the revelation of secrets; silent as to any matter, uncommunicative, close.

c **1440** *Generydes* 720, I haue founde yow..At all tymes full secrete and full trew. **1474** CAXTON *Chesse* II. ii. (1883) 27 That she be secrete and telle not suche thynges as ought to be holden secrete. **1500–20** DUNBAR *Poems* xli. 8 Be secreit, trew, incressing of ȝour name. **1571** CAMPION *Hist. Irel.* II. ix. (1633) 106 Ormond was secret and drifty. **1591** SHAKS. *Two Gent.* III. i. 60, I am to breake with thee of some affaires..wherein thou must be secret. **1599** —— *Much Ado* I. i. 212, I can be secret as a dumbe man. **1600** W. WATSON *Decacordon* (1602) 96 The Nuncio [commanded] them both to be secret of what had past. **1625** BACON *Ess., Simulation* (Arb.) 508 But if a Man be thought Secret, it inuiteth Discouerie;..as in Confession, the Reuealing is not for worldly vse, but for the Ease of a Mans Heart, so Secret Men come to the Knowledge of Many Things, in that kinde. **1732** FIELDING *Miser* v. xiii, Were I not secret, lud have mercy upon many a virtuous woman's reputation in this town. **1825** SCOTT *Talism.* xxviii, 'My master bid me be secret', said the squire. **1874** MOTLEY *Barneveld* I. i. 101 Sully was as secret as the grave. **1893** LELAND *Mem.* I. 242 It was in the hands of so few persons, who were all absolutely secret and trustworthy.

absol. **1785** C. WILKINS tr. *Bhagavad-vita* x. 64 Amongst the secret I am silent.

b. *fig.* of silence, night, etc.

1556 *J. de Flores' Aurelio & Isab.* A 8, The secrete silence of the darcke night. **1592** SHAKS. *Rom. & Jul.* II. iv. 203 Bring thee Cords..Which..Must be my conuoy in the secret night. **1820** SHELLEY *Sensit. Pl.* III. 25 The noonday sun..Mocking the spoil of the secret night.

†**3.** That is entrusted with a person's private or secret affairs; that is a confidant; intimate *with*.

1470–85 MALORY *Arthur* XI. ii. 574 He was receyued worshipfully with suche peple to his semyng as were aboute Quene Queneuer secrete. *c* **1477** CAXTON *Jason* 34 b, The fair Myrro and one woman which was secrete with her, departed from thens. **1533** *Acc. Ld. High Treas. Scot.* VI. 126 To ane secret man quhilk brocht writtingis to the Kingis grace. *a* **1533** LD. BERNERS *Huon* xxix. 90 He was secret with yᵉ duke. **1568** GRAFTON *Chron.* II. 223 He was more secret with Quene Isabell the kings mother, then was to Gods pleasure or the kings honour. **1591** SAVILE *Tacitus, Agricola* (1622) 201 During the time of his sickenesse there came.. both of his secretest seruants and neerest physitians to see him. **1648** [see PRIVATE *a.* 10].

4. In various specific collocations.

a. Secret Council *Sc.*, the Scottish Privy Council: see COUNCIL *sb.* 7.

1546 *Reg. Privy Council Scot.* I. 26 My Lord Governour and Lordis of Secrete Counsel. *c* **1580** *Satir. Poems Reform.* xliii. (*Compl. upon Fortoun*) 205 Sacreit counsell can not be content To suffer lordshippis in equalitie. **1678** FOUNTAINHALL *Hist. Notices* (Bannatyne Club) I. 186 The Secret Councell would have given him ane reprivall.

b. secret seal = *secre seal*: see SECRE *a.* 2. Also = PRIVY SEAL.

1377–93 [see SECRE *a.* 2]. **1378** *Rolls of Parlt.* III. 44/1 Pur Brief, ou lettre de Grant ou Prive Seal, ou del Secret Seal, ou autre mandement. **1445** in *Charters Glasgow* (1906) II. 440 Because I had na sele of myne awn, I have procurit with instance the secrete sele of the burgh of Lithqw to be toput.

c. (*a*) **secret service.** Services rendered to a government, the nature of which cannot be disclosed to the public, but which are paid for from a fund set apart for the purpose; hence an organization which performs this function; *spec.* (*U.S.*) a government department concerned with national security. Also *attrib.*, as ***secret service fund***, ***money***; ***secret-service agent***, ***man***, one employed on secret service by government. Also *transf.*

1737 *Gentl. Mag.* VII. 531/2 The prodigious Increase of secret Service Money in the late Reign. **1808** G. ROSE *Diaries* (1860) I. 256 He would give a sum of 6,000*l*, or 7,000*l.*, out of foreign secret-service. **1809** CANNING *Ibid.* I. 264 The S.S. fund is..for secret services—services that cannot be explained or avowed. **1817** T. L. PEACOCK *Melincourt* III. 140 We shall all be blown up in a body—sinecures, rotten boroughs, secret-service men [etc.]. **1827** HALLAM *Const. Hist.* (1876) III. xv. 189 A large expenditure appeared every year, under the head of secret-service money. **1859** *Atlantic Monthly* Feb. 163/2 The Secret Service was doubled..while half Paris must have been under arrest. **1867** L. C. BAKER *Hist. U.S. Secret Service* 34 There is nothing in the Secret Service that demands a violation of honor, or a sacrifice of principle, beyond the ordinary rules of warfare. **1900** *Westm. Gaz.* 25 May 7/3 Secret-service agent Brown took the accused man in charge [at San Francisco]. **1906** *Daily Chron.* 2 Nov. 10/2 One of the chief racing bodies..has a force of secret-service men to gather information that could never reach the Turf authorities if they sought it as Turf authorities. **1939** T. S. ELIOT *Old Possum's Bk. Pract. Cats* 34 And when the loss has been disclosed, the Secret Service say: 'It *must* have been Macavity!' **1972** *Police Rev.* 10 Nov. 1445/1 The principal mission of the United States Secret Service today is safeguarding the lives of the President of the United States, the Vice-President, and many other important personalities in public life. **1981** A. PRICE *Soldier no More* vii. 93 I've got it... You're in the Secret Service.

(*b*) **secret agent**, a person engaged on secret service, esp. espionage.

a **1715** [see GUARD *sb.* 7 a]. **1837** J. P. HENDERSON *Let.* 5 Nov. in *Diplomatic Corresp. Texas* (Amer. Hist. Assoc.) (1911) III. 827 The Government of the United States ..[sent] a secret agent to Texas to enquire into her situation, power etc. **1893** S. WEYMAN *Gentleman of France* II. xviii. 136 You are here as the secret agent of the King of Navarre. **1907** CONRAD (*title*) The secret agent. **1939** G. GREENE *Confidential Agent* I. ii. 67 In melodrama a secret agent was never tired. **1973** W. FAIRCHILD *Swiss Arrangement* ix. 114 Lisa laughed suddenly. 'I never thought I'd be going to bed with a secret agent,' she said.

(*c*) **secret police**, a police organization operating in secret, *spec.* one owing allegiance to the state or government and used for political purposes. Also ***secret policeman***.

1823 F. BURNEY *Waterloo Jrnl.* in *Jrnls. & Lett.* (1980) VIII. 394 Buonaparte..trusted in the address of that mental diving machine, his secret police, for warding off any hazard. **1863** 'Ouida' *Held in Bondage* I. x. 233 The world has a trick of serving, like the Swiss Guard and the secret police, whichever side is uppermost and pays them best. **1910** A. Bennett *Clayhanger* II. xiv. 257 Some concealed emissary of the Russian secret police. **1938** E. Ambler *Cause for Alarm* vii. 119 The Ovra..has become a regularly constituted secret police force. **1973** D. Miller *Chinese Jade Affair* xviii. 176 The woes of being a secret policeman during the visits of V.I.P. personalities. **1981** G. Priestland *Priestland's Progress* ii. 38 Paul..had begun life as a religious secret policeman commissioned to stamp out the Church.

d. secret society, an organization formed to promote some cause by secret methods, its members being sworn to observe secrecy.

1829 Scott *Anne of G.* xxvi, It was countersigned in red ink, with the badges of the Secret Society, a coil of ropes and a drawn dagger... The extent and omnipresence of these Secret Associations. **1874** C. W. Heckethorn *Secret Societies* 4 Secret societies may be classed under the following heads: 1. Religious... 2. Military... 3. Judiciary. .. 4. Scientific... 5. Civil... 6. Political. **1888** A. Johnston in *Encycl. Brit.* XXIII. 784 A widespread secret society, the 'Ku-Klux-Klan'.

e. secret list chiefly *Mil.*, a register of research work or developments about which information may not be disclosed. Also *transf.*

1933 *Meccano Mag.* Feb. 109/1 As the aeroplane is on the Air Ministry Secret List, performance figures are not yet available for publication. **1949** Koestler *Promise & Fulfilment* II. v. 269 The war research which they are doing ..is still on the secret list. **1955** E. Waugh *Officers & Gentlemen* I. x. 129 There's an agitation..to take you off the secret list. Heroes are urgently required to boost civilian morale. **1977** 'J. D. White' *Salzburg Affair* vii. 63 A missile projector, brand new..and still on the secret list.

f. secret weapon, a weapon (often of potentially decisive force) classified as secret. Also *fig.* and *transf.*

1936 E. Ambler *Dark Frontier* I. vi. 91 He once told me that in these days there was no such thing as a secret weapon. **1939** W. S. Churchill *Into Battle* (1941) 150 The magnetic mine..may perhaps be Herr Hitler's much vaunted secret weapon. **1953** E. Simon *Past Masters* II. 78 See the candid camera at work, that misnamed secret weapon. **1962** *Listener* 2 Aug. 160/2 The formidable Signor Mattei, who is Italy's anything but secret weapon. **1980** A. Scholefield *Berlin Blind* II. 75 Ah, the secret weapons... They are going to bring England to her knees.

5. *attrib.*, as *secret-natured*, *-tongued*.

1596 R. L[inche] *Diella* (1877) 75 When secret-tongued night puts on her mistie sable-coloured vayle. **1728** [Fielding] *Masquerade* 16 'Tis this, which sets the Chymist on, To search that secret-natur'd Stone.

B. *sb.*

I. Something kept secret.

1. Something unknown or unrevealed or that is known only by initiation or revelation; a mystery; chiefly *pl.*, the hidden affairs or workings (of God, Nature, Science, etc.).

1390 Gower *Conf.* III. 54 Was nevere yet so wys a clerk, Which mihte knowe..the secret which god hath set Ayein a man mai noght be let. *c* **1400** tr. *Secreta Secret., Gov. Lordsh.* 84 Glorious Philosophers..to whom ys geuyn þe knowynge of secretez of sciencez, þat were hyd to alle men. **1456** Sir G. Haye *Law Arms* (S.T.S.) 10 That is ane office of ane angel, to revele the secretis of God. **1526** *Pilgr. Perf.* (W. de W. 1531) 7 In the whiche there be innumerable secretes of nature. **1630** Davenant *Just Italian* v. i, Jealous Nature hath lock'd her secrets in a Cabinet. **1667** Milton *P.L.* v. 569 For how shall I..unfold The secrets of another world, perhaps Not lawful to reveal? **1752** Hume *Ess. & Treat.* (1777) II. 35 Nature has kept us at a great distance from all her secrets. **1818** Scott *Hrt. Midl.* xlvii, Many devout ministers and professors in times past had enjoyed downright revelation, like the blessed Peden and Lundie.. wha entered into the secrets. **1850** Tennyson *In Mem.* xxi. 18 When Science reaches forth her arms To feel from world to world, and charms Her secret from the latest moon? **1872** Ruskin *Eagle's Nest* §79 Think of the vain research..of those who have tried to penetrate the secrets of life, or of its support.

2. In Liturgical use: A prayer or prayers said by the celebrant in a low voice after the Offertory and before the Preface. See secreta[1].

1387 Trevisa *Higden* (Rolls) VIII. 33 Sche wolde selden come at cherche, and þan unneþ sche wolde abyde þe secretes of þe messe. **14..** *Pol. Rel. & L. Poems* (1903) 122 And aftur þe fyrste orysoun þer ys an-oþur of gret Renoun þat to þe sowle ys wonþur swete, Menne calle hit þe secrete. *a* **1540** Barnes *Wks.* (1573) 357/2 Pope Gelasius..appointed that the Priestes should say the Secretes, the Cannon, and the Prefaces with their armes stretched abroad. **1844** *Catholic Weekly Instr.* 86 The prayers called *secrets*, (so called because they are silently offered,) follow, and are a second collect.

3. a. Some fact, affair, design, action, etc., the knowledge of which is kept to oneself or shared only with those whom it concerns or to whom it has been confided; something that cannot be divulged without violation of a command or breach of confidence. Frequently with an adj. prefixed, esp. as an intensive, as ***a dead, entire, profound secret.***

1450–80 tr. *Secreta Secret.* lix. 35 þat no man be so prive with him, forto se þe lettris of thi secretz. **1484** Caxton *Fables of Æsop* IV. iii, The shepherd..sayd paye me of that I haue kepte the secrete. **1560** Daus tr. *Sleidane's Comm.* 154 b, Certen Senatours had disclosed their secretes. **1590** Sir R. Williams *Brief Disc. War* 16 There is also one Secretarie..who..knowes all the secret onlie that passeth betwixt the King & the Captain general. **1591** Shaks. *Two Gent.* III. i. 2 Sir Thurio, giue vs leaue (I pray) a while, We haue some secrets to confer about. **1596** Dalrymple tr. *Leslie's Hist. Scot.* I. 152 Quhome he..in al his secreitis admitted. **1601** Shaks. *All's Well* IV. i. 93 O let me liue, And all the secrets of our campe Ile shew, Their force, their purposes. *a* **1700** Evelyn *Diary* 28 June 1683, Who was now again admitted to the councils and cabinet seacrets. **1701** G. Stanhope *Augustine's Medit.* II. iv. (1720) 123 The Gift is evident, and is the Giver a secret? **1743** Lady M. W. Montagu *Let. to Montagu* 20 Nov. (1893) II. 121 Reasons ..for keeping it an entire secret. **1805** [see dead *a.* 31, profound *a.* 3 b]. **1825** Scott *Betrothed* v, The monk, in alluding to the secrets of the confessional, had gone a step beyond what the rules of his order..permitted. **1837** Lockhart *Scott* II. ii. 42 It is an old saying, that wherever there is a secret there must be something wrong. **1854** 'C. Bede' *Verdant Green* II. xi, His writing for the prize poem had been a secret. **1879** Miss Yonge *Cameos* Ser. IV. v. 59 He kept his marriage a secret. **1888** *Encycl. Brit.* XXIII. 450/2 This device has never been patented, but is a secret. **1890** Jean Middlemass *Two False Moves* I. xv. 224 Much that she had heard that day must be kept a dead secret. **1908** R. Bagot *A. Cuthbert* xxvii. 363 If you were to keep this letter a secret from him.

b. In the Biblical phrase, ***the secrets of the (one's) heart.***

Not in Wyclif, who has 'hid thinges' (Vulg. *abscondita*). **1535** Coverdale *Ps.* xliv. 21 Shulde not God fynde it out? for he knoweth the very secretes of the hert. **1548** Udall, etc. *Erasm. Par. John* i. 47–9 Nathanaell..who was perswaded, that the secretes of the hearte was open to god onely. **1601** Shaks. *Jul. C.* II. i. 306 Thy bosome shall partake The secrets of my Heart. **1635** W. Austin *Medit.* 103 The Secrets of his heart none knowes; but he, that made it.

c. ***an open secret***: something which is ostensibly a secret, but which requires little effort or penetration to discover. Also ***secret of Polichinelle*** = secret de Polichinelle.

1828 Carlyle in *Foreign Rev.* II. III. 101 The 'open secret' is no longer a secret to him, and he knows that the Universe is *full* of goodness; that whatever has being has beauty. **1853** C. Brontë *Villette* III. xxiii. 336, I wanted to prove to Miss Lucy that I *could* keep a secret... How many times has she saucily insinuated that all my affairs are the secret of Polichinelle! **1879** F. Pollock in W. K. Clifford *Lect.* Introd. I. 1 It is an open secret to the few who know it, but a mystery..to the many, that Science and Poetry are own sisters. **1882** L. Stephen *Swift* iv. 74 The mask [of anonymity] was..a sufficient protection against legal prosecution, but in reality covering an open secret.

4. a. A method or process (of an art, etc.) hidden from all except the initiated.

1486 *Oath of Barber-Surgeons* in *Vicary's Anat.* (1888) App. xv. 273 And the secretes and counsell of the same arte, ye shall trewlie kepe and Layne. **1555** Eden *Decades* Contents, Of certeyne secreates touchynge the arte of saylynge. **1572** Mascall *Plant. & Graff.* (1592) To Rdr., Declaring of diuers waies of planting and Graffyng,..with shewing of diuers commodities and secrets heerein. *a* **1700** Evelyn *Diary* 14 Dec. 1650, An imposter that had like to have impos'd upon us a pretended secret of multiplying gold. **1742** Hume *Ess. & Treat.* (1777) I. 97 The balance of power is a secret in politics. **1796** H. Hunter tr. *St.-Pierre's Stud. Nat.* (1799) II. 528 What secret did the Asiatics possess to raise cities so vast and so populous? **1819** Scott *Ivanhoe* xxix, Our nation..can cure wounds,..and in our own family, in particular, are secrets which have been handed down since the days of Solomon.

†b. Hence, an infallible prescription, a specific.

1558 Warde tr. *Alexis' Secr.* (1568) 24 a, This is a very rare secrete against suche a disease. **1669** Salmon *Bate's Dispens.* 559/2 It is a Secret against a Gonorrhœa. **1817** Jas. Mill *Brit. India* II. IV. vii. 247 The idea that satiating the servants of the public with wealth is a secret for rendering them honest.

c. (Const. *of.*) That which accounts for something surprising or extraordinary; the essential thing to be observed in order to secure some end.

1738 Swift *Pol. Conversat.* II. 121 Few People know the Secret of this. **1846** Kingsley *Lett.* (1878) I. 146 The only secret of success is to feel and confess yourself nothing, that God may make you everything. **1849** Macaulay *Hist. Eng.* vi. II. 58 So strangely were good and evil intermixed in the character of these celebrated brethren; and the intermixture was the secret of their gigantic power.

†5. A place of concealment; a secret place; a hiding-place, place of retreat. *Obs.*

1530 Palsgr. 268/2 Secrete a prevy place, *requoy*. **1583** *Leg. Bp. St. Androis* 774 in *Satir. Poems Reform.* xlv, Vpon ane dyke doun was he sett Into a secreit out of sicht. **1596** Spenser *F.Q.* VI. xii. 24 Into their cloysters now he broken had..And searched all their cels and secrets neare. **1635** W. Austin *Medit.* 103 God himselfe is an invisible Spirit..he hides himselfe in Clowdes, and dwelleth in Secrets.

†6. *pl.* = *secret parts* (see A. 1 j). Also *sing.*

1535 Coverdale *Deut.* xxv. 11 Yf..the wyfe put forth hir hande, and take him by the secretes. **1552** Lyndesay *Monarche* I. 986 Than..thay..maid thame Breikis of leuis grene, That thair secreitis suld nocht be sene. **1579–80** North *Plutarch, Romulus* (1595) 34 They..run..starke naked (sauing they haue a cloth before their secrets). **1607** Topsell *Four-f. Beasts* 73 Their secret hangeth forth more then at other times. **1656** Heylin *Surv. France* 237 Those.. had the secrets of nature..filled with gun-powder, and so blown into ashes. **1758** J. S. *Le Dran's Observ. Surg.* (1771) Dict. B b 8, The upper Part of a Woman's Secret.

7. *Antiq.* 'A coat of mail concealed under one's usual dress' (Jam.).

1578–9 *Reg. Privy Council Scot.* III. 105 With daggis, pistolettis, Jakis, and secreitis of plait. **1600** *Gowrie Conspiracy* D 2 b, The Earle bade him putte on his secret and plaite sleeues, for he had an hey-land man to take. **1609** Skene *Reg. Maj., Treat.* 151 [They] quha sall resort, or repaire within his Majesteis palace,..armed with Iakis, Secreitis, or corsleits, vnder their coats, doublets, or vtherwaies, sallbe apprehended. **1643** *Sc. Acts Chas. I* (1870) VI. 43/2 That þej provyde jackes or secreites lances and steill bonnettes and swordes. **1820** Scott *Monast.* xxiv, A short doublet of buff, under which was in some places visible that light shirt of mail which was called a *secret*, because worn instead of more ostensible armour, to protect against private assassination. **1825** —— *Talisman* xxviii. **1828** —— *F.M. Perth* iv. **1853** James *Agnes Sorel* (1860) I. 149, I think it were as well if you wore a secret beneath your ordinary dress.

8. Phrases. **a.** (Properly the adj. used *absol.*) ***in secret*** [= L. *in secreto*, F. *en secret*]: in private, not openly or in public; secretly. ***†at one's secret***: to oneself, privately. ***†of secret***: of a secret character.

1474 Caxton *Chesse* II. ii. (1883) 28 And thus euery wyf tolde hit to other in secrete. **1483** —— *G. de la Tour* h vij, And..the kyng..sayd att his secrete that he myght not be wrothe with his wyf. **1526** Tindale *Matt.* vi. 4 Thy father which seith in secret. [So later versions.] **1576** Fleming *Panopl. Epist.* 382 Drunkards..kepe nothing in secrete, but ..blab abroad in the hearing of all men, whatsoever. **1588** Shaks. *L.L.L.* v. ii. 236 One word in secret. **1588** Parke tr. *Mendoza's Hist. China* 143 He..passed alongest, but not in such secret but that hee was discouered. **1611** Shaks. *Cymb.* v. v. 206, I return'd With tokens thus and thus..: nay some markes Of secret on her person. **1616** Chapman *Musæus* 260 Loose acts done In surest secret: in the open Sunne And euery Market place, will burne thine eares. **1781** Cowper *Expost.* 722 My soul shall sigh in secret. **1877** Tennyson *Harold* v. ii, Some held she was his wife in secret.

b. (Chiefly in senses 3–4.) ***to be in*** (rarely ***†on***) ***the secret***, to be one of the participants in a secret; ***†to be of secrets with***, to share the confidence or secrets of (a person); ***to let*** (a person) ***into the secret***, to confide (to him) the secret (*of* an affair, trade); hence *slang* (see quots. *a* 1700[2], 1801); ***to make a secret of*** (something), to make (it) a matter of concealment, to keep (it) to oneself.

1535 *St. Papers Hen. VIII*, II. 228 We have in warde,.. Dam Jenet Ewstace, which was thErle of Kildares aunt, and most of secrets with him. **1680** Burnet *Rochester* (1692) 28 Even those who were on the secret, and saw him in these shapes, could perceive nothing by which he might be discovered. **1697** Vanbrugh *Æsop* II. i, It's a good trade..: let a lad be but diligent, and do what he's bid, he shall be let into the secret, and share part of the profits. *a* **1700** Evelyn *Diary* 22 July 1674, In a short time let him so into the seacret of affaires, that [etc.]. *a* **1700** B. E. *Dict. Cant. Crew, Secret, let into the Secret*, when one is drawn in at Horse-racing, Cock-fighting, Bowling, and other Sports or Games, and *Bit.* **1703** [see let *v.*[1] 11 a(d)]. **1724** *De Foe's Tour Gt. Brit.* (ed. 3) I. 79 Before I was let into the Secret, as 'tis called, which is indeed nothing but the knavish Part of the Sport [of Horseracing]. **1738** Swift *Pol. Conversat.* I. 29 You may make a Secret of it, but we can spell, and put together. **1801** Nelson *Let.* in *Sotheby's Catal.* 15 June 1897, 17 As I am not in the secret, and feel I have a right to speak out. **1849** Macaulay *Hist. Eng.* iv. I. 453 James, who had from the first been in the secret of his brother's foreign politics. **1885** May Peard *Near Neighbours* II. i. 18 Nor had he made the least secret of his intention to use all means to hold her.

9. *attrib.* and *Comb.*, as (objective) ***secret-keeper***, ***-monger***; **secret-graph** (*nonce-wd.*), a code for communicating secrets.

1799 in *Spirit Publ. Jrnls.* III. 329 Instruct ladies to form a perfect *secret-graph by the arrangement of Patches. **1741** Richardson *Pamela* (ed. 3) II. 273 Thou has the Air of a *Secret-keeper of that sort. **1904** *Edin. Rev.* Jan. 56 Earth, the secret keeper of birth and of death. **1754–64** Smellie *Midwifery* I. 257, A selfish *secret-monger. **1756** C. Lucas *Ess. Waters* I. 38 Itinerant empyrics and secret-mongers.

†II. 10. A private counsellor, secret adviser. *Obs. rare*$^{-1}$.

a **1513** Fabyan *Chron.* lxviii. (1533) 25 b/1 When he [*sc.* Constantyne] awoke he called this vysyon to mynde, and tolde vnto his secretes, by whose counsayll he commaunded the sygne of the crosse to be..set in his baners.

†'secret, *v. Obs.* [f. secret *sb.*

In the inflected forms it is not easy to distinguish between '*secret* and secrete *v.*]

trans. To keep secret, conceal, hide.

1595 *Drake's Voy.* (Hakl. Soc.) 25 Your loves, I thinke, can pardon these faltes, and secret them from the vewe of others. **1596** Raleigh *Discov. Guiana* 21 A large chart.. which I shall most humbly pray your Lo. to secret, and not to suffer it to passe your own hands. **1619** W. Sclater *Exp. 1 Thess.* (1630) 398 Things that hee [God] hath pleased to secret vnto himselfe. **1625** Bacon *Ess., Simulation* (Arb.) 506 If a Man..can discerne, what Things are to be laid open, and what to be secretted. **1693** W. Freke *Sel. Ess.* xxvi. 155 The seueral Methods of Secreting our Sense in writing. *a* **1734** North *Exam.* I. i. §xvi. (1740) 23 Can any Thing but a Monster in common Sense argue..that the Earl intended to secret the Sense of his Words.

Hence **'secreting** *vbl. sb.*

1616 Bacon *Adv. to Villiers* Wks. 1872 VI. 41 There is great care to be used for the councillors themselves to be well chosen, so there is of the clerks of the council, for the secreting of their consultations.

‖**secreta**[1] (sɪ'kriːtə). Pl. **secretæ**. *Eccl.* [eccl.L. *sēcrēta* (sc. *ōrātio*), fem. of L. *sēcrētus* secret *a.*] = secret *sb.* 2.

1753 Challoner *Cath. Chr. Instr.* 95 The Prayers called the Secreta, which correspond to the Collects of the Day, and are different every Day. **1859** Neale *Liturgies S. Mark*, etc. p. xxvi *note*, While the *secreta* is being said. **1899** *Lutheran* (Philad.) 6 Apr. 325 The prolonged *secretae* of the priests.

‖**se'creta**[2], *pl.* [Lat.; neut. pl. of pa. pple. of *sēcernĕre*: see SECERN, SECRETE.] Secreted matters; the products of secretion. Cf. EXCRETA.

1877 CHAMBERS in *Encycl. Brit.* VII. 209/2 The actual amount of those elements in the dried solids of the secreta.

secretage ('si:krətɪdʒ). [a. F. *secrétage*, f. *secréter*, SECRETE *v.*[3] and -AGE.] A process of preparing furs for felting: see quot. 1835. Also *attrib.*

1791 HAMILTON *Berthollet's Dyeing* I. I. II. i. 131 The furs of hares.. cannot be employed alone for felting, without having undergone a previous operation which is called secretage. **1835** URE *Philos. Manuf.* 129 The furs of the hare, the rabbit, and the castor, being naturally straight, cannot be employed alone for felting, till they have acquired a curling texture at their points, by the application of nitrate of mercury,—an artifice called secretage. **1839** —— *Dict. Arts* 811 The nitrate of mercury is employed for the secretage of rabbit and hare-skins. **1866** COOLEY *Toilet* 481 Secretage Liquid, Permanent Curling Fluid. **1880** J. PATON in *Encycl. Brit.* XI. 518/2.

secretagogue (sɪ'kri:təgɒg), *sb.* and *a.* *Physiol.* Also (*erron.*) secreto-. [f. SECRET(E *v.*[1] + Gr. ἀγωγός drawing forth.] **A.** *sb.* A substance which promotes secretion. **B.** *adj.* Tending to promote secretion.

1924 *Amer. Jrnl. Physiol.* LXVIII. 143 Secretin solutions prepared from different duodena.. showed variations in their efficacy as pancreatic secretagogues. **1926** *Jrnl. Amer. Med. Assoc.* 28 Aug. 641/1 The acid washings of the upper portion of the small intestine collected from a living dog possess marked secretagogue action on the pancreas when intravenously injected. **1935** *Amer. Jrnl. Physiol.* CXII. 512 An extract of the duodenal mucosa which would possess certain properties, namely, that the intravenous injection of it would cause no secretion of pancreatic juice until acidified or that the secretagogue potency already present would be greatly increased by acidification. **1971** *Nature* 15 Oct. 497/1 We have tested this possibility in rats treated with a combination of two gastric secretogogues (substances which stimulate secretion of gastric juice), pentagastrin and carbachol.

†**secretaire**[1]. *Obs. rare.* Also 5 secretare, 6 secreatore, cecretore. [a. F. *secrétaire.* Cf. SECRETAR.] = SECRETARY.

1390 GOWER *Conf.* II. 31 Fulfild of Slowthes essamplaire Ther is yit on, his Secretaire, And he is cleped Negligence. **1475** *Bk. Noblesse* (Roxb.) 25 Maister Aleyn Chareter.. secretaire to Charlys le bien amée [*sic*]. *c* **1489** CAXTON *Sonnes of Aymon* ix. 210 Thenne sayd the secretare, 'Sire, your commaundemente shall be doon.' **1530** PALSGR. 35 The letters missyves of suche as be secreatores in the sayd countreis. **1556** *Chron. Grey Friars* (Camden) 46 Gardner cecretore un to the byshoppe of Wynchester.

‖**secretaire**[2] (səkretɛr). Also 8 secretare. [F. *secrétaire*: see SECRETARY 5.] **a.** A piece of furniture, usually cabinet-shaped, in which private papers can be kept, with a shelf for writing on, and drawers and pigeon-holes; a bureau.

1771 in *Maryland Hist. Mag.* (1919) XIV. 136 If you have moved it thence it may be in the old secretare in the Chappell. **1792** T. BLAIKIE *Diary Scotch Gardener* (1931) 235 He was forced by them to come to force or break open the Secretaire and drawers. **1818** SCOTT *Hrt. Midl.* xlix, A cracked brown cann, with a piece of leather tied over the top. Its contents seemed to be written papers, thrust in disorder into this uncommon *secrétaire*. **1838** *Civ. Engin. & Arch. Jrnl.* I. 321/2 Description of an improved method of constructing large Secretaires and Writing-tables. **1879** 'E. GARRETT' *House by Works* II. 119 Kate turned to her little secretaire and touched the spring of a secret place.

b. secrétaire à abattant (a abatɑ̃), a variety of fall-front writing cabinet (see quot. 1977).

1920 F. M. ATKINSON tr. *R. de Félice's French Furnit. under Louis XVI & Empire* II. ii. 56 The *secrétaire à abattant* is one of the favourite pieces of this epoch... That is the large drop-front escritoire, a serious, rather masculine piece. **1936** *Burlington Mag.* May p. xvii/1 A magnificent upright Louis Quinze *secrétaire à abattant*, by B.V.R.B. (Boucher, already mentioned). **1967** *Times* 14 Mar. 21/6 Today,.. at 11 a.m. at Blenstock House... Bureau Bookcase.., a Dutch Marquetry Secretaire a abattant. **1977** FLEMING & HONOUR *Penguin Dict. Decorative Arts* 718/1 A *secrétaire à abattant*.. was first made in the C17 and was very popular in late-C18 France. It stands against a wall and looks like a cabinet or cupboard with the fall-front flap closed vertically.

'**secretar.** *Sc.* Also 6 secretare, 6–7 secreter. (See also *Eng. Dial. Dict.*) [Sc. variant of SECRETARY: see -AR[2].]

1. = SECRETARY 2.

c **1450** HOLLAND *Howlat* 126 He..Bad send for his secretar, and his sele sone. **1533** *Acc. Ld. High Treas. Scot.* VI. 122 Alsua deliverit to him be the secretar in Falkland lettrez to the bischopis. **1567** *Reg. Privy Council Scot.* I. 547 The Lordis Regentis.. ordanis the Secretare.. to pas and direct seybrevis in dew and competent forme.. to Sir Williame Murray.. and Sir William Kirkcaldy. **1596** DALRYMPLE tr. *Leslie's Hist. Scot.* II. 448 Quhom we cal the Queines secretar. **1643–4** *Aberd. Acc.* in *Spalding Club Miscell.* V. 107 Quhen the Erll of Kingorne, minister and secreter, wer maid burgessis, 1 lib. 13s. 4d.

2. = SECRETARY 1.

1619 A. SIMSON in *Select Biog.* (Wodrow Soc.) I. 79 He was a faithfull secretar... He said if he thought he should reveall any secret he would wish his tongue cutted out.

secretarial (sɛkrɪ'tɛərɪəl), *a.* [ad. L. type *sēcrētāriāl-is, f. med.L. *sēcrētārius* SECRETARY: see -AL[1].] **a.** Of or pertaining to a secretary or secretaries. Also *spec.* designed for the training of office secretaries, as ***secretarial college, course, school.***

1801 BENTHAM *Mem. & Corr.* Wks. 1843 X. 362 Mr. Rose promised.. to place it with his own secretarial hands.. on.. the table of Mr. Pitt. **1851** DICKENS *Lett.* (1880) I. 244, I would like to have a talk with you about the secretarial duties. **1897** FLOR. MARRYAT *Blood of Vampire* xi, Mr. Milliken would be much occupied with secretarial work. **1922** A. L. CHURCH *Training of Secretary* 193 (Index) Secretarial schools. **1935** R. STRACHEY *Careers & Openings for Women* II. iv. 140 Short six or seven months' secretarial courses to make sure of an early start. **1935** L. H. TURNER *Dict. Careers* 73 A few [scholarships are] given by the leading secretarial colleges. **1941** A. HUXLEY *Let.* 27 Nov. (1969) 473 Sophie has deserted acting for a secretarial school. **1953** B. GORDON-CUMMING *Gentle Rain* 119, I went through secretarial courses and things like that. **1967** K. GILES *Death in Diamonds* i. 7, I finished secretarial school and I speak four languages. **1976** M. MAGUIRE *Scratchproof* vii. 107 She'd left secretarial college bubbling with big job enthusiasm.

b. Of type: = SECRETARY *sb.*[1] 4.

1864 PANIZZI in *Fine Arts Q. Rev.* II. 183 M. Francesco da Bologna.. has devised a new form of letter, called cursive or secretarial.

†**secre'tarian** *a.* *Obs. rare.* [f. med.L. *sēcrētāri-us* SECRETARY + -AN.] = prec.

a **1734** NORTH *Exam.* I. ii. §5 (1740) 33 We may observe in his Book in most Years, a Catalogue of Preferments, with Dates and Remarks, which latter, by the Secretarian Touches, shew out of what Shop he had them. *Ibid.* I. iii. §37. 144 These false Glosses built upon certain Secretarian Expressions in Coleman's Letters. **1801** SOUTHEY *Lett.* (1856) I. 175, I do not receive livery and seisin of the secretarian pen till we reach London.

Secretariat (sɛkrɪ'tɛərɪət). Also **Secretariate**, and with lower-case initial. [a. F. *secrétariat*, ad. med.L. *sēcrētāriāt-us* the office of a secretary, f. *sēcrētārius* SECRETARY: see -ATE[1].] The office or official position of secretary; the body or department of secretaries; the place where a secretary transacts business, preserves records, etc. Also, the administrative and executive department of a government or similar organization (as the United Nations), usu. directed by a Secretary(-General); freq. in Communist use [cf. Russ. *sekretariát*].

α. **1811** WELLINGTON *Let. to C. Stuart* 12 Jan. in Gurw. *Desp.* (1838) VII. 97, I conduct the operations of the Portuguese army as Marshal General, without any reference to the Secretariat. **1849** EASTWICK *Dry Leaves* 116 A series of letters to the Secretariat at Bombay. **1861** MONEY *Java* I. 238 The Secretariat.—The Governor-General is further assisted by a Secretary-General, who has under him three secretaries of Government, and a large staff of clerks. **1884** *Pall Mall Gaz.* 22 Nov. 8/2 The vacancy in the secretariat of the British and Foreign Bible Society. **1908** LD. ROBERTS in Lee-Warner *Mem. Sir H. W. Norman* 310 After the mutiny his career took him to the Military Secretariat. **1926** *Encycl. Brit.* III. 428/1 This 'plenum' elects.. the Secretariat of the Central Committee of five members with two deputies. **1934** B. MAXWELL *Soviet State* iii. 42 The Central Committee of the Union.. is divided into three sections: (1) a Secretariat, which performs the current work of organization and execution. **1934** WEBSTER, *Secretariat*,.. the permanent organ of the League of Nations, comprising the Secretary-General, with officials and secretaries appointed by him. **1949** T. LIE *Road to Peace* 1 Next, I want to thank my staff, the members of the Secretariat. **1955** *Bull. Atomic Sci.* Mar. 85/2 The movement works through its secretariat in Amsterdam where the activities of its national groups are coordinated. **1965** A. NOVE in B. Pearce tr. *Preobrazhensky's New Economics* p. viii, The party secretariat did not yet have the importance it acquired under Stalin. **1977** *Whitaker's Almanack 1978* 957 The real power in the Party [Communist] is vested.. in the Politbureau, the Secretariat and the permanent Departments of the Central Committee.

β. **1858** M. PATTISON *Ess.* (1889) II. 345 Before the beginning of the present century Montaigne's Secretariate to the Queen had become an accredited event. **1910** *Guardian* 22 Apr. 568/3 Claudius.. is regarded as the puppet of dissolute wives and insolent freedmen, not the shrewd organiser of a new Imperial Exchequer and secretariate.

secretary ('sɛkrɪtərɪ), *sb.*[1] (and *a.*) Forms: 4–7 **secretarie**, 5– **-airye**, (**secretrary**), 5–6 **secretarye**, **-ory**, **-orie**, (6 *Sc.* **secrittary**), 5– **secretary**. [ad. med.L. *sēcrētārius* a secretary, notary, scribe, etc., a title applied to various confidential officers (properly an *adj.*), f. *sēcrētum* SECRET *sb.*: see -ARY[1] B. 1. (The equivalent late Latin title was *ā sēcrētīs*.) Cf. F. *secrétaire* (whence SECRETAIRE, SECRETAR), Pr. *secretari*, Sp., Pg. *secretario*, It. *secretario*, *segretario*.]

A. *sb.*

1. †**a.** One who is entrusted with private or secret matters; a confidant; one privy *to* a secret. *Obs.*

1387 TREVISA *Higden* (Rolls) V. 387 Þanne his secretarie [L. *secretarius*] tolde hym what he hadde i-seie and i-doo. *c* **1400** tr. *Secreta Secret., Gov. Lordsh.* cvi, At þe leste be he to þe trewe secretary, no þinge addand, no letiland, in þinges þat þou sendys hym. *c* **1400** LOVE *Bonavent. Mirr.* xl. (Gibbs MS.) lf. 88 Takyng wyth hym hys þre specyall secretaryes þat is to say petyre and james and john. *c* **1440** *Promp. Parv.* 451/1 Secretary, manne of privyte (*v.r.* of priui counsel), *secretarius*. *c* **1440** *Gesta Rom.* xliii. 171 (Harl. MS.), There come to him [the Emperor] a Secretarie, þat was nye of his counseill. **1451** CAPGRAVE *St. Gilbert* xxiii. 97 For to þat pryuyte he desyred no moo secretaries but God and seyntis. **1567** PAINTER *Pal. Pleas.* II. 190 She.. that was the secretarie of hir infortunate marriage. **1590** LODGE *Rosalynde* (1592) N 2 b, Reueale it she durst not, as daring in such matters to make none her secretarie. **1590** GREENE *Fr. Bacon* xii. 75 Raphe tells all, you shall haue a good secretarie of him. **1665** R. BRATHWAIT *Comment Two Tales* 114 This Wife of Bath was too full of Chinks to be a good Secretary. **1815** SCOTT *Guy M.* xvi, My good woman,.. a faithful secretary to her sex's foibles.

†**b.** *fig.* of things personified. *Obs.*

1587 GREENE *Euph. Cens.* (1634) D 1, For they knew if ever (as time is a bad Secretary) their adulterous practises should come to the eares of Polumestor, a worse mishap then death should be allotted for their ingratefull mischiefe [etc.]. **1592** KYD *Sp. Trag.* III. ii. 12 The night, sad secretary to my mones. **1615** DANIEL *Hymen's Tri.* IV. i. Wks. 1718 I. 131 Yonder spreading Beech Which often hath the Secretary been To my sad Thoughts. **1648** CHAS. I *Let.* 31 July *Wks.* (1662) I. 350 Lest it may be imagined that desire of Liberty should now be the only Secretary to My thoughts.

†**c.** Applied to those entrusted with the secrets or commands of God, or of a god. *Obs.*

1599 HAKLUYT *Voy.* II. I. 209 The mercifull God.. commaunded his secretarie Abraham to build him an house in Mecca. **1647** N. BACON *Disc. Govt. Eng.* I. i. 1 Their Priests, whom they [the Britons] accounted the onely Secretaries that God had on earth. **1657** HEYLIN *Eccl. Vind.* II. iii. §14. 164 There was no order and command of Moses, or of any other of Gods Secretaries. *a* **1727** NEWTON *Chronol. Amended* ii. (1728) 210 Thoth, the secretary of Osiris.

transf. **1644** MILTON *Reas. Ch. Govt.* II. Pref. 41 But were it the meanest under-service, if God by his Secretary conscience injoyn it, it were sad for me if I should draw back.

d. ***secretary of nature***: one acquainted with the secrets of Nature.

This doubtless originally belonged to sense 2, being suggested by the title γραμματεὺς τῆς φύσεως, applied (in Suidas) to Aristotle; but in the following examples the word is taken in its etymological sense.

1580 G. HARVEY *Three Proper Lett.* B iij b, The soundest Philosophers in deede, and very deepest Secretaries of Nature, holde.. an other assertion. **1583** GREENE *Mamillia* I. Wks. (Grosart) II. 80, I cannot but maruel that among al these secretaries of nature, there haue neuer byn found any which haue enterprised to search out the essence and perfect nature of loue. **1635** H. VALENTINE *Foure Sea-Sermons* 24 It is reported of Aristotle that great Secretary of Nature, that [etc.]. **1648** *Hunting of Fox* 19 Solinus, and other Secretaries of nature. **1690** C. NESSE *Hist. & Myst. O. & N. Test.* I. 29 Solomons wisdom.. made him natures secretary.

2. a. One whose office it is to write for another; *spec.* one who is employed to conduct or assist with correspondence, to keep records, and (usually) to transact various other business, for another person or for a society, corporation, or public body.

In early use applied almost solely to the officer who conducted the correspondence of a king; app. often employed with some mixture of the etymological sense 1.

private secretary: a secretary employed by a minister of state or other high official for the personal correspondence connected with his official position; also applied to a secretary in the employ of a particular person (as distinguished from the secretary to a society, etc.). Also *spec.* in various civil service and parliamentary sub-ministerial posts: ***Parliamentary Private Secretary***: see PARLIAMENTARY *a.* 1; ***Permanent Secretary***: see PERMANENT *a.* 1 d; ***Second*** (or ***Third***) ***Secretary***: a senior civil servant in the Treasury immediately subordinate to the permanent (or second) secretary. ***Secretary of Embassy*** or ***Legation***: an official of an embassy or diplomatic mission ranking next to the ambassador or envoy, and empowered to some extent to supply his place in his absence.

14.. *Sir Beues* (ed. Kölbing) 58/2 (MS. C) Kyng Armyne ..cawsyd hys secretory a lettyr to make. **1433** LYDG. *S. Edmund* III. 163 Burchardus.. That of seyn Fremund whilom was secretarye. **1455** *Rolls of Parlt.* V. 317/2 For the Office of oure Secretarie of Fraunce. **1465** *Mann. & Househ. Exp.* (Roxb.) 167 My mastyre paid to the Kynges secretory, for makenge of a lettre fro the Kynge into Wales, for my lord, vj. s. viij. d. *a* **1500** *Assembly of Ladies* 553 Tak these billës to the secretary. *a* **1513** FABYAN *Chron.* VI. clxxxvi. (1811) 186 The Kynge was aboute to delyuer this letter to his scribe or secretory. **1540–1** ELYOT *Image Gov.* Pref. 1 Whiche boke was fyrst written in the Greke tonge by his secretarie named Eucolpius. **1576** FLEMING *Panopl. Epist.* 338 *marg.*, He meaneth the Byshop of Yorke, to whom this Burbanco was secretarie. **1613** SHAKS. *Hen. VIII*, II. ii. 116 Cardinall, Prethee call Gardiner to me, my new Secretary. **1706** PHILLIPS (ed. Kersey), *Secretary*, one that is employ'd in Writing Letters, Dispatches, &c. for a Prince, Nobleman, or particular Society: Also one that attends upon an Ambassadour, Envoy, or Resident for that purpose. The *King's Secretaries*, certain Officers that Sign the Dispatches of the Seal; also the Clerks of the King's Chamber and Closet. **1756–7** tr. *Keysler's Trav.* (1760) IV. 424 The secretary of legation to that city. **1819** *Hermit in London* II. 186 We have quill-drivers termed secretaries to such and such a firm. **1821** (*title*) The Secretary's Assistant; exhibiting the various and most correct modes of Superscription, Commencement and Conclusion of Letters to Persons of every degree of Rank. **1838** DICKENS *Nich. Nick.* xvi, Nicholas wanted to know whether there was any such post as secretary to a gentleman to be had. **1845** *Philol. Soc. Trans.* I. 6 The Rules drawn up for the regulation of the Society were then read by the Secretary. **1848** THACKERAY *Van. Fair* xxv, The Secretary of the treasury's antechamber. **1883** 'OUIDA' *Wanda* I. 64 One letter her secretary could not answer for her. **1932** *Whitaker's Almanack 1933* 329/1 Treasury... Permanent Secretary and Head of H.M. Civil Service, Sir Warren Fisher... Second Secretary, Sir Richard V. N. Hopkins. **1939** *Whitaker's Almanack 1940* 433/1 Second Sec., Sir Richard V. N. Hopkins... Joint Third Secretaries, Sir Frederick Phillips..; Sir Alan Barlow. **1964** LD. BRIDGES *Treasury* xv. 145 The next rank in the Treasury is known as Second Secretary, which is the equivalent of a Permanent Secretary in other major departments. *Ibid.* 146 The next rank in the Treasury is Third Secretary which is the equivalent of a Deputy Secretary in a major department. **1976** in R. Crossman *Diaries* II. 200 Philip Allen (K.C.B. 1964) was Second Secretary to the Treasury 1963–6.

b. *transf.* and *fig.*

1561 T. NORTON *Calvin's Inst.* IV. viii. §9. 49b, The Apostles wer ye certaine & authentike secretaries [L. *amanuenses*] of the Holy ghost. **1591** NASHE *Pref. to Sidney's Astrophel*, Fayre sister of Phœbus, and eloquent secretary to the Muses, most rare Countesse of Pembroke. **1642** FULLER *Holy & Prof. St.* v. ii. 364 Charles knew well that Necessity, her Secretary, endited her speech for her. **1665** BOYLE *Occas. Refl.* VI. i. (1848) 341 Those orders of hers, in which she employ'd not Rhetorick for her Secretary, could not be so much as listen'd to, much less obey'd.

†**c.** One who writes (on a particular occasion) for another. *Obs.*

1592 GREENE *Groat's W. Wit* (1617) 9 Words to court her you shall not want, for my selfe will be your Secretary.

†**d.** One skilled in letter-writing. *Obs.*

1586 J. HOOKER *Chron. Irel.* 160/2 in *Holinshed*, The gouernor, who was a verie good secretarie, and could pen a letter verie excellentlie well, did draw a letter.

†**e.** In the titles of books on the art of letter-writing. *Obs.*

1586 A. DAY (*title*) The English Secretorie. Wherein is contayned a perfect method for the inditing of all manner of Epistles and familiar letters, etc. **1715** (*title*) A new Academy of complements; or the Lover's Secretary.. in divers examples of writing and inditing letters.

3. a. In the official designations of certain ministers presiding over executive departments of state.

The occurrence of the title '(Principal) Secretary of State (†Estate)' under Queen Elizabeth may be taken as indicating the beginning of the development by which the king's secretary (in sense 2) became a minister invested with governing functions. Throughout the 17th c. there were two officials jointly holding the office of Secretary of State, and in the 18th c. the number varied between two and three; till near the close of this period the two (or two of the three) were distinguished as 'Principal Secretary of State for the Southern Province' and 'Principal Secretary of State for the Northern Province', with reference to the division between them of the control of foreign relations (see quot. 1755); but with regard to internal administration no division of functions was formally recognized. At the end of the 18th c. there were three Secretaries of State, and shortly afterwards the division of functions between them was recognized in their official designation, as 'Secretary of State for Home Affairs', 'for Foreign Affairs', and 'for the Colonies'. In 1854 a Secretary of State for War was added, and 1858 a Secretary of State for India. The Secretaries of State are often more briefly called the Home Secretary, the Foreign Secretary, etc. The Chief Secretary for Ireland (officially styled the Secretary to the Lord Lieutenant, and informally the Irish Secretary), and the Secretary for Scotland (first appointed in 1885) were not secretaries of state, but had similar functions, and were (c 1911) members of the cabinet. The Secretary at War (down to 1855, when the office was united with that of the Secretary of State for War) was the parliamentary representative of the army, and had some degree of control over its finance. There have been numerous changes (too complex to set down here) in the nomenclature and duties of Secretaries of State since the nineteenth century. Since 1945, principal Secretaries of State have included the Secretary of State for the Home Department (Home Secretary), Foreign and Commonwealth Affairs (Foreign Secretary), Industry, Defence, Employment, and Northern Ireland. The title Chief Secretary (to the Treasury) was introduced in 1961: it is a ministerial appointment as opposed to the various civil servant Treasury Secretaries. The principal Secretary of State (usu. the Home Secretary) is sometimes referred to as the 'First Secretary'.

In the U.S., the Secretary of State corresponds approximately to the British Foreign Secretary. Other cabinet ministers, heads of executive departments, are the Secretary of the Treasury, of War, of the Navy, of the Interior, of Agriculture. Each state of the Union has also its Secretary of State (or a corresponding officer with some other title). In recent years, the nomenclature of senior U.S. cabinet ministers has (as with their counterparts elsewhere) been subject to extensive changes.

1599 HAKLUYT *Voy.* II. I. 175 (transl. of Italian letter) Our Secretarie of estate. **1601** in Rymer *Foedera* (1715) XVI. 421 Sir Robert Cecill Knighte our Principall Secretarie. **1603** *Ibid.* 497 The Right Honorable Sir Robert Cecyll Knight Principall Secretary to her Majestie. **1620** *Ibid.* XVII. 212 Sir Robert Naunton Knight one of our principall Secretaries of State. *a* **1635** NAUNTON *Fragm. Reg.* (Arb.) 30, I now come to the next, which was Secretary William Cecil. **1641** CLARENDON *Hist. Reb.* I. §141 The two Secretaries of State (who were not in those days officers of that magnitude they have been since, being only to make Dispatches upon the conclusion of Councils, not to govern, or preside in those Councils) were Sr John Coke.. and Sr Dudley Carleton. **1693** LUTTRELL *Brief Rel.* (1857) III. 175 Mr. Clerk, secretary at war. **1710–11** SWIFT *Jrnl. to Stella* 17 Jan., I will speak to George Granville, Secretary at War, to make him a captain. **1755** *Chamberlayne's St. Gt. Britain* (ed. 38) I. 85 Secretaries of State... The Correspondence with all Parts of Great Britain is, without Distinction, managed by either of the Secretaries... But as for the Foreign Affairs, all the Nations.. are by them divided into Two Provinces, the Northern, and Southern; of which the Northern is usually under the Junior Secretary, and contains Scandinavia, &c. The Southern under the Senior, and contains Flanders, France, &c. At present (Anno 1752) the Case is just the Reverse. **1774** BURKE *Amer. Tax.* Wks. II. 368 Lord Hillsborough, secretary of state for the colonies. **1789** *Deb. Congr. U.S.* 26 Sept. (1834) 90, I likewise nominate Thomas Jefferson, for Secretary of State. **1846** J. K. POLK *Diary* 20 Mar. (1910) I. 293 Forty or fifty persons.. called; among them the Russian Minister, the Secretary of State, [etc.]. **1863** *Act 26 & 27 Vict.* c. 12 §1 From and after the passing of this Act the Office of Secretary at War shall be.. abolished. **1863** KINGLAKE *Crimea* (ed. 3) II. 72 *note*, According to the practice which was in force up to the summer of 1854, the Secretary of State for the Colonies was also the 'Secretary of War'... In peace-time (thanks to the labours of the 'Horse Guards', the office of the Secretary *at* War, the Ordnance, and several other offices) the duties of the Colonial Secretary, in his character as Secretary of War, were very slight. **1906** 'MARK TWAIN' *Autobiogr.* (1924) I. 236 He had been ambassador, brilliant orator,.. admirable Secretary of State. **1940** W. FAULKNER *Hamlet* I. iii. 74 A gold-filled diploma from the Secretary of State at Jackson saying for all men to know by these presents, greeting, that them twenty thousand goats.. is goats. **1961** *Times* 10 Oct. 12/1 As Chief Secretary (a title used for the first time) Mr. Brooke will come under the general policy direction of the Chancellor. **1962** *Hansard Commons* 19 July 632 The Prime Minister: My right hon. Friend the First Secretary of State will act as Deputy Prime Minister. *a* **1974** R. CROSSMAN *Diaries* (1975) I. 610 Oh dear, it is a panjandrum committee—the Prime Minister, First Secretary, Foreign Secretary, the Minister of Defence, the Minister of Labour for some reason, myself. **1976** *Billings* (Montana) *Gaz.* 20 June 8-A/4 Nixon, whom Bill Rogers (secretary of state from 1969 to 1973) referred to as the world's youngest elder statesman, had acquired enormous stature in world affairs.

b. ***Mr. Secretary***: used before the name of a secretary of state, or as a title instead of his name. Now only *official* and *Hist.*

1576 in Nichols *Progr. Eliz.* (1823) II. 42 Mr. Secretary. Mr. Threasurer. Mr. Comptroller. **1613** SHAKS. *Hen. VIII*, v. iii. 1 [*Scene*, A Councell Table... Cromwell at lower end, as Secretary.] *Chan.* Speake to the businesse, M. Secretary; Why are we met in Councell? **1711** SWIFT *Jrnl. to Stella* 30 Aug., On Saturday I go to Windsor with Mr. Secretary. **1760** *Rhode Island Col. Rec.* (1861) VI. 243 A letter from Mr. Secretary Pitt. **1911** *Times* 23 Feb. 15/5 The Speaker asked who were prepared to bring in the Bill. *Mr. Asquith.*—The Chancellor of the Exchequer, Mr. Secretary Churchill, Mr. Secretary Haldane, Mr. Pease, the Attorney-General, and myself.

4. Short for ***secretary hand, type***: see B.

1771 LUCKOMBE *Hist. Printing* 42 The character itself was a rude old Gothic mixed with Secretary. **1778** MORES *Dissert.* 4 And first Mr Caxton—his letter originally was of the sort called Secretary. **1784** ASTLE *Orig. Writ.* v. 146 In the sixteenth century, the English lawyers engrossed their conveyances and legal instruments in characters called Secretary, which are still in use. **1969** M. B. PARKES *Eng. Cursive Book Hands 1250–1500* p. xx, One of the outstanding features of the history of English handwriting in the fifteenth century is the gradual infiltration of this new script, which in its English form we now call 'secretary', into all classes of books and documents, until by the sixteenth century it had become the principal script in use in this country. **1978** *Bodl. Libr. Rec.* IX. 324 The writing exercises .. are confined in the rectos of the pages, except for practice alphabets in secretary and in a text hand on ff. 30b and 57b respectively.

5. A writing-desk, a secretaire. Now chiefly *U.S.*

After F. *secrétaire*, prob. a transferred use; cf. however SECRETARY *sb.*^{2}

1803 T. SHERATON *Cabinet Dict.* 303 *Secretary*. This term .. among cabinet makers.. is applied to certain pieces of furniture to write at. **1805** *Times* 7 Nov. 4/4 Genuine household furniture, and valuable Effects.. consisting of.. Excellent mahogany secretary and bookcase. **1819** A. CONSTABLE *Let.* 21 Mar. in J. Constable *Corr.* (1962) I. 178 The secretary in the White Room sold for 9 pounds or guineas, I forget which. **1833** LOUDON *Encycl. Archit.* §2096 Writing-Tables, or Secretaries. **1858** G. MACDONALD *Phantastes* i. 2 An old secretary, in which my father had kept his private papers. **1865** G. W. BAGBY *Writings* (1885) II. 27 When you come to open his 'secretary'.. you will find his bonds, accounts.. lying about loose. **1893** LELAND *Mem.* I. 227 My first thought was for this money, so I hurried to get the key of the secretary in which it was. **1975** D. RAMSAY *Descent into Dark* ii. 68 Anita.. was.. stripping the finish from a maple secretary with a blowtorch. **1980** A. N. WILSON *Healing Art* xi. 129 There was a grandfather clock, and a roll-top secretary.

6. The secretary-bird (see 7).

1781 tr. *Sonnerat's Voy. Spice-Isl.* 19 The Secretary, with a crest down back of the neck. **1850** R. G. CUMMING *Hunter's Life S. Afr.* (1902) 144/1 When the tree fell, out from its nest rolled a young secretary.

7. *attrib.* and *Comb.*, as †***secretary-craft, desk*** (now only *U.S.*), ***-interpreter, -office***; (appositively) ***secretary-treasurer, -typist***; **secretary- (†secretaries) bird**, (*a*) a raptorial bird of South Africa, *Serpentarius secretarius*; said to be so called from a tuft of feathers at the back of the head which have a fanciful resemblance to pens stuck behind the ear; also called ***secretary-falcon, -vulture***; (*b*) [BIRD *sb.* 1 d], a punning term for a young woman employed as a secretary; **secretary-general** (see quots. 1701, 1861); also *spec.* the title of the principal official of a Communist party or of some international organizations (as the United Nations); hence **secretary-generalship**.

1797 *Encycl. Brit.* (ed. 3) XVII. 236/2 *Secretaries bird,.. classed by Latham under the genus Vultur. **1824** *Goldsmith's Nat. Hist.* III. Index, Secretary-bird devours serpents. **1870** GILLMORE tr. *Figuier's Reptiles & Birds* 611 The Secretary Bird (*Serpentarius secretarius*,..) has a widely-opening bill, very crooked and very powerful. **1969** W. DOUGLAS-HOME (*title*) The secretary bird. **1974** I. MURDOCH *Sacred & Profane Love Machine* 50 Since Pinn had become what she called a 'secretary bird' she had become much smarter. **1976** DEAKIN & WILLIS *Johnny go Home* xvi. 184 Even London's 'Secretary Birds'.. have problems finding somewhere to live. *a* **1661** FULLER *Worthies, Kent* (1662) II. 75 None alive did better ken the *Secretary Craft, to get Counsels out of others, and keep them in himself. **1798** *Hull Advertiser* 28 July 2/1 Eight fashionable *secretary desks. **1967** MRS. L. B. JOHNSON *White House Diary* 23 Apr. (1970) 509 Mr. Hoes showed me a secret drawer in the secretary desk. **1802** BINGLEY *Anim. Biog.* (1805) II. 185 An engagement between the *Secretary Falcon and a serpent. **1701** *Lond. Gaz.* No. 3713/3 The Sieur de Capistron, *Secretary-General of the French Galleys. **1861** [see SECRETARIAT]. **1934** B. MAXWELL *Soviet State* iii. 42 In theory the Political Bureau is appointed by the Central Committee; in reality the Secretary-General of the Party, if he is powerful enough, makes the selection. This is the case at present, since Stalin is the Secretary-General. **1949** T. LIE *Road to Peace* 1 (*heading*) Secretary-General of the United Nations. **1954** E. H. CARR *Interregnum* 336 Speculating what the secretary-general would report at the next party congress. **1968** *U.N. Security Council Proc.* 10 in *Parl. Papers 1967–8* (Cmnd. 3757) XLII. 229 The Secretary-General deplores any resort to force to settle international problems, wherever it may occur, in contravention of the Charter of the United Nations. **1959** *Economist* 9 May 506/1 According to one view of *secretary-generalship. **1977** *Westindian World* 3–9 June 10/1 The whole trend of his Secretary-Generalship so far.. is to place the Commonwealth firmly in its global setting. **1904** SLADEN *Lovers in Japan* II. xii, The *Secretary-Interpreter at the Legation. **1821** SCOTT *Kenilw.* xl, We will.. place the boy in our *Secretary-office. **1920** *Constitution of Santa Barbara Club* (Santa Barbara, Calif.), Officers.. *Secretary-Treasurer William Wyles. **1979** *Yale Alumni Mag.* Apr. (Suppl.) cn 11/2 He is a past president and secretary-treasurer of the American Association of Law Schools. [**1939** *Daily Tel.* 18 Dec. 13/2 (Advt.), Secretary-shorthand-typist, good correspondent, required immediately for engineer.] **1957** S. SMITH *Not waving but Drowning* 34 Dark was the day for Childe Rolandine the artist When she went to work as a *secretary-typist. **1976** *Milton Keynes Express* 2 July 4/4 His wife, a secretary-typist, had left for work. **1781** LATHAM *Synopsis Birds* I. I. 20 *Secretary Vulture.

B. *adj.* As the distinctive epithet of a style of handwriting used chiefly in legal documents from the 15th to the 17th c. Hence applied to a kind of black-letter type imitating this.

1571 DE BEAU CHESNE & BAILDON (*title*) A booke containing divers sortes of hands, as well the English as French Secretarie, with the Italian, Roman, Chancelry & court hands. **1587** FLEMING *Contn. Holinshed* III. 1370/2 One written in the secretarie hand.. and the other in the Roman hand. **1594** PLAT *Jewell-ho.* 41 The Secretarie small a, hath six partes before it bee made uppe. **1649** DK. NEWCASTLE *Country Capt.* II. i, Papers defild with court hand and long dashes or secretary lines, that straddle, more then Frenchmen. **1705** WANLEY *MSS.* in *Phil. Trans.* XXV. 2000 Like as many Antient People, who do yet continue to write the Roman and Secretary Hands, which were more fashionable 50 or 60 years ago, than now. **1710** HEARNE *Collect.* (O.H.S.) III. 86 The French is printed in a secretary character. **1740** RICHARDSON *Pamela* (1824) I. 127 Don't you see, by the setness of some of these letters, and a little secretary cut here and there,.. that it is the hand of a person bred in the law way? **1845** BLACK *Catal. Ashm. MSS.* 104 The other MS. contained in this volume was written in the time of Q. Elizabeth, in the secretary-hand. **1877** F. C. PRICE *Facsimiles Caxton, Memoir*, When Caxton started in England his whole stock of type consisted of two founts, a church or text type and a secretary type.

†**secretary**, *sb.*^{2} *Obs. rare.* Also secretorie. [ad. late L. *sēcrētārium*, f. *sēcrētum*: see -ARY^{1} B. 2.] A secret chamber or repository. Also *fig.*

c **1440** *Alphabet of Tales* 323 Saynt Martyn.. went in-to his secretorie & doffid his cote. *c* **1440** *Promp. Parv.* 451/1 Secretary, or place in privy councelle (*v.r.* place of privyte or cowncel), *secretarium*. *c* **1450** tr. *De Imitatione* III. xliii. 114 þou owist to fle into þe secretary of þin herte, bisechinge inwardly þe helpe of god.

'secretary, *v.* [f. SECRETARY *sb.*^{1}] **a.** *trans.* To assist (someone) secretarially. *nonce-use.* **b.** *intr.* To work as a secretary (esp. an office secretary). Also const. *to. colloq.* Hence **'secretarying** *vbl. sb.*

1927 *Punch* 26 Oct. 450/1 Poor old Henry.. is in the soup again... He secretaries my uncle,.. and as a rule we lunch together. **1933** WODEHOUSE *Heavy Weather* v. 73 Fellow named Carmody, who has been secretarying there. **1958** *Times Lit. Suppl.* 26 Dec. 749/4 Dish-washing here, secretarying there, finally helping out as Bursar in a school dominated by the headmaster's demented wife. **1971** K. DICK *Ivy & Stevie* 55 Stevie.. secretaried.. to Sir Neville Pearson and Sir Frank Newnes. **1975** P. G. WINSLOW *Death of Angel* vi. 142 She got fed up with secretarying.

secretaryship ('sɛkrɪtərɪʃɪp). [f. SECRETARY *sb.*^{1} + -SHIP.]

†**1.** The duties of a secretary. Also (cf. SECRETARY *sb.*^{1} 2 d), skill or practice in letter-writing.

1530 PALSGR. Introd. 44 He may be able to do servyce in the faict of secretarishype. **1593** G. HARVEY *Pierces Super.* 8 A fine-witted man,.. with a nimble dexterity of liuely conceite, and exquisite secretaryship. **1607** WALKINGTON *Opt. Glass* Ded. ¶2 Wise parly and communication giues the vent and easie flow, and secretariship the sale. *Ibid.* 83 As though they alone were Italian *Magnificoes* and great Turkes for secretariship.

2. The office of secretary.

1550 EDW. VI *Jrnl.* 6 Sept. *Lit. Rem.* (Roxb.) 292 Mr. Wotton gave his secretaryship, and Mr. Cicil toke it. **1670** G. H. *Hist. Cardinals* III. III. 321 He has confirm'd.. Monsignour Piccolomini in his Secretaryship of the Memorials. **1711** SWIFT *Let. to Stella* 19 Apr., Little Harrison the Tatler goes to-morrow to the secretaryship I got him at the Hague. **1796** LD. GRENVILLE in *Paget Papers* (1896) I. 109 This appointment will vacate the secretaryship of Embassy at Madrid. **1809** G. ROSE *Diaries* (1860) II. 402 The Secretaryship-at-War was offered to him. **1885** *Field* 7 Feb. 150/2 Mr. Burton had expressed a wish to retire from the secretaryship [of a hunt]. **1893** *Law Times* XCV. 27/2 In 1858,.. a Secretaryship of State for India was established.

‖**secret de Polichinelle** (səkrɛ də pɔliʃinɛl). [Fr., secret of Polichinelle: see PUNCHINELLO and SECRET *sb.* 3 c.] A supposed secret which is generally known; an open secret.

1857 *Sat. Rev.* 14 Nov. 435/1 The accredited phrase in certain circles about the Court of Spain is, that there is a mystery about it; but the mystery is like the *secret de Polichinelle*. **1908** G. K. CHESTERTON *All Things Considered* 117 There is a..class of things which humanity does agree to hide... But..though they are, in one sense, a secret, they are also always a 'secret [*sic*] de Polichinelle'. **1952** A. CHRISTIE *Mrs McGinty's Dead* xxiv. 171 A *secret de Polichinelle* is a secret that everyone can know. **1979** A. BUCHAN *Scrap Screen* vii. 103 It was a *secret de Polichinelle* in the Grosvenor family that the boy..was not the Dean's.

†**se'crete**, *a. Obs. rare.* [ad. L. *sēcrēt-us*, pa. pple. of *sēcernĕre*: see next.] Separated.

1678 CUDWORTH *Intell. Syst.* I. iv. 307 Numenius and others of the Platonists speak..supposing Two other Divine Hypostases..which were perfectly Secrete from Matter. *Ibid.* 582 This so containeth all things, as not being yet secrete and distinct.

secrete (sɪ'kriːt), *v.*^{1} *Phys.* [f. L. *sēcrēt-*, ppl. stem of *sēcernĕre* to separate: see SECERN. Suggested by SECRETION, from which it might be regarded as derived by back-formation. Cf. F. *sécréter* (1812 in Hatz.-Darm.), Sp. *secretar.*]

1. *trans.* To produce by means of secretion.

1707 [see SECRETED *ppl. a.*^{1}]. **1728** CHAMBERS *Cycl.*, *Animal Secretion* is the Act whereby the divers Juices of the Body are secreted or separated from the common Mass of Blood, by means of the Glands. **1800** E. DARWIN *Phytol.* vi. 72 They [*sc.* glands] secrete, that is, separate or produce, some fluid from the blood; as bile, saliva, urine, milk. **1851** WOODWARD *Mollusca* 6 That part of their integument which contains the viscera and secretes the shell, is termed the mantle. **1877** DARWIN *Forms of Fl.* i. 22 The flowers of the Cowslip..secrete plenty of nectar.

b. *transf.* and *fig.*

1863 KINGSLEY *Lett.* (1878) II. 172 If you won't believe my great new doctrine..that souls secrete their bodies, as snails do shells, you will remain in outer darkness. **1887** LOWELL *Democracy*, etc. 29 Old gold has a civilizing virtue which new gold must grow old to be capable of secreting.

2. *intr.* To perform the act of secretion.

1872 HUXLEY *Physiol.* v. 132 Making the cells secrete just as a nerve when stimulated makes a muscle contract. **1884** BOWER & SCOTT *De Bary's Phaner.* 100 Those delicate,.. umbrella-like scales..secrete on their upper surface.

secrete (sɪ'kriːt), *v.*^{2} [Alteration of SECRET *v.*, after L. *sēcrētus* SECRET *a.*]

1. *trans.* To place in concealment, to hide out of sight, to keep secret.

1741 WARBURTON *Div. Legat.* IV. iv. II. 109 The common Opinion that the Egyptians invented Hieroglyphics to secrete their profound Wisdom. **1768** LADY M. COKE *Jrnl.* 11 July (1889) II. 310 Jane was secreted while the Princess was with me. **1843** LYTTON *Last Bar.* III. ii, How had Sibyll dared to secrete from him this hoard. **1878** HUXLEY *Physiogr.* 74 [It] may be secreted for untold ages in subterranean reservoirs.

b. *refl.*

1764 HARMER *Observ.* XVIII. ii. 79 It appears too that her tent was a much safer place than any other in that encampment in which to secrete himself. **1833** HT. MARTINEAU *Cinnamon & Pearls* i. 5 No shady creek into which a skiff might glide and secrete itself. **1893** LELAND *Mem.* I. 160 A certain French lady..having fallen in love with the said captain, had secreted herself on board the vessel.

2. To remove secretly, to appropriate (the possessions of another) in a secret manner.

1749 FIELDING *Tom Jones* VI. xiii, The secreting of the 500 l. was a matter of very little hazard; whereas the detaining the sixteen guineas was liable to..discovery. **1783** BURKE *Rep. Aff. India* Wks. II. 265 Not the least hint, that he was delivering back to the Company money of their own, which he had secreted from them. **1849** MACAULAY *Hist. Eng.* vi. II. 58 There the bankrupt was taught how he might, without sin, secrete his goods from his creditors.

se'crete, *v.*^{3} *Hat-manuf.* [a. F. *secréter*, f. *secret* SECRET *sb.* (in the sense of 'secret process').] *trans.* To subject to the process of SECRETAGE.

1839 URE *Dict. Arts* 947 After the hairs are properly *secreted*, they are..shorn off by a machine. **1875** KNIGHT *Dict. Mech.*, *Secreting*, a process by which the hairs of hare and rabbit skins are rendered fit for felting.

secrete, obs. form of SECRET *sb.* and *a.*

secreted (sɪ'kriːtɪd), *ppl. a.*^{1} [f. SECRETE *v.*^{1} + -ED^{1}.] Produced by means of secretion.

1707 FLOYER *Physic. Pulse-Watch* 57 The Mass of Blood is chiefly Chyle, chang'd and mix'd with these secreted Humours. **1800** E. DARWIN *Phytol.* vi. 80 Every other secreted fluid in the animal body is in part absorbed again into the system. **1871** GARROD *Mat. Med.* (ed. 3) 413 Diuretics are also administered for the purpose of producing a large flow from the kidneys, so as to enable the secreted urine to hold in solution substances which would otherwise crystallise.

secreted (sɪ'kriːtɪd), *ppl. a.*^{2} [f. SECRETE *v.*^{2} + -ED^{1}.] Concealed, hidden.

1756 AMORY *J. Buncle* (1770) I. 259 Yet it is the small secreted spring that directs, draws, checks, and gives movement to every weight and wheel. **1805** WORDSW. *Prelude* XI. 141 Not in Utopia,—subterranean fields,—Or some secreted island, Heaven knows where!

secretee, obs. form of SECRECY.

‖**'secretement**, *adv. Obs. rare*$^{-1}$. [OF. *secretement*, f. *secret* SECRET *a.*] Secretly.

c **1470** HARDING *Chron.* CC. ii, Then the kyng, him fast to Langley sent There in the Freers to be buryed secretement.

†**se'creter.** *Obs. rare*$^{-1}$. [f. SECRETE *v.*^{2} + -ER^{1}.] One who conceals or hides away.

1755 *Gentl. Mag.* XXV. 184 The gentleman having detected the secreters of the dog..obliged them to give to this charity the money they had received.

secretin (sɪ'kriːtɪn). *Physiol.* [a. G. *secretin* (Bayliss & Starling 1902, in *Centralbl. f. Physiol.* XV. 682); cf. SECRETION and -IN^{1}.] A hormone that is released into the bloodstream from the gut, esp. in response to acidity, and stimulates pancreatic secretion.

1902 BAYLISS & STARLING in *Jrnl. Physiol.* XXVIII. 331 We have already suggested the name 'secretin' for this body, and as it has been accepted and made use of by subsequent workers it is as well to adhere to it. **1927** HALDANE & HUXLEY *Animal Biol.* i. 18 Food..stimulates the intestine chemically, causing it to secrete a special substance from its lining; this passes into the blood, circulates through the whole body, but, though it exerts no effect on most organs, it stimulates the pancreas..to activity. This substance is called secretin. **1962** [see *prosecretin* s.v. PRO-^{2} 1]. **1965** LEE & KNOWLES *Animal Hormones* viii. 121 Hydrochloric acid is not the only substance which induces the secretion of secretin; both digesting fat and bile salts are effective.

†**'secretine.** *Obs. rare*$^{-1}$. [a. OF. *secretin.*] A sacristan.

1607 R. C[AREW] tr. *Estienne's World of Wonders* 264 In which Church there was one which attended vpon these holy Martyrs..the Secretine.

secreting (sɪ'kriːtɪŋ), *ppl. a.* [f. SECRETE *v.*^{1} + -ING^{2}.] That secretes.

1807 *Med. Jrnl.* XVII. 81 High inflammation would only throw out coagulable lymph even on a secreting surface. **1837** P. KEITH *Bot. Lex.* s.v. *Carpellum*, The midrib extended and expanded to a due length and thickness forms the style, and its 'denuded, secreting, and humid apex', forms the stigma. **1871** GARROD *Mat. Med.* (ed. 3) 179 On the Secreting and Excreting Organs, with the exception of the skin, the effect of opium is to lessen their activity. **1899** *Allbutt's Syst. Med.* VIII. 740 The cysts arise from hypertrophy of the secreting part of the sweat-glands.

secretion (sɪ'kriːʃən). [a. F. *sécrétion*, ad. L. *sēcrētiōn-em*, n. of action f. *sēcernĕre* to separate, secrete: see SECERN *v.* Cf. Sp. *secrecion*, Pg. *secreção*, It. *secrezione.*]

1. *Phys.* In an animal or vegetable body, the action of a gland or some analogous organ in extracting certain matters from the blood or sap and elaborating from them a particular substance, either to fulfil some function within the body or to undergo excretion as waste.

1646 SIR T. BROWNE *Pseud. Ep.* III. xiii. 137 It cannot bee called their urine; not onely because they want those parts of secretion; but because it is emitted aversly or backward, by both sexes. **1704** J. HARRIS *Lex. Techn.* I, *Secretion*, is the separation of one Fluid from another in the Body of an Animal or Vegetable, by the means of Glands or something analogous to them. **1717** P BLAIR *Misc. Observ.* (1718) 12 Its being converted into Chyle and under-going the several Secretions throughout the Body. **1839** LINDLEY *Introd. Bot.* II. xii. (ed. 3) 372 Of Digestion, Respiration, and Secretion. **1878** BELL tr. *Gegenbaur's Comp. Anat.* 18 This process of secretion varies in character.

attrib. **1880** BESSEY *Bot.* 128 Intercellular spaces and secretion reservoirs. **1897** *Allbutt's Syst. Med.* IV. 34 Naunyn..concludes then, that the cholesterin of the bile is neither a product of general metabolism nor a specific secretion product of the liver.

2. *concr.* That which is produced by the action of a secreting organ.

1732 ARBUTHNOT *Aliments, Rules of Diet* 271 The Blood may be cleansed..perhaps better by Urine than any other Secretion. **1826** HENRY *Elem. Chem.* II. 433 The solids and fluids, thus produced, are sometimes elaborated by complicated organs called glands, and are then termed secretions. **1832** LINDLEY *Introd. Bot.* 222 A passage through which the peculiar secretions may, when elaborated, arrive at the stations where they are finally to be deposited. **1865** TYLOR *Early Hist. Man.* vii. 177 The milky secretion from a small frog or toad. **1882** VINES tr. *Sachs' Bot.* 568 When pollination takes place it [the Stigma] is covered with a viscid secretion.

b. *transf.* and *fig.*

1727 POPE, etc. *Art of Sinking* iii. 12 Poetry is a natural or morbid Secretion from the Brain. **1822** LAMB *Elia* Ser. I. *Praise of Chimney-Sweepers*, So may thy culinary fires, eased of the o'ercharged secretions from thy worse-placed hospitalities, curl up a lighter volume to the welkin. **1873** SPENCER *Stud. Sociol.* vi. 139 There have come down to us, from a long extinct race of men, those actual secretions of their daily life, which furnish colouring matter for a picture of them.

†**3.** In etymological sense: **a.** Separation. **b.** *Philos.* (= Gr. ἀπόκρισις.) Giving off of particles.

1696 BROOKHOUSE *Temple Open.* 58 The Extrusion of the Poor Reffugies was only an Act of Secretion By Him who has his Fan in his hand, who..dispersed them abroad, not for their Ruine but their Safety. **1678** CUDWORTH *Intell. Syst.* I. i. §5. 8 Generation and Corruption may be sufficiently explained by Concretion and Secretion, or Local Motion, without Substantial Forms and Qualities.

4. *Geol.* (See quot.)

1882 GEIKIE *Text-bk. Geol.* II. II. iv. (1885) 96 In a true concretion, the material at the centre has been deposited first, and has increased by additions from without... Where, on the other hand, cavities..have been filled up by the deposition of materials on their walls, and gradual growth inward, the result is known as a secretion.

Hence **se'cretional**, **se'cretionary** *adjs.*, pertaining to secretion.

1877 BENNETT *Thomé's Bot.* 224 But diseases are also caused through the influence of the soil, depending on an abnormal transformation of those substances out of which the tissue of the plant is constructed. These constitute what are called *secretional diseases.* **1888** TEALL *Brit. Petrogr.* 447 *Secretionary*, a term used to express a growth from without inwards, in contradistinction to *concretionary.*

secretious (sɪ'kriːʃəs), *a.* [f. L. *sēcrētiōn-em* SECRETION + -IOUS. Cf. *captious.*] Characterized by, or having the nature of secretion.

1707 FLOYER *Physic. Pulse-Watch* 151 When the Pulse runs too high..all the Evacuations of the secretious Humours are very violent. **1876** tr. *Wagner's Gen. Path.* 111 Generally possessing a secretious calcareous covering.

†**'secretist.** *Obs. rare*$^{-1}$. [f. SECRET *a.* or *sb.* + -IST. Cf. F. *secrétiste* (18th c. in Littré).] One who has special skill in any matter or special or private information.

1661 BOYLE *Cert. Physiol. Ess.* (1669) 35 Those Secretists that will not part with one Secret but in Exchange for another.

†**secre'titious**, *a. Obs. rare*$^{-1}$. [f. L. *sēcrēt-* (see SECRETE *v.*) + -ITIOUS^{2}.] Produced by secretion.

1696 FLOYER *Humours* Pref., They frequently have a Similitude or contrariety to the Secretitious Humours in taste and Quality.

secretive ('siːkrətɪv, sɪ'kriːtɪv), *a.* Also 5 secretife. [In 15th c. f. SECRET *a.* + -IVE. In mod. use, a back-formation from SECRETIVENESS; but apprehended as f. SECRETE *v.* + -IVE.]

†**1.** = SECRET *a. Obs. rare*$^{-1}$. (Used for rime.)

c **1470** HARDING *Chron.* CLXXVIII. ii, In chambre priuey and secretife [*rime-word* wife].

2. a. Of persons, their feelings, habits, etc.: Addicted or inclined to secrecy; reticent; not frank or open.

1853 C. BRONTE *Villette* ix, These things, contrary to her custom, and even nature—for she was not secretive—were most sedulously kept out of sight for a time. **1884** *Harper's Mag.* June 99/2 She was a shy, secretive maid. **1908** *Hibbert Jrnl.* Oct. 30 So secretive is this tribe that my patient inquiries have not even elicited their true name.

b. *transf.* of things. Also of looks, etc.: Indicating secretiveness.

1865 A. SMITH *Summer in Skye* I. 311 O'er his dark face there flitted A secretive smile. **1866** THORNBURY *Greatheart* I. 320 There was something secretive and sad about the sites of the graves. **1871** LOWELL *Study Wind.* 40 The evening lamps look yellower by contrast with the snow, and give the windows that hearty look of which our secretive fires have almost robbed them. **1892** 'MERRIMAN' *Slave of Lamp* vii, The Citizen Morot raised his secretive eyes.

3. Serving to conceal. *rare.*

1830 I. TAYLOR *Unitar.* 82 The pews.., secretive in their intention.

secretiveness ('siːkrə-, sɪ'kriːtɪvnɪs). [Formed after F. *secrétivité* (Phrenology; Gall, 1808), f. *secret* SECRET; see -IVE and -NESS. Now apprehended as f. SECRETIVE *a.*] The quality of being secretive; disposition to secrecy.

Originally used in Phrenology as the name of a 'propensity' having a special 'bump' allotted to it.

1815 SPURZHEIM *Physiogn. Syst.* (ed. 2) 329 Organ of the propensity to conceal, or Secretiveness. **1878** BAYNE *Purit. Rev.* vii. 265 He had no secretiveness in his nature, and could do nothing by halves. **1897** MARY KINGSLEY *W. Africa* 161 There is a strange sense of secretiveness about all these West African forests.

secretly ('siːkrɪtlɪ), *adv.* [f. SECRET + -LY^{2}.]

1. In a secret manner, in secret, not openly.

c **1386** [see SECRELY]. **1447** BOKENHAM *Seyntys* i. 769 (Horstm.) For lernyd he hadde ful secretlye Of a prest.. whan he shuld dye. **1537** WRIOTHESLEY *Chron.* (1875) I. 43 The King was maried secreatly at Chelsey, in Middlesex, to one Jane Seymor. **1596** SHAKS. *Merch. V.* II. iii. 7 Giue him this Letter, doe it secretly. *a* **1700** EVELYN *Diary* 18 June 1690, The Duke of Savoy.. did seacretly concert measures with, and afterwards declar'd for them. **1766** GOLDSM. *Vic. W.* iv, I still found them secretly attached to all their former finery. **1878** LECKY *Eng. in 18th C.* I. i. 119 He was secretly negotiating with the Pretender.

†**b.** With a hidden meaning. *Obs. rare.*

c **1430** LYDG. *Min. Poems* (Percy Soc.) 119 Poetis of olde fables han contryved,.. By whiche theyr witte was secretely approved. **1632** *Guillim's Heraldry* III. ii. (ed. 2) 115 This did the Poets secretly expresse, when they preferred Pallas to be the Gouernesse of Learning.

†**c.** Indirectly. *Obs. rare*$^{-1}$.

1656 RIDGLEY *Pract. Physick* 227 Antidotes for the Malignity, yet such as secretly respect the disease.

†**2.** In concealment or retirement. *Obs. rare.*

1535 COVERDALE *Ps.* xxx. 20 Thou hydest them priuely by thine owne presence from the proude men, thou kepest them secretly in thy tabernacle, from the strife of tongues. **1599** SHAKS. *Much Ado* IV. i. 205 Your daughter heere the Princesse (left for dead) Let her awhile be secretly kept in.

3. In an inaudible voice.

1608 TOPSELL *Serpents* 161 The dragon..falleth asleepe, the Indians in the meane-season watching, & muttering secretly words of Incantation. **1841** A. R. C. DALLAS *Past. Superintend.* 203 Repeating the Lord's Prayer after the Bishop; and afterwards joining secretly in the prayers which follow.

† 'secretness. *Obs.* [f. SECRET *a.* + -NESS.] The state or condition of being secret.

1. Secrecy, privacy; reticence. ***in secretness***: secretly.

1387–8 T. USK *Test. Love* I. v. (Skeat) 13 A thing enclosed under secretnesse of privyte. *a* **1475** ASHBY *Active Policy* 354 Kepe secretnesse as a secretarye. *Ibid.* 621 Whan any tellethe you any tale,.. than kepe it in secretnesse treuleche. *a* **1533** LD. BERNERS *Gold. Bk. M. Aurel.* (1546) Gj, He.. ought to entre into his owne secretnes, and to thynke profoundely. **1560** DAUS tr *Sleidane's Comm.* 342 Now again muttering something in great secreatnes. **1654** COKAINE *Dianea* 246 Being grown impatient of my timerous secretnesse.. I asked her Advice: If it were better to discover ones flames to a Mistris by Letters, word of mouth, or by the Intercession of others.

2. That which is secret.

c **1425** *Found. St. Bartholomew's* (E.E.T.S.) 13 And begane a litill while to hyde the secretnesse of his soule. *a* **1533** LD. BERNERS *Huon* xcv. 310 Whan ye were prisoner in Babylone I dyscoueryd the secretnes of my mynde to hym, and shewed hym of ye loue betwen you and me. **1623** LISLE *Ælfric on O. & N. T., Serm. Easterday* 13 Then ought we.. not to search rashly of that deepe secretnes aboue the measure of our vnderstanding.

secretor (sɪˈkriːtə(r)). *Physiol.* [f. SECRET(E *v.*¹ + -OR, originally to render G. *ausscheider* (Schiff & Sasaki 1932, in *Klin. Wochenschr.* 20 Aug. 1428/2).] **1. a.** One who secretes appreciable amounts of blood-group antigens with his or her bodily fluids.

1941 *Amer. Jrnl. Obstetrics & Gynecol.* XLII. 933 This applies to about 80 per cent of all individuals (secretors) and if a fetus of Group A belongs to the class of non-secretors (20 per cent).. the maternal iso-agglutinin anti-A may serve as the source of the intrauterine hemolytic process. **1950** *Sci. News* XV. 111 Most people secrete the appropriate blood group substances (antigens) in bodily secretions such as saliva and tears. About one-seventh of the population, however, do not do this, and are called 'non-secretors'... Some cysts, in 'secretors', contain the A and B substances in very high concentration. **1962** R. JEFFRIES *Exhibit No. Thirteen* xi. 112 An examination of the semen enabled a typing to be made... The murderer is from group B and is what is known as a secretor. **1971** J. Z. YOUNG *Introd. Study Man* xl. 585 The secretor genes are quite independent of the ABO genes.

b. *gen.* One who or that which secretes.

1972 *Sci. Amer.* Aug. 46/2 Recently Everitt and his colleagues have learned that when the female monkey's adrenals—the principal secretors of the male hormone androstenedione—are removed, her sexual receptivity is greatly reduced. **1977** *Lancet* 22 Oct. 841/2 Of these secretors, 50% secreted 50 μl of fluid and 10% secreted as much as 400 μl of fluid.

2. *attrib.* **secretor character, status,** the state of being or not being a secretor (sense 1 a).

1956 *Brit. Med. Jrnl.* 29 Sept. 728/1 We have obtained a series of unrelated duodenal ulcer cases and compared their secretor character with controls taken from the general population. **1970** GERSHOWITZ & NEEL in D. Aminoff *Blood & Tissue Antigens* 39 The secretor status of stomach cancer patients should be investigated. **1976** *Proc. R. Soc. Med.* LXIX. 36/2 Attempts have been made to discover whether individuals are carrying the dystrophia myotonica gene by examining their secretor status.

secretorie, -y, obs. forms of SECRETARY.

secretory (sɪˈkriːtərɪ), *a.* and *sb. Phys.* [f. L. *sēcrēt-* (see SECRETE *v.*) + -ORY. Cf. F. *sécrétoire.*]

A. *adj.* Having the function of secreting; pertaining to or concerned with the process of secretion.

1692 RAY *Creation* II. 64 The Glands.. give the Blood time to stop and separate through the Pores of the capillary Vessels into the Secretory ones. **1793** BEDDOES *Calculus* 39 Of all the secretory organs, the kidneys and the mammæ are most certainly and quickly affected by the passions and by food. **1872** HUXLEY *Physiol.* v. 102 The many secretory glands which separate certain substances from the blood at recurrent periods. **1884** BOWER & SCOTT *De Bary's Phaner.* 421 The fibrous strands which surround a secretory passage in the leaves of Pinus and the roots of Philodendron.

B. *sb.* A secreting vessel or duct.

1768 FOOTE *Devil* III. Wks. 1799 II. 276 These are thrown by the digestive powers into the secretory. **1822–29** *Good's Study Med.* (ed. 3) III. 409 Mercury is an universal stimulant and increases the action of all the secretories at one and the same time.

‖ **se'cretum.** *Antiq.* Pl. secreta. [L. *sēcrētum*, neut. of *sēcrētus* SECRET *a.*; in med.L. ellipt. for *sigillum secretum* secret seal.] (See quot. 1886.)

1864 BOUTELL *Her. Hist. & Pop.* xxiv. 399 The same individual also occasionally possessed and sealed with more than one Secretum. *Ibid.* 400 The Seals and Secreta of certain noble families. **1886** *Encycl. Brit.* XXI. 586/2 The aperture [over which a seal was placed] allowed a second matrix to be applied at the back. This was usually a smaller private seal called a *secretum*. **1909** FOX-DAVIES *Compl. Guide Her.* 408 The *secretum* of Isabelle de Flandres (c. 1308) has her shield placed between three lions.

sect (sɛkt), *sb.*¹ Also 4–6 secte, 5 sekte, 6 sekt, seacte, *pl.* sextes, *Sc. pl.* sekkis. [a. F. *secte* (14th c. in Hatz.-Darm.), or directly ad. L. *secta* following (used as cognate object in *sectam sequi*, to follow a particular course of conduct, to follow a person's guidance or example), hence a party or faction, a philosophical sect or school, a class or profession (in med.L. also the distinctive costume of a class or order of men), f. *sequ-* root of *sequī* to follow: for the formation cf. *sectārī* to pursue. The L. word was adopted also in other Rom. langs.: Sp., Pg. *secta*, It. *setta*.

It has been maintained that L. *secta* is the fem. pple. of *secāre* to cut, an ellipsis for *via secta*, from the phrase *viam secāre* (after Gr. τέμνειν ὁδόν) to make (lit. 'to cut') one's way. Formally this would be quite possible; but *secta* does not occur in the physical sense of 'way', nor does it appear that *via secta* was ever in use; and some of the uses of *secta* are more satisfactorily accounted for by derivation from *sequī* than from *secāre*.]

† **1.** A class or kind (of persons). *Obs.*

c **1384** CHAUCER *H. Fame* 1432 (Fairf.) Alderfirste, loo, ther I sighe,.. Hym of Secte saturnyne, The Ebrayke Iosephus. **1393** LANGL. *P. Pl.* C. XVI. 13 How þis couetise ouer-cam alle kynne sectes, As wel lerede as lewede. *c* **1400** *Rom. Rose* 5745 Eke in the same secte are set Alle tho that prechen for to get Worshipes, honour, and richesse. **1430–40** LYDG. *Bochas* III. i. (1494) i viij b, The sect of pouert hath a protection From all statutes to go at lyberte. **1515** BARCLAY *Egloges* iii. (1570) B vj b, Flatterers and hostlers, and other of this sect Are busy in thy chamber. **1540** PALSGR. *Acolastus* II. i. I j, Of whose secte .i. suite or sorte of profession we.. set forth abrode into the market stede many clientes. **1568** GRAFTON *Chron.* II. 932 The which act and priuilege did nourishe and encrease aboundauntly the sect and swarme of theeues and murderers. **1628** BURTON *Anat. Mel.*, Democr. to Rdr. (ed. 3) 15 [Of Physicians] I know many of their Sect [edd. 1, 2, of them] which haue taken Orders, in hope of a Benefice.

† **b.** A religious order. *Obs.*

Properly a use of sense 1; but Wyclif affects to take it in sense 4, as if the orders (esp. the mendicant orders) were new religions, competing with the 'sect' of Christ.

c **1380** WYCLIF *Wks.* (1880) 446 þes foure sectis newe brouȝt in, as emperour clerkis, munkis & chanouns & þes foure ordris freris, disturblen moost þis fiȝtinge chirche & putten it fro þe cours of crist. **1393** LANGL. *P. Pl.* C. XVII. 293 þoȝ men soȝt al sectes [*v.r.* þe sektis] of sistren & of breþeren. **1402** *Jack Upland* 106 Why stele ye mens children for to make hem of youre secte? *c* **1450** *St. Cuthbert* (Surtees) 416 þat he suld be of haly secte. **1533** GAU *Richt Vay* (1888) 104 Our halie fader ye paip and his bischopis giffis ane part of ye spulze quhilk thay reiff fra ye pwir to thir forsaid sekkis. **1574** tr. *Marlorat's Apocalips* 36 Wicked sectes haue bin brought into the worlde vnder the names of Austin, Bernard, Francis, Dominik and others. **1602** WARNER *Alb. Eng.* IX. li. (1612) 231 Ignatius then conceited had his sect, And crau'd Confirmance of the pope. **1779** G. KEATE *Sketches fr. Nat.* (ed. 2) I. 142 As I think that there are only two houses of La Trappe existing, it may not be improper to mention, that this sect was first founded about a century ago, with the sanction of Pope Innocent the Eleventh. **1814** CARY *Dante, Parad.* III. 108, I.. Made promise of the way her sect enjoins.

† **c.** The (human) race. *Obs. rare.*

c **1400** *Rom. Rose* 4859 Ne were ther generacioun Our sectis strene for to save. **1578** BANISTER *Hist. Man* III. 42 The Articulation of the head with the Vertebres.. diuine nature ye mother of humane sect, hath shewed therin more care.

d. Sex. Now only in illiterate use.

A special use of sense 1; possibly suggested by the similarity in sound with SEX. In mod.Eng. it may have originated afresh as an artificial pronunciation of *sek* (a singular evolved from the apparent plural *sex*) on the part of speakers of dialects that have final (k) for (kt).

c **1386** CHAUCER *Clerk's T.* 1171 For the wyues loue of Bathe Whos lyf and al hire secte god mayntene In heigh maistrie. **1387–8** T. USK *Test. Love* II. ii. (Skeat) I. 139 She me hath had so greet in worship, that I nil for nothing in open declare, that in any thing ayenst her secte may so wene. *a* **1592** GREENE *Alphonsus* v. Wks. (Grosart) XIII. 400 Although it be a shame For knights to combat with the female sect. **1608** MIDDLETON *Mad World* II. vi, 'Tis the easiest Art and cunning for our sect to counterfeit sicke. **1624** HEYWOOD *Gunaik.* I. 6 Their controversie was to be determined by Tyresias, (one that had beene of both sects). **1738** [G. SMITH] *Cur. Relat.* II. v. 77 These Robbers without Regard to Sect or Decency, stript all the Company stark naked. **1776** PRATT *Pupil Pleas.* (1777) I. 173 The most artfullest of his sect. **1824** SCOTT *St. Ronan's* xv, 'Ye have skeel of our sect, sir,' replied the dame. **1861** MAYHEW *Lond. Labour* III. 204 [Street-photographer *loq.*] A lady don't mind taking her bonnet off.. before one of her own sect.

† **2.** Distinctive costume (of a class or order). Also *transf.* the 'garb' or guise (of humanity). *Obs.*

1377 LANGL. *P. Pl.* B. XI. 237 Many tyme god hath ben mette amonge nedy peple, þere neuere segge hym seigh in secte of þe riche. *Ibid.* XIV. 258 He bereth þe signe of pouerte, And in þat secte owre saueoure saued al mankynde. **1393** *Ibid.* C. VIII. 130 And sitthe in oure secte as hit semed, þow deydest, On a fryday, in forme of man feledest oure sorwe.

† **3.** Body of followers or adherents. *Obs.*

1450 *Rolls of Parlt.* V. 204/2 The said John Newport and other of his secte.. so thretening the Kingis pepil of the Ile [etc.]. **1512** W. KNIGHT in Ellis *Orig. Lett.* Ser. II. I. 195 Sr William Sands and a few of his secte were in the contrarie opynyon of me. **1523** LD. BERNERS *Froiss.* I. clxxx. 216 The prouost and his sect exhorted hym therto. **1590–91** *Reg. Privy Council Scot.* IV. 562 The.. crafty practizes of Mr James Gordoun, fader bruthir to the Erll of Huntlie, and utheris of his sect. **1621** *Gude & Godlie B.* App. I. 234 Cum heir my Elect, and my awin sweit Sect, ȝour hyre sall not be in weir. [**1647** N. BACON *Disc. Gov. Eng.* I. lxvii. (1739) 169 *Et inde producit sectam suam*; that is, he brings his sect or suit, or such as do follow or affirm his complaint.] **1667** MILTON *P.L.* VI. 147 [Abdiel speaks.] My Sect thou seest, now learn too late How few somtimes may know, when thousands err.

4. A religious following; adherence to a particular religious teacher or faith.

† **a.** Applied to any of the main religions of the world, as Christianity, Judaism, or Islam; the principles, or the adherents collectively, of any one of these faiths. *Obs.*

c **1386** CHAUCER *Sqr.'s T.* 9 (Corpus) As of þe secte of which þat he was born he kepte his lay to which þat he was sworn. **1387** TREVISA *Higden* (Rolls) I. 129 Whan þat false prophete Machometys.. wroot and brouȝt yn þe false lawe and secte of Saracins. **1390** GOWER *Conf.* II. 182 And thus in thilke time tho Began the Secte upon this Erthe, Which of believes was the ferthe. *c* **1450** *Myrr. our Ladye* 85 Of what secte or contre so euer they be, hethen or crysten, sarasen or Iewe. **1483** CAXTON *Gold. Leg.* 73 b/1 Kynge Salamon louyd ouermoche.. straunge wymen of other sectes. **1530** RASTELL *Bk. Purgat.* III. xv. (*fin.*), Wolde to God that thou were of our holy secte and crysten beleve. **1553** EDEN *Treat. New Ind.* (Arb.) 14 Ye Soldan or chefe ruler hereof is of Mahumets secte, as are ye Turkes. *a* **1575** tr. *Pol. Verg. Eng. Hist.* (Camden No. 36) 74 Preaching the woord of Godd and sincere secte of Christe. **1592** KYD *Sol. & Pers.* III. i. 38 How did the Christians vse our Knights? *Bru.* As if that we and they had been one sect. **1600** R. CARR tr. *Mahumetan Hist.* 19 Abagan.. tooke vpon him the superstición of the sect of Mahumet. **1653** H. COGAN tr. *Pinto's Trav.* xx. 73 Whilest these wicked Miscreants [*sc.* Mohammedans] fortifie themselves in their devilish Sect, let us trust in our Lord. **1716** PRIDEAUX *O. & N. Test. Connected* (1718) I. I. III. 139 At this time [an. 522] all the idolatry of the world was divided between two sects, that is, the worshippers of images, who were called the Sabians, and the worshippers of fire, who were called the Magians.

b. †(*a*) A system of belief or observance distinctive of one of the parties or schools into which the adherents of a religion are divided; sometimes *spec.* a system differing from what is deemed the orthodox tradition; a heresy. *Obs.* (*b*) A body of persons who unite in holding certain views differing from those of others who are accounted to be of the same religion; a party or school among the professors of a religion; sometimes applied *spec.* to parties that are regarded as heretical, or at least as deviating from the general tradition.

the Clapham Sect: a name applied derisively early in the 19th c. to a coterie of persons of Evangelical opinions and conspicuous philanthropic activity, some of whom lived at Clapham; among the chief members were Wilberforce, Zachary Macaulay, and Henry Thornton.

13.. *S. Ambrose* 276 (*MS. Vernon*) in Horstm. *Alteng. Leg.* (1878) 12 Wiþ heretykes of þe secte of Arrian. **1382** WYCLIF *Acts* xxvi. 5 For vp [*v.r.* that bi] the moost certeyn secte of oure religioun, I lyuede a Farisee. **1390** GOWER *Conf.* I. 15 This new Secte of Lollardie. *c* **1449** PECOCK *Repr.* v. iii. 497 Aftir the daies of the Apostlis roosen also manye vntrewe sectis of Cristen men, as the sect of Valentynyanys. **1526** TINDALE 1 *Cor.* xi. 19 For there must be sectes amonge you. **1530** CROMWELL in Ellis *Orig. Lett.* Ser. III. II. 187 They wyll not discent from the Lutheran sekt. **1542–3** *Act 34 & 35 Hen. VIII*, c. 1 The damnable opinions of the secte of the anabaptistes. **1560** DAUS tr. *Sleidane's Comm.* 81 They that love sectes are in dede worthy of punyshement. **1577** VAUTROLLIER *Luther on Ep. Gal.* 221 The Jewes assured them selues that the Church.. should shortly be ouerthrowne: the which by an odious name they called a Sect. **1603** DRAYTON *Bar. Wars* IV. liv, And in her Sects, Religion lay confounded. **1613** SHAKS. *Hen. VIII*, v. iii. 81 Doe not I know you [Cromwell] for a Fauourer Of this new Sect? **1625** BACON *Ess., Viciss. Things* ¶ 5 When the Religion formerly receiued, is rent by Discords;.. you may doubt the Springing vp of a New Sect. **1641** J. JACKSON *True Evang. T.* I. 69 The Millenaries, a sect of learned, and criticall Christians, who expect in the last thousand years of the Church, the cream of all militant perfection. *a* **1727** NEWTON *Chronol. Amended* vi. (1728) 349 He reformed the religion of the Persians, which before was divided into many sects. **1788** GIBBON *Decl. & F.* l. V. 170 The church was distracted by the Nestorian and Monophysite sects. **1844** J. STEPHEN in *Edinb. Rev.* LXXX. 251 The Clapham Sect. **1859** FITZGERALD *Omar* xliii, The Grape that can with Logic absolute The Two-and-Seventy jarring Sects confute. **1879** L. STEPHEN *Hours in Library* Ser. III. 288 The Clapham Sect, amongst whom he [Macaulay] had been brought up.

c. In modern use, commonly applied to a separately organized religious body, having its distinctive name and its own places of worship; a 'denomination'. Also, in a narrower sense, one of the bodies separated from the Church. ***the sects***: applied by Anglicans to the various bodies of Dissenters, by Roman Catholics to all forms of Protestantism.

1577–87 HOLINSHED *Hist. Eng.* I. ii. 3/1 They (of all the other sects before specified) were suffered onlie to continue vnabolished. **1651** H. MORE *Mastix his Lett.* in *Enthus. Tri.* etc. (1656) 306 That Sect which are called Quakers. **1673** TEMPLE *Observ. United Prov.* Wks. 1731 I. 58 In Amsterdam.. almost all Sects, that are known among Christians, have their publick Meeting-places. **1676** GLANVILL *Ess.* v. 24 The common practice (at least among the Sects) of declaring against Reason as an Enemy to Religion. **1776** ADAM SMITH *W.N.* v. i. (1869) II. 377 Almost every different congregation might have made a little sect by itself, or have entertained peculiar tenets of its own. **1818** SCOTT *Br. Lamm.* xxxi. But with all the more severe prejudices and principles of his sect, Bide-the-bent possessed a sound judgment. **1828** MACAULAY *Ess., Hallam* ¶ 19 We might say that the massacre of St. Bartholomew was intended to extirpate, not a religious sect, but a political party. **1836** ARNOLD in Stanley *Life & Corr.* (1845) II. 23 Almost all who profess to value Christianity seem when they are brought to the test to care only for their own sect. **1836** H. ROGERS *J. Howe* iii. (1863) 46 It might be said of the latter years of the Commonwealth, that there were almost as many sects as worshippers. **1857** TOULMIN SMITH *Parish* 436 The church is not a building for the service of any sect. **1872** MORLEY *Voltaire* (1886) 4 To each alike of the countless orthodox sects his name is the symbol for the prevailing of the gates of hell.

d. *abstr.* (Cf. PARTY *sb.* 6 b.)

1865 LECKY *Ration.* (1878) II. 104 The spirit of sect, or an attachment not to abstract principles, but to a definite and organised ecclesiastical institution, is a spirit essentially similar to patriotism.

5. The system or body of adherents of a particular school of philosophy.

1387 TREVISA *Higden* (Rolls) III. 359 He [Aristotle] brouȝte up þe secte þat is i-cleped Peripatetica. **1579–80** NORTH *Plutarch, Brutus* (1595) 1070 Cassius being in opinion an Epicurian,..spake..thus. In our sect, Brutus, we haue an opinion, that [etc.]. *a* **1591** H. SMITH *Arrow agst. Atheists* (1637) 18 Three of the most learned that ever professed the Platonicke sect. **1671** MILTON *P.R.* IV. 279 The Sect Epicurean. **1693** DRYDEN *Persius* i. Argt., Our Poet was a Stoick Philosopher; and..all his Moral Sentences..are drawn from the Dogma's of that Sect. **1704** HEARNE *Duct. Hist.* (1714) 399 The Chaldæan Philosophers were divided into Sects, but the Distinction arose from the Nature of their Studies. **1798** FERRIAR *Eng. Historians* 244 Some of the ancient philosophical sects, received their denominations from their places of instruction. **1868** FARRAR *Seekers after God, Seneca* Introd. 5 The purest and most exalted philosophic sect of antiquity was 'the sect of the Stoics'.

6. *transf.* (from senses 4 and 5). A school of opinion in politics, science, or the like; also, more or less jestingly, applied to a group of persons who attach importance to some peculiar crotchet about matters of social custom or the like.

1605 SHAKS. *Lear* v. iii. 18 *Lear*...And wee'l weare out In a wall'd prison, packs and sects of great ones, That ebbe and flow by th' Moone. **1609** B. JONSON *Epicœne* Prol., But in this age, a sect of Writers are, That, onely, for particular likings care, And will taste nothing that is populare. **1692** BENTLEY *Boyle Lect.* iii. 18 The Atheists upon this occasion are divided into Sects. **1712** STEELE *Spect.* No. 479 ¶5 Socrates, who is by all Accounts the undoubted Head of the Sect of the Hen-peck'd, own'd..that [etc.]. **1776** ADAM SMITH *W.N.* v. ii. (1869) II. 420 That sect of men of letters in France who call themselves the economists. **1788** *Trifler* No. 9. 113 The first sect on which I shall recommend you to try your skill..are Old Maids. **1792** JEFFERSON *Writ.* (1859) III. 450 A sect has shown itself among us, who declare they espoused our constitution..as a step to an English constitution. **1821** SHELLEY *Epipsych.* 149, I never was attached to that great sect, Whose doctrine is, that each one should select Out of the crowd a mistress or a friend, And all the rest..commend To cold oblivion. **1821–30** LD. COCKBURN *Mem.* (1856) 367 The Whigs gave him a public dinner on the 21st of February, at which about 300 attended—the largest convocation of the sect that had yet taken place. **1837** WHEWELL *Hist. Induct. Sci.* (1857) I. 175 The doctrine made a sect among astronomers. **1843** R. J. GRAVES *Syst. Clin. Med.* xvii. 197 This I am sure will seem strange to the various sects of pathologists and theorists. **1899** W. S. LILLY *1st Princ. Politics* 135 Socialism is rather a sect than a party.

†**b.** With pseudo-etymological reference: A 'section' of mankind. *Obs.*

1708–9 SWIFT *Let. to Abp. King* 6 Jan., But the world is divided into two sects, those that hope the best, and those that fear the worst. *a* **1764** LLOYD *Poet* 254 There were two sects—the Bad, the Good.

†**c.** *transf.* Way of thinking, turn of mind. *Obs.*

1580–3 GREENE *Mamillia* I. (1592) 2 b, Yet he could haue a quiet conscience, til he might see her of the same sect, and as deadly to hate it [court life], as he did loth it.

†**7.** = SEPT (Irish). *Obs. rare.*

1536 *St. Papers Hen. VIII* (1834) II. 328 There are another sect of the Borkes, and divers of the Irisshery, towardes Slygoo. **1540** *Ibid.* III. 235 Thos sectes of people called the Cavenaghes.

†**8.** Law. *sect of court* (med.L. *secta curiæ*): 'Suit and Service done by Tenants at the Court of their Lord' (J. Harris *Lex. Techn.* 1710, II).

1546 *Yorks. Chantry Surv.* (Surtees) II. 245 To the erle of Comberland for secte of courte for the lande in Skipton. **1546** *Mem. Ripon* (Surtees) III. 13 Sir William Malyory knight for lande in Nunwike and secte of Courte xiij d. John Norton for Fre Ferme and secte of Courte xiij d. **1571** *Reg. Privy Council Scot.* II. 89 With power to..continew court or courtis of Justiciarie..; sectis to mak be callit; absentis to amerchiat. **1578** *Ibid.* III. 13.

9. *attrib.* and *Comb.*, as ***sect-ascendancy***, †***-follower***, ***-founder***, ***-leader***, †***-maker***, †***-master*** (= sect-founder); ***sect-forming***, ***-ridden*** adjs.

1903 *Q. Rev.* Apr. 570 To the pre-Reformation policy of race-ascendency was added, under Elizabeth, that of *sect-ascendency. **1556** OLDE *Antichrist* 102 b, To gratifie his owne *secte folowers. **1891** *Ch. Times* 28 Aug. 824/1 The *sect-forming, dislocating career of the subsequent centuries. **1861** J. EDKINS in Mrs. Edkins *Chinese Scenes* (1863) 273 He receives revelations, becomes a *sect-founder. *a* **1711** KEN *Hymnotheo* Poet. Wks. 1721 III. 389 *Sect-Leaders their own Visions may impose. **1896** *Q. Rev.* Jan. 91 The actual methods adopted by the Hindu sect-leaders. **1530** TINDALE *Prol. 1 Cor.*, Ther came immediatly false Apostles & *sectemakers, drue euery man disciples after hym. **1656** TRAPP *Expos. Acts* xv. 36 Seducers and sect-makers. **1565** ALLEN *Def. Purg.* 14 They doo not folowe these *Secte masters, as scholares moued by any probability of theire teachers persuation. *a* **1708** T. WARD *Eng. Ref.* i. (1716) 73 As if the Holy Isaac were An Heretick or Sect-Master. **1840** MILL *Diss. & Disc.* (1859) I. 444 This *sect-ridden country.

sect, *sb.*[2] *rare.* [? ad. L. *sectum*, neut. pa. pple. of *secāre* to cut. Cf. SET *sb.*] ? A cutting from a plant; in quots. *fig.*

1604 SHAKS. *Oth.* I. iii. 336 Our carnall Stings, or vnbitted Lusts: whereof I take this, that you call Loue, to be a Sect, or Seyen. **1864** SWINBURNE *Atalanta* 1686 The son lies close about thine heart,..Eats thee and drinks thee..thyself, a sect of thee.

†**sect**, *v.*[1] *nonce-word.* [f. SECT *sb.*[1]] **a.** *trans.* To treat as a sect. **b.** *to sect it*: to behave as a sect.

1656 S. H. *Gold. Law* 13 Would you that Prelacy and Priesthood should perk up again, and under pretense of Religion,..be-heretick, and sect you, and then dissect you by persecutions? *Ibid.* 81 The Priests of all sorts sect it, so do all religious persons faction and party it.

†**sect**, *v.*[2] *Obs.* [f. L. *sect-*, ppl. stem of *secāre* to cut.] *trans.* To cut or divide (into equal parts).

1657 TOMLINSON *Renou's Disp.* 245 Its leaves are sected into slender parts. **1697** G. K. *Disc. Geom. Problems* 10 He who understands..to sect any angle into 3. 5. 6. as is above shewed, will by the like Method and Praxis be able to sect any angle into 7. 8. 9. 10. &c. equal parts. *Ibid.*, How a Semicircle may be sected into any number of equal parts. **1882** G. A. SALA *Amer. Revisited* II. ii. 19 Almost every thoroughfare in the city being sected and intersected by lines for horse-cars.

-sect [ad. L. *sect-*, pa. ppl. stem of *secāre* to cut: cf. SECT *v.*[2]], a formative element of vbs. (as *hemisect*, *transect*, *trisect*) and adjs. (as *multisect*); *spec.* in *Bot.* in adjs. denoting forms of leaves (as *palmatisect*, *pedatisect*, *pennatisect*).

†**sectare**, obs. Sc. form of SECTARY.

1563 WINȜET *Bk. Quest.* i. Wks. (S.T.S.) I. 70 *marg.*, Because nane sectare can ansuer heir without manifest confusioun of his errour.

sectarial (sɛk'tɛərɪəl), *a.* [f. SECTARY (or its source med.L. *sectārius*) + -AL[1].] Pertaining to or distinctive of sect. Chiefly used with reference to Indian religions.

1816 G. S. FABER *Orig. Pagan Idol.* I. 137 The doctrine in question was by no means peculiar to the Stoics: it was held also by the philosophers of the other schools. As their sectarial differences however are of no importance in the present inquiry [etc.]. **1832** COLEMAN *Myth. Hindus* 163 Sectarial marks. These symbols are made of ashes, cow-dung [etc.]. **1844** H. H. WILSON *Brit. India* I. viii. I. 545 Numerous sectarial divisions amongst the Hindus. **1886** *Guide Exhib. Galleries Brit. Mus.* 208 They [the Jains] worship chiefly twenty-four sectarial saints or Jins.

sectarian (sɛk'tɛərɪən), *a.* and *sb.* [f. SECTARY + -AN.] **A.** *adj.*

1. Pertaining to a sectary or sectaries; 'belonging to a schismatical sect' (Phillips, ed. Kersey, 1706). *Obs.* exc. *Hist.*

App. first used in the Commonwealth period by the Presbyterians with reference to the Independents; subsequently by Anglicans with reference to Nonconformists.

1649 in *Milton's Wks.* (1738) I. 346 The Sectarian Party in England. **1650** *Rec. Comm. Gen. Assembly* (S.H.S.) III. 92 That Sectarian armie now infesting this Kingdome. **1664** H. MORE *Myst. Iniq.* Apol. 545 Which is..to arm the Sectarian Rabbles, that phansy themselves such Inspiradoes, against the orderly-Reformed Churches. **1687** DRYDEN *Hind. & P.* III. 739 But that unfaithful Test unfound will pass The dross of atheists and sectarian brass. **1822** A. CUNNINGHAM *Tradit. Tales, Placing Scot. Minister* (1887) 89 To all this answered Micah Meen, a sectarian mason. **1828** P. CUNNINGHAM *N.S. Wales* (ed. 3) II. 244 Drawling out the words of Scripture with deep sectarian drone. **1834** SOUTHEY *Doctor* cix. (1862) 265 When a hawker came he had no pestiferous tracts, either seditious or sectarian, for sale.

2. Pertaining to a sect or sects; confined to a particular sect; bigotedly attached to a particular sect.

In recent use, often a pejorative synonym of *denominational*, esp. with reference to education (N.E.D.).

1796 BURKE *Regic. Peace* Wks. VIII. 237 They..have been taught to look on religious opinions as the only cause of enthusiastick zeal, and sectarian propagation. **1836** ARNOLD in Stanley *Life & Corr.* (1845) II. 23 All our education must be Christian, and not be sectarian. **1837** *Ibid.* 91 A Christian, and yet not sectarian University. **1840** CARLYLE *Heroes* iii. (1841) 149 Dante does not come before us as a large catholic mind; rather as a narrow, and even sectarian mind. **1841** E. MIALL in *Nonconf.* I. 1 A natural and invariable tendency..to fall into distinct bodies and become sectarian, both in spirit and in aim. **1876** J. GRANT *Burgh Sch. Scot.* II. 419 The burgh and parish Schools of Scotland were never Sectarian. **1877** CANDLISH in *Encycl. Brit.* VII. 338/2 There are some doctrines in every system that are merely sectarian, adopted by one particular branch of the church, but not recognized by others as correct expressions of Christian faith and life. **1884** LIDDON in J. O. Johnston *Life & Lett.* (1904) 331, I am not at all frightened by the word 'sectarian'. Christianity *is* sectarian as against the non-Christian world. **1903** *Brit. Weekly* 11 June 219/3 He was reluctantly compelled, for conscience sake, to refuse that part of the education rate which would go to the support of sectarian schools. *Ibid.* 219/4 An audience who loudly cheered every declaration of determined resistance to the sectarian rate.

B. *sb.*

1. Originally, an adherent of the 'sectarian party' (i.e. the Independents as designated by the Presbyterians); subsequently, a member of a schismatic sect, a schismatic. Now chiefly *Hist.*

1654 R. WILLIAMS in *Collect. Mass. Hist. Soc.* Ser. III. X. 2 Youre Father and all the people of God in England, formerly called the *Puritanus Anglicanus*, of late Round-heads, now the Sectarians (as more or lesse cut of from the Parishes) they are now in the sadle and at the helme. **1685** BUNYAN *Pharisee & Publ.* 7 The Pharisee was a Sectarian, one that deviated..in his Worshipping from the way of God;..for such an one I count a Sectarian. **1807** SOUTHEY *Espriella's Lett.* III. 79 Charles willingly permitted this, because he dreaded the political opinions of these Sectarians. **1816** —— *Lay of Laureate* liii, The stern Sectarian in unnatural league Joins her to war against their hated foe. **1818** COLERIDGE in *Lit. Rem.* (1838) III. 197 The *Ecclesia* has been an eclipse to the intellect of both Churchmen and Sectarians. **1860** MOTLEY *Netherl.* ii. (1868) I. 25 The Queen of England hated Anabaptists, Calvinists, and other Sectarians.

2. An adherent of a specified sect; a sectary of a particular teacher. Now *rare.*

1819 *Ann. Reg., Chron.* (1820) 273 Shortly after it was agreed, that the family of the plaintiff should become his sectarians, and they accordingly joined the Baptist society and became a part of his congregation. **1828** J. F. COOPER *Notions of Amer.* II. 328 The whole number of the sectarians [*i.e.* Shakers] is, however, far from great. **1836** LYTTON *Athens* (1837) II. 416 A general feeling of alarm and suspicion broke out against the sage [Pythagoras] and his sectarians. **1875** MERIVALE *Gen. Hist. Rome* lxv. (1877) 522 The constancy of these sectarians inflamed, no doubt, the anger of rulers who were accustomed to more pliant submission.

3. A bigoted adherent of a sect; one whose views or sympathies are sectarian.

1827 CARLYLE *Germ. Rom.* IV. 22 Shakspeare is no sectarian: to all he deals with equity and mercy. **1855** *Punch* 27 Jan. 34/2 Sectarians who believe that no good deed can be done, except by a votary of M'Howl and O'Muggins. **1867** EMERSON *Lett. & Soc. Aims, Progr. Cult.* Wks. (Bohn) III. 226 The narrow sectarian cannot read astronomy with impunity.

sectarianism (sɛk'tɛərɪənɪz(ə)m). [f. prec. + -ISM.] The sectarian spirit; adherence or excessive attachment to a particular sect or party, esp. in religion; hence often, adherence or excessive attachment to, or undue favouring of, a particular 'denomination'.

1817 COLERIDGE *Biogr. Lit.* I. xii. 249 The spirit of sectarianism has been..the cause of our failures. We have imprisoned our own conceptions by the lines, which we have drawn, in order to exclude the conceptions of others. **1818** —— in *Lit. Rem.* (1836) I. 89 [In Shakespeare] there is no sectarianism, either of politics or religion. **1833** MILL *Diss. & Disc.* (1859) I. 73 We shall find in that art [Music], so peculiarly the expression of passion, two perfectly distinct stiles; one of which may be called the poetry, the other the oratory of music. This difference, being seized, would put an end to much musical sectarianism. **1850** KINGSLEY *Alt. Locke* i, For art and poetry were tabooed both by my rank and my mother's sectarianism. **1870** *Athenæum* 30 Apr. 573 There is nothing in the poems before us to denote sectarianism in Art or to provoke antagonism from any class of true critics in poetry. **1889** *Spectator* 27 Apr., The book is Roman Catholic, but there is no bigotry or narrow sectarianism about it.

sectarianize (sɛk'tɛərɪənaɪz), *v.* [Formed as prec. + -IZE.]

1. *intr.* To act in a sectarian manner.

1842 FOSTER in *Life & Corr.* (1846) II. 451 We dissenters ..having no prelatical authorities over us, may sectarianize and fight as much as we please. **1874** *Contemp. Rev.* XXIII. 185 They sectarianize, in short, just as naturally as Churches.

2. *trans.* To render sectarian, to reduce to the level of a sect; to imbue with sectarian feelings or principles.

1846–9 S. R. MAITLAND *Ess.*, etc. 279 [tr. Luther.] Human nature when it is sectarianized. **1860** G. P. MARSH *Lect. Eng. Lang.* 643 To revise under present circumstances, is to sectarianise, to divide the one catholic, English Bible,..into a dozen different revelations. **1866** *Ch. Times* 24 Mar., Those who strive to sectarianize the Church. **1883** *Jrnl. Educ.* XVIII. 83 Sectarianizing the schools.

Hence **sec'tarianizing** *vbl. sb.* and *ppl. a.*

1908 *Athenæum* 30 May 666/1 The 'sectarianizing' of the Church, and of any and every form of Christianity. **1909** *Even. Post* (N.Y.) 7 Aug. 6 To strive to catholicise his own communion, that it might become a reconciling power, instead of a sectarianising system of human device.

sectarianly (sɛk'tɛərɪənlɪ), *adv. rare.* [f. SECTARIAN *a.* + -LY[2].] In a sectarian manner.

1853 E. G. HOLLAND *Mem. J. Badger* xix. (1854) 384 Let it not be thought that we speak sectarianly.

sectarism ('sɛktərɪz(ə)m). Now *rare.* [f. SECTAR-Y + -ISM.]

1. The principles, spirit, or practice characteristic of sectaries; sectarianism.

1643 SIR J. SPELMAN *Case of Affairs* 30 Especially now when Schisme and Sectarisme do with such authoritie invade us. **1721** STRYPE *Eccl. Mem.* II. I. xxix. 240 These Checks were given to Sectarism and Popery. **1822** MRS. E. NATHAN *Langreath* III. 195 The charitably religious sentiments of Mrs. Dalton, untainted by the narrow trammels of sectarism. **1835** I. TAYLOR *Spir. Despot.* iv. 125 Sectarism contradicts the first rudiment of Christian combination.

2. A variety of 'sectarism'; a sectarian body.

1821 JEFFERSON *Autob.* Writ. (1892) I. 52 In process of time however, other sectarisms were introduced, chiefly of the Presbyterian family.

†'**sectarist.** *Obs.* [f. SECTAR-Y + -IST.] = SECTARY *sb.* 1.

1618 MIDDLETON *Peacemaker* Wks. (Bullen) VIII. 330 Sectarists and schismatics shall break the peace of God. **1796** MORSE *Amer. Geog.* II. 612 One Hamed, a modern sectarist, and an enemy to the ancient doctrine of the califs. **1802** in Picton *L'pool Munic. Rec.* (1886) II. 401 Any sectarists or dissenting congregation. **1833** I. TAYLOR *Fanat.* viii. 308 The blasphemous arrogance of sectarists.

sectary ('sɛktərɪ), *sb.* and *a.* Also 6 sectorie, 6–7 sectarie. Cf. SECTUARY. [ad. F. *sectaire*, or its source med.L. *sectārius* (Diefenbach), f. *secta* SECT *sb.*[1] Cf. Sp., Pg. *sectario*, It. *settario*.]

A. *sb.*

1. A member of a sect; one who is zealous in the cause of a sect.

1558 MORWYNG tr. *Joseph Ben Gorion's Hist. Jews* (1561) 23 One Dogrus.. whom they slewe, & muche people besides of the auncientes of that sect, so that the Sectaries were in great distresse. **1596** BELL *Surv. Popery* I. v. vi. 144 Thomists, and Jesuites, to be the selfe same sectaries. **1771** *Lett. Junius* lix. (1788) 314 The fundamental principles of Christianity may still be preserved, though every zealous sectary adheres to his own exclusive doctrine. **1780** COWPER *Nightingale & Glowworm* 27 Hence jarring sectaries may learn Their real interest to discern. *a* **1832** BENTHAM *Infl. Time & Place in Legisl.* Wks. 1843 I. 173 The sectary of every religion.. is exposed to the dread of invisible agents. **1861** M. ARNOLD *Pop. Educ. France* 147 It is not as religious sectaries they [school inspectors] have to discharge their duties, but as civil servants. **1869** A. HARWOOD tr. *E. de Pressensé's Early Yrs. Chr.* III. ii. 378 John.. exhibited sometimes the narrow spirit of the sectary. **1883** *Fortn. Rev.* Feb. 199 Many a bitter sectary, thirsting for the discomfiture of his opponents, was tripped up by it.

2. An adherent of a schismatical or heretical sect. In the 17–18th c. commonly applied to the English Protestant Dissenters. Now chiefly *Hist.*

1556 J. CLEMENT in Strype *Eccl. Mem.* (1721) III. App. lxi. 214 All other Heretikes and Sectaries. **1569** BP. PARKHURST *Injunct.* A iv b, Whether you know of any sectaries that vse to make any priuate conuenticles in priuate mens houses. **1590** J. GREENWOOD *Collect. Art.* B j b, They pronounce vs newe sectories. **1605** MARSTON *Dutch Courtezan* III. (end), Now I am discontented, Ile turne Sectarie, that is fashion. **1609** BIBLE (Douay) *Exod.* vii. Annot. 171 Zuinglius, Caluin, Beza, and other Sectaries. **1613** SHAKS. *Hen. VIII*, v. iii. 70 *Gard.* My Lord, my Lord, you are a Sectary. **1656** BLOUNT *Glossogr.*, *Sectary*, one that follows private opinions in Religion, a Ring-leader of a Sect, a seditious, factious person. **1690** CHILD *Disc. Trade* (1698) 213 Their giving liberty.. to all Religions, as well Jews and Roman Catholicks, as Sectaries, gives security to all their Inhabitants. **1762–71** H. WALPOLE *Vertue's Anecd. Paint.* (1786) III. 2 Sectaries have no ostensible enjoyments... The arts that civilize society are not calculated for men who mean to rise on the ruins of established order. **1779** JOHNSON *L.P.*, *Cowley* 5 The omission of his name in the register of St. Dunstan's parish, gives reason to suspect that his Father was a sectary. **1808** SYD. SMITH *Methodism* Wks. 1859 I. 88/1 Mr. Ingram.. has talked a great deal about dissenters, ..we shall endeavour.. to present him [the reader] with a near view of those sectaries, who are at present at work upon the destruction of the orthodox churches. **1812** CRABBE *Tales* xiv. 264 Now, as a sectary, he had all his life As he supposed, been with the Church at strife. **1824** LANDOR *Imag. Conv.*, *Jas. I & Casaubon* Wks. 1846 I. 30 Sectary! Those who dissent from the domineering party have always been thus stigmatized. **1860** MOTLEY *Netherl.* ii. (1868) I. 27 Many sectaries experienced much inhuman treatment. **1864** J. PAYN *Sir Massingberd* i, They had been poachers, or radicals, or sectaries (as Dissenters were then called). **1876** J. GRANT *One of the Six Hundred* ix. 76 The English sectaries warned the General Assembly to begone from Edinburgh. **1903** *Blackw. Mag.* Dec. 757/2 A large boarding-house for sectaries, called a College, has sprung up somewhere behind Holywell.

3. A follower or disciple *of* a particular leader, teacher, party, or school. Now *rare* (with mixture of sense 1). †Also, a votary *of* a particular study, pursuit, etc.

1589 R. HARVEY *Pl. Perc.* 7 It were enough to entitle those Browne sectaries of the Blacke Prince, with the name of traytors. **1591** SPENSER *M. Hubberd* 833 He would scoffe at learning, and eke scorne The Sectaries thereof, as people base And simple men. **1593** G. HARVEY *Pierces Super.* 144 Times alter: and as Fortune hath more sectaries, then Vertue; so Pleasure hath more adherents, then Proffit. **1605** SHAKS. *Lear* I. ii. 164 (Qos.) How long haue you beene a sectary Astronomicall? **1609** HOLLAND *Amm. Marcell.* 109 Aristotle.. sending Calisthenes, a sectarie [*marg.* or disciple] and kinsman of his, unto K. Alexander, gave him [etc.]. **1675** R. BURTHOGGE *Causa Dei* 108 Mr. Hobbs or any of his Sectaries. **1704** N. N. tr. *Boccalini's Advts. fr. Parnass.* III. 146 Which Mahomet so strongly infused into his Sectaries. **1800** *Asiat. Ann. Reg.*, *Misc. Tracts* 79/1 Not votaries of Brahma, but sectaries of Buddha. **1879** FARRAR *St. Paul* I. 269 The Sectaries of an obsolete covenant.

†**4.** A sect. *Obs. rare.*

1643 HOWELL *Twelve Treat.* (1661) 299 One of the fruits of this blessed Parlement, and of these two Sectaries is, that they have made more Jewes and Atheists then I think there is in all Europe besides. **1651** BIGGS *New Disp* Summary § 11 The two grand Sectaries in Physick, and their clashing described. **1764** T. HUTCHINSON *Hist. Mass.* iv. (1765) 431 What they called a sectary sprang up in the Massachusets colony.

B. *adj.* Of or pertaining to a sect; sectarian.

1590 H. BARROW in *Conferences* III. 51 The Apostle.. speaketh of.. sectorie Teachers & people following them. **1602** T. FITZHERBERT *Apol.* 48 A few poor Sectary Caluinists hated & contemned by all other sectes of the same breed. **1638** LD. DIGBY *Lett. conc. Relig.* (1651) 3 A kind of Sectary passion. **1649** HEYLIN *Relat. & Observ.* II. 4 They ..sent them by their Agitators and sectary Priests into all Counties. **1798** EDGEWORTH *Pract. Educ.* (1811) II. 427 Sectary-meta-physicians.. will, we fear be disappointed in our chapters on Memory—Imagination and Judgment. They will not find us the partizans of any system.

sectator (sɛk'teɪtə(r)). Now *rare.* Also 6–7 sectatour. [a. L. *sectātor*, agent-n. f. *sectārī*, freq. of *sequī* to follow: see SECT *sb.*[1] Cf. F. *sectateur*.]

1. A follower, disciple; one who follows a particular school, teacher, or leader; a partisan, sectary.

1541 R. COPLAND *Galyen's Terap.* 2 D ij b, The sectatours of Thessalus, that is to wyt they that obserue his preceptes. **1566** PAINTER *Pal. Pleas.* xxiii. (1569) I. 43 b, It was tolde to the Philosopher Phauorinus, that the wyfe of one of his Sectators and Scholers, was [etc.]. **1585** T. WASHINGTON tr. *Nicholay's Voy.* III. xxii. 112 [He] doth forbid al his sectators Mahometistes to drinke wine. **1614** RALEIGH *Hist. World* I. iii. § 1. 33 Those writers which gaue themselues to follow and imitate others, were in all things so obseruant sectatours of those Masters,.. as [etc.]. **1624** [ABBOTT] *Visibility of True Ch.* 60 And therefore.. as sectators of Wiclife, they were condemned in the Councell of Constance. **1644** DIGBY *Nat. Bodies* xxxviii. 344 The latter sectatours, or rather pretenders of Aristotle. **1664** EVELYN tr. *Freart's Archit.* I. vi. 22 Such markes as clearly shewed him.. to have been a Sectator of these great Masters of Antiquity. **1698** FRYER *Acc. E. India & P.* 53 Not to be remedied by any Panacea of their Esculapian Sectators. **1741** WARBURTON *Div. Leg.* (1846) III. 250 The origin and progress of the folly and the various views of its Sectators in supporting it, are here accounted for and explained. **1804** EARL MALMESBURY *Diaries & Corr.* IV. 286 The sectators of each of them.. increased this sentiment [of personal enmity].. by their virulent and exaggerated reports. **1853** SOYER *Pantroph.* 175 Orpheus, Pythagoras, and their sectators,.. unceasingly recommended in their discourses to abstain from eggs. **1888** DOUGHTY *Arabia Deserta* I. 264 They themselves are fanatic sectators of the old Koran reading.

2. *Law.* One who is bound to 'suit of court'. Now only *Hist.* (Perh. merely Law Latin.)

1860 INNES *Scot. in Mid. Ages* vii. 207 In the court, so composed of all the vassals of a baron—the suitors or sectators of a barony—were discussed the affairs of the barony.

Hence †**sec'tatorship.** *rare*$^{-1}$.

1652 URQUHART *Jewel* Wks. (1834) 213 If a joint and unanimous course were taken to have their noblemen free from baseness, their churchmen from avarice.., their meaner sort from implicit sectatorship.

sectile ('sɛktɪl, -aɪl), *a.* [a. F. *sectile*, ad. L. *sectilem*, f. *sect-*, ppl. stem of *secāre* to cut.] Capable of or suited for being cut. † **a.** *sectile leek* [= L. *sectile porrum* Juv.], a dwarf or stunted variety of *Allium Porrum. Obs. rare*$^{-1}$.

1716 M. DAVIES *Athen. Brit.* II. 349 The Sectile or Cropt Leeks are such as are cut off for the Kitchen.

b. *Min.* (See quot. 1805.)

1805 WEAVER tr. *Werner's External Charac. Fossils* 196 *Sectile* are those fossils whose integrant particles are coherent, but not perfectly immoveable one among another. Sectile is a medium between brittle and malleable. **1839** URE *Dict. Arts* 1141 Bituminous shale is a species of soft, sectile slate-clay. **1879** RUTLEY *Stud. Rocks* x. 157 Distinguished by its inferior hardness, being sectile, while iron pyrites cannot be cut with a knife.

c. *Bot.* (See quot.)

1899 HEINIG *Gloss. Bot. Terms*, *Sectile*, divided into small pieces.

Hence **sec'tility**, sectile quality.

1841 TRIMMER *Pract. Geol. & Min.* 97 A knife is also indispensable for trying the hardness and sectility of minerals.

†**'secting**, *vbl. sb. Obs.* [f. SECT *v.* + -ING[1].]

1. Cutting.

1507 *Acc. Ld. High Treas. Scot.* III. 271 For secting of ane bordour and lynyng of ane goun of blak wellus, xvj s.

2. Dissension, division.

1598 BARRET *Theor. Warres* II. i. 28 If there be any banding, secting, or passionating amongst them, he is to appease.. the same.

section ('sɛkʃən), *sb.* Also 6 sectione, sectioun. [a. F. *section*, or directly ad. L. *sectiōn-em*, f. *sect-*, ppl. stem of *secāre* to cut. Cf. Sp. *seccion*, Pg. *secção*, It. *sezione*.]

1. a. The action, or an act, of cutting or dividing. Now *rare* exc. with reference to surgery or anatomical operations.

1559 tr. *Geminus' Anat.* 4/1 Neyther in man only, is seene the perfecte arte of nature, but in the Anatomie or Section of any other beast, shall you fynde the like wysdome and industrie of the worke master. **1577** HANMER *Anc. Eccl. Hist.* 226 That clause.. The sonne to be of one substance with the father, was.. allowed.. neither to be by diuision of substance neither by section or parting asunder. **1600** HOLLAND *Livy* LV. Brev. 1241 The young prince pined away with the paine of the stone in the bladder, and whiles they would seeme to cut him for it they killed him out of hand in the very section. **1615, 1661** [see CÆSAREAN 2]. **1631** CHAPMAN *Cæsar & Pompey* Ded., The.. section of acts and scenes. [Cf. *ante*, the division of acts and scenes.] **1656** tr. *Hobbes' Elem. Philos.* (1839) 140 Lines and superficies may be exposed by section, namely, a line may be made by cutting an exposed superficies. **1657** J. WATTS *Scribe, Pharisee*, etc. I. 21 He will by a hasty and imprudent Saw, or Razor cut of a part, and make a section, and endanger life. *a* **1682** SIR. T. BROWNE *Tracts* (1683) 58 Their course of mowing seems somewhat different from ours. For they cut not down clear at once, but used an after section, which they called *Sicilitium*. **1836** *Todd's Cycl. Anat.* I. 657/1 Animals have been bled to death by the section of the larger bloodvessels. **1870** M. FOSTER in *Q. Jrnl. Microsc. Sci.* X. 125 The cake with the imbedded object.. in a few minutes is ready for section. *Ibid.*, The sections may then be made either with a microtome or with a hand razor. **1883** BRUNTON in *Nature* 15 Mar. 467 Setchenow explains the increased rapidity of reflex action after section of the cord below the medulla oblongata.

†**b.** Division into parties. *Obs.*

1639 HEYWOOD *Lond. Peaceable Estate* Wks. 1874 V. 371 The Tranquillity of Kingdomes free from Section, tumult, and faction.

†**c.** = CÆSURA. *Obs.*

1585 JAS. I *Ess. Poesie* (Arb.) 60 Remember also to mak a Sectioun in the middes of euery lyne, quhether the lyne be lang or short. **1695** [? WHEELER] *Roy. Gram.*, *Prosodia* 17 This Section of a word just before the last Syllable is call'd Cæsura.

†**d.** The point of cutting or division. *Obs.*

1571 DIGGES *Pantom.* I. xxviii. H iv b, Multiply the portions that are betweene any two sections or places in the distance of your two stations. *Ibid.* I. xxxv. L ij, Cut this last drawen line, and at ye section make a marke. **1599** E. WRIGHT *Err. Navig.* D 1, We may make a table which shall shew the sections and points of latitude in the meridians of the nautical planisphere: by which sections, the parallels are to be drawne.

2. A part separated or divided off from the remainder; one of the portions into which a thing is cut or divided. **a.** *gen.*

1815 J. SMITH *Panorama Sci. & Art* II. 122 It is necessary that the water should begin to fall at BC, with the least possible velocity; and that the height of the water FB should be no more than is necessary to fill the section B. **1876** J. PARKER *Paracl.* I. vii. 106 The theologian is entitled to claim astronomy, geology, botany, agriculture, and chemistry, as sections of theology. **1884** tr. *Lotze's Logic* 178 We have to content ourselves with breaking up the whole series of values into sections and acting as if the conditions were the same throughout each section.

b. A subdivision of a written or printed work, a statute, or the like. Often represented by the symbol § (preceding a numeral figure); also abbreviated *sect.* (rarely *sec.*).

Although in some few books *section* has been adopted as the designation of a division superior to the 'chapter' (cf. G. *abschnitt*), the common practice from the 17th c. onward has been to apply the word to the lowest order of numbered divisions. In most recent books the 'section' (or, at least, the division denoted by the symbol §) either consists of a single paragraph, or, if it extends to several paragraphs, commonly has no head-line separated from the text. In modern Acts of Parliament the 'section' (for which the abbreviations *sect.* and § are both in official use) is a subdivision of the 'chapter' (i.e. Act) containing a specific provision or enactment. In some works (e.g. Bell's *Comment. Laws of Scotland*), the 'Section' (abbreviated 'Sect.' in the table of contents) is the division next below the 'Chapter', and is itself subdivided into numbered portions marked with the symbol §.

1576 FLEMING tr. *Caius' Dogs* (1880) 14 Such Dogges as serue for fowling, I thinke conuenient and requisite to place in this seconde Section of this treatise. **1628** COKE *On Litt.* I. i. § 1. 8 b, Whereof more hereafter in this Section. **1683** MOXON *Mech. Exerc.*, *Printing* ii. 9, § 2. Of the Office of a Master-Printer. *Ibid.* 10 (headed) Sect. II. **1714** CUNN *Doctr. Fractions* 43 The Directions laid down in Sect. 3 of Chap. II. **1738** WARBURTON *Div. Legat.* I. i. I. 1 Book I. Sect. I. **1769** BEATTIE in Dyce *Mem.* (Aldine ed.) p. xxvi, It will be regularly distributed into chapters and sections. **1806** *Med. Jrnl.* XV. 192 Mr. R. has divided his answer into several parts or sections. **1810** BENTHAM *Packing* (1821) 187 In the printed editions (it is true) we see each statute divided into sections, and each section numbered. But this is the work of the printer only or his editor. **1857** *Act 20 & 21 Vict.* c. 25 § 2 Ordinances framed by the Commissioners under Sections Twenty-eight and Twenty-nine of the same Act. **1870** *Act 30 & 34 Vict.* c. 75 § 34 Provided that this section [of the Act] shall not apply to [etc.]. **1874** STUBBS *Const. Hist.* xviii. (1896) III. 250 The preceding sections of this chapter.

c. *Nat. Hist.* Used variously by different writers for a subdivision of a classificatory group, e.g. of a class, order, family, or genus. In *Botany* now chiefly = *sub-genus*; but some writers (as Bentley) use it for a division of a sub-genus.

1720 P. BLAIR *Bot. Ess.* iii. 148 According to Tournefort's Method, *Malva* becomes the Section of a Class. *Althæa*, *Alcæa*, &c. are several Genera of this Section. **1819** MACLEAY *Horæ Entomol.* I. 55 Latreille has.. proposed to make but one genus of them, ascribing to the modern genera the name of sections. **1877** BENNETT *Thomé's Bot.* 238 It is usual to arrange the orders which make up a class into *Series*, the genera which make up a family into *Tribes*, and the species which make up a genus into *Sections*. **1885** *Athenæum* 3 Jan. 20/3 The author.. remarked that amongst the æluroids the section of Viverrina formed a very distinct group. **1899** HEINIG *Gloss. Bot. Terms*, *Section*, a part separated by division; a group of correlated species arranged under genera or sub-genera.

d. A separable portion of any collection or aggregate of persons, e.g. of the population of a country; a group, distinguished by a special variety of opinion, forming part of a political or religious party; one of several groups into which the membership of a learned society is divided according to the various branches of study in which the members are severally interested.

1832 BABBAGE *Econ. Manuf.* xx. (ed. 3) 194 This section consisted of seven or eight persons of considerable acquaintance with mathematics. **1852** ROBERTSON *Serm.* Ser. III. xvi. 205 The question.. whether of the two sections held the abstract right. **1874** GREEN *Short Hist.* vi. § 1. 267 The Church had at this time.. sunk into a mere section of the landed aristocracy. **1884** *Manch. Exam.* 14 May 5/5 To one section of the House Mr. Power's speech gave great delight.

e. (*a*) *French Hist.* One of the electoral districts into which France was divided under the Directory. (*b*) *U.S.* An area of one square mile into which the undeveloped lands are divided. (*c*) Chiefly *U.S.* A district or portion of a town or country exhibiting uniform characteristics or considered as divided from the rest on account of such characteristics. (*d*) *Austral.* and *N.Z.* An area of undeveloped land, variable in size. (*e*) *Austral.* and *N.Z.* A plot of land suitable for building on. (*f*) In various African countries, an administrative district (see quot. 1951).

(*a*) **1837** CARLYLE *Fr. Rev.* II. I. iv, The Sixty Districts shall become Forty-eight Sections.

(*b*) **1785** *Jrnls. Continental Congr. U.S.* (1933) XXVIII. 299 The plats of the townships..shall be marked by subdivisions into sections of 1 mile square. **1809** F. CUMING *Sk. Tour Western Country* (1810) 197 This Crouse is a wealthy man, having..a farm of two sections, containing thirteen hundred acres. **1849** E. CHAMBERLAIN *Indiana Gazetteer* (ed. 3) 420 North of Eel river are about 40 sections of barrens intermixed with small prairies. **1890** *Stock Grower & Farmer* 8 Mar. 5/3 The intervening sections of the Atlantic and Pacific railroad land grant [in Arizona] are owned by the cattle men and are not fenced. **1924** H. CROY *R.F.D. No. 3* 3 He had only one hundred and twenty acres of land, while most of the farmers had a quarter, or a half section, even a section. **1975** *New Yorker* 27 Oct. 114/2 We have six hundred and forty acres—what you call a section—and they wish to flood it to make recreation.

(*c*) **1816** PICKERING *Vocab. U.S.* 170 *Section.* Since the French Revolution this word has been much used here instead of *part, quarter*, &c. Ex. 'In this section of the United States.' It is not thus used in England. **1832** WEBSTER. **1865** E. BURRITT *Walk to Land's End* 171 In estimating the production of a dairy, the farmers of this section do not make much account of the breed, size or color of the cows. **1879** TOURGEE *Fool's Errand* iv. 20 The war is over... For a few months there may be disorders in some sections; but they will be very rare. **1907** *Standard* 19 Jan. 7/2 The northern section of Kingston is deserted.

(*d*) **1836** *S. Austral. Gaz. & Colonial Register* 18 June 4/2 Surveyed land shall be divided, as nearly as may be, into sections of eighty acres each, with the exception of the site of the first town, which shall be divided into acre sections. **1841** W. DEANS *Let.* 25 Mar. in J. Deans *Pioneers of Canterbury* (1937) i. 31 Some part of the rural sections may not just be what could have been wished. **1923** in J. Reid *Kiwi Laughs* (1961) His idea was that he and I should get the firewood rights on a thousand-acre section, up under the mountain reserve. **1950** *N.Z. Jrnl. Agric.* Jan. 26/2 Ten 10-acre sections have been allocated to returned servicemen.

(*e*) **1836** [see (*d*) above]. **1851** *Lyttelton* (N.Z.) *Times* 11 Jan. 5 The immediate choosing of the town acre sections has been a most important and useful measure. **1886** F. HUME *Myst. Hansom Cab* (1887) v. 19 She..purchased a small section at St. Kilda, and built a house on it. **1935** J. GUTHRIE *Little Country* ii. 43 They would much rather have had an eighth-acre section. **1961** B. CRUMP *Hang on Minute Mate* 97 Tony..was paying off a section in Tokoroa and talking about putting in for one of them Government loans to build a house with. **1977** *N.Z. Herald* 8 Jan. 4-6/2 (Advt.), Waiheke Island, sections and batches urgently wanted.

(*f*) **1951** K. L. LITTLE *Mende of Sierra Leone* v. 104 The overall picture..is one of small towns around each of which is spread a number of component villages. This combination of town and villages constitutes a social and political entity which, in the older sense, corresponds to what is officially termed, nowadays, the 'section' of a chiefdom. **1957** M. BANTON *W. Afr. City* viii. 151 He is assisted by seven section chiefs and certain tribal officials. **1977** *Times of Zambia* 7 Sept. 7/7 He has received the reports from all governors in the province on the recent village and section elections.

f. *Bookbinding.* (See quot. 1859.)

1859 *Stationers' Hand-bk.* 81 *Section*, any number of sheets of paper folded together are termed a Section. **1880** ZAEHNSDORF *Bkbinding* 5 The book should be divided into lots or sections of about half-an-inch thick, that will be about 15 to 20 sheets, according to the thickness of paper.

g. *Mil.* Orig., a fourth part of a company or the fourth part of a platoon. Now used of various small tactical units.

1863 KINGLAKE *Crimea* (1877) III. i. 138 The Coldstream broke into open column of sections. **1889** *Infantry Drill* 61 The company..will then be told off into two half-companies and four sections. **1913** *Army Order 323* 1 Oct. 4 The non-commissioned officers and men of the machine-gun section..will be distributed for discipline and administration in peace amongst the four companies. **1915** D. O. BARNETT *Let.* 24 Mar. in *Denis Oliver Barnett* (1915) 100 At first I thought the whole section was done in, as rifles and equipment flew in the air. **1939** J. T. GORMAN *Army of To-Day* iii. 69 All the men in a section or platoon are taught to use the light (Bren) machine-gun *individually*. **1943** *Britain's Mod. Army* ix. 192/2 Columns of threes are now used, each column in a platoon representing a section with the commander at its head. Thus a section can 'peel off' quickly to a threatened flank, without leaving a gap in the column as used to occur when a section left the old column of fours. **1968** R. M. BARNES *Brit. Army of 1914* i. 35 The infantry advanced in small parties—probably sections in fours, spaced out at fairly wide intervals, or in a 'diamond formation' of sections or platoons.

h. *Prosody.* Used by Guest for: A member of a verse, esp. a hemistich of an OE. or ME. alliterative line.

1838 GUEST *Eng. Rhythms* I. vii. I. 149.

i. *Mus.* (See quot. 1866.)

1866 ENGEL *Nat. Mus.* ii. 83 A section consists generally of two phrases; and a simple period consists of two sections.

j. *U.S.* A portion of a sleeping-car containing two berths.

1874 LADY HERBERT tr. *Hübner's Ramble* I. iv. (1878) 38 Each window [in the U.S. railroad cars] allows for two beds, one at the top of the other, unless the traveller has taken a 'section', i.e., the whole space of one window. **1892** GUNTER *Miss Dividends* (1893) 245 Making up his bed in the state-room which is unoccupied, and more roomy than a section.

k. *U.S. Railways.* 'The smallest administrative subdivision of a railroad. It is usually a mile or two in length and is designated by a number.' (*Cent. Dict.* Suppl.; see also quot. 1890.)

1890 E. P. ALEXANDER in *Railways of Amer.* 156 Each of the supervisors of road has his assigned territory divided into 'sections', from five to eight miles in length. At a suitable place on each section are erected houses for a resident section-master and from six to twelve hands. *Ibid.*, At least twice a day track-walkers from the section-gangs pass over the entire line of road. *Ibid.*, The work of the section-men is all done under regular system.

l. One of the component parts of something which is built up of a number of similar portions so as to admit of enlargement when necessary, or which is constructed to be taken to pieces for facility of transport.

1875 KNIGHT *Dict. Mech.*, *Section*,..a detachable portion of a machine or instrument when made up of a number of parts: *e.g.* one of the triangular knives; a row of which is attached to the cutter-bar of a harvesting-machine. *Ibid.*, *Sectional Steam-boiler*, one built up of portions secured together in such a way that the size may be increased by addition of sections. **1897** MARY KINGSLEY *W. Africa* 355 There is always a steamer in sections in every story of a good expedition.

m. *Geol.* (See quot.)

1882 GEIKIE *Text-bk. Geol.* VI. 635 A number of groups or stages similarly related constitute a series, section (Abtheilung) or formation, and a number of series, sections, or formations may be united into a system.

n. *U.S. Railways.* (See quot. 1890.)

1872 *Newton Kansan* 3 Oct. 3/2 The caboose and the next three cars to it of the 1st section was badly smashed up. **1890** *Railways of Amer.* 162 But the more usual way of handling extra trains, when circumstances will permit, is to let them precede or follow a regular train upon the same schedule. The train is then said to be run in 'sections', and a ten minutes' interval is allowed between them. **1948** *Chicago Tribune* 11 Apr. 1 Ho! the second section! And no flagman out from the train we stopped.

o. *Mus.* A group of similar instruments forming part of a band or orchestra; also the players of such instruments. See also *rhythm section* s.v. RHYTHM *sb.* 9a.

1880 GROVE *Dict. Mus.* II. 569/2 The Instrumental Band, as now constituted, naturally divides itself into certain sections, as distinct from each other as the Manuals of an Organ. **1944** W. APEL *Harvard Dict. Mus.* 520/1 It is only in the use of a relatively strong string section that Monteverdi's orchestra is progressive. **1955** KEEPNEWS & GRAUER *Pictoral Hist. Jazz* 103/2 Those two men added were both saxophone players; the total of three, instead of a single clarinetist, made a 'section'. That of course is one of the key words, one of the fundamentals of big-band music. **1977** J. WAINWRIGHT *Do Nothin'* viii. 124 The sax section—Ric.. fills it out, with the tenor.

p. A metal bar, esp. one with a cross-section that is not a simple shape (see quots.).

1881 *Jrnl. Iron & Steel Inst.* 703 A book containing rules and measurements for the construction of various forms of sections of rolled iron, has been drawn up... It is full of formulae applicable to different sizes and forms of sections. **1902** *Ibid.* LXII. 499 Vollkommer suggests an arrangement of plant for the continuous casting and rolling of light sections from fluid metal. **1924** H. J. SKELTON *Econ. Iron & Steel* 278 In Great Britain the product in bars or rods shaped in a rolling mill, when not round or square or flat in cross section, is called a 'section' or sectional material. **1956** A. K. OSBORNE *Encycl. Iron & Steel Industry* 412/2 Structural shapes. (Sections.) Hot rolled steel bars of various cross-sectional contours such as channels, angles, bulb angles, I and H beams, T and Z bars, joists and other complicated contours. **1965** M. H. T. ALFORD tr. *Tselikov & Smirnov's Rolling Mills* ii. 28/2 The second type [of mill] is used for lighter sections nearer in size to the products of medium section mills. **1971** W. K. V. GALE *Iron & Steel Industry* 181 *Section* (*shape*) (*profile*), any rolled product which is not a round, square, or flat. This is British usage. In USA the term is often shape and in Europe, profile.

q. *Austral.* and *N.Z.* A fare stage on a bus or tram route.

1931 V. PALMER *Separate Lives* 285 He had travelled out the two sections to Aunt Rachel's dingy little house in the suburbs. **1948** *Landfall* June 112 He fingered the two pennies that remained from the half-crown... He'd have to walk to the end of the first section, catch the tram there.

3. *Math.* †**a.** A segment of a circle. *Obs.*

1570 BILLINGSLEY *Euclid* I. Def. xix. 4 A section or portion of a circle, is a figure which is contayned vnder a right lyne, and a parte of the circumference, greater or lesse then the semicircle. **1654** H. PHILLIPPES *Purch. Pattern* (ed. 2) 165 The half-Circle and quarter-Circle may be measured also by this rule, but other Sections are very hard and troublesome, and scarce to be found out, without knowing the content of the whole Circle or Semicircle. **1715** LEONI *Palladio's Archit.* (1742) I. 91 If..a perfect semicircle should not be convenient..we must then make use of a lesser section.

†**b.** Intersection. *Obs.*

1667 PRIMATT *City & C. Build.* 159 From the section of these Arches to the point given, a right Line drawn cuts the Line given perpendicularly. **1830** *J. de Vega's Jrnl. Tour* xiii. (1847) 102 A curiously-built cross, situated in the section of the four principal streets.

c. The curve of intersection of two superficies.

1704 J. HARRIS *Lex. Techn.* I. s.v., The common Section of two Planes is always a right Line, being the Line supposed to be drawn on one Plane by the Section of the other, or by its Entrance into it. *a* **1845** LEVY in *Encycl. Metrop.* II. 165 If through a given point..on this surface, we conceive a normal plane, the intersection of this plane with the surface will be a certain curve, which we shall call a normal section. **1887** J. H. SMITH *Geometr. Conic Sect.* 43 For *ab* is the common section of the plane of projection with a plane perpendicular to it and passing through *AB*.

d. The cutting of a solid by a plane; the plane figure resulting from such a cutting; the area of this. (Cf. CONIC *section*.) Hence, of a material object, the figure which would be produced by cutting through it in a certain plane.

1704 J. HARRIS *Lex. Techn.* I., *Section* in Mathematick, signifies the cutting of..a Solid by a Plane. **1715** DESAGULIERS *Fires Impr.* 156 The Passage in the Brick-Work.., whose Section must be 36 Inches, whether it be square or oblong. **1824** TREDGOLD *Strength Cast Iron*, etc. 59 Of the strongest Form of Section for revolving Shafts. **1831** BREWSTER *Optics* xvii. 151 Every plane passing through the axis is called a principal section of the crystal. **1839** G. BIRD *Nat. Philos.* 115 A tube, or channel, whose section is greater at one part than another. *a* **1878** SIR G. SCOTT *Lect. Archit.* (1879) I. 248 Thus, if the normal section of the rib be square, the section of the mouldings is made to fit that figure. **1885** J. CASEY *Analyt. Geom.* 281 Sections of a cone made by parallel planes are similar. **1898** H. R. MILL in *Jrnl. Sch. of Geog.* (U.S.) II. 293 Great screes, which give to the valleys a rounded or U-shaped section.

e. The action of dividing a line into parts. ***golden section***, also ***medial, median section***: the division of a line in extreme and mean ratio.

1820 LESLIE *Elem. Geom. & Pl. Trig.* (ed. 4) 63 It will be convenient..to designate..this remarkable division of a line ..by the term Medial Section. **1898** CHRYSTAL *Introd. Algebra* xxii. 329 To find a point P in the line AB such that $AP^2 = AB, PB$ (Problem of 'Golden Section').

4. a. A drawing representing an object (e.g. a building, a piece of machinery, a portion of the earth's crust) as it would appear if cut through in a plane at right angles to the line of sight.

In strict use, the term denotes a delineation confined to what is in actual contact with the imaginary cutting plane. Sometimes, as in quot. 1793, it is loosely used for what is more properly called a *sectional elevation*.

1669 STAYNRED *Fortif.* 7 They are represented in the Profile, or Section. **1691** T. H[ALE] *Acc. New Invent.* 121 Three perpendicular length-way sections..and..a transverse section of the Hull. **1725** HALFPENNY *Art Sound Building* Pl. 19 The Chamber Plan, and Section. **1793** SMEATON *Edystone L.* §32 The Plate..shews part of the outside and part of the inside, so as to be at once, both an elevation and a section. **1845** DARWIN *Voy. Nat.* xx. (1852) 473 It is a real section (on the scale of ·517 of an inch to a mile) through Bolabola in the Pacific. **1879** *Encycl. Brit.* IX. 422/1 The section or profile is made on a plane perpendicular to the lines of intersection of the planes or slopes, and therefore represents the traces of these planes on the sectional plane.

b. advb. phr. ***in section.***

1860 TYNDALL *Glac.* II. xvii. 321 The portion of the glacier which is shown in section. **1904** R. C. JEBB *Bacchylides* (Proc. Brit. Acad.) 6 The painter's plan was to show both the sea-depths and the upper world in section.

c. *Geol.* A surface exposed by a cutting or by some natural agency, showing the succession of strata.

1858 H. D. ROGERS *Geol. Pennsylv.* II. II. 1027 *Section*, an actual or ideal exposure of any part of the earth's crust, showing the strata edgewise, as if they were laid open by a cut. **1860** TYNDALL *Glac.* I. xxiii. 162 The wall of the Mattmark See is a fine glacier section. **1877** HUXLEY *Physiogr.* 23 Natural sections are frequently exposed in river-beds, sea-cliffs and inland valleys.

5. A thin slice of a vegetable or animal structure, or of an inorganic body, cut off for microscopic examination.

1870 STIRLING in *Jrnl. Anat.* May 234, I can slice such an embryo into from seventy to eighty sections in the long direction. **1874** *Amer. Naturalist* Apr. 252 Mr. Charles Stewart obtains sections of fresh leaves by [etc.]. **1902** G. H. FOWLER in *Encycl. Brit.* XXX. 739/1 The tissue..is cut into sections either by the Rutherford, Cathcart, or some similar section-cutter.

6. *Printing.* The sign §, originally used to introduce the number of a 'section' (sense 2b); subsequently used also as a mark of reference to notes in the margin or at the foot of a page. Also called ***section-mark***.

The primary use of the sign seems to have become rare in the 18th c., and to have been revived in the latter part of the 19th c. under German influence. German printers give to this mark the name of *paragraph*.

1728 CHAMBERS *Cycl.* s.v. *Character*, Characters in Grammar, Rhetoric, Poetry &c...§ Section, or Division. **1770** LUCKOMBE *Hist. Printing* 259 The Sign which implies the word Section, is a Sort..seldom employed, because in Work which is divided into Chapters, Articles, Paragraphs, Sections, or any other Parts, they are commonly put in lines by themselves, either in Large Capitals, Small Capitals, or Italic... But the Sign of Section is sometimes used in (Latin) Notes, and particularly such as are collected from foreign books. **1875** SOUTHWARD *Dict. Typogr.*, *Section* (§), a mark of reference. It stands fourth in order, and immediately after the double dagger. Sometimes it is used to mark the division of a chapter into parts or sections, whence its name. **1894** *Amer. Dict. Printing*, *Section-mark*.

7. *Comb.* **a.** objective; as (sense 5) ***section-cutter, -cutting, -smoother***; (sense 2e(*b*)) ***section corner***; (sense 2g) ***section-commander, -leader***; (sense 2k) ***section boss, crew, -gang, hand, -man, master, work***; (sense 2o) ***section man, work.***

1870 *Daily Territorial Enterprise* (Virginia City, Nevada) 22 Oct. 3/1 The clothes of the *section boss caught upon the brake..as he was in the act of jumping off. **1947** K. D. LUMPKIN *Making of Southerner* 163 The deacon was section boss on the railroad. **1889** *Infantry Drill* 306 During an extension *section commanders will see that the men take their proper intervals. **1817** *Niles' Weekly Reg.* XII. 97/2 At the distance of every mile..*section corners are established. **1947** *Mich. Hist.* Sept. 319 He traced it up to the section corner and discovered that the cruiser had signed his name on the tree. **1884** *Section-crew [see *push-car* s.v. PUSH-]. **1962** W. STEGNER *Wolf Willow* I. ii. 33 Anonymously denounced in the *Leader* for nearly derailing the speeder of a section crew. **1976** *Columbus* (Montana) *News* 1 July 8/4 My sister and her friend thought I should go on the hand-car with the section crew. **1870** STIRLING in *Jrnl. Anat.* May 230 The *section cutter which I am about to describe. **1874** *Amer. Naturalist* Jan. 59 A new section cutter which is principally adapted for preparing sections of soft vegetable tissues and organs. **1878** S. MARSH (*title*) *Section-cutting. **1890** *Section-gang [see 2k]. **1873** *Newton Kansan* 27 Feb. 3/2 A drunked *section hand..laid down upon the railroad track to take a nap. **1904** F. LYNDE *Grafters* xxiii. 284 When the section hands pelt stray dogs with new spikes from the stock keg. **1969** *Islander* (Victoria, B.C.) 2 Nov. 5/2 There are no sectionhands in the pass these days, nature finally triumphed in the thirties, closing the line. **1903** *Daily Chron.* 28 Dec. 3/2 Controlled individual firing, under the direction of group and *section leaders, is the only effective method. **1869** W. H. JACKSON *Jrnl.* 1 Aug. in *Time Exposure* (1940) xi. 182 Got the *section men to take us aboard their handcar. **1890** [see 2k]. **1921** *Daily Colonist* (Victoria, B.C.) 23 Oct. 27/5 A section man..was killed last night while jumping from a moving train. **1936** D. MCCOWAN *Animals Canad. Rockies* viii. 73 In spring..the section men burn the grass along the right-of-way of the railroad. **1955** L. FEATHER *Encycl. Jazz* vii. 194 Reluctant soloist but excellent sectionman. **1872** W. S. HUNTINGTON *Road-Master's Asst.* p. iii, The enormous expense of track repairs..may be greatly reduced by a reform in the every-day practice of the track-layer and *section-master. **1890** Section-master [see 2k]. **1887** *Amer. Naturalist* XXI. 597 Dr. P. F. Mall recommends a *section-smoother constructed on the following principle. **1891** C. ROBERTS *Adrift in Amer.* 71 *Section work is track repairing. **1958** C. FOX in P. Gammond *Decca Bk. Jazz* vii. 91 Its attack and vitality.. made up for any roughness in the section-work. **1977** J. WAINWRIGHT *Do Nothin'* v. 66 Miller's secret? Size, tight section work and damn good arrangers.

b. Special comb.: **section-beam** (see quot.); **Section Eight** (also **8**) *U.S. Mil. slang*, discharge from the Army under section eight of Army Regulations 615–360 on the grounds of insanity or inability to adjust to Army life; hence **section-eight** *v.*, (usu. in *pass.*) to discharge from the Army on such grounds; **section head**, (*a*) the person in charge of a section of an organization; (*b*) the heading of a section of a newspaper or periodical; **section house**, (*a*) (see quot. 1856); (*b*) *U.S.* a house occupied by the men responsible for the maintenance of a section of a railway; **section-line**, (*a*) the boundary of a section (now only *U.S.*); (*b*) a line drawn to indicate the manner of making a section; **section-liner** (see quot.); **section-mark** (see sense 6); **section-plane**, a surface exposed by section; **section-point**, a mark used to indicate the end of a section of a verse; **section sergeant**, a police sergeant in charge of a section.

1875 KNIGHT *Dict. Mech.*, **Section-beam* (Warping, etc.), a roller which receives the yarn from the spools, either for the dressing-machine or for the loom. **1943** *Yank* 23 July 15/2 If it weren't for Yank and its puzzles I'm sure there would be plenty of *Section 8s in places like this. **1945** *Yank* 7 Dec. 8/1 Nobody knew whether he was getting section-eighted out of the Army. **1950** E. HEMINGWAY *Across River & into Trees* xxxiii. 207 You stay in until you are hit badly or killed or go crazy and get section-eighted. **1971** J. AIKEN *Nightly Deadshade* iii. 31 The place..becomes a reservoir of feebles, bullied by the *section heads. **1973** W. H. HALLAHAN *Ross Forgery* ii. 14 Redhaired man with a Sandhurst accent..a former section head of British Military Intelligence. **1977** *Time* 15 Aug. 5/2 The new format includes different section heads, a new type face for headlines, hairline rules to set off columns. **1856** A. WYNTER *Curios. Civiliz.* 465 The *section-house, an establishment generally attached to the chief station of each division, in which the unmarried policemen are lodged. **1869** W. H. JACKSON *Jrnl.* 24 Aug. in *Time Exposure* (1940) xi. 183 Decided to board at the section house rather than cook ourselves. **1890** *Pall Mall Gaz.* 7 July 5/1 This daring disobedience was loudly cheered by the men who crowded the section-house windows as spectators. **1903** *N.Y. Even. Post* 29 Aug. 1/2 Crowbars and tools..were identified as having been taken from the railroad section house. **1976** *Columbus* (Montana) *News* 1 July 8/4, I accompanied my sister and her beau to a dance at a section house near the railroad. **1828** P. CUNNINGHAM *N.S. Wales* (ed. 3) II. 148 The *section-lines being made to run either east and west, or north and south, according as the general course of the river best suits. **1872** *Newton Kansan* 12 Sept. 2/4 The farmers.. are leaving space for a road along the section lines. **1879** *Cassell's Techn. Educ.* I. 100/2 To trace the section-line on this development—that is, to draw the line in which the material is to be cut so as to form both the parts of the cylinder—erect perpendiculars [etc.]. **1948** H. A. JACOBS *We chose Country* 24 We bowled along, climbing past snatches of woods and the straight section-line roads to a high plateau. **1875** KNIGHT *Dict. Mech.*, **Section-liner*, a device for ruling parallel lines. **1889** *Buck's Handbk. Med. Sci.* VIII. 109 The *section-plane, as made by the saw, passed just sinistrad of the meson. **1893** F. THOMPSON *Poems* 55 note, I have..used an asterisk to indicate the caesura in the middle of the line, after the manner of the old Saxon *section-point. [**1956** *Police Jrnl.* XXIX. 1. 52 Sergeants are 'right in the picture'. Supervising each man on his patrol is still an important part of his duties but he is now the head of a team whose job is to police the section.] **1964** M. BANTON *Policeman in Community* ii. 15 The division is divided into four sections, each of which is in the charge of a sergeant... Their *section sergeants use the station as their headquarters and go out from there to supervise their constables. **1973** J. WAINWRIGHT *Pride of Pigs* 12 Sergeant Crawley took some backhanders... And you in favour of section sergeants taking nawpings?

section ('sɛkʃən), *v.* [f. SECTION *sb.*]

1. *trans.* **a.** To divide into sections.

1819 KEATS *Cap & Bells* xi, With special strictures on the horrid crime, (Section'd and subsection'd with learning sage,) Of faeries stooping on their wings sublime To kiss a mortal's lips. **1856** LADY LYTTON in Devey *Life* (1887) 413 The rest was geographically sectioned out for the rest of Europe.

b. To cut through so as to present a section.

1891 G. NEILSON in *Athenæum* 30 May 707/3 The mound, wherever sectioned, invariably shows a steady succession of horizontal layers.

c. With *off*: to make (an area, part of a structure, etc.) into a separate section.

1960 'E. MCBAIN' *Give Boys Great Big Hand* xiii. 156 The Carellas had sectioned off one corner of the house and disconnected the heating to it. **1976** J. SNOW *Cricket Rebel* 72 The authorities sectioned off the stand next to the dressing room for Army marksmen.

2. *intr.* To admit of being cut into sections.

1903 E. H. SELLARDS in *Amer. Jrnl. Sci.* July 89 The spores..are brown in color, somewhat flexible, and section readily on the microtome.

3. *trans.* To cause (a person) to be compulsorily detained in a mental hospital in accordance with the provisions of the relevant section of the Mental Health Act of 1983 or (formerly) that of 1959.

1984 *Brit. Med. Jrnl.* 1 Dec. 1542/3 Before the 1983 Act came into being no social worker ever refused my request to come and see a patient with a view to sectioning the patient under the old section 29. *Ibid.*, I..needed to section a mentally ill patient urgently. **1986** M. DUNBAR *Catherine* vi. 91 Personally, I do not believe that sectioning an anorectic is any answer at all, unless he or she wishes it. **1987** *Openmind* Feb–Mar. 5/1 The author uses the case of Mrs Z as an example. Sectioned by her husband, she was then confined in a secure unit.

Hence '**sectioning** *vbl. sb.* and *ppl. a.*

1887 *Amer. Naturalist* XXI. 595 For the purpose of sectioning, the eggs are transferred from the water used in washing to 50% alcohol. **1900** *Brit. Med. Jrnl.* 5 May 1110 A happy stroke of the sectioning knife, passing through the entire length of the proboscis of a filariated mosquito.

sectional ('sɛkʃənəl), *a.* [f. SECTION *sb.* + -AL[1]. Cf. F. *sectionnel.*]

A. *adj.* **1.** Pertaining to a section or division of a larger part. **a.** Pertaining to a section or sections of a country, society, or population; sometimes (of interests, etc.) with implied opposition to *general*.

1806 *Deb. Congr. U.S.* (1852) 15 Apr. 1042 Let a narrow, selfish, local, sectional policy prevail and struggles will commence. **1816** *Monthly Mag.* XLII. 230 In the sectional or parish assemblies during the revolution a cobbler ascended the tribune. **1856** W. IRVING *Washington* II. 559 The sectional jealousies prevalent among them [*sc.* the troops from the different provinces] were more and more a subject of uneasiness to Washington. **1865** W. C. FOWLER (*title*) The Sectional Controversy; or passages in the political history of the United States, including the courses of the war between the sections. **1881** *Nature* 4 Aug. 325 The sectional meetings are being held in the rooms of the various scientific societies in the Burlington House region. **1886** CAMPBELL-BANNERMAN *Sp.* 13 May in *Hansard's Parl. Deb.* Ser. III. CCCV. 948 Those who anticipate the further embitterment of sectional and sectarian strife [in Ireland]. **1908** *Daily Chron.* 25 Feb. 6/6 The design includes only the Cross of St. George, the sectional emblem of England.

b. *Prosody.* Pertaining to a section or member of a verse.

1838 GUEST *Eng. Rhythms* I. vi. I. 125 Sectional Rhime is that which exists between syllables contained in the same section. *Ibid.* I. vii. 154 Perhaps we may infer, that the sectional pause was originally a stop.

c. Of the nature of a section, incomplete.

1839–48 BAILEY *Festus* xix. 204 Our life is incomplete and sectional.

2. a. Of or pertaining to a section (sense 4), relating to the view of the structure of a body in section.

1825 J. NICHOLSON *Oper. Mech.* 181 Part of the furnace is shown in a sectional view. **1868** HUMBER *Strains in Girders* 67 For sectional area of material, substitute an equivalent strain. **1874** tr. *Lommel's Light* 79 Chief or principal planes or sections, having the same sectional outline.

b. *Geol. sectional line*: the line on the earth's surface through which a section is supposed to be made.

1831 A. SEDGWICK in *Trans. Geol. Soc.* (1836) Ser. II. IV. 87 From Dent the sectional line ranges over the top of Risell to the Garsdale river. **1850** T. BAKER *Mensuration* 121 To draw a sectional line of several points in the earth's surface, the levels of which have been taken.

3. Composed or made up of several sections or parts fitting into one another.

1875 KNIGHT *Dict. Mech.*, *Sectional Steam-boiler.* **1901** *Furniture Rec.* 15 June Suppl. 4 The Gunn K.D. Sectional Book Cases. **1909** 'O. HENRY' *Roads of Destiny* v. 74 A word from me was more to them than a whole deckle-edged library from East Aurora in sectional bookcases was from anybody else. **1937** *Discovery* Feb. 35/1 They had hoped to use a very light sectional building. **1957** *Times* 2 July (Agric. Suppl.) p. vi/2 A typical old barn now houses the grain intake pit, cleaner, pre-dry bin, continuous dryer, and sectional storage bins. **1960** *Which?* Jan. 5 Sectional boiler, coke-fired.

4. Of steel: rolled in the form of sections (sense 2 p).

1881 *Jrnl. Iron & Steel Inst.* 703 The sectional forms given..are intended to supply the requirements of engineers engaged in the construction of railways, warehouses, public buildings, and similar work. **1916** *Ibid.* XCIII. 354 All the sectional material rolled differs from the ideal by not giving equal distribution of stress in the material. **1924** H. J. SKELTON *Econ. Iron & Steel* 279 Wherever practicable, it is desirable that rolled shapes or sectional material in mild steel should be ordered from the list of British Standard Sections.

B. *ellipt.* as *sb.* A piece of furniture composed of sections which can be used separately; *spec.* one which can be used either as a sofa or as a set of chairs. *U.S.*

1961 in WEBSTER. **1972** *Village Voice* (N.Y.) 1 June 3/1 (Advt.), Top quality convertible sofas & sectionals. **1977** *Time* 28 Mar. 50/2 One day Lily and Richard decided that the living-room sofa would look better as a sectional. Practical kids, they picked up a saw and divided it into three pieces. **1980** *Redbook* Oct. 86 (Advt.), Display the sectionals alone or group them with matching modular pieces.

sectionalism ('sɛkʃənəlɪz(ə)m). [f. SECTIONAL *a.* + -ISM.] Confinement of interest to a narrow sphere, narrowness of outlook, undue accentuation of minor local, political, or social distinctions.

1858 *Newark Jrnl.* July (Bartlett 1860), The patriotism and intellect of Massachusetts was represented in a striking contrast with the littleness and sectionalism which now rules the old Bay States. **1872** *Daily News* 23 July, The coalition just cemented at Baltimore seems to mark a new era in American politics, and sectionalism disappears for the first time in the history of the country. **1886** *Manch. Exam.* 17 Mar. 5/3 The scandal of obsolete sectionalism in the attitude of the Liberal party towards the Irish question is brushed away.

sectionalist ('sɛkʃənəlɪst). [f. SECTIONAL *a.* + -IST.] One who advocates sectional aims or interests.

1863 DICEY *Federal St.* II. 86 There were abolition fanatics there, it was true—sectionalists, traitors, brothers of Southern secessionists.

sectionalization (ˌsɛkʃənəlaɪ'zeɪʃən). [f. SECTIONALIZE *v.* + -ATION.] The action or result of dividing into sections.

1904 in WEBSTER. **1920** *Public Opinion* 17 Sept. 268/1 The very formula of 'nationalisation' was a sham, sectionalisation was the object. **1933** *Archit. Rev.* LXXIII. 110/2 What gives interest to London is the diversity of its quarters without extreme sectionalization. **1966** *McGraw-Hill Encycl. Sci. & Technol.* VIII. 490/1 Sectionalization is a method of distributing mine power so that power cables can be isolated..without shutting off the mains supply to several working sections.

sectionalize ('sɛkʃənəlaɪz), *v.* [f. SECTIONAL *a.* + -IZE.]

1. *trans.* To divide into sections. Chiefly as '**sectionalized** *pa. pple.* and *ppl. a.*; also '**sectionalizing** *vbl. sb.*

1854 *Blackw. Mag.* LXXV. 87 Is man really so unlike as a whole, so necessarily subdivided and sectionalised? **1907** *Daily Chron.* 9 Apr. 3/6 In my district [*sc.* in the Upper Congo] there is no such thing as 'unoccupied land'... It is impossible to find a..stream which is not sectionalised for the use of specific communities. **1908** *Install. News* II. 73/2 The catalogue is, as far as practicable, sectionalised not only to facilitate reference, but often because customers are more interested in one particular section than another. **1937** *Discovery* Nov. 360/1 A sectionalised enquiry into the bases of photographic construction. **1957** *Practical Wireless* XXXIII. 357/3 (Advt.), Sectionalised windings ensure low leakage inductance and brilliant top note response. **1965** J. BINGHAM *Fragment of Fear* iv. 67 Luckily I have a sectionalised mind, and my thoughts were now on Juliet. **1976** *Gramophone* Sept. 506/1 It will be seen from the accompanying sectionalized photo..that there are two magnetic gaps. **1977** *Ibid.* Feb. 1343/3 By intelligent sectionalizing, it has been possible to produce modules which can be tested and proved individually before incoporation.

2. To render sectional.

1890–1 A. M. FAIRBAIRN *Cathol. Rom. & Angl.* (1899) 317 The resolute antagonist of those Catholic schemes that so laboured to sectionalize the church he loved. **1971** *Nature* 7 May 2/1 In the event..the foundation may have been lumbered with a number of vested interests which will sectionalize its proceedings.

sectionally ('sɛkʃənəlɪ), *adv.* [f. SECTIONAL *a.* + -LY[2].] In a sectional manner; from a sectional point of view.

1869 *Daily News* 8 Mar., Sectionally the Cabinet is wisely chosen... New England has one, New York one, and Maryland one. **1878** J. S. MORGAN in *N. Amer. Rev.* CXXVI. 316 Less than one-third of the country is united almost solidly and sectionally to oppose the restoration of silver money to its former estate. **1891** MEREDITH *One of our Conq.* xiii, Sectionally social means anything but social.

sectionary ('sɛkʃənərɪ), *a.* and *sb.* [f. SECTION *sb.* + -ARY.] †**A.** *adj. Obs. rare.*

1. Of or pertaining to the sections of a book.

a **1734** NORTH *Life John North* (1744) 259 He gives a short Account of each of the Pieces..and of his adding a sectionary Index to the whole.

2. Of or pertaining to a section (of a party, country, etc.).

1816 PICKERING *Vocab. U.S.* 171 *Sectionary*,..I have never met with this uncommon word except in the following instance: 'This veneration arises not from a little and selfish spirit of sectionary attachment.' **1835** *Tait's Mag.* II. 288 The absence of these is partly compensated by the exclusion of the sectionary leaders.

B. *sb.* A member of a section (of a party, etc.) opposed to the remainder; a partisan.

1835 *Blackw. Mag.* XXXVII. 948 To men who..call them trimmers or waverers, deserters or sectionaries, we have only to say, There is a battle to be fought [etc.]. **1848** W. H. KELLY tr. *L. Blanc's Hist. Ten Y.* II. 257 M. Martin ascended a sort of tribune to address the sectionaries.

sectionist ('sɛkʃənɪst). [f. SECTION *sb.* + -IST.]

1. A member of a section, a partisan.

1893 *Scotsman* 28 June 6 Peculiarly intolerant, therefore, of any interruption on the part of other sectionists anxious to ventilate their special discovery or view.

†**2.** *N.Z.* The owner or occupier of a section (sense 2 e (*d*)) of land. *Obs.*

1841 W. DEANS *Let.* 25 Mar. in J. Deans *Pioneers of Canterbury* (1937) i. 32 The secondary sectionists are to choose their land at Wanganui.

sectionize ('sɛkʃənaɪz), *v.* [f. SECTION *sb.* + -IZE.] *trans.* **a.** To divide into sections or parts. Also *absol.* **b.** To delineate in section. **c.** To cut sections or thin slices from.

a. 1828 *Laws of Texas* Nov. (Bartlett 1860), So much of the vacant lands of the republic shall be surveyed and sectionized, as will be sufficient to satisfy all claims. **1872** *Rep. Indian Affairs 1871* (U.S.) 185 [Various tribes] were induced either to sectionize, or in some way to admit white settlers. **1873** J. H. BEADLE *Undeveloped West* 399 He is the only Choctaw in the district who is in favor of sectionizing and admitting white immigration. **1949** *Surveying & Mapping* Jan.–Mar. 31/2 Long before Florida was sectionized by ranges and townships, rulers of the Old World bestowed favors on a selected few supporters by granting them titles to vast parcels of land in America.

b. 1876 PAGE *Adv. Text-bk. Geol.* vi. 113 Group after group of strata was examined, sectionised, and mapped.

c. 1896 *Naturalist* Jan. 29 John Butterworth..was one of the first to apply successfully the method of sectionising fossil plants to the study of fossil botany.

ˌsectiopla'nography. *Civil Engin.* [f. SECTION *sb.* + PLANE *sb.* + -GRAPHY. Cf. PLANOGRAPHY.] = PLANOGRAPHY.

1837 F. W. SIMMS (*title*) Sectio-Planography. **1842** *Mech. Mag.* XXXVII. 268 A better mode than Sectioplanography for delineating the Drainage and Agricultural Improvements of a Country. **1887** in CASSELL; and in later Dicts.

sectism ('sɛktɪz(ə)m). [f. SECT *sb.*[1] + -ISM.] Devotion to a sect; sectarian spirit.

1864 in WEBSTER. **1879** J. KERR *Ess. Castism & Sectism* 83 An obvious cause of sectism lies in the fact that religious organisations..have a tendency to become corrupt. **1893** J. PULSFORD *Loyalty to Christ* II. 313 Heaven is..humanity delivered from sectism, and come into the liberty and unity of the Spirit.

†**'sectist.** *Obs.* [f. SECT *sb.*[1] + -IST.] One who follows a particular sect, a sectary.

1612 HEYWOOD *Apol. Actors* I. 15 Mooved by the sundry exclamations of many seditious sectists in this age. **1630** BRATHWAIT *Eng. Gentlem.* (1641) 69 Then should wee have no Sectists or Separatists divided from the unity of Faith to disturbe us. **1654** VILVAIN *Theorem. Theol.* iii. 91 St. Austins saying..wil wel suit such Sectists.

sectiuncle, sectiuncule. *rare.* [ad. L. type **sectiuncula*, dim. of *sectiōn-em* SECTION *sb.*]

1. A small section.

1838 GLADSTONE *Let.* in G. W. E. Russell *Life* (1891) 55, I have divided it all through into *sectiuncles*, occupying generally from half a page to a whole one.

2. A small, insignificant religious body.

1851 J. MARTINEAU *Misc.* (1852) 384 The crowd streaming from the conventicle of some new sect or sectiuncle.

†**'sective,** *a. Obs. rare.* [ad. late L. *sectiv-us*, f. *secāre* to cut.] Capable of division or cutting.

1656 BLOUNT *Glossogr.* **1745** tr. *Columella's Husb.* XI. iii, If you would make the leek sective [orig. *sectivum*], or fit for being often cut, the antients directed it to be left very thick sown.

sector ('sɛktə(r)), *sb.* [a. late L. *sector* (Boethius), a special use of L. *sector* (agent-n. f. *secāre* to cut), to translate Gr. τομεύς, lit. 'cutter', but used by Archimedes and later geometers in the senses 1 a and 1 b. Cf. F. *secteur*, Sp. *sector*, It. *settore*.]

I. 1. *Geom.* **a.** A plane figure contained by two radii and the arc of a circle, ellipse, or other central curve intercepted by them.

1570 BILLINGSLEY *Euclid* III. Def. ix. 83 A Sector of a circle. **1660** BARROW *Euclid* III. Def. ix, A sector of a circle is when an angle is set at the center of that circle. **1834** *Nat. Philos.* III. *Hist. Astron.* xvi. 85/1 (U.K.S.) The sector described by its radius vector in a given time round the earth is not changed. **1880** WILLIAMSON in *Encycl. Brit.* XIII. 50/2 The area of the elliptic sector APCP.

b. *sector of a sphere*: a solid generated by the revolution of a plane sector about one of its radii.

1656 tr. *Hobbes' Elem. Philos.* (1839) 371 The centre of equiponderation of the sector of a sphere. **1706** PHILLIPS (ed. Kersey), *Sector of a Sphere*, is a Conical Solid, whose Vertex or Top ends in the Center of the Sphere, and its Base, or Bottom, is a Segment of the same Sphere. **1840** LARDNER *Geom.* 217 The sector of a sphere consists of a cone and a spherical segment.

2. A body or figure having the shape of a sector; hence, a division or part, a unit. **a.** *gen.* Any piece of mechanism so shaped.

1715 DESAGULIERS *Fires Impr.* 122 At the under side of this Trap-Door, on each side have a small portion of a Circle, or a Sector, whose Center is at that part of the Trap-Door where the Hinge is. **1824** R. STUART *Hist. Steam Engine* 145 The double impulse was communicated to the working-beam by the intervention of a sector placed on the end of the pump-rod, working into a sector placed on the end of the working-beam. **1904** *Brit. & Col. Printer* 10 Mar. 14/2 A toothed sector having a pin and slot connection with it gives the required shift to the slide.

b. *Optics.* A division of a disc of paper or other material used in certain demonstrations.

1831 BREWSTER *Optics* vii. 70 The same result will be obtained, if we take a circle of paper and divide it into sectors of the same size as the coloured spaces. **1865** TYNDALL *Fragm. Sci.* (1876) 311 A disk with differently-coloured sectors is caused to rotate rapidly.

c. *Astr.* (See quot. 1863.)

1840 DICK *Sider. Heavens* 447 It appears..that one of these luminous fans or sectors was observed by Sir J. Herschel. **1863** HIND *Introd. Astron.* (ed. 3) 205 *Sector, Luminous*, in the head of a comet, is an emanation from the nucleus brighter than the rest of the coma in the form of a fan or sector.

d. *Electr.* A small piece of ebonite forming part of a Bertsch machine.

1894 BOTTONE *Electr. Instr. Making* 40 This little piece of ebonite (technically known as the 'sector') and its stand must be attached to the base board... Opposite this sector, but on the other side of the glass plate, is a 'comb'.

e. *Path.* A portion of the field of vision cut off in certain diseases of the optic nerve.

1899 *Allbutt's Syst. Med.* VI. 842 There was enormous swelling of the left optic nerve, coupled with loss of a large sector of the temporal portion of the field [of vision].

f. *Ent.* (See quot. 1861.)

1861 HAGEN *Synopsis Neuroptera N. Amer.* 343 *Sectors*, longitudinal nerves which strike the principal nerves at an angle, and usually reach the apex or hind margin of the wing.

g. (*a*) *Mil.* A part or section of a front, corresponding generally to a sector of a circle the centre of which is a headquarters.

1916 'BOYD CABLE' *Action Front* 237 The Colonel was..vainly trying to recall any sap-head within his sector of line. **1917** W. J. LOCKE *Red Planet* xiv. 161 Somewhere in this region—or sector, as we call it nowadays—there was a certain bit of ground that had been taken and retaken over and over again. **1930** S. SASSOON *Mem. Infantry Officer* IV. 61 Rose Trench..and Willow Avenue, were among the first objectives in our sector [of the Somme attack].

(*b*) A part or branch of an economy, or of a particular industry or activity. Freq. in phrases *private sector* (see PRIVATE *a.* 7j), *public sector* (see PUBLIC *a.* 2j).

1937 A. HUXLEY *Ends & Means* xii. 196 The accomplished intellectual understands the relations subsisting between many sectors of apprehended reality. **1950** *Hansard Commons* 7 Mar. 183 Every Member of this House..could point to examples of gross feather bedding both in Government Service, in the socialised sector of the economy and in private industry. **1959** *Listener* 5 Nov. 767/2 Problems of a comparable nature in other sectors of industry. **1964** *Ann. Reg. 1963* 195 The Government's failure to carry out its declared aims—land reform..and planned development in all sectors of the economy—was to some extent caused by the President's readiness to yield too easily to pressure. **1980** *Sci. Amer.* Sept. 134/1 This development is the outcome of an explicit long-term policy to establish an adequate indigenous capacity in all the basic sectors, particularly metals and machinery, heavy chemicals.

(*c*) *gen.* One of the regions or districts into which a geographical area has been divided.

1943 H. A. WALLACE *Century of Common Man* (1944) 82 The ignorance that clouds many communities in many sectors of our own nation. **1958** *Listener* 9 Oct. 547/1 It has recently become fashionable to divide the Middle East into two major entities: the Arab sector and the non-Arab sector. **1971** *Daily Tel.* 12 Apr. 2/1 Experts believe nearly half of the country's daily oil consumption will be produced from the British sector of the sea by 1976.

h. *Computers.* A subdivision of a track on a magnetic drum or disc, or the block of data stored on it.

1958 *Computer Jrnl.* I. 128/1 Information is stored on 'sectors', each capable of containing 32 numbers... There are 1,024 such sectors, two to each track on a drum. **1962** *Gloss. Terms Automatic Data Processing* (*B.S.I.*) 68 *Sector*, a specified part of a track or band on a magnetic disc or drum store: hence, in programming, a deprecated alternative name for a block applied to the group of words stored on a sector. **1976** G. WIEDERHOLD *Database Design* ii. 40 If tracks cannot be divided by hardware into sectors, system software may divide a track into smaller units.

i. *Gram.* The position in a sentence normally occupied by any one of the basic units of which the sentence is composed. Cf. *sector analysis*, sense 3 below.

[**1955** E. H. JORDEN *Syntax Colloq. Jap.* v. 13 Evidence furnished by focus-classes indicates that minor sector boundaries should be observed even here—that the IC division should occur between the gerund of the copula and the following verb, where the sector boundary occurs.] **1966** R. L. ALLEN *Verb Syst. Present-Day Amer. Eng.* iii. 88 An examination of a large number of sequences suggests that in most non-literary sentences there is a kind of 'spectrum' of basic positions, which may be called 'sectors'. **1968** R. CRYMES *Some Syst. Substitution Correlations in Mod. Amer. Eng.* ii. 36 The major positions in the major English sentence, which is a sentence having time orientation [,]..exist in fixed sequence, and they are called sectors. **1974** CHISHOLM & MILIC *Eng. Lang.* VII. lii. 424 According to the grammatical description called Sector Analysis, the English sentence consists of ten sectors.

3. *attrib.* and *Comb.*, as *sector-like*, *-shaped* adjs.; **sector analysis** *Gram.*, the analysis of sentences in terms of the positions occupied by the basic units of which they are composed (cf. sense 2 i above); **sector machine** (see quot. 1888); **sector-piece**, a sector-shaped portion of any object; **sector scanning**, scanning with radar, sonar, or the like in which the detector rotates to and fro through a fixed angle; so **sector scan** *sb.* (freq. *attrib.*, with hyphen).

1966 R. L. ALLEN *Verb Syst. Present-Day Amer. Eng.* iii. 88 The order..of the occupied sectors remains constant... Many of the details of this '*sector' analysis lie beyond the scope of the present study. **1971** D. T. BÌNH *Tagmemic Comparison of Structure of Eng. & Vietnamese Sentences* iii. 66 Sector analysis..primarily emphasizes the positions of units on the sentence, trunk, and predicate..levels. **1977** *Amer. Speech 1975* L. 127 Only the concluding chapters give any attention to the problems of composition, and much of this is a discussion of sector analysis. **1899** *Allbutt's Syst. Med.* VII. 318 Occasionally, instead of complete blindness of one-half of the visual field, *sector, or quadrant-like defects are found in the upper or lower half. **1888** JACOBI *Printers' Voc.*, **Sector machine*, a cylindrical printing machine. **1715** DESAGULIERS *Fires Impr.* 122 Fix a couple of Springs under the Frame, each of which must bear against the Limbs of the *Sector-Pieces. **1902** ORDE-BROWNE *Armour* in *Encycl. Brit.* XXV. 670/2 Before adoption a sector piece was subjected to three blows from projectiles fired from an Elswick 100-ton breech-loading gun. **1946** *Radar: Summary Rep. & Harp Project* (U.S. Nat. Defense Res. Comm.) 143/2 **Sector scan*, motion of the scanner reflector back and forth through a limited angle, instead of through 360°. **1969** R. P. SELBY in C. J. Richards *Mech. Engin. in Radar & Communications* ix. 387 Radar installations used for air-traffic control are sometimes required to operate on demand in sector-scan mode, the area of scan usually not exceeding 20° and the rate of scan approximately 20 scans per minute. **1978** *Nature* 9 Nov. 174/1 A simple sector scan mode is used, at a frequency of 1 Hz, with the target coupled acoustically to the transducer with water. **1946** *Princ. & Applic. of Underwater Sound* (U.S. Nat. Defense Res. Comm.) (1968) xi. 213/1 A plan position indicator is..required for *sector scanning, the CRO spot..tracing a synchronous map of the motion of the active region. **1969** R. P. SELBY in C. J. Richards *Mech. Engin. in Radar & Communications* ix. 386 It is sometimes required to move an antenna system about a vertical axis in an oscillatory mode (sector-scanning), thereby turning the antenna through a limited arc in either direction. **1974** Y. KIKUCHI in G. W. Stroke et al. *Ultrasonic Imaging & Holography* 267 Asberg has been proposing a high speed sector scanning of a focusing mirror system receiver for obtaining an ultrasonic cinematogram of the living heart. **1977** *Navy News* July 18/2 Because the number of wrecks on our continental shelf is so high..modern equipment such as Hydrosearch—the British sector-scanning surveying sonar—is particularly needed. **1902** ORDE-BROWNE *Armour* in *Encycl. Brit.* XXV. 670/2 The joints shown in this figure indicate that the turret roof is built up of fifteen *sector-shaped pieces.

II. 4. A mathematical instrument, invented by Thomas Hood (see quot. 1598) and improved by Edmund Gunter, used for the mechanical solution of various problems.

In its present form it consists of two flat rules stiffly hinged together, inscribed with various kinds of scales. In Hood's form, a graduated arc was an essential part of the instrument, and from some of the inventor's remarks it would appear that the name was given with reference to the form of the apparatus (see sense 1), not, as might be supposed, to its function in performing proportional division of lines.

1598 HOOD *Making & Use of Sector* 1 A Sector is a mathematicall instrument consisting of 2. feete, one moueable, an other fixed, making an angle, and of a circumferentall Limbe. **1624** GUNTER (*title*), The Description and use of the Sector, the Crosse-staffe, and other Instruments. **1673** E. BROWNE *Trav. Germ.*, etc. (1677) 18 By applying an Instrument joynted like a Carpenters Rule, or a Sector, the Skin is held fast. **1766** *Complete Farmer* s.v. *Surveying* 7 G 1/1 If a little error be committed in making up the sector, the most of it goes off again in the substraction of the triangle. **1803** *Phil. Trans.* XCIII. 387 In the sector I am going to describe, Mr. Ramsden has obviated the inconveniences attendant on the use of former sectors. **1884** F. J. BRITTEN *Watch & Clockm.* 233 The sector is really a proportional measuring gauge, suited for nearly all requirements of the watch and clock maker.

attrib. **1664** WAKELY *Mariners-Compass rectified* (1694) 273 All Sector-Lines or Scales, meet at the center of the Head (where the Joint is) at the left-hand, and from thence are figured towards the right, each being twice repeated; that is, one on each Leg or Side of the Sector answering one another. *Ibid.* 274 The Use of the Sector-Lines for Projection.

5. An astronomical instrument consisting of a telescope turning about the centre of a graduated arc. See DIP-*sector*, ZENITH-*sector*.

1711 HEARNE *Collect.* (O.H.S.) III. 129 By my Sector it is but 141. **1755** *Gentl. Mag.* XXV. 511 A sector of six feet radius, whose divided arc was somewhat more than 51 degrees. **1843** *Penny Cycl.* XXVII. 765/2 Bradley's sector as originally made was not reversible, and therefore only fit for measuring differences or variations. **1877** CHAMBERS *Astron.* 920 *Astronomical Sector*, an instrument for finding the distance between two objects whose distance is too great to be measured by means of a micrometer in a fixed telescope.

sector ('sɛktə(r)), *v.* [f. SECTOR *sb.*] *trans.* To divide into sectors; to provide with sectors.

1884 F. J. BRITTEN *Watch & Clockm.* 292 Circularly rounded pinions may be used as drivers if they are sectored large. **1902** W. D. JONES in *Times* 1 Dec. 15/2 It would appear that..the Belle Isle light..is not correctly sectored.

sector, variant of SECUTOR *Obs.*, executor.

sectoral ('sɛktərəl), *a.* [f. SECTOR *sb.* + -AL[1].]

1. Pertaining to a sector. **a.** (See SECTOR *sb.* 4.)

1778 HUTTON in *Phil. Trans.* LXVIII. 768 In this manner were computed all the differences which were necessary to be found, and placed in their proper squares formed by the meeting of the horizontal and vertical lines, or rings and sectoral spaces, in the following set of.. tables. **1828** MOORE *Pract. Navig.* 19 The sectoral lines are like so many similar triangles, namely, that their corresponding sides are proportional.

b. (See SECTOR *sb.* 2 g.)

1969 P. ANDERSON in Cockburn & Blackburn *Student Power* 223 There were various sectoral attacks and refutations of Marx by marginalist economists like Böhm-Bawerk. **1971** *Seminar* Nov. 12/2 The second.. category of English dailies in India is of the more 'professional' dailies. .. Lumped together, they certainly represent what may be called 'a sectoral monopoly'. **1981** *Times* 13 Aug. 16/4 In the sectoral breakdown, the statistics show that the banks have increased their support to manufacturing industry.

2. ***sectoral horn*** (Radio), a horn antenna having a rectangular cross-section and plane sides flared in one dimension only.

1939 W. L. BARROW in *Proc. IRE* XXVII. 41 A horn whose cross section is rectangular and whose sides flare in one direction only.. will be termed a sectoral horn. **1959** K. HENNEY *Radio Engin. Handbk.* (ed. 5) xx. 88 The sectoral horn is flared in one dimension only, either in the plane parallel to the electric vector (*E* plane) or in the plane parallel to the magnetic vector (*H* plane).

sectored ('sɛktəd), *a.* [f. SECTOR *sb.* + -ED[2], or SECTOR *v.* + -ED[1].] Divided into sectors; applied *spec.* to a disc divided into alternate black and white sectors of equal size.

1900 W. M. STINE *Photometrical Measurements* i. 21 Illumination.. viewed through a sectored disk, rotating at a critical speed. **1972** *Nature* 13 Oct. 407/1 He demonstrated this phenomenon by using a black-and-white sectored disk rotated on a phonographic turntable.

sectorial (sɛk'tɔərɪəl), *a.*[1] (and *sb.*) [f. SECTOR *sb.* + -IAL.] Of or pertaining to a sector.

a. Pertaining to the instrument called a sector (SECTOR *sb.* 4, 5).

1803 *Phil. Trans.* XCIII. 387 The principles on which he has founded the several improvements, consist in the means of uniting the sectorial tube to its axis. **1808** TROUGHTON *ibid.* XCIX. 130 The sectorial arc must also be adjusted to its proper radius. **1841** *Penny Cycl.* XXI. 180/1 The others [scales] are merely laid down for convenience on such blank spaces as are left by the converging or sectorial scales.

b. Pertaining to a sector of a circle or a sphere (see SECTOR *sb.* 1 a, 1 b).

1867 THOMSON & TAIT *Nat. Philos.* §781 I. 621 These circles.. are either (1.) all in parallel planes.. and cut the spherical surface into zones, in which case the harmonic is called zonal; or (2.) they.. cut the surface into equal sectors, in which case the harmonic is called sectorial; or (3.) some [etc.]. *Ibid.*, The sectorial harmonics of order *i* [etc.]. **1880** WILLIAMSON in *Encycl. Brit.* XIII. 50/2 If the sectorial area APCP, be represented by S, the preceding result gives [etc.].

c. *Bot.* Applied to a type of chimæra (see quot. 1968). Also as *sb.* [ad. G. *sektorialchimäre* (E. Baur 1909, in *Zeitschr. f. induktive Abstammungs- u. Vererbungslehre* I. 342).]

1927 *Jrnl. Genetics* XVIII. 257 In a sectorial plant a sector (of the stem) is formed of tissue of another species or type. *Ibid.*, Sectorials of the type to which the term is restricted in this paper are of very rare occurrence. **1934** W. NEILSON JONES *Plant Chimaeras & Graft Hybrids* ii. 18 True sectorial chimaeras are relatively uncommon; most of the plants recorded as 'sectorials' were probably mericlinal in structure. **1959** *New Biol.* XXX. 38 The first composite branch to arise had one side producing tomato leaves and the other producing nightshade leaves, and it was, therefore, concluded that the branch was composed half of tomato tissue and half of nightshade tissue. This type of structure is known as a Sectorial chimera. **1968** [see PERICLINAL *a.* 2 b].

Hence **sec'torially** *adv.*, in or into sectors.

1963 *Heredity* XVIII. 266 These plants have.. a sectorially divided growing point.

sectorial (sɛk'tɔərɪəl), *a.*[2] [f. mod.L. *sectōrius* (f. L. *sector* cutter: see SECTOR *sb.*) + -AL[1].] Having the function of cutting; the distinctive epithet of the premolar teeth.

1840-5 OWEN *Odontogr.* I. 475 In most Carnivora one molar tooth on each side of both jaws has its crown modified, .. for reacting upon the opposite tooth, like the blades of scissors,.. whence Cuvier has applied to this tooth the name of '*Dent carnassière*', which I have rendered '*dens sectorius*', sectorial, or scissor-tooth. **1875** BLAKE *Zool.* 22 We perceive in the Lion large pointed canine teeth,.. and a series of sectorial teeth behind them. **1881** MIVART *Cat* 28 The third premolar is yet larger.. and from its trenchant shape is called the upper sectorial tooth.

sectorie, obs. form of SECTARY.

sectorization (ˌsɛktəraɪ'zeɪʃən). *rare.* [f. SECTOR *sb.* + -IZE + -ATION.] Division into sectors; administration or operation on the basis of sectors or local divisions.

1962 *Flight International* LXXXII. 479/1 Traffic growth in recent years has increased the pressure on both pilots and controllers, especially in the sphere of voice communications, so that means have had to be found to reduce their workload. Various alleviating possibilities have been tested, such as 'sectorization', but they in turn usually introduce new difficulties. **1976** *Social Psychiatry* XI. 27 Sectorization of the psychiatric care, which means that all psychiatric care within a geographical area should be under a common management.

sectour(e, var. ff. SECUTOR *Obs.*, executor.

sectroid ('sɛktrɔɪd). [? f. SECTOR + -OID.] The curved surface of two adjacent groins in a vault.

1860 NEWLANDS *Carp. & Joiner's Assist.* 77 To find the covering of the smaller sectroid BPLOD. **1875** in KNIGHT *Dict. Mech.*

† **'sectuary.** *Obs.* [Altered form of SECTARY, after words like *textuary*.] = SECTARY.

1592 NASHE *P. Penilesse* 17 *marg.*, Such Sermons I meane as our sectuaries preach in ditches. *a* **1618** RALEIGH *Mahomet* (1637) 17 God was displeased with the Meccans for the rigorous persecuting of him and his Sectuaries. **1654** E. JOHNSON *Hist. New Eng.* xlii. 99 The pitifull and erronious Doctrines broached by the Sectuaries.

sectur(e, var. ff. SECUTOR *Obs.*, executor.

† **'secture.** *Obs. rare.* [ad. mod.L. type **sectūra*, f. L. *sect-*, *secāre* to cut: see -URE.] A section, cutting, incision.

a **1643** CARTWRIGHT *Comedies & Poems* (1651) 210 Thus would his Horse and all his vectures, Reduc'd to figures and to sectures, Produce new Diagrams and Lectures. **1693** EVELYN *De La Quint. Compl. Gard.* Dict., *Insects*, are all little animals whose bodies are divided by several cuts as 'twere and sectures.

Secuana, var. SETSWANA.

† **secubate**, *v. Obs.*[−0] [a. L. *sēcubāt-*, ppl. stem of *sēcubāre*, f. *sē-* (SE- *prefix*) + *cubāre* to lie down.] (See quot.)

1623 COCKERAM I, *Secubate*, to lie alone [*printed* aboue] by ones selfe.

secular ('sɛkjʊlə(r)), *a.* and *sb.* Forms: 3-6 **seculer**, 4-5 **seculere** (4 **seculeer**, **secler**, 4-5 **seclere**, 5 **seculier**), 5- **secular.** [In branch I, a. OF. *seculer* (mod.F. *séculier*), ad. L. *sæculāris*, f. *sæcul-um* generation, age, in Christian Latin 'the world', esp. as opposed to the church: see SECLE, SIECLE. In branch II, directly ad. L. *sæculāris*, whence mod.F. *séculaire* (which has influenced some of the uses in Eng.). Cf. Sp. *seglar*, *secular*, Pg. *secular*, It. *secolare*.]

A. *adj.*

I. Of or pertaining to the world.

1. *Eccl.* **a.** Of members of the clergy: Living 'in the world' and not in monastic seclusion, as distinguished from 'regular' and 'religious'. ***secular canon***: see CANON *sb.*[2] ***secular abbot***: a person not a monk, who had the title and part of the revenues, but not the functions of an abbot.

In early use frequently placed after the sb., as ***canon secular, priest secular.***

c **1290** *St. Edmund* 393 in *S. Eng. Leg.* I. 442 At salesburi he was i-maket Canoun seculer. **1297-1868** [see CANON *sb.* 1]. *a* **1300** *Cursor M.* 27244 In scrift.. enentes clergis seculers to þe preist at frain it feres o symony. *c* **1380** WYCLIF *Sel. Wks.* I. 73 And þus boþ clerkes seculers and þese newe religiouse forsaken þes two weies. *a* **1400** *Minor Poems fr. Vernon MS.* xxxii. 1054, I þat am in Religioun, I naue no pouwer to ȝiue no mete, Ne drinke.. þerfore me were beter seculer. **1402** *Pol. Poems* (Rolls) II. 23 Why be ye evill apaid that secular priestes should preach the gospell? **1546** *Yorks. Chantry Surv.* (Surtees) II. 426 A seculer man, deane or incombent there. **1673** *Essex Papers* (Camden) I. 138, I made use of some Fryers, who all ways have their litle wrangles wth y[e] secular Clergy. **1716** M. DAVIES *Athen. Brit.* III. 86 Cardinal Rochefaucault being the Secular or Commendatory Abbot thereof. **1782** BURKE *Penal Laws agst. Ir. Cath.* Wks. VI. 235 The secular clergy.. are universally fallen into such contempt, that [etc.]. **1874** STUBBS *Const. Hist.* I. viii. §84 Before the middle of the eighth century.. the secular were synodically divided from the monastic clerks. **1884** *Manch. Exam.* 25 Feb. 5/5 A few secular priests have been invited to co-operate with the resident clergy.

b. Of or pertaining to secular clergy.

1570 FOXE *A. & M.* (ed. 2) 4/2 Reducing regular Monasteries, to a secular state. **1686** tr. *Chardin's Trav. Persia* 96 It differs little from the secular Habit. **1831** SIR W. HAMILTON *Discuss.* (1852) 414 At the commencement of the fourteenth century.. the number of the secular colleges [was], at the highest, only three. **1871** FREEMAN *Norm. Conq.* (1876) IV. xviii. 312 The minster of Saint Werburh, then a secular, but soon to become a monastic, house.

2. a. Belonging to the world and its affairs as distinguished from the church and religion; civil, lay, temporal. Chiefly used as a negative term, with the meaning non-ecclesiastical, non-religious, or non-sacred.

secular arm (= med.L. *brachium seculare*, F. *le bras séculier*): the civil power as 'invoked' by the church to punish offenders.

c **1290** *Beket* 926 in *S. Eng. Leg.* I. 133 And also ȝe bez alȝare In seculer court to demen me: And þat nolde nouȝt wel fare. **1340** *Ayenb.* 215 God.. nele þet me maki uorewerdes ne noyses ne nyedes seculeres þerinne [i.e. His house]. *c* **1380** WYCLIF *Wks.* (1880) 384 þai occupien not siche lordeschipis in propir, as seculer lordis done, but in comoun, like as the apostles. *Ibid.* 385 As prisonynge & hangynge.. the whiche sum-tyme bylongyd oonly to the seculer arme of þe chirche. **1387** TREVISA *Higden* (Rolls) V. 97 þat no man schulde accuse þe ministres of holy chirche to fore a seculer iuge. **1432-50** tr. *Higden* (Rolls) V. 289 Simplicius the pope.. ordeynede that noo clerke scholde receyve investiture.. of the honde of a seculer lay man [*Trevisa* of a lewed man, L. *de manu laici*]. **1456** SIR G. HAYE *Law Arms* (S.T.S.) 93 Kirk men suld pay tailles, tributis and imposiciouns to seclere kingis or princis. **1593** NASHE *Christ's T.* 34 The tongue is the Iudge..; the rest of our faculties and powers, are but the secular executioners of his sentence. *a* **1600** HOOKER *Eccl. Pol.* VII. xv. §14 And divers Councils likewise there are, which have forbidden the Clergy to bear any Secular Office. **1667** MILTON *P.L.* XII. 517 Then shall they seek.. Places and titles, and with these to joine Secular power, though feigning still to act By spiritual. **1673** TEMPLE *Observ. United Prov.* v. 165, I intend not here to speak of Religion at all as a Divine, but as a mere Secular man. **1737** FRANKLIN *Ess.* Wks. 1840 II. 292 Truth never fears the encounter; she scorns the aid of the secular arm. **1765** BLACKSTONE *Comm.* I. 366 The elected bishop could neither be consecrated, nor receive any secular profits. **1853** ROBERTSON *Serm.* Ser. IV. ii. (1863) 20 We stigmatize first one department of life and then another as secular; and so religion becomes a pale, unreal thing. **1873** J. H. NEWMAN *Hist. Sk.* III. III. vi. 333 Bishops now were great secular magistrates, and.. were involved in secular occupations. **1875** TENNYSON *Q. Mary* IV. i, A secular kingdom is but as the body Lacking a soul.

† **b.** *transf.* Of or belonging to the 'common' or 'unlearned' people. *Obs.*

1589 NASHE *Greene's Arcadia* To Gentl. Students A 3 b, Oft haue I obserued.. a secular wit that hath liued all dayes of his life by, what doe you lacke? to be more iudiciall.. then our quadrant crepundios. **1629** B. JONSON *New Inn* V. i, Hang him poore snip, a secular shop-wit!

c. Of literature, history, art (esp. music), hence of writers or artists: Not concerned with or devoted to the service of religion; not sacred; profane. Also of buildings, etc., Not dedicated to religious uses.

c **1450** in Aungier *Syon* (1840) 297 Not medlynge ther speche with seculer fables and fryuoles. **1529** MORE *Dyaloge* IV. Wks. 262/2 One.. neither in holi scripture nor in seculare litteratture vnlerned. **1801** BUSBY *Dict. Mus.*, *Secular-Music.* .. Whatever is composed for the theatre or chamber. An expression used in opposition to that of Sacred-Music. **1801** STRUTT *Sports & Past.* III. ii. 120 The plays mentioned in the preceding pages, and especially the miracles and mysteries, differed greatly from the secular plays.. acted by strolling companies. **1814** CHALMERS *Evid. Chr. Revelation* (1849) I. II. iii. 193 Points in which the historians of the New Testament can be brought into comparison with the secular historians of the age. **1835** I. TAYLOR *Spir. Despot.* III. 85 The education of youth was entrusted not to them [the priests], but to the professors of secular arts—rhetoric and gymnastics. **1860** PUSEY *Min. Proph.* 593 He says that, the bells of the horses, things simply secular, should bear the same inscription as the plate on the high priest's forehead. **1861** STANLEY *East. Ch.* iii. (1869) 97 A secular building was fitted up as a temporary house of prayer. **1874** REYNOLDS *John Bapt.* ii. 79 The supernatural conditions attributed in secular legend to the births of Buddha, Pythagoras and Plato. **1876** ROCK *Text. Fabr.* 63 The excellence of her work in secular silks.

d. Of education, instruction; Relating to non-religious subjects. (In modern use often implying the exclusion of religious teaching from education, or from the education provided at the public expense.) Of a school: That gives secular education.

1526 *Pilgr. Perf.* (W. de W. 1531) 32 b, The argumentes of seculer doctryne be argumentes of reason. **1867** in G. Duff *Pol. Surv.* (1868) 50 This may be hoped for in the increase of liberal sound and secular education in the Ottoman dominions. **1875** MANNING *Mission Holy Ghost* xiii. 377 The Holy See has always laid down.. that secular and religious instruction shall never be parted in Education. **1876** J. GRANT *Burgh Sch. Scot.* II. xiii. 424 These persons maintain that the public Schools should be purely secular.

3. a. Of or belonging to the present or visible world as distinguished from the eternal or spiritual world; temporal, worldly. Also ***secular-minded*** adj.

1597 HOOKER *Eccl. Pol.* v. lxxvi. §5 Religion and the feare of God as well induceth secular prosperitie as euerlasting blisse in the world to come. **1664** H. MORE *Myst. Iniq.* 251 The Sun and Moon have either a Spiritual signification or a Secular. **1875** GLADSTONE in McCabe *Life Holyoake* II. 163, I do not believe that secular motives are adequate either to propel or to restrain the children of our race. **1883** T. H. GREEN *Proleg. Ethics* Introd. 1 Nor does it [moral philosophy] by any means confine itself to what are commonly counted secular or 'positive' considerations.

Comb. **1899** T. VEBLEN *Theory of Leisure Class* xii. 314 The sacerdotal scheme of life.. does not hold good for the clergy of those denominations which have.. diverged from the old established schedule of beliefs or observances... Their manner of life.. does not differ in an extreme degree from that of secular-minded persons. **1930** A. BIRRELL *Et Cetera* 159 An equally veracious, though most secular-minded Presbyterian divine. **1957** N. FRYE *Anat. Criticism* 265 In the Anglo-Saxon congregation of Wulfstan there must have been a few secular-minded highbrows who were thinking.. of the preacher's mastery of alliterative rhythm.

b. Caring for the present world only; unspiritual. *rare.*

c **1425** *Orolog. Sapient.* vii. in *Anglia* X. 388/9 If they were of so harde herte and seculere affeccyone þat [etc.]. **1850** ROBERTSON *Serm.* Ser. III. ii. (1857) 20 Esau.. is called in Scripture a profane, that is, not a distinctly vicious, but a secular or worldly person.

absol. **1883** A. EDERSHEIM *Life Jesus* II. 275 To the secular nothing is spiritual; and to the spiritual nothing is secular.

¶ **4.** Used for: Pertaining to or accepting the doctrine of secularism; secularistic.

secular societies: the designation given to associations formed in various English towns from 1852 onwards to promote the spread of secularist opinions.

1856 R. OWEN in McCabe *Life Holyoake* (1908) I. 292 Your Secular Societies will do well to merge into this movement. **1870** G. J. HOLYOAKE *Princ. Secularism* 47 We believe there is sufficient soundness in Secular principles to make way in the world. **1884** T. COOPER *Men of the Time* (ed. 11) 582/1 Mr. Holyoake is editor of the *Present*, a secular and co-operative review.

II. Of or belonging to an age or long period.

5. Occurring or celebrated once in an age, century, or very long period. ***secular games, plays, shows*** [L. *ludi sæculares*]: in ancient Rome, games continuing three days and three nights celebrated once in an 'age' or period of 120 years. ***secular poem*** [L. *carmen sæculare*], a hymn composed to be sung at the secular games.

1599 PONT *Right Reckoning of Years* 34 Supposing that they celebrate their secular solemnities at the precise end and periode of every hundreth yeare. **1601** HOLLAND *Pliny* VIII. xlii. I. 221 The secular solemnities, exhibited by Claudius Cæsar, in the Circensian games. **1606** —— *Sueton.* 52 He restored againe..the Sæcular playes. **1696** B. KENNETT *Antiq. Rome* II. v. vii. 292 The famous Secular Poem of Horace was compos'd for this last Day, in the Secular Games held by Augustus. **1697** EVELYN *Numism.* iii. 62 To..divert the People..during the Secular Shews. **1706** HEARNE *Collect.* 3 Apr. (O.H.S.) I. 215 A letter sent to our University from the University of Francfort..inviting them to celebrate the secular day of the Foundation of their University, wch will happen in this month, it being now just two Hundred years since that University was Founded. **1716** ADDISON *Free-holder* No. 46 ¶1 When Augustus celebrated the secular year, which was kept but once in a century. **1790** GIBBON *Misc. Wks.* (1814) III. 418 Had a fortnight more been given to the philosopher, he might have celebrated his secular festival [*sc.* his hundredth birthday]. **1862** MERIVALE *Rom. Emp.* lxviii. (1865) VIII. 332 One man asserted that the secular fire would descend at the moment when..he should be seen transformed into a stork. **1869** RAWLINSON *Anc. Hist.* 509 M. Julius Philippus..celebrated the secular games in commemoration of the thousandth year from the founding of the city. **1884** *Q. Rev.* July 1 Changes in..the City..have been going on at a rate..unknown to any former generation, except those distant generations which have witnessed the rare and secular phenomena of siege, fire, and plague.

6. Living or lasting for an age or ages. Now chiefly with reminiscence of the scientific sense 7. Also (of trees, etc., after F. *séculaire*), centuries old.

1629 DONNE *Serm.* cxxxi. Wks. 1839 V. 435 If I had a secular glass, a glass that would run an age.., it would not be enough to tell the godly man what his treasure is. **1671** MILTON *Samson* 1707 And though her body die, her fame survives, A secular bird ages of lives. **1847** EMERSON *Poems, Monadnoc* 311 Slowsure Britain's secular might. **1850** TENNYSON *In Mem.* xli, I shall be thy mate no more, Tho' following with an upward mind The wonders that have come to thee, Thro' all the secular to-be. **1868–9** TYNDALL *Fragm. Sci.* v. (1871) 103 The improvement of man is secular—not the work of an hour or of a day. **1870** LOWELL *Among my Bks.* Ser. I. (1873) 253 We envy the secular leisures of Methusaleh. **1876** R. F. BURTON *Gorilla L.* I. 36 A fern field surrounded by a forest of secular trees. **1879** STEVENSON *Trav. with Donkey* 186 Mankind outlives saecular animosities, as a single man awakens from the passions of a day. **1888** BRYCE *Amer. Commw.* III. VI. cxv. 653 The centripetal forces are permanent and secular forces, working from age to age.

7. In scientific use, of processes of change: Having a period of enormous length; continuing through long ages. **a.** *Astr.* Chiefly of changes in the orbits or the periods of revolution of the planets, as in ***secular acceleration, equation, inequality, variation.*** The terms *secular acceleration, secular variation* were formerly also used (with reference to the sense 'century' of L. *sæculum*) for the amount of change per 100 years; similarly † ***secular precession*** (see quot. 1812). *secular equation* is also used more widely to designate any equation of the form $|a_{ij} - b_{ij}\lambda| = 0$ $(i,j = 1,2, \ldots, n)$, in which the left-hand side is a determinant and which arises in quantum mechanics.

1801 *Monthly Rev.* XXXV. 537 M. De La Place..found the secular equation of the moon to be due to the action of the sun on the moon. **1812** WOODHOUSE *Astron.* ix. 63 The secular precession, that is, the accumulated precessions of 100 years. **1812–16** PLAYFAIR *Nat. Phil.* (1819) II. 275 In the orbit of Mars, the eccentricity is diminishing. The secular variation of the greatest equation of the centre is—37″. **1834** MRS. SOMERVILLE *Connex. Phys. Sci.* iii. (1849) 16 Secular inequalities. **1862** CAYLEY *Math. Papers* (1890) III. 522 On the Secular Acceleration of the Moon's Mean Motion. **1937** E. C. KEMBLE *Fund. Princ. Quantum Mech.* x. 361 Its components must yield a nontrivial (*i.e.*, nonvanishing) solution of the set of *g* equations $\Sigma_n(A_{mn} - a\delta_{mn})x_n = 0$... Such a solution exists only if the determinant of the coefficients vanishes, *i.e.*, if *a* is a root of the so-called 'secular' equation det $(\mathbf{A} - a\mathbf{I}) = ..0$. **1974** GILL & WILLIS *Pericyclic Reactions* i. 21 To obtain the wave functions corresponding to these energies it is necessary to solve the secular equations using the appropriate values of *E*.

b. *Geol., Physical Geogr., Meteorol.*, etc.

1833 LYELL *Princ. Geol.* Gloss., *Secular Refrigeration*, the periodical cooling and consolidation of the globe, from a supposed original state of fluidity from heat. **1856** KANE *Arct. Expl.* I. xxiii. 308 A secular elevation of the coastline. **1861** TYNDALL *Fragm. Sci.* xiii. (1871) 399 The earth's magnetic constituents are gradually changing their distribution. This change is very slow; it is technically called the secular change. **1867** H. MACMILLAN *Bible Teach.* xvi. (1870) 320 Those grand secular tides which have punctually recurred every ten thousand years. **1872** —— *True Vine* v. 176 The earth has its secular seasons as well as its annual. **1880** HAUGHTON *Phys. Geog.* ii. 53 The contraction of the globe due to secular cooling. **1887** ABERCROMBY *Weather* 312 Annual and Secular Variations.

8. *Econ.* and *Statistics.* Of a fluctuation or trend: occurring or persisting over an unlimited period; not periodic or short-term.

1895 A. MARSHALL *Princ. Econ.* (ed. 3) I. v. v. 470 There are secular movements of normal price, caused by the gradual growth of knowledge, of population and of capital, and the changing conditions of demand and supply from one generation to another. **1926** L. D. EDIE *Econ.* II. iv. 49 Economic fluctuations fall into four major types: seasonal, secular, cyclical, and residual. **1971** H. S. SHRYOCK et al. *Methods & Materials Demography* II. xiii. 377/2 If the observations are made at different times of the year, seasonal movements may also be apparent. When we are trying to describe the growth of a population over a relatively longer period of time (for example, India from 1872 to 1961) we are generally interested in the secular trend only. **1973** *Daily Tel.* 15 Jan. 17/6 This is the first time the Government has had to pay so much for money but the secular trend of interest rates will stop rising only if the rate of inflation is brought down. **1976** *Sci. Amer.* Sept. 107/1 The secular trend of workers migrating out of agricultural jobs as a result of technological change in agriculture has recently slackened.

B. *sb.*

1. a. One of the secular clergy, as distinguished from a 'regular' or monk.

c **1290** *Beket* 2205 in *S. Eng. Leg.* I. 169 Ase heo strepten of his cloþes, al a-boue heo founde Clerkene cloþes..and.. Monekene Abite with-Inne..So þat he was Monek with-Inne, and seculer with-oute. *c* **1330** R. BRUNNE *Chron.* (1810) 243, & þer was scho inne four & fifty ȝere, Norised with Wynne, nunne and seculere. *c* **1450** *St. Cuthbert* (Surtees) 6230 He helpid seculers to putt oute Fra þe kirke, and monkes deuoute sette þare. **1544** BALE *Chron. Sir J. Oldcastle* 27 b, The seculars and fryers coude not therin agre. *Ibid.* 39 Both..seculars and relygyouse with dyuerse other expert menne. *a* **1698** T. WHITE *Monitions & Advices* II. (1720) 49 Monks, who despised the settled Clergy, and called them Seculars, giving themselves the glorious Title of Religious. **1864** BRYCE *Holy Rom. Emp.* v. (1875) 67 Endeavours to bring the seculars into a monastic life.

b. A Jesuit lay brother.

1641 R. BROOKE *Eng. Episc.* 10 The others were like the Seculars among the Jesuites, And..did (as the Seculars do) perform the Civill part of those Religious Services.

c. (See quot.)

1801 BUSBY *Dict. Mus.*, *Seculars*, those unordained officiates of any cathedral, or chapel, whose functions are confined to the vocal department of the choir.

2. One who is engaged in the affairs of the world as distinct from the church; a layman.

c **1400** *Apol. Loll.* 77 Now bi new lawis, clerkis propriun to hemsilf temporal þingis as seclereis. *c* **1425** *St. Mary of Oignies* I. i. in *Anglia* VIII. 135/30 Hir fader and modir, as maner is of seculers, wolde haue rayed hir wiþ delycate garmentis. **1483** CAXTON *Gold. Leg.* 115/3 The monkes that goon out of theyr..selles yf they conuerse longe with seculiers they muste nedes lese theyr holynesse. **1509** WATSON *Ship of Fools* ii. (1517) A iij b, In many places be some counsellers & gouernours of courtes, as well seculers as ecclesyastykes. **1596** DALRYMPLE tr. *Leslie's Hist. Scot.* I. 119 *marg.*, The seculars of the Realme in Scotland ar gouerned be the burgesse lawis. **1618** HALES *Lett. fr. Synod Dort* 6 The clergy though that if it pleased the Seculars it might be done. **1710** *Lond. Gaz.* No. 4726/1 All the Inhabitants..as well Seculars as Ecclesiasticks. **1829** LANDOR *Imag. Conv., Miguel & his Mother* Wks. 1853 I. 560/1 Seculars do not know half the wickedness of the world,..until their pastors lead them by the hand and show it them.

†**3.** A centennial anniversary, centenary. *rare.*

1706 HEARNE *Collect.* 20 June (O.H.S.) I. 263 King of Prussia's Letter to ye Queen about ye University's Celebration of ye Secular of Francfurt. **1706** *Ibid.* 27 June I. 267. **1709** *Ibid.* 27 Aug. II. 241, 242.

secularism ('sɛkjʊlərɪz(ə)m). [f. SECULAR *a.* + -ISM.]

1. The doctrine that morality should be based solely on regard to the well-being of mankind in the present life, to the exclusion of all considerations drawn from belief in God or in a future state. **a.** As the name of a definitely professed system of belief, promulgated by G. J. Holyoake (1817–1906). **b.** In wider sense, as denoting a mode of thought more or less implicitly held and acted upon.

1851 G. J. HOLYOAKE in *Reasoner* 10 Dec., I will lay before the meeting the present position of Secularism in the provinces. **1854** —— (*title*) Secularism the practical Philosophy of the People. *Ibid.* 5 The term Secularism has been chosen..as expressing a certain positive and ethical element, which the terms 'Infidel', 'Sceptic', 'Atheist' do not express. **1855** MISS COBBE *Intuit. Mor.* 161 *note*, The earlier Judaism is quite anomalous in its mixture of morality and secularism. **1869** M. PATTISON *Serm.* (1885) 172 Influential leaders of opinion warn us against..materialism, secularism, unbelief. **1884** J. PARKER *Larger Ministry* 28 Secularism cannot be more industrious than Christianity calls upon its followers to be.

2. The view that education, or the education provided at the public cost, should be purely secular.

1872 *Q. Rev.* Apr. 517 The Nonconformists who advocate pure Secularism in national education have in effect come down from their religious position altogether.

secularist ('sɛkjʊlərɪst), *sb.* (and *a.*). [f. SECULAR + -IST.]

1. One of the secular clergy; a secular. *nonce-use.*

1716 M. DAVIES *Athen. Brit.* I. Pref. 62 Of the Modern Fanaticism of Seditious Priests of all the Religions in Europe, viz... Of Secularists and Regularists [etc.].

2. An adherent of secularism.

1851 *Reasoner* 3 Dec., We use the word Secularist as best indicating that province of human duty which belongs to this life. **1859** I. TAYLOR *Logic in Theol.* 219 India..whether governed by Christian men or by secularists, shall feel that it must amend its usages. **1876** GLADSTONE *Relig. Thought* v. in *Contemp. Rev.* June 22 The Secularist..does not of necessity assert anything but the positive and exclusive claims of the purposes, the enjoyments, and the needs, presented to us in the world of sight and experience.

3. An advocate of exclusively secular education.

1872 *Q. Rev.* Apr. 522 The attempt of the 'Secularists' to deprive the poor of religious teaching in the schools.

4. *attrib.* and *appos.* (quasi-*adj.*).

1888 MRS. H. WARD *R. Elsmere* III. VI. xxxviii. 166 The most notorious secularist lecturers held forth. **1890** *Times* 31 Jan. 9/3 This characteristic sample of secularist intolerance. **1904** DOR. P. HUGHES *Life H. P. Hughes* xii. 295 Mr. Jacob Holyoake, the well-known Secularist leader.

secularistic (ˌsɛkjʊlə'rɪstɪk), *a.* [f. SECULARIST + -IC.] Of, pertaining to, or characterized by secularism.

1862 *Westm. Rev.* Jan. 93 People, whose cheap theological literature is..limited to Orthodox tracts and Secularistic periodicals. **1881** *Spectator* No. 2766. 851 Women will imbibe education the more..kindly, that it will have no ostentatiously secularistic aspect. **1899** *Q. Rev.* Apr. 465 The secularistic policy of Gambetta and Jules Ferry.

secularity (sɛkjʊ'lærɪtɪ). Forms: 4 **seculerte**, 6–7 **secularitie**, 6– **secularity**. [a. F. *sécularité* (1332 in Hatz.-Darm; there may have been an AF. **seculerté*, whence Wyclif's form), or directly ad. med.L. *sæculāritās*, f. L. *sæculāris* SECULAR *a.*: see -ITY.]

I. †**1.** Secular jurisdiction or power. *Obs.*

c **1380** WYCLIF *Wks.* (1880) 385 How þai [*sc.* clerks] bissyen hem to be kyngis in her owne, & reioycen hem fulle myche in þat cyuylite or seculerte. **1535** STEWART *Cron. Scot.* II. 458 That kirkmen suld nocht be No way subjectit to secularitie.

2. The condition or quality of being secular.

a. Occupation with secular affairs (on the part of clergymen); secular spirit or behaviour. Also occas. in wider application: Worldliness, absence of religious principle or feeling.

1395 [PURVEY] *Remonstrance* (1851) 147 Seculerte among prelatis and curatis so that oon take to himsilf alle the profitis of a chirche. **1636** *Unbishop. Timothy & Titus* 30 Your Lordly Pompe,..luxury, secularity, suppression of preaching. **1690** E. GEE *Jesuit's Mem.* 123 The Bishop's own Person..[should be far] from..the prophanity and secularity of others, as Hawking, Hunting,..and the like. **1711** G. HICKES *Two Treat.* II. (1847) 231 This secularity of the clergy in complying with the..vanities..of the age. **1835** I. TAYLOR *Spir. Despot.* II. 53 Sloth, pride, and secularity, have crept upon those [clergy] to whom mankind should look up for patterns of purity and heavenly-mindedness. **1843** CARLYLE *Past & Pr.* II. iv. 80 Jocelin, we see, is not without secularity: Our *Dominus Abbas* was intent enough on the divine offices; but then his Account-Books —? **1876** FREEMAN *Norm. Conq.* V. xxiv. 497 The tendency to secularity which beset all the Teutonic Churches from the beginning. **1882** SEELEY *Nat. Relig.* 235 There is a Lower Life, of which the animating principle is secularity, or—in the popular sense of the word—materialism.

†**b.** Lay character (of persons claiming to be in holy orders). *Obs. rare*$^{-1}$.

1616 CHAMPNEY *Voc. Bps.* 152 For the more cleare proofe of the meere secularitie, and pure nullitie of the pretended cleargy of England, as well as of other falsly reformed churches: I will here examine the ordination of them.

c. Secular or non-sacred character; absence of connexion with religion.

1879 *Sat. Mus. Rev.* 6 Sept. 504 At times..the music is really elevating, when suddenly we are back again into secularity. **1910** *Spectator* 25 June 1075/1 To insist..on the secularity of the State can only help to degrade it.

3. A secular matter. Chiefly *pl.* Secular affairs; worldly possessions or pursuits.

1511 COLET *Serm. Conforming* B j, If you haue any secular besynes, ordeyne them to be iuges that be mooste in contemt in ye churche..of this secularitie. **1640** BP. HALL *Episc.* III. viii. 267 How much are we beholden to these kinde friends, who are so desirous to ease us of these unproper secularities? **1828** E. IRVING *Last Days* 144 As to the ordination of elders, or priests, how do men seek the office for mere.. advancement in the secularities of life! **1840** J. J. GURNEY in *Mem.* (1854) II. 228 My secularities afford me many large opportunities of helping others. **1857** KINGSLEY *Two Y. Ago* x, The morning he [the Curate] spent at the school, or in parish secularities. **1877** MORLEY *Crit. Misc.* Ser. II. 401 To throw a golden halo round the secularity of the hour. **1878** R. BRAITHWAITE *Life W. Pennefather* xi. 248 It was a rule with him..that no secularity should be permitted to intrude on the Lord's day.

†**4.** The civil authority or body. *Obs.*

1630 *R. Johnson's Kingd. & Commw.* 380 The chiefe Officer of the Secularitie is the Palatine of Hungaria. **1637** BASTWICK *Litany* I. 11, I intend speedily to write unto the secularity of that ancient city [*i.e.* Babylon], and dedicate my method of Physick to it.

II. 5. The character of having long periods.

1844 EMERSON *Ess.* Ser. II. vi. (1876) 147 Geology has initiated us into the secularity of nature, and taught us to.. exchange our Mosaic and Ptolemaic schemes for her large style.

secularization (ˌsɛkjʊləraɪ'zeɪʃən). [f. SECULARIZE *v.* + -ATION. Cf. F. *sécularisation* (16–17 c. in Hatz.-Darm.).]

1. The conversion of an ecclesiastical or religious institution or its property to secular possession and use; the conversion of an ecclesiastical state or sovereignty to a lay one; an instance of this.

1706 PHILLIPS (ed. Kersey), *Secularization*, The Act of Secularizing. **1742** RICHARDSON *Pamela* III. 273 A Bill for restoring to it all that it had lost by Impropriations and other Secularizations. **1845** LINGARD *Anglo-Sax. Ch.* II. xiv. 343 Till its [*sc.* the abbey of Fulda's] late secularization, its superior was a prince of the empire. **1864** *Realm* 20 Apr. 4 He..wished to accompany the restoration of the Pope by a number of reasonable reforms,..namely,..the secularisation of the administration [etc.]. **1875** GLADSTONE *Glean.* VI. xv. 204 The secularisation of the property of the Religious Orders has been..a more or less rude..operation. **1888** BURGON *12 Gd. Men* I. iv. 428 He resented the secularization of revenues set apart for a..sacred purpose.

b. *transf.*

1822 LAMB *Elia* Ser. I. *Some Old Actors*, But we find him [*sc.* a chorister], after the probation of a twelvemonth or so, reverting to a secular condition, and become one of us... The first fruits of his secularization was an engagement upon the boards of Old Drury.

2. The giving of a secular or non-sacred character or direction to (art, studies, etc.); the placing (of morals) on a secular basis; the restricting (of education) to secular subjects.

1863 E. A. BOND in *Fine Arts Quarterly* I. 87 With this secularization of the art, painting rapidly threw off the conventionalism of the cloister. **1865** LECKY *Ration.* (1878) I. 57 It..thus prepared the way for that general secularisation of the European intellect. **1875** T. HILL *True Order Stud.* 143 Persons who demand the entire secularization of the schools. **1879** H. SPENCER *Data of Ethics* Pref. 4 Now that moral injunctions are losing the authority given by their supposed sacred origin, the secularization of morals is becoming imperative.

3. The alteration of the status of an ecclesiastic from regular to secular.

1882-3 *Schaff's Encycl. Relig. Knowl.* 2146 Secularization means..the legal absolution from ecclesiastical vows.

secularize ('sɛkjʊləraɪz), *v.* [ad. F. *séculariser*, f. L. *sæcular-is* SECULAR: see -IZE.]

1. *trans.* To make secular; to convert from ecclesiastical to civil possession or use; esp. to place (church property) at the disposal of the secular or civil power.

1611 COTGR., *Seculariser*, to secularize; to make secular, lay, temporall. **1657** *Treat. Conf. Sin.* 344 To surprize the possessions of the Church, and to Secularize her patrimony. **1715** *Lond. Gaz.* No. 5345/3 They insist that this Provostship does not come under the Number of Ecclesiastical Benefices, having been Secularized. **1737** OZELL *Rabelais* II. 251 *note*, He was a Monk..[and] he [only] took the liberty to discover his true Name after he had seculariz'd himself, and was become, as it were, a Layman. **1742** RICHARDSON *Pamela* III. 274 Secularizing..the Revenues appropriated to the Church. **1791** MACKINTOSH *Vind. Gallicæ* Wks. 1846 III. 46 The Treaty of Westphalia secularised many of the most opulent benefices of Germany. **1861** BUCKLE *Civiliz.* II. iii. 233 In their opinion, it was impious to secularise ecclesiastical property, and turn it aside to profane purposes.

transf. **1754** PITT *Let.* 7 Mar. in *Grenville Papers* (1852) I. 107 To secularise, if I may use the expression, the Solicitor-General, and make him Chancellor of the Exchequer.

b. To laicize; to deprive of clerical character or remove from clerical control.

1846 *English Rev.* Sept. VI. 150 You will have deprived them of their occupation by secularizing the profession of a teacher. **1885** *Observer* 20 Dec. (Cassell), The work of secularizing the hospitals has been accomplished.

2. To make (a monk or monastic order) secular.

1683 [see SECULARIZED *ppl. a.*]. **1706** PHILLIPS (ed. Kersey), To *Secularize*, to make Secular; as To *Secularize a Monk*. **1773** *Ann. Reg., Hist. Eur.* 9/1 The Bishop of Liege having met with some opposition in his attempts to secularize a convent of monks. **1845** J. H. NEWMAN *Ess. Developm.* 316 The successive Catholics of Seleucia had abolished Monachism and were secularizing the clergy.

3. To dissociate or separate from religious or spiritual concerns, to convert to material and temporal purposes; to turn (a person, his mind, etc.) from a religious or spiritual state to worldliness.

1711 G. HICKES *Two Treat.* II. (1847) 231 So many ministers of late are more than ever secularized in their conversation. **1755** JOHNSON, *Secularize*,.. 2. To make worldly. **1831** SOUTHEY in *Q. Rev.* XLIV. 353 A worldly-minded husband might have secularised and deadened her heart. **1866** LIDDON *Bampt. Lect.* iv. (1875) 190 The Jews secularized the Messianic promises. **1869** M. PATTISON *Serm.* (1885) 173 We hear much of a crisis of the faith, of the perilous errors which are abroad in society, of the aggressions of science, of the attempts to secularise education. **1876** *Times* 8 Nov. 9/3 The policy of those Governments has become secularized. **1877** J. C. COX *Ch. Derbysh.* II. 400 This chapel..had long been secularised, and..used as a malt-house.

4. *intr.* To adopt secular costume or habits.

1864 T. HUGHES in *Reader* 5 Nov. 567/2 Henrietta Caracciolo..secularized in everything except the black veil.

Hence **'secularized** *ppl. a.*, **'secularizing** *vbl. sb.* (in quots. *attrib.*). Also **'secularizer**.

1683 *Apol. Prot. France* iii. 16 The History of Calvinism, by Monsieur Maimbourg, a Secularised Jesuit. **1803** H. REPTON *Observ. Th. & Pract. Landsc. Gard.* xii. (1840) 274 It is..impossible to live in..the secularized abbey.. preserving all the apartments to their original uses. **1825** CHALMERS in Hanna *Mem.* (1851) III. vi. 89, I feel the secularizing effect of worldly company. **1842** MANNING *Serm.* v. (1848) I. 74 We find men..holding out against the secularizing action of worldly things. **1875** E. WHITE *Life in Christ* v. xxxi. (1878) 525 Perhaps there is not a more thoroughly secularised population in Europe than the inhabitants of this 'holy city'. **1886** WILLIS & CLARK *Cambridge* II. 308 The secularized part of the nave. **1887** *Macm. Mag.* Dec. 88 He was..not in the least a secularizer, but..a sanctifier.

secularly ('sɛkjʊləlɪ), *adv.* [f. SECULAR *a.* + -LY².] In a secular manner.

1. As a secular or lay person; in accordance with secular procedure; non-ecclesiastically.

c **1380** WYCLIF *Wks.* (1880) 384 For in sum place..þe clergi occupieþ þe seculer lordeschip seculerli. **1395** [PURVEY] *Remonstrance* (1851) 152 Not oon shal apropre seculerli to himsilf alle the profitis of the chirche. *c* **1440** *Alphabet of Tales* 342 A monke þat was..syttand prowdelie vppon a fayr palfray, and rydyng passand secularelie. **1511** COLET *Serm. Conforming* B iv b, Pristes nat lyuynge pristly but secularly. **1854** H. MILLER *Sch. & Schm.* xxii. (1860) 239 As I held ecclesiastically by the one party, and secularly by the other, I found my position..a rather anomalous one. **1882** STEVENSON *New Arab. Nts.* (1884) 141 One was.. secularly dressed, but with an indelible clerical stamp. **1900** *Nation* 19 Mar. 975/1 Offences with which the Reformers dealt ecclesiastically are now dealt with secularly.

2. In a worldly manner; in a manner characterized by the absence of religion.

1840 G. S. FABER *Regeneration* 180 The youth had received Baptism dissemblingly, secularly, impenitently, unworthily. **1893** E. L. WAKEMAN in *Columbus* (Ohio) *Dispatch* 3 Aug., Possessing no secularly educative or diverting features.

Comb. **1902** *Daily Chron.* 18 Feb. 6/6 A secularly-conducted State school.

3. *Astr.* Over a long period of time.

1971 *Nature* 24 Dec. 453/1 We might expect δf to be secularly dependent in the same way as H_e ($\propto P^{-2}$). **1979** *Ibid.* 20 Sept. 200/1 Even in the worst case of deviation from thermal equilibrium, that is when the fully convective star expands adiabatically,..the system would still be secularly stable against mass exchange.

†**'secularness.** *Obs.* [f. SECULAR *a.* + -NESS.] Secularity, worldliness.

1530 *Proper Dyaloge* in *Rede me*, etc. (Arb.) 143 The landes of lordes and dukes to possesse Thei [the clergy] abasshe not a whit the seculernes Chalengynge tytles of worldly honour. **1730** in BAILEY (fol.). **1755** in JOHNSON.

†**'seculary,** *a.* *Obs. rare*⁻¹. [ad. F. *séculaire* SECULAR: see -ARY.] Secular.

1480 CAXTON *Chron. Eng.* II. (1520) 13/1 So great a charge of seculary thynges, and so pure..a contemplacyon of spyrytuall thynges.

secule ('sɛkjuːl). *Geol. Obsolescent.* [f. L. *sæculum* age, generation.] A period of geological time corresponding to a stratigraphical zone; = MOMENT *sb.* 2 d.

1903 A. J. JUKES-BROWNE in *Geol. Mag.* X. 37 The term hemera may, however, be occasionally convenient to signify the duration of a subzone, as age signifies the duration of a stage, but if we want to avoid confusion we must not speak of the hemera of a zone. For this another word should be coined..I would suggest that the Latin word *seculum* will furnish us with 'secule' which finds an actual French equivalent in *siècle*. **1933** W. J. ARKELL *Jurassic Syst. Gt. Brit.* i. 21 Several hemeræ may be contained in one secule or zone-moment. **1956** *Amer. Jrnl. Sci.* CCLIV. 459 Schindewolf reasserts..his extreme view..that the zone as conceived by Oppel was a purely chronological notion and that the term zone should be used only as a time term (= secule). **1969** [see MOMENT *sb.* 2 d].

seculeer, -er(e, -ier, obs. ff. SECULAR.

secund (sɪ'kʌnd), *a. Bot.* and *Zool.* [ad. L. *secund-us* following: see SECOND *a.*] Arranged on or directed towards one side only; esp. *Bot.* of the flowers, leaves, or other organs of a plant.

1777 ROBSON *Brit. Flora* 21 *Secund*, all the flowers inclining to one side of the stem. *a* **1815** ROXBURGH *Flora Ind.* (1820) I. 299 Spikelets alternate, sessile, secund. **1882-4** COOKE *Brit. Fresh-w. Algæ* I. 142 Branches and branchlets sparse,..often secund.

†**se'cundan,** *a.* and *sb.* *Obs.* [ad. L. *secundānus*, f. *secund-us* SECOND *a.*: see -AN.] **A.** *adj. Path.* Of a fever: Recurring every second day.

a **1400-50** *Stockh. Med. MS.* 114 Þe fyuere secundan.

B. *sb.* in *plural. Math.* (See quot. 1704.)

a **1703** WALLIS in *Misc. Curiosa* (1708) II. 17 And because the first Member doth represent a Series of Equals; the second of Secundans; the third, of Quartans, &c. Therefore the first Member is to be multiplied by S; the second, by ½ S; the third by ⅓ S [etc.]. **1704** J. HARRIS *Lex. Techn.* I, *Secundans*, in Mathematicks, is an infinite series of Numbers, beginning from Nothing, and proceeding as the squares of Numbers in Arithmetical Proportion. **1795** in HUTTON *Math. Dict.*

secundari, -ye, obs. ff. SECONDARY.

†**secundate,** *v. Obs.* [f. L. *secundāt-*, ppl. stem of *secundāre* to direct favourably, f. *secund-us* favourable.] Hence †**secun'dation.** (See quots.)

1656 BLOUNT *Glossogr.*, *Secundate*, to make lucky or prosperous, to make better or amend a thing. **1658** PHILLIPS, *Secundation*, a secunding, forwarding, or making prosperous. **1854** WEBSTER, *Secundation*, prosperity. (*Not used.*)

†**Secundeian,** *a. Obs. rare*⁻¹. [app. f. *Secund-us*: see next.] *Secundeian godhead*: ? the evil deity of the dualistic system of Secundus.

1588 J. HARVEY *Disc. Probl.* 99 May it be deemed..that any higher power, or Secundeian godhead,..presently menaceth any such heinous mischeefes,..as are strongly imagined?

Secundian (sɪ'kʌndɪən). [f. *Secund-us* (see below) + -(I)AN.] A follower of Secundus, a Gnostic heresiarch of the second century.

1765 MACLAINE tr. *Mosheim's Eccl. Hist.* II. II. v. §17 The Secundians, whose chief, Secundus, one of the principal followers of Valentine, maintained the doctrine of two eternal principles, *viz.* light and darkness, from whence arose the good and the evil that are observable in the universe.

se͵cundi'florous, *a. Bot.* [f. L. *secund-us* SECOND *a.* + *flōr-*, *flōs* flower + -OUS.] (See quot.)

1899 HEINIG *Gloss. Bot. Terms*, *Secundiflorous*, with all the flowers of an inflorescence secund.

secundigravida (sɪkʌndɪ'grævɪdə). *Obstetrics.* Pl. idas-, -idæ. Also **secundagravida.** [mod.L., f. as SECUNDIPARA + *gravida*, fem. of *gravidus* GRAVID *a.*] A woman pregnant for the second time.

1904 in STEDMAN *Dunglison's Dict. Med. Sci.* (ed. 23) 1007/1. **1940** *Amer. Jrnl. Obstetr. & Gynecol.* XL. 988 Eighty-seven examinations were upon primigravidas, 61 upon secundigravidas, and 114 upon patients of greater parity. **1977** *Lancet* 22 Jan. 195/2 This policy should be restricted to secundigravidæ and those who have had two babies.

secundine ('sɛkʌndɪn). Also 4-6 **secondyne,** (4 **-dying**), 6-7, 9 **secondine.** [ad. late L. *secundinæ* pl. (for which class. Latin had *secundæ*), f. *secundus* following: see SECOND *a.* and -INE.]

1. *Obstetrics.* The placenta and other adjuncts of a fœtus extruded from the womb after the expulsion of the fœtus in parturition; the afterbirth. Frequently *pl.*

1398 TREVISA *Barth. De P.R.* XVII. xlix. (Tollemache MS.), It is seyde þat it [Dittany]..bryngeþ oute secundine, þe bagge þat þe childe is inne in þe moder. **1490** CAXTON *Eneydos* xxiv. 88 She taketh the lytell skynne that remayneth of the secondyne within the forhed of the lytell foole. *Ibid.* 89 The secondying. **1526** *Grete Herball* xxviii. (1529) B v b, Other saye that it [amber] is yᵉ secondyne that she [a whale] casteth whan she hath spawned. *c* **1550** LLOYD *Treas. Health* (1560) Q j, [It] causeth the delyuerance of the child and of the secondynes, and after burden. **1610** MARKHAM *Masterp.* I. lxxxvii. 171 She cannot auoyd her secundine, which is the skinne wherein the foale is wrapped. **1754-64** SMELLIE *Midwifery* I. 240 All the Secundines ought to be extracted at once. **1855** RAMSBOTHAM *Obst. Med.* 68 And, with the membranes and the cord, the secundines.

b. *transf.* and *fig.*

1643 SIR T. BROWNE *Relig. Med.* 95 Not..till we have once more cast our secondine, that is, this slough of flesh, and are delivered into the last world. **1652** FRENCH *Yorkshire Spa* vi. 55 Every *Sulphur Embroinatum*..is but an impurity of its *Embrio*, and as it were..the secundine thereof. **1656** COWLEY *Pindar. Odes, Muse* iii, Through the firm shell..[thou] do'st spie, Years to come a forming lie, Close in their sacred Secondine asleep, Till hatcht by the Suns vital heat.

†**2.** *Ent.* The inner coat of a cocoon. *rare*⁻¹.

1599 T. M[OUFET] *Silkwormes* 64 Lest..moisture..cause both strings and secundine to rotte.

3. *Bot.* The second of two coats or integuments of an ovule, originally the inner one, later applied to the outer covering: see PRIMINE.

So mod.L. *secundina* (Malpighi 1671, from whom quot. 1683 is a translation).

1671 GREW *Anat. Plants* I. vii. (1682) 47 The Fourth or Innermost Cover we may call the Secondine. The sight of which, by cutting off the Coats of an Infant Bean, at the Cone.., may be obtain'd. **1683** A. SNAPE *Anat. Horse* App. I. i. 10 The first day after it [a grain of wheat] is sown, it grows a little turgid, and the secundine or husk gapes a little. **1832** LINDLEY *Introd. Bot.* 155 The outermost but one of the sacs is called the secondine; it immediately reposes upon the primine. **1875-85** [see PRIMINE b].

secundipara (sɪkʌn'dɪpərə). *Obstetrics.* Pl. -paras, -paræ. [mod.L., f. *secundus*, *secundi-* second + *-para*, fem. of *-parus*, from *parere* to bring forth.] A woman who has twice been delivered of children.

1897 *Lippincott's Med. Dict.* 918/2 *Secundipara*, a woman bearing a child for the second time. **1938** *Nature* 24 Dec. 1121/2 Cases with metastatic tumours were associated with a significant increase in the amount of trimethylamine... In primiparæ, the average amount was 0·30 and in secundiparæ 0·29. **1972** E. C. HUGHES *Obstetr.-Gynecol. Terminol.* vii. 332 A secundipara is a woman who has given birth for the second time to an infant or infants, alive or dead, weighing 500 gm or more.

secundly (sɪ'kʌndlɪ), *adv. Bot.* [f. SECUND *a.* + -LY².] In a secund manner.

1870 HOOKER *Stud. Flora* 305 Spikelets, which are alternately distichously or secundly arranged.

se͵cundo'geniture. [f. L. *secundō*, advb. form of *secundus* SECOND *a.*, after *primogeniture*.] The right of succession or inheritance belonging to a second son; the possession so inherited.

1855 M. BRIDGES *Pop. Mod. Hist.* 412 Tuscany became an archduchy for Francis, the husband of Maria Theresa, and a secundo-geniture in their family afterwards. **1876** BANCROFT *Hist. U.S.* II. xxxv. 387 The kingdom of Naples ..was constituted a secundogeniture of Spain. **1882** *Standard* 28 Sept. 5/5 The restoration of an independent

Poland, even if it were to be placed under Austrian secundogeniture, will..on no account be consented to by Germany. **1910** *Nation* 22 Jan. 672/2 If the same hypnotism could be transferred to the second or the third son, secundogeniture or tertigeniture would rest on a firmer basis than does primogeniture to-day.

‖**secundum** (sɪˈkʌndəm). [L., according to; orig. neut. accus. of *secundus* SECOND *a.*] Used in various med. Latin phrases, sometimes occurring in Eng. contexts. ***secundum artem*** (= Gr. κατὰ τὴν τέχνην): 'according to art', in accordance with the rules of the art (chiefly of medicine; often jocularly *transf.*). ***secundum idem***, 'according to the same argument, calculation, etc.', in the same manner or respect. ***secundum magis et minus*** (= Gr. κατὰ τὸ μᾶλλον καὶ ἧττον): 'according to more and less'; in a quantitative manner or respect; in various degrees. ***secundum naturam*** [Cicero; = Gr. κατὰ φύσιν]: according to nature, naturally. ***secundum quid*** [= Gr. κατά τι]: 'according to something', in some particular respect only (opposed to *simpliciter*, Gr. ἁπλῶς).

1632 B. JONSON *Magn. Lady* III. iv, *Rut.* That is my course with all my Patients. *Pal.* Very methodicall, *Secundum Artem.* **1675** HAN. WOOLLEY *Gentlew. Companion* 68 A Cods-head,..drest *secundum artem.* **1815** SCOTT *Guy M.* iv, He undertook the task [*sc.* of calculating a nativity] *secundum artem.* **1856** 'STONEHENGE' *Brit. Rural Sports* III. iv. 176/2 The kennel-man of the dog will see to everything being done, *secundum artem.*

1696 J. SERGEANT *Method to Sci.* 390 To Affirm that the Atome is Chang'd according to One of those Different Regards or Notions, *viz* the Form, and Not-chang'd according to the Other, viz the Matter, has not the least show of Affirming and Denying *secundum idem*; nor, consequently, the least show of a Contradiction. **1865** S. HODGSON *Time & Space* ii. 140 The two objects are then not limited and unlimited secundum idem. **1882** W. JAMES in *Mind* Apr. 187 The union and the division are not *secundum idem*: it divides them by keeping them out of the space between, it unites them by keeping them out of the space beyond.

1621 BURTON *Anat. Mel.* Democr. to Rdr. 14 Alexander, Gordonius..[and others] confound them, as differing *secundum magis & minus.* [*Note*, More or lesse, some madder then some.] **1837** MACAULAY *Ess., Bacon* (1897) 409 He might have gone on to instances *secundum magis et minus.*

1563 T. GALE *Inst. Chirurg.* 16 Theis .vj. things which are *secundum naturam*, spring of .vij. natural thinges entring the composition of mans body. **1754** *Gray's Inn Jrnl.* No. 76 (1756) II. 153 The modern Hero grafts his Happiness on the Passions..and in that Sense may be said to live *secundum naturam.*

1619 S. NORRIS *Antidote* II. VI. (1622) 232 Our aduersaries make answere..that heauen is called a Crowne, a reward *secundum quid*, and in a respect [;] simply and absolutely it is only a gift, because it is given according to grace. **1693** *Logic or Art of Thinking* (ed. 2) 332 Human form..being a Perfection only *secundum quid*, or in some respect and not simply, it does not follow that it ought to be the shape of God.

‖**secundus** (sɪˈkʌndəs), *a.* [L. *secundus* SECOND *a.*] Appended to a personal name: The second of a name. In some schools used to designate the second in age or seniority of two boys having the same surname.

1826 DISRAELI *Viv. Grey* I. iii, 'What a knowing set out', squeaked Johnson *secundus.* 'Mammy-sick' growled Barlow *primus.* **1827** FLEMING *Brit. Zool.* Pref. 11 The University of Edinburgh possessed, in Dr Monro *secundus*, a comparative anatomist..anxious to inspire [etc.]. **1867** BAKER *Nile Tribut.* xi. 277 Having our party of servants complete, six Tokrooris..with Mahomet,..Mahomet *secundus* (a groom), and Barraké. **1887** *Athenæum* 12 Mar. 350/2 Two excellent volumes... The former contains some sensible advice..by Robert Chambers *secundus.*

secur, obs. form of SICKER *a.*

securable (sɪˈkjʊərəb(ə)l), *a. rare.* [f. SECURE *v.* + -ABLE.] Capable of being secured.

a **1846** *Q. Rev.* (Worcester). **1855** in OGILVIE *Suppl.* **1876** *Tinsley's Mag.* XVIII. 474 Popularity..is always securable by the 'No Popery' cry.

securance (sɪˈkjʊərəns). *rare.* [f. SECURE *v.* + -ANCE.] The action or means of securing; assurance, security.

c **1642** *Contra-Replicant's Compl.* 8 Such securance is not imcompatible with Monarchy. *Ibid.* 22 If the Parliament will undertake to secure the King,..what must that securance be? **1652** BP. HALL *Myst. Godliness* x. (1847) 31 For the securance of thy Resurrection..thou hadst spent forty days upon earth. **1870** MULFORD *Nation* vi. 83 It is only with care and steadiness and tenacity of purpose that those guaranties are forged which are the securance of freedom. **1908** *Protestant Observer* Dec. 182/2 Some provision for the securance of Catholic representation on the Senate at the end of the first five years.

secure (sɪˈkjʊə(r)), *sb.* [f. SECURE *v.*] The position in which a rifle or musket is held when it is 'secured': see SECURE *v.* 2 h.

1802 C. JAMES *Milit. Dict.* s.v. *Secure arms!*, To bring your firelock to the secure, 1st, throw your right hand briskly up [etc.]. *Ibid.*, In order to shoulder from the secure, you must [etc.]. **1847** *Infantry Man.* (1854) 20 Bringing the firelock down to the Secure.

secure (sɪˈkjʊə(r)), *a.* and *adv.* [ad. L. *sēcūrus*, f. *sē-* without (see SE-) + *cūra* care (whence CURE *sb.*).

In the late L. sense 'safe, free from danger', the word passed into the Rom. langs.: F. *sûr* (OF. *sëur*, whence SURE *a.*), Pr. *segur-s*, Sp., Pg. *seguro*, It. *sicuro*; it was also early adopted in WGer., and hence appears in Eng. as SICKER *a.*]

A. *adj.*

I. Feeling no care or apprehension.

1. Without care, careless; free from care, apprehension or anxiety, or alarm; over-confident. Now *arch.* **a.** In predicative use.

In early instances often contrasted with *safe.*

? **1533** LATIMER *Let. to Morice* in Foxe *A. & M.* (1583) 1742/2 But we be secure and vncarefull, as though false Prophets could not meddle with vs. **1579** LYLY *Euphues* (Arb.) 143 And if after these pastimes hee shall seeme secure, nothing regardinge his bookes, I woulde not haue him scourged with stripes, but threatened with wordes. **1587** T. HUGHES *Misf. Arthur* I. iv, Mischiefe is sometimes safe: but n'er secure. **1641** QUARLES *Enchir.* IV. lxiii. (1654) T 1, When the Devil brings thee Oyle, bring thou Vinegar. The way to be safe, is never to bee secure. **1667** D. FOULIS *Let.* in *Slingsby's Diary* (1836) 374 God deliuer us out of these troubles & make us more vigilent & lesse secure for yᵉ future. *a* **1700** EVELYN *Diary* 20 Oct. 1674, He told me 10,000 men would easily conquer all the Spanish Indies, they were so secure. **1758** S. HAYWARD *Serm.* xvii. 543, I had been now amongst the thoughtless crowd,..absolutely ignorant and secure. **1771** WESLEY *Wks.* (1872) V. 99 Because he is blind, he is also secure. **1806** A. MURRAY *Let.* in *Constable & Correspondents* (1873) I. 253 We may expect that he [Bonaparte] will attack us as much as lies in his power. With respect to the issue of that we have not much to fear, and yet we have no cause to be too secure. **1827** KEBLE *Chr. Year, St. Philip & St. James* 25 Youth's lightning flash of joy secure Pass'd seldom o'er His spright. **1841** J. H. NEWMAN *Serm.* vi. 87 Those who have long had God's favour without cloud or storm, grow secure. *a* **1859** MACAULAY *Hist. Eng.* xxiii. (1861) V. 10 They were secure where they ought to have been wary, timorous where they might well have been secure.

b. With various constructions: Free from apprehension *of* (now only *poet.*), †*concerning*; †careless, without anxiety *for.* †Also with indirect question.

1579 LYLY *Euphues* (Arb.) 144 But seeing the father carelesse what they learne, he is also secure what he teacheth. **1608** WILLET *Hexapla Exod.* 838 The Lord therefore biddeth them to be secure for that matter. **1614** RALEIGH *Hist. World* v. ii. §7. 414 The Illyrian Queene was secure of the Romans, as if they would not dare to stirre against her. **1619** HIERON *Wks.* I. 5 There is no man so secure for his way to mill or to market, as hee is for his way to life eternall. **1625** BACON *Ess., Seditions* (Arb.) 401 Neither let any Prince, or State, be secure concerning Discontentments. **1658** ROWLAND *Moufet's Theat. Ins.* 937 The reason why they are so bold and fearlesse, as being secure of any danger. **1697** DRYDEN *Virg. Georg.* I. 427 Ev'n when the Farmer, now Secure of Fear, Sends in the Swains to spoil the finish'd Year:..Oft have I seen a sudden Storm arise. **1700** —— *Cinyras & Myrrha* 277 Secure of Shame because secure of Sight: Ev'n bashful Sins are impudent by Night. **1833** TENNYSON *To J. S.* 76 Lie still, dry dust, secure of change.

c. In attributive use. Now *rare* or *Obs.*

1584 LODGE *Alarum agst. Usurers* 38 b, Alonely lead with carelesse shew of peace, Whereas secure regard doth sinne increase. **1593** SHAKS. *Rich. II*, v. iii. 43 Open the doore, secure foole-hardy King. **1598** —— *Merry W.* II. i. 241. *Ibid.* II. ii. 315. **1612** T. TAYLOR *Comm. Titus* ii. 12 Our common people, whose extream and secure ignorance, loads them with such a burthen of impietie. **1690** C. NESSE *Hist. & Myst. O. & N.T.* I. 116 In the church militant there must neither be an idle soldier nor a secure labourer. *a* **1729** J. ROGERS *Nineteen Serm.* xii. (1735) 249 This is a Reflection which..should strike Terror and Amazement into the securest Sinner. **1773** GOLDSM. *Stoops to Conq.* v, Do you think I could ever catch at the confident addresses of a secure admirer? *Mar.* (kneeling) Does this look like security?

absol. **1659** W. BROUGH *Sacr. Princ.* 79 When the secure and foolish shall be barr'd and excluded the doors of bliss.

d. Said of times, places, actions: In which one is free from fear or anxiety.

1602 SHAKS. *Ham.* I. v. 61 Vpon my secure hower thy Vncle stole With iuyce of cursed Hebenon in a Violl. **1604** —— *Oth.* IV. i. 72 Oh, 'tis the spight of hell, the Fiends Archmock, to lip a wanton in a secure Cowch; And to suppose her chast. **1859** GEO. ELIOT *Adam Bede* xxxvii, The bright hearth and the warmth and the voice of home,—the secure uprising and lying down.

2. a. Free from doubt or distrust; feeling sure or certain. Const. *of*; also with *clause.* ? *Obs.*

1579 LYLY *Euphues* (Arb.) 77 Though he be suspitious of my faire hiew, yet is he secure of my firme honestie. **1595** SHAKS. *John* IV. i. 130 And, pretty childe, sleepe doubtlesse, and secure, That Hubert for the wealth of all the world, Will not offend thee. **1670** DRYDEN *1st Pt. Conq. Granada* v. ii, Give wing to your desires, and let 'em fly, Secure they cannot mount a pitch too high. **1670–1** MARVELL *Corr.* Wks. (Grosart) II. 372 He is secure that nothing will be done by his Majesty. **1688** SHADWELL *Sq. Alsatia* v. 70 How can I be secure you will not fall to your old courses agen? **1713** JOHNSON *Guardian* No. 4 ¶6, I am secure that no man will so readily take them into Protection. **1794** GODWIN *Cal. Williams* 49 He was secure that his animosity would neither be forgotten nor diminished by the interposition of any time or events.

†**b.** Confident in expectation; feeling certain *of* something in the future. Also with *infinitive.*

1653 H. MORE *Antid. Ath.* III. vi. §3 Caesar taking the Omen..enters Italy, secure of success from so manifest tokens of the favour of the Gods. **1667** MILTON *P.L.* IX. 1175 But confidence then bore thee on, secure Either to meet no danger, or to finde Matter of glorious trial. **1686** tr. *Chardin's Trav. Persia* 27 The Grand Vizier, secure of taking Candy..alter'd all Soliman's Titles. **1725** POPE *Odyss.* IX. 498 He..search'd each passing sheep, and felt it o'er, Secure to seize us ere we reach'd the door. **1732** —— *Ess. Man* I. 286 Secure to be as blest, as thou canst bear.

II. Having or affording ground for confidence; safe; (objectively) certain.

3. a. Rightly free from apprehension; protected from or not exposed to danger; safe.

The first quot. is a doubtful example of this sense; the original Gr. ἀμερίμνους is literally 'without care or anxiety' (= sense 1 a above); but the virtual meaning is 'without cause for anxiety, safe'.

1582 N.T. (Rhem.) *Matt.* xxviii. 14 And if the President shal heare of this, we wil persuade him, and make you secure [Vulg. *et securos vos faciemus*]. **1591** SHAKS. *1 Hen. VI*, II. i. 66 Had all your Quarters been as safely kept,..We had not beene thus shamefully surpriz'd. *Bast.* Mine was secure. **1606** WARNER *Alb. Eng.* XIV. lxxxv. (1612) 352 Yeat oft it haps, by how much more high Dignities preferre, So much the more, though lesse secure, men liue irreguler. **1608** SHAKS. *Per.* I. i. 95 Who has a booke of all that Monarches doe, Hee's more secure to keepe it shut, then showne. **1646** SIR T. BROWNE *Pseud. Ep.* I. iv. 15 The divell..would perswade him he might be secure if hee cast himselfe from the pinacle. **1647** COWLEY *Mistr.*, *Writ. Juice of Lemon* ii, Alas, thou think'st thy self secure, Because thy form is Innocent and Pure. **1731** SWIFT *Let.* 10 Sept. in *Pope's Wks.* 1757 IX. 141 Thus I knew myself on the secure side, and it was a mere piece of good manners to insert that clause, of which you have taken the advantage. *a* **1854** LANDOR *Last Fruit of Old Tree* 474 Safe art thou, Louis!..for a time; But tremble..never yet was crime, Beyond one little space, secure. **1889** *Spectator* 21 Dec., England is rich because she has for so many years been secure.

b. Const. *against*, *from*, †*of.*

1588 SHAKS. *Tit. A.* I. i. 152 Repose you heere in rest, Secure from worldly chaunces and mishaps. *Ibid.* II. i. 3 Now climbeth Tamora Olympus toppe, Safe out of Fortunes shot, and sits aloft, Secure of Thunders cracke or lightning flash. **1697** DRYDEN *Virg. Georg.* III. 579 The Men to subterranean Caves retire; Secure from Cold, and crowd the chearful Fire. *Ibid.*, *Æneid* VII. 956 Messapus next,..Secure of Steel, and fated from the Fire, In Pomp appears. **1746** FRANCIS tr. *Horace, Art of Poetry* 360, I stand secure from Censure and from Shame. **1781** COWPER *Charity* 510 No skill in swordmanship, however just, Can be secure against a madman's thrust. **1796** MORSE *Amer. Geog.* I. 168 Secure from those tempestuous winds, by which the adjoining lake is frequently troubled. **1821** SHELLEY *Adonais* xl, From the contagion of the world's slow stain, He is secure. **1825** SCOTT *Betrothed* xxv, The outlaws, secure in their knowledge of the paths,..made an orderly retreat. **1839** LANE *Arab. Nts.* I. 128 Thou art secure from every thing that is not predestined.

c. Of actions or conditions; Involving no danger; safe.

1617 MORYSON *Itin.* III. 9 The most ancient Lawgivers, got the experience, by which they had rule in their Cities, not by secure study at home, but by adventurous travels abroad. **1643** J. M. *Sov. Salve* 9 Such a seeming-secure and supine sleep might have proved a mortall lethargy. **1748** *Anson's Voy.* I. ix. 92 This..would render all that southern navigation infinitely securer than at present. **1819** SHELLEY *Cenci* II. i. 26 He demands at what hour 'twere secure To visit you again? **1881** JOWETT *Thucyd.* I. 134 Inaction is secure only when arrayed by the side of activity.

d. Of an argument, means, agent, etc.: Not liable to fail, trustworthy, safe.

a **1729** J. ROGERS *Seventeen Serm.* v. (1736) 100 But tho' God will accept of a sincere tho' imperfect Obedience, yet this can be no secure Argument to us to remit our Applications. **1823** SCOTT *Peveril* xix, Which made him suspect that the countess had again employed her mute attendant as the most secure minister of her pleasure on this occasion.

e. Of a material thing, a support or fastening: Not liable to be displaced or to yield under strain; firmly fixed, safe.

1841 T. R. JONES *Anim. Kingd.* 95 Armed externally with four circlets of sharp recurved hooks, which, when plunged into the coats of the intestine, serve as secure anchors by which the creature retains itself in a position favourable to the absorption of food. *Mod.* The bridge does not look secure. Do you think the bolt is secure?

f. Of a telephone (line): free from the risk of being tapped (TAP *v.*[1] 2 c).

1961 in WEBSTER. **1975** B. MEGGS *Matter of Paradise* (1976) v. i. 106, I don't want to say anything more right now; this telephone isn't secure.

4. Of a place, also of means of protection or guardianship: Affording safety.

1610 HOLLAND *Camden's Brit.* I. 473 A sure and secure station or place of aboad. **1632** HEYWOOD *2nd Pt. Iron Age* v. i, Hee stands vpon a strict and secure guard. **1634** MILTON *Comus* 327 In a place Less warranted then this, or less secure I cannot be, that I should fear to change it. **1660** F. BROOKE tr. *Le Blanc's Trav.* 30 The Isle hath two good Havens, one in the East, the other in the West, the others are not secure. *a* **1700** EVELYN *Diary* 23 June 1665, His dog sought out absolutely the very securest place in all the vessell [during the fight]. **1745** POCOCKE *Descr. East* II. I. i. 5 The roads would be more secure about the time when the great caravan was passing. ? **1788** COWPER *On Mischiev. Bull* 14, I could pity thee exil'd From this secure retreat. **1818** CRUISE *Digest* (ed. 2) V. 357 It being a common opinion, that a feoffment was the most secure conveyance by which a tenant to the *præcipe* could be made.

5. Predicatively: In safe custody; safely in one's possession or power.

1591 SHAKS. *1 Hen. VI*, I. iv. 49 In Iron Walls they deem'd me not secure. **1766** GOLDSM. *Vic. W.* ii, At least till your son has the young lady's fortune secure. **1791** COWPER *Iliad* XVI. 272 He also kept Secure a goblet exquisitely wrought.

6. Free from risk as to the continued or future possession *of* something; having a safe prospect *of* some acquisition or desirable event. †Also with infinitive: Ensured against failure *to do* something. Cf. 2b.

1664 TILLOTSON *Serm.* i. Wks. (1714) 22 Consider man without the protection and conduct of a superior Being, and he is secure of nothing that he enjoys in this world, and uncertain of every thing that he hopes for. **1700** DRYDEN *Sigism. & Guisc.* 626 For this, she had distill'd, with early Care, The Juice of Simples, friendly to Despair, A Magazine of Death; and this prepar'd, Secure to die, the fatal Message heard. **1705** tr. *Bosman's Guinea* 10 No Body is here secure of Life. **1746** FRANCIS tr. *Horace, Epist.* II. i. 69 Ennius.. Forgets his Promise, now secure of Fame, And heeds no more his Pythagoric Dream. **1758** S. HAYWARD *Serm.* Introd. 17 Oh happy case, when the soul..boldly ventures into eternity, secure of eternal life. **1770** GOLDSM. *Des. Vill.* 288 As some fair female unadorned and plain, Secure to please while youth confirms her reign. **1788** GIBBON *Decl. & F.* xlii. IV. 548 The zeal of Cyril exposed him to the penalties of the Julian law; but in a feeble government, and a superstitious age, he was secure of impunity, and even of praise. **1825** SCOTT *Talism.* vi, When they seemed most secure of victory. **1863** H. BROUGHTON *Let.* in Trevelyan *Compet. Wallah* (1866) 355 For, if they succeed in obtaining her attention, they are secure of her humanity and her justice.

7. Of a possession, acquisition, desirable event, etc.: That may be counted on with certainty; sure to continue or to be attained.

1713 SWIFT *Last Yrs. Q. Anne* Wks. 1902 X. 31 Representing their opinion that no peace could be secure for Britain, while [etc.]. **1819** SHELLEY *Cyclops* 438 Listen then what a punishment I have For this fell monster, how secure a flight From your hard servitude. **1848** THACKERAY *Van. Fair* xxxi, 'If the worse comes to the worst', Becky thought, 'my retreat is secure; and I have a right-hand seat in the barouche'. **1860** TYNDALL *Glac.* I. xviii. 132 We knew that our progress afterwards was secure. **1874** GREEN *Short Hist.* viii. §2 (1882) 461 At the Queen's accession, the success of the Reformation seemed almost everywhere secure.

B. quasi-*adv.* and *adv.* (Chiefly *poet.*)

c **1592** MARLOWE *Edw. II*, IV. vi. 1893 Your grace may sit secure, if none but wee Doe wot of your abode. **1593** SHAKS. *3 Hen. VI*, II. v. 50 All which secure, and sweetly he enioyes. **1596** —— *1 Hen. IV*, I. ii. 145 We may doe it [the robbery] as secure as sleepe. **1611** BIBLE *Judg.* xviii. 7 They dwelt carelesse, after the manner of the Zidonians, quiet and secure. **1633** MASSINGER *Guardian* II. ii, Sleep you Secure on either ear. **1654** FULLER *Two Serm.* 11 The Structure may still stand..by vertue of..such Foundations which still stand secure. **1738** GRAY *Tasso* 15 Against the stream the waves secure he trod. **1784** COWPER *Task* VI. 970 Beneath the shadow of whose vine He sits secure. **1818** SHELLEY *Hymn Venus* 34 Nor mortal men, nor gods Who live secure in their unseen abodes.

secure (sɪˈkjʊə(r)), *v.* [f. SECURE *a.* Cf. med.L. *sēcūrāre, sēcūriāre*, Sp., Pg. *segurar*, It. *sicurare.*]

†**1. a.** *trans.* To make free from care or apprehension; also, to make careless or over-confident. *Obs. rare.*

1604 SHAKS. *Oth.* I. iii. 10, I do not so secure me in the Error, But the maine Article I do approue In fearefull sense. **1605** —— *Lear* IV. i. 22 Full oft 'tis seene, Our meanes secure vs, and our meere defects Proue our Commodities. **1655** FULLER *Ch. Hist.* IX. 82 [tr. Let. Mary Queen of Scots] To obtain of her, that she will let me go out of her country, whither I came, secured by her promises.

†**b.** To free from doubt, to satisfy, convince. Also, to make (one) feel secure *of* or *against* some contingency. *Obs.*

1602 CECIL *Let. to Mountjoy* 7 Aug. in *Moryson's Itin.* (1617) II. 235, I cannot be secured but that he wil stil feede that fier with fewel. **1646** H. LAWRENCE *Commun. & War with Angels* 118 Which should incourage us to fight and secure us of the issue. **1666-7** PEPYS *Diary* 28 Feb., Mr. Holliard [a surgeon] dined with us... I love his company, and he secures me against ever having the stone again. **1668** OWEN *Nat. Indwelling-Sin* viii. 115 Until the soul..begins to secure it self of pardon in course.

2. To make secure or safe.

a. To make (a person, his life, etc.; rarely a thing) secure from danger or harm; to guard, protect.

Obs. exc. with reference to a specific danger mentioned or implied: see c.

1602 WARNER *Alb. Eng.* X. lviii. (1612) 248 And whilst the Writ in reading was [Mary Q. of Scots] no more regarded it, Then if it had secured or concerned her no whit. **1602** SHAKS. *Ham.* I. v. 116 *Mar.* Lord Hamlet. *Hor.* Heauen secure him. *Mar.* So be it. **1624** CAPT. SMITH *Virginia* Ep. Ded. *Wks.* (Arb.) I. 276 The beauteous Lady Tragabigzanda, when I was a slaue to the Turkes, did all she could to secure me. **1639** FULLER *Holy War* II. iv. (1640) 48 Their profession was to fight against Infidels, and to secure Pilgrimes coming to the Sepulchre. *c* **1645** T. TULLY *Siege Carlisle* (1840) 34 Wilson..shot Cholmley in the brest, but his arms secured him. **1697** DRYDEN *Virg. Georg.* IV. 210 His lofty Pines, With friendly Shade, secur'd his tender Vines. *a* **1700** EVELYN *Diary* 22 Sept. 1641, A pass..securing me through Brabant and Flanders. **1706** E. WARD *Wooden World Diss.* (1708) Advt., The Bill..for securing Property in Printed Books. **1707** SIR W. HOPE *New Meth. Fencing* i. 11 For 'tis a general Rule in Fencing..never to present one's Sword, without perfectly Covering, or Securing, as we call it, one side of the Body. **1722** DE FOE *Col. Jack* xix, Any English men-of-war that might be on the coast to secure us to the capes. **1729** TINDAL tr. *Rapin's Hist.* XVII. VIII. 439 They..only helped to secure Elizabeth's Affairs, who thereby was sheltered from the Quarter whence she had most to fear. **1775** JOHNSON *Let. to Mrs. Thrale* 12 May, I really question if at this time my life would not be in danger, if distance did not secure it. **1776** GIBBON *Decl. & F.* xiv. I. 410 Maximian..gave him [Severus] the most solemn assurances that he had secured his life by the resignation of the purple.

†**b.** *refl.* To obtain safety. *Obs.*

1593 SHAKS. *2 Hen. VI*, V. ii. 76 Now is it manhood..To secure vs By what we can, which can no more but flye. **1697** POTTER *Antiq. Greece* I. iv. (1715) 15 Compelled to..secure himself by a dishonourable Flight. **1705** tr. *Bosman's Guinea* 320 Each endeavouring to secure himself by getting away. **1735** JOHNSON *Lobo's Abyssinia, Descr.* ii. 51 We had no way of securing ourselves but by flight. **1760** T. HUTCHINSON *Hist. Mass.* i. (1765) 186 His men had secured themselves in a swamp. **1793** SMEATON *Edystone L.* §313 High wages..did not engage them to secure themselves with a sufficient stock of provisions. **1800** *Asiat. Ann. Reg., Misc. Tracts* 30/2 He accordingly began to secure himself with Shujah al Dowlah, into whose service he entered. **1842** W. C. TAYLOR *Anc. Hist.* xvii. §5 (ed. 3) 515 Though Didius..was able to secure himself in Rome, he could not [etc.].

c. To render safe, protect or shelter *from*, guard *against* some particular danger. Also *refl.*

1634 MILTON *Comus* 618 Care and utmost shifts How to secure the Lady from surprisal, Brought to my mind a certain Shepherd Lad. **1646** J. MAXWELL *Burd. Issachar* 34, I never accounted them as Apostles, men secur'd from error. **1679** MOXON *Mech. Exerc.* ix. 164 The Battlement being.. Man-high, to secure Men from the shot of their enemies. **1685** STILLINGFL. *Orig. Brit.* ii. 71 For when he came against the Bagaudæ, Carausius was employ'd to secure the Seas against the Franks and the Saxons. **1692** LOCKE *Consid. Lower. Interest* 150 That way of Coinage less secures you from having a great part of your Money melted down. **1699** WANLEY in *Lett. Lit. Men* (Camden) 293 Whereby Mr. Benson may secure many old words from being buried in the grave of everlasting oblivion. **1741** WATTS *Improv. Mind* I. vii. §19 [We should] consult the dictionary, which may give us certain information, and thus secure us from mistake. **1748** *Anson's Voy.* III. ix. 386 A very safe road, secured from all winds. **1754** J. BROWN *Barbarossa* v. (1755) 66 Is the Watch doubled? Are the Gates secur'd Against Surprize? **1756** BURKE *Subl. & B.* III. vi. Wks. I 224 The hedge-hog, so well secured against all assaults by his prickly hide. **1784** COWPER *Tiroc.* 119 Neatly secur'd from being soil'd or torn. **1821** SCOTT *Kenilw.* xxxiv, Amy hastily endeavoured to recall what she were best to say, which might secure herself from the imminent dangers that surrounded her, without endangering her husband. **1875** JOWETT *Plato* (ed. 2) V. 30 No possessions seemed to him to have any value which were not secured against enemies.

d. *absol.* To obtain security, take effective precautions *against*.

1658 *Whole Duty of Man* vii. §19. 65 It being much more easie to abstain from all, than to secure against the one, when the other is allowed. **1818** SCOTT *Rob Roy* xxxvi, The extreme strength of the country..made the establishment of this little fort seem rather an acknowledgment of the danger, than an effectual means of securing against it. **1828** —— *F.M. Perth* xx, This guard the burghers will willingly maintain, to secure against the escape of the murderer of their townsman.

†**e.** To take effectual precautions against, to prevent (a danger). Also, to prevent or preclude (a person) *from* doing something dangerous. *Obs.*

1633 P. FLETCHER *Purple Isl.* IV. iv, Which stretching round about his circling arms, Warrants these parts from all exteriour harms; Repelling angry force, securing all alar'ms. **1692** R. L'ESTRANGE *Fables* cciii. 174 Man only is the Creature, that to his Shame, no Benefits can Oblige, no nor Secure, even from seeking the Ruine of his Benefactor. **1697** in Perry *Hist. Coll. Amer. Col. Ch.* I. 33 Such fort can be no security for his Majestys Customs, nor for finding and securing false and illegal trade. **1710** CELIA FIENNES *Diary* (1888) 83 They Wall round the Wells to yᵉ mines to Secure their Mold'ring in upon them. *Ibid.* 140 They Carry much of their Carriages on sledges to secure their pitching in the streetes. **1831** SCOTT *Cast. Dang.* viii, I deprecate no hardship..so I may secure you from acting with a degree of rashness, of which you will all your life repent. **1833** T. HOOK *Parson's Dau.* II. ix, I have secured him from visiting Binford.

†**f.** To render (an action) safe; to free from attendant dangers. Also, to render (a place) safe for transit. *Obs.*

1617 SIR O. ST. JOHN in *Buccleuch MSS.* (Hist. MSS. Comm.) I. 194 The King's ship and pinnace that are appointed for the securing of those seas. **1639** FULLER *Holy War* V. v. (1640) 236 Two hundred and fourteen years.. they [*sc.* the Hospitallers] mainteined this Island, and secured the seas for the passage of Pilgrimes to Jerusalem. **1667** MILTON *P.L.* V. 222 And to him call'd Raphael..that deign'd To travel with Tobias, and secur'd His marriage with the seaventimes-wedded Maid.

g. *Mil.* To render secure from attack or molestation by the enemy; to take defensive means for the safe execution of (a movement, e.g. a retreat, the crossing of a river); to guard efficiently (a pass, a defile).

1617 *Moryson Itin.* II. 66 His Lordship..sent Captaine Edward Blany with 500 foot and 50 horse, to secure their passage through the pace of the Moyrye. **1645** SYMONDS *Diary* (Camden) 242 The out workes, which secured the suburbs. *a* **1671** LD. FAIRFAX *Mem.* (1699) 21 It made us think of securing our retreat, with the prisoners we had got. **1698** FRYER *Acc. E. Ind. & P.* 337 The Passes are easily secured (an Handful of men being able to withstand an Host). **1701** STEELE *Funeral* V. i, Then..you, and your Party, fall in to secure my Rear; while I march off with the Body. **1760** *Cautions & Adv. to Officers of Army* 108 It may be the Means of saving an Army, or securing some Out-post of the utmost Importance. **1831** SCOTT *Ct. Robt.* iv, To take post in the defile..and thus secure it for the passage of the rest of the army. **1849** MACAULAY *Hist. Eng.* ii. I. 261 Making dispositions which, in the worst event, would have secured his retreat. **1869** FREEMAN *Norm. Conq.* (1876) III. xii. 210 The main point in the fortification was to secure the river.

h. *Mil.* ***to secure arms***: 'to hold a rifle or musket with the muzzle down, and lock well up under the arm, the object being to guard the weapon from the wet' (Ogilvie 1882).

1802 C. JAMES *Milit. Dict.* s.v., *Secure arms!* a word of command which is given to troops who are under arms in wet weather. **1892** *Rifle Exerc.* (*L.-M.*) 14 *Secure Arms.*

†**i.** To fence off. *Obs. rare.*

1710 CELIA FIENNES *Diary* (1888) 86 Its vaine to trye yᵉ securing it [*sc.* a hole] round from any falling in. *Ibid.* 90 Water..does often flow yᵉ grounds after Raines, so the Road is secured wᵗʰ a banck and a breast wall of a good Length.

j. To put in safety, 'get in' (a crop).

1885 *Times* (weekly ed.) 11 Sept. 9/1 Shocks of oats, cut, though not yet secured.

3. To make secure or certain.

†**a.** To make (a person) secure *of* a present or future possession, *of* an ally or supporter, etc. Also const. *to* with infinitive. *Obs.*

1610 HEALEY *St. Aug. Citie of God* XXI. xvii. 858 Assigning ..a false blisse, vnto the Saints in heauen, where they.. could neuer be secured to remaine. **1620** BRENT tr. *Sarpi's Counc. Trent* VIII. (1676) 728 And indeed he was secure of France and Germany. For besides his treaty with Lorain which did abundantly secure him of France, he received at the same time a resolution from the Emperour. **1656** EARL MONM. tr. *Boccalini's Advts. fr. Parnass.* II. vi. 218 Since no man can secure himself of the next years plentiful harvest. **1670** DRYDEN *1st Pt. Conq. Granada* V. i, Secur'd of what we hold most dear, (Each other's Love) we'll go—I know not where. **1745** in *Col. Rec. Pennsylv.* V. 5 Had I..been secured of Fund for supplying those Nations with Arms.

†**b.** *refl.* To get possession *of*, make sure *of*.

1675 *Machiavelli's Prince* x. Wks. 71 By..securing himself nimbly of such as appear..turbulent. **1705** *Lond. Gaz.* No. 4158/1, 3 or 4000 of the Inhabitants had taken up Arms,..and had secured themselves of Denia, a good Seaport Town. *Ibid.* No. 4162/1 Those who have declared for his..Majesty having secured themselves of Denia. **1725** BROOME *Notes to Pope's Odyss.* VIII. 239 Ulysses..finds a way..to secure himself of a powerful advocate, by [etc.].

†**c.** To certify, assure (a person) *of* some fact. Also in asseverative phrase, ***I'll secure you.*** *Obs.*

1659 HAMMOND *Ps.* lxxiii. 4 This doth not secure us of the importance of the word in this place. **1672** WYCHERLEY *Love in Wood* II. iv, He spares not the Innocents in Bibs and Aprons (Ile secure you) he has made (at best) some gross mistake concerning Christina. **1674** BOYLE *Excell. Theol.* I. i. 32 For ought reason can secure us of, one of the conditions of that association may be, that the body and soul shall not survive each other. **1689** HICKERINGILL *Ceremony-Monger* vi. 34 But Mum—not a Penny, I'll secure you, to make one Sound, and one Mouth. **1737** WHISTON *Josephus, Antiq.* Diss. ii. §3 The events and consequences of things afterwards always corresponded, and secured them of the truth of such divine revelations.

d. To establish (a person) securely *in* some position, privilege, etc.

1712 SWIFT *Jrnl. to Stella* 27 Dec., Steele I have kept in his place. Congreve I have got to be used kindly, and secured. Rowe I have recommended, and got a promise of a place. **1713** ADDISON *Cato* V. i, The Soul, secur'd in her Existence, smile's At the drawn Dagger, and defie's its Point. **1874** GREEN *Short Hist.* iii. §3 (1882) 125 The towns were secured in the enjoyment of their municipal privileges.

e. To make (something) secure, certain, or reliable. Now only with reference to a prospective possession or result of action: 'To place beyond hazard' (J.), to ensure.

1653 HOLCROFT *Procopius, Goth. Wars* IV. 126 In the Roman army was one Artabanes a Persarmenian, revolted lately to the Roman army, having secured his faith by the killing of a hundred and twenty Persian Souldiers. **1697** DRYDEN *Virg. Past.* vi. 18 For he who sings thy Praise, secures his own. **1746** FRANCIS tr. *Horace, Epist.* I. xvi. 58 Whose Bail secures, whose Oath decides a Cause. **1836** J. GILBERT *Chr. Atonem.* ii. (1852) 39 Yet merely to know that life immortal may be obtained, is not to secure our personal enjoyment of it. **1883** P. H. HUNTER *Story of Daniel* 151 Their manner of building secured a certain air of solidity and grandeur.

f. To make the tenure of (a property, office, privilege, etc.) secure *to* a person.

1736 BUTLER *Anal.* I. iv. Wks. 1874 I. 82 Our whole present interest is secured to our hands, without any solicitude of ours. **1825** SCOTT *Betrothed* Introd., The shareholder might contrive to secure to his heirs a handsome slice of his own death-bed and funeral expenses. **1856** FROUDE *Hist. Eng.* (1858) I. ii. 150 Her right to the succession..would have been readily secured to her by act of parliament.

g. To make (a creditor) certain of receiving payment by means of a mortgage, bond, pledge, or the like.

1677 YARRANTON *Eng. Improv.* 15 The Party lending the Moneys is safe, well and surely secured. **1861** M. PATTISON *Ess.* (1889) I. 41 Some of the large German houses in London..advanced large sums, taking care..to secure themselves by mortgages of parts of the public revenue.

h. To make the payment of (a debt, pension, etc.) certain by a mortgage or charge *upon* certain property.

1818 CRUISE *Digest* (ed. 2) II. 208, 2,000*l.* part of the money secured upon Gidea Hall. *Ibid.* IV. 392 Then such daughter should have 3,000*l.*,..to be secured upon some part of the estate. **1861** M. PATTISON *Ess.* (1889) I. 36 He assigns 1000 marks yearly as pinmoney to his son's wife, secured upon the Swiss possessions of his house.

i. With double obj.: To ensure (a person's) obtaining (something). *rare.* (In quot. *passive.*)

1831 SCOTT *Cast. Dang.* xii, You shall be secured an opportunity of being fully heard.

4. To seize and confine; to keep or hold in custody; to imprison. Now somewhat *rare.*

1645 CHAS. I in Ellis *Orig. Lett.* Ser. I. III. 314 You should beginne with securinge the person of William Legge. **1677** YARRANTON *Eng. Improv.* 3 Some of which Persons..did intend to get me secured for setting out the strength of the Dutch. **1683** WOOD *Life* 6 Sept. (O.H.S.) III. 72 The pro-vice-chancellor would then have secured him [Mr. Parkinson],..till security for his appearance at the assizes should be produced. *a* **1700** EVELYN *Diary* 20 June 1689, Newes of a Plot discover'd, on which divers were sent to the Tower and secured. **1705** [T. WALKER] *Wit of a Woman* III. 32 Secure that Rogue in the Stocks till we have search'd further. **1706** PHILLIPS (ed. Kersey), To *Secure*,..to apprehend or lay hold of one, to clap him into Prison. *a* **1715** BURNET *Own Time* (1724) I. 211 He proposed that about twenty of the chief gentlemen of those Counties might be secured: And he undertook for the peace of the countrey if they were clap'd up. **1799** HT. LEE *Canterb. T., Old Wom. T.* (ed. 2) I. 392 'Let him be secured', said St. Aubert. **1818** SCOTT *Hrt. Midl.* ii, Wilson and Robertson,..each secured betwixt two soldiers of the city guard. **1828–32** WEBSTER, *Secure*,..to inclose or confine effectually; to guard effectually from escape; sometimes, to seize and confine; as, to secure a prisoner. The sherif pursued the thief with a warrant, and secured him.

5. a. To make fast or firm.

1663 GERBIER *Counsel* 97 And so much may suffice for the securing of doores and windowes. **1687** M. SCRIVENER *Will* in Willis & Clark *Cambridge* (1886) III. 437 Chains for the securing the books. **1719** DE FOE *Crusoe* I. 305, I sent Friday with the Captain's Mate to the Boat, with Orders to secure her, and bring away the Oars and Sail. **1753** BARTLET *Gentl. Farriery* xxv. 231 A proper compress of cloth, and a linnen rowler is absolutely necessary both for this purpose, and to secure on the dressings, wherever they can conveniently be applied. **1823** *Mechanic's Mag.* I. 105 On the securing of carriage wheels. **1825** SCOTT *Betrothed* viii, A girdle.. secured by a large buckle of gold. **1867** AUGUSTA WILSON *Vashti* xix, She caught up her hair, twisted it hastily into a knot, and secured it with her comb. **1879** *Cassell's Techn. Educ.* IV. 80/2 These work in nuts secured to the doors. **1894** WEYMAN *Man in Black* 189 A wide-leafed hat, in which a costly diamond secured a plume of white feathers.

b. *Surg.* To close (a vein or artery) by ligature or otherwise, in order to prevent loss of blood.

1662 WISEMAN *Treat. Wounds* I. 35 Having thus secured the Vessels for the present. **1753** BARTLET *Gentl. Farriery* xxvi. 234 Should the wound bleed much from an artery divided, the first step should be to secure that by passing a crooked needle underneath, and tying it up with a waxed thread. **1880** C. HEATH *Man. Minor Surg.* (ed. 6) 34 In the case of an amputation, the main artieries will be secured before the cord is loosened.

6. a. To get hold or possession of (something desirable) as the result of effort or contrivance.

1743 BULKELEY & CUMMINS *Voy. S. Seas* 19 We took Care to secure some Powder, Ball, and a little Bread. **1748** SMOLLETT *Rod. Rand.* xxii, Having thus secured my good opinion, he began [etc.]. **1814** SCOTT *Antiq.* i, The first comer hastens to secure the best birth in the coach for himself. **1824** J. H. NEWMAN *Hist. Sk.* (1873) II. II. i. 246 [The profession] of arms..secures the almost undivided admiration of a rising and uncivilized people. **1855** PRESCOTT *Philip II*, I. II. vii. 219 His cordial manners.. secured the sympathy of all with whom he came in contact. **1873** TRISTRAM *Moab* Pref. 5 The splendid series of 180 photographs which they secured.

b. *Rugby Football.* To get or obtain (a try).

1885 *Field* 31 Jan. 135/2 The last-mentioned secured a try between the posts.

7. *Hort.* (See quot. 1928.)

1928 *Daily Express* 11 Aug. 4/2 The Japanese varieties of the chrysanthemum are now beginning to show their flower buds, and these should be 'secured', as it is called, at the earliest possible moment. This is done by pinching out with the thumb and finger the incipient side shoots or laterals that will be found in process of formation immediately beneath the buds and in the axils of the leaves. **1951** *Dict. Gardening* (R. Hort. Soc.) I. 476/1 It should be possible to secure the first crown bud of many varieties during the last week in July.

secured (sɪ'kjʊəd), *ppl. a.* [f. SECURE *v.* + -ED[1].] In senses of the verb: Assured; firmly fastened; rendered safe. Now chiefly of a debt: For which the creditor holds security. Also of a creditor.

1605 BACON *Adv. Learn.* II. xx. §5 They haue also excellentlye handled it..in the distinction between vertue with reluctation, and vertue secured. **1875** *Act 38 & 39 Vict.* c. 77 §10 The respective rights of secured and unsecured creditors. **1899** *Westm. Gaz.* 28 Aug. 6/3 The companies have no scale by which they regulate their charges, but advance to one man at 4 per cent. and to another at 5 per cent. for a secured loan.

†**se'cureful,** *a. Obs. rare*[−1]. [f. SECURE *a.* + -FUL.] Protecting.

c **1611** CHAPMAN *Iliad* VII. 209, I know..euery sway, of my securefull targe.

securely (sɪ'kjʊəlɪ), *adv.* [f. SECURE *a.* + -LY[2].] In a secure manner (in various senses).

†**1.** In a manner free from care or apprehension; carelessly; confidently; without care or misgiving.

1588 SHAKS. *Tit. A.* III. i. 3 Whose youth was spent In dangerous warres, whilst you securely slept. **1593** —— *Rich. II*, II. i. 266 We see the winde sit sore vpon our sailes, And yet we strike not, but securely perish. **1631** GOUGE *God's Arrows* I. §60 A Priest by vertue of his calling readily and securely admitted lepers to come to him. **1678** BUNYAN *Pilgr.* I. (1900) 67 When I dwelt securely at home. **1707** ATTERBURY *Vind. Doctr. Funeral Serm.* 42 Whether any of the Reasonings..are inconsistent with each other, I securely leave to the Judgment of the Reader. **1768–74** TUCKER *Lt. Nat.* (1834) II. 297 We have nothing but thoughtlessness and insensibility of danger to make us enjoy prosperity securely. **1802** MAR. EDGEWORTH *Moral T.* (1816) I. iv. 25 Trusting securely to the power of his own eloquence.

2. Without danger; in security; safely.

1615 BRATHWAIT *Strappado* (1878) 118 Being vnder shade securely sconst, Which place he had elected for the nonst. **1662** J. DAVIES tr. *Olearius' Voy. Ambass.* 67 This animal [the Reindeer] goes as securely as if it were upon the Ground. **1697** DRYDEN *Virg. Georg.* II. 396 How deep they must be planted woud'st thou know? In shallow Furrows Vines securely grow. *a* **1700** EVELYN *Diary* 11 May 1652, Two cut-throates started out, and..haled me into a deepe thickett some quarter of a mile from the highway, where they might securely rob me. *a* **1701** MAUNDRELL *Journ. Jerus.* 19 Mar. (1732) 43 Princes can never sleep securely but by day. **1784** COWPER *Tiroc.* 808 Tenants of life's middle state, Securely plac'd between the small and great. **1871** GEO. ELIOT *Middlem.* xxi, It was in that way Dorothea came to be sobbing as soon as she was securely alone.

3. Without risk of error; certainly.

1597 HOOKER *Eccl. Pol.* V. lxxviii. §12, I may securely therefore conclude that there are [etc.]. **1877** RUSKIN *Fors Clav.* lxxxii. 297 As I am securely informed. *Ibid.* lxxxiv. 409 The metaphor..I do not yet securely understand.

4. Firmly.

1856 KANE *Arct. Expl.* I. xxiii. 293 They had tied the dogs securely, as they thought: but Toodla and four others had broken loose. **1908** [MISS FOWLER] *Betw. Trent & Ancholme* 14 Those wrought stones..are now securely clamped to the south wall.

securement (sɪ'kjʊəmənt). *rare.* [f. SECURE *v.* + -MENT.] The action or an act of securing. †**a.** Making safe *from* or *against*. *Obs.* **b.** Ensuring or making sure.

1622 in Foster *Eng. Factories Ind.* (1908) II. 108 [Willoughby has also been furnished with money, and left to take his choice of means] for his best securmentt. **1646** SIR T. BROWNE *Pseud. Ep.* I. ii. 7 Cain..grew afraid thereof, and obtained a securement from it [death]. **1658** —— *Let. to Dugdale* 10 Nov., The laborious Aggers, Banks, and Works of Securement against Floods and Inundations. **1883** *Century Mag.* July 475/2 Liberty, however, is so highly prized that society condemns the securement in all cases of perpetual protection by means of perpetual imprisonment.

secureness (sɪ'kjʊənɪs). *rare.* [f. SECURE *a.* + -NESS.] = SECURITY 1, 3.

1591 HARINGTON *Orl. Fur.* VII. xxxvi. 52 To restitution turne your doing wrongs, Your fond securenesse, turne to godly feares. **1618** BOLTON *Florus* IV. xii. (1636) 326 Therefore (O strange securenesse!) as hee sate upon the Tribunall,..they at un-awares assailed him on all hands. **1633** T. ADAMS *Exp. 2 Peter* i. 5 No man perfectly knows his own heart: you think all well; this may be not assurance, but secureness. **1668** TEMPLE *On Approach of Shore of Harwich* 32 Thy sweet Inclosures..Shew thy secureness from thy Neighbours Harms. **1838** MRS. BROWNING *Seraphim* I. (near end), Down-lay Your sweet secureness for congenial fears.

securer (sɪ'kjʊərə(r)). *rare.* [f. SECURE *v.* + -ER[1].] One who or that which secures, in various senses of the verb.

1636 STRAFFORD *Lett.* (1739) II. 18 The Army..was rather to be reinforced..as..the chief Securer..of the.. Plantations. *a* **1704** T. BROWN *Satire upon Fr. King* Wks. 1730 I. 59 Of kings distressed thou art a fine securer. **1820** *Examiner* No. 616. 66/1 He rose early, which is a great securer of health.

securi- (sɪ'kjʊərɪ, ˌsɛkjʊə'rɪ), combining form of L. *secūris* axe, f. *secāre* to cut. Used in various scientific terms. **seˌcuri'cornate** [L. *corn-ū* horn + -ATE] *Ent.*, 'having the antennæ in form of a hatchet' (Mayne *Expos. Lex.* 1858). ‖**se'curifer** [L. *secūrifer* adj., *-fer, ferre* to bear] *Ent.*, one of the *Securifera* or phyllophagous hymenoptera. **secu'riferous** *a.* [-FEROUS], axe-bearing; *spec.* of or pertaining to the *Securifera*. **secu'rigerous** *a.* [-GEROUS] *Bot.* (see quot.). **se'curipalp** [L. *palp-us* PALP] *Ent.*, a beetle of the division *Securipalpi*. **seˌcuri'palpous** *a.* [-OUS] *Ent.*, of or pertaining to the division *Securipalpi*. See also SECURIFORM *a.*

1656 BLOUNT *Glossogr.*, *Securiferous*, that beareth an Axe or Hatchet. **1842** BRANDE *Dict. Sci.* etc., *Securifers*, Securiferi, the name of a tribe of *Terebrantia*, or boring Hymenopterous insects. **1858** MAYNE *Expos. Lex.*, Securiferous. *Ibid.*, *Securigerus*,..applied to the *Montbretea securigera*, from the form of the appendages that garnish the corol: securigerous. **1842** BRANDE *Dict. Sci.* etc., *Securipalps*, Securipalpi, the name of a family of Coleopterous insects, comprehending those in which the maxillary palps terminate in a joint which is elongated and hatchet-shaped. **1858** MAYNE *Expos. Lex.*, Securipalpous.

Securicor (sɪ'kjʊərɪkɔː(r)). [Invented name f. SECURI(TY + COR(PS.] The proprietary name of a private security organization employed in the guarding and safe transport of money, goods, and property. Freq. *attrib.*, esp. as *Securicor man, van*. Also *fig.* (with small initial).

1953 *Change of Name Certificate* 3 Jan. in Dept. of Trade file (354883) Night Guards Limited... Securicor Ltd. **1961** *Security Gaz.* Feb. 64/3 (*caption*) Securicor guards are responsible for the safety of Ireland's greatest art treasure, the 1,000 year old 'Book of Kells'. **1962** *Daily Tel.* 6 Sept. 13/1 An executive of Securicor, the security organization, said..'They were stupid to try to change vehicles.' *Ibid.*, Mr. Norman Negus, 54, a Securicor guard, walked out of the bank..carrying the cash box chained to him. As he approached the armoured Securicor van the ambush was sprung. *Ibid.*, Another Securicor man, locked inside the armoured van, sounded the alarm siren. **1968** *Listener* 12 Dec. 804/3 Unless future student audiences can be screened in advance by the BBC's own securicor, one sees small hope for this series. **1970** *Guardian Weekly* 14 Mar. 9/1 Securicor, Security Express, and Factoryguards—the three main companies which account for about 90 per cent of the manned protection in Britain. **1977** D. BAGLEY *Enemy* xxx. 239 The auctioneer has Securicor men all over the place.

securiform (sɪ'kjʊərɪfɔːm), *a.* [f. SECURI- + -FORM.] Axe-shaped, having the form of an axe or hatchet. **a.** *Bot.* applied to leaves, etc. **b.** *Ent.* applied to a palpus or joint, etc.

1760 J. LEE *Introd. Bot.* III. xviii. (1765) 212 *Securiform*, Hatchet-shaped. **1815** KIRBY & SP. *Entomol.* ix. (1818) I. 299 *note*, Mordellæ will open the anthers with the securiform joints of their palpi to get at the pollen. **1819** SAMOUELLE *Entomol. Compend.* 165 Labial palpi securiform. **1835–6** *Todd's Cycl. Anat.* I. 703/2 *Conchifera*... The foot ..is securiform when its free edge is arched like the cutting face of an axe, as in *Petunculus*. **1852** DANA *Crust.* II. 869 A small hand, slightly oblong, somewhat securiform.

se'curing, *ppl. a. rare.* [f. SECURE *v.* + -ING[2].] That secures, in various senses of the verb.

1643 J. M. *Sov. Salve* 35 The only sure and securing way to follow. **1798** *Times* 28 June 1/1 Drawing papers, pallets, gold and silver paper, copal and securing varnish.

†**se'curitan.** *Obs. rare.* [f. SECURIT-Y + -AN, ? after *Puritan*.] One who is characterized by 'security' or culpable freedom from apprehension.

1623 BP. HALL *Serm. Re-edif. Chapell of Earle of Exeter* Wks. (1625) 529 The sensual Securitan pleases himselfe in the conceit of his owne peace. **1627** R. BERNARD *Isle of Man* 21 One M[r]. Out-side, in the inside a carnall Securitan, [is] a fellow that will come to his Church [etc.].

securite ('sɛkjʊəraɪt). Also -it. [f. SECURE *a.* + -ITE 4, after the Ger. name *sicherit* (*sicher* sure, safe).] A high explosive consisting of a mixture of meta-di-nitro-benzole with nitrate of ammonium (Cundill *Dict. Explosives*, 1889, p. 82); used chiefly in blasting operations.

1888 *Times* 2 Mar. 13/6 Securite consists of nitrated hydro-carbons in admixture with certain oxidizing agents. It is the invention of Herr Schœneweg, who has now rendered it flameless when exploded, by the addition of an organic salt in certain proportions. **1897** *Allbutt's Syst. Med.* II. 958 The symptoms following the use of sicareit (securite or sicherite) resemble those which are caused by roburite.

security (sɪ'kjʊərɪtɪ). Forms: 5 securytye, securite(e, 6–7 securitye, securitie, 6– security. [ad. L. *sēcūritās*, f. *sēcūr-us*: see SECURE *a.* and -ITY. Cf. F. *sécurité* (16th c. in Hatz.-Darm.), Sp. *seguridad*, Pg. *seguridade*.]

I. The condition of being secure.

1. a. The condition of being protected from or not exposed to danger; safety.

1432–50 tr. *Higden* (Rolls) I. 77 Also hit [Paradise] hathe securite, to the whiche seyenge the altitude of the place berrethe testimonye [Lat. *Habet et securitatem cui attestatur loci altitudo*]. **1492** RYMAN *Poems* lxxx. 3 in *Archiv Stud. neu. Spr.* LXXXIX. 249 Thyne eye of grace vpon vs cast, Of helth and of securitee. **1582** STANYHURST *Æneis* I. (Arb.) 25 Therefor No worldly corner can theyme securitye warrant. **1617** MORYSON *Itin.* II. 13 This Earle providing for his securitie, about this time imprisoned the above mentioned sonnes of Shane ONeale. **1745** in *Col. Rec. Pennsylv.* V. 26 Some Provision should be made for the Security of our Frontier Settlements at least. **1781** GIBBON *Decl. & F.* xxxi. III. 229 The emperor and his court enjoyed..the security of the marshes and fortifications of Ravenna. **1861** M. PATTISON *Ess.* (1889) I. 46 The Esterlings..lay in security behind their walls, while the Flemish and other foreign residents fell helpless victims to the rage of the populace. **1903** A. SMELLIE *Men of Covenant* xxxii. (ed. 2) 352 His security lay, of course, in his lord's deafness.

b. The safety or safeguarding of (the interests of) a state, organization, person, etc., against danger, esp. from espionage or theft; the exercise of measures to this end; (the maintenance of) secrecy about military movements or diplomatic negotiations; in espionage, the maintenance of cover. Hence (with capital initial), a department (in government service, etc.) charged with ensuring this. (This sense tends towards 'the condition of making secure'.)

1941 *Times* 16 July 3/1 In order to ensure public security, the occupation of the principal localities in Syria and the Lebanon will be undertaken in accordance with the programme which will allow immediate replacement of French by the occupying forces. **1941** E. JOHN *Lofoten Let.* 34 Major Talbot..prides himself..on the 'security' of this expedition... [*note*] That is the Army term for what normal people call 'secrecy'. **1945** [see LEAKAGE 2]. **1955** *Bull. Atomic Sci.* Apr. 165/3 'Security', as it relates to the continuing struggle between the free world and the Soviet bloc, is an abundantly common yet widely misunderstood word. **1959** *Listener* 8 Oct. 558/1 You can call at offices, clubs, studios, and institutions—anywhere that does not verge on security—and usually they will tell you, foreigner though you are, the telephone numbers of their staff. **1961** R. SETH *Anat. Spying* v. 83 In the spy's vocabulary, Security means doing nothing that is likely to reveal his clandestine rôle... Each separate aspect of Security may be small..but any one aspect neglected is sufficient to cause the spy's downfall. **1965** M. ALLINGHAM *Mind Readers* vi. 59, I thought that might have been what Security told you when they sent for you. **1976** M. DELVING *China Expert* iv. 44 Security persuaded him to leave the army, and a place was found for him in..MI5. **1976** *Daily Tel.* 20 July 2/3 Security at places like the airport is always under review. **1982** *Observer* 6 June 1/7 While Israeli reaction has been to praise the British police..there is some evidence that security outside the hotel was lax.

2. Freedom from doubt; confidence, assurance. Now chiefly, well-founded confidence, certainty.

1597 A. M. tr. *Guillemeau's Fr. Chirurg.* 31 b/2 We may safelye, and with all securitye, vse them. **1646** SIR T. BROWNE *Pseud. Ep.* I. x. 42 Hee begets a security of himselfe, and a carelesse eye unto the last remunerations. **1749** CHESTERF. *Lett.* II. clxxxvi. 193 Negligence would imply either an indifference about pleasing, or else an insolent security of pleasing. **1782** MISS BURNEY *Cecilia* v. i, Rest no security upon yourself, .. since you have no knowledge of the many tricks and inventions by which you may be plundered. **1790** —— *Diary* July, He came .. with an honest, straightforward security of the welcome he really found. **1802** MAR. EDGEWORTH *Moral T.* (1816), I. xix. 154 The .. foreman .. appealed, with assumed security, to the entry in the books. **1849** C. BRONTE *Shirley* xv, She told Mr. Hall they might count on her with security. **1870** LOWELL *Study Wind.* 122 [The articles] are distinguished by a certain security of judgement, remarkable at any time, remarkable especially in one so young.

3. Freedom from care, anxiety or apprehension; a feeling of safety or freedom from or absence of danger. Formerly often *spec.* (now only *contextually*) culpable absence of anxiety, carelessness.

1555 J. BRADFORD in Coverdale *Lett. Martyrs* (1564) 266 Our vayne glory, our viciousness, avarice, ydleness, security. **1575–85** ABP. SANDYS *Serm.* xii. 189 They .. were drowned in sinnefull securitie. **1605** SHAKS. *Macb.* III. v. 32 Security Is Mortals cheefest Enemie. **1647** SPRIGGE *Anglia Rediv.* II. i. (1854) 70 As if he intended to surprise the town, thinking to find them in security. **1679** PENN *Addr. Prot.* I. viii. (1692) 39 His Security (the Effect of his Luxury) was his Ruin. **1726** LEONI *Alberti's Archit.* I. 69/1 The archers may privately annoy the enemy, as he moves about the Field in security. **1774** BURKE *Let. to Marq. Rockingh.* Corr. 1844 I. 496 The supineness, neglect, and blind security of my friend, in that, and every thing that concerns him. **1780** JOHNSON *Let. to Thrale* 30 May, Do not remit your care; for in your condition it is certain that security will produce danger. **1810** MRS. BRUNTON *Self-control* xxv, Lady Pelham smiled at Laura's security, which she did not consider as an infallible sign of safety. **1823** SCOTT *Peveril* xix, The security and carelessness of the sentinels, who had suffered such preparations to be made without observation or alarm given. **1858** *Sat. Rev.* 17 July 51 Every Government knew exactly when there was reason for alarm, and when there was excuse for security. **1876** MOZLEY *Univ. Serm.* iii. (1877) 63 It is an imaginary immortality which encloses him in sevenfold security, even while he stands upon its very last edge. **1977** *Monitor* (McAllen, Texas) 7 June 16A, A feeling of security comes with owning your own home. **1979** R. JAFFE *Class Reunion* (1980) III. i. 305 She knew now it was one of her weaknesses to look for total security.

4. The quality of being securely fixed or attached, stability, fixity.

1849 *Sk. Nat. Hist., Mammalia* IV. 169 Who can mistake the meaning .. of the security of the union of the clavicle to the large scapula?

II. A means of being secure.

5. Something which secures or makes safe; a protection, guard, defence.

a. Const. *against*, *from*, †*for*.

a **1586** SIDNEY *Arcadia* III. (Sommer) 286 b, For your securitie for any treacherie (hauing no hostage woorthie to counteruaile you) take my woorde, which I esteeme aboue all respectes. **1664** TILLOTSON *Serm.* i. Wks. (1714) 23 If the providence of God be taken away, what security have we against those innumerable dangers to which human nature is continually expos'd? **1691** T. H[ALE] *Acc. New Invent.* 21 Universal Practice .. does at this day make Lead the common security of Iron-work against Rust. **1736** BUTLER *Anal.* I. v. Wks. 1874 I. 96 Mankind .. stand in need of virtuous habits, for a security against this danger. **1828–32** WEBSTER s.v., A navy constitutes the security of Great Britain from invasion. **1832** HT. MARTINEAU *Life in Wilds* i. 21 A good fire .. was always a perfect security against the attacks of wild beasts. **1839** LANE *Arab. Nts.* I. 94 And I have no security against thy killing me by a thing that I may smell, or by some other means.

b. Without const.

1641 BAKER *Chron., Hen. I* (1653) 64 Anjou was neighbouring upon Normandy, a great security to it, if a friend; and as great danger, if an enemy. **1658** JER. TAYLOR *Let.* in *12th Rep. Hist. MSS. Comm.* App. v. 5 Nothing is so great a security to love as never to remember any unkindnesse. **1743** TINDAL tr. *Rapin's Hist.* XVII. II. 62/2 She at last formed two Parties in the Court and Kingdom, which proved her security, as she was necessary to Both. **1791** MRS. RADCLIFFE *Rom. Forest* ii, Concealment was his only security. **1817** JAS. MILL *Brit. India* II. IV. vi. 230 He endeavoured to obtain the security of at least a written promise for these terms which had been offered to gain his consent. **1874** GREEN *Short Hist.* viii. §2 (1882) 464 The only security for truth was to draw a hard and fast line between truth and falsehood. **1881** FROUDE *Short Stud.* IV. II. v. 226 Piety, which is a security for good faith, is none against credulity.

†**6.** A means of securing or fixing in position.

1793 SMEATON *Edystone L.* §227 The utility of trenails as a security till the mortar was become hard.

7. a. Ground for regarding something as secure, safe, or certain; an assurance, guarantee.

1623 COCKERAM II, Securitie giuen one for safe comming. *Safe conduite.* **1654** WHITLOCK *Zootomia* 19 To contemne Fame is but a security of doing ill. **1711** SWIFT *Conduct of Allies* Wks. 1901 V. 71 We could have no security for our trade, while that kingdom [Spain] was subject to a prince of the Bourbon family. **1715** ATTERBURY *Serm.* (1734) I. 138 What Security have We, that, abusing and despising the same Mercies, we shall not smart under the same Judgments? **1751** JORTIN *Serm.* (1771) IV. xv. 301 We can have no access to him, no security of His favor, unless we endeavour to conform to His precepts. **1805** WORDSW. *Poems Sent.* xx. *Ode Duty* 20 When love is an unerring light, And joy its own security. **1856** MACAULAY *Biog., Goldsm.* (1860) 71 Both what was good and what was bad in Goldsmith's character was, to his associates, a perfect security that he would never commit such villany. **1863** FAWCETT *Pol. Econ.* II x. 282 What therefore, the poor especially require when they buy their tea and sugar is, the security that they obtain an unadulterated article.

b. *Act of Security*: an Act passed by the Scottish Parliament in 1704, excluding Queen Anne's successor from the throne of Scotland unless conditions of government were enacted which should secure the independence of the kingdom.

1710–11 SWIFT *Examiner* No. 30 Wks. 1902 IX. 192 That unnatural league was afterwards cultivated by another incident; I mean the Act of Security.

8. Property deposited or made over, or bonds, recognizances, or the like entered into, by or on behalf of a person in order to secure his fulfilment of an obligation, and forfeitable in the event of non-fulfilment; a pledge, caution. Phrases, ***to enter*** (***in*** or ***into***), ***find***, ***give*** (***in***), ***go***, † ***put in***, ***take security***.

a. As securing a person's 'good behaviour', his appearance in court at a specified time, or his performance of some undertaking.

1450 *Rolls of Parlt.* V. 181/2 Where securitee of peas was axed bifore you in your said Court. **1611** BIBLE *Acts* xvii. 9 And when they had taken securitie of Iason, and of the other, they let them goe. **1621** ELSING *Debates Ho. Lords* (Camden) 96 Putt in good securitye to fynde out Watson by Monday come sen-night... To remayne in prison untell he putt in securitye here. **1658–9** *Burton's Diary* (1828) IV. 6, I move that he enter security. The person complaining, is a person of as great worth as any person can be. **1668–9** PEPYS *Diary* 5 Mar., Being this day summoned .. to give in security for his good behaviour. **1712** ARBUTHNOT *John Bull* I. iii. 7 You must find sufficient Security to us, our Heirs and Assigns, that you will not employ Lewis Baboon. **1724** SWIFT *Drapier's Lett.* iii. Wks. 1735 IV. 118 Knox .. was obliged .. to enter into Security for so doing. **1790** J. BRUCE *Source of Nile* I. iii. 46 We obliged him to give his son Mahomet in security for his behaviour towards us. **1797** *Month. Mag.* III. 550/1 Where special bail is required, the sheriff may take security of the defendant, by bond, .. for his appearance. **1828–32** WEBSTER s.v., Violent and dangerous men are obliged to give security for their good behavior, or for keeping the peace. **1883** *Act 46 & 47 Vict.* c. 52 §21 (2) The person so appointed shall give security in manner prescribed to the satisfaction of the Board of Trade.

b. As securing the payment of a debt.

1576 *Reg. Privy Council Scot.* II. 539 To subscrive and returne the forme of security. **1592** *Nobody & Someb.* C 2, Without good securitie they will lend Nobody mony. **1607** DEKKER & WEBSTER *Westw. Hoe* IV. i, *Tent.*.. Wel sir, your security? *Amb.* Why sir two Diamonds here. *c* **1613** ROWLANDS *Paire Spy-Knaves* 15 Bonds, Bils, and words, I'le trust none of you three. Bring good securitie to deale with me. *a* **1687** PETTY *Pol. Arith.* Pref., Those who can give good Security, may have Money under the Statute-Interest. **1711–12** SWIFT *Jrnl. to Stella* 22 Mar., The French have offered .. to give us Dunkirk, and the Dutch Namur, for security, till the peace is made. **1724** in *Fasti Aberd.* (1854) 205 Money .. to be laid out .. upon land or upon reall or personal security, and the interest or yearly produce thereof is to be applyed [etc.]. **1766** BLACKSTONE *Comm.* II. 480 The petitioners .. must be bound in a security of 200 *l*, to make the party amends in case they do not prove him a bankrupt. **1818** CRUISE *Digest* (ed. 2) II. 90 The mortgagee holds the estate merely as a pledge or security for the repayment of his money. **1833** HT. MARTINEAU *Manch. Strike* viii. 85 It was frequently necessary to borrow money, .. on the security of what was to come in during the next week. **1868** ROGERS *Pol. Econ.* ix. 107 The reason why this personage [the employer] exists in modern trade and manufacture arises from the facts that he has security on which to borrow [etc.]. **1874** MARKBY *Elem. Law* (ed. 2) §496, I shall also use the word security to express any transaction between the debtor and creditor by which the performance of such a service [*sc.* one capable of being represented in money] is secured.

c. *transf.*

1649 E. REYNOLDS *Hosea* II. 69 We .. stagger and be disheartened, if we have not double securitie from God. *a* **1744** SWIFT *Serm. Testimony Consc.* Wks. 1898 IV. 127 It is impossible for a man who openly declares against religion, to give any reasonable security that he will not be false and cruel. **1825** SCOTT *Talism.* i, But what security dost thou offer that thou wilt observe the truce? **1878** BOSW. SMITH *Carthage* 283 The word of a Gracchus .. was his bond; and a bond which was a first-rate security.

9. One who pledges himself (or is pledged) for another, a surety.

1597 SHAKS. *2 Hen. IV*, I. ii. 38 He said sir, you should procure him better Assurance, then Bardolfe: he wold not take his Bond and yours, he lik'd not the Security. **1627** SIR T. HOPE *Let.* in *Scottish Hist. Soc. Misc.* (1893) I. 93 And for the nott of the Irische landis, it salbe sent with the securities quhen thay go to Irland. **1686** tr. *Chardin's Trav. Persia* 43 He would engage his word and be security for the performance of what the Chancellor had declar'd. **1690** WOOD *Life* 31 Jan. (O.H.S.) III. 324 They were bailed on great security given by each on their owne parts, and on the parts of their security. **1710** SWIFT *Jrnl. to Stella* 13 Nov., When one [of the two people bound] dies, you fall upon the other, and make him add another security. **1721** J. PERRY *Stopping Dagenham Breach* 93 One of my Securitys .. promised to take care of the finishing the work in my Absence. **1786** BURKE *Art. agst. W. Hastings* Wks. 1842 II. 143 Croftes offered the said Richard Johnson as one of his securities for the performance of the said contract. **1844** DICKENS *Mart. Chuz.* xxvii, B wants a loan... B proposes self and two securities. B is accepted. Two securities give a bond. **1908** *Blackw. Mag.* Aug. 213/2 So, with their security and some others, I started in pursuit, and next morning came up with the fugitives.

transf. **1681** LUTTRELL *Brief Rel.* (1857) I. 135 There was .. a motion made that the citty should undertake the businesse of insuring houses from fire, and that the chamber of London should be the security.

10. A document held by a creditor as guarantee of his right to payment. Hence, any particular kind of stock, shares, or other form of investment guaranteed by such documents. Also, in the U.S., such a document issued to investors to finance a business venture. Chiefly *plural.*

1690 CHILD *Disc. Trade* (1698) 7–8 Their keeping up publick registers of all lands and houses, sold or mortgaged, whereby .. the securities of lands and houses [are] rendered indeed, such as we commonly call them, real securities. **1691** LOCKE *Consid. Lower. Interest* (1692) 132 But how Securities will be mended by lowering of Interest, is, I confess, beyond my Comprehension. **1712** ARBUTHNOT *John Bull* III. viii. 33 When I wanted Money, half a dozen of these Fellows were always waiting in my Antichamber with their Securities ready drawn. **1746** LD. HARDWICKE in Atkyns *Chanc. Rep.* (1782) III. 444 Neither South-Sea stock nor Bank stock are considered as a good security. **1788** M. CUTLER in *Life*, etc. (1888) I. 380 Continental Securities have been falling in Boston since my last return from New York. **1848** MILL *Pol. Econ.* I. iv. §3 (1876) 39 He buys from the state what are called government securities; that is obligations on the government to pay a certain annual income. **1848** [see NEGOTIABLE *a.* 1]. **1872** ROGERS *Capital & Lab.* in *Cassell's Techn. Educ.* IV. 14/2 The labour of a stockbroker consists in purchasing securities on behalf of his customers, he receiving a fee in the form of a percentage on the purchase or sale of the security. **1879** *Daily News* 26 May, Liquid Securities, or in other words, those easily convertible into cash when necessity arises. **1899** *Ann. Amer. Acad. Pol. & Soc. Sci.* XIV. 181 The term 'negotiable securities' is applicable in a general sense to many forms of commercial paper, including drafts and bills of exchange, but it is usually employed for the share-capital of corporations and for the bonds of such corporations and of local and state governments. **1925** R. H. MONTGOMERY *Financial Handbk.* VII. 526 The financial executive .. will naturally adapt the securities offered by his company so as best to fit in with the market he is trying to reach. **1937** J. I. BOGEN *Corporation Finance* xiii. 223 Most .. successful enterprises can raise funds .. through the sale of securities. .. So broad has the ownership of stocks and bonds become that the United States has been described as a 'nation of investors'. **1962** *2001 Business Terms* (Alexander Hamilton Inst.) 246 *Securities*, stocks and bonds of business firms used to raise long-term capital. **1970** M. GREENER *Penguin Dict. Commerce* 296 *Security*, a misused term often applied indiscriminately to shares, debentures, etc. In fact a security is something given or guaranteed by the borrower as a safeguard for a loan. The term is often applied to debentures and similar loan stock, and to negotiable instruments. Certificates of liability are known as securities, so sometimes are government stocks or any loans whose repayment is guaranteed. The term should not be applied to shares.

III. 11. *attrib.* as (senses 8, 10) ***security-bond***, ***-writ***; also **security** (also **securities**) **analyst** *U.S.*, a person who analyses the worth of securities, as by measuring the ratio of their cost to their dividends and earnings; **security blanket** orig. *U.S.* [idea popularized by the American cartoonist Charles M. Schulz (b. 1922) in the comic strip 'Peanuts' in which a boy named Linus carries a cot blanket for comfort], an object (esp. a blanket) given to a child to afford reassurance by its familiarity; also *fig.*; see also sense 12 e below; **security-bolt**, a device for securing a motor-tyre to the rim; **security-grinder**, *jocular*, ? an assiduous deviser of securities.

1934 GRAHAM & DODD *Security Analysis* VII. l. 586 There is a fundamental cleavage of viewpoint between the speculator and the *securities analyst. **1937** *N.Y. Times* 18 May 40/4 Plans for the organization of the New York Society of Security Analysts. **1961** 'E. LATHEN' *Banking on Death* iii. 22 One of Robichaux and Devane's security analysts was leaving the firm. **1979** A. MALING *Koberg Link* (1980) xx. 109 I'm a securities analyst. [**1956** C. M. SCHULZ *Good Grief, More Peanuts* 25 (*caption*) This is a 'security and happiness' blanket... *All* little kids carry them.] **1971** *Newsweek* 19 July 48/1 Deferred-admissions plans—a sort of *security blanket that prospective students can carry with them during a year's sabbatical. **1973** *Ladies' Home Jrnl.* Dec. 102 A worn, torn, one-eyed teddy bear about a foot long was my 'security blanket'. **1975** *New Yorker* 21 Apr. 99/1 There's a security-blanket comfort in thinking you have something there in actuarial terms that you can rely on. **1976** *New Society* 28 Oct. 179/2 This [book], to give well deserved recognition to its usefulness .. is already as dog-eared as a security blanket. **1978** *Maledicta* II. 81 The subjunctive mood is his security blanket. **1903** *Motoring Ann.* 304 Fig. 2 shows the *security bolt in the act of pinching the inner tube. **1715** in J. Perry *Stopping Dagenham Breach* (1721) 131 That the *Security Bonds shall be deliver'd up to be cancell'd, when the Conditions are perform'd. **1827** CANNING *Sp.* 6 Mar. (1828) VI. 155 Since the year 1813, I certainly have not meddled in the workmanship of securities; .. I assure my right honourable friend .. that I am perfectly ready to vote for securities; but I am not to be set down as a *security-grinder. **1908** *Carnegie Trust Rep.* 61 The *Security Writs have been exhibited to me.

12. *attrib.* with reference to (the maintenance of) security in military, penal, civil, and commercial contexts (see sense 1 b above).

a. Of devices which assist security, as ***security door***, ***fence***, ***gate***, ***lock***, etc. Also, of areas so protected, as ***security wing***.

1904 A. GRIFFITHS *50 Yrs. Publ. Service* xvii. 232 The locks everywhere, to cells, passages, and in external or 'security' doors [were] of the newest and most approved pattern. **1963** *Security Gaz.* V. 187/2 The main innovation at Blundeston is the 12 ft. high security fence. **1968** *Rep. Work Prison Dept.* 6 in *Parl. Papers 1967–68* (Cmnd. 3774) XXXI. 57 The use of special security wings to house prisoners who require the strictest security is an expedient which poses severe problems. **1971** *Country Life* 10 June

1439/3, I gathered that they [*sc.* four stone figures] once guarded the four corners of Aldgate, one of London's well-known security gates. **1976** 'M. ALBRAND' *Taste of Terror* xviii. 107 I'm going to.. put security locks on every door in the house. **1976** *Washington Post* 19 Apr. c21/2 (Advt.), Will throw in bumper rack, tie downs, security chain & lock. **1976** *Evening Times* (Glasgow) 1 Dec. 3/6 A key that was missing would let anyone escape from the block into the grounds—but it wouldn't let them out of the security gates.

b. Of measures, etc., intended to ensure security, as ***security clearance, measure, pact, rating***, etc.

1925 *Times* 2 Sept. 11/4 The jurists.. are discussing the technical details of the proposed Security Pact at the Foreign Office. **1945** *News Rev.* 10 May 9 The security black-out will be lifted to enable us to print some details about the nation's war effort. **1952** *Ann. Reg. 1951* 424 There were renewed expressions of disquiet from scientists about the encroachment of security measures on personal freedom of speech and action. **1955** M. REIFER *Dict. New Words* 185/1 *Security clearance*, the establishment, by means of investigation and executive determination, that a prospective federal employee or consultant is not a security risk, and may be hired. **1958** *New Statesman* 20 Sept. 365/2 With the off-shore islands and Formosa blanketed by a security screen, it is difficult to know exactly what is happening there. **1963** MRS. L. B. JOHNSON *White House Diary* 2 Dec. (1970) 13 Dr. Henry Smyth, the lone dissenter in the 4-to-1 Commission decision when Dr. Oppenheimer lost his security clearance. **1963** L. DEIGHTON *Horse under Water* xxi. 94 Act grown-up or I'll cut your security rating back. **1976** H. TRACY *Death in Reserve* xv. 118 It's your red area security pass. **1978** R. LUDLUM *Holcroft Covenant* xxxi. 363 Suppose the guards were more alert, security measures more effective.

c. Of persons or organizations charged with the maintenance of security, as ***security guard, man, officer, police, service***, etc. Also ***security van***.

1940 *Hutchinson's Pictorial Hist. War* 4 Feb.–9 Apr. 180 It was quiet on the island at first, the Nazis believing the raiders to be just another security patrol. **1944** P. GIBBS *Battle Within* 135 If one of our Security Police had been in the church to-day he might have tapped you on the shoulder after the service and led you off to Brixton Gaol. **1945** *Daily Express* 4 June 1/1 A double check is being made by security officers on the three Belfast-Dublin trains that stop at Goraghwood daily for Customs examination. **1948** *Straits Times* 20 July 6/2 It is still true that 'the estates, mines and kampongs'—to echo Mr. MacDonald's broadcast again—do not feel that the security forces are doing enough for them. **1951** N. BROOK in *Ld. Denning's Rep.* 79 in *Parl. Papers 1962–3* (Cmnd. 2152) XXIV. 349, I recommend that the Security Service should in future be responsible to the Home Secretary. **1955** EARL WINTERTON *Fifty Tumultuous Years* 74 He had no aide-de-camp with him, no 'security guard' and no police escort, not even a groom. **1958** *New Statesman* 7 June 716/2 But the Socialist Deputies of Nord and Pas de Calais.. replied to these fears by saying openly to Guy Mollet: 'If you're afraid of the paratroops and you can't depend on the security police, arm the miners.' **1959** *Times Lit. Suppl.* 27 Mar. 182/2 Ministers, Civil servants and security men buzzing round the graceless tycoon who is producing a new bomber. **1963** A. DOUGLAS-HOME in *Hansard Commons* DCLXXXVI. 859 If we were to set up a Standing Security Commission, I think, first, that it should have a judicial chairman. **1965** D. FRANCIS *Odds Against* ix. 135 [We] could arrange for some sort of guard on the course. Security patrols, that kind of thing. **1966** M. WOODHOUSE *Tree Frog* xxi. 153 There were no security guards.. there wasn't anywhere to run to. **1970** G. F. NEWMAN *Sir, You Bastard* vii. 198 An attack on a security van. **1973** *Times* 15 May 12/6 Britain's involvement in Northern Ireland was real and earnest, as the security forces knew. **1975** D. LODGE *Changing Places* v. 165 A solitary security man in his shelter lifted a lazy hand in salute. **1975** A. A. THOMPSON *Message from Absalom* iii. 17 Security police carrying rifles. **1976** H. WILSON *Governance of Britain* ix. 167 Until 1952 the Prime Minister was directly responsible for the security service. **1978** R. V. JONES *Most Secret War* liii. 520 One morning just before a weekend, the Security Officer rushed round the M.I.6 offices telling everyone to take down all maps off their walls. **1981** 'W. HAGGARD' *Money Men* xiii. 144 A security van drove up... It contained his loot.

d. With adjs. to form adjs., as ***security-conscious, -minded*** (hence ***-mindedness***).

1943 J. H. FULLARTON *Troop Target* 26 'If you ask me,' said Quigg, 'this Fifth Column palaver is mostly propaganda to make us security-minded.' **1955** I. FLEMING *Moonraker* xv. 149 Drax.. seemed to be meticulously security-conscious. **1955** M. GILBERT *Sky High* v. 69 The Inspector's tone implied exactly what he thought about the security-mindedness of County Councillors. **1960** 'R. EAST' *Kingston Black* xx. 185 In military intelligence it's second nature to be security-minded about public telephones. **1968** M. JONES *Survivor* i. 22 I've always heard they're madly careless in the Air Force. Not security-conscious like the Navy. **1972** M. GILBERT *Body of Girl* xxiii. 200 He decided to test the security-mindedness of the person chiefly concerned. **1976** 'M. BARAK' *Secret List Heinrich Roehm* I. iv. 46 The Israelis are going to be much more security-minded now.

e. Special Combs.: **security blanket**, an official sanction introduced in order to maintain complete secrecy or safety from danger; see also sense 11 above; **security check**, (*a*) a verification of identity or reliability, *spec.* of the loyalty of an official employee, for the purposes of security; (*b*) a phrase incorporated in a broadcast message from a spy to confirm his identity or to indicate that he is not operating under duress; hence **security-check** *v. trans.*, to subject to a security check; **Security Council**, a principal council of the United Nations consisting permanently of the Great Powers of 1945 and temporarily of certain others, charged with the settlement of disputes (and orig. with the threat of military action against aggressors); **security risk**, a person whose tenure of an official position constitutes a possible danger to the security of the state, etc.; also, a situation endangering security.

1955 *New Yorker* 5 Feb. 88/2 The size of the Regular Army is under a security blanket at present. **1972** *Times* 13 Sept. 8/8 At Heathrow.. there was a tight security blanket. **1945** *Daily Express* 4 June 1/1 A security check on their identity cards and permits on the Ulster-Eire border showed that they were apparently in order. **1961** R. SETH *Anat. Spying* vi. 98 The operator is instructed to insert in all his messages what is known as a Security-check. **1966** 'A. HALL' *9th Directive* iii. 31 With the flap on.. they were probably security-checking the Ambassador himself. **1978** R. LUDLUM *Holcroft Covenant* xxxii. 374 Security check requested. **1979** F. FORSYTH *Devil's Alternative* x. 232 The cipher clerks are.. security-checked to the highest level. **1944** *Times* 10 Oct. 5/6 Tentative proposals have been made for the establishment of a general international organization under the title of The United Nations. The proposals.. deal with.. its principal organs, including a General Assembly, a Security Council, and an International Court of Justice. **1968** *Security Council Proc. Czechoslovakia* 3 in *Parl. Papers 1967–8* (Cmnd. 3757) XLII. 229 The Security Council met at 6.30 p.m. (New York Time) on 21st August. After protracted debate, the Council agreed to the inscription of the item on Czechoslovakia on its agenda. **1977** *Whitaker's Almanack 1978* 806/2 The Security Council consists of fifteen Members, each of which has one representative and one vote. **1948** Security risk [see CLEARANCE 5 c]. **1951** *Ann. Reg. 1950* 186 Mr. Acheson was.. asked whether he himself, in view of his friendship for Hiss, could be considered a security risk. **1965** M. SPARK *Mandelbaum Gate* vii. 216 He disapproved of letting young chaps into the Foreign Service who openly professed to have no religion at all. A security risk, Freddy felt decidedly. **1975** *Radio Times* 2–8 Aug. 43/3 He was accused of being a 'security risk' because of his early Communist associations.

† **'secutor, 'sectour.** *Obs.* Forms: 3–4 seketur, 4 sekatur, 4–5 seke-, seka-, secutour, 5 sekka-, seca-, secoutour, seccutur, secutur, -or, seketowr(e, sekiture; 4–6 sectour, 5 sektour, secktur, 5–6 sectur, 6 sekture, sector. [Aphetic form of EXECUTOR.] = EXECUTOR.

a **1300** *Cursor M.* 28322 Ic seketur made of testament, ne folud noght with gode entent þe testament for to fulfill, bot gafe i it gain dedis will. *a* **1330** *Roland & V.* 390 At þe nende of þritti niȝt, To his seketour com þe ded kniȝt, & seyd in þis maner: 'Mi soule [etc.]'. **13..** *Metr. Hom.* (Vernon MS.) in *Archiv Stud. neu. Spr.* LVII. 259 While he lyuede faste preyed he þat þou his sekatur mihte be. **1377** LANGL. *P. Pl.* B. xv. 128 Þe which aren prestes inparfit and prechoures after syluer, Sectoures and sudenes, somnoures and her lemmannes. **1387** *E.E. Wills* (1882) 2, I ordeine Watkyn my sone, secutour. *c* **1425** *Cast. Persev.* 102 in *Macro Plays* 80 He sendith afftyr his sekkatours, ful fekyl to fynde. *c* **1460** *Towneley Myst.* xxxi. 166 Trust neuer freyndys frele Nawthere of childe then wife; ffor sectures ar not lele. *c* **1485** *Early Eng. Misc.* (Warton Club) 41 Ȝefe thi almus with thi hand, trust to no secatour. **1493** *Halyburton's Ledger* (1867) 32 Som that I rest awand to John Twedy or hys wyff and sekituris is 33li. 5s. 5g^s. **1505** *Presentments of Juries* in *Surtees Misc.* (1890) 31 Dyssyryng hym to be hys sektur, and also me to be hys sekture to. **1509** BARCLAY *Ship of Fools* (1874) I. 117 Thou ought nat yet to kepe it nere the more. But to his sectours or heyres it restore. **1567** *Gude & Godlie B.* 30 Sair I suspect, God accuse His sectouris, and him self refuse, That sa vnfaithfullie deceist.

Hence † **'secutorship** *rare* = EXECUTORSHIP.

1553 *Respublica* III. vi. 864 This same I got by sectourshipp of my Mother. *Ibid.* 866 This bag have I kepte of other sectourships whole, whiche the Madde knaves woulde had scettred by penie dole.

sed: see SAD *a.*, SAY *v.*[1], SEED.

† **'sedal**, *a. Obs. rare.* [ad. mod.L. *sēdāl-is*, f. *sēd-ēs* seat, fundament: see -AL[1].] Of or belonging to the fundament.

1681 *Willis's Rem. Med. Wks.*, Vocab., *Sedal veins*, the veins in the fundament. **1684** tr. *Bonet's Merc. Compit.* VI. 197 While they draw [blood] from the sedal Arterie [orig. *ex arteriis sedalibus*].

sedan (siː'dæn, sə-). Also 7 cedan, (? *erron.*) sedam. [Of obscure etymology.

The conjecture (? first in Johnson, 1773) connecting the word with the name of Sedan, a town of NE. France, has nothing to support it, and seems unlikely. In 1634 the exclusive right of supplying 'covered chairs' was granted to Sir Sanders Duncombe; the word *sedan* does not occur in the grant, but the index to the patents of the year has 'covered chairs (called sedans)'. The statement of Evelyn, that Duncombe brought the sedan from Naples may be correct, as the thing had long been in use in Italy (cf. It. *seggietta* in Florio, 1598). It is therefore natural to suppose that the word might be from some South Italian derivative of It. *sede* (L. *sēdēs*) seat, *sedere* to sit; but there seems to be no trustworthy evidence of the existence in It. dialects of any form from which the Eng. word could be derived.]

1. a. A closed vehicle to seat one person, borne on two poles by two bearers, one in front and one behind. In fashionable use during the 17th, 18th, and early 19th cent.

1635 BROME *Sparagus Garden* I. iii. (1640) B4b, What, have you some new project a foot now, to out-goe that of the Hand-barrowes? what call you 'em the Sedams [*sic*]? *Ibid.* IV. x. I 4 b, Shee's now gone forth in one o' the new Hand-litters: what call yee it, a Sedan. *Brit.* O Sedana. **1641** *MSS. Dk. Rutland* (Hist. MSS. Comm.) IV. 531 Payd the men that carried my Lord George in the sedan, 1li. xvjs. **1660** *Trial Regic.* 191 His Majesty was immediately hurried away from the Bar into a Common Cedan. **1666** *Lond. Gaz.* No. 89/2 The Empress.. by reason of her weakness,.. travells in her Sedan. *a* **1700** EVELYN *Diary* 8 Feb. 1645, The streets [of Naples] are full of gallants on horse-back, in coaches and sedans, from hence brought first into England by Sir Sanders Duncomb. **1702** *Lond. Gaz.* No. 3867/1 The Doge was carried in a very rich Sedan. **1737** DUCHESS OF PORTLAND in Mrs. Delany *Life & Corr.* (1861) I. 610 Lady Dunkeron's sedan is yellow velvet, imbroidered and imbossed with silver. **1802** *Anna Seward's Lett.* (1811) VI. 9 Dr. Jones seconded my proposal that he should be brought here in a sedan. **1837** DICKENS *Pickw.* xxv, Mr. Muzzle opened one half of the carriage gate to admit the sedan.

b. *transf.* A litter, palanquin, or the like.

1646 WINTHROP *Hist. New Eng.* (1853) II. 323 He.. presented the governour with a sedan, which (as he said) was sent by the viceroy of Mexico to his sister. **1662** J. DAVIES tr. *Mandelslo's Trav.* 52 Some times, he is carried by several men in a Palanquin, or kind of Sedan. **1737** WHISTON *Josephus, Antiq.* XVIII. vi. §6 As Tiberius lay once at his ease upon his sedan, and was carried about. **1847** PRESCOTT *Peru* (1850) II. 61 Elevated high above his vassals came the Inca Atahuallpa, borne on a sedan or open litter. **1878** J. PAYN *By Proxy* I. iii. 25 All the neighbourhood.. the rich [Chinese] in sedans, the poor on foot, were on their way to do honour to his shrine.

c. = SALOON 4 c. Chiefly *N. Amer.* (Not used in the U.K.)

1912 *Motor World* 14 Nov. 18/1 In the new [Studebaker] cars, there is another coupe, and a 'Sedan', both mounted on a new four-cylinder chassis. **1915** *Literary Digest* (N.Y.) 21 Aug. (cover advt.), A touring car when the windows are down... With the windows raised, a luxurious sedan. **1922** *Short Stories* Feb. 98/1 The sedan had been equipped with an exhaust foot warmer or heater. **1935** M. M. ATWATER *Murder in Midsummer* i. 6 A black sedan was drawn up on the shoulder of the road. **1966** 'A. HALL' *9th Directive* xx. 184 It was a massive black Lincoln sedan; a seven-seater executive-style transport. **1977** *Time* 8 Aug. 23/1 The two were surrounded by four pistol-carrying men and ordered into a nearby Peugeot sedan.

2. *local U.S.* 'A hand-barrow with a deep basket-like bottom made of barrel-hoops, used to carry fish' (*Cent. Dict.* 1891).

3. *Comb.*, as ***sedan-bearer, car, -maker, -man, model***; **sedan clock** *Hist.* = *sedan-chair clock* s.v. SEDAN CHAIR c.

1837 DICKENS *Pickw.* xxv, Mr. Grummer, commanding the *sedan-bearers to halt, advanced. **1931** M. DE LA ROCHE *Finch's Fortune* xxv. 325 A *sedan car stopped before the door. **1957** *N.Z. Listener* 22 Nov. 4/4 New Zealand English has diverged from the English of England more than is generally realised owing to the influence of American usage. 'Sedan' car often appears in the advertisements, where an English advertisement would print 'saloon'. **1950** D. DE CARLE *Watchmakers' & Clockmakers' Encycl. Dict.* 129/1 **Sedan clock*, a small hanging clock usually associated with the period of the Sedan Chair. **1968** —— *Clocks & their Value* 93 The value of a sedan clock depends on the case but can be anything from about £15 to £35. **1641** EARL CORK in *Lismore Papers* Ser. I. (1886) V. 173 Paid Thomas wright, the *sedan maker, dwelling in white ffriers, for my new sedan. **1638** BROME *Antipodes* IV. viii. (1640) I 1, Enter *Sedan-man. **1647** R. STAPYLTON *Juvenal* VI. 110 These Syrians were.. kept by the ladies of Rome.. for their chair-bearers or sedan-men. **1948** *Herald-Press* (St. Joseph, Mich.) 14 Aug. 5/1 Besides making some substantial changes in its present *sedan models it plans to put a hard top convertible into production.

Hence † **se'dan'd** *pa. pple.*, placed or carried in a sedan. † **se'danful** [-FUL], the occupants of a sedan. **sedanier** [-IER], a sedan-bearer.

1647 R. STAPYLTON *Juvenal* I. 6 Sedan-fulls for these hundred farthings throng. **1688** R. L'ESTRANGE *Brief Hist. Times* III. 139 The Body is by This Time Cas'd, Hous'd, Sedann'd, Box'd up, or call it what you will. **1690** EVELYN *Mundus Muliebris* 8 When to the Play 'tis time to go In Pompous Coach, or else Sedan'd With Equipage along the Strand. **1871** MEREDITH *H. Richmond* xliii, By the way, Richie, there will be Sedaniers—porters to pay to-day.

sedanca (sə'dæŋkə). Also **Sedanca**. [f. SEDAN + the name of Count Carlos de *Salaman*)*ca*, Spanish nobleman and Rolls-Royce agent, by whom the word was apparently coined.] In full, ***Sedanca de Ville***. A sumptuously appointed cabriolet de ville mounted on a Rolls-Royce chassis. Cf. (U.S.) *town car* s.v. TOWN *sb.* 10.

1926 *Motor* 26 Oct. 615/3 The other body shown on a Rolls-Royce chassis is styled a Sedanca limousine. It can also be used as a cabriolet, inasmuch as the Barker patent de ville extension over the front seat can be removed completely. **1929** *Motor* 2 July (Suppl.) p. xl/1, 1927 (October) 40–50 hp Phantom Rolls-Royce enclosed-drive Sedanca de Ville. **1937** *Times* 20 Oct. 20/1 The Rolls-Royce Company show a.. Phantom III sedanca at £3,040. **1963** D. SCOTT-MONCRIEFF *Thoroughbred Motor Car 1930–40* ii. 121 (*caption*) Rolls-Royce 20/25 with French-built sedanca-de-ville coachwork, 1935. **1978** *Times* 8 June 28 (Advt.), This magnificent Brewster Salamanca is one of 2 mint Silver Ghosts entered, along with.. Rolls, 220/25 Sedanca, Alvises, Lagondas, [etc.].

sedan chair. Now *Hist.* **a.** = SEDAN 1, 1 b.

1750 *Will* in Payne *Engl. Catholics* (1889) 6 My sedan chair. **1772–84** *Cook's Voy.* (1790) I. 25 The ladies however use a sedan chair,.. which is carried by two negroes on a pole connected with the top of the chair. **1807** *Med. Jrnl.* XXI. 379 To allow the patient to be carried home in a sedan chair. **1840** MALCOLM *Trav.* 52/1 The worst that would probably happen to a proper man making the trial, would be to be placed in a sedan chair, and transmitted to Macao. **1883** S. C. HALL *Retrospect* I. 14 Sedan Chairs.. were the usual modes of conveyance.. to parties, balls [etc.].

b. *transf.* (see quot.).

1869 *Cassell's Househ. Guide* I. 72 Another way of carrying a patient is upon what is known among school-boys as a 'sedan-chair', each bearer grasping his own fore-arm and that of his fellow about its middle . . and the patient grasping the bearers' necks.

c. sedan-chair clock, watch *Hist.*, a large travelling watch of a type supposed to have been hung in sedan chairs.

1904 F. J. BRITTEN *Old Clocks & Watches* (ed. 2) iv. 244 During the eighteenth century watch movements having plain silver dials from three inches to four inches in diameter were fixed in circular frames of wood, polished and with a moulded edge. They were called 'Sedan Chair Watches', though I cannot aver that they were as a rule carried in those useful, but obsolete conveyances. **1951** E. WENHAM *Old Clocks for Mod. Use* vii. 47 It is still possible to obtain one of these . . portable timepieces generally referred to as 'Sedan chair clocks' or, to give them another earlier name, 'post-chaise clocks'. **1960** *House & Garden* Apr. 99/3 Sedan-chair clocks . . reproductions and an antique.

†**'sedant**, *a. Her. Obs. rare*$^{-0}$. [? quasi-Fr. spelling of SEDENT *a.*] = SEJANT.

1688 R. HOLME *Armoury* II. 144/1 Seiant, or Sedant.

†**sedany.** The name of a country-dance.

1651 J. P. *Dancing-master* (1652) 24 Dargason, or Sedany. **1707** *J. Shirley's Tri. Wit* (ed. 5) 206 The Sedany. A pleasant Dance for as many as will in this order, OOO))).

sedate (sɪ'deɪt), *a.* [ad. L. *sēdāt-us*, pa. pple. of *sēdāre* to settle, allay, make calm or quiet, f. root *sĕd-* as in L. *sedēre*: see SIT *v.*]

1. Calm, quiet, composed; cool, sober, collected; undisturbed by passion or excitement.

a. of a person, his disposition, temper, deportment, actions.

1693 LOCKE *Educ.* §86. 100, I think the Chastisement should be a little more Sedate, and a little more Severe. **1700** DRYDEN *Fables* Pref. ¶5 Virgil was of a quiet, sedate Temper. **1704** SWIFT *Tale of Tub* vi. 131 Millions of Stitches, that required the nicest Hand and sedatest Constitution to extricate. **1718** *Free-thinker* No. 17. 113 A Man of Publick Spirit and Sedate Courage. **1768** STERNE *Sent. Journ.* II. 50 (*Le Pâtissier*) He was . . of a sedate look, something approaching to gravity. **1845** SARAH AUSTIN tr. *Ranke's Hist. Ref.* I. 65 They acted with such sedate vigour and cautious determination. **1876** FLOR. MARRYAT *Her Father's Name* xxiv, 'A yellow light!' cried Valera, suddenly. . . 'I never heard of such a thing before', he added a moment after, in a sedater tone. **1908** *Blackw. Mag.* July 146/2 A serious, sedate, and easy-mannered gentleman.

†**b.** of the intellect, and intellectual operations.

1663 J. SPENCER *Prodigies* (1665) 22 When fear hath . . disabled the mind for a cool and sedate judgment and valuation of things. **1665** GLANVILL *Scepsis Sci.* x. 56 Requiring . . a free, sedate, and intent minde. **1701** *Lond. Gaz.* No. 3757/2 The late wise and sedate Resolutions of your Parliament. **1702** *Clarendon's Hist. Reb.* I. Pref. 4 We shall leave them to their own sedate and composed Reflections.

c. *transf.* of literary composition.

1749 HURD *Horace's Ars Poet.* Introd. 14 Such abrupt and violent transitions, as might better agree to the impassioned elegy, than to the sedate didactic epistle.

d. of animals.

1791 COWPER *Retired Cat* 1 A poet's cat, sedate and grave. **1870** DICKENS *E. Drood* ii, That sedate and clerical bird, the rook.

e. Of inanimate objects: not unduly striking in colour or design; quiet and restful in tone.

1924 A. D. SEDGWICK *Little French Girl* I. vi. 48 Sedate chairs with backs and seats embroidered in green and dove-colour were ranged along the wall. **1978** J. CARROLL *Mortal Friends* III. v. 310 Brady stood in the bridge of the window, looking out on the sedate front lawn.

†**2.** Of physical objects: Quiet; motionless, or smooth and steady in motion. *Obs.*

1684 R. WALLER *Nat. Exper.* 57 The Water became sedate, and quiet as at First. **1696** *Phil. Trans.* XIX. 301 If she at any time used any Motion, the Pain would encrease; commonly finding most ease when her Body was sedate. *a* **1727** NEWTON *Chronol. Amended* iv. (1728) 304 The river which was before straight, she made crooked with great windings, that it might be more sedate and less apt to overflow. *c* **1728** EARL OF AILESBURY *Mem.* (1890) 124 His pulse . . was sedate enough.

3. *Comb.*, as ***sedate-looking*** adj.

1925 T. DREISER *Amer. Tragedy* I. II. xxxvii. 411 So clean, modest and sedate-looking a girl. **1977** *Rolling Stone* 19 May 90/5 The sedate-looking trio sings R and B with fervor.

se'date, *v.* [f. L. *sēdāt-*, ppl. stem of *sēdāre*: see prec.] †**a.** *trans.* To make calm or quiet; to assuage, allay. *Obs.*

1646 J. OWEN *Vision Unchang. Free Mercy*, etc. 56 These following lines were intended meerly to sedate and bury such contests. **1652** GAULE *Magastrom.* 204 This was not to procure or excite prophesie, but to sedate passions and affections. **1657–83** EVELYN *Hist. Relig.* (1850) I. 53 Did matter contend with matter, what confusion would it produce? whilst the mind and soul of man sedate the hostility, and bring it to due obedience.

b. *Med.* To make (a patient) sleepy or quiet by means of drugs; to administer a sedative to.

1945 *Richmond* (Va.) *Times-Dispatch* 21 Sept. 1/1 Two capsules are ordinarily considered enough to sedate a person —that is, produce a tendency to sleep. **1961** *Amer. Speech* XXXVI. 145 The informal speech of physicians embodies a great many technical colloquialisms that may be called the argot of medicine... 'He was very apprehensive, so I sedated him heavily.' **1977** *Proc. R. Soc. Med.* LXX. 549/1 He was sedated, intubated and ventilated and full supportive therapy was given with further blood transfusions.

Hence **se'dated** *ppl. a.*, under the influence of a sedative drug; †**se'dating** *vbl. sb.*

1953 R. LEHMANN *Echoing Grove* 129 'How is she?' . . 'Expecting you. Be careful, won't you? She's still sedated —mildly, of course.' **1974** L. DEIGHTON *Spy Story* xi. 107, I was half inclined to give the sedated Miss Shaw a miss. **1976** J. PHILIPS *Backlash* (1977) III. i. 125 Elliot wasn't going to come to. He was heavily sedated.

sedately (sɪ'deɪtlɪ), *adv.* [-LY².] In a sedate manner; without passion or excitement.

1646 TRAPP *Comm. John* xviii. 33 Pilate therefore retires himself into the palace, that he might more sedately set himself to sift the business. *a* **1665** J. GOODWIN *Filled w. the Spirit* (1867) 5 As also those grounds and arguments that are commonly brought . . punctually, sedately, and faithfully answered. **1719** DE FOE *Crusoe* II. *init.* (Globe) 318, I . . began to argue with my self sedately. **1814** BYRON *Lara* I. xxi, And Lara gazed on these, sedately glad. **1840** DICKENS *Barn. Rudge* i, John looked sedately and solemnly at his questioner. **1871** R. ELLIS *Catullus* lv. 8, I had'd each lady promenader, Each, I found, did face me quite sedately.

sedateness (sɪ'deɪtnɪs). [-NESS.] The quality or fact of being sedate (see the adj.).

1647 H. MORE *Song of Soul* Notes 148/2 With inimitable serenity, and sedatenesse of mind. **1655** CROMWELL *Sp.* 22 Jan. ¶17 (Carlyle) There was a very great peace and sedateness throughout these Nations. **1697** LUTTRELL *Brief Rel.* (1857) IV. 176 He behaved himself all the while with great sedatenesse, as became a person under his circumstances. **1730** WATERLAND *Suppl. to Nat. Sacram.* 1 To preserve the Coolness and Sedateness proper to religious or learned Enquiries. **1826** MISS MITFORD *Village* Ser. II. 49 May and myself walking with the sedateness and decorum befitting our sex and age. *a* **1859** MACAULAY *Hist. Eng.* xxiii. V. 5 The sedateness of his deportment and the apparent regularity of his life delighted austere moralists. **1910** *Q. Rev.* Apr. 330 It was an age of sedateness and comparative repose.

sedation (sɪ'deɪʃən). [a. F. *sédation* or ad. L. *sēdātiōn-em*, n. of action f. *sēdāre*: see SEDATE *a.*]

1. The action of allaying, assuaging, making calm or quiet. **a.** *Med.* Now esp. with reference to the use of sedative drugs.

1543 TRAHERON *Vigo's Chirurg.* II. IV. i. 65 It causeth the humours to breath out wyth gentyll resolution, and sedation of payne. **1670** MAYNWARING *Pharm. Phys. Repos.* 53 The Anodyne Pills . . are used in all Cases requiring sedation and allay. **1874** H. C. WOOD *Therap.* 58 In tonic doses quinia produces no perceptible sedation of the circulation. **1897** *Allbutt's Syst. Med.* II. 875 A sedation of certain parts may throw other functions into an eminence which may be positive or may be relative. **1979** *Guardian* 19 Feb. 22/6 The dead youth's parents were under sedation yesterday at their home in Dan-y-Cribyn. **1982** J. PENN *Notice of Death* vii. 65 We may get more in the morning from Mrs H., but at the moment she's under sedation.

†**b.** *gen. Obs.*

1616 *Rich Cabinet* 57 H. 7. who was ledde after the sedation both of forren and domestick encombrances . . to the house of a great Maiestie and Honourable wealth. *a* **1660** *Contemp. Hist. Irel.* (Ir. Archæol. Soc.) II. 70 For the sedation of inquiet . . mindes. **1674** T. TURNOR *Bankers & Creditors* (1675) 41 The King for the sedation of these . . Apprehensions is advised . . to issue forth his Declaration.

†**2.** The state of being settled. *Obs. rare*$^{-1}$.

1627–61 FELTHAM *Resolves* II. lxxxv. 374 The unevenness of the Earth is clearly Providence. For since it is not any fix'd sedation, but a floating mild variety, that pleaseth; The Hills and Valleys in it, have all their special use.

sedative ('sɛdətɪv), *a.* and *sb.* Also 5 sed-, cedatyve. [a. F. *sédatif* adj. and sb., or ad. med.L. *sēdātīv-us*, f. L. *sēdāre*: see prec. and -IVE.]

A. *adj.* **a.** *Med.* That has the property of allaying, assuaging, or soothing.

sedative salt, old name (*sal sedativum*, Homberg 1702) for boracic acid.

c **1425** *Arderne's Treat. Fistula*, etc. 93 Oile roset complete is resolutiue, confortatyue, and conueniently cedatyue of akyng. *Ibid.* 94 It is a conuenient resolutyue, and of akyng sedatyue. **1678** PHILLIPS (ed. 4) s.v., Sedative Medicines . . are such as have power or vertue to allay and asswage pain. **1758** REID tr. *Macquer's Chym.* I. 36 Mr. Homberg called it *Sedative Salt*, on account of its medical effects. **1813** J. THOMSON *Lect. Inflam.* 614 Disputes . . concerning the stimulant and sedative effects of cold. **1862** MILLER *Elem. Chem.*, *Org.* (ed. 2) 492 Morphia . . appears to be the principal sedative constituent of opium.

b. *transf.* and *gen.*

1795 BURKE *Reg. Peace* iv. Wks. IX. 27 Against alarm on their politick and military empire these are the writer's sedative remedies. **1853** KANE *Grinnell Exp.* xxix. (1856) 251 It illustrates the sedative effect of a protracted succession of hazards. **1860** EMERSON *Cond. Life, Illusions* Wks. (Bohn) II. 445 Is not our faith in the impenetrability of matter more sedative than narcotics?

B. *sb.* **a.** *Med.* A sedative medicine.

1797 *Encycl. Brit.* (ed. 3) XVIII. 99/1 Vinegar . . generally acts as a sedative. **1853** C. BRONTE *Villette* xxxviii, The sedative had been administered. In fact, they had given me a strong opiate. I was to be held quiet for one night. **1874** H. C. WOOD *Therap.* (1879) 148 There are certain drugs which are used by practitioners to decrease the activity of the circulation; and it is these which are here considered under the heading of Cardiac Sedatives. **1899** *Allbutt's Syst. Med.* VIII. 604 Sedatives such as bromides and valerian . . must be administered.

b. *transf.* and *gen.*

1785 PALEY *Mor. & Polit. Philos.* III. II. vii. I. 298 Reflections . . which may be called the sedatives of anger. **1840** DICKENS *Barn. Rudge* xv, The lazy influence of a late and lonely breakfast, with the additional sedative of a newspaper. **1864** MRS. RIDDELL *Geo. Geith* xxix, 'Beryl's singing always sends me to sleep'. 'So that I am of some use in the world, if only as a sedative', replied Beryl.

sedche, variant of SIEGE.

†**sede.** *Obs.* [ad. L. *sēdēs* seat.]

1. = SEAT *sb.* 8. *sede celestial*, the throne of God.

a **1300** *Cursor M.* 5320 Of his com þe king was fain, And of his sede [*other texts* sete] him ras again. *a* **1500–34** *Coventry Corpus Chr. Plays* i. 345 The sede seylesteall.

2. = SEAT *sb.* 13.

1387 TREVISA *Higden* (Rolls) I. 183 And at þe laste [þey] cam in to Italia, and . . made þe cheefe sede at Tarentum.

3. = SEAT *sb.* 7.

1552 *Bury Wills* (Camden) 140 Item I do geue for implements to remayne vnto the scholle the hangyns in my chamber, one table, one ioyned forme, one sede.

sede, obs. form of SEED *sb.* and *v.*

se,decimar'ticulate, *a. Ent.* [f. L. *sēdecim* + *articul-us* joint + -ATE².] Having sixteen joints.

1856–8 W. CLARK *Van der Hoeven's Zool.* I. 342 Antennæ porrect, cylindrical, sedecimarticulate.

†**se'decuple.** *Obs.*$^{-1}$ [f. L. *sēdec-im* sixteen, after DECUPLE.] A quantity sixteen times another.

1690 LEYBOURN *Curs. Math.* 349 If any Root be Multiplied by 4 the Product shall be the Root of the Sedecuple.

‖**se defendendo** (siː diːfɛn'dɛndəʊ). *Law.* [Law Latin: *sē* himself, *dēfendendō* abl. gerund of *dēfendere* to defend.] 'In self-defence': a plea which if established is held to remove legal guilt from a homicide.

1548 STAUNFORD *Kinges Prerog.* xvi. (1567) 45 b, In a case where one killed another *se defendendo* or by misaduenture, this offence is felony. **1625** B. JONSON *Staple of N.* v. v. 49 *Mad.* They barke, *se defendendo*. *Shv.* Or for custome, As commonly curres doe, one for another. **1710** *Tatler* No. 256 ¶3 That in consideration . . that his taking the wall was only *Se defendendo*, the prosecutor should let him escape with life. **1728** CHAMBERS *Cycl.* s.v., Though the party justify its being done Se-Defendendo, yet he is driven to procure his Pardon of Course from the Lord Chancellor. **1765** BLACKSTONE *Comm.* I. 126 The law of England . . pardons even homicide if committed *se defendendo*.

subst. use. **1682** DRYDEN *Duke of Guise* Epil. 12 *Se defendendo* never was a Sin.

†**sedeful**, *a. Obs.* Also 1–2 sideful. [OE. *sideful*, f. *sidu* masc. = OS. *sidu* (Du. *zede* fem.), OHG. *situ* (G. *sitte* fem.), Goth. *sidu-s*:—OTeut. **seðu-s* custom, morality (f. root **swedh-*): cf. Gr. ἔθος custom.] Virtuous, moral, chaste.

c **1000** ÆLFRIC in Assmann *Ags. Hom.* iii. 327 Þa heahfæderas haliȝe wæron . . sidefulle on ðeawum. *c* **1200** ORMIN 2175 Ȝho wass . . Shammfasst, & daffte, & sedefull.

‖**sedekah** (sede'ka). [Malay, f. Arab. *ṣadaqa*.] In Malaysia: alms; a voluntary offering.

1839 T. J. NEWBOLD *Straits of Malacca* I. ii. 88 When a boy has gone through the Koran . . his parents give *Sedekah*, or alms. **1900** W. W. SKEAT *Malay Magic* vi. 403 In the case of a Sultan as many as possible bear a hand in sending him to the grave . . partly for the sake of the *sĕdĕkah* or alms given to the bearers. **1972** A. AMIN tr. *Shahnon Ahmad's No Harvest but Thorn* ix. 96 Lahuma need not worry any more, thought Jeha. The feast would be a *sedekah* to all.

sedelinges, obs. form of SIDELINGS *adv.*

sedement, obs. form of SEDIMENT.

sedenes, variant of SEEDNESS. *Obs.*

sedent ('siːdənt), *a.* [ad. L. *sedent-em*, pres. pple. of *sedēre* to sit.] Sitting.

1682 WHELER *Journ. Greece* I. 57 A Fragment of a sedent Figure of a Woman. **1714** *Lond. Gaz.* No. 5286/4 A Griffin Sedent upon a broken Spear. **1832** GELL *Pompeiana* II. xi. 4 The pretty sedent bronze figure. **1889** BRYDALL *Art in Scot.* x. 189 The sedent statue of the very beautiful and handsome Princess Pauline Borghese.

sedentarily ('sɛdəntərɪlɪ), *adv.* [f. SEDENTARY *a.* + -LY².] In a sedentary manner.

1830 *Blackw. Mag.* XXVII. 169 So sedentarily addicted to the composition of verse.

sedentariness ('sɛdəntərɪnɪs). [f. SEDENTARY *a.* + -NESS.] The quality or condition of being sedentary.

1671 L. ADDISON *W. Barbary* 113 Those that live in great Towns . . are enclined to paleness, which may be imputed to their sedentariness, or want of motion. *c* **1740** COLE in *Etoniana* iv. 76 The sedentariness of a scholar. **1822–56** DE QUINCEY *Confess.* (1862) 66 Ratifying and trebling the ruinous effects of this sedentariness. **1898** E. P. EVANS *Evol. Ethics* i. 46 With the beginning of agriculture and sedentariness this relation is reversed.

sedentarization (,sɛdəntəraɪ'zeɪʃən). [f. SEDENTAR(Y *a.* + -IZE: see -ATION.] The settlement of a nomadic people in a permanent homeland or place of habitation.

1960 F. BARTH in *Problems of Arid Zone* (UNESCO) 342 The solution . . favoured by the state authorities . . has been the simple and radical one of sedentarization: the total elimination of nomads by settling them on the land as agriculturalists. **1969** *Times Lit. Suppl.* 21 Aug. 929/2 Both the sedentarization of the tribes and the redistribution of land were thought . . politically desirable. **1979** *West Africa*

13 Aug. 1459/2 Nor, they concluded..would the pastoralists themselves regret such a social and economic transformation once they realised that sedentarisation was good for them.

sedentary ('sɛdəntərɪ), *a.* and *sb.* [ad. F. *sédentaire*, ad. L. *sedentārius*, f. *sedent-em*, pr. pple. of *sedēre* to sit: see SEDENT and -ARY. Cf. Sp., Pg., It. *sedentario*.]

A. *adj.*

1. a. Of habits, occupations, etc.: Requiring continuance in a sitting posture.

1603 FLORIO *Montaigne* I. xxiv. (1632) 66 To divert them from all militarie exercises, and ammuse them to idle, secure, and sedentarie occupations. **1642** FULLER *Holy & Prof. St.* III. xiii. 184 If thy life be sedentary, exercise thy body. **1693** LOCKE *Educ.* §190. 242 Reading and Writing and all other sedentary Studies. **1777** ROBERTSON *Hist. Amer.* (1778) II. VI. 223 The habits of a sedentary and pacific profession. **1817** JEBB *Corr.* (1834) II. 331 The first sedentary morning I have had for weeks. **1863** GEO. ELIOT *Romola* i, A short man..whose bent shoulders told of some sedentary occupation.

b. Of a quality.

1815 KIRBY & SP. *Entomol.* xiii. (1818) I. 428 The sedentary cunning of the lynx.

2. a. Of persons: Accustomed or addicted to sitting still; engaged in sedentary pursuits; not in the habit of taking physical exercise.

1662 WISEMAN *Treat. Wounds* I. 40 A Sedentary young Gentleman of an ill habit of Body. **1693** LOCKE *Educ.* §192. 244 Since..sedentary or studious Men should have some Exercise, that at the same time might divert their Minds, and employ their Bodies. **1711** ADDISON *Spect.* No. 115 ¶4 The Spleen, which is so frequent in Men of studious and sedentary Tempers. **1781** COWPER *Conversat.* 207 But sedentary weavers of long tales Give me the fidgets, and my patience fails. **1809** *Med. Jrnl.* XXI. 322 A Gentleman of Kensington, of middle age, plethoric, and sedentary, but active in his mind. **1816** T. L. PEACOCK *Headlong Hall* vii, Sedentary victims of unhealthy toil. **1840** HOOD *Up Rhine* 263 Fancy a sedentary usher,..suddenly called upon to unlearn all his scholar-like habits. **1844** DICKENS *Mart. Chuz.* xvi, A few sedentary characters..remained at table full a quarter of an hour.

absol. **1732** ARBUTHNOT *Rules of Diet* in *Aliments*, etc. I. 261 The Blood of labouring people is more dense than that of the sedentary. **1813** J. THOMSON *Lect. Inflam.* 433 Thus, the aged, the sedentary, and the dissipated, are known to be more liable to ulcers of the lower extremities, than the young, active, and sober.

†**b.** Slothful, inactive. *Obs.*

1625 HART *Anat. Ur.* I. ii. 17 Our Physitians, being like vnto the lazie sedentarie Physitians of Alexandria,..are ashamed to aske of the patient the..symptomes. **1671** MILTON *Samson* 571 Till length of years And sedentary numness craze my limbs To a contemptible old age obscure. **1707** FLOYER *Pulse-Watch* 160 They are Slothful without Cares or Study, Sedentairy [*sic*], Idle.

†**c.** Not engaged in active business. *Obs.*

1738 WARBURTON *Div. Legat.* I. III. iv. 396 The Egyptians; whose Sages were not sedentary scholastic Sophists, like the Grecian; but employed and busied in the public Affairs of Religion and Government. **1751** CHESTERF. *Lett.* cccxxviii. IV. 116 Abercrombie is to be the Sedentary, and not the acting Commander.

3. a. Remaining in one place of abode; not migratory. Of a tribunal, an assembly, a judge or other official: Established in one place; not moving from place to place in the course of official duty; opposed to *ambulatory*. Now *rare* (in modern use perh. a Gallicism).

1598 DALLINGTON *Meth. Trav.* Q2b, That [Court of Parliament] of Paris..at first was ambulatory: but since Philip le bel, it hath beene sedentary in this Citie. *a* **1628** DODERIDGE *Eng. Lawyer* (1631) 33 As well the Iudges itinerate.., as those that were sedentarie in the King's High Courts of Iustice. **1642** HOWELL *For. Trav.* (Arb.) 11 To bee a Sedentary Traveller only, penn'd up between Wals, and to stand poring all day upon a Map,..is like him, who thought to come to bee a good Fencer, by looking on Agrippa's book-postures only. **1794** HERON *Inform. War* 176 The Convention declares itself sedentary in the capital, and permanent, till the conclusion of a peace. **1803** MALTHUS *Popul.* (1817) I. 184 The sedentary labourer is more exposed to the vicissitudes of fortune than he who leads a wandering life. **1857** *Colton's Atlas, Russia in Asia*, The Tchuktchi..consist of two tribes, one sedentary and the other nomadic. **1891** *Daily News* 16 Mar. 6/1 Does England..in promising to effect the removal of 'sedentary establishments' undertake to forbid her subjects raising any construction, such for example as the lobster factories. **1899** *Ibid.* 13 Nov. 7/7 The remedy consists in adding to the sedentary forces as if we were a State like Switzerland.

†**b.** Of a material thing: Continuing in one place, motionless. *Obs.*

1667 MILTON *P.L.* VIII. 32 And on thir Orbs impose Such restless revolution day by day Repeated, while the sedentarie Earth,..attaines Her end without least motion. **1786-7** BONNYCASTLE *Astron.* ii. 32 The absurdity of supposing the earth a sedentary and immoveable body.

c. *Zool.* Inhabiting the same region through life; not migratory. Also of mollusca, etc.: Confined to one spot, not locomotory. Of spiders: see B.

1851 WOODWARD *Mollusca* 11 The sedentary tribes settle in the place they intend to occupy during the remainder of their lives. **1854** A. ADAMS, etc. *Man. Nat. Hist.* 274 Sedentary Spiders (*Sedentaria*). *Ibid.* 316 Sedentary-Annelids (*Tubicola*). **1872** H. A. NICHOLSON *Palæont.* 241 Most of them [Gasteropods] being free and locomotive, though some are sedentary. **1902** CORNISH *Naturalist on Thames* 153 No one has satisfactorily answered the question why there are sedentary species and migratory species so closely allied in habits and food.

†**4.** Deliberate. *Obs. rare.*

1647 FULLER *Good Th. in Worse T.* II. x. 75 Lord, pardon my cursory, and preserve me from sedentary sinnes. **1673** MARVELL *Reh. Transp.* II. 74 He..proceeded to take away their Lives; not in the hot and Military way..but in the cooler blood and sedentary execution of an High Court of Justice.

5. *Geol.* Of a soil or sediment: = RESIDUAL *a.* 2 f.

1870 S. W. JOHNSON *How Crops Feed* II. iii. 143 Sedentary soils, or Soils in place, are those which have not been transported by geological agencies. **1906** [see RESIDUAL *a.* 2 f]. **1929** *Daily Tel.* 22 Jan. 4/7 The soil being considered 'sedentary' in character. **1943** MILLAR & TURK *Soil Sci.* i. 4 Since they have not suffered the mixing that accompanies transportation by ice and water there are many variations in the characteristics, both physical and chemical, of sedentary materials. **1975** FLEGMANN & GEORGE *Soils* iv. 103 This visual gradation is particularly obvious when a soil has been formed *in situ* by the gradual weathering of parent rock, such soils being referred to as sedentary.

6. *Comb.*, as ***sedentary-looking*** adj.

1937 W. B. YEATS *Vision* (rev. ed.) 37 Aherne..was stout and sedentary-looking.

B. *sb.* [absolute use of A. 3 c.] *Zool.* One of a group of spiders (*Sedentariæ*) which take their prey by means of a web in or near which they remain watching.

1815 KIRBY & SP. *Entomol.* xiii. (1818) I. 425 Walckenaer, ..terming those already mentioned which spin webs and nets, Sedentaries. **1842** BRANDE *Dict. Sci.*, etc., *Sedentaries.*

‖**Seder** ('seɪdə(r)). Also with small initial. [Heb. *sēdher* order, procedure.] A Jewish ritual service and ceremonial dinner held on the first evening of the Passover and repeated on the second evening by Orthodox Jews outside Israel. Freq. *attrib.*

1865 *Chambers's Encycl.* VII. 312/1 At a later period, a certain number of cups of red wine were superadded to this meal, to which, as its special ceremonies and the order of its benedictions were fixed, the name *Seder* (arrangement) was given. **1891** [see HAGGADAH 2]. **1892** I. ZANGWILL *Childr. Ghetto* II. xxii. 166 She would have to..see the sour faces of her little ones round a barren *Seder* table. *Ibid.* xxv. 205 Seder Night was a charmed time. The strange symbolic dishes..the special Hebrew melodies. **1909** *Cent. Dict. Suppl.* s.v., The celebrant, generally the head of the family, begins with the first of the thirteen functions in the seder service. **1932** C. ROTH *Hist. Marranos* vii. 185 The traditional *Seder*-service. **1958** C. P. SNOW *Conscience of Rich* I. iii. 24 We were as good as engaged after seder night in '96. **1970** I. SIEFF *Memoirs* vi. 95 Herbert Samuel..spoke the holy words, the traditional conclusion to the *Seder* service on the eve of the Passover: 'Next year in Jerusalem.' **1978** J. SACKS in P. Moore *Man, Woman, & Priesthood* iii. 39 The best known of these events is the *Seder* on the first nights of Passover. **1982** *Listener* 7 Jan. 13/1, I sat round the Seder table during Passover.

seder, obs. form of CEDAR, SEEDER.

sederunt (sɪ'dɪərənt). *Sc.* [a. L. *sēdērunt* 'there were sitting' (*sc.* the following persons), 3rd pers. pl. pf. ind. of *sedēre* to sit, used subst.]

‖**1.** In minutes of deliberative bodies, used (in its Latin sense) to introduce the list of persons present at a meeting. *Obs.*

The word occurs at least as early as the 15th c. in minutes that are written in Latin, or in which the names or titles of the persons are latinized.

1673 in *Fasti Aberd.* (1854) 339 Sederunt, the earle Marischall, the lord bishop, Mr. Alexander Ross [and others].

2. A sitting of a deliberative or judicial body; now chiefly of an ecclesiastical assembly. *book of sederunt*: a minute-book.

1628 CHAS. I in *Acts of Sederunt* (1790) 39 If you find the said warrant extant in your buikis of sederunt. **1652** *Sess. Rec. of Canisbay* 29 Mar. in *Stat. Acc. Scot.* XV. 25 No session holden, by reasone the Inglishe being quartered in the bounds, the congregation was few in number, and ther was not a sederunt of elders. **1714** *Lond. Gaz.* No. 5262/1 His Majesty was Pleased to Order that One of the said Instruments be Transmitted to the Court of Session, to be Recorded in the Books of *Sederunt*. **1800** A. CARLYLE *Autobiog.* (1860) 108 After many very late sederunts of the Synod, and at last a hearing of the General Assembly, the affair was dismissed. **1856** AITON *Clerical Econ.* 78 The late hours, the long sederunts, and the heats and the colds.

†**b.** The time or occasion of such a sitting or meeting. *Obs. rare*$^{-1}$.

1752 J. LOUTHIAN *Form of Process* (ed. 2) 236 After the Debate, the Judges..delayed the Determination thereof till next Sederunt.

c. *Act of Sederunt*: see quot. 1875.

1672 SIR G. MACKENZIE *Pleadings* Pref. A2 At the first institution of our Senat, It was appointed by an Act of Sederunt, That [etc.]. **1875** *Encycl. Brit.* I. 123 Act of Sederunt, in *Scotch Law*, an ordinance for regulating the forms of procedure before the Court of Session, passed by the judges in virtue of a power conferred by an Act of the Scotch Parliament, 1540 c. 93.

d. *transf.* A sitting for discussion or talk. Also, more loosely, a sitting (of a person) at some occupation, over the bottle, or the like.

1825 T. HOOK *Sayings* Ser. II. *Sutherl.* I. 21 [She] dusted away..sundry furrows of snuff which had gradually accumulated in her lap in the course of a long morning's sederunt. **1829** *Health & Longev.* 143 He was not a drunkard, but at times he took a very long sederunt at his bottle. **1866** GLADSTONE in Morley *Life* v. xiii. (1903) II. 211 Morning sederunt with Lord Russell and Brand on reform and other matters. **1867** MACFARLANE *Mem. T. Archer* vi. 135 Information he had accumulated by his sederunts in the Museum Library.

†**3.** ? A person's record of attendance at a sitting.

1632 *Acts of Sederunt* (1790) 45 Quatsomever Lord shall admit any informer or solliciter within his house..shall loss and forfatt his sederunt of that day, to access to the remanent Lords, observers of this statute.

4. The list of persons present at a 'sederunt' or sitting. ¶ Also *pl.* the persons named on such a list.

1701 *Acts of Sederunt* (1790) 221 The Lords..Do therefore ordain the Lords present at their sitting down in the morning, after the ringing of the Session-bell, to be marked in the sederunt. **1822** GALT *Provost* xliii, Mr. Peevie, one of the very sickerest of all the former sederunts, came to me next morning. **1866** *Leeds Mercury* 4 Apr., He then constituted the meeting by calling over the roll, answered to his own name, and faithfully took down the sederunt. **1910** *U.F. Ch. Miss. Record* Jan. 22/2 The council met with a sederunt of four.

5. *attrib.*: **sederunt book**, a volume containing the record of a sederunt, a minute-book; †**sederunt-day**, a day appointed for a sederunt.

1619 *Reg. Privy Council Scot.* XII. 8 The Lordis of Sessioun and Exchekker, whose names ar insert in the *Sederunt bookis of Sessioun and Exchekquer. **1770** D. HERD *Let.* in *Herd's Songs* (1904) 45 A copy of the Cape [club] sederunt book. **1810** CHALMERS in Hanna *Mem.* (1849) I. 170 Walked to Pittenweem, and got the sederunt-book on Dr. Reid's affairs. **1677** *Acts of Sederunt* (1790) 137 Unless the petition be given in within the space of two *sederunt days, after pronounceing of the decreet. **1753** *Scots Mag.* July 365/1 The first sederunt-day of November. **1754** ERSKINE *Princ. Sc. Law* (1809) 480 A sentence of the inner-house, either not reclaimed against within six sederunt-days after its date,..or adhered to upon a reclaiming bill [etc.].

‖'**sedes.** *Obs. rare.* Pl. sedes. [L. *sēdēs* seat.]

1. = SEAT *sb.* 26 b.

1634 [see SEAT *sb.* 26 b]. **1676** WISEMAN *Chirurg. Treat.* V. ix. 376 Next to these are Wounds made by any sharp Weapon, which, according to the force, cutteth into the Bone many ways, which Cuts are called *Sedes*, and are reckoned amongst the Fractures.

2. = SEAT *sb.* 22.

1662 RAY *Three Itin.* III. 182 A few fibres or stringy roots at the bases or *sedes* of it.

sede vacante ('siːdiː və'kæntiː). [L., 'the seat being vacant'; *sēde* abl. sing. of *sēdēs* seat.]

‖**1.** *Eccl.* In the Latin sense, as advb. phrase: During the vacancy of an episcopal see.

1535 CRANMER in Strype *Memor.* App. xiv. (1694) 20 My Predecessor visited the Dioces of Winchester after the decease of my L. Cardinal, as he did al other Diocesses *Sede Vacante*. **1572** *Act 14 Eliz.* c. 7 Preamble, Under Collectors of the Tenths and Subsidies of the Cleargye appointed by.. Deanes and Chapters (*Sede vacante*). *a* **1900** J. W. LEGG *Ecclesiol. Ess.* 77 We have abundance of documents in Wilkins drawn up *sede vacante*.

¶ **b.** *allusively.*

1608 MIDDLETON *Fam. Love* II. C 1 b, But yet I must not let fall my suite with mistrisse Purge, least (*Cede vacanti*) my friend Gudgin ioyne issue.

2. Used as *sb.*: The vacancy of a see or seat.

1589 PUTTENHAM *Eng. Poesie* I. xxvii. (Arb.) 69 In time of *Sede vacante*, when merry conceited men listed to gibe & iest at the dead Pope. **1670** LASSELS *Voy. Italy* II. 249 The Ceremony of a *Sede Vacante*. **1783** H. WALPOLE *Let. to Mann* 2 Mar., It is not quite new in this country..to see a *sede vacante*: here, I call it an Inter-ministerium.

allusively. **1711** ADDISON *Spect.* No. 72 ¶4 It is a Maxim in this Club That the Steward never dies; for..no Man is to quit the great Elbow-chair..'till his Successor is in a Readiness to fill it; insomuch that there has not been a *Sede vacante* in the Memory of Man.

sedewale, variant of SETWALL.

sedge (sɛdʒ), *sb.*[1] Forms: 1 **sæcg, secg (sech, seic, secgg, segc, segg)**, 3-5 **segge** (? *gg* = (dʒ)), 5 **sege, cegge**, (7 **sage**), 5- **sedge**; *β.* 6-7 **segge** (? *gg* = g), 9 *dial.* **seag**, 5-7, 9 *dial.* **seg(g**. [OE. *sęcg* masc., once neut. (cf. LG. *segge* fem., *Br. Wbuch.*):—OTeut. type **sagjo-z*, f. root **sag-* (:—Indogermanic **sək-*: **sĕk-* in L. *secāre* to cut): cf. SAW *sb.*[2] For the etymological notion cf. quot. 1398 in 1 a below, and the L. *gladiolus*, which the OE. word renders in glosses; also the rare OE. *sęcg* fem. (:—**sagjā*) a sword.

From the same root is OHG. *sahor, sahir, sahar* 'scirpus, juncus, carex' (MHG., mod.G. dial. *saher* sedge, reeds, young shoots of corn). According to some scholars the OCeltic **seskā* sedge (Irish *seisg*, Welsh *hêsg*, Breton *hesq*) is for **sekskā* from the root **sek-*.

The phonology of the *β* forms is somewhat obscure. In most of the words which have parallel forms with final (dʒ) and (g), the latter may be accounted for by Scandinavian influence, and are confined to dialects in which that influence is powerful. The present word, however, is not known in Scandinavian, and its dialectal range extends to the S.W. Counties. Possibly it may be an euphonic variant originating in compounds where the second element began with a spirant. The form *segge*, common from the 13th to the 17th c., is of doubtful phonetic interpretation; probably down to the 15th c. it commonly stands for (sɛdʒ), and in later instances most frequently for (sɛg).]

1. A name for various coarse grassy, rush-like or flag-like plants growing in wet places; also (in different localities) variously applied *spec.*, e.g. to the cyperaceous genera *Carex* and *Cladium*, to the Sweet Flag (*Acorus*) and the Wild Iris (*Iris Pseudacorus*).

In early instances it is often impossible to determine what particular plant is intended; the Latin words which are glossed by 'sedge' were prob. seldom used with any very precise notion of their meaning.

a. As the name of a kind of plant; also *collect. sing.*, plants of this kind growing together in a mass.

α. *c* **725** *Corpus Gloss.* 977 *Gladiolum*, saecg [*Erfurt* secg; *Epinal* segg]. *Ibid.* 371 *Carix*, secg [*Erfurt* sech; *Leiden* seic]. *c* **1000** ÆLFRIC *Gloss.* in Wr.-Wülcker 135 *Carex, uel sabium, uel lisca*, secg. *a* **1250** *Owl & Night.* 18 Þe niȝtingale.. sat up one vaire boȝe,.. in ore waste þicke hegge, imeind mid spire & grene segge. **1398** TREVISA *Barth. De P.R.* XVII. xxxv. (Tollemache MS.), Segge is an herbe most harde and scharpe: þe stalke þerof is þre cornered, and kutteþ and keruеth þe honde þat it holdeþ. *c* **1440** *Promp. Parv.* 451/2 Segge, star of the fenne, *carix*. Segge, of fenne, or wylde gladon.. *accorus*. *Ibid.* 64/2 Cegge, or wylde gladone, *accorus*. *c* **1590** MARLOWE *Jew of Malta* IV. 1814 The Meads, the Orchards, and the Primrose lanes, Instead of Sedge and Reed, beare Sugar Canes. **1622** DRAYTON *Poly-olb.* xx. 139 Some againe.. Of Cat-tayles made them Crownes, which from the Sedge doth grow, Which neatly wouen were. **1660** TATHAM *Roy. Oak* 6 Four Virgins cloathed in white loose garments, and their Brows circled with Sage, representing the Nymphs that frequent Rivers. **1681** CHETHAM *Angler's Vade-m.* iv. §15 (1689) 46 Flags (or, as some call them, Sedges). **1798** COLERIDGE *Anc. Mar.* v. vii, And the coming wind did roar more loud, And the sails did sigh like sedge. **1881** O'SHAUGHNESSY *Songs of a Worker* 137 Close to the canes and swaying sedge Of every dim lake's hidden edge.

β. **1538** TURNER *Libellus*, s.v. *Acorum*, Varie nominant Northumbrienses a seg.. a flag, a yelowe flourdelyce. **1551** TURNER *Herbal* I. H v, Carex is the latin name of an herbe whiche we cal in english segge or shergresse... This herbe that I do take to be carex, groweth in fennes and in water sides. *a* **1552** LELAND *Itin.* (1768) III. 85 Ther be Men alyve that saw almost al the Town of Pole kyverid with Segge and Risshis. **1606** S. GARDINER *Bk. Angling* 34 The bushes and segge in the riuer shall not shrowd them. **1819** H. BUSK *Banquet* I. 414 Lentini's bee would now disdain to crop The scatter'd seg upon Paderno's top. **1899** DICKINSON & PREVOST *Cumberld. Gloss.* s.v. *Mekkins*, Seag, Yellow iris or Corn Flag, *Iris pseudacorus*.

b. *collect. plural.*

α. **1388** WYCLIF *Gen.* xli. 18 Seuene kiyn.. gaderiden grene seggis in the pasture of the marreis. *c* **1440** *Pallad. on Husb.* I. 525 A stondyng.. couered wel with shingil, tile or broom—Or segges ar as gode to my dome. **1549** *Compl. Scot.* vi. 42 Than the scheiphyrdis vyuis cuttit raschis and seggis. **1596** SHAKS. *Tam. Shr.* Induct. ii. 53 Adonis painted by a running brooke, And Citherea all in sedges hid. **1612** *Two Noble K.* IV. i, As I late was angling In the great Lake.., From the far shore, thicke set with reedes and Sedges,.. I heard a voyce. **1770** GOLDSM. *Des. Vill.* 42 No more thy glossy brook reflects the day, But, chok'd with sedges, works its weedy way. **1831** SCOTT *Ct. Robt.* xx, The.. statue of a river deity,.. its front crowned with water-lilies and sedges, and its ample hand half-resting upon an empty urn. **1865** KINGSLEY *Herew.* xxi, A man cutting sedges in a punt in the lode alongside.. leapt on shore.

β. **1594** KYD *Cornelia* III. iii. 15 And on the strond vpon the Riuer side.. I woaue a Coffyn for his corse of Seggs, That with the winde dyd waue like bannerets. **1600** *Weakest goeth to Wall* C 4 b, How first I found thee, being but a child: Hid in the segges fast by a Riuer side. **1631** WIDDOWES *Nat. Philos.* 49 Acorus is a plant growing with leaves like Iris, but smaller, or like segges. **1681** W. ROBERTSON *Phraseol. Gen.* 805 You lay lurking behind the seggs. **1777** LIGHTFOOT *Flora Scotica* II. 1078 *Iris pseudacorus*. Segs, i.e. Sedge. **1853** G. JOHNSTON *Bot. E. Bord.* 194 Bundles of Seggs tied together used to be employed by children learning to swim. **1898** J. A. GIBBS *Cotsw. Vill.* 359 Among the sword-flags and the green rushes and 'segs'.

c. An individual plant or stalk of sedge. *rare.*

a **1450** *Ratis Raving* 1984 To mak.. of a seg a swerd of were. **1591** SHAKS. *Two Gent.* II. vii. 29 Giuing a gentle kisse to euery sedge He ouer-taketh in his pilgrimage. **1761** *Ann Reg.* IV. *Usef. Proj.* 128 Having frequently seen children at play with seggs in their mouths, by bending them in order to make a noise. **1879** JEFFERIES *Wild Life in S. Co.* ii. 22 A few sedges here and there.. betoken that once there was a stream.

d. *Bot.* Formerly, a plant of the genus *Carex*; now usually in wider sense (after Lindley), a plant of the N.O. *Cyperaceæ*.

1785 MARTYN *Rousseau's Bot.* xxviii. (1794) 433 Carex or Sedge, is a most numerous genus of the same order, and the same natural tribe. **1846** LINDLEY *Veg. Kingd.* 117 Order xxx. Cyperaceæ. Sedges. **1869** RUSKIN *Q. of Air* §79 The sedges are essentially the clothing of.. uncultivable soils, coarse in their structure, frequently triangular in stem.. and with their heads of seed not extricated from their leaves.

e. With defining words. †**red sedge**, ? some cyperaceous plant. **sea sedge**, the Sweet Flag, *Acorus Calamus* (Syd. Soc. Lex. 1898); also *Carex arenaria*. **sweet, yellow sedge**, the Wild Iris, *Iris Pseudacorus*. **stinking sedge**, the Gladdon, *Iris fœtidissima*. Also in book-names of various cyperaceous plants: see quot. 1859. Also BROOM-*sedge*.

c **1000** *Sax. Leechd.* II. 102 Wiþ bancoþe þæt is oman nim niȝontyne snæda eolonan & nyȝon ontran & endlefan reades secges. *a* **1490** BOTONER *Itin.* (1778) 288 Shevys de reede segge. **1579** LANGHAM *Gard. Health* (1633) 254 Freckles, seethe the root of stinking segs in Cowes milke, and vse it. **1796** WITHERING *Brit. Plants* (ed. 3) II. 90 Sea Seg. In loose moveable sand on the sea shore. **1839** FR. A. KEMBLE *Resid. in Georgia* (1863) 69 A bed of tall yellow sedges. **1859** MISS PRATT *Brit. Grasses* 27 Order. *Cyperaceæ*.. White sedge. *Ibid.* 29 Great Panicled Sedge. *Ibid.* 30 Great Sedge.. Greater Prickly Sedge.. Grey Sedge.. Sea Sedge. *Ibid.* 32 Hoary Sedge.. Black Sedge.. Common Sedge. *Ibid.* 38 Great Pendulous Sedge. *Ibid.* 42 Great Common Sedge.. Lesser Common Sedge. **1865** KINGSLEY *Herew.* xix, They brought in bundles of sweet sedge.

f. The characteristic greenish- (or reddish-)brown shade of sedge.

1927 *Daily Express* 12 Mar. 3/5 Sedge, a bright shade similar to the always popular almond, but with a tendency towards jade. **1938** J. W. DAY *Dog in Sport* iv. 66 By 1885 the present type had largely evolved, the main differences being that the breed then possessed one colour only, a dark brown shading into a reddish sedge.

†**2.** A leaf shaped like that of a sedge. *Obs.*

1567 MAPLET *Gr. Forest* 73 b, His vse is, to keepe a good while in his mouth the stalke or sedge of Barley.

†**3.** *Her.* A 'spear reed' or flag borne as a charge. Also one of the leaves with which this was figured. *Obs.*

1688 HOLME *Armoury* II. 57/2 He beareth Argent, a Spear Reed, Vert... These are termed also Sedges, Flaggs or Water-flaggs... A[rgent] on a Mount in Base 3 Reed Spears (sans leaves or sedges).

4. Short for *sedge-fly*: see 5. Chiefly *silver sedge*.

1889 HALFORD *Dry-Fly Fishing* 209 A small sedge dressed on a No. O hook, either the silver sedge or an orange sedge with hare's ear body. **1902** S. BUXTON *Fishing & Shooting* 93 To these [flies] I would personally add.. the wickham, the silver sedge [etc.]. *Ibid.* 94 On some rivers, an alder, a sedge, or a caperer,.. is not too large.

5. *attrib.* and *Comb.* **a.** simple attributive, as ***sedge-bed***, †***-bush***, †***-collar***, ***-family***, ***-ground***, ***-peat***, †***-plot***; ***sedge-like*** adj. **b.** instrumental, as ***sedge-choked***, ***-crowned***, ***-embattled***, ***-grown*** adjs.

1871 KINGSLEY *At Last* viii, We hurried on over the water-furrows, and through the *sedge-beds to the further shore. **1551** TURNER *Herbal* I. H v, Thou lurkedest behynde the *sedge bushes. **1647** HEXHAM I, A Sedge-bush, or any place where sedge doth grow, *Een bies-bosch*. **1942** W. FAULKNER *Go down, Moses* 92 The old worn-out brier- and *sedge-choked fields spreading away. **1573** TUSSER *Husb.* (1878) 37 *Sedge collers for ploughhorse, for lightnes of neck. **1749** COLLINS *Ode on Thomson* viii, But thou, lorn stream, whose sullen tide No *sedge-crown'd sisters now attend. **1848** MRS. JAMESON *Sacr. & Leg. Art* (1850) 42 Instead of the winged angel we have the sedge-crowned river God. **1934** E. BLUNDEN *Mind's Eye* 138 We shall see.. the gilt-leaved beechwood and the *sedge-embattled lake. **1847** DARLINGTON *Amer. Weeds* (1860) 358 Order... *Cyperaceæ* (*Sedge Family.) **1667** in *Rec. Town Plymouth* (Mass.) (1889) I. 95 All that pte of the pond or *sedge ground which lyeth between a place there called the Gurnett and the bounds of Samuell Ryders land. **1910** C. HARRIS *Eve's Husband* 30 The poor brown sedge-ground of an old field. **1847** LYTTON *Lucretia* II. i, The whilom chase of Marylebone and the once *sedge-grown waters of Pimlico. **1871** KINGSLEY *At Last* vii, You push on into a bed of strong *sedge-like Sclerias, with cutting edges to their leaves. **1943** G. ERDTMAN *Introd. Pollen Analysis* i. 6 The comparatively low pine pollen frequency of a *sedge-peat was considered to be due to the fact that the pine sheds its pollen at a time when the sedges have attained full growth. **1952** *Chambers's Jrnl.* Jan. 61/2 We propose to.. fork in ample horticultural sedge-peat in the spring. **1977** R. DAVIES *Pract. Gardening Encycl.* ii. 21/1 Sedge (or fen) peats are the remains of reeds and sedges and are dark coloured and well decayed. **1610** HOLLAND *Camden's Brit.* I. 211 This of a *Sedgeplot and of a few fishermen's cotages.. grew to be a mercate town exceeding rich.

6. Special comb., as **sedge-bird** = *sedge-warbler*; †**sedge-boat**, ? a flat-bottomed boat for use in shallow or weed-grown rivers; **sedge-cock** *dial.* = MISSEL-THRUSH; **sedge-fly**, a caddis, or may-fly; also, an imitation of this used in fly-fishing (cf. sense 4); **sedge-grass** = sense 1 (in U.S. variously used *spec.*); †**sedge-hill**, ? an elevation, in the midst of marshy ground, covered with sedge; **sedge reedling** = *sedge-warbler*; †**sedge reek**, ? a stack of cut sedge; **sedge-root**, (*a*) the tuber of various kinds of sedge (*Cyperus esculentus*, *C. bulbosus*, etc.) used in some countries as an article of food; (*b*) = SEDGING; †**sedge-rug**, ? a coarse material woven of sedge and resembling matting; **sedge-warbler**, a small bird, *Acrocephalus schœnobænus*, of the family *Sylviidæ*, common in marshy districts; **sedge-willow**, ? the osier; †**sedge-worm**, some kind of worm used for bait; **sedge-wren** = *sedge-warbler*; also, a small bird native to Australasia.

1738 ALBIN *Nat. Hist. Birds* III. 56 *Sedge Bird. **1883** *Eng. Illustr. Mag.* Nov. 71/2 The sedge-bird commenced its continuous chattering. **1336-7** *Rotuli Scotiæ* I. 480 Ad octo batellos vocatos keles & *seggebotes in partibus de Lenn & Cantebrigg. **1886** R. HOLLAND *Gloss. Words County Chester* 305 *Sedcock,.. the missel thrush... Sedgecock. **1955** E. POUND *Classic Anthol.* I. 75 June's green hopper moves a thigh, 'Sedge-cock' wings it in July. **1965** *Jrnl. Lancs. Dial. Soc.* Jan. 9 Mistle thrush... Sedgecock, Setcock, Sedcock: Oldham; nr. Stockport. **1867** F. FRANCIS *Bk. Angling* vi. 189 The *Sedge Fly.. is a capital fly for all the southern and mid-county rivers.. throughout the summer. **1847** DARLINGTON *Amer. Weeds* 362 *Carex vulpinoidea*... Sedge. *Sedge-grass. **1865** KINGSLEY *Herew.* Prelude ¶30 The cattle waded along their edges after the rich sedge-grass. **1483** *Cath. Angl.* 328/1 A *Segg hylle, *carectum*. **1839** MACGILLIVRAY *Brit. Birds* II. 390 *Calamoherpe phragmitis*. The *Sedge Reedling. *c* **1440** *Promp. Parv.* 451/2 *Segge reeke, *caretum*. **1648** B. PLANTAGENET *Descr. New Albion* 25 Sweet *seg roots. **1850** F. MASON *Nat. Product. Burmah* 142 Sedge root. **1837** *Brit. Husb.* II. xiii. 182 (Libr. Usef. Knowl.), [The oat] is only partially subject to a disease called 'sedge-root, or tulip-root'. **1592** NASHE *P. Penilesse* A 4 b, Dame Niggardize, his wife, in a *sedge rugge kirtle. **1776** PENNANT *Brit. Zool.* II. 672 Index, Warblers, *sedge. **1837** GOULD *Birds Europe* III. Pl. 106 Great Sedge Warbler. *Ibid.* Pl. 112 Rufous Sedge Warbler. **1908** *The Month* Apr. 355 The purple red of the *sedge-willow blossoms. **1839** T. C. HOFLAND *Brit. Angler's Man.* ii. (1841) 11 The *segg-worm. **1802** MONTAGU *Ornith. Dict.* s.v. *Warbler, Sedge*, *Sedge-wren. **1845** *Voy. Port Philip* 53 The cheerful sedge wren and the bald-head friar.

7. quasi-*adj.* (from *attrib.*) Of sedge. *nonce-use.*

1637 MILTON *Lycidas* 104 Next Camus, reverend Sire, went footing slow, His Mantle hairy, and his Bonnet sedge, Inwrought with figures dim.

†**sedge**, *sb.*[2] *Obs. rare.* [ad. It. *seggia* seat, in both senses.] **a.** A hall of assembly. **b.** A sedan chair.

1615 G. SANDYS *Trav.* 258 Most of these [nobles] do live most part of the yeare in the Citie; where they haue five Sedges for the fiue assemblies of Capua, Nido, Montana, Spente and Lespente. *Ibid.* 259 The Sedges not unlike to horse-litters but carried by men.

sedge (sɛdʒ), *v. dial.* [f. SEDGE *sb.*[1]] *intr.* To be affected with SEDGING.

1820 *Farmer's Mag.* XXI. 32 An experienced old farmer.. replied.., 'although I know little about oats seging, I remember well [etc.].' **1876** *Whitby Gloss.* s.v., Our oats are segging.

sedge, var. SAY *v.*[1], SEGGE (man), and SIEGE.

sedged (sɛdʒd), *a.* [f. SEDGE *sb.*[1] + -ED[2].]

†**1.** Woven with sedge. *Obs. rare*$^{-1}$.

1610 SHAKS. *Temp.* IV. i. 129 You Nimphs cald Nayades of yᵉ windring brooks, With your sedg'd crownes.

†**2.** *Her.* Of a 'spear reed' or flag: Having 'sedges' (see SEDGE *sb.*[1] 3). *Obs.*

1688 HOLME *Armoury* II. 57/2 A[rgent] 2 Spear Reeds; single sedged and couped in Salter proper... O[r] on a hill in Base V[ert] 3 Spear Reeds, double sedged or leafed.

3. *Agric.* Of oats: Affected with SEDGING.

1844 H. STEPHENS *Bk. Farm* III. 950, I have cured a piece of land of its constant tendency to grow sedged oats, simply by draining.

4. Bordered with sedge.

1866 M. ARNOLD *Thyrsis* xi, And what sedged brooks are Thames's tributaries.

sedgeyng, obs. form of SAYING *vbl. sb.*

sedging ('sɛdʒɪŋ). *Agric.* Also seg(g)ing. [f. SEDGE *v.* + -ING[1].] A disease incident to oats, characterized by a thickening of the stem near the ground, said to be caused by a grub.

1820 *Farmer's Mag.* XXI. 32 On a Disease in Oats called Seging... This disease.. is known by its soon changing the natural colour of the braird into that of a dark luxuriant green. **1844** H. STEPHENS *Bk. Farm* III. 950 Another complaint of the oat-plant is segging or sedging, so named, in consequence of.. the leaves becoming broad, and the roots thickened like those of the sedge. **1890** MISS ORMEROD *Man. Injur. Insects* (ed. 2) 99 Tulip-root or Segging, caused by Stem Eelworm.

Sedgley ('sɛdʒlɪ). In 7 Seagly, Sedgly, Sedgely. The name of a town in S. Staffordshire: †*attrib.* (see quot.).

a **1625** FLETCHER *Woman's Prize* V. ii, A seagly curse light on him, which is, Pedro; The feind ride through him booted, and spurd, with a Sythe at's back. **1646** SUCKLING *Goblins* I. Wks. (1694) 253 Now the Sedgly curse upon thee. **1655** MENNES & J. SMITH *Mus. Delic.* (1656) 25 But he that hath her I doe wish no worse Then a true Sedgely curse.

sedgy ('sɛdʒɪ), *a.* Also α. 4, 6 seggy, 6 siedgie; β. 9 (dial.) seggy. [f. SEDGE *sb.*[1] + -Y.]

1. Covered or bordered with sedge or sedges.

[*c* **1318** in Wallace James *Deeds East Lothian* (1899) 10 Duas acras ad Seggy-wellis heved.] **1566** *Act 8 Eliz.* c. 8 §1 The Maryshes and Seggie Fenne Groundes wᵗʰin the sayd Isle [of Ely]. **1596** SHAKS. *1 Hen. IV*, I. iii. 98 On the gentle Seuernes siedgie banke. **1666** DRYDEN *Ann. Mirab.* ccxxxii, Deep in his Ooze he sought his sedgy Bed. **1764** *Oxf. Sausage* 100 Charwell, thy sedgy Banks, and glist'ring Streams All laugh and sing at mild Approach of Morn. **1810** SCOTT *Lady of L.* I. xxxi, The bittern.. Booming from the sedgy shallow. **1881** *Harper's Mag.* Sept. 521 The sedgy end Of yonder well-known bight.

b. *transf.* and *fig.*

1659 C. NOBLE *Moderate Answ. to Immod. Queries* To Rdr. 1 Can these rushy and sedgy expressions that are set down in this Paper grow any where, but from marish, myrie grounds and principles? **1862** BURTON *Bk. Hunter* 103 Those terrible folios of the scholastic divines,.. their majestic stream of central print overflowing into rivulets of marginal notes sedgy with citations.

2. Having the nature or properties of sedge.

1625 HEYLIN *Cosmogr.* (ed. 2) 747 On the bankes of this riuer [Nilus] also grew those sedgie weedes called Papyri. **1662** BARGRAVE *Alex. VII* (1867) 124 It was covered, he said, with long sedgy grass growing about it, under the dripp of an higher rock. **1808-13** A. WILSON *Amer. Ornith.* (1831) III. 185 Its flesh, though esteemed by many, tastes somewhat sedgy, or fishy. **1830** LINDLEY *Nat. Syst. Bot.* 284 The herbaceous sedgy habit of the latter [the Bulrush tribe]. **1878** BULLER *New Zealand* I. Introd. 17 A small spider, which is confined to a sedgy grass on the sea-coast.

†**3.** Made of or thatched with sedge. *Obs.*

1624 *Tragedy of Nero* IV. i. (1633) F 3, [Thou] dost rather choose, The smoaky reedes and sedgy cottages, Then the proud roofes.. of Kings. *a* **1835** MRS. HEMANS *Angler* 22 'Tis not the bittern, by the wave Seeking her sedgy nest.

sedigitated, -itism: see SEXDIGITATED, etc.

‖**sedile** (sɪˈdaɪliː). *Arch.* Pl. **sedilia** (sɪˈdɪlɪə). [L. *sedīle* neut., f. root of *sedēre* to sit.] *pl.* A series of seats, usually three in number, either movable or recessed in the wall and crowned with canopies, pinnacles, and other enrichments, usually placed on the south side of the choir near the altar for use by the clergy. Rarely *sing.* one of the sedilia, or a single seat used for this purpose.

1793 *Archæologia* (1794) XI. 335, I shall beg leave to turn the enquiry to..the *sedilia*, so frequently found in our chancels and chauntries. **1848** B. WEBB *Cont. Ecclesiol.* 119 The south wall of the sacrarium contains five sedilia. **1853** ROCK *Ch. of Fathers* III. II. 187 These sedilia were sometimes called, even in smaller churches, the 'presbytery'. **1863** SIR G. SCOTT in *Archæol. Cant.* V. 5 The change..of the chancel into Early Pointed by adding vaulting, inserting lancet windows..and a beautiful Early English sedile. **1866** *Direct. Anglic.* (ed. 3) 360 *Sedilia*, seats for the officiating clergy on the south side of the altar—usually three for Priest, Deacon and Sub-deacon. **1891** *Ch. Times* 27 Nov. 1157/1 The lowest sedile within the sanctuary.

attrib. **1904** *Athenæum* 9 Apr. 473/1 There are sedilia niches in the churches of Witton [etc.].

‖**sedimen.** *Obs. rare.* [L. *sedimen* settlings, sediment, f. *sedēre* to sit, settle.] = SEDIMENT.

1655 in *Hartlib's Ref. Commw. Bees* 21 In Rain-water kept in wooden Troughs..there would in time gather a sedimen of muddy matter to the bottome. **1657** G. STARKEY *Helmont's Vind.* 196 Which precipitates a light sedimen.

sediment (ˈsɛdɪmənt), *sb.* Also 6 **sedyment** (7 **sedement**). [a. F. *sédiment* (16th c. in Hatz.-Darm.), ad. L. *sediment-um* a settling, sinking down, f. *sedēre* to sit, settle.]

1. Matter composed of particles which fall by gravitation to the bottom of a liquid.

1547 RECORDE *Judic. Urine* 16 b, Al thinges in the water, that be of another matter and substaunce particulerly, then is the urine, as the sedyment or grounde. **1659** H. MORE *Immort. Soul* II. ix. 212 The Spirits in the Ventricles of the Brain..will..come to a more course consistency, and settle into some such like moist Sediment as is found at the bottome of the Ventricles. **1676** GREW *Anat. Plants, Salts of Plants* i. (1682) 262 After this white Sedement began to fall to the bottom; there was also gathered on the top, a kind of soft Scum. **1707** *Curios. in Husb. & Gard.* 235 A prodigious Quantity of clear Water must be exhal'd, to get an Ounce of dry Sediments, either saline or earthly. **1743** *Lond. & Country Brew.* II. (ed. 2) 133 But as to this taking Water out of a River, presently after a Flood..;..while such Water is making its Sediments..the Spirit of it dies. **1837** BREWSTER *Magnet.* 302 He poured it out carefully, without disturbing such of the iron sediment as still remained. **1857** *G. Bird's Urin. Deposits* (ed. 5) 189 All the sediments I have met with were amorphous.

2. *spec.* (in *Geol.* etc.). Earthly or detrital matter deposited by aqueous agency.

1684–5 BOYLE *Hist. Mineral Waters* 108 And whether the mud, or Sediment it [*sc.* Mineral Water] leaves, where it passes or stagnates,..have the same..Medicinal vertues. **1696** WHISTON *Th. Earth* II. (1722) 119 Our present upper Earth is factitious, and the Sediment of the Flood. **1794** SULLIVAN *View Nat.* I. 44 These beds are..placed over each other, like matters transported by the waters, and deposited in the form of sediment. **1823** BUCKLAND *Reliq. Diluv.* 40 Had they been washed in by a succession of floods we should have had a succession of beds of sediment and stalactite. **1860** TYNDALL *Glac.* II. xxvi. 372 The snow gradually wasted, but it left its sediment behind. **1865** GEIKIE *Scenery & Geol. Scot.* v. 92 Ordinary marine sediment..sand, gravel, silt, and mud. **1881** A. C. RAMSAY in *Nature* 1 Sept. 420/1 Cosmological geology..must go back to times far anterior to the date of the deposition, as common sediments, of the very oldest known metamorphic strata.

3. *fig.*

1637 SANDERSON *Serm.* (1674) II. 64 Those dregs of Uncharitableness that (as the sediments of depraved nature) lurk in the hearts of the most charitable men. **1691–8** NORRIS *Pract. Disc.* (1707) IV. 44 When the sediment of his troubled spirit was fallen. **1824** BYRON *Juan* XV. iv, The ruby glass that shakes within his hand Leaves a sad sediment of Time's worst sand. **1859** DICKENS *T. Two Cities* II. iv, The last sediment of the human stew that had been boiling there all day, was straining off. **1903** J. C. SMITH in R. Campbell *Life* 124 The late Bailie Colston, a man best known by the criminal sediment of Edinburgh.

4. *attrib.* and *Comb.*, as ***sediment-laden*** adj.; **sediment-collector**, a contrivance for preventing the deposition of sediment in a boiler; **sediment ring** *Astr.*, a ring of rock masses orbiting a planet, regarded as debris from the time of its formation.

1858 R. MURRAY *Marine Engines* (ed. 3) 234 *Sediment collectors*, or *scale pans.* **1886** A. WINCHELL *Walks & Talks Geol. Field* 51 Down its slopes descend the sediment-laden drainage-waters. **1955** *Sci. News Let.* 22 Jan. 53/1 Dr. Kuiper said that the moon, as it sped away from the earth, plowed through a 'sediment ring', a swarm of small satellites moving around the earth. **1970** [see PLANETISMAL *a.* and *sb.*].

sediment (ˈsɛdɪmənt), *v.* [f. SEDIMENT *sb.*]

1. *trans.* To deposit as sediment.

1859 PAGE *Handbk. Geol. Terms* s.v. *Sediment*, Rocks..as shale, clay, sandstone, &c., are termed sedimentary; that is, sedimented from mechanical suspension in water. **1908** *Chambers's Jrnl.* May 396/1 Chemical precipitation was found essential to coagulate the suspended matter and thus enable the greater proportion of it to be sedimented in subsidence basins. **1976** *Nature* 19 Aug. 662/1 We then sedimented the eggs rapidly..in a hand centrifuge.

2. *intr.* **a.** To settle as sediment.

1927 *Brit. Jrnl. Exper. Path.* VIII. 122 In a typical rough culture of *enteritidis*..the bacteria rapidly sediment to the bottom. **1961** *Lancet* 5 Aug. 322/1 The erythrocytes being allowed to sediment within the syringe. **1971** *Nature* 25 June 527/2 Each preparation sedimented in the analytical ultracentrifuge as a single component with a sedimentation coefficient..of about 9·5S.

b. Of a liquid: to deposit a sediment.

1934 in WEBSTER. **1962** LUNTZ & WRIGHT in A. Pirie *Lens Metabolism Rel. Cataract* 319 Blood was collected..in a mixture of 1% sodium ethylenediamine tetra-acetic acid and 5% dextran..and allowed to sediment. **1978** *Nature* 10 Aug. 611/1 (*caption*) Heparinated blood was allowed to sediment at room temperature to separate red cells from plasma.

Hence **ˈsedimented** *ppl. a.* (also *fig.*); **ˈsedimenting** *vbl. sb.* and *ppl. a.*

1901 *Lancet* 1 June 1533/1 Care will..have to be taken not to overlook the sedimented bacteria which may be lying at the bottom of the tube. **1901** DURHAM in *Jrnl. Exper. Med.* 15 Jan. 365 In an afternoon several hundred sedimenting preparations can be put up. **1962** H. BLOEMENDAL et al. in A. Pirie *Lens Metabolism Rel. Cataract* 303 More rapidly sedimenting material is observed, but the shape of the corresponding boundary does not allow calculation of the sedimentation coefficient. **1977** D. L. ALTHEIDE in D. E. Johnson *Existential Sociol.* iv. 149 These tasks become taken for granted as sedimented knowledge for the members.

sedimentable (ˈsɛdɪmɛntəb(ə)l), *a.* [f. prec. + -ABLE.] That may be deposited or obtained as sediment. Hence **ˌsedimentaˈbility**.

1943 *Jrnl. Gen. Physiol.* XXVI. 352 As an elemental volume within the ascending layer is partially or completely cleared of sedimentable material, it has to move only a relatively short distance..before it reaches a region of comparable concentration. **1971** *Jrnl. Insect Physiol.* XVII. 865 Additions of 0·1% Triton..increase..enzymatic activity..without markedly altering the sedimentability of the enzyme. **1978** *Nature* 2 Mar. 55/2 After storing for 1 week at room temperature, at least 50% of the antimony was retained within sedimentable liposomes, the remainder having escaped into solution.

sedimental (sɛdɪˈmɛntəl), *a. rare.* [f. SEDIMENT *sb.* + -AL[1].] Of the nature of sediment. Of rocks: sedimentary.

1614 T. ADAMS *Sinners Passing Bell* Wks. (1629) 253 This drossie, feculent, and sedimentall Earth. **1739** R. BULL tr. *Dedekindus' Grobianus* 222 The Mug may have some sedimental Grout. **1883** *Science* I. 101 A peculiarity of the underlying bed of sedimental rock is its varying thickness.

sedimentarily (ˌsɛdɪˈmɛntərɪlɪ), *adv. rare.* [f. SEDIMENTARY + -LY[2].] In the form of a sedimentary deposit.

1855 *Chamb. Jrnl.* IV. 184 He sees..loose volcanic materials sedimentarily spread over this bed of trap.

sedimentary (sɛdɪˈmɛntərɪ), *a.* and *sb.* [f. SEDIMENT *sb.* + -ARY. Cf. F. *sédimentaire.*]

A. *adj.*

1. Of, pertaining to, or of the nature of sediment.

1846 G. E. DAY tr. *Simon's Anim. Chem.* II. 217 The crisis ..shows itself in the urine by the secretion becoming turbid and sedimentary. **1854** BAKEWELL *Geol.* 33 The sedimentary depositions having taken place after the crust of the earth had been lifted up above the level of the sea. **1860** MAURY *Phys. Geog. Sea* (Low) xiv. 609 Mud and all the light sedimentary matter of river waters. **1876** PAGE *Adv. Text-bk. Geol.* xviii. 351 The sedimentary origin of chalk.

2. *Geol.* Of rocks, etc.: Formed by the deposition of sediment.

1830 LYELL *Princ. Geol.* (1835) I. I. v. 127 Those who endeavoured to explain the formation of sedimentary strata by causes now in diurnal action. **1839** G. ROBERTS *Dict. Geol.* s.v. *Tertiary Strata*, A series of sedimentary rocks. **1880** A. R. WALLACE *Isl. Life* x. 212 The sedimentary rocks of one age are partly formed from the destruction of the sedimentary rocks of former ages.

B. *sb.* A sedimentary formation or deposit.

1878 *Smithsonian Rep.* 70 The older sedimentaries have been entirely removed from the mountain border. **1888** TEALL *Brit. Petrogr.* 418 The zone of contact between the crystalline rocks and the sedimentaries.

sedimentation (ˌsɛdɪmənˈteɪʃən). [f. SEDIMENT *sb.* + -ATION.] **1.** Deposition of sediment; *spec.* in *Geol.* (see SEDIMENT *sb.* 2); also see quot. 1898.

1874 H. A. NICHOLSON in *Trans. Victoria Inst.* IX. 215 There is no proof of any considerable pauses in the process of sedimentation during the same period. **1881** GEIKIE in *Nature* 17 Feb. 358/1 That still comparatively narrow belt of sea to which sedimentation has always been mainly confined. **1896** *Pop. Sci. Monthly* Dec. 243, I am inclined ..to ascribe the greatest potency to the effects of erosion, transportation, and sedimentation on the earth's surface. **1898** *Syd. Soc. Lex.*, *Sedimentation*, production of quick deposition of a sediment, whether in sewage, or urine, &c., by means of some centrifugal apparatus. **1902** *Westm. Gaz.* 20 Dec. 3/1 River water is usually purified by sedimentation and filtration.

2. *Comb.*, as **sedimentation coefficient, constant**, a measure of the size of a microscopic particle, equal to the terminal outward velocity of the particle when centrifuged in a fluid medium divided by the centrifugal force acting on it; (expressed in units of time: cf. SVEDBERG); **sedimentation rate**, the rate of descent of particles suspended in a fluid; *spec.* in *Med.*, of the red cells in drawn blood; **sedimentation tank**, a tank in which sewage is allowed to stand so that the solid matter in suspension may have time to settle.

1962 H. BLOEMENDAL et al. in A. Pirie *Lens Metabolism Rel. Cataract* 300, α-Crystallin, prepared by vertical starch block electrophoresis, has a sedimentation coefficient of 19 S (molecular weight 810,000). **1978** *Nature* 12 Jan. 170/2 Nervous tissue and muscle in rat and chicken contain several molecular forms of acetylcholinesterase.., distinguishable by their sedimentation coefficient in sucrose gradient. **1929** SVEDBERG & KATSURAI in *Jrnl. Amer. Chem. Soc.* LI. 3577 The term 'Sedimentation Constant' has been adopted as a simplified means of expressing the old term 'Specific Sedimentation Velocity'. **1966** B. POLLARA et al. in R. T. Smith et al. *Phylogeny of Immunity* ix. 94/2 The antibody produced by this animal is different from that of the other lower vertebrates, having a sedimentation constant of approximately 9S. **1946** *Nature* 30 Nov. 794/2 In accordance with Stokes's law, sedimentation-rates of such red-cell aggregates will be greater than those of single non-polarized blood cells. **1978** *Ibid.* 12 Oct. 532/1 To predict long-range trends in marsh stability, accurate measurements are needed of both subsidence and sedimentation rates. **1920** *Glasgow Herald* 3 Nov. 13 The sewage passes into a sedimentation tank designed so as to bring down in the form of sludge as much of the suspended solids as possible. **1966** *McGraw-Hill Encycl. Sci. & Technol.* XII. 221/2 In some [sewage] treatment plants screenings are passed through a grinder and returned to the flow so that they will settle out in the sedimentation tank.

sedimentator (ˌsɛdɪmənˈteɪtə(r)). [f. SEDIMENTAT-ION + -OR.] An instrument for expediting urinary sedimentation in diagnosis.

1899 CAGNEY tr. *Jaksch's Clin. Diagn.* vii. (ed. 4) 256 The process [of collection of urinary sediment] may be rendered more certain and expeditious by the use of Stenbeck's sedimentator.

sedimentology (ˌsɛdɪmənˈtɒlədʒɪ). [f. SEDIMENT *sb.* + -OLOGY.] The branch of geology which deals with the nature and properties of sediments and sedimentary rocks. So **ˌsedimentoˈlogical** *a.*, of or pertaining to sedimentology; **ˌsedimentoˈlogically** *adv.*, by means of sedimentology; from the point of view of sedimentology; **ˌsedimenˈtologist**, an expert in sedimentology.

1932 H. WADELL in *Science* 1 Jan. 20/2 Sedimentology is here suggested as a term for the subject taught, retaining sedimentation for the act or process of deposition. The new term and its derivatives sedimentologist, sedimentologic and sedimentological will tend towards clearness. **1957** *Jrnl. Geol.* LXV. 485/1 It might be possible to subdivide further the material in this core from a sedimentological point of view into two components: (1) material of sand size.., and (2) lutite. **1958** *Times* 22 Mar. 8/3 Mr R. J. L. Allen..has been appointed George Martin Lees Research Fellow in Sedimentology. **1961** *Jrnl. Sedimentary Petrol.* XXXI. 207/1 The expression of kurtosis has not been used extensively by sedimentologists. **1966** *Palaeogeogr., Palaeoclimatol., Palaeoecol.* II. 113 The ironstones..mark, sedimentologically, a complete reversal of the trend towards increasing oxygenation. **1967** *New Scientist* 20 July 146/1 A number of grants for further research into sedimentology have been made to the University of Reading. **1970** *Nature* 2 May 425 Sedimentological studies of depositional environments of the modern Omo River delta and floodplain. **1973** *Ibid.* 8 June 342/1 Their [*sc.* marine grasses'] former presence can nevertheless be deduced by sedimentology and palaeontology. **1977** A. HALLAM *Planet Earth* 245/1 The paleoecologist has to be paleobiologist, sedimentologist and biologist.

sedimentous (sɛdɪˈmɛntəs), *a.* [f. SEDIMENT *sb.* + -OUS.] Full of or abounding in sediment.

1869 E. A. PARKES *Pract. Hygiene* (ed. 3) 28 The large tropical streams are much more sedimentous.

sedinge, obs. form of SEETHING *a.*

†**seˈditiary.** *Obs. rare.* [f. SEDITI-ON + -ARY.] A seditious person, a seditionary.

1628 FELTHAM *Resolves* II. lxxxvi. 248 It was onely a few Seditiaries, that hee had commanded to be slaine. **1646** *Mercurius Belgicus* Pref., Seditiaryes and Schismaticks.

sedition (siːˈdɪʃən, sɪ-). Forms: 4 **sedici(o)un, seducioun**, *Sc.* **sedicione, seduccione**, 5 **cedicioun**, 5–6 **sedicion**, 6 **sedycyon, sedytyon**, *Sc.* **sediciounn, sedetione**, 6– **sedition.** [a. OF. *sedition* (mod.F. *sédition*), ad. L. *sēditiōn-em*, f. *sēd-* (see SE-) + *itiōn-em* a going, n. of action f. *īre* to go. Cf. Sp. *sedicion*, Pg. *sedição*, It. *sedizione*.

The ME. spelling *seducioun*, *seduccione* are due to pseudoetymological association with L. *sēdūcĕre* SEDUCE *v.*]

†**1.** Violent party strife; an instance of this, esp. a factious contest attended with rioting and disorder. *Obs.*

c **1375** *Sc. Leg. Saints* ii. (*Paulus*) 163 þe folk of rowme.. Raisit in hym sedicione, and wald have brokyn his palace done. *Ibid.* v. (*Johannes*) 291 Al þa þat mad sacrifice til mawmentis..In þe puple (raisit) seduccione a-gane sancte Iohne. *a* **1380** *S. Ambrose* 113 in Horstm. *Altengl. Leg.* (1878) 10 þei neore not alle in on red, þer ros a gret sediciun Tofore þat ilke elecciun. **1382** WYCLIF *Mark* xv. 7 Barabas, that was boundan with sleeris of men, and that hadde don manslauȝtre in seducioun, that is, debaat in cytee. *Ibid.*, *Acts* xxiv. 5 We han foundun this man..stiringe sedicioun, or dissencioun, to alle Jewis..and auctour of seducioun of the secte of Nazarens. **1402** *Pol. Poems* (Rolls) II. 56 Foure angels singnefien foure general synnes,..cedicioun, superstiscions, the glotouns, and the proude. **1447** BOKENHAM *Seyntys, Agnes* 490 And wyth her wurdys a sedycyoun lo Among þe peple dede grow. *c* **1477** CAXTON *Jason* 77 b, And some ther were couetous desiring their singuler prouffit accorded unto this sedicion. **1529** MORE

Dyaloge I. Wks. 150/2 As though these men were Apostles now specially sent by god to preache heresyes and sow sedicion among christen men. 1536 *St. Papers Hen. VIII*, II. 356 For this cuntrey passith all that ever I sawe, for ministration of sedition and discorde. 1549 *Compl. Scot.* ix. 78 Thair vas gryt sedition and discentione amang al the gryt personagis of grece. 1602 Segar *Honor, Mil. & Civ.* IV. I. iii, When the Romanes were diuided, one faction labouring to oppresse another..such enimitie was called Sedition. 1628 Hobbes *Thucydides* (1822) 87 But there would be thoughts of sedition in one towards another in the city.

2. a. A concerted movement to overthrow an established government; a revolt, rebellion, mutiny. Now *rare*.

1585 T. Washington tr. *Nicholay's Voy.* IV. xxix. 150 Messenie..was giuen to reuolting & seditions. 1607–12 Bacon *Ess., Seditions* (Arb.) 398 The matter of seditions is of two kindes, Much povertye and much discontent. 1689 Locke *Toleration* 50 Seditions are very frequently raised, upon pretence of Religion. 1755 Johnson, *Sedition*, a tumult; an insurrection; a popular commotion; an uproar. 1788 Gibbon *Decl. & F.* xlviii. V. 83 With the dawn of day the city burst into a general sedition. 1842 Elphinstone *Hist. India* II. 65 The tribe had turned into a turbulent democracy..; a sedition had broken out about the property left by Kuttaul. 1875 Jowett *Plato* (ed. 2) V. 327 By reason of inequality, cities are filled with seditions. 1886 *Encycl. Brit.* XXI. 620/1 In the Acts of Congress [of the United States] the word 'sedition' appears to occur only in the army and navy articles. A soldier joining any sedition or who, being present at any sedition, does not use his utmost endeavour to suppress the same is punishable with death.

b. Conduct or language inciting to rebellion against the constituted authority in a state.

1838 W. Bell *Dict. Law Scot.* s.v., Sedition is distinguished from leasing-making, in this respect, that the object of leasing-making is to disparage or prejudice the private character of the Sovereign, whereas sedition is directed against the order and tranquility of the State. 1877 *Act 40 & 41 Vict.* c. 21 §40 [A] prisoner..on conviction for sedition or seditious libel shall be treated as a misdemeanant of the first division. 1883 Stephen *Hist. Crim. Law* II. xxiv. 298 As for sedition itself I do not think that any such offence is known to English law. 1887 Chamberlain *Sp.* 11 Oct. *Sp. Irish Question* (1890) 49 Loyalty in the House of Commons—Irish loyalty—is represented only by seventeen votes, and sedition, on the contrary, enjoys a majority of eighty-six votes.

attrib. 1556 Olde *Antichrist* 92 Murtherous sedicion sowers, and open churche robbers. 1801 A. Hamilton *Wks.* (1886) VII. 193 As to the sedition law, we refer you to the debates in Congress. 1865 *Daily Tel.* 2 Dec. 6/5 Native sedition-mongers. 1886 *Encycl. Brit.* XXI. 620/1 In 1798 an Act of Congress called the Sedition Act was passed, which expired by effluxion of time in 1801. 1898 *Westm. Gaz.* 24 Jan. 9/3 A correspondent at Madras telegraphs to-day that a joint public meeting of Hindoos and Mohammedans was held there..to protest against the sedition law amendments. 1908 *Ibid.* 28 July 9/1 The trial of some sedition-monger in India.

†**3.** Of inanimate things: Tumult, uproar. [After L. *seditio*; in quot. 1640 with allusion to sense 2.]

1640 Habington *Castara* III. 220 When the distracted Ocean Swells to Sedition, and obeys no Law. 1671 R. Bohun *Wind* 12 But what Seditions, Eddies and Undulations must this cause in the whole body of Air.

seditionary (siːˈdɪʃənərɪ, sɪ-), *sb.* and *a.* [f. prec. + -ary.] **A.** *sb.* = seditionist. Now *rare*.

1607 J. Carpenter *Plaine Mans Plough* 216 The factious Schismatike, and the contentious Seditionary. 1634 Bp. Hall *Contempl., N.T., Christ bef. Pilate* 262 Barabbas, a theefe, a murderer, a seditionary. 1640 —— *Rem. Wks.* (1660) 39 Durst the rebellious seditionary lift up his hand against the Lords Anointed..if the fool had not said in his heart, There is no God? 1641 *Ibid.* 71 A Seditionary in a State, or a Schismatick in the Church is like a sulphureous fiery Vapour in the bowels of the Earth. 1865 *Pall Mall Gaz.* No. 192. 6/2 Disposed to shelter seditionaries.

B. *adj.* Of, pertaining to, or characterized by sedition; seditious.

1898 J. Y. Simpson *Side-Lights on Siberia* xi. 346 Seditionary propagandism amongst the soldiers rouses the authorities almost more than anything else. 1909 *Daily News* 23 Apr. 10/1 The Benchers..meet to consider the conduct of one of their Indian members,..in taking an active part in the seditionary movement in his native country.

seditioner (siːˈdɪʃənə(r), sɪ-). *rare.* [f. sedition + -er[1].] = seditionist.

1562 Leigh *Armorie* (1597) 71 When Lucifer with his adherents were expelled heauen, they were disseuered into nine..horrible horrors, as followeth. The first false messengers... The seuenth, sedicioners. 1838 *Times* 8 Nov. 4/1 The Lord High Seditioner [*i.e.* Lord Durham, Lord High Commissioner] has choked the community with indignation.

seditionist (siːˈdɪʃənɪst, sɪ-). [f. sedition + -ist.] One who practises sedition or incites others to sedition; a promoter of disloyalty and factious strife against a government or state.

1786 Mrs. Sarah Trimmer *Œcon. Charity* (1801) I. 151 The endeavours of infidels and seditionists to corrupt the public mind. 1798 Coleridge *Let. to G. Coleridge* Lett. (1895) 243, I therefore consent to be deemed a Democrat and a Seditionist. 1837 *Fraser's Mag.* XVI. 129 Nor..is there any such increase of anarchists and seditionists as other folks are apt to dread. 1907 *Westm. Gaz.* 9 Aug. 7/3 The Maharajahs..dissociating themselves from what is described as the campaign of rancour..pursued by the seditionists.

seditious (siːˈdɪʃəs, sɪ-), *a.* Forms: 5 sedi-, sedycious, seducious, cedicious (ceducious), 6 sedycyous(e, sediciouse, -tiouse, seditius (sedicius, *Sc.* sedetiose), 5– seditious. [ad. OF. *seditieux, -euse* (mod.F. *sé-*), ad. L. *sēditiōsus*, f. *sēditiōnem*: see sedition and -ous.]

1. Of a person or body of persons: Given to or guilty of sedition; in early use, 'factious with tumult, turbulent' (J.); now chiefly, engaged in promoting disaffection or inciting to revolt against constituted authority.

1447 Bokenham *Seyntys, Agnes* 508 þe prefectys vyker, The sedycyous peple assentyng-to, Dede makyn anoon a ryht greth feer. *Ibid.* 564. 1490 Caxton *Eneydos* xviii. 66 O ryght dere eneas, sedycious & ryght cruel, how haste thou had the herte so vntrue, to thynke so grete a treson [etc.]. 1496 *Patent Roll, 12 Hen. VII*, Pt. 2 By instigation of dyvers cedicious and ill-disposed persons. *a* 1513 Fabyan *Chron.* I. (1533) 8 b/2 To which sedycyous persons Margan gyuynge credence,..made warre vpon his sayde brother. 1535 Coverdale 1 *Esdras* iv. 12 That sedicious [Gr. ἀπόστατιν] & wicked cite. 1590 Shaks. *Com. Err.* I. i. 12. 1596 Nashe *Saffron Walden* L 1 b, Thirdly, he is verie seditious and mutinous in conuersation, picking quarrells with euerie man that will not magnifie and applaud him. 1596 *Edw. III*, III. i, England was wont to harbour malcontents, Blood thirsty and seditious Catelynes. 1617 Moryson *Itin.* I. 242 Seditious Ianizaries. 1667 Milton *P.L.* VI. 152 Thou returnst From flight, seditious Angel, to receave Thy merited reward. 1721 Strype *Eccl. Mem.* I. I. xxiii. 171 So one said,..when one asked him, how he liked Latimer's Sermon before King Edward; Even as I liked him always. A seditious Fellow. 1759 Robertson *Hist. Scot.* I. Wks. 1851 I. 22 Reducing to obedience their seditious chieftain. 1820 Shelley *Œd. Tyr.* I. 82 Seditious hunks! to whine for want of grains. 1908 J. O. Dykes *Chr. Minister* xi. 109 An illegal or possibly seditious club. 1909 *Contemp. Rev.* Oct. 498 The Coreans are wrathful and seditious in consequence..and little risings are anticipated.

Comb. 1653 R. Sanders *Physiogr.* 197 A turbulent, seditious-spirited person.

b. *absol.* Seditious persons.

1535 Coverdale *Ecclus.* Contents xlv, The punyshment of the sedicious. *a* 1627 Hayward *Edw. VI* (1630) 65 The seditious in Northfolke were somewhat dangerous. 1796 Burke *Late St. Nat.* Wks. II. 159 Nothing,..but the sending a very strong military, backed by a very strong naval force, would reduce the seditious to obedience.

2. Of, pertaining to, or of the nature of sedition; tending to incite to or provoke sedition.

1455 *Rolls of Parlt.* V. 281/1 For the removyng and overthrawyng of the cedicious and fraudelent blaspheme and defaime untruly..leyed upon us. 1464 *Coventry Leet-bk.* 330 The seid Will. Huet..had then right vnfyttyng, inordinate & ceducious langage sownyng to the derogacion of the kynges lawes & of his peace. 1491 *Act 7 Hen. VII*, c. 15 Certeyn persones of evyll riotous and sedicious disposicions. *c* 1520 Skelton *Magnyf.* 737, I sowe sedycyous sedes of Dyscorde and debates. 1533 More *Debell. Salem* Wks. 932/1 A defence..against yᵉ maliciouse slaunder and..false some sayes in that sediciouse boke. 1560 Daus tr. *Sleidane's Comm.* 55 b, He had made sedicious sermons. 1610 Holland *Camden's Britannia* I. 725 In making complaintes of the misgovernment of the state, spreading seditious rumours, scattering libels abroad [etc.]. 1689 Locke *Toleration* 51 But there is one thing only which gathers People into Seditious Commotions, and that is Oppression. 1718 Prior *Solomon* III. 608 But if she has deform'd this earthly life With murderous rapine, and seditious strife. 1721 Strype *Eccl. Mem.* I. I. xxvii. 192 The Northern Clergy backward. Some of them taken up for seditious Preaching. 1796 *Act 36 Geo. III*, c. 8 (*title*), An Act for the more effectually preventing Seditious Meetings and Assemblies. 1828 D'Israeli *Chas. I*, II. x. 257 To Charles ..the menacing language and the tumultuous acts of the great leaders, appeared seditious. 1845 Sarah Austin *Ranke's Hist. Ref.* II. 399 The disturbed state of the people arose..from seditious writings and discourses. 1883 Stephen *Hist. Crim. Law* xxiv. 298 The second class of offences against internal public tranquility consists of offences not accompanied by or leading to open violence. They may be classified under the general head of seditious offences, and more particularly as seditious words, seditious libels, and seditious conspiracies. All those offences presuppose dissatisfaction with the existing government.

seditiously (siːˈdɪʃəslɪ, sɪ-), *adv.* [-ly[2]] In a seditious manner; so as to cause sedition.

1453 *Rolls of Parlt.* V. 265/1 The..Traitour John Cade.. gaderyng to him youre people in grete nombre by.. sediciously made commotion, rebellion and insurrection. *a* 1513 Fabyan *Chron.* VII. 187/1 Sedyciously the sayde Bysshop hadde by his Letters..wrongfully accused hym that he shuld areyse the kynges people. 1563 Foxe *A. & M.* 1185, I did nothyng sediciously, falsly, or arrogantly, in worde or facte. 1570 T. Norton *Nowel's Catech.* II. 47 They ..that seditiously stirre vp discorde in the Church of God. 1593 Bp. Bancroft *Dang. Posit* IV. xv. 183 To beware of such sectaries as..do thus seditiously endeauour to disturbe the land. 1623 Bingham *Xenophon* 106 In warre,.. whosoeuer..behaueth himselfe seditiously against his Commander, behaueth himselfe seditiously against his owne safetie. 1689 Locke *Toleration* 53 If anything pass in a Religious Meeting seditiously, and contrary to the publick Peace, it is to be punished in the same manner. 1785 Burke *Nabob of Arcot's Debts* Wks. IV. 248 They had no lawful government, seditiously to overturn.

†**se'ditiousness.** *Obs.* [f. seditious + -ness.] Seditious character or condition.

1583 Golding *Calvin on Deut.* cv. 646 He was not minded to let his blessing appeare so soone because of yᵉ peoples seditiousnesse. 1755 in Johnson.

seditty, var. saditty *a.*

Sedobrol (ˈsɛdəʊbrɒl). A proprietary name for a medicinal preparation.

1913 *Trade Marks Jrnl.* 22 Jan. 105 *Sedobrol*... Chemical substances prepared for use in medicine and pharmacy. John Henry Land.., 10, Market Place, Coalville, Leicestershire; Chemist. 1921 R. Macaulay *Dangerous Ages* v. 102 There have been wonderful cures for insomnia lately... Which new thing? Sedobrol? Paraldehyd? 1934 E. Waugh *Handful of Dust* iii. 129 They had boiled water in an electric kettle and were drinking Sedobrol together. 1939–40 *Army & Navy Stores Catal.* 406/3 Sedobrol Tablets 10's 2/–, 30's 5/–.

sedoheptulose (siːdəʊˈhɛptjʊləʊz, -s). *Chem.* [f. sed(um + -o + *hept*)*ose* s.v. hepta- + -ulose[2].] A heptose that is found in the leaves of certain plants of the genus *Sedum* (notably *S. spectabile*), a phosphate of which is involved as an intermediate in carbohydrate metabolism in animals. Formerly called †**sedoheptose**.

1917 La Forge & Hudson in *Jrnl. Biol. Chem.* XXX. 68 Since the analyses of the three crystalline derivatives that have been described show conclusively that the sugar of *Sedum spectabile* contains seven carbon atoms, it will be named, with reference to its origin, sedoheptose. 1938 *Thorpe's Dict. Appl. Chem.* (ed. 4) II. 286/2 The natural ketoheptoses are *d*-mannoketoheptose..; perseulose.., and sedoheptose obtained from *Sedum spectabile*. 1939 *Jrnl. Amer. Chem. Soc.* LXI. 343/2 In the presence of mineral acids, sedoheptulose is transformed to a crystalline anhydride. 1959 [see ribulose]. 1970 R. W. McGilvery *Biochem.* xvi. 325 The only known function for the 7-carbon sedoheptulose-7-phosphate in animals is its participation as an intermediate in the pentose phosphate pathway.

Sedormid (sɪˈdɔːmɪd). *Pharm.* A proprietary term for *N*-(2-isopropylpent-4-enoyl)urea, $C_9H_{16}N_2O_2$, a white crystalline solid employed as a sedative and hypnotic.

1928 *Trade Marks Jrnl.* 9 May 736/2 *Sedormid*... The Hoffman-La Roche Chemical Works Limited..London. 1929 *Official Gaz.* (U.S. Patent Office) 14 May 299/2 *Sedormid.* For sedative and hypnotic. Claims use since Mar. 14, 1929. 1934 *Lancet* 21 Apr. 845/1 Two..cases of thrombopenic purpura were due to prolonged administration of the new hypnotic Sedormid (allylisopropyl-acetylurea). 1964 M. Hynes *Med. Bacteriol.* (ed. 8) vii. 79 In some patients the hypnotic Sedormid combines with the platelets and thrombocytopenic purpura follows. 1974 M. C. Gerald *Pharmacol.* iv. 80 Compare the ease in saying and remembering.. allylisopropylacetylcarbamide vs. Sedormid.

Sedra (ˈsɛdrə). Also **Sedrah, Sidra(h**, and with small initial. [Aram. (via Yiddish *sedre*): cf. Seder.] In Jewish sabbatical liturgy, one of the fifty-four sections of the Pentateuch read in the Synagogue at the Sabbath morning service. Cf. parashah.

Quot. 1909 does not accord with modern usage.

1907 I. Zangwill *Ghetto Comedies* 128 We are reading the *Sedrah* (weekly portion) about Joseph. 1909 *Cent. Dict. Suppl.*, The Pentateuch is divided into fifty-four sedras or sections, which are subdivided into parashoth. The sedras must be read at the morning Sabbath services during the year, but as a year has only 52 weeks, in order to finish the sedras two of them are read on two special Sabbaths. 1962 *New Jewish Encycl.* 370/2 In common usage, the word 'Parashah' also refers to the entire *Sidrah* (or Sedrah), or to any of the various sections or paragraphs in the scroll of the Torah. The Torah is subdivided into *Sidrot* (sections), the reading of which is completed in a one year cycle; and each Sidrah is further subdivided into Parashiyot (sing. Parashah). 1973 *Jewish Chron.* 19 Jan. 18/2 Nehama Leibowitz's studies in the weekly *sidra* have justifiably become renowned as a key for the unlocking of the treasures found among the Jewish Biblical exegetes.

seduce (sɪˈdjuːs), *v.* Forms: 5 seduise, 6 seduse, *Sc.* sedouse, 6– seduce. [ad. L. *sēdūcĕre* to lead aside or away, etc., f. *sē-* (se- *prefix*) + *dūcĕre* to lead. In the earliest examples the proximate source was the F. *séduire* (inflected *séduis-*): see sedue *v.*]

1. *trans.* To persuade (a vassal, servant, soldier, etc.) to desert his allegiance or service.

c 1477 Caxton *Jason* 78 Zethephius seduised the pepel ayenst him by tyraunye al euydent. 1549 *Compl. Scot.* ix. 78 He seducit diuerse grit personagis to rebel contrar athenes. 1562 *Reg. Privy Council Scot.* I. 216 Na persone seducit him fra the obedience of the Quene and magistratis..nor yit seducit him fra his faith. 1601 in Moryson *Itin.* II. (1617) 152 A great Armie..selected out of all the rebels in Ireland, and from all others that he can seduce to his partie. 1667 Milton *P.L.* IX. 307 Suttle he needs must be, who could seduce Angels. *a* 1674 Clarendon *Hist. Reb.* x. §151 Those persons of condition, who..had been seduced to do them service throughout the kingdom. 1718 *Act 5 Geo. I*, c. 27 (*title*), An Act to prevent the Inconveniences arising from seducing Artificers in the Manufactures of Great Britain into foreign Parts. 1745 in *Col. Rec. Pennsylv.* V. 31 Of their being otherwise seduced by, or compelled to join with the Enemy. 1759 Dilworth *Pope* 72 Lord Oxford seduced him over to his side. 1844 Ld. Brougham *Brit. Const.* viii. (1862) 104 To seduce the representatives from their duty to their constituents. 1879 Froude *Cæsar* xxii. 379 He tried to seduce Cæsar's garrison, and was put to death for his treachery.

2. In wider sense: To lead (a person) astray in conduct or belief; to draw away *from* the right or intended course of action *to* or *into* a wrong one; to tempt, entice, or beguile *to do* something wrong, foolish, or unintended.

a. of persons or their action.

1519–20 *Stirling Burgh Rec.* (1887) I. 3 He was nocht compellit, sedoussit nor coacit thar to. 1535 Joye *Apol. Tindale* (Arb.) 27 Lest the reader myght be seduced with you beleuing there is no lyfe of soulis departed. 1581 J. Bell *Haddon's Answ. Osor.* 454 No persuasion will seduce him to thinke, that his Churche may straye .. from the right course. **1596** SPENSER *F.Q.* IV. v. 11 Duessa .. Who with her forged beautie did seduce The hearts of some that fairest her did weene. **1610** HOLLAND *Camden's Brit.* I. 465 But afterwards seduced by his wife, he had in the selfe same Church, .. one Altar for Christ's Religion, and another for sacrifices unto Devils. **1651** HOBBES *Leviath.* II. xix. 96 To be seduced by Orators, as a Monarch by Flatterers. **1673** CAVE *Prim. Chr.* I. iii. 38 They would leave so grave a discipline and suffer themselves to be seduced into a worse. **1711** SWIFT *Jrnl. To Stella* 23 Nov., Leigh .. gives a terrible account of Sterne; he reckons he is seduced by some wench. **1775** BURKE *Let. Mrq. Rockingham* Corr. 1844 II. 41 We have been seduced, by various false representations .. into a war. **1825** SCOTT *Betrothed* xxx, He seduced my simplicity to let him into the castle. **1875** JOWETT *Plato* (ed. 2) III. 92 He is seduced into a life of pleasure.

b. of things, conditions, circumstances.

1526 *Pilgr. Perf.* (W. de W. 1531) 21, & neyther declyneth on the ryght hande, seduced by ony prosperite or worldly delyte: ne on yᵉ lefte hande. **1560** DAUS tr. *Sleidane's Comm.* 76 b, Three, whome povertie, hatred, and hope of better fortune, had seduced. **1599** SHAKS. *Hen. V*, II. ii. 155 For me, the Gold of France did not seduce. **1665** BOYLE *Occas. Refl.* IV. xvii. 109 My natural Curiosity seduc'd me to spend some time in Ranging about the places near the River-side. **1671** J. WEBSTER *Metallogr.* iv. 82 Being seduced by the similitudes taken partly from artificial and manual operations. **1750** JOHNSON *Rambler* No. 34 ¶14 Anthea having wondered what could seduce her to stay so long was eager to set out. **1774** WARTON *Hist. Eng. Poetry* Diss. ii. 85, I am imperceptibly seduced into later periods, or rather am deviating from my subject. **1789** JEFFERSON *Writ.* (1859) III. 124 Could any circumstances seduce me to overlook the disproportion between its duties and my talents. **1826** LAMB *Elia* Ser. II. *Genteel Style in Writing*, On one occasion his wit, which was mostly subordinate to nature and tenderness, has seduced him into a string of felicitous antitheses. **1856** GRINDON *Life* xii. (1875) 151 The embarrassment which often seduces one to an insincere denial.

†**c.** *intr.* To practise seduction, use seductive measures. *Obs. rare*⁻¹.

1597 in *Spalding Club Misc.* (1841) I. 172 The Deuill .. apperit to the .., and than seducit with the, and assurit the, thow suld newir want.

3. *trans.* To induce (a woman) to surrender her chastity. Now said only of the man with whom the act of unchastity is committed (not, e.g., of a pander). Cf. DEBAUCH *v.* 2 b.

Now the prevailing sense. In early use often apprehended as a specific application of sense 1; in Eng. law the plaintiff in an action for seducing a virgin is the parent or master who is supposed to have been deprived of her services.

c **1560** A. SCOTT *Poems* (S.T.S.) iv. 18 The wysest scho may sone Sedusit be and schent. **1601** SHAKS. *All's Well* III. v. 22 Many a maide hath beene seduced by them. **1776** GIBBON *Decl. & F.* xi. I. 355 One of the soldiers had seduced the wife of his host. **1818** SCOTT *Hrt. Midl.* xxii, She was seduced under promise of marriage. **1879** FROUDE *Cæsar* xii. 151 His friend had taken advantage of his absence to seduce his wife.

4. To decoy (*from* or *to* a place), to lead astray (*into*). *Obs.* exc. with notion of sense 2.

a **1668** DAVENANT *Siege* III. i, That employment which seduced me hither. **1679–88** *Secr. Serv. Money Chas. & Jas.* (Camden) 142 In prosecuting Wᵐ Havyland and Abraham Bailey, for seducing, forceing, and transporting his son to Virginia. **1704** SWIFT *Mech. Operat. Spir.* Misc. (1711) 310 That Philosopher, who while his Thoughts and Eyes were fix'd upon the Constellations, found himself seduc'd by his lower Parts into a Ditch. **1745** *Life Bampfylde-Moore Carew* 45 The peculiar Art which Bampfylde had of stealing, or rather seducing, Dogs. **1771** *Ann. Reg.* 78 Mrs. Leggatt had been seduced by her husband, under pretence of taking an airing to Kingston, to the prisoner's house. **1856** KANE *Arct. Expl.* II. xxvi. 259 The rascal, after seducing us a mile and a half out of our way, escaped our guns. **1858** HAWTHORNE *Fr. & It. Note-bks.* I. 229 Interminable staircases which seduce us upwards to no successful result.

†**5.** To win by charm or attractiveness. *Obs. rare.* [? a Gallicism; cf. SEDUCING *ppl. a.*]

1748 CHESTERF. *Lett.* I. cxxxv. 363 That engaging manner, and those graces, which seduce and pre-possess people in your favour at first sight. **1891** T. HARDY *Tess* xiv, One reason why she seduces casual attention is that she never courts it.

seduced (sɪˈdjuːst), *ppl. a.* [f. SEDUCE *v.* + -ED.] In the senses of the verb.

1584 R. SCOT *Discov. Witchcr.* III. xix. 71 They themselues are poore seduced soules. **1610** B. RICH *Descr. Irel.* 87 The papistes of Ireland are (as in other places) of two kinds, the seducers, and the Seduced. **1646** J. WHITAKER *Uzziah* 9 Take heed of a seduced conscience. **1662** *Irish Act 14 & 15 Chas. II*, c. 2 Preamble, To widen the breach between his said Majestie and his seduced subjects in England. **1768** STERNE *Sent. Journ.* (1778) I. 47 (*Remise Door*), Thou [Fancy] art a seduced, and a seducing slut. **1785** BURKE *Sp. Nabob of Arcot's Debts* Wks. (1842) I. 329 These seduced creditors .. may be just objects of compassion. **1842** W. C. TAYLOR *Anc. Hist.* App. VI. (ed. 3) 586 It is more difficult for us, with our feelings, to understand the seduced and returning Helen.

†**seˈducedly**, *adv. Obs.* [f. SEDUCED *ppl. a.* + -LY².] Through seduction or enticement to error.

1642 *Coll. Rights & Priv. Parl.* 6 Such who willfully, or seducedly rejected, .. those Lawes. **1642** T. CASE *Gods Rising* (1644) 9 When they .. sin Ignorantly, seducedly, then, Father forgive them; they know not what they do.

seducee (sɪdjuːˈsiː). *rare.* [f. SEDUCE *v.* + -EE.] One who is seduced.

1602 WARNER *Alb. Eng.* XIII. lxxix. 327 He and his Seducees sinn'd against our Queene and lawes. **1813** *Examiner* 1 Feb. 75/1 The seducer and the seducee seemed worthy of each other. **1819** *Blackw. Mag.* V. 710 You yourself, my fair Mrs. McWhirter, were the seducee, and the ensign the seducer. **1962** GREGOR & NICHOLAS *Moral & Story* iv. 120 The 'innocent' seducee dies a depraved alcoholic, while her seducer is redeemed.

seducement (sɪˈdjuːsmənt). *Obs.* or *rare.* [f. SEDUCE *v.* + -MENT.]

1. The action of seducing.

1586 A. DAY *Eng. Secretary* I. (1625) 32 Persuasion to mischiefe and seducement from the good. **1602** FULBECKE *Pandects* 72 Some Merchants may sowe bad seede, euen the seede of seducement of the Princes lieges. **1642** J. M. *Argt. conc. Militia* 15 Upon the advice and seducement of evill Counsellors. **1646** J. TEMPLE *Irish Rebellion* 54 A multitude .. by the wicked seducement of the first Conspirators had been drawn on to dispoile their English neighbours. **1709** STANHOPE *Paraphr.* IV. 268 In all Seducement the Tempter plays our own Artillery upon us. **1751** HURD *Hor. Ep. ad August.* 19 What contributed to this prostitution of the comic muse, was the seducement of that corruptress of all virtue, the love of money. **1785** T. POTTER *Moralist* II. 2, I will stoutly withstand the seducement of Epicurean companions.

2. Something which seduces or serves as a means of seduction; an insidious temptation.

1644 MILTON *Educ.* 4 Ere any flattering seducement, or vain principle seise them wandering. **1659** *Gentl. Calling* 418 To do this amidst all the seducements of wealth. **1789** MRS. PIOZZI *Journ. France* I. 220 The sweet seducements of a place so pleasing. **1817** JAS. MILL *Brit. India* I. III. iv. 534 The seducements of luxury and ease.

3. The fact or condition of being seduced.

1605 BACON *Adv. Learn.* I. ii. §4 Those particular seducements or indispositions of the minde for policie and gouernement, which learning is pretended to insinuate. *Ibid.* II. xiii. §3. **1642** J. WINTHROP *Hist. New-Eng.* (1826) II. 62 He made a very full and free acknowledgment of his errour and seducement. **1658** T. WALL *Charact. Enemies Ch.* 45 They are roaring Bulls: with what strained throats do they stund the giddy multitude into wonder and seducement? **1690** tr. *Five Lett. Inspiration* 191 The Apostle foretels their Seducement should not long continue.

seducer (sɪˈdjuːsə(r)). Also 6 *Sc.* seducear. [f. SEDUCE *v.* + -ER¹.] One who or something which seduces.

1. One who tempts or persuades (another) to desert his allegiance or service. Now *rare* or *Obs.*

a **1548** HALL *Chron., Hen. IV*, 23 He received a finall reward mete for suche a rebell and sedicious seducer. **1769** BLACKSTONE *Comm.* IV. 160 By statute 23 Geo. II. c. 13. the seducers incur .. a forfeiture of 500*l.* for each artificer contracted with to be sent abroad. **1794** S. WILLIAMS *Hist. Vermont* 236 The spirit of defection, notwithstanding all the arts .. of the seducers, was by no means general.

2. One who or that which entices (a person) into error or wrong-doing.

1545 BRINKLOW *Lament.* 110 Ye blynde guydes and seducers of the people. **1568** GRAFTON *Chron.* II. 352 These seducers, which were about the king, thought they might haue good occasion to put the Duke of Gloucester .. to death. **1611** BIBLE *2 Tim.* iii. 13 Euill men and seducers [Gr. γόητες, *Revised Vers.* impostors]. **1677** DRYDEN *State Innoc.* IV. ii. 33 He, whose firm faith no reason could remove, Will melt before that soft seducer, love. **1848** THACKERAY *Van. Fair* xix, [He] was perverted by Rawdon .., made helplessly tipsy by this abominable seducer and perverter of youth. **1870** THORNBURY *Tour rd. Eng.* I. vii. 153 The mob .. proclaimed him .. a seducer of the King.

3. †**a.** One who tempts (a female child) to leave her parents for marriage or otherwise. *Obs.*

A contextual use of sense 1. Cf. SEDUCTION 3 a.

1769 BLACKSTONE *Comm.* IV. 210 As these stolen marriages, under the age of sixteen, were usually upon mercenary views, this act [4 & 5 Ph. & Mar. c. 8], besides punishing the seducer, wisely removed the temptation.

b. One who seduces a woman. (See SEDUCE *v.* 3.)

1601 SHAKS. *All's Well* V. iii. 146 Grant it me, O King, .. otherwise a seducer flourishes, and a poore Maid is vndone. **1624** FLETCHER *Rule a Wife* II. i, There was no wisdom in't, to bid an Artist, An old seducer to a femal banquet. **1785** PALEY *Mor. Philos.* III. III. iii. 253 *note*, The law has provided no punishment [for seduction] .. beyond a pecuniary satisfaction .. [obtained] by the father's bringing his action against the seducer, for the loss of his daughter's service, during her pregnancy and nurturing. **1818** SCOTT *Hrt. Midl.* x, To all questions concerning the name or rank of her seducer, .. Effie remained mute. **1874** MAHAFFY *Soc. Life Greece* iv. 117 Nay, the peerless beauty Helen excites mere vulgar passion in her seducer.

seducible (sɪˈdjuːsɪb(ə)l), **seduceable** (sɪˈdjuːsəb(ə)l), *a.* [f. SEDUCE *v.* + -IBLE and -ABLE.]

1. Capable of being seduced or led astray.

α. **1629** H. BURTON *Truth's Tri.* 371 Dis-wont thy selfe with this seducible sense. **1646** HAMMOND *Tracts* 59 This easie prostitute seducible sinner. **1782** J. BROWN *Compend. View Nat. & Rev. Relig.* III. i. (1796) 198 It consisted in his being seducible to evil, though he was inclined only to good. **1858** CARLYLE *Fredk. Gt.* x. ii. (1872) III. 231 Friedrich proves little seducible; shows himself laudably indifferent.

β. **1613–18** DANIEL *Coll. Hist. Eng.* (1626) 133 It was a thing vnworthy .. to permit a King, who was so lightly seduceable .. that he should extort so many pretences. **1646** SIR T. BROWNE *Pseud. Ep.* VII. xix. 385 The vicious examples of Ages past, poison the curiosity of these present, affording a hint of sinne unto seduceable spirits.

2. Capable of being won over or attracted.

1815 L. HUNT *Notes Feast Poets* 53 The flowing versification of Fairfax has even drawn some writers into a love of him, who in other respects were not very seducible by the higher species of poetry.

seducing (sɪˈdjuːsɪŋ), *vbl. sb.* [f. SEDUCE *v.* + -ING¹.] The action of the verb.

1561 DAUS tr. *Bullinger on Apoc.* (1573) 8 They flye the seducyng of Antichrist, and abyde in the fayth of Christ. **1651** HOBBES *Leviath.* II. xxii. 122 This is a .. Conspiracy unlawfull, as being a fraudulent seducing of the Assembly. **1721** STRYPE *Eccl. Mem.* I. I. xxvii. 192 They made him [the Pope] a kind of God; to the seducing of the Subject, and bringing the People into Error.

seducing (sɪˈdjuːsɪŋ), *ppl. a.* [f. SEDUCE *v.* + -ING².] That seduces.

1. Tempting to evil.

1575 H. N[ICLAS] *First Exhort.* xvi. §14 Therfore cannot the man .. occupie or use any maner of Freedoms that are falser, wickeder, absurder, seducinger, arroganter nor horribler against God .. then this, &c. **1608** *Convers. Noble Lady of Fraunce* Ded., To those misled Ladies .. of England, whome Seducing Seminaries .. haue too much preuailed withall. **1611** BIBLE *1 Tim.* iv. 1 Giuing heed to seducing spirits [Gr. πνεύμασι πλάνοις]. **1638** E. NORICE *New Gospel* 1 Such a seducing Impostor and cunning Deceiver. **1642** MILTON *Apol. Smect.* Wks. 1851 III. 257 They may .. be mov'd with detestation of their seducing malice. **1701** G. STANHOPE *Augustine's Medit.* II. iv. 122 Impudently prostituting thyself to the lust of seducing strangers. **1831** SCOTT *Ct. Robt.* xxvii, Regarding the imperfect recollection he had .. as the mere suggestion of a deluded imagination, if not actually presented by some seducing spirit.

b. (See quot.)

1780 BENTHAM *Princ. Legisl.* xi. §29 When the act which a motive prompts a man to engage in is of a mischievous nature it may for distinction's sake be termed a seducing or corrupting motive.

2. Alluring, attractive, 'bewitching'. Cf. F. *séduisant.* Now *rare.*

1748 CHESTERF. *Lett.* II. 239 Take great care that the first impressions you give of yourself may be not only favourable, but pleasing, engaging, nay—seducing. **1794** SULLIVAN *View Nat.* I. 9, I shall leave to a future opportunity the consideration of this seducing but erroneous principle. **1818** SCOTT *Rob Roy* ix, Well, it is very seducing to be pitied, after all.

seducingly (sɪˈdjuːsɪŋlɪ), *adv.* [f. SEDUCING *ppl. a.* + -LY².] In a seducing or seductive manner; enticingly, seductively.

1592 CONSTABLE *Diana* VIII. ii. F 4 b, Lesse by some hope seducingly deluded, such thoughts aspyre to fortunate euent. **1602** WARNER *Alb. Eng.* IX. li. 232 Seducingly insisting on performance of their vow. **1866** J. A. SYMONDS *Life* (1895) I. 350 In no other place [than Monaco] could this riotous daughter of hell have set her throne so seducingly.

seducioun, -cious: see SEDITION, SEDITIOUS.

†**seˈducive**, *a. Obs.* [f. SEDUCE *v.* + -IVE.]

1. ? Caused by misleading influences.

1602 WARNER *Alb. Eng.* Epit. 386 King Richard the second .. by his seduciue misgouernment (for his borne-Nature, noble, and debonaire, was too much abused by yong Councell and Parasites) become disgracious with his Princes and People.

2. That leads to error.

1774 *Phil. Trans.* LXV. 28 Analogy, too often seducive in similar matters, leads us to conclude the same of other vulcanic mountains in general.

†**seˈduct**, *v. Obs. rare.* [f. L. *sēduct-*, ppl. stem of *sēdūcĕre.*] *trans.* To seduce.

1490 CAXTON *Eneydos* xxvii. 97 The false & euyl man eneas, that tratoursly hath mocked me, & fraudulently seducted.

Hence †**seˈducted** *ppl. a.*

1773 J. ROSS *Fratricide* v. 449 (MS.), Seducted Eve with her first guilty smile Returning.

seduction (sɪˈdʌkʃən). Also 6 seduccion, -yon. [a. F. *séduction*, ad. L. *sēductiōn-em*, n. of action f. *sēdūcĕre* to SEDUCE. Cf. Sp. *seduccion*, Pg. *seducção*, It. *seduzione.*]

1. The action or an act of seducing (a person) to err in conduct or belief; allurement (*to* some course of action).

1526 *Pilgr. Perf.* (W. de W. 1531) 272 b, Some fooles .. by the seduccyon or illusyon of the ennemy be not ashamed to affirme .. that [etc.]. **1528** ROY *Rede me* (Arb.) 89 Wherfore by their seduccion They haue bene the destruccion Of all true christen liberte. **1536** *St. Papers Hen. VIII*, II. 370 Which Actis bee yit rejectid in the Comon House by the seducyon of certain rynge leaders or belwedders. *Ibid.* 371 And all the styckyng [of the act] is in the Comon House, by seducyon of certain prescrybyd. **1750** JOHNSON *Rambler* No. 171 ¶1 Nothing would more powerfully preserve youth from irregularity or guard inexperience from seduction. **1776** GIBBON *Decl. & F.* ix. I. 239 Every art of seduction was used with dignity, to conciliate those nations. **1796** BURKE *Regic. Peace* Wks. IX. 117 There is no invention of seduction .. that has not been increased; brothels, gaming-houses, every thing. **1848** THACKERAY *Van. Fair* xix, To whom she announced the dreadful intelligence of Captain Rawdon's seduction by Miss Sharp. **1848** MRS. JAMESON *Sacr. & Leg. Art* (1850) 326 Having tried tortures in vain, he determined to try seduction. **1873** HAMERTON *Intell. Life* II. iv. 72 An ambitious man will govern himself .. and withstand the seductions of his senses.

†**b.** The condition of being led astray.

1533 FRITH *Wks.* (1572) 3/1 To Rdr., Knowledge your ignoraunce and seduction, and returne gladly into the right way. **1633** BP. HALL *Hard Texts, N.T.* 112 This ignorant multitude that hath no insight into the Law of God lies open to miserable seduction, and error, and is therein accursed. **1653** HAMMOND *Annot. N.T.* Jude v. 11 (1659) 851/2 For this was the πλάνη τοῦ Βαλαάμ, the seduction into which Balaam brought the Israelites.

2. The persuading (of a subject, soldier, etc.) to desert his allegiance or service.
*a*1700 EVELYN *Diary* 15 July 1685, Monmouth.. acknowledged his seduction by Ferguson the Scot.
3. †a. The action of tempting (a female child) to leave her parents for marriage or otherwise. (Cf. SEDUCER 3 a.) *Obs.*
1769 BLACKSTONE *Comm.* IV. Index, Seduction of women-children.
b. The action of inducing (a woman) to surrender her chastity. (See SEDUCE *v.* 3.)
1785 PALEY *Mor. Philos.* III. III. iii. 250 Seduction is seldom accomplished without fraud; and the fraud is by so much more criminal than other frauds, as injury effected by it is greater. 1794 COLERIDGE *Relig. Musings* 282 O pale-eyed form, The victim of seduction. 1817 W. SELWYN *Law Nisi Prius* (ed. 4) II. 1040 *note*, If the injury of seduction is accompanied with an illegal entry of the house of the parent. 1831 MACKINTOSH *Hist. Eng.* II. 57 Promises of marriage may have been employed as means of seduction. 1886 *Encycl. Brit.* XXI. 621 The action for seduction of an unmarried woman in England stands in a somewhat anomalous position. The theory of English law is that the woman herself has suffered no wrong; the wrong has been suffered by the parent or person *in loco parentis*, who must sue for the damage arising from the loss of service caused by the seduction of the woman.
4. Something which seduces; a cause of error; an allurement.
1554 T. WATSON *Two Serm. bef. Queen* B vij b, The true sense, which is only knowen bi the tradition and consent of the catholike church: so that the one without the other is not a direction, but a seduction, to a symple man. 1817 J. SCOTT *Paris Revisit.* (ed. 4) 255 The Scotchmen, having but small seduction to return to their beds, became quite inclined to talk. 1838 PRESCOTT *Ferd. & Is.* (1846) I. iii. 167 In this abode of pleasure, surrounded by all the seductions most dazzling to youth. 1844 LEVER *T. Burke* vi, Amid every temptation and every seduction.
5. Seductiveness, alluring quality. *rare*⁻¹.
1882 STEVENSON *New Arab. Nts.* (1884) 1 The Prince.. gained the affection of all classes by the seduction of his manner.

seductionist (sɪˈdʌkʃənɪst). [f. SEDUCTION + -IST.] One who practises seduction; one who practises or upholds corruption in public affairs.
1817 BENTHAM *Parl. Reform* Introd. 143 Bribe-offering, bribe-giving, seducer or seductionist, corruptor or corruptionist. 1818 —— *Parl. Reform Catech.* 61 The seductionist, by whose hand.. the instrument of seduction most extensively and conspicuously employed, is that mostly known by the name of bribery, or corruption. 1884 *B'ham Wkly. Post* 15 Nov. 4/6 Cleveland [was depicted] as an 'aristocratic seductionist'.

seductious (sɪˈdʌkʃəs), *a.* *rare*⁻¹. [f. SEDUCTION + -OUS.] Seductive, alluring.
1883 *Harper's Mag.* July 180/1 Dr. Garth.. found conviviality more seductious than duty exacting.

seductive (sɪˈdʌktɪv), *a.* [f. L. type *seductīv-us*, f. *sēduct-*, ppl. stem of *sēdūcĕre*: see SEDUCE and -IVE.]
†1. Tending to seduce or lead astray; that leads to error. *Obs.*
1782 J. BROWN *Compend. View Nat. Rev. Relig.* IV. i. (1796) 249 If Christ be not the Most High God, the language of scripture is most obscure, seductive, impious, and absurd.
2. Alluring, enticing, winning.
176. LANGHORNE *Fables of Flora* i. *Sun-flower & Ivy* x, Go, splendid sycophant! no more Display thy soft seductive arts! 1809–10 COLERIDGE *Friend* (1865) 19 One of the most seductive arguments of infidelity.., asserting the lawfulness of deceit for a good purpose. 1856 W. A. BUTLER *Serm.* Ser. II. xxiv. 348 Every seductive companion who would blind your eyes to this awful fact, is but the active minister of Satan. 1824 DIBDIN *Libr. Comp.* 745 The seductive charms of poetry. 1871 NAPHEYS *Prev. & Cure Dis.* I. iii. 114 The seductive pleasures of opium-eating. 1878 LECKY *Eng. in 18th C.* II. vii. 430 His manners in private life were eminently seductive and insinuating. 1908 *Outlook* 26 Sept. 395/2 It owes something of its beauty to the seductive setting of an autumn morning.

seductively (sɪˈdʌktɪvlɪ), *adv.* [f. SEDUCTIVE *a.* + -LY².] In a seductive manner, enticingly.
1843 MARTINEAU *Chr. Life* (1867) 7 Self and the flesh seductively whisper [etc.]. 1850 MRS. CARLYLE *Lett.* II. 123 To have her kitchen seductively clean for the stranger. 1860 READE *Cloister & H.* lxxix, She.. questioned and cross-questioned him severely and seductively by turns. 1893 SALTUS *Madame Sapphire* 79 Mrs. Carol nodded and smiled seductively.

seductiveness (sɪˈdʌktɪvnɪs). [f. SEDUCTIVE *a.* + -NESS.] Seductive quality.
1816 J. SCOTT *Vis. Paris* 122 The profusion and seductiveness of the *Magazines des Gourmands.* 1822 LAMB *Elia* Ser. I. *Praise Chimney-Sw.*, I am by theory obdurate to the seductiveness of what are called a fine set of teeth. 1879 FROUDE *Cæsar* xii. 152 The same doubt extends to the other supposed victims of Cæsar's seductiveness. 1894 W. B. CARPENTER *Son of Man* i. 28 The world with its seductiveness.. may play the part of Herodias in our lot.

†**se'ductor.** *Obs.* Also 5–6 seductour. [a. OF. *seducteur*, ad. L. *sēductor*, agent-noun f. *sēdūcĕre*: see SEDUCE and -OR.] One who seduces, a misleader, seducer.
In the 15–16th c. frequently in the set phrase ***seductor and deceiver of the people***.
1490 CAXTON *Eneydos* xvi. 60 The whiche seductor of ladies [*sc.* the false Eneas], kepeth himself in maner as a woman,..wyth his longe heres that he maketh to be enoynted & kemed. *Ibid.* 61. 1491 —— *Vitas Patr.* (W. de W. 1495) I. xix. 22 One namyd Phylemon, whyche was moche amyable & debonayr to the peple, & callyd hymself seductour & deseyvour of the peple. 1523 [COVERDALE] *Old God & New* (1534) D ij, Anon he gat certeyn of the Iuwes, whiche did repyne & speake agaynst the doctryne of yᵉ Apostels accusing them to be seductours & deceyuers. 1541 BECON *News out of Heaven* F vij, For they shall reporte him to be.. a seductour and deceyuer of the people. 1588 A. KING tr. *Canisius' Catech.* 111 Yat we diligentlie flie from vthers [*sc.* than those lawfully ordained] as fra our enimies and contagious seductors. 1631 MASSINGER *Believe as You List* II. ii, Since the assurance from one of my place, qualitie, and rancke, is not sufficient with you to suppresse this bold seductor.

seductress (sɪˈdʌktrɪs). [fem. of SEDUCTOR.] A female seducer.
1803 MARY CHARLTON *Wife & Mistress* III. 19 He is accompanied by an army of constables to apprehend the seductress of his nephew. 1891 MEREDITH *One of our Conq.* I. x, They were seductresses for inducing him to drink wine.

†**sedue**, *v. Obs. rare*⁻¹. [a. OF. *seduire*: see SEDUCE *v.*] *trans.* = SEDUCE *v.*
*c*1485 *Digby Myst.* III. 716 O lux vera, gravnt vs ȝower lucense, that with þe spryte of errour I nat seduet be!

sedule, obs. form of SCHEDULE.

sedulity (sɪˈdjuːlɪtɪ). [ad. L. *sēdulitās*, n. of quality f. *sēdul-us* SEDULOUS: see -ITY. Cf. F. *sédulité* (Cotgr.), It. *sedulità*.] The quality of being sedulous; painstaking attention to duty, diligent application, industry.
1542 BECON *Pathw. Prayer* xxxiii. O j b, He deserued this thyng not so much for familiarte & acquayntance sake as for sedulite & careful diligence. 1576 FLEMING *Panopl. Epist.* 175 Their familiaritie is to be sought after with sedulitie and earnestnesse. 1649 JER. TAYLOR *Gt. Exemp.* xiv. §26 He.. tells the offices and sedulity of the clergy. 1659 EVELYN *Chrysostom* Ded. in *Misc. Writ.* (1805) 107, I stood amazed at his sedulity and memory. 1720 J. JOHNSON *Eccl. Laws.* tr. *Const. Othobon* §32 The unquenchable thirst of Ambition chuses neither Mary's better part, nor the sedulity of Martha in ministring. *a*1734 NORTH *Life Ld. Kpr. Guildford* 252 Some of our barbarous Writers call this awaking of the King's Genius to a Sedulity in his Affairs a growing cruel. 1848 THACKERAY *Van. Fair* lvi, It became him to prepare, by sedulity and docility in youth, for the lofty duties [etc.]. 1878 GLADSTONE *Prim. Homer* 44 Even German sedulity has until the present time shrunk from this task.
†b. *pl.* Assiduities, attentions. *Obs.*
1694 tr. *Milton's Lett. St.* 31 That your sedulities in the Reception of our Agent were so cordial and so egregious, we both gladly understand [etc.]. 1696 *Monthly Merc.* VII. 79 On the one side there are never any tender Refusals.. no Submissions, nor Sedulities to please on the other. 1707 tr. *C'tess D'Aulnoy's Wks.* (1715) 10 He thought me unworthy of his Sedulities.

sedull, obs. form of SCHEDULE.

sedulous (ˈsɛdjʊləs), *a.* Also 6 sedulious. [f. L. *sēdulus* careful + -OUS.
The L. word appears to have been evolved from the adv. *sēdulō* sincerely, honestly (hence diligently, assiduously), repr. OLatin *sē dolō* without guile (see SE- *prefix*).]
1. Of persons or agents: Diligent, active, constant in application to the matter in hand; assiduous, persistent.
1593 NASHE *Christ's T.* 24 b, I would gyue thee leaue to hate me, so thy hate woulde make thee industrious & sedulous to harken out & enquire whence I am. 1629 B. JONSON *New Inn* II. ii, There is a chare-woman.. a poore silly foole, But an impertinent, and sedulous one, As euer was. 1667 MILTON *P.L.* IX. 27 Since first this Subject for Heroic Song Pleas'd me long choosing, and beginning late Not sedulous by nature to indite Warrs. *c*1709 PRIOR *1st Hymn Callim.* 56 The sedulous Bee Distill'd her Honey on Thy purple Lips. 1791 COWPER *Iliad* III. 311 They sedulous obey'd. 1836 THIRLWALL *Greece* xxiv. III. 329 He was sedulous in paying court to the people. 1867 PARKMAN *Jesuits N. Amer.* iii. (1875) 21 The.. Algonquins.. of whose language he had been so sedulous a student. 1887 STEVENSON *Mem. & Portraits* iv. 59, I have thus played the sedulous ape to Hazlitt, to Lamb, to Wordsworth [etc.].
2. Of actions: Constant, persistent.
1540 in *Lett. Suppress. Monasteries* (Camden) 281 Thankes for.. your sedulious paynes and labours taken aboute the survey off Cayneham. *a*1631 DONNE *Serm.* lxi. (1640) 612 Admit that preparation.. by an assiduous and a sedulous hearing. 1661 BOYLE *Style of Script.* (1675) 48 That dying Husband-man, who by telling his Sons of a hidden Mass of Wealth he had buried in a nameless place of his Vineyard, occasioned their so sedulous Delving all the Ground, and turning up the Earth about the Roots of the Vines, that they found indeed a Treasure. *a*1778 C. DARWIN *Experiments* (1780) 105 A gentleman of temperate life and sedulous application to business. 1833–48 H. COLERIDGE *North. Worthies* (1852) I. 22 He paid sedulous attention to the interests of his borough. 1859 SMILES *Self Help* iv. (1860) 71 Sedulous attention and painstaking industry always mark the true worker. 1881 WESTCOTT & HORT *Grk. N.T.* Introd. §10 By sedulous cultivation,.. a high standard of immunity from even clerical errors has at times been attained.

sedulously (ˈsɛdjʊləslɪ), *adv.* [-LY².] Diligently, attentively.
1593 NASHE *Unfort. Trav.* (1594) E 2, Surely you would haue sayd they had bin brought vp in hogs academie to learne to eate acornes, if you had seene how sedulously they fell to them. 1634 SIR T. HERBERT *Trav.* 190 The place.. is ..sedulously looked vnto. 1693 OWEN *Holy Spirit* 251 Either not sedulously and duely to Exercise their Ministerial Gifts. 1746 HERVEY *Medit.* (1818) 35 Where find so discreet a counsellor, so improving an example, and a guardian so sedulously attentive to the interests of herself and her children? 1778 MISS BURNEY *Evelina* xxxi. (1791) II. 189 You sedulously avoid my conversation. 1821 SCOTT *Kenilw.* x, His education.. had been too sedulously improved by subsequent study to give way to any imaginary terrors. 1861 THACKERAY *Four Georges* i. (1862) 17 A great brick church which he sedulously frequented. 1885 *Law Times* LXXVIII. 280/1 Any kind of arrangement with creditors is sedulously hedged around.

sedulousness (ˈsɛdjʊləsnɪs). [-NESS.] Care, diligent attention.
1622 FENNER in *Fortescue Papers* (Camden) 183 But have respect to God himselfe by all sedulousnesse in the charge. 1661 BOYLE *Style of Script.* (1675) 99 By their sedulousness and their Erudition they discover'd Difficulties in the Bible that our Quærists could never have dream'd of. 1826 DISRAELI *Viv. Grey* II. xiv, Sir Christopher for half a century has supported in the Senate with equal sedulousness and silence, the constitution and the corn laws. 1884 *Spectator* 4 Oct. 1320/1 Conflicting claims and aims, mustering their forces with swift but sure subtlety and sedulousness for a final decisive combat.

‖**sedum** (ˈsiːdəm). Also 5 cedum. [L. *sedum* houseleek.] †a. A name for certain crassulaceous plants, houseleek, stonecrop, orpine, etc. *Obs.* b. *Bot.* A genus of plants (N.O. *Crassulaceæ*), the British species of which are known as stonecrop.
*c*1440 *Pallad. on Husb.* x. 47 Let mynge Iuce of cedum smal ygrounde With water. 1548 TURNER *Names Herbes* (E.D.S.) 72 Sedum.. the fyrste kynde.. is called in englishe Housleke or syngrene... The seconde kynde is called.. thryft or stoncroppe... The thyrd kinde is called.. Mouse tayle or litle stoncroppe. 1664 EVELYN *Kal. Hort., May* (1679) 16 Syringa's, Sedums, Tulips. 1707 MORTIMER *Husb.* (1721) II. 389 You must never water Aloes or Sedums during the whole Winter. 1760 LEE *Introd. Bot.* App. 326 Sedum, Pyramidal, *Saxifraga*. 1850 MISS PRATT *Comm. Things of Sea-side* i. 48 Several of the Sedums.. were formerly used as medicine. 1882 *Garden* 1 Apr. 213/2 The beautiful yellow mossy Sedum. 1894 FENN *In Alpine Valley* III. 181 He threw himself down upon some bed of sedums, where quite a couch was formed of the tiny rosettes.

sedyl, obs. form of SCHEDULE.

sedyr, obs. form of CEDAR, CIDER.

see (siː), *sb.*¹ Forms: 3–4 ce, 3–5 cee, sce, 3–6 se, 4–5 sey, 6–7 sea, 4– see. [a. OF. *sé*, *sed*, a variant (influenced by the Latin) of *sié*, *sied*:—popular L. **sēdem*, altered form (after *sedēre* to sit) of classical L. *sēdem* (*sēdēs*) a seat.]
†1. A seat, place of sitting.
a. *gen.* (Only in early poetical use.) *Obs.*
*c*1374 CHAUCER *Troylus* IV. 1023 For if þer sit a man yond on a see Than by necessite byhoueth it. *c*1384 —— *H. Fame* III. 120 And smale harpers with her glees Saten vnder hym in sees. *a*1400 *Pistill of Susan* 86 (MS. I.), þe schene briddes in þe schawe þei schappyn in schrowde, On fikes and firres þei fangen her sees, In faye. 1412–20 LYDG. *Chron. Troy* I. 1820 To whom hir fader bad to take hir see Be-syde Iason. *c*1450 LOVELICH *Grail* l. 339 Thilke same se That I inne sat be presomptweste It is that same sege.. Where as God to his disciples made his Sene.
b. A seat of dignity or authority; esp. a royal seat, throne. Hence the rank or position symbolized by a throne. *Obs.*
*c*1290 *Beket* 779 in *S. Eng. Leg.* 129 þe king sat an hei in is sce and a-coupede him wel faste. *c*1306 *Song Exec. Sir S. Fraser* in *Pol. Songs* (Camden) 215 Tho he wes set in see Lutel god couthe he kyne-riche to ȝeme. 1340 HAMPOLE *Pr. Consc.* 4220 And þar sal he [*sc.* Antichrist].. in myddes þe temple make his se. *c*1384 CHAUCER *H. Fame* III. 271 But al on hye, above a dees, Sit in a see imperiall,.. Y saugh, perpetually y-stalled,.. A femynyne creature. 1412–20 LYDG. *Chron. Troy* I. 629 Whan þe schene sonne.. had made in þe crabbis hede His mansioun, and his see ryal. 1489 CAXTON *Faytes of A.* III. ii. 171 A man ydone and hable to the see Imperyall. *a*1522 *World & Child* 22 Lo! here I sette semely in se! I commaunde you all obedyent be. 1590 SPENSER *F.Q.* III. vi. 2 Ioue laught on Venus from his soueraigne see.
c. *transf.* and *fig.* (One's) place of abode; esp. the dwelling-place of a monarch, a god, or the like. *Obs.*
13.. *Cursor M.* 2482 (Gött.) Vnder þe fote of mount mambre þar he ches to sett his se. *c*1430 LYDG. *Min. Poems* (Percy Soc.) 122 Fortune shewithe ay, by chaungyng hir see, How this world is a thurghefare ful of woo. *c*1460 *Wisdom* 132 in *Macro Plays* 40 First, bapteme.. reformyt þe sowll,.. Ande makyt yt.. Crystis own specyall, Hys restynge place, hys plesant see. 1501 DOUGLAS *Pal. Hon.* Prol. 19 The fragrant flouris blomand in thair seis, Ouirspred the leuis of natures tapestries. 1513 —— *Æneis* I. i. 28 Hir native land for it postponit sche Callit Samo; in Cartage set hir se. 1596 SPENSER *F.Q.* IV. x. 30 Nor that [Temple], which that wise King of Iurie framed.. to be th' Almighties see.
2. Ecclesiastical uses.
a. The seat, chair, or throne of a bishop in his church; = CATHEDRA 1. Now only *arch.*
1297 R. GLOUC. (Rolls) 4967 þere sein birin bissop was þe uerste þat was ywis Vor þe se was þere of bissop þo þat at lincolne nou is. *c*1450 *St. Cuthbert* (Surtees) 6665 þe whilk suld haue a bischope se. 1525 LD. BERNERS *Froiss.* II. ccxxxiii. 723 He.. entred into the Consystory, and so came to the pope whyle he sate styll in his see. 1724 *De Foe's Tour Gt. Brit.* I. i. 95 The Cathedral of this City [of Norwich].. is not antient, the Bishop's See having been first at Thetford; from whence it was not translated hither till the Twelfth Century. 1844 LINGARD *Anglo-Sax. Ch.* (1858) I. ii. 76 The archiepiscopal see should never after be fixed in the minster of Litchfield. 1849 ROCK *Ch. of Fathers* II. vi. 255 No church that does not really hold the 'cathedra' or see,

from which a bishop takes his title, can be a cathedral. **1884** E. A. Freeman in *Times* 16 Jan. 8/2 The see of the Bishop of Somerset, his seat—in old English phrase his bishopstool or bishopsettle—was moved more than once between the 11th century and the 13th.

b. The office or position indicated by sitting in a particular episcopal chair; the position of being bishop of a particular diocese.

c **1450** *Bidding Prayer* iii. in *Lay Folks Mass-bk.* 68 Also we sall pray specially for our holy fader þe archbyschop of þis See. **1595** Shaks. *John* III. i. 144 Why thou..dost..force perforce Keepe Stephen Langton chosen Archbishop Of Canterbury from that holy Sea. **1678** Walton *Life of Sanderson* 3 Thomas Rotherham, sometime Archbishop of that Sea. **1680** Godolphin *Repert. Canon.* (ed. 2) 14 The Diocess belonging to the See of York contains [etc.]. **1704** Nelson *Fest. & Fasts* II. iii. (1739) 477 The Office of a Bishop..contains peculiarly the Power of Consecrating Bishops to succeed them in vacant Sees. **1819** Shelley *Cenci* I. ii. 66, I know the Pope Will ne'er absolve me from my priestly vow But by absolving me from the revenue Of many a wealthy see. **1869** *Act 32 & 33 Vict.* c. 111 §5 The bishop shall retain all the temporalities of his see, except the patronage. **1874** Green *Short Hist.* vii. §3. 371 The vacant sees were filled for the med. Latin part with learned and able men.

c. *spec.* Chiefly with defining word, ***the Apostolic, Holy, Papal, Roman See, the See of Rome*** (rarely † *the See*): the office or position of Pope; the Papacy; the authority or jurisdiction belonging to the Pope; occas. the Pope in his official capacity.

The designation *Apostolic See* (in its Latin form, *Sedes Apostolica*) was in patristic use applied more widely to any of the bishoprics founded by apostles; in med.Latin it occurs also (see Du Cange) in the general sense of 'cathedral'.

c **1330** R. Brunne *Chron. Wace* (Rolls) 14946 For he [seint Gregore] was ablest, next pope to be After hym þat held þo þe se. **1529** More *Supplic. Soulys* Wks. 296/2 Nowe if he say ..yt king John made England and Ireland tributary to the pope and the sea apostolike [etc.]. **1559** Abp. Heath in Strype *Ann. Ref.* (1709) I. App. vi. 7 When by the Vertue of this Acte of Supremacye, we must forsake and flee from the Sea of Rome. **1603** Shaks. *Meas. for M.* III. ii. 232, I am a brother Of gracious Order, late come from the Sea, In speciall businesse from his Holinesse. **1616** R. C. *Times' Whistle* (1871) 51 Others..Leave vs, and flie vnto the Sea of Rome. **1656** Earl Monm. tr. *Boccalini's Pol. Touchstone* (1674) 278 The Sea Apostolick was..contented to see the Mauritanian Kings driven out of Spain. **1765** Stonor in E. H. Burton *Life Challoner* (1909) II. 83 They were told that the Society ought to be particularly careful at this juncture not to disgust the Holy See, by being refractory to its orders. **1769** Robertson *Chas. V*, III. Wks. 1813 V. 354 The publishing it by their own authority was highly disrespectful to the Roman see. **1777** Watson *Philip II*, v. (1812) I. 180 Commanding the Catholics every where to have recourse, in all dubious cases, to the Apostolic See. **1788** Jefferson *Writ.* (1859) II. 454 A dispute has arisen between the Papal See and the King of Naples. **1840** Macaulay *Ess.*, *Von Ranke* ¶25 Pius the Fifth..upheld the authority of his see. **1844** Lingard *Anglo-Sax. Ch.* (1858) I. ii. 78 The protection of the Holy See. **1884** *Cath. Dict.* (1897) 93 The bishop speaks of himself as 'N., by the grace of God and of the Apostolic See, Bishop of N.'.

†**d.** The building in which a bishop's throne is placed, a cathedral. *Obs. rare.*

1480 Caxton *Descr. Brit.* 17 The chief moder chirch of alle Wales and the chief see [*Trevisa* chief sete]. *a* **1600** Hooker *Eccl. Pol.* VII. viii. §3 The Church where the Bishop is set with his Colledge of Presbyters about him, we call a Sea. **1665** G. Havers tr. *P. della Valle's Trav. E. Ind.* 78 And lastly, the See or Cathedral, which nevertheless is neither the fairest, nor the greatest Church of that City... The See of Goa at the time of my being there was not finish'd.

†**e.** A city in which the authority symbolized by the throne (of a bishop, etc.) is considered to reside. Cf. siege *sb.* 2. *Obs.*

1534 *Act 26 Hen. VIII*, c. 14 §1 The Townes of Thetforde [etc.] shalbe taken and accepted for Sees of Byshops Suffragans to be made in this Realme. **1673** Ray *Journ. Low C.* 331 Between the monuments..are the arms of the Cities subject to the Great Duke..all Episcopal Seas. **1680** H. More *Apocal. Apoc.* 65 Capernaum, that See as it were of that great Bishop of Souls Jesus Christ. **1756–7** tr. *Keysler's Trav.* (1760) II. 89 Aquapendente is an episcopal see.

†**f.** The territory under the jurisdiction of a bishop, a diocese. *Obs.*

1534 *Act 26 Hen. VIII*, c. 14 §4 No suche Suffragans.. shall..have..any jurisdiccion or Episcopal power..within their said Sees nor within any Dioces or place of this Realme ..but only suche..as [etc.]. *c* **1610** *Women Saints* 64 Archbishop Theodore then ruling the Sea of Canterburie.

fig. **1633** P. Fletcher *Purple Isl.* II. 14 The whole Isle, parted in three regiments, By three Metropolies is joyntly sway'd;..The lowest hath the worst, but largest See.

3. *attrib.* and *Comb.*: simple attributive, as †*see-church, -land* (in Ireland), *-property, -town*; (sense 2) *see-city*; **see-house**, †**-place**, the official residence of the occupant of a see.

c **1449** Pecock *Repr.* III. xiii. 359 The pope and his *see chirche in Rome. **1558** W. Forrest *Grisild the Second* (Roxb.) 59 After whiche great extreme purgation To Yorke (his See Church) dymytted he was. **1937** *Daily Tel.* 28 Aug. 13/3 On this day, very nearly 1,500 years ago, Augustine lay dying in his *see-city of Hippo. **1956** D. E. W. Harrison in D. L. Linton *Sheffield* 199 Meanwhile Sheffield became in 1914 the see-city of a diocese stretching to Goole on the Ouse. **1845** J. H. Newman *Ess. Developm.* (1878) 158 The *see-house at Antioch. **1888** *Ch. Times* 24 Aug. 725/1 The see-house at Bishop Auckland. **1732** Swift *Proposal to pay off Debt of Nation* Misc. (1735) V. 350 The Purchasers of the vacant *See Lands, are to come immediately into Possession of the See he hath left. **1835** Whately in *Life* (1866) I. 326 Bishoprics whose see-lands are..in other dioceses. **1553** *Respublica* III. v. 805 We lefte the best of them a thredebare bisshop:..The beste had but his *see place, that he might kepe home. **1847** Reeves *Eccl. Antiq. Down*, etc. 171 *note*, The half townland of Dundesert is still *see property. **1861** A. J. B. Hope *Eng. Cathedral* 105 It is, I trust, in the process of..being constituted the *see-town of the bishopric. **1895** Rashdall *Universities* II. 359 A city which was neither a capital nor a see-town.

see (siː), *sb.*[2] [f. see *v.*] In nonce-uses: **a.** ***to have a see***, to have a look (*at*); used as a colloq. replacement for look *sb.* (cf. also look-see). **b.** with cognate obj., ***I have seen my see***, I have seen what I wished to see. *rare* or *nonce-use*.

1868 'Holme Lee' *Basil Godfrey's Caprice* xxxiii, Let me have a see at the playbill. **1868** Browning *Ring & Bk.* II. 128 May I depart in peace, I have seen my see. **1927** J. Masefield *Midnight Folk* 251 The son took out a pocket telescope..and handed it to his father. 'Take a see for yourself, pop.' **1938** E. Williams *Corn is Green* I. i. 10 Ought to be 'ere by now, I'll 'ave a see.

see (siː), *v.* Forms and Inflexions: see below. [A Common Teut. str. vb.: OE. *séon* (*seah, sáwon* and *sǽᵹon, ᵹe-sewen*) = OFris. *sîa*, OS. *sehan*, MDu. *sîen* (Du. *zien*), MLG. *sên* (LG. *seen*), OHG. *sehan* (MHG., mod.G. *sehen*), ON. *séa* (Sw. and Da. *se*), *sía* (Fær. *siggja*), *siá* (Icel. *sjá*, Norw. *sjaa*), Goth. *saíhwan* (*sahw, sêhwum, saíhwans*):—OTeut. **sehw-*:—pre-Teut. **sequ-*.

Three distinct Indogermanic roots of the form **sequ-* are commonly recognized; some scholars (as Brugmann) refer the Teut. verb to the root of which an ablaut-variant appears in say *v.*[1]; others (as Kluge) to the root of L. *sequī* to follow; and others (as Fick) to that of L. *secāre* to cut; but each of these views involves a hypothetical sense-development which it is not easy to accept with confidence.]

A. Inflexional Forms.

1. *Infinitive* **see** (siː). Forms: 1 **séon, síon,** *Merc.* **séan, sían,** *Northumb.* **séa,** 2 **syen,** 2–3 **sien,** 2–5 **seo(n,** (2–3 **son,** 3 **so),** 3 **sean,** 3–4 **sei(e,** 3–5 **sen,** 3–6 **se,** 4 **suen, seeyȝen, sey, sy, si,** *Kent.* **zy, zi,** 4–5 **seye,** 4–6 **sene,** 4–6, (8) **seen,** 4 (*north.*), 6–7 (*Sc.*) **sie,** 5 **seene, seyn,** 5–6 **seyne,** (7 **sea),** 7, 9– *dial.* **zee,** 3– **see.** Also *Dative Infinitive* 1 **tó séonne, séanne, séenne,** 2–3 **to siene,** 3 **to seonne, to sene, to sende,** *Kent.* **to zyenne,** (7 **to seene).**

Beowulf 920 Eode scealc moniᵹ swiðhicᵹende to sele þam hean searowundor seon. *c* **950** *Lindisf. Gosp.* Mark x. 51 þætte ic ᵹesii *vel* mæᵹe sea. *c* **1175** *Pater Noster* 110 in *Lamb. Hom.* 61 And cristes wille bo us bitwon neb wið neb for him to son. *c* **1200** Ormin 2845 Her maȝȝ mann sen full opennliȝ þatt [etc.]. *c* **1275** Lay. 8172 One man..þat was þider icome for to se [*c* 1205 i-seon] þis cnihtes game. *a* **1310** in Wright *Lyric P.* xxxvi. 100 When we shule suen thy wounde blede. *c* **1350** *Will. Palerne* 759 William to þe window witterli miȝt sene ȝif [etc.]. **1382** Wyclif *Deut.* xxviii. 10 Alle the puples of erthes shulen seeyȝ en [*MS. A.* seye, **1388** se], that [etc.]. *c* **1450** *Mirk's Festial* 5 Als ferre as he myght seen hit. *c* **1470** Henry *Wallace* VIII. 475 Gyff thai suld battaill seyn. ? *a* **1550** *Droichis Part of Play* 124 in *Dunbar's Poems* (1893) 318 As ȝe may sie. **1611** Mure *Misc. Poems, Confl. Love & Reas.* 18 One quho lothed to sie ye Light. **1638** *Hamilton Papers* (Camden) 3 To publis the proclamatioun fourthwith..and sea itt put in executioun to the best of your pouer.

c **893** [see 16 a (*a*)]. *a* **1225** *Juliana* 47 (Bodl. MS.) Ich.. sohte þe to seonne. **12..** *Moral Ode* 388 (Egerton MS.) in *O.E. Hom.* I. 183 Of him to sene [*c* 1200 Trin. MS. in *O.E. Hom.* II. 232 to isiene] nis no sed. **1340** *Ayenb.* 108 þet he ne is clene ne worþi him to zyenne.

2. *Indicative Present.* **a.** *1st pers. sing.* **see** (siː). Forms: 1 **séom, síum, séo, sío, síe,** 2–5 **seo,** (2–3 **so),** 3–4 *north.* **seis,** 3–6 **se,** (5 **scee),** 6 *Sc.* **sie,** 3– **see.**

a **1000** *Ags. Ps.* v. 3 (Th.) Ic stande on ær-merᵹen beforan ðe æt ᵹebede, and seo þe. *c* **1200** Ormin 7623 Forr her I seo full witerrliȝ þin Hælennd crist onn eorþe. *a* **1250** *Owl & N.* 34 Me is þe wrs þat ich þe so [*Jesus MS.* iseo]. *a* **1300** *Cursor M.* 16327, I wat and seis [*Gött. MS.* seis] þai wel noght fine, be-tuixand þai þe sla. **1377** Langl. *P. Pl.* B. xx. 177 'Now I see' [**1393** *Ibid.* C. XXIII. 178 seo], seyde lyf 'þat [etc.]'. *c* **1400** *St. Alexius* 334 (Cott.) Ys thys my sone þat I here scee? **1471** Caxton *Recuyell* (Sommer) 41 Y shall neuer haue pleasir in my lyf tyll y se hym refrayned of his tyrannye. **1535** Lyndesay *Satyre* 8 All that I sie.

b. *2nd pers. sing.* **seest** (ˈsiːɪst). Forms: α. 1 **seohst, syhst, sihst, sixst, siist, síst,** 3 **sihst, sichst seh[s]te,** 3–4 **seost, sext, syst, sucst, sikst,** 3, 5 **sixst,** 3–5 **sest, sist, sixt,** 4 **suxst, sixte, syxt,** (**sys),** *Kent.* **zixt, zyxt, zist,** 4–5 **suxt,** 5 **sexst, sestt, seist,** 5–6 **seyst,** 4– **seest.** β. (*north.*) 1 **siis,** 3–4 **sais,** 3–5 **se(e)s,** 3–6 **seis,** 4 **seise, seyse,** 4–5 **sese, seys,** 5 **seese, seȝis,** 6 **seyis.**

α. [*c* **888** K. Ælfred *Boeth.* iii. §4 Ðesihst þu nu þæt (etc.).] *c* **1200** *Trin. Coll. Hom.* 137 Wanne þu sest gost cumen [etc.]. *a* **1250** *Owl & N.* 242 (Jesus MS.) Bi daye þu art stare-blynd, þat þu ne syst [*Cott. MS.* sichst] bouh of lynd. *c* **1250** *Ten Abuses* 1 (Cott.) in *O.E. Misc.* 184 Hwan þu sixst on leode King þat is wilful [etc.]. *c* **1320** R. Brunne *Medit.* 212 He þat þou seest yn þe prestes fest. **1393** Langl. *P. Pl.* C. XI. 158 As þow suxt [*v.rr.* sixt, seist, seest, sext] þe sonne som tyme for cloudes May nat shyne. *a* **1400** *How to live perfectly* 1062 in *Minor Poems fr. Vernon MS.* 249 Hem þat þou seost in Meseyse. *c* **1485** *Digby Myst., Mary Magd.* 1542 þis chrisetyn þat here sestt þou. *a* **1586** Sidney *Arcadia* II. (Sommer) 103 Alas my Dorus (said she) thou seest how long [etc.]. **1781** Cowper *Truth* 507 Seest thou yon harlot, wooing all she meets.

β. [*c* **950** *Lindisf. Gosp.* Mark xii. 14 Ne forðon ðu ᵹesiis on onsione monnes.] *a* **1300** *Cursor M.* 14055 'Sais [*Gött.* ses, *Fairf.* sese] þou', he said, 'now þis womman?' *c* **1320** *Sir Tristr.* 2933 No say nouȝt what þou ses. **1375** Barbour *Bruce* IV. 301 Now seis thow I mak na gabbing. *a* **1400–50** *Wars Alex.* 5022 For þi modire nor ȝit Messedon þou seȝis þaim na mare. *a* **1400** in *Relig. Pieces Prose & Verse* 24 The toþer es in Haly Writte whare þou sese what þou doo and what þou sall lefe. **1500–20** Dunbar *Poems* xx. 41 Thow seyis mony thingis variand. **1570** *Ane Tragedie* 26 in *Satir. Poems Reform.* x, We ar cum heir to the..To cause the write that thing thou seis this nycht.

c. *3rd pers. sing.* **sees** (siːz), *arch.* **seeth** (ˈsiːɪθ). Forms: α. 1 **siehð, siohð, seohð, syhð, sihð, sið,** 2 **sicð,** 2–3 **siþ, seoð, seð, siht,** 2–3, 5 **sieþ,** 2–4 **sihþ,** 3 **syhþ,** (**suþ, soþ, seoȝ** error for **seoþ),** 3–4 **sucþ,** 4 **siȝth, sikth, sykþ, syþ, seyþ, syht,** *Kent.* **ziȝþ, zyȝþ, zyþ, zycþ, zykþ, zikþ, zyȝt, ziȝt,** 4–5 **seth,** 5 **sueþ,** 5–6 **sethe, seyth, seith,** 4– (now *arch.*) **seeth.** β. (with ending orig. *north.*) 1 **siis, sís,** 3–6 **seis,** 4 **seise, seos,** 4–5 **ses(e, seys,** 5 **sesse, seȝis, -es,** 6–7 *Sc.* **sies,** 3– **sees.**

[*c* **950** *Lindisf. Gosp.* Matt. vi. 4 Fæder ðin seðe ᵹesiið in deᵹelnisse; *c* **1000** *Ags. Gosp.* ᵹesyhþ; *c* **1160** *Hatton Gosp.* sihð.] **1154** *O.E. Chron.* an. 1124 (Laud MS.) *ad fin.*, Oc ure Laford God ælmihtiᵹ þa eall diᵹelnesse seð & wat, he seoð þæt man læt þæt ærme folc mid ealle un rihte. *c* **1175** *Lamb. Hom.* 29 þe mon þe heleð his sunne aðisse liue ne siht he nefre almihtin drihten. *Ibid.* 157 þe rihtwise Mon þet..sicð þe muchele blisse þet he is to ileðed. *a* **1250** *Owl & N.* 246 Riȝt so hit farþ bi þan un-gode þat noȝt ne suþ [*Jesus MS.* i-syhþ] to none gode. *a* **1310** in Wright *Lyric P.* xxix. 86 Marie wepeth sore, ant siht al this wo. *c* **1315** Shoreham 7 *Deadly Sins* 203 He sykþ gode theawes. *c* **1369** Chaucer *Dethe Blaunche* 595 Who so seeth me firste. *c* **1450** *Mirk's Festial* 62 Holy chyrche..seyth hom all sore seke yn þe sekenes of synne. **1535** Coverdale *Ps.* xvii[i.] 47 Ye God which seyth that I be auenged. *Ibid.* xxxvi[i.] 13 He seith yt his daye is comminge. **1560** *Ovid's Narcissus* C iij b, Ther he seethe the image of his grace. *a* **1629** Goffe *Courag. Turk* v. iv. (1632) H 3 b, Their God seeth their slaughter.

β. [*c* **950** *Lindisf. Gosp.* John iii. 32 þætte ᵹesiis & ᵹehereð.] *a* **1300** *Cursor M.* 862 He wend to hide him amang þa tres, Fra his sight þat al sees [*Gött.* seis, *Fairf.* seise, *Trin.* sees]. *a* **1375** *Joseph Arim.* 258 He seos Jhesu crist in a sad Roode. *a* **1400–50** *Wars Alex.* 2532 Quen he sesse [*Dubl. MS.* seys] vs sike a sowme sare will he drede. *Ibid.* 5583 þe berne blischis on his blonke & seȝes his breth faile. *c* **1614** Mure *Dido & Æneas* II. 120 What all doth boad she sies.

d. *plural* **see** (siː). Forms: α. 1 **séoð, séað, síoð,** 2–4 **seoþ,** (3 **soþ, seoȝ** error for **seoþ),** 3–5 **seþ,** 4 **suþ, seith,** (**seoz** ? error for **seoþ),** *Kent.* **zyeþ** (also written **zyeȝ),** **zeþ,** 5 **seeþ, sethe.** β. 1 **séo,** 3–4 **seo,** 3–6 **se,** 6 *Sc.* **sie,** 3– **see.** γ. *north.* 1 **séas,** 3–4 **sees, sais,** 3–6 **seis,** 4 **seyse, sese.** δ. 3–6 **sen,** 4 **seon,** 4–5 **seen,** 5 **se(e)ne, se(e)yne.**

α. *a* **900** Cynewulf *Crist* 1286 (Gr.) Hy..seoð. *c* **950** *Lindisf. Gosp.* Matt. xiii. 13 Forðon ᵹeseᵹend..ne seað. *a* **1250** *Owl & N.* 884 (Jesus MS.) Hi ne seoþ [*Cott. MS.* soþ] her nowiht bute serewe. [*c* **1290** *Beket* 921 in *S. Eng. Leg.* 133 ȝe i-seoȝ wel echon þat al þe world grat on me one.] **1297** R. Glouc. (Rolls) 2436 In þe firmament beþ Planetes yliche clene sterren someas as ȝe seþ [*v. rr.* iseoþ, seen, sene]. *a* **1325** soez [see B. 9]. **1377** Langl. *P. Pl.* B. I. 41 This and þat sueth þi soule and seith it in þin herte. **1393** —— *P. Pl.* C. v. 154 We seth [*v.rr.* seon, see, seeyne, se] wel syre reson, ..That [etc.]. *c* **1450** *Mirk's Festial* 21 As ȝe here and sethe.

β. [**971** *Blickl. Hom.* 125 Ðeseo we þæt oft swiþe maneᵹum men færlice ᵹelimpeþ þæt he hine wið þas world ᵹedæleþ.] *a* **1300** *Cursor M.* 5335 God men i am, als yee now her se, An old man. **1393** Langl. *P. Pl.* C. x. 244 Oþer sonedays at euesonge seo we wel fewe!

γ. *c* **950** *Lindisf. Gosp.* Matt. xiii. 17 Ða ilco ᵹe seas. *a* **1300** *Cursor M.* 1176 All þat þe sees [*Fairf.* sees, *Gött.* se, *Trin.* seeþ] sal þe not sla. *Ibid.* 21074 þat erth..men sais [*Gött.* seis] vprisand fra þe grund. **1567** *Gude & Godlie Ball.* 89 Quhen my ennemies seis my fall.

δ. *c* **1200** Ormin 18965 Forr swa þeȝȝ mare herenn & sen Off Cristess rihhtwisnesse. **1362** Langl. *P. Pl.* A. III. 210 ȝe seon wel þe soþe. *c* **1450** *Mirk's Festial* 42 þen we seyne þat þou wyll not do þe kyngys byddyng. **1450–80** tr. *Secreta Secret.* xi. 11 Than shalle the kyng be worshipid and dred whan men seyne that he dredith god. *c* **1600** Day *Bednal Gr.* IV. iii. (1659) I 1 b, *Old Stro.* And speak the truth Boy as thou art my Son. *Y. Stro.* And I do not I'll give you leave to call me Cut, sen ye?

3. *Indicative past.* **a.** *1st and 3rd pers. sing.* **saw** (sɔː). Forms: α. 1, 3 **sæh,** 1–3 **seah,** 3 *Ormin* **sahh,** 3–4 **saȝ, sah, sau,** (**saght),** 3–5 **sagh, saȝe, sauȝ,** 4 **saghe, saȝhe, sav, sach,** (*Sc.* **schaw),** 4–5 **saugh, sauh, sawh, sawȝ,** 4–6 **sawe, sauhe, sawhe, sawgh, sauch,** (**saȝ),** **save,** 5–6 **saue, sauȝe,** (5 **saughe),** *Sc.* **sa,** 6 **sae,** *Sc.* **saa,** 3– **saw;** 1–4 **seh,** 3 **sehȝ, seȝh, sæih, sayh, seeh,** 3–4 **seih, seȝ,** 3–5 **sai, sei, saiȝ, seiȝ, seyh, seghe,** 3–5, (7) **say,** 3–6 **saye, sey,** 4 **saiȝe, seiȝe, saih, sayw, seey, seeȝ, seich,** *Kent.* **zeȝ,** 4–5 **seigh(e, seygh, seyȝe, seye, sayȝ, saie, seie, seih, se(e)gh,** 4–6 **se,** 5 **seyhe, seȝhe, sech,** (**seyght),** 3– (now *vulgar*) **see;** 3–4 **sih,** 4 **si, syh, sygȝ,** 4–5 **syȝ, sygh, siȝ(e, sigh(e, syȝe, sihe, sy, sie,** 5 **syg(he, syhe,** 5–6 **sye;** 4 **sugh, sough, sow, sue.** β. *weak forms* (*dial.* and *vulgar*) 8–9 **see'd,** 9 **seed, zeed,** etc. (see also *Eng. Dial. Dict.*).

α. *c* **950** *Lindisf. Gosp.* John xi. 33 Se hælend uutedlice þætte saeh hia hremende. *c* **1200** *Trin. Coll. Hom.* 175 Ure helende..segh þos tweie brodren in þe se on here shipe. *c* **1275** *Passion our Lord* 561 in *O.E. Misc.* 53 þo seyh heo þer twey engles. *c* **1290** *Beket* 167 in *S. Eng. Leg.* 111 Heo saiȝ gilbertus wille þat it was no guod. *a* **1300** *Havelok* 1251 O niht saw she þer-inne a liht. *c* **1325** *Metr. Hom.* 76 When scho on rode sugh hyr son hang. *a* **1330** *Otuel* 738 Rouland was so nyȝ, þat alle foure kinges he syȝ. **1362** Langl. *P. Pl.* A. Prol. 14, I sauh a Tour on a Toft. *c* **1375** *Sc. Leg. Saints* v. (*Johannes*) 250 Paynis..þat he schaw in hell. **1382** Wyclif *Matt.* ix. 23 When Jhesus..seeȝ mynstrelis. *a* **1400** *Pistill of Susan* 316 Vnderr a Cyne..I her se. *c* **1425** Lydg. *Assembly of Gods* 22 When I sy no betterr but I must go. *c* **1450** *Mirk's Festial* 119 He ȝode nygh and sech how an horrybull neddyr..had vmbeclypped a lyon. *c* **1450** *Digby Myst., Mary Magd.* 2051 þe whych I never save þis xxx wynter and more. *a* **1500** *Lancelot* 1225 The lady sauch.. The knychtis worschip which that he haith vroght. **1534** in *Lett. Suppress. Monasteries* (Camden) 36 He was rapte into heven, where he see the Trinite settyng in a pall. **1573** G. HARVEY *Letter-bk.* (Camden) 115 Who ever sae, who ever harde, who ever redd the like to this? **1583** *Leg. Bp. St. Androis* 520 in *Satir. Poems Reform.* xlv, But his commissione na man saa. **1672** WISEMAN *Wounds* I. viii. 73 The Doctor..both see and felt their scars. **1696** DE LA PRYME *Diary* (Surtees) 102 He say an ape, and playing with it, it bit his hand. **1840** THACKERAY *Shabby-genteel Story* iii, But I never, for coolness, see such a man as you. **1874** WHYTE MELVILLE *Uncle John* xiv. II. 91 He see one of 'em ..go by the house this morning.

β. **1746** G. MURRAY *Let.* 17 Apr. in C. Petrie *Jacobite Movement: Last Phase* (1950) v. 113, I never seed him in time of action, neither at Gledsmoor, Falkirk, nor this last. **1777** P. THICKNESSE *Year's Journey* II. xlix. 134 An English servant..told me..that he *seed* her very plain. *a* **1800** PEGGE *Anecd. Eng. Lang.* (1814) 111 The common people of London..will say, for instance,—'I see'd him yesterday'; and 'he was see'd again to-day'. **1818** SCOTT *Hrt. Midl.* xl, I never seed a woman hanged in a' my life. **1833** J. NEAL *Down-Easters* I. i. 14 Never seed sich a fellow since I breathed the breath of life. **1892** KIPLING *Barrack-room Ballads* 51 An' I seed her first a-smokin' of a whackin' white cheroot. **1893** H. A. SHANDS *Some Peculiarities of Speech in Mississippi* 55 *Seed*, Negro and illiterate white for *saw*. **1945** in B. A. Botkin *Lay my Burden Down* 18 He was the ugliest man I ever seed.

b. *2nd pers. sing.* **sawest** (sɔːist), **sawst** (sɔːst). Forms: *α.* 1 **sáwe, 3–4 sagh, 3–5 seȝe, 4 sau, sei(h, sihe, siȝe, 4–5 sey(e, seiȝ e, sawe, sawȝ, saugh, se, siȝ,** *Kent.* **zeȝe, 5 sawhe, say, seghe, see, sye, sogh, 5–6 saw.** *β.* **4–5 seiȝest, -ist, siȝest, seist, 5 sauȝ(e)st, saiest, 5–6 seest, 6 sawyste, -iste, seyst, 7– saw'st, sawst, 5– sawest.**

α. [**971** *Blickl. Hom.* 113 þær þu ær ʒesawe godweb mid golde ʒefaʒod.] *a* **1300** *Cursor M.* 9848 Bot he war ferliful to call if þou it sagh. **1315** SHOREHAM *Hours of Cross* 63 þou seȝe hyne hyder and þyder ycached, Fram pylate to herode. *c* **1350** *Will. Palerne* 276 Sei þou euer þemperour? **1390** GOWER *Conf.* I. 367 Thou sihe nevere thilke place. *a* **1400** *Pistill of Susan* 337 þou sey nou,..Vnder what kynde of tre Semeli susan þou se [*v.r.* see] Do þat derne dede. *c* **1430** *Hymns Virg.* (1867) 12 In hir þou siȝ a semeli sete. **1563** SACKVILLE *Induct. Mirr. Mag.* lxxvi, And nowe behold the thing that thou erewhile, Saw only in thought.

β. **1383** WYCLIF *Dan.* ii. 34 Thou siȝest [*v.r.* sauȝest] thus. —— *Rev.* i. 20 Which thou seiȝest [**1382** siȝe, *v.r.* saiest] in my riȝt hond. *Ibid.* xvii. 8 The beeste which thou seist [**1382** siȝe, *v.rr.* saiest, siȝest; 1534 TINDAL, 1539 CRANMER seest] was, and is not. **1470–85** MALORY *Arthur* III. xii. 113 Sawest thow not..a knyghte rydynge and ledynge aweye a lady. *a* **1536** *Songs, Carols,* etc. (E.E.T.S.) 104 Sawyste thou not myn oxen? *c* **1537** *Thersytes* 501 Seyst thou any man come thys waye? **1592** SHAKS. *Ven. & Ad.* 644 Sawest thou not signes of feare lurke in mine eye? **1602** BRETON *Mother's Blessing* C 2 b, Winke at the world as though thou saw'st it not. **1667** MILTON *P.L.* XI. 603 Those Tents thou sawst so pleasant, were the Tents Of wickedness.

c. *plural.* **saw** (sɔː). Forms: *α.* 1 **sáwun, -an, -en, sáʒon, 1–2 sáwon, 3 sowen, soȝen, saȝen, 3–5 sawen, 5 sauȝen; 1 séʒun, -on, 1–2 sǽʒon, 3** *Ormin.* **sæȝhenn, (sæȝhe we), 3–4 sæ(h)ȝen, 2 seaʒon, 2–4 seȝen, 2–5 seien, 3–4 seiȝen, seh(ȝ)en, seoȝen, 3–5 seiȝen, seghen, seyen, 4 seyȝen, seighen,** *Kent.* **zeȝen, 4–5 saien, say(e)n, seyne, 4–6 seen, 5 seyn, sene, seon, 6 seene; 3–5 siȝen, 4 sihen, syhen, 4–5 sien, sy(ȝ)en, 5 syghen.** *β.* **3 sæȝe, 3–4 sagh, sau, (scau), 3–5 saȝe, 3–6 saue, 4 saghe, sach, 4–5 sawgh, sowe, 4–6 sawe, 5 sawȝ, saugh, sauhe, saȝ, so, 4– saw; 3 seh(ȝ)e, sæȝe, 3–4 seghe, sei(ȝ)e, 3, 5 seȝe, 3–5 say, sei, sey(e, 4 sehe, seih, seygh, saie, seo,** *Kent.* **zeȝe, 4–5 se(i)gh, seiȝ, 5 saye, seyȝe, seyghe, 5–6 se, 5–7, 9 (*vulgar*) see; 3–4 siȝe, 4 syhe, 4–5 sie, sye, siȝ, syȝ(e, sygh(e, sigh(e, 5–6 sy.** *γ.* **8–9** *dial.* and *vulgar* **see'd** (see also *Eng. Dial. Dict.*).

The modern vulgarism (*we, you, they*) *seen* is not connected with the *α* forms above, but is due to substitution of the form of the pa. pple. for that of the pa. t.; so in the sing., *I, he seen* (see d).

α. *a* **900** CYNEWULF *Crist* 536 þonan hy God nyhst up stiʒende eaʒum seʒun. *a* **900** —— *Elene* 1104 (Gr.) þær hie to sæʒon. **1154** *O.E. Chron.* an. 1106 (Laud MS.) Forþam þe we hit sylfe ne sawon. *a* **1225** *Leg. Kath.* 280 For þi þæt ȝe ne sehen ham neauer biginnen. *c* **1250** *Gen. & Ex.* 3522 Ðis forfriȝted folc..Soȝen ðat figer. *a* **1300** *Havelok* 957 Alle him loueden þat him sowen. **1340–70** *Alex. & Dind.* 256 Whan we sihen þi sonde wiþ þi sel prented, We kenden þi couaitise. *c* **1386** CHAUCER *Sec. Nun's T.* 110 Right so men goostly in this mayden free Syen of feith the magnanymytee. *c* **1400** MAUNDEV. (1839) xxviii. 282 Whan that thei seen the Develes visibly and bodyly alle aboute hem. **1440** CAPGRAVE *Life St. Kath.* 1383 Whom ȝe in fleschnow full late sayn. *c* **1450** *Mirk's Festial* 20 þen seon þe byschoppys of mawmetry þat all þe pepul laft hor lawe. **15..** *Scot. Field* 513 in *Chetham Soc. Misc.* II, When the Skottes and the Ketterickes seen our men sketer, They had greate joy of their joyning.

β. *c* **1205** LAY. 11970 þu vmbe stunde ne sæȝe [*c* 1275 sehȝe] heo noht of londe. *c* **1250** *Kent. Serm.* in *O.E. Misc.* 30 Ac fore þe miracle þet hi seghe was here beliaue þe more i-strengþed. *a* **1300** *Cursor M.* 10268 Nu nan [children] we sagh [*Trin.* say, *Laud* sie] þe neuer haue. *Ibid.* 18451 þir war þe priueteis we scau [*Gött.* sau, *Trin.* sawe, *Laud* saw], Ikarius and mi felau. *c* **1330** R. BRUNNE *Chron. Wace* (Rolls) 4670 Men..wel hit sowe. **13..** *Gaw. & Gr. Knt.* 200 So sayd al þat hym syȝe. *c* **1375** *Cursor M.* 21691 (Fairf.) Quen þai sagh [*Edin.* sach] als tai did oft moises lift his hende on loft. *c* **1375** *Sc. Leg. Saints* xvi. (*Magdalena*) 436 For-þi abasit þai var & rad, quhene þai þame-selfine sav sa sted. *a* **1400** *Pistill of Susan* 132 Nou were þis domus men derf drawen in derne, Whiles þei seo [*v.rr.* saw, syghe] þat ladi was laft al hire one. *c* **1420** *Avow. Arth.* xl, Thay so a schene vndur schild. *c* **1450** *St. Cuthbert* (Surtees) 875 All men þat sow and stode by. *c* **1460** *Emare* 869 Alle hym loued þat hym sy. *c* **1550** BALE *K. Johan* (Camden) 81, I am as gentle a worme as ever ye see. **1877** JEFFERIES *Game-keeper at H.* i. (1890) 19 The governor were the haughtiest man as ever you see.

γ. **1752** FOOTE *Taste* II. (1781) 29 The same [gentleman] that we see'd at the Painting Man's.

d. *colloq.* and *dial.* **seen** (chiefly *1st pers. sing.*: see also *Eng. Dial. Dict.*).

1796 *Aurora* (Philadelphia) 30 Sept. 3/3 So fine a sight (says Yankee to his friend) I swear I never seen—you may depend. **1850** *Knickerbocker* July 87 We spoke of Major Andre. 'Oh,' said the old lady, 'I seen him more'n fifty times.' **1861** T. HUGHES *Tom Brown at Oxf.* II. vii. 114 'Hev'ee seed aught o' my bees?'.. 'E'es, I seen 'em.' *c* **1915** in N. I. White *Amer. Negro Folk-Songs* (1928) iii. 146, I seen King Pharoe's daughter seeking Moses on the water. **1976** *Alyn & Deeside Observer* 10 Dec. 12/6 Richardson told Detective Constable Mahoney: 'I seen this Irish bloke and followed him to the Hawarden Castle.'

4. *Subjunctive Present* **see.** Forms: *sing.* **1 sío, séo, sé, see, 3 sio, seȝe, 3–4 seo, 3–5 se, 4** *Kent.* **zi, 5 seye, 3– see.** *Plural.* **1 seon, sen, 3 seon, (so), 3–4 seo, 4–5 se, 3– see.**

[*c* **888** K. ÆLFRED *Boeth.* x, Forðæm mæneʒum men is leofre þæt he ær self swelte ær he ʒesio his wif & his bearn sweltende.] *c* **1200** ORMIN 3842 þohh þatt he grissliȝ deofell seo, Niss he rihht nohht forrfæredd. *a* **1300** *Cursor M.* 1987 Godmen i wil þat ȝee it see. *a* **1340** HAMPOLE *Comm. Canticles* i. 5 in *Psalter* (1884) 504 Depnes of hell sall hill thaim that thai se namare of thaire vanyte. *a* **1400–50** *Wars Alex.* 1846 Sire, if we se with a suth surely me thinke [etc.]. **1426** LYDG. *De Guil. Pilgr.* 5704 Thogh thow seye in me Errour.

5. *Subjunctive Past* **saw.** Forms: (*a*) *sing.* **1 sáwe, 3 sæȝhe, sæȝe, (soȝe, sowe), 3–4 saghe, 3–5 sawe, 4 sau, 4–5 saugh, 5 sauh, 6– saw; 2 seiȝe, 2–4 seie, seȝe, 3 seh(ȝ)e, 3–5 seye, 4 seigh,** *Kent.* **zeȝe, 5 see; 3 siȝe, 4 syhe, sihe.**

[*c* **888** K. ÆLFRED *Boeth.* x, Ðif þu hine ʒesawe on hwelcum eorfodum.] *c* **1200** ORMIN 17425, & þurrh þatt he sæȝhe þærenn He shollde takenn bote. *c* **1220** *Bestiary* 502 Ðat tu wuldes seien get, gef ðu it [the whale] soge wan it flet, ðat it were a neilond. *c* **1230** *Hali Meid.* (Titus) l. 233 Hwa þat sehe þenne hu þe engles beoð isweamed. *a* **1300** *Havelok* 1323, I woth, so wel so ich it sowe, To þe shole comen heye and lowe. **13..** *K. Horn* (Harl. MS.) 985 Rymenild lokede wide by þe see syde ȝef heo seȝe [*a* 1300 *Camb. MS.*, If heo oȝt of horn isiȝe] horn come. **1390** GOWER *Conf.* I. 64 And cast upward his yhe, As thogh he Cristes face syhe.

(*b*) *plural.* **1 sáwon, -an, 4** *Kent.* **zeȝen, 5 seen; 3–5 seie, 4–5 seiȝe, 5 seigh, sey, se, 6– saw.**

[*c* **888** K. ÆLFRED *Boeth.* xvi. §2 Ðif ʒe nu ʒesawan (etc.).] **1297** R. GLOUC. (Rolls) 5023, & vpe þe west ȝate of londone sette hit wel heye..þat men wel wide yseie [*v.rr.* seiȝe, sey, se]. **1340** *Ayenb.* 204 Hy þresten out hare eȝen of þe herte þe hi ne zeȝen þing þet ham miȝte wyþdraȝe uram hire contemplacion. **1377** LANGL. *P. Pl.* B. XIX. 450 For þe comune..counten ful litel þe conseille of conscience..But if þei seiȝe [*v.rr.* seigh, seie, seen] as by syȝte somwhat to wynnynge. **1530** LYNDESAY *Test. Papyngo* 1057 Les skaith it war, with lycence of the Pape, That ilke Prelate one Wyfe had of his awin, Nor se thar bastardis ouirthort the cuntre blawin.

6. *Imperative* **see.** Forms: (*a*) *sing.* **1 sioh, seoh, seh, sih, 3 sih, siȝ, 3–4 seh, sai, 3–6 se, 4 seo,** *Kent.* **ziȝ, 5 say, sey, 5– see.**

a **900** CYNEWULF *Crist* 59 Sioh nu sylfa þe ʒeond þas sidan ʒesceaft [etc.]. *c* **1310** *Marina* 55 in Böddeker *Altengl. Dicht.* (1878) 258 Nou wend & seh wher hit be. **1362** LANGL. *P. Pl.* A. I. 39 For þe Fend and þi Flesch folewen to-gedere, And schendeþ þi soule seo hit in þin herte. *Ibid.* x. 145 So seiþ þe sauter seo hit whon þe likeþ. *c* **1430** *Chev. Assigne* 65 Sone paye þe with þy qwene & se of her berthe. **1508** KENNEDIE *Flyting w. Dunbar* 44 Se sone thow mak my commissar amendis.

(*b*) *plural.* *α.* **1 séoð, síað, 3 seoþ, 4–5 se(e)þ, 5 sethe, seith, seiȝeth.**

[**971** *Blickl. Hom.* 241 Behealdað eow and ʒeseoð hine.] *c* **1350** *Will. Palerne* 1715 Now seþ how sone i haue spedde! **1382** WYCLIF *Matt.* xxviii. 6 Come ȝe, and seeth [1388 se, ȝe] the place. *c* **1425** *Cast. Persev.* 494 in *Macro Plays* 92 Syth & sethe wel to my sawe! *c* **1440** *Gesta Rom.* i. 4 (Harl. MS.) Seith nowe, goode men.

β. **3 seo, 3–6 se, 6** *Sc.* **sie, 3– see.**

a **1300–1400** *Cursor M.* 17288 + 151 (Cott.) He is risen & not here, be-hald þe stede & see! **1567** *Gude & Godlie Ball.* 142 For Christis word se ze stand for it.

γ. *North.* **3–4 sees, 3–5 seis, 4 sese.**

a **1300** *Cursor M.* 17797 Gas, seis [*Trin.* seeþ, *Laud* se] nu, ..And yee sal find þair tumbs tome. *a* **1400–50** *Wars Alex.* 3878 Seis ensampill at myselfe & seke ȝe na ferre.

δ. **5 sene.**

c **1440** *Pallad. on Husb.* I. 410 Hewe hit with an axe and sene If hit be not in thegge.

7. *Present Participle* **seeing** ('siːɪŋ). Forms: **1 síonde, síende, séende, seʒende, 1–2 séonde, 3–4 seant, 3–6 seand, 4 seende, seyinge, siynge,** *Kent.* **zyinde, 4–5 seande, 4–6 seynge(e, seeynge, 5 seenge, s(e)yyng, seond, seinge, seeyng, 6 seing, seying, seeinge, 6– seeing.**

c **950** *Lindisf. Gosp.* Matt. xiii. 13 ðeseʒende *vel* seende. *a* **1300** *Cursor M.* 3950 Bot þou sal be cald israel þat es man seand godd of hel. **1382** WYCLIF *Gen.* xvi. 4 And she [Agar] seynge hir silf that she had conseyued, dispiside hir ladi. **1390** GOWER *Conf.* I. 220 Noght seende This meschief. **1471** CAXTON *Recuyell* (Sommer) 23 Seyng his sorowful maner. *a* **1585** MONTGOMERIE *Cherrie & Slae* 461, I leuir haue euer Ane foule in hand, or tway, Nor seand ten fleand About me all the day. **1596** DALRYMPLE tr. *Leslie's Hist. Scot.* I. I. 100 Seing him self in sandie furdes.

8. *Past Participle* **seen** (siːn). Forms: *α.* **1 (ʒe)sewen, 2 sæwon, sawen, sæʒon, se(o)ʒon, 2–3 sewen, 2–4 seȝen, 3 (i-) sæȝen, sehen, (soȝen),** *Ormin* **seȝhenn, 3–5 sen, seien, 3–7 (8) sene, 4 sewyn, sine, 4–5 seyen, seiȝen, sain, sayn, 4–6 seyn(e, sein, 4–7 seene, 5 saine, sayne, (shene, senene), 5–7 seine, 6 seane, senne, 4– seen.** *β.* **3 seghe, se(i)hȝe, 3–5 sey(e, sei(ȝ)e, 4 seȝe,** *Kent.* **soȝe, zoȝe, 4–5 seyȝ(e, say, se, 5 see, sye, saye, saie.** *γ.* **8–9** *vulgar* **see'd.**

α. [*c* **888** K. ÆLFRED *Boeth.* xxxix. §13 Ac se steorra þe we hatað æfensteorra, þon he bið west ʒesewen, þon tacnnað he æfen.] **11..** *O.E. Chron.* an. 789 (Laud MS.) Heofenlic leoht wæs ʒelome seoʒen ðær þer he [Alfwold] of slaʒen wæs. **1154** *Ibid.* an. 1127 (Laud MS.) *ad fin.*, þis wæs..seʒon on þe selue derfald in þa tune on Burch. *c* **1250** *Gen. & Ex.* 2785 Ic haue min folkes pine soȝen, ðat he nu longe hauen droȝen. *c* **1320** *Sir Tristr.* 466 We and our elders old, þus þan haue we sain. *c* **1350** *Will. Palerne* 1792 þei drow hem to a dern den for drede to be seiȝen. *c* **1375** *Sc. Leg. Saints* xv. (*Barnabas*) 18 To be leile witnes, ewyne of It he had sewyn in hewyn. *c* **1386** CHAUCER *Man of Law's T.* 74 Whan they han this blisful mayden sayn [*v.rr.* seyn, sain, seine]. *c* **1400** *Destr. Troy* 2950 ȝet it ledis vnto laithnes and vnlefe werkes, And shotis into shame as shene has ben ofte. *c* **1420** *Chron. Vilod.* 4136 No blodus drope was senene þo þere. *c* **1450** *Merlin* 21 Neuer was seyen so wyse a man. **1533** GAU *Richt Vay* (1888) 29 Thay ar aluterlie seyne with the eyne of faith. **16..** MURE *Sonn. to Margareit* iii. 3 Wks. (S.T.S.) I. 49 Oght yat my puir eyes hath ewer seine. *c* **1730** RAMSAY *Eagle & Robin* 49 Be nae mair sene At court.

β. [*c* **1250** *Kent. Serm.* in *O.E. Misc.* 32 þo men..hedde i-seghe þo miracle.] *a* **1310** in Wright *Lyric P.* xxxiv. 96 Thestri wæs seie byfore day. **1362** LANGL. *P. Pl.* A. XI. 218 For I haue seiȝe it my-selfe. *a* **1375** *How to hear Mass* 107 in *Minor Poems fr. Vernon MS.* 496 Not Blynt þat day schalt þou not be þat þou þi sauiour hast se. **1387–8** T. USK *Test. Love* I. xii. (Skeat) l. 13 The sonne yeveth light that thinges may be seye. *c* **1450** *Merlin* 26 He hadde neuer seye them before. *a* **1475** *Bk. Noblesse* (Roxb.) 70 It was the joieust and plesaunt sighte that ever the saide citesyn Lisander had see beforne. **1482** *Monk of Evesham* xxxvi. (Arb.) 81 It is seldynne sey yat any man of hem were very penitent. **15..** *Adam Bel* 410 in Hazl. *E.P.P.* II. 156, I had wende yester daye..Thou sholde me never have se.

γ. *a* **1800** [see A. 3 *β*]. **1845** *Great Kalamazoo Hunt* in *Big Bear of Arkansas* 49 Well, after I had looked out for about fifteen minutes or so, and seed the boss begin to get desperately frightened, [etc.]. **1857** A. MAYHEW *Paved with Gold* II. v, Why, it's months since I've seed a sixpence. **1938** M. K. RAWLINGS *Yearling* xvi. 188 Seems to me I've seed it before.

δ. **9–** *U.S. colloq.* and *dial.* **saw.**

1867 C. F. BROWNE *A. Ward in London* II. vii. 123 We have saw a entertainment as we never saw before. **1941** J. FAULKNER *Men Working* ii. 33 How-some-ever, I've saw them.

B. Signification and Uses.

I. The simple verb.

In most of the senses OE. and early ME. used the compound *ʒeséon*, I-SEE, more frequently than the simple verb. Hence the paucity of early examples here.

1. a. *trans.* To perceive (light, colour, external objects and their movements) with the eyes, or by the sense of which the eye is the specific organ.

Beowulf 1365 þær mæg mon..niðwundor seon, Fyr on flode. *a* **1000** *Riddles* lxxxvii. 1 (Gr.) Ic seah wundorlice wiht. **1154** *O.E. Chron.* an. 1122 (Laud MS.), þæt fir hi seaʒon in ðe dæi rime and læste swa lange þæt hit wæs liht ofer eall. *c* **1200** ORMIN 657, & son se Zacariȝe sahh þatt enngless brihhte leome, He warrþ forrfæredd. **1357** *Lay Folks Catech.* (MS. T.) 415 For he that loues noght his brothir,..how suld he loue god almighten that he seis noght. *c* **1450** *Knt. de la Tour* xx. (1906) 29 Atte her dethe was saine a grete clerete & light. **1560** DAUS tr. *Sleidane's Comm.* 465 b, The fourth daye of Marche began to shine a blasing starre, & is sene by the space of twelve dayes. **1590** SHAKS. *Mids. N.* II. ii. 27 What thou seest when thou dost wake, Doe it for thy true Loue take. **1604** DRAYTON *Moyses* II. §2 Darknes is now so palpable and much, That as 'tis seene, as easily is felt. **1614** TOMKIS *Albumazar* I. iii, With this [glass] Ile read a leafe of that small Iliade..as plainly Twelue long miles off, as you see Pauls from Highgate. **1665** *Phil. Trans.* I. 39 In the interim..the other Comet could be seen with the naked eye. **1796** MME. D'ARBLAY *Camilla* I. 376 Sideling towards the window..[she] had heard and seen all that had passed. **1842** TENNYSON *Walking to Mail* 7 Whose house is that I see? **1848** THACKERAY *Van. Fair* xlviii, 'I was in the kitchen making a pudding'. 'I know you were, I saw you through the area railings'. **1873** *Rep. Brit. Assoc.* I. 141 We have seen the third edition. **1896** *Law Times Rep.* LXXIII. 616/2 If he had looked he must have seen the light of the approaching train.

Proverb. *c* **1450** *Mirk's Festial* 230 Hyt ys old Englysch sawe: A mayde schuld be seen, but not herd. **1560** T. BECON *Catechism* in *Works* I. sig. Bbb2, This also must honest maids provide, that they be not full of tongue... A maid should be seen, and not heard. **1773** R. GRAVES *Spiritual Quix.* I. III. xviii. 179 It is a vulgar maxim, 'that a pretty woman should rather be seen than heard'. **1858** GEO. ELIOT *Janet's Repentance* viii, in *Sc. Cler. Life* II. 167 Little gells must be seen and not heard. **1908** L. M. MONTGOMERY *Anne of Green Gables* ii. 22 It's such a relief to talk..and not be told that children should be seen and not heard. **1980** L. LEWIS *Private Life of Country House* v. 63 Two or three children..supposed to be seen and not heard and not to speak unless spoken to.

transf. **1818** KEATS *Endym.* I. 540 This river does not see the naked sky. **1869** TOZER *Highl. Turkey* I. 307 The place only sees the sun for a few hours in winter.

†**b.** Pleonastically, *to see with* (or *at*) *eye(s, with, in sight. Obs.*

For *to see with one's own eyes*, etc., see EYE *sb.*

a **1000** *Riddles* lxxxiv. 31 (Gr.) þæs þe [hio]..ælda bearn eaʒum sawe. *c* **1200** ORMIN 5716 To sen Drihhtin wiþþ ehne. *a* **1300** *Havelok* 1273 þat shalt þu with þin eyne sen. **13**

.. *Gaw. & Gr. Knt.* 1705, & quen þay seghe hym with syȝt, þay sued hym fast. *c* **1380** Wyclif *Wks.* (1880) 384 And if we take hede þus bi þis rule we schal se at yȝe how þe clergie saiþ here oþer-wyse þan it is. *c* **1385** Chaucer *L.G.W.* Prol. 11 But goddis forbode but men schulde leue Wel more thyng than men han seyn with eye. **1418** *Man Beware* 71 in *26 Pol. Poems* 63 For þat ȝe hid, god seeþ in syȝt. **1430–40** Lydg. *Bochas* II. Prol. (1494) fiij b, The rounde droppis of the smoth rayne which that..fall from aloft On stonys harde at the iye as it is seyne Perceth their hardnesse with their fallinge ofte. *c* **1475** *Partenay* 51 A roial gret feste, A more worshipful neuer sayn with eye.

c. predicated of the eye.

a **1225** *Leg. Kath.* 1733 Nan eorðlich ehe ne mei hit seon, ich segge. *a* **1300** *Cursor M.* 4508 Hert sun for-gettes þat ne ei seis. *c* **1421** *Lessons of Dirige* 318 in *26 Pol. Poems* 117 Noon eyȝe hadde sene me after son. **1620** Sir T. Wroth *Destr. Troy*, etc. *Epigr.* 16 *marg.*, That which the eye sees not the heart neuer rues. **1750** Johnson *Rambler* No. 102 ¶4 An expanse of waters..covered with so thick a mist that the most perspicacious eye could see but a little way.

d. To behold (visual objects) in imagination, or in a dream or vision. So ***to see a vision***, †***to see a dream***. Also in phr. ***to see things***, to suffer hallucinations or false imaginings; (usu. *colloq.* as pres. pple.).

c **1200** *Trin. Coll. Hom.* 109 þe holi prophete abacuc..seh suterliche fele of þe wundren þe ure helende dide siðen. *a* **1300** *Cursor M.* 4533 Aiþ er of hus a drem we sau And he us bad til him it scau. **1382** Wyclif *Gen.* xl. 8 A sweuen we han seen [**1388** We seiȝen a dreem], and ther is not that wol vndo it vs. **1387** Trevisa *Higden* (Rolls) III. 99 Here take heed þat Danill seigh ten sightes. *c* **1450** *Myrr. our Ladye* 27 The holy Patryarke Jacob se a vysyon in a place callyd Bethel. **1538** Bale *Thre Lawes* v. F v b, A newe Hierusalem the sayd Johan also se. **1800** Wordsw. *Reverie of Poor Susan* 5 She sees A mountain ascending, a vision of trees. **1848** Dickens *Dombey* xxxii, He saw himself, in his mind's eye, put meekly into a hackney coach. **1859** Helps *Friends in C.* Ser. II. (1877) I. viii. 201, I see, with my mind's eye, a statue of Dunsford raised in Tollerporcorum. **1922** M. A. von Arnim *Enchanted April* iii. 48 Mrs. Fisher..had no wish to find herself shut up..with somebody who saw things... It would be disagreeable..if Mrs. Wilkins were suddenly to assert that she saw Mr. Fisher. Mr. Fisher was dead; let him remain so. **1928** Kipling *Woman in his Life* in *Limits & Renewals* (1932) 47 After a drink or two..he told the tale of a friend who 'saw things'. **1935** A. Christie *Three Act Tragedy* III. vii. 180 Says I imagined it. Says I was 'seeing things'. **1953** B. Glemser *Dove on his Shoulder* ii. 13 'I must be seeing things', the major said... 'You alcoholic bastard.' **1977** 'D Rutherford' *Return Load* ii. 31 Was I seeing things or was that Sally driving your truck?

e. With sb. or pron. and inf. as compound obj.

When *see* is used in the passive the infinitive is normally preceded by *to*; when in the active, the *to* is omitted. In early use, however, exceptions are not uncommon.

In mod. English this construction differs from the use of the pres. pple. as complement (see 1 g) in implying a reference to the ability of the subject to give testimony as to the fact or the manner of the action predicated; compare, e.g. 'I have seen him walk' with 'I have seen him walking'. In early examples the inf. is often found where we should now use the complementary pple.

a **1000** *Riddles* lii. 1 (Gr.) Ic seah wrætlice wuhte feower samed siþian. **1154** *O.E. Chron.* an. 1127 (Laud MS.) *ad fin.*, þa sæȝon & herdon fela men feole huntes hunten. *c* **1200** Ormin 10676 He sahh þære Godess Gast, Inn aness cullfress like, Off heoffne cumenn uppon Crist & upponn himm bilefenn. *c* **1230** *Hali Meid.* (Titus) l. 193 He seð [*MS. Bodl.* sið] þefolhen hire treoden, meiden. *c* **1250** *Gen. & Ex.* 16 Cristene men oȝen ben so faȝen So fueles arn quan he it sen daȝen. **13..** *Seuyn Sages* (W.) 1258 And do als tou sest me do. *a* **1352** Minot *Poems* (ed. Hall) vii. 70 þat fire ful many folk gan fere, When þai se brandes o ferrum flye. *c* **1381** Chaucer *Parl. Foules* 211 Vndyr a tre be-syde a welle I say Cupide oure lord hise arwis forge & file. **1382** Wyclif *Gen.* xxxvii. 25 And sittynge for to eet breed, thei seen Ysmaelitis weie-goers to comen fro Galaad. **1382** —— *Mark* ix. 37 Maistir, we syȝen [**1388** sayn] sum oon for to caste out fendis in thi name. **1471** Caxton *Recuyell* (Sommer) 34 Whan Iasius sawe hys broder come all in armes, all his blood began to chaunge. **1542** Udall *Erasm. Apoph.* Table Y ij b, Phocion was never seen laugh ne wepe. **1576** Turberv. *Venerie* xxx. 80 But here he shall marke one secrete: that he go not aboute to herbor an Harte an houre at least after he see him go to layre. **1577** Kendall *Flowers of Epigr.* 28 That thou wilt not be seen to talke with any others wife. **1596** Shaks. *Tam. Shr.* I. i. 179, I saw her corrall lips to moue. **1596** Danett tr. *Comines* (1614) 159 But some of them reported that he was seen flie, and was escaped. **1731** Medley *Kolben's Cape G. Hope* II. 101 When you see him [the elephant] march, you are amazed at the Ground he rids. **1779** *Mirror* No. 27 As he looked at it, I saw the tears start from his eyes. **1805** Scott *Last Minstr.* VI. xxiii, O'er Roslin all that dreary night A wondrous blaze was seen to gleam. **1862** Thackeray *Philip* iii, I could see the diamond twinkle on his pretty hand. **1894** 'Max O'Rell' *John Bull & Co.* 2, I have seen French people laugh side-splittingly.

†**f.** With ellipsis of indefinite obj. (*some one*) before the infinitive. *Obs. rare.* (A Gallicism.)

c **1350** *Will. Palerne* 5071 Whan bordes were born adoun & burnes hade waschen, Men miȝt haue seie to menstrales moche god ȝif. *c* **1489** Caxton *Blanchardyn* xxix. 110 What so euer goode sporte & pleysure that blanchardyn sawe ther make for his sake.

g. With obj. and compl. (adj., pple., or phrase).

a **900** Cynewulf *Crist* 1270 Hy. grim hellefyr, ȝearo to wite ondweard seoð. *c* **1200** Ormin 3829 Forr Godess enngell rofreþþ mann, 3iff þatt he seoþ himm færedd. *c* **1275** *Passion our Lord* 495 in *O.E. Misc.* 51 þo heo comen to ihesu crist and seyen hine ded. *a* **1375** *Joseph Arim.* 269 þenne he sauh Ihesu crist I-strauȝt vppon þe Roode. *c* **1386** Chaucer *Frankl. T.* 122 Where as she many a shipe and barge seigh Seillynge hir cours where as hem liste go. *c* **1400** Maundev. (1839) iv. 24 Though thou see me hidouse and horrible to loken onne. **1470–85** Malory *Arthur* III. xii. 113 Sawest thow not saide Pellinore a knyghte rydynge and ledynge aweye a lady. **1536** *Primer Eng. & Lat.* 64 b, Sone after none thys mother..Sawe from the body [of her son], the soule departynge. **1621** G. Sandy *Ovid's Met.* II. (1626) 39 Saw'st thou no cattel through these fields conuay'd? **1709** Pope *Let. to Cromwell* 7 May, In which time all the verses you see added, have been written. **1821** Scott *Kenilw.* xxiv, They.. had just seen the little party..crossing the summit of a gentle hill. **1862** Mrs. H. Wood *Mrs. Hallib.* III. vi, They are acquiring self-respect... They wouldn't be seen in the street now in rags, or the worse for drink. **1865** Swinburne *Chastelard* II. i. 52, I say what I saw done.

h. To distinguish by sight *from.*

c **1450** *Brut* 591 Kyng Herry..leete cere hym [K. Richard]..in a fayre cheste, closyd alle in lynnyn clothe, saaf his visage, whiche was lefte opyn, þat men myht see & knowe his persone from alle othir men. **1862** Mrs. H. Wood *Mrs. Hallib.* II. iv, I can't see one sort from another; we must have candles.

i. In various phrases (some of which occur chiefly in figurative use), ***to see the colour of*** (a person's money), ***to see double, to see the light, to see one's way***: see the associated words; ***to see red***: see red *sb.*[1] 1 f. ***to see*** (a person) ***coming***, to make out one who can be fooled or deceived. Also in proverbial phrase ***when you've seen one, you've seen them all***; a conjuror's phrase ***now you see him, now you don't***, and varr.

c **1811** Blake *Public Address* in *Writings* (1978) II. 1046 When you have seen one of their Pictures you have seen all. **1869** 'Mark Twain' *Innocents Abr.* xxiii. 177 To me it seemed that when I had seen one of these martyrs I had seen them all. **1931** T. R. G. Lyell *Slang, Phrase & Idiom* 671 D'you mean to say you paid £100 for that car? My dear fellow, they must have seen you coming! As scrap iron, it's worth perhaps £10—not a penny more!! **1949** G. Davenport *Family Fortunes* II. iv. 145 'If you've seen one you've seen them all,' said Sam. **1967** T. Stoppard *Rosencrantz & Guildenstern are Dead* II. 62 It's just a man failing to reappear, that's all—now you see him, now you don't. **1973** *Illustr. London News* May 100/4, I know many people who feel that once you've seen one Jancso film, you've seen them all. **1980** G. M. Fraser *Mr American* xix. 370 If the American..had subsequently proved to be of moderate means, would he have been quite so welcome?.. Old Man Clayton had seen him coming. **1980** P. G. Winslow *Counsellor Heart* xx. 221 The only way is to.. have them think it's something else. Now you see it, now you don't.

j. *transf.* or *fig.* of radar equipment, cameras, artificial satellites, etc.

1923 E. W. Marchant *Radio Telegr. & Teleph.* iv. 36 The method that was described by Hertz for detecting or 'seeing' radio waves was to use a spark gap in a circuit which was tuned to the frequency of the waves. **1945** *Rev. Sci. Instruments* XVI. 46/1 The photo-tube camera is mounted beneath the photofluorograph hood and 'sees' the object image on the screen which is 'seen' by the photographic camera at the apex of the hood. **1952** E. Larsen *Radar works like This* 9 Thus the picture of what the waves 'see' is built up from glowing blobs on the screen. **1957** T. Adler *Seeing Earth from Space* v. 126 The earth satellite Vanguard II.. looks down on the earth from a much greater height than 86 miles. So it can see more of the earth than the camera that took this picture did. **1975** D. G. Fink *Electronics Engineers' Handbk.* xxv. 4 When connected to the antenna, the receiver sees a low-noise background of empty space, modified by surrounding terrain or sea surfaces and atmosphere, [etc.].

2. a. *absol.* and *intr.* To perceive objects by sight. Formerly often, to have the faculty of sight, not to be blind (now commonly expressed by *can see*).

can see often means to have sufficient light or power of vision to see as clearly as is necessary for some contextually implied purpose. Sometimes an inf. of purpose follows, as 'I can see to read, but not to paint'.

c **1250** *Gen. & Ex.* 3108 He adden liȝt and sowen wel. *a* **1300** *Cursor M.* 6706 Qua smites vte his thains eie, And mas him vn-mighti for-to seie,..He sal [etc.]. **1382** Wyclif *John* ix. 11, I wente, and waischide, and syȝ [**1388** say; *the O.E. versions have* ȝeseah]. **1387** Trevisa *Higden* (Rolls) II. 191 Tiberius Cesar sigh more clereliche in derkenesse þan in liȝt. **1426** Lydg. *De Guil. Pilgr.* 3306 To sen, myn Eyen ben to blynde. *c* **1450** *Mirk's Festial* 54 And when he layde his hondys on his hed, anon he segh. *a* **1586** Sidney *Arcadia* III. (Sommer) 268 b, The first had his eyes cut out so, as he could not see to bid the neare following death welcome. **1596** Shaks. *Merch. V.* III. ii. 124 But her eies, How could he see to doe them? **1596** Dalrymple tr. *Leslie's Hist. Scot.* Prol. I. 5 The beimes of the Sone, al Scotland throuch, the hail nychte ar sein, the space of twa monethis..in sik brichtnes that esilie thay may sie to reid and wryte. **1607** Topsell *Four-f. Beasts* 466 Lions, Beares, Tygres, and their whelpes are not able to see, stand or goe, for many monthes. **1712** Lady M. W. Montagu *Let. to W. Montagu* 9 or 11 Dec., I write and read till I can't see, and then I walk. **1743** Pococke *Descr. East* I. II. ii. 80 We could not see before us any further than in a very thick fog. **1749** Fielding *Tom Jones* VII. iv, When he repaired to her bed he was generally so drunk that he could not see. **1774** Goldsm. *Nat. Hist.* (1776) II. 153 He was, at first, couched only in one of his eyes; and, when he saw for the first time, he was so far from judging of distances, that [etc.]. **1820** Keats *St. Agnes* xxxix, There are no ears to hear, or eyes to see. **1820** Scott *Abbot* xix, Why, man, it was but a switch across the mazzard —blow your nose, dry your eyes, and you will see all the better for it. **1861** Whyte Melville *Mkt. Harb.* xxv, It was a bad day to see; a bad day to hear; above all, a bad day to ride.

Prov. **1546** Heywood *Prov.* I. x. Wks. (1562) C iij, She thought..she had seene far in a milstone. **1718** Mrs. Centlivre *Bold Stroke for Wife* II. 31, I am sorry such a well-invented Tale should do you no more Service. We old Fellows can see as far into a Mill-stone, as him that picks it. **1862** H. Kingsley *Ravenshoe* II. ix. 80 He could see through a brick wall as well as most men. **1885** C. M. Yonge *Two Sides of Shield* II. i. 16 He should defer his letter till he had ..talked to his sister Jane, who could see through a milestone any day. **1920** 'Sapper' *Bull-Dog Drummond* v. 127 He could see farther into a brick wall than most of the people who called him a fool. **1978** A. Price *'44 Vintage* xviii. 204 I had a grandma could see clear through me and a brick wall both, so it's no surprise you can figure us.

b. With ellipsis of an obj. implied by the context.

c **1160** *Hatton Gosp.* John xx. 29 þu ȝe-lyfdest for-þan þu me ȝe-seaȝe. þa sænden eadiȝe þe ne seaȝen [*c* **1000** *Ags. Gosp.* ȝe-sawon] & ȝe-lyfdon. *a* **1310** in Wright *Lyric P.* ix. 36 The water that it wetes yn, Y-wis hit wortheth al to wyn, that seȝen seyden so. **1382** Wyclif *Ezek.* viii. 10 And I gon in, seeȝ; and loo! **1832** Tennyson *Sisters* 163 The sweet dwelling of her eyes Upon me when she thought I did not see. **1888** Kipling *Soldiers Three, In Matter of a Private*, People who have seen say that one of the quaintest spectacles of human frailty is an outburst of hysterics in a girls' school.

3. a. (*fig.*) *trans.* To perceive mentally (an immaterial object, a quality, etc.); to apprehend by thought (a truth, the answer to a question), to recognize the force of (a demonstration). Often with reference to metaphorical light or eyes. Also, to foresee or forecast (an event, trend, etc.); *U.S.*, to understand (a person). Also, ***to see*** (something) ***coming***: to foresee or anticipate.

As the sense of sight affords far more complete and definite information respecting external objects than any other of the senses, mental perceptions are in many (perh. in all) languages referred to in visual terms, and often with little or no consciousness of metaphor.

c **1200** Ormin 13590 Whamm þu þurrh Drihhtin sest nuȝȝu Wiþþ innsihht off þin herrte. *a* **1225** *Leg. Kath.* 477 Ah sone se ich seh þe leome of þe soðe lare þæt leadeð to eche lif, ich leafde al þæt oðer. *a* **1250** *Owl & N.* 950 Heo..so forleost al hire liht, þat heo ni siþ [*Jesus MS.* syhþ] soð ne riht. *c* **1330** *Spec. Gy de Warw.* 657 If þu couþest knowe and se þe uertu of humilite [etc.]. *a* **1400** Chaucer *Merciles Beaute* 10 For with my deeth the trouthe shal be sene. **1426** Lydg. *De Guil. Pilgr.* 2739 Now haue I told (ye sen yt wel,) Touchyng thys swerd eueryde1. *c* **1537** *Thersytes* 59 Your mynde now I se. *c* **1553** Earl of Bath *Let.* in Gage *Hengrave* (1822) 141 And except the bishop wold wincke at the same, and wold not see it, there is no law can assure it before he were priest. **1594** Lyly *Mother Bombie* II. iii, We gird them and flout them out of all scotch and notch, and they cannot see it. **1609** Carleton in *Crt. & Times Jas. I* (1848) I. 95 He may well be deceived, for I see no better benefice for him at his return than to serve as a clerk. **1651** Hobbes *Leviath.* II. xxvi. 148 From seeing the Extraordinary wisdome..of his Actions. **1721** Lady M. W. Montagu *Let. to C'tess Mar* (1893) I. 457 The first of those ladies is on the brink of Scotland for life. She does not care; to say truth, I see no very lively reasons why she should. **1768** Whately in *Grenville Papers* (1853) IV. 294 Lord Temple says that he sees no objection to your coming up. **1825** T. Hook *Sayings* Ser. II. *Passion & Princ.* ix. III. 164 She saw nothing before her but distress and misery. **1827** Scott *Chron. Canongate* Introd., I did not immediately see the purpose of his lordship's question. **1849** Macaulay *Hist. Eng.* vi. II. 63 Nor did he ever see his error till [etc.]. **1872** E. Eggleston *End of World* xxiii. 158 '[I] see yer,' said Bill, trying in vain to draw his coat. **1873** J. H. Beadle *Undevel. West* xx. 369 'Marshal's got a good thing, though.' I see you; best place to make money in the United States. **1884** *Manch. Exam.* 10 May 5/4 As soon as the question was put it was easy to see the course which the Government would take. **1888** 'J. S. Winter' *Bottle's Childr.* ix, Then why didn't you tell Geoffrey you didn't see the good of sending so many? **1946** G. B. Shaw *Geneva* Pref. 7 Historians and newspaper editors can see revolutions three centuries off but not three years off. **1966** M. Woodhouse *Tree Frog* xxii. 161 'Let me guess... I know radar and guidance.'.. I nodded. I could see it coming a mile off. **1971** *Times* 16 June 21/5 Boost in gas reserves seen... The Soviet Union will expand production of oil..and of natural gas.. over 'the coming years'. **1974** 'E. Lathen' *Sweet & Low* xv. 149 Thatcher sympathized with him. This was one he had not seen coming, either.

b. With obj. a clause or an indirect question.

a **1000** *Ags. Ps.* lvii. 9 (Gr.) Soðfæst blissað, þonne he sið onȝan hu þa arleasan ealle forweorðað. *c* **1200** Ormin Introd. 47 Nu mihht tu sen þatt tatt wass rihht þatt mannkinn for till helle. *a* **1300** *Cursor M.* 1165 'Lauerd,' he said, 'now see i well Mi sin me has seit in vnsell.' *c* **1385** Chaucer *L.G.W.* 795 That whan sche say hire tyme myghte be At nygh sche stal a wey ful pryuyly. **1470–85** Malory *Arthur* XIII. xix. 639 Now I see and vnderstande that myn old synne hyndereth me and shameth me. *a* **1533** Ld. Berners *Huon* lvii. 191, I can not se but we are lyke to dye. **1551** R. Robinson tr. *More's Utopia* I. (1895) 102 Wherby I can not see what good they haue doone, but that men may more sickerlye be euell. **1606** Shaks. *Ant. & Cl.* III. xiii. 33, I see mens Iudgements are A parcell of their Fortunes. *c* **1645** Howell *Lett.* (1655) II. xviii. 30 Therefore I do not see how she could support a war long to any purpose if Castile were quiet. **1716** Addison *Freeholder* No. 22 ¶2, I only answered, that I did not see how the badness of the weather could be the King's fault. **1778** *Geraldina* I. 30 You see how rusticated I am, by writing on such uninteresting subjects. **1813** *Sketches of Character* (ed. 2) I. 123, I dont see what there is for me to say. **1856** J. H. Newman *Serm. Var. Occ.* i. (1881) 8 And thus you see, my brethren, how that particular temptation comes about. **1875** Jowett *Plato* (ed. 2) III. 219, I see that you are speaking your mind. **1895** E. B. Rowlands in *Law Times* XCIX. 464/2 It is at the first look hard to see why the Court of Appeal should ever have been troubled with Wegg-Prosser *v.* Evans.

c. With obj. and infinitive or †compl.

1435 Misyn *Fire of Love* 82 Vnwerily it byrnys þo þingis to fulfil þat it seys & knawes plesynge to god. *c* **1449** Pecock *Repr.* I. vii. 34 That what he siȝe to be trewe bifore in doom of resoun and lawe of kinde he toold out to hise herers. **1584** B. R. tr. *Herodotus* II. 101 b, But seeyng hym-selfe in these braakes, hee called hys brother [etc.]. *a* **1700** Evelyn *Diary* 25 July 1673, Besides he saw the Dutch warr..very unprosperous. **1700** Dryden *Sigism. & Guisc.* 276 The Youth, who saw His forfeit Life abandon'd to the Law. **1743** J. Morris *Serm.* vii. 190 But surely every one must see this to be highly absurd.

d. In literary use, expressions like 'we have seen', 'we shall see', 'the reader has now seen', etc., are common with reference to what has been or is to be narrated or proved in the book.

1422 tr. *Secreta Secret., Priv. Priv.* ii. 128 But whate myschefe folwyth of chynchry and folargesse, ye schal sene hit aftyr in this boke. **1560** WHITEHORN *Machiavel's Arte of Warre* v. 72 You shall see.. howe moche trouble and disease an armie and a capitaine is auoided of. **1820** KEATS *Lamia* I. 201 Why this fair creature chose so faerily By the wayside to linger, we shall see. **1846** CARPENTER *Man. Phys.* §843 We shall presently see reason to believe, that a very large proportion of the movements of many of the lower animals are of this reflex character. **1869** RUSKIN *Q. of Air* i. §38 We saw before the reason why Hermes is said to be the son of Maia. **1893** KIPLING *Many Invent., Lost Legion*, What.. the English did will be seen later on [in the story].

†**e.** Phrase, ***all things seen***: all things being duly considered. *Obs.*

c **1449** PECOCK *Repr.* II. viii. 186 Wherfore, alle thingis seen, this present v^e^. reule, or supposicion is trewe.

f. *absol.* Often with virtual ellipsis of obj.-clause, esp. in parenthetic use, or preceded by *as* or *so*. Also as figurative application of sense 2 and *colloq.* with omission of the second person subj. pronoun, appended parenthetically to a statement, freq. implying refusal to tolerate dissent, or as a mere filler; also standing alone (= 'do you see?') as an interrogative, with similar force.

I see: often used *colloq.* in assenting to an explanation or argument. *you see*: sometimes appended parenthetically to a statement of a fact known to the hearer which explains or excuses something that provokes surprise or blame.

a **1300** *Cursor M.* 2137 O þis thre com all, as þou sais, Has bene in werld and yeit beis. **1390** GOWER *Conf.* III. 251 Bot thei weren blinde, And sihen noght so fer as he. *c* **1485** *Digby Myst., Mary Magd.* 507 Lady, þis man is for ȝow, as I se can. **1570** T. WILSON tr. *Demosth. Orat.* vii. 98 And as farre as I can see, the daunger that we are in, is farre different from other folkes. **1657** CROMWELL *Sp.* 21 Apr. in Carlyle *Lett. & Sp.* (1845) II. 582 Because, you see, the present Government has 1,900,000 l.; and [etc.]. **1706** FARQUHAR *Recruiting Officer* I. i, Look'ee Serjeant, no Coaxing, no Wheedling, d'ye see. **1741–2** CHALLONER *Missionary Priests* (1803) II. 19 All the sanguinary laws enacted by queen Elizabeth were from time to time put in execution by this king,.. as we shall see anon. **1753** RICHARDSON *Grandison* (1754) III. xviii. 246 Surely.. a man of common penetration may see to the bottom of a woman's heart. **1802–12** BENTHAM *Ration. Judic. Evid.* (1827) II. 578 A man who.. if he saw to the bottom of his own mind, would acknowledge [etc.]. **1818** BYRON *Juan* I. xcvii, Whether it was she did not see, or would not, Or, like all very clever people, could not. **1823** SCOTT *Quentin D.* v, 'I see,' answered his uncle—'I comprehend. Cunning rogues—very cunning!' **1855** BROWNING *Bp. Blougram* 3 We ought to have our Abbey back, you see. **1859** HELPS *Friends in C.* Ser. II. (1877) I. viii. 216 The man who sees too widely is nearly sure to be indecisive, or to appear so. **1873** F. HALL *Mod. Eng.* 344 He replies, as we have seen, that he had anticipatively considered and rejected every view that I present. **1892** *Macmillan's Mag.* July 229 A few corns of wheat must always drop off, you see, before one can get the harvest. **1952** J. BINGHAM *My Name is Michael Sibley* xv. 183 You and me have got to understand each other right, see? **1959** N. MAILER *Advts. for Myself* (1961) 39 Listen, bud, you ain't talkin' to Joe Crap, see; you watch what you say with me. **1968** *Listener* 19 Dec. 810/3, I believe in having a go, see, so long as there's some fun in it, see. **1976** T. SHARPE *Wilt* v. 45 There was this student all dressed up like a waiter see.

g. *trans.* To have a particular mental view of; to perceive, apprehend, or appreciate in a particular manner. Also *absol.* esp. in ***to see with*** = to agree in opinion with another person.

For *to see eye to eye*, see EYE *sb.* 5.

a **1586** SIDNEY *Arcadia* II. (Sommer) 173 Alas, incomparable Philoclea, thou euer seest me, but dost neuer see me as I am. **1786** BURNS *To a Louse* viii, O wad some Pow'r the giftie gie us To see oursels as others see us! **1892** KIPLING in *Sun* (N.Y.) 28 Aug. II. 6/2 Each, in his separate star, Shall draw the Thing as he sees It for the God of Things as they are! *a* **1911** *Mod.* I now see the matter in a new light. I wish you could see with me on this question. **1934** E. O'NEILL *Days without End* III. ii. 113 He sees it clearly as a throwback to boyhood experiences. **1976** M. MACHLIN *Pipeline* xi. 135 Dad's idea of an oil man is a financier in a starched collar... I see it more like the way you did things Gramps.

h. To perceive (good or attractive qualities) *in* a person or thing, often in an interrogative clause; to perceive (a certain characteristic or type) *in* a person or thing.

1832 SCOTT *Ct. Robert* in *Tales of my Landlord* 4th Ser. I. iv. 113 Hereward, though flattered by the unusual degree of attention which the Princess bestowed upon him, saw in her only the daughter of his Emperor. **1835** BROWNING *Paracelsus* III. 419 A professorship At Basil! Since you see so much in it. **1863** 'OUIDA' *Held in Bondage* I. viii. 193 What could De Vigne possibly see in that woman? **1864** J. BRYCE *Holy Rom. Emp.* 62 He put to death the rebel Crescentius, in whom modern enthusiasm has seen a patriotic republican. **1916** 'TAFFRAIL' *Pincher Martin* vii. 114 Can't think what he sees in her. **1927** A. P. HERBERT *Plain Jane* 95 I'm not a jealous woman, But I *can't* see what he sees in her. **1971** P. O'DONNELL *Impossible Virgin* v. 107 She said quietly, 'Don't ask me what I see in him, please... Don't make judgments.'

i. To recognize the rightness or desirability of (an idea or thing); to give credence to, believe, accept; to consent to (a proposal). Usu. with *it. colloq.* (orig. *U.S.*).

1850 *California Courier* (San Francisco) 14 Nov. 2/2 This may be all right—but if it is, we cannot see it. **1860** R. NICHOLSON *Autobiogr.* 67 'Get up, my man, and let us go on,' said the stranger, almost throttling Cracroft. That worthy gentleman, however, 'could not see it', as we now say in modern slang. With a struggle he stammered that he had lost the wager. **1864** HOTTEN *Slang Dict.* 223 In street parlance, 'to see' is to know or believe; 'I don't see that,' i.e., 'I don't put faith in what you offer, or I know what you say to be untrue.' **1877** H. RUEDE *Sod-House Days* (1937) 8 The hack driver wanted us to go with him to Osborne, but the fare was $3.50 (trunks extra) and we 'could not see it'. **1890** KIPLING in *United Service Mag.* June 236, I said.. 'I don't keep a canteen up my sleeve.' They couldn't see it. **1934** G. B. SHAW *Too True to be Good* II. 60 But the old man never could be brought to see it. He said the proper profession for me was the bar. **1945** J. L. MARSHALL *Santa Fe* vii. 98 Fred then tried to interest the Burlington in his idea... But the Burlington couldn't see it. **1971** 'E. LATHEN' *Longer the Thread* (1972) vi. 65, I know that's what it looks like... But, for the life of me, I can't see it.

j. Usu. in negative or interrogative context with personal obj. (esp. *refl.*) and compl. (pple. or phrase): to perceive in one's mind's eye; to envisage as possible or acceptable.

1875 L. TROUBRIDGE *Jrnl.* 2 June in J. Hope-Nicholson *Life amongst Troubridges* (1966) x. 117 My dreadful yellow that I don't see myself wearing at all. **1915** R. BROOKE *Let.* 26 Jan. (1968) 657, I don't 'see' Viola [Tree] as the Lithuanian. **1926** CHESTERTON in W. R. Titterton *G. K. Chesterton* (1936) II. vii. 169, I do not quite see myself as the President of the League of Little People. **1955** R. BANNISTER *First Four Minutes* 16, I could not see myself in the winning place. **1962** M. TREVOR *Newman* 441 He stuck to his opinion that Bayswater was not the place for them; he could not see Faber going there. **1976** M. MACHLIN *Pipeline* iv. 45, I can't see dying because of your feelings about conservation.

4. a. *trans.* With mixed literal and figurative sense: To perceive by visual tokens. With obj. a sb. (denoting a fact, quality, state of things), more frequently a clause or an indirect question. Also with obj. and predicative complement (now usually introduced by *to be*).

c **1200** ORMIN 2930 He sahh þatt ȝho wiþþ childe wass, & nisste he nohht whæroffe. **1362** LANGL. *P. Pl.* A. VI. 15 Moni Cros on his cloke.. And þe vernicle bi-fore for men schulde him knowe, And seo be his signes whom he souht hedde. *c* **1400** LOVE *Bonavent. Mirr.* (1908) 23 Sche was sad and invariable: so ferforth that as sche profited better and better, so was there none that euere syhe or herde hir wrooth. **1426** LYDG. *De Guil. Pilgr.* 24272 Thou mayst se by my lokkes hore And by ryvels of my visage How that I am called 'Age'. **1432–50** tr. *Higden* (Rolls) V. 439 This man instructe in astronomy, see in the firmament þat his realme scholde be destroyede. *c* **1489** CAXTON *Sonnes of Aymon* iv. (1885) 120 'Syres', answered Reynawde, 'ye enquere over moche; see ye not what folke we ben'. **1513** DOUGLAS *Æneis* VIII. xii. 73 Actius Appollo, seand in the skye Off this melle the doutsum victorie. **1622** MABBE tr. *Aleman's Guzman d'Alf.* I. 34 Perceiuest thou not how impatient I am? Seest thou not that I can not containe my selfe? **1765** FOOTE *Commissary* I, Don't you see I am tired to death? **1848** THACKERAY *Van. Fair* xlvi, She was never seen angry but twice or thrice in her life.

b. The construction with sb. or pron. as obj. is sometimes combined with that with an obj.-clause. Now only *poet.*

Common in the Bible as literal rendering of a Heb. idiom, but app. also developed independently in Eng.

1382 WYCLIF *Gen.* xii. 14 Egipciens sawen the woman that she was ful fayre. *c* **1430** *Chev. Assigne* 26 Se ȝe þe ȝonder pore womman how þat she is pyned Withe twynlenges two. *c* **1440** *Alphabet of Tales* 427 Þe knyghtis of Rome saw Vaspasyan, at he was a nobyl man and a redy to cowncell. **1575** *Gammer Gurton* I. iv. 15 Here is a prety matter, to see this gere how it goes. **1842** TENNYSON *Morte d'Arthure* 123, I see thee what thou art.

c. To learn by reading.

Often idiomatically in present tense, *I see* = I have just read (esp. in a newspaper) *that* something has happened.

1426 AUDELAY *Poems* 6 In the gospel thou sist. **1612** SKELTON *Don Quixote* IV. v. (1620) 338 What then can you say to me of the good Don Cirongilio of Thracia, who was so animous and valiant as may be seene in his booke? **1651** HOBBES *Leviath.* II. xxvi. 150, I could never see in any Author, what a Fundamental Law signifieth. **1765** H. WALPOLE in Jesse *Selwyn & Contemp.* (1843) II. 11 *A propos*, I see by the papers, that the Bishop of London is suppressing mass-houses. **1847** THACKERAY *Lett.* (1887) 8 Did you see her death in the paper? **1881** SAINTSBURY *Dryden* 13 One thing in particular I have never seen fairly put as accounting for the complete royalization of nearly the whole people.

d. *intr.* To read music. *colloq.*

1955 L. FEATHER *Encycl. Jazz* 347 *See*, read (music). 'He doesn't see too well' refers to a performer who reads music slowly. **1970** C. MAJOR *Dict. Afro-Amer. Slang* 101 *See*,.. to read music.

5. a. *trans.* To direct the sight (literal or metaphorical) intentionally to; to look at, contemplate, examine, inspect, or scrutinize; to visit (a place); to attend (a play, etc.) as a spectator. (Cf. *to see on*, 21.) Also ***to see and (to) be seen***; hence ***see-and-be-seen*** attrib. phr.

a **1225** *Leg. Kath.* 2085 Þæt alle weren isihen hider for to seon þis feorlich. *a* **1300** *Havelok* 1021 For it ne was non horse-knaue,.. þat he ne kam þider, þe leyk to se. **1362** LANGL. *P. Pl.* A. II. 163 Soþnesse sauh hem wel and seide bote luyte, Bote prikede on his palfrey and passede hem alle. *c* **1386** CHAUCER *Wife's Prol.* 552, I hadde the bettre leyser for to pleye And for to se and eek for to be seye Of lusty folk. **1471** CAXTON *Recuyell* (Sommer) 281 Whan they had seen and beholde the monstre ynowh they departed thens. *c* **1590** *Faire Em* II. i. 97 Two gentlemen.. Oft times resort to see and to be seene Walking the streete fast by thy fathers dore. **1592** NASHE *P. Penilesse* F 3, Gameing,.. drinking, or seeing a play. **1600** SURFLET *Country Farm* I. vi. 27 Let him not goe to see the towne, except it be vpon his earnest affaires. **1604** SHAKS. *Oth.* II. i. 37 Let's to the Sea-side (hoa) As well to see the Vessell that's come in, As to throw-out our eyes for braue Othello. **1642** D. ROGERS *Naaman* 113 Their answer was, I am to goe see a farme, I haue bought oxen. **1645** SYMONDS *Diary* (Camden) 221 One of the statues was serjeant-at-law, the other a soldjer. See the fashion of the serjeant's habit. **1693** RYMER *Short View Trag.* i. 6 Some go to see, others to hear a Play. **1697** DRYDEN *Virg. Georg.* II. 704 Whose Mind, unmov'd, the Bribes of Courts can see, Their glitt'ring Baits, and Purple Slavery. **1710** SWIFT *Jrnl. to Stella* 13 Dec., [We] set out.. to the Tower, and saw all the sights. **1721** DE FOE *Mem. Cavalier* (1840) 148 By their faces,.. they durst see an enemy. **1738** SWIFT *Polite Conv.* 41 Her Ladyship went to see, and to be seen. **1828** W. SCOTT *Jrnl.* 3 May (1972) 468 After the dinner I went to Mrs. Scott of Harden to see and be seen by her nieces. **1848** THACKERAY *Van. Fair* li, My father took me to see a show at Brookgreen Fair. **1878** *Athletic World* 17 May 79/1 The finish was one worth going miles to see. **1881** FREEMAN in W. R. W. Stephens *Life & Lett.* (1895) II. 236 We have trotted about, been into Canada, and seen the sights. *a* **1911** W. S. GILBERT *Lost Bab Ballads* (1932) 31 To see and be seen is for what we pay At Islington on the half-crown day. **1960** *Times* 3 June 6/5 London audiences to which the social see-and-be-seen set attaches itself. **1961** *Economist* 25 Nov. 770/1 This mixing of 'blind' traffic with see-and-be-seen aircraft is particularly dangerous in overcrowded terminal areas.

b. With sb. or pron. as obj. and complementary pple. or inf. Cf. 1 g.

1903 F. M. CRAWFORD *Uncanny Tales* (1911) 146 (*Man Overboard!*) So I wrote to Jack that I would come down and see him married.

†**c.** *absol.* To look. *Obs.* (Cf. 17–25.)

c **1250** *Gen. & Ex.* 2169 It semet wel ðat ȝe spies ben, And in-to ðis lond cumen to sen. *a* **1300** *Cursor M.* 17288 + 447 Gropes & sees oueralle, and knaw þat it be. *c* **1425** *Seven Sag.* (P.) 781 Toward the credyl as he saythe, The good grew-hond lay and syȝe. **1484** CAXTON *Fables of Alfonce* xiii, He.. sawe and serched al aboute here and there.

d. *trans.* To look at, read (a book, document, etc.). ***seen and allowed, seen and approved***, etc.: a formula used in certifying the official inspection of a document.

a **1300** *Cursor M.* 26593 Þe quilk [circumstances] grathli þe sal be kend, If þou þis bok will se till end. **1377** LANGL. *P. Pl.* B. II. 70 Thanne.. lyer.. preide cyuile to se and symonye to rede it. *c* **1386** CHAUCER *Man of Law's T.* 711 And what þat he this pitous lettre say ffull ofte he seyde Allas and weylaway. **1426** LYDG. *On Eng. Title to Crown of France* Prol. in *Pol. Poems* (Rolls) II. 133 Tho that shalle hit sene or rede. *c* **1450** *Godstow Reg.* (1905) 206 After sche had say the charters. **1523** FITZHERB. *Husb.* §152 For I haue seen bokes of accompte of householde.. & I doubte not, but [etc.]. **1576** GASCOIGNE *Spoyle of Antw.* title-p., Novem. 1576. Seene and allowed. Printed at London by Richard Jones. **1594** NASHE *Unfort. Trav.* Ded., Least anie man should challenge these my papers as goods vncustomd.. to the seale of your excellent censure loe here I present them to bee seene and allowed. **1609** SKENE *Reg. Maj.* 89 We charge and command zou, thir present letters being sene, ze cause lawfully summone *A.* to compeir before vs. **1621** *Shuttleworths' Acc.* (Chetham Soc.) 258 [At end of an account.] Seene and allowed by mee, Ric. Shuttleworthe. **1662** *Acts of Sederunt* (1790) 85 The defender's advocat shall return the proces, and shall write on the back the day of the return, (*seen and returned*), and sett his name thereto. **1818** CRUISE *Digest* (ed. 2) II. 215 No man would advance money upon an estate without seeing the title deeds.

e. The imperative *see* is used in books to a passage in the same or some other work in which information will be found. Cf. mod.L. *vide*, F. *voyez, voir*, G. *siehe*.

1608 PLAT *Garden of Eden* (ed. Bellingham 1653) 50 See more of this in Numb. 30. *Ibid.* 88 See before, Numb. 67. **1704** J. HARRIS *Lex. Techn.* I, Period, in Chronology, signifies a Revolution of a certain Number of Years; as the *Metonick Period*, the *Julian Period*, and the *Calippick Period*; which see in their proper places. **1753** CHALLONER *Cath. Chr. Instr.* 21 See *St. Dionysius, L. de Eccles.* **1769** FALCONER *Dict. Marine* (1780), *Rim*, or *Brim*, a name given to the circular edge of any of the *tops*. See that article. **1818** SCOTT *Rob Roy* ix, See twenty-third of Queen Elizabeth, and third James First, chapter twenty-fifth. **1849** MACAULAY *Hist. Eng.* iii. I. 339 *note*, The population of Derby was 4000 in 1712. See Wolley's MS. History, quoted in Lyson's Magna Britannia. **1861** PALEY *Æschylus* (ed. 2) *Persians* 741 *note*, ὅστις, *quippe qui*. See on Prom. 38. **1868** BROWNING *Ring & Bk.* VIII. 812 For pregnant instance let us contemplate The luck of Leonardus,—see at large Of Sicily's Decisions sixty-first.

f. The imperative is often employed exclamatorily, either with obj. a sb. or a clause introduced by *what* or *how*, or *absol.* as quasi-*int.* = Behold! Also ***see here***, a brusque form of address used to preface an order, expostulation, reprimand, etc. Cf. *look here* s.v. LOOK *v.* 4 a.

In OE. accompanied by the dative *þe*, a use which, though unrecorded in ME. or mod.Eng. literature, survives in dialects: see *sithee* in *Eng. Dial. Dict.* The corresponding plural *see you!* also occurs in dialects, but is apt to be confused with the interrogative *see you?* do you see?

c **825** *Vesp. Psalter* xxxii. 18 Sehðe [*ecce*] eȝan dryhtnes ofer ða ondredendan hine ȝehyhtende soðlice in mildheortnisse his. *c* **975** *Rushw. Gosp.* Matt. xxiv. 25 Sihþe ic sæcge eow [*ecce praedixi uobis*]. *a* **1325** *Prose Psalter* l[i.] 6 Se! for ich am conceiued in wickednesses. *c* **1440** *Alphabet of Tales* lxxix. 61 Se! yonder gois a fayr yong man! *c* **1440** *Gesta Rom.* i. 4 (Harl. MS.) Seith nowe, goode men; þis emperour I call owre lord ihesu Criste. **1500–20** DUNBAR *Poems* xliv. 28 Se quhat wirschep wemen suld haif than. **1522** *World & Child* 79 Lo my toppe I dryue in same, Se it torneth rounde. *c* **1570** W. WAGER *The longer thou livest* 684 (Brandl), Se, se, woulde you iudge him a foole So sadly as he readeth on his booke! **1671** WOODHEAD *St. Teresa* I. xiv. 88 See how these Trees begin to button. *c* **1690** LD. HALIFAX *Epist. to Earl Dorset* 89 See, see! Upon the Banks of Boyne he stands. **1734** POPE *Ess. Man* IV. 327 See the sole bliss Heav'n could on all bestow! **1739** C. WESLEY *Hymn, 'Hail the Day'* v, See! He lifts his Hands above! See! He shews the Prints of Love!

a **1744** POPE (J.), See what it is to have a poet in your house. **1755** JOHNSON, *See*, interjection. Lo; look; observe; behold. **1807** WORDSW. *Mother's Return* xii, But see, the evening star comes forth! **1818** SCOTT *Hrt. Midl.* xxx, See there!—that was the gait my auld joe used to cross the country. **1821** —— *Kenilw.* xii, 'See you, sir!' said he, 'I have changed my garb from that of a farrier to a serving-man.' **1871** R. ELLIS *Catullus* lv. 12 See! what bowery roses; here he hides him. **1898** G. B. SHAW *Mrs. Warren's Profession* II. 185 Now see here, George: what are you up to about that girl? **1925** F. SCOTT FITZGERALD *Great Gatsby* vii. 152 'Now see here, Tom,' said Daisy, turning around from the mirror. **1941** J. D. CARR *Case of Constant Suicides* ii. 29 'See here,' pursued Alan... 'Let us get this straight.' **1974** G. JENKINS *Bridge of Magpies* ix. 148 'See here,' I said. 'There's been another death. I want you to signal the fisheries frigate.'

6. a. With indirect question as obj.: To ascertain by inspection, inquiry, experiment, or consideration.

In modern use, a promise 'to see what one can do', or 'to see if one can do (so and so)' commonly implies a promise to use one's best endeavours to secure the desired result.

1373 BARBOUR *Bruce* v. 126 A quhill in Carrik lendit he, To se quha frend or fa vald be. *c* **1425** AUDELAY *XI Pains of Hell* 5 in *O.E. Misc.* 210 Hou mychael and poule þay went in fere To se what payns in hel were þer. *c* **1440** *Pallad. on Husb.* I. 410 As tymber, hewe hit with an axe and sene If hit be not in thegge. **1561** *Maitland Club Misc.* III. 277 The superintendent beand in ye sayd kyrk..seand gyf ye kyrk wes repared conform to ye act of his visitacion. **1575** *Gammer Gurton* I. v. 51 Breake it, foole, with thy hand, and see and thou canst fynde it. **1582** ALLEN *Martyrd. Campion* (1908) 87 This Havard..went furth into the citie with another in his company to see if he could meet with M. Cottam. **1613** TAPP *Pathw. Knowl.* 8 And when you haue all added them, see what remaines besides the nynes, and drawing a short line [etc.]. **1676** T. MACE *Musick's Monum.* 59 [In making a lute] First bring your Back and Belly together, and see if they will fit. **1743** POCOCKE *Descr. East* I. II. iii. 105 The people had come rudely to the boat when I was absent, and had said that they would see whether this stranger would dare come out another day. **1766** EARL MARCH in Jesse *Selwyn & Contemp.* (1843) I. 62, I am just going to ride out to see if air and exercise will get me a stomach. **1821** SCOTT *Kenilw.* iv, Follow yonder fellow, and see where he takes earth. **1835** DICKENS *Sk. Boz, Mr. J. Dounce*, 'Can you open me half-a-dozen more [oysters], my dear?' inquired Mr. John Dounce. 'I'll see what I can do for you, Sir', replied the young lady in blue. *a* **1853** ROBERTSON *Serm.* Ser. IV. iv. (1876) 46 He will look at the fact in every way to see if he cannot get it into a position where it shall be seen no longer. **1865** H. KINGSLEY *Hillyars & B.* ii, Cut away, old chap, and see who it is.

b. *absol.* or with ellipsis of indirect question. Sometimes used as a formula for not giving a direct answer on the spot.

a **1300** *Cursor M.* 14310 'And quar haf yee his bode laid?' 'Sir', said mari, 'cum forth and se'. **1568** GRAFTON *Chron.* II. 773 As for this gentleman my sonne, I mind he shal be where I am till I see further. **1581** EARL MORTON in *Cal. Scott. Papers* VI. 14, I was purposed to have banished my self againe and turned my backe upon Scotland while I had sene further. **1851** HAWTHORNE *Ho. Sev. Gables* xx, Ah, something terrible has happened! I must run and see! **1851** I. SPENCER *Let.* 11 Jan. in U. Young *Life I. Spencer* (1933) III. iii. 181 About going to France, we shall see. **1861** *Two Cosmos* I. 283 'But what ails you to tell him I am here now?' ..She shut the door, looked inquiringly at him, and left him standing, with 'I'll see'. **1898** G. B. SHAW *Arms & Man* III. 62 We shall see. And you shall wait my pleasure. **1925** F. SCOTT FITZGERALD *Great Gatsby* vii. 137 What he really said was: 'Yes... Yes... I'll see.' **1959** R. MATTHEWS tr. *J. Steinmann's Saint Jerome* I. xi. 49 He would tell his friend about it, and later they would see.

c. To make sure by inspection (before taking action) *that* certain conditions exist. Cf. sense 8.

c **1440** *Alphabet of Tales* 78 He þat giffis it [the benefice] suld se þat he þatt he gaff it to war able for to take it. **1523** FITZHERB. *Husb.* §57 Se that they be soft on the fore-croppe, and upon the hucbone. **1821** SCOTT *Kenilw.* xxiii, He looked sharply around to see that there was nothing in sight which might give the lie to his words.

7. †a. To keep in view; to watch over; chiefly in favourable sense, to protect, take care of, tend.

c **1250** *Gen. & Ex.* 1663 Laban bi-taȝte him, siðen to sen, His hirdenesse ðat it wel ben. *a* **1300** *Cursor M.* 16488 'Ha we noght þar-of to do', coth þai, 'þou sal þi-self it se'. *c* **1307** *Song Exec. Sir S. Fraser* in *Pol. Songs* (Camden) 216 Sire Edward of Carnarvan, Jhesu him save ant see! *c* **1374** CHAUCER *Troylus* II. 85 Quod Pandarus ma dame god yow see. **1426** LYDG. *De Guil. Pilgr.* 4824 And to Seyn Iohan I leve also, That he may han perseueraunce To sen me in my gret suffraunce. *c* **1440** *York Myst.* viii. 77 Luke þat þi semes be suttilly seyn. *Ibid.* xvii. 33 Sirs! god yowe saffe ande see. *c* **1460** *Towneley Myst.* ix. 127 Mahowne the saue and se, sir syryne! *a* **1535** *Frere & Boy* 64 in Ritson *Anc. Pop. Poetry* 37 Sone, he sayde, god the se. **1563** *Child-Marriages* 132 This deponent..went home againe to se his busines. **1607** NORDEN *Surv. Dial.* v. 230 If he be an inferior, he may be his owne Bayly, and see the managing and manuring of his owne reuenewes, and not to leaue it to the discretion and diligence of lither swaines.

b. With adv. or phrase: To escort (a person) *home*, *to the door*, etc. ***to see*** (a person) ***off***: to be present at (his) starting for a journey. ***to see*** (a person) (***all***) ***right***: to ensure (his) well-being or safety; ***to see*** (a person) ***over***, ***through***: of a thing, to be sufficient for (his) needs; also with prep. *over* or *through* (a period of time or difficulty). Also, ***to see*** (a book) ***through the press***.

1607 SHAKS. *Cor.* III. iii. 137 Go see him out at Gates,.. Giue him deseru'd vexation. **1693** CONGREVE *Old Bach.* IV. xix, *Læt.* Oh! Won't you follow, and see him out of Doors, my Dear? *Fond.* I'll shut this door, to secure him from coming back. **1698** FRYER *Acc. E. India & P.* 1 For your singular Favour, in seeing me Aboard-ship. **1770** C. JENNER *Placid Man* I. II. v. 104 When he had seen her safe into her chair, he went home. **1775** SHERIDAN *Duenna* I. ii, But, hark ye, Ferdinand, did you leave your key with them? *Don Ferd.* Yes; the maid who saw me out, took it from the door. **1809** W. IRVING *Knickerb.* II. iv. (1820) 119 Escorted by a multitude of relatives and friends, who all went down, as the common phrase expresses it, 'to see them off'. **1819** KEATS *Let.* 16 Apr. (1958) II. 92 Do you..get groggy..so as to be obliged to be seen home with a Lantern. **1884** RIDER HAGGARD *Dawn* xlii, 'Where have you been to, Lady Florence?' he said. 'To see my brother off', she answered. **1884** W. C. SMITH *Kildrostan* 50 Do not trouble to bring back the boat; I'll see Miss Ina home. **1886** MISS L. TOULMIN SMITH *Bk. Brome* Pref. 1, I willingly undertook, at her request, to see it through the press. **1888** FLOR. WARDEN *Witch of Hills* II. xviii. 104 We saw the ladies into the brougham. **1894** 'MARK TWAIN' in *St. Nicholas* Mar. 393/1 Thirty camel-loads of treasures was enough to see a dervish through, because they live very simple. **1899** RIDER HAGGARD in *Longm. Mag.* Apr. 125, I opened the door to see out some friends. *a* **1914** 'SAKI' *Beasts & Super-Beasts* (1914) 217 If you'll lend me three pounds that ought to see me through comfortably. **1959** *Times* 19 Mar. 5/5 He said he would see me all right if I said I saw the two police strike the boy. **1965** *Listener* 25 Nov. 865/1 Although Louis MacNeice was a fluent and sometimes facile poet, his sense of fact generally saw him through. *a* **1966** 'M. NA GOPALEEN' *Best of Myles* (1968) 87 To be saddled with the task of 'seeing' an inebriated friend 'right'. **1966** M. STEEN *Looking Glass* iii. 52 He..wrote me a cheque for twenty pounds—'to see me over'. **1971** *N.Z. Listener* 22 Mar. 13/1 Tell yer, I'll see you right at a boardin' place until you get jacked up. **1974** S. B. HOUGH *Fear Fortune, Father* i. 15, I could remember Lawson saying to me, 'I'll see you all right.' **1976** M. BUTTERWORTH *Remains to be Seen* vi. 89, I stopped the milk till Monday... But if you want a couple of pints to see you over the weekend.

8. To ensure by supervision or vigilance that something shall be done or not done. **a.** with clause as obj. Often with reference to action on the part of the subject: To take care, see to it (cf. 25 c) *that* one does so and so. (In this use rarely †with dative of pron. used *refl.*)

a **1300** *K. Horn* (Camb. MS.) 452, & se he holde foreward. *c* **1400** *Apol. Loll.* (Camden) 41 And se hem religious, þat þei feyn not falsly pouert... And see þei þat þei oblesche no man to the maner of pouert, but þat God haþ callid þer to. *c* **1422** tr. *Secreta Secret., Priv. Priv.* xxxiv. 187 See that thou can lyue Of Lytill mette and Drynke. *c* **1449** PECOCK *Repr.* II. xvii. 253 Se ȝe that in ȝoure vndirnymyng ȝe bere ȝou discreetli. **1468** [see MAN *sb.*[1] 4 f]. **1502** ATKYNSON tr. *De Imitatione* III. viii. (1893) 202 Se, therfore,..that no strong fantasies of any mater trouble the. *c* **1530** H. RHODES *Bk. Nurture* in *Babees Bk.* 67 See ye haue Voyders ready for to auoyd the Morsels that they doe leaue on their Trenchours. **1535** LYNDESAY *Satyre* 52 And sie the burgessis spair not for expence, Bot speid thame heir, with Temporalitie. **1560** DAUS tr. *Sleidane's Comm.* 1 b, It is the propre office of a Byshop to see that the people be rightly instructed. **1575** *Gammer Gurton* II. i. 77 Now, Hodge, see thou take heede And do as I thee byd. **1632** HOLLAND *Cyrupædia* 197 See then quoth he, you order the matter so, and provide against that time. **1639** W. C. *Italian Convert* xxx. 222 Shee was never from about him, and saw that hee wanted nothing which the world could yeeld for the recovery of his health. **1685** BAXTER *Paraphr. N.T., Mark* iv. 23 Let him that hath ears and understanding see that he hear God's word regardfully. **1741** RICHARDSON *Pamela* III. 214 Only when your worthy Parents have perused them, see that I have every Line of them again. **1873** BLACK *Pr. Thule* xxi. 341 Mrs. Lavender would see that she was properly looked after. **1884** *Manch. Exam.* 17 May 4/7 It behoves us to see that we are not outstripped by our rivals abroad. **1886** PEARSON in *Law Rep. 32 Chanc. Div.* 48 The landlord..is interested in seeing that the liquidators discharge their duty properly.

b. with obj. a sb. or pronoun, and pa. pple. or adj. (rarely infinitive) as complement.

1558 Q. MARY *Will* in J. M. Stone *Mary I* (1901) 515 That they to the uttermost of ther powers and wyttes, shall see this my present Testament & last will perform'd and executed. **1583** SIR C. HATTON in Kempe *Losely MSS.* (1836) 268 W[ch] I thought good to advertise you of, that in the meane whyle you myght see every thinge well ordered. **1586** A. DAY *Eng. Secretary* I. (1625) 66 And if my opinion may at all prevaile with you should quickly call him home from hence, and see him more better to be provided for. **1607** SHAKS. *Cor.* IV. vi. 47 Go see this Rumorer whipt. **1672** R. MONTAGU in *Buccleuch MSS.* (Hist. MSS. Comm.) I. 517, I think seeing an Ambassador's debts paid when he comes away belongs to your province. **1697** DRYDEN *Virg. Past.* IX. 29 O Tity'rus, tend my Herd, and see them fed. **1704** *Milit. Dict.* (ed. 2), *Major of a Regiment*..is to convey all Orders to the Regiment..to see it march in good order [etc.]. **1824** SCOTT *St. Ronan's* xxxviii, I will see her avenged on every one of them! **1899** in *Law Times* XCII. 92/2 We undertake to see you paid the said sum of £526.

c. Coupled by *and* with another verb: To be careful to (do something). *colloq.*

a **1766** MRS. F. SHERIDAN *Sidney Bidulph* IV. 69 David.. told me he'd see and get me another every jot as pretty. **1825** T. HOOK *Sayings* Ser. II. *Passion & Princ.* xi. III. 257 If you get your letters ready early in the day, I will see and get them franked.

9. a. To view or regard as, to judge, deem. With complementary adj., *good*, *fit*, *proper*, or the like, the object being an infinitive phrase (less frequently a clause), which is sometimes suppressed by ellipsis or represented by *it*.

a **1325** *MS. Rawl. B.* 520 b, Þat..suuche enquestene..be after þat te Iustises soez best to doinde to þe wille of þe reaume. *Ibid.* 31 b, To ben..ipubliste, in schirene, in Citees ..ant in oþere sollempne studes, þare þe seost best forte spede. *c* **1375** *Lay Folks Mass Bk.* 393 (Royal MS.) Þo froytes of þo erthe make plenteuus, als þou sees best. **1558** *Will* in *Berks, Bucks, & Oxon N. & Q.* (1905) II. 48 W[t] suche armes in money as myne executours shall thinke and see requysite in charitie to be gyven to the poore. **1581** PETTIE tr. *Guazzo's Civ. Conv.* III. (1586) 150 The father by his authoritie ought to distribute his fauoures as he seeth good, to one more, to another lesse. **1663** BUTLER *Hudibras* I. iii. 275 Others may doe as they see good. **1818** SCOTT *Hrt. Midl.* xii, To abide the dispensation that the Lord sees meet to send us. **1829** —— *Anne of G.* xxxiv, The Duke for once saw it necessary to alter his purpose of instant battle. **1837** CARLYLE *Fr. Rev.* I. v. i, The only thing one sees advisable is to bring up soldiers. **1860** RUSKIN *Unto this Last* i. §24 Supposing the master of a manufactory saw it right..to place his own son in the position of an ordinary workman.

†b. Passive, ***to be seen***: (*a*) to seem, appear [= L. *videri*]; (*b*) *ellipt.* to seem good, approve itself. *Obs.*

1382 WYCLIF *Gen.* xix. 14 And he was seen to hem as pleiynge to speke. *c* **1400** tr. *Secreta Secret., Gov. Lordsh.* xiii. 55 With discrecion do he hit noght ouer latly ne ouer hastly, þat he be noght sen hastyf ne slowe. **1466** *Dunfermline Reg.* (Bannatyne) 356 To mak a mylne within my said grunde..giff it be sene spedfull till ws. **1473** *Rental Bk. Cupar-Angus* (1879) I. 178 Rychswa the myl to be fychit gif it be sein to ws profitabile fra the place it standis up til ane place of mair eysmentis and profitis. *Ibid.* 182 Anens the pairtyn of the town it is seyn to the Abbot and the Conuent for al pairtis that the town stand vnpairtyt as it standis and allegis tham of that condicion. **1484** in *Exch. Rolls Scot.* IX. 603 To prolong and continew takkis of thaim for the space of fyve yeris or within as salbe sene speidfull to thaim. **1548** UDALL, etc. *Erasm. Par. Matt.* xvii. 1–8 These thynges wer seene to the Apostles as to men newely waked from slepe. **1549** *Bk. Comm. Prayer, Visit. Sick* Prayer, Consider his contricion, accept his teares, aswage his payne as shalbe seen to thee moste expediente for hym. **1574** M. STOKES in G. Peacock *Observ. Stat. Cambr.* (1841) App. A. p. xxxvi, When the Father hathe arguyde att hys Plesure the Bachelars of Arte shall replye, as many as shall be seene to the Father.

10. a. To know by observation (ocular and other), to witness; to meet with in the course of one's experience; to have personal knowledge of, to be a contemporary of and present at the scene of (an event); to be living at (a certain period of time). Also, to experience (a specific age in life): usu. in negative context. Phrases, ***to see life, the world***: see the sbs. ***to have seen everything, it all***: to have experienced all the possible events and situations of life (often used as an expression of resignation or boredom); ***to see the New*** (***Old***) ***Year in*** (***out***): see YEAR 7.

Sometimes with mixture of sense 11, as in ***to have seen better days***, to have been formerly better off or (of a thing) in better condition than now; ***to have seen one's day***, ***one's best days***, to be no longer in one's prime.

Beowulf 2014 Ne seah ic..meduaream maran! *c* **1200** *Trin. Coll. Hom.* 139 And teh folc to him to heren his wise word, and to sende his wunderliche liflode. **1297** R. GLOUC. (Rolls) 1611 Vol vewe kinges me sucþ þat it wolde do. **1375** BARBOUR *Bruce* XVI. 179 In-till all the weir of Irland So hard ane fechting wes nocht seyne. **1412–20** LYDG. *Troy Bk.* I. 1133 He schal þe tyme se þat he par-avnter schal mow þanked be. *a* **1533** LD. BERNERS *Huon* lxi. 213, I haue longe desyryd to se ye day that I nowe do se. **1575** *Gammer Gurton* I. iv. 2, I may well cursse and ban This daie, that euer I saw it. *c* **1590** *Sir T. More* IV. v. 86 But we..Hauing seene better dayes, now know the lack Of glorie that once rearde eche high-fed back. **1593** SHAKS. *Lucr.* 380 O had they in that darkesome prison died, Then had they seene the period of their ill. **1679** DRYDEN *Limberham* Prol. 1 True Wit has seen its best days long ago. **1686** tr. *Chardin's Coronat. Solyman* 35 One who had never seen the world. *a* **1700** EVELYN *Diary* 27 Jan. 1658, He declaim'd against the vanities of the world before he had seene any. **1712–13** SWIFT *Jrnl. to Stella* 16 Feb., I never saw such a continuance of rainy weather. **1759** JOHNSON *Rasselas* xxxix, They had seen nothing, for they had lived from early youth in that narrow spot. **1763** *Brit. Mag.* IV. 372, I, being elevated with liquor, could not pass by a night-house, always being fond of seeing life, as the term is. **1806** To have seen better days [see DAY *sb.* 13 a]. **1821** SCOTT *Kenilw.* xxxvii, The wisest men whom the world has seen. **1848** THACKERAY *Van. Fair* lxi, I never saw his equal for pluck and daring. **1870** MORRIS *Earthly Par., Lovers of Gudrun* 40 Kiartan now had seen His eighteenth spring. **1876** FLOR. MARRYAT *Her Father's Name* xxv, The truth is, the old housekeeper had seen her day, and was thankful for the prospect of any help in her duties. **1883** R. W. DIXON *Mano* I. viii. 21 And this I say Who have seen much that mighty love can do. **1899** H. JAMES *Awkward Age* I. i. 3 He had..doubled the Cape of the years—he would never again see fifty-five. **1925** F. SCOTT FITZGERALD *Great Gatsby* i. 21 I've been everywhere and seen everything and done everything. **1930** W. S. MAUGHAM *Cakes & Ale* v. 72 'But she's not as old as you are,' I said... 'She'll never see thirty again.' **1941** F. THOMPSON *Over to Candleford* x. 144 Laura [wore] a green smock which had seen better days. **1957** 'M. M. KAYE' *Shadow of Moon* xiv. 216 'I escorted her out from England.' '*What*!.. Now I have seen everything!' **1959** N. MAILER *Advts. for Myself* (1961) 209 Pot gave me a sense of something new about the time I was convinced I had seen it all. **1973** G. GREENE *Honorary Consul* II. iii. 80 She's not twenty, and, you know, I won't see sixty again. **1973** 'E. MCBAIN' *Hail to Chief* i. 6 Men..with..eyes that had seen it all, seen it all: Monoghan and Monroe from Homicide. **1977** G. TINDALL *Fields Beneath* vi. 90 The workhouse itself was a 'handsome brick edifice' that had seen better days. **1978** T. WILLIS *Buckingham Palace Connection* viii. 161 'A boat race,' said Tremayne... 'Now I've seen everything!' said Story.

b. With clause, obj. and inf., or obj. and complement: To observe, find. Also (chiefly in the future tense), to find, come to know in the course of events.

1390 GOWER *Conf.* I. 3 For now upon this tyde Men se the world on every syde In sondry wyse so diversed, That [etc.]. *c* **1425** *Cast. Persev.* 3227 in *Macro Plays* 173 Þer schal we sone se what þat his Iugement schal be. **1500–20** DUNBAR *Poems* iv. 45, I see that makaris amang the laif Playis heir ther pegeant, syne gois to graif. ? **1533** HEYWOOD *Pard. & Frere* 611 Thou shall se What I shall do by and by. **1536**

CRANMER in Ellis *Orig. Lett.* Ser. III. III. 27, I had dayly prayed unto God that I might se the power of Rome destroyed, and that I thanked God that I had now sene it in this Realme. **1551** T. WILSON *Logic* (1563) 6 b, We see heate in other thynges to bee seperated from the subiecte. Whereupon we Iudge that the heate is an other thyng then the very substaunce of Fire. **1611** BIBLE *Transl. Pref.* ¶2 He gaue foorth, that hee had not seene any profit to come by any Synode. **1764** GOLDSM. *Trav.* 397 Have we not seen, round Britain's peopled shore, Her useful sons exchanged for useless ore? **1821** SCOTT *Pirate* xxvi, We shall soon see how the old spell-mutterer will receive us. **1825** T. HOOK *Sayings* Ser. II. *Passion & Princ.* v. III. 6 At length he came to a resolution..to 'wait and see' what would turn up for the best. **1847** TENNYSON *Princess* III. 244 There is nothing upon earth More miserable than she that has a son And sees him err. **1856** FROUDE *Hist. Eng.* (1858) I. iii. 244 The astonished church authorities saw bill after bill hurried up before the Lords.

absol. **1456** SIR G. HAYE *Law Arms* (S.T.S.) 102 As men seis, naturaly ilke wilde beste and tame defend the self. **1823** COLERIDGE *Table-t.* 28 Apr., 'The Spaniards are absolutely conquered; it is absurd to talk of their chance of resisting'.—'Very well, my lord', I said, 'we shall see'. **1865** KINGSLEY *Herew.* xxi, You will see some day. Now, I will tell you but one word.

c. In *passive*. Formerly often impersonal, *it is seen*, it is observed, experience shows *that*.

1390 GOWER *Conf.* I. 15 But ofte is sen that mochel slowthe, When men ben drunken of the cuppe, Doth mochel harm. *c* **1400** *Master of Game* ii. 32 (MS. Digby 182) The other hertes..renne vponn hym and sle hym. And þat is see and sothe. **1451** CAPGRAVE *Life St. August.* iii. 6 And as often is sene þei make sumtyme debate betwyx wif and husband. **1545** in I. S. Leadam *Sel. Cases Crt. Requests* (1898) 86 Whiche..was never vsid nor senne in his tyme to be one. **1576** GASCOIGNE *Compl. Philom.* ad fin., The sonnes of such rash sinning sires, Are seldome sene to runne a ruly race. **1580** FRAMPTON *Dial. Yron & Steele* 168 For it is seene that a cuppe of colde water beeing dronke, that commeth foorth of a well..hurteth. **1607** NORDEN *Surv. Dial.* I. 13 There grew such emulation among Farmers, that one would outbid another, (which in the beginning was little seene). **1638** JUNIUS *Paint. Ancients* 38 So is it seldome or never seene that the workes of one man should fit our humour in all things.

d. Willingness (or unwillingness) *to see* an event is often predicated as equivalent to willingness (or unwillingness) that the event should occur. Hence the vb. sometimes assumes the sense: To allow (something to happen).

So in colloquial expressions of emphatic refusal: ***I'll see him hanged*** (***damned, further***, etc.) ***first***.

c **1400** *Cato's Morals* 92 in *Cursor M.* 1670 Qua-sim-euer þou be þat wille þi-self safe se..loke..þou kepe þi corage fra ille tecchis rife. *c* **1400** *Gamelyn* 146 Be thou nought wroth, For to seen thee have harm it were me right loth. *c* **1420** *Avow. Arth.* xxxvii, But I nolde, for no lordeshippe, se þi life lorne. *c* **1489** CAXTON *Sonnes of Aymon* ix. 228 Reynawde is my cosin, & I oughte not to see his dethe nor his dommage. **1554** in Warden *Burgh Laws Dundee*, etc. (1872) 333 Ȝe salbe ane obedient and trew servand to ȝour maister. And sall nether heir nor sie his skaith. **1596** SHAKS. *Tam. Shr.* II. i. 301 Vpon sonday is the wedding day. *Kate.* Ile see thee hang'd on sonday first. **1631** HEYWOOD *2nd Pt. Fair Maid West* I. B 2 b, Ile see you damn'd as deep as the black father of your generation the devill first. **1709** FELTON *Diss. Classics* (1718) 50, I am ambitious, my Lord, to see You Master of a fine Pen. **1736** AINSWORTH *Lat. Dict.* IV. s.v. *Amata*, She hanged herself that she might not see Æneas her son in law. **1756–7** tr. *Keysler's Trav.* (1760) I. 459 To Ansaldo Grimaldo, who with regret sees himself alone. **1779** *Mirror* No. 44 ¶1 The old man hoped..to join their hands, and see them happy before he died. **1797** [see FIRST *adv.* 26]. **1831** SCOTT *Ct. Robt.* xvi, It is with no small confidence that I desire to see us set forth in quest of my beloved Countess. **1849** MACAULAY *Hist. Eng.* v. I. 598 He would see Bristol burned down, he said,..rather than that it should be occupied by traitors. **1867** AUGUSTA WILSON *Vashti* xviii, You ought to be willing to see me do anything honest, that will secure my dependent brother and sister from want.

e. *transf.* Of things, places, etc.: To be contemporary with and in the neighbourhood of, to be the scene of (an event); to be in existence during (a period of time). Also of a period of time: To be marked by (an event).

1739 C. WESLEY *Hymn*, Hail the Day that sees Him rise, Ravish'd from our wishful Eyes. **1839** DIGBY *Mores Cath.* IX. i. (1847) III. 13/1 These are the funeral and Tartarean years of which St. Augustin speaks, like that when Rome saw five consuls. **1849–50** ALISON *Hist. Europe* VIII. l. §62. 187 Eighteen rivers have seen their navigation improved. **1895** WORKMAN *Alger. Mem.* 77 A bright cold morning saw us in the saddle at 6.15. **1907** A. LANG *Hist. Scot.* IV. 408 In 1906 Cambridge saw three or four of her most learned men compete for the Greek chair.

11. To experience in one's own person; to undergo, enjoy, or suffer. Now *rare*. (For *to have seen service*, see SERVICE *sb.*)

The use is app. native, but coincides with a Biblical Hebraism: see, e.g. Luke ii. 26 (in all Eng. versions).

Beowulf 1180 þonne ðu forð scyle metodsceaft seon! *a* **900** CYNEWULF *Crist* 1611 Ðær sceolan þeofas..ond mansworan morþorlean seon. **1297** R. GLOUC. (Rolls) 6236 We fiȝteþ & beþ ouercome & no maistrie we ne seþ. *a* **1310** in Wright *Lyric P.* xxxiv. 96 Crist leve us alle with that wymman that joie al forte sene. *a* **1300** *K. Horn* (Camb. MS.) 650 Heo ferde in to bure To sen auenture. **1387** TREVISA *Higden* (Rolls) IV. 61 He schavede nevere his heed, noþer his berde, ..he wolde have no worschepe, er he seigh wreche of Hanybal. **1470–85** MALORY *Arthur* IV. xviii. 141 They ansuerd hym that they cam from kynge Arthurs courte for to see auentures. *c* **1530** G. CROMWELL in Ellis *Orig. Lett.* Ser. III. I. 339 His Lorchyp..mad us good schere; and lett us see schuch game and plesure as I never saye in my lyfe. **1611** BIBLE *Tobit* iv. 4 Remember, my sonne, that shee saw many dangers for thee. **1738** WESLEY *Psalms* XCIII. ii, How sure establish'd is thy Throne; Which shall no Change or Period see. **1799** WORDSW. *Fountain* 42 They see A happy youth, and their old age Is beautiful and free. **1894** SIR J. ASTLEY *Fifty Yrs. Life* II. 7, He [a horse] was a very clever hunter and I saw a lot of sport on him.

12. a. To be in the company of, to meet and converse with (a person). ***to go*** or ***come to*** (or ***and***) ***see***: to visit, call upon. ***to see a man*** (***about a dog***) and varr. (orig. *U.S.*), a joc. form of excuse or explanation used to avoid giving the real reason for one's absence or departure; *spec.* (*euphem.*) to obtain an alcoholic drink; to go to the lavatory. ***to see much*** or ***little of*** (a person): to be often or seldom in his society.

a **1300** *K. Horn* (Camb. MS.) 1356 'Childre', he sede, 'hu habbe ȝe fare? þat ihc ȝou seȝ hit is ful ȝare.' *c* **1320** R. BRUNNE *Medit.* 232 Y go and come to ȝow aȝen, Forsoþe eftsones y wyl ȝow sen. **1470–85** MALORY *Arthur* XI. iii. 575 Thenne she said my lord sir launcelot I biseche yow see me as soone as ye may. *a* **1548** HALL *Chron., Hen. VIII* 111 He made muche suite to come into Englande, to see and speake with the kyng. **1609** CARLETON in *Crt. & Times Jas. I* (1848) I. 95 You will hear of Sir Thomas Smith by your servant, who went the last night to see him. **1662** J. DAVIES tr. *Mandelslo's Trav.* 280 There came along with them the President's Lady, whom he had not seen in seven years before. **1670** LADY MARY WORTLEY in *12th Rep. Hist. MSS. Comm.* App. v. 21, I have been twice to see my lady Northampton but could not find her at hom. **1710** SWIFT *Jrnl. to Stella* 18 Sept., When you see Joe, tell him [etc.]. **1762** G. COLMAN *Musical Lady* I. 6 Come! I have been in search of you this hour—and thought I should have been obliged to go back again without seeing you. **1800** GEO. IV in *Paget Papers* (1896) I. 181 In short, the more I see of her and the more I probe her Heart the more perfect I see her. **1848** THACKERAY *Van. Fair* xl, Mrs. Bute and Lady Southdown never could meet without battles, and gradually ceased seeing each other. **1849** MACAULAY *Hist. Eng.* v. I. 531 He saw little of any Whigs. **1867** *Ball Players' Chron.* 12 Sept. 3/1 The rest of our nine having gone to see a man there was nobody to take the bat. **1872** DASENT *Three to One* III. 241 Have either of you seen anything of Mr. Fortescue in town? **1882** MOZLEY *Remin.* (ed. 2) I. 57, I was seeing very little of Blanco White. **1890** BARRÈRE & LELAND *Dict. Slang* II. 216 *To see a man* (American), to go and have a drink at the bar. **1927** *Amer. Speech* III. 221 *See a man about a dog*, to go out and buy liquor. **1931** T. R. G. LYELL *Slang, Phrase & Idiom* 670 Excuse me a moment,—I shan't be long; I just have to go and see a man about something! **1945** *Richmond* (Va.) *Times-Dispatch* 25 Oct. 14/5 Greet the home-coming hero with a load of this and he will immediately find that he has to go somewhere else and see a man about a dog. **1969** *Private Eye* 28 Mar. 14, I got to see a man about a dog! **1977** A. C. H. SMITH *Jericho Gun* v. 63 I've got to dash. Must see a man about a horse.

b. To obtain an interview with, call upon, or meet in order to consult or confer with, give directions to or receive directions from. In U.S. *colloq.* 'To interview or consult in order to influence, esp. improperly, as in order to bribe' (Webster 1911).

1782 MISS BURNEY *Cecilia* I. x, She therefore went..to enquire among the servants if Mrs. Hill was yet come? Yes, they answered, and had seen their master, and was gone. **1848** THACKERAY *Van. Fair* xliv, She promised to see her man of business immediately. **1867** *Ball Players' Chron.* 12 Dec. 4/2 This, that or the other 'professional' is 'seen'—that is the professional term for the act of bribery—and lo and behold! the second game between the rival clubs is marked by a signal defeat. **1875** JOWETT *Plato* (ed. 2) I. 11, I want him to come and see a physician about the illness of which he spoke to me. **1888** BRYCE *Amer. Commw.* xv. I. 213 The class of professional 'lobbyists', men, and women too, who make it their business to 'see' members and procure..the passing of bills..which involve gain to their promoters. *Ibid.* c. III. 411 The president of a great rail-road..must have adroit agents at the State capitals..ready to 'see' leading legislators [etc.]. **1891** 'J. S. WINTER' *Lumley* xiii, I have to see a lady in Queen's Gate about a sitting. **1908** R. BAGOT *A. Cuthbert* xii. 140 Kindly send a waiter to find my servant. I must see him directly.

c. To receive as a visitor; to admit to an interview. Phrases, ***to see company***; †***to see masks*** = to hold a masquerade.

c **1500** *Melusine* xxxvii. (1894) 298 For he knew wel that Raymondyn his brother wold neuer loue hym nor see hym. **1710** SWIFT *Jrnl. to Stella* 1 Nov., I..went..to see Mr. Harley, who could not see me for much company; but sent me his excuse, and desired I would dine with him on Friday. **1712** STEELE *Spect.* No. 429 ¶8 Lady Lydia cannot see Company. **1744** LADY M. W. MONTAGU *Let. to Montagu* (1893) II. 125 The vice-legate has a court of priests, and sees little other company. **1761** COLMAN *Jealous Wife* I. (1775) 13 Assert your Right boldly, Man!..see what Company you like; go out when you please; return when you please. **1770** FOOTE *Lame Lover* II. 29 *Serjeant.* How often have I told you, that I will see none of these sort of folks but at chambers? **1779** *Mirror* No. 25 She replied, that Mrs. Dimmity, my Lady ——'s gentlewoman, told her all the maids at —— had tea, and saw company of an afternoon. **1782** MISS BURNEY *Cecilia* VI. vii, When Mr. Harrel saw masks in Portman-square, my curiosity to behold a lady so adored, and so cruel, led me thither. **1802** MAR. EDGEWORTH *Moral T., Forester* (1806) I. 2 My master is just going to dinner, and can't see anybody now. **1804** BP. PRETYMAN in *G. Rose's Diaries* (1860) II. 94 Mr. Pitt saw Lord Harrowby ..for an hour and a half. **1883** *Daily News* 31 Oct. 5/3 Lord Derby will not be able to see the Transvaal delegates.. during the present week. **1885** *Encycl. Brit.* XIX. 751/1 It was easy [for prisoners] to get drink and tobacco, and see friends from outside.

euphemistically **1749** FIELDING *Tom Jones* XVI. ii, He felt the same compunction with a bawd, when some poor innocent..falls into fits at the first proposal of what is called seeing company.

†**d.** absol. ***to see*** (***together***): to meet one another, have an interview. *Obs.*

a **1548** HALL *Chron., Hen. VIII* 200 After this day, the kyng and she neuer saw together. **1578** WHETSTONE *Promos & Cass.* II. IV. ii, Wees see at the sport. **1611** SHAKS. *Cymb.* I. i. 124 When shall we see againe? **1613** —— *Hen. VIII*, I. i. 2. How haue ye done Since last we saw in France?

e. ***see you***: colloq. formula of farewell, often in weakened sense without reference to an anticipated meeting (in full ***I'll see you***). Also with advbs. and other extensions, as *around*, *soon*, etc. Also, (***I'll***) ***be seeing you***. Cf. F. *au revoir*, G. *auf Wiedersehen*.

1891 S. WEYMAN *New Rector* II. i. 25 He waved an awkward farewell to Jack, muttered 'See you soon!' and went off. **1906** 'O. HENRY' in *McClure's Mag.* Aug. 392/1 Now lift your hat and come away, while you receive Lou's cheery 'See you again'. **1932** J. W. HARRIS *Days of Endeavour* xiii. 228 The boys..follow it with no more than a cheery, 'So-long, old son; see you in Liverpool!' **1937** D. & H. TEILHET *Feather Cloak Murders* ii. 33 He waved cheerfully to the Baron, said, 'I'll be seeing you.' **1945**, etc. [see HOORAY *int.*]. **1951** M. KENNEDY *Lucy Carmichael* v. i. 239 'Well..be seeing you.'.. 'Be seeing you,' agreed Owen without enthusiasm. **1959** I. FLEMING *Goldfinger* xix. 264 'See you around.' He grinned at Bond and moved off down the room. **1962** L. DEIGHTON *Ipcress File* xi. 71 Thanks, chief. See you. **1970** J. PORTER *Rather Common Sort of Crime* ii. 24 Well, ta ever so! Be seeing you! **1975** I. McEWAN *First Love, Last Rites* 96 'See you tomorrow, then.'.. 'Yes, tomorrow.' **1978** J. IRVING *World according to Garp* xiii. 253 'See ya,' she called, and drove off... 'See ya,' Garp mumbled after her.

13. *Gaming.* **a.** To meet (a bet), or meet the bet of (another player), by staking an equal sum. Now chiefly in *Poker* (see also quot. 1885). †**b.** In *Brag*: see quot. 1804.

1599 MINSHEU *Sp. Dial.* iii. 16 *M.* Giue me fower cards, Ile see as much as he sets. *R.* See heere my rest, let euery one be in. *M.* I am come to passe again... *O.* I set my rest. *M.* Ile see it. **1804** *New Pocket Hoyle, Brag*, Or if either party lay down a stake, saying *Let me see you*, or *I'll see it*, in which case both the hands are to be shown, and the strongest wins. **1880** [see BET *sb.* 1 b]. **1885** H. JONES in *Encycl. Brit.* XIX. 283/1 [Poker.] The next in rotation to say must either (1) go out of the game; or (2) see the raise, i.e., put up an equal amount; or (3) go better, i.e., increase the raise. *Ibid.*, The last to stake, who makes his raise equal to that of each of the others, *sees* them, i.e. the player to the left has to show his hand... The next..then similarly shows his hand..; and so on all round; the holder of the best hand takes the pool.

transf. **1890** *Sat. Rev.* 15 Feb. 183/2 A rather discreditable attempt to 'see' other Pretenders and 'go one better' in patriotism. **1890** *Spectator* 20 Sept., He 'saw' the enemy's veteran, in fact, and went 599 better.

14. *Mil.* To command or dominate (a position). Said of a fortification, artillery, etc. [So F. *voir.*]

1829 NAPIER *Penins. War* v. ii. (Rtldg.) I. 234 The guns.. saw it [a convent] in reverse. **1834–47** J. S. MACAULAY *Field Fortif.* (1851) 43 In proportion as the height of the parapet is increased the danger of being seen by enfilade, slant, or reverse fire, diminishes. *Ibid.* 142 An interior intrenchment should therefore be formed; it will generally be the church and cemetery, or the strongest house in the village, if.. placed so as to see the principal streets.

15. let see. a. ***to let*** (a person) ***see***: to show, bring to the sight or knowledge of. With sb. or clause as obj. Formerly often with ellipsis of personal obj. †***to let see***.

c **1320** *Sir Tristr.* 501 Houndes on hyde he diȝtes, Alle he lete hem se. *Ibid.* 554 Who better can, lat se. **1338** R. BRUNNE *Chron.* (1810) 18, & Ethelbert in the felde his fader lete he se, How Dardan for his lance doun to the erth went, & smote his hede of, his fader to present. **1377** LANGL. *P. Pl.* B. XVII. 9 'Late se þi lettres' quod I 'we miȝte þe lawe knowe'. *c* **1400** *Laud Troy Bk.* 2865 Lete se now, what ȝe say? **14..** W. PARIS *Cristine* 152 (Horstm.) Sire, make theme hole! late se, cane ye? *c* **1430** *Hymns Virg.* (1867) 58 How many foolde Hast þou brouȝt richesse? now late se. *c* **1450** *Merlin* xx. 357 'Now let se', quod Merlin, 'what ye will do, for now is ther oon lesse'. *c* **1485** *Digby Myst., Mary Magd.* 1738 Lett se whatt I xall have, Or elles I woll nat wend. **1535** COVERDALE *2 Kings* xviii. 23, I will geue yᵉ two thousande horses, let se yf thou be able to man them. **1596** DALRYMPLE tr. *Leslie's Hist. Scot.* Prol. I. 10 To lat sie quhan danger is, thay kendle bleises in tour heidis. **1601** Q. ELIZ. *Let. to Mountjoy* 12 Jan. in *Moryson's Itin.* (1617) II. 197 Wee could not forbeare to let you see, how sensible we are of this your merit. **1725** P. WALKER *Life Peden* in *Biogr. Presbyt.* (1827) I. 79 The Lord has letten me see the Frenches marching..thorow..the Land. **1752** FOOTE *Taste* II. (1781) 25 Gentlemen, here is a Jewel. *All.* Ay, ay, let's see.

†**b.** The imperative *let see* was sometimes used with indirect question (= 'let us see *if*'); also *absol.* prefixed to a request (= 'come', 'go to'); also to a question asked in soliloquy. *Obs.*

c **1470** HENRY *Wallace* I. 442 'Uncle', he said, 'I will no langar bide; Thir Southland hors latt se gif I can ride'. **1513** DOUGLAS *Æneis* XII. xi. 49 Quhat sall I do, lat se; quhar sall I now? [L. *nam quid ago*]. **1525** LD. BERNERS *Froiss.* II. cxxvii. [cxxiii.] 359 That is trouthe, quod the duke, let se, name a wyfe for him. *Ibid.* clxvii. [clxiii.] 464 Well, syrs, quod the bretons, lette se laye forthe the money.

c. ***let me see, let us see***: indicating that the speaker is trying to recall something to memory, or finds it necessary to reflect before answering a question.

c **1520** SKELTON *Magnyf.* 595 Abyde—lette me se—take better hede—Cockes harte! it is Cloked Colusyon! **1533** J. HEYWOOD *Merry Play Johan* (1909) A ij, But abyde a whyle, yet let me se Where the dyuell hath our gyssypry begon. **1599** SHAKS. *Hen. V*, III. vii. 168 It is now two a Clock: but let me see, by ten Wee shall haue each a hundred English men. **1599** NASHE *Lenten Stuffe* 42 Let me see, hath any bodie in Yarmouth heard of Leander and Hero? **1693** CONGREVE *Old Bach.* IV. vi, A Prayer-Book? Ay, this is the Devil's *Pater-noster*. Hold let me see; The Innocent Adultery. **1741** RICHARDSON *Pamela* IV. 101 Let me see, then, can I give you the brief History of this Comedy? **1761** FOOTE *Liar* I. Wks. 1799 I. 282 Where do we open?.. Let us see—one o'clock—it is a fine day: the Mall will be crouded. **1921** G. B. SHAW *Back to Methuselah* II. 83 That would be —let me see—five times three hundred and sixty-five is—um.

16. Special uses of the gerundial infinitive.

a. Formerly often appended, with the sense 'in visible aspect', to various predicates, esp. adjs. descriptive of appearance, as *fair*, *foul*, *terrible*, etc. Three varieties of this use have been current: †(*a*) (*fair*, etc.) *on to see*. (The only form recorded from OE. times: cf. 21). (*b*) (*fair*, etc.) *to see*. (The surviving use, now only *poet.*; common from the 14th c.) †(*c*) (*fair*, etc.) *to see to* (rarely *unto*). (Occurs from the 16th to the 18th c.)

(*a*) *c* **893** K. ÆLFRED *Oros.* I. iii, Ða syndon swyþe fæȝere ..on to seonne. *c* **1200** *Trin. Coll. Hom.* 163 Hire handcloðes, and hire bord cloðes [ben] makede wite, and lustliche on to siene. *c* **1250** *Gen. & Ex.* 2659 So faiȝer he was on to sen. *a* **1300** *Cursor M.* 7446 Gret he [Goliath] was wit-all, and hei, And semed sathan on to sei. *c* **1369** CHAUCER *Dethe Blaunche* 1177 That swete wyght That is so semely on to see. **1430–40** LYDG. *Bochas* I. xiv. (1494) d viij b, Vpon the mounteyne callyd auentyne..There is a wode..Right fresshe of sight and goodly on to se. **1500–20** DUNBAR *Poems* lxxxvii. 36 Moir semely na is the sapheir one to seyne.

(*b*) *a* **1310** in Wright *Lyric P.* xxv. 71 Jhesu, al that is fayr to see..me Graunte for the love of the. **1340** *Ayenb.* 150 Þe þridde him makeþ briȝte to zyenne and uol of wytte. *c* **1380** *Sir Ferumb.* 1700 A geant ys maked briggeward þat symeþ þe fend to see. *c* **1400** *Sowdone Bab.* 39 With many a Baron & Kniȝtis ful boold, That roialle were and semly to sene. **1437** *Libel Eng. Policy* in *Pol. Poems* (Rolls) II. 179 And wee to martis of Braban charged bene Wyth Englyssh clothe, fulle gode and feyre to seyne. *c* **1500** *Flower & Leaf* 157 It was a noble sight to sene. **1503** DUNBAR *Thistle & Rose* 88 The Lyone..most fair to sene. **1563** SACKVILLE *Induct. Mirr. Mag.* ii, The soyle that earst so seemely was to seen. **1607** R. C[AREW] tr. *Estienne's World of Wonders* 236 More gay to seene Then some Atturney's clarke, or George a Greene. **1833** TENNYSON *Sisters* i, O the Earl was fair to see!

(*c*) **1542** UDALL *Erasm. Apoph.* 296 A cypres tree goodly to see to, but in deede unfruitefull. **1552** *Elyot's Dict.*, *Anagyris*, an herbe or shrub verie pleasant to see to. *a* **1586** SIDNEY *Arcadia* III. (Sommer) 268 In one place lay disinherited heades, dispossessed of their naturall seignories: in an other, whole bodies to see to, but that their harts wont to be bound all ouer so close, were nowe with deadly violence opened. **1601** HOLLAND *Pliny* XI. xviii. I. 320 There is a kind of rusticall and wild Bee: and such are more rough and hideous to see to. **1610** —— *Camden's Brit.* I. 86 Now was the State everie where in a most wofull and pitious plight to see unto. **1634** MILTON *Comus* 620 A certain Shepherd Lad Of small regard to see to, yet well skill'd In every vertuous plant. **1671** H. M. tr. *Erasm. Colloq.* 144 The ceremonies being indeed very goodly to see to. **1737** WHISTON *Josephus*, *Antiq.* XVIII. ix. §4 He was a little man to see to.

b. As predicate (= the more usual 'to be seen'). †(*a*) Visible, evident. *Obs. rare.* (*b*) Remaining to be seen.

1456 SIR G. HAYE *Law Arms* (S.T.S.) 271 For it is to se that the provour has begunnyn his clame ferr ynouche quhen [etc.]. **1577** KENDALL *Flowers of Epigr.* 39 Once woodden Challices there were, Then golden priests were euery where: Now golden chalices there be, And woodden priestes eache where to see. **1818** SHELLEY *Lett.* Pr. Wks. (1888) II. 231 But Rome and Naples—even Florence, are yet to see. **1846** BROWNING *Soul's Trag.* I Shame Fall presently on who deserves it most! Which is to see.

II. Phraseological combinations.

* *intransitive uses with prepositions.*

17. see about ——. To attend to; to take steps with reference to; also, to take into consideration, see what can be done with regard to. *I'll see about it*: often used *colloq.* to evade giving an immediate decision.

1839 DICKENS *Let.* Feb. (1965) I. 510 Will you dine with us at 5 — and see about a box without loss of time? **1848** BARTLETT *Dict. Amer.*, *See about*, to attend to; to consider. **1858** HAWTHORNE *Fr. & It. Note-bks.* (1871) I. 48, J—— and I then went to the railway station to see about our luggage. **1869** 'WAT BRADWOOD' *The O.V.H.* xxxiv, Yes—I don't know—perhaps I'll go with you. We'll see about it.

18. see after ——. To ascertain the condition of; to attend to the wants or safety of; also, to take means to obtain.

1727 [E. DORRINGTON] *Philip Quarll* (1816) 28, I feared that..another accident had befallen him.., so I went to see after him. **1775** S. J. PRATT *Liberal Opin.* liv. (1783) II. 142, I shan't be able to answer it to my conscience if I don't see after it. **1782** MISS BURNEY *Cecilia* II. iii, Pretty dove,..be of good heart! sha'n't be meddled with; come to see after you. **1872** H. KINGSLEY *Hornby Mills* etc. II. 46 Here Tom, Tom, see after the luggage.

19. see for ——. **a.** To look for, try to find. Now *rare* or *Obs.* Also †*see out for* (obs.).

1535 STEWART *Cron. Scot.* I. 558 And mony saikles ȝit sall suffer deid, Without richt sone ȝe se for sum remeid. **1670** NARBOROUGH *Jrnl.* in *Acc. Sev. Late Voy.* I. (1694) 32 My Lieutenant went up the River in the Boat nine or ten miles to see for People that way. **1719** DE FOE *Crusoe* I. (Globe) 203, I..went to the West End..of the Island, almost every Day, to see for Canoes, but none appear'd. **1775** S. J. PRATT *Liberal Opin.* l. (1783) II. 120 Adding, that, against my next excursion she would see out amongst her young friends for a more suitable companion. **1778** MISS BURNEY *Evelina* lxxvi, [She] begged me to see for some books she had left in the parlour. **1789** CHARLOTTE SMITH *Ethelinde* (1814) IV. 84 Montgomery..went down himself to see for a coach. **1802** MAR. EDGEWORTH *Moral T.* I. viii. 55, I was just coming to see for you. **1812** J. GROOM in *Examiner* 31 Aug. 552/1 He searched the..lodging-houses.., to see for suspicious persons. **1848** THACKERAY *Van. Fair* lxiv, Little Bob Suckling, who..would walk a mile in the rain to see for her carriage in the line at Gaunt House.

†**b.** To provide for, act for the benefit of. *Obs.*

1548 UDALL etc. *Erasm. Par. Matt.* i. 19 He began to cast in his mynde, by what meanes he myght bothe see for the good name, & also the lyfe of his wyfe.

20. see into ——. To perceive (by physical or mental sight) what is below the surface of.

1593 SHAKS. *2 Hen. VI*, III. i. 42 Well hath your Highnesse seene into this Duke. **1615** SIR J. THROCKMORTON in *Court & Times Jas. I* (1848) I. 382 Then we shall undoubtedly be able to see into the bottom of this and their other wicked practices. **1798** WORDSW. *Poems Imag.* xxvi. *Tintern Abb.* 49 While with an eye made quiet by the power Of harmony,.. We see into the life of things. **1824** MISS L. M. HAWKINS *Annaline* I. 295 He could see no farther into the affair than before. **1863** KINGSLEY in *Lett.* etc. (1877) II. 179 We must send up one of our F.G.S.'s to see into the matter.

†**21. see on, upon** ——. To look on, look at. (Cf. sense 5.) *Obs.*

Beowulf 2863 Seah on unleofe. *c* **1250** *Gen. & Ex.* 2664 So was hem lef on him to sen. *a* **1300** *Cursor M.* 12343 Bot fra þe leons on him sau Wel þai can þair lauerd knau. *a* **1310** in Wright *Lyric P.* v. 26 That syht upon that semly, to blis he is broht. *c* **1330** *Spec. Gy de Warw.* 389 Hit greueþ euere mannes eiȝe, Inwardliche on hire [the sun] to se For hire grete clerte. *c* **1400** *Rom. Rose* 3597 Ye not wolde upon him see. **1513** DOUGLAS *Æneis* XIII. viii. 62 At the first blenk astonyst half wolx he, And musyng hovirris styll on hir to se.

22. see over ——. (See also sense 2 and OVER *prep.*). †To look over, peruse (a book) (*obs.*); to have a comprehensive view of. Now chiefly, to go over and inspect (a building).

1490 CAXTON *Eneydos* I To my hande came a lytyl booke ..whiche booke I sawe ouer and redde therin. **1513** DOUGLAS *Æneis* v. Prol. 5 The clerk reiosis his buikis our to seyne. **1765** J. INGERSOLL *Lett. relat. Stamp-Act* (1766) 34 There must be some one Eye to see over, and some one Hand to guide and direct, the Whole of it's Defence and Protection. **1793** J. WOODFORDE *Diary* 23 June (1929) IV. 36 We took a walk to Weston House and saw it all over. **1830** MOORE in *Mem.* (1854) VI. 108 Took Miss Macdonald to see over new Athenæum. *c* **1869** TAYLOR & DUBOURG in M. R. Booth *Eng. Plays of 19th Cent.* (1973) III. 245 Mr. Secker's card for a friend of his to see over the ruins. **1909** M. BEERBOHM *Yet Again* (ed. 5) 3 If I were 'seeing over' a house. **1920** 'O. DOUGLAS' *Penny Plain* v. 62, I was going to ask if I might see over the house. **1977** 'M. YORKE' *Cost of Silence* i. 9 The house..was..up for sale... People saw over it and were dashed by the need to replumb and repair.

23. see round ——. To have views beyond, to perceive the limitations of. *rare.*

1879 M. PATTISON *Milton* 83 Milton, though he had come to see round Presbyterianism, had not, in 1644, shaken off all dogmatic profession.

24. see through ——. **a.** *lit.* To see objects on the other side of (an aperture, or something transparent). Hence *fig.* to penetrate (a disguise, fallacious appearance), to detect (an imposture), to perceive the real character or aims of (a person).

1400 *Love God* 95 in *26 Pol. Poems* 4 God seeth thurgh euery bore. *Ibid.* 103 God seeth thurgh eche mysse. *a* **1548** HALL *Chron.*, *Hen. VIII* (1550) 187 b, His graces sight was so quicke and penetrable, that he saw him, ye and saw through him, both within and without. **1599** B. JONSON *Cynthia's Rev.* v. ii, He is a mere peece of glasse, I see through him, by this time. *c* **1610** *Women Saints* 160 There was not to be seene on her riche garments,..so thinne as that you might see throughe. **1623** COCKERAM II, To be Seene thorow. *Translucent, Transparent.* **1679** J. GOODMAN *Penit. Pard.* II. ii. (1713) 198 Alexander the great..had the luck or the sagacity to see through and despise the empty pageantry and shew. **1719** H. BARHAM in *Phil. Trans.* XXX. 1036 When held against the Light, they [the silkworms] might be seen through as you may an Egg. **1751** LABELYE *Westm. Bridge* 93 The Board seeing thro' all this, enforced the Directions I had given. **1784** BURNS *Ep. to J. Rankine* ii, And then their failings, flaws, an' wants, Are a' seen thro'. **1863** COWDEN CLARKE *Shaks. Char.* xvi. 394 He saw through their insufficiency. **1885** *Manch. Exam.* 6 Nov. 5/3 The object of the Commission was seen through at a glance.

†**b.** To have a clear notion of. *Obs.*

1729 BUTLER *Serm.* Pref., Wks. 1874 II. 7 Any one may.. know whether he understands and sees through what he is about.

c. *colloq.* To 'get through' (a meal).

1863 W. C. BALDWIN *Afr. Hunting* ix. 440, I need hardly say I had a bilious headache all the following day, as I was ravenously hungry, and saw through most of it [a meal of many dishes].

25. see to (or †**unto**) ——. †**a.** To be solicitous about. *Obs.*

1389 *Eng. Gilds* (1870) 51 Also afterward, men seende to þe deuocioun don in holy chirche,..askynd [*read* askyd] þe fraternite..to mayntene..þe forseyd ymage.

b. To attend to, do what is needful for; to provide for the wants of; to charge oneself with (a duty, a business).

a **1400–50** *Wars Alex.* 754* (Dubl. MS.) Þan says he to hys seruand to see to þis capyll. **1406** *E.E. Wills* (1882) 13 Yef outgh come to Thomas Roos, than y pray Iohan Wodcok to se to my son, that he be nat lost. **1470–85** MALORY *Arthur* XIX. vi. 781 That they were layde within draughtes by her chamber vpon beddes and pylowes that she her self myght see to them that they wanted no thynge. **1529** WOLSEY in Ellis *Orig. Lett.* Ser. I. II. 8 Alas M^r. Secretary, ye with other my lordys shewyd me that I shuld otherwyse be furnyshyd, and seyn unto. **1535** COVERDALE *Jer.* xl. 4, I will se to the, and prouyde for the. **1570–6** LAMBARDE *Peramb. Kent* 283 If the matter were well and in season seene vnto, there was no doubte [etc.]. **1642** C. VERNON *Consid. Exch.* 39 The Chiefe Vsher..seeth to all places of the Court, that all Doores, Chests, Records and things be in safety from fire, water, or other spoile. **1844** ALB. SMITH *Mr. Ledbury* vii, I leave everything to you, and thank you into the bargain for seeing to it. **1861** FLOR. NIGHTINGALE *Nursing* (ed. 2) 41 If a patient has to see, not only to his own but also to his nurse's punctuality. **1884** W. C. SMITH *Kildrostan* 73 What is there to arrange with her? O yes! About her shootings—I will see to that.

c. To take special care about (a matter.) Chiefly, *to see to it*, to make sure *that* (something is done).

1474 CAXTON *Chesse* III. iii. (1883) 103 Also they ought to see well to that they be of one Acorde in good. **1481** —— *Reynard* xii. (Arb.) 27 Here is the theef the wulf, see wel to that he escape vs not. **1865** RUSKIN *Sesame* ii. §89 See to it that your train is of vassals whom you serve and feed, not merely of slaves who serve and feed *you*. **1874** BLACKIE *Self-Cult.* 43 What a student should specially see to..is not to carry the breath of books with him wherever he goes. **1891** MORRIS *Poems by the Way* (1896) 69 Lay me aboard the bastard's ship, And see to it lest your grapnels slip!

†**d.** To respect, look up to. *Obs. rare.*

1579 TOMSON *Calvin's Serm. Tim.* 222/2 The ministers of the word must marke why this office is given them,..it is not because a few should be sene vnto, and that they should speake, and others hold their peace.

†**e.** In physical sense: To look towards. *Obs.*

1669 STURMY *Mariner's Mag.* II. xiii. 80 The eye maketh (seeing now to the lower, and then again to the upper end of the Cross) greater motion in looking up and down.

** *transitive uses with adverbs.*

26. see away. To spend (money) in seeing. *nonce-use.*

1613 SHAKS. *Hen. VIII*, Prol. 12 Those that come to see Onely a show or two..may see away their shilling Richly in two short houres.

27. see off. a. To put to flight, chase off (esp. of a dog). Also *trans.* and *fig.*, to get the better of, defeat, put down. *colloq.* (orig. *Mil.*). Cf. sense 7 b.

1915 H. BRUCKSHAW *Diary* Aug. in *Times* (1976) 7 Feb. 12/6 We had at last cleared the place except for sundry stragglers who would no doubt be seen off later. **1919** W. LANG *Sea Lawyer's Log* xi. 137 You may 'see off' a messmate by overwhelming him with violence, outpointing him in cunning or overcoming him with policy. **1929** *Times* 21 Feb. 11 When he and another detective went to arrest the men Hughes called to the Alsatian. 'See 'em off.' **1944** R. P. FLEMING *Jrnl.* in D. Hart-Davis *Peter Fleming* (1974) xii. 293 An unusually well-found fighting patrol..perfectly capable of seeing-off the small parties from L. of C. **1961** *Sunday Express* 10 Dec. 5/2 (*caption*) Fast as I tell him to 'See 'em off' they tell him to 'Sit'. **1969** Y. CARTER *Mr. Campion's Farthing* ix. 86, I know an audience of stuffed shirts when I see one. Besides—I just had to see that pompous bastard off. **1981** 'M. YORKE' *Hand of Death* x. 90 He'd..been rebuffed... She'd seen him off good and proper.

b. Cricket. *to see off the new ball*: to bat until the shine has been removed from the ball (esp. at the start of an innings).

1969 J. ARLOTT *Crickett: Great All-Rounders* vii. 108 Bailey was the intractable substance which..made a good innings better by seeing off a new ball down the order to give the tail-enders a chance. **1977** *Observer* 20 Mar. 1/4 The openers had batted for a while and had seen a lot of the new ball off.

28. see out. †**a.** ? To let (a person) have his say, to see how far he will go.

1715 ADDISON *Freeholder* No. 22 ¶2 He [a fellow-traveller] affirmed roundly, that there had not been one good law passed since King William's accession to the throne, except the Act for preserving the game. I had a mind to see him out, and therefore did not care for contradicting him.

b. In a drinking contest, to outlast.

1756 *Connoisseur* II. 555 Tom Buck..can *see out* the stoutest freeholder in England. **1837** DICKENS *Pickw.* xlviii, I have heard him say that he could see the Dundee people out any day, and walk home afterwards without staggering. **1862** THACKERAY *Philip* vii, Pass the bottle!..we intend to see you all out.

c. To go through with to the end.

1782 *Let.* 12 Feb. in *Essex Inst. Hist. Coll.* (1859) I. 13/2, I am Detarmend as I have beene so long in the servis to se it out. **1783** H. NEWDIGATE *Let.* 23 Mar in A. E. Newdigate-Newdegate *Cheverels* (1898) iv. 50 Y^e Opera..is to be wonderfully shewy & the last Dance ye best, so we must see it out. **1794** GOUV. MORRIS in Sparks *Life & Writ.* (1832) II. 453, I conceived my honor concerned in seeing the thing out. **1879** FROUDE *Cæsar* xx. 333 The engagement had been entered into that he was to see his term out. **1860** F. W. ROBINSON *Grandm. Money* II. viii, [I] wish he'd stop another week [at Hastings] and see the five and twenty pounds out. **1889** J. K. JEROME *Three Men in Boat* v. 73 He evidently meant to see this thing out.

d. To survive.

1825 SCOTT *Diary* 7 Dec. in *Lockhart* VI. 151 My dear wife..is, I fear, frail in health—though I trust and pray she may see me out.

e. Of a thing (esp. one's personal property): to last (at least) as long as (a person or his lifetime); to outlast or suffice to the end.

1969 M. PUGH *Last Place Left* xix. 143 The suits I have will see me out. **1976** *Guardian* 10 Apr. 10/8, I imported a German car, a convertible Beetle... No more of these are being imported, but I expect it to see me out.

29. see through. To continue to watch or take part in (a matter) until the end (cf. 28 c); to take care that (a person) comes successfully through his difficulties.

1828 L. HUNT in *Companion* 6 Feb. 48 *William III.* The Dutchman, call'd to see our vessel through. **1872** H. KINGSLEY *Hornby Mills* etc. II. 60 O'Flaherty..told him that he would see the bonfire through and the captain to bed, and take the consequences. *Ibid.* 68 We will see him through if he were to burn the college down. **1913** J. VAIZEY *College Girl* xviii. 250 Her thoughts flew off to Ralph Percival..

recalling with pleasure his promise to 'see her through'. **1916** H. G. Wells (*title*) Mr. Britling sees it through. **1939** *War Illustr.* 14 Oct. 147 (*heading*) Mr. Briton'll see it through. **1977** G. Butler *Brides of Friedberg* v. 129 Don't worry.. I'll see you through.

III. 30. *Comb.* **see-everything**, one who sees everything.
1853 [see say *v.*[1] B. 14].

see, obs. form of sea *sb.*[1]

seeable ('si:əb(ə)l), *a.* and *sb.* [f. see *v.* + -able.]
A. *adj.* Capable of being seen, visible. Also *fig.*
?*a* **1400** in *Hampole's Wks.* (1895) I. 165 Forwy, a saule þat is ȝit ruyde & fleshle, knaws not ȝitt bot bodele ynges [= þynges], & no yng comes ȝitt to þe mynde bot seabull ynges. *c* **1449** Pecock *Repr.* II. v. 162 Marie Magdalen..vsid the oynement as a seable and a smelleable rememoratijf signe. **1548** Geste *Agst. Pr. Masse* B v b, These therfore be named sacramentes, for that in them one thyng is seable, and another vnderstande. **1624** Bp. Mountagu *Gagg* 49 That which cannot be seene, if it be seeable, is no where at all, nor in being. **1829** Jas. Mill *Hum. Mind* (1869) I. 13 In that case, we should have no idea of objects as seeable, as hearable, as touchable, or tasteable. **1874** Tyndall *Presid. Addr. Brit. Assoc.* 81 This, as a purely mechanical process, is seeable by the mind. **1896** Dk. Argyll *Philos. Belief* 43 We cannot even think of it as seen or seeable.

†**B.** *sb.* (absolute use of the *adj.*) A thing capable of being seen. *Obs. rare*$^{-1}$.
1812 Southey *Lett.* (1856) II. 271 We shall make a march of it, seeing all the seeables on the way.

Hence '**seeableness**, visibility; †'**seeably** *adv.*, visibly. *Obs. rare*$^{-1}$.
1548 Geste *Agst. Pr. Masse* H iv b, Manye dyd worshyp.. Christ as beyng seably conuersant emonge them. **1865** J. Grote *Explor. Philos.* I. 123 These qualities which we perceive, seeableness or colour, handleableness or shape, taste, smell, &c.

seeal, seeay, obs. forms of seal *sb.*[2], say *sb.*[1]

Seebeck ('zeɪbɛk). *Physics.* [The name of Thomas Johann *Seebeck* (1770–1831), Russian-born German physicist, who discovered the effect (*Abhandl. der K. Akad. der Wissensch. zu Berlin: Phys. Klasse* (1822–23) 265).] **Seebeck effect**, the phenomenon whereby an e.m.f. is generated in a circuit containing junctions between dissimilar metals if these junctions are at different temperatures; the phenomenon of thermoelectricity.
1903 *Whittaker's Electr. Engineer's Pocket Bk.* 99 If a junction between two dissimilar metals be heated or cooled, a flow of electricity will take place across the junction. If a current be passed through such a junction, a change of temperature will be produced. The former phenomenon is known as the Seebeck effect, the latter as the Peltier effect. **1906** *Sci. Abstr.* A. IX. 481 The Thomson-, Peltier-, and Seebeck-effects may be combined in one diagram, and the author does this for the case of iron and silver. **1964** S. H. Avner *Introd. Physical Metall.* i. 6 The total emf in a thermoelectric pyrometer, sometimes called the Seebeck effect, is therefore the algebraic sum of four emf's, two Peltier emf's at the hot and cold junctions and two Thomson emf's along each of the wires. **1973** J. G. Tweeddale *Materials Technol.* I. iv. 97 If an electric circuit is suitably completed a current will flow between the materials (the Seebeck effect).

see-bright ('si:braɪt), *sb.* [f. see *v.* + bright *a.* A rendering of *clear-eye*, a perversion of *clary*.]
= clary.
1863 Prior *Plant-n.* 201 See-bright, from its supposed effect on the eyes. **1866** *Treas. Bot.*, Seebright, *Salvia Sclarea*.

seecatch ('si:kætʃ). Pl. seecatchie. [? Aleutian Indian; the pl. is Russian in form.] The male of the Alaska fur-seal, *Callorhinus ursinus*.
1881 H. W. Elliott *Seal Isl. Alaska* (1884) 42 The 'seecatchie' which have held the harems from the beginning to the end of the season, leave [etc.]. *Ibid.* 175 Gloss., *Seecatch*, pl. seecatchie (Russian), male fur-seal and sea-lion, full grown. **1896** Kipling *Seven Seas* 71 (Three Sealers) What time the scarred see catchie lead their sleek seraglios.

seece, seeche, obs. forms of cease, seek.

seech, dial. variant of sitch (swamp).

seed (si:d), *sb.* Forms: 1 sǣd, Anglian sēd, 2–5 sed, (2–3 sad(e), 2–6 sede, 3, 6 side, 4 seod, *Kent.* zed, *Sc.* seiyde, 4–6 *Sc.* seid(e, 4–7 seede, 5 seyde, ceed, ced, 6 siede, sead(e, 4 -seed. [OE. *sǣd* neut. = OFris. *sêd*, OS. *sâd* neut. (MLG. *sât*), MDu. *saet* neut. (Du. *zaad*), OHG., MHG. *sât* fem. (mod.G. *saat*), Goth. *-sêþ-s* (in *manasêþ-s* fem., mankind), ON. *sáð* neut., whence *sǽði* in the same sense (Sw. *säd* fem., Da. *sæd*):—OTeut. **sǣdi-*, *sǣđo-*, f. root **sǣ-* to sow.]

1. a. That which is or may be sown (often as cognate obj. to sow *v.*); the ovules of a plant or plants (chiefly, when in the form of 'grains' or small roundish bodies) esp. as collected for the purpose of being sown. Also, in *Agriculture* and *Horticulture*, applied by extension to other parts of plants (e.g. tubers, bulbs) when preserved for the purpose of propagating a new crop. In *plural*, kinds of seed. Phr. *to go to seed* (go *v.* 44 b): to cease flowering as seeds develop; *fig.*, to become habitually unkempt, ineffective, etc.; to deteriorate; ***to run to seed*** (see run *v.* 69 e); also † ***to grow to seed*** (obs.), ***to be in seed***.
c **825** *Vesp. Psalter* cxxv. 6 Gongende eodon & weopun sendende sed [etc.]. *c* **1000** *Ags. Gosp.* Mark iv. 3 Ut eode se sædere his sæd to sawenne. *c* **1200** Ormin 15905 Swa þatt itt muȝhe takenn wel Wiþþ sed to berenn wasstme. *c* **1250** *Prov. Ælfred* 93 in *O.E. Misc.* 108 And þe cheorl beo in fayþ his sedes to sowen, his medes to mowen. *a* **1300** *Cursor M.* 5230 His suns all and þair flitting.. In weynis war þai don to lede, þat ioseph wit ful of side. **1362** Langl. *P. Pl.* A. vi. 34, I haue.. Boþe I-sowed his seed and suwed his beestes. *c* **1381** Chaucer *Parl. Foules* 328 But foul that lyuyth be sed sat on the grene. **1520** Nisbet *N.T.* I. 10 Christ..schewe the parrabile of the seide. **1526** *Grete Herball* xlvii. (1529) C v b, Auena is an herbe, the sede of it is called otes. **1602** Shaks. *Ham.* I. ii. 136 Oh fie, fie, 'tis an vnweeded Garden That growes to Seed. **1611** Bible *Gen.* i. 29 Every herb bearing seed. **1675** Evelyn *Fr. Gard.* 244 When it [the onion] is in seed, 'tis very subject to be over-thrown by the wind. **1729** *Fog's Wkly. Jrnl.* 30 Aug. 2/2 To hinder the forestalling of Markets, by the Farmers selling Wheat..at home, or by buying Wheat for Seed. **1760** Brown *Compl. Farmer* II. 15 All seed degenerates, if long sown upon any land. **1817** J. K. Paulding *Lett. fr. South* I. xvii. 188 His white dimity could not last for ever, and he gradually went to seed. **1831** Loudon *Encycl. Agric.* (1857) §4856 The only small seeds the farmer has to sow on a large scale, are the clovers, grasses, the different varieties of turnip, and probably the mangold wurzel and carrot. **1839** Stonehouse *Axholme* 32 Those [potatoes] grown upon the warp land are generally disposed of for seed to the market gardeners and others. **1856** Glenny *Gard. Everyday-bk.* 174/1 Cut down the old plants that have rambled and are past their prime, unless you are saving seed. **1859** [see go *v.* 44 b]. **1929** G. Ade *Let.* 8 Feb. (1973) 139 We have ridden for miles and miles [in Peking], visiting temples and palaces of incredible size and beauty, some of them slightly gone to seed and others filled with the most wonderful museum displays of Chinese art. **1951** E. Paul *Springtime in Paris* ii. 33 Clients, mostly young and disreputable, or old and gone to seed. **1967** G. F. Fiennes *I tried to run Railway* iv. 42 He seemed to be going to seed a bit; to be a bit slow.

b. An individual grain of seed. In *Bot.*, technically restricted to the fertilized ovule of a phanerogam. Popularly applied also to the 'spore' of a cryptogam, and to certain 'fruits' (in the scientific sense of the word) which have the appearance of seeds, e.g. that of the strawberry.
c **1000** *Ags. Gosp.* Mark iv. 31 Hit is ealra sæda læst þe on eorðan synt. *a* **1300** *Cursor M.* 22875 þat mighti godd þat all waldes, qua can sai me hu of a side He dos an hundret for to brede? **1340** *Ayenb.* 113 þet zed o mostard is wel small. *c* **1440** *Promp. Parv.* 64/2 Ceede of corne, as kyrnel, *granum*. *c* **1450** Holland *Howlat* 31 Under the Cirkill solar thir sauoruss seidis War nurist be dame Natur. **1592** Shaks. *Rom. & Jul.* v. i. 46 A beggerly account of emptie boxes, Greene earthen pots, Bladders, and mustie seedes. **1712** tr. *Pomet's Hist. Drugs* I. 38 Little, thin, black Seeds, each one having a spiral head. **1797** Wordsw. *Poems Old Age* i. *Old Cumb. Beggar* 86 Like the dry remnant of a garden flower Whose seeds are shed. **1811** A. T. Thomson *Lond. Disp.* (1818) 568 Seeds are to be collected when they are ripe, and before they drop from the plant. **1875** E. White *Life in Christ* I. i. (1876) 11 Each seed possessing a life originating in the life of the plant, but capable of an independent survival.

c. *pl.* (*a*) Land sown with corn. (*b*) Clover and 'artificial' grasses raised from seed.
1794 R. Lowe *Agric. Notts* 9 Artificial grasses, (generally called here, simply seeds). **1885** *Field* 31 Jan. 118/1 Some seeds came in the line, and, with the ground in the state it was in just after frost, of course it was incumbent on all to.. avoid crossing them as much as possible. **1910** *Daily News* 4 July 6/4 Yet it is those who have had 'seeds' to cut that have come off best this haysel.

d. *collect. sing.* and *pl.* Various kinds of grain suitable as the food of a cage-bird. Cf. *bird-seed* s.v. bird *sb.* 9.
1897 F. Thompson *New Poems* 175 When the bird quits the cage, We set the cage outside, With seed and with water, And the door wide.

e. *pl.* Particles of bran. Now *dial.* Cf. sid.
1598 *Sc. Acts Jas. VI* (1816) IV. 179/2 þe haill subiectis susteinis greit lose and skayth in paying alss deir for dust and seidis as gif þe samyn wes guid meill. *a* **1779** D. Graham *Writings* (1883) II. 36 Your groat meal, and gray meal, sand dust and seeds. **1799** H. Mitchell *Scotticisms* 73 'I have got a seed in my throat', is a phrase very common among the Scots. They mistake a piece of the husk for the seed. **1814** *Abstract, Proof, Mill of Inveramsay* 2 (Jam. s.v. *Dust*) Some of the dust and sheeling seeds..is left at the mill. **1815** *Pennecuik's Wks.* 87 These shells thus separated, and having the finer particles of the meal adhering to them, called mill seeds, are preserved for sowins... The seeds from the different makings of meal are preserved till the potatoes are exhausted.

2. a. *fig.* (often with reference to a metaphorical 'sowing', 'soil', or the like). The germ or latent beginning of some growth or development. Also, with allusion to the Parable of the Sower, applied to religious or other teaching, viewed with regard to its degree of fruitfulness.
sing. *a* **1000** *Boeth. Metr.* xxii. 37 þeah bið sum corn sædes ȝehealden symle on þære saule soðfæstnesse. *c* **1200** *Trin. Coll. Hom.* 151 þe sed þat he sew were soðe wordes. *a* **1300** *Cursor M.* 21226 In all þe stedes quar he yede, O godds word he sceued þe sede. ?*a* **1366** Chaucer *Rom. Rose* 1617 For venus sone daun Cupido Hath sowne there of loue the seed. *c* **1480** Henryson *Test. Cress.* 137 The seid of luf was sawin in my face, And ay grew grene throw your supply and grace. **1596** Spenser *F.Q.* v. i. 1 Yet then like-wise the wicked seede of vice Began to spring. **1646** Sir T. Browne *Pseud. Ep.* I. x. 37 Beside..the seed of error within our selves.. there is an invisible Agent. **1732** Berkeley *Alciphr.* vi. §18 The advantages which we experience from the seed of the gospel sown in good ground. **1840** Jolly *Sunday Serv.* 309 The blood of the martyrs, in Tertullian's expression, proved the seed of the Church.
pl. **1605** Shaks. *Macb.* I. iii. 58. **1608** —— *Per.* IV. vi. 93. **1692** R. L'Estrange *Fables* xxxviii. 38 We have the seeds of Virtue in us, as well as of Vice. *a* **1729** J. Rogers *Twelve Serm.* viii. (1730) 238 Some Seeds of Grace are yet alive in him. **1751** Johnson *Rambler* No. 168 ¶8 The seeds of knowledge may be planted in solitude, but must be cultivated in publick. **1821** Lamb *Elia* Ser. I. *Old Benchers*, The seeds of exaggeration will be busy there.

b. *Chem.* A small crystal of the desired substance introduced into a liquid in order to promote crystallization and to provide a nucleus for crystal growth. Orig. *spec.* in sugar manufacture. Also *fig.*
1909 in *Cent. Dict.* Suppl. **1915** H. C. Prinsen-Geerligs *Pract. White Sugar Manuf.* II. i. 80 White sugar destined for direct consumption should not only be white and brilliant, but should also possess a regular form and a rather large size; this latter desideratum makes it preferable to start the building up of the grain from a well-developed seed. **1959** *Engineering* 13 Feb. 219/2 Seeds can be cut to provide grown crystals that can be sawn in the most efficient manner. **1966** *McGraw-Hill Encycl. Sci. & Technol.* III. 601/1 A small crystal of the desired substance is added to the solution as a 'seed' to induce the formation of the first crystals. **1973** *Nature* 12 Oct. 294/1 Some cardinal topics in evolutionary biology were adopted as 'seeds' on which other constituents of the programme might crystallise: protein polymorphism, for example.

3. *Sport*, esp. *Lawn Tennis*. [f. sense 11 of the vb.] One of a number of seeded players in a tournament.
1933 M. D. Lyon in *Aldin Bk. Outdoor Games* 509 'But why put my beloved lawners last?' wails the Thibetan 'seed'. **1954** *Sun* (Baltimore) 22 June 17/3 The remaining four men's seeds won just the way they were supposed to due to the sudden decision by Wimbledon to seed 12 instead of the traditional eight. **1958** *Times* 20 Mar. 16/5 (*heading*) Badminton seeds dislodged. **1963** *Times* 12 June 5/6 Mr. McKinley, the United States number one and runner-up at Wimbledon in 1961, is top seed in the men's event. **1977** *Western Morning News* 30 Aug. 12/8 Fiona Moffitt, the number five seed from Dawlish, is Devon's main hope for the title.

4. = semen. Now *rare*.
c **1290** *S. Eng. Leg.* 319/700 A swyþe foul þing is þat sed of ȝwan Man is i-spreind. **1340** Hampole *Pr. Consc.* 445 He was geten aftir, als es knawen, Of vile sede of man with syn sawen. **1471** Caxton *Recuyell* (Sommer) 103 She..also conceyued of his seed a sone that was named Abas. **1548** Vicary *Anat.* ix. (1888) 78 The which seede of generation commeth from al the partes of the body, both of the man and the woman. **1608** Topsell *Serpents* 293 When the male [Viper] hath filled her with all his seed-genitall. **1668** Culpepper & Cole *Barthol. Anat.* I. xvii. 48 Others have attributed to the Kidneys the preparation of Seed, because hot Kidneys cause a propensity to fleshly lust. **1713** Cheselden *Anat.* IV. i. (1726) 290 The office of the Testes, is to separate the seed from the blood. **1847–9** *Todd's Cycl. Anat.* IV. 472/1 This fluid, so indispensably necessary as the medium of sexual generation, is the seed or semen. **1914** J. London *Let.* 24 Feb. (1966) 415, I have never wantonly scattered my seed. **1973** K. A. Sey *Ghanaian English* vii. 84 *To take seed*, to become pregnant.

5. Offspring, progeny. Now *rare* exc. in Biblical phraseology.
c **825** *Vesp. Psalter* xxxvi. 28 Ða unrehtwisan soðlice bioð wicnade & sed arleasra forweorðeð. *c* **950** *Lindisf. Gosp.* Mark xii. 22, & onfengon ða ilca ȝelic ða seofona & ne forleorton vel ne læfdon sed vel team. *c* **1175** *Lamb. Hom.* 133 Vre drihten cleopede monnes streon sed. *c* **1250** *Gen. & Ex.* 1613 And ðis lond ic sal giuen ðin sed. *a* **1340** Hampole *Psalter* xxi. 23 þe sede of iacob is þe folke of cristen men. *c* **1366** Chaucer *A.B.C.* 182 Sithe þou canst and wilt Ben to þe seed of Adam merciable. **1480** Caxton *Chron. Eng.* lxxv. 61 His seed shal bycome faderles in straunge lond for euermore. **1596** Dalrymple tr. *Leslie's Hist. Scot.* I. 80 *marg.*, The seid and successione of Simon Brechus stil inherited Irland. **1618** Chapman *Hesiod's Georg.* I. 398 Iustice is seed to Ioue. **1644** *Directory for Publ. Worship* 11 The rest of the Royal Seed. **1715** Pope *Iliad* II. 724 'Till, vain of Mortal's empty Praise, he strove To match the Seed of Cloud-compelling Jove. **1739** C. Wesley *Hymn*, '*Hark how all the Welkin rings*' vii, Rise, the Woman's Conqu'ring Seed, Bruise in Us the Serpent's Head. **1842** Tennyson *Godiva* 5 Not only we, the latest seed of Time,..have loved the people well. **1864** Pusey *Lect. Daniel* 397 Certain of the seed-royal and of the nobles were carried to Babylon.

6. a. *sing.* and *pl.* The ova of the lobster (cf. berry *sb.*[1] 3) and of the silkworm moth. **b.** Oyster-spat (cf. *seed oyster* in 9 below).
a. **1620** *Observ. Making Fit Rooms Silkworms* 5 The Silkwormes comming of ten ounces of seed [etc.]. **1662** J. Davies tr. *Olearius' Voy. Ambass.* 313 In the Spring..the Persians begin to hatch their Silk-worms. To do this, they carry the Seed in a little bag under the arm-pit. **1778** Mrs. Raffald *Eng. Housekpr.* 41 Take all the red seeds and the meat of a lobster. **1870** Yeats *Nat. Hist. Comm.* 334 The eggs in this state are called by the silk cultivators seed.
b. **1721** *Phil. Trans.* XXXI. 251 From the Spat or Seed of which, it is most probable,..all the Bottom at length,.. became covered with Oysters. **1887** Goode, etc. *Fish. Industr. U.S.* v. II. 524 The cultivation of oysters transplanted when young (termed 'seed') from the natural reefs where they were spawned to inshore [etc.].

7. a. *Glass-making.* A minute bubble arising in glass during fusion.
1856 H. Chance in *Jrnl. Soc. Arts* IV. 226/2 A piece whose beginning was miraculous,—no seed, no blisters; it prospered under the hands of the gatherer and blower, and left the glass-house a perfect cylinder.

b. *Med.* A small container for holding a radioactive material such as radon when it is placed in body tissue in radiotherapy. Cf. *radon seed* s.v. RADON 2.

1925 *Glasgow Herald* 26 Mar. 9 To capture the gas emanating from radium, purify it, and bottle it in tiny tubes called from their shape seeds. 1974 R. M. KIRK et al. *Surgery* iv. 66 The gas radon ^{222}Rn, a product of radium decay, with a half-life of four days, can be sealed in gold tubes or 'seeds' and implanted into the tissues. 1980 *Daily Tel.* 4 Dec. 6/8 It can implant radioactive seeds by needle when surgery has failed to remove malignancy or patients can no longer sustain external radiation therapy.

8. *attrib.* and *Comb.*: **a.** simple attrib. (*a*) (sense 1) ***seed catalogue, -crop, -fall, -farm, -garden, -growth*** (in quot. *fig.*), ***-gutter, -house, -market,*** †***-month, -oil*** (also *attrib.*), ***packet, rate, -season, set, -shop, tray, weight,*** etc.; also SEED-FIELD, -FURROW, -PLOT, -TIME; (*b*) (sense 1 b) ***seed-ball, -branch, -capsule,*** †***-case, -cone, -cover, -down,*** †***-embryo, -glume, -head, -pod, -speck, -spike, -stalk, -stem,*** †***-umbel,*** etc.; also SEED-CROWN 2; (*c*) in the sense of grain, etc. preserved for raising new crops, as ***seed-barley, -grain, -maize, -oats, -potatoes, -wheat;*** also SEED-CORN; (*d*) in names of agricultural implements or their component parts used in the sowing of land with seed, as ***seed-barrel, -basket, -drill, -funnel, -harrow,*** †***-plough*** (also *fig.*), ***-slide, -tube, -vent;*** also SEED-BOX.

1917 D. H. LAWRENCE *Look! We have come Through!* 119 The *seed-ball of the sun Is broken at last. 1540 *Test. Ebor.* VI. 95 One strike of *sede barlie. 1844 H. STEPHENS *Bk. Farm* III. 790 The true seed-box..is in form of a small barrel, and is hence called the *seed-barrel. 1831 *Seed-basket [see SEED-CARRIER 2]. 1671 GREW *Anat. Plants* I. vii. (1682) 47 In this Inner Coat in a Bean the Lignous Body or *Seed-Branch is distributed. 1844 *Zoologist* II. 451 The seed-branches of field grasses. 1860 GOSSE *Rom. Nat. Hist.* 21 Ever and anon the *seed-capsule of some forest-tree bursts with a report like that of a musket. 1677 GREW *Anat. Plants, Anat. Fruits* v. (1682) 186 The *Seed-Case, whether it be called a Cod, Pod, or by any other name. 1724 P. BLAIR *Pharmaco-Bot.* II. 68 The Top of the flowering Foot-stalk, supports the Ovarium or Seed-case. [1760 J. WEBB (*title*) A catalogue of seeds and hardy plants.] 1901 L. H. BAILEY *Princ. Veg. Gardening* v. 168 The differences..might be of such a character that they could not be definitely described in a *seed catalogue. 1938 N. MARSH *Death in White Tie* xxv. 266 He hastily gathered up..parish magazines, *Church Times*, and seed catalogues. 1973 K. GILES *File on Death* v. 138 'Do you get much mail?'.. 'Today there were three letters and a seed catalogue.' 1842 LONGF. *Hiaw.* xviii. 44 So they gathered cones together, Gathered *seed-cones of the pine tree. 1796 WITHERING *Brit. Plants* (ed. 3) I. 80 *Seed-cover (calyculus) the real cover of the seed. 1868 *Rep. U.S. Commissioner Agric.* (1869) 204 When the orange-colored capsules open, and show the scarlet seed-covers. 1824 LOUDON *Encycl. Gard.* (ed. 2) §7484 In cases where a partial failure has taken place in the *seed crop. 1829 T. CASTLE *Introd. Bot.* 87 The less essential parts of a seed are, the pellicle, the tunic, the *seed-down [etc.]. 1883 *Good Words* Dec. 790/1 Thus, as seed-down is to dandelion and thistle..so is this adhesive pulp to the Mistletoe. 1792 W. RUTHERFORD *Let.* 28 Feb. in *Trans. Soc. Promotion of Useful Arts* (N.Y.) I. 121 Some years ago a farmer in Somerset county, in New Jersey, first introduced a *seed-drill of his invention. 1850 *Mary Wedlake's Priced List Farming Implements* 14 (*heading*) Improved corn and seed drill. 1941 [see COMBINE *sb.* c]. 1973 L. RUSSELL *Colonial Canada* iii. 38 The seed drill was invented in the 1850s; in this the seeds were not just dropped into the furrows, but were inserted into the soil through flexible tubes with a cutting edge in front. 1671 GREW *Anat. Plants* I. vii. (1682) 49 The Sap being thus prepared in the Inner Coat, as a Liquor now apt to be the Substratum of the future *Seed-Embrio; by fresh supplies, is thence discharg'd. 1968 *Jrnl. Forestry* LXVI. 422/2 The estimated *seedfall..averaged..almost 1 pound per acre. 1981 *Country Life* 16 July 184/1 My fear of the allium menace..prompts me to dead-head every species before seed-fall. 1824 LOUDON *Encycl. Gard.* (ed. 2) §7361 *Seed-gardens, or *seed-farms, require a dry soil. 1844 H. STEPHENS *Bk. Farm* II. 596 The bearing or platform of the *seed-funnels. 1840 J. BUEL *Farmer's Comp.* 228 It may be known by its..*seed-glumes resembling a cock's-foot. 1805 R. W. DICKSON *Pract. Agric.* I. 447 The steeping of *seed-grain may be useful in other respects. 1840 CARLYLE *Heroes* i, This seems to me the primary seed-grain of the Norse Religion. 1852 MUNDY *Antipodes* (1857) 23 They were furnished with..implements of husbandry, seed-grain, live-stock. 1876 GEO. ELIOT *Dan. Der.* xxvi, Yet in the dark *seed-growths of Consciousness a new wish was forming itself. 1831 LOUDON *Encycl. Agric.* (1857) §2714 Two cast-iron wheels, for the purpose of impressing two small *seed gutters or drills on the furrow slices turned over by the common plough. *Ibid.* §2704 Gray's *seed-harrow for wet weather promises to be useful..in a tenacious retentive soil. 1823 *Trans. Soc. Arts* XLI. 103 Eight bunches of straw, having the *seed-heads on. 1902 CORNISH *Naturalist Thames* 91 Goldfinches flying from seed-head to seed-head. 1912 'C. F. BENTON' *Fairs & Fetes* 116 Give to every purchaser a catalogue, which will be donated by any *seed-house on request. 1941 *Sun* (Baltimore) 6 Aug. 16/7 Gray's standard manual apparently *versus* a Philadelphia seed-house. 1809 A. HENRY *Trav.* 233, I distributed *seed-maize among the Indians here, which they planted accordingly. 1824 LOUDON *Encycl. Gard.* (ed. 2) §7515 The *seed-market is held twice a-week..in a large roofed space in Mark-lane. 1898 *Daily News* 9 June 7/5 To-day's seed market..was most thinly attended. 1647 HEXHAM I, *Seed-moneth, *Zaey-maent*. 1707 MORTIMER *Husb.* (1721) II. 360 This [Febr.] is a principal Seed Month, for such as they commonly call Lenten Grain. 1801 *Farmer's Mag.* Aug. 272 The same premium..to be given for ascertaining the proper quantity of *seed oats dibbled on a lay, or on old pasture ground. 1858 SIMMONDS *Dict. Trade*, **Seed-oil*, an indefinite name for several kinds of oil, which enter into commerce. 1881 *Harper's Mag.* Oct. 726/2 There are now fifty-nine seed-oil mills in the South. 1935 A. G. L. HELLYER *Pract. Gardening* v. 43 Beginners are safe in following the directions printed on the *seed packet. 1981 'M. YORKE' *Hand of Death* xvi. 143 Ronald..sorted through old seed packets. 1552 LATIMER *Serm. Lincolnsh.* i. (1584) 186 Vppon the Sabboth day Gods *seede plough goeth. 1764 *Ann. Reg.* 76 At York: †a newly invented seed plough ..on two wheels. 1718 R. BRADLEY *Gentl. & Gard. Kal.* 35 Pulling up the whole Plants, and setting them upright in a Green-house till the *Seed-Pods are dry. 1831 LOUDON *Encycl. Agric.* (1857) §2741 A machine for reaping the heads or seed-pods of clover. 1742 J. SAVAGE in *New Hampshire Probate Rec.* (1916) III. 115, I Give to my Dear and Loving Wife..Ground..for to plant one bushel of *Seed pertators. 1901 L. H. BAILEY *Cycl. Amer. Hort.* III. 1419/2 The seed Potatoes are cut to one eye, and dropped about 12 to 15 in. apart. 1977 *Belfast Tel.* 22 Feb. 22/4 (Advt.), Foundation stock seed potatoes for sale. 1960 *Times* 28 Nov. 16/5 The recommended *seed-rate [for maize] is 30 to 35 lb. an acre. 1977 J. L. HARPER *Population Biol. Plants* viii. 250 Seed of *T[rifolium] repens* was sown together with varying seed rates of *Lolium perenne*. 1617 PURCHAS *Pilgrimage* v. ix. (ed. 3) 619 Which [feastings] they vse to doe in all their feasts, marriages, childe-births, and their haruest and *seed-seasons. 1805 R. W. DICKSON *Pract. Agric.* I. 461 In very wet seed seasons too, it must, perhaps, give way in many cases to the broadcast method. 1946 *Nature* 12 Oct. 519/2 The reactions based on pollen-tube growth and *seed-set determinations of these two groups of plants are given in the accompanying table. 1978 *Ibid.* 7 Sept. 54/2 In artificial field bean pollination, manual stripping of open flowers is a recommended practice for increasing seed set in autosterile lines. 1700 T. BROWN *Amusem. Ser. & Com.* iii. 33 A Red-Headed Monkey lost from a *Seed-Shop in the Strand. 1866 *Chamb. Encycl.* VIII. 600/2 In sending a parcel from a seed-shop to a neighbouring garden. 1875 KNIGHT *Dict. Mech.* s.v. *Seed-planter*, The rod-shaft, which communicates by rods with the *seed-slides of the separate hoppers, which discharge into the seed-tubes of the shares. 1917 D. H. LAWRENCE *Look! We have come Through!* 59 Rose-leaves that whirl in colour round a core Of *seed-specks kindled lately. 1840 J. BUEL *Farmer's Comp.* 228 It may be known by its coarse appearance, both of the leaf and *seed-spike. 1744 W. ELLIS *Mod. Husbandman* Jan. ii. 32 A Turnep runs up a *Seed-stalk sometimes near seven Feet high. 1846 J. BAXTER *Libr. Pract. Agric.* (ed. 4) II. 19 They will shoot in summer in single tall seed-stalks. 1813 VANCOUVER *Agric. Devon* 355 In summer, it chiefly subsists on the tops and *seed-stems of thistles. 1875 *Seed-tube [see *seed-slide* above]. 1953 E. R. JANES *Sweet Peas* vii. 53 Standard *seed trays give little trouble. 1971 P. D. JAMES *Shroud for Nightingale* vi. 183 A small stack of seed trays, pruning shears, a trowel and small fork. 1786 ABERCROMBIE *Gard. Assist.* 201 Dill—if now advanced in *seed-umbels, may be pulled up for use. 1844 H. STEPHENS *Bk. Farm* II. 538 A register screw..by which the sower could at once fix upon the extent of opening in the *seed-vents. 1927 HALDANE & HUXLEY *Animal Biol.* x. 219 They will produce plants each of which will have the same range of *seed-weight as did its parent. 1977 J. L. HARPER *Population Biol. Plants* vii. 203 The year to year variation in seed weight is quite large. 1592 *Shuttleworths' Acc.* (Chetham Soc.) 78 Foure mettes of *side wheite which was soune at Eclestone, xij^s iiij^d. 1801 *Farmer's Mag.* Aug. 271 The proper quantity of seed-wheat to be used per acre.

b. Objective and objective genitive, as ***seed-bearer, -crusher, -grower, planter,*** †***-saver, -seller, -serving, sower, -sowing, -testing; seed-bearing, -eating*** adjs.; also SEED-CARRIER.

1883 'ANNIE THOMAS' *Mod. Housewife* 19 John had cut certain heads of asparagus that were intended for *seed-bearers. 1766 *Complete Farmer* Z 2/2 s.v. *Hemp*, This other species,..which is commonly termed male hemp, should be called *seed-bearing hemp, or female hemp. 1877 HEATH *Fern World* 25 These beautiful plants, however, though flowerless, are seed-bearing. 1858 SIMMONDS *Dict. Trade*, **Seed-crusher*, one who expresses oil from seeds; a machine with rollers. 1927 HALDANE & HUXLEY *Animal Biol.* x. 205 If..a tame sea-gull is fed on corn instead of fish, the whole lining of its stomach alters, becoming thicker and more like that of *seed-eating birds. 1977 J. L. HARPER *Population Biol. Plants* xx. 629 A plague of seed-eating mammals, birds or insects may prevent regeneration. 1824 LOUDON *Encycl. Gard.* (ed. 2) §7390 *Seed growers are as frequently farmers as gardeners. 1850 *Rep. Comm. Patents 1849* (U.S.) I. 151 Having thus fully described my improved grain and *seed planter. 1585 HIGINS *Junius' Nomencl.* 513 *Seminaria*,..a *seedesauer: a woman that gathereth and preserueth the seedes of herbs. 1562 J. HEYWOOD *Prov. & Epigr.* (1867) 212 We *seede sellers must sell seedes one with an other. 1848 *Commerc. Rev.* VI. 133 *Seed-Sowers, &c.—These machines are quite ingenious and labor-saving in their contrivance, [etc.]. 1977 *Young's Sporting Appliances* (S. Young & Sons Ltd.) 5 Seed sower. 1865 *Rep. Maine Board Agric.* X. 65 The use of the drill for general *seed-sowing is at present considered too expensive. 1896 *U.S. Dept. Agric. Yearbk. 1895* 175 The importance of *seed testing is recognized not only by professional seedmen, but also by intelligent farmers. 1910 *Chambers's Jrnl.* Oct. 685/1 Next comes seed-testing under the microscope, which shows the weed, seeds, and rubbish amongst them. 1950 *N.Z. Jrnl. Agric.* Mar. 243/1 Some 80 years ago the first seed-testing station was established in Saxony by Professor Nobbe. 1973 *Country Life* 15 Mar. 714/2 Work on onions at the Cambridge Official Seed Testing Station.

c. Similative, as ***seed-coral, -egg;*** also ***seed-like*** adj.; SEED-PEARL.

1879 SIMMONDS *Commerc. Products of Sea* 441 The Chinese..used to prepare strings of small rows of *seed-coral beads for embroidery. 1835 URE *Philos. Manuf.* 235 Under favourable circumstances, one ounce of *seed-eggs will produce eighty pounds of cocoons, and even more. 1715 *Phil. Trans.* XXIX. 351 These *seedlike Bodies may be the *Ovaria* of some Insects. 1887 PHILLIPS *Brit. Discomyc.* 110 A number of small, hard, seed-like bodies.

d. Instrumental, as ***seed-borne*** adj.

1931 *Bull. W. Virginia Agric. Exper. Station* No. 245. 5 The economic losses occasioned by these few seed-borne parasites..are enormous. 1968 *Times* 16 Dec. 7/1 A seed-borne fungus disease.

9. Special combinations: **seed-bag** (see quot.); **seed bank,** (*a*) a place where seeds of different plant varieties and species are stored as a safeguard against their possible extinction; (*b*) the seeds that have accumulated naturally in a given area of ground; **seed-bird,** (*a*) the Pied Wagtail, *Motacilla lugubris* or *alba*; (*b*) any sea-fowl, esp. the Common Gull, *Larus canus*; †**seed-bone** *Anat.* = SESAMOID *sb.*; †**seed-bringer** *Anat.* (see quot.); **seed-bud** *Bot.* (see quot. 1796); **seed bull,** a bull kept to serve cows; **seed-coat** *Bot.* = TESTA; †**seed-cob,** †**-cod,** †**-cot** = SEED-LIP; **seed-cotton,** cotton in its native state, with the seed not separated; **seed crystal** = sense 2 b above; **seed dressing,** a preparation applied to seed in order to protect it against pests; the practice or an instance of employing this; †**seed-earth** [EARTH *sb.*^{2}], the side of a seed-furrow; **seed-eater, -feeder,** any granivorous bird, *spec.* the Grass-quit, *Phonifara bicolor*; **seed fat,** a fat obtained from seeds; **seed-finch, -fish** (see quots.); †**seed-fowl,** a granivorous bird; †**seed-horse,** a stallion; †**seed-land,** ground capable of raising crops (in quot. *fig.* and *attrib.*); **seed-leaf,** (*a*) = COTYLEDON 3 (but see quot. 1793 for *seed-lobe*); also **seed-lobe**; (*b*) used *attrib.* and *absol.* to designate a kind of tobacco grown in the northern United States and used chiefly for wrapping cigars (so called because it was first grown from imported seed); **seed metering,** automatic control of the numbers of seeds sown or planted by a machine; **seed money** *U.S.*, money allocated (esp. from public funds) for the initiation of a project and designed to stimulate the independent economic expansion of the project; †**seed-nest** *Bot.* = OVARY 2; **seed orchard,** a group of trees cultivated for the production of seed; †**seed-ore,** ore found in the form of grains; **seed oyster,** oyster-spat; †**seed-pair,** a pair, male and female, regarded as primogenitors; **seed-pan,** a pan of red earthenware used for the raising of plants from seed; **seed parent,** in hybridization, a plant whose seed is fertilized by pollen from a different plant; **seed-plant,** (*a*) a plant grown from a seed, a seedling; (*b*) a plant grown for its seed; **seed-pot,** a pot in which a plant is raised from seed; †**seed-seam,** a seed-furrow (cf. SEAM *sb.*^{1} 4 e); **seed-snipe,** a bird of the S. American genus *Thinocorys*; †**seed-spark,** the germ of a fire (in quots. *fig.*); **seed stitch** *Needlework* = SEEDING *vbl. sb.* 4; **seed-thought,** thought comparable to seed, fruitful or suggestive thought; **seed-tick,** a mite of the family *Ixodidæ*, esp. the young of *Ixodes bovis*; †**seed-trough** *Anat.*, ? the *vas deferens*; †**seed-vein,** ? the spermatic cord; **seed-vessel** = PERICARP (also *fig.*); †**seed-water,** a decoction of coriander and caraway seeds mixed with sack and sugar; **seed-weed,** a weed that propagates itself by seeding, as distinguished from one that spreads by its roots; **seed year,** one of the years in which a particular tree produces a good crop of seeds. See also SEED-CAKE, SEED-LAC, etc.

a 1864 GESNER *Coal, Petrol.*, etc. (1865) 32 To prevent communication between any particular portion of the well and the pumping tube, a bag of linseed, called a '*seed bag', is sent down to the required place. This bag, encircling the tube, soon swells.., and forms a water-tight joint. 1958 *Economist* 25 Oct. 328/2 In America's first central *seed bank, which has recently been opened at Colorado State University, there is space to store supplies of several hundred thousand basic seed stocks. 1974 *Nature* 24 May 303/2 As part of a worldwide effort to conserve this fast disappearing genetic resource, a seed bank had already been set up. 1977 J. L. HARPER *Population Biol. Plants* iv. 83 The store of seeds buried in soil (the seed bank) is composed in part of seeds produced on the area and partly of seeds blown in from elsewhere. 1678 RAY *Willughby's Ornith.* 237 Moreover it [the white Wagtail] follows the Plough..: As.. our Husbandmen have told me of their own observation; who therefore call it the *Seed-bird, as Mr. Johnson informed me. 1791 SIR J. SINCLAIR *Statist. Acc. Scot.* I. 67 Sea fowls appear here in great numbers in the spring, about seed-time; they follow the plough and are thence called seed-birds. 1634 T. JOHNSON tr. *Parey's Wks.* VI. xxvii. 220 The *Ossa Sesamoidea*, or *seed bones: these are 19 in number. 1545 RAYNALD *Byrth Mankynde* I. ix. (1552) 13 b, The *sede bringers, called in Latyn *Vasa semen adferentia*, be two vaines & two artyres. 1776 WITHERING *Bot. Arrangem. Veget.* I. 2 Hippuris... *Seed-bud oblong; superior. 1796 —— *Brit. Plants* (ed. 3) I. 61 *Germen*, or *Seed-bud*, the lower part of a Pistil. It is the rudiment of the seed-vessel, or of the embryo fruit. 1837 P. KEITH *Bot. Lex.* 43 A little gnat, *Cynips Ficus Caricæ*, which lays its egg in the seed-bud of the Wild Fig. 1932 E. HEMINGWAY *Death in Afternoon* xi. 118 The usual ranch has two hundred cows and four *seed bulls. 1796 WITHERING *Brit. Plants* (ed. 3) I. 80 *Seed-coat (*arillus*) the proper coat of a seed which falls off spontaneously. 1766 *Complete Farmer* K 3/2 s.v. *Cob*, A *seed-cob, or seed-lip. 1235–52 *Rentalia Glaston.* (Somerset Rec. Soc.) 113 Unum *sedcod plenum frumenti. 1407 in Kennett *Par. Antiq.* (1818) II. 213 Et pro uno Seedcod empto, iij[d]. **1733** W. Ellis *Chiltern & Vale Farm.* 58 Some will dress.. this Chalk.. with Rags chop'd small.. and then sown out of a *Seed Cot all over the Ground. **1797** F. Baily *Jrnl. Tour N. Amer.* 285 The *seed-cotton loses three-fourths of its weight by jenning. **1835** Ure *Philos. Manuf.* 113 One hundred and six pounds of wool from the first kind of seed-cotton. **1934** *Industr. & Engin. Chem.* Nov. 1201/1 The initial formation of crystal nuclei is profoundly influenced by the chance presence of very small *seed crystals of the solute. **1962** [see melt *sb.*[3] 2]. **1974** *Encycl. Brit. Macropædia* V. 337/1 If the structure and interatomic spacing of the surface.. approximate that of the crystal, growth on the surface can resemble growth on a normal seed crystal. **1926–7** *Army & Navy Stores Catal.* p. lxxi/2 *Seed Dressings, Liquid. **1955** E. Holmes *Pract. Plant Protection* iv. 31 By far the most important fungicidal seed-dressings are those based on chemicals known as the organo-mercury products. **1977** M. B. Green et al. *Chemicals for Crop Protection & Pest Control* xii. 103 The convenience and economy of seed-dressing makes it.. a clear choice when the disease can be controlled this way. **1805** R. W. Dickson *Pract. Agric.* I. 10 Ley-grounds cannot be laid too flat, or *seed earths too much on an edge. **1879** G. N. Lawrence in *Proc. U.S. Nat. Mus.* I. 355 *Phonipara bicolor* (Linn.)... 'Mangeur des herbes'. *Seed-eater. **1884** J. Burroughs in *Century Mag.* Dec. 220/1 Even the slate-coloured snow-bird, a seed-eater, comes and nibbles. **1940** T. P. Hilditch *Chem. Constitution of Natural Fats* i. 18 However varied the fatty acids in *seed fats may be, the resulting triglycerides are.. fundamentally similar in type. **1949** *Thorpe's Dict. Appl. Chem.* (ed. 4) IX. 8/2 In many seed fats.. the main component acids are confined to palmitic, oleic, and linoleic in varying proportions. **1963** *Times* 22 May (Suppl.) p. iv/2 The main sources of edible oils and fats are vegetable fats—particularly palm oil; seed fats, notably those of groundnut, coconut, soya bean, palm kernel and cotton seed; [etc.]. **1853** *Zoologist* II. 4025 The *seed-feeders are far more likely to escape observation. **1888** P. L. Sclater *Argentine Ornith.* I. 69 *Sycalis lutea*... (Yellow *Seed-finch). *Ibid.* 71 *Orospina pratensis*... (Meadow Seed-finch.) **1891** *Century Dict.*, **Seed-fish*, a fish containing seed, roe, or spawn; a ripe fish. *c* **1381** Chaucer *Parl. Foules* (MS. Seld.) 328 Bothe watere foule and *sede foule on the grene That so fele were þat wonder was to sene. *c* **1450** Holland *Howlat* 238 All Se fowle and Seid fowle was nocht for to seike. **1794** Morse *Amer. Geog.* 485 The gentlemen.. have taken much pains to raise a good breed of horses... They will give 1000l. sterling for a good *seed horse. **1607** Chapman *Bussy d'Ambois* I. i. 124 But his unsweating thrift is policy, And learning-hating policy is ignorant To fit his *seed-land soil. **1693** Evelyn *De La Quint. Compl. Gard.* Dict., *Seed Leaves, are the first Leaves that Spring up like ears on each side, at the first cleaving or sprouting of any Seed. **1852** *Hunt's Merch. Mag.* XXVII. 555 The 'seed leaf' is raised on the Miami River. **1877** Huxley & Martin *Elem. Biol.* 71 The cotyledons of the contained embryo swell, burst the seed coat, and, becoming green, emerge as the fleshy seed leaves. **1888** *Encycl. Brit.* XXIII. 425/2 The 'seed-leaf' tobacco of Pennsylvania, Connecticut, and Ohio, grown from Havana seed, is devoted to cigar-making in the United States. **1910** 'Mark Twain' *Speeches* 267, I bought what was called a seed-leaf cigar with a Connecticut wrapper. **1946** W. W. Garner *Production of Tobacco* ii. 35 The process of fermenting the leaf in cases in preparation for manufacture.. began about 1845 and gave great impetus to the manufacture of the 'Seed and Havana' cigar, composed of Cuban filler and Connecticut Seedleaf wrapper. **1968** B. C. Akehurst *Tobacco* xi. 266 The current U.S. Department of Agriculture classification is as follows: Class 4...Type 41 Pennsylvania Seed Leaf. **1793** Martyn *Lang. Bot.* s.v. *Cotyledon*, In English we commonly call this part the *Cotyledon* or **seed-lobe*, when we speak of it as a portion of the seed, in a quiescent state—and the *seed-leaf*, when the seed is in a growing state. **1796** Withering *Brit. Plants* (ed. 3) I. 80 Seed-lobes (cotyledone) the perishable parts of a seed, designed to afford nourishment to the young plant when it first begins to expand. **1871** H. Macmillan *True Vine* iii. 76 The embryo of the seed is provided with two seed-lobes. **1955** R. Bainer et al. *Princ. Farm Machinery* xi. 225 Most *seed-metering devices may be classified as: (*a*) those having cells on a moving member, the cells being sized to accommodate single seeds or groups of a few seeds each, (*b*) the so-called 'force-feed' devices.., (*c*) stationary-opening units. **1971** *Power Farming* Mar. 29/4 The gearing.. has been improved to give greater precision in seed metering. **1966** *N.Y. Times* 21 Aug. F15/2 The bonds would have enabled the state to gain $17-million, to be used as *seed money to set up the loan guarantee rotary fund. **1970** *Sat. Rev.* (U.S.) 10 Jan. 27/1 This has been seed money in the best sense of the term. As President Nixon pointed out to Congress last month, every dollar of Foundation money has stimulated the donation of three dollars from other sources. **1977** *Time* 12 Dec. 33/2 It calls for $120 million in federal seed money to create 14,000 new jobs and rehabilitate four neighborhoods. **1728** Bradley *Dict. Bot.* Introd. 15 In these [lilies] the *Seed-nests are at the Bottom of the Pistillum. **1951** H. McKusick in *Tree Planters' Notes* VIII. 8 It.. seems logical that we should explore the possibility of establishing *seed orchards. **1979** *Beautiful British Columbia* Fall 40 Others are from seed orchards maintained by the province and the forest companies. **1796** Morse *Amer. Geog.* I. 683 In the cavities between [large rocks of iron ore] lie an ochre and *seed ore. **1885** *Encycl. Brit.* XVIII. 109/2 Under proper restriction.. mature oysters, and seed oysters as well, may be taken from any region. **1591** Sylvester *Du Bartas* I. ii. 1210 Noah.. sav'd a *seed-pair of all living things. **1731** Miller *Gard. Dict.* s.v. *Tulipa*, There should be provided a Parcel of shallow *Seed-Pans or Boxes. **1882** *Garden* 7 Jan. 10/3 When sufficiently large the plants should be pricked into seed-pans. **1902** *Jrnl. R. Hort. Soc.* XXVII. 209 We suggested.. crossing our common Wood Anemone.. with the scarlet *Anemone fulgens*, making the Wood Anemone the *seed parent. **1970** R. Gorer *Devel. Garden Flowers* 19, I have tried to follow the convention in which the seed parent is the first named and the pollen parent the second. **1707** Mortimer *Husb.* (1721) II. 251 It is necessary to remove *Seed-plants often as well as Forest-trees, because by that means they get good Roots. **1878** J. Inglis *Sport Nepaul Frontier* xvi. 187 The planters advance about four rupees a beegah to the ryot, who cuts his [indigo] seed-plant, and brings it into the factory threshing ground. **1846** J. Baxter *Libr. Pract. Agric.* (ed. 4) II. 71 Turn the young plants carefully out of the *seed-pot, breaking the fibres as little as possible. **1778** [W. Marshall] *Minutes Agric., Observ.* 94, I will endeavour to bury the Surface for Pease; leaving the *Seed-Seams as open and deep as possible. **1889** P. L. Sclater *Argentine Ornith.* II. 176 *Thinocoridæ*, or *Seed-snipes. **1611** Speed *Hist. Gt. Brit.* IX. ix. §92. 618 These were.. the *seede-sparkes of those factious fires which afterward brake forth. **1858** Sears *Athan.* xviii. 158 The seed-spark of our resurrection-body will not appear till Gabriel blows after it with his trumpet and kindles it up somewhere. **1934** M. Thomas *Dict. Embroidery Stitches* 182 Tiny stitches taken at all angles and in any direction but of more or less even length produce a surprisingly effective filling, as the diagram of *Seed Stitch shows. **1964** *McCall's Sewing* xiii. 246/2 *Seed stitch*,.. a very tiny chain stitch tightly drawn and scattered in all directions to fill an open area. **1863** *N. & Q.* Ser. III. III. 379 Aird's volume is full as a pomegranate of *seed-thought. **1895** *Educ. Rev.* Sept. 107 Hegel.. coming early to an appreciation of the seed-thought of Plato. **1705** Beverley *Hist. Virginia* IV. xix. (1722) 267 *Seed-Tick and Red-Worms are small Insects, that annoy the People by Day, as Musketaes and Chinches do by Night. **1893** E. B. Custer *Tenting* 88 Two pests of that region, the seed-tick and the chigger. **1615** Crooke *Body of Man* 207 Moreouer in copulation or coition they draw them back, that the *seed trough becomming shorter, the seed may more easily and readily be supplyed. *Ibid.* 201 The hollow veine where the right *seede-veine arose. **1668** Wilkins *Real Char.* II. iv. §5. 96 Herbs considered according to their *Seed-vessel. **1857** A. Gray *First Less. Bot.* (1866) 127 A simple fruit consists, then, of the Seed-vessel (technically called the Pericarp), or the walls of the ovary matured, and the seeds contained in it. **1869** J. Martineau *Ess.* II. 22 The code is the seed-vessel of all the virtues. **1747** Mrs. Glasse *Cookery* x. 120 *Seed Water. **1765** A. Dickson *Treat. Agric.* (ed. 2) 270 When the design of plowing is to.. destroy *seed-weeds [etc.]. **1805** R. W. Dickson *Pract. Agric.* I. 415 Where seed-weeds are to be eradicated, the surface should constantly be.. made as fine and smooth as the nature of the land will admit. **1889** W. Schlich *Man. Forestry* I. II. ii. 173 The quantity of seed is governed by two things:—(1.) The average yield of each *seed-year; and (2.) The frequency of seed-years. **1979** H. W. Hocker *Introd. Forest Biol.* ii. 55 Heavy seed years do not occur at frequent intervals, but are usually offset by succeeding years of light to very light crops.

seed (siːd), *v.* Forms: see the sb. [f. seed *sb.* Cf. OFris. *sêdia*, WFris. *siedsje.*]

I. *intr.*

1. a. To produce seed; to run to seed. Also *fig.*

c **1374** Chaucer *Anel. & Arc.* 306 Youre chere floureth but hit will not sede. *a* **1400–50** *Wars Alex.* 3725 Ȝoure saule sa full of sapient sedis & floures. **1523** Fitzherb. *Husb.* §20 Drake is lyke vnto rye, till it begynne to sede. **1600** Bodenham *Belvedere* 227 First doe we bud, then blow; next seed, last fall. **1606** Dekker *Seven Sins* v. (Arb.) 36 This flower when it first came into the Citie, had a prettie scent, .. hath bene let to run so high, that it is now seeded. **1617** Markham *Country Housew. Gard.* viii. (1623) 12 Hollyhocke riseth high, seedeth and dyeth. **1713** Petiver in *Phil. Trans.* XXVIII. 190 It flowers and seeds with us in May, June, &c. **1821** Southey *Ode King's Vis. Irel.* ix, Labours of love remain; To weed out noxious customs rooted deep In a rank soil, and long left seeding there. **1880** C. R. Markham *Peruv. Bark* 345 The tea plants are now three or four feet high, and seeding freely.

b. To develop *into* something undesirable.

1898 B. Gregory *Side Lights* 205 The egotism.. had not seeded into the fanatical distension of your genuine demagogue. **1909** *Sat. Rev.* 17 Apr. 487/1 In Persia it [Parliamentary government] soon blossomed out into civil war, and now is seeding into anarchy.

†**2.** To beget children. *Obs. rare*$^{-1}$.

1393 Langl. *P. Pl.* C. XI. 251 And god sente to seth.., That for no kyne catel ne no kyne byheste Suffren hus seed seeden with caymes seed hus broþer.

†**3.** To be born *of*. *Obs. rare*$^{-1}$.

c **1450** *Cov. Myst.* (Shaks. Soc.) 393 The voys of my moder me nyhith ful ny I am dyssend on to here of whom I dede sede.

†**4.** To gather seed. *Obs. rare*$^{-1}$.

1573 Tusser *Husb.* (1878) 112 Slack neuer thy weeding.., And specially where ye doo trust for to seede.

II. *trans.*

†**5.** To stock with inhabitants. *Obs. rare*$^{-1}$.

13.. *Cursor M.* 1627 (Gött.) Here bigines at noe þe lede þe toþer world for to sede.

6. a. To sow (land) with seed. Also *absol.*

c **1440** *Pallad. on Husb.* VI. 71 The spaces that in heruest sowe or sede Me wol, may best ha now their pastynynge. **1482** *Paston Lett.* III. 293 Weche absenting of the tenauntes is to them a greet hurt and los, for lak of sedyng ther londes with ther wynter corn. **1598** Dallington *Meth. Trav.* N 4 b, He giues them also Wheat to seed their land. **1610** W. Folkingham *Art of Survey* I. x. 32 They will Marle, Till, and Seede it for halfe the increase. **1707** *Curios. in Husb. & Gard.* 120 A third part less than usual will sufficiently seed the Ground. *a* **1814** *Apostate* II. iv. in *New Brit. Theatre* III. 320 You taught us arts—divided us in bands, These for the chace, and those to seed the soil. **1888** *Vermont Agric. Rep.* X. 48, I.. then seed broadcast with grass-seed. **1895** *Outing* (U.S.) XXVII. 254/1 The field was plowed, seeded and rolled. **1979** [see plant *v.* 1].

b. *transf.* and *fig.*

1647 C. Harvey *Schola Cordis* Epigr. xxviii, Manure the ground [of my heart], then come Thyself and seed it, And let Thy servants water it and weed it. *a* **1670** Hacket *Abp. Williams* II. (1693) 6 And the Keeper understood that no Peace was to be had from an Adversary seeded with such Qualities. **1898** *Westm. Gaz.* 12 Jan. 10/2 We know that a cow suffering from tuberculosis may yield milk seeded with the germs of consumption.

spec. (i) To introduce a crystal or small particle into (a liquid or apparatus) so as to induce crystallization. Cf. seed *sb.* 2 b.

1909 in *Cent. Dict.* Suppl. **1921** *Jrnl. Physical Chem.* XXV. 534 Points on the stable curve.. were then easily determined by seeding the proper mixtures.. with small crystals from this lot of hydrate. **1930** *Amer. Speech* VI. 14 Sometimes a crystallizer is seeded with a nest egg of sugar. **1936** H. L. Alling *Interpretative Petrol. Igneous Rocks* iv. 41 Supercooled water, left undisturbed, is stable if not in contact with ice. 'Seeding' it with the solid phase produces crystallization. **1964** G. H. Haggis et al. *Introd. Molecular Biol.* iv. 94 It has further been possible recently to study this process *in vitro* by 'seeding' near-saturated solutions of calcium phosphate with collagen fibres.

(ii) To introduce crystals of a substance such as silver iodide into (a cloud, etc.) in order to cause precipitation.

1947 *Sun* (Baltimore) 9 Sept. 3/3 Today's storm developed too close to the Florida West Coast to be seeded with dry ice or other crystals by Army and Navy planes. **1958** *Observer* 12 Jan. 6/3 The nearest thing to weather control so far is 'seeding' clouds with ice or silver iodide to persuade them to give up their rain. **1974** *Nature* 11 Oct. 461/3 Potential hail clouds are observed by radar, and then seeded by lead iodide from a rocket fired into the cloud's centre. **1975** *Daily Colonist* (Victoria, B.C.) 16 July 3/3 The United States government did not seed hurricane Fifi, nor was it ever contemplated.

(iii) *Biol.* To inoculate (a culture vessel) *with* cells from a culture which is to be propagated.

1960 *Virology* X. 387 One hundred-millimeter petri dishes were seeded with cells from primary cultures of normal mouse. **1978** *Nature* 23 Mar. 372/2 The procedure was repeated using cultures of Wi-38 cells prepared in.. eight-compartment chamber slides.. that had been seeded three days earlier with 15,000 cells in each compartment.

c. const. *to*.

1887 *Blackw. Mag.* CXLI. 813 The estate.. had been seeded largely to grass and clover, the very acme of high farming in the South. **1908** *Standard* 29 Apr. 2/5 Reliable authorities place the area to be seeded to wheat in Western Canada this year at six million acres.

d. ***to seed down***: to sow grass or clover seeds amongst (a crop of oats, wheat, etc.). Cf. *sow down* s.v. sow *v.* Also *fig.*

1846 *Jrnl. R. Agric. Soc.* VII. II. 505 It is the practice of one farmer.. to seed down without a crop: his custom is to fallow. **1864** *Ibid.* XXV. II. 527, I seed down the oat-crop for clover. **1873** Will Carleton *Farm Ball.* 30 And I'll plough her grave with hate, and seed it down to scorn!

7. a. To sow (a particular kind of seed) upon land. † Also with cogn. obj., ***to seed seed*** (a Hebraism).

1560 Bible (Geneva) *Gen.* i. 12 The budde of the herbe, that sedeth sede according to his kinde. **1614** Raleigh *Hist. World* I. i. §7. 11 The Earth.. brought forth the budde of the hearbe that seedeth seede. **1814** J. Taylor *Arator* (ed. 2) 154 When the wheat was seeded on high and narrow ridges. **1851** C. Cist *Cincinnati* xv. 317 The cotton crop is seeded in the spring. **1894** *Times* 14 Aug. 15/2 In the course of another week or two, English farmers.. will be seeding 'trifolium' upon the wheat stubble.

b. *transf.*

1602 Rowlands *Greenes Ghost* 8, I wish.. he had also looked into other grosse sinnes, which are seeded in the hearts of sundrie persons. **1844** S. Wilberforce *Hist. Prot. Episc. Ch. Amer.* (1846) 408 Division has grown up in all its rankness, and seeded freely on every side a new crop of errors.

c. *refl.* of a plant: To sow itself.

1909 *Eng. Rev.* Feb. 403 There is no further need of planting, for they [the pines] seed themselves.

d. *Biol.* To inoculate (cells from a culture) *into* a culture vessel or medium.

1965 *Proc. Nat. Acad. Sci.* LIV. 1585 The cells were.. seeded into 60-mm plastic dishes at a density of $2{\cdot}5 \times 10^6$ cells per dish. **1973** *Nature* 22 June 450/1 Cells (10^7) were seeded into each 100-mm Petri dish (Falcon Co.) and incubated at 37°C in a humidified incubator with 5% CO_2 in air.

†**8.** *pass.* To run to seed, to mature. *Obs.*

1593 Shaks. *Lucr.* 603 How will thy shame be seeded in thine age When thus thy vices bud before thy spring?

†**9.** To sprinkle or cover a surface lightly with; so, to decorate the material of a garment with powdering of small ornament. *Obs.*

1598 Dallington *Meth. Trav.* L 4, The Constable.. as the Grand Escuyer,.. hath the Sword in the scabberd *D'Azure, semé de fleurs de Lys d'or*: Azure seeded with flowers de Lyce. **1603** B. Jonson *King's Entertainm.* Wks. 1616 I. 844 Theosophia, or diuine Wisedome, all in white, a blue mantle seeded with starres. **1633** Shirley *Tri. Peace* 4 In the next Chariot of equall glory, were placed on the lowest staires foure in skie-coloured Taffata Robes seeded with starres. **1678** Jordan *Triumphs of Lond.* 4 Vigilancy, in a Silver Robe, a French green Mantle, seeded with waking Eyes.

10. To remove the seeds from (fruit), to 'stone'.

1904 *Daily Chron.* 9 June 8/5 Seed a pound of raisins, cut them in quarters, and mix them with six ounces of shredded citron. **1908** *Ibid.* 5 Mar. 8/3 The currants should be cleaned, raisins seeded, and citron shredded.

11. *Sport*, esp. *Lawn Tennis.* To assign (to several of the better competitors) a position in an ordered list, so that those most highly ranked do not meet until the later stages of an elimination competition; to arrange (a draw or event) to this end. Cf. seed *sb.* 3. orig. *U.S.*

1898 *Amer. Lawn Tennis* 13 Jan. 4/2 Several years ago, it was decided to 'seed' the best players through the championship draw, and this was done for two or three years. **1900** *Spalding's Lawn Tennis Ann.* 78 It is generally advisable to 'seed' the draw in handicap tournaments so that the players in each class shall be separated as far as possible one from another. **1911** *Spalding's Off. Lawn Tennis Guide* 55 Unlike many big events, Longwood is never seeded, and in consequence the possibility of an uneven draw materialized. **1924** *Times* 23 June 4/4 This year, for the first time, the draw has been 'seeded'; how little seeding accords with British notions may be gathered from there being no reference in the Oxford Dictionary—at any rate in the smaller one... In some countries the seeding is designed to keep the better players apart until the final stages. **1929** *Times* 29 June 4/4 Three of the women who had been 'seeded' for the draw were defeated during the day. **1953** *Sunday Graphic* 7 June 22/4 Rose, likely to be seeded in the first four at Wimbledon, did not play up to his reputation. **1955** *N.Y. Times* 10 May 33/5 Joe Burk's Red and Blue eight, which beat Navy and Harvard Saturday for the Adams Cup, was seeded first in the draw for the tenth annual regatta. **1972** D. DELMAN *Sudden Death* (1973) i. 17 Timmy was up against a big Australian kid who'd given me fits at Wimbledon... Timmy..would probably go into the tournament seeded second behind Cole. **1982** *Guardian* 8 June 22/8 She is seeded 14th and is not particularly worried that a seeding at Wimbledon is unlikely.

†**'seedage.** *Obs. rare.* [f. SEED *v.* + -AGE.]

1. A sowing.

1610 W. FOLKINGHAM *Art of Survey* I. x. 27 The shaked corne seruing..for the second seedage. *Ibid.* I. xi. 35 Wheat craues a fat Clay (and dry to make it hard and compact) and durty Seedage.

2. Production of seed.

1891 L. H. BAILEY *Nursery-bk.* (1896) 1 Chapter I. Seedage. *Ibid.*, Moisture is the most important factor in seedage.

'seed-bed.

1. A bed for sowing seeds; also, the seedlings growing there.

1660 SHARROCK *Vegetables* 25 In seeds that are long in coming up, the seed bed is not to be digged up the first winter. **1723** P. BLAIR *Pharmaco-Bot.* I. 38 Like a Fir-tree, when in the Seed Bed, but much less. **1846** J. BAXTER *Libr. Pract. Agric.* (ed. 4) I. 265 They should never be allowed to remain more than two years in the seed-bed, for in that case they will be completely spoiled. **1852** C. W. H[OSKINS] *Talpa* 178 He will cut up the soil into a seed-bed of the pattern required.

b. *transf.* and *fig.*

1826 E. IRVING *Babylon* II. VIII. 312 The Church hath been set into action to prepare the seed-bed of the truth over the earth. **1884** *Pall Mall Gaz.* 9 July 2/1 There must have been seed-beds of disease to have produced leprosy in houses and in people.

†**2.** *Bot.* = PLACENTA 2. *Obs. rare*$^{-1}$.

1720 P. BLAIR *Bot. Ess.* ii. 54 As the Seeds ripen, and separate from the proper Placentæ or Seed-beds.

'seed-box.

1. The receptacle for the seed in a grain-drill or seed-sowing-machine.

1733 TULL *Horse-Hoeing Husb.* xxii. 315 Of these [parts of the Drill] the Seed-Box is the chief; it measures (or rather numbers) out the Seed which it receives from the Hopper. **1831** LOUDON *Encycl. Agric.* (1857) §2679 The seed-box being elevated or depressed accordingly, so as to render the distribution of the seed regular. **1875** *Encycl. Brit.* I. 320/1 [In the machine for broadcast sowing] motion is communicated to a spindle which revolves in the seed-box, and expels the seed by means of cogs or brushes.

2. *U.S.* A plant of the genus *Ludwigia*, so called from its cubical pod.

1821 BARTON *Flora N. Amer.* I. 49 *Ludwigia macrocarpa.* Large-capsuled Seed-box, or Ludwigia. **1856** GRAY *Man. Bot.* (1860) 33 *Ludwigia alternifolia.* (Seed-box.)

'seed-cake. A cake flavoured with caraway seeds and more or less sweetened. Cf. CAKE *sb.* 1 c.

The 'seed-cakes' formerly eaten at the rustic festival celebrating the end of sowing-time may have been of this kind, though the custom prob. had an allusive reference to SEED *sb.*

Warton's statement (quoted in the 1878 ed. of Tusser) that the name was applied to the festival itself, seems doubtful; cf., however, quot. 1726.

1573 TUSSER *Husb.* (1878) 181 Wife, some time this weeke, if the wether hold cleere, an end of wheat sowing we make for this yeere. Remember you therefore though I do it not: the seede Cake, the Pasties, and Furmentie pot. **1710** P. LAMB *Royal Cookery* 84 To make a Seed-Cake. **1726** AYLIFFE *Parergon* 8 It was a..customary thing..for every Man in the Parish..to give to the Church a certain Measure of Wheat..on St. Martin's Day; and this in our ancient Books is called Church-Seed, from whence came the Rise of our Seed-Cakes. **1755** in W. Macgill *Old Ross-sh.* (1909) 154 Sugar biscake..plumbcake..seedcake. **1833** HT. MARTINEAU *Berkeley the Banker* II. viii. 143 Mrs. Pye's seed-cake and currant-wine. **1850** DICKENS *Dav. Copp.* xlii, I cut and handed the sweet seed-cake.

'seed-carrier.

1. One who carries seed. †**a.** *fig.* One who disseminates the tenets of another. *Obs. rare*$^{-1}$.

1600 W. WATSON *Decacordon* (1602) 101 The seed-cariers of these contentions are either close Iesuits, and so will not be knowne, or at least..Iesuited faultors of their pollicies.

b. In sowing corn, etc.: An assistant who replenishes the seed-baskets of the sowers.

1844 H. STEPHENS *Bk. Farm* II. 506 If the sacks of seed are conveniently placed, one active seed-carrier will serve two sowers.

†**2.** = SEED-LIP. *Obs.*

1831 LOUDON *Encycl. Agric.* (1857) §2526 The seed-carrier or seed-basket is sometimes made of thin veneers of wood, bent into an irregular oval, with a hollow to fit the seedsman's side.

3. Applied to various animals with reference to the part which they play in the dispersion of seeds.

1880 A. R. WALLACE *Isl. Life* xii. 238 The dispersal of seeds—Birds as seed-carriers. **1906** *Athenæum* 12 May 581 Bats and insects may be active seed-carriers.

'seed-corn. **1.** Grain (or *occas.* a grain of corn) for sowing in order to produce a new crop.

1592–3 *Shuttleworths' Acc.* (Chetham Soc.) 79 Roberte Aspeden for to bestowe upone side corne and other charges ..x^{s}. **1645** QUARLES *Sol. Recant.* Sol. xi. 70 Stay not for showres; The soile, if overflowne, Will drown thy seed-corn, and return thee none. **1719** DE FOE *Crusoe* I. (Globe) 119 Even after I had got the first Handful of Seed-Corn. **1844** H. STEPHENS *Bk. Farm* II. 283 All seed-corn should be sifted.

fig. **1800** W. TAYLOR in *Monthly Mag.* VIII. 598 Some of these seed-corns of superstition, it is expected, must strike root. **1870** EMERSON *Soc. & Solit.* ix. 199 We know that *l'homme de lettres* is a little wary, and not fond of giving away his seed-corn. **1962** *Economist* 19 May 688/1 The loans and grants from his agency are 'seed corn'; they stimulate local initiative and self-help. **1977** *Times* 20 Dec. 10/8 The IBA should be prepared to use the secondary rental income from these established stations which are already well into profit, as seedcorn money to help establish and run independent stations in smaller townships.

2. seed-corn maggot *U.S.*, the yellowish-white larva of a fly, *Hylemya platura*, which infests the seed of many vegetables and other crop plants, preventing sprouting or causing the seedlings to be weak and sickly; also, the adult fly.

1869 C. V. RILEY *First Ann. Rep. Noxious Insects Missouri* 154 (*heading*) The seed-corn maggot. **1902** *Bull. Div. Entomol. U.S. Dept. Agric.* XXXIII. 84 The Seed-Corn Maggot..has received no less than seven Latin names. **1949** *Jrnl. Econ. Entomol.* XLII. 77/1 The seed corn maggot..injures bean, pea and corn seedlings before the plants emerge. **1975** *Nature* 7 Aug. 487/1 Larvae of the seedcorn maggot..may damage or kill young plants of many crop species by feeding on the cotyledons and plumules.

'seed-crown.

†**1.** *nonce-use.* (See quot.)

1607 CHAPMAN *Bussy d'Ambois* I. i. 122 What will he send? Some crownes? It is to sow them Upon my spirit, and make them spring a crown Worth millions of the seed-crownes he will send.

2. *Bot.* = CORONA 7 a.

1807 J. E. SMITH *Phys. Bot.* 457 In every case the partial calyx is distinguished from the chaffy seed-crown observable in several genera of the other Orders,..either by being inferior, or by the presence of a seed-crown, or feathery down, besides.

seede, obs. pa. pple. of SAY *v.*^{1}

1515 in *Coll. Surrey Archæol. Soc.* (1858) I. 182.

seeded ('siːdɪd), *ppl. a.* [f. SEED *v.* and *sb.* + -ED.]

1. Sown with seed.

1591 SPENSER *Ruins of Rome* 407 Like as the seeded field green grasse first showes. **1894** *Times* 16 Apr. 7/2 All recently seeded areas have responded promptly and vigorously to an abundance of moisture on a warm soil.

2. Furnished with a seed or seeds; run to seed, matured.

1610 FLETCHER *Faithf. Shepherdess* IV. i, In some hollow tree or bed Of seeded Nettles. **1763** J. MILLS *Pract. Husb.* III. 222 It requires some experience to know at what degree of ripeness it is best to cut the seeded sainfoin. **1830** TENNYSON *Poems* 108 The seeded summerflowers. **1875** BLACKMORE *Alice Lorraine* xxx, The gossamer floats idly over the sere and seeded grass.

fig. **1593** NASHE *Christ's T.* X iij, London, thou art the seeded Garden of sinne. **1606** SHAKS. *Tr. & Cr.* I. iii. 316 The seeded Pride That hath to this maturity blowne vp In ranke Achilles, must or now be cropt.

3. *Her.* Of flowers: Having seeds of a specified tincture.

1611 [see BARBED *ppl. a.*^{1} 3]. **1777** PORNY *Elem. Her.* Dict., *Seeded a.* This is said of Roses and other Flowers, to express the tincture of their seed. **1868** CUSSANS *Handbk. Her.* (1893) 104 *Seeded*, applied chiefly to roses, in blazoning the Seeds in the centre.

4. ? Covered with dots.

1893 *Atlantic Monthly* Feb. 231/1 It [her best dress] was a purple, seeded silk, adorned with lapels that hung in wrinkles across her flat chest.

5. Of fruit, esp. dried fruit: having the seeds removed.

1921 *Daily Colonist* (Victoria, B.C.) 1 Apr. 6/1 (Advt.), Sun-Maid seeded raisins, bulk, packets of 15 oz.

6. *Sport*, esp. *Lawn Tennis.* Of a competitor: assigned a position in a list of seeds (SEED *sb.* 3) in an elimination competition. Also of a draw arranged in such a manner. Also *transf.*

1922 *Spalding's Tennis Ann.* 30 Commencing in 1922, all championships and other sanctioned tournaments except handicap events shall have a seeded draw. *Ibid.* 31 Seeded men in the top half of the draw. **1954** *New Yorker* 28 Aug. 57/1 The semifinals had the No. 1 and No. 2 seeded teams in each division. **1961** *Listener* 21 Sept. 437/1 One more look at the seeded players, a convincing warts-and-all likeness of Wingate, Stilwell an 'unmitigated disaster', and some memorable marginalia to the saga of Slim.

seeder ('siːdə(r)). Also 1 sǽdere, sédere, 4 seder. [OE. *sǽdere*, f. *sǽd* SEED *sb.*: see -ER^{1}.]

†**1.** One who sows seed; a sower. Also *fig. Obs.*

c **950** *Lindisf. Gosp.* Mark iv. 3 Herað heono eode ðe sawende *vel* sedere to sawenne. *c* **1000** ÆLFRIC *Hom.* (Thorpe) II. 88 Sum sædere ferde to sawenne his sæd. **1398** TREVISA *Barth. De P.R.* IX. xviii. (Tollemache MS.), [October] is payntid in þe liknesse of a seder [1495 sower] þat soweþ his corne. *a* **1500** *Sayings of Philosophers* (Tollemache MS.), [Socrates] seide to his dissiples: I am the Seeder [*Caxton* tilman], and the vertues of the soule bene seedis.

2. A mechanical contrivance for sowing seed.

1868 *Rep. Iowa Agric. Soc. 1867* 226 The seeder can be adjusted in five minutes. **1875** KNIGHT *Dict. Mech.*, *Seeder*, ..a seed-sower for gardens. **1883** *Sci. Amer.* 3 Mar. 139/4 Seeder and cultivator. **1899** *Daily News* 13 July 4/6 The modern seeder leaves to the sower no heavier work than the guidance of his team from the waggon seat.

3. *cloud seeder*: one who or that which seeds clouds.

1953 *Jrnl. Amer. Water Works Assoc.* XLV. 1144/1 The skilled commercial cloud seeder is qualified by training and experience to undertake the large-scale operations that make cloud seeding economically worthwhile. **1958** *Ann. Reg. 1957* 485 Experiments with an electrostatic cloud seeder consisting of an aircraft trailing two 300 ft. cables carrying a 50,000 volt charge of electricity. **1975** *Nature* 28 Aug. 690/3 The responsibility..rests as much with the policy makers as it does with the plant breeders, the climatologists and the cloud seeders. **1981** *Economist* 20 June 55/1 Utilities that hire cloud-seeders, hoping to increase water-flow into their reservoirs, may cause the heavens to fall on the tourist industry.

'seed-field. [f. SEED *sb.* Cf. G. *saatfeld*, *samenfeld.*] A place wherein seed is sown. Also *fig.*

1615 W. BEDWELL tr. *Moham. Impost.* II. §70 The wiues of men are as it were the seedfields of the men. **1831** CARLYLE *Sart. Res.* I. ii, For a speculative man, 'whose seedfield', in the sublime words of the Poet, 'is Time', no conquest is important but that of new ideas. **1832** —— *Remin.* (1881) I. 46 Our country was all altered; browsing knowes were become seed-fields. **1865** KINGSLEY *Herew.* ix, A folk, poor and savage;..often without cattle or seed-field.

seedful ('siːdfʊl), *a. rare.* [f. SEED *sb.* + -FUL.] Full of seed, productive. Also *fig.*

1591 SYLVESTER *Du Bartas* I. v. 626 She [Phœnix] sits all gladly-sad expecting Some flame..To burn her sacred bones to seedfull cinders. **1859** CHR. G. ROSSETTI *Poems* (1904) 346/2 Love moves the subtle fountain-rills To fertilize uplifted hills, And seedful valleys fertilize.

'seed-furrow. Also seed-fur.

1. A furrow for the reception of seed.

1523 FITZHERB. *Husb.* §4 And yf he wyll haue his plough to go a narowe forowe, as a sede-forowe shulde be, than he setteth his fote-teame in the nycke nexte to the ploughe-beame. **1764** *Ann. Reg.* 76 A..seed plough..which makes three seed-furrows at once, at any distance from each other. **1844** H. STEPHENS *Book of Farm* II. 503 Land should only receive one furrow, the seed-furrow, for spring-wheat.

2. The process of producing a seed-furrow. Phrases, *to get, give the seed-furrow.*

1610 W. FOLKINGHAM *Art of Survey* I. xi. 43 Their seuerall orders and seasons for fallowing, twifallowing, trifallowing and seed-furre. **1743** R. MAXWELL *Select Trans. Impr. Agric. Scot.* 83 In the Spring give a Steering-fur, as it is called; then the Seed-fur; then sow Barley or Bear with Grass-seeds. **1765** A. DICKSON *Treat. Agric.* (ed. 2) 271 A much less quantity is taken off when land gets the seed-furrow, the chief design of which is to enlarge the pasture. **1805** FORSYTH *Beauties Scot.* II. 217 It is neither practicable nor prudent to give the seed-furrow to much of that land in winter. *a* **1830** *Glouc. Farm Rep.* 7 in *Libr. Usef. Knowl., Husb.* III, If the land requires another ploughing before the seed-furrow.

3. *attrib.*

1764 J. RANDALL in *Gentl. Mag.* XXXIV. 515/1, I find you have done me the honour of taking notice of my Seed-furrow plough.

Hence **'seed-furrow** *v. trans.*, to 'give the seed-furrow' to (land). **'seed-furrowing** *vbl. sb.*

1812 SIR J. SINCLAIR *Syst. Husb. Scot.* I. 217 Another ploughing must be given, previous to the application of manure, after which it ought to be seed furrowed, by the end of August. **1844** H. STEPHENS *Bk. Farm* II. 501 They are always formed on ridges, never on the flat, and only used in seed-furrowing.

seedge, obs. form of SIEGE.

seedily ('siːdɪlɪ), *adv.* [f. SEEDY *a.* + -LY^{2}.] In shabby, impecunious fashion.

1879 F. W. ROBINSON *Coward Consc.* II. vi, One tall man, seedily attired. **1909** MAX BEERBOHM *Yet Again* 22 He was an excellent actor... But, like many others of his kind, [he] drifted seedily away into the provinces.

seediness ('siːdɪnɪs). [f. SEEDY *a.* + -NESS.] The attribute of being seedy.

1. Untidiness, squalid shabbiness.

1837 DICKENS *Pickw.* xliii, A casual visitor might suppose this place to be a Temple dedicated to the Genius of Seediness. **1853** R. S. SURTEES *Sponge's Sp. Tour* xl. 218 The seediness of the blue cloth was relieved by a velvet collar. **1889** TROLLOPE *What I remember* III. xiii. 200 An appearance of seediness in poor fallen Venice is by no means an inexplicable characteristic.

2. Slight indisposition, general want of 'tone' in the physical system.

1874 BLACKIE *Self-Cult.* 74 What is called 'seediness', after a debauch, is a plain proof that nature has been outraged, and will have her penalty. **1894** ASTLEY *50 Years Life* I. 323 Slight fits of seediness from time to time.

3. *nonce-use.* (See quot.)

1893 G. D. LESLIE *Lett. Marco* xii. 71, I take great interest ..in the seediness of my garden; seeds and seed-cases are perhaps the most wonderful of any of the parts of plant life.

seeding ('siːdɪŋ), *vbl. sb.* [f. SEED *v.* + -ING^{1}.]

1. a. The production of seed.

a **1300** *Cursor M.* 386 Alkin things grouand sere þat in þam self þaire seding bere. **1398** TREVISA *Barth. De P.R.* XVII. i. (1495) 591 A tree hath vertue in itself of sedynge: and maye therby brynge forth a nother lyke itself in kynde. **1563** HYLL *Art Garden.* (1593) 161 If that the stems or stalkes after they be well come, be then broken off or cut away, they wil continue the longer greene and without seeding. **1675** EVELYN *Fr. Gard.* 178 Tread down the Stem, till the Cabbage inclines to one side; this will much impede its seeding. **1760** BROWN *Compl. Farmer* II. 69 Before they are near seeding.

†**b.** *concr.*

1650 H. VAUGHAN *Silex Scint., Repentance* 34 The trees, their leafs; the flowres, their seeding;..I summon'd to decide this strife.

2. a. The sowing of seed; the sowing (of land) with seed. Also *fig.*

1542 in J. H. Glover *Kingsthorpiana* (1883) 81 And the rent, sowyng, arying, foldyng, and sedynge of an acre of rey wyll cost the tenant therof fyve shillings and above. **1609** BIBLE (Douay) *Ps.* cxxv. 5 Comm., His seruants shal make their seeding..with teares..and reape a plentiful haruest..in the next life. **1623** W. LAWSON *New Orchard* iv. 8 The labour and seeding of your Corne-fields. *a* **1629** T. ADAMS *Serm. Man's Seed-time* Wks. 648 You see the wickeds Seeding and Haruest... The godly haue also their Seeding and their Haruest. **1647** C. HARVEY *Schola Cordis* Epigr. xxvii, Mine heart's a field; Thy crosse a plow; be pleas'd Dear Spouse, to till it, till the mould be rais'd Fit for the seeding of Thy Word. **1810** JEFFERSON *Writ.* (1853) V. 509, I talk of ploughs and harrows, of seeding and harvesting, with my neighbors. **1842** LANCE *Cottage Farmer* 15 Horses often..execute the drilling, hoeing, seeding, haymaking, &c. in a wasteful and expensive manner, compared to manual labour properly directed. **1875** *Encycl. Brit.* I. 320/1 Openings [in the seed-box] which can be graduated to suit the required rate of seeding. **1892** *Times* (weekly ed.) 2 Feb. 89/3, 800 acres were ready for seeding.

†**b.** *concr.* The seed sown. *Obs. rare.*

1814 MRS. J. WEST *Alicia de Lacy* III. 241 Twice the seasons were against us, and the seeding and the earing might go into the same sack.

c. *transf.* (Cf. SEED *v.* 6 b.)

1926 *Jrnl. Chem. Soc.* II. 2774 Crystallisation could be easily induced by 'seeding'. **1935** J. N. FRIEND *Physical Chem.* II. v. 128 This cannot be done even by careful seeding as the hydrate is too soluble to be reached in this way. **1939** E. LILJENCRANTZ *Cancer Handbk. of Tumor Clinic* xi. 94 Medulloblastoma is distinguished by its tendency toward subarachnoid dissemination or 'seeding' along the entire cerebrospinal axis. **1947** *Sun* (Baltimore) 8 Sept. 3/2 The Miami plane will fly above the storm to photograph the effects of 'seeding' by the weather-science plane. **1958** S. M. BROOKS *Basic Facts Med. Microbiol.* i. 29 Inoculation means the seeding of a culture medium with an organism..using a sterile platinum wire (straight or looped) or a sterile glass pipette. **1966** WRIGHT & SYMMERS *Systemic Path.* II. xxxiv. 1248/1 The ability of a glioma to spread by seeding is of considerable practical importance. **1972** *Materials & Technol.* V. xx. 713 This process may be induced by the introduction of a few crystals of ephedrine oxalate—a process known as 'seeding'. **1977** *Jrnl. R. Soc. Arts* CXXV. 160/1 By far the largest and most sustained effort to modify weather deliberately has involved the artificial seeding of clouds in an attempt to increase the rainfall or suppress damaging hailstorms.

3. The separation of flax-seed from the straw. = RIPPLING *vbl. sb.*[1]

1853 URE *Dict. Arts* I. 789 The time occupied..in the processes, from the seeding of the flax to the commencement of the scutching.

4. A stitch in embroidery (see quot. 1960). Cf. SEED *v.* 9; *seed-stitch* s.v. SEED *sb.* 9.

c **1840** LADY WILTON *Art of Needlework* xx. 317 There is slabbing—veining—and button stitch; seeding—roping—and open stitch. **1960** B. DEAN in G. Lewis *Handbk. Crafts* 24 Stem stitch..and seeding.., which consists of a small back stitch with another worked over it, to form an irregular filling, are also useful.

5. *Sport*, esp. *Lawn Tennis.* The placing of competitors in a list of seeds (SEED *sb.* 3); (also *pl.*) the order or ranking so produced.

1912 A. F. WILDING *On Court & Off* 140 Arranging or 'seeding' is a distinction without any material difference. **1937** P. B. HAWK *Off Racket* i. 13 'Seeding' was believed to be unfair to certain contestants and to make for a less interesting tournament by eliminating..the probability of thrilling matches in the early rounds. **1955** *N.Y. Times* 10 May 33/5 (*heading*) Penn crew tops sprint seedings. **1958** *Oxford Mail* 15 Jan. 8/1 For the first time, seeding is to be introduced into the Amateur Golf Championship being played at St. Andrews in the week beginning June 2. **1978** *Times* 4 July 19/3 Another clay court specialist, Miss Jausovec, upset the seedings by beating Wendy Turnbull.

6. *attrib.* and *Comb.*, as (sense 1) ***seeding-season, -stage***; (sense 2) ***seeding rate***; (sense 5) ***seeding(s)-committee, system***; **seeding felling** (see quot. 1928); **seeding-house**, an apartment in a rettery, in which the flax-seed is separated from the straw; †**seeding-time** = SEED-TIME; also *fig.*; †**seeding-top**, the seed-vessels borne upon a stalk.

1936 *Times* 22 June 7/4 If six of the chosen eight come through the *seeding committee will have guessed well. **1960** *Times* 4 July 15/6 In spite of the skilful pruning of the seedings committee. **1976** *Liverpool Echo* 7 Dec. 17/7 Mrs. Marshall had a tough fight in her semi-final..as the girls battled to give the seeding committee for the finals an idea of current form. **1928** R. S. TROUP *Silvicultural Systems* iv. 32 The *seeding felling, under which the canopy is opened out in order to afford sufficient light to ensure the survival for a short time of seedlings springing from seed shed by the overhead trees. **1968** CHAMPION & SETH *Gen. Silviculture for India* v. 269 The overwood may be removed in only two fellings, first the main seeding felling. **1867** *Ure's Dict. Arts* (ed. 6) II. 328 The *seeding-house requires to be of large size. **1930** L. S. DICKINSON *Lawn* iv. 34 The *seeding rate 3½ pounds per 1,000 square feet of lawn. **1949** G. H. ALGREN *Forage Crops* xxiv. 241 The seeding rates shown for certain crops..are too high. **1876** HARDY *Ethelberta* ii, He was taking them home to his sister Faith, who prized the lingering blossoms of the *seeding season. **1885** *Manch. Exam.* 16 June 5/1 No plants, after entering the *seeding stage..are good for green fodder. **1929** *Times* 24 June 7/1 The '*seeding' system undoubtedly has its merits. **1613** in Picton *L'pool Munic. Rec.* (1883) I. 184 Harvest and *seeding tyme. **1790** GOUV. MORRIS in Sparks *Life & Writ.* (1832) II. 42 We are yet but in the seeding time of national prosperity, and it will be well not to mortgage the crop before it is gathered. **1676** BEAL in *Phil. Trans.* XI. 586 The Lilly of the Valley (which propagates it self by the weight of its *seeding tops, descending into the earth) is much esteem'd on the Elbe.

seeding ('si:dɪŋ), *ppl. a.* [f. SEED *v.* + -ING[2].] That seeds; running to seed.

1868 MORRIS *Earthly Par., K. Acrisius* 211 Though the birds see them, and the seeding grass Harsh and unloving over them may pass, When carelessly through rough and smooth they run. **1892** RIDER HAGGARD *Nada the Lily* v. 34 Their plumes bent in the breeze; like a plain of seeding grass they bent.

seed-lac ('si:dlæk). [f. SEED *sb.* + LAC[1].] See LAC[1] 1. Also *attrib.*

1703 *Art's Improv.* I. 37 And lastly, bestow Eight or Ten Washes of your best Seed-Lack-Varnish. *c* **1790** IMISON *Sch. Art* II. 91 To make Seed-lac Varnish. Take spirits of wine, one quart;..add thereto eight ounces of seed-lac. **1882** *Encycl. Brit.* XIV. 182/1 The resin crushed to small fragments and washed free from colouring matter constitutes 'seed lac'.

seedless ('si:dlɪs), *a.* [f. SEED *sb.* + -LESS.] Devoid of seed or seeds.

1598 SYLVESTER *Du Bartas* II. i. II. 479 In stead of sweet fruits which she selfly yeelds Seed-less, and Art-less, over all thy fields, With thorns and burs shall bristle up her brest. **1870** HOOKER *Stud. Flora* 21 Lower joint slender, seedless. **1871** H. MACMILLAN *True Vine* iv. 167 Seedless oranges and seedless grapes are often met with. **1890** *Pall Mall Gaz.* 29 Sept. 2/1 They might give loans to seedless tenants for seed to anticipate another season of want next year.

Hence '**seedlessness.**

1905 *Westm. Gaz.* 6 Feb. 3/1 The permanency of the seedlessness of the Spencer apple is beyond dispute.

seedlet ('si:dlɪt). [-LET.] A small seed.

1863 JEAN INGELOW *Poems* 50 The goldfinch on a thistle-head Stood scattering seedlets while she fed. **1899** G. ALLEN *Story of Plants* ii. 25 A little grain of pollen produced by the male plant unites with a little ovule or seedlet produced by the female.

seedling ('si:dlɪŋ), *sb.* and *a.* [f. SEED *sb.* + -LING[1].]

A. *sb.*

1. A young plant developed from a seed, esp. one raised from seed as distinct from a slip, cutting, etc.

1660 SHARROCK *Vegetables* 9 Divers..persons affirm, that they have seen the small Plants, or Seedlings at a distance all round the Mother-plant. **1664** EVELYN *Kal. Hort., Nov.* 79 Prepare also Mattresses, Boxes, Cases, Pots, &c. for shelter to your tender Plants and Seedlings newly sown. **1672** GREW *Anat. Plants, Anat. Roots* I. i. (1682) 59 The Roots of most Seedlings grow Downward and Upward, or shoot out in length at both Ends, at the same time. **1723** P. BLAIR *Pharmaco-Bot.* I. 7 The Seedlings (as they are called, viz.) such as have naturally sprung forth from their Seeds, accidentally dispers'd. **1781** COWPER *Yardley Oak* 61 Through all the stages thou hast push'd Of treeship—first a seedling hid in grass; Then twig; then sapling. **1859** DARWIN *Orig. Spec.* i. (1873) 22 This amount of change may have suddenly arisen in a seedling. **1882** VINES tr. *Sachs' Bot.* 508 The terminal bud of the stem of the seedling grows more rapidly..than the lateral shoots which arise subsequently.

fig. **1760** GRAY *Let. to Wharton* 22 June, The prophetic eye of taste..when it plants a seedling, already sits under the shadow of it. **1860** MOTLEY *Netherl.* ii. I. 27 It was thought indispensable to execute as traitors those Roman seedlings—seminary priests and their disciples—who [etc.].

†**2.** The young of an animal hatched from an egg resembling a seed in appearance. *Obs.*

1705 BEVERLEY *Hist. Virginia* IV. xix. (1722) 268 They [*sc.* Ticks] produce a kind of Egg, which lies about a Fort-night before the Seedlings are hatch'd. **1754** BRANDER in *Phil. Trans.* XLVIII. 808 In the spring..a thousand small fish appear in the water to one grown to maturity, or seedlings on the shores of shell-fish, to one at full growth.

3. A small seed. In quots. *fig.*

1809 MALKIN *Gil Blas* x. i. ¶3 Whether any seedlings of ambition were scattered among the fallows of your philosophy. **1876** HARDY *Ethelberta* vi, Not a kiss—not so much as the shadow, hint, or merest seedling of a kiss.

4. *attrib.* and *Comb.*, as ***seedling-bed, -stock***; **seedling blight**, a disease of seedlings, esp. a seedborne, sometimes fatal disease of flax that affects esp. seedlings and is caused by the fungus *Colletotrichum lini*; **seedling leaf** = *seed-leaf*, a cotyledon.

1757 J. HILL *Eden* 167 And let him..take off the Mats..from..his *Seedling Beds. **1763** MILLS *Syst. Pract. Husb.* IV. 179 If they are transplanted directly from the seedling-bed. **1919** PETHYBRIDGE & LAFFERTY in *Jrnl. Dept. Agric. & Technical Instr. Ireland* XX. 327 It is usually not recognised in the brairding crop until the seedlings are one or two inches high... It is during these early stages that the disease causes most damage, and it is for this reason that we have proposed the name '*Seedling-blight' for it, although the trouble is not entirely confined to plants in the seedling stage. **1980** F. HOPE *Recognition & Control of Pests & Dis. Farm Crops* (ed. 2) 159/1 Seedling Blight *Colletotrichum lini* can be a destructive disease of flax seedlings. **1771** G. WHITE *Selborne, Let. to Pennant* 30 Mar., The insect that infests turnips..(destroying often whole fields in their *seedling leaves). **1664** EVELYN *Kal. Hort., Aug.* (1699) 102 Inoculate..at the commencement of this Month, upon *seedling Stocks of four Years growth.

B. *adj.* [From the appositive uses of the sb.]

1. Developed or raised from seed.

1693 EVELYN *De La Quint. Compl. Gard.* Dict., A Seedling Orange-Tree. **1707** MORTIMER *Husb.* (1721) II. 384 Remove Seedling Digitalis, and plant the Slips of Lychnis. **1786** ABERCROMBIE *Gard. Assist.* 215 Seedling biennials and perennials, raised from seed this year. **1808** J. WALKER *Hist. Hebrides & Highl. Scot.* II. 229 The seedling firs are to be had in great quantities in the natural woods in the north. **1825** *Greenhouse Comp.* I. 229 A seedling lemon or orange of a year old being procured as a stock. **1884** BROWNING *Ferishtah* 83 Some five pippins from the seedling tree.

fig. **1810** SCOTT *Lady of L.* II. xx, O that some seedling gem Worthy such noble stem, Honour'd and bless'd in their shadow might grow.

2. Of the nature of a small seed; existing in a rudimentary state. In quots. *fig.*

1886 RUSKIN *Præterita* I. x. 332 He saw that I..had some seedling brains which would come up in time. **1891** LECKY *Poems* 105 Some Scattered seedling thoughts that flew Farther than their authors knew.

3. Of oysters: Hatched from 'seed'.

1862 ANSTED *Channel Isl.* IV. xxii. (ed. 2) 509 *note*, Luxuriant branches, to which the seedling oyster may become attached.

seed-lip ('si:dlɪp). Forms: 1–2 **sǽdléap**, 2 **sed læp**, 3 **sedelip, sedlep**, 4 **sedelep, seed-leep**, 5 **sedlepe, seedlep(e, -leppe, ceed(eleep(e**, 6 **seede-leape**, (7 **seed-lappe, -lop, sydlop**), 7–8 **seed-leap**, (8 *dial.* **sidlup**), 7– **seedlip.** Also SEBLET. [OE. *sǽdléap*; see SEED *sb.* and LEAP *sb.*[2]] A basket in which seed is carried in the process of sowing by hand.

c **1100** *Gerefa* in *Anglia* IX. 264/13 Man sceal habban..windlas, systras, syfa, sædleap, hriddel, hersyfe [etc.]. **1154** *O.E. Chron.* an. 1124, Swa þæt be tweonen Cristes messe & Candel messe man sælde þæt acer sæd hwæte þæt is twegen sed læpas to six scillingas. **1235–52** *Rentalia Glaston.* (Somerset Rec. Soc.) 57 Unum sedelip plenum de frumento. *c* **1340** *Nominale* (Skeat) 861 *Herce et semyloun.* Harewe and sedelep. *c* **1440** *Promp. Parv.* 64/2 Ceed lepe or hopyr, *satorium.* *c* **1565** ABP. PARKER *Ps.* cxxvi. 376 Who goeth from home: all heavily—With his seede-leape: his land to try. **1607** J. CARPENTER *Plaine Mans Plough* 81 God hath..sent forth..his holy Prophets with this soueraigne Seed in the spirituall seed-lappe. **1620** MARKHAM *Farew. Husb.* iv. 36 To euery bushell of that seede you shall adde a bushell of Bay salt and mixe them very well together in your Hopper or Sydlop. **1669** WORLIDGE *Syst. Agric.* xi. §4. 275 A Seed-lop, or Seed-lip, the Hopper, or Vessel wherein they carry their Seed at the time of Sowing. **1766** *Complete Farmer* 5 D 1/1 s.v. *Lucern*, The labourer, if he makes use of a peat-ash spoon and seed-lip, may sprinkle the rows of an acre in four or five hours. **1800** HURDIS *Fav. Village* 163 From the seedlip [he] scatters wide around The fruitful grain. **1884** JEFFERIES *Life of Fields* 150 A seed-lip, which is a vessel like a basket used in sowing corn.

†'**seedly**, *a. Obs. rare*[−1]. [f. SEED *sb.* + -LY[1].] Existing in the state of seed.

1699 *Phil. Trans.* XXI. 271 When a Cod hath shot his Masculine Seed, there doth still remain in his Soft Rows, a great deal of Seeding Matter, where out more Seedly Animals are produced, then were shot out of it the Year before.

†'**seedman.** *Obs.* [f. SEED *sb.* or *v.* + MAN *sb.*[1]]

1. = SEEDSMAN 1.

In 16–17th c. often *fig.* with etym. allusion to SEMINARY. **1583** *Exec. for Treason* (1675) 5 These Seminaries, or Seedmen, and Jesuits,..have..laboured..to perswade the people. *c* **1615** *God & the King* (1663) 6 Wherewith these seed-men of sedition were no way suppressed. **1686** GOAD *Celest. Bodies* II. ii. 161 Just as two Seed-men in a Field, that sow more ground at convenient distance, than if they walked together in the same Furrow.

2. = SEEDSMAN 2.

1652 BLITHE *Eng. Improv. Impr.* xxvi. (1653) 179 Much that is sold in the Seed-mens shops in London. **1670** MEAGER *Eng. Gard.* 191 In the first place you are to endeavour to be furnished with such sorts of Seed as are of best account..either at the hand of Friend, Gardener, or Seed-man. **1719** LONDON & WISE *Compl. Gard.* Pref. 2 At the Seed-Mens Shops.

†'**seedness.** *Obs.* [f. SEED *v.* + -NESS.]

1. The action of sowing, the state of being sown. Also *fig.*

c **1440** *Pallad. on Husb.* I. 256 Trymenstre sednes [*v.r.* seedis; orig. *satio*] eke is to respite To placis colde, of wyntir snowis white. **1549** COVERDALE, etc. *Erasm. Par. Phil.* i. 3–11 So perseuer styll vnto the daye of Christes commynge, that you maye than appeare..aboundauntlye ful of good workes, wherof in this world you make as it wer a seedenesse, and shal reape yᵉ frute therof at yᵉ day. **1601** HOLLAND *Pliny* XIX. v. II. 18 The manner is to plant them..at both times of Seednes, to wit, the Spring and the Fall. **1603** SHAKS. *Meas. for M.* I. iv. 42 As blossoming Time That from the seednes, the bare fallow brings To teeming foyson. **1609** HOLLAND *Amm. Marcell.* XXII. viii. 200 The vast wildernesse (which never felt the plough, nor know [*sic*] what seednesse [orig. *sementem*] is, but lye desert, and subject to many frosts). **1661** P. HENRY *Diaries & Lett.* (1882) 85 Barley much abused in Drunknes, and now Barley seedness hindred, God is Righteous. **1710** M. HENRY *Comm. Isa.* xvii. (1848) II. 531 Look upon it at the time of seedness and it shall be like a garden.

b. *concr.* The thing sown, seed. In quot. *fig.*

1597 J. PAYNE *Royal Exch.* 19 As the corne must fyrst be sowen and dye in the yerthe before yt receyve a new bodye, ..so must we be the lords sedenes before the happie harvest.

2. Seed-time.

1668 R. STEELE *Husbandm. Calling* iii. (1672) 26 From seedness to harvest, he is bound to a constant dependance on God, and from harvest to seedness again. **1793** *Trans. Soc.*

Arts (ed. 2) V. 83 At Wheat seedness in 1785, having purchased a Machine, I drilled eighty acres with Wheat.

† **seedow**, var. SIDDOW *a.*, tender, mellow.

Holland seems to have supposed the word to mean 'fit to serve as seed'.

1601 HOLLAND *Pliny* XIX. vii. II. 23 But they [the seeds] must be all throughly dried before they be seedow and fruitfull. [Fr. *pour rendre les graines bonnes à semer, il les fault toutes secher.*]

seed-pearl ('siːdpɜːl). [f. SEED *sb.*] A minute pearl having the appearance of a seed, usually drilled and fastened to some material to be worn as an ornament. **a.** *collect. sing.*

1553 *Inv. Ch. Goods York*, etc. (Surtees) 168 Garnished with..an edge of smale seede pearle sett round abowte the same. **1573–4** *New Yrs. Gifts* in Nichols *Progr. Eliz.* (1823) I. 380 Item, a fayre gyrdle of pomaunder and seede perle garnets and pomaunders. **1624** CAPT. SMITH *Virginia* v. 198 Some seed Pearle they got. **1710** STEELE *Tatler* No. 245 ¶2 Bracelets of braided Hair, Pomander, and Seed-Pearl. **1879** E. ARNOLD *Lt. Asia* IV. (1881) 105 A golden net, With tassels of seed-pearl and silken strings.

b. *pl.*

1598 FLORIO, *Perlette*, little, small, seede pearles. **1619** tr. *Mexia's Treas. Anc. & Mod. Times* II. 976/2 Some [pearls] are found to be so little, that they can not bee drilled by any meanes; and therefore they call them Seede-pearles. **1799** G. SMITH *Laboratory* I. 132 Take oriental seed-pearls; reduce them into a fine powder. **1877** STREETER *Prec. Stones* 235 According to their size they [Pearls] receive certain names;..small, Piece Pearls; smaller, Seed Pearls; smallest, Dust Pearls.

seed-plot ('siːdplɒt). [f. SEED *sb.* + PLOT *sb.*] A piece of ground in which seed is or may be sown, a seed-bed. Now only *transf.* and *fig.*

1561 T. NORTON *Calvin's Inst.* Pref., Should they not.. rather alltogether haue geuen ouer and forsaken the Gospell which they sawe to be the sedeplott [orig. Fr. *semence*] of so many contentions. **1587** FLEMING *Contn. Holinshed* III. 1311/2 This gentleman had..a regard for the seed-plots of learning, to haue them watered with the springs of his bountie. **1604** R. C. *Table Alph.*, *Seminarie*, a seede plot for young trees or grafts, a nurserie. **1641** MILTON *Animadv.* xiii. 52 The honest Gardener that..had wrought painfully about his bankes and seed-plots. **1702** *Pres. St. Jacobitism* 13 The contrary Practise..was nothing else but a Seed-plot of Destruction. **1731** MILLER *Gard. Dict.*, A *Seminary* is a Seed-Plot, which is adapted or set apart for the sowing of Seeds. **1759** BP. HURD *Moral Dialogues* iii. 114 A nursery of brave men, a very seed-plot of warriors and heroes. **1865** LECKY *Ration.* (1878) II. 279 It has been the seed-plot of poetry and romance. **1901** *Edin. Rev.* July 77 The dim nebulous seed-plots of worlds that strew the sidereal heavens.

seedsman ('siːdsmən). [f. genitive of SEED *sb.* + MAN *sb.*[1] Cf. SEEDMAN.]

1. A sower of seed.

1601 HOLLAND *Pliny* XVIII. xiii. I. 571 Moreover, they would haue the seeds-man to be naked when he soweth them. **1606** SHAKS. *Ant. & Cl.* II. vii. 24. **1657** J. WATTS *Scribe, Pharisee*, etc. I. 115 A plain and ordinary man, a Plough-man and Seedsman. **1764** J. RANDALL in *Gentl. Mag.* XXXIV. 515/1 The seedsman can easily lift it [*sc.* the seed plough] up by the handles, even when the hopper is quite full. **1787** BURNS *Song, 'Again rejoicing Nature sees'* iii, The merry Plough-boy cheers his team, Wi' joy the tentie Seedsman stalks. **1854** MARY HOWITT *Pict. Calendar* 107 A ..train of ploughmen and seedsmen preparing the ground for fresh harvests. **1882** J. WALKER *Jaunt to Auld Reekie*, etc. 24 The seedsman had scattered the handfu's abroad.

fig. **1592** NASHE *P. Penilesse* K 2, The second kind of Diuels..called..the authors of massacres, & seedsmen of mischiefe. **1726** PENN *Tracts* Wks. I. 537 It is granted by all that I know of, that the Seeds-Man is Christ. **1833** TENNYSON *Poems* 123 The seedsman, memory, Sowed my deepfurrowed thought with many a name [etc.].

2. A dealer in seed.

1691 WOOD *Ath. Oxon.* II. 33 *note*, The Wife of..Bury, a Seeds-man, living at the Frying-pan in Newgate Market. **1742** *De Foe's Tour Gt. Brit.* (ed. 3) I. 162 From this Place also the Seedsmen in London are furnished with the greatest Quantity of their Seeds. **1801** *Farmer's Mag.* Nov. 443 The ground would be sufficiently filled with roots, not to be purchased in the seedsman's shop. **1891** S. C. SCRIVENER *Our Fields & Cities* 148 Eliminate the stimulus given by manufacturers of implements, of artificial manures, and by the numerous competing seedsmen, and our agricultural shows would simply be a series of cattle fairs.

† **'seedster.** *Obs. rare.* [f. SEED *v.* + -STER.] A sower; *fig.* a disseminator, an originator.

1598 SYLVESTER *Du Bartas* II. ii. IV. *Columnes* 606 Mars (the Seedster of debate). **1606** WARNER *Alb. Eng.* XV. xciii. 375 Yet, though against the Welsh-kings will, our royall Surname now..It Seedster from that kingly Streene deriues.

seed-time ('siːdtaɪm). Also 7 **seeds-time.** [f. SEED *sb.* + TIME *sb.*] The season of sowing seed.

1400 *Langland's P. Pl.* A. Prol. 21 (Univ. Coll. MS.) In seed tyme and in Sowynge. *c* **1450** *Mirk's Festial* 253/20 Bytwyx heruest and syde-tyme. **1570** *Satir. Poems Reform.* xii. 59 In beir seid tyme ȝour burrow rudis ly Cause of this murther laitly maid amang ȝow. **1611** BIBLE *Gen.* viii. 22 While the earth remaineth, seed-time and haruest..shall not cease. **1647** FULLER *Good Th. in Worse T.* 17, I saw in seed-time an Husbandman at Plow. **1767** A. FERGUSON *Ess. Hist. Civ. Soc.* II. ii. (1793) 137 After they have shared the toils of the seed-time, they enjoy the fruits of the harvest in common. **1844** H. STEPHENS *Bk. Farm* II. 484 Harrowing, an operation which is executed by an implement that will be particularly described when it comes to be spoken of in seed-time.

fig. **1614** R. HARRIS *Samuel's Funerall* (1618) 8 Now is the seeds-time, sowe apace, as yet you haue all aduantages from grace and nature. **1776** PAINE *Com. Sense* 60 Youth is the seed time of good habits. **1860** GUTHRIE (*title*) Seed-Time and Harvest of Ragged Schools.

seedy ('siːdɪ), *a.* [f. SEED *sb.* + -Y[1].]

1. a. Abounding in seed, full of seed.

1574 J. JONES *Nat. Beginning* 25 The second alteration is partly good, partly euell.., good because it endeth in a seedy qualitie, euel because it is made of some parte corrupted. *c* **1586** C'TESS PEMBROKE *Ps.* LXXVIII. xx, That rich land, where over Nilus trailes Of his wett robe the slymy seedy train. *c* **1611** CHAPMAN *Iliad* XXIV. 402 Forthwith they reacht the Tent..A shaggie roofe of seedy reeds, mowne from the meades. **1733** W. ELLIS *Chiltern & Vale Farm.* 298 They.. run up with a great Stalk, and large, high, seedy, white, yellow Head. **1821** CLARE *Vill. Minstr.* II. 97 Thistles shake their seedy heads.

b. Used to designate the male hop-plant.

1848 *Jrnl. R. Agric. Soc.* IX. II. 546 Difference of opinion exists among experienced planters as to the utility of the seedy or male plant.

2. a. Shabby, ill-looking.

App. in allusion to the appearance of a flowering plant that has run to seed.

1739 *Joe Miller's Jests* No. 158 A seedy (poor) half-pay Captain. **1768** GOLDSM. *Good-n. Man* 111, He is a little seedy, as we say among us that practise the law. Not well in clothes. **1831** SCOTT *Ct. Robt.* Introd. Addr. ¶8 The outward man of the stranger was, in a most remarkable degree, what mine host of the Sir William Wallace, in his phraseology, calls seedy. **1837** DICKENS *Pickw.* xxx, 'Devilish cold', he added pettishly, 'standing at the door, wasting one's time with such seedy vagabonds.' **1845** *Punch* VIII. 78 A very seedy coat will ruin the effect of a new hat. **1861** HUGHES *Tom Brown at Oxf.* xii, It's a bore to have been caught in so seedy an affair. **1868** *Less. Midd. Age* 123 A very seedy little railway station, on the outskirts of a large and horribly ugly town. **1892** 'F. ANSTEY' *Voces Pop.* Ser. II. 30 Seated on a Bench beside a Seedy Stranger.

b. Unwell, poorly, 'not up to the mark', *spec.* as a result of excessive eating or drinking; = CROP-SICK *a.*

1729 R. SAVAGE *Author to be Lett* 7 After an Evening's hard boozing, my brother Bards..have been what we call Seedy or Crop-sick. **1845** *Punch* IX. 40/2 Young Oxford eats a wondrous meal, And drinks a lot of beer, And in the morning oftentimes, Full seedy does appear. **1858** DICKENS *Lett.* (1880) II. 55 This morning I was very dull and seedy. **1866** *Mysteries of Isis* 35, I shall go to bed, for I feel very seedy after this knocking about. **1889** JEROME *Three Men in Boat* 1 We were all feeling seedy, and we were getting nervous about it. **1902** BUCHAN *Watcher by Threshold* 169 A man who is a bit seedy.

† **3.** (See quot.) *Obs.*

1753 *Chambers' Cycl.* Suppl. s.v. *Seedy*, The French suppose that these brandies obtain the flavour which they express by this name from the weeds which grew among the vines, from whence the wine, of which this brandy was made, was pressed.

4. *Glass-making.* Containing 'seed' or minute bubbles (see SEED *sb.* 7).

1856 H. CHANCE in *Jrnl. Soc. Arts* IV. 225/1 Perhaps the glass has been badly melted, and is seedy, full (that is) of little vesicles, to which the rotary motion has given a circular shape. **1883** —— in H. J. Powell, etc. *Glass-making* 121 The glass is..seedy, for the seed has not the power to collect itself into bubbles and reach the surface of the pot.

5. Of wool: Not cleared from adhering seeds.

1895 *Daily News* 13 Nov. 9/4 Since the opening of the sales, seedy, and burry, and crossbred wools have declined ⅛d. per lb.

6. *Comb.*, as ***seedy-looking*** adj.; **seedy-toe**, a diseased condition of a horse's foot (see quot. 1849).

1837 DICKENS *Pickw.* xx, A precious seedy-looking customer. **1849** PERCIVALL *Hippopathol.* IV. 492 Seedy Toe ..is a disease of foot consisting in a mouldering away, as though through decay, of the toe of the hoof. **1898** *Encycl. Sport* II. 519/1 'Seedy-toe', another disease of the [horse's] foot, is sometimes accompanied by lameness.

see-er, seeër ('siːə(r)). *rare.* [f. SEE *v.* + -ER[1].] One who sees or beholds. (Used to avoid the customary suggestions of SEER.)

1882 R. L. STEVENSON in *Longman's Mag.* I. 79 He was a great daydreamer, a seeër of fit and beautiful and humorous visions. **1904** FINDLAY in *Expositor* Oct. 314 That implies.. a likeness of character, a moral congruity and conformity between the see-er and the Seen.

seegar. Representing a U.S. colloq. or dial. pronunciation of CIGAR, with stress on the first syllable.

1935 Z. N. HURSTON *Mules & Men* (1970) I. v. 119 Settin' by de fire smokin' uh seegar. **1976** W. GOLDMAN *Magic* III. viii. 171 'Got any of them jazzy see-gars?' Fats wondered. **1976** *Time* 27 Sept. 46/1 Carter does not fit many Southern stereotypes. He is not a hard drinker, poker player, or profane and garrulous see-gar-chomping raconteur.

seege. *Obs.* exc. *dial.* Also 7 **sedge, sege, seydge,** 9 *dial.* **seech, sych.** [Of obscure origin: perh. identical with the OE. *sęcg* sea (only in the early glossaries, rendering *salum* and *mare*, and as the second element in *gársęcg* ocean).] The rush of the waves upon the shore; surf.

a **1609** SIR F. VERE *Comm.* (1657) 120 The seege of the sea [was] such, that no shipping could lie there unbroken. **1622** R. HAWKINS *Voy. S. Sea* xii. 26 All these Ilands are perilous to land in, for the seege caused by the Ocean sea. *Ibid.* xiv. 33 My Boates could not discover any landing place,..for that the sedge was exceedingly great and dangerous. *Ibid.* xli. 97 Certaine of my people standing to defend the Boates with their Oares, for that there went a bad sege, were forced to lay downe their Musketts. **1625** MARKHAM *Farew. Husb.* (ed. 2) 71 Your Hemp-weede, or any other weede which groweth neere the seydge of the Sea. **1823** BOND *E. & W. Looe* 148 The waves, as they come into the river, occasion the water to rush up the street with great violence... This run of the water is locally called The Seech—they say, the Seech is coming, or the Seech is going back. **1880** COUCH *E. Cornw. Gloss.*, *Sych*, the edge or foaming border of a wave as it runs up a harbour or on the land.

seege, obs. f. SIEGE; var. SEGGE, man.

seegh, seeh, obs. pa. t. sing. of SEE.

see-ho. Also 6 **se-howe,** 7 **seehoo.** [? f. SEE *v.* + HO *int.*; but cf. SA-HA, SOHO.] A cry used in coursing, on first view of the hare.

a **1500** *Mourn. Hare* 20 in Hartshorne *Anc. Metr. Tales* (1829) 166 The furste man that me may see Anon he cryes, 'se howe, se howe'. *a* **1700** B. E. *Dict. Cant. Crew*, *Sohoe*, *Seehoo*, said aloud at the starting a hare. **1841** HEWLETT *Par. Clerk* I. 128 'Seeho!' called out the squire, as if he'd found a hare sitting. **1862** H. KINGSLEY *Ravenshoe* xiii, At this moment there came a 'See Ho!' from Charles; in the next a noble hare had burst from a tangled mass of brambles at his feet.

seeine, variant of SENE, synod.

seeing ('siːɪŋ), *vbl. sb.* Forms: see the vb. [f. SEE *v.* + -ING[1].]

1. a. The action (*rarely* an act) of the vb. SEE. *Proverb*: *seeing is believing*.

Often in phrase ***worth seeing*** (formerly † ***worth the seeing, worthy seeing***).

1375 BARBOUR *Bruce* XVII. 88 Swa thai vroucht than That, but seying of ony man, Outane Sym of Spaldyne allane. *c* **1450** *Mirk's Festial* 171 The secund cause þat þe sacrament is vset in þe auter is, forto make man by ofte seynge to haue þe sadur mynde of Cristis passion in his hert. **1538–9** in *Lit. Rem. Edw. VI* (Roxb.) p. cclxiv, A cuppe gevon by my Lorde of Wynchester at his first seeyng of the Prince grace. *a* **1586** SIDNEY *Ps.* XLII. i, Ah, when comes my blessed being, Of thy face to have a seeing. **1629** CARLIELL *Deserv. Favourite* 534 Madame, will it please you walke into the gallery, There are some pictures will be worth your seeing. **1670** RAY *Prov.* 140 Seeing is believing. *a* **1700** EVELYN *Diary* 17 Aug. 1654, But most remarkable and worthy seeing is St. Peter's Cathedrall. **1712** J. ARBUTHNOT *Lewis Baboon* iv. 21 There's nothing like Matter of Fact; Seeing is Believing. **1756–7** *Keysler's Trav.* (1760) I. 468 There is another church of the same name..which is also very well worth seeing. **1807** WORDSW. *Ode Intimat. Immortality* 156 Those shadowy recollections, Which, be they what they may,..Are yet a master-light of all our seeing. **1848** J. C. & A. W. HARE *Guesses at Truth* 2nd Ser. 497 *Seeing is believing*, says the proverb... Though, of all our senses, the eyes are the most easily deceived, we believe them in preference to any other evidence. **1859** RUSKIN *Two Paths* iv. §108 But your architectural designing leads you into no pleasant journeys,—into no seeing of lovely things. **1909** *Times Lit. Suppl.* 28 May 198/2 Seeing is believing;..only art can make history really credible, or a great name more than a label to an abstraction. **1975** A. PRICE *Our Man in Camelot* v. 84 'Show him the stuff.'..'Okay. Maybe you're right... Seeing is believing, I guess.'

b. *pl.*

1832 J. P. KENNEDY *Swallow B.* Introd. Ep. (1860) 13 A particular account of all my doings, or rather my seeings and thinkings. **1870** *Athenæum* 2 July 8 Enough would have remained, despite many errors, many seeings of things which cannot be seen, to leave the book..interesting.

2. The faculty of seeing, sight, vision.

c **1375** *Sc. Leg. Saints* x. (*Mathou*) 82 As to defe men þe herynge, & to blynd men þe seynge. **1426** AUDELAY *Poems* 7 Thi v. wyttis thou most know,..Thi heryng, thi seyng, as I the schewe [etc.]. **1426** LYDG. *De Guil. Pilgr.* 8235 My helm hath rafft me my syyng And take a-way ek myn heryng. *a* **1704** LOCKE *Elem. Nat. Phil.* xi. (1754) 41 The organ of seeing is the eye. **1785** REID *Intell. Powers* 520 Seeing and hearing by philosophers are called senses. **1820** KEATS *Isabella* ii, He might not in house, field, or garden stir, But her full shape would all his seeing fill. **1860** TYNDALL *Glac.* II. i. 229 The range of seeing is different in different persons. **1897** WATTS-DUNTON *Aylwin* IV. iv, Hunger gives a new seeing to the eyes.

3. *Astr.* The quality of telescopic observation; the extent to which a stellar image remains steady and free from twinkling, or a planetary image sharp.

In modern usage seeing is quantified as the apparent angular diameter of a point source as seen in a powerful telescope.

1903 *Phil. Mag.* V. 674 Observatories are put even on high mountains to get rid of the disturbances in this atmosphere, which tend to make the image of every object tremulous.., and to prevent what the astronomer terms 'good seeing'. **1969** N. CALDER *Violent Universe* 21 The best 'seeing' at any working observatory is said to be that at Cerro Tololo, in Chile. **1977** *Nature* 21 Apr. 693/2 The seeing during the observations was generally between 1″ and 2″.

4. *attrib.* and *Comb.*, as † ***seeing power***; **seeing-glass** (now *dial.*), a mirror; † **seeing-shop** *nonce-wd.*, one's faculty of sight; † **seeing-stone**, a crystal used for scrying; also *fig.*

1565 JEWEL *Repl. Harding* xii. (1611) 336 Now we see as thorow a *seeing glasse in a riddle: but then we shall see face to face. **1662** HIBBERT *Body of Div.* I. 184 Men of repute are as seeing-glasses by which most men dresse them-selves. **1731** *Inventory of G. Bamforth, Sheffield*, A stand, a large seeing glass. **1855** ROBINSON *Whitby Gloss.*, *Seeing-glass*, the old-fashioned term for a mirror, formerly a surface of polished metal. *c* **1449** PECOCK *Repr.* I. xiv. 74 And ȝit what othere iȝen or *seing power hath God ȝouen to man-kinde forto therwith se, than which at sumtyme wolen faile and erre? **1577–82** BRETON *Flourish Fancy*, etc. (Grosart) 25/2 With that I winckte for feare, And shut the windowes of my *seeing shoppe. **1849** ROCK *Ch. of Fathers* I. 295 A globe of crystal was employed by the Druids in their divinations as a *seeing-stone. *Ibid.*, They must look into that true seeing-stone, the teaching of Christ's Church.

seeing ('siːɪŋ), *ppl. a.* Forms: see the vb. [f. SEE *v.* + -ING[2].] **1.** That sees, in various senses of the vb.; having the faculty of sight; †discerning, possessing insight (*obs.*); †gifted as a seer.

a **1300** *Cursor M.* 14804 Quen seand men him herd and sagh, Of him þam stod selcut gret agh. **1382** WYCLIF *Isa.* xxx. 10 That seyn to men seende [1388 profetis], Wileth not see. **1440** CAPGRAVE *Life St. Kath.* IV. 1386 'Thei that see', he seyth, 'shul be ful blynde',.. The seeynge men be-tokene ȝow, I-wis. **1592** TIMME *Ten Eng. Lepers* B 1 b, So David had his seeing Gad to be his watchman. **1655** FULLER *Ch. Hist.* v. iii. §10 (191) Strange that a Foraigner should be more seeing herein, then any of our Native Authors and Records that I ever could behold. **1825** COLERIDGE *Aids Refl.* (1848) I. 5 This seeing light, this enlightening eye, is reflection. **1887** *Athenæum* 17 Dec. 818/3 The tendency is.. for more and more seeing people to be imported into institutions, until at last they receive more wages than the blind people.

2. ***seeing eye***: in various senses of the vb. SEE, the faculty of seeing; ***seeing-eye dog*** (U.S.): a guide-dog trained to lead the blind.

Seeing eye is registered in the U.S. as a proprietary name for guide-dogs trained to lead the blind.

1921 P. LUBBOCK *Craft of Fiction* x. 146 The 'seeing eye' to which it is presented is not his, but the reader's own. **1930** *Official Gaz.* (U.S. Patent Off.) 26 Aug. 553/2 The Seeing Eye, Nashville, Tenn... *The Seeing Eye* for trained dogs. Claims use since Mar. 30, 1929. **1938** *Sun* (Baltimore) 18 May 8/7 Many people.. will be much moved by the story of how the first of the now famous 'seeing-eye' dogs has been carried by plane back to the Seeing Eye School at Morristown, N.J., there to spend its last days quietly. **1948** J. CANNAN *Little I Understood* viii. 101, I don't pretend to be able to draw. I've just got the seeing eye. **1950** P. BOTTOME *Under Skin* xvi. 137 He had bought her [*sc.* a blind woman] a 'Seeing Eye' dog, who took her wherever she wished. **1969** K. M. WELLS *Owl Pen Reader* II. 210 You see, Grandpa had the seeing eye and grandma hadn't. **1979** 'A. HAILEY' *Overload* III. xiii. 267 The interior [of the bar] was dark and smelled of mildew. 'Christ!' Nancy said. 'We need a seeing-eye dog.'

seeing ('siːɪŋ), quasi-*conj.* [orig. the pres. pple. of SEE *v.*; the use in concord with the subject was developed into the conjunctional use as in *considering*, *excepting*, *providing*, *supposing*, etc. Cf. SEEN *prep.* and *conj.*

The first quot. is a doubtful or transitional example, as the pple. admits of being construed as in concord with the subject, in the sense 'recognizing, perceiving'. The development of the conjunctional use may have been aided by the similarity of sound with SEN, SIN *conj.*]

seeing that, hence ellipt. ***seeing***: considering the fact that; inasmuch as; since, because. Also (*colloq.*) with *as* (*how*).

1503 *Paston Lett.* III. 401, I wol.. exhorte you to take it as .. paciently as ye can, seeyng that we al be mortal and borne to dey. **1526** TINDALE *John* ii. 18 What token shewest thou vnto vs, seynge that thou dost these thinges? [So most later versions.] **1537** CRANMER in Ellis *Orig. Lett.* Ser. I. II. 77 As towching the house of the Charterhouse I pray.. that it may be turned into a better use (seing it is in the face of the world). **1601** SHAKS. *Jul. C.* II. ii. 36 Of all the Wonders that I yet haue heard, It seemes to me most strange that men should feare, Seeing that death.. Will come, when it will come. **1669** STURMY *Mariner's Mag.* I. ii. 17 The Top-mast being aloft the Ship.. maketh better way.., seeing we have Sea-Room. **1711** PUCKLE *Club* (1817) 35 Seeing Great Britain affords so many lawyers,.. he is doubly a fool that.. applies himself to a scab. **1796** H. HUNTER tr. *St.-Pierre's Stud. Nat.* (1799) III. 578 It must be of importance to accustom young people to it [*sc.* vegetable diet], seeing it's influence is.. so happy on beauty of person and tranquillity of soul. **1833** DICKENS *Let.* 18 Mar. (1965) I. 17 Seeing as I cannot fail to do that I have engaged in a pursuit. **1842** TENNYSON *Morte d'Arthur* 94 Deep harm to disobey, Seeing obedience is the bond of rule. **1857** HUGHES *Tom Brown* II. viii, Which isn't to be wondered at, seeing that he has just finished six weeks of examination work. **1895** *Dialect Notes* I. 399 Seein' as how it's you, I'll do so-and-so. **1952** M. LASKI *Village* vii. 121, I suppose—seeing as how we've both been let down—you wouldn't care to come in with me? **1974** S. GULLIVER *Vulcan Bulletins* 29 Seeing as how you're always short of £sd, I thought you could maybe earn a bit.

seek, *sb.* [f. SEEK *v.*] † **1.** A series of notes upon a horn calling out hounds to begin a chase. Usually ***to blow a seek*** (BLOW *v.*[1] 14 c). Also *fig. Obs.*

c **1500** *Coucher-bk. Tutburye* in Blount *Anc. Tenures* (1679) 170 At the said Crosse in the Towne the formast keper shall blow a Seeke. **1576** TURBERV. *Venerie* 139 Lo now he blowes his horne, euen at the kennell dore, Alas, alas, he blowes a seeke, alas yet blowes he more. *Ibid.* ad fin., The measures of blowing set downe in the notes... The Seeke, with twoo windes. **1624** BP. MOUNTAGU *Immed. Addr.* 35 There are.. that loose themselues often, and their Desires in their Deuotions: and may very well goe blow the seeke for them. **1826** HOR. SMITH *Tor Hill* (1838) I. 292 The foremost keeper blew a seek, to which all the others replied.

2. *Computers.* The movement of a read/write head to a new position on a storage device; **seek-time**, the time taken by this, as part of the total access time.

1965 *IEEE Trans. Computers* XIV. 580/2 No more than three concurrent seek operations per data channel are justified for System I. **1967** *AFIPS Conf. Proc.* XXX. 11/1 Suppose that secondary memory is a disk... The operation of moving the arm is known as a seek; but the policy shortest seek time first.. is unsatisfactory. **1974** *Communications Assoc. Computing Machinery* XVII. 139/2 The objective of optimally scheduling a sequence of requests on the DASD to minimize seektime or rotational delays. **1980** *Sci. Amer.* Aug. 118/3 First the head must be positioned over the proper track. This requires a 'seek time'.

seek (siːk), *v.* Pa. t. and pa. pple. sought (sɔːt). Forms: **a.** *Inf.* α. 1 **sœ́can, sécan, sécean, séocan, 2–5 sieche, 2–6 seche,** 4 *Kent.* **zeche,** 3 **sæche, 3–5 siche, sheche, suche, 5 sech, seeche,** 6 (9 *dial.*) **seech.** β. 2–7 **seke,** (2–3 *imper.* **siec**), 3–5 *north.* **sek,** 4–6 **sieke, sike, syke,** (chiefly *Sc.*) **seyk,** 4–7 **seeke,** 4–8 *Sc.* **seik,** 5 **ceke,** *Sc.* **seike,** 6 **seyke, seick, seake,** 5– **seek.** **b.** *3rd sing. Pres. Indic.* α. 1 **sœ́ceð, -as,** 1–2 **séceð,** 2 **sechð,** 3 **schecheð,** 2–5 **secheth,** 4–5 **-ith, -yth, -es.** β. 1–2 **sécð,** 2–3 **secþ, sekþ,** 4 *Kent.* **zekþ,** 3–6 **seketh, -es, -is,** 4–5 **-ith, -ez,** 6 *Sc.* **seik(k)is,** 6–7 **seekes,** 6– **seeketh, seeks.** **c.** *Pa. t.* 1 **sohte,** *pl.* **sohtun, -on, -an,** 2–4 **sohte,** (3 **soðte, soþte, soch,** *Orm.* **sohhte**), 3–4 **sohut(e, soghut, soht,** *north.* **sochte,** (**sogtht**), 3–5 **souhte, souȝte, soȝte, soght(e,** 3–6 **sowte,** 4 **saȝte,** (**southe, southte, souch**), *Kent.* **zoȝte,** 4–5 **soughte, sowhte, souȝt, soȝt, sowght, sout(e, sowt, saght,** *pl.* **souȝtten,** *Sc.* **sowcht, schocht,** 4–6 *Sc.* **socht, soucht,** 5 **sowȝte, souȝhte,** 6 *Sc.* **souchte,** 6–7 *Sc.* **soght,** 7 **saught,** 4– **sought.** Also 5 **sekyd,** 7 **seekt.** **d.** *Pa. pple.* 1 **ᵹesoht,** 3 **i-soht, i-soȝt, i-souht,** (**y-soþt**), *Orm.* **sohht,** 3–4 **soht,** 3–5 **soȝt, souȝt,** 3–6 **soght,** 4 **sohut, sowght,** 4–5 **souht, sout, sowt, soȝte, souȝte,** (5 **south, sowth, soyght**), 4–6 **sowȝt(e,** *Sc.* **socht, soucht,** (4 **sochte,** 5 **soacht**), 6 **sowghte,** 6–7 **saught,** 5– **sought.** Also 8 **seeked.** [A Com. Teut. weak verb: OE. *sécan*, pa. t. *sǒhte*, corresp. to OFris. *sêka*, *sêza*, pa. t. *sôchta*, OS. *sôkian*, pa. t. *sôhta* (MLG. *sôken*), MDu., mod.Du. *zoeken*, OHG. *suohhan*, *suohhen*, pa. t. *suohta* (MHG. *sûchen*, mod.G. *suchen*), ON. *søkja*, pa. t. *sótte* (Sw. *söka*, Da. *søge*), Goth. *sôkjan*, pa. t. *sôkida*, f. OTeut. **sōk*-:—pre-Teut. **sāg*-: cf. L. *sāgīre* to perceive by scent, Gr. ἡγεῖσθαι to lead.

The normal modern form of OE. *sécan* would be *seech*, which survives *dial.* in Lancashire, Cheshire, and Derbyshire (cf. *beseech*); the form with *k* is prob. due to the ME. *sēcþ*, 3 pers. sing. pres. ind., which shows the regular phonetic development of OE. palatal *c* before a spirant; but it is not clear why the *k* form should have been generalized in *seek* and not in *teach*, unless indeed the tendency was supported in the former instance by the influence of the ON. form.]

I. Transitive uses.

1. a. To go in search or quest of; to try to find, look for (either a particular object—person, thing, or place—whose whereabouts are unknown, or an indefinite object suitable for a particular purpose).

In most parts of England the vb. in this sense is no longer colloquially current, being superseded by *look for*.

c **888** K. ÆLFRED *Boeth.* xxxii. §3 Hwæðer ᵹe nu secan gold on treowum? *c* **1000** *Ags. Gosp.* Luke ii. 48 þin fæder & ic sariᵹende þe sohton. *c* **1175** *Lamb. Hom.* 27 þe unclene gast ..secheð reste hwer he mei wunian. *c* **1200** ORMIN 7308 Herode king let sekenn Crist. *a* **1225** *Ancr. R.* 324 A wummon þet haueð forloren hire nelde, oðer a sutare his el, he secheð hine anonriht. *a* **1250** *Owl & N.* 380 [The hare] secheþ paþes to þe groue. *a* **1300** *Cursor M.* 22901 An hungre leon mete he son, Vp and dun his prai sekand. *c* **1374** CHAUCER *Former Age* 30 Corsed was the tyme.. þat men.. in þe Ryuerys fyrst gemmys sowhte. *c* **1440** *Gesta Rom.* 118 He yede abowte in the gardin, and soute the clewe, & fonde it. *a* **1450** *Knt. de la Tour* 48 He dede seche her a man of holy lyff. *c* **1450** *Merlin* 41 And ther was Merlyn longe tyme, till that the sones of Constance lete seche hym in many contrees. **1471** CAXTON *Recuyell* (Sommer) 110 He.. so wente and cam sechyng the tour of darayn, whiche he fonde in an euenyng. **1549** *Compl. Scot.* To Rdr. 12 Ane hen that seikis hyr meyt in the mydding. **1600** *Weakest goeth to Wall* G 2, Sexton, I haue sought thee in euery seate in the Church. **1606** SHAKS. *Ant. & Cl.* IV. vi. 37, I will go seeke Some Ditch, wherein to dye. **1618** BOLTON *Florus* III. iii. (1636) 167 The Cimbrians, Theutons, and Tigurins,.. sought new habitations. *c* **1730** RAMSAY *Vision* xx, Nor scour about to seik a wench. **1768** STERNE *Sent. Journ.* (1778) I. 155 (*Paris*), I called La Fleur to go seek me a barber directly. **1780** BURKE *Corr.* (1844) II. 366 Other persons should be sought who can do the necessary business with more skill. **1816** SCOTT *Old Mort.* xxxvii, I am seeking a place called Fairyknowe. **1818** —— *Hrt. Midl.* xxvi, Ye may be seeking a father to another wean for onything I ken. **1818** —— *Rob Roy* xvii, 'I only sought the Orlando.' 'It lies there,' said Miss Vernon, pointing to the table. **1842** TENNYSON *Ulysses* 57 Come, my friends, 'Tis not too late to seek a newer world. **1852** R. FORTUNE *Tea Countries of China* 86 Travellers who seek Sunglo tea may now search in vain. **1865** MRS. L. L. CLARKE *Seaweeds* iv. 89 Wade into the sea, and seek them in the shadow of a rock under water. **1871** R. ELLIS *Catullus* lv. 3 You I sought on Campus. **1888–91** BLANFORD *Mammalia India* 121 The Mungooses are terrestrial animals, seeking their prey on the ground.

b. with adv., esp. *out*, *up*, †*forth*.

c **1290** *S. Eng. Leg.* 390/27 Men leten heom sechen wel widen out and bringue þere into place. **1338** R. BRUNNE *Chron.* (1810) 22 þe body son þei fonde, þe hade was in doute. Up & doune in þe felde þei souht it aboute. **1375** BARBOUR *Bruce* XIX. 602 His men.. Myssit thar lord quhen thai com thar... Than can thai consale sammyn ta, That thai to sek hym vp wald ga. **1530** PALSGR. 708/2 Throw your glove where you wyl and my dogge shal seke it out. **1536** *MS. Acc. St. John's Hosp., Canterb.*, Payd to a man to helpe me to syke vp Byngis mare ij d. **1575–85** ABP. SANDYS *Serm.* viii. 137 Let vs seeke vp Christ and prouide for him. He sought vs and found vs, when we [etc.]. **1605** SHAKS. *Lear* III. iv. 157 Yet haue I ventured to come seeke you out. **1616** T. SCOT *Philomythie* II. B 8 b, Those Serpents which you run from, I seeke forth. **1818** SCOTT *Br. Lamm.* xxix, Lucy arose, and opening a little ivory-cabinet, sought out the ribbon the lad wanted. **1837** CARLYLE *Fr. Rev.* I. IV. iv, The Deputies have mostly got thither, and sought out lodgings. **1875** JOWETT *Plato* (ed. 2) I. 104 Every one of us should seek out the best teacher whom he can find. **1889** R. A. KING *Passion's Slave* III. xxix. 61 With this hope, she sought up Herbert in his smoking den.

†**c.** In *imper.* as a direction to a reader: Look or search for (in a book, table, etc.). Also used = refer to, look up, see, *vide*. *Obs.*

1362 LANGL. *P. Pl.* A. XI. 55 And so seiþ þe psauter, sech hit In *Memento*. **1599** E. WRIGHT *Err. Navig.* E e 4 b, Seeke the signe and degree of the Sunne in the vpper Margine of the Table. **1611** COTGR., *Loinceau*. Seeke *Loinseau*. **1694** J. SELDEN *Trades-man's Help* 142 Seek the Month among the rank of Months. **1730** MALCOLM *New Syst. Arith.* 342 If the given Number is even, seek in the Table the odd Number next lesser. **1828** *Moore's Pract. Navig.* 22 Seek under the column o.. the next less logarithm.

d. Sporting. ***to seek dead***: chiefly in the imperative, as an order given to a dog to search for and retrieve killed game.

1850 HUTCHINSON *Dog Breaking* (ed. 2) 162 If you wish to establish for ever a confirmed perseverance in 'seeking dead', you must sacrifice *hours*.. rather than give up any of the first wounded birds. *Ibid.* 163 The pertinacity with which some dogs will 'seek dead' is really surprising.

2. To try to discover or find out (something unknown). Also with *out*, *up*. Now *rare* or *Obs.*

c **900** tr. *Bæda's Hist.* I. xxvii. (1890) 78 Wið untrymnesse Iacedom secan. *c* **1200** ORMIN 16325 All all swa summ þu findenn mahht, ȝiff þatt tu willt itt sekenn, þe tale off sexe & fowwerrtiȝ þurh Adam all bitacnedd. *a* **1300** *Cursor M.* 1542 For-þi lete god þam lijf sua lang þat þai moght seke and vnderfang þe kynd o thinges þat þan were dern. *c* **1327** *Poem Evil Times Edw. II* in *Pol. Songs* (Camden) 332 Bringe hire to the constorie ther treuthe sholde be souht. *c* **1374** CHAUCER *Boeth.* I. met. ii. (1868) 8 He was wont to seche þe causes whennes þe sounyng wyndes moeuen. **1382** WYCLIF *Ecclus.* xxiv. 47 Not to me alone I trauailede, but to alle sechende out the treuthe. *c* **1386** CHAUCER *Can. Yeom. Prol. & T.* 310 The Philosophres stoon Elixer clept, we sechen faste echoon. *c* **1425** *Crafte Nombrynge* (E.E.T.S.) 30 þat nounbur þat þou secheste. ? *c* **1450** CAPGRAVE *St. Augustine* ii. 4 And þouȝ þat he telle not her names þere, we haue sout hem oute of oþir of his bokis. *c* **1485** *Digby Myst.*, *Mary Magd.* 307 Yf þe trewth be sowth. **1530** TINDALE *Answ. More* Wks. (1573) 257/1 If ye signification were once lost, we must of necessitie either seeke vp the signification or put some signification of Gods word therto. **1604** E. G[RIMSTONE] *D'Acosta's Hist. Indies* II. xi. 105 We are forced to seeke out other reasons, whence this great diversitie should proceede in the burning Zone. **1610** HOPTON *Baculum Geod.* VI. xl. 217 To seeke the distance of any place from you. **1714** CUNN *Doctr. Fractions* 16 Multiply all the Numbers continually, and the Product is the Number sought. **1803** *Med. Jrnl.* X. 128, I believe that its cause must be sought in the state and variations of the atmosphere. **1828** *Moore's Pract. Navig.* 167 The height of the elevated pole or latitude sought.

3. a. With object-clause introduced by a conjunction or by an interrog. pron. or adv.: To try to find or discover (*if*, *how*, *whether*, *what*, etc.). ? *Obs.*

a **1000** *Juliana* 571 Sohte synnum fah hu he sarlicast þurh þa wyrrestan witu meahte feorh-cwale findan. *c* **1290** *S. Eng. Leg.* 339/527 Gredinde heo orn and longue souȝte a-boute bi þe se-side, ȝif þe se him hadde up i cast. **1340** *Ayenb.* 80 þe yealde filozofes þet zuo byzylyche desputede and zoȝten huet wes þe heȝeste guod ine þise lyue. *c* **1375** *Sc. Leg. Saints* xx. 14 þare-fore I.. set me rycht besyly to seke quhat man he was & of quhat land. **1382** WYCLIF *Lev.* xiii. 36 He shal na more seche, wher the heer be chaungid in to ȝalow colour. **1390** GOWER *Conf.* I. 85 Ayein hir will yit mot I bowe, To seche if that I myhte have grace. *c* **1440** *Gesta Rom.* 136 He rode aboute this forest, & sowte wher this harpe myght be founde. **1574** H. BAKER *Well-spring Sci.* (1617) 29 First, I must seek how many times the diuisor is contayned in the higher number. **1591** SHAKS. *1 Hen. VI*, III. iii. 91 Now let vs on, my Lords, and ioyne our Powers, And seeke how we may preiudice the Foe. **1613** TAPP *Pathw. Knowledge* 311 Which product beeing 1587, I seeke how often it may be had in 3201. **1738** in Boswell *Johnson* (1816) I. 92 What mean the servile imitating crew.. Ne'er seek.

b. with *how* (etc.) followed by infinitive. ? *Obs.*

1526 TINDALE *Mark* xi. 18 The scribes and hye prestes.. sought howe to destroye him [1611 how they might destroy him]. **1593** SHAKS. *3 Hen. VI*, v. iv. 2 Wise men ne'r sit and waile their losse, But chearely seeke how to redresse their harmes. **1621** T. WILLIAMSON tr. *Goulart's Wise Vieillard* 120 As a hote furious horse,.. seekes how to cast his rider. **1667** MILTON *P.L.* IX. 75 Satan.. then sought Where to lie hid. **1671** —— *Samson* 795, I.. sought by all means therefore How to endear, and hold thee to me firmest.

4. a. To go to, visit, resort to (a place). *arch.*

†In early use also: to take to (the sea); to fall on (the ground); to fall into (the water). (Cf. 14.) ***to seek a saint*** or ***hallow***: to visit his shrine.

Beowulf 1450 Se þe meregrundas mengan scolde, secan sundᵹebland. **971** *Blickl. Hom.* 47 þæt hi Sunnandaᵹum & mæssedaᵹum Godes cyrican ᵹeorne secan. *c* **1200** ORMIN 7574 Forrþrihht se time comm þærto þatt ure laffdiȝ Marȝe, Affterr Judisskenn laȝhess boc, þe minnstre shollde sekenn. *a* **1225** *Ancr. R.* 350 Oðre pilegrimes goð mid swinke uorte sechen one holie monnes bones. *c* **1275** LAY. 7938 þar Cesares folk þane grunde sohte [*c* 1205 folden isohten]. *Ibid.* 23490. *Ibid.* 14739 þar þe Saxesse men þare see sohte [*c* 1205 þæ sæ isohten]. *a* **1300** *Cursor M.* 13252 þe sinagogs all soght he Ouer all þe land of galilee. **13..** *E.E. Allit. P.* C. 249 A wylde walterande whal.. was war of þat wyȝe þat þe water soȝte. *c* **1386** CHAUCER *Prol.* 17 To Caunturbury they wende The hooly blisful martir for to seke. —— *Wife's Prol.* 657 Who so.. suffreth his wyf to go seken halwes. *c* **1400** *Beryn* 632 As he souȝt his logging. **1422** YONGE tr. *Secreta Secret.*, *Priv. Priv.* 245 [In autumn] the byrdys shechyn hote regions. **1576** GASCOIGNE *Philomene* (Arb.) 95 You haue desire Your sisters court to seech. **1697** DRYDEN *Virg. Past.* vii. 14 Your lowing Heifers, of their own accord, At wat'ring time will seek the neighb'ring Ford. **1798** WORDSW. *Goody Blake & Harry Gill* 64 And, now and then, it must be said, ..She left her fire, or left her bed, To seek the hedge of Harry Gill. **1847** TENNYSON *Princess* II. 429 At last a solemn grace Concluded, and we sought the gardens. **1871** R. ELLIS *Catullus* xxxv. 4 Come from Larius,..seek Verona.

†**b.** Naut. *to seek up*: to make for (a place). *Obs.*

14.. *Sailing Directions* (Hakl. Soc. 1889) 12 Goo south southwest, and seke up Tenet, and seke up vj. fadome on the brakis.

5. a. To come or go to (a person) in order to see or visit him; to approach or resort to (for help, or the like). *Obs.*

Beowulf 2380 Hyne wræcmæcgas ofer sæ sohtan, suna Ohteres. *c* **893** K. ÆLFRED *Oros.* I. i. §17 He hæfde þaȝyt, ða he þone cyningc sohte, tamra deora unbebohtra syx hund. *c* **1200** ORMIN 16781 He nass nohht derrf inoh All opennliȝ to sekenn þe Laferrd Crist biforr þe follc. *a* **1250** *Owl & N.* 1759 To seche hine is lihtlich þing, he naueþ bute one woning. *a* **1300** *K. Horn* 465 Aþelbrus he soȝte [*Harl.* sohte, *Laud* sowte] & ȝaf him þat he broȝte. **1362** LANGL. *P. Pl.* A. VIII. 149 We schulle..seche þe for neode. *c* **1375** *Sc. Leg. Saints* iii. 97 þane sante andro sone scho schocht. *c* **1386** CHAUCER *Friar's T.* 113 Where is now youre dwellyng, Another day if þat I sholde yow seche? **1447** BOKENHAM *Seyntys* x. 165 (Horstm.) And where myht I fynd þat man? quod he; If þat I wyst, I wold hym seche. **1522** *World & Child* 571 (Manly) *Foyle.* But, syr, in London is my chefe dwellynge. *Manh.* In London? Where, yf a man the sought? **1530** PALSGR. 708/1 We wyll seke you there as we go, *nous demanderons apres vous en chemyn.* **1538** LONDON in *Lett. Suppress. Monasteries* (Camden) 218 He ys moch sowȝt for the agow.

b. *spec.* To approach, draw near to (God), in prayer, etc. [A Hebraism.] Said also of God's visiting the soul. *arch.*

971 *Blickl. Hom.* 87 Sec nu þinne þeow, Drihten. *c* **1000** *Ags. Ps.* xiii. 3 Drihten..hawað hwæðer he ȝeseo æniȝne þæra, þe hine sece. *a* **1340** HAMPOLE *Psalter* xiii. 3 þat he see if any is vndirstandand or sekand god. *c* **1366** CHAUCER *A.B.C.* 114 To enquere Wherfore and whi þe holi gost þee souhte. **1535** COVERDALE *Ps.* lxii[i]. 1 O God..early wil I seke the. **1611** BIBLE *Ezra* iv. 2, *Ps.* xxiv. 6, cxix. 2, *Zeph.* ii. 3, etc. *a* **1674** CLARENDON *Hist. Reb.* VIII. §191 They agreed therefore..that they would have a solemn fast-day, in which they would *seek God* (which was the new phrase they brought from Scotland with their Covenant), and desire his assistance.

†**6. a.** To pursue with hostile intention (a person; also, in Biblical phrase, his soul or life); to go to attack, advance against (an army, country); to persecute, harass, afflict. Also ***to seek out, to seek to death.*** *Obs.*

Beowulf 801 Sawle secan. *c* **825** *Vesp. Ps.* lxix. 3 Fiond mine ða ðe soecað sawle mine. *O.E. Chron.* an. 894, Ond hi mon eac mid oþrum floccum sohte. *c* **1205** LAY. 31724 Oswi iherden suggen þat Penda hine sohte..& fusde toȝæines Pendan. *c* **1275** —— 6940 þat neuere onleode ne sohte his riche [*c* 1205 þis lond ne iseoðten], ac þis lond was in paise. **1297** R. GLOUC. (Rolls) 11361 þe king hom sende word aȝen ..þat he wolde hom seche out as is pur fon. *a* **1300** *Cursor M.* 13307 To man þai wroght neuer vn-pes, þof man þam soght wit gret males. *a* **1352** MINOT *Poems* vii. 65 Inglis men with site þam soght. **1375** BARBOUR *Bruce* v. 102 Thai with so felloun will thaim socht, That thai slew thame euirilkane. *a* **1400-50** *Wars Alex.* 2020, I sall þe seke [Dubl. MS. seche] with a sowme of seggis enarmed. *c* **1470** HENRY *Wallace* VIII. 441 Lordis, he said, thus is King Eduuard set, In contrar rycht to sek ws in our land. **1561** UNDERHILL in *Narr. Reform.* (Camden) 169 Methynkes you do moore then the parte off a jentyllemane thus to seke hym. **1583** GRINDAL in Strype *Life* (1710) 281 Tending to the Defence of so notable and sincere a Church, dangerously sought and distressed by many mighty Enemies. **1588** ALLEN *Admon.* 34 Elias being sought to death by Achab and Iesabell. **1606** SHAKS. *Ant. & Cl.* II. ii. 161-2 Of vs must Pompey presently be sought, Or else he seekes out vs.

b. Of sin, disease, etc.: To attack. *Obs.*

a **1300** *Cursor M.* 11833 On ilk side him soght þe sare. *Ibid.* 27543 Sines..þat clerkes clepes veniale, þe quilk sua hali man es noght þat he ne vmquil wit þaim es soght. **1390** GOWER *Conf.* II. 118 Mi sorwe is everemore unteid, And secheth overal my veines. *a* **1450** *Le Morte Arth.* 870 Lord, suche syttes me haue sought! *c* **1470** HENRY *Wallace* IX. 1531 Seknes hyr had so socht in to that sted, Decest scho was.

7. a. To try to obtain (something advantageous); to try to bring about or effect (an action, condition, opportunity, or the like). Also with *out.*

c **1000** *Ags. Gosp.* John v. 44 þe..ne seceaþ þæt wuldor þe is frame gode syluum. *a* **1200** *Moral Ode* 215 in *Lamb. Hom.* 173 þa þe godes milce secheð [*other texts* sechð, secð, sekþ], he iwis mei ha ifinden. *a* **1225** *Ancr. R.* 390 Ich chulle.. aredden þe of ham þet schecheð þine deað. *a* **1300** *Cursor M.* 7239 Hir time sco soght, bad þam be nere. *c* **1375** *Sc. Leg. Saints* i. 315 þe prefet..socht Ithandly occasione To bring hym to confusione. *c* **1400** *Destr. Troy* 531 A sure knyghte, þat ayres into vnkoth lond auntres to seche. **1471** CAXTON *Recuyell* (Sommer) 43 Ye..muste seke remedye and retorne to Epire. **1572** *Memorial* in *Buccleuch MSS.* (Hist. MSS. Comm. 1899) I. 22 To seik refuge againe in England. **1644** VICARS *God in Mount* 209 Seeking-out new occasions still to crosse the Parliaments desires of a faire Accomodation. *a* **1697** AUBREY *Lives* (1898) II. *Sir T. Morgan* 87 At which he tooke pett, and seek't his fortune (as a soldier). *a* **1700** EVELYN *Diary* 14 Jan. 1682, How earnestly the late E. of Danby..sought his friendship. **1798** FERRIAR *Illustr. Sterne* i. 19 Mary sought relief from the tiresome uniformity. **1831** SCOTT *Ct. Robt.* x, Those adventures which it is the business of errant-knights to be industrious in seeking out. **1845** M. PATTISON *Ess.* (1889) I. 19 The king sought the ruin of Praetextatus. **1835** *Field* 7 Feb. 147/3 [The fox] once more sought refuge in a drain. **1908** R. BAGOT *A. Cuthbert* i. 2 She sought consolation in district visiting.

†**b.** Phr. ***to seek one's best***, to seek one's advantage. Cf. OF. *querre son mieilz.* (Later, ***to seek one's best avail.***) *Obs.*

1297 R. GLOUC. (Rolls) 940 Oþer half ȝer we abbeþ now iwend wiþ oute reste In þe grete se of occean vorto seche oure beste. *a* **1300** *K. Horn* 770 'Cutberd', he sede, 'ihc hote, Icomen vt of þe bote, Wel feor fram biweste To seche mine beste'. *a* **1300** *Cursor M.* 2456 For þai wit þaim moght haf na rest, þai most þan scail and seke þair best. **1553** T. WILSON *Rhet.* Pref. A iij b, Menne lyued Brutyshlye in open feldes, hauiug neither house to shroude them in,..nor yet anye regarde to seeke their best auayle.

†**c.** *refl.* To aim at one's own advantage. (Cf. *self-seeking.*) *Obs.*

c **1450** tr. *De Imitatione* I. xiv. 16 Many priuely sekiþ hemself [L. *se ipsos quaerunt*] in þinges þat þey done. **1645** CALAMY *Indictm. England* 19 These men seeke themselves and not the publique... These seeke their owne belly.

†**d.** To invent, contrive. Also with *out, up.*

1340 *Ayenb.* 38 Kueade lordes..þet be-ulaȝeþ þe poure men..be tayles,..oþer be oþre wones þet hy zecheþ oþer beþencheþ hou hi moȝe habbe of hiren. *c* **1400** *Destr. Troy* 1623 The chekker.., The draghtes, the dyse, and oþer dregh gamnes [*printed* gaumes]. Soche soteltie þai soght to solas hom with. **1548** FORREST *Pleas. Poesye* 46 By moste honeste meanys of lawes ordynaunce sought owte wondreslye by witt polytike. **1593** G. HARVEY *Pierce's Super.* D d 2 b, When I haue sought-vp my day-charmes and night-spelles.

†**e.** To pursue, try to practise (virtue). *Obs.*

1340 *Ayenb.* 74 Ac hit ne is naȝt ynoȝ to lete þe kueades, ..bote yef me zeche þe uirtues.

f. To plan, or try to work (evil) *on* or *to* (a person).

c **1250** *Gen. & Ex.* 3130 Oc among ȝu, dredeð ȝu noȝt, to ȝu ne sal non iuel ben soȝt. *a* **1300** *Cursor M.* 688 þe hund ne harmed noght þe hare, ne nane soght on oþer sare. *Ibid.* 16629 þe scam þai on þair lauerd soght, ful tor it war to tell! **1390** GOWER *Conf.* II. 120 As he which of his lif ne rowhte, His deth upon himself he sowhte.

8. a. To ask for, demand, request (*from* a person); to inquire, try to learn by asking. Const. *from,* †*at,* †*of,* in OE. †*to.*

971 *Blickl. Hom.* 137 Hwæt secestu minne naman? *a* **1000** *Juliana* 170 Gif þu..þe to swa mildum mundbyrd secest. *c* **1200** ORMIN 16212 þeȝȝ sohhtenn..Att Jesu Crist summ takenn. *c* **1205** LAY. 3571 Wenne þu wult more suluer sæche hit at me suluen. *a* **1300** *Cursor M.* 3138 þat child þat was sa mani yere, Ar it was send, soght wit praiyer. **1340** *Ayenb.* 184 'Vayre zone', zayþ he, 'zech euremo red of wyse men'. ..Alsuo tekþ þe writinge þet me ssel zeche red ate yealden, and naȝt mid þe yonge. *c* **1380** WYCLIF *Wks.* (1880) 56 God schal seke þe synful mannus bloode..of þe prelatis hondis. *c* **1450** *Merlin* 10, I come to seche youre counseill. *c* **1470** HENRY *Wallace* I. 54 Foly it was..Succour to sek of thar alde mortale fa. **1526** TINDALE *Luke* xi. 16 And other tempted hym sekynge of hym a signe from heven. **1535** COVERDALE *Bible* To Rdr., In the Psalmes we lerne how to resorte onely vnto God in all oure troubles, to seke helpe at him. **1596** LODGE *Marg. Amer.* D 4 b, You best were rather..to beseech for life then to seech loue. **1604** SHAKS. *Oth.* IV. ii. 203, I will seeke satisfaction of you. **1848** DICKENS *Dombey* xx, Before I sought a word of confidence from him. **1908** R. BAGOT *A. Cuthbert* x. 113 Nothing would have induced her ever again to seek help or counsel from a priest.

†**b.** With *up*: To try to recover (a debt). *Obs.*

1581 RICH *Farew.* D ij, To seeke vp suche small sommes as were due vnto hym. **1607** R. JOHNSON *Pleas. Conceites Old Hobson* (Percy Soc.) 8 Maister Hobson comming into Kent, to seeke up some desperate debts.

†**c.** With *in*: (*a*) To invite (a person); (*b*) to call in (rent). *Sc. Obs.*

1675 in *Fasti Aberd.* (1854) 339 Upon the occasion of the regents ther soliciting for and seeking in of scollars throw the countrey. *Ibid.* 340 None of the regents of the saids colledgis shall..seek in or solicite..for any schollers to enter this present year. **1725** RAMSAY *Gentle Sheph.* I. ii. 130 With glooman brow the laird seeks in his rent.

d. In *passive*, of a person: To be 'sought for' (see 16); to be courted, to be 'in request' as a companion. Of a woman: to be wooed or asked in marriage.

1671 MILTON *P.R.* III. 342 His daughter, sought by many Prowest Knights. **1825** T. HOOK *Sayings* Ser. II. *Man of Many Fr.* I. 208 She beheld him sought and courted. **1835** MACAULAY *Ess., Mackintosh* ¶34 Charles was not imposed on his countrymen, but sought by them.

e. Of things: †To demand, call for (*obs.*); to invite. *rare.*

1656 EARL MONM. tr. *Boccalini's Advts. fr. Parnass.* I. lxxxii. (1674) 110 Injuries written by loquacious Poets, did not touch to the quick,..Truths did only nettle and seek revenge. **1883** *Century Mag.* Oct. 929/1 The fashion..of printing verse attractively and in a shape that seeks the hand.

†**9.** To entreat, beseech (a person) *to do* something; also *of* (the thing asked for). *Obs.*

a **1300** *Cursor M.* 19590 For drightin has þou soght wit wogh þe to for-giue. *Ibid.* 19786 Til-ward þat like he turnd his face, And kneland soght godd of his grace. **1362** LANGL. *P. Pl.* A. IV. 49 Wrong was a-Fert þo and Wisdam souhte To Make his pees with pons. **1385** in *3rd Rep. Hist. MSS. Comm.* 410/2 The forsayde personaris..souch hym nother with grace lufe na with lauch, to delay his dome. *a* **1400-50** *Wars Alex.* 163 Him þai supplyed & soȝt & him ensence castis. **1562** A. SCOTT *Poems* (S.T.S.) i. 149 Be thai vnpayit, thy pursevandis ar socht To pund pure communis corne, and cattell keir. **1629** MAXWELL tr. *Herodian* III. 171 Plautian [the traitor]..fell on his knees, and sought them not to misdeeme him.

10. a. To search, explore (a place) in order to find something. (Sometimes coupled with *search.*)

With this and 10 b, c, d, cf. THROUGH-SEEK *v.*

a **1225** *Ancr. R.* 314 Hwoso haueð ȝeorne isouht alle þe hurnen of his heorte & ne con of-sechen more ut. *a* **1300** *Cursor M.* 7379 Samuel went secand þe land Til he þe hus o iesse faand. **1375** BARBOUR *Bruce* II. 62 Thai fand nocht, The quhethir the chambre hale thai socht. *c* **1400** MAUNDEV. (1839) xxi. 226 Thei wenten and soughten the Wodes, ȝif ony of hem had ben hid in the thikke of the Wodes. *c* **1400** *Sowdone Bab.* 225 Lukafere, kinge of Baldas, The countrey hade serchid and sought, Ten thousande maidyns faire of face Vnto the Sowdan hath he broghte. *c* **1440** *Promp. Parv.* 65/1 Cekyn, or serchyn, *scrutor.* **1530** PALSGR. 708/1, I have sought all the cofers I have for your writynge. *a* **1548** HALL *Chron., Hen. VIII* 32 The kyng contynually sent foorth his light horses to seke the countrey, and to se yf any apparaunce were. *a* **1578** LINDESAY (Pitscottie) *Chron. Scot.* (S.T.S.) I. 214 [He] bad them searche and seik his schipis at thair awin plesour. **1596** SPENSER *F.Q.* VI. iv. 16 Seeking all the woods both farre and nye For herbes to dresse their wounds. **1827** SCOTT *Highl. Widow* v, They sought brake, rock, and thicket, in vain.

†**b.** To search, examine, consult (a book, register, etc.). Cf. 1 e. *Obs.*

? *a* **1500** *Chester Pl.* viii. 233 Looke vp thy Bookes of prophesie... Seeke each leafe, I thee pray. **1523** LD. BERNERS *Froiss.* I. xlii. 23 b, Robert of Cicyle..a great astronomyer..had often tymes sought his bokes on thestate of the kynges of England and of france: & he founde by his astrology [etc.]. **1654** *Caldwell Papers* (Maitland Club) I. 123 For seiking of ye register, to get ye auld gift of ye ward 0120.

†**c.** To probe (a wound); cf. SEARCH *v.* 8. *Obs.*

a **1300** *Cursor M.* 26641 Alsua þe sin quen it es wroght, Bot it be son wit saluing soght, it reches wide and rotes ai. *a* **1400-50** *Wars Alex.* 3132 (Dubl. MS.) He gart seke þair sarys & þaim salue. *c* **1400** *Laud Troy Book* 9437 To him come fycisiens,..And soughte his woundes on eche halue, And leyde ther-to plastres & salue. *c* **1435** *Torr. Portugal* 1730 Lechis sone his woundis sought.

†**d.** With immaterial object: To examine, investigate, scrutinize; to try, test. Also with *out, through. Obs.*

a **1300** *Cursor M.* 26671, I haue mi hert soght ilk a delle. *c* **1380** WYCLIF *Wks.* (1880) 231 Kyngis & lordis schulden.. wiþ most diligence sike þe cause þat þei knowe not [cf. *Job* xxix. 16]. **1408-9** *26 Pol. Poems* viii. 6 Wheþer hast þou serued pyne or blisse, Seche þy werkis and assaye. **1533** GAU *Richt Vay* 31 Faith is socht and prouine in aduersite as the gold is prouine in the fyr. **1535** COVERDALE *Ps.* lxxvi[i]. 6, I commoned with myne owne herte, and sought out my sprete. **1552** LYNDESAY *Monarche* 5201 Wer thare fals lawis weill soucht out. **1611** SHAKS. *Cymb.* IV. ii. 160, I would Reuenges..wold seek vs through And put vs to our answer.

11. a. Const. *inf.*: To make it one's aim, to try or attempt *to* (do something). †Also with *for to*; rarely with plain inf. (without *to*).

c **1000** *Ags. Gosp.* John vii. 30 Hiȝ hine sohton to nimanne. *a* **1225** *Ancr. R.* 130 Uor to huden him urom Saul þet him hatede & souhte uorte slenne. **1297** R. GLOUC. 1325 Mid þe emperour & me pes he secþ drawe. *a* **1300** *Cursor M.* 3768 He soght his broþer for to sla. *Ibid.* 4076 þai soght him ai to greue wit wrang. *c* **1450** tr. *De Imitatione* III. xxv. 95 Seke euer þe lower place & to be under all. *a* **1586** SIDNEY *Arcadia* II. (Sommer) 129 The King of Phrygia..sought by force to destroy the infant. **1667** MILTON *P.L.* XI. 148 Since I saught By Prayer th' offended Deitie to appease. **1848** THACKERAY *Van. Fair* xxxii, He sought to drown his sorrow for the defeat in floods of beer.

b. said of a thing.

1610 SHAKS. *Temp.* III. i. 80 But this is trifling, And all the more it seekes to hide it selfe, The bigger bulke it shewes. **1871** R. ELLIS *Catullus* lxix. 3 Not tho' a gift should seek, some robe most filmy, to move her. **1879** *Cassell's Techn. Educ.* IV. 93/1 The compass having free movement, is always seeking to point to the magnetic north.

c. In indirect passive const., in which the object of the inf. becomes the subject of the main verb, followed by the passive inf.

c **1380** WYCLIF *Wks.* (1880) 368 Whan he was sowȝte to be made a kynge, & to take in hym worldly lordeschip. **1891** *Law Times* XCII. 106/2 Persons who have any interest in land which are sought to be registered can lodge a caution with the registering officer.

†**d.** With a clause expressing desire or purpose, introduced by *that. Obs.*

c **1200** *Vices & Virtues* 59 Siec ðat tu haue pais aȝeanes gode. **1382** WYCLIF *1 Cor.* xiv. 12 To edificacioun of the chirche seke that ȝe be plenteuous [*and similarly in later versions*]. **1526** *Pilgr. Perf.* (W. de W. 1531) 3 b, Seke euer yt ye may se his blessed..face.

II. Intransitive uses.

12. a. *absol.* To make search.

c **1000** *Ags. Gosp.* Luke xv. 8 Heo..secð ȝeornlice oð heo hine fint. *a* **1225** *Leg. Kath.* 975 Heo ne sohte nawiht, an seide ananriht aȝein. *c* **1250** *Gen. & Ex.* 1533 Ðor quiles esau soȝte and ran. *a* **1300** *Cursor M.* 19499 Fra hus to hus secand he ran. *c* **1300** *Havelok* 1085 þou y southe heþen in-to ynde, So fayr, so strong, ne mithe y finde. *c* **1391** CHAUCER *Astrol.* II. §1, I sowhte in the bakhalf of myn astrelabie, and fond the sercle of the daies. *c* **1450** *Mankind* 770 in *Macro Plays* 28 Yf ȝe wyll haue hym, goo, & syke, syke, syke! **1500-20** DUNBAR *Poems* liii. 13 To seik fra Sterling to Stranawer, A mirrear Daunce mycht na man see. **1568** GRAFTON *Chron.* II. 774 If examples be sufficient to attaine priuilege for my childe, I nede not farre to seeke. *c* **1570** *Pride & Lowl.* (1841) 9 Which in its furniture dyd so exceede As hardly shal ye find yf that ye seech. **1872** TENNYSON *Gareth & Lynette* 1247 'Seek, till we find'. And when they sought and found [etc.].

indirect passive. **1847** C. BRONTE *Jane Eyre* xxxiii, The pocket-book was again..sought through.

b. In *imper.* as a call to a dog to search for game, etc. Also *seek out!* (See quots.) Cf. SICK *v.*[2]

1840 BLAINE *Encycl. Rural Sports* 805 *Back!* returns the dog to your heels. *Seek out!* sends him off again in quest of game... *Go seek!* should be impressed on the dog's memory as an order to look for something supposed to be actually lost, or a bird you think is wounded. **1848** Hutchinson *Dog Breaking* 21 Then say 'seek' and, without your accompanying him he will search for what you have previously hidden. **1928** Kipling *Limits & Renewals* (1932) 64 Go seek, boy! It's Dinah! Seek! **1968** P. N. Walker *Carnaby & Gaolbreakers* xix. 178 'Seek,' and the two police dogs were cast about the mini car.

†**c.** Cricket. *to seek out*: to field. *Obs.*

1840 Blaine *Encycl. Rural Sports* 135 The whole party, who are seeking out..change their positions.

d. Phrase, *to have far to seek (for)*. Cf. 19.

1780 Bentham *Princ. Legisl.* xix. §9 Where then is the line to be drawn? We shall not have far to seek for it. **1828** Carlyle *Burns* Misc. 1840 I. 340 The poet, we imagine, can never have far to seek for a subject.

13. a. To go, resort, pay a visit (*to, unto, †till* a person, *to, into* a place). *Obs.* exc. *arch.*

c **1200** *Trin. Coll. Hom.* 127 Ðo..bigan þat folc sechen to his wunienge. *c* **1205** Lay. 28782 And he gon sechien to his twam susteren. *c* **1250** *Owl & N.* 538 Hi boþ hoȝ-ful & uel arme, an secheþ ȝorne to þe warme. *a* **1300** *Cursor M.* 13457 Fra full ferr can þai till him seke. *Ibid.* 28432 Þe nedy sekand to my hus I haue wit-draun wit almus. **1377** Langl. *P. Pl.* B. xv. 392 In-to Surre he souȝte. *c* **1470** Henry *Wallace* I. 282 Quha sperd, scho said to Sanct Margret thai socht. **1513** Douglas *Æneis* xii. Prol. 184 Litill lammys Full tayt & tryg socht bletand to thar dammys. **1590** Greene *Orl. Fur.* (1599) F 1 b, Sith we haue..found the rich and wealthie Indian clime, Sought to, by greedie mindes, for hurtfull Gold. **1596** Bp. W. Barlow *Three Serm.* i. 129 To seek into strange places for sustenance. **1630** Bp. Hall *Occas. Medit.* xxxiii. (1633) 83 Give me that Bird which will..seeke to my window in the hardest frost. **1632** Lithgow *Trav.* iii. 99 The tempest continuing..we were constrained to seeke into a creeke..for safety of our liues. **1634** Milton *Comus* 376 Wisdoms self Oft seeks to sweet retired Solitude. **1856** R. A. Vaughan *Mystics* (1860) I. vi. vii. 252 If he is always to be thus sought unto methinks he is as far from his longed-for seclusion as ever. **1883** R. W. Dixon *Mano* ii. vi. 86 And in those days Sir Mano to him sought, And held with him much converse. **1887** Morris *Odyss.* xi. 190 But a-winter he sleeps in the feast-hall whereto the thrall-folk seek.

b. To apply, have recourse *to* or *unto* (a person, *for* something); to pay court, make request or petition *to*. Often in indirect passive. *Obs.* exc. *arch.*

c **1366** Chaucer *A.B.C.* 78 To whom j seeche for my medicyne. **1465** *Paston Lett.* II. 200, I can not seke to no man, nor will not but only to yow. *a* **1555** Hooper in Coverdale *Lett. Martyrs* (1564) 152 Prayer..is the meanes wherby god will be saught vnto for his gifts. **1560** Bible (Geneva) *2 Chron.* xvi. 12 *marg.*, It is in vaine to seke to yᵉ Phisitians, except first we seke to God to purge our sinnes. **1584** Lodge *Alarum agst. Usurers* 10 My friends now disdain thee, the day shall come that they shall seeke to thee. *a* **1616** Beaum. & Fl. *Custom of Country* v. i, I may shine out againe And as I have been, be admired and sought to. **1656** Earl Monm. tr. *Boccalini's Advts. fr. Parnass.* ii. liv. 316 No ..Souldier, could receive a greater affront, than being sought unto, to do an unworthy action. **1740** Richardson *Pamela* II. 53 And you know you have been sought to by some of the first Families in the Nation, for your Alliance. **1746** Hervey *Medit.* (1818) 224 The dead cannot seek unto God. **1818** Scott *Hrt. Midl.* xxxiii, If the wicked will turn from their transgressions, and seek to the Physician of souls. **1853** Lynch *Lett. to Scattered*, etc. (1872) 349 The Bereans ..sought to the Referee; they searched the Old Scriptures. **1865** Swinburne *Atalanta* 32 Who then sought to thee? who gat help?

†**c.** To resort *to, unto, till* (a remedy, means of help, an action). *Obs.*

a **1300** *Cursor M.* 26678 Sekand til an sakful dede. *c* **1350** *Will. Palerne* 5519 Of alle bales was he brouȝt..& so schal euerich seg þat secheþ to þe gode. *c* **1400** *Rule of St. Benet* (Verse) 988 The fift degre es to be swift Eftir our sin to seke to schrift. **1621** Burton *Anat. Mel.* ii. i. i. 289 Cunning men, Wisards, & white-witches,..that if they bee sought vnto, will helpe almost all infirmities of body & mind. **1679** Penn *Addr. Prot.* i. x. (1692) 54 'Twas his Reproof..that they should seek to the stratagems of Heathen Nations. **1819** Scott *Ivanhoe* xxvii, Seek to prayer and penance, and mayest thou find acceptance!

†**d.** To make a hostile approach *to, till* (a person). *Obs.* (Cf. senses 6 and 17 a.)

1375 Barbour *Bruce* vi. 625 The kyng met thame that till hym socht. *c* **1400** *Destr. Troy* 5903 He soght to on Symagon, a sad man of armys,..He bere to þe bold with a big sworde.

†**14. a.** To go, move, proceed (in a specified direction). Widely used in ME.; e.g. *to seek up*, to rise (from a sitting posture); *to seek asunder*, to part; *to seek to the earth* or *ground*, to fall; *to seek out of life*, to die. *Obs.*

c **1000** Ælfric *Hom.* (Thorpe) I. 504 Hi ða syððan ȝewunelice þider sohton. **1297** R. Glouc. (Rolls) 1810 Þe luþer maximian westward hider soȝte. *c* **1330** R. Brunne *Chron. Wace* (Rolls) 12734 Wyþ þat strok to þe erþe he sought. *c* **1350** *Will. Palerne* 5455 Þei..soute seþe on-sunder, þouȝh it hem sore greued. *a* **1375** *Joseph Arim.* 655 Þat þou miȝt seo him þi-self ar þow henne seche. *a* **1400-50** *Wars Alex.* 2962 With þat he sleȝly vp soȝt & his sete leuys. *c* **1400** *Destr. Troy* 6644 He seyt to þe soile & soght out of lyue. *a* **1450** *Le Morte Arth.* 2952 They brake sege and homward sought. *c* **1470** Henry *Wallace* vi. 201 War nocht for schayme he had socht to the ground. *a* **1500** *Lancelot* 3428 And he goith one, and frome the feld he socht.

b. said of a thing. *Obs.*

a **1300** *Cursor M.* 3106 Þe smel was suette þat soght til heuen. **13..** *E.E. Allit. P.* B. 563 Quen þe swemande sorȝe soȝt to his hert. *c* **1384** Chaucer *H. Fame* 744 Ryght so sey I be fire or sovne Or smoke or other thynges lyght Alwey they seke vpwarde on hight. *c* **1400** *Destr. Troy* 1091 Er the sun vp soght with his softe beames. *c* **1435** *Torr. Portugal* 1619 The giaunt hym ayen smate, Thorough his sheld and his plate, Into the flesh it sought. *c* **1470** Henry *Wallace* vi. 200 The paynfull wo socht till his hart full sone. **1567** Maplet *Gr. Forest* 43 Another Fig tree called Ægiptiaca, being throwen into the water, it straight waye discendeth and seeketh to the bottom.

c. Sometimes conjugated with *be*, in the perfect and pluperfect tenses. *Obs.*

c **1250** *Gen. & Ex.* 3707 In-to cades ðe folc was sogt. *a* **1300** *Cursor M.* 4320 For sua þou mai þe driue to ded.. Quen þou art soght fra þi succur. **13..** *Guy Warw.* (1891) 502 Swiche sorwe icham in souȝt. *a* **1400-50** *Wars Alex.* 3003 Or he was soȝt to þe side. **1513** Douglas *Æneis* ix. i. 23 Eneas..Is till Evander socht.

15. seek after ——. To go in quest of, look for; to try to find, reach, or obtain; †to pursue in order to hurt. Now chiefly in passive: To be desired or in demand; to be courted, to have one's presence desired.

c **1200** *Trin. Coll. Hom.* 9 Sech after þing þe ðe beð biheue. *c* **1200** Ormin 6273, & all forrwerrp þu towarrd himm To sekenn affterr wræche. *c* **1290** *S. Eng. Leg.* i/6 Eleyne, þat was is moder, to Ierusalem he sende to sechen after þe holie rode. *c* **1374** Chaucer *Boeth.* ii. pr. v. (1868) 47 Þan is it no nede þat þou seke after þe superfluite of fortune. **1377** Langl. *P. Pl.* B. xvi. 178, I seke after a segge þat I seigh ones. *c* **1449** Pecock *Repr.* i. ix. 48 Bifore eer he eny suche causis fyndeth, and eer he aftir eny suche causis sechith. **1482** *Monk of Evesham* (Arb.) 53 Yef they..sekyd after the mercye of god and alsoo after the helpe of his holy seyntys. **1535** Coverdale *Ps.* xiii. (xiv.) 2 To se yf there were eny, that wolde vnderstonde & seke after God. *Ibid.* lxix. [lxx.] 2 Let them be shamed & confounded that seke after my soule [*and so* **1611**]. **1597** Shaks. *2 Hen. IV*, ii. iv. 405 You see (my good Wenches) how men of Merit are sought after. **1615** W. Bedwell *Moham. Impost.* iii. §97 We..do not seeke after those bookes. **1638** Baker tr. *Balzac's Lett.* (vol. II.) 44, I will never believe that ill fortune any more than good will seeke after me as far as this. **1709** Steele *Tatler* No. 11 ¶ 5 They have been always seek'd after by the Ladies. **1850** Scoresby *Cheever's Whalem. Adv.* vi. (1859) 77 The first four, only, of this catalogue are much sought after for their oil. **1856** R. A. Vaughan *Mystics* (1860) I. vi. viii. 262, I was aware that he had been greatly sought after as a preacher.

16. seek for ——. a. To look for, try to find or obtain, etc. (An equivalent for the transitive senses 1, 2, 7.)

c **1250** *Owl & N.* 1508 Ich not hu mai eni freo-man for hire sechen after þan. **1390** Gower *Conf.* I. 208 And yit therfore With al his wit he hath don sieke. *c* **1430** Lydg. *Min. Poems* (Percy Soc.) 133 For more pasture I will nat stryue Nor seche for my foode no more. **1526** Tindale *Mark* i. 37 All men seke for the. **1563** *Homilies* ii. *Rogation Week* iii. 247 b, If we be colde, we seke for cloth. **1600** E. Blount tr. *Conestaggio* 18 They went therefore seeking heere and there for money. **1748** *Anson's Voy.* ii. iv. 161 Our disappointment and their security were neither to be sought for in their valour nor our misconduct. **1860** Tyndall *Glac.* i. xxv. 182 The group..broke up, seeking in all directions for a means of passage. **1875** Jowett *Plato* (ed. 2) V. 362 The true life should neither seek for pleasures, nor.. entirely avoid pains.

†**b.** Naut. *to seek up for*: to 'bear up for', sail towards. *Obs. rare.*

1632 Lithgow *Trav.* ii. 44 The tempest increasing.., we were constrained to seeke vp for the Port.

†**17. seek on, upon ——.** [Cf. onseek *v.*] **a.** To approach with hostile intention; to advance against, set on, attack, assail. Also in indirect passive. Similarly, *to seek again(s* (= against). (Cf. sense 6.) *Obs.*

c **1205** Lay. 8433 Herigal him soðte on mid hehær strengðe. *c* **1230** *Hali Meid.* 22 Leccherie anan riht greideð hire wið þet to weorrin o þi meiðhad, & secheð erst upon hire, nebbe to nebbe. *a* **1300** *Cursor M.* 4411 Ioseph soght [*Gött.* sohut] on me in bour. *c* **1386** Chaucer *Friar's T.* 196 And somtyme be we suffred for to seke Vp-on a man, and doon his soule vnreste. **1390** Gower *Conf.* I. 190 And he with pouer goth to seke Ayein the Scottes forto fonde the werre which he tok on honde. *a* **1400-50** *Wars Alex.* 1735 For þou has samed..a selly nounbre..to seke vs agaynes. *c* **1430** *Syr Gener.* (Roxb.) 84 My lord the Sowdon vpon me soght In grete wrathe. *c* **1470** Henry *Wallace* iii. 304 Vndyr my seylle I sall be bound to the For Inglismen, that thai sall do him nocht, Nor to no Scottis, less it be on thaim socht. **1470-85** Malory *Arthur* iii. xiii. 115 He is..ful lothe to fyghte with ony man but yf he be sore souȝt on. *a* **1500** *Lancelot* 3311 One thar fois ful fersly thai soght. **1525** Ld. Berners *Froiss.* II. xlv. 150 Better it were for vs to seke batayle then to be sought on. **1542** Udall *Erasm. Apoph.* 341 Alcibiades..so came home highly welcomed, although thei had by necessitee been forced to seeke vpon hym.

b. To approach, apply to (a person) in order to obtain something. *Obs.*

a **1300** *Cursor M.* 13726 Quen þai þis wais on iesu soght, Well he wist all quat þai thoght. **1470-85** Malory *Arthur* xxi. i. 840 Than Syr Mordred sought on quene Gueneuer by letters & sondes..for to haue hir to come oute of the toure of london. **1523** Ld. Berners *Froiss.* I. cccxlviii. 556 When Johan Lyon sawe himselfe sought on by them whom he desyred to haue their good wylles and loue, he was greatly reioysed. **1536** Cromwell in Merriman *Life & Lett.* (1902) II. 5 They..seke only uppon hym for theyr ouun commodytye. **1560** Daus tr. *Sleidane's Comm.* 12 b, Seyng that we seke upon straungers [L. *quando peregrinos euocamus*].

†**18.** To make inquiry or request. Const. *of* (the thing inquired for). *Obs.*

1390 Gower *Conf.* I. 80 Bot of here entre whan thei soghte, The gates weren al to smale. *Ibid.* III. 373 This have I for thin ese cast, That thou nomore of love sieche.

III. Uses of the gerundial infinitive *to seek.*

19. a. Predicated of a thing or person that needs to be sought or looked for; = not to be found or not yet found, not at hand, absent, missing, lacking. *far to seek*, far out of reach, a long way off.

c **1386** Chaucer *Can. Yeom. Prol. & T.* 321 The Philosophres stoon..I warne yow wel, it is to seken euere. *c* **1540** J. Heywood *Four PP.* 294 Who may not playe one daye in a weke May thincke his thrift farre to seke. **1561** Awdelay *Frat. Vacab.* (1869) 13 When his Maister nedeth him, he is to seeke. **1573-80** Tusser *Husb.* (1878) 21 With some vpon Sundaies, their tables doe reeke, and halfe the weeke after, their dinners to seeke. **1612** Rowlands *Knave of Harts* B 4 b, With trauellers monie may be to seeke. *a* **1668** Lassels *Voy. Italy* ii. (1670) 317 Lest they should grow idle, and have their strength to seek when the war should break out. **1775** *Tender Father* I. 205 Amelia..was still to seek, and, perhaps, in reality, totally lost to him. **1874** Sidgwick *Meth. Ethics* iii. v. §6. 262 This supposes that we have found the rational method of determining value: which, however, is still to seek. **1904** Weyman *Abb. Vlaye* xi, The end she knew; the means were to seek.

b. With negative: Not needing to be sought or looked for, not hard to find, not absent or wanting. Also *not far, †not long, to seek.*

c **1386** Chaucer *Prol.* 784 Oure conseil was nat longe for to seche. **1390** Gower *Conf.* I. 160 My sorwe is thanne noght to seche. *Ibid.* 236 Whan Deianyre hath herd this speche, Ther was no sorwe forto seche. *c* **1450** Holland *Howlat* 238 All Se fowle and Seid fowle was nocht for to seike. ? *a* **1550** *Freiris of Berwik* 26 in *Dunbar's Poems* (1893) 26 The four ordouris wer nocht for to seik, Thay wer all in this toun dwelling. **1860** Gen. P. Thompson *Audi Alt.* III. cxxxiv. 102 The extreme answer, for which examples are not to seek. **1876** W. H. Pollock in *Contemp. Rev.* June 57 The reason is not far to seek.

20. Of a person, his faculties, etc.: **a.** At a loss or at fault; unable to act, understand, etc.; puzzled to know or decide. *Const.* indirect question introduced by *how, what,* etc.; also *to* (do). *Obs.* or *arch.*

Also *much, far, all to seek*; † *new to seek*, utterly at a loss.

1390 Gower *Conf.* I. 61 Thi wittes ben riht feer to seche. **14..** Hoccleve *Min. Poems* xxiv. 514 With him ther hath been many a sundry leeche..but al to seeche Hire art was. *a* **1500** *Flower & Leaf* 234 And hardily, they were nothing to seke How they on hem shuld the harneys set. **1523** Skelton *Garl. Laurel* 893 Zeuxes, that enpicturid fare Elene the quene, You to deuyse his crafte were to seke. *a* **1529** —— *Agst. Garnesche* ii. 37 To turney or to tante with me ye ar to fare to seke. **1581** Rich *Farew.* B b j, Thus Emelya was now [*read* new] to seeke. **1583** Golding *Calvin's Deut.* lxxii. 445/1 Insomuch that..they wote not where they bee, but are newe to seeke in their imaginations. **1597** Hollyband *Fr. Littleton* Ep. Ded. (1625) 5 Saying, that the learner is newe to seeke, when he cometh to a booke without such marks. **1602** Warner *Alb. Eng.* xii. lxxix. (1612) 325 Yea far he is to seeke of what his proper Nature is. **1603** Knolles *Hist. Turks* (1621) 847 The Gouernour..who alwaies brought vp in ciuile affaires, was to seeke how to defend a siege. **1667** Duchess of Newcastle *Life Duke of N.* (1886) iii. 192 Whereas now he should be to seek to do the like, his estate being so much ruined by the late Civil Wars. **1698** M. Lister *Journ. Paris* (1699) 27 Whence this great Liberty of Sculpture arises, I am much to seek. **1709** Shaftesb. *Moralists* ii. i. 47 But what real Good is, I am still to seek. **1803** tr. *P. Le Brun's Mons. Botte* I. 48 Charles passed the night in..forming projects, abandoning them [etc.]. In the morning he was as much to seek as ever. **1886** Stevenson *Kidnapped* xx, For the details of our itinerary, I am all to seek.

b. Wanting or deficient *in*, †*of*; without skill or learning *in*. With *for*: Badly off or at a loss for, unable to find. *arch.*

c **1522** Skelton *Why nat to Courte* 314 Sergyantes of the coyfe eke, He sayth they are to seke In pletynge of theyr case At the Commune Place. **1545** Raynald *Byrth Mankynde* Prol. D j, So be there agayne many mofull vndiscreate, vnreasonable, chorlishe, and farre to seke in such thinges. **1579** Lyly *Euphues* (Arb.) 89 Greece is..neuer void of some Synon, neuer to seeke of some deceitful shifter. **1614** B. Jonson *Barth. Fair* ii. ii, I that haue dealt so long in the fire, will not be to seek in smoak, now. **1625** Bacon *Ess., Usury* (Arb.) 544 For if you reduce Vsury, to one Low Rate,..the Merchant wil be to seeke for Money. **1633** Bp. Hall *Hard Texts, Dan.* iii. 16 O King Nebuchadnezzar, wee are not to seeke of a ready answer to this charge of thine. **1670** Wood *Life* (O.H.S.) II. 199 He being to seek for a version that would please the Doctor, it was a long time before he could hit it. **1704** Swift *T. Tub* v. 118 Does he not also leaue us wholly to seek in the Art of Political Wagering? **1771** Foote *Maid of Bath* iii. Wks. 1799 II. 238, I promise you she sha'n't be to seek for the means. **1803** Porson in *Museum Crit.* (1814) I. 332 The Germans in Greek Are sadly to seek. **1835** H. J. Rose in *Newman's Lett.* (1891) II. 107 Our good clergy are sadly to seek in the great points, viz. Church authority, &c. **1886** Besant *Childr. Gibeon* i. ix, The Cause, which is at present sadly to seek in the matter of young ladies.

†**c.** Astray from the truth, mistaken. *not to seek*: not ignorant, well aware (*that*). *Obs.*

1569 Sir N. Throckmorton *Let.* in Robertson *Hist. Scot.* App. No. 32 You are not to seek that some will use cautions, some neutrality, some delays. **1639** T. de Gray *Compl. Horsem.* 347 Yet are they very much to seeke in that they doe so much exclaime against taking up of veyns. **1657** Heylin *Ecclesia Vind.* Gen. Pref. c 1 b, Which if it be not a restraining of the Gift of Prayer, I am much to seek.

IV. 21. *Comb.* **a.** of the verb + object, as †**seek-sorrow, -trouble**, one who seeks sorrow, etc. **b. seek-no-farther** (or **-further**), a kind of apple.

a **1586** Sidney *Arcadia* i. (1598) 88 A field they go, where manie lookers be, And thou seek-sorrow Klaius them among. **1611** Florio, *Cattabriga*, a make-bate, a busie-bodie, a pick-thanke, a seeke-trouble. **1670** Meager *Eng. Gard.* 86 [Apples.] Seek no farther. **1845** Downing *Fruits Amer.* 93 Autumn Apples... Rambo. Seek-no-further, of New Jersey. **1850** Miss Warner *Wide Wide World* xxii, 'Seek-no-further!' said Ellen;—'what a funny name. It ought to be a mighty good apple'. **1875** Hogg *Fruit Man.* (ed. 4) 134 This is the true old *Seek-no-farther*.

seek, obs. f. SICK; var. SIKH.

'seekable, *a.* *rare*⁻⁰. [f. SEEK *v.* + -ABLE.] † Capable of investigation. *Obs.*

1483 *Cath. Angl.* 328/1 Sekabylle, *scrutabilis.*

seeke: see SICK *a.* and *v.*[1]

seeker ('siːkə(r)). Forms: 4 secher, sekere, 5 seker, 6 seaker, *Sc.* seiker, 6– seeker. [f. SEEK *v.* + -ER[1].]

1. a. One who seeks, in various senses of the verb; a searcher, an explorer, one who endeavours to find something hidden or lost. Const. as the vb. Also in phr. ***seeker after truth.***

Often used as the second element in objective combinations, such as OFFICE-SEEKER, PLEASURE-SEEKER.

c **1330** *Arth. & Merl.* 1196 (Kölbing) On a day, as ich ȝou telle, Þo ich Þre sechers snelle Þat were ysent fram Þe king. **1387–8** T. USK *Test. Love* Prol. 117 Knowing of trouth in causes of thinges was more hardyer in the first sechers.. and lighter in us that han folowed after. **1483** *Cath. Angl.* 328/1 A Seker, *scrutator.* **1567** PALFREYMAN *Baldwin's Mor. Philos.* VII. vii. (1600) 129 Neither slaunder nor flatter, nor bee no seeker out of other mens matters. **1596** DALRYMPLE tr. *Leslie's Hist. Scot.* I. 136 He trett mekle the seikeris of wylde beistes. *a* **1686** CLARKSON *Serm.* (1696) 150 He rewards all seekers. **1818** BYRON *Juan* I. cxliv, 'Tis odd, not one of all these seekers thought.. Of looking in the bed as well as under. **1840** [see SCIENTIST]. *a* **1850** CALHOUN *Wks.* (1874) IV. 302 As soon as the government becomes the mere creature of seekers of office, your free institutions are nearly at an end. **1868** FARRAR *(title)* Seekers after God. **1881** LADY D. HARDY *Through Cities & Prairie Lands* 131, I fancy they are searching for the bride... But nobody attempts to put the clue in the hands of the seekers. *a* **1968** A. FARRER *Interpret. & Belief* (1976) 138 Madame Blavatsky, than whom few women have been more remarkable for the power of making solid objects fade into thin air among the mountains of India, and crystallize back to physical solidity in the middle of English drawing-room cushions, thence to be hacked out with scissors by delighted seekers after truth.

b. *Eccl. Hist.* (With capital S.) As the designation assumed by a class of sectaries in the 16–17th c.: see quot. 1645.

The date and authorship of the first quotation seem to be highly questionable. The passage quoted from Pagitt 1645 appears to contain the earliest known example of the use of the word as the designation of a sect, though the opinion there described was held by the three brothers Legate (*c* 1600), whose followers were called Legatine-Arians. (See C. Burrage, *The Early English Dissenters*, 1912, I. 214–6, 259–61, and App. A.)

1617 J. MORTON in R. Barclay *Inner Life Relig. Soc. Commw.* (1876) 412 Oh, ye Seekers, I would ye sought aright, and not beyond the Scriptures, calling it carnal. **1645** PAGITT *Heresiogr.* (ed. 2) 141 Many.. go under the name of Expecters and Seekers & doe deny that there is any true Church, or any true Minister, or any Ordinances: some of them assume the Church to be in the wildernesse, and they are seeking it there: others say it is in the smoke of the Temple, & that they are groping for it there. **1651** CLEVELAND *Poems* 1, I saw a Vision yesternight Enough to sate a Seekers sight: I wisht my self a Shaker there, And her quick pulse my trembling sphear. *a* **1720** SEWEL *Hist. Quakers* (1795) I. 10 Many separate societies, and amongst the rest also, such as were called Seekers. **1795** SEWARD *Anecd.* (ed. 2) I. 318 Sir Henry Vane, so sagacious and resolute as to daunt and intimidate even Cromwell himself, yet so visionary and so feeble-minded as to be a Seeker and Millennist. **1836** H. ROGERS *J. Howe* iii. (1863) 47 From the Papists, who clung to every particle of ancient error, to the Seekers, who wandered about [etc.].

†**c.** ***seeker-out***: a fielder at Cricket. *Obs.*

1744 J. LOVE *Cricket* (1770) 18 The Seekers-out change Place. **1748** in *Waghorn's Cricket Scores* (1899) 41 Smith.. being allowed a seeker-out.

2. An instrument used in seeking or searching. **a.** A kind of slender probe or tracer used in dissections. Cf. SEARCHER 3 a.

1658 A. FOX *Wurtz' Surg.* I. vi. 22 The small iron [surgical] instruments, which by reason of seeking, are called the seekers or searchers. **1882** WILDER & GAGE *Anat. Technol.* 72 The tracer is apparently similar to the 'seeker' of the English anatomists... This instrument was introduced into the laboratory of Cornell University [etc.]. **1888** HUXLEY & MARTIN *Elem. Biol.* (ed. 2) 281 Insert a seeker into it [the pedal gland of the common snail]—it can be readily introduced for a distance of more than an inch.

b. Part of an astronomical telescope; cf. SEARCHER 3 e, FINDER 3 b.

1892 *Athenæum* 9 Apr. 473/2 Prof. Lamp at Kiel found it easily visible to the naked eye.., with a tail which in the seeker appeared about 2° in length.

Hence (sense 1 b) **'seekerism**, † **'seekerness.**

1657 J. WATTS *Scribe, Pharisee*, etc. I. 58 Is it to shew your unsetled and scrupulous seeker-nesse? **1884** *Ch. Quarterly Rev.* XIX. 57 It [Independency] was continually losing its younger adherents by the ceaseless drift to Anabaptism, to Seekerism, to Quakerism [etc.].

Seekh, variant of SIKH.

seeking ('siːkɪŋ), *vbl. sb.* For forms see the vb. [f. SEEK *v.* + -ING[1].] The action of the vb. SEEK in its various senses.

(*it is*) *of my own seeking*: said of a misfortune that has been brought about by one's own fault. Also negatively, *it is not* (colloq. *it is none*) *of my seeking*: said of an honour or success, or of a quarrel or the like, which the speaker disclaims having sought.

1303 R. BRUNNE *Handl. Synne* 5930 Þan asswyÞe pers Þey soght, But al here sekyng was for noȝt. **1470–85** MALORY *Arthur* x. lii. 500 Fyrste to the vncoupelynge, to the sekynge, to the rechate,.. and many other blastes and termes. *c* **1500** *Lancelot* 2503 And gawan, which was in the seeking ȝhit Of the gud knycht, of hyme haith got no wit. **1535** COVERDALE *Job* xi. 7 Wilt thou fynde out God with thy sekynge? *a* **1643** CARTWRIGHT *Siedge* II. iii, You hear the Tyrant's wonderfully taken With us: It was none of our seeking; Fortune Hath thrown the Dignity into our Lap. **1668** [BETHEL] *World's Mistake in O. Cromwell* 13 Instead of answering his seekings, the Marchants remonstrated to him, the great prejudice that a Warr with Spain would be to England. **1671** MILTON *P.R.* III. 151 Of glory as thou wilt, said he, so deem, Worth or not worth the seeking, let it pass. **1718** MOTTEUX *Quix.* (1733) II. 23 Why that's well quoth Sancho: a happy Seeking and a happy Finding. **1825** T. HOOK *Sayings* Ser. II. *Sutherl.* I. 98 The misfortune is entirely of my own seeking. **1878** BOSW. SMITH *Carthage* 288 They had been involved in hostilities which were not of their own seeking.

†**b.** The object of seeking. *Obs. rare.*

a **1340** HAMPOLE *Psalter* xxvi. 13 And fra now .i. sall seke Þi face lastandly til my ded and Þat .i. fynd my sekynge. *c* **1375** *Sc. Leg. Saints* xii. (*Mathias*) 437 Þane socht Þay hyme dais thre.. til hyme-self one Þe thryd day askyt Þare sekyne. **1607** SHAKS. *Cor.* I. i. 192 What's their seeking? *Men.* For Corne at their owne rates, wherof they say The Citie is well stor'd.

seeking ('siːkɪŋ), *ppl. a.* [f. SEEK *v.* + -ING[2].] That seeks, in various senses of the vb.

1483 *Cath. Angl.* 328/2 Sekynge, *querens, scrutans.* *a* **1586** SIDNEY *Arcadia* III. (Sommer) 249 Pamela only casting a seeking looke, whether she could see Dorus. **1656** *Sibbes' Confer. Christ & Mary* To Rdr. 4 Christ, (who is never far absent from a seeking soul). **1715** E. ERSKINE *Wks.* (1871) I. 51 Wind is of a very seeking penetrating nature. **1859** R. H. HUTTON *Ess.* v. (1871) I. 122 Inspirations addressed to the seeking intellect of the philosopher.

seekle, seekly: see SICKLE, SICKLY *adjs.*

†**seel**, *sb. Naut. Obs.* Also 7 seele. [f. SEEL *v.*] A sudden heeling over of a vessel in a storm.

1625 GLANVILLE *Voy. Cadiz* 117 Our shipp did rolle more, and fetch deeper and more dangerous Seeles then in the greatest storme. **1644** MANWAYRING *Sea-mans Dict.* s.v., The Lee-seele, is when she rowles to Leeward; there is no danger in this seele, though [etc.]. **1688** HOLME *Armoury* III. 165/2 Seele, or seeling, is a sudden turning aside of a ship, forced by the motion of the Sea and fearful Winds. **1753** *Chambers' Cycl.* Suppl. s.v. *Seeling*, When a ship thus tumbles to lee-ward, they call it *lee-seel.*

†**seel**, *v.*[1] *Naut. Obs.* [Of obscure origin.] *intr.* Of a ship: To make a sudden lurch to one side. Hence †**'seeling** *vbl. sb.* and *ppl. a.*

a **1618** RALEIGH *Royal Navy* 24 When a Ship seels or roules in foule weather. **1621** G. SANDYS *Ovid's Met.* XI. 487 They plie their tasks: some seeling yards bestry'd And take-in sailes. **1644** MANWAYRING *Sea-mans Dict.* s.v. *Seele*, So that seeling is but a suddaine heeling, forced by the motion, and feare of the sea or wind. **1692** *Smith's Seaman's Gram.* I. xvi. 81 *The Ship seels*, that is, when on a sudden she lies down on her side, and tumbles from one side to the other. **1753** *Chambers' Cycl.* Suppl. s.v. *Seeling*, If she rowls or seels to windward, there is fear of her coming over too short or suddenly.

seel (siːl), *v.*[2] Forms: 5 sele, 6 cele, 6–7 siel, 6–9 seal, 7 ceel, seele, seile, 6– seel. [Later form of SILE *v.*[3]]

1. *trans.* To close the eyes of (a hawk or other bird) by stitching up the eyelids with a thread tied behind the head; chiefly used as part of the taming process in falconry. Also, to stitch *up* (the eyes of a bird).

a **1500** in Harting *Perf. Bk. Sparhawkes* (1886) Introd. 12 Take the outsyd of her ye and put thorgh ye nedell and the threde [etc.]... And then thou maist sey she is a seled. **1530** PALSGR. 479/1, I cele a hauke or a pigyon whan I sowe up their eyes for caryage or otherwyse. **1611** B. JONSON *Catiline* II. i, He, tame Crow,.. would haue kept Both eyes, and beake seal'd vp, for sixe *sesterces.* **1641** R. BROOKE *Eng. Episc.* 5 Your Faulkners seele a Pigeons eye (when they would haue her soare high) to prevent a Vertigo. **1647** HEXHAM I. (Birds), To seile a Hawke. **1797** *Encycl. Brit.* (ed. 3) s.v. *Falconry*, Care ought to be taken, not to seel her too hard. **1818** SCOTT *Rob Roy* v, You cannot.. reclaim a hawk .. or direct his diet when he is sealed. **1852** R. F. BURTON *Falconry in Valley Indus* vi. 68 A bird of the same colour with eyes seeled and wings shortened. **1897** *Encycl. Sport* I. 373/1 (Falconry) *Seel*, to sew up the upper eyelids of a hawk, and tie the threads behind the head. An obsolete practice now superseded by the hood.

fig. **1584** LYLY *Campaspe* IV. i. 41 Al conscience is sealed at Athens.

2. *transf.* To close (a person's eyes). Also *fig.* to make blind, to prevent from seeing, hoodwink.

1591 SYLVESTER *Du Bartas* I. iv. 766 Thy light is darkned, and thine eyes are siel'd. **1604** SHAKS. *Oth.* III. iii. 210 Shee that so young could giue out such a Seeming To seele her Fathers eyes vp. **1606** —— *Ant. & Cl.* III. xiii. 112 But when we in our viciousnesse grow hard.. the wise Gods seele our eyes In our owne filth. **1633** T. ADAMS *Exp. 2 Peter* i. 18 It is bad to have the eyes seeled, but worse to have the ears sealed up. **1814** SOUTHEY *Roderick* XVI. 240 A life-long night Seel'd his broad eye.

Hence **seeled** (siːld) *ppl. a.*; **'seeling** *vbl. sb.* and *ppl. a.*

a **1586** SIDNEY *Arcadia* I. (Sommer) 65 b, Now she brought them to see a seeled Doue, who the blinder she was, the higher shee straue. **1605** SHAKS. *Macb.* III. ii. 46 Come, seeling Night, Skarfe vp the tender Eye of pittiful Day. **1625** QUARLES *Sions Sonets* XV. iii, These seiled eyes that slept So soundly fast, awak'd, much faster wept. **1661** BOYLE *Style of Script.* (1675) 186 Lovers like ceel'd Pidgeons flying the Higher for having been Blinded. **1797** *Encycl. Brit.* (ed. 3) s.v. *Hawking*, Then cast out a sealed duck. **1852** R. F. BURTON *Falconry in Valley Indus* iv. 48 The seeling threads are cut short. **1859** TENNYSON *Merlin & V.* 123 Their talk was all of training, terms of art, Diet and seeling.

†**seel**, *v.*[3] *Obs.*⁻⁰ [ad. F. *ciller*, f. *cil* eyelash, orig. also eyebrow.] (See quot.)

1728 CHAMBERS *Cycl.* s.v. *Seeling*, A Horse is said to *Seel*, when upon his Eye-brows, there grows about the Breadth of a Farthing of white Hairs, mixed with those of his natural Colour; which is a Mark of Old Age.

seel: see CEIL *v.*, SEAL *sb.* and *v.*, SELE, SELL *v.*

seelapak, var. SILLAPAK.

seeld(e, var. ff. SELD; obs. pa. t. of SELL *v.*

seelden, seeldome, obs. forms of SELDOM.

†**seele.** *Obs.* Also 5 cele, seill. [? a. F. *ciel* sky, canopy.] A canopy.

1485 *Rutland Papers* (Camden) 5 In this wise the King shall ride opyn heded vndre a seele of cloth of gold baudekyn. *Ibid.* 7 A cele of white damaske. **1494** in *Househ. Ord.* (1790) 127 A seill of bawdkyne of gould lyned with bawdkyne.

seele, obs. f. CEIL *v.*, SEAL *sb.* and *v.*; var. SELE.

seeled, obs. form of CEILED, canopied.

1643 *Farington Papers* (Chetham Soc.) 99, 1 Seeled Bed with ffurniture.

†**'seelihead.** *Obs.* In 5 selyhede. [f. SEELY *a.* + -HEAD.] Happiness.

14.. *Voc.* in Wr.-Wülcker 582/31 *Felicitas*, selyhede.

†**'seelily**, *adv.* *Obs.* Forms: 1 séliȝlíce, 3 seliliche, seliliȝ, 4 selily, 5 selyly. [ONorthumb. *séliȝlíce* (= WS. *ȝesǽliȝlíce*): see SEELY *a.* and -LY[2].] Happily.

[*c* **888** K. ÆLFRED *Boeth.* XI. §1 Maniȝe habbað ȝenoȝ ȝesælilice ȝewifod.] *a* **1000** *Rituale Eccl. Dunelm.* (Surtees) 79 Seliȝlice, *feliciter.* *c* **1200** ORMIN 17318 Þurrh whatt himm comm swa seliliȝ To findenn Godess are. *c* **1374** CHAUCER *Boethius* II. pr. iv. 64 (Addit. MS.) Som man is wel and selily maried but he haÞ no children. *c* **1425** *Eng. Conq. Irel.* (Dubl. MS.) xviii. 42 Yn hys lyf of thys world, chaunged wel selyly for Þe lyf that euer shal lest without end.

†**'seeliness.** *Obs.* Forms: 4 selines, sellines, 4–5 selynes(s(e, 4, 7 selinesse, 7 seelinesse. [f. SEELY *a.* + -NESS. OE. had *ȝesǽliȝnes.*]

1. Happiness, blessedness.

a **1300** *Cursor M.* 10816 All cristen men Þat was and es, Has thorut hir Þair selines. *c* **1374** CHAUCER *Troylus* III. 813 So worldly selinesse,.. Y-medled is with many a bitternesse! **1387–8** T. USK *Test. Love* I. x. 79 For thou wenest thilke joye to be selinesse or els ese. **1447** BOKENHAM *Seyntys, Agnes* 135 Swetter Þe loue, feyrere Þe face, And of selynes mych gretere Þe grace. *c* **1470** HARDING *Chron.* XXX. iv, In mykill ioye and worldly selynesse.

2. Simplicity; silliness. *rare.*

1642 D. ROGERS *Naaman* 45 As old Eli overrules Samuels seelinesse. **1653** GATAKER *Vind. Annot. Jer.* 164 Any simple Reader may easily discry the selinesse of your Arguments.

seeling, obs. f. CEILING.

seeling, *vbl. sbs.* and *ppl. adjs.*: see SEEL *v.*[1] and *v.*[2]

seely ('siːlɪ), *a.* *Obs.* (exc. *dial.*). Forms: 3 seoly, 3–6 seli(e, 3–7 sely, 4 sele (celly, selli), 4–5 cely, (selly), 5 cele, 6 sealie, -y, seally(e, seilie, -ye, selle, sellie, sel(l)ye, sielie, -y, zelie, 6–7 seeley, seelye, 6–7, 9 seelie, 5– seely. See also I-SELI, and the later SILLY *a.* [Com. WGer.: OE. **sǽliȝ* (implied in the synonymous *ȝesǽliȝ* I-SELI *a.*, and in the adv. *séliȝlíce* SEELILY) = OFris. *sêlich* (mod.NFris. *salig*, WFris. *sillich*), OS. *sâlig*, MDu. *sâlech* (Du. *zalig*), OHG. *sâlig* (MHG. *sælic*, mod.G. *selig*):—OTeut. type **sæligo-* f. **sæli-z* luck, happiness (Goth. *sêls*, OE. *sǽl*: see SELE). In ordinary mod. English the word is represented by SILLY, a form which arose in the 15th c. from a shortening of the vowel, the pronunciation of which had changed from (eː) to something approaching (iː).]

1. (Cf. SELE *sb.* 2). ? Observant of due season, punctual.

c **1200** *Trin. Coll. Hom.* 13 Đe ðridde [werke of brihtnesse] is Þat man be waker and liht and snel and seli and erliche rise and ȝernliche sech chireche.

2. Happy, blissful; fortunate, lucky, well-omened, auspicious.

c **1250** *Gen. & Ex.* 31 Almiȝtin louerd,.. ðu giue me seli timinge To thaunen ðis werdes biginninge. *Ibid.* 2546 And egipte folc adden nið, for ebris adden seli sið. *a* **1272** *Luue Ron* 143 in *O.E. Misc.* 97 Nere he mayde ful seoly Þat myhte wunye myd such a knyhte. *a* **1300** *Cursor M.* 3362 Til his behoue haue i Þe soght, In seli time. *c* **1374** CHAUCER *Troylus* IV. 503 For sely is that deeth,.. That, ofte y-cleped, cometh and endeth peyne. **1387–8** T. USK *Test. Love* II. x. 108 Than, say I, thou art blisful and fortunat sely, if thou knowe thy goodes that thou hast yet beleved. *c* **1400** *Melayne* 392 The by-tide a cely chaunce, thi lyfe was savede this daye. **1423** JAS. I *Kingis Q.* 185 In gude tyme and sely to begynne Thair prentissehed. *c* **1440** *Promp. Parv.* 452/1 Sely, or happy, *felix, fortunatus.* **1468** *Medulla* in *Cath. Angl.* 56 *Felicio*, to make sely. **1483** *Cath. Angl.* 56/1 Cele, *vbi* happy.

3. Spiritually blessed, enjoying the blessing of God. Said of persons, their condition or experiences.

a **1225** *Leg. Kath.* 1421 Þurh seli martirdom. *a* **1225** *Ancr. R.* 108, & tu seli ancre, Þet ert his seli spuse, leorne hit ȝeorne of him þet [etc.]. *a* **1240** *Lofsong* in *O.E. Hom.* 205 Bisech for me þine seli sune Milce and merci and ore. *c* **1340** *Abbey of Holy Ghost* in *Hampole's Wks.* (1895) I. 326 A Jhesu, blyssede [es] þat abbaye and cely es þat religione. *c* **1375** *Sc. Leg. Saints* xxiv. (*Alexis*) 74 In pathmos als þe angel brycht Schawyt hyme ful sely sycht. *c* **1400** *Primer* in Maskell *Mon. Rit.* (1846) II. 11 Resp: Cely [orig. *felix*] art thou, hooli virgyne marie, and worthiest al maner preisyng.

4. Pious, holy, good.

a **1225** *Leg. Kath.* 1453 Tac read, seli meiden, to þe seoluen. *c* **1250** *Gen. & Ex.* 1986 Ðor was in helle a sundri stede, wor ðe seli folc reste dede;.. Til ihesu crist fro ðeden he nam. *c* **1275** *On Serving Christ* 53 in *O.E. Misc.* 92 Þureh his [John the Baptist's] sely sermun serewe him wes byþouht. *c* **1450** *Mankind* 426 in *Macro Plays* 16 Lady, helpe! sely darlynge, vene, vene!

absol. *a* **1225** *Ancr. R.* 64 Þis is nu inouh of þisse witte iseid et tisse cherre, to warnie þeo selie.

Proverb. *c* **1290** *Beket* 216 in *S. Eng. Leg.* 112 Seli child is sone i-lered. *c* **1386** CHAUCER *Prioress' T.* 60 For sely [*v.r.* cely] child wold alday soone lere. *a* **1450** *Ratis Raving* III. 3265 For sely barnis are eith to leire.

5. Innocent, harmless. Often as an expression of compassion for persons or animals suffering undeservedly.

c **1290** *S. Eng. Leg.* 453/138 'Alas', he seide, 'þis seli best: þat no-þing ne doth a-mis!' **1297** R. GLOUC. (Rolls) 6453 To þe king of hongri þis seli children twie He sende uor to norisi þat he wardede hom wel beye. *a* **1300** *Havelok* 499 Withdrow þe knif, þat was lewe Of þe seli children blod. *c* **1386** CHAUCER *Man of Law's T.* 584 Gret was.. the repentance Of hem that hadden wronge suspecioun Vpon this sely Innocent Custance. *c* **1475** HENRYSON *Orpheus & Eurydice* 336 Acab and quene iesabell, Quhilk sely nabot.. For his wyne yarde wyth outyn pitee sleue. *a* **1529** SKELTON *Col. Cloute* 578 And thus the loselles stryues, And lewdely sayes by Christ Agaynst the sely preest. **1545** JOYE *Exp. Dan.* vi. M v, Sely innocent Daniell was caste into the lyons. **1551** ROBINSON tr. *More's Utopia* II. vi. (1895) 200 To see a seely innocent hare murdered of a dogge. *a* **1604** HANMER *Chron. Irel.* (1633) 114 And murther the poore and seely people, which God wot, meant no harme. [**1884** SYMONDS *Shaks. Predec.* iii. 135 A racy sense of what such seely shepherds may have gathered from an angel's song.]

6. Deserving of pity or sympathy; pitiable, miserable, 'poor'; helpless, defenceless. Cf. SILLY *a.* 1, 1 b.

1297 R. GLOUC. (Rolls) 781 Þis word dude muche wo to þis seli olde king. *a* **1300** *Cursor M.* 13972 A seli sin-ful sco was an, And first als a comun womman. *c* **1374** CHAUCER *Troylus* II. 683 To helpen sely Troilus of his wo. **1423** JAS. I *Kingis Q.* 44 Quhy lest god mak ȝou so, my derrest hert, To do a sely prisoner thus smert. *c* **1470** HENRY *Wallace* II. 201 Sely Scotland, that of helpe has gret neide. **1530** PALSGR. 323/2 Sely or fearfull, *paoureux*. Sely wretched, *meschant*. *a* **1542** WYATT in *Tottel's Misc.* (Arb.) 86 At the threshold her sely fote did trippe. **1551** ROBINSON tr. *More's Utopia* II. ix. (1895) 301 But thies seilie poore wretches be presently tormented with barreyne and vnfrutefull labour. **1573–80** TUSSER *Husb.* (1878) 113 Grasse, thistle and mustard seede, .. Are very ill neighbours to seely poor hop. **1590** C'TESS PEMBROKE *Antonie* 1466 The seelie man [Fr. *le miserable*].. Me battaile gaue. **1602** CAREW *Cornwall* II. 112 The seely Gentlewomen, without regard of sexe or shame, were stripped from their apparrell to their verie smockes. **1609** BIBLE (Douay) *Isa.* x. 30 Attend Laisa, seelie poore [Vulg. *paupercula*] Anathoth. [**1858** KINGSLEY *Misc.* (1859) I. 148 The famous castle of Malepartus which beheld the base murder of Lampe, the hare, and many a seely soul beside.]

b. Often of the soul, as in danger of divine judgement.

1310 *St. Brendan* (Bälz) 584 Þe develen come blaste To lede to helle þis seli [*c* **1290** *S. Eng. Leg.* sori] gost. *c* **1330** *Spec. Gy Warw.* 576 Þu most.. þenke þat god it þe sende, þi seli soule to amende. **1508** DUNBAR *Tua Mariit Wemen* 502 My sely saull salbe saif, quhen sa bot [? *read* Sabaot] all iugis. **1529** MORE *Supplic. Soulys* Wks. 321/2 The paynes that selye soules feele when they be departed thence.

7. Insignificant, trifling; mean, poor; feeble.

1297 R. GLOUC. (Rolls) 2528 Of an holi prechors word hii nolde noȝt so ofte þenche As of þe murye word.. of the seli wenche. *a* **1300** *Expos. Cross* 458 (Ashm.) in *Leg. Rood* (1871) 54 Vp an seli asse he rod. *a* **1400** MAUNDEV. (1839) xxix. 293 And for to apparaylle with oure bodyes wee usen a sely litylle clout, for to wrappen in our careynes. **1461** *Paston Lett.* II. 22, I se his slouthe and sely labour, which is no labour. *c* **1540** tr. *Pol. Verg. Eng. Hist.* (Camden) 193 Egbertus.. in moste ample wise hadde enlarged the seelie littell kingdom. **1563** *Homilies* II. *Agst. Gluttony* 107 Holophernes.. hadde his head strycken from his shoulders by that sely woman Iudith. **1568** *Jacob & Esau* II. i. C j, And not one siely bitte we got since yesterday. **1577** KENDALL *Flowers of Epigr.* 75 b, Lerned Luther.. how far doth he both twayn Surmount, who with his seely pen to yeld doth both constraine. **1583** STUBBES *Anat. Abus.* II. (1882) 56 Whilst the mountains doe trauell, a seely mouse will be brought forth. **1593** SHAKS. *Lucr.* 1812 He with the Romians was esteemed so As seelie ieering idiots are with Kings, For sportiue words, and vttring foolish things. **1603** FLORIO *Montaigne* II. xv. 358 There is a Nation, where the enclosures of Gardens and Fields they intend to keep several, are made with a seely twine of cotton. **1613–16** W. BROWNE *Brit. Past.* I. ii. 40 Hauing layne Her in a Boate like the Cannowes of Inde, Some seely trough of wood, or some trees rinde. **1642** D. ROGERS *Naaman* 67 Commonly the Lord effects those things which are of greatest consequence, by poore and seely meanes. [**1839** KINGSLEY *Poems, In Illum. Missal* 7 My love, my song, my skill, my high intent, Have I within this seely book y-pent.]

b. Frail, worn-out, crazy.

1562 BULLEIN *Bulwarke, Dial. Sorenes & Chir.* 24 b, We see the like effecte in olde selie bodies whiche.. bee continually eaten up of ulcers. **1587** TURBERV. *Trag. T., To R. Baynes* 32 The Pilot.. Beset with stormes,.. knowes not howe to saue His sielie barke, but lets the rudder goe. [**1847** KINGSLEY *Poems, Red King* 67 By Mary's grace a seely boat On Christchurch bar did lie afloat.]

8. Foolish, simple, silly.

a **1529** SKELTON *Col. Cloute* 1246 Nor of theyr noddy polles, Nor of theyr sely soules. **1573–80** TUSSER *Husb.* (1878) 107 With such seelie huswiues no penie is found. **1583** BABINGTON *Commandm.* (1590) 265 In pride wee speake it, or at least inwardlie thinke it, wee are not as those seely Idiotes are. **1605** CAMDEN *Rem., Wise Sp.* 224 The fellow seemed but a seely soule, and sate still, and sayde nothing. **1622** MABBE tr. *Aleman's Guzman d'Alf.* I. 127 Holding those that deale more honestly.. to be.. poore seely fooles, that want wit.

seem, *sb.* ? *Obs.* or *dial.* (chiefly *Sc.*) [f. SEEM *v.*[2]] Seeming, semblance, appearance.

c **1440** *Promp. Parv.* 452/2 Semynge, or semys, *apparencia*. **1549** *Prayer Bk. Troubles* (Camden) 147 The innocent that have been seduced under the colour and seame of good. **1596** GRIFFIN *Fidessa* (1876) 58 The fairest good in seeme, but fowlest ill. **1730** A. RAMSAY *Tea-Table Miscellany* (ed. 5) 213 His seim in Thrang of fiercest Stryfe, When Winner ay the same. **1812** JANE AUSTEN *Let.* 29 Nov. (1952) 499 It [*sc.* a cloak] is to be Grey Woollen & cost ten shillings. I hope you like the *sim* of it. **1837** J. M. WILSON *Tales of Borders* III. 131/1 There comes slowly, as if frae the womb o' a cloud o' mountain mist, the seim o' a turreted abbey. **1913** H. P. CAMERON tr. *T. à Kempis's Imit. Christ* II. vii. 63 Ye'se sune be begunkit, gin ye regaird allenarlie the ootrin seim o' men.

†**seem**, *a.* *Obs.* In 4–5 **seme**. [a. ON. *sém-r*: see SEEM *v.*[2]] Seemly, proper, fitting.

13.. *Gaw. & Gr. Knt.* 1085 Let þe ladiez be fette, to lyke hem þe better þer was seme solace by hem-self stille. **13..** *E.E. Allit. P.* B. 1810 Ande clannes is his comfort, and coyntyse he louyes, & þose þat seme arn & swete schyn se his face. *c* **1400** *Cursor M.* 28015 (Cott. Galba) Ȝe ladys.. þat stodis hals and hare to hew,.. for to mak ȝow seme [*earlier MS.* semle] and quaint.

b. quasi-*adv.*

13.. *E.E. Allit. P.* A. 190 Þat gracios gay with-outen galle, So smoþe, so smal, so seme slyȝt.

†**seem**, *v.*[1] *Obs. rare.* In 3 **seme**. [OE. *séman* (:—prehist. **sōmjan*), f. *sóm* agreement. (More commonly *ȝeséman*: see I-SEME *v.*)] *trans.* **a.** To settle (a dispute), reconcile (contending parties). **b.** To ratify, confirm (an agreement).

a **1000** *Canons Edgar* vii. in Thorpe *Ags. Laws* II. 246 Nan sacu þe betweox preostan si ne beo ȝescoten to world-manna some, ac seman & sibbian heora aȝene ȝeferan. *c* **1205** LAY. 4259 Heo makeden ane sætnesse and mid aȝe [*read* aþe] heo semde. *a* **1250** *Owl & Night.* 187 (Jesus MS.) Þo quaþ þe vle, Hwo schal vs seme?

seem (siːm), *v.*[2] Forms: 3–5 **sem**, 3–6 **seme**, 4 **syme**, **sieme**, 4–7 **seeme**, 5 **ceme**, 5–7 (9 *dial.*) **seime**, 6 **seym(me**, **semme**, 6–7 **seame**, 6, 8 *Sc.* **seim**, 5– **seem**; *Pa. t.* 3–4, 6 **semde**, 5 **sempt(e**, 6 **semt**. [ME. *sēme*, a. ON. *sǿma* (mod.Icel. *sæma* to honour, conform to, MSw. *söma* to befit, beseem, Da. *sømme* refl. to beseem), f. *søm-r* (:—prehistoric **sōmi-*) fitting, seemly; cf. the cognate ON. *sóma* (pa. t. subj. *sǿmðe*) to beseem, befit.

From the same grade of the root are OE. *sóm* reconciliation (whence *séman* SEEM *v.*[1]); the ablaut-variant **sam-* appears in SAME *a.*, SAMEN *adv.*, together.]

†**I. 1.** To be suitable to, befit, beseem. Often with adv., *well*, *best*, *fair*, etc. **a.** quasi-*trans.* with obj. originally dative. (*a*) *impersonal* and quasi-*impers.* with the real subject expressed by a clause or infinitive phrase.

a **1200** ORMIN Ded. 66, & te bitæche icc off þiss boc, Heh wikenn alls itt semeþþ, Al to þurrhsekenn illc an ferrs. *a* **1240** *Wohunge* in *O.E. Hom.* I. 271 For he þurh þe þat wisdom art al þis world wrahte and dihteð hit and dealeð as hit best semeð. *c* **1300** *Havelok* 2916 Hire semes curteys forto be, For she is fayr so flour on tre. **1350–1400** *Sir Beues* (E) 1746 He took hys scheeld & hys spere As it semyd a good rydere. *c* **1400** *Secreta Secret., Gov. Lordsh.* xx. 58 It semes a kynge to haue discrescioun. *a* **1425** *Arderne's Treat. Fistula*, etc. 6 It semeth any discrete man y-cladde with clerkis clothing for to occupie gentil mennez bordez. *a* **1470** GREGORY *Chron.* in *Hist. Coll. Cit. Lond.* (Camden) 129 As hyt syttythe and semyþe so worthy a prynce and a pryncesse. **1513** DOUGLAS *Æneis* XI. iii. 37 Gif he pretendis in batale with a brand To end the weyr,.. heir semyt hym vnder scheyld With wapynnis to recontre me in feyld. *a* **1529** SKELTON *Agst. Garnesche* iv 89 It semyth nat thy pyllyd pate Agenst a poyet lawreat To take vpon the for to scryue. **1601** WEEVER *Mirr. Mart.* A viii, But ill it seem'd me them to blame, though I Censur'd myselfe like mine owne enemy.

(*b*) with person or thing as subject.

a **1300** *Cursor M.* 3311 Bot ai þe quils he ne fan To be-hald þat leue maidan, How all hir dedes can hir seme. *c* **1330** R. BRUNNE *Chron. Wace* (Rolls) 11914 Nys non on lyue, cayser ne kynge. Þat semeþ so wel his beryng. *a* **1375** *Joseph Arim.* 564 Þenne he seiȝ a whit kniht comynge him a-ȝeines.. A red cros on his scheld seemed him feire. *c* **1450** *St. Cuthbert* (Surtees) 7355 Him semyd wele his abyte. **1584** LODGE *Alarum agst. Usurers* Ep. A iij, Who.. delighted in such clothing as seemed ye place where he soiourned. **1591** SPENSER *M. Hubberd* 35 A good old woman.. who did farre surpas The rest in honest mirth, that seem'd her well. **1615** BRATHWAIT *Strappado* 16 Bid them seeke, Actions that seeme them better.

b. const. *to*, *for*, *with*.

c **1205** LAY. 10207 Preostes heo þer setten ase þer to mihte semen. *a* **1300** *Cursor M.* 9111 He wald men raf it al to dust, Quar-thoru it semes wel wit þis Þat he wan merci of his mis. *c* **1400** tr. *Secreta Secret., Gov. Lordsh.* xiv. 56 Þerfore a kynge sholde vse cleþynge and ornementz dere, fayre, and straunge, for it semes to a kynges prorogatyue to passe oþer, so þat his dignite þerby be maad fairer. **1533** BELLENDEN *Livy* v. xx. (S.T.S.) II. 215, I wald nane of ȝow belevit þat I am cumin as Ignorant or mysknawing sic thingis as semys to my estate.

c. *absol.*

a **1375** *Joseph Arim.* 115 He seiȝ þe peple þorw peine passen in-to helle.. and þe fader þouȝte þat hit seemede nouȝt. *c* **1400** *Secreta Secret., Gov. Lordsh.* cv. 106 And right as þe Skryueyn ys enterpretour of þy wyl... So it nedys .. þat he besye hym to þy profyt and to þy worschipe as it semys. *c* **1440** *Promp. Parv.* 66/1 Cemyn or becemyn, *decet*. *c* **1510** BARCLAY *Mirr. Gd. Manners* (1570) E vj, It seemeth not in streete as palfray to praunce. **1533** GAU *Richt Vay* (1888) 37 Thane he is veralie God for that seemis noth that ony suld be placit at the richt hand of God the fader bot giff he war God. **1579** SPENSER *Sheph. Cal.* May 158 Nought seemeth sike strife. **1605** BACON *Adv. Learn.* I. *To the King* §2 For it seemeth much in a King, if.. he can take hold of any superficiall Ornaments and shewes of learning.

†**2.** *refl.* and *intr.* To vouchsafe, deign. [So MSw. *söma* (refl.).] *Obs.*

a **1300** *Cursor M.* 11042 Blisced be þou ai, marie!.. Þat þou ne [? *read* þe] seme wald me to se. *Ibid.* 12445 'Na', sco said, 'þat es na nede, For he þat sent him vs a-mang To be born, he wald him seme, Fra wick men ai wel him yeme.' *Ibid.* 17622 Wald þou me leif freind te seme For to cum wit us to mele. *Ibid.* 23913, I prai leuedi if þou wald seme, To tak þis littel werc to quem.

II. To have a semblance or appearance.

Normally with indirect object of the person to whom the appearance is presented; where no object is expressed one may ordinarily be supplied. In the present tense, 'seems' is often equivalent to 'seems to me', which expresses belief in the truth of the appearance predicated. Where the object expressed or implied is not in the first person, or where the verb is in the past tense, there is usually, on the other hand, the notion of *mere* appearance as opposed to fact.

* *As personal verb.*

3. With sb., adj., or phrase as complement: To appear to be, to be apparently (what is expressed by the complement).

Very often, esp. when the complement is a sb. or a phrase, it is introduced by the infinitive *to be*: see examples in 4 a.

a. without object expressed.

a **1225** *St. Marher.* 9 His grisliche teeð semden of swart irn, ant his twa ehnen steappre þene steorren. *a* **1225** *Ancr. R.* 112 So ful of anguise was þet ilke ned swot.. þet hit þuhte [*v.r.* semde] read blod. **1340** HAMPOLE *Pr. Consc.* 1322 For welthes, þat men has here at wille, Semes tokenyng of endeles pyn. ? *a* **1366** CHAUCER *Rom. Rose* 1011 As the mone lyght, Ageyn whom all the sterres semen But smale candels. **1390** GOWER *Conf.* I. 62 He.. doth to seme of gret decerte Thing which is litel worth withinne. *c* **1450** LOVELICH *Merlin* 1000 And with-jnne tho x mounthes he was so bold that thyke tyme he semede two ȝeres old. **1526** *Pilgr. Perf.* (W. de W. 1531) 38 Makyng bodyes of ayre to compasse a man & make hym seme a hors or another beest. **1570** T. WILSON *Demosth. Orat.* iii. 63 That thing which I shall say, though it seeme against the opinion of all men: yet it shal be true for all that. **1667** MILTON *P.L.* II. 672 What seem'd his head The likeness of a Kingly Crown had on. **1667** PEPYS *Diary* 27 June, A silly rogue, but one that would seem a gentleman. *a* **1700** EVELYN *Diary* 23 Apr. 1646, Trees on which Bacchus seems riding as it were in triumph every autumn. **1742** LADY M. W. MONTAGU *Let. to Montagu* 22 Mar. (1893) II. 104 Mr. Gibson says.. that he seems another man. **1807** CRABBE *Birth of Flattery* 33–4 What seem'd the door, each entering guest withstood, What seem'd a window was but painted wood. **1837** DICKENS *Pickw.* xxxiv, Mr. Justice Stareleigh.. seemed all face and waistcoat. **1884** R. W. CHURCH *Bacon* ix. 220 Easy and unstudied as his writing seems, it was [etc.].

b. const. *to*; formerly also †with simple dative.

a **1513** DUNBAR *Poems* lxxxi. 13 This seimes to me ane guidlie companie. **1598** SYLVESTER *Du Bartas* II. i. I. 368 But, of all sights, none seemes him yet more strange Then the.. Exchange. **1871** R. ELLIS *Catullus* lxxxiii. 2 This to the fond weak fool seemeth a mighty delight.

c. Followed by †*as*, *as if*, *as though*.

a **1300** *Cursor M.* 2863 Þar.. es noght now bot a stinkand see, Þat semes als a lake of hell. *Ibid.* 9928 Þe thrid [colour] Als ros þat es als in springing, And semes als a brennand thing. **1584** B. R. tr. *Herodotus* I. 3 b, The Lady seyng the fond and vndiscrete treacherye of her husband made little adoe, and seemed as though shee had seene nothing. **1673** DRYDEN *Love in Nunnery* III. ii, Stay, there's a Dance beginning, and she seems as if she wou'd make one. **1730** A. GORDON *Maffei's Amphith.* 320 It is probable that the Roofs of these Lodges were under the great Windows... I dare not however affirm it, for the Medals seem as if they came up even to the very Top of all. **1908** R. BAGOT *A. Cuthbert* xviii. 223 Having yielded to his persuasions and arguments, Sonia seemed as though she were only anxious to forget past troubles.

4. With infinitive: To appear *to be* or *to do* something. **a.** with *to be.* (Cf. 3.) Also in weakened sense (chiefly interrogative).

a **1300** *Cursor M.* 5698 A yongman Þat semed to be an egypician. **1388** WYCLIF *Acts* xvii. 18 And othere seiden, He semeth to be a tellere of newe fendis. *c* **1450** *Mirk's Festial* 230/18 This fayth hade our lady passyng all oþer; for þeras hit was semyng forto be ynpossybull þat scho schuld conceyue wythout cowpule of man [etc.]. **1560** DAUS tr. *Sleidane's Comm.* 4 Luther.. hath preached also some thinges that seme to be hereticall. **1651** HOBBES *Leviath.* II. xxviii. 165 Exile.. seemeth not in its own nature, without other circumstances, to be a Punishment. **1756** FRANCES BROOKE *Old Maid* No. 29. 172 Young women are not the angels they seem to be. **1812** J. WILSON *Isle of Palms* I. 223 Fair creature! Thou dost seem to be Some wandering spirit of the sea. **1848** THACKERAY *Van. Fair* xviii, Of all Sedley's opponents.. the most determined and obstinate seemed to be John Osborne. **1875** JOWETT *Plato* (ed. 2) IV. 247 Many .. think that you should follow virtue in order that you may seem to be good. **1901** A. K. MCCLURE '*Abe' Lincoln's Yarns & Stories* 65 'What seems to be the matter?' inquired Lincoln with all the calmness and self-possession he could muster. **1958** B. W. ALDISS *Non-Stop* IV. iii. 219 'What seems to be the trouble?' he asked. **1974** WODEHOUSE *Aunts aren't Gentlemen* xvi. 134 My voice shook a bit as I applied for further details. 'What seems to be the trouble?' I asked.

1977 G. MARKSTEIN *Chance Awakening* xix. 55 He dialled 100..'What seems to be the trouble?' asked the operator.

b. with other verbs.

a **1300** *Cursor M.* 5749 Als did þe tre þat semed to bren, And þan was þar na fir wit-in. *c* **1400** *Apol. Loll.* 21 And al oþer lawis þat semen to sey, þat man how to curse for crime of vowtre, þeft, and swilk oþer. *a* **1557** *Tottel's Misc.* (Arb.) 267 Of Venus stocke she semde to spring, the rote of beauties grace. **1603** SHAKS. *Meas. for M.* I. i. 4 Of Gouernment, the properties to vnfold, Would seeme in me t'affect speech & discourse. **1697** DRYDEN *Virg. Georg.* III. 54 The Parian Marble, there, shall seem to move, In breathing Statues. **1712** STEELE *Spect.* No. 472 ¶3 The following Letter seems to be written by a Man of Learning. **1781** COWPER *Conversat.* 714 The Christian dares not feign a zeal, Or seem to boast a fire, he does not feel. **1849** MACAULAY *Hist. Eng.* iii. I. 417 These facts are in perfect accordance with another fact which seems to deserve consideration. **1895** ESHER in *Law Times Rep.* LXXIII. 701/2 The statute..does not seem upon a true construction of it to support the assertions for which it was cited.

¶ With omission of *to*. *Obs. rare.*

c **1374** CHAUCER *Troylus* I. 747 Eek som-tyme it is craft to seme flee Fro thing which in effect men hunte faste. **1513** DOUGLAS *Æneis* XI. xvi. 2 Ane huge clamour that tyde did rys on hycht, That semyt smyte the goldin starnis brycht.

c. Occas. ***would seem***: cf. the impersonal use 7 f.

1754 WARBURTON *View Bolingbr. Philos.* II. 94 He has refused no arms, we see, to combat the Revelations God hath *actually given*. He would seem to relax a little of his severity, as to those which God may *possibly give*.

d. In modern use, the combination of *seems* with an infinitive is often equivalent to the finite verb qualified by 'probably', 'if the evidence may be trusted.'

1841 *Penny Cycl.* XXI. 484/2 Sicily seems to contain no iron. **1874** GREEN *Short Hist.* ii. §8. 102 Henry's policy seems, for good or evil, to have been throughout his own.

e. To appear to oneself; to imagine oneself, or think one perceives oneself, *to* (do something). Also (*colloq.*), in negative contexts (preceded by *can*): to seem unable.

1638 JUNIUS *Paint. Ancients* 22 These Images doe follow us so close, that wee seeme to travell, to saile, to bestirre our selves mightily in a hot fight. **1704** POPE *Windsor For.* 265, I seem through consecrated walks to rove. **1799** WORDSW. *Poems on Affect.* ix. 7 Still I seem To love thee more and more. **1810** SHELLEY *Marg. Nich., Melody* 40, I seem again to share thy smile, I seem to hang upon thy tone. **1874** HARDY *Far from Madding Crowd* II. xiii. 168 Troy could hardly seem to believe her to be his proud wife Bathsheba. **1875** JOWETT *Plato* (ed. 2) V. 10 On such occasions Plato seems to see young men and maidens meeting together. **1898** G. GISSING *Human Odds & Ends* 57 As a lad, I couldn't stick to anything—couldn't seem to put my heart into any sort of work. **1937** I. BAIRD *John* xix. 229 He couldn't seem to get the boy out of his head. **1969** M. PUGH *Last Place Left* vii. 44 Somehow I can't seem to get warm.

¶ **f.** *confused construction.* Instead of the infinitive, a clause was in the 14–16 c. sometimes used, as if the verb were impersonal. (Cf. 7.) *Obs.*

1375 BARBOUR *Bruce* III. 168 And tournys sa mony tyme his stede, That semys off ws he had na dred. **1565** STAPLETON *Fortr. Faith* 77 b, Well furnished with all such bookes as Caluin had writen or any other which semed might serue their purpose. **1614** GORGES *Lucan* v. 206 She ..Durst not..seeme she did his teares discerne.

5. To appear to exist or to be present. Chiefly in the inversion ***there seems*** (followed by the subject); otherwise *poet.* or *rhetorical*. Also, in the same sense, ***there seems to be***.

c **1391** CHAUCER *Astrol.* II. §25 Now yif so be þat the semith to long a tarienge..thanne whaite whan the sonne is in any other degree of the zodiak. *c* **1400** *Beryn* 2775 They make semen (as to a mannys sight) Abominabill wormys. *Ibid.* 446 So wele they make seme soth, when þey falssest ly. *a* **1533** LD. BERNERS *Huon* xxi. 64 He shall make to seme before you a grete rynnynge riuer. *a* **1674** TRAHERNE *Poet. Wks.* (1903) 61 Men's Hands than Angels' Wings Are truer wealth..For those but seem. **1766** BLACKSTONE *Comm.* II. II. xiv. 232 So far as the inheritance can be evidently traced back, there seems no need of calling in this presumptive proof. **1831** SCOTT *Ct. Robt.* xxx, 'I regret', said Achilles, 'that there should have seemed any cause for such precautions'. **1883** *Law Times* 20 Oct. 409/1 Some fifteen years ago..there seemed a general consensus of opinion that inventors were a nuisance.

†**6.** Of a real existence: To be manifested, come to view, be seen; = APPEAR *v.* 1, 9. *Obs.*

1340 HAMPOLE *Pr. Consc.* 6022 Bot many other þar [at the day of doom] sal seme, þat sal nouther be demed ne deme. *c* **1374** CHAUCER *Boethius* III. met. xi. (Sk.) 18 And thanne alle the derknesse of his misknowinge shal seme more evidently to sighte of his understondinge thanne the sonne ne semeth to sighte with-oute-forth. *c* **1440** *York Myst.* iii. 20 For loue made I þis worlde alone, Therfore my loue shalle in it seme. **1575** J. SMITH *Myst. Dev., Jeremy's Epist. to Jews*, My Angel shall be with you.., And I myselfe will surely seeme for all your soules to care.

** *Impersonal uses.*

7. ***it seems.*** (In all uses, admitting a construction with *to* or †simple dative.) **a.** with the real subject expressed by a clause: = It appears, it is apparently true (*that*); it is seen (*that*).

it seems not (†*nay*) = 'it seems that it is not so'. *it seems so, so it seems* = 'it seems that it is so'.

a **1225** *St. Marher.* 5 Lauerd..salue me mine wunden þat hit ne sem nowðer ne suteli omi samblant þat ich derf drehe. *c* **1250** *Gen. & Ex.* 2169 It semet wel ðat ȝe spies ben, And in-to ðis lond cumen to sen. *a* **1300** *Cursor M.* 10441 Ne wat þou noght, it semes nai, Quat a fest it es to dai? *c* **1386** CHAUCER *Melib.* ¶355 And al be it so þat it seme that thou art in siker place, yet shaltow alwey do thy diligence in kepynge of thy persone. *c* **1400** MAUNDEV. (1839) xvii. 184 And righte as it semethe to us, that thei ben undre us, righte so it semethe hem, that wee ben undre hem. *c* **1489** CAXTON *Sonnes of Aymon* xxii. 480 Yf it semeth you that I have doon amys, soo take ye amendes vpon me. **1530** TINDALE *Pract. Prelates* I vij. It semeth me, that it might be dispensed with in certayne cases. **1590** SHAKS. *Mids. N.* IV. i. 198 It seemes to mee, That yet we sleepe, we dreame. **1638** BAKER tr. *Balzac's Lett.* (vol. II) 52 It seemes you thought not our walks pleasant enough for you. **1687** LADY R. RUSSELL *Let.* 5 Oct., It seems I must remit seeing you, as you once kindly intended. **1747** *Gentl. Mag.* XVII. 541/1 It seems also that capt. Callis..fell in with and engaged this Spanish ship. **1833** TENNYSON *Lady Clara Vere de V.* 53 Howe'er it be, it seems to me, 'Tis only noble to be good. **1908** R. BAGOT *A. Cuthbert* ix. 86 It seems to me..that looking into holes is a monotonous occupation.

b. with complementary predicate or infinitive, the real subject being expressed by a clause or infinitive phrase. (Also with ellipsis of the subject clause.)

1439 *E.E. Wills* (1882) 128 Like as in that partye after their conscience and good discrecions it shall seme hem necessarie for to be done and executed for the most ease of his entent. **1512** *Knaresb. Wills* (Surtees) I. 4 As it shall seym to my said feoffees mooste expediente. **1584** B. R. tr. *Herodotus* I. 6 b, He besought them humbly yt since it semed them best to deale so roughly wt him they would graunt him liberty in his richest aray, to sing a song. **1651** HOBBES *Leviath.* II. xxix. 169 No man dare to obey the Soveraign Power farther than it shall seem good in his own eyes.

c. followed by *as if, as though*.

c **1320** *Sir Tristr.* 2097 It semeþ by his lat As he hir neuer had sene Wiþ siȝt. *Ibid.* 2131 Wende forþ in þi way, It semes astow were wode, To wede. **1853** J. H. NEWMAN *Hist. Sk.* (1873) II. I. iii. 132 It seemed as though the Turks had come to their end and were dying out. **1908** R. BAGOT *A. Cuthbert* vii. 63 It seemed to Jim as though the hour would never arrive at which the steamer was timed to get under way.

d. Parenthetically. Now often with somewhat of the sense 'So I am informed', or 'As it appears from rumour or report'.

1377 LANGL. *P. Pl.* B. XVIII. 117 Her suster, as it semed, cam softly walkynge. **1447** BOKENHAM *Seyntys, Agatha* 369 For in hys conscyence ful confuse ys he And, as yt semyth, at hys wyttys ende. **1525** SAMPSON in Ellis *Orig. Lett.* Ser. I. I. 263 His moderacion off gesture, cowntenance, and os it semyd allso of inwarde intente and mynde. **1598** B. JONSON *Ev. Man in Hum.* III. i, Then you were a seruitor at both, it seemes. **1662** J. DAVIES tr. *Olearius' Voy. Ambass.* 285 They were provided, it seems, only for the Ambassador Brugman, and his Ladies. **1712** ADDISON *Spect.* No. 305 ¶8 Six Professors, who it seems, are to be Speculative Statesmen. **1829** MACAULAY *Mill on Govt.* in *Edin. Rev.* Mar. 175 There is still, however, it seems, a hope for mankind. **1876** GLADSTONE *Homeric Synchr.* 167 Who lived before the close, as it seems, of the sixteenth century B.C.

†**e.** = 'it seems good'. *Obs. rare.*

1557 NORTH *Gueuara's Diall. Pr.* 157 This case was so horrible, that it seemed to many not to speake it.

f. ***it should seem, it would seem***: used to express somewhat more of hesitation or uncertainty than is expressed by *it seems*.

The older form, *it should seem*, is perh. slightly *arch.*, and is now chiefly used to express a guarded (or sometimes an ironical) acceptance of statements made by others. *It would seem* does not appear in our quots. before the 19th c. (but cf. the cognate use 4 c).

1525 BP. CLERK in Ellis *Orig. Lett.* Ser. II. I. 310 As for the maters off France, it shold seim that his Holynes rekonythe not gretly howe your determyn them. **1606** HOLLAND *Sueton.* Annot. 31 For it should seeme that the Game of Tali heere mentioned was Pleistoboleuda [*sic*]. **1776** ADAM SMITH *W.N.* v. ii. II. i. (1869) II. 438 It should not, however, seem very difficult to distinguish those two parts of the rent from one another. **1816** WORDSW. *Pr. Wks.* (1876) II. 11 It should seem that the ancients thought in this manner. **1826** R. H. FROUDE *Rem.* (1838) I. 154 But, with regard to writings, as it would seem, the case is different. **1829** WHEWELL in *Life* (1881) 129 All official papers were brought there: and among the rest it would seem these Cologne ones. **1875** SWINBURNE *Ess. & Stud.* Pref. 10 The accident of personal intimacy, it should seem, deprives you of all right to express admiration of what you might allowably have found admirable in a stranger. **1902** GAIRDNER *Hist. Eng. Ch. 16th C.* iv. (1903) 54 From all this it would seem that he could not have been much under fifty when he was compelled to abjure.

†**g.** ? Perfect tense with *is*; ? or passive. *Obs.*

1442 BP. BEKYNTON *Offic. Corr.* (Rolls) II. 191 Sir, hit is semed right expedient unto suche as loveth the wele of the king [etc.]. *Ibid.* 219 As soon as hit shall be seemed unto you and hym to be doon.

8. The *it* of the impersonal verb is sometimes omitted. **a.** with the dative preceding the verb, ***thee seemeth, us seemed***, etc. See also MESEEMS and cf. METHINKS. *Obs.* or *arch.*

c **1386** CHAUCER *Pars. T.* ¶123 Right so the synful man that loueth his synne, hym semeth, that it is to him moost sweete of any thyng. **1413** *Pilgr. Sowle* (Caxton 1483) IV. v. 60 That other shalle answere as hyr semeth good. **1512** R. COPLAND *Helyas* in Thoms *Pr. Rom.* (1828) III. 116 And than her semed that the two fyrst had [etc.]. **1594** CAREW *Huarte's Exam. Wits* xv. (1596) 278 Eue fixed her eies on the tree forbidden, and her seemed that it was sweet in tast. **1870** MORRIS *Earthly Par., Hill of Venus* 656 Still awhile himseemed That of that fair close, those white limbs he dreamed. **1871** D. G. ROSSETTI *Blessed Damozel* iii, Herseemed she scarce had been a day One of God's choristers.

¶ **b.** The prefixed dative sometimes was used (? by confusion) with reference to the subject of the appearance, so that the impersonal ***him, her seems*** became = *he, she seems* (senses 3–4). *Obs.*

a **1300** *Cursor M.* 3284 þe formast was vnlaghter milde, Hir semed na wight to be wilde. **1375** BARBOUR *Bruce* XII. 147 Thame semyt men forsuth, I hicht, That had fayndit thair fayis in ficht. **1413** *Pilgr. Sowle* (Caxton) I. xxxiii. (1859) 37 Hyr semed wel a lady of ful huge estate, as duchesse, or pryncesse. *c* **1440** *Ipomydon* 280 The lady byheld Ipomydon, Hym semyd wele a gentil man. *a* **1500** *Chester Pl.* (Shaks. Soc.) II. 51 Hym seemes wearye on his waye.

†**c.** with dative following. *Obs. rare.*

c **1386** CHAUCER *Knt.'s T.* 2112 Thanne semed me ther was a parlement At Atthenes vpon certein poyntz and caas. *a* **1400–50** *Wars Alex.* 3196 Semes ȝow noȝt it suffice my sorowe with-out, þat as a bitand brand me brettens with-in.

†**d.** ***what, how seemeth you?*** = what do you think? *Obs.*

c **1450** *Merlin* ii. 28 Lete eche man by hymself telle me what hym semeth in this mater. **1485** CAXTON *Paris & V.* (1868) 85 What seemeth you of the wysedom of my fader. *c* **1530** LD. BERNERS *Arth. Lyt. Brit.* lxxx. (1814) 377 How semeth you by the knightes of this countre?

e. After *as* or *than*.

1570 T. WILSON *Demosth. Orat.* vi. 69 As seemeth to me. *c* **1600** T. PONT *Topogr. Acc. Cunningham* (Maitland Club) 22 The forsaid Richard being, as vald seime, touched vith compunctione. **1611** BIBLE *Jer.* xviii. 4 So he made it againe another vessell as seemed good to the potter to make it. *Mod.* If he did so, as seems likely enough, he was excusable. He spoke more strongly than seemed justifiable.

†**f.** *poet.* in occasional uses. *Obs.*

1303 R. BRUNNE *Handl. Synne* 11764 Yn tyfed wurdys þat slyked are, Semeþ þy synnes þat þey noȝt were. **1591** SPENSER *M. Hubberd* 216 But neither sword nor dagger he did beare, Seemes that no foes reuengement he did feare. **1614** GORGES *Lucan* III. 84 And yet now seemes that he doth meane, From cares of warres his thoughts to weane.

g. *colloq.* or *vulgar*, esp. in ***seems to me***.

1888 'J. S. WINTER' *Bootle's Childr.* viii, Seems to me women get like dogs—they get their lessons pretty well fixed in their minds after a time.

†**III. 9. a.** *trans.* To think, deem, imagine. With obj.-clause, obj. and inf. or complement; also *absol.* ***to seem good*** = to think good (see GOOD *a.* 4 b). *Obs.*

The early examples in which the subject is a sb. might be referred to 8 a, from which this sense arose by conversion of the prefixed indirect object into the subject; but unequivocal instances with nom. pron. occur often in the 15th c.

c **1386** CHAUCER *Sqr.'s T.* 193 It was a ffairye, as al the peple semed. **1428** *E.E. Wills* (1882) 79 The residue of all my godes..I be-quethe to be distribued..like as myn executours seme best. *c* **1430** *Syr Gener.* (Roxb.) 8054 She semed Darel Iusted wel. *c* **1485** *Digby Myst., Mor. Wisd.* 610 These thynges be now so conuersaunt, we seme it no shame. **1492** ? MYLL *Spect. Luf* in *Bannatyne Misc.* (1836) II. 128 Ane askit him quhat he semyt of a woman? **1493** *Festivall* (W. de W. 1515) 57 Euer whan the bysshop loked on her he semed her so fayre yt he was gretely tempted on her. **1512** R. COPLAND *Helyas* in Thoms *Pr. Rom.* (1828) III. 24 If you seme it good, I shal make her to waste and sle the childe. *a* **1533** LD. BERNERS *Gold. Bk. M. Aurel.* Kk 7 b, Fynally, seyng that Rome was Rome, he was demanded how he semed therby. **1627** HAKEWILL *Apol.* I. ii. §3. 17 *Possunt, quia posse videntur.* They can, because they seeme they can.

b. To think fit. *Obs.*

c **1450** in Aungier *Syon* (1840) 258 The unresonable grudgers schalle abstayne them from that kende of mete [etc.] that they grudge aȝenste, after that the presidente semethe it for to be doon. **1471** PASTON *Lett.* III. 17, I wolle spende xxd or as ye seme to have the sertayn off every thyng her in. **1610** B. JONSON *Alch.* I. iii, And Beneath your threshold, bury me a load-stone To draw in gallants, that weare spurres: the rest, They'll seeme to follow.

seem, obs. form of SEAM *sb.*²

†**'seemable**, *a. Obs. rare.* In 5 **seameable**, 6 **semabill**. [f. SEEM *v.*² + -ABLE. Cf. SEMBLABLE.] Like, similar.

1501 in *Surtees Misc.* (1890) 51 As þei wold we did to thaym or thayrez in a cause seameable. **1513** DOUGLAS *Æneis* I. Prol. 394 Rycht so, by about speche oft in tymes, And seuthable [*MS. C.* semabill] wordis we compile our rymes.

Hence †**'seemably** *adv.*, in like manner.

1535 CROMWELL in Merriman *Life & Lett.* (1902) I. 398 For your goodnes herein to be shewed vnto hym..ye shalbe well assured to fynd me as redy semably to requyte you.

seemble, obs. form of SEEMLY *a.*

seemer ('siːmə(r)). [f. SEEM *v.*² + -ER¹.] One who seems, or makes a pretence or show.

1603 SHAKS. *Meas. for M.* I. iii. 54 Lord Angelo..scarce confesses That his blood flowes: or that his appetite Is more to bread than stone: hence shall we see If power change purpose, what our Seemers be. **1647** TRAPP *Comm. 1 Cor.* x. 12 If he be no more then a seemer, he will fall at length into hell-mouth. **1875** JOWETT *Plato* (ed. 2) III. 297 When the guardians of the laws and of the government are only seemers and not real guardians.

seeming ('siːmɪŋ), *vbl. sb.* For Forms see the verb. [f. SEEM *v.*² + -ING¹.] The action of SEEM *v.*² in various senses.

1. The action or fact of appearing to be (to the mind or to bodily sense), appearance.

1398 TREVISA *Barth. De P.R.* XI. xiv. (Tollemache MS.), By his [lightning's] sodeyne semynge he smyteþ here syȝte þat lokeþ þeron, and makeþ hem drede. **1413** *Pilgr. Sowle* (Caxton 1483) v. xi. 102 The cursid Sathanas with a shepes symplenes in semyng come and hurteled with hym. *c* **1440** *Promp. Parv.* 66/1 Cemynge, or a cemys (*P.* or cemys), *apparencia*. **1581** PETTIE tr. *Guazzo's Civ. Conversation* II. (1586) 72 The more we consider the sayde sentence of Socrates, the more wayes we finde out to auoide this vaine seeming. **1613** SHAKS. *Hen. VIII*, II. iv. 108 My Lord, my Lord,..You signe your Place and Calling, in full seeming,

With Meekenesse and Humilitie. **1678** CUDWORTH *Intell. Syst.* I. i. §7. 10 Sensible Qualities..are called after *τίνα ἐν ἡμῖν Φάσματα*, certain Phansies, seemings, or Appearances in us. **1845** R. W. HAMILTON *Pop. Educ.* x. (ed. 2) 330 The events which are the most threatening in their seeming, speak to us of hope.

b. † ***by seeming***, † ***to seeming***, ***in seeming***, ***in all seeming***, to all appearance.

c **1369** CHAUCER *Dethe Blaunche* 944 Wyth-outen hole or canel boon As be semynge had she noon. **1470–85** MALORY *Arthur* XVII. vii. 699 Thenne they lefte vp a clothe whiche was aboue the ground & there fond a ryche purse by semynge. *c* **1532** LD. BERNERS *Huon* xxiii. 68 On euery toure a clocher of fyne golde be semynge. **1612** J. CHAMBERLAIN in *Crt. & Times Jas. I* (1848) I. 168 [His wife] would have accompanied him to the King's Bench, taking his cause, to seeming, very heartily. *a* **1639** W. WHATELEY *Prototypes* III. xxxix. (1640) 20 All this was done in seeming, only to bring them to thorough repentance for their sin. **1871** R. ELLIS *Catullus* lxiv. 83 Ere his country to Crete freight corpses, a life in seeming.

† **c.** ***to (my) seeming***, as it seems or appears to (me), as (I) think, in (my) opinion or judgement. Also ***in my seeming***. *Obs.*

c **1386** CHAUCER *Prioress' T.* 196 Tel me, what is thy cause for to synge Sith þat thy throte is kut to my semynge. *c* **1440** *Generydes* 4986 Right Inly fayre she was to his semyng. *c* **1530** LD. BERNERS *Arth. Lyt. Bryt.* lv. (1814) 202 Incontynente the ymage tourned towarde him, and, to his seming, it blusshed as red as sendall. **1604** HIERON *Preachers Plea* Pref. *Wks.* I. 476 A very good way (in my seeming) to help the vnderstanding of common men. **1617** MORYSON *Itin.* II. 176 This night our horsemen set to watch, to their seeming did see Lampes burne at the points of their staves or speares in the middest of these lightning flashes. **1667** MILTON *P.L.* IX. 738 He ended..and in her ears the sound Yet rung of his perswasive words, impregn'd With Reason, to her seeming, and with Truth.

2. The form in which a person or thing seems or appears; look, aspect.

c **1400** tr. *Secreta Secret., Gov. Lordsh.* 47 For oon sect þat er namyd ypatetiks affermes þat he steigh to þe emperien heuene yn þe semynge of fir. **1484** CAXTON *Fables of Æsop* IV. xi, We must kepe our self fro all them whiche vnder fayre semynge haue a fals herte. **1632** BROME *Northern Lasse* II. iv, I present her to your judgment, whether her out-ward seeming may deserve such scorn. **1765** H. WALPOLE *Otranto* i, Your behaviour is above your seeming. **1813** BYRON *Corsair* II. xii, He slept in calmest seeming, for his breath Was hush'd so deep—Ah! happy if in death! **1874** GREEN *Short Hist.* vi. §4. 305 Words which show the tenderness that lay beneath the stern outer seeming of the man.

3. External appearance considered as deceptive, or as distinguished from reality; an illusion, a semblance.

1576 GASCOIGNE *Steele Gl.* 229 And since myselfe (now pride of youth is past) Do love to be, and let al seeming passe, Since I desire, to see my selfe in deed [etc]. **1603** SHAKS. *Meas. for M.* III. ii. 41 That we were all, as some would seeme to bee From our faults, as faults from seeming, free. **1816** BYRON *Sketch* 59 A plain blunt show of briefly-spoken seeming, To hide her bloodless heart's soul-harden'd scheming. **1891** F. THOMPSON *Sister-Songs* (1895) 35 Even so Its lovely gleamings Seemings show Of things not seemings.

seeming (ˈsiːmɪŋ), *ppl. a.* For Forms see the verb. [f. SEEM *v.*² + -ING².] That seems, in various senses of the verb.

† **1.** Suitable, beseeming, fitting; according. *Obs.*

1338 R. BRUNNE *Chron.* (1810) 51 Bataile bituene vs wille not be semand. **1377** LANGL. *P. Pl.* B. xv. 386 For sarasenes han somewhat semynge to owre bileue. For þei loue and bileue in o persone almiȝty. *c* **1440** *York Myst.* xvii. 274 Insens to þi seruis is semand. ? **1548** tr. *Viret's Expos. XII Art. Chr. Faith* B viij b, The name of father..is semynge vnto hym [God] for dyuers causes and reasons. **1687** DRYDEN *Hind & P.* 1176 The Buzzard..Invites the feather'd Nimrods of his Race, To hide the thinness of their Flock from Sight, And all together make a seeming, goodly Flight.

† **2.** Probable, likely. *Obs.*

c **1450** *St. Cuthbert* (Surtees) 6517 Sa Eata, it is semand, Was þan bischop of haly eland. **1655** EARL ORRERY *Parthenissa* Pref. A 2, And where I have found any contradictions..I have gone according to the seeming'st Truth.

3. Apparent to the senses or to the mind, as distinct from what *is*.

1340 HAMPOLE *Pr. Consc.* 5290 Þis taken, als I trowe, sal noght be þe sam cros, ne þe sam tre,..Bot a taken of þat cros semande. *a* **1400–50** *Wars Alex.* 1252 Sa stithe a steuyn in þe stoure of stedis & ellis, As it was semand to siȝt as all þe soyle trymbled. *a* **1557** *Tottel's Misc.* (Arb.) 215 Oft craft can cause the man to make a semyng show Of hart with dolour all distreined, where griefe did neuer grow. **1653** H. MORE *Antid. Ath.* II. Philos. Writ. (1712) 11 The seeming Ashes may be no Ashes. **1700** DRYDEN *Sigism. & Guisc.* 46 A seeming Widow, and a secret Bride. **1766** GOLDSM. *Vic. W.* xix, Miss Wilmot's reception [of him] was mixed with seeming neglect, and yet I could perceive she acted a studied part. **1857** H. MILLER *Test. Rocks* v. 194 That his seeming argument was no argument, but merely a sort of verbal play. **1875** JOWETT *Plato* (ed. 2) I. 263 He asserts the seeming paradox that [etc.] **1883** R. W. DIXON *Mano* II. iv. 74 We came upon him riding loftily, Clad in his knightly arms without disguise, No seeming pilgrim now.

b. In comb. with sbs.

1598 MARSTON *Pygmal. Sat.* ii. 144 Diomedes Iades were not so bestiall As this same seeming-saint, vile Canniball. **1654** W. STREAT (*title*) The dividing of the Hooff: or, Seeming-Contradictions throughout sacred Scriptures. **1870** LOWELL *Among my Bks.* Ser. I. iii. 163 Those astronomic wonders of poise and counterpoise, of planetary law and cometary seeming exception, in his metres.

4. Used adverbially with other adjectives to form hyphened compounds with the sense of 'having a (specified) appearance'.

In some of these formations the writers may have intended *seeming* as pres. pple. with the second adj. as predicate, though such a use would be grammatically abnormal.

[*c* **1400** tr. *Secreta Secret., Gov. Lordsh.* xii. 55 And if he oonly shew hym semand religious, and yn his werkys be an euyl doere..he shal be refusyd of god and of þe folk despysed.] **1590** SPENSER *F.Q.* I. ii. 27 With chaunge of cheare the seeming simple maid Let fall her eyen. *a* **1641** BP. MOUNTAGU *Acts & Mon.* (1642) 401 As commonly all seeming-religious Hypocrites bee, they are charged to have beene devourers of Orphans goods. **1742** YOUNG *Nt. Th.* IX. 1113 What knots are ty'd! How soon are they dissolv'd, And set the seeming marry'd planets free! **1812** BYRON *Ch. Har.* II. xxxiii, Little knew she that seeming marble heart,..Was not unskilful in the spoiler's art. **1817** SHELLEY *Rev. Islam* III. x, Whilst I had watched the motions of the crew With seeming-careless glance. **1850** TENNYSON *In Mem.* xlviii, But blame not thou the winds that make The seeming-wanton ripple break. **1899** MACKAIL *W. Morris* II. 205 He was continually seeking refuge from it in dreams of some settled and seeming-changeless order.

seemingly (ˈsiːmɪŋlɪ), *adv.* Also 5 semeinly, 6 semyngly. [f. SEEMING *ppl. a.* + -LY².]

1. Fittingly, becomingly. Now somewhat *rare*.

1483 *Cath. Angl.* 329/1 Semeinly, *decenter, conuenienter, eleganter, & cetera.* *c* **1630** RISDON *Surv. Devon* § 112 (1810) 117 The tenant..is to come seemingly apparelled. **1702** *Lond. Gaz.* No. 3804/2 The Temporal Lords, did their Homage, and seemingly kissed Her Majesty's Left Cheek. **1883** *Harper's Mag.* Dec. 93/1 Try and bear yourselves more seemingly.

2. To external appearance, apparently. (Distinguished from but not necessarily opposed to *really*.)

1598 SHAKS. *Merry W.* IV. vi. 33 To this her Mothers plot She seemingly obedient likewise hath Made promise to the Doctor. **1634** SIR T. HERBERT *Trav.* 196 One of these seemingly deuout *Abdals*. **1692** R. L'ESTRANGE *Fables* xi. 10 Now the City-Dame was so well bred, as seemingly to take All in Good Part. **1736** BUTLER *Anal.* I. vii. Wks. 1874 I. 132 Things seemingly the most insignificant imaginable. **1802** MAR. EDGEWORTH *Moral T., Angelina* ii, A young lady seemingly not more than sixteen years of age. **1868** E. EDWARDS *Ralegh* I. vii. 109 A combination of circumstances seemingly more favourable to the enterprise..could scarcely be looked for. **1893** *Law Times* XCV. 28/1 The Director..managed to get the better of the Lord Chief Justice..and is seemingly desirous that the facts of the victory should be fully known.

† **b.** ? *nonce-use.* ? So as to seem real. *Obs.*

1602 *Kyd's Sp. Trag.* III. xii. A. 123 Canst paint a dolefull crie? *Paint.* Seemingly, sir.

3. So far as it appears from the evidence; so far as one can judge by circumstances.

1715 DE FOE *Fam. Instruct.* (1841) I. 62 Well, it must be done, however difficult, however seemingly fruitless, and to no purpose. **1748** HARTLEY *Observ. Man* II. iii. §6. 293 Where they are opposite, or seemingly so, we may suppose them to..restrain one another. **1856** FROUDE *Hist. Eng.* (1858) II. ix. 307 Through French influence the rupture with Scotland had been seemingly healed. **1875** JOWETT *Plato* (ed. 2) I. 434 The seemingly true belief that God is our guardian. **1892** *Speaker* 3 Sept. 279/1 The prisoners..were cheered on leaving, but seemingly only by their own *claque*.

b. In combinations (usually hyphened) with adjectives in the sense of 'apparently ——'.

1725 *Pope's Odyss.* v. Notes II. 49 This seemingly-trifling circumstance is an instance. **1753** RICHARDSON *Grandison* (1754) III. xviii. 158 What excellence shines out in full lustre, on this unaffected and seemingly little occasion. **1853** KINGSLEY *Hypatia* viii, More than once some..question of his had..opened up ugly depths of doubt, even on the most seemingly-palpable certainties.

c. *parenthetically*. As it seems.

1702 S. PARKER tr. *Cicero's De Finibus* v. 285 Not that there is any Thing Material wherein they vary or disagree, tho' seemingly they may teach us inconsistent Lessons. **1828** SCOTT *F.M. Perth* xi, The contending parties, seemingly, were partizans of Douglas, known by the cognizance of the Bloody Heart, and citizens of the town of Perth. **1863** MRS. WHITNEY *Faith Gartney's Girlh.* xxix, Some women..have done this, and, seemingly, done well.

seemingness (ˈsiːmɪŋnɪs). [f. SEEMING *ppl. a.* + -NESS.]

1. The quality or fact of seeming to be something; unreal pretence; plausibility.

1640 G. ABBOTT *Job Paraphr.* vi. 21, I put my confidence in you, because of your former seemingnesse. **1644** DIGBY *Nat. Bodies* vi. §7. 45 Were it not for the authority of Aristotle and of his learned followers, that presseth vs on the one side, and for the seemingnesse of those reasons we haue already mentioned, which persuadeth vs on the other side. **1647** TRAPP *Comm. Matt.* vi. 16 There is a great deal of seemingnesse, and much counterfeit grace abroad. **1830** LAMB *Let. to Rev. J. Gillman* 8 Mar., In the silken seemingness of his nature there is that which offends me.

2. Semblance, seeming existence or presence.

1656 *Disc. Auxil. Beauty* 91 Under the seemingnesse or appearance of evill. **1702** SHERBURNE *Seneca's Trag.* Ep. Ded. A 3 b, I must confess, there is not a little Seemingness of Incongruity between [etc.]. **1851** MEREDITH *Poems, Sleeping City* 14 The seemingness of Death, not dead.

seemlaunte, variant of SEMBLANT *Obs.*

ˈseemless, *a.* *Obs.* exc. *arch.* Also 6–7 se(e)meless, (7 seeme-les). [f. SEEM *v.*² (assumed to be the source of SEEMLY *a.*) + -LESS.] Unseemly; shameful; unfitting.

1596 SPENSER *F.Q.* v. ii. 25 Thence he her drew By the faire lockes, and fowly did array..That Artegall him selfe her seemelesse plight did rew. **1609** B. JONSON *Case is Altered* III. vii, And here I vow, Neuer to dreame of seemeles amorous toyes. **1615** CHAPMAN *Odyss.* xx. 397 The Prince..did his Father place..in a Seate Seemelesse, and abiect. **1855** SINGLETON *Virgil* II. 116 Maimed with seemless wound [L. *inhonesto vulnere*].

seemlihead (ˈsiːmlɪhɛd). *arch.* (written *-hed* after Spenser). [f. SEEMLY *a.* + -HEAD.] The condition of being seemly; seemliness.

? *a* **1366** CHAUCER *Rom. Rose* 777 Ful fetis damiselles two, Right yonge, and fulle of semlihede. *Ibid.* 1130 A yong man ful of semelihede. *c* **1403** CLANVOWE *Cuckow & Night.* 157 Lowliheed, and trewe companye, Seemliheed, largesse, and curtesye. **1596** SPENSER *F.Q.* IV. viii. 14 She..by his persons secret seemlyhed Well weend that he had beene some man of place. **1818** KEATS *Endym.* IV. 950 And then his tongue with sober seemlihed Gave utterance.

† **ˈseemlihood.** *Obs. rare*⁻¹. In 5 semely hode. [f. SEEMLY *a.* + -HOOD.] = SEEMLIHEAD.

c **1440** *Partonope* 6274 A gentyllmaun whens euer ye come Be youre semely hode a man may deme.

† **ˈseemlily**, *adv.* *Obs.* Forms: 4 semlyly, semblely, 5 semlely, semelily, 6 semelely, 7 seemlily. [f. SEEMLY *a.* + -LY².] In a seemly manner; so as to present a seemly appearance; pleasingly, handsomely, nobly, elegantly.

13.. *Gaw. & Gr. Knt.* 622 He braydez hit by þe bauderyk, aboute þe hals kestes, þat bisemed þe segge semlyly fayre. *c* **1400** *Sc. Trojan War* (Horstm.) I. 96 Thane to þe messenger ine hye He turnyt ande saide hyme semblely [etc.]. *c* **1420** *Anturs of Arth.* 24 (Thornton MS.) Hir sadille..Semelely sewede with sylke. **1567** DRANT *Horace Ep.* I. xviii. F v, Who can then the more semelily Thy manlike armoure weelde? **1615** W. BEDWELL *Moham. Impost.* I. §6 He is also that word or soule which created the heauens vaultwise most seemlily.

seemliness (ˈsiːmlɪnɪs). Forms: see the adj. [f. SEEMLY *a.* + -NESS.]

† **1.** Pleasing appearance; elegance or handsomeness of form (of the body or its parts); gracefulness, attractiveness (of things, actions, etc.). *Obs.*

c **1385** CHAUCER *L.G.W.* 1041 If that god..Wolde han a loue for beute & goodnesse And womanhod & trouthe & semelynesse, Whom schulde he louyn but this lady swete? *c* **1440** *Promp. Parv.* 452/2 Semelynesse, yn syghte, *decencia*. Semelynesse, or comelynesse of schappe, *elegancia*. *c* **1460** J. METHAM *Wks.* 155 He that ys born that day schuld be dysposyd..gretly to be louyd off women for semlynes off persone and beute off face. **1545** ASCHAM *Toxoph.* II. (Arb.) 149 Therfore to drawe easely and vniformely,..vntil you come to the rige or shouldringe of ye head, is best both for profit and semelinesse. **1578** T. PROCTER *Gorg. Gallery* G iv b, In boddy seemelynesse doth shew,..All partes of her doth prayse deserue. **1584** B. R. tr. *Herodotus* II. 108 Yet for the sightly grace and seemelynesse of building, there is none comparable vnto it. *c* **1595** R. CAREW *Excell. Eng. Tongue* in *Camden's Rem.* 43 When substantialnesse combineth with delightfulnesse,..seemelinesse with portlinesse, and currantnesse with stayednesse, how can the language..sound other then most full of sweetnes? **1633** P. FLETCHER *Purple Isl.* VIII. ix, Strip thou their [*sc.* vices'] meretricious seemlinesse,..That we may loath their inward uglinesse.

2. Propriety, becomingness, fitness; decorum in behaviour or demeanour.

1548 UDALL, etc. *Erasm. Par. Matt.* iii. 13–15 Obseruing & marking a meruaylouse semelynes and honesty apperyng in his iyes, in all his countenaunce, & in his maner of going. *c* **1550** N. SMYTH tr. *Herodian* VI. 66 But thadministracion of all affayres..appertained to the women: who endeuored to reduce all thinges to their pristinate semelynes and modesty. **1577** tr. *Bullinger's Decades* II. vii. 188/1 Which thinck..they may vtterly abolish good lawes, and liue against all lawe and seemelinesse [*contra jus & decorum*]. **1627** P. FLETCHER *Locusts* III. xii, The second beast..Comes on the stage, and with great seemelinese Acts his first scenes. **1752** CARTE *Hist. Eng.* III. 95 The dispensation relating only to the affinity between the parties, and not to the publick honesty or seemliness of the marriage. **1803** WORDSW. *Mem. Tour Scot., To Highl. Girl* 36 And seemliness complete, that sways Thy courtesies, about thee plays. *a* **1806** HORSLEY *Serm.* xxi. (1816) II. 189 The natural seemliness of one action and unseemliness of another. **1871** PALGRAVE *Lyr. Poems* 24 But thou art ever equal to thy fate, Robed in all seemliness, lady complete. **1878** BAYNE *Purit. Rev.* iii. 86 He had in view chiefly the rational decoration and seemliness of worship.

† **b.** Something becoming *to*. *Obs. rare*⁻¹.

1577–87 HOLINSHED *Chron.* III. 412/2 Of face..manlike,..in age bald, but so as it was rather a seemelinesse to those his ancient yeares than any disfiguring to his visage.

† **ˈseemlity.** *Obs. rare*⁻¹. In 5 semelyte. [f. SEEMLY *a.* + -TY.] Seemliness.

c **1440** *York Myst.* xxv. 116 He þat is rewler of al right,..kepe ȝou in ȝoure semelyte And all honoure.

seemly (ˈsiːmlɪ), *a.* Forms: *α.* 3–4 semliche, (3 somlich, semlyche, sem(e)like), 3–4 sem(e)li, (3 semele, 3, 5 semle, 4 seemeli), 4 semelich(e, seem(e)lich, 4–5 semlich, 5 semelych, 4–6 semly, 5–6 semelie, (5 cemely, semly, seymely), 4–7 semely, (5–6 -ye), 5–7 seemely, (6 seemlie), 4– seemly. *β.* 4–6 sembly, (4 sembbly, sembli, semblych, 6 seemble). *Compar.* 4 semeliere, semloker, 5 semelyar, 6 seemelyer, 6– seemlier. *Superl.* 4 semelieste, 4–5 sem(e)lokest,

semlyest(e, (semelest, semylyeste), 5 sem(e)liest, sem(e)list, seymliast, 5–6 semelyest, 7 seemelyest, 6– seemliest. [a. ON. *sœmilig-r* (MSw. *sömeleker*, Da. *sømmelig*), f. *sœm-r* becoming: see SEEM *v.*[2] and -LY[1].]

1. Of a person, his figure, etc.: Of a pleasing or goodly appearance, fair, well-formed, handsome, 'proper'. *Obs.* exc. *dial.*

In early use chiefly applied to a person of high rank or lineage. Frequently used alliteratively, as *seemly to see, seemly in* or *to sight.*

α. *a* **1225** *Leg. Kath.* 449 Ah þischene nebscheft & tisemliche schape schaweð wel þæt tu art freo monne foster. *c* **1250** *Gen. & Ex.* 1007 Siðen,..saȝ abraham figures ðre, Sondes semlike kumen fro gode. *a* **1300** *Cursor M.* 18830 Of heght he [Christ] was meteli man,.. And wonder semli was wit-al. *c* **1350** *Libeaus Desc.* 125 Þer nas countesse ne quene So semelich on to sene, þat miȝte be her pere. **13..** *E.E. Allit. P.* B. 816 His [Lot's] two dere doȝterez..wer semly & swete, & swyþe wel arayed. *c* **1386** CHAUCER *Manciple's T.* 15 Therto he was the semelieste man That is or was sith þat the world bigan. *c* **1400** *Sowdone Bab.* 39 A Baron & Kniȝtis ful boold, That roialle were and semly to sene. **1432–50** tr. *Higden* (Rolls) I. 263 That peple is stronge and of semely stature. **1483** CAXTON *Gold. Leg.* 237/1 He sawe an auncient man of noble stature wyth a long berd wyth a semely vysage. *c* **1510** MORE *Picus* Wks. 2/2 He was of feture and shappe semely, and bewteous. **1540** CROMWELL in Merriman *Life & Lett.* (1902) II. 269 She is nothing so Fayre as she hathe bene reportyd, howbeit she is well and semelye. **1548–77** VICARY *Anat.* iii. (1888) 25 The Heire..maketh the forme.. of the head to seeme more seemelyer or beautyfuller. **1596** SPENSER *F.Q.* v. iv. 4 And them beside two seemely damzells stood. **1900** E. PHILLPOTTS in *Pall Mall Mag.* Apr. 436 He was a man of seemly outward parts.

β. *c* **1380** *Sir Ferumb.* 834 Þanne was Olyuer þat sembbly knyȝt al-one among is fon. *Ibid.* 5884 Hure vysage was fair & tretys, Hure body..semblych of stature. **1382** WYCLIF *Gen.* xxiv. 16 Rabecca..a ful sembly damysel, and moost fayr mayden. *Ibid.* *1 Sam.* xvi. 12 Forsothe he was rodi.. and sembli in face. *c* **1470** HENRY *Wallace* IX. 1920 In schuldrys braid was he, Rycht sembly, strang, and lusty for to se. **1513** DOUGLAS *Æneis* VI. XV. 37 A sembly springald, a fayr ȝowng galland, Rycht schaply maid.

†**b.** *absol.* (quasi-*sb.*) A 'seemly' person. *Obs.*

a **1300** *Cursor M.* 13371 Þat gadring þar was ful gret And mani semli sett in sete. *a* **1310** [see SAD *a.* 1]. *c* **1350** *Will. Palerne* 732 But certes þat semly sat so in his hert..þat..a-wai wold it neuer. *c* **1440** *York Myst.* xlvii. 6 And to þat semely schall ȝe saye Off heuene I haue hir chosen quene. *a* **1450** *Le Morte Arth.* 639 Is noon of vs but wold be blithe Suche a semely for to see.

2. Of things: Pleasant (*esp.* to the sight); handsome in appearance; of fine or stately proportion.

a **1310** in Wright *Lyric P.* v. 25 Ase beryl so bryht, Ase saphyr in selver semly on syht. *c* **1320** *Sir Tristr.* 12 Þis semly somers day. **1340–70** *Alex. & Dind.* 115 Þere sai he semliche tres wiþ þe sonne woxe. **1380** CHAUCER *To Rosemounde* 11 Your seemly voys that ye so smal out-twyne. **1387–8** T. USK *Test. Love* Prol. (Skeat) l. 11 This book, that nothing hath of the greet flode of wit ne of semelich colours, is dolven with rude wordes and boystous. **1432–50** tr. *Higden* (Rolls) I. 81 There be trees of so semely stature that vnnethe the altitude of theym may be atteynede by the schote of an arowe. **1563** SACKVILLE *Induct. Mirr. Mag.* ii, The soyle that earst so seemely was to seen. **1585** T. WASHINGTON tr. *Nicholay's Voy.* II. vii. 37 Their gownes.. white or of other seemlie colour. **1615** W. LAWSON *Country Housew. Gard.* (1626) 12 You must therefore plant in such a soile, where you may prouide a conuenient, strong, and seemely fence. *a* **1661** FULLER *Worthies, Chester* (1662) I. 292 He erected a seemly waterwork built Steeplewise..by his own ingenious industry. **1826** E. IRVING *Babylon* I. IV. 294 This seemly fabric which he had built up, of arms, of arts, of elegance,..began to crumble. **1870** ROCK *Textile Fabrics* Introd. 86 From such a prohibition we are not to draw as a conclusion that fustian was at the time a mean material; quite the contrary, it was a seemly textile. **1884** *Manch. Exam.* 18 Sept. 4/6 He..like a skilful architect, builds them into a fair and seemly edifice.

β. *c* **1305** *Land Cokayne* 66 Þer is a cloister fair and liȝt Brod and lang, of sembli siȝt. *c* **1470** HENRY *Wallace* VIII. 1008 A sembly place so fand thai..Quhilk Ramswaith hecht.

3. Of conduct, speech, appearance: Conformable to propriety or good taste; becoming, decorous.

a **1225** *Ancr. R.* 94 Ant forþui hit is riht & somlich [*v.r.* semlich] þæt ancren þes two morhȝiuen habben biuoren oðre. *c* **1380** WYCLIF *Wks.* (1880) 41, I conseile..my freris ..þat þei ben..homly & meke, spekynge of al þingis as it is semely. *c* **1400** *Destr. Troy* 2962 Hit were sittyng for sothe, & semly for wemen, þaire houses to haunt & holde hom with in. **1545** JOYE *Exp. Dan.* vii. 124 A fayer decent semely shewe of vtwarde deuocion. **1579** TOMSON *Calvin's Serm. Tim.* 139/1 That our liues be honest and semely, not dissolute and lawlesse. **1657** J. SMITH *Myst. Rhet. Unvail'd* 70 Such like formes of speaking are used for modesties sake; for it were not so seemly to say..that he is a fool. **1708** J. PHILIPS *Cyder* II. 484 May we..enjoy Our humid Products, and with seemly Draughts Enkindle Mirth. **1785** COWPER *Task* I. 729 It is not seemly, nor of good report, That she is slack in discipline. **1805** WORDSW. *Prelude* III. 398 And over all A healthy sound simplicity should reign, A seemly plainness, name it what you will, Republican or pious. **1817** COLERIDGE '*Blessed are ye that sow*' 72 To be..industrious, useful, and of seemly bearing, are qualities presupposed in the gospel code. **1865** DICKENS *Mut. Fr.* II. xv, Take a little time..to make your eyes seemly [after weeping]. **1871** BLACKIE *Four Phases Mor.* i. 153 It were not seemly in me to follow their example. **1877** J. D. CHAMBERS *Div. Worship* 346 Let the Priest set down the Chalice in front of him in a seemly way.

absol. *a* **1806** HORSLEY *Serm.* xxi. (1816) II. 187 A system of morality in which the formal nature of the moral good should be traced to the original idea of the seemly and the fair.

β. **1554** in Strype *Eccl. Mem.* (1733) III. xvi. 139 For it was not meet nor seemble, that the Bishop being occupied with other weightier Affairs..should debase himself to such petit Functions.

†**4.** Suitable to the person or the occasion; appropriate. Const. *to, for. Obs.*

c **1350** *Will. Palerne* 568, I sayle now in þe see as schip boute mast,..or ani semlyche sayle. *Ibid.* 1882 Þei ete.. boute salt oþer sauce or any semli drynk. **1568** GRAFTON *Chron.* II. 302 He commaunded the Citezens of London to prepare themselues and their Citie, and to make the same seemely and meete to receyue..the French king. **1586** A. DAY *Eng. Secretary* I. (1625) 15 The very lowest margent of paper shall doe no more but beare it, so be it the place be seemely for the same. **1586** T. B. *La Primaud. Fr. Acad.* I. 623 Artaxerxes said, that it was a great deale more seemlier for the majestie of a king to give, than to take. *c* **1600** SHAKS. *Sonn.* xxii. 6 For all that beauty that doth couer thee, Is but the seemely rayment of my heart, Which in thy brest doth liue. **1601** B. JONSON *Poetaster* IV. vi, And are these seemely companie for thee, Degenerate monster? **1611** BIBLE *Prov.* xix. 10 Delight is not seemely for a foole. **1634** SIR T. HERBERT *Trav.* 146 The heeles [of shoes] shod with thin Iron, and end with small nailes in seemely order.

†**5.** [Influenced by SEEM *v.*[2]]

a. Likely. **b.** Apparent, seeming. *Obs.*

a. *c* **1400** MAUNDEV. (Roxb.) xxxi. 140, I dare noȝt say þat þai ware all verray bodys:..for it es noȝt semely þat so grete a multitude of folk schuld verrayly hafe bene deed so resch withouten..corrupcioun. *c* **1425** *Cursor M.* 9781 If aungel had take monnes kynde þenne were he leþyere þen he was ere..And semelyer was for to doun falle. **1496** *Dives & Pauper* (1534) II. xiii. 98 b, He sholde not haue made that oth..for it was semely, that moche dysease myght come therof, yf it were kepte.

b. *c* **1440** LOVE *Bonavent. Mirr.* viii. (Gibbs MS.),[Christ giving us example that] we schulden not go fro þe ground of trew mekenesse by colour of any semelych profyte or gode [L. *apparentis boni*]. **1800** SOUTHEY *Thalaba* II. 370 And still the wily man With seemly kindness, to the eager Boy Directs his winning tale.

seemly ('siːmlɪ), *adv.* Forms: **3 semelike, semele, semili, 4 sem(e)liche, semeli, (semeely), 4–5 sem(y)ly, 4–6 semely, 5 cemely, (6 semelie, -ye, 7 seemlie), 6– seemly.** [a. ON. *sœmiliga* (Icel. *sæmiliga*, MSw. *sömelika*), f. *sœm-r*: see prec. and -LY[2].]

1. In a pleasing manner; so as to present a fair, handsome, or stately appearance. Now *arch.*

c **1250** *Gen. & Ex.* 1504 Ðe firme sune at offrende sel Was wune ben scrid semelike and wel. *a* **1300** *Cursor M.* 8322 It sal be precius and prude, þe werc he [Solomon] sal sua semele scrude. *Ibid.* 9880 A castell bath god and gett, Strenthed well and semili sett. *c* **1350** *Will. Palerne* 1432 Þemperour ful semly seide to hem þanne [etc.]. **13..** *E.E. Allit. P.* B. 1442 Þe iueles..Bi þe syde of þe sale were semely arayed. *c* **1386** CHAUCER *Prol.* 123 Ful weel she soong the seruice dyuyne, Entuned in hir nose ful semely. *Ibid.* 151 Ful semyly hir wympul pynched was. *c* **1400** tr. *Secreta Secret., Gov. Lordsh.* 73 A spouse semly dighte of ryche ornements. **1470–85** MALORY *Arthur* XVII. vii. 699 Gyrdels which were semely wroughte with golden thredys. **1526** *Pilgr. Perf.* (W. de W. 1531) 257 Those blessed lockes of heare and beerd, whiche in lyfe moost semely did become that graacyous heed and face. **1553** BRENDE *Q. Curtius* D d vj, Whiche beyng menne of goodly personages, rydde in wagons semely appareyled. **1671** MILTON *P.R.* II. 299 A man before him stood, Not rustic as before, but seemlier clad. **1876** SWINBURNE *Erechtheus* 379 Look on this child, how young of years, how sweet;..her eyes How seemly smiling.

2. Fittingly, appropriately; decently, becomingly.

c **1320** R. BRUNNE *Medit.* 387 Þat mannes soule, þat lyþ yn helle, May nat semely to blys be broȝt, But þey with hys blode be fyrst oute boȝt. **1387** TREVISA *Higden* (Rolls) VIII. 87 Þe bisshop of Durham, þat schulde more skilfulliche and semeliche occupie hym self in Goddis service þan in þe kynges service. *c* **1440** *Astron. Cal.* (MS. Ashm. 391), Þan meve þe cercle semyly aboute þ[t] hath þe moonþes and signes writen in hym. **1552** *Godly Prayers* in *Psalter* (1560) N ij, That..we maye..decently and semely walke (as in the day time) beyng pure and cleane from the workes of darkenes. **1593** *Wills & Inv. N.C.* (Surtees 1860) 218 My bodye I commytt to the earth, to be semelye buried at the discretion of my frendes. **1594** R. ASHLEY tr. *Loys le Roy* 94 For we haue..their domestical, and familiar affaires, better, and seemlier ordered. **1643** MILTON *Divorce* II. x. Wks. 1851 IV. 88 Nor is it seemly or piously attributed to the justice of God,..that [etc.]. **1725** POPE *Odyss.* XIX. 21 These swarthy arms among the covert stores Are seemlier hid. **1875** MORRIS *Æn.* XII. 210 E'en as this sceptre..A tree once, but the craftsman's hand hath wrapped it seemly now With brass about.

†**3.** In a moderate degree, 'fairly'. *Obs. rare.*

c **1460** J. METHAM *Wks.* 90 And yff this lyne be semely longe and pase noght the hylle off the schewyng ffynger, yt sygnyfyith hardynes. **1647** N. BACON *Disc. Govt. Eng.* I. xlvii. (1682) 79 Henry the first..recontinued the liberty of publick Consultations, and yet maintained his Dignity and Honour seemly well.

4. Apparently, seemingly. *dial.*

1821 CLARE *Vill. Minstr.* II. 77 The shrieking bat, Who, seemly pleas'd to mock our treacherous view, Would even swoop and touch us as he flew. **1901** ELEANOR G. HAYDEN *Trav. round Village* i. 16 We yeard a girt hollerin' as comed simly from unner our fit.

seen (siːn), *ppl. a.* [pa. pple. of SEE *v.*]

1. In senses of the verb. Now *rare* exc. in antithesis with *unseen* (cf. SENE *a.*).

1434 MISYN *Fire of Love* II. xii. 129 Als we in dyrknes standand seys noþinge, so in contemplacione þat vnsemly lightis þe saule, noo seyn light we see. **1561** NORTON & SACKV. *Gorboduc* II. ii. 9 Ne bring I to my lorde reported tales Without the ground of seen and searched trouth. **1585** JAS. I *Ess. Poesie* vii. (Arb.) 66 It is best that ȝe inuent ȝour awin subiect, ȝour self, and not to compose of sene subiectis. *a* **1586** SIDNEY *Arcadia* II. (Sommer) 127 By a more felt then seene maner of proceeding. **1615** CHAPMAN *Odyss.* XX. 291 Philætius tooke note in his repaire, Of seene Vlysses. **1636** HEYWOOD *Chall. Beauty* II. C 3, And should I not in unseene Vertue strive To equall that seene beautie you so prayse. *Ibid.* IV. F 4, Let not thy seene griefe please him. **1837** CARLYLE *Fr. Rev.* I. VI. i, Sanctioned..if not by a seen Deity, then by an unseen one. **1858** T. GUTHRIE *Christ & Inher. Saints* (1860) 162 They cannot stand *seen* death.

b. *absol.* That which is seen or visible as contrasted with that which is unseen or invisible.

1848 LOWELL *Biglow P.* Ser. I. (1859) p. xxxiv [Burlesque of Carlyle], He shall paint the Seen, since the Unseen will not sit to him. **1897** F. THOMPSON *New Poems* 61 Man! swinging-wicket set Between The Unseen and Seen.

†**c.** Provided, furnished. (Cf. *beseen* s.v. BESEE *v.* 9.) *Obs. rare.*

c **1450** *Merlin* xiv. 204 A-noon thei lighten and yede vp in-to the halle that was right feire and welle seyn.

2. *to be* (*well, ill,* etc.) *seen*: to be (well, ill, etc.) versed *in* some art or science.

Very common in the 16th and 17th centuries. Now *arch.*

1528 TINDALE *Obed. Chr. Man* Pref. 16 b, A man must fyrst be well sene in Aristoteles yer he can vnderstonde the scripture saye they. **1528** ROY *Rede me* (Arb.) 49 In sondrye sciences he is sene. **1561** T. HOBY tr. *Castiglione's Courtyer* (1900) 369 To be meanly seene in the play at Chestes, and not overcounninge. *a* **1577** SIR T. SMITH *Commw. Eng.* II. xxix. (1633) 177 A man seene in the Lawes of the Realme. **1594** CAREW *Huarte's Exam. Wits* (1616) 311 They are slenderly seene in naturall Phylosophie. **1596** SHAKS. *Tam. Shr.* I. ii. 134 A schoole-master Well seene in Musicke. *a* **1612** HARINGTON *St. Church* (1653) 174 A man well spoken, properly seen in Languages. **1620** E. BLOUNT *Horæ Subs.* 286 Men of mature yeares, and seene in the warres. **1759** BP. HURD *Moral Dialogues* iv. 165 *note*, This was frank. But Sir James Melvil was too well seen in courts to have used this language, if he had not understood it would be welcome. **1786** BURNS *Ep. to J. Smith* viii, There's ither Poets, much your betters, Far seen in Greek, deep men o' letters. **1886** A. LANG in *Longman's Mag.* Feb. 443 The bibliophile..was extremely well seen in the naughty little novels of the eighteenth century.

†**b.** rarely with other prepositions. *Obs.*

1583 STOCKER *Civ. Warres Lowe C.* III. 124 b, There were some, who thought themselues very well seene about these field bankes. **1650** H. MORE *Observ.* in *Enthus. Tri.*, etc. (1656) 81 This new Writer is the onely man, that is both deeply seen into the Center of Nature, and as willing also to publish these spiritual mysteries.

†**c.** Hence without *const. Obs.*

1577–87 HOLINSHED *Chron.* III. 1254/1 Better seene antiquaries than my selfe.

†**seen**, quasi-*prep.* and quasi-*conj.* *Obs.* [pa. pple. of SEE *v.*, in absolute construction with following sb. Cf. F. *vu.*] **a.** quasi-*prep.* Seeing, considering. **b.** quasi-*conj.* (More fully *seen that.*) Seeing, considering, since, inasmuch as.

a. **1470–85** MALORY *Arthur* V. viii. 175 For his [Arthur's] myght and prowesse is most to be doubted seen the noble kynges and grete multytude of knyghtes of the round table. **1489** CAXTON *Faytes of A.* I. i. 1 To put it forth without other thyng seen the lytylhed of my persone. **1559** *Mirr. Mag., Earl Salisb.* ii, But seen the date so doubtful and so short,.. I can not chuse but prayse the princely minde That preaseth for it.

b. **1484** CAXTON *Curiall* 8 Seen that it is [not] a thyng more free in a man than to lyue naturelly. *c* **1500** *Melusine* xix. (1891) 107 Seen & considered that the Cite is strong. *a* **1533** LD. BERNERS *Huon* ix. 26, I am sory therof, but seen it is done, yf [etc.]. **1577–86** HOLINSHED *Hist. Scot.* 309/1 Therefore seene you thinke it not gude to inuade, my councell is that we campe still on the bordures.

seende, obs. form of SEND *v.*

seene, var. SENE *a.*, SENE *sb.*[2], synod *Obs.*

seene, seenie, obs. ff. SENNA, SENVY, mustard.

seenil, -le, variant forms of SENDLE *adv.*

se'ennight, variant of SENNIGHT.

seens, obs. form of SINCE *adv.*

1553 *Respublica* II. ii. 532 And behold where he is returned againe seens.

seeny, obs. variant of SENVY, mustard.

seep (siːp), *sb.* Also **seip.** [Related to SEEP *v.* (Perh. repr. OE. *sipe*: see SIPE, SIP *sbs.*)]

1. Moisture that drips or oozes out. *dial.*

1825 JAMIESON *Suppl., Sipage,..Seip*, leakage. **1834** *Brit. Husb.* I. 414 In Ireland..every peasant..bottoms his dung-stead with stuff drawn from the bogs, that he may thus preserve the seep or gooding, as he terms it, of his stable-manure. **1871** P. H. WADDELL *Psalms* Pref. 1 Thar's the saft seep o' the cluds an' the dour chirt o' the cranreuch.

2. A small spring; *U.S.*, a place where petroleum oozes out slowly (Webster, 1911).

1824 MACTAGGART *Gallovid. Encycl.* 424 *Seeps*, sypes or sykes, trivial springs. **1902** *Nature* 4 Dec. 113/1 At Comanche Spring, a small 'seep',..the limestone bluffs have been covered in a number of places with rude paintings of characteristic Indian design. **1903** *Bull. U.S. Geol. Survey* No. 212. 97 In this well small seeps or pockets of petroleum were found at several depths. **1966** *McGraw-Hill Encycl. Sci. & Technol.* X. 60/2 Almost without exception, seeps are at topographically low spots where water has accumulated. Oil..rises to the surface of the water, covering it with an iridescent film. **1972** *Science* 16 June 1257/2 The existence of submarine seeps is often mentioned in discussions of oil pollution.

3. A sip of liquor. *dial.*
1897 LD. E. HAMILTON *Outlaws* xvii. 187 I've mair than a mind to rin doun..and see if I canna light on a stolum o' bread and a seip o' milk maybe. **1901** R. BUCHANAN *Poems* 157 (E.D.D.) Anither bit seep, wi' her han' below the glass in case o' ony scaling.

seep (siːp), *v.* Formerly *dial.* and *U.S.* Also seap, seip. [Perh. repr. OE. *sipian*: see SIPE *v.*] *intr.* To ooze, drip, trickle: = SIPE *v.* Also *fig.*
1790 A. WILSON *Ep. to Brother Pedlar* Poet. Wks. 173 Rain seeps through the thack. **1818** SCOTT *Hrt. Midl.* xvii, That canna hinder the bluid seiping through. **1882** CABLE *Dr. Sevier* xv, Water seeps up through the side-walks. **1922** H. CRANE *Let.* 6 May (1965) 85 A new literary magazine.., *Secession*, which is (first number) just seeping into this country. **1931** W. G. MCADOO *Crowded Years* xviii. 284 The..emotions generated by the European struggle seeped into American thought. **1942** *R.A.F. Jrnl.* 13 June 13 The Commandos had been part of the British Army for about eight months before they seeped into print. **1955** A. L. ROWSE *Expansion Elizabethan England* iv. 141 In 1585 a plan for peopling Munster was drawn up... Meanwhile the Irish came seeping back. *a* **1974** R. CROSSMAN *Diaries* (1976) II. 453 One thing I learnt from my brief visit was how well-informed the Transport House staff are about internal Cabinet affairs and how they seep with anti-Government gossip.
Hence **'seeping** *ppl. a.*
1927 M. EIKER *Over Boat-Side* xi. 161 The nagging, monotonous, unessential, seeping harassments that sap a man of achievement.

seep, obs. form of SHEEP.

seepage ('siːpɪdʒ). orig. *Sc.* and *U.S.* Also seipage, sepage. [f. SEEP *v.* + -AGE. Cf. SIPAGE.]
1. Percolation or oozing of water or fluid; leakage; *spec.* the slow movement of water into or out of the ground (as distinct from percolation through it); the slow movement of water through the ground under the action of gravity. Also, that which oozes.
1825 JAMIESON *Suppl.*, *Sipage, Seipage*,..leakage. **1874** RAYMOND *6th Rep. Mines* 324 To allow for evaporation and seepage. **1892** GUNTER *Miss Divid.* (1893) 190 There is no seepage at this season, and we are way above the water level. **1913** V. B. LEWES *Oil Fuel* 61 The surface indications, apart from seepages of oil, escape of natural gas from the soil, [etc.]..are practically nil. **1923** *U.S. Geol. Survey Water-Supply Paper* No. 494. 43 Seepage may be divided..into influent seepage..and effluent seepage. **1950** *N.Z. Jrnl. Agric.* June 559/2 Placing concrete 'seep collars' round the pipe reduces the possibility of seepage. **1967** R. C. WARD *Princ. Hydrol.* viii. 311 Most of the rainfall which percolates through the soil layer to the underlying groundwater will eventually reach the main stream channels as groundwater runoff (sometimes referred to as..effluent seepage). **1974** *Daily Tel.* 4 Apr. 17 An extensive seepage of fuel oil from a fractured feed pipe. **1976** RAUDKIVI & CALLANDER *Analysis Groundwater Flow* i. 1 The motion of groundwater can be subdivided as follows: seepage; capillary rise and capillary flow; percolation, which occurs..under the action of a hydraulic gradient; turbulent groundwater flow.
fig. **1883** CABLE *Old Creole Days* (Edinb. ed.) 104 The Anglo-American flood..had thus far been felt only as slippery seepage which made the Creole tremble for his footing. **1952** *Time* 14 Apr. 17/2 *Seepage* (n.), small net decrease in circulation, resulting from temporary suspension of subscriptions. (Opposite of *creepage*.) **1961** L. MUMFORD *City in History* x. 285 The 'law of cultural seepage': the making of innovations by a favored minority and their slow infiltration..into the lower economic ranks. **1976** *National Observer* (U.S.) 17 July 3/1 So far the seepage has had minimal effect on the multibillion-dollar Social Security system.
2. *attrib.*, as ***seepage flow, loss, spring, water, well***; **seepage lake**, a lake that loses water chiefly by seepage into the ground containing it.
1939 A. K. LOBECK *Geomorphology* v. 159 Run-off.. occurs in two ways: (*a*) as surface run-off..; and (*b*) as ground-water run-off,..often called seepage flow. **1976** RAUDKIVI & CALLANDER *Analysis Groundwater Flow* i. 2 This movement is complicated by the presence of ground air, most of which is expelled from the ground or dissolved in the seepage flow. **1934** *Ecol. Monogr.* IV. 441 These lakes may be classified into..those with outlets and those without them... The movement of water through lakes of the second type is entirely under ground and they are named seepage lakes. **1975** R. G. WETZEL *Limnology* iv. 40 In seepage lakes the lake seal is..likely to be effective over much of the deeper portions of the basin. **1902** *U.S. Geol. Survey Water-Supply & Irrigation Paper* No. 67. 42 C. E. Grunsky has measured the seepage loss in King River and the Fresno canal. **1937** C. F. TOLMAN *Ground Water* vii. 169 Seepage loss from this river is less than 5 per cent of the total flow. **1908** T. C. HOPKINS *Elem. Physical Geogr.* ii. 60 Sometimes..the water..seeps or trickles out along the line of outcrop of the layer in sufficient quantities to keep the surface wet,..forming a swamp or bog on the hillside. This is called a seepage spring. **1964** G. B. SCHALLER *Year of Gorilla* (1965) x. 264 We came upon six elephants pawing the soil of a seepage spring. **1876** RAUDKIVI & CALLANDER *Analysis Groundwater Flow* i. 1 The capacity of the soil to hold suspended capillary water and water in the attached films is called field capacity and it is the excess over the field capacity which is free to travel downwards as gravity or seepage water. **1883** *Century Mag.* July 421/2 Rills of seepage water wet the road. **1969** N. W. PARSONS *Upon Sagebrush Harp* xviii. 103 Later that winter the farm papers began to tell of farm dugouts and seepage wells for the well-less prairie.

seepy ('siːpɪ), *a. U.S.* [f. SEEP *v.* + -Y.] (See quot.)
1860 BARTLETT *Dict. Amer.* (ed. 3), *Seepy*, seepy land is land under cultivation that is not well drained.

seer[1] (sɪə(r), in sense 1 also 'siːə(r)). Forms: 4 seere, 5 scere, 5–6 sear, 6 seear, 7 seare, 4– seer. [f. SEE *v.* + -ER[1]. Cf. G. *seher.*]
1. a. *gen.* One who sees. *rare.* † ***seldom seer***, one who sees seldom. Cf. SEE-ER.
c **1425** *Found. St. Bartholomew's* (E.E.T.S.) 59 A certeyne childe that hadde lost hys sight..receyued hit ageyne. And he, seygne with othir seers the mercy of God..gretly he magnyfied and prechid. *c* **1440** *Jacob's Well* 102 Þanne alle þe scerys weryn astonyed. **1562** A. BROOKE *Romeus & Iuliet* 1070 And seemely grace that wonted so to glad the seers sight. **1656** JER. TAYLOR *Let. to Evelyn* 16 Apr., Strangers & seldome seers feel the beauty of them more than you who dwell with them. **1701** G. STANHOPE *Augustine's Medit.* I. xiii. (1720) 25 God, the searcher and seer of Hearts. **1736** BUTLER *Anal.* I. i. 22 His Eyes are the Seers or his Feet the Movers. **1833** LAMB *Elia* Ser. II. *Productions Mod. Art*, Or what associating league to the imagination can there be between the seers and the seers not, of a presential miracle? **1873** M. ARNOLD *Lit. & Dogma* (1876) 376 Seer of the vision of peace, that yet couldst not see the things which belong unto thy peace.
b. Comb. ***seer-off***: cf. SEE *v.* 7b. (*nonce-use.*)
1909 MAX BEERBOHM *Yet Again* 25 Giving the date of their departure, and a description by which the seer-off can identify them on the platform.
2. One to whom divine revelations are made in visions. In mod. use occas. *transf.*, applied to a person gifted with profound spiritual insight.
Originally rendering L. *videns* (Vulg.), Gr. βλέπων (LXX), Heb. *rōēh*, said in 1 Sam. ix. to have been an earlier synonym of *prophet*.
1382 WYCLIF *1 Kings* ix. 9 Cometh, and goo we to the seer. **1526** *Pilgr. Perf.* (W. de W. 1531) 216 b, And therfore (sayth scripture) they that now be called prophetes, in olde tyme were called seers. **1667** MILTON *P.L.* XII. 553 How soon hath thy prediction, seer blest, Measur'd this transient world. **1718** POPE *Iliad* I. 93 That sacred Seer whose comprehensive View The past, the present, and the future knew. **1835** THIRLWALL *Greece* I. iv. 111 The king..sought the aid of the seer Melampus. **1884** *Contemp. Rev.* Mar. 311 The admiration..for Maurice as a thinker and seer.
attrib. **1844** MRS. BROWNING *Sounds* iii. 6 The seer-saint of Patmos. **1851** CARLYLE *Sterling* II. vi. (1872) 137 Here actually is a real seer-glance..of an eye that is human.
3. A magician; one who has the power of second sight. Also a crystal-gazer, a scryer.
1661 'MONTELION' *Don Juan Lamberto* II. xi. N 4 b, Now as soon as Pacolet the Dwarf espyed him [the Necromancer]; Quoth he unto the Seer [etc.]. **1691** WOOD *Ath. Oxon.* I. 244 Dee..appointed his Friend Kelley to be his Seer or Skryer or Speculator, that is to take notice what the spirits did. **1763** 'THEOPHILUS INSULANUS' *Second Sight* 78 A number of Seers whose predictions have exactly tallied with circumstances of time and place. **1889** *Proc. Soc. Psych. Research* XIV. 502 The seer in this case was a girl,..whose visions were perceived by means of a glass of water.
†4. An overseer; an inspector. *Obs.*
1498 *Reg. Privy Seal Scot.* I. 28/1 Settar and sear of skinnys within the said burgh. **1604** *Stirling Burgh Rec.* (1887) I. 111 James Short and Duncane Patersoun to be seares of the wark.
5. Comb. ***seerlike*** adj.; **seercraft**, the prophetic art.
1883 R. C. JEBB *Sophocles* I. 139 Thus did the messages of seer-craft [*Oedipus Tyrannus* 723 φῆμαι μαντικαί] map out the future. **1913** G. MURRAY tr. *Euripides' Rhesus* 6 Sage and prophet, learned in the way of seercraft. **1849** J. G. WHITTIER *Proem* in *Poems* p. iv, Nor mine the seer-like power to show The secrets of the heart and mind. **1975** *New Yorker* 21 Apr. 96/2 One indication of the seer-like quality of these underwriting judgments can be glimpsed in the Continental Insurance underwriters' manual concerning the accident probabilities of drivers.
Hence **'seerhood.**
1884 M. BOOLE in *Jrnl. Educ.* 1 Sept. 344 Certain individuals have had a special tendency to inspirations of sudden perception of new truth... It is variously called Intuition, Genius, or Seerhood.

‖**seer**[2] (sɪə(r)). *Anglo-Ind.* Forms: 7 ceer, sear, seere, sera, serre, 9 ser (*erron.* sir), 8– seer. *Pl.* seer, seers. [Hindi *ser.*] A denomination of weight varying in different parts of India from over 3 lb. to 8 ounces. In districts under British rule it was officially equal to a kilogramme, or 2·2 lb. avoirdupois. Also used as a measure of capacity; the official regulation (see quot. 1871) made it equal to a litre, or 1·76 pint.
1618 in Foster *Eng. Factories Ind.* (1906) 47, 52½ tole make a seere of 30 pices. **1662** J. DAVIES tr. *Mandelslo's Trav.* 85 There is but one kind of weight all over the Kingdome of Guzuratta, which they call Maon,..which weighs fourty Ceers, and makes thirty pounds and a half. **1698** FRYER *Acc. E. India & P.* 209, 1 Cattee is $2\frac{1}{16}$ Sear. **1787** W. CHAMBERS tr. *Short Acc. Marratta St.* 30 Rice..is sold for ten or twelve Seer for a Rupee. **1816** 'QUIZ' *Grand Master* VIII. 217 His master had not one Fanam, To purchase half a seer of gram. **1819** F. HAMILTON *Nepal* 216, 72 Paises = 1 Ser = lb. avoirdupois 1·666. **1842** VIGNE *Trav. Kashmir* I. 196 The ser at Lodiana is equal to about 2 lbs. English. **1845** STOCQUELER *Brit. India* (1854) 209 A *seer* (a full quart) of the best [rose-water] may be obtained for eight *annas*. **1849** EASTWICK *Dry Leaves* 33 He refused the cash, and bartered his milk to us for a sir of rice. **1871** *Indian Weights*, etc. *Act* in *Unrepealed Gen. Acts* (1876) II. 1426 The units..shall be —for weights, the said ser [previously prescribed to be equal to the French Kilogramme des Archives]; for measures of capacity, a measure containing one such ser of water at its maximum density, weighed in a vacuum. **1902** *Man* II. 60 Bringing with him one and a quarter seer of rice.

seer(e, variant forms of SERE *sb.*[1], SERE *a.*

seer: see SEIR-FISH, SEER-FISH.

'seeress. [f. SEER[1] + -ESS.] A female seer.
1845 MRS. CROWE *Kerner's Seeress of Prevorst* 330 Last days and death of the Seeress. **1897** WATTS-DUNTON *Aylwin* I. vi, Fenella Stanley seems in her later life to have set up as a positive seeress.

seer-fish: see SEIR-FISH.

seerge, obs. form of SEARCH *v.*, SERGE.

seering, variant of CERING *vbl. sb.*
1572 in Feuillerat *Revels Q. Eliz.* (1908) 158 For seering Candell vi lb.

seerou, variant of SEROW.

‖**seerpaw** ('sɪəpɔː). *Indian.* Also 7 serapah, serpow, 7–8 serpaw. [Urdū *saropā*, a. Pers. *sarāpā*, head to foot, cap-a-pie, f. *sar, sir* head + *pā* foot.] 'A complete suit, presented as a *khilat* or dress of honour by the sovereign or his representative' (Y.).
1671 tr. *Bernier's Partic. Events Gt. Mogul* II. 4 That which they call Ser-Apah, that is, an habit from head to foot. **1698** FRYER *Acc. E. India & P.* 87 Sir George Oxendine.. had a Collat or Serpaw, a Robe of Honour from Head to Foot, offered him from the Great Mogul. **1715** in J. T. Wheeler *Early Rec. Brit. India* (1878) 171 We were met by Padre Stephanus, bringing two seerpaws. **1763** ORME *Milit. Trans.* I. 163 Serpaws..are garments which are presented sometimes by superiors in token of protection, and sometimes by inferiors in token of homage.

seership ('sɪəʃɪp). [f. SEER[1] + -SHIP.]
1. ***your seership***: a mock title of address to a 'seer'.
1784 *New Spectator* ix. 6 Which [certain phrases], therefore, we request your Seership to explain in such a manner as that we may give an account thereof.
2. The office or function of a seer.
1835 MISS SEDGWICK *Linwoods* I. i. 17 Isabella was nettled at Herbert's open contempt of Effie's seership. **1881** J. G. HOLLAND in *Scribner's Monthly* XXII. 142 Would these men in any way distinguish seership and prophecy from imagination. **1884** P. B. RANDOLPH (*title*) Seership! The Magnetic Mirror. A practical guide to those who aspire to clairvoyance, etc.

seersucker ('sɪəsʌkə(r)). Also 8 sea sucker, seesucker, sirsakas, 9 searsucker. [East Indian corruption of Pers. *shīr o shakkar* lit. 'milk and sugar', transf. 'a striped linen garment' (Vullers *Lex. Pers.-Lat.*).] A thin linen, or sometimes cotton, fabric, striped and with a crimped or puckered surface, of Indian manufacture. Also (and now chiefly) applied to imitations made elsewhere. Also, a garment made of seersucker. Also *attrib.* or as *adj.*
1722 C. CARROLL in *Maryland Hist. Mag.* (1925) XX. 64 To Corded Dimothy..To I Sea Sucker D°. **1736** *Virginia Gaz.* 15 Oct. 4/2 Ran away..a Servant Woman..took..a Seesucker Gown. **1757** *Guyon's New Hist. E. Indies* II. 145, 600 pieces sirsakas. **1757** in *Dalrymple's Oriental Repertory* (1793) I. 203, I have with me..as a present for the King of Ava..2 Pieces of Seersuckers. **1866** *Daily Tel.* 29 Jan. 5/3, I have made acquaintance with the Spanish soldier..in Havana, where in summer he is sensibly clad in a suit of seersucker. **1872** HOWELLS *Wedd. Journ.* vi. (1882) 145 The clerk, in a seersucker coat. **1901** ESTHER SINGLETON *Furniture of Our Forefathers* II. 631 The materials used for upholstering in the seventeenth century were camak,.. searsucker [etc.]. **1958** B. MALAMUD *Magic Barrel* 124 He dried himself and dressed. When he came forth in his seersucker, she offered salami. **1964** *Punch* 29 Apr. p. xiv/2 For men, striped cotton seersucker jackets. **1975** B. GARFIELD *Hopscotch* vii. 77 A trim sandy man..in the regulation seersucker. **1981** L. STEPHAN *Murder or Not* vi. 40 Her seersucker shift..with its thin blue and white stripes.

sees, obs. form of CEASE *v.*

see-safe, *a.* and *adv.* [f. SEE *v.* + SAFE *a.*] (See quot. 1960.)
1926 S. UNWIN *Truth about Publishing* vi. 180 Some firms occasionally seek to protect themselves when buying books of doubtful saleability by marking their order..'see safe'. If this condition is passed..the publisher can be called upon.. to exchange any surplus copies. *Ibid.*, If the firm has bought fifty-two copies of a new novel and marked the order 'twenty-six see safe', the publisher..may find himself obliged to take twenty-six back and to supply some more saleable work in their place. **1939** F. D. SANDERS *Brit. Bk. Trade Organisation* 42 The Committee recommended..that books ordered as a result of such information be treated on the 'see safe' principle. **1959** *Bookseller* 24 Oct. 728/3 After say, 20 evening class students have called at a bookshop, all asking for the same title, the bookseller may be moved to telephone an order, three copies firm and three see-safe. **1960** G. A. GLAISTER *Gloss. Book* 372/2 *See safe*, said of books bought by a bookseller from a publisher..with the understanding that at some future date the publisher may be asked to exchange the bookseller's surplus for copies of another title. **1974** I. NORRIE in Mumby & Norrie *Publishing & Bookselling* (ed. 5) II. 423 As the paperback boom gathered force it was increasingly difficult to sell new novels ..by unknown writers... What was known as the 'see safe' system (titles which did not sell could be swopped for those which did) was adopted.

see-saw ('siːsɔː), *int.*, *sb.* and *a.* [A reduplicating formation symbolic of alternating movement;

the particular form may be suggested by SAW *v.*, to which the oldest example refers. Cf. SITISOT.]

A. *int.* Used as part of a rhythmical jingle, apparently sung by sawyers, or by children imitating sawyers at their work. Hence in nursery songs serving as accompaniment to alternating movements in games.

1640 BROME *Antipodes* II. ii, Let me not see you act now, In your Scholasticke way, you brought to towne wi' yee, With see saw sacke a downe, like a Sawyer. *c* **1685** *MS. Douce* 357 lf. 124 See saw, sack a day; Monmouth is a pretie Boy. **17..** in *Ritson's Gammer Gurton's Garl.* (1783) 48 See Saw, sacaradown, Which is the way to London town? *Ibid.* 51 See saw, Margery Daw Sold her old bed to lay on straw. **18..** in Halliwell *Nursery Rhymes* (1842) 88 See saw, Margery Daw, Jackey shall have a new master.

B. *sb.*

1. The motion of going up one moment and down the next, or of swaying backwards and forwards. *to play (at) see-saw*: a sport or child's amusement in which children sit one or more at each end of a board or piece of timber balanced so that the ends move alternately up and down.

A wholly different game, a form of CAT'S CRADLE, is known in some parts of England as *see-saw*, with reference to the backward and forward movements of the hands.

1704 SWIFT *Mechan. Operat. Spirit* Misc. 297 Then, as they sit, they are in a perpetual Motion of See-saw. **1712** —— *Let. to Mrs. Hill* July, One who knows your constitution very well, advises you by all means against sitting in the dusk at your window, or on the ground, leaning on your hand, or at see-saw in your chair. **1792** MME. D'ARBLAY *Diary* Jan., I thought by his see-saw he was going to interrupt the speech. *a* **1806** H. K. WHITE *Lett.* (1837) 338 The delicious see-saw of a post-chaise. **1821** CLARE *Vill. Minstr.* II. 77 Play at see-saw on the pasture-gate. **1877** BLACKMORE *Erema* liv. III. 237 The butt-ends of the three old streets.. were dipped as if playing see-saw in the surf.

b. *transf.* and *fig.*

1714 SHAFTESB. *Charac.* (1737) III. 25 The common Amble or Canterbury is not, I am persuaded, more tiresom to a good Rider, than this See-saw of Essay-Writers is to an able Reader. **1748** RICHARDSON *Clarissa* III. 99 To see.. what can be done by the amorous See-saw; now humble; now proud; now expecting, or demanding [etc.]. *Ibid.* IV. 280. **1827** DISRAELI *Viv. Grey* v. xiii, He had persisted obstinately against a run on the red; then floundered and got entangled in a see-saw, which alone cost him a thousand. **1838** SIR W. HAMILTON *Logic* xxiv. (1860) II. 18 The ancients called the circular definition also by the name of Diallelon... In probation there is a similar vice which bears the same names. We may, I think, call them by the homely English appellation of the Seesaw. **1860** EMERSON *Cond. Life* i. *Fate* (1860) 39 If a man has a seesaw in his voice, it will run into his sentences. *a* **1870** W. STUBBS *Lect. Europ. Hist.* I. i. (1904) 8 Charles's wars with France are a regular see-saw.

c. *Whist.* = CROSS-RUFF *sb.* 2.

1746 HOYLE *Whist* (ed. 6) 36 See-Saw, is when each Partner trumps a Suit, and they play those Suits to one another to trump. **1876** A. CAMPBELL-WALKER *Correct Card* (1880) *Gloss.*, *See-saw.*—Partners trumping each a suit, and leading to each other for that purpose.

2. A plank arranged for playing see-saw.

1824 CARLYLE *Wilhelm Meister, Trav.* xvii[i], A large swing-wheel.. other see-saws [etc.]. **1844** LOUISA S. COSTELLO *Béarn & Pyr.* I. x. 177 Swings and see-saws for the exercise of youthful bathers after their dips. **1884** *Harper's Mag.* Apr. 771/1 The long cemented play-ground below, with a seesaw for the children.

fig. **1855** THACKERAY *Newcomes* II. 140, I began by siding with Mrs. Grundy and the world and at the next turn of the seesaw have lighted down on Ethel's side.

3. *nonce-use.* ? One whose life is passed in monotonous repetition of the same incident.

1753 RICHARDSON *Grandison* (1754) III. xviii. 159 Let me alone Harriet: Now a quarrel; now a reconciliation; I warrant I shall be happier than any of the yawning see-saws in the kingdom. Everlasting summers would be a grievance.

C. *adj.* Moving up and down, or backwards and forwards, in the manner of a see-saw. Also *fig.*

1735 POPE *Prol. Sat.* 323 His wit all see-saw, between *that* and *this*, Now high, now low, now master up, now miss. **1760** LLOYD *Actor* 148 When desperate heroines grieve with tedious moan, And whine their sorrows in a see-saw tone. **1772** MASON *Her. Epist. to Sir W. Chambers* 22 Let D**d H*e, from the remotest North, In see-saw sceptic scruples hint his worth. **1796** E. DARWIN *Zoon.* II. 389 Some elderly people acquire a see-saw motion of their bodies from one side to the other, as they sit, like the oscillation of a pendulum. **1812** BYRON *Waltz* To Publisher, Turning round to a d——d see-saw up-and-down sort of tune. **1854** H. MILLER *Sch. & Schm.* (1858) 375, I lived on for years in a sort of uneasy, see-saw condition, without any middle ground between the two extremes, on which I could at once reason and believe. **1878** S. WALPOLE *Hist. Eng.* II. 434 They did not tolerate a see-saw Government.

'see-saw, *v.* [f. SEE-SAW *sb.*]

1. *intr.* **a.** *lit.* To move up and down, or backwards and forwards; to undergo a see-saw motion; also to play see-saw.

1712 ARBUTHNOT *John Bull* IV. vii, So they went see-sawing up and down, from one End of the Room to the other. **1778** MME. D'ARBLAY *Diary* 23 Aug., 'Why, ay, true', cried the doctor [Johnson], see-sawing very solemnly. **1835** WILLIS *Pencillings* I. xxiii. 161 A decrepid nun was see-sawing backwards and forwards. **1853** KANE *Grinnell Exp.* xlix. (1856) 469 It see-sawed with him a good deal, but he jumped for it safely. **1860** GEO. ELIOT *Mill on Floss* I. vi, She was seesawing on the elder bough. **1898** FRASER in *Daily News* 15 June 5/2 Our way lay east, over a road see-sawing continuously between altitudes of 5,000 and 8,000 feet.

b. *fig.*

1826 JAS. MILL in *Westm. Rev.* VI. 259 To see-saw between these two horrible conditions, with one half of our population always in misery, is a grand item in the present state of the nation. **1835** LADY GRANVILLE *Lett.* 7 Sept. (1894) II. 195 He.. then has to see-saw between Peel and the Ultras. **1856** DE QUINCEY *Confess.* (ed. 2) Wks. V. 135 Dialogues that loitered painfully, or see-sawed unprofitably. **1894** G. PARKER *Trail of Sword* xx. (1897) 280 It is curious how their fortunes had see-sawed one against the other for twelve years.

2. *trans.* To cause to move in a see-saw motion.

1754 RICHARDSON *Grandison* VI. 285 Your nurse, in your infancy *see-sawed* you. **1801** in *Spirit Publ. Jrnls.* IX. 377 He sits cocking his chin, and see-sawing his right arm. **1813** COLERIDGE *Remorse* II. i, A poor idiot boy.. See-saws his voice in inarticulate noises. **1832** LYTTON *Eugene A.* I. ix, He ponders, he see-saws him-self to and fro. **1873** MISS BRADDON *Str. & Pilgr.* III. xiii, Dr. Cameron see-sawed the matter in his most delicate way. **1873** MISS BROUGHTON *Nancy* iv, Bobby, stop see-sawing that chair, it makes me feel deadly sick.

Hence **'see-ˌsawing** *vbl. sb.* and *ppl. a.*

1793 *Laity's Directory* 20 The shameful act of see-sawing in their chairs. **1827** CARLYLE *Germ. Rom.* III. 246 To mount a plank over a beam, and commence seesawing. **1832** LYTTON *Eugene A.* I. ii, A certain lolling, see-sawing method of balancing his body upon his chair. **1876** A. J. EVANS *Through Bosnia* ii. 50 Two Croats.. imparted a see-sawing motion to it. **1906** BARONESS VON HUTTEN *What became of Pam* II. viii. 166 He seemed.. so above all mental see-sawing.

seese, obs. form of CEASE; variant of SEISE *v.*

seesee ('siːsiː). Also see-see, sisi. [Echoic: see quot. 1969.] In full, *seesee partridge*. A small sand partridge, *Ammoperdix griseogularis*, found in parts of western Asia.

1851 J. GOULD *Birds of Asia* VII. Pl. 1 Sportsmen reckon it very easy to kill, and it is said to be delicious eating: the name Seesee expresses its call. **1858** *Proc. Zool. Soc.* XXVI. 503 It [sc. *Ammoperdix bonhami*] is known by the name of 'Sisi' in the Punjab. **1864** T. C. JERDON *Birds of India* III. 567 (*heading*) The Seesee partridge. *Ibid.* 568 The Seesee is only found in the Punjab. **1923** *Blackw. Mag.* July 125/2 Game abounded—black partridge and sisi, hare and pigeon. **1928** *Ibid.* Apr. 544/2 We had an exciting and noisy hunt after a see-see partridge. **1969** ALI & RIPLEY *Handbk. Birds India & Pakistan* II. 8 Seesee Partridge... A small sandy grey-brown, concealingly desert-coloured partridge... When flushed on a hillside the birds invariably fly downhill, the wings producing the characteristic high-pitched squeaking *see-see* noise.. which has given the bird its name.

seesen, -in, obs. forms of SEISIN.

seesoo, seesu, variant forms of SISSOO.

seet, obs. pa. t. of SET and SIT.

seet(e, obs. forms of SEAT *sb.*

seete, obs. pa. pple. of SET *v.*[1]; var. SETE, suitable.

seeth, variant of SAITHE, SEATH, SETHE *Obs.*

seethe, *sb.* [f. SEETHE *v.*] Seething, ebullition (of waves); intense commotion or heat. Also *fig.*

1816 W. TAYLOR in *Monthly Mag.* XLI. 330 A rush of wandering winds, a seethe of waves, is heard. **1856** DORELL *Eng. in Time of War* 66 Nigher comes the seeth of fields on fire. **1865** A. SMITH *Summer in Skye* I. 200 The seethe of the wave on the rock. **1901** H. TRENCH *Deirdre Wed* 45 He choked at his own spirit's seethe.

seethe (siːð), *v.* Pa. t. seethed, †sod. Pa. pple. seethed, †sodden. Forms: α. *Inf.* 1 séoþan, 3–5 seoþe(n, 3–5 seþe(n, 3–6 sethe, 4–6 seth, (5 cethyn, sith, sede, syede), 6 seith(e, seeith, syeth, seath, 6, 9 seathe, 5–9 seeth, 4– seethe. Also *3rd sing. Pres. Ind.* 1 sýþ, 4 seþ. β. *Pa. t. sing.* 1 séaþ, 3 seð, 3–5 seþ, seth, 4–5 seeth, sethe; *pl.* 1 sudon, 3 sude(n, 3–4 sodun, 3–6 sode(n, 4–5 sothe(n; *sing.* and *pl.* 6–7 sod, sodd(e; *weak form* 4–5 sethed(e, -ide, -it, seethede, 7– seethed. γ. *Pa. pple.* 1 soden, 3–4 i-sode, i-zode, 4–5 sode, sodun, -yn, y-soden, sooden, 4–7 soden, 5 soddyn, 6 sodene, sodne, sod(d)in, soddyne, 7 sudden, 4– sodden (see SODDEN); 5–7 sodde, 7 sodd, 5–9 sod; 3 siþen, 3–5 soþen, (4 soiþen), 4–5 soþin, -yn, -un, y-sothe(n, y-soothe, soothen, 5 soþe; *weak form* 8–9 seethed. [A Common Teut. strong verb (wanting in Gothic): OE. *séoðan* (pa. t. *séað*, pl. *sudon*, pa. pple. *soden*) corresponds to OFris. *siatha* (WFris. *siede*), OS. **sioðan* (in pa. pple. *gesodenemo* 'recocto'), MLG. *sêden* (LG. *seden*), Du. *zieden*, OHG. *siodan* (MHG., mod.G. *sieden*), ON. *sióða* (Sw. *sjuda*, Da. *syde*). The root, OTeut. **seuþ-* (: **sauþ-* : **suð-*) occurs in Goth. *sauþ-s* sacrifice (? originally 'boiled flesh'), with which ON. *sauð-r* sheep is probably identical. From the weak grade **suð-* appears to have been developed the parallel root **sweþ-* (: **swaþ-*: **suð-*) in OHG. *swedan* to smoulder, MHG. *swaden* smoky vapour (mod.G. *schwadem* fire-damp), ? OE. *swaþul* smoky vapour. Brugmann refers the root to an Indogermanic type **kpeut-*, found in Lith. *szuntù* (pret. *szuntau*) 'I smoulder, stew'.

The original pa. t. (ME. *seeth*) was superseded by the form *sod* taken from the pa. pple. The verb is now conjugated weak, *sod* being obsolete, and *sodden* having ceased to be associated with this verb.]

1. *trans.* To boil; to make or keep boiling hot; to subject to the action of boiling liquid; *esp.* to cook (food) by boiling or stewing; also, to make an infusion or decoction of (a substance) by boiling or stewing. *Obs.* or *arch.*

OE. had certain figurative uses not found later: To try as by fire; to afflict with cares.

c **1000** *Sax. Leechd.* II. 276 Gif mon syþ garleac on henne broþe. *c* **1205** LAY. 20978 þat orf þat heo nomen al heo sloȝen,.. and suden and bradden. *c* **1250** *Gen. & Ex.* 1487 Iacob An time him seð a mete ðat man callen lentil ȝete. **1297** R. GLOUC. (Rolls) 8447 So muche honger hii adde þer,.. þat hii sode þe saracens & þat fless ete. *a* **1300** *Cursor M.* 6081 It sal noght siþen be bot bred, þis lamb þat þai of sal be fedd. **1382** WYCLIF *Gen.* xxv. 29 Jacob.. hadde sothun [**1388** Jacob sethide, **1611**, **1884** sod] potage. *c* **1386** CHAUCER *Clerk's T.* 171 Wortes or othere herbes.. The whiche she shredde and seeth for hir lyuynge. **1398** TREVISA *Barth. De P.R.* XVII. ix. (1495) 608 The floure of Anetum sod wyth wyne dooth away heed ache. *c* **1440** *Gesta Rom.* (1879) 247 þe Emperour smote oute fire of a stone, and seþe his mete, as welle as he myȝt. **1470–85** MALORY *Arthur* VI. ix. 196 And so that veneson was rosted baken and soden. **1509** BARCLAY *Shyp of Folys* (1874) II. 6 Progne.. whiche sode hir oune childe after she had hym slayne. **1540** MOULTON *Mirr. Health* f iv, Take hemlocks and seth them tyll they be softe as pappe. **1579** T. STEVENS in *Hakluyt's Voy.* (1599) II. II. 101 We saw crabs swimming on the water that were red as though they had bene sodden. **1607** *Relat. Disc. River* in *Capt. Smith's Wks.* (Arb.) Introd. 42 Wee sodd our kettle by y[e] water syde. *Ibid.* 43 He.. gave vs a Deare roasted; which according to their Custome they seethed againe. **1648** GAGE *West Ind.* xii. (1655) 61 From the root of this tree cometh a juyce like unto a syrup, which being sod will become Sugar. **1653** H. MORE *Antid. Ath.* II. vi. §4 (1712) 56 The Lye in which it is sodden or infus'd is good to wash the Head. **1713** *Guardian* No. 139 Androcles, having sodden the flesh of it by the sun. *a* **1779** COOK *Voy. Pacific* IV. iii. (1784) II. 321 This operation they repeat till they think the contents are sufficiently stewed or seethed. **1828** SCOTT *F.M. Perth* xxviii, Others were cut into joints and seathed in cauldrons made of the animal's own skins. **1835** WILLIS *Pencillings* I. ii. 19 Cold meat, seethed, Italian fashion, in nauseous oil. **1849** MACAULAY *Hist. Eng.* v. I. 634 A poor man whose loyalty was suspected.. was compelled to ransom his own life by seething the remains of his friends in pitch.

absol. *c* **1386** CHAUCER *Prol.* 383 He coude roste, and sethe, and broille, and frye. **1577–82** BRETON *Flourish Fancy*, etc. (Grosart) 15/2 And what kinde cookes she hath, and how they make their fyre To roast, to seeth, to broile, to bake, and what you will desire.

†**b.** With adv., *to seethe out, away* (also *fig.*). Also, to separate *from* (a part) by boiling.

1382 WYCLIF *Isa.* i. 25, I shal sethen out [Vulg. *excoquam*] to the pure thi dros. *c* **1440** *Gesta Rom.* (1879) 385 Than the ij. deuyls.. Caste hem into a Cawderon and helde hem there, till the fleshe was sothyn fro the bone. **1561** T. NORTON *Calvin's Inst.* III. 172 In continually sething out and burning vp the vices of our lust. **1567** HARMAN *Caveat* (1867) 22 Then was.. a great fat oxe sod out in Furmenty. **1595** DUNCAN *App. Etym.* (E.D.S.), *Excoquo*, to seathe away, to fyne.

†**c.** To prepare or produce by boiling. *Obs.*

? *a* **1500** *Chester Pl.* vii. 73 To seeth salve for our sheepe. **1598** GRENEWEY *Tacitus, Ann.* XIII. iv. [xv.] (1622) 183 A poison was sod [L. *decoquitur virus*] strong & violent.

†**d.** To digest (food). Hence perh. the use in OE. for: To brood over (care, anxiety): cf. Gr. κήδεα πέσσειν. *Obs.*

Beowulf 190 Swa ða mælceare maga Healfdenes singala seað. *Ibid.* 1993 Ic ðæs modceare sorhwylmum seað. **1398** TREVISA *Barth. De P.R.* III. xiv. (1495) 59 The fode is sodde and defyed by werkynge of kynde. *c* **1400** tr. *Secreta Secret., Gov. Lordsh.* xl. 71 Wherfore þe stomak.. losyth his strengthe to fully sethe þe mete. **1628** [see SEETHING *vbl. sb.* 3].

2. *intr.* (for passive). To be boiled; to be subjected to boiling or stewing; to become boiling hot. Said of a liquid, or a substance boiled in a liquid; also of the pot or other receptacle. Also *to seethe over*.

13.. *Sir Beues* 3455 He let felle a led Ful of pich and of bremston, And hot led let falle þer on; Whan hit alþer swiþer seþ, þemperur þar in a deþ. *Ibid.* 3460 Hire lord seþen in þe pich þe sai. *a* **1400** *Vis. St. Paul* 133 in *Minor Poems fr. Vernon MS.* 255 þer he sauh.. Blake Maydens in Blac cloþing, And þei sodun euerichon In wellyng pich and Brumston. *c* **1430** *Two Cookery Bks.* I. 6 Let hem sethe to-gederys a whyle. *c* **1481** CAXTON *Dialogues* viii. 30 Make the ynche to seethe... *Fais bouillir lencre.* **1541–72** *Schole-house of Women* 628 in Hazl. *E.P.P.* IV. 129 [He] Bad her take the pot, that sod ouer the fire. **1609** C. BUTLER *Fem. Mon.* (1634) 165 When it hath sod a while, and is thorowly melted, take it off the fire. **1646** CRASHAW *Sospetto d' Herode* 37 And while the black soules boile in their own gore, To hold them down, and looke that none seeth o're. **1801** *Med. Jrnl.* V. 367 The water begins to seeth. **1827** LAMB *Remin. Sir J. Dunstan* in *Hone's Every-d. Bk.* II. II. 843 The scent of horse-flesh seething into dog's meat.

3. *trans.* To reduce to a condition resembling that of food which by boiling or stewing has lost its flavour or crispness; to soak or steep in a liquid; to dissipate the vitality or freshness of (the brain, blood, spirits, etc.) by excessive heat or by intoxicating liquor. Chiefly in passive; for special developments of the pa. pple. see SOD and SODDEN.

1599 NASHE *Lenten Stuffe* 45 This piteous spectacle of her loue [*sc.* Leander drowned], sodden to haddocks meate. **1615** HEYWOOD *Four Prentises* K 1, Such as shrinke not to haue their blouds sod with the dog-daies heat. **1621** BURTON *Anat. Mel.* II. ii. VI. 380 They drown their wits, seeth their brains in ale [etc.]. **1650** BULWER *Anthropomet.* 47 By heate, whence the Spirits are dissipated and the braine as it were sod. **1813** COLERIDGE *Remorse* II. ii. 188 His weak eyes seeth'd in most unmeaning tears. **1842** W. C. TAYLOR *Anc. Hist.* xvii. §9 (ed. 3) 557 They [the Huns] lived on raw flesh, or at best only sodden by being placed under their saddles and pressed against the backs of their steeds during a sharp gallop. **1844** MRS. BROWNING *Rime Duchess May* v, And the castle, seethed in blood, fourteen days and nights had stood. *a* **1851** D. JERROLD *St. Giles* xxii, There was a man..still alive; though seethed in drink, and looking like death.

4. *intr.* (transf. from 2). Of a liquid, vapour, etc.: To rise, surge or foam up, as if boiling; to form bubbles or foam. Said also of a receptacle thus filled with foam or vapour; also of a flatulent stomach, of the heart or blood. Also with *up*.

1535 COVERDALE *Job* xxx. 27 My bowels seeth with in me & take no rest. *a* **1552** LELAND *Itin.* VI. 7 Sidingburne,..so caullid by reason of many springges that in the Chalke Hilles about it doth seeth and boyle oute. **1623** WEBSTER *Duchess Malfi* II. i, She puykes, her stomacke seethes. **1633** FORD *'Tis Pity* III. vii. 19 My belly seeths like a Porridge-pot. **1679** DRYDEN *Œdipus* IV. i, A thousand frantick Spirits Seething, like rising Bubbles, on the Brim. **1797** COLERIDGE *Kubla Khan* 17 And from this chasm, with ceaseless turmoil seething,..A mighty fountain momently was forced. **1860** TYNDALL *Glac.* I. §18. 126 Vapour..came seething at times up the sides of the mountain. **1873** G. C. DAVIES *Mount. & Mere* xvi. 133 The white surf which broke over their bows and seethed along the decks.

5. *fig.* To be in a state of inward agitation, turmoil, or 'ferment'. Said of a person in trouble, fever, etc.; of plans, elements of discontent or change; also of a region filled *with* excitement, disaffection, etc.

1606 SHAKS. *Tr. & Cr.* III. i. 43, I will make a complementall assault vpon him, for my businesse seethes. **1820** KEATS *Isabella* xv, For them alone did seethe A thousand men in troubles wide and dark. **1845** DISRAELI *Sybil* v. viii, 'All the north is seething', said Gerard. 'We must contrive to agitate the metropolis', said Maclast. **1856** MRS. BROWNING *Aur. Leigh* III. 1141 She lay and seethed in fever many weeks. **1874** GREEN *Short Hist.* iv. §4. 194 The city had all through the interval been seething with discontent. **1882** J. H. BLUNT *Ref. Ch. Eng.* II. 506 The elements of that war had been seething in English society. **1894** MRS. DYAN *All in Man's Keeping* xxv. (1899) 348 His brain had no respite either. Plans seethed there incessantly.

seethe, variant of SAITHE.

†**seethed**, *ppl. a. Obs. rare.* Cf. SODDEN *ppl. a.* [f. SEETHE *v.* + -ED[1].] Boiled.

1775 ADAIR *Amer. Ind.* 407 They..boil them well, as they do every kind of seethed food.

seethence, variant of SITHENCE *Obs.*

†**'seether.** *Obs.* [f. SEETHE *v.* + -ER[1].]

1. One who is employed in boiling.

1377 *Durham Acc. Rolls* (Surtees) 46 Stipendia..It., Pro Sether, 3*s.* 4*d.* **1389** *Ibid.* 49 In ij[bus] garniamentis pro fyssman et Le Sether, 11*s.* 6*d.*

2. A utensil for boiling. *nonce-use.*

1700 DRYDEN *Baucis & Philemon* 57 She sets the Kettle on, (Like burnish'd Gold the little Seether shone).

seething ('siːðɪŋ), *vbl. sb.* [f. SEETHE *v.* + -ING[1].] The action of SEETHE *v.*

1. The state of being boiling hot.

c **1300** *St. Margarete* 31 He let hete water oð seoþinge & þo hit boillede faste, He let nyme þis holi maide & þer amidde hire caste.

b. *transf.* and *fig.* Ebullition, intense inward agitation. Also with *up*.

1593 NASHE *Christ's T.* O 2, This Vaine-glory..is (as I may call it) the froth and seathing vp of Ambition. **1851** LONGF. *Gold. Leg.* IV. *Convent Cellar*, But within, what a spirit of deep unrest! What a seething and simmering in his breast! **1873** BLACK *Pr. Thule* xxiii. 388 Nothing was visible but a wild boiling and seething of clouds and waves.

†**2.** The action or an act of keeping a liquid boiling hot, of cooking in boiling water, or of submitting anything to the action of boiling liquid.

1387 TREVISA *Higden* (Rolls) IV. 439 Biggynge and sellynge cesede, and so dede rostynge and seþinge [MS. γ seoþyng] and greyþinge of mete. **1398** —— *Barth. De P.R.* VI. xxi. (1495) 210 Salte is made by grete sethynge of water. **1585** T. WASHINGTON tr. *Nicholay's Voy.* III. xi. 91 The seething together of plummes..and other lyke fruits. **1622** MABBE tr. *Aleman's Guzman d' Alf.* II. 327 The better to secure the seething of the Pot. **1725** *Bradley's Fam. Dict.* s.v. *Potage*, When this Mixture has been season'd, let it have five or six Seethings in a Stew-pan.

†**b.** *concr.* Something boiled or in process of boiling. *Obs.*

1382 WYCLIF *Gen.* xxv. 30 3if to me of this brown sething [Vulg. *Da mihi de coctione hac rufa*]. *c* **1400** tr. *Secreta Secret., Gov. Lordsh.* lxviii. 85 Sethe hem softly to þe half, and after lat þe sethinge be steryd and strenyd.

†**c.** *Comb.*, as *seething-house, -pot. Obs.*

1459–60 *Durham Acc. Rolls* (Surtees) 89 In coquina sunt, viz. in le *sethynghowse, ij magne olle in furnis. *c* **1500** LACY *Wyl Bucke's Test.* a iij b, Then caste all togeter in a faire *sething-pott with water. **1668** CULPEPER & COLE *Barthol. Anat.* I. ix. 18 So we cover it as we do our seething-pots with a potlid, to keep in the fumes.

†**3.** Digestion. *Obs.*

1398 TREVISA *Barth. De P.R.* v. xl. (Bodl. MS.), þe galle by heete þereof helpeþ þe seeþing of mete and drinke. **1628** BURTON *Anat. Mel.* I. i. II. v. (ed. 3) 20 Elixation is the seething [edd. 1, 2 boyling] of meat in the stomacke.

seething ('siːðɪŋ), *ppl. a.* [f. SEETHE *v.* + -ING[2].]

1. Originally, of liquids, a cauldron, etc.: Boiling. In mod. use, a somewhat rhetorical expression for: Intensely heated (said of solids, the atmosphere, etc., as well as of liquids).

a **1300** *Leg. Rood* 60 A caudron he let fulle Wiþ seþing oile vol Inouȝ. **1481** CAXTON *Reynard* xlii. (Arb.) 114 [They] were aferd of that syedyng water. **1535** COVERDALE *Jer.* i. 13, I do se a seethinge pot. **1662** J. DAVIES tr. *Olearius' Voy. Ambass.* 413 There is a Spring of seething Water, which falls into a Pool. **1825** MACAULAY *Ess., Milton* ¶36 The hooks and the seething pitch of Barbariccia and Draghignazzo. **1848** LYTTON *Harold* v. iii, But did he try the ordeals of God?..did his hand grasp the seething iron?

b. quasi-*adv.*, esp. in phrase *seething hot.*

1489 CAXTON *Faytes of A.* II. xxxvii. 155 Yf..the watre might be sedinge hote. *a* **1635** CORBET *Poems* (1807) 138 That 'tis so seething hott in Spaine, they sweare They never heard of a raw oyster there. **1870** TYNDALL *Fragm. Sci.* (1879) I. vi. 197 The whole surface of which [the sea] was seething white.

2. *transf.* and *fig.* Of waves, etc.: Ebullient, tumultuous. Also, pervaded by intense and ceaseless inner agitation: often with reference (*lit.* and *fig.*) to the condition characteristic of corruption or putrefaction.

1588 MARLOWE *2nd Pt. Tamburl.* IV. i. 3818 Whose scalding drops wil pierce thy seething braines. **1590** SHAKS. *Mids. N.* v. i. 4 Louers and mad men haue such seething braines [etc.]. **1868** J. H. BLUNT *Ref. Ch. Eng.* I. 433 The seething spirit of controversy. **1868** G. DUFF *Pol. Surv.* 73 [He] plunged into the seething gulf of insurrection which was raging in Eastern Turkestan. **1871** R. ELLIS *Catullus* lxiv. 156 Seething sand [L. *Syrtis*]. **1877** L. MORRIS *Epic Hades* I. 37 One white sea Of churning, seething foam. **1875** S. HADEN *Earth to Earth* 66 To avoid the seething suburban cemeteries and to bury their dead at Woking. **1879** FARRAR *St. Paul* (1883) 238 Amid this seething corruption.

Hence **'seethingly** *adv.*

1887 *Temple Bar* Oct. 199 He explained to his seethingly angry friend.

see-through ('siːθruː), *a.* and *sb.* Also (chiefly *U.S.*) see-thru. [f. vbl. phr. *to see through*: SEE *v.* 24 a.] **A.** *adj.* That can be seen through; transparent, diaphanous; having spaces allowing the passage of light. **a.** Of a fabric or (usu. woman's) garment.

1950 *Life* 10 Apr. 100 (*heading*) See-through fabrics bring undercovering to the surface. **1951** *Sunday Pictorial* 21 Jan. 2/1 'See-through' nighties..may be heavenly for women, but they have many disadvantages. **1960** J. IRONSIDE *Fashion Alphabet* 30 The present trend towards see-through dresses and no-bras indicates that it [*sc.* the bare breast] is only one step away. **1968** B. NORMAN *Hounds of Sparta* xix. 143 Some slinky girl spy in a see-through nightdress. **1979** M. HEBDEN *Death set to Music* iii. 24 You don't normally come down dressed in a see-through robe to answer the door. **1980** *Quilt World* Sept./Oct. 63/1 'Mirror' or 'See-Thru' quilt, make in one day, instructions 50c.

b. in other contexts.

1956 *Sun* (Baltimore) 5 Sept. 19/3 The 40 by 80-foot building at the northwest corner of Light and Cross streets is of the 'open' or 'see-through' style of architecture that reveals the revolution that banking in all its phases has been undergoing. **1966** *Punch* 5 Oct. 506/2 Each resident is given a few square feet of privacy, enclosed by see-through fencing. **1967** 'G. BAGBY' *Corpse Candle* (1968) ix. 122 'With a glass house..there's no place a man could go there to take his pants off.' 'It's not all that see-through,' I assured him. **1975** G. SEYMOUR *Harry's Game* ii. 22 The troops..with..the medieval Macron see-through shields. **1978** J. IRVING *World according to Garp* xv. 314 He cleared a see-through spot on the dusted and caked rear window.

B. *sb.* **1.** The quality of allowing the passage of light; the extent to which it is possible to see clearly through something; unimpeded vision.

1954 *Sun* (Baltimore) 21 Dec. 5/6 (Advt.), In opaque nylon tricot for less see thru. **1957** *Jrnl. Optical Soc. Amer.* XLVII. 785/2 A material with good 'see-through' qualities may, in fact, be quite hazy. **1959** *Motor Man.* (ed. 36) xiii. 273 The driver has a clear 'see-through' if the towing angle is correct. **1969** C. O. RASPOR in W. R. R. Park *Plastics Film Technol.* iv. 97 Transparency or 'see through' refers to the capability of seeing objects through a film without loss of detail caused by blurring or distortion. **1974** E. CASTAGNA in P. F. Bruins *Packaging with Plastics* 126 Contact clarity, i.e., see-through to contained liquids, is excellent for copolymers.

2. A see-through fabric or garment.

1962 G. CALLINGFORD *Third Party Risk* iii. 42 Might buy 'erself..brushed nylon if she don't fancy the see-through. **1971** *Guardian* 1 June 9/2 Conditioned as we are to seeing hot pants and cool see-throughs worn in city streets. **1974** P. HAINES *Tea at Gunter's* xiv. 149 You know—a rented place, Lu; and me in one of those flimsy see-throughs, lying about on the settee.

seeve, seew, seex: see SIEVE, SEW, SEX.

seey, obs. pa. t. sing. of SEE *v.*

seeyne, obs. pres. ind. pl. of SEE; var. SENE.

sef, obs. form of SAVE quasi-*prep.*

sef, sefen, seff(e(n, sefne, obs. ff. SEVEN.

sefende, seffnde, sefnthe, sefth, obs. ff. SEVENTH.

sefenneghte, -nahht, sefniht, obs. ff. SENNIGHT.

‖**Sefer Torah** ('seɪfə 'tɔərəʊ). Also **Sepher Torah**; *pl.* **Sifrei Torah** (sɪ'freɪ). [ad. Heb. *sēper tōrā* book of (the) Law; cf. TORAH.] = *Scroll of the Law* s.v. SCROLL *sb.* 1 e.

1650 E. CHILMEAD tr. *L. Modena's Hist. Rites, Customes, & Manners of Jews* x. 29 And there are in this Ark, or Chest, sometimes Two, sometimes Four..of these Books: and they are called..Sepher torah, The Book of the Law. **1893** I. ZANGWILL *Ghetto Tragedies* 9 The *Sepher Torah* is to the Jew at once the most precious and the most sacred of possessions. **1936** S. M. LEHRMAN *Jewish Festivals* 139 The Megillah is completely unrolled..to distinguish it from the 'Sefer Torah'. **1960** *Commentary* June 495/2 Anyone who inscribes even one letter on a Sefer Torah earns a *mitzvah*. **1973** *Jewish Chron.* 18 May 39/1 (Advt.), Wanted for immediate purchase..two Sifrei Torah. Must be first-class condition. **1976** B. WILLIAMS *Making of Manch. Jewry* x. 242 The warden..encouraged them to purchase a *Sepher Torah*.

sefte, obs. form of SIFT *v.*

Sefton ('sɛftən). [From the title of the Earl of *Sefton.*]

1. *Cookery.* (In two applications: see quots.)

[App. invented by L. E. Ude, cook to the Earl of Sefton.] **1845** ELIZA ACTON *Mod. Cookery* (ed. 2) 352 A Sefton, or Veal Custard. *Ibid.* 363 Ramekins à l'Ude, or Sefton Fancies.

2. (In full *Sefton landau.*) A kind of landau.

1885 *Coach Builders' Art Jrnl.* Aug. Suppl. 93 Our drawing represents Messrs. Hooper & Co.'s 'Sefton Landau' for one horse. **1889** DUKE OF BEAUFORT *Driving* 385 Those with curved lines are known as 'Sefton' landaus, from the present Earl of Sefton, who had the first one built for his own use. **1898** *Times* 12 Jan. 9/5 The Prince of Wales..drove in the Queen's 'Sefton' and four to the Windsor Station.

seg (sɛg), *sb.*[1] *dial.* Also 7 **sag(ge**, 8 **saig**. [Of obscure origin.] An animal which has been castrated when fully grown.

1600 *Shuttleworths' Acc.* (Chetham Soc.) 131 In Blakburne, for one fat sagge for the howse use, iiij[s] x[d]. **1641** *Watertown (Mass.) Rec.* (1894) 7 No Steers or Sags of three yeares old shalbe herded with the Dry Cattle. **1641, 1820** Bull-seg [see BULL *sb.*[1] 11]. **1788** W. H. MARSHALL *Yorksh.* II. 350 *Seg*, or *Bullseg*; a castrate bull. **1789** DAVIDSON *Seasons* 46 The saig, poor dowy beast! nae pleasure kens Aboon a gowan tap. **1844** H. STEPHENS *Bk. Farm.* II. 129 An aged bull that is castrated is called a segg. **1856** MORTON *Cycl. Agric.* II. 725 *Seg.* (Suff., Yorks., Norf.), any animal castrated when full grown.

Hence **seg** *v. dial. trans.* (See quots.)

1886 *Cheshire Gloss.*, *Segged*, castrated, but only applied when the operation is performed on full-grown animals. **1887** *S. Chesh. Gloss.*, *Seg*, to castrate a full-grown animal.

seg (sɛg), *sb.*[2] *dial.* (See Eng. Dial. Dict.) [a. ON. *sigg* neut., hard skin (Norw. *sigg*, Ross).] A callosity, esp. on the hand.

1865 B. BRIERLEY *Irkdale* I. vii. 130 They startn o'feighten ..an' never gi'en o'er till they'n segs ole o'er 'em. **1902** *Brit. Med. Jrnl.* 15 Feb. 378 Callosities (called planker's 'segs') on the thenar and hypothenar eminences.

seg (sɛg), *sb.*[3] [Abbrev. of SEGMENT *sb.*] A metal stud attached to the toe or heel of a shoe (or boot) to strengthen or protect from wear.

1958 *Shoe & Leather Trades Buyers Reg., Brands Directory & Diary* 100/1 Blakey's Boot Protectors Ltd.,... Boot protectors..all sorts and sizes, malleable cast hob nails, segs & studs, cricket spikes. **1970** *Guardian* 24 Dec. 9/3 The boys made indoor slides across the hall..scoring great weals in the polish with their segs and blakeys. **1976** A. HILL *Summer's End* viii. 123 Might be metal segs, them half-moons of metal you hammered into the heels and sole-tips of your boots to stop 'em wearing out quick.

seg (sɛg), *sb.*[4] **a.** Also **seggie**. U.S. colloq. abbrev. of SEGREGATIONIST *sb.* Cf. OUTSEG *v.* **b.** Slang (chiefly *U.S.*) abbrev. of SEGREGATION 1 g.

1965 *Britannica Bk. of Year* 869/2 *Seg*,..a segregationist. Also *seggie*. **1970** *New Yorker* 12 Dec. 107 Fulbright for the first time openly appealed for black votes, because he believed that he couldn't win without them and that the 'seggies'..would vote against him no matter what he did. **1971** *Harper's Mag.* Jan. 35 When people wore the American flag then it was to show that they were not segs, because the segs of course wore the Confederate flag. **1974** *Guidelines to Volunteer Services* (N.Y. State Dept. Correctional Services) 43 *Seg*, segregation unit. **1977** *New Society* 23 June 616/2 He went straight into the segregation unit [at Wormwood Scrubs]... He continued his [hunger] strike simply in order to prevent an early return to 'seg'.

seg, obs. or dial. form of SEDGE.

‖**segador.** *Obs.*[—0] [Sp., agent-n. f. *segar* to reap.] 'A reaper, a Mower, a Harvest-man' (Blount *Glossogr.* 1656).

segamore, obs. form of SAGAMORE.

Segan, variant of SAGAN *Jewish Antiq.*

segar: see CIGAR.

†**segara.** *Obs.* [quasi-Sp. form of *segar*, CIGAR (Sp. *cigarro*).] A cigar.

1785 R. CUMBERLAND *Observer* No. 88 ¶1 Taking the segara from his mouth. *Ibid.* ¶4 In his pockets he had..a small bundle of segaras.

segashuate, var. SAGACIATE.

segathy, variant of SAGATHY.

sege, obs. form of SEDGE, SEGGE, SIEGE.

segement, obs. form of SEGMENT.

segeneration (siːdʒɛnəˈreɪʃən). *rare*⁻¹. [f. L. *sē* SE- + GENERATION.] (See quot.)
1888 GULICK in *Linn. Soc. Jrnl. (Zool.)* XX. 200 Many species are now divided into two or more intergenerants, between which there is little or no intercrossing. This state of freedom from crossing I call segeneration.

Seger (ˈzeɪgə(r)). [The name of Hermann August *Seger* (1839–93), German ceramics technologist.] *Seger* (also *seger*) *cone*: each of a series of small numbered cones or pyramids made of different mixtures of refractory material and flux so that they melt at different known temperatures, used to indicate the temperature inside kilns, etc.
[**1890** *Jrnl. Iron & Steel Inst.* II. 680 Professor Seger's 'normal' clay pyramids..should find extended application. **1894** *Ibid.* XLV. 432 Le Chatelier's pyrometer was used.., as Seger's cones did not appear to exactly meet all requirements.] **1895** *Ibid.* XLVII. 304 These Seger cones give the temperatures with quite sufficient accuracy. **1931** G. W. TYRRELL *Volcanoes* iv. 115 He used a stout iron pipe within which seger cones were fastened at regular intervals, and thrust it into the lava as far as he could. **1964** H. HODGES *Artifacts* i. 40 There are several series of pyrometric cones of which the Seger cones are, perhaps, the most commonly used. **1971** *Materials & Technol.* II. v. 271 The plaque..is heated above 1000°C at about 10°C per minute, and the end point is taken as the temperature (as indicated by the condition of the Seger cones) at which the tip of the test cone is on a level with the base.

segerstane, -ston(e, etc., obs. forms of SEXTON.

segg, obs. or dial. form of SEDGE.

seggar: see SAGGAR.

†ˈ**seggard.** *dial. Obs.* = SAFEGUARD *sb.* 8.
1746 *Exmoor Scolding* (E.D.S.) 34 Th'art olways a vustled up in an old Jump, or a Whittle, or an old Seggard. **1790** GROSE *Provinc. Gloss.* (ed. 2) Suppl., *Seggard*, safeguard. A kind of riding surtout so called. West.

†**segge**[1]. *poet. Obs.* Forms: 1 secg, 3 sæg, 3–4 (6) seg, 3–6 segge, 4–6 sege, 4 segg, (seegge, 5 seege, seghe, seige), 6 sedge. [OE. *sęcg* = OS. *segg*, ON. *segg-r*:—OTeut. **sagjo-z*.] A man. (In the 16th c. only *contemptuous*.)
Beowulf 208 (Gr.) Secg wisade, laȝucræftiȝ mon, landȝemyrcu. *Ibid.* 633 Þa ic on holm ȝestah, sæbat ȝesæt mid minra secga ȝedriht. *c* **1205** LAY. 7991 Heo ledden in heore scipen..moni forhfulne sæg sare iwunded. *Ibid.* 5109 Þer weore segge songe [*c* 1275 gleomenne songe]. *Ibid.* 20854 Þene siȝeð him to segges vnder beorȝen. **1340–70** *Alex. & Dind.* 165 Of þe seggus þat he sai bi-ȝonde þe side stronde. **1377** LANGL. *P. Pl.* B. xx. 333 'I am a surgien', seide þe segge 'and salues can make'. *a* **1400** *Morte Arth.* 1574, I had leuer see hym synke one the salte strandez, Than the seegge ware seke, that es so sore woundede. *c* **1470** HENRY *Wallace* III. 53 Robert Boid, quhilk wald no langar bide Vndir thrillage of segis of Ingland. *c* **1475** *Rauf Coilȝear* 713 Thair was seruit in that saill Seigis semelie. **1508** DUNBAR *Flyting* 13 For and I flyt sum sege for schame sould sink. **15..** *Scot. Field* 113 in *Chetham Soc. Misc.* II, Then sumoned he his sedges, in sondry places. **1557** GRIMALD *Death Zoroas* 98 in *Tottel's Misc.* (Arb.) 122 Wherwith a hole route came of souldiours stern, And all in peeces hewed the silly seg. **1567** DRANT *Horace, A.P.* B vij, Through this and such the sillie segge lay plasde in puddle still. *Ibid., Ep.* I. ii. C iij, Duke Nestor, sillie carkinge segge.

†**segge**[2]. *Obs. rare*⁻¹. [? a. OF. *seiche* (:—L. *sēpia*).] ? A cuttle-fish.
c **1300** [see LAX *sb.*[1]]

segge, obs. form of SAY *v.*[1], SEDGE, SIEGE.

segged (sɛgd), *a. dial.* [f. *seg*, dial. var. of SEDGE.] Seated with sedge or rushes; rush-bottomed. Also Comb. *segged-seated* adj.
1872 MRS. H. WOOD *Within the Maze* xii, The plain segged-seated chairs stood pretty thick. **1873** —— *Master of Greylands* xvi, A small apartment looking to the kitchen-garden, with an old carpet on its floor, painted segged chairs, and a square piano against the wall.

†ˈ**segger.** *Obs. rare.* [f. *segge* SAY *v.* + -ER[1].] One given to 'talking', a boaster, braggart.
c **1440** *York Myst.* xxviii. 201 Ȝone segger [*sc.* Christ] þat callis hym-selffe a sire.

segger, seggerson, Obs. ff. SAYER[1], SEXTON.

seggie: see SEG *sb.*[4]

†ˈ**segging.** *Obs. rare.* Used in echoes of the Du. proverb *zeggen is goedkoop*, 'saying is cheap.'
1546 J. HEYWOOD *Prov.* K iij, The Ducheman saieth, that seggyng is good cope. **1613** F. ROBARTS *Revenue Gosp.* 104 Alasse, alasse, segging is no good coping.

†ˈ**seggon.** *Obs. rare*⁻¹. [Of obscure origin; connexion with SEGGE seems unlikely.] A term of depreciation or pity (meaning uncertain).
1573–80 TUSSER *Husb.* (1878) 174 Poore seggons halfe starued worke faintly and dull.

seggrum (ˈsɛgrəm), *dial.* Also 8 seagrim. The Common Ragwort, *Senecio jacobæa.*
1633 JOHNSON *Gerarde's Herbal* II. xxviii. 281 The first is called in Latine, *Herba S. Iacobi*..: in English, S. James his Wort... In Holdernesse in Yorke-shire they call it Seggrum. **1766** *Museum Rust.* VI. 450 Ragwort,..Seggrum, or Seagrim. **1788** W. H. MARSHALL *Yorksh.* II. 350 Seggrums; *senecio jacobæa*; ragwort.

seggy, obs. or dial. form of SEDGY.

segh(e, obs. forms of SEE *v.*, SIEGE, SIGH *v.*

segholate, variant of SEGOLATE.

segment (ˈsɛgmənt), *sb.* Also 6 **seagment**, 7 **segement**. [ad. L. *segment-um*, f. *sec-* (euphonically *seg-* before *m*), *secāre* to cut: see -MENT.]

1. A piece cut or broken off; a fragment. *rare.*
1586 FERNE *Blaz. Gentrie* II. 98 Antichrist..deuiseth by councels and synods hat all signes, images, seagments or reliques of holy men..should be adored. *c* **1620** A. HUME *Brit. Tongue* II. v, This s sum haldes to be a segment of his, and therfoer now almost al wrytes his for it, as if it wer a corruption. **1704** RAY *Creation* I. (ed. 4) 58 The Segments and Cuttings of some Plants. **1832** LYTTON *Eugene A.* I. i, He also quarrelled with him the oftenest and testified the least forbearance at the publican's segments of psalmody. **1837** CARLYLE *Fr. Rev.* I. VII. xi, The truest segment of Chaos seen in these latter Ages!

2. a. *Geom.* A plane figure contained by a right line and a portion of the circumference of a circle. In full ***segment of a circle***. Also, see quot. 1728.
In quot. 1626 loosely used for *arc*.
1570 BILLINGSLEY *Euclid* III. Def. v. 81 b, A section or segment of a circle, is a figure comprehended vnder a right line and a portion of the circumference of a circle. **1626** DONNE *Serm.* lxvii. (1640) 677 The earth it selfe being round, euery step we make upon it, must necessarily bee a segment, an arch of a circle. **1738** CHAMBERS *Cycl.* (ed. 2), *Segment* is sometimes also extended to the parts of ellipses, and other curvilinear figures. **1806** HUTTON *Course Math.* (ed. 5) I. 42 To find the Area of any Elliptic Segment. Find the area of a corresponding circular segment.

b. ***segment of a sphere***: a solid figure bounded by a portion of the surface of a sphere and an intersecting plane.
1570 BILLINGSLEY *Euclid* XII. Prop. xvi. 376 Of segmentes, some are greater then the halfe sphere, some are lesse. **1704** J. HARRIS *Lex. Techn.* I, *Segment of a Sphere*, is a part of it cut off by a Plane;..therefore the Base of such a Segment must always be a Circle, and its Superficies a part of the Surface of the Sphere.

c. A segmental portion of anything having a circular or spherical form.
1646 SIR T. BROWNE *Pseud. Ep.* VII. iv. 346 Even unto..such as live under the pole, for halfe a yeare some segments [of a rainbow] may appeare at any time under any quarter. **1700** DRYDEN *Ceyx & Alcyone* 265 Indu'd with Robes of various Hew she flies, And flying draws an Arch (a segment of the Skies). **1837** BREWSTER *Magnet.* 326 A frame..contains the segment of a glass cylinder.

d. *Her.* A bearing representing a portion of a circular object.
1828–40 BERRY *Encycl. Her.* I, *Segment*, one side only of a coronet, &c.

3. a. *Geom.* The finite part of a line between two points; a division of a line.
1617 SPEIDELL *Geom. Extract.* 24 Let BA be the greater segement giuen, and the whole line is required. **1885** LEUDESDORF *Cremona's Proj. Geom.* 53 Let us examine the relation which exists between the lengths of two corresponding segments *AB, A'B'* [of two straight lines].

b. *Acoustics.* Each of the portions into which the length of a vibrating string, wire, etc. is divided by the nodes.
1863 ATKINSON *Ganot's Physics* 160 The part vibrating between two nodal points is called a ventral segment. **1870** EVERETT *Deschanel's Nat. Philos.* 832 The division into segments is often distinctly visible when the string of the sonometer is strongly bowed. **1879** [see NODE *sb.* 6 a].

4. a. Each of the parts into which a thing is or may be divided; a division, section.
1762 BP. LOWTH *Introd. Eng. Gram.* 157 A sentence or Member is again subdivided into Commas, or Segments. **1847** LEWES *Hist. Philos.* (1867) I. 236 By the second segment of the intellectual world understand me to mean all [etc.]. **1847** L. HUNT *Men, Women & B.* I. ii. 22 Being unable to divide the orange into its segments, he ventures upon a great liquid bite. **1886** RUSKIN *Præterita* I. x. 307, I must..cease talk of pictorial and rhythmic efforts..and go back to give account of another segment of my learning.

b. *Anthrop.* An autonomous sub-branch of a lineage group which remains within the larger tribal or clan structure.
1940 M. FORTES in Fortes & Evans-Pritchard *Afr. Polit. Systems* 243 A maximal lineage has an hierarchical structure. It consists of two or more major segments, each of a lesser span than the (inclusive) maximal lineage... Each major segment comprises lesser segments constituted on the same principle. **1950** M. GLUCKMAN in A. R. Radcliffe-Brown *Afr. Systems of Kinship* 169 The lineages within the clan are usually residential units. Their segments are cores of villages. **1977** HUNTER & WHITTEN *Stud. Cultural Anthrop.* xviii. 397/1 A hierarchical type of authority structure that rests on levels of increasingly inclusive tribal segments.

c. *Linguistics.* A unit forming part of a continuum of speech or (less commonly) text; an isolable unit in a phonological or syntactic system.
1943 K. L. PIKE *Phonetics* vii. 107 A *segment* is a sound (or lack of sound) having indefinite borders but with a center that is produced by a crest or trough of stricture during the even motion or pressure of an initiator. **1946** B. BLOCH in *Language* XXII. 237 A segment is a word or a sequence of words that does not occur alone as a pause-group in a major sentence. **1953** C. E. BAZELL *Linguistic Form* 7 Morphemic segments may frequently be classed together under one morpheme in the American sense, and considered from this standpoint are regarded as allomorphs. **1960** E. SIVERTSEN *Cockney Phonol.* iv. 122 /ð/ may be manifested, not as a separate segment, but in the dental quality of a preceding apical segment whose phonemic norm is otherwise alveolar. **1964** E. PALMER tr. *Martinet's Elem. Gen. Linguistics* i. 26 The word *puerum*, adequately characterized by the segment *-um* as the object of the verb. **1972** W. LABOV *Language in Inner City* iii. 99 As a rule the ordering of variable constraints within a segment is more regular than ordering across segments.

d. *Computers.* (See quot. 1954.)
1954 *Computers & Automation* May 18/2 *Segment*, a part of a complete specific routine, which can be entirely stored in the internal storage and contains the coding necessary to automatically call in and transfer control to other segments. **1963** *Communications ACM* VI. 391/2 Segments of a program could not be treated as independent entities. In general, a symbol name, if used in one segment, could not be used in another segment with a different meaning. **1969** [see OVERLAY *sb.* 6]. **1977** HUGHES & MICHTOM *Structured Approach to Programming* v. 107 A segment is both a logical and physical subdivision of a module. Logically, it is a subfunction of the module's function. Physically, it is limited to the number of source-code lines that will fit on one printer page of source output (50 to 60 lines).

5. *Bot.* Each of the portions into which a leaf or other plant-organ is divided by long clefts or incisions.
1713 P. BLAIR *Misc. Observ.* (1718) 104 Flowers..divided into five Segments. **1723** —— *Pharmaco-Bot.* I. 18 The Bottom Leaves generally consist of five Pair of Segments. **1796** WITHERING *Brit. Plants* (ed. 3) I. 80 *Segment* (lacinium), the small parts of a leaf, cup, or petal, included between the incisions. **1877** HULME *Wild Flowers* I. Summary 6 Borage... Calyx of five segments, very deeply cleft. **1880** A. GRAY *Struct. Bot.* iii. §4. 98 When a leaf is divided or parted and these primary lobes again lobed or cleft, the lobes of first order are called Segments (sometimes divisions or partitions), and the parts of these, Lobes.

6. *Biol.* and *Embryol.* **a.** Each of the longitudinal divisions composing the body in some animals, esp. in the Articulata; a somite, metamere.
1826 KIRBY & SP. *Entomol.* IV. 297 Segment (*Segmentum*). The great inosculating joints of the body. **1828** STARK *Elem. Nat. Hist.* II. 127 Articulata. The third great division of the Animal Kingdom consists of animals which have their body or members composed of segments or articulated rings. **1872** H. A. NICHOLSON *Palaeont.* xiv. 143 The body [in Arthropods] is composed of a series of segments or 'somites', arranged along a longitudinal axis.

b. A cell formed by segmentation.
1862 DARWIN *Orchids* v. 207 The three proper ovule-bearing cords or segments. **1882** VINES *Sach's Bot.* 139 The other daughter-cell..appears..like a piece cut off from the back or side of the apical cell,..and is hence called the Segment.

7. *Anat.* **a.** Each complete series of bones forming a vertebra of the spinal column; also, each of the three annular divisions of the cranium proper.
1844 OWEN *Anat. Vertebr. Anim.* iii. 42, I define a vertebra, as one of those segments of the endo-skeleton which constitute the axis of the body [etc.]. **1880** GÜNTHER *Fishes* iv. 64 There is no trace of vertebral segments or ribs.

b. A division of the spinal cord and nerves.
1855 H. SPENCER *Psychol.* (1872) I. I. ii. 16 We find the nervous system formed of a series of centres, each sending fibres to the different organs of its own segment. **1899** *Allbutt's Syst. Med.* VIII. 623 Zoster on the face tends to follow the distribution of the three main peripheral branches of the ganglion rather than to be distributed over the supply of 'root areas' or segments'.

8. = *segment* (or SEGMENTAL) *arch* (see 9 b).
1836 PARKER *Gloss. Arch.* (1850) s.v. *Arch*, The only forms used by the ancients were the semicircle, the segment, and ellipse, all of which continued prevalent till the pointed arch appeared. *a* **1878** SIR G. SCOTT *Lect. Archit.* (1879) I. 146 The pointed arch had obtained universal predominance, though without involving the rejection of the semicircular or the plain segment.

9. *attrib.* and *Comb.* **a.** simple attrib., as (sense 6) ***segment-boundary***, (sense 5) ***segment-leaf***; **segment-shell** (see quot. 1862).
1893 J. TUCKEY *Amphioxus* 119 Thereby is introduced the later characteristic curvature of the *segment boundaries [of the mesoblastic somite]. **1731** MILLER *Gard. Dict.*, **Segment-leaves*, are Leaves of Plants divided or cut into many Shreds. **1862** F. A. GRIFFITHS *Artil. Man.* (ed. 9) 192 The *Segment Shell consists of thin cast iron cylinders, enclosing a series of segments of the same metal, cast separately, and built upon an iron disc.

b. In many combinations with the meaning SEGMENTAL (sense 1), esp. in the names of mechanical appliances, parts of machinery, etc., indicating the shape of the essential or working part, as ***segment-arch, -rack, -roof, vault*** (see quots.); ***segment-gear, -saw, -valve, -wheel, -window*** (see Knight *Dict. Mech.* 1875 and Suppl. 1884).
1887 *Archit. Publ. Soc. Dict.*, **Segment arch.* **1835** URE *Philos. Manuf.* 196 The..stretching-roller has its axle mounted in the *segment-racks. **1838** *Civ. Engin. & Arch. Jrnl.* I. 225/2 From these springs a *segment roof. **1776** G. SEMPLE *Building in Water* 123 Erect a competent Number of Pillars..and thereon turn *segment Vaults and Arches.

c. In *Linguistics* (see sense 4 c above).
1961 F. W. HOUSEHOLDER in Saporta & Bastian *Psycholinguistics* 20/2 Exact boundaries were not as

important as some early workers thought; location of segment-centers is in general adequate. **1969** *Language* XLV. 303 They would be stated in terms of component-sized entities (hypophonemes), however, not in terms of segment-sized entities (classical phonemes). **1971** *Archivum Linguisticum* II. 135 The features of articles and the features of suffixes are extracted from this complex and distributed in their proper places by 'segment transformations' or 'segmentalization'. **1978** *Language* LIV. 47 Cf. Eng. *svelte*, *sphere* etc., whose initial clusters violate the segment-sequence constraints of English.

segment (sɛgˈmɛnt, ˈsɛgmənt), *v.* [f. SEGMENT *sb.*]

1. *trans.* To subject to the process of segmentation or division and multiplication of cells; to produce (new cells) by this process.

1859 *Todd's Cycl. Anat.* V. 79/2 The whole yolk is segmented in mammalia. **1877** HUXLEY & MARTIN *Elem. Biol.* 50 The new cells which are successively segmented off from the terminal cell.

2. a. *intr.* Of a cell or ovum: To divide or split up and give origin to one or more new cells by the process of SEGMENTATION.

1888 ROLLESTON & JACKSON *Anim. Life* Introd. 24 In some *Rotifera*, *Crustacea*, and *Insecta* one polar body only is formed, and the ovum then proceeds to segment.

b. *Anthrop.* Of a lineage group or clan: to divide into smaller autonomous branches within the larger social structure. Cf. sense 4 b of the sb.

1940 E. E. EVANS-PRITCHARD in Fortes & Evans-Pritchard *Afr. Polit. Systems* 284 In the diagram below, A is a clan which is segmented into maximal lineages B and C. **1965** P. C. LLOYD in M. Banton *Polit. Systems & Distrib. Power* 66 The Ngoni have a lineage structure which continually segments. **1974** L. MAIR *Afr. Societies* x. 127 All lineages segment in the course of generations.

3. *trans.* To divide into segments. Cf. senses 4 c, d of the sb.

1872 HUMPHRY *Myology* 5 The caudal muscles therefore consist of a 'dorsal' and 'ventral' muscle on each side,.. transversely segmented by the membranous septa and the vertebral processes running into it. **1878** A. H. GREEN, etc., *Coal* iv. 121 The axis, prefiguring what in most vertebrates becomes segmented and ossified into the centra,..retains [etc.]. **1959** E. M. GRABBE et al. *Handbk. Automation, Computation, & Control* II. ii. 130 A discussion of an automatic system which faces the problem of segmenting a program, either data or instructions, into pieces is given by this group. **1962** C. O. FRAKE in Gladwin & Sturtevant *Anthrop. & Human Behavior* 75 How do we segment the stream of speech into category-designating units? **1969** P. B. JORDAIN *Condensed Computer Encycl.* 202 No matter how much central memory is provided for a computer, it will always be possible to write a program too large to fit. The most common way to handle this situation is to segment the program into overlays. **1972** W. LABOV *Language in Inner City* ii. 50 Young black children frequently find it difficult to segment *I'm* into *I am.* **1977** HUGHES & MICHTOM *Structured Approach to Programming* vi. 122 A module..is segmented in the same hierarchical fashion that a system or program is developed.

Hence **segˈmenting** *ppl. a.* and *vbl. sb.*

1912 J. S. HUXLEY *Individual in Animal Kingdom* vi. 149 The blastomeres or separate cells of the segmenting egg. **1959** E. M. GRABBE et al. *Handbk. Automation, Computation, & Control* II. ii. 130 It is imperative that a programmer be allowed to override any automatic segmenting and allocation system in order to provide increased efficiency. **1977** HUGHES & MICHTOM *Structured Approach to Programming* vi. 122 Segmenting is best handled at the stepwise refinement stage.

segmentable (sɛgˈmɛntəb(ə)l), *a.* [f. SEGMENT *v.* + -ABLE.] Capable of being divided into segments (*Linguistics* in quots.). Hence **segmentaˈbility**.

1957 TRAGER & SMITH *Outl. Eng. Structure* 52 The phenomena that are segmentable were analyzed as phonemes of one kind or another. **1962** H. C. CONKLIN in Householder & Saporta *Probl. Lexicogr.* 122 Unitary lexemes may be either *simple* (unsegmentable) or *complex* (segmentable). **1964** *Language* XL. 207 The 'segmentability' and the quantum mechanics available to linguists strikes these other workers as very rigorous. **1979** *Trans. Philol. Soc.* 82 The 'weak' adjective endings are clearly segmentable suffixed formatives.

segmental (sɛgˈmɛntəl), *a.* [f. SEGMENT *sb.* + -AL[1].]

1. a. Having the form of a segment (or, loosely, of an arc) of a circle.

1837 *Fraser's Mag.* XVI. 151 Giving its point a segmental sweep from Penlee Point..to the Mew-stone. **1856** 'STONEHENGE' *Brit. Sports* II. I. viii. §5. 346/1 This segmental form is better than the straight bit. **1869** RANKINE *Machine & Hand-tools* Pl. N 1, A segmental bevel wheel.

b. *Arch.* Of an arch, a pediment, window-head, etc. Hence *segmental-arched, -headed* adjs.

1816 RICKMAN *Archit.* in J. Smith *Panorama Sci. & Art* I. 131 A segmental arch has its centre lower than the spring. **1849** FREEMAN *Archit.* 350 The segmental arch..is both more horizontal and less elegant than the four-centred. **1851** —— *Window Tracery* 253 Of Segmental-Headed Windows. *Ibid.* 254 By a segmental head I of course understand one in which the centre (or centres) is very much below the line of the constructive impost. *Ibid.* 255 Segmental windows filled with Reticulated tracery. **1867** A. BARRY *Life Sir C. Barry* iii. 84 Angular and segmental pediments. **1867** *Church News* 31 July 327/2 A small chamber with a segmental arched vault.

2. a. Of, pertaining to, or composed of segments or divisions. In various applications (*Anat.*, *Biol.*, *Acoustics*, etc.). ***segmental apparatus***, the brain-stem of a vertebrate.

1854 OWEN in *Orr's Circ. Sci., Org. Nat.* I. 172 Giving the first indication of the segmental character of the skeleton. **1856** T. WILLIAMS in *Phil. Trans.* (1859) CXLVIII. 93 Under the appellation of the 'segmental organ', accordingly, it is proposed to describe that viscus upon the basis of which ..are always ingrafted the true generative structures [in Annelids]. **1870** EVERETT *Deschanel's Nat. Philos.* 1067 *Index*, Segmental vibration, 832. **1879** F. M. BALFOUR in *Q. Jrnl. Microsc. Sci.* XIX. 8 The first part of the urino-genital system to develop is the segmental duct (Vornieregang of Fürbringer), which is formed by a groove-like invagination of the peritoneal epithelium. **1888** HUXLEY & MARTIN *Elem. Biol.* i. 169 The prorenal (segmental) duct. **1888** [see SEGMENTALLY]. **1898** *Syd. Soc. Lex.*, *Segmental organ*, an organ consisting of a primitive epithelium-lined tubule opening at one end on the body-surface, and at the other into the cœlom or body-cavity. It is the type of the primitive kidneys. **1917** [see PALÆENCEPHALON]. **1974** D. & M. WEBSTER *Compar. Vertebr. Morphol.* xi. 240 Segmentation in the developing brain is neither as regular nor as apparent as it is in the spinal cord. However, during early development (at least), segmentation can be determined in the basal portion, which is, therefore, known as the 'segmental apparatus'.

b. *Path.* Characterized by segmentation or division into segments.

1896 *Allbutt's Syst. Med.* I. 189 Segmental degeneration of the nerves.

c. *Linguistics.* Of, pertaining to, or designating the division of speech or (less commonly) text into segments (cf. SEGMENT *sb.* 4 c). Freq. in phr. ***segmental phoneme***, a consonant or vowel phoneme, which can occur as one of the units in a sequence of such phonemes.

1938 B. L. WHORF *Lang., Thought, & Reality* (1964) 126 Timbre phonemics (segmental): Table of phonemes. Pattern congruity. Allophones or probitional variants. Allophonic constellation. **1942** C. F. HOCKETT in *Language* XVIII. 8 Features..which clearly extend over a series of several segmental groupings are suprasegmental. **1950** R. A. HALL in *Ibid.* XXVI. 12 Forty-seven segmental phonemes is not an excessive number to posit for a language. **1958** *English Studies* XXXIX. 104 The segmental sounds are almost exclusively transferred from indigenous languages of the area. **1966** *Amer. Speech* XLI. 225 Pitch levels are not always suprasegmental features. When they are short enough, they can be considered one of the distinctive features of a segmental phoneme. **1976** *Word 1971* XXVII. 57 The speech rhythms and patterns and intonations of the pregnant mother will [not] generate..'segmental phonemes', or anything so phonetically sophisticated relatedly. **1981** *Canad. Jrnl. Linguistics* XXVI. 74 The initial portions of the word have the same segmental values and the same relative prominence as the base word.

segmentalization (sɛgˌmɛntəlaɪˈzeɪʃən). [f. next + -ATION.] Division into segments; *spec.* in *Linguistics*, transformation of a grammatical feature into a distinct segment of speech or text. Cf. SEGMENT *sb.* 4 c.

1964 E. BECKER in I. L. Horowitz *New Sociology* 115 There is another kind of confusion..in complex society, which Mills called attention to as a 'segmentalization of conduct'. **1969** *Language* XLV. 718 The auxiliary *be* is introduced by a segmentalization transformation from features of the following element. **1970** *Canad. Jrnl. Linguistics* XVI. 17 Their [*sc.* linguistic features'] eventual extraposition (or 'segmentalization') is blocked in the case of participles.

segˈmentalize, *v.* [f. SEGMENTAL *a.* + -IZE.] *trans.* To divide into segments. Hence **segˈmentalized, segˈmentalizing** *ppl. adjs.*; **segˈmentalizer**.

1956 H. WHITEHALL et al. in *Kenyon Rev.* XVIII. 413 The constructive features must necessarily serve a descriptive grammar as *segmentalizers*—they are our chief scissors of linguistic perception. **1956** *Ibid.* 417 Both the rhythm-pointing and the segmentalizing functions of the three interrelated configurational features are of basic prosodic importance. **1968** *Language* XLIV. 774 Even when the feature is segmentalized, like *should* in Modern English, it remains an 'auxiliary' of the main verb. **1976** *Brit. Jrnl. Sociol.* XXVII. 317/1 The teaching practice of academic sociology..presents its subject matter in segmentalized courses on stratification, organization, politics, religion, etc.

segmentally (sɛgˈmɛntəlɪ), *adv.* [f. SEGMENTAL *a.* + -LY[2].] In a segmental manner.

1888 HUXLEY & MARTIN *Elem. Biol.* iii. 244 These [excretory] organs, being thus segmentally arranged, are termed segmental organs or nephridia. **1900** MIALL & HAMMOND *Harlequin Fly* ii. 84 Tracheal gills..may be ventral,..caudal,..segmental (i.e. segmentally repeated). **1957** S. POTTER *Mod. Linguistics* v. 105 Sentences may be analyzed *segmentally* into phonological units called *phonemes* and *syllables*; into morphological units called *morphemes* and *words*; and into syntactic units called *phrases* and *clauses*. **1964** R. H. ROBINS *Gen. Linguistics* vi. 262 Stress and pitch are just as fit to serve as the markers or exponents of grammatical categories and of syntactic relations as are segmentally represented morphemes.

segmentary (sɛgˈmɛntərɪ), *a.* [f. SEGMENT *sb.* + -ARY. Cf. F. *segmentaire.*]

1. Of the nature of or resembling a segment or an arc of a circle; segmental.

1853 KANE *Grinnell Exp.* xxxv. (1856) 314 Clouds, assuming a segmentary or arch-like form. *Ibid.* 321 Attracting attention by..its well-defined segmentary character.

2. Pertaining to segments or divisions; composed of segments. Cf. SEGMENT *sb.* 4 b.

1898 *Syd. Soc. Lex.*, *Segmentary*, made up of segments. **1899** *Allbutt's Syst. Med.* VIII. 99 Such a segmentary anæsthesia could not be produced by lesion of either the cord nerve-roots, or nerve-trunks. **1940** E. E. EVANS-PRITCHARD in Fortes & Evans-Pritchard *Afr. Polit. Systems* 284 Fission and fusion are two aspects of the same segmentary principle. **1957** V. W. TURNER *Schism & Continuity in Afr. Soc.* x. 291 Overlapping of territorial and kinship groupings such as one finds in segmentary societies. **1977** HUNTER & WHITTEN *Stud. Cultural Anthrop.* xviii. 396/1 Like other Bedouin tribes, Mutayr have what is called a segmentary tribal structure.

segmentate (ˈsɛgmənteɪt), *a.* [f. SEGMENT *sb.* + -ATE[2]. (L. had *segmentātus* ornamented with strips of cloth.)] Formed of segments, segmented.

1875 *Encycl. Brit.* II. 292/2 The abdomen [of an Araneid] is covered with a continuous integument neither annulate nor segmentate.

segmentation (ˌsɛgmənˈteɪʃən). [f. SEGMENT *v.* + -ATION.]

†**1.** 'A cutting into small pieces, an embroidering' (Blount *Glossogr.* 1656). *Obs.*—[0]

2. a. The process of division into segments; *spec.* in *Embryology*, the process by which, in the Metazoa, the germinal cell or protoplasmic mass is converted by division into a multitude of cells, which become metamorphosed into the tissues of the body; cf. also SEGMENT *sb.* 4 c, d.

1851 CARPENTER *Man. Phys.* (ed. 2) 487 The first change ..in the Mammalian ovum, is the 'segmentation' of the yolk; the entire mass of which..resolves itself..into.. segments. **1880** A. GRAY *Struct. Bot.* iii. §4. 98 Lobation or Segmentation. **1882** VINES *Sachs' Bot.* 293 The leaves undergo a segmentation similar to that of the stem. **1884** A. SEDGWICK in *Q. Jrnl. Microsc. Sci.* XXIV. 43 On the Origin of Metameric Segmentation [etc.]. **1910** *Spectator* 30 July 173/1 This segmentation of the tribe into clans would lead us to the discussion of exogamy. **1943** M. SCHLAUCH *Gift of Tongues* 254 French has its own formulas of segmentation like *quant à.* **1950** A. R. RADCLIFFE-BROWN *Afr. Systems Kinship* 40 For structures having successive segmentations the term 'polysegmentary' has been suggested. **1953** C. E. BAZELL *Linguistic Form* p. i, Space has been found to touch on several aspects of linguistic form which pass unnoticed in more extensive treatments of the subject... The problem of segmentation..has for this reason been left in the background. **1962** C. O. FRAKE in Gladwin & Sturtevant *Anthrop. & Human Behavior* 76 The segmentation of speech into the grammatically functioning units revealed by linguistic analysis is a necessary, but not sufficient, condition for terminological analysis. **1962** *Spring Joint Computer Conf.* 307/1 Segmentation is the process of dividing a single program into pieces. This is done to permit the operation of programs that are too large to completely fit into memory. **1971** W. WILDER in R. Needham *Rethinking Kinship & Marriage* 213 It might well be possible to decide whether local segmentation among the Purum appeared to lead to the formation of alliance groups. **1973** C. W. GEAR *Introd. Computer Sci.* vi. 243 The process of breaking a program into a number of smaller segments is called *segmentation.*

b. *attrib.*, as **segmentation cavity** = BLASTOCELE; **segmentation sphere**, see quot. 1898.

1888 HUXLEY & MARTIN *Elem. Biol.* i. 166 The cleavage cavity (segmentation cavity); small and central. **1898** *Syd. Soc. Lex.*, *Segmentation sphere*, one of the cells of a fertilized ovum that has undergone segmentation. **1909** *Contemp. Rev.* Apr. 447 Each segmentation sphere contained all the characters necessary to produce the entire organism.

segmentative (sɛgˈmɛntətɪv), *a. Linguistics.* [f. SEGMENT *sb.* + -ATIVE.] = SEGMENTAL *a.* 2 c (see also quot. 1936).

1936 *Language* XII. 127 Punctual and segmentative aspects of verbs in Hopi... The segmentative aspect is formed by final reduplication of this root plus the durative suffix *-ta.* **1961** *Amer. Speech* XXXVI. 159 This and other such 'segmentative' analyses fail to explain a number of other grammatical facts about nominals.

segmented (ˈsɛgməntɪd, sɛgˈmɛntɪd), *ppl. a.* [f. SEGMENT *v.* + -ED[1].]

1. a. *Anat.*, *Zool.*, etc. Consisting of segments or similar parts arranged in a longitudinal series.

1854 OWEN in *Orr's Circ. Sci., Org. Nat.* I. 176 In the cod-fish..it forms no part of the segmented neuroskeleton. **1870** ROLLESTON *Anim. Life* Introd. 124 The segmented Vermes.

b. *Bot.* Of a leaf: Divided into segments or lobes.

1883 G. ALLEN in *Nature* 15 Mar. 466 The divided but more broadly segmented leaves of those tall open-field species, cow-parsnip..and Alexanders.

2. *Embryol.* Of an ovum, a cell: Divided or split up by segmentation into cells.

1875 *Encycl. Brit.* III. 682/2 [Biology.] In the segmented body, the segments may or may not give rise to symmetrically or asymmetrically disposed processes. **1877** HUXLEY & MARTIN *Elem. Biol.* 106 The segmented ovum: composed of a large number of small cells.

3. *Archæol.* Of a prehistoric gallery (grave): divided into sections or segments; having compartments.

1920 *Glasgow Herald* 9 Mar. 9 Vestiges of a segmented central gallery were disclosed. **1939** V. G. CHILDE *Dawn Europ. Civilization* (ed. 3) xii. 206 On the slopes of the Pyrenees, [etc.]..gallery graves are divided into a series of intercommunicating compartments by low, transverse slabs... Such tombs are known as *segmented cists.* **1954** S.

PIGGOTT *Neolithic Cultures* vi. 160 In the typical form of 'segmented gallery' a number of such slabs divide the chamber into a series of compartments.

4. *gen.*

1950 *Sci. News* XV. Pl. 5 (*caption*) The segmented appearance of the flame is due to the shock wave which is formed in the jet as it leaves the nozzle. **1967** *Jane's Surface Skimmer Systems 1967–68* 59/2 The pockets, based on the segmented skirts of a hovercraft, form a seal around the body.

segmenter (sɛg'mɛntə(r)). *Zool.* [f. SEGMENT *v.* + -ER[1].] A fully developed sporozoan schizont ready to divide into a number of merozoites.

1929 R. W. HEGNER et al. *Animal Parasitol.* xi. 144 (*caption*) *Plasmodium vivax.* 1, Ring stage; 2, schizont; 3, segmenter; 4, gametocyte. **1946** P. F. RUSSELL et al. *Practical Malariol.* ii. 31 (*caption*) A large segmenter in an endothelial cell in the brain. **1978** *Jrnl. Protozool.* XXV. 449/1 In schizonts and segmenters knobs often obscure the unit membrane structure.

segne, obs. form of SEINE.

segnior, -orie, -y: see SEIGNIOR, SEIGNIORY.

'segnitude. *rare*[−0]. [ad, med.L. *segnitūdo*, f. L. *segnis*: see next and -TUDE.] = SEGNITY.

1818 in TODD; hence in later Dicts.

†**'segnity.** *Obs.*[−0]. [ad. L. *segnitāt-em*, f. *segnis* slow, sluggish: see -ITY.] (See quots.)

1623 COCKERAM II, Slothfulnes..*Segnity.* **1656** BLOUNT *Glossogr.*, *Segnity*, negligence, slowness, slothfulness; also barrenness.

[**segnotic**, erron. form of STEGNOTIC *a.* and *sb.*]

segnoury, -nurie, -nyorye: see SEIGNIORY.

sego ('si:gəʊ). *U.S.* [Said to be Ute Indian.] A showy-flowered plant, *Calochortus Nuttallii*, of the western United States, with an edible bulb. Also *sego lily*.

1851 H. HOWE *Hist. Coll. Gt. West* 432 Hogs fatten on a succulent bulb or tuber, called the Seacoe, or Seegose Root, which is highly esteemed as a table vegetable by the Mormons. **1852** H. STANSBURY *Expl. & Survey Gt. Salt Lake* 160 Sego..is much used by the Indian tribes as an article of food. **1875** *Amer. Naturalist* IX. 18 The general Indian name of 'Sego' is applied indiscriminately to all the edible bulbs of this region [*sc.* Utah]. **1883** *Harper's Mag.* 709/2. **1915** ARMSTRONG & THORNBER *Western Wild Flowers* 64 [The mariposa] is called Sego Lily..in Utah and is the 'State flower'. **1963** J. J. CRAIGHEAD et al. *Field Guide to Rocky Mt. Wildflowers* 18 Sego Lily... A white tuliplike flower with a triangular cup-shaped appearance.

segolate, segholate ('sɛgələt), *a.* and *sb.* *Heb. Gram.* [a. mod.L. *seg(h)olātus*, f. Heb. *seˢgōl*, the name of the vowel-point ֶ and of the sound (ɛ) which it represents.

The name *seˢgōl* means lit. 'bunch of grapes', alluding to the shape of the character.]

a. *adj.* Originally, of a disyllabic noun: Having the vowel *seˢgōl* in both syllables. Now commonly in extended sense, as the distinctive epithet of the class of disyllabic nouns having an unaccented short vowel (normally *seˢgōl*) in the last syllable. **b.** *sb.* A segolate noun.

1831 M. STUART *Gram. Hebr.* §100. 46 All Segholate forms, i.e. those which have a furtive vowel in their final syllable. *Ibid.* §119. 56 *Aleph penult*, in words that would regularly be Segholates. **1837** G. PHILLIPS *Syriac Gram.* 25 One of the old forms of segolate nouns in Hebrew. **1884** CHEYNE *Isaiah* I. 291 The word is a so-called 'Segolate' in form.

segoon (sɪ'gu:n). *Fencing. Obs.* or *arch.* Also 8 sec(c)oon, sagoone. [a. F. *seconde*, pronounced (səgɔ̃d).] = SECONDE 2.

1721 D'URFEY *Two Queens Brentf.* II. i, Straight, in Seccoon, grim Death shall be his Lot. **1730** H. B[LACKWELL] *Compl. Fencing Master* 9 Which seven [thrusts] are these following: Carte, Tierce, Sagoone [etc.]. **1777** SHERIDAN *Sch. Scand.* v. ii, Sir Peter is dangerously wounded—By a thrust in segoon quite through his left side. **1903** *Longm. Mag.* Apr. 530 A thrust in segoon.

segra ('si:grə). [Perh. a native W. Indian name.] = SEQUA.

1864 GRISEBACH *Flora W. Ind. Islands* 787 Segra-seed: *Feuillea cordifolia.* **1891** in *Century Dict.*

segreant ('sɛgri:ənt), *a.* *Her.* Forms: 6–7 sergreant, 8 *Dicts.* sergreiant, 7– segreant. [Originally *sergreant*, of obscure etymology; probably corrupt; *s'érigeant* ('erecting itself') has been conjectured.] An epithet applied to a griffin (in quot. *a* 1695, perh. erroneously, to a falcon).

The real meaning of the term seems to be unknown. In some examples it is combined with *passant*; if this be not an error, the explanation in modern books, 'Rampant with wings expanded', cannot be correct.

?*a* **1550** in Baring-Gould & Twigge *West. Armory* (1898) 5 *Bligh*: Azur a griffon sergreant arg. **1562** LEGH *Armory* 106 A Griffin sergreant Or.—Wherefore saye you Sergreante? —For that he is halfe byrd, half beast. **1610** GUILLIM *Heraldry* III. xxvi. 181 Hee beareth Argent, a Griffon Passant, his wings displaied Sable... Leigh in his Blazon of this Beast, addeth this word Sergreant, in regard of his two-fold forme. *c* **1630** RISDON *Surv. Devon* §95 (1810) 91 A Griffin, segreant, or. **1682** GIBBON *Introd. Lat. Blasoniam* 60 Segreant..is the proper term for a Griffon displaying his Wings, *Segreant ses aisles*, as ready to fly. *a* **1695** WOOD *Oxford* (O.H.S.) III. 146 Armes are 'parted per chevron azure and argent, in chief two falcons sergreant or'. **1763** *Brit. Mag.* IV. 415 On a wreath, a gryphon passant, segreant, sable.

segregable ('sɛgrɪgəb(ə)l), *a.* [f. L. *sēgregā-re* SEGREGATE *v.*: see -ABLE.] That may be segregated.

1905 *Rep. Evol. Comm. R. Soc.* II. 124 An extracted type ..may carry on segregable determinants, whereby the individuals may, in reality, differ from each other, though outwardly alike. **1907** *Contemp. Rev.* June 908 Where the parent types differ in more than one pair of segregable characters we have new combinations of the parental characters. **1978** P. SUTCLIFFE *Oxf. Univ. Press* vi. 241 Milford tried to divide his business into 'segregable categories'.

'segregant, *a.* and *sb.* [ad. L. *sēgregant-em*, pres. pple. of *segregāre* to SEGREGATE.]

A. *adj.* †**1.** Separated, divided. *Obs. rare*[−1].

1647 WARD *Simple Cobler* 5 Tolerations of divers Religions, or of one Religion in segregant shapes.

2. *Genetics.* Having or being a genotype derived by segregation; usu., one different from that of either parent.

1936 *Discovery* May 161/1 The earlier investigators of heredity emphasised the discontinuous nature of inheritance... This is understandable when it is remembered that the segregant types, with which the earlier work was done, were of a very sharply contrasted nature. **1971** *New Scientist* 8 July 92/1 When certain chromosomes were eliminated, the malignant phenotype reappeared and the segregant cells were again able to produce tumours. **1974** *Nature* 27 Sept. 322/1 So called 'tritypes' involving any three of the four segregant genotypes should also be recovered frequently.

B. *sb.* *Genetics.* A segregant organism.

1955 *Genetics* XL. 894 No instances of adenineless segregants were obtained. **1976** *Nature* 29 Apr. 785/1 All 28 haploid segregants of strain DP62..were indistinguishable from strain NP73.

segregate ('sɛgrɪgeɪt), *a.* and *sb.* [ad. L. *sēgregātus*, pa. pple. of *sēgregāre*: see SEGREGATE *v.*]

A. *adj.*

1. Separated, set apart, isolated. Now *rare*.

In early use often †as pa. pple.

1426 LYDG. *De Guil. Pilgr.* 9399 The Body..Whan yt ys fro the segregat, Dysseueryd & separat. *c* **1480** *St. Ursula* (Roxb.) A j, So were the nobles from Brytayne segregate. **1532** MORE *Confut. Tindale* Wks. 428/1 Those holye consecrate companyes, the tone segregate from paynims by the sacrament of baptysme, the tother segregate fro the laye peple by the sacrament of order. **1563** FOXE *A. & M.* (1596) 1004/2 He was *segregatus a peccatoribus*—clean segregate from all kind of uncleanness. **1670** G. H. *Hist. Cardinals* III. II. 279 Two or three Cardinals, segregate from the other Factions. **1685** BAXTER *Paraphr. N.T.* 2 Cor. vi. 17–18 A holy people segregate to the Lord. **1865** *Spectator* 14 Jan. 32 It is true they have been celebrating their defeat..in a more morose and segregate manner than is here suggested.

2. *spec.* (*Zool.*, *Bot.*, etc.). Separated (wholly or partially) from the parent or from one another; not aggregated.

1793 T. MARTYN *Lang. Bot.*, *Segregata Polygamia.* Segregate Polygamy... When several florets comprehended within a common calyx are furnished also with their proper perianths. **1846** DANA *Zooph.* iv. (1848) 82 *Segregate*, when the buds are separate from the parent, except at base, each forming a distinct shoot or branch. **1882–4** COOKE *Brit. Fresh-w. Algæ* I. 29 Either single, segregate, or associated in families.

B. *sb.*

1. *Math.* One of a smallest select aggregate of products of irreducible covariants which suffices to provide by linear combination all covariants of every degree and order.

1878 CAYLEY *Math. Papers* X. 339 The effect of this was to enable me to establish for any given degree in the co-efficients and order in the variables..a selected system of powers and products of the covariants, say a system of 'segregates'. *Ibid.* 345 The terms in the expansion of the R.G.F. [*i.e.* Real Generating Function] may be called 'segregates', and the terms not in the expansion 'congregates'.

2. *Bot.* (See quot. 1900.)

1871 BRITTEN in *Trans. Newbury Field Club* I. 36 In this first enumeration aggregate species only..are entered; the segregates being noticed in the second..list. **1900** B. D. JACKSON *Gloss. Bot. Terms* s.v., A Segregate is a species separated from a super-species.

Hence **'segregateness.**

1668 WILKINS *Real Char.* II. i. 34.

segregate ('sɛgrɪgeɪt), *v.* Also 6–7 segregat. [f. L. *sēgregāt-*, ppl. stem of *sēgregāre* to separate from the flock, hence to set apart, isolate, divide, f. *sē-* (see SE-) + *greg-*, *grex* flock.]

1. a. *trans.* To separate (a person, a body or class of persons) from the general body, or from some particular class; to set apart, isolate, seclude.

In early use often with allusion to the Vulgate renderings of Heb. vii. 26, *segregatus a peccatoribus*, and of Jude 19, *qui segregant semetipsos.*

1542 BECON *News out of Heaven* G j, Your Bysshop shalbe godly, innocent, fautles, segregated from synners. **1552** LATIMER *4th Serm. Lord's Pr.* (1584) 145 b, This is the cause wherefore he will haue hys flocke segregated from the wicked. **1552** —— *Serm. 5th Sund. Epiph.* ibid. 322 So the Anabaptistes in our time..segregated themselues from the companye of other men. **1582** N. T. (Rhem.) *Jude* 19 These are they which segregate them selves, sensual, having not the Spirit. **1602** T. FITZHERBERT *Def.* 54 The Apostles.. were commanded by the holy ghost to segregat Paul and Barnabas. **1678** CUDWORTH *Intell. Syst.* 891 Nature absolutely Dissociates and Segregates men from one another, by reason of the Inconsistency of those Appetites of theirs. **1749** FIELDING *Tom Jones* XIII. ii, He rambled about some time before he could even find his way to those happy mansions, where fortune segregates from the vulgar, those magnanimous heroes. **1799** COLERIDGE in Mrs. H. Sandford *T. Poole & Fr.* (1888) I. 299 But dear Wordsworth appears to me to have hurtfully segregated and isolated his being. **1852** LD. COCKBURN *Jeffrey* I. 200 Certain peculiarities, or habits, which segregated him from the whole human race. **1884** *Law Rep.* *14 Q.B. Div.* 178 Mr. Newitt has.. segregated himself from Mr. Saffery in the trust. **1904** DOR. P. HUGHES *Life H. P. Hughes* xxii. (1907) 632 That innate instinct which ever aimed at uniting, not segregating groups of Christians.

b. To subject (people) to racial segregation; to enforce racial segregation in (a community, institution, etc.). Cf. DESEGREGATE *v.*, INTEGRATE *v.* 2 b.

1908 R. S. BAKER *Following Color Line* III. xiv. 299 All through my former chapters I have been showing how the Negroes are being segregated. So are the Chinese segregated, and the blacks in South Africa. **1930** *Economist* 27 Sept. 563/1 It is not surprising that a South African Nationalist politician should..proclaim his preference for his own party's policy of 'segregating' the natives and safeguarding 'the natural superiority' of the whites. **1948** *Rep. Native Laws Commission 1946–48* (Dept. Native Affairs, South Africa) 33/1 This effect was accentuated by the policy which sought to segregate the Africans as far as possible in specially demarcated 'Reserves'. **1958** *N.Y. Post* 20 Apr. 11. 7/3, I guess the DAR is not so much for segregating the colored as it is against doing you-know-what with them.

2. a. To separate or isolate (one thing from others or one portion from the remainder); to place in a group apart from the rest; *esp. Chem.*, *Geol.*, etc. (of natural agencies) to separate out and collect (certain particular constituents of a compound or mixture). In scientific classification: To remove (certain species) etc. from a group and place them apart.

1579 FULKE *Conf. Sanders* 662 Christe vouchsafed to segregate it from other wood, to make it the instrument of his passion. **1625** JACKSON *Creed* v. xxxiv, The prototype is conspicuous in the image, it is not segregated from it. **1691** TAYLOR *Behmen's Theos. Phil.* 73 Like a Refiner's fire which segregates Metals. **1744** BP. BERKELEY *Siris* §190 The pure fire is to be discerned by it's effects alone; such as..the segregating heterogeneous bodies, and congregating those that are homogeneous. **1831** D. E. WILLIAMS *Sir T. Lawrence* I. 167 Had these superb paintings been segregated in a national gallery. **1842** GROVE *Corr. Phys. Forces* (ed. 6) 100 The energy of the rays having been used up in decomposing the carbonic acid. The carbon thus segregated by the sun's rays is ready to give out heat and light, whenever it may be recombined with oxygen. **1872** W. S. SYMONDS *Rec. Rocks* x. 360 The limestone must have been segregated in deeper and tranquil waters. **1872** C. KING *Sierra Nevada* vii. 134 By an Act of Congress, the Yosemite Valley had been segregated from the public domain. **1911** *Q. Rev.* Jan. 290 In a true reference to the people the issue would be segregated.

b. *Mining.* (*U.S.*) See quot.

1881 RAYMOND *Mining Gloss.*, *Segregate*, Pac. To separate the undivided joint owership of a mining claim into smaller individual 'segregated' claims.

3. a. *intr.* for *refl.* To separate from a main body or mass and collect in one place.

1863 BATES *Nat. Amazon* vii. (1864) 169 The Mauhés are considered..to be a branch of the great Mundurucú nation; having segregated from them at a remote period. **1870** PROCTOR *Other Worlds* xi. 261 Whether clusters of them will eventually segregate from their neighbours..it is as yet.. impossible to judge. **1877** *Fraser's Mag.* XVI. 401 Most of the provinces had segregated into independent principalities.

b. *Genetics.* To undergo or display segregation (sense 1 e).

1904 W. BATESON et al. in *Rep. Evol. Comm. R. Soc.* II. 120 The fern-leaved type is recessive to the palm-leaved, segregating from it perfectly. **1930** R. A. FISHER *Genetical Theory Nat. Selection* i. 9 Mendel also demonstrated what a theorist could scarcely have ventured to postulate, that the different factors examined by him in combination, segregated in the simplest possible manner, namely independently. **1974** *Encycl. Brit. Macropædia* XIV. 775/1 The once-separate genes have been brought together..to produce a tightly packed unit of several genes sufficiently near each other on the chromosome that they segregate together.

Hence **'segregated** *ppl. a.*; *spec.* of institutions, groups, etc.: divided or separated on the basis of race (cf. SEGREGATE *v.* 1 b); **'segregating** *vbl. sb.*

a **1628** PRESTON *New Covt.* (1629) 221 My Word is as fire; It is a segregating thing, that differenceth, and puts a separation betweene the scum, and the liquor. **1652** *News fr. Low-Countr.* 1 Those four segregated forms. **1844** DISRAELI *Coningsby* IV. x, To the segregating genius of their great Lawgiver, Sidonia ascribes the fact that they had not been long ago absorbed among those mixed races. **1855** J. R. LEIFCHILD *Cornwall* 127 By the segregating power of electric action. **1855** J. PHILLIPS *Man. Geol.* 513 We may collect masses of true granite,..compact felspars, and many other segregated varieties. **1874** RAYMOND *6th Rep. Mines* 518 That the extensions, bought by Raymond..were..on segregated ground far to the south. **1948**, **1956** [see INTEGRATED *ppl. a.* c]. **1958** *Listener* 11 Dec. 982/1 Nine-tenths of the Negro children in the whole Southern region still go to segregated schools. **1960** *Guardian* 22 Mar. 13/7 San Antonio, Texas, launched its campaign against segregated lunch-counters. **1971** *Graphic* (Durban) 7 May

4/5 You are the future Black citizens of this segregated Republic.

segregation (ˌsɛgrɪˈgeɪʃən). [ad. late L. *sēgregātiōn-em*, n. of action f. L. *sēgregāre*: see SEGREGATE *v.*]

1. The action of segregating. **a.** The separation or isolation of a portion of a community or a body of persons from the rest.

1615 N. BYFIELD *Coloss.* i. 18 (1628) 122 The Church..is Holy by segregation from the sinnefull world. *a* **1677** MANTON *Serm. Ps. cxix*, cxxx. (1725) 600 Mat. 25. 32, 33... There is a congregation and then a segregation. **1829** SOUTHEY *Sir T. More* (1831) I. 384 There would be that segregation from the community into particular societies. **1849** A. BRYSON *Med. Statist.* in *Man. Sci. Enq.* 455 The utter impossibility of complete segregation [of fever patients], even in the most roomy vessel. **1859** TENNENT *Ceylon* II. VII. iii. 158 The social segregation is carried to such an extreme, that members of the several classes.. refuse to associate together. **1861** BERESF. HOPE *Eng. Cathedr. 19th C.* vi. 215 The provision which the early Eastern Church made, with true Oriental feeling, for the segregation of women into galleries. **1904** *Brit. Med. Jrnl.* 17 Sept. 631 Manson has also declared segregation to be the first law of hygiene for the Europeans in the tropics.

b. Dispersion, break up (of a collective unity).

1604 SHAKS. *Oth.* II. i. 10 What shall we heare of this [*sc.* a storm]? A segregation of the Turkish Fleet.

c. The separation of a portion or portions of a collective or complex unity from the rest; the isolation of particular constituents of a compound or mixture.

1612 WOODALL *Surg. Mate* Wks. (1653) 273 Segregation is the solution of that which was whole and perfect into parts divided, which flow not together as colliquables dissolved. **1634** T. JOHNSON *Parey's Chirurg.* XXVII. viii. (1678) 668 Vinegar is made by the corruption of Wine, and the segregation of the fiery and airy parts. *a* **1734** NORTH *Exam.* III. x. §1 (1740) 658 Now I have but one Matter more to work up,..which is a Segregation of Libel from History, which this Author has blended together. **1798** W. TAYLOR in *Monthly Mag.* V. 190 These observations..tend to authorize the segregation of a very fine set of oracles from those of Isaiah, Jeremiah, and Ezekiel. **1836** BUCKLAND *Geol. & Min.* xxi. (1837) I. 551 A fourth hypothesis considers veins to have been slowly filled by Segregation, or infiltration... Segregation of this kind may have taken place from electro-chemical agency, continued during long periods of time. **1878** BELL *Gegenbaur's Comp. Anat.* 43 Ontogenetic facts point to the primitive segregation of the nervous system from the ectoderm. **1886** LD. COLERIDGE in *Law Times* LXXXI. 65/2 The general costs of the action, which remain after the segregation of these separate costs.

Comb. (*Geol.*). **1875** J. W. DAWSON *Dawn of Life* ii. 28 Many of the veins are not true fissures but..segregation veins. **1888** TEALL *Brit. Petrogr.* 447 *Segregation vein*, a vein which has been produced by the segregation of the component mineral matter of a rock along fissures.

†**d.** *spec.* Separation from a church or ecclesiastical organization: chiefly in reproachful sense, schism. *Obs.*

1555 PHILPOT in Coverdale *Lett. Martyrs* (1564) 219 If we behold through yͤ iniquity of tyme, segregations to be made wyth counterfayt religion. **1662** H. HIBBERT *Body Divin.* II. 36 Let the seperatist..through his sullen segregation..be a thief to himself. **1683** CORBET *Nonconf. Plea* 26 There is a great difference between inimical segregation, like sedition in a Commonwealth; and a going severally upon weighty reasons.

e. *Genetics.* The separation of pairs of homologous alleles or chromosomes, esp. as occurs at meiosis in the formation of gametes by a heterozygous organism, to whose progeny different traits may consequently be transmitted.

1902 W. F. R. WELDON in *Biometrika* I. 229 If the hybrids of the first generations [of two races of peas]..be allowed to fertilise themselves, all possible combinations of the ancestral race-characters will appear in the second generation with equal frequency... Characters intermediate between those of the ancestral races will not occur... This may be called the Law of Segregation. **1904** *Rep. Evol. Comm. R. Soc.* II. 128 The balance of evidence is in favour of the belief that gametic segregation takes place at the reduction-division. **1930** R. A. FISHER *Genetical Theory Nat. Selection* i. 8 The segregation of single pairs of genes, that is of single factors, was demonstrated by Mendel in his paper of 1865. **1954** *Genetics* XXXIX. 432 The..abnormal segregation of *s* has been observed whenever C 602/λ has been used as the *F*-parent in cross. **1970** *Watsonia* VIII. 48 We hope that the present investigation will show clearly that the concept of segregation following allopolyploidy (intergenomic segregation, Jones 1967) can offer another possible explanation of this phenomenon.

f. The enforced separation of different racial groups in a country, community, or institution. Cf. APARTHEID.

1903 T. T. FORTUNE in B. T. Washington et al. *Negro Problem* vii. 215 The Afro-American people have been held together rather by the segregation decreed by law..than by ties of consanguinity. **1916** *Virginia Rep.* CXVII. 692 The cities and towns of this State have the power.. to pass segregation ordinances separating the places of residence of white and colored citizens, respectively. **1927** [see EURAFRICAN *a.* and *sb.* 3]. **1947** *Forum* (Johannesburg) 17 May 29/1 Political segregation is only possible where territorial segregation is in force. **1952** [see DESEGREGATE *v.*]. **1957** *Times* 18 May 6/3 The ruling of the Supreme Court that racial segregation in public schools [in South Africa] was unconstitutional. **1974** *Spartanburg* (S. Carolina) *Herald* 25 Apr. A1/6 The black majority has the franchise in tribal homelands under South Africa's race segregation policy.

g. The isolation or separate confinement of dangerous or troublesome prisoners. Hence *concr.* (also ***segregation unit***) a part of a prison designated for this purpose. Chiefly *U.S.*

1952 K. J. SCUDDER *Prisoners are People* 82 We set aside a few cells at Chino for segregation... If some man at Chino becomes defiant or refuses to work, he is placed in segregation. **1955** T. E. GADDIS *Birdman of Alcatraz* x. 91 The rear half of the structure held eighteen segregation cells... It was a prison within a prison. **1964** D. GLASER *Effectiveness of Prison & Parole System* viii. 174 The duration of disciplinary segregation is much briefer in federal prisons than in most state prisons... Men in segregation now receive the regular inmate food. *Ibid.* 175 Such units, usually called 'administrative segregation' in federal prisons, resemble the regular disciplinary section of a prison... The inmate may be restricted to quarters temporarily without being transferred to the segregation unit. **1974** P. W. KEVE *Prison Life & Human Worth* ix. 158 The segregation unit needs intensive service. *Ibid.* 162 A man..cannot get out of segregation unless he meets certain good behavior standards. **1977** *New Yorker* 24 Oct. 114/3 Such sentences often included a certain number of days in segregation.

2. The condition of being segregated.

1668 WILKINS *Real Char.* IV. ii. 407 To which [companionship] the opposite..is being in a state of Segregation from others. **1718** BP. T. WILSON in Keble *Life* xi. (1863) 386 Sooner than unite with her [the church of Rome]..I should rather choose to live in a state of segregation. **1841** L. HUNT *Seer* (1864) 81 To show the selectness and segregation of their accomplishments.

3. *concr.* Something segregated; in early use, †a schismatic body.

1563 WINȜET *Bk. Quest.* Wks. (S.T.S.) I. 98 Ȝe dissent fra the..haly Kirk vniuersall, and als fra the segregatioun of all heretikis afoir ȝow. **1605** in *10th Rep. Hist. MSS. Comm.* App. v. 372 The schismatick uniting himselfe unto their congregations, or rather, as this Sainct sayeth, unto their segregations. **1859** MURCHISON *Siluria* xix. (ed. 3) 493 Vein-stones or original segregations of gold. **1869** F. GALTON *Heredit. Genius* 376 We must..consider each human or other personality..as a segregation of what already existed. **1877** RAYMOND *Mines* 146 Number of feet in claim is 600, being a segregation of the north end of the Ophir Mine.

segregational (ˌsɛgrɪˈgeɪʃənəl), *a.* [-AL[1].] Of, pertaining to, or characterized by segregation.

1875 *Ure's Dict. Arts* (ed. 7) I. 812 Clays..from which the oxide of iron has been abstracted; partly by a segregational process, drawing together the iron into ferruginous nodules of hydrous sesquioxide.

segregationist (sɛgrɪˈgeɪʃənɪst), *a.* and *sb.* [f. SEGREGATION + -IST.] **A.** *adj.* Of, pertaining to, or designating persons or policies advocating or supporting political or racial segregation. Cf. INTEGRATIONIST *a.*

1954 W. K. HANCOCK *Country & Calling* vi. 171 Segregationist theory had partial relevance in that it emphasized South Africa's diversity of cultural inheritance. **1957** *Economist* 30 Nov. 774/2 One has to go as far to the right as Senator Ellender, the segregationist Democrat from Louisiana. **1961** *Encounter* XVI. 7/1 There is no segregationist legislation in Algeria. **1976** *National Observer* (U.S.) 21 Feb. 6/1 He could not accept its [*sc.* a club's] 'segregationist policy prohibiting any black guest'.

B. *sb.* An adherent or advocate of segregation. Cf. INTEGRATIONIST *sb.* and SEG *sb.*[4] a.

1955 [see INTEGRATIONIST *sb.*]. **1957** P. WORSLEY *Trumpet shall Sound* x. 206 One of their spokesmen..posed the 'sixty-four dollar' question of the segregationist 'Would you let a native marry your daughter or sister?' **1962** *Daily Tel.* 2 Apr. 12/2 This is because Southern segregationists are yielding to the inevitable, or at least refraining from militant resistance. **1977** *Time* 24 Jan. 27/1 Joseph Rauh..charged that Bell had given 'aid and comfort to segregationists' while an Atlanta attorney.

segregative (ˈsɛgrɪgeɪtɪv), *a.* [ad. med.L. *sēgregātīvus*, f. L. *sēgregāre*: see SEGREGATE *v.*]

1. Having the power or effect of separating. †**a.** *Gram.* and *Logic.* A general designation for adversative (or †discretive) and disjunctive conjunctions. Hence of a proposition, Consisting of members joined by a segregative conjunction.

1588 FRAUNCE *Lawiers Log.* II. vii. 95 b, The segregative axiome is that whose conjunction is segregative, and therefore is fittest to dispose disagreeable arguments which must be severed. The segregative is either disjunctive or discretive. **1626** A. WOTTON *Art Logick* II. vii. 142 That word is a conjunction Segregatiue, which severeth or divideth the parts of speech each from other.

b. Having the property of separating the elements or constituent parts of matter.

1674 T. FLATMAN *Belly God* 95 The Vintner..With segregative things as Pigeons eggs Strait purifies, and takes away the dregs. **1858** *Sat. Rev.* 20 Nov. 502 Iron-stone nodules..are..probably the result of a segregative power.

2. Of persons: Given to separation or disunion. Of an individual: Unsociable.

1685 H. MORE *Refl. Baxter* 24, I leave him..to consider what a pleasant thing it is to Flesh and Blood to be a Segregative Rabboni. **1875** WHITNEY *Life Lang.* ix. 158 The influences of barbarism, beyond narrow limits, are prevailingly segregative, a wild race..breaks up into mutually jealous and hostile divisions. **1888** MRS. H. SANDFORD *T. Poole & Fr.* I. 157 Coleridge was as social as Wordsworth was segregative in his tendencies.

†**segregator** (ˈsɛgrɪgeɪtə(r)). *Med. Obs.* [f. SEGREGATE *v.* + -OR.] An instrument for obtaining the urine from one kidney unmixed with that from the other.

1903 *Ann. Surg.* XXXVII. 30 The segregator could not possibly have attained the results given thus by catheterism and the strong aspiration. **1919** W. C. PEDERSEN *Urology* xiii. 704 The development of segregators corresponds with that of catheterization cystoscopes.

†**'segstar.** *Sc. Obs.* [Prob. repr. med.L. *sacristārius*, through some OF. form.] = SEXTON.

1531 *Aberdeen Reg.* (1844) I. 143 And the segstar and his seruand to ansuer for the keiping of the kirk zard to the maisteris of kirk vark.

segue (ˈsɛgweɪ), *v. Mus.* [a. It. *segue*, 3rd pers. sing. pres. of *seguire* to follow.] *intr.* ‖**1.** (See quot. 1959.)

1740 J. GRASSINEAU *Mus. Dict.* 214 *Segue*, it follows, or comes after; this word is often found before *aria, alleluja, amen.* **1801** T. BUSBY *Compl. Dict. Mus.* p. xxxii, The Italian word *Segue*, set against any of these abbreviations, signifies a repetition of the same notes, or passage. *Ibid. s.v. Segue*, (Ital.) it follows: as *Segue Coro*, the chorus follows. **1876** STAINER & BARRETT *Dict. Mus. Terms* 390/1 *Segue* (It.), follows, succeeds, comes after; as, *segue il coro*, the chorus follows; *segue l'aria*, the aria follows. **1959** *Collins Mus. Encycl.* 592/2 *Segue*,..'Follows'. Used as a direction (1) to proceed to the following movement without a break, and (2) to continue a formula which has been indicated, such as arpeggiating of chords or doubling in octaves.

2. *slang.* Of a person or music: to move without interruption from one song or melody to another. Freq. const. *into.* Also *transf.* and *fig.*

1958 D. HALPERIN in P. Gammond *Decca Bk. of Jazz* xx. 250 Then, without stopping, the guitarist and Ellington segued into *Body and soul.* **1962** 'K. ORVIS' *Damned & Destroyed* (1966) iii. 26 The Haydn selection reached the oboe part—melody segued and started to build. **1967** A. ARENT *Gravedigger's Funeral* (1968) xii. 190 Just then the orchestra segued into something I recognised. **1970** *New Yorker* 12 Sept. 32/2 The first started off with some flourishes from a Bach organ toccata and segued into 'She Comes in Colors'. **1976** C. LARSON *Muir's Blood* (1978) xxv. 135 The organist..*segued* resonantly from 'In the Garden' to 'Rock of Ages'.

transf. and *fig.* **1972** G. BAXT *Burning Sappho* v. 78 The crowds..let up a roar which soon segued into a mixture of cheers, jeers, jests, gibes. **1977** *Time* (Chicago) 17 Oct. 79/3 Bertolucci abruptly and wisely segues from the festivities to an epilogue, set in the present, that brings the enormous film full circle. **1978** LOGAN & WOFFINDEN *Illustr. New Musical Express Encycl. Rock* 199/1 How do the world's most celebrated adolescents [*sc.* the Rolling Stones] segue into middle age?

segue (ˈsɛgweɪ), *sb. Mus. slang.* [f. prec.] An uninterrupted transition from one song or melody to another. (Used of both live and pre-recorded music.)

1937 *Printers' Ink Monthly* May 42/1 *Segue*, the transition from one musical number to another without break or announcements. **1952** B. ULANOV *Hist. Jazz in Amer.* (1958) xix. 240 We could be doing 'Limehouse Blues' way up in tempo, look at the clock, and do a direct segue into the theme. **1977** *Rolling Stone* 13 Jan. 19/1 The band plays an hour straight, moving fluidly from one number to another; indeed, Parker calls Edwards the 'King of Segue'. **1980** S. BRETT *Dead Side of Mike* xv. 162 'He just does a long sequence of slow, sexy numbers, so they can dance real close... Straight *segue.*' 'What's a *segue*?' 'Record to record, no chat.'

‖**seguidilla** (segiˈdiʎa). Also 8 sequedilla, 8–9 **seguedilla**; 9 (after Fr.) **segua-, seguidille.** [a. Sp. *seguidilla* (whence F. *séguidille, séguedille*), f. *seguida* following, sequence, f. *seguir*(:—L. *sequī*) to follow.] A Spanish dance in $\frac{3}{4}$ or $\frac{3}{8}$ time; also the music for such a dance.

1763 *Court & City Mag.* Apr. 191/2 (Stanf.) He joined the others and danced a Sequedillas. **1775** R. TWISS *Trav. Portugal & Sp.* 167 A seguedilla is only a part of a tonadilla [*sic*]. **1782** *Ann. Reg.* II. 11 A monotonous drawling seguidilla that serves the nurses as a lullaby to put their children to rest. **1811** SCOTT *Don Roderick* II. xxxiv, And rung from village-green the merry seguidille. *a* **1852** MOORE *Oh! remember the time* 5 When I taught you to warble the gay seguadille, And to dance to the light castanet. **1854** THACKERAY *Newcomes* xxiii. I. 222 Percy sings a Spanish seguidella, or a German lied [etc.].

‖**seguiriyas** (segiˈrias). Also **seguiriya**, etc. [Andalusian-Gypsy var. of Sp. *seguidilla* SEGUIDILLA.] In full, ***seguiriyas gitana*** [Sp. *gitano*, fem. *gitana* gypsy]: a regional variety of flamenco music; the song or dance which accompanies this.

1922 I. BROWN *Nights & Days on Gypsy Trail* iv. 86 Silverio asked the guitar player to strike up a Gypsy seguirya, and throwing back his head..he sang..the very song that one of the cantadores present had improvised years before. **1926** J. B. TREND *Mus. Sp. Hist. to 1600* 7 The more modern forms (*flamenco*) often sound more 'oriental' than the older, traditional *Cante hondo*; and the oldest, the *Siguiriya gitana*, seems..less tinged with superficial orientalism than any. **1936** W. STARKIE *Don Gypsy* xix. 289 The *siguiriya gitana*..is full of tears and tragedy and for that reason is often called *playera* (the weeping poem). **1948** 'LA MERI' *Sp. Dancing* vii. 92 Of the flamenco estilos which are more distinctly song than dance, the *Seguidillas Gitano* (seguiriyas gitana) is the most typical. It is composed of four lines as against the seven which go to make up the Spanish Seguidillas. **1967** CHUJOY & MANCHESTER *Dance Encycl.* (rev. ed.) 856/1 Rhythm-forms of flamenco dances are: Alegrias, Soleares, Bulerias, Farruca, Zapateado, Tango, Zambra, and Seguiriyas. **1972** H. MACINNES *Message from Malaga* ii. 40 Once, she too had danced the *seguiriyas.*

segundo (sɪˈgʌndəʊ). [f. the name of Juan *Segundo*, the author of a book on bridle bits.
The British Museum has a copy in Spanish dated 1855, and one in French dated 1829. An English translation, 'from the original Spanish MS. which was dedicated to George IV. in 1832', was printed in Latchford's book cited below.]
A kind of bridle bit. Also *attrib.*
1860 WHYTE MELVILLE *Mkt. Harb.* xvii, An animal that may have the pace of a race-horse, but requires a segundo bridle, and a hundred-acre field to turn him in. **1871** B. LATCHFORD *The Loriner* List of Engravings, *Segundo Bit*, No. 41. Buxton Segundo, No. 81.

segur, obs. form of SAGGAR.

‖**Seguridad** (seguriˈðað). [Sp., security.] The Spanish security service.
1937 F. BORKENAU *Sp. Cockpit* ii. 120, I soon found out that these people belonged to the Seguridad, in other words the ordinary police of the old régime. **1938** E. HEMINGWAY *Fifth Column* (1939) II. i. 47 A room in Seguridad headquarters. **1977** *Guardian Weekly* 3 Apr. 13/1 From time to time it's learned that this or that army officer has been replaced by a liberal, or that new police and Seguridad chiefs have been appointed.

seh(e, sehel, obs. ff. SEE *v.*, SEAL *sb.*[2]

†ˈ**sehelich**, *a. Obs. rare.* [? f. stem of SEE *v.* + -*lich*, -LY[1]. Cf. the synonymous OE. *ȝesewenlic*, f. the pa. pple.] That may be seen, visible.
a **1225** *Leg. Kath.* 249, & hereð & hersumeð seheliche schaftes. *a* **1225** *St. Marher.* 11 Glistinde gimstan of all seheliche þing ant untsehelich baðe.

sehen, -ene, obs. ff. SEE *v.*, SENE *a.*

Sehna (ˈsɛnə). Also **Sena, Senne**, etc. The name of a town (now Sanandaj) in Kurdistan, used *attrib.* and *absol.* to designate a variety of finely-woven Persian rug or a knot used in weaving some oriental carpets (see quot. 1910). Also *Comb.*, as **Sehna-Kurd** (see quot. 1931[2]).
1901 J. K. MUMFORD *Oriental Rugs* xi. 183 In most of the Sehnas the diaper of small patterns covers the entire field. *Ibid.*, A few Sehna rugs have the pear pattern wrought upon a large scale. *Ibid.* 198 The genuine Mir Sarabands are tied in the Sehna knot. **1910** *Encycl. Brit.* V. 393/2 The second traditional knot is the Persian or Sehna knot, which..is tied so that from every space between the warp-threads one end of the knot protrudes. **1931** A. U. DILLEY *Oriental Rugs & Carpets* iv. 102 Sehna (Senneh or Senna) rugs..are distinguished by masterful accomplishment in small pattern. *Ibid.* 103 Sehna-Kurd is the name applied to rugs woven by the Kurds in emulation of the Sehnas. **1957** [see GHIORDES]. **1962** C. W. JACOBSEN *Oriental Rugs* 289 The finest old Sena with silk warp will often have 500 to 600 knots to the square inch. A good average new Sena with cotton warp will have from 150 to 250 knots to the inch. *Ibid.* 291 We class many of the better rugs from Hamadan district (woven in small villages) and superior to the usual Hamadan, Sena-Kurds. **1975** 'E. LATHEN' *By Hook or by Crook* xviii. 167 A very nice, versatile Sena... This Sena is ..twenty-six hundred dollars. **1975** *Oxf. Compan. Decorative Arts* 612/1 The Ghiordes knot is quite commonly used in western districts [of Persia] but a fine Sena knotting predominates. **1978** *Times* 13 Oct. 19/4 One expensive carpet, an unsold Senna at £40,000.

‖**Sehnsucht** (ˈzeːnzʊxt). [Ger.] Yearning, wistful longing.
[**1847** THACKERAY *Van. Fair* (1848) iv. 28 It is no blame to them that after marriage this *Sehnsucht nach der Liebe* subsides.] *a* **1861** A. H. CLOUGH *Poems* (1869) II. 193 (*title*) Sehnsucht. **1862** J. A. SYMONDS *Let.* 9 Dec. (1967) I. 372 Today I had a wondrous Sehnsucht to hear our choir once more. **1902** W. JAMES *Varieties Relig. Exper.* xvi. 383 An excellent old German Lady..used to describe to me her *Sehnsucht* that she might yet visit 'Philadelphia', whose wondrous name had always haunted her imagination. **1911** G. BELL *Let.* 6 May (1927) I. xii. 303 When the 1st of May came I had a great 'Sehnsucht' for the daffodils and the opening beech leaves at Rounton. **1941** [see RADIO *sb.* 3]. **1955** C. S. LEWIS *Surprised by Joy* i. 14 The Castlereagh Hills..taught me longing—*Sehnsucht*; made me..a votary of the Blue Flower. **1972** J. I. M. STEWART *Palace of Art* xiv. 141 The stickiest romance of all attends, of course, upon gondolas by moonlight, and Gloria felt she must by no means counter or abridge this small enclave of adolescent *Sehnsucht* in her almost undeviatingly rational friend.

sei, obs. f. SAY *v.*[1], SEE *v.*; var. SEY *sb.*[2]

seiannte, seiant(e, obs. forms of SEJANT.

‖**seicentismo** (seitʃenˈtizmo). Also **secentismo** and with cap. initial. [It., f. *seicento* SEICENTO.] = SEICENTO; also, the character or quality of works produced during this period.
1881 *Encycl. Brit.* XIII. 511/1 This period [*sc.* the hundred and forty years from the treaty of Cateau Cambresis to the war of the Spanish succession] is known in the history of Italian literature as the Secentismo. Its writers ..tried to produce effect with every kind of affectation, with bombast, with the strangest metaphors, in fact, with what in art is called mannerism, 'barocchism'. **1923** *Oxf. Broom* Apr. 17 Timid critics..excusing themselves on the ground that Seicentismo is analogous to the modern spirit, Fascismo, nay—Futurism even. **1926** R. FRY *Transformations* 95 A more guarded enthusiasm for these works than altogether suits recent converts to Seicentismo.

seicentist (seɪiːˈtʃɛntɪst), *sb.* (*a.*). Also *pl.* ‖**se(i)centisti** and with cap. initial. [ad. It. *seicentisti* pl., f. *seicento*: see next.] An Italian artist or man of letters of the seventeenth century. Also *attrib.* or as *adj.*
1841 W. SPALDING *Italy & Ital. Islands* II. III. iv. 414 The *seicentisti*, or artists of the seventeenth century. **1881** *Encycl. Brit.* XIII. 511/2 The 'Secentisti' erred by an overweening desire for novelty, which made them always go beyond the truth. **1905** *Athenæum* 25 Mar. 376/3 The rest of the Italian School is of minor importance, though one or two of the Seicentists are here..well represented. **1931** A. HUXLEY *Music at Night* i. 38 The bright reassuring Heaven,..the stage immensities and stage mysteries, all the stock-in-trade of the *seicentisti*, are absent from his [*sc.* El Greco's] pictures. **1938** L. MACNEICE *Mod. Poetry* i. 7 Theocritus is more escapist than Euripides..the Seicentist poets than Dante.

‖**seicento** (seiˈtʃɛnto). Also **Seicento**. [It.: short for *mil seicento* one thousand six hundred.] The seventeenth century considered as a period of Italian art. Also *attrib.*
1908 R. BAGOT *A. Cuthbert* iv. 29 Beautiful specimens of Italian cabinets of the cinquecento and seicento. **1926** E. HUTTON tr. *A. Venturi's Short Hist. Ital. Art* vii. 339 The glory of the *Seicento* at Milan is summed up in the names of Feraro and Cairo. **1938** *Burlington Mag.* Aug. 82/2 To pass from the seicento to the settecento is inevitably to experience a slackening of tension which the impressive body of Solimenas..do little to check. **1947** D. MAHON *Studies in Seicento Art & Theory* 1 The writer was primarily interested in discovering why this occurred, and became involved..with certain aspects of Seicento art theory. **1972** *Listener* 7 Sept. 317/2 Festive scraps from the Seicento. **1979** *Now!* 21–27 Sept. 116/1 Two outstanding *seicento* marble busts..remind the viewer of J. Pierpont Morgan's greater collection of sculpture formed in America with the help of Henry Duveen.
Hence **seiˈcentoist** (*rare*) = SEICENTIST.
1830 *Fraser's Mag.* I. 146 The architect..has thought proper to have recourse to the 'seicentoists'.

seich, obs. pa. t. of SEE *v.*

seiche (seɪʃ). *Physiogr.* [a. Swiss Fr. *seiche*, perh. a graphic adoption of G. *seiche*, sinking (of water).
Not connected, as is usually stated, with F. *seiche, sèche*, 'a portion of the sea-bottom left uncovered at low tide'.]
A short-lived standing oscillation of a lake or other body of water (as a bay or basin of the sea), somewhat resembling a tide, which may be caused by abrupt changes in atmospheric conditions or by small earth tremors.
1839 G. ROBERTS *Dict. Geol.*, *Seiches* (Swiss term); an occasional undulation of the water of lakes, like a tide wave, sometimes to the height of five feet, supposed to be caused by the unequal pressure of the atmosphere. **1852** TH. ROSS *Humboldt's Trav.* I. i. 24 M. Vaucher thinks that the tides in the lake of Geneva, known by the name of the seiches, arise from the same cause. **1898** G. H. DARWIN *Tides* ii. 37 Although, then, it is possible to indicate causes competent to produce seiches, yet we cannot as yet point out the particular cause for any individual seiche. **1905** *Geogr. Jrnl.* XXVI. 46 A seiche was observed..within the shelter of the pier at the east end of Loch a' Chroisg... The amplitude was a quarter of an inch, and the period about $11\frac{1}{2}$ minutes. **1932** *Geogr. Rev.* XXII. 476 The strongest current caused by the seiches was found in the south-east corner of Great Bear Lake. **1957** G. E. HUTCHINSON *Treat. Limnol.* I. v. 299 The phenomenon has long been recognized locally in the Lake of Geneva, and the term seiche was recorded by Fatio de Duillier (1730) as applied to the oscillation in that lake. **1962** *New Scientist* 13 Sept. 560/1 Wind can also cause whole lakes and bays to oscillate..and these movements, called 'seiches', can communicate energy to the ground. **1971** *Nature* 4 June 306/2 The dominant internal seiche has a wavelength twice the length of the Loch, and a marked asymmetry.
Hence ˈ**seiching**, the occurrence of a seiche; the motion occurring in a seiche; **seiˈchometer** [-METER] an instrument for measuring seiches.
1903 *Nature* 23 Apr. 599/2 Sir John Murray..exhibited a seichometer with which he hoped in the coming season to get a more definite and precise record of these oscillations. **1955** *Sci. Amer.* Jan. 2/2 The extreme heights reached by the water in specific locations is due to another phenomenon known to oceanographers as 'seiching', which is similar to the sloshing of water in a bathtub. **1967** *Oceanogr. & Marine Biol.* V. 27 In contrast, Corkan..and Rossiter..found.. little evidence of North Sea seiching. **1971** *Nature* 4 June 308/1 It is likely that the effect of the Earth's rotation is principally to cause a small alternating transverse tilt of the isotherms across the Loch during the seiching motion.

seicle, obs. Sc. form of SIECLE.

seid(e: see SAYYID, SAID *ppl. a.*, SEED.

Seidel[1] (ˈzaɪd(ə)l). *Ophthalm.* [The name of Erich *Seidel* (1882–1946), German ophthalmologist, who described the sign (see below) in 1914 (*Archiv f. Ophthalm.* LXXXVIII. 102).] Used in the possessive, as **Seidel's sign**, the occurrence of one or two hooked scotomata extending from the blind spot.
1918 R. H. ELLIOT *Glaucoma* iv. 220 Should the condition of increased intra-ocular pressure continue, Seidel's sign will pass on into Bjerrum's sign. **1932** *Optician* LXXXIII. 398/1 With 2/1,000 white definite Seidel's signs were evident as horns extending about $1\frac{3}{4}$ in. both above and below the projected blind-spot. **1964** S. DUKE-ELDER *Parsons' Dis. Eye* (ed. 14) xxi. 305 Occasionally there is a sickle-shaped extension of the blind-spot above or below, or both, with the concavity of the sickle directed towards the fixation point (Seidel's sign); this is of more doubtful significance [as a symptom of glaucoma].

‖**seidel**[2] (ˈzaɪd(ə)l). [Ger., orig. a liquid measure varying locally between about a third and a half litre.] A beer mug or glass (in quot. 1930 used *loosely*); the quantity that such a vessel will contain.
1922 E. E. CUMMINGS *Enormous Room* iv. 92 Such..hands as might have grasped six seidels..on 13th street. **1930** D. RUNYON in *Collier's* 1 Feb. 12/1 Wilbur Willard all mulled up to a million, what with him having been sitting out a few seidels of Scotch with a friend. **1957** M. SWAN *British Guiana* xi. 180, I was welcomed with a seidel of Pilsener. **1980** G. V. HIGGINS *Kennedy for Defense* ii. 14 Knackwurst, German potato salad, couple seidels of Jake's Special Dark.

seidg(e, obs. forms of SIEGE.

Seidlitz (ˈsɛdlɪts). Also 8 **seydlitz**, 9 **sedlitz**. The name of a village in Bohemia, where there is a spring impregnated with magnesium sulphate and carbonic acid. Used *attrib.* in †**Seidlitz salt**, magnesium sulphate; †**Seidlitz water**, an artificial aperient water of the same composition as the water of the Seidlitz spring. Hence in **Seidlitz powder** (arbitrarily named, merely on account of its aperient property), a dose consisting of two powders, one of tartaric acid and the other of a mixture of potassium tartrate and sodium bicarbonate, which are to be dissolved separately, and the solutions mixed and drunk during effervescence.
1784 CULLEN tr. *Bergman's Phys. & Chem. Ess.* I. 439 The Seydlitz, Seydschutz, or Epsom salts are got by evaporation from the water of fountains in the places from whence they borrow their names. **1802** *Med. Jrnl.* VIII. 491 The Sedlitz water is another sort of artificial mineral water introduced by Mr. Paul in this country... This water consists of vitriolated magnesia,..and is so powerfully impregnated with carbonic acid, as to render the bitterness of the salt scarcely discoverable. **1815** *Specif. Savory's Patent* No. 3954, The combination of a neutral salt or powder which possesses all the properties of the medicinal spring at Seidlitz, in Germany, under the name of the Seidlitz Powders. **1837** DICKENS *Pickw.* xx, Another clerk..was mixing a Seidlitz powder, under cover of the lid of his desk. **1872** BAKER *Nile Tribut.* viii. 112 The simple effect of mixing a seidlitz powder was a source of amusement.

seie(n, obs. ff. SAY *v.*[1], SEE *v.*

seif (siːf, seɪf). *Physical Geogr.* Also **sif**. [ad. Arab. *saif*, lit. 'sword'.] A sand dune having the form of a narrow ridge elongated in a direction parallel to that of the prevailing wind. Also *seif dune*.
1925 W. J. H. KING *Myst. Libyan Desert* xxiii. 221 In front of us..was a high three-headed *sif*, or longitudinal sand dune. **1931** *Geogr. Jrnl.* LXXVIII. 16 In form it is a typical *sif* dune, a long straight ridge of sand with a single longitudinal chain of crests rising to billowy pyramids set at regular intervals, in silhouette something like huge saw-teeth. **1933** *Ibid.* LXXXII. 107 The Prince's map of this area shows a sudden change in the direction of the straight parallel lines of *seif* dunes which cross the country. **1941** R. A. BAGNOLD *Physics of Blown Sand & Desert Dunes* xv. 234 The early observers..held that it blew at right angles to the dune direction, whereas later observations over a longer period show that it blows parallel to the dunes... Both are right, since cross-winds are essential for seif formation. **1953** *Sci. News* XXVII. 16 The greatest height recorded for a *seif* dune is 210 metres... Their lengths vary from about 60 to 120 kilometres. **1975** *Nature* 20 Feb. 617/2 Until the recent drought, seif dunes were mainly active in this region north of the 150-mm isohyet. **1976** *Ibid.* 26 Feb. 654/1 Nearby, near the oasis of Bilma, a small dune field of seifs and barchans again indicates that the wind at right angles to the barchans would be to the left of the main trend.

seif: see SIEF *Obs.*

seige, var. SIEGE.

seigh(e, etc.: see SAY *v.*[1], SEE *v.*, SIGH *v.*

seigne, variant of SENYE *Obs.*

Seignette (sɛɲɛt). Also 8 **Saignette**. The name of a French chemist of the seventeenth century used attrib. in *Seignette salt*, (earlier †*Seignette's salt*, F. *sel de Seignette*), a name for potassium and sodium tartrate, Rochelle salt.
1753 *Chambers' Cycl.* Suppl., *Seignette's salt*, a name given in France to a kind of sal polycrestus [etc.]. **1758** REID tr. *Macquer's Chym.* I. 126 This salt is another sort of soluble Tartar. It is called Saignette's Salt, from the inventor's name. **1863** FOWNES *Chem.* (ed. 9) 566 Tartrate of potassa and soda; Rochelle or seignette salt.

seigneur (sɛɲœr). Also 8 *erron.* **seignieur**. [Fr.:—L. *seniōr-em*: see SENIOR, and cf. SEIGNIOR and SIGNOR.] **a.** In *French History*, a feudal lord; a noble taking his designation from the name of his estate. Also *transf.* in extended use.
1592 *Surv. France* To Rdr., William of Saluste Seigneur of Bartas. **1876** LOWELL *Ode 4th July* II. i, The lands no serf or seigneur ever trod. **1883** R. W. DIXON *Mano* IV. vii. 155 They whom distress and poverty constrain Against the seigneurs and their heavy dues To meet in conjuration, and complain. **1907** F. W. RAFFETY *Burke's Wks.* IV. Pref. 10 Every newspaper recalled the murder of a seigneur; but on the other side the sufferers were too ignoble to be known. **1924** WODEHOUSE *Ukridge* vii. 156 'Yes, yes, yes,' said Ukridge, with testy impatience, quite the seigneur resenting interference from an underling. **1978** A. MORICE *Murder by Proxy* i. 20 They used to own all the land... He still sees himself as the Seigneur of the neighbourhood.

b. In Canada, the holder of a SEIGNEURY; one of the landed gentry.

1775 JEFFERSON *Let.* Writ. 1892 I. 489 This St. Luc is a great Seigneur amongst the Canadians and almost absolute with the Indians. **1776** C. CARROLL *Jrnl.* (1845) 79 These are the rich men in Canada: the seigneiurs are in general poor. **1888** LIGHTHALL *Young Seigneur* 2 'Oh, the seigneurs have not yet altogether disappeared', said the Montrealer to the Ontarian.

c. In the Channel Islands, the lord of the manor; *spec.* the overlord of Sark.

1694 P. FALLE *Acct. Isle of Jersey* iv. 114 The place of Bailly being lately become vacant by the..death of Sir Philip de Carteret,..Seigneur of St. Ouen,..the States of the Island..have..chosen for Judge Delegate Philip le Geyt. **1815** T. QUAYLE *Agric. Islands on Coast of Normandy* 298 Some small specimens of copper ore are said to have been discovered... Little hope is entertained by the Seigneur of the fief [*sc.* Sark], that the quantity of ore will be found considerable. **1835** H. D. INGLIS *Channel Islands* 313 The lord of Serk is the sole lay impropriator of tithes. The tithe paid to the seigneur is the tenth sheaf of wheat, barley, oats, beans, &c. **1856** C. LE QUESNE *Constitut. Hist. Jersey* ii. 31 At the Assize d'Héritage, or first day of sitting, the principal feudal seigneurs, or lords holding *in capite* from the Crown, are bound to appear. **1885** A. EDWARDES *Girton Girl* I. v. 118 He had come to be Seigneur of Tintajeux through the inheritance of his Guernsey wife. **1935** E. PLATT *Sark as I found It* ix. 67 Mr. Collings, the late Seigneur, had more than one offer during his lifetime to restart the mines. **1957** *Encycl. Brit.* V. 231/1 In Jersey, if a land-owner dies without a direct heir, the *seigneur* claims for a year and a day the income of his estate; the *seigneurs* of St. Ouen's and La Motte still license taverners. **1976** *Times* 10 Mar. (Channel Islands Suppl.) p. ii/3 You can cross to Sark where buying a freehold property depends simply on availability and the consent of the island's Seigneur.

d. *Comb.*

1873 BROWNING *Red Cott. Nt.-cap* 139 To sit free and take tribute seigneur-like.

seigneurage: see SEIGNIORAGE.

seigneuress ('seɪnjʊərɪs). [a. F. *seigneuresse*, fem. of SEIGNEUR.] A woman who exercises feudal authority; also, the wife of a seigneur.

1849 [MRS. WILDE] tr. *Meinhold's Sidonia Sorc.* II. 130 Your feudal lady and seigneuress, Sidonia Bork. **1888** LIGHTHALL *Young Seigneur* 118 How is Monsieur the Seigneur? And how is Madame the Seigneuresse?

seigneurial (seɪ'njʊərɪəl), *a.* Also *erron.* 7 signeural, 8–9 seigneural. [a. F. *seigneurial*, f. *seigneur*, influenced by *seigneurie* (Hatz.-Darm.). Cf. SEIGNORAL.] Pertaining to a seigneur; sometimes used in wider sense = SEIGNORIAL. Also *fig.*, lordly; authoritative.

1656 HEYLIN *Surv. France* IV. ii. 174 So did the Vidames disclaim their relation to the Bishop, and became Signieural or honorary also. **1673** TEMPLE *Observ. United Prov.* i. 7 Seigneurial Jurisdiction over the Inhabitants. **1757** BURKE *Abridgm. Eng. Hist.* III. vi. Wks. 1812 V. 650 From them [the clergy] were often taken the bailiffs of the seigneurial courts. **1792** A. YOUNG *Trav. France* I. 259, I was sorry to see, at the village, a *carcan*, or seigneural standard, erected, to which a chain and heavy iron collar are fastened, as a mark of the lordly arrogance of the nobility, and the slavery of the people. **1834** K. H. DIGBY *Mores Cath.* V. vi. 156 In the seigneural chapel of the church of Mery-sur-Oise. **1865** *Q. Rev.* July 17 There was a something repugnant to the just pride of the Highland gentleman in the very idea of parting with his seigneurial rights, even for a season. **1887** *Spectator* 5 Nov. 1514/2 Canada could never have made much real progress under the seigneurial system. **1970** *Times Lit. Suppl.* 23 July 787/2 In the United States, Linguistics has long derived authority from the presence there of the two most seigneurial of living linguists, Roman Jakobson and Noam Chomsky. **1972** A. FRIEDMAN in Cox & Dyson *20th-Cent. Mind* I. xii. 428 Conrad's irony is heavy and fuming, his seigneurial distance from his madmen..woefully great.

seigneury ('seɪnjʊərɪ), ‖**seigneurie** (sɛɲœri). *Hist.* Also 9 seignurie, -ury. [ad. F. *seigneurie*, later form of *seignorie* (see SEIGNORY), assimilated to *seigneur*.]

1. a. *Fr. Hist.* A territory under the government of a seigneur. **b.** In Canada, a landed estate held (until 1854) by feudal tenure.

1683 *Apol. Prot. France* ii. 22 They have turn'd out of all Jurisdictions and Seignuries (which are almost infinite in France) all Protestants who had been admitted Officers in those Jurisdictions. **1763** LD. HOLLAND in Jesse *Selwyn & Contemp.* (1843) I. 269 Here is a large and good house..in the midst of a most extensive seigneurie. **1825** J. NICHOLSON *Oper. Mech.* 453 The chatelleine or seigneurie of Lille alone makes annually between 30,000 and 40,000 barrels. **1871** MISS YONGE *Cameos* (1877) II. viii. 100 The seigneurie of Garre, which lay near his own castle of Blein. **1903** *Times* 12 Dec. 8/6 His father, from whom he inherited the seigneurie, was the most prominent French leader of the rising of 1837.

2. a. In Canada, the mansion of a seigneur.

1895 G. PARKER *When Valmond came* vi. (1896) 115 The old sergeant went to the Seigneury, knocked, and was admitted to a room where were seated the young Seigneur, Medallion, and the avocat. **1895** *Outing* (U.S.) XXVI. 415/2 As he passed one of the cottages within half a mile of the seigneurie, the sound of a piano made him stop short.

b. In the Channel Islands, the residence of a Seigneur (sense c).

1935 E. PLATT *Sark as I found It* ix. 65 The Seigneurie must always be the centre of entertaining in Sark. **1978** *Times Lit. Suppl.* 26 May 572/5 There is a nice photograph of him in a group of them outside the Seigneurie, looking as if there is a nasty smell under his nose.

seignior ('seɪnɪə(r)). Forms: 4 segnour, seynour, seignoure, 4–5 seignour, seynowre, seyngnour, seynȝowre, senyowr, -owr, seinoure, sene-, senei-, senȝe-, senyeour, 5, 7 seniour, 6 senȝ-, seneȝe-, seinȝeour, senȝe-, senyor, senȝeoure, senior, 7 seignor, seigniour, 7–9 seignior. [a. AF. *segnour*, OF. *seignor*, *-eur* (mod.F. *seigneur*, a Com. Rom. word = Pr. *senhor*, Sp. *señor*, Pg. *senhor*, It. *signore*:—L. *seniōrem*, acc. of *senior* elder (see SENIOR). Cf. SEIGNEUR, SEÑOR, SIGNOR, SIR, SIRE, all ultimately of the same etymology.]

1. In early use, synonymous with LORD; a person high in rank or authority, a ruler, a feudal superior; the lord of a manor. Now *rare*, and chiefly as a more vernacular substitute for SEIGNEUR in speaking of a French feudal noble.

13.. *K. Alis.* 1455 (Laud MS.), Þe keyes hij token in his honde Of her Cites of her honoure And maden hym her liege seignoure. **1393** LANGL. *P. Pl.* C. XII. 269 Now beeþ þese seintes, as men seyen, and souereynes [*v.r.* seynours] in heuene. *c* **1400** *Destr. Troy* 13056 Then the Seniour [*i.e.* Menelaus] full sone, with seasonable windes, Cairet fro Crete with his clene nauy. **1552** LYNDESAY *Monarche* 5758 Thare sall our Senȝeouris of the cessioun Off all thare faltis mak cleir confessioun. **1648** GAGE *West Ind.* 39 A hundred thousand men of Warre..were sent by the Seniours of Mexico and Tezcuco to encounter Cortez. **1656** BLOUNT *Glossogr.* **1706** PHILLIPS (ed. Kersey), *Seignior* or *Signior*,.. Lord, Master. In a Law Sense, the Lord of the Fee, or of the Manour. **1809** A. HENRY *Trav.* 9 Late in the evening, I reached Les Cèdres, and was carried to the house of M. Leduc, its seignior. **1834** K. H. DIGBY *Mores Cath.* V. vii. 218 In the year 1245, was buried..a pious seignior, de Romilly, who dwelt at Romilly-sur-Seine. **1876** BANCROFT *Hist. U.S.* V. lii. 113 They denied the authority of the French nobility as magistrates, and resisted their claim of a right as seigniors to command their military services.

b. As a title of address. *Obs.* exc. *arch.*

c **1330** *Arth. & Merl.* 3607 (Kölbing) Merlin com þe king to & to hem seyd: Bieu segnours [*MS.* sengours], ȝe ben yswore to king Arthours. *c* **1440** *York. Myst.* xxx. 73 [To Pilate] My seniour, will ye see now þe sonne in youre sight. *c* **1460** *Towneley Myst.* xx. 8 Seniours, seke to my sawes, ffor bryssyng of youre bonys. **1528** ROY *Rede me* (Arb.) 67 Worsshipful seniours we must theym call Requyrynge that we shulde to theym obeye. **1823** SCOTT *Quentin D.* xix, 'Surely not, good seignior', answered the burgher.

†**2.** Used to represent It. SIGNOR or F. SEIGNEUR in designations of Italians or Frenchmen. *Obs.*

a **1578** LINDESAY (Pitscottie) *Chron. Scot.* (S.T.S.) II. 187 Seinȝeour Dauid the Italian secriter. **1588** *Rot. Scacc. Reg. Scot.* XXI. 410 For chalmer maill and bedding to Senyeour Du Barras, Francheman. **1718** *Free-thinker* No. 15. 101 Seignior Camillo and Seignior Alessandro..entered.

seignior, obs. form of SENIOR.

seigniorage, seignorage ('seɪnjərɪdʒ). Also 6 s(e)ignowrage, 8 seignourage, 5, 9 seigneurage. [a. OF. *seignorage*, *seigneurage* (mod.F. has *seigneuriage*), f. *seigneur*: see SEIGNEUR, SEIGNIOR, and -AGE. Cf. It. *signoraggio*.]

†**1.** Lordship, dominion. *Obs.*

1656 BLOUNT *Glossogr.* **1798** W. TAYLOR in *Monthly Mag.* V. 353 Opinions of hereditary right..must either be allowed to establish their superstitions (the monarchy or seigniorage of certain families),..or must be coerced in the exercise of their claims. **1820** WIFFEN *Aonian Hours* (ed. 2) 47 Her [Europe's] throne has been an armed seignorage.

2. A duty levied on the coining of money for the purpose of covering the expenses of minting, and as a source of revenue to the crown, claimed by the sovereign by virtue of his prerogative.

1444 *Rolls of Parlt.* V. 109/1 Wherof our Soverein Lord to have and take for his Seigneurage vii d in nombre. **1543** tr. *Act 9 Hen. V* Stat. II. c. 2 Payeng yᵉ seignowrage & cunage of golde after the rate of .v.s. for the pounde of the tower. *Ibid.*, With the signowrage and coynage as afore is sayde. **1658** PHILLIPS. **1695** LOCKE *Further Consid. Money* 84 This at least they were not mistaken in, that they brought Work to the Mint, and a Part of the Money coined to the Crown for Seigniorage. **1797** *Monthly Mag.* III. 352 Delivering out, without deduction for seignorage, duty, workmanship, or even waste, the full value of all bullion brought in to be coined. **1805** EARL LIVERPOOL *Treat. Coins* 102 Augmentation of revenue was expected from the additional profits, which would in such case arise, from the right of Seigneurage. **1880** DEL MAR *Hist. Prec. Metals* 125 The royalties, seignorages, convoy-duties, and other impositions ..which the Portuguese monarchs levied upon the gold product of Brazil. **1885** *Manch. Exam.* 7 Apr. 4/5 The proposal often made of deducting a seigniorage from the intrinsic value of the coinage. **1891** *Daily News* 6 Nov. 3/5 Any profit which the State gets from note circulation, seigneurage, and the like.

3. A duty claimed by the over-lord upon the output of certain minerals, a royalty.

a **1859** MACAULAY *Hist. Eng.* xxv. V. 265 With that domain they had as little to do as with the seignorage levied on tin in the Duchy of Cornwall.

¶**4.** Alleged to signify: 'Profit' (Webster 1847–54); 'The money paid on a copyright by a publisher to an author' (Webster 1864, marked '*Eng.*'). Cf. LORDSHIP *sb.* 6, ROYALTY 6 e.

†**5.** *attrib.* **seigniorage fine**, a royalty paid to the over-lord in return for the concession of a privilege. *Obs.*

1800 *Asiat. Ann. Reg.* 318/1 Perhaps a seigniorage fine to government for permission to sink a new well.

†'**seignioresse.** *Law. Obs.* Also 7 segnioresse, seignoresse, signioresse. [a. OF. *seignoresse*, var. of *seigneuresse*.] = SEIGNEURESS.

a **1604** HANMER *Chron. Irel.* (1809) 386 If the eldest sister should take homage of the yonger, she should be as a segnioresse to them all. **1642** tr. *Perkins' Prof. Bk.* vi. §459. 200 If a woman be seignoresse and a man be tenant. **1651** tr. *Kitchin's Courts Leet* (1653) 313 If a Woman Signioresse take her Tenant to Husband.

†**seigni'ority, sei'gnority.** *Obs.* [a. OF. *seignourité*, f. SEIGNEUR: see -ITY.] Lordship, governance.

1525 LD. BERNERS *Froiss.* II. ccxxiv. 291 They..founde a great nombre of Ladyes and damosels, who had the sygniorite of that isle. **1596** LODGE *Marg. Amer.* 10 Your couetous longing after riches, your ambitious hunting after seignioritie, haue occasioned this warre. **1598** SPENSER *Brief Note Irel.* Wks. (Grosart) I. 540 Then was he..to loose that seignoritie wᶜʰ he claimed of that land.

'**seigniorship.** *rare.* [f. SEIGNIOR + -SHIP.] The rank or condition of a seignior. In quot. used as a form of address.

1823 SCOTT *Quentin D.* xiv, Your seigniorship.

seigniory, seignory ('seɪnjərɪ), *sb.* Forms: 3–4 senurre, 4–5 senurie, senery, 5 senowrye; 4 *Sc.* senȝhory, senȝeroy, senȝhowry, 4–5 senyoury (*Sc.* senȝoury, senȝory), seniourie, 5–7 seniory, seniorie, (5 seniore), senȝowry, 6 senȝeory, -ie, 6–7 senyeory; 3 seynorye, 4 seynu(r)rye, 4 seynore, seinuri, 5 seynourye; 4 seinȝnery, 4–5 sengnurie, syngnory; 4 segnoury, 6 segnorie, segniory, 6–7 segniorie, 6 segnyorye; 3–6 seygnery, seignori(ȝ)e, seiȝnory, 4–5 seignurie, 4–6 seignorye, seygno(u)rye, seignourie, -y(e, seygnourie, 4–7 seigniorie, (7 seigniore, siegniory, seignieurie), 4– seignory, 6– seigniory. [a. OF. *seignorie* (mod.F. refashioned *seigneurie*), f. *seigneur*: see SEIGNIOR. Cf. Sp. *señoría*, Pg. *senhoria*, It. *signoria*. See also SEIGNEURY, SIGNORY.]

†**1.** Lordship, domination, sovereignty. *Obs.*

c **1290** *S. Eng. Leg.* 115/320 ȝif he hadde of is owene flesche al-ovt þe seignorie. **1297** R. GLOUC. (Rolls) 3858 He wolde wende Vor to winne seygnorie aboute in oþer ende. **13..** *K. Alis.* 597 (Laud MS.) He shal habbe seignorye Of þis rounde myddell erd. **1375** BARBOUR *Bruce* XII. 298 Covaitiss of senȝhory. *c* **1400** *Laud Troy Bk.* 3159 Thei made lettres.. To eche a lond and prouynce That Gregeys hadde in seygnorye. **1456** SIR G. HAYE *Law Arms* (S.T.S.) 209/11 Mony has jurisdiccioun and seignoury be way of dede, and nocht be way of lawe. **1474** CAXTON *Chesse* II. v. (1883) 66 Whan thou haste moste seignourye and lordships than shalt thou [etc.]. *a* **1547** SURREY *Æneid* II. 467 That many yeres did hold such seignorie. *a* **1548** HALL *Chron.*, *Hen. IV* 1 The Turke..by the discord of christen princes hath amplified greatly his seigniory and dominion. **1638** SIR T. HERBERT *Trav.* (ed. 2) 66 If hee would..do homage to him, he should re-accept his seniory. **1649** G. DANIEL *Trinarch.*, *Hen. IV* ccclxi, The more Politicke Molls, (who in fatter Soyles, have Seigneiorie). **1684** *Contempl. St. Man* I. ii. 20 What were.. the Seignory of the World, but Vanity of Vanities?

b. quasi-*arch.* ***your seignorie*** = 'your lordship': attributed to a foreign speaker.

1829 SCOTT *Anne of G.* xxix, 'It may be your seignorie is right', answered the guide. *Ibid.* xxx.

2. *spec.* Feudal lordship or dominion; the authority, rights, and privileges of a feudal lord.

1464 *Rolls of Parlt.* V. 524/1 Articles of Liberteez to Seignorie apperteynyng. **1567** in F. J. Baigent *Crondal Rec.* (1891) 171 With suche segnyorye and preferment of the said under tenauntes as the personne so atteyncted had before the said atteyndour. **1620** J. WILKINSON *Coroners & Sherifes* 3 Alwaies saving to the King and to other Lords their Seigniories and Franchises. **1834** PRINGLE *Afr. Sk.* xiv. 473 Reserving to the chiefs certain rights of seigniory over the respective domains. **1851** DIXON *W. Penn* xxii. (1872) 188 James thought..the rights of seigniory too large.

b. A particular feudal lordship; in *English Law* chiefly, the relation of the lord to the tenants of a manor.

seigniory appendant, seigniory in gross: see quot. 1886. By some writers *seigniory* has been used as equivalent to 'seigniory in gross'.

1466 *Paston Lett.* II. 283 Their ancestors had been possessed of a court and seniory in the town of Paston. **1482** *Rolls of Parlt.* VI. 204/2 Any Tenaunt holdyng..by Knyghts service, by reason of any Seignorie or Lordshipp. **1553** *Act 1 Mary* Stat. II. c. 5 Any person..having a Seignorie by reason of any Castells,..[etc.]..of him.. holden by Knightes service. **1586** J. HOOKER *Hist. Irel.* 113/1 in *Holinshed*, Matthew did..seeke to vsurpe the name of a segniorie of the Oneiles, and the dominions apperteining to that segniorie and surname. **1597** SHAKS. *2 Hen. IV*, IV. i. 111 Were you not restor'd To all the Duke of Norfolkes Seignories, Your Noble, and right well-remembred Fathers? **1607** J. NORDEN *Surv. Dial.* II. 43 He may haue thereby a kind of seignory, a Lordship or gouernement in grosse ouer his Tenants by contract or couenant, but no Mannor. *c* **1600** BACON *Elem. Com. Law* ii. (1630) 7 If tenant in ancient demesne be disseised by the Lord, whereby the seigniory is suspended,..Francke fee is no plea. **1652** tr. *Fitzherbert's New Nat. Brev.* 6 If a man hold of a Lord, as of Seigniory in gross, which is not any Manor, for which Seigniory he cannot keep any Court. **1730** M. WRIGHT *Tenures* 30 Neither could the Lord alien or transfer his Seigniory or Superiority to another, without the Consent of his Feudatary. **1844** J. WILLIAMS *Real Prop.* (1879) 322 By the grant of an estate in fee simple, he necessarily parted with the feudal possession... The grantee, however, became his tenant... This simply having a free tenant in fee simple was called a seignory. **1875** Digby *Real Prop.* i. §3 (1876) 50 *note*, If the lord retained no lands in his own hands, but all the lands within the manor were held by free tenants, he was said to have a seignory, or a seignory in gross. **1886** *Encycl. Brit.* XXI. 623/2 They [seignories] are regarded as incorporeal hereditaments, and are either appendant or in gross. A seignory appendant passes with the grant of the manor; a seignory in gross—that is a seignory which has been severed from the demesne lands of the manor to which it was originally appendant—must be specially conveyed by deed of grant.

3. The territory under the dominion of a lord; *esp.* a feudal domain. Sometimes used for SEIGNEURY with reference to France or Canada.

1338 R. Brunne *Chron.* (1810) 49 Whan Knoute had resceyued boþe þe seignories, He parted þe lond in foure parties. **1489** Caxton *Faytes of A.* I. i. 6 To recoure londes, seignoryes or ther thynges. **1532-3** *Act 24 Hen. VIII*, c. 7 Prouided alwayes, that euery lorde marcher haue the forfaytes..within their seygnories, liberties, aed [*sic*] frauncheses royall. **1601** Holland *Pliny* v. xxix. I. 107 A third Seignorie or Shire there is that goeth to Apamia. **1603** Knolles *Hist. Turks* (1638) 71 The Venetians; by whom it was holden as a part of their seignorie almost an hundred yeares. **1646** Bp. Maxwell *Burd. Issach.* 7 Crime.. committed, within the Seignory of this pettie Principality. **1818** Cruise *Digest* (ed. 2) I. 3 The codes of the Germans.. were superseded by these local customs: each seignory and province had its own. **1839** Stonehouse *Axholme* 144 The Lord of the Manor..could search for stolen goods within the extent of his seignory.

fig. **1579** Northbrooke *Dicing* Ep. Ded., I will poure out prayers vnto the Lord of heauen & earth to sende you..after this life neuer ceassing, and endlesse ioyes in the heauenlie Seignorie. *a* **1586** Sidney *Arcadia* III. (Sommer) 268 In one place lay disinherited heades, dispossessed of their naturall seignories.

4. A body of 'seigniors' or lords. Often with reference to Italy, = SIGNORIA, SIGNORY 4.

1485 Caxton *Chas. Gt.* 88 Ye myght be blamed, seen that your seygnorye ne your lordes be not here now present. **1517** Torkington *Pilgr.* (1884) 12 The Duke..with all the Senyorye went in ther Archa triumphali. **1603** Knolles *Hist. Turks* (1638) 84 Ouer all which, the seignorie neuertheless had a generall care. **1872** Lowell *Dante* Wks. 1890 IV. 134 The new decree by which the seigniory of Florence recalled a portion of the exiles.

seigniour, obs. form of SENIOR.

†'**seignorable**, *a.* *Obs.* *rare*$^{-1}$. In 5 **senȝeorabill.** [a. OF. *seignorable*, f. *seigneur*: see SEIGNEUR and -ABLE.] Pertaining to or characteristic of a lord, lordly.

c **1475** *Rauf Coilȝear* 717 Thair was seruit in that saill Seigis semelie, Mony Senȝeorabill Syre on ilk syde seir.

seignoral ('seɪnjərəl), *a.* *Hist.* Also 7-9 **seignioral.** [f. SEIGN(I)OR + -AL^{1}.]

= SEIGNORIAL; cf. SEIGNEURIAL.

1627 in Rushw. *Hist. Coll.* (1659) I. 508 And yet it was by him thus said.. That the Kings of England always have had a Monarchy Royal and not a Monarchy Seignoral. **1658** Cleveland *Rustick Rampant* 149 A Tyrannie after the Turkish mode, a Monarchy seignioral. **1790** Burke *Fr Rev.* (ed. 2) 219 The bishopricks and cures, under kingly and seignoral patronage,..are sometimes acquired by unworthy methods. **1809** *Ann. Reg., St. Papers* 733/2 All seignioral courts of justice are abolished in Spain. **1886** *Pall Mall Gaz.* 5 June 4/1 The history of Chantilly as a seignoral residence goes back to a very early period.

seignorial (seɪ'njɔərɪəl), *a.* Also **seigniorial.** [f. *seignor*, SEIGNIOR + -IAL. Cf. F. *seigneurial.*] Pertaining to a seignior or seigniors.

1818 Hallam *Mid. Ages* (1872) I. 209 Several other small emoluments of himself and his successors,..were in that age rather seigniorial than royal. **1823** Southey *Penins. War* I. 721 Provincial custom-houses were abolished, and all seignorial courts of justice. **1877** Mrs. Oliphant *Makers Flor.* vi. 158 This liberal and almost splendid existence, with its seignorial amusements of hunting and hawking.

†'**seignorize**, *v.* *Obs.* [f. *seignor*, SEIGNIOR + -IZE (in early use after F. †*signoriss-*, *signorir*). See also SIGNORIZE *v.*] *intr.* To hold sway, act as lord. Const. *in*, *over*.

1634 W. Tirwhyt tr. *Balzac's Lett.* I. 26 Those Statesmen, who made accompt to Seignorize in all Assemblies. **1799** W. Taylor in Robberds *Mem.* (1843) I. 283 A woman may be..a Mrs. Arlberry in the art of Seignorizing over men.

†'**seignorous**, *a.* *Obs.* [ad. OF. *seignoureux*: see SEIGNEUR and -OUS.] Lordly, noble. Hence †'**seignorously** *a.*, in the same sense.

c **1477** Caxton *Jason* 121 b, And in fauour of youre seignoureuse gentilnesse..I shal renewe you as sayd is. **1481** —— *Godfrey* clxxxvii. 274 In to thynner part of the temple were fledde moche grete peple of the toun by cause it was the moost seynorously and rial place of the toun.

seignory, *sb.*: see SEIGNIORY.

†'**seignory**, *v.* *Obs.* *rare.* [a. OF. *seignorier*, *seigneurier*, f. *seigneur*: see SEIGNIOR.]

1. *intr.* To exercise mastery.

1474 Caxton *Chesse* III. iv. g 2 b, Hit is sayd in prouerbe that a man ought to seignorie ouer the riches, and not to serue hit. **1483** —— *Gold. Leg.* 306/1 Thordre of domynacion whiche seygnoryeth aboue other that ben lower.

2. *trans.* To govern.

c **1475** *Partenay* 5090 Terry seignóried A full large contre.

seih, seihȝe, obs. ff. SEE *v.*

seihtle, variant of SAUGHTEL *v.* *Obs.*

c **1200** *Vices & Virtues* 3 Ga arst and seihtle wið ðine broðer.

seik: see SACK *sb.*^{1}, SICK *a.*, SIKH.

seil, obs. f. CEIL *v.*, SAIL *sb.*^{1}; *Sc.* var. of SILE *v.*^{2}

‖**Seilbahn** ('zaɪlbaːn). [Ger., f. *seil* cable, rope + *bahn* way, road.] A cable railway; an aerial cableway.

1963 I. Fleming *On Her Majesty's Secret Service* ix. 99 Together with the Gemeinde, the local authorities, he constructed the Seilbahn. **1972** *Daily Tel.* 12 Feb. 14/7 Sonntag, a delightful old village clustered round a tall-spired church has a *seilbahn* from which the venturesome may 'sail' across the deep ravine in a cable cab to Stein.

seilde(n, -in(e, -yn, obs. ff. SELD and SELDOM.

seile, obs. f. CEIL *v.*, SAIL *v.*^{1}, SEEL *v.*^{2}

†'**seiler.** *Obs.* *rare.* [f. *seil* var. CEIL *v.* + -ER^{1}.] One who 'ceils' (CEIL *v.* 2); a house-painter or plasterer.

1672 in E. B. Jupp *Carpenters' Co.* (1887) 303 The Company of Joyners and Seilers London. **1688** Holme *Armoury* III. 148/2 Seiler or House Painter.

seili(en, obs. forms of SAIL *v.*^{1}

seill: see SEELE, canopy, SELE, happiness.

seille, seily, obs. forms of SAIL *sb.*^{1}, *v.*^{1}

seilye, variant of SEELY *a.* *Obs.*

seim(e, seiment, obs. ff. SEEM *v.*^{2}, CEMENT.

†**sein**, *v.* *Obs.* Also 6 **seyn.** [a. OF. *seignier*:—L. *signāre* to SIGN.] *trans.* To sign, seal.

1258 *Procl. Hen. III* in *Trans. Philol. Soc.* 1868-9, 21 We senden ȝew þis writ open iseined wiþ ure seel. **1549** in R. G. Marsden *Sel. Pleas Crt. Admir.* (1897) II. 70, I have written and seynidde this presentt with myne owne proper handde. **1638** *Hamilton Papers* (Camden) 3 We command you expreslie..to publis the proclamatioun fourthwith drauen up with your oune hand, which we have seined. *a* **1660** *Contemp. Hist. Irel.* (Ir. Archæol. Soc.) I. 136 He seined his fiat to the conformation of the said requeste.

sein, obs. f. SAINT, SAY *v.*^{1}

seind, obs. f. SEND *v.*

seindell, -dill, -dl(e, variant ff. SENDLE *adv.*

seine (seɪn), *sb.*^{1} Forms: α. 1 **segne**, 3-8 **seyne**, 4-7 **sayne**, 5 **seyn**, 7-8 **sayn**, **sain(e**, **sein**, 7- **seine**. β. 7 **seene**, 7- **sean.** [OE. *segne* wk. fem. = OS., OHG. *segîna*:—WGer. **sagīna*, a. L. *sagēna* (whence F. *seine*), a. Gr. σαγήνη.] **a.** A fishing net designed to hang vertically in the water, the ends being drawn together to inclose the fish. (See quot. 1874 in β.)

Also with defining word denoting the kind of seine, as ***cod***, ***herring***, ***pilchard***, ***shad***, ***drift-***, ***drag-***, ***tuck-seine***, etc.

α. *c* **950** *Lindisf. Gosp.* John xxi. 11 Næs ðiu segni tosliten [Vulg. *non est scissum rete*]. *a* **1000** *Cædmon's Exod.* 584 Hi ongunnon sælafe segnum dælan. *c* **1300** *K. Horn* (Laud MS.) 700 þe fis þat brac þi seyne. *a* **1400-50** *Wars Alex.* 4270 Set we na saynes in þe see, ne sese we na fischis. **1483** *Cath. Angl.* 328/1 A Seyn, *sagena*. **1602** Carew *Cornwall* I. 30 The Sayne is a net, of about fortie fathome in length, with which they encompasse a part of the Sea, and drawe the same on land by two ropes, fastned at his ends, together with such fish, as lighteth within his precinct. **1657** R. Ligon *Barbadoes* 35 He hath of his own a Saine to catch fish withall. **1726** Shelvocke *Voy. round World* 55 They have almost every where the best conveniences for hauling the seyne. **1797** Polwhele *Hist. Devon* I. 120 Herrings..are taken in seines—three tons have been caught at a hawl. **1883** Moloney *W. Afr. Fisheries* (Fish. Exhib. Publ.) 28 A manatee had been caught in a drift-seine near Ajedé.

β. **1607** Cowel *Interpr.*, *Seane fish*,..seemeth to be that fish which is taken with a very great and long net called a seane. *a* **1656** Bp. Hall *Rem. Wks.* (1660) 193 These two holy Epistles are as some seene, or large drag-net. **1745** P. Thomas *Jrnl. Anson's Voy.* 11 We had very good Fishing with a Sean. **1874** Holdsworth *Deep-Sea Fishing* 156 Seans may be divided into three classes, namely, the sean proper..the 'tuck-sean', and the 'ground or foot-sean'. All these nets have the same general character... The back or upper edge of the net is buoyed up by corks..; and the foot is weighted with lead to keep it down, so that the net may hang perpendicularly in the water. **1880** Mrs. Parr *Adam & Eve* II. 75 Barnabas had a share in a pilchard sean.

b. ***to blow up the seine***: of a fish, 'to press against the lead-line in the endeavour to escape' (*Cent. Dict.* 1891). ***to shoot a seine*** (or ***seine-net***): to throw it out into position.

1698 *Act 10 Will. III*, c. 14 §12 No Person..shall..shoot his..Sayn or Sayns within or upon the Sayn or Sayns of any other Person. **1893** *Act 36 & 37 Vict.* c. 71 §14 Any person who shall shoot or work any seine or draft net for salmon in a river across the whole width.

c. *attrib.* and *Comb.*, as ***seine fishery***, ***fishing***, ***-hauling***, ***line***, ***trawl***, ***trawler***, ***trawling***, ***twine***; **seine-boat**, a boat adapted for carrying and throwing out a seine; †**seine-fish**, a fish caught in a seine, *spec.* in Jamaica, the Saury Elops; **seine-gang**, 'a body of men engaged in seining, together with their boats and other gear' (*Cent. Dict.*); **seine-man**, one of a seine-gang; **seine-needle**, a needle with which the meshes of a seine are netted; **seine-net** = sense 1; also as *v.* *intr.*, to fish with a seine; hence **seine-netter**, **seine-netting**, *vbl. sb.*; **seine-roller** (see quot.); **seine-shooting**, the casting of the nets in seine-fishing; **seine-tender** (see quot.).

1602 Carew *Cornwall* I. 27 b, They haue..*Sayn-boats for taking of Pilcherd. **1874** Holdsworth *Deep-Sea Fishing* 159 The other rope and the whole of the net are put into the stern of the sean-boat. **1603-4** *Act 1 Jas. I*, c. 23 §1 Herringes, Pilchardes and *Seane Fishe. **1725** Sloane *Jamaica* II. 284 *Saurus maximus*... The Sein-Fish, or Sea-Gally-Wasp. **1874** Holdsworth *Deep-Sea Fishing* 188 St. Ives is especially famous for the extent of its *sean-fishery. **1834** *Tait's Mag.* I. 125/2 The difference between drift and *seine fishing. **1883** Joncas *Fish. Canada* (Fish. Exhib. Publ.) 23 Seine-fishing for herrings is chiefly carried on by fishermen of Nova Scotia. **1909** Moresby *Two Admirals* 111 Oh, the shooting, the *seine-hauling, the picnics of those enchanted coasts [of Chili]. **1794** *Rigging & Seamanship* I. 65 *Sean-lines, for fixing the sean-nets, have 18 threads, 6 in a strand. **1879** G. B. Goode *Catal. Anim. Resources U.S.* 97 Seine lines. **1879** Holdsworth in *Encycl. Brit.* IX. 254/2 The *seanmen receive certain wages in money and a share of the fish. **1879** G. B. Goode *Catal. Anim. Resources U.S.* 131 *Seine-needle. **1603** Owen *Pembrokesh.* (1891) 117 Taken.. in a *sayne nette, drawne after euerye tide. **1898** S. Evans *Holy Graal* 41 A fetch that will bring them all safe home with a seine-net full of fish. **1961** *Seine-net v. [see NEPHROPS]. **1947** A. C. Hardy *Seafood Ships* vii. 99 The *seine netter..is invariably under 100 ft. long and of wooden construction. **1970** *Cape Times* 28 Oct. (S.A. Fishing Rev.) 1/2 The days when trawlers and seine-netters could make maximum hauls virtually on their doorsteps are over. **1905** J. Johnstone *Brit. Fisheries* p. xxviii, This latter method of *seine-netting brings us to the consideration of the methods of the inshore or longshore man. **1977** *Grimsby Even. Tel.* 14 May 7/7 A list of..stretches of water to be closed to trawling and seine netting. **1887** Goode, etc. *Fish. Industr. U.S.* v. I. 249 A *seine-roller..is a wooden roller.. which revolves on pivots in its ends... The use of this roller is to lessen the friction between the rail of the vessel and the seine, as the latter is being hauled on deck. **1864** Mrs. Lloyd *Ladies of Polecarrow* 29 The first successful *seine-shooting for several long needy years. **1856** Olmsted *Slave States* 351 There are two large seine-boats, in each of which there is one captain, two *seine-tenders, and eight or ten oarsmen. *Ibid.*, The seine-tenders throwing off, until the seine is all cast between them. **1874** Holdsworth *Deep-Sea Fishing* 323 The drift-men may therefore frequently have a chance of success when *sean-trawlers have none. *Ibid.* 323 An Act was passed to put an end to *sean-trawling for herrings on the coast of Scotland. **1770** *Boston Gaz.* 13 Mar. 4/2 (Advt.), The right sort of three-threaded *Sein Twine. **1875** Bedford *Sailor's Pocket Bk.* v. (ed. 2) 158 Seine twine.

†**seine**, *sb.*^{2} *Obs.* *rare.* [OE. *segn*, ad. L. *signum* SIGN *sb.*] A banner.

Beowulf 2958 þa wæs æht boden Sweona leodum, segn Higelace. *c* **1275** Lay. 9282 Nam he his seine and his sceald briþte.

†**seine**, *a.* *Obs.* *rare*$^{-1}$. [ME. *seine* (disyllable), perh. a. OF. *sené* wise, assimilated to the rime-word *meyne* MEINY.] ? Grave, sober.

c **1330** R. Brunne *Chron. Wace* (Rolls) 11447 Faire þey come..Wyþ softe pas & fulle seine [Wace, *Petit pas, ordeneement*] Gret þei Arthur & his meyne.

seine (seɪn), *v.* Also **sean.** [f. SEINE *sb.*^{1}] **a.** *intr.* To fish or catch fish with a seine. **b.** *trans.* To catch with a seine, also to use a seine in.

1836 [implied in SEINING, *vbl. sb.*] **1863** *Rep. Sea Fisheries Comm.* (1865) II. 432/1 Were you in the habit of seining for herrings every season? **1887** Goode, etc. *Fish. Industr. U.S.* v. I. 260 The fact of mackerel being seined at night could not long be kept a secret. **1890** *Pall Mall Gaz.* 29 May 1/2 To send a fleet..to 'seine' the bay for herring for bait.

Hence **seined** *ppl. a.*; '**seining** *vbl. sb.* and *ppl. a.*

1836 *1st Rep. Ir. Fisheries* 152 Seaning seldom commences before June or July. **1874** Holdsworth *Deep-Sea Fishing* 189 The seaning ground is on the western side of the bay. **1876** Goode *Fishes of Bermudas* 10 Row-boats filled with small seined fish may be found at the quay. **1887** Goode, etc. *Fish. Industr. U.S.* v. I. 267 A seining schooner. **1900** *Field* 18 Aug. 297/3, I was anxious to follow up my seining operations.

seine: see SEE *v.*, SENE *a.* *Obs.*, SYNE.

seiner ('seɪnə(r)). Also **seaner.** [f. SEINE *sb.* + -ER^{1}.] A fisherman who uses a seine, or one employed to haul in a seine. Also a seine-boat.

α. **1602** Carew *Cornwall* I. 32 The Sayners complayne.. that these drouers worke much preiudice to the Commonwealth of fishermen and reape thereby small gaine to them-selues. **1776** *Act 16 Geo. III*, c. 36 §25 The Hewer of such Seyne or Master Seyner thereof. **1848** Johns *Week at Lizard* 173 The labours of the seiners..are rewarded by a catch of mackerel. **1884** Goode, etc. *Nat. Hist. Aquatic Anim.* 571 A gentle ripple indicates their position..and is of great assistance to the seiners in setting their nets. **1906** J. B. Connolly *Out of Gloucester* 8 She's a seiner out of Gloucester.

β. **1874** Holdsworth *Deep-Sea Fishing* 189 Then is the seaner's opportunity. **1879** —— in *Encycl. Brit.* IX. 254/1 Besides these there is a small boat..from which the master seaner directs all the proceedings.

seinle, variant of SENDLE *adv.*, seldom.

seint(e: see SAINT, SEYNT *Obs.* (girdle).

seintefie, -ifie, obs. ff. SANCTIFY *v.*

seintewarie, -tuarie, etc.: see SANCTUARY.

seinye, -zie, var. ff. SENE *sb.*², SENYE *Obs.*

seip, -age, -ing, var. ff. SEEP, SEEPAGE, SEEPING.

‖**se ipse** (seɪ ˈɪpseɪ). [Eng. adaptation of L. *se ipsum*; cf. IPSE *pron.*] Himself: used emphatically with preceding sb.

1853 W. JERDAN *Autobiogr.* IV. xiii. 238 It was Wordsworth *se ipse*... The ideal was complete. **1943** G. COPE *Democracy within Church* 8 The then Archbishop of Canterbury did not hesitate to rebuke his sovereign.. and so demonstrated that the clerical oath of allegiance is not to the monarch *se ipse*.

seipter, obs. form of SCEPTRE *sb.*

seir, obs. f. SERE *a.*; obs. Sc. f. SORE *a.*

seirce, seirch(e, obs. Sc. forms of SEARCH *v.*

seire, obs. form of SERE *a.*

seir-fish, seer-fish (ˈsɪəfɪʃ). [The first element is a corruption of the Pg. name *serra* lit. 'saw'.] An East Indian scombroid fish, *Cybium guttatum*. Also *ellipt.* as **seer**.

1727 A. HAMILTON *New Acc. E. Ind.* I. xxx. 379 In November and December they have great Plenty of Seer-fish, which is as savory as any Salmon or Trout in Europe. **1813** J. FORBES *Oriental Mem.* I. 53 The robal, the seir-fish, the grey mullet, and some others, are very good. **1883** DAY *Indian Fish* (Fish. Exhib. Publ.) 12 Drift-nets.. are used for taking these two descriptions of fish, as well as for the seir fish (*Cybium*). **1913** C. F. HOLDER *Game Fishes of World* viii. 83 The Seer.. leaps eight feet and has a fighting weight of fifteen pounds. **1971** *Fashion Panorama* (Ceylon) Apr.-June (Advt., verso front cover), 12 lbs. comprising Seer, Crabs or Prawns.

seirs, obs. form of SEARCH *v.*

seis, obs. form of CEASE *v.*, SYCE.

seisant, erron. form of SEJANT.

1612 PEACHAM *Gentl. Exerc.* III. 168. (Also in edd. 1634, 1661.)

†**seise**, *sb. Obs.* [f. *seise*, SEIZE *v.*] = SEISIN.

1607 J. CARPENTER *Plaine Mans Plough* 241 Who.. hath taken seise and possession for man in the kingdome of his Father.

seise, *v. Law.* The usual spelling of SEIZE *v.* in the sense: To put in possession, invest with the fee simple *of*. (See SEIZE *v.* 1, 2.)

†**ˈseiser**. *Law. Obs.* Also 6 seasor, -er, 7 seisor. [a. AF. *seiser* (inf.) = F. *saisir* to SEIZE.] = SEIZURE.

1550 *Rutland MSS.* (Hist. MSS. Comm. 1905) IV. 354 Ryding from Anwyke to Raylye (sic) to make a seasor. **1558** *Act 1 Eliz.* c. 12. §3 The Shire or Place where the Seaser was made. *c* **1560** in Strype *Ann. Ref.* (1709) I. II. App. VIII. 21 Temporalities of Bishoppes seisid; and of the seiser of the Goodes of the Clergie. *a* **1625** SIR H. FINCH *Law* (1636) 11, A. erects a Shop vpon the Kings Freehold, the King grants the land to B. in fee; A. before entry or seisor of the shop by the Kings Patentee, continueth his possession and dieth seised.

‖**seises** (ˈseises), *sb. pl.* [Sp., (*los*: also used) *seises* (the) sixes, pl. of *seis* six.] The choristers (formerly six, now usu. ten) in certain Spanish cathedrals, esp. Seville, who perform a ritual dance with castanets before the altar during the octave of Corpus Christi and certain other festivals.

1845 R. FORD *Hand-bk. for Travellers Spain* I. ii. 255/2 At this Octave and at Corpus, the Quiresters or *Seises* (formerly they were six in number) dance before the high altar [of Seville Cathedral] with castanets and with plumed hats on their heads... They are dressed as pages of the time of Philip III. They wear blue and white for the Virgin, red and white for Corpus. **1885** E. DE AMICIS *Spain & Spaniards* ix. 324 The most curious privilege.. of the Seville Cathedral, is the.. dance of *los seises*, which takes place every evening.., for eight consecutive days, after the festival of *Corpus Domini*. **1903** A. SYMONS *Cities* 128, I returned to the Cathedral to see the dance of the Seises... The sixteen boys .. came forward and knelt before the altar. **1926** J. B. TREND *Mus. Sp. Hist. to 1600* v. 85 The ten little *Seises* who dance, sing, and clack their castanets before the high altar of Seville Cathedral for the festivals of Corpus Christi and the Immaculate Conception. **1938** B. SCHÖNBERG tr. *C. Sachs's World Hist. Dance* vii. 337 The classical number of participants in the *Morris Dance*, six, was once the same for the Spanish cathedral dance..—and even today, although there are ten performers, they are still known as *los seises*, 'the sixes'. **1941** G. CHASE *Music of Spain* xvi. 256 The *seises* (choirboys) of Seville Cathedral, who every year, during the octave of Corpus Christi, dressed in quaint costumes of the time of Carlos III.., dance before a special altar to the sound of their own castanets and the accompaniment of an orchestra. **1969** S. SITWELL *Gothic Europe* xii. 132 Dancing with castanets before the high altar.. is performed by the *seises* or choristers.

seisin (ˈsiːzɪn), *sb.* Forms: 3-4 sesin, 4-5 sesyn(e, sesine, 3-7 sesyng(e, 4-7 sesing, 5 sesun, seson, sesen, sesynn, 6 *Sc.* sessing, 7 sezin; 4-5 cesoun, 5 cesone; 4 saysyne, sayzine, 5 saisine, 6 saysing, saising, 7 *Sc.* saseing; 5 seasyng, 6 seasyne, 5-7 season, 6 seasen, 6-7 seasin, 6 ceassing, 7 seasing, seasin; 3-5 seysyn(e, 3-8 seisine, 3-5 seisyn(e, 5-6 seising, 6 seissin, seizine, 6-7 seizon, seison, 7 seizen, seisen, seysin, 3- seisin. Also *Sc.* SASINE. [a. F. *saisine* (from 13th c.) = Pr. *sazina* (whence It. *sagina*), f. F. *saisir*, Pr. *sazir*: see SEIZE *v.*]

1. In early use, Possession: chiefly in phrases, ***to have, take seisin*** (***in, of***). Now only in *Law*, Possession as of freehold.

1297 R. GLOUC. (Rolls) 6431 King knout of edmondes londes anon seisine nom. *a* **1300** *Cursor M.* 3360 He drogh hir ner and still spak 'Yon es mi lauerd ysaac,.. Of him now sal þou ha sesin'. **1303** R. BRUNNE *Handl. Synne* 6012 Yn alle here landes he toke sesyne, And was þan a ryche lordyng. *c* **1330** —— *Chron. Wace* (Rolls) 7621 Of prest was þer no benisoun,.. In sesyn þe kyng had hure þat nyght. **1340** *Ayenb.* 144 And þervore zayþ oure Lhord þet þe kingdom of hevene is hare, naȝt wyþoute more be beheste, ac be saysyne zykere. **1375** BARBOUR *Bruce* VI. 496 He had him in his sesing. *c* **1400** MAUNDEV. (1839) xxi. 222 Theise 3 Bretheren had Cesoun in alle the Lond. *c* **1412** HOCCLEVE *De Reg. Princ.* 1812 Wolde honest deth come, and me ouerterue, And of my graue me put in seisyne. *c* **1425** *Cast. Persev.* 767 in *Macro Plays* 100 In all þis worlde.. here I ȝyfe þee with myn honde, syr, an opyn sesun. *c* **1425** *Eng. Conq. Irel.* (1896) 82 Reymond went ouere yn-to Walys to take seysyne yn hys fadyr landys. *c* **1440** *Promp. Parv.* 67/1 Cesone in londe, or oþyr go(o)d takynge, *seisina*. **1525** LD. BERNERS *Froiss.* II. clxvii. [clxiii.] 463 To entre and take season of the castell. **1611** SPEED *Hist. Gt. Brit.* IX. viii. §50 The Legate (hauing after fiue dayes seysin re-deliuered the Crowne, but not yet released the Censures, till conditions were performed). **1628** COKE *On Litt.* 31 Here this word (seised) extendeth it selfe as well to a seison in law, or a ciuill seison, as to a seison in deed, which is a naturall seison... For a woman shall be endowed of a seison in Law. **1647** N. BACON *Disc. Govt. Eng.* I. lxii. (1739) 123 The Heir of a Free-man shall by descent be in such seisin as his Ancestor had at the time of his death, doing service, and paying relief; and shall have his Chattels. **1766** BLACKSTONE *Comm.* II. v. 66 Immediately upon the death of a vasal the superior was intitled to enter and take seisin or possession of the land. **1818** CRUISE *Digest* (ed. 2) III. 371 The law vested the seisin in law in the daughters upon the death of the father. **1869** BLACKMORE *Lorna D.* lvi, The Grange had only devolved to him by will, at the end of a long entail,.. and.. he had gone abroad, without taking seisin. **1875** DIGBY *Real Prop.* i. (1876) 50 *note*, The proper meaning of the word 'seisin' is possession as of freehold; i.e. the possession which a freeholder has.

b. The phrases ***to give, take seisin*** are sometimes used with special reference to the symbolical acts called ***livery of seisin*** (see LIVERY *sb.* Sc.). Hence, in popular language, *seisin* has been occas. applied loosely to the object (e.g. a turf, a key, a staff) handed over in 'livery of seisin' as a token of possession.

1523 FITZHERB. *Surv.* 14 The stewarde.. shall delyuer to hym yᵗ shall haue the lande the same yerde or another in the name of season. *c* **1600** BACON *Use Com. Law* (1630) 52 And in Seisin thereof, hee deliuereth to him a Turfe, twig, or Ring of the doore. **1762** HUME *Hist. Eng.* I. iii. 136 A soldier .. plucked some thatch, which, as if giving him seizine of the kingdom, he presented to his general [William]. **1863** KEBLE *Bp. Wilson* v. 168 Giving a kind of seizin by the delivery of a straw.

fig. **1602** MARSTON *Ant. & Mel.* II. D 2 *Gal.* Thy lips, and loue, are mine. *Mell.* You nere tooke seizin on them yet. **1609** BP. ANDREWES *Serm.* iv. (1629) 30 He sends the Spirit of his Sonne, to give us seisin of this our Adoption. **1861** PEARSON *Early & Mid. Ages Eng.* 243 The story that he [William the Conqueror].. stumbled on the shore and converted it into an omen of good luck, by professing to take seisin of the new territory. **1868** E. EDWARDS *Ralegh* I. xxi. 462 His horse fell with him, and forced him to take seisin of the soil in the roughest fashion.

c. ***primer*** (also ***premier, †first***) ***seisin***: see PRIMER *a.* 3 b. Now only *Hist.*

1459 *Rolls of Parlt.* V. 362/1 And the seid Edward.. used to have and had.. the furst seisine of all Londes.. of every Tenaunt that held of them in chief. **1622** BACON *Hen. VII* 210 Wardships, Liueries, Primier Seisines, and Alienations. **1875** CURTIS *Hist. Eng.* 396 All wardships, forfeitures for marriage.., premier seisins.. for alienation.

2. *Scots Law.* The act of giving possession of feudal property by the delivery of symbols; infeftment. Also, the instrument by which the possession of feudal property is proved.

14.. *Chalmerlan Ayr* §4 (Sc. Acts I), Item at þai gif seising heratabill or of lang tym of ony baronagis [etc.]. **1498** *Reg. Privy Seal Scot.* I. 30/2 Quhil the lauchfull are or aeris thairof optene lachfull state and sesing of the sammyn. **1499** *Ibid.* 60/2 Confirmand a letter of sessing mad and gevin thairuppon to the said Wilȝame. **1521** *Stirling Burgh Rec.* (1887) I. 13 Sir James Akman, chep-lane,.. produsit.. ane attentic chartour and seissin of twa markis of obit silver to be upliftit.. to the feft chaplanis yeirly. **1540** *Sc. Acts Jas. V* (1814) II. 375/1 The persoun.. havand privait stait & saising of þe saidis landis. **1592** in *Oppress. Orkney & Zetld.* (1859) 101 But charter or seasing. **1604-5** *Aberd. Acc.* in *Spalding Club Miscell.* V. 78 Ane skyn of parchement to wreit the sesing of the said chartour of mortificatioun. **1609** SKENE *Reg. Maj.* 2 Item, for ane precept of saising, conforme to the chartour, to the Chan-cellar for the fie of the seale, ane mark. **1693** STAIR *Instit. Law Scot.* II. iii. §16 (ed. 2) 199 These Charters.. never become a real Right till they be compleated by Seasin, which imports the taking of Possession. *Ibid.* §19. 201 Albeit the most ordinar Warrant of Seasins be the Superiors Precept ingrossed or related to in the Seasin. **1696** *Lond. Gaz.* No. 3228/2 Act anent the Registration of Seasings. **1733** J. INNES *Idea Juris Scotici* 77 And the Seisin itself is nothing else but an Instrument (of a settled Style).. setting forth that upon such a Day.. the Disponee was seized and invested in the Feu in Virtue of his Disposition. **1754** ERSKINE *Princ. Sc. Law* (1809) 266 Apprisings were, by the former practice, preferable, according to the dates of the seisins following upon them, where the debtor himself was infeft.

b. *Comb.*: †**seisin-ox**, an ox formerly due as a perquisite to the sheriff when he gave infeftment to crown lands.

1567 *Sc. Acts Jas. VI* (1814) III. 40/1 That na saising ox .. be gevin or takin for na maner of saising tobe takin. *a* **1768** ERSKINE *Inst. Law Scot.* III. viii. §79 (1773) 585 The sheriff who thus gives seisin, was by our old customs intitled to a seisin-ox as his fee.

†**ˈseisin**, *v. Obs.* Forms: 5 seysne, ceson, cesun, seysonne, sesyn, seson, seisyne, 6 season, seasne, seizon. [f. SEISIN *sb.*; cf. med.L. *sesināre*; there may have been an AF. **seisiner*: cf. OF. *seisineor* (agent-n.) and *seisinement* (n. of action).]

1. *trans.* To give seisin of (property).

13.. *Guy Warw.* (Caius) 8590, I will season into thyn hande Evyn halfen deale of my lande.

2. To invest with the seisin of property; to put in possession; = SEIZE *v.*¹

c **1450** *Godstow Reg.* 135 þei preied.. þat [they] wold.. commaund to seysonne hem in hit. *Ibid.* 661 Bernarde of Seynt Walerye yaf the forsaid towne.. and graunted hit to kyng henry and seisyned hym (by a silken cloth, wherof was a chesible I-made) with the lordship and the right of the Avowery of the same Abbey.

3. To confiscate (property); to apprehend (a prisoner); = SEIZE *v.* 5.

c **1425** *Found. St. Bartholomew's* (E.E.T.S.) 57 Yf he wolle denay hit the kyngis officer hym as a theyf may holde and sesyne And for to be condempnyd betake hym to the Iugys. *c* **1450** *Godstow Reg.* 155 He nother his heires shold never.. sesyn the lond of the same for the defaute of the same Robert. **1535** COVERDALE *1 Esdras* vi. 32 All his goodes shalbe seasoned to yᵉ kynge.

4. To seize, take hold of; to take *root*.

1568 SKEYNE *Pest* (Bannatyne Cl.) 15 Quhan all apperis to succede weill than the tirane [the Plague] sessinis rute and slayis sonest.

5. *intr.* To seize *upon*.

c **1540** tr. *Pol. Verg. Eng. Hist.* IV. (Camden No. 36) 178 Cerdicius bie littell and litell seasoned on the weaste partes of the Ile. **1563-87** FOXE *A. & M.* (1596) 188/2 The kings officers came.. to seizon upon his goods in the kings behalfe. **1587** *Mirr. Mag., Wolsey* xlv, One Wealsh, a Knight, came downe in good aray, And seasned sure,.. On Wolsey wolfe, that spoiled many a lambe. **1587** FLEMING *Contn. Holinshed* III. 1548/1 Such, as vpon whom the infection was seizoned.

Hence †**ˈseisining** *vbl. sb.*, chiefly = SEISIN *sb.* Also †**ˈseisiner** *Sc.*, lawful possessor (of lands).

c **1450** LOVELICH *Grail* lv. 214, I schal.. Corowne hym kyng be My levenge, & Of Alle My londis to ȝeven him sesenynge. **1498** *Reg. Privy Seal Scot.* I. 35/1 The letter made to him be his said fader makand him sessonar and assignay to al his landis of Mᶜkaristonn. **1523** LD. BERNERS *Froiss.* I. ccxiv. 266 Thus the kyng of England had the possession and sesenynge of the duchie of Aquitayne. **1547** in J. H. Glover *Kingsthorpiana* (1883) 88 Such as have landes by will or testament, shall paye for their sesianynge vis. **1623** COCKERAM II, A Seazning of goods to the kings vse. *Confiscation.*

seism (ˈsaɪz(ə)m). *rare.* [f. Gr. σεισμ-ός: see SEISMIC *a.* Cf. F. *sisme*.] An earthquake.

1883 MILNE *Earthquakes* i. (1886) 9 To be consistent with a Greek basis for seismological terminology, some writers have thrown aside the familiar expression 'earthquake', and substituted the awkward word 'seism'. **1904** C. E. DUTTON *Earthquakes* xiv. 238 The average intensity of the quakes or 'seisms' as De Montessus terms them.

seismal (ˈsaɪzməl), *a. rare.* [f. Gr. σεισμ-ός: see SEISMIC *a.* + -AL¹.] Seismic.

1864 in WEBSTER. **1977** A. HALLAM *Planet Earth* 78/3 Gravimetric, seismal and geothermal investigations of several rift zones.

seismic (ˈsaɪzmɪk), *a.* [f. Gr. σεισμ-ός earthquake (f. σεί-ειν to shake) + -IC.

The normal form would be **sismic*: cf. F. *sismique*.]

1. a. Pertaining to, relating to, characteristic of, connected with, or produced by an earthquake, earthquakes, or earth-vibration. Also, pertaining to or involving earth vibrations produced artificially by explosions. ***seismic survey***, †(*a*) a survey of an area in connection with its liability to earthquakes; (*b*) a survey (for oil and gas) employing seismic methods.

1858 MALLET in *Rep. Brit. Assoc.* I. 7 The period of the year at which seismic action appears to be greatest. *Ibid.* 18 Whether, as a seismic region, Northern Africa have a centre disturbance of its own [etc.]. **1877** RUDLER in *Encycl. Brit.* VII. 611/1 The depth of the seismic focus is easily determined. For since the waves radiate from this focus, any two wave-paths when produced backwards will meet at the seismic centre. **1887** G. H. DARWIN in *Fortn. Rev.* Feb. 267 Regions subject to earthquakes, or seismic areas. **1887** *Trans. Seismol. Soc Japan* X. 36 The first method of avoiding earthquake motion in a given district is to make a seismic survey of that area. **1935** *Geol. Natural Gas* (Amer. Assoc. Petroleum Geologists) 664 Seismic surveys isolated a relatively small area with structural closure on the upthrown side of the fault. **1941** *Bull. Amer. Assoc. Petroleum Geologists* XXV. 1261 The unsolved problems in the field of seismic surveying require for their solution a more complete understanding of the properties of the earth strata. **1944** A. HOLMES *Princ. Physical Geol.* xii. 206 Near the middle of the sheet the ice has been shown by seismic methods.. to be over 8,000 feet thick. **1969** *Times* 16 July 4/2 The scientific equipment bay where the seismic experiment and the laser rangefinding device are stowed. **1972** *Daily Tel.* 1 May 2/7 Seismic studies show these areas could be almost as rich in oil and gas as the North Sea. **1979** *Jrnl. R. Soc. Arts* CXXVII. 405/1 The first stage in oil and gas exploration is usually in the form of seismic surveys.

b. *fig.*

1962 S. E. FINER *Man on Horseback* xii. 222 These bands of successor-states form so many seismic zones of preternatural military eruption. **1979** A. DRAPER *Fish* 10 Churchill's seismic decision to empty the national coffers in one bold operation..was only taken when the Germans were hammering at the door.

2. Special collocations: **seismic prospecting**, prospecting by investigating the propagation in rock of artificially created elastic waves; **seismic reflection**, the reflection of elastic waves at boundaries between different rock formations; usu. *attrib.*; **seismic refraction**, the refraction of elastic waves on passing between formations of rock having different seismic velocities; usu. *attrib.*; **seismic sea-wave** = TSUNAMI; **seismic velocity**, the velocity of propagation of elastic waves in a particular rock; **seismic wave**, an elastic wave in the earth produced by an earthquake or by artificial means.

1929 *Trans. Amer. Inst. Mining & Metall. Engineers* LXXXI. 626 In seismic prospecting in general, fewer data are employed than in pure seismology. **1963** C. A. HEILAND *Geophysical Exploration* ix. 439 Uses of seismic prospecting in mining have been few. **1932** *Trans. Amer. Inst. Mining & Metall. Engineers* XCVII. 469 A second application of the method of least squares is the outlining of a buried structure by seismic reflections. **1940** *Bull. Amer. Assoc. Petroleum Geologists* XXIV. 1391 The sequence of methods of examination..is likely to be that of reconnaisance geology, detailed geologic mapping,..and core-drilling or seismic reflection examination. **1977** A. HALLAM *Planet Earth* 29/2 In the search for oil-bearing strata, geophysicists make use of the seismic-reflection technique to the virtual exclusion of all other exploration methods. **1934** *Trans. Amer. Inst. Mining & Metall. Engineers* CX. 473 (*heading*) Seismic refraction methods as applied to shallow overburdens. **1979** *Nature* 3 May 56/2 In 1977 an 800-km long seismic refraction profile was shot across Iceland and along the south-eastern flank of the Reykjanes Ridge. **1905** C. DAVISON *Study of Recent Earthquakes* vi. 163 (*heading*) Seismic sea-waves. **1944** A. HOLMES *Princ. Physical Geol.* xvii. 362 Strong submarine earthquakes are followed by seismic sea waves. **1966** *McGraw-Hill Encycl. Sci. & Technol.* XIV. 355/1 Explosions or collapses taking place under water may cause water waves, sometimes of great size. These fall within the class of tsunamis (seismic sea waves). **1935** *Bull. Amer. Assoc. Petroleum Geologists* XIX. 1 The idea that the longitudinal seismic velocity of sediments increases with the age of the sediments has been held rather generally for some time. **1977** A. HALLAM *Planet Earth* 11/1 Observed seismic velocities..allow the variation of density with depth in the Earth to be determined. **1900** H. NAGAOKA *Elastic Constants of Rocks & Velocity of Seismic Waves* (Publ. Earthquake Investigation Comm. in Foreign Languages No. 4) 65 The investigation of the seismic waves affords the best means of feeling the pulse of the interior of the earth. **1925** M. MÜHLBERG in I. A. Stigand *Outl. Occurrence & Geol. of Petroleum* 217 The transmissive velocity for seismic (as also acoustic) waves is different in various media. **1966** *McGraw-Hill Encycl. Sci. & Technol.* XII. 147/1 Seismic waves from explosions and earthquakes occur in the frequency range from about 100 to 1/3000 cps.

So **ˈseismical** *a.*, in the same sense; **ˈseismically** *adv.*, with regard to earthquakes; by seismic methods.

1858 MALLET in *Rep. Brit. Assoc.* I. 67 A third..volcanic region, of which I am not aware that anything is known seismically. **1869** *Spectator* 6 Nov. 1291 Considerable atmospheric and seismical disturbance. **1904** C. E. DUTTON *Earthquakes* xiv. 245 *note*, This locality is certainly a seismically sensitive one to-day. **1905** *Athenæum* 29 July 137/3 The cartography, geological, magnetical, seismical, &c., of Italy. **1941** *Bull. Amer. Assoc. Petroleum Geologists* XXV. 1258 The average depth to which the Gulf Coast has been seismically surveyed. **1978** *Nature* 27 Apr. 791/2 The absence of a seismically detectable Tertiary-Quaternary sediment cover.

seismicity (saɪzˈmɪsɪtɪ). [f. SEISMIC *a.* + -ITY. In Fr. *sismicité* (De Montessus de Ballore).] The frequency per unit area of earthquakes of a particular country; the number representing this.

1902 MILNE in *Encycl. Brit.* XXVII. 603/1 If we pick out the well-marked earthquake districts of the world, and give to each of them a seismicity or earthquake frequency per unit area of one-third of that of Japan, the conclusion arrived at is [etc.]. **1904** C. E. DUTTON *Earthquakes* xiv. 243 This statement..greatly facilitates the way toward a numerical measure of seismicity.

seismics (ˈsaɪzmɪks), *sb. pl.* [f. SEISMIC *a.*: see -IC 2.] Seismic exploration techniques, esp. such techniques considered as a whole.

1934 *Trans. Amer. Inst. Mining & Metall. Engineers* CX. 462 Roman has developed the application of the method to seismics very satisfactorily. **1976** D. MCLEOD tr. *Beckmann's Geol. Petroleum* II. iv. 64 Reflexion seismics are the most frequently-used, but also the most expensive of all methods used in petroleum exploration.

seismism (ˈsaɪzmɪz(ə)m). [f. Gr. σεισμ-ός (see SEISMIC *a.*) + -ISM.] The phenomena of earthquake movements collectively.

1902 in *Webster's Suppl.* **1910** in *Century Dict. Suppl.*

ˈseismo-, combining form f. Gr. σεισμό-ς (see SEISMIC *a.*). **ˌseismo-ˈchronograph** (see quot.).

1876 *Catal. Sci. Apparatus S. Kensington* 424 Seismochronograph, apparatus for determining the exact time of an earthquake.

seismocardiography (ˌsaɪzməʊkɑːdɪˈɒgrəfɪ). [f. SEISMO- + CARDIOGRAPHY.] The analysis of movements of the chest as a means of studying those of the heart. So **seismoˈcardiogram**, the record made by this process; **ˈseismocardioˈgraphic** *a.*, of or pertaining to seismocardiography.

1962 *Probl. Space Biol.* I. 461 The constructional details of a seismocardiographic transducer on dogs are given. *Ibid.* 463 Seismocardiography is a form of ballistocardiography. *Ibid.*, The recording of the seismocardiograms is impossible during movements. **1965** *Proc. 14th Internat. Astronaut. Congr., 1963* III. 38 During weightlessness the animal showed an absolute and relative increase of the first cycle of the seismocardiogram. **1970** L. I. KAKURIN et al. in D. E. Busby *Rec. Adv. Aerospace Med.* 43 Biomedical monitoring was carried out by means of a unified sensor system. It comprised seismocardiographic (SCG) and pneumographic (PG) sensors. **1979** *Human Physiol.* V. 542 The use of seismocardiography in clinical, athletic, and space medicine, ..and for mass examinations of the population is..a promising development.

seismogram (ˈsaɪzməʊgræm). [f. SEISMO- + -GRAM.] The record of a seismograph.

1891 in *Century Dict.* **1897** *Nature* 16 Dec. 156/1 Seismograms have already been received from Toronto.

seismograph (ˈsaɪzməʊgrɑːf, -æ-), *sb.* and *v.* Also **sismo-**. [f. SEISMO- + -GRAPH. Cf. It. *sismografo* (Palmieri), F. *sismographe.*] An instrument for recording automatically the phenomena of earthquakes.

1858 C. V. WALKER tr. *De la Rive's Electricity* III. 508 An apparatus..which he [Palmieri] has designated, under the name of Electro-magnetic Seismograph. **1862** *Times* 6 Jan. 10/2 How long the eruption might continue Palmieri had no means of calculating; it was going on as violently as ever, and his sismograph was always registering. **1887** G. H. DARWIN in *Fortn. Rev.* Feb. 262 Instruments by which the motion of the ground during an earthquake is recorded on an accurate scale of time..are called seismographs, or recording seismometers.

transf. **1879** G. MACDONALD *Sir Gibbie* III. xi. 176 His soul..like a delicate spiritual seismograph, responded at once to the least tremble of a neighbouring soul.

attrib. **1904** BROWNELL *Hrt. Japan* xxvi. 88/2 Thousands of seismograph records.

Hence **ˈseismograph**, *v. trans.* and *intr.*, to study (a region) by means of seismography; to prospect for oil by seismic methods; **seisˈmographer**, a seismologist (*Cent. Dict.* 1891); **seismoˈgraphic, seismoˈgraphical** *adjs.*, connected with, furnished by, or relating to a seismograph; of or pertaining to seismography; **seismoˈgraphically** *adv.* (*fig.* in quot. 1964); **seisˈmography**, the descriptive science of earthquakes; also, the use of the seismograph in recording disturbances of the crust of the earth.

1858 MALLET in *Rep. Brit. Assoc.* I. Pl. 11 Seismographic Map of the World. **1865** PAGE *Handbk. Geol. Terms* (ed. 2), *Seismography.* **1905** *Edin. Rev.* Apr. 310 Mr. Oldham distinguishes three types of pulsation in the seismographic records of distant shocks. **1925** M. MÜHLBERG in I. A. Stigand *Outl. Occurrence & Geol. of Petroleum* 218 The times of arrival are recorded seismographically. **1940** *Trans. Amer. Inst. Mining & Metall. Engineers* CXXXVIII. 305 (*heading*) Continuous profiling method of seismographing for oil structures. **1964** *New Statesman* 10 Apr. 577/1 In the quintessential Hanley lodging-house, every creak or whisper registered seismographically. **1968** C. HELMERICKS *Down Wild River North* xxvi. 423 They go 'seismographing' right overland through the wilderness. **1969** J. MAVOR *Voyage to Atlantis* ix. 203 Dr Marinatos suggested we seismograph the whole field in order to determine whether the Minoan layer was relatively level and therefore a logical town site.

seismoˈlogic, *a.* = next.

1904 C. E. DUTTON *Earthquakes* xiv. 239 Seismologic observations.

seismological (saɪzməʊˈlɒdʒɪkəl), *a.* [f. SEISMOLOGY + -ICAL.] Of or pertaining to seismology.

1850 MALLET in *Rep. Brit. Assoc.* I. 89 Seismological books. **1880** (*title*) Transactions of the Seismological Society of Japan. Vol. I. **1887** G. H. DARWIN in *Fortn. Rev.* Feb. 263 A seismological observatory.

Hence **seismoˈlogically** *adv.*; also *fig.*

1891 in *Century Dict.* **1955** *Sci. Amer.* Sept. 59/1 Seismologically speaking, the crust differs from the underlying part of the mantle in the fact that P and S waves travel in it more slowly and with more variable speed. **1970** *Nature* 15 Aug. 649/2 This earthquake was a nice reminder that Britain is not as seismologically quiet as people believe. **1977** H. GREENE *FSO—1* xix. 171 In an arm of government as seismologically sensitive as the Foreign Service,.. Friburn's sudden resignation was a shock on the level of six or seven on the diplomatic Richter scale.

seisˈmologist. [f. SEISMOLOGY + -IST.] An investigator or student of seismology.

1859 R. MALLET in *Rep. Brit. Assoc. 1858* 133 The subject appears to me worthy of more examination at the hands of Vulcanologists and Seismologists. **1868** R. A. PROCTOR in *Chamb. Jrnl.* 7 Nov. 710/1 The most eminent seismologists. **1902** *Encycl. Brit.* XXVII. 604/1 The ordinary apparatus employed by seismologists. **1955** *Sci. Amer.* Sept. 168/2 Our values agree well with those obtained by seismologists, who measure the thickness of the crust by the travel time of earthquake waves. **1973** *Nature* 27 July 195/2 This region of northern California, highly populated with seismologists and seismometers, is proving to be quite a testing ground for prediction.

seismologue (ˈsaɪzməʊlɒg). *rare*$^{-1}$. [f. SEISMO- + -LOGUE.] A catalogue of earthquake observations; a detailed account of earthquake phenomena.

Wrongly explained in some Dicts. as 'a seismologist'.

1858 MALLET in *Rep. Brit. Assoc.* I. 1 The labour of collecting and calculating further and future *Seismologues* will be in a great degree thrown away, unless [etc.].

seismology (saɪzˈmɒlədʒɪ). [f. SEISMO- + -LOGY. Cf. late Gr. σεισμολόγιον a treatise on earthquakes.] The science and study of earthquakes, and their causes and effects and attendant phenomena.

1858 MALLET in *Rep. Brit. Assoc.* I. 1 The few physicists who are engaged in Seismology. **1879** RUTLEY *Stud. Rocks* iii. 9 The branches of physical geology known as Vulcanicity and Seismology.

seismometer (saɪzˈmɒmɪtə(r)). [f. SEISMO- + -METER.] An instrument for measuring the intensity, direction, and duration of earthquakes.

All practical seismometers now record their observations automatically, hence the name is used almost interchangeably with *seismograph* (q.v.).

1841 J. D. FORBES in *Edin. Phil. Trans.* XV. I. 220 The self-registering part of the apparatus, which Mr. David Milne has termed a Seismometer. **1886** J. A. EWING in *Encycl. Brit.* XXI. 626/2 *Seismometer.* This name was originally given to instruments designed to measure the movement of the ground during earthquakes. *Ibid.* 627/1 The term 'seismometer' may conveniently be extended (and will here be understood) to cover all instruments which are designed to measure movements of the ground.

seismometric (saɪzməʊˈmɛtrɪk), *a.* [f. SEISMOMETRY + -IC.] Of or pertaining to seismometry, or to a seismometer.

1858 MALLET in *Rep. Brit. Assoc.* I. 72 Twelve years ago ..the construction of seismometric instruments seemed a comparatively easy matter. **1879** LE CONTE *Elem. Geol.* I. iii. 125 If *c* and *b* be the position of two seismometric observatories.

So **seismoˈmetrical** *a.* [See -ICAL.]

1885 *Athenæum* 7 Mar. 315/3 The occurrence of long-continued earthquake disturbances in Tasmania.. suggested to Mr. Ellery the propriety of instituting at the observatory some sort of seismometrical apparatus.

ˈseismoˈmetrograph. [f. SEISMOMETER (comb. form *-metro-*) + -GRAPH.] A seismograph.

1894 *Nature* 9 Aug. 362/1 The new continuous-record seismometrograph of the Collegio Romano.

seismometry (saɪzˈmɒmɪtrɪ). [f. SEISMO- + -METRY.] The scientific study, determination and recording of earthquake phenomena, esp. by means of the seismometer; the scientific study, theory, and application of the seismometer.

1858 MALLET in *Rep. Brit. Assoc.* I. 72, I therefore proceed to some observations upon instrumental seismometry, and the construction of seismometers. **1902** MILNE in *Encycl. Brit.* XXVII. 602/2 The seismometry developed in Japan revolutionized the seismometry of the world.

seismonasty (ˈsaɪzməʊnæstɪ). *Bot.* [f. SEISMO- + NASTY *sb.*[2]] A nastic movement made in response to a mechanical shock. Hence **seismoˈnastic** *a.*, of or pertaining to a movement of this kind.

1912 W. H. LANG tr. *Strasburger's Text-bk. Bot.* I. 323 (*heading*) Seismonasty. *Ibid.*, Every disturbance resulting from a mechanical shock acts as a stimulus... These movements are termed seismonastic. **1951** [see NASTIC *a.*]. **1965** BELL & COOMBE tr. *Strasburger's Textbk. Bot.* (new ed.) 382 A whole series of plants displays movements of this kind after touching, a phenomenon termed seismonasty. *Ibid.* 383 Many petals, stamens and stigmata show seismonastic reactions.

seismoscope (ˈsaɪzməʊskəʊp). [f. SEISMO- + -SCOPE.] A simple form of seismometer; a contrivance for detecting or indicating the occurrence of an earthquake shock, sometimes also indicating (without measuring) the intensity or direction of the earthquake wave.

1851 MALLET in *Rep. Brit. Assoc.* I. 278 This instrument I have named the Seismoscope. **1887** G. H. DARWIN in *Fortn. Rev.* Feb. 263 An instrument which tells only that there has been a shock, without giving a record of the nature of the movement, is called a seismoscope.

Hence **seismoˈscopic** *a.*

1882 MILNE in *Nature* 26 Oct. 627/2 The records of most of the older forms of seismographs and seismometers,..can only be regarded as seismoscopic.

seismotectonic (ˌsaɪzməʊtɛkˈtɒnɪk), *a.* [f. SEISMO- + TECTONIC *a.*] Of, pertaining to, or designating features of the earth's crust, such as faults, which are associated with or revealed by earthquakes; † *seismotectonic line* (see quots. 1907, 1924).

1907 W. H. HOBBS in *Beiträge zur Geophysik* VIII. 224 A tendency of the damaged communes to be arranged in essentially right lines (seismotectonic lines) is noteworthy. **1907** —— *Earthquakes* ii. 32 Buried planes may, however, often be traced as lines of destruction especially marked out upon the surface of the ground. Such straight lanes of special damage from earthquake have been called seismotectonic lines, or structure lines revealed by earthquakes. **1924** *Bull. Seismol. Soc. Amer.* XIV. 31 Hobbs, 1907, describes as seismotectonic lines certain structure-lines which he believes to be revealed by earthquakes. **1974** *Nature* 19 Apr. 661/2 Here, we describe three additional earthquake faults found during recent seismotectonic field studies in Iran. **1980** *Ibid.* 19 June 529/2 An aftershock study was begun..in an effort to examine seismotectonic processes near Mt. St. Helens.

seismotherapy (saɪzməʊˈθɛrəpɪ). *Path.* [f. Gr. σεισμό-ς a shaking (see SEISMIC) + THERAPY.] (See quot.)

1901 DORLAND *Med. Dict.* (ed. 2), *Seismotherapy*, the treatment of disease by mechanic vibration.

seismotic (saɪzˈmɒtɪk), *a. rare.* [f. Gr. σεισμ-ός (see SEISMIC *a.*) + -OTIC.] Seismic.

1889 KINGSFORD *Canada* III. 207 *note*, The assumption that Canada is beyond seismotic influences is not borne out by fact.

seison, seisor: see SEISIN, SEISER.

seiss, seissure: see CEASE, SEIZURE.

Seistan (ˈsiːstɑːn). Also seistan. [The name of a low-lying region of eastern Iran and south-western Afghanistan.] A strong north-westerly wind prevalent in this region in the summer months. Also *attrib.*, as ***Seistan wind***.

1906 *Geogr. Jrnl.* XXVIII. 224 The extraordinary frequency and violence of the Seistan wind, and the regularity with which it blows from the same quarter, are very remarkable. **1940** *Chambers's Techn. Dict.* 754/1 *Seistan*, the 120-day summer north wind in E. Persia. **1959** R. E. HUSCHKE *Gloss. Meteorol.* 503 The seistan is associated ..with the deep summer-time low over northwest India. **1967** R. W. FAIRBRIDGE *Encycl. Atmospheric Sci. & Astrogeology* 1155/2 The 'seistan' or 'Wind of 120 days' is the characteristic wind of Seistan in eastern Iran, which blows from late May till the end of September, from north-northwest, sometimes with velocities from 70–120 mph.

seistar, variant of SISTRE *Obs.*, sistrum.

c **1590** J. BURELL *Queen's Entry* in Sibbald *Chron. S.P.* (1802) III. 468 Trumpets and timbrels maid gret beir, With instruments melodious: The seistar and the sumphion [etc.].

seisure, seisz: see SEIZURE, CEASE.

seit, obs. 3rd sing. ind. pres. of SAY *v.*[1]

seit, obs. f. SET, SIT *v.*

seite, obs. f. SEAT *sb.*

seith, var. SAITHE.

1711 *Extracts Rec. Convent. Burghs Scot.* (1880) IV. 515 There has been a trade of barrelled codd, ling, and seith fish.

seith, obs. form of SCYTHE.

seity (ˈsiːɪtɪ). *rare.* [ad. med.L. *sēitās*, f. L. *sē* oneself: see -ITY.] That which constitutes the self, selfhood.

1709 STEELE *Tatler* No. 174 ¶1 Scotus, to distinguish the Race of Mankind, gives every Individual of that Species what he calls a Seity, something peculiar to himself. **1733** BUDGELL *Bee* IV. 347 For, these were Parts, of Dennis, Born, to Die! But, there's a Nobler Se-ity, behind; His Reason dies not. **1761** G. COLMAN *Crit. Refl. Dram. Writers* in *Massinger's Wks.* (1779) I. p. xxiv, Our Old Writers thought no Personage whatever, unworthy a Place in the Drama, to which they could annex what may be called a *Seity*; that is, to which they could allot Manners and Employments peculiar to itself. **1906** W. T. SEEGER in *Hibbert Jrnl.* Oct. 83 [In Hindu theology] Seity is the power of infinite self-manifestation, man's being the same essentially as God's.

Seitz (zaɪts). [See quot. 1944: a proprietary term in the U.S.] Used *attrib.* and in *Comb.* with reference to filtration, as **Seitz disc**, a small disc of compressed asbestos fibres, used for filtration; **Seitz filter**, a type of filter in which liquids are purified by passage through a readily replaceable Seitz disc; so as *v. trans.*; **Seitz-filtered** *ppl. a.*, **Seitz filtration**; **Seitz pad**, a Seitz disc.

1925 *1st Progress Rep. Foot-&-Mouth Dis. Res. Comm.* (Min. of Agric. & Fisheries) App. II. 20 A routine form of asbestos filter of German manufacture, the Seitz filter, has been employed with success. **1928** T. M. RIVERS *Filterable Viruses* ii. 59 Smaller filters with Seitz discs have been made for use in experimental work. [**1944** *Official Gaz.* (U.S. Patent Office) 4 Apr. 12/2 Republic Filters, Inc., Paterson, N.J... *Seitz*. The trade-mark is a facsimile of the signature of Mr. Seitz, the late inventor of the basic construction of the filtering apparatus manufactured and sold by applicant.] **1946** *Nature* 31 Aug. 293/2 After the fungus has grown in the liquid medium for about two weeks, the culture medium is Seitz-filtered and collected in autoclaved tubes and ampoules. **1947** *Ann. Rev. Microbiol.* I. 378 The second experiment..involved thirty-six men who were divided into three groups of twelve each and sprayed, respectively, with untreated sputum and throat washings, with the material filtered through sintered glass or Seitz pads, or with the same material autoclaved. **1956** *Nature* 21 Jan. 134/1 Another 2 ml. of the same medium, containing 0·05 per cent aesculin sterilized by Seitz-filtration, [was] added. *Ibid.* 10 Mar. 481/2 (*caption*) Curve *B* shows the results in Seitz-filtered artificial duodenal contents alone. **1961** *Lancet* 29 July 227/2 The pH was adjusted to 7·4 and the medium sterilised by Seitz filtration. **1964** M. HYNES *Med. Bacteriol.* (ed. 8) ii. 25 The Seitz filter has almost entirely replaced all other types of filter... Filtration is carried out through an asbestos pad clamped to the bottom of a metal container.

seive, seiyde, obs. ff. SIEVE, SEED *sb.*

sei whale (seɪ weɪl). Also sejhval; (*erron.*) seivhal. [Anglicization of Norw. *sejhval*, f. *sei* coal-fish + *hval* WHALE *sb.*] A blue-grey rorqual, *Balænoptera borealis*.

1912 *Rep. Brit. Assoc.* 158 The Right whales and Sejhvals are said to appear only during the earlier part of the season. **1916** R. S. ANDREWS in *Mem. Amer. Mus. Nat. Hist.* I. 295 The vernacular term Sei Whale (*Sejvhal*), adopted in this memoir, is the name by which *Balænoptera borealis* is known to the Norwegians. **1919** R. W. CLARK in E. Shackleton *South* I. 364 The sperm-whale and the sei-whale have shown a good deal of seasonal variation. **1923** *Chambers's Jrnl.* Jan. 112/1 The lesser rorqual, the seivhal, and the humpback, another whalebone whale, take some small fish. **1939** *Nature* 16 Dec. 999/2 (*caption*) Species..Sei, Right, Sperm. **1958** *Times* 12 Nov. 11/6 A unit is defined as equalling one blue whale..or six sei whales. **1974** *Country Life* 11 Apr. 866/1 With the cessation of whaling in the Faeroes and Norway the numbers of fin and sei whales in those areas..will..increase.

seizable (ˈsiːzəb(ə)l), *a.* Forms: 5 seisible, seasible, seisable, 6 seisibill, seizeabil, 7– seizable. [f. SEIZE *v.* + -ABLE; an AF. *seisable* occurs A.D. 1361.] Capable of being seized (in various senses of the verb). Chiefly of property, that may lawfully be seized.

1461 *Rolls of Parlt.* V. 479/2 Not forfeited nor forfeitable ..nor seisible into any of their handes. **1483** *Ibid.* VI. 248/1 That all Castelles..be not forfeited..to the Kyng..nor be seiseble into his handys by this present Acte. **1574** in *Exch. Rolls Scot.* XX. 467 To sell..and put away his landis, heretagis [etc.]..sua that sche sall get nathing seizeabil thairfore. **1652** *Obs. Orig. Govt.* 19 It was alienable by the Parent, and seizable by an usurper as other goods are. **1768** *Woman of Honor* III. 129 Private property..was transferable and seizable on private suit. **1815** MME. D'ARBLAY *Diary* (1876) IV. lxv. 335 Carts, waggons, and every..seizable vehicle were unremittingly in motion. **1846** RUSKIN *Mod. Paint.* II. III. II. ii. §28 *note*, It is the characteristic of truth to be in some way tangible, seizable, distinguishable, and clear. **1870** *Daily News* 25 July 4 The principles laid down in the Declaration of the Congress of Paris of 1856..are as follows:—..3d. Merchandise of neutrals, except contraband of war, sailing under an enemy's flag is not seizable. **1885** *Law Times* LXXVIII. 229/1 The personal liability of the official receivers for mistakes as to property seizable as assets of the estate.

seize (siːz), *v.* Forms: 3–8 **saise**, 3–4 **sayse**, 3–9 **seise**, 3–5 **seyse**, 4 *Sc.* **seyss**, 4–5 **sese**, **sess**, 5–8 **sease**, 6 *Sc.* **sase**, **seysse**, 6–7 **seaze**, (7 **seaz**), 6–8 **sieze**, 7 **siese**, (8 *Naut.* **size**); 5 **cess**, 6–7 **cease**, **ceaze**, (7 **ceize**, **ceese**); 6– **seize**. [a. OF. *saisir*, *seisir* (mod.F. *saisir*) to put in possession, to take possession of, to take hold of = Pr. *sazir* (whence It. *sagire*):—Frankish Latin (8th c.) *sacīre* in the phrase *ad propriam* (or *ad proprietatem*) *sacire*, to take into one's own possession, to appropriate. As the word *sacire* is replaced by *ponere* in another example of the formula, its source is commonly believed to be the Teut. **satjan* to place: see SET *v.*[1]]

I. To put in possession.

1. *Law.* **a.** (In technical use written seise.) *trans.* To put (a person) in legal possession *of* a feudal holding; to invest or endow *with* property; to establish *in* a holding or an office or dignity.

c **1290** *Beket* 1695 in *S. Eng. Leg.* 155 Þe king..wende in-to engelonde, For to saisi sir henri is sone mid al is kinedom. *Ibid.* 1708 Þe fader seruede þe sone at þe mete a-dai, And with reaume saisede him. **1297** R. GLOUC. (Rolls) 8991 To ..saysi þer wiþ willam Roberdes sone courtehese. *a* **1300** *Havelok* 2518 Her ich sayse þe In al þe lond, in al þe fe. **13** .. *K. Alis.* 7951 (Laud MS.), Darries heir I make þee And seise þee wiþ al his fee. *c* **1400** *Destr. of Troy* 119 Of Septur and soile he sesit his brothir. *c* **1400** *York Manual*, etc. (Surtees) 221* *note*, Wiþ my body y the worschipe, and wiþ my worldliche catel iche þe sese. **14..** *Beryn* 1549 Beryn first was sesid in the Shippis fyve. *c* **1440** *Ipomydon* 1592 Ipomydon sesyd hym in his lande And yaffe hym the profyte for his sake. **1471** CAXTON *Recuyell* (Sommer) II. 693 For as moche as Pirrus my right dere nevewe is the nexte eyer I sease hym now therin. **1480** —— *Chron. Eng.* clxvi. k4b, The lordes of Scotland..come to kyng Edward of englond & seised hym in all the land of Scotland as hir chief lord. *c* **1500** *Melusine* lix. 358 Wilt thou denye my trybute that of ryght I ought to haue vpon the pommel of this toure of the which I was seasyd & enpocessid by thy fader? **1526** SKELTON *Magnyf.* 1554 In my fauour I haue you feffyd and seasyd. **1559** *Fabyan's Chron.* (1811) 711 Al whiche tyme doctour Ponet was ceased in that bisshoprike. **1836** *Penny Cycl* V. 226/2 Borthwick had acquired various lands..but having seised his son James in several of them, he [etc.].

b. Passive. *to be seised of* or *in*: to be the legal possessor of. Phrases, *to be seised in fee*, *to be seised of* (a manor, etc.) *in his demesne as of fee*: to be the holder of the fee-simple.

seised is sometimes used *simply* = seised of the property in question.

13.. *E.E. Allit. P.* A. 417, & sesed in alle hys herytage Hys lef is. *a* **1400** in *Eng. Gilds* (1870) 362 Þe tenemens of weche he deyd y-seysed. **1427** *Rolls of Parlt.* IV. 318/2 Every persone..beeyng seysed of Londes.., in his demesne as of freehold. **1473–5** *Cal. Proc. Chanc. Q. Eliz.* (1830) II. Pref. 61 Richard Saunder was thenne therof seised in his demene as of fee symple. **1502** *Reg. Privy Seal Scot.* I. 115/1 Lanndis..quhilk his grantschir..deit last vestit and sesit in. **1558** *Mortgage* in *Vicary's Anat.* (1888) App. v. 183 That he the said Thomas Dunkyn, the daye of the makyng herof, is lawfully seased in his demeane as of fee. **1602** SHAKS. *Ham.* I. i. 89 Who by a Seal'd Compact,..Did forfeite..all those his Lands Which he stood seiz'd on. **1603** T. M. *True Narr. Entert. Jas. I* B 2 b, The saide Bishop being thus seized of all the authoritie to the Kings Maiesties vse. **1607** DAVIES *1st Let. to Earl of Salisbury* (1787) 225 It was found that Sir John O'Relie was seized of the country in fee, and died seized. **1716** M. DAVIES *Athen. Brit.* II. 77 It appears that he died seiz'd of Lands in Slacksted in Hampshire. *a* **1768** ERSKINE *Inst. Law. Scot.* III. viii. §83 (1773) 587 This holds though the lands had been adjudged from the ancestor during his life,..if the ancestor died seised, and in the possession of the lands. **1827** JARMAN *Powell's Devises* II. 103 If a devisor, being seised of both Blackacre and Whiteacre, devise Blackacre to A. in fee. **1844** WILLIAMS *Real Prop.* (1877) 105 The person last seized (or feudally possessed). *a* **1845** POLSON *Eng. Law* in *Encycl. Metrop.* II. 827/1 The Statute of Uses..which provides, that where one is seised of lands, &c. to the use of another, he who has the use shall become seised of the lands. **1872** 'MARK TWAIN' *Roughing It* xxii, We were land-owners now, duly seised and possessed.

†**c.** Without const.: To endow, dower. *Obs.*

c **1430** *How Wise Man taught Son* in *Babees Bk.* (1868) 51 For ritchesse take hir neuere þe more þouȝ sche wolde þee boþe feffe & ceese.

2. *transf.* **a.** in Passive, *to be seized* (*seised*) *of* or †*with*: to be in possession of. Now only *arch.* and with conscious allusion to the legal use. Formerly often influenced by sense 5, 6, or 7, †to have seized, to hold as the result of seizing.

c **1477** CAXTON *Jason* 81 b, And thus..thou mayst retourne with glorie in to thy countre and be seased with the noble fliese of gold. *a* **1533** LD. BERNERS *Huon* xxxi. 94 Whan Huon sawe that he was sessyd of his horne of Iuorey he was ioyfull. **1590** SPENSER *F.Q.* I. v. 8 As when a Gryfon, seized of his pray, A Dragon fiers encountreth in his flight. **1594** CAREW *Huarte's Exam. Wits* xiv. (1596) 257 Temperat men are seized of the wisdom and knowledge requisit to the calling of a king. **1612** BREREWOOD *Lang. & Relig.* (1614) Pref. ¶¶1 b, Those (as they vsually stile them) of the Religion..are seased of aboue 70 Townes. **1628** HOBBES *Thucydides* (1629) 58 The Outlawes of Bœotia being seazed of Orchomenus and Chæronea,..the Athenians made Warre vpon those places. **1653** H. COGAN tr. *Pinto's Trav.* xxx. 122 If any that sell Goose Eggs do chance to be taken siesed with Hens eggs..they are presently punished with thirty lashes. **1659** T. PECKE *Parnassi Puerp.* 159 Seventy six years his Lungs were seis'd of Breath. **1710** HEARNE *Leland's Itin.* I. Pref. 13 By this means Sir John became seiz'd of far the largest parcel of this great man's writings. **1713** ADDISON *Cato* III. vii, So Pluto, seiz'd of Proserpine, convey'd To hell's tremendous gloom th' affrighted maid. *a* **1715** BURNET *Own Time* (1766) I. 6 Being seized of his Mother's Crown, while she was an exile and a prisoner. **1885** GLADSTONE *Sp.* in *Standard* 14 Apr., I have no doubt that in due time Parliament will be seised of that correspondence. **1896** A. J. BALFOUR *Sp.* in *Daily News* 18 Mar. 3/3 So far as I am seised of the case..it appears to me that [etc.].

†**b.** *refl.* To take possession *of*, to seize *on*; = senses 6, 7, 9. [So F. *se saisir de*.]

1579 J. STUBBES *Gaping Gulf* C 4 b, The French king was not ashamed to excite John the brother of England to seize himselfe of the crowne. *a* **1586** SIDNEY *Arcadia* I. (Sommer) 81 b, The Lion..was ready to seaze him selfe on the pray. *Ibid.* III. 295 b, Death began to seaze him selfe of his harte.

†**3. a.** To settle, establish in a place; to place, seat, fix. *Obs.*

a **1400–50** *Wars Alex.* 5637 Twyse sex Semylacris sesid he þar-vndire. **14..** *Siege of Jerusalem* (E.E.T.S.) 1/2 Sir Sesar hym sulf seysed in rome. *c* **1430** in *Pol. Rel. & L. Poems* (1866) 165 For þee y suffride greet repreef, In hiȝ heuene þi soule to ceese Y was an-hangid as a þeef. **1513** DOUGLAS *Æneis* XIII. ii. 106, I sall ȝou seis and induce now, but weir, In far largear rewardis mychtely. **1535** STEWART *Cron. Scot.* I. 118 The lordis..Hes seisit him syne in his sepulture. *Ibid.* II. 247 Tha buir his bodie to Ecolumkill..Syne sesit him thair into sepultiur. **1535** LYNDSAY *Satyre* 8 The Father and founder of faith and felicitie..Gif ȝow all that I sie seasit in this place [etc.]. **1589** R. BRUCE *Serm.* (1843) 118 He makes his Son to come down, to sease himself in the womb of the Virgin. **1594** ALEX. HUME *Epist. to Rdr.* 19 The filthie vice and corruption that naturallie is seased in the harts of all men. **1600** in T. Stafford *Pac. Hib.* I. xvii. (1633) 104 Considering the Gentleman was ceased in my Countrie, and had my word. **1633** T. STAFFORD *Ibid.* II. x. 190 The Soveraigne with his white rod in his hand, going to billet, and cease them in severall houses.

b. Of a beast of prey: To fasten (its claws) upon. *Obs.*

1590 SPENSER *F.Q.* I. iii. 19 When that disdainfull beast.. him suddaine doth surprize, And seizing cruell clawes on trembling brest Vnder his Lordly foot him proudly hath supprest. *Ibid.* I. viii. 15 The cruell beast Who on his necke his bloudie clawes did seize. **1596** *Ibid.* v. iv. 40 As when a Beare hath seiz'd her cruell clawes Vppon the carkasse of some beast too weake.

†**4.** To give possession of, grant. *Obs.*

a **1400–50** *Wars Alex.* 5220 Þe maistir out of Messedone ȝow maynly enjoynes, If ȝe ȝoure cite will saue to sese him his brid. *c* **1450** *Erle Tolous* 1199 He made hym steward of hys londe, And sesyd agayne into hys honde That he had rafte hym froo. *c* **1450** *St. Cuthbert* (Surtees) 8230 All betwene tyne and teese, To durham mynster þai þaim seese.

II. To take possession.

5. a. Of a feudal superior or a sovereign (or one acting on his behalf): To take possession of, confiscate (the property of a vassal or subject). Also, to annex (a country) to one's own dominions. Phrases, *to seize into one's hands*, †*to one's behoof*.

c **1290** *Beket* 705 in *S. Eng. Leg.* 126 Þe king sende is men sone to saisi al is lond And al-so al is bischopriche ase is traitores, In-to is hond. **1297** R. GLOUC. (Rolls) 10125 Þe king of france orn vpe þe king Ion, & is londes biȝonde se seisede anon, Aquitayne & normandie. *a* **1300** *Havelok* 2513 Þanne he was ded..Sket was seysed al þat his was In þe kinges hand il del, Lond and lith, and oþer catel. *c* **1330** R. BRUNNE *Chron. Wace* (Rolls) 2703 For first he slow þe kyng Pyncer, & seysed þe lond til his byhoue. **1387** TREVISA *Higden* (Rolls) VIII. 287 þe kyng made seyse into his hond al þe temporalte of clerkes. **1447–8** SHILLINGFORD *Lett.* (Camden) 96 The said Citie..was seised into the saide King Edward's hondes. **1610** HOLLAND *Camden's Brit.* I. 677 Roger Mortimer..seised also this Chirck, into his possession. **1613** R. C. *Table Alph.* (ed. 3), *Seize*, to forfaite to the prince. **1723** *Lond. Gaz.* No. 6174/3 A Grey..Horse ..was..seized into the Hands of the Lord of the Manor.. as Felons Goods. **1750** CARTE *Hist. Eng.* II. 231 Three of his principal castles were, for his contempt of the court, to be seized into the King's hands. **1763** J. BROWN *Poetry & Music* viii. 161 It was held an Act of Sacrilege to seize their Estates, even for the public Service. **1829** SCOTT *Anne of G.* xix, The Duke of Burgundy's attempt to seize that fief into his own hands. **1871** FREEMAN *Norm. Conq.* (1876) IV. xvii. 34 The estates of the fallen King..were no doubt at once seized into the King's hands.

b. To take possession of (goods) in pursuance of a judicial order.

1482 in Leadam *Star Chamber Cases* (1903) 9 One Robert Bonyfaunt as one of the clerkes..in the Superuysershipp of your Custumes..shold sease and arreste..to your vse at Topsam..a hundreth peces of cresscloth. **1581** LAMBARDE *Eiren.* II. vii. (1588) 207 Every Iustice of the Peace may.. seaze all the goods of any outlandish persons (calling themselves Egyptians) that shall come into this Realme. **1716** HEARNE *Collect.* (O.H.S.) V. 186 James Newlin was put into yᵉ Ground last night, for fear they should seize his Body. **1733** *Gentl. Mag.* May 266/2 The Watchmen.. seized 1100 Weight of uncustom'd Tea. *c* **1733** J. P. DU PLESSIS in *Pepys' Diary* (1879) VI. 259 Being quite moneyless, and in danger of having my goods seized for rent. **1782** MISS BURNEY *Cecilia* v. viii, The house was seized before ever I could get nigh it. **1878** *22nd Rep. Customs Comm.* 58 The tobacco seized on these several occasions weighed 2,601 lbs. **1885** BRETT in *Law Rep. 14 Q.B.D.* 878 Goods..which the sheriff could rightfully seize under the writ.

c. To arrest, apprehend (a person). Cf. 6 b.

1471 *Little Red Bk. Bristol* (1900) 131 That ye sease the persones of thaim alle as ferforthly as ye may sette hand vpon thaim. **1910** *Daily Mail* 8 Feb. 7/5 The rare occurrence of 'seizing' a jury..was witnessed at Manchester Assizes yesterday.

6. a. To take possession of by force; to capture (a city); to take as plunder.

1338 R. BRUNNE *Chron.* (1810) 47 Knoute & Edrik þei seised [Langtoft *ont pris*] þorgh tresone Bokyngham & Bedford, þe toun of Huntyngtone. **1375** BARBOUR *Bruce* x. 108 The king in hy gert sess the pray Off all the land. **1390** GOWER *Conf.* II. 248 The flees of gold he shulde sese. *a* **1400–50** *Wars Alex.* 1452 Gase forth to gaza ane othre grete cite, And he settes on a sawte and seses it beliue. **1481** CAXTON *Myrr.* I. v. 25 The riche haue now in thise dayes seased somoche that the poure abide naked. **1607** HEYWOOD *Woman kild with Kindnes* Wks. 1874 II. 146 There, take her to thee, if thou hast the heart To ceize her as a rape or lustfull prey. **1687** A. LOVELL tr. *Thevenot's Trav.* II. 149 There they would have seized our Mules to carry Provisions for the king to Ispahan. **1864** BRYCE *Holy Rom. Emp.* xii. (1875) 184 Posen and Galicia were seized by Prussia and Austria, A.D. 1772. **1883** R. W. DIXON *Mano* II. vii. 93 Robbers, who seized church goods without remorse.

b. To take prisoner, to catch.

a **1400–50** *Wars Alex.* 4119 His seggis sesid of þam [*sc.* the bearded women] sum & to him-selfe broȝt. *c* **1400** *Destr. Troy* 1513 He was enformyt..how his towne was takon..his suster sesyd and soght into syde londis. **1609** HEYWOOD *Brit. Troy* IV. xxix, Nor can his troubled sences be appeas'd Till as a Traitor he Prince Ioue hath ceas'd. **1682** BUNYAN *Holy War* To Rdr. 92, I heard the Prince bid Boanerges go Up to the Castle, and there siese his foe. **1777** WATSON *Philip II*, III. I. 72 The inhabitants..seized his person, and confined him in the castle. **1827** *Hist. Mod. Europe* II. lii. 14 By putting to death all the Turks whom they had seised before the battle.

7. a. To take hold of with the hands, claws, teeth, etc.; in mod. use, to take hold of suddenly or eagerly, to clutch.

13.. *Coer de L.* 78 Her men aborde gunne to stande, And sesyd that other. **13..** *Gaw. & Gr. Knt.* 822 Sere seggez hym sesed by sadel, quel he lyȝt. *c* **1350** *Will. Palerne* 1236 He sesed a spere, & dressed him to þe duk presteli to iuste. *c* **1374** CHAUCER *Compl. Mars* 240 And lyke a fissher as men alday may se Bateth hys angle-hoke with summe plesaunce Til mony a fissch ys wode to that he be Sesed therwith. **1390** GOWER *Conf.* I. 260 This knyht..hath him be the bridel sesed. *c* **1450** *Merlin* xxxii. 649 He stombeled on his clubbe, and it sesed. **1513** DOUGLAS *Æneis* III. ii. 15 Delos..Quham ..Apollo..Sesit and band betuix vther ilis twa. **1591** SHAKS. *Two Gentl.* v. iv. 33 Had I beene ceazed by a hungry Lion, I would haue [etc.]. **1609** HEYWOOD *Brit. Troy* IV. lxxxvi, The Crones his bounty praise, And in their hands two costly Iewels cease. **1717** POPE *Iliad* XII. 260 Allow'd to seize, but not possess the Prize. **1797** HT. LEE *Canterb. T., Old Wom. T.* (1799) I. 373 Lothaire abruptly seized him by the arm. **1875** JOWETT *Plato* (ed. 2) I. 477, I seized the books and read them as fast as I could. **1879** LUBBOCK *Sci. Lect.* 36 If you touch an ant with a needle or a bristle, she is almost sure to seize it in her jaws.

b. *transf.* of inanimate things.

1673 TEMPLE *Observ. Un. Prov.* iii. 122 The Sea.. yielding up what it had seized, and seizing what it had yielded up. **1818** ACCUM *Chem. Tests* 261 The barytes seizes the acid.

†**c.** *to seize up*: ? to haul up (a sail). *Obs.*

c **1400** *Destr. Troy* 3241 þai shot into shippe..sesit vp þere sailes, set hom to wyndes. *Ibid.* 4619 All the company..knyt vp hor ancres, Sesit vp hor sailes in a sad hast.

d. *to seize hold of*: to take hold of suddenly and roughly: cf. TAKE *v.* 69, HOLD *sb.*[1] 2.

1839 FR. A. KEMBLE *Resid. in Georgia* (1863) 84, I was seized hold of by a hideous old negress.

8. In various figurative uses. **a.** With impersonal subject, e.g. death, disease, calamity: To oppress or attack suddenly. Also of a fear, a belief, etc.: To take sudden possession of (a person, his mind). In passive often const. *with* (less frequently *by*).

c **1381** CHAUCER *Parl. Foules* 481 Til that deth me sese, I wele ben heris. *c* **1425** *Cast. Persev.* 246 in *Macro Plays* 84 þou synne my sowle sese, I ȝeue not a myth. *c* **1585** MONTGOMERIE *Sonnets* xxxv. 7 Suppose my silly saull with sin be seasde. **1644** MILTON *Areopag.* (Arb.) 42 A fantasm bred by the feaver which had then seis'd him. **1659** HAMMOND *On Ps.* lxxxix. 48 We are borne miserable, and pass through a succession of miseries here, and are shortly seised with death. **1700** DRYDEN *Sigism. & Guisc.* 205 A welcome Heaviness that seiz'd his Eyes. **1732** BERKELEY *Alciphr.* III. §3 Seized and rapt with this sublime idea. **1757** GRAY *Bard* I Ruin seize thee, ruthless King! **1797** HT. LEE *Canterb. T., Old Wom. T.* (1799) I. 372 [He] was seized with dizziness. **1830** R. KNOX *Béclard's Anat.* 67 Putrefaction always..seizes it at the end of a short period. **1845** M. PATTISON *Ess.* (1889) I. 7 A nation, indifferent to the creeds, is seized with a sudden passion for ecclesiastical art. **1849** MACAULAY *Hist. Eng.* vii. II. 171 The young prince..was seized by the small pox. **1871** R. ELLIS *Catullus* lxxxiv. 10 Sudden a solemn fright seized us.

b. Of an object of perception, a fact, etc., hence of a speaker, writer, or artist: To arrest, hold (the attention), to impress irresistibly (the mind, etc.).

1772 SIR J. REYNOLDS *Disc.* v. (1876) 374 Carlo Maratti.. rarely seizes the imagination by exhibiting the higher excellencies. **1865, 1886** [see SEIZING *ppl. a.* 2].

c. To avail oneself eagerly or dexterously of, take advantage of (an opportunity). Also, to take (a resolution) decisively.

1618 CHAPMAN *Hesiod's Georg.* II. 487 Thy selfe, if well in yeares; thy wife take home, Not much past thirtie; But being yong thy selfe; Nuptialls that sease, The times best season in their acts are these [that follow]. **1642** FULLER *Holy & Prof. St.* IV. xv. 317 Where her resolutions once seis'd, she would never let go her hold. **1809** ROLAND *Fencing* 86 At the instant, therefore, I perceive him turn his wrist, I seize the moment he expects to strike my blade. **1855** MACAULAY *Hist. Eng.* xx. IV. 433 Whether the opportunity should be seized or lost it did not belong to him to decide. **1861** HUGHES *Tom Brown at Oxf.* vi, The latter seized the occasion to propound this question.

d. To grasp with the mind or perceptive faculties; to apprehend.

1855 BAIN *Senses & Int.* II. ii. §8 Its peculiar character or tone cannot be seized by any descriptive phrase. **1861** BUCKLE *Civiliz.* (1873) III. v. 290 The reader must firmly seize and keep before his eyes the essential difference between deduction..and induction. **1865** M. ARNOLD *Ess. Crit.* viii. (1875) 321 A beauty which a foreigner cannot perfectly seize. **1873** BROWNING *Red Cott. Nt.-cap* 1019 Sit on the little mound here, whence you seize The whole of the gay front sun-satisfied. **1877** E. R. CONDER *Bas. Faith* ii. 69 It is the infinite which the intellect can seize but not embrace.

9. *intr.* with various constructions. **a.** *to seize on* or *upon* = to seize (in senses 6–8). Also, in the same sense, † *to seize of* (*obs. rare*).

1399 LANGL. *Rich. Redeles* III. 49 Thanne cometh þer a congioun..And sesith on hir sete with hir softe plumes. **1546** in *Sel. Pleas Crt. Admiralty* (1894) I. 148 The sayde Leonard Sumpter..toke and seased uppon the same as lawfull wayff and thynge forsaken. **1600** W. WATSON *Decacordon* (1602) 64 The English: a nation apt to ceaze of euery noueltie. **1600** HOLLAND *Livy* XXXIII. 835 With these forces Pausistratus encamped in the territorie of Stratonicea, and there hee seized of a commodious place. **1672** *Essex Papers* (Camden) 2 Yᵗ at any Time 40 desperat fellows may either ceese on it or blow it up. **1672** STILLINGFL. *Serm.* xi. Wks. 1710 I. 151 We find the best of men in Scripture seized on with a very unusual consternation at any extraordinary divine appearance. **1768** EARL CARLISLE in Jesse *Selwyn & Contemp.* (1843) II. 276, I make a point of seizing upon every leisure moment to thank you for your constant attention. **1800** tr. *Lagrange's Chem.* I. 217 The liquid carbonates contained in the bottles, which are decomposed in proportion as the sulphurous acid expels the carbonic acid to seize on the bases. **1842** BORROW *Bible in Spain* xxxiv, A morbid melancholy seized upon the Irishman. **1899** E. CALLOW *Old Lond. Tav.* II. 302 The Gardens were demolished and the jerry builder seized upon the ground.

†**b.** Of a stroke, a weapon: To penetrate deeply *in*. *Obs.*

1590 SPENSER *F.Q.* I. xi. 38 The mortall sting his angry needle shot Quite through his shield, and in his shoulder seasd. *Ibid.* II. viii. 38 But th'other on his hacqueton did lyte, The which diuiding..It seizd in his right side, and there the dint did stay. **1600** FAIRFAX *Tasso* VII. xli. 125 The wicked steele seaz'd deepe in his right side.

c. To grasp or clutch *at*. *rare.*

1848 THACKERAY *Van. Fair* lxvi, Then he..gave him a note. William seized at it rather eagerly.

III. Technical senses.

10. *trans.* (*Naut.*). †**a.** To reach, arrive at (= MAKE *v.* 65 b). Also with *in*. *Obs.*

1588 FENNER in *Defeat Sp. Armada* (Navy Rec Soc.) II. 41 Thereby the enemy was able neither to seize England, Ireland, Scotland, Flanders, and hardly the out isles of Scotland. **1590** SPENSER *F.Q.* I. xii. 17 Since now safe ye seised haue the shore, And well arriued are. **1628** DIGBY *Voy. Medit.* (Camden) 75, I seeing that the great sattia could not worke to seaze the shore, I bore up to her. **1635** L. FOXE *N.-W. Fox* 127 The wind would not permit him to seize in that N. shore.

b. To fasten (two ropes or parts of a rope) together, or to attach (a rope) to something else, by binding with marline, yarn, or the like. *to seize up*: to fasten (a man) by the wrists to the shrouds, in preparation for a flogging.

[A use of F. *saisir*; the proximate source may be Du. *seizen*; the word was adopted in other Teut. langs.: G. *seisen*, Sw. *sejsa*, Da. *seise*. The use 7 c seems unconnected.]

1644 MANWAYRING *Sea-mans Dict.*, To *Sease* or *Seasing*, is to make fast..any roapes together with some small roape-yarne, marling or any line. **1747** *Gentl. Mag.* XVII. 486 By the time the new breachings were all seized, I was got almost alongside the *Trident*. **1778** [see GAMMET]. **1817** J. MARTIN *Tonga Isl.* I. 4 They were seized up and received a dozen lashes each. **1840** R. H. DANA *Bef. Mast* xv, Sam..was seized up, as it is called, that is, placed against the shrouds, with his wrists made fast to them, his jacket off, and his back exposed. **1875** BEDFORD *Sailor's Pocket Bk.* vi. 227 Boat-hooks fitted with a stout lanyard, ending in an eye, secured to the hook, and seized two-thirds down the staff. **1895** *Outing* (U.S.) XXVI. 47/1 Next, seize the luff of the sail to the mast hoops with marline.

11. *intr.* (*Mech.*) Also with *up*. Of a machine or mechanism: to stick, jam, or lock fast; to become unworkable, as by reason of undue heat or friction. Also *fig.*

1878 A. RIGG *Steam Engine* 128 The surfaces of motion blocks and side bars are found to wear exceedingly well when..efficient lubrication exists; but in the event of failure in this respect the metallic surfaces become dry, and their friction engenders so much heat that there is a liability of a kind of union taking place between the two surfaces, technically called 'seizing'. **1908** *Westm. Gaz.* 28 Sept. 10/3 We were given..paraffin for lubricating oil. Through this one of the bearings of our crank-axle 'seized'. **1917** *Blackw. Mag.* May 807/1 Our engine recovered slightly now that its recovery was not so important, and it behaved well until it seized up for better or worse when we had landed. **1963** *Listener* 31 Jan. 198/2 As for the camera itself, at 40 below zero the wind-on mechanism jammed and the range-finder seized up. **1981** P. AUDEMARS *Gone to her Death* ii. 44 Better we should find the trouble on our hoist rather than having something seize up on the main road.

fig. **1955** CORMACK & MCDOUGALL in C. Morris *Social Case-Work in Gt. Britain* (ed. 2) i. 35 When the social service system was primitive it could do without case-work: the more elaborate modern machine would seize up. **1960** C. DAY LEWIS *Buried Day* ix. 182, I read the book; then, for hour after hour, I sat trying to think of something to say about it. I could not... My brain had seized up. **1976** DEXTER & MAKINS *Testkill* 100 Any exercise..might make me seize up.

Hence **seize-up** *Mech.*, the action or state of seizure (cf. sense 11 of the vb.).

1912 *Motor Man.* (ed. 14) vi. 232 Unless one makes quite certain that every bearing and cylinder be properly relubricated before starting up again, a 'seize-up'..is not improbable.

seize, variant of SESS *v.*, *Obs.*

seized (siːzd), *ppl. a.* [f. SEIZE *v.* + -ED[1].] In senses of the verb.

1837 CARLYLE *Fr. Rev.* I. VII. v, The seized cannon are yoked with seized cart-horses. **1911** E. W. WALFORD *Maintenance of Motor Cars* ii. 30 The procedure is to allow the parts to cool down..and to inject a copious supply of oil to the seized part. **1977** F. DURBRIDGE *Passenger* iii. 154 He walked the six miles into Reading..told a story about a seized engine.

†**'seizement.** *Obs.* [f. SEIZE *v.* + -MENT.] An act of seizing, a seizure.

1581 *Apol. Will. of Orange* H 1, They..pursued me with ..seasementes of goodes.

seizement, variant of SESSMENT *Obs.*

seizer ('siːzə(r)). Also 5 sesour, 6 seysere, -our. [f. SEIZE *v.* + -ER[1].] One who or that which seizes; *spec.* †**a.** a canine tooth (*obs.*); **b.** a person authorized to seize persons or certain goods, = SEIZOR; **c.** a sporting dog trained to seize the animal hunted.

c **1400** *Master of Game* (MS. Digby 182) xv, A good alaunt shuld renne also faste, as a grehounde, and any that he may comme to, he shulde holde wele with his sesoures and not leue it. **1531–2** *Act 23 Hen. VIII*, c. 16 One halfe of the price of the saide horse..shalbe to the vse of the seysour and arrestour of the same. **1693** *Dryden's Juvenal* iv. (1697) 80 The Boatman than shall a wise Present make, And give the Fish before the Seizers take. **1718** ROWE tr. *Lucan* IV. 1162 Full at his [the Serpent's] Throat the nimble Seizer flies. **1809** SIMOND *Jrnl. Gt. Brit.* (1815) I. 2, I overheard the head seizer asking the Captain whether he preferred having his wine or his spirits seized. **1854** BAKER *Rifle & Hound in Ceylon* viii. 200 The pack..comprising..a few couple of immense seizers, a cross between bloodhound and greyhound.

seizing ('siːzɪŋ), *vbl. sb.* [f. SEIZE *v.* + -ING[1].]

1. The action of the verb SEIZE. Also Comb. *seizing-up* (see SEIZE *v.* 10 b and 11).

c **1400** *Destr. Troy* 2463 Iff tylmen toke tent what shuld tynt worth, Of sede þat is sawen, be sesyng of briddes, Shuld neuer corne for care be caste vppon erthe. *c* **1400–50** *Wars Alex.* 3490 þai [*sc.* the Macedonians] said, it miȝt be sufficient þe sesyng of Persy... 'Quat sulde we fonde any ferre?' **1615** LATHAM *Falconry* Expl. Words, *Ceasing*, is when a Hawke taketh any thing into her foot, and gripeth or holdeth it fast. **1736** *Gentl. Mag.* VI. 434/1 The seizing of any Place in Lorrain by France, was always looked on as a Declaration of War. **1840** R. H. DANA *Bef. Mast* xv, They had never heard before of a regular seizing-up and flogging. **1911** E. W. WALFORD *Maintenance of Motor Cars* ii. 30 An engine may suddenly pull up, and it be found impossible to turn the crankshaft with the starting handle. The popular expression for this is 'seizing'. **1925** *Morris Owner's Man.* 29 Neglect of this results in harsh running and an overheated engine, loss of power, and finally 'seizing-up' of pistons or connecting rods.

2. *concr.* (*Naut.*) †**a.** A rope for attaching a boat to a ship (*obs.*). **b.** A small cord for 'seizing' two ropes together, or a rope to something else. **c.** Cordage or yarn used for 'seizing'; also *seizing-stuff*.

F. *saisine* (see SEISIN) has this sense, but it is not clear what is the relation between the Eng. and the Fr. word.

1336 in Nicolas *Hist. Royal Navy* (1847) II. 471 [For 15 stone of hempen cordage to make] peyntours [and] seysynges [15 *s*.]. **1615** E. S. *Britain's Buss* B 3, Each net must haue a rope five or six Fathom long and an inch through,..called a Seazing, to fasten the net vnto the Warroape. **1627** CAPT. SMITH *Seaman's Gram.* v. 25 There is also a rope by which the Boat doth ride by the ships side, wch we cal a Seasen. **1634** W. WOOD *New Eng. Prosp.* I. xl, The Tyde being very strong, they are constrayned to goe ashore, and hale their Boats, by the seasing, or roades [see RODE *sb.*[2]]. **1711** W. SUTHERLAND *Shipbuild. Assist.* 141 The Seizings may be 1/6 of the Rope they seize. **1836** MARRYAT *Midsh. Easy* xiii, In a few minutes they had prepared a great many seizings to tie the men with. **1840** R. H. DANA *Bef. Mast* iii, Marline and seizing-stuffs. **1877** HOLDSWORTH *Sea Fisheries* 57 The warp..to which each net is made fast by two small ropes called 'seizings'. **1903** *Pall Mall Gaz.* 28 Mar. 2/2 A length of fine steel wire seizing.

seizing ('siːzɪŋ), *ppl. a.* [f. SEIZE *v.* + -ING[2].]

1. That seizes, takes possession, or lays hold on something.

1835 *App. Munic. Corpor. Rep.* II. 1027 (Romney Marsh) The Seizing Officer of wrecks, fines and forfeitures,..is remunerated by his charges for business done. **1887** L. OLIPHANT *Episodes* viii. 144 The rest of the pack, with the seizing hounds and their owner, had apparently gone off upon some other scent.

2. That seizes the attention; arresting, powerfully impressive. [After F. *saisissant*.]

1865 *Pall Mall Gaz.* 27 Mar. 8/2 One [woman] being exceedingly lovely, and the other of a very seizing ugliness. **1886** STEVENSON *Dr. Jekyll* 100 There was something abnormal..in the very essence of the creature that now faced me—something seizing, surprising and revolting.

†'**seizling.** *Obs.*[−0] [Corruptly a. G. *setzling* in the same sense.] (See quot.)

1688 HOLME *Armoury* II. 325/2 A Carpe, first a Seizling, then a Sproll or Sprall, then a Carbe or Karbe.

†'**seizor.** *Law. Obs.* Also 6 seisor. [f. SEIZE *v.* + -OR.] A person authorized to seize persons or goods.

1555 *Cal. Anc. Rec. Dublin* (1889) 449 All that he shall soo bye to be solde shalbe forfaict, halfe to the seisor or accuser. **1626** *Proclam.* 29 Sept., All the Tobacco which, uppon any Seizure shall become forfeyted, shall be brought to our Custom House..where the seizor thereof shall deliver the same to our use. **1702** *Guide for Constables* 27 Any person may make such seizures..and..the seizors shall..cause the said cattle..to be killed; and the hides and tallow shall be to the seizor.

seizure ('siːʒ(j)ʊə(r)). Forms: 5 seasur, seissure, 5–6 seasour, 6 seasor, ceazure, seysure, 6–7 seasure, 7 ceasure, 6–9 seisure, 6- seizure. [f. SEIZE *v.* + -URE.]

1. The action or an act of seizing, or the fact of being seized; confiscation or forcible taking possession (of land or goods); a sudden and forcible taking hold.

1482 in Leadam *Star Chamber Cases* (1903) 9 The xxvjth day of Auguste..your sayde seruaunt shuld come to Topsam..and founde the same seasur as ys in forme afor rehersid and ratified the same seasur. **1492** *Rolls of Parlt.* VI. 456/1 The Banishment of Scotts out of England by a certeyne day, under loss and seissure of theyr Goodes. **1545** in Leadam *Sel. Cases Crt. Requests* (1898) 172 Onles some iuste cause of forfeiture and seasour of and in the same demesne landes..shall growe to the said defendauntes. **1592** *No-body & Some-body* F 3 b, Lets..make ceazure of the Crowne. **1600** SHAKS. *A.Y.L.* III. i. 10 Thy Lands and all things that thou dost call thine, Worth seizure, do we seize into our hands. **1666** BUNYAN *Grace Abound.* §99 These suggestions..make such a seizure upon my Spirit. **1701** in *10th Rep. Hist. MSS. Comm.* App. v. 516 His Majestie's Attornie-Generall..moved..for a seisure of the premises. **1793** BURKE *Corr.* (1844) IV. 143 The seizure of the estates of the church. **1831** SCOTT *Ct. Robt.* xiii, His grasp..is like the seizure of a vice! **1844** H. H. WILSON *Brit. India* III. iv. III. 131 The burning of villages and the seizure of the inhabitants as slaves. **1862** MRS. H. WOOD *Mrs. Hallib.* III. xxiv, We called in at your office as we came by, and found a seizure was also put in there. **1878** *22nd Rep. Customs Comm.* 56 A seizure of 108 lbs. of un-customed tobacco was effected.

†**b.** Grasp, hold; a fastening. *Obs.*

1595 SHAKS. *John* III. i. 241 And shall these hands.. Vnyoke this seysure? **1621** G. SANDYS *Ovid's Met.* VII. (1626) 132 With spels and charmes I break the Vipers iaw, Cleaue solid rocks, okes from their seasures draw.

c. A sudden attack of illness, esp. a fit of apoplexy or epilepsy. Also, a sudden visitation (of calamity).

1779 JOHNSON *Let. to Mrs. Thrale* 14 June, The seizure was, I think, not apoplectical. **1805** *Med. Jrnl.* XIV. 203 If a person is incommoded by nausea or vomiting, on his seizure with this fever. *a* **1881** D. G. ROSSETTI *House of Life* vi, What..seizure of malign vicissitude Can rob this body of honour. **1899** *Allbutt's Syst. Med.* VIII. 347 The character of the seizures in general paralysis also varies.

†**2.** Possession, SEISIN. *Obs.*

1592 LODGE *Euph. Shadow* (1882) 16 When chillie age had seasure of this earth. **1611** W. SCLATER *Key* (1629) 303 As he [Satan] hath giuen Rome seizure of the keyes of heauen, so [etc.]. **1612** —— *Ministers Portion* 44 Such consecration giues him seizure of them in fee. **1625** GILL *Sacr. Philos.* iv. 56 It hath thereby..a seisure and delivery of those heavenly joyes, which it had here onely in assurance of hope. **1641** BRATHWAIT *Penit. Pilgr.* xix. 101 So dangerous is the custome of sinne, when it has taken seazure, or possession of the soule. **1658** SLINGSBY *Diary* (1836) 202 On whom these inferiour contentments have taken Seasure.

3. *Mech.* The action of SEIZE *v.* 11.

1903 COOPER-KEY *Rep. Explos. Lowwood* 7 Partial 'seizure' took place at times between the ram and the U-leather.

sejant ('siːdʒənt), *a. Her.* Forms: 6 seand, seiaunte, seiante, 7 seijant, 7–9 seiant, 7- sejant. [Properly *seiant*, a. OF. **seiant* var. of *seant* (mod.F. *séant*), pres. pple. of *seoir* to sit:—L. *sedēre*.] In a sitting posture; *esp.* of a quadruped: Sitting with the fore-legs upright.

c **1500** *Sc. Poem on Her.* 129 in *Q. Eliz. Acad.* 98 First, a lionne statant;..the v. seand. **1562** LEGH *Armory* 79 b, A Lion seiaunte, Sable. **1610** HOLLAND *Camden's Brit.* I. 396 A falcon Seiant vpon a gloue. **1644** SYMONDS *Diary* (Camden) 17 Creast, a dog sejant. *c* **1791** *Encycl. Brit.* VIII. 459/1 Two Squirrels sejant adossée Gules. **1864** BOUTELL *Her. Hist. & Pop.* xxi. §7 (ed. 3) 365 A lion sejant affronté gu.

‖**Sejm** (seɪm). Also **Seym**. [Pol.] In Poland: a general assembly or diet; a parliament; *spec.* (since 1921) the lower house of the Polish parliament.

[**1698** B. CONNOR *Hist. Poland* II. II. iii. 83 The Grand Diet or Parliament of Poland, by the Natives call'd Seym Walny.] **1893** W. R. MORFILL *Poland* v. 40 Ladislaus had assembled the first known *Seym*, or Diet, at Checiny... It consisted of the princes..prelates, barons and knights. **1916** G. E. SLOCOMBE *Poland* ix. 85 Their [*sc.* the nobles'] first step was to obtain a revival of the *sejm* or general Diet of Poland. **1924** A. E. TENNANT *Studies in Polish Life & Hist.* ix. 162 The new Sejm is a democratic assembly in which all classes are represented. **1934** E. J. PATTERSON *Poland* iii. 83 Under the constitution the powers of the Seym were very great... In case of a disagreement between the two houses the Senate could be over-ridden by a majority of 11/20 in the Seym, in ordinary session. **1959** Z. PELCZYNSKI in D. E. Butler et al. *Elections Abroad* ii. 125 The Sejm had been evolving and adapting itself to the policy of 'democratisation'. **1981** *Financial Times* 13 Jan. 1/3 It will be discussed at a special Polish Communist Party congress this spring, then go for approval to the Sejm (Parliament).

sejoin (sɪ'dʒɔɪn), *v. rare.* Also 6 seajoyn, 6–7 sejoyn(e. [f. SE- + JOIN *v.*, after L. *sējungĕre*: see SEJUNCT.] *trans.* To separate, disjoin.

1568 tr. *P. Mart. Vermil. Comm. Rom.* viii. 207 b, Wherfore in godly men feare is neuer seioyned from faith. **1584** LODGE *Alarum agst. Usurers* 22 Though perhaps my tearmes by distance be Seaioyned from thee. **1651** HOWELL *Venice* 184* Which Councells though they be sejoynd in Colleges and Offices, yet when the quality of the affair requires, they all consociat. *a* **1754** W. HAMILTON *Poems, To Gentl. going to travel* 173 Thou wanderest into foreign realms, from this Far, far sejoined. **1844** SIR W. HAMILTON *Logic* App. II. 333 That it may appear whether they are to be conjoined or sejoined.

†**se'joint,** *pa. pple. Obs. rare*[−1]. [f. SE- + JOINT *a.*, after L. *sējunctus*, pa. pple of *sējungĕre*: see SEJUNCT.] Separated, disjoined.

c **1440** *Pallad. on Husb.* IV. 370 Deuyde hem that pith be fro pith seioynt [gl. *seiuncta*].

‖**séjour** (seʒur). [Fr., f. *séjourner* to SOJOURN. Cf. SOJOUR.]

1. The act of staying or sojourning in a place (for a longer or shorter period).

1755 *Mem. Capt. P. Drake* I. ix. 63 We now had a Sejour, or Day's Rest. **1759** CHESTERF. *Let. to Son* 30 Mar., In the meantime, make the best of your *séjour* where you are. **1840** BARHAM *Ingol. Leg.* Ser. I. *Spectre Tapp.*, Mrs. Simpkinson preferred a short *séjour* in the still-room.

2. A place of sojourn or residence.

1769 LD. HOLLAND in Jesse *Selwyn & Contemp.* (1843) II. 375 You will have a better opinion of the *séjour* of Nice. **1770** H. ST. JOHN ibid. III. 6 Then comes the melancholy passage to Mahon; then the charming *séjour* of Minorca. **1824** SCOTT *St. Ronan's* xxv, Edinburgh..in autumn is the most melancholy *sejour* that ever poor mortals were condemned to.

sejourne, obs. form of SOJOURN *v.*

sejugate ('sɛdʒʊgeɪt), *v. rare.* [f. L. *sējugāt-*, ppl. stem of *sējugāre*, f. *sē-* SE- + *jugāre* to yoke, join.] *trans.* To separate, disjoin.

1623 in COCKERAM. **1656** in BLOUNT *Glossogr.* **1839–52** BAILEY *Festus* 534 His infallible eye,..The darkness from the light shall sejugate.

sejugous ('sɛdʒəgəs), *a. Bot.* [ad. mod.L. *sējugus* (f. *sex* six + *jug-um* yoke or pair of cattle) + -OUS. L. had *sējugis* adj. and sb. (a chariot) drawn by six horses.] (See quot.)

1793 MARTYN *Lang. Bot.*, *Sejugum folium*, a sejugous leaf; or a pinnate leaf having six pairs of leaflets.

†**se'junct,** *a. Obs. rare.* [ad. L. *sējunctus*, pa. pple. of *sējungĕre* to separate, f. *sē-* SE- + *jungĕre* to join.] Separated, separate.

1602 WARNER *Alb. Eng.* Epit. (1612) 351 The seiunct Territories of the English, Welch, and Scots. **1648** N. ESTWICK *Treat. Holy Ghost* 90 Hereby is noted a peculiar manner of the original of one Person from another.., as the Son from the Father, which is sejunct from the Father. **1922** JOYCE *Ulysses* 378 Images, divine and human, the cogitation of which by sejunct females is to tumescence conducive.

sejunction (sɪ'dʒʌŋkʃən). *rare.* [ad. L. *sējunctiōn-em*, f. *sējungĕre*: see prec.] Separation.

In quot. *c* 1530 as a term of rhetoric, after Cicero.

c **1530** L. COX *Rhet.* (1899) 74 This diuision is deuyded into seiunction and distribucion. Seiunction is whan we shewe wherin our aduersaries and we agre, and what it is, wherupon we stryue. **1653** R. SANDERS *Physiogn.* I. i. 4 Amongst the Mathematicians the Lines are considered under divers species, as Right or Straight..; as also is considerable..their Application and Sejunction, their Conjunction and Separation. **1654** Z. COKE *Logick* 26 Difference restraineth not the Genus, but by a kind of opposition and sejunction of the Species. **1831** I. TAYLOR *J. Edwards' Freedom of Will* Introd. Ess. 86 The sounds *good, nice, pleasant*,..&c. so fix themselves in the memory in connexion with qualities, as to admit of sejunction from their concretes. **1867** *Transmut. Species* xiv. 262 An efficient rule for dissociation and sejunction.

†**se'junctively,** *adv. Obs. rare*[−2]. [f. **sejunctive* adj. (as if ad. L. **sējunctīv-us*, f. *sējunct-us* SEJUNCT) + -LY[2].] Separately.

1602 WARNER *Alb. Eng.* XIII. lxxviii. (1612) 322 As holesome Plants and poysonous, light, darkenesse, Heat, and Cold, That Contraries of Creatures, seiunctiuely, should holde. **1650** CHARLETON *Paradoxes* 28 Neither vitrioll nor Galls are sejunctively black.

†**se'junctly,** *adv. Obs. rare*[−1]. [f. SEJUNCT *a.* + -LY[2].] Separately.

1586 WARNER *Alb. Eng.* III. xv. (1612) 68 Fower Dukes at once, in ciuil broyles, seiunctly after raine [= reign].

†**se'jungate,** *v. Obs. rare*[−1]. [? Misprinted for SEJUGATE; or badly f. L. *sējungĕre* SEJUNGE *v.* + -ATE.] = SEJUGATE *v.*

1578 BANISTER *Hist. Man* I. 7 b, These bones are seiungated on eche side, in their endes and borders. *Ibid.* I. 9 b, The eight bone of the head is..seiungated from the Cuneale bone..by the vij. Suture.

†**se'junge,** *v. Obs. rare*[−2]. [ad. L. *sējungĕre*: see SEJUNCT *a.*] *trans.* To separate, disjoin.

1597 A. M. tr. *Guillemeau's Fr. Chirurg.* 23/1 Then must the seiunged and separated partes, ioyn and heale together agayn. **1599** —— tr. *Gabelhouer's Bk. Physicke* 311/1 By which occasione these little bones soe will separate and seiunge themselves from the other fleshe and Bones.

†**se'jungible,** *a. Obs. rare*[−1]. In 7 sejungeable. [ad. L. type **sējungibilis*, f. *sējungĕre* to separate: see SEJUNGE *v.* and -IBLE, -ABLE.] That may be separated or sejoined.

1659 PEARSON *Creed* I. 105 The spawn and egge are sejungeable [*so ad edd.* 1659–92] from the fish and fowl, and yet still retain the prolifick power of generation.

sek, obs. f. SACK *sb.*[1]; obs. pa. t. of SUCK.

sek, seke, obs. forms of SEEK, SICK.

seken, seker, obs. forms of SICKEN, SICKER.

‖**sekere** (seke're). Also **shekere**. [Yoruba.] A Yoruba gourd-rattle.

1921 S. & O. JOHNSON *Hist. Yorubas* I. viii. 121 The Calabash drum—ornamental with strings of cowries—is called *Sèkèrè*. **1937** I. O. DELANO *Soul of Nigeria* xiii. 160 The acrobatic dancers..tour the Yoruba land... They have their beaters, and what they beat is called 'Sekere'. These are not drums, but gourds to which a number of cowries have been attached, so that they make a noise when shaken. **1963** W. SOYINKA *Lion & Jewel* 61 Distant music. Light drums, flutes, box-guitars, 'sekere'. **1975** *New Yorker* 29 Sept. 41/2 The other instruments are..and two shekeres—large West African calabashes strung with beads.

sekil, sekir(e, obs. ff. SIECLE, SICKER.

sekk, obs. form of SACK *sb.*[3]

†**sekke,** *v. nonce-wd.* [Back-formation from *seketur* SECUTOR, with allusion to *sekke* SACK *sb.*[1]]

1303 R. BRUNNE *Handl. Synne* 6235 þe whyles þe executours sekke [*gloss*, fyl þe bag] Of þe soule þey ne rekke.

sekke, sekklath, obs. ff. SACK, SACKCLOTH.

‖**sekos** ('siːkɒs). *Egyptology.* Also secos. [a. Gr. σηκός pen, enclosure.] A sacred enclosure in an ancient Egyptian temple.

1820 G. BELZONI *Narr. Egypt & Nubia* III. 291 Having observed, that the part where the sekos and cella must be was not touched, I set the men to work there. **1837** *Penny Cycl.* IX. 316/2 Facing its entrance was that leading into the *sekos* or shrine containing the figure of the deity. **1887** *Dict. Architecture* (Architectural Publ. Soc.) VII. 45/1 In the Egyptian temples the *secos* was the same as the *adytum* of the Greeks and Romans.

‖**Sekt** (zɛkt). [Ger.; cf. SACK *sb.*[3]] A German sparkling white wine or champagne.

1920 G. SAINTSBURY *Notes on Cellar-bk.* vi. 84 The 'Cabinet *Sekt*'..was 'a very *German*' champagne. **1924** [see FLUTE *sb.*[1] 3 a]. **1951** R. POSTGATE *Plain Man's Guide to Wine* v. 96 A horrible German imitation [of champagne] called Sekt. **1962** P. PURSER *Peregrination 22* xvi. 72 Do you remember the time in Berlin you were so sick after drinking too much sekt? **1971** 'M. SINCLAIR' *Sonntag* xxii. 129 The bottle of *Sekt* in front of them was good though.

sekur, sekyl, sekkul: see SICKER, SICKLE *a.*

sel, obs. form of CELL *sb.*[1]

c **1375** *Sc. Leg. Saints* xxxiv. 329 þe thryd day he come agane..to þe sel, quhare frere pelagius can duel. **1546** BALE *Eng. Votaries* I. (1560) 38 b, The sel of an holy Nun.

sel, obs. f. SEAL, SELL *v.*; variant of SELE *Obs.*

selachian (sɪˈleɪkɪən), *a.* and *sb. Zool.* Also **selacian**, **selacean**. [f. mod.L. *Selachē* (a. Gr. σελάχη, pl. of σέλαχος, shark) or its derivative *Selachii* + -IAN. Cf. F. *sélacien* (Cuvier).] **a.** *adj.* Of or belonging to the genus *Selache* (Cuvier) of sharks, or to the group *Selachii*, the sharks and their allies. **b.** *sb.* A shark or allied fish.

1835 KIRBY *Hab. & Inst. Anim.* II. xxi. 391 The Selacians. **1857** AGASSIZ *Contrib. Nat. Hist. U.S.* I. 82 *note*, I would, therefore, propose the name of Selachians for a distinct class embracing the Sharks, Skates and Chimæras. **1859** DARWIN *Orig. Spec.* xi. (1873) 308 The selaceans or sharks. **1870** ROLLESTON *Anim. Life* 38 A few Selachian fishes.

selachyl (sɪˈleɪkaɪl, -kɪl). *Chem.* [a. G. *selachyl* (Tsujimoto & Toyama 1922, in *Chem. Umschau auf dem Gebiete der Fette*, etc. XXIX. 36): see SELACHIAN *a.* and *sb.* and -YL.] ***selachyl alcohol***: an oily liquid, α-glyceryl *cis*-9-octadecenyl ether, $C_{21}H_{42}O_3$, found in the liver oils of elasmobranch fishes.

1922 *Chem. Abstr.* XVI. 1513 The formula $C_{20}H_{40}O_3$ [*sic*] was selected to represent this unsatd. alc. and the name selachyl alcohol given to it. **1944** *Jrnl. Biol. Chem.* CLV. 448 Selachyl alcohol has been isolated from natural sources so far only as an oil. **1964** *Oceanogr. & Marine Biol.* II. 177 The most abundant alcoholic component of the alkoscydiglycerides is invariably selachyl alcohol, followed by chimyl alcohol and then by batyl alcohol.

selad, obs. form of SALAD.

seladang (səˈlɑːdæŋ). Also **saladang**, **salandang**, **sladang**. [Malay, in Borneo *seladang*, in Sumatra *saladang*.] = GAUR; also, formerly, the Malayan tapir, *Tapirus indicus*.

1821 T. S. RAFFLES in *Trans. Linnean Soc.* XIII. 270 It [sc. *Tapirus Malayanus*] is known by different names in different parts of the country [*sc.* Sumatra]. By the people of Limun it is called Saladang. **1839** T. J. NEWBOLD *Straits of Malacca* I. vii. 435 The Seladang is supposed by some zoologists to be identical with the Tapir. **1868** *Proc. Asiatic Soc. Bengal* 194 The Malayan bison, an animal well known to the Malays under the name of *Sladang*..[is] more formidable when wounded than the tiger. **1875** E. BLYTH *Cat. Mammals & Birds of Burma* 47 In the Malayan peninsula, where it is known as the *Salandang*, this animal [*sc.* the Gaur] would appear to be becoming extremely rare. **1905** T. R. HUBBACK *Elephant & Seladang Hunting* 44 The seladang has no dewlap and no hump. *Ibid.* 47 Seladang are only found in little-inhabited districts. **1927** H. M. TOMLINSON *Gallions Reach* xxxv. 263 A likely corner for sladang, the instantaneous bull which does not wait for trouble but makes it when you are not looking. **1933** L. AINSWORTH *Confess. Planter in Malaya* 219 The Seladang or Malayan Bison is diminishing in numbers, and is now found almost exclusively in Negri Sembilan and Pahang. **1965** R. MCKIE *Company of Animals* viii. 130 Seladang (this spelling will be used for both singular and plural) are among the largest of the ox tribe and are remote relatives of domestic cattle. **1974** R. BUTLER *Buffalo Hook* iv. 28 The seladang is the wild buffalo of Malaysia.

seladony, -dyne, var. ff. CELIDONY[1] *Obs.*

seladyne (also **seledyne**), ? var. CELIDONY[2] *Obs.* Cf. SALADINE *sb.*[2]

c **1420** *Anturs of Arth.* 22 (Douce MS.) With saffres and seladynes [*Ireland MS.* seledynis] set by þe sides.

Selaginella (sɪleɪdʒ-, sɪlædʒɪˈnɛlə). *Bot.* [mod.L., dim. of SELAGO.] A genus of cryptogams; also (with *pl.*) a plant of this genus.

1865 GOSSE *Land & Sea* 350 A carpet of lovely green *Selaginella*. **1891** L. H. BAILEY *Nursery-bk.* (1896) 24 Ferns, lycopodiums and selaginellas are often grown from spores.

Selago (sɪˈleɪgəʊ). *Bot.* [L. *selāgo*.] †**a.** The club-moss *Lycopodium Selago* (*obs.*). **b.** A Linnæan genus of S. African herbs or undershrubs.

[**1601** HOLLAND *Pliny* XXIV. xi. II. 193 Much like unto this hearbe Savine, is that which they call Selago.] *a* **1627** MIDDLETON *Witch* III. iii. (1778) 70 Heer's Pannax too... And Selago, Hedge hisop too.

‖**Selah** (ˈsiːlə). Also 6–7 **sela**. [Heb. *'selāh*.] A Hebrew word, occurring frequently at the end of a verse in the Psalter and thrice in Hab. iii, by the LXX rendered διάψαλμα; supposed to be a musical or liturgical direction of some kind, perhaps indicating pause or rest. Hence in various allusive uses (see quots.).

1530 tr. *Bucer's Psalms* iii. A 5, This worde *Selah* signifyeth yͤ sentence before to be pond'red with a depe affecte, longe to be rested upon and the voyce there to be exalted. **1623** S. WARD *Peace-off.* (1624) 50 Record, not all and euery fauour, which is impossible, but the most memorable and thankworthy; putting a special Selah of thankes vpon them. **1826** MRS. BROWNING *Ess. Mind* II. 629 Then comes the Selah! and the voice is hush'd. **1872** O. W. HOLMES *Poet Breakf.-t.* iv, But you need not think I am going to tell you every time his popgun goes off, making a Selah of him whenever I want to change the subject. **1906** J. LONDON *Let.* 1 Dec. (1966) 229, I want an answer... I want it to the point... Selah. **1924** E. E. CUMMINGS *Let.* 13 May (1969) 107 The Independants found me not incapable of a 40′ × 50′ '*abstract*' canvas which..hung very well (by itself)—this lidel effut cost me 9 days work and was dry on time, selah-sounds. **1947** W. STEVENS in *Q. Rev. Lit.* III. 110 The dove in the belly builds his nest and coos, Selah, tempestuous bird. **1975** *New Yorker* 26 May 33/3 Then I can go back to doing what every really dedicated writer wants to do. Nothing. Selah, Phil.

selam(e, selander: see SALAAM, SALLENDER.

‖**selamlik** (sɛˈlɑːmlɪk). Also with capital initial. [Turk., lit. 'place of greeting', f. *selâm* a. Arab. *salām* SALAAM *sb.*) + *-lik* place.]

1. A room in a Muslim house set aside for business or the reception of male friends; the part of such a house reserved for men. Cf. HAREMLIK.

1838 D. URQUHART *Spirit of East* I. xxi. 392 The European arrives... Some of the attendants, in reply to his inquiries, point to the door of the Selamlik. **1854** R. CURZON *Armenia* 79 We went into the selamlik (or reception room) together. **1888** 'BEY KESNIN' *Evil of East* vii. 127 Every Turkish house is divided into two distinct parts:—the *selamlik* for men, and the *haremlik* for women. **1900** 'ODYSSEUS' *Turkey in Europe* vii. 331 One feels that..their existence is really divided into the departments of Selamlik and Harem, which means the difference, not only between the men's and the women's part of the house, but between formal and domestic life. **1936**, **1941** [see HAREMLIK]. **1965** J. FLEMING *Nothing is Number* I. i. 15 The *selamlik*, or male reception room, is inviolate.

2. The public procession of the Sultan to a mosque on Friday at noon. Now *Hist.*

1888 'BEY KESNIN' *Evil of East* vi. 125 On Fridays, for Selamlik, the soldier makes himself as smart as possible to escort his sovereign to the mosque. **1905** *Globe* (N.Y.) 21 July 1/2 It is reported here officially from Constantinople that during to-day's selamlik an attempt was made to assassinate the sultan. **1935** H. EDIB *Clown & his Daughter* ix. 45 Selim Pasha decided to speak about Rabia's musical training to the Imam after the Selamlik—the Friday ceremony of His Majesty's going to the mosque. **1955** H. LUKE *Old Turkey & New* (rev. ed.) vii. 166 On Friday, the 10th November, 1922 Vahid ed-Dîn attended his last *selamlik*. **1980** J. LEES-MILNE *Harold Nicolson* 56 The First Balkan War had begun. That day [*sc.* 17 Oct. 1912] Harold witnessed the ceremony of the Selamlik.

selandine, -yne, obs. forms of CELANDINE.

selar, variant of CELURE *Obs.*, canopy.

1470–85 MALORY *Arthur* XVII. vi. 698 The selar of the bedde.

selar(e, obs. forms of CELLAR.

c **1425** *Voc.* in Wr.-Wülcker 670/14 *Hoc selarium*, selare.

selblack, variant of SELFBLACK *Obs.*

Selbornian (sɛlˈbɔːnɪən), *a.* Also **Selburnian**. [f. *Selborne*, the name of a village in Hampshire + -IAN.] **1.** Of, pertaining to, or connected with Selborne, the parish described in *The Natural History and Antiquities of Selborne* (1789) by Gilbert White (1720–93). Also as *sb.*, an inhabitant of Selborne or an admirer of the writings of Gilbert White.

1869 J. R. LOWELL in *Atlantic Almanac* 32/1 How pleasant is his innocent vanity in adding to the list of the British, and still more of the Selbornian, *fauna*! **1928** *Observer* 26 Feb. 8/5 Another book about 'Gilbert White',.. a book full of pleasures for all Selbornians. **1938** H. J. MASSINGHAM *Writings of Gilbert White* I. p. x, He writes of the Selburnian echo. *Ibid.* p. xxii, How absorbed the greatest and most typical of Selburnians was with gardening. **1954** R. M. LOCKLEY *Gilbert White* i. 9 Already he was able to convey his love of the Selbornian scene.

2. *Geol.* A name given by A. J. Jukes-Brown (see quot. 1900) to the Upper Greensand and Gault beds in the Albian stage of the Cretaceous in Southern England, from the prominent occurrence of these deposits near Selborne. Also *absol.* Now *rare* or *Obs.*

1900 A. J. JUKES-BROWN *Cretaceous Rocks Brit.* I. 1 The Selbornian comprises the beds which are generally known as the Gault and the upper Greensand. *Ibid.* 31 Gault clay and greensand are only two of the different kinds of deposits that make up the group for which the name Selbornian is now proposed. **1910** [see ALBIAN *a.* and *sb.*]. **1922** J. C. HUGHES *Geol. Story of Isle of Wight* vi. 37 Some prefer to call the Lower Greensand Vectian, from Vectis, the old name of the Isle of Wight, and the Upper Greensand Selbornian, a name generally adopted, because it forms a marked feature of the country about Selborne.

selch(e, selcht, obs. forms of SEAL *sb.*[1]

selcitud, obs. form of CELSITUDE.

†**ˈselcouth**, *a.*, *adv.*, and *sb. Obs.* Forms: 1 **seld-**, (**selt-**), **selcúð**, 2–3 **sel-**, **seolcuð**, 3 **sel-**, **seolkuð**, *Orm.* **sellcuþ**, (**selkeð**, **sulcuð**, **-kuð**, **sæl-**, **salcuð**), 3–5 **selcuþ**, **-cuth**, **-kuth**, **-couþ**, **-kouþ**, 4–5 **selcuþe**, **-couþe**, **-cowþ(e**, **-kowþ**, **-coþ(e**, (4 **selcut**, **-cutt**, **-cuht**, **silkouth**, 5 **selcowgh**, **-kow**, **-cought**, **-chouth**, **seelcowth**), 3–6, 9 **selcouth**. [f. OE. *seld-an* SELDOM + *cúð* known: see COUTH *a.*]

A. *adj.*

1. Unfamiliar, unusual, rare; strange, marvellous, wonderful.

c **888** K. ÆLFRED *Boeth.* xxxv. §7 He wæs oflyst ðæs seldcuðan sones. *c* **1200** ORMIN 19217 Forr þatt wass wiss sellcuþ mecle33c, & sellcuþ ædmodnesse. *c* **1205** LAY. 3894 From heouene her com a sulcuð flod. **1338** R. BRUNNE *Chron.* (1810) 33 Þis was þe selcouthest cas, þat haf herd neuen. *c* **1440** *Promp. Parv.* 452/1 Selkow, or seeldam seyne [*v.rr.* selcowthe, seelcowth], *rarus.* *c* **1460** *Towneley Myst.* viii. 103 Yonder I se a selcowth syght. **1596** SPENSER *F.Q.* IV. viii. 14 She..wondred much at his so selcouth case. **1815** SCOTT *Ld. of Isles* IV. xii, Deep import from that selcouth sign Did many a mountain Seer divine.

2. Various, different, not of one kind.

a **1000** *Colloq. Ælfric* in Wr.-Wülcker 96 *Varias uestes*, selcuþe reaf. *a* **1175** *Lamb. Hom.* 41 Seofe leies uwil[c]an of seolcuðre heowe. *a* **1300** *Cursor M.* 23 Sanges sere of selcuth [*Gött.* diuers] rime, Inglis, frankys and latine. **1340–70** *Alex. & Dind.* 490 Þer-inne..we sen selcouþe kindus Of þe fletinge fihs [L. *ibi varia genera piscium contemplamur*]. *c* **1425** *Eng. Conq. Irel.* xii. 28 Aftyr many selcouth & dyuers redes [orig. *post multa variaque consilia*].

B. *adv.* Wonderfully.

a **1300** *Cursor M.* 1060 Þis abel was a hird for fee, Selcuth hali man was he. *Ibid.* 24093 Mi sun þat was sa selcut suete.

C. *sb.* Something wonderful; a marvel.

c **1200** ORMIN 16156, & tatt wass wunnderrli3 sellcuþ, & wunnderrli3 forrtakenn. *c* **1220** *Bestiary* 556 In ðe se senden selcuðes manie. *c* **1350** *Will. Palerne* 2579 Se wich a selcouþ þis semliche best worcheþ. **1377** LANGL. *P. Pl.* B. XI. 355 Many selcouthes I seygh. *c* **1470** HENRYSON *Mor. Fab.* ix. (*Fox, Wolf & Cadger*) xvii, Sic ane selcouth saw I not this seuin ʒeir.

b. In phrases, as ***what selcouth***, ***no selcouth***, what wonder, no wonder. ***me*** (***him*** etc.) ***thinks selcouth***, ***I have selcouth*** = I wonder.

a **1225** *Ancr. R.* 8 Gif him þuncheð wunder & selkuð of swuch onswere. *a* **1300** *Cursor M.* 1238 Adam had pastd nine hundret yere, Nai selcut þof he wex vn-fere. *Ibid.* 13902 Selcut me thinc [*Trin.* Selcouþe I haue] yee hatte me sua. **1377** LANGL. *P. Pl.* B. XI. 358 And how amonge þe grene grasse grewe so many hewes, And somme soure and some swete, selcouthe me þouȝte.

Hence †**ˈselcouthness** *Obs.*[-0]

c **1440** *Promp. Parv.* 452/1 Selcowtnesse [*Winch. MS.* Selcowthnesses, Seelcowthnesses], *raritas.*

†**ˈselcouth**, *v. Obs. rare.* [f. SELCOUTH *a.*] *trans.* To make wonderful; to show as marvellous.

a **1300** *E.E. Psalter* iv. 4 And wites þat lauerd his halign selkouþede [*v.r.* selcuþed] he [Vulg. *mirificavit*]. *a* **1340** HAMPOLE *Ps.* xv. 2 He selcouthid alle mi willes [Vulg. *mirificavit omnes voluntates meas*].

†**ˈselcouthly**, *adv. Obs.* [f. SELCOUTH *a.* + -LY[2].] Strangely, wonderfully.

c **1200** ORMIN 2586 Forr nære ȝho nohht Drihhtin Godd Swa sellcuþlike cweme, ȝiff [etc.]. *c* **1330** R. BRUNNE *Chron. Wace* (Rolls) 7333 So waxynge folk..Ne so gendryng, ne so pleyntyue..In no londe scholde men fynde, Ne selcouþloker so to gendre. *c* **1475** *Rauf Coilȝear* 680 Selcouthly in seir he was set suttelly.

†**seld**, *sb. Obs.* Forms: 1 **seld**, 2 **selt**, 3 **seld**, 5 **selde**, 6 *Hist.* **silde**. [OE. *seld* neut., metathetic form of *setl* SETTLE *sb.*

(A distinct word from OE. *sęld*, *sæld* mansion, hall.)]

1. A seat, throne.

c **825** *Vesp. Psalter* x. 5 In heofene seld his. *c* **1175** *Lamb. Hom.* 93 Ða apostoli siððan..isetten iacob þet wes ihaten rihtwis on cristes selt [*Ælfric* setle]. *c* **1205** LAY. 25988 And þa six swin he gon æten alle ær he arise of selde.

2. A shop. (In L. records *selda* or *silda*; also in AF. form *seude*.) Also, a stand for spectators.

[**1407** *Maldon* (Essex) liber A, lf. 14 b, Pro parcella terre de communi super quam finis unius seude in le draperie est edificatus.] *c* **1450** *Godstow Reg.* 96 And ij. seldis in the market of Wycombe. **1461** *Ibid.* 508 One selde, with a solar ouer the same selde I-bilde. **1598** STOW *Surv.* 206 After which time the king caused this silde or shede to bee made, and strongly to bee builded of stone, for himself, the Queene, and other estates to stand in, and there to behold the iustings. *Ibid.* 207 The men of Bredstreete ward contended with the men of Cordwayner street ward for a selde or shede.

†**seld**, *adv.* and *a. Obs.* Forms: 3–7 **selde**, 4–7 **seld**; 3 **sealde**, 3–6 **sielde**, 4 **sylde**, 4–5 **seyld(e**, 4–6 **seild(e**, **silde**, **seelde**, 4–7 **seeld**, 5 **zelde**, 6 **sield**, **sealde**, 6–7 **sild**. [Early ME. *selde*, formed as positive to *seldor*, *seldost*, in OE. used as compar. and superl. of *seldan* SELDOM.]

A. *adv.* = SELDOM *adv.*

c **1000** ÆLFRIC *Gram.* xxxviii. (Z.) 240 *Raro* seldan, *rarius* seldor, *rarissime* ealra seldost. *c* **1200** *Trin. Coll. Hom.* 207 He haueð..gon..seldere þene he sholde to his chirche. *c* **1205** LAY. 17940 For selde [*c* **1275** sealde] he aswint þe to him seolue þencheð. *c* **1290** *S. Eng. Leg.* 474/424 ȝwane he is wroth, he doth wreche, ake þat fallez ful sielde. *c* **1386** CHAUCER *Clerk's T.* 371 The peple hym heelde A prudent man, and that is seyn ful seelde. **1387** TREVISA *Higden* (Rolls) I. 131 Egypt is silde bereyne. **1483** CAXTON *Gold. Leg.* 175 b/2 He wente ofte barefote and selde ware ony gyrdle. **1529** MORE *Dyaloge* III. Wks. 225/2 It is pytye that we see suche lyghte so sielde. **1590** GREENE *Never too Late* Wks. (Grosart) VIII. 158 Report that sild to honour is a friend. **1591** HARINGTON *Orl. Fur.* IX. xxiv, A weapon strange, before this seen but seeld. **1652** C. B. STAPYLTON *Herodian* iv. 26 Though such a fall hath heard of been but seeld.

b. *predicatively.* (Cf. SELDOM *adv.* d.)

1390 GOWER *Conf.* II. 78 For sielde it is that love alloweth The gentil man withoute god. *c* **1460** FORTESCUE *Abs. & Lim. Mon.* xiii. (1885) 141 Wherfore it is right selde þat Frenchmen be hanged ffor robbery.

B. *adj.* = SELDOM *a.*

1398 TREVISA *Barth. De P.R.* v. xxxvi. (1495) k j, Yf the herte be to dreye & colde he makyth..slowȝ brethe and selde [L. *respiratio tarda est & rara*]. **1534** MORE *Comf. agst. Trib.* II. Wks. 1172/1 Let vs..make those kyndes of recreacion as shorte and as silde as we can. **1603** FLORIO *Montaigne* III. v. 530 Therefore hath nature bestowed..on vs a seld and vncertaine abilitie. **1607** TOURNEUR *Rev. Trag.* IV. H 2 b, Honest women are so sild and rare.

C. *Comb.*, as ***seld-heard-of***, ***-known***, ***-shaven***, ***-shown*** adjs.; **seld-speech**, taciturnity; **seld-**

time, -when (also *-whens*), **-where, -while** *advs.*, rarely. Also SELDSEEN *a.*

1597 *Cert. Prayers* in *Liturg. Serv. Q. Eliz.* (Parker Soc.) 671 Thy rare-seen, unused, and *seeld-heard-of goodness. 1603 FLORIO *Montaigne* II. xii. 256 Strange and *seld-knowne opinions. 1800 LAMB *Let. to Coleridge* 14 Aug., Please to blot out 'gentle-hearted', and substitute.. *seld-shaven, odd-eyed, stuttering, or any other epithet. 1607 SHAKS. *Cor.* II. i. 229 *Seld-showne Flamins Doe presse among the popular Throngs. *a* 1225 *Ancr. R.* 76 Nouhware ine holi write, ne ivinde we þet heo spec bute uor siðen; auh for þe *seldspeche hire wordes weren heuie. *c* 1386 CHAUCER *Clerk's T.* 90, I me reioysed of my liberte, That *seelde [*v.r.* selden] tyme is founde in mariage. *c* 897 K. ÆLFRED *Gregory's Past. C.* xliii. 313 Ðonne cymð sio blis *seldhwanne. *a* 1225 *Ancr. R.* 428 Swuch ouh wummone lore to beon—luuelich & liðe, and seldhwonne sturne. 1387 TREVISA *Higden* (Rolls) I. 333 Men of that lond haueþ no feuere, but onliche þe feuere agu, and þat wel silde whanne. 1422 tr. *Secreta Secret., Priv. Priv.* 157 Thow shalte Preyse and commende scarsly and seldewannes. 1546 J. HEYWOOD *Prov.* (1867) 40 Meete shall they seelde when, or haply neuer. 1390 GOWER *Conf.* III. 234 Chastete, which *sielde wher Comth nou adaies into place. 1387 TREVISA *Higden* (Rolls) I. 389 þey.. eteþ wel *seelde while.

seld, obs. pa. t. and pa. pple. of SELL *v.*

†**seldall.** *Obs. rare.*

1560 in *Coventry Corpus Chr. Plays* (1902) 86 A selldall for God xij d. *a* 1585 *Ibid.* 82 A seldall for God xij d.

selde, obs. pa. t. of SELL *v.*

seldom ('sɛldəm), *adv.* and *a.* Forms: α. 1 **seldan, -on, -un, 3–6 selden,** (3 *Orm.* **seldenn**), 4–5 **-ene, -on(e, -yn(e, -ine,** 4–6 **-in,** 5 **-ing, -an, celdane;** 4–5 **sild-, sylden,** 5 **-un, -yn,** 4–6 **-on;** 4–5 **sielden, seelden, -yn, seilden, -yn,** 4–6 **-in,** 5 **seyldyn.** Also SENDLE. β. 1, 3, 5 **seldum,** 4–7 **-ome,** 5 **celdom, seldoum,** 6 **selldome,** 4– **seldom;** 5–7 **sildom(e,** 6 **syldome, sildam;** 4–7 **seeldome,** 5 **-am, -em, ceeldam,** 6 **seeldom, sealdome,** 6–7 **sieldome.** [OE. *seldan* (altered to *seldum* by the analogy of advb. datives plural like *hwílum*: see WHILOM) corresponds to OFris. *sielden*, MLG., MDu. *selden* (mod.Du. *zelden*), OHG. *seltan* (MHG., mod.G. *selten*), ON. *sialdan* (Da. *sjelden*, Sw. *sällan*), f. OTeut. **seldo-* (prob. an adj.) represented in Goth. *sildaleik-s* wonderful (whence *sildaleikjan* to be astonished). The ulterior affinities are unknown.]

A. *adv.* **a.** On few occasions, in few cases or instances, not often; rarely, infrequently.

α. *c* 897 K. ÆLFRED *Gregory's Past. C.* ix. 57 Seldun mon ȝeleornað on miclum rice eaðmodnesse. *c* 1200 ORMIN 8468 Forrþi þatt Arrchelaw þe king þær munnde cumenn seldenn. 1398 TREVISA *Barth. De P.R.* XIII. ii. (1495) 441 Also in wynter selden or neuer pytte water fresyth. *c* 1460 FORTESCUE *Abs. & Lim. Mon.* iii. (1885) 114 Thai eyten no flesshe but yf it be right seldon a litle larde. *a* 1510 DOUGLAS *K. Hart* I. 142 For seildin had thai sene sic folkis befoir. 1538 STARKEY *England* I. iii. 85 Pryncys and lordys syldon loke to the gud ordur and welth of theyr subiectys.

β. *a* 1000 [see b]. *c* 1220 *Bestiary* 241 Ðe mire.. resteð hire seldum. 1340 HAMPOLE *Pr. Consc.* 756 For seldom a man þat has þat held, Hele has, and him-self may weld. *c* 1440 *Promp. Parv.* 65/1 Ceeldam (*P.* celdom), *raro.* *c* 1449 PECOCK *Repr.* I. xiv. 77 Seeldem fallith the contrarie. 1589 NASHE *Anat. Absurd.* A 4 b, That face [is] most faire, which seldommest comes into the open ayre. 1615 G. SANDYS *Trav.* 47 Or oftner, or seldomer, as occasion required. 1678 RAY *Prov.* (ed. 2) 348 Listners seldome hear good of themselves. 1748 LADY M. W. MONTAGU *Let. to Montagu* 2 Feb. (1893) II. 159 Complainers are seldom pitied, and boasters yet seldomer believed. 1867 MILL *Subj. Women* (1869) 142 Women, it is said, seldomer fall under the penal law.. than men.

Proverb. 1546 HEYWOOD *Prov.* I. iv. Wks. (1562) A iv b, Seldome comth the better. 1594 SHAKS. *Rich. III*, II. iii. 4. 1650 H. PARKER *True Portr. Kings Eng.* 32 Yet (as we say) Seldom comes a better; when one is cut off, another like the Hidra's head springs up in his place.

b. With *ever* added pleonastically. (Cf. EVER 7 c, RARELY 2 b.) ? *Obs.*

a 1000 *Sal. & Sat.* 269 Seldum æfre his leoma licggað. 1643 TRAPP *Comm. Gen.* iv. 17 They seek to immortalize themselves upon their possessions; but the third heire seldome ever owns them. 1813, 1828 [see EVER 7 c].

†**c.** ***seldom or ever***: by confusion of 'seldom if ever' and 'seldom or never'. (Cf. EVER 7 b, RARELY 2 c.)

1752 A. MURPHY *Gray's Inn Jrnl.* No. 14 ¶2 The Players seldom or ever throw out the Voice with any Vehemence. 1827 D. JOHNSON *Ind. Field Sports* 100 It is what they seldom or ever do.

d. ***it is seldom that***... (Cf. RARELY 2 d.) Also †***it is seldom when***... (Cf. *seldom-when* in C.)

1390 GOWER *Conf.* I. 30 Ful selden is that welthe Can soffre his oghne astat in helthe. *c* 1430 *Pilgr. Lyf Manhode* II. lviii. (1869) 98 Seelden it was þat j sih hire. 1597 SHAKS. *2 Hen. IV*, IV. iv. 79 'Tis seldome, when the Bee doth leaue her Comb In the dead Carrion. 1812 COLERIDGE *Lett.* (1895) 599 It is seldom that want of leisure can be fairly stated as an excuse for not writing. *a* 1859 MACAULAY *Hist. Eng.* xxiv. V. 229 It was seldom indeed that a white freeman.. was employed in severe bodily labour.

B. *adj.* Rare, infrequent. Now chiefly *U.S.*

1483 *Cath. Angl.* 328/2 Seldome [*MS.* seldone], *jnfrequens, rarus, rariter.* 1528 TINDALE *Obed. Chr. Man* 71 b, Chastite is an exceadinge selden gyfte. 1585 Q. ELIZ. in *Holinshed's Chron.* (1587) III. 1396/2 Yet amongst my manie volumes, I hope Gods booke hath not beene my sildomest lectures. 1587 in *10th Rep. Hist. MSS. Comm.* App. v. 445 Yf at seldom tymes he should chaunce to play at lawfull games. *c* 1600 SHAKS. *Sonn.* lii, Blunting the fine point of seldome pleasure. 1650 JER. TAYLOR *Holy Living* ii. §2 (1727) 59 A suppressed and seldom anger. 1658 *Whole Duty Man* v. §14. 45 We should think it wisdom to be as frequent as we are ordinarily seldom in it. 1797 ANNA SEWARD *Lett.* (1811) IV. 302 His 'nor did not', used as an affirmative at seldom times by Milton, is frequent here. 1822 LAMB *Elia* Ser. II. *Books & Reading*, Seldom-readers are slow readers. 1865 MRS. WHITNEY *Gayworthys* xix, They.. watched, with grieved hearts and seldom speech. 1883 'MARK TWAIN' *Life on Mississippi* xxi. 222 The seldomest spectacle on the Mississippi to-day is a wood-pile. 1891 *Pall Mall Gaz.* 18 Nov. 1/2 On evenings reserved.. to the seldom speakers. 1959 W. GOLDING *Free Fall* i. 26 My seldom night terrors. 1961 E. WILSON in WEBSTER s.v., With her small seldom smile.

C. *Comb.*, as ***seldom-comfortless, -seen*** (cf. SELDSEEN), ***-trodden*** adjs.; **seldom-time(s, -when, -while** *advs.*, rarely.

a 1586 SIDNEY *Arcadia* II. (Sommer) 229 His *seldom-comfortlesse flatterers. *c* 1440 *Promp. Parv.* 452/1 Selkow, or *seeldam seyne, *rarus.* 1600 J. PORY tr. *Leo's Africa* I. 22 So woorthie and so seldome-seene guests. 1386 *Selden time [see *seld-time*, SELD C.]. *c* 1450 *St. Cuthbert* (Surtees) 2289 Ful seldyn tyme speke he walde. 1557 NORTH *Gueuara's Diall Pr.* 106 It *seldome times chaunceth but that one of the parties are deceived. *c* 888 K. ÆLFRED *Boeth.* xxxvii. §4 þeah hi *seldum hwonne beswemde weorðen. 1390 GOWER *Conf.* III. 237 He duelte evere in chambre stille,.. That selden whanne in other stede If that he wolde wenden oute. 1603 SHAKS. *Meas. for M.* IV. ii. 89 Sildome when The steeled Gaoler is the friend of men. 1876 LANIER *Poems, Ps. West* 107 Solemn wings that wave but *seldomwhile.

†'**seldomly**, *adv.* *Obs.* [f. SELDOM *a.* + -LY[2].] Rarely.

1549 LATIMER *5th Serm. bef. Edw. VI* (Arb.) 143 So that it be vsed rarely, seldomly. 1620 VENNER *Via Recta* Introd. 8 The aire is for the most part pure, seldomely corrupted with noysome vapours. *c* 1864 E. DICKINSON *Poems* (1955) II. 610 The ships.. That touch how seldomly Thy Shore?

seldomness ('sɛldəmnɪs). [f. SELDOM *a.* + -NESS.] Infrequency, rareness.

1561 T. HOBY tr. *Castiglione's Courtyer* II. L iv b, The sildomenesse of suche as are seen to attain to that point. 1682 SIR T. BROWNE *Chr. Mor.* II. i. (1716) 44 The strength of delight is in its seldomness or rarity. 1792 ANNA SEWARD *Lett.* (1811) III. 172 Suffer the length of my letters to attone for their seldomness. 1861 LD. PALMERSTON *Sp.* in *Times* 9 Jan. 6/4 In proportion to the seldomness of those occasions.. is the gratification which they afford.

†'**seldseen**, *a.* *Obs.* Forms: 1 **seldsíene, -sýnde,** 3 **seldcene, seltsene, -scene,** 6 **seld-, seildsene, seeldseene,** 6–7 **seldseen(e.** [OE. *seldsíene* = MDu. *seltsiene*, OHG. *seltsâni* (MHG. *seltsæne*, mod.G. with change of suffix *seltsam*), ON. *sialdsénn* (Sw. has *sällsam* after Ger.):—OTeut. **seldosewnjo-, -sǣwnjo-*: see SELDOM and SENE *a.*] Seldom to be seen or met with; rare. (By 16th c. writers sometimes analysed as *seld seen.*)

c 893 K. ÆLFRED *Oros.* II. iv. (1883) 76 Cirus ȝeahsade.. þæt þæm folce seldsiene & uncuðe wæron wines dryncas. *c* 959 in Kemble *Cod. Dipl.* (1845) III. 450 Ælc seldsynde fisc ðe weorðlic byð. *a* 1225 *Ancr. R.* 80 Our speche schal beon seldcene. *c* 1230 *Hali Meid.* 37 Hit is selt sene on eorðe. 1547 BALDWIN *Mor. Philos.* I. viii. C iv b, Thales.. was asked what was the most difficill and seldest seen thing? He aunswered: an olde Tyrant. A selde sene thing in dede. *c* 1590 MARLOWE *Jew of Malta* I. 63 Seildsene costly stones. 1616 T. SCOT *Philomythie* D 5 b, The most precious-seld-seen Vnicorne. 1916 E. BLUNDEN *Pastorals* 30 Even as she flung the seld-seen gaud away.

sele (siːl), *sb.* *Obs.* exc. *dial.* Forms: 1 **sǽl** (*dat. pl.* **sælum, sálum**), **seel,** 3 **sæl, seale, sil,** 3–5 **sel,** 4 **sell,** 4–5 **cele, seele,** 4–8 **seel,** 4, 9 **seyle,** 5 **ceele, ceyl(l)e,** 5–6 **seill, seyll(e,** 5, 9 **sale,** 7 **ceile,** 7–9 **seal, seil,** 3– **sele.** [OE. *sǽl* masc. and fem.:—OTeut. type **sǣli-z*, app. a subst. use of the adj. found in Goth. *sêl-s* good (whence *sêlei* goodness), ON. *sǽll* happy (whence *sǽla* wk. fem., *sǽld* str. fem., happiness); in WGer. outside Eng. preserved only in derivatives, OS. *sâlig*, OHG. *sâlîg* (see SEELY *a.*), MHG. *sâllîche* fortunately, OS. *sâlda*, OHG. *sâlida* happiness (see SELTH). An ablaut-variant **sōl-* occurs in OE. *sél* adv.: see etymological note to SELE *a.*]

1. Happiness, prosperity, good fortune. ***on sele, a sele*** (OE. *on sǽlum, on sálum*): happy.

Beowulf 607 þa wæs on salum sinces brytta. *Ibid.* 1170 þu on sælum wes. *c* 1200 *Trin. Coll. Hom.* 183 þu ware a sele gief ich was wroð. *c* 1200 ORMIN 14304 All middellærdess sellþe & sel. *c* 1205 LAY. 10040 Bruttes heo gretten.. beden heom beon on sele [*c* 1275 seale]. *a* 1240 *Ureisun* in *Cott. Hom.* 183 Ihesu min heorte Mi sel mi saule hele. *a* 1300 *Cursor M.* 2905 þar neuer man sank þat was o sele. *Ibid.* 3962 He is vm-sett all wit sell. 13.. *Gaw. & Gr. Knt.* 2409 Sele yow bytyde. *c* 1375 *Sc. Leg. Saints* xl. (*Ninian*) 1117 Lord, sa haf I sele, in galouay we haf don rycht wele. *c* 1485 *Digby Myst.* IV. 72 How rewfully he hinges here, That set you first in ceile! 1513 DOUGLAS *Æneis* V. i. 46 So haif I seill. 1668 R. B. *Adagia Scot.* 47 Seil comes not while sorrow be gone. 1875 W. ALEXANDER *Sk. Ain Folk* 82 Seil upo' them, they're a winsome pair.

2. Favourable or proper time, opportune moment; occasion, opportunity; season, time of day. Cf. BARLEY-*sele*, HAYSEL.

With OE. *sǽl and mǽl* (Beowulf) cf. quot. *a* 1825. ***to give the sele of the day***: 'to pass the time of day,' to give a friendly greeting in passing.

Beowulf 1008 þa wæs sæl and mæl, þæt to healle gang Healfdenes sunu. *c* 1000 *Sax. Leechd.* I. 112 þas wyrte man mæȝ niman on ælcne sæl. *c* 1200 *Trin. Coll. Hom.* 185 Ðos feawe word seide ure drihten.. at sume sele, þo þe he wunede licamliche on eorðe. *c* 1250 *Gen. & Ex.* 1095 Loth and his doȝtres two Ledden ðis angeles ut in sel. 1303 R. BRUNNE *Handl. Synne* 5779 Now whom Myȝt y fynde, þys yche sele, To whom y myȝt selle Pers wele. 1375 *Creation* 770 in Horstm. *Altengl. Leg.* (1878) 133 þo wente he aȝen in þat sel And tolde Miȝhel his cas. *c* 1440 CAPGRAVE *Life St. Kath.* 682 þat alle þese þingys at euery tyme & seele schuld be redressed. *a* 1450 *Mankind* (Brandl 1898) 354 He hath mett wyth the goode man mercy in a schroude sell. 1662 GURNALL *Chr. in Arm.* III. verse 18. I. xxx. §1. 385 At what ceile of the day or night soever it be. 1674 RAY *S. & E.C. Words* 76 It is a fair *seel* for you to come at, i.e. a fair season or time; spoken ironically to them that come late... What Seel of day? What time of day. 1787 W. H. MARSHALL *Norfolk* (1795) II. 387 *Seel*, or *Seal*, time or season; as, 'hay-seel', hay-time; 'barley-seel', barley seed-time; 'wheat-seel', wheat seed-time; 'bark-seel', the barking season. *a* 1825 FORBY *Voc. E. Anglia* s.v. *Seal*, Of an idle and dissipated fellow, we say that he 'keeps bad seals';.. of a sober, regular, and industrious man.. that he 'keeps good seals and meals'. 1857 BORROW *Romany Rye* I. xxi. 249 As I passed.., I gave the man the sele of the day.

b. A period of time.

a 1250 *Owl & Night.* 953 He mihte bet speken a sele. *c* 1330 R. BRUNNE *Chron. Wace* (Rolls) 7005 Ȝyf Constant had lyued ani sel He schuld haue mended þe lond ful wel. 1338 —— *Chron.* (1810) 80 þer duelled þei non seel. 1447 BOKENHAM *Seyntys, Mary Magd.* 1026 In ful short seel.

†**sele**, *a.* *Obs.* Forms: *Compar.* 1 **sélra, séllra, sélla,** 2–3 **selre,** 3 **selere;** *Superl.* 1 **sélest,** 3 **selest;** *Positive* 3 **sæl, sel, seal,** *accus.* **seolne.** [The OE. *sélra, sélla*, better, *sélest* best, represent OTeut. types **sōlizon-*, **sōlisto-* (cf. OE. *sél*, older *sœ́l* adv. better:—**sōliz*), f. **sōl-*, ablaut-variant of **sœ́l-*: see SELE *sb.* The positive *sel(e* in early ME. is a back-formation from the other degrees; whether there is mixture of an adoption of ON. *sǽll* happy is uncertain.] Good.

Beowulf 2890 Deað bið sella eorla ȝehwylcum þonne edwitlif! *c* 950 *Lindisf. Gosp.* Matt. x. 31 Sellra [L. *meliores*]. *c* 1000 *Ags. Gosp.* ibid., ðe synt selran. *Ibid.* Luke x. 42 Maria ȝeces þæne selestan dæl. *c* 1205 LAY. 3955 He ferde awi ouer sæ þat him þuhte selest. *Ibid.* 17679 þæt vther his broðer hæfde him þider i-send seolne læche. *Ibid.* 21166 Ne isæh næuere na man selere cniht nenne. *Ibid.* 24954 þus andswærede Walwain þe sele. *c* 1230 *Hali Meid.* 67 In al þat euer sel is. 13.. *K. Alis.* 7430 For ben yee sele, ben ye wrothe, Ynde and Perce buth myn bothe.

sele, obs. form of CEIL *v.*

a 1400–50 *Wars Alex.* 1519 Sylours of sendale to sele ouire þe gatis.

sele: see SEAL *sbs.*, SEEL *v.*[2], SEELY *a.*, SELL *v.*

select (sɪ'lɛkt), *a.* (and *sb.*). Also 6 **selecte.** [ad. L. *sēlect-us* select, chosen, pple. of *sēligĕre* to choose out, select, f. *sē-* apart, SE- + *legĕre* to collect, choose, etc. Cf. Sp., Pg. *selecto.*]

A. *adj.*

1. Selected, chosen out of a larger number, on account of excellence or fitness; picked.

select committee, see COMMITTEE 3. ***select meeting***, (amongst Quakers) a meeting of ministers and elders. ***select vestry***, see VESTRY.

1565 COOPER *Thesaurus*, *Selectus*, chosen from amonge other: chief amonge other: selecte. 1571 DIGGES *Pantom.* Ep. + ij b, When they shall perceiue your Lordshippe.. doth allow and accepte them as fragrante floures selecte and gathered out of the pleasant gardynes Mathematicall. 1580 *Lease* in *Collect.* (O.H.S.) I. 237 These twelve select trees. 1606 WARNER *Alb. Eng.* XIV. Ded., Whom my Muse Doth its select Mecænas chuse. 1667 MILTON *P.L.* XI. 819 No sooner hee with them of Man and Beast Select for life shall in the Ark be lodg'd. 1676 HALE *Contempl.* II. *Medit. Lord's Pr.* 167 Not only at the select and solemn times of Prayer, but in the general Frame of our conversation. *a* 1700 EVELYN *Diary* June 1647, He married us in Sir Richd. Browne's Chapell.., some few select freinds being present. 1712 in T. W. Marsh *Early Friends in Surrey & Sussex* xv. (1886) 140 Its Unanimusly agreed.. that a Select Meeting be Held in each Weekly Meeting.. concerning the good order and Discipline of the Church. 1718 PRIOR *Solomon* III. 653 Select from vulgar Herds, with Garlands gay, A hundred Bulls ascend the Sacred Way. 1731 *Gentl. Mag.* I. 159 In the Parish where I serve, the Vestry is compos'd of thirty select Members besides the Rector. 1744 DODSLEY (*title*) A select Collection of Old Plays. 1782 PRIESTLEY *Corrupt. Chr.* II. VI. i. 4 The more secret parts of the heathen worship, to which select persons only were admitted. 1819 SHELLEY *Œdipus* I. 217 Every gibbet says its catechism And reads a select chapter in the Bible Before it goes to play. 1835 *App. Munic. Corpor. Rep.* III. 1496 (Doncaster) The mayor, aldermen and capital burgesses form the Select Body or common council. 1855 MACAULAY *Hist. Eng.* xxi. IV. 649 To the smaller plot.. only a few select traitors were privy. 1873 (*title*) Cornelius Nepos. Select Lives. With notes by Edward Walford.

2. Hence, Choice, of special value or excellence; composed of or containing the best, choicest or most desirable; superior. **a.** Of things, material or immaterial.

1590 SPENSER *F.Q.* III. vi. 12 Whence all the world deriues the glorious Features of beautie, and all shapes select, With which high God his workmanship hath deckt. 1602 SHAKS. *Ham.* I. iii. 74 And they in France of the best rank and station, Are of a most select and generous cheff in that. 1623 LD. HERBERT in Ellis *Orig. Lett.* ser. I. III. 164, I will come from the ordinarie voice to the selecter judgement of the

Ministers of State, and more intelligent people in this Kingdome. **1656** RIDGELEY *Pract. Physick* Pref. 3 Most select Remedies for every Disease. **1667** MILTON *P.L.* VIII. 513 And happie Constellations on that houre Shed their selectest influence. **1709** STEELE *Tatler* No. 142 ¶5 He has spent his most select Hours in the Knowledge of them. *a* **1822** SHELLEY *Def. Poetry* Pr. Wks. 1888 II. 19 The Romans appear to have considered the Greeks as the selectest treasuries of the selectest forms of manners. **1848** THACKERAY *Van. Fair* xxxviii, His senior..had consigned a quantity of select wines to him. **1868** JOYNSON *Metals* 99 If what is called the 'best select' copper is required, the refining process is gone through a second time.

b. Of persons, company, etc. Now often: Unexceptionable with regard to social standing or estimation.

1602 MARSTON *Ant. & Mel.* Prol. 3 Select and most respected Auditours. **1603** DRAYTON *Bar. Wars* VI. xvi, Men most select, of speciall worth and sort. **1677** LADY CHAWORTH in *12th Rep. Hist. MSS. Comm.* App. v. 36 The Venetian Embassador made a ball to Lord Ossery and his family and Lord Arlington and his, and some other select company last weeke. **1770** MISS BURNEY *Early Diary* (1889) I. 84 The party though small were select. **1838** LYTTON *Alice* II. ii, The Reverend Charles Merton..kept up all the most select of his old London acquaintances. **1840** MACAULAY *Ess., Ranke* 559 Persecution of that sort which bows down and crushes all but a very few select spirits. **1855** —— *Hist. Eng.* xix. IV. 266 He [the Elector of Saxony] had ..a great desire to be a member of the most select and illustrious orders of knighthood. **1871** CARLYLE in *Mrs. Carlyle's Lett.* II. 278 Company at first aristocratic and select.

absol. **1828** P. CUNNINGHAM *N.S. Wales* (ed. 3) II. 112 The first of our subscription-concerts..was attended by one hundred and twenty of the select, admittances being decided by ballot. **1831** SCOTT *Ct. Robt.* ii, The public games..where, in the select of their own countrymen, they saw the handsomest specimens of the human race.

3. Careful in selection. Hence, (of a society or association) admitting only persons of a high class, esp. with regard to social station; exclusive; (of a place of resort) frequented only by persons of good social position.

1842 A. COMBE *Physiol. Digestion* (ed. 4) 23 The appetite becomes less keen and more select in its choice. **1875** JOWETT *Plato* (ed. 2) I. 316 You are select in your acquaintance. **1876** GEO. ELIOT *Dan. Der.* I. iii. 54 And I have spoken for Gwendolen to be a member of our Archery Club—the Brackenshaw Archery Club—the most select thing anywhere. **1888** *Lady* 25 Oct. 374/1 Such a sweet, select watering-place. All the best people go there.

B. *sb.* **a.** A selected person or thing. †**b.** A selected class or group, a selection. **c.** See quot. 1881.

a. **1610** HEALEY *St. Ang. Citie of God* VII. iii. 261 If therefore felicity bee not to bee placed amongst those selects, because they gotte their places rather by chance then desert: yet surely fortune should bee one amongst them. *a* **1733** NORTH *Life Ld. Kpr. Guilford* (1742) 29 In Town, he had his Select of Friends and Acquaintance. *a* **1733** —— *Exam.* I. ii. §2 (1740) 32 Borrow of the profligate Speech-makers, or Lyars of the Time in Print, and make a Select out of a Select of them to adorn a Party. *Ibid.* II. iv. §144. 308 He..sets forth a Select of the Rye-Plot Papers. **1805** T. HOLCROFT *Bryan Perdue* I. 159, I appeared to be the inmate and select of his soul, and almost as necessary to him as his horses and dogs. **1881** INGERSOLL *Oyster-Industr.* (Hist. Fish. Industr. U.S.) 248 *Selects*, oysters of the first quality, *i.e.* selected; applied wholly to opened stock. **1961** S. TAYLOR in WEBSTER s.v., It is possible to buy ware that is composed wholly of selects. **1968** *Globe & Mail* (Toronto) 15 Jan. 17/6 The All-Star game tomorrow night with the selects meeting the Stanley Cup defending champions from Toronto.

select (sɪˈlɛkt), *v.* [f. L. *sēlect-*, ppl. stem of *sēligĕre* (see prec.).]

1. *trans.* To choose or pick out in preference to another or others. Also *to select out.*

1567 MAPLET *Gr. Forest* 25 To select or choose forth amongst many things what is heade and principall. **1597** DANIEL *Civ. Wars* VI. lxxxvii. (1609) 165 Haue you then selected me To be the man whom you would haue displac't Out of the roule of Immortalitie? **1607** SHAKS. *Cor.* I. vi. 81 A certaine number..must I select from all. The rest shall beare the businesse in some other fight. **1615** G. SANDYS *Trav.* 141 Of some [reeds] the Arabians make darts and jauelins..; others they select to write with. **1706** POPE *Let. to Wycherley* 10 Apr., You desire me to select..some Things from the first Volume of your Miscellanies, which may be altered so as to appear again. **1754** WARBURTON *View Bolingbr. Philos.* ii. 135 Men..were not always sufficiently careful in selecting their arguments. **1825** COLERIDGE *Aids Refl.* (1843) I. 187 A power of selecting and adapting means to proximate ends according to circumstances. **1838** DICKENS *Nich. Nick.* xiv, The party was admirably selected. **1839** EARL SPENCER in *Jrnl. R. Agric. Soc.* (1840) I. 22 The importance of selecting good male animals [for breeding purposes]. **1849** MACAULAY *Hist. Eng.* v. I. 657 In selecting rebels for punishment. **1867** *Jrnl. R. Agric. Soc.* Ser. II. III. II. 464 He then soon begins to select out fine days for this purpose. **1875** JOWETT *Plato* (ed. 2) V. 25 Would a forger have had the wit to select the most..characteristic thoughts of Plato?

b. Said of impersonal agencies. Cf. SELECTION 3.

1859 DARWIN *Orig. Species* Introd. 5 Any being, if it vary however slightly in any manner profitable to itself,..will have a better chance of surviving, and thus be naturally selected. **1899** *Allbutt's Syst. Med.* VIII. 494 The eruption ..not selecting any special nerve territories.

c. To choose and dedicate *to. nonce-use.*

1715 POPE *Iliad* II. 504 The Limbs they sever from th' inclosing Hyde, The Thighs, selected to the Gods, divide.

2. *intr.* To choose or pick out something from a number; to make a selection.

1833 T. HOOK *Parson's Dau.* III. ix, 'The next dinner you give, George, we will select better', said Lady Frances. 'We will have up the local lawyer who knows the country politics, and all the friends and foes of the district.' **1859** DARWIN *Orig. Species* iv. 102 In man's methodical selection, a breeder selects for some definite object, and free intercrossing will wholly stop his work.

selectable (sɪˈlɛktəb(ə)l), *a.* [f. SELECT *v.* + -ABLE.] Worthy or fit to be selected; capable of being selected.

1836 HOOD in *Mem.* (1860) I. 239 Each going into his own quarters..though some next door houses were infinitely to appearance more selectable than their neighbours. **1975** *Gramophone* Nov. 950/3 Low and high pass filters..with two selectable cut-off points for bass and treble are also featured.

Selectasine (sɪˈlɛktəsiːn). The proprietary name of a colour-printing process which uses a single silk screen for each of the colours (see quot. 1934).

1918 *Official Gaz.* (U.S. Patent Office) 29 Jan. 1075/1 Method of delineating or reproducing pictures and designs. .. Assignors to Selectasine System, San Francisco, Cal., a Corporation of California. Filed Dec. 1, 1915. **1926** H. L. HIETT *Man. Stencil Screen Process Work* 79 Invented by Edward A. Owens, San Francisco, Cal., assignor to Selectasine System, Inc., San Francisco. **1934** H. CURWEN *Processes of Graphic Reproduction in Printing* I. 40 Selectasine is best suited to showcards of very bold design. .. A sheet of fabric ready impregnated with wax is the basis, and one sheet is used for each colour of the design. The wax filling is removed from the fabric following the shape of the colour to be worked, and a stencil is thus formed. **1948** H. MISSINGHAM *Student's Guide in Commercial Art* II. 137 (*heading*) Silk screen or Selectasine process.

seˈlected, *ppl. a.* [f. SELECT *v.* + -ED[1].]

1. Specially chosen, picked out.

1590 MARLOWE *2nd Pt. Tamburl.* v. ii. 4381 For we haue here the chiefe selected men Of twenty seuerall kingdomes at the least. **1629** QUARLES *Argalus & Parth.* III. Wks. (Grosart) III. 277/1 Sometimes (for change of pleasure) he would read Selected stories, whilst her eares would feed Upon his lips. **1729** T. COOKE *Tales* etc., *Knts. Bath* 14 He thrice twelve gallant Youths, of high Renown, Selected Souls, of all the Land the Flowr, Appointed to adorn the bridal Hour. **1818** SCOTT *Hrt. Midl.* vii, For an instant this man quitted the prisoner, whom he consigned to a selected guard. **1865** TYLOR *Early Hist. Man.* x. 273, I give some selected cases of the Argument from similar customs.

†**2.** Choice, 'select'. *Obs. rare.*

1598 B. JONSON *Ev. Man in Hum.* I. ii, To his most selected [*Qo.* elected] friend, master Edward Knowell. **1605** BACON *Adv. Learn.* VII. §4 To keepe still the Lawe of breuitie, by vsing the most eminent and selected examples. **1655** H. VAUGHAN *Silex Scint.* 180 The first true worship of the world's great king From private and selected hearts did spring.

Hence †**seˈlectedly** *adv.*

1637 HEYWOOD *Royal Ship* (1638) 48 All of them in their severall faculties being knowne to bee the prime Workmen of the Kingdome, selectedly imploy'd in this Service.

selectee (sɪlɛkˈtiː). *U.S.* [f. SELECT *v.* + -EE.] A person selected for military service under the Selective Service system; a draftee. Now chiefly *transf.*

1940 *Army & Navy Register* (U.S.) 30 Nov. 7/2 The public considers the percentage of rejections of selectees high. **1942** *Newsweek* 27 Apr. 41/3 The Selectee is to be given a furlough up to ten days to arrange his personal affairs. **1958** *Optima* Mar. 47/2 The suspicion remains that the selectee is being favoured because he is regarded as the 'comer'—the man most likely to succeed in the immediately foreseeable future. **1979** *Tucson* (Arizona) *Citizen* 20 Sept. 10A/3 Most of Carter's selectees..passed in a breeze.

selecting (sɪˈlɛktɪŋ), *ppl. a.* [f. SELECT *v.* + -ING[2].] That selects, chooses, or picks out.

1871 BLACKIE *Four Phases Mor.* i. 100 A reasonable result always implies some principle of selection and a selecting agency. **1880** R. H. HUTTON in *Fraser's Mag.* May 665 The ..conception of will as a selecting power between two alternatives.

selection (sɪˈlɛkʃən). [ad. L. *sēlectiōn-em*, n. of action f. *sēligĕre*: see SELECT *v.*]

1. The action of selecting or choosing out; also the fact of being selected or chosen.

1646-58 SIR T. BROWNE *Pseud. Ep.* III. xxv. (ed. 4) 211 While we single out several dishes, and reject others, the selection seems but arbitrary, or upon opinion. **1744** HARRIS *Three Treat.* Wks. (1841) 83 It should seem, then,..that the essence of right conduct lay in selection and rejection. **1825** COLERIDGE *Aids Refl.* (1843) I. 187 There is [in the instinctive action of insects] selection, but not choice; volition rather than will. **1890** A. J. BELL *Why does Man exist?* xi. 75 Can selection of food-materials by plants be accounted for without consciousness? **1893** J. A. HODGES *Elem. Photogr.* (1907) 113 The careful selection of the point of view.

2. a. A particular choice; choice of a particular individual or individuals; *concr.* the (†person or) thing selected; a number of selected (†persons or) things. Often, a passage or a number of extracts from one or more literary works; a musical passage or a sequence of selected musical extracts.

1805 W. COOKE *Foote* II. 7 His company generally consisted of men of rank and fashion, some literary characters, and a selection from the stage. **1828** B. OAKLEY (*title*) Selections from Shakspeare. **1837** DICKENS *Pickw.* xxxvii, At this, the assembled selections laughed very heartily. **1857** W. ACTON *Prostitution* vii. 103 [We].. enjoyed in a grim kind of way the 'selection' from some favourite opera. **1865** (*title*) A Selection from the Works of Alfred Tennyson. **1878** C. STANFORD *Symb. Christ* i. 27 They make a selection from His laws, choosing some and rejecting others. **1887** TRAILL in *Contemp. Rev.* Oct. 479 The English public..does not pretend to care for poetry except in 'selections'. **1899** *Observer* 1 Oct. 5/3 The 'selection', which always begins the second part of the concert, was the familiar fantasia on English airs. **1929** *Radio Times* 8 Nov. 411/1 Selection of Songs by T. C. Sterndale Bennett. **1945** S. HUGHES in C. Madge *Pilot Papers* I. 94 The brass band repertoire..consists principally of marches..waltzes and light opera selections. **1968** M. BALL (*title*) Selections from the classics for chime bar music making.

b. *Sporting.* The horse or horses selected by a racing prophet as likely to win or obtain a place.

1901 *Scotsman* 12 Mar. 5/2 In 1897..the sporting selections of a highly respectable newspaper..the individual race prophecies numbered 1739.

c. in *pl.* 'In tobacco-culture, the choicest leaves and the highest grades of tobacco' (*Funk's Stand. Dict.* 1895).

3. a. Applied *spec.* to the action of a breeder in selecting individuals from which to breed, in order to obtain some desired quality or characteristic in the descendants. **b.** Hence in *Biology*, used by C. Darwin (*Origin of Species*, 1859) and subsequent writers, to designate any process, whether artificial or natural, which brings about a particular modification of an animal or vegetable type by ensuring that in successive generations the individuals that reproduce their kind shall be those that have transmissible variations from the ancestral form in the direction of this modification.

natural selection: the operation of natural causes by which those individuals of a species that are best adapted to the environment tend to be preserved and to transmit their characters, while those less adapted die out, so that in the course of generations the degree of adaptation to the environment tends progressively to increase. ***sexual selection***: that kind of natural selection which arises through the preference by one sex of those individuals of the other sex that have some special characteristic, in consequence of which that characteristic tends to be transmitted, with progressive enhancement in succeeding generations.

a. **1837** YOUATT *Sheep* iii. 60 That which enables the agriculturist not only to modify the character of his flock, but to change it altogether..—the principle of selection. **1844** H. D. RICHARDSON *Pigs* 51 In the selection of a boar and sow for breeding, much more attention and consideration are necessary.

b. **1857** DARWIN *Lett.* (1887) II. 123 There is such an unerring power at work, or *Natural Selection* (the title of my book), which selects exclusively for the good of each organic being. **1859** —— *Orig. Species* iv. 81 This preservation of favourable variations and the rejection of injurious variations, I call Natural Selection. *Ibid.* iv. 88 And this leads me to say a few words on what I call Sexual Selection. This depends, not on a struggle for existence, but on a struggle between the males for the possession of the females; the result is not death to the unsuccessful competitor, but few or no offspring. **1868** —— *Var. Anim. & Plants Domest.* (1875) II. 177 The principle of selection may be conveniently divided into three kinds. Methodical selection ..Unconscious selection..Natural selection. **1878** TAIT & STEWART *Unseen Universe* v. §170 Thus the struggle for existence bears to natural selection the same relation as man bears to artificial selection. **1882** VINES tr. *Sachs' Bot.* 929 The struggle for existence acts therefore in a certain sense similarly to the selection of the breeder; as the breeder developes only that which is suited to his own purposes... Thus,..through what may be termed metaphorically *Natural Selection* by means of the struggle for existence, —forms are produced which are as well or even better adapted for the purpose of self-preservation than cultivated plants are for the purpose of man.

transf. **1860** O. W. HOLMES *Elsie V.* xix, That is the way ..physiological democracy is enabled to fight against the principle of selection which would disinherit all the weaker children. **1869** *Fortn. Rev.* June 644 By a sort of critical selection, the cultivated class improves the breed of literary egotists; it suppresses all but the best specimens.

4. *Austral.* **a.** = FREE-SELECTION. Also *attrib.*

1866 ROGERSON *Poems* 22 Heathcote never was so gay As on the land selection day. **1880** *Victorian Rev.* I. 628 It is surprising that the selectors themselves have not prayed the Government to stop selection for some years at least.

b. A piece of land selected or taken up through 'free-selection'.

1875 *Melbourne Spect.* 21 Aug. 189/3 Jumping selections ..is said to be very common now in the Winmera district. **1881** MRS. C. PRAED *Policy & P.* I. 50 He has a selection down the Koorong.

5. a. *attrib.* as (sense 1) ***selection board, committee, panel, test***; **selection pressure** *Biol.*, differential mortality or fertility such as tends to make a population adapt genetically; **selection restriction** *Linguistics*, a syntactic or semantic restraint on the concurrence of dependent lexical items; **selection rule** *Physics*, any of a number of rules which describe, within certain limits, which particular quantum transitions can occur in an atom, molecule, etc., and which are 'forbidden'; **selection value**, value (of a variation or peculiarity) as affecting natural selection.

1940 R. S. LAMBERT *Ariel & all his Quality* xi. 302 Methods of appointing new staff..by advertising vacancies and setting up selection boards. **1976** L. DEIGHTON *Twinkle, twinkle, Little Spy* xvi. 162 Douglas was sent to a swanky private school..but was still unable to pass the U.S. Army officers' selection board. **1909** *Daily Graphic* 26 July 6/3 It is safe to believe that the Selection Committee has done its best, the players will do their best, Australia will do its best. **1932** Q. D. Leavis *Fiction & Reading Public* i. ii. 22 The Book Society...was started..in 1927..with a Selection Committee of five novelists and journalists. **1978** J. Pudney *Thank Goodness for Cake* 97, I was short-listed and looked over by a selection committee. **1974** *BP Shield Internat.* Oct. 8/1 Conference members..were screened by a selection panel. **1944** J. S. Huxley *On living in Revolution* 79 [In the Australian area] there is less scope for variation,..so that general selection-pressure never became so intense. **1977** J. L. Harper *Population Biol. of Plants* ii. 46 Groups of species caught in different evolutionary pathways may face the same selective forces, e.g. a selection pressure to disperse. **1964** Katz & Postal *Integrated Theory of Linguistic Descriptions* ii. 15 Each reading in the dictionary entry for a lexical item must contain a *selection restriction*, i.e., a formally expressed necessary and sufficient condition for that reading to combine with others. **1976** *Word 1971* XXVII. 133 One reason is that the selection restrictions of the verb *throw* require an animate subject. **1931** H. P. Robertson tr. *H. Weyl's Theory of Groups & Quantum Mech.* iv. 198 The selection rule for the inner quantum number *j* is obtained in an analogous manner. **1977** I. M. Campbell *Energy & Atmosphere* viii. 218 The origin of the selection rules for radiative transitions between electronically excited states and the ground state lies in fundamental quantum theory. **1935** *Discovery* Jan. 17/2 The most anxious moment in the design of a selection test now comes. If we take a group of workers..can the new test sort them into their correct relative order? **1967** Wills & Yearsley *Handbk. Managem. Technol.* xi. 202 Are we right to ignore *selection tests*? **1892** Romanes *Darwin & After* I. 275 We cannot speak of adaptations as due to natural selection, without thereby affirming that they present what I have elsewhere termed a 'selection value'.

b. *Forestry.* Used *attrib.* with reference to a system of forest management under which there is a continuing selection of individual trees for felling over the whole area, on the basis of their saleability.

1891 W. Schlich *Man. Forestry* II. 133 The term *selection system* was introduced into India; it is perhaps not an ideal term, since a certain amount of selection is practised in all systems; it has been retained, as none better is at present available. **1911** H. S. Graves *Princ. handling Woodlands* ii. 72 The development of the individual trees in a selection stand is somewhat different than in an even-aged stand. **1935** N. C. Brown *Gen. Introd. Forestry U.S.* viii. 105 The selection method is likely to be best adapted to general silvicultural and economic conditions found in this country. **1950** *Q. Jrnl. Forestry* XLIV. 15 Rabbits are probably the greatest drawback to the selection system or any irregular system in this country. **1979** O. Kuthanova tr. *Jenik's Pict. Encycl. Forests* 451 (*caption*) Diagram showing selection felling in a high forest; four stages of forest with alternating generations of trees in man-made clearings.

selectional (sɪˈlɛkʃənəl), *a.* [f. selection + -al.] Of or pertaining to selection. Freq. in *Linguistics*; ***selectional restriction*** = *selection restriction* s.v. selection 5 a.

1961 R. B. Long *Sentence & its Parts* ii. 40 Predeterminer modifiers generally are adverbial in function, and mensurant, selectional..or adjunct-like in force. **1964** *Language* XL. 38 There are, then, selectional restrictions between determiners and relative clauses. **1968** *Ibid.* XLIV. 579 On the other hand, there are cogent observations about the role of 'suffixoids' such as *-er* of *hammer* as selectional factors favoring the development of homophonous derivational affixes. **1971** *Nature* 9 Apr. 410/2, I identified all the maxima and minima of PDS for a given population and summed the successive absolute differences to give me an index that combined both selectional and random factors. **1977** *Word 1972* XXVIII. 89 The NP analysis of copular predicates can be retained for comparatives if *nios* is viewed as some sort of denominalizing particle which makes a comparative adjective compatible with the selectional restrictions of *tá*.

So **se'lectionally** *adv.*

1958 P. Maas *Textual Crit.* 13 The task of proving the existence of the conjecturally (or 'selectionally'..) presupposed errors plays a considerable..role in textual criticism. **1965** N. Chomsky *Aspects of Theory of Syntax* ii. 116 We label as Noun the one that is selectionally dominant.

selectionism (sɪˈlɛkʃənɪz(ə)m). [f. selection + -ism.] The belief that evolution proceeds by natural selection; opp. to Lamarckism.

1912 A. Tridon tr. *Delage & Goldsmith's Theories Evol.* xi. 163 (*heading*) A discussion of Roux's theory; its merits.—Its relation to selectionism and Lamarckism. **1944** J. S. Huxley *On Living in Revolution* vi. 70 In the last twenty-five years..an enormous amount of new facts about evolution have been discovered, and the balance has now swung over heavily, and, I think, permanently, in favour of Darwinism or selectionism. **1982** *New Scientist* 15 Apr. 162/1 Neutralism never seriously claimed to do more than ride piggyback on selectionism.

selectionist (sɪˈlɛkʃənɪst), *sb.* and *a.* [f. selection + -ist.] **A.** *sb.* **a.** One who believes in or supports the theory of natural selection. †**b.** One who believes that evolution proceeds primarily by natural selection for small differences (*Obs.*); opp. mutationist. **c.** One who holds a selectionist view of genetic variation (cf. sense B. b below).

1892 *Nation* 6 Oct. 266/3 Extreme selectionists like Wallace and Weismann. **1899** J. L. Tayler in *Nat. Sci.* Sept. 190 A pure or nearly pure selectionist hypothesis. **1909** W. Bateson *Mendel's Princ. Heredity* i. 3 If species had really arisen by the natural selection for impalpable differences,..the limits between species should be.. indefinite... The selectionists believe..that it represents the facts of nature. **1911** [see mutationist]. **1959** *Encounter* Sept. 62/2 The selectionist must assume..that consciousness is *useful*. **1979** *Sci. Amer.* Nov. 96/3 Selectionists maintain that for a mutant allele to spread through a species it must have some selective advantage.

B. *adj.* **a.** Pertaining to or connected with the theory of natural selection. **b.** Of or pertaining to the belief that the majority of observed genetic variation is maintained by natural selection rather than by random effects.

1944 J. S. Huxley *On Living in Revolution* vi. 69 By Darwinism..was meant the selectionist theory of the method of evolution. **1971** *Nature* 13 Aug. 487/1 They maintain that a selectionist hypothesis would predict radical changes to be favoured over conservative changes. **1974** *Ibid.* 1 Nov. 62/2 A selectionist interpretation of the more rapid rate of molecular evolution in a living fossil is possible. **1978** *Sci. Amer.* Sept. 45/1 Selectionist evolution..is neither a chance phenomenon nor a deterministic phenomenon but a two-step tandem process combining the advantages of both.

selective (sɪˈlɛktɪv), *a.* [f. select *v.* + -ive. Cf. F. *sélectif.*] **1. a.** Having the quality or faculty of selecting; characterized by choice or selection.

1625 Bp. Hall *Contempl.* xviii. *Elijah with Sareptan* Wks. 1332 Who can enough wonder at the pitch of this selectiue prouidence of the Almighty? **1853** Whewell *Grotius* I. p. iv, The translation is thus rather a selective than an abridged translation. **1875** Ruskin *Lect. Art* iii. 72 The selective and ordinant energy of the brain.

b. Applied to physical processes or agencies which result in the selection of some elements or factors and the exclusion of others.

1843 Carpenter *Anim. Phys.* i. 39 The selective absorption of nutritious matter. **1889** A. R. Wallace *Darwinism* vii. 171 The isolation of varieties by selective association.

c. *Wireless Telegraphy.* 'Designating a system by which two or more messages can be sent or received simultaneously without interference' (Webster 1911).

1906 Eichhorn *Wireless Telegr.* v. 23 A system of selective electric wave telegraphy, *i.e.* wireless multiplex telegraphy. **1906** Kennelly *Wireless Telegr.* 173 The Problem of Selective Signaling.

d. *Psychol.* Applied to the capacity for, or process of, selection manifested by the mind or senses in reacting to certain stimuli and not to others, esp. ***selective attention.***

1875 W. James in R. B. Perry *Thought & Char. W. James* (1935) I. 528 The *whole* mass of impressions falling on any individual are chaotic, and become orderly only by selective attention and recognition. **1935** G. Murphy *Briefer Gen. Psychol.* xii. 210 From the point of view..of what takes the most prominent place in consciousness, there is a further selective function to be considered. **1958** D. E. Broadbent *Perception & Communication* ii. 15 The performance of selective listeners seems to vary with information as defined by communication theory, rather than with amount of stimulation in the conventional sense. **1968** Trabasso & Bower *Attention in Learning* i. 18 Our primary goal is to offer new theory and new results regarding selective attention in discrimination learning. **1978** G. Underwood *Strategies of Inform. Processing* vii. 237 The selective rehearsal of some members of the memory set in preference to others.., the selective 'forgetting' of some items previously encoded.

e. *Educ.* (See quot. 1960–1.) Also applied to any school within the selective (as opposed to the comprehensive) system. Cf. comprehensive *a.* 1 d.

1926 *Educ. of Adolescent* (Board of Educ. Consult. Comm.) iii. 79 As post-primary education develops, the schools dealing with the post-primary or secondary stage of education should include..schools of the type of the existing selective Central Schools, which give at least a four years' course from the age of 11+. **1955** O. Banks *Parity & Prestige in Eng. Secondary Educ.* viii. 97 Both the selective central school and the junior technical school originated in the period before the first world war. **1960–1** *Where?* Winter 17/1 *Selective school*, a school for which pupils have been selected (usually at 11 plus) on the grounds that they can benefit from a more academic education. **1974** *Times* 17 Apr. 1/5 Over half of our secondary school pupils are still in selective schools. **1978** *Jrnl. R. Soc. Arts* CXXVI. 335/1 The decision to change our schooling from a selective to a comprehensive system.

f. *Philos.* Applied to a doctrine of realism put forward in the early 20th century which maintained that sense-data exist in material objects and that the senses of the perceiver select those which are appropriate to be registered.

1932 H. H. Price *Perception* ii. 40 Now let us turn to the *selective* interpretation. According to this, the somatic data ..merely..enable us to be conscious of environmental data. **1944** W. T. Stace in P. A. Schilpp *Philos. B. Russell* 365 The view of selective realism is quite different... The sense-qualities actually exist in the object, whether it is perceived or unperceived, just as common sense supposes. What the sense-organ does is to *select* which of the sense-qualities we shall perceive. **1967** *Encycl. Philos.* VII. 78/2 Their.. attempt..to deal with illusions..is a version of what is often called the selective theory.

2. Special collocations: ***selective breeding***; ***selective employment tax*** (also with capital initials), a tax levied by the British Government between 3 May 1966 and 1 Apr. 1973, payable on all employees at varying rates and refunded to employers in selected branches of manufacturing industry; cf. S.E.T. s.v. S 4 a; ***selective service*** (U.S.), a system of military service (from 1917 to 1973) under which draftees were selected from those persons required to enrol; ***selective strike***, a form of industrial action in which union labour is not totally withdrawn but withheld in chosen sectors; ***selective weedkiller***, a substance which kills some plant species without harming others.

1931 J. S. Huxley *What dare I Think?* i. 40 Selective breeding I have just touched upon. **1971** F. Hamilton *World Encycl. Dogs* 354 Selective breeding down through the last 150 years has produced the Foxhound of today. **1966** *Times* 4 May 1/1 A selective employment tax payable by employers only is to be introduced by the Government from September 5 to divert manpower from the service industry into manufacturing. **1973** *Guardian* 13 Apr. 13/5 Selective Employment Tax ended on 1 April 1973. As an employer, you may be eligible for a refund of S.E.T. **1978** *Jrnl. R. Soc. Arts* CXXVI. 405/1 The next phase was the indictment of the so-called 'candyfloss industries' and their punishment through the Selective Employment Tax. **1917** *New Republic* 9 June 148/2 The New Republic advocated the principle of selective service for this emergency. **1920** E. H. Crowder *Spirit of Selective Service* v. 119 There were to be two phases to Selective Service, the one, enrollment, the other selection. **1969** G. L. Wamsley *Selective Service & Changing Amer.* i. 1 A step can be taken toward understanding why Selective Service has come under attack after years of anonymity. **1976** N. Thornburg *Cutter & Bone* vii. 157 Nor did he meekly submit to his Selective Service draft notice. **1959** *Wall St. Jrnl.* 29 Dec. 2/2 Selective strikes would be expedient to the union, since they would concentrate pressure on individual companies. **1979** *Arizona Daily Star* 1 Apr. A1/5 The powerful Teamsters union early today called 'selective strikes' against a portion of the trucking industry. **1928** H. Martin *Sci. Princ. Plant Protection* ix. 170 The peculiar virtues of the metallic sulphates as selective weedkillers. **1965** *Listener* 22 July 142/1 Historically, selective weedkillers have been used since 1895 when solutions of copper sulphate were used to destroy charlock in cereal crops. **1976** *Field* 18 Nov. 1040/2 Base fertilizer for lawns should be applied in March or early April..and the selective weedkiller a week or two later.

selectively (sɪˈlɛktɪvlɪ), *adv.* [f. selective *a.* + -ly[2].] In a selective manner; by selection.

1651 Biggs *New Disp.* ¶ 113 They..cannot selectively separate and draw forth one humour, from another. **1897** *Allbutt's Syst. Med.* II. 826 The respiratory centre is not selectively affected.

selectiveness (sɪˈlɛktɪvnɪs). [f. selective *a.* + -ness.] The attribute of being selective.

c **1850** Clough *Poems*, etc. (1869) I. 320 A certain withdrawal and separation, a moral and almost religious selectiveness,..are essential to Wordsworth's being.

selectivist (sɪˈlɛktɪvɪst). [f. selective *a.* + -ist.] One who supports a selective theory or policy. Hence **se'lectivism.**

1932 H. H. Price *Perception* ii. 44 The Selectivist is asked to say *which* colour belongs to the rose when nobody is looking at it. **1944** W. T. Stace in P. A. Schilpp *Philos. B. Russell* 365 There are grave objections to selectivism, but that is not the present point. **1967** *Guardian* 4 Sept. 14/8 The selectivists are right in saying that much more should be done to channel social benefits to the people who need them most. **1969** *Physics Bull.* Mar. 108/1 They are apt to ignore work not published in their country's journals, a selectivism matched by the singlemindedness of the articles.

selectivity (ˌsɛlɛkˈtɪvɪtɪ). [f. selective *a.* + -ity.] **1.** *Radio.* The ability of a receiver to tune separately to signals of adjacent frequencies, measured by the frequency difference between the half-power points of the pass-band of the receiver.

1903 *Electr. World & Engin.* 1 Aug. 173/2 The system of selectivity devised by Sir Oliver [Lodge] was the outcome of a series of classical experiments based upon his syntonic Leyden jars in which one jar is caused to discharge through a circuit by the sparks of another jar, provided the two circuits are of equal electrical dimensions. **1930** *Manch. Guardian* 20 Sept. 15/7 It is no exaggeration to say that.. four-valve sets are more than equal in power and selectivity to a six or seven-valve set of the old type. **1943** C. L. Boltz *Basic Radio* viii. 131 The sharper is the resonance curve the better it will select, for supplies at frequencies quite near the resonant one will have very much less effect. The sharpness of the curve is therefore a measure of the selectivity. **1976** *Which?* Sept. 203/2 If you want to receive particularly weak signals, you need a set which has good selectivity.

2. *gen.* The quality of being selective.

1948 E. G. Boring et al. *Found. Psychol.* x. 218/1 This selectivity of perception amounts to giving one sense impression a clear track. **1951** Ruesch & Bateson *Communication* iii. 84 An alternate solution of the psychiatrist is to abstract and condense his observations before writing them down; selectivity, therefore, becomes an unavoidable issue. **1969** *Computers & Humanities* III. 278 The main program was the Formatting Program in which the two files were used as input to produce six indexes, four of which were selective. A 'selectivity module' had been introduced to make the selections possible. *a* **1974** R. Crossman *Diaries* (1976) II. 471 We were able to discuss one of the minor sensations of the recess—Ray Gunter's speech in August, in which he said we must be realistic and brave and face up to the need for selectivity and the means test. **1978** G. Underwood *Strategies of Information Processing* vii. 235 To information processing theory.. attention and selectivity are central features.

selectly (sɪˈlɛktlɪ), *adv. rare.* [f. select *a.* + -ly[2]] By selection; in a select manner.

1689 E. Howard *Caroloiades* 196 If from their Numbers they'd Scelectly [*sic*] take Men that, by zeal, their valours fiercer make. **1865** Dickens *Mut. Fr.* iv. iv, The Minister speaking, as directed by the Rubric, to the people, .. selectly represented .. by G. & G. above mentioned.

se'lectman. *U.S.* [f. SELECT *a.* + MAN *sb.*[1]] One of a board of officers elected annually to manage various local concerns in a 'town' or 'township' in New England.

1646 in *Gen. Laws Massachusetts* (1672) 122 The Select men of Boston, Charlstown [etc.]. **1792** BELKNAP *Hist. New Hampsh.* III. 282 Three or five Selectmen are annually chosen in each town, who are entrusted with its general concerns. **1888** BRYCE *Amer. Commw.* III. lxiv. II. 468 *note,* The 'selectmen' of a New England Town are not paid.

transf. **1858** O. W. HOLMES *Aut. Breakf.-t.* x. (1859) 233 The select-men of an African kraal-village would have had more respect for their ancestors.

selectness (sɪ'lɛktnɪs). [f. SELECT *a.* + -NESS.] The quality of being select.

1727 BAILEY (vol. II.), *Selectness,* Chosenness, Choiceness. **1755** JOHNSON, *Selectness,* the state of being select. **1816** JEFFREY *Swift* Wks. (1853) 77/1 Goldsmith .. had the harmony of Pope without his quaintness, and his selectness of diction without his coldness and eternal vivacity. **1852** R. S. SURTEES *Sponge's Sp. Tour* xxix. (1893) 158 The Flat Hat Hunt had relapsed into its wonted quiet, or 'selectness', as its members called it, and Beggar-my-Neighbour Hill saw none but the regular attendants.

selector (sɪ'lɛktə(r)). [f. SELECT *v.* + -OR.] One who or something which selects. **a.** *gen.*

1782 V. KNOX *Ess.* CV. [civ.] II. 93 Like all inventors and selectors of their own systems, they have been hurried to excess. **1797** (*title*) The Selector. Being a new .. collection of Visions, Tales [etc.]. **1809** HEBER in *Q. Rev.* II. 294 Given from Dr. King's work, with sundry comments by the ingenious selector. **1867** S. WILBERFORCE *Ess.* (1874) I. 67 Why should she [nature] become a selector of varieties? **1887** *Law Rep., Weekly Notes* 48/2 Here both parties were selectors or importers of cigars, not manufacturers.

b. *Austral.* = FREE-SELECTOR.

1875 *Melbourne Spect.* 12 June 70/2 A public meeting of non-resident selectors has been held at Rushworth. **1890** 'R. BOLDREWOOD' *Miner's Right* xxvii. 242 She was the daughter of one of the selectors at Blue Gum Flats.

c. As a name for various appliances in metallurgy, telegraphy, motor-car machinery, etc. *spec.* (*a*) in a gearbox, the part that moves the gearwheels into and out of engagement; (*b*) *Teleph.*, a mechanism which automatically establishes electrical connection with one of a group of available contacts according to the number of impulses in the incoming signal; (*c*) in a motor vehicle with automatic transmission, the control by which the driver selects the mode of operation of the transmission.

1890 *Nature* 7 Aug. 357/1 A device [in a horsehair-cloth loom] .. known as the selector .. picks up one hair, and only one, to present to the jaws of the shuttle. **1903** *Electr. Rev.* (Chicago) XLIII. 583/1 Each subscriber is connected to the exchange by two lines which end in what is called a first selector switch... The first selector consists of a couple of relays. **1907** *Westm. Gaz.* 9 Nov. 15/2 The selector or operating mechanism is placed in the bottom of the gear-box; so that all the gears can be removed without disturbing any part of it. **1908** *Ibid.* 16 Nov. 14/2 A selector-gate change has been installed [in the motor-car]. **1926** H. T. RUTTER *Mod. Motors* II. vii. 262 By moving the gear lever by hand it actuates what are termed selector rods, which are forked rods that slide the gear wheels on the gear-shaft one at a time into a position to mesh with the respective gear wheels on the lay-shaft. **1930** *Bell System Tech. Jrnl.* IX. 22 By placing several selectors in series a network of central offices may be built up, each office serving 10,000 telephones. **1961** *Listener* 16 Nov. 832/1, I would have been waiting, like some predetermined selector, for the necessary keys to fall into position. **1967** K. H. BRINKMANN tr. *K. Trautman's Design of Automatic Telephone Exchanges* 16 Each selector has a relay set which controls the switching functions... Ten final selectors would suffice to serve 100 subscribers since each switch interconnects two subscribers. **1967** *Times* 31 Mar. 3/7 The coroner said the selector lever must have been in 'drive'. **1973** D. BARNES *See the Woman* (1974) I. 9 Conrad stopped, pushed the selector to park .. and opened the car door. **1973** H. FANTEL *True Sound of Music* (1974) vii. 105 To start with, any amplifier has a selector switch. As its name implies, it lets you pick the program source you want to hear: radio, record player, or tape. **1976** L. THOMAS *Dangerous Davies* ii. 13 The record .. swooped again onto the turntable at her touch of the selector button.

d. *Sport.* One of a number of officials appointed to select a team.

1928 *Daily Mail* 2 Apr. 14/1 The selectors could not find in England a team good enough to stop this very perfect Scottish machine. **1934** F. J. C. GUSTARD *Eng. v. Austral.* 9 His action may have saved the selectors a certain amount of embarrassment. **1953** B. HARRIS *Cricket Triumph* i. 19 Laker did not come into the side until the third test match, for in the selectors' minds he and Roy Tattersall .. were of equal talent. **1976** J. SNOW *Cricket Rebel* 138, I said somewhere in a newspaper article that 1974 summer that the selectors would have to be shot before I made a Test comeback. I think my assessment was right.

Hence **selec'torial** *a.*, of or pertaining to a team selector (sense d above).

1959 *Times* 12 Oct. 15/4 The manner of its achievement cannot but raise some doubts in selectorial minds. **1963** A. ROSS *Australia 63* 13 Selectorial opinion, for one reason or another, was hardening against Sheppard. **1975** *Cricketer* May 37/1 Mr Holloway .. seems to feel (as indeed I do) that selectorial bias in favour of the southern and more particularly Home counties is an inescapable fact.

selectorate (sɪ'lɛktərət). [Blend of SELECTOR and ELECTORATE.] That section of a political party which has the effective power to choose a representative.

1967 P. PATERSON *Selectorate* i. 27 Within the Conservative selectorate there are almost as many grades and ranks and classifications as in a masonic order. **1969** *Daily Tel.* 10 Dec. 14 Most [primaries], while broadening the selectorate, are still open to the criticism that the many are brought in only at the final stage, to exercise a choice over a few candidates chosen by a committee. **1980** *Times* 20 June 14/4, I favour confining the selectorate to MPs.

Selectric (sɪ'lɛktrɪk). Also **selectric.** [Blend of SELECT *v.* and ELECTRIC *a.* and *sb.*] A proprietary name for a kind of electric typewriter.

1964 *Official Gaz.* (U.S. Patent Office) 29 Sept. TM 211/2 International Business Machines Corporation, Armonk, N.Y. Filed May 15, 1964. *Selectric* for typewriters. First use July 21, 1961. **1967** *Trade Marks Jrnl.* 8 Nov. 1716/2 *Selectric...* Electrically operated typewriting machines; electrically operated machines... International Business Machines Corp... New York... 23rd February 1967. **1970** [see *golf ball* s.v. GOLF *sb.* b]. **1971** *Computers & Humanities* V. 2/3 If a magnetic tape selectric typewriter (MT/ST) or a keypunch is used, the sorting and page-entering processes can be eliminated. **1977** J. WAMBAUGH *Black Marble* vi. 76 They can also .. start operating *your* Selectric.

selectron (sɪ'lɛktrɒn). Also **Selectron.** [f. SELECT *v.* + -T)RON.] A kind of cathode-ray tube formerly used in computers as a means of storing digital information.

1947 *Math. Tables & Other Aids to Computation* II. 229 'The selectron—a tube for selective electrostatic storage' by Dr. Jan Rajchman. **1947** [see INSTRUCTION 4 c]. **1950** W. W. STIFLER *High-Speed Computing Devices* xiv. 370 The Selectron utilizes the fact that an insulated secondary-electron emitter can be made to 'float' at either of two stable potentials. **1957** R. K. RICHARDS *Digital Computer Components & Circuits* vi. 265 Among the more important forms of electrostatic storage are the 'Williams tube', the 'barrier-grid tube', the 'holding-gun tube', and the Selectron, each of which has at one time or another been successfully used in a digital computer.

seledyne : see SELADYNE.

selen- ('sɛlən), *prefix.*

1. *Min.* [After G. *selen* selenium.] In names of certain minerals containing or formerly supposed to contain selenium, as †**,selen'cuprite** = BERZELIANITE. †**,selen'palladite, -pa'lladium** = ALLOPALLADIUM. †**,selen'silver** = NAUMANNITE. **,selen'sulphur,** a native variety of elemental sulphur containing a small proportion of selenium. **,selente'llurium,** a native compound of selenium and tellurium.

1835 C. U. SHEPARD *Treat. Min.* (ed. 2) II. 177 Selen-cuprite. *Ibid.*, Selenpalladite. **1849** J. NICOL *Man. Min.* 506 Selen-sulphur. **1857** DANA *Man. Min.* (1862) 327 Another seleniferous ore, from the Hartz, called selensilver. **1882** [see HIERATITE]. **1890** E. S. DANA & H. L. WELLS in *Amer. Jrnl. Sci.* Ser. III. XL. 79 We propose to call it Selen-tellurium. **1944** C. PALACHE et al. *Dana's Syst. Min.* (ed. 7) I. 142 Old specimens of reddish brown selensulfur from Vulcano gave *n* [*sc.* refractive index] 2·544–2.675 indicating 83–90·5 per cent Se; but this high Se content lacks confirmation.

†**2.** *Chem.* [For *seleno-*, SELENIO-.] Formerly used (before a vowel or *h*) in names of certain compounds containing selenium. **sele'naldine** [ALD(EHYDE) + -INE[5]], a basic substance produced by the action of hydrogen selenide on ammonium aldehydate. **selenethyl,** ethyl selenide. **selenhydric** *a.* = *hydroselenic* (*acid*): see HYDRO-. **selenhydrate** (see quot. 1858).

1848 BRANDE *Chem.* (ed. 6) II. III. 173 With seleniuretted hydrogen aldehyde-ammonia yields Selenaldine. **1853** WATTS tr. *Gmelin's Hand-bk. Chem.* VIII. 356 Selenide of Ethyl or Selenethyl. **1858** MAYNE *Expos. Lex., Selenhydrate,* term by Berzelius for the combinations of hydric selenide with the metallic seleniurets which contain the radicals of alkalis and alkaline earths. **1868** WATTS *Dict. Chem.* V. 218 Selen-hydric Acid.

selenate ('sɛlɪnət). *Chem.* Also **-iate.** [f. SELEN-IUM, after SELENIC *a.*] A salt of selenic acid.

1818 tr. *Berzelius* in *Ann. Philos.* XI. 293 The selenates of barytes and of lime are soluble in water. **1819** *Ibid.* XIII. 406 The acid obtained by the decomposition of the seleniate of tin. **1857** DANA *Man. Min.* (1862) 285 Selenate of lead. **1867** BLOXAM *Chem.* 220 The seleniates closely resemble the sulphates. **1880** CLEMINSHAW *Wurtz' Atom. Theory* 139 The sulphate and selenate of silver.

selendang, var. SLENDANG.

selenders (*pl.*), obs. form of SALLENDER.

selendine, -yne, obs. forms of CELANDINE.

selenes, variant of SEELINESS.

selenescope, obs. form of SELENOSCOPE.

selenetic, obs. form of SELENITIC *a.*

selenetted, var. *seleniettted* s.v. SELENIET *Obs.*

selenian (sɪ'liːnɪən), *a. rare.* [f. Gr. σελήνη moon + -IAN.] Of or pertaining to the moon considered as a world.

1669 FLAMSTEED in Rigaud *Corr. Sci. Men* (1841) II. 84 There are yet abundant laurels to be won in the Selenian games. **1864** *Intell. Observer* V. 525 They will have a right .. for regarding creation, the earth included, as especially made for the Selenian race. **1866** *Ibid.* IX. 136 Numerous tracts of selenian scenery.

selenic (sɪ'lɛnɪk), *a.*[1] *rare.* [Formed as prec. + -IC.] Of, pertaining to, or derived from the moon.

1816 BENTHAM *Chrestom.* Wks. 1843 VIII. 132 Selenic, Selenigenous, or simply mechanical source of motion. **1849** OTTÉ tr. *Humboldt's Cosmos* I. Index s.v. *Chladni,* On the selenic origin of aërolites.

selenic (sɪ'lɛnɪk), *a.*[2] *Chem.* [f. SELEN-IUM + -IC.] ***selenic acid,*** an acid formed when selenium is oxidized by fusion with nitre.

1818 tr. *Berzelius* in *Ann. Philos.* XI. 293 The selenic acid is soluble in water and in alcohol. **1867** BLOXAM *Chem.* 220 Selenic acid (SeO_3) is not known in the anhydrous state.

selenide ('sɛlɪnaɪd). *Chem.* Also **-id.** [f. SELEN-IUM + -IDE.] A combination of selenium with an electro-positive element or with a radical.

1849 D. CAMPBELL *Inorg. Chem.* 62 Selenide of hydrogen gas (prepared from the selenide of iron or potassium by decomposition with an acid, as in the sulphide of hydrogen). **1857** DANA *Man. Min.* (1862) 280 Clausthalite, or selenid of lead. **1873** WATTS *Fownes' Chem.* (ed. 11) 212 Insoluble selenides are thus produced.

†**se'leniet.** *Chem. Obs.* [f. SELENI-UM + *-et* as in *sulphuret.*] = SELENIURET. So †**seleniettted** (also **selenetted**) *a. Obs. rare.* = SELENIURETTED.

1831 T. THOMSON *Chem.* (ed. 7) I. 293 Selenium combines with hydrogen, and forms a gaseous substance, which has been distinguished by the name of seleniettted hydrogen gas. *Ibid.* 597 This precipitate is probably a seleniet of copper. **1854** DANA *Syst. Min.* (ed. 4) II. 42 Clausthalite... Seleniet of Lead. **1866** ODLING *Anim. Chem.* 13 Sulphuretted, selenetted, and telluretted hydrogen. **1867** BLOXAM *Chem.* 220 Hydroselenic acid, or seleniettted hydrogen (HSe).

seleniferous (sɛlɪ'nɪfərəs), *a.* [f. SELENI-UM + -FEROUS.] Containing or yielding selenium.

1823 W. PHILLIPS *Introd. Min.* (ed. 3) 219 Seleniferous Iron Pyrites. **1867** BLOXAM *Chem.* 219 To extract selenium from the seleniferous deposit of the vitriol works.

sele'nigenous, *a. rare*[−1]. [f. Gr. σελήνη moon + -GENOUS.] Produced by the moon.

1816 [see SELENIC *a.*[1]].

se'lenio-. *Chem.* Also **seleno-.** Used as a combining form of SELENIUM.

1831 T. THOMSON *Chem.* (ed. 7) II. 249 Seleniocyanogen .. was discovered by Berzelius. **1836** BRANDE *Chem.* (ed. 4) 570 Seleniocyanuret of Potassium. [**1848** *Ibid.* (ed. 6) I. 602 Seleniocyanide.] **1853** WATTS tr. *Gmelin's Hand-bk. Chem.* VIII. 122 Selenocyanide of lead. *Ibid.*, Selenocyanide of Ammonium. **1868** —— *Dict. Chem.* V. 219 Seleniocyanates. *Ibid.*, Seleniocyanic Acid.

selenious (sɪ'liːnɪəs), *a. Chem.* [f. SELEN-IUM: see -OUS *suffix* c.] ***selenious acid,*** a dibasic acid H_2SeO_3, forming salts called *selenites.*

1827 MITSCHERLICH & NITZSCH in *Q. Jrnl. Sci., Lit. & Art* II. 471 The acid is isomorphous with the sulphuric acid, and may with propriety be called selenic acid, that described by M. Berzelius being considered as the selenious acid. **1834** E. TURNER *Elem. Chem.* (ed. 5) 326 Selenious acid. **1869** ROSCOE *Chem.* 144 Selenium dioxide is .. capable of dissolving in water, and thus forming selenious acid.

seleniscope, obs. form of SELENOSCOPE.

selenite[1] ('sɛlɪnaɪt). *Min.* and *Chem.* Forms: 6 **silenite,** (7 **silonite**), 7– **selenite.** [ad. L. *selēnītēs* SELENITES.]

1. A stone described by ancient writers; apparently to be identified with the mineral now so called (see 2), though the accounts of its properties are inconsistent and partly fabulous. (In the 17–18th c. often identified with stones described by travellers or existing in collections.)

1567 MAPLET *Gr. Forest* 19 Silinite the Stone is seene in Persia in colour like to the jasper, or like to a fresh and flourishing greene herb. **1605** DRAYTON *Man in Moone* 321 That stone [*side-note* the Selenite of σελήνη] that doth the name derive From me, with me that lesseneth or doth thrive. **1623** COCKERAM III, *Selenite,* a stone wherein is a white, that decreaseth and encreaseth as the Moon groweth. **1686** GOAD *Celest. Bodies* I. vi. 17 Some pretious Stones are Natural Moon-Dials; the Selenite, which Pope Clement the VIII .. had among his Rarities [etc.]. **1688** HOLME *Armoury* II. 41/2 The Silonite .. is a stone in Persia. **1738** CHAMBERS *Cycl.* (ed. 2) s.v., There are some of these selenites preserved in the palace of Peking, valued at an incredible rate. **1855** SMEDLEY *Occult Sciences* 358 Selenite is supposed to give the faculty of prediction, and to reconcile lovers.

2. *Min.* Sulphate of lime (gypsum) in a crystalline or foliated form. Also, a slip or film of this mineral used for the polarization of light.

1668 WILKINS *Real Char.* II. iii. §2. 62 Selenite, Muscovia glass, Isingglass, Sparr, Talc. **1691** RAY *Creation* (1701) 119 Those rhomboideal selenites found near St. Ives. **1789** E. DARWIN *Bot. Gard.* I. ii. 219 Hence silvery Selenite her chrystal moulds And soft Asbestus smooths his silky folds. **1799** G. SMITH *Laboratory* I. 334 There is another kind of marble made of the flaky selenite. **1851** MAYNE REID *Scalp Hunters* xxxvi, I had recognised the sparkling scales of the selenite. **1867** J. HOGG *Microsc.* I. ii. 139 Used in combination with a superposed film of selenite or not as required.

attrib. **1839** G. BIRD *Nat. Philos.* 367 (*head-line*) Colours exhibited by selenite analyzing plate. **1888** RUTLEY *Rock-*

Forming Min. 116 In the case of nosean very few or no selenite crystals are formed.

†**b.** *Chem.* Sulphate of lime, without regard to structure. *Obs.*

1756 C. LUCAS *Ess. Waters* I. 94 Many waters are charged with selenite; as those of Pyrmont..and others. **1776** WOULFE in *Phil. Trans.* LXVI. 617 The acid of vitriol forsakes its alkaly to unite, and form a selenite with the calcareous earth. **1816** ACCUM *Chem. Tests* (1818) 293 Thus sulphate of lime, or selenite, may be precipitated by alcohol from water which contains this salt. **1823** P. NICHOLSON *Pract. Build.* 334 Water may be found naturally free from fixable gas, selenite, or clay.

Selenite[2]. [f. Gr. σεληνίτης (*pl.* Σεληνῖται men in the moon), f. σελήνη moon.] A supposed inhabitant of the moon.

c **1645** HOWELL *Lett.* (1655) III. ix. 18 The sphear of the Moon is peepled with Selenites or Lunary men. **1652** URQUHART *Jewel* Wks. (1834) 268 Leaving the new Baronets to search for land amongst the Selenits in the Moon, or turn Knights of the Sun. **1864** T. W. WEBB in *Intell. Observer* V. 200 Gruithuisen fancied that certain rows of hillocks might contain the habitations of Selenites!

selenite[3] (ˈsɛlɪnaɪt). *Chem.* [f. SELEN-IUM + -ITE.] A salt of selenious acid.

1831 T. THOMSON *Chem.* (ed. 7) I. 290 The analyses of two selenites given by Berzelius. *Ibid.* II. 44 The selenites (as the salts which it forms are called). **1842** PARNELL *Chem. Anal.* (1845) 258 Seleniates and selenites give the characteristic odour of selenium. **1869** ROSCOE *Chem.* 145 Selenic Acid is best prepared by fusing a selenite with nitre.

‖**selenites** (sɛlɪˈnaɪtiːz). *Obs.* In 4–5 silenites. Also 7 selenitis. [L. *selēnītēs* (also *selēnītis*) = Gr. σεληνίτης λίθος (*lit.* 'moonstone'; so called because it was supposed to wax and wane with the moon), f. σελήνη moon: see -ITE.]

1. = SELENITE[1] 1.

1398 TREVISA *Barth. De. P.R.* XVI. xci. (1495) 584 Silenites is a stone of Perse grene as grasse and shineth with a white specke and this stone foloweth the mone and wexyth and waneth as the mone dooth. **1601** HOLLAND *Pliny* XXXVII. x. II. 629 Selenites is a precious stone, white and transparent. **1610** HEALEY *St. Aug. Citie of God* XXI. v. 843. **1738** CHAMBERS *Cycl.* (ed. 2), *Selenites*, among the ancient naturalists, denotes a white, or transparent figured stone; thus called from its representing the moon as in a glass... Some give the same appellation to Muscovy-talc, from an opinion, that its brightness increases and diminishes with the moon.

2. *Min.* = SELENITE[1] 2.

1681 GREW *Musæum* III. §i. v. 309 A lump of the Talk-rock near Spiral..consisteth of broken pieces, like those of the Selenites. **1695** WOODWARD *Nat. Hist. Earth* IV. 172 A Body, that has the shape and appearance of a Diamond, may prove, upon Examination, to be nothing but Crystal, or Selenitis [(1713) Selenites]. *a* **1728** —— *Nat. Hist. Fossils* I. (1729) I. 73 A pretty large Piece of a Selenites. **1753** *Chambers' Cycl.* Suppl. s.v., *Selenites*,..the name of a large class of fossils. *Ibid.*, Of this class there are seven orders... The *selenitæ* of the first order are those composed of horizontal plates, and approaching to a rhomboidal form. **1820** *Gentl. Mag.* Apr. 308/2 Quarries of Heddington yield fine selenitæ.

selenitic (sɛlɪˈnɪtɪk), *a.*[1] Also 8 selenetic. [f. SELENITE[1] + -IC. Cf. F. *sélénitique.*] Of, pertaining to, resembling or containing selenite. †Of water: impregnated with sulphate of lime (cf. SELENITE[1] 2 b).

1756 P. BROWNE *Jamaica* (1789) 51 The Stalactite seems to be but a meer sparry, or selenetic matter. **1794** SCHMEISSER *Syst. Min.* I. 243 Selenitic-Spar. **1802** BEDDOES *Hygeia* VI. 66 Hard selenitic and calcareous waters. **1851** MANTELL *Petrifactions* ii. § I. 78 A remarkably fine group of selenitic crystals. **1889** CUNDILL *Dict. Explosives* 61 Selenitic Powder is a mixture of nitroglycerine with plaster of Paris.

seleˈnitic, *a.*[2] *rare.* [f. Gr. σεληνίτης, SELENITE[2] + -IC.] Of or pertaining to the moon; also (*nonce-use*) said of a flower which opens when the moon shines.

1863 R. F. BURTON *Abeokuta* I. 39 A large white flower, said to be selenitic, and opening only to the moon. **1882** OGILVIE, *Selenitic*, pertaining to the moon.

†**seleˈnitical**, *a. Obs.* [f. SELENITE[1] + -ICAL.] Resembling, containing, or composed of selenite.

1755 *Phil. Trans.* XLIX. 156 Their shells break with a selenitical appearance. **1799** W. TOOKE *View Russian Emp.* I. 113 Some few crystal-gypsum or selenitical nodules.

selenitiferous (sɛliːnɪˈtɪfərəs), *a.* [f. SELENITE *sb.*[1] + -FEROUS.] Containing selenite.

1891 in *Century Dict.*; and in later Dicts.

selenitish, *a. rare*[−1]. [f. SELENITE *sb.*[1] + -ISH[1].] Selenitic or somewhat selenitic.

1839 URE *Dict. Arts* 305 If the waters be selenitish, it would be a reason for adding a little alkali.

†**selenitous**, *a. Obs. rare*[−1]. [f. SELENITE *sb.*[1] + -OUS.] = SELENITIC *a.*[1]

1794 SULLIVAN *View Nat.* I. 319 A strongly impregnated selenitous water.

selenium (sɪˈliːnɪəm). *Chem.* [mod.L., f. Gr. σελήν-η moon: see -IUM. Cf. G. *selen.*

Named in 1818 by Berzelius, the discoverer (*Journal für Chemie u. Physik* XXIII. 316), who explains that the name was chosen to indicate the resemblance of the properties of the new element to those of tellurium.]

a. One of the rarer elements, closely resembling tellurium in properties, and, like that element, formerly classed among the metals, but now regarded as non-metallic. Symbol Se; atomic weight 79.

Like sulphur, to which it is in many respects analogous, it has several allotropic forms; one of these, still sometimes known as ***metallic selenium***, is a dark grey or black solid with metallic lustre.

An important property of selenium is that its electrical resistance is greatly decreased by exposure to light: hence its use in the photophone or radiophone of A. Graham Bell.

1818 tr. *Berzelius* in *Ann. Philos.* XI. 292 The analogy of tellurium has induced me to give it the name of selenium. **1826** HENRY *Elem. Chem.* I. 464 Phosphuret of Selenium. **1849** D. CAMPBELL *Inorg. Chem.* 61 Selenium when distilled is of a reddish-brown colour, when reduced to powder it is red; when fused in a mass, it is of a lead grey colour and metallic lustre. **1881** A. G. BELL *Sound by Radiant Energy* 23 But the selenium was very inconstant in its action.

b. *attrib.* as **selenium cell**, a photoconductive or photovoltaic cell containing selenium; **selenium eye** (see quot. 1893).

1880 A. G. BELL in *Jrnl. Franklin Inst.* Oct. 243 The resistance of selenium cells employed by former experimenters was measured in millions of ohms. **1893** SLOANE *Stand. Electr. Dict.*, *Selenium eye*, a model eye in which selenium in circuit with a battery and galvanometer takes the place of the retina of the human eye. **1929** [see PHOTOCONDUCTIVE *a.*]. **1946** *Nature* 20 July 88/1 In the early days of his training he [*sc.* J. L. Baird] devised an improved pattern of selenium cell, which led him to develop a crude form of television. **1977** J. HEDGECOE *Photographer's Handbk.* 32 Your meter may use a selenium cell which generates a minute current of electricity, measured on a galvanometer.

seleniuret (sɪˈliːnjʊərɛt). *Chem.* Now *rare.* Also †selenuret. [f. SELENI-UM + -URET.] A compound of selenium with hydrogen or a metal: now usually SELENIDE.

1818 tr. *Berzelius* in *Ann. Philos.* XI. 292 The selenuret of potassium dissolves in water without evolving any gas. *Ibid.* 293 The selenurets of barytes and of lime are also red. **1822** CLEAVELAND *Min. & Geol.* (ed. 2) II. 539 Cupreous Seleniuret of Silver. Eukairite. **1823** W. PHILLIPS *Introd. Min.* (ed. 3) 294 Seleniuret of silver and copper. **1869** RANKINE *Machine & Hand-tools* App. 60 Seleniurets of arsenic, antimony, lead, and other metals.

seleniuretted (sɪˈliːnjʊərɛtɪd), *a. Chem.* Now *rare.* Also †selenuret(t)ed. [Formed as prec. + -ED[1].] Combined with selenium. ***seleniuretted hydrogen***: a gaseous compound of hydrogen and selenium, SeH_2, formerly also called *hydroselenic* or *selenhydric acid*, and now *hydrogen selenide*.

1818 tr. *Berzelius* in *Ann. Philos.* XI. 292 If we pour diluted muriatic acid upon the selenuret of potassium, a selenuretted hydrogen gas is disengaged. **1826** HENRY *Elem. Chem.* II. 502 Selenureted hydrogen may be recognized by its odour. **1836** BRANDE *Chem.* (ed. 4) 530. **1947** *Electronic Engin.* XIX. 363/1 On exposure to a moist atmosphere, sulphuretted, seleniuretted and telluretted hydrogen can be detected.

seleno- *Chem.*: see SELENIO-.

selenocentric (sɪliːnəˈsɛntrɪk), *a.* [f. Gr. σελήνη moon + CENTRIC *a.*] Having relation to the centre of the moon or to the moon as a centre; as seen or estimated from the centre of the moon.

1852 HIND *Astron. Vocab.* 52. **1867–76** G. F. CHAMBERS *Astron.* 920. **1970** N. ARMSTRONG et al. *First on Moon* v. 118 On July 17 at 1300 Moscow time the probe was placed in a selenocentric orbit. **1973** *Nature* 2 Nov. 7/2 [They] have detected increases of up to 100% in the density of picogram particles, in this case in selenocentric space, by using microphone sensors on board the satellites.

selenod. [f. Gr. σελήν-η moon.] See OD[2] b.

selenodesy (sɛliːˈnɒdɪsɪ). *Astr.* [f. Gr. σελήν-η moon + -O, after GEODESY.] The study of the shape and features of the moon. Hence **selenoˈdetic** *a.*, of or pertaining to selenodesy.

1962 Z. KOPAL *Moon* p. ix, The contents of the present volume..have been divided into five parts: I. Rocket exploration of the moon... II. Selenodesy and mapping of the moon. **1962** D. W. G. ARTHUR in *Ibid.* 102 The simplest of the two major selenodetic problems is the determination of the Moon's geometrical figure. **1962** *Flight International* LXXXII. 251/1 Selenodetic measurements of the Earth-Moon distance. **1967** J. RÖSCH in Kopal & Goudas *Measure of Moon* 71 Our task in starting up Selenodesy is not to determine the shape of a fictitious surface, but simply to establish reference points on the surface of the Moon to which we can refer the positions of other points. **1977** R. W. KING et al. in J. D. Mulholland *Sci. Applications Lunar Laser Ranging* 51 (*heading*) Lunar dynamics and selenodesy.

selenodont (sɪˈliːnəʊdɒnt), *a.* and *sb.* [f. Gr. σελήν-η moon + ὀδοντ- tooth.] **a.** *adj.* Of molar teeth: Having crescentic ridges on the crowns. Also, having such teeth, of or pertaining to the *Selenodonta*. **b.** *sb.* A selenodont animal.

1883 FLOWER in *Encycl. Brit.* XV. 429/2 The grinding surfaces of the molar teeth either of a distinctly tubercular (bunodont) or of a crescentic (selenodont) form. *Ibid.* 430/1 The Selenodont Artiodactyles. **1891** FLOWER & LYDEKKER *Introd. Mammals* 294 These features being unknown in any other Selenodonts.

selenograph (sɪˈliːnəʊgrɑːf, -æ-). [f. Gr. σελήν-η moon + -GRAPH.] A photograph of a part of the surface of the moon.

1868 J. PHILLIPS in *Proc. Roy. Soc.* XVI. 232 With this excellent arrangement I was enabled to use photography very successfully, and to obtain selenographs 2 inches across in 5^s of time.

selenographer (sɛliːˈnɒgrəfə(r)). [f. SELENOGRAPH-Y + -ER[1].] One engaged in selenography.

1670 H. STUBBE *Plus Ultra* 32 [He] represents the ansulae of Saturn, differently from what Fontana and the Dantiscan Selenographers do write. *a* **1700** EVELYN *Diary* 28 Aug. 1655, He [Oughtred] believ'd the sunn to be a material fire, the moone a continent, as appears by the late Selenographers. **1795** *Phil. Trans.* LXXXV. 122 The.. selenographer Hevelius. **1881** PROCTOR *Poetry of Astron.* iv. 176 The astronomer Schmidt, a selenographer of selenographers.

selenographic (sɪliːnɒˈgræfɪk), *a.* [f. SELENOGRAPH-Y + -IC.] Belonging to selenography.

1675 SHERBURNE tr. *Manilius* Pref. 3 Of the Moon and of her Spots, whereunto we have added the Selenographick Schemes of Hevelius and Grimaldi. **1796** MORSE *Amer. Geog.* II. 663, 1647 the first Selenographick maps made by Hevelius. **1874** tr. *Jules Verne's Fur Country* (1881) 18 Results so interesting for selenographic science.

selenoˈgraphical, *a.* [Formed as prec. + -ICAL.] = SELENOGRAPHIC.

1669 FLAMSTEED in *Phil. Trans.* IV. 1107 Over what Spots of the Moon, the seeming way of the Star would pass, I do not here shew, because I dare not rely on our Selenographical Tables. **1876** NEISON *Moon* Pref. 9 In the final chapter a complete series of selenographical formulæ is given.

seleˈnographist. [f. SELENOGRAPH-Y + -IST.] A selenographer.

1864 in WEBSTER.

selenography (sɛliːˈnɒgrəfɪ). [ad. mod.L. *selēnographia* (Bacon *Nov. Org.* II. xxxix), f. Gr. σελήνη moon: see -GRAPHY.] **a.** A description of the moon's surface. **b.** The description and delineation of the moon's surface; the descriptive science relating to the moon, 'lunar geography'.

a. 1650 SIR T. BROWNE *Pseud. Ep.* VI. xiv. (ed. 2) 288 The learned Hevelius in his accurate Selenography, or description of the Moon. **1667** SPRAT *Hist. R. Soc.* 315 He has essay'd to make a true Selenography by measure. **1696** WALLIS *Acc. own Life* in *R. Brunne's Chron.* (1810) p. clxiii, We there discoursed of..the Inequalities and Selenography of the Moon, the several Phases of Venus and Mercury [etc.].

b. 1784 WESLEY *Wks.* (1872) XIII. 490 Some men have.. carried selenography to so great perfection, as to give us a complete map of the moon. **1852** HIND *Astron. Vocab.* 52 *Selenography*, the description and delineation of the surface of the moon. **1876** NEISON *Moon* Pref. 5 This work was undertaken with the view of promoting the study of Selenography.

selenology (sɛliːˈnɒlədʒɪ). [f. Gr. σελήν-η moon + -OLOGY.] The science relating to the moon; chiefly, the science of the movements and astronomical relations of the moon (or, occasionally, the science of the formation of the moon's crust, lunar 'geology'), in contradistinction to *selenography*. Hence **selenoˈlogical** *a.*, of or pertaining to selenology; so **selenoˈlogically** *adv.*; **seleˈnologist**, one versed in selenology.

1821 *Blackw. Mag.* IX. 85 The Welshmen are correct in their Selenology, except as to colour. **1860** J. BROWN *Horæ Subs.* Ser. II. *Let. to Cairus* (1861) 242 Mathematics, astronomy, and especially what may be called selenology, or the doctrine of the moon,..he knew more or less thoroughly. **1865** T. W. WEBB in *Intell. Observer* VIII. 374 We may distinguish, then, three clearly marked selenological epochs. **1868** LOCKYER *Guillemin's Heavens* (ed. 3) 166 Observations of the geologically or rather selenologically recent formations. **1881** W. R. BIRT in *Observatory* Feb. 48 Before we can obtain a clear insight into the operation of selenological forces we need a greatly extended topography of the moon's surface. **1890** *Nature* 2 Jan. 197/2 Neither is he the only selenologist who thinks that these crater-rings consist more or less of frozen water.

selenoscope (sɪˈliːnəʊskəʊp). *rare.* Also 7 *erron.* seleniscope. [f. Gr. σελήν-η moon + -SCOPE.] An instrument for observing the moon.

1651 R. CHILD in *Hartlib's Legacy* (1655) 70 The Selenoscope, which discovereth mountains in the Moon, divers Stars, and new Planets, never seen till our days. *Ibid.* 161 They are found by the Selnescope [sic] to increase and decrease as the Moon doth. **1660** R. H. *New Atlantis* II. 68 He next showed me a selenoscope to view the Moon. *a* **1700** EVELYN *Diary* 9 June 1653, Mr. Henshaw..presented me with a seleniscope. **1876** *Catal. Sci. Apparatus S. Kensington Mus.* 71 *Selenoscope*, to demonstrate the kinematic effects of the three hypotheses of the moon's motion.

seˌlenotoˈpography. *rare.* [f. Gr. σελήν-η moon + TOPOGRAPHY.] The topography of the moon. Hence **selenotopoˈgraphic, -ical** *adjs.*

1792 *Phil. Trans.* LXXXII. 335 According to my Selenotopographical Observations. *Ibid.* 337 Referring to my Selenotopographic Fragments for the proofs I there adduced of the real existence of a lunar atmosphere. **1795** *Ibid.* LXXXV. 147 *note*, I contrived it for my purpose of a selenotopography, and constructed it myself. **1864** T. W. Webb in *Intell. Observer* V. 194 Schröter introduced the use of the letters of the Roman and Greek alphabets for the minor details of his 'selenotopographical' plates.

selenotropic (siːliːnəʊˈtrɒpɪk), *a. Bot.* Also selene-, selenio-. [f. Gr. σελήν-η moon + -τροπος turning + -IC, after F. *sélénetropique* (sic: Ch. Musset, 1883).] Bending or turning under the influence of moonlight. So **seleˈnotropism** (Musset *sélénetropisme*), **seleˈnotropy**.

1883 *Nature* 15 Mar. 476/2 Selenetropism of plants, by M. Musset. **1883** *Times* 27 Mar. 3/4 Such movements of plants in moonlight M. Musset proposes to call selenetropic. [**1883** *Sci. Amer.* 27 Oct. 263/3 Selenotropic.] **1883** *Nat. Educ.* XXIV. No. 6. 6 The branches almost immediately became curved toward the moon... The author [C. Musset] applies the name selenotropy to these motions. **1884** *Hardwicke's Sci. Gossip* XX. 64 The stalks at once grew seleniotropic, that is, they turned towards and followed the moonlight.

selenuret(t)ed, obs. forms of SELENIURETTED.

selenyl (ˈsɛlɪnɪl). *Chem.* [f. SELEN-IUM + -YL.] A compound radical consisting of one atom of selenium and one of oxygen.

1910 *Encycl. Brit.* XXIV. 602/2.

seler, obs. var. CELURE, SALER, SELLER[2], SOLER; obs. f. CELLAR, SEALER *sb.*[1]

selerer, obs. form of CELLARER.

seleri, obs. form of CELERY.

1695 Ray in *Phil. Trans.* XIX. 635 The Root of Seleri, or Sweet Smallage. **1707** Sloane *Jamaica* I. Pref. 3.

selerite, -itie, selestial, obs. ff. CELERITY, CELESTIAL.

selette, obs. form of SELLETTE.

Seleucian (sɪˈl(j)uːsɪən), *a. rare.* [f. *Seleuc-us*: see SELEUCID *a.* + -IAN.] = SELEUCID *a.*

1715 Prideaux *Conn. O. & N.T.* I. VIII. (1718) 450 Which can be understood only of the Seleucian, or new Babylon, and not of the old. **1886** *Guide Exhib. Galleries Brit. Mus.* 42 Dated in the Seleucian and Arsacean eras (113–93 B.C.).

Seleucid (sɪˈl(j)uːsɪd), *sb.* and *a.* [f. L. *Seleucid-ēs*, Gr. Σελευκίδης descendant of Seleucus, f. Σέλευκος: see below.] **a.** *sb.* One of the Seleucidæ, or members of the dynasty founded by Seleucus Nicator (one of the generals of Alexander the Great) which reigned over Syria from 312 to 65 B.C., and subjected a great part of Western Asia. **b.** *adj.* Pertaining to the Seleucidæ.

1851 Conybeare & Howson *St. Paul* v. (1868) I. 133 'Seleucia by the Sea' was a place of great importance under the Seleucids and the Ptolemies. **1904** W. M. Ramsay *Lett. to Seven Ch.* xix. 254 Smyrna was struggling to maintain its freedom against the Seleucid power.

So **Seleucidan, -ean, -ian, -ic** *adjs.*, of or pertaining to the Seleucidæ; Seleucid.

Seleucidan, etc. *era*, an era usually reckoned as dating from 1st Sept. 312 B.C., formerly widely used in the East, and still used by Syrian Christians.

1803 [Gough] *Coins of Seleucidæ* Pref. 15 The Seleucidan Æra. **1849** *Smith's Dict. Grk. & Rom. Biog.* III. 776/1 The later Seleucidan kings. **1849** Otté tr. *Humboldt's Cosmos* II. 536 The traffic carried on in the Seleucidean kingdom was besides more an inland one. **1853** Horner tr. *Lepsius' Lett. fr. Egypt*, etc., *Chronol.* 455 The Seleucidic Era. **1882-3** *Schaff's Encycl. Relig. Knowl.* I. 752 The Christians of the East continued to use the Seleucidian era.

self (sɛlf), *pron.*, *a.*, and *sb.* Forms: 1- self; 1-4 silf, 1-3 sylf, seolf, (2 solf, suelf), 2-3 sulf, 5-7 selfe, 6 silfe; 5-6 selph, (6 sealf, seylffe, sill); 1 selfa, silfa, etc., 2 seolve, silve, 2-5 selve, 3 sulfe, sulve; 2-5 (*orig. oblique cases*) selven, (4 selvin, selfine, selwyn), 9 *dial.* sen, 6- *Sc.* sell. *Plural*: 1 selfe, silfe, etc., *wk.* selfan, etc., 2-5 selven, selve, (2 seolve), 5-6 selfs, (6 selfis, selfes), 9 *dial.* sens, 6- selves. [Com. Teut.: OE. *self* str., *selfa* wk., corresponds to OFris. *self* str., *selva* wk., OS. *self* str., *selbo* wk. (MLG. *sulf*, *self*, *silf*, *solf*), Du. *zelf*, wk. *-zelve*, *-zelfde*, OHG. *selp* str., *selbo* wk. (MHG. *selp*, *selbe*, mod.G. *selb*, *selbe*), ON. only str. *sialf-r* (Icel. *sjálfr*, Sw. *sjelv*, Norw. *sjøl*, *sjølv*, Da. *selv*), Goth. *silba* wk.:—OTeut. **selbo-*, *selbon-*. The ultimate etymology is obscure; many scholars regard the word as a compound of the pronominal stem *se-* (in Goth. *s-ik*, G. *sich*; cf. L. *sē*).

In Goth. and Scandinavian the primary sense (= L. *ipse*) is the only one that exists; the sense of 'same', found in Eng. and the other WGer. langs., was developed from this in collocations where the notion of identity implied by a demonstrative was emphasized by the additon of *self* (thus the OE. *se selfa man þe* may be rendered either 'the *very* man who' or 'the *same* man who').]

A. *pronoun* and *pronominal adj.* In the sense of the L. *ipse*. In concord with a sb. or pron., to indicate emphatically that the reference is to the person or thing mentioned and not, or not merely, to some other.

1. With sb. *Obs.* exc. *arch.*; superseded by the use of the 'emphatic pronouns', *himself*, *herself*, *itself*, *themselves*, or, after a def. art. or demonstrative, by (*the*, *this*, *that*) *very*. †**a.** following the sb. (immediately or with interposed words).

In OE. the strong and the weak declension were both common in this use, and traces of the twofold inflexion remain even in early mod.Eng. From the 12th c. the uninflected form (prob. apprehended as adv.) was often used after a sb. in an oblique case.

a **900** Cynewulf *Crist* 11 Nu is þam weorce þearf þæt se Cræftga cume and se Cyning sylfa and þonne ȝebete..hus under hrofe. *Ibid.* 134 Nu is rodera Weard, God sylfa mid us. *c* **1055** *Byrhtferth's Handboc* in *Anglia* VIII. 320 þæt we ȝearnion æt criste sylfum ece mede. *c* **1175** *Pater Noster* 234 in *Lamb. Hom.* 67 He fondede god self mid his wrenche. *c* **1175** *Lamb. Hom.* 107 We maȝen..habban us on ende þene eche wurðment a mid gode seoluan. *a* **1225** *Ancr. R.* 186 Ase dude ure Louerd sulf, & alle his haluwen. *a* **1225** *Leg. Kath.* 58 Euchan bi his euene, biforen Maxence seolf, wurðgede his maumez. *a* **1300** *Cursor M.* 11985 And o lame o þaa lakes selue Wit handes made he sparus tuelue. **1340** Hampole *Pr. Consc.* 236 Þe bygynnyng of alle þis proces Ryght knawyng of a man self es. **13..** *Gaw. & Gr. Knt.* 51 With all þe wele of þe worlde þay woned þer samen, þe most kyd knyȝtez vnder kryste seluen. **1377** Langl. *P. Pl.* B. I. 202 Loue is leche of lyf and nexte owre lorde selue. *c* **1450** *Godstow Reg.* 365 By the auctorite I-yove to them of the pope self. **1509** Fisher *Fun. Serm. Hen. VII*, Wks. (1876) 274 Tyl he came vnto the place selfe where he receyued the sacrament. **1532** More *Confut. Tindale* Wks. 473/2 Thys is the thing selfe that is in debate. **1541** Wyatt *Declar. to Privy Council* Wks. (1816) 282 In searching Mason's papers, the minute thereof was found; and after..the letter self came to his hands. **1548** Geste *Agst. Priv. Masse* H iv b, Dyd not christ selue alwaye pray to hys father. **1566** in Ellis *Orig. Lett.* Ser. I. II. 208 We fynde the same confirmed by the parties self that were their present. **1579** E. K. *Spenser's Sheph. Cal.* June 18 *gloss.*, This is..spoken of the Poete selfe.

b. Preceding the sb. (immediately or with interposed words). Now only *arch. rare.*

c **900** tr. *Bæda's Hist.* I. Introd. (1890) 26 Under þam sylfum norðdæle middanȝeardes. *a* **1000** *Elene* 69 Þa wearð on slæpe sylfum ætywed þam casere, þær he on corðre swæf. *a* **1250** *Owl & Night.* 746 (Jesus MS.) Ich graunti þat þu go to dome To-vore the sulve [*Cotton MS.* sulf] Pope of Rome. *a* **1300** *Cursor M.* 22597 Þe self angels [*Gött.* þe seluen angelis] sal quake vnqueme for dute of him þat all sal deme. *c* **1374** Chaucer *Boeth.* I. pr. i. (1868) 5 And when sche hef hir heued heyer sche perced[e] þe selue heuene. *c* **1375** *Sc. Leg. Saints* v. (*Johannes*) 508 Quhen sancte Iohne ..for selfe eld ves sa wery þat [etc.]. *c* **1375** Barbour *Bruce* VII. 126 (Edin. MS.) Thai persauit..That he wes the selwyn Robert King. **1387** Trevisa *Higden* (Rolls) VII. 151 Oþer elles oþere hadde possessioun, in so moche þat þe self offrynges were reft fro þe autters under naked swerdes. *c* **1430** *Syr Gener.* (Roxb.) 3857 Thurgh [Generides] shelde ..He smote it in to the sokett, That the Iren with the hawberk met Right ageyn the self brest. *c* **1450** *Myrr. our Ladye* 197 *Vere caritatis.* God ys the louer of very charite, and god is the selfe charyte. **1472-3** *Rolls of Parlt.* VI. 34/1 That the said copie of the said Recorde be taken, demed, and had for the self Recorde. *a* **1483** *Liber Niger Domus Edw. IV* in *Househ. Ord.* (1790) 61 Also they have oversyght for the Thesaurers partie in every office, bothe of the selfe stuffe, and the ministration, how it passith. **1526** *Pilgr. Perf.* (W. de W. 1531) 155 b, In theyr olde age before yᵉ houre of deth, or in the selfe poynt of deth. **1531** Elyot *Gov.* I. xxv. (1880) I. 267 *Discretio* in latine..as it is communely used, it is nat only like to Modestie, but it is the selfe Modestie. *a* **1569** Kingesmyll *Man's Est.* x. (1580) 61 Christ hath hereby approved hymselfe the true anointed, the self Saviour, and verie Jesus. **1610** Gwillim *Heraldry* I. viii. (1660) 46 If a man do perform any praiseworthy Action the self deed will sufficiently commend him though he hold his peace. *c* **1730** Ramsay *Address of Thanks* xii, Even sell K. T. that gart us ban, And eke that setting-dog his man. **1848** Lowell *Biglow Papers* Ser. I. ix. *ad fin.*, I confess to a satisfaction in the self act of preaching.

†**c.** (? As adv.: cf. Ger. *selbst.*) Used, uninflected, before an article or poss. pron. *Obs. rare.*

c **1250** *Gen. & Ex.* 1806 Wulde he non senwe siðen eten Self his kinde nile ðat wune forgeten. *Ibid.* 2610 God haued swilc fair-hed him geuen, ðat self ðe fon it leten liuen.

†**2.** With pers. pronoun in the nominative. *Obs.*; *rare* after OE.

c **897** K. Ælfred *Gregory's Past. C.* xvi. 104 Oft eac ȝebyreð ðonne se scrift onȝit ðæs costunga þe he him ondetteð ðæt he eac self bið mid ðæm ilcum ȝecostod. *c* **1000** *Ags. Gosp.* Luke xxiv. 39 Ic sylf hit eom. *c* **1000** *Ags. Ps.* lxvii. 4 Doþ siðfæt ðæs..rihtne ðe he sylfa astah, þam [etc.]. *a* **1175** *Cott. Hom.* 229 Ne michti hi alle hin acwelle ȝef he sylf nold. *a* **1300** *Cursor M.* 6096 In mining sal ye hald þis dai, Yee-self and your oxspring ai. *Ibid.* 2559 Þou wat child haue i self nan. *Ibid.* 19432 And siþen spak he o þair lagh, þat þai it cuth noght seluen knau. **1633** P. Fletcher *Pisc. Ecl.* IV. xx, Self did I see a swain not long ago.

3. Following a pron. in oblique case. *Obs.* exc. in HIMSELF, HERSELF, THEMSELVES. **a.** *refl.*

c **897** K. Ælfred *Gregory's Past. C.* xxxiii. 220 Ðurh þa we forlætað ðone anwald ure selfra. *c* **1175** *Lamb. Hom.* 95 Erest he scal hine seolfne wið sunnan isteoran, and seoððan his heorde. *c* **1200** *Vices & Virtues* 125 Bute ðu neme riht of ðe seluen of ðe misdedes ðe ðu mis-dest. *a* **1225** *Ancr. R.* 108 He seið bi him seluen,..'Et factus sum sicut homo non audiens'. *a* **1300** *Cursor M.* 335 For of him self he toke his euen. *Ibid.* 16653 Wepe yee noght for me, Bot on yur childer and on yow-self. *c* **1380** Wyclif *Sel. Wks.* I. 172 But oo firstnesse of love shulde we have to us silf, and to oure fadir and oure modir. *c* **1386** Chaucer *Wife's Prol.* 812 But atte laste..We fille acorded by vs seluen [*Camb. MS.* seluyn] two. *c* **1400** *Destr. Troy* 6322 He..louyt hym no lesse þen hym lefe seluyn. **1426** Lydg. *De Guil. Pilgr.* 7762 For to make the sylue strong. *c* **1460** Fortescue *Abs. & Lim. Mon.* xi. (1885) 135 Wherby we bith lerned þat it shal-not only be goode to owre prince, but also to vs selff, that he be well indowed. **1576** Fleming *Panopl. Epist.* 24 Wilt thou, Seruius, stay thee selfe.

b. Emphasizing a non-reflexive pron.

c **893** K. Ælfred *Oros.* III. xi. §5. 146 Þa sende Antigones hiene selfne [Neoptolemus] & his oþerne þeȝn Polipercon. *c* **1175** *Lamb. Hom.* 15 Eower lond ic wulle friþian and eow selfe meȝhan and bi-werian. *c* **1205** Lay. 493 Mine þralles i mire þeode me suluen þretiað. *a* **1300** *Floriz & Bl.* (Hausknecht) 550 þat he þe helpe in alle helve, Ase he wolde me selve. **1535** Coverdale *1 Macc.* viii. 7 How they discomfited greate Antiochus..: how they toke him self alyue.

†**c.** In agreement with a possessive genitive (expressed or implied by poss. pron.), the word may be rendered 'own'. Hence the use of the uninflected *self* in 16-17th c. for: Own, peculiar.

Beowulf 1115 Het ða hildeburh, at hnæfes ade hire selfre suna sweoloðe befæstan. **1516** *Will of R. Peke* 4 June, She wer fully agrede to for her sill parte, and they agreid to receyve for hir childes part. **1539** Cromwell in Merriman *Life & Lett.* (1902) II. 175 As he knoweth right well, who at his being here sawe her self visage. **1579** Spenser *Sheph. Cal.* Sept. 176 Colin clout I wene be his selfe boye. *c* **1580** Sidney *Ps.* xxxv, Let their sly witts unwares destruction gett Fall in self pitt, be caught in their own nett. **1585** T. Washington tr. *Nicholay's Voy.* IV. xxxi. 153 b, He forbad the often attempting of warres agaynst ones self party or enemies. *a* **1586** Sidney *Arcadia* I. (1622) 3 A thing which floated drawing neerer and neerer to the banke; but rather by the favourable working of the sea, then by any selfe industry. **1598** Chapman *Hero & L.* iv. 185 What her hart Did greatest hold in her selfe greatest part. **1601** R. Johnson *Kingd. & Commw.* (1603) 163 A people having many selfe fashions and strange kinds of behaviour differing from the rest. **1605** Shaks. *Macb.* V. viii. 70 His Fiend-like Queene; Who (as 'tis thought) by selfe and violent hands, Tooke off her life. **1632** Lithgow *Trav.* IV. 158 They Gormandize at their selfe pleasures. **1654** Earl Monm. tr. *Bentivoglio's Warrs Flanders* 316 He considered that many Towns in Picardy were under the self Forces of Spain.

†**4.** In OE. and ME., the nom. *self* in agreement with the subject of the sentence (sb. or pron.) was often preceded by the dative of a pronoun referring to the subject, used pleonastically (the so-called ethic dative); subsequently, *self* was often put in the dative, agreeing with the pers. pron. This use is now historically represented by certain uses of HIMSELF, HERSELF, THEMSELVES; some examples of *me self*, *thee self*, are given s.vv. MYSELF, THYSELF.

c **888** K. Ælfred *Boeth.* xxi, Hi..weorþaþ him selfe to nauhte. *c* **1175** *Lamb. Hom.* 35 Nis þas weorld nawiht ȝe hit iseoð eow seluen. *c* **1205** Lay. 3315 Vs selve we habbet cokes to quecchen to cuchene, vs sulue we habbet bermen & birles inowe. *Ibid.* 28484 Þa heo here seolf weore isunken in þe watere. *a* **1300** *K. Horn* 45 And þe selue riȝt anon Ne schaltu to dai henne gon. *c* **1380** *Sir Ferumb.* 2810 We ous self buþ feynt & pal for hungre & for þerst. *c* **1380** Wyclif *Sel. Wks.* II. 125 Pilat seide to hem, Tak ȝe him ȝou self, and do ȝe him on þe cross. *c* **1430** *Chev. Assigne* 20 Þey wente vp-on a walle ..Both þe kynge & þe qwene hem selfen to-gedere.

†**5.** Used *absol.* as independent pronoun (= he himself, I myself, etc.). After OE. almost exclusively with pleonastic dative of pronoun, a use now represented by HIMSELF 3.

Beowulf 895 Þæt he beahhordes brucan moste selfes dome. *a* **900** Cynewulf *Crist* 1115 Eall þis maȝon him sylfe ȝeseon þonne. *c* **1205** Lay. 5246 Al þa kinges þus duden swa heom self demmeden. *a* **1300** *Cursor M.* 26738 Hast noght þi scrift on þiskin wis, Bot ilk-a sin be self þou schau. **1585** Jas. VI in *Holinshed's Hist. Scot.* (1587) 445/2 A thing hurtfull to none, profitable for selfis, acceptable to God, and vise in the sight of the varld. **1616** B. Jonson *Volpone* I. ii. Song *Wks.* I. 454 Selues [*ed.* 1607 Themselues], and others merry-making.

†**6.** Used indefinitely (= *oneself*) in a proverb.

1546 Heywood *Prov.* I. viii. Wks. (1562) B iv b, For I did it my selfe: and selfe do, selfe haue. **1579** Gosson *Sch. Abuse* (Arb.) 46. **1707** J. Stevens tr. *Quevedo's Com. Wks.* (1709) 339.

7. In commercial use (hence *jocular* or *colloq.*) substituted for *myself*, or occas. for *himself*. *spec.* written on a cheque or counterfoil.

1758 Johnson *Idler* No. 33 ⁋21 Mr. H. and self agreed at parting to take a gentle ride. **1829** Lamb *Let. to Gillman* 30 Nov., He hath..served for self or substitute the greater parish offices. **1841** Thackeray *Gt. Hoggarty Diam.* vi, I am, dear Sirs, for self and partners, Yours most faithfully, Samuel Jackson. **1844** Dickens *Mart. Chuz.* xxvii, B wants a loan... B proposes self and two securities. B is accepted. Two securities give a bond. **1863** S. Hibberd in *Intell. Observ.* IV. 267 Self and friend took train..for Leatherhead. **1866** Crump *Banking* iv. 88 With the exception of those payable to 'self', drawn at the bank counter, or paid to an authorised person for the use of the drawer. **1873** D. G. Rossetti *Let.* 14 July (1967) III. 1192 If however you would prefer the cheque made out to *Self* as usual..I will send you another. **1894** Sir J. Astley *Fifty Yrs. Life* II. 31 As both self and wife were fond of seeing life, ..we decided a trip to Baden Baden would be a nice change for us. **1905** *Macm. Mag.* Dec. 107 Faro..much resembled the Self and Company still played by children. *a* **1911** *Mod.* (*Cheque*) Pay self or order, Ten Pounds. **1935** G. Heyer *Death in Stocks* vi. 74 He drew a cheque for a hundred pounds to self on Friday. **1967** C. Watson *Lonely Heart 4122* ii. 23 He turned back the counterfoils... The uppermost..was marked 'Self', a withdrawal of four hundred pounds.

B. *adj.*

I. = SAME (and in derived senses).

†**1.** = SAME *a.* 1-3. **a.** Preceded by dem. pron. or definite article. *Obs.*

c 900 tr. *Bæda's Hist.* iv. xxiii. (1890) 338 þa wæs in þære seolpan nihte, þætte [etc.]. *Ibid.* 340 Wæs in þæm seolfan mynstre sumu haligu nunne. c 1000 *Ags. Ps.* cvii. 10 [cviii. 11] Hwæt! þu eart se sylfa god, þe us synnige iu adrife fram dome. 1297 R. Glouc. (Rolls) 5318 Tueye batayles her after in þis sulfe ȝere Hii smite & at boþe þe heþene maystres were. c 1330 *Arth. & Merl.* 7396 (Kölbing) [They] helden hem a litel bi hest Vnder þe selue forest. c 1380 *Sir Ferumb.* 1997 þay schulleþ haue þe selue dome. a 1400 *Prymer* (1891) 47 We by sechith, þt by the sadnesse of that selue byleue we be ..defended of alle aduercetees. c 1420 *Lessons of Dirige* 183 in *26 Pol. Poems* 113 He..fleeþ as shadow,..Dwelleþ neuere in þe self stat of ouris. 1426 Lydg. *De Guil. Pilgr.* 3396 Ryht in the sylue wyse. c 1489 Caxton *Blanchardyn* xv. 51 Thenne the proude pucelle..vnderstode..that he was that self knyght that the kisse had taken of her. 1513 Douglas *Æneis* x. Prol. 31-2 The Son the self thing with the Fader is; The self substans the Haly Gaist, I wys. 1525 Tindale *N.T.* Prol., That selfe good thynge. c 1530 —— *Pathw. Script.* Wks. (1573) 378/1 In the Gene. iii. God sayth to the Serpent: I wil put hatred betwen thee and the woman, betwen thy seede and her seede, that selfe sede shall treade thy head vnder foote. 1530 Palsgr. Epist. 7 Instructour to your noble grace in this selfe tong. 1540 Brereton in *St. Papers Hen. VIII*, III. 206 The Satterday folowing I.. arryved at Tryme, whiche selffe day Occhonor invading thEnglishe pale, burnte Kyldare. 1563 *Homilies* II. *Comm. Pr. & Sacram.* 149 b, To pray commonly is for a multitude to aske one & the selfe thyng with one voyce [etc.]. 1581 J. Bell *Haddon's Answ. Osor.* 285 b, [He] was requited with the selfe trechery that he offered before. 1588 Shaks. *Tit. A.* iv. ii. 123 He is your brother Lords, sensibly fed Of that selfe blood that first gaue life to you. 1594 Carew *Huarte's Exam. Wits* (1616) 118 Of this selfe opinion with Plato, was a Spanish Gentleman; who [etc.]. c 1611 Chapman *Iliad* v. 379 Pluto sustaind no lesse By that selfe man, and by a shaft of equall bitternesse. 1632 Lithgow *Trav.* ix. 387, I neuer saw any of that selfe Nation, to begge bread.

b. With article omitted. *Obs.*; *rare* after OE.

c 1000 *Sax. Leechd.* II. 72 Wiþ swile ȝenim gate tyrdlu on scearpum ecede ȝesoden & on selfe wisan on ȝedon. c 1375 *Lay-Folks Mass-Bk.* (*MS.* B.) 563 On selue manere. 1599 Nashe *Lenten Stuff* 39 As he was troubled with the falling sicknesse, in his life time, in selfe manner it tooke him in his mounting vp to heauen.

c. Combined for emphasis with the synonymous *ilk*, *same*. Also strengthened by *very* prefixed. *Obs.* Cf. same *a.* 4 and selfsame.

a 1300 *Signs bef. Judgem.* 96 in *E.E.P.* (1862) 10 No no tre in erþ so fast..þat ne sal adun to-berst þilk silue dai er hit be niȝt. a 1300 *Cursor M.* 22948 O þat ilk seluin euen. 1338 R. Brunne *Chron.* (1810) 61 þat ilk self ȝere. 1426 Lydg. *De Guil. Pilgr.* 20934 The same sylue carpenter. c 1460 *Towneley Myst.* xxviii. 95 Thou grauntt vs for to se The self body and the same the which that died on tre. 1526 Tindale *Rom.* ii. 1 For thou that iudgest doest euen the same silfe thynges. 1543 *Necessary Doctr.* L j b, This coniunction..is the very selfe thing, whiche is signified..by [etc.]. 1606 Bryskett *Civ. Life* 80 Two gentlemen, subiect to the selfe and same lawes.

d. *one self*: one and the same. *Obs.*

1491 Caxton *Vitas Patr.* (W. de W. 1495) i. cviii. 135 a/2 He commaunded that in one selfe mesure & weighte all manere of marchaundyses sholde be solde. 1523 Ld. Berners *Froiss* I. Auth. Pref. 1 Albeit, that mortall folke are marueylously separated,..yet are they..compact togyder by thistographier, as it were, the dedes of one selfe cyte. 1561 T. Hoby tr. *Castiglione's Courtyer* iv. (1577) X iv b, And it maye be sayd, that Good and beautifull be after a sorte one selfe thing. 1598 Florio, *Germano*, a brother of one selfe father and mother. 1601 Shaks. *Twel. N.* i. i. 39. 1607 R. C[arew] tr. *Estienne's World of Wonders* 131 They will not quite despaire, that one selfe man should be a lawyer and a Christian. 1624 Quarles *Job Milit.* Med. xvii. N 3, Whirling like fire-balles in their restlesse spheares, At one selfe-instant mooving seuerall wayes. [1877 Tennyson *Harold* v. ii, Of one self-stock at first, Make them again one people—Norman, English; And English, Norman.]

†**2.** *absol.* With def. art. (The) same person or thing. *Obs.*

c 897 K. Ælfred *Gregory's Past. C.* xliv. 322 Ne laða ðærto no ðine friend,..ne ðine weleȝan neahȝeburas, ðylæs hie ðe don ðæt selfe. c 1000 Ælfric *Metr. Lives Saints* IV. 352 Nelle þu leng beon hohful be þinre dohter eufrosinan soðlice ic earme eom sio sylfe. 1390 Gower *Conf.* I. 84 He..is that selve of whom men speke, Which wol noght bowe er that he breke. a 1400-50 *Bk. Curtasye* 776 in *Babees Bk.* 325 3if þe baken mete be colde, as may byfalle, A gobet of þo self he sayes with-alle. 1423 Jas. I *Kingis Q.* clxi, A mantill..That furrit was with ermyn full quhite, Degoutit with the self In spottis blake. 1486 *Bk. St. Albans, Hunting* e i b, And when he hath in the toppe .iii. of the selue Then ye shall call hym trochid an hert of .xij. 1532 *Acc. Ld. High Treas. Scot.* (1905) VI. 76 Ane doublat with ane lang geit of the self.

3. a. Of a colour: The same throughout, uniform. (See also self-colour.) Often prefixed to adjs. denoting colour (sometimes hyphened), as ***self russet, self silver***. Cf. self-black.

1601 Holland *Pliny* xxxii. vii. II. 439 In a peece of selfe russet cloth (such as is made of blacke wooll as it came in the fleece from the sheepe). 1851 *B'ham & Midl. Gardeners' Mag.* May 71 A third [prize], to Mr. Sharp, for one [*sc.* seedling] named Purity, a self-white. 1898 *Ladies' Field* 6 Aug. 378/2 The chinchillas or self-silvers [i.e. cats]; the latter is undoubtedly the correct name... The self-silvers are a fine collection. 1905 *Daily Chron.* 12 July 3/2 The border carnation Miss Willmott, a beautiful self brick-red flower of a quite distinct shade. 1906 *Westm. Gaz.* 10 May 2/1 Not in one self-tint, not spotted, but in tiny squares.

b. Self-coloured.

1852 *Beck's Florist* 200 A stand of finely-grown Carnations..was disqualified, owing to its having a self petal. 1902 *Westm. Gaz.* 29 Mar. 4/3 A new variety of self carnation. 1930 R. A. Fisher *Genet. Theory Nat. Selection* vii. 165 In rats, the hooded (black and white) pattern is a simple recessive to the 'self' or 'solid' coloration. 1950 *Sun* (Baltimore) 7 Jan. 22/7 The 'self' pigeon..has a solid color while the 'barred' has a blue background with black bars across the wing.

4. Of whiskey: Not blended.

1904 *Dundee Advertiser* 20 Aug. 5 In the market for self-whiskies there has been a pronounced want of activity.

II. Senses related to the pronominal use.

5. a. Of a portion of an instrument: Of one piece with the instrument itself.

1888 Bell *Later Age of Stone* 19 The second is a solid tool with a self-handle and is well able to make holes in wood.

b. Of a trimming: Of the same material as the garment itself; *spec.* in ***self belt, -fabric***.

1904 *Daily Chron.* 3 May 8/2 A new..crêpe that is being shown..is striped with its own material, and the stripe has a knot a frequent intervals which..makes, as it were, a self-trimming. *Ibid.* 5 May 8/3 Finished with self-ruffles edged with narrow lace. 1960 *Times* 21 Jan. 14/4 Jackets had either let-in or low-placed self belts. 1961 *Guardian* 28 Feb. 7/4 Jacket caught at the hips by a self-fabric belt. 1969 *Sears Catal.* Spring/Summer 10 Shower-resistant coat features self-fabric yoke for added protection. 1979 *Daily Tel.* 13 Feb. 15/1 (Advt.), Soft shirt dress..—no waist seams and self belt.

6. Of a bow: Made all of one piece: in contradistinction to *backed*. Also in quasi-comb. (usually hyphened) ***self-lance, self-yew***, applied *attrib.* to designate a self bow made of lance or yew (also with ellipsis of *bow*).

1801 T. Roberts *Eng. Bowman* 135 Back'd bows..were deemed so much preferable to self-bows, that [etc.]. *Ibid. note*, Yet many excellent archers give the preference to the self-yew-bow. 1840 G. A. Hansard *Bk. Archery* 344 In selecting a bow, whether backed or self, the modern archer has little occasion to exercise critical acumen. 1897 *Encycl. Sport* I. 40/2 (Archery.) Bows are called 'Self' if made of one piece of wood, and 'Backed' if made of two or more strips of wood glued together. Self-bows are generally made of yew or lance, though the term as applied to those made of the former wood is misleading, as they are almost invariably spliced at the handle. Self-yew is the dearest bow made, self-lance the cheapest.

†**7.** *Mining.* Of a rock, etc.: Detached, of material different from its surroundings. *Obs.*

1747 Hooson *Miner's Dict.* Q 4, Many times a Vein will carry two Ribbs, and softness between them, and often self Lumps. 1824 Mander *Derbysh. Miners' Gloss.* 60 A self rock or stone that often lies in the middle of a vein so as to cut or divide it into two branches. 1829 Glover *Hist. Derby* I. 49 Large stones, rounded by attrition, are called bolders; but if they retain the original shape and angles of the block, they are called self-stones. 1855 Phillips *Geol.* Gloss., *Self-stone*, blocks of stone lying detached at, or not far below, the surface. A north of England term sometimes applied to solitary boulders = 'earth-fast'.

†**8.** Own, peculiar. (See A. 3 c.) *Obs.*

C. *sb.*

I. From the pronoun.

[This use originated in early ME., when *mi(n, þi(n, his self* (see myself, thyself, himself) began to be substituted for the two varieties of combinations of pers. pron. + *self* which were current in OE. (see A. 2-4).

The subst. use appears to have been developed chiefly from collocations in which the OE. masc. and neut. genitive *selfes* admitted of being taken as the genitive of a neuter sb. Thus in *his selfes, Godes selfes*, it was easy to interpret *selfes* as a sb. governing the preceding genitive, instead of as a pronominal adj. in concord with it. The same liability to change in the grammatical apprehension of the word existed also in the examples of the curious construction (shared by OE. with ON. and OHG.) by which a poss. pron. when followed by the genitive of *self* became assimilated in inflexion to that word, instead of retaining the form demanded by the syntax of the sentence: e.g. in *ic ontýne mínes* (for *mínne*) *sylfes múð*. (The same 'attraction' occurred in the fem., as in *minre selfre*, and in the plural, as *úrra selfra*; but this has no bearing on the origin of *self* sb.)

Another influence which contributed to the development of the sb. was that of ME. *her self*, in which *her*, originally dative, was coincident in form with the genitive.

Although the subst. use of the pronoun thus appears to have originated in morphological processes, it came to supply a need of expression which has been felt and variously supplied in some other langs.; cf., e.g. Ger. *selbst* sb., which is an application of *selbst* adv. (earlier *selbes*, orig. the genitive of the pron.).]

1. (The pronominal notion expressed subst.) **a.** Preceded by a possessive pronoun, with which it forms a combination serving as a reflexive or an emphatic personal pronoun. Often qualified by an adj., either emphasizing, as ***my own self, his very self***, or descriptive, as ***your dear self, her sweet self, our two selves***, etc.

For examples of *my, thy, her, our, your self* (*selves*), see myself, thyself, etc. The 16th c. use of *myself, thyself*, with a vb. in the 3rd person seems to belong more properly to the sb. than to the compound pron. (Cf. myself 4.) For *his self, their selves*, see himself, themselves.

c 1205 [see myself 1 β]. 12.. *Moral Ode* 15 (Egerton MS.) in *E.E.P.* (1862) 23 Ne beo þe leure þan þi [*older texts* þe] self þi mei ne þi moȝe [etc.]. a 1300 *E.E. Psalter* (Surtees) xxxv. 2 þe un-rightwis saide with tunge hisse, þat in his self noght gilt in isse. c 1400 *Rule of St. Benet* (verse) 577 Oure awn self we sal deny, And folow oure lord god al-myghty. c 1450 *Mirk's Festial* 4 As moche þonke I kan you for þat ȝe dydden to þe lest of myn, as ȝe hadden don hit to myn owne selfe. c 1475 *Rauf Coilȝear* 638 Gif thow will not seik him, my awin self sall. c 1530 Tindale *Pathw. Script.* Wks. (1573) 381/2 As a stone cast vp into the ayre commeth downe naturally of his owne selfe with all the violence and swyng of his owne wayght. 1587 W. Gifford in *Cath. Rec. Soc. Publ.* V. 143 Premised commendations to your good self & to the bulchen my cousin. c 1590 Greene *Fr. Bacon* x. 78 Give me but ten days' respite, and I will reply, Which or to whom myself affectionates. 1596 Spenser *F.Q.* vi. vii. 39 And eeke that angry foole..did with his smarting toole Oft whip her dainty selfe. 1601 Shaks. *Jul. C.* i. ii. 96 But for my single selfe, I had as liefe not be, as [etc.]. 1651 Stanhope in *Prestwich's Poems* To Author, But why translate, gild, hatch, why not appear Thy solid self. 1690 Norris *Beatitudes* (1692) 46 There are some men..that would see the whole World in Flames without any concern, were but their own little selves secure from the Ruin. 1732 Mandeville *Enq. Orig. Hon.* 39 There is nothing which he has so constantly before his eyes as his own dear self. 1737 Whiston *Josephus, Antiq.* xix. i. § 19 He lies now dead, as perishing by his own self. 1745 *Life Bamfylde-Moore Carew* 64 Entertaining them in a most florid Manner with the sovereign Virtues of his Pills, Plaisters, and Self. 1749 C. Wesley *Hymns, 'And have I measur'd'* xii, Till He his glorious Self reveals, The Veil is on my Heart. 1816 Scott *Antiq.* xxiv, We'll gang quietly about our job our twa sells, and naebody the wiser for't. 1824 Byron *Juan* xvi. ciii, Their hideous wives, their horrid selves and dresses. 1846 Tennyson *Literary Squabbles* iii, Who..strain to make an inch of room For their sweet selves. 1875 Jowett *Plato* (ed. 2) I. 233 If the discussion were confined to your two selves. 1884 C. F. Woolson in *Harper's Mag.* Feb. 375/2 The installment of our twelve selves in these..carriages.

b. Preceded by a sb. in the possessive, with which it forms a combination having the sense now expressed by the sb. + *himself, herself, itself*, etc., and formerly by the sb. + *self* in concord with it.

Self may be qualified by an adj. as in 1 a.

a 1300 *Cursor M.* 12248 A tregetur i hope he be, Or elles godds self [*later MSS.* god him self] es he. 1473 *Acc. Ld. High Treas. Scot.* I. 33 Deliuerit to the Qwenis selue be Andro Balfour. 1536 Wriothesley in *St. Papers Hen. VIII*, I. 490 His Grace..liketh both thordre therof, and the thinges self, excedingly wel. 1542 Udall *Erasm. Apoph.* 141 For that thei abused the kynges selfes. 1590 Spenser *F.Q.* iii. iii. 46 Ne shall the Saxons selves all peaceably Enioy the crowne. 1607 Cowell *Interpr.*, Purgation (*Purgatio*) is a cleering of a mans selfe from a crime, whereof he is probably and publiquely suspected. 1634 Milton *Comus* 375 And Wisdoms self Oft seeks to sweet retired Solitude. 1667 —— *P.L.* ix. 388 She..like a Wood-nymph..of Delia's Traine, Betook her to the Groves, but Delia's self In gate surpass'd. 1704 Pope *Windsor For.* 223 Not Neptune's self from all her streams receives A wealthier tribute than to thine he gives. 1785 Burns *Epist. to J. L——k* 1 Apr. viii, Yet crooning to a body's sel, Does weel eneugh. 1814 Scott *Ld. of Isles* v. iv, 'Tis Edith's self!—her speechless woe, Her form, her looks, the secret show! 1816 J. Wilson *City of Plague* i. i. 405 Though dark his brain It has, thou seest, an heavenly visitor That comfort brings when reason's self is gone. 1837 Carlyle *Fr. Rev.* II. i. i, Nay, Sire, were it not better you, your Majesty's self, took the children? 1855 Kingsley *Westw. Ho!* xvi, Elizabeth's self consecrated her solemnly. 1871 R. Ellis *Catullus* xliv. 21 Not me That read the volume—no, but him, The man's vain self.

†**c.** ***the self*** = itself. Chiefly *Sc. Obs.*

a 1340 Hampole *Psalter* iv. 6 þe offrand of rightwisnes is a sorowful gast, punyschand þe self for synne. c 1400 Maundev. (Roxb.) vii. 24 In Egipte er bot fewe castelles, for þe cuntree es strang ynogh of þe self. 1409 in *Exch. Rolls Scot.* IV. p. ccix, This endenture..purportis in the self and beris witnes that [etc.]. 1434 Misyn *Mending of Life* i. (1896) 107 For fayrnes soyne is lufyd, & qwhen it felis þe self lofyd, lightly it is chirischyd. 1475 in *3rd Rep. Hist. MSS. Comm.* 418/1 The dowme..is false, and rottyn in the self, be cause it is gyffyn expresse in the contrare of the cursse of comone lawe. 1492 *Rolls of Parlt.* VI. 446/2 It is a doubt, whedre, the said V mark, be parcell of the Manor of Haveryng, or a somme by the self, and no parcell of the said Manor. 1513 Douglas *Æneis* i. Pref. 119 Nocht for our toung is in the selfin scant. 1525 Sampson in Ellis *Orig. Lett.* Ser. iii. I. 355 And as concerning the interception off the lettirs they esteme it, Sir, for a very grevos matir, as well for the deade off the selff, as the rumor that schuld aryse off the sam to the enemies. 1526 *Pilgr. Perf.* (W. de W. 1531) 269 But this hye ioye and iubile of the spiryt..can not be expressed with tonge, as it is in the selfe, but the effect that it leueth behynde it sheweth..what it was. 1570 in *R. Bannatyne's Memor.* (1836) 56 Becaus I sie..my voce is not able to straicht the self vnto the earis of the multitud heir convenit, I wilbe content [etc.]. 1580 in *Sc. Bks. Discipl.* etc. (1621) 18 The whole Assembly of the Kirk..declares the same pretended office [of bishop]..unlawfull in the selfe. 1605 *His Majesty's Sp.* etc. E 4, To so hatefull and vnheard of inuention there can be no greater enemy than the selfe. c 1614 Mure *Dido & Æn.* i. 470 The subtle air..In solide substance did the self congeale.

d. Sc. ***the sell o' it***, itself. ***the sell o' ye***, yourself. ? *Obs.*

1818 Scott *Rob Roy* xxvi, The College didna get gude £600 a-year out o' bishops' Rents..nor yet a lease o' the Archbishoprick o' Glasgow the sell o't. 1818 —— *Hrt. Midl.* ix, I ken nae friend..that's been sae like a father to him as the sell o' ye, neibor Deans.

e. In generalized sense.

1826 Disraeli *Viv. Grey* i. ix, Self is the only person whom we know anything about.

2. *transf.* in various uses, †*esp.* a person whom one loves as oneself or is a counterpart of oneself (*obs.* exc. in ***other self, second self***: see second *a.*).

1605 *1st Pt. Jeronimo* ii. iv. 49 Welcome, my selfe of selfe. 1671 H. M. tr. *Erasm. Colloq.* 4 Heavens grant you a safe return. God keep thee my half self. a 1700 Ken *Hymnotheo* Poet. Wks. 1721 III. 115 But when the Babe breaks out into the Light, Soon as her little self is in her sight,..She feels a Mother's Bowels yearn within. 1763 C. Johnston *Reverie* II. 133 The tender connexions of nature, which, as it were, multiply a man into many selfs for the safety of each dear particular of whom, his anxiety is greater than for his own. 1771 H. Walpole *Vertue's Anecd. Paint.* (1786) III. 139 My dear heart and self and son Charles. 1827 Hood *Mids. Fairies* xliv, We shall not die nor disappear, But in these other selves ourselves succeed. 1858 Stanley *Life Arnold* I. iii. 89 Our 'great self', the school.

3. Chiefly *Philos.* That which in a person is really and intrinsically *he* (in contradistinction to what is adventitious); the ego (often identified with the soul or mind as opposed to the body); a permanent subject of successive and varying states of consciousness.

a **1674** TRAHERNE *Poet. Wks.* (1903) 49 A secret self I had enclos'd within, That was not bounded with my clothes or skin. **1682** SIR T. BROWNE *Chr. Mor.* I. §24 The noblest Digladiation is in the Theater of our selves. **1690** LOCKE *Hum. Und.* II. xxvii. §9 Since consciousness always accompanies thinking, and 'tis that, that makes every one be, what he calls self. *Ibid.* §17 Self is that conscious thinking thing, whatever Substance, made up of Spiritual, or Material, Simple, or Compounded, it matters not, which is sensible, or conscious of Pleasure and Pain,..and so is concern'd for it self, as far as that consciousness extends. **1713** BERKELEY *Hylas & P.* iii. Wks. 1871 I. 329, I, one and the same self, perceive both colours and sounds. **1862** SPENCER *First Princ.* I. iii. §20 (1875) 65 If, then, the object perceived is self, what is the subject that perceives? or if it is the true self which thinks, what other self can it be that is thought of? **1865** J. H. NEWMAN *Dream Ger. 5th Choir, Praise to the Holiest*, God's Presence and His very Self And Essence all-divine. **1865** MILL *Exam. Hamilton* 207 Reid seems to have imagined that if I myself am only a series of feelings, the proposition that I have any fellow-creatures, or that there are any selves except mine, is but words without a meaning. **1866** DK. ARGYLL *Reign of Law* i. (1867) 8 But these selves of ours do belong to Nature. **1871** MEREDITH *H. Richmond* lv, In reality the busy little creature within me, whom we call self, was digging pits for comfort to flow in, of any kind, in any form. **1877** E. R. CONDER *Bas. Faith* iv. 184 But Self does not come and go; it abides. Self, therefore, is not a phenomenon, nor yet a bundle of phenomena. **1899** *Allbutt's Syst. Med.* VIII. 267 Insanity has been already defined as defect or disorder of the process of adjustment of self to circumstances. *Ibid.* 288 So long as the 'self' is not implicated in what is done by the body, the self is not responsible and cannot justly be punished. **1909** CHESTERTON *Orthodoxy* iii. 63 You cannot call up any wilder vision than a city in which men ask themselves if they have any selves.

4. a. What one is at a particular time or in a particular aspect or relation; one's nature, character, or (sometimes) physical constitution or appearance, considered as different at different times. Chiefly with qualifying adj., (*one's*) *old*, *former*, *later self*.

1697 DRYDEN *Virg. Georg.* III. 160 In vain he burns..And in himself his former self requires. *a* **1711** KEN *Div. Love* Wks. (1838) 282 My duty of loving those best, which either in blood are nearest my natural self, or in grace nearest my Christian self. **1746** FRANCIS tr. *Horace, Epist.* I. x. 66 If e'r, forgetful of my former Self, I toil to raise unnecessary Pelf. **1841** C. FOX *Jrnl.* 30 Sept. (1972) 115 Dr. Calvert..was quite his old self, talking on his old subjects in his old way. **1858** O. W. HOLMES *Aut. Breakf.-t.* ix. (1859) 211 How pleasant it would be, if in another state of being we could have shapes like our former selves for playthings. **1910** 'MARK RUTHERFORD' *Pages fr. Jrnl.* (ed. 2) 268 The self of two hours before seemed to confront him. **1975** H. FLEETWOOD *Picture of Innocence* x. 177 You seem quite like your old self again.

b. An assemblage of characteristics and dispositions which may be conceived as constituting one of various conflicting personalities within a human being. ***better self***: the better part of one's nature.

1595 SPENSER *Amoretti* xlv. 3 And in my selfe, my inward selfe I meane, Most liuely lyke behold your semblant trew. *a* **1703** BURKITT *On N.T.* Mark xii. 34 Every man may, yea, ought to love himself: not his sinful self, but his natural self: especially his spiritual self, the new nature in him. **1820** KEATS *Lamia* 170 In self despite, Against his better self. **1849** SIR J. STEPHEN *Eccl. Biog.*, *I. Taylor* II. 389 So, indeed, resolved the Self inhabiting one of the phrenological hemispheres within me. But the resolution was ultimately reversed by the superior energy of the Self who reigned over the opposite hemisphere. **1866** G. MACDONALD *Ann Q. Neighb.* vii. (1878) 125 Whatever your lowest self, and not your best self may like. **1867** GOLDW. SMITH 3 *Eng. Statesmen* (1882) 45 Our nation..had to go through greater trials, and be thrown more upon its nobler self, before it could deserve victory. **1908** R. BAGOT *A. Cuthbert* x. 116 Sonia di San Vico was asking herself whether this were love. .. For the first time in her life that other self of hers gave no satisfactory reply.

5. One's personal welfare and interests as an object of concern; chiefly in bad sense, selfish or self-interested motives, selfishness.

a **1680** CHARNOCK *Attrib. God* (1682) 70 Self is the great Anti-Christ and Anti-God in the World. **1725** WATTS *Logic* II. iii. §3 Were it not for this Influence of Self and a Bigotry to our own Tenets, we could hardly imagine that so many.. wicked..Principles should pretend to support and defend themselves by the Gospel of Christ. **1782** MISS BURNEY *Cecilia* VIII. iii, But self will still predominate. **1842** TENNYSON *Locksley Hall* 34 Love..Smote the chord of Self, that, trembling, passed in music out of sight. **1855** KINGSLEY *Westw. Ho!* ii, One who had long since learned to have no self, and to live not only for her children, but in them. **1859** GEO. ELIOT *Adam Bede* liv, She's better than I am—there's less o' self in her, and pride. **1870** MOZLEY *Univ. Serm.* iii. (1877) 67 This respect to self and its ultimate good pertains to the very nobility of man's nature. **1906** CHARL. MANSFIELD *Girl & Gods* xix, Self is their god and Selfishness their religion.

II. From the adjective.

6. (Cf. B. 3 b.) **a.** A 'self-coloured' flower: esp. applied to carnations.

1852 G. W. JOHNSON *Cottage Gard. Dict.*, *Self*, a flower with petals of only one colour. **1869** *Contemp. Rev.* XI. 149 Some of her characters are too much what a florist would call 'selfs'—all one colour. **1892** *Garden* 27 Aug. 194/2 The majority of present-day kinds [of Carnations]—I allude chiefly to garden selfs—are..scentless.

b. Something (as an animal or garment) of a single colour.

1930 R. A. FISHER *Genet. Theory Nat. Selection* vii. 165 Rats of both selected lines were bred back to unselected selfs. **1978** *Lochaber News* 31 Mar. 2/1 (Advt.), 'Dereta' coats, superb collection of tweeds and selfs in a variety of fabrics, designs and colours.

7. A self bow. (See B. 6.)

1856 H. A. FORD *Archery* iii. 14 Ascham..mentions none other than selfs.

D. -self in compound pronouns. For the diverse grammatical character (partly adj., partly sb.) of this element in *myself*, *thyself*, *himself*, *herself*, *itself*, *ourselves*, *yourselves*, *themselves*, *oneself*, and for illustration of the emphatic and the reflexive functions of these words, see the several articles. Certain phraseological uses common to the whole group in their capacity of reflexive pronouns may conveniently be noticed here.

1. *to be* ——*self*: **a.** *colloq.* To be in (one's) normal condition of body or mind; to be in (its) accustomed state. Also ***to feel like*** ——***self***.

For other examples see HIMSELF 3 b, MYSELF 4 b, THEMSELVES 2 b.

1849 MACAULAY *Hist. Eng.* v. I. 644 The chief justice was all himself. His spirits rose higher and higher as the work went on. **1884** *Daily News* 23 May 5/3 Mr. Grace was all himself [at cricket].

b. To act according to one's true character, without hypocrisy or constraint.

1864 [see MYSELF 4]. **1896** 'M. FIELD' *Attila* I. 26 Only the courage seems impiety For just a girl to dare to be herself.

2. The refl. pron. assumes in certain contexts the sense: The normal condition (of the person or thing). So ***to come to*** ——***self*** (COME *v.* 45 h), ***to bring, restore to*** ——***self. out of*** ——***self*** (? now *rare*), †***from*** ——***self, beside*** ——***self*** (see BESIDE *prep.* 5 a): out of (one's) mind or senses, deranged.

a **1450** *Knt. de La Tour* iii. (1906) 6 And he was so sore afraied and aferde, that he ranne awaie as he had be oute of hym selff. *c* **1489** CAXTON *Blanchardyn* xii. 43 She fell doune from her ain beere as a woman from her self and in a swone. **1659** B. HARRIS *Parival's Iron Age* 17 France being.. restored to her self, as well by the help of forreigners, as of her Neighbours. **1727** SWIFT *Furth. Acc. E. Curll* Misc. 1732 III. 30, I never perceived he was out of himself, till that melancholy Day that he thought he was poison'd in a Glass of Sack. **1846** DIGBY *Broad Stone Hon.* II. *Tancredus* 301 A novice of the order of St. Francis being now almost out of himself, struggling with death cried out [etc.]. **1856** MISS YONGE *Daisy Chain* I. xix. (1879) 192 But Tom, who seemed fairly out of himself, would not stir.

3. *by* ——*self*: alone, without society; unaided; separately. See BY *prep.*

c **888** K. ÆLFRED *Boeth.* xxxv. §6 Ne mæȝ nan oðru ȝesceaft be him selfum bion. *a* **1300** *Cursor M.* 1714 Þe meke [beist] be þam ai tua and tua, Þe wild do be þam-self al-sua. *c* **1386** CHAUCER *Reeve's T.* 222 Noght from his owene bed ten foot or twelue His doghter hadde a bed al by hir selue Right in the same chambre by and by. **1448** in Willis & Clark *Cambridge* (1886) II. 8 All the bemes that lyen by hemself. *c* **1449** PECOCK *Repr.* v. xv. 564 Aȝens this..is maad a book by him silf clepid the Book of Faith. **1573** *Treas. Hid. Secrets* xiii, This wise you may make Marmalade of wardens, peares, apples &c..everyone by himself. **1581** G. PETTIE tr. *Guazzo's Civ. Conv.* I. (1586) 17 b, It is dailie seene that a man being by himselfe is fearefull, and being in companie, is couragious. **1610** SHAKS. *Temp.* I. ii. 221 The Kings sonne haue I landed by himself. **1711** ADDISON *Spect.* No. 12 ¶3, I am mistaken if he ventures to go to Bed by himself this Twelve-month. **1857** MRS. CARLYLE *Lett.* II. 308 Mr. C. dines all by himself at present, I merely looking on. **1889** SAINTSBURY *Ess. Eng. Lit.* (1891) 65 If Hogg in some lucky moment did really 'write it all by himself', as the children say.

self (sɛlf), *v.* [f. prec.] *trans.* To fertilize by means of pollen from the same plant; = SELF-FERTILIZE *v.*

1905 R. C. PUNNETT *Mendelism* 61 When this, the normal mode of fertilisation, takes place, the flower is said to be selfed. **1924** E. W. MACBRIDE *Study of Heredity* vi. 143 When the recessive green peas are sown they give rise to plants which, when 'selfed', bear only green peas. **1949** H. L. MENCKEN in Kirby & Woolf *Philologica* 316 So far I have heard of no verb made of what appears to be a pronoun save *to self*. **1970** *Watsonia* VIII. 142 Rousi selfed a number of plants.

Hence **selfed** (sɛlft) *ppl. a.*; **'selfing** *vbl. sb.*, fertilization in this manner (in quot. 1924: a plant grown from seed so derived).

1924 *Genetics* IX. 30 Two such selfings of plants in family J were grown. **1927** *Technical Bull. N.Y. State Agric. Exper. Station, Geneva* No. 127. 4 Four selfed varieties of P[*runus*] *salicina* gave no seed. **1942** *Jrnl. Genetics* XLIII. 312 Their doubly heterozygous progeny will on selfing produce a range of genotypes with phenotypic differences. **1953** *Heredity* VII. 185 This mating system occurs in plants which have an imperfect selfing mechanism. **1977** M. ALLAN *Darwin & his Flowers* xv. 256 Nine of the original selfed plants had died. **1978** *Nature* 2 Feb. 441/1 Experimental selfings and crossings each lead to similar and relatively high levels of fruit set.

self-, the word SELF used as a prefix [OE. *self-*, *sylf-*, ? occas. instr. *selfe-*, corresp. to OS. *self-*, MLG. *sulf-*, MDu. *self-* (Du. *zelf-*), OHG., MHG. *selb-*, *selp-* (Ger. *selb-*, also genitive *selbs-*, later *selbst-*), ON. *sialf-* (MSw. *sialf-*, also genitive *sialfs-*, Sw. *sjelf-*, Norw. *sjølv-*, Da. *selv-*), Goth. *silba-*] with reflexive meaning = 'oneself', 'itself' in various relations with the second element of the compound.

The basis of compounds falling under headings 1 and 2 (below) is normally a reflexive verbal phrase; thus, from 'to accuse oneself' is formed a series of formally related words, *self-accusation*, *self-accusatory*, *self-accusing*, *self-accused*, any of which may arise independently of the others.

In OE. the number of recorded compounds is 13, of which half exhibit the prefix in the objective relation. The only survivals of the OE. compounds in ME. are SELF-WILL and its cognates; these, together with the plant-name SELF-HEAL (which may also have been common Germanic) are the only representatives in that period of the prefix-formation. *Self-* first appears as a living formative element about the middle of the 16th cent., probably to a great extent by imitation or reminiscence of Greek compounds in αὐτο-. The number of *self-* compounds was greatly augmented towards the middle of the 17th cent., when many new words appeared in theological and philosophical writing, some of which had apparently a restricted currency of about 50 years (e.g. 1645–1690), while a large proportion became established and have a continuous history down to the present time. The latter, with the compounds formally related to them, are for the most part treated in this Dictionary as Main words, together with all such as require specific definition. With regard to the remainder, since the prefix is of unlimited application, no attempt has been made to represent with fullness the extent to which it has been employed either in early or in recent times, and in the present article only a typical selection is given from the hundreds of compounds for which evidence is forthcoming.

In the Elizabethan period the imperfect union of *self-* with the second element of the compound appears to be evident from the occasional correlation of the prefix with an adj., as *strange and self-abuse* (Shaks.), *wilful and self-murder* (Foxe); cf. *self and vain conceit* (Shaks.).

1. Compounds in which *self-* is in the objective relation to the second element: **a.** with nouns of action; as ***self-abandonment*** = abandonment by oneself of oneself, one's power, position, rights, desires, ambitions, or the like.

1901 'L. MALET' *Hist. Sir R. Calmady* I. ix. 74 Her mother love..had none of the sweet *self-abandon..which that earlier passion had. **1818** SCOTT *Br. Lamm.* xvii, The.. generous *self-abandonment with which the Master of Ravenswood renounced his feudal enmity. **1958** R. KNOX *Priestly Life* ix. 96 Self-abandonment has been preached by writers of undoubted orthodoxy. **1690** NORRIS *Beatitudes* (1692) 23 To descend into the lowest Abyss of *Self-abdication. *a* **1763** *Mem. G. Psalmanazar* (1764) 21 The duties of self-denial, *self-abhorrence, fasting. **1750** RICHARDSON *Let.* 29 Mar. (1964) 157 The place allows the latter [*sc.* conversationalists] to sit far enough from the [card-] tables not to be interrupted with remarks, blames, *self-acquittals, of the engaged. **1892** 'MARK TWAIN' *Amer. Claimant* xiv. 132 You can't get the best of all verdicts, self-acquittal. **1848** J. S. MILL *Pol. Econ.* I. II. xi. 406 Population had exercised its power of *self-adjustment. **1962** A. BATTERSBY *Guide to Stock Control* v. 51 This capacity for self-adjustment is a necessary part of *any* practical control system. **1606** SHAKS. *Tr. & Cr.* II. iii. 176 With-out.. respect of any, In will peculiar, and in *selfe admission. **1806** BYRON *On a Distant view of Harrow* vi, Fired by loud plaudits and *self-adulation, I regarded myself as a Garrick revived. **1707** NORRIS *Treat. Hum.* v. 205 To accomplish this *self-advancement. **1840** J. S. MILL in *Edin. Rev.* LXXII. 27 What is saved in the workmanship may be more profitably expended in *self-advertisement. **1891** Self-advertisement [see SELF-CENTREDNESS]. **1854** GEO. ELIOT tr. *Feuerbach's Essence Christianity* iii. 45 The exclusive *self-affirmation of the human nature. **1924** W. B. SELBIE *Psychol. Relig.* 53 That desire for..self-affirmation..is so characteristic of man at all stages of his development. **1979** *Dædalus* Summer 92 We are thrown back on our own truth and to the act of self-affirmation that constitutes our personal identity. **1842** MANNING *Serm.* xx. (1848) I. 305 Fasting, and *self-affliction. **1799** *Monthly Rev.* XXX. 228 That the system of this prince is founded on views of *self-aggrandizement. **1937** *Discovery* July 225/2 A Board of Directors seeking only self-aggrandisement. **1716** POPE *Wks.* (1751) I. Pref. p. iv, The agreeable power of *self-amusement when a man is idle or alone. **1819** SHELLEY *Cenci* II. ii, Such *self-anatomy shall teach the will Dangerous secrets. **1764** GOLDSM. *Trav.* 280 Nor weighs the solid worth of *self-applause. **1856** GROTE *Greece* II. xcvi. XII. 518 This song is curious, as..affording a measure of their *self-appreciation. **1751** EARL ORRERY *Rem. Swift* ix. (1752) 73 With the smiles of *self-approbation upon her equals. **1863** A. BLOMFIELD *Mem. C. J. Blomfield* II. viii. 173 Had he been given to self-approbation, [he] might have claimed no small part of the credit. **1812** CRABBE *Tales* xix. 166 He began to feel Some *self-approval on his bosom steal. **1857** GEO. ELIOT *Ess.* (1884) 37 The *self-betrayal that runs through all his works. **1931** G. F. STOUT *Mind & Matter* 174 Each blindly strives towards its own self-maintenance and *self-betterment. **1977** A. GIDDENS *Stud. in Social & Polit. Theory* i. 39 He criticizes Comte along with Spencer for..treating the impulse to self-betterment as if it were a general cause of the evolution of society. *a* **1711**

Ken *Preparatives* Poet. Wks. IV. 52 Confusion, Terrour, Trembling, Shame, And fierce *Self-blame. **1934** R. Campbell *Broken Record* vii. 161 Amongst the average English literary men, it is usual for them to go soft at thirty (the moral *self-castration of the exoletus). **1845** Maurice in *Encycl. Metrop.* II. 615/2 To a first cause we necessarily attribute *self Causation. **1950** R. Ames in *Science & Society* XIV. 195 The obvious need of the oppressed..for *self-censorship of his social ideas. **1604** Shaks. *Oth.* II. iii. 202 Vnlesse *selfe-charitie be sometimes a vice. **1834** *Tracts for Times* No. 21 p. 1 In reward for his *self-chastisements. **1835** James *Gipsy* xix, With the common *self cheatery of fear, she loved not to give her apprehensions voice. **1848** Poe *Eureka* Wks. 1865 II. 131 The finest quality of Thought is its *self-cognizance. **1583** Lyly in T. Watson *Poems* (Arb.) 29 Your *selfe commendations. **1779** Johnson *L.P., Dryden* (1868) 156 His [*sc.* Dryden's] self-commendations. **1904** K. C. Thurston *John Chilcote* xi. 119 He had..a feeling of bitter *self-commiseration that for the moment outweighed all other considerations. **1862** G. P. Marsh *Eng. Lang.* x. 161 A cautious desire of avoiding embarrassing *self-committals. **1605** Shaks. *Macb.* I. ii. 55 Till that Bellona's Bridegroome..Confronted him with *selfe-comparisons, Point against Point. **1734** Watts *Reliq. Juv.* (1789) 104 A vain self-comparison with creatures. **1909** W. James *Pluralistic Universe* i. 36 It may be a supreme reaction of the universe upon itself by which it rises to *self-comprehension. **1935** *Mind* XLIV. 94 The Delphic Γνῶθι σεαυτὸν..counsels self-knowledge *versus* his [*sc.* Nietzsche's] and every Power-Man's need for *self-concealment. **1963** Auden *Dyer's Hand* 109 A capacity for self-disclosure implies an equal capacity for self-concealment. **1885** W. James *Lit. Remains H. James* 19 Society is the same Creator, with the nothingness saved, determined to transparency and *self-confession. **1923** F. G. Ellerton *Let.* 4 Nov. in *John Bailey* (1935) 236, I take it that the *pargoletta* passage is of the nature of a self-confession on Dante's part. **1961** *New Statesman* 23 June 1010/3 'Mellowness' becomes a means of avoiding the self-confrontations he says he has funked all his life. *a* **1711** Ken *Urania* Poet. Wks. IV. 471 She to *Self-conquest me dispos'd. **1862** Lytton *Str. Story* I. 255 Whenever it schemed or aimed at the animal *self-conservation, which now made its master-impulse. **1883** F. H. Bradley *Logic* III. I. vi. 450 Synthesis..would not force its parts into violent conjunctions, but, itself in each, by the loss of *self-constraint would embrace its own fulfilment. **1953** D. F. Pocock tr. *Durkheim's Sociol. & Philos.* ii. 36 The act..cannot be accomplished without effort and self-constraint. **1594** Southwell *Marie Magd. Fvnerall T.* 80 A submitted soul..the deeper it sinketh in a *self contempt [etc.]. **1842** Tennyson *Locksley* 96 Perish in thy self-contempt! **1653** H. More *Antid. Ath.* I. iv. (1712) 15, I conceive the intire Idea of a Spirit..to consist of..Self-penetration, Self-motion, *Self-contraction. **1710** Norris *Chr. Prud.* v. 238 Repentance is an act of *Self-correction. **1965** *Math. in Biol. & Med.* (Med. Res. Council) III. 85 The use of computers in diagnosis will need provision for..*self-correction by new data, and for questioning unusual or missed signs. **1959** E. Pulgram *Introd. Spectrogr. Speech* 7 Switching from one linguistic code to another is conducive to *self-critique. **1897** W. J. Locke *Derelicts* II. xxiii. 413 The tragic futility of such *self-crucifixion. **1858** J. Martineau *Stud. Christ.* 333 The palsy of will, the incapacity of *self-cure. *a* **1711** Ken *Hymnarium* Poet. Wks. II. 86 Themselves must their own *Self-damnation rue. *a* **1711** —— *Hymns Festiv.* ibid. I. 359 Of God offended, the sad Thought Deep *Self-debasement wrought. **1695** Rokeby *Mem.* 15 Sept. (Surtees) 56 This covenant and *selfe-dedication was..renewed by me. **1943** J. S. Huxley *Evolutionary Ethics* 67 The desire for self-dedication..should be available to society's common pool. **1957** M. J. Huntingdon in R. K. Merton *Student-Physician* 181 First-year students..think of each other primarily as students. This is reflected in their *self-definitions. **1980** S. Brett *Dead Side of Mike* ii. 19 Definition, and particularly self-definition is very important to me as an artist. **1903** 'Mark Twain' in *N. Amer. Rev.* Apr. 510 She..has carried *self-deification to a length which has not before been ventured in ages. **1962** E. Snow *Other Side of River* xvii. 122 Chiang made a fair start toward self-deification. **1698** Norris *Pract. Disc.* (1707) IV. 147 Humility and *self-dejection. **1935** T. S. Eliot *Murder in Cathedral* ii. 66 Dominated by the lust of *self-demolition. **1924** W. Holtby *Crowded Street* xxxv. 260 Don't you think that this *self-deprecation of yours was a little like cowardice? **1977** A. Giddens *Stud. in Social & Polit. Theory* ix. 307 Suicide represents an extreme on a range of possible forms of self-aggression, which extends from relatively minor forms such as verbal self-deprecation to actual self-destruction. **1827** Hare *Guesses* Ser. II. (1873) 503 *Self-depreciation is not humility. **1902** W. James *Var. Relig. Exper.* xvi. 415 In spite of their repudiation of articulate *self-description, mystical states in general assert a pretty distinct theoretic drift. **1978** J. Dunn in Hookway & Pettit *Action & Interpretation* 157 Two main difficulties follow from this centrality of the human capacity for self-description in specifying the field of the sciences of man. **1796** F. Burney *Camilla* V. 454 Thy afflicting, however blamable *self-desertion. **1823** Lamb *Elia* II. *Stage Illusion*, The imbecility, helplessness, and utter self-desertion [of the coward]. **1817** Coleridge *Biog. Lit.* I. xii. 275 Intelligence is a *self-development. **1895** W. J. Locke *At Gate of Samaria* i. 7 She read books with the eagerness only exhibited by the young girl craving for self-development. **1977** Warren & Ponse in Douglas & Johnson *Existential Sociol.* x. 285 The Goffmanic masked self..comes into play when the audience is..to be manipulated rather than for such motives as self-development, [etc.]. **1660** Boyle *New Exp. Phys. Mech.* i. 23 [Hairs] endow'd with a Power..of *Self-Dilatation. **1663** Power *Exper. Philos.* II. 102 To fill up the aerial interstices (which must needs be considerable in so great a *self-dilation). **1798** R. Watson *Addr. People Gt. Brit.* 29 The physical strength of the bulk of a nation is irresistible, but it is incapable of *self-direction. **1880** J. Caird *Introd. Philos. Relig.* ix. 285 We cannot, if we would effect any such..forced *self diremption. **1699** Shaftesb. *Charac., Inq. conc. Virtue* II. II. §1 The more Contradiction and *Self-disapprobation he must incur. **1876** Geo. Eliot *Dan. Der.* lvi, That *self-disapproval which had been the awakening of a new life within her. **1796** Ld. Glenbervie *Diary* 15 Oct. (1928) I. 87 Every young person..should be conducted to form himself to such habits of *self-discipline. **1838** Pusey *Let. to B. Harrison* 13 Aug., His careful self-discipline is..calculated in this self-indulgent age to do much immediate good. **1946** *Nature* 27 July 113/1 The man who pursues truth for its own sake and studies science in an impersonal way, with rigorous self-discipline, is really showing his belief in a religion and is taking up a religious attitude. **1866** J. Martineau *Ess.* I. 191 Here you deny the power of *self-disclosure. **1655** Fuller *Ch. Hist.* I. i. §1 Called Picti, from their *self-discoloration. **1965** J. A. Michener *Source* 532 The Arabs arrived when they were strongest, in the throbbing flush of *self-discovery and unification. **1709** Shaftesb. *Charac., Freed. Wit* IV. §1 An alternate Disquiet and *Self-dislike. **1795–1814** Wordsw. *Excurs.* IV. 475 Inward *self-disparagement. **1744** Birch *Life of Boyle* 41 Nothing but the forbiddenness of *self-dispatch hindered his acting it. **1838** J. S. Mill in *Westm. Rev.* Apr. 7 M. de Vigny,..a man..of a rare simplicity of heart, and freedom from egotism and *self-display. **1885** *Manch. Exam.* 12 Jan. 6/2 Self-bedizenment is one of the forms of self-display. **1652** J. Wright tr. *Camus' Nat. Paradox* IV. 195 Beeing in full capacity of Understanding and *Self-disposall. *a* **1885** G. M. Hopkins *Poems* (1918) 78 One part, Reason, selfdisposal, choice of better or worse way, Is corpse now, cannot change. **1795–1814** Wordsw. *Excurs.* IV. 475 There is a luxury in *self-dispraise. **1677** Gale *Crt. Gentiles* IV. 209 What more potent principe of *self-dissolution is there than Division? *a* **1586** Sidney *Arcadia* v. (1622) 449 Till it..runne it selfe vpon the rockes of *selfe-diuision. **1857** Gosse *Omphalos* vii. 177 The whole of this immense structure [a tree] originated in a single cell, which, by repeated acts of self-division..has gradually built up the mass. **1933** *Week-end Rev.* 11 Feb. 151/1 Like Hamlet, he had an incurable habit of *self-dramatization. **1959** *Encounter* July 66/2 It was not so much insincerity as self-dramatisation. **1817** Coleridge *Biog. Lit.* I. xii. 268 A perpetual *self-duplication of one and the same power into object and subject. **1953** J. S. Huxley *Evol. in Action* i. 16 They [*sc.* the chromosomes] have divided longitudinally after self-duplication. **1831** J. S. Mill *Let.* 22 Oct. (1910) I. 8 The only thing which I can usefully do at present,..is to work out..principles of morals, government, law, education, above all *self-education. **1846** Lytton *Lucretia* II. i, He [*sc.* a poet] must employ his intellect, and his self-education must be large and comprehensive. **1664** H. More *Myst. Iniq.* II. xvii. 435 The Impious *Self-elation of the Bishop of Rome. **1844** W. H. Mill *Serm. Tempt. Christ* v. 133 The grounds of self-elation..were..the revelations with which he had been favoured by God. **1745** J. Mason *Self-Knowl.* I. viii. (1853) 60 He must have been a great stranger indeed to the Business of *Self-Employment. **1976** *Times* 13 Aug. 13/7 In the poorest parts of the country..self-employment is frequently the only manner in which a living income can be put together. **1649** Milton *Eikon.* xv. 144 His *self Encomiums. **1699** Shaftesb. *Charac., Inq. conc. Virtue* II. I. ad fin., To have the chief Means and Power of *Self-Enjoyment. **1870** D. G. Rossetti *Let.* 7 Nov. (1965) II. 914 That sense of the poet's self-enjoyment which is indispensable to the enjoyment of the reader. **1960** H. Read *Forms of Things Unknown* III. ix. 149 No explanation of art as 'objectified self-enjoyment'..can account for the facts of art history. **1920** B. Russell *Pract. & Theory Bolshevism* II. i. 127 *Self-enrichment seemed the natural aim of a man's political actions. **1710** Shaftesb. *Advice to Author* I. § 2 Neither Lover, Author, Mystick, or Conjuror,..can..be intitl'd to a Share in this *Self-entertainment. **1683** J. Corbet *Free Actions* II. 19 And that the Power in Man is not brought into act, it is for want of *Self-excitation. **1884** *Leeds Merc.* 30 Apr. 4/6 Her *self-exclusion from that great movement. **1859** Geo. Eliot *Adam Bede* xxvii, All screening *self-excuse..forsook him. **1939** A. Huxley *After Many a Summer* I. ii. 24 Jeremy made his mannequin's gesture of apologetic *self-exhibition. **1939** *Mind.* XLVIII. 238 He sees that the root motive of mysticism is *self-expansion—though he does not use this expression. **1839** De Quincey *Wordsworth* Wks. 1862 II. 182 Read..of the *self-expatriation..as a measure of despair on the part of myriads. **1611** Shaks. *Cymb.* III. iv. 8 A thing perplex'd Beyond *self-explication. **1742** Young *Nt. Th.* VII. 152 Why beats thy bosom with illustrious dreams Of *self-exposure, laudable, and great? **1921** D. H. Lawrence *Tortoises* 40 Doomed to partiality,..Want, Self-exposure, hard humiliation, need to add himself on to her. **1979** J. Rathbone *Euro-Killers* ii. 22 Neither man was prepared to risk possible self-exposure by offering his ideas. **1892** *Nation* 7 Apr. 263/2 This doctrine of unbounded self-indulgence—or, as his [Walt Whitman's] admirers would prefer to call it, *self-expression. **1846** Lytton *Lucretia* II. xiv, He had to listen..to her haughty *self-felicitations. *a* **1845** Barham *Ingol. Leg.* Ser. III. *Brothers of Birchington* x, Oh, such a knout!! For his *self-flagellations. **1624** Wotton *Archit.* II. 82 Every Mans proper Mansion House and Home, being..the Seate of *Selfe fruition. **1936** *Mind* XLV. 242 He affirms the awareness of God to be 'rooted in' the human interest of *self-fulfilment. **1981** R. Barnard *Sheer Torture* x. 109 Cultivating your ego, aiming at total self-fulfilment, doing your own thing. **1950** *Essays & Studies* III. 37 Everything in his poetry goes to suggest that it was created..by a largely spontaneous..process of *self-generation. **1677** Gilpin *Dæmonol.* III. xx. 169 It may..be..for themselves that they work, in a *self-gratification of their natural Zeal for their way. **1859** R. F. Burton *Centr. Afr.* in *Jrnl. Geogr. Soc.* XXIX. 330 His egotism renders him parsimonious even in self gratification. **1634** Bp. Hall *Occas. Medit.* xxxix, A *selfe-humiliation. **1848** Thackeray *Van. Fair* l, That timorous debasement and self-humiliation of a woman. **1817** Lady Morgan *France* III. (1818) I. 308 The ready *self-immolation of Madame La Valette. **1845** Stocqueler *Handbk. Brit. India* (1854) 74 The suttee, or self-immolation of widows upon the funeral pile. **1898** G. B. Shaw *Perfect Wagnerite* 95 Her self immolation on the pyre. **1961** D. G. James *Matt. Arnold* iii. 57 The omission of it [*sc.* *Empedocles*] from the 1853 volume..was a fine piece of self-immolation. **1850** Robertson *Serm.* Ser. III. vii. (1853) 100 Creation itself is sacrifice—the *self-impartation of the divine Being. **1836–9** *Todd's Cycl. Anat.* II. 411/2 The process of copulation..does more than stimulate each individual to *self-impregnation. **1911** *U.S. Reports* (U.S. Supreme Court) CCXXI. 388 The clear and simple directness of the privilege against *self-incrimination. **1977** 'E. McBain' *Long Time no See* xv. 267 You are warned of your right to counsel and your privilege against self-incrimination. *a* **1711** Ken *Christophil* Poet. Wks. I. 462 Honours in him no *Self-inflations raise. **1898** *Syd. Soc. Lex., Self-inflation*, a method of rendering one's self buoyant in water when in danger of drowning. **1948** *Commentary* Nov. 417/2 Intelligence, humor, and charm is often humiliatingly exploited..as entertainment and *self-ingratiation. **1963** *Times* 9 Feb. 4/2 The pallid self-ingratiation of Sally Logan's performance. **1699** Shaftesb. *Charac., Inq. conc. Virtue* II. II. §1 Nor are the greatest Favourites of Fortune exempted from this Task of *Self-Inspection. *a* **1854** J. S. Mill *Draft Autobiogr.* (1961) 122 Let..your scrutiny, your *self interrogation exhaust themselves on that. **1870** J. H. Newman *Gram. Assent* II. vii. 195 That palpitating *self-interrogation. **1873** Hamerton *Intell. Life* II. i. 44 That the reading of poetry..was clearly *self-intoxication. **1818** Scott *Br. Lamm.* x, I am obliged to you..for breaking the ice at once, where circumstances..rendered *self-introduction peculiarly awkward. **1754** Richardson *Grandison* VI. 68 We then endeavoured to recollect the words of his *self-invitation hither. **1805** Jane Austen *Let.* 24 Aug. (1952) 162, I defy her to accept this self-invitation of mine, unless it be really what perfectly suits her. **1963** *English Studies* XLIV. 144 Here, however, he will not allow himself to feel the *self-laceration in the final stanzas of that canto. **1853** C. Bronte *Let.* in Gaskell *Life* (1857) II. 287 No charge of *self-laudation can touch her. **1977** *Jrnl. Protozool.* XXIV. 9/2 Pattern formation by *self-linkage. **1656** Owen *Mortif. Sin* xiv. (1668) 170 The rigidest Means of *self-maceration. *a* **1866** J. Grote *Exam. Utilitarian Philos.* (1870) vi. 116 Good *self-management his highest aim. **1977** Warren & Ponse in Douglas & Johnson *Existential Sociol.* x. 277 There is a difference in degree between the problems and self-management of gays and most other people. **1949** M. Mead *Male & Female* x. 216 The female child's genitals are less exposed..to *self-manipulation. **1964** E. H. Mizruchi in I. L. Horowitz *New Sociol.* 257 Mental self-manipulation appears to be characteristic of the assembly-line work process. *a* **1680** Butler *Char., Obstinate Man* (1908) 177 He will rather suffer *Self-Martyrdom than part with the least Scruple of his Freehold. **1954** Koestler *Invisible Writing* iii. 40 Amiable Hans was a bald, moon-faced little man with a wealth of humour and *self-mockery. **1823** Bentham *Not Paul but Jesus* 287 Terror and *self-mortification. **1931** J. S. Huxley *What dare I Think?* v. 169 He [*sc.* the humanist] finds the desire for a sacrifice and self-mortification just as natural..as the desire for achievement and self-assertion. **1864** G. O. Trevelyan *Compet. Wallah* 380 What is there in common between the faith of Heber and Swartz and a creed which enjoins suicide and *self-mutilation. **1980** *Jrnl. R. Soc. Arts* Feb. 137/2 It represents self-mutilation, it can only lead to genocide and biocide. **1628** Feltham *Resolves* II. xxxvii. 113 The vilenesse of a wilfull *selfe-neglect. **1876** Miss Yonge *Womankind* xv, The hopeless dejection of self-neglect. **1933** *Times Lit. Suppl.* 16 Mar. 174/1 His book is one long and infinitely various act of self-discovery, *self-objectification, made possible only by self-forgetfulness. **1969** T. F. Torrance *Theol. Sci.* i. 42 We are frequently engaged in mythological self-objectifications of this sort. **1898** G. B. Shaw *Perfect Wagnerite* 11 The..*self-organization of life. **1967** *Oceanogr. & Marine Biol.* V. 274 Ecological succession is a process of self-organization. **1656** Earl Monm. tr. *Boccalini's Advts. fr. Parnass.* I. xl. (1674) 54 Vain-glorious pomp, and *self-ostentation. **1726** Amherst *Terræ Fil.* App. 327 The poignancy of the satire, and artfulness of *self-panegyric. **1958** S. Spender *Engaged in Writing* 89 He [spoke]..in the comic manner which was half-serious *self-parody. **1978** *New York* 3 Apr. 64/3 The majesty of our landscape has its own built-in note of self-parody, and it has eluded these artists. **1682** H. More *Annot. Glanvill's Lux O.* 217 They demonstrate still their Spirituality by *Self-Penetration, haply a thousand and a thousand times repeated. **1678** Cudworth *Intell. Syst.* I. iii. 160 If the souls of Men and Animals be at any time without Consciousness and *Self-perception, then..Clear and Express Consciousness is not Essential to Life. **1972** M. Argyle *Social Psychol. of Work* iv. 60 The self-image also includes self-perceptions such as being 'intelligent' or 'lively'. **1850** L. Hunt *Autobiogr.* II. xii. 98 The strange *self-permission of a man like Walter Scott..to countenance the border-like forages of his friends. **1843** J. S. Mill *Logic* II. III. xv. 32 A permanent effect..possessing the property of *self-perpetuation. **1906** W. G. Sumner *Folkways* 473 They show how deep is the interest of human beings in the sex taboo, and in the self-perpetuation of society. **1962** F. I. Ordway et al. *Basic Astronautics* vi. 247 We think of life as a system or aggregate of chemical reactions that possess the inherent capability of self-perpetuation. **1704** Steele *Lying Lover* v. i, We may feel Comfort by our *Self-persuasion. **1914** G. B. Shaw *Dark Lady of Sonnets* 121 Self-betrayal is one thing; and *self-portrayal, as in Hamlet and Mercutio, is another. **1890** *Spectator* 3 May 614/1 Fortitude, endurance, *self-postponement. **1803** T. Scott *Funeral Serm.* iii. Wks. 1807 III. 111 Was he not tempted to *self-preference, and to trust in his own righteousness? **1868** *Rep. U.S. Comm. Agric.* (1869) 140 This bridge between *self-preparation and the university course. **1879** Geo. Eliot *Theo. Such* i. 8 This naive veracity of *self-presentation. **1901** Gore *Body of Christ* iv. 219 The heavenly intercession and self-presentation of Christ. **1880** Sanday in *Expositor* XI. 353 A certain *self-projection of the commentator into a different order of ideas. **1872** Geo. Eliot *Middlem.* III. li. 354 The divine tribunal had changed its aspect for him; *self-prostration was no longer enough. **1834** J. S. Mill in *Monthly Repos.* VIII. 838 This is..the best sort of *self-protection. **1860** Froude *Hist. Eng.* V. 101 In self-protection he had been obliged to arm his household. *a* **1586** Sidney *Arcadia* (1622) 194 The *selfe-punishment for others fault. **1798** Sotheby tr. *Wieland's Oberon* (1826) II. 67 Son! by self-punishment thy guilt atone. **1974** R. H. S. Crossman *Diaries* (1975) I. 14 My own generalizations and predictions..sometimes provide an exercise in self-punishment since some of them read very foolishly today. **1924** W. B. Selbie *Psychol. Relig.* x. 202 A longing for *self-purification. **1902** *Class. Rev.* XVI. 148/1 These are examples of coincident language, not of *self-quotation. **1871** Geo. Eliot *Middlem.* I. iii. 41 Dorothea checked herself suddenly with *self-rebuke for the presumptuous way in which she was reckoning on uncertain events. **1927** T. Wilder *Bridge of San Luis Rey* II. 15 Each..was on the point of losing her mind under the alternations of self-rebuke and the outbursts of passion. **1955** *Essays & Studies* VIII. 75 Emma is shown as incapable of *self-recognition. **1873** M. Arnold *Lit. & Dogma* (1876) 101 The time had come for inwardness and *self-reconstruction. **1961** Webster, *Self-recrimination. **1965** J. A. Michener *Source*

700 He was thrown into a world of self-recrimination and remorse. 1642 H. MORE *Song of Soul* II. ii. II. xxxiii, One spirit goes Through all this bulk, not by extension But by a totall *self-reduplication. 1892 J. TAIT *Mind in Matter* 271 In *self-reformation the vicious become wretched by their abstentions. 1918 W. S. CHURCHILL in M. Gilbert *Winston S. Churchill* (1977) IV. Compan. I. 366 They should by..a real act of *self-regeneration make a definite break with the system. 1962 E. SNOW *Red China Today* (1963) xlviii. 373 In prison there is the omnipresent *threat* of force and humilitation, combined with the demand for self-regeneration. 1959 B. & R. NORTH tr. *Duverger's Pol. Parties* I. ii. 87 One of the constant features of the French Communist party is its perpetual *self-renewal. 1971 J. Z. YOUNG *Introd. Study Man* xi. 147 They [*sc.* 'post-mitotic' cells] are provided with especially active mechanisms for self-renewal. 1848 POE in *Graham's Mag.* Feb. 131/1 Apparent plagiarisms..arise from an author's *self-repetition. 1959 *New Biol.* XXVIII. 93 The most characteristic property [of life], that of *self-replication, has been studied theoretically by certain mathematicians. 1892 J. TAIT *Mind in Matter* 5 In judging of men, acts form an incomparably higher standard than *self-representation. 1926 J. S. HUXLEY *Essays of Biologist* vii. 256 The attributes of living matter which mark it off from inorganic matter become dominant—its capacity for *self-reproduction, [etc.]. 1964 *Sci. Amer.* Sept. 154/2 Seen in this light, crystal growth is self-reproduction. 1676 OWEN *Serm.* Wks. 1851 IX. 379 *Self-reputation in the exercise of gifts. 1668 — *Expos. 130th Ps.* iv. 120 Unspeakable are the Advantages which a soul obtains by this *self Resignation. 1824 JAS. NICHOLS *Calvinism & Armin.* I. 376 *note*, The British Constitution..contained within itself copious materials for *self-restoration. 1842 MANNING *Serm.* xii. (1848) I. 169 In all these acts of *self-restriction. 1898 *Month* Sept. 237 To learn independence and *self-rule. 1900 G. B. SHAW *Let.* 14 Mar. (1972) II. 156 The definite intention to clear out of India as soon as the natives are capable of self rule is the most pious of superfluities. 1978 *Times* 5 May 6/8 There is apprehension..that Israel will impose its own peace plan which offers a measure of self-rule for the West Bank. *a* 1711 KEN *Christophil* Poet. Wks. I. 464 Frequent *self-scrutinies the Humble makes. 1865 D. G. ROSSETTI *Let.* 21 Nov. (1965) II. 581 This [feeling of rage]..leads not to envy in the least, but to self-scrutiny. 1979 *Dædalus* Summer 3 Genuine charity and a constant and severe self-scrutiny are psychologically unthinkable without the moral pride that is all but inseparable from spiritual energy. 1840 DICKENS *Master Humphrey's Clock* I. 47, I..have no power of *self-snatchation (forgive me if I coin that phrase) from the yawning gulf before me. 1947 C. GRAY *Contingencies* 37 The voluntary *self-starvation of the rich. 1904 W. JAMES in *Mind* XIII. 466 Can there be *self-stultification in urging any account whatever of truth? Can the definition ever contradict the deed? 1855 DICKENS *Dorrit* II. xxvii, Patience, self-denial, *self-subdual. 1863 KAVANAGH *Q. Mab.* III. vi, They prefer self-indulgence to *self-subjection. 1853 GROTE *Greece* II. lxxxvii. XI. 387 Spartan *self-suppression and rigour of life. 1642 H. MORE *Song of Soul* II. I. xliv, When she doth with *self-sway Thus change herself. 1841 MERIVALE *Lect. Coloniz. & Col.* I. iv. 101 A right to self-government and *self-taxation. 1959 *Spectator* 11 Sept. 336/3 He came to each [session] with notes on the successive steps in his '*self-therapy'. 1809–10 COLERIDGE *Friend* (1865) 31 The hideous practices of *self-torture. 1949 KOESTLER *Promise & Fulfilment* II. iv. 253 This difference..was demonstrated by Irgun's..*self-transformation into a *bona fide* democratic party. 1640 T. H[OOKER] *title*, The Christians two chiefe lessons; viz. Selfe-deniall, and *Selfe-tryall. 1872 YEATS *Techn. Hist. Comm.* 33 Cultivation and refinement, apparently acquired by *self-tuition. 1709 SHAFTESB. *Charac., Moralists* III. §2 *Self-valuation supposes Self-Worth. 1946 P. BOTTOME *Lifeline* xxxix. 297 Their self-valuation was threatened. 1854 MILMAN *Lat. Christ.* III. v. (1864) II. 13 *Self vendition into slavery. 1854 GEO. ELIOT tr. *Feuerbach's Essence Christianity* i. 6 Consciousness is *self-verification. 1975 T. P. WHITNEY tr. *Solzhenitsyn's Gulag Archipelago* II. III. i. 11 Prisoners, wherever possible, were to be brought into self-verification and self-supervision. 1654 WHITLOCK *Zootomia* 28 *Selfe-vexations..may by no way better be blowne over, then by reckoning Impossibles not to concerne our Desires. 1690 C. NESSE *Hist. & Myst. O. & N. Test.* I. 314 Jacobs silence..was far better than his son's *self-vindication. 1831 CARLYLE *Sartor Res.* III. x, That primeval Superstition, *Self-worship.

b. With vbl. sbs.; as ***self-abominating*** = self-abomination.

1829 J. MACDONALD in Tweedie *Life* (1849) 131 On the very back of this *self-abominating, I rear another monument of self-exaltation. 1762 GOLDSMITH *Life of Richard Nash* 13 Little Things..without merit..by *self-advertizing, attract the attention of the day. 1909 BANK *Myst. F. Farrington* 280 Contain yourself in the matter of self-advertising. 1768–74 TUCKER *Lt. Nat.* (1834) II. 571 Humiliations and *self-afflictings. 1840 CARLYLE *Heroes* iv. 215 No sophistry, *self-blinding or other dishonesty. 1876 GEO. ELIOT *Dan. Der.* lxiii, *Self-checking and suppression. 1702 HOWE *Self-ded.* 16 Our dedicating our selves, to God, is a *self-committing. 1890 W. JAMES *Princ. Psychol.* I. vi. 158 *Self-compounding of mental facts is inadmissible. 1649 ROBERTS *Clavis Bibl.* 367 Without carkings, covetousnesse, or other *self-disquietings. 1817 JANE AUSTEN *Sanditon* v, in *Minor Wks.* (1954) 388, I can be no Judge of what the habit of *self-doctoring may do. 1951 C. R. ACTON *Dog Annual* 143 The all-important power of..self-doctoring. 1754 RICHARDSON *Grandison* VI. 115 She embraced me,..and cleared up all my *self-doubtings. 1882–3 *Schaff's Encycl. Relig. Knowl.* II. 992/2 A *self-emptying of himself, and the assumption of human nature. 1842 MANNING *Serm.* iii. (1848) I. 44 Nothing so wears down the sharpness of conscience..as *self-excusing. 1720 T. BOSTON *Hum. Nat. Fourfold St.* (1784) 88 *Self-jealousing well becomes Christians. 1758 S. HAYWARD *Serm.* 53 To keep us ever humble, and to fill us with *self-loathing. 1899 *Allbutt's Syst. Med.* VIII. 366 Perversion of self-feeling may culminate in self-loathing or hatred. 1971 P. O'DONNELL *Impossible Virgin* ix. 176 She..was filled with self-loathing because it was she who had trapped him. 1599 SHAKS. *Hen. V*, II. iv. 75 Selfe-loue..is not so vile a sinne, As *selfe-neglecting. 1850 ROBERTSON *Serm.* Ser. III. vii. (1853) 101 That one offering..repeated in the life and *self-offering of all. 1902 *Westm. Gaz.* 11 Apr. 10/1 The habit of *self physicking, often with powerful drugs, is on the increase. 1907 W. JAMES in *McClure's Mag.* (1908) Feb. 420/2 Democracy as a whole may undergo *self-poisoning. 1968 *Times* 28 Oct. 3/1 Professor Kessel..has found that 34 per cent of 511 patients admitted for self-poisoning gave warning. 1960 *Times* 13 May 18/5 Unless some *self-policing is done in the American film industry. 1977 *Jrnl. R. Soc. Arts* CXXV. 450/1 Self-policing by the data storage industry is simply not an adequate safeguard. 1649 LIGHTFOOT *Battle with Wasp's Nest* Wks. 1825 I. 421 Pride, blind zeal, and *self-prizing. 1856 BAGEHOT in *National Rev.* Apr. 370 He has no passionate *self-questionings, no indomitable fears, no asking perplexities. 1862 LYTTON *Str. Story* II. 199 My self-questionings halted here. 1884 *Encycl. Brit.* XVII. 96/2 He was under a continuous course of *self-schooling. 1825 HALKETT *Hist. Notes Indians N. Amer.* xvi. 376 The..*self-scourgings publicly exhibited by the Indian Pigarouick in the church of Montreal. 1916 G. B. SHAW *Androcles & Lion* p. xx, Saints amazed the world with their austerities and self-scourgings. 1681 OWEN *Humble Test.* 139 This *Self-Searching is the first Duty we are..called unto. 1978 J. SACKS in P. Moore *Man, Woman, & Priesthood* iii. 28 It has led to considerable self-searching in the Jewish community in recent years. 1571 GOLDING *Calvin on Ps.* xi. 8 Howsoeuer the vngodly beguyle themselues with their *selfesoothing. 1891 *Self-teaching [see *nursery school* s.v. NURSERY 8 c]. 1967 G. JACKSON *Let.* 31 Jan. in *Soledad Brother* (1971) 107 A good self-teaching book on Arabic. 1868 *Rep. U.S. Comm. Agric.* (1869) 250 Good management may postpone the '*self-thinning', by the inside, shaded, and weak bottom branches dying out. 1903 G. B. SHAW *Man & Superman* III. 129 Life's incessant aspiration to higher organization, wider, deeper, intenser, self-consciousness, and clearer *self-understanding. 1977 A. GIDDENS *Stud. in Social & Polit. Theory* i. 57 In the philosophy of science, as contrasted to the methodological self-understanding of the social sciences, the 'orthodox model' has long since become subject to broad-ranging attack. 1882 ROSSETTI *Poems* (1904) 262/1 Lord, undo Our *self-undoing. 1902 J. SMITH *Integr. Script.* i. 9 The *self-unveiling of God. *a* 1700 KEN *Hymnotheo* Poet. Wks. III. 105 He *self-upbraidings felt his Spirit gore. 1840 MRS. CARLYLE *Lett.* (1883) I. 124 Overcome by her tears and promises and self-upbraidings. 1671–2 R. WILD *Let.* 14 The..*self-whippings of the Popish Priests.

c. With agent-nouns; as ***self-advertiser***, one who advertises himself, one given to self-advertisement.

1890 *Pall Mall Gaz.* 21 Aug. 1/3 These safeguards..would make it rather more difficult for the *self-advertiser and the bore to inflict themselves upon the House. 1654 WHITLOCK *Zootomia* 296 Aquinas dareth do it to the proudest *Mihi plaudo*, *Selfe-approver of them all. 1841 *Penny Cycl.* XX. 270/2 The *Samokreshchennikee*, or '*self-baptisers',..baptise themselves by repeatedly diving into a river. 1658 ROWLAND tr. *Moufet's Theat. Ins.* 890 In Greek αὐτοπάτορες, or *Self-begetters. 1598 SYLVESTER *Du Bartas* II. ii. II. 16 Who (*self-commanders) rather sin suppresse By self-examples then by rigorousnesse. 1758 JOHNSON *Idler* No. 88 ¶8 If I had ever found any of the *self-contemners much irritated..by the consciousness of their meanness. 1672 BAXTER *Bagshaw's Scandals* ii. 16 What a forgetful *self-contradicter is this man? 1818 BYRON *Juan* I. xv, An all-in-all sufficient *self-director. 1936 A. THIRKELL *August Folly* viii. 247 'She is a *self-dramatiser,' said Charles. 1948 *Medium Ævum* XVII. 1 (*title*) A medieval *self-educator. 1970 P. DICKINSON *Seals* ii. 35 Great self-educators, these Pibbles. *a* 1793 J. HUNTER in *Catal. Mus. Coll. Surg.* (1833) I. 259 It is most probable that all Barnacles are of both sexes, and *self-impregnators. 1657 J. WATTS *Scribe, Pharisee*, etc. I. 118 To take you off..from being a self-ordainer, or a *self-intruder. 1699 SHAFTESB. *Charac., Inq. conc. Virtue* II. §2 Such a one is in reality a *Self-Oppressor, and lies heavier on himself than he can ever do on Mankind. 1840 DISRAELI *Misc. Lit.* 45/2 The letters of..Gray, Cowper, and Walpole..., *self-painters. 1598 SYLVESTER *Du Bartas* II. i. II. 451 A blade Wherewith vain Man and his inveigled Wife (*Self-parricides) have reft their proper life. 1780 MME. D'ARBLAY *Diary* May, A *self-piquer upon immense good breeding. 1894 WEYMAN *Man in Black* x, The *self-poisoner had done his work well. 1668 DRYDEN *Dram. Poesy* Ess. (ed. Ker) I. 48 [Terence's] *Heautontimorumenos*, or *Self-Punisher. 1966 'J. BERRISFORD' *Wild Garden* viii. 99 One of the most..accommodating *self-seeders is a biennial evening primrose—*Oenothera lamarckiana*. 1742 YOUNG *Nt. Th.* v. 711 Man is a *self-survivor ev'ry year. 1899 *Dublin Rev.* Apr. 250 When he..becomes not a *self-teacher but a disciple. 1876 T. HARDY *Ethelberta* xxiii, If I could only turn *self-vivisector, and watch the operation of my heart. 1729 C. MIDDLETON *Let. fr. Rome* 51 That..Penance of the Flagellantes or *Self-whippers. 1819 KEATS *Fall of Hyperion* I. 207 Large *self worshipers.

d. With nouns of state or condition; as ***self-awareness***, the condition of being aware of oneself, ***self-mastery***, mastery of oneself, self-command.

Some of the combinations illustrated under this head and the next might with equal propriety have been referred to 3; they are placed here because the relation of *self-* to the second element may be conveniently defined as objective.

1880 CYPLES *Human Exp.* ii. 34 The egoistic consciousness—that is, our *self-awareness. 1682 SIR T. BROWNE *Chr. Mor.* I. §23 (1716) 24 *Self-credulity, pride, and levity lead unto self-Idolatry. 1671 HOWE *Let.* in *Life* (1836) 185 A mean and inglorious *self-despiciency. 1921 E. M. HULL *Sheik* v. 160 A *self-disgust seized him. He had been within an ace of betraying the man. 1977 *Listener* 28 Apr. 552/4 George Grosz..the master of self-disgust. 1853 J. BROWN *Let.* (1912) 132 Dr. Scott's illness and death, and my own profound *self-disrespect and indifferent health and overwork,—altogether I was in a sorry condition. 1938 LD. LYMINGTON *Famine in Eng.* 74 They are waiting to be led to salvation, and out of the slough of self-disrespect into which they have been driven. 1885 *Athenæum* 26 Dec. 832 The duty of *self-dominance. 1847 C. BRONTË *J. Eyre* ii, My habitual mood of humiliation, *self-doubt. 1930 E. WAUGH *Vile Bodies* vi. 106 Magically, self-doubt began to spread in the audience. 1980 J. MCCLURE *Blood of Englishman* xv. 142 His hunch..drifted dangerously towards the jagged reef of self-doubt. 1677 GALE *Crt. Gentiles* III. 41 Pressing men to spiritual povertie, *self emtinesse. 1734 WATTS *Reliq. Juv.* (1789) 121 By the influence of the same native principle of flattery and *self-fondness. 1927 J. S. HUXLEY *Relig. without Revelation* iv. 130 'My country, right or wrong'..words which are immortal as the fittest inscription on the pedestal of the golden calf of *self-hero-worship. 1948 L. SPITZER *Linguistics & Lit. Hist.* iv. 156 An enthusiasm inspired by *self-infatuation. 1973 M. AMIS *Rachel Papers* 16 Thinking back, actually, 'self-infatuation' strikes me as a rather ill-chosen word. It isn't so much that I like or love myself. Rather, I'm sentimental about myself. 1673 FLAVEL *Saint Indeed* 12 Quick-sighted *self-jealousie is an excellent preservative from sin. *a* 1860 BAYNE (Worc.), A sustained *self-mastery. 1933 *Burlington Mag.* Dec. 260/1 The art of self-mastery, the grand style. 1979 *Dædalus* Summer 90 One must be..forever inaccessible to the seductions that distract or subtract from the forces necessary for self-mastery and self-defense. ? 1809 WORDSW. *Poems to Nat. Indep.* II. xvii, Happy occasions oft by *self-mistrust Are forfeited. 1946 DYLAN THOMAS *Let.* 30 May (1966) 288 Inevitable moments of depression and self-mistrust. 1661 GLANVILL *Van. Dogm.* A 6 We came into the world, and we know not how; we live in't in a *self-nescience. 1868 LOWELL *Among my Bks., Dryden* (1870) 40 He had more of that good luck of *self-oblivion than most men. 1842 in H. W. S[mith] *Secret of Happy Life* vii. (1886) 79 A relinquishment of the principle of *self-ownership. 1668 H. MORE *Div. Dial.* I. xxx. I. 129 The last Attribute..that of *Self-penetrability. 1977 R. HOLLAND *Self & Social Context* i. 20 From Freud they need clinical methods which give such primacy to the individual case but they dislike the 'pathological' *self-picture. 1809 R. HALL *Wk. Holy Spirit* (1813) 21 That *self-recollection and composure, which are so essential to devotion. 1832 *Selfreverence [see SELF-CONTROL 1]. 1647 J. HALL *Poems* II. 104. 5 Lest from my selfe my owne *selfe-ruine bee. 1745 J. MASON *Self-Knowl.* I. i. (1853) 6 With what..Care we are to..examine ourselves..in order to acquire this important *Self-Science. 1861 E. B. BROWNING *Mother & Poet* in *Last Poems* (1862) 95 Some women bear children in strength, And bite back the cry of their pain in *self-scorn. 1804 WORDSW. *Small Celandine* 8 In close *self-shelter, like a Thing at rest. *c* 1645 HOWELL *Lett.* II. li. (1650) II. 66 Hee is too much given to his study and *self-society. 1646 FULLER *Wounded Consc.* ix. 67 *Selfe-suspition of hypocrisie, is a hopefull symptome of sincerity. 1964 M. HYNES *Med. Bacteriol.* (ed. 8) vii. 74 An animal will not normally form antibodies to its own tissues, even though these may be powerfully antigenic to a litter-mate. The mechanism of this *self-tolerance and the consequences of its breakdown are discussed later. 1977 I. M. ROITT *Essent. Immunol.* iv. 109 Although we are uncertain of the mechanism, the idea that deletion of specific clones is responsible for tolerance induction is attractive. For example, it can account for the development of self-tolerance. 1807 JEBB *Let. to Knox* 20 Aug., Encouragement is held out, to prayer, and to *self-watchfulness. 1748 MELMOTH *Fitzosborne Lett.* lxxi. (1749) II. 210 *Self-weariness is a circumstance that ever attends folly.

e. With adjs.; as ***self-adaptive***, capable of adapting oneself or itself, (hence, by extension) pertaining to, involving, or characterized by self-adaptation, ***self-fond***, fond of oneself.

1903 F. W. H. MYERS *Human Pers.* I. 216 Typical of life is its *self-adaptive power. 1864 PUSEY *Lect. Daniel* viii. 550 Earnest *self-afflictive prayer. 1943 H. READ *Educ. through Art* iii. 42 It may be that such eidetic individuals are more *self-analytical than an eidetic person without creative gifts would be. 1924 R. GRAVES *Mock Beggar Hall* 28 Alert, with both eyes open, *self-aware. 1979 A. CHISHOLM *Nancy Cunard* viii. 75 An intelligent, imaginative, self-aware young man. 1698 NORRIS *Pract. Disc.* (1707) IV. 180 God, who is such a Good, Bountiful, *Self-communicative, Self-diffusive, Universalized Being. 1909 WEBSTER, *Self-corrective. 1934 *Mind* XLIII. 506 The inductive method is self-corrective. *a* 1812 J. BENTHAM *Rationale Judicial Evid.* (1827) III. v. xv. 224 We must..express the distinction between the two opposite kinds of evidentiary chains: styling the one, for example, the *self-infirmative* chain, we may style the other the **self-corroborative.* 1909 W. JAMES *Meaning of Truth* xiii. 267 The hypothesis will, in short, have worked successfully all round the circle and proved self-corroborative. 1936 *Mind* XLV. 98 This suggestion that art, like religion, is self-critical in its activity. 1979 B. MALAMUD *Dubin's Lives* ix. 346 The tone of the book was self-critical. 1867 J. R. LOWELL *Fitz Adam's Story* in *Poems* (1912) 575 He went on with a self-derisive sneer. 1928 D. H. LAWRENCE *Woman who rode Away* 172 His rather hooked nose self-derisive. 1698 *Self-diffusive [see *self-communicative* above]. 1884 HOWELLS *Silas Lapham* (1891) I. 267 A *self-disdainful air. 1934 *Essays & Studies* XIX. 28 The most seemingly *self-expressive 'human document'. 1977 R. HOLLAND *Self & Social Context* v. 102 He must develop an autonomous aspect of self to account for the more self-expressive or impulsive actions. *a* 1797 WALPOLE *Geo. II* (1847) I. 222 The *self-fondest and greatest of poets. 1845 R. W. HAMILTON *Pop. Educ.* x. (ed. 2) 271 All popular opinion and information, which is wholesome and enduring, is *self-generative. 1745 J. MASON *Self-Knowl.* I. i. (1853) 7 Condemning others for the very crimes we ourselves are guilty of, which a *self-ignorant Man is very apt to do. 1949 KOESTLER *Promise & Fulfilment* I. xiii. 149 [He]..refused to testify..on the grounds that his testimony would be *self-incriminatory. *a* 1812 *Self-infirmative [see *self-corroborative* above]. 1875 A. SWINBOURNE *Picture Logic* (ed. 2) xxii. 142 Self-infirmative inference is where each fresh fact weakens the conclusion. *a* 1711 KEN *Hymns Evang.* Poet. Wks. I. 326 We from our proneness to backslide, *Self-jealous, shou'd in Thee confide. *a* 1863 WHATELY *Comm.-pl. Bk.* (1864) 173 [A party] that assumes some *self-laudatory title. 1897 G. B. SHAW *Let.* 10 Aug. (1965) I. 795 It is sheer want of practice that makes actors *self-mistrustful when they are asked to..tell a story on the stage. 1699 SHAFTESB. *Charac., Inq. conc. Virtue* I. §3 If a Creature be *self-neglectful, and insensible of Danger. 1816 SHELLEY *Daemon* I. 89 *Self-oblivious solitude. 1889 MIVART *Orig. Hum. Reason* 45 Ideas are abstract, reflective and *self-perceptive. 1849 RUSKIN *Seven Lamps* i. §8. 17 There is no need to offend by importunate, *self-proclaimant splendour. 1890 W. JAMES *Princ. Psychol.* II.

xxiii. 381 The tendency to contract is the source of all the *self-protective impulses and reactions which are later developed. **1979** B. Malamud *Dubin's Lives* ix. 337 Some people complicate their feelings in self-protective ways. **1852** Bailey *Festus* 407 Its self consuming fate, *self-punitive. **1678** Cudworth *Intell. Syst.* I. v. 846 A..*Self Recollective Power. **1943** J. S. Huxley *Evolutionary Ethics* v. 34 The capacity for self-reproduction, or better *self-reproductive evolution. **1847** Tennyson *Princess* vii. 274 *Self-reverent each and reverencing each. *a* **1914** Joyce *Stephen Hero* (1944) xvi. 36 Stephen, as he looked contemptuously at the laughing faces, thought of a *self-submersive reptile. **1888** R. F. Horton *Inspir. Bible* vi. 153 The author is entirely *self-suppressive. **1918** G. Frankau *One of Them* in *Poet. Works* (1923) II. 75 Goddess indeed! A *self-sure, jade-eyed, slim puss, of life's each latest luxury impassioned. **1954** *Numbers* (N.Z.) July 1/5 Paul was lying on his bed, reading. Twenty-five; good-looker; self-sure. **1668** J. Corbet *2nd Disc. Relig. Eng.* 16 Modestly..*self-suspicious. **1884** Tennyson *Becket* v. ii, We are *self-uncertain creatures. **1903** *Speaker* 6 June 232/2 Nothing exists..to keep together a body of weary and *self-weary men.

f. With ppl. adjs. in *-ing*; as ***self-abandoning***, abandoning oneself, (hence, by extension) pertaining to, involving, or characterized by self-abandonment. (For the extended meaning cf. sense 2 note, below.)

1818 Scott *Rob Roy* xxxvii, The wo-begone and *self-abandoning note in which he uttered the disconsolate words. **1922** Joyce *Ulysses* 718 The selfprolonging tension of the thing proposed to be done and the *selfabbreviating relaxation of the thing done. **1836** Keble *Lyra Apost.* (1849) 57 When the *self-abhorring thrill Is past. **1864** Pusey *Lect. Daniel* ii. 65 The then most stirring and *self-adapting people. **1848** J. S. Mill *Pol. Econ.* II. iii. xx. 154 There is a *self-adjusting power in the variations of the exchange itself. **1894** *Pop. Sci. Monthly* June 184 Nature is..more self-adjusting than his system contemplates. **1900** *Daily News* 15 Nov. 4/7 An advertising and..a *self-advertising age. **1607** Tourneur *Rev. Trag.* iii. i. F j b, Euery proud and *selfe-affecting Dame. **1856** Grote *Greece* ii. xcii. XII. 118 His own *self-aggrandising impulse. **1922** W. B. Yeats *Trembling of Veil* iii. 144 The subtle torture of *self-analysing passion. **1980** A. Wilson *Setting World on Fire* iii. i. 264 Find a play..which has a thoughtful, self-analysing part for an old actor like me. **1734** Pope *Ess. Man* iv. 255 One *self-approving hour whole years out-weighs Of stupid starers. **1857** Hughes *Tom Brown* i. iii, A self-approving smile. **1598** Sylvester *Du Bartas* ii. i. i. 123 Their new *Self-arching arms in thousand Arbours grew. **1713** Derham *Phys.-Theol.* ii. i. (1714) 40 *note*, Therein gravity doth so far over-power their *self-attracting Power. **1935** H. H. Farmer *World & God* i. ix. 158 Our interest is in the Christian experience of God as personal, which in the nature of the case must be *self-authenticating. **1976** H. Montefiore in *Christian Believing* 151 His character is to me self-authenticating. **1698** Norris *Pract. Disc.* (1707) IV. 34 Love is so *self-betraying a Passion. **1907** A. French *Bk. Vegetables* 78 Varieties [of celery] are many, and classify chiefly as to height, color (red tint), and '*self-blanching' properties. **1976** 'D. Halliday' *Dolly & Nanny Bird* xi. 138 Simon had turned the colour of self-blanching celery. *a* **1711** Ken *Hymnarium* Poet. Wks. II. 3 In thy own *Self-comprehending Thought. **1647** C. Harvey *Schola Cordis* xxxi. 12 Or doth thy *self-confounding fancy feare thee, When there's no danger neare thee? **1817** Coleridge *Biog. Lit.* (1907) II. 229 A *self-consoling grin. **1590** Spenser *F.Q.* iii. xi. 1 Fowle Gealosie, that..mak'st the louing hart ..feed it selfe with *selfe-consuming smart? **1655–87** H. More *App. Antid.* (1712) 185 How it comes to pass that the Soul cannot withdraw her self from pain by her *Self-contracting faculty. **1944** *Mind* LIII. 212 The last topic with which Hr. von Wright deals is Reichenbach's contention that induction is a *self-correcting process. **1979** *Dædalus* Summer 150 The idea of a developing and self-correcting body of scientific inquirers offered what seemed to him a more satisfactory model. **1650** Baxter *Saint's R.* iii. v. §4 (1651) 92 Those *self-couzening, formal, lazie Professors of Religion. **1909** W. M. Urban *Valuation* xiv. 413 In this concept of the *self-defeating process we have a negative test of validity. **1949** M. Mead *Male & Female* ix. 196 The Weimar Republic's self-defeating practice of giving..jobs..to older men. **1979** B. Malamud *Dubin's Lives* ix. 336 Their talk was self-defeating. **1968** *Self-defining [see literal *sb.* 3]. **1856** R. A. Vaughan *Mystics* (1860) I. 42 The *self-deifying tendency. **1908** W. B. Yeats *Poetry & Ireland* 10 None other has a continual deliberate *self-delighting happiness. **1958** *Times Lit. Suppl.* 17 Jan. 30/1 Mr Amis, seen by himself in a way in which ironical, *self-deprecating people do see themselves. **1971** S. Hill *Strange Meeting* ii. 111 Barton turned his head and smiled, and then his face changed again, the old, self-deprecating expression over it. **1864** Bagehot in *National Rev.* Nov. 34 Such *self-describing poets describe what is *in* them, but not *peculiar* to them. **1978** J. Dunn in Hookway & Pettit *Action & Interpretation* 156 Between a describer and a self-describing object there exist relations which are peculiar. **1865** *Self-developing [see self-changing *ppl. a.* 1]. **1980** N. Marsh *Photo-Finish* iii. 79 The lens cap..produced instant self-developing results. *a* **1586** Sidney *Apol. Poetry* (Arb.) 34 The *selfe-deuouring crueltie in his Father Atreus. **1877** E. Caird *Philos. Kant* ii. xi. 465 Whenever we conceive any object as *self-differentiating. **1781** Cowper *Conversat.* 735 Shame upon a *self-disgracing age. **1945** Koestler *Yogi & Commissar* iii. iv. 242 Koehler assumes that there are *self-distributing electromagnetic currents between the cortical projections of retinal points. **1966** *English Studies* XLVII. 201 Only the second look of recent criticism has shown how homosexual were those claims, and how *self-doubting and despairing. *a* **1974** R. Crossman *Diaries* (1975) I. 339, I had noticed already that Ray Gunter was a dramatic, *self-dramatizing kind of chairman. **1598** Sylvester *Du Bartas* ii. i. iii. 670 Foule-squinting Envie, that *selfe-eating Elfe. **1692** W. Marshall *Gosp. Myst. Sanctif.* iv. (1764) 65 What a *self-emptying grace faith is. **1945** Auden *Coll. Poetry* 120 That through his self-annulment the real world Of *self-enduring instants may endure Its final metamorphosis. **1965** F. Sargeson *Memoirs of Peon* viii. 265 The *self-enhancing aim of endeavouring to ameliorate the lot of the family. **1854** Geo. Eliot tr. *Feuerbach's Essence Christianity* ii. 40 The understanding alone..is the *self-enjoying, self-sufficing existence. **1951** Auden *Enchafèd Flood* iii. 102 All it desires is to be in equilibrium, a self-enjoying, self-sufficient self. **1634** R. Bolton (*title*) A Three-fold Treatise: containing the Saints ..*Selfe-enriching Examination. **1947** *Mind* LVI. 58 The problem of a *self-equilibrating physical system can now be attacked with both vigor and generality. **1974** W. Rees-Mogg *Reigning Error* iv. 81 A gold system is a self-equilibrating system operating on a constant world money supply. **1962** *Listener* 15 Mar. 455/1 Not all the provisions of the treaty [*sc.* Treaty of Rome] are of this so-called '*self-executing' character. **1903** J. Joyce *Let.* 9 Mar. (1966) II. 35, I enclose you *self-explaining documents. **1868** Lowell *Among my Bks., Shaks. once more* (1870) 217 Our *self-exploiting nineteenth century. **1646** Fuller *Wounded Consc.* iv. 24 A wounded Conscience, *selfe-fearing, selfe-frighted. **1865** H. Maudsley *Meth. of Study of Mind* 18 It is ridiculous to suppose that the man of genius is ever a fountain of *self-generating energy. **1968** H. Harris *Nucleus & Cytoplasm* vi. 122 On any model..we are forced to consider how a set of conditions, initially produced in a cell by external stimuli, can become self-generating. **1887** A. Seth *Hegelianism* vi. 205 Hegel, like Plato, seeks reality not in the actual world, but in the eternal realm of an absolute and *self-guaranteeing thought. **1961** J. Wilson *Reason & Morals* iii. 164 What is irrational is that such people take their feelings as self-guaranteeing, that they treat them as carrying their own justification with them. **1590** Shaks. *Com. Err.* ii. i. 102 *Selfe-harming Iealousie. **1977** *New Yorker* 29 Aug. 82/3 Perhaps there was the same sort of *self-hating or fearful motive behind Hitler's orders to murder the most helpless patients in the hospitals of the Third Reich. **1828–32** Webster s.v., The *self-healing power of living animals and vegetables. *a* **1711** Ken *Hymns Festiv.* Poet. Wks. I. 289 *Self-humbling View. **1938** R. Graves *Coll. Poems* p. xiii, It is an exorcism of physical pretensions by self-humbling honesties. **1915** D. H. Lawrence *Rainbow* ii. 52 A burst of religious, *self-hurting fervour had passed over the country. **1939** R. Campbell *Flowering Rifle* vi. 150 And better maimed Of a self-hurting member so inflamed. *a* **1922** T. S. Eliot *Waste Land Drafts* (1971) 101 line 26 One soul,..*Self-immolating on the Mound. **1925** T. Dreiser *Amer. Tragedy* I. i. iii. 16 Any self-abnegating and self-immolating religious theory. **1687** Norris *Coll. Misc.* 322 God..must needs be..*self-imparting and communicative. **1836–9** *Todd's Cycl. Anat.* II. 377/1 In many [orders] the sexes are..*self-impregnating. **1925** T. Dreiser *Amer. Tragedy* I. ii. xxi. 303 He was not without the *self-incriminating thought that in seeking this..he was driving toward a relationship which was not legitimate. **1964** *Harvard Law Rev.* Nov. 219 Implicit..is the proposition that in a pretrial police interrogation the accused has a right to remain silent, which he must waive intelligently before any self-incriminating statements will be admissible at trial. **1925** T. Dreiser *Amer. Tragedy* I. ii. xxiii. 313 Clyde..now approached, his manner the epitome almost of a *self-ingratiating..dog of high breeding and fine temperament. **1778** J. Brown (*title*) The *self-interpreting Bible. **1935** A. C. Baugh *Hist. Eng. Lang.* vii. 266 One further habit which was somewhat weakened [in Middle English], although by no means broken, was that of combining native words into self-interpreting compounds. **1876** Geo. Eliot *Dan. Der.* xxxv, *Self-lacerating penitents. *a* **1613** Overbury *A Wife*, etc. (1638) 101 *Selfe-lashing Penitentiaries. **1834** J. Macdonald in Tweedie *Life* iii. (1849) 228 In a very degraded and *self-loathing state of mind. **1868** J. H. Newman *Verses on Var. Occas.* 23 Her heart's *self-mastering power. **1966** *English Studies* XLVII. 204 The *self-mocking,..witty, ironical, comic Whitman. **1685** Boyle *Salubr. Air* 34 A kind of propagative of *self-multiplying power. **1963** L. Trilling in N. Frye *Romanticism Reconsidered* 83 One of Keats's boldest expressions of his sense that there is something perverse and *self-negating in the erotic life. **1745** J. Mason *Self-Knowl.* iii. i. (1853) 167 O my wandering, *Self-neglecting Soul. **1960** Koestler *Lotus & Robot* ii. xi. 243 The split between the acting self and the *self-observing self disappears. **1961** *Times* 23 Mar. 17/2 The anti-hero, oddly likable and self-observing. **1860** Trench *Serm.* xv. 170 All acts of *self-offering love. **1961** D. Gabor et al. in C. Cherry *Information Theory* xxvii. 348 (*heading*) A *self-optimizing non-linear filter, predictor and simulator. **1968** *Brit. Med. Bull.* XXIV. 251/1 Priban and Fincham..have been examining the adjustment of the rate and depth of breathing and the generation of individual breaths, using a 'self-optimizing' model. **1923** J. S. Huxley *Essays of Biologist* vi. 217 A universe which the march of knowledge is showing us ever more clearly as self-ordered and *self-ordering. **1958** R. Williams *Culture & Society* iii. 298 The development of an organized and *self-organizing working class. **1946** P. Larkin *Jill* 13 Never having heard before this *self-parodying Southern coo. **1958** S. Spender *Engaged in Writing* 14 Asphalt's..blotched face with its self-parodying leer. **1825** J. Neal *Bro. Jonathan* III. 119 All the bad passions of our nature have a..*self-perpetuating power. **1938** Huxley & Haddon *We Europeans* iii. 8 The gene is then as self-perpetuating in its new type as it was in its old. **1971** N. Stacey *Who Cares?* viii. 139 It was quite obvious that few of our efforts looked like being self-generating and self-perpetuating. **1955** G. Gorer *Exploring Eng. Character* xv. 296 The English character became, to a very marked degree, '*self-policing'. **1922** *Self-prolonging [see *self-abbreviating* above]. **1843** J. S. Mill *Logic* I. iii. xiii. 565 It is..upon such substances that the *self-propagating power of chemical action is likely to exert itself in the most marked manner. **1868** *Rep. U.S. Comm. Agric.* (1869) 265 In any soil congenial to its growth, the atocha is self-propagating. *a* **1586** Sidney *Arcadia* iii. (Sommer) 315 b, To witnesse a *selfe-punishing repentaunce. **1978** H. McLeave *Borderline Case* (1979) i. 14 A bloody-minded, self-punishing type. **1827** Pollok *Course of T.* vii. 84 *Self-purifying, unpolluted sea! **1964** *Punch* 20 May 760/3 His..reaction.. is bitterly *self-recognising. **1921** J. McTaggart *Nature of Existence* I. iv. xxxi. 299 Every substance which is a *self-reflecting unity possesses two sorts of unity—organic unity and unity of self-reflection. **1857** Gosse *Omphalos* xii. 349 *note*, The very supposition which he considers as *self-refuting is an indubitable physiological fact. **1953** J. S. Huxley *Evolution in Action* iv. 91 The organization..of large groups of nerve-cells and their connecting outgrowths into *self-reinforcing circuits of excitation. **1875** J. R. Lowell in *Cambridge in Centennial Proc.* 30 The wingëd years, that winnow praise and blame, Blow many names out: they but fan to flame The *self-renewing splendors of thy fame. **1977** J. L. Harper *Population Biol. Plants* 306 The food of an animal is self-renewing. **1871** Morley *Condorcet* in *Crit. Misc.* Ser. i. (1878) 73 They move in a constant and *self-repeating orbit. **1946** *Nature* 21 Sept. 406/1 Alternatively..some *self-replicating cytoplasmic constituent of a complex cell, such as a plasmagene, may become capable of multiplying when transferred to a new environment. **1926** J. S. Huxley *Ess. Pop. Sci.* 230 The chromosomes are *self-reproducing. **1964** *Sci. Amer.* Sept. 149 (*caption*) The little red and blue 'creatures' in the photograph..are the two kinds of part of an elementary self-reproducing machine designed by..L. S. Penrose. **1825** Hazlitt *Spirit of Age* 186 A lofty and *self-scrutinising ambition. **1838** W. E. Channing *Self-Culture* 12 There are two powers of the human soul which make self-culture possible, the *self-searching and the self-forming power. **1978** P. Griffiths *Conc. Hist. Mod. Music* iii. 34 Both have a public rhetoric which was..foreign to Schoenberg in his profoundly self-searching form of Expressionism. **1827** J. Bentham *Rationale Judicial Evid.* III. vi. ii. 415 The probability, of mendacity, *self-serving mendacity, and consequent deception, attached to the admission of the testimony of the party in his own behalf. **1896** *Southwestern Reporter* XXXIII. 791/1 On a criminal trial, self-serving acts of the defendants are properly excluded. **1904** J. H. Wigmore *Treat. Syst. Evidence* III. lvii. 2273 There is no principle of evidence especially excluding 'self-serving' statements by an accused or by any one else. **1958** *Listener* 18 Sept. 412/2 How far would the majority go in applying the general rule excluding what are sometimes called self-serving statements to conduct? **1972** J. Philips *Vanishing Senator* (1973) ii. iii. 76, I always thought he was a kind of cheap, self-serving jerk. **1904** W. James in *Mind* XIII. 474 It seems to me to illustrate beautifully how *self-stultifying the conception of a truth that shall merely register a standing fixture may become. **1955** J. L. Austin *How to do Things with Words* (1962) iv. 51 This commits you to it and refuses to commit you to it. It is a self-stultifying procedure. **1842** E. FitzGerald *Let.* 16 Aug. (1960) 37 When I read of your ..riding into Naples with huge *self-supplying beakers full of the warm South I am sure you had best stay where you are. **1946** *Nature* 2 Nov. 606/1 A permanent self-supplying community of professional miners. **1807** Wordsw. *White Doe* 1630 A *self-surviving leafless oak. **1964** J. Z. Young *Model of Brain* v. 69 In particular we are interested in a *self-teaching homeostat, that is to say, one whose information and instructions are not entirely built in by heredity. **1668** Owen *Indwelling Sin* 297 Penances, and *self-torturing Discipline. **1816** Byron *Ch. Har.* iii. lxxvii, The self-torturing sophist, wild Rousseau. **1849** Dana *Geol.* ii. (1850) 107 The *self-triturating sands of the reefs. *a* **1711** Ken *Edmund* Poet. Wks. II. 83 Past vices gall his *self-upbraiding Mind. **1945** *Mind* LIV. 46 These beliefs were after all cases of immediate knowledge which would therefore be *self-validating and so require no further explanation. *a* **1586** Sidney *Arcadia* ii. (Sommer) 202 With a certaine sincere boldenesse of *selfe-warranting friendship. **1652** Crashaw *Carmen Deo Nostro* Wks. (1904) 247 O soft *self-wounding Pelican! *a* **1656** Bp. Hall *Let. Person Qual.*, Our exposedness to the danger of *self-wronging consequences.

†**g.** With vb.-stems, forming adjs., as ***self-tire*** = self-tiring. Also self-kill. *Obs.*

1615 Chapman *Odyss.* xvi. 5 The *selfe-tyre barking Dogs.

h. With vbs. (? *obs.*) and pres. pples.

1609 W. M. *Man in Moone* (1849) 13 This pretious weede ..doth so *selfe-besot those which take it. *a* **1618** Sylvester *Mottoes* 204 What Beautie's This..*Self-blinds, *self-bindes, and self it self bewitches? *Ibid.* 286 In Fire, Air, Earth, Water, The world *self-drowns, *self-burns, *self-hangs, *self-slaies. **1820** Keats *Lamia* i. 138 She..cower'd ..*self-folding like a flower that faints into itself at evening hour. **1738** Wesley *Ps.* xxxvi. i, He..*Self-soothing in his lost Estate Sleeps on secure. **1858** Longf. *M. Standish* vii. 58 Then stood Pecksuot forth, *self-vaunting.

i. With advs. related to actual or possible formations in e and f (above).

1899 *Westm. Gaz.* 8 June 2/1 The figure seems..*self-cognisably burthened with the griefs of all the generations. **1890** *Pall Mall G.* 24 Mar. 5/2 He *self-consolingly exclaimed, 'Le roi me reverra.' **1924** W. Holtby *Crowded Street* xxxv. 259 She laughed *self-deprecatingly. **1966** S. Beer *Decision & Control* xiv. 346 More typically, and more '*self-organizingly', we say that energy evens out. ? **1629** Donne *Serm.* vii. (1640) 65 To come..so *selfe proditoriously, as to betray himselfe..to his enemies. **1909** R. Law *Tests of Life* xi. 220 He who *self-tolerantly commits sin. **1933** Auden *Dance of Death* 32 *Self-understandingly I come. **1901** *Academy* 14 Dec. 585/2 Only intense feeling can use it [a metre] *self-vindicatingly.

2. Compounds with pa. pples. and ppl. adjs. in which *self-* denotes the agent or what is conceived as the agent; = by oneself or itself, by one's own (unaided) efforts or action, without help from others. Also with related advs., as ***self-confessedly***, and occas. with other adjs., as ***self-adhesive***.

Such compounds may qualify the designation of: (*a*) a person or thing that is the subject and object of the action, as ***self-appointed censors*** = censors appointed by themselves; (*b*) a thing that is operated upon, performed, produced, etc. by oneself, as ***self-appointed duties*** = duties appointed by the person himself; (*c*) a thing conceived as operated upon by itself, as ***self-arched rocks*** = rocks formed into arches of themselves without human or mechanical agency, ***self-balanced*** = balanced without external support; cf. 3 b below.

When transferred from a person to his actions, etc., compounds of this class (like those of 1 f) acquire a wider meaning; thus, ***self-abandoned*** = abandoned by oneself, hence, full of or marked by self-abandonment.

In some cases the formations are analogical and scarcely admit of analytical explanation; e.g. †self-assured from self-assurance, self-denied from self-denial, ***self-mortified*** from *self-mortification*.

1791 COWPER *Iliad* XII. 138 Nor expected less Than that ..the host Should *self-abandon'd fall an easy prey. 1813 BYRON *Giaour* 1006 The *self-accorded grave Of ancient fool and modern knave. 1809–10 COLERIDGE *Friend* (1865) 25 *Self-acknowledged beasts. 1814 F. BURNEY *Wanderer* III. xlv. 107 Their honour was *self-acquitted and their generosity was self-applauded. 1825 SCOTT *Betrothed* xxii, When she stood self-acquitted to her own mind. 1958 *Engineers' Digest* XIX. 244/1 (*heading*) *Self-adhesive nameplates. 1977 *Lancashire Life* Dec. 80/1 Products range from a reproduction of a timbered English pub for a Paris shoe exhibition to self-adhesive stickers for confectionery packets. 1924 W. B. SELBIE *Psychol. Relig.* 55 They [*sc.* primitive religions]..become *self-adjusted to man's growing intellectual capacity and needs. 1908 *Daily Chron.* 6 Nov. 5/3 An overdose of morphia *self-administered. 1593 SHAKS. *Rich. II*, III. ii. 53 His Treasons will sit blushing in his face, Not able to endure the sight of Day; But *selfe-affrighted, tremble at his sinne. 1799 *Hull Advertiser* 21 Sept. 3/2 Some of them [pilots] are *self-appointed. 1892 ZANGWILL *Bow Myst.* 172 His engrossing self-appointed duties. 1762 CHURCHILL *Night* 114 Where Virtue, *self-approv'd, reclines her head. 1598 SYLVESTER *Du Bartas* II. i. I. 537 Rocks *self-arched by the eating Current. 1818 SCOTT *Hrt. Midl.* v, His *self-assumed profession of the law. 1833 J. H. NEWMAN *Arians* I. iii. (1876) 55 The *self-authorised, arbitrary doctrines of the heretics. 1667 MILTON *P.L.* VII. 242 Earth *self-ballanc't on her Center hung. 1890 'R. BOLDREWOOD' *Colonial Reformer* (1891) 348 Crutchless and self-balanced. 1700 DRYDEN *Ovid's Met.* xv. 78 *Self-banish'd from his native shore. *a*1716 SOUTH *Serm.* (1717) IV. 156 *Self-befooled Sinners. 1784 *New Spectator* No. I. 7 The *self-be-paragraphed, the self-puffed and the self-adoring Mother Abington. 1784 COWPER *Tiroc.* 171 *Self-betray'd, and wilfully undone. 1644 DIGBY *Nat. Soul* Concl. 455 To transforme me totally into a *selfe-blessed creature. 1640 BASTWICK *Lord Bps.* ix, If the Prelates were not *selfe-blinded, they might discerne the reason. 1865 DICKENS *Mut. Fr.* II. xvi, Her pompous self-blinded father. 1846 BROCKETT *N.C. Words* s.v., *Adder-stone*, a perforated stone—the perforation imagined by the vulgar to be made by the sting of an adder... They are also called *self-bored stones. 1838 E. B. BROWNING *Seraphim* 50 The winding, wandering music that returns Upon itself in starry course, *self-bound To praise, and praise, and praise. 1935 T. S. ELIOT *Murder in Cathedral* i. 29 Cabined in Canterbury, realmless ruler, Self-bound servant of a powerless Pope. 1845 J. R. LOWELL in *Broadway Jrnl.* 8 Mar. 154/2 A guess At the spirit's deathlessness, Which ye entertain with fear In your *self-built dungeon here. 1970 A. G. FRANK in I. L. Horowitz *Masses in Lat. Amer.* vi. 220 In Mexico City 30 per cent of the population lives in self-built housing. 1784 COWPER *Task* v. 88 *Self-buried ere they die. 1748 RICHARDSON *Clarissa* IV. 347 Evils *self-caused..admit not of palliation. 1839 HALLAM *Lit. Eur.* IV. iii. §74 Every substance therefore is self-caused; that is its essence implies its existence. *a*1649 DRUMM. OF HAWTH. *Poems* Wks. (1711) 5 To ease *self-chosen pain. 1856 BAGEHOT *Coll. Works* (1965) I. 408 Anything free refers to the people; anything elected seems self-chosen. 1972 *Guardian* 19 Jan. 2/7 Vienna's self-chosen image of 'Schlamperei', roughly translated as carefree sloppiness. 1952 A. G. L. HELLYER *Sanders' Encycl. Gardening* (ed. 22) 240 *H[ydrangea] petiolaris*, *self-clinging climbing species, white. 1718 POPE *Iliad* XIV. 196 *Self-clos'd behind her shut the valves of gold. 1844 P. HARWOOD *Hist. Irish Reb.* 25 Hosts of armed citizens, self-paid and *self-commissioned. 1856 AYTOUN *Bothwell* v. xiv, Bold in his self-commissioned cause. 1922 JOYCE *Ulysses* 712 Ever would he wander, *selfcompelled, to the extreme limit of his cometary orbit. 1599 JONSON *Cynthia's Rev.* I. ii, To beare too deepe a sense Of her owne *selfe-conceiued excellence. *c*1900 H. A. JONES *Mrs. Dane's Defence* IV. 83, I intend that Mrs. Bulsom-Porter shall stay ..as a *self-confessed scandal-monger. 1981 M. UNDERWOOD *Hand of Fate* II. 91 Even a self-confessed liar is capable of telling the truth. 1977 A. GIDDENS *Stud. in Social & Polit. Theory* i. 72 Lakatos's sophisticated methodological falsificationism is *self-confessedly an attempt to reconcile a version of Popper's philosophy of science with some of the major difficulties created for the latter by the works of Kuhn and others. 1699 BENTLEY *Phal.* 69 This lame and *self-confuted Story. 1809 J. ORROK *Let.* 28 Sept. (1927) 110 Here, and at every other Station, they had *self-constituted Committees and carried everything their own way. 1818 SCOTT *Br. Lamm.* ix, The old gentleman, his self-constituted companion. 1634 MILTON *Comus* 597 It shall be in eternal restless change Self-fed, and *self-consum'd. 1644 —— *Divorce* II. iii. 39 Mans own will *self-corrupted. 1742 YOUNG *Nt. Th.* VI. 495 Learn, and lament, thy *self-defeated scheme. 1856 E. B. BROWNING *Aurora Leigh* I. 28 Books, that prove God's being so definitely, that man's doubt Grows *self-defined the other side the line, Made atheist by suggestion. 1977 R. HOLLAND *Self & Social Context* v. 95 There is a strong sense of tension between socially given role demands and self-defined role demands. 1667 MILTON *P.L.* III. 130 The first sort by thir own suggestion fell, Self-tempted, *self-deprav'd. 1784 COWPER *Task* I. 259 *Self-depriv'd Of other screen. 1846 J. D. MORELL *Hist. Philos.* II. v. 117 We..come, at length, at the end of the process, to a self-produced, or rather a *self-developed, *subject-object*. 1808 LAMB *Adv. Ulysses* vii. (1848) 74 Some have said..that they [*sc.* our vessels] move instinctively, *self-directed. 1894 *Pop. Sci. Monthly* XLIV. 516 Self-directed acts of perception. 1596 SPENSER *F.Q.* IV. viii. 14 *Selfe disliked life. 1598 SYLVESTER *Du Bartas* II. i. II. 393 Their *self-doom'd soules. 1789 COWPER *On the Queen's Visit to London* 14 And rockets flew, *self-driven. 1818 MRS. SHELLEY *Frankenstein* ii, It is a still greater evil to me that I am *self-educated. 1898 'MARK TWAIN' in *Harper's Mag.* Mar. 533/2 When an Austrian is called Doctor it means that he is either a lawyer or a physician, and that he is not a self-educated man. 1977 *Listener* 15 Dec. 783/1 From his self-educated mother, Trilling inherited a love of English literature. 1871 FRASER *Berkeley* ix. 351 His unborrowed, evidently *self-elaborated thought. 1797 SOUTHEY *Vis. Maid of Orleans* iii, The little glow-worm's *self-emitted light. 1947 *Hansard Commons* 15 Dec. 1441 Mr. Amory asked the Minister of Food why persons who would qualify otherwise for the extra cheese are ineligible if they are *self-employed. 1978 *Jrnl. R. Soc. Med.* LXXI. 768 'Persons' include both salaried and self-employed, including those self-employed persons established in one country who provide services in another. 1860 TYNDALL *Glac.* I. i. 2 A diamond is a crystal *self-erected from atoms of carbon. 1859 J. S. MILL in *Fraser's Mag.* LX. 767/1 An enemy, or a *self-fancied rival. 1634 *Self-fed [see *self-consum'd* above]. 1881 O. WILDE *Poems* 123 That holocaust, That self-fed flame. 1960 *Farmer & Stockbreeder* 1 Mar. 72/2 He had heard a lot of farmers expressing disappointment in the..meat yield from self-fed silage. 1611 SHAKS. *Cymb.* II. iii. 124 To knit their soules..in *self-figur'd knot. 1590 C'TESS PEMBROKE *Antonie* 742 Unhappy he, in whome selfe-succour lies, Yet *selfe-forsaken wanting succour dies. 1621 G. SANDYS *Ovid's Met.* I. (1626) 17 She starts: and from her selfe, *self-frighted, fled. 1591 SYLVESTER *Du Bartas* I. vi. 332 Who, still *self-furnisht, needest borrow never Diana's shafts. 1935 M. LOWENFELD *Play in Childhood* i. 37 Play..is taken as applying to all activities in children that are spontaneous and *self-generated. 1965 J. D. CHAMBERS in Glass & Eversley *Population in Hist.* xiii. 333 The increase in the industrial population was partly self-generated. *a*1667 COWLEY *Ret. Scotl.* Wks. 1711 III. 40 The *self-gotten Phœnix. 1820 KEATS *Hyperion* I. 161 The Titans fierce, *self-hid, or prison-bound. 1774 GOLDSM. *Nat. Hist.* (1824) III. 121 The oyster..is *self-impregnated. 1815 *Zeluca* III. 44 She never knew the *Self-incurred Catastrophe. 1938 (*title*) The Oxford companion to music: *self-indexed and with a pronouncing glossary. 1978 *Canad. N. & Q.* Dec. 1/2, I am in the process of preparing a bibliography of Canadian periodicals that are self-indexed, or which have been indexed externally. 1879 G. M. HOPKINS *Poems* (1967) 81 What the heart is! which, like carriers let fly..To its own fine function, wild and *self-instressed. 1654 OWEN *Doctr. Saints Persev.* xiii. 313 A vaine, superstitious, *selfe-invented Worship of God. 1748 RICHARDSON *Clarissa* VII. 288 Some other more distant relations.., *self-invited..attended. 1813 SCOTT *Rokeby* v. xvi, This self-invited guest. 1979 C. MACLEOD *Family Vault* (1980) xviii. 162 The first of the self-invited guests slumped into a wooden chair. 1700 DRYDEN *Pal. & Arc.* III. 253 And left one altar dark, a little space, Which turned *self-kindled, and renewed the blaze. 1889 *Spectator* 28 Dec. 922/1 A tax..*self-levied. 1625 K. LONG tr. *Barclay's Argenis* IV. xviii. 306 The *selfe-maim'd Thracian King. 1903 A. R. WALLACE *Man's Place in Universe* iii. 44 By the use of the photographic plate the exact positions of..thousands of stars can be *self-mapped simultaneously. 1849 M. ARNOLD *Mycerinus* 28 When the duped soul, *self-mastered, claims its meed. 1849 C. BRONTE *Shirley* vii, The thoughts were *self-matured. 1594 SHAKS. *Rich. III*, IV. iv. 376 Thy Selfe, is *selfe-misvs'd. 1809 MALKIN *Gil Blas* XI. xiii. ¶13 You are become highly moral and *self-mortified. 1819 WORDSW. *Waggoner* IV. 64 The vapours sweep Along..Like fleecy clouds *self-multiplied. *a*1704 T. BROWN *Lond. & Lacedem. Oracles* Wks. 1709 III. III. 135 *Self-nam'd Athenians. 1955 S. SPENDER *Making of Poem* I. iv. 67 The observer is *self-observed. *a*1700 KEN *Hymnotheo* Poet. Wks. III. 112 Lord, I *self-offer'd, am not mine. 1923 *Self-ordered [see *self-ordering*, sense 1 f above]. 1959 I. & P. OPIE *Lore & Lang. Schoolch.* xii. 252 A contributor..gives a vivid description of a particular party of *self-organized jollyboys. 1855 MILMAN *Lat. Christ.* XIV. ii. (1864) IX. 53 Those who were *self-outlawed, or outlawed by the dominant authority. *c*1865 G. M. HOPKINS *Poems* (1967) 120, I storm and shock you. So I fail. And like a *self-outwitted blast Fling to the convent wicket fast. 1962 H. C. WESTON *Sight, Light & Work* (ed. 2) iii. 76 Persons of average vision are able to perform *self-paced tasks requiring the perception of detail. 1835 J. S. MILL in *Lond. Rev.* I. II. iv. 360 The unpaid is apt to become the *self-paid. 1844 Self-paid [see *self-commissioned* above]. 1864 BRYCE *Holy Rom. Emp.* x. (1866) 171 Lewis the Pious, submitting to a fresh coronation, admitted the invalidity of his former *self-performed one. 1821 LAMB *Elia* I. *Witches & other night-fears*, Had I never met with the picture, the fears would have come *self-pictured in some shape or other. 1822 S. ROGERS *Italy* (1823) 55 An ancient grove *Self-planted. 1830 TENNYSON *Dirge* v, Round thee blow, *self-pleached deep, Bramble roses. 1868 TYNDALL *Fragm. Sci.* (1879) II. vi. 81 These molecular blocks of salt are *self-posited. 1642 FULLER *Holy & Prof. St.* v. v. 374 A private maid, how highly soever *self-pretended. 1943 A. V. BARBER *Let.* 8 Feb. in W. Temple *Lett.* (1963) 58 Their arguments reveal elementary, and sometimes even *self-proclaimed, ignorance of the monetary mechanism. 1979 A. CHISHOLM *Nancy Cunard* xi. 103 John Banting..was to become England's sole self-proclaimed Surrealist painter. 1647 C. HARVEY *Schola Cordis* iv. 8 Why dost thou hugge thy *self-procured woes? 1774 GOLDSM. *Nat. Hist.* IV. ii. (1824) III. 82 Their shell is *self-produced. 1977 *Lancet* 30 July 207/2 A large proportion of the food consumed is self-produced. 1851 *Illustr. Catal. Gt. Exhib.* III. 542/1 Complete phonological English alphabet constructing *self-pronouncing words with the proper orthography. 1931 (*title*) The Royal Webster dictionary for home and school, self-pronouncing. 1678 *Self-punish'd [see SELF-ACCUSED]. 1738 LILLO *Marina* III. ii. 50 *Self-resign'd to silence and despair. 1667 MILTON *P.L.* IX. 183 [The Serpent] In Labyrinth of many a round *self-rowld. 1849 M. ARNOLD *Shakespeare* 10 *Self-school'd, *self-scann'd, self-honour'd, self-secure. 1970 P. Y. CARTER *Mr Campion's Falcon* ix. 68 A belt of *self-seeded larches. 1924 G. B. SHAW *St Joan* Pref. p. xlii, The saints and prophets..are always really self-selected, like Joan. 1977 J. D. DOUGLAS in Douglas & Johnson *Existential Sociol.* i. 17 At first the recruits to this rationalized segment of society were self-selected. 1828 JOLLY *Sunday Services* (1840) 276 False and *self-sent teachers. 1865 G. M. HOPKINS *Poems* (1967) 169 Will no one show I argued ill? Because, although *Self-sentenced, still I keep my trust. *a*1957 R. CAMPBELL tr. *Camões's Lusiads* in *Coll. Poems* (1960) III. 129 Like Canace, self-sentenced and undone. 1785 MME. D'ARBLAY *Lett.* 25 Aug., So hard and dangerous a *self-set task. 1956 *Nature* 10 Mar. 490/1 The distribution of this *self-set seed mainly on the more heterozygous members of the population restricts the rate of fixation of genetic variability under these conditions. 1977 *Times Lit. Suppl.* 28 Jan. 94/2 Downright despair over his herculean, self-set task. 1837 CARLYLE *Fr. Rev.* III. II. vii, Guardsman Pâris..will be found some months after, *self-shot in a remote inn. 1856 J. G. WHITTIER *Panorama* 23 The *self-sold knaves of gain and place. 1924 G. B. SHAW *Saint Joan* Pref. p. lii, We do not..rush to the opposite extreme in a recoil from her as from a witch self-sold to the devil. 1816 BYRON *Ch. Har.* III. 80 His life was one long war with *self sought foes. 1862 *All Year Round* 13 Sept. 8 A rough kind of grass,..on the sharp points of whose rigid blades flies and beetles are often *self-spitted. *a*1700 KEN *Hymnotheo* Poet. Wks. III. 295 Matter self-form'd, self-mov'd, *self-steer'd. 1899 *Allbutt's Syst. Med.* VIII. 210 *Self-stimulated thoughts, in place of those implanted from without. 1823 BENTHAM *Not Paul but Jesus* 206 The sort of connection..between the undoubted Apostles, and this *self-styled one. 1907 *National Church* 15 Oct. 263/1 The self-styled 'Free Churches'. 1605 SHAKS. *Lear* II. ii. 129 He..got praises of the King, For him attempting, who was *selfe-subdued. 1801 SOUTHEY *Thalaba* I. xxx, Here *self-suspended hangs in air,..The living carbuncle. 1667 *Self-tempted [see *self-depraved* above]. 1922 JOYCE *Ulysses* 344 A neat blouse of electric blue, *self-tinted by dolly dyes. 1810 SCOTT *Lady of L.* II. xv, Thy father's battle-brand..Did, *self-unscabbarded, foreshow The foot-step of a secret foe. 1866 *Ch. Times* 3 Feb., A *self-vaunted 'friend of the working classes'. *a*1763 SHENSTONE *Past. Ode to Lyttleton* xxv, To see the babbling floods Thro' *self-worn mazes flow. 1823 BENTHAM *Not Paul but Jesus* 110 In comparison of *self-written biography, scarcely does any other biography deserve the name.

(*b*) Rarely, with adjs. in *-able*; as ***self-impairable*** = liable to be impaired by one's own action, ***self-irrecoverable*** = not recoverable by oneself (whence ***self-irrecoverableness***).

1678 CUDWORTH *Intell. Syst.* I. iv. §36. 565 Endowed with ..Freewill, and consequently..*Self-improvable and *Self-impairable. 1782 J. BROWN *View of Nat. & Rev. Relig.* v. iv, We are altogether guilty, polluted, miserable and *self-irrecoverable. *Ibid.* VI. i, Their sinfulness, misery, and *self-irrecoverableness. 1769 —— *Dict. Bible* s.v. *Gospel*, *Self-irreformable transgressors.

b. With nouns of action, as ***self-selection*** (see also SELF-ASSEMBLY 1, etc.). Similarly with verbs (usu. forming adjs., occas. sbs.), as ***self-build***, ***-erect***, ***-feed*** (see also SELF-DRIVE *a.*).

1952 *Times* 5 Mar. 5/6 The first self-build society put up its first houses over three years ago. There are now several scores of societies with hundreds of houses built or building. 1976 *Eastern Even. News* (Norwich) 13 Dec. 13 (Advt.), Renta-tower lightweight self-build staging. 1924 *Motor* 28 Oct. 697/1 The open tourer, with its self-erect transparent side screens. 1960 *Farmer & Stockbreeder* 16 Feb. 20/2 (Advt.), Self-erect cattle shelter. 1897 *Sears, Roebuck Catal.* 127/1 Self-feed Base Burner... A neat, attractive stove. 1951 *Sun* (Baltimore) 31 May 9/5 Mixing salt with cottonseed meal enables livestock growers to self-feed controlled amounts of protein supplement to their beef cattle. 1958 *Times* 1 July (Suppl.) p. viii/7 For up to 20 cows the trailer can be a home-made self-feed rack standing on an ordinary farm trailer. 1969 *Times* 24 Feb. 12/2 Larger farmers have taken advantage of improvement grants to erect concrete-and-asbestos covered yards and silos, generally using a combination of self-feed and easy-feed. 1975 *N.Z. Jrnl. Agric.* Sept. 63/1 We self-fed our grass silage. 1962 E. GODFREY *Retail Selling & Organization* i. 7 Members..can..obtain..financial assistance in the conversion of their shops to self-service or self-selection. 1979 *Guardian* 5 Nov. 22/2 A half of all Jobcentre placements are made as a result of the self-selection of a job by a job-seeker.

3. Compounds in which *self-* is adverbial:

a. with sbs., adjs., vbs., advs. = for, in, into, on or upon, to or towards, with oneself or itself, the prep. to be supplied being that required in the construction taken by the word which forms the second element; e.g. ***self-absorbed*** = absorbed in oneself, ***self-acquaintance*** = acquaintance with oneself, ***self-addressed*** = addressed to oneself, ***self-compassion*** = compassion for oneself.

1847 HELPS *Friends in C.* I. v. 85, I do not mean that people are to be *self-absorbed. 1903 SOMERVILLE & 'ROSS' *All on Irish Shore* 132 His face was pale and strange and entirely self-absorbed. 1980 D. NEWSOME *On Edge of Paradise* 8 One can admit to being self-absorbed... Arthur was genuinely self-critical. 1745 J. MASON *Self-Knowl.* I. vii. (1853) 50 *Self-acquaintance shews a man the particular Sins he is most..addicted to. 1855 BROWNING *Old Pictures in Florence* xix, To become now *self-acquainters. 1642 FULLER *Holy & Prof. St.* IV. xvi. 323 Sullennesse and *self-addiction, things ill beseeming his noble spirit. 1847 C. BRONTE *Professor* xxiii, A voice..so low, so *self-addressed. 1904 *Delineator* Dec. 1084 If you will send a stamped self-addressed envelope, we will tell you where you can take a course. 1976 *Oxford Consumer* Mar. 11/1 Sending a stamped self-addressed envelope (6 × 3½) to the Chief Superintendent, St Aldate's Police Station. 1880 *Q. Rev.* CXLIX. 285 The honourable and..*self-advantageous task. 1606 SHAKS. *Tr. & Cr.* II. iii. 250 *Vlis.* If he were proud... *Dio.* Or strange, or *selfe affected. 1656 EARL MONM. tr. *Boccalini's Advts.fr. Parnass.* II. xxvii. (1674) 177 *Self-affectionate people..prove perfidious. 1964 M. ARGYLE *Psychol. & Social Probl.* iv. 55 There is some evidence that *self-aggression is a result of displaced aggression. *a*1593 MARLOWE *Ovid's Eleg.* III. viii. [ix.] 10 And knocks his bare brest with *selfe-angry hands. 1697 BURGHOPE *Disc. Relig. Assemb.* 114 Reflection, and *self-application. 1597 SHAKS. *Lover's Compl.* 76 If I had *self-applied Love to myself. 1663 OWEN *Vind. Animadv.* Wks. 1851 XIV. 405 Such *self-assumings are many of the old papal epistles stuffed withal. 1837 TENNENT *Vis. Glencoe* 58 The self-assuming smile. 1606 SHAKS. *Tr. & Cr.* II. iii. 133 In *selfe-assumption greater Then in the note of iudgement. 1784 COWPER *Task* I. 616 A school in which he learns..Mean *self-attachment. 1862 MERIVALE *Rom. Emp.* lxv. VII. 392 Held firmly together by its inherent *self-attraction. 1649 ROBERTS *Clavis Bibl.* 184 Luxury, Vain-glory, *Self-attributions. 1894 MRS. OLIPHANT *Autobiogr.* (1899) 81, I have fallen back into my own way of *self-comment. 1898 T. HARDY *Wessex Poems* 2 'Life is roomy yet, and the odds unbounded'. So *self-communed I. 1863 I. WILLIAMS *Baptistery* I. xi. (1874) 130 With silence and with *self-communing fear. 1927 E. M. FORSTER *Aspects of Novel* iii. 67 The..self-communings which politeness and shame prevent him from mentioning. **1963** *Times Lit. Suppl.* 11 Jan. 21/3 A seven-year-old girl's self-communings. **1818** Byron *Don Juan* I. xci. 48 His *self-communion with his own high soul. **1916** Joyce *Portrait of Artist* (1969) 160 The impression which effaced his troubled selfcommunion was that of a mirthless mask reflecting a sunken day from the threshold of the college. *a* **1634** Chapman *Rev. for Honour* II. i. 202 *Self-compassion, soothing us to faith Of what we wish should hap. **1875** Lowell *Lit. Ess., Wordsw.* Wks. 1890 IV. 406 *His self-concentrated nature. **1862** Lytton *Str. Story* II. 53 Intense *self-concentration is..a mighty magician. **1816** H. G. Knight *Ilderim* 577 Some deep dream of *self-concenter'd thought. **1680** J. Quarles (*title*) *Self-Conflict: or, the Powerful Motions between the Flesh and Spirit. **1819** Shelley *Prometheus Unbound* IV. 259 Its intense yet self-conflicting speed. **1848** R. I. Wilberforce *Doctr. Incarnation* xiv. (1852) 423 The partial, *self-conflicting, uncertain views. **1725** Pope *Odyss.* VI. 170 The King ..*self-considering, as he stands, debates. **1710** Shaftesb. *Charac., Advice to Author* I. §1 Our Exercise of *Self-Converse. **1591** Sylvester *Du Bartas* I. ii. 866 *Self-cruell Mothers. **1643** Milton *Divorce* 37 Those commands.. which compell us to *self-cruelty above our strength. **1725** Pope *Odyss.* xx. 36 Ulysses..In *self-debate the Suitors doom resolv'd. **1661** Glanvill *Van. Dogm.* 133 *Self-designers are seldom disappointed. **1872** Geo. Eliot *Middlem.* III. lviii. 290 His endurance was mingled with a *self-discontent. **1853** Kingsley *Hypatia* xiii, He continued talking to himself aloud after the manner of restless *self-discontented men. **1671** Milton *Samson* 514 *Self-displeas'd For self-offence. **1640** Bp. Reynolds *Passions* (1658) 1047 A *self-displicency and severity towards our own errors. **1802** Mrs. J. West *Infidel Father* III. 239 The earl..endeavoured to conceal his chagrin and *self-dissatisfaction. **1891** W. James *Let.* 6 July (1920) I. 310 You've been saved many forms of self-dissatisfaction and misery. **1981** V. Canning *Boy on Platform One* ii. 30 She felt a rare mood of self-dissatisfaction. **1809–10** Coleridge *Friend* (1865) 1 The *self-dissatisfied race of men. **1964** *Language* XL. 226 Syntactically complex *self-embedded constructions in English. **1963** *Self-embedding [see push-down *a.* 1]. **1978** *Language* LIV. 171 Yngve is probably best known as the man who erroneously attributed to left-branching the effects of self-embedding. **1727** Somerville *Use of Looking-Glass* 14 On her the *self-enamour'd chit Was very lavish of his wit. **1814** F. Burney *Wanderer* IV. lxxi. 240 Juliet passed three days, *self-inclosed. **1876** Geo. Eliot *Dan. Der.* xxvi, Its self-enclosed unreasonableness and impiety. **1599** Shaks. *Much Ado* III. i. 56 She cannot loue..Shee is so *selfe indeared. **1848** Dickens *Dombey* xxx, [She] in her *self-engrossment did not trouble herself about the nature of this agitation. **1818** Scott *Br. Lamm.* xxv, The *self-exultation with which he was, as it were, distended. **1647** H. More *Philos. Poems* Addit. *Exorcismus* 18 You *self-exulting sprights. **1647** Bp. Hall *Sel. Th.* §34 The *self-felony of a wilful sinner. **1842** Tennyson '*Of old sat Freedom*' ii, *Self-gather'd in her prophet-mind. **1601** Shaks. *All's Well* IV. v. 78 A *selfe gracious remembrance. **1817** Coleridge *Biog. Lit.* I. xii. 265 We are to seek..for some absolute truth..a truth *self-grounded, unconditional and known by its own light. **1940** *Mind* XLIX. 171 All demonstration leads back to indemonstrable bases, and grounds must themselves be grounded on what is self-grounded. **1691** South *12 Serm.* (1697) II. 484 A fatal *Self-imposture. **1920** 'K. Mansfield' *Let.* 27 Oct. (1977) 190 Don't you feel that what English writers lack today is experience of Life. I don't mean that superficially. But they are *self-imprisoned. **1876** L. Stephen *Eng. Th. 18th C.* II. 30 Every vicious action must be *self-injurious. **1864** Pusey *Lect. Daniel* vii. 433 To secure the poor sufferer from *self-injury, or from injuring others. **1667** Milton *P.L.* XI. 93 His heart I know, how variable and vain *Self-left. **1922** Joyce *Ulysses* 212 Amused Buck Mulligan mused in pleasant murmur with himself, *self-nodding. **1876** Mrs. Oliphant *Phœbe Jun.* xxvi, His *self-occupation was an offence to the girl. **1795–1814** Wordsw. *Excursion* I. 798 The careless stillness of a thinking mind *Self-occupied. **1818** *Art Pres. Feet* 128 A mode of cure, less dangerous in the hands of a *self-operator than the knife. **1900** B. D. Jackson *Gloss. Bot. Terms*, **Self-parasitism*, parasitic on its own species. **1819** Byron *Mazeppa* xvii. 80 At times sought with *self-pointed sword. **1959** 'M. Ainsworth' *Murder is Catching* xv. 173 The sublime *self-preoccupation of so many actors. *a* **1592** T. Watson *Poems* (Arb.) 179 Vnwise they were their sorrowes *selfe procuring. **1654** Whitlock *Zootomia* 440, I will not think men that want Bread, do therefore want Wisdome (even that of *Self-provision). **1883** F. H. Bradley *Logic* III. I. vi. 448 The analysis in the end is hence *not* synthesis, if that means *self-relation. **1906** D. H. MacGregor in *Hibbert Jrnl.* July 800 The fact of self-distinction from the world is as ultimate as that of self-relation to it. **1870** J. H. Newman *Gram. Assent* II. vi. 197 The enjoyable *self-repose of certitude. **1856** Mrs. Carlyle in Froude *Carlyle* (1890) II. 197 Then I should be going as part of your luggage without *self-responsibility. **1820** Keats *Isabella* xvii, *Self-retired In hungry pride and gainful cowardice. **1671** Milton *Samson* 513 Who *self-rigorous chooses death as due. **1591** *Self-rumineth [see rumine]. **1671** Milton *Samson* 827 Impartial, *self-severe, inexorable. **1891** T. Hardy *Tess* xxxvii, *Self-solicitude was near extinction in her. *a* **1586** Sir P. Sidney *Arcadia* III. (1598) 346 These doubtful *selfe-speches. **1715** *Wodrow's Corr.* (1843) II. 37 My *self-tenderness will not allow me to spend time at night on the records. **1687** Norris *Coll. Misc.* 234 Since he [man] is not a Central and *self-terminating Being. *Ibid.* 303, I conclude that I am not..a Central or *self-terminative Being. **1865** Grote *Plato* I. vii. 293 Individual, *self-thinking minds. **1598** Sylvester *Du Bartas* II. ii. I. 99 Wishing already to dis-throne th'Eternall, And *selfe-usurp the Majesty supernall. **1882–3** *Schaff's Encycl. Relig. Knowl.* III. 2507/1 The *self-witness of Jesus to his divinity. **1849** Grote *Greece* II. xlviii. VI. 145 The Peloponnesians were a *self-working population with few slaves. **1590** Shaks. *Com. Err.* III. ii. 168 Least my selfe be guilty to *selfe wrong.

b. with adjs. and related sbs., vbs., pples. = of or in oneself or itself, of or in one's or its own nature or power; e.g. ***self-apparent*** = apparent of itself, ***self-desirable*** = desirable in itself. Also (after self-fertile), ***self-impotent***, ***-sterile*** adjs., ***-sterility***.

1845 *Florist's Jrnl.* 107 The utility of such a book..is *self-apparent. **1847–54** Webster, **Self-attractive*, attractive by one's self. **1605** Sylvester *Du Bartas* II. iii. III. 574 [He] Hardens the King, and blinding him (*selfe-blinde) Leaves him to Lusts of his own vicious minde. **1857** E. B. Browning *Aurora Leigh* VII. 289 Both faces leaned together like a pair Of folded innocences, *self-complete. **1882** H. S. Holland *Logic & Life* xviii. 273 The Holy Church..must..be also self-complete. *Ibid.*, By faith, spirit shows its self-mastery, its *self-completeness. *c* **1586** C'tess Pembroke *Ps.* LVIII. ii, The aspick..*self-deaf and unaffected lies. **1710** Norris *Chr. Prud.* v. 200 The end having an intrinsic Goodness of its own, and so being *Self-desirable. **1642** H. More *Song of Soul* II. i. II. xlvi, Whiles *self-flowing sourse I here detect In plants. **1591** Sylvester *Du Bartas* I. v. 834 And on shamefull Tree (*Self-guiltless) shed his blood. *a* **1586** Sidney *Arcadia* (1622) 148 *Selfe-guiltie folke most prone to feele compassion. **1869** Darwin *Orig. Spec.* viii. (ed. 5) 333 They have become *self-impotent, whilst still retaining the capacity of fertilising. **1704** Norris *Ideal World* II. v. 280 In the head of these *Self-intelligible objects let us..place the great.. God. **1798** Sotheby tr. *Wieland's Oberon* (1826) II. 173 To eclipse the *self-resplendent blaze. **1598** Sylvester *Du Bartas* II. iv. II. 392 Whether the Sun *self-shine. **1882** G. M. Hopkins *Lett. to R. Bridges* (1955) 165 This seems in English a point..insisted on, that words shall be single and specific marks for things, whether *self-significant or not. **1735** Somerville *Chase* III. 286 The unweildly Beast *Self-sinking, drops into the dark Profound. **1876** Darwin *Cross & Self Fertilisation* ix. 329 *Self-sterile Plants. **1913** Self-sterile [see incompatibility 4b]. **1876** Darwin *Cross & Self Fertilisation* ix. 346 The belief that *self-sterility has been acquired to prevent self-fertilisation. **1645** Rutherford *Tryal & Tri. Faith* (1845) 392 Peter is *self-strong. **1642** H. More *Song of Soul* II. i. II. xlv, All humane souls be *self-vivacious. **1695** Owen *Faith of God's Elect* Wks. 1851 V. 453 Those *self-whole, jolly professors which these days abound with.

c. with pples. = from or out of oneself or itself (as a source or point of origin); e.g. ***self-arising*** = arising from or out of oneself.

a **1871** Grote *Eth. Fragm.* i. (1876) 20 This inward and *self-arising determination. **1744** J. Harris *Three Treat.* III. II. (1765) 192 Those other Preconceptions—being Durable, *Self-derived, and Indeprivable. **1613** Shaks. *Hen. VIII*, I. i. 63 But Spider-like Out of his *Selfe-drawing Web. **1864** Bryce *Holy Rom. Emp.* xviii. (1866) 360 It was proclaimed that the individual spirit..had..an independent existence as a centre of *self-issuing force. **1684** Howe *Redeemer's Tears* Wks. (1846) 84 The Christians of our age deceive themselves with a *self-sprung religion. **1855** Bailey *Mystic*, etc. 113 Begetting and conceiving and self-sprung.

4. In technical use, forming compounds to designate machines, appliances, or processes by or in which certain operations are performed without human or animal agency or special manipulation or adjustment for the purpose; usually = automatic, automatically. Also self-acting, etc.

1959 H. Barnes *Oceanogr. & Marine Biol.* 168 Our attention will, therefore, be focussed on remotely controlled or *self-actuating underwater cameras. **1834–6** Barlow in *Encycl. Metrop.* (1845) VIII. 175/1 To some boilers are also attached *self-adjusting feeders to supply the fuel to the furnace. **1893** *Outing* XXII. 145/2 Thus making the boat *self-bailing. **1908** *Harrod's Stores* Price List 950 *Self-basting Roaster. **1883** *Fisheries Exhib. Catal.* 32 Permanent *self-bury Anchor. **1825** Lunn in *Encycl. Metrop.* (1845) IV. 95/1 Cavallo's *self-charging jar. **1903** *Daily Chron.* 25 Feb. 10/4 *Self-clamp cutting machine. **1875** Knight *Dict. Mech.*, **Self-closing Bridge*, a pivot bridge opened by canal-boats in passing. **1931** *Times Educ. Suppl.* 27 June 249/4 Noise is minimized by the use of self-closing double doors. **1971** *Oxf. Univ. Gaz.* 18 Feb. 671/1 The barrier must be self-closing after a car has passed through. **1888** Papworth *Gwilt's Encycl. Archit.* §4148*a*, Laths of wood rebated together, having numerous mortices, through which pass a series of tempered steel bands, causing the shutter to be *self-coiling. **1960** *Times* 7 Mar. 13/5 Refrigerators..*self defrosting. **1912** *Proc. Physical Soc.* XXIV. 342 (*heading*) The *self-demagnetisation of annealed steel rods. **1855** in *Brit. Alm. & Comp.* (1856) 50 Quick *self-discharge of water. **1825** J. Nicholson *Oper. Mech.* 35 The *self-disengaging coupling. **1886** *Sci. Amer.* LV. 373/2 A *self-dropping two-horse planter. **1825** J. Nicholson *Oper. Mech.* Index 790 *Self-easing coupling. **1869** Rankine *Machine & Hand-tools* Pl. L 6, Enabling the machine to drill or bore at any angle whatever with a *self-feed. **1877** Raymond *Statist. Mines* 48 The adoption of *self-feeders. **1834–6** Barlow in *Encycl. Metrop.* (1845) VIII. 178/1 *Self-feeding furnace. **1908** *Daily Chron.* 27 Feb. 7/3 *Self-Filling Pens. **1869** Rankine *Machine & Hand-tools* Pl. L 6, *Self-friction feed motion. **1884** *Self-going [see self-fluxing]. **1906** *Self-hardening [see *air-hardening a.* s.v. air *sb.*[1] B. II]. **1865** M. Mackenzie *Laryngoscope* 85 The *Self-holder, or *fixateur* for holding the laryngeal mirror after introduction. **1856** *Farmer's Mag.* Jan. 64 The *self-holding lever plough. **1865** *Naval & Mil. Gaz.* 16 Sept. 589/2 *Self-igniting cartridges. **1948** L. Spitzer *Linguistics & Lit. Hist.* iv. 167 Diderot has experienced to the bitter end the self-annihilation of the self-igniting mind. **1927** *Automobile Engineer* XVII. 500/1 Compression ignition stands out clearly as the one factor controlling the onset of detonation in engine practice, this simultaneous activation of compressed combustion being what is understood by the '*self-ignition temperature' of a combustible. **1969** *Gloss. Terms assoc. with Fire (B.S.I.)* 1. 7 *Self-ignition temperature*, the temperature at which a flammable gas/air mixture will ignite without an external source of ignition. **1842** *Mech. Mag.* XXXVI. 155/1 *Self-inking Printing Press. **1960** *Farmer & Stockbreeder* 16 Feb. 47/3 (Advt.), Patent *self-levelling linkage ensures uniform depth of cultivation despite ground variations. **1965** *Sun* 28 Sept. 6/2 Citroen.. continue their anti-flash campaign. They are fitting 'self-levelling' headlights to a new..version of their Drop-head Coupe. **1977** *Observer* 8 May 33/3 Low-roll cornering and self-levelling rear suspension keep the handling predictable under all loads. **1864** Atkinson *Stanton Grange* 299 A *self-lighting hydrogen lamp. **1899** *Kynoch Jrnl.* Oct.–Nov. 2/2 Jones's *self-loading cartridge case. **1973** *Country Life* 28 June 1907 Self-loading forage machines, used primarily for handling loose hay. **1977** *R.A.F. News* 8–21 June 5/3 Their equipment includes..self-loading rifles and Sterling sub-machine guns. **1976** V. Canning *Doomsday Carrier* i. 6 The door swung back to *self-lock. *a* **1884** E. H. Knight *Pract. Dict. Mech.* Suppl. 795/2 **Self locking hook*, one which automatically closes. **1938** *Archit. Rev.* LXXXIII. p. lx/3 The glass is held by a continuous self-locking spring aluminium cover strip. **1980** D. Bloodworth *Trapdoor* xxx. 185 The door was self-locking and he could not force his way in. **1967** M. Chandler *Ceramics in Mod. World* v. 154 Among the many highly-specialized uses of graphite refractories is the making of *self-lubricating piston rings. **1947** M. M. Lewis *Language in Society* 136 The machines of war are its *self-operating weapons. **1962** A. Nisbett *Technique Sound Studio* 260 '*Midget' recorder*,..a *self-powered recorder which is light enough to be carried about without too much difficulty. **1853** Whyte-Melville *Digby Grand* x, Heavy and light guns, *self-primers, revolvers, and other deadly weapons. **1899** *Daily News* 3 May 10/6 The *Self-Propelled Traffic Association. **1928** C. F. S. Gamble *Story N. Sea Air Station* xxii. 428 To clear out the stores and take them by sea to other stations,..a large, self-propelled concrete lighter (*R.A.F. 110*) was used. **1945** *Finito! Po Valley Campaign* 31 Tanks and self-propelled guns were captured intact. **1977** J. Stern in *Winter's Tales 23* 178 Of his last years several were spent..in a self-propelled wheelchair on the roads..of Dorset. **1862** *Times* 7 Apr. 9/4 A *self-propelling bathing-machine. **1895** *Daily News* 11 June 7/5 Very little is known in England of what is being done in France with self-propelling carriages. **1866** *Trans. Brit. Assoc. 1865* 20 (*heading*) Description of the magnetic storm of the beginning of August 1865, as recorded by the *self-recording magnetographs at the Kew and Lisbon observatories. **1875** *Chamb. Jrnl.* 2 Jan. 7/2 Self-recording observatories. **1895** *Army & Navy Soc.* Price List 15 Sept. 1639 Self-Recording Aneroid Barometer and Clock. **1885** *Arch. Ophthalmol.* XIV. 54 The advantages offered by a perimeter with *self-register are too evident to be overlooked. **1836** Brande *Chem.* 140 The *self-registering thermometers..showing the maximum and minimum of temperature during the absence of the observer. **1847** *Phil. Trans. R. Soc.* CXXXVII. 111 It would be superfluous to speak of those proposals..for self-registering, photographically, the variation of the declination magnet. **1847** *Rep. Brit. Assoc. Adv. Sci. 1846* II. 11 In order to adapt it for *self-registration, a light conical brass tube..was affixed to the lower side. **1908** *Sears, Roebuck Catal.* 37/2 The shuttle is the most perfect self threading cylindrical shuttle... The needle is *self setting. **1948** W. E. Stephens et al. *Nuclear Fission & Atomic Energy* ix. 128 An interesting possible mechanism for *self-stabilization of a chain reaction in the presence of a cadmium absorber was suggested by Adler and von Halban. **1953** *Jrnl. Inst. Electr. Engineers* C. I. 101/1 The *self-stabilizing effect is so important in establishing an inherently safe and stable plant [*sc.* nuclear reactor]..that it should always be carefully studied. **1853** Ure *Dict. Arts* II. 697 His invention of the *self-strippers for the main cylinders. **1868** Joynson *Metals* 61 The *self-subsidation of the iron on the hearth. **1908** *Self-threading [see *self-setting* above]. **1964** *Discovery* Oct. 67/2 The Rank Organisation has recently marketed a 16 mm projector which is self-threading. **1864** *Trans. Highl. Soc.* Jan. 135 A *self-tipping platform. **1902** *Westm. Gaz.* 7 Apr. 4/2 Considerable practical advantage has been derived by the photographer from the *self-toning papers which are being so widely adopted. **1956** R. Sheckley in Aldiss & Harrison *Decade 1950s* (1976) 189 The portable sub-space set was *self-tuning. **1960** *Farmer & Stockbreeder* 16 Feb. 72/3 He could load five tons of chopped silage from the barn silo into two *self-unloading trailers to feed 180 cows in three-quarters of an hour. **1964** *New Scientist* 4 June 596/2 The self-unloading ship is not new but economic factors have until recently restricted its operation. **1825** *Mechanics' Mag.* III. 293/2 M. Recordon..proceeded to England, where he obtained a patent for his invention of *self-winding watches, which were then in great request. **1884** F. J. Britten *Watch & Clockm.* 239 Self-winding..[is] a watch or clock fitted with apparatus for winding it automatically.

5. Compounds in which *self-* is in the adjective relation: †**a.** = relating to oneself, one's own, personal, individual, private, intimate. *Obs.* Cf. self *pron.* 3c.

1661 Glanvill *Van. Dogm.* 134 *Self-advantage can as easily incline some, to believe a falshood, as profess it. **1590** Shaks. *Mids. N.* I. i. 113 Ouer-full of *selfe-affaires. **1604** —— *Oth.* III. iii. 200, I would not haue your free, and Noble Nature, Out of *selfe-Bounty, be abus'd. **1606** —— *Tr. & Cr.* II. iii. 182 He..speakes not to himselfe, but with a pride That quarrels at *selfe-breath. **1611** —— *Cymb.* III. iv. 149 By *selfe-danger, you should tread a course Pretty, and full of view. **1717** Fenton *Poems* 203 Sickly'd with Age, and sow'r with *Self-disgrace. **1598** Sylvester *Du Bartas* II. ii. II. 17 Who..rather sin suppresse By *selfe-examples, then by rigorousnesse. **1616** B. Jonson *Epigr.* ii, Thou art not couetous of least *selfe fame. **1640** D. Cawdrey *Three Serm.* (1641) 8 *Selfe-guiltinesse commonly makes men partiall, in judging others. **1598** Sylvester *Du Bartas* II. i. I. 54 Sufficient rich in *self-invention. **1613** Shaks. *Hen. VIII*, I. i. 134 Anger is like A full hot Horse, who being allow'd his way *Selfe-mettle tyres him. **1668** H. More *Div. Dial.* v. xxxvii. II. 436 Quitting all *Self-relishes he became an entire Servant of God. **1658** Earl Monm. tr. *Paruta's Wars Cyprus* 29 Whereby he might plead necessity of *selfe-safety for what he did. **1748** Richardson *Clarissa* II. 12, I am concerned, that you ever wrote at all to him..It was adding to his *self-significance. **1603** Florio *Montaigne* III. ix. 575 Yet is it safe by *selfe-waight [*pondere tuta suo*], and will last. **1678** R. Barclay *Apol. Quakers* xi. §10 (1729) 365 The *Self-workings and Motions of his own Mind.

b. = inherent in, depending upon, or proceeding from oneself (itself), one's nature, etc.; belonging to oneself (itself) as an independent creature; in the 17th cent. often

spec., dependent or relying upon one's own efforts or merits apart from the grace of God.
1596 NORDEN *Progr. Pietie* (1847) 28 A slumber which procureth many drowsy dreams of *self-ability to wade through all adverse things of the world. **1626** LAUD *Serm. 5th July* 32 No deserting the cause though no selfe-ability could hold it vp. **1598** SYLVESTER *Du Bartas* II. i. IV. 301 The other loud-resounded Heart-wanting Hymns, on *self-deserving founded. **1668** H. MORE *Div. Dial.* I. xxix. I. 119 By *Self-disunity I understand nothing else but that Matter has no *Vinculum* of its own to hold it together. **1660** INGELO *Bentiv. & Ur.* II. (1682) 217 Check the first Relishes of *self-excellency which you find in your Souls. **1678** BUNYAN *Pilgr.* I. (ed. 2) 254 Their pitiful old *self-holiness. **1858** BUSHNELL *Nat. & Supernat.* iv. (1864) 95 A soul..acting by its own free *self-impulsion. **1867** G. EASTON *Autobiogr.* vii. 81 Never had I felt such a deep sense of *self-insignificance. **1640** BP. REYNOLDS *Passions* xvi. (1647) 169 A Vacuity, Indigence, and *selfe-insufficiency of the Soule. **1745** ELIZA HAYWOOD *Fem. Spect.* x. (1748) II. 162 Vanity, and a high opinion of *self-merit, sometimes renders one party easy and contented. **1773** BERRIDGE *Wks.* (1864) 182 Self-will, *self-potence, and self-righteousness. *a* **1688** R. CUDWORTH *Treat. Freewill* (1838) 62 God Almighty could not make such a rational creature as this is..which had no *self-power, no hegemonic or ruling principle. **1896** W. JAMES *Let.* 24 July (1920) II. 41 Full of swelling and bursting *Weltschmerz* and religious melancholy, yet no more flexibility or self-power in his mind than in a boot-jack. **1964** E. BECKER in I. L. Horowitz *New Sociol.* 123 This is the basic phenomenology of alienations: the failure to develop self-powers by transacting with the world of things. **1668** OWEN *Expos. 130th Ps.* 380 The..infinite *self-purity of this Eternal Immense Being. **1701** NORRIS *Ideal World* I. i. 7 Any *self-stability, aseity, or essential immutability of its own. **1656** OWEN *Mortif. Sin* i. (1668) 5 Mortification from a *self-strength, carried on..unto the End of a self-Righteousness. **1880** G. M. HOPKINS *Sermons & Devotional Writings* (1959) 125 Above all my shame, my guilt, my fate are the very things in feeling, in tasting, which I most taste that *selftaste which nothing in the world can match. **1642** H. MORE *Song of Soul* II. ii. II. ix, Indispers'd, quick, close with *selfe-union. **1668** —— *Div. Dial.* I. xxx. I. 124 By the *Self-unity of a Spirit I understand a Spirit to be immediately and essentially one. **1633** FORD *Broken H.* I. i, So much out of a *selfe-vnworthinesse, His feares transport him. **1959** *Guardian* 28 Aug. 4/3, I did meet Colin Wilson, and..I found that with him I received my sense of my *self-value in its fullness. *a* **1631** DONNE *Poems* (1669) 86 My *self-want of sight. **1944** *Horizon* Feb. 104 The feeling of *self-worth experienced by contented individualists. **1978** M. PUZO *Fools Die* xlvii. 501 The lack of self-worth, the desire to please someone that they thought really cared about them. **1639** W. SCLATER *Worthy Commun.* 14 We must lay by all thoughts of honour, of place, of all kind of *selfe-worthinesse. *a* **1889** G. M. HOPKINS *Poems* (1967) 101 *Selfyeast of spirit a dull dough sours.

c. = having an independent existence, position, or authority; †pristine, original.
1839 E. A. POE *William Wilson* Wks. 1864 I. 434 Natural rights of *self-agency. **1657** HEYLIN *Hist. Ref.* I. ii. §5. 84 The Clergy of this Realm had a *Self-authority in all matters which concerned Religion. **1629** W. SCLATER *Expos. 2 Thess.* 169 Are Churches, Councels, Popes Authentique, of *selfe credit? **1643** LD. DIGBY *Obs. Relig. Med.* 34 Hee being in his proper nature *Selfe-Entity, all being must immediately flow from him. **1606** SYLVESTER *Du Bartas* II. iv. II. 1327 *Self-Eternitie, Infinite, All in all, yet out of all. **1612** SELDEN *Illustr. Drayton's Poly-olb.* viii. 125, I dare follow none of the Moderne erroniously transcribing Relaters..but haue..tooke it from the best *selfe-fountaines. **1610** G. FLETCHER *Christ's Vict.* I. lxiii, Thou *self-Idea of all joyes to come. *c* **1616** FLETCHER *Thierry & Theod.* I. i, A *selfe-peece from the touch of power and Iustice. **1905** *Athenæum* 1 Apr. 396/3 The full *self-sovereignty of Japan.

d. = having self as the object or aim; self-centred.
1654 WHITLOCK *Zootomia* 367 This thread of *Self-aime runnes through the whole Peece of what men do. **1687** NORRIS *Coll. Misc.* 262 Neither does he [God] govern the Rational part of it by the Precepts of Religion out of any *Self-design, as if he feasted his nostrils with the perfumes of the Altar. **1647** H. MORE *Philos. Poems* Addit. 35 Save me, God! from *Self-desire. **1841** GLADSTONE in Morley *Life* (1903) I. 233 Men hurrying this way and that for gold, or pleasure, or some self-desire. **1621** BARGRAVE *Serm. agst. Selfe Policy* (1624) 28 This wicked sibi, this *selfe-doctrine. **1778** [W. MARSHALL] *Minutes Agric., Digest* 4 Nor was actuated by any other motive than *Self-Emolument. **1587** GOLDING *De Mornay* xvi. (1592) 257 What else is the whole societie of man..but a *self-gaine? **1624** BARGRAVE (*title*) A Sermon against *Selfe Policy, preached at White-Hall in Lent. 1621. **1654** WHITLOCK *Zootomia* 177 The *Ratio formalis*, essentiall of a Suist, or *selfe-politician. **1832** TENNYSON *Œnone* 156 Unbias'd by *self-profit.

e. = caused by oneself, of one's own making.
This use is rare; the mod. examples are due to analysis of compounds illustrated under 2; e.g. *self-chain* from 'self-chained'.
1652 CRASHAW *Carmen Deo Nostro* To C'tess Denbigh, Fetter'd, & lockt up fast they ly In a sad *selfe-captivity. **1882** ROSSETTI *Poems* (1904) 262/2 Who from thy *self-chain shall set thee free? **1845** E. WARBURTON *Crescent & Cross* II. 163 The *self-outlaws of humanity.

self-a'based, *ppl. a.* [SELF- 2.] Full of self-abasement.
a **1748** WATTS *Att. Pract. Relig.* [II.] iii, Are you more penitent and self-abased under a sense of your sins?

self-a'basement. [SELF- 1 a.] Humiliation of oneself.
1656 OWEN *Mortif. Sin* xii. (1668) 128 Such Meditations as may serve to fill thee..with self-abasement. **1710** SHAFTESB. *Charac., Adv. Author* III. iii. (1727) I. 331 The method of Self-abasement may perhaps be thought the properest to make Approaches to the sacred Shrines. **1860** MOZLEY *Univ. Serm.* vii. (1877) 160 Self-abasement, as illustrated by the parable of the sanctified Publican. **1883** WACE *Gospel & its Witnesses* iv. 76 The Church's daily Confession, with its keen self-abasement.

self-a'basing, *ppl. a.* [SELF- 1 f.] Marked by, involving, or requiring self-abasement.
1656 OWEN *Mortif. Sin* xii. (1668) 128 This self-abasing Consideration. **1793** COWPER *Let. to J. Johnson* Wks. 1837 XV. 253 The self-abasing doctrines of the gospel. **1822** JAS. MACDONALD *Mem. Jos. Benson* 330 Their joyful and self-abasing reflections.

self-abne'gation. [SELF- 1 a.] Self-renunciation.
1657 *Baker's Sancta Sophia* II. II. iii. §6 (1908) 249 The smallest act of love and service to God, performed with a perfect self-abnegation. DOVE *Logic Chr. Faith* IV. ii. §5. 226 In the Christian missionary..we have some of the noblest specimens of..self-abnegation. **1873** B'NESS BUNSEN in Hare *Life* (1879) I. ii. 57 Her true humility and self-abnegation.

So **self-'abnegating** *ppl. a.*, **self-'abnegator** (*rare*), **self-'abnegatory** *a.*
1864 PUSEY *Daniel* i. 22 Amid this *self-abnegating silence, what is the self-laudation? **1874** H. R. REYNOLDS *John Bapt.* iv. §5. 257 The recklessness of self-abnegating love. **1907** G. B. SHAW *John Bull's Other Island* p. xix, The Catholic is theoretically a Collectivist, a *self-abnegator, a Tory. **1897** MARY KINGSLEY *W. Africa* 680 A *self-abnegatory religion.

self-ab'sorption. 1. [SELF- 3 a.] Absorption in one's own emotions, interests, or situation; self-preoccupation.
1862 LYTTON *Str. Story* I. 131 That self-absorption which the habit of reverie had fostered. *a* **1930** D. H. LAWRENCE *Last Poems* (1932) 94 The lovely and self-absorbed girl Looked back at the handsome and self-absorbed young man And thrilled. And in that thrill he felt: Her self-absorption is even as strong as mine. **1979** V. S. NAIPAUL *Bend in River* xi. 188, I did not wish to lose myself in the..self-absorption of that fantasy.

2. *Physics.* [SELF- 2 b.] Absorption of radiation by the material emitting it. Cf. SELF-SHIELDING *vbl. sb.*
1938 *Proc. Cambr. Philos. Soc.* XXXIV. 600 With radium E, strong sources may be obtained showing negligible self-absorption. **1950** *Atomics* Nov. 334/2 The self-absorption of β-rays in radioactive films..has been investigated. **1978** H. H. BAUER et al. *Instrumental Analysis* x. 265 At too high a current, Doppler broadening and self-absorption (absorption of part of the emitted radiation by the dense cloud of atoms in the source itself) will occur.

self-a'buse. [SELF- 1 a.]
1. Self-deception. (Cf. ABUSE *sb.* 4.)
1605 SHAKS. *Macb.* III. iv. 142 My strange and self-abuse Is the initiate feare, that wants hard vse.

2. Abuse or revilement of oneself.
1795–1814 WORDSW. *Excurs.* VII. 910 Those cold humours ..That..had sometimes urged To self-abuse a not ineloquent tongue. **1865** TROLLOPE *Belton Est.* xx. 238 He abused himself for his own selfishness. But such self-abuse [etc.].

3. Masturbation. Hence **self-a'buser**.
1728 CHAMBERS *Cycl.* s.v. *Abuse*, Self-Abuse, is a Phrase used by some late Writers for the Crime of Self-Pollution. **1829** *Good's Study Med.* (ed. 3) III. 242 The evils that haunt the worn-out debauchee, and especially the self-abuser. **1899** *Allbutt's Syst. Med.* VIII. 373 Eroticism and self-abuse.

self-accu'sation. [SELF- 1 a.] Accusation of oneself.
1662 E. LAKE (*title*) Memoranda: touching the Oath Ex Officio, pretended Self-accusation, and Canonical Purgation. *a* **1716** WYCHERLEY *Posth. Wks.* I. (1728) 35 His Self-Accusation calls his Sense in Question. **1740** RICHARDSON *Pamela* (1824) I. l. 380 Too liberal self-accusations are generally but so many traps for acquittal with applause. **1842** MANNING *Serm.* xvi. (1848) I. 229 The depth of his self-accusation and repentance,..in a time of severe sickness.

So **self-a'ccusatory** *a.*, **self-a'ccused** *ppl. a.*, **self-a'ccuser**, **self-a'ccusing** *vbl. sb.* and *ppl. a.*
1836 J. FOSTER in *Life & Corr.* (1846) II. 309 This *self-accusatory recollection. **1678** DRYDEN *All for Love* IV. 51 This *self-accus'd, self-punish'd Criminal. **1872** C. J. VAUGHAN *Earnest Words* (1878) 54 Self-accused, self-emptied, self-condemned. *a* **1631** DONNE *Epigrams* Poems (1639) 69 A *selfe-accuser. **1642** FULLER *Holy & Prof. St.* V. iii. 366 The *self-accusing of some is as little to be credited, as the self-praising of others. **1894** A. WHYTE *Sam. Rutherford* i. 7 His self-discoveries and self-accusings. *a* **1586** SIDNEY *Arcadia* II. (Sommer) 179 Then held she her tongue, and cast downe a *self-accusing looke. **1839** HALLAM *Lit. Eur.* III. iv. §5 The walls of the confessional are privy to the whispers of self-accusing guilt.

† **self-'acted**, *pa. pple. Obs.* [SELF- 2.] Moved to action of their own accord.
1763–5 CHURCHILL *Gotham* I. 8 All Instruments, self-acted,..Shall pour forth harmony.

self-'acting, *ppl. a.* [SELF- 3 b, 4.]
1. Acting independently, without external impulse or influence. Also applied to motion characterized by such action.
1740 CHEYNE *Regimen* 2 A Self-moving, self-acting secondary Agent. **1856** GROTE *Greece* II. xcvii. XII. 612 Self-acting Hellas. **1890** A. R. WALLACE *Darwinism* 12 This self-acting process which..brings about change in the organic world.

2. *Mech.* Acting automatically without the manipulation (or mechanism) which would otherwise be required. Also said of the operation.
1824 R. STUART *Hist. Steam Engine* 84 The..self-acting mechanism of the Atmospheric Engines. *Ibid.* 85 Their simultaneous (rather than self-acting) operation. **1834–6** BARLOW in *Encycl. Metrop.* (1845) VIII. 175/1 For the prevention of this [the unnecessary destruction of fuel], the self-acting damper has been invented. *Ibid.* 700/2 The machinery in the self-acting mule. **1869** RANKINE *Cycl. Mach. & Hand-tools* Pl. F 3 The self-acting motion is obtained from the lever. *Ibid.* L 2 Self-acting radial drilling machine. **1875** KNIGHT *Dict. Mech.* s.v., *Self-acting Valve*, one moved by the fluid, in contradistinction to one moved by the application of mechanical devices.

self-'action. [SELF- 5 c.] Independent action; action uninfluenced by external impulse.
1819 SCOTT *Ivanhoe* xxiv, At the feet of my Superior I have laid down the right of self-action—the privilege of independence. **1833** J. H. NEWMAN *Arians* I. ii. (1876) 34 The existence of moral self-action or free-will. **1856** GROTE *Greece* II. xcviii. XII. 613 The Hellenic world while yet in the period of full life, in freedom and self-action.

self-'active, *a.* [SELF- 3 b.] Acting of itself without external impulse.
1642 H. MORE *Song of Soul* II. I. II. xxiv, Some souls at least are self-active Withouten body having Energie. **1692** BENTLEY *Boyle Lect.* ii. 17 Intrinsecally moved by an immaterial self-active Substance. **1906** G. H. HOWISON *Let.* 9 Feb. in R. B. Perry *Tht. & Char. W. James* (1935) I. 776 The self-active unity of consciousness. **1936** ALLPORT & ODBERT in *Psychol. Monogr.* XLVII. I. 17 It was customary for psychologists to conceive some 'power of the mind'..and by naming it to regard the power as fixed and self-active.

So **self-ac'tivity.**
1644 DIGBY *Nat. Soul* Concl. 455 A selfe actiuity, and vnbounded extent, and essence free from time and place. *a* **1761** LAW *Comf. Weary Pilgr.* (1809) 72 Stop..all self-activity. **1864** BOWEN *Logic* i. 3 The spontaneity, or self-activity, of the intellect. **1889** MIVART *Truth* 190 Whenever we act, we have a certain vague feeling of our self-activity. **1932** C. S. MYERS *Absurdity of Mind-Body Rel.* 4 All conscious mental activity is self-activity; only the self is conscious—conscious, at first, solely of self-activity (conation) and of modifications of that self-activity (affects). **1961** R. C. TUCKER *Philos. & Myth in Marx* viii. 134 'Self-activity'.., by which Marx means free creativity in which a person feels thoroughly at home with himself..and experiences his energies as his own.

self-'actor. *Mech.* [SELF- 4.] A self-acting mule in a spinning-machine.
1835 URE *Philos. Manuf.* 40 One horse power drives 500 on the fine hand-mule, 300 on the self-actor mule. **1892** *Pall Mall Gaz.* 24 Aug. 2/1 Fine spinning, for which self-actors cannot as yet be profitably introduced.

self-actuali'zation. Chiefly *Psychol.* [SELF- 1 a.] Realization or fulfilment of oneself, esp. considered as a drive or need.
1939 H. ANSBACHER tr. *Goldstein's Organism* v. 197 Experiences..teach us that we have to assume only one drive, the drive of self-actualization. **1943** A. H. MASLOW in *Psychol. Rev.* L. 382 What a man *can* be, he *must* be. This need we may call self-actualization. **1957** C. ARGYRIS *Personality & Organization* vii. 181 The degree of self-actualization increases sharply for individuals as their dependence..and submissiveness are decreased. **1975** *Ecologist* V. 123/1 The evolving form of marriage seems to aim at what might be called 'self-actualization' of the persons.

Also **self-'actualize** *v. intr.*; **self-'actualized** *ppl. a.*, **self-'actualizing** *ppl. a.* and *vbl. sb.*; **self-'actualizer**.
1874 W. WALLACE *Hegel's Logic* §20. 30 Thought may be called a self-actualising universal. **1943** A. M. FARRER *Finite & Infinite* xi. 119 Will is the self-actualising potency of (the process of) a project. **1954** A. H. MASLOW *Motivation & Personality* xii. 223 The creativeness of the self-actualized man. *Ibid.* 230 A firm foundation for a value system is automatically furnished to the self-actualizer. **1959** H. B. ANDERSON *Creativity* xv. 242 To do this much would..appear to be a step toward self-actualizing. **1961** H. C. SMITH *Personality Adjustment* xiv. 381 Somerset Maugham shows..the qualities of spontaneity..and self-acceptance that are found in self-actualizers. **1977** R. HOLLAND *Self & Social Context* iv. 61 Arguing that there is a given 'instinctoid' tendency for the human being to self-actualise, that is to go beyond the satisfaction of the more basic needs to seek satisfaction of the higher needs. **1980** *Redbook* Oct. 58/1 Once I had seen close up what Friedan labeled the 'self-actualized woman', I was damned if I would take a chance with anything else.

self-admi'ration. [SELF- 1 a.] Admiration of oneself, self-conceit.
1661 BOYLE *Style of Script.* (1675) 197 The quiet Enjoyment of their unenvi'd Self-admiration. *a* **1761** LAW *Comf. Weary Pilgr.* (1809) 83 They..full of self-esteem, and self-admiration, for their own progress in them. **1888** F. COWPER *Captain of Wight* (1889) 58 At first the sense of shyness had kept this feeling of self-admiration down.

So **self-ad'mired** *ppl. a.*, **self-ad'mirer**, **self-ad'miring** *ppl. a.*
1785 G. A. BELLAMY *Apol.* (ed. 3) VI. 98 My *self-admired person. **1863** I. WILLIAMS *Baptistery* I. ii. (1874) 17 Folding his in self-admir'd repose. **1690** C. NESSE *Hist. & Myst. O. & N. Test.* I. 204 A contrary state and temper of the heart in self-admiration secludes such *self-admirers. **1621** SANDYS *Ovid's Met.* III. (1632) 92 Deaths cold hand shuts his *selfe-admiring eyes. **1711** SHAFTESB. *Charac., Misc. Refl.* III. 300 The self-admiring Wits. **1871** GEO. ELIOT *Middlem.* (1872) I. I. i. 7 Dorothea..was open, ardent, and not in the least self-admiring. **1951** M. MCLUHAN *Mech. Bride* (1967) 141/1 Is this little tough the twin brother of any self-patting, self-admiring deb? **1981** J. CAREY *John Donne* iv. 99 His poems..though self-absorbed ..are not self-admiring.

self-alie'nation. *Philos.* and *Social Sci.* [SELF- 1 a.] Alienation that takes place within the self, esp. in *Marxism*. Cf. ALIENATION 1 c.

1906 J. B. BAILLIE *Outl. to Idealistic Construct. Exper.* vii. 242 For this Self-alienation is itself regarded as necessary, as the very expression of free self-consciousness. **1926** H. J. STENNING tr. *Marx's Sel. Ess.* 13 The immediate task of philosophy, when enlisted in the service of history, is to unmask human self-alienation in its unholy shape. **1938** K. KORSCH *Marx* II. xi. 158 The actual 'self-alienation' of the wage-labourer. **1964** S. M. JOURARD *Transparent Self* ii. 11 It often comes to pass..that our public selves become so estranged from our real selves that the net consequence is self-alienation. **1977** A. GIDDENS *Stud. in Social & Polit. Theory* v. 199 For Marx..money is the epitome of human self-alienation under capitalism, since it reduces all human qualities to quantitative values of exchange.

self-a'ligning, *ppl. a. Mech.* [SELF- 4.] Capable of aligning itself automatically. Of a bearing or the like: having a degree of flexibility as regards alignment. Hence **self-a'lignment**.

1904 *Science* 29 Jan. 164/1 Where the ends of the polar axis are supported on separate piers the bearings can be made self-aligning. **1905** *Daily Chron.* 15 Feb. 4/6 The new patent self-aligning, self-adjusting roller axle-bearings. **1930** *Engineering* 26 Sept. 394/3 A self-aligning double roller feed for vertical double-spindle moulders. **1960** *Farmer & Stockbreeder* 15 Mar. 148/1 All-steel welded construction with self-aligning ball bearings throughout. **1962** G. A. T. BURDETT *Automatic Control Handbk.* iv. 9 A method of maintaining self-alignment.

self-a'nalysis. [SELF- 1 a.] Analysis by or of oneself; *spec.* Psychol., psychoanalysis of oneself undertaken by oneself.

1860 A. J. MUNBY *Diary* 12 Mar. in D. Hudson *Munby* (1972) 54 Self analysis helps one... I am sensible of a feeling of placid halfcontemptuous indifference. **1862** SPENCER *First Princ.* II. iv. §53 (1875) 177 Careful self-analysis shows this to be a datum of consciousness. **1911** E. JONES in *Amer. Jrnl. Psychol.* XXII. 520 The greatest value is to be attached to self-analysis, a fact to which attention cannot too often be called. *a* **1930** D. H. LAWRENCE *Last Poems* (1932) 28 Self-analysis Which goes further and further, and yet never finds an end. **1958** K. MENNINGER *Theory of Psychoanal. Technique* vii. 159 The process of self-analysis continues automatically..with increasing freeing and expanding of ego functions. **1977** M. JAHODA *Freud & Dilemmas of Psychol.* iii. 52 The self-analysis is important beyond this and..stakes the claim for psychoanalysis to be a reflexive psychology. **1981** B. MASTERS *Georgiana* viii. 204 With time on her hands, Georgiana gave way to self-analysis, introspection, regret.

Hence **self-'analyst**.

1929 SHEEHAN & GAFFNEY *Tristram Lloyd* III. i. 187 He was a self-analyst, and he carried the principle into every-day life, sorting, sifting, examining motives and principles. **1958** B. W. ALDISS *Non-Stop* III. iv. 184 He was not enough of a self-analyst to see it was a quality he had..himself.

self-annihi'lation. [SELF- 1 a.] Annihilation or obliteration of self.

1647 TRAPP *Comm. Matt.* xix. 17 Here then our Saviour learns this *yonker* humility, and self-annihilation. **1713** ADDISON *Guardian* No. 153 ⁋2 To sink the Soul into the lowest State of Humility, and what the School-men call Self-Annihilation. **1860** R. A. VAUGHAN *Mystics* (ed. 2) I. 119 The mystical death, self-annihilation, and holy indifference of the Quietists.

So **self-a'nnihilated** *pa. pple.*

1794 COLERIDGE *Relig. Musings* 43 Till by exclusive consciousness of God All self-annihilated it shall make God its identity.

self-a'pplauding, *ppl. a.* [SELF- 1 f.] Given to or marked by self-applause.

1654 WHITLOCK *Zootomia* 296 The Toiles of Selfe-applauding Husbandry. *a* **1680** CHARNOCK *Attrib. God* (1834) I. 94 Self-applauding confidences in our own wisdom and strength. **1781** COWPER *Truth* 58 The self-applauding bird, the peacock. **1818** SCOTT *Rob Roy* iv, With the chuckle of a self-applauding wit. **1867** MRS. WHITNEY *L. Goldthwaite* iii. (1873) 42 A little matter, nothing to be self-applauding about.

self-a'pplause. [SELF- 1 a.] Approval or commendation of oneself.

1678 MARVELL *Def. John Howe* Wks. (Grosart) IV. 202 Its insolent boasting and self-applause upon no occasion. **1728** POPE *Dunc.* I. 82 She..With self-applause her wild creation views. **1748** SMOLLETT *Rod. Rand.* xliv, He addressed himself to me..with a smile of self-applause. **1880** BURTON *Reign Q. Anne* II. xi. 228 The exulting and abounding current of his self-applause.

So **self-a'pplausive** *a.* = SELF-APPLAUDING.

1807 D. GILSON *Serm.* vii. 136 A mind already wounded with self-applausive, unnecessary advice.

self-a'ssembly. **1.** [SELF- 2 b.] Subsequent assembly of something bought in the form of a kit; usu. *attrib.*, denoting items (e.g. furniture) sold in this form.

a **1966** in G. N. Leech *Eng. in Advertising* (1966) xv. 137 Peerless brings within your reach..the luxury of a Built-in Bedroom at a price you can really afford With Dovetail Self-assembly Units. **1978** *Dumfries Courier* 20 Oct. 27/1 (Advt.), Broom unit for self assembly £10. **1980** *Daily Tel.* 9 July 2/1 A subsidiary..which makes self-assembly garages and prefabricated home extensions.

2. *Biol.* [SELF- 1 a.] The spontaneous formation of a sub-cellular particle from its components, e.g. that of a ribosome or of a virus in a medium containing the appropriate RNA and proteins. Hence **self-a'ssemble** *v. intr.*

1969 *Jrnl. Molecular Biol.* XL. 412 We feel that the general principle of self-assembly revealed in the present *in vitro* system also operates *in vivo*. **1977** *Jrnl. Protozool.* XXIV. 9/1 Self-assembly of a restricted number of different macromolecular subunits to form comparatively simple structures such as a rhizoplast, a pelta, or a trichocyst. **1978** *Sci. Amer.* Nov. 53 (*caption*) The virus 'self-assembles' spontaneously in the test tube from its constituent RNA molecule and protein subunits, giving rise to infective virus particles indistinguishable from those found in nature.

self-a'ssertion. [SELF- 1 a.] The action of asserting one's individuality, or insisting upon one's claims or one's supremacy.

180. FOSTER *Ess.* II. vi. (1806) I. 205 They [*sc.* passions which inspirit men to resistance] put the mind in the habitual array of defence and self-assertion. **1847** LD. LINDSAY *Sk. Hist. Chr. Art* I. p. ccix, The self-assertion of the Teutonic over the classic element of modern Europe. **1856** MERIVALE *Rom. Emp.* xliii. (1871) V. 188 A class whose intense self-assertion was inflamed by family names [etc.].

So **self-a'sserting, self-a'ssertive** (also **self-a'ssertingly** *adv.*, **self-a'ssertiveness**), **self-a'ssertory** *adjs.*, full of or characterized by self-assertion.

1837 J. S. MILL in *Westm. Rev.* XXVIII. 98 Carrel's manner was not of the *self-asserting kind. **1869** TROLLOPE *He Knew*, etc. lvi. (1878) 311 Some specially self-asserting American. **1865** DICKENS *Mut. Fr.* II. xvi, A *self-assertingly temporary and nomadic air. *Ibid.* I. iv, Unwilling to own to the name of Reginald, as being too aspiring and *self assertive a name. **1884** *Truth* 13 Mar. 374/1 A refreshing individuality and *self-assertiveness. **1866** ALGER *Solitudes of Nature & Man* IV. 381 This *self-assertory language.

self-a'ssessment. [SELF- 1 a.] Assessment or evaluation of oneself, one's actions or attitudes by oneself; an instance of this; *spec.* calculation of taxable liability by oneself.

1954 *Brit. Jrnl. Med. Psychol.* XXVII. 142/1 The psychiatric inventory described here (to be known as the Tavistock Self-assessment Inventory) is one which has been developed over the past few years in the Tavistock Clinic. **1960** *Spectator* 1 July 34 In the study of myth, Professor Kerényi explained in a 'self-assessment' written ten years ago, one must accept the 'axiom' of depth psychology. **1972** *Accountant* 12 Oct. 441/2 Special arrangements will secure for them the equivalent of tax credits, and self-assessment is waiting in the wings. **1979** *Internat. Rehabilit. Med.* I. 53/1 They were asked to assess the ability with which they performed a variety of activities during the preceding few weeks..self-assessments.

self-a'ssurance. [SELF- 1 d.] Feeling of security as to oneself; self-confidence.

1594 SPENSER *Amoretti* lix, Thrise happie she! that is so well assured Unto her selfe [etc.]... Such selfe-assurance need not feare the spight Of grudging foes. **180.** FOSTER *Ess.* III. ii. (1806) II. 22 The flattering self-assurance simply of a life of singular felicity. **1818** SCOTT *Rob Roy* xii, Lightness, gallantry, and something approaching to well-bred self-assurance. **1891** T. HARDY *Tess* vi, Going about her business with some self-assurance in the thought [etc.].

So **self-a'ssured** *a.*, self-confident.

1711 G. HICKES *Two Treat. Chr. Priesth.* (1847) II. 3 He is so very self-assured as to affirm that [etc.]. **1880** MᶜCARTHY *Own Times* xlviii. IV. 12 His style was far too self assured.

self-'balancing, *ppl. a.* [SELF- 1 f, 4.] **1.** In technical use: capable of balancing itself automatically; automatically producing balance.

1912 *Chambers's Jrnl.* Sept. 638/1 An upright position is always assured when the car is stationary, a continuous self-balancing motion being given to the vehicle. **1954** D. E. CARRITT in Isaacs & Iselin *Oceanogr. Instrumentation* 182 Snodgrass et al. have constructed a self-balancing photoelectric filter photometer.

2. *Accounting.* Designating that in which the debit side of the accountable items is equal to the credit side; ***self-balancing ledger*** (see quot. 1970).

1898 S. S. DAWSON *Accountant's Compendium* 350/2 The Customers' Ledger..is self-balancing because of the operation of the Controlling Account. **1931** *Economist* 3 Jan. 7/2 The gross figures, including self-balancing revenue, show receipts from all sources amounting to £486·5 millions. **1953** *Chambers's Jrnl.* June 343/1 Catering generally is a profitable or at least self-balancing item in the seaside resort budget. **1964** R. B. NOTESTEIN in I. L. Horowitz *New Sociology* 52 The economy was self-balancing, with authority exerted by impersonal regional markets. **1970** M. GREENER *Penguin Dict. Commerce* 297 *Self-balancing ledger*, an accounting term for a personal ledger containing a control account.

self-be'got, *pa. pple.* [SELF 2.] Begotten of oneself by one's own power.

1667 [see SELF-RAISED]. **1845** [see SELF-BORN 1].

So **self-be'gotten** *pa. pple.* and *ppl. a.*; also †**self-be'gottenly** *adv.*

1671 MILTON *Samson* 1699 That *self-begott'n bird In the Arabian woods embost. **1797** *Monthly Mag.* III. 511 Souls of this kind..possess a self-begotten and self-vital essence. **1833** J. H. NEWMAN *Arians* II. iv. (1876) 195 Iamblichus calls the Son self-begotten. **1678** CUDWORTH *Intell. Syst.* 574 Its Own-Parent, and its Own-Ofspring, and said to have sprung out, αὐτογόνως *Self-begottenly.

self-'being. Now *rare.* [SELF- 5 c.] Independent existence; also †*concr.* a self-existent being.

1587 GOLDING *De Mornay* xiv. (1592) 199 So is reason or vnderstanding the very forme or Selfbeeing of the Soule of man. *a* **1619** FOTHERBY *Atheom.* II. iii. §3 (1622) 219 One certaine power or Nature of Selfe-being. *a* **1656** BP. HALL *Medit. Love of Christ* §10 Let me set all my soul upon Thee ..who art the eternal and absolute Self Being. **1880** G. M. HOPKINS *Sermons & Devotional Writings* (1959) 122 And this whether I speak of human nature or of my individuality, my selfbeing. **1915** A. VONIER *Personality of Christ* v. 31 The scholastic maintains that self-being underlies self-consciousness, as the cause underlies the effect. **1977** R. HOLLAND *Self & Social Context* ii. 41 He attributes the non-disclosure to role-playing, which is placed in sharp contrast with real self-being.

So †**'self-being** *ppl. a.*, self-existent.

1599 DAVIES *Nosce Teipsum* 17 Her selfe being Nature shines in this, That she performes her noblest works alone.

self-'bias. *Electronics.* [SELF- 1 d.] Bias applied to the grid of a valve by means of a resistor in the cathode circuit or the grid circuit. So **self-'biased** *ppl. a.*, **self-'biasing** *vbl. sb.*

1931 MOYER & WOSTREL *Radio Handbk.* xiii. 708 (*heading*) Self-biasing grid-glow tube. **1932** F. E. TERMAN *Radio Engin.* xi. 389 (*caption*) Self-bias circuits for obtaining a negative grid bias..by utilizing the voltage drop across a resistance in series with the cathode. *Ibid.*, When an anode detector is self-biased by the arrangement shown.., the detector characteristics are quite different from those obtained with a bias derived from a battery. **1939** H. J. REICH *Theory & Application Electron Tubes* vi. 161 (*caption*) Impedance-capacitance—coupled amplifier, showing the use of self-biasing resistors. **1945** [see PUSH-PULL *a.* 2]. **1960** *Practical Wireless* XXXVI. 319/1 This condenser discharges through the grid leak.., building up the self bias for the valve.

self-'binder. orig. *U.S.* [SELF- 4.] **1.** A reaping-machine which has an apparatus for binding the corn into sheaves automatically.

1882 *Evening Star* 28 June, The country has more wheat growing than it could reap save for self-binders. **1884** *Pall Mall G.* 25 Nov. 2/1 The regular price now paid in the States for a self-binder is 160 dols., say £33.

2. (See quot.)

1950 *Times* 26 July 6/5 A self-binder for *The Times*, which takes one month's issues on sprung cords, is now available.

So **self-'binding** *ppl. a.*

1883 *Sci. Amer.* 3 Mar. 138/3 A self-binding harvester. **1884** *Pall Mall Gaz.* 29 Nov. 3/2 Self-binding reapers.

self-bi'ography. *rare* or *Obs.* [SELF- 1 d.] = AUTOBIOGRAPHY.

1796 I. D'ISRAELI *Miscellanies or Lit. Recreations* 95 (*heading*) Some observations on diaries, self-biography and self-characters. **1813** J. F. STANFIELD *Essay on Study & Composition of Biography* I. i. 2 Our supply of genuine self-biography is but scanty.

self-black. Chiefly northern. Also 6 selblack(e. [SELF B. 3.] **a.** Of a uniformly black colour. **b.** Of a naturally black colour, not dyed. Also *sb.*, a colour of this description; †a stuff of such a colour.

1558 *Will of Rolandson of Kendal* (Somerset Ho.), A selblacke jerkin. **1562** *Richmond Wills* (Surtees) 152 Inprimis, iij. mellyd russetts, xlij s. Item ij. other selblacks, xx s.. Blacke woulle, xx s. Selblacke woulle, xij s. **1573** *Ibid.* 235 To Sybbel yᵉ doghter of Robart my soon a browne cote, a pare of selblacke slevys. **1595** *Aberdeen Reg.* (1848) II. 117 Ane gown of selfblak. **1621** *Sc. Acts Jas. VI* (1816) IV. 626/2 Selffblak Claithe maid in Scotland. **1828** [W. CARR] *Craven Gloss.* II. 109 My stockins er self black.

self-'blimped, *a.* [SELF- 4; cf. BLIMP 1 b.] Of a ciné camera: fitted with a sound-proof cover; insulated from sound by its own housing.

1961 in WEBSTER. **1965** R. FIELDING *Technique Special-Effects Photogr.* x. 269 The projector must be somehow silenced... Either the machine must be self-blimped or installed within a sound-proof projection room. **1969** *Focal Encycl. Film & Television* 74/2 Sound cameras of recent design are..self-blimped..so that mechanical noise is reduced to an absolute minimum. **1979** D. CHESHIRE *Bk. Movie Photogr.* 174 The camera must run as silently as possible to avoid disturbing the animals. You may need a 'self-blimped' camera.

†**self-blood.** *Obs.*

1. [SELF- 1 a.] Self-murder.

c **1616** FLETCHER *Thierry & Theod.* IV. i. (1621) H 2 b, Do you feele What followes a selfe blood, whither you venter, And to what punishment?

2. [SELF- 5 a.] One's own blood relations.

1603 B. JONSON *Sejanus* III. i. (1605) E 4 b, Though he had proper Issue of his owne, He would no lesse bring vp, and foster these, Then that selfe-bloud.

self-'boasting, *vbl. sb.* [SELF- 1 b.] Boasting about oneself. So **self-'boasted** *ppl. a.*, boasted of as one's own.

1599 *Broughton's Lett.* iv. 15 Importunate selfe-boasting. *Ibid.* vii. 23 Thy great selfe-boasted learning. *a* **1653** GOUGE *Comm. Heb.* xii. 10 This taketh away all ground of self-boasting from them. **1850** O. WINSLOW *Inner Life* 92 Self-confidence, self-seeking, self-boasting.

self-born, *ppl. a.* [SELF- 3 b.] Born of or originating from oneself or itself.

1587 GOLDING *De Mornay* vi. (1592) 79 Selfeborne, and father of himself. *a* **1644** QUARLES *Sol. Recant.* Sol. xi, And leave to morrow To beare the burden of her self-borne sorrow. **1700** DRYDEN *Ovid's Met.* xv. *Pythag. Philos.* 580 From himself the Phœnix only springs: Self-born. **1845** BAILEY *Festus* 120 The self-begot, self-wedded, and self-born. **1875** BAIN *Ment. & Mor. Sci.* III. xi. §7 The pleasure of the original or self-born feeling.

⁋In Shaks. *Wint. T.* IV. i. 8 'one self-borne howre' = one and the same hour (see SELF B. 1 d); in *Rich. II*, II. iii. 80

'self-borne Armes' is of disputed meaning (some mod. edd. read *self-born* = indigenous).

self-bow: see SELF B. 6.

self-bred, *ppl. a.* [SELF- 3 b.]
†1. = SELF-BORN. *Obs.*
1587 GOLDING *De Mornay* iii. 30 Plato..calleth God..the Beer..the self bred, who also made yᵉ Heauen.
†2. Native. *Obs.*
1590 R. W. *Three Lords & Ladies* B, Of selfe bred soile, of London is her race.
3. *Bot.* Applied to the offspring of self-fertilized flowers.
1900 B. D. JACKSON *Gloss. Bot. Terms.*

self-'cancelling, *ppl. a.* [SELF- 1 f, 4.] That cancels itself; that negate each other. 1. In technical use: designed to stop working automatically when no longer required; applied esp. to traffic indicators of motor vehicles.
1935 [see DIPPER 8]. **1945** *Autocar Handbk.* (Autocar Techn. Staff) (ed. 18) x. 196 Some form of 'self-cancelling' arrangement is..fitted, to avoid drivers unknowingly going along with an indicator extended. **1960** *News Chron.* 6 May 8/8 They have omitted..to make the traffic indicators self-cancelling. **1963** *Times* 15 Jan. 12/1 By flicking in the self-cancelling overdrive in third and top the motorway cruising speed went up to about 80. **1972** *Daily Tel.* 12 July 10/5 Not only is the stalk on the column very flimsy and mounted on the wrong side..but the indicators are not self-cancelling.
2. *gen.*
1943 *Mind* LII. 295 It has been made a *self-cancelling* expression like the expression 'ride a motor cycle' as used by someone who is determined to use 'ride' only where what you ride is something living. **1965** *Spectator* 15 Jan. 60/1 The concept of fighting for export orders has become largely self-cancelling.

self-ca'pacitance. *Electr.* [SELF- 5 b.] The inherent capacitance of a circuit or component. Also **self-ca'pacity.**
1923 E. W. MARCHANT *Radio Telegr. & Teleph.* v. 66 Such coils have a considerable inductance, and 'self-capacity'. **1937** L. D. WELD *Gloss. Physics* 207/2 *Self-capacitance*, distributed capacitance of an electric circuit due to its containing closely wound coils of insulated wire, the adjacent turns of which have a condenser effect. **1958** *Practical Wireless* XXXIV. 22/2 This was found to be essential since the timebase was affecting the appearance of the trace due to the self-capacity of the X switch. **1960** *Ibid.* XXXVI. 397/2 A small capacitance which is in fact the self-capacitance of the crystal.

self-care (stress variable). [SELF- 1 a, 2 b, 3 a.] Care for oneself; self-interested behaviour; freq. used *attrib.* to denote an institution in which patients and convalescents attend to many of their own needs.
1904 in WEBSTER. **1932** AUDEN *Orators* II. 41 The second law of thermodynamics—self-care or minding one's own business. **1962** *Punch* 7 Nov. 658/1 Recovering your strength you're passed to the Self-Care Unit. **1979** *Internat. Rehabilit. Med.* I. 59/1 Assessment of the competence of patients in essential activities of daily living (A.D.L.), such as mobility, self care, and domestic activities.

self-'catering, *vbl. sb.* [SELF- 3 a.] Catering for oneself; *spec.* providing one's own domestic services (as meals and cleaning) in rented holiday accommodation. Chiefly *attrib.* of holidays and vacation accommodation.
1970 *Country Life* 1 Oct. 802/1 There has also been a discernible movement towards self-catering holidays, in farmhouses, chalets, caravans and cottages. **1972** *Guardian* 9 Dec. 13/2 Holiday camps are increasingly turning to self-catering. **1973** *Times* 25 Jan. (Channel Islands Suppl.) p. v/3 Self-catering accommodation is..increasing rapidly. **1977** *Western Morning News* 1 Sept. 6/5 (Advt.), Comfortable all-electric self-catering Farm-house; 2 double bedrooms week 3/10 September. **1981** *Daily Tel.* 27 Jan. 12/5 Two redundant stone-built barns..have been converted into self-catering bunkhouses for walkers.

†**self-'central**, *a. Obs.* [SELF- 3 a.]
= SELF-CENTRED 1, 2.
1647 H. MORE *Song of Soul* IV. xx, A self-centrall essence. *a* **1652** J. SMITH *Sel. Disc.* VII. vi. (1821) 367 This sensual, brutish, and self-central life.
So **self-'centralism**, self-centredness; †**self-cen'trality**, the quality of being 'self-central'; **self-centrali'zation**, **self-cen'tration** (Webster, 1864), the state or quality of being self-centred.
1903 *Month* July 33 Proud *self-centralism. **1647** H. MORE *Song of Soul* IV. xix, Which doth all souls into one centre strain, And make them void of *self-centrality. **1903** *Q. Rev.* Oct. 407 The *self-centralisation of Latin politics.

self-'centre, *v. rare*⁻¹. [SELF- 3 a.] *trans.* To centre in oneself.
1794 COLERIDGE *Relig. Musings* 91 What thirsty cares Drink up the spirit and the dim regards Self-centre.

self-'centred, *ppl. a.* [SELF- 3 a.]
1. Fixed or stationary, as a centre round which other things move.
1676 DRYDEN *State Innoc.* II. i. (1677) 12 There hangs the ball of Earth and Water mixt, Self-Center'd, and unmov'd. **1687** NORRIS *Coll. Misc.* 84 He is one unmov'd self-center'd Point of Rest. **1737** POPE *Hor. Ep.* I. vi. 6 Self-center'd Sun. **1872** BROWNING *Fifine* lxxx. 11 Your steadying touch of hand Assists me to remain self-centred, fixed amid All on the move.
2. Of persons, their activities, etc.: Centred in oneself (or itself); independent of external action or influence.
a **1764** LLOYD *Whim* Poet. Wks. 1774 II. 166 Genius self-center'd feels alone That merit he esteems his own. **1828** SEWELL *Oxford Prize Ess.* 43 Self-centred circles of commercial employments, professions, and amusements. **1877** E. CAIRD *Philos. Kant* II. 15 The self-centred life that makes itself independent of everything but the individuality in which it is imprisoned. **1895** ZANGWILL *Master* III. viii, He would be fixed at last, swinging steadily on a pivot of happiness... Now at last he would be self-centred.
b. In an unfavourable sense, passing into that of: Engrossed in self, selfishly independent.
1783 JOHNSON *Let. to Mrs. Thrale* 20 Nov., A stubborn sufficiency self-centered. **1873** MORLEY *Rousseau* I. 126 He was both too self-centred and too passionate for warm ease and fulness of life in all things, to be truly sympathetic [etc.]. **1884** W. H. WHITE *Mark Rutherford's Deliv.* vii. (1892) 97 That self-centred satisfaction which makes life tolerable.
Hence **self-'centredness.**
1891 F. PAGET *Spirit of Discipline* iii. 98 The absurdity of self-centredness and self-advertisement. **1894** *Athenæum* 21 July 94/2 With nearly as strong a belief as his master's in the self-centredness of man.

self-'centring, *ppl. a.* (and *vbl. sb.*)
†1. [SELF- 3 a.] = SELF-CENTRED 1, 2. *Obs.*
1693 NORRIS *Pract. Disc.* IV. 186 The Self-Ending, Self-Centring Man does in a very true..Sense Idolize himself. **1701** —— *Ideal World* I. vi. 398 Truth being of the Divine essence..is really a ground and foundation to itself, even as that self-centring essence is. **1809–10** COLERIDGE *Friend* (1865) 217 They pursue the interests of freedom steadily, but with narrow and self-centring views.
2. *Mech.* [SELF- 4.] a. Applied to chucks, etc., which hold the object in a central position without the necessity of tentative adjustments.
1884 F. J. BRITTEN *Watch & Clockm.* 237 These self-centring chucks. **1908** *Westm. Gaz.* 17 Nov. 5/2 The clutch is of the self-centring type.
b. Of the steering of a motor vehicle: tending to return automatically to a central alignment. Also as *vbl. sb.*
1926 H. T. RUTTER *Mod. Motors* II. ix. 331 The steering gear is arranged to be self-centring, so that little pressure is required to maintain the car in a straight line. **1963** *Times* 5 Feb. 7/5 At first, the powerful self-centring action of the steering makes the car feel heavy and slightly unstable. **1975** *Drive* New Year 102/3 The tail certainly wags the Beetle, especially in the wet when even the responsive, self-centring steering won't help to avoid trouble. **1977** *Times* 18 Aug. 23/3 The main criticisms of steering were..stiffness of operation, and lack of self-centring.

self-'changing, *ppl. a.*
1. [SELF- 1 f.] Causing a change in the self.
1865 GROTE *Plato* I. i. 5 A self-changing and self-developing force.
2. [SELF- 4.] Of a gearbox: preselective.
1930 [see *fluid flywheel* s.v. FLUID *sb.* 3]. **1939** *Country Life* 11 Feb. p. xxx/3 The self-changing gear box and the special anti-snatch Armstrong Siddeley transmission.

selfcide. *nonce-wd.* [f. SELF + -CIDE².] Suicide.
1692 WOOD *Ath. Oxon.* II. 479 Hobbes..saith..that no Homicide, or Selfcide,..is against the law of nature.

self-'cleaning, *ppl. a.* (*vbl. sb.*) [SELF- 1 b, f, 4.] Designed to keep itself clean automatically. Also as *vbl. sb.*, the action or capability of doing this.
1898 L. S. ROBERTSON tr. *Bertin's Marine Boilers* iv. 91 Self-cleaning grates with movable bars have been used in America. **1930** *Daily Express* 6 Oct. 7/5 (Advt.), The Ewbank Success sweeper is fitted with ball bearings, a self-cleaning brush and rubber protectors. **1960** *Farmer & Stockbreeder* 15 Mar. 119/2 The self-cleaning action of the slats has not been particularly evident. **1971** *Engineering* Apr. 31/1 So far, cost and complexity have ruled out self-cleaning [for vending machines]. **1979** *Arizona Daily Star* 5 Aug. (Advt. Section) 17/7 Self-cleaning patio pool, landscaped, block wall.

self-'cleansing, *ppl. a.* (*vbl. sb.*) [SELF- 1 b, f, 4.] Tending automatically to keep itself clean. Also as *vbl. sb.*
1911 H. S. WATSON *Sewerage Systems* iii. 41 All sewers should be self-cleansing. **1921** T. GOODHUGH *Operative Dental Surg.* xviii. 262 Food in mastication cleans the teeth on the exposed surfaces, which are called 'self-cleansing surfaces'. **1963** J. OSBORNE *Dental Mech.* (ed. 5) viii. 147 The resin..may then be lightly polished to give a surface that is readily self-cleansing. **1978** *Jrnl. R. Soc. Med.* LXXI. 718 In these situations, self-cleansing is less common and keratin may accumulate.

self-'cocking, *ppl. a.* (*vbl. sb.*) [SELF- 4.] Of a firearm: cocked and fired by pulling the trigger; double-action. Also *fig.*, and as *vbl. sb.*
1862 [see BACK-ACTION]. **1880** *News & Press* (Cimarron, New Mexico) 23 Dec. 3/1 Mr. T. O. Boggs of Tramperos, while in the act of drawing a self-cocking pistol from his pocket, accidentally discharged it. **1892** GREENER *Breech-loader* 65 The self-cocking of the locks is..an immense advantage. **1902** W. D. HULBERT *Forest Neighbors* 161 Four shots, as fast as the self-cocking revolver could pour the lead into his body. **1964** H. L. PETERSON *Encycl. Firearms* 17/1 The revolver patented by Robert Adams in 1851 was the English challenge to the Colt revolver, but unlike the latter it was made with a solid frame and a self-cocking action.
Hence **self-'cocker**, a firearm thus cocked and fired.
1863 *Battle-fields of the South* I. 125 An Adam's self-cocker (unloaded). **1902** S. E. WHITE in *McClure's Mag.* Apr. 552/2 It was wonderful work, rattling fire, quicker than a self-cocker even.

self-co'incidence. [SELF- 3 a.] The fact or state of coinciding with its former position following a displacement.
1904 *Knowledge* June 110/1 Every molecule of the medium..is brought by certain so-called 'movements' into the position previously occupied by some other molecule of the medium (the medium is said to be 'brought to self-coincidence' by such a movement). **1966** [see ISOMETRIC *a.* 7].

self-co'llected, *ppl. a.* [SELF- 3 a.]
= COLLECTED 2.
a **1711** KEN *Hymnarium* Poet. Wks. II. 12 O may I self-collected here, Live all at once in filial fear. **1831** SCOTT *Ct. Rob.* xiv, The features, with their self-collected composure. **1842** MANNING *Serm.* ii. (1848) I. 23 Look at the penitent sinner, calm and self collected.
So **self-co'llectedness, self-co'llection.**
1834 GODWIN *Necromancers* 18 Boldness and *self-collectedness. **1842** FABER *Styrian Lake*, etc. 292 With solemn *self-collection did he slay Himself upon the barrow newly raised. **1871** MORLEY *Vauvenargues* in *Crit. Misc.* Ser. I. (1878) 29 The self-collection, the feminine solicitude, that [etc.].

self-'colour. [SELF B. 3.]
1. One uniform colour; orig. used of flowers (cf. next). Also, a colour belonging to the same series as another.
1665 REA *Flora* 177 These self-colours [in Columbines] are not valued. **1731** MILLER *Gard. Dict.* s.v. *Tulipa* 8 C 3/1 These do, in time, break into various beautiful Stripes, according to the Ground of their former Self-colour. **1849** *Q. Rev.* Mar. 414 The cattle of mountainous countries..are always of self-colours—black, red, or dun. **1859** GULLICK & TIMBS *Painting* 19 The system of shading with a 'self-colour', as pink with crimson. **1888** SANSONE *Dyeing* vii. 154 Madder is still employed..in wool dyeing, both as self-colour and in combination with other dyewoods. **1927** T. WOODHOUSE *Artificial Silk* ix. 86 Knitted garment of a self-colour are made, in this simplest form, by the manipulation of a single continuous thread. **1950** *Sun* (Baltimore) 9 May 18 (Advt.), Barbara Lee leg-contour proportioned-fit sheer nylons with contrast or self-color seams. **1964** A. BUTLER *Teaching Children Embroidery* II. iv. 35 Free experimenting, with stitches used in some areas, in which self-colour is worked as a texture. **1976** *Morecambe Guardian* 7 Dec. 1/1 (Advt.), 100% wool skirt suit with self-colour embroidery.
2. The natural colour.
1851 MAYHEW *Lond. Labour* I. 440/2 The Scotch boxes [*sc.* snuff-boxes], called 'Holyroods'..are generally the 'self-colour' of the wood.

self-'coloured, *ppl. a.* [f. prec. + -ED. Cf. MHG. *selpvar* having the natural colour or aspect.]
1. Of one uniform colour.
1759 MILLER *Gard. Dict.* (ed. 7) s.v. *Tulipa* 13 Q 4/1 The Stripes should be small and regular, arising from the Bottom of the Flower, for if there are any Remains of the former self-coloured Bottom, the Flower is in Danger of losing its Stripes again. **1862** *Chamb. Encycl.* IV. 784/1 Pieces of self-coloured glass. **1889** MRS. PANTON *Nooks & Corners* 29 The darkest brown self-coloured linoleum put down all over the passages and halls.
2. Of the natural colour. (In mod. Dicts.)

self-co'mmand. [SELF- 1 a.] Control of one's actions or feelings, self-control.
1699 SHAFTESB. *Charac., Inq. conc. Virtue* II. §2 The Advantages..of a contrary Sobriety, and Self-Command. **1818** SCOTT *Rob Roy* ii, My father had, generally speaking, his temper under complete self-command. **1898** J. MORLEY *Let.* in *Westm. Gaz.* 14 Dec., Your..self-command under the provocation of those 'unworthy insinuations'.

self-com'patible, *a.* and *sb. Bot.* [SELF- 3 b.]
A. *adj.* Able to be fertilized by means of its own pollen. B. *sb.* A self-compatible plant or species. Opp. SELF-INCOMPATIBLE *a.* and *sb.*
1922 *Bot. Gaz.* LXXIII. 111 There are in the feebly self-compatible plants of these species no specially marked tendencies to self-compatibility at any definite phase of the blooming period. **1938** [see SELF-INCOMPATIBLE *a.* and *sb.*]. **1955** *Heredity* IX. 70 The trees he tested could be divided on their setting capacity into those which were self-compatible and those which were self-incompatible. **1969** *Ibid.* XXIV. 165 We may suppose that dioecy here evolved recently from hermaphroditism in a *self-compatible* ancestor. **1979** *Nature* 20–27 Dec. 837/2 The usual explanation that dioecy arises in a self-compatible taxon as a way of ensuring outcrossing is certainly possible.
So **self-compati'bility**, the state of being self-compatible.
1917 *Jrnl. Genetics* VII. 78 The behaviour of the various series indicates an irregular inheritance of the characteristics of self-compatibility. **1969** *Heredity* XXIV. 613 Different self-compatibility alleles may occur localised in different habitats.

self-com'placence, -'complaisance. [SELF- 3 a.] = COMPLACENCE 1.
1748 RICHARDSON *Clarissa* I. xiii. 73 The self-complaisance which an imagin'd happy thought can be supposed to give the speaker. **1781** COWPER *Charity* 468 Extravagance and av'rice shall subscribe, While fame and self-complacence are the bribe. **1821** SCOTT *Kenilw.* xli, Foster..pointed with self-complacence to a piece of concealed machinery in the wall. **1827** CARLYLE *Germ. Rom.* IV. 73 Self-complaisance over the concealed destroys its concealment.

self-com'placency. [SELF- 3 a.] = prec.

1687 NORRIS *Coll. Misc.* 302 Acts of self-complacency, whereby I delight and please my self in the perfections of my Nature. **1694** SOUTH *Serm. 1 Cor. ii.* 7 Wks. 1823 II. 396 To check those self-complacencies which it is apt to grow into. **1707** NORRIS *Treat. Humility* 26 To receive it modestly, without any expressions of self-complacency. **1817** COLERIDGE *Statesm. Man.* 36 In the blindness of self-complacency. **1879** FROUDE *Cæsar* xxviii. 490 About himself and his own exploits there is not one word of self-complacency.

self-com'placent, *a.* [SELF- 3 a.] = COMPLACENT 2.

1763 CHURCHILL *Rosciad* 161 With a self-complacent jutting air, It smil'd, It smirk'd. **1849** MACAULAY *Hist. Eng.* v. I. 543 Selfcomplacent stupidity. **1878** GLADSTONE *Prim. Homer* 148 The wisdom of Nestor is amusingly accompanied with self-complacent reflection.

self-compla'cential, -com'placing *adjs.*, self-complacent; **self-com'placently** *adv.*

a **1711** KEN *Hymnarium* Poet. Wks. II. 109 Thy Love *self-complacential. **1806** KNOX *Let. to Jebb* 27 Oct., The sweet, rational, self-complacential, yea, direct, disinterested, delight. *a* **1700** KEN *Hymnotheo* Poet. Wks. III. 304 God.. Self-knowing, *Self-complacing on his Throne. **180.** FOSTER *Ess.* I. iii. (1806) I. 49 As polemics most *self-complacently avow their opinions to be more firmly established by all that the opponent has objected.

self-con'ceit. [SELF- 1 a.]

1. One's opinion or estimate of oneself; *esp.* high or exaggerated opinion of oneself, one's talents, attainments, etc.

1588-9 MARLOWE *Faustus* Chor. 20 Till swolne with cunning, of a selfe conceit [etc.]. **1603** HOLLAND *Plutarch's Mor.* 84 To confirme that good selfe-conceit and opinion of his owne. **1608** D. T[UVILL] *Ess. Pol. & Mor.* 62b Not tainted with anie humorous Selfe-conceit. **1651** HOBBES *Leviath.* I. viii. 35 Vaine-Glory; which is commonly called Pride, and selfe-conceipt. **1781** COWPER *Charity* 374 Philosophy, without his heav'nly guide May blow up self-conceit. **1875** JOWETT *Plato* (ed. 2) V. 185 He remarks the self-conceit of a younger generation of philosophers.

†**2.** One's own opinion; wilful thought. *Obs.*

1602 WARNER *Alb. Eng.* IX. lii. 234 Our Mindes doe wauer still Our selfe-Conceits be winged and we flie from good to ill. **1642** D. ROGERS *Naaman* 98 [Naaman] had a self-conceit of the way of curing him.

self-con'ceited, *ppl. a.* Now somewhat *rare*; freq. in 17th c. [f. prec.] Full of or marked by self-conceit; having an overweening opinion of oneself; = CONCEITED 3.

1595 *Polimanteia* in Brydges *Brit. Bibl.* I. 285 Any male-contented selfe-conceited, vnregarded malicious subiect. **1597** THYNNE in *Animadv.* (1875) Introd. p. xcix, The selfe conceyted m^r Savile, prouoste of Eatone. **1611** *Bible, Transl. Ep.* ¶5 If..we shall be maligned by selfe-conceited brethren, who runne their owne wayes. **1653** W. RAMESEY *Astrol. Rest.* 211 Lulled asleep with self-conceited ignorance. **1741** tr. *D'Argens' Chinese Lett.* i. 2 The French ..seem to me to be as self-conceited as the Japonese. **1818** SCOTT *Rob Roy* xxiv, This troublesome, pedantic, self-conceited coxcomb. **1887** BESANT *The World Went* xv. 122 Dwarfs..are the most vainglorious and self-conceited persons imaginable.

¶ With predicative adj. = thinking oneself to be (so-and-so).

1616 R. C. *Times' Whistle* (1871) 34 Others..which, selfe-conceited wise, Take a great pride in their owne vaine surmise.

Hence **self-con'ceitedly** *adv.*, **self-con'ceitedness** (freq. in 17th c.).

1603 FLORIO *Montaigne* III. ix. 566 *Selfe-conceitedly to ouer-esteeme what they possesse aboue others. *c* **1616** S. WARD *Coal from Altar* (1627) 21, I feare most of them be sicke of *selfe-conceitednesse, new-fanglenesse, and desire of mastership. **1661** BAXTER *Mor. Prognost.* 67 Self-Conceitedness in their Controversies. *a* **1721** PRIOR *24 Songs* xxiii, But self-conceitedness does reign In every mortal mind.

self-'concept. *Soc. Psychol.* [SELF- 1 d.] A person's concept or idea of himself. Also **self-con'ception.**

1934 in WEBSTER. **1938** *Psychol. Abstr.* XII. 770/1 (Index) Self-concept, adolescence. **1947** *Amer. Psychologist* Sept. 365/2 Our observations of psychotherapeutic experience would seem to indicate that absence of any threat to the self-concept is an important item in the problem. **1957** *Amer. Sociol. Rev.* XXII. 218/2 The following analysis is limited to the executives' and the supervisors' self-conceptions and conceptions of each other. **1968** *Internat. Encycl. Social Sci.* XIV. 150/1 Since the 1940s, problems related to self concept have surged forth as indispensable..topics for scientific study in psychology and sociology. **1977** M. EDELMAN *Polit. Lang* ii. 29 The self-conceptions that are a part of these contradictory cognitive structures.

self-con'cern. [SELF- 5 a.] Personal interest. So **self-con'cerned,** †**-con'cerning** *ppl. adjs.*, self-interested; †**self-con'cernment,** self-interest.

1681 OWEN *Φρονημα του Πνευματος* I. iv. Wks. 1852 VII. 302 Confined almost in their thoughts unto themselves,..and their *self-concerns. **1972** P. D. JAMES *Unsuitable Job for a Woman* iv. 148 Even their compassion had been overlaid with self concern. **1982** J. O'FAOLAIN *Obedient Wife* i. 23 It says something about the way you see me. Forgive my self-concern. **1662** J. DAVIES tr. *Olearius' Voy. Amb.* 367 The most *self-concern'd person of all that ever had the management of publick affairs. **1941** *Mind* L. 179 The self is part 'psyche' and part 'spirit': the psyche or animal soul self-concerned and partial, the spirit disinterested and catholic. **1656** COWLEY *Pindar. Odes, Nemeæan* v, For *self-concerning ends. **1644** MILTON *Divorce* To Parlt. of Eng. A 3, It is incredible how cold..we are, without the spurre of *self-concernment. **1699** SHAFTESB. *Charac., Inq. conc. Virtue* II. §2 A more than ordinary Self-Concernment, or Regard to private Good.

self-condem'nation. [SELF- 1 a.]

Condemnation by oneself of one's own action.

1703 [J. HAY] *title*, Self-Condemnation: or the author of the second edition of the Debate in the Shop, condemned out of his own mouth. **1757** W. THOMPSON *R.N. Adv.* 31 It must have produced not only Self-conviction, but Self-condemnation. **1858** LONGF. *M. Standish* IV. 26 Shame.. and abasement and self-condemnation.

So (all *rare*) **self-con'demnable** *a.*, carrying with it its own condemnation; **self-con'demnant, self-'condemnating, self-con'demnatory** = SELF-CONDEMNING.

1728 R. MORRIS *Ess. Anc. Archit.* 70 They become *self-condemnable, by being the Result of human Productions. **1846** G. S. FABER *Lett. Tractar. Secess.* 234 If the spurious *self-condemnant reading *salvatur* be adopted. **1863** CARLYLE *Let.* 18 Mar., A wonderful *self-condemnating MS. by Frk. the Great. **1823** BENTHAM *Not Paul but Jesus* 111 He states the *self-condemnatory mental facts.

self-con'demned, *ppl. a.* [SELF- 2.]

Condemned by one's own action or words.

1623 N. ROGERS *Strange Vineyard* 6 Had he knowne on whom the sentence would haue light, it should not haue beene so heauie; but now he is selfe-condemned. **1736** BUTLER *Anal.* I. vii. 131 Which we cannot violate without being Self-condemned. **1836** SIR H. TAYLOR *Statesman* xvii. 126 In adopting it [a course of conduct] they stand self-condemned without reason. **1856** FROUDE *Hist. Eng.* II. 90 Self-condemned in his wretchedness.

Hence **self-con'demnedly** *adv.*, so as to condemn oneself.

1679 PENN *Addr. Prot.* 216 Obstinately and Self-condemnedly maintaining inconsisting Things with the Faith.

self-con'demning, *pple.* and *ppl. a.* [SELF- 1 f.] Condemning oneself, one's way of life, etc.

1647 C. HARVEY *Schola Cordis* xxx. 27 That self-condemning shamefastnesse. **1667** MILTON *P.L.* IX. 1188 They in mutual accusation spent The fruitless hours, but neither self-condemning. **1729** LAW *Serious Call* iii. 37 A self-condemning conscience. **1791** BOSWELL *Johnson* an. 1777, Johnson laughed heartily at this good Quietist's self-condemning minutes [= Dr. Rutty's Spiritual Diary]. **1816** BYRON *Ch. Har.* III. lix, And could the ceaseless vultures cease to prey On self-condemning bosoms.

Hence **self-con'demningly** *adv.*, in self-condemnation.

1681 BAXTER *Answ. Dodwell* iv. 37 Mr. Dodwell, self-condemningly saith, that [etc.].

self-conden'sation. *Chem.* [SELF- 1 a.] A condensation reaction between two molecules of the same compound. Also **self-con'dense** *v. intr.*, to undergo such a reaction.

1946 *Nature* 12 Oct. 514/1 The highly reactive bi-functional compound, γ-bromopropylamine,..would immediately undergo self-condensation. **1959** A. ALBERT *Heterocyclic Chem.* vii. 269 β-Keto-esters..self-condense to pyrones, e.g. ethyl acetoacetate gives 2-methyl-5-acetyl-6-hydroxy-γ-pyrone. **1964** N. G. CLARK *Mod. Organic Chem.* xxiii. 478 The self-condensation of acetophenone provides one of the rare examples of the carbonyl group of an aromatic ketone participating in a condensation reaction. **1976** *Austral. Jrnl. Chem.* XXIX. 1039 Self-condensation of cyanoacetamides under the influence of phosphorus oxychloride leads to pyridines and pyridinium salts in high yield.

self-'confidence. [SELF- 3 a.] Confidence in oneself; often in an unfavourable sense, arrogant or impudent reliance on one's own powers.

1653 GAUDEN *Hierasp[i]stes* 69 A matter..of self-confidence and intolerable boastings. **1691** HARTCLIFFE *Virtues* 405 Self-confidence and Self-Conceit render Men Fools. **1779** JOHNSON *L. P., Pope* (1868) 375 Self-confidence is the first requisite to great undertakings. **1825** SCOTT *Talism.* i, The calm self-confidence belonging to the victor in many contests. **1849** ALISON *Hist. Eur.* II. vii. 135 Self-confidence, or, in plainer language, impudence, was the great secret of his success. **1875** GLADSTONE *Glean.* (1879) VI. 120 Both rather abounded in self-confidence.

So **self-'confident** (hence **-'confidently** *adv.*, Webster, 1847–54).

a **1617** P. BAYNES *Christian Lett.* (1620) sig. C5, O Lord.. thou has promised that thou wilt circumcise our selfe-confident hearts, so that we shal haue no trust in the flesh, but haue all our reioycing in thee. **1837** WHEWELL *Hist. Induct. Sci.* III. 310 Shallow and self-confident persons. **1921** E. O'NEILL *Diff'rent* I, in *Emperor Jones* 221 Her face ..attracts the eye by a certain boldly-appealing vitality of self-confident youth. **1951** in M. McLuhan *Mech. Bride* (1967) 72/1 It's a self-confident look.

self-con'fiding, *ppl. a.* [SELF- 3 a.] Trusting in oneself, marked by self-confidence.

1654 GATAKER *Disc. Apol.* 52 An haughtie, bold, out-stretching, and selfe-confiding spirit. **1725** POPE *Odyss.* XIII. 174 The thoughtless self-confiding train. **1823** SCOTT *Quentin D.* xiii, Free, and fearless, and self-confiding.

self-congratu'lation. [SELF- 1 a.]

Congratulation of oneself.

1712 ADDISON *Spect.* No. 381 ¶11 How many self-congratulations naturally rise in the mind. **1810** SCOTT *Let.* in *Lockhart* (1837) II. ix. 321 A sort of self-congratulation, a little tickling self-flattery. **1870** DICKENS *E. Drood* iv. 22 The honor is mine and the self-congratulation is mine.

So **self-con'gratulating, -con'gratulatory** *adjs.*

1784 COWPER *Task* v. 622 The puny child Of self-congratulating pride. **1877** MRS. FORRESTER *Mignon* iii, A very pleasant, self-congratulatory frame of mind.

self-'conjugate, *a. Math.* [SELF- 3 a.]

a. Applied to a figure each side of which is, relatively to some conic, the polar of the opposite vertex. Of a function (see quot. 1873). Hence **self-conjugation**, the state of being self-conjugate.

1866 HAMILTON *Quaternions* §349 Where the function $\phi\rho$ is its own conjugate, or is the common self-conjugate part of $\phi\rho$ and $\phi'\rho$. *Ibid.* §353 When this condition of self-conjugation is not satisfied. **1873** MAXWELL *Electr. & Magn.* I. 12 In Quaternion language, the one vector is said to be a linear and vector function of the other, and when there are three pairs of equal coefficients the function is said to be self-conjugate. **1885** J. CASEY *Analyt. Geom.* 305 Let the conics be referred to their common self-conjugate triangle. **1893** in Cayley *Math. Papers* (1897) XIII. 269 Of course, here a self-conjugate term such as *bcd* is put in evidence.

b. Of a subgroup: having the property that for any elements h in the subgroup and g in the group, the product ghg^{-1} is in the subgroup.

1888 G. G. MORRICE tr. *Klein's Lectures on Ikosahedron* I. i. 7 Every group contains..two self-conjugate subgroups: viz., in the first place, the totality of all its operations, *i.e.*, the group itself, and, in the second place, that simplest group which consists of the identical operation alone. **1937** A. A. ALBERT *Mod. Higher Algebra* vi. 131 We call $\mathfrak{H}$ a normal divisor (or invariant subgroup, or self-conjugate subgroup) of $\mathfrak{G}$. **1979** PAGE & WILSON *Introd. Computational Combinatorics* iv. 74 A partition whose Ferrers graph reads the same by rows and by columns is called self-conjugate.

Hence **self-'conjugately** *adv.*, as a self-conjugate subgroup.

1897 W. BURNSIDE *Theory of Groups* x. 208 If two of these sub-groups have a common subgroup of order 4, it must be contained self-conjugately..in a sub-group of order 24 or 56. **1901** L. E. DICKSON *Linear Groups* p. vii, Largest subgroup containing the Abelian group self-conjugately.

self-'conscious, *a.* [SELF- 1 e.]

1. a. *Philos.* Having consciousness of one's identity, one's actions, sensations, etc.; reflectively aware of one's actions. Also said of action, thought, etc.

a **1688** CUDWORTH *Treatise of Freewill* (1838) 71 We are certain by inward sense that we can reflect upon our-selves and consider ourselves, which is a reduplication of life in a higher degree; for all cogitative beings as such are self-conscious. [**1690**, etc.: cf. SELF-CONSCIOUSNESS 2.] **1817** COLERIDGE *Biog. Lit.* 97 An infinite yet self-conscious Creator. **1871** R. H. HUTTON *Ess.* i. (1888) 4 So far as human action is self-conscious as well as voluntary. **1907** ILLINGWORTH *Doctr. Trin.* vii. 136 A person is..essentially a self-conscious subject.

†**b.** Of which one is conscious in oneself. *Obs.*

1697 DRYDEN *Æneid* VIII. 174 My self-conscious Worth. **1824** BENTHAM *Bk. Fallacies* I. i. §2 Wks. 1843 II. 392 Self-conscious and self-avowed imbecility.

2. Marked by undue or morbid pre-occupation with one's own personality; so far self-centred as to suppose one is the object of observation by others.

1834 J. S. MILL *Let.* 12 Jan. in *Wks.* (1963) XII. 208, I begin to think that instead of being, as I once thought I was, the most self-conscious person living, I am much less self-conscious *now*..than almost anybody. **1837** CARLYLE *Fr. Rev.* II. III. vii, Self-conscious, conscious of a world looking on. **1848** THACKERAY *Van. Fair* xxiv, Their..innocence so self-conscious and self-satisfied. **1882** J. HAWTHORNE *Fort. Fool* xxxix, He was singularly free from self-consciousness; and she was so exquisitely self-conscious as completely to conceal it. **1937** 'G. ORWELL' *Road to Wigan Pier* xiii. 255 Self-conscious Socialists dutifully addressing one another as 'Comrade'. **1974** J. IRVING *158-Pound Marriage* ii. 42 She had never been self-conscious about what she wore.

Hence **self-'consciously** *adv.*

a **1834** COLERIDGE *Shaks.* Lit. Rem. (1836) II. 68 A genial understanding directing self-consciously a power and an implicit wisdom deeper even than our consciousness.

self-'consciousness. [SELF- 1 d.]

†**1.** The condition of being privy *to* a thing. *Obs.*

1675 J. SMITH *Chr. Relig. App.* II. 5 Self-consciousness to the closest Villany.

2. *Philos.* Consciousness of one's own identity, one's acts, thoughts, etc.; = CONSCIOUSNESS 4.

1690 LOCKE *Hum. Und.* II. xxvii. §16 Appropriated to me now by this self-consciousness. **1692** BENTLEY *Boyle Lect.* ii. 15 A distinct Animal, endued with self-consciousness and personal sensation of its own. **1722** WOLLASTON *Relig. Nat.* 184 That, which in man is the subject or *suppositum* of self-consciousness, thinks, and has the foresaid faculties, must be something different from his body or carcass. **1836-7** SIR W. HAMILTON *Lect. Metaph.* xxix, Perception is the power by which we are made aware of the phænomena of the external world; Self-consciousness the power by which we apprehend the phænomena of the internal. **1874** G. H. LEWES in *Contemp. Rev.* Oct. 689 Philosophy must be regarded in the light of a continuous history of Self-consciousness.

3. Internal knowledge or conviction *of* a thing; = CONSCIOUSNESS 2.

1751 EARL ORRERY *Rem. Swift* xiii. (ed. 5) 114 With only the self consciousness of deserving a rank among the companions of Brutus in the Elysian fields.

4. The condition of being self-conscious (sense 2).

1833 J. S. MILL *Let.* 25 Nov. in *Wks.* (1963) XII. 195 A man singularly free, if we may trust appearances, from self-consciousness. **1851** KINGSLEY *Yeast* ii, It sweeps away that infernal web of self-consciousness, and absorbs me in outward objects. **1876** FARRAR *Days of thy Youth* xxxvii. 373 If he is not free from the self-consciousness which is usually called being nervous. **1932** G. GREENE *Stamboul Train* I. i. 5 Her body..even while stumbling..retained its self-consciousness.

self-'consequence. [SELF- 5 a.] Self-importance.

1778 MISS BURNEY *Evelina* xxxiv. (1791) II. 225 By no means wanting in pride and self-consequence. **1829** SCOTT *Anne of G.* xviii, To..enhance the self-consequence of a powerful ecclesiastic. **1873** M. ARNOLD *Lit. & Dogma* (1876) 101 Warped by personal pretensions and self-consequence.

So **self-'consequent** *a.*, self-important.

1878 MRS. H. WOOD *Pomeroy Abbey* III. viii, Jupiter, seated on Olympus,..never felt more self-consequent than does Jeffs feel, perched on his box-seat to-day.

self-con'sistency. [SELF- 3 a.] = CONSISTENCY 5, 5 b.

1692 NORRIS *Curs. Reflect.* 13 How then can he with any tolerable Self-consistency say [etc.]. **1770** LANGHORNE *Plutarch* (1879) I. 66/1 Lycurgus..considered happiness..as flowing from virtue and self-consistency. **1858** J. MARTINEAU *Stud. Chr.* 270 You deny the self-consistency of the Church of England and call it a compromise. **1876** GLADSTONE *Homeric Synchr.* 40 Such facts do not..destroy ..the self-consistency of the objects themselves.

self-con'sistent, *a.* [SELF- 3 a.]

a. = CONSISTENT 6 b, 7.

1704 NORRIS *Ideal World* II. ii. 60 They are also so self-consistent as in consequence of their common principle to hold that they do not think. **1817** COLERIDGE *Statesm. Man.* 5 Imposture, organized into a comprehensive and self-consistent whole. **1843** *Penny Cycl.* XXVII. 199/2 An accurate and self-consistent system of weights and measures.

b. *Physics.* Of a trial solution of Schrödinger's equation for a nucleus with more than one electron: consistent with its own postulates (see quots.).

1928 D. R. HARTREE in *Proc. Cambr. Philos. Soc.* XXIV. 113 If the final field is the same as the initial field, the field will be called 'self-consistent'. **1958** SYKES & BELL tr. *Landau & Lifshitz' Quantum Mechanics* x. 232 Schrödinger's equation for atoms containing more than one electron cannot be directly solved in practice, even by numerical methods. Approximate methods of calculating the energies and wave functions of the stationary states of the atoms are therefore important. The most important of these methods is what is called the self-consistent field method. The idea of this method consists in regarding each electron in the atom as being in motion in the 'self-consistent field' due to the nucleus together with all the other electrons. **1974** EISBERG & RESNICK *Quantum Physics* ix. 347 It might seem that there is no way to find the net potential of an atom at intermediate distances from its center... But it can be taken care of by demanding that the net potential be self-consistent.

Hence **self-con'sistently** *adv.*

1953 F. J. WHITFIELD tr. *L. Hjelmslev's Prolegomena to Theory of Lang.* 9 We require of linguistic theory that it enable us to describe self-consistently and exhaustively all conceivable or possible Danish texts. **1973** *Physical Rev.* B. VII. 674 Energy bands, Fermi surfaces, and densities of states of calcium as a function of lattice constant have been calculated self-consistently by the augmented-plane-wave method.

self-con'tained, *ppl. a.* [SELF- 3 a.] Having all that one (it) needs in oneself (itself); independent of external means or relations; esp. (of persons) not dependent upon, or communicating oneself to, others; reserved or restrained in behaviour.

1591 SYLVESTER *Du Bartas* I. vii. 694 Our own Bodie's self-containèd motions. **1839** BAILEY *Festus* 360 The self-contained Perfection. **1843** DICKENS *Chr. Carol* i. 3 Secret, and self-contained, and solitary as an oyster. **1860** RUSKIN *Mod. Painters* V. VI. ix. §7. 84 The pine rises in serene resistance, self-contained. **1865** MEREDITH *R. Fleming* viii, A beauty has all the world with her when she is self-contained. **1890** 'R. BOLDREWOOD' *Col. Reformer* (1891) 290 The vast, surging, excited, but self-contained crowd. **1905** CHESTERTON *Heretics* 181 When London was smaller, and the parts of London more self-contained and parochial.

b. Of a house, or (now more usually) of a flat, or suite of rooms, within a house: Of which the apartments and the approaches are restricted to the use of one family or household; having a private entrance. Orig. *Sc.*

1827 SCOTT *Chron. Canongate* v, It is a house 'within itself', or, according to a newer phraseology in advertisements, self-contained. **1861** BERESF. HOPE *Eng. Cathedr. 19th C.* iv. 126 The Englishman has a weakness..to rent a self-contained house rather than an apartment. **1910** *Bradshaw's Railway Guide* Apr. 1174 The only Hotel in the Town having self-contained Suites. **1928** E. A. ROBERTSON *Cullum* xi. 206 We came back in the evening to what was practically a self-contained flat—no one else slept on that landing. **1977** *Wandsworth Borough News* 16 Sept. 15/1 Planning Proposals..7 Eckstein-road, Clapham Junction—conversion to form two self-contained flats.

allusive. **1829** CARLYLE in Froude *Life* (1882) II. iv. 73 We are a world 'within ourselves', a 'self-contained house'.

c. Of a machine or device: Complete in itself.

1828 SCOTT *Aunt Margaret's Mirr.* ii, [The mirror] no longer simply reflected the objects placed before it, but, as if it had self-contained scenery of its own, objects began to appear within it. **1839–47** [see *self-containedness* below]. **1869** RANKINE *Cycl. Mach. & Hand-tools* Pl. K 3, It [*sc.* shearing-machine] is self-contained, is easily fixed, requires ..but moderate skill to work it. **1875** KNIGHT *Dict. Mech.* s.v., *Self-contained engine*, an engine and boiler attached together complete for working. **1893** J. A. HODGES *Elem. Photogr.* (1907) 133 A self-contained mechanical device for exposing the plates automatically.

Hence **self-con'tainedly** *adv.*, **self-con'tainedness**; so **self-con'taining** *vbl. sb.* and *ppl. a.*; **self-con'tainment**, the condition of being self-contained.

1884 G. ALLEN *Philistia* III. 268 Ernest and Edie..went their own way as *self-containedly as usual. **1839–47** TODD *Cycl. Anat.* III. 348/2 All the advantage of Mr. Holland's microscope, except its *self-containedness. **1879** A. W. WARD *Chaucer* 147 That self-containedness (very different from self-contentedness) which distinguishes Chaucer. **1882** *Expositor* Aug. 140 The self-containedness, the incommunicableness of God. **1847** EMERSON *Repr. Men, Montaigne* Wks. (Bohn) I. 340 This, then, is the right ground of the sceptic—this of consideration, of *self-containing. **1856** *N. Brit. Rev.* XXVI. 101 The nation was to be free, self-helping, *self-containing, unconquerable. **1850** *Tait's Mag.* XVII. 734/1 Their whole condition is..one of unsociability, *self-containment, and isolation. **1866** VISCT. STRANGFORD *Selection* (1869) I. 108 A country the very essence of whose positon is self-containment.

self-con'tempt. [SELF- 1.] Contempt of self.

1600 in Farr *S.P. Eliz.* (1845) II. 446 An humble soule that sincks in selfe-contempt. *a* **1711** KEN *Christophil* Poet. Wks. I. 504 Thou Self-contempt didst practise and instil. **1821** SHELLEY *Adonais* xxxvii, Remorse and Self-contempt shall cling to thee. **1861** WHYTE MELVILLE *Good for Nothing* II. 157 An expression in which joviality, recklessness, and a certain sorrowing self-contempt were strangely mingled.

self-con'tent, *sb.* [SELF- 3 a.] Self-satisfaction.

1654 WHITLOCK *Zootomia* 367 If even in self-vexation, something of self-content is sought. **1694** CONGREVE *Double Dealer* III. ad fin., If Happiness in Self-content is plac'd. **1820** SHELLEY *Prometh. Unb.* I. i. 487 Like a vain loud multitude Vexing the self-content of wisest men. **1852** THACKERAY *Esmond* II. x, This self-content of his kept him in general good-humour.

self-con'tent, *a. rare.* [SELF- 3 a.] = next.

1857 E. FITZGERALD *Lett.* (1889) I. 257 Frenchmen are so self-content and superficial.

self-con'tented, *ppl. a.* [SELF- 3 a.] Self-satisfied. So **self-con'tentedly** *adv.*; **self-con'tentedness**, **self-con'tentment**, self-satisfaction; † **self-con'tenting** *a.*, self-satisfying.

1819 SHELLEY *Rosalind & Helen* 29 Men, women, children, slunk away, Whispering with *self-contented pride. **1862** THORNBURY *Turner* I. 16 One of those self-contented fussy men. **1844** MRS. BROWNING *Early Rose* xlvi. Poems (1850) II. 299 Ye to yourselves suffice,..*Self-contentedly approve you Unto Him who sits above you. **1691** NORRIS *Pract. Disc.* (1711) III. 168 What an inward sufficiency and *Self-Contentedness. **1897** W. C. HAZLITT *Ourselves* 34 The wide prevalence of self-contentedness and self-complacency. **1647** H. MORE *Exorcismus* ii, Whose inward like Is *self-contenting joy. **1647** TRAPP *Comm. Luke* ii. 16 He would chuse to live and dye in his self-contenting secresie. **1815** JANE AUSTEN *Emma* III. xiv. 374 He..talked on with much *self-contentment. **1866** GEO. ELIOT *F. Holt* I. x. 232 Esther felt herself seriously shaken in her self-contentment.

self-contra'diction. [SELF- 1 a.] The act or fact of contradicting oneself (or itself); also, a statement which contains elements that contradict one another.

1658 OWEN (*title*) A Defence of Mr. John Cotton from the imputation of Selfe Contradiction. **1661** BOYLE *Style of Script.* (1675) 95 As if there were a great many Self-contradictions to be met with in the Scripture. **1736** BUTLER *Anal.* I. vii. 125 The most palpable Self-contradictions. **1865** KINGSLEY *Herew.* xxxvi, With the strange self-contradiction of human nature. **1876** MELLOR *Priesthood* v. 250 The superlocal presence of a body is a phrase which involves a self-contradiction, inasmuch as it excludes an essential property in the definition of body.

So **self-contra'dicting** *ppl. a.* (hence **self-contra'dictingly** *adv.*), † **self-contra'dictious**, **self-contra'dictory** *adjs.*, (hence **self-contra'dictorily** *adv.*).

1655–87 H. MORE *App. Antid.* (1712) 221 It is an incongruous and *self-contradicting position to hold. **1672** BAXTER *Bagshaw's Scandals* ii. 15 The self-contradicting man. **1866** *Macm. Mag.* Feb. 383 An authority thus divided, and thus self-contradicting. **1653** BAXTER *Christian Concord* 30 To say we deal *self-contradictingly. **1660** H. MORE *Myst. Godl.* I. v. 12 A Mystery which they hold impossible and *self-contradictious. **1943** *Mind* LII. 313 We remember the man who never said, 'To see an event we should have to see it in an instant', thus self-contradictorily misdescribing our use of 'see an event'. **1959** P. F. STRAWSON *Individuals* i. 34 The standard..is set self-contradictorily high. **1981** G. MACBETH *Kind of Treason* ii. 17 The Clapham Center, as it was rather self-contradictorily called. **1657** BAXTER *Agst. Quakery* 8 Their Doctrines are *self-contradictory. **1864** BURTON *Scot Abr.* I. iv. 162 The Florentine's precepts were ..so self-contradictory..that he was supposed to be in jest.

self-con'trol. [SELF- 1 a.]

1. Control of oneself, one's desires, etc.

1711 SHAFTESB. *Charac.* III. 260 *note*, The Perfection of Virtue is from long Art and Management, Self-Controul. **1799** WORDSW. *Ruth* 154 A Man who without self-control Would seek what the degraded soul Unworthily admires. **1832** TENNYSON *Œnone* 142 Selfreverence, selfknowledge, selfcontrol. **1859** GEO. ELIOT *A. Bede* xxxix, As if all self-control had forsaken him, [he] grasped Adam's arm.

2. Self-government. *rare.*

1850 MARSDEN *Early Purit.* (1853) 26 If it be not only an independent but a national church, the right of self-control is one that it cannot part with without disloyalty.

Hence **self-con'trolled**, **-con'trolling** *adjs.*

1875 MANNING *Mission Holy Ghost* viii. 210 The human frame, so strong, so dignified, so *self-controlled in its perfections. **1835** LYTTON *Rienzi* I. iv, The deep and *self-controlling mind of Adrian. **1873** SPENCER *Study Sociol.* vi. 131 A comparatively self-controlling nature, capable of sacrificing present ease to future good.

self-con'victed, *ppl. a.* [SELF- 2.] Convicted by one's own words or action.

1729 SAVAGE *Wanderer* III. 306 Pale Guilt starts self-convicted, when arraign'd. **1821** SCOTT *Kenilw.* xxi, I should stand self-convicted of villainy, were I to urge such a deceit. **1867** FREEMAN *Norm. Conq.* I. App. (1877) 738 Such a document is self-convicted.

self-con'viction. [SELF- 1 a.] Conviction of oneself by one's own words or action.

1640 R. BAILLIE (*title*) Ladensivm Αὐτοκατακρισις, The Canterbvrians Self-Conviction. **1751** SMOLLETT *Per. Pic.* lxxxi. (1779) III. 163, I began to hate him in proportion to the self-conviction I felt. **1798** SOTHEBY tr. *Wieland's Oberon* (1826) I. 90 Too late at last the self-conviction came.

self-cre'ated, *ppl. a.* [SELF- 2.] Created, brought into existence, or constituted by oneself.

1677 GILPIN *Dæmonol.* (1867) 403 That God promiseth to keep him in his ways, but not in self-created dangers. **1802** MRS. E. PARSONS *Myst. Visit* III. 198 The self-created distinction of polished society. **1815** W. PRICE *Hist. Oswestry* 78 Napoleon Buonaparte, the self-created emperor of the French. **1871** R. H. HUTTON *Ess.* iv. I. 72 The particular, partly self-created, character of Gibbon's mind.

So **self-cre'ate** *ppl. a.* (*rare*) = prec.; **self-cre'ation; self-cre'ating, -cre'ative** *adjs.*, capable of self-creation.

1875 LIGHTFOOT *Comm. Col.* (1886) 270 They divided the universe into..the uncreate, the *self-create and the created. **1774** GOLDSM. *Nat. Hist.* (1824) III. 119 As the muscle is thus furnished with a kind of *self-creating power. **1862** SPENCER *First Princ.* I. ii. §11 (1875) 32 The hypothesis of *self-creation, which practically amounts to what is called Pantheism. **1898** ILLINGWORTH *Div. Immanence* i. §1 This capacity of self-determination, and therefore of self-creation, compels us to place will in a category by itself. **1845** BAILEY *Festus* 12 Thy might is *self-creative. **1898** ILLINGWORTH *Div. Immanence* i. §1 We are, in a measure, self-creative, causes of ourselves.

self-'criticism. [SELF- 1 a.] **1.** Criticism of oneself.

1857 GEO. ELIOT *Ess.* (1884) 8 The self-criticism which prompted the suppression of the dedication. **1926** J. S. HUXLEY *Essays in Popular Science* 162 The normal tendency of strongly-felt religious emotion to..set itself up as an absolute standard untempered by tolerance or by the self-criticism of reason. **1937** O. JESPERSEN in *S.P.E. Tract* XLVIII. 269 While one pronounces the beginning of an utterance the mind is busy preparing the rest, not only what to say, but how to say it. But most of this linguistic self-criticism is..lost to the world. **1956** H. KURNITZ *Invasion of Privacy* ii. 20 In this last phrase of good-natured self-criticism, Stradling's voice shifted into a glacial gear. **1977** *Lancet* 13 Aug. 357/1 Dr Bartsch reiterates our self-criticism that the two groups of patients were not comparable in all respects.

2. *Pol.* Criticism undertaken publicly by oneself of one's actions, attitudes, or policies, considered as a duty in order to ensure conformity with communist party doctrine. Also *transf.*

1933 E. & C. PAUL tr. *Stalin's Leninism* II. 122 An abyss divides the self-criticism of the opposition..from Bolshevik self-criticism, the purpose of which is to *strengthen* the Party spirit. **1966** J. BINGHAM *Double Agent* vii. 101 Colonel Golchenko has performed an act of self-criticism in accordance with the principles of our party. **1976** M. MACHLIN *Pipeline* x. 116 Finally, after a scathing self-criticism session in the collective's skid row tenement in Seattle, Sonia decided she had had enough. **1978** D. BLOODWORTH *Crosstalk* x. 84 She was in trouble—public accusations that she was a counterrevolutionary, self-criticism sessions, denunciations,..the works.

self-culti'vation. [SELF- 1 a.] = SELF-CULTURE.

1873 J. S. MILL *Autobiogr.* iv. 119, I did not neglect other modes of self-cultivation. **1964** R. MILIBAND in I. L. Horowitz *New Sociology* 80 A society..where man's social ..setting would encourage self-cultivation and craftsmanship.

self-'culture. [SELF- 1 a.] The cultivation or development by one's own efforts of one's mind, faculties, manners, etc.

1829 J. STERLING *Let.* 10 Nov. in Carlyle *Life John Sterling* (1851) I. vii. 56, I have no doubt that, by practice and self-culture, she will be a far finer actress. **1847** EMERSON *Repr. Men, Goethe* Wks. (Bohn) I. 394, I suppose the worldly tone of his tales grew out of the calculations of self-culture. **1872** LOWELL *Among my Bks., Dante* Wks. 1890 IV. 149 From being the slave of his imaginative faculty, he rose by self-culture and force of will to that mastery of it which is art. **1926** B. WEBB *My Apprenticeship* ii. 60 A device of my own for self-culture—reading the books of my free choice.

† **self-dead,** *a. Obs.* [SELF- 3 a.] Dead to self.

1647 H. MORE *Philos. Poems, Addit.* 332 That pure fire Wherewith thou wontest to inspire All self-dead souls. **1688** NORRIS *Lett.* 187 To be thus self-dead and self-annihilated. **1798** SOTHEBY tr. *Wieland's Oberon* VI. xxxi. (1805) I. 194 Self-dead, for him alone to be, to breathe, to move.

Hence † **self-'deadness.**

1647 H. MORE *Song of Soul* Notes 147/2 The most profound and spirituall humility,..and a perfect self-deadness.

†**self-death.** *Obs.* [SELF 1 a.] Self-murder.
1659 *Leg. Capt. Jones* in *Archæologist* Feb. (1842) 281 Brutus, I am a brute, and have thy spirit, Thy fortune and self-death I will inherit.

self-de'ceit. [SELF- 1 a.] Self-deception.
1679 FLAVEL *Saint Indeed* II. 16 Evidences of self-deceit in matters of Religion. **1712** ADDISON *Spect.* No. 399 ⁋2 This fatal Hypocrisie and Self-deceit. **1828** D. STEWART *Philos. Powers of Man* II. ii. I. 157 Our moral powers are warped by the influence of self-partiality and self-deceit. **1832** MISS MITFORD *Village* Ser. v. *Incendiary* 6 They show to the human heart its own desperate self-deceit.

So **self-de'ceitful** *a.*, **-de'ceitfulness**.
1818 BYRON *Juan* I. cvi, How *self-deceitful is the sagest part Of mortals whom thy [*sc.* Love's] lure hath led along. **1850** W. H. GOOLD *J. Owen's Wks.* I. Pref. 9 The *self-deceitfulness of the heart.

self-de'ceived, *ppl. a.* [SELF- 2.] Deceived by oneself, marked by self-deception.
1671 MILTON *P.R.* IV. 7 Who self deceiv'd And rash, before-hand had no better weigh'd The strength he was to cope with. **1746** FRANCIS tr. *Hor., Sat.* I. i. 75 Some, self-deceived, who think their lust of gold Is but a love of fame. **1831** COLERIDGE *Table-talk* 30 July, An intense half self-deceived humorism.

So **self-de'ceiver, -de'ceiving** *vbl. sb.* and *ppl. a.*
a **1614** DYKE *Myst. Selfe-deceiving* iv. (ed. 8) 65 And so much for the three former *selfe-deceiuers. KEBLE *Chr. Y., 6th Sund. Epiph.*, The self-deceiver's dreary theme. *a* **1614** DYKE (*title*) The Mystery of *Selfe-Deceiving. **1668** OWEN *Expos. 130th Ps.* (1669) 165 All their profession is but a miserable self-deceiving. **1734** WATTS *Reliq. Juv.* (1789) 121 Thus we begin to learn and practise early this art of self-deceiving. **1597** HOOKER *Eccl. Pol.* v. lx. §3 (1617) 315 A *selfe-deceiuing vanitie. **1690** C. NESSE *Hist. & Myst. O. & N. Test.* I. 212 We are poor, empty self-deceiving and self-defiling creatures. **1827** KEBLE *Chr. Y., 14th Sund. Trin.*, What sadder scene can angels view Than self-deceiving tears? **1865** PUSEY *Truth Eng. Ch.* 119 Easy and self-deceiving ways, by which to deny Christ.

self-de'ception. [SELF- 1 a.] The action or fact of deceiving oneself; self-delusion.
1677 GILPIN *Dæmonol.* (1867) 53 It may be said a man complies with those things which are intended for his delusion, and so improperly by his negligence may fall under blame of self-deception. **1745** J. MASON *Self-Knowledge* I. xi. (1758) 75 Of all impostures Self-Deception is the most dangerous, because least suspected. **1827** SCOTT *Surg. Dau.* v, With all a lover's power of self-deception. **1907** RALEIGH *Shakespeare* 175 Self-deception is a male weakness.

So **self-de'ceptious, -de'ceptive** *adjs.*
1809 KNOX *Let. to Jebb* 8 Mar., A *self-deceptious substitution of a lower..good, in the place of the highest. **1894** *Athenæum* 3 Nov. 599/1 [They] showed themselves theatrical, self-conscious, and *self-deceptive.

self-de'fence. [SELF- 1 a.] The act of defending oneself, one's rights or position; *spec.* in *Law* (see quot. 1769).
1651 HOBBES *Leviath.* II. xxi. 113 The offer of pardon taketh from them, to whom it is offered, the plea of self-defence. **1681** DRYDEN *Abs. & Achit.* I. 458 Self-defence is Nature's eldest law. **1733** POPE *Ess. Man* III. 279 Forc'd into virtue thus by Self-defence, Ev'n Kings learn'd justice and benevolence. **1769** BLACKSTONE *Comm.* IV. 183 Homicide in self-defence, or *se defendendo*, upon a sudden affray, is.. excusable rather than justifiable, by the English law. **1855** MACAULAY *Hist. Eng.* xvii. IV. 26 He deduced the doctrine that selfdefence against pirates and assassins is unlawful. **1876** BANCROFT *Hist. U.S.* IV. xv. 420 The settler..trusted for security in the forest to his perpetual readiness for self-defence. **1886** *Field* 9 Oct. 535/2 [Football] Each team scored a goal, and each touched down in self-defence.

b. ***the (noble, manly) art of self-defence***: †(*a*) fencing; (*b*) pugilism, boxing. (Cf. DEFENCE *sb.* 4, NOBLE *a.* 9.)
1724 SIR W. HOPE (*title*) A Vindication of the true art of self-defence... To which is annexed, a short..memorial for sword-men. **182.** *Art & Pract. Boxing* Pref., A knowledge of the art of Self-Defence. **1849** COBDEN *Speeches* 76 Are the men the most peaceful in society, who have studied the 'noble art of self-defence?' **1887** W. P. FRITH *Autobiogr.* I. i. 5 A little knowledge of the manly art of self-defence.

self-de'fended, *ppl. a.* [SELF- 2.] Defended by oneself (or itself).
1775 in ASH. **1845** *Athenæum* 11 Jan. 37 A system should either be self-defended or not at all.

self-de'fensive, *a.* [SELF- 1 e.] Of, pertaining to, or involving the principle of, self-defence. So **self-de'fensory** *a.*
1828 *Lights & Shades* I. 6 A habit of *self-defensive refusal to all similar propositions. **1905** *Q. Rev.* Oct. 473 The next self-defensive artifice is that of accommodation and compromise. **1872** H. W. BEECHER *Lect. Preaching* ii. 33 A man of..peaceableness,..though of high spirit and *self-defensory power when required.

self-de'light. [SELF- 3 a.] Delight in oneself, one's being or existence.
1594 SOUTHWELL *M. Magd. Funerall Teares* 76 b, Least you loose your selues in too much selfe delight. **1665** BRATHWAIT *Comm. Two Tales* 123 Seeing it affords such sweet self-delight to the Sense. *a* **1711** KEN *Hymnarium* Poet. Wks. II. 41 God sits unchang'd in glorious Height, Self-life, Self-love, and Self-delight. **1891** T. HARDY *Tess* xv, The invincible instinct towards self-delight.

self-de'liverance. [SELF- 1 a.] Suicide by an incurable patient who finds his suffering intolerable.
This euphemism is not yet (1982) in wide currency. The related expression ***self-deliveration*** has also been used.
1975 M. R. BARRINGTON in M. Kohl *Beneficent Euthanasia* 214 Taking one's own life..would be more readily comprehended as responsible behavior if it were expressed as 'self-deliveration'. *Ibid.* 245 *Self-deliverance*, accession to deliverance. *Self-deliveration*, suicide where deliverance has or might have been given. **1975** *Hansard Lords* 4 Dec. 47/2 Self-deliverance to be regarded as death by misadventure. **1980** *Daily Tel.* 12 Aug. 6/2 The decision not to publish [a guide to suicide] would mean 'tragedy and continued distress..for many who wish to bring about their own self-deliverance'.

self-de'livery, [SELF- 4.] Automatic delivery: **a.** by a reaping-machine of the corn in swaths or sheaves; **b.** of a pattern from the mould in founding. Also *attrib.* So **self-de'liverer**, a self-delivery reaping-machine; **self-de'livering** *ppl. a.*
1864 *Trans. Highl. Soc.* Jan. 133 The self-delivering machinery now consisting of a series of four (formerly six) rakes attached to an upright shaft in such a manner as to admit of a free ascending, descending, and horizontal motion. *Ibid.* 143 Of the self-delivery reapers, Crosskill's Bell did its work most satisfactorily. **1908** *Chamb. Encycl.* VIII. 596/1 [Reaping-machines] delivered by mechanical labour, or self-deliverers. **1908** J. G. HORNER *Encycl. Pract. Engin., Self-Delivery*, the delivery of a pattern from the mould without requiring the use of cores.

self-de'luded, *ppl. a.* [SELF- 2.] Deluded by oneself, suffering from self-delusion.
1766 LD. MANSFIELD in *Hansard's Parl. Hist.* XVI. 312 What the self-deluded and self-destroyed king said deceitfully. **1784** COWPER *Task* III. 316 Self-deluded nymphs and swains, Who dream they have a taste for fields and groves. **1884** *Leeds Merc.* 24 Oct. 4/4 He had warned the self-deluded members of the Conservative party.

So **self-de'luder, -de'luding** *ppl. a.*
1748 RICHARDSON *Clarissa* VII. xv. 61 Poor mistaken creature!—Unhappy *self-deluder! **1817** KEATS *Let. to Haydon* May, If one be a self-deluder. **1903** *Edin. Rev.* Apr. 325 Impostors or at best self-deluders. **1650** BAXTER *Saint's Rest* III. v. §2 (1651) 86 Their own *self-deluding folly. **1667** FLAVEL *Saint Indeed* (1673) 184 Thou self-deluding hypocrite. **1955** *Bull. Atomic Sci.* Apr. 168/1 It is shortsighted and self-deluding to ascribe more than a small part of Russian success to efficient espionage. **1980** D. FRANCIS *Reflex* xii. 142 He was a pernicious self-deluding little egotist.

self-de'lusion. [SELF- 1 a.] The act of deluding oneself; an instance of this.
1634 MILTON *Comus* 365 If they be but false alarms of Fear, How bitter is such self-delusion? **1794** MRS. RADCLIFFE *Myst. Udolpho* xxxvii, Pitying the self-delusion which disarmed him of the will to depart. **1818** SCOTT *Br. Lamm.* xv, Covering with no unusual self-delusion his interested views with a hue of virtue. **1880** *Fortn. Rev.* Feb. 229 To go on as we do now..in the vague hope that some day we may begin to do our duty..is..mere self-delusion.

self-de'nial. [SELF- 1 a.] Denial or abnegation of oneself; sacrifice of one's personal desires.
1642 D. ROGERS *Naaman* To Rdr. §1 This notion of Selfe and her opposite Self-deniall. **1683** TRYON *Way to Health* 62 This excellent state is not obtainable without Self-denial, and suffering now and then a little gentle Hunger. **1711** STEELE *Spect.* No. 248 ⁋1 The great Foundation of civil Virtue is Self-Denial. **1718** LADY M. W. MONTAGU *Let. to C'tess Mar* 10 Mar., I have not written to you..these many months; a great piece of self-denial. **1834** J. H. NEWMAN *Par. Serm.* I. v. 79 Let your very rising from your bed be a self-denial; let your meals be self-denials.

self-de'nied, *ppl. a.* [SELF- 2.] Given to, or characterized by, self-denial; self-denying.
1693 *Apol. Clergy Scot.* 9 They could not be so self-denyed as to be willingly deprived of the honour. *a* **1715** BURNET *Own Time* (1766) I. 270 He..was a mortified and self-denied man, that delighted in nothing so much as in the doing good. **1818** SCOTT *Hrt. Midl.* xxxiii, The undaunted and self-denied manner in which he sacrificed himself. **1850** J. BROWN *Disc. & Sayings of our Lord* (1852) II. xvi. 206 Are we following him in self-denied service?

Hence **self-de'niedly** *adv.*
1676 ROW *Contn. Blair's Autobiogr.* xii. (1848) 379 Mr. Blair did seriously and self-deniedly bestir himself.

self-de'nier. [SELF- 1 c.] A practiser of self-denial.
1654 WHITLOCK *Zootomia* 366 The greatest Arnautists, Selfe-denyers in shew. **1865** M. ARNOLD *Ess. Crit.* Ser. I. vii. (1886) 262 These saintly self-deniers, these resigned sufferers.

†**self-de'nying,** *vbl. sb. Obs.* [SELF 1 b.] Self-denial.
1661 FELTHAM *Resolves* II. iii. 181 To undergo a self-denying or some Sufferance. **1664** BUTLER *Hud.* II. ii. 134 Breaking of an Oath, and Lying, Is but a kind of Self-denying. **1878** TROLLOPE *Is he Popenjoy?* I. xiii. 174, I hate all kind of strictness and duty and self-denying.

self-de'nying, *ppl. a.* [SELF- 1 e.] That denies himself; characterized by or involving self-denial.
self-denying ordinance (Eng. Hist.), 'an Ordinance appointing, That no Member of either House, during the Time of this War, shall have or execute any Office or Command, Military or Civil' (Jrnl. Ho. Commons, Dec. 11, 1644); also transf. (colloq.) applied to any course of action by which a person deprives himself of some advantage or benefit.
1632 E. SYMONDS *Eccles. Self-seeking* (1712) 1 A most learned, loving, faithful, and self-denying Man. **1644** WHITELOCKE *Mem.* (1732) 118 They could find no other way than by passing a self-denying ordinance, (as they called it,) which would serve their turn. **1693** LUTTRELL *Brief. Rel.* (1857) III. 3 The lords were this day in a long debate on the commons selfe denying bill. **1784** COWPER *Task* v. 328 Whence springs Your self-denying zeal? **1795** SCOTT *Let.* in *Lockhart* (1837) I. vii. 233, I anticipate with pleasure their marvellous adventures, in the course of which Dr. Black's *self-denying ordinance* will run a shrewd chance of being neglected. **1832** —— *Ct. Rob.* x, A benevolent individual, who, self-denying to himself, is liberal to all others. **1853** C. BRONTE *Villette* xx, The self-denying and self-sacrificing part of the Catholic religion. **1878** EMERSON *Sov. Ethics* Wks. (Bohn) III. 382 A self-denying, ardent church.

Hence **self-de'nyingly** *adv.*
1649 ROBERT *Clavis Bibl.* 340 To submit silently and self-denyingly to the Lords chastisements. **1671** BAXTER *Power of Mag.* I. 15 Most impartially and self-denyingly faithful to Christ. **1876** STUBBS *Study Med. & Mod. Hist.* iii. (1886) 57 The labours self-denyingly and generously tendered of hard-worked tutors.

self-de'pendence. [SELF- 3 a.] Dependence entirely upon oneself, one's own efforts, etc.
1759 TOPLADY *Hymn, 'Lord, I feel a carnal mind'*, A submissive heart, From pride and self-dependence free. **1837** HT. MARTINEAU *Soc. Amer.* III. 177 The children of America have the advantage of the best possible early discipline; that of activity and self-dependence. **1857** J. H. NEWMAN *Serm. Var. Occas.* (1881) vi. 81 The Omnipotence, the Self-dependence, the Self-sufficiency..of the Eternal God. **1876** BANCROFT *Hist. U.S.* V. xvi. 522 His haughty self-dependence and force of will.

So **self-de'pendency**.
1853 PULSFORD tr. *J. Müller's Chr. Doctr. Sin* II. 53 Custom..regarded as determining power, may be very well reconciled with spiritual self-dependency.

self-de'pendent, *a.* [SELF- 3 a.] Possessing or characterized by self-dependence.
1677 GALE *Crt. Gentiles* IV. 93 The excellence of the Angelic nature could not preserve them when self-dependent. **1764** GOLDSM. *Trav.* 341 The self-dependent lordlings. **1833** J. H. NEWMAN *Arians* II. iv. 201 The existence of an irresponsible self-dependent Being. **1848** R. I. WILBERFORCE *Doctr. Incarnation* vi. (1852) 162 Salvation rests on the supernatural gift of God, and not on the self-dependent exertions of human excellence. **1861** GOSCHEN *For. Exch.* 14 A nation, rich in capital and very self-dependent.

Hence **self-de'pendently** *adv.*; so **self-de'pending** *ppl. a.*, self-dependent.
1853 PULSFORD tr. *J. Müller's Chr. Doctr. Sin* II. 57 In so far as it..*self-dependently works and is active from out the very inmost of its essence. **1855** *Self-depending [see SELF-WROUGHT b].

self-de'spair. [SELF- 1 d.] Despair of oneself.
1677 GALE *Crt. Gentiles* IV. 526 An holy self-despair and humble trembling dependence on Divine grace. **1742** C. WESLEY *Wrestling Jacob* viii. Hymns 116, I am weak But confident in Self-despair. **1858** GEO. ELIOT *Scenes Cler. Life, Janet's Rep.* xv, No human soul had..understood her self-despair. **1884** *Encycl. Brit.* XVII. 130/2 The widespread feeling of self-despair and the longing for divine illumination.

self-de'stroyed, *ppl. a.* [SELF- 2.] Destroyed by one's own act.
1766 [see SELF-DELUDED]. **1805-6** CARY *Dante, Inf.* XXVI. 84 In what clime death o'ertook him self-destroyed.

self-de'stroyer. [SELF- 1 c.] One who is the cause of his own destruction.
1657 BAXTER *Call to Unconverted* (1666) 215 It's apparent that you are self-destroyers, in that you draw the matter of your sin and destruction even from the blessed God himself. **1713** [see SELF-FLATTERER].

b. A suicide.
1654 WHITLOCK *Zootomia* 376 No man is Master of his own Body, and therefore selfe-destroyers have not common buriall. **1826** W. E. ANDREWS *Fox's Cal. Prot. Saints* 473 Fox being in want of a saint-martyr thought proper to canonize a self-destroyer. **1886** STEVENSON *Dr. Jekyll* viii. (1895) 84 By the crushed phial in the hand..Utterson knew that he was looking on the body of a self-destroyer.

So **self-de'stroying** *vbl. sb.* and *ppl. a.*
1612 W. SCLATER *Sick Souls Salve* 29 Lust, murther, *selfe destroying. **1687** BOYLE *Martyrd. Theodora* Pref. (1703) 21 St. Jerome..speaks of the unlawfulness of self-destroying. **1645** RUTHERFORD *Tryal & Tri. Faith* 127 To kill high thoughts of a *self-destroying sinner. *a* **1699** J. BEAUMONT *Psyche* VII. cxxviii. (1702) 96 Driving the self-destroying Trade of Sin. **1713** M. HENRY *Ordination Serm.* Wks. 1857 II. 501/1 This perishing self-destroying people. **1820** SHELLEY *Prometh. Unb.* IV. 249 With the force of self-destroying swiftness.

self-de'struct, *v.* orig. *N. Amer.* [f. SELF- 1 a, h: cf. DESTRUCT *v.*]

1. *intr.* Of a thing: to destroy itself automatically. Also *fig.*
1969 *Daily Colonist* (Victoria, B.C.) 30 Mar. 43/4 This message will self-destruct in 10 seconds but the printed message is the one that lives on. **1970** *New Yorker* 28 Nov. 58 Our definition of 'history' is going to change as we raise our consciousness. Our definition's going to—it's going to self-destruct. **1973** *Guardian* 18 June 4/6 Watergate came from within. The system itself has begun to self-destruct. **1977** D. FRANCIS *Risk* xiv. 188 He's programmed to self-destruct before the end of the season... He'll go bust to the bookies. **1979** R. PERRY *Bishop's Pawn* i. 14 The tape would automatically self-destruct after twenty minutes.

Hence as *sb.*; **self-destructing** *ppl. a.*

1970 *New Scientist* 27 Aug. 406 (*title*) Self-destructing proteins may tick away our years. **1972** *Village Voice* 1 June 25/3 These are finally not poems or plays or stories, but self-destructs. **1977** *Daily Tel.* 21 May 12/4 Built into the whole modernist adventure was a kind of self-destruct. **1978** J. McNeil *Consultant* xxxvi. 295 Alloway's program has done a convenient self-destruct.

2. *attrib.* as *adj. phr.*

1966 R. W. Taylor *Doomsday Sq.* iii. 36 There's a double safeguard in a self-destruct system that would operate automatically in case of navigational error. **1969** M. Crichton *Andromeda Strain* x. 108 At the lowest level of this laboratory is an automatic self-destruct device. **1975** J. Grady *Shadow of Condor* xvi. 250 He flicked the last strap holding him to the machine. He also punched the delayed self-destruct switch.

self-de'struction. [self- 1 a.] Destruction of oneself, one's life; *esp.* self-murder, suicide.

a **1586** Sidney *Arcadia* (1622) 144 To frame of Earth a vessell of the minde, Where it should be to selfe-destruction bound. **1667** Milton *P.L.* x. 1016 Self-destruction therefore saught, refutes That excellence thought in thee. **1751** Mason *Elfrida* (1752) 77 Ye need not fear it, She means not self-destruction. **1821** Scott *Kenilw.* xv, To give gold to youth is..furnishing them with the means of self-destruction. **1899** *Allbutt's Syst. Med.* VIII. 371 Very commonly attempts at self-destruction or self-injury are made.

self-de'structive, *a.* [self- 1 e.] Having the property of destroying or annulling itself (or each other).

1654 H. L'Estrange *Chas. I* (1655) 80 The Commons..imagined it would make the Petition so much Royalist, as it would signifie nothing..and would prove *felo de se*, self-destructive. **1699** Shaftesb. *Charac., Inq. conc. Virtue* ii. §2 How mischievous and self-destructive Anger is. **1723** Blackmore *Alfred* Pref. p. xvii, Moral Evil and the divine Nature are contradictory and self-destructive Idea's. **1864** Bowen *Logic* xiii. 420 Any Reasoning..by which we might attempt to doubt or deny the validity of our Intuitions, would be self-destructive.

Hence **self-de'structively** *adv.*, **self-de'structiveness.**

1851 Kingsley *Yeast* v, They cannot be intended to compete self-destructively with each other. **1733** A. Baxter *Enq. Human Soul* vi. xlv. 267 Nothing is a mark of impossibility, but a self-destructiveness in the idea. **1977** J. D. Douglas in Douglas & Johnson *Existential Sociol.* i. 46 Self-hatred and the resulting self-destructiveness pervades the lives of the poor.

self-determi'nation. *Metaph.* [self- 1 a.]

1. Determination of one's mind or will by itself towards an object.

1683-6 J. Scott *Chr. Life* ii. vii. §5 Wks. 1718 I. 406 As necessary Agents, that have no Free-will or Principle of Self-determination. **1690** Locke *Hum. Und.* iv. xvii. §4 The ideas of men and self-determination appear to be connected. **1842** Manning *Serm.* iv. (1848) I. 59 Our fearful and wonderful inward nature..has a power of self-determination. **1870-2** Liddon *Some Elem. of Relig.* iii. 89 It is your will which, by a voluntary self-determination, caused the movement of the muscles of your arm.

2. *Pol.* The action of a people in deciding its own form of government; free determination of statehood, postulated as a right (see quot. 1929).

1911 *Encycl. Brit.* XXIII. 653/1 The more enlightened of the emperors..made a genuine endeavour to give a due share in the work of government to the various subject races. But nothing could compensate for the lack of self-determination. **1917** *Times* 28 Dec. 8/1 According to the declarations of..the quadruple alliance, protection of the right of minorities forms an essential component part of the constitutional right of peoples to self-determination. **1918** Woodrow Wilson in *N.Y. Times* 12 Feb. 1/5 National aspirations must be respected; peoples may now be dominated and governed only by their own consent. 'Self-determination' is not a mere phrase. It is an imperative principle of action, which statesmen will henceforth ignore at their peril. **1929** W. S. Churchill *World Crisis* V. xi. 203 Although the expression 'Self-determination' will rightly be forever connected with the name of President Wilson, the idea was neither original nor new. The phrase itself is Fichte's 'Selbst bestimmung'. **1946** D. L. Sayers *Unpopular Opinions* 100 Eire demanded self-determination. .. Northern Ireland also wanted self-determination, and was determined to remain with England. **1959** E. H. Carr *Socialism in One Country* II. iv. xxi. 278 It was not only in Soviet Russia that a potential clash could be discerned between the claims of national self-determination and the claims of economic progress. **1968** 'J. le Carré' *Small Town in Germany* x. 162 The Yanks are going crazy about self-determination. Why don't they try it in East Germany? **1976** Ld. Home *Way Wind Blows* xii. 168 'Self-determination' was a slogan to which the Soviet leaders paid lip-service.

So **self-de'termined** *ppl. a.*, determined by oneself; having the quality of self-determination; **self-de'termining** *vbl. sb.*, = self-determination 1; **self-de'termining** *ppl. a.*, determining one's own acts; possessing self-determination.

1732 Berkeley *Alciphr.* vii. §22 It is not doubted that man is accountable, that he acts, and is *self-determined. **1898** Illingworth *Divine Immanence* i. §1 We are self-determined; since, from the objects that occur to us, we can choose the one which we shall make our own. **1683** J. Corbet *Free Actions* ii. 15 The Natural Liberty of the Will is..an Indetermination with a Power of *self-determining. **1853** Pulsford tr. *J. Müller's Chr. Doctr. Sin* II. 33 The self-determining of the free will. **1662** Stillingfl. *Orig. Sacræ* iii. iii. §7 To give man the freedom of his actions, and a *self-determining power. *c* **1714** Arbuthnot, etc. *Mem. M. Scribl.* i. xii. Pope's Wks. 1741 II. 44 Every animal is conscious of some individual self-moving, self-determining principle. **1853** Grote *Greece* ii. xc. XI. 700 A free self-determining political aggregate. **1864** Pearson *Div. Pers.* (1865) 1 Is God a self-determining agent apart from the world? **1874** Carpenter *Mental Phys.* i. i. (1879) 28 We have within us a self-determining Power which we call Will.

self-de'vised, *ppl. a.* [self- 2.] Devised or invented by oneself.

1606 Sylvester *Du Bartas* ii. iv. iii. 169 The while this Priest-King sacrifiz'd To's clov'n-foot God in Bethel (self-devis'd). **1671** Baxter *Power of Mag.* i. 9 Self-devised Worship and Religion. **1683** Owen *Chamb. Imagery* Wks. 1851 VIII. 590 Unlawful vows, self-devised rules. **1846** Trench *Mirac.* viii. (1862) 201 To worship God not with self-devised services, but after the pattern that He has shown them.

self-de'voted, *ppl. a.* [self- 2.] Characterized by self-devotion.

1713 Addison *Cato* iv. iv, For him the self-devoted Decii died. **1814** Wordsw. *Laodamia* 48 And forth I leapt upon the sandy plain; A self-devoted chief. **1817** Lady Morgan *France* ii. (1818) I. 260 Self-devoted patriotism. **1831** Scott *Ct. Rob.* iv, These bold and self-devoted men.

So **self-de'votedness,** † **-de'votement,** † **-de'voting** *vbl. sb.* (*rare*) = self-devotion; **self-de'voting** *ppl. a.* = self-devoted.

1823 Lamb *Guy Faux* Misc. Wks. (1871) 368 Heroic *self-devotedness and true Christian martyrdom. **1800** *Characters* in *Asiat. Ann. Reg.* 23/1 To acquiesce cheerfully to this species of *self-devotement. **1819** G. S. Faber *Dispensations* (1823) II. 293 That Jehovah..through a mysterious self-devotement shadowed out by the rite of sacrifice,..would reconcile man to God. **1702** Howe *Self-Ded.* 35 Solemn, personal *self-devoting. *Ibid.* 44 This *self-devoting disposition. **1832** Downes *Lett. Cont. Countries* I. 171 The self-devoting prowess of Arnold von Winkelried.

self-de'votion. [self 1 a.] Devotion of oneself, one's life, etc.

1815 Kirby & Sp. *Entom.* (1818) I. xi 372 The self-denial and self-devotion of these admirable creatures. **1855** Kingsley *Glaucus* (1878) 46 The very essence of true chivalry, namely, self-devotion.

Hence **self-de'votional** *a.* = self-devoted.

1838 Dickens *O. Twist* i, The latter of whom invariably swore whatever the parish wanted; which was very self-devotional.

self-differenti'ation. [self- 1 a.] Differentiation arising from within oneself or itself; *spec.* in *Biol.*, that of embryonic tissue occurring more or less independently of other parts of the embryo.

1891 W. J. Greenstreet tr. *Guyau's Educ. & Heredity* ix. 288 We are capable of self-imitation, self-differentiation, or self-modification. **1902** *Encycl. Brit.* XXVIII. 150/2 This partial independence has been called self-differentiation (*Selbstdifferenzierung*) by Roux, and is entirely a characteristic feature of ontogeny. **1926** [see differentiation 1 a]. **1972** *Jrnl. Embryol. & Exper. Morphol.* XXVIII. 547 The capacity of Henson's node for self-differentiation and induction.

self-'diffidence. [self- 1 d.] Self-distrust.

1658 Baxter *Saving Faith* §12 Yet is it with a mixture of self-diffidence, when I think what a person I dissent from. **1712** M. Henry *Life of P. Henry* iv. (1765) 91 His great Modesty and Self-diffidence. **1872** J. L. Sanford *Est. Eng. Kings* 334 This reserve was caused much less by self-diffidence than by self-conceit.

So **self-'diffident,** † **-di'ffiding** *adjs.*, self-distrustful.

a **1791** Wesley *Serm.* xlix, This very consideration..would make all who now speak upon the subject, exceedingly wary and *self-diffident. **1654** Gataker *Disc. Apol.* 52 A low, bashful,..*self-diffiding..disposition.

self-di'ffusion. *Chem.* [self- 3 a.] Migration of constituent atoms or molecules within the bulk of a substance, esp. in a crystalline solid.

1924 *Chem. Abstr.* XVIII. 2632 By mixing such comps. with AgI interchange of ions (self-diffusion) can be effected. **1938** R. W. Lawson tr. *Hevesy & Paneth's Man. Radioactivity* (ed. 2) xviii. 173 Not until the introduction of radioactive indicators was it possible to open up to observational study the phenomenon of self-diffusion. **1958** *New Scientist* 2 Jan. 24/2 Autoradiograph (*a*) shows the self-diffusion after treatment at 800°C—this has occurred mainly along the boundaries of the grains or crystals of metal that make up bulk iron. **1974** D. M. Adams *Inorg. Solids* ix. 286 Self-diffusion work with silver isotopes confirms that these ions move freely between the available sites in the iodine lattice.

self-dissoci'ation. *Chem.* [self- 1 a, d.] = self-ionization. So **self-di'ssociated** *a.*, that undergoes self-ionization.

1905 *Jrnl. Physical Chem.* IX. 178 The conductivity of the pure solvents is explained by assuming 'self-dissociation' and considerable space is devoted to mere speculation as to what the composition of the ions might be in the various individual cases. **1973** Schmidt & Siebert in J. C. Bailar et al. *Comprehensive Inorg. Chem.* II. xxiii. 873 Sulphuric acid is also slightly self-dissociated into sulphur trioxide and water. *Ibid.*, The complete self-dissociation reaction in the sulphuric acid solvent system can be described..by the above equation.

self-dis'trust. [self- 1 d.] Distrust of oneself, one's powers, etc.

1789 Burke *Lett., to Dupont* (1844) III. 105 It would become me, least of all, to be so confident, who ought..to have well learned the important lesson of self-distrust. **1847** Keble *Serm.* Pref. 19 Self-distrust is a temper so suitable to us.., that [etc.]. *a* **1890** Liddon *Life Pusey* (1893) I. xviii. 441 Keble's habitual self-distrust made him at times of less service as an adviser than he might have been.

Hence **self-dis'trustful** *a.*, **-dis'trusting** *ppl. a.*

1860 J. Cairns *Mem. J. Brown* viii. 263 This lady..of mature, though *self distrustful piety. **1834** Mrs. Hemans *Sc. & Hymns of Life* 58 A lowly, fearful, *self-distrusting heart.

selfdom ('sɛlfdəm). [f. self *sb.* + -dom.] The realm or domain of self: **a.** a condition of things of which self is the centre; **b.** what constitutes a man's self.

1863 Cowden Clarke *Shakesp. Char.* xvi. 396 These phrases, he says, are 'the delight of Noodledom'... Ay, and they are the delight, too, of selfdom. **1885** J. Martineau *Types Eth. Th.* II. 373 If death should..put his selfdom to the test of loneliness. **1888** —— *Study of Relig.* II. iv. ii. 350 This durable selfdom attaches to us..as personal beings.

'self-drive, *a.* [self- 2 b.] Designating a motor vehicle hired to be driven by oneself, not by a chauffeur, or an agency which supplies such vehicles. Also *ellipt.* as *sb.*, a self-drive car or van, and **'self-driven** *ppl. a.*

1929 *Star* 21 Aug. 13/3 (Advt.), Motor-cars for hire. Self-drive Sal[oon]s, tourers fr. 17/6 day. **1932** Kipling *Limits & Renewals* 80 A natty little grey and black self-driven coupé came from Brighton way. **1953** R. Macaulay *Last Lett. to Friend* (1962) 97, I have hired a self-drive car, as there seems no other way of getting about Cyprus. **1969** J. Leasor *They don't make them like that any More* vi. 194 We could hire a self-drive from some-where. **1972** L. P. Bachmann *Ultimate Act* xvi. 125 At the international self-drive agency I handed over my credit card. **1978** N. Freeling *Night Lords* ii. 14 French show-offs in Jaguars.. Americans in self-drives. **1982** 'W. Haggard' *Mischief Makers* xi. 132, I have hired a self-drive removal van... We will load those crates.

self-ease. [self- 5 a.] Personal comfort.

1604 Rowlands *Looke to it* 12 Regarding nothing but selfe-ease and health. **1849** Rock *Ch. of Fathers* I. v. 334 Churchmen..more thoughtful of self-ease, than of what was becoming and dignified, cut away the folds of the old chasuble. **1854** Whittier *Voices* xi, Self-ease is pain; thy only rest Is labor for a worthy end.

self-edge, obs. form of selvage.

self-e'ffacement. [self- 1 a.] The keeping of oneself out of sight or in the background.

1866 Visct. Strangford *Selections* (1869) II. 319, I am..content to remain unknown, and successful in self-effacement. **1883** J. Hawthorne *Fort. Fool* i. i, The completest private humility and self-effacement. **1889** *Spectator* 14 Dec. 847 The skill and self-effacement which mark the book.

So **self-e'ffacing** *ppl. a.* (hence **-e'ffacingly** *adv.*), **-e'ffacive** *a.*, retiring; **self-e'ffacingness.**

1902 'H. S. Merriman' *Vultures* vi, Miss Netty Cahere was a vision of pink and *self-effacing quietness. **1900** *Academy* 25 Aug. 147/1 [He] *self-effacingly pulls the curtain aside, and intrudes not at all. **1883** Caird *Edin. Lect. Hume* 23 Nov., In society he was the most *self-effacive of men. **1951** S. Spender *World within World* 167 Forster's strange mixture of qualities—his *self-effacingness combined with a positive assertion of his views.

selfegre(e)ne: see sengreen.

self-e'lect, *a.* [self- 2.] = self-elected.

1842 Miall in *Nonconf.* II. 97 In virtue of trusteeship to which they are self-elect. *a* **1885** Sir Jas. Paget *Mem.* iii. (1901) 42 Some self-elect of the pupils, making themselves into a kind of club.

self-e'lected, *a.* [self- 2.] Elected by oneself, (of a body) elected by its members; *transf.* of an office to which a person has appointed himself.

1818 Scott *Rob Roy* xxxix, The connivance of Government to his self-elected office of Protector of the Lennox. **1849** Macaulay *Hist. Eng.* ii. I. 216 Self-elected Town Councils. **1886** C. E. Pascoe *Lond. of To-day* xxvi. (ed. 3) 248 Nominally, the election of the directors is in the hands of the stockholders; virtually, they are self-elected.

self-e'lection. [self- 1 a.] Election of oneself by oneself.

1790 *Bystander* 129 Whether or not Alexander was conscious that this self election..would not equally hold good with posterity. **1835** *Penny Cycl.* III. 476/1 Their weakness..lay in the system of self-election of those magistrates.

So **self-e'lecting** *ppl. a.*, **self-e'lective** *a.*, having the right of electing oneself.

1787 Jefferson *Writ.* (1859) II. 228 The violent Aristocrats would have wished..that these [the Regents] should remain self-elective. **1855** Bagehot in *National Rev.* Oct. 271 In the towns, the franchise belonged to a close and self-electing corporation. **1863** H. Cox *Instit.* iii. ix. 728 Boroughs constituted with self-elective Councils. **1980** D. Francis *Reflex* vii. 76 That they [*sc.* the Jockey Club] were also self-electing meant in practice that the members were almost all..upper-class.

†**self-end.** *Obs.* Chiefly *pl.* (Very common 1650-1700.) [f. self- 5 a, d + end *sb.* 14.] Personal or private end or object; selfish aim or purpose.

a **1628** Grevil *Life of Sidney* ii. (1652) 33 These were not complements, self-ends, or use of each other. **1633** —— *Let. to Hon. Lady* iii. Wks. 1870 IV. 254 My self-end being nothing but your favor, and my true end your good. **1691** Norris *Pract. Disc.* 118 He that loves God, loves him for his own good..; but he that Praises him..does it not upon any self-end, but meerly because he thinks it just. **1709** Mrs.

MANLEY *Secret Mem.* (1720) IV. 257 Having no Treachery, no Self-ends in his own Breast. **1728** R. MORRIS *Anc. Archit.* 11 They had some sinister View and Self-end.

†**self-ended**, *ppl. a. Obs.* [f. prec. + -ED.] Of merely private or selfish aims; characterized by self-centred actions or desires.

1645 W. GOODE *Discov. Publ. Spirit* 17 Publique spirits delight in their worke more then their wages, but self-ended men love their wages better then their worke. **1682** SIR T. BROWNE *Chr. Mor.* III. §17 (1716) 104 Narrow self-ended Souls make prescription of good Offices. *a* **1693** *Urquhart's Rabelais* III. xliv. 361 Self ended Lawyers. **1716** M. DAVIES *Athen. Brit.* III. 10 That self-ended occasional Conformity. **1731** BAILEY vol. II, *Self-ended*, for one's own advantage.

Hence †**self-'endedness**.

1664 H. MORE *Myst. Iniq.* I. II. viii. 131 Displaying the Frauds and Self-endedness of all their Errours and Mispractices. **1697** R. PIERCE *Bath Mem.* Pref. 5, I find a Physician of great Name..blaming the Bath..not without just Suspition of some Self-endedness.

†**self-ending**, *ppl. a.* [analogical after SELF-ENDED; cf. *self-centred, self-centring*.] = SELF-ENDED.

1698 NORRIS *Pract. Disc.* (1707) IV. 114 The Self-ending, Self-centring Man does in a very true..sense idolize himself.

self-'energy. *Physics.* [SELF- 5 b.] The energy possessed by a particle in isolation from other particles and fields; the energy of interaction of a particle, quasi-particle, or current with its own field.

1883 O. HEAVISIDE in *Electrician* 10 Mar. 390/1 We have next..to consider the potential energy of a current system on itself, as distinguished from its energy with respect to another system. The last being called the mutual energy, we may for brevity term the former the self-energy. **1933** *Nature* 30 Dec. 1004/2 The use of the classical function *L* gives infinite values of self energy and other physical quantities which are, in fact, certainly finite. **1956** E. H. HUTTEN *Lang. Mod. Physics* iii. 97 The electron as a point-particle would possess infinte self-energy: this must occur when a finite charge is concentrated into a point—thus making the charge density, or charge per unit volume, infinite. **1962** CORSON & LORRAIN *Introd. Electromagn. Fields* vi. 243 The first two terms on the right are self-energies arising from the interaction of each current with its own field. **1977** *Dædalus* Fall 25 Just as the exchange of virtual photons between two electrons produces an energy of interaction between them, so also in quantum field theory the emission of virtual photons and their reabsorption by the same electron produces a self-energy.

†**self-'essence.** *Obs.* [SELF- 5 c.] Self-existent being. So **self-e'ssential, -e'ssentiated** *adjs.*, self-existent.

1644 DIGBY *Nat Soul* Concl. 463 That..proceedeth..from the bounteous hand of the nothing annihilating *selfe essence. **1642** H. MORE *Song of Soul* III. II. xxxiv, By her own centrall self-vitality Which is her *self-essentiall omniformity. **1668** HOWE *Bless. Righteous* xi, This eternal and self-essential Being, the infinitely blessed God. **1653** H. MORE *Antid. Ath.* I. viii. (1712) 23 If any Thing may be *Self-essentiated besides God.

self-e'steem. [SELF- 1 a.] Favourable appreciation or opinion of oneself.

1657 *Baker's Sancta Sophia* II. II. ii. §2 Independence, Selfe-esteem, Selfe-judgment, & Selfe-will. **1667** MILTON *P.L.* VIII. 572 Oft times nothing profits more Then self-esteem, grounded on just and right Well manag'd. **1745** J. MASON *Self-Knowledge* I. i. (1853) 10 Thou wilt find nothing here that will flatter thy self-esteem. **1851** D. JERROLD *St. Giles* xii. 121 The larger the man's self-esteem the surer is he of putting it off in the world's mart. **1884** *Manch. Exam.* 11 Nov. 5/2 There are plentiful grounds for an honest self-esteem.

b. *Phrenology.* One of the mental faculties with which an 'organ' or 'bump' in the cranium is associated; the 'bump' itself.

1815 SPURZHEIM *Physiogn. Syst.* III. ii. 332. **1825** COMBE *Syst. Phrenol.* 154 Self-esteem. This organ is situated at the vertex or top of the head, a little above the posterior or sagittal angle of the parietal bones. *c* **1835** W. D. COOLEY *Phrenol.* in *Encycl. Metrop.* (1845) XXIII. 326/2 Self-esteem..occupies the middle of the upper posterior part of the head immediately above the Inhabitiveness..of Gall's system.

So **self-e'steeming** *ppl. a.*

1658 BAXTER *Saving Faith* §6 Learned self-esteeming men.

self-'estimate. [SELF- 1 a.] Estimate or valuation of oneself.

1837 HT. MARTINEAU *Soc. Amer.* III. 22 The event decides this matter of self-estimate. **1878** GROSART *More's Poems* Mem. Introd. 36/1 More's Wordsworthian self-scrutiny and lofty self-estimate.

So **self-esti'mation**.

1790 CATH. GRAHAM *Lett. Educ.* 504 Such an arrogant self estimation tends to weaken that strong sense of allegiance and dependance which is due from the creature to the Creator. **1856** GROTE *Greece* II. xciv. XII. 355 An exorbitant personality and self-estimation.

self-e'strangement. *Social Psychol.* [SELF- 1 a; cf. G. *selbstentfremdung*.] Estrangement from one's natural self, esp. such as is thought to result from the alienating development of consciousness or from involvement in a complex industrialized culture. Hence **self-e'stranged** *ppl. a.*

1878 A. C. BRACKETT *Science of Educ.* 43 [The mind's] first stage of development is self-estrangement—it is absorbed in the observation of objects around it... This process of self-estrangement and its removal belongs to all culture. **1910** J. B. BAILLIE tr. *Hegel's Phenomenol.* II. vi. 488 (*heading*) Spirit in self-estrangement—the discipline of culture. *Ibid.* 490 The equilibrium of the whole..rests on the alienation of its opposite. The whole is, therefore, like each particular moment, a self-estranged reality. **1951** P. TILLICH *Systematic Theol.* I. ii. 74 A second part of the system must give an analysis of man's existential self-estrangement..and the question implied in this situation. **1972** M. ARGYLE *Social Psychol. of Work* ix. 226 Self-estrangement—failure to regard the work as a central life interest or means of self-expression, experiencing a depersonalized detachment while at work. **1978** J. UPDIKE *Coup* (1979) iv. 138 You can't talk about that without talking about the self-estrangement induced by forced labor.

self-evalu'ation. *Psychol.* [SELF- 1 a.] Appraisal of one's actions or attitudes, esp. in relation to an objective standard. Hence **self-e'valuative, -e'valuatory** *adjs.*

1933 *Psychol. Abstr.* VII. 473/2 To attain self-evaluation, psycho-physiological and psychotechnical methods must be supplemented by introspection. **1957** N. FRYE *Anat. Criticism* 179 The hero Denis comes to a point of self-evaluation. **1957** R. B. CATTELL *Personality & Motivation* vi. 220 Self-evaluatory methods of gathering personality data include questionnaires, biographical inventories, [etc.]. **1966** J. FLESCHER *Dual Therapy* vii. 154 The self-evaluative recording seems to promote the therapist's training as well as the patient's progress. **1979** A. CHISHOLM *Nancy Cunard* xxx. 315 A nightmare crisis of self-evaluation.

self-'evidence. [SELF- 1 d.] **a.** Evidence of its own truth. **b.** The quality or condition of being self-evident.

1682 BUNYAN *Holy War* 16 There is not a word but carries with it self-evidence in its Bowels. **1690** LOCKE *Hum. Und.* IV. vii. §3 'Tis plain, that several other Truths, not allow'd to be Axioms, partake equally with them in this Self-evidence. **1692** NORRIS *Curs. Reflect.* 5 He resolves that ready..assent which is given to certain Propositions upon their Proposal, into the Self-Evidence of them. **1796** COLERIDGE *Let.* in *Biog. Lit.* (1847) II. 352 He deems that there is a certain self-evidence in Infidelity, and becomes an Atheist by intuition. **1885** J. MARTINEAU *Types Eth. Th.* II. 478 [Hutcheson's] writings..fetched back into the light of self-evidence many a generous trait of inward experience. **1898** ILLINGWORTH *Div. Immanence* iv. §3. 87 The personality of Jesus Christ is its own self-evidence.

So **self-'evidencing** *ppl. a.*, providing itself the evidence of its own truth; hence **self-'evidencingly** *adv.*

1658–9 OWEN (*title*) Of the Divine Originall, Authority, *Self-Evidencing Light, and Power of the Scriptures [etc.]. **1681** FLAVEL *Meth. Grace* vi. 118 The native clearness of self-evidencing principles. **1862** M'COSH *Supernat. in relat. to Natural* II. i. §3. 133, I believe that the truths revealed in Scripture are so self-evidencing [etc.]. **1890** *Spectator* 6 Sept., The self-evidencing character of intrinsic divinity. **1882–4** GROSART *Spenser* I. 191 The Poet was *self-evidencingly a man of moods.

self-'evident, *a.* (*sb.*) [SELF- 3 b.] Evident of itself without proof; axiomatic.

1690 LOCKE *Hum. Und.* I. ii. §14 These general and self-evident Maxims. *Ibid.* II. i. §10 Whether this, That the Soul always thinks, be a self-evident Proposition. **1736** BUTLER *Anal.* II. Concl. 290 The Truth of revealed Religion,..is not self-evident. **1809** W. IRVING *Hist. New York* (1861) 115 He never suffered even a self-evident fact to pass unargued. **1861** PALEY *Æschylus' Persians* 578 *note*, This is one of those happy emendations which at once commend themselves by a self-evident propriety. **1875** JOWETT *Plato* (ed. 2) I. 405 The self-evident fact that growth is the result of eating and drinking.

b. as *sb.* A self-evident proposition.

1868 *Athenæum* 22 Aug. 241/3 The relations of premise and consequence which exist between self-evidents.

So **self-evi'dential** *a.*, resting upon self-evidence; **self-'evidentism**, the character of being self-evident; **self-'evidently** *adv.*, in a self-evident manner.

1872 SANDAY *4th Gosp.* i. 1 Its *self-evidential force at once ceases. **1825** *New Monthly Mag.* XIII. 336 Two propositions, which she is ready to back for *self-evidentism against any two in Euclid. **1696** LORIMER *Rem. on Goodwin's Disc.* vii. 40 The Major Proposition is *self evidently false, when stript of its Identical dress. **1768–74** TUCKER *Lt. Nat.* (1834) II. 684 All voluntary labour..appears an oddity and strangeness, and by that mark must needs be self-evidently wrong. **1886** *Law Times* LXXXII. 77/1 Any alteration in the terms of a contract which is not self-evidently for the benefit of the surety.

self-evo'lution. [SELF- 1 a.] Evolution of oneself (itself) by one's (its) own power.

1857 KINGSLEY *Lett.* (1877) II. 39 The idea of self-evolution in a story. **1883** *Bible Myths* (ed. 2) 369 In the progress of still further self-evolution, he [Brahma] willed to invest himself with the second quality of goodness, as Vishnu.

So **self-e'volved, -e'volving** *ppl. adjs.*

1856 R. A. VAUGHAN *Mystics* (1860) I. 34 Their *self-evolved inexplicable explanations of everything. **1862** SPENCER *First Princ.* I. ii. §11 (1867) 32 A symbolic conception of a self-evolved Universe. **1852** BAILEY *Festus* 526 Each heart lit up with *self evolving joy. **1871** *Times* 5 Apr. 3/1 The presumption that Man is but a term in this self-evolving series.

self-exal'tation. [SELF- 1 a.] Exaltation of oneself, one's personality or claims.

1677 GALE *Crt. Gentiles* IV. 132 Proud self-exaltation brings down the soul. **1726** AMHERST *Terræ Fil.* Pref. p. xxiii, To indulge the natural vanity of an author, by applying to my own performance the self-exaltation of the celebrated Horace. **1856** GROTE *Greece* II. xciv. XII. 328 That exorbitant self-exaltation which formed the leading feature in his character. **1864** PUSEY *Lect. Daniel* vi. 337 It is not self-exaltation to speak the simple truth.

So **self-e'xaltative** *a.*, **-e'xalted** *ppl. a.*, **-e'xalting** *vbl. sb.* and *ppl. a.* (whence **-e'xaltingly** *adv.*).

1810 BENTHAM *Packing* (1821) 23 Of these two branches of the art of deception, the first mentioned may be termed the depressive or humiliative; the other the *self-exaltative. **1905** HOLMAN-HUNT *Pre-Raphael.* I. 376 The arrogant self-taught and *self-exalted umpires. **1685** BAXTER *Paraphr. N.T.* 1 Tim. iii. 6 The Errour of *Self-exalting. *a* **1688** BUNYAN *Of the Trinity* Wks. 1767 I. 690 Those high towering and *self-exalting imaginations. **1781** COWPER *Hope* 530 If self-exalting claims be turn'd adrift. **1874** SPURGEON *Treas. David* lxxxvi. 5 So *self-exaltingly indignant at the injuries done them by others.

self-exami'nation. [SELF- 1 a.] Examination of oneself with regard to one's conduct, motives, etc., esp. as a religious duty.

1647 C. HARVEY *Schola Cordis* Introd. 5 Resume thy long-neglected liberty Of selfe-examination. *a* **1700** EVELYN *Diary* 16 Sept. 1655, Preach'd at St. Gregories one Darnell on 4 Psalm 4. concerning the benefit of selfe examination. **1712** ADDISON *Spect.* No. 317 ¶10 This kind of self-examination would give them a true state of themselves. **1875** KEBLE *Lett. Spir. Counsel* lxiv. (ed. 3) 128 Let your self-examination..turn upon the government of your thoughts..towards your fellow-creatures.

So **self-e'xaminant, self-e'xaminer, self-e'xamining.**

1825 COLERIDGE *Aids Refl.* 164 If the *Self-examinant will ..exchange the safe circle of Religion..for the shifting Sand-wastes..of Speculative Theology. **1710** SHAFTESB. *Charac., Adv. to Author* I. i, 'Tis the hardest thing in the world to be a good Thinker, without being a strong *Self-Examiner. *Ibid.* III. iii, There is something valuable in this *self-examining Practice.

self-ex'citing, *ppl. a.* [SELF- 1 f.] **a.** *Electr.* Designating a dynamo-electric machine that excites its own field. Also *transf.*, with reference to the hypothesis that the earth's magnetic field is generated in the earth's core by a mechanism analogous to that of a dynamo.

1884 C. G. W. LOCK *Workshop Rec.* Ser. III. 119/1 Self-exciting machines. **1922** GLAZEBROOK *Dict. Appl. Physics* II. 195/1 The great advantage of direct-current machines is that: (i) They can be made self-exciting. **1954** E. BULLARD in G. P. Kuiper *Earth as Planet* iii. 129 The possibility that the motion of the material of the core could cause it to act as a self-exciting dynamo. **1971** *Sci. Amer.* Dec. 80/1 The influence of the Coriolis force on the motions of the outer core is thought to be critical to the operation of the self-exciting dynamo that generates the main magnetic field of the earth.

b. *Radio.* Self-oscillating; (see quot. 1943).

1922 *Proc. IRE* X. 251 The basis of super-regeneration was the discovery that a variation in the relation between the negative and positive resistances prevented a system which would normally oscillate violently from becoming self-exciting. **1943** *Gloss. Terms Telecomm.* (*B.S.I.*) 69 *Self-exciting sender*, a radio sender in which the oscillator determining the frequency also generates the radio-frequency power.

So **self-excitation; self-ex'cite** *v. intr.* and *trans.*; **self-ex'cited** *ppl. a.*, self-exciting.

1908 J. G. HORNER *Encycl. Pract. Engin.*, *Self-Excitation*, the characteristic of a dynamo which enables it to build up a magnetic field upon the rotation of its armature from the residual magnetism of its magnet poles. **1921** J. H. MORECROFT *Princ. Radio Communication* vi. 562 A possible arrangement of self-excitation, in which the phase of the voltage impressed on the grid is adjustable. *Ibid.* 563 (*caption*) Conditions occurring in the self-excited tube. **1922** GLAZEBROOK *Dict. Appl. Physics* II. 196/2 It is also necessary that the winding should have a sufficiently low resistance, otherwise self-excitation will not occur. *Ibid.*, At this speed..the machine will not self-excite. **1940** *Amateur Radio Handbk.* (ed. 2) xvii. 245/1 Developments during the few years prior to the war tended to relegate self-excited transmitters into the background. **1962** *Newnes Conc. Encycl. Electr. Engin.* 672/2 An induction generator can be self-excited by means of a capacitor. *Ibid.* 673/1 Unwanted self-excitation with dangerously-high voltages may occur in induction generators. **1977** *Jrnl. R. Soc. Arts* CXXV. 764/1 Before the appearance of the self-excited dynamo in 1867 it was by no means obvious that magneto-electric induction would power the world's industries.

self-'exile. [SELF- 1 a.] Voluntary exile.

1827 *Buckham's Theat. Greeks* 137 The motives for this self-exile are obscure. **1852** H. W. PIERSON *Miss. Mem.* 168 Duty to our Lord required self-exile from home.

So **self-'exiled** *pa. pple.*

1737 SAVAGE *Of Public Spirit* 191 Must self-exil'd roam Never to hope a friend, nor find a home. **1813** SCOTT *Trierm.* II. Interl. v, Arthur must..Self-exiled seek some distant shore. **1903** KIPLING *5 Nations* 60 Self-exiled from our grass delights.

self-e'xist, *v. rare.* [Back formation from next.] *intr.* To be self-existent.

1697 [see next].

self-e'xistence. [SELF- 5 c.] Existence of a being by virtue of his inherent nature independently of any other being.

1697 J. SERGEANT *Solid Philos.* 84 Even Self-existence signifies a kind of Form or Mode of the Subject that Self-exists. **1712** BLACKMORE *Creation* III. 102 'Tis plain, it then may absent be from all; Who then will this a Self-existence call? **1860** PUSEY *Min. Proph.* 325 That Name which He [God] vouchsafed to give to Himself, expressed His Self-existence. **1862** SPENCER *First Princ.* I. ii. §11 (1867) 31 Even were self-existence conceivable, it would not in any sense be an explanation of the Universe.

So †**self-e'xistency.**

1631 GOUGE *God's Arrows* III. §72. 317 Jehovah..sets out ..the eternity and selfe-existency of God. *a* **1653** —— *Comm. Heb.* i. 10 Christ in regard of his self-existency giveth to himself this title, 'I am that I am'.

self-e'xistent, *a.* [SELF- 3 b.]

1. Having the property of self-existence; existing of or by oneself (itself).

1701 [see SELF-MOVENT]. **1726** WATTS *Logick* II. v. §2 (ed. 2) 258 The Argument for the Existence of God, derived from the Idea of a most perfect and self-existent Being. **1848** R. I. WILBERFORCE *Doctr. Incarnation* vi. (1852) 147 The self-existent Godhead. **1862** SPENCER *First Princ.* I. ii. §11 (1867) 35 Those who cannot conceive a self-existent universe.

2. Having a primary or independent existence.

1779 BURKE *Sp.* in *Ann. Reg.* (1780) 142/1 Property was not made by government, but government by and for it. The one is primary and self-existent; the other is secondary and derivative. **1876** BANCROFT *Hist. U.S.* VI. lvi. 441 The hatred of America as a self-existent state.

So **self-e'xisting** *ppl. a.*

1701 GREW *Cosm. Sacr.* I. i. 1 This Self-existent Being hath the Power of Perfection, as well as of Existence, in Himself. **1747** LYTTELTON *Obs. Conv. St. Paul* Wks. (1774) 328 If..we have recourse..to the independent existence of matter, then we must admit two self-existing principles. **1795–1814** WORDSW. *Excurs.* IV. 80 Self-existing cause and end of all.

self-ex'perience. [SELF- 5 a.] Personal trial or experience.

1645 BP. HALL *Rem. Discontent.* §26. 159 Meere ignorance, and want of self-experience, is guilty of this errour. **1650** TRAPP *Comm. Deut.* xi. 2 Those that have such evidence and selfe-experience, are usually more affected, then those that have things by hear-say only. **1778** [W. MARSHALL] *Minutes Agric., Observ.* 164 The Self-Experience I have..had with respect to the Weather. **1846** JOWETT in *Life & Lett.* v. (1897) I. 132 Whether all this self-experience and over-sensibility ends in a morbid consciousness. **1886** M. F. TUPPER *Life as Author* 159 It is a volume of self-experiences, to be read 'through the lines'.

So **self-ex'perienced** *ppl. a.*

1782 J. BROWN *Compend. View Relig.* Introd. p. vi, What stock of self-experienced truths.

self-ex'plained, *ppl. a.* [SELF- 2.] Explained by itself, understood without specific explanation.

1725 POPE *Odyss.* XIX. 651 The vision self-explain'd. *a* **1843** SOUTHEY *Comm.-Pl. Bk.* Ser. II. (1849) 209 The excellence of the German language is its independence; its compound words being like the Greek, self-explained.

So **self-ex'plaining** *ppl. a.*, **-ex'planatory** *a.*

1864 WEBSTER, *Self-explaining. **1898** *Philos. Mag.* Ser. v. XLV. 73, I have drawn the diagrams for the various methods, which are nearly *self-explanatory.

self-faced, *ppl. a.* [f. after SELF-COLOURED; cf. SELF B. 3.] Of a paving-stone: Retaining its natural face or surface, undressed or unhewn.

1850 in OGILVIE. **1876** *Encycl. Brit.* IV. 473/1 Ordinary paving is of self-faced or of tooled York.

self-feeling, *sb.* [SELF *sb.* and SELF- 1 d, 5 d. Cf. G. *selbstgefühl.*]

1. Used to render CŒNÆSTHESIS.

1835 J. YOUNG *Lect. Intell. Philos.* ix. 81 Dr. Crichton gives an account of a sense called by some German writers Cœnesthesis or self-feeling.

2. Feeling centred in oneself, egoistic feeling.

1879 MAUDSLEY *Path. Mind* v. 241 This extreme development of..selfhood or self-feeling among the insane. **1895** *Pop. Sci. Monthly* Sept. 653 Self-feeling, a germ of the feeling of 'my worth' enters into this early passionateness. **1899** *Allbutt's Syst. Med.* VIII. 194 There is often an exaggerated 'self-feeling' which may give rise to hypochondriasis, or to false ideas of self-importance.

3. The sense of one's individual identity.

1908 G. A. COE in *Hibbert Jrnl.* Jan. 365 [In self-hypnosis] First, the bodily sensations were modified... Second, the self-feeling underwent an equally marked change. It seemed as if the self melted into its object.

†**self-feeling,** *ppl. a. Obs.* [SELF- 1 f.] Self-conscious.

1642 H. MORE *Song of the Soul* I. II. xxv, Self-feeling *Autæsthesia.*

self-'fertile, *a. Bot.* [SELF- 3 b.] Of a flower: Having the property of fertilizing itself by the action of its pollen on its pistil. Of a plant: Fertilized by the pollen of its own flowers alone. Also applied to hermaphrodite animals. So **self-fer'tility, self-'fertilizable** *a.*, **-fertili'zation, -'fertilize** *v.*, **-'fertilized** *ppl. a.*, **-'fertilizer,** a self-fertilizing plant, **-'fertilizing** *ppl. a.*

1859 DARWIN *Orig. Spec.* iv. 98 The contrivance seems adapted solely to ensure self-fertilisation. *Ibid.* 100 Of aquatic animals, there are many self-fertilising hermaphrodites. **1865** —— in *Life & Lett.* (1887) III. 276, I conjectured that the Spider and Bee-orchids might be a crossing and self-fertile form of the same species. **1871** A. W. BENNETT in *Jrnl. Linn. Soc., Bot.* XIII. 149 It is very commonly the case in closed self-fertilized flowers for the pollen-tubes to penetrate the substance of the anther itself. **1877** A. GRAY in *Amer. Jrnl. Sci.* Ser. III. XIII. 135 Many ..flowers which are frequented by insects are none the less self-fertilizable. *Ibid.* 126 The flowers of this species self-fertilize, but must also be habitually cross-fertilized. **1879** G. HENSLOW in *Pop. Sci. Rev.* XVIII. 8 Scrophulariaceæ furnishes several self-fertilisers. **1917** *Genetics* II. 525 That some of his families arising from selfed seed behaved exactly as the families arising from crossed seed shows that he is often (at least) dealing with a pseudo self-fertility. **1924** *Ibid.* IX. 16 The self-fertile plants differed among themselves in the expression of their self-fertility. **1956** *Nature* 10 Mar. 490/1 On hybridization, spontaneous self-fertility was restored. **1970** *Bot. Gaz.* CXXXI. 139/2 Species were rated for self-fertility by their ability to set seed under isolated conditions.

'self-field. *Physics.* [SELF- 5 b.] A field intrinsically associated with a charged particle, particle beam, or current, esp. as contrasted with any externally applied field that may be present.

1934 *Proc. R. Soc.* A. CXLIII. 437 The usual quantum mechanics is the limiting case in which the self-field is regarded as rigidly bound to the centre. **1970** *Particle Accelerators* I. 1/1 If the self-fields are large enough to trap the ions,..the cluster can be accelerated. **1976** *Nature* 19 Aug. 651/1 In the vicinity of the disk there is a small toroidal self-field B_ϕ from the proton beams.

self-fi'nancing, *ppl. a.* [SELF- 1 f.] That finances itself; *spec.* (of a programme of development, etc.) that pays for its own implementation or continuation. Also as *vbl. sb.* and (as a back-formation) **self-fi'nance** *v. trans.*

1957 A. C. L. DAY *Outl. Monetary Econ.* xxiii. 312 Such self-financing by large-scale industry has been very important in recent years. **1962** H. E. BEECHENO *Introd. Bus. Stud.* xvi. 150 The whole body of these policies must therefore be set on a self-financing basis. **1962** E. SNOW *Other Side of River* (1963) lix. 448 Cadres working in the brigade..'penetratingly explained' the necessity to 'self-finance' next year's development program. **1964** *Financial Times* 12 Mar. 5/8 It is becoming harder to rely principally on self-financing in order to raise capital for expansion. **1972** *Accountant* 19 Oct. 489/2 The Canadian company has maintained its contribution to group earnings and at the same time is self-financing its own expansion. **1979** *Jrnl. R. Soc. Arts* CXXVII. 656/1 They discuss the Society's miscellaneous activities, such as..the establishment in 1851–2 of self-financing public lavatories. **1980** I. ST. JAMES *Money Stories* II. i. 42 Can't you sell some diamonds and plough the cash back into fresh equipment? Make the project self-financing?

self-'flattered, *ppl. a.* [SELF- 2.] Flattered by oneself.

1742 YOUNG *Nt. Th.* VIII. 180 Self-flatter'd, unexperienc'd, high in hope.

So **self-'flatterer** [SELF- 1 c.]

1713 M. HENRY *Folly Desp. own Soul* Wks. 1855 I. 160 Self-flatterers and self-deceivers will prove self-destroyers. **1787** J. HOWIE *Ref. Princ. re-exhibited* Pref. p. xli, [We may] incur the suspicion of self-flatterers.

self-'flattering, *ppl. a.* [SELF- 1 f.] Flattering oneself, encouraging oneself in a lofty opinion of one's achievements, powers, or influence.

a **1586** SIDNEY *Arcadia* III. (Sommer) 302 Which (like a self-flattering woman) she conceiued was done for her sake. **1667** FLAVEL *Saint Indeed* (1673) 148 The damning sin of the self-flattering Hypocrite. **1728** R. MORRIS *Ess. Anc. Archit.* 70 Those self-flattering Companions, Novelty and Singleness. **1795–1814** WORDSW. *Excurs.* VII. 1007 The hopes And expectations of self-flattering minds. **1842** MANNING *Serm.* viii. (1848) I. 110 The indulgence of.. some self-flattering and sensitive vanity.

So **self-'flattery.**

1680 ALLEN *Peace & Unity* 83 In danger of being betrayed into such a self-flattery. **1745** J. MASON *Self-Knowl.* I. vii. (1853) 55 It is dangerous Self-flattery to give soft and smoothing Names to Sins. **1842** MANNING *Serm.* xiv. (1848) I. 191 It is only the vain self-flattery of the day to talk as if we had less need now of the daily service.

self-'fluxing, *ppl. a.* [SELF- 4.] Of iron ore: capable of being smelted without the addition of a flux, usu. because it contains a high proportion of lime. Also as *vbl. sb.*

1884 W. H. GREENWOOD *Steel & Iron* vi. 104 The ore is accompanied by a sufficient quantity of calcareous matters to yield the necessary flux without any further addition of fluxing materials to the charge; such ores are..known as 'self-going' or 'self-fluxing'. **1923** HARBORD & HALL *Metall. of Steel* (ed. 7) II. xxvi. 504 A few ores have an excess of lime, and if unable to secure self-fluxing ores the blast furnace manager endeavours to mix siliceous and calcareous ores when obtainable to form a self-fluxing mixture. **1973** *Times* 12 Feb. (Anchor Project Suppl.) p. ii/5 To have constructed an integrated plant..near the ore terminal would have entailed..the transport of a considerable amount of local ore in the reverse direction (or the loss of 'selffluxing' economies).

self-for'getful, *a.* [SELF- 1 e.] Forgetful of one's self or one's own individuality; having or characterized by no thought of self.

1848 J. G. WHITTIER *Pæan* in *Poet. Works* (1898) 336/1 They died, their brave hearts breaking slow, But self-forgetful to the last..Their breath upon the darkness passed. **1864** PUSEY *Lect. Daniel* vii. 438 The quick, honest, self-forgetful acknowledgment of the truth. **1897** 'A. HOPE' *Phroso* xvii, One, fierce, uncalculating, self-forgetful triumph. **1981** F. INGLIS *Promise of Happiness* I. ii. 37 Many arts and crafts..offer an occasion for self-forgetful joy and peace.

Hence **self-for'getfully** *adv.*, **self-for'getfulness;** so **self-for'getting** *ppl. a.*

1859 RUSKIN *Two Paths* i. §15 Art, devoted humbly and *self-forgetfully to the clear statement..of the facts of the universe. **1805–6** WORDSWORTH *Prelude* (1959) IV. 294 The quiet stream Of *self-forgetfulness. **1832** DISRAELI *Cont. Fleming* I. xix, All that I can recommend you now is to practise self-forgetfulness. **1864** PUSEY *Lect. Daniel* i. 14 Daniel, in noble self-forgetfulness. **1942** C. S. LEWIS *Screwtape Lett.* xiv. 72 Let him think of it not as self-forgetfulness but as a certain kind of opinion..of his own talents and character. **1847** MRS. TROLLOPE *Three Cousins* xv. I. 250 Her *self-forgetting kindness to every being that approached her. **1908** *Expositor* July 35 A self-forgetting idealist.

self-for'mation. [SELF- 1 a.] Formation or production without extraneous aid; self-development of the mind or character.

a **1713** SHAFTESB. *Charac.* (1723) III. 139 *note,* The natural Production, and Self-Formation of the Arts. **1837** [C. LOFFT] (*title*) Self-Formation; or, the history of an individual mind.

So **self-formed** *ppl. a.*

a **1700** [see *self-steer'd,* SELF- 2 a]. **1711** SHAFTESB. *Charac.* III. 139 With them every noble Study and Science was.. self-form'd [tr. αὐτοσχεδιαστική]. **1787** HAWKINS *Life Johnson* 52 A character self-formed, as owing nothing to parental nurture, and scarce anything to moral tuition. **1834** NEWMAN in *Lyra Apost.* (1849) 55 Whose spirits live..Each in his self-formed sphere of light or gloom. **1844** W. H. MILL *Serm. Tempt. Christ* v. 125 A vain and self-formed assurance. **1876** BANCROFT *Hist. U.S.* VI. I. 319 Self-formed bands of volunteers started into being.

†**'selfful,** *a. Obs.* [f. SELF *sb.* + -FUL.] Full of 'self', self-centred, selfish.

1654 [J. SPARROW] tr. *Behmen's Myst. Magn.* xxix. §18 A Source out of the Centre of the fiery desire, a selfefull will of the fiery might of the Soule. *Ibid.* 167 A Source of selfefull Lust. **1692** MATHER *Pref. to Owen's Holy Spirit* (1693) A 3 Untimely Abortions of a Self-full, Distempered Spirit.

self-ful'filling, *ppl. a.* orig. *Social Sci.* [SELF- 1 f.] In phr. ***self-fulfilling prophecy***: a prophecy or prediction which gives rise to actions that bring about its fulfilment (see quot. 1949).

1949 R. K. MERTON *Soc. Theory & Soc. Structure* vii. 181 The self-fulfilling prophecy is, in the beginning, a *false* definition of the situation evoking a new behavior which makes the originally false conception come *true.* **1962** BLAKE & MOUTON in M. Sherif *Intergroup Rel.* v. 113 Another dynamic, the self-fulfilling prophecy, also operates to cause one to misplace motivation. **1973** *Times* 7 Dec. 18/8 Panic buying of spirits..caused largely by forecasts of the shortage—a self-fulfilling prophecy. **1979** D. GURR *Troika* ix. 60 '*Wonderful*..to meet again. Didn't I tell you that we should? *Vodka!*'.. 'A self-fulfilling prophecy, Alexey Ilyich.'

†**self-'full,** *a. Obs.* [f. SELF- 3 b + FULL *a.*] = SELF-SUFFICIENT 1. So †**self-'fullness** = SELF-SUFFICIENCY 1.

1642 H. MORE *Song of Soul* II. iii. IV. xxii, [God's] being is self-full, self-joy'd, self-excellent. **1672** OWEN *Disc. Evang. Love* 25 His [*sc.* God's]..Communicative Love, from his own infinite self-fulness.

'selffulness. Now *rare.* [f. prec. + -NESS.] Selfcentredness, selfishness.

1654 [J. SPARROW] tr. *Behmen's Myst. Magn.* xxix. §18 A Sprout..out of the first Principle, in which..the first Principle, did in an especiall manner prevaile and would Sever it selfe into a selfe-fulnesse [orig. *ein eigenes*]. **1658** OWEN *Of Tempt.* viii. 172 Selfe-fulnesse as to principles, and selfishness as to ends. **1660** GAUDEN *Brownrig* 233 Savouring of self-fulness and conceit. **1887** BP. MOULE *Thoughts Spir. Life* iii. 54 Nothing does the world's Microscope discover more keenly than selffulness in a Christian man.

self-given, *a. rare* [SELF- 2.] Emanating or derived from oneself (itself).

1742 YOUNG *Nt. Th.* I. 219 Virtue's sure, Self-given, solar, ray of sound delight. **1751** J. BROWN *Shaftesb. Charac.* 123 A self-given and original beauty. **1909** R. KANE *Sermon of Sea* viii. 120 This object of intuitive consciousness must have its moral kind, its spiritual character, its self-given growth in evil or in good. **1934** T. S. ELIOT *Rock* ii. 84 Those who prize the serpent's golden eyes, The worshippers, self-given sacrifice of the snake.

self-'giving, *vbl. sb.* [SELF- 1 b.] The giving of oneself for others; self-devotion, self-sacrifice.

1850 ROBERTSON *Serm.* Ser. III. vii. (1857) 114 To give rather than to receive—the blessedness of self-giving. **1888** PIERSON *Evang. Wk.* xviii. 183 His self-giving to the cause of the poor.

So **self-giving** *ppl. a.*, self-sacrificing.

1850 ROBERTSON *Serm.* Ser. III. vii. (1857) 113 A flow of this divine self-giving charity.

†**self-glori'ation.** *Obs. rare.* [SELF- 3 a.] Self-boasting.

1672 H. MORE *Brief Reply* Pref. A 2 b, That I ought to be utterly dead to all Self-joy and Self-gloriation.

self-glorifi'cation. [SELF- 1 a.] Glorification or exaltation of oneself.

1838 J. S. MILL in *Westm. Rev.* Apr. 37 Those antique characters which, without self-glorification or hope of being appreciated, 'carry out..the sentiment of duty to its extremest consequences'. **1848** DICKENS *Dombey* xvii, The unconscious Captain walked out in a state of self glorification. **1885** G. RAWLINSON *Egypt & Bab.* iii. 50 The great King Nebuchadnezzar,..his grandeur, his pride, his cruelty,..his self-glorification. **1953** *Encounter* Oct. 49/1 It was..only Stalin who was thus hymned in the inevitable major key of Soviet self-glorification.

self-'glorious, *a.* [SELF- 3 a.] Marked by vain-glory or boasting.

1599 SHAKS. *Hen. V,* v. Prol. 20 Free from vain-nesse, and selfe-glorious pride. **1611** BEAUM. & FL. *King & No K.* IV. ii, Your too self-glorious temper.

So **self-'glory, self-'glorying** *vbl. sb.* and *ppl. a.*

1647 tr. *Behmen's XL Quest.* i. §66 Covetousnesse, Pride, *Selfe-glory and Arrogancy. **1729** LAW *Serious C.* xvi. 299 If such a creature pretends to self-glory for any thing that he is, or does. **1878** GOSSE *Rivers of Bible* 118 Self-indulgence, self-glory..hide Christ from the soul. **1848** W. R. WILLIAMS *Lord's Prayer* ix. (1854) 326 To slay this *self-glorying. **1860** PUSEY *Min. Proph.* 500 These are only *self-glorying records of victories.

'self-good. [SELF- 5 a.] Personal benefit or advantage.

1618 *Barnevelt's Apol.* C 3 All men are bound their selfe-good to procure. **1699** SHAFTESB. *Charac., Inq. conc. Virtue* II. §1 Nor has for Object any Self-Good or Advantage of the private System. **1832** TENNYSON *Œnone* 155 Good for selfgood doth half destroy selfgood.

self-'governed, *ppl. a.* [SELF- 2.]

1. Acting or living according to one's own desires uninfluenced by others; independent.

1795–1814 WORDSW. *Excurs.* v. 386 How few who mingle with their fellow-men And still remain self-governed, and apart. **1797** SOUTHEY *Comm.-pl. Bk.* Ser. IV. (1851) 273 When, a self-governed man, No laws exist to thee. **1847** MRS. GORE *Castles in Air* i, New works derived from the London library, to which my self-governed sisters were subscribers.

2. Of persons: Marked by self-control. Of a state: Having self-government.

1709 SHAFTESBURY *Moralists* II. 150, I suppose you will send your Disciple to seek for Deity in Mechanism; that is to say, in some exquisite System of self-govern'd Matter. **18..** *Brit. Rev.* (Worc.), A self-governed state is a strong state, for it is made up of self-governed citizens. **1848** J. S. MILL *Pol. Econ.* II. IV. vii. 320 They will require that their conduct and condition shall be essentially self-governed. **1859** J. BROWN *Let.* 19 Aug. (1912) 171 Frankfort is a little Republic, self-governed, and a thriving, handsome, well-conditioned town. **1883** M. MORRIS *Bk. Health* 378 Reasonably self-governed beings. **1886** DICEY *Eng. Case agst. Home Rule* vii. 198 The constitutional relations existing between England and a self-governed colony.

So **self-'governing** *ppl. a.*, autonomous.

1845 J. S. MILL in *Edin. Rev.* LXXXI. 511 For two centuries, the Scottish peasant..has been a reflecting, an observing, and therefore naturally a self-governing, a moral and a successful human being. **1880** A. TODD *Parl. Gov. in Brit. Col.* iv. I. 161 Matters affecting the internal administration of a self-governing colony. **1886** DICEY *Eng. Case agst. Home Rule* vii. 198 Victoria..is..for some purposes..an independent, self-governing community. **1933** *Discovery* Feb. 68/1 The greatest problem facing British Statesmen of modern times—the problem of transforming that India, in which society is organized on a religious basis, into a self-governing community on modern democratic lines. **1976** *Glasgow Herald* 26 Nov. 6/6 What business man in his right mind would prefer minimum lending rate of 14¾% to one in the 5–7% range which a self-governing Scotland would..achieve.

self-'government. [SELF- 1 a.]

1. Self-control, self-command. Now *rare.*

1734 WATTS *Reliq. Juv.* (1789) 201 Self-government is an eternal duty. **1736** BUTLER *Anal.* I. iii. 47 His natural Faculty of Self-Government impaired by Habits of Indulgence. **1821** SCOTT *Kenilw.* xxxviii, He had but sense and self-government enough left to prevent his stabbing to the heart the audacious villain. **1878** GLADSTONE *Prim. Homer* xi. 128 Intensity of Achilles... Any degree of self-government is a wonder, when exercised over such volcanic forces.

2. Administration by a people or state of its own affairs without external direction or interference.

1798 JEFFERSON in Lieber *Civil Lib.* (1853) 205 *note,* The residuary rights are reserved to their (the American States) own self-government. **1870** J. E. T. ROGERS *Hist. Glean.* Ser. II. 4 The towns gained charters of self-government. **1886** DICEY *Eng. Case agst. Home Rule* ii. 22 Home Rule does not mean Local Self-Government.

self-gratu'lation. = SELF-CONGRATULATION.

1802 MRS. E. PARSONS *Myst. Visit* II. 125 The self-gratulation of her insidious guardian. **1829** LYTTON *Devereux* III. iv, The wisdom of a choice which has brought you self-gratulation. **1870** J. H. NEWMAN *Gram. Assent* II. vi. 196 It [certitude] is a feeling of satisfaction and self-gratulation.

So **self-'gratulating** *ppl. a.*, **-'gratulatingly** *adv.*, **-'gratulatory** *a.*

1876 GEO. ELIOT *Dan. Der.* xlii, The *self-gratulating ignorant prosperity of the Cohens. **1835** *Tait's Mag.* II. 533 Amusements and dissipations are *self-gratulatingly denounced as gross follies and sins. **1859** BAIN *Emotions & Will* vii. 136 Those various forms of *self-gratulatory feeling. *Ibid.* 140 The self-gratulatory pleasures.

self-gravi'tation. *Astr.* [SELF- 3 a.] The gravitational forces acting among the components of a massive body.

1962 K. H. PRENDERGAST in L. Woltjer *Distribution & Motion Interstellar Matter* 233 In our own galaxy, if you consider the terms in the equations of motion, other than the gravitational field of all the matter, then there are three: the random velocities, some sort of ordered magnetic field, and the self-gravitation of the gas. **1968** R. A. LYTTLETON *Mysteries Solar Syst.* i. 36 Self-gravitation within the disk can far exceed the solar disruptive effect. **1977** *Dædalus* Summer 36 Roughly speaking we can attribute this change from Newtonian theory to the greater self-gravitation which matter possesses according to general relativity.

Hence **self-gravi'tational** *a.*; **self-'gravitating** *ppl. a.*, influenced by self-gravitation; **self-'gravity,** self-gravitation.

1962 P. O. LINDBLAD in L. Woltjer *Distribution & Motion Interstellar Matter* 223 A massive ring in a central force field ..can carry two different kinds of bisymmetrical waves by self-gravitational action. **1962** G. B. FIELD in *Ibid.* 318 Is the system a self-gravitating one in the sense that the gas acts on the gas, or is it not? **1972** *Sci. Amer.* Apr. 43/2 The restoring forces that limit the height of the tides are due to the planet's elasticity and self-gravity. **1976** *Nature* 11 Nov. 114/1 Ultimately, self-gravity must drive the enormous contractions which convert diffuse gas into new stars. **1979** *New Scientist* 3 May 424/2 A self-gravitating mass of gas, cohering under its self-attraction, would adopt spherical symmetry.

†**self-guard.** *Obs. rare.* In 6 -gard. [SELF- 1 a.] Reserve.

a **1586** SIDNEY *Arcadia* (1622) 87 Selfe-gard with mildnesse, Sport with Maiestie.

self-hate. [SELF- 1 d.] = next.

1947 F. FRENAYE tr. *C. Levi's Christ stopped at Eboli* (1948) iv. 28 To the hates of the gentry he added self-hate. **1951** K. HORNEY *Neurosis & Human Growth* v. 110 Pride and self-hate are actually one entity. **1979** R. BLYTHE *View in Winter* ix. 289 Creeping indifference is a large factor in the self-hate of the aged.

self-'hatred. [SELF- 1 d.] Hatred of oneself, esp. of one's actual self when contrasted with one's imagined self. Cf. prec.

1865 D. G. ROSSETTI *Let.* 21 Nov. (1965) II. 581 Ambition, i.e. the feeling of pure rage and self-hatred when any one else does better than you do. **1896** A. THOROLD tr. *Dialogue of St. Catherine of Siena* lxiii. 134 Digging up the root of self-love, with the knife of self-hatred and the love of virtue. **1942** C. S. LEWIS *Screwtape Lett.* xiv. 72 All the abjection and self-hatred are designed, in the long run, solely for this end. **1975** G. ST. GEORGE *Proteus Pact* (1976) iii. 95 He descended vertiginously into utter self-loathing.. paralyzed by..self-hatred.

self-heal ('sɛlfhiːl). Also 4 selfhele, 5 selhele, sulfhele, selfhol (?), 6–7 selfeheale. [f. SELF- 1 + HEAL *v.*; cf. OHG. *selbheila* 'euphrasia' (see EUPHRASY).] A name for various plants believed to have great healing properties, esp. *Prunella vulgaris* (Common S.), *Sanicula europæa*, and formerly *Pimpinella Saxifraga* (see PIMPERNEL 3).

a **1387** *Sinon. Barthol.* (Anecd. Oxon.) 11 *Armoniaca,* i. Self-hele. *Ibid.* 13 *Betonica major,* i. Selfhele. *Ibid.* 33 *Oxyndrele,* i. Selfhele. *Ibid.* 43 *Unctuosa,* Self hele. *a* **1400–50** [see MORECROP]. *c* **1450** *Alphita* (Anecd. Oxon.) 193 Unctuosa..an..selhele uel smerwrt. *c* **1450** *M.E. Med. Bk.* (Heinrich) 201 Tak crowsope, penywort, sulfhele. **1526** *Grete Herball* ccclv. (1529) T vj, De pinpinella. Selfe heale or pympyrnell. **1568** TURNER *Herbal* III. 61 Selfe heale is good to heale grene woundes. **1664** DR. BURNET in Pepys *Diary* 1 July, Take..of Selfeheale, of Red Roses, of each one Handfull. **1760** J. LEE *Introd. Bot.* App. 326 Self-heal, *Sanicula.* **1844** H. STEPHENS *Bk. Farm* III. 944 The seeds.. of the common self-heal, *Prunella vulgaris,* mix themselves with those of clover. **1880** JEFFERIES *Gt. Estate* 132 In the grass the short selfheal shows.

self-'heating, *vbl. sb.* (*ppl. a.*) [SELF- 1 b, f, 4.] The action of becoming heated spontaneously or automatically. Also as *ppl. a.*, that is designed to heat itself automatically; (of food) held in a self-heating container.

1929 *Chem. Abstr.* XXIII. 1561 The effect..of self-heating of metals after previous chilling is attributed here to establishment of equil[ibrium] in a metastable system. **1952** KOESTLER *Arrow in Blue* v. xxxii. 272 Some new 'colossal' project like the radioactive soap or the self-heating bricks. **1959** P. CAPON *Amongst Those Missing* 23 They found several battered cans of self-heating soup. *Ibid.* 24 The fuses on the self-heating cans did not burn too well. **1961** *Guardian* 29 May 2/3 Tins of self-heating cocoa fell from their appointed places into the bilges. **1965** PHILLIPS & WILLIAMS *Inorg. Chem.* I. xvi. 576 As a result of self-heating effects, polonium and polonium compounds are always at temperatures markedly above their surroundings. **1981** J. R. L. ANDERSON *Death at High Latitude* ix. 135, I opened three more cans of our self-heating soup, the only means we had of getting a hot drink.

self-'help. [SELF- 1 a.]

1. The action or faculty of providing for oneself without assistance from others.

1831 CARLYLE *Sart. Res.* II. iii, In the destitution of the wild desert does our young Ishmael acquire for himself the highest of all possessions, that of Self-help. **1860** SMILES (*title*) Self-help. **1865** KINGSLEY *Herew.* ix, Free, with the divine instinct of freedom, and all the self-help and energy which spring thereout. **1870** ROLLESTON *Anim. Life* p. lv, Birds which are possessed, immediately after hatching, of the faculty of self-help.

attrib. **1887** (*title*) Self-Help Emigration Society. **1908** (*title*) Self-help exercises in English.

2. *Law.* Redress of one's wrongs by one's own action, without recourse to legal process.

1875 POSTE *Gaius* III. (ed. 2) 476 The inducement to abstain from self-help..is still required.

Hence **self-'helper, self-'helpful** *a.* (whence **-'helpfulness**), **self-'helping** *ppl. a.*, **self-'helpless** (whence -'helplessness).

1891 G. B. SHAW *Quintessence of Ibsenism* ii. 34 No one ever feels helpless by the side of the *self-helper. **1976** W. GOLDMAN *Magic* III. vii. 165 'How come you have all these same kind of books?'.. 'That's my self-help collection. I'm an addict.'.. 'Why're you such a self-helper?' **1855** KINGSLEY *Westw. Ho!* viii, A pig of *self-helpful and serene spirit..fatting fast. **1890** *Athenæum* 11 Oct. 476/3 The self-helpful quality which enables a man..to secure comforts and luxury without deserving..them. **1855** KINGSLEY *Westw. Ho!* xxvii, His body, pampered with easily-obtained luxuries,..loses its *self-helpfulness. **1840** CARLYLE *Heroes* ii. (1858) 239 He is a rough *self-helping son of the wilderness. **1855** D. J. BROWNE *Amer. Poultry Yd.* 242 The young are active, self-helping little things. **1848** KINGSLEY *Yeast* ii, I am miserable, self-disgusted, *self-helpless. **1881** *Daily News* 1 Feb. 3/2 Apathy, or at least what I would call *self-helplessness.

self-'heterodyne, *a. Radio.* [SELF- 1 e.] Being or employing a heterodyne receiver in which the same valve is used for the generation and rectification of local oscillations. Hence **self-'heterodyning** *ppl. a.* and *vbl. sb.*

1918 [see AUTODYNE]. **1922** *Proc. IRE* X. 245 In the various forms of self-heterodyne circuits a free oscillation of constant amplitude is maintained in the system and the circuit may be considered as having zero resistance, but only for that particular amplitude of current. **1929** DUNCAN & DREW *Radio Telegr. & Teleph.* xii. 344 The circuit is commonly known as a self-heterodyning detector because the tube functions both as an oscillator and detector. *Ibid.* 351 (*heading*) The phenomenon of self-heterodyning.

self-'homicide. Now *rare.* [f. SELF- 1 a + HOMICIDE *sb.*[2]] Self-murder, suicide.

1621 HAKEWILL *David's Vow* 308 Selfe homicide, the destroying of a mans selfe. *a* **1631** DONNE (*title*) *ΒΙΑΘΑΝΑΤΟΣ.* A Declaration of that Paradoxe, or Thesis, That Selfe-homicide is not so naturally Sinne, that it may never be otherwise. **1651** CHARLETON *Eph. & Cimm. Matrons* (1668) 20 Of all Murders, the most detestable was self-Homicide. **1899** *Allbutt's Syst. Med.* VIII. 371 Self-homicide occasionally occurs in melancholia.

selfhood ('sɛlfhʊd). [f. SELF *sb.* + -HOOD.

Orig. representing G. *selbheit*, but rendering also *ichheit, meinheit,* and *eigenheit* (Jacob Behmen or Boehme, 1575–1624); see quots. 1649, etc. There is no evidence of the continuity of the word from the 17th cent., and it appears as a new formation in the middle of the 19th. Blake's use of the word, in 'the Great Selfhood Satan', *Jerusalem* (1804) 33, seems to be isolated.]

1. The quality by virtue of which one is oneself; personal individuality; ipseity; that which constitutes one's own self or individuality; (one's) self.

1649 J. E[LLISTONE] tr. *Behmen's Ep.* i. §23, I live to him & not to my selfehood [orig. *Meinheit*]. *Ibid.* ii. §19, I cannot ascribe, or arrogate any thing unto my selfe, as if my selfehood [orig. *Ichheit*] were, or understood, any thing. *Ibid.* vi. §35 The Separator of the naturall selfe-hood [orig. *Eigenheit*] hath no true Ens. *Ibid.* x. §8 [A child's] naturall understanding of selfehood [orig. *Selbheit*]. **1682** HOWE *Prayer from Name of God* Wks. 1862 IV. 247 My single personality, ipseity, self-hood, call it what you will.

1858 BUSHNELL *Nat. & Supernat.* ii. (1864) 57 Their glorious self-hood and immortal liberty. **1869** *Contemp. Rev.* XI. 250 To act, to originate action, there must be.. something of selfhood—a self. **1892** W. S. LILLY *Gt. Enigma* 239 The perception of selfhood is the very fundamental interior fact of which I am conscious.

2. Oneself as the centre of one's life and action; hence, self-centredness; devotion to self, selfish life or conduct.

1649 J. E[LLISTONE] tr. *Behmen's Ep.* x. §2 Antichrist.. acteth selfe-hood [orig. *Eigenheit*] and the lust of the flesh. **1661** SPARROW tr. *Behmen's Rem. Wks., Apol. conc. Perf.* 148, I wish that I yet might totally dye to self-hood. **1683** TRYON *Way to Health* 403 To destroy all the mischievous Works of Self-hood and the Devil. *a* **1763** BYROM *Poet. Vers. Let. Behmen* xiii, When the Soul has tasted of the Love,.. Still in its Self-hood it wou'd seek to shine.

1860 J. YOUNG *Prov. Reason* 205 The..stubborn selfhood of men. **1884** *Ch. Times* 16 May 373/1 The destruction of self-hood and the entire indwelling of the Holy Ghost.

3. One's personality, one's personal interests or character.

1854 LADY LYTTON *Behind the Scenes* I. II. i. 160 They had connexions, or money, which served as a pretty relief.. to the mosaic of his self-hood. **1867** LOWELL *Among my Bks.* Ser. I. *Rousseau* (1873) 377 Originality does not consist in a fidgety assertion of selfhood. **1886** *Century Mag.* XXXI. 440 In cultivating manhood we develop selfhood.

self-hyp'nosis. *Psychol.* [SELF- 1 a, d.] = *autohypnosis* s.v. AUTO-[1] a. Also **self-'hypnotism, -hypnoti'zation, -'hypnotized** *ppl. a.*, **-'hypnotizer.**

1852 J. BRAID *Magic* 20, I stated that I had found in the writings.., 'many statements corroborative of the fact, that the eastern saints are all self-hypnotizers.' *Ibid.* 108 Special gifts imparted to them in token of the great superiority of their religious system, of inducing a state of self-hypnotism, or ecstatic trance. **1891** G. C. KINGSBURY *Practice Hypnotic Suggestion* vi. 91 It would be..interesting..to try if suggestions written out by ourselves, and used as the object of our fixed gaze for the purpose of self-hypnotization, would have any after influence. **1902** H. B. WOOLSTON in *Amer. Jrnl. Psychol* XIII. 71 This sort of self-hypnosis may lead even to an identification of the individual with the ideal form that absorbs his mind. **1925** A. S. M. HUTCHINSON *One Increasing Purpose* III. xvi. 333 He..gazed up, up, into cloudless perfect blue until, selfhypnotised, he seemed to himself to be rising up there. **1939** G. GREENE *Lawless Roads* x. 252 He had listened to the pilgrims' tales. It couldn't be self-hypnotism. **1959** *House & Garden* July 32/1 The wondrous and covetable gift of self-hypnotism. **1960** *Times* 11 Feb. 13/2 He [*sc.* McCarthy] was not a self-hypnotized genius of hate like Hitler. **1976** M. V. KLINE in E. Dengrove *Hypnosis & Behav. Therapy* x. 139 The use of self hypnosis and..of audio tape recordings.

self-i'dentical, *a. Philos.* [SELF- 3 a.] Identical with itself.

1877 E. CAIRD *Philos. Kant* II. xix. 660 We cannot determine the soul as a pure self-identical nature. **1884** tr.

Lotze's Logic IV. ii. 441 The eternally self-identical significance of Ideas. **1898** ILLINGWORTH *Div. Immanence* iii. 68 As self-conscious, self-identical, self-determined, we possess qualities which transcend or rise above the laws of matter.

self-identifi'cation. [SELF- 1 a.] Identification with something outside oneself.

1941 *Manch. Guardian Weekly* 14 Mar. 214/3 Are we to sympathise with the young? Certainly... But need this be called 'Self-identification with the experience, interests, and problems of other young people?' **1959** *Twentieth Cent.* June 629 The great admiration which James..felt for the work of Sainte-Beuve..in many ways a matter of self-identification. **1973** C. SAGAN *Cosmic Connection* (1975) i. 6 There is a serious question whether such a global self-identification of mankind can be achieved before we destroy ourselves with the technological forces our intelligence has unleashed.

Hence **self-i'dentifying** *ppl. a.*

1963 N. FRYE *Romanticism Reconsidered* 14 The self-identifying admiration which so many Romantics expressed for Napoleon. **1976** H. WILSON *Governance of Britain* iv. 92 His post-box will include hundreds of letters a week from self-identifying officials or members of local organizations of his party.

self-i'dentity. *Philos.* [SELF- 3 a.] The identity of a thing with itself.

1866 J. MARTINEAU *Ess.* I. 229 Emotion and change..are incompatible with immutable self-identity. **1877** E. CAIRD *Philos. Kant* II. xv. 544 Consciousness may pass through many states without losing its self-identity. **1899** J. CAIRD *Fundam. Ideas Christ.* II. xv. 161 That separate, solitary self-identity, which makes each human spirit..the bearer of its own burden.

self-i'dolater. [SELF- 1 c.] One who idolizes or worships self. So **self-i'dolatry, self-'idolized** *ppl. a.*, **self-'idolizing** *vbl. sb.* and *ppl. a.*

1844 LD. LEIGH *Walks in C.* 125 And *self-idolaters in drawling tone Whine about 'brethren dear', yet care for none. **1682** SIR T. BROWNE *Chr. Mor.* I. §23 (1716) 24 Self-credulity, pride, and levity lead unto *self-Idolatry. **1864** PUSEY *Lect. Daniel* ii. 94 A self-idolatry, a self-deifying, which shall compete with the true God. **1781** COWPER *Expost.* 94 The pharisee the dupe of his own art, *Self-idoliz'd. **1651** BAXTER *Inf. Bapt.* 193 Knowing such motions to come from pride and *self-Idolizing. **1860** PUSEY *Min. Proph.* 441 From Isaiah, Zephaniah adopts that characteristic picture of self-idolising. **180.** J. FOSTER *Ess.* III. iv. (1805) II. 76 The *self-idolizing men who dream.

†**self-ill,** *a. Obs. rare.* [f. SELF- 3 a + ILL *a.*] Harmful to oneself.

1633 P. FLETCHER *Hymn Marr. Cousins* xiii, Live each of other firmly lov'd, and loving; As farre from hate, as self-ill, jealousie.

self-'image. [SELF- 1 d.] An image or conception of oneself, esp. considered in relation to others.

1939 S. SPENDER *Still Centre* 101 The self-image Lifted in light against the lens Stares back with my dumb wall of eyes. **1951** M. MCLUHAN *Mech. Bride* (1967) 66/1 She embodies that self-image of a knight in shining armor. **1969** C. FREMLIN *Possession* xiv. 117 The way into these cloying, stagnant emotional pools is smooth... You come out..with your self-image in shreds. **1977** *Church Times* 14 Jan. 10 It stresses..the Vatican's self-image as the centre of Christian prayer and charity and of work for justice and peace.

self-im'portance. [SELF- 5 a.] The sense of one's importance; bearing or conduct arising from this.

1775 in ASH. **1779** *Mirror* No. 43 ¶1 She found in him nothing of that self-importance which superior parts, or great cultivation of them, is apt to confer. **1818** SCOTT *Hrt. Midl.* xii, The worthy burgher, in the plenitude of self-importance. **1825** —— *Betrothed* xxii, Solitude is favourable to feelings of self-importance. **1872** SANFORD *Est. Eng. Kings* 331 The dignity of bearing in Charles..was sustained by a profound sense of self-importance and superiority.

self-im'portant, *a.* [f. prec.] Marked by self-importance; having an exaggerated opinion of one's own importance.

1775 in ASH. **1783** O'KEEFFE *Birth-Day* 30 A little self-important court gadder. **1793** SMEATON *Edystone L.* §281 Five of our best hands being grown self-important, demanded an increase of wages. **1842** MANNING *Serm.* iii. (1843) 39 The imposing comments of self-important people.

So **self-im'portantly** *adv.*

1961 in WEBSTER. **1977** T. HEALD *Just Desserts* vi. 134 A police sergeant who arrived self-importantly. **1981** *London Rev. Bks.* 19 Nov.–2 Dec. 7/1 Marilyn Butler..is importantly and not self-importantly a citizen of the world.

self-im'posed, *ppl. a.* [SELF- 2.] Imposed on one by oneself.

1781 COWPER *Conversat.* 350 Of needless shame, and self-impos'd disgrace. **1838** DICKENS *O. Twist* xlii, Upon the night when Nancy..hurried on her self-imposed mission to Rose Maylie. **1877** FREEMAN *Norm. Conq.* II. App. 651 There is no reason to think that the pilgrimage was other than a self-imposed one.

self-im'provable, *a.* [SELF- 2 b.] Capable of self-improvement.

1678 CUDWORTH *Intell. Syst.* I. iv. xxxvi. 565 Endowed with..Freewill, and consequently..self-improvable and self-impairable. *a* **1866** J. GROTE *Exam. Utilit. Philos.* iv. (1870) 83 Some sentient beings..(of whom is man) imaginative and self-improvable.

self-im'provement. [SELF- 1 a.] Improvement of oneself, one's character, etc., by one's own efforts.

1745 J. MASON *Self-Knowl.* I. ix. (1853) 66 Had I such a temper by Nature, I should perhaps, with all my Self-Improvement find it a difficult Thing to manage. **1841** HELPS *Ess., Self-discipline* (1842) 21 The whole energies of the man devoted to self-improvement. **1879** R. K. DOUGLAS *Confucianism* iv. 94 Self-improvement and the knowledge of one's own faults.

So **self-im'prover, self-im'proving** *ppl. a.*

1853 T. T. LYNCH *Self-Improvement* 1 The *self-improver is both a labourer and a field of labour; a labourer in his own field. **1709** SHAFTESB. *Charac., Moralists* III. §2 Neither is this Knowledg [of ourselves] acquir'd by..the View of Pageantrys, the Study of Estates and Honours: nor is He to be esteem'd that *self-improving Artist, who makes a Fortune out of these. **1869** W. P. MACKAY *Grace & Truth* (1874) 41 A long series of self-improving processes.

self-incom'patible, *a.* and *sb. Bot.* [SELF- 3 b.] **A.** *adj.* Unable to be fertilized by means of its own pollen. **B.** *sb.* A self-incompatible plant or species. Opp. SELF-COMPATIBLE *a.* and *sb.*

1922 *Bot. Gaz.* LXXIII. 119 Plants may be completely self-incompatible throughout. **1938** CRANE & LAWRENCE *Genetics of Garden Plants* ix. 188 Self-compatibles crossed with self-incompatibles will give both self-compatibles and self-incompatibles in the proportion 1:1 or 2:1 according to the constitution of the self-incompatible plants used. **1944** *Nature* 5 Aug. 164/2 The nuclear and cytoplasmic systems of self-incompatible plants are mutually and constructively related. **1968** *Times* 23 May 17/5 In some species more individuals are self-incompatible than in others. **1979** *Nature* 25 Oct. 671/2 This species is self-incompatible.

So **self-incompati'bility.**

1917 *Genetics* II. 506 The words self-incompatibility and self-impotence have been substituted for self-sterility by various writers. **1952** *Heredity* VI. 286 The primary function of self-incompatibility is the avoidance of self-fertilisation. **1970** *Watsonia* VIII. 142 The failure of fruit production following self-pollination results from self-incompatibility rather than sterility.

self-incon'sistency. [SELF- 3 a.] = INCONSISTENCY 2, 4.

1698 NORRIS *Pract. Disc.* (1707) IV. 113 To acquit himself from the imputation of Absurdity and Self-inconsistency. **1778** R. SMITH *(title)* Self-inconsistency Exemplified. **1844** J. JAMIESON *Real Infl. Holy Spirit* iii. 62 This objection cannot be made without obvious self-inconsistency.

So **self-incon'sistent** *a.*, = INCONSISTENT 3, 4.

1668 G. C. *More's Div. Dial.* To Rdr. A 3, As if the more perplext and self-inconsistent the Nature of God were, it were the more..adorable. **1745** WESLEY *Answer to Church* 12 They are, I believe, the most self-inconsistent People.

self-in'duced, *pa. pple.* and *ppl. a. Electr.* [SELF- 1.] **1.** Produced by self-induction.

1886 *Science* 14 May 442/2 An extra current of opposite name self-induced in the wire. **1897** L. WRIGHT *Induction Coil* i. 20 The self-induced current in the coil from 'make' is inverse.

2. *gen.* Induced by oneself or itself.

1949 WELLEK & WARREN *Theory of Lit.* iii. 21 What it articulates is superior to their own self-induced reverie or reflection. **1954** G. I. M. SWYER *Reprod. & Sex* 246 This often happens in clumsy attempts at self-induced criminal abortion. **1981** J. BRABAZON *Dorothy L. Sayers* xx. 267 The pressures on Patrick McLaughlin, some of them self-induced.

self-in'ductance. *Electr.* [SELF- 3 b.] = next. Also, the coefficient of self-induction.

[**1883**: see INDUCTANCE.] **1897** *Amer. Jrnl. Sci.* Ser. IV. IV. 431 We can always determine the mutual inductances in terms of the self-inductances. **1903** *Times* 6 Feb. 9/6 In self-inductance electricity had a property resembling inertia.

self-in'duction. *Electr.* [SELF- 3 b.] The production of an induced current in a circuit by means of a variation in the current of that circuit (see INDUCTION 10, INERTIA 1 b). Also, the coefficient of self-induction.

1865 J. C. MAXWELL in *Phil. Trans. R. Soc.* CLV. 472 The equation of the current x in a circuit whose resistance is R, and whose coefficient of self-induction is L, acted on by an external electromotive force ξ, is $\xi - Rx = d(Lx)/dt$. *Ibid.* 475 Hence the effect..is to increase the apparent resistance and diminish the apparent self-induction of the circuit. **1873** —— *Electr. & Magn.* II. 291 The self-induction of a round wire doubled on itself. **1876** CHRYSTAL in *Encycl. Brit.* VIII. 76/2 What has been called the coefficient of self-induction of a circuit he [Neumann] calls the potential of the circuit on itself. **1886** *Science* 14 May 443/1 The electromotive force of self-induction currents. **1902** *Encycl. Brit.* XXVIII. 56/1 The circuit in the jar C is provided with a sliding piece, F, by means of which the self-induction of the discharging circuit..can be adjusted. **1958** CONDON & ODISHAW *Handbk. Physics* IV. i. 17/1 If the current in the circuit increases for any reason, the flux through the circuit must also increase, and this gives rise to an emf of self-induction which acts to oppose the increase in the current by Lenz's law.

So **self-in'ductive** *a.*, produced by self-induction.

1834 FARADAY *Exp. Res.* (1844) II. 208 Self-inductive action of a current. **1886** *Science* 14 May 442 The self-inductive capacity of non-magnetic wires of different metals.

self-in'dulged, *ppl. a.* [SELF- 2.] Indulged, gratified, or humoured by oneself.

1846 H. G. ROBINSON *Odes of Horace* II. ii, Fell dropsy, self-indulg'd, is nurst, Nor drives away its growing thirst. **1881** 'RITA' *My Lady Coquette* i, Spoilt..and self-indulged.

self-in'dulgence. [SELF- 1 a.] Indulgence of one's desires, etc.; = INDULGENCE 2 b.

1753 MISS COLLIER *Art Torment.* II. iii. (1811) 159 That you do not believe that ill-health comes to any but through their own self-indulgence. **1779** JOHNSON *L.P., Garth* (1868) 215 The author never slumbers in self-indulgence; his full vigour is always exerted. **1869** TROLLOPE *He knew,* etc. xviii. (1878) 98 One finds so few people that will do any duty that taxes their self-indulgence.

So **self-in'dulgent** *a.* (cf. INDULGENT 2), **self-in'dulger, self-in'dulging** *ppl. a.*

1791 BOSWELL *Johnson* 27 Mar., an. 1776, A capricious and *self-indulgent valetudinarian. **1833** J. H. NEWMAN *Arians* I. i. (1876) 11 Those festive, self-indulgent habits. **1847** MRS. TROLLOPE *Three Cousins* xxvii. II. 186 All the articles ever invented by the ingenuity of man for rendering the retired hours of an aged *self indulger luxurious. **1687** NORRIS *Misc.* (1699) 275 Our most forward and *Self-indulging Opinions. **1795–1814** WORDSW. *Excurs.* II. 311 Steeped in a self-indulging spleen.

self-in'flicted, *ppl. a.* [SELF- 2.] Inflicted by oneself or one's own hand.

1784 COWPER *Task* IV. 430 Poverty, with most who whimper forth Their long complaints, is self-inflicted woe. **1814** BYRON *Lara* I. xvii, Self-inflicted penance. **1885** *Law Times* LXXVIII. 270/2 The injury was self-inflicted.

So **self-in'fliction.**

1860 PUSEY *Min. Proph.* 583 Self-infliction was characteristic of the idolatrous cuttings. **1892** ZANGWILL *Bow Myst.* 36 In the absence of any theory as to how the cut could possibly have been made by that other hand, we should be driven back to the theory of self-infliction.

self-in'structed, *ppl. a.* [SELF- 2.] Self-educated, self-taught. So **self-in'struction; self-in'structor** (used as a title for a manual of self-instruction).

1833 J. S. MILL in *Tait's Mag.* III. 348 Narrowness and self-conceit..are the..failings of the *self-instructed. *a* **1704** T. BROWN *Lond. & Lacedem. Oracles* Wks. 1709 III. III. 136 The Desire of *Self-Instruction. **1729** LAW *Serious C.* xviii. 326 Had we continued perfect, as God created the first man, perhaps the perfection of our nature had been a sufficient self-instruction for every one. **1848** THACKERAY *Van. Fair* x, What instruction is more effectual than self-instruction? **1905** *Athenæum* 7 Jan. 21/2 To assist officers in self-instruction in tactics. **1807** *(title)* The *Self Instructor, or Young Man's Best Companion; being an introduction to all the various branches of useful learning and knowledge. **1883** *(title)* Ward and Lock's Self-instructor; or, Every Man his own Schoolmaster.

self-in'surance. [SELF- 1 a.] Insurance of oneself or one's interests by maintaining a fund to cover possible losses. Hence **self-in'surer, -in'suring; self-in'sured.**

1905 *Ann. Amer. Acad. Polit. & Social Sci.* XXVI. 452, I am informed by the managers and officers of the largest steamship lines that self-insurance is practiced extensively by their companies in one form or another. **1909** WEBSTER, Self-insurer. **1932** *Sun* (Baltimore) 8 Sept. 4/4 Self-insuring might be permitted to employers or industrial groups who can guarantee maintenance of a benefit system equal or superior to the standards of the State system. **1934** WEBSTER, Self-insured. **1972** *Accountant* 5 Oct. 422/1 Premiums..are tax-deductible... This is an important advantage for the self-insurer... The company with a poor loss record has most to gain from self-insurance.

†**self-'interessed,** *ppl. a. Obs.* [See INTERESSED.] = SELF-INTERESTED.

1656 EARL MONM. tr. *Boccalini's Advts. fr. Parnass.* I. xi. (1674) 14 The self-interessed and perfidious heart of Man. **1707** *Lond. Gaz.* No. 4324/1 Those narrow Self-Interessed Notions which..had so long cramp'd and fetter'd them.

self-'interest. [SELF- 5 a.]

1. One's personal profit, benefit, or advantage. (Cf. INTEREST *sb.* 2 b.) Now *rare* or *Obs.*

1658 T. WALL *Charact. Enemies Ch.* 35 Self interest..is the second end. *a* **1662** DUPPA *Holy Rules Devot.* II. (1675) 162 Hast thou set up nothing in competition with him [*sc.* God],..no Profit, no Self-love, no Self-Interest of thine own? **1726** BUTLER *Serm. Rolls Chapel* xi. 202 Greater Regards to Self-interest. **1801** *Farmer's Mag.* Aug. 332 An enlightened sense of self-interest. **1831** SCOTT *Ct. Rob.* xiii, He holds his own self-interest to be the devoted guide of his whole conduct. **1833** LYTTON *Godolphin* I. ii. 22 Like Lysander, he loved plotting, yet neglected self-interest.

b. A private or personal end. ? *Obs.*

1658 SLINGSBY *Diary* (1836) 208 It admitted no alloy or mixture with By-respects or self-interests. **1712** PRIDEAUX *Direct. Church-W.* (ed. 4) 91 They have a By-end and Self-interest of their own. **1867** BAGEHOT *Engl. Const.* viii. 277 The self-interests, the jobbing propensities of the assembly.

2. Regard to, or pursuit of, one's own advantage or welfare, *esp.* to the exclusion of regard for others. (Cf. INTEREST *sb.* 5.) For the favourable sense, cf. SELF-LOVE 2.

1649 J. E[LLISTONE] tr. *Behmen's Ep.* x. §4 He must mortify the Antichrist in his soule..and become the poorest creature in the owne-hood (selfenesse or selfe interest) of his mind. **1657** *Baker's Sancta Sophia* II. II. ii. §5 (1908) 245 So absolute a purity and freedom from self-interest. **1693** DRYDEN *Exam. Poet.* Ded., Ess. (ed. Ker) II. 2 The same jugglings in State, the same hypocrisy in religion, the same self-interest and mismanagement. **1780** COWPER *Expost.* 439 The priestly brotherhood, devout, sincere, From mean self int'rest and ambition clear. **1790** BURKE *Fr. Rev.* Wks. V. 271 An enlightened self-interest, which, when well understood, they tell us, will identify with an interest more enlarged and publick. **1865** LOWELL *Reconstruction* Wks. 1890 V. 236 The..weak good-nature inherent in popular government, but against which monarchies and aristocracies are insured by self-interest. **1878** EMERSON *Sov. Ethics* in *N.*

Amer. Rev. CXXVI. 407 In spite of malignity and blind self-interest..necessity is always bringing things right.

self-'interested, *a.* [f. prec. + -ED.] Characterized by self-interest; actuated solely by regard for one's personal advantage or welfare.

1657 *Narr. late Parlt.* in *Harl. Misc.* (1809) III. 462 Men, standing under such mercenary and self-interested obligations. **1688** LD. CHURCHILL *Let. to King* ibid. IV. 59 Those unhappy designs, which inconsiderate and self-interested men have framed against your Majesty's true interest. **1707** HEARNE *Collect.* 19 Sept. (O.H.S.) II. 48 A.. stingy self-interested Fellow. **1784** J. POTTER *Virtuous Villagers* II. 69 The gifts of Fortune..applied to..self-interested purposes. **1834** K. H. DIGBY *Mores Cath.* v. x. 360 The zeal of the middle ages had..nothing to recommend it to the favour of..self-interested reformers. **1863** MRS. OLIPHANT *Salem Chapel* v, I must learn to be prudent and self-interested for your sakes.

Hence **self-'interestedness;** so †**self-'interesting** *ppl. a.* = SELF-INTERESTED.

1727 BAILEY vol. II, *Sinisterness*, Unfairness, *Self-Interestedness. *a* **1734** NORTH *Life Dudley North* (1744) 6 Experience of Mens ordinary Self-Interestedness and Treachery. **1870** MOZLEY *Univ. Serm.* iii. (1877) 67 This charge of self-interestedness against the motive of a future life. **1699** SHAFTESB. *Charac., Inq. conc. Virtue* II. 79 All social Love, Friendship [etc.]..does by its nature take place of the *self-interesting Passions. **1710** —— *Adv. Author* I. 201 The self-interesting Partys [viz. the reader and the author] both vanish at once.

self-invo'lution. [SELF- 3 a.] The condition or fact of being self-involved.

1817 COLERIDGE *Biog. Lit.* xxiii. (1907) II. 183 The self-involution and dreamlike continuity of Richardson. **1888** *Amer. Jrnl. Psychol.* I. 630 Heraclitus..seemed to appreciate the dangers of self-involution.

self-in'volved, *ppl. a.* [SELF- 3 a.] Wrapped up in oneself or one's own thoughts.

1842 TENNYSON *Day-Dream* 261 The pensive mind..all too dearly self-involved. **1847** JAMES *Russell* I. ix. 175 That peculiar sort of self-involved business air. **1869** RUSKIN *Q. of Air* i. §21 Coiling and recoiling and self-involved returns of some sickening famine and thirst of heart.

self-ioni'zation. *Chem.* [SELF- 1 a, d.] Spontaneous dissociation of a proportion of the molecules of a liquid into ions.

1931 *Chem. Rev.* VIII. 201 Bishop..used the hydrogen electrode for titrations in ethanol and emphasized the effect of the low self-ionization of the solvent on the titration curves. **1972** COTTON & WILKINSON *Adv. Inorg. Chem.* (ed. 3) v. 181 Pure H_2SO_4 shows extensive self-ionization resulting in high conductivity.

selfish ('sɛlfɪʃ), *a.* Also 7 self(e)-ish, selvish. [f. SELF *sb.* + -ISH[1] 2.

In Hacket's life of Archbishop Williams, *Scrinia Reserata* (1693) II. §136, the word is said to be of the Presbyterians' 'own new mint'; it is used in reference to events of the year 1641. Synonyms current in the 17th cent. are *self-ended* and *self-ful*.]

1. a. Devoted to or concerned with one's own advantage or welfare to the exclusion of regard for others.

1640 W. BRIDGE *True Souldiers C.* 74 A carnal selfe-ish spirit is very loathsome in what is spirituall. **1645** T. HILL *Olive Branch* (1648) 27 When you are so selfish in your designs and undertakings, and so far prefer your self-ends before the Publique. **1656** JEANES *Mixt. Schol. Div.* 14 It is a selvish fear, proceeding from an..adulterous love of ourselves. **1753** JOHNSON *Advent.* No. 62 ¶5 Want makes almost every man selfish. **1775** SHERIDAN *Duenna* I. iv, Anywhere to avoid the selfish violence of my mother-in-law. **1838** DICKENS *Nich. Nick.* xiv, 'Well, but what's to become of me?' urged the selfish man. **1863** GEO. ELIOT *Romola* xxv, The subjection of selfish interests to the general good. **1870** MOZLEY *Univ. Serm.* iii. (1877) 65 He necessarily wishes his own good; the wish..is no more selfish in him than it is selfish in him to be himself.

Comb. **1666** BP. S. PARKER *Free & Impart. Censure* (1667) 139 We cannot imagine him so selfish-spirited as to effect it. **1863** HAWKER in Byles *Life* (1905) 462 A downlooking lying selfish-hearted throng.

b. Used (by adversaries) as a designation of those ethical theories which regard self-love as the real motive of all human action.

[**1663** W. LUCY *Observ. Hobbes* 178 To use the Phrase of the time, this Gent. [Hobbes] is very selfish.] **1847** *London Univ. Cal.* (1848) 157 The different systems to which the term 'selfish' has been applied. **1868** BAIN *Ment. & Mor. Sci.* 638 The Epicurean, or Selfish, System.

c. *Genetics.* Of a gene or genetic material: tending to be perpetuated or to spread although of no effect on the phenotype.

1976 R. DAWKINS *Selfish Gene* i. 3 Let us understand what our own selfish genes are up to, because we may then at least have the chance to upset their designs. **1979** *Human Genetics* (Ciba Symp.) 41 It seems to me that repetitive DNA is the only true selfish gene. **1981** *Nature* 13 Aug. 648/1 Selfish DNA, which contains no genetic information but which is perpetuated in eukaryote genomes, has attracted a lot of attention recently.

¶**2.** By etymological re-analysis used for 'pertaining to or connected with oneself'.

1835-6 *Todd's Cycl. Anat.* I. 72/2 The sensation excited on the skin is less *selfish*, if we may use the term in this sense. **1899** *Westm. Gaz.* 3 May 3/2 To pursue this self-ish ideal.

selfishly ('sɛlfɪʃlɪ), *adv.* [f. prec. + -LY[2].] In a selfish manner.

1735 POPE *Prol. Sat.* 293 Who can your merit selfishly approve. **1809** PINKNEY *Trav. France* 140 Who was never known to forget himself, and act otherwise than selfishly.

selfishness ('sɛlfɪʃnɪs). Also 7 selvish-. [f. SELFISH + -NESS.] The condition or quality of being selfish; selfish disposition or behaviour; regard for one's own interest or happiness to the disregard of the well-being of others.

1643 W. GREENHILL *Axe at Root* A iij b, It's domesticknes of spirit, selvishnesse, which is the great let to Armies, Religions, and Kingdomes good. **1645** T. HILL *Olive Branch* (1648) 26 As long as ever you are full of Envy..or full of Selfishness, it argues you want love. **1709** SHAFTESB. *Charac.* (1711) I. 115 The Opposite of Sociableness is Selfishness. **1790** BURKE *Fr. Rev.* 333 A tax by which luxury, avarice, and selfishness were screened, and the load thrown upon productive capital. **1839** JAMES *Louis XIV*, I. 406 Passion, vanity, interest, and all the other species of selfishness.

selfism ('sɛlfɪz(ə)m). [f. SELF *sb.* + -ISM.] Devotion to or concentration upon one's own interests; self-centredness. Also, the 'selfish theory' of morals.

1791-1823 D'ISRAELI *Cur. Lit.* (1866) 524 In the pride of luxury and selfism. **1832** DISRAELI *Cont. Fleming* II. x, That nothing could tempt me to compromise my absorbing selfism. **1860** EMERSON *Cond. Life* (1861) 79 By treating the patient tenderly, to shut him up in a narrower selfism. **1871** BLACKIE *Morals* i. 50 Hobbes and the other advocates of selfism. **1894** [see OTHERISM].

selfist ('sɛlfɪst). Also 7 selfeist. [f. SELF *sb.* + -IST.] A self-centred or selfish person.

1649 J. E[LLISTONE] tr. *Behmen's Ep.* i. §62 [It] covetously desireth to draw their life and maintenance to it selfe, and to make it selfe a Lord over it, and will be a Selfeist [orig. *ein eigenes*].

1829 I. TAYLOR *Enthus.* ix. 223 The anchoret is a selfist by his very profession. **1857** J. HAMILTON *Less. fr. Biogr.* (1859) 270, I have been a mere selfist, living for men's praise.

self-judged, *ppl. a.* [SELF- 2.] Judged by oneself. So **self-'judging** *vbl. sb.* and *ppl. a.*

1798 SOTHEBY tr. *Wieland's Oberon* (1826) II. 10 Who but the wretch *self-judg'd, has cause to fear? **1850** S. DOBELL *Roman* iii. Poet. Wks. (1875) 49 Each self-judged helot, pleased to toil. *a* **1680** CHARNOCK *Self-Exam.* Wks. 1684 II. 825 With a power of self-tryal and *self-judging. **1847-54** WEBSTER, **Self-judging*, judging one's self.

self-'judgement. [SELF- 1 a.]

†**1.** Self-opinion. *Obs.*

1657 *Baker's Sancta Sophia* II. II. xi. §10 (1908) 296 An obstinate self-judgment in this.

2. Judgement passed upon oneself.

1745 J. MASON *Self-Knowl.* I. xiv. (1853) 108 The Want of this previous Act of Self-judgment is the cause of so much Self-Deception. **1868** GLADSTONE *Juv. Mundi* x. (1870) 384 Nemesis is self-judgment by the inward law.

†**self-ju'sticiary.** *Theol. Obs.* [SELF- 1 c.] = JUSTICIARY *sb.*[1] 5.

1644 PRYNNE & WALKER *Fiennes's Trial* 115 He professeth himselfe no Delinquent, but a just person... (O strange self-Iusticiary, O most impudent affronter of Iustice!) **1661** SOUTH *Serm.* (1823) II. 333 The arrogant assertions of self-justiciaries on the one hand, and the wild opinions of the Antinomians on the other. **1692** *Christ Exalted* 79 The Apostle concludes, to the shame of self-justiciaries, Rom. 3. 27. Where is boasting then? it is excluded.

self-justifi'cation. [SELF- 1 a.] The action of justifying or excusing oneself.

1775 in ASH. **1826** MISS MITFORD *Village* Ser. II. (1863) 359 The total absence of sullenness and self-justification towards her superiors. **1876** BANCROFT *Hist. U.S.* III. vi. 371 He abounded in repetitions and explanatory self-justification.

self-'justifier. [SELF- 1 c.]

†**1.** = SELF-JUSTICIARY.

1655 BAXTER *Quaker's Catech.* 9 And yet was he counted a proud self-justifier.

2. *Printing.* A self-justifying type-machine.

In recent Dicts.

So **self-'justified** *ppl. a.* (*Printing*), arranged by means of automatic justifying mechanism; **self-'justifying** *ppl. a.* (whence **-'justifyingly** *adv.*).

1897 *Brit. Printer* 268 When followed by a like variation of the three remaining spaces between words in the line, the latter, when assembled, will be *self-justified. **1740** RICHARDSON *Pamela* (1824) I. xxiii. 275 What *self-justifying minds have the meekest of these women! **1860** PUSEY *Min. Proph.* 595 What have we spoken against Thee? is the self-justifying question which Malachi records of them. **1895** *Funk's Stand. Dict.* s.v., A self-justifying type-setting machine. **1891** MEREDITH *One of our Conq.* II. x. 257 She thought, as an observer; and *self-justifyingly thought on.

†**self-kill,** *a. Obs.* [f. SELF- 1 g + KILL *v.*] Mutually slaughtering.

a **1618** SYLVESTER *Mirac. Peace* xxxii, With self-kill Swords to cut each other's throat.

self-'killed, *pa. pple.* [SELF- 2.] Killed by one's own hand; self-destroyed.

c **1600** SHAKS. *Sonn.* vi. 4 Treasure thou some place, With beauties treasure ere it be selfe kil'd. **1671** MILTON *Samson* 1664 And now ly'st victorious Among thy slain self-kill'd.

So **self-'killer,** a suicide; **self-'killing,** self-murder, suicide.

1658 SIR T. BROWNE *Hydriot* 37 No relicks of traitors to their country, *self-killers or sacrilegious malefactors. **1618** BOLTON *Florus* (1636) To Rdr., Heathen, with whom ..*self-killing, to avoyd disgrace, seemed an high point of true magnanimity. *a* **1721** SHEFFIELD (Dk. Buckhm.) *Wks.* (1729) I. 149 In those Times Self-killing was not rare.

self-'knowing, *vbl. sb.* = SELF-KNOWLEDGE.

1817 COLERIDGE *Biog. Lit.* xii. (1907) I. 186 Whether abstracted from us there exists any thing higher and beyond this primary self-knowing.

self-'knowing, *ppl. a.* [SELF- 1 f, 3 b.]

1. Knowing oneself; having self-knowledge.

1667 MILTON *P.L.* VII. 510 And upright with Front serene Govern the rest, self-knowing. **1745** J. MASON *Self-Knowl.* II. iii. (1853) 146 A self-knowing man can easily distinguish between these two. **1890** W. T. HARRIS *Hegel's Logic* ii. 23 (Funk) That this is meant for a personal Reason, we may know from the fact that Aristotle calls it self-knowing Reason.

2. Knowing of oneself, without help from another (Webster, 1828-32).

self-'knowledge. [SELF- 1 a, d.] Knowledge of oneself, one's character, capabilities, etc.

a **1613** OVERBURY *Newes* Wks. (1856) 174 That a courtier never attaines his selfe-knowledge, but by report. **1647** C. HARVEY *Schola Cordis* Concl. 7 Self-knowledge is an everlasting taske. **1745** J. MASON *Self-Knowl.* I. i. (1853) 10 Self-Knowledge is that Acquaintance with ourselves, which shews us what we are, and do, and ought to be. **1855** MACAULAY *Hist. Eng.* xx. IV. 455 It is a remarkable proof of his selfknowledge that, from the moment at which he began to distinguish himself in public life, he ceased to be a versifier. **1869** MOZLEY *Univ. Serm.* ii. (1876) 35 Self-knowledge is the first condition of repentance.

self-known, *ppl. a.* [SELF- 2.] Possessing self-knowledge.

1782 COWPER *Glory to God Alone* 17 Oh lost in vanity till once self-known!

self-lance: see SELF B. 6.

†**self-law.** *Obs.* [SELF- 5 e.] A law of one's own making or to suit oneself.

1654 WHITLOCK *Zootomia* 365 It is Selfe-Law, or if you will, love God, so as not to lose by him, and thy Neighbour for thy selfe. *a* **1680** CHARNOCK *Mercy for Chief of Sinners* (1846) 16 [They] are so much a law to themselves, that it is difficult to persuade them..to part with this self-law in matter of justification.

So †**self-lawed** *a.*, that is a law to himself.

1635 QUARLES *Embl.* III. iii. 134 It raignes in ev'ry part, But playes the selfe-law'd Tyrant in my heart.

selfless ('sɛlflɪs), *a.* [f. SELF *sb.* + -LESS.]

1. Having no regard for or thought of self; not self-centred; unselfish.

1825 COLERIDGE *Aids Refl.* 83 Holy instincts of maternal love detached and in selfless purity. **1859** TENNYSON *Vivien* 293 They never mount As high as woman in her selfless mood. **1894** LD. WOLSELEY *Marlborough* II. xci. 445 The noble, selfless word 'duty'.

2. Not identifiable with a man's self. *rare.*

1853 PULSFORD tr. *J. Müller's Chr. Doctr. Sin* II. 49 Instead of the will being merely the self-less means for calling the natural individuality into activity.

Hence **'selflessly** *adv.*, **'selflessness.**

1853 VAUGHAN in *Guardian* 3 Jan. 18/2 That selflessness which God requires in His servant. **1903** *Contemp. Rev.* Mar. 411 A pious priest selflessly devoted to his church. **1904** *Hibbert Jrnl.* Oct. 122 With a worthy selflessness he throws himself into the life of the people.

self-life.

1. [SELF- 5 c.] = SELF-EXISTENCE.

1613 DONNE *Good Friday* Poems (1639) 353 Who sees Gods face, that is selfelife, must die. *a* **1711** KEN *Hymnarium* Poet. Wks. II. 41 A co-eternal Force, Co-boundless with its Source, Could in no Moment idle rest, But in pure Act self-life express'd.

2. [SELF- 5 d.] Life lived for oneself; life devoted to selfish ends.

1848 BAILEY *Festus* 324 Let then mere self-life cease. **1893** *New Church Mess.* (N.Y.) 19 Apr. 242 In this self-laudation we are indulging ourselves in the vanities of self-life.

†**'self-like,** *a.* and *adv. Obs.* [In A. 1, f. SELF *a.* + LIKE *a.*; cf. SELFSAME; in A. 2 and B., f. SELF *sb.* + LIKE.] **A.** *adj.*

1. 'Very like', similar, of the selfsame kind.

1556 *Aurelio & Isab.* G 3 You men be of the same selfe lyke qualite. *a* **1586** SIDNEY *Arcadia* I. Ecl. i. (1622) 95 Till Strephons plaining voice him nearer drew, Where by his words his selfe-like case he knew. **1594** H. WILLOBIE *Avisa* 19, I little thought to find you so:..Such selfe like wench I neuer met. **1596** LODGE *Marg. Amer.* 114 This other in the selfe like passion, but with more government, he wrote.

2. Like oneself.

1606 SYLVESTER *Du Bartas* II. iv. IV. Decay 1143 And so God bless your lawfull-loved womb With Self-like Babes [orig. *enfans pareils à vous*]. **1621** G. SANDYS *Ovid's Met.* I. (1626) 6 His selfe-like jawes still grin [orig. *ab ipso colligit os rabiem*].

B. *adv.* Even; = SELFLY *adv.* 1 a.

1556 *Aurelio & Isab.* H 7 In tyme & in place where they be not requiered, selfe lyke in the presence of so grete a Kinge & Quene.

† **self-liked**, *a. Obs.* [f. next. Cf. OE. *selflíce* self-conceited, self-satisfied.] Self-conceited.
1599 *More's Life* in Wordsw. *Eccl. Biogr.* (1853) II. 106 That he should not be so obstinate and self-liked, as to persevere still in one minde.

† **self-'liking**, *vbl. sb. Obs.* [SELF- 1. Cf. OE. *selflíce* self-love, self-satisfaction.] Self-love; attachment to one's own opinion, self-conceit.
1561 T. HOBY tr. *Castiglione's Courtyer* Zz iv b, Giue her self to vnderstand the full troth in euery thyng, without entring into self leeking and ignorance. **1594** HOOKER *Eccl. Pol.* Pref. vi. §3 So full of wilfulnes and selfe liking is our nature. **1623** CAMDEN *Rem.* (1637) 230 So over-gulled with selfe-liking, that they are more then giddy in admiring themselves. **1638** JUNIUS *Paint. Ancients* 191 It is not amisse there should be perceived some kind of selfe-liking and hardnesse in the works of excellent Artificers. **1714** MANDEVILLE *Fab. Bees* (1729) II. 134 The Reasons why this Self-liking, give me Leave to call it so, is not plainly to be seen in all Animals that are of the same Degree of Perfection, are many.
So † **self-'liking** *ppl. a.*
a **1586** SIDNEY *Arcadia* III. (1605) 337 Spacious romes, such as the self-liking men, haue..found out the most easeful.

self-limi'tation. [SELF- 1 a.]
1. The limitation of oneself, one's nature, etc.
1847 J. D. MORELL *Hist. View Philos.* (ed. 2) II. v. 105 The idea of the objective arises from the self-limitation of our own free activity. **1853** PULSFORD tr. *J. Müller's Chr. Doctr. Sin* II. 204 A self-limitation of God. **1902** J. SMITH *Integrity of Scripture* iii. 106 There must have been a marvellous self-limitation in the Incarnation. **1907** J. R. ILLINGWORTH *Doct. Trin.* x. 191 Virtue is rooted in self-control, self-discipline, that is, voluntary self-limitation.
2. *Med.* The property of being self-limited.
1879 FLINT in *Arch. Med.* (N.Y.) June, Self-limitation in Cases of Phthisis.
So **self-'limiting** *ppl. a.*; *spec.* in *Med.* = SELF-LIMITED *ppl. a.* 2.
1863 E. V. NEALE *Analogy of Thought & Nature* 43 By a first cause we mean a self-limiting will, while by the secondary causes derived from it, we mean powers thought of as limited by their effects. **1954** S. DUKE-ELDER *Parsons' Dis. Eye* (ed. 12) x. 125 The factor dominating the prognosis ..is the recurrence of relapses on its cessation unless the malady is eradicable or self-limiting. **1965** J. POLLITT *Depression & its Treatment* v. 71 Premenstrual depression is a short-lived, self-limiting depressive illness. **1977** *Lancet* 19 Mar. 648/2 Whooping-cough is a self-limiting infection which should never be fatal with proper medical care.

self-'limited, *ppl. a.* [SELF- 2.]
1. Limited by oneself or itself.
1845 LEWES *Hist. Philos.* I. 92 They held The One to be spherical:..having neither beginning, middle, nor end: and yet self-limited. **1879** P. BROOKS *Infl. Jesus* ii. (1883) 86 The ..self-limited character of the love of Jesus for His native land.
2. *Med.* Of a disease: That runs a definite course, being little modified by treatment.
1855 DUNGLISON *Med. Lex.* **1885** J. F. PAYNE in *Encycl. Brit.* XIX. 166/1 The disease [*sc.* plague] was in fact, as in other cases, self-limited. **1897** *Allbutt's Syst. Med.* II. 781 Catarrhal dysentery..is a self-limited disease.

self-'liquidating, *ppl. a. Comm.* (orig. *U.S.*). [SELF- 1 f.] Of, pertaining to, or designating credit, or a loan, that repays itself with the money accruing within a certain period after its investment. Also of a premium similarly offered.
1915 *U.S. Fed. Reserve Board 1st Ann. Rep. 1914* 9 It is recommended that the Federal Reserve Banks confine themselves strictly to dealing in short-term, self-liquidating paper growing out of commercial, industrial, and agricultural operations. **1928** *Burroughs Clearing House* May 32/3 If the purpose is a constructive one, stimulating production and of a self-liquidating character..then the loan should be made. **1939** *Construction & Financing of Self-Liquidating Projects* (U.S. Congr. House Comm. on Banking & Currency) 2 In view of this splendid repayment record there can be little doubt that the tenancy program has been established on a sound, self-liquidating basis. **1942** W. B. TAYLOR *Financial Policies of Bus. Enterprise* IV. xiii. 288 Short-term loans, commonly made for less than a year, are usually self-liquidating and hence not adapted to the raising of fixed capital. **1967** *Economist* 10 June p. xxxi/2 The traditional role of providing short term, self-liquidating trade finance to a nation of shopkeepers is too narrow. **1971** R. L. WILLSMER *Directing Marketing Effort* II. xviii. 292 A self-liquidating premium looks good because it theoretically costs nothing.
Also **self-'liquidator**, a self-liquidating premium.
1944 *Premium Practice* Mar. 8/2 Mr. Cahill mentioned the following: (a) self-liquidators. **1948** *Ibid.* Oct. 30/1 The juvenile field was once the objective of the self-liquidator. Now it is the adult thing. **1962** G. MEREDITH *Effective Merchandising with Premiums* II. iv. 37 It would be impossible to identify one promotion as the beginning of modern self-liquidator practice. **1970** R. WILLSMER in G. Wills *New Ideas in Retail Managem.* xii. 170 Self-liquidating premium offers continue to lead the field... Only eight store-promoted self-liquidators were recorded.

self-liqui'dation. [SELF- 1 a.] **1.** *Comm.* (orig. *U.S.*). The action or process of repaying a self-liquidating loan. Cf. SELF-LIQUIDATING *ppl. a.*
1932 *Burroughs Clearing House* Mar. 23/1 The idea of self-liquidation, of having a definite source of repayment in sight, of inquiring into the purpose of the loan with a view to finding out how far the money is to be sunk in fixed assets, all these relate to the liquidity of loans. **1949** H. V. PROCHNOW *Term Loans & Theories of Bank Liquidity* i. 5 The belief that commercial banks..should extend credit only for short periods and for purposes which result in the self-liquidation of the credit. **1951** *Banco Nazionale del Lavoro Q. Rev.* July–Sept. 135/2 In the last few decades the theory of 'self-liquidation' has been gradually set aside and replaced by the 'shiftability theory'.
2. The destruction or elimination of oneself by oneself. Also *fig.* Cf. LIQUIDATION 3 b.
1949 KOESTLER *Promise & Fulfilment* II. iv. 253 This difference..was demonstrated by Irgun's voluntary self-liquidation..as opposed to the Stern Group's persistence in terrorism. **1964** I. L. HOROWITZ *New Sociology* 17 The recent work in some quarters..seems to point precisely in the direction of the self-liquidation of sociology. **1977** *Canadian Jrnl. Sociology* II. 106 The inevitable self-liquidation of science is another way of speaking of science's tie to life.

self-lived, *a. rare.* [f. SELF- 2 a + LIVED or SELF-LIFE + -ED.]
† **1.** Animated by oneself. *Obs.*
1598 SYLVESTER *Du Bartas* II. i. III. 197 Nor craftie Jugglers, can more eas'ly make There self-liv'd Puppits (for their lucre's sake) To skip..and play.
† **2.** Having an independent life. *Obs.*
1642 H. MORE *Song of Soul* III. I. xxxii, The soul then works by 't self, and is self-liv'd.
3. Living for oneself.
1855 BAILEY *Mystic*, etc. 66 Malignant, uncreate, inert, self-lived.

† **self-'living,** *a. Obs.* [SELF- 3 b.] Self-existent.
1682 H. MORE *Annot. Glanvill's Lux O.* 236 They are immediately Self-living.

'self-loop. [SELF- 3 a.] In a graph or network, a line that returns to the node it leaves.
1964 S. E. SALMAGHRABY in *Managem. Sci.* X. 499 We shall reserve the terms 'self-loop' to designate a branch that leads from a node to itself. **1980** *Sci. Amer.* Mar. 18/1 In graph theory a graph is defined as any set of points joined by lines, and a simple graph is defined as one that has no self-loops (lines that join a point to itself) and no parallel lines (two or more lines joining the same pair of points).

self-loss. [SELF- 1 a, d.] Loss of oneself, one's being or personality.
1826 LAMB *Ess.*, *Sanity of True Genius* (1860) 292 He wins his flight without self-loss through realms of chaos. **1860** R. A. VAUGHAN *Mystics* (ed. 2) I. 119 That transformation and utter self-loss in which we love ourselves only for the sake of God.

self-lost, *a.* [SELF- 2.] Lost through one's own action, fault, etc. In first quot., lost in one's own estimation.
1645 RUTHERFORD *Tryal & Tri. Faith* 108 It is one thing to be lost, and a sinner, and another thing to be self-lost. **1667** MILTON *P.L.* VII. 154, I can repaire That detriment, if such it be to lose Self-lost. **1792** R. CUMBERLAND *Calvary* v. 214 Rush'd into sin prepense, self-will'd, self-lost. **1796** MME. D'ARBLAY *Camilla* II. 149 The infatuated blindness of that self-lost young man. **1856** E. FITZGERALD *Salámán* I. 23 Thyself Self-Lost, and Conscience-quit of Good and Evil.

self-lough. *local.* [f. SELF- 3 b + LOUGH[1].] See quot.
1700 C. LEIGH *Nat. Hist. Lanc.*, etc. I. 71 There are sometimes Cavities in the Body of this [Spar]..which are impleted with Water, tho there are no apparent Aqueducts leading to them; these by the Miners are stiled *Self-Loughs*.

self-'love. [SELF- 1 a, d.]
1. Love of oneself; in early use most freq. = partiality to oneself, AMOUR-PROPRE; later, usually = regard for one's interests or well-being; chiefly with definitely opprobrious implication, self-centredness, selfishness.
1563 *Mirr. Mag.*, *Hastings* ii, In Læthes floud, long since, in Stigian vale Selfe love I dreynt. *a* **1586** SIDNEY *Apol. Poetry* (Arb.) 19 Selfe-loue is better then any guilding to make that seeme gorgious, wherein our selues are parties. *c* **1600** SHAKS. *Sonn.* lxii. 1 Sinne of selfe-loue possesseth al mine eie. **1655** CULPEPPER, etc. *Riverius* To Rdr., I, who never had the thought (being very free from Self-Love,) that my writings were of so much worth. **1733** POPE *Ess. Man* III. 281 Self-love forsook the path it first pursu'd, And found the private in the public good. **1837** HT. MARTINEAU *Soc. Amer.* III. 35 That kind of self-love which takes the form of family pride. **1861** *Sat. Rev.* 14 Sept. 269 Bear irritations, nuisances, what not, rather than inflict any sudden wound on your friend's self-love. **1875** MANNING *Mission Holy Ghost* v. 130 Self-love..is the abuse and perversion of that love of self which is a divine law.
attrib. **1596** NASHE *Saffron Walden* N 3 b, In thys innouating selfe-loue Age.
2. *Philos.* Regard for one's own well-being or happiness, considered as a natural and proper relation of a man to himself.
1683 D. A. *Art Converse* 1 A rational and lawful sort of Self-love. **1688** NORRIS *Love* I. v. 51 That special sort of Benevolence which we call self-love. **1726** BUTLER *Serm. Rolls Chapel* iii. 55 Conscience and Self-love, if we understand our true Happiness, always lead us the same Way: Duty and Interest are perfectly coincident. **1727** POPE *Thoughts Var. Subj.* in *Misc.* I. 400 Religion is allow'd to be the highest Instance of Self-Love. **1828** D. STEWART *Philos. Powers of Man* II. i. I. 145 Self-love..is inseparable from our nature as rational and sensitive beings. **1883** MAUDSLEY *Body & Will* 166 Self-love is not despicable, but laudable, since duties to self, if self-perfecting..must needs be duties to others.

† **self-'loved,** *ppl. a. Obs.* [SELF- 2.] Loved or cherished by oneself; marked by self-love.
1590 SPENSER *F.Q.* II. iii. 5 Puffed vp with smoke of vanitie, And with selfe-loued personage deceiu'd. **1602** CAMPION *Art Eng. Poesie* 6 Bring before me now any the most selfe-lou'd Rimer. **1621** G. SANDYS *Ovid's Met.* III. Argt., Scorn'd Eccho pines t' a voice: Selfe-lou'd Narcissus to a Daffadill. **1820** SHELLEY *Prometh. Unb.* III. iv. 43 Men ..with..the dull sneer of self-loved ignorance.

† **self-'lover.** *Obs.* [SELF- 1 c.] A lover of self; one who cares for his own interests alone.
1573 L. LLOYD *Marrow of Hist.* (1653) 167 The self lover [doth glory] in some part of his body more then in other. **1594** T. B. *La Primaud. Fr. Acad.* II. 239 Saint Paul [2 Tim. iii. 2] speaking of wicked men that should be in the latter times, saieth first, that they shoulde bee selfe-louers. **1677** GALE *Crt. Gentiles* IV. 120 Self is the last end of self-lovers even in their highest acts of self-denial. **1741** RICHARDSON *Pamela* (1785) IV. 10 A Nurse.. may be careless, and a Self-lover; while a Mother prefers the Health of her Child to her own private Satisfactions.

self-'loving, *ppl. a.* [SELF- 1 f.] Loving or devoted to oneself; seeking one's own interests or advantage; characterized by self-love.
1590 *Broughton's Lett.* ii. 8 Looking your selfe..in this Selflouing glasse. **1607** SHAKS. *Cor.* IV. vi. 32 Insolent, O'recome with Pride, Ambitious, past all thinking Selfe-louing. **1616** B. JONSON *Cynthia's Rev.* ad. fin., From..all selfe-louing humours. *Chorvs.* Good Mercvry defend vs. **1712** STEELE *Spect.* No. 515 ¶1 An happy self-loving dame, that takes all the admiration she can meet with. **1816** BYRON *Sketch* 83 Feel for thy vile self-loving self in vain. **1842** MANNING *Serm.* xxiii. (1848) I. 346 All shallow, petulant, self-loving, boastful men!
Hence † **self-'lovingness.**
a **1628** F. GREVIL *Let. Hon. Lady* i, Those humble natures, that passe away the Fee-simple of themselues, either with Selfe-louingnesse, or superstitious opinion of Duty.

self-'luminous, *a.* [SELF- 3 b.] Possessing in itself the property of emitting light.
1791 HERSCHEL in *Phil. Trans.* LXXXI. 85 If..this matter is self-luminous, it seems more fit to produce a star by its condensation than to depend on the star for its existence. **1831** BREWSTER *Optics* Introd. 1 Self-luminous bodies, such as the stars, flames of all kinds, and bodies which shine by being heated or rubbed. **1876** TAIT *Rec. Adv. Phys. Sci.* x. (ed. 2) 253 The tail of the Comet is not self-luminous.
Hence **self-lumi'nosity.**
1901 *Nature* 4 July 244 Bodies like radium that exhibit self-luminosity in the dark.

† **'selfly,** *a. Obs. rare.* [f. SELF + -LY[1].] **a.** (One's or its) own. **b.** *a* or *one selfly*, one and the same.
1591 SYLVESTER *Du Bartas* I. iii. 402 Severally, and of a selfly motion. *Ibid.* v. 647 [The phœnix] re-ingendred of it's selfly seed. **1598** *Ibid.* II. ii. IV. 730 Where, as (by Art) one selfly blast breath'd out From panting bellows passeth all-about.

† **'selfly,** *adv. Obs.* [f. SELF + -LY[2].]
1. a. Even. **b.** Specially.
c **1532** DU WES *Introd. Fr.* in *Palsgr.* 922 We knowe selfely (*neiz*) the soveraygne lyghtnesse to be darked of a lyght cloude. **1556** *Aurelio & Isab.* M 3 Selfley at this owre whan plaintes and wepinges seakes my.
2. Of or by oneself (or itself); of one's (or its) own accord or motion; spontaneously.
Several times in Sylvester, Sclater, and S. H. *Golden Law.*
1591 SYLVESTER *Du Bartas* I. ii. 1176 Selfly too weak for the least weights foundation. **1595** SOUTHWELL *St. Peter's Compl.* (1602) 8 Selfely dismayd, I neyther fought nor lost, I gaue the field. **1598** SYLVESTER *Du Bartas* II. i. I. 587 A Forrest thick..Which, selfly op'ning [etc.]. **1610** FOLKINGHAM *Art of Survey* I. viii. 18 That ground..which attracts humors and selfely expels them. **1629** W. SCLATER *Expos. 2 Thess.* 211 There is in God, what selfely inclines him to giue, without, and against merit. *Ibid.* 272 He monisheth them, selfely to correct their errors. **1656** S. H. *Golden Law* 4 His Right to the Crown is not Natural, or selfly Hereditary.

self-made, *ppl. a.* [SELF- 2.] Made by oneself, one's own action or efforts; of one's own making.
self-made man, one who has risen from obscurity or poverty by his own exertions. (orig. U.S.)
1615 DANIEL *Hymen's Tri.* Poems (1717) 119 Worshipping A Nothing, but his self-made Images. **1832** *Reg. Deb. Congr. U.S.* 2 Feb. 277 In Kentucky,..every manufactory..is in the hands of enterprising self-made men. **1854** DICKENS *Hard Times* I. iv. 18 Mr. Bounderby.. could never sufficiently vaunt himself a self-made man. **1858** C. C. B. SEYMOUR (*title*) Self-made Men. **1860** PUSEY *Min. Proph.* 422 Self-made blindness. **1870** LOWELL *Study Wind.*, *Gt. Publ. Char.*, We are fond in this country of what are called self-made men. **1870–2** LIDDON *Elem. Relig.* iv. §1 (1904) 136 As a self-made devil differs from an angel. **1890** *Spectator* 25 Jan., Wealth, if it be self-made.
¶ Used as pa. pple. with predicative sb.
1784 COWPER *Tiroc.* 837 Men..Design'd by nature wise, but self-made fools.
Hence **self-'making** *vbl. sb.* and *ppl. a.*
1883 *Blackw. Mag.* 247 The process of self-making..is one of the most interesting at which it is possible to look. **1892** *Q. Rev.* Oct. 326 The ideal to which the average self-making Englishman continues to look up.

self-'mailing, *a. U.S.* [SELF- 1 f.] Designating postal matter that may be folded or otherwise secured, and sent by post without enclosure in an envelope. Also **self-'mailer.**
1950 *Self-mailer, -mailing* in WEBSTER Add. **1963** *Publishers' Weekly* 2 Sept. 28/1 Two types of mailing pieces

have been prepared for the book trade: a self-mailer and a statement enclosure. For the self-mailer, which is a full-color, four-piece unit, the print order is 650,000.

self-main'taining, *ppl. a.* [SELF- 1 f.] That maintains or sustains itself or (oneself); *spec.* = HOMŒOSTATIC *a.*

1879 [see *race-maintaining* s.v. RACE *sb.*² 11]. **1890** W. JAMES *Princ. Psychol.* II. xxvi. 582 If this were the entire nervous mechanism, the movement, once begun, would be self-maintaining. **1933** *Mind* XLII. 146 Immortality demands self-maintaining effort and formed character. **1959** G. D. MITCHELL *Sociol.* vi. 101 It can thus be seen that witchcraft as a system of beliefs and practices is self-maintaining. **1971** J. Z. YOUNG *Introd. Study Man* viii. 115 The whole mass constitutes one single self-maintaining system.

Also **self-'maintenance**.

1867 H. SPENCER *Princ. Biol.* II. VI. ix. 454 Increased cost of self-maintenance entailed decreased power of propagation. **1909** W. JAMES *Pluralistic Universe* iii. 121 The problem of understanding how the complete coherence of all things in the absolute should involve as a necessary moment in its self-maintenance the self-assertion of the finite minds. **1942** *R.A.F. Jrnl.* 13 June 18 Every man has to know something about cooking as a part of his self-maintenance in the field. **1971** J. Z. YOUNG *Introd. Study Man* xi. 143 Continuous replacement is the absolutely necessary condition of self-maintenance.

self-'mass. *Physics.* [SELF- 5 b.] The mass of a particle arising relativistically from its self-energy.

1955 O. KLEIN in W. Pauli *Niels Bohr* 112 Since we are neglecting the interaction between electrons and electromagnetic fields the question of the self-mass does not appear. **1977** *Dædalus* Fall 27 Thus the electron mass found in tables of physical data.. would have to be identified with the bare mass *plus* the infinite 'self mass', produced by the interaction of the electron with its own virtual photon cloud.

self-mate, *sb. Chess.* [SELF- 1 a.] Checkmate produced by the side that is mated. Also as *vb.*

1867 *Chess Player's Mag.* III. 45 The self-mate, though not difficult, is very prettily conceived. **1888** J. A. MILES, etc. (*title*) Chess-stars: a galaxy of self-mates. **1902** *Encycl. Brit.* XXVI. 754/4 White to play and self-mate in three moves.

self-medi'cation. [SELF- 1 a.] Medication carried out on oneself.

1942 *Horizon* June 371 *Le vice anglais* is most certainly and typically self-medication. **1961** *New Scientist* 5 Jan. 16/3 In spite of the National Health Service British pharmacists continue to sell large quantities of preparations for self-medication.

†**self-'minded**, *ppl. a.* [SELF- 3.] Obstinate in one's opinion. So †**self-'mindedness**.

1530 TINDALE *Answ. More* III. xiii. Wks. (1575) 315/1 Opinatiue, selfe-mynded and obstinate. **1579** W. WILKINSON *Confut. Fam. Love* 39 b, The imagination which proceedeth out of the selfemindednes of the outward man.

self-'motion. [SELF- 5 c.] Motion produced by inherent power apart from external impulse; voluntary or spontaneous motion.

[**1591** SYLVESTER *Du Bartas* I. iv. 145 As Car-nails fastned in a wheel (without Selfs-motion) turn with others turns about.] *a* **1619** FOTHERBY *Atheom.* Pref. (1622) p. iij, Ascribing that his inclination, not vnto his owne selfe-motion; but vnto Gods prouidence. **1677** GALE *Crt. Gentiles* IV. 99 By how much the more spontaneous.. the self-motion is, by so much the more free it is judged to be. **1715** CHEYNE *Philos. Princ.* I. 10 Matter is not endow'd with Self-motion. **1788** T. TAYLOR *Proclus* I. Diss. 13 A self-motive nature, which is nothing besides self-motion, is the cause of motion to all things. **1868** BAIN *Ment. & Mor. Sci.* IV. xi. 417 This theory [*sc.* Samuel Clarke's] of self-motion has been severely criticized by Sir W. Hamilton.

self-'motivated, *ppl. a.* [SELF- 2.] Motivated by oneself; *spec.* stimulated to work by one's own enthusiasm and ambition. Also **self-'motivating** *ppl. a.*; **self-moti'vation**.

1973 *Daily Tel.* 27 July 13 (Advt.), Applicants should be ..self-motivating, enthusiastic and determined to succeed. **1974** *Spartanburg* (S. Carolina) *Herald Jrnl.* 20 Apr. B5/1 Secretary. Must be good typist, have good personality and be self-motivated. **1978** *Detroit Free Press* 16 Apr. F6/6 (Advt.), Nationwide meat wholesaler looking for self-motivated people. **1980** *West Lancs. Evening Gaz.* 6 Nov. 15 (Advt.), If you're over 21 with a car and possess the self-motivation and determination to succeed [etc.].

self-'motive, *a.* [SELF- 3 b.] Moving by inherent power, endowed with self-motion.

1676 GLANVILL *Ess. Philos. & Relig.* IV. 9 Beings, self-motive, penetrable and indivisible. **1788** [see prec.]. **1836** I. TAYLOR *Phys. The. another Life* (1857) 55 The most elastic gas is not in itself at all more self-motive than a block of granite.

self-moved, *a.* [SELF- 3 b.] Moved of itself without external agency.

a **1711** KEN *Hymnarium* Poet. Wks. II. 41 What is self-mov'd is unconfin'd. **1831** SCOTT *Ct. Rob.* xiv, As if self-moved, the mystic curtain arose. **1845** LEWES *Hist. Philos.* I. 69 The Soul, being a self-moved monad, is One.

So †**self-'movable** *a.*, = SELF-MOTIVE; †**-'movably** *adv.*; **self-'movement**, = SELF-MOTION; †**self-'movent** *a.*, = SELF-MOTIVE; †**self-'mover**, something that moves itself; an automaton; †**self-'moving** *vbl. sb.*, (*a*) spontaneous motion; (*b*) an automaton; **self-'moving** *ppl. a.*, moving spontaneously or automatically, capable of self-motion.

1642 H. MORE *Song of Soul* II. i. II. xxvi, All these be substances *self-moveable. **1678** CUDWORTH *Intell. Syst.* I. iv. 565 Beings in their own nature Selfmoveable, and Active. *Ibid.* 582 Πάντα ψυχικῶς, All things Animally; that is, *Self-movably, Actively and Productively. **1883** F. H. BRADLEY *Princ. Logic* 448 Want of individuality in the *datum* that we began with, absence of *self-movement and impossibility of self-development, this is the first defect. **1885** *New Engl. Dict., Automaton*... Something which has the power of.. self-movement. **1905** *Athenæum* 1 July 21/2 Self-movement, which has been suggested [as the real touchstone of life]. **1701** GREW *Cosmol. Sacra* I. i. 5 To suppose Body to be Self-Existent..is as absurd, as to suppose it to be *Self-Movent. **1648** WILKINS *Math. Magick* II. i. [heading], The divers kinds of *Automata*, or *Self-movers. *a* **1688** CUDWORTH *Immut. Mor.* IV. ii. §8 The.. Essence and Idea of this Self-Mover, Watch or Horologe. **1740** LAW *Answ. Trapp's Disc.* Wks. 1756 VI. 305 Every intelligent Creature is its own Self-mover. **1583** GOLDING *Calvin on Deut.* ii. 26–37 Their sinnes come of nothing else than their owne *selfemouing. **1587** —— *De Mornay* vii. 100 Things.. which men as thou art doe deeme to be without end, as straunge Milles and Trindles, and such other kind of selfmouings. **1607** J. DAVIES *Summa Totalis* E, Siluer *selfe-mouing we call Siluer-quick. **1655** STANLEY *Hist. Philos.* II. (1687) 64/2 That God is an infinite self-moving mind. **1674** BOYLE *Excell. Theol.* II. iv. 169 A great Automaton or self-moving engine. **1715** CHEYNE *Philos. Princ.* I. 115 Allowing Matter to be self-existent and self-moving. **1825** J. NICHOLSON *Oper. Mech.* 236 A self-moving valve. **1837** KEITH *Bot. Lex.* 341 The self-moving leaves of *Hedysarum gyrans.* **1880** MUIRHEAD *Gaius* iv. §16 Moveable and self-moving things that could be carried or brought into court.

self-'murder, *sb.* [SELF- 1 a.] The taking of one's own life; self-destruction; suicide.

1563–83 FOXE *A. & M.* 2114/1 The wilfull and selfe murder of Pauyer, of Richard Long,.. besides infinite other. **1632** LITHGOW *Trav.* VI. 282 Where Iudas hanged him-selfe ..there is a vault erected.. in memory of his selfe murther. *a* **1715** BURNET *Own Time* III. (1724) I. 553 He [Lord Essex] was found dead; his throat cut... The Coroners Jury found it self-murder. **1741** RICHARDSON *Pamela* (1785) IV. 68 In such a gloomy, saturnine Nation as ours, where Self-murders are more frequent than in all the Christian World besides. **1843** MACAULAY *Ess. Addison* (1865) II. 338 The disciple [Budgell].. closed a wicked and unhappy life by selfmurder. **1898** WATTS-DUNTON *Aylwin* xii, To save me from dying of self-murder or of a broken heart.

transf. *a* **1631** DONNE *Div. Poems, Letanie* i. Wks. (Grosart) II. 298 My hart is by dejection clay, And by selfe-murder redd. **1710** STEELE *Tatler* No. 251 ¶2 We should think it the most unnatural Sort of Self-Murther to sacrifice the Sentiment of the Soul to gratify the Appetites of the Body. **1721** AMHERST *Terræ Fil.* No. 15 (1726) I. 76 When a whole civil society.. destroys itself, it is civil self-murder.

So †**self-'murder** *v.*, **-'murdered** *pa. pple.*, **-'murdering** *ppl. a.*

1648 GAGE *West Ind.* 153 Some have died under their own whipping, and have *selfe murthered themselves. **1716** OLDMIXON in *Ovid's Ep.* 180 My dear Mother there *Self-murder'd lyes. **1725** POPE *Odyss.* XI. 337 The wife self-murder'd from a beam depends. **1590** SPENSER *F.Q.* III. x. 57 Through long anguish, and *selfe-murdring thought. **1692** W. MARSHALL *Gosp. Myst. Sanct.* x. (1764) 166 The wicked, persecuting, self-murdering jailor [Acts xvi. 27].

self-'murderer. [SELF- 1 c.] One who commits self-murder, a suicide, *felo de se.*

The OE. words were *selfbana, selfmyrþra.*

a **1614** DONNE *Βιαθανατος* (1644) 92 He is bound in conscience to steal, and were, in some opinions,.. a selfe-murderer if he stole not. *a* **1674** CLARENDON *Hist. Reb.* XV. §144 His Body was.. buried.. with a Stake driven through him, as is usual in the Case of Self Murtherers. **1769** BLACKSTONE *Comm.* IV. 189 The same argument would prove every other criminal *non compos*, as well as the self-murderer. **1865** BRADDON *Sir Jasper's T.* xviii, You would be sorry that one more self-murderer had gone red-handed to his doom.

'selfness. [f. SELF *sb.* + -NESS.]

1. Self-centredness; egoism; selfishness; †occas. *pl.* selfish acts or manifestations. Rarely in a neutral sense, Due regard for oneself.

a **1586** SIDNEY *Astr. & Stella* Sonn. lxi, Wholly hers all selfenesse he forbeares. *a* **1628** F. GREVIL *Of Hum. Learn.* cxlv. Wks. (1633) 50 A sound foundation, not on sandy parts Of light Opinion, Selfenesse, Words of men. *a* **1628** —— *Sidney* xvii. (1652) 240 This Noble Secretary.. moved, but not removed with those selfenesses of my opinion. **1665** WITHER *Lord's Prayer* 158 That selfness which made the Temptation [of Adam and Eve] prevalent.

1857 EMERSON *Poems* 30 Now, to a savage selfness grown, Think nature barely serves for one. **1883** BEECHER in *Chr. World Pulpit* XXIV. 404 Religion is the power to deliver men from sinful, animal selfishness into a benevolent and other-seeking selfness. **1899** *Q. Rev.* Apr. 433 The magnificent 'self-ness' of his [Byron's] poetry.

2. Individuality, personality, essence. *rare.*

1611 COTGR., *Mesmeté*, selfenesse. **1642** H. MORE *Song of Soul* IV. xxxvi, The most profound and centrall energie, The very selfnesse of the soul. **1651** J. E[LLISTONE] tr. *Behmen's Sign. Rerum* xi. §89 The expressed Mercury must again come unto the End of its selfness [orig. *Selbheit*].

self-'noise. [SELF- 5 b.] Noise generated directly by a particular object.

1953 *Jrnl. Acoustical Soc. Amer.* XXV. 314/2 The self-noise characteristics of this [wind]screen were measured at two wind speeds as a function of the frequency. **1954** L. L. BERANEK *Acoustics* vi. 174 The self-noise produced by an electrostatic microphone is that produced by the d-c resistance of the crystal or dielectric shunted by the capacitance. **1960** *McGraw-Hill Encycl. Sci. & Technol.* XII. 504/1 Self-noise increases rapidly with the speed of the ship. **1975** D. G. FINK *Electronics Engineers' Handbk.* xxv. 125 Self-noise has many directional characteristics..; ambient noise generally has an omni-directional distribution.

†**self-'nothingness.** *Obs.* [SELF- 1 d.] Self-annihilation, self-abasement.

1647 H. MORE *Song of Soul* Notes 373 This valley of *Ain* is nothing else but self deadnesse, or rather self-nothingnesse. **1677** GALE *Crt. Gentiles* IV. 31 It doth lift the heart above al things create and yet at the same time depresse it at the lowest centre of self-nothingnesse.

self-noughting. Also **-naughting.** [SELF- 1 b.] Depreciation or effacement of oneself, as manifested in the lives of saints and mystics. (Probably derived by E. Underhill from Hilton's *Scale of Perfection*: see quot. *a* 1400 s.v. NOUGHTING *vbl. sb.*)

1911 E. UNDERHILL *Mysticism* ix. 477 The 'self-naughting' or 'purification of the will', which here takes place, is the struggle to resolve that disharmony. **1937** *Mind* XLVI. 91 We remember what has been written by writers such as those cited above about self-surrender, submission and self-noughting or annihilation. **1959** *Month* Dec. 331 This is the true self-noughting, to know oneself incapable of any good. **1976** H. A. WILLIAMS *Tensions* v. 89 Through this discovery of our true identity in God and the self-naughting which inevitably accompanies it, we become truly ourselves.

self-observation. [SELF- 1 a.] Objective observation of one's attitudes, reactions, or thought processes.

1832 J. S. MILL in *Monthly Repos.* VI. 652 The knowledge of supersensual things, of man's mental and moral nature, where the appeal is to internal consciousness and self-observation. **1865** —— *Comte* 63 It is clear to him that we can learn very little about the feelings, and nothing at all about the intellect, by self-observation. **1948** *Mind* LVII. 511 [Social scientists].. making use of.. official statistics.., interviews of various types.., and new techniques of self-observation. **1977** METTEE & SMITH in Suls & Miller *Social Comparison Processes* iv. 98 A theory.. based on self-observation of one's own behavior rather than on observation and comparison with.. others.

†**selfode, selfoder.** *Obs. local.* [Of obscure origin.] A class of tenant in Northumberland and Cumberland.

In quot. 1290–1 *selfode* is app. fem. and may denote the holding, not the tenant.

1271 *Inquis. post mortem* 55 *Hen. III*, N. 33 in Vinogradoff *Vill. in Eng.* 250 Redditarii qui vocantur selfoders. **1290–1** in *N. & Q.* Ser. IX. VII. 89/1 [Eglingham, Nhbld.] De qualibet selfode iij dietas vel iij denarios, exceptis selfod' propriis Joh'i de Somervile in terra sua comorantibus. **1378** *Rentale de Tynemuth* in Brand *Hist. Newcastle* (1789) II. 594 Omnes selfodes facient quilibet tres precar' tantum.

self-o'ffence. *rare.*

1. [SELF- 3 a.] Damage or injury to oneself.

a **1628** F. GREVIL *Cælica* c, Feare.. Confounds all powers, and thorough selfe-offence, Doth forge and raise impossibility. **1671** MILTON *Samson* 515 Self-displeas'd For self-offence, more then for God offended.

b. Attack upon oneself.

1819 SHELLEY *Cenci* V. i. 101 A word ? which those of this false world Employ against each other, not themselves; As men wear daggers not for self-offence.

2. [SELF- 5 a.] One's own offence.

1603 SHAKS. *Meas. for M.* III. ii. 280 More, nor lesse to others paying, Then by selfe-offences weighing.

†**self-o'ffender.** *Obs.* [SELF- 5.] A self-willed offender.

c **1661** *Papers on Alter. Prayer-bk.* 70 Will you call men obstinate self offenders that differ from you?

†**self-one**, *a. Obs. rare.* [SELF- 3 a.] ? Alone with itself.

1602 MARSTON *Antonio's Rev.* II. iii, A selfe-one guilt doth onely hatch distrust.

self-'open. *northern.* [SELF- 3 b. Cf. OPEN *sb.* 1 d.] A miners' term for a natural cavity met with in digging.

1683–4 LISTER in *Phil. Trans.* XIV. 512 That the Earth is more or less hollow is made probable, by what is found every where in the Mountains; viz. Natural Cavities or Chambers, which the Miners of the North call *Self-opens.* [**1748** *Earthquake Peru* i. 118.] **1824** MANDER *Derbysh. Miner's Gloss.*, Self-opens. Natural Fissures in the stone.

self-'opened, *pa. pple.* [SELF- 3 b.] Opened of its own accord.

1667 MILTON *P.L.* v. 254 The gate self-opend wide On golden Hinges turning. *c* **1820** S. ROGERS *Italy* (1839) 13 The door which ever, as self-opened, moves To them that knock. **1824** HOOD *Two Swans* xix, A little casement... Widens self-open'd into the cool air. **1855** BAILEY *Mystic*, etc. 162 Self-opened like a magic book.

So **self-'opening** *ppl. a.*

1833 LOUDON *Encycl. Archit.* Index, Self-opening gate. **1895** *Army & Navy Soc. Price List* 15 Sept. 1403 The 'Ideal' patent self-opening pocket knife.

self-o'piniated, *ppl. a.* [Formed after SELF-OPINION.] = SELF-OPINIONATED.

1627 SIR S. D'EWES *Jrnl.* (1783) 63 He being proud and selfe-opiniated, tooke his owne way. **1868** J. H. BLUNT *Ref. Ch. Eng.* I. 84 Such conceited and self-opiniated men.

Hence **self-o'piniatedly** *adv.*; so †**self-o'piniating** *a.*; **self-o'piniativeness** (cf. SELF-OPINIONATIVENESS).

1651 HOBBES *Govt. & Soc.* Author's Pref., [I] would rather chuse to brooke with patience some inconveniences.. then *selfe opiniatedly disturb the quiet of the publique.

1632 LITHGOW *Trav.* x. 490 Peeuish and *selfe-opiniating Puritanes. **1889** SKRINE *Mem. Thring* 120 Disputants put this down to *self-opiniativeness.

self-o'pinion. Now *rare.* [SELF- 1 d.] High opinion of oneself, self-esteem; esp. overweening estimate of oneself, self-conceit; obstinacy in one's own opinion.

1579-80 NORTH *Plutarch, Coriol.* (1595) 243 Wilfully giuen to a selfe opinion and obstinate minde. **1586** A. DAY *Eng. Secretary* I. (1625) 11 Rather equity than selfe-opinion must and ought chiefly to be weighed. **1676** DRYDEN *Aurengz.* Ep. Ded. 7, I have labour'd.. to divest my self of the self-opinion of an Author. **1712** STEELE *Spect.* No. 443 ¶5 Fortunatus is stocked with Ignorance, and consequently with Self-Opinion. **1818** SCOTT *Rob Roy* vi, I should be sorry to shock your self-opinion, but you were never more mistaken. **1858** BUSHNELL *Serm. New Life* xxi. (1860) 297 The veils of pride are rent, the rock of self-opinion is shattered. **1876** GEO. ELIOT *Dan. Der.* xxiii, Her self-opinion rallied,..she was tempted to think that his judgment was not only fallible but biassed.

†**self-o'pinionate,** *ppl. a. Obs.* = next.

1602 MARSTON *Ant. & Mel.* III. Wks. 1856 I. 36 Th' other learned, but selfe-opinionate. **1651** BP. HALL *Soliloquies* xliv, We all are born proud and selfopinionate.

self-o'pinionated, *ppl. a.* [f. SELF-OPINION.]

1. Having an exaggerated opinion of oneself; self-conceited.

1671 STILLINGFL. *Serm.* viii. Wks. 1710 I. 114 There never was a nation more self-opinionated as to their wisdom, goodness, and interest with God. **1674** BOYLE *Excell. Theol.* II. v. 187 Most men are so self-opinionated, that they will easily believe themselves masters of things, if they do but half understand them. **1825** HAZLITT *Spirit of Age* 372 He is no formalist, not he! All is crude and chaotic, self-opinionated, vain.

2. Obstinate in one's opinion.

1770 LANGHORNE *Plutarch* (1879) II. 590 A body of Germans, who were so rash and self-opinionated as to separate from the troops of Spartacus. **1857** TOULMIN SMITH *Parish* 148 Self-opinionated doctrinairism. **1868** J. H. BLUNT *Ref. Ch. Eng.* I. 538 The young priest was far too self-opinionated to yield to argument.

Hence **self-o'pinionatedness**; so **self-o'pinionative** *a.*, **self-o'pinionativeness.**

1730 BAILEY (fol.), *Affectation*, Affectedness, Conceitedness, *Self-opinionatedness. **1888** GORE *R.C. Claims* viii. 119 The temper of self-opinionatedness. **1904** H. BLACK *Pract. Self-Culture* viii. 225 A man *self-opinionative and harsh. **1857** PUSEY *Real Presence* i. (1869) 65 Whose docility, unspoiled by any *self-opinionativeness.

self-o'pinioned, *ppl. a.* [f. SELF-OPINION.] = SELF-OPINIATED.

1624 MASSINGER *Parlt. Love* III. i, This self-opinioned fool. **1692** SOUTH *Serm.* (1697) 355 A bold, self-opinion'd Physician. **1794** ELLIOT in *14th Rep. Hist. MSS. Comm.* App. v. 578 He argues closely, but is long-winded and self-opinioned. **1822** SCOTT *Nigel* i, An ingenious, but whimsical and self-opinioned mechanic. **1903** *Westm. Gaz.* 2 Dec. 12/1 Nobody could have been less self-opinioned, and indeed if he made a suggestion it was with a half-apology.

Hence **self-o'pinionedness.**

1879 *Daily News* 22 Oct. 6/5 A peculiar kind of religious self-opinionedness sprang up.

self-orien'tation. [SELF- 1 a.]

1. The orientation or directing of one's actions or attitudes for oneself or by oneself.

a **1896** G. DU MAURIER *Martian* (1897) vi. 250 The feeling of self-orientation which was so necessary to him. **1936** WIRTH & SHILS tr. *Mannheim's Ideol. & Utopia* i. 22 To the extent that mechanistic psychology and..the social impulsion towards all-embracing mechanization, negated these values, they destroyed an important element in the self-orientation of human beings in their everyday life.

2. *Social Psychol.* Underlying motivation that orients one's behaviour primarily towards what concerns oneself.

1951 PARSONS & SHILS *Toward Gen. Theory of Action* i. 77 We maintain that there are only five basic pattern variables. .. They are..2. Self-orientation—Collective orientation. **1964** GOULD & KOLB *Dict. Soc. Sci.* 489/1 In applying the moral mode of value-orientation, the actor must choose between action for private goals (self-orientation) and action on behalf of collective goals (collectivity-orientation).

Also **self-'oriented** *ppl. a.*

1936 *Mind* XLV. 72 Mr Leon holds, with Butler if not with Plato, that all the natural appetites, though self-oriented, are in themselves innocent. **1975** R. H. RIMMER *Premar Experiments* (1976) i. 49 At first the child is completely self-oriented, autistic, hedonistic.

self-o'riginal, *a.* [SELF- 3 b.] Having its origin in itself.

1704 S. CLARK *Demonstr. Being & Attrib. God* (1760) 27 Self-original Independent Existence.

†**self-o'riginate,** *ppl. a. Obs.* = next.

1668 HOWE *Bless. Righteous* xi, Its perfections were not self-originate. **1732** BERKELEY *Minute Philos.* I. 160 The.. independent, self-originate Cause and Source of all Beings.

self-o'riginated, *pa. pple.* and *ppl. a.* [SELF- 2.] Originated by oneself (itself).

1677 GALE *Crt. Gentiles* IV. 229 That they are not self-originated, but had some beginning in prime Motors. *a* **1711** KEN *Hymnarium* Poet. Wks. II. 47 O Self-originated Might, Thou All-creating Infinite. **1852** GROTE *Greece* II. lxx. IX. 103 A..self-originated stimulus. **1871** FRASER *Berkeley* ii. 27 Thoughts, self-originated, or immediately occasioned by reading.

So **self-o'riginating** *ppl. a.*; **self-origi'nation**; **self-'origined** *pa. pple.*, = SELF-ORIGINATED.

1833 J. H. NEWMAN *Arians* I. v. (1876) 127 To discriminate between the Son and His underived *self-originating Father. **1854** MILMAN *Lat. Chr.* I. 129 A personal, spontaneous, self-originating and self-maintained surrender to evil influences. **1715** CHEYNE *Philos. Princ.* I. 175 By Self-existence here I mean *Self-origination. *a* **1866** J. GROTE *Exam. Utilit. Philos.* xi. (1870) 177 The view..that there can be nothing in it [*sc.* moral action] of free self-origination. *a* **1711** KEN *Hymnarium* Poet. Wks. II. 40 From God *self-origin'd.

self-osci'llation. *Electronics.* [SELF- 3 b.] The generation of continuous oscillations in a circuit, amplifier, etc., in circumstances of excessive positive feedback.

1921 J. SCOTT-TAGGART *Thermionic Tubes* vi. 204 The potentiometer..if suitably adjusted, will effectually prevent self-oscillation. **1943** K. R. STURLEY *Radio Receiver Design* I. viii. 394 As the coupling between anode circuit and input is increased a point is reached where self-oscillation occurs. **1963** B. FOZARD *Instrumentation Nuclear Reactors* x. 118 Feedback may be defined as positive, in which case it produces an increase in gain and may lead to instability and self-oscillation.

Hence **self-'oscillate** *v. intr.*, to display self-oscillation; **self-'oscillating** *ppl. a.*

1928 L. S. PALMER *Wireless Princ. & Pract.* ix. 328 Similar trouble arises when unstable receiving circuits self-oscillate accidentally. **1962** SIMPSON & RICHARDS *Physical Princ. Junction Transistors* xviii. 459 Such a circuit..is called a self-oscillating mixer or a frequency converter stage.

†**self-'partial,** *a. Obs. rare.* [SELF- 3 a.] Favourable to one's own interests.

1591 SYLVESTER *Du Bartas* I. vii. 702 O do not, through self-partiall zeal, With light-brain'd Counsels vex your Common-weale.

self-parti'ality. Now *rare*; common *c* 1725–1865. [SELF- 3 a.] Partiality or favourable disposition towards oneself; excessive regard for one's own interests; self-love.

1628 FELTHAM *Resolves* II. xxxix. 119, I know not what selfe-partialitie, makes vs thinke our selues behind-hand, if wee offer not repayment in the same coine wee receiu'd it. **1658** OSBORN *Q. Eliz.* Ep. A 4 b, Any acquired advantage.. self-partiality or others indulgence hath..been able to estate me in. **1726** BUTLER *Serm. Rolls Chapel* x. 189 Hardness of Heart with respect to others, joined with this Self-partiality. **1802-12** BENTHAM *Ration. Judic. Evid.* (1827) IV. 418 Self-partiality draws from each of them such of the facts as promise to operate in favour of his claim. **1868** BAIN *Ment. & Mor. Sci.* 600 We have our self-partialities, but have learnt the value of equity.

self-'perfect, *a.* [SELF- 3 b.] Perfect in oneself.

1610 HEALEY *St. Aug. Citie of God* 308 Alcinous saith that God is supreme, eternall, ineffable, self-perfect.

self-per'fecting, *vbl. sb.* [SELF- 1.] = SELF-PERFECTION 2. So **self-per'fecting** *ppl. a.*, leading to self-perfection.

1883 [see SELF-LOVE 2]. **1908** *Daily Chron.* 6 Jan. 4/4 In self-perfecting there is something personal, something gratifying to self-love.

self-per'fection.

†**1.** [SELF- 5 a.] Inherent perfection. *Obs.*

1628 FELTHAM *Resolves* II. ix. 22 Shee was of such a selfe-perfection; that she might very well embleme, whatsoeuer omnipotency could make most rare.

2. [SELF- 1 b.] The perfecting of one's character, life, etc. *U.S.*

1837 HT. MARTINEAU *Soc. Amer.* III. 49 In the days when mutual and self-perfection will be the prevalent idea which the civilisation of the time will express. **1905** E. B. HOLT tr. *Münsterberg's Americans* 355 In Puritan America the soul's welfare stood in the foreground, and only secondarily was the striving for self-perfection, self-searching, and self-culture made to contribute to the advance of objective culture.

Hence **self-per'fectionating** *ppl. a.*, **self-per'fectionment** (in recent Dicts.).

1858 J. MARTINEAU *Stud. Chr.* 144 No self-perfectionating process..has warmth enough to ripen the soul's diviner fruits.

self-'pity. [SELF- 1 d.] Pity or tender feeling for oneself.

1621 G. SANDYS *Ovid's Met.* v. (1632) 182 She tare, Without selfe-pitty, her dis-heueled haire. **1647** H. MORE *Philos. Poems, Insomn. Philos.* xxii, They would forsake This work of God, and out of dear self-pitty Fly from the creatures. *a* **1711** KEN *Christophil* Poet. Wks. I. 504 Not thy pure Will, not thy nice Sense of Pain, Cou'd Self-indulgence, or Self-pity gain. **1859** BAIN *Emotions & Will* viii. 135 Self-pity,..often very strong in the sentimentally selfish, but quite real in all who have any tender susceptibilities. **1885-94** R. BRIDGES *Eros & Psyche* Apr. viii, Disconsolate, and with self-pity pined. **1899** CROCKETT *Kit Kennedy* xxx, Self-pity is bad at any time. It is fatal at twelve.

attrib. *a* **1628** F. GREVIL *Alaham* v. ii, This innocent.. With his selfe-pitty teares, drew teares from vs.

So **self-'pitiful** *a.*, **-'pitifulness; self-'pitying** *ppl. a.*; **self-'pityingly** *adv.*

1754 RICHARDSON *Grandison* V. xxxiv. 217, I should have thought myself concerned,..to have expatiated on the self-pitying reflexion conveyed in these words. **1880** G. MEREDITH *Tragic Com.* viii, The necessity for draining her of her self-pitifulness. *Ibid.*, In the morning she was a dried channel of tears, no longer self-pitiful. **1899** MACKAIL *W. Morris* II. 66 'I feel a lonely kind of a chap', he says of himself..half self-pityingly. **1927** C. CONNOLLY *Let.* 1 Jan. in *Romantic Friendship* (1975) 205 Propertius too self-pitying and conceited really to suffer. *a* **1974** R. CROSSMAN *Diaries* (1976) II. 266 Over the weekend I'd been a bit self-pitying and not merely defeatist but defeated.

self-pleased, *ppl. a.* [SELF- 3 a.] Pleased with oneself; self-complacent.

1748 RICHARDSON *Clarissa* VI. lxxxvi. 311 How, self-pleased, she could smile round. **1825** T. HOOK *Sayings* Ser. II. *Man of Many Fr.* I. 283 She quitted the sofa she had been unwillingly sharing with the self-pleased beau. **1904** DOWDEN *Browning* 56 The self-pleased, keen-sighted Legate.

†**self-'pleaser.** *Obs.* [SELF- 1 c.] One who does his own 'pleasure'.

1582 *Bible* (Rheims) 2 Pet. ii. 10 Them whiche.. contemne dominion, bold, self-pleasers [Vulg. *sibi placentes*, Gr. αὐθάδεις, 1611 selfe willed]. **1632** SANDERSON *Serm.* II. 18 S. Peters word..signifieth as much as self-pleasers.

self-'pleasing, *vbl. sb.* [SELF- 1 b.]

1. Doing one's own 'pleasure' or will.

1681 OWEN *Humble Test.* 89 All Self-seeking, and Self-pleasing,..must utterly be cast away. **1842** MANNING *Serm.* vii. (1848) I. 98 The greater number of men live lives of mere self-pleasing.

2. Self-complacency.

1856 EMERSON *Eng. Traits, Cockayne*, Their culture generally enables the travelled English to avoid any ridiculous extremes of this self-pleasing.

So **self-'pleasing** *ppl. a.*

1590 SPENSER *F.Q.* III. iv. 6 With such selfe-pleasing thoughts her wound she fed. **1607-12** BACON *Ess., Marriage & Single Life* (Arb.) 266 Self pleasing, and humorous mindes. **1735** POPE *Prol. Sat.* 90 Who shames a Scribbler? break one cobweb thro', He spins the slight, self-pleasing thread anew. **1818** *Brit. Rev.* XII. 191 His vanity and self-pleasing activity. **1855** KINGSLEY *Westw. Ho!* xi, All the trickeries of self-pleasing sorrow.

self-poise. *U.S.* [f. next: cf. POISE *sb.*[1]] The condition or property of being self-poised.

1854 'GRACE GREENWOOD' *Haps & Mishaps* 3 A maturity of thought.., a self-poise about him, which impress you. **1860** EMERSON *Cond. Life, Worship* Wks. (Bohn) II. 394 A self-poise belongs to every particle. **1884** *Century Mag.* Jan. 453/2 Excellent qualifications for either soldier or citizen —self-poise, a quick intelligence, close application.

self-poised, *ppl. a.* [SELF- 3 b.] Poised or balanced by its own unaided power or without support. Also *fig.* of persons, their actions, etc.

1621 G. SANDYS *Ovid's Met.* I. (1626) 1 Nor hung the selfe-poiz'd Earth in thin Ayre plac't. **1776** MICKLE tr. *Camoens' Lusiad* x. 442 Each movement still beginning, still compleat, It's Author's type, self poised, perfection's seat. **1802** WORDSW. *To a Butterfly* 2 I've watched you now a full half-hour, Self-poised upon that yellow flower. **1838** TUPPER *Proverb. Philos.* Ser. I. *Of Subjection* 7 The self-poised character of God. **1875** LONGF. *Masque of Pandora* iv, Thy form Self-poised as if it floated on the air.

Hence **self-'poisedness.**

1848 *Westm. Rev.* XLIX. 339 This favourite notion of man's self-poisedness.

self-polli'nation. [SELF- 1 a.] The deposition on a stigma of pollen from stamens within the same flower or another flower on the same plant.

1872 *Jrnl. Bot.* X. 25 Hildebrand has shown that sometimes, where at first sight self-pollenation [*sic*] (a better word, I think for '*Bestäubung*', than 'pollenization', suggested by Mr. Bennett) seems to be the intention of Nature, this is not followed by fertilization. **1876** G. HENSLOW in *Nature* 19 Oct. 544/1 The pistil recovers itself, and its growth is equal to or precedes that of the stamens, the result issuing in a synchronous maturity, and consequently self-pollination. **1974** A. HUXLEY *Plant & Planet* xiii. 124 A fail-safe device, such as..self-pollination as a last resort.

Hence **self-'pollinate** *v. trans.*; **self-'pollinated** *ppl. a.*, **-'pollinating** *vbl. sb.* and *ppl. a*; **self-'pollinator**, a species which commonly shows self-pollination.

1890 J. R. A. DAVIS *Flowering Plant* ix. 130 Regularly self-pollinated flowers are characterized by inconspicuousness. *Ibid.*, All this [*sc.* absence of scent and nectar, inconspicuousness, etc.] is carried to the extreme in cleistogamous flowers, i.e., minute self-pollinating ones, which never open. **1933** *Jrnl. R. Hort. Soc.* LVIII. 283 At first the trees were too young to yield reliable results by crossing and self-pollinating. *Ibid.* 358 Hips developed freely, but even in those which were self-pollinated rarely more than one achene was formed. **1960** *McGraw-Hill Encycl. Sci. & Technol.* VIII. 223/1 A second generation, bred by self-pollinating the hybrid. **1961** WEBSTER, Self-pollinator. **1977** *Nature* 2 June 402/2 It was suggested that some of the Mediterranean floras..evolved..from cross-into self-pollinators because insects could not have followed the new hardy plants into the hot dry environment. **1979** *Ibid.* 25 Oct. 671/2 This species is self-incompatible (1978 seed sets of self-pollinated flowers on five bagged plants compared with those of open-pollinated flowers on eight unbagged plants were 0.3 ± 0.08 ($n = 256$) compared with 7.1 ± 0.71 ($n = 43$)).

self-po'llution. [SELF- 1 a.] Masturbation, self-abuse.

1626 R. BERNARD *Isle of Man* (1627) 77 Fornication, Selfe-pollution, &c. **1733** *Ordinary of Newgate* No. 1 Advt., Self-Pollution (that cursed School Wickedness). **1829** *Good's Study Med.* (ed. 3) III. 240 Two young men who had induced the same disease by a habit of self-pollution.

Hence **self-po'lluter.**

1797 *Encycl. Brit.* (ed. 3) XIII. 214/1 In scripture..we find self-polluters termed *effeminate, unclean.*

self-'portrait. [tr. G. *selbstbildnis, selbstporträt*; cf. SELF- 1 d.] A self-made portrait of oneself. Cf. PORTRAIT *sb.* 1 b and 3 b.

1831 *Fraser's Mag.* Mar. 129/1 The two self-portraits, so far as they are filled up, may be looked upon as real likenesses. **1896** *Academy* 25 Apr. 350/3 A self-portrait of the artist in the act of drawing. **1919** *Q. Rev.* Oct. 322 The high society of the 17th century had shown their taste for an analysis of this kind in their self-portraits. **1975** *Amer. N. & Q.* XIV. 58/2 G. C. Williamson, *English Conversation Pictures of the Eighteenth and Early Nineteenth Centuries*.. provides a self-portrait of an era. **1977** R. L. WOLFF *Gains & Losses* vii. 413 As an authentic portrait (and self-portrait) of the late 1840's.. *Oakfield* has no equal.

Also **self-'portraiture**.

1847 BAGEHOT in *Prospective Rev.* III. 532 Nor without the will can the self-scrutinizing power show to men those startling self-portraitures. **1979** *Dædalus* Summer 89 The self-portraiture is but the further elaboration of a thought that was from the outset oriented toward personal life.

self-po'ssessed, *ppl. a.* [Formed after SELF-POSSESSION; see SELF- 2.] Characterized by self-possession.

1818 SCOTT *Heart Midl.* I. vii. 228 He.. came forward to meet him, with a self-possessed, and even dignified air. **1838** LYTTON *Alice* I. v, Tall, self-possessed, and dressed plainly indeed. **1848** DICKENS *Dombey* xxi, She was not embarrassed, but wholly self-possessed. **1897** 'H. S. MERRIMAN' *In Kedar's Tents* iii, The voice was clear and low, remarkably self-possessed.

Hence **self-po'ssessedly** *adv.*

1893 *Cornh. Mag.* July 2 She received the ovation self-possessedly.

self-po'ssessing, *ppl. a. rare.* [f. after next.] = SELF-POSSESSED.

1789 BURKE *Corr.* (1844) III. 20 To dare to be fearful, when all about you are full of presumption and confidence.. discovers a self-possessing and collected character. **1863** M. BRYDIE *Tabl. Geol.*, etc. 54 A quiet, self-possessing mind.

self-po'ssession. [SELF- 1 d.] Command of one's faculties or feelings; self-command, composure.

1745 J. MASON *Self-Knowl.* II. i. (1853) 135 To preserve an Equanimity and Self-possession under all the various scenes of Adversity and Prosperity. **1821** SCOTT *Kenilw.* xv, The youth underwent the gaze of Majesty, not the less gracefully that his self-possession was mingled with embarrassment. **1878** GLADSTONE *Prim. Hom.* 112 The self-possession and self-command of every Greek are perfect.

transf. **1859** LANG *Wand. India* 314 A low flight of steps on which the ponies pass up and down with extraordinary self-possession.

self-praise. [SELF- 1 a.] Praise or commendation of oneself.

1549 CHALONER *Erasm. on Folly* A ij, Unles perhaps some be better acquainted with me, then this my self-prayse (as me seemeth) I maie well take vpon me. **1662** *Mr. Hobbes considered* 57 That part of his self-praise which most offends you is in the end of his Leviathan. **1725** *Pope's Odyss.* VIII. Notes II. 225 Self-praise is sometimes no fault. **1826** *Cobbett's Reg.* LVIII. 743/1 In general it is a good rule.. that self-praise is no commendation. **1848** THACKERAY *Van. Fair* xxxv, Osborne broke out into a rhapsody of self-praise and imprecations. **1856** GROTE *Hist. Greece* II. xciv. XII. 260 These and other self-praises disparaging to the glory of Alexander.

So **self-praised** *pa. pple.*

1621 G. SANDYS *Ovid's Met.* VI. (1626) 110 A Stork; who, with white pinions rais'd, Is euer by her creaking bill selfe-prais'd.

self-preser'vation. [SELF- 1 a.] The preservation of one's existence; *esp.* applied to the natural law or instinct which impels living creatures to take measures to prolong life and avoid injury.

a **1614** DONNE *Βιαθανατος* (1644) A A, It is onely upon this reason, that selfe-preservation is of Naturall Law. **1671** MILTON *Samson* 505 If the punishment Thou canst avoid, self-preservation bids. **1681** DRYDEN *Span. Friar* IV. ii, Self-preservation is the first of laws. **1776** GIBBON *Decl. & F.* ii. I. 40 Against such internal enemies.. the most severe regulations, and the most cruel treatment, seemed almost justified by the great law of self-preservation. **1875** GLADSTONE *Glean.* (1879) III. 172 Both the instinct of self-preservation and the laws of duty combine in prompting them to put off the evil day.

So **self-pre'servative, self-pre'servatory** *adjs.*, **self-pre'serving** *ppl. a.*; †**self-pre'servingly** *adv.*, so as to save oneself trouble.

1839 *Times* 29 July 4/2 Every creature has its *self-preservative instinct. **1871** R. H. HUTTON *Ess.* iii. (1877) I. 45 The self-preservative correspondence between internal and external changes. **1885** H. O. FORBES *Natur. Wand.* III. viii. 254 My rower righted it by a *self-preservatory act. **1669** HOPKINS *Serm. 1 Pet.* 13, 14 (1685) 34 Upon.. *self-preserving Principles, Submission may sometimes be yielded to the lawful Commands of an unlawful.. Power. **1735** SOMERVILLE *Chace* II. 503 Others, whom Fear Inspires with self-preserving Wiles. **1837** CARLYLE *Fr. Rev.* III. II. v, A traitorous self-preserving Court. **1654** GAYTON *Pleas. Notes* III. viii. 123 It was.. more *selfe-preservingly done to leave him to the Sarcasmes of his Book, then by a shoulder-experience to have learn'd how to write a literall invective against him.

self-pride. [SELF- 3 a.] Pride in oneself, one's achievements, one's position; personal pride.

a **1586** SIDNEY *Arcadia* (1622) 289 Puffing them vp by being besought, with such a selfe-pride of superiority. **1632** STRAFFORD in Browning *Life* (1891) 301 That self pride which hath to our owne esteeme, represented vs much bigger.. then in deed ther is cause for. **1729** LAW *Serious C.* xviii. 341 Banish.. every thought of self-pride and self-distinction. **1822** COLTON *Lacon* II. cxxxviii. 104 This Self-pride is the common friend of our humanity. **1865** FLOR. MARRYAT *Love's Confl.* xxxix, George Treherne's self-pride came to his aid in this place, and stood him in the stead of virtue. **1907** *Ch. Q. Rev.* July 471 To gratify private pride and self-interest in the first case, then the self-pride of the Suprema.

self'quained, *ppl. a. nonce-wd.* [SELF- 2; cf. QUAIN *v.*²] Having natural angles or corners.

1888 G. M. HOPKINS *Poems* (1967) 199 A coffer, burly all of blocks Built of chancequarriéd, selfquainèd, hoar-huskèd rocks.

self-'quenching, *ppl. a.* (*vbl. sb.*) [SELF- 1 f, b.] Having within itself a cause of quenching. Also as *vbl. sb.*, quenching that occurs spontaneously. Also **self-'quenched** *ppl. a.*, self-quenching.

1936 *Rev. Sci. Instruments* VII. 31/1 When the discharge is self-quenched, the total charge passed through the counter is directly proportional to the primary ionization. **1940** *Physical Rev.* LVII. 1035/2 All counters are self-quenching if they overshoot, and if they do not, the inherent instability of the discharge will cause the discharge to be extinguished. **1946** *Ibid.* LXIX. 689/2 A study was made of the characteristics of self-quenched G-M counters filled with mixtures of argon and 28 different organic vapors. **1959** F. W. WILSON *Tool Engineer's Handbk.* (ed. 2) xv. 27 With extremely rapid heating rates and shallow heating, the mass of the part may conduct heat away fast enough to quench the part suitably. This is termed 'self-quenching'. **1963** B. FOZARD *Instrumentation Nuclear Reactors* v. 51 If bromine.. is added to the neon-argon mixture, satisfactory operation as a self-quenching counter is achieved. **1970** D. L. HORROCKS in E. D. Bransome *Liquid Scintillation Counting* 36/2 Self-quenching seems to occur in molecules that have unprotected, coplanar chromophores so that there can be a complete mirror image overlap of the chromophores of the excited and unexcited solute molecules. **1971** *Gloss. Electrotechnical, Power Terms (B.S.I.)* III. i. 32 *Self-quenching oscillator*, a generator of short trains of oscillations, the trains being separated by intervals of quiescence caused by the accumulation of electric charge in a capacitor in the circuit.

self-raised, *pa. pple.* and *ppl. a.* [SELF- 2.] Raised by oneself, by one's own power; (of a plant) grown without human aid.

1647 tr. *Behmen's Clavis* §54 The most Inward ground, wherein, the selfe raised [*marg.* Or owne arisen] will bringeth it selfe, by a reception, into somethingnesse. **1667** MILTON *P.L.* I. 634 That all these puissant Legions.. shall faile to re-ascend Self-rais'd. *Ibid.* 858 Self-begot, self-rais'd By our own quick'ning power. **1852** G. W. JOHNSON *Cottage Gard. Dict.* s.v. *Rosemary*, When the plants are self-raised on an old wall. **1872** MORLEY *Voltaire* (1886) 6 The self-raised spontaneous products of some miraculous soil.

self-'raising, *ppl. a.* [SELF- 3 b.] Applied to a kind of flour which causes dough or paste to rise without the addition of baking-powder, etc.

1854 *Daily Placer Times & Transcript* (San Francisco) 7 Mar. 1/4 Among the advantages of the Self-Raising Flour, are: The saving of time in preparing it for the oven, [etc.]. **1869–71** *Cassell's Househ. Guide* IV. 14 Richardson's Tryphena, or Self-raising Flour. **1875** *Encycl. Brit.* III. 256/1.

self-'rating, *vbl. sb. Psychol.* [SELF- 1 b.] Rating of one's own attributes, feelings, or behaviour; an instance of this.

1938 G. W. ALLPORT *Personality* xvi. 444 In self-rating there is a tendency to overestimate those qualities considered desirable and to underestimate those considered undesirable. **1945** *Jrnl. Clin. Psychol.* I. 297/1 The second approach to verbal self-ratings.. consists simply in the.. assertion that a 'self-rating' constitutes an intrinsically interesting and significant bit of verbal behavior. **1958** M. ARGYLE *Relig. Behaviour* x. 124–5 Several investigators have examined the factors associated with marital happiness or 'adjustment'—this being measured by means of self-ratings. **1972** *Jrnl. Social Psychol.* LXXXVI. 121 Some researchers have gone beyond this correlational approach to include self-ratings and peer ratings.

selfre: see SILVER.

self-reali'zation. *Philos.* [SELF- 1 a.] The fulfilment by one's own efforts of the possibilities of development of the self.

1874 W. WALLACE *Logic of Hegel* xxi. p. clx, This process.. may be called self-realisation (or development). **1876** F. H. BRADLEY *Eth. Studies* ii. 59 What remains is to point out the most general expression for the end in itself, the ultimate practical 'why'; and that we find in the word *self-realization*. *Ibid.* 75 There is self-realization in all action. **1907** ILLINGWORTH *Doctr. Trin.* xii. 245 This realisation for which the Christian looks, while it is the realization of himself, is not self-realisation. For.. it is not in the last resort his own achievement, but the gift of God.

self-'reference. [SELF- 3 a.] Reference to oneself or itself; the direction of one's attention at oneself, esp. in forming a comparative assessment of one's characteristics or experience; *spec.* in *Philos.*, the characteristic or quality of referring to itself contained in certain paradoxes, propositions, or statements.

1910 WHITEHEAD & RUSSELL *Principia Math.* I. ii. 64 In all the above contradictions.. there is a common characteristic, which we may describe as self-reference or reflexiveness. **1943** *Mind* LII. 20 Man is a microcosm of *Natura*, and his self-reference involves him therefore only in partial impotence. **1952** *Psychol. Abstr.* XXVI. 31/2 (*title*) The use of a new experimental autokinetic situation in the evaluation of self reference. **1960** E. H. GOMBRICH *Art & Illusion* vii. 239 The perplexing effect of this self-reference is very similar to the paradoxes beloved of philosophers. **1966** G. N. LEECH *Eng. in Advertising* viii. 81 Only in a few stereotyped contexts.. is third person address and self-reference still used. **1978** M. HESSE in Hookway & Pettit *Action & Interpretation* 7 Self-reference of social theorising as part of its own subject matter. **1981** *Sci. Amer.* Apr. 6/2 One has only to watch the Muppets or Monty Python on television to see dense and intricate webs of self-reference.

Also **self-'referent, -refe'rential (-ially** *adv.*) *adjs.*; **self-re'ferring.**

1943 *Mind* LII. 20 Man's power over.. himself as he appears in the self-referent perspective. **1946** *Mind* LV. 65 If a theory is included in its own subject-matter, we say that it is a *self-referential* theory. *Ibid.* 67 Complete doubt of everything led to a self-referentially inconsistent view and so had to be abandoned. **1958** A. PAP *Semantics & Necessary Truth* ix. 263 The kind of self-referential proposition forbidden by the theory of types. **1969** *Mind* LXXVIII. 9 A partly self-referring sentence, such as art. 88 of the Danish constitution. **1979** *Sci. Amer.* Nov. 29/3 These irreducible questions tend, however, to be rather artificial and self-referent. **1980** *Times Lit. Suppl.* 5 Sept. 957/2 The self-referential and profoundly paradoxical late novels.

self-re'ferral. [SELF- 1 a.] The referring of oneself to an expert or (esp. medical) specialist for advice or treatment. Cf. REFERRAL b.

1971 *New Society* 14 Jan. 65/1 Fewer of its clients died in the high-risk first year after self-referral. **1975** *Language for Life* (Dept. Educ. & Sci.) xix. 281 There was an immediate and large increase in the number of self-referrals. **1979** *Internat. Rehabilit. Med.* I. 75/2 Some of the outcome measures to which numbers can be applied are.. responses to stress (e.g. self-referral to social services).

Also **self-re'ferred** *ppl. a.*

1960 *Cambr. Rev.* 7 May 506/2 'Self-referred' patients generally turn out to be at least as ill as those who are referred by their tutors or general practitioners.

self-re'flection. [SELF- 1 a, 3 a.]

†**1.** Reflection or image of oneself. *Obs.*

1636 DAVENANT *Plat. Lovers* II. i. D4, The fam'd Antipheron, whom once the learned Stagerite Admir'd so for the selfe-reflection that He wore like to his perfect Image still where hee mov'd.

†**2.** Censure or reproof of oneself. *Obs.*

1681 OWEN *Φρονημα του Πνευματος* I. iv. Wks. 1852 VII. 307 We can omit and lose such.. opportunities.. without regret or self-reflection. **1697** BURGHOPE *Disc. Relig. Assemb.* Ded., They can hear the call to church, and see others go, and yet stay at home without any self-reflections.

3. Reflection, meditation, or serious thought as to one's character, actions, motives, etc.

c **1670** O. HEYWOOD *Script. Fast* in *Autobiog.* (1881) II. 332 How usefull is this self-reflexion in order to a fast. **1691** HARTCLIFFE *Mor. & Int. Virtue* 285 Self-Reflection, the best means to an impartial judgment of things, will take place, and the true voice of Conscience will be heard. **1809–10** COLERIDGE *Friend* (1865) 99 A moment's steady self-reflection will show us, that in the simple determination 'black is not white'.. all the powers are implied that distinguish man from animals. *a* **1882** T. H. GREEN *Proleg. Ethics* §94 Self-reflection is the only possible method of learning what is the inner man or mind that our action expresses.

So **self-re'flective** *a.*, disposed to or characterized by self-reflection.

1879 *Expositor* X. 87 In opposition to the Buddhist spirit of self-annihilation, he declares that the sympathetic are the most self-reflective.

self-reflexive, *a.* [SELF- 3 a.]

†**1.** = SELF-REFLECTIVE *a.*

1677 GALE *Crt. Gentiles* IV. 6 These self-reflexive Acts of Conscience.

2. Characterized by reflexive action on itself; containing a reflection or image of itself.

1933 A. KORZYBSKI *Science & Sanity* xx. 323 All human 'knowledge' is structurally circular and self-reflexive, and so depends on some conscious or unconscious theory of knowledge and undefined terms. **1957** *Essays in Criticism* VII. 46 When everything is worked in to comprise part of a highly involute and self-reflexive symbolic pattern, there is just too much of it for poetry; it becomes mainly a complex intellectual parlour game. **1977** *Dædalus* Fall 105 The best way to illustrate the complex and self-reflexive progress of a semiotic enterprise is to consider what semiotics has done and promised to do for the study of the most complex of sign systems, literature. **1980** *San Francisco Bay Guardian* 16–23 Oct. 17/3 We all know about Vladimir Nabokov and self-reflexive writing.

So **self-re'flexiveness,** the quality or condition of being self-reflexive.

1933 A. KORZYBSKI *Science & Sanity* iv. 58 A word *is not* the object it represents; and languages exhibit also this peculiar self-reflexiveness, that we can analyse languages by linguistic means.

self-re'gard. [SELF- 1 a, 3 a.]

1. Regard of or consideration for oneself.

1595 SPENSER *Col. Clout* 682 But selfe-regard of priuate good or ill, Moues me of each, so as I found, to tell. **1691–8** NORRIS *Pract. Disc.* (1711) III. 185 Without being sway'd by any by, private, or self-regards. **1705** POPE *Let. to Wycherley* 30 Apr., The friendship.. is the more likely to be true and unmixed with too much self-regard. **1890** *Spectator* 11 Jan. 43/2 Effectually fusing the indifference and cool self-regard of others.

2. = SELF-RESPECT 3.

1811 BYRON *Hints fr. Hor.* 741 If friendship's nothing, self-regard might teach More polish'd usage of his parts of speech. **1856** EMERSON *Eng. Traits, Cockayne* 83 This little superfluity of self-regard in the English brain, is one of the secrets of their power.

So **self-re'gardant** *a.*, **-re'garding** *ppl. a.*, looking towards or centring upon oneself, marked by self-regard; watchful of oneself; **self-re'gardless** *a.*, **-re'gardlessness**.

1840 C. H. TOWNSHEND *Facts in Mesmerism* III. ii. 294 To be *self-regardant and watchful of our own sensations as they arise. **1895** *N. Amer. Rev.* Aug. 237 Man is not only a self-regardant but a sympathetic..being. **1789** BENTHAM *Princ. Legisl.* p. xxxviii *note*, The pleasures and pains of amity and enmity are of the *self-regarding cast. **1868** BAIN *Ment. & Mor. Sci.* IV. x. 393 The application of Prudential or self-regarding motives. **1907** ILLINGWORTH *Doctr. Trin.* vii. 140 Certain personal or self-regarding virtues.. consisting chiefly in habits of propriety and self-control. **1899** *Daily News* 2 Oct. 6/4 The courage and *self-regardless patriotism of youth. **1870** BLACK *Kilmeny* xxvi, Wonderful self-possession and *self-regardlessness.

self-'regulated, *ppl. a.* [SELF- 2, 4.] Regulated from within or automatically.

1847 in WEBSTER. **1903** *Edin. Rev.* Oct. 517 The Colleges were isolated, self-regulated and self-contained.

So **self-'regulating** *ppl. a.*

1837 *Penny Cycl.* IX. 26/2 A self-regulating thermostat or heat-governor. **1839** SELBY in *Proc. Berw. Nat. Club* I. vii. 191 A self regulating thermometer. **1840** *Mech. Mag.* XXXIII. 274 Chesterman's Patent Self-regulating Stove. The principal novelty..is the mode adopted for regulating the rate of combustion..by means of the vaporization of water. **1846** J. D. MORELL *Hist. Philos.* I. iv. 323 The human mind..is a spontaneous self-regulating existence. **1975** *Listener* 11 Sept. 328/3 This new ideal of the self-regulating individual.

self-regu'lation. [SELF- 1 a.] Regulation, control, or direction by or of oneself (itself); *spec.* in *Biol.* = HOMŒOSTASIS.

1693 NORRIS *Pract. Disc.* (1707) IV. 196 'Tis a very considerable degree of Self-regulation for a Man to proceed thus far, not to *enjoy*, but only to *use* the World. **1879** DOWDEN *Southey* ii. 29 His chief lesson was the large one of self-regulation. **1896** *Allbutt's Syst. Med.* I. 110 The muscular coats of the small arteries are..capable of self-regulation. **1912** J. S. HUXLEY *Individual in Animal Kingdom* i. 18 Protoplasm has primitively a great power of self-regulation. **1957** —— *Relig. without Revelation* (rev. ed.) ix. 215 There has been an enormous rise in level of harmonious organisation—think of a bird or a mammal as against a flatworm or a jellyfish; inflexibility and the capacity for self-regulation.

So **self-'regulative** *a.*, **self-'regulator, self-'regulatory** *a.*

a **1866** WHEWELL (Ogilvie), *Self-regulative. **1896** *Allbutt's Syst. Med.* I. 110 The endothelium of the capillaries is..self-regulative. **1862** BURTON *Bk.-Hunter* 11 Any..peculiarity which may transfer them from the class of free *self-regulators to that of persons 'under treatment'. **1899** *Allbutt's Syst. Med.* VI. 239 An..adaptive *self-regulatory capacity.

self-rein'forcement. *Psychol.* [SELF- 1 a.] The reinforcement or strengthening of one's own response to a stimulus or situation. Also *transf.* Also **self-rein'forcer; self-rein'forcing** *ppl. a.* Cf. REINFORCEMENT 3 c.

1963 *Jrnl. Experim. Psychol.* LXVI. 245/1 This procedure [*sc.* switching on a light for oneself] was called self-reinforcement. *Ibid.*, The frequency and accuracy of self-reinforcing responses..increased with more learning. **1973** *Jrnl. Genetic Psychol.* Sept. 86 Generally self-reinforcement studies have not attempted to deal with the classroom learning situation. **1977** P. F. SECORD in T. Mischel *Self* ix. 261 Positive self-reinforcers are seen as increasing the frequency of desirable behavior, and aversive self-reinforcers are thought to reduce undesirable behavior. **1979** *Sci. Amer.* Sept. 52/1 The process is self-reinforcing: the flow of sodium ions through the membrane opens more channels and makes it easier for other ions to follow.

self-re'liance. [SELF- 3 a.] Reliance upon oneself, one's own powers, etc. (*rarely* with unfavourable implication.)

1833 J. S. MILL *Let.* 25 Nov. in *Works* (1963) XII. 195 Combining perfect self-reliance with the most unaffected modesty. **1837** HT. MARTINEAU *Soc. Amer.* III. 117 In as far as they exchange self-reliance for reliance on anything out of themselves. **1862** GOULBURN *Pers. Relig.* 203 If we have failed again and again in meeting Temptation..it will be well to examine whether there be not some particle of self-reliance lurking at the bottom of our hearts. **1879** M. ARNOLD *Mixed Ess., Democracy* 18 A self-reliance which disposed each man to act individually and independently.

So **self-re'liant** *a.*, **self-re'lying** *ppl. a.*

1848 LYTTON *Harold* VIII. iv, *Self-reliant hath Hilda called me. **1878** BOSW. SMITH *Carthage* 292 Publius was sent off to Spain with a..force, which a less courageous and self-reliant people would have been unwilling to spare. **1829** SCOTT *Anne of G.* iii, The *self-relying resolution of a mind too virtuous to suspect evil. **1880** MCCARTHY *Own Times* xl. III. 225 An independent, quiet, self-relying man.

selfren, obs. form of SILVERN.

self-re'nounced, *ppl. a.* [Formed after SELF-RENUNCIATION; see SELF- 2.] Full of self-renunciation. So **self-re'nouncement**, = SELF-RENUNCIATION; **self-re'nouncing** *ppl. a.* (hence **-re'nouncingly** *adv.*).

1838 MRS. BROWNING *Virgin Mary to Child Jesus* vi, I knelt down..Too *self-renounced for fears. **1842** MANNING *Serm.* v. (1848) I. 75 To take shelter in a secret life of *self-renouncement. **1873** M. ARNOLD *Lit. & Dogma* (1876) 93 Self-examination, self-renouncement, and mildness. **1781** COWPER *Truth* 568 That *self-renouncing wisdom. **1858** GEO. ELIOT *Sc. Cler. Life, Janet's Rep.* xix. II. 285 The self-renouncing faith which has soothed that conflict into rest. **1859** —— *A. Bede* I. iv, Such a woman as Lisbeth..at once patient and complaining, self-renouncing and exacting. **1842** MRS. BROWNING *Grk. Chr. Poets* 196 Trustfully as child before mother, *self-renouncingly as child after sin.

self-renunci'ation. [SELF- 1 a.] Renunciation of oneself, one's own will, etc.

1791 [HANNAH MORE] *Relig. Fashion. World* 63 He..who does not live in a regular course of self-renunciation, will not be likely..to perform acts of beneficence. **1842** MANNING *Serm.* xii. (1848) I. 160 They who followed Him..had to make the same..act of self-renunciation. **1861** MILL *Utilit.* ii. 24 The only self-renunciation which it [*sc.* utilitarian morality] applauds, is devotion to the happiness..of others.

So **self-re'nunciatory** *a.*

1901 W. MACINTOSH *Rabbi Jesus* 232 Jesus..asks for a love as self-renunciatory as His own.

self-re'pellency. ? *Obs.* [SELF- 1 d.] The quality (possessed by gases) of being made up of mutually repelling molecules or atoms. So **self-re'pellent** *a.*, **self-re'pelling** *ppl. a.*

1803 JOS. BLACK *Lect. Chem.* I. 34 We may expect to find the matter of heat..rarefied, in consequence of its own ..*self-repellency. *Ibid.* 49 Heat depends on the abundance of a subtile matter highly elastic, or *self-repellent. **1828–32** WEBSTER, **Self-repelling*, repelling by its own inherent power.

self-re'port. *Psychol.* [SELF- 3 a.] A report about oneself or aspects of one's behaviour made by oneself. Freq. *attrib.*

1970 *Jrnl. Gen. Psychol.* Oct. 169 Self-report statements of awareness are influenced by the same independent variables as other verbal behaviors. **1972** *Jrnl. Social Psychol.* LXXXVI. 124 The LSQ was designed to elicit a self-report of actual behaviour. **1977** J. D. DOUGLAS in Douglas & Johnson *Existential Sociol.* 305 My theoretical variables..could not be directly related to the experience of the people killing themselves by anything except my own imagination and a few snatches of self-report data.

self-re'pression. [SELF- 1 a.] Repression of oneself, one's desires, opinions, etc. So **self-re'pressed, self-re'pressing** *ppl. adjs.*, characterized by self-repression.

1870 DICKENS *E. Drood* xix, Rosa, I am *self-repressed again. **1904** W. M. ROSSETTI in *Chr. Rossetti's Poems* Pref. p. x, One finds in her verse a noticeable combination of the outspoken with the *self-repressing. **1866** *Ch. Times* 27 Jan., His whole official career has displayed a capacity for *self-repression which [etc.]. **1890** HENTY *With Lee in Virg.* ii, The habitual self-repression of a slave.

self-re'proach. [SELF- 1 a.] Reproach of oneself.

1754 RICHARDSON *Grandison* III. 3 Dear Miss Grandison, don't give me cause for self-reproach. **1779** *Mirror* No. 50 ¶4 A conscious blush of shame and self-reproach. **1797** WORDSW. *Old Cumb. Beggar* 136 Men who can hear the Decalogue and feel No self-reproach. **1876** BANCROFT *Hist. U.S.* II. xxxiv. 354 The English monopolist had no self-reproach for prohibiting the industry of the colonists.

So **self-re'proached** *ppl. a.*, **self-re'proachful** *a.*, **self-re'proaching** *ppl. a.* (hence **self-re'proachingly, -re'proachingness**).

1829 SOUTHEY *Sir T. More* II. 111 Such a man may live *self-reproached. **1869** P. LANDRETH *Adam Thomson* ii. 77 Disappointed, depressed, desponding, and fiercely *self-reproachful. **1784** COWPER *Task* v. 600 *Self-reproaching conscience. **1848** KEBLE *Serm.* Pref. p. xxix, To help him to assuage his self-reproaching thoughts. **1847–54** WEBSTER, **Self-reproachingly*, by reproaching one's self. **1850** *Fraser's Mag.* XLII. 139 The weary..loathsome *self-reproachingness of idleness. **1890** TALMAGE *From Manger to Throne* 306 His *self-reproachment for doubting the words of Christ.

self-re'proof. [SELF- 1.] Reproof of oneself. So **self-re'proval, self-re'proved** *ppl. a.*, **self-re'proving** *vbl. sb.* and *ppl. a.*

1775 ASH, **Self-reproof*, the reproof of conscience. **1827** SCOTT *Chron. Canongate* iii, The anguish produced by this self-reproof was so strong, that I put my hand suddenly to my forehead. **1847** HELPS *Friends in C.* I. iii. 42 All that part of worldly trouble which consists of *self-reproval. **1828–32** WEBSTER, **Self-reproved*, reproved by consciousness or one's own sense of guilt. **1605** SHAKS. *Lear* v. i. 4 He's full of alteration, And *selfereprouing. **1775** ASH, **Self-reproving*, reproving one's self.

self-re'pugnance. Now *rare.* [SELF- 1 d.] Self-contradictory quality or character. So **self-re'pugnancy; self-re'pugnant** *a.*, self-contradictory.

1649 MILTON *Tenure of Kings* 5 The ignorance or the notorious hypocrisie and *self-repugnance of our dancing Divines. **1674** BOYLE *Corpusc. Philos.* 16 They..have recourse to agents, which..involve no *self-repugnancy in their very notions, as many of the judicious think substantial forms and real qualities do. **1701** NORRIS *Ideal World* I. vi. 339 For necessary truth to be the effect of God is a most inconsistent *self-repugnant notion. **1835** BROWNING *Paracelsus* I. 398 An arbitrary, self-repugnant scheme. **1836–7** SIR W. HAMILTON *Metaph.* xii. (1859) I. 218 This, at first sight, may appear like paradox: I trust you will soon admit that the counter doctrine is self-repugnant.

self-re'pulsion. ? *Obs.* [SELF- 1 a.] The action of self-repellent molecules or substances. So **self-re'pulsive** *a.*, self-repellent.

1834 PROUT *Chem. Meteorol.* App. 563 The individual molecules of the gas..are thus enabled to assume those positions..in which their mutual self-repulsion is the greatest possible. *Ibid.* 70 A given volume of steam,.. contains the same number of self-repulsive molecules, as a similar volume of air. *Ibid.* 73 The molecules..may..be supposed to exert a self-repulsive influence on each other. **1837** WHEWELL *Hist. Induct. Sci.* III. 17 Æpinus devised a method of examining the nature of the electricity..by means of which he ascertained its distribution, and found that it agreed with such a law of self-repulsion.

self-rescuer. *Coal-mining.* [SELF- 1 c.] A safety device carried by coal-miners to give protection against noxious gases (see quot. 1977).

1961 in WEBSTER. **1962** *Guardian* 31 Oct. 5/5 A new safety apparatus known as a 'self-rescuer', which gives a miner 30 minutes to reach a fresh-air area. **1977** *Guardian Weekly* 4 Dec. 19/3 Both the lamp..and the self-rescuer (a steel box containing a mask to refine dangerous gases, also hung from the waist) were heavy. **1979** *Daily Tel.* 13 July 6/8 The miners also carry safety equipment called a 'self-rescuer' and have automatic gas detectors.

self-re'spect. [In sense 1, SELF- 5 a, d; in senses 2 and 3, SELF- 1 d.]

†**1.** A private, personal, or selfish end. (Chiefly *pl.*; cf. SELF-END.) *Obs.*

1613 BP. HALL *Serm.* Wks. (1625) 468 Men; subiect to all passions, infirmities, self-respects. **1668** H. MORE *Div. Dial.* II. 30 Impartial Rectitude and Uprightness, without all Self-respects. **1675** HOWE in H. Rogers *Life* (1863) v. 141 Have I not an undue design or self-respect in it?

†**2.** Self-love, self-conceit. *Obs.*

1657 HAWKE *Killing is M.* Pref., Most men are transported with a philauty or self-respect, and have envious ..ears, to hear ill reports of others.

3. Proper regard for the dignity of one's person or one's position.

1795–1814 WORDSW. *Excurs.* VI. 353 To her guilty bowers Allured him, sunk so low in self-respect As there to linger. **1849** MACAULAY *Hist. Eng.* v. I. 619 The fortitude of Monmouth was not that highest sort of fortitude which is derived from reflection and from selfrespect. **1873** F. HALL *Mod. Engl.* 363 Much too cheap for any person of proper self-respect to indulge in. **1881** BESANT & RICE *Chapl. Fleet* I. vi, Things which, if left undone, would cause a gentlewoman to lose her self-respect.

So **self-re'spectful** (hence **-re'spectfulness**), **self-re'specting** *ppl. a.*

1890 *Academy* XXXVIII. 192/2 His style, while firm.., is *self-respectful with that reticence which in manners we call breeding and in art distinction. **1903** *19th Cent.* Dec. 1003 There was a dignity, a '*selfrespectfulness' in her demeanour that was most impressive. **1786** BURNS *Despondency* iv, The lucky moment to improve, And just to stop, and just to move, With *self-respecting art. **1828** SEWELL *Oxford Prize Ess.* 23 For the humiliation of habitual mendicity, it substituted an honourable and self-respecting industry. **1864** BURTON *Scot Abr.* I. ii. 102 The well-becoming pride and self-respecting gravity.

self-re'straint. [SELF- 1 a.] Restraint imposed by oneself upon one's actions, etc.

1775 ASH, *Self-restraint*, a restraint from one's self. **1848** MILL *Pol. Econ.* I. x. §3 (1876) 99 A prudent and conscientious self-restraint. **1871** JOWETT *Plato* II. 253 Those invalids who, having no self-restraint, will not leave off their habits of intemperance.

So **self-re'strained, self-re'straining** *ppl. adjs.*, marked by or involving self-restraint.

a **1700** DRYDEN *Iliad* I. 398 Power, *self-restrain'd, the people best obey. **1861** WHYTE MELVILLE *Good for Nothing* II. 195 Her tone was softened, and her bearing more self-restrained. **1828–32** WEBSTER, **Self-restraining*, restraining or controlling itself. **1844** MARG. OSSOLI *Woman in 19th Cent.* (1862) 65 Not [capable] of a steadfast wisdom, nor self-restraining virtue.

self-re'vealed, *ppl. a.* [SELF- 2.] Revealed by one's own action. So **self-re'vealing** *vbl. sb.* and *ppl. a.*, **self-re'vealment**.

1839 HALLAM *Lit. Eur.* III. iv. §3 By sanctioning the guilt of the self-revealing party. **1877** E. CAIRD *Philos. Kant* II. xviii. 645 The doctrine that God as a spirit is necessarily self-revealing. **1897** DOWDEN *Fr. Lit.* IV. ii. 277 The *Esprit des Lois*..must always be precious as the self-revealment of a great intellect. **1907** W. H. HADOW *Shaks. Sonn.* Introd. p. xi, Of all poetic forms the lyric..is the most self-revealing. **1908** *Outlook* 10 Oct. 462/1 Seeing all its strange beauty and listening to its mysterious self-revealing. **1923** J. W. HARVEY tr. *Otto's Idea of Holy* xx. 175 For the abyss between creature and Creator.., sin and holiness, is.. increased by that deeper knowledge that comes from the Gospel of Christ: and, as a result of the emotion..stirred in the recognition of it, that in which 'the holy' stands self-revealed is taken here..both as the refuge from, and the means by which to approach, Holiness. **1978** *Church Times* 11 Aug. 6/3 Barth's God is God self-revealed not as a doormat but as Father, Son and Spirit.

self-reve'lation. [SELF- 1 a.] Revelation of oneself.

1852 PULSFORD tr. *J. Müller's Chr. Doctr. Sin* I. 98 A self-revelation of God. **1853** W. JERDAN *Autobiogr.* III. 51 The self-revelations I have deemed essential to my life-story. **1898** ILLINGWORTH *Div. Immanence* iv. §3. 88 This then was the primary proof, the essential evidence of the Incarnation; the self-revelation of a person to persons.

So **self-'revelative, self-'revelatory** *adjs.*

1888 *Encycl. Brit.* XXIII. 312/2 *Self-revelative passages are frequent. **1890** *Advance* (Chicago) 23 Oct., I suppose that in the *self-revelatory character of these notes, I am bound to say that..I am lazy.

self-re'versal. [SELF- 3 b.] **1.** Reversal (of motion) by agency of the mover itself.

1886 R. WORMELL *Electr. in Service of Man* 61 This [induction] machine is exceedingly powerful in favourable weather, but has an important defect, in a tendency to self-reversal, which is apt to occur at a stoppage.

2. *Physics.* The darkening of the middle of a bright spectral line as a result of radiation emitted by a hot gas being partly reabsorbed as it passes through parts of the gas that are cooler.

1905 E. C. C. BALY *Spectroscopy* xii. 384 The lines generally were sharper than in the case of the arc in air,.. and there were fewer self-reversals. **1934** H. E. WHITE *Introd. Atomic Spectra* xiv. 250 The centers of the potassium-doublet, the calcium-singlet, and the copper-doublet lines show self-reversal due to absorption. **1977** A. CORNEY *Atomic & Laser Spectrosc.* x. 313 Systematic errors are difficult to avoid in these experiments since the profile.. is usually considerably distorted by self absorption or even self reversal.

3. *Geol.* The postulated reversal of the magnetization of some rocks by intrinsic means, rather than by reversal of the Earth's magnetic field (see quot. 1971).

1952 T. NAGATA et al. in *Jrnl. Geomagnetism & Geoelectr.* IV. 22 An experimental proof of self-reversal of thermo-remanent magnetism of igneous rocks is obtained. **1971** *Nature* 5 Feb. 378/1 At this point [*sc.* the early 1950s] an alternative to field reversal began to receive serious consideration. This was self-reversal, the possibility that some rocks possessed an intrinsic property whereby they could acquire a magnetization antiparallel to the ambient field, or whereby an originally parallel magnetization could reverse spontaneously.

self-re'ward. [SELF- 5 b.] Reward derived from or inherent in itself. So **self-re'warded, -re'warding** *ppl. adjs.*

1742 YOUNG *Nt. Th.* VII. 236 Who virtue's *self-reward so loud resound, Would.. virtue, while they compliment, betray. **1824** MISS MITFORD *Village* Ser. I. 229 Her sweet and loving temper was *self-rewarded. **1740** BP. RUNDLE in J. Duncombe *Lett.* (1773) II. 140 To perform to you all the *self-rewarding duties of good neighbourhood. **1868** BAIN *Mental & Moral Sci.* III. v. 245 If benevolent actions, instead of being a tax, were self-rewarding. **1876** MOZLEY *Univ. Serm.* xv. 259 Gratitude is.. a self-rewarding virtue.

self-'right, *v.* [Back-formation f. SELF-RIGHTING.] *intr.* To right iself. So **self-'righted; self-'righter,** a self-righting boat.

1881 *Daily News* 21 Jan. 5/8 The 'Norfolk Lifeboats'.. will not *self-right if upset. **1901** H. TRENCH *Deirdre Wed.* etc. 101 He.. From storm and mutiny emerged alone *Self-righted from the dreadful self-surrender. **1867** *Routledge's Ev. Boy's Ann.* 636 When a '*self righter' is upset by a heavy sea, her crew may be thrown out.

self-'righteous, *a.* [SELF- 3 b.] Righteous in one's own esteem.

a **1680** CHARNOCK *Mercy for Chief of Sinners* (1847) 15 This self-righteous temper is like an external heat got into the body, which produceth an hectic fever. *a* **1820** I. MILNER *Serm.* iii. I. 118 Pharisaical, self-righteous views and motives. **1854** C. HODGE *On Romans* vii. 200 Legal or self-righteous strivings after holiness. **1892** J. TAIT *Mind in Matter* 259 His severity was reserved for the self-righteous.

So **self-'righteously** *adv.*; **self-'righteousness,** the condition of being self-righteous; righteousness for which one gives oneself credit.

1901 *Westm. Gaz.* 1 July 7/3 A vigilant police are *self-righteously discussing whether they should enforce the lodging-house law. **1656** OWEN *Mortif. Sin* To Rdr. (1668) A3b, The deplorable Issues of Superstition, *self-righteousness and Anxiety of Conscience. **1833** WHATELY in *Life* (1866) I. 209, I understand the disease which you call self-righteousness: though the word is hardly yet good English. **1893** SWINBURNE *Stud. Prose & Poetry* (1894) 27 The unconscious malevolence of self-righteousness which distorted the critical appreciations.. of Lord Macaulay.

self-'righting, *vbl. sb.* [SELF- 1 b.] Of a boat: The action of righting itself after being upset. So **self-'righting** *ppl. a.*

1855 *Art. Life-boat Inst.* (Paris Exhib.) in *Brit. Alm. & Comp.* (1856) 50 The power of self-righting if upset. **1858** *Merc. Marine Mag.* V. 115 The new class of self-righting life-boats. **1882** *Encycl. Brit.* XIV. 573/1 Surf-boats, incapable of self-righting.

fig. **1891** *Times* 14 Jan. 5/3 The self-righting power which British constitutions derive from the absolute freedom of the people.

self-rising, *ppl. a. U.S.* [SELF- 3 b.] = SELF-RAISING *ppl. a.*

1865 *Chicago Tribune* 10 Apr. 1/6 Rogers' Self Rising Flour. The best, cheapest and most convenient Flour. **1930** *Randolph* (W. Va.) *Enterprise* 20 Nov. 4/3 Girls love to make 'skillet biscuits' with a self-rising flour when out camping. **1976** *Encycl. Brit. Micropædia* IV. 195/1 The wide variety of wheat flours generally available includes.. self-rising flour, refined and bleached with added leavening and salt.

self-'sacrifice. [SELF- 1 a.] Sacrifice of oneself; the giving up of one's own interests, happiness, and desires, for the sake of duty or the welfare of others.

1805 WORDSW. *Poems Sentim., Ode to Duty* 54 Give unto me, made lowly wise, The spirit of self-sacrifice. **1843** KINGSLEY *Lett.* (1878) I. 101 What a strange mystery is that of mutual self-sacrifice! to exist for one moment for another. **1885** J. MARTINEAU *Types Eth. Th.* I. I. i. §7. 226 Absolute self-sacrifice of the passions and imagination.

So **self-'sacrificed** *pa. pple.*; **self-'sacrificer,** a self-sacrificing person; **self-sacri'ficial** *a.*, = next; **self-'sacrificing** *ppl. a.*, making a sacrifice of one's life, etc. (whence **-'sacrificingly** *adv.*, **-'sacrificingness**).

a **1711** KEN *Preparatives* Poet. Wks. IV. 83 *Self-sacrific'd, his Father's Will, And our Redemption to fulfil. **1900** *Inscr. in Postmen's Park, Aldersgate St., London,* Mary Rogers, stewardess of the Stella, March 30, 1899, self-sacrificed by giving up her life-belt, and voluntarily going down in the sinking ship. **1668** H. MORE *Div. Dial.* III. xxv. I. 467 Martyrs and *Self-sacrificers to but so faint a Shadow.. of the first uncreated Perfection. **1903** *Sat. Rev.* 4 Apr. 421/2 It is usual for the self-sacrificer to be a consistently melodramatic person. **1855** BAILEY *Mystic,* etc. 98 The painful pelican *Self-sacrificial. **1893** H. R. REYNOLDS in *Life* (1898) 473 Your self-sacrificial love to a great duty. **1817** MOORE *Lalla Rookh, Parad. & Peri* (ed. 2) 149 That precious sigh Of pure, *self-sacrificing love. **1897** GLADSTONE *E. Crisis* 14 In the midst of a high and self-sacrificing enthusiasm, the Greek Government and people have shown good sense. **1882** *Advance* (Chicago) 5 Oct., *Self-sacrificingly non-denominational in all directions. **1871** SMILES *Charac.* ix. (1876) 239 In *self-sacrificingness, ..in the ordinary intercourse of life, mainly consists the difference between being well and ill bred.

†**self-said,** *ppl. a. Obs.* [= SELF *pron.* or *a.* + SAID *ppl. a.*] Selfsame.

1548 UDALL *Erasm. Par. John* x. 15–18 To sende furth this lyfe out of the bodye, and to cal agayn the same into the very selfsayd bodye [orig. *hoc ipsum corpus*]. **1579** LYLY *Euphues* (Arb.) 129 Euen in the selfe said moment it is borne.. to deliuer to a straunge nurse.

selfsame ('sɛlfseɪm), *a.* (*sb.*). Now *literary.* [orig. two words (see SELF A. 1 b, B. 1 c, and SAME A. 4); subsequently written as a compound with a hyphen, now as one word. Cf. Norw., Da. *selvsamme*; OHG. *selbsama* adv., in just the same way.]

A. *adj.* (The) very same, very identical.

c **1407** LYDG. *Reson & Sens.* 3992 She.. With the selve same suerde.. Karf hyr hart even atweyn. **1539** BIBLE (Great) *Matt.* viii. 13 Hys seruaunt was healed in the selfe same houre [TINDALE 1526 that same, 1534 the selfe, *Rheims* 1582 the same]. **1573** L. LLOYD *Marrow of Hist.* (1653) 87 The self same day that Adrian was made Emperour of Rome. **1593** SHAKS. *3 Hen. VI,* III. iii. 161 Both of you are Birds of selfe-same Feather. **1637** MILTON *Lycidas* 23 We were nurst upon the self-same hill, Fed the same flock. **1664** BUTLER *Hud.* II. iii. 213 And still he's in the self-same place, Where at his setting out he was. **1710** STEELE *Tatler* No. 177 ¶2 The very self-same Action done by different Men can not merit the same Degree of Applause. **1781** COWPER *Table-t.* 388 He trod the very self-same ground you tread. **1819** G. S. FABER *Dispens.* (1823) II. 331 In the Greek original, the self-same phrase occurs in each place without the least difference. **1833** TENNYSON *Miller's Dau.* iv, Pray, Alice, pray, my own sweet wife, That we may die the selfsame day. **1893** EARL DUNMORE *Pamirs* II. 333, I could hardly believe it was the same Jura Bek who had been such a bitter enemy to Russia... But it was the selfsame man.

b. *one and the selfsame* (arch.), †*one selfsame*.

1570 BILLINGSLEY *Euclid* bk. I. post. vi. 7 Thinges which are double to one and the selfe same thing, are equall the one to the other. **1587** GOLDING *De Mornay* ii. (1592) 19 One selfesame Creature, which at one selfesame instant, by one selfesame course, and with one selfesame qualitie of heate, doth all the said things. **1588** SHAKS. *L.L.L.* I. ii. 4 Sadnesse is one and the selfe-same thing... How canst thou part sadnesse and melancholy? **1611** BIBLE *1 Cor.* vii. 11 All these worketh that one and the selfe same spirit [WYCLIF one and the same, TINDALE, etc. the silfe same]. **1630** *R. Johnson's Kingd. & Commw.* 93 Having in one selfe-same field.. both Corne, Vines, and Fruit-trees. *Ibid.* 117 This River (as Severne) ariseth.. from one and the self-same Mountaine.

c. in predicative use. Now *rare.*

1582 *N. T.* (Rheims) Heb. i. 12 Thou art the self same, and thy yeres shal not faile [*earlier versions and* 1611 the same]. **1633** P. FLETCHER *Purple Isl.* I. iii, Their souls self-same in nearer love did grow. *c* **1680** BEVERIDGE *Serm.* (1729) I. 16 The case is the self-same here. **1860** PUSEY *Min. Proph.* 77 That we should believe in Him.. as He Who Is, the self-existing, the self-same. **1870** EMERSON *Soc. & Solit.* vii. 148 Always selfsame, like the sky.

†**B.** *absol.* or *sb.* The selfsame person or thing; rarely as *sb., pl.* identical things. *Obs.*

1421 HOCCLEVE *Minor Poems* 136/731 Let noon housbonde thynke it shame.. Thogh his wyf do to him þat selue same. *c* **1550** COVERDALE *Treat. Sacr.* Transl. Pref., So dyd he ordayne his apostles and in them all that shoulde succede them: priestes to offer vp the selfe same. **1574** tr. *Marlorat's Apocalips* 15, I the Lord am the firste, and euen I the selfsame am also with the last. **1582** WATSON *Centurie of Loue* (Arb.) 41 The Author.. varieth from that sense, which Chawcer vseth in translating the selfe same. **1638** QUARLES *Mildreiados* Ded., You shall receive but the selfe-same by Number and by Measure; which, before, you had by Waight. **1701** NORRIS *Ideal World* I. ii. 50 That they seem to be as so many self-sames, so many reproductions of one thing.

Hence **self'sameness,** identicalness, identity.

1577 *Bullinger's Decades* (1592) 629 The immutable self-same-nesse of the Trinitie. **1587** GOLDING *De Mornay* vi. 87 There must needes be euer both a selfesamenesse and also an othernesse. **1639** LD. DIGBY, etc. *Lett. conc. Relig.* (1651) 132 Sweet, happie, and I think sole, is the self-sameness which arises from pure principles of nature. **1876** F. H. BRADLEY *Eth. Studies* 5 The first condition.. is my self-sameness; I must be throughout one identical person. **1893** —— *Appear. & Real.* x. 113 Self-sameness exists as a fact, and.. hence somehow an identical self must be real.

self-satis'faction. [formed after next.] The condition or quality of being self-satisfied.

1739 HUME *Treat. Hum. Nature* II. I. 32 We are not much satisfy'd with the thing itself; and are still less apt to feel any new degrees of self-satisfaction upon its account. **1793** BEDDOES *Math. Evid.* 117 We differ from one another in every circumstance of conduct, taste, and sentiment with perfect self-satisfaction. **1848** THACKERAY *Van. Fair* xxviii, Following his chief, who rode away in great state and self-satisfaction. **1885** PATTISON *Mem.* 254, I have never enjoyed any self-satisfaction in anything I have ever done.

self-'satisfied, *ppl. a.* [SELF- 3 a.] Satisfied with oneself, one's achievements, etc.; marked by self-satisfaction.

1734 POPE *Ess. Man* IV. 42 No Bandit fierce, no Tyrant mad with pride, No cavern'd Hermit, rests self-satisfy'd. **1823** SCOTT *Quentin D.* ix, Hurried away, as the most cautious sometimes are, by the self-satisfied humour of the moment. **1838** DICKENS *O. Twist* xxv, The self-satisfied smirk of flash Toby Crackit. **1876** GEO. ELIOT *Dan. Der.* III. xxxvi. 74 One must care for them more than for the comfortably self-satisfied.

self-'satisfying, *ppl. a.* [SELF- 1 f.] That satisfies oneself; affording self-satisfaction.

1671 MILTON *Samson* 306 They ravel more, still less resolv'd, But never find self-satisfying solution. **1781** COWPER *Truth* 7 Then farewell all self-satisfying schemes, His well-built systems, philosophic dreams! **1823** KEBLE *Serm.* (1848) II. 42 Those self-satisfying thoughts, which the doctrine of assurance.. is continually fostering among Christians.

self-'sealing, *ppl. a.* [SELF- 4.] Becoming gas- or liquid-tight automatically; used esp. of a type of fuel tank.

1895 *Montgomery Ward Catal.* Spring & Summer 545/3 Owing to frequent inquiries for a self-sealing jar.. we decided to purchase the Globe Glass Top Jar. **1920** *Flight* XII. 605/2 A tank of his design was dropped from a height of approximately 400 ft... Although badly battered and bent, it is stated that no leakage of petrol occurred. The tank is a metal one and designed to be self-sealing. **1978** R. V. JONES *Most Secret War* x. 78 The single bomber that we had shot down was found to have self-sealing tanks.

self-se'cure, *a.* [SELF- 1 e.] Sure of oneself, one's position, etc.

a **1700** KEN *Hymnotheo* Poet. Wks. III. 17 He self-secure thought he should neither need. **1834** *Tait's Mag.* I. 661/1 The most frugal and self-secure of sovereigns. **1849** M. ARNOLD *Shakespeare* 10 Self-schooled, self-scanned, self-honoured, self-secure.

So **self-se'curity.**

1766 BLACKSTONE *Comm.* II. iv. 50 This new polity.. seems.. to have been.. adopted.. upon the same principle of self-security. **1768** H. WALPOLE *Hist. Doubts* 33 Self-security prompted the princes and lords to guard against this reverse. **1905** *Speaker* 8 Apr. 32/1 Bunyan's self-security of opinion.

self-'seeker. [formed after next.] **1.** One who seeks his own welfare; one given to self-seeking.

1632 SYMONDS *Eccles. Self-seeking* 6 No Self-seeker, but faithful for Christ. **1816** SCOTT *Old Mort.* i, Self-seekers all of them, strivers after wealth, power, and worldly ambition. **1852** TENNYSON *Ode Death Wellington* 187 Self-seekers trampling on the right. **1894** WOLSELEY *Marlborough* I. 257 William, like most men of the time, was a self-seeker.

2. A push-button device on a radio for automatic tuning to the desired station. Cf. SELF-SEEKING *ppl. a.* (*b*).

1960 *News Chron.* 22 Apr. 11/3 If the programme displeases you, press the button again and the self-seeker will move on to the next station.

self-'seeking, *vbl. sb.* [SELF- 1 b; cf. SEEK *v.* 7 c.] The seeking after one's own welfare before that of others, prosecution of selfish ends.

a **1586** SIDNEY *Arcadia* II. (Sommer) 202 Who by the rules of his own mind could construe no other end of mens doings but self seking. **1654** WHITLOCK *Zootomia* 364 Further than Selfe-destruction, none can drive this Selfe-seeking. *a* **1680** BUTLER *Charac., State-Convert,* He has so much of a Saint left as to.. denounce against Self-seeking, until he is sure to find what he looks for. **1705** STANHOPE *Paraphr.* I. 55 Partiality and a corrupt principle of Self-seeking. **1860** WHITTIER *Quaker Alumni* 7 All your petty self-seekings.

So **self-'seeking** *ppl. a.*, (*a*) characterized by self-seeking; (*b*) (of a radio) fitted with a self-seeker (sense 2).

a **1628** F. GREVIL *Let. Hon. Lady* i. Wks. (1633) 259 Those selfe-seeking Arts, which teare vp the bowels of the earth for the priuate vse of more than milke, and hony. **1668** H. MORE *Div. Dial.* IV. viii. II. 29 The Reign of mere self-seeking Nature. **1712** ARBUTHNOT *John Bull* II. xv, He is a Tradesman, a self-seeking Wretch. **1823** BYRON *Age of Bronze* xiv. 83 To pamper the self-seeking wants, And prop the hill of these agrarian ants. **1878** BOSW. SMITH *Carthage* 233 The.. least self seeking Roman of his time. **1972** *Times* 14 Sept. 31/8 At 90 mph it is still quiet enough to enjoy the self-seeking radio. **1976** *Drive* Jan.–Feb. 82/2 Electric quarter lights, self-seeking radio with automatic electric aerial, two cigarette lighters.

self-'service. [SELF- 1 a.] **1.** A system whereby customers in a shop, restaurant, etc., serve themselves instead of being attended to or waited on by the staff, usu. paying for all purchases in one place. Also, an establishment or department where this system obtains.

1919 *Ladies' Home Jrnl.* Jan. 65/2 The Duffy-Powers Company, operating a full-fledged department store in Rochester, New York, inaugurated self-service—that is, the customers, not the store, provide the service—in its grocery department. **1928** *Daily Mail* 7 Aug. 3/3 This same principle of self-service has.. been successfully applied to food shops. **1944** M. PANETH *Branch Street* 6 The outing ended in a 'Lyons' with 'self-service'. **1952** *Economist* 29 Nov. 636/1 Food shops.. may soon be turning over to self-service. **1961** *Listener* 7 Dec. 983/1 Big stores, self-services, cinemas losing business. **1962** H. O. BEECHENO *Introd. Bus. Stud.* xi. 101 Self-service is.. a very suitable form of retailing for pre-weighed or measured, pre-packed goods which the customer can select for himself and pay for at a cash-taking position as he leaves the shop. **1972** J. MANN *Mrs Knox's Profession* v. 31 She had pulled into the motorway café.. and had gone into the self-service to buy a cup of tea.

2. *attrib.* or as *adj.* Designating: **a.** A place where customers may serve themselves.

1919 *Ladies' Home Jrnl.* Jan. 65/3 After several months.., not only are all the self-service departments reported on a self-supporting basis, but with sales increasing. **1950** 'N. SHUTE' *Town like Alice* xi. 330, I sat on the veranda with Jean, studying her drawing of the layout of the self-service grocery. **1952** D. RIESMAN in *Antioch Rev.* Dec. 430 The self-service supermarket, with its abundance of foods capably displayed. **1967** *Times* 16 May 21/1 The situation with self-service filling stations is a classic case. **1977** B. PYM *Quartet in Autumn* ii. 24 Letty did her shopping.. at a small self-service store run by Uganda Asians that stayed open till eight o'clock in the evening.

b. A system of this nature.

1919 *Ladies' Home Jrnl.* Jan. 65/2 It [*sc.* a department store] followed this with an even greater inauguration—the self-service system in the sale of shoes.. and women's wearing apparel. **1969** *Which?* Nov. 338/2 For clothes, some people liked self-service arrangements... Older women preferred the help.. of an assistant.

c. A facility operated by the customer or user.

1952 S. KAUFFMANN *Philanderer* (1953) xiv. 240 Then he walked back into the house and went up in the self-service elevator. **1960** [see *coin-operated* adj. s.v. COIN *sb.* 8].

d. Merchandise bought by self-service.

1958 *Spectator* 18 July 118/1 Packaging for 'self-service' retailed goods. **1967** M. DRABBLE *Jerusalem the Golden* viii. 194 They.. collected themselves a large self-service meal.

Also **self-'serve** *attrib.* (chiefly *N. Amer.*).

[**1916** *Amer. Mag.* Oct. 69/1 'We told the customers to make their own selection, which they did.' 'It was a sort of serve-self arrangement, like a restaurant,' I said. '*Serve self* ..,' repeated Garner. '*Serve-Self Sale.* I have it.'] **1931** W. FAULKNER *Sanctuary* xxxi. 305 A self-serve place, where the customers moved slowly along a railing in single file. **1981** *Univ. Coll. London Bull.* Dec. 4/2 Self-serve counters would replace the current type.

self-'shielding, *vbl. sb.* Chiefly *Nucl. Physics.* [SELF- 1 b.] Shielding of the interior of a body as a result of the outer parts' absorbing radiation coming from the exterior; also = SELF-ABSORPTION 2.

1958 *Proc. 2nd U.N. Internat. Conf. Peaceful Uses Atomic Energy* XIII. 435/1 As the poison becomes depleted, its self-shielding decreases and the poison burns out faster than the fuel, causing a reactivity rise. **1963** B. FOZARD *Instrumentation Nucl. Reactors* i. 3 In many practical cases difficulties [in measuring the radioactivity of a source] arise due to such phenomena as self-shielding. **1977** J. MOTEFF in J. Weisman *Elem. Nucl. Reactor Design* v. 143 The receptor is shielded from each point source not only by interposed shielding material but also by materials within the source itself. This second contribution to the total shielding is called self-shielding or self-absorption.

So **self-'shielded** *ppl. a.* (quot. 1964 refers to shielding from electromagnetic fields).

1958 *Proc. 2nd U.N. Internat. Conf. Peaceful Uses Atomic Energy* XIII. 433/2 The analytical treatment of self-shielded or lumped poisons. **1964** R. F. FICCHI *Electr. Interference* vii. 119 A self-shielded distributor cap is available commercially that makes use of the same physical configuration as a nonshielded cap. **1973** P. F. ZWEIFEL *Reactor Physics* ix. 248 The center of the resonance line is strongly self-shielded.

†'selfship. *Obs. rare.* [f. SELF *sb.* + -SHIP.] Selfhood, personality, individuality.

1668 H. MORE *Div. Dial.* I. xxxiv. I. 143 Can you compare your distinct Selfship with this immense compass, and yet not conceive your self surrounded?

self-'similar, *a.* [SELF- 3 a.] Similar to itself; having no variety within itself, uniform; *spec.* in *Math.* similar to itself at a different time, or to a copy of itself on a different scale.

1867 R. W. EMERSON *May-Day* 48 Stumbling on through vast self-similar woods. **1956** A. A. TOWNSEND *Struct. Turbulent Shear Flow* v. 101 The rate of strain in shear flow is self-similar everywhere. **1967** *Science* 5 May 636 Many [geographical curves] are statistically 'self-similar', meaning that each portion can be considered a reduced-scale image of the whole. **1978** *Sci. Amer.* Apr. 22/3 A coastline, for example, may be self-similar when viewed from a height of several miles down to several feet, but below that the fractal property is lost. **1978** *Amer. Scientist* LXVI. 713/1 The flow tends toward a self-similar solution, i.e. a flow in which the profiles of the physical quantities behind the shock wave remain constant in time.

Hence **self-simi'larity**.

1967 *Science* 5 May 636/1 Seacoast shapes are examples of highly involved curves such that each of their portion can —in a statistical sense—be considered as a reduced scale image of the whole. This property will be referred to as 'statistical self-similarity'. **1978** *Sci. Amer.* Apr. 22/2 Unlike these striking artificial curves the fractals that occur in nature—coastlines, rivers, trees, star clustering, clouds and so on—are so irregular that their self-similarity (scaling) must be treated statistically.

self-slain, *pa. pple.* and *ppl. a.* [SELF- 2.] Slain by one's own hand.

1814 BYRON *Devil's Drive* i, Sausages made of a self-slain Jew. **1883** L. MORRIS *Songs Unsung* 27 Being self-slain and numbered with the dead.

So **self-'slayer**, self-murderer.

1690 C. NESSE *Hist. & Myst. O. & N. Test.* I. 212 Thou art.. a felo-de-se or self-slayer. **1823** in Cobbett *Rur. Rides* (1885) I. 390 They have, since Castlereagh cut his throat, relieved self-slayers from the disgrace of the cross-road burial. **1845** BAILEY *Festus* 254 Let it not be said He sought his God in the self-slayer's way.

self-'slaughter. [SELF- 1 a.] = SELF-MURDER.

1602 SHAKS. *Ham.* I. ii. 132 Oh.. that the Euerlasting had not fixt His Cannon 'gainst Selfe-slaughter. **1649** *Vindic. Hammond's Addr.* 10 §26 Those Lawes of our Land, which have look'd on this selfe-slaughter, as an inhumane crime. **1743** BLAIR *Grave* 410 Just reeking from Self-slaughter, in a Rage To rush into the Presence of our Judge! **1842** I. WILLIAMS *Baptistery* v. 69 All the shapes of death were seen, Robbers, fell beasts, disease, Self-slaughter's murderous mien. **1897** *Daily Tel.* 6 Oct. 10/6 The horrible self-slaughter by religious fanatics.

So **self-'slaughtered** *ppl. a.*, self-murdered.

1593 SHAKS. *Lucr.* 1733 Till Lvcrece Father that beholds her bleed, Himselfe, on her selfe-slaughtred bodie threw. **1621** G. SANDYS *Ovid's Met.* VII. (1626) 132 Selfe-slaughtred. **1837** R. WILSON *Pleas. Piety* VI. 142 Dying self-slaughter'd that she may obtain Eternal bliss!

self-sowed, *ppl. a. rare.* = next.

1759 *Phil. Trans.* LI. 300 In the middle of January, I had self-sowed marigolds and violets in bloom.

self-sown, *pa. pple.* and *ppl. a.* [SELF- 2. Cf. ON. *sjálfsáinn*.] Sown by itself without human or animal agency. Hence **self-sow** *v. intr.*, to propagate itself by seed.

1608 PLAT *Garden of Eden* (ed. Bellingham 1653) 78 These seeds will also come up well, being self-sowen. **1664** EVELYN *Sylva* Introd. 3 Oaklings, young Beeches, Ash,.. spring from the self-sown mast and keys. *a* **1746** HOLDSWORTH *Rem. & Diss. Virgil* (1768) 85, I rather believe, he means self-sown plants, and adds—'Nullis hominum cogentibus', —to explain his meaning. **1853** O. W. HOLMES *Poem Amer. Med. Assoc.* 50 The bud that came Self-sown in your poor garden's borders. **1908** [MISS FOWLER] *Betw. Trent & Ancholme* 379 The annuals being self-sown year by year. **1909** *Country Life in Amer.* Aug. 394/1 Annuals that 'self-sow' are welcome. **1980** *Country Life* 3 July 52/2 The milk thistle.. might self-sow over-exuberantly.

self-'starter. [f. next.] **1.** An electrical device for starting the engine of a motor vehicle without the need to crank it. Also *fig.*

1894 *Work* 17 Feb. 73/3 The many improvements made in recent years in the use of ignition tubes, self-starters. **1902** A. C. HAWKSWORTH *Motors & Motor-Driving* vii. 137 In the case of cars with two or more cylinders various self-starters have also been introduced. **1927** *Sat. Even. Post* (N.Y.) 24 Dec. 15/3 Conversation with him was never a self-starter; you had to crank it. **1973** M. RUSSELL *Double Hit* xxv. 190 There was the squawk of a self-starter, a roar, a piping of tyres.

2. A person who acts on his own initiative (*spec.* at work). *colloq.*

1960 *Times* 1 Feb. 2/4 (Advt.), The Man: Must be a self-starter yet able to work within references given to him. **1964** MRS. L. B. JOHNSON *White House Diary* 15 Nov. (1970) 203 Luci describes herself as a 'self-starter'. **1971** *Sunday Times* (Johannesburg) 28 Mar. 30/4 (Advt.), Suitable applicants will be self-starters in the 24–35 year age group. **1979** *Arizona Daily Star* 5 Aug. (Advt. Section) 4/2 Must be self-starter with project management experience.

self-starting, *ppl. a.* [SELF- 4.] That comes into operation automatically or semi-automatically. Of a motor vehicle: fitted with a self-starter. Also *fig.*

1866 *Proc. Inst. Mech. Engineers* 268 An arrangement for rendering the self-adjusting injector also self-starting has been contrived at the writer's works. **1887** *Encycl. Brit.* XXII. 500/1 Another form of the self-starting injector. **1910** *Daily Mail Year Bk.* 157/1 A few non-dazzling headlights, and one or two dual ignition and self-starting devices. **1912** *Chambers's Jrnl.* Aug. 556/2 Self-starting motor-cars. **1927** M. ASQUITH *Lay Sermons* i. 22 After making elaborate notes on all his self-starting symptoms, he wrote a long prescription. **1965** *Wireless World* July 56/1 (Advt.), Synchronous electric clock movements... Self starting.

self-'steering, *vbl. sb. Naut.* [SELF- 4.] The steering or directing of a vessel on a predetermined course by automatic means; **self-steering gear** (also **sails**), apparatus by which this is achieved; also *absol.*

1950 E. C. HISCOCK *Cruising under Sail* II. xix. 363 For a single-handed or short-handed ocean passage I consider that self-steering sails are most necessary. **1956** P. JOHNSON in J. Morwood *Sail Evolution* (A.Y.R.S. Publ. No. 3) 22 It is not only to the single-handed ocean voyager that self steering is useful. **1957** T. HERBERT *Self Steering* (A.Y.R.S. Publ. No. 13) 6 *Self Steering* may be defined as the ability of a sailing boat to stay on a set course relative to the wind... The various types of self steering gears fall into two broad categories: 1. Those gears which convert variations in wind pressure on the sails into rudder movements [etc.]. **1971** J. R. L. ANDERSON *Reckoning in Ice* viii. 153, I had no self-steering on Gudrid, but she was a beautifully balanced boat. **1976** *Southern Even. Echo* (Southampton) 1 Nov. 3/6 The 29-year-old blonde Lymington girl.. expressed her admiration for.. the winner—'one of the greatest sailors who have ever been, because he sailed without self-steering gear.'

self-stimu'lation. *Psychol.* [SELF- 1 a.] Stimulation of oneself for pleasure or excitement; *spec.* masturbation. Also, stimulation of its own pleasure centres effected in an animal by means of implanted electrodes (see quot. 1956).

1947 M. M. LEWIS *Lang. in Society* i. 18 There, at that level [*sc.* babbling]—as a form of play, of self-stimulation, of narcissism—it [*sc.* language] might remain. **1951** FORD & BEACH *Patterns of Sexual Behav.* ix. 155 American men who begin to masturbate.. discontinue the practice.. because self-stimulation is replaced by heterosexual intercourse. **1956** J. OLDS in *Sci. Amer.* Oct. 114/3 In the rhinencephalon the effects were milder, producing self-stimulation at rates around 200 times per hour. **1964** J. Z. YOUNG *Model of Brain* xiv. 234 With stimulating electrodes implanted in them animals can be made either to seek self-stimulation from one centre or to avoid it if the electrode is in.. one nearby. **1977** R. HOLLAND *Self & Social Context* iv. 62 Olds' study of self-stimulation by rats with implanted electrodes.

self-'study. [SELF- 1 a, 2 b.] **1.** Study or contemplation of oneself.

1683 TRYON *Way to Health* 669 Self-study and Heart-knowledge. **1936** L. PEARSALL SMITH *Reperusals & Re-Collections* i. 6 He found moral profit also in the self-study, for how, he asked, can we correct our vices if we do not know them.

2. Study by oneself; private study.

1958 *Practical Wireless* XXXIV. 1 (Advt.), Designed and arranged for self-study at home. **1962** E. SNOW *Other Side of River* (1963) xviii. 130 Mao had already made wide-ranging contacts and done omnivorous reading in the Changsha library. In his self-study he was guided by his favorite professor. **1977** P. STREVENS *New Orientations Teaching of English* ii. 13 The adult who works on his own with a self-study course is still, though in an extended way, learning with a teacher.

self-sub'sistence. [SELF- 5 b.] The quality or condition of subsisting alone without dependence on or support of anything external.

1629 DONNE *Serm.* xxiv. (1640) 240 We banish all self-subsistence, all attributing of any power, to any faculty of our own. **1677** GALE *Crt. Gentiles* IV. 339 This Independence and Self-subsistence of the Divine Wil. **1701** NORRIS *Ideal World* I. vi. 333 Whence has it [Truth] this self-subsistance and independency of being? **1853** J. MARTINEAU *Ess.* (1869) II. 268 The belief.. that causality.. has an absolute self-subsistence. **1904** *Edin. Rev.* Jan. 172 It is the height of absurdity for an advocate of self-subsistence to measure prosperity by the export trade.

So **self-sub'sistency; self-sub'sistent** *a.*, **-sub'sisting** *ppl. a.*

1657 HEYLIN *Ecclesia Vind.* I. ii. §2. 55, I look upon the Musarabick Liturgie.. for as unquestionable a character of *self-subsistency as the Ambrosian Office was in the Church of Millain. **1825** COLERIDGE *Aids Refl.* (1848) I. 325 The attribute of self-subsistency vanishes from the soul on the same grounds, on which it is refused to the mind. **1844** EMERSON *Ess.* Ser. II. vii. (1876) 173 'Lynch-law' prevails only where there is greater hardihood and self-subsistency in the leaders. **1647** H. MORE *Song of Soul* II. *App.* Pref. 1 Any actuall and *self-subsistent Being. **1704** NORRIS *Ideal World* II. iii. 250 Those sensible qualities.. such as heat, cold, sweetness.. are not self-subsistent beings. **1827** COLERIDGE *Const. Church & State*, etc. (1839) 269 *note*, The self-subsistent Reason or *Logos.* *a* **1676** HALE *Prim. Orig. Man.* IV. iv. 321 Their Souls are not of a *self-subsisting nature, they cannot exist out of them. **1837** WHEWELL *Hist. Induct. Sci.* I. 61 Those [Platonic] ideas were described as eternal and self-subsisting, forming an 'intelligible world', full of the models or archetypes of created things.

self-sub'stantial, *a. rare.* [SELF- 3 b.] Derived from one's own substance.

c **1600** SHAKS. *Sonn.* i, Thou.. Feed'st thy lights flame with selfe substantiall fewell.

self-su'fficed, *ppl. a. rare.* [formed after next; see SELF- 2.] = SELF-SUFFICIENT 1.

1706 WATTS *Horæ Lyricæ* I. *To Mitio* II. 87 How self-suffic'd Lives their Eternal Maker, girt around With Glories!

self-su'fficience. [formed as next: see -ENCE.] = next.

1706 WATTS *Horæ Lyricæ* I. *Creator & Creatures* ii, Thou art thine own Original, Made up of uncreated Things, And Self-sufficience bears them all. **1867** SWINBURNE *Ess. & Studies* (1875) 133 This is the gospel of αὐτάρκεια, the creed of self-sufficience.. [*Footnote*] I take leave to forge this word, because 'self-sufficingness' is a compound of too barbaric sound, and 'self-sufficiency' has fallen into a term of reproach. **1873** MORLEY *Rousseau* II. 221 This cardinal doctrine of limitation of desire, with its corollary of self-sufficience.

self-su'fficiency. [f. next (see -ENCY); in sense 1 a rendering Gr. αὐτάρκεια.]

1. The quality or condition of being SELF-SUFFICIENT: **a.** in sense 1 a, formerly *esp.* as an attribute of God; now freq. in sense 1 b.

1623 R. CARPENTER *Conscionable Christ.* 59 A good.. conscience is a.. principall part of Gods Image in man, whereby he doth most resemble the selfe-sufficiency of God. **1701** NORRIS *Ideal World* I. iii. 157 The excellent perfections of the Divinity, especially those of His self-sufficiency and independency. **1847** F. W. NEWMAN *Hist. Heb. Mon.* 22 The land of Israel, for so very small a tract, possessed an unusual self-sufficiency for all physical well-being. **1897** J. MORLEY *Machiavelli* 26 Self-sufficiency, military strength, force, flexibility, address. **1932** *World Agriculture* (R. Inst. Internat. Affairs Study Group) viii. 133 A measure of self-sufficiency in food is regarded as one of the primary elements in natural defence. **1953** G. E. & K. R. FUSSELL *Eng. Countrywoman* iii. 90 The canopy of self-sufficiency that covered all the needs of the manor house. **1973** J. & S. SEYMOUR *Self-Sufficiency* i. 9 What I am interested in is *post*-industrial self-sufficiency: that of the person who has gone through the big-city-industrial way of life.. and wants to go on to something better. **1974** *News & Courier* (Charleston, S. Carolina) 7 Apr. A-12/2 They argue that the 1985 target date for self-sufficiency is unrealistic, and that.. some oil and gas still must be imported. **1980** 'M. INNES' *Going it Alone* iv. 31 She had persuaded herself.. that self-sufficiency must now be the prime concern of the small rural gentry.

b. in sense 2.

1693 DRYDEN *Disc. Satire* Ess. (ed. Ker) II. 18 An author of your own quality..has given you all the commendation which his self-sufficiency could afford to any man. *a* **1704** T. BROWN *Praise of Poverty* Wks. 1730 I. 89 Such a self-sufficiency, such an overweaning conceit. **1745** J. MASON *Self-Knowl.* II. v. (1853) 147 An Eagerness and Zeal for Dispute on every subject, and with every one, shews great Self-sufficiency. **1825** T. HOOK *Sayings* Ser. II. *Doubts & F.* vii. II. 211 Astonished even with all his self-sufficiency at the triumphant success of his enterprise. **1885** *Manch. Exam.* 21 Jan. 5/2 We threw him off, and acted..with arrogant inconsiderateness and self-sufficiency.

†**2.** A sufficiency for oneself. *Obs. rare.*

1650 FULLER *Pisgah* I. iv. 10 Commodities..whereof that Countrey had not only a self-sufficiency, but also sent plenty thereof to Tyre.

self-su'fficient, *a.* [SELF- 3 b; in sense 1 rendering Gr. αὐτάρκης.]

1. a. Sufficient in or for oneself (itself) without aid or support from outside; able to supply one's needs oneself. Not now of persons.

1589 PUTTENHAM *Eng. Poesie* I. xii. 22 One God Almightie, euerlasting, and in euery respect selfe suffizant (*autharcos*). *c* **1645** HOWELL *Lett.* (1890) I. 41 A compleat self-sufficient Country, where there is rather a Superfluity than Defect of anything. **1702** S. PARKER tr. *Cicero's De Finibus* IV. 228 Vertue, it seems, is Self-sufficient to render us as Happy as 'tis possible for us to be. *a* **1706** EVELYN *Hist. Relig.* (1850) I. 411 These books..[which] if they be not written by the dictate of the Holy Spirit,..St. Athanasius assures us are self-sufficient. *a* **1711** KEN *Hymnarium* Poet. Wks. II. 1 Thou self-originated Deity,..Thou Self-sufficient, by thy self didst reign. **1803** W. TAYLOR in *Ann. Rev.* I. 427 The proportion of paupers to self-sufficient persons, is larger in villages than in cities. **1869** F. W. NEWMAN *Misc.* 184 Syria is a very self-sufficient region. **1897** tr. *Fichte's Sci. Ethics* 223 The truly free and self-sufficient Ego. **1899** INGE *Christ. Myst.* vii. 267 Physical science..while it keeps to its proper subject..is self-sufficient, and can receive nothing on external authority.

b. *spec.* Of persons, groups, or nations: able to provide enough of a commodity (as food, oil) to supply one's own needs, without obtaining goods from elsewhere; self-reliant, self-supporting, independent. Freq. const. *in*.

1932 [implied at SELF-SUFFICIENCY 1 a]. **1955** K. A. H. MURRAY *Agriculture* iii. 40 For countries that are practically self-sufficient in their food requirements.., war or the threat of war may necessitate little or no change in agricultural effort or output. **1973** J. & S. SEYMOUR *Self-Sufficiency* i. 10 More and more people, in all the highly industrial societies, are trying partially to opt out of the big-industry set-up and become less specialized and more self-sufficient. **1977** *Undercurrents* June–July 11/2 If we are to become self-sufficient in food production in Britain we are told that we must eat more grain and less meat. **1978** *Lancs. Life* July 54/2 He was soon back in the Lake District .., becoming self-sufficient through selling his paintings and wood sculptures, doing odd jobs and growing his own food.

2. In an unfavourable sense: Having excessive confidence in oneself, one's powers, etc.; characterized by overweening or self-conceited opinion or behaviour.

1734 tr. *Rollin's Anc. Hist.* II. II. (1827) 96 Haughty and self-sufficient behaviour. **1824** R. C. DALLAS *Corr. Byron* (1825) I. 51 Self-sufficient free-thinkers and witty sophs. **1842** LOVER *Handy Andy* vii, A self-sufficient jackanapes.

Hence as *sb.* (*rare*), one that is sufficient in itself (oneself); **self-su'fficientness,** = SELF-SUFFICIENCY 1 a.

1889 LOWELL *Let. to Mrs. Mitchell* 9 Mar., [Philadelphia] was very sweet in its provincial valley of self-sufficientness and contentment. **1909** W. JAMES *Meaning of Truth* xiv. 276 Mr. Russell, and also Mr. Hawtrey..seem to think that in our mouth also such terms..are self-sufficients with no context of varying relation that might be further asked about. **1926** I. BROWN *H. G. Wells* iii. 43 They have the Cockney's superb self-mastery, his power to rise to an occasion... Bert Smallways in *The War in the Air* is another of these admirable self-sufficients.

self-su'fficing, *ppl. a.* [formed after SELF-SUFFICIENT.] = SELF-SUFFICIENT 1 and 2.

1687 NORRIS *Coll. Misc.* 84 Why not indulge his self-sufficing state, Live to himself..A wise eternal Epicure? **1799** WORDSW. *Poems Sentim., Poet's Epit.* 31 A reasoning, self-sufficing thing, An intellectual All-in-all. **1840** CARLYLE *Heroes* iii. (1858) 260 So great, quiet, complete and self-sufficing is this Shakspeare. **1874** O'SHAUGHNESSY *Music & Moonlight* 157 In spite of some fond fit Of self-sufficing thoughts. **1893** TRAILL *Soc. Eng.* Introd. p. xix, It is..in its earliest stages that Art is most distinctly independent and self-sufficing.

self-su'fficingness, = SELF-SUFFICIENCY 1 a.

1844 EMERSON *Ess., Character* 65 The face which character wears to me is self-sufficingness. **1847–8** DE QUINCEY *Protestantism* Wks. 1858 VIII. 95 *note*, The Greek autarkeia.., self-sufficiency, or, because that phrase, in English has received a deflection towards a bad meaning, the word self-sufficingness might answer. **1881** MYERS *Wordsw.* 13 A picture..of hardy English youth,—its proud self-sufficingness and careless independence of all human things.

self-su'ggested, *ppl. a.* [SELF- 2.] Suggested by oneself; caused by self-suggestion.

1856 GROTE *Greece* II. xciii. XII. 145 The self-suggested illusion of untaught men. **18..** *Alien. & Neurol.* X. 444 (Cent. Dict.) Such self-suggested paralysis.

self-su'ggestion. [SELF- 3 b.]

1. A suggestion arising of its own accord.

1892 J. TAIT *Mind in Matter* 247 Although sin overflows so as to embrace others besides the guilty, the idea of substitution by blood-shedding would scarcely come as a self-suggestion.

2. Suggestion to oneself; the voluntary fixing in one's own mind some idea in order that it may afterwards operate subconsciously or automatically.

1893 A. LANG in *Folk-Lore* IV. 433 But I am not my own dupe. Others may be more fortunate or more amenable to self-suggestion. **1899** *Two Worlds* 6 Jan. 2/1 Self-suggestion will, I believe, prove a great aid in counteracting many of the evils of life. **1903** F. W. H. MYERS *Human Pers.* I. p. xxi, Self-suggestion..means a suggestion conveyed by the subject himself from one stratum of his personality to another, without external intervention.

So **self-su'ggestive** *a.*; **self-su'ggester,** one who performs self-suggestion.

1848 BAILEY *Festus* 248 Who taking pleasure in all reason find The science of self-suggestive wisdom in themselves. **1903** F. W. H. MYERS *Human Pers.* I. 139 Some self-suggestive machinery by which the patient cures his toothache himself. *Ibid.* 213 The task is quite as difficult for the self-suggester as for the hypnotist.

self-su'pport. [SELF- 1 a.] The act of supporting oneself (itself) without external assistance; the fact of being self-supporting. So **self-su'pported** *ppl. a.* (hence **self-su'pportedness**); **self-su'pporter** (see quot.); **self-su'pporting** *ppl. a.*, supporting oneself (itself) without external aid, (of a physical object) not requiring the usual support, (of an enterprise) paying its way; **self-su'pportless** *a.*

1774 GOLDSM. *Nat. Hist.* (1824) I. 197 The children, not long after they are born, appear possessed of a greater share of *self-support. **1856** GROTE *Hist. Greece* II. xcvii. XII. 611 Hellenic power and interests become incapable of self-support, and sink into a..subservient position. **1896** *Daily News* 19 Dec. 8/2 To encourage self-support as far as possible, but not to plant a missionary down in a place, give him no salary [etc.]. **1768–74** TUCKER *Lt. Nat.* (1834) II. 679 They appear to need no foundation, being *self-supported by an inherent certainty. **1784** COWPER *Task* III. 657 Few self-supported flow'rs endure the wind Uninjur'd. **1862** F. HALL *Hindu Philos. Syst.* 256 [tr. Sanskrit] Nor may *self-supportedness here be charged. **1897** *Westm. Gaz.* 24 June 10/1 '*Self-supporters'— that is, men out on ticket-of-leave in the settlement. These men are allowed to marry. **1829** *Lond. Med. & Surg. Jrnl.* II. 341 (*heading*) Atherstone *self-supporting dispensary. **1836** BUCKLAND *Geol. & Min.* xv. §4 (1837) I. 340 The recent application of thin plates of corrugated iron to the purpose of making self-supporting roofs. **1845** J. S. MILL in *Edin. Rev.* LXXXI. 521 It is an indispensable condition that there be a reasonable prospect of their being at some future time self-supporting. **1868** *Rep. U.S. Comm. Agric.* (1869) 320 This establishment..is self-supporting, the sale of fish more than paying the expenses. **1893** G. B. SHAW *Widowers' Houses* II. 52 *Trench*: We must do the best we can with seven hundred. I think we ought to be self-supporting. **1895** *Army & Navy Soc. Price List* 15 Sept. 683 Self-supporting portfolio. **1936** N. STREATFEILD *Ballet Shoes* iii. 46 You will at least have taken a step towards trying to make them self-supporting. **1972** *Guardian* 1 Sept. 1/1 Britain took a giant stride towards becoming self-supporting in oil yesterday. *a* **1834** COLERIDGE *Lit. Rem.* (1836) II. 186 The *self-supportless leaning for all pleasure on another's breast.

self-su'rrender. [SELF- 1 a.] The surrender or giving up of oneself to an influence, emotion, or the like.

1702 J. HOWE *Self-Ded.* 12 This must be the Sense of the sincere Soul, intreating the Matter of its Self-surrender, and Dedication, with the great God. **1854** DE QUINCEY *Murder as One of the Fine Arts* Postscr. (ed. Masson) XIII. 101 In blind, passive, self-surrender to panic. **1859** O. W. HOLMES *For Burns Centen. Celebr.* 32 We love him, even in his wrong,—His wasteful self-surrender. **1900** W. L. COURTNEY *Idea of Trag.* 75 The absolute self-surrender of a middle-aged man who ought to be conquering the world.

Hence **self-su'rrendering** *ppl. a.*

1878 J. G. WHITTIER *Vision Echard* 12 Its [*sc.* love's] self-surrendering freedom, Its loss that gaineth all. **1903** W. H. GRAY *Our Div. Sheph.* 199 The Lamb of God, innocent and self-surrendering.

self-su'stained, *a.* [SELF- 2.] Sustained by one's own power or efforts; (*rarely* in a physical sense) held up without support.

1742 YOUNG *Nt. Th.* VIII. 926 False pleasure from abroad her joys imports; Rich from within, and self-sustain'd, the true. **1768–74** TUCKER *Lt. Nat.* (1834) I. 538 Whether we suppose this chain upholden by an intelligent being, or self-sustained. **1845** MRS. JAMESON *Early Ital. Painters, M. Angelo* II. 65 *note*, The dome of the Pantheon, which appears self-sustained. **1870** J. H. NEWMAN *Gramm. Assent* II. vi. 160 We assented to them, we still assent, though we have forgotten what the warrant was. They are self-sustained in our minds. **1873** B. HARTE *Fiddletown* 11 A certain self-sustained air which is apt to come upon children who are left much to themselves.

So **self-su'staining** *ppl. a.* (hence **self-su'stainingly** *adv.*); **self-su'stainment; self-'sustenance; self-susten'tation.**

1844 EMERSON *Emancip. Negroes* 28 The *self-sustaining class of inventive and industrious men. **1868** *Rep. U.S. Comm. Agric.* (1869) 354 The earth-banks..should..be sufficiently sloped to be self-sustaining. **1905** TUCKWELL *Remin. Rad. Parson* xii. 173 Healthily, happily, *self-sustainingly at work. **1840** DARLEY *Beaum. & Fl.'s Wks.* I. Introd. p. xxviii, Where is the single character delineated by our authors with the force,..and uniform *self-sustainment, of any principal portrait by Ben? **1867** LOWELL *Rousseau* Wks. 1890 II. 256 Souls capable of self-sustainment. **1862** TROLLOPE *Orley F.* xlv, Though she was ..frail-looking, there was within her a great power of *self-sustenance. *a* **1866** J. GROTE *Exam. Utilit. Philos.* xi. (1870) 174 Impartial nature..in proportion to the freedom of attack by others, has made difficulty of self-sustenance. **1845** MAURICE in *Encycl. Metrop.* II. 617/1 Whether the life in each plant..must be considered as the active or only the passive instrument in *self-sustentation. **1890** H. SPENCER in *Pop. Sci. Monthly* May 22 During early life, before self-sustentation has become possible.

self-'system. *Psychol.* [SELF- 5 b.] The organized complex of drives and responses pertaining to (an aspect of) the self; the final choice of potentialities which the individual seeks to develop.

1897 W. JAMES *Let.* 1 Feb. (1920) II. 57 It is a case of the conflict of two *self-systems* in a personality up to that time heterogeneously divided, but in which..the higher loves and powers come definitively to gain the upper-hand. **1940** H. S. SULLIVAN *Psychiatry* III. 9/1 Along with the learning of language, the child is experiencing many restraints on the freedom which it had enjoyed..and from these restraints there comes the evolution of the self system. **1977** R. HOLLAND *Self & Social Context* ii. 31 Anxiety is the special 'dynamism' that attaches to the development of a 'self-system'.

self-'tapping, *ppl. a.* *Mech.* [SELF- 4.] Designating a hardened screw that will cut its own thread in a hole in metal that would otherwise need tapping. Also **self-'tapper** (*colloq.*).

1936 R. T. KENT *Mech. Engineers' Handbk.* (ed. 11) III. ix. 36 Self-tapping screws are screws that may be driven into an untapped hole, forming the thread in the hole as they are driven. **1955** *Archit. Rev.* CXVII. 213/1 From the point of view of large-scale production of sheet metal components, the greatest design change has been brought about by the Parker-Kalon or self-tapping screw. **1970** K. BALL *Fiat 600, 600D Autobook* viii. 99/1 Slightly tighten the self-tapping bushes. **1978** *Hot Car* June 98 (Advt.), A spoiler which needs only six self tappers to secure it to withstand heavy impact.

self-taught, *ppl. a.* [SELF- 2.] Taught by oneself without aid from others; self-educated.

1725 POPE *Odyss.* XXII. 383 Self-taught I sing. **1791** BOSWELL *Johnson* 26 Oct., an. 1769, Mr. Fergusson, the self-taught philosopher. **1840** R. H. DANA *Bef. Mast* xxiii, Like most self-taught men he over-estimated the value of an education. **1847** H. MILLER *First Impr. Eng.* xiv. (1857) 235 Every great writer..whether he be a learned Milton or an unlearned Burns, is self-taught.

b. Of that which is learnt: Acquired by one's own unaided efforts.

1774 GOLDSM. *Nat. Hist.* VI. xii, All the arts of inferior animals are self-taught, and scarce one acquired by imitation. **1828** MISS MITFORD *Village* Ser. III. 123 She had much of the self-taught knowledge, which is, of all knowledge, the surest and the best. **1903** *19th Cent.* Apr. 651 His scholarship was self-taught.

self-'timer. *Photogr.* [SELF- 1 c or 4.] A mechanism that introduces a delay between the operation of the shutter release and the opening of the shutter, so that the photographer can photograph himself.

1951 L. A. MANNHEIM et al. *Rollei Way* 53 To make exposures with the self-timer..pull the button outwards. **1968** M. WOODHOUSE *Rock Baby* xvii. 173 He had..a self-timer on the camera and there were pictures of the two of us together. **1978** *Detroit Free Press* 5 Mar. A14 (Advt.), The Polaroid Prontol RF Land Camera..comes with self timer and tripod.

self-'torment. [SELF- 1 a.] Tormenting of oneself. So **self-tor'mented** *ppl. a.*; **self-tor'menting** *vbl. sb.* and *ppl. a.*; **self-tor'mentor** (occas. used to render the title of Terence's play, *Heautontimorumenos*).

1671 FLAVEL *Fount. Life* iv. Wks. 1701 I. 32/2 The Self-revenges, the *Self-torments, which the Damned suffer for this their Folly. **1819** SCOTT *Ivanhoe* xxxix, The stupid self-torments of an ascetic. **1713** ROWE *Jane Shore* v. i, So wakes my Soul, Restless and *self-tormented. *a* **1711** KEN *Hymns Evang.* Poet. Wks. I. 115 Though all her *self-tormentings are in vain, She no Alleviation can obtain. **1841** HELPS *Ess., Aids Contentm.* (1842) 8 To suggest some antidotes against the manifold ingenuity of self-tormenting. **1648** CRASHAW *Steps to Temple, Sospetto d'Herode* lii, Tyranny And *selfe-tormenting sin. **1712** BLACKMORE *Creation* III. 687 Tim'rous Minds with self-tormenting Care Create those awful Phantoms. **1865** DICKENS *Mut. Fr.* IV. xiv, The many wills made by my unhappy self-tormenting father. **1667** FLAVEL *Saint Indeed* (1754) 41 Mourners in Sion, you may, and ought to be; but *self-tormentors you must not be. **1712** STEELE *Spect.* No. 521 ¶6 The Play of the *Self-Tormentor* of Terence's. **1825** SOUTHEY *Tale of Paraguay* IV. xv, Poor, erring, self-tormentor that thou art, O Man!

self-tran'scendence. [SELF- 1 a, d.]

Transcendence or surpassing of oneself or one's limitations; the achievement of or capacity to achieve a higher level of awareness, compassion, etc. Also **self-tran'scendency.**

1885 W. JAMES in *Mind* X. 27 We are not to ask, 'How is self-transcendence possible?' **1895** —— in *Psychol. Rev.* II. 110 Those mysterious notions of self-transcendency and presence in absence which are such essential parts of the ideas of knowledge, both of common men and of philosophers. **1946** J. S. HUXLEY *Unesco* ii. 62 Individuals.. can only achieve fullest self-development by self-transcendence. **1956** *Essays in Criticism* VI. 17 An irony of a more darkly moral colouring, a sardonic self-transcendence, was known to Friedrich Schlegel. **1975** P. BAELZ *Forgotten Dream* iii. 46 To place such emphasis on the possibility of creative self-transcendence..at once suggests that we have escaped from sober reality into a world of our own make-believe.

So **self-tran'scendent** *a.*, **self-tran'scending** *ppl. a.*

1884 W. JAMES in R. B. Perry *Tht. & Char. of W. James* (1935) I. xxxvi. 579 A consciousness not self-transcendent in form is inconceivable. **1904** —— in *Jrnl. Philos.* I. 538 Common-sense theories left the gap untouched, declaring our mind able to clear it by a self-transcending leap. **1948** J. L. ADAMS tr. *Tillich's Protestant Era* v. 67 Self-transcending realism is a universal attitude toward reality . . combines two elements, the emphasis on the real and the transcending power of faith. **1975** P. BAELZ *Forgotten Dream* ii. 25 Man also has the ability to distance himself from what is immediately presented to him as himself. . . He is self-transcending.

self-trust. [SELF- 1 a.] = SELF-CONFIDENCE.

1583 GOLDING *Calvin on Deut.* ii. 12 Let vs vnderstand that there is no strength in vs, and that we must rid our selues of all selfetrust. **1593** SHAKS. *Lucr.* 158 Then where is truth if there be no selfe trust? **1841** EMERSON *Ess., Heroism* 253 Self-trust is the essence of Heroism. **1862** GOULBURN *Pers. Relig.* 145 Those . . who in one and the same act of faith have renounced both self-will and self-trust. **1875** LOWELL *Among my Bks.* Ser. II. *Wordsworth*, Wordsworth had that self-trust which in the man of genius is sublime.

So **self-'trusting** *vbl. sb.* and *ppl. a.*

1685 BAXTER *Paraphr. N.T.* Matt. vi. 32 By *self-trusting and self-seeking [they] are drowned in worldly love and care. **1842** MANNING *Serm.* x. (1848) I. 144 The more learned, toilsome, and *self-trusting it [*viz.* the world] has become. **1868** J. H. NEWMAN *Verses on Var. Occas.* 157 Men close the door, and dress the cheerful hearth, Self-trusting still.

self twist. [SELF- 4.] A method of spinning in which the yarn is twisted by the lateral movement of a roller. Usu. (with hyphen) *attrib.*

1970 SELLING & LORD in P. R. Lord *Spinning in '70s* vii. 96 The second section deals with the so-called *self-twist yarns* such as those produced experimentally in Australia. **1972** *Sci. Amer.* Dec. 55/1 Self-twist spinning was developed in Australia, where a great deal of research is done on wools. **1974** [see *open end* adj. s.v. OPEN *a.* 22 c]. **1980** *Jrnl. R. Soc. Arts* May 364/1 Perhaps our most notable success has been the development of the wool spinning method called 'Self-twist'.

†**self-uned,** *pa. pple.* [f. SELF- + F. *uni* united.] United or made one with itself.

1598 SYLVESTER *Du Bartas* II. i. I. 408 When no more the soules chiefe faculties, Are 'sperst to serve the body many wayes, When all self-uned, free from days disturbers, . . she finds a quiet harbor.

†**self-'violence.** *Obs.* [SELF- 3 a.] The laying of violent hands upon oneself: a euphemistic term for SELF-MURDER.

1671 MILTON *Samson* 1584 Self-violence? what cause Brought him so soon at variance with himself Among his foes? **1721** YOUNG *Revenge* IV. i, I . . Exact your solemn Oath, that you'll abstain From all Self-Violence. **1787** HAWKINS *Life of Johnson* 231 Whether he resigned himself to the slow operation of that disease, or precipitated his end by an act of self-violence.

So †**self-'violent** *a.*

1747 MALLET *Amyntor & Theod.* II. 358 Stay Thy hand self-violent.

selfward ('sɛlfwəd), *adv.* and *a.* Chiefly *U.S.* [f. SELF *sb.* + -WARD.] **A.** *adv.* Towards or in the direction of oneself.

1887 *Springfield* (Mass.) *Republ.* 8 Oct., Contrary to the beneficent law of his being, he [*viz.* man] exercised this choice selfward.

B. *adj.* Tending or directed towards oneself.

1888 *Advance* (Chicago) 15 Nov., I wonder if other ministers are prone to fall into this habit of selfward praying. **1888** GIBSON *Christ. acc. to Chr.* (1889) 3 The relative proportions of the Godward and selfward sides of the Christian life. **1907** R. J. CAMPBELL in *Hibbert Jrnl.* Jan. 340 Every possible activity of human nature is either wholeward or selfward.

Hence **'selfwardness.**

1889 *Advance* (Chicago) 28 Mar., The selfwardness of piety which Lent emphasizes.

'selfwards, *adv.* [-WARDS.] = SELFWARD *adv.*

1890 W. A. WALLACE *Only a Sister* xxvi, When the eyes look self-wards.

†**self-'weening,** *vbl. sb. Obs.* [SELF- 1 b.] Self-opinion, self-conceit. So **self-'weening** *ppl. a.*, self-opinioned, self-conceited.

1583 GOLDING *Calvin on Deut.* v. 30 Wee must ridde ourselues of all selfweening and couet nothing but to goe vnto God. **1594** T. B. *La Primaud. Fr. Acad.* II. 300 Wise in themselues, that is to say, arrogant and selfe-weening. **1664** H. MORE *Myst. Iniq.* xi. 149 Eeked and patched out by the Supplements of such self-weening wretches. **1679** J. GOODMAN *Penit. Pard.* III. vi. (1713) 370 Those . . self-weaning persons who would ingross all God's favours to themselves.

self-will, *sb.* [Com. Teut.: OE. *selfwill* = MLG. *sulfwille*, OHG. *selb-*, *selpuuillo*, *-uuilli* (cf. mod.Ger. *selbstwille*), ON. *sjálfvili* (cf. MSw. *sialfsvili*): see SELF- and WILL *sb.*, and cf. SELF-WILLY *a.*]

†**1.** OE., ME. *selfwilles* (advb. gen.), voluntarily, of one's own accord; ME. *of selfwill*, without cause (cf. SELF-WILLY *adv.*). *Obs.*

Cf. OHG. *pî selpwillin* 'ultro', ON. *með* or *at sjálfvilja*.

c **960** ÆTHELWOLD *Rule St. Benet* (Schröer) vii, Se gæð sylfwilles twa mila, to anre ʒeneadod. *c* **1000** ÆLFRIC *Gram.* xxxviii. (Z.) 234 *Sponte*, sylfwilles. *Ibid.* 237 *Ultro*, sylfwilles. *a* **1100** *Leg. Rood* (1871) 17 Drihten . . þe on hire self willes þrowode. *a* **1340** HAMPOLE *Psalter* lxviii. 5 Multiplide thai ere abouen the hares of my heued: that hatid has me of self-will. *c* **1380** *Sir Ferumb.* 221 Sire, wat hast þow þoȝt? Wilt þu silf willes lete þe slen? *c* **1420** LYDG. *Assembly of Gods* 120 Of verrey pure malyce and sylfe wyll.

†**2.** One's own will or desire. *Obs.*

In OE. only in phr. with prep.

c **888** K. ÆLFRED *Boeth.* xi. §1 Ðetæc me nu sumne mann þara ðe þe ʒesæleʒost þince & on his selfwille sy swiðost ʒewiten. *a* **1000** *Boeth. Metr.* iv. 50 ðif ðu nu, waldend, ne wilt wirde steoran ac on selfwille siʒan lætest. *c* **1430** *Syr Gener.* (Roxb.) 3009 Whan I can not accused be By noo man but by your selfwil. **1456** SIR G. HAYE *Law Arms* (S.T.S.) 199/23 We say . . that a monk has na self will, bot anerly the will of his abbot.

3. Wilful or obstinate persistence in following one's own desires or opinions.

14.. *Why I can't be a Nun* 195 in *E.E.P.* (1862) 143 Where that selfe-wylle ys reygnyng, The whyche causethe dyscord and debate, And resun hathe none enteryng. **1489** CAXTON *Faytes of A.* I. xix. 61 So blynded that thy sellfwylle letteth the to submytte thy self to reason. **1514** BARCLAY *Cyt. & Uplondyshm.* (Percy Soc.) 28 All in selfewyll without reason they fyght. **1590** SIR J. SMYTH *Disc. Weapons* 48 They are growen to such a selfe-wil and liking of their owne opinions. **1657** *Baker's Sancta Sophia* II. II. iii. §5 All the comfort of Nature lies in Selfe will. **1780** COWPER *Progr. Err.* 543 First appetite enlists him truth's sworn foe, Then obstinate self-will confirms him so. **1818** SCOTT *Hrt. Midl.* l, So totally unacquainted with contradiction, that she did not even use the tone of self-will. **1860** PUSEY *Min. Proph.* 201 All idolatry is self-will, first choosing a god, and then enslaved to it.

†**self-will,** *a. Obs.* [In OE. *selfwille*; in mod.E. prob. an adjectival use of SELF-WILL *sb.* (cf. attrib. uses of SELF-LOVE, SELF-PITY).]

Self-willed.

1. (in OE.) Voluntary.

a **1100** *Gloss. Aldhelm De Laudibus Virg.* (Napier) 236 *Uoluntarie seruitutis*, sylfwilles þeowdomes. *Ibid.* 1394 *Spontaneo*, .i. *uoluntario*, mid sylfwilre.

2. Self-willed.

1552 ASCHAM *Germany* 9 Contemnyng easely all aduise of others (which selfe will condition doth commonly follow). **1562** COOPER *Answ. Priv. Masse* 122 They be selfwill moichers, they be not diligent scholers. **1581** W. CLARKE in *Confer.* IV. (1584) Ccij b, All vnwritten and selfe will worshippings. **1598** GRENEWEY *Tacitus, Ann.* IV. v. 96 To single out a course . . betweene selfewill stubbornes, and filthy flattery. [**1719** J. T. PHILIPPS tr. *Thirty-Four Conf.* 83 Their pretended meritorious Performances of Self-will Worship.]

self-willed, *a.* Also 5 **-willyd**, *Sc.* **-willit**, 6 **-wyld**, 6–7 **-wild**, 7 **wil'd**; 5 **selwillyd**. [f. SELF-WILL *sb.* + -ED². Cf. SELF-WILLY.] Wilful or obstinate in the pursuit of one's own desires or opinions; characterized by self-will.

G. Campbell *Philos. Rhet.* (1776) I. 421 mentions the word as being 'now little used'.

c **1470** ASHBY *Active Policy* 366 Kepe no selfe-willed oppunion, But to all reason bethe appliable. *c* **1475** *Promp. Parv.* 452/1 Selwillyd . . *Effrenatus.* **1590** SPENSER *F.Q.* I. vi. 17 The lad . . pynd away in anguish and selfe-wild annoy. **1611** *Bible*, Tit. i. 7 A Bishop must be blameles . . not selfe-willed, not soone angry. **1618** BRETON *Court & Country* ad fin., I will pray for your better wit, then you haue showne in a selfe wild humour. **1736** BUTLER *Anal.* I. ii. 39 If, during the Opportunity of Youth, Persons are indocile and selfwill'd; they suffer greatly in their future Life. **1808** SCOTT in *Lockhart* I. i. 25 Habits of self-willed caprice and domination. **1848** THACKERAY *Van. Fair* xliii, The little boy . . is . . forward and inclined to be saucy and self-willed. **1893** LIDDON *Pusey* II. xx. 29 Keble's faith in God's presence and guidance made all high-handed, self-willed action on man's part appear . . irreverent.

Hence †**self'willedly.** *Obs. rare*⁻⁰.

1530 PALSGR. 841/2 Selfwylledly, *testyfuement.*

self'willedness. [f. prec. + -NESS.] The quality or condition of being self-willed.

1509 BARCLAY *Shyp of Folys* (1570) 18 Hector also by his selfwilledness, Was slayne with payne for all his doubtynes. **1530** PALSGR. 269/1 Selfewyldenesse, *obstination.* **1646** P. BULKELEY *Gospel Covt.* I. 111 To suppresse our inordinate passions . . self-willednesse, emulation. **1677** HUBBARD *Narrative* (1865) II. 36 Like sullen Dogs, that would rather in their Self-willedness and Madness sit still to be shot through or cut in Pieces, than receive their Lives for the asking. **1826** E. IRVING *Babylon* III. I. 176 In order that I may not be accused of any self-willedness of interpretation. **1863** SPEKE *Discov. Nile* 389 The capricious restlessness and self-willedness of this despotic king. **1888** *Jrnl. Educ.* Apr. 184 Suppose he . . could sympathise with *our* self-willedness.

†**self-'willing,** *ppl. a.* [f. SELF- + WILLING, after SELF-WILL. Cf. *ill-willing.*] Spontaneous.

c **1000** *Lamb. Ps.* lxvii. 10 Ren sylfwillendne, *Pluuiam uoluntariam.* **1571** GOLDING *Calvin on Ps.* li. 14 Yᵉ free and selfwilling [orig. *vltroneum*] spirit from which hee was almost quyte falne away.

So †**self-'willingness,** spontaneity.

1674 N. FAIRFAX *Bulk & Selv.* 8 'Tis enough there, for the freedom of the will to stand alone in *spontaneitate ad bonum*, or self-willingness to good.

†**self-'willy,** *a. Obs.* Also 5 **sel(f)wylly**, **cel(f)wyl(l)y**. [f. SELF-WILL *sb.* + -Y¹. Cf. *good-willy*, *ill-willy*, and MDu. *selfwilligh*, MLG. *sulfwillich*, OHG. *selbuuillich* (cf. early MHG. *selbswillig*), ON. *sjálfviljugr*, Goth. *silbawiljis* 'αὐθαίρετος'.] Self-willed.

c **1440** *Jacob's Well* 70 Whan a man folwyth his owyn wyll for pompe, & . . euere is selfwylly. *c* **1440** *Promp. Parv.* 65/2 Celwylly [*Winch. MS.* Celf-wylly] . . *effrenatus. Ibid.* 452/1 Selwylly . . [*Winch. MS.* selfe wyly], *effrenatus.* **1471–3** FORTESCUE *Decl. Certayn Wrytinges* Wks. 1869 I. 533 Yf I do not as ye move me I dred that men shall holde me selfewylly. **1611** COTGR., *s'Aheurter*, to be wilfull, . . headie, selfewilly. **1631** WEEVER *Anc. Funeral Mon.* 212 Of a violent selfe-willie disposition.

Hence †**self'williness.** *Obs. rare*⁻⁰.

1611 COTGR., *Teste* . . headinesse, obstinacie, selfewillinesse.

†**self-'willy,** *adv. Obs.* Also 4 **selwilli.** [f. as prec.] Without cause. (Cf. SELF-WILL *sb.* 1.)

a **1300** *E.E. Psalter* cviii 3 With wordes of hatred mikel Um-gaf þai me witerli, And over-wonnen me selwilli. *a* **1400** *Gloss.* in *Rel. Ant.* I. 7 *Gratis*, selfwylly, i. sine causa.

self-'wisdom. [formed after next; cf. SELF- 5 b.] The condition of being self-wise.

1571 GOLDING *Calvin on Ps.* ii. 10 The fond swelling of self-wysdome wherewith they are puffed up. **1625** BACON *Ess., Wisd. Man's Self* (Arb.) 187 They become in the end themselves Sacrifices to the Inconstancy of Fortune; whose Wings they thought, by their Self-Wisedome, to haue Pinnioned. **1657** F. COCKIN *Div. Blossomes* 46 By crucifying All earthly members, to self-wisdome dying. **1729** LAW *Serious C.* xxii. 448 His own self-will and self-wisdom, is of more weight with him, than the will and wisdom of God. **1877** W. BRUCE *Comm. Rev.* iii. 82 Happy are those who have so completely conquered their own self-love and self-wisdom. **1889** M. E. BAMFORD *Up & down the Brooks* 215 Those who know but little about them being much more elated with self-wisdom than those who know more.

self-wise, *a.* [SELF- 3 b.] Wise in one's own conceit, relying on one's own wisdom.

1561 DAUS tr. *Bullinger on Apoc.* (1573) 267 b, Selfwilled and selfewyse men, keeping a rule and a lawe of their owne making. *a* **1586** SIDNEY *Apol. Poetrie* (Arb.) 67 A selfe-wise-seeming schoolmaster. **1646** CRASHAW *Steps to Temple, Sospetto d'Herode* x, How lost Art thou unto thyself, thou too self-wise Narcissus! **1834** J. H. NEWMAN *Par. Serm.* I. xvii, The Self-wise Inquirer. **1836** —— *Lyra Apost.* lxxxvii. 11 Then keep good heart; nor take the self-wise course Of Thomas, who must see ere he would trust.

absol. **1579** W. WILKINSON *Confut. Fam. Love* Bj, No selfe-wise, or enuious scripture learned could or can euer attaine vnto it.

Hence †**self-'wiseling** [see -LING], one who is wise in his own conceit.

1649 *Test. conc. Jacob Beme* i. §13 Hidden unto the high and self-wiselings.

†**self-wit.** *Obs.* [SELF- 3 b.] Self-wisdom. So **self-'wittedness.**

1647 WARD *Simple Cobler* 19 Bred of the Exhalations of their owne pride and selfe-wittednesse. **1657** [J. ELLISTONE] tr. *Behmen's Sign. Rerum* Pref. sub fin., By Glosses, Comments, Curiosity and Self-wit, none shall be able to reach or apprehend it in his own ground.

self-wrought, *ppl. a.* [SELF- 2.] Produced or brought about by oneself.

a **1593** MARLOWE *Ovid's Eleg.* II. xiv. 3 If without battell selfe-wrought wounds annoy them. **1742** YOUNG *Nt. Th.* VIII. 682 Can man outwit Omnipotence? strike out A self-wrought happiness unmeant by him. **1830** TENNYSON *Tears of Heaven* Poems 118 The earth hath made her state forlorn With selfwrought evils of unnumbered years.

b. self-wrought-out.

1656 OWEN *Mortif. Sin* To Rdr. (1668) A 3 b, [They] have anew imposed the Yoke of a self-wrought-out Mortification on the Necks of their Disciples. **1855** MILMAN *Lat. Christ.* XIV. x. VI. 632 Teutonic Christianity, more self-depending, more self-guided, more self wrought out.

self-yew: see SELF B. 6.

selghe, obs. form of SEAL *sb.*¹

selham, var. SULHAM.

seli, variant of SEELY *a.* and of SELLY *a.*, etc.

selibub, obs. form of SILLABUB.

‖**selicha** (sɪ'li:xə, sɪli:'xɑ:). Also **seliha**; pl. **selichot**, **-oth**, etc. [a. Heb. *səlīḥā*, pl. *səlīḥōṯ* penitential prayer.] A Hebrew liturgical poem recited in penance on fast days, before Rosh Hashanah, and before and on Yom Kippur.

1864 *Chambers's Encycl.* VI. 155/1 The *Selichoth*, or Penitential Prayers. **1909** *Cent. Dict.* Suppl. 1194/2 The selihot are acrostically arranged, many containing not only the alphabet but also the names of the composer and his father. **1925** W. O. E. OESTERLEY *Jewish Background Christ. Liturgy* ii. 76 What are called the *Selichôth* (i.e. prayers for forgiveness; the word comes from the root *salach* 'to forgive') form an important element in the Jewish liturgy. **1960** S. BECKER tr. *A. Schwarz-Bart's Last of Just* (1961) I. 9 He is the author of the famous Seliha, Oh God, cover not our blood with thy silence. **1974** *Jewish Chron.* 13 Sept. 34/3, I was at selichot the other morning (none of your midnight revels for me) with my soul on high. **1976** B. WILLIAMS *Making of Manch. Jewry* xii. 304 In October 1870 the congregation agreed on minor ritual changes—including the abbreviation of the *Piyyutim* and *Selicoth.*

‖**se'lictar.** *Obs.* Also 7 **selihhtar.** [repr. Turkish pronunciation of Pers. *silaḥdār*, f. Arab. *silāḥ* (pl. of *silḥ* weapon) + Pers. *-dār* having.] The sword-bearer of a Turkish chieftain.

1684 *Lond. Gaz.* No. 1985/1 The Selictar Aga, or the Great Sword-Bearer, attended with a great number of Spahees. **1687** LOVELL tr. *Thevenot's Trav.* I. 161 After him came his Selihhtar and Tchoadar, each with his long tail'd Cap hanging down behind his back. **1696** *Lond. Gaz.* No. 4236/1 He was Selictar Aga to the late Sultan. **1812** BYRON *Ch. Har.* II. lxxii, Selictar! unsheathe then our chief's scimitar. **1820** T. S. HUGHES *Trav. Sicily* II. 148, 3000 Albanian troops under the selictar or sword-bearer of the vizir.

†**'selidone.** *Obs.* Also 4 **salidoine,** 5 **salidone.** [a. OF. *celidoine*, ad. med.Lat. *c(h)elidonius*: see CELIDONY[2].] = CELIDONY[2].

13.. *Owain Miles* (1837) 37 Ribes and salidoines, Onicles and causteloines. *c* **1400** *Beryn* 3302 A saphir, & a salidone, & a rich ruby. *c* **1400** *Laud Troy Bk.* 8057 In hem stode many a riche ston, Saphur riche, and selidone.

selie, variant of SEELY *a.*

seligmannite ('sɛlɪgmənaɪt). *Min.* [ad. G. *seligmannit* (H. Baumhauer 1901, in *Sitzungsber. d. K. Preuss. Akad. d. Wissensch. zu Berlin* 110), f. the name of Gustav *Seligmann* (1849–1920), German mineral collector: see -ITE[1].] An arsenic sulphide of lead and copper, $PbCuAsS_3$, occurring as brittle, dark grey to black, orthorhombic crystals having a metallic lustre.

1902 *Mineral Mag.* XIII. 205 Seligmannite... Of this mineral,.. only five crystals, varying in size from ½ to 4 mm., have been found. **1969** *Zeitschr. für Krist.* CXXX. 224 The structure of seligmannite is built up essentially of a framework or CuS_4 tetrahedra and AsS_3 pyramids, with lead atoms inserted in the large holes.

selihe, obs. form of SALLOW *sb.*

seliliche, -ly, seliness: see SEELILY, -NESS.

selion ('sɛlɪən). *Hist.* and *local.* Forms: 5 **sellion, seylon,** 6 **selyon,** 7 **selione, sillyon,** 4– **selion.** [ad. Anglo-L. *seliōn-em*, *seilōn-em*, AF. *seilon* = OF. *seillon*, mod.F. *sillon* furrow.] **1.** A portion of land of indeterminate area comprising a ridge or narrow strip lying between two furrows formed in dividing an open field, a 'narrow-land'.

c **1450** *Godstow Reg.* 215, xx. seylons & j. of hys arable londe. *c* **1460** *Oseney Reg.* 68, ij. sellions or buttes of lond to a wey to be made at northoseney. **1542** *Conveyance* in Willis & Clark *Cambridge* (1886) II. 398 Foure selyons of lande arrable conteynyng two acres. **1628** COKE *On Litt.* 5 b, By the grant of a selion of land, a ridge of land which containeth no certainty, for some be greater and some lesser, doth pass. **1669** *Will of R. Mayor* in *Blk. Bk. Dioc. Lichf.* I. 87 Four lands or rudges or sillyons of arrable land. **1695** KENNETT *Par. Antiq.* ix. 368 A croft.. containing five selions or ridges of land. **1839** STONEHOUSE *Isle of Axholme* 302 Two selions of land containing one acre, lying in a furlong called Foxholes. **1894** *Times* 19 May 7/3 The land is for the most part in open fields, cut up into numerous narrow strips, or 'selions' as they are locally termed, and cultivated by small farmers.

2. A furrow turned over by the plough. *nonce-use.*

1877 G. M. HOPKINS *Poems* (1967) 69 No wonder of it: shéer plód makes plough down sillion Shine.

Selish, var. SALISH.

Seljuk ('sɛldʒuːk), *a.* and *sb.* Also 9 **Seljouk.** [f. Turk. *seljūq*, the name of the reputed ancestor of the Seljuk dynasties.] **A.** *adj.* **1.** The distinctive epithet of certain Turkish dynasties which ruled over large parts of Asia from the 11th to the 13th c. Hence used to designate the branch of the Turkish people to whom these dynasties belonged (in contradistinction to *Ottoman* or *Osmanli*).

1834 J. B. FRASER *Acc. Persia* vi. 214 His heir Musaood was defeated ten years after by the Seljuk Turkomans, in Khorasan. **1879** FREEMAN *Hist. Ess.* Ser. III. 268 A new enemy appeared in the form of the Seljouk Turks. **1904** W. M. RAMSAY *Lett. Seven Churches* xvii. 216 The coins of a Seljuk principality.. bear the legend in mediaeval Latin.

2. Designating a style of oriental carpet.

1931 A. U. DILLEY *Oriental Rugs & Carpets* xiii. 267 Seljuk, lifted out of Turkish history, and Dinar.. are the names of oriental rugs produced in Greece. **1952** B. MIALL tr. *H. Jacoby's How to know Oriental Carpets & Rugs* 13 The oldest known Oriental carpets, the so-called Seljuk carpets of the thirteenth century, which came originally from the Ala-eddin Mosque at Konia, are now preserved, with other magnificent examples, in the Evkaf Museum at Istanbul. **1963** I. SCHLOSSER *European & Oriental Rugs & Carpets* 118 The Seljuk carpets.. in the Evkaf Museum.. have small but very interesting geometric patterns.

B. *sb.* (or absol. use of the adj.). A member of the Seljuk tribe or dynasty.

1841 *Penny Cycl.* XXI. 211/1 A dynasty which.. overturned that of the Iranian Seljuks. **1899** F. M. CRAWFORD *Via Crucis* xxii. 351 A full hour the Seljuks slew and slew.

Seljukian (sɛl'dʒuːkɪən), *a.* and *sb.* Also 7 **Selzuccian,** (**Salghucian**), **Zelzuckian,** 9 **Seljookian, Seljucian.** [f. SELJUK + -IAN.]

A. *adj.* = SELJUK *a.* 1

1603 KNOLLES *Hist. Turks* (1638) 3 Tangrolipix, Chiefetaine of the Selzuccian Familie. **1634** SIR T. HERBERT *Trav.* 84 The Zelzuckian Family. **1788** GIBBON *Decl. & F.* lvii. V. 656 The first of the Seljukian sultans was conspicuous by his zeal and faith. **1840** *Penny Cycl.* XVII. 484/1 The descent from Central Asia of the Seljookian Turks. **1875** BUNBURY in *Encycl. Brit.* II. 712/2 The whole country.. continued subject to the Byzantine empire, until it was overrun by the Seljukian Turks in 1074 A.D.

B. *sb.* (or absol. use of adj.) = SELJUK *sb.*

1638 SIR T. HERBERT *Trav.* (ed. 2) 284 The Salghucian.. commanded Persia. **1818** HALLAM *Mid. Ages* vi. (1819) II. 181 The Seljukians of Rûm. **1841** *Penny Cycl.* XXI. 210/1 Seljukides, or Seljucians, a dynasty originally Tartar, and descended from a captain named Seljuk. **1845** J. E. RIDDLE in *Encycl. Metrop.* XII. 276/1 Ortogrul acquired the confidence of the Seljukians.

selk(e, selken, obs. ff. SILK, SILKEN *a.*

†**'selkhorn.** ? *Sc. Obs. rare*⁻¹. [Of obscure origin: the mod. dial. forms are *shill-corn*, *shilf-corn* (E.D.D.).] An incrustation of the sebaceous matter of the skin, producing a small maggot-like mass.

1681 COLVIL *Whigs Supplic.* (1751) 20 A mountain rather than a nose; Upon which savage beasts did feed, As worms and selkhorns.

selkin, -yn, obs. forms of SILKEN *a.*

selkouþ, selkowþ, selkuð: see SELCOUTH *a.*

Selkup (sɛl'kuːp). Also **Sel'kup.** [Native name.] A member of a Samoyedic people of northern Siberia; the language of this people belonging to the Uralic family of languages. (Formerly known as 'Ostyak Samoyed': cf. OSTYAK; SAMOYED *sb.* and *a.*)

1962 [see NENETS]. **1964** in S. P. Dunn *Levin & Potapov's Peoples of Siberia* 597 The summer dwelling of the Northern Sel'kups was the birchbark tent. **1967** D. S. PARLETT *Short Dict. Languages* 107 The Southern languages include Ostyak Samoyed (Sel'kup), and Kamassian. **1972** *Language* XLVIII. 206 Of the southern group, only Sel'kup ('Ostyak Samoyed') can be considered a living language. **1974** *Encycl. Brit. Macropædia* XVIII. 1022/2 The fourth language, Selkup, lies to the south in a region between the central Ob and central Yenisey. **1975** G. F. CUSHING tr. *Hajdu's Finno-Ugrian Languages & Peoples* iii. 215 The only representatives of the southern group of Samoyeds still extant are the Selkups.

sell (sɛl), *sb.*[1] Now only *arch.* Forms: 4–5, 9 **selle,** 6 **scell,** 7 **cell,** 7–8 **selly,** 7– **sell.** [a. F. *selle*:—L. *sella*:—prehistoric **sedla* f. *sed-*, *sedēre* to sit; the Teut. form corresponding (except in declension) occurs in OE. *setl* SETTLE *sb.*]

†**1.** A seat, a low stool; a seat of dignity. *joint sell* = JOINT-STOOL. *Obs.*

1382 WYCLIF *2 Macc.* xiv. 21 To eche sellis [Vulg. *sellæ*], or smale setis, ben brouȝt forth and putt. *c* **1425** *Cast. Persev.* 1749 in *Macro Plays* 129 Heyl, set in þyn selle! **1531** *Rec. St. Mary at Hill* (1904) 37 Item, iiij Joyntes scells, at iiij d the pesse. Some xvj d. **1627** MAY *Lucan* III. 114 But empty stand those honor'd Sells.

2. A saddle.

c **1425** *Thomas Erceld.* 49 Hir selle it was of roelle bone. **1590** SPENSER *F.Q.* II. viii. 31 Yet was the force so furious and so fell, That horse and man it made to reele aside; Nath'lesse the Prince would not forsake his sell. **1600** FAIRFAX *Tasso* VI. xxxii, Downe from his steed the Christian backward fell; Yet his proud foe so strong and sturdie was That he nor shooke, nor staggered in his cell. **1803** SCOTT *Cadyow Cast.* xxx, From gory selle, and reeling steed, Sprung the fierce horseman with a bound. **1855** BAILEY *Mystic* 140 Then to horse; the gallant knighthood lift their ladies to the sells. **1886** R. F. BURTON *Arab. Nts.* (abr. ed.) I. 175 He bade one of his pages saddle him his Nubian mare-mule with her padded selle.

sell (sɛl), *sb.*[2] [f. SELL *v.*]

1. An act of betraying or giving up to justice.

1838 DICKENS *O. Twist* xxvi, I say,.. what a time this would be for a sell! I've got Phil Barker here: so drunk, that a boy might take him.

2. *slang.* **a.** A contrivance, fiction, etc., by which a person is 'sold': a planned deception, hoax, take-in. Also, something that utterly disappoints high expectations.

1838 *Actors by Daylight* 4 Aug. 179 (*heading*) Editorial consequence—Specimens of wit—A decided sell. **1853** 'C. BEDE' *Verdant Green* I. vii, Mr. Verdant Green having swallowed this, his friend was thereby enabled not only to use up old 'sells', but also to draw largely on his invention for new ones. **1857** GEN. P. THOMPSON *Audi Alt. Part.* I. ii. 5 The thing is what in the language of the turf is called a sell. **1890** R. F. D. PALGRAVE *Cromwell* xiv. 298 The Insurrection proved, in vulgar phrase, 'a thorough sell'. **1898** R. BLAKEBOROUGH *Wit, Char.*, etc. *N.R. Yorks.* 79 The last sell I heard was sending a lad from one place to another for a bucket of steam.

b. The technique of selling by advertising or persuasive salesmanship; the practice or fact of this. Usu. with qualifying word: cf. *hard sell* s.v. HARD *a.* 23 a; *soft sell* s.v. SOFT *a.* 29.

1952, etc. [see *hard sell* s.v. HARD *a.* 23 a]. **1970** G. GREER *Female Eunuch* 11 The main force of their energy filtered away.. through the sexual sell of the fifties. **1976** SCOTT & KOSKI *Walk-In* (1977) xiii. 81 He was like an encyclopedia salesman moving into the soft, memorized sell.

3. (See quot. 1911.)

1911 *Webster's Dict.*, *Sell.* 2. A stock that should be sold. *Stock Exchange Cant.* **1981** *Times* 20 July 20/1 Cooke, Lumsden waver between a hold and sell recommendation for Dowty Group. *Ibid.* 27 July 20/1 Woodside Petroleum is a sell. **1981** *Sunday Times* 2 Aug. 43/6 We rated them a sell ahead of the disappointing figures last month.

4. sell-out. orig. *U.S.* **a.** An agreement or contract corruptly made by a public body, involving sacrifice of public to private interest. Also *gen.*, (one who makes) a sacrifice of principle or betrayal.

1862 M. B. CHESNUT *Diary* 6 May in C. V. Woodward *M. Chesnut's Civil War* (1981) 336 Another sellout to the devil. It is this giving up that kills me. **1883** J. HAY *Bread-Winners* 151 How much did the Captain give you for that sell-out? **1890** *Advance* (Chicago) 1 Feb. 3 The proposed sell-out of the State of North Dakota to the infamous Louisiana Lottery Company. **1906** *Tom Watson's Mag.* Jan. 362 (Cent. *Suppl.*) The Tariff Act.. was an ungodly and unblushing sell-out to the Sugar Trust,.. [and to] the greedy manufacturing interests generally. **1940** 'G. ORWELL' *Jrnl.* 24 June in *Coll. Essays* (1968) II. 354 High-up influences in England are preparing for a similar sell-out [to Pétain's]. **1953** *Landfall* (N.Z.) Dec. 283 This film could have ended with a punch; but this would have been running counter to the sacrosanct Hollywood tradition of the inevitable happy ending. So there is a sell-out. **1959** *Economist* 11 Apr. 134/2 Specially elected members (reference to whom the wilder parts of the audience had greeted with familiar African cries of 'stooges', 'sell-outs'). **1960** J. LEHMANN *I am My Brother* 4 A gigantic sell-out to the Nazis. *a* **1974** R. CROSSMAN *Diaries* (1975) I. 182 Then Maurice Edelman made an inflammatory half-hour attack on the Government, charging me and Frank Cousins with every kind of crime, including a sell-out to the Americans. **1980** *Times* 19 Feb. 6 Mr. Robert Mugabe's Zanla guerrillas infiltrated the region.. maiming or murdering those who were considered sell-outs.

b. A card game otherwise called *auction pitch*: cf. PITCH *sb.*[2] 4 b.

c. The disposal of a commodity because of great demand; also, a completely disposable commodity. Also *transf.*, an event for which all tickets have been sold; the occasion of such an event.

1859 *N.Y. Herald* 11 July 6/5 (Advt.), Our goods shall be sold cheap!! In this great sellout. **1923** *Variety* 11 Oct. 17/4 Business at 'Give and Take' at the Adelphi was generally big last week... Wednesday.. was a virtual sell-out. **1933** *Sun* (Baltimore) 29 Aug. 8/3 The [actor's] interpretation may not be art, and it may not even be O'Neill, but it may easily be a sellout and it will almost assuredly be entertaining. **1945** *Ibid.* 27 Apr. 10-o/1 On a sharp sell-out of rails and steels after the opening, dealings were relatively heavy. **1945** S. LEWIS *C. Timberlane* (1947) xliii. 289, I have four tickets... They're absolutely impossible to get, show is a sell-out, but the agent is a friend of mine. **1950** *Sport* 22–28 Sept. 2/1 The Cup Final.. is always a sell-out but crowds at other games are always below maximum. **1962** *Listener* 27 Dec. 1095/1 The shortage of shopping times for working people.. causes overcrowding, queuing, poor service and sell-outs on Saturday. **1968** *Globe & Mail* (Toronto) 15 Jan. 17/2 A sellout crowd of 75,546 watched.. Vince Lombardi's National Football League champions. **1977** *Time* 19 Dec. 41/2 Such delicacies are instant sellouts.

5. sell-off. *Stock Exchange* (orig. and chiefly *U.S.*). A sale or disposal of bonds, shares, or commodities, usu. causing a fall in price.

1937 *Sun* (Baltimore) 6 Feb. 19/1 The sell-off was less pronounced than that of the share market and was slower in developing. **1941** *Ibid.* 16 Oct. 21/1 Adverse war news was blamed in most quarters for the selloff in stocks and commodities. **1958** *Time* 8 Dec. 98/3 The sell-off did not alarm most market experts. **1981** *Times* 21 May 24/1 The recent sell-off by a major institution has done much to cloud market sentiment.

sell (sɛl), *v.* Pa. t. and pa. pple. **sold** (səʊld). Forms: see below. [A Com. Teut. wk. verb: OE. *sęllan*, pa. t. *sealde*, pa. pple. *seald*, corresponds to OFris. *sella* to give, sell, OS. *sellian* to give, pa. pple. *gisald* (MLG., LG. *sellen* to sell by retail, huckster; hence in Ger. dialects), OHG. *sellen* to deliver up, pa. t. *salta*, pa. pple. *kasalt*, *giselit* (MHG. *sellen*), ON. *selja* to give up, sell, pa. t. *selda*, pa. pple. *seld* (Sw. *sälja*, Da. *sælge* to sell), Goth. *saljan* to offer (sacrifice):—OTeut. **saljan*, f. **salā* gift, delivery, SALE *sb.*

It has been suggested by Osthoff that OTeut. **sal* (:—pre-Teut. **sol*) may be an ablaut-variant, with causative sense, of **sel-* to take (Irish *selaim*, Gr. ἑλεῖν).

The difference of vowel between the pres. stem and the pa. t. and pa. pple. arises from the fact that the *i* in OTeut. **salidō*, **salido-* was lost in W.Ger., and the root-syll. therefore has no umlaut except in the pres. stem. Cf. TELL *v.*

The OE. form (**siellan*) *syllan* (beside the normal *sęllan*: cf. *tęllan* TELL *v.*) is difficult to account for, as the breaking before *ll* otherwise occurs only when the gemination is of OTeut. date. Possibly the sibilant may in some way have affected the following vowel.]

A. Illustration of Inflexional Forms.

1. Present stem. *Inf.* 1 **sellan, sillan, syllan,** (*Northumb.* **sealla, sella**), 1–2 **syl(l)e,** 2 **sillen,** 2–3 **sullen,** (3 **seollen**), 3 *Ormin* **sellenn,** 3–5 **selle(n, sulle,** 3–7 **sel,** 4–5 **sill(e,** 4 *Kent.* **zelle, suylle,** 5 **syll(e, (sile), seel(l,** *Promp. Parv.* **ceele, cellyn, sellyn,** 3– **sell.** Also 1 *imper.* **sele, syle;** *3rd pers. pres. ind.* 4 *Kent.* **zelþ.**

c **950** *Lindisf. Gosp.* Luke xi. 7 Ne mæȝe ic arisa & sealla ðe [*c* **1000** *Ags. Gosp.* ibid., & syllan þe, *c* **1160** *Hatton Gosp.* ibid., & sillen ðe]. *c* **1000** *Ags. Gosp.* Matt. xx. 23 [It] nys me inc to syllanne [*c* **1160** *Hatton Gosp.* ibid., to sellenne]. *c* **1000** Sylle [See B. 1]. *c* **1200** *Trin. Coll. Hom.* 213 þe sullere .. swereð þat he hit nele lasse selle. *c* **1205** LAY. 29057, & we wulleð.. to ȝislen sullen þe ure sunen. *Ibid.* 31053 And he wulle.. to ȝisle seollen þe his sune. *c* **1250** Sel [see B. 3]. **1340** *Ayenb.* 36 Huanne me zelþ þet þing. *Ibid.* 138 þet hi hit moȝe yeue and zelle. **1362** LANGL. *P. Pl.* A. III. 189 And beere heor bras on þi Bac to Caleys to sulle [**1377** B. III. 195 to selle]. **1382** Wyclif *Gen.* xlvii. 22 Thei ben not nedid to sellen [**1388** to sille] her possessiouns. *c* **1400** *Apol. Loll.* 113 þei do uniustly, & silun God & þe peple. **1422** *Secreta Secret., Priv. Priv.* xxvi. 159 He the kyngedome of hewyn sillyth for a lytill price. *Ibid.* 169 Sylle [see B. 7a]. **1574** Shell, shyll [see B. 3]. **1649** Bp. Reynolds *Hosea* ii. 77 Judas ..at once sels a soul, and a Saviour.

2. *Pa. t.* α. 1–2, 4 sealde, 2 sælde, 4 seelde, *Kent.* zyalde, 5 seeld.

a **1000** *Cædmon's Gen.* 857 (Gr.) Wiste forworhte þa he ær wlite sealde. *a* **1175** *Cott. Hom.* 227 þes cenne god sælde & ȝesette æ. *c* **1315** Shoreham *Poems* i. 1287 He..bet out..þo þat bouȝte and sealde ine godes hous. **1340** *Ayenb.* 215 He wrek þo þe zyalde and boȝte ine þe temple. *c* **1449** Pecock *Repr.* III. vi. 309 Thei seelden possessiouns and catel.

β. 1–2, 3 salde, 3 sald, saald, 6, 9 *Sc.* sauld.

c **950** *Lindisf. Gosp.* John xix. 9 Uutudlice ondsuare ne salde him. *c* **1200** Ormin 15960 þa menn þatt saldenn cullfress þær. *a* **1300** Saald [see B. 3]. *a* **1300** *Cursor M.* 3518 Esau his forbirth sald [*c* **1375** *Ibid.* (Fairf.) salde]. *c* **1400** *Ywaine & Gaw.* 1703 The ermyte..salde the skinnes that he broght. **1562** Winȝet *Cert. Tractates* Wks. (S.T.S.) I. 6 The Disciplis..sauld thair landis. **1600** J. Hamilton *Facile Traictise* 280 Whair euer the pape sauld indulgencis.

γ. 3–6 solde, (4 soold), 6 soulde, 7–8 (9 *dial.*) sould, 4– sold.

a **1225** *Ancr. R.* 398 þet ase ofte ase me euesede him me solde his euesunge. **13..** *Cursor M.* 3550 (Gött.), As a wreche he sold his eritage. **1526** *Pilgr. Perf.* (W. de W. 1531) 14 They solde theyr possessyons. **1597** Hooker *Eccl. Pol.* v. lxxviii. §7 They soulde their possessions. **1710** Prideaux *Orig. Tithes* iii. 142 The first Christians..sould all, that they had.

δ. 3–5 selde, 4 sillide, 5 sellid, seld, 6 selled; 9 *dial.* (see Eng. Dial. Dict.) selled, sell'd, seld; *Sc.* and *north.* sell't, sellt, selt.

c **1380** Wyclif *Sel. Wks.* I. 286 He..selde al þat he hadde. **138.** Sillide [see B. 7a]. *c* **1440** *Alphabet of Tales* 64 Constancius..sellid his hors for xiȷ d of gold. **1451** Capgrave *Life St. Gilbert* 77 For he seld hem nowt. **1562** Selled [see B. 3].

3. *Pa. pple.* α. 1 seald, 2 iseald, 3 isæld, iseold, 4 seeld.

a **1000** *Ags. Ps.* cxix. [cxx.] 3 (Gr.) Hwæt bið þe ealles seald ..yflan tungan? *c* **1175** *Lamb. Hom.* 13 And ȝe beoð iseald eower feonde to prisune. *c* **1205** Lay. 11998 Seoððen þis world wes astald & monnen an honde isælde. *Ibid.* 29459 Heo scolden beon iseolde. **1388** Wyclif *Isa.* xlii. 19 Who is blynd, no but he that is seeld [Vulg. *venundatus*]?

β. 3 sald, (saald), isald, 4 salde; *Sc.* 4–6 sald, 6 salde, 5–9 sauld.

c **1205** Lay. 29471 And we weoren ut isalde of Anglene londe. *a* **1300** *Cursor M.* 142 How þat ioseph was boght and sald. *Ibid.* 4241 He was eftursons saald. *c* **1375** *Ibid.* 6755 (Fairf.) He salle be salde. *c* **1470** Sald, sauld [see B. 7c]. **1596** Dalrymple tr. *Leslie's Hist. Scot.* I. 26 The fowlis..ar sent to the nerrest tounes to be salde.

γ. 4 i-sold(e, 4–6 solde, (5 swolde), 7 sould, (soald), 4– sold.

1382 [see B. 3e]. **1387** [see B. 3]. *c* **1451** *Pol. Poems* (1859) II. 230 Suffolk Normandy hath swolde. **1615** R. Cocks *Diary* (Hakl. Soc.) I. 68 Our pepper..was soald long since. **1618** Raleigh in *Four-Cent. Eng. Lett.* 38, I might elsewhere have sould my shipp and goods.

δ. 4–5 seld, 5 *Promp. Parv.* celde; *Sc.* 6 sellit, 8–9 sell'd, seld, selt; 9 *dial.* selled. (See E.D.D.)

13.. *Cursor M.* 13182 (Gött.) Bot þis dede was seld ful dere. **1549** Sellit [see B. 2]. **1815** Scott *Guy M.* xii, It will be sell'd the morn to the highest bidder.

B. Signification.

I. The simple verb.

†**1.** *trans.* To give, in various senses; esp. to hand over (something, esp. food, a gift) voluntarily or in response to a demand or request; to deliver up (a person, esp. a hostage) to the keeping of another; to grant (forgiveness, etc.); also, rarely of an impersonal agent, to yield. (Chiefly OE.)

Beowulf 1161 (Gr.) Byrelas sealdon win of wunderfatum. *c* **950** *Lindisf. Gosp.* Matt. vi. 11 Hlaf userne ofer wistlic sel us todæȝ. *c* **1000** Ælfric *Exod.* vi. 8 (Gr.) þat land..ic sylle eow to aȝenne. *Ibid.* xxii. 29 Sylle me þin forme bearn. *a* **1175** *Cott. Hom.* 223 And se eorðe his awiriȝd on þine weorcum, sylðe þornes and brembles. *a* **1200** *12th Cent. Hom.* 132 Ic ȝeafe heom mine milse; & sylle heom forȝefenesse. *c* **1205** Lay. 13437 Vortiger heom salde al þat heo wolden. *Ibid.* 23779 Me salde him an honde enne scaft stronge. *c* **1275** *Serving Christ* 63 in *O.E. Misc.* 92 Seynt thomas wes biscop & barunes him quolde..For þe dute of þe dom he þet lif solde. *a* **1300** *Cursor M.* 17042 And sua to mak vs ranscuning, for vs him-self he sald.

2. a. To give up (a person) treacherously to his enemies; to betray (a person, a cause, country, etc.).

Chiefly, with mixture of sense 3, to betray for a price or in order to obtain some advantage for oneself. In early use often with reference to the betrayal of Christ by Judas.

c **950** *Lindisf. Gosp.* John vi. 71 Cuæð uutedlice iudam ..ðes forðon uæs sellend hine [Vulg. *traditurus eum*]. *c* **1275** *Passion our Lord* 115 in *O.E. Misc.* 40 He com to þe Gywes ..And chepte heom to sullen vre helare. **1375** Barbour *Bruce* v. 610 'Tratour', he said, 'thou has me sald'. **1549** *Compl. Scot.* 72 Tha deserue as grite reproche as tha hed sellit traisonablye the realme to there enemeis. **1574** Hellowes *Gueuara's Fam. Ep.* (1577) 154 In things of common libertie, he that shall seeme most to serue you, the same is he that most will sell you. **1599** Shaks. *Hen. V,* II. ii. 10 That he should for a forraigne purse, so sell His Soueraigne's life to death and treachery. **1654** tr. *Martinius' Conq. China* 48 But when the Emperour had perused the Treatie, he presently found his Plenipotentiarian had sold him. **1692** R. L'Estrange *Fables* cxxxii. 123 Those that Sell their Country..for Mony. **1791** Burns *Such a Parcel of Rogues* iii, We're bought and sold for English gold. **1816** 'Quiz' *Grand Master* II. 36 Have you e're met a faithless friend, That sold you to effect his end? **1820** J. W. Croker *Diary* 12 Apr. in *C. Papers* (1884) I. 172 Brougham, it is said, grossly, has sold the Queen. **1895** Wolseley in *United Serv. Mag.* Aug. 475 There can be no moral doubt..that there were traitors in the Turkish ranks, and that the Turkish Army was more or less sold.

b. *transf.* Of a thing: To betray, 'give away', inform against.

1831 *Ann. Reg., Law Cases* (1832) 325/2 Bishop..said to May, 'It was the blood that sold us'.

3. (The chief current sense.) **a.** To give up or hand over (something) to another person for money (or something that is reckoned as money); esp. to dispose of (merchandise, possessions, etc.) to a buyer for a price; to vend. Const. †*with, for* (the price), †*at, to* (the buyer). Also, in habitual sense, of a shopkeeper, etc.: To deal in, keep for sale (a particular commodity).

c **1000** *Ags. Gosp.* John xii. 5 Hwi ne sealde heo þas sealfe wiþ þrim hundred peneȝon. *c* **1175** *Lamb. Hom.* 91 And þa ..fuleden þam apostles and salden heore ehte and þet feh bitahten þam apostles. *c* **1200** Ormin 15557, & he fand i þe temmple þær Well fele menn þatt saldenn þærinne baþe nowwt & shep. *c* **1250** *Gen. & Ex.* 1495 'Broðer', quad he [*sc.* Esau], 'sel me ðo wunes'. *a* **1300** *Cursor M.* 5407 þai saald þair landes þan for nede. *a* **1330** *Roland & V.* 386 þe hors was seld..For to hundred schillinges. **1387** Trevisa *Higden* (Rolls) VIII. 237 A busshel of corn was i-solde for twelf schillynges þat ȝere. *c* **1440** *Alphabet of Tales* 216 He sellid a noder hors & spendid þe price þer-of. **1562** Legh *Armory* (1597) 77 b, So when they die, their wiues..selled for a little money, their books of visitations. **1574** in *10th Rep. Hist. MSS. Comm.* App. v. 424 The inhabitance..shall not..shell any kynd of flesh..to any of the bucheares. **1595** Shaks. *John* I. i. 153 Yet sell your face for fiue pence and 'tis deere. **1615, 1618** [see A. 3γ]. **1625** Bacon *Ess., Seditions* (Arb.) 405 There be but three Things, which one Nation selleth vnto another; The Commoditie as Nature yeeldeth it; The Manufacture; and the Vecture or Carriage. **1728** Young *Love Fame* II. 202 As pedlars with some hero's head make bold, Illustrious mark! where pins are to be sold. **1732** Pope *Ep. Bathurst* 212 Last, for his Country's love, he sells his Lands. **1821** Scott *Kenilw.* xxii, I bought you some books, madam,..from a lame fellow who sold them in the Market-place. **1883** Howells *Woman's Reason* v. 98 The auctioneer intoned his chant..varied with a quick 'Sold!' as ..he knocked off this lot or that. *Ibid.* 106, I won't sell this property at that price. *Mod.* Many grocers sell wines and spirits.

fig. **1742** Young *Nt. Th.* VIII. 787 Heav'n sells all pleasure; effort is the price.

b. To dispose of (one's commission in the army) by sale under the purchase system. Now only *Hist.* Also †*to sell* one's ***company, regiment***, etc., and *absol.* (Cf. *sell out*, 12c. below.)

1713 Swift *Jrnl. to Stella* 8 Apr., Lieutenant-general Palmer will be obliged to sell his regiment. **1749** Fielding *Tom Jones* I. x, The half-pay officer having quarrelled with his colonel, was by his interest obliged to sell. **1852** Thackeray *Esmond* III. iv, An old army acquaintance of Colonel Esmond's..had sold his company.

c. *causatively.* To promote the sale of.

1709 Swift *Vind. Bickerstaff* 8 Or, perhaps, a Name can make an Almanack, as well as it can sell one. **1793** *Trans. Soc. Arts* XI. 8 Every costermonger knows it is the fine fruit which sells the orchard.

d. *Comm.* In passive with adv.: To have one's stock (well, etc.) disposed of.

1882 *Daily News* 4 Mar., The market will be better later on in the season, and hence makers who are fairly sold are not much inclined to do business for forward delivery. **1898** *Ibid.* 8 Nov. 2/7 Makers have but a small surplus to dispose of as they are well sold.

e. To hand over (a person, a people) into slavery or bondage for a sum of money. In Biblical use (after Heb.) often merely (without reference to a price received), To hand over to the dominion of another, to enslave. Hence *fig.*

a **1000** Ælfric *Gen.* xxxvii. 27 Selre ys, þat we hine syllon to ceape Ysmahelitum. **1382** Wyclif *Ps.* civ. [cv.] 17 And into a thral Joseph is sold. **1388** *Ibid.*, Joseph was seeld in to a seruaunt. *Ibid. Rom.* vii. 14 Sothli we witen, for the lawe is spiritual, or goostli; forsoth I am fleischly, sold vndir synne. **1390** Gower *Conf.* I. 215 Mi brother hath ous alle sold To hem of Rome. *c* **1400** *Mirr. St. Edm.* in *Hampole's Wks.* (Horstm.) I. 221 Whene þou was saulde with syne þan he boghte þe. **1576** *Gude & Godlie B.* 122 My Mother als did eik the same, And I to sin was sald. **1576** Fleming *Panopl. Epist.* 282 Othersome, being as it were bought & sould to that laborious kind of life, spend their days in that allotted torment of toile, as in their natural countrie. **1611** Bible *2 Kings* xvii. 17 And they..sold themselues to doe euill in the sight of the Lord. **1638** Sanderson *Serm.* (1681) II. 99 Behold for your iniquities have you sold your selves. *Ibid.* 100 We must..see if we can leave it upon Adam: for did not he sell us many a fair year before we were *in rerum naturâ*? **1683** *Col. Rec. Pennsylv.* I. 63 He had sould a Servt to Henry Bowman. **1788** Cowper *Negro's Compl.* i, Men from England bought and sold me, Paid my price in paltry gold.

f. ***to sell his soul, himself,*** etc., ***to the devil***: to make a contract with the devil ensuring him possession of one's soul after death, as the price of his help in attaining some desired end. Also *transf.* of one who sacrifices conscience for worldly advantage.

c **1570** *Buggbears* v. ii. 72 *Tra.* Loue youe money so well? *Ame.* What a question ys that? do not very manye sell their soules & all for monye? **1677** Horneck *Gt. Law Consid.* iv. 125 They sell their Souls to the Devil, for 2, 3, or 400 l. **1859** Geo. Eliot *Lifted Veil* i, It is an old story, that men sell themselves to the tempter, and sign a bond with their blood, because it is only to take effect at a distant day.

g. ***to sell down the river***: see river *sb.*[1] 4a.

h. To advertise or publish the merits of (a commodity, idea, etc.); to persuade (a person) to accept or buy. Also, to convince (someone) of the worth of (something). (Variously with direct and indirect object.) *colloq.* (orig. *U.S.*).

1916 *Amer. Mag.* Mar. 50/1 I'd make my readers want to enlist. I'd 'sell' them the army. **1925** *Publishers' Weekly* 5 Dec. 1863 An advertising campaign to sell New York as the printing center of the world. **1931** W. G. McAdoo *Crowded Years* iii. 41, I had to 'sell' the idea to men like the elder J. P. Morgan. **1938** E. Bowen *Death of Heart* III. iii. 362 They forget Major Brutt has come here to get a job... Oh dear, oh dear, I shall never sell him at all. **1942** *R.A.F. Jrnl.* 2 May 30 My work—in horrid modern commercial terms—is to 'sell' the R.A.F. to the Army. **1951** H. MacInnes *Neither Five nor Three* I. v. 77 The people of France were sold such ideas as..'Patriotism is for the rich'. **1956** B. Holiday *Lady sings Blues* (1973) xix. 158 It seemed like a crazy idea, but he sold me. And what's more important, he sold a lot of other people. **1960** *Guardian* 9 Nov. 6/4 We have to sell to the public the idea that being a foster mother is a service..to the community. **1976** J. I. M. Stewart *Memorial Service* iv. 60 It's just no good your trying to sell me those rotten dons.

i. Const. *on.* To make (someone) enthusiastic about, or convinced of the worth of, something. Freq. *pass. colloq.* (orig. *U.S.*).

1918 *Maclean's Mag.* Mar. 52/2 The writer believes it is possible to finally 'sell' the Teutons on the advantages of peace as compared with war. **1928** Wodehouse *Money for Nothing* vii. 133 Come to think of it. I'm not too sold on this thing, anyway. **1932** E. Wilson *Devil take Hindmost* x. 112 He rarely mentions Communism, but..he is as much sold on it as any..party member. **1948** *Manch. Guardian Weekly* 9 Dec. 8 He is not selling anybody on America. **1950** *Newsweek* 1 May 45/1, I am going to..sell her on the idea of picking up the option for another 25 years. **1969** L. Hellman *Unfinished Woman* xii. 177 He had been doing his thesis on modern American novelists... I tried hard to sell him on Faulkner and Fitzgerald. **1970** J. Earl *Tuners & Amplifiers* iii. 72 If you are sold on a medium price ceramic cartridge it would pay to look for an amplifier with a 2MΩ ceramic (piezo) input of around 50mV sensitivity. **1978** A. Price *'44 Vintage* iv. 46 I've never been absolutely sold on the classics.

j. *refl.* use of sense 3h above.

1938 L. Bemelmans *Life Class* I. v. 73 He told me that what was most important in life was..the ability to 'sell' oneself, to call [hotel] guests by their correct names and to remember their faces. **1968** *Globe & Mail* (Toronto) 3 Feb. 11/3 Supersalesmanship is used to sell to adolescents, who must also learn to sell themselves. **1978** H. Jobson *To die a Little* ii. 36 Sales gimmicks are out. We don't need them. The scheme sells itself.

4. a. *absol.* and *intr.* (Often in phrase ***to buy and sell***; more rarely ***to sell and buy.***)

c **1200** *Trin. Coll. Hom.* 213 þat is ure alre wune þe biggeð and silleð. **1338** R. Brunne *Chron.* (1810) 287 þat our merchantz mot go forto bie & selle. **1458** *Cal. Anc. Rec. Dublin* (1889) 300 And he sel or by in maner above sayd. **1596** Shaks. *Merch. V.* I. iii. 36 *Iew.* I will buy with you, sell with you, talke with you..: but I will not eate with you. **1611** Bible *Gen.* xlii. 6 And hee it was that sold to all the people of the land. *a* **1700** Evelyn *Diary* 5 Feb. 1657, They..were permitted to sell to the friends of their enemies. **1818** Cruise *Digest* (ed. 2) IV. 467 The testator had no power to sell.

b. ***to sell short***: see short *adv.* 11.

5. ***to sell*** (gerundial inf. used predicatively): on sale, offered for sale. Now *rare.*

a **1300** *Cursor M.* 2399 Abram to sell moght find na sede. ? **1370** *Robt. Cicyle* 243 in Horstm. *Altengl. Leg.* (1878) 215/1 Wher such cloþ was to selle, Ne ho hit made, couþe noman telle. *c* **1386** Chaucer *Wife's Prol.* 414 Winne whoso may, for al is for to selle. **1426** Lydg. *De Guil. Pilgr.* 21262 Folkys for to telle, That, with-inne, ys wyn to sell. *a* **1500–20** Dunbar *Poems* xxxi. 23 Now quhill thair is gude wyne to sell, He that dois on dry breid virry, I gif him to the Devill. **1896** A. E. Housman *Shropsh. Lad* vi, Buy them, buy them: eve and morn Lovers' ills are all to sell.

6. a. *intr.* in passive sense. Of a commodity: To find purchasers. ***to sell for, at*** = to fetch (a price). †***made to sell***: manufactured or contrived to secure a ready sale without regard to quality.

1606 Shaks. *Tr. & Cr.* I. iii. 360 Let vs (like Merchants) shew our fowlest Wares, And thinke perchance they'l sell. **1616** B. Jonson *Epigr.* iii, To my Book-seller. Thou, that.. Call'st a booke good, or bad, as it doth sell, Vse mine so, too. **1656** Earl Monm. tr. *Boccalini's Advts fr. Parnass.* I. i. 4 There is no Merchandize in this Ware-House which sels better, then certain Fans. **1711** Swift *Jrnl. to Stella* 24 Sept., Prior's *Journey* sells still. **1827** P. Cunningham *Two Yrs. New South Wales* (ed. 2) I. xvii. 297, I..seized a musket 'made to sell', and sallied out. **1833** Ht. Martineau *Brooke Farm* v. 63 They sell at about a shilling a dozen. **1851** Lytton *Not so bad* IV. i. 77, I found a bookseller to publish my treatise. It sold well. **1855** P. H. Delamotte *Pract. Photogr.* (ed. 2) 42 In some cameras, 'made to sell', no care is taken to adjust this plane. **1860** *Cassell's Illustr. Family Paper* Apr. 300/3 We shall hear fewer complaints of seed, unless it be from those who obtain packets which are only 'made to sell'. **1896** Wells *Wheels of Chance* i. 7 This, madame,..is selling very well.

b. *transf.* with personal subj.

1915 R. Fry *Let.* 21 Nov. (1972) II. 391 My show is turning out a great success..as far as attendance goes... Of course I don't sell—I never expected to. **1966** C. Achebe in *Black Orpheus* Mar. 45, I had a Raleigh bicycle, brand new, and everybody called me Jolly Ben. I was selling like hot bread.

7. *trans.* In various figurative uses. **a.** To take money or reward for (something that should be freely bestowed or done); to make subservient to monetary considerations (something which should not be so influenced); to make profit or gain of.

c **1175** *Lamb. Hom.* 135 *Quatuor modis uenditur elemosina.* .. An fower cunne wise mon sulleð his elmesse. *c* **1200** ORMIN 15968 He sellepp Haliȝ Gast forr fe & biggepp hellepine. **1390** GOWER *Conf.* I. 364 Lich as it was be daies olde, Whan men the Sennes boghte and solde. *c* **1400** MAUNDEV. (Roxb.) iii. 10 þai sell benificez of haly kirk. **1422** tr. *Secreta Secret., Priv. Priv.* 169 Whan Iusticia..hit for Penyes sylle and Sauyth gilti men. **1474** CAXTON *Chesse* II. iii. (1883) 38 And oftetymes they [aduocates and men of lawe] selle as welle theyr scilence as theyr vtterance. **1593** SHAKS. *2 Hen. VI*, IV. i. 41 Therefore, when Merchant-like I sell reuenge, Broke be my sword. *a* **1605** MONTGOMERIE *Sonn.* vi. 9 Quhat justice sauld! vhat pilling of the pure! **1622** FLETCHER *Beggar's Bush* II. iii, Do not your Lawyers Sell all their practice, as your Priests their prayers? **1781** COWPER *Table-t.* 419 When perjury..Sells oaths by tale, and at the lowest price. **1864** TENNYSON *Aylmer's F.* 483 But..Her worldly-wise begetters, plagued themselves To sell her.

b. To give up or part with one thing in exchange *for* another; esp. (after Gen. xxv. 29–34) to barter away (something of value) *for* (a trifle).

a **1225** *Ancr. R.* 148 Hware þuruh me buð þene kinedom of heouene, & sulleð hit for a windes puf of wordes hereword. *Ibid.* 398 Me sulleð wel luue uor luue. **1422** tr. *Secreta Secret., Priv. Priv.* 159 He..the kyngedom of hewyn Sillyth for a lytill price, lyke as esau didd, that [etc.]. **1526** *Pilgr. Perf.* (W. de W. 1531) 18 These maner of people sell paradyse for an apple, with Adam and Eue. **1593** SHAKS. *2 Hen. VI*, III. i. 92 But I will remedie this geare ere long Or sell my Title for a glorious Graue. **1650** B. *Discolliminium* 48, I will sell my Esquireship to any honest man for a good People-ship. **1785** COWPER *Task* II. 229 Effeminates..Who sell their laurel for a myrtle wreath, And love when they should fight. **1813** SHELLEY *Q. Mab* v. 210 Whose applause he sells For the gross blessings of a patriot mob. **1859** FITZGERALD *Omar* lxix, [They] Have..sold my Reputation for a Song.

†**c.** To make an offender 'pay for', to inflict vengeance for (an injury). Chiefly qualified by *dear*, *dearly*, or an equivalent advb. phrase. *to sell* (another's act, an offence) *dear*, to exact a heavy penalty for. *to be dear* or *dearly sold*, to be attended with great cost. *Obs.*

a **1300** *Cursor M.* 13182 [Herod] þat godman dos wit tresun sla. But þis ded was sald full dere. *c* **1400** *Laud Troy Bk.* 7864 Ector sclees and Ector felles; His hors takyng dere he selles. *c* **1470** HENRY *Wallace* VII. 22 But wald ye do rycht as I wald you ler, This pes to thaim it suld be sald full der. *Ibid.* IX. 1068 Till Inglismen thar cummyng was sauld full der. **1483** CAXTON *G. de la Tour* k ij, Alas how this folysshe enuye..shalle to them be dere sold. *a* **1533** LD. BERNERS *Huon* clxii. 630 That aquayntauns shall be derely solde for with myne owne handes I shall sle her.

d. *to sell one's life* (rarely †*death*) *dear*, *dearly*, etc., to destroy many of one's adversaries before giving up one's life in an encounter; to make the enemy pay dearly for one's death.

1297 R. GLOUC. (Rolls) 4569 Sulle we he sede vure lif dere ar we be ded. *Ibid.* 4570, 8177. **13..** *Guy Warw.* 1342 (MS. A) Sir Gij..seyd..'Dere we schul our deþ selle'. *Ibid.* (MS. C.), Full deere oure liffis we selle shall. *a* **1548** HALL *Chron.*, *Hen. VI*, 139 The French kyng..slewe to the nombre of four hundred, whiche derely sold their lifes. **1603** *North's Plutarch, Cæs. Aug.* (1612) 1163 P. Naso was betrayed by his slaue freed... But he sold his death [Amyot *mais il vendit sa mort*], for he killed the traytor with his owne hands. **1608** D. T[UVILL] *Ess. Pol. & Mor.* 69 With a resolution to sel their liues at as high a rate as possibly they can. **1623** MASSINGER *Bondman* III. iii. Better expose Our naked breasts to their keene Swords, and sell Our liues with the most aduantage. **1682** DRYDEN *Dk. Guise* Epil. 10 For what should hinder Me to sell my Skin, Dear as I cou'd, if once my Hand were in? **1893** SELOUS *Trav. S.E. Africa* 191 The brave beast was..doing his utmost to sell his life dearly.

e. *refl.* *to sell oneself*: to dispose of one's services for money; to enslave oneself. Also *pass.*

1771 *Junius Lett.* lii. 265 You have sold yourself to the ministry. **1781** COWPER *Expost.* 375 Hast thou..brought home the fee, To tempt the poor to sell himself to thee? **1837** CARLYLE *Fr. Rev.* II. II. iv, Is Bouillé a traitor then, sold to Austria? **1849** MACAULAY *Hist. Eng.* vi. II. 64 Money could be..obtained from the court of Versailles; and Sunderland was eager to sell himself to that court.

f. To lose (a match, game) for a bribe. *to sell one's back*, (*Wrestling*) to be bribed to allow oneself to be thrown. *to sell one's stone*, (*Curling*) 'to throw away the advantage of a well-placed stone' (Eng. Dial. Dict.).

1805 G. MᶜINDOE *Poems & Songs* 55 (E.D.D.) Dinna ride Nor sell your stane by playing wide. **1862** *Lillywhite's Cricket Scores & Biogr.* I. 341 This match was said to have been 'sold' by the England side. **1880** *W. Cornw. Gloss.* s.v. *Faggot*, In wrestling, a man who 'sells his back' is said 'to faggot'.

g. Phrase. *to sell the pass* (see quots.).

1850 OGILVIE s.v., *To sell the pass*, to betray one's countrymen, by giving information to the authorities. (*An Irish phrase.*) **1865** *Athenæum* 22 July 106/3 An Irish plotter invariably fancies that his companions will 'sell the pass' on him. **1897** *Westm. Gaz.* 6 Dec. 7/1 He now warned the men that by accepting the proposal they would be 'selling the pass' for all other trades. **1903** *Daily Chron.* 16 Nov. 5/1 He ..accepted the settlement, and at once fell from his pre-eminence,..being viewed by his followers..as one who had 'sold the pass'.

†**8.** To cry up, praise, recommend (a person) as if a saleable commodity. *Obs. rare.* [= L. *vendere*, *venditare*.]

1540 PALSGR. *Acolastus* G iij b, Who here happye selleth hym selfe .i. who is he here that setteth hym selfe out to the sale, for a fortunate or lucky man? [*margin* Phra. Beatum sese uenditare.] **1622** SIR R. HAWKINS *Voy. S. Sea* 126 Had our Gunner beene the man he was reputed to be, and as the world sould him to me, shee had receiued great hurt by that manner of bourding.

9. *slang.* To cheat, trick, deceive, take in.

The two earliest examples suggest development from sense 2; the mod. slang use, however, may be partly ellipt. for the older phrase *to sell a person a bargain*: see BARGAIN *sb.*[1] 7.

1607 B. JONSON *Volpone* Argt., Volpone, childlesse, rich, faines sick,..Offers his state to hopes of seuerall heyres,.. His Parasite receaues Presents of all..Then weaues Other crosse-plots,..New tricks for safety, are sought; They thriue: When, bold, Each tempt's th'other againe, and all are sold. **1733** FIELDING *Quixote in Eng.* I. viii, *Mayor.* I begin to smoke a Plot. I begin to apprehend no opposition, and then we're sold, Neighbour. *Voter.* I would ride all over the Kingdom for a Candidate if I thought Sir Thomas intended to steal us in this manner. **1849** ALB. SMITH *Pottleton Legacy* xv. 123, I've sold them, though! **1852** SMEDLEY *Lewis Arundel* xxiv, You're not going to try and cut out Bellefield by proposing for my cousin Annie, are you? I wish you would, it would sell Bell so beautifully. **1861** HUGHES *Tom Brown at Oxf.* xxxvii, I'll bet you a sovereign you never see a poacher, and then how sold you will be in the morning. **1893** LELAND *Mem.* I. 113 Nor was I 'selling' him, for I certainly had read the works.

Phrase. **1859** *Hotten's Slang Dict.* s.v., 'Sold again, and got the money', a costermonger cries after having successfully deceived somebody.

II. Combined with adverbs.

10. sell away. **a.** *trans.* To dispose of, or dispossess oneself of, by selling, *lit.* and *fig.* ? *Obs.*

c **1230** *Hali Meid.* 36 (MS. Bodl.) Wa wurðe þet cheaffeare, for ei hwilinde weole sullen meiðhad awei. **1387** TREVISA *Higden* (Rolls) IV. 425 An hondred þowsand were i-take prisoners and i-solde awey, þritty for a peny. ? **1600** SIR R. BOYLE in *Lismore Papers* Ser. II. (1887) I. 35, I..haue lefte heer..xxxix papers of Sylck..; which..I praie sell awaie to paie your self. **1611** BIBLE *Tobit* i. 7 The first tenth part of al increase, I gaue to the sonnes of Aaron..another tenth part I sold away. **1639** S. DU VERGER tr. *Camus' Admir. Events* 309 Our wary Thyrse shall not sell away his power or mastery.

b. *absol.* To go on selling.

1878 A. L. PERRY *Elem. Pol. Econ.* 543 'Never mind', says England, 'sell away, and I will make up your loss by a bounty!'

11. sell off. *trans.* To dispose of by sale; to sell the whole of (one's stock, possessions, etc.).

a **1700** EVELYN *Diary* 18 Jan. 1671, He answer'd he [Grinling Gibbons] was yet but a beginner, but would not be sorry to sell off that piece. **1780** *Mirror* No. 106 He.. wound up his business, sold off his stock, and purchased an estate in the country. **1816** SCOTT *Bl. Dwarf* v, You should ..set up shop, and sell off all the goods you do not mean to keep for your own use. **1856** READE *Never too Late* xxxviii. A farmer who was selling off his sheep. **1871** *Routledge's Ev. Boy's Ann.* Mar., Suppl. 2 Selling off! Bargains!

absol. **1871** R. ELLIS *Catullus* lxxix. 3 Only let all your tribe sell off, and follow, Catullus.

12. sell out. **a.** *trans.* To distribute by sale.

1648 GAGE *West Ind.* xii. 42 The Herbes and Salets.. which were sold out, brought in a great Rent yeerely. **1705** ADDISON *Italy, Switzerl.* 506 The Corn being sold out at a much dearer Rate than 'tis bought up.

b. To dispose of (stock, shares, etc.) by sale. Also *absol.*

1721 LADY M. W. MONTAGU *Let. to C'tess Mar* (1893) I. 450, I advised him..to sell out the subscription [for South Sea stock]. **1772** FOOTE *Nabob* II. (1778) 40 Then sell out till you sink it [*sc.* stock] two and a half. **1834** MARRYAT *P. Simple* III. xxiii. 300, I wrote..sending her a power of attorney to him [*sc.* the agent], to sell out the stock. **1862** MISS BRADDON *Lady Audley* iv, He made arrangements for selling out a couple of hundred pounds worth of consols. **1893** CORDINGLEY *Guide to Stock Exch.* 61 Should a purchaser fail to take up his securities..when the Certificate and Transfer are presented to him, the seller has the right to instruct an official to 'sell out' at once by auction.

c. *intr.* To dispose of one's commission in the army by sale. Now only *Hist.* (Cf. B. 3 b above.)

1787 *Minor* 13 After some campaigns;..his creditors allowing him the alternative of rotting in a jail, or selling out. **1860** THACKERAY *Lovel* iv. (1861) 133 His regiment was ordered to India, and he sold out.

d. *trans.* To dispose of the whole of (one's stock, property, etc.) by sale. Also *absol.*, and *intr.* for *pass.*

Also *colloq.* in passive, to have sold one's whole stock *of* some article.

1796 JANE AUSTEN *Sense & Sens.* xxxiv, In spite of its [*sc.* an estate's] owner having once been within some thousand pounds of being obliged to sell out at a loss. **1823** J. BADCOCK *Dom. Amusem.* 155 Three young women went to market with eggs... All three sold out, and at the same rate. **1898** *Daily News* 8 Aug. 2/5 [He] sold out his licensed premises. **1907** *Daily Chron.* 9 Sept. 3/1, I produced two one act operas ..and our takings were no more than £57. In Germany or Italy the house would have been sold out. **1914** *Daily Mail* 31 Jan. 1/2 My first parcel from you sold out very quickly. **1974** M. BIRMINGHAM *You can help Me* ii. 39 The Friday flower stall was rapidly selling out.

e. colloq. (orig. *U.S. political slang*). *trans.* and *intr.* To betray a person or cause for gain (cf. *sell-out* s.v. SELL *sb.*[2]). Also *trans.*, to betray (a candidate) by secret bargains (*Cent. Dict.* 1891).

1888 BRYCE *Amer. Commw.* III. IV. lxxxiii. 110 When this transfer of the solid vote of a body of agitators is the result of a bargain with the old party which gets the vote, it is called 'selling out'. **1903** G. B. SHAW *Man & Superman* III. 78 He has sold out to the parliamentary humbugs and the bourgeoisie. **1946** KOESTLER *Thieves in Night* 112 The English are going to sell out on us. **1976** *Survey* Winter 86 Barbé called for tactics of disobedience to the colonial administrators and to the traditional chiefs who had 'sold out' to the French government.

1857 *Lawrence* (Kansas) *Republican* 2 July 1 If the *Times* has not been 'sold out' to the Border Ruffian party, it looks very much as if it had been 'chartered'. **1867** *Oregon State Jrnl.* 19 Jan. 3/1 The writer thinks the officers were 'badly sold out'. **1936** M. MITCHELL *Gone with Wind* ix. 189 Why quibble about the Yankees earning an honest penny selling out the Union? **1940** J. B. PRIESTLEY *Postscripts* 45 It let the old hands, the experts,..speak for it, and they sold it out. **1967** *Times* 17 Nov. 8/6 With shouts of 'They sold us out, the bastards', the meeting moved to 'the moment of truth'. **1976** 'J. CHARLTON' *Remington Set* xxviii. 141 What happened is, Rog sold us out.

13. sell over. *trans.* †**a.** To sell again. *Obs.* **b.** To transfer by sale. *lit.* and *fig.*

1596 DANETT tr. *Comines* VII. vii. Note 5. 287 It was sold to this John Galeas, and he sold it ouer to the Florentines. **1837** J. H. NEWMAN *Par. Serm.* (ed. 2) III. xxiii. 372 A man is sold over into bondage to this world.

14. sell up. **a.** *trans.* To dispose of the whole of (a person's stock, goods, etc.) by sale. ? *Obs.*

c **1480** *Childe of Bristowe* 209 in Hazl. *E.P.P.* (1864) I. 118 Al the catel his fader hade, he sold it up, and money made. **1566** STOWE in *Three 15th Cent. Chron.* (Camden) 140 He sold up his movable goods and went to Rie. **1784** R. BAGE *Barham Downs* I. 55 He..had determined to sell all up.

b. To dispose of the whole or a portion of the goods of (an insolvent or bankrupt person) for the benefit of his creditors. Also with the goods as obj.

1825 C. M. WESTMACOTT *Eng. Spy* (1907) I. 149 Being much averse to dunning, I was soon sold up. **1848** THACKERAY *Van. Fair* ix, He..would..drink his glass with a tenant and sell him up the next day. *Ibid.* xviii, The house and furniture of Russell Square were seized and sold up. **1862** MISS BRADDON *Lady Audley* xxviii, I was obliged to sell him up..for he owed me fifteen months' rent.

c. *intr.* To dispose of (a house, business, etc.) by sale.

1862 *Manch. Examiner & Times* 8 July 6/2 We hed a varra good heawse i' Stanley-street, once; but we hed to sell up an' creep hitherto. **1977** E. DEWHURST *Curtain Fall* xviii. 216 She would be coming home only in order to sell up.

III. 15. *Comb.* with a sb. as **sell-soul**, **sell-truth**, one who sells a soul, the truth. *nonce-use.*

c **1680** HICKERINGHILL *Hist. Whiggism* Wks. 1716 I. II. 140 Is it not enough that this Kingdom..should be once in one Age undone by the same kind of Men, the same Sell Truths? **1681** —— *Black Non-Conf.* Postscr. (1682) X 2, These little Sell-souls do the feat.

b. sell-by date, a date marked on food packaging to indicate the latest recommended date of sale, esp. for perishable goods; also *fig.* Cf. *pull-date* s.v. PULL- 2.

[**1972** *Which?* Sept. 266/2 Waitrose already have *sell by such-and-such a date* on dairy produce, bacon,..fish, cakes and crisps... Marks and Spencer..are going to include *sell by* in the future.] **1973** *Which?* Mar. 96/1 Most of the date stamps will be 'Sell by...' dates [*sic*]. **1976** *Grocer* 8 May 72/3 The printing of sell-by dates. **1984** *Oxford Consumer* Autumn 10/2 Perishable foods, like yogurt, which the manufacturer intends you to eat within six weeks of packing, may..be marked with the words 'Sell by' followed by the latest recommended date of sale. **1987** *Daily Tel.* 13 Mar. 16/2 (*heading*) Socialism: the package that's passed its sell-by date.

sell, obs. f. CELL, SILL *sb.*[1]; var. SELE *sb.*

‖**sella** (ˈsɛlə). *Anat.* [L. *sella* seat, saddle.] A saddle-shaped portion of the sphenoid, more fully ***sella equina***, ***sphenoidalis*** or ***turcica***.

1693 tr. *Blancard's Phys. Dict.* (ed. 2), *Sella Equina, seu Turcica*, it is compounded of four Processes of the Bone *Sphenoeides*, or Wedge-like Bone... *Sella Sphenoeides*, the same with *Sella Equina*. **1843** *Penny Cycl.* XXVII. 278/1 Internally the cerebral cavity [of a dolphin] is very remarkable... The sella is but slightly marked. **1854** OWEN *Skel. & Teeth* in *Orr's Circ. Sci., Org. Nat.* I. 232 The sella turcica is shallow. **1881** MIVART *Cat* 70 The upper surface of the posterior sphenoid exhibits, on each side of the sella, a faintly-marked groove.

sellable (ˈsɛləb(ə)l), *a.* Also 4 sillable, 6 sellabill. [f. SELL *v.* + -ABLE.] That may be sold, saleable. Hence ˈ**sellably** *adv.*

1382 WYCLIF *Ecclus.* x. 10 This forsothe hath his soule sillable, or able to be sold. **1561** *Extracts Aberd. Reg.* (1844) I. 334 Quhatsumewir schip of gudis sellabill arrywis to the port..of this burght. **1611** COTGR., *Venalement*, vendibly, salably, sellably. **1620** J. MASON *Disc. Newfoundland* 6 Fish being a staple commoditie with us, and so sellable in other countries. **1633** *Sc. Acts Chas. I* (1870) V. 37/2 To sett downe the pryces of sellable teinds According to the worth thairof. **1886** *Dict. Nat. Biog.* V. 371/1 The..villein regardant—attached to the soil, and sellable with it.

b. Venal.

1650 in Row *Hist. Kirk* (1842) 424 Those were sellable, vendible men, (πρασιμοι,) to be sold for money.

selladine, obs. form of CELANDINE.

1610 MARKHAM *Masterp.* I. xcvi. 190 Generall Drenches. Take of selladine two handfuls, both root and leaues.

sellaite (ˈsɛləaɪt). *Min.* [a. It. *sellaite* (Strüver 1868, in *Atti d. R. Accad. d. Sci. di Torino*: *Classe di Sci. fis.*, etc. IV. 35), f. the name of Q. *Sella* (1827–84), Italian mining engineer and mineralogist: see -ITE[1].] Native magnesium fluoride, MgF_2, occurring as fibrous aggregates of colourless tetragonal crystals.

1872 G. J. BRUSH *Dana's Syst. Min.* (ed. 5) App. I. 14 Sellaite... Found with anhydrite at Geibroula in Piedmont. **1923** J. W. MELLOR *Comprehensive Treat. Inorg. & Theoret. Chem.* IV. xxix. 296 Warm crystals of sellaite show a faint violet luminescence with cleavage. **1933** *Mineral. Abstr.* V.

238 Microscopical examination of the dolomite of bore-cores from the southern Harz showed the presence of sellaite as minute (0·04–0·075 mm.) tetragonal prisms. **1968** I. Kostov *Mineralogy* 189 Sellaite is isostructural with rutile .., the chain type of structure explaining its perfect {110} cleavage, prismatic to acicular habit, and optically positive character.

sellak, sellander, obs. ff. SILLOCK, SALLENDER.

† **'sellary**[1]. *Obs.* [ad. L. *sellārius* (Tac. *Ann.* VI. i.), f. *sella* seat, couch.] A male prostitute.

1603 B. Jonson *Sejanus* IV. v, Others Are rauish'd hence ..and..dealt away Vnto his Spintries, Sellaries, and Slaues. **1603** Grenewey *Tacitus, Ann.* VI. i. (1622) 121 Then first of all were those vnknowen words of Sellaries and Spintries found out of the filthines of the place.

† **'sellary**[2]. *Obs. rare*$^{-1}$. [ad. It. *sellaria.*]

1650 Howell *Giraffi's Rev. Naples* I. 65 It was discover'd ..that the waters..were poison'd..specially in those Cisterns which receive the raine water, as in the Sellaries, the publick Markets [etc.].

sellary, obs. form of CELERY.

1727 Swift *Let. Sheridan* 1 July, We eat it like Sellary, either with or without Oil, &c.

sellat, obs. form of SALLET.

selle, obs. f. CELL, SILL *sb.*[1]; var. SEELY, SELLY.

selleir, obs. Sc. form of CELLAR.

1500–20 Dunbar *Poems* xxxiv. 47 Thair is sic wyne in my selleir As neuir come in this cuntrie.

sellender, obs. form of SALLENDER.

Sellenger's round. *Obs.* exc. *Hist.* Also 6 Sellengars, 6–7 Sellingers, 7 Selingers, Sal(l)enger(s, Salinger's, Sallingers. [*Sellenger* represents the pronunciation of the surname *St. Leger*; cf. *Sellinger* as the popular name of the race called St. Leger (SAINT *sb.* 3 c). See conjectures in quot. 1855.] An old country dance; also, the music for this dance.

1567 Pikeryng *Horestes* 305 (Brandl), Entrithe and singeth this song to yᵉ tune of 'haue ouer yᵉ water to floride' or 'selengers round'. **1593** 'P. Foulface' *Bacchus' Bountie* C 3 b, The fidler he fidled, and the pots danced for ioy the old hop about, commonly called Sellengars round. **1597** Morley *Introd. Mus.* III. 119. **1604** Middleton *Ant & Night.* D 4, Dauncing of Sallingers-round in Moone-shine nights about May Poles. **1607**, *c* **1645** [see ROUND *sb.*[1] 11 c]. *a* **1683** Oldham *Wks.* (1686) 55 Fairies dancing Salenger a Nights. **1698** [see ROUND *sb.*[1] 11 c]. **1855** W. Chappell *Pop. Mus.* I. 69 Sellenger's Round, or The Beginning of the World. *Ibid.* 70 This tune..is to be found in Queen Elizabeth's and Lady Neville's Virginal Books,..&c... It might be from 'Sir Thomas Sellynger', who was buried in St. George's Chapel, Windsor, before the year 1475..; or from Sir Antony St. Leger,..Lord Deputy of Ireland in 1540.

seller[1] ('sɛlə(r)). Forms: 3–4 sullere, 4 suller, -ar, *Kent.* zeller, 4–5 siller(e, 5 sellere, -ar(e, -our, 5–6 syller, 4– seller. [f. SELL *v.* + -ER[1].]

1. a. One who sells.

c **1200** *Trin. Coll. Hom.* 213 Þe sullere loueð his þing dere. .. Ðe beger bet litel þar fore. *c* **1380** Wyclif *Wks.* (1880) 90 Most principale sillere of benefices & veyn indulgencis. *a* **1400** *Old Usages Wynchestre* in *Eng. Gilds* 355 Euerych sullere of bred in þe heyȝestrete of Wynchestre. **1444** *Rolls of Parlt.* V. 116/2 To damage of the beyour or sellour. **1540** *Sel. Pleas Crt. Admiralty* (1894) I. 98 Having a byll of sale ..delyvered to hym by the seller. **1588** Shaks. *L.L.L.* IV. iii. 240 To things of sale, a sellers praise belongs. **1692** Locke *Lower. Interest* 132 And so[to] raise the Price of Land, by making more Buyers than Sellers. **1776** Adam Smith *W.N.* IV. ii. 46 By diminishing the number of sellers, therefore, we necessarily diminish that of buyers. **1855** Dickens *Dorrit* I. xii, The Plaintiff was a chaunter, not a singer of anthems, but a seller of horses. **1866** W. Reed *Hist. Sugar* 159 Whilst sellers advanced their claims to be heard on the ground, that if [etc.]..the Americans would immediately become strong buyers. **1884** J. Gilmour *Mongols* xxxi. 365 After the two busy seasons there are a few buyers and sellers. **1900** *Daily News* 20 June 9/1 The number of easy sellers in cloth is again on the increase.

fig. **1697** G. Burghope *Disc. Relig. Assemblies* xii. 121 His Ears itch, and he runs after the Canting Seller of Breath.

b. *seller-up*: see SELL *v.* 14 b.

1894 A. Morrison *Tales Mean Streets* 294 A professional rent-receiver and seller-up.

c. *Business.* In various phrases, as: (*a*) ***seller four*** (***ten, twenty, the year***, etc.): a form of contract in which the seller has the right to effect delivery within the specified number of days (four, ten, etc.); ***seller's option***: the right of the seller to specify the number of days after which a sale is effected.

1849 *Merchants' Mag.* (U.S.) XX. 670 Fifty-six, buyer 20; 3rd broker—55⅝, seller 10. **1857** *Ibid.* XXXVII. 134 Sales at seller's option are generally a fraction below the current cash price. **1869** 'Mark Twain' *Innocents Abr.* xxxiv. 369 Sales of one lot Circassians, prime to good, 1852–1854..; one forty-niner—damaged—at £23, seller ten, no deposit.

(*b*) ***seller's market***: a market in which there is excess demand at the going rate so that it is easy to effect additional sales. Also *fig.*

1934 in Webster. **1948** G. Crowther *Outl. Money* (ed. 2) v. 163 The raw material markets may be transformed overnight from 'seller's markets' (i.e. where buying is insistent and the seller is in the strategic position) into 'buyer's markets', while the opposite movement is much slower. **1965** Zigrosser & Gaehde *Guide to Collecting Orig. Prints* vi. 91 In boom times and a seller's market, almost anyone can set up as a dealer and make a success of it. **1979** R. Jaffe *Class Reunion* III. vii. 275 Everybody..here seems to be going to some shrink. They're all into self-help,..or screaming sessions, or group therapy... It's a seller's market.

2. A thing to be sold.

1831 *Sutherland Farm Rep* 80 in *Libr. Usef. Knowl., Husb.* III, The packs, or shepherds' lambs, are divided into two sorts, sellers and keepers.

3. Something with a (wide, poor, etc.) sale; also, without qualification, something that sells well. Also used of other commodities.

1895 *Montgomery Ward Catal.* Spring & Summer 6/2 Brocaded Brilliantines... This line we expect will be one of the greatest sellers of the season. **1900** *Century Mag.* LIX. 646/2 But tragic novels are poor sellers. **1903** *Munsey's Mag.* XXIX. 764 What are known as 'sellers'—meaning books that enjoy a wide sale. **1905** *Athenæum* 9 Sept. 330/3 Fortunately the 'best sellers' are the worst survivors. **1925** *Daily Tel.* 13 May 20/7 (Advt.), Traveller Wanted.—We offer the latest new line. Big seller. Live men can earn £10 week. **1976** *Times* 1 May (Food Suppl.) p. ii/6 On tinned meat he said: 'My advice is to stock the major sellers, such as stewed steak.'

4. A selling race. *colloq.*

1922 *N. & Q.* 12th Ser. XI. 207/1 *Seller*,..a selling race—one in which the winner is bound to be offered by public auction. **1927** *Daily Express* 23 June 12/2 The game little Congou colt took another seller. **1928** *Daily Sketch* 7 Aug. 22/4 Another interesting proposition at the Midland meeting is the Loud Report filly in the juvenile seller.

† **'seller**[2]. *Obs. rare.* Also 4 seler. [a. OF. *seller, selier* (mod.F. *sellier*), f. *selle* saddle: see SELL *sb.*[1]] A saddler.

1311 in *Cal. Let.-Bk. Lond.* D 64 [The same day, Richard de Gloucestre], seler, [admitted]. **1415** in *York Myst.* Introd. 26 Sellers [*foot-n.* 'Sadellers' is written above].

seller, obs. f. CELLAR, CELURE; var. SOLER.

sellerage, -edge, -idge, obs. ff. CELLARAGE.

1611 Cotgr., *Droict de Cellerage*, Sellerage; a duetie.. paied..at the laying of wines into sellers.

sellerar, obs. form of CELLARER.

c **1450** Holland *Howlat* 180 The Goule was a gryntar, The Suerthbak a sellerar. **1530** Palsgr. 269/1 Sellerar of a relygious place, *bovtelier.*

selleri(e, obs. forms of CELERY.

sellery, obs. form of SILLERY.

1770 Hooper *Baron Bielfeld's Lett.* III. viii. 101 A large glass of water, which the princess..had ordered to be emptyd, and had filld it with sellery wine.

‖ **sellette** (sɛlɛt). Also 7 selette. [Fr., dim. of *selle* seat: see SELL *sb.*[1]] The stool upon which a prisoner in France sits during his examination.

1670 Cotton *Espernon* II. VII. 315 His Host..demanded his Name, Surname, Country, Quality, and Age, with many other interrogatories, as if he had been upon the Selette. **1841** James *Brigand* III. iii. 63 The prisoner was brought forward and placed on the elevated seat called the scellette [*sic*], where he was interrogated..by his judges.

selli, sellie, var. forms of SEELY *a.*

sellic, -ich(e, -ick, etc., var. ff. SELLY *Obs.*

sellid, obs. pa. t. of SELL *v.*

selliform ('sɛlɪfɔːm), *a.* [f. L. *sella* saddle: see -FORM.] Saddle-shaped.

1898 in *Syd. Soc. Lex.*

sellines, variant of SEELINESS.

selling ('sɛlɪŋ), *vbl. sb.* [f. SELL *v.* + -ING[1].]

a. The action of the verb SELL; an instance of this.

a **1325** *MS. Rawl. B.* 520 lf. 29 Þoru þe foreseide sullinges ore buchginges of londes. *c* **1440** *Pol. Rel. & L. Poems* 225 Biynge & sillynge þou not forsakist. **1591** *Child-Marriages* 151 And that yow doe not..make.. any order.. concerninge the sellinge of your Victualls. **1676** Phillips *Purchasers Pattern* 1 The buying and selling of Land. *a* **1700** Evelyn *Diary* 3 Sept. 1683, His late purchas'd house at Chelsey, which I once had the selling of. **1772** R. Graves *Spir. Quixote* (1783) III. 282 He excelled in smart repartees, and selling of bargains, as they call it. **1885** *Athenæum* 29 Aug. 269/1 The buyings and sellings of land.

b. With an adverb.

1852 Mundy *Antipodes* I. 58 During the first year or two of my residence in Sydney, the selling off of families going home or into retirement were very numerous. **1872** *Punch* 1 June 232/2 The notices of pretended sellings-off of swindling bankrupts' stock. **1903** *Westm. Gaz.* 29 May 11/1 Selling-out is going on in a desultory manner round the Stock Exchange to-day.

c. *attrib.* and *Comb.*, as ***selling invoice, job, -power, rights, title, value***; **selling-point**, a place at which sales may be effected (cf. *point-of-sale* s.v. POINT *sb.*[1] D. 17), a retail outlet; **selling price**, the price at which an article is offered for sale; **selling race**, a race for horses which are to be sold after the race; so ***selling chase, handicap, plate*** (hence ***selling plater***), ***stakes, sweepstakes***: see the sbs.

1965 D. Francis *For Kicks* iii. 44 The horses had all won *selling chases—races where the winner was subsequently put up to auction. **1809** R. Langford *Introd. Trade* 60 A *selling Invoice. **1963** Mrs. L. B. Johnson *White House Diary* 23 Nov. (1970) 8, I will have to..see about getting Lynda Bird to come back and live in Washington with us and go to school somewhere up here (and that will be a *selling job!). **1976** I. Levin *Boys from Brazil* iii. 77 He's never been as sure as the rest of us that the project will work. .. The selling job we had to do! **1888** *Selling plate [see PLATE *sb.* 17]. **1886** *Selling plater [see PLATER 3]. **1898** *Encycl. Sport* II. 219/2 This is another risk run by owners who wish to gamble on selling platers. **1953** *Chambers's Jrnl.* June 343/1 In recent years some seaside resorts have entered the catering business... Margate, starting with nothing in 1946, now has fifty-two *selling-points. **1960** R. Williams *Border Country* 158 Within a month..he would have all the selling-points he needed. **1904** J. London *Let.* 11 July (1966) 161 My *selling-power has increased. **1960** C. S. Lewis *Studies in Words* 104 The literary innovators want to retain the prestige, almost the 'selling-power', of the consecrated word. **1815** *Selling price [see PRICE-CURRENT]. **1848** Leon *On Sugar Cultiv.* I. 68 The selling price of sugar delivered on board ship. **1898** *Encycl. Sport* II. 219/1 *Selling races are the lowest forms of contest recognised by the rules of racing; and selling handicaps, the lowest of all. *Ibid.* 219/2 The winner of a selling race has..to be sold by auction; the owner receives no more than the entered selling price. **1908** *Westm. Gaz.* 2 Apr. 4/3 [They] have secured the sole *selling rights in this country..for the Autoclipse lamps. **1839** *Sporting Mag., Racing Cal.* 3 The *Selling Stakes of 5 sovs. each..for horses of all ages. *Ibid.* Ser. II. XX. 71 A *Selling Sweepstakes of 10 sovs. each. **1884** *Law Times Rep.* 1 Mar. L. 20/1 The consent of the parties entitled for life was not necessary to enable the trustees to make a good *selling title. **1803** *Ann. Rev.* I. 383/1 The singularity of the parody has given to such notes a *selling value analogous to current value.

selling ('sɛlɪŋ), *ppl. a.* [f. SELL *v.* + -ING[2].]

1. That readily finds buyers, saleable.

1771 Luckombe *Hist. Print.* 227 Irregular Bodied Letter of the smaller sizes sometimes serves the ends of proprietors of standing and selling Copies. **1854** *Jrnl. R. Agric. Soc.* XV. II. 241 He will find nothing more selling than a carefully selected lot of young stock. **1896** *Westm. Gaz.* 6 Feb. 3/3 International quarrels unfortunately make the most selling 'copy'.

2. That is engaged in selling.

1848 Mill *Pol. Econ.* III. xvii. §4. 116 The authors and leaders of opinion on mercantile questions have always hitherto been of the selling class.

3. That helps to effect a sale; esp. in phrr. ***selling point, title.***

1875 Trollope *Way We live Now* II. lxxxix. 248, I don't believe that anything like real selling praise is ever given to anybody, except to friends. **1959** *Times* 4 Mar. 11/7 The educational usefulness of television in backward areas depends on a firm grasp of the staffing problem. Otherwise it will be a selling-point, not a reality. **1963** P. Phillips in Sissons & French *Age of Austerity* 148 The old selling phrase 'pre-war value' lost some of its attraction. **1965** W. Haggard *Hard Sell* ii. 12 'A delightful name for an aeroplane, isn't it?'.. 'I'd call it a selling title.' **1978** *Times* 27 Jan. 13/7 A French name is still a selling point for clothes.

sellock, sellok, variant forms of SILLOCK.

sell-off: see SELL *sb.*[2] 5.

sellondine, sellor, obs. ff. CELANDINE, CELLAR.

sellore, variant of CELURE *Obs.*

c **1474** *Paston Lett.* III. 406 Item, a sellore, xij d.

Sellotape ('sɛləʊteɪp), *sb.* Also **sellotape, cellotape.** [f. CELL(ULOSE *sb.* + -O + TAPE *sb.*[1]] The proprietary name of a cellulose or plastic self-adhesive tape, freq. dispensed from reels for domestic use. Also *gen.*

1949 *Trade Marks Jrnl.* 9 Nov. 1002/2 Sellotape... Adhesive tape (stationery). Adhesive Tapes Limited, 8, Brunel Road, Acton, London, W.3; Manufacturers and Merchants. **1957** *Landfall* (N.Z.) XI. II. 169 Does she want to come a cropper, dashed earthward by wings casually fastened with sellotape? **1960** P. A. Bennett in J. Pudney *Pick of Today's Short Stories* XI. 16 A wind..blew down all the pictures stuck with cellotape to the wall. **1960** H. Pinter *Birthday Party* 76 There's some Sellotape somewhere. We can stick them together. **1971** *Petticoat* 24 July 3/1 It's certainly a lot less painful than ordinary cellotape which we've been using up till now. **1974** J. Cooper *Women & Super Women* 19 They always talk about having 'stuck together because of the children', as though the little blighters have been using glue and sellotape on them. **1980** *Guardian Weekly* 3 Feb. 20/5 So far he has largely run on string and Sellotape.

Hence as *v. trans.*, to fasten with Sellotape; **'sellotaped** *ppl. a.*, **'sellotaping** *vbl. sb.*

1960 P. A. Bennett in J. Pudney *Pick of Today's Short Stories* XI. 16 She..cellotaped them [*sc.* pictures] to the wall. **1964** A. Wilson *Late Call* iii. 113 He continued to sellotape Beth's caricatures to the walls. **1965** M. Drabble *Millstone* 178 Lydia really did have to rewrite two whole chapters as well as doing a lot of boring sellotaping. **1969** E. McGirr *Entry of Death* iii. 56 An assortment of cellotaped cartons. **1976** *Daily Tel.* (Colour Suppl.) 14 May 36/3 There are four pictures (one bought in Piccadilly, the others from *Elvis Monthly*) Sellotaped to the wall.

sellour, ? obs. form of CELLAR.

1558 in Feuillerat *Revels Q. Eliz.* (1908) 47 One Roome below..the same gate used for A Sellour.

sell-out: see SELL *sb.*[2] 4

sellt, sell't, Sc. and north. pa. t. of SELL *v.*

† **'selly,** *a., adv.* and *sb. Obs.* Forms: 1 sellic, syllik, seldlik, 2 sullic, 3 sellic, -lik, sellich(e, (sælliche), seollic(h(e, sillich, sullich, (4 sellike), 3–4 selli, seli, (3 selle), 4 celly, (celli, solly), 4–5 selly, 4–6 sely. [OE. *sellic* (adv. *sellíce*), *seldlic*,

corresp. to Goth. *sildaleik-s* strange:—OTeut. **seldoliko-*: see SELDOM and -LY[1].]

A. *adj.* Strange, marvellous, wonderful.

Beowulf 3038 (Gr.) Ær hi þær ʒeseʒan syllicran wiht, wyrm on wonge wiðerræhtes þær laðne licʒean. *a* **1000** *Boeth. Metr.* xxviii. 53 (Gr.) Is þæt sellic ðincg þæt hi ne wundriað, hu [etc.]. *c* **1205** LAY. 6438 Wnder þon hær com tidinde..þat wes icumen of þær sæ a deor swiðe sellich [*c* **1275** sullich]. *Ibid.* 7328 Sillich [*c* **1275** seollich] us þuncheð Cezar. *c* **1250** *Gen. & Ex.* 466 Sella..bar tubal, a sellic smið. *a* **1300** *Cursor M.* 26010 And it agh be sa selle wonder Als þof his hert him brest in sunder. **13..** *Seuyn Sag.* (W.) 248 Herkneth nou a selli tiding! **13..** *Gaw. & Gr. Knt.* 1439 Þenne þay beten on þe bushez, &..On þe sellokest swyn swenged out þere. *c* **1330** R. BRUNNE *Chron. Wace* (Rolls) 15171 Þat estre þat we on Englische calle Roucestre; Byforn hit hadde a name selly In Breton, Dorciberni. *c* **1384** CHAUCER *H. Fame* 513 For now at erste shul ye here So selly an avisioun, That Isaye..Ne mette swich a dreem as this! *c* **1400** *Destr. Troy* 8713 The sorow þat ho suffert were solly to here. *c* **1400** *Ywaine & Gaw.* 3513 Of tham this was a selly case, That nowther wist what other wase.

B. *adv.* Wonderfully, marvellously, strangely.

a **1000** *Sal. & Sat.* 149 (Gr.) Næfre hie ðæs syllice bleoum breʒdað æfter bancofan federhoman onfoð. *Ibid.* 269 Se fuʒel..singgeð syllice. *c* **1205** LAY. 20179 Þat he com to Eouerwic riden swiðe sellic [*c* **1275** sellich]. *Ibid.* 30579 He igrap a nail sax selliche kene and wel iwhæt. *c* **1250** *Gen. & Ex.* 1315 Sellik ðu art on werlde cumen, Sellic ðu salt ben heðen numen. *a* **1290** *Pains of Hell* (MS. Digby 86) 191 For fendes hem stondeþ bi and pineþ hem swiþe selli. *a* **1300** *Cursor M.* 2271 Þis tour was selli mad vpright, Fiue thusand steppes it had on hight. *c* **1325** *Metr. Hom.* (1862) 72 This womane yode wit chylde full lange, And tholed paynes sely strang. *a* **1375** *Joseph Arim.* 94 He lette sle for his sake selli mony children. *a* **1450** *Le Morte Arth.* 3387 Hys brodyr..Was sely seke and sore vnsounde. *Ibid.* 3482 That shall thou rew sely sore.

C. *sb.* Marvel, wonder; something wonderful. Phrase, ***to have selly***.

a **1200** *Moral Ode* 181 in *Lamb. Hom.* 171 Nis na sullic [*v.rr.* sellic, sellich, seollich] þech hom bo wa and hom bo uneade. *c* **1205** LAY. 18730 Nu ihere ich muche seollic [*c* **1275** sellich]. *c* **1250** *Gen. & Ex.* 3260 Ð is bode herde king pharaon And him ðuhte sellic ðer-on. **13..** *Childh. Jesus* 176 in *Archiv Stud. neu. Spr.* LXXIV. 329 No celly þof þai chaunged chere. **13..** *Gaw. & Gr. Knt.* 239 For fele sellyez had þay sen, bot such neuer are. *Ibid.* 475, I haf sen a selly. *c* **1400** *St. Alexius* (Vernon MS.) 104 Þat chirche was of vr ladi, þer-inne was a gret celli [*Laud MS.* 108 selly], an ymage of hire sone. *c* **1400** *Destr. Troy* 5153 All the souerayns hade selly..Of priam, the price Kyng, þat prudly hade saide. *a* **1400-50** *Wars Alex.* 2551 He sall vs sett on a-saute & surely encounbre If þai were sary & so na selly [*Dubl. MS.* no selly] me thingke.

Hence †**ˈsellyly** *adv. Obs.*

13.. *Gaw. & Gr. Knt.* 963 Þe tweyne yʒen, & þe nase, þe naked lyppez, & þose were soure to se, & sellyly blered.

selly(e, variant forms of SEELY *a.*

selm (ˈsɛl(ə)m). *dial.* Also 6 selme, 9 sellem. [Of obscure origin.] A bar of a gate.

1591 *Mem. St. Giles' Durh.* (Surtees) 16 Paid for one selme to the yeate iij^d. **1893-4** *Northumb. Gloss.*, *Selm, Sellem.*

†**ˈselondyn.** *Obs. rare*$^{-1}$. [Corrupt form of OF. *celidoine*: see SELIDONE.] A precious stone.

c **1400** *Beryn* 2723 The keueryng of-bove, is of selondyn; And the pament be-neth, of gold & asure fyne.

‖**selon les règles** (səlɔ̃ le rɛgl), *phr.* [Fr.] According to the rules (of polite society). Also *fig.*

Victorian writers frequently wrote the third word with an acute accent.

1825 H. WILSON *Mem.* IV. 30 Our's bid fair to grow into a strong mutual fancy, if not to real true love, selon les régles. **1837** G. H. LEWES *Let.* in A. T. Kitchel *G. Lewes & G. Eliot* (1933) i. 12 In spite of its not being *selon les régles* of this most artificial of worlds..I take the shortest and easiest way I can think of for our better acquaintance. **1864** C. M. YONGE *Trial* II. iv. 74 He thinks he is proceeding *selon les régles*. **1893** —— & COLERIDGE *Strolling Players* xxv. 225 There was so much laughter around that George thought a jest quite *selon les règles*. **1921** L. STRACHEY *Q. Victoria* iii. 73 Was not such a course of conduct..simply *selon les règles*?

selour(e, selowyr, var. forms of CELURE *Obs.*

s'elp. Also 9 swelp. [Cf. MHG. *selftir = so helfe dir.*] Contraction of 'So help', in the oath 'So help me God'. Now only *vulgar*, often in jocularly altered forms.

a **1330** *Otuel* 308 Quaþ roulond, þar he stod on grounde, 'Selpe me gode'. *Ibid.* 879 3ef ani sarazin wiþ eie, Comeþ to lette me of mi weie, Selp me god & þis day, He sschal abugge, 3ef ich may. **1842** BARHAM *Ingol. Leg.*, *Dead Drummer* xlii, His jaw-work would never, I'm sure, s'elp me Bob, Have come for to go for to do sich a job. **1888** KIPLING *Soldiers Three*, *In Matter of a Private*, Slane knelt down and murmured: 'S'elp me, I believe 'e's dead'.

†**selrife**, *a. Obs. Sc.* [f. SELL *v.* + RIFE *a.* Cf. mod.Sc. *salerife* in the same sense (Jam.).] That can be sold, marketable.

1517-42 *Reg. Mag. Sig. Scot.* 644/2 Yeirlie confluence of our..subditis with merchandice and selrife gudis at the toun.

Selsdon man (ˈsɛlzdən). *Pol.* [The name of the *Selsdon* Park Hotel near Croydon, Surrey (see below) + MAN *sb.*[1]: after *Piltdown man*, etc.] Used orig. and chiefly by political opponents to denote an imagined person or persons believed to be pursuing the policies outlined at a conference of Conservative Party leaders held at the Selsdon Park Hotel 30 Jan.–1 Feb. 1970.

1970 H. WILSON in *Labour Govt.* (1971) xxxvii. 759 Selsdon Man is designing a system of society for the ruthless and the pushing. **1971** BUTLER & PINTO-DUSCHINSKY *Brit. General Election of 1970* vi. 131 To Mr. Wilson, these were demonstrations of atavistic Conservative instincts, which he summed up in a phrase he repeated time and again: 'Selsdon man'. **1974** *Times* 31 Dec. 12/4 Selsdon man went wrong because it appeared to make the Conservative Party into a set of decimalized economic liberals. **1979** *Internat. Jrnl. Sociol. of Law* Feb. 102 'Selsdon Man' climbed into office..by exploiting the traditional staple stuff of postwar British electoral politics—prices, unemployment and speculation about the 'economy'.

selsyn (ˈsɛlsɪn). Also **Selsyn**. [f. SEL(F- + SYN(CHRONOUS *a.*] A kind of electric motor closely resembling a magslip and employed similarly in pairs in order esp. to transmit and receive information about the position or motion of mechanical equipment. Also ***selsyn motor***.

Formerly a proprietary term in the U.S.

1926 *Official Gaz.* (U.S. Patent Office) 27 Apr. 802/1 General Electric Company, Shenectady, N.Y... *Selsyn*... Electrical apparatus for transmitting and receiving motion. Claims use since April, 1921. **1930** *Gen. Electr. Rev.* July 378/2 A distinct possibility exists in the application of Selsyn motors to remote control. **1945** *Rev. Sci. Instruments* XVI. 132/2 The Central Scientific Company announces the availability of a limited supply of a.c. Selsyn motors. **1948** *Electronic Engin.* XX. 17 A recorder..was modified..by removing the motor and replacing it by a gear train driven by a selsyn. **1962** J. BELL in G. A. T. Burdett *Automatic Control Handbk.* iv. 11 In the German Navy of the 1914–18 war an early form of a.c. synchronous transmission was used; this was copied by U.S.A. in the G.E. 'Selsyns', the forerunners of the present U.S.A. synchros. **1967** [see MAGSLIP].

selt, pa. t. of SALT *v.*[1]

selt, Sc. and north. pa. t. and pa. pple. of SELL *v.*

†**selth.** *Obs.* Forms: 1 sǽlþ, 2 sielþ, 2–3 selðe, 2–4 selþ, 3 sealþe, selhðe, selðhe, selehðe, seleʒehðe, seluhðe, *Ormin* seollþe, sellþe, 3–4 selthe, 4–5 selth. [OE. *sǽlþ* str. fem. = OS. *sâlda*, OHG. *sâlida*, ON. *sǽld*:—OTeut. **sǽlipā*, f. **sǽli-* good, happy: see SELE *sb.*] Prosperity, good fortune, happiness.

In OE. chiefly *plural*.

c **888** K. ÆLFRED *Boeth.* x, Ic nu hæbbe onʒiten þæt þa mine sælþa & seo orsorʒnes ðe ic ær wende þæt ʒesælþa beon sceoldan nane sælþa ne sint. *a* **1175** *Cott. Hom.* 233 Of wam we alle and us sielþe habbeð. *c* **1200** ORMIN 2823 Þin seollþe iss all unnseʒʒenndlic. *c* **1205** LAY. 32059 Selehðe him wes ʒiueðe. *a* **1225** *Ancr. R.* 354 Vor þis is þe meste seluhðe on eorðe hwose mei, uor Godes luue, habben scheome & teone. *c* **1315** SHOREHAM I. 394 Þe bisschop þese wordes seþ, And beþ wordes of selþe. *c* **1425** *Eng. Conq. Irel.* xx. 50 Euery gladnesse ys endet wyth sorowe, & euery selth hath wnselth at þe end.

†**ˈselthelike**, *adv. Obs. rare*$^{-1}$. [f. SELTH(E + -LIKE.] Successfully, prosperously.

c **1250** *Gen. & Ex.* 1372 'Louerd god', quað he mildelike, 'min erdne ðu forðe selðhelike'.

seltron, variant of SHELTRON.

seltzer (ˈsɛltzə(r)). Also 8 selters, 9 selzer. [Alteration of G. *Selterser*, f. *Selters*, the name of a village in Hesse-Nassau, Prussia. Cf. F. *seltz, selz.*] (In full ***seltzer-water***.) An effervescent mineral water obtained near Nieder-Selters, containing sodium chloride and small quantities of sodium, calcium, and magnesium carbonates. Also an artificial mineral water of similar composition.

1741 POTT in *Phil. Trans.* XLI. 618 To drink the Selters Water, and keep to a cooling Regimen. **1775** SHERIDAN *St. Patrick's Day* I. i, Then she was such a hand at making foreign waters!—for Seltzer, Pyrmont, Islington, or Chalybeate, she never had her equal. **1784** CULLEN tr. *Bergman's Phys. & Chem. Ess.* I. 242 Seltzer water..excites upon the tongue a taste gently salt, and mildly alkaline. **1847** MRS. GORE *Castles in Air* xix, Neither soda-water, however, nor seltzer-water..inspired me with courage to look Sir Robert in the face. **1871** M. COLLINS *Marq. & Merch.* I. ix. 277 A great gulp of brandy and seltzer.

seltzogene (ˈsɛltsədʒiːn). [a. F. *sel(t)zogène*, f. *seltz, selz* (see prec.) + *-gène*: see -GEN.] An apparatus for the production of artificial Seltzer and other mineral and aerated waters.

1860 *Chamb. Encycl.* I. 55/1 Carbonic acid water..prepared in the apparatus known as the gazogène or seltzogène. **1868** W. S. GILBERT *Bab Ball.*, *Capt. Reece* 18 Did they with thirst in summer burn? Lo, seltzogenes at every turn. **1870** *Eng. Mech.* 11 Feb. 537 My seltzogene cost only 14*s.* 6*d.*

selure, var. CELURE *Obs.*; obs. f. SILVER.

‖**selva** (ˈsɛlvə). *Physical Geog.* Also erron. silva. [Sp. and Pg.:—L. *silva* wood.] A tract of densely wooded country lying in the basin of the river Amazon. Usually *pl.*

1849 MRS. SOMERVILLE *Phys. Geog.* ix. (ed. 2) 177 The Silvas of the river of the Amazons, lying in the centre of the continent, form the second division of the South American low lands. **1868** G. DUFF *Pol. Surv.* 175 Next we come to the great wood-covered plains known as the Selvas of the Amazons. **1870** YEATS *Nat. Hist. Comm.* I. xi. (1872) 109 The selvas or woody plains of the Amazon.

selvage, selvedge (ˈsɛlvɪdʒ), *sb.* Forms: [? 5 *corruptly* sultviche], 6 silvadge, 6–7 silvage, selvege, 7 selvedg, self edge, 7–9 selvidge, selfedge, self-edge, 8–9 salvage, 5– selvage, 7– selvedge. [Apparently f. SELF + EDGE *sb.*, after the equivalent early mod.Du. *selfegghe* (Kilian), now *zelfegge* = LG. *sulfegge*. Cf. the Du. synonyms cited by Kilian, *selfkant*, now *zelfkant* (*kant* = border), *selfende*, now *zelfeinde* (*einde* end) = G. *selbende*, by popular etymology *salband*.]

1. a. The edge of a piece of woven material finished in such a manner as to prevent the ravelling out of the weft. Also, a narrow strip or list at the edge of a web of cloth, which is not finished like the rest of the cloth, being intended to be cut off or covered by the seam when the material is made up.

c **1460** *Bk. Curtasye* 657 in *Babees Bk.*, The ewerer schal hele his lordes borde With dowbull napere at on bare worde, The seluage to the lordes syde withe wine. **1537** BIBLE (Matthew's) *Exod.* xxvi. 4 Then shalt thou make loupes of Jacyncte coloure, a longe by the edge of the one curtayne euen in the seluege of the couplinge courtayne. **1597** A. M. tr. *Guillemeau's Fr. Chirurg.* 44/1 Nether must they [*sc.* bandages] have any silvages. **1665** HOOKE *Microgr.* 9 The two edges or silvages. **1725** *Bradley's Fam. Dict.* s.v. *Clear Starching*, The two Selvages put together, then the Ends together, and wash it the Way the Selvage goes, to prevent the Fraying. **1878** BARLOW *Weaving* 198 The application of gauze to the formation of selvages may now be readily understood. **1888** *Encycl. Brit.* XXIV. 466/1 These prongs come in contact with the weft thread between the selvedge of the web and the shuttle box.

fig. *a* **1633** AUSTIN *Medit.* (1635) 282 Now when wee thus let slip these heavenly Thred Lines, that should bee the Selvedge, to bound in all our Worke, wee fall to tangling, tying, and knitting. **1864** *Spectator* 27 Feb. 244/2 Almost every-thing is left with what seamstresses call raw selvidges,—some loose threads just sticking out that the reader feels inclined to lay hold of and pull away.

b. *transf.* A marginal tract, border, edge.

1650 FULLER *Pisgah* IV. ii. 34 Thus though for his disobedience forbidden the entrance of the land of Canaan, yet he came to the selvedge or out-skirt thereof. **1663** SIR G. MACKENZIE *Relig. Stoici* 149 It should not have been thrust out upon the selvage and border of time. **1698** PETIVER in *Phil. Trans.* XX. 321 The Seed..of a brown Colour, and hem'd about with a rusty colour'd List or Selvedge. **1850** CLOUGH *Dipsychus* II. iv. 59 This narrow interspace, this marge, This list and selvage of a glorious time. **1854** H. MILLER *Sch. & Schm.* xiii. (1857) 292 The population..now exists as a miserable selvedge. **1893** STEVENSON *Catriona* xi, I..threaded through the midst of it [the wood], and returned to the west selvage.

c. *Tin-plating.* = LIST *sb.*[3] 7 d.

1834 [see LIST *sb.*[3] 7 d].

d. A waste strip on either side of a piece of wall-paper.

1901 BLACK *Carp. & Build.*, *Home Handicr.* 40 The handy man first cuts the salvage from all his paper on the same side, and then cuts his paper into lengths. **1904** SIR A. GEIKIE *Scott. Remin.* xi. 295 The paper had been stuck on the walls just as it came, without the selvages being cut off.

†**2.** The selvages of cloth cut off for use as a bandage. *Obs.*

1599 A. M. tr. *Gabelhouer's Bk. Physicke* 102/2 Take two peeces of silvadge, and..tye him therwith above his knees as stiffely as is possible.

3. An ornamental border or edging. ? *Obs.*

1481–90 *Howard Househ. Bks.* (Roxb.) 467 Item, for xxiiij. ellys of sultviche to the same coverlett, the elne iiij.d. summa viij.s. **1513** DOUGLAS *Æneis* XII. Prol. 16 As fresch Aurora.., Ischit of hir safron bed..In crammysin cled and granit violat, With sanguyne cape, the selvage purpurat. **1827–35** N. P. WILLIS *David's Grief* 20 The golden selvedge of his robe was heard Sweeping the marble pavement.

4. *Naut.* and *Mil.* = SELVAGEE.

1711 W. SUTHERLAND *Shipbuild. Assist.* 133 Salvages for Shrowds, worn. **1769** FALCONER *Dict. Marine* (1780), *Selvage*, a sort of hank or skein of rope-yarn tied together at several distances. It is used to fasten round any rope, as a shroud or stay, so that a tackle may be hooked in it, to extend the said shroud or stay, which is called setting it up. **1859** F. A. GRIFFITHS *Artill. Man.* (1862) 318 A block..attached to a selvage, answers the same purpose.

5. a. *Mining.* A thin layer of clayey or earthy matter surrounding a metalliferous vein.

1757 tr. *Henckel's Pyritol.* 61 The vein, which has its selvages entire and close. **1897** T. H. HOLLAND in *Rec. Geol. Surv. India* XXX. 18 Each group is represented by microcrystalline and hemicrystalline types occurring either as thin veins, or as selvages to larger masses.

b. *Geol.* An alteration zone at the edge of a rock mass.

1934 [see PARAGENESIS 2]. **1958** *Econ. Geol.* LIII. 292 Selvages of hydrothermal alteration of quartz monzonite along the contacts of some larger aplite-pegmatite bodies. **1979** *Nature* 5 Apr. 511/2 That some basic dykes have conspicuous charnockite selvedges might indicate metasomatic interchange between acid and basic rocks as a primary cause of the conversion, except that many dykes..have no such marginal alteration. **1981** *Cambr. Encycl. Earth Sci.* 211/1 The majority of M[id-]O[cean]R[idge]B[asalt] lavas have a pillow form..and glass selvages—characteristics of rapid cooling in seawater.

6. (See quot.)

1875 KNIGHT *Dict. Mech.*, *Selvage* (Locksmithing), the edge-plate of a lock through which the bolt shoots.

7. *attrib.* and *Comb.*, as *selvage-thread*; **selvage-motion**, ? the motion of a shuttle in forming a selvage; **selvage-protector** (see quot.); **selvage-strop** (sense 4); **selvage-way** *adv.*, in a direction parallel to the selvage.

1893 J. T. TAYLOR *Cotton Weaving* 98 Another kind of *selvedge motion is that used for producing a plain selvedge on a loom weaving satteens with tappets. **1863** J. WATSON *Weaving* 160 The *selvage protector..to prevent the warp yarn from being broken by the weft shot drawing it too tightly. *c* **1860** H. STUART *Seaman's Catech.* 33 Put on the *selvage strop over the parcelling, and hook the single block of the luff tackle to both parts of the selvage. **1863** J. WATSON *Weaving* 161 They allow the pins to fall into position at the selvage, taking hold of the *selvage threads. **1875** *Plain Needlework* 13 Half a yard should be snipped *selvage-way into twelve portions.

selvage, selvedge (ˈsɛlvɪdʒ), *v.* [f. SELVAGE *sb.*] *trans.* To form a boundary or edging to.

1704 PETIVER *Gazophyl.* iv. 35 This has no blue above, but selvidg'd with Golden Eye-like Spots. **1774** GOLDSM. *Nat. Hist.* VI. 37 Where the stream is selvaged with sedges, or the pond edged with shrubby trees. **1849** D. JERROLD *Man of Money* xi, One of the Primrose Places to be found selvaging London. **1899** *Blackw. Mag.* Feb. 180 Where the little grey towns cluster Deep in the hills or selvedging the sea.

Hence **ˈselvaged** *ppl. a.*, **ˈselvaging** *vbl. sb.*

1611 COTGR., *Orlement*, a hemming, seluidging. **1750** G. HUGHES *Barbados* 150 The outside is divided into five selvaged seams, the inside containing three blackish seeds.

selvagee (ˈsɛlvədʒiː). *Naut.* and *Mil.* Also 8–9 salvagee, 9 silvagee. [app. f. SELVAGE *sb.* (sense 5).] (See quot. 1867.)

1750 BLANCKLEY *Nav. Expos.*, *Salvagees* are made with three flat Strands breeded, or by a small Turn put into several Rope Yarns cut into proper Lengths. **1800** J. MITCHELL *Cursory Observ. Modes Manuf. Cables* Pref., Selvagee..is generally pronounced by seamen Salvagee. **1867** SMYTH *Sailor's Word-bk.*, *Selvagee*, a strong and pliant hank, or untwisted skein of rope-yarn marled together, and used as a strap to fasten round a shroud or stay, or slings to which to hook a tackle to hoist in any heavy articles. **1879** *Man. Artill. Exerc.* 392 Selvagees are used for slinging projectiles of the abovementioned natures [i.e. of R.M.L. guns, 9-in. to 12-in., of 25 tons] when loading.

b. *attrib.*

1860 ALSTON *Seamanship* 193 A *Selvagee Strop is made of spun-yarn, or small rope, according to the size required, warped off, and marled down. **1904** in *Dixon Kemp's Yacht & Boat Sailing* (ed. 10). **1882** NARES *Seamanship* (ed. 6) 46 The pendant, having two *selvagee tails, is secured to the bight. **1799** *Specif. J. Mitchell's Patent* No. 2333. 3 *Selvagee twists are of two sorts. **1843** A. SMITH in *Trans. Soc. Arts* XXXIV. 164 *Selvagee wire ropes are made of wires laid parallel and without twist.

selvatic: see SYLVATIC, SILVATIC *a.* 2.

selve (sɛlv), *v. rare.* [f. SELF *sb.*] *intr.* (only G. M. Hopkins) and *trans.* (To cause) to become and act as a unique self. Hence **selved** *ppl. a.*, **ˈselving** *vbl. sb.* Also *Comb.*, as *selved-up*.

1880 G. M. HOPKINS *Sermons & Devotional Writings* (1959) 122 Human nature, being more highly pitched, selved, and distinctive than anything in the world. *Ibid.* 123 Nothing else in nature comes near this unspeakable stress of pitch, distinctiveness, and selving, this selfbeing of my own. *Ibid.* 125 Nothing can..exercise function and determination before it has a nature to 'function' and determine, to selve and instress, with. *Ibid.*, I may treat the question from the side of my being, which is said to be compounded, selved-up, or identified with this universal mind. **1953** K. RAINE *Coll. Poems* (1956) 166 Ceasing to trouble the flowing of things with the fleeting Dream and hope and despair of this transient perilous selving. **1976** H. A. WILLIAMS *Tensions* v. 87 Around that dim and dull awareness of our identity with God we begin, gradually and instinctively, to centre and selve the rest of what we are. That centring and selving takes the whole of our life.

selve, obs. form of SALVE *sb.*[1]

c **1400** *Beryn* 3588.

selvyt (ˈsɛlvɪt). [An arbitrary name.] A kind of duster or polishing cloth.

1891 *Patent Specif.* No. 21,399. **1898** *Cycling* 76 Plating is best cleaned of rust by hard rubbing with paraffin and polished with chamois leather or Selvyt.

sely, selybube: see SEELY, SILLABUB.

selydoyne, variant of CELIDONY[1].

selye, obs. form of SEELY.

†**ˈselyer.** *Obs. rare*⁻¹. [ad. OF. *celier* (mod.F. *cellier*):—L. *cellārium* receptacle for food: see CELLAR.] A storehouse, larder. In quot. *fig.*

1483 CAXTON *Gold. Leg.* 346/2 The holy bodyes were the selyers of god temple of Jhesu crist.

selyng(e, obs. ff. CEILING, SEALING *vbl.*

Sem (sɛm). *Egyptology.* Also **sam.** [Egyptian.] An Egyptian officiating priest who wore a distinctive robe made from a leopard's skin. Also *attrib.* as *sem priest.* Cf. SETEM.

1882 G. RAWLINSON *Hist. Anc. Egypt* I. xi. 438 The 'Sem',..or officiating high-priest, wore, as his costume of office, a complete leopard-skin, with head, claws, and tail. **1898** E. A. W. BUDGE tr. *Bk. Dead* cxvi. 181 The goddess Maāt is carried by the arm of him who eateth the Eye, and who is its divine judge, and the Sem priest carrieth me over upon it. **1910** *Hastings's Encycl. Relig. & Ethics* III. 538/1 Canonical part of the dress of the *sam* priest. **1927** H. CARTER *Tomb of Tut-ankh-amen* II. 28 Ay as king with royal insignia, clad in a leopard's skin of the *Sem* priest.

sem, obs. form of SEAM, SEEM.

sema (ˈsiːmə, ˈseɪ-). *Linguistics.* Pl. ˈsemas, ˈsemata. [a. G. *sema* (V. Skalička *Zur ungarischen Grammatik* (1935) 13), f. Gr. σῆμα sign.] = SEME. Also *transf.*

1938 C. E. BAZELL in *Trans. Philol. Soc.* 112 It is only from the standpoint of their formatives that these morphemes behave like the 'cellules' (we should say the semata) of a single morpheme. *Ibid.* 113 There seems no reason to doubt that the smallest element in grammar, as Skalička holds, is the sema. **1973** D. OSMOND-SMITH tr. *Bettetini's Lang. & Technique of Film* i. 4 One must take into account..the so-called 'semas'—that is, signs whose signifieds correspond to a verbal proposition.

Semainean (səˈmaɪniːən), *a. Archæol.* Also **Semainian.** [f. the name of *Semaine(h*, a village in Upper Egypt + -AN.] A term used by W. M. F. Petrie to designate the last period of predynastic culture in Egypt. Also *absol.* as *sb.*

? **1925** *Catal. Egyptian Antiquities found at Badari in 1925* 3 Approximate dates..9,000 B.C....Gerzean Age...7,000 B.C....Semainean Age...5,500 B.C....First Dynasty. **1928** [see GERZEAN *a.*]. **1939** W. M. F. PETRIE *Making of Egypt* vii. 55 We now reach the last of the ages, the Semainean, best represented at Semaineh, 17 miles west of Qena. **1958** V. G. CHILDE *New Light on Most Anc. East* v. 99 Petrie..postulated a 'dynastic race' and interpolated a Semainian period to contain the conquest and a Semainian culture to result from it. **1964** *Jrnl. Near Eastern Studies* XXIII. 274 Sir Flinders Petrie..divided the Naqadian into three principal phases, named, with reference to the sites of El Amrah, Gerzeh, and Semaineh, the 'Amratian', the 'Gerzean', and the 'Semainean' and otherwise known as Naqada I, Naqada II, and Naqada III.

semal, semul, var. of SIMOOL.

‖**Semana Santa** (seˈmana ˈsanta). [Sp.] In Spain: = HOLY WEEK.

1910 S. L. BENSUSAN *Home Life in Spain* vi. 73 The *feria* persists for a full fifteen days, starting on the Sunday before Easter and only beginning to pass when the last day of Semana Santa is a week old. **1966** E. MCGIRR *Funeral was in Spain* 56 That's Semana Santa in Spain. The week before Easter Sunday. **1979** A. SCHOLEFIELD *Point of Honour* 73 The flames and the smoke reminded me of a *semana santa* procession.

Semang (səˈmaŋ), *sb.* and *a.* Also **Samang.** [Mal.] **A.** *sb.* (A member of) a Negrito people inhabiting the interior of the Malay peninsula. **B.** *adj.* Of or pertaining to this people.

1812 [see POLYNESIAN *a.*]. **1814** [see PAPUAN *sb.* 1]. **1839** T. J. NEWBOLD *Brit. Settlements in Straits of Malacca* II. xv. 377 It would appear that the Semang does not differ much in personal appearance from the Jakun. *Ibid.* 379 The Semang women..are said to be in common. **1860** MAYNE REID *Odd People* 415 The Samangs—a tribe inhabiting the mountainous parts of the Malayan peninsula—are also a negro or negrillo race. **1902** *Encycl. Brit.* XXVI. 485/2 The Vaalpens represent..a state of arrested development analogous to that of the Samangs and other Negritoes of the Malay Peninsula. **1920** R. J. WILKINSON *Hist. Peninsula Malays* (ed. 2) i. 2 The word Semang..has come to be regarded as contemptuous. No negrito will answer to it. *Ibid.* i. 3 For practical purposes a Semang is a nomadic primitive Peninsular negrito whose numeral system stops at two. **1948** A. L. KROEBER *Anthropol.* (ed. 2) x. 424 Asia is particularly rich in tribal societies with 'internally marginal' cultures. Examples are..Palaung, Kachin, Moi, Semang, Sakai, and many others in the states of Farther India and Malaya. **1974** *Encycl. Brit. Micropædia* IX. 46/2 *Semang*, Negrito people of the Malay Peninsula... In the 1970s their population was estimated to be less than 3,000, with only about 100 in Thailand (where they are known as Ngok, or Ngo).

semanteme (siːˈmæntiːm). *Linguistics.* [a. F. *sémantème*, f. Gr. σημαντικός significant, after *morphème* MORPHEME, *phonème* PHONEME.] A unit of meaning; a linguistic element which expresses a concept; = SEMEME. Hence **semanˈtemic** *a.*

1925, etc. [see MORPHEME]. **1933** *S.P.E. Tract* XXXVIII. 596 We already have plenty of synonyms for rumour, news, report, &c., to which semantemes the word *khubber* does not add any new shade of meaning. **1938** I. GOLDBERG *Wonder of Words* xvi. 324 If, in addition to its phonemic and semantemic elements, a word has another element, that element is morphemic. **1949** C. E. BAZELL in E. P. Hamp et al. *Readings in Linguistics II* (1966) 213 The inflections of tense..are naturally always determinants of the verbal semanteme. **1960** G. THOMSON *Greek Lang.* 1 The words composing a sentence may be divided into two kinds: those which express concepts ('full words' or semantemes) and those which express relationships between concepts ('empty words' or morphemes). **1977** A. SHERIDAN tr. *J. Lacan's Ecrits* iii. 63 The effects would no longer be produced, thus revealing that they do not depend even conditionally on the semanteme.

semantic (sɪˈmæntɪk), *a.* and *sb.* [ad. Gr. σημαντικ-ός significant, f. σημαίνειν to show, signify. Cf. F. *sémantique.*] **A.** *adj.*

†**1.** Relating to signs of the weather. *Obs.*

1665 J. SPENCER *Prodigies* v. §1 (ed. 2) 300 'Twere easie to shew how much this Semantick Philosophy..was studied.

2. a. Relating to signification or meaning.

1894 E. W. FAY in *Amer. Jrnl. Philol.* XV. 433 Freedom of interchange between *r* and *l* is limited by semantic considerations. **1895** BLOOMFIELD in *Amer. Jrnl. Philol.* XVI. 412 The semantic value of the older reduplications. **1901** H. OERTEL *Lectures on Study of Lang.* i. 72 He was the first to distinguish clearly between the *formal* and the *semantic* side of a word. *Ibid.* v. 297 In the discussion of all semantic changes the logical aspect must be carefully kept separate from the psychological aspect. **1920** B. MALINOWSKI in *Bull. School Oriental Studies London Inst.* I. iv. 62 Sound semantic definitions valid for a wide range of linguistic types are needed before any grammatical analysis of native languages is possible. **1943** *Time* 22 Nov. 99/3 U.S. intellectuals in 1943 went out and ratified the Constitution all over again. But some of them had semantic reservations. **1968** *N.Y. Post* 15 Jan. 45/3 Each day passes with some new semantic quibble emanating from Washington. **1976** J. S. GRUBER *Lexical Structures in Syntax & Semantics* 1 We would acknowledge the necessity for interpretive semantics of some sort (e.g. a semantic calculus), but not one based on the interpretation of words and phrases.

b. In weakened uses.

1959 W. R. FISHEL in *New Leader* 2 Nov. 13/1 We do ourselves and our Asian neighbors a distinct disservice when we insist on stretching them or shrinking them to fit our particular semantic bed. **1971** L. KOPPETT *N.Y. Times Guide Spectator Sports* ii. 41 Lesson No. 1 must be clung to through all the semantic storms.

B. *sb. pl.* **1. a.** = SEMASIOLOGY. Also, (the study or analysis of) the relationships between linguistic symbols and their meanings. Const. as *sing.* and *pl.*

Now the usual word in this sense.

[**1883** M. BRÉAL in *Études Grecques en France* XVII. 133 Cette étude..nous l'appellerons la *Sémantique*..c'est-à-dire la science des significations.] **1893** E. WILLIAMS tr. M. Bréal in *Trans. Amer. Philol. Assoc.* XXIV. 27 All, or almost all, the chapter of linguistics treating of Semantics, or the science of meanings, has yet to be written. **1895** C. R. LANMAN in *Ibid.* XXVI. p. xi, The doctrine of the principles that underlie the processes of the development of the meanings of words may be called semantics or semasiology. **1900** MRS. H. CUST (*title*) Semantics: Studies in the Science of Meaning. [tr. M. Bréal *Essai de Sémantique.*] **1901** *Athenæum* 13 July, As applied to language, psychology is not easily distinguishable from semantics or semasiology. **1912** E. WEEKLEY *Romance of Words* 79 The convenient name semantics has been applied of late to the science of meanings, as distinguished from phonetics, the science of sound. **1920** B. MALINOWSKI in *Bull. School of Oriental Studies London Inst.* I. iv. 35 All these works..are résumés of the present state of linguistics, and they reflect the insufficient attention hitherto given to Semantics. **1933** L. BLOOMFIELD *Language* viii. 138 When the phonology of a language has been established, there remains the task of telling what meanings are attached to the several phonetic forms. This phase of the description is *semantics*. It is ordinarily divided into two parts, *grammar* and *lexicon*. **1941** J. RANSOM *New Criticism* i. 5 *The Meaning of Meaning* is in terms of the new philosophy of language; the authors refer to the latter as Symbolism, but since their book the name of it appears to have become standardized as Semantics. **1952** *Economist* 21 June 813/2 Professor Hayakawa says nothing about..the importance of semantics in the determination of word-origins and word-history. **1964** E. A. NIDA *Toward Sci. Transl.* iii. 35 While semantics deals with the relationship of symbols to referents, syntactics is concerned with the relationship of symbol to symbol. **1972** HARTMANN & STORK *Dict. Lang. & Linguistics* 204/2 *Linguistic semantics* has studied meaning more in terms of the connexions between speech acts and the physical and intellectual environment of the speaker. **1980** *Times Lit. Suppl.* 7 Mar. 268/1 Frege's goal was not to provide a semantics for natural language as he found it.

b. In weakened uses.

1944 M. RYSKIND in *Sat. Rev. Lit.* 23 Dec. 4/1 The technique of character-assassination instead of arguments is ..standard totalitarian semantics. **1966** *N.Y. Post* 3 Aug. 6/4 Sen. Pastore said that everybody was engaged in semantics. 'It comes down to a very fine point,' he said, stating the obvious in a nutshell. **1978** K. HUDSON *Jargon of Professions* 16 Almost daily in the press briefing, whenever a newsman raises his hand to ask for clarification of some mealy-mouthed statement: 'I am not going to debate semantics with you,' the spokesman replies.

2. *transf.* The interpretation of signs in general.

1946 C. MORRIS *Signs, Lang. & Behavior* viii. 219 *Semantics* deals with the signification of signs in all modes of signifying... When so conceived, pragmatics, semantics, and syntactics are all interpretable within a behaviorally oriented semiotic. **1962** *Listener* 11 Jan. 70/2 Exposure to art, erroneous notions mixed with some accurate ones of history, the private struggle with semantics and meaning. **1970** G. GREER *Female Eunuch* 33 The notion of a curve is so closely connected to sexual semantics that some people cannot resist sniggering at road signs.

C. Special collocations. **semantic aphasia** *Path.*, disturbance in understanding the significance of any but the simplest forms of words or speech caused by disorder in the cerebral cortex; **semantic differential** *Psychol.*, a technique devised to measure the distribution of meaning that a person attaches to a concept, by rating descriptive words selected by him from an evaluated list; a scale or test to achieve this; **semantic paradox** *Logic*, a paradox caused by ambiguity of meaning in the language of a statement, rather than by its logical reasoning; **semantic poetry** (see quot. 1969).

1926 H. HEAD *Aphasia* II. 259 A case of Semantic Aphasia. **1958** *Lang. & Speech* I. 26 This symptom, appearing distinctly in cases where the affection damages the most complex and most recently formed zones of the parieto-occipital region at its border with the temporal region, constitutes a basic symptom of so-called 'semantic aphasia'. **1974** L. F. SIES *Aphasia Theory & Therapy* i. 51 Semantic aphasia produces an inability to perceive the complex relationships by which language classifies separate concepts. **1953** C. E. Osgood *Method & Theory in Exper. Psychol.* xvi. 713 The distribution of his [*sc.* the subject's] judgments on a standardized series of such scales serves to differentiate the meaning of this concept from others; for this reason this measuring instrument has been called a 'semantic differential'. **1962** *Listener* 11 Jan. 62/1 Identification with parents was measured by the similarity of children's description of their parents, and of the kind of person they would most like to be themselves, on a series of seven-point rating scales known as the 'semantic differential'. **1962** U. Weinreich in Householder & Saporta *Probl. Lexicogr.* 26 Semantic-differential tests. **1979** T. Shapiro *Clinical Psycholinguistics* iii. 26 Procedures such as the semantic differential offer valid and important experimental properties to understand meaning. [**1939** *Mind* XLVIII. 358 This semantico-empirical paradox can easily be solved by the ramified theory of types without using the simple theory of types. **1948** H. C. Brodie tr. *Chwistek's Limits of Sci.* ii. 40 Logical paradoxes must be distinguished from semantical paradoxes.] **1960** P. Ziff *Semantic Anal.* iv. 134 The fact that the semantic paradoxes can be formulated in English has led some philosophers, primarily logicians, to the conclusion that English is in a muddled state. **1978** T. J. Smiley in F. P. Ramsey *Foundations* 8 Ramsey transforms the problem by drawing the now standard distinction between the logical and semantic paradoxes. **1949** S. Themerson (*title*) Bayamus and the Theatre of Semantic Poetry. **1951** *Times* 5 Apr. 5/1 Nothing could prevent Mr. Vyshinsky or Mr. Acheson from discussing Etruscan pottery or semantic poetry if they really wished to do so. **1969** *Poetry Rev.* LX. 274 Semantic Poetry is based on the idea that words such as *moon, night, heart, flower*, etc., having become clichés have become devalued and devoid of affective effect. SP avoids all forms of rhetorical device and relies upon a text derived from traditional language by replacing each word by its dictionary definition... Semantic Poetry does not rarefy the verbal material to condense the meaning.

Hence **se'mantical** (also **-ly** *adv.*) *a.*; **seman'tician, se'manticist**, a student of semantics; **seman'ticity**, the quality of being semantic or possessing meaning derived from signs.

1895 M. Bloomfield in *Amer. Jrnl. Philol.* XVI. 409 Every word, in so far as it is semantically expressive, may establish, by hap-hazard favoritism, a union between its meaning and any of its sounds. **1917** *Jrnl. Eng. & Gmc. Philol.* XVI. 472 The professional semanticist is visualized in his work-shop,.. feverishly fingering the leaves of a host of lexical tomes, standard and dialect, old, middle and new. **1921** H. E. Palmer *Princ. Lang.-Study* 62 The lexicologist or semantician will study the meanings. **1926** C. M. Doke *Phonetics of Zulu Lang.* 217 (*caption*) Words semantically alike but differing in tone. **1936** *Mind* XLV. 272 Chwistek, a semanticist and metamathematician noted for his work on the theory of types. **1941** J. Ransom *New Criticism* iv. 282 All discourse consists in signs.., there is the *semantical* dimension proper, involving the reference of a sign to an object. **1960** *Sci. Amer.* Sept. 90/2 The dog's panting [does not] exhibit the design-feature of 'semanticity'... The calls of gibbons.. possess semanticity. **1960** *Economist* 15 Oct. 251/1 In Natal.. there has been some talk of secession—semantically disguised because secession today bears a stigma it did not carry ten years ago. **1973** J. M. Anderson *Structural Aspects Lang. Change* 186 Many of the outstanding semanticists have been optimistic about finding some kind of regularity behind semantic processes. **1975** *Language* LI. 207 This distinction [between competence and performance].. is constantly attacked.. by the 'semanticians'. **1975** I. Robinson *New Grammarians' Funeral* viii. 165 He says that music hasn't semanticity because 'Vivaldi's *Four Seasons* is stylized away from the reality it pretends to imitate'. **1978** C. Hookway in Hookway & Pettit *Action & Interpretation* 26 The semantical and intentional discourse of the subjects provides an additional control.

semanticize (siː'mæntɪsaɪz), *v. Linguistics.* [f. SEMANTIC *a.* + -IZE.] *trans.* To invest (something) with meaning; also, to analyse semantically. So **se'manticized** *ppl. a.*, **se'manticizing** *vbl. sb.*

1942 *Sat. Rev. Lit.* 10 Jan. 14 (*heading*) Semanticizing. **1961** Webster, Semanticize. **1964** P. Meadows in I. L. Horowitz *New Sociol.* 450 The straitlaced purity of semanticized communication-theory. **1976** *Times Lit. Suppl.* 31 Dec. 1631/2 Lotman appears to be over-eager to semanticize, in his own words, 'any element on the parole level'.

semantico- (siː'mæntɪkəʊ), also **se'manto-**, combining form f. Gr. σημαντικός of SEMANTIC *a.*, used with adjs. and advbs. in sense 'semantic(ally) and..'.

1932 W. L. Graff *Lang. & Languages* 277 All linguistic change is a process pertaining to.. semanto-phonetic expression. *Ibid.* 420 Archaic Chinese seems to have had a system of.. semanto-phonetically changeable radicals. **1939** Semantico-empirical [see *semantic paradox* s.v. SEMANTIC *a.* C.]. **1971** *Language* XLVII. 80 These structures are semanto-syntactic, which means that the semantic properties or bundles of properties are arranged not in a linear order but in a hierarchical one. **1976** *Word 1971* XXVII. 268 Semantico-intentionally there are two stages of development. **1977** P. Strevens *New Orientations Teaching of English* ii. 25 *Semantico-grammatical categories*—expressing universal concepts of time, quantity, space and matter, as well as expressing grammatical concepts of *case* ('who did it, who it happened to, and what got changed').

semantron (sɪ'mæntrɒn). *Gr. Orthodox Ch.* Also **simandro, simantron**; pl. **semantra**. [med.Gr. use of Gr. σήμαντρον sign, mark.] A wooden or metal bar struck by a mallet used to summon worshippers to service.

1849 R. Curzon *Visits to Monasteries of Levant* p. i, Interior of the Court of a Greek Monastery. A monk is calling the congregation to prayer, by beating a board called the simandro.. which is generally used instead of bells. **1850** J. M. Neale *Hist. Holy Eastern Ch.* I. II. ii. 217 The word *semantra*.. properly signifies.. the instruments.. by which the people were called together before bells were introduced into the east... They are of two kinds, wooden and iron. The wooden semantron is generally a long, well planed piece of timber. **1912** W. G. Holmes *Age Justinian & Theodora* I. i. 110 At the boom of the great *semantron*.. the various congregations issue forth to attend their respective places of worship. **1939** *Archit. Rev.* LXXXV. 289/1 Round the church.. is a broad path along which a monk walks summoning the faithful to prayer by hammering on a simantron, a long piece of wood which he balances in one hand. **1958** *Times Lit. Suppl.* 10 Oct. 581/5 The simantron .. which summons the monks of Athos to prayer is a wooden not a brass instrument.

semaphore ('sɛməfɔə(r)), *sb.* [f. Gr. σῆμα sign, signal + -PHORE. Cf. F. *sémaphore* (1812 in Hatz.-Darm.).] **1. a.** An apparatus for making signals, consisting of an upright post with one or more arms moving in a vertical plane.

Orig. used for transmitting telegraphic messages; = TELEGRAPH *sb.* 1. Now used on railways and at sea.

1816 *Ann. Reg., Chron.* 85/2 The improved Semaphore has been erected on the top of the Admiralty. **1832** *Act 2 & 3 Will. IV*, c. 64 Sched. O. 33 In a straight line towards Worplesdon semaphore. **1886** *Encycl. Brit.* XX. 238/1 The semaphore has been almost universally adopted for fixed signalling on railways.

b. *attrib.*, as ***semaphore house, lamp***. Also, in recent use, applied to a special form of flag-signalling.

1821 *Lond. Gaz.* 7 Apr. 787/1 Building a Semaphore House at each of the following places. **1855** D. K. Clark *Railway Mach.* 327/1 The semaphore lamps are lighted, to give signals, at night, by white, green, and red lights as required.

2. This method of signalling; *spec.* a system for conveying messages by a code whereby the arms are moved through certain positions in a vertical plane relative to the body.

1904 *Army Signalling Regul.* 25 Semaphore alphabet. *Ibid.* 32 Semaphore drill. **1918** E. S. Farrow *Dict. Mil. Terms* 544 *Semaphore*, a method of signalling in which the letters depend on the position of one or both arms in relation to the body. When sending semaphore, the signaller always faces the distant station. **1975** *Scout Handbk.* (1976) 124/1 Semaphore uses a different position of the arms for each letter.

Hence **'semaphore** *v.* (*trans.* and *intr.*), to signal by semaphore; also *fig.*

1893 *Daily News* 3 July 5/6 The Commander-in-Chief semaphored to me to know 'what I was waiting for?' **1893** *Times* 30 Dec. 9/6 To semaphore to the Commander-in-Chief his doubt as to the signal. **1957** R. Campbell *Coll. Poems* II. 32 The lonely hamlets semaphore their loss. **1981** *Economist* 24 Jan. 88/1 American firms are nervously semaphoring price rises after a strong recovery at the end of 1980.

semapho'retic, *a. Math.* Suggested as a var. of SIGNALETIC (where see quot. 1853).

semaphoric (sɛmə'fɒrɪk), *a.* [f. SEMAPHORE *sb.* + -IC. Cf. F. *sémaphorique*.] Relating to, of the nature of, a semaphore.

1808 Cochrane in *Naval Chron.* XXI. 73 The newly constructed Semaphoric telegraphs.. have been blown up. *a* **1872** B. Harte *Waiting for Ship* Wks. (Hotten) 415 Near this place formerly arose a great semaphoric telegraph with its gaunt arms tossed up against the horizon.

Hence **sema'phorical** *a.* = SEMAPHORIC (Ogilvie Suppl. 1855); **sema'phorically** *adv.* (Webster, 1847). Also **se'maphorist**, one who has charge of a semaphore (Ogilvie, 1882).

†**se'mar.** *Obs.* Also **semmar, -er, semeare, samare**. [var. of SIMAR.] A loose coat or mantle worn by women, *c* 1670–80.

1673 in *12th Rep. Hist. MSS. Comm.* App. VII. 384 A semmar for my wife. **1674** T. Duffett *Span. Rogue* Prol., Here's many a Spark, I fear, That has been lewdly Chous'd in fine Semar. **1688** Holme *Armoury* III. 19/1 A Semeare.. is a kind of loose Garment.., and was a great fashion for Women about the Year 1676, some call them Mantua's. *Ibid.* 95/2 A Semmer, or Semare.

semasiology (ˌsiːmeɪsɪ'ɒlədʒɪ). [f. Gr. σημασί-α signification, meaning + -LOGY.] That branch of philology which deals with the meanings of words, sense-development, and the like.

[*a* **1829** C. K. Reisig *Vorlesungen über Lateinische Sprachwissenschaft* (1839) II. 286 (*heading*) Semasiologie oder Bedeutungslehre.] **1847** J. W. Gibbs *Philol. Studies* (1857) 18 The development of intellectual and moral ideas from physical, constitutes an important part of *semasiology*, or that branch of grammar which treats of the development of the meanings of words. **1877** R. Martineau tr. *Goldziher's Mythol. Hebrews* iii. 43 Some phenomena in the semasiology of Arabic words. **1884** *Athenæum* 27 Sept. 395/1 Philology is now advancing towards a new branch having intimate relations with psychology, the so-called semasiology of Abel and others.

Hence **semasio'logic** *a. rare* = SEMASIOLOGICAL *a.*; **semasio'logical** *a.*, belonging to semasiology; **semasio'logically** *adv.* Also **semasi'ologist**, one who studies semasiology.

1889 F. Haverfield in *Academy* 7 Dec. 374/2 It is phonetically quite possible that.. *aestimo* is connected with αἰσθάνομαι, but semasiologically (as the phrase now is) it is improbable. **1890** *Athenæum* 4 Oct. 450/1 Semasiological solecism. **1899** *Ibid.* 5 Aug. 185/3 The semasiologist.. has to trace the vicissitudes which the history of forms, words, and phrases presents with respect to signification. **1909** L. Bloomfield in *Mod. Philol.* VII. 248 A number of examples are here given of secondary Germanic ablaut forms exhibiting a.. feature of semasiologic differentiation.

semat, obs. form of SEMMIT *Sc.*, under-vest.

sematic (sɪ'mætɪk), *a.* [f. Gr. σηματ-, σῆμα sign + -IC.] **1.** *Biol.* Of mimetic colours: Serving for signal or warning.

1890 Poulton *Colours of Animals* xvii. 336 Sematic or Warning and Signalling Colours.

†**2.** = SEMANTIC *a. Obs. rare*$^{-1}$.

1855 J. W. Powell in *Trans. Anthropol. Soc. Washington* III. 189 While in the present state of knowledge it is perhaps not possible to set forth clearly the resultant sematic and structural effects upon any language, in linguistic arts important effects are discovered.

sematography (siːmə'tɒgrəfɪ). [f. Gr. σηματ-, σῆμα sign + -GRAPHY.] The use of signs or symbols (instead of letters) in writing. So **semato'graphic** *a.*, of or pertaining to sematography.

1902 F. W. G. Foat in *Jrnl. Hellen. Stud.* XXII. 135 (*title*) Sematography of the Greek Papyri. *Ibid.* 144 The sematographic condensation of the ordinary cursive letters. *Ibid.* 154 Perhaps the most striking feature of the sematography of the Roman period is the prominence of that sign or mark.

sematology (siː-, sɛmə'tɒlədʒɪ). [f. Gr. σηματ-, σῆμα sign + -LOGY.]

1. Used by Smart for: The doctrine of the use of 'signs' (esp. words) in relation to thought and knowledge.

1831 [Smart] *Outline of Sematology* 1 If we might call the whole body of instruction which acquaints us with τὰ φυσικά by the name *Physicology*, and that which teaches τὰ πρακτικά by the name *Practicology*,—all instruction for the use of τὰ σήματα, or the signs of our knowledge, might be called *Sematology*. **1839** Smart *Way out* 40 Sematology, or the doctrine of the relation of lingual signs to thought.

2. = SEMASIOLOGY.

1880 Sayce *Sci. Lang.* I. (*Contents-table*) Chapter IV. The Physiology and Semasiology of Speech (Phonology and Sematology). *Ibid.* iv. 336 But by its very nature a science of meanings, sematology, as it has been named, can never have the same certitude, the same exactness, as a science of sounds. **1884** J. A. H. Murray in *Trans. Philol. Soc.* 1882–4, 511 The writing of the Morphology, and of the Sematology, must go hand in hand.

Hence **semato'logical** *a. rare.*

1882 J. A. H. Murray *Let.* 27 Mar. in K. M. E. Murray *Caught in Web of Words* (1977) x. 190 All that you urge against phonetic statements, can be urged with far greater force against sematological ones.

sembel: see SEMBLE *v.*^{1} and *v.*^{2}

sembelande, -ant, etc.: see SEMBLANT.

semblable ('sɛmbləb(ə)l), *a.* (and *sb.*). Also 5 **semlable, (semalable), sembleabil, semblabyll**, 6 **-yl, -il, -ell, sembleable, simblable**. See also SEMNABLE, SIMILABLE. [a. F. *semblable* (13th c.), f. *sembler* to seem, appear: see SEMBLE *v.* and -ABLE. Cf. SEEMABLE.] **A.** *adj.*

†**1. a.** Like, similar. Const. *to. Obs.*

c **1374** Chaucer *Boeth.* II. pr. v. (1868) 48 ȝe men þat ben semblable to god by ȝoure resonable þouȝt. **1477** Earl Rivers (Caxton) *Dictes* 98, I finde hem all so semblable that I can not knowe one from the other. **1576** Fleming *Panopl. Epist.* 17 If so be my discredit, and want of honestie, had been equal or semblable to theirs. **1597** Shaks. *2 Hen. IV*, v. i. 72 It is a wonderfull thing to see the semblable Coherence of his mens spirits, and his. **1609** G. Benson *Serm.* 7 May 60 Semblable vnto Ephraim are many, who know too much and too little. **1658** Osborne *Tradit. Mem. Jas. I*, §17. 55 He owning a Countenance not in the least regard semblable to any my eyes ever met with. **1686** Goad *Celest. Bodies* II. i. 125 God who has made Light to move for thousands of Miles in an instant, by a streight Line, may make it move a semblable space through a Circle, if the use of the World requires it. **1840** *Fraser's Mag.* XXI. 214 Semblable to this is the story of the mad waggery, by which [etc.].

b. Resembling something already mentioned or implied; the like, such-like. Also ***the semblable, such semblable***. *Obs.*

c **1386** Chaucer *Merch. T.* 256, I seye the same, or elles thing semblable. *a* **1470** Tiptoft *Cæsar* x. (1530) 11 These and such semblable things. **1544** tr. *Littleton's Tenures* 50 b, To yelde to his lorde yerely at suche a feaste a horse, or a hauke, or such thynge semblable. **1571** Fortescue *Forest* 164 b, The fallyng evill also with others many the semblable and like infirmities. **1606** Shaks. *Ant. & Cl.* III. iv. 3 That and thousands more Of semblable import. **1653** H. Cogan tr. *Pinto's Trav.* xxxviii. 151 As is the custom in semblable occasions.

c. ***in semblable manner, wise, sort***, in like manner; ***semblablewise***, likewise. Also ***in semblable case(s, in case(s semblable***. *Obs.*

1390 Gower *Conf.* I. 63 And riht so in semblable cas This vice hath ek his officers Among these othre seculers. *c* **1410** Lydg. *Reas. & Sens.* 157 And thus in semblable wise The erthe did him self disgise. **1511–2** *Act 3 Hen. VIII*, c. 23 §7 As thei have doon.. in cases semblable. **1549** Coverdale, etc. *Erasm. Par. Eph.* iv. 14–16 And in semblable wyse vnto this, there is a lyke procedyng in the ordre of godlinesse. **1607** Walkington *Opt. Glass* 10 The heavenly soule of man .. semblablewise, doth feele.. the ill affected crasis of the body. **1624** Bp. Mountagu *Immed. Addr.* 79 We may therefore Call vnto Holy Saints as well, and in semblable sort.

†2. a. Corresponding, proportional, accordant, suitable. *Obs.*

1513 *Life Hen. V* (1911) 19 And that hath bin..the vtter impouerishinge and vndooeinge not of a fewe men w[th]in this Realme, w[ch] haue not bin able to make semblable intercessors and aduocates to theire Prince. *Ibid.* 145 The Kinge continewed by treatie trustinge to finde the way of peace, w[ch] was semblable enoughe had not the Dolphine [etc.]. **1632** LITHGOW *Trav.* II. 52 Their..legges [were] of a great growth, not semblable to their age, being but sixe and thirty dayes old. **1681** WITTIE *Surv. Heav.* 44 Whether it be not most suitable..to the Wisdom, and Power of God.., and semblable to the plain course of his Providence. **1817** PENNIE *Roy. Minstr.* II. 504 But who can paint In language semblable, the blissful scene.

†b. Seemly, becoming. *Obs.*

1647 N. BACON *Disc. Govt. Eng.* I. lx. 188 Neither could Monarchy, Aristocracy, nor Democracy, attaine any semblable condition in any place so long as the Church held its designe apart.

3. Apparent, seeming, not real. †Of treason: Presumptive, constructive. *rare.*

1627 W. SCLATER *Exp. 2 Thess.* (1629) 264 Imitation implies three things: 1 *Factum*, semblable, or rather reall acting of what we pretend to imitate. **1642** D. ROGERS *Naaman* 244 Here is no actuall, but an appearing and semblable concurrence. **1660** *Trial Regic.* 124 That there shall be no semblable Treasons made by presumptions or straines of wit, but those Treasons specified there. **1696** PHILLIPS, *Semblable*, seeming, likely or probable. **1874** FARRAR *Christ* (1894) 122 What is gained..by supposing..the miracle was only semblable, not real?

†4. quasi-*adv.* = SEMBLABLY *adv. Obs.*

1490 CAXTON *Eneydos* xv. 54 For to make semblable [orig. *semblablement*] his aunsuers duryng the syx monethes of the somer. **1568** GRAFTON *Chron.* II. 817 Semblable my Cosin the Erle of Richmonde,..will surely attempt..to pierce me on the other syde.

B. *sb.*

†1. *absol.* and quasi-*sb.* (occas. pl. *semblables*): Something that is like or similar. ***the semblable*** = the like (see LIKE C. 3); as, ***to do the semblable*** (= F. *faire le semblable*). *Obs.*

c **1400** *Rom. Rose* 6759 In al this caas, and in semblables, If that ther ben mo resonables, He may begge, as I telle you here. **1471** CAXTON *Recuyell* (Sommer) 115 He that doeth shewe loue and curtoisie ought to be thankyd by semblable. **1521** WOLSEY in Ellis *Orig. Lett.* Ser. III. I. 283 Who..herin geueth vnto you herty thanks, like as I do the semblable. **1528** *Instruct. P. Vannes* in Burnet *Hist. Ref.* (1679) I. II. Rec. 48 Studying how they may acquite this your Ingratitude..with the semblable. **1560** in J. Scott *Berwick-upon-Tweed* (1888) 448 Yf any soldiers of the garrison be appointed to keep scourage or any such semblables as their course shall come about. **1627** HAKEWILL *Apol.* IV. vi. §4. 343 Long before their time, Clodius..practised the semblable in pearles of great price.

2. With qualifying possessive: (One's) like, (one's) fellow. (So F. *son semblable.*) (Revived in 20th cent. use.)

c **1400** *Rom. Rose* 4855 For he shulde setten al his wil To geten a likly thing him til, And to sustene, if he might, And kepe forth, by kindes right, His owne lyknesse and semblable. ?*a* **1412** LYDG. *Two Merch.* 83 Vnto his semblable thus euery thyng can drawe. **1533** ELYOT *Cast. Helthe* (1541) 6b, Every natural complexion delyteth in his semblable. **1602** SHAKS. *Ham.* v. ii. 124 (1604 Qo.) To make true dixion of him, his semblable is his mirrour. **1607** —— *Timon* IV. iii. 22 His semblable, yea himselfe Timon disdaines.

1922 JOYCE *Ulysses* 377 It behoves every most just citizen to become the exhortator and admonisher of his semblables. [**1923** T. S. ELIOT *Waste Land* i. 8 You! hypocrite lecteur!—mon semblable,—mon frère!] **1941** V. WOOLF *Between Acts* 242 There was Dodge, the lip-reader, her semblable, her conspirator. **1979** *Dædalus* Summer 30 These thoughts picture Othello as, in various ways, a semblable of yours.

†3. A similitude or parable. *Obs.*

1547 BALDWIN *Mor. Philos.* I. iv. (1550) A vj, Parrables, Semblables & examples, (though differing in sumwhat) drawe al to one ende.

†**'semblableness.** *Obs. rare.* [f. SEMBLABLE *a.* + -NESS.] Likeness; congruity.

c **1550** in Strype *Eccl. Mem.* (1721) III. App. XI. 30 For doo but conferre thys Masse of Mans makyng, wyth the Supper of Christs Institution; and see that sembleablenes ys betwene them. *a* **1638** MEDE *Wks.* (1672) 95 This Congruity or semblableness of our Actions and Affections one towards another with God's Favour and Mercy towards us.

semblably ('sɛmbləblɪ), *adv.* Also 5 **semlably, sem(e)blabilly, semblabelie,** (5–7 **-blaby**), 6 **-billabillie, -blablye,** 6–7 **-blablie,** (7 **-bably**). [f. SEMBLABLE *a.* + -LY[2].]

†1. In like manner, similarly. *Obs.*

1420 HEN. V in Rymer *Fœdera* (1709) IX. 907/1 Th' Accorde..was there Sworne by both the sayde Commissaires, yn name of our foresaid Fader; And semblably by Us in oure owne Name. **1520** *St. Papers Hen. VIII*, II. 34 That all other shall take fearfull example by hym, semblably to offende hereafter. **1596** SHAKS. *1 Hen. IV*, v. iii. 21 A gallant knight he was, his name was Blunt, Semblably furnished like the king himselfe. **1601** HOLLAND *Pliny* XXII. xxiii. II. 133 Semblably, good showres doe breed Silphium. **1693** J. EDWARDS *Author. O. & N. Test.* I. 167 The Idolatrous Tabernacle was called the Tabernacle of Moloch *i.e.* the King: Semblably the Mosaick Tabernacle was..held to be the Palace..of the Highest King, *i.e.* God.

2. Seemingly, apparently, speciously. *rare.*

1889 FARRAR *Lives Fathers* I. x. 635 Martin saw through his semblably orthodox language.

semblance ('sɛmbləns). Also 4–6 **-aunce,** (5 **sembal-, sembelaunce,** 6 **sembleaunce**). [a. F. *semblance*, f. *semblant*: see SEMBLANT. Cf. Sp. *semblanza*, It. *sembianza*.]

†1. The fact of appearing to view. ***in semblance***, apparent, visible, to be seen. *Obs.*

c **1300** *Cursor M.* 21638 Sin first þe werld was wroght, Meracles o þe cros might Has ben in semblance and in sight.

2. The appearance or outward aspect of a person or thing.

?*a* **1366** CHAUCER *Rom. Rose* 425 Ful lyk to hir was that image, That maked was lyk hir semblaunce. *a* **1400–50** *Wars Alex.* 4098 A burly best..Of sembalaunce as a see-bule. *c* **1477** CAXTON *Jason* 40b, They jugged him with his mayntene and semblaunce to be a moche noble knight. **1591** SPENSER *M. Hubberd* 200 Be you the Souldier, for you likest are For manly semblance, and small skill in warre. **1593** SHAKS. *2 Hen. VI*, III. ii. 162 A timely-parted Ghost, Of ashy semblance. **1631** MILTON *Sonn.* ii. 5 Perhaps my semblance might deceive the truth, That I to manhood am arriv'd so near. **1741–2** GRAY *Agrippina* 120 By Juno, It bears a noble semblance. On this base my great revenge shall rise. **1806** WORDSW. *Ode Intim. Immortality* 108 Thou whose exterior semblance doth belie Thy Soul's immensity. **1865** M. ARNOLD *Ess. Crit.* x. (1875) 417 It may be the vulgar part of human nature which busies itself with the semblance and doings of living sovereigns.

b. The form, likeness or image *of* a person or thing, considered in regard to another that is similar. Chiefly in phrases, as ***to the semblance of; to have*** or ***take the semblance of; in (the) semblance of***, in likeness of, so as to resemble; †***of one's semblance***, resembling him.

c **1374** CHAUCER *Boeth.* IV. pr. vi. (1868) 142 þe þinges þat he haþ maked in to hys semblaunce [L. *in sui similitudinem*]. **1377** LANGL. *P. Pl.* B. XVIII. 285 And in semblaunce [*v.r.* semblaunt] of a serpent sat on þe appeltre. *c* **1400** *Pilgr. Sowle* (Caxton) v. xiv. (1859) 80 And sodenly was sente doune the hooly ghoost in semblaunce of fyry tonges. *c* **1450** *Merlin* v. 91 He hadde take the semblaunce of a moche olde man. **1471** CAXTON *Recuyell* (Sommer) 245 This childe had hooly the veray semblance and liknes of kynge Iupiter. **1513** *Life Hen. V* (1911) 37 Whereby the water gathered and arised..to the semblaunce of a little sea. *Ibid.* 65 Smale children apparrelled in the semblance of Angels. **1598** SHAKS. *Merry W.* v. v. 11 A fault done first in the forme of a beast..and then another fault in the semblance of a Fowle. **1772** MACKENZIE *Man of World* II. v. (1823) 471 To assume her semblance, is a tribute which vice must often pay to virtue. **1807** WORDSW. *White Doe* I. 277 'Twas said that She all shapes could wear; And oftentimes before him stood,.. In semblance of a lady fair. **1867** PARKMAN *Jesuits N. Amer.* xvi. (1875) 218 And now the lake narrowed to the semblance of a tranquil river.

3. A person's appearance or demeanour, expressive of his thoughts, feelings, etc., or feigned in order to hide them. (Cf. SEMBLANT *sb.* 1 b, c, d.)

a **1400–50** *Wars Alex.* 5192 Bot lat þi semblance be sadd quen þou þi saȝe ȝildis. **1514** BARCLAY *Cyt. & Uplondyshm.* (Percy Soc.) 21 What is fayre semblaunce, with thought & hevynes? Forsothe nought elles but cloked folysshness! **1600** SHAKS. *A.Y.L.* I. iii. 124 Weele haue a swashing and a marshall outside, As manie other mannish cowards haue, That doe outface it with their semblances. **1606** J. CARPENTER *Solomon's Solace* i. 4 He was neuer of the mind or semblance, to be couetous towards his subiects, whiles he was bountifull to himselfe. **1633** BP. HALL *Hard Texts, Prov.* xi. 9 A dissembling friend with faire and false words and semblances draweth his neighbour into some dangerous inconvenience. **1726** POPE *Odyss.* XVII. 77 Him, gath'ring round, the haughty Suitors greet With semblance fair, but inward deep deceit. **1805–6** CARY *Dante, Inf.* IV. 78 Four mighty spirits toward us bend their steps, Of semblance neither sorrowful nor glad.

†b. Phr. ***to make*** or ***show*** (a specified) ***semblance***. (Cf. SEMBLANT *sb.* 3 a, b, f.) *Obs.*

1387 TREVISA *Higden* (Rolls) II. 421 Ȝif þe Grees..comeþ þeder, þe bryddes makeþ hem good semblaunce [*MS. a* semblaunt]. *a* **1450** *Knt. de la Tour* 161 What chere or what sembelaunce that men make vnto suche women in thaire presence. **1568** GRAFTON *Chron.* II. 778 Of truth the Protectour and the Duke of Buckingham made very good sembleaunce vnto the Lord Hastinge's and kept him much in their company. **1596** SPENSER *F.Q.* IV. vii. 44 He..humble homage did vnto him make, Midst sorrow shewing ioyous semblance for his sake.

4. An appearance or outward seeming *of* (something which is not actually there or of which the reality is different from its appearance).

1599 SHAKS. *Hen. V*, II. ii. 117 With patches, colours, and with formes being fetcht From glist'ring semblances of piety. **1647** CLARENDON *Hist. Reb.* II. §39 They had the appearance of a good body of men, there being all the semblance of great bodies behind on the other side of the hill. **1667** MILTON *P.L.* I. 529 With high words, that bore Semblance of worth not substance. **1797** GODWIN *Enquirer* I. xi. 96 Where the parent is not prepared to grant a real and *bona fide* equality..he should avoid the semblance of it. **1799** HT. LEE *Canterb. T., Frenchm. T.* (ed. 2) I. 288 [She] was not duped by this semblance of tranquillity. **1822** LAMB *Elia* Ser. II. *Books & Reading*, To reach down a well-bound semblance of a volume. **1855** MACAULAY *Hist. Eng.* xiii. III. 298 Carstairs was forced to content himself with the substance of power, and to leave the semblance to others. **1855** DICKENS *Dorrit* II. xiii, On the door..appeared the semblance of a brass-plate. **1861** BUCKLE *Civiliz.* (1873) III. i. 21 Any thing which bore even the semblance of wealth was an irresistible excitement to their cupidity. **1889** JESSOPP *Coming of Friars* ii. 89 In many cases oiled linen cloth served to admit a feeble semblance of light.

b. An apparition or vision (*of* a person, etc.).

1489 CAXTON *Faytes of Armes* III. i. 168 Appiered byfore me the semblaunce of a creature hauyng the fourme of a stately man. *a* **1717** FENTON *Odyss.* XI. *in Milton's Style* Poems 125, I last the visionary Semblance view'd Of Hercules, a shadowy Form; for He The real Son of Jove, in Heav'ns high Court Abides. **1813** SCOTT *Trierm.* II. xxviii, And her semblance oft will seem, Mingling in a champion's dream, Of her weary lot to 'plain, And crave his aid to burst her chain. **1870** O'SHAUGHNESSY *Epic of Women* 202, I saw Him some time by the flickering light, As the one in my dream who was playing my part; Till his semblance grew dim and was gone from my sight.

c. With negative (or equivalent): Even the appearance, the bare appearance.

1828 MACAULAY *Ess., Hallam* ¶29 When the Protector wished to put his own brother to death, without even the semblance of a trial. **1847** R. W. HAMILTON *Rewards & Punishm.* vii. (1853) 320 Where is the semblance of proof that Christ visited disembodied spirits of the wicked? **1874** GREEN *Short Hist.* viii. §6. 524 The fall of Strafford had put an end to all semblance of rule.

d. ***in semblance***, in seeming, in appearance (only).

1864 BRYCE *Holy Rom. Emp.* v. (1866) 78 So was his government Roman in semblance rather than in fact.

e. In generalized sense and quasi-personification.

1839 CARLYLE *Chartism* v. (1840) 44 It is the heyday of Imposture; of Semblance recognising itself and getting itself recognised, for Substance. **1840** —— *Heroes* vi. (1841) 382 The..return of mankind to Reality and Fact, now that they were perishing of Semblance and Sham.

5. A person or thing that resembles another; a likeness, image, or copy *of*.

1513 *Life Hen. V* (1911) 143 Maruelouslie imbordered wth signes and semblances of Lillies and of Roses. **1593** SHAKS. *Lucr.* 1246 No more then waxe shall be accounted euill, Wherein is stampt the semblance of a Deuill. **1762–71** H. WALPOLE *Vertue's Anecd. Paint.* (1786) I. 88 John Rous, the antiquary of Warwickshire, who drew his own portrait and other semblances. **1824** CAMPBELL *Theodric* 155 The painting long in that sweet mansion drew Regards its living semblance little knew. **1846** RUSKIN *Mod. Paint.* II. III. I. xi. §4 The fact of our deriving constant pleasure from whatever is a type or semblance of divine attributes.

6. The fact or quality of being like something; likeness, resemblance.

1576 FLEMING *Panopl. Epist.* 236 There is suche affinitie and semblaunce in the matter, that we could not doe amisse to ioyne them all together. **1648–99** J. BEAUMONT *Psyche* iii. 67 The Reins were cloath'd in whitest silk, to hold Some 'semblance to the Hand that them controll'd. **1684** BUNYAN *Pilgr.* II. 122, I thought no body had been like me, but I see there was some Semblance 'twixt this good Man and I. *a* **1864** FERRIER *Grk. Philos.* (1866) I. iv. 92 Construct our skeleton as we best may, and..give it..some semblance to the remains of an organic creature. **1900** J. G. CAMPBELL *Superstit. Scott. Highl.* 78 The student..will recognize in them a semblance to the Fairy tales of the North of Ireland.

†7. Likelihood, probability. *Obs.*

1548 GESTE *Agst. Pr. Masse* F iv, It is expressely wrytten..(say our catholiques) that they sacrificed to thee Lorde. Therfore by al sembleaunce they sacrificed his body and bloud. **1647** N. BACON *Disc. Govt. Eng.* I. lxxi. (1739) 189 Yet some semblance there is, that it was yet more ancient.

8. Phr. ***to make semblance***: to make an appearance or pretence. Const. *of* (something, doing something); also with clause introduced by *that, as if, as though*; also with inf. (Cf. SEMBLANT *sb.* 3 c, d.)

c **1450** *Merlin* ii. 39 He that shewed yow that, made yow semblance that ye sholde be deed for me. **1585** T. WASHINGTON tr. *Nicholay's Voy.* I. xx. 24 He should make a semblance as though he would remayne there in hostage. **1602** MARSTON *Antonio's Rev.* v. i. Wks. 1856 I. 132 They all make semblance of loathing Piero. **1610** HOLLAND *Camden's Brit.* I. 813 A souldior..making semblance to deliver unto him the keies of the Castle. **1649** MILTON *Eikon.* xxvii. 224 His words make semblance as if hee were magnanimously exercising himself. **1670** —— *Hist. Eng.* II. 51 Who, by his Father banish'd,..made semblance of marching toward Britain. **1850** GLADSTONE *Glean.* (1879) V. 213 Did she, or did she not, ever make a semblance of surrendering it?

†**'semblant,** *sb. Obs.* Forms: 3 **samblant,** 3–5 **semblaund,** 3–6 **sembland, -blaunt,** 4 **sembelande, -aund, -aunt, semblont,** 4–5 **semblaunde,** 5 **sembelant, -blande,** 5–6 **-blaunte,** 6 **-blante,** 3–7 **semblant;** also 4 **semelant,** 4–5 **semlaunt, -land(e,** 4–6 **semlant,** 5 **semeland(e, -awnt, seemlaunte, seymland, semlante.** Also SEMENAUNT. [a. F. *semblant* (11th c.), sb. use of pr. pple. of *sembler* SEMBLE *v.*

The corresponding forms in the other Rom. langs. (see SEMBLANT *a.*) are likewise used subst.]

1. A person's outward aspect or appearance.

a **1225** *St. Marher.* 5 Salue me mine wunden þat hit ne sem..o mi samblant þat ich derf drehe. *c* **1290** *S. Eng. Leg.* 322/799 þe eiȝene stareinde, And þe mouth of foul semblaunt. **1297** R. GLOUC. (Rolls) 3985 þer come in tuelf olde men wiþ euene pas þere, Men of wel vair semblant. *c* **1330** *Arth. & Merl.* 5537 (Kölbing) Alle his barouns him seyd, ywis. It sembled men of gret priis, Her semblaunt hem bar witnisse. *c* **1440** *Generydes* 4019 By hir semlante he thought it shuld be she. *a* **1529** SKELTON *P. Sparowe* 936 His foule semblaunt All displeasaunte. **1594** R. C[AREW] *Godfrey* (1881) 109 And with a semblant braue and nobellest, (As lightning wonts) he in his armour shines. **1595** SOUTHWELL *Poet. Wks.* (1856) 118 In springing locks lay crouched hoary wit, In semblant young, a grave and ancient port.

b. esp. as betokening the thoughts, feelings, mood, disposition, etc.: Demeanour, air, look, expression.

a **1240** *Sawles Warde* in *Cott. Hom.* 247 Nis hare nan þe ne..gulteð ilome, oðer ifol semblant oder in vuel dede. **13..** *Coer de L.* 3464 Kyng Richard..Abouten hym gan loke ful yerne With wrathful semblaunt and eyen sterne. **1387** TREVISA *Higden* (Rolls) III. 275 Socrates..drank venym wiþ stedfast semblaunt [L. *constanti vultu*]. 1390 GOWER *Conf.* III. 253 And thei hire sihe of glad semblant, Al full of merthes and of bordes. c1460 *Towneley Myst.* iii. 211 With seymland full sory, wryngand both my handis ffor drede. 1531 ELYOT *Gov.* III. xi. (1880) II. 277 Pacience is a noble vertue,..retayninge all wayes glad semblaunt in aduersitie and doloure. 1596 SPENSER *F.Q.* IV. x. 31 Therein sate an amiable Dame, That seem'd to be of very sober mood, And in her semblant shewed great womanhood. 1651 *Life Fr. Sarpi* 4 Being in himselfe..of a semblant or meane, alwaies thoughtfull, and rather melancholique then serious.

c. The demeanour or 'countenance' which a person exhibits towards others; ***good*** or ***fair semblant***, favourable countenance, favour. Also, a look or glance cast upon another. Cf. 3 b.

c1330 R. BRUNNE *Chron. Wace* (Rolls) 6434 He tok sire Conan by þe hond, & on hym low wyþ god semblaunt [*Petyt MS.* faire semblande]. 1387 TREVISA *Higden* (Rolls) VI. 87 Som wikked men sighe þat Berthericus hadde good semblant of meny men [L. *quod Bercaricus a multis esset salutatus*]. 1387–8 T. USK *Test. Love* II. xii. 3 And she, aperceyving this fantasyse in myne herte, gan her semblaunt goodly on me caste. 1470–85 MALORY *Arthur* II. xvii. 96 He sawe an hondred ladyes and many knyghtes that welcommed hym with fayr semblaunt. c1477 CAXTON *Jason* 61 And Ysiphile on that other syde alwaye in her amerouse semblants and regardes. a1586 SIDNEY *Arcadia* III. (Sommer) 278 A minde which could cast a carelesse semblant vppon the greatest conflictes of Fortune. 1598 YONG *Diana* 49 Whereupon Doria with a gratious semblant answered her thus againe.

d. With contextual implication that the appearance is deceitful or misleading. Often ***false*** or ***fair semblant*** (= F. *faux, beau semblant*).

a1225 *Ancr. R.* 128 Ant te valse ancre..habbeð efter þe uoxe a simple semblaunt sume cherre, & beoð þauh ful of gile. 1390 GOWER *Conf.* I. 7 The word was lich to the conceite Withoute semblant of deceite. 1401 *26 Pol. Poems* 13/122 The world is like a fals lemman, ffayre semblaunt, and moche gyle. 1591 SAVILE *Tacitus, Hist.* IV. xlvii. 204 Shortly after the necessity ceased, or the false semblant [L. *simulatio*]. 1600 O. E. *Repl. to Libel* I. v. 121 In outward semblant they are sheepe, but inwardly they are goates.

e. The face, countenance. (= L. *vultus.*)

c1315 SHOREHAM *Poems* II. 57 Hy..By-spet hym þat swe[t]e semblant þat heuene and erþe a-lyȝte [L. *Vultum Dei conspuunt, lumen caeli gratum*]. c1380 WYCLIF *Last Age Ch.* (1840) 36 Jhūs wente into heuene to apere to þe semlant of God for us [Heb. ix. 24 *ut appareat nunc vultui Dei pro nobis*]. 1382 —— *Luke* xxiv. 5 Whenne thei dredden, and bowiden her semelant [1388 semblaunt, sembland, Vulg. *declinarent vultum*] in to erthe. c1425 *St. Mary of Oignies* I. xii. in *Anglia* VIII. 147/43 In swote of þy semelande þou schalte ete þy mete. c1440 *Promp. Parv.* 452/1 Semelawnt [*Winch. MS.* Seemlaunte], *vultus.* 1483 *Cath. Angl.* 329/1 A Semlande (*v.r.* Semblande), *vultus.*

2. *gen.* Appearance, seeming, outward aspect; also, an appearance or show (whether true or false) *of* some quality, etc. Also, something that exists only in appearance or pretence.

a1225 *Ancr. R.* 416 Vnder semblaunt of gode is ofte i-heled sunne. c1386 CHAUCER *Clerk's T.* 872 No pompe, no semblant of roialtee. 1554 PHILPOT *Exam. & Writ.* (Parker Soc.) 388 So that I dare say that the temples of the cruel barbarous nations have more semblant of religion. 1590 SPENSER *F.Q.* III. iv. 54 And thousand fancies bett his ydle brayne With their light wings, the sights of semblants vaine. 1591 —— *Virg. Gnat* 93 Ne measures all things by the costly rate Of riotise, and semblants outward braue. 1624 *Brief Inform. Palatinate* 42 Counterfeit Embassades sent here and there, vnder false pretexts and semblants.

b. ***by semblant***, in appearance or aspect (cf. OF. *par semblant*). Also ***in semblant***, in seeming.

?a1366 CHAUCER *Rom. Rose* 152 And ful of gyle, and felle corage, By semblaunt [F. *par semblant*] was that ilke ymage. c1386 —— *Sqr.'s T.* 508 Right so this god of loue, this ypocryte..kepeth in semblant alle hise obseruances That sowneth in to gentillesse of loue. c1400 *Brut* I. 120 He saw a wonder faire ymage, & wel made, & in semblant as it were an Archire. 1513 DOUGLAS *Æneis* I. xi. 43 As Cupide hingis abowt Eneas hals,..fenȝeand luif full fals, By sembland as he his fader hed bene.

3. to make semblant [= F. *faire semblant*].

a. To have or assume a (specified) expression, look, or demeanour.

c1290 *S. Eng. Leg.* 322/797 Ȝwane huy i-seoz heore felawe to torment i-brouȝt, Luþur semblaunt huy makiez boþe, as it ne likede heom nouȝt. 1375 BARBOUR *Bruce* IX. 250 Thai ..maid gude sembland for the ficht. 1474 CAXTON *Chesse* III. vii. (1883) 141 Allway where he wente he made heuy and tryste semblant. 1561 RANDOLPH *Let. to Cecil* (MS. Cott. Calig. B. 10 lf. 32), It is said..what semblant somever the noble men do make, that they are grieved with their queen's refusal. 1603 KNOLLES *Hist. Turks* (1621) 803 Valetta although his mind..was inwardly attainted with exceeding griefe, yet made semblant otherwise. 1624 *Brief Inform. Palatinate* 49 Where yet neuerthelesse was made all manner of faire semblant, and seeming to haue a desire to giue satisfaction.

b. To show a (good or ill) countenance (to any one); to give (a person) a welcome, reception, or entertainment (of a specified character, friendly or unfriendly). Cf. 1 c.

a1225 *Ancr. R.* 90 His eie euer bihalt te ȝif þu makest ei semblaunt, oðer eni luue lates touward unðeauwes. c1290 *S. Eng. Leg.* 41/256 þe schrewe heom made fair semblaunt, ..þat huy were for-dronke beie and a-slepe leiȝen sone. c1430 *Syr Tryam.* 1142 The kyng toke hym be the hande, And made hym glad semelande. a1450 *Knt. de la Tour* 24 Y praie you..that ye make me never the worse chere..nor that ye make me not the worse semblaunt.

c. To make a show, appearance, or pretence *of*; to appear *to do* or *be* something; to seem likely, threaten, *to do*. (Cf. F. *faire semblant de*). Also occas. without const.

1375 BARBOUR *Bruce* VIII. 238 Lordingis, now ȝhe se How ȝon men, throu thar gret pouste, Wald, and thai mycht fulfill thar will, Slay vs, and mak sembland thar-till. 1470–85 MALORY *Arthur* VII. viii. 224 And therwith al he made a semblaunt to slee hym. 1481 CAXTON *Myrr.* III. xvi. 171 They..make semblaunt to be moche grete clerkis & experte. a1533 LD. BERNERS *Huon* lix. 205 Whan they saw them comynge, they made semblaunt to returne to the cyte a soft pace. 1573 *New Custom* Prol., Making semblant of antiquitie in all that they did. 1602 DOLMAN *La Primaud. Fr. Acad.* (1618) III. 830 He will make semblant to despise and scorne the hounds. 1629 MAXWELL *Herodian* App. 98 Seeing what was done, could not be vndone, they..made semblant of reioycing, as others did.

d. With clause introduced by *that, as, as if, as though.* Also rarely with obj. + inf.

a1300 *Cursor M.* 17288 + 389 Iesus made hom semblant as he wald ferrer goo. c1340 *Ayenb.* 137 þe wel couaytouse wrechche, þet..makeþ alneway semblont þet he ne heþ naȝt. c1386 CHAUCER *Pars. T.* ¶570 þay make semblaunt as þough þay speke of good entencioun. c1450 *Merlin* xi. 25 When Vortiger wiste he was ded, he made semblaunt as he hadde be right wroth. 1548 UDALL, etc. *Erasm. Par. Mark* vi. 45–52 Jesus..made semblaunte as though he would haue passed by them. 1561 T. HOBY tr. *Castiglione's Courtyer* I. E ij b, Some Oratours..dissemblinge their cunning, made semblant their orations to bee made very simply. 1609 HOLLAND *Amm. Marcell.* XIV. vii. 15 Making faire semblant, That himselfe was much disquieted.

e. With negative (or its equivalent): Not to let one's thoughts, feelings, etc. appear; to show no sign (*of*); not to seem (or not to seem likely) *to be* or *do* something. (So in Fr., esp. in phr. *ne faire semblant de rien*, to take no notice.)

c1230 *Hali Meid.* 44 (MS. Bodl.) Me þeo þe best luuieð, ham to-beoreð ofte þrin, þah ha na semblant [*MS. Titus* þerof na semblaund] ne makien ine marhen. 13.. *Guy Warw.* 2290 þurch his bodi þe blod ran; Tirri made no semblaunt of þan. a1330 *Otuel* 467 To smiten made he semblant non, Er otuwel was risen & gon. a1450 *Knt. de la Tour* xiv. 19 Her suster, that had lost atte the plaie as well as she, made no semblaunt of her losse.., but made as good chere as she hadd wonne. 1471 CAXTON *Recuyell* (Sommer) 65 Whan saturne sawe that his enemyes made no semblant to meue. a1533 LD. BERNERS *Huon* lxxxii. 256 Whan Gerard vnderstode the kynge he was ioyfull ther of in his herte, but he made no semblant of ioy by cause of the lordes that were there present. 1559 *Mirr. Mag., Dk. Glouc.* xxii, Yet openly in shewe made he no semblaunt, By worde nor by deed to beare displeasure. 1603 KNOLLES *Hist. Turks* (1621) 368 For all that, Moses neither word or countenance made any semblant of liking, or disliking the message.

f. In similar phrases with other vbs., as ***to show*** or ***kithe semblant; to give a semblant*** (*of*). ***to let no semblant be seen***: cf. e.

13.. *Cursor M.* 29067 (Cott. Galba) þot when ȝe fast, þan sall ȝe schaw Meri sembland with glad chere. 13.. *Guy Warw.* 2214 Al togider þai gun smite; Semblant of loue þai kidde bot lite. 13.. *Gaw. & Gr. Knt.* 468 þaȝ Arþer þe hende kyng at hert hade wonder, He let no semblaunt be sene. c1500 *Melusine* 252 The whiche esquyer with his companye came with amyable contenaunce, shewyng no semblaunt but as frendes. 1618 BOLTON *Florus* IV. ii. (1636) 288 Had not five cohorts of the Pompeian horse..given a semblant of flying [orig. *nisi cohortes hostium quinque..fugae speciem praebuissent*].

4. A likeness or resemblance, an image or portrait (*of*).

a1400 *Relig. Pieces fr. Thornton MS.* 84/21 Hys semblant he sete my saule with-in. 1422 YONGE tr. *Secreta Secret.* lvi. 217 Phylomon..sayde, 'who-so Is this ymage?' They sayden, 'this ys the Semblaunt of the wyse ypocras'. 1590 SPENSER *F.Q.* I. ii. 12 But he the knight, whose semblaunt he did beare, The true Saint George was wandred far away. 1614 T. WHITE *Martyrd. St. Geo.* D 3, Here's thy clay-frame,—God, doe with it thy pleasure; Here's thine owne semblant by my sinnes abased. 1617 COLLINS *Def. Bp. Ely* II. x. 416 While we lay downe the old man, and take vp the new, there is a semblant of our dying, as well as of our rising againe.

5. By extension from 3 b (where cf. quot. c1290): Entertainment furnished to guests. (For the sense-development cf. CHEER.)

1297 R. GLOUC. (Rolls) 7167 He ber þe croune & huld þe deis mid oþer atil al so, & mid gret semblant þe feste huld. 13.. *Seuyn Sag.* 404 (W.) Thai..maked at ese the messagers, With god semblant, and glade chers. 13.. *E.E. Allit. P.* B. 131 He..Solased hem with semblaunt & syled fyrre.

semblant ('sɛmblənt), *a.* Now *rare* or *Obs.* Forms: 4, 6 sembland, 5 semland, samblant, 6 semblante, 6–9 semblant. [a. Of. *semblant*, pres. pple. of *sembler* SEMBLE *v.*, used as adj. Cf. Sp. *semblante*, It. *sembiante*.]

†**1.** Like, similar. Const. *to.* Obs.

1377 [see SEMBLABLE *a.* 1]. 1485 CAXTON *Chas. Gt.* 240 O comforte of my body,..resemblyng to Iudas machabeus in prowesse, samblant to sampson in strengthe. 1513 DOUGLAS *Æneis* X. xii. 130 Bot siclike chancis and semblant [*v.r.* sembland] ennoy Abydis the. 1607 J. CARPENTER *Plaine Mans Plough* 15 They had..followed after strange and false gods, as semblant to the Heathens. 1612 W. SCLATER *Minister's Portion* 1 In other semblant imployments. 1725 POPE *Odyss.* IV. 33 Two youths approach, whose semblant features prove Their blood devolving from the source of Jove. 1729 SAVAGE *Wanderer* II. 24 This figure tender grief, like mine, implies, And semblant thoughts, that earthly pomp despise.

†**b.** Of a portrait: Resembling the original.

1714 PRIOR *Ep. Desiring Queen's Picture* 18 That as their Eyes survey The semblant Shade, Men yet unborn may say: Thus Great, thus Gracious look'd Britannia's Queen.

†**2.** That simulates an appearance. *Obs.*

1725 W. HAMILTON *To C'tess Eglinton* 68 in Ramsay *Gentle Sheph.*, And semblant falsehood puts on truth's disguise.

3. Seeming, apparent, counterfeit.

1840 *Blackw. Mag.* XLVII. 776 This alliance between Rome and a wide semblant indifference towards all creeds is the most characteristic and portentous sign of the times. 1840 CARLYLE *Heroes* v. (1841) 284 Thou art not *true*; thou art not extant, only semblant. 1843 —— *Past & Pr.* I. ii. 16 A just real union as of brother and brother, not a false and merely semblant one as of slave and master.

'semblative, *a. rare.* [f. SEMBLE *v.* + -ATIVE, after SEMBLANT.] Coined by Shaks. (if the text is sound) to mean 'like, resembling', or perh. 'seeming, appearing'. In the later quots.: Seeming; simulating the appearance (*of*).

1601 SHAKS. *Twel. N.* I. iv. 34 Thy small pipe Is as the maidens organ, shrill, and sound, And all is semblatiue a womans part. 1814 A. BECKET *Genii* i. in *New Brit. Theatre* I. 500 Well, young Marcellus, soon shall it be known If thine be actual worth, or merely semblative. 1816 TOWNE *Farmer & Grazier's Guide* 60 The..ague-stricken Appearance which is betrayed in Oxen, when they become Hidebound, is semblative of an autumnal, or intermitting fever.

'semble, *a. Obs.* (exc. *arch. poet.*) [a. OF. *semble*:—L. *similis*: see SIMILAR *a.*] Like, similar.

1449 *Verulam MSS.* (Hist. MSS. Comm. 1906) 4 The seide place without delaye to be abated in semble wyse. a1450 *Knt. de la Tour* 87 Thanne the quene after kneled tofore her lorde, and besought hym that men shulde do semble iustice to Amon the seneschall. 1546 LANGLEY tr. *Pol. Verg. de Invent* VI. iv. 118 b, Also he did in semble wise consecrate the Table. 1584 HUDSON *Du Bartas' Judith* I. (1608) 16 A tyrant vile, Of name and deed that bare the semble stile, That did this king. 1965 AUDEN *About House* (1966) 40 Six lenient semble sieges, None of them perilous, Is now a Perfect Social Number.

†**'semble,** *v.*[1] *Obs.* Forms: 3–4 semele, 4 sembul, 4–7 semble, sembyll. *Pa. t.* and *Pa. pple.* 4 semblet, -blyt, semlit, 5 sembelet, sembild, semblyde, semled, semlyd, semyld. [Aphetic var. of ASSEMBLE *v.* (Godefr. has a few instances of OF. *sembler* in the same sense.)]

1. *trans.* **a.** To bring together (persons) into one place or company; = ASSEMBLE *v.*[1] 1.

c1250 [see ASSEMBLE *v.*[1] 1]. a1300 *Cursor M.* 7410 His scepe þam-self war [*read* wald] sembel samen. a1352 MINOT *Poems* (ed. Hall) iii. 87 He sembled all his men full still. a1500 *Beket Prophecy* in *Bernard. de cura rei fam.* (E.E.T.S.) 25 And þen thomas semblise sone seyue skore masons. 1603 DEKKER & CHETTLE *Grissil* v. ii. 2984 Heare you now, awl that bee sembled heere.

b. *spec.* (See quot.) Cf. SEMBLING *vbl. sb.*[2] 2.

1870 *Hardwicke's Sci. Gossip* 153 A group [of moths], the females of many of which are noted for the peculiar property they possess of collecting, or, as the old entomologists named it, 'sembling', the males from long distances.

2. To bring together (things) into one place or mass, to collect; = ASSEMBLE *v.*[1] 2.

a1400 *Relig. Pieces fr. Thornton MS.* 55 Scho sall gedyre and sembyll gude whete and oþer gud cornnes to-gedir. c1470 HARDING *Chron.* LXV. i, That made a wall well wrought of lyme and stone, Where Seuer made of turues & soddes sembled.

3. *intr.* To come together; = ASSEMBLE *v.*[1] 5.

13.. *Guy Warw.* (1891) 452 þer sembled a fair ferred. c1375 *Sc. Leg. Saints* xxxvi. (*Baptista*) 800 þe sarazenis semlit ilkane. 1389 in *Eng. Gilds* (1870) 47 Eueriche broþer & sister..shuln semelyn in a certayne place. c1420 *Avow. Arth.* lxx, Hor lordis sembelet to a syȝte. 1497 BP. ALCOCK *Mons Perfect.* C iij, Ye people semblid togydre to ouercome vyce. 1535 STEWART *Cron. Scot.* I. 67 Ten thousand men.. Syne semlit hes togither on ane da.

4. To meet in conflict; = ASSEMBLE *v.*[1] 6. Also, to make an attack *on.*

c1350 *Will. Palerne* 3811 þan aswiþe þei sembled to-gader. ?a1400 *Morte Arth.* 967 Siche sex ware to symple to semble with hyme one. *Ibid.* 3746 Now they..Sembles one the sowdeours, and settys theire dyntys. 1456 SIR G. HAYE *Law Arms* (S.T.S.) 164 Men may..geve thame the werr felde, outhir lawar or in a myre, quhare thai may nocht wele semble, na to help thame selff. 1513 DOUGLAS *Æneis* VIII. Prol. 60 To semble wyth thair schaftis.

5. *trans.* To assail, attack; = ASSEMBLE *v.*[1] 7.

a1400–50 *Wars Alex.* 1333 þan bowes he to þe baistall & brymly it semblis.

†**'semble,** *v.*[2] *Obs.* Also 4 sembel, 5 cemble, cem(e)lyn, 5–6 sembil. [a. F. *semble-r*:—L. *similāre, simulāre* (cf. SIMULATE *v.*), f. *simil-is* like. Cf. Pr., Sp. *semblar*, It. *sembiare, sembrare.*]

1. a. *trans.* To be like, resemble.

c1330 *Arth. & Merl.* 8853 (Kölbing) He no sembled no more him oȝan, þan doþ a child oȝain a man. 1340 *Ayenb.* 176 þo þet makeþ zuo greate hornes of hare here..þet hi sembleþ wel fole wyfmen. 1483 CAXTON *Gold. Leg.* 117/1 And to that other she said thou were lyke and semblest wel thy fader. 1630 I. CRAVEN *God's Tribunall* (1631) 33 Let no man dissemble himselfe out of policy, or semble another in hypocrisie. 1650 BULWER *Anthropomet.* iii. 61 A broad forehead which in a manner sembles a quadrangle may be somewhat suitable. 1713 *Yarhell's Kitchen* 2 With..Eyes that darted Fire, And a Proboscis, sembling Sarum's Spire.

b. *intr.* To be like, to have a resemblance *to.*

c1400 *Rule of St. Benet* (prose) 3 Til þe wyis man sembils he þat fundes his hus opon þe stan. a1450 *Knt. de la Tour* 125 She sembled not vnto the doughter of a senatour of Rome that had so cursed a father that [etc.]

2. *intr.* To seem, appear.

c1325 *Metr. Hom.* 136 And forthi that Crist tholes this, Ite sembeles that he slepand is. c1330 *Arth. & Merl.* 5547 (Kölbing) Ac ȝe semble so wiȝt & fre, þat ȝe beþ welcome to me. **1526** *Pilgr. Perf.* (W. de W. 1531) 263 Then he wyll semble to go with vs to counseyle, & directe vs in our purpose.

b. To be likely *to do* something.

a **1300** *Cursor M.* 9781 If angel had tan mans kind þan war he wayker mad þan ar, þat he suld haue na pouer þar; And sembel lightli for to fall.

3. To assume an appearance, make oneself seem, to pretend. (Very common in Udall's writings.)

1542 UDALL *Erasm. Apoph.* 128 Diogenes sembleyng to have no greate witte ne knowlage. *Ibid.* 214 b, He sembleed & made as though he tooke not indignacion. *Ibid.* 319 Sembleyng that he graunted his saiyng. *c* **1550** L. WAGER *Marie Magd.* 1502, I pray you do your diligence, And semble rather to loue hym than to hate.

4. *trans.* To simulate, feign; *absol.* to practise simulation.

1530 TINDALE *Pract. Prelates* G iv b, Vtterlye appoynted to semble and dissemble, to haue one thinge in the harte and a nother in the mouth. **1537** tr. *Latimer's Serm. Convoc.* ii. C j b, Al be it they swere.. that they knowe not theyr father, nor mother,.. as in dede they can semble & dissemble all thynges. **1570** LEVINS *Manip.* 60/5 To semble, *simulare.* *c* **1570** W. WAGER *The longer thou livest* 1074 (Brandl), *Stage direct.*, Semble a goyng out. **1584** R. W. *Three Ladies Lond.* II. A iij b, Ile tell thee what, thou wilt euen semble and cog with thine own father, A couple of false knaues togither. **1590** *Humble Motion with Submission* 57 By these couloured offices a man may haue a popish schoole-maister, especially if he can semble a little.

¶ Used for DISSEMBLE *v.*

1603 DEKKER & CHETTLE *Grissil* v. ii. 2769 *Sir Ow.* [a Welshman]. Ian Niclas is honest man: hee does not flatter, and sembles, but tell his intentions.

5. To liken, compare.

a **1440** *Promp. Parv.* 66/1 Cemelyn' or lykyn' [*v.rr.* cemlyn, cemblen], *assimulo.* **1563** SHUTE *Archit.* E iv b, Whiche piller for his strength is likned or to be sembled vnto Tuscana.

6. To represent, picture.

1610 G. FLETCHER *Christ's Vict. Earth* xlii, The azure fields of heav'n wear sembled right In a large round. **1627** W. SCLATER *Exp. 2 Thess.* (1629) 94 The terrible sound of the last trumpe which Hierome so continually sembled to himselfe, how it made him feare where he was most secure. *Ibid.* 163 Semble to your selues a Papist prostrate before his breaden God. **1706** [see SEMBLING *ppl. a.* 2]. **1755** JOHNSON, *Semble*, to represent, to make a likeness.

Hence †**'sembling** *vbl. sb.*[1]

c **1440** *Promp. Parv.* 452/2 Semlynge, or lykenesse, *assimilacio.* **1567** *Gude & Godlie B.* 235 To thair sembling tak gude sicht, How that thay pas away sa bair.

‖**semble** ('sɛmbl(ə)l), *v.*[3] *impers. Law.* [Fr., 3rd pers. sing. pres. ind. of *sembler* to seem.] = 'It seems'; used in judicial utterances to introduce the incidental statement of an opinion on a point of law which it is not necessary to decide authoritatively. In reports abbreviated *sem.*, *semb.*

1817 SELWYN *Law Nisi Prius* (ed. 4) II. 1294 And *semble*, under these circumstances, an eviction might be pleaded to the whole demand. *a* **1859** AUSTIN *Jurispr.* (1879) II. 850 It is essential to the character of a real servitude that there should be a 'prædium serviens', and a 'prædium dominans'. *Semble* that a personal servitude.. can hardly exist over a movable.

semble, variant of SEMBLY *Obs.*

†**'semblesse.** *Obs. rare*[−1]. [? f. SEMBLE *v.* + -*esse*, -ESS[2].] Seemliness.

14.. in *Hist. Coll. Citizen Lond.* (Camden) 53 A famos knyght and of grete semblesse.

†**'sembling,** *ppl. a. Obs.* [f. SEMBLE *v.*[2] + -ING[2].]

1. That feigns or simulates.

1557-8 *Jacob & Esau* v. iv. (1568) F iv b, Ah hypocrite, ah hedgecreeper, ah sembling wretche. **1583** *Leg. Bp. St. Androis* 916 in *Satir. Poems Reform.* xlv, They knew him for a sembling baird. **1612** T. TAYLOR *Comm. Titus* i. 16 Counterfeit and sembling professors. **1642** S. W. *Parl. Vind. Answ. Rupert* 3 In this not sembling but suffering age.

2. That depicts or represents.

1706 PRIOR *Ode to Queen* xxviii, Where sembling Art may carve the fair Effect.

sembling ('sɛmblɪŋ), *vbl. sb.*[2] Also **symbolling.** [See SEMBLE *v.*[1]] The action of the verb.

1. *gen.*

a **1300** *Havelok* 1018 Þere was sembling i-now! *a* **1400-50** *Wars Alex.* 769 Þe same day at was sett þe sembling of bathe. *c* **1420** *Anturs of Arth.* 661 With owttene more lettynge, Was dighte there thiere semblynge. *c* **1440** *Promp. Parv.* 452/2 Semlynge, or metynge to-geder, *concursus.*

2. *Ent.* The coming together of a male and a female moth; *spec.* a method of trapping male moths by using a captive female to attract them.

1748 J. DUTFIELD *New Nat. Hist. Engl. Moths & Butterflies* s.v. Emperor Moth. What is called Symbolling, or, the Coming together, is particularly observable of this Species. **1894** *Science* 23 Mar. 156/2 The sembling of a large native moth. **1924** *Contemp. Rev.* Sept. 364 Collectors of lepidoptera have long known the trick of 'sembling' to obtain a large series of males of certain moths.

semblont, variant of SEMBLANT *sb. Obs.*

†**'sembly.** *Obs.* Forms: 3–6 semble, 4–5 semblé, semblee, 6 sembla, semblay, semely, semlay, semle, semly, 5–6 semblie, 6 samble, semblye, 6, 8 sembly. [Aphetic form of ASSEMBLY. (AF. had *semblé, semblée.*)]

1. A gathering of people; an assembly. *to do, to make sembly*, to meet, to be present at an assembly.

a **1300** *Cursor M.* 6408 Moyses þan cald sir iosue, And mad him maister o þat semble. *Ibid.* 14489 Wit þis þai mad a gret semble. **1375** BARBOUR *Bruce* II. 380 In the stour sa hardyly He ruschyt, that all the semble schuk. **1389** in *Eng. Gilds* (1870) 31 Qwo-so be somouned to don semble er to congregacioun. *c* **1400** *Master of Game* (MS. Digby 182) xxxii, The semble, þat men clepeth gaderynge, shulde be maked in þis manere. *c* **1400** MAUNDEV. (1839) Prol. 3 For a semblee of Peple withouten a Cheventeyn, or a chief Lord, is as a Flock of Scheep withouten a Schepperde. *a* **1450** *Knt. de la Tour* 63 A fest and a gret semble of ladies and gentilwomen. *c* **1470** HENRY *Wallace* II. 415 A blyth semblay was at his lychtyn doun. *a* **1542** WYATT *Penit. Ps.* cii. 72 But to this samble running in the way, My strength failed to reach it at the full. **1562** in *Cal. Anc. Rec. Dublin* (1891) II. 25 Yf thenheritors.. do not show sufficient title.. this side the next quarter sembly after Cristenmas. **1715** LEONI *Palladio's Archit.* (1742) II. 60 A Council of.. Fathers; whose sembly was called the Senate.

2. Suite, retinue.

14.. *Sir Beues* 3963/23 (MS. E.) Now wendiþ sere B. wiþ hys semble To Hampmyngforde, þat goode cyte. *c* **1430** *Syr Gener.* (Roxb.) 105 To come to Mountanar that feir Citie, And eche a Prince bring his semble.

3. Hostile meeting, conflict; = ASSEMBLY 3.

a **1400-50** *Wars Alex.* 797 Sa sare was þe semble þire seggis be-twene. *a* **1400** *Relig. Pieces fr. Thornton MS.* 92 At a semle þat segge in certayne was slayne. **1456** SIR G. HAYE *Law Arms* (S.T.S.) 117 He that departis fra the ost in the tyme of semble, that is feid and wrytyn. **1535** STEWART *Cron. Scot.* II. 454 Ane scharpar sembla ȝit wes thair neuer sene.

4. *attrib.*, as *sembly-house.*

c **1400** *Wyclif's Bible* Prol. I. 51 The iij. orrible synne is symonie, and forswering in the semble hous. **1447** *Epist. Acad. Oxon.* (O.H.S.) I. 260 In a tym of a convocation in our semble house.

‖**sembra'dor.** *Obs.* exc. *Hist.* [Sp. *sembrador*, f. *sembrar* to sow:—L. *sēmināre*, f. *sēmin-*, *sēmen* seed.] (See quot. 1670.)

1670 EVELYN in *Phil. Trans.* V. 1055 The Spanish Sembrador or New Engin for Ploughing, and Equal Sowing all sorts of Grain, and Harrowing, at once. *a* **1700** —— *Diary* 25 Nov. 1668, I waited on Lo. Sandwich, who presented me with the Sembrador he brought out of Spaine.

sembreefe, -brief(e, obs. forms of SEMIBREVE.

semde, obs. pa. t. of SEEM *v.*[2]

seme (siːm). *Linguistics.* [ad. Gr. σῆμα sign: cf. SEMA.] **a.** A sign. **b.** A unit of meaning; *spec.* the smallest unit of meaning. Cf. PHEME, RHEME.

a **1866** J. GROTE in *Jrnl. Philol.* (1872) IV. 158 The noematism of it [*sc.* a language] might be.. written.. by symbols naturally suggesting themselves for the visual percepts, and by others agreed upon for abstract terms and those related to other senses than the eye. It might be well to call such quasi-writing or exhibition to the eye by other than vocal elements, *sematism*, and the symbols *semes*. **1906** C. S. S. PEIRCE in *Monist* XVI. 506 By a *Seme*, I shall mean anything which serves for any purpose as a substitute for an object of which it is, in some sense, a representative or Sign. .. The term 'The mortality of man' is a Seme. **1923**, **1931** [see PHEME]. **1951** E. A. NIDA in *Word* VII. 5 The simple term *seme* identifies any minimal feature of meaning. **1966** D. G. HAYS in *Automatic Transl. of Lang.* (NATO Summer School, Venice, 1962) 163 These semes are more nearly the units wanted in translation than the morphs or morphemes that comprise them. **1973** *Screen* Spring/Summer 18 [Eric Buyssens].. established a certain number of notions and distinctions (*seme* and *semic act*, *intrinsic* and *extrinsic semes*, *direct* and *substitutive semes*).

seme: see SEAM, SEEM.

semeare: see SEMAR.

semeblabilly, obs. form of SEMBLABLY *adv.*

‖**semée** ('sɛmiː, ‖səme), *a.* and *sb. Her.* Forms: 6 semie, 6–7 semi, 7 seme, semy, 8–9 semé, 8– semée. [a. F. *semée* fem. of *semé*, pa. pple. of *semer* to sow.] **A.** *adj.* = POWDERED *ppl. a.* 3. †Also in AF. phrases, *semi de crosses, semi de luces* = Semée of crosses, of lilies.

1562 LEGH *Armory* 63 b, He bereth Geules, semi de crosses flourte, Or. If there were but vii, and that the half of some of them, were out of the fielde.. yet it sholde be called Semi. **1586** FERNE *Blaz. Gentrie* I. 194 The chief: which is Or:.. semie of teares, which is signified heere, by this colour of Azure. **1611** SPEED *Hist. Gt. Brit.* IX. xii. §51 The golden Lillies of France, which now are borne in triangle, were in those dayes born, and aduanced Semi. **1641** BAKER *Chron., Hen. V* 47 First therefore he begins to alter in his Arms the bearing of Semy-de-Luces, and quarters the three Flower Deluces, as the Kings of France then bare them. *a* **1700** EVELYN *Diary* 7 Sept. 1651, Heralds in blew velvet semèe with fleurs de lys. **1718** A. NISBET *Ess. Armories* Index Terms, *Semee*, that is sown when many small Figures are irregularly disposed in a Field. **1823** RUTTER *Fonthill* Introd. 22 Morville, Azure, Semée of Fleurs de Lys, and fretty, Or. **1873** MRS. PALLISER tr. *Jacquemart's Ceramic Art* 51 Blue ground semé with red and lilac splashes.

B. *sb.* = POWDERING 3 b.

In recent Dicts.; in quot. perh. adj. with plural ending.

1562 LEGH *Armory* 50 Geules, a playne crosse, Frette Azure, As ye haue this Frette: So shall you haue some Diaper & some Semies, of dyuers thynges, that I can not speake of here.

seméed ('sɛmiːd), *ppl. a. Her.* Forms: 6 semyed, 7, 9 seméed, semied, 9 semé'd. [Anglicized f. prec.] = SEMÉE *a.*

1572 BOSSEWELL *Armorie* 26 There are also to bee founde and seene in armes Crosses double partited, semyed, quartered of the fielde wherein they stande. **1652** EVELYN *St. France* Misc. Wks. (1825) 61 A casque of blew velvet seméed with fleurs de lys. **1862** H. MARRYAT *Year in Sweden* II. 149 *note*, This chapel has been restored, the vaulting semé'd with gold stars on a blue ground. **1879** WATERTON *Pietas Mariana* 223 She wears a purple garment, seméed with leaves of Shamrock.

semeiography, semeiologic, etc. (etymologically correct, and formerly the preferred forms): see SEMIOGRAPHY, SEMIOLOGIC, etc.

†**'semel.** *Obs. rare.* In 7 semell, semill. [a. Du. *semele* (now *zemelen* pl.) fine wheat flour, fine wheaten bread = OHG. *semala*, *simula*, a. L. *simila*: see SIMNEL.] A cake of fine wheat flour.

1643 in Warden *Burgh Laws Dundee*, etc. (1872) 350 As also in beakinge of bunnes, semells, oat lowes, kaikis [etc.]. **1697** *Ibid.* 352 Any semill, or wastill or pis of beakin meat.

semeland(e, -ant, -awnt: see SEMBLANT *sb.*

semeld: earlier form of SAMEL.

1601 HOLLAND *Pliny* XVIII. x. I. 565 A fragment or peece of a broken semeld brick.

semele, obs. form of SEEMLY *a.*, SEMBLE *v.*

semelfactive (siːmɛl'fæktɪv), *a. Slav. Gram.* [f. L. *semel* once + *facĕre* to do: see FACTIVE.] (See quot. 1827.)

1827 J. HEARD *Gram. Russ. Lang.* v. §1. 142 The semelfactive [verb] expresses the sudden and single occurrence of an action. **1843** *Proc. Philol. Soc.* I. 100 The author considered the 'semelfactive verbs', as Heard calls them, to represent the Sanskrit verbs of the fifth, seventh, and eighth conjugations. **1894** *19th Cent.* May 816 Semelfactive perfect aspect of unity.

semeli, semelich(e, obs. forms of SEEMLY *a.*

semeline ('sɛmɪlaɪn). *Min.* Also **semelin, semelina.** [Named in Fr. by Fleurian de Bellevue (*Jrnl. de Physique* LI. 450, 1800) '*sémélinite*, and by abbreviation *séméline*', f. L. *sēmen līnī* seed of flax, referring to the appearance of the crystals.] A variety of titanite found in the Eifel.

c **1830** H. J. BROOKE *Min.* in *Encycl. Metrop.* (1845) VI. 518/1 Silico-titaniate of Lime. Sphene. Spinthere. Semeline. **1836** T. THOMSON *Min., Geol.*, etc. I. 151 Sphene. [Varieties:] Brunon, semelin, spinellane [etc.]. **1869** PHILLIPS *Vesuvius* x. 300 Sphene—Semelina—occurs in ejected blocks with icespar.

semelitude, semely: see SIMILITUDE, SEEMLY.

sememe ('siːmiːm). *Linguistics.* [f. Gr. σῆμ-α sign + -EME.] A unit of meaning; *spec.* the smallest unit of meaning. Cf. SEME.

[**1904** A. NOREEN *Vårt Språk* V. III. 6 Detta sålunda definierade abstrakta begrepp 'betydelse' uppträder in concreto alltid i någon viss språklig dräkt, som ofta kan efter omständigheterna vara mycket varierande, och det kallas då semem, hvilken term alltså kan definieras som: ett visst bestämdt idéinnehåll, uttryckt i någon språklig form, likgiltigt hvilken. **1911** A. L. ELMQUIST in *Jrnl. Eng. & Gmc. Philol.* X. 321 Semology [in Noreen's *Vårt Språk*] deals with the 'semem' and Morphology with the 'morfem'.] **1913** *Jrnl. Eng. & Gmc. Philol.* XII. 87 This need not have been the only or even perhaps the usual sememe associated with the morpheme *flik* in O. Scand. **1926** L. BLOOMFIELD in *Language* II. 157 The sememes.. which stand in one-to-one correspondence with the morphemes, cannot be further analyzed by linguistic methods. **1933** —— *Language* x. 162 The meaning of a morpheme is a *sememe*. The linguist assumes that each sememe is a constant and definite unit of meaning, different from all other meanings, including all other sememes, in the language. **1949** [see CONTRASTIVENESS]. **1954** C. E. BAZELL in E. P. Hamp et al. *Readings in Linguistics II* (1966) 329 At the European Semantic Conference, held at Nice in March, 1951.. it was agreed to call the fundamental unit of content (in the linguistic norm) the sememe. **1965** N. CHOMSKY *Aspects of Theory of Syntax* 230 We could perfectly well state the facts .. in terms of such new notions as 'semantic subject', 'semantic object', various kinds of 'sememes', etc., but such proliferation of terminology contributes nothing toward clarifying the.. issues. **1973** *Screen* Spring/Summer 234 Greimas analyses the units of content (lexemes) into constant minimal semantic nuclei (semes) and contextual semantic units (sememes).

Hence **se'memic** *a.*, **se'memically** *adv.*

1953 C. E. BAZELL *Linguistic Form* 81 The sememic level is approached when several congruent morphemes of this type are regarded as a single unit, for commutation is then usually possible. *Ibid.*, Sememically the unit may normally be taken as zero. **1968** P. M. POSTAL *Aspects Phonol. Theory* viii. 198 The four current properly linguistic strata are, in hierarchical order from 'top' to 'bottom', the sememic, the lexemic, the morphemic, and the phonemic. **1973** *Archivum Linguisticum* IV. 119 By a 'semantic base' Hutchins means a set of 'sememic graphs'.

semen ('siːmɛn, -ən). [a. L. *sēmen* seed (of plants and animals), f. root **sē-* (: **sa-*) of *serĕre* to sow.] **1.** The impregnating fluid of male animals; the seed or sperm.

1398 TREVISA *Barth. De P.R.* XVIII. i. (1495) 743 The synewe.. by the whyche semen sholde come downewarde to effecte of generacyon. **1725** P. DUDLEY in *Phil. Trans.* XXXIII. 266 Some took it to be the true and proper Semen, being only found in the Bull [whale], at the Root of the Penis. **1880** GÜNTHER *Fishes* 164 The mode of passage of the semen into the funnel is not known.

2. *attrib.*, as **semen bank**, a store of semen which is kept available for artificial insemination.

1954 *Fertility & Sterility* V. 28 A semen bank could be organized and maintained, with the same scientific attitude and spirit of research as is found in all other therapies for helping the infertile. **1972** *Sat. Rev.* (U.S.) 10 June 40/3 Semen banks..are gaining popularity among vasectomy candidates as a solution to the irreversibility problem.

†**semenaunt.** *Obs. rare*$^{-1}$. [var. SEMBLANT. Cf. the converse variation in *remlant* for REMNANT.] Appearance, 'false semblant'.

c **1450** *Songs & Carols* (Warton Club) 86 Semenaunt is a wonder thing, It begylyt bothe knyȝt and kyng. *Ibid.*, Semenaunt is a sly peyntour.

'semence. [a. F. *semence* (= Pr. *semensa*, It. *semenza*):—pop.L. **sēmentia*, f. L. *sēmenti-s* a sowing, f. *sēmen* seed.]

†**1.** Seed; in quots. = SEMEN. *Obs.*

1480 CAXTON *Ovid's Met.* XIV. xiii, Which [Pallas] was conceyved and born of the semence of the fader w[t]oute semence carnal. *a* **1693** *Urquhart's Rabelais* III. xxxi. 257 Which..do..benumb..with Cold the prolifick Semence.

¶**2.** Used for: A sowing. *rare*$^{-1}$.

1859 R. F. BURTON *Centr. Afr.* in *Jrnl. Geog. Soc.* XXIX. 401 The ground is rarely weeded unless wanted for a second and different semence.

semend, semond, ? obs. forms of SALMON.

c **1480** *Cely Papers* (Camden) 189 Item ij jollys sallt semend xviij d... Item a jowlle freshe semond.

†**semendacy.** *Obs.* [Corruption of mod.L. *sēmen daucī* (*sēmen* seed, *daucī* genit. of *daucus* some umbelliferous plant, perh. carrot or parsnip).] The seeds of the sweet chervil (*Myrrhis odorata*), formerly used in medicine.

1714 *Fr. Bk. of Rates* 97 Semendacy per 100 Weight.

semeniferous, -ivorous: see SEMIN-.

sement, obs. form of CEMENT.

?*c* **1600** *Distr. Emperor* I. i. in Bullen *Old Pl.* (1884) III. 174 Our acquayntance is Too oulde, and as I hope frendshypp too fyrme To be nowe semented.

†**semen'tation.** *Obs.*$^{-0}$ [ad. late L. *sēmentātiōn-em*, f. L. *sēmentāre* to sow seed, f. *sēmen* seed.] 'A bringing forth seed' (Blount *Glossogr.* 1656).

sementation, erron. form of CEMENTATION.

1592 LYLY *Gallathea* II. iii. 13 Circination, Sementation.

†**'sementine,** *a. Obs.* [f. L. *sēment-is* sowing + -INE[1].] 'Belonging to sowing, continuing to seed time' (Blount *Glossogr.* 1656).

se'mese, *a. rare.* [ad. L. *sēmēs-us*, f. *sēmi-* + *ēsus*, pa. pple. of *edĕre* to eat.] Half-eaten.

1859 FARRAR *Julian Home* vii. 86 They're sons of gyps and that sort of thing, who feed on the semese fragments of the high table.

semester (sɪ'mɛstə(r)). [a. G. *semester*, ad. L. (*cursus*) *sēmēstris* (period) of six months, f. *sē-*, *sex* six + *mēns-is* month.] A period or term of six months, esp. in German and U.S. universities and colleges, the college half-year.

1827 *Lancet* 17 Nov. 251/2 The student..attends it daily during two semesters. **1852** H. ROGERS *Ecl. Faith* (1864) 146 A young Englishman..fresh from Germany, after sundry semesters at Bonn and Tübingen. **1888** BRYCE *Amer. Commw.* III. cii. 450 Graduates who..spend a semester or two at a German university. **1895–6** *Cal. Univ. Nebraska* 33 The year is divided upon the semester plan. Each semester has eighteen weeks.

semester, obs. form of SEMPSTER.

semestrial, semestral (sɪ'mɛstrɪəl, sɪ'mɛstrəl), *a.* [f. L. *sēmēstr-is* (see SEMESTER) + -IAL, -AL[1].] Half-yearly; taking place every six months; lasting for six months. Of persons: holding office for six months; exercising office every six months.

1701 J. SAGE *Vind. Princ. Cypr. Age* iii. 118 Neither was the change..made only from weekly, or monthly, or semestrial, or annual, to constant Moderators. **1726** AYLIFFE *Parergon* 332 As they may in their Semestral Visitations inform themselves touching such Churches as are become void. **1844** W. KAY in *Fleury's Eccl. Hist.* III. 406 *note*, The old canonical semestral council. **1847** THACKERAY *Barnwell* in *Punch* XII. 136/2 Speeding to the Bank for her semestrial pittance. **1894** *Westm. Gaz.* 18 Dec. 1/2 The ideal state of things, Lord Salisbury's argument implies, would be not Triennial but Semestral Parliaments.

Hence **se'mestrially** *adv.*, every six months.

1891 *Sat. Rev.* 9 May 573/2 [He] continues..semestrially ..to furnish his quota of sensational *aventures parisiennes.*

†**'semet.** *Bot. Obs.* [f. L. *sēm-en* seed + -ET[1]. Corrupted by later writers into SUMMIT.]

Term used by Grew for an ANTHER.

1671 GREW *Anat. Veget.* v. (1672) 140 The Attire I find to be of two kinds, Seminie and Florie: That which I call Seminie, is made up of two general parts, Chives and Semets, one upon each Chive. These Semets have the appearance (especially in many flowers) of so many little Seeds; but are quite another kind of Body: For upon enquiry we find, that these Semets, though they seem to be solid, and for some time after their first formation, are entire. **1725** *Bradley's Fam. Dict.* s.v. *Attire*, The Semini-form Attire consists of two parts, viz. Chives, or the Stamina as some call them, and Semets or Apices.

semeterrie, obs. form of SCIMITAR.

semetory, obs. form of CEMETERY.

c **1502** *Joseph Arim.* 379 In the holy grounde called the semetory.

semi[1] ('sɛmɪ). *Sc.* Also 7–8 **semie.** [app. short for *semi bejanus* 'half a bejan'; A. Dalzel *Hist. Univ. Edin.* (1862) II. 10 cites 'Classis Semi Bejanorum' from a document of *c* 1590.] In Scottish universities (latterly at Aberdeen and St. Andrews), a student in his second year; also called **semi-bachelor** and **semi-bejan.** So **semi-class,** the class of second-year students; **semi-regent,** the regent in charge of the semi-class; **semi-year,** a student's second year.

1661 RAY *Itin.* in *Sel. Rem.* (1760) 203 [At Glasgow] about 40 Students of the first Year, which they call Obedients [*i.e.* bejants]; near so many of the Second, which they call Semies. **1688** in Dalzel *Hist. Univ. Edin.* (1862) II. 197 If they find him to have any competent skill in the Greek language, they are to signify the same..unto the Semi Regent. **1695** in *Fasti Aberd.* (1854) 374 That none be admitted or received into the semi-class, but upon strict tryall of their proficiencie in the Greek tongue. *c* **1700** *Dom. Details D. Hume* (1843) 5 In my semie year I was boarded in one Mr. Nisbet's. *Ibid.* 6 At this time, the 11th of March was solemnly keeped by the semies, in going to the foot-ball on the Borrow Moor. **1704** in Macgill *Old Ross-sh.* (1909) 63 If he be readie for colledge to enter a semie and not com in this year. **1843** *Dom. Details D. Hume* Notes p. xv, The students of the second year continuing under the same regent, were called the *semi* class, or the *semi-bachelors.* [*Note,* Sometimes called the *semi-bajan* class.] **1857** [see TERTIAN *sb.* 3]. **1884** SIR A. GRANT *Story Univ. Edin.* I. 152 [*c* 1590] At the final examination..The Magistrands came before the Regents of the Bachelor, Semi-Bajan, and Bajan classes. **1889, 1891** [see MAGISTRAND].

semi[2] ('sɛmɪ). Colloq. abbrev. of: **1.** SEMI-DETACHED house.

1912 R. MACAULAY *Views & Vagabonds* xvi. 292 To settle down in the new semi and 'do for' her Ben,..what had heaven to offer more than that? **1939** R. FERGUSON in *Queen's Bk. of Red Cross* 234, I wish my girl could see it, but ..it might spoil her for a little semi on a housing estate. **1958** J. SYMONS *Gigantic Shadow* ii. 8 These were the moments when the watchers in their suburban semis wriggled most deliciously in their overstuffed armchairs. **1977** B. PYM *Quartet in Autumn* iii. 28 That house which, in the estate agents' language, was on its way to becoming a 'twenty thousand semi'.

2. *semi-evening dress* s.v. SEMI- 9. Now *rare.*

1927 N. COWARD *Sirocco* II. i. 38 Miss Johnson is wearing what might technically be described as a 'semi'. Mrs Breeze is in a tea-gown. **1934** C. L. ANTHONY *Touch Wood* II. ii. 57 Mrs McCrossan and Mr Berridge enter. Mrs McCrossan is in her semi.

3. *semifinished* (steel): see SEMI- 9. Usu. in *pl. Industry.*

1931 *Economist* 5 Dec. 1054/2 If Continental exporters of 'semis'..feel that a high tariff is likely to be imposed in the ..Budget, steel imports..are likely to increase. **1950** *Engineering* 21 July 59/2 Home produced steel semies are reaching the re-rolling mills in very large quantities. **1975** 'D. JORDAN' *Black Account* xii. 62 Have you ever thought that the next stage would be a semis plant?

4. *semi-final* s.v. SEMI- 9.

1942 BERREY & VAN DEN BARK *Amer. Thes. Slang* §643/6 Next to last event...*semi.* **1976** *Star* (Sheffield) 29 Oct. 2/5 Last heat of the TV sheepdog trials and it's no secret that Scotland meet England West in the first semi.

5. SEMI-TRAILER; *semi-truck* s.v. SEMI- 9. *U.S.* (with pronunc. ('sɛmaɪ)) and *Austral.*

1942 BERREY & VAN DEN BARK *Amer. Thes. Slang* §81/16 *Semi*,..a two-wheeled truck. **1961** *Amer. Speech* XXXVI. 272 It is common to call..a trailer a *semi.* **1968** J. M. ULLMAN *Lady on Fire* (1969) viii. 102 They..rolled past a row of semis lined up at an unloading dock. **1969** *Northern Territory News* (Darwin) *Focus '69* 97/2 The Stuart Highway..has become increasingly busy with road trains and semis to meet the needs of the increased population. **1976** B. BOVA *Multiple Man* (1977) iv. 49 The Beltway..was almost always jammed with..heavy semis delivering the daily bread.

6. *semi-submersible* (rig, barge, etc.): see SEMI- 9. *Oil Industry.*

1975 *Offshore* Aug. 19/1 We will operate three semis of the Aker H-3... These rigs are well published in various publications. **1977** *Offshore Engineer* Apr. 51 (*caption*) Drillships closely follow semis in the oversupply stakes.

semi, obs. form of SEMÉE.

semi- ('sɛmɪ, *U.S.* 'sɛmaɪ), *prefix.* Also 4–7 **semy-,** 5–6 **seme-,** 6–7 **semie-.** [repr. L. *sēmi-* (whence F., It., Sp., Pg. *semi-*) = Skr. *sāmi-*, Gr. ἡμι-, OHG. *sâmi-*, OS. *sâm-*, cogn. w. OE. *sam-* (see SAM-):—Indogerm. **sēmi-*.] = HALF-; cf. DEMI-, HEMI-.

L. *sēmi-* (occas. shortened to *sēm-* before a vowel, e.g. *sēmanimis*) is, esp. in post-classical Latin, compounded freely with adjs. and pples., less commonly with nouns; in med. and still more in mod.L. the prefix is extensively employed in technical terminology. The compounds of earliest date in English are: the adjs. SEMICIRCULAR (1432–50), SEMI-MATURE (*c* 1440), SEMIVIF (Piers Plowman) direct from L., and SEMI-BOUSY (*c* 1400); the sbs. SEMICICLE (*c* 1440), SEMI-COPE (Chaucer), SEMIGOD (1417), SEMI-SOUN (Chaucer). In the 16th–18th c., the number of permanent compounds was increased mainly by the accession of terms more or less technical (many of them adapted or imitated from Latin), such as SEMIBREVE, SEMICIRCLE, SEMIDIAMETER, SEMILUNAR, SEMI-PELAGIAN, SEMIVOWEL. At the same time there was gradual enlargement of the scope of the prefix in the formation of general nonce-compounds, which became very frequent in the 19th c., and of which it is possible to illustrate but a small proportion in the present article (branch I).

I. In general use.

1. a. Compounded with adjs. and pples., with the meaning 'half, partly, partially, to some extent'. A few are used *ellipt.* as sbs.

From the early part of the 19th c. it has been not uncommon to substitute '*semi-...semi-...*' for '*half-... half-...*' (HALF *adv.* 2); hence arise certain quasi-compounds that only occur in correlative pairs, as 'semi-chemical semi-mechanical'.

1871 BAGEHOT in *Fortn. Rev.* 1 Aug. 158 A *semi-abstract discussion of practical topics. **1974** K. CLARK *Another Part of Wood* ii. 52 From behind the semi-abstract clouds there appeared the same sexy girls. **1816** *Edin. Rev.* XXVII. 464 Nature seems..to have afforded this level space for a *semi-aerial dwelling. **1848** MILL *Pol. Econ.* I. xi. §3 The *Semi-agriculturalised Indians. **1860** TRISTRAM *Gt. Sahara* xxi. 354 It was a magnificent *semi-alpine, semi-tropical scene. **1840** CARLYLE *Heroes* iv. (1858) 293 It is a country as yet without a soul: nothing developed in it but what is rude, external, *semi-animal. *Ibid.* i. 205 This Odin, in his rude *semi-articulate way, had a word to speak. **1963** W. R. ROSE in Wyndham Lewis *Lett.* 558 René Harding, the uncompromising, *semi-autobiographical hero of *Self Condemned.* **1926** J. M. KEYNES *End of Laissez-Faire* iv. 41, I suggest, therefore, that progress lies in the growth and the recognition of *semi-autonomous bodies within the State. **1974** tr. *Wertheim's Evolution & Revolution* 371 This semi-autonomous activity by living beings..is increasingly determining the course of nature on earth. **1828** MISS MITFORD *Village* Ser. III. 63 A simpering *semi-bald apothecary. **1822** HOOD *To Celia* iv, Once it happ'd that, *semi-blind, He [Love] met thee on a summer day. **1869** G. LAWSON *Dis. Eye* (1874) 74 Blows on the eye..with some blunt or *semi-blunt instrument. **1837** DICKENS *Pickw.* xxviii, A *semi-cannibalic leer. **1837** CARLYLE *Fr. Rev.* I. VI. v, How thou glitterest with a fallen, rebellious, yet still *semi-celestial light. **1839** DE LA BECHE *Rep. Geol. Cornwall*, etc. viii. 227 A *semi-chemical, semi-mechanical origin. **1847** PRESCOTT *Peru* (1850) II. 248 Brought in contact with *semi-civilised man. **1838** DICKENS *Nich. Nick.* ii, The second resolution was moved by a grievous gentleman of *semi-clerical appearance. **1587** FLEMING *Contn. Holinshed* III. 1453/1 His heart brought to Ludlow, and buried..in the *semi-collegiat parish church there. **1952** C. P. BLACKER *Eugenics: Galton & After* 178 The countries of Asia are rapidly emerging from their colonial or *semi-colonial status. **1974** tr. *Wertheim's Evolution & Revolution* 67 The colonial or semi-colonial backyards which capitalism..was exploiting in such a way as to provoke strong popular counter-forces. **1721** BAILEY, **Semi-combust*, (*semi-combustus*, L.) half-burned. **1818** LADY MORGAN *Autobiogr.* (1859) 172 He looked semi-tragic, *semi-comic, like a mask with two sides. **1838** DICKENS *O. Twist* xliii, A look of *semi-comical woe. **1965** *Math. in Biol. & Med.* (Med. Res. Council) I. 7 A service for the collection and recording of this information is also being made available on a *semi-commercial basis to any hospital in the United States. **1839** DE QUINCEY in *Tait's Edin. Mag.* Sept. 573/2 This..*semi-conscious feeling..taught them to feel the extremity of their danger. **1977** J. D. DOUGLAS in Douglas & Johnson *Existential Sociol.* i. 22 Most of our experiences in everyday life are only semiconscious. **1721** BAILEY, **Semi-conspicuous*, (*semiconspicuus*, L.) half or partly visible. **1890** 'R. BOLDREWOOD' *Col. Reformer* (1891) 215 The *semi-coöperative community at Rainbar. **1891** *Anthony's Photogr. Bull.* IV. 130 A short *semi-dark passage between the studio and dark room. **1937** *Discovery* Sept. 277/2 The comfort and interest with which the [television] pictures may be viewed in a *semi-darkened room. **1680** T. BROWNE *Let.* 6 Sept. (1946) 181 Esquire Mildmay..a melancholy & *semi-delirious person, yet fayre condition'd. **1975** M. AMIS *Dead Babies* xiii. 67 His strangled shout had been a semi-delirious reply to Quentin's courtly knock. **1879** *St. George's Hosp. Rep.* IX. 531 A *semi-demented old epileptic patient. **1864** BOWEN *Logic* xi. (1870) 370 This half latent *semi-developed state. **1881** *Nature* XXIII. 382 The coarse and *semi-diagrammatic figures which..occupy a.. place in the text-books of histology. **1859** DARWIN *Orig. Spec.* i. 25 Some *semi-domestic breeds. **1847** W. C. L. MARTIN *Ox* 6/2 The *semi-domesticated buffalo. **1868** *Rep. U.S. Comm. Agric.* (1869) 276 To maintain in the hive throughout the winter a uniform temperature, which will keep the bees in a continuous *semi-dormant state. **1895** *Pop. Sci. Monthly* Aug. 444 The interests of the stage and the *semi-dramatic music-hall. **1942** E. PARTRIDGE *Usage & Abusage* 91/2 *Conditional clauses* have always caused trouble to the *semi-educated and the demi-reflective. **1954** KOESTLER *Invisible Writing* IV. xxxiv. 371 There is a character in *The Magic Mountain*, the semi-educated Frau Stoehr, who is always trying to be refined. **1920** T. S. ELIOT *Sacred Wood* 49 You see..how completely any *semi-ethical criterion of 'sublimity' misses the mark. **1943** V. SACKVILLE-WEST *Eagle & Dove* II. ix. 138 A *semi-experimental perception of God, in very varying degrees of intensity and clarity. **1861** BERESF. HOPE *Eng. Cathedr. 19th C.* v. 158 The narthex or *semiexternal vestibule. **1854** A.

ADAMS, etc. *Man. Nat. Hist.* 55 The *semi-fabulous monster of our own times, the celebrated Sea-Serpent. **1938** H. NICOLSON *Diary* 22 Aug. (1966) 356 Russia has no sympathy for the *semi-fascist systems established in the Balkans. *a* **1974** R. CROSSMAN *Diaries* (1977) III. 299 This semi-fascist reaction has been accompanied by a general lack of credibility in the whole establishment. **1905** *Westm. Gaz.* 30 Sept. 9/1 The 9.13 from London Bridge was a *semi-fast train to Brighton. **1956** *Railway Mag.* Feb. 113/2 When travelling from Cologne to Wiesbaden in a semi-fast, we left Cologne 20 min. late. **1937** KOESTLER *Spanish Testament* iii. 63 Spain was still, when the People's Front came into power in 1936, a *semi-feudal country, with sharp social contrasts. **1970** C. FURTADO in I. L. Horowitz *Masses in Lat. Amer.* ii. 31 As an instrument for domination over a society where some forms of semi-feudal decentralization prevailed, the State emerged in colonial times as a strong bureaucracy. **1897** *Westm. Gaz.* 8 July 3/2 The *semi-fitting coat is more usual than the Eton form. **1930** *Daily Express* 8 Sept. 7/5 (Advt.), Semi-fitting bodice, with belt forming waist-line. **1960** *Farmer & Stockbreeder* 26 Jan. 66/2 Any kind of fixed or *semi-fixed equipment..will be considered. **1872** HOWELLS *Wedding Journey* ix, Some *semi-forbidding commissary of police. **1906** E. JOHNSTON *Writing & Illuminat. & Lettering* xv. 317 The writing approaches the *stylographic*... It may conveniently be termed **Semi-formal*. **1977** *Stornoway Gaz.* 27 Aug. 1/7 The possibility of formal or semi-formal competitions could not be discounted. **1830** *Edin. Rev.* LI. 459 A flighty *semi-Frenchified coquette. **1821** BYRON *Sardanap.* I. ii, Like my ancestor Semiramis, A sort of *semi-glorious human monster. **1947** A. KOESTLER in *Partisan Rev.* XIV. 144 The unions become more and more absorbed into *semigovernmental, managerial functions. **1849** EASTWICK *Dry Leaves* 29 A more miserable race of starved, or *semi-human, beings I never beheld. **1950** B. RUSSELL *Unpopular Essays* iv. 64 A rare moment of self-knowledge must have inspired the initial aphorism, which was made bearable to its author by its *semi-humorous form. **1859** R. F. BURTON *Centr. Afr.* in *Jrnl. Geogr. Soc.* XXIX. 54 Study..seems to make these weak-brained races *semi-idiotic. **1860** R. D. in *Galton's Vac. Tour.* (1861) 108 The *semi-independent existence of Montenegro. **1851** MILL *Logic* (ed. 3) II. v. v. 352 As the former is the error of sheer ignorance, so the latter is especially that of *semi-instructed minds. **1955** J. BURNABY *Christian Words & Christian Meanings* iii. 62 The same tendency in modernised form is to be observed in much semi-instructed Christian thinking of our own time. **1841** H. MILLER *Old Red Sandstone* x. (1887) 206 Notwithstanding the advantages of its *semi-insular situation, it was suffered to lie as an unclaimed common. **1921** F. SCOTT FITZGERALD *Let.* 25 Aug. (1964) 148 I'm sick of the flabby *semi-intellectual softness in which I flounder with my generation. **1957** J. KEROUAC *On Road* (1958) II. 176 In Frisco eager crowds of young semi-intellectuals sat at his feet and listened to him. **1851** H. MELVILLE *Moby Dick* III. xl. 230 Most mariners cherish a very superstitious feeling about seals, arising..from..the human look of their round heads and *semi-intelligent faces. **1861** MAINE *Anc. Law* iv. (1876) 95 The *semi-juridical, semi-popular opinions which were fashionable in France. **1871** MORLEY *De Maistre* in *Crit. Misc.* Ser. I. 128 There is a certain *semi-latent quality of hardness lying at the bottom of De Maistre's style. **1949** KOESTLER *Promise & Fulfilment* I. viii. 90 Haganah had a kind of *semi-legal status which varied according to the political constellation. **1979** *Dædalus* Winter 157 The strength of the 'second' or 'parallel' market within the economy—in reality an entire spectrum of legal, semilegal, and illegal markets. **1878** STUBBS *Const. Hist.* III. xviii. 71 A *semi-legendary belief that he was still alive. **1909** O. LODGE *Survival of Man* vi. 86 Public performances ..often tend to obscure a phenomenon by covering it with *semi-legitimate contempt. **1624** WOTTON *Archit.* II. 121 *Semi-liberall Arts. **1850** *Blackw. Mag.* May 515 The semi-Liberal semi-Tory Governments from 1815 to 1830. **1927** *Mod. Philol.* Nov. 221 Even the *semi-literate speaker actually obtains some of his speech material by linguistic borrowing from written records. **1957** E. PARTRIDGE *English gone Wrong* I. 5 The best English of the semi-literate. **1976** P. CAVE *High Flying Birds* i. 10 Those who have perused my semi-literate journals masquerading as novels in the past may be familiar with some of my previous exploits. **1656** BLOUNT *Glossogr.*, **Semimarine* (*semimarinus*), belonging partly to the Sea, and partly to the Land. **1885** *Times* (weekly ed.) 11 Sept. 9/4, I should be much inclined to envy him his semi-marine residence. **1924** W. B. SELBIE *Psychol. Relig.* 269 The persistence of the belief in such a *semi-material ghost soul is a most interesting fact. **1924** *Econ. Jrnl.* XXXIV. 346 Meanwhile I got a good deal interested in the *semi-mathematical side of pure Economics. **1839** *Semi-mechanical [see *semi-chemical*]. **1837** CARLYLE *Fr. Rev.* VI. VI. iii, *Semi-military costume. **1859** DARWIN *Orig. Spec.* viii. 275 Varieties often suddenly produced and *semi-monstrous in character. **1902** W. JAMES *Var. Relig. Exper.* iii. 69 Here is the abridged record of another mystical or *semi-mystical experience. **1951** S. ULLMANN *Princ. Semantics* iii. 158 The somewhat abstruse and occasionally semi-mystical jargon in which his views are often couched has given rise to a number of misinterpretations. **1962** H. R. LOYN *Anglo-Saxon England* i. 26 The *semi-mythical island of Brittia, to which..the souls of the dead were ferried. **1962** Y. MALKIEL in Householder & Saporta *Probl. Lexicogr.* 5 Perspective essentially involves the deliberate or *semi-naïve attitude of the collector toward the chosen slice of material. **1841** W. SPALDING *Italy & It. Isl.* II. 255 The *semi-oriental aspect of its costumes. **1890** W. JAMES *Princ. Psychol.* II. xxiv. 420 In ordinary fear, one may either run, or remain *semi-paralyzed. **1922** JOYCE *Ulysses* 302 The semiparalysed *doyen* of the party..had to be assisted to his seat by the aid of a powerful steam crane. **1895** *Pop. Sci. Monthly* Apr. 764 The head of the hoactzin is ornamented with a *semi-pendent crest. **1895** *Outing* XXVI. 398/2 *Semi-permanent telegraph lines. **1857** HUGHES *Tom Brown* Pref. (1871) p. xvi, A *semi-political semi-sacerdotal fraternity. **1653** GATAKER *Vind. Annot. Jer.* 19 An obtrusion upon their Nation of a *Semipopish Book of Common-Prayer. **1860** ADLER *Prov. Poet.* viii, The transition from the *semi-popular poetry in monkish Latin to a decidedly popular poetry in the pure Romansh. **1973** *Morning Star* 16 Jan. 5/3 There [is] a much better and wider distribution of shops selling *semi-prepared foods [in Moscow now]. **1876** BLACK *Madcap Violet* ii, The..*semi-private throughfare. **1804** *Edin. Rev.* IV. 23 Delicts, according to him [Bentham], are..*Semipublic, or against some class or description of persons. **1875** JEVONS *Money* xviii. 217 It may allow private individuals, or semi-public companies..to undertake the work. **1931** E. H. MORRIS *Temple of Warriors* i. 5 A more than life-size sculpture of a *semireclining human figure. **1864** J. H. NEWMAN *Apol.* i. (1904) 6/1 On subjects *semi-religious and semi-scholastic. **1841** MERIVALE *Lect. Coloniz. & Col.* I. ii. 50 A singular race, of *semi-republican habits. *a* **1974** R. CROSSMAN *Diaries* (1976) II. 742, I am *semi-retired. **1849** *Westm. Rev.* L. 423 The *semi-Romanized Britons. **1834** BECKFORD *Italy* II. 25 The abode of these *semi-royal sober personages. **1835** DICKENS *Let.* (1965) I. 56 You would prefer living in Chambers to remaining in your present *semi-rural tranquility. **1864** *Realm* 23 Mar. 6 The most semi-rural of suburbs. **1930** AUDEN *Poems* 75 And I, stung by the sun, Think, *semi-satisfied That, 'ere the smile is done, The eye deliberate May qualify the joy. **1954** S. DUKE-ELDER *Parsons' Dis. Eye* (ed. 12) vi. 86 (*caption*) *Semi-schematic diagram showing the correspondence of the structures seen in the normal eye by gonioscopy with those of a microscopic section. **1864** *Sat. Rev.* 31 Dec. 812/1 Scientific or *semi-scientific observations. **1865** DICKENS *Mut. Fr.* IV. xii, A *semi-seafaring man. **1955** D. W. MAURER in *Publ. Amer. Dial. Soc.* XXIV. 4 The language [of criminal subcultures] is usually secret or *semisecret. **1939** *Daily Tel.* 18 Dec. 12/8 (Advt.), Audit clerk, *semi-senior, able to work without supervision. **1951** *Sport* 16–22 Mar. 9/2 Alec Talbot..finished his career with another semi-senior club, Stourbridge. **1976** *Eastern Daily Press* (Norwich) 16 Dec. 5/4 (Advt.), Applicants from ambitious semi-seniors would be welcome. **1840** POE *Autobiogr.* in *Graham's Mag.* Nov. 225/1 The design was never more than *semi-serious. **1977** J. F. FIXX *Compl. Bk. Running* xiv. 167, I don't know of a single even semiserious runner who smokes. **1848** MILL *Pol. Econ.* 22 The immediate cultivators of the soil..ceased to be in a servile or *semi-servile state. **1875** POSTE *Gaius* II. (ed. 2) 174 Tenant farmers of a semi-servile condition. **1896** T. W. SANDERS *Encycl. Gardening* (ed. 2) 35 Place plants in *semi-shady position outdoors June to Aug. **1973** M. AMIS *Rachel Papers* 67 *Semi-shaven, dishcloth hair, *duffle*-coat, baggy brown Farmer-Giles corduroys. **1873** WHITNEY *Or. & Ling. Studies* 293 A long and tedious climb upward from a miserable *semi-simious state. **1899** *Daily News* 19 Sept. 6/7 A hilly, cross-country, *semi-single line railway. **1927** CARR-SAUNDERS & JONES *Soc. Struct. Eng. & Wales* v. 50 It is not usual to think of those occupied in retail dealing as divided into skilled, *semi-skilled, and unskilled. **1940** W. S. CHURCHILL *Into Battle* (1941) 166 We have to make a huge expansion of our labour force, and especially of those capable of performing skilled or semi-skilled operations. **1976** E. STEWART *Launch!* (1977) 16 In 810—semiskilled—they were playing Tensor beams across eight-by-five-inch printed circuits. **1780** BENTHAM *Princ. Legisl.* xi. §18 Where..the motive..is a *semi-social one, the love of reputation. **1925** T. DREISER *Amer. Trag.* (1926) I. II. viii. 206 They were in the midst of one of those semi-religious, semi-social and semi-emotional church affairs, the object of which was to raise money for the church. **1620** BP. HALL *Hon. Marr. Clergie* I. §3 Their Vow is but *semi-solemne. **1922** JOYCE *Ulysses* 659 A noggin and a quarter of soured adulterated milk, converted by heat into water, acidulous serum and *semi-solidified curds. **1874** WHYTE-MELVILLE *Uncle John* xiv. II. 95 That *semi-sporting appearance which is attainable by means of scanty trousers [etc.]. **1922** JOYCE *Ulysses* 680 A series of static, *semistatic and peripatetic intellectual dialogues. **1962** J. T. MARSH *Self-Smoothing Fabrics* xxiii. 382 Variations of the crumpling method have produced a few *semi-subjective tests. **1880** FROUDE *Bunyan* i. 14 A *semi-supernatural being. **1943** *List Retail Controlled Prices* (Ministry of Food) (ed. 3) 6 Biscuits, sweet or *semi-sweet. **1972** *Times* 15 Nov. (Ital. Wine Suppl.) iv./3 Est! Est!! Est!!!..comes in both dry and semi-sweet. **1954** W. K. HANCOCK *Country & Calling* viii. 227 There are..many words of technical or *semi-technical origin which have lodged themselves.. firmly in everyday speech. **1976** *Classical Q.* XXVI. 216 Both lines, as Nicolaus notes..allude to a semi-technical legal term. *a* **1974** R. CROSSMAN *Diaries* (1976) II. 27 It was a reasoned, *semi-theoretical speech and it produced an amazingly good response. **1850** *Semi-Tory [see *semi-Liberal* above]. **1884** *Manch. Exam.* 9 July 4/6 The swamping of the agricultural labourers by the *semi-urban population. **1780** JOHNSON *Let. to Mrs. Thrale* 21 June, A *semivegetable diet. **1851** H. MELVILLE *Moby Dick* II. xliii. 294, I am convinced that from the heads of all ponderous profound beings, such as Plato,..Dante, and so on, there always goes up a certain *semi-visible steam, while in the act of thinking deep thoughts. **1749** HARTLEY *Observ. Man* II. ii. 140 The automatic and *semivoluntary Exertions of the Organs of Speech. **1847** W. C. L. MARTIN *Ox* 74/1 A noble *semi-wild race.

b. Compounded with a sb. to form an adj. phr.

1899 *Daily News* 26 Aug. 7/5 Some fancy woollen fabric, only too ready to betray its *semi-cotton derivation. **1897** *Ibid.* 24 Apr. 2/5 A posting landau converted into a *semi-dress landau. **1906** *Daily Chron.* 5 Oct. 4/5 Her dress..was of *semi-Empire shape. **1896** *Daily News* 28 Oct. 3/2 Five *semi-gala carriages with Royal scarlet liveries. **1955** KEEPNEWS & GRAUER *Pict. Hist. Jazz* xi. 117 They made much use of jazz and *semi-jazz conceptions in their dance music. **1938** *New Statesman & Nation* 23 July 143/2 What is needed is an extended application of the Trade Board method over a wide range of growing trades which mass-produce luxury or *semi-luxury goods. **1962** H. E. BEECHENO *Introd. Bus. Stud.* xi. 98 The more expensive type of goods..which are not the subject of so much branding and national advertising—the luxury and semi-luxury goods. **1837** CARLYLE *Fr. Rev.* II. v. xi, What Un-Patriot or *Semi-Patriot Ministry. **1837** DICKENS *Pickw.* xxvii, A *semi-rattlesnake sort of eye. **1886** *Pall Mall Gaz.* 10 June 4/2 Since his father's death the Prince of Wales and the Princess have done the *semi-state honours. **1901** *Scotsman* 2 Mar. 9/7 One of the King's semi-State landaus. **1935** *Discovery* Aug. 220/1 Subsistence or *semi-subsistence farming was the rule, the settlers eked out a bare existence from such poor land. **1975** *Sci. Amer.* May 76/3 Most of them work as semi-subsistence farmers and live according to Mayan cultural patterns.

2. Compounded with sbs.: **a.** with nouns of action or condition, as ***semi-allegiance*** = partial, imperfect, or incomplete allegiance; **b.** with descriptive sbs., as ***semi-acquaintance*** = one with whom one is partially acquainted, † ***semi-body*** = an imperfect body.

1872 HOWELLS *Wedding Journey* vii, Isabel had found among the passengers her *semi-acquaintances of the hotel parlour. **1689** D. GRANVILLE *Lett.* (Surtees No. 37) 117 An universall semi-conformity would end in as universall *semi-allegiance. **1948** D. DIRINGER *Alphabet* II. iv. 286 Groups of 'Assyrians'..developed a *semi-autonomy, owing allegiance only to their *maliks*. **1874** J. S. MILL *Ess. Relig.* 70 An argument for the utility of religion is an appeal ..to *semi-believers to make them avert their eyes from what might possibly shake their unstable belief. **1643** SIR T. BROWNE *Relig. Med.* II. §14 There is under..these mutilate and *semi-bodies [*sc.* of beggars], a soule of the same alloy with our owne. **1646** —— *Pseud. Ep.* IV. v. 189 One [testicle] sufficeth unto generation, as hath beene observed in *semicastration. **1964** L. MACNEICE *Astrol.* vii. 230 The *semi-charlatan who may not subscribe to any code of ethics. **1962** E. SNOW *Other Side of River* iv. 36 China's major ocean and river ports fell under foreign control and she became a *semicolony not of one nation but of all the major industrial and naval powers. **1865** J. S. MILL *Exam. Hamilton's Philos.* vii. 104 But such a *semi-concession.. cannot save him. *a* **1631** DONNE *Serm.* lvii. (1640) 581 All *Semi-confitents, that confesse them [*sc.* their sins] to halfs, without purpose of amendment. **1865** BAGEHOT *Eng. Const.* i. 19 A *semi-connection has grown up between the legislature and the executive. **1929** *Evening News* 18 Nov. 4/5 His weariness was so heavy that it bore him into a state of *semi-consciousness. **1641** J. JACKSON *True Evang. T.* I. 72 Such are the blots and spots of our *semi-conversions. **1751** SMOLLETT *Per. Pickle* lii, In the transports of his zeal he wrung this *semi-convert's hand. **1825** T. HOOK *Sayings* Ser. II. *Passion & Princ.* x. III. 191 [She] was led out of the room in a sort of *semi-convulsion. **1835** DICKENS *Sk. Boz, Charac.* iv, That description of *semi-curls usually known as 'haggerawators'. **1958** T. STANWELL-FLETCHER *Clear Lands* 89 That cold, beautiful *semidark of the Arctic night. **1849** LEVER *Roland Cashel* li, The vast apartment is in *semi-darkness. **1914** W. S. CHURCHILL *Let.* 8 Oct. in M. Gilbert *W. S. Churchill* (1972) III. *Compan.* I. 182 We must not be led into frittering away resources by keeping half a dozen anchorages in a state of *semi-defence. **1977** *Financial Times* 7 Oct. 23/3 Mr Wedgwood Benn's silky semi-defence of Government strategy from the platform. **1963** *Times* 7 Feb. 4/4 A Prime Minister with the support of the House of Commons may be in a stronger position than a President who has not got the support of Congress, but he is not the sole executive officer as a President is, or a dictator such as Khrushchev, or a *semidictator such as de Gaulle. **1817** PEACOCK *Nightmare Abbey* i, Nightmare Abbey..in a highly picturesque state of *semi-dilapidation. *a* **1835** MCCULLOCH *Attributes* (1837) III. 134 A state of *semidomestication. **1825** T. HOOK *Sayings* Ser. II. *Man of Many Fr.* (Colburn) 128 Mrs. Abberly moved in that class of *semi-fashion, which..never exceeds a certain circle. **1907** *Westm. Gaz.* 12 Oct. 13/2 Something between a sac and a *semi-fit. **1871** *Fair France* v. 160 That perpetual state of *semi-fuddle, peculiar to our beer-drinking agricultural labourer. *a* **1667** COWLEY *Sylva, Poeticall Revenge* 10 A *semi-gentleman of th' Innes of Court. **1938** *New Statesman & Nation* 20 Aug. 288/2 They operated in a twilight of *semi-illegality. **1949** KOESTLER *Insight & Outlook* vi. 84 The comic effects of *misspelling* in the letters of children or *semi-illiterates. **1850** ROBERTSON *Serm.* Ser. III. ix. (1853) 114 The oratory of the statesman in the senate has been kindled by *semi-intoxication. **1952** E. GRIERSON *Reputation for Song* vii. 58 She lived with an aunt, a *semi-invalid. **1864** TENNYSON *Aylmer's F.* 189 A flash of *semi-jealousy. **1974** *Howard Jrnl.* XIV. 78 Sir Cyril Burt defined *semi-literates as those 'who cannot make effective use of reading or writing'. **1688** D. GRANVILLE *Lett.* (Surtees No. 37) 229, I censure my censurers more for their *semi-loyalty. **1920** J. M. KEYNES *Econ. Consequences Peace* 95 Germany is threatened with a deluge of luxuries and *semi-luxuries from abroad. **1875** TENNYSON *Q. Mary* II. i, A *semi-mad-man..So fancy-ridd'n. **1961** tr. Zhou Enlai in *Look* 31 Jan. 104/2 A considerable period is needed before China can surpass the norm with regard to mechanization and *semimechanization. **1788** *Phil. Trans.* LXXIX. 157 The loins of the *semi-monster. **1884** 'H. COLLINGWOOD' *Under Meteor Flag* 102 The branches met overhead, veiling the path in *semi-obscurity. **1774** J. BRYANT *Mythol.* I. 453 In short, till we recollect ourselves, we are *semi-pagans. **1894** *Daily News* 4 Oct. 2/1 The condition of *semi-panic which lasted for some hours. **1906** E. DYSON *Fact'ry 'Ands* xiii. 169 He smote himself on the breast..leaving the packer in a condition of *semi-paralysis. **1873** F. HALL *Mod. Eng.* Pref., A motley cluster of philologists, *semi-philologists, and entire philologasters. **1713** POPE *Let. to Caryll* 31 Aug., A letter of yours has infinitely more charms to me, than the newest mail to the most ardent *semi-politician. **1958** F. NEWTON in P. Gammond *Decca Bk. Jazz* v. 65 Variety songs, effect-catching numbers and calculated *semi-pornography. *a* **1930** D. H. LAWRENCE *Phoenix* (1936) v. 597 Some sort of *semi-profession, such as school-teaching. **1626** BP. HALL *Contempl., O.T.* XXI. i. 356 Those sparkes of piety which he descryed in this *semi-proselite. **1805–6** WORDSW. *Prelude* (1850) v. 113 This Arab phantom, which my Friend beheld, This *semi-Quixote. **1866** *Macm. Mag.* XIII. 274 The *semi-rebellion of the Gallicans against the despotism of the Pope. **1835** J. S. MILL in *London Rev.* II. 272 A last desperate attempt of the Tories to creep back into power as *semi-reformers. **1935** *Mind* XLIV. 524 Retirement (or shall we say *semi-retirement) has given Dr. Schiller increased leisure. **1971** D. J. SMITH *Discovering Railwayana* viii. 47 After the grouping..many of the relics were consigned to semi-retirement in backyard and basement. **1653** WITHER (*title*) The dark Lantern, containing a dim discoverie, in riddles..parables and *semi-riddles. **1867** LADY HERBERT *Cradle L.* iii. 103 It soon fell into decay, and remained a *semi-ruin. **1878** MRS. H. WOOD *Pomeroy Abbey* II. xv, That for which Leolin had been working for years in *semi-secrecy. **1952** A. G. L. HELLYER *Sanders' Encycl. Gardening* (ed. 22) 40 Position, *semi-shade or north aspect. **1900** W. S. CHURCHILL in *Morning Post* 20 July 5/7 It was not possible for the conquering army to allow the capital..to be in a state of *semi-siege. **1841** LYTTON *Nt. & Morn.* IV. iii, A doleful and doubtful *semi-smile of welcome. **1825** JOS. BLACK *Capillary Circ.*, etc. 163 *Semi-stagnation may deteriorate into more complete deprivation of the materia vitæ. **1855** THACKERAY *Char. Sk.* Wks. 1898 III. 535 Tolerably cheerful in the midst of his *semi-starvation. **1929** *New Yorker* 12 Oct. 25/3 It is like the *semi-stupor of an habitual intoxication. **1977** *Proc. R. Soc. Med.* LXX. 689/1 High alcohol intake probably meets this need as well as providing them with an intermittent refuge in sedation and semistupor. **1865** KNIGHT *Passages Work. Life* II. 10 In the *semi-thoroughfare of Pall Mall East. **1863** J. S. MILL *Let.* 7 Jan. (1910) I. 273 He has triumphed wonderfully over the difficulty of rendering the thoughts or *semi-thoughts of Plato. **1878** MRS. H. WOOD *Pomeroy Abbey* III. ii, Something in the very words, in what she undoubtedly knew to be their *semi-truth. **1678** NORRIS *Misc.* (1699) 135 Tho seriousness be generally reckon'd only as a *Semi-Virtue, and by some as no Virtue at all. **1886** RUSKIN *Præterita* I. 424 Wasted affection, and rewardless semi-virtue. **1867** J. S. MILL *Let.* 19 Oct. (1910) II. 90 Parliamentary *semi-work or idleness.

3. Compounded with vbs., as ***semi-castrate*** = to castrate partially, ***semi-close*** = to shut in partly.

1828–32 WEBSTER, **Semi-castrate*, to deprive of one testicle. **1858** BARROW in *Merc. Marine Mag.* V. 13 The bays which these headlands *semi-close. **1902** MONKSHOOD & GAMBLE *Kipling* (ed. 3) 240 [In 'Stalky & Co.'] he chose to *semi-conceal his purposes behind a lattice-work of farce. **1845** JOWETT in *Life & Lett.* (1897) I. 120 If you will resign yourself to be *semi-humbugged by a semi-humbug. **1973** M. AMIS *Rachel Papers* 102 Kiss and *semi-lick throat and neck. **1962** *Times* 9 Apr. (Suppl.) p. iii/3 The dispensation of powdered lime with oxygen is used to *semi-refine molten iron before final treatment.

4. Compounded with advs., as ***semi-adjectively*** = in a function partly adjectival.

1810 COLERIDGE in *Lit. Rem.* (1839) IV. 368 And is not 'Scripture' as often used *semi-adjectively? **1945** *Plastics* IX. 143/1 Practical mechanical [safety] devices capable of functioning either fully or *semi-automatically. **1861** MAINE *Ancient Law* v. 146 A duty *semi-consciously followed.

5. The prefix used *absol.* as an advb., in sense 'partly, to some extent'. *colloq.*

1979 K. M. PEYTON *Marion's Angels* vi. 102 'I thought you were on holiday.' 'Semi.'

II. In special and technical use.

6. a. With designations of quantity, extent of space or time, and the like, as ***semi-amplitude***, ***-arc***, ***-century*** (= 50), †***-cotyle***, †***-cubit***, †***-dole*** (see DOLIUM), ***-drachm***, ***-duration***, ***-lunation***, ***-molecule***, ***-phase***, ***-revolution***, ***-span***, ***-tour***, ***-vibration***; †**semi-hore** [L. *sēmihōra*], half an hour; **semi-interquartile range** *Statistics*, half of the interquartile range.

1831 BREWSTER *Optics* x. 94 By exposing the north pole of a needle a foot long, the *semi-amplitude of the last oscillation was 6° more than the first. **1794** ATTWOOD in *Phil. Trans.* LXXXIV. 151 The balance commencing its vibration at the extremity of the arc B, after having passed the *semiarc BO with an accelerated motion. **1858** HUXLEY in *Proc. Roy. Soc.* (1859) IX. 428 Each distal portion of the hæmal semi-arc. **1650** J. GOLDOLPHIN (*title*) The Holy Limbeck, or a *Semi-Century of Spiritual Extraction. **1693** tr. *Blancard's Phys. Dict.* (ed. 2), **Semicotyle*, half a Cotyla. **1623** COCKERAM I, **Semicubit*, halfe a cubit. **1656** BLOUNT *Glossogr.*, **Semidole* (*semidolium*), a vessell containing half a Tun, a Pipe. **1827** ROBINSON *Archæol. Græca* V. xxvi. (ed. 2) 549 A *semi-drachm. **1719** POUND in *Phil. Trans.* XXX. 1032 The *Semi-duration of the Eclipse. **1867** G. F. CHAMBERS *Astron.* I. i. 8 Longer than the semi-duration of the Sun's rotation. **1623** COCKERAM I, **Semi-hore*, halfe an houre. **1911** G. U. YULE *Introd. Theory Statistics* viii. 134 There are three such measures in common use—the standard deviation, the mean deviation, and the quartile deviation or *semi-interquartile range. **1971** T. R. HARSHBARGER *Introd. Statistics* v. 91 The semi-interquartile range is half the quartile range: $Q = \frac{1}{2}(Q_3 - Q_1)$. Q is also called the quartile deviation. **1790** *Phil. Trans.* LXXX. 564 Each *semi-lunation is distinguished into fifteen equal portions, or lunar days. **1862** MILLER *Elem. Chem., Org.* (ed. 2) iii. §4. 238 Wurtz's double radicles would therefore be merely compounds in which the place of the *semi-molecule of hydrogen, or of the ethyl was supplied by a different hydrocarbon. **1863** *Intell. Observer* IV. 368 In this case the first *semi-phase of the vibration affected her room, and the second semi-phase operated more especially below. **1715** tr. *Gregory's Astron.* (1726) I. 131 A *Semi-revolution of the Earth about the Sun. **1884** HIGGS *Magn. Dyn. Electr. Mach.* 242 The current changes its direction with every semi-revolution of the spindle. **1772** C. HUTTON *Bridges* 62 A circular arc whose . . versed sine . . = the *semi-span. **1890** *Anthony's Photogr. Bull.* III. 187 A *semi-tour of the horizon is taken at a single exposure. **1825** J. NICHOLSON *Oper. Mech.* 517 The pendulum, moving down the arch of *semi-vibration.

b. With adjs., advs., and sbs. expressing periodical recurrence or duration, *semi-* denotes that the period is halved (after SEMI-ANNUAL); **semi-centenarian**, a person of 50 years of age; **semi-centenary**, the fiftieth anniversary; so **semi-centennial** *a.*; **semi-daily** *a.* and *adv.*, (occurring) twice daily; **semi-horal** *a.*, half-hourly; **semi-jubilee**, a twenty-fifth anniversary; **semi-menstrual**, **-mensual** *adjs.*, recurring twice a month; of tides (see quot. 1863); **semi-millenary** *a.*, lasting 500 years; **semi-monthly** *a.* and *adv.*, (occurring, issued, etc.) twice a month; also *sb.* a fortnightly periodical; so **semi-weekly**.

1828 *Lights & Shades* II. 36 Off the two *semi-centenarians started with a duet. **1870** ANDERSON *Missions Amer. Bd.* II. xxvii. 235 The *semi-centenary of the mission. **1859** (*title*) Memorials of the *semi-centennial celebration of the founding of the Theological Seminary at Andover. **1868** *Rep. U.S. Comm. Agric.* (1869) 335 This process of impregnating and depositing in the hatching-house was repeated *semi-daily. **1903** *Westm. Gaz.* 19 Oct. 7/1 Semi-daily attacks of epilepsy. **1847–54** WEBSTER, **Semi-horal*. **1893** *Miss. Herald* (Boston) Mar. 114 *Semi-Jubilee of the Mardin Church. **1901** *Nature* 27 June 210 His semi-jubilee as a doctor of physics. **1842** AIRY in *Encycl. Metrop.* V. 382* The observed *semimenstrual irregularities. **1863** HARBORD *Gloss. Navig.*, *Semimenstrual Inequality*, an inequality (of the tide) which goes through its changes every half month. **1857** WHEWELL *Hist. Induct. Sci.* (ed. 3) II. 195 The laws of a great number of the tidal phenomena—namely, of the *Semi-mensual Inequality of the Heights. **1727** EARBERY tr. *Burnet's St. Dead* II. 24 A long millenary or *semi-millenary Life. **1851** C. CIST *Sk. & Statistics Cincinnati* 75 These are *semi-monthlies. **1860** *Ex. Doc. 36th U.S. Congr. 2 Sess. Senate* No. 1. 435 The present contract . . provides for an additional monthly trip between New York and San Francisco, making the service tri-monthly instead of semi-monthly as heretofore. **1895** *Cal. Univ. Nebraska* 250 The Hesperian is the pioneer paper of the University, published semi-monthly. **1791** T. JEFFERSON *Let.* 21 July in A. A. Lipscomb *Writings T. Jefferson* (1903) XIX. 79 Besides this, Fenno's being the only weekly or *semi-weekly newspaper. **1833** A. H. TRACY *Let.* 10 June in T. W. Barnes *Mem. T. Weed* (1884) iv. 49 Put Millard Fillmore on your list for the Semi-Weekly. **1843** *Penny Cycl.* XXVI. 14/2, 138 daily, 1141 weekly, and 125 semi- or tri-weekly newspapers. **1851–6** (*title*) Semi-weekly courier and New York enquirer. **1926** *Jrnl. Biol. Chem.* LXIX. 92 The weights of the rats and of their food intake were recorded semiweekly.

c. *Music.* (*a*) Designating a note, etc. of half the length, as †***semi-crotchet***, †***-minim***, †***-tact***; also SEMIBREVE, SEMIQUAVER, SEMITONE; †(*b*) = IMPERFECT, DIMINISHED 4 a, as ***semi-diapason***, ***-diapente***, ***-ditone***, etc. (Cf. DEMI- 9, HALF- II. g.)

[**1688** HOLME *Armoury* III. 158/2 *Semi*, it is not to be taken for the half of such a Note or Interval in Musick, but only imports a dificiency, as wanting something of perfection.] **1598** FLORIO, *Semicrome*, a *semie crochet in musike. **1609** DOWLAND *Ornith. Microl.* 21 *Semidiapason Is an imperfect eight. **1694** W. HOLDER *Princ. Harmony* 172 The greatest [seventh], called Semidiapason, whose Ration is 48 to 25; . . wanting Hemitone Minor of Diapason. **1609** DOWLAND *Ornith. Microl.* 20 *Semidiapente Is an Interuall by an imperfect fift. **1694** *Phil. Trans.* XVIII. 73 The false fifth, or Semidiapente, made of a Fourth and Hemitone major, *i.e.* 64 to 45. **1730** *Treat. Harmony* 7 The Leaps of the False Relations, viz. of a Tritonus, and of a Semidiapente are absolutely forbidden. **1728** CHAMBERS *Cycl.*, **Semi diatessaron*, in Music, a defective Fourth, call'd, properly, a false Fourth. **1609** DOWLAND *Ornith. Microl.* 18 A *Semiditone . . is an Interuall of one Voyce from another by an imperfect third. **1598** FLORIO, *Semiminima*, a *semi-minime in musicke. **1795** MASON *Ch. Mus.* IV. 248 The . . Semiminim now called Crotchet. **1883** ROCKSTRO in Grove *Dict. Mus.* s.v. *Semiminim*, Sometimes the head of the greater Semiminim was 'void'—that is to say, open or white. **1609** DOWLAND *Ornith. Microl.* 46 Tact is three-fold, the greater, the lesser, and the proportionate. . . The lesser Tact, is the halfe of the greater, which they call a *Semitact.

d. *Astron.* †**semi-quadrate** (? erron. **-quadrant**), †**-quartile**, **-quintile**, **-sextile**, †**-sixth**, denoting aspects of planets when they are 45°, 36°, 30°, respectively, distant from one another; **semi-square** = *semi-quadrate*.

1721 BAILEY, **Semi-quadrant*, *Semi-quartile* (in Astronomy), an Object invented by Kepler, when two Planets are distant 45 Degrees from each other. **1647** LILLY *Chr. Astrol.*, etc. c. 511 You find in the directions of this Nativity, the *Semisextill, *Semiquintill, *Semiquadrate, Quintill, Sesquiquintill, Byquintill and Sesquiquadrate, mentioned. **1674** JEAKE *Arith.* (1696) 11 [Aspects.] . . *Semiquartil. **1835** 'ZADKIEL' *Introd. Astrol.* 24 Evil aspects are the *semi-square, square, sesquiquadrate, and opposition. **1728** CHAMBERS *Cycl.* s.v. *Semi-Sextile*, The *Semi-sixth was added to the ancient Aspects by Kepler.

7. a. Designating a (geometrical) form derived from another by bisection (usually) in a vertical or longitudinal direction, as ***semi-canal***, ***-cone***, ***-conic(al*** adj., ***-conoidal*** adj., ***-cup***, ***-disk***, ***-dodecagon***, ***-egg***, ***-fistular*** adj., ***-hexagon***, ***-hexagonal*** adj., ***-lens***, ***-octagonal*** adj., †***-orb*** [L. *sēmiorbis*], ***-ovoidal*** adj., ***-pyramidical*** adj., ***-rotund*** adj. (Cf. c, d.)

1836–9 *Todd's Cycl. Anat.* II. 390/2 A *semi-canal formed by a fold of the right side of the mantle. **1877** HUXLEY *Anat. Inv. Anim.* viii. 496 The duct of the ovotestis . . incompletely divided into two semicanals. **1899** *Daily News* 14 July 6/4 A silver-gilt chalice . . of *semi-cone form. **1756** P. BROWNE *Jamaica* 84 Sharp *semiconic leaves. **1822** J. PARKINSON *Outl. Oryctol.* 299 The inner surface [of the teeth], which is round, or rather *semiconical. **1865** LUBBOCK *Preh. Times* 64 The fracture is at first *semi-conoidal or nearly so. **1779** FORREST *Voy. N. Guinea* 28 Edible birds nests. . . I have taken them from the face of a perpendicular rock, to which they strongly adhered, in rows like *semi-cups, the one touching the other. **1784** HERSCHEL in *Phil. Trans.* LXXIV. 265 The *semi-disk, which is full, is evidently part of an oblate spheroid. **1849** *Guardian* 733/2 This roof is boarded . . , and its section forms a *semidodecagon. **1805** R. W. DICKSON *Pract. Agric.* I. 17 Cavities resembling the form of a *semi-egg when cut longitudinally. **1796** MORSE *Amer. Geog.* I. 528 A handsome court-house 100 feet by 50, with a *semi-hexagon at each end. **1843** BLOXAM *Gothic Archit.* (ed. 5) 87 A *semihexagonal one [string-course], as at Hampton-in-Arden. **1832** *Nat. Philos., Optic. Instr.* xvii. 57 (U.K.S.) The divided object-glass micrometer is composed of two *semilenses. **1751** LABELYE *Westm. Bridge* 23 A *Semi-octagonal rusticated Turret. **1615** CROOKE *Body of Man* 371 The belly of the partition which is like a *semiorbe stands out into it. **1851** MADDEN *Shrines & Sep.* I. 229 The interior assumes a *semi-ovoidal shape, or that of which the section will be a parabola. **1843** BLOXAM *Gothic Archit.* (ed. 5) 133 A *semi-pyramidical projection. **1652** *News fr. Low Countr.* 2 As an Ecliptick Line doth go, To the Antartick Pole, and frames Two *semi-Rotunds. **1856** W. CLARK *Van der Hoeven's Zool.* I. 813 Shell elliptical . . with aperture semirotund.

b. *Math.* Designating a bisected line, arc, area, segment, etc., or the half of a definite quantity, as ***semi-angle***, ***-base***, ***-circumference***, ***-circumvolution***, ***-cycloid***, ***-perimeter***, †***-perimetry***, ***-periphery***, ***-quadrangle***, ***-segment***; (in conic sections) ***semi-ordinate***, ***-parameter***, ***-transverse***; also **semi-convergent** *a.*, applied to a series the sum of whose terms converges while the sum of the moduli of its terms diverges; hence **semi-convergence**; **semi-difference**, half the difference between two quantities; **semi-infinite** *a.*, limited in one direction and extending to infinity in the other; **semi-major (-minor) axis**, half of the length of the longest (shortest) diameter of an ellipse; **semi-quadrantally** *adv.*, from 0° to 45°; **semi-regular** (see quot.); **semi-sum**, half the sum of two or more quantities; **semi-tangent**, the tangent of half an arc.

1765 LUDLAM in *Phil. Trans.* LV. 213 Let the *semi-angle of the lever be 84°:03'. **1666** COLLINS in Rigaud *Corr. Sci. Men* (1841) II. 461 The *semibase of a cylinder. **1796** HUTTON *Math. Dict.* s.v. *Cycloid*, The semi-circumf[erence] DGC = semi-base AC. **1661** S. PARTRIDGE *Double Scale Prop.* 80 First get the Semidiameter, which in this example is 3, 5 inches, and also the *Semicircumference, which here is 11. **1825** J. NICHOLSON *Oper. Mech.* 83 Such a resistance will stop the wheel, as it is equal to the effort of all the buckets in one semi-circumference filled with water. **1761** *Brit. Mag.* II. 642 Two *semi-circumvolutions, or segments, of this curve. **1902** E. T. WHITTAKER *Mod. Anal.* 12 Absolute convergence and *semi-convergence. **1872** *Monthly Notices R. Astron. Soc.* XXXII. 262 Most functions are expansible in an ascending (convergent) series of the form $A_0 + A_1x + A_2x^2 + \ldots$, and a descending (*semi-convergent) series of the form $B_1/x - B_2/x^2 + B_3/x^3 - \ldots$ **1959** A. ZYGMUND *Trigonometric Series* (ed. 2) II. iv. 175 If f is continuous, and $S[f]$ is uniformly semi-convergent to f from below, then $S[f]$ converges uniformly. **1695** WALLIS in *Phil. Trans.* XIX. 111 The *Semicycloid Figure. **1796** HUTTON *Math. Dict.* s.v. *Cycloid*, Two equal semicycloids OP, OQ. **1765** LUDLAM in *Phil. Trans.* LV. 210, ACK is the semi-sum, and DAI the *semi-difference of the angles CAI, CIA. **1873** *Rep. Brit. Assoc.* I. 23 The semi-sum and semidifference of the numbers to be multiplied. **1903** *Proc. R. Soc.* LXXII. 128 A '*semi-infinite' isotropic elastic solid, *i.e.*, a solid bounded only by a plane. [**1850** J. HAAN *Analytical Geom. & Conic Sections* v. 45 The equation to the ellipse [is] . . $y^2/b^2 + x^2/a^2 = 1$ . . , a and b being termed respectively the semi-axis major and the semi-axis minor.] **1899** GRACE & ROSENBERG *Coordinate Geom.* iv. 50 Find the length of the ordinates of each of the curves in Ex. 3 corresponding to the middle points of the *semi-major axis. **1977** *Whitaker's Almanack 1978* 156/1 The squares of the periodic times vary as the cubes of the semi-major axes. **1909** C. N. SCHMALL *First Course in Analytical Geom.* viii. 191 Prove that the *semi-minor axis is a mean proportional between the parts of tangent cut off. **1962** CORSON & LORRAIN *Introd. Electromagn. Fields* iv. 175 A charge Q is uniformly distributed throughout the volume of an ellipsoid of revolution whose semi-major axis is a and whose semi-minor axes are b. **1704** HARRIS *Lex. Techn.* I, *Ordinate* . . a Line in any Conick Section drawn at Right Angles to, and bissected by the Axis, and reaching from one side of the Section to the other; the half of which is properly the *Semi-ordinate. **1728** CHAMBERS *Cycl.* s.v. *Parabola*, The Squares of the Semi-ordinates are to each other as the Abscisses. **1759** STERNE *Tr. Shandy* II. iii, He found . . that the parameter or *latus rectum*, of the conic section of the said path . . and that the *semi-parameter [etc.]. **1816** PLAYFAIR *Nat. Phil.* II. 43 The solid contained by the radius of curvature, at any point in an ellipsis, and the square of the semiparameter of the greater axis, is equal to the cube of the normal at the same point. **1819** HUTTON *Course Math.* (1828) II. 328 Let p denote the *semiperimeter. **1571** DIGGES *Pantom.* IV. iii. V j b, From the *Semiperimetry of the triangle deducte euery side. **1610** FOLKINGHAM *Art of Survey* II. viii. 61 Multiply the *semiperipherie by the perpendicular. **1770** LANDEN in *Phil. Trans.* LX. 443 The semi-periphery of the circle. **1789** T. TAYLOR *Proclus* II. 32 That which has the vertical angle double of each at the base, as a *semiquadrangle. **1873** *Rep. Brit. Assoc.* I. 69 Logarithmic sines, tangents, and secants, *semi-quadrantally arranged, to every minute, to five places. **1867** BRANDE & COX *Dict. Sci.*, etc. s.v. *Polyhedron*, The *semi-regular polyhedrons of Archimedes, the corners of which are equal and similar to one another, but formed by regular polygons of different kinds. **1743** EMERSON *Fluxions* 226 Distance of the Center of Gravity of the *Semi-segment *PADQ* from *QD*. **1765**, **1873** *Semi-sum [see *semi-difference* above]. **1743** EMERSON *Fluxions* 203 In the Hyperboloid *BM*, described by revolving about *AP*, let the Semi-conjugæ = *b*, *Semi-transverse *AB* = *a*. **1816** PLAYFAIR *Nat. Phil.* II. 177 The semi-transverse axes of the orbits. **1823** J. MITCHELL *Dict. Math.* s.v. *Projection*, Any arc EMF of a great circle is projected into the sum of its *semi-tangents.

c. *Nat. Hist.* With adjs. and sbs. descriptive of shape in the contour or marking of natural objects; **semi-annular**, of the form of a half-ring; **semi-collar**, **-coronet**, **-fascia** (hence ***-fasciated***), **-ring**, a band, etc. roughly semicircular or extending halfway round a part or an organ; **semi-coronate(d**, having a semicircle of spikes, bristles, etc.

1681 GREW *Musæum* I. ii. 27 Another Boar-Tusk, somewhat slenderer, and of *semiannular Figure. **1844** WILKINSON tr. *Swedenborg's Anim. Kingd.* II. iii. 91 The semiannular cartilages. **1869** *Ibis* (N.S.) V. 409 The throat is a pure white, which is met below by a rufous *semicollar. **1826** KIRBY & SP. *Entomol.* IV. 354 *Semicoronate Prolegs. **1843** *Penny Cycl.* XXVI. 446/1 Shell turreted, fusiform, costated, and *semi-coronated. 1817 Kirby & Sp. *Entomol.* xxi. (1818) II. 253 Several larvæ of butterflies, distinguished at their head by a *semicoronet of strong spines. 1861 Hagen *Synopsis Neuroptera N. Amer.* 45 A large, hyaline, oblique *semi-fascia about the middle on the anal margin. 1803 Shaw *Gen. Zool.* IV. 472 *Semifasciated Sparus. 1706 Phillips (ed. Kersey), **Semifistular Flowers*, are such, whose upper-most part resembles a Pipe, cut off obliquely; as in Aristolochia or Birth-wort. 1841 Miller *Old Red Sandstone* vii. (1887) 134 This huge *semi-ring of fossiliferous clays. 1896 Newton *Dict. Birds* IV. 941 The first and second bronchial semirings.

d. *Nat. Hist.* Denoting that a part has a certain form or character (*a*) for half the extent, or along half the length, etc. of an organ, 'half-way,' as ***semi-adherent***, ***-adnate***, ***-amplexicaul***, ***-appressed***, ***-bifid***, ***-costiferous***, ***-equitant***, ***-erect***, ***-quinquifid***, ***-sexfid***; **semi-anatropal, -ous** (see quot. 1839); (*b*) on one side only, or so as to exhibit the half of a particular figure, as ***semi-cordate(d***, ***-crescentic***, ***-hastate***, ***-lanceolate***, ***-lenticular***, ***-orbicular***, ***-orbiculate***, ***-pectinate(d***, ***-penniform***, ***-pinnate***, ***-reniform***, ***-sagittate(d***, ***-terete***.

Sometimes represented by $\frac{1}{2}$, as $\frac{1}{2}$-hastate, $\frac{1}{2}$-sagittate.

1857 A. Gray *First Less. Bot.* (1866) Gloss., **Semiadherent*, as the calyx or ovary of Purslane. 1876 Harley *Mat. Med.* 431 Ovary *semi-adnate. 1753 *Chambers's Cycl.* Suppl. s.v. *Leaf*, **Semamplexicaule Leaf*, one resembling the *amplexicaule*, but with its lobes at the base too small to entirely surround the stalk. 1877 Hulme *Wild Flowers* Ser. I. p. xiv, The upper [leaves]..sinuate, semi-amplexicaul. 1846 Lindley *Veget. Kingd.* 368 Ovules ..amphitropal or *semi-anatropal. 1839 —— *Introd. Bot.* I. ii. (ed. 3) 215 There is the amphitropous ovule, whose foraminal and chalazal ends are transverse with respect to the hilum, which is connected with the latter by a short raphe; and the *semianatropous, which is only different from the last, in the ovule being parallel with the funiculus instead of being at right angles with it. 1857 T. Moore *Handbk. Brit. Ferns* (ed. 3) 43 Scales..*semi-appressed. 1775 J. Jenkinson *Brit. Plants* Gloss., **Semibifid*, half way divided into two. *Ibid.*, **Semi-cordate*, half cordate. 1826 Kirby & Sp. *Entomol.* xxxv. III. 641 The wings..in several of the Heteropterous *Hemiptera*..may..be termed semicordate or semiovate. 1845 *Encycl. Metrop.* XXIII. 640/2 The posterior pair [of the lamina in *Pseudoboa Cœrulea*] large, semicordate. 1877 Coues *Monogr. N. Amer. Rodentia* 549 Seventh cervical *semicostiferous, without vertebrarterial canal. 1836–9 *Todd's Cycl. Anat.* II. 390/1 A *semi-crescentic membrane. 1900 B. D. Jackson *Gloss. Bot. Terms*, **Semiequitant*, half-equitant. 1822 J. Parkinson *Outl. Oryctol.* 221 *Chama..unicornaria*: sub-imbricated, rough, with unequal, *semierect, vaulted squamæ. 1851 Carpenter *Man. Phys.* (ed. 2) 556 The semi-erect Apes. 1853 Royle *Mat. Med.* (ed. 2) 402 Stipules..*semihastate, spreading, minute. 1900 B. D. Jackson *Gloss. Bot. Terms*, **Semilanceolate*, half-lanceolate, longitudinally divided. 1794 Kirwan *Elem. Min.* (ed. 2) I. 99 A dark blue limestone, of a conchoidal or *semilenticular form. 1775 J. Jenkinson *Brit. Plants* Gloss., **Semiorbicular*, half orbicular. 1860 L. Reeve *Elem. Conchol.* I. 185 Aperture semiorbicular. 1816 T. Brown *Elem. Conchol.* 163 **Semi-orbiculate*, in the shape of a half globe. 1847 Johnston in *Proc. Berw. Nat. Club* II. v. 228 The 5th [joint]..furnished beneath with three or four pairs of neat *semi-pectinate processes. 1848 *Ibid.* vi. 308 A pair of *semipectinated processes or combs. 1826 Kirby & Sp. *Entomol.* xliii. IV. 178 A pair of *semipenniform muscles. 1878 Bell tr. *Gegenbaur's Comp. Anat.* 338 The right gill is generally developed on one side only, so that it is *semi-pinnate, owing to the disappearance of the second row of lamellæ. 1775 J. Jenkinson *Brit. Plants* Gloss., **Semi-quinquifid*, half way divided into five. 1866 *Treas. Bot.* 1048 **Semi-reniform*, reniform on one side only. 1806 J. Galpine *Brit. Bot.* 329 Stipulæ *semi-sagittate. 1804 Shaw *Gen. Zool.* V. 361 *Semisagittated teeth. 1819 *Pantalogia*, **Semisexfid Calyx*, in botany, half-six-cleft. 1857 Moore *Handbk. Brit. Ferns* (ed. 3) 186 Stipes ..*semiterete.

e. In *Building*, designating structural forms of half the full width, breadth, or girth, resulting from (usually) vertical or longitudinal bisection, as ***semi-arch***, ***-barrel vault***, ***-bay***, ***-channel***, ***-counter-arch***, ***-cross-rib***, ***-cupola***, ***-groove***, ***-roll***, ***-rotunda***, ***-shaft***, ***-transept***, ***-vault***; **semi-basement**, a basement sunk only part of its depth below the ground surface; **semi-beam** = CANTILEVER 2; **semi-engaged** *a.*, (of a column) attached to a wall so that half its diameter projects; **semi-girder** = *semi-beam*; **semi-relief**, half-relief, mezzo-rilievo; so **semi-ball, -urn**, a ball, an urn in half-relief.

1823 P. Nicholson *Pract. Builder* 295 To determine the centre of gravity of the *semi-arch. 1875 Brash *Eccl. Archit.* 99 A bold label..bearing a line of *semi-balls. 1905 *Daily Chron.* 18 Mar. 3/4 In the *semi-basement are carpenters' shops, laboratory, &c. *a* 1878 Scott *Lect. Archit.* I. 118 Not, as usual, embracing two bays, but two of these *semi-bays. 1850 E. Clark *Britannia & Conway Bridges* I. 276 The *semi-beam, or cantilever,..has to support half the weight of the beam..suspended from its extremity. 1908 J. G. Horner *Encycl. Pract. Engin.*, *Semi-Beam.*—A beam supported at one end only. A cantilever. 1728 R. Morris *Ess. Anc. Archit.* 52 The two outward, or *Semi-Channels. 1751 Labelye *Westm. Bridge* 83 Two *Semicounter Arches butting against the opposite Side of the..Piers. 1835 R. Willis *Rem. Archit. Mid. Ages* vii. 79 The *semi-cross rib. 1869 Tozer *Highl. Turkey* I. 79 In the transepts are *semi-cupolas. 1886 Willis & Clark *Cambridge* II. 533 A hexastyle portico of *semi-engaged columns. *Ibid.* I. 273 The *semi-groove or 'rebate' which is cut..along the.. edge. 1703 T. N. *City & C. Purchaser* 30 Embossments, which resembles ..Beads in *Semi-relief. *a* 1878 Scott *Lect. Archit.* (1879) II. 80 The rib may be amplified by a central *semi-roll moulding. 1797 Holcroft tr. *Stolberg's Trav.* II. xlii. (ed. 2) 138 It rested on two *semi rotundas. 1853 Ruskin *Stones Ven.* III. 247 Small pilasters with *semi-shafts at their sides. 1783 T. Warton *Hist. Kiddington* (ed. 2) 2 There is a proportionable lateral projection, or southern *semitransept. *a* 1734 North *Life Ld. Kpr. North* (1742) 84 A Monument of white Marble.. being an oblong *Semiurn upon a large Face of a Cube. 1798 Hutton *Course Math.* (1828) II. 176 The centre of gravity of the *semi-vault. *a* 1878 Scott *Lect. Archit.* I. 59 The continuous semi-vault would do away with clerestory windows.

f. *Cryst.* **semi-prismated, -tesseral, -tessular** *adjs.* (see quots.).

1805 R. Jameson *Char. Min.* (1817) 197 A crystal is named *semi-prismated, when only half of the edges on the common basis are obliterated by lateral planes. 1883 Heddle in *Encycl. Brit.* XVI. 355/2 Two *semitesseral forms with parallel faces occur... The two other semitesseral forms, the pentagonal dodecahedron and the pentagonal icositetrahedron, both bounded by irregular pentagons, have not yet been observed in nature. 1858 Mayne *Expos. Lex.*, **Semi-tessular*, term applied to a combination of the tessular system, into which the forms enter with only half the number of their faces.

g. *Her.* = DEMI- B. 1, HALF- II. b; as ***semi-chevron***, ***-saltire***.

1864 Boutell *Her. Hist. & Pop.* xiv. (ed. 3) 147 The Dexter *semi-chevrons are shown in combination with the sinister *semi-saltire. 1688 Holme *Armoury* III. 371/2 A *semi-Quadrant, of some called a demi-Quadrant.

h. *Printing.* †**semi-quadratures**, crotchets, square brackets; **semi-quotes** *colloq.*, single quotation-marks (' ').

1764 *Behmen's Wks.* I. Advt., Synonymous Expressions are placed..betwixt two *Semiquadratures [ ] in the Body of the Work.

8. = to the extent of (only) a half, imperfect(ly), incomplete(ly). **a.** With adjs. and sbs. expressing kinds or degrees of composition, consistency, texture, colour, as ***semi-coagulated***, ***-concrete***, ***-digested***, ***-ductile***, ***-friable***, ***-fused***, ***-fusion***, ***-grainy***, ***-liquid***, ***-lucent***, ***-matt***, ***-membranous***, ***-moist***, ***-opalescent***, ***-pasty***, ***-pellucid***, ***-pellucidity***, ***-petrified***, ***-plastic***, ***-purulent***, ***-putrid***, ***-resinous***, ***-translucent***, ***-volatile***. (See also d, f, i.)

1833 *Cycl. Pract. Med.* I. 386/1 *Semi-coagulated, in respect to consistence. 1876 Gross *Dis. Bladder* (ed. 3) 154 Nodules, of a *semiconcrete consistence. 1842 G. Bird in *Urin. Deposits* (1853) 254 The vomiting of the meal in a *semi-digested state. 1796 Kirwan *Elem. Min.* (ed. 2) II. 453 A grey *semi-ductil Regulus. 1834 J. Forbes *Laennec's Dis. Chest* (ed. 4) 157 An opaque, very dry, *semi-friable matter. 1876 in *Ure's Dict.* (1878) IV. 599 By grinding the *semi-fused mass and treating it with water. 1791 Macie in *Phil. Trans.* LXXXI. 372 A *semi-fusion, or softening of the whole mass. 1855 J. Phillips *Man. Geol.* 260 The induration and semifusion of sandstones. 1756 P. Browne *Jamaica* 387 Thin, fleshy, or *semigelatinous lips. 1893 *Times* 13 Dec. 3/5 *Semi-grainy brownish crystallized. 1684 T. Burnet *Th. Earth* I. 125 While the mass was liquid or *semiliquid. 1963 D. W. & E. E. Humphries tr. *Termier's Erosion & Sedimentation* x. 193 Some marly deposits still contain 41·3% of water, which results in numerous landslips in this plastic, semi-liquid material. 1818 Keats *Endym.* IV. 385 Smooth *semilucent mist. 1919 V. Woolf *Night & Day* xi. 138 Rodney's windows..were a semilucent red colour. 1967 *Semi-matt [see MATT *a.*]. 1846 Dana *Zooph.* (1848) 625 Thin, *semi-membranous partitions. 1967 E. Chambers *Photolitho-Offset* xvii. 259 The soft, tacky gelatinous Everdamp paper makes for easier working, being *semi-moist and ready for use. 1830 Lyell *Princ. Geol.* I. 213 This sinter has often a beautiful *semi-opalescent lustre. 1851 *Art Jrnl. Illustr. Catal.* p. iij*, At a temperature but just sufficient to maintain it in a *semi-pasty state. *a* 1728 Woodward *Nat. Hist. Fossils* (1729) I. I. 32 A light grey *Semi-pellucid Flint, 'Tis of much the same Complexion with the common Indian Achate. 1867 H. Macmillan *Bible Teach.* xii. (1870) 247 The purest agates ..are not perfectly transparent; they are only semi-pellucid. 1828–32 Webster, **Semipellucidity*, the quality or state of being imperfectly transparent. 1853 Kane *Grinnell Exp.* xxvi. (1856) 211 As they strike her, the *semi-plastic mass is impressed with a mould of her side. 1734 Burton in *Phil. Trans.* XLII. 103 By a *semipurulent cancerous *Sanies.* 1762 Lysons ibid. LII. 639 The kidneys, in one of the subjects, are said to have been found putrid, in the other, *semiputrid. 1862 *Jrnl. Soc. Arts* X. 330/2 The *semi-resinous material would..resume..the form it was in prior to solution. 1832 *Nat. Philos. Thermom. & Pyrom.* i. 9 (U.K.S.), It consists of a ball and tube of *semitranslucent porcelain, highly baked. 1738 *Gentl. Mag.* VIII. 140/2 The grateful Bitter is of a middle Nature, *Semivolatile.

b. In designations of heresies, sects, and schools of thought, expressing partial adherence to the tenets or theories connoted by the second element of the compound, as ***semi-antiministerial***, ***-Apollinarism***, ***-atheist***, ***-Augustinian***, ***-catholicism***, ***-Christianity***, ***-conformist***, ***-Darwinian***, ***-infidel***, ***-Jesuit***, ***-Judaizer***, ***-Manicheanism***, ***-nonconformist***, ***-Pythagorean***, ***-quietism***, ***-quietist***, ***-revolutionist***, ***-Romanism***, ***-Sadducee***, ***-Sadduc*(e)*-ism***, ***-separatist***, ***-socialism***, ***-socialist***, ***-Socinian***, ***-Tychonic***, ***-universalist***.

1653 Gauden *Hierasp.* 190 These *Semiantiministeriall adversaries. 1855 Mozley *August. Doctr. Predest.* iii. 100 A *semi-Apollinarism in a soul imperfectly connected with the flesh, a *semi-Manicheanism in a flesh imperfectly connected with the soul of our Lord. *a* 1619 Fotherby *Atheom.* I. xii. §1 (1622) 123 This is to be, but a *Semi-Atheist. 1879 M. Pattison *Milton* xi. 126 The two first Stuarts, coquetting with *semi-catholicism at home. 1882 J. Snodgrass tr. *H. Heine's Relig. & Philos. in Germany* II. 67 Leibnitz..was well able to defend Christianity in its integrity. I say, in its integrity, for he defended it against *semi-Christianity. 1961 C. S. Lewis *Let.* Feb. (1966) 297 For some people at some moments what I call semi-Christianity may be useful. 1685 D. Granville *Lett.* (Surtees No. 37) 210 A breach..which I do as much dread, as the phanatick and *semi-conformists do our union. 1903 (*title*) Doubts about Darwinism. By a *Semi-Darwinian. 1861 J. G. Sheppard *Fall of Rome* xii. 683 The..*semi-Gnostic notions [of the Templars]. 1833 J. H. Newman *Arians* I. v. (1876) 124 The change to the second position, or *semi-humanitarian, may be detected in the Sabellians. 1735–6 Gibson in Fraser *Berkeley* vii. (1871) 244 We have.. little trouble from professed infidels, but a great deal from *semi-infidels. *a* 1631 Donne *Serm.* xii. (1640) 113 A Jesuit, or a *Semi-Jesuit, a practising Papist, or a Sesqui-Jesuit. 1765 Maclaine tr. *Mosheim's Eccl. Hist.* XVI. II. iv. §23 This little sect is branded by the Socinian writers, with the ignominious appellation of *Semi-Judaizers. 1655 Fuller *Ch. Hist.* IX. xvi. 161 How he interceded to qualifie the Arch-Bishop, for a *Semi-non conformist. 1857 Pusey *Real Presence* iii. (1869) 247 Parker, whom, for his belief in the sacraments, his adversaries called 'Lutheran or *Semi-Papist'. 1865 Grote *Plato* I. i. 15 *note*, Alkmæon, a *semi-Pythagorean. 1876 Sweeney in *Baker's Sancta Sophia* (1908) 493 The Quietism of Molinos, and the *semi-Quietism of Madame Guyon. 1882 McClintock & Strong *Cycl. Bibl. Lit.* VIII. 847 (Cassell) Fénelon and Madame Guyon .. are .. usually called *semi-Quietists. 1812 Coleridge in *Lit. Rem.* (1836) I. 298 Curio, the *quondam* patriot, reformer, and *semi-revolutionist. 1847 *Edin. Rev.* Oct. 325 Church architecture has been set up under our own eyes as the banner of a more than *semi-Romanism. 1690 Baxter *Kingd. Christ* (1691) 46 You brand all that dissent from you as *Semi-Sadducees of the Apostacy. *Ibid.* 42 He that accuseth others of *Semi-Sadduceism of the Apostasie. 1691 Beverley *Thousand Years' Kingd.* 4 Antichristian Semi-Sadducism. *a* 1628 F. Grevil *Disc. Nat. Episc.* II. vi. (1641) 90 The *Separist* is subdivided too (as they say) into *Seperatist*, and **Semi-seperatist*. 1647 Pagitt *Heresiogr.* (ed. 4) 81 There is a sort of Semi-separatists, that will heare our Sermons, but not our Common-prayers. 1886 W. Morris in Mackail *Life* (1899) II. 167, I have a long letter from W. Birchall..about *semi-Socialism. 1930 W. K. Hancock *Australia* xi. 225 The Liberal party still continued to tread ..the familiar path of semi-socialism. 1939 N. & S. Weyl *Reconq. Mexico* iv. 110 Mexico's long indoctrination with *semisocialist theory..made leftist political candidates almost a political inevitability. 1976 N. O'Sullivan *Conservatism* i. 30 A great body of conservative thought.. has itself tended to move in a semi-socialist or collectivist direction. 1834 *Tracts for Times* No. 22. 4 A *semi-socinian or five-quarter latitudinarian. 1786–7 Bonnycastle *Astron.* iv. 63 He was abandoned by some of his followers, who chose rather to save this immense labour to the spheres, by ascribing a diurnal motion to the earth; on which account they were distinguished by the name of *Semi-Tychonics. 1794 G. Adams *Nat. & Exp. Philos.* IV. xxxiii. 2 [Aristotle] speaks of a set of men, who held a system essentially similar to that of the modern Semitychonic. 1765 Maclaine tr. *Mosheim's Eccl. Hist.* XVII. II. II. ii. §12 The Reformed Church was immediately divided into Universalists, *Semi-universalists, Supralapsarians, and Sublapsarians.

c. *Gram.*, as ***semi-compound*** (also as *sb.*), ***-grammatical***, ***-nasal***, ***-phonetic*** adjs.; **semi-consonant** = SEMIVOWEL; **semi-deponent**, a verb in Latin of which the tenses of the present group have active forms and those of the perfect group passive forms, as *gaudeo*, *gavisus sum*; †**semi-pause**, a slight pause or cæsura; **semiphonotypy**, printing in a 'reformed' spelling intermediate between the traditional and purely phonetic spelling; **semi-predicative** *a.*, quasi-predicative; forming part of a predicate; **semi-rhythm**, free-rhythm verse; **semi-sentence**, a statement or utterance which possesses some of the features of a sentence; †**semi-spiritous** *a.*, (of a consonant) voiced; **semi-telic** *a.*, partially final or expressing purpose.

1963 F. T. Visser *Hist. Syntax* I. iv. 389 An older *semi-compound verb of the type *overpass*. 1964 *English Studies* XLV. 50 Some combinations..can therefore be considered as compounds or semi-compounds. 1820 F. Bopp in *Ann. Oriental Lit.* I. 6 The letter *y*..in Sanskrit or Gothic words ..is always to be considered as a *semi-consonant. 1828 Walker *Pron. Dict.* 17/1 These two letters [*w* and *y*] are so far from being simple vowels, that they may more properly be called semi-consonant diphthongs. 1888 Kennedy *Revised Lat. Primer* (1900) §6. *Ibid.* §127 Some Verbs have a Perfect of Passive form with a Present of Active form; they are called **semi-deponents*. 1964 P. Strevens *Papers in Lang. & Lang. Teaching* (1965) iv. 61 The body of data..includes grammatical, *semi-grammatical and non-grammatical features. 1863 A. M. Bell *Princ. Speech* 178 The Englishman's difficulty in giving the Gallic effect to the French *semi-nasal elements. 1762 Kames *Elem. Crit.* xviii. (1774) II. 127 A *semipause..being short and faint, is not sensibly disagreeable when it divides a word. 1824 [see *demi-cæsura*, DEMI- 11]. 1933 L. Bloomfield *Language* xvii. 290 *Semi-phonetic devices, such as rising combinations of letters for a single phoneme. 1964 *Language* XL. 302 He had to depend mainly on the semiphonetic materials recorded by H. Paasonen. 1914 O. Jespersen *Mod. Eng. Gram.* II. 386 It is used in that sense as a *semi-predicative post-adjunct. 1933 L. Bloomfield *Language* xii. 206 Some numeratives are used also in other syntactic positions, as..*all*, *both* as semi-predicative attributes (*the boys were both there*). 1876 Max Müller *Sel. Ess.* (1881) I. 259 A style of spelling will now be introduced which has received the name of *Semiphonotypy. 1893 G. A. Greene *Italian Lyrist, Luigi Capuana* 54 The exact metre,..is, as might be expected from '*semi-rhythms', somewhat difficult to ascertain. 1954 *Acta Universitatis Carolinae* VII. 35 In the present article, the term '*semi-sentence' constructions covers both participial and infinitive phrases as well as those having neither of these, but which, owing to their binary character, have a distinct predicational form (e.g. *If lawful*.). **1969** *Word* XXV. 195 A sentence which contains no predicate is a semi-sentence. **1975** N. Chomsky *Logical Struct. Linguistic Theory* viii. 244 We are building a system of phrase structure only for first-order grammatical sentences, a category that presumably excludes such semisentences as 'sincerity appointed the table'. **1668** Wilkins *Real Char.* 369 By *Semi-spiritous or halfbreathed Consonants, are meant such as are accompanied with some kind of vocal murmure, as B, D, G. **1865** Alford *Grk. Test.* III. 285 When we are speaking of the divine proceedings, the tendency involves the purpose, and there is no need for a *semi-telic force.

d. *Nat. Hist.* = imperfectly, incompletely, partly (of a certain habit, form, texture, etc.), as ***semi-aquatic***, ***-arborescent***, ***-articulate***, ***-complete***, ***-complicated***, ***-connate***, ***-coriaceous***, ***-corneous***, ***-crustaceous***, ***-erect***, ***-granulate***, ***-heterocercal***, ***-horny***, ***-hyaline***, ***-imbricated***, ***-immersed***, ***-internal***, ***-osseous***, ***-oviparous***, ***-permeable***, ***perspicuous***, ***-petaloid***, ***-radiate***, ***-recondite***, ***-retractile***, ***-revolute***, ***-septate***, ***-sessile***, ***-social***, ***-spiral***, ***-staminate***, ***-striate***, ***-striated***, ***-terrestrial***, ***-valvate***, ***-verticillate***; **semi-evergreen**, normally evergreen but shedding some leaves if conditions become severe.

1833 Hooker in J. E. Smith *Eng. Flora* V. I. 112 Among *Sphagnum* and other *semi-aquatic mosses. **1910** Roosevelt *Afr. Game Trails* 126 They [buffalo] are semi-aquatic beasts. **1880** C. R. Markham *Peruv. Bark* 236 The vegetation . . is of a *semi-arborescent character. **1815** Kirby & Sp. *Entomol.* I. 68 Those of the Linnean order Hemiptera, which resemble the perfect insect, except in having only the rudiments of wings, and to which the name of *semi-complete pupæ was applied by Linnè. **1822** J. Parkinson *Outl. Oryctol.* 225 Valves *semicomplicated. **1900** B. D. Jackson *Gloss. Bot. Terms*, **Semiconnate*, applied to such structures as the half-united filaments of certain willows. **1852** Th. Ross tr. *Humboldt's Trav.* II. xxiv. 451 The *semi-coriaceous leaves. **1835–6** *Todd's Cycl. Anat.* I. 703/1 A brownish and *semi-corneous filament. **1771** *Encycl. Brit.* III. 364/1 The Hemiptera have four wings, the two superior ones being *semicrustaceous, and incumbent. **1894** R. B. Lee *Hist. & Descr. Mod. Dogs of Gr. Brit. & Ireland* (*Terriers*) xv. 353 Ears . . if not cut, to be small V-shaped and carried *semi-erect. **1931** A. G. L. Hellyer *Sander's Encycl. Gardening* (ed. 21) 409 *S*[*milax*] *herbacea*, greenish, bluish-black fruits, twining or semi-erect, N. America. **1952** *Ibid.* (ed. 22) 10 Adenocarpus. . . Deciduous or *semi-evergreen shrubs or small trees. **1978** *Detroit Free Press* 16 Apr. (Parade Suppl.) 32/2 (Advt.), The lush, semi-evergreen foliage erupts in massive clusters of star-shaped, fiery red blooms. **1815** Burrow *Elem. Conchol.* 185 Shell 8-valved, *semi-granulate. **1787** Hunter in *Phil. Trans.* LXXVII. 404 A *semi-horny substance. **1819** Samouelle *Entomol. Compend.* 230 *Asiraca clavicornis* . . elytra *semihyaline. **1840** tr. *Cuvier's Anim. Kingd.* 280 The scales are square, thick, and *semi-imbricated. **1871** W. A. Leighton *Lichen-Flora* 417 Apothecia large, . . *semi-immersed in thalline elevations. **1843** Kirby & Sp. *Entomol.* (ed. 6) I. 289 This insect is a *semi-internal parasite. **1822** J. Parkinson *Outl. Oryctol.* 191 The ligament internal or semi-internal. **1841** H. Miller *Old Red Sandstone* iv. (1887) 95 The *semi-osseous . . icthyolites of the Lower Old Red Sandstone. **1897** *Pop. Sci. Monthly* Nov. 7 The oöticoids or *semi-oviparous mammals. **1900** W. Ramsay in *Smithsonian Rep.* 253 A vessel the walls of which are permeable to the solvent, but not to the dissolved substance ('*semipermeable membrane'). **1681** Grew *Musæum* III. iv. 288 Of the colour of yellow Amber, and *semiperspicuous. **1830** Lindley *Nat. Syst. Bot.* 86 Cycnia has a *semipetaloid irregular calyx and no petals. **1900** B. D. Jackson *Gloss. Bot. Terms*, **Semiradiate*, when only a portion of the outer florets of a Composite are radiant and different from those of the disk. **1826** Kirby & Sp. *Entomol.* IV. 306 *Semirecondite. . . When the head is half covered by the shield of the thorax. **1883** Flower in *Encycl. Brit.* XV. 440/2 Claws short, compressed, acute, curved, often *semi-retractile. *a* **1843** South in *Encycl. Metrop.* VII. 289/1 Sometimes, as in the *semi-revolute Shells, the whorls are perfectly distinct from each other. **1866** *Treas. Bot.*, **Semi-septate*, half-partitioned; having a dissepiment which does not project into the cavity to which it belongs sufficiently to cut it off into two separate cells. **1962** D. Nichols *Echinoderms* xii. 156 These facts suggest that the animal remained *semi-sessile on the sea-bottom and searched the surrounding area with its tentacles. **1962** *Sci. Survey* XVII. 285 Numbers of insects are affected [by sounds] . . which are related, not to sexual activity, but to social or *semi-social activities. **1828** Stark *Elem. Nat. Hist.* II. 33 Shell ovate, inflated, *semispiral. **1900** B. D. Jackson *Gloss. Bot. Terms*, **Semistaminate*, when part of the stamens are changed into petals. **1815** Burrow *Elem. Conchol.* 131 Shell 8-valved, *semistriate. **1932** J. S. Huxley *Probl. Relative Growth* i. 33 Twenty-four grams is a very small weight for many crabs, including forms of *semi-terrestrial and burrowing habits. **1964** *Oceanogr. & Marine Biol.* II. 302 The semi-terrestrial hermit crab, *Coenobita perlatus*, . . varies the frequency with which it visits water of different salinities. **1900** B. D. Jackson *Gloss. Bot. Terms*, **Semivalvate*, when the valves of a fruit are only partially dehiscent. **1847–54** Webster, **Semi-verticillate*, partially verticillate.

e. Designating an animal or vegetable form, class, species, etc., which has only some of the characteristics of that denoted by the second element, or is intermediate between that and another, as ***semi-ape*** (= half-ape, lemur), ***-avocet***, ***burrower***, ***-dwarf*** (also as *adj.*), ***-egret***, ***-lichen***, ***-looper*** (cf. half-looper), ***-parasite*** (whence ***-parasitic*** adj., ***-parasitism***), ***-pupa*** (whence ***-pupal*** adj.), ***-rapacious*** adj., ***-stilt***; similarly in anglicized forms of L. names of zoological groups, etc., as ***semi-digitigrade***, ***-phyllidian***, ***-plantigrade*** = belonging to (or a member of) the groups *Semidigitigrada*, *Semiphyllidiana*, *Semiplantigrada*; **semi-nymph** [= F. *semi-nymphe*], a nymph of such insects as undergo only a slight change in passing to the imago state.

1886 Kipling *General Summary* in *Departmental Ditties*, We are very slightly changed From the *semi-apes who ranged Pre-historic India. **1886** Seebohm in *Ibis* July 227 The four groups of which we are in search are Stilts, Semi-stilts, Avocets, and *Semi-avocets. **1864–5** Wood *Homes without H.* ii. (1868) 76 Among the *semi-burrowers we may rank the Starling . . as this bird invariably lays its eggs in a hollow of some kind. **1864** *Reader* 23 Apr. 525/3 They [*sc.* the *Lemurini*] are all plantigrade or *semi-digitigrade. **1931** *Semi-dwarf [see Peter Pan 2]. **1959** *Sci. News Let.* 22 Aug. 120/3 Stiff-stemmed semidwarf wheat may be the answer for Pacific Northwest growers whose wheat suffers extensively from lodging. **1979** *Nature* 3 May 7/1 In India . . rice research has tended to focus on light-yielding semi-dwarfs for irrigated land. **1880** Newton in *Encycl. Brit.* XI. 760/2 The group of *Semi-egrets, containing some nine or ten forms. **1900** B. D. Jackson *Gloss. Bot. Terms*, **Semilichen*, Zukal's term for forms which when destitute of their appropriate Alga can subsist as saprophytes. **1880** *Libr. Univ. Knowl.* I. 706 The larva [of southern army-worm or cotton-worm] is a *semi-looper. **1899** D. Sharp *Insects* vi. 415 When the abdominal legs are reduced in number (*Plusia*, e.g.) the larvae are said to be Half-loopers, or Semi-loopers, as they assume to some extent the peculiar mode of progression of the Geometrid larvae, which are known as Loopers. **1815** Kirby & Sp. *Entomol.* iii. (1818) I. 68 Those of the Linnean order Hemiptera . . to which the name of semi-complete pupæ was applied by Linné, and that of *semi-nymphs by some other authors. **1868** Watts *Dict. Chem.* IV. 354 Green perfect parasites (*Viscum*), and more or less coloured *semi-parasites (*Melampyrum arvense*). **1878–80** Brady (*title*) Monograph of the Free and *Semi-parasitic Copepoda of the British Islands. **1894** *Proc. Boston Soc. Nat. Hist.* XXVI. 338 The head . . is without a labrum or epipharynx, a loss due to adaptation to its suctorial habits and *semiparasitism. **1839** *Penny Cycl.* XIV. 322/1 Inferobranchians (Phillidians and *Semi-phillidians). **1870** H. A. Nicholson *Man. Zool.* lxxix. (1875) 634 The second family of the *Semi-plantigrade Carnivores is that of the Viverridæ. **1668** Wilkins *Real Char.* 145 *Semirapacious; feeding commonly either on Carrion, or other things, and more seldome on living Animals. **1886** *Semi-stilt [see *semi-avocet* above].

f. In *Anatomy*, chiefly in names (in Latin form, but occas. anglicized) of muscles (*a*) situated partly in a certain region, as ***semi-interrosseus***, ***-spinalis***, or (*b*) being partly of a certain texture or shape, as ***semi-membranosus*** (also ***-membranous***), ***-nervosus***, ***-orbicularis*** (also ***-orbicular***), ***-tendinosus*** (also ***-tendinous***, ***-tendinose***); also ***semi-decussation***, ***-intercostal***, ***-mucous***, ***-sarcodic***; **semi-bulb**, the bulbus vestibuli, either of two vascular bodies on either side of the entrance of the vagina.

1855 Dunglison *Medical Lexicon*, *Semi-bulb of the female, *Bulbus vestibuli*. **1855** Brewster *Newton* I. x. 226 The *semi-decussation of the optic nerves. **1733** Douglas *Winslow's Anat.* (1756) II. 24 *Semi-intercostal Arteries. *Ibid.* I. 202 The Antithenar or Internal *Semi-Interosseus of the Thumb. *Ibid.* 216 *Semi-Membranosus. This is a long thin Muscle, partly Tendinous, from whence it has its name. **1875** Turner in *Encycl. Brit.* I. 841/1 The biceps [is inserted] into the head of the fibula, and semi-tendinosus and semi-membranosus into the upper end of the tibia. **1896** Treves *Syst. Surg.* II. 31 An enlargement of the bursa between the semi-membranosus and inner head of the gastrocnemius. **1758** J. S. *Le Dran's Observ. Surg.* (1771) Dict. Cc8 *Semimembranosus*, the *Semi-membranous Muscle that serves to move the Leg. **1843** Graves *Syst. Clin. Med.* xxvii. 350 The external skin or *semimucous membrane of the male. **1693** tr. *Blancard's Phys. Dict.* (ed. 2), *Seminervosus Musculus*, the *Semi-nervous Muscle. **1704** J. Harris *Lex. Techn.*, **Semi-nervosus, seu Semi-tendinosus*, a Muscle of the Thigh, which is so called from its being half Tendinous and Nerve-like. **1733** Douglas *Winslow's Anat.* (1756) II. 346 The superior *Semi-Orbicular Muscle is oftentimes broader than the inferior. *Ibid.*, The *Semi-Orbiculares are commonly looked upon as one Muscle, surrounding both Lips, from whence it is called Orbicularis. **1879** tr. *De Quatrefages' Hum. Spec.* 4 The *semi-sarcodic substance which surrounds their siliceous or horny skeleton. **1753** *Chambers's Cycl.* Suppl., **Semispinalis*, a muscle, called also *transverso-spinalis dorsi*. **1875** Turner in *Encycl. Brit.* I. 835/1 The semispinales, multifidi and rotatores spinæ muscles. **1704** *Semitendinosus [see *seminervosus*]. **1733** Douglas *Winslow's Anat.* (1756) I. 215 This Tendon is inserted . . above the Semi-Tendinosus. **1875** Turner in *Encycl. Brit.* I. 841/1 The action of the sartorius, gracilis and semi-tendinosus, which are inserted close together into the tibia. **1733** Douglas *Winslow's Anat.* (1756) I. §677 The Muscles which move the Vertebræ of the Back and Loins . . were they to be reckoned separately as Vertebral or *Semi-Vertebral Muscles.

g. In *Pathology* and *Therapeutics*, as ***semi-albinism***, ***-coma***, ***-comatose***, ***-confluent***, ***-fluctuant***, ***-fluctuating***, ***-hepatization***, ***-luxation***, ***-malignant***, ***-narcosis***, ***-pectoral***, ***-prone*** (whence ***-pronation***), ***-recumbent***, ***-supination***.

1898 *Syd. Soc. Lex.*, **Semi-albinism*, a half-white condition of the skin, sometimes occurring in negroes. **1897** *Allbutt's Syst. Med.* II. 202 Delirium . . verging into *semi-coma. **1878** A. M. Hamilton *Nervous Dis.* 36 She complained of vertical headache, became *semi-comatose. **1887** *Cassell's Encycl. Dict.*, **Semiconfluent*, half confluent. Used spec. of a kind of small-pox. **1897** *Allbutt's Syst. Med.* II. 1137 An elastic *semifluctuant sensation on percussion. **1872** T. Bryant *Pract. Surg.* 734 Fixed *semifluctuating growths. **1879** *St. George's Hosp. Rep.* IX. 73 *Semi-hepatization of left lung. **1898** *Syd. Soc. Lex.*, **Semi-luxation*, a syn. for *Sub-luxation*. **1864** Erichsen *Sci. & Art Surg.* (ed. 4) 469 *Semi-Malignant Tumours. **1937** Koestler *Spanish Testament* ii. 235 That merciful state of *semi-narcosis induced by . . spinning illusions. **1965** J. Pollitt *Depression & its Treatment* v. 67 In very severe cases, continuous sleep (continuous narcosis) or continuous semi-narcosis with chlorpromazine and small amounts of Sodium Amytal must be given. **1881** *Trans. Obstetr. Soc. Lond.* XXII. 284 The patient resting either in the *semi-prone or *semi-pectoral position. **1898** *Syd. Soc. Lex.*, **Semipronation*, the Semi-prone position, or the assuming of that position. **1875** Bedford *Sailor's Pocket Bk.* viii. (ed. 2) 308 The individual should be placed in a *semi-recumbent position. **1889** *Buck's Handbk. Med. Sci.* VIII. 534 When the hand is *semisupinated, *i.e.*, with the radius and ulna parallel. **1898** *Syd. Soc. Lex.*, **Semisupination*, half-supination. A position halfway between supination and lying on the side.

h. In *Chemistry*, as ***semi-acid***, ***-acidified***, ***-carbonization***, †***-oxidated***, ***-oxidized***, ***-oxygenated***, ***-oxygenized***, †***-phlogisticated***, †***-saline***, ***-reduced***; in the designation of a class of compounds, as ***semi-benzidam***, ***-glutin*** (see quot. 1879), ***semi-naphthalidine***; also **semialdehyde**, a derivative of a compound containing two identical functional groups (e.g. a dicarboxylic acid) in which one of the groups has been converted into an aldehyde group; †**semi-carbonate**, a subcarbonate; **semi-combined** *a.*, partially or loosely combined; **semi-covalent** *a.*, having some covalent character; **semi-normal** *a.* (see quot.).

1880 *Webster's Suppl.*, **Semiacid*. **1796** Kirwan *Elem. Min.* (ed. 2) II. 91 The Calx which is certainly *semi-acidified. **1942** *Jrnl. Biol. Chem.* CXLV. 69 In the presence of this enzyme . . α-ketoglutaric acid formed succinic *semi-aldehyde and CO_2. **1976** *Nature* 16 Dec. 652/2 GABA concentrations were measured using GABA transferose and succinic semialdehyde dehydrogenase to generate NADH, which was measured spectrofluorometrically. **1868** Watts *Dict. Chem.* V. 233 *Semibenzidam, this name was given by Zinin to a compound produced by the action of sulphide of ammonium on dinitrobenzene. **1808** *Phil. Trans.* XCVIII. 98 A saturated soda . . becomes a true *semi-carbonate by being exposed . . to a red heat. **1804** *Ibid.* XCIV. 400 Woody fibre in a state of *semicarbonization. **1965** Phillips & Williams *Inorg. Chem.* I. v. 156 *Semi-covalent bonding involving *d* orbitals may also be expected to lead to high coordination numbers for early members of the transition series. **1879** *Encycl. Brit.* X. 132/2 Two distinct substances could be separated, one precipitable by perchloride of platinum, which he [Hofmeister] calls *semiglutin, and the other . . which he calls hemicollin. **1852** W. Gregory *Handbk. Org. Chem.* 344 *Seminaphtalidine, $C_{10}H_5N$, is obtained when nitronaphtalèse is treated by Zinin's process. **1868** Watts *Dict. Chem.* V. 233 *Seminaphthylamine, $C^{10}H^8N^2$ . .; also called Seminaphthalidine, Semi-naphthalidam, and Azonaphthylamine. . . A base produced by the action of sulphydrate of ammonium on dinitronaphthalene. **1896** Gould *Student's Med. Dict.*, **Seminormal Solution*, one containing in solution half the quantity of the substance contained in the normal solution. **1965** *Semi-oxidized [see *semi-reduced* below]. **1794** Kirwan *Elem. Min.* (ed. 2) I. 365 Moist *semi-oxygenated calces of iron. *a* **1846** Ure (cited by Worcester), **Semi-oxygenized*. **1805** Saunders *Min. Waters* 556 A very soluble *semi-oxydated calx. **1828–32** Webster, **Semiphlogisticated*, partially impregnated with phlogiston. **1965** Phillips & Williams *Inorg. Chem.* I. x. 386 The anaerobic system . . tends to yield acetic acid, alcohol, and similar semi-oxidized and *semi-reduced compounds. **1799** *Med. Jrnl.* I. 379 The neutral and *semi-saline combinations before specified.

i. In *Geology*, *Mineralogy*, and *Geography*, as ***semi-aluminous***, ***-calcareous***, ***-compact***(***ed***, ***-deltaic***, ***-desert***, ***-extinct***, ***-fossil***, ***-granitic***, ***-hard***, ***-indurated***, ***-lapidified***, ***-mineralized***, ***-porphyritic***, ***-stratified***, ***-volcanic*** adjs.; **semi-anthracite**, **semi-bituminous** *a.* (see quot.); †**semiprimigenous** *a.*, applied by Kirwan to formations intermediate between the primary and the secondary; †**semiprotolite** (Kirwan), a 'semi-primigenous' fossil.

1841 Miller *Old Red Sandstone* vi. (1887) 127 The stratified clay is mottled by layers of *semi-aluminous, semi-calcareous nodules. **1858** H. D. Rogers *Geol. Pennsylv.* II. II. 990 The Anthracites being properly separable into Hard Anthracites and *Semi-anthracites; the Bituminous Coals into dry or *Semi-bituminous, and fat or true Bituminous Coals. **1841** *Semi-calcareous [see *semi-aluminous*]. **1794** Kirwan *Elem. Min.* (ed. 2) I. 158 A *semicompact mass of the nature of porcelain. **1796** *Ibid.* II. 348 A *semi-compacted coagulated mass. **1849** Dana *Geol.* vii. (1850) 433 The *semi-continent New Holland. **1898** *Engineering Mag.* XVI. 106 Rivers may be divided into four great classes: (1) the tidal; (2) the deltaic; (3) the *semi-deltaic; and (4) the torrential. **1849** Dana *Geol.* ix. (1850) 455 The *semi-desert of California. **1903** W. R. Fisher tr. *Schimper's Plant Geog.* 163 Transition forms between desert on the one hand, and woodland or grassland on the other, are termed semi-deserts. **1839** G. Roberts *Dict. Geol.*, *Solfatara*, a *semi-extinct volcano, emitting only gaseous sulphurous exhalations, and aqueous vapours. **1896** H. Woodward *Guide Fossil Reptiles Brit. Mus.* 93 Teeth of Sharks . . in a *semi-fossil state. **1791** Beddoes in *Phil. Trans.* LXXXI. 50 *Semi-granitic, porphyritic, and common whinstone. **1811** Pinkerton *Petral.* II. 197 A little more than *semi-hard, only being capable of being scratched with the point of a knife. **1794** Kirwan *Elem. Min.* (ed. 2) I. 76 Mild Calx in a loose or *semi-indurated form. **1799** Kirwan *Geol. Ess.* 236 Hills of *semi-lapidified marl. **1802** Playfair *Illustr. Hutton. Theory* 153 This *semi-mineralized coal. **1839** De la Beche *Rep. Geol. Cornwall*, etc. iii. 83 Some very remarkable rocks with a *semi-porphyritic character. **1799** Kirwan *Geol. Ess.* 44 *Semi-primigenous strata (Todliegendes). *Ibid.* 307 After this shale and coal alternate until all terminate in red *semiprotolite. **1890** Dana

Charact. Volcanoes 23 The eruptions are only *semi-volcanic.

j. In names of articles or processes of manufacture: **semi-china, -porcelain**, ware resembling china, etc., but having an inferior glaze, finish, etc.; **semi-coke**, a smokeless fuel that leaves little ash, made from coal by carbonization at a low temperature (usu. 500–600°C); **semi-coking** *a.*, designating a coal that is intermediate between a good coking coal and one that does not produce coke; **semi-steel**, a low-carbon cast iron produced by melting mild steel with pig iron in a furnace; **semi-water-gas**, a fuel gas made by blowing a mixture of steam and air into a producer.

1786 Cavallo in *Phil. Trans.* LXXVII. 9 The *semi-calcined part floats at the top. **1825** J. Nicholson *Oper. Mech.* 482 The blue printed tea-ware has recently obtained the name of *semi-china, owing to its being, when well fired, very fine, white and neat, and possessing some degree of transparency. **1918** *Chem. & Metallurgical Engin.* XIX. 580/1 Charles Howard Smith..proposed to get an intermediate soft 16 to 20 per cent volatile *semi-coke. **1972** Harker & Allen *Fuel Sci.* v. 70 The tar and most of the volatile matter are driven off leaving a material known as 'semi-coke'. **1915** *Iron & Coal Trades Rev.* XCI. 421/2 No serious attempts have hitherto been made to utilise in the low-temperature system non-coking and *semi-coking coals for the production of oils. **1977** *Jrnl. R. Soc. Arts* CXXV. 64/2 High grade coke can be made from a coal mixture including a proportion of only semi-coking coal. **1892** *Labour Commission* Gloss., **Semi-dried bricks*, bricks manufactured from clay, one half dry and the other half damp. **1878** *Encycl. Brit.* VIII. 188/2 The *semi-dry or 'dust' process of manufacturing encaustic tiles. **1897** Sparkes & Gandy *Potters* 40 The kind of *semi-glaze known as a 'smear'. **1893** Barber *Pottery & Porcel.* 391 The *semi-glazed old-gold color of the adjacent terra-cotta. **1886** *Guide Exhib. Galleries Brit. Mus.* 210 The pottery *semi-porcelain, and porcelain known as Kutani ware, made in the province of Kaga. **1908** *Ch. Times* 20 Mar. 394/2 Pretty novelties in semi-porcelain. **1858** *Q. Jrnl. Chem. Soc.* X. 145 Mr. Bessemer claims the production..of a particular product called *semi-steel. **1861** Fairbairn *Iron* 141 What he [Bessemer] calls semi-steel. **1929** *Iron & Steel Industry* III. 35 The metallurgist has long regarded the term 'semi-steel' as a misnomer, although the use of the term within the foundry business is harmless when it is simply made to imply the use of steel in a cast iron mixture... Instead, we have at present the innuendo that 'semi-steel' is more or less a definite iron-carbon alloy of superior properties compared to cast iron, whereas it is in reality an 'unknown quantity'. **1958** *Engineering* 21 Mar. 384/2 The bottom grate is of heat resistant 30 per cent chrome semi-steel and is reversible for burning coal or coke. **1910** *Encycl. Brit.* (ed. 11) XI. 286/1 *Semi-water gas is especially adapted for the purpose of driving gas-engines on the explosive principle (gas motors).

k. Denoting styles of architecture having only some of the features connoted by the second element, as ***semi-classic, -Gothic, -Norman***.

1843 Bloxam *Gothic Archit.* (ed. 5) 219 Key-stones after the Roman or Italian *semi-classic style. **1768** *Acct. Denmark* 94 The royal palace of Rosenburg..is a handsome structure in the *semi Gothic taste. **1925** F. Madan *Oxf. outside Guide-Books* (ed. 2) 186 The Firm's premises..were entirely rebuilt and included the present 'semi-Gothic' elevation. **1829** Bloxam *Gothic Archit.* 31 *Semi-Norman Pointed Arch.

l. In names of mechanical contrivances (see quots.). Cf semi-automatic *a.*

1884 Knight *Dict. Mech.* Suppl. 796 **Semifixed*, said of a steam engine bolted to an iron foundation piece on which it may be moved intact. *Ibid.*, **Semi-multi-flue Boiler*, a flue-plate is fixed in the flue a short distance behind the furnace, and a number of wrought-iron or brass flues pass from this to the back of the boiler. *Ibid.*, **Semi-multi-tubular Boiler*, a term applied to those boilers in which a portion of the cylindrical shell is occupied by flues. **1753** *Chambers's Cycl.* Suppl., **Semireverberatory fire*, in chemistry, a term used to express such a reverberatory fire, in which the flame is only beaten back upon the bottom of the vessel.

9. Miscellaneous: **semi-active** *a.*, designating a method of missile guidance in which the missile responds to a signal transmitted from elsewhere and reflected by the target; **semi-antique** *a.*, of a rug or carpet: between fifty and one hundred years old; also *absol.* as *sb.*; **semi-armour-piercer, -piercing**, applied to a kind of shell for perforating some thickness of armour plate; **semi-Bantu** *a.*, of or pertaining to a number of languages in Central and West Africa closely related to the Bantu family; also as *sb.*; **semi-basement**, a basement room or rooms set only partially below ground level; †**semi-brick** [after L. *sēmilater*], a half-baked brick; **semi-broch** *Archæol.*, in the Hebrides and western mainland of Scotland: a hollow-walled fort-like structure representing a stage of development between the galleried dun and the broch; **semi-bull** *R.C. Ch.*, a bull issued by a pope before his coronation (Cass.); **semi-cardinal**, applied to the points of the compass half-way between the cardinal points, as NE.; **semi-cell** *Bot.*, each of the two parts of a cell which is constricted in the middle, as in desmids; **semi-chemical** *a.*, applied to (wood pulp made by) a pulping process in which wood chips are subjected to mild chemical delignification followed by mechanical processing; †**semi-cipher**, *fig.* a nothing or nobody; **semi-classical** *a.*, (*a*) *gen.*, esp. in *Music*; (*b*) *Physics*, designating a theory that is intermediate in its assumptions and methods between the classical, or Newtonian, description and that of modern physics, esp. in quantum mechanics and relativity; hence **semi-classically** *adv.*; **semi-closed** *a.*, (*a*) *Fortif.* (see quot.); (*b*) *Med.*, applied to methods of administering anæsthetics employing a gas supply that is closed from the atmosphere and in excess of the patient's needs, the excess being vented to the atmosphere; (cf. open *a.* 11 h, semi-open *a.*); †**semi-commoner**, a demy of Magdalen College, Oxford; **semi-cretin**, 'a variety of cretin who can speak in a rudimentary way and can appreciate his everyday bodily necessities' (*Syd. Soc. Lex.* 1898); **semi-cursive** *a. Palæogr.*, of or pertaining to one of various scripts combining cursive features with elements of a more formal style; also *absol.* as *sb.*; **semi-definite** *a. Logic*, implying 'some but not all'; **semi-diesel, -Diesel** *a.*, of an engine: (see quot. 1974); also as *sb.*, an engine of this type; **semi-display** *Typogr.*, a lay-out (for advertisements, etc.) intermediate between the run-on and displayed styles; hence **semi-displayed** *a.*; **semi-documentary** *a.*, of or pertaining to a film that presents factual or semi-factual material in fictional form; also as *sb.*; **semi-empirical** *a.*, that derives in part from theoretical considerations and in part from the results of experiment; so **semi-empirically** *adv.*; **semi-evening dress** (also **gown**, etc.), (a) fashionable dress (gown, etc.) of less than fully formal design suitable for both afternoon and evening wear; also *ellipt.* as **semi-evening** *sb.*; **semi-fabricated** *a.*, (of a material) formed into some standard shape for use in the making of finished articles; so **semifabricator**, a manufacturer of semifabricated goods; **semi-final**, in football and other contests, the match or round immediately preceding the final one; **semi-finalist**, a competitor in a semi-final; **semifinished** *a.*, (of a material, esp. steel) manufactured or treated for use in the making of finished articles; **semi-gloss** *a.*, designating a finish intermediate between matt and glossy; **semi-grand** *a.* and *sb.*, a modified form of the grand piano; **semi-high** *a.* = *half-high* (see half- 4); **semi-hoop**, a semicircular arc or arch; **semi-intensive** *a. Agric.*, of or pertaining to a method of rearing livestock that includes features of intensive farming; **semi-island, -islet**, a piece of land that becomes insular at high tide; **semileptonic** *a. Particle Physics*, involving both leptons and hadrons; hence **semileptonically** *adv.*; **semi-logical** *a.* (see quot.); **semi-main** *U.S.* = repêchage; **semi-manufacture**, a product made from raw materials and used in the manufacture of finished goods; **semi-mute** *a.* and *sb.*, applied to those who, through deafness, speak only imperfectly; **semi-portal** *a.*, applied to a crane mounted on a frame consisting essentially of a horizontal member supported at one end by an upright; **semi-precious** *a.*, (of stones) that may be cut and polished but are not of sufficient value to rank as gems; **semi-proletariat** *Communism* [tr. Chinese *bànwúchǎnjiējí* (1926 Mao Zedong)], the class of poor peasants and others intermediate between the proletariat and the petty bourgeoisie; **semi-proof**, proof depending on the evidence of a single witness; **semi-psychic** *adv.* and *a. Bridge*, (see quot. 1964); **semi-quantitative** *a.*, partly quantitative; approximate; based on or yielding approximate figures; hence **semi-quantitatively** *adv.*; **semi-reflecting** *a.*, designating a material of low reflectivity (usu. a film deposited on a transparent base) which permits partial reflection and partial transmission; hence **semi-reflection**; **semi-reflective** *a.*; **semi-reflector**; **semi-scale**, half or some fraction of full-scale; usu. *attrib.*; **semi-sequitur** [after *non sequitur*], an inference or conclusion which is related only indirectly to the premisses; **semi-sub**, short for *semi-submersible* sb.; **semi-submersible** *a.* and *sb.*, (applied to) an offshore drilling platform or barge equipped with submerged hollow pontoons that can be flooded with water when the vessel is anchored on site in order to give it stability against waves and wind; **semi-synthetic** *a.*, that is a mixture of synthetic and natural materials, or has been prepared by artificial modification of a natural material; that is a combination of synthetic and natural processes; †**semi-time**, 'half a time' (see Rev. xii. 14 and cf. Dan. vii. 25, xii. 7); **semi-tint** (see quot. 1752; = *half-tint*); **semi-tropic(al** *a.*, subtropical; so **semi-tropics**; **semi-truck** *U.S.*, = semi-trailer; **semi-variable** *a. Econ.*, of a cost (see quot. 1965); **semi-works** *U.S.*, a manufacturing plant used to develop and perfect a new product or process after testing in a pilot plant and before full-scale production; usu. *attrib.*

1954 K. W. Gatland *Devel. Guided Missile* (ed. 2) iii. 83 Final guidance is obtained by the technique known as '*semi-active homing', the missile responding to target reflection from the ground radar. **1945** G. G. Lewis *Pract. Bk. Oriental Rugs* (ed. 6) v. ii. 304 Antique or *semi-antique Chinese rugs are as scarce as hen's teeth. **1970** J. Franses *European & Oriental Rugs* 3 Its wool is hand-spun on all the early carpets and semi-antiques. **1979** *Tucson Mag.* Apr. 23/1 The semi-antique Iranian prize rug was rolled up. **1895** *Daily News* 14 Nov. 6/5 This company was supplying *semi-armour-piercers, built to perforate a considerable thickness of armour and to burst sufficiently inside. **1898** *Westm. Gaz.* 9 June 5/1 *Semi-armour piercing shell and other ammunition. **1919** H. H. Johnston *Compar. Study Bantu & Semi-Bantu Languages* ii. 17 The *semi-Bantu languages on this north-west borderland have a vocabulary which contains a greater or smaller amount of Bantu roots. *Ibid.* 814 The Indiki language of the southern Maneñguba country [is an]..interesting form of Semi-Bantu. **1977** *Language* LIII. 291 Bantu and Semi-Bantu classifiers do have meaning. **1934** in Webster, *Semi-basement. **1963** *Punch* 20 Nov. 729/1 Desks crowded among filing cabinets in semi-basement. **1974** *Country Life* 7 Mar. (Suppl.) 32l/1 Semi-basement boiler/drying room, playroom. **1601** Holland *Pliny* xix. x. II. 32 Water wherein the pouder of a *semi-bricke or halfe-baked tile is mingled. **1903** E. Beveridge *Coll & Tiree* x. 73 *The *Semi-broch type.* It may be bold to introduce a new name in our description of the Tiree Duns, but a type seems to occur here which is.. distinct from the ruder Hill-Forts. **1963** *Times* 16 Feb. 10/4 Tiree has some 20 dun sites, of which four appear to be hollow-walled semi-brochs. **1980** *Glasgow Archaeol. Jrnl.* VII. 73/1 There are only three semibrochs on the whole of the NW coast of Scotland. **1653** R. G. tr. *Bacon's Hist. Winds* 20 Let Cardinall windes be those which blow from corners or Angles of the World: *Semi-cardinall, those which blow in the halfe wards of those. **1872** H. C. Wood *Contrib. Hist. Fresh-Water Algæ N. Amer.* 101 Divided into two symmetrical *semi-cells. **1927** West & Fritsch *Treat. Brit. Freshwater Algæ* 259 The young semicells are clearly recognisable and nuclear division is complete before any change takes place in the chloroplasts of the parent. **1969** F. E. Round *Introd. Lower Plants* ii. 27 Each mature semicell is ornamented or produced into spines and looked at from the apices is constructed on a bilateral..or triangular basis. **1925** *Paper Trade Jrnl.* 15 Oct. 57/1 The various processes ..for the production of semi-cellulose as above defined may conveniently be termed *semi-chemical inking processes, as they consist essentially of some chemical treatment combined with a mechanical disintegration of the partially cooked wood. **1961** *Times* 2 June 26/2 A new semi-chemical pulp mill to use indigenous woods. **1974** *Sci. Amer.* Apr. 56/3 Semichemical processes are applied mainly to hardwoods because of the lower content of lignin in such wood. ?**1550** R. Bieston *Bayte Fortune* A iij, Loe there goeth a *semesypher in algorisme, There goeth a wretch, a foole, and a barat bringer. **1949** *Billboard* 2 Apr. 34/3 Albums listed are those classical and *semi-classical albums selling best in the nation's retail record stores. **1964** J. W. Linnett *Electronic Struct. Molecules* i. 6 In quantum mechanics the orbits of the Bohr-Sommerfeld semi-classical methods are replaced by orbitals. **1970** G. K. Woodgate *Elem. Atomic Struct.* i. 4 Another important quantity corresponds *semi-classically to the speed of the electron in the first Bohr orbit as a fraction of the speed of light. **1888** *Pall Mall Gaz.* 12 June 3/2 The works in which these guns should..be mounted..must be of the kind known technically as '*semi-closed', strong enough to prevent a detachment taking them in the rear. **1914** J. T. Gwathmey *Anesthesia* vi. 272 Semi-Closed method.—Martin Ware has reported one or two thousand cases without a fatality. **1977** *Proc. R. Soc. Med.* LXX. 784/2 Anaesthesia with spontaneous breathing usually employs a semi-closed circuit. **1691** Wood *Ath. Oxon.* I. 14 William Lilye was.. Elected one of the Demies or *Semi-commoners of St. Mary Magd. Coll. in 1486. **1715** M. Davies *Athen. Brit.* I. 36 The foresaid William Grocyn, became a Divine or Semicommoner of St. Mary Magdalen College, Oxon. **1927** *Bull. Bezan Club* IV. 11 These lines, on both the Greek and Latin sides, are written not in a stiff, formal book-script, but in an easy-going *semi-cursive. **1948** D. Diringer *Alphabet* II. x. 545 The Italian semi-cursive minuscule..developed from the Roman minuscule, was employed throughout Italy from the seventh to the ninth century, and continued to be used in Tuscany until the twelfth century. **1968** *PMLA* LXXXIII. 23/1 The script..may be described as an upright, bold but somewhat ungainly *cursiva* (*anglicana*) *formata*, or semi-cursive in older and looser nomenclature. *a* **1856** Sir W. Hamilton *Logic* App. (1860) II. 279 Here *some* may mean *some only—some not all.* Here *some*, though always in a certain degree indefinite, is definite so far as it excludes omnitude,—is used in opposition to all. This I would call its *Semi-definite meaning. **1864** Bowen *Logic* v. 137 Whenever we predicate a Genus of a Species, the Predicate is obviously quantified as Particular; and *some*, which is the predesignation of particularity, must then be thought in its semi-definite sense. **1911** *Engineer* 7 June 27/1 (*caption*) *Semi-Diesel oil engine. **1920** R. A. McMillan *Guide to B.O.T. Exam. for Extra First-Class Engineers* xv. 396 A common type of Semi-Diesel is the Bolinder engine. **1960** G. Blanchet *Search in North* i. 19 From the engine exhaust came the hollow staccato of the semi-diesel. **1974** *McGraw-Hill Dict. Sci. & Techn. Terms* 1323/2 *Semidiesel engine.* 1. An internal combustion engine of a type resembling the diesel engine in using heavy oil as fuel but employing a lower compression pressure and spraying it under pressure, against a hot (uncooled) surface or spot, or igniting it by the precombustion or supercompression of a portion of the charge in a separate member or uncooled portion of the combustion chamber. 2. A true diesel engine that uses a means other than compressed air for fuel injection. **1971** *Cabinet Maker & Retail Furnisher* 24 Sept. 537 Run-on and *Semi-display Announcements are set only in Times Bold and Times Roman. **1976** *Horse & Hound* 10 Dec. 65/1 (Advt.), Advertisers wishing to take a smaller space may use semi display with a minimum size of 2 cms but no blocks or illustrations are permissible in this style. **1972** *Daily Tel.* 5 July 6 *Run-on* (minimum setting) and **semi-displayed* (with lines of white space, indents, or double-line capitals)—£1.40 per line. **1939** L. Jacobs *Rise of Amer. Film* 413 Allied in spirit to the *semi-documentary films were the realistic regional dramas. **1948** L. Levy *Music for Movies* xiii. 131 (*heading*) The semi-documentary. **1958** *New Statesman* 3 May 567/3 Granada's main achievement is to prove that serious semi-documentary or discussion programmes (*Under Fire, Youth wants to Know, What the Papers Say*) can be successful entertainment. **1935** Condon & Shortley *Theory of Atomic Spectra* i. 9 The results.. were obtained in *semi-empirical ways from consideration of a formulation of the theory that was only true in the limit of large quantum numbers. **1970** Semi-empirical [see *pre-exponential* s.v. pre- B. 1 d]. **1976** *Physical Rev. Lett.* XXXVI. 375/1 We may now *semiempirically incorporate the major factor neglected so far. **1917** *Vogue* Early Apr. 3/1 *Semi-evening or Afternoon Gown in best quality Chiffon Taffetas and Ninon de Soie. **1923** A. Huxley *Antic Hay* x. 156 For semi-evening dress, shell rims with gold ear-pieces. **1923** B. Ruck *Dancing Star* i. vi. 117 Ripple's frock was the kind of garment dear to the compromise-loving British heart. It was '*a semi-evening*', which, to a purist, means that the dress is appropriate neither to evening or afternoon. **1938** E. Bowen *Death of Heart* i. ix. 155 She asked me to come to Peter Jones's with her to help her choose a semi-evening dress. *a* **1976** A. Christie *Autobiogr.* (1977) iii. iv. 155, I had a pale grey *crêpe de Chine* semi-evening dress. **1947** J. Newton *Introd. Metallurgy* (ed. 2) v. 238 Rolling not only produces finished shapes such as plates, sheets,.. and rails, but many *semifabricated shapes such as steel, copper, and brass rod for wire drawing; steel billets for forging and piercing. **1976** *Scotsman* 24 Dec. 4/5 Alcan (US), are also to raise prices for their semifabricated aluminium products. **1967** *Economist* 29 July 425/3 Hitherto most of this east European aluminium has been bought by the giant non-American producers... It has then either been passed on to their own *semi-fabricators or sold to the independent semi-fabricators at the official producers' price. **1884** *Truth* 13 Mar. 369/2 The *semi-final tie between Notts County and the Blackburn Rovers. **1895** *Daily News* 21 Feb. 5/5 Sunderland, the favourites for the trophy,..are pretty certain to obtain a place in the semi-final. **1898** *Semi-finalist [see -ist 4 b]. **1922** *Daily Mail* 24 Nov. 11 Beaten semi-finalists. **1972** D. Delman *Sudden Death* (1973) ii. 39 The year before he'd been champion at Wimbledon and a semi-finalist at Forest Hills. **1942** *R.A.F. Jrnl.* 16 May (*verso rear cover*), Germany would have to supply raw materials and *semi-finished products. **1959** [see *forge-master* s.v. forge *sb.* 6 b]. **1972** *Daily Tel.* 9 Feb. 2/4 The plastics industry expects that about 50 per cent. of finished and semi-finished products will be wholly or partially metricated by mid-1971. **1963** *Times* 8 Jan. 11/2 A mid-tone matt or *semi-gloss single colour. **1835** *Court Mag.* VI. 220/2 Several *semi-grands were also shown to us: these were equal in power to ordinary grand piano-fortes, but with a lengthened undulation of sound. **1842** *Penny Mag.* 30 Apr. 172/1 The semi-grand pianoforte. **1875** Browning *Inn Album* ii. 45 A brand-new bore she calls a 'semi-grand'. **1905** *Daily Chron.* 2 Nov. 3/5 *Semi-high bodices. **1687** Wood *Life* (O.H.S.) III. 226 They caused.. the forefront..of the arches of the several gates to be trimmed up with bowes and green leaves tied to a *semi-hoop. **1835-6** *Todd's Cycl. Anat.* I. 283/2 In the true *Rasores* ..the posterior lateral processes pass backwards exterior to the ribs, supporting them in the Capercailzie, like a semi-hoop. **1935** J. S. Hicks *Encycl. Poultry* II. 509 A *semi-intensive house may be of any size from one, say, 6 ft. by 6 ft. by 6 ft., capable of housing ten or a dozen birds, to a mammoth affair for the accommodation of 500 or more layers. **1966** *Economist* 1 Oct. 72/2 Beef growers are turning to what is termed 'semi-intensive' beef rearing instead. This combines intensive grazing with fattening on high protein compounds to produce a 15- to 18-month-old beast for market. **1870** F. R. Wilson *Ch. Lindisf.* 20 The Venerable Bede writes of Lindisfarne as a *semi-island. **1867** Smyth *Sailor's Word-bk.*, **Semi-islet*, an old term for *bridge-islet*. **1965** *Physical Rev. Lett.* XIV. 51 (*heading*) SU(6) and *semileptonic interactions. **1979** *Nature* 14 June 588/2 If the D decays *semi-leptonically some of its energy is taken by the unobserved neutrino. **1827** Whately *Logic* (ed. 2) 138 The other kind [of Logical Fallacies] may be most properly called *semi-logical; *viz.* all the cases of ambiguous middle Term except its non-distribution. **1968** *Surfer Mag.* Jan. 48/1 Overland finally got into the finals by winning the men's *semi-main. **1979** *Tucson* (Arizona) *Citizen* 28 Apr. 2b/5 The top two finishers in the consolation and 25-lap semi-main will qualify for the final run for the lion's share of the $12,000 purse. **1935** *Economist* 16 Feb. 353/1 Japan is exporting more finished goods and manufactured foodstuffs, importing more raw materials and *semi-manufactures. **1979** *Shell Trade in Eastern Europe* (Shell Internat. Petroleum Co.) 3 Historically, Eastern European exports to the West have been principally raw materials, semi-manufactures, fuels and agricultural produce. **1864** Webster, **Semi-mute*. **1896** *Godey's Mag.* Feb. 163/1 The oral work which was at first only done for the benefit of semi-mutes. **1908** A. Tolhausen tr. *Böttcher's Cranes* vi. 256 (*heading*) *Semi-portal travelling crane, with central steam supply station. **1958** *Times Rev. Industry* Oct. 20/3 Electric semi-portal cranes serving three transit sheds. **1905** *Bookman* June 83/1 Metal clasps set with *semi-precious stones. **1951** tr. M. Litvinoff in J. Degras *Soviet Documents on Foreign Policy* I. 136 This new apparatus of power should embody the dictatorship of the working class (and in some places also the rural *semi-proletariat, i.e. the poor peasants). **1965** J. Ch'ên *Mao & Chinese Revolution* (1967) i. v. 110 The semi-proletariat, according to Mao, consisted of the overwhelming majority of the semi-tenant peasants, poor peasants, handicraftsmen, shop assistants and pedlars. **1975** J. De Bres tr. *Mandel's Late Capitalism* xi. 362 Many of the producers in the export branch are recruited from the stratum of the semi-proletariat who engage in wage labour only to obtain a supplementary income to eke out their means of subsistence in agriculture. **1728** Chambers *Cycl.*, **Semiproof*, an imperfect Proof. The Depositions of a single Evidence only make a Semi-proof. **1856** Bouvier *Law Dict.* (ed. 6), *Semi-proof*. Presumptions of fact are so called. **1960** T. Reese *Play Bridge with Reese* 118 Unless he has opened *semi-psychic he should have both the minor suit Queens. **1962** *Listener* 3 May 790/3 North opened with a semi-psychic One Club. **1964** *Official Encycl. Bridge* 493/2 *Semi-psychic*, a departure from normal bidding methods which is not a complete bluff but is still intended to deceive the opponents. The term usually refers to an opening bid well below minimum values, but lead-inhibiting bids belong in the same category. **1929** Parker & Crozier in C. Murchison *Found. Exper. Psychol.* viii. 362 The comparison of odors is possible, in an empirically *semi-quantitative way, by the use of several such instruments. **1977** *Sci. Amer.* May 39/2 The first semiquantitative step in generalizing the theory of crystalline semiconductors to amorphous materials was taken by Sir Nevill Mott of the University of Cambridge. **1956** *Nature* 21 Jan. 127/1 The intermediate products formed in the hydrolysis of the cyclic oligomers of ϵ-caprolactam..have been identified and *semi-quantitatively determined. **1927** *Jrnl. Sci. Instruments* IV. 491 (*heading*) *Semi-reflecting surfaces. **1946** *Nature* 20 July 101/2 For glass surfaces that have not been made semi-reflecting these [interference patterns] do not have the contrast of reflected interference patterns. **1976** Z. Knittl *Optics of Thin Films* ix. 374 A common feature of many synthesis problems is the condition for $\tau(\omega^2)$ to be flat in a certain range about $\omega = 0$ and at a certain level. Depending on this level we have the anti-reflection or the *semireflection problem. **1973** *Sci. Amer.* June 69/1 The devices can be made transmissive for rear-lighting applications,..or *semireflective for both kinds of operation. **1945** *Jrnl. Sci. Instruments* XXII. 103/1 Before 1936, the majority of *semi-reflectors were made by chemical deposition of silver. **1976** Z. Knittl *Optics of Thin Films* ix. 397 Chebyshev-type semireflectors..may be only one of the ways of achieving a broad-band maximum. **1946** *Nature* 7 Sept. 337/2 It is impossible in chemical engineering and many other branches of applied science to conduct research entirely in the laboratory; full-scale or *semi-scale plant must be used. **1973** *Ibid.* 2 Feb. 319/1 In 'semi-scale' tests (about a tenth the size of a real reactor) water failed..to stay in the test vessel. **1965** *Punch* 24 Nov. 779/1 The discords between received Edwardian fiction and child-observed fact work as poignantly as ever, as do the *semi-sequiturs: 'He was broad and stout and had a manful way of carelessly swinging his arms that gave him many friends.' **1975** *Offshore Engineer* Sept. 55/1 *Staflo*..and *Sea Quest*..along with the ill-fated *Ocean Prince*, are the only *semi-subs built in the UK. **1962** *World Oil* Sept. 96/3 The rig is an all weather, *semi-submersible which is submerged to the 40 foot level in normal drilling operations. **1963** *World Petroleum* Aug. 47/1 The semi-submersible vessels give a desired balance between cost, safety and performance. **1975** *North Sea Background Notes* (Brit. Petroleum Co.) 11 Semi-submersibles can be used for drilling when resting on the sea bottom, but they are generally employed in the floating position. **1980** *Christian Sci. Monitor* (Mid-western ed.) 4 Dec. 11/1 A third delineation well..was spudded on Nov. 14 five miles west of P-15 by the newly arrived semi-submersible drilling rig. **1946** *Nature* 7 Sept. 350/2 The method may give still better results if..*semi-synthetic mediums are used for the toxin production. **1974** *Ibid.* 19 Apr. 706/2 Rats..were fed a semisynthetic diet for 3 months. **1664** H. More *Exp. 7 Epist.* vi. 105 Those people that keep my works to the end, to the last *semi-time of the Seven, they shall have power over the Pagan Christians. **1685** —— *Paralip. Prophet.* 236 A Semi-time (which I call also, in one word, an Hexamenon). **1752** Chambers *Cycl.*, *Teints*, and **Semi-Teints*, in painting, denote the several colours used in a picture, considered as more or less high, or bright, or deep, or thin, or weakened, and diminished. **1773** *Gentl. Mag.* XLIII. 216 The great lights..are well enough coloured, but the semi-tints..are..without grace or variety. **1853** Kingsley *Hypatia* ix, The balmy *semi-tropic night. **1896** *Yearbk. U.S. Dept. Agric.* 191 The citrus and other semi-tropic fruits. **1856** J. C. Patteson *Let.* 18 June in C. M. Yonge *Life J. C. Patteson* (1874) I. 258 Many New Zealand and many *semi-tropical plants. **1860** [see *semi-alpine* in 1 above]. **1890** 'R. Boldrewood' *Col. Reformer* (1891) 214 The growth of certain semi-tropical crops. **1908** R. W. Chambers *Firing Line* x, These quaint little black quail of the *semi-tropics. **1975** J. Grady *Shadow of Condor* viii. 130 The bus parked between two idling *semi-trucks. **1965** H. K. Compton *Gloss. Purchasing & Supply Managem. Terms.* 123 **Semi-variable cost*, a cost which is partly fixed and partly variable, such as the cost of placing orders, carrying stock, etc., each of which has a fixed cost content, and a variable cost proportional to the volume of throughput. **1971** D. C. Hague *Managerial Econ.* ii. v. 104 Depreciation is a semi-variable cost. **1935** *Industr. & Eng. Chem.* XXVII. 863/2 The main purpose of the *semi-works is the development to a financially profitable stage of those processes which have been initiated in the laboratory. **1945** H. D. Smyth *Gen. Acct. Devel. Atomic Energy Mil. Purposes* vii. 74 These include all aspects of the research, development and semi-works studies necessary for the design, construction, and operation of chain-reacting piles. **1956** A. H. Compton *Atomic Quest* 152 A 'semi-works' installation where they could train the men needed for the final operation and where they could make preliminary tests of their equipment and processes.

semi-'animate, *a.* [f. semi- + animate *a.*, after L. *sēmianimis, -us.*] Half-alive. Also *fig.*

1815 Kirby & Sp. *Entomol.* (1818) I. 58 Should your greenhouse be infested with Aphides, or your grapery by the Semianimate Coccus. **1887** *Pall Mall Gaz.* 27 May 1/1 There are Bills before Parliament... They will remain in their present semi-animate condition. **1908** Saintsbury in *Cambr. Hist. Eng. Lit.* II. 209 The semi-animate condition of the final *-e*.

So **semi-'animated** *a.*

1886 P. Robinson *Teetotum Trees* 96 A cloudy day [will] tempt them out for a semi-animated inspection of the world.

semi'animous, *a. rare.* [f. L. *sēmianim-is, -us* (*anima* life) + -ous.] = prec.

1825 Syd. Smith *Bentham's Bk. Fallacies* Wks. 1859 II. 70/2 Punished by semianimous semicadaverous judges. **1837** —— *2nd Let. Singleton* ibid. 275/1 Semianimous on its back, or vigorous on its legs.

semi-'annual, *a.* (and *sb.*) [semi- 6 b. Cf. L. *sēmi-annus* in sense 2, and F. *semi-annuel.*]

1. Recurring every half-year; half-yearly.

1794 [see semi-diurnal 2]. **1803** *Phil. Trans.* XCIII. 470 Semi-annual solar Equation, Precession, and Refraction. **1860** (*title*) Semi-Annual United States Register. **1866** Crump *Banking* i. 33 Merchants are not in the habit of placing a semi-annual or even annual statement of their position before the public. **1868** *Rep. U.S. Comm. Agric.* (1869) 260 [Esparto] becoming more vigorous and abundant with yearly or semi-annual gathering.

2. Lasting for half a year (only); esp. of plants. Also *sb.* = semi-annual plant.

1882 *Encycl. Brit.* XIV. 857/1 The higher plants may be classed, according to duration of life, as follows:—annuals, or semi-annuals..biennials. **1888** Dawson *Geol. Hist. Plants* 258 Arctic semi-annual days and nights.

So **semi-'annually** *adv.*, every half-year, once in every six months.

1828-32 in Webster. **1889** Farmer *Americanisms* s.v. *Papabotte*, It visits the Western prairies in large numbers semi-annually; early in the spring and late in the summer.

Semi-'Arian, *a.* and *sb.* [ad. eccl. L. *sēmiariānus*: see semi- 8 b and Arian.]

a. *adj.* Partially Arian; used chiefly with reference to a sect which arose in the 4th cent. A.D., holding that the Son is of like substance (ὁμοιούσιος) but not of the same substance (ὁμοούσιος) with the Father. **b.** *sb.* One who holds Semi-Arian views.

a **1616** T. Rogers *39 Art.* v. (1625) 23 Some affirme the holy Ghost to be but a meere creature, as did Arius, the Semiarians [etc.]. **1667** H. More *Div. Dial.* Schol., Wks. (1713) 549 The Semiarians, who affirm'd the Son to be in no wise of the same Substance with the Father, but allowed him in all things to be like him in Substance and Being. **1756-9** A. Butler *Lives of Saints, S. Meletius*, Eustathius, bishop of Sebaste, a semi-Arian. **1781** Gibbon *Decl. & F.* xxi. (1787) II. 267 The Arian and Semi-Arian factions. **1833** J. H. Newman *Arians* iv. ii, The Semi-Arian Creed.

Hence **Semi-'Arianism.**

1819 *Brit. Rev.* XIV. 81 From Calvinism, through the intermediate states of Arianism and Semi-Arianism, into Socinianism, or Unitarianism. **1884** *Cath. Dict.* 50/2 In 359 the Emperor did his utmost to establish Semiarianism, but his efforts were in vain.

semi-'arid, *a.* [semi- 8 i.] Having slightly more precipitation than an arid climate, grasses being the characteristic vegetation.

1898 *Pop. Sci. Monthly* LII. 466 In the semiarid region the struggle for existence is so great. **1916** *Daily Colonist* (Victoria, B.C.) 22 July 4/2 Irrigation is being more and more applied to cultivated lands that are neither arid nor semi-arid. **1941** J. S. Huxley *Uniqueness of Man* ii. 61 The semi-arid bush country provides but scanty nutriment. **1976** *Sci. Amer.* Sept. 99/2 The wheat plant, which dominates the semiarid croplands of the world, fills the need in this area for a cultivated crop with a lower demand for water and a great tolerance of drought.

semi-a'ttached, *ppl. a.* [semi- 1.] Partially or loosely attached; also, = semi-detached (mod. Dicts.).

1860 Thackeray *Lovel* ii, I say, why didn't I say this to her? She would have come, I feel sure she would. We would have been semi-attached as it were. **1860** [Emily Eden] (*title*) The Semi-Attached Couple.

semi-auto'matic, *a.* and *sb.* [semi- 1 a, 8 l.]

A. *adj.* Partially automatic; *spec.* designating a system, device, or machine whose function is not completely automatic.

1890 W. James *Princ. Psychol.* I. 5 The performances of animal *instinct* seem semi-automatic, and the *reflex acts* of self-preservation certainly are so. **1908** J. G. Horner *Encycl. Pract. Engin., Semi-Automatic.*—This is practically identical in meaning with the term self-acting. It signifies a machine, some of the movements only of which are automatic, and which therefore requires constant attendance. **1937** [see chrome *sb.* 1 b]. **1970** *Computers & Humanities* IV. 351 *Scope*: To make more specific and semiautomatic the testing technique of scientific works, intensive critique of books and other lengthy works.

2. Specialized uses. **a.** Of a type of lathe: that can perform a number of distinct operations on a given work-piece without intervention from an operator.

1903 T. R. Shaw *Lathes, Screw Machines, Boring & Turning Mills* xii. 505 A semi-automatic lathe, having four spindles, is illustrated. **1950** S. J. Gibson in A. W. Judge *Centre, Capstan & Automatic Lathes* II. iv. 181 The 'Maximatic'..is semi-automatic only in the sense that the loading is done by hand.

b. *Mil.* Of a firearm: that loads itself or performs part of the loading operation automatically, but does not fire continuously.

1911 H. A. Bethell *Mod. Artillery in Field* i. 15 Semi-Automatic Actions.—In these the breech opens automatically during the run up, and ejects the cartridge case. **1945** C. E. Balleisen *Princ. Firearms* i. 2 Most 'automatic' pistols are only *semiautomatic*. **1976** J. Wainwright *Walther P. 38* 7 The Luger..was a *semi*-automatic pistol... Its trigger had to be squeezed for each shot.

c. Applied to a telephone system of which the operation is automatic except that dialing of the required number is done by an operator (see quots.).

1912 J. POOLE *Pract. Telephone Handbk.* (ed. 5) xxxii. 536 Semi-automatic systems are in use on the Continent, and also in some towns in America, but not to any great extent. **1927** C. W. WILMAN *Man. Automatic Telephony* xxii. 219 It is claimed for semi-automatic systems that many of the advantages of automatic systems, such as the rapidity of connection and instantaneous clearing, are retained, while the subscribers are relieved of the duty of dialling. **1976** T. H. FLOWERS *Introd. Exchange Systems* iii. 65 It was asserted that if a subscriber paid for service as he did, it was not right and was even dishonest to make him do his own operating, so semi-automatic exchanges with operators to do the dialling was the right thing.

B. *sb.* **1.** A semi-automatic lathe.

1902 *Lockwood's Dict. Mech. Engin.* (ed. 3) 444 *Semi-automatics*, these constitute a large class of machines which occupy a middle position between the..'full' automatic machines and those which involve the constant attendance of an operator. **1963** N. WEINSTEIN tr. *Boguslavsky's Automatic & Semi-Automatic Lathes* i. 32 If internal surfaces are to be machined in addition to external surfaces, semi-automatics having a central end-working toolslide, or a turret are employed.

2. A semi-automatic firearm.

1964 H. L. PETERSON *Encycl. Firearms* 31/2 In 1916, the Germans introduced a limited number of Mauser semi-automatic rifles. The French followed in 1917, with the Saint-Étienne gas-operated semi-automatic. **1978** S. BRILL *Teamsters* vi. 239 The gunman reached down, held the High Standard semiautomatic against Mrs. Rand's chin and fired three more shots.

†**semi-axe.** *Obs.* [f. SEMI- 7 b + AXE.] = next.

1728 tr. *Newton's Treat. Syst. World* 53 Put the semi-axe of the Earth's orbit 100000. **1780** LUDLAM in *Phil. Trans.* LXX. 379 An ellipse, whose first semi-axe is CA.

semi-'axis. [SEMI- 7 b.] The half of the axis of an ellipse, etc.

1743 *Phil. Trans.* XLII. 360 The Semiaxis of the Spheroid. **1816** PLAYFAIR *Nat. Phil.* II. 215 If a fixed star had an annual parallax that was sensible, it would appear to describe an ellipsis, of which the greater semi-axis was equal to that parallax. **1866** HERSCHEL *Fam. Lect. Sci.* v. §40. 213 The period of their mutual circulation may be stated at about ninety-six years, and the semiaxis of their mutual ellipse in angular measure at 4″·8. **1867** SMYTH *Sailor's Word-bk., Mean Distance*, the average distance of a planet from the sun; it is equal to half the longer axis of the ellipse, and hence is..termed the semi-axis-major.

semi-bar'barian. [SEMI- 2; cf. L. *sēmibarbarus.*] One who is half-barbarian.

1692 BENTLEY *Boyle Lect.* vi. 4 The rude and simple Semi-barbarians of Lycaonia. **1774** GOLDSM. *Nat. Hist.* (1824) I. 204 The sensual pleasures are the only study of the semi-barbarian. **1853** WHYTE-MELVILLE *Digby Grand* x, Those semi-barbarians of the north.

So ˌ**semibar'barianism, -bar'baric** *a.*, **-'barbarism, -'barbarous** *a.*

1828 *Examiner* 122/2 An intention on the part of the Sultan to proceed to extremities in the usual headlong style of haughty..*semi-barbarianism. **1864** WEBSTER, **Semibarbaric*,..as semibarbaric display. **1817** JAS. MILL *Brit. India* I. II. iv. 164 The age of false refinement, which is that of *semibarbarism. **1798** A. F. M. WILLICH *Elements Crit. Philos.* p. cxxii, The ancient Britons were as little acquainted with the art of writing, as any of the rude and *semi-barbarous nations of those times. **1817** JAS. MILL *Brit. India* I. II. x. 437 Had the Hindus remained fixed from the earliest ages in the semibarbarous state. **1894** J. T. FOWLER *Adamnan* Introd. p. xxv, Its Latin is rude and semibarbarous in grammar and spelling.

†**semi-bousy,** *a. Obs.* [SEMI- 1.] Halfdrunk.

c **1400** *Beryn* 706 Som vnlusty persone, þat were nat wele awakid, or semybousy ouyr eve.

ˌ**semibrachi'ation.** *Zool.* [SEMI- 2 a.] A mode of progression exhibited by certain monkeys in which the forelimbs may be used both as legs in a quadrupedal gait and as arms by which to grasp and swing.

1961 J. R. NAPIER in *Symp. Zool. Soc. Lond.* V. 127 The twist [of the head] is generally seen in Primates that combine a quadrupedal gait with the specialized arboreal locomotor patterns of brachiation and semi-brachiation. [*Note*] The term semibrachiation has been devised by the author in association with Dr E. H. Ashton to describe the highly arboreal and acrobatic activities of certain of New and Old World monkeys. **1972** W. C. O. HILL *Evolutionary Biol. Primates* ix. 65 Old World exponents of semibrachiation include the six or more genera of the family Colobidae (the Asiatic leaf monkeys and the African *Colobus*).

Hence **semi'brachiating** *ppl. a.*; **semi'brachiator**, an animal that exhibits semibrachiation.

1963 J. R. NAPIER in *Symp. Zool. Soc. Lond.* X. 186 The mode of locomotion of semibrachiators is basically that of an arboreal quadruped but, in addition, a variable amount of time is spent in swinging by the arms and leaping with the forelimbs outstretched to grasp a hand-hold. *Ibid.* 188 The African semibrachiating *Colobus* shows a decided preference for the higher strata of the forest canopy. **1973** *Nature* 10 Aug. 373/2 With respect to locomotion, the first component separates quadrupedal cercopithecoids from both knuckle-walkers..and the quadrupedal arm-swinger (so-called 'semi-brachiator') *Ateles*.

semibreve ('sɛmɪbriːv). *Mus.* Also α. 6–7 semibriefe, -7 -eefe, 7–9 -ief. β. 6 sembreefe, 6–7 -iefe, 7 -ief, -eefe, -eve. [f. SEMI- 6 c + BREVE *sb.* 2, BRIEF *sb.* 8, after obs. F. *semibreve* (14th c.) or mod.L. *sēmibrevis.*] A note having half (†in the greater prolation, one third) the length of a breve: in modern music the longest note in ordinary use. (Its figure is now an open oval ○.)

α. **1594** BARNFIELD *Sheph. Content* (Arb.) 25 No Briefes nor Semi-Briefes are in my Songs. **1601** HOLLAND *Pliny* x. xxix. I. 286 [The nightingale] one while, full or her largs, longs, briefes, semibriefes, and minims; another while in her crotchets, quavers, semiquavers, and double semiquavers. **1696** DERHAM *Artif. Clock-maker* ii. 49 The first note in the 100th Psalm is a Semibrief. **1779** SHERIDAN *Critic* I. i, The signors and signoras..sliding their smooth semibreves, and gargling glib divisions. **1849** W. IRVING *Goldsm.* xxxiv. 290 He pretended to score down an air as the poet played it, but put down crotchets and semi-breves at random. **1883** W. S. ROCKSTRO in *Grove's Dict. Mus.* III. 459/2 Until the beginning of the 17th century, the Semibreve represented one third of a Perfect Breve, and the half of an Imperfect one.

β. **1591** J. FARMER *Diuers Waies* B i, 2. parts in one in the fourth, a sembriefe after the other. **1602** CAMPION *Art Eng. Poesie* 1 In Musick we do not say a straine of so many notes, but so many sem'briefes. **1609** *Ev. Woman in Hum.* I. i. in Bullen *O. Pl.* IV, I spend my breath to thee, and thou answerest me an houre after in a sembreve. *a* **1646** J. GREGORY *Posthuma* (1649) 48 If there stood Minim or Sembrief in the upper part, there stood another against it in the lower and inner parts. **1678–1706** in PHILLIPS.

b. The 'space' of a semibreve.

1845 S. JUDD *Margaret* I. xvii, Great red coals roll out on the hearth, sparkle a semibrief,..and then dissolve into brown ashes.

c. *attrib.*, as ***semibreve rest***; † **semibreve time**, (*a*) common time with two beats in a bar; (*b*) the time occupied by a semibreve.

1591 J. FARMER *Diuers Waies* C iij, The plainsong beneath beginning at the end, & so forward sembreefe time. **1598** E. GUILPIN *Skial.* (1878) 14 All his talke's of crotchets and of quauers, His very words to sembriefe time doe fall. **1609** DOWLAND *Ornith. Microl.* 88 A perfect Mood is inwardly noted by a rest of 3. times. A perfect time by 2. Semibreefe Rests, placed with a Semibreefe. **1661** BLOUNT *Glossogr.* (ed. 2), *Sembrief*, a slow time in Musick. **1662** PLAYFORD *Skill Mus.* I. x. (1674) 34 The Dupla or Semibreve Time (but many call it the Common Time, because most used). **1669** COKAINE *Poems* 79 His Life was but a Minum, till his prime; When as old Age should last out Sembrief-time. **1818** BUSBY *Gram. Mus.* 70 *note*, A Semibreve Rest forms.. a whole bar's rest in any time, or measure.

Hence †**'semibreved** *a.*, punctuated as with semibreve rests.

1631 BRATHWAIT *Whimzies, Yealous Neighbour* 189 He fetcheth a deepe sigh, semi-brev'd in these words. **1641** —— *Eng. Gentlew.* 288 Their discourse is semibrev'd with sighes, their talke with teares.

semicarbazide (sɛmɪ'kɑːbəzaɪd). *Chem.* [f. SEMI- 8 h + CARB- + AZ(O- + -IDE.] A colourless, crystalline, basic solid, $NH_2{\cdot}CO{\cdot}NH{\cdot}NH_2$, derived from urea by substitution of a hydrazino group for one of the amino groups, which reacts with carbonyl compounds to form semicarbazones. Also, a derivative of this.

1892 *Jrnl. Chem. Soc.* LXII. II. 1297 When amidoguanidine is treated with dilute acids, or with caustic alkalis, and is first converted into semicarbazide with liberation of ammonia. **1938** G. H. RICHTER *Textbk. Org. Chem.* xiii. 224 Semicarbazide is a valuable reagent for..the Wolff-Kishner reduction of the carbonyl group. **1968** R. O. C. NORMAN *Princ. Org. Synthesis* x. 315 In order to obtain derivatives for the characterization of the carbonyl compound it is more satisfactory to use a monosubstituted hydrazine; semicarbazide, phenylhydrazine, and 2,4-dinitrophenylhydrazine are commonly chosen.

semicarbazone (sɛmɪ'kɑːbəzəʊn). *Chem.* [f. prec. + -ONE.] Any of a class of (usu. crystalline) compounds of general formula $RR'C{:}N{\cdot}NH{\cdot}CO{\cdot}NH_2$ which are prepared by the condensation of semicarbazide with carbonyl compounds, in order to characterize the parent carbonyl or to protect the carbonyl group in synthesis.

1896 *Jrnl. Chem. Soc.* LXX. I. 343 Mesityl oxide semicarbazone melts at 156°. **1938** G. H. RICHTER *Textbk. Org. Chem.* vii. 102 The semicarbazones may be converted into hydrazones by the action of sodium ethylate. **1973** H. J. E. LOEWENTHAL in J. F. W. McOmie *Protective Groups in Org. Chem.* ix. 340 In general, and in the steroid field in particular, ease of semicarbazone formation from different types of carbonyl groups follows the order observed with other protecting groups.

semi-carti'laginous, *a.* [SEMI- 8 a.] Of a texture approaching that of cartilage. Of fishes: Having a semi-cartilaginous skeleton.

1806 A. HUNTER *Culina* (ed. 3) 109 It is a singular circumstance, that those strong semi-cartilaginous substances should have the power of coagulating milk. **1829** *Good's Study Med.* (ed. 3) V. 374 Such [diseased] kidneys have generally a lobulated form and semicartilaginous hardness. **1841** MILLER *Old Red Sandstone* iv. (1887) 95 The semi-cartilaginous..fishes. **1865** LYELL *Elem. Geol.* 553 Exchanged a..semi-cartilaginous spinal cord for an ossified one.

†**semi-'caseate,** *a. Obs.* [f. SEMI- 1 + L. *cāseus* cheese + -ATE².] Half converted into cheese.

1651 BIGGS *New Disp.* ¶141 A lacteous semi-caseate & semi-petrified juice.

semicha (sɛ'miːxə). *Judaism.* Also **semichah, semikhah**, and with capital initial. [Heb. *sᵉmīkhāh*, lit. leaning.] The laying-on of hands by which a rabbi is ordained; the ordination of a rabbi. Also, a diploma of rabbinical ordination.

The laying-on of hands, practised only in antiquity, was later replaced by a proclamation (also called *semicha*).

1866 *Chambers's Encycl.* VIII. 70/1 Out of the number of the regular disciples (Talmidim) were chosen the Chaberim (Colleagues), who, again, were elected to the dignity of a rabbi by the 'Semichah', or imposition of hands by three members of the Sanhedrim. **1914** J. HASTINGS *Encycl. Relig. & Ethics* VII. 604/2 Among these Rabbis there grew up the desire to re-establish the old Rabbinic supremacy of Palestine. They desired to institute once more the *sᵉmīkhāh*, or ordination, and thus ordain a Sanhedrin which would be recognized throughout the world. **1962** *New Jewish Encycl.* 438/2 Technically, Semikhah ceased some two thousand years ago, and was not established anew until the 14th or 15th century. In modern times rabbinical students are granted Semikhah, that is, they receive a rabbinical diploma and become ordained as rabbis upon graduation from a rabbinical school or *Yeshivah*. **1973** *Jewish Chron.* 9 Feb. 22/1 The principal..accepts the fact that some of his best students go on to Gateshead for their semicha, not merely with resignation, but with positive approval. **1976** B. WILLIAMS *Making of Manch. Jewry* vii. 184 The possession of Rabbinical *semikhah* endorsed by European rabbis of unquestioned repute.

semi-'choric, *a.* [f. next + -IC.] Pertaining to or of the nature of a semi-chorus.

In mod. Dicts.

semi-'chorus. [mod.L., rendering Gr. ἡμιχόριον.] **a.** One of two parts into which the main body of a chorus is divided; chiefly *Mus.* **b.** A piece of music to be performed by a company of singers selected from a chorus.

1797 *Pope's Wks.* (ed. Warton) I. 159 Chorus of Youths and Virgins. Semichorus. **1820** SHELLEY *Prom. Unb.* II. ii, Semichorus I. of Spirits. **1828** R. WARNER *Psalter* p. xxiii, When..one band began the hymn thus..the chorus, or semi-chorus, took up the corresponding versicle. **1847–54** WEBSTER, *Semi-chorus*, a short chorus performed by a few singers. **1897** *Daily News* 15 June 7/5 The number..will be rendered..by a semi-chorus consisting of the basses of the St. Paul's, Westminster Abbey, and Chapel Royal chorus.

†**semicicle.** *Obs.* In 5 semycycle. [ad. med.L. **sēmicicla*, in Du Cange *semissecla*, f. *sēmi-* SEMI- + *sicla* = *siclus* a liquid measure.] Half a pint.

c **1440** *Pallad. on Husb.* VIII. 148 A sester and a semycicle [orig. *sextarii unius et semis*] take Of senuey seede.

semicircle ('sɛmɪsɜːk(ə)l). [ad. L. *sēmicirculus*: see SEMI- 7 b and CIRCLE *sb.*]

1. The half of a circle divided by a diameter, or the half of its circumference.

1526 *A C. mery talys* 3 b, [Oxford scholar loq.] Cobler I pray the set me .ii. tryangyls & .ii. semy cercles vppon my subpedytals. **1551** RECORDE *Pathw. Knowl.* I. Defin., If that part be separate from the rest of the circle..And if it be parted juste by the centre..then is it called a semicircle, or halfe compasse. **1571** DIGGES *Pantom.* I. B ij, A Semi-circle or halfe Circle, doth conteine both the Dimetient and Centre of his circle, with the precise halfe of his circumference. **1610** HOLLAND *Camden's Brit.* I. 208 A very antient towne..situat amidst hilles in forme of a semicircle. **1667** PRIMATT *City & C. Builder* 164 The measuring of a Semi-circle, is the multiplying half the Diameter..by a quarter of the Circle. **1798** HUTTON *Course Math.* I. 301 An Angle in a Semicircle, is a Right Angle.

2. A set of objects or an arrangement in the form of a half-circle; a semicircular form, formation, structure, etc.

1597 A. M. tr. *Guillemeau's Fr. Chirurg.* 27/1 We must file of all such teeth which will not be contayned in the semicircle of the other teeth. **1636** B. JONSON *Eng. Gram.* II. i. (1640) 70 Apostrophus..should, and of the learneder sort hath his signe and marke, which is such a Semicircle ' placed in the top. *a* **1674** CLARENDON *Hist. Reb.* xv. §54 The smaller ships..lay in a semicircle moored along the shore. **1726** SWIFT *Gulliver* I. i, The Chains..gave me..the Liberty of walking backwards and forwards in a Semicircle. **1817** SHELLEY *Rev. Islam* I. 168 The pallid semicircle of the moon. **1831** in *Jrnl. Frankl. Inst.* VIII. (N.S.) 195 The teeth being placed on a fixed semi-circle. **1837** *Penny Cycl.* IX. 129/1 The semicircle of the orchestra. **1874** BLACK *Pr. Thule* ii, The harbour was overlooked by a semicircle of hills.

fig. *a* **1619** BEAUM. & FL. *Q. Corinth* IV. i, Has he given the lye In circle, or oblique, or semi-circle, Or direct parallel? you must challenge him.

3. A semicircular instrument or one marked with a semicircle; now only = GRAPHOMETER.

1594 BLUNDEVIL *Exerc.* IV. (1597) 209 Another Circle of brasse plate..called the semi-Circle of position, which serueth chiefly for matters of Astronomie, as to find out the twelu houses of heauen. **1701** MOXON *Math. Instr.* 18 *Semicircle*, made of Brass, with an Index and sights, Box and Needle, Ball and Socket, and Staff; containing 180 Degrees, being half the Theodolet. **1712** J. JAMES tr. *Le Blond's Gardening* 81 Instruments made use of for tracing upon the Ground..are the Graphometre, or Semi-circle. *a* **1859** MACAULAY *Hist. Eng.* xxiv. V. 133 They meet at the corner of his park with paper and pencils, a pole, a chain and a semicircle, measure his fields.

Hence **'semicircle** *v. trans.*, to surround with a semicircle; *intr.* to form a semicircle.

1813 SHELLEY *Q. Mab* I. 235 An immense concave..semicircled with a belt Flashing incessant meteors. *a* **1864** HAWTHORNE *Amer. Note-bks.* (1879) II. 124 A broad streak ..semicircling beneath either eye.

semicircled ('sɛmɪsɜːk(ə)ld), *ppl. a.* Chiefly *poet.* [f. SEMICIRCLE *sb.* + -ED.] Of the form of a semicircle; arranged as in a semicircle.

1586 MARLOWE *1st Pt. Tamburl.* III. i, When the Moone begins To ioine in one her semi-circled hornes. **1598** SHAKS. *Merry W.* III. iii. 68 A semi-circled farthingale. **1616** SURFL. & MARKH. *Country Farm* II. xlviii. 241 Seeds, which as soone as they are ripe, are like Marigold seeds, white, rough, and semicircled. **1629** QUARLES *Argalus & Parth.* III. Wks. (Grosart) III. 277/1 Now and then a kisse Would interpose like a parenthesis, Betweene their semicircled armes, inclos'd. **1834** DISRAELI *Rev. Epick* I. i. 9 Rank above rank in semicircled grace.

semicircular (sɛmɪ'sɜːkjʊlə(r)), *a.* Also 5 -er. [ad. med.L. *sēmicirculāris*, f. L. *sēmicircul-us* SEMICIRCLE. Cf. F. *semi-circulaire*.] Of the form of a semicircle.

1432–50 tr. *Higden* (Rolls) IV. 101 After auctores theatrum is proprely a flore semicirculer, in the myddes of whom was an howse whiche was callede scena. **1615** CROOKE *Body of Man* 984 The figure of the ribs is semicircular like a Bow. **1624** WOTTON *Archit.* I. 50 Semicircular Arches, or Hemisphericall Vaults, being raised vpon the totall Diameter. **1708** J. CHAMBERLAYNE *St. Gt. Brit.* (1710) 417 The Lords.. when in the Inner House sit on a Semicircular Bench.. to hear Petitions. **1776** GIBBON *Decl. & F.* xi. I. 300 Disposing the legions in a semicircular form, he advanced the two horns of the crescent across the Danube. **1864** BRYCE *Holy Rom. Emp.* iv. (1875) 48 Behind in the semicircular apse sat the clergy, rising tier above tier. *a* **1878** SIR G. SCOTT *Lect. Archit.* (1879) I. 49 The arches [in the Romanesque style] always either semi-circular or segmental.

Comb. **1766** *Complete Farmer* s.v. *Mouldiness* 5 P 4/2 Two twigs of ozier put semicircular-wise into holes made in the handle of the scythe. **1828–9** NARRIEN in *Encycl. Metropol.* (1845) V. 284/2 Semicircular-headed apertures serving as entrances. **1897** *Ch. Times* 20 Aug. 186/1 Small semicircular-headed windows of one light.

b. *Anat.* Designating †(*a*) the orbicular muscle of the eyelid; (*b*) the three canals of the internal ear.

1706 PHILLIPS (ed. Kersey), *Semicircular Muscles*, the same as *Claudent Muscles*. **1748** HARTLEY *Observ. Man* I. ii. §5. 224 Vibrations communicated to the Cochlea, and semicircular Canals. **1843** CARPENTER *Anim. Phys.* §518 The three semicircular canals are passages, excavated in the solid bone, and lined by a continuation of the same membrane as that which lines the vestibule [of the ear]. **1885** *Encycl. Brit.* XIX. 38/2 The horizontal semicircular canal in the internal ear of a pigeon.

Hence **semicircu'larity, semi'circularness.**

1731 BAILEY, *Semicircularness*, half circularness. **1863** READE *Hard Cash* i, Observing his semicircularity and general condition.

semi'circularly, *adv.* [f. SEMICIRCULAR + -LY².] In a semicircular form; in a half-circle.

1615 CROOKE *Body of Man* 770 The vse of this seueenth paire is semicircularly to mooue the head. **1705–30** S. GALE *Tour through Engl.* (1790) 15 A narrow passage between two stone walls.. built semicircularly. **1756** PENNANT in *Phil. Trans.* XLIX. 514 The flat or upper part is striated semi-circularly. **1839** *Sat. Mag.* Sept. 127/2 The semicircularly-formed vault. **1888** *Century Mag.* XXX. 882 The 'belt', or rainbow, of fertile land Swept semicircularly round.

semi'circulating, *ppl. a. rare*⁻¹. [Cf. L. *sēmicirculātus*.] Semicircular.

a **1700** KEN *Hymnotheo* Poet. Wks. III. 4 A Gulf.. Whose fertile semicirculating Head, With Temples and with Palaces is spread.

semicirque ('sɛmɪsɜːk). *poet.* [f. SEMI- 7a + CIRQUE.] A semicircle.

1795–1814 WORDSW. *Excurs.* III. 50 Upon a semicirque of turf-clad ground, The hidden nook discovered to our view A mass of rock. **1831** *Blackw. Mag.* XXIX. 328 The skater there, with motion nice, In semicirque and graceful wheel. **1872** A. DE VERE *Leg. St. Patrick* 153 Above the semicirque of grassy seats.

semicolon (sɛmɪ'kəʊlən). [f. SEMI- + COLON².] A punctuation-mark consisting of a dot placed above a comma (;): see quots.

In present use it is the chief stop intermediate in value between the comma and the full stop; usually separating sentences the latter of which limits the former, or marking off a series of sentences or clauses of co-ordinate value.

1644 HODGES *Eng. Primrose* N 3, At a comma, stop a little .. At a semi-colon, somewhat more. **1692** *B. Jonson's Eng. Gram.* Wks. 690 A Semicolon is a distinction of an imperfect Sentence, wherein with somewhat a longer Breath, the Sentence following is included. **1771** LUCKOMBE *Hist. Printing* 267 The semicolon is a point of great use to enforce and illustrate what has been advanced, and digested by the Comma... The Semicolon is used as an Abbreviation, in the word Esquire. **1800** L. MURRAY *Eng. Gram.* 227 The semi-colon is sometimes used, when the preceding member of the sentence does not of itself give a complete sense, but depends on the following clause.. and sometimes when the sense of that member would be complete without the concluding one.

'semi-column. *Arch.* [SEMI- 7e; cf. med.L. *semi-columnium* (Isidore).] The half of a column cut longitudinally.

1715 LEONI *Palladio's Archit.* (1742) I. 52 Halls.. surrounded with semi-columns. **1862** *Parthenon* 26 July 400 The walls projecting from the *cella* terminated in two semi-columns, instead of square pilasters. **1875** BRASH *Eccl. Archit. Irel.* 99 The flank walls.. are.. divided by semi-columns.

Hence **,semico'lumnar** *a.*, of the form of a semi-column; *Bot.* applied to stems, etc. shaped like half a cylinder cut lengthwise.

1793 MARTYN *Lang. Bot.* (1796), *Semiteres*, semicolumnar. **1849** DANA *Geol.* iii. (1850) 274 Walls of semi-columnar lava.

†semi-concave. *Obs.* [SEMI- 7a.] Applied to the half of a hollow cylinder bisected longitudinally. (See CONCAVE *sb.* 1 b.)

1626 BACON *Sylva* §131 As the Enclosure, that is Round about and Entire, preserueth the Sound; So doth a Semi-Concaue. **1734** *Builder's Dict.* s.v. II. B 7, A Semi-Concave-Cylinder.

semicon'ducting, *a. Physics.* [SEMI- 8a.] Having the properties of a semiconductor.

1782 tr. A. Volta in *Phil. Trans. R. Soc.* LXXII. p. xii, The surface of those bodies does not contract any electricity, or if any electricity adheres to them, it vanishes soon, on account of their semi-conducting nature. **1787** CAVALLO in *Phil. Trans.* LXXVIII. 7 A semi-conducting or imperfectly insulating plane. **1884** J. T. SPRAGUE *Electricity* (ed. 2) xiii. 573 A semi-conducting incandescent material compounded of infusible earths and carbon or metals. **1975** D. G. FINK *Electronics Engineers' Handbk.* VII. 31 By far the most widely used semiconducting materials are germanium and silicon.

Also **semicon'ductive** *a.*, in the same sense; **semicon'duction, ,semiconduc'tivity.**

1931 *Proc. R. Soc.* A. CXXXIII. 469 To explain the general outlines of semi-conduction. **1953** *Jrnl. Inst. Electr. Engineers* C. I. 76/2 The value of semi-conductive glaze lies in its use in situations where trouble is expected due to flashover of insulators under adverse weather.. conditions. **1954** R. P. TURNER *Transistors* i. 8 Many.. elements and compounds have been found to possess semiconductivity in varying amounts. **1960** *Cambr. Rev.* 27 Feb. 394/1 Although a Cambridge physicist, A. H. Wilson, put forward the basic theory of their behaviour in 1931, it is really only in the last ten years that the phenomena of semiconductivity have been clearly understood. **1973** K. SEEGER *Semiconductor Physics* i. 2 Semiconduction is specified by the following properties: [etc.].

semicon'ductor. *Physics.* [SEMI- 8a.]

1. a. A material whose capacity to conduct electricity is intermediate between that of a good conductor and an insulator. *Obs.* exc. as in next sense.

1838 *Ann. Electr., Magn., & Chem.* III. 316 Lichtenberg .. observes.. 'it is deserving of a trial also whether phosphorus would not become ignited at points whence a stream [of electricity] is issuing, on a semi-conductor being inserted between them'. **1863** E. ATKINSON tr. *Ganot's Elem. Treat. Physics* IX. iv. 592 The retardation which electricity experiences in traversing a semi-conductor, such as a wet string. **1879** G. PRESCOTT *Sp. Telephone* iv, Carbon and certain other semi-conductors. **1900** *Engineering* 28 Sept. 412/3 Semi-conductors like iron filings.

b. *spec.* Such a material in which there is a narrow gap between permitted energy bands, so that the only current carriers are electrons thermally excited from the valence band into the conduction band (*intrinsic semiconductor*: see INTRINSIC *a.* 3e) or into intermediate energy levels provided by impurity ions (*extrinsic semiconductor*).

1931 *Proc. R. Soc.* A. CXXXIII. 459 It is not possible to maintain that the difference between good and bad conductors is one of degree only... There is an essential difference between a semi-conductor, such as germanium, and a good conductor, such as silver, which must be accounted for by any theory which attempts to deal with semi-conductors. **1946** *Electronic Engin.* XVIII. 66/2 It is well known that 'semi-conductors', such as carbon, silicon .., etc., possess negative temperature coefficients of resistance at ordinary temperatures. **1961** G. R. CHOPPIN *Exper. Nuclear Chem.* iii. 41 The semiconductor detectors.. are made from thin (approximately 1mm) wafers of semiconductor silicon. **1970** J. SHEPHERD et al. *Higher Electrical Engin.* (ed. 2) xx. 623 In an extrinsic or doped semiconductor, impurities are added to the intrinsic material to give a predominance of either electrons (in *n*-type material) or holes (in *p*-type material) as charge carriers. **1979** *Jrnl. R. Soc. Arts* Oct. 692/2 Sometimes a significant advance in technology may itself create a new market, as did the advent of the semiconductors to the small 'transistor radio' market.

2. Special Combs.: **semiconductor diode**, a diode whose rectifying action depends on the properties of a junction between a semiconductor and either a metal or another type of semiconductor; cf. *junction diode* (s.v. JUNCTION *sb.* 4); **semiconductor junction** = JUNCTION *sb.* 2b; **semiconductor rectifier**, a semiconductor diode, usu. one intended for large currents; **semiconductor triode**, a junction transistor having two junctions.

1954 *Trans. IRE Prof. Group Broadcast & Television Receivers* July 34 (*heading*) Semiconductor diodes for TV receivers. **1975** FINK & MCKENZIE *Electronics Engineers' Handbk.* VII. 34 One of the highest-volume uses of the semiconductor diode is in computers. *Ibid.* 35 When a semiconductor junction is exposed to light, photons generate hole-electron pairs. **1946** *Physical Rev.* LXIX. 42/2 This effective contact e.m.f. is one important parameter in the theory and practice of semi-conductor rectifiers. **1962** *Times* 14 May 14/7 Semiconductor rectifiers on heavy-duty electric railway locomotives. **1948** *Physical Rev.* LXXIV. 230/1 (*heading*) A semi-conductor triode. **1970** D. F. SHAW *Introd. Electronics* (ed. 2) xii. 262 The transistor is a semiconductor triode possessing characteristics which are similar in many respects to those of thermionic triodes.

semi-'conjugate, *a.* (*sb.*) *Math.* [SEMI- 7b.] *semi-conjugate axis, diameter* = conjugate semiaxis, semidiameter: see CONJUGATE *a.* 6a, and cf. quot. 1680 there, and 1885 s.v. SEMI-DIAMETER. Also *ellipt.* (as *sb.*) for these.

1743 EMERSON *Fluxions* 187 Let *AD* be an Hyperbola, *B* the Center, *BA* = *a*, Semi-conjugate = *b*. **1790** *Phil. Trans.* LXXX. 536, CV and CW being a kind of semitransverse and semiconjugate axes to the elliptic track on the spherical surface. **1882** MINCHIN *Unipl. Kinemat.* 130 An ellipse referred to two semi-conjugate diameters, *pa*, *pb*, as axes.

,semi-con'servative, *a. Biochem.* [SEMI- 1.] Of the replication of nucleic acid: such that one complete strand of each double helix is directly derived from its parent.

The term was originally proposed (see quot. 1957) to designate a class of models of the replication of DNA; it is now accepted that its true mechanism of replication falls in this class.

1957 DELBRUCK & STENT in McElroy & Glass *Chem. Basis of Heredity* 707 The considerable number of proposed schemes may be divided into three general classes as conservative, semi-conservative, and dispersive. *Ibid.* 709 Semi-conservative mechanisms are those which conserve the atomic identity of single chains of the parental DNA duplex, although effecting a permanent separation of the two chains from each other in the course of replication. **1970** *Nature* 7 Nov. 522/1 There is good evidence that DNA replication is semi-conservative and involves separation of the two strands which then act as templates. **1976** P. COLLARD *Devel. Microbiol.* viii. 106 Semi-conservative replication thus provided a possible answer to the riddle of the stability of the genome from generation to generation.

Hence **,semicon'servatively** *adv.*

1966 *Jrnl. Molecular Biol.* XV. 372 Since all the DNA is replicated semiconservatively.. such a segregation pattern could arise most simply if every chromosome contained all its DNA within a single molecule. **1979** *Nature* 3 May 75/2, pBR322 DNA replicates semiconservatively and completely in a crude lysate of *E. coli*.

†semicope. *Obs.* [f. SEMI- + COPE *sb.*¹] A short cloak.

c **1386** CHAUCER *Prol.* 262 Of double worstede was his semycope That rounded as a belle out of the presse.

semi-'crystalline, *a.* [SEMI- 8a.] Having or being a structure of crystals embedded in an amorphous groundmass; having or being a structure possessing crystalline character to some extent.

1816 *Edin. Rev.* XXVI. 163 Primitive limestone of a.. semi-crystalline grain. **1871** *Phil. Mag.* XLII. 404 This silica forms a series of semi-crystalline bands parallel with the walls of the fissure. **1882** GEIKIE *Text-bk. Geol.* II. II. §4. 104 Truly vitreous rocks tend to graduate into the.. semi-crystalline type. **1927** *Proc. Physical Soc.* XXXIX. 370 In 1924 I [*sc.* Rutherford] put forward a suggestion that the central nucleus was a closely ordered arrangement of α particles and electrons in a semi-crystalline formation. **1975** *Sci. Amer.* Dec. 99/2 Representative values for the percentage by volume of crystals in a number of semicrystalline polymers are high-density polyethylene, 75 percent; low-density polyethylene, polypropylene and nylon, 50 percent.

semi-'cubic, *a. rare.* = next.

1797 *Phil. Trans.* LXXXVIII. 390 A conic parabola being given, a semicubic one may be found.

semi-'cubical, *a. Math.* [SEMI- 7b.] Applied to the curve of the third degree with a cusp referred to rectangular axes, the equation to which can always be reduced to the form $ay^2 = x^3$.

The exponent of the power of the abscissa which is proportional to the ordinate is $^3/_2$, whence the name.

1677 WALLIS in Rigaud *Corr. Sci. Men* (1841) II. 609 That [invention] of Mr. Neale is straightening the semi-cubical parabola without supposing the squaring an hyperbola. **1704** J. HARRIS *Lex. Techn.* I, *Semi-cubical Paraboloid*, is a Curve whose Ordinates are in Subtriplicate of the Duplicate proportion of the Diameter. **1855** G. SALMON *Conic Sect.* xiii. (ed. 3) §251 The equation of the evolute of a parabola represents a curve called the semicubical parabola.

†semi'cupium. *Obs.* Also erron. -'cubium; and anglicized **semicupe.** [med.L., f. *sēmi-* SEMI- + *cūpa* tun.] A bath in which only one's legs and hips are covered; a hip-bath.

1634 T. JOHNSON *Parey's Chirurg.* 1049 Bags, Fumigations, Semicupiums, Baths. **1661** BLOUNT *Glossogr.* (ed. 2), *Semi-cupe*, is a half Bath, up to the navel of the patient. **1684** tr. *Bonet's Merc. Compit.* III. 58 Many Lithotomists immediately after the operation clap the Patient in a Semi-cupe. **1706** PHILLIPS (ed. Kersey), *Semicubium*. **1785** GARTHSHORE in *Med. Commun.* II. 44 Fomentations, and the Semi-cupium.. were of no avail. **1799** UNDERWOOD *Dis. Childhood* (ed. 4) II. 255 Oily embrocations, a blister, leeches, and the semicupium were had recourse to.

semi-'cylinder. [SEMI- 7a.] The half of a cylinder divided longitudinally.

1666 COLLINS in Rigaud *Corr. Sci. Men* (1841) II. 461 In the concave of the said semicylinder. **1777** G. FORSTER *Voy. round World* I. 228 This and the first trumpet were both made of two hollow semicylinders of wood. **1841** S. CLEGG *Manuf. Coal-Gas* 60 The scoop is a semi-cylinder made of thin plate iron. **1880** C. & F. DARWIN *Movem. Pl.* 81 One of the two cotyledons failed to produce a petiole, whilst the other produced one consisting of an open semi-cylinder ending in a sharp point.

Hence **semicy'lindric, -cy'lindrical** *adjs.*, of the form of a semi-cylinder.

1731 BAILEY (ed. 2), *Semicylindrical.* **1760** LEE *Introd. Bot.* III. v. (1765) 185 *Semicylindric*, like a halved Cylinder; when they are round on one side, and flat on the other. **1793** *Phil. Trans.* LXXXIV. 10 The semicylindric cavity. **1801** *Ibid.* XCI. 131 The thermometer, having its scale-board.. of a semicylindrical form. **1842** GWILT *Archit.* §217 Semicylindrical vaults. **1870** HOOKER *Stud. Flora* 147 Water-Purslane..placentas semicylindric.

semi-'deity. [SEMI- 2.] = SEMIGOD.

c **1612** CHAPMAN *Homer's Hymn to the Moone* 27 Men whose states the Deities did raise To Semideities. **1685** BOYLE *Enq. Notion Nat.* 15 A certain Semi-Deity, which they call Nature. **1848** BAILEY *Festus* (ed. 3) 190 Adieu! ye semideities! **1860** PUSEY *Min. Proph.* 2 As if nature were a sort of semi-deity, or creation were its own Creator.

semi-demi-, used (1) = half-half, i.e. quarter, in **semidemisemiquaver**, a note the 64th part of a semibreve; (2) vaguely in a diminutive sense, as ***semi-demi-dinner***. (Cf. DEMI-SEMI.)

a **1661** FULLER *Worthies* (1662) II. 246 [Rabbits'] wool is.. used in making of hats, commonly..called half-beavers, though many of them hardly amount to the proportion of semi-demi-castors. **1826** J. F. DANNELEY *Mus. Gram.* 4 The Semidemisemiquaver has four hooks. **1836** T. HOOK *G. Gurney* (1850) III. iii. 351 She..at last appeared to expect me at luncheon as regularly as she looked for that semi-demi-dinner itself. **1876** STAINER & BARRETT *Dict. Mus. Terms*, *Semidemisemiquaver*, a half demisemiquaver, the 64th part of a semibreve.

semi-det (ˈsɛmɪdɛt), *sb.* Short for SEMI-DETACHED house.

1960 J. STROUD *Shorn Lamb* x. 110 An unexpected footpath in between a couple of semi-dets. **1978** J. MCNEIL *Consultant* xx. 174 A neat semidet with a bay window.

ˌsemi-de'tached, *a.* (and *sb.*) [SEMI- 1.]

A. *adj.* **a.** Partially detached.

1859 *Archaeol. Cant.* II. p. xxxix, The foundations of the villa were very extensive including one semi-detached apartment. **1862** ANSTED *Channel Isl.* I. v. 93 Large semi-detached masses of rock. **1907** *Daily Chron.* 28 Oct. 7/4 The miserable semi-detached life you and I have been living.

b. *spec.* Designating either of a pair of houses joined together and forming a block by themselves.

1859 [EMILY EDEN] (*title*) The Semi-Detached House. **1871** *Punch* 9 Sept. 100/1 A lot of semi-detached Cockney villas. **1882** *Brit. Med. Jrnl.* 16 Sept. 517/1 No drain should pass beneath a detached or semi-detached house.

B. *absol.* as *sb.* A semi-detached house. *colloq.*

1928 D. H. LAWRENCE *Lady Chatterley's Lover* xi. 188 New little streets of semi-detacheds were run up. **1957** M. & A. POTTER *Interiors* 43/2 The garden city notions.. blotting the green countryside everywhere with varieties of the popular 'semi-detached'. **1979** C. DEXTER *Service of All Dead* iii. 23 He'd found a quiet little semi-detached to rent.

ˌsemidi'ameter. [late L. (Boethius): see SEMI- 7 b.] The half of a diameter.

1551 RECORDE *Pathw. Knowl.* I. Defin., Diameters, whose halfe, I meane from the center to the circumference any waie, is called the semidiameter, or halfe diameter. **1625** N. CARPENTER *Geogr. Del.* I. v. (1635) 117 Astronomers measure the magnitude of the Starres by Diameters and Semi-diameters of the Earth. **1648** WILKINS *Math. Magick* I. vi. 38 That dis-proportion of distance, which there is betwixt the Semidiameter of the Cylinder AB, and the Semidiameter of the rundle with the spokes FA. **1709** BERKELEY *Th. Vision* §44 Fifty or Sixty Semidiameters of the Earth distant from me. **1763** *Ann. Reg.* 106 A curious halo appeared round the moon. Its semidiameter, from the lower limb of the planet to the opposite arch of the phenomenon, was very near twenty-one degrees and a half. **1816** PLAYFAIR *Nat. Phil.* II. 213, 23659 semidiameters of the Earth, or 93595000 miles. **1885** J. CASEY *Analyt. Geom.* 188 If any tangent meets two conjugate semidiameters of an ellipse.

fig. **1614** JACKSON *Creed* III. xii. 224 By so much doth the Pope..make his authoritie..greater then Christs, which is the semidiameter of this mouth of blasphemies.

b. *Fortif.* (See quot. 1704).

1669 STAYNRED *Fortification* 1 The Semidiameter of the Outward Polygon. **1704** J. HARRIS *Lex. Techn.* I, *Semi-diameter*..is two-fold, *viz.* the Greater and Lesser: The former being a Line composed of the Capital, and the Small Semi-diameter of the Polygon: And the other, a Line drawn to the Circumference from the Centre thro' the Gorges.

Hence **semidi'ametral** *a.*, that is a semidiameter.

1678 MOXON *Mech. Exerc.* v. 86 The Semi-Diametral line proceeding from the Center.

ˌsemi-di'aphanous, *a.* Now *rare.* [SEMI- 8 a.] Partially or imperfectly transparent.

1663 BOYLE *Exp. Hist. Colours* I. iii. 22 We should not judge it Opacous, but either Translucid, or at least Semi-diaphanous. *a* **1728** WOODWARD *Nat. Hist. Fossils* (1729) I. I. 87 A yellowish semidiaphanous Crust. **1826** KIRBY & SP. *Entom.* xxxv. III. 606 Those [tegmina] of the Manes that resemble dry leaves are only semidiaphanous.

Hence † **semi-diapha'neity.**

1663 BOYLE *Exp. Hist. Colours* I. iii. 73 The Transparency or Semi-diaphaniety of the Superficial Corpuscles of Bigger Bodies.

semidine (ˈsɛmɪdiːn). *Chem.* [ad. G. *semidin* (P. Jacobson 1893, in *Ber. d. Deut. Chem. Ges.* XXVI. 700), f. *semi-* SEMI- + *benzi-din* benzidine (s.v. BENZO-).] Any compound which is either (*a*) an *ortho-* anilino-derivative, or (*b*) an *N-para*-aminophenyl derivative, of a *para*-substituted aniline (distinguished as *ortho-* and *para*-semidines respectively); also ***semidine base***; ***semidine reaction, transformation***, etc., the rearrangement of *para*-substituted hydrazobenzenes in the presence of acid to yield *ortho-* and *para*-semidines (in proportions governed by the nature of the substituents).

1893 *Jrnl. Chem. Soc.* LXIV. I. 330 The hydrazo-compound..undergoes molecular change yielding two compounds, derivatives of ortho- and of para-amido-diphenylamine. It is proposed to call this reaction the semidine reaction, and to designate the orthamido-diphenylamine bases thus obtained by the name orthosemidines; the paramidodiphenylamine bases by the name parasemidines. **1898** *Ibid.* LXXIV. I. 441 Only 50 per cent. of the total semidines obtained. **1938** A. J. MEE tr. *P. Karrer's Org. Chem.* xxxiv. 498 If a *para*-position in hydrazobenzene is already occupied by a substituent, there are still further possibilities of isomerization. In addition to a diphenyline base and benzidine compounds.., two diphenylamine derivatives are formed in which only one of the benzene nuclei has rotated, the so-called *p*-semidine and *o*-semidine bases. The transformation is known as the semidine transformation. **1959** E. S. GOULD *Mech. & Structure in Org. Chem.* xv. 658 The rearrangements of hydrazobenzenes to benzidines, to diphenylenes, and to *o*-semidines are third-order reactions, first order in substrate and second order in hydrogen ion. **1975** R. F. BROWN *Org. Chem.* xxii. 772 A small amount of *o* shift occurs anyway, as well as a halfway shift to give semidines.

semi-di'rect, *a.* [SEMI- 1 a.] Not wholly direct; *spec.* (of lighting) so disposed that most but not all of the light reaches the illuminated area without first being reflected.

1914 S. C. BATSTONE *Electr. Light Fitting* viii. 166 If a frosted glass bowl or something of a similar nature be placed between the lamps and the surface or space to be illuminated, the result is 'semi-direct lighting'. **1926** J. S. HUXLEY *Essays of Biologist* i. 15 We can learn a great deal from the semi-direct methods of paleontology. **1957** *Encycl. Brit.* XIV. 107/2 Semidirect [lighting equipment]..10–40 [% upward]... 60–90 [% downward]. **1971** POWELL & HIGMAN *Finite Simple Groups* viii. 294 We form the semi-direct product *GI*.

ˌsemi-di'urnal, *a.* [SEMI- 6 a.]

1. *Astron.* Pertaining to, consisting of, or performed in, half the time between the rising and setting of a celestial body. Chiefly in ***semi-diurnal arc***.

1594 BLUNDEVIL *Exerc.* III. xviii. (1597) 154 It deuideth the artificial day and artificiall night each of them into two parts, that is to say, into two semi-diurnall and into two seminocturnall parts. *Ibid.* I. 176 b, There will remaine 9. houres 4'8. which is the length of the artificiall day, when the Sunne is in the first degree of Scorpio, the one halfe wherof is called the semi-diurnall Arke of that artificial day. **1664** WAKELY *Mariners-Compass rectified* (1694) 93 Astronomical Tables of Semidiurnal and Seminocturnal Arches. **1725** WATTS *Geog. & Astron.* xix, The difference between the sun or star's semidiurnal arc and a quadrant or ninety degrees. **1852** HIND *Astron. Vocab.* 52 *Semi-diurnal Arc*, is half the arc described by a heavenly body between its rising and setting. **1867** G. F. CHAMBERS *Astron. Vocab.* 801.

2. Occurring every twelve hours. Chiefly of the tides.

1794 SULIVAN *View Nat.* I. 414 The tides are semi-diurnal polar effusions, as the general currents of the ocean are semi-annual. **1813** J. FORBES *Oriental Mem.* I. 309 The sole cause then of these semidiurnal breezes, being the capacity which the earth has for acquiring a higher temperature than that of the sea. **1866** LOCKYER *Guillemin's Heavens* 59 The semi-diurnal oscillatory movement of the waters of the ocean,—the tides.

3. *Ent.* Partly diurnal, flying at twilight.

In recent Dicts.

ˌsemi-di'vine, *a.* [SEMI- 1.] Half divine; that is a demigod.

1600 W. WATSON *Decacordon* (1602) 95 All whatsoeuer is ..brought in by those outcasts of Moses, staine of Solon, and refuse of Licurgus, must be reputed for Metaphisicall, semie Diuine. **1846** GROTE *Greece* I. iv. I. 110 Either the common god whom they worshipped, or some semi-divine being closely allied to him. **1874** LISLE CARR *Jud. Gwynne* I. vii. 226 The new governess was actually attempting to level sarcasm at the semi-divine head of her mistress.

'semi-dome. [SEMI- 7 a.] Half a dome, usually one formed by vertical section.

1788 GIBBON *Decl. & F.* xl. IV. 94 The inside of St. Sophia, the cupola, the two larger, and the six smaller, semi-domes [etc.]. **1841** *Penny Cycl.* XX. 74/1 A large semicircular..apsis, covered by a semi-dome. **1874** *Contemp. Rev.* Oct. 161 The..figure of Christ in the semi-dome of the apse.

Hence **'semi-domed, semi-'domical** *adjs.*, having the form of a semi-dome.

1864 LADY EASTLAKE *Hist. Our Lord* I. 19 The semi-domed tribune or apse. *a* **1878** SIR G. SCOTT *Lect. Archit.* (1879) II. 250 Other semi-domical projections branching out from the walls which support the great semi-domes. **1888** *Gd. Words* 238 The..semi-domed nest [of the willow wren].

semi-'double, *a.* (*sb.*) [SEMI- 1. So Fr.]

1. *Liturg.* (See quots.) Also *sb.* = semi-double feast. [tr. med.L. *sēmiduplex*.]

1728 CHAMBERS *Cycl.* s.v., The Semidouble office has double Vespers and Nine Lessons at Mattins; but the Anthems are not re-doubled. **1850** *Vesper Bk.* Pref. p. xii, Sundays and Days within an Octave are Semi-doubles. **1884** *Cath. Dict.* 344/1 On semi-doubles, half of the antiphon was repeated before, the whole after the psalm. **1909** *Cath. Encycl.* VI. 23/1 In the Mass, the semidouble has always at least three orationes or prayers.

2. Of flowers: Having the innermost stamens perfect, while the outermost have become petaloid.

1720 P. BLAIR *Bot. Ess.* iv. 294 The double Roses seldom fructify, but if you shall take the Hip of one that's semi-double [etc.]. **1796** *New Ann. Reg.* 146, I had collected my opium from double or semi-double poppies. **1861** BENTLEY *Man. Bot.* 366 Cultivated semi-double flowers.

semie, obs. f. SEMÉE.

semied, var. SEMÉED.

ˌsemi-e'llipse. [SEMI- 7 a.] The half of an ellipse bisected by one of its diameters (usually the transverse).

1733 TULL *Horse-Hoeing Husb.* xxii. 344 The two Semi-Ellipses, which are on the Fore-sides of their longest Axes or Diameters. **1841** MILLER *Old Red Sandstone* viii. (1887) 150 The convex or sharpened edge is elongated into a semi-ellipse cut in the line of its shortest diameter. *a* **1878** SIR G. SCOTT *Lect. Archit.* (1879) I. 57 To make the section of the narrower vault an upright semi-ellipse.

So **ˌsemi-e'llipsis** (hence **ˌsemi-e'lliptic, -e'lliptical** *adjs.*); **semi-ellip'soidal** *a.*, of the form of half an ellipsoid.

1767 FERGUSON in *Phil. Trans.* LVII. 392 Right lines.. shall cut the *semi-ellipsis in those points through which the hour-lines must be drawn. **1833–4** J. PHILLIPS in *Encycl. Metrop.* (1845) VI. 703/1 The Yorkshire flagstone is..used, to make curb stones of two feet in height, the laminæ being placed vertically, and the block worked above to a *semi-ellipsoidal figure. **1900** B. D. JACKSON *Gloss. Bot. Terms*, **Semielliptic*, half-elliptic, the division being longitudinal. **1907** *Westm. Gaz.* 11 Nov. 6/3 The suspension of the rear part of the chassis is now by three-quarter elliptical springs instead of semi-elliptics. **1762** *Ann. Reg.* 75 A bright semicircular or *semielliptical arch over the moon. **1841** MILLER *Old Red Sandstone* viii. (1887) 166 They remind one ..of pieces of ancient iron armour, fitted into semi-elliptical scales. **1866** R. TATE *Brit. Mollusks* iv. 128 The aperture is oblique, semielliptical, thin.

semi-'feral, *a.* [SEMI- 2; cf. L. *sēmifer*, and see FERAL *a.*[2], FERINE.] Half-wild.

1887 FLOWER in *Encycl. Brit.* XXII. 774/1 The semiferal pigs of New Granada. **1906** *Westm. Gaz.* 29 Dec. 4/1 A stag in Warnham Park, one of a semi-feral herd.

So **ˌse'miferine, semiferous** (*rare*—⁰) *adjs.*

1854 KEIGHTLEY *Mythol.* (ed. 3) 233 The she-dragon Delphýné, a *semi-ferine maid. **1858** GLADSTONE *Homer* III. 605 [Achilles] is represented as having owed everything to the peculiar training of Chiron; whose semi-ferine life he shared. **1656** BLOUNT *Glossogr.*, *Semiferous*, half wilde.

semi-fidel, *a.* [f. SEMI- + *-fidel* in INFIDEL.] That is a half-believer.

1834 SOUTHEY *Doctor* xv. (1862) 37 Some of the infidel, some of the semi-fidel, and some of the super-fidel schools.

'semi-field. *Math.* [SEMI- 8 a.] Used variously to denote a set, together with operations answering to addition and multiplication, that has certain specified properties of a field but not all of them.

1923 *Ann. Math.* XXIV. 240 A set *D* which satisfies these postulates will be called a semi-field. **1966** *Math. Rev.* XXXI. 39/2 A semifield is essentially an algebraic structure which satisfies all field axioms except perhaps associativity and commutativity of multiplication; the more customary terminologies are 'division ring' (not necessarily associative) and 'distributive quasifield'.

'semiflex, *v.* [SEMI- 3.] *trans.* To bend into a position halfway between that of extension and that of complete flexure.

1835–6 *Todd's Cycl. Anat.* I. 805/2 Supposing that a muscular effort equal to 20 would completely bend the elbow, one equal to 10 would semiflex it. **1846** BRITTAN tr. *Malgaigne's Man. Oper. Surg.* 224 Semiflex the limb, to extend the parts and enlarge the articular line.

So **'semiflexed, ˌsemi'flexion, -'flexure.**

1836–9 *Todd's Cycl. Anat.* II. 78/1 The whole limb remains habitually in the *semiflexed position. **1879** *St. George's Hosp. Rep.* IX. 323 The right knee was semiflexed; the joint was greatly distended. **1828** *Lancet* 12 Apr. 64/1 The fingers are constantly in a state of *semiflexion. **1767** GOOCH *Treat. Wounds* I. 91 *Semiflexure is the proper position to keep the limb in, the muscles being then in a state of relaxation.

semi-'floret. *Bot.* [SEMI- 7 c.] A floret having a ligulate corolla, as in the dandelion.

1731 BAILEY (ed. 2), *Semi-floret* (with Florists), an half-flourish, is tubulous at the beginning like a Floret, and afterwards expanded in the form of a tongue. **1785** MARTYN *Rousseau's Bot.* vi. 68 You have observed two sorts of florets in the Daisy: the yellow ones, which occupy the middle..of the flower, and the little white tongues..which surround them... We shall leave to the first the name of Florets, and to distinguish the second we shall call them Semi-florets.

So **semi-'floscule**, in Latin form **-'flosculus**; hence **semi-'floscular, -'flosculose, -'flosculous** *adjs.*, having semi-florets (cf. LIGULATE *a.* 1).

1753 *Chambers's Cycl.* Suppl. s.v. *Scorzonera*, The flower is of the *semifloscular kind. **1727** P. BLAIR *Pharmaco-Bot.* v. 210 All the *Semifloscles or half Flourishes have a Capillamentum and Vagina. *Ibid.* 227 The yellow radiated large Flowers..have their Corona, consisting of two or three Rows of very small Semifloscules. **1720** —— *Bot. Ess.* i. 30 Each of these *Flosculi*, and **Semiflosculi*, are situated upon the top of an Embryo seminis. **1760** J. LEE *Introd. Bot.* III. xx. (1776) 232 The *Semiflosculose Flowers of Tournefort. **1866** *Treas. Bot.*, *Semiflosculose*, having the corolla split and turned to one side, as in the ligule of composites. **1720** P.

BLAIR *Bot. Ess.* iii. 128 *Semiflosculous Flowers. **1797** *Encycl. Brit.* (ed. 3) III. 422/2 One naked seed, and compound flowers semiflosculous.

semi'fluid, *a.* (and *sb.*) [SEMI- 8 a.] **A.** *adj.* Of a consistency midway between fluid and solid.

1775 ASH, *Semifluid*, imperfectly fluid. **1791** BEDDOES in *Phil. Trans.* LXXXI. 174 Workman keeps stirring and turning over the metal; in 3 m. it becomes soft and semi-fluid. **1833** N. ARNOTT *Physics* (ed. 5) II. 37 The reason why thick soups, pies, puddings, and all semifluid masses, retain their heat..so much longer than equal bulks of mere fluid. **1834** M. SCOTT *Cruise Midge* xix, Semifluid, as if composed of earth and water. **1880–1** SAVILLE KENT *Man. Infusoria* I. 234 *Monas fluida*... Body soft and semifluid, exceedingly variable in shape.

B. *sb.* A semi-fluid substance.

1731 ARBUTHNOT *Aliments* vi. vii. §7 (1735) 189 Phlegm, or Pituite, is a sort of Semi-fluid. **1873** GEIKIE *Ice Age* iii. 33 What property does ice possess which enables it to creep upon slopes adown which only fluids and semi-fluids can move?

Hence ˌ**semiflu'idity**.

1807 T. THOMSON *Chem.* (ed. 3) II. 455 The semifluidity of tar. **1860** TYNDALL *Glac.* II. xxv. 365 A proof of the semi-fluidity of the glacier.

'semi-form, *sb.* [SEMI- 2, 7 f.] An imperfect form; *Cryst.*, a hemihedral form.

1836 SMART, *Semi-form*. **1895** STORY-MASKELYNE *Crystallogr.* §137 A form of the hemi-symmetrical kind will be termed a semiform or a hemihedron.

semi-form, *a.* *rare*$^{-0}$. [ad. L. *sēmiformis*, f. *sēmi-* SEMI- + *forma* FORM *sb.*] 'Half formed, imperfect' (Bailey, 1721).

semi-formed, *a.* [SEMI- 1, ? partly after L. *sēmiformis* (see prec.).] Half-formed.

1828–32 WEBSTER, *Semi-formed*, half-formed; imperfectly formed; as, semi-formed crystals. **1897** MARY KINGSLEY *W. Africa* 44 Transparent semi-formed images of his own delirium.

semi-globe. [SEMI- 7 a.] The half of a globe; a hemisphere or hemispherical form, structure, etc.

1748 *Anson's Voy.* III. ii. 312 A semi-globe, with the flat part upwards. **1776** G. SEMPLE *Building in Water* 142, I do not..determine, whether Semi-globes, or common square Lamps, will prove most commodious. **1792** A. YOUNG *Trav. France* I. 17 The hills..swell in beautiful semi-globes. **1867** G. F. CHAMBERS *Astron.* VI. vi. 550 Diodorus conceived it [*sc.* the Milky Way] to be a dense celestial fire, shewing itself through the clefts of the starting and dividing semi-globes. **1875** BRASH *Eccl. Archit. Irel.* 43 The next order is enriched with a line of semiglobes.

So **semi-'globose, -'globular** *adjs.*, of the form of a semi-globe or hemisphere.

1721 BAILEY, **Semiglobular*, of the Form of half a Globe. **1818** KIRBY & SP. *Entomol.* vi. (ed. 3) I. 199 The red *semi-globose bodies of the gravid females. **1822** J. PARKINSON *Outl. Oryctol.* 100 The central semiglobular ventricular cavity. *Ibid.* 159 A semiglobose univalve. **1891** T. HARDY *Tess* xlii, The irregular chalk table-land or plateau, bosomed with semi-globular tumuli.

'semigod. [SEMI- 2; freq. used to render L. *sēmideus*, Gr. ἡμίθεος.] A demigod.

1417 CAPGRAVE *Chron.* (Rolls) 50 Thei had doute, whan he was ded, whethir thei schuld a noumbir him among the hie goddis or semigoddes. **1596** FITZ-GEFFREY *Sir F. Drake* (1881) 16 Some semi-God, more then a mortall creature. **1615** B. JONSON *Golden Age Rest.* Wks. (1616) 1013 Yonder soules..in Elysian bowres..That for their liuing good, now semigods are made. **1618** CHAPMAN *Hesiod* I. 254 Diuine Heroes; That the surnames bore Of Semigods. **1726** LEONI *Alberti's Archit.* II. 21/2 Semi-Gods and Heroes to be Guardians over Cities. **1831** KEIGHTLEY *Mythol.* II. i. 259 The divine race of heroes, in former times called Semigods. **1860** EMERSON *Cond. Life, Culture* Wks. (Bohn) II. 363 Can rules or tutors educate The semigod whom we await?

'semi-group. *Math.* [ad. F. *semi-groupe* (J.-A. de Séguier *Élem. de la Théorie des Groupes Abstraits* (1904), i. 8); cf. SEMI- 8.] A set together with an associative binary operation under which it is closed.

1904 *Bull. Amer. Math. Soc.* XI. 160 The author [*sc.* de Séguier] introduces..a semigroup *G* in connection with any subset *S* containing a system of generators of *G*. The postulates defining *G* are: (1) associativity; (2) for any *a* in *S* and *b* in *G*, there is at most one solution (*n* in *G*) of $an = b$; (3) similarity for $na = b$. **1905** *Trans. Amer. Math. Soc.* VI. 205 The correct theorem involves the concept semi-group, which reduces to a group when there is a finite number of elements, but not in general for an infinitude of elements. **1968** P. A. P. MORAN *Introd. Probability Theory* ii. 66 The convolution operation..has some of the properties of multiplication in that it is associative..and commutative,.. but division is not in general possible. With this operation the set of all discrete distributions on (0, 1, ...) is therefore said to form a 'semi-group'. **1972** A. G. HOWSOW *Handbk. Terms Algebra & Anal.* v. 25 A semigroup..possessing..an identity element..is called a monoid. **1979** *Proc. London Math. Soc.* XXXVIII. 335 First we find exactly when the resolvent operators and the semigroup operators are strong Feller operators.

semi'hiant, *a.* *rare*$^{-1}$. [ad. L. *sēmihiant-em*, f. *sēmi-* SEMI- 1 + *hiant-em*, pres. pple. of *hiāre* to gape.] Of lips: Half-open.

1873 M. COLLINS *Miranda* xxx, He stooped and softly kissed the semihiant lips.

ˌ**semi-indi'rect**, *a.* [SEMI- 1 a.] Of lighting: so disposed that most but not all of the light reaches the illuminated area indirectly, after having been reflected or scattered by some surface. Cf. SEMI-DIRECT *a.*

1914 J. ECK tr. *Högner's Light, Radiation & Illumination* (*table facing p.* 44), Ordinary direct-current arc lamp with standard arrangement of carbons and opal glass bowl below the arc producing semi-indirect illumination. **1964** S. DUKE-ELDER *Parsons' Dis. of Eye* (ed. 14) xxxvii. 559 In semi-indirect lighting the use of opalescent bowls permits a certain amount of direct illumination.

semi-in'variant. *Math.* Also **seminvariant.** [f. SEMI- + INVARIANT.] **1.** A function of the coefficients of a binary quantic which remains unchanged, except for a constant factor, when $x + \lambda$ is substituted for x, but not when $y + \lambda$ is substituted for y.

1860 in Cayley *Math. Papers* (1891) IV. 241 The coefficients of the equation of differences, *quâ* functions of the differences of the roots of the given equation, are leading coefficients of covariants, or (to use a shorter expression) they are 'Seminvariants'. [*Note*, The term 'Seminvariant' seems to me preferable to M. Brioschi's term 'Peninvariant'.] **1882** SYLVESTER in *Amer. Jrnl. Math.* V. 79 On Sub-invariants, i.e. Semi-Invariants to Binary Quantics of an Unlimited Order.

2. *Statistics.* Any of a set of functions of a statistical distribution, each expressible as a polynomial in the moments.

[**1903** T. N. THIELE *Theory of Observations* vi. 24 From the sums of powers we can easily compute also another serviceable collection of symmetrical functions, which for brevity we shall call the half-invariants.] **1922** A. FISHER *Math. Theory Probabilities* (ed. 2) xiv. 191 (*heading*) Semi-invariants of Thiele. **1930** *Biometrika* XXII. 225 Thiele, in 1889, after defining the semi-invariants, used symmetric functions of the observations of a sample which are the same functions of the sample moment coefficients as the population semi-invariants are of the population moment coefficients. He supplied an expression covering all the semi-invariants of the mean. **1968** P. A. P. MORAN *Introd. Probability Theory* vi. 267 The κ_n ($n \geq 2$) are dependent only on μ_2, μ_3,.. and are the same for all distributions of the form $F(x + d)$ ($-\infty < d < \infty$). They are therefore sometimes known as 'semi-invariants' since they are invariant under translation.

semikhah, var. SEMICHA.

semi-'lethal, *a.* and *sb.* *Genetics.* [SEMI- 8 a.] **A.** *adj.* Of an allele or a chromosomal abnormality: causing impaired viability of most of the individuals homozygous for it.

1917 *Proc. Nat. Acad. Sci.* III. 621 The viability of the three sex-linked dominants was..already known; the remaining six dominants were tested. In all, it was found that three of the nine are not lethal, one..is semi-lethal, and five..are completely lethal when homozygous. **1927** *Brit. Jrnl. Exper. Biol.* V. 124 This mutation appears to be semi-lethal, as the animals homozygous for it are delicate and difficult to rear. **1937** *Genetics* XXII. 471 A group of nine changes obtained from male 8..proved to be semilethal. **1962**, **1973** [see LETHAL *a.* 1 d].

B. *sb.* A semi-lethal gene.

1919 *Proc. Soc. Exper. Biol. & Med.* XVII. 12 Four of the lethals (perhaps five) are more strictly speaking 'semi-lethals', as they occasionally allow the male possessing them to live. **1944** *Proc. Nat. Acad. Sci.* XXX. 174 *Fu* is a tail mutation closely resembling *Ki*. It acts as a semi-lethal, some *Fu Fu* being viable. **1974** *Nature* 2 Aug. 451/3 Most of such populations in North America and Europe proved to be polymorphic for variant genes, usually embryonic lethals or semilethals, belonging to the T series.

semili, obs. form of SEEMLY *adv.*

Sémillon (semijɔ̃). Also **Semillon** and with small initial. [Fr. dial. (Midi), ult. ad. L. *semen* seed.] A white grape of France; also a similar one grown abroad; the white wine made from this grape.

1875, etc. [see SAUVIGNON a]. **1926** [see MONBAZILLAC]. **1963** *Times* 12 Mar. (Austral. Suppl.) p. xv/7 The best dry whites are made from the riesling and the semillon. **1978** *Courier-Mail* (Brisbane) 16 Nov. 20/5 If you think you know semillon, you may be surprised by the flavour of Huntington Estate's Mudgee semillon, 1978.

semi-log (stress variable), *a.* [Shortened f. next: cf. LOG *sb.*^{3} and *a.*] = next.

1921 W. C. MARSHALL *Graphical Methods* ii. 16 It often happens that log-log or semi-log paper would be preferable to rectangular ruled paper. **1941** *Trans. Amer. Soc. Mech. Engineers* LXIII. 539/2 We may expect..information on just why actual log curves do not plot straight on semilog paper. **1978** *Sci. Amer.* Mar. 150/3 A plot of the data on a semilog graph is shown.

ˌ**semi-loga'rithmic**, *a.* Also **semilogarithmic.** [SEMI- 8.] Having or being a scale that is linear in one direction and logarithmic in the other. Cf. prec.

1919 A. C. HASKELL *How to make & use Graphic Charts* iv. 20 The semi-logarithmic chart has a wide use for the plotting of comparative statistics of similar kind but dissimilar magnitude. **1930** R. PEARL *Med. Biometry & Statistics* (ed. 2) vi. 183 The scale of the ordinates is divided not in arithmetic progression but in proportion to the logarithms of numbers in arithmetic progression. Such a ruling is called an arithlog or semi-logarithmic grid. **1977** J. L. HARPER *Population Biol. of Plants* xv. 458 Some of these are redrawn in Fig. 15/1 on a semi-logarithmic scale to show the change in range of dispersal if the seed crop is halved.

Hence ˌ**semi-loga'rithmically** *adv.*

1919 A. C. HASKELL *How to make & use Graphic Charts* iv. 18 This is shown very clearly by charting the same data on both arithmetically and semi-logarithmically ruled paper. **1976** *Nature* 11 Mar. 153/2 Figure 1 is an action spectrum obtained by plotting semi-logarithmically the reciprocal of retinal irradiance ($1/W\ cm^{-2}$) against wavelength (nm) for each exposure duration.

'semilor, alteration of SIMILOR by association with SEMI-, *quasi* 'half-gold'.

1866 G. STEPHENS *Runic Mon.* I. 321 An inner smooth unbroken tube of semilor [*printed* semidor]. **1874** KNIGHT *Dict. Mech.* I. 63 Jeweller's Alloys..Semilor.

semilunar (sɛmɪ'l(j)uːnə(r)), *a.* (*sb.*) [ad. mod.L. *sēmilūnāris*, f. **sēmilūna* half-moon (cf. late L. *sēmilūnium*); see SEMI- 7 a and LUNAR. Cf. F. *semi-lunaire.*] **A.** *adj.* Half-moon-shaped; crescentic. (Cf. LUNAR *a.* 3.) **a.** in general use.

1597 A. M. tr. *Guillemeau's Fr. Chirurg.* 17 b/1 The Knife is of the Latinistes callede 'Culter excisorius lunatus', in Englishe a semi-lunare cutting Knife. **1717** *Phil. Trans.* XXX. 556 Some exactly Square, some oblong Square, some Semi-lunar. **1774** PENNANT *Tour Scotl. in 1772*, 188 A beautiful semilunar bay. **1795** *Anna Seward's Lett.* (1811) IV. 102 A semilunar seat, beneath its boughs, admits four people. **1865** LUBBOCK *Preh. Times* 74 It is probable that the semi-lunar instruments were fixed in wooden handles, and then used in cleaning skins.

b. *Zool.*, *Bot.*, and *Anat.* (e.g. ***semilunar cartilage, fold, ganglion, valve***: see quots.).

1681 GREW *Musæum* I. ii. 103 The Snout [*sc.* of the River-Whale] flat. Both the Chaps before of a Semilunar figure. **1719** QUINCY *Phys. Dict.* (1722), *Semilunar Valves*, thus called from their resemblance in shape to a half moon. **1728** CHAMBERS *Cycl.*, *Semilunar Valves*..are little Valves or Membranes of a Semilunar Figure, placed in the Orifice of the Pulmonary Artery, to prevent the Relapse of the Blood into the Heart at the time of its Dilatation. **1753** *Chambers' Cycl.* Suppl. s.v., All the species of the semi-lunar shells have few convolutions. **1763** *Phil. Trans.* LIV. 180 In the abdomen this nerve unites with the par vagum of the right side, and together form the great semi-lunar Ganglion. **1768** PENNANT in *Ibid.* LVIII. 93 Between the toes is a strong semilunar membrane. **1831** KNOX *Cloquet's Anat.* 133 The Semilunar Bone (*os Lunatum*), is smaller and less elongated than the scaphoid. Its upper surface is convex and smooth. **1839–47** *Todd's Cycl. Anat.* III. 84/2 The lacrymal caruncle and semilunar fold. **1840** W. J. WILSON *Anat. Vade M.* (1842) 69 The semilunar bone may be known by having a crescentic concavity, and a somewhat crescentic outline. **1852** DANA *Crust.* I. 474 The nasal opening in males is irregularly semilunar. **1871** DARWIN *Desc. Man* I. i. 23 In man..[the third eyelid] exists..as a mere rudiment, called the semilunar fold. **1873** MIVART *Elem. Anat.* v. 183 Two inter-articular cartilages, called semilunar, are..interposed between the cartilaginous articular surfaces of the femur and those of the tibia.

B. *sb.* A semilunar bone, valve, etc.

1893 S. GEE *Auscult. & Percuss.* I. iii. 50 That the closure of the aortic semilunars precedes that of the pulmonary semilunars.

semi'lunary, *a.* Now *rare* or *Obs.* [Formed as prec.: see -ARY.] = prec. adj.

1638 SIR T. HERBERT *Trav.* (ed. 2) 13 The Soldania Bay is of a semi-lunary forme. **1653** H. MORE *Antid. Ath.* II. xii. §6 Schol., The semilunary Valvulæ. **1678** *Phil. Trans.* XII. 1037 They both made but one continued semilunary Body. **1715** *Ibid.* XXIX. 328 The semilunary Valves in the Mouth of the Aorta. **1748** RICHARDSON *Clarissa* (1811) VI. 111 Semilunary rays darting from gilded clouds, surrounding an achievement motto, In Coelo Salus.

semi'lunate, *a.* [As prec.: see -ATE^2.] = LUNATE.

1841 JOHNSTON in *Proc. Berw. Nat. Club* I. ix. 266 Operculum semilunate. **1847–9** *Todd's Cycl. Anat.* IV. I. 402/2 Semilunate pancreatic glands. **1882–4** COOKE *Brit. Fresh-w. Algæ* I. 47 Cells semilunate, with the cusps either expanded or curved inwards.

So ˌ**semi-'lunated** *a.*

1726 MONRO *Anat. Bones* 106 We remark on the occipital Bone a small Rising and semilunated Excavation of each Side. **1785** LATHAM *Gen. Synopsis Birds* III. I. 293 Avoset. ..Feet palmated; the webs deeply semilunated between each toe.

'semi-lune. [As if ad. L. **sēmilūna* half-moon: see SEMI- 7 a and LUNE^3.] A semilunar or crescent-shaped form, structure, etc.; *Fortif.* = DEMI-LUNE 2.

1858 HOLDEN *Hum. Osteol.* (1878) 162 The 'semilunar' bone may be told by its two 'semilunes' below. **1862** RAWLINSON *Anc. Mon. Assyria* iv, Between this outer barrier and the City moat were interposed a species of semilune. **1880** V. HARRIS & POWER *Man. Physiol. Lab.* 46 Granular semilunar bodies, the semilunes of Heidenhain. **1905** *Daily Chron.* 18 Oct. 4/4 The vast semi-lune along the Strand.

semi-mature, *a.* [ad. L. *sēmimātūrus*: see SEMI- 1, MATURE *a.*] †**a.** Half ripe. *Obs.* *rare*$^{-1}$.

c **1440** *Pallad. on Husb.* IV. 529 Semymature also me may hem glene.

b. [SEMI- 8 a.] Partially mature.

1928 *Bull. Amer. Soil Survey Assoc.* IX. 39 Semimature soil. **1976** *Southern Even. Echo* (Southampton) 16 Nov. 2/8 Semi-mature trees are to be planted in Station Road.

semi-'metal. [ad. mod.L. *sēmi-metallum*: see SEMI- 2, 8 i.] Orig. a non-malleable metal. Now usu. signifying incomplete metallic character in other physical properties, esp. electrical conductivity; *spec.* an element (as arsenic, antimony, bismuth) or other substance having properties intermediate between those of true metals and those of semiconductors.

1661 LOVELL *Hist. Anim. & Min.* Introd. f 2 b, Semi-mettals, &c. which are mineral bodies, neere in nature unto mettals. **1671** J. WEBSTER *Metallogr.* 89 [A Metal] may comprehend both those that are strictly called Metals (not excluding common *argent vive* to be one) and those that are also called semi-metals, as Antimony and the like. **1732** *Hist. Lit.* III. 349 Fossils are divided into Metals, Salts, Sulphurs, Stones, Semi-Metals, and Earths. **1754** LEWIS in *Phil. Trans.* XLVIII. 680 Regulus of antimony, the most difficultly fusible of the semi-metals. **1812** J. SMYTH *Pract. Customs* 26 Crude Antimony, or the Ore of Antimony,.. is a semi-metal. **1831** T. P. JONES *New Convers. Chem.* Gloss., *Semi-metal.* This term is now obsolete. **1835** POE *Adv. Hans Pfaall* Wks. 1864 I. 8 A particular metallic substance or semi-metal. **1912** W. E. FORD *Dana's Man. Mineral.* (ed. 13) iv. 115 The semimetals—tellurium, arsenic, antimony and bismuth—belong together in a crystal group, all of them showing rhombohedral crystals with closely agreeing fundamental angles. **1952** *Chem. Abstr.* XLVI. 1187 Semimetals with continuous properties between metals and ceramics. **1972** *Science* 19 May 753/1 There is a clear trend both with increasing pressure and with atomic number from a semiconductor to a semimetal with a distorted simple cubic structure to a metallic, simple cubic phase.

ˌsemi-meˈtallic, *a.* [SEMI- 8 i.] Partly metallic; *spec.* of the nature of a semi-metal. Cf. SEMI-METAL.

1748–52 J. HILL *Mat. Med.* (J.), The semimetallick recrements. **1794** KIRWAN *Elem. Min.* (ed. 2) I. 164 Lustre, of the grey part, silky, verging to the semimetallic. **1804** *Edin. Rev.* III. 393 Semi-metallic matter. **1974** D. M. ADAMS *Inorg. Solids* v. 88 In contrast, the heaviest elements of the same groups (Pb, Bi, Po) are metallic or semimetallic as revealed by a progressive change down the group in properties such as electrical conductivity and optical behaviour, as well as by changes of structure type.

semimicro- (sɛmɪˈmaɪkrəʊ), *prefix* and quasi-*adj. Chem.* [f. SEMI- 1 a + MICRO- 2 a, 8 b.]

a. Formative element denoting a scale of quantitative analysis between micro-scale and macro-scale (commonly 0·01–0·1 gramme), as in ***semimicroanalysis***, ***-analytical*** adj., ***-determination***, ***-method***.

1951 A. I. VOGEL *Text-Bk. Quantitative Inorg. Analysis* (ed. 2) xi. 814 Semi-micro-analysis is concerned with the manipulation of 10–100 mg. of material, whilst micro-analysis deals with 1–10 mg. of material. **1938** *Jrnl. Soc. Chem. Industry* Dec. 464/1 (*heading*) The determination of free and saline ammonia using a semi-microanalytical method. **1937** *Industr. & Engin. Chem.* (*Analytical Ed.*) 15 June 296 (*heading*) Micro-, semimicro-, and macro-determination of halogens in organic compounds. **1933** *Ibid.* Nov. 402/1 Northrop.. has used a semi-micromethod with an accuracy of 0·2 per cent. **1963** tr. *Alexeyev's Quantitative Analysis* i. 16 The main advantages of the micro- and semimicromethods are their high speed and the need for only very small amounts of material.

b. Used without hyphen as an independent word.

1935 *Industr. & Engin. Chem.* (*Analytical Ed.*) Nov. 432/1 Semi-micro adaptations of the classical Kjeldahl method.. have been reported. **1946** F. SCHNEIDER *Qualitative Organic Microanalysis* ii. 39 Bernhauer describes several types of micro or semi-micro receivers for vacuum distillations. *Ibid.* vii. 195 A test for the nitro group carried out on a semi-micro scale. **1974** [see MICRO- 8 b]. **1976** *Lancet* 13 Nov. 1091/2 Plasma creatinine (semi-micro alkaline-picrate method) and urea (diacetyl-monoxime method) concentrations were measured.

semi-ˈmonocoque. [SEMI- 8 a.] **a.** *Aeronaut.* A fuselage or other structure having a rigid outer skin and a framework of longerons or stringers, so that stresses are shared between the skin and the framework. Usu. *attrib.*

1918 *Flight* 28 Feb. 224/2 This semi-*monocoque* structure would retain its strength even after damaging some of the longitudinal members. **1931** WARNER & JOHNSTON *Aviation Handbk.* 653 The semimonocoque has the skin reinforced by longerons and vertical bulkheads but has no diagonal web members. *Ibid.*, For the semimonocoque type the verticals should be designed as for the true monocoque designs. **1948** [see MONOCOQUE a]. **1960** C. H. GIBBS-SMITH *Aeroplane* xii. 93 As many of the so-called 'monocoque' structures came to include internal stiffening members—the skin bearing most but not all of the loads—the term 'stressed-skin' is better, implying a 'semi-monocoque' rather than a wholly unaided 'shell' structure. **1980** R. C. MIKESH *Albatros D.Va* i. 13 Their semi-monocoque, smoothly contoured plywood fuselage was a radical change from the boxy, fabric-covered structures then in general use.

b. In a motor vehicle, a body or chassis combining features of the monocoque and space-frame types. Usu. *attrib.*

1966 *Publ. Amer. Dial. Soc.* 1964 XLII. 8 *Semi-monocoque, adj.*, applied to a chassis which combines constructions of both monocoque and space frame, such as that of the Jaguar. **1973** C. CAMPBELL *Design Racing Sports Cars* viii. 134 The Formula 1 solution is usually called 'semi-monocoque' since the typical design has a centre section that is more like a bath-tub than an egg.

†**seminair(e.** *Obs. rare.* [a. F. *séminaire* (16th c. in Hatz.-Darm.), ad. L. *sēminārium* SEMINARY *sb.*[1]] = SEMINARY *sb.*[1]

c **1440** *Pallad. on Husb.* VI. 64 The semynair is doluen in this mone Al bisily.

seminal (ˈsɛmɪnəl), *a.* and *sb.* Also 4–5 **semynall**, 5–6 **seminall**. [a. F. *séminal* (14th c. in Hatz.-Darm.), = Pr., Sp., Pg. *seminal*, It. *seminale*, ad. L. *sēmināl-is*, f. *sēmin-*, *sēmen* seed, SEMEN: see -AL[1].] **A.** *adj.* Of or pertaining to seed; of the nature of seed.

1. a. Of or pertaining to the seed or semen of men and animals (applied *Phys.* and *Anat.* to structures adapted to contain or convey semen); of the nature of semen.

1398 TREVISA *Barth. De P.R.* XVII. i. (Bodl. MS.), þe humoure seminal. **1477** NORTON *Ord. Alch.* v. in Ashm. (1652) 90 Then is the Marriage perfect..; And ye maie trewly know.. How the seminall seed Masculine, Hath wrought and won the Victory, Upon the menstrualls worthily. **1620** VENNER *Via Recta* vii. 154 They notably strengthen the seminall vessels. **1673** *Phil. Trans.* VIII. 6047 Animals, of spontaneous and seminal generation. **1774** GOLDSM. *Nat. Hist.* (1776) II. 19 The seminal liquor, not only of males, but of females also, abounds in these moving little animals. **1853** G. BIRD *Urin. Deposits* §345 (ed. 4) 360 Some time after a seminal emission. **1861** T. R. JONES *Anim. Kingd.* (ed. 3) 51 We regard the former as an ovary and the second as a testicle or seminal capsule. **1880** HUXLEY *Crayfish* 351 The seminal matter is poured out.

†**b.** Begotten of the seed (of a person). *Obs.*

1646 SIR T. BROWNE *Pseud. Ep.* I. x. 43 Some deny his Divinity, that he was begotten of humane principles, and the seminall sonne of Joseph.

2. a. With reference to plants: Pertaining to or of the nature of seed. *Bot.* Of organs or structures: Serving to contain the seed.

† ***seminal plant*** (= mod.L. *plantula seminalis*): the future plant as contained in the seed, the embryo. † ***seminal root*** = RADICLE 1. ***seminal leaf*** = COTYLEDON.

1658 SIR T. BROWNE *Gard. Cyrus* iii. 125 The seminal spike of Mercurie weld. **1660** SHARROCK *Vegetables* 56 Every small particle of that imperfect plant being rather beleived seminall.. than [etc.]. **1671** GREW *Anat. Pl.* I. i. (1682) 5 If you take the Lobe of a Bean, and lengthwise pare off its Parenchyma by degrees, and in extreme thin slices, many Branches of the Seminal Root.. will appear. **1691** RAY *Creation* I. (1692) 99 Most Seeds having in them a seminal Plant perfectly formed. **1704** J. HARRIS *Lex. Techn.* I, Seminal Leaves. *c* **1770** A. HUNTER *Georg. Ess.* (1777) 262 The seminal root serves the purposes of an anchor. **1833** HOOKER in Smith *Eng. Flora* V. I. 10 The inner membrane (or seminal bag) is attached by numerous threads or veins to the inside of the outer covering. **1837** P. KEITH *Bot. Lex.* 119 The former [epigean cotyledons] springing up during the process of germination, and being converted into seminal leaves.

†**b.** Produced from seed. *Obs.*

1731 MILLER *Gard. Dict.* s.v. *Crocus*, There are several other Varieties of the Spring Crocus.., which are seminal Productions. **1766** *Complete Farmer* s.v. *Pease* 5 Z 1/1 Several of the above-mentioned.. are.. only seminal variations, which will degenerate into their original state in a few years, if they are not very carefully managed. **1796** C. MARSHALL *Gardening* v. (1798) 68 A seminal variety of any tree, or shrub, that is remarkably different from the original.

3. *gen.* Of or pertaining to the seed or reproductive elements existing in organic bodies, or attributed in pre-scientific belief to inorganic substances. Formerly often in ***seminal power***, ***virtue***: the power of producing offspring.

1605 TIMME *Quersit.* II. iv. 117 Gold phylosophicall,.. having gotten a more perfect vegetation and seminal vertue, may be dissolued into any liquor. **1651** BIGGS *New. Disp.* ¶73 The Earth hath of herself a seminall vertue of producing herbs. **1662** STILLINGFL. *Orig. Sacræ* III. ii. §17. 463 And consequently different appearances and effects may be caused in the same bodies, though it results from seminal principles. **1692** BENTLEY *Boyle Lect.* 122 To prove our assertion about the seminal production of all living creatures,.. we appeal to observation and experiment. **1701** SWIFT *Contests Nobles & Comm.* v. Misc. (1711) 74 We cannot prolong the Period of a Commonwealth beyond the Decree of Heaven, or the Date of its Nature, any more than Humane Life beyond the Strength of the Seminal Virtue.

4. a. *fig.* Having the properties of seed; containing the possibility of future development. Also, freq. used of books, work, etc., which are highly original and influential; more loosely: important, central to the development or understanding of a subject.

a **1639** WOTTON *Surv. Educ.* in *Reliq.* (1672) 77 In divers Children their ingenerate and seminal powers (as I may call them) lie deep. **1651** BAXTER *Inf. Bapt.* 294 Conferring upon them Seminal and Initial Grace, which doth not presuppose Faith, but is it self the seed of Faith. *a* **1703** BURKITT *On N.T.* Acts viii. 25 Sinful thoughts are radical and seminal evils. **1751** JOHNSON *Rambler* No. 184 ¶1 A careless glance upon a favourite author,.. is sufficient to supply the first hint or seminal idea. **1779** —— *L.P., Milton*, It is pleasant to see great works in their seminal state, pregnant with latent possibilities of excellence. **1838** MILL *Bentham* in *Westm. Rev.* Aug. 468 Jeremy Bentham and Samuel Taylor Coleridge—the two great seminal minds of England in their age. **1883** A. ROBERTS *O.T. Revision* v. 105 The Book of Job.. seems to abound in those seminal thoughts which were developed and exhibited clearly in the later books. **1889** J. M. ROBERTSON *Ess. towards Crit. Method* 30 It was due to no seminal virtue in him that French literature later flowered afresh. **1947** *Partisan Rev.* XIV. 409 To be sure, Engels' more specialized *Anti-Dühring* and *Feuerbach*, if less seminal are more systematized, more apposite to Lenin's immediate purposes. **1957** D. J. ENRIGHT *Apothecary's Shop* 233 The seminal works of modern literary criticism (such as Eliot's earlier essays and Leavis's *Revaluation*). **1960** *Guardian* 14 Oct. 8/6 Everything he says is of real value... This is what academics call a seminal book. **1960** *Twentieth Century* Nov. 438 Since the war there has been.. no seminal poet in the younger generation. **1977** *New Yorker* 6 June 122/2 That the two pianists, each seminal, agreed to play together at all was startling.

b. *nonce-use.* Concerned with the 'seeds' of future growth.

1827 HARE *Guesses* Ser. I. (1873) 199 The true reformer is the Seminal Reformer, not the Radical.

†**B.** *sb. Obs.*

1. A seminal particle; a seed, germ. Also *fig.*

1646 SIR T. BROWNE *Pseud. Ep.* VII. xvii. 379 Perhaps they containe the seminals of Spiders, and Scorpions. **1661** GLANVILL *Van. Dogm.* 155 Did it [the Peripatetic Philosophy] suppose any thing of the form to pre-exist in the matter, as the seminal of its being; 'twere a tolerable sense to say it were educed from it. **1671** R. BOHUN *Disc. Wind* 175 The seminals of heat. **1682** SIR T. BROWNE *Chr. Mor.* IV. §4 Mother-vices, which carry in their Bowels the seminals of other Iniquities.

2. *Phys.* A seminal vessel or duct.

1733 *Ordinary of Newgate* No. 1. Advt., By.. replenishing the Reins and Seminals.

†**semiˈnality.** *Obs.* Also **seminalty.** [f. SEMINAL *a.* + -ITY.] Seminal quality, principle, or condition.

1646 SIR T. BROWNE *Pseud. Ep.* I. iii. 11 As though there were a seminalitie in Urine. **1651** in Biggs *New Disp.* Verses to Author c 2, My Quill Is to seek the Seminalty of things That's cover'd in these Lines. **1665** NEEDHAM *Med. Medicinæ* 141 The Seminality or Ferment of the Disease being lodged in the Seed.

b. *pl.* Seminal properties; seminal particles, germs. *lit.* and *fig.*

1651 BIGGS *New Disp.* ¶215 Alien humours and seminalities. **1665** NEEDHAM *Med. Medicinæ* 62 The Influence which the Seminalities of the Pox have by intermixture with other Maladies. **1679** J. GOODMAN *Penitent Pardoned* I. iv. (1713) 87 Such kind of mutinous thoughts, such jealousies and suspicions are.. the seminalities of all rebellion against God. **1681** SIR T. BROWNE *Chr. Mor.* I. §28 Like the dispersed Seminalities of Vegetables at the Creation, scattered through the whole Mass of the Earth.

seminally (ˈsɛmɪnəlɪ), *adv.* ? now *rare.* [f. SEMINAL *a.* + -LY[2].] In a seminal state or manner; as a seed, germ, or reproductive element; in the form or state of seed; as regards germination or reproduction. Chiefly *fig.*

1634 JACKSON *Creed* VII. vii. Wks. VII. 35 All prediction of contingents to come, or of events not as yet seminally extant in their natural causes was from divine inspiration. **1640** BP. REYNOLDS *Passions* xxxii. 394 If the Soule be seminally traduced, it must be either from the body, or from the soule of the Parents. **1675** BAXTER *Cath. Theol.* II. v. 105 Why am I guilty of what Adam did, but because I have a nature that was seminally in him? **1772** FLETCHER *Logica Genev.* 150 If we all received an unspeakable injury by being seminally in Adam when he fell.. we all received also an unspeakable blessing by being in his loins when God spiritually raised him up. **1847** A. M'LEAN *Comm. Hebr.* I. vii. 264 Levi.. may be said to have been seminally in the loins of Abraham when Melchisedec met him. **1887** GLADSTONE in *19th Cent.* Jan. 2 Homer.. is.. also a great dramatist, and contains within him seminally the drama of his country.

†**ˈseminant.** *Obs. rare*[−1]. [ad. L. *sēminant-em*, pres. pple. of *sēmināre* to sow.] A sower of seed; applied allusively to a seminary priest: cf. SEEDMAN and SEMINARY *a.* 2 and *sb.*[2] 2.

c **1588** SEGAR *Blazon of Papists* C 3, A Papist Seminant. Ioyn'd with the rest of this pernicious broode, Are Seminants calde Iesuistes of some.

†**ˈseminar**[1]. *Sc. Obs.* [ad. L. *sēminārium*: see -AR[2].] = SEMINARY *sb.*[1]

1573 TYRIE *Refut. Knox* 44 b, But he of his prouidence hes reseruit sindrie, as ane seminar, be quhome he hes prorogat his doctrine to the posteritie.

seminar[2] (ˈsɛmɪnɑːr). [Ger., ad. L. *sēminārium* SEMINARY *sb.*[1]] **1. a.** In German universities (hence in certain British and American universities), a select group of advanced students associated for special study and original research under the guidance of a professor. Also *transf.*, a class that meets for systematic study under the direction of a teacher.

1889 A. S. HILL *Our English* v. 209 In New York and Washington, if I am not misinformed, 'seminars' are periodically held, at which a clever woman coaches other clever women in the political, literary, and ethical topics of the day. **1892** *Daily News* 3 Aug. 6/1 [University Extension meeting at Oxford] A seminar is being organised in connection with the economic course, and the students will write essays and have tutorial supervision. **1893** *Chicago Advance* Apr. 27 The Seminar.. is a society for the prosecution of independent work in some chosen field. There are to be eight of these Seminars next year. **1911** *Expositor* July 16 It has been well dealt with in the brilliant volume of Essays from Dr. Sanday's Seminar.

b. A conference of specialists; also, more generally, a course of instruction for managers, etc. orig. *U.S.*

1944 *Sun* (Baltimore) 21 Sept. 6/2 Problems of condemnation for the temporary war use of property will be featured at a seminar conducted by the American Institute of Real Estate Appraisers. **1969** *Listener* 10 Apr. 482/2 For the first time in its history, the Conservative Party has held a one-day seminar, not on Exports, or on Trade Unions, or on Defence, but on the Arts. **1982** *REMARC Database News* July 1 Key members of the Scottish Library Network.. attended a REMARC seminar at the Carrollton Press data-entry facility at Irvine, Scotland.

2. *attrib.*

1948 *Sun* (Baltimore) 12 May 12/3 Two years ago he started the personal campaign that took him into large communities and small, and he developed a sort of '*seminar*' method of question-and-answer discussion at luncheons, meetings of students and similar gatherings. **1959** Seminar-paper [see *fence-sitting* s.v. FENCE *sb.* 11]. **1977** J. D. DOUGLAS in Douglas & Johnson *Existential Sociol.* i. 27 One can even see the feelings leading to important actions, such as separating from a lover or starting a seminar workshop to deal with the feelings. **1981** *Times Lit. Suppl.* 6 Feb. 136/4 The names of these daunting authors . . make an occasional modest appearance on reading-lists and in seminar-rooms.

seminarial (sɛmɪˈnɛərɪəl), *a. rare.* [f. SEMINARY *sb.*[1] + -AL[1].] Of or pertaining to a seminary.

1762 tr. *Busching's Syst. Geog.* V. 180 Four are invested with the government of seminarial convents. **1870** DICKENS *E. Drood* iii, Miss Twinkleton, in her seminarial state of existence.

seminarian (sɛmɪˈnɛərɪən), *a.* and *sb. rare.* [f. SEMINARY *sb.*[1] + -AN.] †**A.** *adj.* = SEMINARY *a.*

1584 in Foley *Rec. Eng. Prov. S.J.* (1880) VI. 722 Martin Array, a Seminarian priest.

B. *sb.* †**a.** A seminary priest (*obs.*). **b.** A student at a seminary or Jesuit school, a seminarist.

1584 in Foley *Rec. Eng. Prov. S.J.* (1880) VI. 721 Lane, of Fisheborne receiveth Correy, a Seminarian. **1794** tr. *Barruel's Hist. Clergy Fr. Rev.* III. 27 At eight o'clock in the morning the clergymen of St. Nicholas . . were dragged with their seminarians to the house of St. Firmin. **1908** G. TYRRELL in *Hibbert Jrnl.* Jan. 254 In protecting the seminarian from the knowledge of awkward facts.

Hence **semiˈnarianism**, the mannerism of a seminarian.

1879 W. M. BAKER *His Majesty Myself* xviii. (1880) 139 (Funk) 'He, at least, has no seminarianism about him' she said, incidentally to Revel.

seminarist (ˈsɛmɪnəˌrɪst). [f. SEMINAR-Y *sb.*[1] + -IST. Cf. F. *séminariste* (1690 in Hatz.-Darm.), Sp., Pg., It. *seminarista*, Du., Ger., Sw., Da. *seminarist.*]

1. A Roman Catholic priest educated in a foreign seminary in the 16th and 17th c., esp. at Douay for the English mission. Now *Hist.*

1583 FULKE *Def. Tr. Script.* v. 147 One who hath more profited the Church of God, with his sincere translation, and learned annotations, than all the popish Seminaries, and Seminarists, shall be able to hinder it. **1679** EVERARD *Popish Plot* 1, I surprized her with two of the chief Scotch Seminarists of Paris. **1716** M. DAVIES *Athen. Brit.* III. *Diss. Drama* 4 The Romish regular *Clerici*, Cannon Regulars, Theatins, Oratorians, Seminarists, Chapterists, &c. **1826** J. R. BEST *Four Yrs. France* 6 The story of the poor seminarist of Douay. **1841** D'ISRAELI *Amen. Lit.* (1867) 424 The seminarists were universally revered as candidates of martyrdom.

2. a. A student in a seminary; chiefly, a student in a seminary for the training of Roman Catholic priests.

1835 BECKFORD *Alcobaça & Batalha* 90 A tide of monks, sacristans, novices, seminarists . . appeared all of a sudden flowing forth from every cell and cloister. **1862** *Westm. Rev.* Jan. 185 The greatest stress is laid [in Prussian training-colleges] on learning by heart. The seminarist must be able to repeat without book all the Scripture histories read in the school. **1877** D. M. WALLACE *Russia* iv. 52 The Bishop does the same for all the seminarists who wish to be ordained.

b. *pl.* The teaching staff in a seminary.

a **1668** LASSELS *Voy. Italy* II. (1670) 119 This Church now belongs to the Seminarists of the German Colledge. **1873** MORLEY *Rousseau* I. 56 Shortly the Seminarists reported that, though not vicious, their pupil was not even good enough for a priest, so deficient was he in intellectual faculty. **1886** *Encycl. Brit.* XXI. 24/1 He was sent to the seminarists of St. Lazare to be improved in classics.

3. A member of a SEMINAR[2].

1865 M. PATTISON *Ess.* (1889) I. 347 A Göttingen student could not carry with him into the world any better recommendation than to have been one of Heyne's seminarists. **1882–3** *Schaff's Encycl. Relig. Knowl.* 2497/2 [Wessenberg] sent his seminarists to Pestalozzi to learn the new method of instruction. **1972** *Daily Tel.* 14 Jan. 17 For a fee of £60, seminarists will be impressed with the need for strategic plans for growth . . over the next decade, fed but not accommodated.

Hence **seminaˈristic** *a.*, of or pertaining to a seminary priest.

1841 *Fraser's Mag.* XXIV. 299 The mixture of seminaristic modesty and nautical devil-may-care-ishness . . caused me to laugh outright.

†**seminarize**, *v. Obs. rare*[−1]. [f. SEMINAR-Y *sb.*[1] + -IZE.] *trans.* To sow.

1593 NASHE *Christ's T.* G iij, Eleazer . . was the first that seminarizd thys hope of signiorizing and freedome amongst them. **1623** COCKERAM I, *Seminarize*, to sow or plant.

seminary (ˈsɛmɪnərɪ), *sb.*[1] Forms: 5 **seminari, semynari**, 5–6 **semynary**, 5–7 **seminarie**, 6 **seminarye**, (**semenarie, -ye, semynarie, seameanary**, *pl. Sc.* **seminareis**), (7 **semenary**), 6– **seminary**. See also SEMINAIR(E, SEMINAR[1]. [ad. L. *sēminārium* seed-plot (also *fig.*), orig. neut. of *sēminārius* SEMINARY *a.* Cf. F. *séminaire*, Sp., Pg., It. *seminario*, G. *seminar.*]

†**1.** A piece of ground in which plants are sown (or raised from cuttings, etc.) to be afterwards transplanted; a seed-plot. *Obs.*

c **1440** *Pallad. on Husb.* III. 480 Let set in to thy semynari bliue Oliues bowis vj feet long or fiue. *Ibid.* III. 489, IV. 558. **1601** HOLLAND *Pliny* XVII. x. I. 510 Concerning seminaries and nource-gardens. **1658** EVELYN *Fr. Gard.* (1675) 46 Then taking your grafted trees out of the seminary, you shall transplant them into this nursery. **1719** LONDON & WISE *Compl. Gard.* 185 For Apple-tree Seminaries, plant the Wildings grown from the Kernels... For a Seminary of Plumbs, plant the Suckers of their several kinds. **1778** R. WESTON *Gard. & Planter's Cal.* (ed. 2) 80 The Nursery and Seminary. **1829** SOUTHEY *Sir T. More* (1831) II. 47 They have become mere seminaries . . and for raising dwarf trees.

†**b.** *transf.*

1590 SPENSER *F.Q.* III. vi. 30 In that same Gardin all the goodly flowres, Wherewith dame Nature doth her beautifie, . . Are fetcht: there is the first seminarie Of all things, that are borne to liue and die [etc.]. **1660** SHARROCK *Vegetables* 29 The ground itself from its own seminary sent out the supposititious crop of oates.

†**2.** *transf.* A place where animals are bred; a region which supplies (some kind of animal). Also, a stock or breed (of animal). *Obs.*

1607 TOPSELL *Four-f. Beasts* 21 He that will haue a good flocke of Asses, must looke that the male and female be sounde, . . and out of a good seminary, as of Arcadia or Rea. *Ibid.* 69 Very great and large oxen, which the inhabitants cal *Pyrhicæ*, because that their first stocke or seminary were kept by King Pirrhus. **1612** SELDEN *Illustr. Drayton's Poly-olb.* vi. 99 The whole tract is a Seminary of Horses. **1665** NEEDHAM *Med. Medicinæ* 197 Man's rotten Carcase becomes a Seminary of Worms.

3. *fig.* **a.** A place of origin and early development; a place or thing in which something (e.g. an art or science, a virtue or vice) is developed or cultivated, or from which it is propagated abundantly.

1592 R. D. *Hypnerotomachia* 79 b, My insatiable and wanton eyes . . whome I founde the seminaries and moovers of all so great strife and trouble, in my . . heart. **1596** R. L[INCHE] *Diella* viii, Thyne eyes (those Semynaries of my griefe). **1625** JACKSON *Creed* v. xx. Wks. IV. 177 That the seminaries of poetry should be the chief nurses of idolatry argues how apt the one is to bring forth the other. **1646** SIR T. BROWNE *Pseud. Ep.* VI. vii. 308 God . . hath with variety disposed the principles of all things; wisely contriving them in their proper seminaries, and where they best maintaine the intention of their species. *a* **1656** USSHER *Power of Princes* II. (1683) 156 The bloud of this noble Army of Martyrs became the fruitful seminary thereof. **1659** *Gentl. Calling* (1696) 114 If Gentlemen's families were so ordered, as to become Seminaries of Industry and Sobriety. **1696** WHISTON *Th. Earth* (1722) 88 The Chaos, that known fund and seminary of the Six Days Creation. **1744** BERKELEY *Siris* §141 Wks. 1871 II. 415 All which demonstrates the air to be a common seminary and receptacle of all vivifying principles. **1830** MACKINTOSH *Ethical Philos.* Wks. 1846 I. 113 The virtues which guard the natural seminaries of the affections are their only true and lasting friends. **1849** MACAULAY *Hist. Eng.* vi. II. 112 The Council chamber at Edinburgh had been . . a seminary of all public and all private vices. **1864** LOWELL *Study Windows, Libr. Old Authors* end, We are profoundly thankful for the omission of a glossary. It would have been a nursery and seminary of blunder.

b. A place, country, society, condition of things, or the like, in which some particular class of persons are produced or trained.

a **1604** HANMER *Chron. Irel.* (1633) 53 The seminarie or bee hive of many thousands of Monkes. **1615** E. S. *Britain's Buss* E 2 By which meanes euery Busse shall be a Seminary of Saylors and Fishers also, for so shall euery busse breede and make Sixe new Marriners. *a* **1626** BACON *Notes Sp. conc. War Spain* Wks. 1826 V. 234 There is not in the world again such a spring and seminary of military people as is England, Scotland, and Ireland. *a* **1635** NAUNTON *Fragm. Reg.* (Arb.) 33 Those Netherland wars were the Queens Seminaries, and the Nurseries of very many brave Souldiers. **1750** CARTE *Hist. Eng.* II. 762 The north used to be the seminary of Henry's and Margaret's forces, supplying them constantly with fresh recruits. **1756–9** A. BUTLER *Lives of Saints, S. Wasnulf*, In the seventh century St. Vincent . . invited many holy monks from Ireland and Scotland, then seminaries of saints, into the Netherlands. **1876** BLACKIE *Lang. & Lit. Scott. Highl.* v. 309 What had once been . . the seminary of a stout Celtic people, and the nursery of a brave British army.

†**c.** A continuous supply (of a class of persons).

1652–62 HEYLYN *Cosmogr.* III. (1673) 166/1 And from hence supply themselves with a perpetual Seminary of Slaves and Souldiers.

4. A place of education, a school, college, university, or the like; often explicitly (cf. 3 a) ***seminary of learning, science***, etc. Also in more specific sense (cf. 3 b) an institution for the training of those destined for some particular profession.

'In the earlier half of the 19th c. 'Seminary for Young Ladies' was very common as the designation of a private school for girls. This use is perhaps not wholly obsolete, but is no longer in repute.' *N.E.D.*

1585 *Reg. Privy Council Scot.* Ser. I. IV. 2 Universiteis and seminareis for instructioun of craftie personis. **1607** *Statutes in Hist. Wakefield Gram. Sch.* (1892) 62 This schole is principallie ordained a seminarie for bringinge up of christian children. **1611** CORYAT *Crudities* 378 A Schoole which hath beene a most fruitfull seminarie of many excellent learned men. **1628** WOTTON *Life & Lett.* (1907) II. 307 This Royal Seminary [Eton]. **1642** FULLER *Holy & Prof. St.* II. xxiii. 146 He was preferred to be Master of Westminster School a most famous seminarie of learning. *a* **1700** EVELYN *Diary* 10 Mar. 1687, I . . much admir'd the order, œconomy, and excellent government of this most charitable seminary [Christ's Hospital]. **1709** SWIFT *Advancem. Relig.* 30 As for the Inns of Court, . . they must needs be the worst instituted Seminaries in any Christian Country. **1757** BURKE *Abridgm. Eng. Hist.* II. ii. Wks. (1812) 281 That a nation . . should . . have established so flourishing a seminary of learning. **1774** J. BRYANT *Mythol.* I. 436 They were made use of for seminaries, where young people were educated. **1800** HT. LEE *Canterb. T.* (ed. 2) III. 9 The seminary to which Mr. Cavendish conducted his son could not properly be termed a school. **1802** BEDDOES *Hygeia* VIII. 71 A lady who believes herself to have been the favourite of the heads of one of the most numerous seminaries in England. **1815** SCOTT *Guy M.* xvii, To place his daughter in a seminary for female education. **1817** *Sporting Mag.* L. 13 The modern metaphorical refinement of styling a school a seminary which may be now seen in many a blind alley of London. **1831** BREWSTER *Newton* i. 4 At the usual age he was sent to two day-schools at Skillington and Stoke, where he acquired the education which such seminaries afforded. **1837** LOCKHART *Scott* I. iii. 102 Young Walter spent one hour daily at a small separate seminary of writing and arithmetic. **1840** DICKENS *Old C. Shop* viii, Whereon appeared, in circumambient flourishes, the words 'Ladies' Seminary'. **1840** JOS. QUINCY *Harvard Univ.* II. 452 The interests of society demand, that the number of the greater seminaries of science should be few. **1876** J. GRANT *Burgh Sch. Scot.* II. v. 201 That famous seminary [Aberdeen University]. **1885** W. S. GILBERT *Mikado* I. Trio, Three little maids who, all unwary, Come from a ladies' seminary, Freed from its genius tutelary—Three little maids from school!

5. *R.C. Ch.* A school or college for training persons for the priesthood. In 16–17th c. often used with reference to those institutions engaged in the training of priests for the English mission.

1581 J. HAMILTON *Cath. Traict.* Epist. 9 He hes not neglectit ye occasion offrit to plant sindrie learnit and godlie ȝong men in a publik seminarie. **1582** ALLEN *Martyrd. Campion* (1908) 6 Hearing that there was a Seminary not longe before begonne in Doway. **1589** NASHE *Pasquill & Marforius* A iij, At the last, hearing the Schollers of the English Seminarie merrie, as they returned from their Vineyarde . . I stole out of Rome by night [etc.]. **1678** PHILLIPS (ed. 4), *Seminary* . . a Colledge approved for the education of Priests of the Romish Church, who were to propagate their Doctrine in England, or other Parts of a different perswasion. **1716** in Payne *Rec. Eng. Catholics of 1715* (1889) 148 John is now in some Popish seminary abroad. **1868** G. DUFF *Pol. Surv.* 16 For monasteries, we should read convents, mission-houses, and seminaries.

b. *attrib.*, as in ***seminary †college, -man, -priest.***

1581 in *Cath. Rec. Soc. Publ.* V. 20 William thorley . . was brought uppe in a Semynary College at Reames iij yeares. **1582** ALLEN *Martyrd. Campion* (1908) 99 Confessing boldly himself to be a Catholike, a Priest, and a Seminarie man of Rhemes. **1582** in *Cath. Rec. Soc. Publ.* V. 26 He is now w[th]in this moneth returned a Seameanary preest from Rheames. **1693** *Mem. Ct. Teckely* I. 5 [The Emperors of the House of Austria] filled their Countreys with Missionaries, or Seminary Priests, as we call them. **1759** ROBERTSON *Hist. Scot.* I. Wks. 1813 I. 542 He drove many of the seminary priests out of the kingdom. **1821** SCOTT *Kenilw.* i, Giles Gosling . . was at one time inclined to suspect his guest of being a Jesuit, or seminary priest.

6. = SEMINAR[2]. Also *attrib.*

1889 *Academy* 17 Aug. 103/2 The 'seminary' system seems to be making way [at Harvard]... The seminary is an association of the teachers, fellows, and scholars . . for the prosecution of original studies by means of discussion and criticism. **1891** *Century Dict.* s.v., Seminary course.

†**7.** Short for *seminary priest* (see 5 b). *Obs.*

1581 W. CHARKE *Replie to Censure* I iii, This should be a note not only to those Iesuites, but to al whatsoeuer they be, Iesuites, or Seminaries or massepriestes, or what persons soeuer. **1593** NASHE *Christ's T.* Q iii b, The Romish Seminaries haue not allured vnto them so many good wits as Atheisme. **1614** B. JONSON *Barth. Fair* II. i, A while agone, they made mee, yea me, to mistake an honest zealous Pursiuant, for a Seminary. **1685** WOOD *Life* Sept. (O.H.S.) III. 162 M[r] Ll. Jenkyns was imprison'd for a seminary.

¶**b.** Often treated as a subst. use of SEMINARY *a.*, with the sense 'one who sows the seed' (of Romish doctrine). See SEMINARY *a.* 2 and *sb.*[2] 2.

1583 [see SEEDMAN 1]. **1610** J. DOVE *An Advert.* 2 Their yong frye of Seminaries and seed-men, which are trained up under them, see not with their owne eyes.

†**ˈseminary**, *a.* and *sb.*[2] *Obs.* [ad. L. *sēminārius*, f. *sēmin-* seed: see SEMEN.] **A.** *adj.*

1. = SEMINAL *a.*

1592 NASHE *P. Penilesse* H ii, They [spirits] so comprehend those seminarie vertues to men vnknown, that those thinges which, in course of time, . . Nature of it selfe can effect, they . . can contriue and compas in a moment. **1602** DOLMAN *La Primaud. Fr. Acad.* (1618) III. 727 That which the point is in the Mathematicks, the same is the seminarie power in the Phisickes. **1615** CROOKE *Body of Man* 219 Aristotle . . would haue that humor which is auoyded by the necke of the matrix not to be a seminarie or seedy humour. **1650** BULWER *Anthropomet.* 233 The Testes and seminary vessels. **1671** J. WEBSTER *Metallogr.* ii. 33 Especially in declaring the root and seminary power of Metals. **1720** P. BLAIR *Bot. Ess.* iv. 306 The Seminary Particles in the Ova. *a* **1742** G. MARTIN in *Med. Ess. Edin.* V. 231 The seminary Blood-vessels.

2. Occupied in sowing seed. *fig.* with allusion to SEMINARY *sb.*[1] 7.

1609 BIBLE (Douay) To Rdr. †6 And so [he] . . calleth the other Apostles *Messores*, Reapers, and S. Paul, being specially sent to the Gentiles, *Seminatorem* a Sower, or Seminarie Apostle. **1640** GAUDEN *Love of Truth* 25 Fortifying truth, against the Seminary incursions of those, that seeke to encroach upon its ancient bounds.

B. *sb.* (From absolute uses of the adj.)

1. a. A germ, embryo, seminal particle. **b.** *spec.* The morbific matter or principle (of a disease); *pl.* germs (of infection). Cf. SEMINAL *sb. Obs.*

a. 1671 J. WEBSTER *Metallogr.* III. 40 Plants were not created perfect at first, but only in their seminaries.

b. 1604 F. HERING *Mod. Defence* A iiij, The four windes bring diuers affections of the aire, and especially contagious seminaries. **1650** BULWER *Anthropomet.* 244 In whom there lies hid the Seminary of a disease. **1665** G. HARVEY *Adv. agst. Plague* 9 Houses built upon a clay and foggy ground are more subject to conceive pestilent Seminaries. **1684** tr. *Bonet's Merc. Compit.* VI. 202 The Plague, whose *fomes*, seminary, or contagion you will never cast out of the Body, except by [Alexitericks or Sudorificks]. **1694** SALMON *Bate's Dispens.* (1713) 191/2 Dedicated to the Kidneys and Bladder, not only to evacuate what is viscous and sandy in them, but also to move the Seminary thereof, and hinder.. the farther Generations of Sand, Gravel, or Stones.

2. A sower of seed. Only *fig.*, chiefly with punning allusion to SEMINARY *sb.*[1] 7.

[**1583, 1610**: see SEMINARY *sb.* 7 b.] *a* **1680** BUTLER *Charac.* in *Rem.* (1759) II. 450 A Pettifogger..is a Law-seminary, that sows Tares amongst Friends to entangle them in Contention with one another.

†**'seminate,** *a. Obs. rare*$^{-1}$. [ad. L. *sēminātus*, pa. pple. of *sēmināre*: see SEMINATE *v.*] Disseminated.

a **1560** ROLLAND *Crt. Venus* II. 851 The suaue odour Was seminate about that blisfull tour.

seminate ('sɛmɪneɪt), *v.* Now *arch.* [f. L. *sēmināt-*, ppl. stem of *sēmināre* to sow, bring forth, propagate, etc., f. *sēmin-*: see SEMEN and -ATE[3].]

1. *trans.* To sow; chiefly *fig.* to promulgate or disseminate.

1535 HEN. VIII in Strype *Eccl. Mem.* (1733) I. App. liv. 141 Who..intended to seminate, engender, & breed, among our people & subjects, a most mischievous & seditious Opinion. **1597** A. M. tr. *Guillemeau's Fr. Chirurg.* fiv b, I am not entred into this matter to sowe and seminate the same in an infertille grownde. **1652** GAULE *Magastrom.* 60 If naturall, where are the innate principles, primely seminated, common to all men? *a* **1734** NORTH *Life Dr. J. North* (1742) 248 He shewed an innate Hatred of popular Faction; as well that which had been seminated all over England..as also [etc.]. **1796** W. H. MARSHALL *West Eng.* I. 164 The method of seminating the Wheat crop.

†**b.** *Her.* (Cf. SEMÉE *a.*, SEMINED.)

1610 GUILLIM *Heraldry* III. x. (1611) 115 If they were strowed, or (as I may better terme it) seminated all over the field, then were it not a bend betweene but upon or over them.

2. *intr.* To produce seed. *rare*$^{-1}$.

1676 HALE *Contempl.* I. 430 The secret spark of life that is in it, that Attracts, increaseth, Groweth, Seminateth, preserves it self and its kinds.

Hence **'seminated** *ppl. a.*

1662 J. CHANDLER *Van Helmont's Oriat.* 236 Wherefore the whole muckie and phlegmatick Doctrine of Galen, hath been dried up in a seminated or seedied Stone.

semination (sɛmɪ'neɪʃən). [a. L. *sēminātiōn-em*, f. *sēmināre* to sow: see SEMINATE *v.*]

1. The action or process of sowing. Chiefly *fig.*

1531 CROMWELL in Merriman *Life & Lett.* (1902) I. 338 The semynacyon and sowing such euill seedes of dampnable and detestable heresies. **1664** EVELYN *Sylva* ii. 8 But to make an Essay what Seed is most agreeable to the Soil, you may by the thriving of a promiscuous Semination make a judgement of it. **1737** L. CLARKE *Hist. Bible* II. 195 From a slender Semination of the Gospel there was likely to be a vast Harvest. **1797** J. LAWRENCE in *Monthly Mag.* XLVIII. 314 It is beginning to be sown with the seeds of such as we fashionably style French principles: in a few years, the semination will be universal and complete.

†**b.** A mode of grafting. *Obs. rare*$^{-1}$.

1589 FLEMING *Virg. Georg.* II. 21 *note*, Semination, insition, inoculation or implastration, the three kindes of grafting.

†**c.** (See quot.) *Obs.*

1722 QUINCY *Lex. Physico-Med.* (ed. 2), *Semination*, is called by Blasius the Immission of the Male-Seed into the Womb in Coition.

2. The production of seed or semen.

1658 PHILLIPS, *Semination*, or *Sementation*, a sowing, or bringing forth seed. *a* **1676** HALE *Prim. Orig. Man.* III. iv. (1677) 267 And therefore such Herbs, if their Semination be prevented by being cut, survive to the next Year. **1822–29** *Good's Study Med.* (ed. 3) V. 112 The generic term Prœotia or Prœotes is copied from Theophrastus... It is, however, peculiarly applied to premature semination. **1853** G. JOHNSTON *Nat. Hist. E. Borders* I. 124 All the Hieracia are erect throughout the process of florescence and semination.

3. The natural dispersion of seeds.

1765 JOHNSON *Shaks. I Hen. IV*, II. i. *note*, Those who perceived that fern was propagated by semination, and yet could never see the seed.

†**4.** = INOCULATION. *Obs. rare*$^{-1}$.

1747 *Gentl. Mag.* XVII. 527 We are informed (by the learned Maitland) that this method of Semination of the small pox has been in use above 100 years among the Chinese.

seminative ('sɛmɪneɪtɪv), *a. rare.* [Formed as SEMINATE *v.* + -IVE.] Having the function of sowing or propagating; capable of sowing seeds (of thought). †*seminative power, virtue*: cf. SEMINAL *a.*

1398 TREVISA *Barth. De P.R.* XVII. cxlii. (Bodl. MS.), Vertu semynatife of Rewe is in þe sede in the stalke in spraie and in rote. **1651** BIGGS *New Disp.* ¶73 The seminative power is taken from the Earth. **1818** G. S. FABER *Horæ Mosaicæ* I. 22 Lastly, the whole frame of seminative nature was, by all the gods, distributed in proper order. **1889** LOWELL *Latest Ess., Stud. Mod. Lang.* (1891) 143 There have been men of genius, like Emerson, richly seminative for other minds.

†**seminator.** *Obs.* [a. L. *sēminātor*, agent-n. f. *sēmināre*: see SEMINATE *v.*] A sower, a scatterer of seed. (With quot. 1609 cf. SEMINARY *sb.*[2] 2.)

1609 WOTTON *Life & Lett.* (1907) I. 462 Here hath been scattered a report by the Pope's seminators that his Majesty had [etc.]. **1651** PRESTWICH tr. *Seneca's Hippol.* I. ii. 7 The Gods fruitfull Seminator, who As he his Thunder brandishes, doth shake The trembling world.

†**'semined,** *pple. Obs.* [f. *semine vb., ad. L. *sēmināre*: see SEMINATE *v.*] = SEMÉE *a.*

1603 B. JONSON *King's Entertainm.* (1604) C 2 Irene, or Peace... Her attire White, semined with Starres. *a* **1616** —— *Hymenæi* B 2 Reason, seated in the top of the Globe.. her Garments blew, and semined with Starres. **1611** SPEED *Hist. Gt. Brit.* IX. xii. §47 Philip de Valoys sate crowned in violet veluet, semined with golden lillies. **1672** T. JORDAN *Lond. Triumph.* 6.

†**se'minial,** *a. Obs. rare*$^{-1}$. [f. SEMINI-UM + -AL[1].] Of or pertaining to a 'seminium'.

a **1676** HALE *Prim. Orig. Man.* III. iv. (1677) 271 The Seminial Particles of Insects.

semi'niferal, *a. rare.* [f. L. *sēmin-* SEMEN + *-fer* (f. *ferre* to bear) + -AL[1].] = SEMINIFEROUS *a.* 2.

1840 G. V. ELLIS *Anat.* 502 Between the seminiferal tubes.

seminiferous (sɛmɪ'nɪfərəs), *a.* Also 8 semen-. [f. L. *sēmin-*, *sēmen* SEMEN + -(I)FEROUS.]

1. *Bot.* Bearing or producing seed.

seminiferous scale, in *Coniferæ* the scale above the bract-scale bearing the ovules, and ultimately the seeds.

1692 RAY in *Lett. Lit. Men* (Camden) 198 Because, being seminiferous, I deferred it when I entred the Lenticulæ. **1707** *Monthly Miscell.* Dec. I. 230 Seminiferous Cup Mushroom. **1720** P. BLAIR *Bot. Ess.* iii. 192 There is a Difference among the Flowers of this Valerian, for some are Seminiferous, more compactly united, like the Heads of Scabiosa. **1784** TWAMLEY *Dairying Exemp.* 172 Most of the seminiferous, or Seed tribe. **1821** W. P. C. BARTON *Flora N. Amer.* I. 109 Seminiferous dissepiment parallel with the valves. **1882** VINES *Sachs' Bot.* 518 The seminiferous scales ..appear to be axillary structures in the axils of bracts.. which spring from the axis of the cone.

2. *Anat.* Containing or conveying the seminal fluid; bearing or producing semen.

1831 R. KNOX *Cloquet's Anat.* 808 These filaments are the seminiferous vessels or ducts. **1860** TANNER *Pregnancy* i. 33 In the male we have the bundles of seminiferous tubules enclosed in a fibrous capsule.

seminific (sɛmɪ'nɪfɪk), *a. rare*$^{-0}$. [f. L. *sēmin-* SEMEN + -(I)FIC.] Producing semen or seed.

1696 PHILLIPS (ed. 5), *Seminific*, producing seed for generation. **1706** —— (ed. Kersey), *Seminifick*, that makes or breeds Seed. **1898** *Syd. Soc. Lex.*, *Seminific*, semen-producing. **1900** B. D. JACKSON *Gloss. Bot. Terms.*, *Seminific*, forming or producing seed.

†**semi'nifical,** *a. Obs. rare*$^{-1}$. [Formed as prec. + -AL[1].] = prec.

1646 SIR T. BROWNE *Pseud. Ep.* VI. viii. 317 We are made to beleeve that the fourteenth yeare males are seminificall and pubescent. **1656** in BLOUNT *Glossogr.*

seminifi'cation. *rare*$^{-1}$. [f. L. *sēmin-* SEMEN + -(I)FICATION.] Production of seed.

a **1676** HALE *Prim. Orig. Man.* I. ii. (1677) 45 The Faculties or Operations of this *Anima vegetabilis* are these; 1. Attraction of aliment:..6. Seminification and propagation from the seed or seminal parts. **1900** B. D. JACKSON *Gloss. Bot. Terms*, *Seminification*, propagation from seed.

seminiform (sɪ'mɪnɪfɔːm), *a. Bot. rare.* [Formed as SEMINIFIC *a.*: see -FORM.] Having the form of seeds. †**a.** ***seminiform attire***, a name given by Grew to the stamens. See ATTIRE *sb.* 8. *Obs.*

1676 GREW *Anat. Pl.* I. v. §13 (1682) 37 The Attire, I find to be of two kinds, Seminiforme, and Florid. *Ibid.* IV. II. iii. 167 That sort of Attire, which may be called Seminiform, being usually, as it were, a little sheaf of seed-like Particles, standing on so many Pedicills, as the Ear doth upon the End of the Straw.

b. Bory's epithet for the reproductive bodies of Fungi, Polypi, Confervæ, and other vegetable or animal organisms which have no specialized generative organs.

1858 MAYNE *Expos. Lex.* s.v. *Seminiformis.*

seminist ('sɛmɪnɪst). *Biol.* [a. F. *séministe* (18th c.), f. L. *sēmin-* SEMEN: see -IST.] (See quot. 1876.)

1857 DUNGLISON *Med. Lex.*, *Seminist*, animalculist. **1876** *Ibid.*, *Seminist*, animalculist. The term was, also, used for one who belived that the new being was formed by an admixture of the seed of the male with the supposititious seed of the female.

‖**seminium** (sɛ'mɪnɪəm). *rare.* Pl. seminia. [L. *sēminium* procreation, also race, stock, breed, f. *sēmin-*, *sēmen*: see SEMEN.] The first principle (of anything), germ, etc. = SEMINARY *sb.*[2] 1.

a **1676** HALE *Prim. Orig. Man.* III. iv. (1677) 271 The first Seminium of these *Insecta*. **1720** tr. *Hodges' Loimologia* 52 There is an Efflux of the contagious Seminium. *Ibid.* 55 Hence it comes strongly to be conjectured, how the pestilential Seminium comes to be hid so secretly in the Porosities of the Air. **1723** MAITLAND *Acc. Inoc. Small Pox* (ed. 2) 15 But in effect, to cleanse Nature from the latent *Fomes* or *Seminium*; and to secure against that popular Contagion. **1753** *Chambers's Cycl.* Suppl., *Seminium*, a term used by the writers on fossils to express a sort of first principle, from which the several figured stones..are supposed to have their origin. *Ibid.*, The *seminia* of fossils may be as easily sustained in the air, as those of plants and animals. **1822–9** *Good's Study Med.* (ed. 3) IV. 426 It is difficult if not impossible, to account..for the quickening of the lurking seminium of the poison at this time rather than at any other. [**1858** MAYNE *Expos. Lex.*, *Seminium*,..applied (nom. pl.) to the seeds or predisposing causes of disease.]

seminivorous (sɛmɪ'nɪvərəs), *a. rare.* Also 7 semenivorous. [f. mod.L. **sēminivor-us* (f. L. *sēmin-* SEMEN + -(*i*)*vorus* devouring) + -OUS.] Eating or feeding on seeds.

1688 HOLME *Armoury* II. 310/1 Semenivorous Birds, such as feed upon Seeds, as the Linnet, Jacknicco, and..Finches. **1819** G. S. FABER *Dispens.* (1823) I. 59 The whole race of graminivorous and seminivorous and fructivorous animals.

semi-noc'turnal, *a. Astr.* [SEMI- 6 b.] Pertaining to, or accomplished in, half a night.

1594, 1664 [see SEMI-DIURNAL 1]. **1660** H. MORE *Myst. Godl.* VII. xv. 342 The seminocturnal archs of the Ascension of the Eclipick. **1679** MOXON *Math. Dict.* 87 By the help thereof [the Meridian], is found..the..Seminocturnal Arch of any Star. **1819** J. WILSON *Dict. Astrol.* 49 Subtract the seminocturnal arc of the star from its oblique ascension.

Seminole ('sɛmɪnəʊl), *sb.* and *a.* Also 8 Seminollie, 8–9 Siminole, etc. [ad. Creek *simanó:li* wild, runaway, earlier and dial. *simaló:ni*, f. Amer. Sp. *cimarrón* (cf. CIMARRON).] **A.** *sb.* **1.** A member of any of several groupings of North American Indians that comprise or comprised Creek Confederacy emigrants in Florida, or their descendants now resident in Florida and Oklahoma, esp. the present-day Florida Indians, who speak the Muskogee and Mikasuki languages of the Muskogean family. Also as *collect. sing.*

1763 W. G. DE BRAHM in *Amer. Indian Ethnohist.: S. & S.E. Indians: Florida Indians* (1974) I. 244 The Surveyor General..must have fallen in with many Hunting Ganges of Semiolilies. **1771** in *Ibid.* III. 17 The Seminolies or East Florida Creeks had frequent inter-course with Spaniards.. by means of Fishing vessels. **1789** *Amer. State Papers: Indian Affairs* (1832) I. 15 Some of the most southern towns of the Lower Creeks, or Seminoles, are within the territory of Spain. **1866** 'F. KIRKLAND' *Pict. Bk. Anecdotes* 318/2 He fainted at the spectacle, and was soon after butchered by a Seminole. **1910** F. W. HODGE *Handbk. Amer. Indians* II. 500/2 While still under Spanish rule the Seminole became involved in hostility with the United States. **1946** *Nat. Geogr. Mag.* Jan. 53/2 The later Seminole, who were primarily an offshoot of the Creeks and Hitchiti, were also a Muskhogean people. **1972** *Listener* 28 Dec. 904/3 Hidden here in the Everglades..a race of forgotten, proud but degenerate Seminoles.

2. An Eastern Muskogean language of the Seminoles.

1848 *Southern Lit. Messenger* XIV. 482/2, I concluded at the time [that the opera] was written in Seminole, as the only word which I distinctly heard was *en ca.* **1933** [see CREEK *sb.*[3]]. **1972** J. L. DILLARD *Black Eng.* iv. 153 The sentence is in fact Pidgin English with some relexification by Seminole.

B. *adj.* **1.** Of, pertaining to, or designating any of the Seminole groupings, or these peoples collectively.

[**1774**: see sense 2 below.] **1775** W. BARTRAM in *Trans. Amer. Philos. Soc.* (1943) XXXIII. 160 These were Seven likely Young Siminole Fellows all elligantly dresst & painted after the Indian fashions. **1797** J. MORSE *Amer. Gazetteer* s.v. *Calos*, Not far from this is a considerable town of Seminole Indians. **1837** H. MARTINEAU *Society in Amer.* II. 71 The Seminole fathers would not deliver them up. **1881** *Rep. Indian Affairs* (U.S.) p. lv, [They] were willing to incorporate the whole Seminole tribe into their nation. **1945** L. R. TRYON *Poor Man's Doctor* 3 The belt-like stone-crop, symbol of fertility to the original Seminole inhabitants of this paradise. **1973** A. H. WHITEFORD *North Amer. Indian Arts* 96 Seminole patchwork is unique among Indians of North America.

2. Special collocations: **Seminole horse**, a small horse belonging to a feral stock once found in south-eastern North America and locally domesticated by Indians and others; **Seminole war**, any of three wars waged by the U.S. against the Seminole Indians in 1817–18, 1835–42, and 1855–58.

1774 W. BARTRAM in *Trans. Amer. Philos. Soc.* (1943) XXXIII. 148 Here we saw herds of deer bounding before the chace of the naked active Floridian mounted on his fleet Siminole horse. **1806** P. WAKEFIELD *Excursions N. Amer.* xvi. 107 Extensive savannahs..maintain innumerable herds of deer, cattle, and Siminole horses, which are of a small breed. **1931** F. HARRISON *John's Island Stud (South Carolina) 1750–1788* 170 The Seminole (or Creek) horse, small in size and capricious in nature, having its origin in Florida. **1818** *Repub. Constellation* (Winchester, Va.) 11 July 2/1 Gen. Jackson..obtained full proof that the Spanish authorities at Pensacola had been active in fomenting the Seminole war. **1837** H. MARTINEAU *Society in Amer.* II. II. i. 71 Probably few of the United States troops who fell in the late Seminole war knew how the strife arose. **1948** *Florida Hist. Q.* July 35 Had not the Seminole war intervened, there is little question that the settlement of the present Taylor county would have begun ten years earlier than it did. **1973** D. AARON *Unwritten War* IV. xi. 171 Sergeant Weber.. veteran of the Seminole War.

seminoma (sɛmɪ'nəʊmə). *Path.* [mod.L., ad. F. *seminome* (M. Chevassu *Tumeurs du Testicule* (1906) i. 15), f. L. *sēmin-*, *sēmen* SEMEN: see -OMA.] A malignant tumour of the testis, now acknowledged to derive from spermatogenic tissue.

[**1919** J. EWING *Neoplastic Dis.* xl. 773 (*caption*) Embryonal carcinoma of testis. ('Seminome of Chevassu').] **1931** *Amer. Jrnl. Obstetrics & Gynecol.* XXII. 697 The term seminoma was chosen because this testicular new-growth in parts of its structure resembles seminal tubules. **1966** WRIGHT & SYMMERS *Systemic Path.* I. xxvi. 820/1 Between 40 and 50 per cent of all testicular tumours are seminomas. **1974** J. D. MAYNARD in R. M. Kirk et al. *Surgery* viii. 190 The seminoma is a firm uniform mass of sheets of polyhedral cells with a tendency to undergo central necrosis.

semi-no'madic, *a. Anthrop.* [SEMI- 1 a.] Of a people, way of life, etc.: partially nomadic and partially settled. Freq. applied to a social group that depends largely on seasonal pasturing.

1843 J. C. PRICHARD *Nat. Hist. Man* xxx. 316 The Kafirs are associated together in large communities under chiefs, or kings... They are semi-nomadic, although living in towns of considerable size..which they occasionally move. **1918** G. BELL *Let.* 17 Mar. (1927) II. xvii. 450 They were men of the Ghazzi, a semi-nomadic tribe near Nasiriyeh. **1954** KOESTLER *Invisible Writing* x. 110 The natives were left to their semi-nomadic existence. **1960** J. BRIGHT *Hist. Israel* ii. 73 The patriarchs..were semi-nomadic stockbreeders such as we know from the Tale of Sinuhe (twentieth century) or the Mari texts.

Hence **semi-'nomad** *a.* and *sb.*

1948 in D. Diringer *Alphabet* II. iv. 277 Semi-nomad Arabs may have had their settlements round the natural wells from time immemorial. **1960** J. BRIGHT *Hist. Israel* ii. 72 The patriarchs are portrayed as seminomads living in tents. **1972** *Catholic Bibl. Q.* Apr. 231 A seminomad sheep-farmer.

semi-'nude, *a.* [SEMI- 1.] Half naked.

1856 SMYTH *Rom. Family Coins* 209 A seminude Victoria alata in a rapid biga. **1880** 'OUIDA' *Moths* i, She had floated and bobbed and swum and splashed semi-nude. **1886** *Guide Exhib. Galleries Brit. Mus.* 110 A semi-nude figure of a saint holding an ensign.

b. *Bot.* (see quot. 1849).

1849 BALFOUR *Man. Bot.* §576 In mignonette, the seed-vessel opens early, so as to expose the seeds, which are called seminude. **1887** BENTLEY *Man. Bot.* (ed. 5) 325 True Gymnospermous plants..should be carefully distinguished from those with seminude ovules.

Hence ˌ**semi-'nudity,** the condition of being half naked; *concr.* a semi-nude figure.

1859 SALA *Tw. round Clock* (1861) 417 The glittering semi-nudities gyrating here. **1896** *Daily News* 12 June 5/1 Then there were the Revolutionary semi-nudity, and the sham Greek dress.

seminule ('sɛmɪnju:l). *Bot.* [f. mod.L. *sēminulum*, diminutive of L. *sēmin-, sēmen*: see SEMEN and -ULE.] A reproductive corpuscle of cryptogamous plants; also a small seed, a spore. Hence ˌ**seminu'liferous** *a.*, bearing seminules.

1858 in MAYNE *Expos. Lex.*

seminvariant: see SEMI-INVARIANT.

†'**seminy,** *a. Obs. rare.* In 7 seminie. [irreg. f. L. *sēmin-* (see SEMEN).] = SEMINIFORM.

1671 [see SEMET].

ˌ**semi-o'ccasional,** *a. U.S.* [SEMI- 1.] Occurring once in a while. Hence ˌ**semi-o'ccasionally** *adv.*

1850 'Dow jr.' in Jerdan *Yankee Hum.* (1853) 113 Semi-occasional intoxication. **1854** *Putnam's Monthly* May 459/2 A newspaper published semi-occasionally. **1861** LOWELL *Biglow P.* Ser. II. i, They jest work semioccashnally, or else don't work at all.

ˌ**semi-o'fficial,** *a.* [SEMI- 1.] Partly official; depending to some extent upon official authority or knowledge.

1806 *Deb. Congr. U.S.* 6 Mar. (1852) 597 Must we have semi-official authority, even for a title-page? **1859** *Habits of Gd. Society* 292 Unless the dinner was a semi-official one. **1868** G. DUFF *Pol. Surv.* 2 The semi-official and opposition press has done its best to increase difficulties which required no increasing. **1897** *Westm. Gaz.* 23 Feb. 5/1 The Central News asserts that there is semi-official reason for stating that [etc.]. **1901** *Scotsman* 8 Mar. 6/1 The semi-official 'North German Gazette'.

So ˌ**semi-o'fficially** *adv.*, in a semi-official manner.

1859 LANG *Wand. India* 191 That a civilian in power had a quarrel with the Commissary-General, and had represented, semi-officially, that great frauds had been committed. **1861** M. PATTISON *Ess.* (1889) I. 38 The Bishop of Basle..writes semi-officially to the King a letter of excuse.

semiography (si:mɪ'ɒgrəfi, sɛmɪ-). Also **semeiography** (si:maɪ-). [f. Gr. σημεῖο-ν sign + -GRAPHY. (Gr. had σημειογράφος short-hand writer.) Cf. F. *séméiographie*.]

†**1.** Symbolic notation: in quot. with reference to the symbols of the planets. *Obs.*

1706 THWAITES in *Hearne's Collect.* 8 Mar. (O.H.S.) I. 201 A dispute about Semeiography causes you this trouble.

2. *Path.* A description of symptoms; the art of describing symptoms.

1855 DUNGLISON *Med. Lex., Semeiography.. Semiography.* **1890** BILLINGS *Nat. Med. Dict., Semeiography.*

semiologic (si:mɪəʊ'lɒdʒɪk, sɛmɪ-), *a.* Also semeiologic (si:maɪ-). = next.

In recent Dicts.

semio'logical, *a.* Also semei-. [f. SEMIOLOGY + -ICAL.] Pertaining to semiology.

1839 SPILLAN tr. *Schill's Outl. Pathol. Semeiol.* 8 These semeiological works. **1862** *New Syd. Soc. Year-bk.* 382 Remarks on the Semeiological Value of the Pulse in Child-bed. *a* **1911** *N.E.D.*, Semiological ['In Dicts.']. **1932** W. L. GRAFF *Lang. & Languages* 303 What is called change of meaning is essentially a semeiological phenomenon. **1968** JACOBSON & SCHOEPF tr. *Levi-Strauss's Structural Anthrop.* xvii. 364 Anthropology aims to be a semeiological science, and takes as a guiding principle that of 'meaning'. **1968** *Listener* 25 Jan. 122/1 The wide-awake analogue to this use of television is the employment of the medium for basic communication—infralinguistic and, if semiological at all, concerned with the most primitive human signals. **1973** D. OSMOND-SMITH tr. *Bettelini's Lang. & Technique of Film* i. 1 The basic material that the Barthes group take as a starting-point for their semiological and aesthetical observations is not their own. **1978** *Guardian Weekly* 5 Feb. 21/4 In semiological parlance, the film's lacunae often seem rather more important than what's actually happening on screen.

semiologist (si:mɪ'ɒlədʒɪst, sɛmɪ-). Also **semeiologist** (si:maɪ-). [f. next + -IST.] One skilled in sign-language.

1848 LOWELL *Biglow P.* Ser. I. ii. Comment., Yet must he be a semeiologist the most expert, making himself intelligible to every people and kindred by signs.

semiology (si:mɪ'ɒlədʒɪ, sɛmɪ-). Also 7 erron. semæology, 9- **semeiology** (si:maɪ-). [f. Gr. σημεῖο-ν sign + -LOGY. Cf. F. *séméiologie* (1762), in Dicts. *sémiologie* (in sense 2).]

†**1.** Sign language. *Obs.*

[**1641** WILKINS *Mercury* ii. (1694) 14 The particular ways of discoursing were before intimated to be threefold...3. By Signs or Gestures. According to which variety, there are also different ways of Secrecy...3. Semæologia.] **1694** MOTTEUX *Urquhart's Rabelais* Pref. 98 These ways of signifying our Thoughts by Gestures, called by the Learned Bishop Wilkins Semæology, are almost of infinite Variety.

2. The branch of medical science which is concerned with symptoms.

1839 SPILLAN tr. *Schills' Outl. Pathol. Semeiology* 1 Semeiology constitutes the doctrine of the relations in which the phenomena in the human system stand with respect to the vital state which causes them. **1855** DUNGLISON *Med. Lex., Semeiology,..Semiology.* **1876** tr. *Wagner's Gen. Pathol.* 8 The knowledge of these signs constitutes semeiology or symptomatology. **1887** *Homœopathic World* 1 Nov. 496 At first glance, the semiology suggested cancer.

3. The branch of science concerned with the study of linguistic signs and symbols. Also in extended use.

[**1916** F. DE SAUSSURE *Cours de Linguistique Générale* iii. 34 On peut donc concevoir une science qui étudie la vie des signes au sein de la vie sociale; elle formerait une partie de la psychologie sociale, et par conséquent de la psychologie générale; nous le nommerons *sémiologie* (du grec *sēmeîon* 'signe').] **1923** OGDEN & RICHARDS *Meaning of Meaning* i. 8 The initial recognition of a general science of signs, 'semiology', of which linguistic would be a branch, was a very notable attempt in the right direction. **1932** W. L. GRAFF *Lang. & Languages* 72 Semeiology, the science of signs and symbols, is only in its infancy. **1947** *Word* III. 29 [According to de Saussure] there is a science of semiology, hitherto unrecognized... This semiology is differentiated by definition from semantics. **1959** *Times Lit. Suppl.* 20 Nov. 669/2 Joyce has become an inexhaustible hunting ground for hermeneutical exegesists to whom semeiology.. is a science beside which plain criticism offers no excitements. **1967** *Economist* 14 Oct. 156/2 The tired businessman who refreshes himself with courses like 'Structural Linguistics, Semiology and Criticism'. **1972** *Times Lit. Suppl.* 21 July 833/1 He has written..about literature and about the semiology of the cinema. **1976** T. EAGLETON *Crit. & Ideology* v. 166 Literature must indeed be re-situated within the field of general cultural production; but each mode of such production demands a semiology of its own.

Hence **semi'ologist**.

1973 D. OSMOND-SMITH tr. *Bettelini's Lang. & Technique of Film* i. 3 There exists a certain confusion in the use of terms recently coined by semiologists. **1975** *Listener* 20 Mar. 367/3 Though the 'synchronic' approach of the semiologists is for the moment more fashionable, it is impossible not to be interested in the history of social myths. **1979** *Dædalus* Summer 111 It has proved much more elusive to disclose the overall intention underlying their visual assembly in any way that an anthropologist or semiologist would recognize as coherent.

ˌ**semi-o'pacity.** [SEMI- 2; cf. next.] The condition or quality of being semi-opaque.

1688 BOYLE *Final Causes* iv. 147 The Opacity of the Uvea, and the Semi-opacity of the Retina. **1836-9** *Todd's Cycl. Anat.* II. 117/2 The membrane of the cyst is thin, delicate, transparent, or with a certain pearly semi-opacity.

ˌ**semi-o'pacous,** *a. rare*$^{-1}$. [SEMI- 1.] = SEMI-OPAQUE *a.*

1663 BOYLE *Exp. Hist. Colours* III. iii. 189 Semi-opacous Bodyes, and those such as look'd upon in an ordinary Light, and not held betwixt it and the Eye, are not wont to be Discriminated from the rest of Opacous Bodyes.

semi-'opal. [transl. G. *halbopal* (Werner, 1788).] An inferior variety of opal harder and more opaque than common opal.

1794 KIRWAN *Elem. Min.* (ed. 2) I. 290 Semi Opal..much resembles flint. **1857** DANA *Man. Min.* (1862) 139 Common opal has the hardness of opal and is easily scratched by quartz, a character which distinguishes it from some silicious stones often called semi-opal.

ˌ**semi-o'paque,** *a.* [SEMI- 1.] Partly opaque; only partially transparent.

1691 RAY *Creation* II. (1692) 198 The Element of Water being semi-opake. **1765** *Phil. Trans.* LV. 31 *note*, It looks like a piece of yellowish glass, semiopaque and brittle. **1834** MRS. SOMERVILLE *Connex. Phys. Sci.* xiv. (1849) 114 Certain semi-opaque minerals and other substances becoming transparent when plunged in water. **1871** GARROD *Mat. Med.* (ed. 3) 340 Semi-opaque Socotrine and Barbadoes aloes.

semi-'open, *a.* [SEMI- 1 a, 8 a.] Partially open; *spec.* in *Med.*, applied to methods of administering anæsthetics in which the inspired gas is atmospheric air partially restricted or controlled by some device. Cf. OPEN *a.* 11 h, *semi-closed* adj. (*b*) s.v. SEMI- 8.

1914 J. T. GWATHMEY *Anesthesia* vi. 276 If ethyl chlorid [*sic*] is administered to adults from an open or semi-open inhaler large quantities of the drug will be needed to bring about even partial anesthesia. **1972** [see OPEN *a.* 11 h].

semiosis (si:mɪ'əʊsɪs). Also **semeiosis.** [a. Gr. σημείωσις sign, inference from a sign.] The process whereby something functions as a sign (see also quots. 1971 and 1981).

c **1907** C. S. PEIRCE *Coll. Papers* (1934) V. III. i. 332 It is important to understand what I mean by *semiosis*. All dynamical action..either takes place between two subjects ..or..is a resultant of such actions between pairs. But by 'semiosis' I mean, on the contrary, an action, or influence, which is, or involves, a coöperation of *three* subjects, such as a sign, its object, and its interpretant. **1938** A. HUXLEY *Let.* 18 Nov. (1969) 438 It interests me a lot and has set me reading along a number of interesting lines—Carnap, Neurath, Morris and Korzybski on the problems of semiosis. **1963** J. WIESENFARTH *H. James* v. 97 The novel.. is, rather, a study in logic and semiosis. **1971** HEATH & PRENDERGAST tr. J. Kristeva in *Signs of Times* 3 What we call semeiosis is not the signifying activity in all its complexity, but only one of the signifying acts such as the structure of judgement allows it to filter through. **1981** M. WARNER *Joan of Arc* I. i. 28 Elements of mimesis..cling to..accounts of her..death, while..an accretion of semiosis, the search for inner meaning, covers their story.

semiotic (si:mɪ'ɒtɪk, sɛmɪ-), *a.* (and *sb.*) Also 7 **semioticke, semeiotic** (si:maɪ-). [a. Gr. σημειωτικός significant; also, concerned with the interpretation of symptoms (chiefly fem. ellipt.: see SEMIOTICS), f. σημειοῦν to interpret as a sign, f. σημεῖον sign.]

A. *adj.* **1.** Relating to symptoms.

1625 HART *Anat. Ur.* I. i. 13 The chiefe..part of Physicke diagnosticke or semioticke, which teacheth vs to know the nature, causes, and substance of the disease by the signes and grounds of the same. **1876** DUNGLISON *Med. Lex., Semiotic*, symptomatic. **1898** *Syd. Soc. Lex., Semeiotic.*

†**2.** Symbolic, serving to convey meaning. *Obs.*

1797 *Monthly Mag.* III. 269/1 That the Egyptians were not acquainted with the alphabet, till the time of Psammeticus, and that commerce alone gave birth to semeiotic signs.

3. Of or pertaining to semiotics or the use of signs. Cf. SEMIOTICS 2.

1923 H. G. BAYNES tr. *Jung's Psychol. Types* i. 82, I say 'semiotic' in contradistinction to 'symbolic'. What Freud terms symbols are no more than *signs* for elementary instinctive processes. **1957** *Publ. Amer. Dial. Soc.* XXVIII. 4 It is an utterance that 'craves' a verbal or other semiotic (e.g., a nod) response. **1973** AKHMANOVA & MARČENKO *Meaning Equivalence & Linguistics Expression* 7 The Morse code is a semiotic system *par excellence*, for in it every unit of content and every unit of expression are in regular one-to-one correspondence... The same applies..to all the other semiotic systems such as, for instance, notation in music, or chemical formulae, or mathematical signs. **1974** S. MORAWSKI *Inquiries into Fundament. of Aesthetics* viii. 302 The fourth approach..considers the artistic communication itself and its semiotic connections. **1978** J. UPDIKE *Coup* (1979) vii. 257 No doubt this semeiotic treasure-lode [*sc.* a wallet] enriches the arcana of some light-fingered ex-nomad.

B. *absol.* as *sb.* = SEMIOTICS 2.

[**1690** LOCKE *Hum. Und.* IV. xx. 361 The third Branch may be called σημιωτική, or *the Doctrine of Signs*, the most usual whereof being words, it is aptly enough termed also λογική, Logick.] *c* **1897** C. S. PEIRCE *Coll. Papers* (1932) II. II. ii. 134 Logic, in its general sense, is..only another name for *semiotic* (σημειωτική), the quasi-necessary, or formal, doctrine of signs. **1937** C. MORRIS *Logical Positivism, Pragmatism, & Sci. Empiricism* 4 Semiotic being the general science which includes all of these [dimensions] and their interrelations. **1953** F. J. WHITFIELD tr. *Hjelmslev's Prolegomena to Theory of Lang.* 76 The so-called metalanguage (or, we should say, *metasemiotic*), by which is meant a semiotic that treats of a semiotic. **1973** R. JAKOBSON *Sci. of Lang.* ii. 32 The subject matter of semiotic is the communication of any messages whatever, whereas the field of linguistics is confined to the communication of verbal messages.

Hence **semio'tician**.

1946 C. MORRIS *Signs, Lang., & Behavior* I. i. 4 At some point the semiotician must say: 'Henceforth we will recognize that anything which fulfills certain conditions is a sign.' **1946** *Mind* LV. 46 Other groups of workers in the same field, as, for example..the Semioticians (*e.g.* Carnap, Morris). **1960** H. READ *Form of Things Unknown* I. ii. 34 In general, semioticians have confined themselves to the study of the various types of discourse which make use of language. **1976** *Visible Language* X. 68 It is possible, in the case of some 'auto-illustrations', to follow those semioticians who prefer to view iconic motivation as a special case of metonymic *pars pro toto*.

semiotical (si:mɪ'ɒtɪkəl, sɛmɪ-), *a.* Also semei- (si:maɪ-). [Formed as prec. + -AL[1].] **1.** = SEMIOTIC *a.* 1.

1588 J. HARVEY *Disc. Probl.* 79 Looke into the semeioticall or presignificative iudgements of phisitions. **1623** HART *Arraignm. Ur.* II. iv. 59 He maketh moreover this semeioticall part of Physicke, concerning the signes of diseases, to depend altogether upon conjecture. **1703** *Art's Improv.* p.

xxv, Thirdly, Semeiotical. Treating of the Crisis of Diseases. **1825** BEDDOES *Let.* 4 Dec. in *Poems* p. li, It still remains for some one to exhibit the sum of his experience in mental pathology and therapeutics, not in a cold, technical, dead description, but a living semiotical display.

2. = SEMIOTIC *a.* 3.

1938 C. MORRIS in *Internat. Encycl. Unified Sci.* I. II. 29 'Rules of sign usage', like 'sign' itself, is a semiotical term and cannot be stated syntactically or semantically. **1946** *Mind* LX. 146 As a semiotical psychiatrist, a Therapeutic Positivist has to hand a technique for the resolution of philosophical problems and disputes.

Hence **semi'otically** *adv.*

1916 C. E. LONG tr. *Jung's Analytical Psychol.* p. vii, The Vienna School interprets the psychological symbol semiotically, as a sign or token of certain primitive psychosexual processes. **1972** W. C. STOKOE *Semiotics & Human Sign Lang.* i. 15 Semiotically considered the difference between fingerspelling and a sign language could hardly be greater.

semiotics (siːmɪ'ɒtɪks, sɛmɪ-). Also **semeiotics** (siːmaɪ-). [ad. Gr. σημειωτική, ellipt. use (sc. τέχνη) of the fem. of σημειωτικός SEMIOTIC. See -IC 2.] **1.** The branch of medical science relating to the interpretation of symptoms.

1670 H. STUBBE *Plus Ultra* 75 Semeiotics, method of curing, and tried..medicines. **1793** HOLCROFT tr. *Lavater's Physiog.* iii. 27, I shall now proceed to consider Medicinal Semeiotics, or the signs of Health and Sickness. **1867** CORFE in *Med. Times & Gaz.* 7 Sept. 252/1 Semeiotics may be construed as the doctrinal language of pathology. **1873** WAGNER tr. *Teuffel's Hist. Rom. Lit.* II. 26 The second [treats] of semiotics and general pathology and therapy.

2. The science of communication studied through the interpretation of signs and symbols as they operate in various fields, esp. language (see SEMIOTIC *sb.* for parallel form). Cf. SEMIOLOGY.

1880 G. MALLERY *Introd. Study Sign Lang. among N. Amer. Indians* 4 Our native semiotics will surely help the archæologist in his study of native picture-writing. **1911** A. M. LUDOVICI tr. *F. Nietzsche's Antichrist* in *Twilight of Idols* xxxii. 169 One should guard against seeing anything more than a language of signs, semeiotics, an opportunity for parables in all this. **1955** A. HUXLEY *Genius & Goddess* 42 He kissed her—kissed her with an intensity of passion..for which the semiotics and the absent-mindedness had left her entirely unprepared. **1964** T. SEBEOK et al. *Approaches to Semiotics* 5 Margaret Mead proposed semiotics..as a term which might aptly cover 'patterned communication in all modalities'. **1973** D. OSMOND-SMITH tr. *Bettelini's Lang. & Technique of Film* i. 2 Some talk of a universal semiotics, capable of including within itself all aspects of the film as sign-system. **1980** *Semiotica* XXIX. 185 (*heading*) A firework for the semiotics of visible human action.

semi-'oval, *a.* Chiefly *Nat. Hist.* [SEMI- 7 a.] Of the form of half an oval cut longitudinally, semi-elliptical.

1703 MOXON *Mech. Exerc.* 273 Semi-Oval Arches. **1756** G. DOUGLAS *Winslow's Anat.* II. §554 The Semi-Oval Fibres of the upper Palpebra. **1775** J. JENKINSON *Brit. Plants* Gloss. **1856-8** W. CLARK *Van der Hoeven's Zool.* I. 798 Aperture entire, semioval. **1875** W. MCILWRAITH *Guide Wigtownshire* 100 The whole garden-ground is included in a semi-oval hollow.

So **,semi-'ovaloid** *a.*

a **1843** J. F. SOUTH in *Encycl. Metrop.* (1845) VII. 314/2 The Skink has the anterior end of the [upper arm] bone very wide, with a semiovaloid head, looking upwards.

semi-'ovate, *a. Nat. Hist.* [SEMI- 7 a.] Of the shape of half an egg divided lengthways, ovate on one side only.

1760 J. LEE *Introd. Bot.* III. v. (1765) 176 *Semiovate*, half Egg-shaped. **1775** J. JENKINSON *Brit. Plants* Gloss. **1822** J. PARKINSON *Outl. Oryctol.* 211 Opening semiovate.

So †**,semi-o'vated** *a.*

1757 *Phil. Trans.* L. 66 The germen is of a semiovated figure.

semi-'palmate, *a. Zool.* [SEMI- 8 d.] Partly palmate, half-webbed.

1828-32 WEBSTER, *Semi-palmate, Semi-palmated*, half palmated or webbed. **1856-8** W. CLARK *Van der Hoeven's Zool.* II. 249 Anterior feet cloven, posterior semipalmate. **1872** COUES *Key N. Amer. Birds* 51 This constitutes the semipalmate (½-webbed, that is,) foot.

So **semi-'palmated** *a.*; hence **,semi-pal'mation**, the condition of being semi-palmate.

1785 PENNANT *Arctic Zool.* II. 502 Avoset... Feet *semi-palmated. **1808-13** A. WILSON & BONAPARTE *Amer. Ornith.* (1831) III. 63 *Tringa semipalmata*... Semipalmated Sandpiper. **1839-47** *Todd's Cycl. Anat.* III. 439/1 The Caymans are semipalmated. **1872** COUES *Key N. Amer. Birds* 51 They [webs] run out to the end of the first, or along part of the second joint, constituting true *semipalmation.

,semipa'rabola. *Math.* [SEMI- 7 b.]

1. Half of a parabola.

1656 HOBBES *Six Lessons* iv. 34 You ought to have made a Semiparabola on the Diameter AC. **1668** *Phil. Trans.* III. 809 When Comets describe a Semi-parabola only. **1745** BAILEY (ed. 10) vol. II, *Parabolick Conoid*, a solid figure generated by the rotation of a Semi parabola about its Axis.

2. 'A curve of such a nature that the powers of its ordinates are to each other as the next lower powers of its abscissas' (Hutton, *Math. Dict.*).

1728 CHAMBERS *Cycl.* s.v. *Parabola*, Those Curves are likewise used to be referred to Parabola's wherein $ax^{m-1} = y^m$. as *E. gr.* $ax^2 = y^3$, $ax^3 = y^4$, which some call Semi-parabola's. **1815** HUTTON *Math. Dict.* II. 150/1 Parabolas, that are expressed by the general equation $ax^{n-1} = y^n$..are called semi-parabolas.

,semi-para'bolic, *a.* [In sense 1, f. SEMI-PARABOLA + -IC; in 2, f. SEMI- 1 + PARABOLIC *a.*]

1. (See quot.)

1775 ASH, *Semiparabolic*, comprising half a parabola.

2. Partly of the nature of parable.

1876 STEWART & TAIT *Unseen Univ.* (1880) 31 Semi-parabolic representation of spiritual truths.

,semi-para'bolical, *a.* [f. SEMIPARABOLA + -ICAL.] = prec. 1.

1656 tr. *Hobbes' Elem. Philos.* xvi. 170 The Body will be carried through the Semipa[ra]bolical crooked line AGD. **1656** HOBBES *Six Lessons* iv. 36 Two Movents, one uniform, the other uniformly accelerated, make the Body describe a Semiparabolical line. **1775** in ASH.

'semi-ped, -pede. *Pros.* [ad. L. *sēmiped-, -pēs*, f. *sēmi-* SEMI- + *ped-, pēs* foot.] A half-foot.

1756 T. SHERIDAN *Brit. Educ.* (1761) 317 An English heroick verse is composed of ten semipeds, or syllables. **1824** L. MURRAY *Eng. Gram.* (ed. 5) I. 387 'Day' or the sweet approach of even or morn'. Here the cæsura after the first semipede *Day*, stops us unexpectedly. **1907** OMOND *Eng. Metrists* 12 The first six lines of *Paradise Lost*, each of which consists of ten 'semi-peds'.

So **semipedal** *a. rare*$^{-0}$ [L. *sēmipedālis*].

1658 PHILLIPS, *Semipedal*, consisting of half a foot in measure.

,semi-Pe'lagian, *a.* and *sb.* [ad. eccl. L. *Sēmipelagiānus*: see SEMI- 8 b and PELAGIAN *a.*[1]]

A. *adj.* Pertaining to the semi-Pelagians or semi-Pelagianism.

1626 *Second Parallel* A iij b, No better then an halfe-faced groat of the Semipelagian alloy. **1626** PYM in Rushw. *Hist. Coll.* (1659) I. 341 A Semipelagian and a Popish Faction set on foot to the danger of this Church and State, whose Tenets are Liberty of Free-will. **1765** MACLAINE tr. *Mosheim's Eccl. Hist.* Cent. v. II. v. §27 They had embraced the Semi-Pelagian doctrine before Cassian. **1807** SYD. SMITH *Lett. Cath.* i, [They] enabled every sublapsarian, and supralapsarian, and semi-pelagian clergyman, to build himself a neat brick chapel. **1845** *Encycl. Metrop.* XI. 346/2 Yet to Cassian is generally attributed the honour or disgrace of founding the Semipelagian School.

B. *sb.* An adherent of semi-Pelagianism.

a **1600** HOOKER *Wks.* (1888) II. 540 If his grace did no otherwise draw our minds than Pelagians and Semi-Pelagians imagined. **1607** HIERON *Wks.* I. 420 Some papists, who are in this point (as they are rightly called) semi-pelagians; they, acknowledging originall corruption, yet doe limit it. **1744** TINDAL *Contin. Rapin* III. 511 *note*, The Semipelagians think, that an assisting Grace is necessary, but that the first turn of the will to God is the effect of a man's own choice. **1885** MARCUS DODS in *Encycl. Brit.* XVIII. 472/2 A similar scheme was adopted by Cassian of Marseilles (hence Semi-pelagians are often spoken of as Massilians).

,semi-Pe'lagianism. [f. prec. + -ISM.] A doctrine intermediate between Augustinianism and Pelagianism, taught by Cassian of Marseilles in the 5th century.

1626 DONNE *Serm.* (1640) 675 Not disposed by preventing grace, without use of subsequent grace, by Antecedent and anticipant, without concomitant and auxiliant grace; that is Semi-pelagianisme. **1728** CHAMBERS *Cycl.* s.v. *Jansenism*, It is Semi-pelagianism to say, that Jesus Christ died, or shed his Blood, for all Men in general. **1885** MARCUS DODS in *Encycl. Brit.* XVIII. 472/2 The differentia of Semipelagianism is the tenet that in regeneration..the divine and the human will are co-operating (synergistic) coefficient factors.

semi-'perfect, *a. rare.* [SEMI- 1; in L. *sēmiperfectus.*] Imperfect, incomplete.

1623 COCKERAM I, *Semiperfect*, halfe formed. **1626** BACON *Sylva* §107 The Concords in Musick which are Perfect, or Semiperfect, betweene the Vnison, and the Diapason are the Fifth, which is the most Perfect; the Third next; And the Sixth which is more harsh.

semi'permeable, *a.* [tr. G. *halbdurchlässig* (J. H. van't Hoff 1887, in *Zeitschr. für physik. Chem.* I. 482), f. *halb-* HALF, semi- + *durchlässig* pervious, permeable.] Of a membrane or other structure: selectively permeable to certain atoms and molecules; *spec.* permeable to molecules of water but not to those of any dissolved substance. Also in extended use.

1888 W. RAMSAY tr. J. van't Hoff in *Phil. Mag.* XXVI. 82 The porous membrane..will be termed in the following pages a 'semipermeable membrane'. **1895** W. C. D. WHETHAM *Solution & Electrolysis* iv. 34 These semi-permeable membranes are made by filling a porous pot with the solution of a salt such as potassium ferro-cyanide, and surrounding the outside with another solution..which gives an insoluble precipitate when in contact with the first. **1930** *Engineering* 28 Nov. 670/1 Each droplet [of sap] being subject to forces equivalent to the osmotic pressure acting on a plant cell within a semi-permeable membrane. **1974** L. THOMAS *Lives of Cell* (1975) 162, I am glad to have a semi-permeable memory after getting into this. **1978** P. W. ATKINS *Physical Chem.* viii. 222 The chemical potential of the solvent on both sides of the semipermeable membrane must be equal.

Hence **,semipermea'bility**, the property or condition of being semipermeable.

1900 W. H. HOWELL *Text-bk. Physiol.* (ed. 2) I. ii. 66 The semi-permeability is only approximately complete. **1974** L. THOMAS *Lives of Cell* (1975) 173 Oxygen filters out the very bands of ultraviolet light that are most devastating for nucleic acids and proteins, while allowing full penetration of the visible light needed for photosynthesis. If it had not been for this semipermeability, we could never have come along.

semi-'pro, *a.* and *sb. colloq.* (orig. and chiefly *U.S.*). **A.** *adj.* **a.** = SEMI-PROFESSIONAL *a.* 1 b. *spec.* of sports.

1908 *Spalding's Official Base Ball Guide* 368 (Advt.), The 'Semi-Pro' League Ball; regulation size and weight..Price, $1.00. **1910** *Baseball Mag.* Apr. 4/2 The semi-pro league flourishes. **1969** *Wall St. Jrnl.* 30 Sept. 28/2 Sam turned to umpiring..working in semipro and minor leagues. **1972** J. MOSEDALE *Football* viii. 116 He was playing semi-pro ball on Sundays. **1980** *Washington Post* 15 Aug. D2/1 The Metro Buccaneers, a first-year semipro football team, will play an exhibition game..Sunday.

b. = SEMI-PROFESSIONAL *a.* 1 a. Chiefly in *Music* and *Photography*.

1927 *Melody Maker* Aug. 757/3 This competition will be open to amateur, semi-pro. or full pro. combinations. **1934** S. R. NELSON *All about Jazz* iv. 82 There are thousands of 'semi-pro' dance bands, the members of which work at their ordinary occupations during the day and play in their leisure. **1965** *Melody Maker* 17 July 15, I am forming a semi-pro trio to play at weddings. **1977** *Time* 26 Sept. 43/1 She is a semipro photographer.

B. *sb.* = SEMI-PROFESSIONAL *sb.*

1910 *Baseball Mag.* Apr. 4/2 The despised semi-pros were drawing big crowds. **1912** *N.Y. Tribune* 7 Oct. 8/5 Enste, of the semi-pros, connected with his slow ball..for a home run wallop. **1966** *Melody Maker* 15 Oct. 6 Semi-pros have always played an important role on the jazz scene.

semi-pro'fessional, *sb.* and *a.* [SEMI- 1 a, 2 b.]

A. *sb.* One who receives payment for an occupation or activity but does not rely on it for subsistence.

1897 *Sporting News* (St. Louis, Missouri) 27 Mar. 1 Doheny was only a semi-professional before he joined the New Yorks. **1971** *Daily Tel.* 4 Oct. 11/2 From the beginning ..semi-professionals and professionals swooped down on the city's many basements..where they offered new drama.

B. *adj.* **1. a.** Designating a person or group receiving payment for an occupation or activity but not relying on it for subsistence.

1900 G. BELL *Let.* 21 Mar. (1927) I. v. 70 He is a photographer, semi-professional. **1951** KOESTLER *Age of Longing* i. 8 Gaston..had become a semiprofessional dancer and near-gigolo. **1972** *Daily Tel.* 22 May 1/8 The Storm are a semi-professional group formed about nine months ago.

b. Applied to an organization, activity, etc., involving semi-professionals.

1976 *Eastern Even. News* (Norwich) 9 Dec. 19/5 They would have to take drastic measures to keep the club within the semi-professional Magnet League any longer. **1978** *Homes & Gardens* Oct. 166 As each new instrument is made ..it is tested in one of the semi-professional concerts given by the group.

2. Of or pertaining to an occupation considered intermediate in standing between a learned or skilled profession and a trade or handicraft.

1950 T. H. MARSHALL *Citizenship & Social Class* 150 They [*sc.* techniques] lend themselves in the same way to the establishment of semi-professional associations. **1965** *Word Study* Oct. 3/1, I wonder, however, if most of us have not observed an equally wanton use of the word *type* among various professional and semiprofessional groups in our country.

3. Of equipment: of a kind or quality close to that appropriate for professional use.

1953 E. T. CANBY *Home Music Systems* xiii. 229 The semi-professional machines come with two or three speeds. **1975** *Gramophone* Sept. 531/2, 3M announced a new line.. called the CTR series, featuring..a semi-professional 8-track recorder-player.

semiquaver ('sɛmɪkweɪvə(r)), *sb. Mus.* [SEMI-6 a.] A note half the length of a quaver, the sixteenth part of a semibreve. (Also *attrib.*)

1576 GASCOIGNE *Grief of Joye* iv. Wks. 1870 II. 296 Whiles I searcht the semyquaver toyes, the glancing sharpes, the halfenotes. **1597** MORLEY *Introd. Mus.* Annot. ¶4 Who inuented the Crotchet, Quauer, and Semiquauer is vncertaine. **1669** [see DEMI- 9]. **1706** A. BEDFORD *Temple Mus.* xi. 227 The Author had never heard of a Semiquaver. **1848** RIMBAULT *Pianoforte* 57 When groups of Quavers, Semiquavers, &c. are to be repeated several times in succession. **1884** G. MOORE *Mummer's Wife* xiii, Kate, who did not know a crotchet from a semiquaver.

†**b.** *allusively.* A very short space of time. ***the brief and the semiquaver***, jocular amplification of 'the brief' (see BRIEF B b.). *Obs.*

1602 MARSTON *Ant. & Mel.* II. C3 b, The breefe and the semiquauer is, wee must haue the descant you made vpon our names, ere you depart. **1635** QUARLES *Emblems* IV. xv, Till then, earth's Semiquaver, mirth, farewell.

Hence **semiquaver** *v. nonce-wd.*, to drive *away* with playing semiquavers.

1780 COWPER *Progr. Err.* 127 With wire and catgut he concludes the day, Quavering and semiquavering care away.

semiquinone (sɛmɪ'kwɪnəʊn). *Chem.* [SEMI-8 h.] A molecule or ion derived from a quinone and having one of the two oxygen atoms ionized or bonded to a hydrogen atom.

1931 L. MICHAELIS in *Jrnl. Biol. Chem.* XCII. 213 The difference between 1 molecule of each of the two successive steps will be proved to be only 1 electron (*i.e.* hydrogen atom) without any change in molecular size. The intermediary form will in this case be designated as a semiquinone. **1956** *Nature* 10 Mar. 483/1 Alcohols are attacked by photo-excited anthraquinones A^* with the production of semiquinones AH. **1973** B. J. HAZZARD tr.

Organicum vi. 380 Since..the semiquinone and *p*-benzoquinone are not resistant to alkali, the oxidation is carried out in acid solution and then takes place via quinhydrones.

Hence **semi'qui(no)noid** *a.*, having or being a structure resembling that of a semiquinone; also *absol.* as *sb.*

1932 *Jrnl. Biol. Chem.* XCVI. 704 Let us designate the three forms of the substance as *R* (the reduced form), *S* (the semiquinoid or intermediary form), and *T* (the totally oxidized, or quinoid, or holoquinoid form). **1935** *Chem. Rev.* XVI. 265 Among the three constituents of a two-step system it is not always the semiquinoid that exhibits the greatest instability. **1964** J. W. Linnett *Electronic Struct. Molecules* vii. 110 The two members are such that the transfer of one electron from one of the molecules to the other (e.g. from diamine to chloranil) will produce two semiquinonoid-type radicals.

semi-rect, *sb.* Anglicized form of **semi-recta**, corruption of *cyma recta*: see CYMA 1.

1776 G. Semple *Building in Water* 13 A Cornice.. consisting of a Semirect and a Semirevers and Tuscan Blocks. **1841** Miller *Old Red Sandstone* viii. (1887) 162 Mouldings somewhat resembling the semi-recta of the architect.

semirect, *a.* [ad. mod.L. *sēmirectus*: see SEMI- and RECT *a.*] Half a right angle.

1656 tr. *Hobbes' Elem. Philos.* xxiv. 285 If the angle of Inclination be semirect.

semi-revers. Corrupt anglicized form of *cyma reversa*: see CYMA 1.

1776 [see SEMI-RECT *sb.*].

[**semi-rife.** In forms *semyryfe, -rife*, error for *semyvyf* (see SEMIVIF) in Bailey's Dict. 1728, etc.]

semi-'rigid, *a.* and *sb.* [SEMI- 1, 8 l.] **A.** *adj.* **a.** Of an airship: having a flexible gas container to which is attached a stiffened keel or framework.

1908 *Daily Chron.* 6 Aug. 1/2 The so-called semi-rigid airships. **1919** H. Shaw *Text-bk. Aeronautics* xvii. 200 The semi-rigid type includes the Forlanini, Lebaudy, etc., of which the envelopes are not rigid, but are stiffened longitudinally by a framework, running the whole length of the envelope. **1935** C. G. Burge *Compl. Bk. Aviation* 148/2 As with non-rigid and semi-rigid airships, a rigid at the start of a journey has its gas space about 90–95 per cent full of hydrogen. **1955, 1974** [see KEEL *sb.*[1] 3 b].

b. *gen.* Somewhat rigid; having a certain amount of rigidity; ***semi-rigid theory*** (see quot. 1959).

1929 *Rep. & Mem. Aeronaut. Res. Comm.* No. 1155. 19 (*heading*) Specification of a simple type of semi-rigid wing. **1937** *Jrnl. R. Aeronaut. Soc.* XLI. 723 It was..possible to deduce from the semi-rigid theory design recommendations. **1946** *Nature* 30 Nov. 798/2 Rigid frames of triangular and square shapes, and semi-rigid frames. **1959** J. L. Nayler *Dict. Aeronaut. Engin.* 234 *Semi-rigid theory*, an approximate theory of elastic structure in which the theoretical infinite number of degrees of freedom is represented by a finite number, each being associated with an invariable mode. **1963** C. R. Cowell et al. *Inlays, Crowns, & Bridges* xi. 118 The retainer which is united to a pontic by a semi-rigid joint is called the 'minor' retainer.

B. *sb.* A semi-rigid airship.

1920 [see RIGID *sb.* 2]. **1925** E. H. Lewitt *Rigid Airship* i. 1 The airship may be divided into three classes: non-rigids, semi-rigids, and rigids. **1935** C. G. Burge *Compl. Bk. Aviation* 148/2 The semi-rigid is very similar in operation to the non-rigid.

semi-'rotary, *a.* [SEMI- 8.] Partly rotary.

1850 in Woodcroft *App. Specif. Pat. Reaping Machines* (1853) 99 The part N moves by a lateral and semi-rotary motion. **1884** Knight *Dict. Mech.* Suppl. 796 *Semi-rotary Engine*, an engine between a reciprocating and rotary one.

So **ˌsemi-ro'tating, -'rotative, -'rotatory** *adjs.*

1881 T. Wardle *Wild Silks of India* 30 A *semi-rotating brush is placed over them [cocoons], which quickly catches the exterior fibres of each cocoon. **1846** *Mech. Mag.* 3 Oct. 314 Soutter's Patent *Semirotative Pump. **1826** Kirby & Sp. *Entomol.* xxxv. III. 671 Upon these the tibia turns, with a *semirotatory motion up and down as upon a pair of pivots. **1851** Mantell *Petrifactions* iii. 233 *note*, There are some of the large Monitors which can give a semi-rotatory motion to the back teeth.

‖**semis**[1] ('sɛmɪs). *Rom. Antiq.* [L., app. reduced f. *semi-* SEMI- + *as* AS *sb.*] A Roman coin, equivalent under the Republic and the early Empire to half an as, and under the later Empire to half a solidus. Cf. TREMIS.

1853 H. N. Humphreys *Coin Collector's Man.* I. xxi. 260 The *Semis, Semisis*, or *Semi-as*, has an S upon it to denote its weight, as half that of the 'as'; it represented six ounces, and the type most usual in the Roman *series* is the head of Jupiter. **1949** *Oxf. Class. Dict.* 210/2 The coinage [of the early Empire] comprised *aureus* and half-piece in gold, *denarius* and half-piece in silver, *sestertius, dupondius*, and *semis* in orichalcum (brass), *as* and *quadrans* in copper. **1962** R. A. G. Carson *Coins* 180 Gold solidi were issued with some frequency, the semis or half-piece only rarely in the reign of the three brothers. *Ibid.* 197 In keeping with the earlier fifth-century tradition the obverse of the semis and the tremissis showed the diademed and cuirassed bust of the emperor in profile. **1979** *Nature* 5 July 46/2 The magnetisation of an orichalcum semis of the Roman Emperor Tiberius remained below the noise level up to the maximum fields available.

‖**semis**[2] (sə'miː). [F., lit. 'sowing'; cf. SEMÉE *a.* and *sb.*] A form of decoration used in bookbinding, in which small ornaments are repeated regularly.

1926 R. Glazier *Man. Historic Ornament* 155 Some French bindings for Henry IV. are tooled with a *semis* of monograms on flowers. **1960** G. A. Glaister *Gloss. Book* 323/2 *Powdered*, the effect obtained on a book cover when small flower ornaments are repeated regularly in rows over it. Early examples date from 1560 on books bound for Charles IX of France. Also known as *semis* or *semé*. **1960** H. Hayward *Antique Coll.* 253/1 *Semis*,..a repeating pattern of small ornaments used by bookbinders, 'sown' over the covers of books. **1977** Fleming & Honour *Penguin Dict. Decorative Arts* 719/1 *Semis*, an heraldic term also used in bookbinding for a diaper design made by the repetition of one or more small tooled ornaments.

semi-'savage, *a.* and *sb.* [SEMI- 1, 2.] = SEMI-BARBARIAN.

1807 J. Barlow *Columb.* vi. 528 The semisavage sees his tribes retire. **1833** J. H. Newman *Arians* i. iii. (1876) 77 The rude and semi-savage state in which they are considered to have lived. **1884** *Manch. Exam.* 27 May 5/1 Semi-savage tribes who lived by pillaging caravans.

Hence **ˌsemi-'savagedom, -'savagery.**

1882 Miss Braddon *Mt. Royal* I. ii. 41 That unsophisticated semi-savagery which Hamleigh had expected in a place so remote. **1887** H. Knollys *Life in Japan* 321 The spirit of semi-savagedom apparent amongst all [classes].

Semi-'Saxon, *a.* and *sb.* [SEMI- 1, 2. Cf. mod.L. *Sēmisaxonicus* (Hickes 1689).]

A. *adj.* Intermediate between 'Saxon' and 'English'; formerly used by philologists to designate the first period of Middle English, from *c* 1100–50 to *c* 1250. **B.** *sb.* The 'Semi-Saxon' language; Early Middle English.

1735 Shelton tr. *Wotton's View Hickes' Thes.* 100 The Nicene..Creed, translated into Semi-Saxon. **1813** Whitaker *Langl. P. Pl.* Introd. p. vii, From the extinction of the pure Saxon..to the reign of Edward the Third, the language of our country, which, during that period, may be called Semi-Saxon, had scarcely been reduced to any standard. **1847** (*title*) Layamon's Brut, or Chronicle of Britain; a poetical semi-Saxon Paraphrase of the Brut of Wace. **1853** Morton *Ancr. R.* Pref. p. x, A few passages in the Latin which are not in the semi-Saxon.

'semisection. [SEMI- 2.] = HEMISECTION.

1889 *Lancet* 13 Apr. 720/2 After semisection of the cervical region in dogs.

†**semi-semi-** = DEMI-SEMI-.

1611 Cotgr., *Fredon*, a..Semie-semie-quauer.

semi-'solid, *a.* [SEMI- 8 a.] Half-solid, extremely viscous.

1834 M. Scott *Cruise Midge* ii, The gun..was now useless, from sinking in the semisolid black soil. **1853** Kane *Grinnell Exp.* xlviii. (1856) 451 The semi-solid character of the ice. **1857** Miller *Elem. Chem., Org.* (1862) iv. §1. 259 Sperm oil becomes semisolid at about 45°. **1897** *Trans. Amer. Pediatric Soc.* IX. 152 The tumor was excised..and a semi-solid mass..was removed.

semi'somnous, *a. rare.* [f. L. *sēmisomn-is, -us*, f. *sēmi-* SEMI- + *somnus* sleep.] Half asleep.

1873 H. Rogers *Orig. Bible* viii. 321 While his sister Oblivion reclineth semisomnous on a pyramid.

†**semi-soun.** *Obs.* [f. SEMI- 2 + *soun* SOUND. Cf. late L. *sēmisonus.*] A slight or gentle sound.

a **1386** Chaucer *Miller's T.* 511 And softe he knokketh with a semy soun [*MS. Lansd.* seme sowne].

'semispecies. *Biol.* [SEMI- 8 e.] A subdivision of a species regarded as having more individuality than does a subspecies.

1940 E. Mayr in *Amer. Naturalist* LXXIV. 256 The taxonomist finds it sometimes useful for practical purposes to treat as full species what should be regarded as subspecies on the basis of the definition. Groups of such 'semi-species' are called superspecies in the subsequent discussion. **1953** J. S. Huxley *Evolution in Action* iii. 71 The borderline of incipient species or semi-species. **1978** *Sci. Amer.* Sept. 60/1 Semispecies from the same locality will not crossbreed in the laboratory but semispecies from different localities will.

'semisphere. Now *rare.* [f. SEMI- + SPHERE. Cf. late L. *sēmisphæra, -ium.*] A hemisphere.

1659 Torriano, *Semi-sphéra*, a semy sphear. **1773** Brydone *Tour through Sicily* ix. 81 These are all..of a regular figure, either that of a cone or a semisphere. **1792** *Baron Munchausen's Trav.* xxiii. 99 The summit of the mountain, in the form of a semisphere. **1798** [see SEMI-SPHEROID]. **1849** *Sk. Nat. Hist., Mamm.* III. 44 In the two-horned rhinoceros the disc which bears the anterior horn is a semisphere.

Hence **semi'spheric, -'spherical** *adjs.*

1661 Lovell *Hist. Anim. & Min.* Introd. e 8 b, Semi-spherical, as callai, astroitæ. **1664** Power *Exp. Philos.* i. 37 You shall in the Microscope see those 2. black spots to be semi-spherical eyes. **1896** Vizetelly tr. *Zola's Rome* 198 A spacious round chamber with semispherical ceiling.

ˌsemi'spheroid. [SEMI- 7 a.] Half a spheroid.

1775 Ash, *Semispheroid.* **1798** Hutton *Course Math.* II. 325 In the semisphere, or semispheroid; the distance from the centre is $\frac{3}{8}r$, or $\frac{3}{8}$ of the radius.

Hence **semisphe'roidal** *a.*, of the form of a semispheroid.

1664 Power *Exp. Philos.* i. 6 The Gray, or Horse-Fly. Her eye..'tis of a semisphaeroidal figure. **1822** J. Parkinson *Outl. Oryctol.* 48 Semi-sphæroidal masses. **1839** *Proc. Amer. Philos. Soc.* I. 71 Semi-spheroidal cavities.

semi-'sports. [SEMI- 1 b.] Used *attrib.*: **1.** Of articles of attire: somewhat informal or casual.

1929 *Footwear Organiser* July 25/1 There is no doubt that semi-sports shoes in two-colour effects will be largely worn. **1973** Schoeffler & Gale *Esquire's Encycl. 20th Cent. Men's Fashions* 194 By the early forties not only was a semisports outfit acceptable for town wear but, according to *Esquire*, it was 'smart to be sporty'.

2. Of a motor car: possessing some of the characteristics of a sports car.

1933 *Motor* 10 Oct. 513/1 The 20 h.p. Daimler semi-sports saloon. **1966** 'E. Peters' *Piper on Mountain* iii. 56 Half the world buys British when it comes to cars, especially semi-sports jobs like this.

semi-'sterile, *a. Biol.* [SEMI- 8 d.] Reduced in fertility by approximately 50 per cent.

1914 J. Belling in *Jrnl. Heredity* V. 71/1 The plants with perfect pollen have also perfect ovules; the plants with semi-sterile pollen have also half their ovules sterile. **1927** *Ibid.* XVIII. 267/1 Ears produced on semi-sterile individuals bear only 50 per cent of the normal number of seeds irrespective of the source of the pollen used, since the lethal operates prior to fertilization. **1956** *Nature* 10 Mar. 452/2 The cytological properties of a series of semi-sterile stocks. **1978** *Ibid.* 20 July 253/1 Using this method, dieldrin-resistant sterile or semisterile males would be released into the field.

Hence **semi-ste'rility.**

1914 J. Belling in *Jrnl. Heredity* V. 73/1 These plants are favorable for an investigation of semi-sterility since no complications arise from self-sterility, incompatibility, or intercrossing by insects. **1978** *Nature* 20 July 253/1 A release programme involving..males carrying genetic aberrations that give high semisterility.

‖**semita** ('sɛmɪtə). *Zool.* [mod.L. use of L. *sēmita* narrow way or path.] A band of minute close-set tubercles which bear ciliated clubbed spines, characteristic of the spatangoid sea-urchins.

1877 Huxley *Anat. Inv. Anim.* ix. 574 These bands of peculiarly modified spines are called *semitæ* or *fascioles*. **1888** Rolleston & Jackson *Anim. Life* 558.

Hence **'semital** *a.* [cf. L. *sēmitālis* belonging to footpaths], of or pertaining to a semita.

1877 Huxley *Anat. Inv. Anim.* ix. 573 Fig., Semital tubercles... Semital spine.

semitar(ie, obs. forms of SCIMITAR.

†**'semitate,** *v. Obs. rare*[−0]. [f. L. *sēmita* path + -ATE.] *intr.* 'To make pathes, to divide into pathes or ways' (Blount *Glossogr.* 1656).

†**semitaur.** *Obs.* In 6 -tawre. [ad. L. **sēmitaurus*, f. *sēmi-* SEMI- 2 + *taurus* bull.] A creature shaped half like a bull.

1592 Breton *Pilgr. Parad.* (Grosart) 8/2 Some Semi-tawres, and some, more halfe a Beare. **1614** Sylvester *Bethulian's Rescue* vi. 108 He sees Chimeras, Gorgons, Mino-Taures, Medusas, Haggs, Alectos, Semi-Taures.

Semite ('sɛmaɪt). [ad. mod.L. *Sēmīta*, f. late Latin *Sēm*, Gr. Σήμ Shem: see -ITE. Cf. the earlier SHEMITE.] A person belonging to the race of mankind which includes most of the peoples mentioned in Gen. x. as descended from Shem son of Noah, as the Hebrews, Arabs, Assyrians, and Aramæans. Also, a person speaking a Semitic language as his native tongue.

1848 C. Bunsen in *Rep. Brit. Assoc. Advancem. Sci. 1847* XVII. 266 The country which, according to the most ancient traditions of the Semites, was the cradle of mankind. **1875** Whitney *Life & Growth Lang.* xii. 247 None but the Semites have, since the dawn of the historic period, seriously disputed with our family the headship of the human race. **1882** Farrar *Early Chr.* II. 199 The mutual aversion of Semites and Aryans thus finds ample illustration in the literature of both. **1886** Ragozin *Chaldea* ii. v. (1891) 237 Nor did the Semites preserve a separate existence.

semiter(e, -erie, obs. forms of SCIMITAR.

semitertian (sɛmɪ'tɜːʃən), *a.* (*sb.*) *Old Path.* [ad. mod.L. *sēmitertiāna (febris)*, rendering Gr. ἡμιτριταία HEMITRITÆAN; see SEMI- and TERTIAN.] Applied to an intermittent fever which combines the symptoms of a quotidian and a tertian fever, consisting of a paroxysm occurring every day with a second stronger one every other day.

1611 Florio, *Hemitritéa fébbre*, a Semitertian feauer. **1656** Ridgley *Pract. Physick* 138. **1749** Short *Hist. Air*, etc. I. 223 In some Places few recovered who had it [*sc.* Peripneumony] accompanied with a violent Fever. Semi-tertians were next dangerous. **1888** Fagge & Pye-Smith *Princ. Med.* (ed. 2) II. 165 The 'hemitritæus', i.e. semi-tertian, a form of ague mentioned by Galen.

Semitic (sɪ'mɪtɪk), *a.* and *sb.* Also 9 Semmetic. [ad. mod.L. *Sēmīticus*, f. *Sēmīta* SEMITE. Cf. F. *sémitique*, Sp., Pg., It. *semitico*, G. *semitisch*. Cf. SHEMITIC.] **A.** *adj.* Of or pertaining to the Semites. (In recent use often *spec.* = Jewish.)

1826 Pritchard *Res. Phys. Hist. Mankind* II. 210 The Semitic nations. **1835** J. B. Robertson tr. *Schlegel's Philos. Hist.* vi. (1846) 206 The people of the Semitic race. **1839** T. Mitchell *Frogs of Aristoph.* Add. 411 *note*, The Semitic origin of this worship. **1885** FLOWER in *Jrnl. Anthrop. Inst.* XIV. 382 Hamitic and Semitic Melanochroi. **1886** [see SEMITISM 1 b].

b. In linguistic sense: The distinctive epithet of that family of languages of which Hebrew, Aramæan, Arabic, Ethiopic, and ancient Assyrian, are the principal members. Hence (in *Semitic scholar, studies, grammar, philology,* etc.) concerned with the Semitic languages.

1813 *Q. Rev.* X. 267 (Adelung's *Mithridates*) The Arabian family is called by our author Semitic. **1827** BUCKINGHAM *Trav. Mesopot.* II. 385 In any of the Semmetic languages. **1850** DONALDSON *New Cratylus* (ed. 2) §100. 150 These arguments of the great Semitic scholar have been violently combated by one of his countrymen. **1877** *Smith & Wace's Dict. Chr. Biog.* I. 470/1 (*Chosroes*), There is a large Semitic element in the Pehlvi language.

B. *sb.* **a.** A Semite (*rare*). **b.** The Semitic family of languages; *occas.* the Semitic language of Babylon in opposition to Sumerian. **c.** *pl. U.S.* The scientific study of the language, literature, etc. of Semitic peoples.

1875 WHITNEY *Life & Growth Lang.* xii. 251 The scale of dialectic differences is much less in Semitic than in Indo-European. **1879** tr. *Brugsch's Hist. Egypt* II. 107 *note,* A very remarkable word which shows a full knowledge of Semitic in the writer. **1886** *Athenæum* 21 Aug. 238 [Pauli's] view that the Etruscans were neither Indo-Europeans nor Semitics. **1895** *Min. 9th Nat. Council Congr. Ch.* (U.S.A.) 239 With the growing interest in Semitics.. it is not easy to get the time for study which these subjects demand. **1899** SIR H. HOWORTH in *Eng. Hist. Rev.* Oct. 626 Written in the primitive language of Babylonia and in Semitic.

Hence **Se'miticism** = SEMITISM.

1907 *Expositor* Nov. 434 The number of real Semiticisms is therefore smaller than was supposed. **1908** *Spectator* 18 Apr. 625/1 Further, he discusses the 'semiticism' of the Greek Bible,—what it is, and what it is not.

Semiticize (sɪ'mɪtɪsaɪz), *v. trans.* [f. SEMITIC *a.* + -IZE.] = SEMITIZE *v.*

1859 R. F. BURTON *Centr. Afr.* in *Jrnl. Geog. Soc.* XXXIX. 48 The.. Sawahili races, mulattos, originally African, but semiticised like the Moplahs of Malabar by Yemeni or Omani blood [etc.]. **1881** *Athenæum* 9 July 48/1 The word became Semiticized by the Assyrians into Dumuzu.

Hence **Se'miticized** *ppl. a.*; **Se'miticizing** *vbl. sb.*

1863 R. F. BURTON *Wand. W. Africa* I. 188 With.. faces like the Semiticized negroids generally. **1887** *Athenæum* 28 May 698/3 He informs us.. that Anu was a Semitic god, whereas it is only a Semiticized form of the Accadian Anna. **1885** *Academy* 3 Jan. 15/1, I used to watch with much interest the Semiticising of foreign names in Syria.

†**semi-tile.** *Obs.* In 5 semy tyll. ? Alteration of *samel tile (see SAMEL) = half-baked tile, by association with SEMI-.

1448 *Cov. Leet Bk.* 232 That no tyler frohensfurth ley no semy [*MS.* seny] tyle ne crased tyle. **1454** *Ibid.* 279 Quod non vendant aliquam Semy tyll, nec illi qui tegulant ponant huiusmodi semytyll.

Semitism ('sɛmɪtɪz(ə)m). [f. SEMITE + -ISM.]

1. The attributes characteristic of the Semitic peoples. Also, the fact of being Semitic.

1851 LATHAM *Man & his Migrations* 146 The amount of Semitism in certain families. **1863** W. L. BEVAN in *Smith's Dict. Bible* II. s.v. *Philistines,* A period when the distinctive features of Hamitism and Semitism were yet in embryo.

b. In recent use, Jewish ideas or Jewish influence in politics and society.

1885 *Guardian* 6 May 697/3 The rivalry which exists with Catholicism and Semitism. **1886** W. J. TUCKER *E. Europe* 198 The Church of Rome will never countenance semitic innovations of any sort. The Catholic party must be propped up by staunch opponents to semitism.

2. A Semitic word or idiom; also (*nonce-use*) Semitic speech.

1869 FARRAR *Fam. Speech* iii. (1870) 114 The soberest conclusion seems to be.. for the present to exclude Egyptian from the dignity of being a kind of ante-historic Semitism. **1886** HUXLEY in *19th Cent.* Apr. 498 The Egyptian language, during the period of the nineteenth dynasty, is said by Brugsch to be as full of Semitisms as German is of Gallicisms. **1898** SIR H. HOWORTH in *Eng. Hist. Rev.* Jan. 11 These Semitisms [in Egyptian], moreover, are partly popular, partly literary in origin.

Semitist ('sɛmɪtɪst). [f. SEMITE + -IST.] One versed in Semitic languages, literature, etc.; a Semitic scholar.

1885 *Athenæum* 10 Jan. 46/2 It will be for Semitists to decide if these words were borrowed from Hebrew. **1902** *Ibid.* 30 Aug. 282/2 The majority of Semitists consider the word to be connected with Sin, the Babylonian Moon-god.

Semitize ('sɛmɪtaɪz), *v.* Also †Semetize. [f. SEMITE + -IZE.] *trans.* To render Semitic in character, language, or religion.

1869 BALDWIN *Preh. Nations* iv. (1877) 159 The language of Phoenicia is said to have been Semetized. **1880** CHEYNE *Isa.* xx. I. 118 The name is.. therefore non-Semitic, but the Assyrians.. Semitised it into Sarru-kinu. **1895** *Athenæum* 6 Apr. 447/3 We have a school who would roundly semitize the whole Greek civilization.

Hence **'Semitized** *ppl. a.*; **'Semitizing** *ppl. a.* Also **Semiti'zation,** the action of the verb.

1885 W. R. SMITH in *Encycl. Brit.* XVIII. 756/1 [The Philistines] were a Semitic or at least a thoroughly Semitized people. **1886** *Encycl. Brit.* XXI. 656/1 The partial Semitization of the southern districts of Abyssinia. **1884** CHEYNE *Isa.* xix. (ed. 3) I. 119 The political history of Palestine assisted this Semitising process.

Se,mito-Ha'mitic, *a.* and *sb.* = HAMITO-SEMITIC *a.* and *sb.* Also **Semitic-Hamitic** *a.* and *sb.*

1879 E. S. ROBERTS tr. *D. Pezzi's Aryan Philol.* I. i. 46 Hence the Southern and Central African dialects, the Erythræan (Semito-Hamitic) and the Aryan. **1910** *Encycl. Brit.* XII. 894 The development of a grammatical gender, this principal characteristic of Semito-Hamitic, in Bari and Masai, may be rather accidental than borrowed. **1928** *Language* IV. 129 If there is a Semitic-Hamitic language-group, then not primitive Semitic, but primitive Semitic-Hamitic must be correlated with primitive Indo-European. **1949** W. F. ALBRIGHT *Archaeol. Palestine* iii. 61 Since very similar human skeletons have been found in the Badarian of Egypt as well as in late chalcolithic Gezer and Byblus, it seems to follow that these folk belonged to the ancestral Semito-Hamitic stock. **1964** *Jrnl. Semitic Studies* IX. 137 The Semito-Hamitic family, for which the very apt term Erythraic has been recently proposed by A. N. Tucker and M. A. Bryan. **1974** *Encycl. Brit. Macropædia* VIII. 589/2 Also known as the Semito-Hamitic, Erythraean, Afro-Asiatic, and Afrasian language group, it [*sc.* Hamito-Semitic] is the main language family of northern Africa.

semitonal ('sɛmɪtəʊnəl), *a.* [f. SEMITONE + -AL[1].] = SEMITONIC.

1863 OUSELEY in *Guardian* 18 Nov. 1082/1 It is.. improbable that they would ever have abandoned a semitonal scale.. in order to adopt so very different a system as their present one. **1891** *Athenæum* 17 Oct. 524/3 Double-basses.. maintaining a semitonal trill.

Hence **'semitonally** *adv.,* = SEMITONICALLY.

1876 STAINER & BARRETT *Dict. Mus. Terms* s.v. *Descant,* Notes altered semitonally by accidentals. **1885** *London & Prov. Mus. Trades Rev.* 15 Sept. 7 The trumpet calls are accompanied by the violins rising semitonally.

semitone ('sɛmɪtəʊn). [f. SEMI- + TONE *sb.*; cf. late L. *sēmitonium,* OF. *semithon* and Gr. ἡμιτόνιον HEMITONE. Senses 2 and 3 (usually written *semi-tone*), are new formations distinct from 1.]

1. *Mus.* An interval approximately equal to half a tone, the smallest interval in the ordinary scales; a minor second.

Semitones are *chromatic* or *minor, diatonic* or *major,* and *enharmonic*: see these words.

1609 DOWLAND *Ornith. Microl.* 17 A Semitone.. is a rising from one Voyce to another, (by an imperfect second) sounding flatly: and it is onely betwixt the Voyces *Mi, fa.* It is called a Semitone, not because it is halfe a Tone.. but because it is an imperfect Tone. *a* **1620** CAMPION *Counterpoint* Wks. (1909) 192 A lesser Third consists of a Tone, and a Semi-tone. **1753** *Chambers' Cycl.* Suppl. s.v. *Interval,* The lesser flat seventh is equal to the sixth major and semi-tone major. **1811** BUSBY *Dict. Mus.* (ed. 3), The Semitone-Major is produced by rising a degree... The Semitone-Minor, by passing from a natural note to its sharp. **1848** RIMBAULT *Pianoforte* 33 A tone always includes both a Chromatic and a Diatonic semitone. **1876** tr. *Blaserna's Sound* vii. 133 Raising a note a semi-tone signifies raising that note to its sharp, as lowering it a semi-tone signifies lowering it to its flat.

2. *Art.* An intermediate tone or tint in a picture; = HALF-TONE 2. (Cf. *semi-tint* s.v. SEMI- 9.)

1782 *Mrs. Delany's Life & Corr.* III. 97 *note,* The greatest harmony of colouring from the various semi-tones of tint laid on. **1821** CRAIG *Lect. Drawing,* etc. iii. 155 The semi-tones, formed by the reflected lights in his pictures, appear scarcely distinguishable. **1906** *Daily Chron.* 5 Apr. 8/1 The soft tones and semi-tones seem to melt.. into one another. *fig.* **1911** CHESTERTON *Crit. & Apprec. Dickens* 154 Anyone who thinks that Dickens could not describe the semi-tones and the abrupt instincts of real human nature.

3. A soft or gentle tone of voice; an undertone.

1818 'T. BROWN' *Brighton* I. i. 39 'Yes, my lord,' said Zephyr, and, in a semi-tone, muttered, 'he'll overlook many things.' **1837** DISRAELI *Venetia* I. vi, Speaking in a semi-tone. **1894** *Advance* (Chicago) 4 Oct., Preachers should pray less in semi-tones, and preach more in thunder tones.

semitonic (sɛmɪ'tɒnɪk), *a. Mus.* [f. SEMITONE + -IC.] Pertaining to or consisting of a semitone or semitones; (of a scale) chromatic.

1728 CHAMBERS *Cycl.* s.v. *Scale,* This, then, is the present Scale for Instruments, *viz.* Between the Extremes of every Tone of the natural Scale is put a Note, which divides it into two unequal Parts, called Semi-tones, whence the whole may be called the *Semitonic scale.* **1760** STILES in *Phil. Trans.* LI. 706 In the diatonic genus, the diapason consisting of five tonic and two semitonic intervals. **1833** RUSH *Philos. Human Voice* (ed. 2) 332 *note,* It is the diatonic shake, the semitonic not being found in his [*sc.* the mocking-bird's] song. **1838** G. F. GRAHAM *Mus. Comp.* 7/1 The chromatic scales formed from these consist of a semitonic (or so-called semitonic) series between the key-note and its octave.

Hence **semi'tonically** *adv.,* by a semitone or semitones.

1838 G. F. GRAHAM *Mus. Comp.* 25/1 The cadence is complete, from the third of dominant rising semitonically.. to the tonic itself. **1867** MACFARREN *Harmony* iii. 113 Chromatic notes, which must always be quitted semitonically.

semitor, -orie, obs. forms of SCIMITAR.

semi-'trailer. [SEMI- 8 a.] A road trailer that has a wheel system at the rear only and is coupled to a suitable tractor to form an articulated lorry. Freq. *transf.,* an articulated lorry made up in this way.

1919 *Engineering* 28 Nov. 718/2 With the semi-trailer the tractor partly carries and partly hauls the load, the front end of the two-wheeled vehicle being carried on a platform directly over the rear or driving wheels. **1926** *Encycl. Brit.* II. 987/2 This semi-trailer was a two-wheeled construction, the forward end of which was supported on the tractor frame by means of a swivelling fifth wheel. This end of the semi-trailer could be supported by means of jacks. **1949** *Automobile & Carriage Builders' Jrnl.* CIII. III. 38/1 Probably the world's most curvaceous semi-trailer. **1956** 'N. SHUTE' *Beyond Black Stump* 44 The diesel semi-trailer.. ground to a standstill in a swirl of red dust. **1962** *Coast to Coast 1961–62* 141 A loaded semi-trailer stood beside the kerb in front of the hotel.. and Keppler started towards it, hoping for a lift. **1978** O. WHITE *Silent Reach* xv. 154 His car collided with a semi-trailer.

,semi-trans'parency. [f. next: see -ENCY.] The quality or condition of being semi-transparent; partial transparency.

1787 J. WEDGWOOD *Let.* 16 June (1965) 308 The original artist availed himself of the semitransparency of the white glass. *c* **1793** *Encycl. Brit.* (1797) XI. 434/1 This ore is so called from its colour and semitransparency, by which it resembles horn or colophony. **1860** GOSSE *Rom. Nat. Hist.* 161 The obscure semi-transparency of the texture of the animal.

,semi-trans'parent, *a.* Chiefly *scientific.* [SEMI- 8.] Partially or imperfectly transparent.

c **1793** *Encycl. Brit.* (1797) XI. 434/1 Corneous ore.. is foliated and semitransparent. **1857** MILLER *Elem. Chem., Org.* (1862) iv. §1. 253 They possess the property of rendering paper semitransparent, producing what is well known as a greasy stain. **1870** DICKENS *E. Drood* iv, Her semi-transparent hands were clasped together. **1883** *Encycl. Brit.* XVI. 390/1 Common Opal: semitransparent, vitreous.

semitte, obs. form of SEMMIT *Sc.*

†**semitune.** *Obs.* Also 5 -toyn. [early f. SEMITONE: see TUNE *sb.*] = SEMITONE 1.

1486 *Bk. St. Albans* d iij b, Of hawkys Bellys.. Looke.. that thay be.. not both of oon sowne: bot that oon be a semytoyn vnder a noder. **1607** HEYWOOD *Wom. Killed w. Kindn.* I. iii, Her Bels.. had not both one waight, Nor was one semi-tune aboue the other.

semi-'uncial, *a.* (*sb.*) *Palæography.* [SEMI- 6 a.] Name of a style of writing intermediate between uncial and minuscule. Cf. *half-uncial* s.v. HALF- II. n.

a **1734** NORTH *Life Ld. Kpr. North* (1742) 16 It is not well to write, as the Fashion now is, uncial or semiuncial Letters, to look like Pigs Ribs. **1815** SCOTT *Guy M.* xlix, The letters are uncial or semi-uncial, as somebody calls your large text-hand, and in size and perpendicularity resemble the ribs of a roasted pig. **1883** I. TAYLOR *Alph.* v. ii. 173 [Irish script] is usually called the Irish uncial or semi-uncial.

†**semi'ustulate,** *pa. pple.* [ad. L. *sēmiustulātus*: see SEMI- 1 and USTULATE.] Half-burnt; also **semi'ustulated**; so **semiustu'lation,** a half burning.

1621 BURTON *Anat. Mel.* I. i. II. v. (1651) 21 Assation is a concoction of the inward moisture by heat, his opposite is a semiustulation. **1623** COCKERAM I, *Semiustulated,* halfe burnt. **1721** BAILEY, *Semiustulate,* (*semiustulatus* L.) half burnt or consumed by fire.

†**semivif,** *a. Obs.* In 4–5 semi-, semy-, seme-, -uyf, -uijf. [ad. L. *sēmivīvus,* f. *sēmi-* SEMI- 1 + *vīvus* alive.] Half alive, half dead.

1377 LANGL. *P. Pl.* B. XVII. 55 Semiuyf he semed [C. xx. 55 *semivivus, v. rr.* semiuyf, semeuijf]. *a* **1400** *Beryn* 2202 He sat hym down sofftly on a stall, Semyvif for sorow.

semi-'vitreous, *a.* [SEMI- 8 a.] Partially vitreous.

1782 WEDGWOOD in *Phil. Trans.* LXXII. 317 By a very strong fire, they are changed to a porcelain or semi-vitreous texture. **1807** T. THOMSON *Chem.* (ed. 3) II. 339 Semi-vitreous oxide of lead. **1813** BAKEWELL *Introd. Geol.* (1815) 421 Semivitreous lava. **1890** *Q. Jrnl. Geol. Soc.* XLVI. I. 74 Finely vesicular rhyolitic rock with compact semivitreous green-grey base.

So **,semi-vitrifi'cation, -'vitrified** *ppl. a.*

1753 *Chambers's Cycl.* Suppl., *Slacken,*.. a term used by the miners to express a spungy and semivitrified substance. **1791** E. DARWIN *Bot. Gard.* I. Notes 52 The semivitrification, which constitutes porcelain. **1794** KIRWAN *Elem. Min.* (ed. 2) I. 396 That which produces enamels and semi-vitrifications. **1841** *Proc. Amer. Philos. Soc.* II. 4 The semi-vitrified quartz rock of the western part of the Hoosae mountain. **1889** C. T. DAVIS *Pract. Treat. Bricks,* etc. (ed. 2) 78 A degree of heat when semi-vitrification and shrinkage take place.

†**semivocal,** *a.* and *sb. Obs.* [ad. L. *sēmivocālis* (in sense A. 2, B., transl. of Gr. ἡμίφωνος): see SEMI- and VOCAL *a.*]

A. *adj.* **1.** Applied to the sound of trumpets, drums, etc. (see quots.).

1614 ADAMS *Divell's Banket* 28 By vocall speeches, semivocall Drummes and Trumpets, mute Ensignes. **1688** HOLME *Armoury* III. xix. (Roxb.) 167/2 A Semivocall signe, is that which is distinguished by the Trumpett, or other warlike Instrument.

2. That is a semivowel.

1828–32 WEBSTER, *Semivocal,* pertaining to a semivowel; half-vocal; imperfectly sounding.

B. *sb.* A semivowel.

1530 PALSGR. Introd. p. xxiii, Theyr consonantes be devyded in to mutes and liquides or semivocalles.

semivowel (ˈsɛmɪvaʊəl). [f. SEMI- 8 c + VOWEL, after L. *sēmivocālis*: see prec. Cf. F. *semi-voyelle*.] A vocal sound that partakes of the nature of a vowel and of a consonant; a letter representing such a sound.

The general literary use echoes that of the Roman grammarians, who applied the term to the spirants and liquids (including nasals), *f, l, m, n, r, s, x*. As a technical term the word now most commonly denotes only *w* and *y*, but sometimes it includes these together with the liquids and nasals, chiefly in their non-syllabic values.

1530 PALSGR. Introd. p. xxiii, The latines in soundyng of theyr liquides or semi vowelles begyn with *e*. **1552** HULOET s.v. *X*, X is a semiuowell, and hathe the voice of a double consonante for the which in olde writinges *cs* and *gs* was vsed. **1656** BLOUNT *Glossogr.*, *Semivowels*, certain Consonants so called, because they have the sound of Vowels, As *f, l, m, n, s*. **1668** WILKINS *Real Char.* III. xii. 369, (*S*) the correspondent mute (though it be commonly reckoned for a semivowel). **1726** BROOME *Notes Pope's Odyss.* XVII. 46 When Homer.. paints a beautiful face, or an engaging object, he chuses the softest vowels, and most smooth and flowing semivowels. **1751** JOHNSON *Rambler* No. 88 ¶3 By tempering the mute Consonants with Liquids and Semivowels. **1841** LATHAM *Eng. Lang.* II. ix. 165 The Semivowel *y*. **1876** BANCROFT *Hist. U.S.* II. xxxvi. 409 The whole Iroquois family never use the semivowel *m*.

attrib. **1860** O. W. HOLMES *Elsie V.* xix. (1891) 261 The foam-flowers dropping as the grass-flowers drop,—with sharp semivowel consonantal sounds,—*frsh*.

semland(e, -ant(e, -aunt, var. ff. SEMBLANT.

semlar, var. SOMLER *Sc. Obs.*, butler.

semle, obs. f. SEEMLY *a.*; var. SEMBLE *v. Obs.*

semli, -lich(e, -like, obs. forms of SEEMLY.

semly, obs. f. SEEMLY; var. SEMBLE *sb.* and *v.*

semmar, -er, var. forms of SEMAR *Obs.*

semme, semmetic: see SEEM *v.*[2], SEMITIC *a.*

semmit (ˈsɛmɪt). *Sc.* Forms: 5 semat, 6 semitte, 9 semmit, -et. An under-shirt or vest.

1456 SIR G. HAYE *Law Arms* (S.T.S.) 64 Cesar brocht with him nouthir wapyn na armuris na othir defence bot in his semat. **1562–3** *Act 5 Eliz.* c. 22 §1 Unles suche person.. doo make..therof tawed..Leather or Parchement or otherwise converte the same into Semittes Panelles [etc.]. **1888** *Glasgow Even. Times* 15 Oct. 3/5 Offering a petticoat and semmit in pledge. **1904** *C.T.C. Gaz.* Feb. 91 A tight-fitting woollen semmit next the skin (thin and light)... I also carry a semmit made of Welsh flannel, made wide and of full size... I wear this semmit during the evenings, and also sleep in it under my nightshirt.

†ˈ**semnable** *a.*, †ˈ**semnably** *adv.* Used by Fuller = SEMBLABLE *a.*, SEMBLABLY *adv.*

1651 FULLER *Abel Rediv.*, *Huss* 19 That semnably with rhetoricall flusculations I should endevour to adorne his memoriall. **1659** —— *Appeal Injured Innoc.* III. 57 As Marriners..are fain to fetch a compass; Semnably, I..was faine to go about. *a* **1661** —— *Worthies, Northumb.* (1662) II. 302 From Berwick to Dover three hundred miles over: That is from one end of the land to the other. Semnable the Scripture expression, From Dan to Ber-sheba.

‖**Semnopithecus** (ˌsɛmnəpɪˈθiːkəs). [mod.L. *semnopithēcus*, f. Gr. σεμνός revered, holy + πίθηκος ape.] A genus of long-tailed, long-limbed Asiatic monkeys. Also, a monkey of this genus: often in anglicized form **Semnopiˈthec** (-ˈθɛk), or **-thece** (-ˈθiːs). Hence **Semnopiˈthecine** *a.*, pertaining to the subfamily *Semnopithecinæ*, or to the genus *Semnopithecus*; *sb.*, a semnopithecine monkey. ˌ**Semnopiˈthecoid** *a.* and *sb.* = prec.

1824 HORSFIELD *Zool. Res. Java* 9 The comparisons which I have been enabled to make of the skulls of various Semnopitheci and of Gibbons. **1838** [? RENNIE] *Nat. Hist. Monkeys*, etc. (Libr. Entert. Knowl.) 216 The tails, likewise, are much longer in the semnopithecs than in any of the ordinary monkeys. **1891** *Century Dict.*, Semnopithece... Semnopithecine [*a.* and *sb.*]... Semnopithecoid [*a.* and *sb.*].

semo- (ˈsiːməʊ), combining form of Gr. σῆμα sign, used as the first element in **semoleˈxemic** *a.*, of linguistic rules: governing the conversion of units of meaning into lexical items; **semoˈlogical** *a.*, of or pertaining to semology; hence **semoˈlogically** *adv.*; **seˈmology**, the study of meaning as an aspect of language; = SEMANTIC *sb.* 1 a; **semoˈtactic** *a.*, of or pertaining to the ordering of units of meaning; hence **semoˈtactically** *adv.* Cf. SEMANTICO-.

1968 *Language* XLIV. 578 The last four pages of chapter 6 are devoted to a discussion of '*semolexemic rules', which map sememic networks onto lexemic trees. **1913** *Jrnl. Eng. & Gmc. Philol.* XII. 78 The change may be purely *semological. **1928** C. BERGENER *Contribution to Study of Conversion of Adjectives into Nouns* iv. 170 *Light, dark*, and *dusk* form a semological association-group. **1975** M. A. K. HALLIDAY in S. Rogers *Children & Lang.* IV. 225 This is an analysis at the semological level in which the elements of structure are functional in character. **1913** *Jrnl. Eng. & Gmc. Philol.* XII. 78 Morphologically and *semologically the stem *flik* exhibits types of word-formation and meaning development that are representative. **1911** A. L. ELMQUIST in *Ibid.* X. 318 The grammar [of Noreen's *Vårt Språk*] is in four parts..(3), *Semology, a new term for semasiology. *Ibid.*, The grammar offers a large number of new features, the Semology, perhaps, most of all. **1928** C. BERGENER *Contribution to Study of Conversion of Adjectives into Nouns* i. 7 We are not only concerned with the semology but also with the morphology of converted adjectives. **1958** G. L. TRAGER in *Studies in Linguistics* XIII. 8 There seems to be no subdivision of either kinesics or paralinguistics exactly analogous to the phonology-morphology-semology of language. **1970** *Canadian Jrnl. Linguistics* XVI. 22 Below each disjunction each wire leads (though not necessarily immediately) to an inverse conjunction, the other wire of which leads up to the semology. **1966** S. M. LAMB *Outl. Stratif. Gram.* 14 *Semotactic patterns differ from tactic patterns for lower strata in having considerable numbers of upwards ANDS. **1967** D. G. HAYS *Introd. Computational Linguistics* xiii. 215 If parsing is performed after this dictionary lookup, its object is to determine semotactic well-formedness. **1969** *Language* XLV. 491 The principal area of stylistic concern is the discourse, not primarily the pleasing sound patterns or the juxtaposition of *semotactically felicitous phrases.

semola (ˈsɛmələ). [a. It. *semola* bran.] A trade name for a special variety of semolina.

1853 [see SEMOLETTA]. **1858** SIMMONDS *Dict. Trade*, *Semola*, an Italian name for bran; but often erroneously applied by grocers, and other vendors, to semolino. **1882** in OGILVIE; and in later Dicts. **1895** *Stores' Price-list*, Gluten Preparations for Special Dietary... Semola.

‖**semoletta** (sɛməˈlɛtə). *rare.* (In some Dicts. *erron.* **semolella.**) [It. *semoletta*, dim. of *semola*: see SEMOLA.] A variety of semolina.

1844 T. WEBSTER *Encycl. Dom. Econ.* 767 Semolina..is called also *soojee*: and a still smaller kind, called semoletta, is sifted out of the other. **1853** T. C. ARCHER *Pop. Econ. Bot.* 86 Semolina, Semoletta, Semola, Semola rarita, Soojee, and Urena, are names used to designate a product of wheat.

semolina (sɛməˈliːnə). Also **semoulina**, ‖**semolino.** [Altered form of It. *semolino*, dim. of *semola* bran: see SEMOLA.] An article of food consisting of those hard portions of 'flinty' wheat which resist the action of the millstones, and are collected in the form of rounded grains. (See also quot. 1858.) Also *attrib.*, as ***semolina pudding.***

1797 UNDERWOOD *Dis. Children* III. 82 To broth may be added light puddings, made of bread, semolina, tapioca, or rice. **1845** ELIZA ACTON *Mod. Cookery* (ed. 2) 395 A good Semoulina pudding. **1858** SIMMONDS *Dict. Trade*, *Semolino*. .. The commercial name for the fine hard parts of wheat rounded by attrition in the millstones, imported chiefly from Italy... In France the name semolino is given to the large hard grains of wheat retained in the bolting machine, after the fine parts have been pressed through its meshes. **1884** *Bath Herald* 27 Dec. 6/4 It is sought, while dividing the bran from the interior of the grain, to break up the latter, not into flour but into fragments known as 'semolina', or 'middlings'. **1904** 'E. NESBIT' *Phœnix & Carpet* xii. 219 When lunch came it was just hashed mutton and semolina pudding.

semon (ˈsiːmɒn). *Linguistics.* [Irreg. f. Gr. σῆμα: cf. -ON[1].] In stratificational grammar: an element of meaning or one which combines with others to make up a sememe.

1965 S. M. LAMB in *Amer. Anthropol.* LXVII. II. 46 Turning now to semology, the elementary unit is the semon, and a sememe is a unit composed of one or more semons. In a clause such as *he found his brace and bit* all the sememes are simple, but the following expressions contain or are complex sememes, i.e. sememes composed of multiple semons: *she put all her eggs in one basket.., don't give up the ship.* **1968** *Language* XLIV. 576 Hockett divides the 'semons' (the labels on the nodes in the sememic networks) into three classes, called 'links', 'kernels', and 'modifiers'. **1973** *Archivum Linguisticum* IV. 119 Within his general model the speaker makes a selection of 'semons' (elementary semantic features) on the basis of his 'awareness of a "cognitive experience"'.

semond: see SEMEND *Obs.*, salmon.

semonde, semoom: see SIMMON *sb.*[1], SIMOOM.

†**semoted**, *a. Obs. rare*[−1]. [f. L. *sēmōt-us*, pa. pple. of *sēmovēre* to separate, f. *sē-*, apart, SE- + *movēre* to move: see -ED[1].] Separated, removed.

1542 BECON *Pathw. Prayer* vii. D iv, Is it ynough yf I pray with my mynde, the herte beynge semoted from mundane affayres?

semoulina, obs. form of SEMOLINA.

†**seˈmovedly**, *adv. Obs.* [f. SE- + MOVED *ppl. a.* + -LY[2]. Cf. SEMOTED.] Separately.

1593 NASHE *Christ's T.* 38 b, None I will semouedly allude to, but onely attaint vice in generall. **1623** COCKERAM I, *Semouedly*, meaning one alone.

sempect (ˈsɛmpɛkt). *Hist. rare*[−1]. [ad. med.L. *sempēcta*, *senpecta*, *sympæcta*, ad. Gr. συμπαίκτης playfellow.] A term formerly used in the Benedictine Order, according to Pseudo-Ingulf applied to monks over fifty years old, who were allowed special privileges on account of age.

This seems to be a misapprehension. In the Benedictine Rule itself (cap. xxvii) *senpectæ* denotes the elder monks chosen by the abbot to visit (secretly) an excommunicated brother and to encourage him if likely to fall into despair.

1865 KINGSLEY *Herew.* xx, Only the ancient sempects—some near upon a hundred and fifty years old—wandered where they would.

‖**semper-** (ˈsɛmpə(r)), the L. adv. *semper* always, used in various nonce-combinations (in imitation of SEMPERVIRENT, etc.), as **semper-annual** *a.*, unceasing in annual succession; **semper-green**, an evergreen; **semper-identical** *a.* [after L. phrase *semper idem*, always the same]; **semper-juvenescent** *a.*, always growing younger; **semper-lenity**, unvarying gentleness.

1623 COCKERAM II, Accustomed Gentlenesse, *Semperlenity*. **1694** WESTMACOTT *Script. Herb.* 18 The common Bay-tree, which is a sempergreen, is now commonly found in most Gardens. **1820** ? WAINEWRIGHT *Ess. & Crit.* (1880) 98 That perfectly semperidentical display of idiosyncratic egotism which runs through..all his varieties. **1830** *Fraser's Mag.* I. 342 Blisses of an immortal and semperjuvenescent life. **1861** G. MEREDITH *Evan Harrington* xxviii, Supposing Lord Mayor's footmen to be plumed like estridges... What must Lord Mayors be and semperannual Lords?

sempervirent (sɛmpəˈvaɪrənt), *a.* (*sb.*) [f. L. *semper* always + *virent-em*, pr. pple. of *virēre* to be green.] Evergreen. Also *absol.* as *sb.*, an evergreen plant (*rare*).

1668 WILKINS *Real Char.* II. iv. §6. 109 Bacciferous sempervirent shrubs. **1693** *Phil. Trans.* XVII. 762 It is sempervirent, and grows in sandy places. **1857** A. GRAY *First Less. Bot.* (1866) Gloss., *Sempervirent*, evergreen. **1957** J. D. SALINGER in *New Yorker* 4 May 42/1 She nudged an unopened box of Sal Hepatica..to align it with the other sempervirents in its row.

sempervirid (sɛmpəˈvɪrɪd), *a. Bot.* [Formed as prec. + L. *virid-is* green, VIRID *a.*] = prec.

1911 in WEBSTER. [*Obs.* or *rare.*]

†**sempervive.** *Obs.* Also 8 (after Sp.) **sempre vive.** [Anglicized form of SEMPERVIVUM. Cf. F. †*sempervive* (Cotgr. 1611), Sp. *siempreviva*.] The houseleek.

1625 PURCHAS *Pilgrims* I. 277 An herbe (which for his forme is scarce to be discerned from a Semperuiue). **1626** BACON *Sylva* §29 The greater Sempervive..will put out Branches, two or three yeares. **1764** GRAINGER *Sugar Cane* IV. 124 With sempre vive Unload their bowels.

attrib. a **1722** LISLE *Husb.* (1752) 257 Purge them with aloes, or sempervive leaves cleared of their outward skins.

‖ˌ**semper-ˈvivens.** *Obs. rare*[−1]. [mod.L., f. L. *semper* always + *vīvens*, pr. pple. of *vīvēre* to live.] The houseleek.

1672 W. HUGHES *Amer. Physit.* 98 Of Semper-Vivens.

‖**sempervivum** (sɛmpəˈvaɪvəm). [L. *sempervīvum* neut. of *sempervīvus* ever-living. The fem. *sempervīva* (sc. *herba*) was also used.] **a.** The houseleek. **b.** A genus (Linnæus 1737) of crassulaceous plants containing the houseleek, *S. tectorum* and about 50 other species; a plant of this genus.

1591 PERCYVALL *Span. Dict.*, *Yerva puntera*, semperuiuum, *Aizous*. **1655** FULLER *Hist. Cambr.* 134 Two Serpents, erected, azure,..having a branch of semper vivum proper betwixt their heads. **1666** J. DAVIES tr. *Rochefort's Caribby Isl.* 62 *Semper-vivum*. There are in these Islands several kinds of Herbs that never dye or wither. **1882** *Garden* 3 June 306/1 To see the pleasing tints and forms of the Sempervivums at the present season makes one wonder why these plants are not grown in every rock garden.

sempill, obs. Sc. form of SIMPLE *a.*

sempitan, obs. f. SUMPITAN, Malay blow-gun.

sempitern (ˈsɛmpɪtɜːn), *a. arch.* Forms: 4–7 **sempiterne**, 6 **sempyterne**, 6– **sempitern.** [a. OF. *sempiterne*, ad. L. *sempiternus*, f. *semp-er* always (cf. *æviternus*: see ETERNE *a.*).] = next.

1390 GOWER *Conf.* III. 88 That is the god, whos mageste Alle othre thinges schal governe, And his beinge is sempiterne. *c* **1440** CAPGRAVE *Life St. Kath.* IV. 1586 Than is oure feyth grounded on noo lye, But on swiche thyng whiche is sempiterne. **1535** STEWART *Cron. Scot.* I. 505 In sempiterne rememberance to be Of Christis deith and Cristianitie. **1624** DARCIE *Birth of Heresies* Ded., Vnder whose Sacred Sempitern Defence Long liue, Chast Star. **1683** E. HOOKER *Pordage's Myst. Div.* Pref. Ep. 107 The only True, semper eadem, sempitern, ever-adorable and super-benedict Tri-une Deitie. **1866** BLACKMORE *Cradock Nowell* xxviii, That asylum is inviolable and sempitern, I hope. **1876** J. ELLIS *Caesar in Egypt* 66 Those unexampled Temples sempitern.

sempiternal (sɛmpɪˈtɜːnəl), *a.* Also **sempiternall**, **sempyternal, -el**, 5–7 **sempiternall**, 6 **sempyternall**, 6–7 **sempeternal.** [a. F. *sempiternel* (13th c. in Hatz.-Darm.), or ad. late L. *sempiternāl-is*, f. L. *sempitern-us*: see SEMPITERN *a.* and -AL[1].] Enduring constantly and continually; everlasting, eternal.

14.. *Pol. Rel. & L. Poems* (1903) 113 As thou art cyte of god, & sempiternal throne, Here now, blessyd lady, my wofulle mone. **1432–50** tr. *Higden* (Rolls) III. 183 Trawthe is immortalle, immutable, and sempiternalle. **1566** PAINTER *Pal. Pleas.* xxvii. (1569) 55 A miraculous acte, and worthie (in deede) of sempiternall remembraunce. **1579–80** NORTH *Plutarch, Camillus* (1595) 152 Some writers say, that they [*sc.* the Vestals] had nothing els in keeping but the sempiternall fire. **1632** LITHGOW *Trav.* x. 437 Queene Elizabeth of sempiternall renowne. *a* **1730** G. GUTHRIE *Monogr.* (1900) 66 Fearing it might be a sempiternal work to him. **1784** COWPER *Task* II. 499 All truth is from the sempiternal source Of Light Divine. **1831** J. JEKYLL *Corr.* 18 July (1894) 274 Dull dinners..with the sempiternal saddle of mutton. **1860** GEN. P. THOMPSON *Audi Alt.* III. cxxiv. 75 Two sources of war are sempiternal. **1884** *World*

20 Aug. 8/1 We have discovered the elixir of sempiternal juvenility.

sempi'ternally, *adv.* [f. prec. + -LY².] Everlastingly, eternally.

1509 BARCLAY *Shyp of Folys* (1874) I. 27 God is aboue and regneth sempiternally [**1570** sempeternally] Whiche shall vs deme at his last Jugement. **1635** PAGITT *Christianogr.* App. 22 The Word and his Spirit sempiternally proceed from God, and are sempiternally in him. *a* **1693** *Urquhart's Rabelais* III. v, That is to be done infinitely and sempiternally. **1879** ESCOTT *England* xi. (1881) 161 The filthy back-kitchen of the den, sempiternally reeking with the fumes of bad drink and vile tobacco. **1895** ZANGWILL *Master* II. x. 245 It wore a sempiternally festive air.

sempi'ternity. [ad. late L. *sempiternitās*, f. L. *sempitern-us*: see SEMPITERN *a.* and -ITY.] Duration without end; perpetuity.

1599 NASHE *Lenten Stuffe* 22 Or thou wilt commend thy muse to sempiternity, and haue images and statues erected to her after her vnstringed silent interment. *a* **1676** HALE *Prim. Orig. Man.* (1677) 227 A Supposition of a future Sempiternity would produce the same difficulty, without such interposition of the Divine Wisdom and Providence. **1802** in *Spirit Publ. Jrnls.* VI. 261 All concurred in the sempiternity of merit that they were determined to discover in him in all time forthcoming. **1933** *Mind* XLII. 309 Spinoza did not mean by 'eternity' either endless future duration or endless past and future duration ('sempiternity'). **1980** *Dædalus* Spring 255 The fraternal impulse of the heroic youth in the barque unsettles the moral ground of Hell's sempiternity.

† **sempiternize**, *v. Obs. rare*⁻¹. [f. SEMPITERN *a.* + -IZE.] *trans.* To perpetuate.

a **1693** *Urquhart's Rabelais* III. viii, The sempiternizing of Human Race.

† **sempiternly**, *adv. Obs.* [f. SEMPITERN *a.* + -LY².] = SEMPITERNALLY *adv.*

c **1450** *Mirour Saluacioun* (1888) 140 The gude entre in the joye of thaire lord sempiternely.

sempi'ternous, *a.* ? *Obs. rare.* [ad. OF. *sempiterneux*, f. L. *sempitern-us*: see SEMPITERN *a.* and -OUS.] Sempiternal.

1653 URQUHART *Rabelais* II. xv, A sempiternous Crone and old Hag. *Ibid.* II. xvii, Great old sempiternous trots [Fr. *grandes vieilles sempiterneuses*]. **1809** W. IRVING *Knickerb.* VI. iv. (1849) 335 A race of pestilent sempiternous beldames.

‖ **sempiternum** (sɛmpɪ'tɜːnəm). *Obs.* [L. *sempiternum*, neut. of *sempiternus* SEMPITERN.] A quality of woollen cloth made in the 17th c. and similar to PERPETUANA. Cf. EVERLASTING *sb.*

1633 in *Naworth Househ. Bks.* (Surtees) 295 For one yearde and a halfe of Sempiternum iiij. vj^d. *Ibid.* 300. **1665** BRATHWAIT *Comm. Two Tales* 65 She would have her Husband's Life of any Stuff rather than *Perpetuano* or *Sempiternum*.

semplar, obs. form of SAMPLER.

1685 BOYLE *Salubr. Air* Pref. 1 To give a Semplar or Specimen of what may be done upon the other Heads of the designed History.

Semple ('sɛmp(ə)l). *Med.* The name of Lt.-Col. Sir David *Semple* (1856–1937), English bacteriologist, used *attrib.*, *absol.*, in *Comb.*, and in the possessive to designate a vaccine against rabies described by him in 1911 (*Sci. Mem. by Officers of Med. & Sanitary Depts. of Govt. of India* No. 44), and the techniques of preparing and administering it.

1934 *Q. Bull. Health Organisation* III. 615 Killed phenol vaccines...4000 mg. Semple. *Ibid.* 618 Semple's modification of Fermi's original method (*i.e.*, the phenol vaccine is incubated at 37°C. for twenty-four hours) is employed. **1938** *Jrnl. Amer. Med. Assoc.* 20 Aug. 690/2 The Semple modification of the Pasteur treatment is commercially available and should be given twice daily. **1939** *Ibid.* 29 July 392/1 The Alabama State Health Department distributes Semple vaccine without charge to physicians for the treatment of those exposed to rabid animals. **1949** *New Gould Med. Dict.* 920/2 The vaccine used is made from 4% inoculated rabbit brain attenuated with 0·5% phenol; called *Semple's vaccine.* **1971** E. S. TIERKEL in Nagano & Davenport *Rabies* 3 The Semple vaccine eventually became the biologic of choice in many countries. **1977** C. KAPLAN *Rabies* vii. 108 A Semple-type vaccine was first used in 1921 for the successful mass vaccination of dogs in Japan.

semple, obs. form of SIMPLE.

‖ **semplice** ('sempliʧe), *a.* and *adv. Mus.* [It., simple.] **A.** *adj.* Simple. **B.** *adv.* Simply. (Chiefly as a direction.)

1740 GRASSINEAU *Mus. Dict.* 218 *Semplice*, simple, not doubled, compounded, or composed of any thing else, as *cadenza simplice*, is a cadence in which all the notes are equal in all the parts. **1801** BUSBY *Dict. Mus.* s.v., *Semplice*, (Ital.), a word implying that the movement before which it is placed is to be performed with chasteness and simplicity. **1883** GROVE *Dict. Mus.* III. 461/1 *Semplice*, 'simple'; a direction denoting that the passage so marked is to be performed without any adornment or deviation from the time, used particularly in passages of which the character might possibly be misunderstood. **1976** *Gramophone* Nov. 786/2 The moment I suggest as a prime sample of Zukerman's profound insight is the third theme in that same movement with its rising phrases marked *pianissimo* and *semplice*.

‖ **sempre** ('sempre), *adv. Mus.* [It.] Always, still: used to qualify an adj. or advb. Also *transf.*

1801 BUSBY *Dict. Mus.* s.v., *Sempre*, (Ital.), always, or throughout: as *sempre piano*, soft throughout. **1816** in G. Thomson *Sel. Collection Irish Melodies* 139 Judy Lovely Matchless Creature *Sempre dolce.* **1883** GROVE *Dict. Mus.* III. 461/2 *Sempre*, 'always'; a word used in conjunction with some other mark of time or expression to signify that such mark is to remain in force until a new direction appears. **1959** *Collins' Mus. Encycl.* 594/1 *Sempre*, 'always, still', as in *sempre piano*, still softly. **1959** E. POUND *Thrones* xcvii. 29 Earth under Fortuna, each sphere hath its Lord, with ever-shifting change, sempre biasmata.

sempre vive, variant of SEMPERVIVE *Obs.*

sempster, sempstress, etc.: see SEAMSTER, SEAMSTRESS.

‖ **semsem** ('sɛmsɛm). [Arab. *simsim*, prob. ad. Gr. σήσαμον.] = SESAME. Also *attrib.*

1866 LIVINGSTONE *Jrnl.* i. (1873) I. 17 Some sorghum, sem-sem seed [etc.]..constitute the commerce of the port. **1896** *Daily News* 24 Nov. 11/2 The valleys..were covered with plantations of Indian corn,..tobacco, semsem oil, and banana. **1899** *19th Cent.* Aug. 273 An interminably long stretch of dhurra cultivation appears, varied by sem-sem plants.

semseyite ('sɛmsiːaɪt). *Min.* [ad. Hung. *semseyit* (J. S. Krenner 1881, in *Magyar tudományos Akad. Értes.* XV. 113), f. the name of Andor *Semsey* (1833–1923), Hung. nobleman and amateur mineralogist: see -ITE¹.] A monoclinic sulphide of lead and antimony, $Pb_9Sb_8S_{21}$, found usu. as grey or black tabular or prismatic crystals with a metallic lustre.

1886 *Jrnl. Chem. Soc.* L. 313 Semseyite from Felsöbánya; small, grey tabular crystals. **1920** *Brit. Mus. Return* 142 in *Parl. Papers* XXXVI. 673 Semseyite from Dumfriesshire. **1955** [see ROSETTED *a.* 1 a]. **1976** *Mineral. Abstr.* XXVII. 306/2 Genetic antagonism between semseyite..and boulangerite..may have been caused by variation in oxidizing power of sulphur between the two media.

semster, -stress(e, obs. ff. SEAMSTER, -STRESS.

semulacre, obs. variant of SIMULACRE.

‖ **semuncia** (siː'mʌnʃ(ɪ)ə). *Rom. Antiq.* Pl. -iæ (siː'mʌnʃiː). [L. *sēmuncia*, f. *sēmi-* SEMI- + *uncia* OUNCE *sb.*¹] A half-ounce, the twenty-fourth part of an *as*. Also anglicized † **semunce** (*rare*⁻⁰). Hence **se'muncial** *a.* [ad. L. *sēmunciāl-is*].

1656 BLOUNT *Glossogr.*, *Semuncial*, of or belonging to half an ounce. **1658** PHILLIPS, *Semuncial*, belonging to a semunce, *i.* half an ounce. **1887** HEAD *Hist. Nummorum* 43 Bronze coins of Uncial and Semuncial weight, B.C. 217–89.

† **semy**, *a. Obs.* Also **cemy**. [Of obscure origin; possibly an inference from some compound of SEMI-.] (See quot.) Hence † '**semyly** *adv.*

c **1440** *Promp. Parv.* 66/1 Cemy, or sotelle.., *subtilis.* Cemely, or sotely, *subtiliter. Ibid.* 452/2 Semy.., *subtilis.* Semyly.., *subtiliter.*

semy, semyed, obs. ff. SEMÉE, SEMÉED.

semylacre, -ylytude, obs. ff. SIMULACRE, SIMILITUDE.

semyld, pa. t. of SEMBLE *v.*¹ *Obs.*

† '**semys**, *a. Obs. rare*⁻¹. [App. = G. *sämisch* (15th c. also *semisz*) a kind of soft leather.] The distinctive epithet of some kind of leather.

1508 *Acc. Ld. High Treas. Scot.* (1902) IV. 25, iiij skinnis of blak semys leddir to be ane doublat to the King.

‖ **sen** (sɛn), *sb.*¹ Also †**seni**, † **senni.** [Japanese.] A Japanese copper or bronze coin (see quot. 1897), now a hundredth part of a yen. Chiefly *collect.* as *plural.*

1727 J. SCHEUCHZER tr. *Kæmpfer's Hist. Japan* I. 17 The use of silver Money was forbid, and in its stead brass Sennis coin'd. **1802** PINKERTON *Mod. Geog., Japan* iii. II. 166 The Seni, of copper or iron, are strung like the Chinese pieces of a similar value. **1839** *Penny Cycl.* XV. 326/1 *Sennis*, or *Cashes*, are small pieces of iron, copper, or brass, having a square hole in the middle, through which, as in China, they are strung on a wire or thread. **1875** BEDFORD *Sailor's Pocket Bk.* ix. (ed. 2) 316, 10 Rin = 1 Sen = ½d. **1895** C. HOLLAND *My Japanese Wife* 75 To be English spells generosity in Japanese eyes in the matter of sen for her own little pocket. **1897** *Daily News* 27 Sept. 5 The sen..is nominally equal to a halfpenny, though in fact only worth half that coin.

‖ **sen** (sɛn), *sb.*² [Indonesian, etc., repr. CENT¹.] In Indonesia, Malaysia, and other countries of the Far East: a coin or unit of currency valued at one hundredth of the principal measure.

1957 *Whitaker's Almanack 1958* 965 Indonesia...*Rupiah* of 100 *Sen.* **1959** *Ibid.* *1960* 961 Cambodia...*Riel* of 100 *Sen.* **1962** R. A. G. CARSON *Coins* 557 The islands became the independent republic of Indonesia in 1950. The unit of the new coinage is the rupiah of 100 sen.

sen (sɛn), *adv.*, *prep.*, and *conj.* Now *rare.* Chiefly *Sc.* and *north.* Also 5 **senne**, 6 **senn.** [Contracted form of *sethen*, SITHEN: cf. SENE, SIN, SYNE, and SINCE.]

A. *adv.* Then, afterwards; also ago. *rare.*

c **1460** *Towneley Myst.* xx. 259 She weshyd hym with hir terys weytt, and sen dryed hym with hir hare. **1867** J. P. MORRIS *Siege o' Brou'ton* 3 (Lanc. Gloss.) That's a conny lang time sen now.

B. *prep.* From, after; subsequent to.

c **1330** R. BRUNNE *Chron. Wace* (Rolls) 24 Sen þe tyme of sir Noe. *c* **1400** MAUNDEV. (Roxb.) xvi. 74 þe kyng..had.. ay were, sen þat tyme. **1456** SIR G. HAYE *Law Arms* (S.T.S.) 32 Sen the passioun of Crist,.. the haly kirk was never ȝit in pes. *c* **1460** *Towneley Myst.* xx. 714 It has bene told, sen many a day, sayngys of hym full sare. **1577** FULKE *Confut.* 7 There was neuer greater store in the church of Christ, sen Christ his time. **1593** (*title*), Actis of Parliament, past sen the Coronatiovn of the Kingis Maiestie.

C. *conj.* **1.** From or since the time that.

1338 R. BRUNNE *Chron.* (1810) 28 þe tend ȝere of his regne sen he was crouned Kyng. **1375** BARBOUR *Bruce* III. 496 Sen the king discumfyt was At Meffan, he herd neuir thing [etc.]. *c* **1400** MAUNDEV. (Roxb.) i. 4 It es lang sen it fell oute of þe hand. *c* **1421** *Lessons of Dirige* 231 in *26 Pol. Poems* 114 Trowest þou ouȝt þat y..Shal..ȝelde rekenyng sen y bygan? **1552** LYNDSAY *Monarche* 329 Sen I could ryde. **1599** ALEX. HUME *Hymns* ii. 219 Sa great a wonder was not heard, sen first the warld began. **1829** BROCKETT *N.C. Gloss.* (ed. 2) s.v., Its lang syne, sen he left us. **1871** J. RICHARDSON *Cummerland Talk* Ser. I. 18 (E.D.D.) Theer's been a deal o' ups an' doons sen I went to scheul.

2. Seeing or considering (*that*). [Cf. SEEN *conj.*, which may have been partly confused with this.]

13.. *Gosp. Nicod.* 53 Sen he to blind has gifen þe sight.., whi suld he vnto ded be dight? *a* **1340** HAMPOLE *Psalter* lxxxiv. 8 Sen þat he is turnyd away fra þe vnrest of þis life. **1423** JAS. I *Kingis Q.* cxliv, 'Now wele,' quod sche, 'and sen that It is so, That In vertew thy lufe is set with trueth [etc.].' *c* **1460** *Towneley Myst.* xxvi. 292 Sen I for luf, man, boght the dere,..I pray the hartely,..luf me agane. *a* **1500** *Lancelot* 1019 Bot, hart, sen at yow knawith she is here,.. Now is thi tyme. *a* **1533** LD. BERNERS *Huon* xviii. 49 Huon, sen thou woldest be agreed with me, Then [etc.]. **1588** A. KING tr. *Canisius' Catech.* 122 Sen we have sufficientlie according to our present purpose spokin hitherto. *a* **1756** PENNECUIK *Coll. Sc. Poems* 48 Sen your'e gotten out o's grips, Gi'e John a bucky.

Sen., sen., abbrev. of SENIOR *a.* 1 a. Cf. JUN.

1676 WISEMAN *Chirurg. Treat.* VII. v. 491 Doctour Chamberlain Sen. **1708** *Lond. Gaz.* No. 4475/4 Tho. Crabb, Sen. and Tho. Crabb, Jun. of Malborrow. **1837** [see JUN.]. **1862** *Lillywhite's Cricket Scores & Biogr.* I. 449 It will sometimes be found impossible to distinguish his performances in this work from those of his son, owing to sen. and jun. being omitted. **1955** *Times* 8 July 6/7 In two suits in another bedroom was found £115 10s., which Thomas Foote, sen., said was his. **1960** *Bedside 'Guardian'* IX. 140 It was an old tradition, Professor Arthur M. Schlesinger, sen., has said, [etc.].

Sen., abbrev. of SENATOR 1 f. *U.S.*

1857 WEBSTER & GOODRICH *N. Webster's Explanatory & Pronouncing Dict. Eng. Lang.* App. 462/1 *Sen.*, Senator. **1972** *Guardian* 3 July 1/2 (*heading*) Sen McGovern fights on. **1974** *Sumter* (S. Carolina) *Daily Item* 23 Apr. 1B/1 She has written Sen. Thomas O. Bowen..several times.

sen: see SAINT, SAY *v.*¹, SEE *v.*, SEND *v.*, SENE *a.*

sena, obs. form of SENNA.

Sena, var. SEHNA.

Senacar, var. SENECA.

[**senacion**, anglicized form of med.L. *senaciōn-em*, for L. *senecīōn-em* groundsel, SENCION.

1526 *Grete Herball* ccccviii. (1529) Y ij b, Whan receptes expresseth Senacions in the plurell nombre it is to wyte cresses. But yf senacion be wryten in the synguler nombre, it is an other herbe.]

† '**senage.** *Obs.* Also 4 **synage**, 6 **senagy.** [a. OF. *senage* (f. *sene* synod: see SENE and -AGE) or its med.L. form *senagium* (1292 in *Durh. Acc. Rolls*, Surtees Soc., p. 490).] Money paid for synodals, a tribute due to the bishop or archdeacon (or bursar) at Easter.

c **1380** WYCLIF *Wks.* (1880) 249 And whanne bischopis & here officeris comen & feynen to visite,..wrecchid curatis ben nedid to festen him richely & ȝeue procuracie & synage. *Ibid.* 456 þis is a foul offis of a prest to robbe his puple to ȝyue to bischop or erchedekene godis þat god biddiþ not, as senage & procurasies. **1546** *Yorks. Chantry Surv.* (Surtees) 30 Paiable yerely to the archebysshope of Yorke for proxies and senagies. **1684** *Cowel's Interpr.* (ed. Manley), *Senege*, There goes out ȝearly in Proxege and Senege 33*s.* 6*d.*

senaite (seɪ-, 'sɛnəaɪt). *Min.* [f. the name of Joachim de Costa *Sena*, 19th-cent. Brazilian mineralogist + -ITE¹.] A rhombohedral titanate of iron, lead, and manganese, found as rough black crystals and rounded fragments in diamond-bearing sands in Brazil.

1898 HUSSAK & PRIOR in *Mineral. Mag.* XII. 30 (*heading*) Senaite, a new mineral belonging to the ilmenite group, from Brazil. **1976** *Acta Crystallographica* XXXII. B. 1509/1 Senaite, crichtonite, and davidite form a closely related series of minerals with similar morphologies and chemical compositions.

senarian (siː'nɛərɪən). *Ancient Prosody. rare.* [f. L. *sēnār-ius*: see next + -IAN.] = next.

1803 PORSON *Let. to A. Dalzel* in *Mus. Crit.* (1826) I. 330 The fifth foot of a Senarian. **1895** *Q. Rev.* Oct. 34 The great Greek Iambic line is of course the Senarian, consisting of six Iambics or their equivalents.

‖ **senarius** (siː'nɛərɪəs). *Prosody.* Pl. senarii. [L. *sēnārius* adj., consisting of six each, f. *sēnī* adj. pl.

six each, f. *sex* six; used subst. by ellipsis of *versus* verse.] (More fully, ***iambic senarius.***) A (Greek or Latin) verse consisting of six feet, each of which is either an iambus or some foot which the law of the verse permits to be substituted; an iambic trimeter.

1540 PALSGR. *Acolastus* I. i. C iij b, All the versis of this scene be *Senarii*. **1811** ELMSLEY in *Edin. Rev.* XIX. 80 The fifth foot of a tragic senarius cannot be a spondee, except in three cases. **1832** [see PYTHIAMBIC]. **1869** H. SNOW *Theocritus, Epigr.* xvi. Notes (1873) 219 The lines are alternately iambic senarii and hendecasyllables.

senarmontite (sɛˈnɑːməntaɪt). *Min.* [Named after H. de *Senarmont*, who first described it + -ITE[1].] A native tri-oxide of antimony, crystalizing in colourless or greyish-white octahedrons.

1851 DANA in *Amer. Jrnl. Sci.* Ser. II. XII. 209.

†ˈ**senary**, *sb. Obs.* [ad. L. *sēnārius* adj. (see next) used subst. by ellipsis.]

1. [= *senarius* (*numerus*).] The number six; a set or sequence of six things; in the 17th c. often, the six days of the Creation.

1570 BILLINGSLEY *Euclid* x. lxx. 280 b, Hetherto hath bene spoken of sixe Senaryes, of which the first Senary [*sc.* of propositions] contayneth the production of irrationall lines by composition. *Ibid.* lxxiii. 282 b, Here beginneth the Senaries by substraction. **1653** H. MORE *Conject. Cabbal.* (1713) 16 Wherefore God having thus compleated his work in the Senary, comprehending the whole Creation in Six orders of things, he ceased from ever creating any thing more. **1686** GOAD *Celest. Bodies* II. xiv. 339 They will bring you Cold and Heat, Calm and Storm,..in one Senary of Days. **1693** PASCHALL in *Phil. Trans.* XVII. 816, I divided the *Νυχθήμερον* into four Senaries of Hours.

2. *Prosody.* = SENARIUS.

1579 G. HARVEY *Two other Lett.* (1580) 64 This foote [*sc.* the trochee]..is..quite thrust out of doores in a pure and iust Senarie. **1828** *Classical Jrnl.* XXXVII. 127 *Ἀλλ' ὅμως* are words frequently employed by Euripides at the end of an Iambic senary.

senary (ˈsiːnərɪ, ˈsɛnərɪ), *a.* [ad. L. *sēnārius*: see SENARIUS.] Pertaining to the number six. ***senary scale***: the scale of arithmetical notation of which the radix is six. ***senary division***: division into six parts.

1661 BLOUNT *Glossogr.* (ed. 2), *Senarie*, that contains or belongs to the number six. **1721** BAILEY, *Senary*, that which consists of Six. **1755** JOHNSON, *Senary*, belonging to the number six; containing six. **1810** P. BARLOW in *Nicholson's Jrnl.* XXV. 183 Thus, in the binary scale only two characters are wanted, namely 1 and 0; in the senary, six; in the decimal, ten. *Ibid.* 186 Transform 11111 to the senary scale. **1830** LINDLEY *Nat. Syst. Bot.* 81 The Cephalotus of Labillardière, offers a remarkable exception to the usual characters..in the senary division of its flower [etc.]. **1881** BAUERMAN *Syst. Min.* 11 The only other class of symmetry possible in crystals is senary or hexagonal, corresponding to a rotation of one-sixth of a revolution, such as that of a regular hexagonal prism about its axis.

senassee, obs. var. SANNYASI, Indian ascetic.

senate (ˈsɛnət). Forms: 3 **senaht**, 4 **senas**, 4–7 **senat**, 6 **cenate**, *pl. Sc.* **senat(t)is**, 4– **senate**. [a. F. *senat*, *senaz* (mod.F. *sénat*), ad. L. *senātus* (*u*-stem), lit. council of old men, f. *sen-em* (nom. *senex*) old (see SENIOR *a.*), absol. old man: see -ATE[1]. Cf. Pr. *senet*, Sp., Pg. *senado* It. *senato*, G. *senat*, Du. *senaat*.]

1. An assembly or council of citizens charged with the highest deliberative functions in the government of a state. **a.** In ancient Rome: A legislative and administrative body, consisting originally of representatives elected by the patricians, and in later times composed partly of appointed members and partly of the actual and former holders of certain high offices of state.

c **1205** LAY. 25388 þis weoren þa sixe þe þat senaht al biwusten. **13..** *K. Alis.* 1477 His lettres come Into þe cite of grete Rome. Þe riche people, & þe senas, Spaken togedres of þis cas. *c* **1375** *Sc. Leg. Saints* xxix. (*Placidas*) 352 Al þe hale senat [of Rome]. *c* **1460** FORTESCUE *Abs. & Lim. Mon.* xvi. (1885) 149 The Romaynes, while thair counsell callid þe senate was gret, gate, through þe wysdome off that counsell, the lordschippe off gret partye of the world. **1531** ELYOT *Gov.* I. ii. (1880) I. 20 The Senate..which was fyrste ordayned by Romulus. **1614** GORGES *Lucan* v. 166 The Consuls both did then decree The Senate should assembled be. **1775** HARRIS *Philos. Arrangem.* Wks. (1841) 247 Cato.. used to read philosophy in the senate-house, while the senate was assembling. **1879** FROUDE *Cæsar* viii. 79 The Senate was..a body composed of men of any order who had secured the suffrages of the people.

b. Applied to bodies having more or less similar functions in other states of the ancient world, esp. as the equivalent of Gr. *γερουσία* (lit. 'body of elders') and *βουλή* (lit. 'council').

a **1586** SIDNEY *Arcadia* I. (Sommer) 21 b, By the king and Senat of Lacedæmon, Demagoras was..banished the countrie. **1607** SHAKS. *Timon* v. i. 132 Th' Athenians By two of their most reuerend Senate greet thee. **1658** HARRINGTON *Prerog. Pop. Govt.* I. xii. 108 The Senate of the Beane being the proposing-Assembly (for that of the Areopagites, called also a Senate, was a Judicatory) consisted of four hundred Citizens chosen by Lot, which was performed with beanes. **1738** GLOVER *Leonidas* I. 408 Lacedæmon's senate now approach'd. **1842** *Smith's Dict. Grk. & Rom. Antiq.* s.v. *βουλή*, This senate of 500 [at Athens] was divided into ten sections of fifty each, the members of which were called prytanes (*πρυτανεῖς*), and were all of the same tribe.

c. In the Middle Ages, and subsequently, used as the official title of the governing body in various free cities of Europe.

c **1374** CHAUCER *Boeth.* I. pr. iv. (1868) 19 At þe citee of verone whan þat þe kyng gredy of comune slauȝter caste hym to transporten vpon al þe ordre of þe senat þe gilt of his real maieste. **1530** in Ellis *Orig. Lett.* Ser. III. II. 193 The day after our coming the Senate [at Nuremberg] sent gentilmen to shew us their provision of harneis, ordinance, and corne. **1838** *Murray's Hand-bk. N. Germany* 444/1 In the election chamber (Wahlzimmer), the Senate of Frankfort now holds its sittings. **1841** W. SPALDING *Italy & It. Isl.* III. 344 On the mainland there are four Supreme Tribunals, called Senates, placed at Turin, Chambery, Nice, and Genoa. **1880** H. A. WEBSTER in *Encycl. Brit.* XI. 404/1 According to the present constitution [of Hamburg] .., the legislative power is in the hands of the senate [of 18 members] and the general body of citizens, and the executive is committed to the senate alone.

d. *gen.* The governing or legislative assembly of a nation. Often applied, more or less rhetorically, to the British parliament.

1560 DAUS tr. *Sleidane's Comm.* 15 b, That he appointe a Cenate or counsell within the empire. **1584** D. FENNER *Def. Ministers* (1587) 12 At the table of whose Hon. Senat [app. of Privy Council], our supplications were..read. **1659** MILTON *Let. Friend* Wks. 1738 I. 583 Being now in Anarchy, without a counselling and governing Power..the first thing to be found out with all speed, without which no Commonwealth can subsist, must be a Senate, or General Council of State. **1718** PRIOR *On Corrup. Man.* vi, And senates vote, as armies fight, for pay. **1742** *Johnson's Debates* (1787) II. 139 (Ld. Hervey) It declares, my Lords, that there is now an enquiry depending before the Senate. **1775** ABIGAIL ADAMS in *Fam. Lett.* (1876) 227 Whether you are in the American Senate [*i.e.* Congress] or on board the British fleet, is a matter of uncertainty. **1787** *J. Lewis's Mem. Dk. Glocester* 58 *note*, [The Duke of Buckingham] was..an eloquent orator in the British Senate. **1809–10** COLERIDGE *Friend* (1865) 22 The pernicious influence of this lax morality extends from the nursery and the school to the cabinet and senate. **1848** THACKERAY *Van. Fair* lviii, He says there is no place in the bar or the senate that Georgy may not aspire to.

†**e.** Applied (perh. in passages translated from Latin) to the Corporation of London. *Obs.*

a **1548** HALL *Chron., Hen. V* 52 b, The Mayre of London and the Senate appareled in orient grayned Skarlet. **1568** GRAFTON *Chron.* II. 633 Continuall watch was kept by the Maior and senate of London,..for the preseruacion of the peace, and continuance of good order.

f. In the 18th and 19th c. adopted as the official name for the upper and smaller branch of the legislature in various countries, as the United States (and each of the separate states of the Union), France, Italy, etc.

1776 A. ADAMS *Let.* 15 Sept. (1875) 227 Whether you are in the American Senate or on board the British fleet, is a matter of uncertainty. **1780** ABIGAIL ADAMS in *Fam. Lett.* (1876) 388 Hancock will be Governor, by a very great majority; the Senate [of Massachusetts] will have to choose the Lieutenant-governor. **1789** *Constit. U.S.* Art. I. § 3 The Senate of the United States shall be composed of two senators from each state. **1796** T. TWINING *Trav. Amer.* (1894) 52 From the hall of the Representatives, I went to that of the Senate, or Upper Chamber. *a* **1817** DWIGHT *Trav. New Eng.* (1823) IV. 159 New Hampshire... The legislature consists of a senate and house of representatives, chosen annually by ballot. **1887** W. C. FORD *Amer. Citizen's Man.* I. 11 In all the States the upper or smaller House is known as the Senate.

g. *transf.* and *fig.*

1540 PALSGR. *Acolastus* v. i. Y ij, Suerly the senate of my harte is sedicious. **1735** POPE *Prol. Sat.* 209 Like Cato give his little Senate laws And sit attentive to his own applause. **1820** COMBE *Syntax, Consol.* II. (Chandos) 152 Sometimes my bosom's senate sits In silent thought. **1821** SHELLEY *Hellas* Prol. 73 The senate of the Gods is met, Each in his rank and station set.

2. a. In the University of Cambridge, and in some other British universities, the official title of the governing body. Cf. SENATUS.

The Senate of the University of Cambridge corresponds to the Convocation of Oxford University, and consists of all Doctors, Masters of Arts, Law, and Surgery, and Bachelors of Divinity, who keep their names on the books. In the newer English universities, Durham, London, Liverpool, Birmingham, etc., the senate is a smaller body, its composition being different in different universities. In Scotland, the Latin form *Senatus* (*Academicus*) is commonly employed.

1736 *Charter* etc. *Coll. Will. & Mary, Virginia* 78 Concerning the College Senate. **1748** SALMON *Foreigner's Comp. Cambr.* 16 All Graces intended to be proposed to the Senate, must first pass the *Caput*. **1797** *Cambr. Univ. Cal.* 147 By the senate is meant all the doctors and masters of arts in the university, who have their names on the boards of their college. **1804** *Med. Jrnl.* XII. 286 Regulations enacted by the Senate of the University of Glasgow, respecting Degrees in Medicine. **1829** R. GILBERT *Liber Scholast.* 50 The Senate [of Cambridge], in 1818, decreed the foundation of three scholarships.

b. *U.S.* In some American colleges, a council composed of members of the faculty and elected students, having the control of the discipline, etc., of the students.

1891 in *Century Dict.*

†**3.** A senate-house. *Obs. rare.*

1616 BULLOKAR *Eng. Expos.*, *Senat*, the Counsell house, where the Magistrates of a citie assemble themselues. **1623** COCKERAM I. **1700** tr. *Danet's Dict. Grk. & Rom. Antiq.* s.v. *Senatus*, The Tribunes of the People at first stood at the Door of the Senate to know their Deliberations.

¶**4.** Misused for: A senator. *Obs. rare.*

157. SEMPILL *Compl. Fort.* 87 in *Satir. Poems Reform.* xliii, Of Julius Cesar..Slaine be his Senatis,.. By his awin kinsmen Brutus and Cassus. *Ibid.* 210 To keip sic senattis it sall decore ȝour land. **1609** *Ev. Woman in Hum.* C 4 b, The olde Senate has put on his spectacles, and Lentulus and hee are turning the leaues of a dog-hay, leaues of a worme eaten Chronicle, and they want Tullies iudgement.

5. *attrib.* as ***senate-chamber***, ***-fight***, ***-hall***, etc.

a **1700** EVELYN *Diary* June 1645, The Senate-hall [at Venice]. **1736** THOMSON *Liberty* v. 568 In the warm struggles of the senate-fight. **1737** SAVAGE *Of Public Spirit* 161 Bid Courts of Justice, Senate-chambers join, Till various All in one proud Work combine! **1855** DICKENS *Dorrit* II. vii, The rugged remains of temples and tombs and palaces and senate halls and theatres.

ˈ**senate-house.** [HOUSE *sb.*[1]]

1. A house or building in which a senate meets.

c **1550** N. SMYTH tr. *Herodian* II. 18 He wente too the Senate house. **1601** SHAKS. *Jul. C.* II. ii. 52 Wee'l send Mark Antony to the Senate house. **1634** MILTON *Comus* 389 Musing meditation most affects The pensive secrecy of desert cell,..And sits as safe as in a Senat house. *a* **1700** EVELYN *Diary* 4 Oct. 1641, The Senate-house of this city [Antwerp] is a very spacious and magnificent building. **1709** ADDISON *Tatler* No. 162 ¶7 It was usual for them to expel a Senator who had been guilty of great Immoralities out of the Senate-House. **1886** *Encycl. Brit.* XX. 815 The Curia or senate-house.

transf. *a* **1586** SIDNEY *Arcadia* II. (Sommer) 129 b, The senate house of the planets was at no time so set, for the decreeing of perfection in a man, as at that time all folkes skilful therin did acknowledge. **1608** SHAKS. *Per.* I. i. 10. **1821** SHELLEY *Hellas* Prol. 2 It is the day when all the sons of God Wait in the roofless senate-house, whose floor Is Chaos.

2. *spec.* The building which serves for the meetings of the senate of a university, esp. of Cambridge.

1748 SALMON *Foreigner's Comp. Cambr.* 15 The Senate-House is a magnificent and elegant Building; the Length [etc.]. **1769** GRAY (*title*), Ode performed in the Senate-House at Cambridge. **1797** *Cambr. Univ. Cal.* 148 In the senate-house the elections of all the officers of the university take place, the appointments of the magistrates, the admissions to degrees, congregations, and consultations upon important matters by the senate, and by a statute of the university, no language is to be spoken therein but Latin. **1862** CALVERLEY *Verses & Transl.* (1894) 43 Past the Senate-house I saunter.

b. *attrib.* **senate-house examination**, examination for degrees in Cambridge University; so **senate-house examiner**; **senate-house problem**, a mathematical problem proposed in a Senate-house examination.

1837 *Math. Probl. fr. Senate-House Exam. Papers* Pref. 7 Questions which have actually been set from time to time, at the Senate-House examinations. **1855** *Househ. Words* 8 Dec. 442/2 He harassed me with questions about the book as pertinaciously as any senate-house examiner. **1875** CAYLEY *Math. Papers* (1896) IX. 246 A Senate-house Problem.

†**senatical**, *a. Obs. rare.* [f. SENATE + -ICAL.] Of or pertaining to a senate.

1651 *Animadv. Macdonnel's Answ. Eng. Ambass.* 48 Or incroach upon the Senaticall part and right of the people. **1652** PEYTON *Catastr. Ho. Stuarts* (1731) 49 That which overthrows Monarchy, the same overthrows a Senatical Government.

†**senatoire.** *Obs. rare*$^{-1}$. [a. OF. *senatoire*, ad. med.L. *senātōrium*, f. L. *senātor*.] A senate-house.

1474 CAXTON *Chesse* II. ii, Whan he was comen home from the senatoire. [Cf. SENATORY *sb.*[1] 2.]

senator (ˈsɛnətə(r)). Forms: 3–5 **senatur**, 3–7 **senatour**, 4–5 **cenatour**, **sinatour**, 4–6 **senatoure**, 5 **cenatoure**, **senatowre**, (6 **sanatour**), 6– **senator**. [a. OF. *senateur* (mod.F. *sénateur*), ad. L. *senātor*, f. *sen-em*, *senex* old, old man; a parallel formation with *senātus* SENATE. Cf. Sp., Pg. *senador*, It. *senatore*.]

1. A member of a senate. **a.** A member of the ancient Roman senate.

In some of the early examples (*c* 1290, *c* 1386, 1390, and perhaps others) the writers evidently attribute to antiquity the usage of their own time, according to which 'the senator of Rome' was the title of a single high official. See sense 2.

c **1205** LAY. 25337 þat was þurh þa senaturs þa þet sinað heolden. *c* **1290** *St. John* 81 in *S. Eng. Leg.* 404 For þe senatour him a-slovȝ: þat was þo of rome, In contek þat heom was bi-twene. **13..** *Seuyn Sag.* 1267 Amorewe aros that sinatour. *c* **1386** CHAUCER *Man of Law's T.* 863 For which this Emperour hath sent anon His senatour..And othere lordes..On Surryens to taken heigh vengeance. **1390** GOWER *Conf.* I. 199 This Lord, with whom sche scholde go, Of Rome was the Senatour. *c* **1400** *St. Alexius* 65 þerfore þe riche Emperoure Of þe Cite made hym Cenatoure. **1422** YONGE tr. *Secreta Secret.* xxxi. 178 The Sinatouris of the Cite [of Rome]. **1475** *Bk. Noblesse* 1 The noble cenatoure of Rome Kayus son. **1513** DOUGLAS *Æneis* Comm., Wks. II. 292 Quhen Cesar was slayn by the Sanatouris. **1540–1** ELYOT *Image Gov.* xxxix. (1544) 101 b, For thy pacience, wysedom and temperance, we deeme the worthy to be admitted into the college of Senatours. **1696** B. KENNETT *Romæ Antiquæ* II. III. ii. (1717) 101 The right of naming Senators belong'd at first to the Kings; afterwards the Consuls chose, and refer'd them to the People for their Approbation: But at last the Censors engross'd the whole Privilege of conferring this Honour. **1834** LYTTON *Pompeii* I. vii, 'The emperor has been giving a splendid supper to the senators,' answered Sallust.

b. A member of the senate or governing council in other states of antiquity.

1586 Sir E. Hoby *Pol. Disc. Truth* viii. 23 The Ephores, hauing chosen a Senator that was very true, commanded him [etc.] **1607** Shaks. *Timon* v. i. 139 The Senators of Athens, greet thee Timon. **1656** Stanley *Hist. Philos.* v. *Plato* iii. (1687) 159/2 That he was a Senator, implies he was full thirty years old at that time, according to Solon's Law. **1790** Cowper *Odyss.* viii. 56 He..led the way, whom follow'd all The sceptred senators. **1837** Thirlwall *Greece* xxxv. IV. 379 The senators, ephors, and other magistrates [at Sparta].

c. A member of the senate or governing body in certain mediæval and modern cities of Europe. Cf. SENATE 1 c.

1560 Daus tr. *Sleidane's Comm.* 79 b, The bishop of Strausborough writeth letters to divers of the senatours. **1604** Shaks. *Oth.* iv. i. 230 The Duke, and the Senators of Venice greet you. **1682** *Lond. Gaz.* No. 1737/2 The Count d'Archinto has received his Patent from Spain, to be first Senator of Milan. **1741** Lady M. W. Montagu *Let. to Montagu* 25 Aug. (1893) II. 95 The senators [at Genoa] can converse with no strangers during the time of their magistracy. **1762** *New Biogr. Dict.* IX. 222 s.v. *Peiresc*, They..were sent to Aix to their uncle Claude Fabri, their father's elder brother, who was senator there. **1782** J. Adams in *Fam. Lett.* (1876) 404 [At the Hague] I am going to dine with..a number of Ambassadors and Senators. **1860** Motley *Netherl.* i. (1868) I. 12 The Sage-Men chose annually a board of senators.

d. *gen.* A member of a governing body or parliament. Often applied (unofficially and sometimes rhetorically) to a member of either House of the British Parliament.

1387 Trevisa *Higden* (Rolls) VII. 35 Þerfore was i-made a counsaile of þe real strete of Calne..þere seten in an hiȝe hous þe senatoures of Engelond. *a* **1513** Fabyan *Chron.* vi. ccxvi. (1811) 234 A nyce folysshe couenaunte ought nat to be holden,..without the hole assent of the senatours of the same lande. **1553** Eden *Treat. New Ind.* (Arb.) 17 The Magistrates..are no lesse estemed then amonge vs Senatoures or Lord of the Counsayl. **1628** A. Leighton *App. Parlt.* Ep. Ded., To the right Honourable & High Court of Parliament. Right Honorable and High Senators. Such hath beene the care [etc.]. **1660** Tatham *Roy. Oak* 8 Holding..in the other [hand] a statute Book as a Senator and maintainer of laws. **1708** Swift *Predict. for 1708*, 6 At home, the Death of an old famous Senator will happen on the 15th. *a* **1763** W. King *Lit. & Polit. Anecd.* (1819) 35 [The Duke of Wharton's] speech..was indeed not unworthy of the oldest and most accomplished senator..in either House of Parliament. **1776** J. Adams in *Fam. Lett.* (1876) 215, I had rather build stones upon Penn's hill, than to be the first Prince in Europe, or the first General or Senator in America. **1849** Macaulay *Hist. Eng.* ii. I. 171 He had, during the first year of the Long Parliament, been honourably distinguished among the senators who laboured to redress the grievances of the nation. **1894** Sir J. Astley *Fifty Yrs. Life* II. 123 How those forty senators [*sc.* the Irish M.P.'s] (or their successors) have been going on since, is notorious.

e. In vaguer sense: A counsellor, statesman; †a leader in State or Church. Also *fig.*

c **1400** *Rom. Rose* 4999 Peyne and Distresse, Syknesse and Ire, And Malencoly, that angry sire, Ben of hir paleys senatours. **1535** Coverdale *Ps.* civ. [cv.] 22 That he might enfourme his prynces after his wil, and teach his Senatours wysdome. ?**1548** tr. *Viret's Expos. XII Art. Chr. Faith* M vj b, Euen so hathe the churche hys spirituall policie..and hys pastures, ministers, and senatoures. **1597** Hooker *Eccl. Pol.* v. lxxvi. §6 That which children might haue seene, their grauest Senators could not discerne. **1656** Blount *Glossogr.*, *Muncerians*, a sort of Anabaptists, so called from Tho. Muncer, who was their Prophet, Senator and General, when they rose in Rebellion in Suevia and Franconia, &c. **1820** Keats *Hyperion* i. 73 Those green-rob'd senators of mighty woods, Tall oaks.

f. The official title of a member of the senate or upper house of the legislature in the United States, in modern France, Italy, etc.

In the U.S., *Senator* prefixed to the surname denotes a member of the federal Senate, not of the Senate of a particular state.

1788 J. Stokes in *M. Cutler's Life*, etc. (1888) II. 275 The Constitution of the United States pleases me much, but you ought to allow the people to have the power of appointing Senators-extraordinary in cases of exigency, as of war, or national distresses. **1837** Carlyle *Fr. Rev.* I. iii. viii, The long-gowned Senators of France. **1863** Bright *Sp., Amer.* 30 June (1876) 139 He has been for many years a Senator from the State of Mississippi. **1877** *Encycl. Brit.* VII. 347/1 He [Dombrowski] was named in 1815 general of cavalry and senator palatine of the new kingdom of Poland. **1905** R. Bagot *Passport* iii. 17 He was a well-known scientist,..and, in recognition of his work in the domain of physical science, had been created a senator of the Italian kingdom.

2. In Papal Rome: The title given at various periods from the 12th c. onwards to the civil head of the city government, appointed by the Pope.

[*c* **1290**, *c* **1386**, **1390**: see sense 1 a, and the note.] **1832** G. Downes *Lett.* xxvi. I. 427 In this [Senatorial] palace are held the sittings of Rome's one senator, and of the Judges of the Tribunal. **1841** W. Spalding *Italy & It. Isl.* II. 153 Anarchy of Rome..induced Innocent in 1354 to send him [Rienzi] back as a governor with the title of Senator.

3. ***Senator of the College of Justice***: in Scotland, the official designation of a Lord of Session.

1540 *Sc. Acts Jas. V* (1814) II. 371/2 Þe president vice-president and senatores [of the College of Justice]. **1562** in *Acts of Sederunt* (1790) 4 The Senators, ordinaris of our College of Justice, instituted be our maist nobill fader of gude memorie. **1905** *Westm. Gaz.* 3 Jan. 8/2 One of the Senators of his Majesty's College of Justice in Scotland.

†**4.** ***The Senators***: a convivial London club in the 18th c. *Obs.*

1761 *Ann. Reg.* IV. ii. 51/1 He was a respectable member of The Killers of Care,..The Senators [etc.].

5. The Ivory Whale-gull.

[*a* **1713** Ray *Syn. Avium* 126 Raths-herr i.e. Senator *Friderici Martens*.] **1852** Macgillivray *Brit. Birds* V. 508 *Cetosparactes eburneus*. The Ivory Whale-Gull... Senator.

senatorial (sɛnəˈtɔərɪəl), *a.* [f. L. *senātōri-us* (f. *senātōr-em* SENATOR) + -AL¹. Cf. F. *sénatorial* (1727 in Hatz.-Darm.).]

1. Of or pertaining to a senator or senators; characteristic of or befitting a senator; consisting of senators. **a.** With reference to ancient Rome, or to other states of antiquity.

senatorial order: the highest of the three ranks of citizens in the later Roman republic.

1791 Cowper *Iliad* x. 490 Hector, with all the Senatorial Chiefs [x. 414 ὅσοι βουληφόροι εἰσί]. **1842** *Smith's Dict. Grk. & Rom. Antiq.* 851/1 It has been supposed by Niebuhr..that a senatorial census existed at Rome at the commencement of the second Punic war. **1850** Merivale *Rom. Emp.* ii. (1865) I. 53 Whole cities and states placed themselves sometimes under the protection of a senatorial patron. *a* **1859** De Quincey *Aelius Lamia* Wks. 1860 X. 306 A Roman noble, a man..of senatorial rank.

b. With reference to modern senates.

1740 *Johnson's Debates* (1789) I. 19 (Sir R. Walpole), The authority which can be conferred only by senatorial sanctions. **1765** Blackstone *Comm.* I. ii. 175 Not as at Venice, and many other senatorial assemblies. **1796** Coleridge *Watchman* No. 1. 20 The attack on the Duke of Bedford, for enjoying the senatorial office by hereditary right. **1855** Thackeray *Newcomes* ii, He eschewed honours senatorial. **1897** *Edin. Rev.* Jan. 145 The senatorial leader.

2. Of a Roman province under the Empire: Administered by the senate (not by the emperor).

1841 W. Spalding *Italy & It. Isl.* I. 102 Into those provinces which were senatorial, the senate continued to send pro-consuls or prætors as Governors. **1879** Farrar *St. Paul* (1883) 342 Bithynia [was] at that time a senatorial province.

3. *U.S.* 'Entitled to elect a Senator: as, a *Senatorial* district' (*Cent. Dict.* 1891).

1785 T. Jefferson *Notes Virginia* App. 2 Let each county at the time of electing its delegates, chuse senatorial electors. .. Let the senatorial districts be divided into two classes. **1864** *Harper's Mag.* Mar. 568/2 Mrs X——..resides in our senatorial district. **1948** *Daily Ardmoreite* (Ardmore, Oklahoma) 23 July 14/6 This Senatorial district of Carter county is the birthplace and home of Joe.

Hence **sena'torially** *adv.*, in a senatorial manner.

1754 A. Drummond *Trav.* i. 17 The mother was chearful; the father senatorially grave. **1821** *Examiner* 83/1 Whatever may be thought senatorially of the modest assertion,..the people at large may laugh at it.

senatorian (sɛnəˈtɔərɪən), *a.* (and *sb.*). [f. L. *senātōri-us* (see prec.) + -AN. Cf. OF. *senatorien* (Godef.), mod.F. *sénatorien* (1690 in Hatz.-Darm.).]

A. *adj.*

1. Of or pertaining to a senator; = SENATORIAL *a.* 1. Now chiefly as applied to the senatorial order of ancient Rome, its members, their privileges, etc.

1614 Gorges *Lucan* v. 167 The Senatorian ordred state Is neuer chang'd by place or date. *Ibid.*, That great Senatorian traine. **1629** Maxwell *Herodian* 74 Yet was he far exceeded in Birth by many of the Senatorian Order. **1665** Manley *Grotius' Law C. Wars* 940 Janinus, having setled himself into a Senatorian Gravity, began thus to speak. **1781** Gibbon *Decl. & F.* xxxi. III. 199 The dignity of the senatorian rank. **1830** J. H. Monk *Bentley* (1833) II. 327 This distinguished prelate had already displayed his senatorian talents in the discussion on the Pension Bill, and other occasions. **1880** R. Owen *Sanctorale Cathol.* 12 Mar. 136 He was of a high senatorian family at Rome.

2. = SENATORIAL *a.* 2.

1842 G. Long in *Smith's Dict. Grk. & Rom. Antiq.* 801/1 The Senatorian provinces.

B. *sb.* ? *nonce-use.* A partisan of the senate.

1869 Seeley *Ess. & Lect.* (1870) 21 [Augustus] began as a professed Senatorian;..he became ultimately emperor.

†**sena'torical**, *a.* *Obs.* [f. SENATOR + -ICAL.] = SENATORIAL *a.*; also ruled over by a senate.

a **1618** Raleigh *Maxims of State* vi. Rem. (1664) 9 And so that State is Senatorical or Aristocratical. **1655** tr. *Com. Hist. Francion* v. 10 The Advocate marched in magnificent array, with a Senatorical countenance.

†**senatorious**, *a.* *Obs.* *rare*⁻¹. [f. L. *senātōri-us* (see SENATORIAL *a.*) + -OUS.] = SENATORIAL *a.*

1664 H. More *Myst. Iniq.* 280 This Head of the Roman Hierarchy with his purple Cardinals are so Emperour-like and of such a Senatorious splendour.

senatorship (ˈsɛnətəʃɪp). [f. SENATOR + -SHIP.] The office or dignity of a senator.

1602 Carew *Cornw.* ii. 120 From which step his courage and wisedome raysed him by degrees to..the Senatorship of Rome. **1837** Carlyle *Fr. Rev.* III. iii. ix, We have got to the last scene of all, that ends this history of the Girondin Senatorship. **1909** *Contemp. Rev.* Aug., *Lit. Suppl.* 12 The senatorship conferred on him by Napoleon.

†**senatory**, *sb.*¹ *Obs.* [ad. med.L. *senātōrium*, f. L. *senātōr-ius* (see SENATORIAL *a.*): see -ORY¹.]

1. The senatorial order or body.

Chaucer's use is due to mistaking the adj. for a sb.

c **1374** Chaucer *Boeth.* iii. pr. iv. (1868) 74 Þe rente of þe senatorie [is noþing but] a gret charge [L. *et senatorii census gravis sarcina*]. **1528** Roy *Rede me* (Arb.) 40 As for the comens vniuersally And a greate parte of the senatory Were of the same intencion. **1614** Raleigh *Hist. World* v. ii. §6. 400 The Achaians..by a Senatorie and two Prætors, ordered all things in their Commonweale.

2. A senate-house. (Cf. SENATOIRE.)

1474 Caxton *Chesse* ii. ii, And thus hit happend anone after that alle the wyues of rome cam to the senatorye.

senatory (ˈsɛnətərɪ), *sb.*² *French Hist.* Also -orie. [ad. F. *sénatorerie*, f. L. *senātor* SENATOR: see -ERY.] The landed estate granted to a senator under the consulate and the first empire.

1804 *Revol. Plutarch* III. 164 Lucien was..afterwards ordered to visit his senatories on the Rhine. **1810** *Ann. Reg.* 503 A senatory shall be established in the departments of Rome and Trasimene. **1827** Scott *Napoleon* xxix. Wks. 1870 XI. 349 Monsieur Fargues, senator of the district of Bearn, whom these plots..interested as having his senatorie for their scene. **1898** J. B. Rye in *Eng. Hist. Rev.* July 490 You leave in twenty-four hours, to live in your senatory.

†**senatory**, *a.* *Obs.* *rare.* [ad. L. *senātōri-us* (see SENATORIAL *a.*): see -ORY². Cf. OF. *senatoire*.] = SENATORIAL *a.*

1523 [Coverdale] *Old God* (1534) Hj, The comen people was taught to say, that Charles was of the senatorie stocke gouernour of Rome. **1612** Selden *Illustr. Drayton's Polyolb.* viii. 124 By senatory authority P. Sulpitius..was committee to transact with the enemy for leaving the Roman territory. *a* **1618** Raleigh *Maxims of State* ii. Rem. (1664) 5 Aristocracy, or Senatory State. **1684** tr. *Bonet's Merc. Compit.* xviii. 646 A Gentleman..of the Senatory Order, being subject to Diseases in his Spleen.

senatour(e, obs. forms of SENATOR.

senatress (ˈsɛnətrɪs). *rare.* [f. SENATOR + -ESS. Cf. OF. *senatresse* wife of a senator (Godef.).] A female senator; a female of senatorial dignity.

1731 Gurdon *Hist. Parlt.* I. 200 Heliogabalus..made the first Senatress, he created a little Senate of Women, which met on *Collis Quirinalis*. **1793** Murphy *Tacitus* IV. 319 There were no terms in the Latin language to signify senatress, dictatress or even empress.

‖**senatus** (sɪˈneɪtəs, -ˈnɑː-). [L.: see SENATE.] The title given to the governing body in certain universities. More explicitly **senatus academicus**: see SENATE 2.

1835 Malden *Orig. Universities* 165 The government of the university [of Glasgow] is administered by the senatus academicus. **1839** W. Chambers *Tour Holland* 26/1 The senatus [of Leyden University]..employs a set of travellers to gather rare specimens from Africa. **1845** McCulloch *Brit. Emp.* (1854) II. 367 [In Scotch universities] The superintendence of their respective professors, and of the Senatus, does not extend farther.

‖**se'natus con'sultum.** Pl. consulta. Also anglicized **senatus consult.** [L.; *senātūs* genit. of *senātus* SENATE, *consultum* CONSULT *sb.*¹]

a. A decree of the ancient Roman senate. **b.** A decree of the 'senate' in certain modern states, e.g. France under Napoleon I and Napoleon III.

1696 B. Kennett *Romæ Ant. Not.* ii. iii. ii. (1717) 103 A *Senatus-Consultum* was accordingly wrote by the publick Notaries. **1758** Chesterf. *Lett. to Son* cxiv. (1774) II. 418, I will lay out twelve ducats for twelve bottles of the wine..if you can obtain a *senatus consultum* for it. **1813** *Examiner* 4 Jan. 4/1 [tr. French] The *Senatus Consultum* of last September. **1875** Poste tr. *Instit. Gaius* i. §4 A senatus-consult is a command and ordinance of the senate. **1886** Muirhead in *Encycl. Brit.* XX. 704/2 In the imperial council, where the drafts of the senatus consults were prepared.

senaw, obs. form of SINEW *sb.*

sence, var. CENSE; obs. f. SENSE, SINCE.

senceall, sencer: see SENESCHAL, CENSER.

†**sench**, *v.* *Obs.* Also 4 sinche; *pa. pple.* 4 seint. (See also ASENCH *v.*) [OE. *sęncan* = OS. *senkian*, OHG. *senchan* (MHG., mod.G. *senken*), ON. *søkkva* (Sw. *sänka*, Da. *sænke*), Goth. *sagqjan*:—OTeut. *sankwjan, causative of *siŋkwan SINK *v.*] *trans.* To sink, plunge.

c **1000** *Ags. Gosp.* Luke x. 15 And þu cafarnaum oð heofon upahafen, þu byst oþ helle ȝesenced. *c* **1230** *Juliana* 32 (MS. Roy.) Þu..hare fan senchtest [*MS. Bodl.* asenchtest] þat ham efter sohten. *a* **1310** in Wright *Lyric P.* iv. 24 In sunne and sorewe y am seint. *c* **1310** *S. Margaret* 307 in Horstm. *Altengl. Leg.* (1881) 233 In a fat ful of water, he bad men schuld hir sinche [*rimes with* drenche].

senche, obs. variant of SHENCH *sb.* and *v.*

senchip, sencial: see SHENDSHIP, SENESCHAL.

sencion (ˈsɛnʃən). *Obs.* exc. *dial.* Forms: 5 **chynchone, chymchon, cyn-, synchone, (synyon, synthon), 6 senechon, (synthone), 7 senchion, 9 sension, sinsion, senshon, sencion.** [a. OF. *senechion* (mod.F. *seneçon*):—L. *senecīōn-em*, perh. f. *senex* old man (cf. *senectūs* old age), with reference to the white down of the inflorescence.] Groundsel.

c **1440** *Promp. Parv.* 77/2 Chynchone, herbe [*v.r.* cynchone]. *Ibid.* 456/1 Synchone, herbe (*v.rr.* synyon, synthon), *senecion, camadreos*. *c* **1460** *Ibid.* (Winch.) 83/1 Chymchon, herbe: *Cenacion et cambidreos*. *Ibid.* 411/1

Synyon, herbe: *Senecion*: *Camadreas*. **1526** *Grete Herball* ccccix. (1529) Yiij, De senacionibus. Grownswell. Senechon is an herbe called sellechon. **1530** PALSGR. 270/2 Synthone, an herbe. *a* **1500** *Rel. Ant.* I. 324 Take groundis walle, that ys senchion. *a* **1825** FORBY *Voc. E. Anglia*, *Sencion*. **1882** *Hardwicke's Sci. Gossip* 214 Suffolk Names.. Sinsion (groundsel).

senct, obs. form of SAINT.

sencyal, obs. form of SENESCHAL.

send (sɛnd), *sb.*[1] [f. SEND *v.*[1]]

†**1.** *Sc.* The action of sending; dispensation (of God). *Obs.*

1551 ABP. HAMILTON *Catech.* (1884) 137 Thair is na evil of payne or trubil in the pepil, bot it cummis be the send of God.

b. *Sc.* A message.

1825 *Gay Goss-hawk* x. in Child *Ballads* II. 360 Ye're bidden send your love a send.

c. An accelerating impulse; impetus. Cf. SEND *sb.*[2]

1890 *Illustr. Lond. News* 6 Dec. 714/1 That piston that with a mighty send gives before them and spins the great wheel above. **1894** *Northumb. Gloss.*, *Send*, impetus. 'It cam' wi' sic a send'. **1899** SOMERVILLE & ROSS *Exper. Irish R.M.* xi. 273 Sultan came at it [*sc.* a wall] with the send of the hill behind him, and jumped it.

2. *Sc.* A messenger sent to the bride in advance of the bridegroom (see quots.); also, the bridal party. (See *Eng. Dial. Dict.*)

1814 MARY BRUNTON *Discipline* xxii. (1852) 191 The harbingers of the bridegroom, (or, to use Cecil's phrase, the send,) a party of gay young men and women, arrived. **1818** *Edin. Mag.* Nov. 412 A couple of envoys (Scot. *sends*) arrive from the bridegroom, who lead the bride to the temple of Hymen.

send (sɛnd), *sb.*[2] *Naut.* Also scend. [Belongs to SEND *v.*[2] Cf. SEND *sb.*[1] 1 c.]

1. The carrying or driving impulse of a sea or wave; more fully *send of a* or *the sea*.

1726 SHELVOCKE *Voy. round World* 65, I have frequently thought it impossible to escape striking upon them on every send of a sea. **1805** SIR R. LAWRIE in *Naval Chron.* XIII. 409 Much Sea running, appearing to cut us asunder at every send. **1885** R. F. BURTON *Arab. Nts.* I. 141 We found ourselves much nearer the Loadstone Mountain, whither the waters drave us with a violent send. **1901** CLARK RUSSELL *Ship's Advent.* v, To each foaming scend the ship drove in a curtsey of fury.

2. A sudden plunge (of a boat) *aft*, *forward*, etc.

1836 MARRYAT *Midsh. Easy* xix, Both fell with the send aft of the boat. **1859** J. C. ATKINSON *Walks Two Schoolboys* xvii. 367 With many a forward send..she threw up showers of spray. **1882** NARES *Seamanship* (ed. 6) 143 The bows will.. give a send in against the ship's side.

send (sɛnd), *v.*[1] *Pa. t.* and *pa. pple.* sent (sɛnt). Forms: *Infin.* 1 sendan, 2–3 senden, (3 seind, siende, sent), 2–6 sende, 4 *Kent.* zende, 5 sendyn, cendyn, *Sc.* sen, 3– send. *3rd sing. pres. ind.* 1–3 sendeþ, 1–5 sent, 3 seint, *Kent.* zent, 4–5 sendith, 5 -yth, 5– sendeth; 3–7 sendes, (5 sendez, sendis), 6 sends. *Pa. t.* 1–6 sende, 2–3 seonde, (2 sænde, sænte), *Ormin* sennde, 3–6 sente, 4 seende, 3–7 send, (5 sont), 3– sent; 3, 6 sendet, 4 sendyd, seended, 5 sended. *Pa. pple.* 1 sended, 2 (ȝe) seond, (ȝe) send, 3 ysend, iseind, 3–4 isend(e, ysent, 3–6 send(e, 3 *Ormin* sennd, 4 i-sente, 4–5 isent, sente, (4 seynte), 5 ysende, 3– sent. [Com. Teut. wk. verb: OE. *sęndan* = OFris. *senda*, *sanda*, pa. t. *sante*, OS. *sendian*, pa. t. *senda*, *sanda* (LG. *senden*, Du. *zenden*), OHG. *senden*, *senten*, pa. t. *santa* (MHG. *senden*, pa. t. *sante*, *sande*, mod.G. *senden*, pa. t. *sandte*, *sendete*), ON. *senda* (Sw. *sända*, Da. *sende*), Goth. *sandjan*:—OTeut. **sandjan*, f. **sand-* (:—**sanþ-*) ablaut-variant (of the grade usual in causative verbs) of the root **senþ-* (:—OTeut. *sent-*) to go, found in Goth. *sinþ-s*, OE. *sīð* way, journey (see SITHE *sb.*[1]).] General sense: To cause to go.

I. To order or direct to go or to be conveyed.

* *with a person as object.*

1. a. *trans.* To commission, order, or request (a person) to go *to* or *into* a place or *to* a person. Chiefly, to dispatch as a messenger or on an errand.

Const. *about* (a business), *after*, *for* (something to be fetched), *on*, †*of*, †*in* (an errand, quest; the prep. is sometimes omitted). See also MESSAGE *sb.*[1] 2 b.

c **950** *Lindisf. Gosp.* Matt. x. 16 Heonu ic sendo iuih suæ scip in middum uulfa. *c* **1175** *Lamb. Hom.* 153 He sende his patriarken and propheten for to bodien his tokume. *c* **1200** ORMIN 17034 He sennde dun Hiss aȝhenn Sune ankennedd, To wurrþenn mann. *c* **1205** LAY. 26367 He sent þe his sonde wið uten gretinge. *c* **1290** *St. Barnabas* 34 in *S. Eng. Leg.* 27 Iesu cristes man icham, þat me gan hidere sende. *a* **1300** *Cursor M.* 711 Bot adam son was send a saand. *Ibid.* 14846 Þan said an þat was his frend, Hight nichodem, was sent in saand,..'Me think' [etc.]. **1382** WYCLIF *Matt.* x. 5 Jhesus sente [*v.r.* seended] these twelue. **1456** SIR G. HAYE *Law Arms* (S.T.S.) 11 The sone of God..was send in erde for salvacioun of man. **1591** SHAKS. *Two Gent.* IV. iv. 120 Oh: he sends you for a Picture. **1599** —— *Hen. V*, IV. i. 155 A Sonne that is by his Father sent about Merchandize. **1599** —— *Much Ado* II. i. 274, I will goe on the slightest arrand..that you can deuise to send me on. **1611** BIBLE *Gen.* l. 16 And they sent a messenger vnto Ioseph, saying [etc.]. **1636** MASSINGER *Gt. Duke Flor.* II. i, I am sent..On a how doe you, as they call't. **1655** tr. *Com. Hist. Francion* II. 26 If she were sent of an errand. **1722** DE FOE *Col. Jack* i, If he was sent of an errand he would forget half of it. **1744** BIRCH *Life Boyle* 23 A gentleman of his father's, sent to convey them thither. **1776** EARL CARLISLE in Jesse *Selwyn & Contemp.* (1844) III. 144, I by no means approve of your sending a physician to her, except she is really ill. I hate the tribe. **1821** SCOTT *Kenilw.* vi, Workmen sent from London..had converted the apartments..into the semblance of a royal palace. **1834** MARRYAT *P. Simple* xv, Luff now..quarter master... Send the men aft directly. **1848** THACKERAY *Van. Fair* xvi, Send her to me, the instant she comes in. **1859** TENNYSON *Elaine* 626 To whom the Prince Reported who he was, and on what quest Sent. **1907** 'Q.' *Poison Isl.* xiv, Did he send you with that message to Captain Branscome?

fig. **1591** SHAKS. *Two Gent.* III. i. 141 My thoughts do harbour with my Siluia nightly, And slaues they are to me, that send them flying. **1722** WOLLASTON *Relig. Nat.* ix. 187 Commands his own thoughts, sends them to this or that place.

b. With specified destination considered as a place of residence, or connoting a sphere or kind of employment; e.g. in ***to send to school, college***, etc. (sometimes with the notion of defraying the expense of the person's education); ***to send*** (one or more members) ***to Parliament*** (said of a constituency).

1531 ELYOT *Gov.* I. xiii. (1880) I. 113 Where theyr parentes wyll nat aduenture to sende them farre out of theyr propre countrayes. **1568** GRAFTON *Chron.* II. 434 The king ..sent to the sea, Lord Edmond Holland Erle of Kent, as Chefetaine of that Crewe. **1575** GASCOIGNE *Glasse Govt.* I. ii, So that we are partely perswaded to send them vnto some vniuersity. **1737** POPE *Ep. Hor.* I. i. 119 Send her to Court, you send her to her grave. **1769** *De Foe's Tour Gt. Brit.* (ed. 7) II. 49 Heightsbury, a Town..sending two Members to Parliament. **1784** COWPER *Tiroc.* 240 T' ensure the perseverance of his course,..Send him to college. *Ibid.* 872 Then..send him not to school. No—guard him better. **1834** MARRYAT *P. Simple* lii, He was sent to sea to be got rid of. **1859** *Habits of Gd. Society* 57 The haberdasher sits in Parliament, and sends his son to Oxford. **1882** *Encycl. Brit.* XIV. 835/1 The education [at Christ's Hospital] is chiefly commercial, but four boys are annually sent to the universities.

c. In wider sense: To occasion or induce to go to a place or in a particular direction; to recommend or advise to go to a place or a person; *fig.* to refer (a reader) to some author or authority.

c **1449** PECOCK *Repr.* I. x. 52 Tho ij. textis seruen and remytten or senden into other Scripturis. *Ibid.* I. xx. 127, Y remytte and send ech man desiring forto it leerne..into the firste parti of the book. **1550** BALE *Apol.* 68 He sendeth vs ther to the pedigrew of the Leuites. I. Paralip. vi. **1751** JORTIN *Serm.* (1771) I. i. 11 Those who send the blind out of their way. **1844** LINGARD *Anglo-Sax. Ch.* (1858) I. iv. 144 Writers who have sent us to the laws of the Christian Emperors.

d. *fig.* To describe (a person) in narrative as going (to a specified place).

1776 MICKLE tr. *Camoens' Lusiad* Introd. 125 Voltaire has corrected his error in sending Camoens to the East Indies.

e. With complementary sb. (now only, introduced by *as*) indicating the capacity in which a person is sent.

1605 *1st Pt. Jeronimo* I. i. 77 So, so, Andrea must be sent imbassador? **1613** SHAKS. *Hen. VIII*, III. ii. 260 You sent me Deputie for Ireland. **1711** *Lond. Gaz.* No. 4903/1 Signior Bentivoglio..is to be sent Nuncio into France. **1756–7** tr. *Keysler's Trav.* (1760) III. 220 [They] sent the noble Julian and Martin ambassadors from..Japan to pope Gregory XIII.

f. *to be sent* (*into the world*): said of a child as born for some divine purpose, or as a gift to the parents. Cf. sense 7.

c **1560** A. SCOTT *Poems* (S.T.S.) xxxvi. 22 By syn maternall I am send, With vyce I vaneiss. **1594** SHAKS. *Rich. III*, I. i. 20, I, that am..sent before my time Into this breathing World. **1831** SCOTT *Ct. Robt.* xx, Being the only child..and sent late in life to bless their marriage bed. **1839** THACKERAY *Stubbs's Cal.* Nov. *Comic Tales* (1841) II. 360, I..wore my red coat as naturally as if I had been sent into the world only for the purpose of being a letter-carrier.

g. Without the notion of a destination or errand: To cause or order to depart *from* one; to dismiss. Chiefly with advs., *away*, *off*. ***to send packing***: see PACK *v.*[1] 10 b.

a **1533** LD. BERNERS *Gold. Bk. M. Aurel.* (1546) L vj, As an ydell vacabunde man they dyspatched and sent hym awaie. **1608** SHAKS. *Per.* IV. vi. 148 Shee sent him away as colde as a Snoweball. **1611** BIBLE *Luke* i. 53 And the rich hee hath sent emptie away. **1668** PEPYS *Diary* 13 Nov., It is intended to..try them for a sum of money; and, if they do not like it, then to send them going, and call another [parliament]. **1796** MME. D'ARBLAY *Camilla* I. I. iv. 85 There was no other way for him to get rid of his tutoring, without sending off Dr. Orkborne. **1908** R. BAGOT *A. Cuthbert* xvi. 215, I will not take no from you,..and if you send me away from you I will not go! *Ibid.*, The moment was fast coming when I should not have the strength to send him from me.

2. a. To compel or force to go; to drive, impel. Also *transf.* of a circumstance, impulse, etc. Also with *up*.

c **950** *Lindisf. Gosp.* Mark ix. 21, & symble hine [*sc.* one possessed of a devil] & in fyr & on wætro sende [Vulg. *misit*] þætte hine losade *vel* fordyde. *c* **1205** LAY. 14840 He hafð.. isend heom [*sc.* his foes] ouer sæ stran. **1712–14** POPE *Rape Lock* IV. 64 Hail, wayward Queen!.. Who..send the godly in a pet to pray. **1849** MACAULAY *Hist. Eng.* v. I. 609 The royal troops instantly fired such a volley of musketry as sent the rebel horse flying in all directions. **1886** STEVENSON *Treasure Isl.* xiii, The plunge of our anchor sent up clouds of birds.

b. To drive (a person) *into* some state or condition, to cause to go *to* (sleep); also with adj. complement.

1831 *Society* I. 179 You, both of you, will send me distracted between you. **1848** THACKERAY *Van. Fair* ii, Rebecca laughed in her face, with a horrid sarcastic demoniacal laughter, that almost sent the schoolmistress into fits. **1852** —— *Esmond* III. vii, He..sent the Colonel to sleep, with a long, learned, and refreshing sermon. **1892** TENNYSON *Foresters* IV, I had despair'd of thee—that sent me crazed.

c. *slang* (orig. *U.S.*). To transport or arouse emotions in (a person); to enthral, delight (esp. of popular music). Also *absol.* Hence **ˈsending** *ppl. a.*

1932 *Melody Maker* Oct. 836/1, I enclose the following wire which Louis (Musicmouth) Armstrong sent to Big John... 'My boy Earl was marvellous as ever yessir he sent me.' **1935** *Vanity Fair* (N.Y.) Nov. 71/3 Hot artists or bands that can put across their licks successfully are '*senders*'; they '*send*'. **1937** *Amer. Speech* XII. 47/1 The action of this trumpet really sends me and that's no jive. **1943** *N.Y. Times* 9 May II. 5/4 There has [*sic*] been some really solid trumpet players who can really send; some like Louis Armstrong who had a trumpet like heaven. *Ibid.*, Jimmy has a sending band and when he plays, brother, even the seats jump. **1955** V. NABOKOV *Lolita* I. xxiv. 138, I do not know if in these tragic notes, I have sufficiently stressed the peculiar 'sending' effect that the writer's good looks..had on women of every age and environment. **1956** B. HOLIDAY *Lady sings Blues* (1973) ix. 86 Meade Lux Lewis knocked them out; Ammons and Johnson flipped them..Newton's band sent them. **1959** C. MACINNES *Absolute Beginners* 16 A film we went to ages ago that rather sent us. **1975** N. MITCHISON *All change Here* iv. 39 So much modern poetry is ironic or deliberately held on a low note; that may be artistically admirable, but it doesn't send the reader.

3. To cause (a person) to be carried or conducted to a destination. **a.** To direct to be conveyed as a prisoner or a slave; to commit or consign officially *to* prison, the gallows, death, etc.

971 *Blickl. Hom.* 237 Mid þy þe hie me sendon on þis carcern. *c* **1205** LAY. 26981 Petreiun heo nomen & heore inume allen and mid þreo hundred sweinen in to wude senden. *a* **1300** *Cursor M.* 4445 Was tua men in þe kinges hus To prisun sent for þair misdede. *a* **1380** in Horstm. *Altengl. Leg.* (1878) 38/2, I am sent hider to beo slayn. *a* **1500** *Contin. Brut* 509 Þe Mair..sont þo þat cried so to Newgate. **1591** SHAKS. *1 Hen. VI*, II. iii. 42 [Thou] That hast..slaine our Citizens, And sent our sonnes and Husbands captiuate. **1687** A. LOVELL tr. *Thevenot's Trav.* I. 76 They took him, and with other Slaves sent him to Constantinople. **1706** E. WARD *Wooden World Diss.* (1708) 2 [A ship of war is] the New-Bridewell of the Nation, where all the incorrigible Roages [*printed* Viages] are sent. **1834** MARRYAT *P. Simple* lvi, Miller was sent on board of the frigate, and under surveillance. **1848** THACKERAY *Van. Fair* lxvii, I tell you they are rascals; men fit to send to the hulks.

b. To consign (a departed spirit) *to* (a place or condition).

c **1400** *Rule St. Benet* (Prose) Prol. iii. 3 For þi he giuis us respit, þat we sal mende ure sinne and siþin to þe ioy be sent. **1671** MILTON *P.R.* IV. 632 To torment sent before thir time. **1831** SCOTT *Ct. Robt.* v, The abode to which departed spirits are sent after this life.

c. In various phrases with the meaning to kill, put to death.

a **1586** SIDNEY *Arcadia* II. (Sommer) 211 b, I..sent him to feede fishes. **1592** *Soliman & Pers.* v. ii. 110 What, is thy hand to weake? then mine shall helpe To send them down to euerlasting night. **1599** MASSINGER, etc. *Old Law* v. i. (1656) 59 He must make yong [judges] or none, for all the old ones Her father he hath sent a fishing. **1602** SHAKS. *Ham.* I. v. 78 Thus was I..sent to my account With all my imperfections on my head. **1634** SIR T. HERBERT *Trav.* 102 Ere they could strangle him, he sent three of them to the Deuill. **1711** W. KING tr. *Naude's Ref. Politics* iii. 100 Quintus Fabius sent a hundred thousand Gauls into the other world.

** *With a thing as object.*

4. a. To cause (a thing) to be conveyed or transmitted by an intermediary to another person or place.

Beowulf 471 (Gr.) Sende ic Wylfingum ofer wæteres hrycȝ ealde madmas. *a* **1225** *Ancr. R.* 416 Gif heo mei sparien eni poure schreaden, sende ham al derneliche ut of hire woanes. *a* **1300** *Cursor M.* 4162 His kyrtil sal we..til his fader seind. *c* **1386** CHAUCER *Prol.* 426 Ful redy hadde he his Apothecaries To sende him [*i.e.* the sick man] drogges. **1471** MARG. PASTON in *P. Lett.* III. 25, I shal sende yw mony to bye wyth soch stwfe as I wull have. **1536** CROMWELL *Let.* 30 Apr. in Merriman *Life & Lett.* (1902) II. 11, I sende your lordship certain Crampe ringes to be bestowed there amonges your Freendes. **1663** BOYLE *Usef. Exp. Nat. Philos.* Advt., Though it come not forth before, divers parts were sent to the Press in 1660, or 1661. **1670** MARVELL *Corr.* clxiv. Wks. 1875 II. 353, I sent my letter to the post. **1743** BULKELEY & CUMMINS *Voy. S. Seas* 5 We sent on Board the Pearl twelve Butts..of Water. **1825** T. HOOK *Sayings* Ser. II. *Passion & Princ.* viii, Stages go every hour..by which Mr. W. may send his trunk with safety. **1826** *Museum Criticum* I. 137 Mr. Blomfield's edition of the *Persæ* of Æschylus will very shortly be sent to Press. **1859** TENNYSON *Elaine* 544 Since the knight Came not to us, of us to claim the prize, Ourselves will send it after. **1871** R. ELLIS *Catullus* xii. 11 Or most speedily send me back the napkin.

b. To cause (food, wine) to be handed (to a guest).

1770 FOOTE *Lame Lover* III. 52 Why, Madam..—shan't I send you a biscuit? **1825** T. HOOK *Sayings* Ser. II. *Passion & Princ.* v, Perhaps, Miss Rodney, you will let me send you wine... What wine do you take? *Ibid.*, General,..you eat nothing; let Mr. Rodney send you some lamb.

c. To serve up (food, a course, meal): only with *in*, *up*, and in phr. *to send to table*.

1662 J. DAVIES tr. *Olearius' Voy. Ambass.* 64 The Countrey cannot produce Apples or other Fruits that are worth sending up to the Table. **1687** MIEGE *Gt. Fr. Dict.* II. s.v. *Send*, Bid the Steward to send in Dinner. **1806** A. HUNTER *Culina* (ed. 3) 25 It should..be sent in hot and hot. **1825** T. HOOK *Sayings* Ser. II. *Passion & Princ.* v, What paper is that, in which those cutlets have been sent to table? **1888** 'J. S. WINTER' *Bootle's Childr.* ii, He found the cook just resting after sending up the late dinner.

d. Of a country: To export.

1596 DALRYMPLE tr. *Leslie's Hist. Scot.* I. 16 It sendes to the Easte cuntreyes verie fatt Rye. **1785** COWPER *Task* III. 583 Those [*sc.* greenhouse plants] Ausonia claims,..th' Azores send Their jessamine.

e. *transf.* and *fig.* Also with *up*.

a **1200** *Moral Ode* 51 in *O.E. Hom.* I. 163 Al þet beste þet we hefden þider [*sc.* to heaven] we hit solde senden. **1340** *Ayenb.* 73 Todel þine zaule uram þe bodye be þoȝte, zend þine herte in-to þe oþre wordle. **1595** SHAKS. *John* II. i. 409 We from the West will send destruction Into this Cities bosome. **1667** MILTON *P.L.* IX. 195 When all things that breath,..send up silent praise To the Creator. **1687** A. LOVELL tr. *Thevenot's Trav.* II. 67 The sky overcast with Clouds, that now and then sent us some drops of Rain. **1780** COWPER *Progr. Err.* 256 Has some sickly eastern waste Sent us a wind to parch us at a blast? **1825** SCOTT *Talism.* i, That sea which holds no living fish..and..sends not, like other lakes, a tribute to the ocean.

5. To dispatch (a boat, carriage, etc.). Also with *out*.

a **1122** *O.E. Chron.* (Laud MS.) an. 1101, And se cyng syððan scipa ut on sæ sende his broðer to dære & to lættinge. *c* **1200** ORMIN 8701, & Drihhtin sennde an karrte himm [*sc.* Helyas] to. *a* **1352** MINOT *Poems* (ed. Hall) i. 19 Þai sent þaire schippes on ilka side With flesch and wine. **1594** KYD *Cornelia* III. iii. 182 The Merchant, that for priuate gaine, Doth send his Ships to passe the maine. **1743** BULKELEY & CUMMINS *Voy. S. Seas* 3 The Commodore sent out a Privateer Sloop. **1836** MARRYAT *Midsh. Easy* xi, There would be two boats sent for them.

6. a. To dispatch (a message, letter, telegram, etc.) by messenger, post, or other means of communication. So *to send cards* (of invitation).

c **897** K. ÆLFRED *Gregory's Past. C.* xxxii. 213 Ne ðeah eow hwelc ærendȝewrit cume, suelce hit from us send sie. *c* **1200** ORMIN 2851 Þatt Drihhtin haffde sennd hiss word Till hire. *a* **1225** *Ancr. R.* 422 Ȝe ne schulen senden lettres..buten leaue. **1340–70** *Alex. & Dind.* 972 *rubric*, How dindimus sendyd an answere to alixandre by letter. *c* **1460** FORTESCUE *Abs. & Lim. Mon.* xiv. (1885) 143 Þat all supplicacions wich shalbe made to þe kynge..be sende to the same counsell. **1513** DOUGLAS *Æneis* XIII. vi. *title*, Kyng Latyne till Eneas send message For peax. **1615** G. SANDYS *Trav.* 86 The Embassador..sent intelligence of the same into England. **1711** SWIFT *Jrnl. to Stella* 13 Apr., I sent my excuses, adorned with about thirty compliments, and got off as fast as I could. **1770** FOOTE *Lame Lover* II. 49 She very well knows that I have not sent cards but twice the whole season. **1842** W. C. TAYLOR *Anc. Hist.* xvii. §5 (ed. 3) 519 Heliogabalus being thus victorious, sent intelligence of his success..to the senate. **1859** LYTTON *What will he do* XII. xi, I sent a telegram. **1908** R. BAGOT *A. Cuthbert* xviii. 225, I sent him a line..just to say that I had succeeded in finding you.

b. *to send* (a person) *word*: to transmit a message (to a person); to inform, notify. Const. *of*, clause, or inf.

c **1205** LAY. 25309 Bi us he sende word þe þat he wule to þisse londe. **1375** BARBOUR *Bruce* I. 145 And syne till Scotland word send he, That thai suld mak ane assemble. *a* **1450** *Knt. de la Tour* 13 And so God sent worde to the kinge and the citee bi the profete Ionas, but yef [etc.]. **1570** in Kempe *Losely MSS.* (1836) 235, I pray yow send me worde by this bearer what yow thinke. **1598** SHAKS. *Merry W.* III. v. 59 He sent me word to stay within. *Ibid.* IV. iv. 18. **1655** STANLEY *Hist. Philos.* I. (1687) 35/2 You send me word of an expedition you are preparing. **1711** SWIFT *Jrnl. to Stella* 1 Dec., Whenever you would have any money, send me word three weeks before. **1886** STEVENSON *Treasure Isl.* xii, Not long after, word was sent forward that Jim Hawkins was wanted in the cabin.

c. With the message expressed by a clause †or inf.

a **1122** *O.E. Chron.* (Laud MS.) an. 656, Ða seonde se kyning æfter þone abbode þet he æuestlice scolde to him cumon. **1297** R. GLOUC. (Rolls) 1239 Þis erl..to þe king ofte sende þat he ssolde..is herte somdel amende. *c* **1435** *Torr. Portugal* 2209 The Soudan sent to sir Torent than, With honger that thes people be slan. **1592** KYD *Sp. Trag.* III. ii. 88 Ile send to him to meet The Prince and me. *Ibid.* III. xii. 58 Although he send not that his Sonne returne. *a* **1700** EVELYN *Diary* 12 Feb. 1672, We tooke order to send to the Plantations that none of their ships should adventure homeward single.

†d. *to send greeting*: see GREETING *vbl. sb. Obs.*

c **900** tr. *Bæda's Hist.* II. x. (1891) 124 Bonefatius papa sende Eadwine greting. *c* **1205** LAY. 27885 And efte wolde heom alswa senden heom gretinge ma. **1483** *Cal. Anc. Rec. Dublin* (1889) 489 Baillifes of the same cite..senden gretyng in oure Lorde Jhesu Criste. **1535** [see GREETING *vbl. sb.*]. **1611** BIBLE *Acts* xxiii. 26.

e. In complimentary formulæ, *to send* (one's) ***compliments, love, respects***, etc. †Also, *to send* ***health, happiness***, etc.

1474 CAXTON *Chesse* Ded., Your most humble servant william Caxton..sendes unto you peas helthe Joye and victorie upon your Enemyes. **1732–3** LD. CARTERET *Let.* 24 Mar. in *Swift's Lett.* (1767) III. 36 The whole family of my ladies send their compliments. **1779** MISS M. TOWNSHEND in Jesse *Selwyn & Contemp.* (1844) IV. 100 My father is very well, and sends his love to you. **1833** T. HOOK *Parson's Dau.* II. xiii, My aunt desires to send her affectionate regards to you. **1848** THACKERAY *Van. Fair* lxvii, She made George write.., and persisted in sending Mamma's kind love in a postscript. **1852** —— *Esmond* III. xi, The man said..that his young mistress had sent her duty.

7. a. Of God, fate, chance, etc.: 'To grant as from a distant place' (J.); to cause to happen or come into existence; to ordain as a blessing or a punishment.

c **825** *Vesp. Psalter* xix. 3 Ðehere ðe dryhten..send ðe fultum of halȝum. *a* **1175** *Cott. Hom.* 225 Ic wille senden flod. *c* **1200** ORMIN 5531, & aȝȝ to þannkenn innwarrdliȝ Drihhtin all þatt he senndeþþ. *a* **1300** *Cursor M.* 1592 Forþi in forme of iugement God thoght a neu wengaunce to sent. *c* **1400** *Rule St. Benet* (Verse) 162 Euil dedes er of oure awn entent, And all gude dedes fro god er sent. **1584** B. R. tr. *Herodotus* II. 72 b, If yᵉ gods did not vouchsafe to send them raine in due season. **1601** SHAKS. *Twel. N.* III. i. 51 Now Ioue in his next commodity of hayre, send thee a beard. **1697** DRYDEN *Virg. Georg.* IV. 774 The Nymphs..have..sent a Plague among thy thriving Bees. **1734** POPE *Ess. Man* I. 113 God sends not ill. **1825** SCOTT *Betrothed* vi, I..appoint thee to be kept in ward in the western tower, till God send us relief. **1877** W. S. GILBERT *Sorcerer* II. Quintette, Bless the thoughtful fates that send him Such a wife to soothe his years. **1896** A. E. HOUSMAN *Shropshire Lad* v, Ah, spring was sent for lass and lad.

Proverbial. **1545** ASCHAM *Toxoph.* II. (Arb.) 132 He maye chaunce haue cause to saye so of his fletcher, as..is..spoken of Cookes: and that is, that God sendeth vs good fethers, but the deuyll noughtie Fletchers. **1668** R. B. *Adagia Scot.* 20 God sends never the mouth, but the meat with it. *Ibid.* 21 God sends meat, and the Devil sends Cooks.

b. In the phrase ***God, Heaven, Lord send***; (also simply *send*); esp. with clause as obj. and †with obj. and compl.

† ***God send*** (a person) ***safe, victorious***, etc. = God grant that he may be safe, etc. † ***God send*** (you, us, etc.) with inf. or subjunctive = God grant that you, we, etc. may do (what is indicated by the vb.).

c **1470** HENRY *Wallace* IV. 146 Gret God sen we had euir with him past! **1530** PALSGR. 701/1 God sende him good spede. **1556** LAUDER *Tractate* 330 Grit God we pray, sen Prencis wald perceaue,..How be tha [etc.]. **1568** GRAFTON *Chron.* II. 773 God send grace they hurt not. **1601** SHAKS. *All's Well* I. i. 190 God send him well. **1649** W. DUGDALE in *Lett. Eminent Men* (Camden) 176 God send him well recover. **1653** WALTON *Angler* I. ii. 45 God keep you all, Gentlemen; and send you meet this day with another bitch Otter. **1690** CROWNE *Eng. Friar* III. 28 *Sr. Tho.* I have a great fancy I shall do well in the Country. *La. C.* Ah! send thou dost. ? **1740** *Thesaurus Musicus* in W. H. Cummings *God Save the King* (1902) 83 God save our Lord the King. .. Send him victorious, Happy and Glorious. **1776** FOOTE *Capuchin* III. (1778) 136 Lord send us safe to Old England, say I! **1829** SCOTT *Anne of G.* xxxii, God send my poor people may have no cause to wish their old man back again. **1833** T. HOOK *Parson's Dau.* III. viii, Heaven send him happy, but I fear for the success of my prayers. **1841** DICKENS *Barn. Rudge* vi, Heaven forgive me if I am wrong, and send me just thoughts.

****** absolute uses.***

8. a. *absol.* To send a message or messenger. Const. *after*, *to*.

971 *Blickl. Hom.* 205, & [he] hie lærede þæt hie raðost to Rome sendon to ðæm papan. *a* **1122** *O.E. Chron.* (Laud MS.) an. 1011, Her on þissum ȝeare sende se cyng & his witan to ðam here. **1132** *Ibid.*, Sua ðet te king..sende efter þe muneces. **1297** R. GLOUC. (Rolls) 261 To þe king of grece he sende. *a* **1300** *Cursor M.* 10737 Wit þis þai sent sun vp and don, And bad þam at a dai be bon. *c* **1386** CHAUCER *Man of Law's T.* 1047 And hastifly he sente after Custaunce. *c* **1425** ? LYDG. *Assembly of Gods* 734 He bade him nat long Tary to sende aftyr more socour. *c* **1489** CAXTON *Sonnes of Aymon* iv. 149 He sent thrughe all the londe and made com all the maysters masons [etc.]. *a* **1533** LD. BERNERS *Huon* xcv. 309 He sende & commaundyd hym that he sholde no more fyght with me. **1591** SHAKS. *Two Gent.* IV. ii. 132 Send to me in the morning. *a* **1700** EVELYN *Diary* 25 Aug. 1660, Coll. Spencer..sent to me and intreated that I would take a Commission. **1833** T. HOOK *Parson's Dau.* II. v, When your lordship—wants me again, send. You know where I live. If you don't send I shan't come. **1841** THACKERAY *Gt. Hoggarty Diam.* ix, John, send to Mrs. Hoggarty in the shrubbery. **1873** *Independent Defender* (San Francisco) 15 Nov. 3/1 The operator..excitedly telegraphed back, don't send so d——d fast. **1924** *Radio Times* 19 Dec. 585/3 This is only a receiving station. We can't send. We can only listen. **1929** *Amer. Speech* IV. 288 The sender's task is to 'move it', ..—or simply 'send'. **1974** W. GARNER *Big Enough Wreath* xi. 140 What if he'd asked to see the print-out? What if he'd gone over to see you send?

b. Followed by inf. (or, *rarely*, by *and* with a co-ordinated verb) indicating the purpose.

a **1225** *Leg. Kath.* 151 Ha sende swiðe for to witen hwet wunder hit were. **1297** R. GLOUC. (Rolls) 7125 To þe duc he sende sone to helpe him in þat cas. **1482** *Monk of Evesham* (Arb.) 54 Myne soule was gonne and paste out of my bodye yere my wyfe knewe hit or sende to calle for the pryste. **1599** SHAKS. *Hen. V*, III. v. 62 And let him say to England, that we send To know what willing Ransome he will giue. **1692** R. L'ESTRANGE *Fables* xci. 86 His Wife sent up and down to look after him. *a* **1700** EVELYN *Diary* 29 Aug. 1678, The D. of Norfolk..sent to me to take charge of the bookes. **1710** SWIFT *Jrnl. to Stella* 16 Sept., Sir John Holland..has sent to desire my acquaintance. **1748** RICHARDSON *Clarissa* VII. 207, I have sent every half hour to know how she does. **1835** WILLIS *Pencillings* III. x. 121 He inquired whether there was not a morsel left... Mr. R. was not sure. 'Send and see', said Lamb. **1863** COWDEN CLARKE *Shaks. Char.* ix. 218 He sent to invite her to supper with him.

c. Of a shop: to deliver goods ordered.

1871 G. H. LEWES *Let.* 27 Aug. in *Geo. Eliot Lett.* (1956) V. 181 Take care the Stores people send on Thursday. **1968** *Observer* (Colour Suppl.) 22 Dec. 17/4 The shops won't send and now they've stopped the bus.

9. send for ——. **a.** To send a messenger or message for; to send (a person) to fetch ——.

1338 R. BRUNNE *Chron.* (1810) 19 He sent for alle þe kynges, fro Berwik vnto Kent. **1387** TREVISA *Higden* (Rolls) VII. 237 He hadde nouȝt i-send for more help. *c* **1450** *Merlin* xxviii. 566 Than com Merlin to Arthur, and bad hym sende for all his power in all haste. **1562** MACHYN *Diary* (Camden) 282 Ther was a grett frey and my lord mare..was send fore. **1672** WISEMAN *Treat. Wounds* I. 38 The next day ..it burst out impetuously; I was sent for, and found it bleeding with a strong impulse. *a* **1674** CLARENDON *Hist. Reb.* XI. §123 The guard..sent for drink. **1748** RICHARDSON *Clarissa* VII. 213, I send by poor Lovelace's desire, for particulars of the fatal breviate. **1847** TENNYSON *Princess* IV. 220 She sent for Blanche to accuse her face to face. **1908** R. BAGOT *A. Cuthbert* xxviii. 373 Would you not like me to send for one of your priests?

b. With adv. qualifying 'to come' or 'be brought' understood.

1592 *Arden of Feversham* Epil. 3 The one tooke Sanctuary, and being sent for out, Was murthred in Southwark. *c* **1643** LD. HERBERT *Autobiog.* (1824) 34 My mother thought fit to send for me home. **1703** *Rules of Civility* 40 You must go away without seeing him, unless he sends for you in. **1714** SWIFT *Imit. Hor.* II. vi. 16 Send for him up, take no Excuse. **1753** MISS COLLIER *Art Torment.* I. ii. (1811) 60, I shall not send for you back. **1833** T. HOOK *Parson's Dau.* II. vii, The Squire was sent for home.

c. Of a sovereign: To command the attendance of; *esp.* to summon a leader or prominent member of a political party, for the purpose of offering him the office of prime minister.

1744 BIRCH *Life Boyle* 154 He was then by his Majesty's order sent for to Whitehall. **1765** G. WILLIAMS in Jesse *Selwyn & Contemp.* (1843) I. 382 The King declared to his ministers that he had no further occasion for their services, but had sent for Mr. Pitt. **1806** G. ROSE *Diaries* (1860) II. 227 The King could do no better than to send for Lord Grenville. **1880** MCCARTHY *Own Times* IV. 512 The Queen sent for Lord Hartington, she then sent for Lord Granville; but everyone knew in advance who was to come into power at last.

II. To cause to go, by physical means or by direct volition.

10. a. *trans.* To discharge and direct (a missile); to throw or propel in a particular direction; occas. †to thrust (a dagger). Also said of a missile weapon.

c **825** *Vesp. Psalter* xvii. 15 [xviii. 14] Sende strele his & tostencte hie. *c* **1205** LAY. 6483 And he lette fuse him to flan swuðe kene and alle him to sende. **1627** DRAYTON *Agincourt* 20 As thick againe their Shafts the English send. **1646–7** BOYLE in Birch *Life* (1744) 74 Which [wind-gun]..would.. send forth a leaden bullet..with force to kill a man at twenty five..paces. **1667** MILTON *P.L.* VI. 836 In his right hand Grasping ten thousand Thunders, which he sent Before him. **1687** SETTLE *Refl. Dryden* 83 To send a Dagger to a Mans heart is an expression older than thou art. *a* **1700** EVELYN *Diary* Sept. 1646, He was sending a brace of bullets into the poore beast. **1717** ADDISON tr. *Ovid's Metam.* III. 91 Cadmus..Then heav'd a stone, and rising to the throw, He sent it in a whirlwind at the foe. **1780** COWPER *Progr. Err.* 570 None sends his arrow to the mark in view, Whose hand is feeble. **1784** —— *Task* III. 803 And the whistling ball Sent through the trav'llers temples! **1842** BARHAM *Ingol. Leg.*, *St. Medard*, As the cannon recoils when it sends its shot. **1852** THACKERAY *Esmond* I. xiv, 'I fling the words in your face, my lord', says the other; 'shall I send the cards too?' **1857** HUGHES *Tom Brown* I. viii, Flashman..sent an empty pickle-jar whizzing after them.

fig. *a* **1854** H. REED *Lect. Eng. Lit.* xii. (1878) 392 The Duke of Wellington uses words with a strange frugality, and sends them straight to their mark.

b. To deliver (a blow). †Formerly const. *dative*. Also *to send home* (see HOME *adv.* 10 b).

a **1626** MIDDLETON *Mayor Queensb.* II. i, How am I serv'd in this? I offer a vexation to the King, He sends it home into my bloud with vantage. **1628** FELTHAM *Resolves* II. vii. 16 Hadrian sent his inferiour seruant a box on the eare, for walking but betweene two Senators. **1861** H. C. PENNELL *Puck on Pegasus* 111 Right to his dexter optic The Champion sent a blow. **1894** KIPLING *Jungle Bk.* 59 Kaa..sent home half-a-dozen full-power smashing blows.

c. To drive (a ball).

1782 *Kentish Gaz.* 20–23 Nov., Now the Batsman..Sends the Ball Over all. **1887** *Field* 5 Nov. 714/1 Lawrence then, by a well-judged kick, sent the ball between the [goal] posts.

11. To emit, give forth as a source. **a.** To give off or out (light, heat, odour, etc.); to discharge, pour out (liquid). Chiefly with advs., *forth*, *off*, *out*.

971 *Blickl. Hom.* 245 Nu þonne, anlicnes,..sænd mycel wæter þurh þinne muþ. *a* **1425** *Arderne's Treat. Fistula*, etc. 56 If þai sende out blode þai ar seid ryȝtfully emeroydez. **1535** COVERDALE *Jas.* iii. 11 Doth a fountayne sende forth at one place swete water and bytter also? **1567** *Gude & Godlie B.* (S.T.S.) 145 He is the Morning Star, His bemis send he hes out far. **1574** HYLL *Art Garden.* lvii. (ed. 3) 115 By the watring on this wise, the roote sendeth such bitternesse as then remayneth in the same. **1584** B. R. tr. *Herodotus* II. 74 b, I demaunded..the reason..why this streame..neuer sent foorth any miste or vapour. **1611** BIBLE *Eccl.* x. 1 Dead flies cause the oyntment..to send foorth a stinking sauour. **1614** GORGES *Lucan* VI. 241 And with the very breath she sends The healthy aire taints and offends. **1662** J. DAVIES tr. *Olearius' Voy. Ambass.* 204 Many Springs send forth their Water with such violence, that [etc.]. **1667** MILTON *P.L.* VIII. 141 That light Sent from her through the wide transpicuous aire. **1820** SHELLEY *Sensit. Pl.* I. 15 And their breath was mixed with fresh odour, sent From the turf, like the voice and the instrument. **1840** H. SMITH *Oliver Cromwell* II. 239 Several pipes of trinidado were sending forth their powerful fumes. **1862** BORROW *Wild Wales* xxiii. (1901) 71/1 A white farm-house—sending from a tall chimney a thin misty reek up to the sky.

b. To give *forth* or *out* (sound); to utter (a cry, groan, etc.). Cf. 13.

c **1200** *Trin. Coll. Hom.* 211 Muð sent ut þe stefne. **1535** COVERDALE *Ps.* lxvii[i]. 33 He shal sende out his voyce, yee and that a mightie voyce. *a* **1586** SIDNEY *Arcadia* III. (Sommer) 274 Or such a noise it was, as highest thunders sende. 1621 BRATHWAIT Nat. Embassie, etc. 233 Rather then for her I'de shed one teare,..or send one grone. 1688 HOLME Armoury II. 134/1 An Hart, when he sendeth forth his Cry, is said to Bellow. 1725 POPE Odyss. IX. 469 He sends a dreadful groan. 1784 COWPER Task v. 821 When ev'ry star ..Sent forth a voice. 1813 BYRON Corsair I. xv, But still her lips refused to send—'Farewell!' 1847 TENNYSON Princess IV. 373 The lost lamb at her feet Sent out a bitter bleating for its dam. 1859 —— Geraint & Enid 728 Then Enid..Sent forth a sudden sharp and bitter cry.

c. To throw out as a branch or offshoot. Chiefly with *off*, *out*, †*forth*.

1715 CHEYNE Philos. Princ. Relig. I. 297 The Aorta,.. bending a little upwards, sends forth the Cervical and Axillary Arteries. 1723 P. BLAIR Pharmaco-Bot. I. 34 Sending forth here and there several Leaves. 1732 A. MONRO Anat. Nerves 3 The Nerves..send off their Branches at more acute Angles..than the Blood-vessels do. a1767 —— Wks. (1781) 312 The lymphatic vessel which enters its superior arch, is often sent from the thyroid gland. 1812 New Bot. Garden I. 90 It sends out several stems from the root. 1837 P. KEITH Bot. Lex. 395 Each [bronchial tube] dividing and subdividing, and sending off secondary branches. 1870 ROLLESTON Anim. Life 131 A minute mesial stomato-gastric ganglion, which..sends nerves to the..jaw and its muscles.

12. To direct (a thought, look, glance).

?c1420 26 Pol. Poems 74 God askeþ of the:..þy swete þou3tes (þou) me sende. 1592 KYD Sp. Trag. II. iii. 35 Send thou sweet looks, ile meete them with sweete lookes. 1782 COWPER Alex. Selkirk 37 My friends, do they now and then send A wish or a thought after me? 1831 SCOTT Ct. Robt. x, Many were the glances which the Princess sent among her retinue. 1890 CLARK RUSSELL Marr. at Sea vii, Never can I forget the expression of her face..when..she sent a look at the yacht.

13. To cause (sound, one's voice) to 'carry' or travel. Chiefly *poet.* Cf. 11 b.

1593 SHAKS. Rich. II, III. iii. 33 Through Brazen Trumpet send the breath of Parle Into his ruin'd Eares. 1667 MILTON P.L. v. 548 When Cherubic Songs by night from neighbouring Hills Aereal Music send. 1749 FIELDING Tom Jones VII. iii, The squire..sent after his sister the same holla which attends the departure of a hare. 1842 TENNYSON Talking Oak 123 And livelier than the lark She sent her voice thro' all the holt Before her. 1892 HENLEY Song of Sword 76 The cry of a gull sent seaward.

14. To drive by pulsation, impulse, etc.

a1767 A. MONRO Wks. (1781) 378 The liquors sent from the umbilical arteries to be mixed with the uterine blood, resemble the..liquors separated from the..blood. 1835–6 Todd's Cycl. Anat. I. 638/2 The cavities..on the right side of the heart send the blood to the lungs for the purposes of respiration. 1873 F. JENKIN Electr. & Magn. xxii. §4 (1881) 300 A simple key, which the operator depresses when he wishes to send a current. 1874 W. K. CLIFFORD in Fortn. Rev. Dec. 719 Like the wave which you send along a string and which comes back. Ibid., There is a physical excitation or disturbance which is sent along two different nerves.

15. Of a blow or something having the effect of a blow, also of the agent, a weapon: To cause to go or fall violently. Also with *down*.

1822 A. THORNTON Don Juan II. ii. 25 But the contest was suddenly arrested..by a colossal fist which sent two or three of the combatants sprawling among the wine buts. 1840 THACKERAY Barber Cox Aug., His lance took Tagrag on the neck, and sent him to the ground like a stone. 1848 —— Van. Fair lxii, My lord nearly sent Jos off his legs with the most fascinating smile. 1855 SMEDLEY H. Coverdale ii, He struck his antagonist a crashing blow, which..sent him down like a shot. 1879 [see FLY v.¹ 9]. 1887 'MARK RUTHERFORD' Revol. Tanner's Lane i. (ed. 8) 8 In an instant it was sent flying to the other side of the road. 1898 Daily News 24 Nov. 7/3 Sharkey..put a right hand smash on the jaw, sending Corbett down.

16. To cause (a thing) to go *down*, *up*, etc. Also *transf.* with immaterial object, e.g. prices, one's spirits.

1657 W. COLES Adam in Eden ix. 20 Lavender..heateth the Belly, and sendeth down the Terms. 1794 Rigging & Seamanship I. 213 The Jack-block is used for sending top-gallant-yards up or down. 1823 J. BADCOCK Dom. Amusem. 108 Tartar emetic..solution being heated with sulphuret of ammonia, sends down a copious gold coloured precipitate. 1830 SCOTT Introd. to Ld. of Isles, I sent up another of these trifles, which, like schoolboys' kites, served to show how the wind..was setting. 1841 R. H. DANA Seaman's Man. 30 If the topgallant sail is to be bent aloft, send it up to the topmast cross-trees by the clewlines. 1860 H. STUART Seaman's Catech. 50 Reeve a topgallant mast rope, and send the mast on deck. 1895 DOYLE Stark Munro Lett. xvi. 332 We could manage very well on that—the more so as marriage sends a doctor's income up.

17. To cause to move or travel; to cause to work. Cf. *send along* 21.

1864 TENNYSON En. Arden 532 The breath of heaven came continually And sent her [sc. a ship] sweetly by the golden isles. 1885 Pall Mall Gaz. 12 Jan. 7/2 The order was given to send the engines full speed astern. 1893 F. F. MOORE Gray Eye or So III. 205 Harold..sending his horses at a pretty fair pace into the square.

III. In idiomatic combination with adverbs. (For the obvious combinations see the simple senses and the adverbs.)

†18. send about. *trans.* To dispatch (messengers) here and there; also *absol.* *Obs.*

c1330 King of Tars 146 He sente aboute on uche a syde Alle that he mihte of seende. 1604 SHAKS. Oth. I. ii. 46 The Senate hath sent about three seuerall Quests, To search you out.

19. send abroad. **a.** *trans.* To publish, make known widely; also, to cause (a sound) to be heard far and wide. *arch.* or *poet.*

1681 W. ROBERTSON Phraseol. Gen., To send abroad or to publish, edere, evulgare. 1706 E. WARD Wooden World Diss. (1708) 79 He has a thousand pretty Phrases which he never sends abroad. 1821 SCOTT Kenilw. xxxiii, The great bell of the Castle..began to send its pealing clamour abroad. 1864 TENNYSON E. Arden 764 He..fear'd To send abroad a shrill and terrible cry.

b. *absol.* To send out notices widely.

1611 BIBLE 1 Chron. xiii. 2 Let vs send abroad vnto our brethren euery where.

†20. send against ——. *pass.* To be met. (Cf. *go against*, GO *v.* 51 a.) *Obs.*

1541 SIR T. WYATT Def. in Poet. Wks. (1858) p. xxxiii, He [Pole] was neither sent against, being the Bishop of Rome's legate, neither received,..nor accompanied out again.

21. send along. *trans.* To cause to travel rapidly; *fig.* to accelerate the progress or growth of.

1867 Jrnl. R. Agric. Soc. Ser. II. III. II. 533 If they have been 'sent along' with Indian corn [etc.] they will make up to nearly 2 lbs. heavier. Mod. The coachman sent his horses along at a good rate.

22. send away. **a.** *trans.* To dispatch (a messenger, message, boat, etc.). Also *absol.*

1597 SHAKS. 2 Hen. IV, II. iv. 408 If I be not sent away poste, I will see you againe, ere I goe. 1612 SIR R. NAUNTON in Buccleuch MSS. (Hist. MSS. Comm.) I. 118, I am in some haste, for fear Mr. More should send away before this comes to him. a1779 COOK 3rd Voy. III. viii. (1784) II. 128 Before we got near enough to send away a boat to sound the entrance.

†b. See quot. *Obs.* Cf. *send down* b.

1714 Spectator No. 596 ⁋3 Upon which I was sent away, or in the University Phrase, Rusticated for ever.

23. send back. *trans.* (*Cricket.*) To cause (one who has come out to bat) to return; to 'put out'.

1870 Baily's Mag. Aug. 359 A good catch..sent him back when only a few runs were wanted. 1882 Daily Tel. 19 May, The first ball..sent back Mr. Greenfield.

24. send before. *trans.* To cause to go in advance. Now *rare.*

1538 ELYOT Dict., Emissarius,..signyfieth hym, whiche is sent before in battayle to espie. 1590 [see BEFORE adv. 1]. 1596 SHAKS. Tam. Shr. IV. i. 4, I am sent before to make a fire, and they are coming after to warme them. 1646 BOYLE in Birch Life (1744) 55 At Salisbury I overtook my trunks I had sent thither before. 1740 [see BEFORE adv. 1]. 1744 BIRCH Life Boyle 34 To make his addresses to this lady, Mr. F. was sent..before up to London. 1819 SHELLEY Mask of Anarchy 82 So he sent his slaves before To seize upon the Bank and Tower.

25. send down. **a.** To dispatch from the King or the Lords to the Commons, from the capital, a city, one's headquarters, etc. into the country. Also *absol.*

1455 Rolls of Parlt. V. 303/1 That than the seid provisions and exceptions be sende doune unto us, to that ende that we may gife oure assentz therto. a1513 FABYAN Chron. VII. (1533) II. aa iij b/2 Wherfore in all haste he [Richard I] sent downe, gyuyng strayte commaundement that they shuld cease of the ryot. 1585 T. WASHINGTON tr. Nicholay's Voy. I. ii. 1 b, [He] sent downe his traine by water: and himselfe went by land. 1671, 1678 [see DOWN adv. 2]. 1884 ANNIE S. SWAN Dorothea Kirke xviii. 164 If we meet any poor shop-girl..we'll send her down..to wonder at the blueness of the sky. 1891 'J. S. WINTER' Lumley xi, I'm going to send down for Ruth to come up to help to nurse you.

b. To compel (an undergraduate) to leave the University (permanently or for a specified time), as a punishment. = RUSTICATE *v.* 2.

1853 [see DOWN adv. 2]. 1894 Times 16 May 10/4 Some 17 members of Christ Church..have been heavily fined and 'sent down'.

c. *Cricket.* To bowl (a ball, an over).

1871 Baily's Mag. Oct. 415 At times, no bowler in England sends down such utterly unplayable balls. 1882 Daily Tel. 19 May, Nine overs were then sent down for half a dozen runs.

d. To dispatch or commit to prison by sentence. Freq. *pass. slang* (orig. *U.S.*).

1840 Picayune (New Orleans) 2 Aug. 2/5 She scorned to find surety in $500 to keep the peace, so she was sent down. 1880 G. A. SALA Amer. Revisited (1882) I. v. 85 They were 'sent down' for ten days. 1941 'R. WEST' Black Lamb II. 315 We caught the murderer..and he was sent down for a long sentence. 1960 G. BUTLER Death lives Next Door vi. 118 I'm Ted Springer's missus. Sent him down for three years, you did. 1976 'P. B. YUILL' Hazell & Menacing Jester iii. 39 'Is there any chance he could go to gaol?' 'You'd like him sent down, would you?'

e. To cause to accompany someone (to dinner).

1888 MRS. H. WARD R. Elsmere II. II. xvii. 74 They would be sent down to dinner together to a certainty. 1892 'A. HOPE' Mr. Witt's Widow viii. 98 That lady..sent Laura down to dinner with him.

f. ***send her down, Davy*** (also ***Hughie***, etc.) and varr.: phr. expressing a wish for rain to fall. Cf. HUGHIE. *slang* (chiefly *Austral.* and *N.Z.*).

1919 W. H. DOWNING Digger Dial. 44 Send her down, Steve!, let it rain on. 1925 FRASER & GIBBONS Soldier & Sailor Words & Phrases 72 David (or Davy), send it down, a soldier's greeting to a shower of rain likely to postpone a parade. 1928 L. H. NASON Sergeant Eadie xi. 321 Hurray! Send her down, Davie; no drill today! 1937, 1958 [see HUGHIE]. 1975 Panorama (Austral.) Nov. 2/5 'Send 'er down, Hughie!' An expression in nationwide use since the turn of the century, which is..an invocation to Heaven..to send rain.

26. send forth. *trans.* To produce, yield; also, of a country, to export; of the press, to issue, publish.

1626 BACON Sylva §567 The Water also doth send forth Plants, that haue no Roots. 1819 BYRON Juan I. i, I want a hero: an uncommon want, When every year and month sends forth a new one. 1825 SCOTT Betrothed x, I have.. cyprus, such as the East hath seldom sent forth. 1849 MACAULAY Hist. Eng. iii. I. 415 The press now often sends forth in a day a greater quantity of discussion..than was published [etc.]. 1885 Field 4 Apr. 426/2 Skeffington Wood sent forth the first [fox].

27. send in. **a.** *trans.* To give (one's name), hand (one's card) to a servant when making a call.

1748 RICHARDSON Clarissa VII. 204 The Colonel..sent in his name; and I..introduced the afflicted gentleman. 1897 WATTS-DUNTON Aylwin v. ii, On sending in my card I was shown at once into the studio.

b. To cause (a thing) to be delivered at its destination, to the person entitled to receive it or to the appointed receiver; esp. to render (an account, a bill).

to send in one's jacket: see JACKET sb. 1 b. *to send in one's papers*: see PAPER sb. 7 d.

1715 DE FOE Fam. Instruct. II. i. (1841) I. 169 At Church there are bills sent in for the Minister to pray for folks. 1772 FOOTE Nabob I. (1778) 22 Sir Robert Bumper's butler is to send in the wine. 1834 MARRYAT P. Simple lxi, My father's bills had been sent in, and amounted to twelve hundred pounds. 1887 ESHER in Law Rep. 19 Q.B. Div. 518 It is suggested that to send in a bill is not to demand payment of it, but this is a fanciful view. 1895 SAINTSBURY Corr. Impr. 179 An editorial notice of a poem which had been sent in.

c. *Cricket.* To send (a batsman) into the field to bat. Also, to send (the opposing side) in to bat first.

1857 HUGHES Tom Brown II. viii, Arthur is sent in, and goes off to the wicket. 1898 GIFFEN With Bat & Ball viii. 111 Bonnor was sent in third wicket down. 1912 P. F. WARNER England v. Australia vi. 48 Trumper beat Douglas in the toss, and sent us in. 1930 C. G. MACARTNEY My Cricketing Days iii. 18 They might have given us a good game had not our captain..won the toss and sent them in on a bad wicket. 1969 Wisden Cricketers' Almanack 478 Although Lancashire were without..their opening bowlers, Leicestershire sent them in on winning the toss.

28. a. send off. *trans.* To cause to start on a mission from oneself; to see to the departure of (a person or thing, a message, etc., that is to be conveyed somewhere).

1666 DRYDEN Ann. Mirab. lxxiv, His wounded men he first sends off to shore. 1782 MISS BURNEY Cecilia VII. ix, When she had sent off this letter. 1896 R. S. S. BADEN-POWELL Matabele Campaign vi, We..sent off some native runners to go and find him.

absol. 1848 THACKERAY Van. Fair xix, The trembling old lady sent off for her doctor.

†b. = sense 25 b. *Obs.*

1843 [see FACULTY 9 b].

c. *Sport.* To order (a player) to leave the pitch as a punishment.

1906 W. PICKFORD in Gibson & Pickford Association Football III. XVI. 6 A referee may send a player off at once and without any previous caution, if he is guilty of violent conduct. 1976 Milton Keynes Express 2 July 43/4 Newton.. suffered a severe setback in the first half when they had a player sent off.

29. send on. **a.** *trans.* To dispatch (a person or thing) in advance; also *absol.* for 'to send on one's horse'.

a1700 EVELYN Diary 11 June 1652, Having sent my man on before, I rode negligently under favour of the shade. 1848 THACKERAY Van. Fair xli, Pitt accompanied them.. having sent on their baggage in a cart previously. 1895 DOYLE Stark Munro Lett. xvi. 342, I work a town at a time. I send on an agent to the next to say that I am coming.

absol. 1854 R. S. SURTEES Handley Cross xxxii, Because Sir Yawnberry Dawdle, who lies long in bed, sends on, Mr. Larkspur..must needs do the same.

b. To cause (a person) to go onward.

1877 SPURGEON Serm. XXIII. 357, A asks B to help him, and B, in his wonderful charity, does him the great favour of sending him on to C.

c. To dispatch (a letter, etc.) forward from the place to which it was addressed.

1833 S. SMITH Life & Writings J. Downing liii. 183 Dear sir, I want you to send this on to cousin Jack. 1879 GEO. ELIOT Let. 7 July (1956) VII. 179, I have had 2 letters from him which Miss Gibson sent on. 1895 'G. MORTIMER' Like Stars that Fall xiv. 198 Didn't you get the letter sent on?

30. send out. *trans.* To issue (†a commandment, an invitation); †to proclaim *that*.

c1400 Three Kings Cologne 26 Whan Octouianus had sent houte a commaundement..þat euery man and woman scholde go to his cite. a1450 Mirk's Festial 22 þan was send out a mawndement. a1700 EVELYN Diary 11 May 1652, I rode to Coll. Blount's..who sent out hue and cry immediately.

31. send over. *trans.* To dispatch across the sea, or (in later use) from one place to another (cf. OVER *adv.* 5). Also *absol.*

1483 Cely Papers (Camden) 140, I beseche yowre master-schypp to remember to send ower the pampelett. 1594 KYD Cornelia III. i. 94 Send Sextus over to some forraine Nation. 1646 BOYLE in Birch Life (1744) 65 Some of the least bad of which [verses] I shall venture to send you over. a1700 EVELYN Diary 9 Mar. 1652, I..meditated sending over for my wife. 1888 'J. S. WINTER' Bootle's Childr. ix, Hothouse blooms and delicate ferns and tall palms, which had been sent over by cartloads.

32. send round. **a.** *trans.* To circulate.

1839 THACKERAY Stubb's Cal. Dec. Comic Tales (1841) II. 366 'Never mind, my boys', I used to say, 'send the bottle round'. 1841 PUSEY in Newman's Lett. (1891) II. 370 note, A circular is being sent round to all the members of Convocation.

b. ***to send round the hat***: see HAT sb. 5 b.

c. *colloq.* To send (something; also *absol.* to send a message) to some one in the neighbourhood.

Mod. I will leave the basket; you can send it round anytime. I will send round tomorrow to inquire how the patient is.

33. send up. a. *trans.* Of things: To emit, give off, shoot out (something that rises or travels upwards).

1584 B. R. tr. *Herodotus* II. 76 The countrey is exceeding hote and parching, being altogether vnfit to sende vp any vapours. **1667** MILTON *P.L.* XI. 738 The Hills..Vapour, and Exhalation dusk and moist, Sent up amain. **1711** ADDISON *Spect.* No. 62 ¶5 It is a Flame that sends up no Smoke. **1817** SHELLEY *Rev. Islam* 2928 [It] Passed like a spark sent up out of a burning oven. **1837** P. KEITH *Bot. Lex.* 104 If a bean is planted..it will immediately begin to send up a stem.

b. To cause (a person) to go or (a thing) to be taken 'upstairs' (from the kitchen, entrance hall, etc.); esp. to serve up (a meal), to send in (one's name or card as a visitor).

1836 MARRYAT *Midsh. Easy* xi, The master of the inn.. sent up the bill by the waiter. **1884** *Graphic* 29 Nov. 578/3 Gerald..sent up his name to Lord Whitby.

absol. **1862** MISS BRADDON *Lady Audley* xxxvi, Poor Tomlins has sent up three times to say the fish will be spoiled.

c. To send (a bill) from the Commons to the Lords.

1832 GREVILLE *Mem.* 6 Apr. (1874) II. 282 That could not be *now* in the Bill, as it was sent up from the Commons.

d. *Public Schools.* To send (a boy) to the headmaster (*a*) for reward, (*b*) for punishment.

1821 *Salt-Bearer* (Eton Coll.) 129 He more than once had the honour of being 'sent up for good', *i.e.* having his verses read over by the head master as being worthy of commendation. **1849** THACKERAY *Pendennis* xxxiv, I remember poor Shelley at school being sent up for good for a copy of verses. **1857** HUGHES *Tom Brown* I. vii, 'What if we're late?' said Tom. 'No tea, and sent up to the Doctor', answered East. *Ibid.* II. vii, He sent me up to be flogged for it. **1881** *Everyday Life in Public Sch.* (ed. Pascoe) 322 *Sent up*, Eton. An honour due usually to distinction in verses. *Ibid.* 323 The Head Master exercised the power of sending up 'for play', which was counted as three times 'sent up for good'. Every third occasion of being sent up for good the boy could claim a book from the Head.

e. To put in prison.

1852 JUDSON *Myst. N.Y.* III. 7 (Farmer) They'd blow on me for some of my work, and I'd be sent up. **1897** *Westm. Gaz.* 30 Apr. 10/1 Only two prisoners, men, occupied the prison-van... Burns was being 'sent up' for wife-beating, and Tannahill for theft.

f. To mock, make fun of (a person or thing); to parody.

1931 T. R. G. LYELL *Slang, Phrase & Idiom in Colloq. Eng.* 673 The last time he came in, he was sent up unmercifully by half the room. **1957** 'N. BLAKE' *End of Chapter* 68 Who's Johnnie Ray? He's—go on! you're sending me up! **1962** *John o' London's* 29 Nov. 506/3 The effect..is as if he is attempting to 'send up' the whole picture. **1969** *Times* 13 Dec. p. v/2 These represented the British sense of humour, our genius for sending ourselves up, but they seem to me rather to be reinforcements of such attitudes. **1977** P. G. WINSLOW *Witch Hill Murder* II. xvii. 220, I wasn't sending you up the other night. I was *afraid*.

IV. 34. The infin. used: a. to describe the position of a switch for transmission.

1876 *Jrnl. Soc. Telegr. Engineers* V. 494 The switch has been put on 'send'. **1976** C. EGLETON *State Visit* ix. 88 Because he kept the switch on 'send', they could just hear the band.

b. *attrib.* in the sense 'sending', as the name of a part.

1973 C. BONINGTON *Next Horizon* xiii. 194 He ended up by telling me to press the send switch of the radio three times as affirmative and twice for negative, in reply to his questions. **1976** K. THACKERAY *Crownbird* ix. 198 He pulled his microphone towards him..and depressed the send button.

send (sɛnd), *v.*² *Naut.* Pa. t. **sended**. Also 7–9 **scend**, (8 **sand**). [Belongs to SEND *sb.*²; possibly a mere application of SEND *v.*¹ Often written '*scend*, as if aphetic for *descend* or *ascend*.] (See quot. *a* 1625.)

a **1625** *Nomenclator Navalis* (Harl. MS. 2301), When a shipp falls (whether under saile or at Anchor) with her head or with her sterne deepe into the Trough of the Sea it is said she Sends much either a sterne or a head. **1691** T. H[ALE] *Acc. New Invent.* 122 An uneven and unlevel keel drooping forwards, or sending aft. *Ibid.* 127 What makes her pitch and scend too much. **1794** J. H. MOORE *Pract. Navig.* (ed. 10) 286 *She sands* or *sends.* When the ship's head or stern falls deep in the trough of the sea. **1769** FALCONER *Dict. Marine* (1780), *Sending*, the act of pitching precipitately into the hollow, or interval, between two waves. **1833** M. SCOTT *Tom Cringle* ii, She sended forward, heavily and sickly, on the long swell.—She never rose to the opposite heave of the sea again.

transf. **1896** R. S. S. BADEN-POWELL *Matabele Campaign* i, All day and all night we go rocking and pitching, rolling and 'scending' along in the creaking, groaning old coach.

¶ b. Apparently misapplied from incorrect notion of the etymology.

1867 SMYTH *Sailor's Word-bk.*, '*Scending* (from *ascend*), the contrary motion to pitching. **1889** WELCH *Text Bk. Naval Archit.* iii. 50 The motion is termed..pitching or 'scending according as the bow of the ship moves downward and the stern upward or vice versâ.

sendable (ˈsɛndəb(ə)l), *a.* [f. SEND *v.*¹ + -ABLE.] That may be sent.

1483 *Cath. Angl.* 329/2 Sendabylle, *missilis.* **1791** BENTHAM *Mem. & Corr.* Wks. 1843 X. 263, I have it before me, but not in a sendable state. **1901** *Chambers's Jrnl.* July 464/1 We have become so used to connecting the convenient little slips of sendable money with the Post-Office. **1965** P. WYLIE *They both were Naked* I. iii. 150 She had been sendable because she wanted to be sent.

Sendai (ˈsɛndaɪ). *Biol.* and *Med.* The name of a city in northern Honshu, Japan, used attrib. as **Sendai virus**, a paramyxovirus (first identified in Sendai) which causes disease of the upper respiratory tract in mammals, and is used in the laboratory to produce cell fusion.

[**1953** T. SANO et al. in *Yokohama Med. Bull.* IV. 215 We consider this disease a new form of virus pneumonitis and have termed it 'Newborn Virus Pneumonitis (Type Sendai)'.] **1958** *Ann. Rev. Microbiol.* XII. 66 Similar to the influenza virus, one of the new agents, Sendai virus, propagates sufficiently well in eggs to permit primary isolation by amniotic inoculation. **1970** *Nature* 25 July 339/2 The possibility of introducing alien genetic material into mammalian eggs by fusion with somatic cells using Sendai virus. **1976** *Ann. Rev. Microbiol.* XXX. 29 The transcriptive complex of a representative paramyxovirus, Sendai virus, contains a major structural polypeptide, NP..a less abundant polypeptide, P..and a high-molecular-weight polypeptide that is present in minute amounts.

sendal (ˈsɛndəl). Now only *Hist.* Forms: 3–4 **cendal**, 3–5 **cendel, sendell**, 4–5 **sandelle**, 4–6 **sendel, sendale**, (4 **cendale, -dele, sandale**), 5 **sandel, sendelle**, 5–6 **sendalle, syndall**, (5 **sendyll(e**, 5–7 **sandall**, 6 **sindal**, 6–7 **sindall**, (6 **cendell, sandell, syndale**, *Sc.* **san-, sendill**), 5–9 **sendall**, 4– **sendal**. [a. OF. *cendal*, = Pr. *zendal-s*, *sendat-z*, Sp., Pg. *cendal*, It. *zendale*, *sendale*, *zendado*; a Com. Rom. word, whence MHG. *zendâl*, *zindal*, mod.G. *zindel*.

It is probable that the word is ultimately derived from Gr. σινδών fine linen, which it renders in OF. translations of the New Testament; but the history of the form is obscure.]

1. A thin rich silken material; also, a covering or garment of this material.

a **1225** *Juliana* 9 (MS. Bodl.) Al þe cure ouertild..wið purpres & pelles, wið ciclatuns & cendals & deorewurðe clathes. *a* **1300** *Cursor M.* 14984 Þair lauerd was noþer cledd Wit silk ne yeitt cendel. **1362** LANGL. *P. Pl.* A. VII. 19 And ȝe, loueli Ladeis.., Þat habbeþ selk, and sendel souweþ. *c* **1386** CHAUCER *Prol.* 440 In sangwyn and in pers he clad was al Lyned with Taffata and with Sendal. **1395** *E.E. Wills* (1882) 4 A keuerlet of red sendel. **1523** LD. BERNERS *Froiss.* I. 740 There was pyght vp a pauilyon of crymasyn sendall, right noble and riche. *c* **1530** —— *Arth. Lyt. Bryt.* (1814) 202 The ymage..blusshed as red as sendall. **1558** in Feuillerat *Revels Q. Eliz.* (1908) 82 Gowlde & sylver sendalls narrowe at xxᵈ the yarde. **1599** THYNNE *Animadv.* (1875) 41 'Sendale'..was a thynne stuffe lyke sarcenette, and of a rawe kynde of sylke or sarcenett, but courser and narrower, then the Sarcenett nowe ys. **1679** BLOUNT *Anc. Tenures* 117 Which horse shall have a saddle..covered with a sendal of the same armes. **1850** LONGF. *By Seaside, Secret of Sea* ii, Sails of silk and ropes of sendal, such as gleam in ancient lore. **1881** F. T. PALGRAVE *Vis. Eng.* 46 One girdled with the vervain-red, And three in sendal gray.

†**2.** As a rendering of L. *sindon*, the word was often understood (even before it became obsolete in sense 1) in the original Gr. and L. sense: Fine linen, lawn; a piece of this, used esp. as a shroud and as a dressing for wounds, etc. *Obs.*

a **1300** *Gosp. Nicod.* (Galba) 722 He wand þat cors..in sendell new and clene. **1382** WYCLIF *Matt.* xxvii. 59 And the body taken, Ioseph wlappide it in a clene sendel, or lynnen cloth. **1470–85** MALORY *Arthur* v. viii. 174 Syxty senatours of Rome..whome the kynge dyd do bawme and..do cere them in syxty fold of cered clothe of Sendale. **1530** PALSGR. 203/2 Cendell thynne lynnen, *sendal.* **1606** HOLLAND *Sueton.* 147 A loose mantle of fine Sendall [*margin* Lawne or Tiffanie].

sendaline (ˈsɛndəlaɪn). *rare*⁻¹. [Extension of SENDAL: see -INE.] = SENDAL.

1865 SWINBURNE *Poems & Ball., Ball. Death* 41 Upon her raiment of dyed sendaline [*rime-word* wine] Were painted all the secret ways of love.

sendee (sɛnˈdiː). [f. SEND *v.*¹ + -EE.] The person to whom a thing is sent.

1806 COLERIDGE *Lett.* (1895) 502 All transmission of papers..highly dangerous both to the sender and sendee. **1869** LUSH in *Law Rep. 4 Q.B. Div.* 714 There is nothing in their [the telegraph company's] special Act which affects their relation either to the sender or the sendee of a message.

sendel, -dell: see SANDAL *sb.*¹, SENDAL.

sender (ˈsɛndə(r)). [f. SEND *v.*¹ + -ER¹.]

a. One who or something which sends (in the various senses of the verb).

c **1200** *Trin. Coll. Hom.* 111 Eft sone he is sendere of alle holie heten. **1587** in Picton *L'pool Munic. Rec.* (1883) I. 115 The bringers and senders thereof. **1642** T. GOODWIN *Heart of Christ* 65 The Sender and Bestower of the holy Ghost. **1667** MILTON *P.L.* IV. 852. **1727** DE FOE *Syst. Magic* I. i. (1840) 4 The gift sent was not suited to the prophet so much as to the sender; he gave as a king. **1885** *Manch. Exam.* 16 Sept. 5/2 The sender of a telegraph message has hence-forth to bear in mind..that [etc.]. **1908** *Q. Rev.* Oct. 303 The countries which are large senders of produce to our markets.

b. One who signals a message.

1904 *Army Signalling Regul.* 123 The Sender..will pay attention to his heliograph, lamp or flag... He will send each word or group as ordered by the caller.

c. The transmitting instrument of a telephone or telegraphic apparatus. = TRANSMITTER.

1879 tr. *Du Moncel's Telephone* 128 Its primary wire is traversed by a current from the local battery, and so also is the sender. **1906** EICHHORN *Wireless Telegr.* vi. 36 Closely-coupled Sender and Receiver.

d. One who or that which moves or enthrals, esp. a popular musician. Also in phr. ***solid sender*** (cf. SOLID *a.* 20). Cf. SEND *v.*¹ 2 c. *slang* (orig. and chiefly *U.S.*).

1935 *Vanity Fair* (N.Y.) Nov. 38/1 None of these plates will be senders. *Ibid.* 71/3 Hot artists or bands that can put across their licks successfully are '*senders*'. **1938** *Metronome* Apr. 26/2 A really solid sender is the third record from the right in my collection. **1938** *Amer. Speech* XIII. 314/2 *Sender*, one who is extremely well-dressed or witty. **1954** [see DRAG *sb.* 3 d]. **1960** *Spectator* 7 Oct. 523 Fabian, the teenagers' sender, indistinguishable from Cliff Richards. **1978** G. VIDAL *Kalki* vi. 147 Arlene was addicted to the slang of her youth. 'A solid sender!' she added, nicely dating herself to World War II during which she entertained the troops.

sendge, obs. form of SINGE *v.*

sendill, obs. form of SENDAL, SENDLE *adv.*

sending (ˈsɛndɪŋ), *vbl. sb.* [f. SEND *v.*¹ + -ING¹.]

1. a. The action of the verb SEND.

c **1400** *Laud Troy Bk.* 15293 He wolde neuere of sendyng blyn, Til he of me answere myȝt wyn. **1450** *Rolls of Parlt.* V. 178/2 By cause of his fals messages, sendynges and writynges. **1627** ABP. ABBOT in Rushw. *Hist. Coll.* (1659) I. 461 Thus..to quicken my remembrance, I have laid down the Cause and the Proceedings of my sending into Kent, where I remain. **1793** BURKE *Corr.* (1844) IV. 153 The sending of the troops..to extirpate our friends in Poitou. **1882** E. R. LANKESTER in *Linn. Soc. Jrnl.* XVI. *Zool.* 460 For repeated sendings of a large number of Italian Scorpions.. I am indebted to [etc.].

b. With adverbs, expressing the action of the verbal combinations: see SEND *v.* Also *attrib.*

c **1375** *Sc. Leg. Saints* xii. (*Mathias*) 301 Be-twene þe ascencione of criste & þe spryte sendynge-done, all þe apostolis semblyt vare. **1456** SIR G. HAYE *Law Arms* (S.T.S.) 142 At the sending for of the Pape. **1540** PALSGR. *Acolastus* II. i. Hiv, After we shall haue assembled our felowshyp togyther (by the sendynge aboute of oure bedyll). **1646** SIR T. BROWNE *Pseud. Ep.* III. xxv. 173 There is little intermission..betweene the drawing in and sending forth of their breath. **1748** *Anson's Voy.* II. xiii. 278 The sending away our prisoners was our last transaction. **1858** *Chamb. Jrnl.* 2 Oct. 209/1 Sending-in Day [Royal Academy]. **1938** *Times* 17 Feb. 15/6 The great expense of the traditional sending-off parties for soldiers called to the colours. **1978** *Rugby World* Apr. 7/3 The laws..make no provision for a foul committed *before* a try—unless it be sending off. **1982** 'W. HAGGARD' *Mischief-Makers* vi. 65 The referee, white, had sent off a black... There was a code which governed sendings-off, particularly in amateur [football] matches.

2. The transmission of a telegraphic or telephonic message. Also *attrib.*

c **1865** *Wylde's Circ. Sci.* I. 271/2 One..ribbon may be carried..over any number of sending machines. **1876** PREECE *Telegraphy* 115 The sending of a clerk after a time loses clearness and legibility. **1906** KENNELLY *Wireless Telegr.* 110 A wireless-telegraph sending station.

3. Something sent.

1599 SHAKS. *Much Ado* II. i. 25 Too curst is more then curst, I shall lessen Gods sending that way. **1842** MRS. CARLYLE *Lett.* I. 138 You ask me how I like your last sendings? **1896** KIPLING *Seven Seas* 117 For I send east and I send west,..And syne my Sendings return to me. They come wi' news [etc.].

4. [ON., in same sense.] An unpleasant or evil thing supposed to be sent by a wizard, or through a wizard at the request of another party, as a punishment or act of revenge.

1864 POWELL & MAGNUSSON *Icel. Legends* 238 If he did not return to them by Christmas-day next, they would despatch a Sending to him who should kill him. **1888** KIPLING *In Black & White* 68 A Sending..is a Thing sent by a wizard. **1915** *Hastings's Encycl. Relig. & Ethics* VIII. 218 A phenomenon analogous to that of the werwolf is that of the 'sending'—a thing or animal, sometimes animated or even created by the sorcerer, or some part of the sorcerer himself (his soul, etc.) and sent out by him to annoy or injure people. **1980** G. HOUSEHOLD *Sending* v. 68 What your Norse shamans and the sagas called a 'sending'..a sort of portable ghost.

sendle, *adv. Sc.* Forms: 6 **sendill, -yll, sindall, -ill, seindill, -ell, seyndil(l, sendle, seindl**, 6–9 **seindle, sindle**, 7–9 **sinle**, 8 **sinal, -ile, synle, seenly**, 8–9 **seenle, senil, seenil**, 9 **seinle, sennil, -el**. [Metathetic alteration of *selden*, SELDOM *adv.*] = SELDOM. Also ***sendle-times*** = seldom-times.

c **1470** HENRYSON *Mor. Fab.* VIII. (*Preach. Swallow*) xxviii, His pray full sindill tymes will be mis. **1501** DOUGLAS *Pal. Hon.* I. xl, I knew that was the court sa variabill Of eirdly lufe, quhilk sendill standis stabill. **1549** *Compl. Scot.* xv. 130 It is rycht seyndil sene that he eschapis the deith. **1588–[89]** *Reg. Privy Council Scot.* IV. 342 The like barbarous and shamefull crueltie hes sendle bene hard of amangis Christeanis. **1644** R. BAILLIE *Lett. & Jrnls.* (1841) II. 191 Only the Saturday free [from exercise], and that for Sunday's preaching, when sinle times any of us does vacke. *c* **1730** RAMSAY *Betty & Kate* iv, Sindle times they e'er come back. **1815** G. BEATTIE *John o' Arnha'* (1826) 24 Frail man, alack! but seenil thinks..That [etc.]. **1862** HISLOP *Prov. Scot.* 8 A gentle horse should be sindle spurr'd.

†ˈ**sendman.** *Obs.* [a. ON. *sendimann-* (nom. *-maðr*), f. stem of *senda* to SEND.] An envoy,

messenger. Cf. *sand-man* (SAND *sb.*[1]), SANDESMAN.

a **1300** *Cursor M.* 21408 þan sent þe king constantin, Send men til his moder eline.

send-off.

1. *colloq.* A friendly demonstration on the occasion of a person's starting on a journey or the like. (Originally *U.S.*) Also *transf.* and *fig.*

The earliest sense of the word appears to be 'a sending off or starting of contestants in a race'.

1841 *Spirit of Times* 18 Dec. 499/2 Sleepy John was the favorite against the field; by bad management of the groom John got a miserable send off and lost at least fifty yards. **1867** *Harper's Mag.* Dec. 135/1 As they say at Jerome Park, a 'good send off' at life's outset is, for one, better than a 'false start'. **1872** 'MARK TWAIN' *Roughing It* (1900) II. vi. 63 One of the boys has passed in his checks, and we want to give him a good sendoff. **1875** *Chicago Tribune* 15 July 1/3 There was considerable jockeying, and..an even send-off [in the boat-race] was not obtained. **1882** *Times* 27 Mar. 4/1 When General Grant went to Europe, he..had a grand 'send-off' on the Delaware. **1899** *Ibid.* 13 Dec. 12/1 The medical officers..gave the slip to the medical students and other admirers who intended to give them an enthusiastic send-off. **1908** G. G. GREENWOOD *Shakespeare Problem Restated* xv. 483 If we could only get to the back of his [*sc.* Jonson's] mind, we should find that there was some efficient cause operating to induce him to give the best possible send-off to that celebrated venture. **1934** [see CASH *v.*[2] 2 c]. **1977** J. MCCLURE *Sunday Hangman* ii. 19 Every warder has to witness at least one little send-off.

attrib. **1876** BESANT & RICE *Gold. Butterfly* xviii, After the funeral Huggins..wrote a beautiful send-off notice. **1889** *Pall Mall Gaz.* 16 Nov. 6/1 Adelina Patti's 'send off' concert.

2. Consignment (of goods).

1909 *Westm. Gaz.* 14 July 4/2 A well-known gang [of bird-catchers for the London market], whose send-off had averaged 500 birds a week.

sendony, variant of SINDONY *Obs.*

†**'sendre**, *v. Obs. rare.* [app. repr. (in Kentish form) OE. *syndrian* to separate, f. *sundor*: see SUNDER *adv.*] *trans.* To purify.

1340 *Ayenb.* 251 Þe ilke welle is zuo clier and zuo y-zendred þet þe herte hire y-knauþ..ane nayre welle wel yzendred.

sendri, obs. form of SUNDRY.

senduolliche, ME. variant of SHENDFULLY.

'send-up. *colloq.* [f. vbl. phr. *to send up*: see SEND *v.*[1] 33 f.] An act of mocking or teasing; a parody, a satire.

1958 A. WILSON *Middle Age of Mrs. Eliot* 355 If she teased him a bit maliciously, it was with such caressing malice that the ragging was more like a flirtation than a 'send up'. **1962** *Guardian* 24 Dec. 4/6 'Merry Christmas You Suckers'.., according to the record company, is 'a send-up of the whole commercialised business'. **1970** G. F. NEWMAN *Sir, You Bastard* iii. 108 Gordon moved away, accepting his opinion as infallible, and never suspecting the blatant send-up. **1976** J. I. M. STEWART *Young Patullo* xi. 256 What had taken place would have been describable a decade later as a send-up.

Sendzimir ('sɛndzɪmɪə(r)). The name of Tadeusz or Thaddeus K. *Sendzimir* (b. 1894), Polish-born American engineer, used *attrib.* with reference to a type of rolling mill developed by him for cold rolling of steel, in which each of two working rolls is supported by two larger rolls, which are themselves backed by three still larger rolls (a further tier of four larger rolls is sometimes used).

1936 *Jrnl. Iron & Steel Inst.* CXXXIV. 166P, In the case of cold rolling mills for wide strip, simpler designs could be developed, like those described by Mr. Nöll. In these forms, however— as in the Sendzimir mill which he described—it was essential to avoid at all costs friction on the pulling drum, which might entail damage to the upper surface of the strip. **1956** W. D. HARGREAVES in D. L. Linton *Sheffield* 294 A Sendzimir mill, which uses work rolls of only 2¼ inches diameter in conjunction with a cluster of backing rolls, operates for the production of thin gauges without intermediate annealing. **1967** A. H. COTTRELL *Introd. Metallurgy* xxii. 442 Long slender rolls are too elastically flexible to compress the metal unless they are supported by heavy backing rolls... This principle has been particularly developed in Rohn and Sendzimir mills for rolling thin foil. **1975** C. M. BLACK tr. *Thelning's Steel & its Heat Treatment* vi. 290 To a large extent the steels are used for tools for shaping and forming. The so-called Sendzimir rolls, i.e. rolls forming a cluster-roll mill, constitute an example of such use.

†**sene**, *sb.*[1] *Obs.* [OE. *séen, sín, séon, sýn*, str. fem. = OS. *siun*, ON. *sión, sýn*, Goth. *siun-s*:—OTeut. **sewni-z*, f. **sew-*: **sehw-* to SEE.] Vision, power of sight. Cf. EYESENE, ONSENE.

a **1000** *Juliana* 468 (Gr.) Oft ic syne ofteah, ablende bealoþoncum beorna unrim. *c* **1000** *Sax. Leechd.* II. 26 Wiþ eagna miste monige men..lociað on ceald wæter..ne wyrt þæt þa seon. *c* **1200** ORMIN 9394 ȝiff þatt tin eȝhe iss all unnhal Wiþþinnenn o þe sene. *a* **1250** *Owl & Night.* 240 Þu hauest a-niȝt wel briȝte sene.

†**sene**, *sb.*[2] *Obs.* Also 5 cene. [a. OF. *sené*:—L. *senātus* SENATE.

The word should etymologically be disyllabic; the metre appears (doubtfully) to indicate a monosyllable, and probably the OF. word was merely adopted in its written form. Even in Fr. some confusion arose between *sené* 'senatus' and *sene* 'synodus' (see next): Cotgr. explains *sené* as synod, and quotes a proverb in which it has clearly that sense.]

= SENATE.

c **1330** R. BRUNNE *Chron. Wace* (Rolls) 3311 Þe Sene seide þey were affrayed. **1422** YONGE tr. *Secreta Secret.* xxix. 168 Therefor hit was cried in the Sene of the Senatowres of Rome. *a* **1470** TIPTOFT *Tulle on Friendship* (Caxton 1481) 4 b, By the lawe that Cassius made, me semeth that I see the people dissevered from the Cene.

†**sene**, *sb.*[3] *Obs.* Forms: 4–5 seyne, 4–6 sene, 5 senne, seeine, seeyne, sean, ceene, 5–6 cene, seyn, seene, seane, 6 seeane, 7 seing. [a. F. *sene, senne*, etc.:—eccl. L. *synodus*, a. Gr. σύνοδος SYNOD. Cf. SENYIE.] A synod, a meeting of clergy for deliberation. Often applied to the bishop's or the archdeacon's visitation; the form *seing* in this use is prob. due to the identification of the word with *seeing* vbl. sb.

1380 *Antecrist* in Todd *Three Treat. Wyclif* (1851) 147 Bi peter pens gederynge bi sute and servyse þat þei owen to seynes and to chapitres. *c* **1425** *Eng. Conq. Irel.* 120/15 Theder he made come to-for hym al the bysshoppes & the clergye of Irland & held hys senne. **1432–50** tr. *Higden* (Rolls) VI. 171 The V[the] vniversalle seeine or cownesayle was kepede..at Aquileia. *c* **1440** *Promp. Parv.* 66 Ceene of clerkys, *sinodus.* **1513** BRADSHAW *St. Werburge* I. 2435 The Seyn was kepte at a place called Alue. **1526** R. WHYTFORD *Martiloge* 100 He kept a generall counseyle or sene at constantynople. **1536** *Act 28 Hen. VIII*, c. 10 §4 Al..archebishops bishops and archedeacons..in euery their visitacion and seanes shall make diligent insearche. **1581** MARBECK *Bk. of Notes* 678 Anselme then Archbishop of Canterbury in a Seane that he helde at London, did make a Decree, that Priests should forsake their wiues.

attrib. **1596** *Churchw. Acc. Pittington*, etc. (Surtees) 270 For our apperance upon the seane daye. **1609** *Ibid.* 61 Item payed when we where before Mr Hutton at the Seing day, xvj d.

†**sene**, *sb.*[4] *Obs.* Also 6 seene, seny, 7 senie. [a. OF. *sené, cené, senet*: see SENNA.] = SENNA.

c **1400** *Lanfranc's Cirurg.* 192 Take xx. damascenes & xij. figis, & vj. datis, sene ʒj. **1436** *Libel Eng. Policy* in *Pol. Poems* (Rolls) II. 173 Wee shulde have no nede to skamonye, ..Rubarde, sené, and yet they bene to nedefulle. **1585** HIGINS *Junius' Nomencl.* 149 *Colutea*..the trifolie tree, or (as some thinke) the sene tree. **1597** GERARDE *Herbal* Table Eng. Names, Bastard Sene or Sene tree. **1625** HART *Anat. Ur.* II. v. 79, I had..drunke of an infusion wherein was some quantitie of Sene leaues. **1651** BIGGS *New Disp.* ¶ 104 Allayed with aloes, rubart, sene,..and the like. **1658** PHILLIPS, *Senie*, the leaf of a medicinable herb which purgeth cholerick and melancholick humours [1671 adds:—see *Sena*].

†**sene, i-sene**, *a. Obs.* Forms: α. 1 ȝesíene, -séne, -sýne, 3 i-sene, 4 a-sene, ysene; β. 3 sen, 4 seine, 4–5 seene. [OE. *ȝesíene, ȝeséne*:—prehistoric **gisewnjo-*, f. **gisewen*, pa. pple. of **sehan, séon* to SEE. The dropping of the prefix was prob. hastened by the influence of the corresponding ON. *sýnn.*] Easy to see, visible, evident, manifest. (In later use blended with *seen* pa. pple. of SEE *v.*)

α. *Beowulf* 1403 Lastas wæron æfter waldswaþum wide ȝesyne. *c* **1205** LAY. 9548 Ȝet hit is isene þat heo wes her quene. **13..** *K. Alis.* 847 Who me loveth now worth a-sene [*Bodl. MS.* ysene]! *c* **1386** CHAUCER *Prol.* 592 Ful longe were his legges and ful lene,..ther was no calf ysene.

β. *c* **1200** ORMIN 2547 Þær wass full sene þatt ȝho wass All full off soþ clænnesse. *c* **1310** *Song agst. Retinues* in *Pol. Songs* (Camden) 239 Sene is on is browe Ant on is eȝebrewe, That he louseth a losynger, And shoyeth a shrewe. *c* **1369** CHAUCER *Dethe Blaunche* 413 And that was sene, For all the woode was waxen grene. *c* **1402** LYDG. *Compl. Bl. Knt.* 437 As it is sene by myn oppressed chere. *c* **1440** *Promp. Parv.* 66/2 Cene, or besene, *apparens, manifestus.* *c* **1480** HENRYSON *Test. Cresseid* 353 'Lo! quhat it is', quod she, 'With fraward langage for to mufe and steir Our crabbit goddis, and sa is sene on me! **1513** DOUGLAS *Æneis* II. x. 27 Hir self scho hid thairfor, and held hir quoye, Beside the altar sittand vnethis sene.

b. Used pleonastically in verse.

1340 HAMPOLE *Pr. Consc.* 7684 And þat ilka myle fully contene A thowsand pases or cubites sene. **13..** *Gaw. & Gr. Knt.* 341, I be-seche now with saȝez sene, Þis melly mot be myne.

c. *well sene*, easy to see; *evil sene*, hard to see.

The former continued as *well seen*(*e* down to the 16th c.; it is still familiar from the example in the Prayer Book, but is now apprehended as a use of the pa. pple.

α. *c* **1205** LAY. 24277 Summe bokes suggeð to iwisse þat þa burh wes biwucched. And þat is wel isene.

β. *a* **1300** *Havelok* 656 Þre dayes þer-biforn, i wene, Et he no mete, þat was wel sene. *a* **1352** MINOT *Poems* (ed. Hall) vii. 104 Sir Philip wanted all his will, þat was wele on his sembland sene. *c* **1386** CHAUCER *Knt.'s T.* 66 Now be we caytyues, as it is wel seene. **1470–85** MALORY *Arthur* II. viii. 85 It is euyl sene..that thou art a true man that thou wolt not telle thy name. **1535** COVERDALE *Ps.* lxvii[i]. 24 It is well sene (o God) how thou goest. [So in Prayer-bk.]

†**sene**, *adv.* and *conj. Sc.* and *north. Obs.* [Var. of SEN, SIN, SYNE *advs.*, etc.] = SINCE.

adj. *c* **1375** *Sc. Leg. Saints* viii. (*Philip*) 62 Quhene he had a ȝer dwelte þare, In asya sene canne he fare. *c* **1470** *Gol. & Gaw.* 286 Thair gat he nane homage,..Of lord of yone lynage, Nor neuer none sene.

conj. **13..** *Gosp. Nicod.* (Galba) 439 Slike sotell talkinges ..was neuer ȝit sene þe world bigan sene in prophecy. *c* **1470** HENRY *Wallace* v. 511 Mony hundreth,..Sene he begane, ar lost with out ramede.

sene, variant of CENE *Obs.*, supper.

c **1450** LOVELICH *Grail* xlviii. 31 Whanne that Iesus his Sene Made.

sene, obs. Sc. form of SAIN *v.*

1691 R. KIRK *Secret Commw.* i. (1815) 3 Who..have made it a Custome..to keep Church duely evry first Sunday of the Quarter to sene or hallow themselves,..from the Shots and Stealth of these wandring Tribes.

sene: see SENYE, SHEEN *a.*, SEE *v.*

Seneca ('sɛnɪkə), *sb.* and *adj.* Also †Senacar, Senecke, Sineque, etc. [ad. N. Amer. Du. *Sennecas, Sennecaas*, collect. name for the Upper Iroquois tribes, perh. orig. a Mahican name for the Oneida or their village.]

A. *sb.* (A member of) one of the five (later, six) tribes of the Iroquois Confederacy of North American Indians; their language. **B.** *adj.* Of or pertaining to this tribe.

Formerly used also to designate the four Upper Iroquois tribes, and the Iroquois collectively.

[*c* **1616** in *Documents Colonial Hist. N.Y.* (1856) I. *facing* p. 11 Sennecas.] **1664** J. WINTHROP *Let.* 6 Feb. in *Mass. Hist. Soc. Coll.* (1863) 4th Ser. VI. 531, 3000 of the Seneckes, a people in league with the Mohawkes beyond them, are gathered together. **1684** *New-Hampshire Hist. Soc. Coll.* (1827) II. 199 The sd Mohauck, Senacar, or other Indians, [shall] be paid out of such monies as shall be raised in the sd Province. **1684** [see ONONDAGA]. **1709** S. SEWALL *Jrnl.* 12 Aug. in *Mass. Hist. Soc. Coll.* (1879) 5th Ser. VI. 262, 300 Eastern Indians..were gon to the 5 Nations to pray leave to dwell with them; and..others refusing them, they were gon to the Senecas. **1724** H. JONES *Pres. State Va.* I. i. 5 The Senecaa Indians in their War Dress may appear as terrible as any of the Sons of Anak. **1775** J. ADAIR *Hist. Amer. Indians* 393 A party of the Senekah Indians came to war against the Katahba. **1823** [see CAYUGA]. **1874** [see ONONDAGA]. **1895** [see SIX *a.* 1 d]. **1900** *Congress. Record* (U.S.) 26 Jan. 1232/2 Among the Seneca Indians a singularly beautiful belief prevailed. **1910** KIPLING *Rewards & Fairies* 187 Senecas aren't Hurons, they're Iroquois, of course, and Toby told him so. **1933** L. BLOOMFIELD *Language* iv. 72 The languages of the Iroquois type ..*Seneca.* **1969** *Observer* (Colour Suppl.) 25 May 61/1 The Iroquois leader Sagoyewatha, known as Red Jacket, was one of the Seneca tribe who fought alongside the British during the American War of Independence. **1976** T. A. SEBEOK *Native Lang. Americas* I. 537 Wright at one time devised a unique set of letters to be used in printing Seneca, but they were never adopted.

C. *attrib.* in **Seneca grass**, a name for Northern holy-grass (*Hierochloa borealis*); **Seneca oil**, a name for crude petroleum (see quot. *a* 1864): now only *Hist.*

1814 J. BIGELOW *Florula Bostoniensis* 245 *Seneca grass. .. An erect, early grass, with a small panicle of short flowers. **1846–50** A. WOOD *Class-bk. Bot.* 608 Seneca grass. **1795** J. SCOTT *U.S. Gazetteer* s.v. *Allegany*, In this county is Oil creek: It flows from a spring much celebrated for a bitumen resembling Barbadoes tar, and is known by the name of *Seneca Oil. **1826** HILDRETH in *Amer. Jrnl. Sci.* X. 5 The other [well] discharges..vast quantities of petroleum, or, as it is vulgarly called 'Seneka oil'. **1833** —— *Ibid.* XXIV. 64 This oil..acquired its name of Seneca oil,..from having been first found in the vicinity of Seneca Lake, N. York. *a* **1864** GESNER *Coal, Petrol.*, etc. (1865) 16 Under the name of 'Seneca Oil' which it derived from an Indian tribe, petroleum was formerly collected in Chatauque County, N.Y., and in Crawford County, Pennsylvania, and sold for medicinal purposes. **1910** KIPLING *Rewards & Fairies* 161 He took orders for that famous Seneca Oil which he had the secret of from Red Jacket's Indians. **1959** *Chambers's Encycl.* X. 619/1 In North America crude oil was undoubtedly used by the Indians, and Seneca oil skimmed from the surface of water near Lake Seneca..utilized for rheumatism, coughs, burns, sprains etc.

'Senecal, *a.* Now only in allusion to Chapman's use (see quot. 1612). [f. *Seneca* + -AL[1].] Characteristic of, or conformable to the principles of the Stoic philosopher L. Annæus Seneca (died A.D. 65). Also as *sb.*: a writer of drama in the Senecan manner; *spec.*, one of a group of early seventeenth-century playwrights (see quot. 1926).

1600 W. WATSON *Decacordon* (1602) 102 Euery word when it comes to a pragmaticall practise, hath close couched in it the energy of a Senecall sentence. **1612** CHAPMAN *Rev. Bussy d'Ambois* IV. iv. 42 In short, this Senecal man is found in him,..To whom the day and fortune equal are..Fix'd in himself, he still is one to all. **1926** T. S. ELIOT in *Times Lit. Suppl.* 9 Dec. 906/3 In the effort to 'place' Davies, who appears anomalous, critics have compared him..to the Senecals, to Chapman and Daniel and Greville... The type of his thought..separates him from the Senecals. **1934** H. ELLIS *Chapman* 62 Chapman often refers to Seneca and the 'Senecal men', and he was also influenced by Epictetus. **1954** E. REES *Tragedies of George Chapman* iv. 114 Chapman was too much of a humanist to forget that even a 'Senecal man' is human.

Senecan ('sɛnɪkən), *a.* [f. *Seneca* + -AN.] Pertaining to Seneca (see prec.) and the tragedies written by him and his imitators. Hence **'Senecanism**.

1885 J. M. HART in *Nation* 26 Mar. 264/2 The Senecan spirit of the 'Gorboduc' writers. **1903** SECCOMBE & ALLEN *Age of Shaks.* I. 52 In 1594 appeared his [Daniel's] Senecan tragedy *Cleopatra*. **1934** T. S. ELIOT *Elizabethan Essays* 40 Much of Chapman's Senecanism has lately been shown..to be directly borrowed from Erasmus. **1978** *Studies in Eng. Lit.: Eng. Number* (Tokyo) 173 Jonson's use of Hoskyns' essay as a foundation for his own brand of Senecanism looks back to the past as well as to the future in the development of English prose.

'Senecaster. *nonce-wd.* [-ASTER.] An imitator of Seneca.

1884 SYMONDS *Shaks. Predecessors* 227 Though.. written by Senecasters of the purest water, both [plays] are founded upon ancient English fables.

senechal, variant of SENESCHAL.

senecio (sɛ'niːʃɪəʊ, -sɪəʊ, -'ɛkɪəʊ). [L. *senecio* old man, groundsel, in reference to the hairy pappus of the plant: adopted by Linnæus (*Hortus Cliffortianus* (1737) 406) as the name of a genus: cf. SENCION.] An annual or perennial herb or shrub of the large genus so called, which belongs to the family Compositæ and includes many cultivated plants and a few poisonous ones. Cf. GROUNDSEL *sb.*[1] 1, JACOBÆA 1, RAGWORT[1] 1.

1562, 1657 [see GROUNDSEL *sb.*[1] 1]. **1784** J. ABERCROMBIE *Propagation & Botanical Arrangement Plants & Trees* II. 678 *(heading) Senecio longifolius.* Long-leaved Cape Senecio. **1859** D. BUNCE *Travels with Dr. Leichhardt* ix. 105, I obtained specimens of.. a.. new species of *Stackhousia*, and a yellow, flowering *Senecio*. **1896** E. J. VON DADELSZEN *N.Z. Year-Bk.* 470 There are several kinds of ranunculus, and a bewildering variety of celmesias.. and senecios also flourish. **1902** L. H. BAILEY *Cycl. Amer. Hort.* IV. 1656/1 A distinguishing mark of the Senecios lies in the character of the involucre. **1920** *Lancet* 23 Oct. 848/2 Senecio disease, or cirrhosis of the liver due to senecio poisoning... We have called the condition about to be described 'senecio disease' for want of a more appropriate name. **1954** *New Biol.* XVII. 14 The unique African alpine flora of giant Senecios (members of the same genus as common groundsel). **1975** P. LIVELY *Going Back* i. 4, I came out.. past the buddleias and senecios past the iris garden hedge.

senectitude (sɪ'nɛktɪtjuːd). [ad. med.L. *senectitūd-o* (*c* 800 in Du Cange), irreg. f. *senectūs*: see SENECTUTE and -TUDE.] Old age.

1796 *Mod. Gulliver* 49 Persons, of all ages, from twenty to extreme senectitude. **1898** B. GREGORY *Side Lights* 482 Replete with the mild wisdom of senectitude.

senectude (sɪ'nɛktjuːd). [Badly f. L. *senectūs*: see prec. and -TUDE.] = prec.

1756 H. JOHNSON in J. Duncombe *Lett.* (1773) III. 50 The word 'senectude', which you enquire after, is derived from *senex, senectus*. **1831** *Fraser's Mag.* III. 485 Did you think to conceal the heinousness of your tergiversation under the mask of senectude? **1863** READE *Hard Cash* III. iv. 103 The Archbold had not deigned to make him safe; senectude [**1868** xli, senectitude] had done that.

†**se'nectute.** *Obs. rare.* [ad. L. *senectūt-em*, f. *senex* old man: see SENIOR *a.*] Old age.

1481 CAXTON *Tulle of Old Age* Pref., And in especial unto them that.. ben approchid unto senectute callyd olde and auncient eage. **1533** ELYOT *Cast. Helthe* (1541) 13 Ages be foure: Adolescency to xxv yeres:.. Senectute unto lx yeres.

senefee, variant of SENVY *Obs.*, mustard.

senega ('sɛnɪgə). Also 8 senegaw, senekka, 8–9 seneka, seneca. [app. identical with SENECA (see quot. 1738); the forms with *g* may be due to association with *(gum) senega = gum Senegal*.] The N. American plant *Polygala Senega*. Also a drug obtained from the root of this plant, formerly used as an antidote for snake-bite. Also *attrib.*

1738 TENNENT *Epist. to Mead* 5 At last I was informed.. that there was a Root discovered by the Seneca Indians which was a certain Remedy against the Bite of the Rattle-snake,.. and was distinguished.. by the Name of Seneca Rattle-snake Root. **1748** W. LEWIS *Pharmacopoeia* 63 Seneka, the root. Senegaw rattle-snake-root. **1753** *Chambers's Cycl.* Suppl. s.v. *Polygala*, The trials.. made of the virtues of the Senekka rattlesnake root, recommended by Dr. Tennent. **1799** *Med. Jrnl.* II. 170 He prescribed the taraxacum, senega, and radix graminis, in decoctions. **1877** F. T. ROBERTS *Handbk. Med.* (ed. 3) I. 390 Ammonia and senega may be given, if there is much debility. **1896** BRANNT *Anim. & Veg. Fats* (ed. 2) II. 458 Senega oil..., Senega, *Polygala Senega*... The root contains fat oil, resin [etc.].

Senegal ('sɛnɪgɔːl, senɪ'gɔːl). [The name of a river and a republic, formerly a French overseas territory, in western Africa.] **1.** Used *attrib.* in names of local animals and plants.

1783 J. LATHAM *Gen. Synopsis Birds* IV. 456 Senegal Warbler, *Motacilla Senegalensis*. Length five inches and a quarter... Inhabits Senegal. **1781** T. PENNANT *Hist. Quadrupeds* I. 91 Antelope.. Senegal. *Antilope Bubalis*.. with horns almost close at the base, a little above bending out greatly... Inhabits Senegal. **1833** *Penny Cycl.* I. 187/1 The Senegal custard apple (*Anona Senegalensis*). **1896** H. A. BRYDEN *Tales S. Afr.* 60 Great spur-heeled Senegal cuckoos flapped heavily from one reed-bed to another. **1952** MACKWORTH-PRAED & GRANT *Birds E. & N.-E. Afr.* I. 516 Senegal Coucal. *Centropus senegalensis.* **1966** C. SWEENEY *Scurrying Bush* xi. 158 The Senegal galago is one of the commonest mammals in the Nuba Mountains in southern Kordofan.

2. Special Comb. *Senegal gum* = *gum-senegal* s.v. GUM *sb.*[2] 3 a.

1867 P. L. SIMMONDS *Dict. Trade* (rev. ed.) Suppl. 454/1 *Senegal gum*, an African gum obtained from *Acacia Senegalensis*. **1951** KIRK & OTHMER *Encycl. Chem. Technol.* VII. 332 Kordofan gum is the finest gum obtainable... Senegal gum ranks second in importance and is much used for technical purposes although some of the better grades are used in pharmaceutical work.

Senegalese (ˌsɛnɪgə'liːz, -gɔː'l-), *sb.* and *a.* [f. prec. + -ESE.] **A.** *sb.* A native or inhabitant of Senegal. **B.** *adj.* Of or pertaining to Senegal.

Formerly applied loosely to an inhabitant of any French colony in West or Central Africa.

1917 *19th Cent.* Feb. 313 The Senegalese were in the fight with us. **1919** H. H. JOHNSTON *Compar. Stud. Bantu & Semi-Bantu Langs.* p. vi The facilities accorded to me in 1915 to visit the camps and hospitals of the 'Senegalese' soldiers in France. This assemblage of negroes from all parts of French West and West-Central Africa was a singularly fortunate circumstance. **1926** *Blackw. Mag.* Oct. 501/1 His French was fluent,.. the French of the Senegalese troops. **1938** L. BEMELMANS *Life Class* II. ii. 131 In the Ballroom kitchen, Kalakobé the Senegalese is dragging the huge casseroles up out of the elevator. **1978** *Black World* May 93/1 The struggle of the Senegalese against the invading French forces nearly a century ago. **1980** *Times Lit. Suppl.* 24 Oct. 1200/2 The belligerent exchange between the Senegalese writers at Frankfurt was symbolic of larger antagonisms.

Senegambian (sɛnə'gæmbɪən), *sb.* and *a.* [f. *Senegambia* (see below) + -AN.]

A. *sb.* A native or inhabitant of Senegambia, former name of the region surrounding the Senegal and Gambia rivers in West Africa (cf. SENEGAL, GAMBIA); *U.S. colloq.*, applied to a Black American. **B.** *adj.* Of or pertaining to Senegambia; also used of Black Americans.

Senegambia is the name of a confederation of Senegal and Gambia, formed for military and trade purposes in February 1982; both countries retain their sovereignty; the president of Senegal is president of the confederation.

1900 *Dialect Notes* II. 58 *Senegambian*, a negro or negress. **1902** *Encycl. Dict.* Suppl. 646/3 Senegambian. **1911** *Encycl. Brit.* XXIV. 642/2 The conquest of the Senegambian region by the French followed. **1920** W. C. WITWER in *Collier's* 11 Dec. 21/1 A little bimbo.. is struttin' around and bellerin' about the undaunted white race to a big fat grinnin' Senegambian porter. **1942** W. FAULKNER *Go down, Moses* 49 What the hell kind of Senegambian Montague and Capulet is this any-how? **1943** G. S. SCHUYLER in *Pittsburgh Courier* 11 Sept. 13/7 There are thousands of Negroes living in similar or better houses, despite the race hustling talk about the 'horrible houses' of Harlem. All the civilized Senegambians live in good homes. **1947** *Publ. Amer. Dial. Soc.* VIII. 36 *Senegambian.* I am acquainted with this word as meaning a Negro from Senegambia—whether ten, fifteen, or fifty years old. Used as a term of contempt. **1970** P. OLIVER *Savannah Syncopators* 70 The importance of the Senegambian slave trade lies in the accessibility of these parts to the Sudan savannah interior.

senegin ('sɛnɪgɪn). Also 9 seneg(u)ine. [f. SENEGA + -IN.] An amorphous glucoside, consisting of sapogenin and sugar, obtained from senega.

1830 LINDLEY *Nat. Syst. Bot.* 146 A peculiar vegetable principle, called Senegin, has been discovered by Gehlen in the root of *Polygala senega*. **1845** W. GREGORY *Outl. Chem.* II. 459 Seneguine is an acrid.. substance, found in *Polygala senega*. **1853** ROYLE *Man. Mat. Med.* (ed. 2) 329 The Polygalic acid, Senegine of Gehlen, and Polygaline of others.

senegog, obs. form of SYNAGOGUE.

senei, var. SENVY.

seneiour: see SEIGNIOR.

†**'senek(e.** *Obs. rare*[−1]. [ad. L. *senex* old man.] An 'elder', one of authority on account of the dignity proper to his age.

a **1400** *Pistill of Susan* (MS. P.) 301 And sodenly a seneke [*MS. C.* þat senek] þei broght in to sale.

seneour, obs. form of SEIGNIOR, SENIOR.

senesce (sɪ'nɛs), *v.* [ad. L. *senēsc-ĕre*, f. *sen-em* (*senex*) old: see -ESCE.] *intr.* To grow old.

1656 BLOUNT *Glossogr.* **1894** STEVENSON *Lett.* (1899) II. 321 It gets a little stale, and my work will begin to senesce. **1909** G. B. SHAW *Let.* 22 June (1972) II. 847, I am not adolescing but senescing. **1955** *New Biology* XVIII. 12 If they [*sc.* experimental animals] do not senesce, they will tend to decrease in number exponentially. **1965** J. D. SALINGER in *New Yorker* 19 June 34/1 Few of these.. boys will mature. The majority.. will merely senesce. **1979** *Nature* 5 July 55/2 The secondary compounds that deter grazers while the plants are alive do not disappear immediately when plants senesce and die.

senescence (sɪ'nɛsəns). [f. SENESCENT: see -ENCE.] The process or condition of growing old.

1695 WOODWARD *Nat. Hist. Earth* I. 61 The Earth, Sea, and all natural things will continue in the state wherein they now are, without the least Senescence or Decay. **1757** MRS. GRIFFITH *Lett. Henry & Frances* (1767) III. 138 The several Seasons of Life, open, with Novelty, to Childhood, to Youth, to Manhood, to Senescence. **1887** A. H. CUMMINS *Gram. O. Fries.* 17 In the senescence of the language.

b. *Biol.* (See quot.)

1879 MINOT *Probl. Age*, etc. App. v. (1908) 270 *Senescence*. With each successive generation of cells the power of growth diminishes... This loss of power I term senescence.

†**se'nescency.** *Obs.* [f. next: see -ENCY.] Senescence.

1669 *Addr. Hopef. Young Gentry Eng.* 132 We may guess .. the worlds age not so full of the aggravated Symptoms of its Senescency.

senescent (sɪ'nɛsənt), *a.* [ad. L. *senēscent-em*, pr. pple. of *senēscĕre* to grow old: see SENESCE *v.* and -ENT.] Growing old, elderly.

1656 BLOUNT *Glossogr.*, *Senescent*, waxing old, growing in age, wearing away, drawing to the wain. *a* **1843** SOUTHEY *Doctor* cxci. (1848) 505 Senescent spinsters and dowagers. **1878** STUBBS *Lect. Med. & Mod. Hist.* (1886) 153 It is not a dead but a living language, senescent, perhaps, but in a green old age. **1893** *Nation* 13 July 33/3 Great convenience to scholars, especially to those with senescent eyesight, would be secured by such a restoration.

seneschal ('sɛnɪʃəl). Forms: 4–5, 7 senescal(l, 4–7 seneschall, 5 senescha, senesshawle, senceall, sencial, sencyal, 5, 9 seneshall, 6–8 seneshal, 7 scenechal, 4– seneschal. [a. OF. *seneschal* (mod.F. *sénéchal*) = Pr. *senescal-s*, Sp., Pg. *senescal*, It. *siniscalco, sescalco*; a Com. Rom. word ad. Teut. **seniscalc* (latinized *seniscalcus, siniscalcus*, in the Frankish and Alamannic laws), f. OTeut. **seni-* old (in Goth. *sinista* superl. of *sineigs* old) + **skalko-z* servant (Goth. *skalk-s*, OHG. *scalc*, OE. *scealc*). The Fr. word was adopted in MHG. as *seneschalt, scheneschlant*.]

1. An official in the household of a sovereign or great noble, to whom the administration of justice and entire control of domestic arrangements were entrusted. In wider use: a steward, 'major-domo'.

1393 LANGL. *P. Pl.* C. I. 93 Somme aren as seneschals and seruen oþere lordes. *a* **1450** *Knt. de la Tour* (1868) 86 Amon was seneschalle of the king. **1470–85** MALORY *Arthur* I. xiv. 55 Thenne syr kay cam vnto syr Morganore sencial with the king of the C knyghtes. **1596** SPENSER *F.Q.* VI. i. 15 Which to prouide, she hath this Castle dight, And therein hath a Seneschall assynd. **1612** DAVIES *Why Ireland*, etc. 221 These great Lordes.. managed their estates heere, by their Seneschals and Seruants. **1667** MILTON *P.L.* IX. 38 Then marshal'd Feast Serv'd up in Hall with Sewers, and Seneshals. **1725** POPE *Odyss.* IV. 47 The Seneshal rebuk'd, in haste withdrew. **1818** SCOTT *Hrt. Midl.* li, The respectable gentleman who acts as seneschal on the Duke's domains. **1875** MAINE *Hist. Instit.* v. 139 Whence came this great exaltation of.. great Seneschal or Steward.

fig. **1854** EMERSON *Lett. & Soc. Aims* Wks. (Bohn) III. 176 For example, what a seneschal and detective is laughter!

b. A cathedral official in England.

1882 *Standard* 31 Aug. 3/5 Mr. H. G. Austin, the Cathedral seneschal, said the Chapter [Canterbury] did not press for a heavy penalty.

2. As the title of a governor of a city or province, and of various administrative or judicial officers. Now only *Hist.* exc. with reference to the Channel Islands.

c **1400** *Brut* 232 To bene Senescal and wardein of Gascoigne. **1539** in Hore *Hist. Wexford* (1900) I. 239 Wm. Seyntlow.. beyng chief officer of the said shire by the name of Seneschall. **1580** HOLLYBAND *Treas. Fr. Tong*, *Seneschaux*,.. Seneschals, Bailifs, other officers or stewardes of courtes. **1586** *Cal. St. Papers, Irel.* 1586–1588, 41 Nicholas Dawtrey, gent., Seneschal of Claneboy. *c* **1630** RISDON *Surv. Devon* (1810) 13 The High Seneschal of the Dutchy of Cornwall.. in English.. is termed Lord Warden. **1675** *Essex Papers* (Camden) I. 309 All is forfited & taken up by the Shiriffe or Senescall. **1862** ANSTED *Channel Isl.* IV. xxiii. (ed. 2) 537 The court at Sark consists of the seneschal, or judge, or his deputy, the prevôt and the greffier.

3. *attrib.*

1756 *Gentl. Mag.* XXVI. 333 The officers of the seneschal jurisdiction of Auvergne.

†**'seneschally.** *Obs. rare.* [a. OF. *seneschallie*, f. *seneschal*: see prec.] The territory under the government of a seneschal.

1700 J. BROME *Trav. Eng., Journ.* iii. (1707) 179 These [Counties] are subdivided.. into divers Seneschallies or Sheriffdoms. **1708** J. CHAMBERLAYNE *St. Gt. Brit.* II. II. v. (1710) 413 After the Seneschally came to the Crown, these Officers were called *Magistri Hospitii Regis*.

seneschalship ('sɛnɪʃəlˌʃɪp). *Hist.* Also 6 senshalship. [f. SENESCHAL + -SHIP.]

1. The office and functions of a seneschal.

1580 HOLLYBAND *Treas. Fr. Tong*, *Seneschaussée*, Seneschalship, or Stewardship. **1612** DAVIES *Why Ireland*, etc. 278 Graunts of Captaine-shippes or Seneschal-shippes, in the Irish Countries. **1878** SIMPSON *Sch. Shaks.* I. 57 The Seneschallship of Wexford.. was worth but £20 Irish a year.

†**2.** = SENESCHALSY 1. *Obs.*

1586 T. B. *La Primaud. Fr. Acad.* I. 561 One citie and political communion, compounded of manie.. Provostships, Bailiweekes, Senshalships [etc.]. **1741** tr. *D'Argens' Chinese Lett.* vi. 35 A Man, who has lost his Cause before the Judges of the Bailywic, appeals to those of the Seneschalship. **1804** tr. *Picquenard's Zoflora* II. 63 The tribunals of the seneschalships, and all the superior councils of the island. **1837** W. F. SKENE *Highlanders* II. v. 153 One branch possessed the seneschalship, and another branch the office of baillie of the Abthainrie of Dull.

seneschalsy ('sɛnɪʃəlsɪ). *Fr. Hist.* Forms: 5 seneschalcie, 7 seneschalsie, 7, 9 seneschalcy, 7– seneschalsy. [a. OF. *seneschalcie*, ad. med.L. *seniscalcia*, f. *seniscalcus* SENESCHAL.]

1. A territory under the government of a seneschal. Cf. SENESCHALTY.

1475 *Bk. Noblesse* (Roxb.) 38 [So he] toke the homages of alle the vassallis and subgettis in the seneschalcie of Agenois. **1700** TYRRELL *Hist. Eng.* II. 707 Out of whose hands he had taken.. the Seneschalsy of Anjou. **1837** CARLYLE *Fr. Rev.* I.

IV. ii, By Bailliages, by Seneschalsies, in whatsoever form men convene.

2. a. The administrative seat of a seneschal. **b.** The office of seneschal.

1652 HEYLIN *Cosmogr.* I. 181 An Episcopall See, and the Seneschalsie for all the Countrie of Begorre. **1898** *Eng. Hist. Rev.* Jan. 137 He believes the evidence may be trusted..of the Count of Anjou's claim to the seneschalcy.

seneschalty (ˈsɛnɪʃəltɪ). *Fr. Hist.* [f. SENESCHAL + -TY.] = SENESCHALSY 1.

1577 *F. de L'isle's Legendarie* G v, The deputies of about fourty baylywickes and Seneschaltyes of the realme. **1880** *Sat. Rev.* 25 Dec. 808/1 The Lieutenant-General of the Seneschalty.

ˈseneschaunce. *Obs. rare*$^{-1}$. [erroneous form of next.] = SENESCHALSY 1.

1525 LD. BERNERS *Froiss.* II. clx. 178 The gouernyng of Languedocke was taken awaye fro the duke of Berrey, and deuyded in to Seneschaunces in the kynges profyte [orig. *remys par membres & seneschaussees au prouffit du roy*].

†**ˈseneschausee.** *Obs.* [a. F. *sénéchaussée*, irreg. f. *sénéchal* SENESCHAL.] = SENESCHALSY 1.

1647 COTTERELL *Davila's Hist. Fr.* II. 66 These being divided into 30 Precincts or Jurisdictions, which they call Baillages or Seneschausees.

senester, -tre, obs. forms of SINISTER *a.*

senet, senett: see SENNIGHT, SINET.

seneuei, seneuey(e, seneuy, var. ff. SENVY.

senew(e, senewy, obs. ff. SINEW, SINEWY.

‖**senex** (ˈsɛnɛks). Pl. **senes.** [L., old man.] In literary contexts, the stock figure of an old man. Also in various L. phrases. Cf. OLD MAN 1 g.

1898 E. P. MORRIS *Captives & Trinummus of Plautus* p. xxxvi, Hegio becomes in part the *comicus stultus senex*, chiefly concerned with the humiliation of having been deceived. **1923** G. NORWOOD *Art of Terence* v. 76 How much better to collect the necessary funds permanently and elegantly from the *senes*! *Ibid.* vii. 128 Micio has gone back to his normal position of a *lepidus senex*. **1957** N. FRYE *Anat. Criticism* 172 Central to the *alazon* [*sc.* imposter] group is the *senex iratus* or heavy father. **1957** F. N. ROBINSON *Wks. Chaucer* (ed. 2) 684/1 The Oxford carpenter is an example of the familiar figure of the 'senex amans'. **1968** E. SEGAL *Roman Laughter* iv. 119 Plautus makes the inversion of status still more meaningful for his countrymen by presenting as comic butts *senes* who are also *senatores*. **1975** H. A. KELLY *Love & Marriage in Age of Chaucer* xi. 271 William Langland, writing when he himself was admittedly a *senex non potens*, shows that the sentiment could be held seriously in a less absurd match than that between January and May. **1977** *Times Lit. Suppl.* 20 May 623/3 An archetypal comedy plot, deprecating December/May marriages and involving the victory of the young man over the *senex*... The emotions of a comic *senex*.

seneyt, obs. form of SENNIGHT.

senfte, senfulle, obs. ff. SEVENTH, SINFUL.

senge: see SENYE *Obs.*, SIGN *sb.*, SINGE *v.*

sengeley, -ell(e, -il(l, obs. ff. SINGLY, SINGLE *a.*

senȝe, senȝhe, senȝie: see SENYE, SENYIE.

†**ˈsengilbond.** *Obs. rare*$^{-1}$. [? f. *sengle* = CINGLE + BOND *sb.*[1]] An encircling band.

1479 *Inv.* in *Paston Lett.* III. 272 Another mater sownde in the botom and a sengilbonde viij unc.' & j quarter.

sengle, obs. f. CINGLE (girth), SINGLE *sb.* and *a.*

sengler, senglet: see SINGLER *a.*, SINGLET.

sengreen (ˈsɛngriːn). Now *dial.* (see *Eng. Dial. Dict.* s. vv. *Sengreen, Silgreen, Singreen*). Forms: α. 1 **singréne**, 3, 6 **sin-**, (5 **sine-**), 5–6 **sen-**, (6 **sene-**), **syngrene**, (5 **sygryme**, 6 **singren**), 6–7 **sengreene**, (7 **sean-**, **sem-**, **syngreen**), 7– **sengreen**. β. 5 **silfgrene**, 6 **selfegre(e)ne**, 9 *dial.* **sil(l)green**, etc. [OE. *singréne*, subst. use of *singréne* adj., evergreen:— OTeut. **sengrōnjo-*, f. **sen-*:—pre-Teut. **sem-* one, always (in Goth. *sin-teins* daily, OE. *sin-niht* eternal night; cogn. w. L. *semel* once, *semper* always, *sim-plex* simple, Gr. εἷς:—**sems*, etc.) + **grōnjo-* GREEN *a.* Cf. MLG. *singrone*, MDu. *sindegroen* (mod.Du. *senegroen*), MHG. *singrüen* (mod.G. *sinngrün*), names for periwinkle and other evergreen plants; ON. *sígrǿnn* adj., evergreen.]

1. The houseleek, *Sempervivum tectorum.*

α. *c* **1000** *Sax. Leechd.* I. 152 Ðeos wyrt þe man singrene nemneð..ys swyðe fremful. *c* **1265** *Voc. Plants* in Wr.-Wülcker 558 *Iouis barba*, iubarbe, singrene. *a* **1425** tr. *Arderne's Treat. Fistula*, etc. 64 Rubarbe [*read* iubarbe], i. sengrene. *c* **1440** *Pallad. on Husb.* I. 853 Thy seed with Iuce of rukel or syngrene To wete, vp sleeth the rukel. **1601** HOLLAND *Pliny* XXVI. vii. II. 247 Or els to take Iubarbe, *i.* Sengreene, to the same effect. **1641** FRENCH *Distill.* iv. (1651) 104 Macerate them in water of Sengreen. **1874** HARDY *Far fr. Mad. Crowd* ix, The houseleek or sengreen.

β. *c* **1475** *Pict. Voc.* in Wr.-Wülcker 787 *Hoc jurbarium*, a silfgrene. **1526** *Grete Herball* ccclxxxi. (1529) Xij, De semper viua Howsleke or selfegrene. **1570** LEVINS *Manip.* 69/43 Selfegreene, *semper viuum.* **1825** E. HEWLETT *Cottage Comforts* xi, Mallow..and houseleek, (or sillgreen).

b. *Her.* Used as a bearing.

c **1550** *Arms of Caius* in J. W. Clark *Cambridge* (1881) 69 In the mydelle of the cheyfe sengrene resting vppon the heades of ii serpentes in pale.

2. Applied to other plants, *esp.* **a.** the sedums; **b.** varieties of saxifrage; **c.** the periwinkle, *Vinca minor*; **d. water sengreen**, *Stratiotes aloides.*

c **1000** *Sax. Leechd.* II. 54 þa smalan singrenan. **1555** EDEN *Decades* (Arb.) 175 That which is commonly cauled Sengrene or Orpin. **1578** LYTE *Dodoens* I. lxxvii. 114 Amongst the kindes of Sengreene also, at this time there is conteyned, the herbe (called *Crassula minor*) whiche is great stone Crop, called of some wilde Prickmadam, or wormegrasse. **1597** GERARDE *Herbal* II. cclxxxv. 677 Water Sengreene, or fresh water Soldier. **1629** PARKINSON *Parad.* 231 *Sedum serratum flore rubente maculato.* The Princes Feather. This kinde of Sengreene is composed of heads of larger..leaues. **1731** MILLER *Gard. Dict.* s.v. *Saxifraga, Saxifraga Alpina ericoides, flore cæruleo...* Mountain Heath-like Sengreen with a blue Flower. **1777** JACOB *Plantæ Faversh.* 102 White Saxifrage, or Sen-green. **1796** WITHERING *Brit. Plants* (ed. 3) II. 402 *Chrysosplenium alternifolium...* Alternate-leaved Sengreen. *a* **1851** W. A. BROMFIELD *Flora Vect.* (1856) 306 *Vinca minor*, L. Lesser Periwinkle. Vect. Sengreen.

sengyl, obs. form of SINGLE *a.*

‖**senhor** (seˈɲor). [Pg. *senhor* = Sp. *señor*, It. *signor*, F. *seigneur*:—L. *seniōr-em*, acc. of *senior* SENIOR *a.* and *sb.*] In Portuguese use, or with reference to Portuguese: A term of respect placed before the name of a man in addressing him or speaking of him, equivalent to the English 'Mr.' Also used without the name as a form of address, equivalent to 'sir' in English. Hence, a Portuguese gentleman.

1795 J. MURPHY *Trav. Portugal* 31, I am sorry, Senhors, (said she,) that you have not rested well. **1830** *Portugal; or Yng. Travellers* 56 Senhor Macedo..turning to Mr. Grey, said, smilingly: 'This is good policy, is it not, Senhor?' *Ibid.*, The lively sallies of the Senhor. **1853** A. R. WALLACE *Amazon & Rio Negro* 198 Though Senhor L. is well acquainted with the river, we here almost lost our way.

‖**senhora** (seˈɲora). [Pg. *senhora* = Sp. *señora*, It. *signora*, a fem. formed upon *senhor*, etc.; see SENHOR.] A term of respect applied to Portuguese ladies; hence (with *a, the*, etc.) a Portuguese lady.

1802 SOUTHEY *Lett.* (1856) I. 193 To Miss Barker. Senhora Barkeriana,—it is but an awkward way of expressing the tune of those words. *Ibid.* 194 And do you, Senhora, instruct yourself in the Creed [etc.]. **1841** LEVER *Chas. O'Malley* xl, It was the Senhora's voice. **1874** LADY JACKSON *Fair Lusitania* 82 A staid middle-aged senhora.

‖**senhorita** (seɲoˈrita). [Pg. dim. of prec.] A term of respect applied to a young Portuguese lady; hence, a young Portuguese lady.

1874 LADY JACKSON *Fair Lusitania* 61 There is..perhaps a furtive kiss, and the senhora, or senhorita, glides off quickly by the bye-paths to a *coupé* that awaits her.

Senhouse (ˈsɛnhaʊs). *Naut.* [Origin unknown.] In full, ***Senhouse slip.*** A slip (SLIP *sb.*[3] 3 e) designed to secure the end of a cable.

1923 *Man. Seamanship* (Admiralty) II. ix. 163 The special towing Senhouse slip is inserted between the first and second shackle of the cable. **1948** R. DE KERCHOVE *Internat. Maritime Dict.* 648/2 *Senhouse slip*, a short length of chain of the same strength as the anchor cable, with a slip hook at one end and a shackle at the other. It is shackled to the cable clench, its purpose being to allow the bitter end of the cable to be easily slipped in case of emergency. **1961** F. H. BURGESS *Dict. Sailing* 183 *Senhouse*, a large slip in the cable locker near the clench bolt for holding the cable should it have to be unbolted and slipped. **1963** P. J. ABRAHAM *Last Hours* 135 He remembered knocking the Senhouse slip on one of the gripes away. **1976** *Oxf. Compan. Ships & Sea* 126/2 *Senhouse slip...* Its normal place in a ship used to be in the cable lockers where the inboard end of the cable is secured, but in several modern ships the end of the cable is shackled on to a deck bolt in the locker, no Senhouse slip being used. Smaller Senhouse slips are used in many smaller vessels and yachts to hold the ends of the guard-rails to the stanchions.

senical, erron. form of SINICAL.

ˈsenicide. *rare.* [f. L. *seni-*, *senex* old man + -CIDE 2.] The killing of the old men of a tribe, etc.

1889 H. H. JOHNSTON in *Fortn. Rev.* XLV. 24 Although they are never accused of superadding cannibalism to 'senicide', still the ancient Sardi of Sardinia regarded it as a sacred..duty for the young to kill their old relations. **1931** R. R. MARETT in W. Rose *Outl. Mod. Knowledge* 419 One must not make too much of the occasional cases of..senicide, namely, the putting away of the old.

senie, variant of SENE *sb.*[3]

senight(e, senil: see SENNIGHT, SENDLE.

senile (ˈsiːnaɪl), *a.* [ad. L. *senīlis*, f. *sen-em*, *senex* old man: see -ILE. Cf. F. *sénile* (16th c.).]

1. a. Belonging to, suited for or incident to old age. Now only of diseases, etc.: Peculiar to the aged.

1661 BOYLE *Style of Script.* To Rdr. 2 A Person in whom Nature, Education, and Time have happily Match'd a Senile Maturity of Judgement with a Youthfull Vigour of Phansie. **1797** JEFFERSON *Writ.* (1859) IV. 192 To exchange the roar and tumult of bulls and bears, for the prattle of my grand-children and senile rest. **1866** A. FLINT *Princ. Med.* (1880) 284 The form of emphysema distinguished as atrophous or senile. **1874** MAUDSLEY *Mental Dis.* iii. 83 Senile insanity. **1875** B. W. RICHARDSON *Dis. Mod. Life* 108 There is local death, or what is called senile gangrene.

b. *Path.* **senile dementia**, a severe form of senile deterioration, in which loss of memory, disorientation in time and space, and inability to cope with everyday life are strongly marked. Hence **senile dement**, one who suffers from this. Cf. DEMENTIA.

1851 R. DUNGLISON *Dict. Med. Sci.* (ed. 8) 276/1 *Senile dementia, Insanity of the aged*, a form of moral insanity, in which the whole moral character of the individual is changed. **1902** A. R. DEFENDORF *Kraepelin's Clin. Psychiatry* viii. 273 Senile dementia includes those forms of mental disease appearing in the period of involution. **1948** W. A. O'CONNOR *Psychiatry* xii. 269 The senile dement exhibits to a profound degree the characteristic failings of the deteriorated senile person. **1954** W. MAYER-GROSS et al. *Clin. Psychiatry* xi. 482 The two pictures of senile dementia and normal ageing are qualitatively different and must be distinguished. **1976** *Scotsman* 20 Nov. (Weekend Suppl.) 3/4 Laing comments on this: 'I am sure he was not suffering from senile dementia, nor was it a slip of the pen.'

2. Exhibiting the weakness of old age.

1848 THACKERAY *Van. Fair* xx, Dobbin was not a little affected by the sight of this once kind old friend,..raving with senile anger. **1882** MISS BRADDON *Mt. Royal* I. iii. 73 Your snaky Vivien, and your senile Merlin. **1902** MONKSHOOD & GAMBLE *Kipling* 289 Certain supposedly effective ships of battle are senile, and others are yet unborn.

3. *Phys. Geog.* Approaching the end of a cycle of erosion.

1902 WEBSTER Suppl., *Senile stream*,..a stream whose valley is reduced so nearly to base level that its longitudinal profile is flat and its current feeble. *Senile topography*,..the configuration of land which prolonged degradation has reduced nearly to a base-level plain.

Hence **ˈsenilely** *adv.*

1898 *Punch* 2 July 309/2 Yet he never whineth, he'll senilely say.

senile (ˈsiːnaɪl), *sb.* [f. the adj.] An aged person; one who exhibits the weakness or diseases of old age.

1938 N. CAMERON in *Amer. Jrnl. Psychol.* LI. 664 The seniles..exhibited..the loose cluster-form of organization (*asyndesis*). **1962** *Lancet* 8 Dec. 1212/2 Of every 100 potential long-stay male patients, 30 were schizophrenics, 21 seniles, and 12 manic-depressives. **1981** J. B. HILTON *Playground of Death* v. 67 The old girl was well into her eighties... You never know where you stand with these so-called seniles.

senility (sɪˈnɪlɪtɪ). [f. SENILE *a.* + -ITY. Cf. F. *sénilité.*] The condition of being senile; old age or the mental and physical infirmity due to old age.

1791 BOSWELL *Johnson* an. 1778, Apr., Mr. Edwards..again recurred to his consciousness of senility. **1821** LAMB *Elia* Ser. I. *Old Benchers* (end), He is yet in green and vigorous senility. **1899** *Allbutt's Syst. Med.* VI. 361 The weakness of the wall [of the heart] implied in the fact that the disease is one of senility.

senilize (ˈsiːnɪlaɪz), *v.* [f. SENILE *a.* + -IZE.] *trans.* and *intr.* To make or become senile. Hence **ˈsenilizing** *ppl. a.*

1823 *New Monthly Mag.* VII. 18 Hence, senilising tribe! avaunt, ye piecemeal destroyers! **1841** HOR. SMITH *Moneyed Man* III. xi. 320 Often, as I began to senilise, did I reiterate Horace's prayer.

senior (ˈsiːnɪə(r)), *a.* and *sb.* Forms: 4–6 **senyour(e**, 4, 6–7 **seniour**, 5–6 **seniore**, **senyor**, 6 **senioure**, **seneour**, 7 **seigniour**, 8 **seignior**, 5– **senior.** [a. L. *senior*, compar. of *sen-em*, *senex* old, cogn. w. Gr. ἕνος old (in ἕνη last day of the moon), OIrish *sen*, Lith. *séna-s*, Skr. *sána* old. The subst. use of the Latin word (cf. B. below) is the source of SEIGNEUR, SEIGNIOR, SENHOR, SEÑOR, SIGNOR.] **A.** *adj.*

1. a. Older, elder; esp. used after a person's name to denote the elder of two bearing the same name in a family; also (after a simple surname) the elder of two boys of the same surname in a school, etc. Abbreviated SEN., SEN. (*U.S.* SR. 3).

1432–50 tr. *Higden* (Rolls) II. 103 Kynge Edwarde the senior. **1496** *Rolls of Parlt.* VI. 518/1 Johannes Robynson de Boston Sen'. **1577** KENDALL *Flowers of Epigr.* 6 Widowes old, and senior chuffs. *c* **1630** RISDON *Surv. Devon* §311 (1810) 321 Edward, surnamed Senior, a nurse-father of the church. **1668** STEELE *Husbandm. Calling* vi. (1672) 138 The grass sprung lately of the ground, and so did he, only he is the senior grass. **1825** T. HOOK *Sayings* Ser. II. *Man of Many Fr.* I. 201 The senior four children re-appeared in the drawing-room. **1893** LELAND *Mem.* I. 21 An infant school ..kept by the Misses Donaldson... Miss Donaldson, senior, sat at a desk [etc.].

†**b.** Anterior in date, superior in antiquity *to.*

1655 FULLER *Ch. Hist.* II. vii. §87 Plain-song is much seniour to all Descanting. **1699** BENTLEY *Phal.* 362 He must be senior to Zaleucus himself.

c. ***senior citizen***, a term for an elderly person, esp. one who is past the age of retirement. orig. *U.S.*

Freq. used in official communications and by the media as a euphemism for 'old-age pensioner'.

1938 *Time* 24 Oct. 12/2 Mr. Downey had an inspiration to do something on behalf of what he calls, for campaign purposes, 'our senior citizens'. **1956** *School & Society*

(U.S.) 12 May 169 As a basis for their education, it [*sc.* pragmatism] is good for the young, the middle-aged, and our senior citizens. **1962** *British Advent Messenger* 28 Sept. 30/2 Owing to the extensive alterations to be done it was October 27, 1958, before we could welcome any of those dear senior citizens who were so anxiously waiting to enter the Home. **1966** T. PYNCHON *Crying of Lot 49* iv. 90 Vesperhaven House, a home for senior citizens that Inverarity had put up. **1969** *Listener* 23 Jan. 101/2 More organised resistance came from the 'senior citizen'—or 'old age pensioners'—lobby. **1974** H. MACINNES *Climb to Lost World* iv. 56 We staggered up the bank to the village like senior citizens en route to the post office to collect their pensions. **1977** B. PYM *Quartet in Autumn* xxi. 192 She *is* a retired person, a senior citizen, you might say.

2. a. That ranks before others in virtue of longer service or tenure of a position; superior *to* others in standing. ***the senior service***: the navy as distinguished from the army.

1513 BRADSHAW *St. Werburge* I. 2164 Bycause that Werburge in order was senyoure, Her mother Ermenylde gaue her the sufferaynte. **1811** WELLINGTON in Gurw. *Desp.* (1837) VII. 245 You are aware that he is senior to Marshal Beresford. **1886** C. E. PASCOE *London of To-day* xxiv. (ed. 3) 225 The Inner and Middle Temple..are the two senior Inns. **1899** HOPE HUNTLY *Our Code of Honour* xxii, 'It was my heart's desire in boyhood to enter the senior service'. 'Then why did you not?' 'Oh, I yielded to my mother; she was keen on the army.' **1911** *London Mag.* Oct. 264 The Admiral turned round... 'The Army', he said gaily, 'comes to the rescue of the senior Service'.

b. In school and college use.

(*a*) Applied to a pupil or student who has been longer under tuition than another (const. *to*). (*b*) Applied to a student who is no longer a freshman; in the U.S. to a student in his last year or term. (*c*) In certain universities, used in designations connoting a specific standing, as *senior* SOPHISTER. Also ***Senior Fellow***, a term applied at Cambridge and Dublin to a select number of the fellows of longest standing in a college, in whom the whole or the greater part of its government was formerly vested; at Oxford in the 18th c. sometimes applied to those fellows who had graduated, as distinguished from the undergraduate fellows. ***senior student*** (Christ Church, Oxford): see STUDENT[1].

1651 [LANGBAINE] *Found. Oxford* 4 Merton Colledge.. twelve Schollers, whereof nine should serve the nine seniour Fellows. **1651** —— *Found. Cambridge* 9 Kings Colledge... In which Colledge at this present is a Provost, 70 Fellows and Scholars,..besides 12 servitors to the seniour Fellows, 6 poor Scholars, with other Students. **1698** FARQUHAR *Love & Bottle* III. ii, Your father was a senior fellow and your mother was an air-pump. **1721** AMHERST *Terræ Fil.* xl. (1726) 212 He would give his vote, that every senior-fellow in the college should have a living tack'd to his fellowship. **1744** BIRCH *Life Boyle* 69 Mr. Tallents..became senior fellow and president or vice-master of his college [Magdalene, Cambridge]. *a* **1763** MARTYN & KIPPIS *Life of 1st Earl Shaftesb.* (1836) I. 42 On a particular day, the senior undergraduates, in the evening, called the fresh-men to the fire, and made them hold out their chins. **1877** in *Worthington's Pract. Physics* (1881) Introd. 1, I should be inclined to discontinue Physical Laboratory work in schools, except in the case of senior boys.

c. In quasi-superlative sense, applied to the officer, student, etc. who is highest in seniority among those of his own grade.

1848 THACKERAY *Van. Fair* xxx, The stout senior Major, who led the regiment into action. **1863** 'OUIDA' *Held in Bondage* i, The senior pupil was standing with his back to the fire.

d. In commercial use, applied to the partner in a firm who (whether on account of length of standing or for other reasons) has precedence of the rest in the formal enumeration of the members.

1864 R. W. KIMBALL *Was he Successful?* 209 (Hoppe) Mr. Tenant..was..the senior member of the house of Allwise, Tenant & Co.

e. *Stock Exch.* Applied to securities the owners of which have first claim to be repaid by the issuing company. Cf. *junior stock* s.v. JUNIOR *a.* (*sb.*) 5.

1914 H. HALFORD *Dict. Stock Market Terms* (ed. 2) 79 Senior stocks. Debentures and Preference Stocks carrying a fixed rate of interest and ranking for dividend in priority to the Ordinary and Deferred Stocks. **1925** H. PARKINSON *ABC of Stocks & Shares* 63 Among the 'senior' securities of the large railway companies the investor may roam at will. **1939** MEAD & GRODINSKY *Ebb & Flow of Investment Values* i. 5 Granted these formal requirements in ratios, priorities, and margins of safety, the senior securities of certain industries secured by certain forms of property,..are recommended. **1964** P. WYCKOFF *Dict. Stock Market Terms* 238 Senior Securities. Bonds and preferred stock which receive prior consideration when a corporation fails or is being dissolved.

3. In certain Cambridge University terms, used to connote a pre-eminence in rank having no relation to length of standing. **senior wrangler**, the head of the 'wranglers', i.e. of the first class of those who are successful in the Mathematical Tripos at Cambridge (hence **senior-wranglership**); similarly, **senior classic, senior moralist**, the student who takes the first place in the Classical and the Moral Sciences Tripos respectively. (In consequence of the reforms of 1906–9, the status indicated by these titles has ceased to exist, the class-lists being now arranged not in order of merit but alphabetically). **senior optime**, one who is placed in the second class in the Mathematical Tripos. (See OPTIME.)

1831 GREVILLE *Mem.* 2 Jan. (1874) II. 101 Maule was senior wrangler and senior medallist at Cambridge, and is a lawyer. **1859** FARRAR *Julian Home* v, Of course you intend to be senior classic, or senior wrangler? **1862** CALVERLEY *Verses & Transl.* (1894) 44 Each perambulating infant Had a magic in its squall, For my eager eye detected Senior Wranglers in them all. **1878** LATHAM in *Encycl. Brit.* VIII. 778 The *éclat* attaching to the 'tripos list' and the senior wranglership.

4. Of institutions, associations, etc. reserved for the senior members of a body, as ***senior common-room, senior mess***, etc.

1774 J. WOODFORDE *Diary* 14 Jan. (1924) I. 122 We all went into the Senr Common Room. **1959** M. BRADBURY *Eating People is Wrong* i. 28 As Treece was leaving the Senior Common Room..the Vice-Chancellor appeared in the doorway. **1981** E. NORTH *Dames* iii. 41 They were in the Senior Common Room standing by the first school photograph.

5. Special collocations: **senior class** *U.S.*, a class in college or high school made up of students in their fourth year of academic study; **senior college** *U.S.*, a college in which the last two years' work for the bachelor's degree is done; **senior high (school)** *N. Amer.*, a secondary school comprising the three (or four) upper high school grades (cf. *junior high* (*school*) s.v. JUNIOR *a.* (*sb.*) 5); **senior school**, a school, or part of a school, for older children; **senior year** *U.S.*, the fourth and last year of a high school or college course.

1766 T. CLAP *Ann. or Hist. Yale College* 14 The *Senior Class were removed to Milford. **1837** *Stat. Harvard Univ.* 11 The third vacation for the Senior Class shall begin one day before the general vacation. **1900** C. W. WINCHESTER *Victories of Wesley Castle* 25 Wesley and Chester went to the city of Dorchester on some business for the senior class. **1980** *Redbook* Oct. 231/2, I couldn't go on the senior-class trip to Washington. **1899** *Univ. of Chicago Reg.* 37/1 The Faculties of the Schools of Arts, Literature, and Science have been organized as follows:..(2) The Faculty of the *Senior Colleges [etc.]. **1942** *Bull. Vanderbilt Univ.* 15 May 69 The College is divided, for certain purposes, into the Junior College and the Senior College. **1977** *Information Please Almanac for 1978* 826 (*heading*) Accredited U.S. Senior Colleges and Universities. **1909** *Ann. Rep. Bd. Educ.* (Columbus, Ohio) 29 You have established a Junior High School..leaving the tenth, eleventh and twelfth grades for the *Senior High Schools. **1949** *Los Angeles Times* 23 June II. 5/1 Then they enter senior high school, and become 'juniors' and then seniors. **1955** [see COMPOSITE *a.* 6 e]. **1974** *Encycl. Brit. Macropædia* VI. 422/1 The elementary-secondary sequence overall is 12 years in length.., but the subdivisions of these years are various:..six-three-three (elementary school, junior high school, and senior high school), [etc.]. **1871** *Senior school [see *junior school* s.v. JUNIOR *a.* 5]. **1930** *Times* 26 Mar. 12/1 The first step in reorganization is to group all the senior children from 11 upwards in separate senior schools or departments or 'senior tops'. **1963** [see DJEBBA, JIBBAH]. **1963** BARNARD & LAUWERYS *Handbk. Brit. Educ. Terms* 175 *Senior School*, (1) An obsolete term used to describe the free non-selective post-primary schools (age-group 11–14) established under the pre-1944 elementary code. They provided a course of general studies with some vocational bias... (2) A term sometimes used to describe the top classes/forms of a grammar or public school. **1796** J. MORSE *Amer. Univ. Geogr.* (ed. 3) I. 420 The undergraduates are not permitted to attend them [*sc.* medical lectures] till their *senior year. **1924** S. S. COLVIN *Introd. High School Teaching* 12 A number of high schools offer in their senior year a vocational course.

B. *sb.* An elder person. *lit.* and *fig.*

1. a. One superior or worthy of deference and reverence by reason of age; one having pre-eminence in dignity by priority of election, appointment, etc.

c **1380** WYCLIF *Wks.* (1880) 303 Non drede siche seniours ben fendis þat speken lying in ypocrisie. *c* **1440** *York Myst.* xli. 78 Symeon, that senyour. **1482** *Monk of Evesham* (Arb.) 31 When the bretheren had begunne matens y mette with a senyor that ye knowe wele in the chirche porch. **1513** BRADSHAW *St. Werburge* I. 1175 Folowynge the counseyll and mynde of a senyor. **1615** CROOKE *Body of Man* 360 The diuine senior Hippocrates. **1725** POPE *Odyss.* III. 23 Meet then the Senior far renown'd for sense, With rev'rent awe, but decent confidence. **1823** SCOTT *Quentin D.* xvi, His conversation, tricks, and songs, were..entertaining to the.. younger brethren, and so unedifying in the opinion of the seniors of the fraternity, that [etc.]. **1905** TUCKWELL *Remin. Radical Parson* xii. 159 Its castellan was a dignified, sweet-visaged senior.

b. With possessive.

c **1425** *Found. St. Bartholomew's* (E.E.T.S.) 17 In the begynnynge of this areysed frame oure senyoures tellid vs that one a day at evensong tyme whan derkenys drew vpon ther was seyn a light from heuyn. **1678** CUDWORTH *Intell. Syst.* 211 [tr. Herodotus]. Hesiod and Homer, were..not above four hundred years my Seniors [orig. μευ πρεσβυτέρους]. **1782** MISS BURNEY *Cecilia* I. i, Though much her senior, he was by no means of an age to render his addressing her an impropriety. **1818** SCOTT *Hrt. Midl.* xxii, His senior at the bar. **1862** F. W. ROBINSON *Owen* IV. vi, She was a year or two my senior.

†**2.** In early translations of the New Testament, used to render L. *senior*, Gr. πρεσβύτερος, in various applications, where the later versions have *elder*. Hence occas. used as the designation of the class of ministers called 'elders' or 'presbyters' in the primitive church, or in communities professedly formed on the model of this. *Obs.*

1382 WYCLIF *Rev.* vii. 11 And alle aungels stoden in cumpas of the trone and of [the] senyouris or eldre. *c* **1440** *Alphabet of Tales* 233/26 þan prayed for þis childe þe xxiiij seniores; and so þis childe was forgyffen his tryspas. **1526** TINDALE *Matt.* xxvi. 59 The chefe prestes, and the seniours, and all the counsell sought false witnes ageinste Jesus. **1564** *Brief Exam.* *****iij, Whence were Seniours in the primitiue Churche? **1572** [J. FIELD, etc.] *Admonit. Parl.* A vj, And to these three ioyntly, that is, the Ministers, Seniors, and deacons, is the whole regimente of the churche to be committed. **1582** N. T. (Rheims) *Rev.* iv. 4 Upon the thrones foure and twentie seniors sitting.

3. a. In school and college use: One of the more advanced students; also one no longer a freshman. In *U.S.* a student in his fourth year.

1612 BRINSLEY *Lud. Lit.* xxvi. (1627) 272 That the two or foure Seniors in each fourme, be as Ushers in that fourme. **1741** *Customs of Harvard* in Hall *College Words* (1851) 318 No Freshman shall be saucy to his Senior. **1836** O. W. HOLMES *Song Centenn. Celebr. Harvard* 39 Lord! how the seniors knocked about The freshman class of one. **1888** BRYCE *Amer. Commw.* VI. cii. III. 453 In an American college the students..of the fourth year [are called] seniors.

b. A senior fellow of a college; a member of a council or deliberative assembly for managing the internal affairs of a college. Cf. SENIORITY 3.

1645 *Ordin. Parl. Regul. Univ. Cambr.* 3 The Government of Trinity Colledge is setled in the Master and eight Seniors. **1648** WINYARD *Midsummer-Moon* 3 Doctors and Seniors are too tough for continuall cramming, he must have Batchellers of art [etc.]. **1717** E. MILLER *Acc. Cambr.* 109 The 11th and 12th Statutes [Trin. Coll.] concern the Election of Officers, Lecturers, Seniors, College Preachers, and Fellows; and appoints first, That the Master read this Statute before the eight Seniors; then he and the Seniors are to take an Oath, That they will elect no-body to any Office by Favour, &c. but him only whom [etc.]

4. With *the*. The familiar name of the United Service and Royal Aero Club.

1906 G. W. E. RUSSELL *Social Silhouettes* xxviii. 195 If he is an old soldier, he is eligible for 'The Senior', and may make free with the Duke of Wellington's dry sherry and Dugald Stewart's still drier library. **1974** *Financial Times* 29 June 15/3 Commander James Allen, secretary of the United Services and Royal Aero (which is widely known in club circles as the Senior), [etc.]. **1974** R. MCDOUALL *Clubland Cooking* 11 Going west from Trafalgar Square we come first to the United Service Club, known as 'The Senior', because it was for senior officers of the Army and Navy. **1975** *Sunday Times* 25 May 24/1 The closure of the Senior will shake all the generals and admirals who have taken it for granted since 1815.

5. *Comb.*: †**senior-junior**, a person old and young at the same time.

1588 SHAKS. *L.L.L.* III. i. 182 This signior Iunior gyant drawfe [*read* dwarf], don Cupid.

senior, obs. form of SEIGNIOR.

seniority (siːnɪˈɒrɪtɪ). Forms: 5–6 seniorite, 6 senyoryte, segniorite, 6–7 senioritie, 6– **seniority**. [a. med.L. *seniōritās*, f. L. *seniōr-em* SENIOR; see -ITY.]

1. The state or quality of being senior; priority by reason of birth, superior age.

1533 MORE *Apol.* xv. Wks. 875/2 Sometime some one religion haue had some question and dysputed as it were a probleme, vpon thantiquitie or senioritie of their institucion. **1674** *Govt. Tongue* iv. 46 The first provoker has, by his seniority and primogeniture a double portion of the guilt. **1737** *Gentl. Mag.* VII. 100 A sage Lady observ'd to them, that in this Assembly Respect and Precedence were only due to Seniority. **1838** THIRLWALL *Greece* V. 343 It had been agreed among the envoys that they should address the king in the order of seniority; and Demosthenes happened to be the youngest. **1863** 'OUIDA' *Held in Bondage* i, The senior pupil..gave me his hand, cordially and frankly, for all his hauteur and seniority.

†**b.** The senile period of life. *Obs. rare*$^{-1}$.

a **1688** BUNYAN *Mr. Badman* To Rdr., The minority, flower, and seniority of his Age.

†**c.** ? Numerical position in order of age. *Obs.*

1776 T. PERCIVAL *Ess.* III. 342 In the second column is the surname and seniority of the infant, also in large characters.

2. Priority or precedence in office or service; esp. *Mil.* Superiority in standing to another of equal rank by reason of earlier entrance into the service, or an earlier date of appointment.

c **1450** in Aungier *Syon* (1840) 366 Eche in hys order after their seniorite in religion. **1592** NASHE *Strange Newes* D 4, Where in an honorable Index they shall be placed according to their degree and segnioritie. **1600** J. PORY tr. *Leo's Africa* II. 75 We were certaine yeeres fellow-students together at Fez, where being of one standing and seniority we [etc.]. **1668** PEPYS *Diary* 13 Oct., That places of preferment may go according to seniority and merit. **1704** *Milit. Dict.* (ed. 2). **1769** *Junius Lett.* iv. (1804) I. 33 Let me ask Junius, if he knows any one nobleman in the army who has had a regiment by seniority? **1853** BRIGHT *Sp., India* 3 June (1876) 3 To go on from beginning to end in a system of promotion from seniority. **1908** *Q. Rev.* July 238 The fetish of seniority is responsible for many a muddle.

3. The body of seniors or senior fellows of a college.

1678 A. FARMER in *Magd. Coll.* (O.H.S.) 69, I..do acknowledge before the Seniority that I have deservedly received..my..admonition. **1717** E. MILLER *Acc. Cambr.* 129 That 'tis the first Instance that ever appear'd in the College Books..That any By-Law..was enter'd, or made in the Master's Name, without the Consent of the Seniority. **1843** WHEWELL *Jrnl.* in Willis & Clark *Cambr.* II. 627 If the Fellows were dissatisfied I regretted that the matter had not been brought before the Seniority. **1859** FARRAR *Julian Home* xxiii. 300 Kennedy..rushed back to the Seniority, who were already beginning to wonder at his long absence.

†**4.** Used for SIGNORITY, in the sense 'body of signors'. *Obs.*

1517 TORKINGTON *Pilgr.* (1884) 14 The Duke Satt in Seynt Markes Churche in ryght hys [*read* hye] astate in the Qwer on the ryght syd with senyoryte which they call lords.

† **'seniorize**, *v. Obs. rare*⁻¹. [f. SENIOR *a.* + -IZE. Cf. SIGNORIZE *v.*] *intr.* To assume the position of a senior or superior, to have or exercise dominion, to rule, to lord it.

1593 G. HARVEY *Pierce's Super.* 88 Alas, that wise men.. should once imagine, to finde it a matter of as light consequence, to seniorise in a realme, ouer the greatest Lordes,..as in a towne, ouer a company of meane marchantes.

seniorship ('siːnɪəʃɪp). [f. SENIOR + -SHIP.] The position of 'senior' or head boy of a school.

1862 MRS. H. WOOD *Channings* I. xi. 156 It is a shame if Pye has promised the seniorship to Yorke over my head.

† **'seniory**. *Obs.* Also 6 **seign(i)orie**, 6–7 **sign(i)orie**, 7 **signeurie**. [f. SENIOR + -Y.]

1. Seniority.

1594 SHAKS. *Rich. III*, IV. iv. 36 If ancient sorrow be most reuerent, Giue mine the benefit of signeurie [*Qq.* sign(i)orie].

2. *Eccl.* A body of 'elders', a presbytery.

1572 [J. FIELD, etc.] *Admonit. Parl.* A vj, In steade of Chancelors, Archdeacons,..churchwardens and such like: You haue to plant in euery congregation a lawfull and godly seignorie. **1583** STUBBES *Anat. Abus.* II. (1882) 100 Though a seigniorie or eldership then in euerie particular church were necessarie. **1589** T. L. *Advt. to Q. Eliz.* (1651) 50 That the magistracy whereunder he is placed, whether it be of one of few, or many is his allowed seniory and lawfull presbytery.

seniour(e, obs. forms of SEIGNIOR, SENIOR.

senister, senit: see SINISTER, SENNIGHT.

senith, senjaque: see ZENITH, SANJAK.

senium ('siːnɪəm). *Med.* [a. L. *senium* debility of age, f. *senēre* to be feeble, f. *senex* old.] The period of old age. Usu. with *the*.

1911 STEDMAN *Med. Dict.* 786/1 *Senium*, old age, especially the debility of the aged. **1932** F. M. LIPSCOMB *Dis. Old Age* p. v, I have included only..those maladies which have a high incidence in the senium. **1968** J. G. HOWELLS *Family Psychiatry* ii. 23 Individual members of the family..may be of any age, from infancy to senium. **1977** T. R. HARRISON *Princ. Internal Med.* (ed. 8) 8/2 In the absence of disease there is a steady falloff [of nerve and muscle cells] which begins at about the end of the growth period and continues at an accelerated pace into the senium.

‖ **senn** (sɛn). *rare.* [G. *senn(e.*] A herdsman in the Alps. Also *Comb.* **senn-cabin, sennhutt**, repr. G. *sennhütte*, a herdsman's chalet.

c **1822** MRS. HEMANS *League of Alps* 1 'Twas night upon the Alps. The Senn's wild horn,..had pour'd its last long tone. *c* **1822** —— *Alp-Horn Song* 16 The low sen-cabins and pastures free. **1868** KINGSLEY *Hermits* 131 During that short period of the year when the maidens in the sennhutt watch the cattle upon the upland pastures.

senn, obs. form of SEN *adv.*, *prep.*, and *conj.*

senna ('sɛnə). Also 6–8 **sena**. [mod.L. *senna*, *sena*, a. Arab. *sanā*; cf. SENE *sb.*[4]]

1. *Bot.* A shrub of the genus *Cassia*, native in tropical regions, bearing yellow flowers and flat greenish pods. Cf. CASSIA.

American, Wild, or Maryland senna, *Cassia marilandica*.

1543 TRAHERON *Vigo's Chirurg.* Interpr., Sena hath lytle braunches, and the leafe of fenugreke [etc.]. **1601** CHESTER *Loves Martyr* (1878) 84 Mugwort, Sena and Tithimailes [etc.]. **1782** J. SCOTT *Poet. Wks.* 261 In vain the senna waves its glossy gold. **1811** A. T. THOMSON *Lond. Disp.* (1818) 92 The best senna, named in Nubia *guebelly*, or *sena mekki*, grows wild, and yields two crops of leaves, the abundance of which depends on the periodical rains. **1847** DARLINGTON *Amer. Weeds* (1860) 109 Maryland Cassia. Wild, or American Senna.

b. Applied with defining word to shrubs of other genera which have similar medicinal properties; as **bastard senna** = next; **bladder senna**, *Colutea arborescens*, see BLADDER *sb.* 10; **Chile senna**, *Myoschilos oblongus*; **scorpion senna**, *Coronilla Emerus*, see SCORPION 8 c; **wild senna**, *Poinciana pulcherrima* or *Globularia Alypum*, formerly †the genus *Colutea*.

1705 DALE *Pharmacol.* Suppl. 318 Colutea... Bastard Sena. **1750** G. HUGHES *Barbados* 204 The Wild Sena, or the Wild Cassia Fistula; Lat. *Colutea*. **1866** *Treas. Bot.* s.v. *Senna*, Wild Senna, *Poinciana pulcherrima*; also an American name for *Cassia marilandica*. **1874** *Ibid.* Suppl., Chili Senna, *Myoschilos oblongus*.

2. *Pharm.* The dried leaflets of various species of *Cassia*, used as a cathartic and emetic.

1571 *Wills & Inv. N.C.* (Surtees 1835) 363, ½ a lb ½ a qⁿ of sen'a xxᵈ. *a* **1618** *Rates Marchandizes* F 4, Druggs... Sena the pound xviij.d. **1794** GODWIN *Cal. Williams* 29, I shall hate you as bad as senna and valerian. **1830** LINDLEY *Nat. Syst. Bot.* 91 The Senna of the shops consists, according to M. Delile, of Cassia acutifolia, Cassia Senna, and Cynanchum Argel. **1880** J. W. LEGG *Bile* 172 Senna was found by Röhrig to have an active effect on the secretion of bile.

b. The many varieties of the drug are commercially distinguished by defining words (now often used loosely), as ***Alexandrian***, ***Aleppo***, ***Arabian***, ***Indian***, ***Tinnevelly***, etc., ***senna***.

1693 DALE *Pharmacol.* 502 Senna Alexandrina *Offic*... Alexandrian Sena. **1693** tr. *Blancard's Phys. Dict.* (ed. 2), Senna, Alexandrine, Ægyptian, Syriac. **1845** *Encycl. Metrop.* VII. 508/1 The Tinnevelly Senna consists of the leaflets of *Cassia Elongata*. **1861** BENTLEY *Man. Bot.* 527 Bladder-Senna.—The leaflets have been used on the continent to adulterate Alexandrian Senna.

3. *attrib.* and *Comb.*, as ***senna leaf***, ***leaflet***, ***shrub***; **senna-draught**, **-tea**, an infusion of the drug taken as a purgative.

1879 *St. George's Hosp. Rep.* IX. 190 A dose of calomel.. followed by a *senna draught in the morning. **1699** GARTH *Dispens.* v. 103 A Folliage of dissembl'd *Senna Leaves Grav'd round its Brim. **1887** BENTLEY *Man. Bot.* (ed. 5) 532 They are at once distinguished from *Senna leaflets by their regularity at the base. **1766** STORK *Acc. E. Florida* 48 The vines, the *senna shrub, sarsaparilla, China-root,..are indigenous plants of East-Florida. **1753** CHESTERF. *Lett. to Son* (1774) II. lxxiv. 307 Chewing a little rhubarb, when you go to bed at night, or some *senna-tea in the morning.

Senna, etc., varr. SEHNA.

sennachie ('sɛnəxɪ). Forms: 6 **shannaghe**, 7 **sanachie**, 8 **senachi**, **seanachie**, **sennachai**, 9 **sennachy**, **shan(n)achie**, **shanachy**, **seannachie**, 8– **sen(n)achie**. [a. Gael. *seanachaidh* (= OIrish *senchaidh*), f. *sean* old: cf. *seanachas* (OIrish *senchas*) ancient legend.] In Ireland and the Scottish Highlands: One professionally occupied in the study and transmission of traditional history, genealogy, and legend; now chiefly *Sc.* a Gaelic teller of legendary romances.

1534 *St. Papers Hen. VIII* (1834) II. 215 That no Yryshe mynstrels, rymours, shannaghes, ne bardes, unchaghes, nor messangers, come to desire any goodes of any man dwellinge within the Inglyshrie. **1685** STILLINGFL. *Orig. Brit.* Pref. 40 Nay, why should the British History be questioned? since no doubt the Britains had Druids, Sanachies, and Bards as well as the Scots or Irish. **1775** JOHNSON *West. Isl.* 258 A great family had a Bard and a Senachi, who were the poet and historian of the house. **1827** SCOTT *Highl. Widow* iv, Her stores of legendary history..were augmented by an unusual acquaintance with the songs of ancient bards, and traditions of the most approved Seannachies and tellers of tales. **1863** J. F. CAMPBELL *Pop. Tales W. Highl.* (1893) IV. 15 A Shanachie means a teller of old tales and traditions. **1873** BURTON *Hist. Scot.* VI. lxv. 32 He was surrounded by a court or staff of sennachies—the bards and historians of his race. **1898** J. MACMANUS *Bend of Road* 53 Shanachy.

senne, obs. form of SEN *adv.*, etc.

sennegrass ('sɛnɪgrɑːs, -æ-). [a. Norw. *senegras*: cf. ON. *sina*, Sw. dial. *sena* withered grass.] An Arctic sedge, *Carex vesicaria*.

1897 tr. *Nansen's Farthest North* II. 95 Turn them [*sc.* Finn shoes] inside out, fill them with sennegraes [*sic*] or sedge,..and creep into the sleeping bag. **1919** E. SHACKLETON *South* xii. 229 Oil mixed with reindeer hair, bits of meat, sennegrass, and penguin feathers form a conglomeration which cements the stones together.

sennel, sennen: see SENDLE *adv.*, SINEW.

sennere, sennest, obs. ff. SOONER[1], SOONEST.

'sennet[1]. *Obs.* exc. *Hist.* Forms: 6 **senet**, **(sonnet)**, 7 **sennit**, **sennate**, **sinet**, **synnet**, **cynet**, **signate**, **sennet**. [app. a variant of SIGNET, in the sense 'sign, token' (see SIGNET *sb.* 5).

The forms *senet*, *sinet*, and others, occur in OF. as variants of *signet*, which, however, seems not to occur either in the sense below or in the wider sense of token. The word may possibly be Anglo-French.]

A set of notes on the trumpet or cornet, ordered in the stage-directions of Elizabethan plays, apparently as a signal for the ceremonial entrance or exit of a body of players.

c **1590** MARLOWE *Faust* 862 Sound a Sonnet [**1609**, **1611** Sinet], enter the Pope and the Cardinall of Lorraine to the banket, with Friers attending. **1593** SHAKS. *3 Hen. VI*, I. i. 205 Senet. Here they come down. **1602** DEKKER *Satirom.* F 4, Trumpets sound a florish, and then a sennate. Enter King [etc.]. **1602** MARSTON *Ant. & Mel.* I. B 2 b, The Cornets sound a Synnet. *Ibid.* B 3 b, The Cornets sound a Cynet. **1605** *1st Pt. Ieronimo* I. i, Sound a signate, and passe ouer the stage... After a long signate is sounded, enter all the nobles. **1613** SHAKS. *Hen. VIII*, II. iv, Trumpets, Sennet, and Cornets. *a* **1619** FLETCHER *Valentinian* V. viii, A Synnet with Trumpets. **1922** JOYCE *Ulysses* 471 Four buglers on foot blow a sennet. **1942** E. BLOM *Music in Eng.* iii. 49 Shakespeare was much attached to music, and it would be rash to conclude from the mere evidence of printed texts that he contented himself in his plays with a few songs and an occasional tucket (*toccata*) or sennet (*sonata*) for trumpets behind the scenes.

sennet[2] ('sɛnɪt). *Nat. Hist.* Also 7–8 **sinnet**. [? From some W.-Indian lang.] A West-Indian fish; = BARRACUDA.

1671 J[OHN] H[ARDIE] in *Lefroy's Mem. of Bermudas* (1879) II. 344 Which [fish] the people store As Pilchards, Sinnets [etc.]. **1756** P. BROWNE *Jamaica* 451 *Perca?* I. *Minor subargentea*. The Sinnet. **1859** J. M. JONES *Nat. in Bermuda* 105 The Sennet is likewise a common fish in the waters of Bermuda, and sells freely in the market. **1876** GOODE *Fishes of Bermudas* 62 *Sphyræna Picuda*... Sennet.

Senni ('sɛnɪ). The name of a tributary of the River Usk, Powys, S. Wales, used *attrib.* as **Senni Bed**, any of a series of fossiliferous sandstones in the Lower Old Red Sandstone of S. Wales, well seen in the valley of the Senni. Usu. *pl.*

1904 A. STRAHAN *Geol. S. Wales Coalfield* V. i. 3 Nearly all the remainder of the Old Red [Sandstone] tract is occupied by the red sandstones of the Brownstone division, but a thick and persistent group of sandstones and marls with cornstones, generally characterised by a green colour, appears in some of the deeper valleys, among others that of the Senni, from which fact the name of Senni Beds has been applied to them. **1927** *Q. Jrnl. Geol. Soc.* LXXXIII. 197 The plant-remains are entombed in sage-green arenaceous shales, which are intercalated among the typical sage-green sandstones of the Senni Beds of this locality. **1970** R. M. BLACK *Elements Palaeont.* xix. 302 (*caption*) A psilophyte; a primitive vascular plant from the Lower Old Red Sandstone (Senni Beds), South Wales.

sennight ('sɛnaɪt). Now *arch.* Forms: α. see SEVEN and NIGHT; β. 2–3 **soveniht**, 3 **seoveniht**, **-niþt**, 3–4 **seve-**, **sove-niȝt**, **-nyȝt**, 4 **seovenyght**, **sefnight**, **seve-nyht**, **-niȝth**, 4–5 **sevenyght(e**, **sevenyȝt**, 5 **seve-nyth**, **-nyut**, 6 **sevenighte**, 6–8 **sevenight**, 7 **seue'night**, 7–8 **sev'night**; γ. 5 **sennyȝt**, **synyght**, **sennett**, **sennyt**, **senit**, 5–6 **senyght**, **sennet**, 6 **senighte**, **senyghte**, **seneyt**, 6–7 **sennyght**, 7 **senight**, **senet**, **senith**, **sennit**, **sinnitt**, **s'ennight**, 7, 9 (*dial.*) **se'night**, 7–9 **se'ennight**, **se'nnight**, 8 (*dial.*) **zennet**, 8–9 **sen'night**, 6– **sennight**. [Originally two words: OE. *seofon* SEVEN, *nihta* pl. of *niht* NIGHT *sb.* OE. had the derivative *seofonnihte* adj., seven days old (of the moon). Cf. FORTNIGHT.] A period of seven (days and) nights; a week.

α. *a* **1000** *Elene* (Gr.) 694 Heht þa..scufan scyldiȝne..in dryȝne seað, þær he duȝuða leas siomode in sorȝum seofon nihta fyrst. *c* **1200** ORMIN 545 Hiss sefennnahht To þewwtenn i þe temmple. *c* **1386** CHAUCER *Nun's Pr. T.* 53 Curteys she was..and bar hyr self so faire Syn thilke day þat she was seuen nyght oold. **1415** SIR T. GREY in *43rd Rep. Dep. Kpr. Rec.* (1882) 582 A sefenneghte after that Murdok of Fyche was take away. *a* **1586** SIDNEY *Arcadia* II. (Sommer) 194 b, Iusts, both with sword and launce, mainteined for a seuen-night together. *a* **1641** FINETT *Observ.* (1656) 133 The crosse windes..held him in the Downes almost a seavennight before they would blow him over. **1653** W. RAMESEY *Astrol. Restored* 319 They never appear a shorter time than a seven-night.

β. *c* **1205** LAY. 4434 Seoueniht he wes þære. *c* **1350** *Will. Palerne* 766 Swiche a sorwe he suffred a seue-niȝt fulle. **1461** *Paston Lett.* II. 19, I prey ȝow..lat me have an awnswer within this sevenyut. **1553** T. WILSON *Rhet.* (1580) 94 A notable waister, to daie full of money, within seuenight after not worthe a grote. **1652** H. L'ESTRANGE *Amer. no Jewes* 23 Owr own usuall reckoning by nights, as Sevenight, Fortnight.

γ. *c* **1420** *Avow. Arth.* xlviij, A sennyȝt duellut he thare. *a* **1529** SKELTON *E. Rummyng* 394, I dranke not this sennet A draught to my pay. **1604** SHAKS. *Oth.* II. i. 77 The bold Iago, Whose footing heere anticipates our thoughts, A Senights speed. *a* **1746** *Exmoor Scolding* (E.D.S.) 42 Nif won zey the le-ast Theng out, tha wut purtee a Zennet arter. **1851** TENNYSON *E. Morris* 30 My love for Nature is as old as I; But thirty moons, one honeymoon to that, And three rich sennights more, my love for her. **1894** K. GRAHAME *Pagan P.* 139 A luscious treat that had been specially reserved for me, a sennight past, by the gardener's boy.

b. ***this day***, ***Sunday***, † ***Sunday come*** (***a***) or ***was*** (***a***), etc. ***sennight***: a week from (this day, etc.).

c **1205** LAY. 5457 Ȝif ȝe spekeð mid rihte, comeð to dæi a seouen nihte. *a* **1350** *S. Stephen* 295 in Horstm. *Altengl. Leg.* (1881) 31 It fell efter on þat day seuyn night Of al þis same þan had he sight. **1486** *Plumpton Corr.* (Camden) 68 Upon tewsday come a sennyt. **1549** LATIMER *6th Serm. bef. Edw. VI* (Arb.) 158 What doctrine is written for vs in the .viii. Chapter of the fyrst boke of the kynges, I dyd partely shewe vnto you..this day sennight. **1566** *Eng. Ch. Furniture* (1866) 59 Item one cope one vestment & one albe—sold to Thomas Inman for the some of Vs vpon sondaie was a sevenighte. **1633** W. MULSHO in *Buccleuch MSS.* (Hist. MSS. Comm.) I. 274 They propose to..set forth on Tuesday sevennight. **1644** SYMONDS *Diary* (Camden) 50 Newes..That Waller was at Abingdon on Tuesday last was sevenight. **1727** [E. DORRINGTON] *Philip Quarll* 87 Bidding him not fail coming there again that Day Sev'night. **1741** RICHARDSON *Pamela* (ed. 3) II. 153 Every one names Thursday come Sev'nnight for our Nuptials. **1771** PENNANT *Tour Scot.* I. (1774) 96 An assignation, at that very hour, that day sevenight. **1861** MAY *Const. Hist.* (1863) I. i. 95 Mr. Canning stated that Lord Eldon's visit to Windsor had taken place on Saturday se'nnight, preceding the change of ministry.

c. *attrib.* as in ***sennight space***; † **sennight day**, the space of a week; also, the same day in the following week.

? *a* **1400** *Morte Arth.* 380 Within a seuenyghte daye..I salle be seene on the see. *c* **1440** *Alphabet of Tales* I. 233 Þis wulfe come agayn vppon þe sennet day. **1601** HOLLAND *Pliny* VIII. xlvi. I. 226 And this is one thing to be wondred at, That in that seven-night space there is not one that taketh hurt by Crocodiles.

sennil, variant of SENDLE *adv. Sc.*

‖ **sennin** ('sɛn,nɪn). Also **sennen**. [Jap., wizard, recluse, f. Chinese *hsien-jên* an immortal man.] In Oriental mythology: originally in Taoism, an elderly recluse who has acquired immortality through meditation and self-discipline; hence, a human being with supernatural powers, a recluse embodying the spirit of nature.

1875 AUDSLEY & BOWES *Keramic Art of Japan* II (caption to plate X, division 1), Figure of a Buddhist *Sennen*, playing the *Koto*, and seated on the back of a fish. **1908** [see KIRIN]. **1912** F. H. DAVIS *Myths & Legends of Japan* xxix. 356 The

Sennin are mountain recluses, and many are the legends told in connection with them. Though they have human form, they are, at the same time, immortal, and adepts in the magical arts. **1915** E. POUND *Cathay* 19 In the storied houses of San-Ko they gave us more Sennin music. **1930** —— *XXX Cantos* iv. 17 Père Henri Jacques would speak with the Sennin, on Rokku.

sennit (ˈsɛnɪt). *Naut.* Also 9 sennet. [var. of SINNET.] **a.** = SINNET. **b.** (See quot. 1858.)

1769 FALCONER *Dict. Marine* (1789), *Sennit.* **1858** SIMMONDS *Dict. Trade, Sennit*,..plaited straw or palm leaves, &c., of which grass hats are made. **1881** *Chequered Career* 92 These young gentlemen are to be seen..making sennet, the latter amusement being on a par with picking oakum.

attrib. and *Comb.* **1882** NARES *Seamanship* (ed. 6) 79 A sennit eye is worked in. *c* **1898** J. CHALMERS in Lovett *Life* (1902) 146 The long sennit hawser kept on deck had been passed ashore to natives on the reef.

sennit, -nyght, -nyȝt, -nyt, obs. ff. SENNIGHT.

sennon, -oun, -own, obs. forms of SINEW *sb.*

senny, variant of SENYE *Obs.*

senocular (sɪˈnɒkjʊlə(r)), *a.* [f. L. *sēnī* six each + *oculī* eyes + -AR.] Having six eyes.

1713 DERHAM *Phys.-Theol.* VIII. iii. (1727) 361 *note*, Most Animals are binocular..and some senocular. **1898** *Syd. Soc. Lex., Senocular.*

senoculate (sɪˈnɒkjʊleɪt), *a.* [Formed as SENOCULAR + -ATE[2]; cf. F. *sénoculé.*] Having six eyes.

1858 MAYNE *Expos. Lex., Senoculatus*,..senoculate.

senofegia, obs. variant of SCENOPEGIA.

Senoi (sɛˈnɔɪ). [Native name, meaning 'man'.] **A.** *sb.* The name of a people inhabiting the provinces of Perak, Kelantan, and Pahang in West Malaysia; the language of this people. **B.** *adj.* Of or pertaining to this people. Cf. SAKAI *sb.* (and *a.*).

1891 *Jrnl. Straits Branch R. Asiatic Soc.* Dec. 14, I shall deal chiefly with the Sĕn-oi dialect. *Ibid.* 16 The country South of this line being inhabited by Sĕn-oi, and the northern division by Tĕm-be. *Ibid.* 22 There are two distinct *r*'s in Sĕn-oi. **1910** R. J. WILKINSON *Papers on Malay Subjects: Aboriginal Tribes* 21 The Northern Sakai of the Plus valley, a different race, also speak of them-selves as *Senoi* and *Mai Darat. Ibid.* 23 The true 'Senoi' quiver is plain. **1923** I. H. N. EVANS *Studies in Religion, Folk-Lore & Custom in Brit. N. Borneo & Malay Peninsula* II. 202 A Senoi man told me the following legend. **1958** J. SLIMMING *Temiar Jungle* 3 The largest of the three racial divisions, the Senoi, is divided linguistically into..the Semai-Senoi who are scattered across southern Perak & North Pahang and the Temiar-Senoi living to the north of the Semai. **1972** E. A. NIDA *Bk. of Thousand Tongues* 386/2 Senoi is spoken by 15,000 to 20,000 people in the South Perak, Ipoh, Tanjong Malim, and Central Pahang states of Malaya. *Ibid.*, The Senoi moved into the higher inland areas during the early 19th century. *Ibid.*, Now speakers of different Senoi dialects can understand one another only with great difficulty.

senon, north. variant of SINEW *sb.*

Senonian (sɪˈnəʊnɪən), *a. Geol.* [ad. F. *sénonien*, f. L. *Senonēs*, a people of central Gaul.] D'Orbigny's subdivision of the Cretaceous in France and Belgium corresponding to the 'Upper Chalk with flints' of British geologists. Also *absol.*

1850 ANSTED *Elem. Geol., Min.*, etc. 336 Senonian division of D'Orbigny (*Craie blanche*). **1879** GEIKIE in *Encycl. Brit.* X. 360/1 The uppermost member of the Senonian series contains in like manner a blending of well-known Upper Chalk organisms with the Tertiary genera *Cypræa, Oliva*, and *Mitra.* **1882** —— *Text-bk. Geol.* VI. iii. §3 (1903) 1205 The Senonian stage of N.W. Germany. *Ibid.*, The Lower Senonian is marked by the abundance of *Actinocamax.* **1885** ETHERIDGE *Stratigraph. Geol. & Palæontol.* 517 Senonian (Upper Chalk with Flints).

senoper, variant of SINOPER *Obs.*

‖**señor** (seˈɲor). Pl. señores (seˈɲores). Also 7 sennor. [Sp. *señor*:—L. *seniōrem*: cf. SIGNOR, SEIGNEUR and SEIGNIOR.]

1. In Spanish use or with reference to a Spaniard: A title of respect placed before the name of a man, equivalent to 'Mr.'

1622 MABBE tr. *Aleman's Guzman d'Alf.* I. 129 How now (Sennor few-clothes) what winde draue you hither? **1868** MISS M. B. EDWARDS *Through Sp.* 166 Señor Bensaken.. would wait upon the Señoras at once, was the reply.

b. Used without the name as a form of address.

1832 W. IRVING *Alhambra* I. 196 'But have you ever met with it yourself?'.. 'No, Señor, God be thanked!' **1884** F. BOYLE *Borderland* 372 Now, señores! What was the creature that pursued me thus, in broad daylight?

c. A Spanish gentleman.

1868 MISS M. B. EDWARDS *Through Sp.* 189, I am..but a humble Señor, of little account.

2. A feudal lord, seigneur (in Spain).

1845 FORD *Handbk. Spain* II. 938 Castro Urdiales of which the Black Prince was Señor, has its bay [etc.].

‖**señora** (seˈɲora). [Sp. *señora*, a fem. formed on SEÑOR. Cf. SIGNORA.] A title of respect prefixed to the name of a Spanish lady, or used without the name in addressing her; hence, a lady of Spanish nationality.

1579 G. GILPIN tr. *Rabbotem's Bee-Hive Rom. Ch.* ii. (1580) 17 A worthie matrone of Spaine called Senora Maria Osorio. **1818** LADY CHARLEVILLE in Lady Morgan *Passages Autobiog.* (1859) 244 He was not aware how you quizzed the unlucky Senora. **1840** LONGF. *Sp. Student* II. iv, Señora, pardon me! **1844** KENDALL *Texan Santa Fé Exped.* II. 336 The Mexican senoras have a frankness of deportment.. which [etc.]. **1860** ANDROS *Pen & P. Sk. Spain* 64 The lovely señora sees it not, nor does the handsome Abigail.

‖**señoria** (seɲoˈria). *rare.* [Sp. *señoría*, f. *señor*: see SEÑOR. Cf. *Signoria.*] A lordship, fief. (In quot. 1634 used for SIGNORIA.)

1634 G. BARRY *Milit. Discipl.* I. i. 2 The Senoria of Venecia was governed by Francisco Carmanola. *a* **1859** W. IRVING *Span. Papers* (1866) 401 (Stanf.) A prince of Portugal..held the señoria of Serpa.

‖**señorita** (seɲoˈrita). [Sp., dim. of SEÑORA.]

1. a. A Spanish title of respect prefixed to the name of a young lady, or used without the name in addressing her.

1850 MAYNE REID *Rifle Rangers* xxvi, 'Do not be alarmed, señorita', said I, approaching.

b. A young Spanish lady.

1823 J. A. QUITMAN *Let.* 23 Aug. in J. F. H. Claiborne *Life & Corr. J. A. Quitman* (1860) I. iv. 85 The belles..'tote' their fans with the air of Spanish señoritas. **1845** DARWIN *Voy. Nat.* xii. 263 In the evening we reached a comfortable farm-house, where there were several pretty señoritas. **1848** LOWELL *Biglow P.* Ser. I. *A Letter*, Caleb hain't no monopoly to court the seenoreetas. **1886** *Athenæum* 28 Aug. 276/1 The artist..filled up his foreground with a group of Spanish señoritas.

2. A name given to a small labroid fish, *Pseudojulis* or *Oxyjulis modestus*, native in Californian waters. Also ***senorita-fish.***

1882 JORDAN & GILBERT *Fishes N. Amer.* 604 *Pseudojulis* Bleeker. Señoritas. *Ibid., P. modestus*... Señorita; Pesce Rey. **1888** GOODE *Amer. Fishes* 299 The Senorita-fish, of Monterey, *Pseudojulis modestus*, is known as 'Pesce-rey'; southward it is called 'Senorita'.

senou, -ow(e, senown, obs. ff. SINEW *sb.*

Senousian, Senoussi, etc., see SENUSSI.

senple, obs. form of SIMPLE.

senr., abbrev. of SENIOR *a.* 1 a. Cf. SEN., SEN.

1763 J. BELL *Trav. from St. Petersburg* p. v/1 Peter Bell, senr. Esq. **1885** T. HARDY *Let.* 18 Mar. (1978) I. 131 The arrangement I made with Mr Macmillan Senr & Mr Craik. **1932** BLUNDEN *Face of England* 73 John Bowers, senr., came through the clap-gate.

‖**senryu** (ˈsɛnriːu). The name of Karai *Senryu* (1718–90), a Japanese poet, used to denote a type of Japanese verse, similar in form to HAIKU but more intentionally humorous or satirical in content and usually without seasonal references.

1938 T. KUNITOMO *Jap. Lit. since 1868* II. i. 156 His submissive attitude which he likened to the spirit of *senryû* increased in his later writings. **1958** *Japan: its Land, People & Culture* xiii. 665/2 By applying the rule of 5.7.5. but disregarding other rigid rules *senryu* (satirical poems) were written in a freer spirit and with humour. **1977** G. GRIGSON *Faber Bk. Epigrams & Epitaphs* p. viii, Both *haiku* and *senryu* are epigrams—if epigram is taken to mean brevity; but a *haiku* has been defined as expressing a moment of vision into the nature of the world and a *senryu* as expressing a moment of satirical insight into the nature of ourselves... With us, rather unfortunately, 'epigram' has come only to suggest something like *senryu*, short and sharp.

sens, variant of CENSE *sb.*[1], incense.

a **1400–50** *Wars Alex.* 4184 Þan knelis doun oure conquirour & callis on his driȝtins, Giffe þam siluir & so & sens at þaim castis. **1473** *Acc. Ld. High Treas. Scot.* I. 64 Item for a pund of sens, iiij s.

sens, variant of CENSE *sb.*[2]

1458 in *10th Rep. Hist. MSS. Comm.* App. v. 299 Ther sholde no manere of man be recevid sensers to passe fre of thar custumes over the sea at sens makyng in no manner wise save [etc.]. **1466** *Ibid.* 303.

sens, obs. form of CENSE *v.*[1]

16.. *Funeral in Popish Times* in *Q. Eliz. Acad.* 33 Att the West dore of the Church, A prælat shall sens the Corps.

sens, obs. form of SINCE.

†**ˈsensable,** *a.*[1] *Obs. rare.* In 5 sensabul. [a. OF. *sensable*, incorrect spelling of *censable*, f. *cense* tax, assessment + -ABLE; see CENSE *sb.*[2]] Capable of assessment or taxation.

1450 *Rolls of Parlt.* V. 204/2 The pepul is forsake the Ile, so at this dai is not xv pepul sensabul. *Ibid.*, Seyng no more stuf of men, nor no stuf of arcerie sensabul left.

†**ˈsensable,** *a.*[2] *Obs. nonce-wd.* [f. SENSE *sb.* + -ABLE.] Of figures of speech: Consisting in an alteration of the sense of words.

1589 PUTTENHAM *Eng. Poesie* III. x. (Arb.) 171 Your second [sort of figures] serues the conceit onely and not th'eare, and may be called sensable, not sensible nor yet sententious.

sensal (ˈsɛnsəl), *a. Philos. rare.* [f. SENSE *sb.* + -AL.] Of or pertaining to sense or meaning (opp. *verbal*), or to the senses.

a **1866** J. GROTE *Treat. Moral Ideals* (1876) xxi. 518 Part of our sensal organization. **1896** V. WELBY in *Mind* V. 29 We might be allowed to coin a new derivative and speak of 'sensal' where we often now speak of 'verbal' questions. **1927** J. M. E. MCTAGGART *Nature of Existence* II. v. xxxviii. 116 We rejected the existence of matter and of sensa, because material and sensal qualities, as ordinarily defined, would not permit the determination, within the substances possessing them, of an infinite series of parts within parts. **1938** C. D. BROAD *Exam. McTaggart's Philos.* II. VII. xxxiii. 249, I conclude then that McTaggart's argument against the possibility of extended particulars, whether material or sensal, breaks down at the fourth step in my synopsis of it.

sensament, var. form of SENSEMENT *Obs.*

sensar, obs. form of CENSER.

1573–80 BARET *Alv.*, A Sensar, *thuribulum.*

sensate (ˈsɛnsət), *a.* [ad. late L. *sensāt-us* gifted with sense, f. *sensus* sense: see -ATE[2] 2.]

1. Endowed with physical sensation.

c **1500** MEDWALL *Nature* (Brandl) 536 Sensualyte..by whom I haue power To do as all sensate bestys do.

†**2.** Of the nature of or involving sensation. *Obs.*

1677 GALE *Crt. Gentiles* III. 86 In his Theætetus he [Plato] laies down this as his opinion,.. It seems to me, that he who knows any thing has a sensate cognition of what he knows. **1813** T. BUSBY *Lucretius* I. III. 290 That Fourth Principle.. From whose power all sensate motions [orig. *sensiferos motus*] flow.

†**3.** ? Endowed with sensibility. *Obs.*

1796 MRS. M. ROBINSON *Angelina* II. 264 Give me the sensate mind, that knows The vast extent of human woes!

4. Perceived by the senses.

1847 in WEBSTER. [Hence in later Dicts.] **1898** *Westm. Gaz.* 27 Sept. 3/1 Mr. Merriman, it would seem, is of those who hold that poetry co-exists with the least congenial of elements, being common to all sensate things.

5. *Sociol.* In the theory of P. A. Sorokin, a type of culture in which the satisfaction of material needs and desires is the main objective. Cf. IDEALISTIC *a.* 2 and IDEATIONAL *a.* 2.

1937 [see IDEATIONAL *a.* 2]. **1959** C. C. ZIMMERMAN in J. S. Roucek *Contemp. Sociol.* 18 In sensate culture the main outlook for the individual is for extra-person stimuli, for articles which appeal to the ordinary untrained tastes, such as is seen in a quantity consumption culture. **1967** T. PARSONS *Sociological Theory & Mod. Society* IV. xii. 388 The idealistic synthesis has then proceeded to break down into an increasingly sensate phase. **1977** J. D. DOUGLAS in Douglas & Johnson *Existential Sociol.* i. 69 Most men have distinguished between such sacred thought and everyday, practical thought. (It is important, however, to note that rarely has this distinction been as sharp and important as in our increasingly sensate or secular culture.)

sensate (sɛnˈseɪt), *v.* [f. L. *sens-us* SENSE *sb.* + -ATE[3], after SENSATION.]

1. *trans.* To perceive by sense; to have a sensation of.

a **1652** J. SMITH *Sel. Disc.* IV. iv. (1821) 93 These corporeal motions, as they seem to arise from nothing else but merely from the *machina* of the body itself; so they could not at all be sensated but by the soul. **1665** HOOKE *Microgr.* 179 Each of them can distinctly sensate or see onely those parts which are very neer perpendicularly oppos'd to it. **1889** *Academy* 16 Nov. 323/2 We find an irresistible impulse to find strain ..or motion..of the ether wherever we sensate anything electrical.

†**2.** *intr.* To have sensation. *Obs.*

1672 PENN *Spir. Truth Vind.* 24 No man can live, move, sensate, or act but from the original Heat, Life, Motion and Action of that which did beget him. **1687** A. LOVELL tr. *Bergerac's Com. Hist.* 112 When it finds only such, as are proper for sensation, it sensates.

Hence **senˈsating** *vbl. sb.* and *ppl. a.*

a **1652** J. SMITH *Sel. Disc.* v. 149 Indeed, without such a universal sensating faculty as this is, we should never know when our souls are in conjunction with the Deity. **1888** H. W. PARKER *Spir. Beauty* 58 Sir John Lubbock's experiments proved nothing but the simple sensating of certain crude colors by bees.

sensation (sɛnˈseɪʃən). [ad. med.L. *sensātiōn-em*, f. L. *sens-us* SENSE *sb.*, after late L. *sensātus* SENSATE *a.*: see -ATION. Cf. F. *sensation* (OF. *sensacion*, Oresme 14th c.), Sp. *sensacion*, Pg. *sensação*, It. *sensazione.*]

1. a. An operation of any of the senses; a psychical affection or state of consciousness consequent on and related to a particular condition of some portion of the bodily organism, or a particular impression received by one of the organs of sense. Now commonly in more precise use, restricted to the subjective element in any operation of one of the senses, a physical 'feeling' considered apart from the resulting 'perception' of an object.

Often const. *of* with sb. defining the nature of the sensation, as in *a sensation of giddiness, nausea, cold*, etc.

1615 CROOKE *Body of Man* 525 Finally, that our Motions and Sensations should not be rash or phanaticall as they are in such as are phreneticall, that is, haue their braines inflamed. **1646** SIR T. BROWNE *Pseud. Ep.* I. iii. 8 Their understanding..submitteth unto the fallacies of sence, and is unable to rectifie the error of its sensations. **1759** PORTERFIELD *Eye* II. 343 The smallest or most refrangible Rays will excite the shortest and weakest Vibrations for making a Sensation of deep Violet. **1785** REID *Intell. Powers* 599 When I grasp an ivory ball in my hand, I feel a certain sensation of touch. **1804** ABERNETHY *Surg. Obs.* 192 He said his sensations were such as would induce him to believe that his brain was loose. **1845** R. WILLIAMS in *Encycl. Metrop.* VII. 544/2 An uneasy sensation and tension of the præcordia. **1892** BIERCE *In the Midst of Life* 23 The familiar sensation of an abraded shin recalled his dazed faculties.

b. In generalized use: The operation or function of the senses; 'perception by means of the senses' (J.). Now commonly (esp. in philosophical language) the subjective element in the operation of the senses; physical 'feeling'.

1642 H. MORE *Song of Soul* II. ii. II. xi, O sunken souls, slaves of sensation. **1677** GALE *Crt. Gentiles* III. I. iv. 86 As it now appears, science is nothing else than sensation, or a particular experimental feeling knowledge. **1739** HUME *Hum. Nat.* I. i. §2 (1888) 7 Impressions may be divided into two kinds, those of Sensation and those of Reflexion. **1812** SHELLEY *Q. Mab* I. 24 Or is it only a sweet slumber Stealing o'er sensation? **1876** MAUDSLEY *Physiol. Mind* iv. 221 Sensation expresses merely the state of simple feeling, without reference to an external cause.

†**c.** Observation by the senses, actual seeing or hearing. *Obs.*

1657 J. SERGEANT *Schism Dispach't* 104 The testimony of others founded in their several sensations being faithfully conveyed to us by undeniable tradition, are as unquestionably certain as if we had seen them ourselves.

d. Faculty of perceiving by the senses, physical sensibility.

1799 *Med. Jrnl.* II. 451 When excitement is produced in this system..then a corresponding change is occasioned in the nervous system, and sensation returns. **1869** *Lancet* 18 Dec. 842/2 The woman is of an older age than in other described cases [of scleroderma]. The sensation seemed not to be impaired.

†**e.** Effect produced on the senses; in quots. = appearance. *Obs.*

1662 EVELYN *Chalcogr.* Table, How to express the sensation of the Relievo or Extancie of objects, by the Hatches in Graving. **1663** BOYLE *Exp. Colours* ii. 10 Colour may be considered, either as it is a quality residing in the body that is said to be coloured, or to modifie the light after such or such a manner; or else as the Light it self, which so modifi'd, strikes upon the organ of sight, and so causes that Sensation, which we call Colour.

f. A popular name for the *aura epileptica*, the physical premonition of an epileptic seizure.

1899 *Allbutt's Syst. Med.* VII. 770 Attacks [of Epilepsy] may consist only of the 'warning' or 'sensation'... This has led to the popular use of the word 'sensation' as a synonym for the minor attacks.

2. a. A mental feeling, an emotion. Now chiefly, the characteristic feeling arising in some particular circumstances.

1755 SHEBBEARE *Lydia* (1769) II. 421, I feel a sensation of distress in my bosom which is intolerable. **1758** JOHNSON *Idler* No. 100 ¶8 She smiles not by sensation, but by practice. **1809–10** COLERIDGE *Friend* (ed. 3) III. 312 How distinct and different the sensation of positiveness is from the sense of certainty. **1821** SCOTT *Kenilw.* xl, All other sensations were, for the time, lost in the agony which his haughty spirit felt. **1883** FR. M. PEARD *Contrad.* iii, 'At last I have realized a dream', she said. 'Do you know the sensation?'

b. Mental apprehension, sense or 'realization' *of* something.

1639 ROUSE *Heav. Univ.* (1702) 157 To have a continual sensation of thee. **1753** HOGARTH *Anal. Beauty* xi. 82 The nice sensation we naturally have of what certain quantities.. are fittest. **1775** JOHNSON *Tax. no Tyr.* 9 Those who look but little into futurity, have perhaps the quickest sensation of the present. **1817** COLERIDGE *Biog. Lit.* I. iv. 85 Therefore is it the prime merit of genius..so to represent familiar objects as to awaken..freshness of sensation. **1864** BAGEHOT *Lit. Stud.* II. 139 Men of ordinary nerves who feel a little of the pains of society, who perceive what really passes..could well observe how keen was Thackeray's sensation of common events.

†**c.** Capacity for (moral) feeling, sensibility.

1742 *Johnson's Debates* (1787) II. 247 (*St. Aubyn*) He has undoubtedly a most passionate love for his native country, a passion which a man of any sensation can hardly divest himself of.

†**d.** What is felt or thought; sentiment, opinion.

1788 JEFFERSON *Writ.* (1859) IV. 127 You would of course, however, wish to know the sensations here on those facts.

3. An excited or violent feeling. **a.** An exciting experience; a strong emotion (e.g. of terror, hope, curiosity, etc.) aroused by some particular occurrence or situation. Also, in generalized use, the production of violent emotion as an aim in works of literature or art.

1808 PIKE *Sources Mississ.* (1810) 237 We may be supposed to have also had our sensations. **1859** GEO. ELIOT *Adam Bede* lii, He..was free from that periodicity of sensations which we call post-time. **1863** MANSEL *Lett., Lect.*, etc. (1873) 242 The cheap publications which supply sensation for the million in penny and halfpenny numbers. **1867** LOWELL *Among my Bks.* Ser. I. *Rousseau* (1870) 346 [Petrarch was] an intellectual voluptuary, a moral *dilettante*, the first instance of that character, since too common, the gentleman in search of a sensation. **1905** C. WHITNEY *Jungle Trails* xi. 303, I knew it was a tiger..; and as the jerky roar grew nearer and nearer, I stood there having sensations—I do assure you.

b. A condition of excited feeling produced in a community by some occurrence; a strong impression (e.g. of horror, admiration, surprise, etc.) produced in an audience or body of spectators, and manifested by their demeanour.

1779 EARL MALMESBURY *Diaries & Corr.* I. 257 What had passed already caused a great sensation in foreign Courts. **1818** SOUTHEY in *Q. Rev.* XVIII. 10 His death produced what in the phraseology of the present day is called, a great sensation. **1837** DICKENS *Pickw.* xxxiv, A slight sensation was perceptible in the body of the court. **1855** MACAULAY *Hist. Eng.* xvii. IV. 46 The sensation produced by this work was immense. **1879** MCCARTHY *Own Times* III. xliv. 333 His death created a profound sensation. **1885** HALL CAINE *Shadow of Crime* xlii, Amid much sensation, the witness gave the name of the Sheriff of Cumberland.

c. An event or a person that 'creates a sensation'.

1864 *Times* 11 Apr. 1/4 The greatest sensation of the day: grand Incantation Scene from Der Freischütz. **1884** *St. James's Gaz.* 29 Nov. 6 The sensation of a London season was the appearance of a new ballerina in a new ballet.

4. *colloq.* and *slang.* A 'taste', small quantity.

1859 F. FOWLER *South. Lights* 52 A Sensation. [*i.e.*] Half-a-glass of sherry. **1859** *Hotten's Slang Dict.*, *Sensation*, a quartern of gin.

5. *attrib.* and *Comb.* (chiefly in sense 3 a).

a. simple attrib., as ***sensation drama***, ***-novel***, ***novelist***, ***-paragraph***, ***-scene***, ***story***, etc.; **b.** objective, as ***sensation-monger***, ***-seeker***; ***sensation-giving***, ***-hungry***, ***-mongering***, ***-seeking*** adjs. **c.** Special comb.: †**sensation cell**, a sense-cell (*obs.*).

1892 LIEW & BEYER tr. *Ziehen's Introd. Physiol. Psychol.* 160 He has lost the acoustic memory-cells, but retained the acoustic *sensation-cells. **1904** E. B. TITCHENER tr. *Wundt's Physiol. Psychol.* I. 289 It thus becomes necessary to posit the existence of two sorts of cortical cells: sensation cells and idea cells. **1860** MRS. S. COWELL *Jrnl.* 13 Mar. in M. Willson Disher *Cowells in Amer.* (1934) 36 We..saw Matilda Heron ..in a 'new *sensation Drama' called 'Mathilde'. **1861** THACKERAY *Round. Papers, On Two Round. Papers*, At the theatres they have a new name for their melodramatic pieces, and call them 'Sensation Dramas'. **1863** TREVELYAN *Compet. Wallah* (1866) 336 When we see in Piccadilly a file of men with blank boards on their shoulders, we become aware that a sensation drama has been put in hand at one of the leading theatres. **1865** MILL *Exam. Hamilton's Philos.* xxvii. 526 The knowledge-giving and the *sensation-giving properties of an impression of sense. **1951** KOESTLER *Age of Longing* v. 86 She was sorry to disappoint the expectations of *sensation-hungry journalists. **1882** A. MATHESON in *Macm. Mag.* XLVI. 496 What mere *sensation-monger would have chosen this morally obtuse old Pharisee? **1925** W. DEEPING *Sorrell & Son* xvi. 147 It wasn't..our hard work, Stephen, that saved us, but luck, and the noise made by a section of a *sensation-mongering press. **1937** *Downside Rev.* LV. 402 The idea of his indulging in 'sensation-mongering' of any sort or kind was ridiculous. **1980** *Times Lit. Suppl.* 24 Oct. 1210/5 They have given a..sober account of..the trial, leaving all the sensation-mongering to frequent interspersions from newspaper headlines. **1863** *Q. Rev.* Apr. 486 A *sensation novel, as a matter of course, abounds in incident. **1864** *Edin. Rev.* July 53 Two or three years ago nobody would have known what was meant by a Sensation Novel. **1863** *Sensation novelist [see PURPOSE *sb.* 3]. **1932** Q. D. LEAVIS *Fiction & Reading Public* II. iv. 154 Mrs. Radcliffe makes an appeal less to the nerves than to the imagination... The sensation novelists make a brute assault on the feelings and nerves in quite another way. **1861** *Illustr. Lond. News* 25 May 485/1 The local inditers of 'screamers' and '*sensation' paragraphs. **1861** H. MORLEY *Jrnl. London Play-goer* (1866) 282 Mr. Falconer's 'Peep o' Day'.. deserves full houses..for what is called, according to the new term in theatrical slang, which Mr. Boucicault imported for us from the other side of the Atlantic, its '*sensation' scene. **1865** EARLE *Sax. Chron.* 340 One of the established sensation scenes of History. **1976** D. FRANCIS *In France* i. 21 All day..cars..disgorged crowds of reporters, photographers and plain *sensation-seekers. **1923** R. MACAULAY *Told by Idiot* IV. 296 It was a queer affair, born of the emotionalism and *sensation-seeking that beset many people at that time. **1869** L. M. ALCOTT *Little Women* II. xi. 157 She took to writing *sensation stories—for..even all-perfect America read rubbish. **1862** *Athenæum* 23 Aug. 233 Much of his pamphlet is mere '*sensation' writing.

d. *Audiometry.* **sensation level**, the number of sensation units by which the loudness of a sound (supposedly proportional to its pressure amplitude) exceeds the loudness at which it would be barely perceptible; **sensation unit**, the unit of loudness by which two sounds differ if one is louder by a factor $10^{0.05}$. (Both terms are disused.)

If loudness were truly proportional to pressure (or displacement) amplitude, and hence to the square root of power, a sensation unit would be equal to a decibel.

1925 J. C. STEINBERG in *Physical Rev.* XXVI. 508 By sensation level is meant the number of units that the amplitude of any sound wave must be reduced in order to reach the threshold. **1927** *Ibid.* XXIX. 597 A unit of loudness somewhat better for our purpose would have been the least perceptible increment of loudness of a 700 cycle tone compared with its sensation level. **1929** H. FLETCHER *Speech & Hearing* iii. 68 A change of the power level of a sound by one decibel is approximately the smallest that the ear can detect. When this unit is used in this connection the term 'sensation unit' has come into use. The sensation level of any sound reaching the ears is the number of sensation units it is above the threshold level for audition. **1931** STEWART & LINDSAY *Acoustics* ix. 224 For the sake of convenience several authors are using the terms sensation unit and sensation level.

sensational (sɛn'seɪʃənəl), *a.* [f. SENSATION + -AL[1].]

1. Of or pertaining to or dependent upon sensation or the senses.

1840 WHEWELL *Philos. Induct. Sci.* (1847) II. 651 No apprehension of things is purely ideal: no experience of external things is purely sensational. **1860** FARRAR *Orig. Lang.* (1865) 98 If the entire lexicon of every language be capable of being reduced to a number of sensational roots,.. Grammar always remains as the indisputable result of the pure reason. **1877** E. CAIRD *Philos. Kant* II. i. 219 Hume had actually attempted to reduce mathematical truth within the limits of sensational experience. **1893** PULSFORD *Loyalty to Christ* II. 348, I am persuaded that the Divine-human life as much includes sensational pleasure, as intelligence, righteousness, purity, and goodness.

absol. **1854** LOWELL *Among my Bks.* Ser. II. *Keats* (end), The sensational was elevated into the typical by the control of that finer sense which underlies the senses and is the spirit of them.

2. Of philosophical theories: Regarding sensation as the sole source of knowledge.

1854 A. G. HENDERSON tr. *Cousin's Philos. of Kant* iii. 32 The sensational philosophy..pretends to deduce all knowledge from experience. **1855** *Dubl. Rev.* XXXVIII. 198 The Sensational School [of Philosophy], as it has been called. **1860** YOUNG *Prov. Reason* 292 In opposition to a mere sensational, materialistic, positive philosophy.

3. a. Of works of literature or art, hence of writers: Dealing in 'sensation' (see SENSATION 3 a), aiming at violently exciting effects. Also of incidents in fiction or in real life: Calculated to produce a startling impression.

1863 MANSEL *Lett., Lect.*, etc. (1873) 242 The above samples may be considered as belonging to the aristocratic branch of sensational literature. **1864** *Times* 11 Apr. 8/3 Astley's... Stupendous sensational effect, never equalled on any stage. **1868** JAS. YORK tr. *Juan Manuel's C'nt Lucanor* (1888) Pref. 7 An age surfeited with the sensational novels that pour from our circulating libraries in an uninterrupted stream. **1879** B. TAYLOR *Germ. Lit.* 190 The 'sensational' element which has crept into English and American literature is worse than the affected classicism of the 17th century. **1885** *Diary of Actress* 131 Rehearsing all the morning: a most sensational piece.

b. *absol.* Also *U.S.* as *sb.*, a sensational journal or journalist.

1899 H. WRIGHT *Depopulation* 90 In modern life, where the electric waves of the sensational vibrate through a continent rapidly. **1901** *Scribner's Mag.* Apr. 407/2 The sensationals had been encouraging cranks to remember the rights of labor.

sensationalism (sɛn'seɪʃənəlɪz(ə)m). [f. SENSATIONAL *a.* + -ISM.]

1. *Philos.* The theory that sensation is the only source of knowledge.

1846 J. D. MORELL *Hist. Philos.* I. p. x, There are four expressions which occupy a very prominent place throughout the whole work, and those are—sensationalism, idealism, scepticism, and mysticism. Now of these four, the first, I believe, is a word entirely new, and, therefore, demands some apology for its introduction. **1867** LEWES *Hist. Philos.* II. 228 Here is stated, in the broadest manner, the principle of sensationalism. **1877** E. CAIRD *Philos. Kant* Introd. ii. 13 Sensationalism necessitates..a materialistic explanation of the Universe.

2. Addiction to what is sensational in literature or art.

1865 *Sat. Rev.* 4 Feb. 145/2 That well of sensationalism pure and undefiled, the 'London Journal'. **1886** FROST *Remin. Country Journalist* 215 Without the vicious sensationalism which renders so objectionable a large portion of the cheap periodical literature of the day.

sensationalist (sɛn'seɪʃənəlɪst). [f. SENSATIONAL + -IST.]

1. *Philos.* One who regards the senses as the ultimate source of all knowledge.

1847 J. D. MORELL *Hist. Philos.* (ed. 2) I. i. 118 Sensationalists have attempted to contravene this view. **1855** *Dubl. Rev.* XXXVIII. 199 Locke himself did not profess to be a thorough-going Sensationalist. **1867** LEWES *Hist. Philos.* II. 228 [Hobbes] is the precursor of modern sensationalists [1846 ed. Materialism].

attrib. **1860** FARRAR *Orig. Lang.* (1865) 150 We are not surprised to find that Locke was claimed as the founder..of a sensationalist school. **1877** E. CAIRD *Philos. Kant* Introd. iv. 60 The sensationalist view of the development of knowledge. *Ibid.* 61 A sensationalist theory of knowing.

2. One whose aim is to make a sensation; a sensational writer. Also *attrib.* or as *adj.*

1868 PAGET *Lucretia* 309 The circumstances of most people's every-day life are as unlike those depicted by the sensationalists as anything that can be imagined. **1884** *Pall Mall Gaz.* 2 Aug. 3/1 The most dangerous of modern criminals..is above all a great sensationalist. **1979** *Guardian* 24 Aug. 8/6 A sensationalist and grossly misrepresentative newspaper story. **1980** *Times Lit. Suppl.* 18 Apr. 443/5 Compared with the style of Lady Falkender, Joe Haines *et toute cette galère*, so effectively convicted by their own sensationalist memoirs, the Garden Suburb was distinctly civilized in tone.

Hence **sensationa'listic** *a.*, pertaining to or of the nature of sensationalism.

1882 *Pall Mall Gaz.* 18 Nov. 7 His moral sense is blunted by his sensationalistic views. **1886** *Encycl. Brit.* XXI. 40/2 The dominant sensationalistic materialism of France.

sensationalize (sɛn'seɪʃənəlaɪz), *v.* [f. SENSATIONAL *a.* + -IZE.] *trans.* To make sensational.

1. *nonce-use.* To restrict (concepts) to what is given in sensation.

1851 MANSEL *Proleg. Log.* 33 Individualize your concepts, does not mean sensationalize them, unless the senses are the only sources of presentation.

2. a. To subject to the influence of 'sensation' or factitious emotion. **b.** To exaggerate in a sensational manner.

1863 *Reader* 31 Oct. 507/2 Possibly we should learn in time to imitate the German example [in establishing dramatic academies], and another generation might refuse to be sensationalized, elevated and generally educated by upholstery, 'headers', and ghosts. **1869** *Athenæum* 18 Dec. 824 But in that class of specimens..are none of the merits of the above, while all their faults are vulgarized and sensationalized. **1900** *Daily News* 18 Dec. 5/6 The Paris Press as a whole does not sensationalise De Wet's raid, and the recent success of Delarey.

Hence **sen,sationali'zation**.

1955 *Times* 15 Aug. 7/5 By silence, and by mistrust of any publicity save that in the jargon of scientific journals, science has succeeded (in the words of Rutherford) in its own 'sensationalization'. **1977** *Lancet* 27 Aug. 449/1 It fell into disuse with..the sensationalisation of the 'opium vice' by writers such as De Quincey.

sensationally (sɛn'seɪʃənəlɪ), *adv.* [f. SENSATIONAL *a.* + -LY[2].] In a sensational manner.

1. With respect to sensation or feeling.

1865 *Pall Mall Gaz.* 3 Apr. 11 It is an old subject, argumentatively as well as sensationally. **1886** L. OLIPHANT in *Mem.* (1891) II. 335 For this cause He came into the world, that he might unite us sensationally to His Father.

2. In a manner intended to make a sensation.

1894 *Rev. of Rev.* (Amer. ed.) Oct. 356/1 Saratoga..has been sensationally exposed in the newspapers as the most reckless..gambling resort of all this year's watering-places.

sensationary (sɛn'seɪʃənərɪ), *a. rare.* [f. SENSATION + -ARY[2].] = SENSATIONAL 2.

1864 *Realm* 18 May 5 It has lately been urged that Shakspeare is sensationary—that Hamlet, Lear, Macbeth, Othello, are heroes of strange and wild adventure.

sen'sationish, *a. nonce-wd.* [f. SENSATION + -ISH[1].] Bordering on the sensational.

1863 *Reader* 31 Oct. 497 The subject is a repulsive one, the treatment of it somewhat sensationish, and the plot is not well kept in hand.

sensationism (sɛn'seɪʃənɪz(ə)m). [f. SENSATION + -ISM.] **1.** = SENSATIONALISM 2.

1863 MANSEL *Lett., Lect.*, etc. (1873) 242 (art. *Sensation Novels*) In them we have sensationism pure and undisguised. **1878** *Scribner's Monthly* Nov. 144/2 Sensationism is a grievous vice of the pulpit... But sensationism is only an insurrection..against conventionality.

2. = SENSATIONALISM 1.

1846 J. D. MORELL *Hist. Philos.* I. p. xi, Next, I thought of sensism and sensationism, as being terms well adapted to describe the philosophy which builds itself up upon sense, or sensation; but these seemed to fail in respect to taste and euphony. **1936** *Brit. Jrnl. Psychol.* July 96 Stout saw the futility of associationism and sensationism forty years ago. **1948** W. McDOUGALL *Social Psychol.* (ed. 29) 427 The essential novelty (for German psychology) of the teaching of this [sc. *Gestalt*] school is the repudiation of atomistic sensationism.

sensationist (sɛn'seɪʃənɪst). [f. SENSATION + -IST.] **1.** One who deals in sensation; a sensational novelist, dramatist, or journalist.

1861 W. H. RUSSELL in *Times* 24 Sept., '*Vult decipi, decipiatur*' is the motto of the Sensationists. **1863** MANSEL *Lett., Lect.*, etc. (1873) 248 (art. *Sensation Novels*) To these specimens of the sensationist's power of making, may we venture to add one more as a sample of his ability in marring? **1864** DASENT *Jest & Earnest* (1873) II. 27 Of late we have been handed over..to the tender mercies of the sensationists both on and off the stage.

2. = SENSATIONALIST 1. Also *attrib.*

1890 W. JAMES *Princ. Psychol.* I. ix. 277 Now most believers in the ego make the same mistake as the associationists and sensationists whom they oppose. **1942** E. G. BORING *Sensation & Perception* i. 4 An empiricist is apt to be a sensationist, because it is by way of the senses that the mind has experience of the external world. **1953** K. BRITTON *J. S. Mill* vi. 192 From Locke to James Mill, there continued a complicated debate about the way in which we know physical objects; Reid and Hamilton providing an intelligent opposition to the sensationist school.

Hence **sensatio'nistic** *a.*

1936 *Brit. Jrnl. Psychol.* July 97 The agreement, in principle, to discard the sensationistic hypothesis.

sensationless (sɛn'seɪʃənlɪs), *a.* [f. SENSATION + -LESS.] Without sensation.

1874 TYNDALL *Presid. Addr. Brit. Assoc.* 81 Imagine them [*sc.* atoms] separate and sensationless.

sensative: see SENSITIVE.

†**sen'sator.** *Obs. rare.* [f. SENSATE *v.* + -OR.] An agent concerned in sensation.

1615 CROOKE *Body of Man* 41 The Braine therefore, not the Heart, is the first Mouer, and first Sensator. *Ibid.* 288 The Philosopher calleth sleepe ἠρεμία τοῦ πρώτου αἰσθητικοῦ, the rest of the first sensator.

sensatorial (sɛnsə'tɔərɪəl), *a.* [f. SENSATE *v.* + -ORIAL.] Of or pertaining to sensation.

1890 J. SULLY in *Academy* 16 Aug. 136/2 [Weber's] psychophysical theory of sensatorial intensity.

†**'sensatory**, *a. Obs. rare*[−1]. [f. SENSATE *v.* + -ORY[2].] = SENSORY.

1741 A. MONRO *Anat. Nerves* Wks. (1781) 331 The objections against the sensatory nerves acting by vibration.

senscer, obs. form of CENSER.

senschepe, -chip(e, var. ff. SHENDSHIP.

sense (sɛns), *sb.* Forms: 6 **cense, sens**, 5–8 **sence**, 7 *Sc.* **senss**, 5– **sense**. [a. F. *sens* or ad. L. *sensus* (*u* stem), perception, feeling, faculty of perception, meaning, f. *sentire* to feel. Cf. Pr. *sens, sentz*, Sp. *seso*, Pg. *siso*, It. *senso*.]

I. Faculty of perception or sensation.

1. a. Each of the special faculties, connected with a bodily organ, by which man and other animals perceive external objects and changes in the condition of their own bodies. Usually reckoned as five—sight, hearing, smell, taste, touch. Also called ***outward*** or ***external sense*** (cf. 8).

Earlier called *the five wits*: see WIT.

1526 *Pilgr. Perf.* (W. de W. 1531) 127 Eyther within or withoutforth, that is to saye eyther in the conscyence, or in the outwarde censes. **1553** T. WILSON *Rhet.* 112 The common sense..is therefore so called, because it geueth iudgement, of al the fiue outwarde senses. **1647** COWLEY *Mistr., Not Fair* 21 My Reason strait did to my Senses shew, That they might be mistaken too. **1669** HOLDER *Elem. Speech* 1 Of the Five Senses, Two are usually and most properly called the Senses of Learning..; And these are Hearing and Seeing. **1690** LOCKE *Hum. Und.* IV. xix. §10 How is he prepared easily to swallow, not only against all Probability, but even the clear Evidence of his Senses, the Doctrine of Transubstantiation? **1698** FARQUHAR *Love & Bottle* I. i, I must have the evidence of more senses than one to confirm me of its truth. **1739** HUME *Hum. Nature* II. i. (1874) I. 336 A, The only defect of our senses is, that they give us disproportion'd images of things. **1753** MISS COLLIER *Art Torment.* Concl. (1811) 221 With various inventions of disagreeableness for offending some or all of the senses! **1835** BECKFORD *Alcobaça & Batalha* 111 My sense of hearing is painfully acute. **1841** T. R. JONES *Anim. Kingd.* (1871) 860 The sense of touch in Mammalia is diffused over the whole surface of the body.

†**b.** Used for: An organ of sense. *Obs.*

1526 *Pilgr. Perf.* (W. de W. 1531) 7 Wyssheth that he neuer had had eyes to se..neyther eares to here..ne other senses to haue knowen [etc.]. **1538** STARKEY *England* 48 To the hede, wyth the yes, yerys, and other sensys therin. **1604** SHAKS. *Oth.* IV. ii. 154 Mine Eyes, mine Eares, or any Sence.

c. *pl.* The faculties of physical perception or sensation as opposed to the higher faculties of intellect, spirit, etc.

1841 EMERSON *Ess.* vii. *Prudence* ¶2 Prudence is the virtue of the senses. It is the science of appearances. *Ibid.* ¶3 The world of the senses is a world of shows. **1865** M. ARNOLD *Ess. in Crit.* Ser. I. vi. (1886) 215 The life of the senses has its deep poetry.

d. Applied to similar faculties of perception, not scientifically delimited, or only conjectured to exist.

muscular sense: see MUSCULAR *a.* 1. ***sixth sense***: see quot. 1829; also, the feelings connected with sexual pleasure.

1690 LOCKE *Hum. Und.* II. ii. §3 Had Mankind been made with but four Senses, the Qualities then, which are the Object of the Fifth Sense, had been as far from our notice, Imagination, and Conception, as now any belonging to a Sixth, Seventh, or Eighth Sense, can possibly be. **1699** MAUNDRELL *Acc. Turks* in *Journ. Jerus.* (1721) T 2b, They know hardly any Pleasure but that of the sixth Sense. **1768** TUCKER *Lt. Nat.* I. 405 We may possibly be capable of twenty senses, but being provided with inlets only for five, have no more conception of the others than a blind man has of light. **1822–9** *Good's Study Med.* (ed. 3) IV. 22 The bat appears to be sensible of the presence of external objects.. that are neither seen, smelt, heard, touched, or tasted... And hence many naturalists have ascribed a sixth sense to this animal. *Ibid.* 23 In Germany it has of late been attempted to be shown that every man is possessed of a sixth sense [viz. a bodily feeling of health and elasticity, or of lassitude and fatigue]. **1858** HAWTHORNE *Fr. & It. Note-bks.* (1871) II. 121 Certainly it was in God's power to create beings who should communicate with nature by innumerable other senses than those few which we possess.

e. That one of the senses which is indicated by the context. Now *rare* or *Obs.*

1607 SHAKS. *Cor.* II. ii. 120 When by and by the dinne of Warre gan pierce His readie sence. **1626** B. JONSON *Staple of N.* III. iv, Ha? I am somewhat short In my sense too... My hearing is very dead, you must speake quicker. **1683** MOXON *Mech. Exerc., Printing* xi. ¶23 The process of making Inck being..noysom and ungrateful to the Sence. **1733** POPE *Ep. Cobham* 53 So Darkness strikes the sense no less than Light. *a* **1774** GOLDSM. *Surv. Exp. Philos.* (1776) I. 319 Salts, metals, plants, ordures of every kind..make one mass of corruption, equally displeasing to the sense, and injurious to the health. **1794** MRS. RADCLIFFE *Myst. Udolpho* xliv, As he gazed, he perceived the countenance of the knight change and begin to fade, till his whole form gradually vanished from his astonished sense! **1819** SCOTT *Ivanhoe* xliii, The fearful picture of a vision, which appals my sense with hideous fantasies, but convinces not my reason. **1833** TENNYSON *Two Voices* 285 That heat of inward evidence, By which he doubts against the sense.

f. With defining word: the intuitive knowledge or appreciation of what action or judgement is appropriate to a given situation or sphere of activity. (Closely related to sense 1 d.)

1879, 1880 [see *colour-sense* s.v. COLOUR, COLOR *sb.* 19]. **1923** G. ATHERTON *Black Oxen* vii. 23 The reportorial news-sense died painlessly. **1926**, etc. [see *dress sense* s.v. DRESS *sb.* 4a]. **1932**, etc. [see *clothes-sense* s.v. CLOTHES *sb. pl.* 4]. **1932** E. V. LUCAS *Reading, Writing & Remembering* i. 29 Had he [*sc.* Dickens] been possessed of more prudence or money-sense..his last years would have been more leisurely and peaceful. **1957** H. READ *Tenth Muse* xxii. 182 The producer, and the actor, are firmly convinced that there is some sixth sense, a feeling for what is possible in the theatre, a 'stage-sense'.

2. *transf.* An instinctive or acquired faculty of perception or accurate estimation. Now chiefly const. *of* (locality, distance, etc.).

1567 MAPLET *Gr. Forest* 82b, There is saith Tullie, in the Dogge a merueylous perceiuerance and sharpe sense to know who doth him good. *a* **1586** SIDNEY *Arcadia* I. (Sommer) 84b, This Basilius (hauing the quicke sense of a louer) tooke, as though his Mistres had giuen a secret reprehension. **1590** SPENSER *F.Q.* II. Introd. iv, Ne let him then admire, But yield his sence to be too blunt and bace, That no'te without an hound fine footing trace. **1599** SHAKS. *Hen. V*, IV. i. 308 Take from them now The sence of reckning. **1606** —— *Tr. & Cr.* IV. v. 54 A woman of quick sence. **1888, 1889** [see LOCALITY 8].

3. In generalized use: The senses viewed as forming a single faculty in contradistinction to intellect, will, etc.; the exercise or function of this faculty, sensation.

1538 STARKEY *England* 48 Al wyt, reson, and sens, felyng, lyfe, and al other natural powar, spryngyth out of the hart. **1553** EDEN *Treat. Newe Ind.* (Arb.) 9 Nothinge is in vnderstandinge, but the same was fyrst in sense. **1643** SIR T. BROWNE *Relig. Med.* II. §15. 180 Thus we adore vertue, though to the eyes of sense shee bee invisible. **1690** LOCKE *Hum. Und.* IV. xi. §6 Though mathematical demonstrations depend not upon sense. **1732** POPE *Ess. Man* I. 226 What thin partitions Sense from Thought divide. **1794** PALEY *Evid.* (1825) II. 324 A body is a real thing, an object of sense. **1794** S. WILLIAMS *Vermont* (1809) I. 208 The only objects, on which the Indian had employed his reason, were those of external sense. **1827** WORDSW. *Eccl. Sonn.* II. xxx. 2 The Soul, freed from the bonds of Sense, And to her God restored by evidence Of things not seen. **1877** E. CAIRD *Philos. Kant* Introd. v. 91 The doctrine that sense is confused thought.

4. a. *pl.* The faculties of corporeal sensation considered as channels for gratifying the desire for pleasure and the lusts of the flesh. Also *sing.*, any one of such faculties so regarded.

1597 *Pilgr. Parnassus* IV. 480 Ile bringe you to sweet wantoninge yonge maides Wheare you shall all youre hungrie sences feaste. **1608** *Yorkshire Trag.* IV. 69 That heauen should say we must not sin, and yet made women! giues our sences waie to finde pleasure, which being found confounds vs. *a* **1657** MURE *Sonn.* vi. 5 Thy beutyes did my sensses suire suppryse, Or eir thy sight my ravischt eyes did blesse. **1720** MRS. MANLEY *Power of Love* (1741) 239 To take in whole Nature,..and have her every Sense gratify'd with the agreeable Feast of Variety! **1819** SHELLEY *Cenci* I. i. 69 Seeing I please my senses as I list. **1820** BYRON *Juan* IV. xxvii, Love was born *with* them, *in* them, so intense, It was their very spirit—not a sense.

b. *collect. sing.*

a **1586** SIDNEY *Arcadia* I. (Sommer) 52b, This bastard Loue..vtterly subuerts the course of nature, in making reason giue place to sense. **1603** SHAKS. *Meas. for M.* II. ii. 169 Can it be, That Modesty may more betray our Sence Then womans lightnesse? **1657–83** EVELYN *Hist. Relig.* (1850) I. 230 She [the soul]..oft has..escaped the inescations of sense. **1738** WESLEY *Hymn*, '*Infinite Power, Eternal Lord*' v, But Flesh and Sense, enslav'd to Sin Drawing best Thoughts away. **1764** GOLDSM. *Trav.* 123 But small the bliss that sense alone bestows, And sensual bliss is all the nation knows. **1852** M. ARNOLD *Empedocles* II. 374 Some bondage of the flesh.., Some slough of sense. **1871** J. R. MACDUFF *Mem. Patmos* xviii. 249 The life of sense—the life of selfish and sensuous pleasure.

†**5.** Capability of feeling, as a quality of the body and its parts; liability to feel pain, irritation, etc. ***to the sense***, to the quick. *Obs.*

1563–83 FOXE *A. & M.* 2083/1 He did lye..with his heeles so hye, y[t] by meanes the bloud was fallen from his feete, his feet wer almost without sense for a long time. **1604** SHAKS. *Oth.* V. i. 11, I haue rub'd this yong Quat almost to the sense, And he growes angry. **1612** BACON *Ess., Death* (Arb.) 384 For the most vitall parts are not the quickest of sence. **1672** WISEMAN *Wounds* II. x. 69 The wound.. extinguished both Sence and Motion of the Member. **1691** RAY *Creation* I. (1692) 150 A..nervous Ligament..apt to stretch and shrink again as need requires, and void of sence. **1759** T. WALLIS *Farrier's Dict.* s.v. *Teeth*, But all within the sockets of the jaws is..covered with a thin membrane of exquisite sense. **1771** J. S. *Le Dran's Observ. Surg.* (ed. 4) 313 He was without Sense, and cold all over his Body.

6. a. *pl.* A general term for the faculties of perception (including the 'five senses': see 1), which are in abeyance when their owner is asleep or otherwise unconscious. Also *sing.*, any one of these faculties. Cf. 10.

1597 SHAKS. *2 Hen. IV*, III. i. 8 O Sleepe..how haue I frighted thee, That thou no more wilt weigh my eye-lids downe, And steepe my Sences in Forgetfulnesse? **1700** DRYDEN *Sigism. & Guisc.* 749 The creeping Death Benum'd her Senses first, then stopp'd her Breath. *c* **1742** GRAY *Ignorance* 18 Dost thou..dews Lethean through the land dispense To steep in slumbers each benighted sense? **1762** LLOYD *Poems* 115 And gently lull my senses all the while With placid poems in the sinking stile! **1849** MACAULAY *Hist. Eng.* iii. I. 439 Before ten his senses were gone. **1892** BIERCE *In Midst of Life* 109 He seated himself on a log, and, with senses all alert, began his vigil.

b. *collect. sing.* The perceptive faculty of a conscious animate being.

1585 T. WASHINGTON tr. *Nicholay's Voy.* II. xx. 57 Pictures..are but dead things, & in whom there is no sence or feeling. **1635** LAUD *Diary* 26 Oct., I found him past sense, and giving up the ghost. **1667** MILTON *P.L.* VIII. 289 There gentle sleep..with soft oppression seis'd My drousèd sense. *a* **1699** LADY HALKETT *Autobiog.* (1875) 8 With that hee fell downe in a chaire..as one without all sence. **1768** PENNANT *Brit. Zool.* I. Pref. 10 Through every species of animal life, ..to that point where sense is almost extinct, and vegetation commences. **1805–6** CARY *Dante, Inf.* VI. 1 My sense reviving, that erewhile had droop'd With pity for the kindred shades.

7. a. Applied to faculties of the mind or soul compared or contrasted with the bodily senses; usually with some defining word, as ***inner***, ***interior***, ***internal***, ***inward sense***. ***moral sense***: see MORAL *a.* 1 d.

1566 ALDAY tr. *Boaistuau's Theat. World* T iv, Knowing that he had to exercise his fancie and other interior senses. **1635** PAGITT *Christianogr.* I. iii. (1636) 102 Not sensibly champing it with their teeth but partaking it by the sence of the soule. **1672** HOOLE *Comenius' Vis. World* xlii. 87 The inward Senses are three. The Common-sense... The

Phantasie... The Memory. **1690** LOCKE *Hum. Und.* II. i. §4 This Source of Ideas, every Man has wholly in himself: And though it be not Sense, as having nothing to do with external Objects; yet it is very like it, and might properly enough be call'd internal Sense. But as I call the other Sensation, so I call this Reflection. **1732** LAW *Serious C.* xiv. (ed. 2) 256 They would soon see that the spirit of devotion was like any other sense or understanding. **1779** *Mirror* No. 48 ¶3 The truth of perception, in our internal senses, employed in morals and criticism. **1809–10** COLERIDGE *Friend* (ed. 4) I. 239 *note*, His sensations, and impressions, whether of his outward senses, or the inner sense of imagination. **1847** HELPS *Friends in C.* I. 10 All the senses, if you might so call them, of the soul..that is, the affections and the perceptions. **1870** [see ILLATIVE *a.* 3].

b. ***reprobate sense***: used to render the Vulgate version of Rom. i. 28 *in reprobum sensum* (Gr. *εἰς ἀδόκιμον νοῦν*, A.V. 'to a reprobate minde').

1550 CROWLEY *Way to Wealth* 418 He hath geuen the ouer into a reprobate sence. **1680** BURNET *Rochester* (1692) Pref. 11 It is much to be feared they are given up to a reprobate sense.

†**8.** Capacity for mental feeling; sensibility. *Obs.*

1602 MARSTON *Antonio's Rev.* IV. i, I should be deade of sense, to viewe defame Blur my bright love. **1608** *Yorkshire Trag.* IV. 42 Sir, you haue much wrought with mee. I feele you in my soule... I neuer had sence til now.

9. Capacity for perception and appreciation *of* (beauty, humour, some quality, etc.). Rarely const. *for*. Formerly also without const.: †Feeling or sensibility in matters of artistic taste.

1604 SHAKS. *Oth.* II. i. 71 Tempests themselues, high Seas, and howling windes..As hauing sence of Beautie, do omit Their mortall Natures, letting go safely by The Diuine Desdemona. *a* **1704** T. BROWN *Imit. 1st Sat. Persius* Wks. 1730 I. 54 His sense is smothered, and his judgement dies. *a* **1704** —— *Praise of Poverty* ibid. 97 They have no taste of wit, and sense of arts and sciences. **1715** POPE *Let. to J. Craggs* 15 July, We talk much of fine Sense, refin'd Sense, and exalted Sense. **1851** RUSKIN *Stones Ven.* (1874) I. App. 373 The sense of beauty I consider a mixture of the senses of the body and soul. **1875** M. ARNOLD *God & Bible* v. 244 The sense which English people have for fact and for evidence will tell them that [etc.]. **1878** C. STANFORD *Symb. Christ* i. 4 The Bible..delights our sense of the picturesque. **1885** J. PAYN *Talk of Town* I. 222 William Henry, who had a strong sense of humour. **1962** A. NISBETT *Technique Sound Studio* vi. 106 The live broadcast seems to have a greater sense of occasion. **1974** R. ADAMS *Shardik* lvi. 472 From natural awe and sense of occasion, they did not press forward.

10. a. *pl.* The mental faculties in their normal condition of sanity; one's 'reason' or 'wits'. (Cf. 6.) ***in one's (right) senses***, in one's right mind. ***to bring*** (a person) ***to his senses***: to cure of his folly (one who is behaving 'madly'). (***to frighten***, etc.) ***out of one's (seven) senses***: out of one's wits.

1568 GRAFTON *Chron.* II. 638 His senses were moued, and his wittes disturbed. **1585** T. WASHINGTON tr. *Nicholay's Voy.* I. xv. 16 As cleane bereft of sences [he] made towardes his enemies. **1692** R. L'ESTRANGE *Fables* lxviii. 67 What Man in his Right Senses..would make himself a Slave for Superfluities! **1694** MOTTEUX *Rabelais* IV. xiii, The Filly was ..scar'd out of her seven Senses. **1727** GAY *Begg. Op.* III. xlii, You shall..mortify yourself into reason, with..a little handsome discipline to bring you to your senses. **1787** MME. D'ARBLAY *Diary* May, I asked him whether he was really in his senses? **1794** MRS. RADCLIFFE *Myst. Udolpho* xli, Sometimes he would be in such fits of violence, that we almost thought he had lost his senses. **1835** CORRIE in Holroyd *Mem.* (1890) 17, I thought with myself that the dog ought to be flogged out of his seven senses if he were not happy. **1893** DUNMORE *Pamirs* I. 187 The public..would think that the artist had taken leave of his senses.

†**b.** *sing.* (with the same meaning). *Obs.*

1590 GREENE *Orl. Fur.* (1599) H2, Ne're was the Queene of Cypresse halfe so glad, As is Angelica to see her Lord, Her dear Orlando, settled in his sense. **1605** SHAKS. *Lear* IV. iv. 9 In the restoring his bereaued Sense. **1694** PENN *Rise & Progr. Quakers* v. 99 He had the Comfort of a short Illness, and the Blessing of a clear Sense to the last.

11. a. Natural understanding, intelligence, esp. as bearing on action or behaviour; practical soundness of judgement.

See also COMMON SENSE 2, 2b, GOOD SENSE, HORSE-SENSE.
1684 ROSCOMMON *Ess. Tr. Verse* 162 Pride..Proceeds from want of Sense or want of Thought. **1690** NORRIS *Refl. Cond. Hum. Life* (1691) 44 For first, 'tis reckon'd a notable point of Learning to understand variety of Languages. This alone gives a Man a Title to Learning without one Grain of Sense. **1727** ARBUTHNOT *John Bull* I. viii, The Parson of the Parish preaching one Day with more Zeal than Sense [1712 a little sharply] against Adultery. **1779–81** JOHNSON *L.P., Prior* Wks. III. 131 If we can suppose him [Dryden] vexed, it would be hard to deny him sense enough to conceal his uneasiness. **1782** MISS BURNEY *Cecilia* VI. i, You speak, ma'am, like a lady of sense. **1849** MACAULAY *Hist. Eng.* ii. I. 169 The facility of Charles was such as has perhaps never been found in any man of equal sense. **1880** MEREDITH *Tragic Com.* (1881) 291 Alvan had a saying, that want of courage is want of sense.

b. ***to have the sense***: to be wise enough *to do* something. Similarly, ***to have too much sense to***, ***to have more sense than to*** do something.

a **1701** MAUNDRELL *Journ. Jerus.* (1732) 56 Which if they should have the sence to do..they might shake off the Turkish yoak. **1735** POPE *Donne Sat.* ii. 2 As early as I knew This Town, I had the sense to hate it too. **1735** —— *Ep. Lady* 87 Flavia's a Wit, has too much sense to Pray. **1800** PAGET in *P. Papers* (1896) I. 184 My courier had the good sense to make two men with lanterns precede the carriage. **1826** LAMB *Juke Judkins*, He had slipped away to an eminent fruiterer's, about three doors distant, which I never had the sense to think of. **1847** EMILY BRONTE *Wuthering H.* iv, They [the children] entirely refused to have it [a foundling] in bed with them,..and I had no more sense, so, I put it on the landing of the stairs. *Mod.* He has more sense than to go where he is not wanted.

II. Actual perception or feeling.

12. A feeling or perception *of* (something external) through the channels of touch, taste, etc.; the feeling or consciousness *of* some bodily affection, as pain, fatigue, comfort or discomfort, etc. †Also (rarely) *absol.* a sensation.

a **1586** SIDNEY *Arcadia* II. (Sommer) 186 He..beating her with wandes he had in his hande, she crying for sense of payne, or hope of succour. *Ibid.* III. 306b, Fire, burne me quite till sense of burning leaue me. **1607** TOPSELL *Four-f. Beasts* 289 The Lybian horsses..have no sence of their labors. *a* **1628** PRESTON *Breastpl. Faith* (1630) 13 Before you will be healed, you must have a sense of your sickness. **1669** H. STUBBE in Birch *Life Boyle* (1744) 192 It creates in the throat such a sense, as remains after drinking pepper-posset. **1675–6** BOYLE in *Phil. Trans.* No. 122. 522 The immediate contact of the Ingredients and the skin produc'd a sense of heat. **1709** FLOYER *Cold Bathing* I. iv. 98 The way to prepare our Body for Cold Baths..is to wash it all over in warm Water first..and so every Morning use cooler till it can bear the Sense of very Cold Water. **1820** KEATS *Isabella* xxxiv, Like a lance, Waking an Indian..With cruel pierce, and bringing him again Sense of the gnawing fire at heart and brain. **1843** R. J. GRAVES *Syst. Clin. Med.* xxiv. 305 Astringent injections, so weak that when used, they may produce merely a sense of titillation. **1879** GEO. ELIOT *Theo. Such* x. 182 An idle craving without sense of flavours.

13. A more or less vague perception or impression *of* (an outward object, as present or imagined).

1596 SPENSER *F.Q.* VI. x. 42 Lightned..with continuall candlelight, which delt A doubtfull sense of things, not so well seene, as felt. **1647** C. HARVEY *Schola Cordis* xxxiv. 12 And by Thy light Possesse my sight With sense of an eternall day. **1798** WORDSW. *Poems Imag., Tintern Abb.* 95 A sense sublime Of something far more deeply interfused. **1855** BAGEHOT *Biogr. Stud.* 334 He [Cobden] excited a personal interest; he left what may be called a *sense* of himself among his professed enemies. **1876** HENLEY *Life & D.* xxxiv. *Bk. Verses* (1888) 100 And the darkening air Thrills with a sense of the triumphing night. **1887** W. JAMES in *Mind* XII. 209 Such expressions as the abysmal vault of heaven, the endless expanse of ocean,..give the sense of an enormous horizon.

14. a. A more or less indefinite consciousness or impression *of* (a fact, state of things, etc.) as present or impending.

1604 SHAKS. *Oth.* III. iii. 338 What sense had I, in [*Q.* 1, 2 of] her stolne houres of Lust? **1722** DE FOE *Plague* (1756) 285 Perhaps it may be thought by some, after the Sense of the Thing was over, an officious canting of religious Things. **1742** GRAY *Eton* 53 No sense have they of ills to come. **1759** HURD *Moral Dial.* iv. 133 Her parliaments were disposed to wave all disputes about the stretch of her prerogative, from a sense of their own and the common danger. **1849** HELPS *Friends in C.* II. i. (1854) I. 266 The keenness of pursuit thus engendered [in reading]..takes away the sense of dulness in details. **1849** MACAULAY *Hist. Eng.* x. II. 592 In a very few days the confusion..was at an end, and the kingdom wore again its accustomed aspect. There was a general sense of security. **1874** L. STEPHEN *Hours in Library* (1892) II. 67 There are few books..that do not sadden us by a sense of incompleteness. **1874** GREEN *Short Hist.* viii. §2. 466 His words..startled English ears with a sense of coming danger to the national liberty.

b. *const.* a dependent statement or question.

1683 *Pennsylv. Arch.* I. 83 He gave Me a kind of cold Answer.., and I had a real sence upon Me, that he is not Right to thy Interest. **1698** A. BRAND *Emb. Muscovy into China* 22 The Resurrection (which they believe, without the least sense whither they are to go afterwards). **1713** JOHNSON *Guardian* No. 5 ¶4 Which gives the Mother an uneasie Sense, that Mrs. Jane really is what her Parent has a mind to continue to be. **1859** GEO. ELIOT *Adam Bede* x, Seth, always timid in his behaviour towards his mother, from the sense that he had no influence over her. **1888** BRYCE *Amer. Commw.* III. lxxxii. 84 The spirit of Puritanism, with..its sense..that there are times when Agag must be hewn in pieces before the Lord.

15. a. Mental apprehension, appreciation, or realization *of* (some truth, fact, state of things). Also, †comprehension, perception of the meaning *of*.

a **1540** BARNES *Wks.* (1573) 360/2 Chrisostome sayth, Behold I see men that haue no trew sence of holy Scripture: yea they vnderstand nothyng at all therof. **1612** BACON *Ess., Praise* (Arb.) 350 The common people vnderstand not many excellent vertues:..but of the highest vertues they haue no sense or perceiuing at all. **1692** R. L'ESTRANGE *Fables* ccxlvii. 214 The True Intent of This Fable is to Possess us with a Just Sense of the Vanity and Folly of these Craving Appetites. **1758** S. HAYWARD *Serm.* xiv. 402 To have a just sense of the worth of a soul. **1853** J. H. NEWMAN *Hist. Sk.* II. I. ii. 43 He seemed visited by a sense of the vanity of all things. **1871** MORLEY *Carlyle* in *Crit. Misc.* Ser. I. (1878) 175 The same sense of the puniness of man in the centre of a cruel and frowning universe.

b. The recognition *of* (a duty, virtue, etc.) as incumbent upon one, or as a motive or standard for one's own conduct.

1604 SHAKS. *Oth.* I. i. 132 Do not beleeue That from the sence of all Ciuilitie, I thus would play and trifle with your Reuerence. **1722** DE FOE *Col. Jack* (1840) 145 These fellows have no sense of gratitude. **1779** *Mirror* No. 35, I was conscious of an inclination to oblige, and a quick sense of propriety. **1802** MAR. EDGEWORTH *Moral T.* (1816) I. 223 They would suffer no motives to influence them but a sense of truth and justice. **1848** J. MITCHEL in *State Trials* VI. 697, I have acted in this business, from the first, under a strong sense of duty. **1869** FREEMAN *Norm. Conq.* III. xiii. (1876) 296 He appealed to their sense of feudal honour.

†**c.** (*one's*) ***sense of things***: perception or judgement of what is right, fitting, etc. *Obs.*

a **1715** BURNET *Own Time* (1823) I. 327 He went into the humours of that high sort of people beyond what became him, perhaps beyond his own sense of things. **1719** DE FOE *Crusoe* I. (Globe) 98 Whenever they come to a true Sense of things, they will find Deliverance from Sin a much greater Blessing, than Deliverance from Affliction.

16. a. Emotional consciousness of something; a glad or sorrowful, grateful or resentful recognition *of* (another person's conduct, an event, a fact or a condition of things).

1604 SHAKS. *Oth.* V. i. 32 O braue Iago, honest, and iust, That hast such Noble sense of thy Friends wrong. **1643** BAKER *Chron., Edw. II* 149 The King in a calmer humour, beganne to have a sense of the Earle of Lancasters execution. **1642** *Lanc. Tracts Civil War* (Chetham Soc.) 6 Shewing.. our heart-breaking sence, and sorrow, for the unhappy.. Distraction in your Majesties Dominions. **1662** *Bk. Com. Prayer, Gen. Thanksgiving*, Give us that due sense of all thy mercies. **1664** MARVELL *Corr.* Wks. 1872–5 II. 172 He declared the sence his Master had of the great Expressions of kindness which he had received. **1726** BROOME *Pope's Odyss.* xxiv. Notes V. 286 The sense I have of this, and other instances of that friendship. **1821** COMBE *Syntax* III. iv. (Chandos) 343 He spoke at once his grateful sense Of her warm friendship and regard. **1825** SCOTT *Betrothed* xi, While he expressed his sense of the honour with which she now graced him. **1856** HAWTHORNE *Eng. Note-bks.* (1870) II. 164 No better way of showing our sense of his hospitality ..has occurred to us.

†**b.** ***with (great,*** etc.) ***sense***: with (much) emotion, feelingly. *Obs.*

1666 BUNYAN *Grace Abound.* §276 Now this part of my Work I fulfilled with great sense... I preached what I felt, what I smartingly did feel. **1676** LADY FANSHAWE *Mem.* (1830) 247 Then I did my duty to the Queen, who with great sense condoled my loss. *a* **1715** BURNET *Own Time* (1823) II. 170 He knew, he had led a bad life; (of which he spoke with some sense).

17. A consciousness or recognition *of* (some quality, condition, etc.) as attaching to oneself; esp. such as is accompanied by inward feeling or emotion, or acts as a motive for conduct.

1614 EARL STIRLING *Doomsday* v. lxxxiv, Who have no sence of sinne, nor care of fame. **1662** *Bk. Com. Prayer, Visit. Sick*, That the sense of his weakness may add strength to his faith. **1692** R. L'ESTRANGE *Fables* lix. 59 The smart brings him to a sense of his Errour. **1719** DE FOE *Crusoe* I. (Globe) 97 For now I pray'd with a Sense of my Condition. **1777** SHERIDAN *Sch. Scand.* III. i, Who..has done everything in his power to bring your nephew to a proper sense of his extravagance. **1791** COWPER *Retired Cat* 109 Beware of too sublime a sense Of your own worth and consequence! **1833** HT. MARTINEAU *Three Ages* II. 44 The nation was growing bold under a sense of injury. **1867** RUSKIN *Time & Tide* ii. §7 The healthy sense of progress, which is necessary to the strength and happiness of men. **1872** SANFORD *Estim. Eng. Kings, Chas. I*, 331 The dignity of bearing in Charles..was sustained by a profound sense of self-importance and superiority. **1888** LOWELL *Heartsease & Rue* 178 Giving Eve a due sense of her crime. **1908** R. BAGOT *A. Cuthbert* vi. 51 To confess herself mistaken was altogether opposed to her sense of personal dignity.

18. An opinion, view, or judgement held or formed †**a.** by an individual. ***to speak*** or ***give one's sense***, to express one's opinion. ***to abound in one's own sense***: see ABOUND *v.*[1] 5. *Obs.*

1552–1775 [see ABOUND *v.*[1] 5]. **1620–55** I. JONES *Stone-Heng* (1725) 24 These Monuments..I have not seen, otherwise I would give my Sense upon them. **1650** EARL MONM. tr. *Senault's Man bec. Guilty* 13 If I may be permitted to speak my sense. **1656** STANLEY *Hist. Philos.* v. (1687) 171/2 Not engaging himself in publick Affairs;.. because the Athenians were accustomed to Laws different from his sense. *a* **1734** NORTH *Exam.* I. ii. §138 (1740) 107 Under the Banner of &c. comes the Earl of Shaftsbury, and the Lords of his Sense. **1747** DR. HOADLY *Suspicious Husb.* I. i, My Lord Coke, in a Case I read this Morning, speaks my Sense. **1761** HUME *Hist. Eng.* II. xxiv. 80 The entail of the Crown was drawn according to the sense of the king, and probably in words dictated by him.

b. by an assemblage of persons (or by a majority of their number). Now somewhat *arch.* ***to take the sense of***, to ascertain the general feeling or opinion of.

1654 GODDARD in *Introd. to Burton's Diary* (1828) I. 96 Which had been otherwise declared by this Parliament, and seemed still to be the general sense of us all. **1691** WOOD *Athen. Oxon.* II. 315 Prynne afterwards was called in again to receive the sense of the House. **1778** WARNER in Jesse *Selwyn & Contemp.* (1844) III. 343 Pray let us take the sense of the University;—not that they are the judges whom I most admire. **1793** BURKE *Observ. Conduct Minority* §44 A House of Commons which does not speak the sense of the people. **1817** [see TAKE *v.* 32a]. **1849** MACAULAY *Hist. Eng.* vi. II. 81 He soon found that he had against him almost the whole sense of Westminster Hall. **1855** *Ibid.* xv. III. 533 He spoke, he told the King, the sense of a great body of honest gentlemen.

†**c.** ***in one's sense***, in one's opinion, according to one's judgement. *Obs.*

1604 SHAKS. *Oth.* V. ii. 290, I am not sorry neither, Il'd haue thee liue: For in my sense, 'tis happinesse to die. *a* **1628** PRESTON *New Covt.* (1634) 10 But because in his sence, the object is too narrow, there is something he would have more. **1771** LUCKOMBE *Hist. Printing* 24 Merit, that in the sense of all nations, gives the best Title to True Praise. **1832** GREVILLE *Mem.* 24 Feb. (1874) II. 263 The petition turned out to be one for a moderate Reform, more in their sense than in the Duke's own.

†**d.** const. *of* (a person, a matter), and with clause introduced by *that*. Also, favourable opinion, high estimate *of*. *Obs.*

1565 T. STAPLETON *Fortr. Faith* 122 b, Let vs see what sence he had of monasticall religion. **1638** STRAFFORD *Lett.* (1739) II. 195 Your Lordship's of the 27th of June expresseth more Sense of me than I am worthy of. *c* **1650** DENHAM *Of Old Age* 813 Now you, my friends, my sense of Death shall hear. **1687** *Lond. Gaz.* No. 2342/1 It is..Our constant Sense and Opinion..that Conscience ought not to be constrained. **1744** WESLEY *Wks.* (1872) VIII. 39, I will now simply tell you my sense of these matters. **1760** T. HUTCHINSON *Hist. Col. Mass. Bay* i. 64 A letter, wrote from New England, shews the sense they had of him after they had made trial. **1778** MISS BURNEY *Evelina* (1794) I. 148 Pardon the earnestness with which I write my sense of this affair. **1785** JEFFERSON *Writ.* (1859) I. 497 Congress have studiously avoided giving to the public their sense of this institution.

III. Meaning, signification.

19. a. The meaning or signification of a word or phrase; also, any one of the different meanings of a word, or that which it bears in a particular collocation or context.

1530 PALSGR. 792 Where *re* signyfyeth in our tonge agayne, he is very moche used in this sence in the composycion of verbes. **1538** ELYOT *Dict.* Pref. A iij, As well for the difficultie in the true expressynge the lyuely sence of the latine wordes. **1581** PETTIE tr. *Guazzo's Civ. Conv.* I. (1586) 22 We give a large sense and signification to this word (Ciuile). **1611** BIBLE *Transl. Pref.* ¶16 There bee some wordes that bee not of the same sense euery where. **1681** DRYDEN *Abs. & Achit.* I. 965 Gull'd with a Patriot's name, whose Modern sense Is one that woud by Law supplant his Prince. **1729** BUTLER *Serm.* Wks. 1874 II. 22 Here then are two different senses of the word nature. **1802** MAR. EDGEWORTH *Moral T.* (1816) I. 6 Education, in the enlarged sense of the word. **1884** W. C. SMITH *Kildrostan* 78 Cheating conscience so With words depleted of their natural sense.

b. A meaning recorded in a dictionary, etc.

1755 JOHNSON *Dict.* Pref., The solution of all difficulties.. must be sought in the examples, subjoined to the various senses of each word. **1818** TODD, *Largeheartedness*... See the fourth sense of *Largeness*. **1887** SKEAT *Gosp. S. Matt. in Ags.* Pref. 7 See the fifth sense of the verb *bield* in Murray's New English Dictionary.

20. a. The meaning of words in connected or continuous speech; the meaning of a passage or context. Also, one of two or more meanings which the words naturally bear or are held to bear.

1513 *Balade to Author* in *Bradshaw's St. Werburge* (1887) 201 O frutefull histore..With termes exquised and sence retoriall. **1530** PALSGR. *Introd.* 15 Thoughe we shulde gyve worde for worde, yet the sens shulde moche differ betwene our tong and theyrs. **1549** *Compl. Scot.* x. 83 Cayphas..spak treu prophesye; bot ȝit he and the iueis interpret it to the vrang sens. **1560** *Ovid's Narcissus* A iv, Thou speakest words, the sence whereof, myne eares can not deserne. **1611** BIBLE *Neh.* viii. 8 So they read in the booke, in the Law of God distinctly, and gaue the sense, and caused them to vnderstand the reading. *a* **1674** CLARENDON *Hist. Reb.* VIII. §79 The King's letter would not bear that sense. **1684** ROSCOMMON *Ess. Tr. Verse* 346 The sound is still a Comment to the Sense. **1699** BENTLEY *Phal.* 141 We must read *προπομπῶν*, as the learned Mr. Stanley guess'd from the Sense of the place. **1768** GRAY in *Corr. w. Nicholls* (1843) 73 In the second letter, he is conscious he had gone too far in his expressions, and tries to give them a sense they will not bear. *a* **1768** SECKER *Serm.* (1770) I. iii. 66 And lastly, Abstain from all Appearance of Evil. It might be translated, from every Kind of Evil. But even then, the Sense would be much the same. **1863** GEO. ELIOT *Romola* I. vii, He had barely enough Greek to make out the sense of the epigram. **1885** *Diary of Actress* 87 How I got the words, or the sense of the words, into my head I don't know.

b. The meaning or interpretation of a dream, or of anything cryptic or symbolical.

1584 B. R. tr. *Herodotus* I. 11 It is needfull then yt..I lay open vnto you the true meaning and sence of the dreame. **1601** B. JONSON *Poetaster* Prol. 12 'Gainst these, haue we put on this forc't defence: Whereof the allegorie and hid sence Is, that a well erected confidence Can fright their pride, and laugh their folly hence. **1650** FULLER *Pisgah* I. iv. 9 Which passage may serve as a parable, whereof our Saviour himself is the sense.

c. The gist, upshot, or general purport of words spoken or written. † *to that sense*, to that effect.

1596 DALRYMPLE tr. *Leslie's Hist. Scot.* II. 268 With lettres to the Gouernour..; Quhairof this was the sence, that thay suld remayne constant and true in thair promise. *a* **1700** EVELYN *Diary* 18 Aug. 1673, Where he read..that he should not long enjoy it, but should die, or expressions to that sense. **1777** SIR W. JONES *Poems, Ess.* i. 166 This is the general sense of his remark. **1855** MACAULAY *Hist. Eng.* xxi. IV. 575 They proceeded to pass several votes, the sense of which was finally summed up in an address to the King. **1883** R. W. DIXON *Mano* I. iv. 9 Of this epistle Mano made the sense Ampler by various tidings that he brought.

21. Any of the various meanings or interpretations (*literal*, *mystic*, *anagogic*, *moral*, †*ghostly*, *spiritual*, etc.) of which, according to the principles of patristic and mediæval exegesis, a word or passage of Holy Scripture was considered to be susceptible. Hence *transf.* with reference to similar methods of interpretation as applied to other writings.

c **1400** *Prol. Wyclif Bible* xiii. 52–3 And of these iiij. sensis, either vndirstondingis, may be set ensaumple in this word Jerusalem; for bi the literal vndirstonding Jerusalem singnefieth a cyte..; bi moral sense..bi sense allegorik..bi sence anagogik [etc.]. *Ibid.* xiv. 54 The historial, either literal sense, and the mystik, either goostly sense, is taken vndir the same lettre. **1446** LYDG. *Nightingale* I. 16 Commandyng theym to here wyth tendernesse Of this your nightyngale the gostly sense. **1509** HAWES *Past. Pleas.* vii. (Percy Soc.) 28 To moralise thy lytterall censes trewe. **1549** COVERDALE, etc. *Erasm. Par. 1 Cor.* xiii. 1–3 The gyft of prophecie, wherby I know all the secrete senses of the scriptures. **1617** MORYSON *Itin.* I. 232 These Greekes, as in this point, so in all other, follow the literall sense of the Scriptures. **1751** JORTIN *Serm.* (1771) I. i. 2 The ancient Christians imitated the Jews in finding out Senses in the Scriptures, which were never intended.

22. ***in a*** (specified) ***sense***, according to a particular acceptation or interpretation (of a word, phrase, etc.). Often in phrases, ***in a sense***, ***in some sense***, ***in any sense***, ***in no sense***, ***in all senses*** (which sometimes come to mean 'in some degree', 'in no respect', 'on every account', etc.).

1593 SHAKS. *Lucr.* 324 He in the worst sence consters their deniall. **1596** —— *Tam. Shr.* v. ii. 141 It blots thy beautie. .. And in no sence is meete or amiable. **1660** R. COKE *Justice Vind.* 22 Resistance is usually taken in an ill sence, as when the subordinate resists his superior. **1664** BUTLER *Hud.* II. ii. 82 Not that they really cuff or fence, But in a Spiritual Mistique sence. **1719** W. WOOD *Surv. Trade* 317 Tho' we destroyed so many capital Ships of France the two last Wars, yet..in some sence, the Naval Strength of France is rather encreased than diminished. **1719** DE FOE *Crusoe* I. (Globe) 97–8 Yet the Island was certainly a Prison to me, and that in the worst Sense in the World; but now I learn'd to take it in another Sense. **1745** LADY M. W. MONTAGU *Let. to C'tess Oxford* 1 June (1893) II. 140 This is the first prize that ever came to my share, and that is owing to your ladyship in all senses. **1853** MAURICE *Proph. & Kings* ii. 22 All is, in the strictest sense of the word, dramatical. **1871** FREEMAN *Norm. Conq.* (1876) IV. xviii. 228 That one among the Conqueror's children who alone could be looked on as in any sense an Englishman. **1878** C. STANFORD *Symb. Christ* i. 10 Abram, whose vocation was so high,..bows to him as one whose vocation was in some sense higher than his own. *a* **1881** A. BARRATT *Phys. Metempiric* (1883) 110 The consciousness of the body is of course in a sense its inner nature. **1910** J. SARGEAUNT *Dryden's Poems* Introd. 21 If no poet in the highest sense of the word, he was at least a surpassing rhetorician.

†**23.** The meaning of a speaker or writer; the substance, purport, or intention of what he says.

c **1400** *Prol. Wyclif Bible* xv. 59 Austyn seith..that if equiuok wordis be not translatid into the sense, either vndurstonding, of the autour, it is errour. **1540** PALSGR. *Acolastus* Prol. B ij b, Our play..vnder whose couert or darke meanyng, thou haste a secrete sence or hydde intent. **1596** SHAKS. *Tam. Shr.* v. ii. 18 You are verie sencible, and yet you misse my sence: I meane Hortentio is afeard of you. *a* **1619** FOTHERBY *Atheom.* II. viii. §5 (1622) 290 His Expositor, Elias Cretensis, deliuereth his sense in the same hight of words. **1700** DRYDEN *Pref. to Fables* ¶3 Where I have been wrongfully accus'd and my Sense wire-drawn into Blasphemy or Bawdry. **1710** LADY M. W. MONTAGU *Let. to Bp. Salisbury* 20 July (1893) II. 2, I endeavoured at no beauty of style, but to keep as literally as I could to the sense of the author [Epictetus]. **1735** POPE *Donne Sat.* ii. 126 Let no Court Sycophant pervert my sense.

24. ***in a*** (specified) ***sense***: with a particular aim or purpose (in speaking or writing); to a (given) effect.

1837 CARLYLE *Fr. Rev.* I. II. iv, France..is now beginning to speak also; and speaks in that same sense. **1837** MOORE *Diary* 8 Aug. in *Mem.* VII. 196 The Fireworshippers, he told me, had been translated in Poland in a Polish sense. **1883** L. OLIPHANT *Altiora Peto* II. 118 He had no scruple in writing to the Baroness in the above sense.

25. A connected series of ideas expressed in words; the substance of a passage.

a **1568** ASCHAM *Scholem.* II. (Arb.) 93 *Metaphrasis* is, to take some notable place out of a good Poete, and turn the same sens into meter, or into other wordes in Prose. **1582** T. WATSON *Centurie of Love* lxxxvi. (Arb.) 122 The sense of this Sonnet is for the most part taken out of a letter, which Æneas Syluius wrote vnto his friend. **1748** RICHARDSON *Clarissa* VII. 197 She took the pen, and..supported by Mrs. Lovick, wrote the conclusion... You will find the sense surprizingly intire, her weakness considered.

26. A passage, context, or set of sentences, expressed in bare prose, used as material for the composition of Latin or Greek verses. Also allusively. Also *attrib.*, as ***sense verses***.

1693 LOCKE *Educ.* §171 It is usual in such Cases for the poor Children to go to those of higher Forms with this Petition, *Pray give me a little Sense.* **1743** CHESTERF. *Lett.* xcviii. (1792) I. 275 As you are now got into sense verses, remember, that it is not sufficient to put a little common sense into hexameters and pentameters. **1765** G. WILLIAMS in Jesse *Selwyn & Contemp.* (1843) I. 361 When you write next to me, give me some *sense*, as the boys say, that I may answer for you as often as you are attacked. **1892** W. CORY *Lett. & Jrnls.* (1897) 564 Write a paper on governesses. I can give you 'sense', as the boys say about verses.

27. Discourse that has a satisfactory and intelligible meaning. Phr. ***to talk***, ***speak***, ***write*** (***good***) ***sense***. ***to make sense of***, to find a meaning in. Of discourse: ***to give***, ***have***, ***make sense***, to be intelligible. ***to make sense***: also in extended use (freq. in neg. contexts).

1598 SHAKS. *Merry W.* II. i. 129 Beleeue it (Page) he speakes sence. **1671** MILTON *P.R.* IV. 296 A third sort doubted all things, though plain sence. **1682** DRYDEN *Mac Flecknoe* 20 The rest to some faint meaning make pretence, But Sh[adwell] never deviates into sense. **1685** in *Verney Mem.* (1899) IV. 344 Hot-headed people that can't speak sense, hate to hear it. **1686** [ALLIX] *Dissert.* iv. in *Ratramnus' Body & Bl.* (1688) 68, I must needs say, that I cannot make sence of him, if he mean not as the French Translator hath rendered him. **1721** A. MALCOLM *Treat. Mus.* 538 This, to make any Sense, must signify that [etc.]. **1746** FRANCIS *Hor. Epist.* II. ii. 190 Rather..Than write good Sense, and smart severely for't. **1857** RUSKIN *Pol. Econ. Art* i. §8 That is a wholly barbarous use of the word..for it is not English, it is bad Greek, and it is worse sense. **1870** J. H. NEWMAN *Gram. Assent* 264 In the first authentic edition..the words, I believe, ran, 'and a table of green fields', which has no sense. **1910** J. SARGEAUNT *Dryden's Poems* Introd. 23 This is the only reading that gives any sense. *a* **1912** *Mod.* Now you are talking sense. **1921** G. B. SHAW *Back to Methuselah* IV. 148 She spoke to me without any introduction, like any improper female... Improper female doesnt make sense. **1936** *Punch* 12 Feb. 170/2 It can't be right, it can't be. Spats and a bowler-hat, but no umbrella—it doesn't make sense.

28. What is wise or reasonable. ***there is no sense*** (***in*** doing something): it is unreasonable or useless (to do it). † ***it is to*** (***good***) ***sense*** (obs.), ***it stands to sense*** (colloq.): it is reasonable, it stands to reason.

1600 W. WATSON *Decacordon* (1602) 98 He [Cardinal Allen] was often wont to say, that seeing England was lost and gone from her ancient faith..it was to good sense that we and all their posterity should be punished. **1603** SHAKS. *Meas. for M.* v. i. 226 As there is sence in truth, and truth in vertue. *Ibid.* 438 Against all sence you doe importune her. **1639** N. N. tr. *Du Bosq's Compl. Woman* II. 73 There is no sense I should leave out this goodly vertue. **1847** EMILY BRONTE *Wuthering H.* ix, 'Aw sud more likker look for th' horse', he replied. 'It 'ud be tuh more sense'. **1859** *Habits of Gd. Society* 54 The more fashionable..were distinguished for the smartness, not the sense of their conversation. **1859** GEO. ELIOT *Adam Bede* xxi, There's a good deal o' sense in what you say, Mr. Massey. *Ibid.* xxiii, It stands to sense.. as old Mr. Poyser, as is th' oldest man i' the room, should sit at top o' the table. **1897** KIPLING *Capt. Cour.* iii. 65 'What's the sense o' wastin' canvas?'

29. a. [After F. *sens.*] A direction in which motion takes place. *rare.*

1797 SIR G. STAUNTON *Acc. Embassy* (1798) II. 5 Cords were attached to the canvas, with a contrivance to enable persons underneath to move it in any sense that was necessary. **1900** H. C. JONES *Theory Electrolytic Dissoc.* 61 If the reaction is reversible..then there will exist a force which tends to stop the original reaction, and to set up one in exactly the opposite sense.

b. Chiefly *Math.* That which distinguishes a pair of entities which differ only in that each is the reverse of the other.

1894 H. W. L. HIME *Outl. Quaternions* I. i. 2 No two vectors are equal unless they have, first, equal lengths, and, secondly, similar directions—the phrase 'similar directions' meaning 'parallel directions with the same sense'. **1947** COURANT & ROBBINS *What is Math.?* (ed. 4) iii. 159 Although inversion preserves the *magnitude* of angles, it reverses their *sense*; i.e. if a ray through *P* sweeps out the angle *x*. in a counterclockwise direction, its image will sweep out angle *y*. in a clockwise direction. **1950** [see ORIENTED *ppl. a.* 1]. **1962** A. NISBETT *Technique Sound Studio* 251 The doublet [microphone] can become bi-directional, cardioid or omnidirectional, simply by varying the size and sense of the potential on one of the diaphragms. **1977** HOLLAND & TREEBY *Vectors* i. 10 The vector (1/*a*)**a** is a unit vector in the direction and sense of **a**.

IV. 30. *attrib.* and *Comb.*, as ***sense-appearance***, ***-apprehension***, ***-awareness***, ***-cell***, ***-consciousness***, ***-element***, ***-feeling***, ***-idea***, ***-impression***, ***-impulse***, ***-knowledge***, ***-life***, ***-material***, ***-modality***, ***-object***, ***-observation***, ***-organ***, ***-percept***, ***-perception***, ***-phenomenon***, ***-picture***, ***-presentation***, ***-symbolism***, ***-verification***; (senses 19 and 20) ***sense-assimilation***, ***-change***, ***-development***, ***-group***, ***-link***, ***-linkage***, ***-loan***, ***-unit***, ***-word***; objective, as ***sense-pleaser***; ***sense-bereaving***, ***-confounding***, ***-confusing***, ***-ravishing*** adjs.; instrumental, etc., as ***sense-besotted***, ***-bound***, ***-distracted***, ***-given*** adjs. Also **sense aerial** = *sense-finder* below; **sense-box** *jocular*, the head; **sense-carrier** *Anglo-Irish*, one who expresses the collective opinion of a group or party; **sense-content**, (*a*) *Philos.*, whatever is present to one of the senses; a sense-datum; (*b*) the sense or meaning contained in an idea or literary passage; **sense-experience**, experience that is derived from the senses; **sense-field** *Philos.* (see quot. 1925); **sense-finder**, an aerial designed for sense-finding; **sense-finding**, with some radio direction-finders: the operation of determining which of two indicated directions 180° apart is correct; **sense history**, (*a*) *Philos.* (see quot. 1923); (*b*) the history of the development of meaning attached to a word; **sense-quality** *Philos.* and *Psychol.*, the quality of the sensory properties inherent in an object; **sense-withdrawal** *Yoga* = PRATYAHARA; **sense-world**, the external world as it is known through the senses; the 'world' of experience that is derived from one of the senses.

1941 W. J. D. ALLAN *Radio Navigation* ii. 42 The third method of finding sense is by means of a *sense aerial. **1970** TAYLOR & PARMAR *Ground Studies for Pilots* vii. 245 By adjusting the phasing of the loop and sense aerials, the cardioid and its image are produced in rapid alterations. **1894** A. C. FRASER in *Locke's Essay Hum. Und.* II. IV. xi. 328 When ideas, or qualities of things, are..not merely revived in memory or imagination, in the absence of the actual *sense-appearances. **1947** *Mind* LVI. 300 A chief begetter of the sense-datum theory was the problem set by illusory sense-appearances. *a* **1902** R. ADAMSON *Devel. Mod. Philos.* (1903) II. II. i. 229 Leibniz..maintains that our *sense-apprehension of the colour green is a confused sense-apprehension of the two colours blue and yellow. **1921** HANNAY & COLLINGWOOD tr. *Ruggiero's Mod. Philos.* 206 The first 'something' is mere sense-apprehension. **1935** M. E. HOUTZAGER *Unconscious Sound- & Sense-Assimilations* i.

26 Place-names..change according to sound-laws, but also ..through unconscious sound- and *sense-assimilations. **1922** A. N. Whitehead *Princ. Relativity* ii. 20 Divest consciousness of its ideality, such as its logical, emotional, aesthetic and moral apprehensions, and what is left is *sense-awareness. **1978** *English Jrnl.* Dec. 57/2 The second group of students did get to try to drink from a water fountain which was truly a unique experience in sense-awareness. **1597** Drayton *Heroic Ep., Isabel to Mortimer* 29 Those *sence-bereauing stalkes That grow in shadie Proserpines darke walkes. **1647** C. Harvey *Schola Cordis* iv. 7 Poore, silly, simple, *sense-besotted soule. **1620** Quarles *Feast for Wormes* (1638) 13 His *sense-bound heart relents not. **1853** Kingsley *Hypatia* viii. 99 The coarse and sense-bound tribe who can appreciate nothing but what is palpable to sense and sight! **1808** E. S. Barrett *Miss-led General* 132 Spun from my own *sense-box. **1879** McCarthy *Own Times* I. xvi. 401 Thenceforward he was really the mouth-piece and the *sense-carrier of his party. **1887** Dowden *Shelley* I. vi. 247 Eliza..had..evidently been assigned the position of sense-carrier to the others. **1908** *Practitioner* Oct. 548 In the case of all our senses, the effects are produced by reponsive protoplasmic movements of the specially adapted *sense-cells. **1953** N. Tinbergen *Herring Gull's World* iii. 19 The sense-cells in the retina are the units of vision. **1976** H. R. Schiffman *Sensation & Perception* ix. 125/2 (*caption*) The tips of the sense cells extend into a pit. **1931** G. Stern *Meaning & Change of Meaning* x. 261 Clippings seldom give rise to *sense-changes. **1951** W. Empson *Structure Complex Words* 26 The cause of a sense-change need have nothing to do with the use made of it after it has been pushed through. **1600** Tourneur *Trans. Metamorph.* xlvii, Amazed with *sence-confounding wretchednesse. **1837** Carlyle *Fr. Rev.* III. i. viii, One *sense-confusing tumult. **1858** A. C. Fraser *Rational Philos.* 94 So-called **sense*-consciousness can be analysed. **1874** Reynolds *John Bapt.* iii. §3. 201 The prophet's ordinary sense-consciousness was suspended. **1896** L. T. Hobhouse *Theory of Knowl.* ii. 42 It is quite enough for our purpose that *some* *sense-contents should be complex. **1902** W. James *Varieties Relig. Experience* iii. 55 The words 'soul', 'God', 'immortality', cover no distinctive sense-content. **1962** W. Nowottny *Lang. Poets Use* v. 111 The action of the poem..is not something agglomerated out of the successive sense-contents of each line. **1975** W. S. Robinson in H. N. Castaneda *Stud. in Sellars' Philos.* 105 An analogue..designed to apply specifically to sensing sense contents, is presupposed. **1882** J. A. H. Murray *Let.* in K. M. E. Murray *Caught in Web of Words* (1977) x. 190 Nobody exc[ept] my predecessors in specimens of the Dicty has yet *tried* to trace out historically the *sense-development of English words. **1960** C. S. Lewis *Studies in Words* 29 Indeed the sense-development of the word *proper* itself..is a striking instance. **1621** G. Sandys *Ovid's Met.* iii. (1632) 97 With that, in-rush the *sense-distracted Crew. **1889** J. Venn *Empirical Logic* vi. 150 The adhesive power between the *sense-element and the notion is particularly strong in the case of..smell. **1862** A. C. Fraser in *Macm. Mag.* VI. 194/2 The steady reference to *sense-experience.. distinguished Locke. **1871** Sense-experience [see preperception]. **1923** T. P. Nunn *Educ.* xiii. 171 All that constitutes..the quantitative as distinguished from the qualitative aspects of sense-experience. **1968** *Listener* 30 May 685 Principles native to the mind which we utilise in grasping sense-experience. **1890** W. James *Princ. Psychol.* II. xx. 268 The *education* of our space-perception consists largely of two processes—reducing the various *sense-feelings to a common *measure*, and *adding them together* into the single all-including space of the real world. **1925** C. D. Broad *Mind & its Place* iv. 195 A sensum is not something that exists in isolation; it is a differentiated part of a bigger and more enduring whole, viz., of a *sense-*field*. **1971** A. J. Ayer *Russell & Moore* iii. 65 To obtain the equivalent of sensibilia, on the basis of our primitive percepts, all that is needed, I believe, is the projection of spatial and temporal relations beyond the sense-fields in which they are originally given. **1934** Webster, *Sense finder. **1953** C. H. Cotter *Elem. Navigation* xlvii. 485 The principle of the sense finder is as follows. Depending on whether the transmitting station lies in a certain direction or the opposite direction, the e.m.f. in the loop aerial will be altered in phase by 180°. **1937** D. C. T. Bennett *Compl. Air Navigator* iv. 134 A *sense-finding arrangement is usually incorporated in Fixed Loop Direction Finders. **1957** R. Watson-Watt *Three Steps to Victory* lviii. 361 Our Radio Research Station work ..had included 'sense-finding', the removal of the direction-finding ambiguity between one compass bearing and its exact opposite. **1871** A. C. Fraser *Life of Berkeley* x. 369 We may even, with Berkeley, call these *sense-given phenomena 'sensations'. **1933** *Mind* XLII. 292 A great variety of sense-given shapes—squares, parallelograms, trapezia, etc.—would then..all be either portions or distortions of the surface of this cube. **1928** C. Bergener *Contrib. to Study of Conversion of Adjectives into Nouns* 1, I have..made an attempt.., after arranging the material in *sense-groups, to ascertain the productivity of this mode of word-formation during the different periods of the language. **1966** G. N. Leech *Eng. in Advertising* viii. 89 One of the skills of writing formal English consists in..arranging one's ideas so as to make the end of each sense-group..as far as possible the appropriate place for emphasis. **1923** C. D. Broad *Sci. Thought* x. 362 Let us call the whole series of sensible fields which an observer O senses in the course of his life, O's **sense-history*. **1933** *Oxf. Eng. Dict.* I. p. v, The aim of this Dictionary is to present..the words that have formed the English vocabulary..with all the relevant facts concerning their form, sense-history, pronunciation, and etymology. **1954** A. J. Ayer *Philos. Ess.* iv. 95 The occurrence, within a given sense-history, of a series of sense-fields. **1871** A. C. Fraser *Life of Berkeley* iii. 75 *Sense-ideas are with Berkeley real and presentative; not representative images. **1900** B. Russell *Philos. Leibniz* xiv. 161 Sense-ideas must..be distinguished by their own nature. **1862** Spencer *First Princ.* i. iv. §22 (1875) 69 The illusiveness of *sense-impressions. **1896** L. T. Hobhouse *Theory of Knowl.* ii. 56 A felt total impression resulting from the forty separate *sense-impulses. **1847** Lewes *Biog. Hist. Philos.* I. 111 The distinction between *sense-knowledge and reflective knowledge. **1894** A. C. Fraser in *Locke's Essay Hum. Und.* II. iv. xi. 332 For it is not metaphysically impossible that there may be a *dream*, continuous and orderly, like the actual *sense-life of a man. **1964** M. McLuhan *Understanding Media* i. i. 19 Money has reorganized the sense life of peoples just because it is an *extension* of our sense lives. **1957** N. Frye *Anat. Criticism* iv. 272 The poetic creation..is an associative rhetorical process, most of it below the threshold of consciousness, a chaos of paronomasia, sound-links, ambiguous *sense-links, and memory-links very like that of the dream. **1962** W. Nowottny *Lang. Poets Use* i. 15 The *sense-linkage effected by rhyme is an effect of which Arnold was well aware. **1931** *Sense-loan [see *cross-influence* s.v. cross- B.]. *a* **1902** R. Adamson *Devel. Mod. Philos.* (1903) II. 68 Nor does inner *sense-material lend itself even to the less complete theoretical form of natural science. **1894** Creighton & Titchener tr. *Wundt's Hum. & Anim. Psychol.* vii. 119 The individual sensation is estimated by the relation in which it stands to other sensations of the same *sense-modality. **1977** P. Strevens *New Orientations Teaching of Eng.* ix. 115 The sense-modalities of vision and hearing. **1908** W. James *Meaning of Truth* (1909) xii. 239 Our private concepts represent the *sense-objects to which they lead us, these being public realities independent of the individual. **1920** A. N. Whitehead *Concept Nat.* viii. 170 The appearance of sense-objects is conditioned by the adventures of material objects. **1949** *Mind* LVIII. 58 The position will be, as Mr. Russell in fact saw, that the constituents of physical constructs are not simply sense-*objects* but sensations or sense-experiences. **1909** W. James *Pluralistic Universe* iv. 145 Hypotheses, and deductions from these, controlled by *sense-observations and analogies with what we know elsewhere, are to be thanked for all of science's results. **1956** E. L. Mascall *Christian Theol. & Nat. Sci.* ii. 48 Scientific theories need for their expression technical terms..whose definition in terms of sense-observations is extremely complicated and remote. **1854** Owen *Skel. & Teeth* (1855) 13 Brain and *sense-organs. **1907** W. James *Pragmatism* vi. 218 Some part of a system that dips at numerous points into *sense-percepts. **1846** J. D. Morell *Hist. Philos.* I. ii. 205 In doing this, Kant took it for granted, as a thing lying altogether beyond the region of proof, the reality of our *sense-perceptions. **1868** N. Porter *Hum. Intellect* §102 (1872) 119 We define Sense-perception as that power of the intellect by which it gains the knowledge of material objects. **1971** R. I. Aaron *Knowing & Function of Reason* iv. 79 This conclusion is reinforced by arguments from the change induced in sense-perception by drugs, such as mescaline. **1871** A. C. Fraser *Life of Berkeley* x. 371 There is no evidence that an unperceived sensation or *sense-phenomenon exists. **1971** R. I. Aaron *Knowing & Function of Reason* iv. 79 What is sensed has been variously described as idea, impression,..sense-phenomenon, sensum, and so on. **1920** A. S. Eddington *Space, Time & Gravit.* ii. 32 It would be unreasonable to limit our thought of nature to what can be comprised in *sense-pictures. **1600** Sir W. Cornwallis *Ess.* i. xiv. I. 5, When these *sence-pleasers haue come from any of their sports. **1884** S. H. Hodgson *Let.* 14 Feb. in R. B. Perry *Thought & Char. W. James* (1935) I. 625 The answer must, for me, be given by a 'what' which is at least a *possibility* of *sense presentation. **1932** W. T. Stace *Theory of Knowl.* iii. 34 The images of hallucination and dream are just as much part of the given as are sense presentations. **1896** L. T. Hobhouse *Theory of Knowl.* ii. 38 The idea of sensation as giving these simple *sense-qualities and nothing else. **1954** R. Wells in Saporta & Bastian *Psycholinguistics* (1961) 280/2, I refer to the fact that they are all names of sense-qualities. **1638** Sir T. Herbert *Trav.* (ed. 2) 266 The ayre is a compound of *sense-ravishing odours. **1871** A. C. Fraser *Life of Berkeley* x. 375 The substantiality and causality of matter thus resolve into a Universal *Sense-symbolism, the interpretation of which is the office of physical science. **1892** H. Sweet *New Eng. Gram.* i. 20 A word may be defined as an ultimate independent *sense-unit. **1974** R. Quirk *Linguist & Eng. Lang.* vi. 97 We are dealing with languages whose structures differ so much that..translation..is possible only if we deal in large sense-units. **1907** W. James *Pragmatism* vi. 209 Their relations are perceptually obvious at a glance, and no *sense-verification is necessary. **1937** K. T. Behanan *Yoga* xiii. 215 In *pratyahara* or the *sense-withdrawal stage, a deliberate effort is made to diminish the impulses streaming in through the sense organs. **1960** J. Hewitt *Yoga* viii. 116 Sense-Withdrawal is something which you must do for yourself, your 'I' must be in complete control. *c* **1874** *Sense-word [see *rhythm-word* s.v. rhythm 9 a]. **1911** W. James *Some Probl. Philos.* viii. 139 Monism usually treats the *sense-world as a mirage or illusion. **1932** W. T. Stace *Theory of Knowl.* ix. 212 Those characters of the 'thing'..are in different sense-worlds.

sense (sɛns), *v.* Also 6–7 sence, 7 sens. [f. the sb.]

†**1. a.** *trans.* To perceive (an outward object) by the senses; also, to feel (pain). *Obs.*

1598 Rowlands *Betray. Christ* D j, Could sinnes-besotted, hell-path wrandrers, see The horrours on an out-cast wretch imposed, Or sence the inward worme that gnaweth me. **1682** Flavel *Fear* 129 They loved their lives, and sensed their pains as well as you. **1873** Will Carleton *Farm Ball.* 33 O God! if you want a man to sense the pains of hell, Before you pitch him in just keep him in a heaven a spell!

b. To feel, be conscious of (an inward state, etc.).

1685 W. Adams *Dedham Pulpit* 86 The man that does duly sense his spiritual poverty. **1755** Amory *Mem.* (1769) I. Ded. 6 Your books and philosophy..hinder you from ever sensing the irksomeness of solitude and indolence.

†**c.** To test, make trial of. *Obs.*

a **1688** Bunyan *Christ Compl. Saviour* Wks. 1852 I. 221/1 To sense smell and taste what saving is..is a rare thing kept close from most. *a* **1688** —— *Expos. Gen.* iii. ibid. II. 431/1 She took Satan's arguments into consideration and sensed or tasted them; not by the word of God, but her own natural or rather sore-deluded fancy.

†**2.** To expound the sense or meaning of; to ascribe a meaning to; to take or understand in a particular sense. Also, to explain (*to be something*). *Obs.*

1623 Ailesbury *Serm.* 4 The first [exposition]..is Origens, who hath sensed the bodie to be the church. *a* **1631** Donne *Polydoron* (1650) 88 The word good fellow as it is now senced by the vulgar, imports a drunkard. **1643** Trapp *Comm. Gen.* xx. 16 Some sense the text thus. **1687** Stillingfl. *Doctr. Trin. & Transubst.* ii. 2, *Pr.* How doth it [*sc.* the Doctrine of the Trinity] appear? *P.* By the Scripture sensed by the Church. **1726** Wodrow *Corr.* (1843) III. 261 Dr. Clarke at first tried to reconcile his doctrine to that of the Church of England, by sensing the Articles.

3. To perceive, become aware of, 'feel' (something present, a fact, state of things, etc.) not by direct perception but more or less vaguely or instinctively. (Often app. a nonce-word, adopted by the writer to express a particular shade of meaning.)

1872 L. Oliphant *Let.* in *Life* (1891) 101 He 'senses' the least coldness towards himself, and it stops everything. **1885** Hornaday *2 Yrs. in Jungle* xvii. 189 The herd sensed the danger and made off. **1904** M. Hewlett *Queen's Quair* i. vii. 102 Queen Mary watched her closely, sensing an enemy. **1904** S. E. White *Forest* iii. 28 You must travel three or four days from such a place before you sense the forest in its vastness.

4. To understand, comprehend, grasp, 'take in'. Chiefly *U.S.* and *dial.*

1841 A. M. Maxwell *Run through U.S.* I. 102 The noun *sense* they convert into a most comical verb—'I sense', or 'She sensed him to do it'. **1849** *Knickerbocker* XXXIII. 201 'Do you sense what you are doing, Jack?' said she. 'Sense it, Suzy?' replied B.,—'I do, to the letter.' **1860** Bartlett *Dict. Amer.* (ed. 3), *To sense*, to comprehend; as, 'Do you sense that?' New England. **1885** Merriam in *Century Mag.* XXX. 832 He..got at the plans of the leaders, the temper of the crowd, sensed the whole situation. **1891** Hardy *Tess* xlviii, I cannot sense your meaning sometimes. **1893** E. D. Fawcett *Riddle of Universe* Proem 2 He should sense how this spectacle belittles the theology of his fellows.

5. *Philos.* To have a sense-perception of. Also *absol.*, to experience sensations.

1661 Glanvill *Van. Dogm.* xxii. 218 Is he [the Sciolist] sure, that objects are not otherwise sensed by others, then they are by him? **1704** Norris *Ideal World* ii. ii. 81 All that we sense or experience are the outward actions and motions which proceed from them. **1884** [Laurie] *Metaph. Nova & Vet.* 91 But we did not then *perceive* extension or space as such, although it was *felt* in the very first breath which consciousness drew, and was afterwards *sensed.* **1904** Titchener tr. *Wundt's Physiol. Psychol.* I. 14 We may sense in dreams, or in a state of hallucination, as intensively as we sense under the operation of actual sensory stimuli. **1909** *Q. Rev.* Oct. 434 The impossible assumption that there are sensations which are not 'sensed'.

6. Of a machine, instrument, etc.: to detect (some circumstance or entity).

1946 *Ann. Computation Lab. Harvard Univ.* I. 22 In the event that one or both of the factors involved in a multiplication are negative numbers, this fact is sensed and stored by the multiply unit. **1962** F. I. Ordway et al. *Basic Astronomics* v. 197 After arrival on the Moon the fluid is vented, an operation sensed by a pressure switch. **1978** *Sci. Amer.* June 54/3 In general particle detectors operate by sensing the ionization of atoms caused by the passage of a charged particle.

Hence **sensed** *ppl. a.*

1884 [Laurie] *Metaph. Nova & Vet.* 26 The subject as Will..itself goes out and seizes the sensed object.

sense, obs. form of cense *sb.*[1], *v.*[1], *sb.*[2], *v.*[2]

c **1550** *Disc. Common Weal Eng.* (1893) 77 In paiment of theire rentes, customes and senses. **1623** tr. *Favine's Theat. Honour* i. vi. 54 The sonnes..are not sensed and reputed to be noble [F. *ne sont censez et reputez Nobles*]. **1657** W. Morice *Coena* Pref. 1 The Ministery, whose honor and maintenance I have ever sensed to be very much of the interest of Religion.

sensed, *a.* [f. sense *sb.* + -ed[2]. Cf. F. *sensé*, L. *sensātus*: see sensate *a.*] Only with defining word (adj. or adv.).

1. Having a specified sense or meaning.

1577 B. Googe *Heresbach's Husb.* iii. (1586) 147 b, This olde englishe *Distichon*, better sensed, then footed. **1624** H. Mason *New Art Lying* v. 90 They call it Equiuocall, because it is a double-sensed Proposition. **1670** Eachard *Contempt of Clergy* 10 The committing of such high and brave sens'd Poems to a School-boy. *a* **1850** Rossetti *Dante & Circle* i. (1874) 236 His words are wonderfully deep, Oft doubly sensed, asking interpreter.

†**2.** Having wits or senses. *Obs.*

1582 Hester *Secr. Phiorav.* i. xxii. 23 Feuer corrupteth also the sences, so that the sicke is not stable senced.

sense-datum ('sɛns,deɪtəm). *Philos.* Pl. -data. [f. sense *sb.* 1 + datum.] Whatever is the immediate object of any of the senses, usually, but not always, with the implication that it is not a material object.

1882 J. Royce in *Mind* VII. 44 What relation does the external reality bear to the sense-datum? **1890** W. James *Princ. Psychol.* II. xx. 146 It is no wonder if some authors have gone so far as to think that the sense-data have no spatial worth at all. **1912** B. Russell *Probl. Philos.* i. 12 Let us give the name of 'sense-data' to the things that are immediately known in sensation: such things as colours, sounds, smells, hardnesses, roughnesses, and so on. **1938** W. S. Maugham *Summing Up* 260 The sense-datum, on which I thought all knowledge was based, seemed to me something given, which had to be accepted whether it suited the convenience or not. **1956** A. J. Ayer *Probl. Knowl.* 85 What..is immediately given in perception is an evanescent object called an idea, or an impression, or a presentation, or a sense-datum, which is not only private to a single observer but private to a single sense. **1980** *Dædalus* Spring 11 From the point of view of strict empiricism, the attempt to go beyond sense data..seems to fail.

senseful ('sɛnsfʊl), *a.* [f. sense *sb.* + -ful.]

1. Full of sense or meaning; significant.

1591 SYLVESTER *Du Bartas* I. vi. 997 And gave thee power (as Master) to impose Fit sense-full Names unto the Hoast that rowes In watery Regions. **1596** SPENSER *F.Q.* VI. iv. 37 The Ladie hearkning to his senseful speach, Found nothing that he said, vnmeet nor geason, Hauing oft seene it tryde, as he did teach. **1683** D. A. *Art Converse* 44 Not sharp enough to conceive at the first..a senseful and witty word. **1865** CARD. WISEMAN *Shaks.* 9 It is not like that of the printer, who, from a chaotic heap of seemingly unmeaning lead, draws out letter after letter, and so disposes them that they shall make senseful..lines.

†**2.** Intelligent. *Obs.*

1598 MARSTON *Pigmalion*, etc. Sat. iv. 70 Prometheus who celestiall fier Did steale from heauen, therewith to inspire Our earthly bodies with a sencefull minde. *c* **1700** NORRIS (J.), Men, otherwise senseful and ingenious, quote such things out of an author as would never pass in conversation.

‖**sensei** (sɛn'seɪ). [Jap.] In Japan: a teacher or instructor; a professor; a respectful title, occasionally with ironic connotations, for one skilled in an art. Also *transf.*

1884 tr. *J. J. Rein's Japan* II. i. 378 The Ban-i (foreign barbarian) of yesterday was the Ijin-san (foreign gentleman) of to-day, and in the mode of address even a sen-sei (worthy scholar). **1934** E. BLUNDEN *Mind's Eye* 93 A copy of some newly acquired book, or a Japanese clay figure for the sensei's table. **1959** *Times Lit. Suppl.* 10 July 411/1 The ordinary reader begins to feel that he cannot get very far in poetry without a *sensei* or a *guru*. **1972** J. BALL *Five Pieces of Jade* iii. 35 My karate sensei tells me that I should learn Japanese. **1981** J. MELVILLE *Sort of Samurai* i. 7 I'm afraid your colleague my father never really forgave me, Horiguchi-sensei.

senseless ('sɛnslɪs), *a.* Forms: see SENSE *sb.* Also *superl.* 6–7 **sense-, sencelest.** [f. SENSE *sb.* + -LESS.]

1. Of persons, their bodies or organs: Destitute or deprived of sensation; physically insentient.

1557 GRIMALDE *Cicero's Death* in *Tottel's Misc.* (Arb.) 125 Popilius flyeth, therwhyle: and, leauyng there The senslesse stock, a gryzely sight doth bear Vnto Antonius boord, with mischief fed. **1590** SHAKS. *Com. Err.* IV. iv. 25, I would I were senselesse sir, that I might not feele your blowes. **1607** TOPSELL *Four-f. Beasts* 306 His cheekes must not be pinched by the bridle, least the skin grow sencelesse. **1621** G. SANDYS *Ovid's Met.* II. (1626) 37 And stifning cold benums her senselesse lims.

transf. **1883** R. W. DIXON *Mano* II. ii. 67 One that among us was in company Felt his knees smitten with a senseless cold.

b. That is in a state of unconsciousness.

1585 FORMAN *Diary* (1849) 18, I was sensles eight howares. **1595** *Caxton's Blanchardyn* liv. 212 More to hasten on deathes speedy pace to this sencles olde man. **1778** MISS BURNEY *Evelina* xxxiii, I was almost senseless with terror. **1820** BYRON *Juan* IV. xxx, Strange state of being! (for 'tis still to be) Senseless to feel, and with seal'd eyes to see. **1849** MACAULAY *Hist. Eng.* iv. I. 433 His wife..was carried senseless to her chamber. **1889** GRETTON *Memory's Harkback* 109 Where the poor fellow was lying senseless from his fall.

†**c.** Said of sleep, death, the grave, etc. *Obs.*

1576 FLEMING *Panopl. Epist.* 67 What harme can there be in death? which if it were not senselesse, might much rather be termed immortalitie, then death. *a* **1586** SIDNEY *Arcadia* III. (Sommer) 343 With that, he stabbed himselfe into diuers places of his breast and throte, vntill those wounds.. brought him to the senselesse gate of death. **1627** BERNARD *Guide Grand-Jury* I. ii. 13 In another disease..the sicke are ..surprized with a senselesse trance. *a* **1674** TRAHERNE *Poet. Wks.* (1903) 71 Those joys and praises must repair To us, which 'tis a sin To bury in a senseless tomb.

d. Of things: Incapable of sensation or perception.

1577 tr. *Bullinger's Decades* II. ii. (1592) 123 What needest thou any more hereafter, to hunt after senselesse Idoles? **1579** SPENSER *Sheph. Cal.* Feb. 205 Semed, the sencelesse yron did feare, Or to wrong holy eld did forbeare. **1602** SHAKS. *Ham.* II. ii. 496 Then senselesse Illium, Seeming to feele his blow, with flaming top Stoopes to his Bace, and with a hideous crash Takes prisoner Pyrrhus eare. **1610** TOFTE *Hon. Acad.* 15 Love doth willing draw The hardest hearts and sencelest rocks of Epyr with great awe. **1720** A. HILL *Zara* III. i. (near end), I stand, immoveable, like senseless marble! **1825** T. HOOK *Sayings* Ser. II. *Passion & Princ.* viii. III. 105 As he reflected whither the senseless paper [a letter] was soon to be conveyed. **1871** R. ELLIS *Catullus* lxiv. 165 The brutish winds..senseless, voiceless, inhuman Utter'd cry they hear not, in answers hollow reply not.

2. Destitute of mental sensibility, incapable of feeling or perception. Also, having no sense, feeling, or consciousness *of* something. Now *rare* or *Obs.*

1561 T. NORTON *Calvin's Inst.* I. iv. 4b, Those that chokyng the light of nature, do of purpose make them selues senselesse [F. *s'abrutissent*]. **1581** PETTIE tr. *Guazzo's Civ. Conv.* II. (1586) 50b, Which is a signe not onelie of presumptious arrogancie, but also of senseless brutishnesse. **1602** MARSTON *Antonio's Rev.* I. i, Piero..is no nummed lord, Senselesse of all true touch. **1611** SHAKS. *Cymb.* I. i. 135, I am senselesse of your Wrath. **1612** PEACHAM *Gentl. Exerc.* I. xvii. 59 To draw Mars like a yong Hippolitus with an effeminate countenance..proceedeth of a sencelesse & ouercold a iudgement. **1680** OTWAY *Orphan* v. vii. 2068 Why wert thou Deaf to my Cries and senseless of my Pains. **1784** COWPER *Task* I. 516 Not senseless of its charms. **1796** COLERIDGE *Lett.* (1895) 171 Your poor father is, I hope, almost senseless of this calamity. **1818** SHELLEY *Eugan. Hills* 36 Senseless is the breast, and cold, Which relenting love would fold.

†**b.** Unconscious *that*. *Obs.*

1603 DRAYTON *Bar. Wars* v. xiii, As though he thought not on it, As he were senseless that it should forgoe him.

3. Of a person, etc.: Devoid of sense or intelligence, stupid, silly, foolish.

1565 CALFHILL *Answ. Martiall's Treat. Cross* ii. 42b, I think there is none so senslesse as yourselfe, but consters his words otherwise than you. **1580** LUPTON *Sivquila* 55 Far more senselesse, than the senselest or brutest beast in the world. **1602** MARSTON *Antonio's Rev.* IV. i, An honest senselesse dolt, A good poore foole. *a* **1660** *Contemp. Hist. Irel.* (Ir. Archæol. Soc.) II. 99 Will both churche and laitie be soe senclesse as not to disclaime against such a Nero. **1670** COTTON *Espernon* II. VIII. 400 His Lieutenant..being so senseless as to come upon the draw Bridge of the Castle to talk with them. *a* **1716** SOUTH *Serm.* (1737) IV. 47 To hold forth, and harangue the multitude,..wheresoever, and howsoever they could clock the senseless and unthinking rabble about them. **1819** SHELLEY *Cenci* v. iii. 36 What! Will you give up these bodies to be dragged At horses' heels, so that our hair should sweep The footsteps of the vain and senseless crowd. **1855** BREWSTER *Newton* II. xxiv. 345 But when Eusebius asked her if she knew the man, she answered that she would not be so senseless as to accuse such men.

†**b.** quasi-*adv.* Unreasonably. *Obs. rare*$^{-1}$.

1594 SHAKS. *Rich. III*, III. i. 44 You are too sencelesse obstinate, my Lord, Too ceremonious, and traditionall.

4. Of actions, words, dispositions, etc.: Proceeding from lack of sense or intelligence, foolish. Also, without sense or meaning; unmeaning, meaningless, purposeless.

The two uses, related to different meanings of SENSE *sb.*, are often blended; unequivocal examples of the sense 'meaningless' are rare.

1579 E. K. in *Spenser's Sheph. Cal.* Ep. Ded. §1 What so they vnderstand not, they streight way deeme to be sencelesse. **1588** *Marprel. Epist.* (Arb.) 3, D. Bridges hath written in your defence, a most senceless book. **1613** PURCHAS *Pilgrimage* (1614) 627 The Rabbines haue another as senselesse a dreame that Phineas was Elias. **1645** USSHER *Body Div.* (1647) 419 Which thing yet were senslesse to doubt of. **1647** CLARENDON *Hist. Reb.* II. §86 Cheap senseless libels were scattered about the city. **1693** LOCKE *Educ.* §11 (1699) 16, I cannot but conclude there are other Creatures, as well as Munkeys, who, little wiser than they, destroy their young Ones by senseless fondness, and too much embracing. **1709** STEELE *Tatler* No. 26 ¶10 Putting all my Force against the horrid and senseless Custom of Duels. **1839** FR. A. KEMBLE *Resid. Georgia* (1863) 129 Cheerful music and senseless words. **1849** MACAULAY *Hist. Eng.* iv. I. 441 The senseless and dastardly wickedness of mixing noxious drugs with the food of a young girl whom he had no conceivable motive to injure. **1864** PUSEY *Lect. Daniel* (1876) 150 It is senseless to bring the Ptolemies into the line of Syrian kings. **1884** BRETT in *Law Rep. 14 Q.B. Div.* 799 If that argument be true, the clause..was an absolutely futile and senseless one.

senselessly ('sɛnslɪslɪ), *adv.* [-LY².] In a senseless manner, foolishly, irrationally. Also, †in a senseless or unconscious condition.

1611 COTGR., *Stupidement*, Sencelessly, dully. **1621** SIR W. ALEXANDER in *Sidney's Arcadia* III. (1629) 332 He was lying downe senslesly on his senslesse friend. **1660** R. COKE *Justice Vind.* 7 And then most senselessly he [White] confounds the offices of command and obedience. **1742** WESLEY *Jrnl.* 26 June, A drunken man..was so senselesly impertinent, that even his comrades were quite ashamed of him. **1860** SALA *Lady Chesterf.* Pref. 3 The most brilliant achievements of human genius have been impudently and senselessly caricatured.

senselessness ('sɛnslɪsnɪs). [-NESS.]

1. Absence of or incapacity for feeling (physical or mental); insensibility, impassibility. Also, unconscious or insensible condition, as in sleep, coma, etc. Now *rare*.

1577 tr. *Bullinger's Decades* III. iii. (1592) 302 Which cannot choose but happen to them which of pacience doo make a kinde of sencelesnesse. **1583** B. GOOGE *Let.* in *N. & Q.* Ser. III. III. 243 The people (exceptynge theyr blindnesse, or rather senselessnesse in relygyon) live in as goodd order as maye bee. **1601** DEACON & WALKER *Answ. Darel* 36 Besides this sencelessnes of bodie: he foamed at the mouth like an Horse. **1643** *Orkney Witch Trial* in *Abbotsford Club Miscell.* I. 173 He was brocht in to Jonet Sklateris hous in Cogare, heavilie diseasit with a senslesnes, that he knew not quhat was said or done to him. **1677** PLOT *Oxfordsh.* 198 Using divers remedies respecting her senselessness, Head, Throat, and Brest, in so much that within 14 hours, she began to speak. **1697** BURGHOPE *Disc. Relig. Assemb.* 75 The true cause of this carelessness and neglect is a senselessness in religion. **1813** SHELLEY *Q. Mab* IX. 86 Unchecked by dull and selfish chastity, That virtue of the cheaply virtuous, Who pride themselves in senselessness and frost. **1822–9** *Good's Study Med.* (ed. 3) IV. 602 [They] fall down instantly in a state of senselessness and apparent death. **1839** BAILEY *Festus* (1848) 43 A swimming, swollen senselessness of soul.

†**b.** Absence of sense or appreciation *of* something. *Obs.*

1618 TOWNSON in Gutch *Coll. Cur.* (1781) II. 422 Out of an humour of vain-glory or..senselessness of his own estate. **1796** MME. D'ARBLAY *Camilla* IV. ii. 37 A hasty challenge.. was accepted with a horse laugh of brutal senselessness of danger.

2. Foolishness, irrationality.

1611 COTGR., *Stupidité*, stupiditie, sencelesnesse. **1621** T. WILLIAMSON tr. *Goulart's Wise Vieillard* 48 It is a brutish stupiditie and sencelessenesse, both in yong and old men, to promise to themselues to morrow. **1681** GREW *Musæum* I. II. iii. 44 The senselesness of the tradition of the Crocodiles moving his upper Jaw, is plain from [etc.]. **1847** C. BRONTE *Jane Eyre* xvi, He said something in praise of your eyes, did he? Blind puppy! Open their bleared lids and look on your own accursed senselessness! **1903** MORLEY *Gladstone* VIII. iii. (1905) II. 262 In a boundless coil of mischief pure senselessness will entangle you.

†'**sensement.** *Sc. Obs.* Forms: 5 **sensment,** 6 **sensyment, -iment, censement, sens(i)ament, sensement.** [a. OF. *sensement*, pseudo-etymological spelling (as if f. *sens* SENSE *sb.*) of **censement*, f. *cense-r* to give a decision: see -MENT.] A decision, judgement.

1488 in Pitcairn *Crim. Trials* I. *11 Forsamekle as it is fundin be sensment of Parliament. **1513** DOUGLAS *Æneis* XI. v. 89 Mony sensymentis For Turnus schawis evident argumentis. **1567** Q. MARY in R. Keith *Hist. Aff. Scot.* (1734) 394 He wes acquite to oure Lawis, and be the Sensament of Parlament. **1567** *Sc. Acts Jas. I* (1814) III. 28 Our Souerane Lord..thairfor be censement of this present Parliament, authorisis [etc.]. **1582** *Reg. Privy Council Scot.* III. 514 The said Sir James standis forfaltit be the sensiament of the Thre Estaittis in Parliament. **1582–8** *Hist. Jas. VI* (1804) 37 As concerning the honor, I refer it to the sensement of the indifferent reedar. *Ibid.* 51.

Sen-Sen ('sɛnsɛn). *N. Amer.* Also **sen-sen.** The proprietary name of a breath-sweetener, freq. used to disguise the smell of drink or cigarettes.

1911 *Official Gaz.* (U.S. Patent Office) 30 May 1273/2 Sen-Sen Chiclet Company, New York, N.Y. Filed Mar. 23, 1911... Chewing-Gum and Cachous. Claims use since on or about the month of March, 1894. **1936** J. DOS PASSOS *Big Money* 497 He was waiting..in the lobby..chewing sensen to take the smell of three whiskeys..off his breath. **1947** J. STEINBECK *Wayward Bus* vii. 98 He took a few grains of sen-sen out of his inner shirt pocket and threw them in his mouth. **1951** P. BRANCH *Lion in Cellar* i. 8 He was eating sen-sen cachous. **1972** *Even. Telegram* (St. John's, Newfoundland) 28 June 12/1 Imbibers chewed Sen Sen to take the odor of liquor off their breath.

senser, obs. f. CENSER *sb.*¹, var. CENSER *sb.*²

sensewalite, obs. form of SENSUALITY.

senshalship, obs. form of SENESCHALSHIP.

‖**senshaw** ('sɛnʃɔː). [prob. repr. Chinese *siensha* (*sien* thread, *sha* gauze).] A Chinese gauze-like silk fabric.

1848 S. W. WILLIAMS *Middle Kingd.* II. xv. 123 The common people wear pongee and senshaw, which they frequently dye in gambier to a dust or black color.

sensiament, variant of SENSEMENT *Obs.*

‖**sensibile** (sɛn'sɪbɪleɪ). *Philos.* Usu. in pl. **sensibilia** (sɛnsɪ'bɪlɪə). [L., neut. of *sensibilis* SENSIBLE.] A term popularized by Bertrand Russell to denote the kind of thing which, if sensed, is a sense-datum.

1856 J. HINTON *Sel. from MSS.* (1871) II. 159 The matter of the schools, the substratum that underlies and is to be distinguished from the 'properties' or 'sensibilia', must be the 'actualistic', eternal (or spiritual.) That is, it is the eternal *not seen*..i.e. it is the hypothesis. **1906** J. A. STEWART in *Mind* Oct. 521 The Ideas [of Plato]..are 'known'.. only as performing their function of making *sensibilia* intelligible. **1918** B. RUSSELL *Mysticism & Logic* viii. 148, I shall give the name *sensibilia* to those objects which have the same metaphysical and physical status as sense-data, without necessarily being data to any mind. Thus the relation of a *sensibile* to a sense-datum is like that of a man to a husband: a man becomes a husband by entering into the relation of marriage, and..a *sensibile* becomes a sense-datum by entering into the relation of acquaintance. **1921** tr. *Ruggiero's Mod. Philos.* 324 On this basic duality Varisco builds his theory. On the one side there exists the reality of sensibilia. **1940** A. J. AYER *Found. Emp. Knowl.* ii. 71 We shall have to take as a criterion for the existence of a sensibile the truth of a single hypothetical proposition. **1962** J. L. AUSTIN (*title*) Sense and sensibilia.

‖**sensibilité** (sɑ̃sibilite). *rare.* [Fr.] = SENSIBILITY.

1926 D. H. LAWRENCE *Plumed Serpent* v. 90 And in all the crowd, a sense of guardedness..a curious soft *sensibilité*. **1960** *Encounter* XV. II. 64 It was a matter of being formed alike, of having the same *sensibilité*.

sensibilitous, *a. nonce-wd.* [f. SENSIBILITY + -OUS.] Cultivating 'sensibility'.

1811 BYRON in *Mem. F. Hodgson* (1878) I. 177 But you are a sentimental and sensibilitous person, and will rhyme to the end of the chapter.

sensibility (sɛnsɪ'bɪlɪtɪ). [ad. L. *sensibilitās* (-*tātem*), f. *sensibilis*: see SENSIBLE *a.* and -ITY. Cf. F. *sensibilité* (1314 in Hatz.-Darm.), Pr. *sensibilitee*, Sp. *sensibilidad*, Pg. *sensibilidade*, It. *sensibilità, sensibilitade, -tate*.

Rare until the middle of the 18th century.]

†**1. a.** *pl.* Sensible species; the emanations from bodies, which were supposed to be the cause of sensation. **b.** Capability of being perceived by the senses. *Obs. rare.*

a. **1374** CHAUCER *Boeth.* v. met. iv. (1868) 166 Philosophers þat hyȝten stoiciens þat wenden þat ymages & sensibilites [*sensus et imagines*] þat is to sein sensible ymaginacious..weren inprentid in to soules fro bodies wiþ oute forþe.

b. **1616** R. C. *Times' Whistle* I. 496 That's only good In their grosse braines, whose visibility And appetituall sensibility Lies open to their sence.

2. a. Power of sensation or perception; †the specific function of any of the organs of sense (*obs.*). Now often, the (greater or less) readiness of an organ or tissue to respond to sensory stimuli; sensitiveness.

c **1400** tr. *Secreta Secret., Gov. Lordsh.* xci. 97 Þe sensibilitez of þe Eres er harkenyng of souns. *Ibid.* xcii. 97 Þe sensibilyte of þe tonge ys by way of tastynge & sauour. **1412–20** LYDG. *Troy Bk.* III. 5687 Comparysownyd..To a sowle þat were vegetable, þe whiche, with-oute sensibilite Mynystreth lyf in herbe, flour, and tre. **1533** ELYOT *Cast. Helthe* (1541) 52 The sinewes which make sensibilitie, the rootes of whom are in the braine. **1769** COOK *1st Voy.* I. iv. in Hawkesworth *Voy.* (1773) II. 51 Having now been exposed to the cold and the snow near an hour and an half, some of the rest began to lose their sensibility. **1789** W. BUCHAN *Dom. Med.* (1790) 557 The great sensibility of their [children's] organs. **1794** PALEY *Nat. Theol.* xxvi. (1819) 431 An increased, no less than an impaired sensibility, induces a state of disease and suffering. **1807** *Med. Jrnl.* XVII. 523 The anatomically non-corresponding points of the two eyes may be possessed of equal sensibility. **1834** McMURTRIE *Cuvier's Anim. Kingd.* 16 Sensibility resides in the nervous system. **1875** W. S. WATSON *Dis. Nose* 21 Common sensation or tactile sensibility. **1879** *Cassell's Techn. Educ.* I. 350/1 A more than normal sensibility in the retina is an inconvenience.

b. *Philos.* Power or faculty of feeling, capacity of sensation and emotion as distinguished from cognition and will.

1838 [HAYWOOD] tr. *Kant's Crit. Pure Reas.* 57 If we will term the receptivity of our mind for receiving representations..sensibility, so is..the faculty of itself bringing forth representations, or the Spontaneity of the cognition, the Understanding. **1858** O. W. HOLMES *Aut. Breakf.-t.* x. 96 A man's body..is whatever is occupied by his will and his sensibility. **1861** MILL *Utilit.* iv. 59 Even though these pleasures are much diminished by..decay of his passive sensibilities. **1877** E. CAIRD *Philos. Kant* II. iii. 233 Our assertions must be based on the very nature of our own sensibility, and not on the nature of the objects affecting it.

c. ***dissociation of sensibility***: T. S. Eliot's term for a separation of thought from feeling which he held to be first manifested in poetry of the later seventeenth century.

1921 T. S. ELIOT in *Times Lit. Suppl.* 20 Oct. 669/4 The poets of the seventeenth century..possessed a mechanism of sensibility which could devour any kind of experience... In the seventeenth century a dissociation of sensibility set in, from which we have never recovered. **1930** E. M. W. TILLYARD *Milton* 356 Some sort of dissociation of sensibility in Milton, not necessarily undesirable, has to be admitted; but that he was responsible for any such dissociation in others (at least till this general dissociation had inevitably set in) is untrue. **1943** L. C. KNIGHTS *Explorations* (1963) 93 It is as a contribution to our understanding of the seventeenth century 'dissociation of sensibility'—from which, as Mr. Eliot remarked,..'we have never recovered'—that I wish to consider some of the work of Francis Bacon. **1947** T. S. ELIOT *Milton* 7, I wish first to mention another reproach against Milton, that represented by the phrase 'dissociation of sensibility'... I believe that the general affirmation represented by the phrase 'dissociation of sensibility'.. retains some validity, but I now incline to agree with Dr. Tillyard that to lay the burden on the shoulders of Milton and Dryden was a mistake. **1957** F. KERMODE *Romantic Image* viii. 143 The theory of the dissociation of sensibility is, in fact, the most successful version of a Symbolist attempt to explain why the modern world resists works of art that testify to the poet's special, anti-intellectual way of knowing truth.

†**3.** Mental perception, awareness *of* something.

c **1412** HOCCLEVE *De Reg. Princ.* 5009 þei erren foule, & goon out of þe wey; Of trouth haue þei scant sensibilite. *a* **1635** NAUNTON *Fragm. Reg.* (Arb.) 37 That he said unto the Queen, with some sensibility of the Spanish designs on France: Madam, I beseech you be content not to fear [etc.].

4. a. Emotional consciousness; glad or sorrowful, grateful or resentful recognition of a person's conduct, or of a fact or a condition of things.

1751 ORRERY *Rem. Swift* iii. (ed. 5) 21 The treatment was thought injurious, and Swift expressed his sensibility of it in a short, but satyrical copy of verses entitled *The Discovery*. **1760–72** H. BROOKE *Fool of Qual.* (1809) II. 83, I am very sensible..of your friendship.., and that sensibility constitutes..my happiness. **1776** JOHNSON *Let. to Mrs. Thrale* 1 Apr., I was on Saturday at Mrs. Montague's, who expressed great sensibility of your loss. **1779** FORREST *Voy. N. Guinea* 250, I expressed my sensibility of his many marks of favour to myself. **1790** DUCHÉ *Discourses* II. xvii. 363 A sensibility of our own weakness. **1818** LADY CHARLEVILLE in Lady Morgan *Passages Autobiog.* (1859) 244, I will only speak of my real sensibility of Sir Charles's kind politeness.

†**b.** *pl.* A person's feelings of gratitude. *Obs.*

1753 RICHARDSON *Grandison* (1781) IV. xxii. 168, I cannot speak my grateful sensibilities.

†**c.** A mark of appreciation or consideration; a delicate attention. *Obs.*

1795 SIR J. DALRYMPLE *Let. to Admiralty* 9 Every sensibility that we can shew to our brave Officers and Seamen..is too little for what they do for us.

5. a. Quickness and acuteness of apprehension or feeling; the quality of being easily and strongly affected by emotional influences; sensitiveness. Also, with const., sensitiveness *to*, keen sense *of* something.

1711 ADDISON *Spect.* No. 231 ¶7 Modesty..is a kind of quick and delicate Feeling in the Soul... It is such an exquisite Sensibility, as warns a woman to shun the first Appearance of every thing which is hurtful. **1741** HUME *Ess.* i. 2 There is a certain Delicacy of Passion, to which some People are subject, that makes them extremely sensible to all the Accidents of Life... And when a Person, that has this Sensibility of Temper, meets with any Misfortune, his Sorrow or Resentment takes intire Possession of him. **1756** BURKE *Subl. & B.* Introd. (1759) 34 It frequently happens that a very poor judge, merely by force of a greater complexional sensibility, is more affected by a very poor piece, than the best judge by the most perfect. **1779–81** JOHNSON *L.P., Philips* Wks. 1787 IV. 197 He had great sensibility of censure. **1794** GODWIN *Cal. Williams* 101 My life has been spent in the keenest and most unintermitted sensibility to reputation. **1799** SICKELMORE *Agnes & Leonora* II. 9 Her feelings, which had been so acutely wounded..as almost to hurry sensibility to madness, now assailed her with renovated force. **1802–12** BENTHAM *Ration. Judic. Evid.* (1827) V. 655 A man's sensibility to pecuniary influence. **1810** W. WILSON *Hist. Dissent. Churches* III. 50 He discovered great sensibility and grief on this occasion. **1815** JANE AUSTEN *Emma* II. vi, More acute sensibility to fine sounds than to my feelings. **1822** HAZLITT *Table-t.* Ser. I. ix. 192 That trembling sensibility which is awake to every change and every modification of its ever-varying impressions. **1832** W. IRVING *Alhambra* I. 203, I have often remarked this sensibility of the common people of Spain to the charms of natural objects. **1843** RUSKIN *Mod. Paint.* I. II. §6. iii. §4. 410 A sensibility to colour..being very different from a sensibility to form. *a* **1859** MACAULAY *Hist. Eng.* xxiv. V. 197 From Charles neither the remains of his mother nor those of his grandfather could draw any sign of sensibility. **1874** SHERMAN *Mem.* (1875) II. xxiv. 395, I would define true courage to be a perfect sensibility of the measure of danger, and a mental willingness to incur it.

b. *pl.* Emotional capacities; †instincts of liking or aversion.

1634 W. TIRWHYT tr. *Balzac's Lett.* 36 It is fitting that reason convince our Sensibilities, causing us to agree to what is otherwise distasteful unto us. **1858** O. W. HOLMES *Aut. Breakf.-t.* xii. 111 Something intensely human, narrow, and definite pierces to the seat of our sensibilities more readily than huge occurrences and catastrophes. **1892** BIERCE *In Midst of Life* 109 Doubtless this feeling was due to his unusually acute sensibilities—his keen sense of the beautiful, which these hideous things outraged.

c. *sing.* and *pl.* Liability to feel offended or hurt by unkindness or lack of respect; susceptibilities.

1769 GRAY in *Corr. w. Nicholls* (1843) 85, I wish he would not give too much way to his own sensibilities, and still less (in this case) to the sensibilities of other people. **1778** LAURENS in Sparks *Corr. Amer. Rev.* (1853) II. 203 The Count's sensibility was much wounded. **1806–7** J. BERESFORD *Miseries Hum. Life* (1826) VII. xli, Grating the sensibility, the prepossessions..of the person to whom you are speaking, by some unguarded words. **1855** PRESCOTT *Philip II*, II. i. (1857) I. 156 The sensibilities of a commercial people.

6. In the 18th and early 19th c. (afterwards somewhat *rarely*): Capacity for refined emotion; delicate sensitiveness of taste; also, readiness to feel compassion for suffering, and to be moved by the pathetic in literature or art.

1756–82 WARTON *Ess. Pope* I. v. 262 The force of the repetition of the significant epithet 'foreign', need not be pointed out to any reader of sensibility. **1762** COWPER *To Miss Macartney* 68 Oh! grant, kind heav'n, to me, Long as I draw ethereal air, Sweet Sensibility. **1768** STERNE *Sent. Journ., Bourbonnois*, Dear sensibility! source unexhausted of all that's precious in our joys, or costly in our sorrows! **1807** BYRON *To Romance* v, Where Affectation holds her seat, And sickly Sensibility. **1827** CARLYLE *Richter* Misc. I. 12 Unless seasoned and purified by humour, sensibility is apt to run wild. **1843** PRESCOTT *Mexico* III. v. (1850) I. 401 Those monuments of Oriental magnificence, whose light, aërial forms still survive after the lapse of ages, the admiration of every traveller of sensibility and taste. **1848** THACKERAY *Van. Fair* lxii, This lady had the keenest and finest sensibility, and how could she be indifferent when she heard Mozart?

7. (*transf.* from 2.) Of plants and their organs, also of instruments (esp. a balance, magnetic needle, etc.) or other inorganic objects: Aptness to be affected by external influences; sensitiveness. Const. *to* (rarely *of*).

1662 SIR S. TUKE *Adv. Five Hours* I. 6 Your Story (I confess) is strangely moving; Yet if you could my Fortune weigh with yours, In scales of equal Sensibility, You would not change your Sufferings, for mine. **1783** CULLUM in *Phil. Trans.* LXXIV. 417 As the two last are solstitial, and rather delicate plants, I wondered the less at their sensibility. **1793** SMEATON *Edystone L.* §184 Mortar made up with salt-water, might equally discover its sensibility of moisture. **1825** NICHOLSON *Oper. Mech.* 42 Thus a receptacle is given to the fluid [mercury], which would otherwise disturb the centrifugal force and impair the sensibility of the instrument. **1841** R. HUNT *Art Photogr.* 3 The want of sensibility in the preparation..rendered it necessary that the prepared plate should be exposed..from seven to twelve hours. **1866** R. M. FERGUSON *Electr.* (1870) 21 The sensibility of the [magnetic] needle. **1879** THOMSON & TAIT *Nat. Phil.* I. I. §431 Qualities of a balance:..Sensibility... The definite measure of the sensibility is the angle through which the beam is deflected by a stated difference between the loads in the pans. **1880** C. & F. DARWIN *Movem. Pl.* 193 Here then we have a case of specialized sensibility, like that of the glands of Drosera. **1882** VINES tr. *Sachs' Bot.* 877 The differing sensibility of leaves to variations of temperature on the one hand, and to variations in the intensity of light on the other.

sensibilize ('sɛnsɪbɪˌlaɪz), *v.* [f. late L. *sensibil-is* SENSIBLE + -IZE, after F. *sensibiliser.*] *trans.* To render sensitive. Hence **'sensibiˌlizing** *ppl. a.*; **'sensibiˌlizer. a.** *Phys.* (see quot. 1900); **b.** *Photogr.* = SENSITIZER.

1900 *Lancet* 25 Aug. 564/2 To this specific body [a certain substance in the serum of an immunized animal] M. Bordet gave the name of 'sensibiliser', because it renders the blood-disc or the specific micro-organism susceptible to the attack of the normally present hæmolytic ferment. **1904** *Knowledge* May 98/1 A sheet of silver bromide jelly to which a sensibiliser absorbing the yellow and green rays was added.

sensible ('sɛnsɪb(ə)l), *a.* (and *sb.*). Also 4–6 sencyble, sensyble, 5 sensibill, -yll, censible, 6 sensybul, sensibil, 6–7 sencible, (sensable, 8 senceible). [a. F. *sensible*, ad. late L. *sensibilis*, f. *sens-* (:—**sentt-*), ppl. stem of *sentire* to perceive, feel: see -IBLE. Cf. Sp. *sensible*, Pg. *sensivel*, It. *sensibile.*] **A.** *adj.*

I. That can be felt or perceived.

1. a. Perceptible by the senses. (In *Philos.*, opposed to INTELLIGIBLE 3: in this use now *rare.*).

c **1374** CHAUCER *Boeth.* v. pr. iv. (1868) 165 For it [intelligence] knoweþ þe vniuersite of resoun and þe figure of þe ymaginacioun and þe sensible material conseiued. *c* **1380** WYCLIF *Wks.* (1880) 302 Cristis religion telliþ lityl bi siche sensible habitis [of religious orders], but now takiþ oon & now an oþer as dide crist on good fryday. *Ibid.* 341 Iche good sensible dede þat we don..may be callid a sacrament. **1434–5** MISYN *Fire of Love* 2 When I felt fyrst my hert wax warme, and treuly, not ymagynyngly, bot als it wer with sensibyll fyer, byrned. **1534** [see INTELLIGIBLE 3]. **1538** STARKEY *England* II. i. 165 The gudnes of God (wych only therby mouyd made thys sensybul world). **1631** WIDDOWES *Nat. Philos.* 7 Fixed are the starres of the firmament, whose motion is not sensible. **1638** [see INTELLIGIBLE 3]. **1670** R. COKE *Disc. Trade* Ded., Carnal copulation, killing another, and taking from another, are sensible Actions, and cannot be defined: but Murder, Justice, Adultery, Theft, &c. may be defined..but can never be perceived by the sences. **1690** LOCKE *Hum. Und.* III. ii. §1 The Use then of Words is to be sensible Marks of Ideas. **1704** NORRIS *Ideal World* II. iv. 271 By sensible objects, I mean those objects which the understanding has a perception of by the mediation of the senses. **1732** ARBUTHNOT *Rules of Diet* in *Aliments* (1735) 261 Taste and other sensible Qualities. **1796** KIRWAN *Elem. Min.* (ed. 2) I. 2 The other sensible appearances of earths. **1805** T. WEAVER tr. *Werner's Ext. Charac. Fossils* 1 External characters..are also called Sensible Characters, the use of our senses being sufficient for their discovery. **1805** WORDSW. *Prel.* XIV. 106 In a world of life they live By sensible impressions not enthralled. **1851** WESTCOTT *Introd. Study Gosp.* vi. (ed. 5) 333 St. Matthew alone notices..the earthquake, the sensible ministry of the divine messenger. **1865** GROTE *Plato* I. i. 10 Some primordial and fundamental nature, by and out of which the sensible universe was built up and produced. **1880** J. MILNE in *Trans. Seismol. Soc. Japan* I. II. 53 The earthquake of which we write had certainly a radius over which it was sensible of 120 miles.

b. Const. *to.*

1605 SHAKS. *Macb.* II. i. 36 Art thou not, fatall Vision, sensible To feeling, as to sight? or art thou but A Dagger of the Minde. **1733** ARBUTHNOT *Ess. Effects Air* i. 1 Air is sensible to the Touch by its Motion, and by its Resistance to Bodies moved in it. *a* **1854** H. REED *Lect. Eng. Lit.* i. (1878) 36 All of earth and sky that..is sensible to us.

c. Specific collocations in scientific use. ***sensible horizon***: see HORIZON 1. ***sensible heat*** (†*caloric*): used in contradistinction to *latent heat*: see HEAT *sb.* 2c. ***sensible perspiration***: sweat as distinguished from the emission of vapour through the pores.

1642 Sensible horizon [see RATIONAL *a.* 5b]. **1764** J. FERGUSON *Lect.* 156 The sensible horizon is that circle.. where the heaven and earth seem to meet. **1815** J. SMITH *Panorama Sci. & Art* II. 335 The sensible caloric of adjacent bodies is incessantly employed in maintaining each others equilibrium of temperature. **1830** KNOX tr. *Béclard's Anat.* 152 The cutaneous perspiration, whether sensible or insensible, is to be considered as one of the most important secretions of the organic structure. **1839** URE *Dict. Arts* 444 Heat..perceived by the touch and measured by the thermometer, which is called sensible heat.

†**d.** Of or pertaining to the senses or sensation.

1602 SHAKS. *Ham.* I. i. 57, I might not this beleeue Without the sensible and true auouch Of mine owne eyes. *a* **1619** FOTHERBY *Atheom.* II. ii. §3 (1622) 200 As it is in naturall appetites: so is it, in sensible appetites too. **1793** BEDDOES *Math. Evid.* 7, I will subjoin an instance which perhaps may give the reader an idea how the pronouns arise, and what is their primary sensible signification.

†**e.** quasi-*adv.* Perceptibly. *Obs.*

1590 SWINBURNE *Testaments* 167 Although his childe did neuer crie, so that it did sensible breath or moue.

2. Perceptible by the mind or the inward feelings.

1597 MORLEY *Introd. Mus.* 100 This waie is so well, as I perceiue no sensible fault in it. **1701** *Stanley's Hist. Philos.* Biog. 11 He affirms that it bears sensible marks of its Newness. **1734** tr. *Rollin's Anc. Hist.* (1827) I. Pref. 13 The visible and sensible connexion of sacred and profane history. **1782** J. BROWN *View Nat. & Rev. Relig.* v. v. 498 Sensible assurance of God's love. **1854** C. HODGE *Comm. Rom.* vii. 201 Conversion is a great change, sensible to him that experiences it, and visible to others. **1875** MANNING *Mission Holy Ghost* iv. 104 But the love of God does not mean..the sensible love which we feel towards human friends.

3. Easy to perceive, evident.

a **1586** SIDNEY *Arcadia* III. (Sommer) 319 Their smart being more sensible to others eyes, then to their owne feeling. **1604** T. WRIGHT *Passions* v. §2. 166 In some musick there is to be noted a manifest loose effeminatenesse: and the experience is so sensible, that it were superfluous to proceed any farther in proofe. **1604** R. CAWDREY *Table Alph.*, *Sensible*, easily felt or perceiued. **1690** LOCKE *Hum. Und.* III. v. §8 These are too sensible proofs to be doubted. **1692** —— *Let. to Molyneux* Lett. (1708) 10 We had here..a very sensible earthquake. **1702** C. MATHER *Magn. Chr.* VI. vii. 78 In this present Evil World, it is no Wonder that the Operations of the Evil Angels are more sensible than of the Good ones. **1736** BUTLER *Anal.* I. v. 125 Under the more immediate, or if such an expression may be used, the more sensible government of God. **1794** S. WILLIAMS *Vermont* 57 It..is most of all sensible and apparent in a new country. **1816** P. CLEAVELAND *Min.* 539 It yields a white smoke and a very sensible odor of garlic. **1831** BREWSTER *Nat. Magic* vi. (1833) 142 A tremulous and perfectly transparent vapour was particularly sensible and profuse. **1853** PHILLIPS *Rivers Yorks.* v. 150 The warming influence of the sea air begins to be very sensible in October.

4. Large enough to be perceived or to be worth considering; appreciable, considerable. Now only of immaterial things (as quantities, magnitudes, etc.).

1398 TREVISA *Barth. De P.R.* XVIII. cv. (1495) 849 And though a moughte be a sencyble beest: yet he hydeth hymselfe wythin the clothe that vneth he is seen. **1581** LAMBARDE *Eiren.* IV. xx. (1588) 619 If our Gaoles in Englande were more often swept and emptied, I doubt not, but that wee also should finde a sensible profite to arise thereby. **1646** SIR T. BROWNE *Pseud. Ep.* IV. vii. 196 We could discover no sensible difference in weight. **1755** B. MARTIN *Mag. Arts & Sci.* 116 A very sensible Distance Eastward. **1792** JEFFERSON *Writ.* (1859) III. 340 You will perceive that the Indian War calls for sensible exertions. **1825** *Q. Jrnl. Sci.*, etc. XVIII. 398 It re-dissolves, especially if the muriatic acid added be in sensible excess. **1843** PORTLOCK *Geol.* 215 Both contain a sensible amount of Strontian. **1860** TYNDALL *Glac.* I. i. 4 A fine mud, composed of particles of sensible magnitude. **1877** *Encycl. Brit.* VI. 33/2 Epicycloidal cams described as follows..may be used without any sensible error. **1880** C. R. MARKHAM *Peruv. Bark* III. xv. 436 [It will] effect a sensible reduction in these figures.

†**5.** Of discourse, etc.: Easily understood; suited to make a strong impression on the mind; striking, effective. *Obs.*

c **1530** COX *Rhet.* (1899) 42 To be techars of goddes worde in suche maner as maye be moste sensible and accepte to their audience. **1558** BONNER in Foxe *A. & M.* (1583) 2041/1 It doth appeare vnto me thou art of a good memorie & of a very sensible talke, but something ouerhastie. *a* **1568** ASCHAM *Scholem.* II. (Arb.) 100 He..therefore imployed thereunto a fitte, sensible, and caulme kinde of speaking and writing. *a* **1586** SIDNEY *Arcadia* II. (Sommer) 219 b, That as her wordes did paint out her minde, so they serued as a shadow, to make the picture more liuely and sensible. **1684** R. WALLER *Nat. Exp.* To Rdr., Wherefore he judges it an Undertaking worthy of his great Mind to confront with the most Accurate, and sensible Experiments, the force of their Assertions. **1715** DESAGULIERS *Fires Impr.* 22 If such a Tube be bent, the Experiment will be much more sensible. **1744** HARRIS *Three Treat.* Wks. (1841) 40 The ideas, therefore, of poetry, must needs make the most sensible impression, when the affections, peculiar to them, are already excited by the music.

quasi-*adv.* **1665** HOOKE *Microgr.* 68, I shall endeavour to explain my meaning a little more sensible by a Scheme.

†**6.** Such as is acutely felt; markedly painful or pleasurable. Const. *to*. *Obs.*

1593 SHAKS. *Lucr.* 1678 My woe too sencible thy passion maketh More feeling painfull. **1598** YONG *Diana* 63, I felt so sensible griefe, to see my selfe forgotten of him, who had so great reason to loue me, and whom I did loue so much. **1640** tr. *Verdere's Rom. of Rom.* III. ix. 34 The fall of this young Prince..was so sensible to the Emperour, that had he not feared the anger of Brustafard..the Jousts had been at an end. **1655** TERRY *Voy. E. India* iv. 122 Scorpions..whose stinging is most sensible, and deadly. *a* **1674** CLARENDON *Hist. Reb.* VIII. §136 This very sensible mortification transported him so much, that [etc.]. **1711** in *10th Rep. Hist. MSS. Comm.* App. v. 184 His..death proved very sensible to the languishing King. **1781** J. MOORE *View Soc. It.* (1790) II. lvii. 148 [The King] can inflict a punishment highly sensible to them, by not inviting them to the amusements of the Court. **1796** PEGGE *Anonym.* 445 The circumambient air, when a man is so hot within, is very sensible to him, and ..makes him chill, and liable to colds. **1819** SCOTT *Ivanhoe* ix, The time and place prevented his receiving..more sensible marks of his master's resentment.

II. Capable of feeling or perceiving.

7. Endowed with the faculty of sensation.

†**a.** Of living beings, their nature or mode of existence.

c **1374** CHAUCER *Boeth.* v. pr. iv. (1868) 166 A man is ymaginable and sensible. **1601** HOLLAND *Pliny* XXXI. xi. II. 423 That spunges have life, yea and a sensible life, I have prooved heretofore. **1613** PURCHAS *Pilgrimage* (1614) 536 A tree..hauing..on each side of the leafe, as it were, two feete with which (as if it had bin mouing and sensible) it would stirre and go vp and down. **1621** BURTON *Anat. Mel.* III. ii. I. i. 528 Loue..extends and shewes it selfe in vegitall and sensible creatures. *a* **1676** HALE *Prim. Orig. Man.* I. i. (1677) 39 That Sensible Natures should enjoy a life of Sense. **1690** LOCKE *Hum. Und.* I. i. §1 It is the Understanding that sets Man above the rest of sensible Beings. **1755** B. MARTIN *Mag. Arts & Sci.* 79 Can it be possible for any sensible Beings to endure that Intensity of Cold, and live?

b. of organs, tissues, or parts of the body.

c **1400** *Lanfranc's Cirurg.* 24 From þe brayn comen .vij. peire cordes & þei ben clepid sensible senewis. *Ibid.* 28 Þe skyn..is maad of smale þredis of veynes, senewis, & arteries, þat makiþ him censible, & ȝeueþ him liȝf & worchinge. **1547** BOORDE *Brev. Health* xcvii. 38 A tothe is a sencyble bone, the whiche beynge in a lyvyng mans heade hath felynge. **1831** YOUATT *Horse* (1843) 378 Between the coffin-bone and the horny sole is situated the sensible sole. **1849** NOAD *Electricity* (ed. 3) 234 The pain is of a sharper kind on those sensible parts of the body included in the circuit, which are on the negative side of the pile. **1850** SCORESBY *Cheever's Whalem. Adv.* v. (1859) 69 Outside of the sensible skin.

†**c.** ***sensible virtue, wit***, later ***sensible faculty, capacity***: faculty of sensation. *Obs.*

1398 TREVISA *Barth. De P.R.* III. xii. (1495) 55 The vertue sensyble that meuyth is departed on thre, One partye hyghte Naturalis, and the other Vitalis, and the other Animalis. *c* **1407** LYDG. *Reson & Sens.* 716 Whiche vertu namyd ys sensible, And is, as y reherse kan, Yove to beste and eke to man. **1594** HOOKER *Eccl. Pol.* I. vi. §2 Beasts are in sensible capacitie as ripe euen as men themselues, perhaps more ripe.

erroneous use. *c* **1400** *Beryn* 2621 Wherfor wee must, with al our wit sensibill Such answers vs purvey, þat þey been insolibil.

†**8. a.** Having (more or less) acute power of sensation; sensitive. *Obs.*

1526 *Pilgr. Perf.* (W. de W. 1531) 205 Whose blessed flesshe was moost tender sensible and lyuely. **1543** TRAHERON *Vigo's Chirurg.* II. ii. 16 After the digestyve, ye must clense the place wyth a mundificatyve of syrupe of Roses, cheyfelye whan the aposteme is aboute very sensible places. **1600** SURFLET *Country Farm* II. xlvi. 299 The stomacke being easie and inclined to vomit, as hauing a verie sensible orifice. **1610** SHAKS. *Temp.* II. i. 174 These Gentlemen, who are of such sensible and nimble Lungs, that they alwayes vse to laugh at nothing. **1644** MILTON *Areop.* (Arb.) 54 An imposition which I cannot believe how he that values time, and his own studies, or is but of a sensible nostrill should be able to endure. **1662** R. MATHEW *Unl. Alch.* 54 A Woman comes to me sorely afflicted a long time in all her limbs..; the woman I perceived was exceeding sensible, and in most grievous extremity cryed out. **1679** G. R. tr. *Boaistuau's Theat. World* II. 318 A Faggot burning hot, applyed to the most sensible parts about him. **1758** J. S. *Le Dran's Observ. Surg.* (1771) 324 The Flesh at the Bottom of the Wound was very sensible. **1766** GOLDSM. *Vic. W.* iii, Physicians tell us of a disorder, in which the whole body is so exquisitely sensible, that the slightest touch gives pain. **1813** J. THOMSON *Lect. Inflam.* 45 Parts, which in the sound state have little or no sensibility, become exquisitely sensible in the inflamed. **1831** BREWSTER *Nat. Magic* ix. (1833) 229 The human ear is so extremely sensible as to be capable of appreciating sounds which arise from about twenty-four thousand vibrations in a second.

fig. phrase. **1705** HEARNE *Collect.* 14 Sept. (O.H.S.) I. 44 Who have touch'd 'em in yᵉ sensible pᵗ by..making Scotch men Aliens. *a* **1715** BURNET *Own Time* (1823) I. 416 And, to touch the King in a sensible point, he said, the covenant stuck so deep in their hearts, that no good could be done till that was rooted out. **1817** JAS. MILL *Brit. India* III. VI. i. 46 The dignity of the Directors was now touched in a most sensible part. **1818** SCOTT *Br. Lamm.* xv, He had alarmed his fears in a most sensible point.

†**b.** Liable to be quickly or acutely affected by (some object of sensation); sensitive *to* or *of*. *Obs.*

1601 SHAKS. *Jul. C.* I. iii. 18 Yet his Hand, Not sensible of fire, remain'd vnscorch'd. **1774** GOLDSM. *Nat. Hist.* II. 169 Dogs are well known to be very sensible of different tones in music. **1779–81** JOHNSON *L.P.*, *Pope* Wks. 1787 IV. 90 Extremely sensible of cold. **1822–29** *Good's Study Med.* (ed. 3) I. 51 The gum is often extremely sensible. *Ibid.* IV. 202 Albinoes..are painfully sensible to light.

9. Capable of or liable to mental emotion.

†**a.** Having sensibility; capable of delicate or tender feeling. *Obs.*

1675 R. BURTHOGGE *Causa Dei* 13 A person of a tender, sensible and compassionate Temper. **1734** WATTS *Reliq. Juv.* (1789) 182 Preserve your Conscience always soft and sensible. **1749** FIELDING *Tom Jones* v. vi, Thus his backwardness..wrought so violently on her sensible and tender heart, that she soon felt for him all those gentle sensations which are consistent with a virtuous and elevated female mind. **1760** STERNE *Serm.* III. 405 St. Peter certainly was of a warm and sensible nature.

†**b.** Sensitive; easily hurt or offended. *Obs.*

1759 CHESTERF. *Lett.* IV. ccclv. 170 You will say..that if a person is born of a very sensible gloomy temper..they cannot help it. **1792** GOUV. MORRIS *Diary & Lett.* (1889) II. 3 These [titles] should be properly placed, you know, because monarchs are very *sensible* on that subject.

c. Sensitive or readily accessible *to* some specified emotional influence. Also const. *of*. Now *rare*.

1791 BOSWELL *Johnson* an. 1734, Johnson had, from his early youth, been sensible to the influence of female charms. **1845** GRAVES *Rom. Law* in *Encycl. Metrop.* II. 738/2 The Roman mind seems to have been always sensible to the claims of justice. **1849** MACAULAY *Hist. Eng.* iv. I. 450 Work was to be done, however, which could be trusted to no man who reverenced law or was sensible of shame. *Ibid.* vi. II. 65 Even Sunderland, though not very sensible to shame, flinched from the infamy of public apostasy.

10. *transf.* **a.** Of material things or substances, esp. of instruments of measurement, as a balance, a thermometer: Readily affected by physical impressions or influences, sensitive. Const. *to*. Now *rare*.

Also in † ***sensible plant, weed*** = SENSITIVE *plant*, where the adj. has, strictly speaking, sense 8, the movements of the plant having been formerly regarded as evidence of real sensation.

1661 FELTHAM *Resolves* II. xxiv. (ed. 8) 231 Like the sensible plant, when the hand of flesh does touch it, she shrinks in all her leaves. **1678** LOCKE *Let. to Boyle* in Bourne *Life* (1876) I. 399 A very sensible hygrometer. **1684** R. WALLER *Nat. Exper.* 5 The Third [thermometer]..is more sensible, and swifter near four times. **1725** SLOANE *Jamaica* II. 58 Sensible Grass. It is so very sensible that..I have on horseback wrote my name with a rod in a spot of it which continued visible for some time. **1742** BURGESS in *Phil. Trans.* XLII. 4 The Antidote is, the Root of the Sensible Weed, as it is commonly called, or *Herba Sensitiva*. **1769** E. BANCROFT *Guiana* 225 From the Sensible Plant to the scarce vegetable Moss, all are exquisitely adapted. **1819** J. G. CHILDREN *Chem. Anal.* 372 This balance is sensible to the 1/100dth part of a grain when loaded with 1000 grains in each pan. **1834** MRS. SOMERVILLE *Connex. Phys. Sci.* xxxi. 330 This instrument [the galvanometer] is rendered much more sensible by neutralizing the effects of the earth's magnetism on the needle. **1835–41** BRANDE *Man. Chem.* 72 Nitrate of mercury is a prevaricating test, but very sensible to a variety of substances that may exist in mineral waters.

†**b.** *Music.* ***sensible note.*** [tr. F. *note sensible*.] = *leading note* (see LEADING *ppl. a.*). Cf. SENSITIVE. *Obs.*

1797 *Encycl. Brit.* (ed. 3) XII. 521/1 This third major, which with the generator forms a semitone, has for that reason been called the sensible note, as introducing the generator. **1801** BUSBY *Dict. Mus.*, *Sensible*, the appellation given to the sharp seventh of any key. **1827** HONE *Every-day Bk.* II. 965 The first note..has the effect of that which our musicians call sensible. **1830** *Examiner* 340/2 (Review of Drouet's *Method of Flute-Playing*) [Condemns the term as not English].

III. Actually perceiving or feeling.

11. a. Cognizant, conscious, aware of something. Often with some tinge of emotional sense: Cognizant of something as a ground for pleasure or regret. Const. *of*, †*to*; also with *clause*. Now somewhat *rare*.

c **1412** HOCCLEVE *De Reg. Princ.* 1566 Art þou oght, sone myn, sensible In whiche cas þat þou oghtest the for-bere, And in whiche nat? **1625** BACON *Ess.*, *Great Place* (Arb.) 293 Be not too sensible, or too remembring, of thy Place, in Conuersation. *Ibid.*, *Greatn. Kingd.* (Arb.) 481 Nay, it seemeth at this instant, they [the Spaniards] are sensible of this want of Natiues. **1662** J. DAVIES *Olearius' Voy. Ambass.* 200 The Birds, which were not yet sensible of the Cold,.. continued their Chirping and Singing till near the middle of December. **1666–7** PEPYS *Diary* 14 Feb., Which shows how little we are sensible of the weight of the business upon us. **1676** TEMPLE *Let. to Sir J. Williamson* 12 June, I went to Monsieur Mauregnault, and made him sensible, how all these Exceptions of the Resident were expresly provided against. **1683** TRYON *Way to Health* (1697) 92 The learned Prophet Moses was sensible that the common and frequent eating of Flesh was very dangerous. **1699** BENTLEY *Phal.* 309, I am sensible how long I have detain'd the Reader upon this Subject. *a* **1700** EVELYN *Diary* June 1645, I think I was never sensible of so burning a heate as I was this season. **1700** DRYDEN *Sigism. & Guisc.* 270 The gloomy Sire, too sensible of Wrong To vent his Rage in Words. **1711** HEARNE *Collect.* (O.H.S.) III. 209, I am very sensible that I deserve none of those Favours. **1721** LADY M. W. MONTAGU *Let. to C'tess Mar* (1893) I. 452, I would have you then..try to make the wretch sensible of the truth of what I advance. **1739** SHERIDAN tr. *Persius' Sat.* iv. 63 You will soon be sensible how short your Abilities are. **1741–2** CHALLONER *Missionary Priests* (1803) II. 18 The catholics were made sensible that, however the persecution might in some measure be abated, it was not to cease. **1744** LADY M. W. MONTAGU *Let. to C'tess Oxford* 13 Apr. (1893) II. 129 My health..is extremely good; I thank God I am sensible of no distemper or infirmity. **1765** A. DICKSON *Treat. Agric.* 466 If these salts and oils actually fly off from it in such quantities, as to make us sensible of them by smell. **1782** MISS BURNEY *Cecilia* VII. iii, Cecilia, sensible of the truth of this speech,..now summoned her utmost courage to her aid. **1806** R. CUMBERLAND *Mem.* (1807) II. 160, I was not sensible to the extent of my danger. **1813** T. BUSBY *Lucretius* I. I. *Comm.* p. xxxvi, [Lucretius] sensible to the difficulty of the subject on which he is engaged. **1819** BYRON *Juan* I. cli, That sublime of rascals, your attorney, Whom I see standing there, and looking sensible Of having play'd the fool. **1821** LAMB *Elia* Ser. I. *Grace bef. Meat*, We may be gratefully sensible of the deliciousness of some kinds of food beyond others. **1825** SCOTT *Betrothed* ii, He was sensible that the alliance which he meditated might indeed be tolerated, but could not be approved, by his subjects. **1837** HALLAM *Lit. Eur.* I. I. iii. 168, I am sensible that the mention of such a circumstance may appear trifling.

†**b.** Mindful *of* a person. *Obs.*

1643 CHAS. I in Ellis *Orig. Lett.* Ser. II. III. 309 The perticuler persons whoe in this our extremity are soe sensible of us. **1646** H. LAWRENCE *Comm. Angells* Ded. 2 b, As we usually are more sensible of our enemyes than our friends.

12. a. Emotionally conscious; having a pleasurable, painful, grateful or resentful sense *of* something. In later use almost exclusively: Gratefully conscious *of* (kindness, etc.). Also const. *to* (? *obs.*), †*for*, and with *clause*.

1634 W. TIRWHYT *Balzac's Lett.* I. 26 They stood amazed to see a servant..Who was as sensible of the least evils of his country as of his proper sorrows. **1656** BRAMHALL *Replic.* 11 God seemeth to be more sensible of the injuries done unto his church and to his servants, then of the dishonor done unto himself. **1680** BUTLER *Rem.* (1759) II. 74 His Pleasures require a larger Proportion of Excess and Variety, to render him sensible of them. **1711** ADDISON *Spect.* No. 166 ¶8 He found that he was so very sensible of his Fault, and so sincerely repented of it. **1715** HICKES *Let. to Hearne* (MS. Rawl. Lett. f. 15) 75, I am as sensible & sorry for the great Loss of Mr. Urry, as any Friend he hath left behind him. **1775** EARL CARLISLE in Jesse *Selwyn & Contemp.* (1844) III. 108 Lady Carlisle desires to be remembered to you; she is, indeed, very sensible of your goodness to us all. **1823** SCOTT *Quentin D.* xxxvi, He was sensible to the indignity of serving with his noblest peers under the banners of his own vassal. **1831** —— *Ct. Robt.* xvi, The creature seemed sensible of the clemency. **1856** CARLYLE *Let. to J. Knight* 19 Apr., Surely I am very sensible to the kindness of the President and Council in this matter. **1895** *N. Amer. Rev.* Aug. 149 They are always sensible to kindness and sympathy.

†**b.** Without const. *Obs.*

1748 RICHARDSON *Clarissa* (1768) III. 62, I kissed her, and she made me a courtesy for my condescension; and blushed, and seemed sensible all over.

13. Conscious, free from physical insensibility or delirium.

1732 LEDIARD *Sethos* II. IX. 283 The governor was not yet sensible. **1743** BULKELEY & CUMMINS *Voy. S. Seas* 32 Where we saw Mr. Cozens..alive, and to Appearance sensible, but speechless. **1835** *Comic Almanack* (1870) 2 *Nurse.* Speak softly, Sir; my master's turning blue, He's not been sensible since last November. *Rig. Fun.* (*aside*) Nor ever was, that I can remember. **1862** MRS. H. WOOD *Mrs. Hallib.* III. vi, 'And now the doctor says he has not many hours to live.' 'I am sorry to hear it,' cried William. 'Is he sensible?' **1891** 'J. S. WINTER' *Lumley* xiii, He's asking for you and is quiet and sensible.

IV. 14. a. Endowed with good sense; intelligent, reasonable, judicious.

Stigmatized by Johnson 1755 as used only 'in low conversation'. In some of the early instances the sense may perh. be rather 'capable of mental perception'.

1584 R. SCOT *Discov. Witchcr.* III. viii. (1886) 40 If they were sensible, they would saie to the divell: Whie should I hearken to you? **1586** A. DAY *Eng. Secretary* I. (1625) 111 These (the more sensible they are with whom wee deale, and of greater capacity) the more vehemently may we enforce by all sorts of forcible arguments. **1596** SHAKS. *Merry W.* II. i. 151 'Twas a good sensible fellow. **1597** —— *2 Hen. IV*, I. ii.

220 For the boxe of th'eare that the Prince gaue you, he gaue it like a rude Prince, and you tooke it like a sensible Lord. **1598** W. PHILLIP tr. *Linschoten* I. xlvi. 85 In the Island of Seylon there are also great numbers [of Elephants], which are esteemed the best and sensiblest of all the worlde. *c* **1600** BACON *Elem. Com. Laws* (1630) Pref. B 3 b, And that Ciuilians, States-men, Schollers, and other sensible men might not haue beene barred from them. **1711** ADDISON *Spect.* No. 130 ¶ 3 Sir Roger.. knew several sensible People who believed these Gypsies now and then foretold very strange things. **1747** H. WALPOLE *Let. to Mann* 1 Sept., You will, I think, like Sir James Grey; he is very civil and good-humoured, and sensible. **1766** GOLDSM. *Vic. W.* xxxi, My loveliest, my most sensible of girls. **1768** SIR P. FRANCIS *Let.* 26 Apr. *Mem.* (1867) I. 210 The woman.. is honest and intelligent, or in the cant word, sensible. **1781** COWPER *Convers.* 193 A moral, sensible, and well-bred man Will not affront me, and no other can. **1849** MACAULAY *Hist. Eng.* vi. II. 97 He was too sensible a man not to know that he might at some future time be called to a serious account by a parliament. **1860** *Proc. Zool. Soc.* 184 It [a young female Gorilla] was tame, lively, sensible, and not near so noisy or dirty as a Chimpanzee. **1876** MISS BRADDON *J. Haggard's Dau.* II. 9 'They're all glad to get a husband; even the sensiblest of them', chuckled the farmer. **1885** O. W. HOLMES *Mortal Antipathy* iv. (1886) 65 No sensible person in Arrowhead village really believed in the evil eye.

b. Of action, behaviour, discourse, etc.: Marked by, exhibiting, or proceeding from good sense.

1653 H. MORE *Antid. Ath.* I. xiii. (1662) 126 The manner of this Genius his sensible Converse. *a* **1699** TEMPLE *On Health & Long Life* Wks. 1720 I. 277 He had been a Soldier in the Cales Voyage.. of which He gave me a sensible Account. **1778** MME. D'ARBLAY *Diary* Sept., She has a sensible and penetrating countenance. **1801** *Farmer's Mag.* Aug. 362 A very sensible paper, on the use of lime. **1822** LAMB *Elia* Ser. I. *Some Old Actors*, His rebuke to the knight and his sottish revellers, is sensible and spirited. **1849** MACAULAY *Hist. Eng.* ii. I. 221 *note*, The most sensible thing said in the House of Commons, on this subject, came from Sir William Coventry.

Comb. **1895** J. G. MILLAIS *Breath Veldt* (1899) 116 Oom Paul's mode of government is entirely unpopular amongst the more sensible-minded Dutch.

c. Of clothing, footwear, etc.: practical rather than attractive or fashionable.

1855 MRS. GASKELL *North & South* xii. 146 Margaret was busy embroidering a small piece of cambric... Mrs. Thornton.. liked Mrs. Dale's dull knitting far better; that was sensible of its kind. **1888** KIPLING *Under Deodars* 8 Nice, large, sensible shoes for all couples to stumble over as they go into the verandah! **1907** *Yesterday's Shopping* (1969) 339/3 The 'Sensible' carrier bag.. is the only paper Bag with a firm bottom. **1924** A. CHRISTIE *Man in Brown Suit* xx. 169 Forty, if she's a day, wears pince-nez and sensible boots and an air of brisk efficiency that will be the death of me. **1944** AUDEN *For Time Being* ii. 36 The river on this side of which initiative and honesty stroll arm in arm wearing sensible clothes. **1959** *Observer* 22 Mar. 1/1 Chintz curtains and no-nonsense bundles of flowers in sensible pots. **1978** R. HILL *Pinch of Snuff* x. 100 Genuine English county.. unobtrusively elegant.. in simple twinset and sensible shoes.

B. *absol.* and *sb.*

1. That which produces sensation; that which is perceptible; an object of sense, or of any one of the senses.

1589 PUTTENHAM *Eng. Poesie* III. xxiii. (Arb.) 269 This louely conformitie.. betweene the sence and the sensible hath nature.. most carefully obserued in all her owne workes. **1656** STANLEY *Hist. Philos.* v. *Plato* iv. (1687) 160/2 In Sensibiles (saith Plato) neither magnitude nor quality is permanent. **1665** GLANVILL *Scepsis Sci.* ix. 50 A blind man conceives not colours, but under the notion of some other sensible. *a* **1704** T. BROWN *London & Lacedem. Oracles* Wks. 1730 III. 131 By Phenomena's we understand Sensibles, which we oppose to Intelligibles. **1788** T. TAYLOR *Proclus* I. 44 *note*, All the ancient theologists.. affirmed that the soul was of a certain middle nature and condition between intelligibles and sensibles. **1856** R. A. VAUGHAN *Mystics* (1860) I. 54 Those.. who think they can storm the Intelligible by the Sensible.

†**2.** A being that is capable of sensation. *Obs.*

a **1676** HALE *Prim. Orig. Man.* I. i. (1677) 17 The Life that is in Vegetables..; the Life and Sense that is in Sensibles. **1682** CREECH *Lucretius* Notes (1683) 33 This agrees to Plants as well as Sensibles, They are nourisht grow and live alike.

†**3.** The element (in a spiritual being) that is capable of feeling. *Obs.*

1667 MILTON *P.L.* II. 278 Our torments also may in length of time Become our Elements,.. our temper chang'd Into their temper; which must needs remove The sensible of pain.

4. One possessing good sense, a judicious person.

1747 W. HORSLEY *Fool* (1748) II. 323 The Sensibles are desired to confine theirs to Masquerades and Playhouses.

5. *the sensibles*, sensible views of things. *nonce-use.*

1880 BLACKMORE *Mary Anerley* xli, After the sensitive age was past, and when the sensibles ought to reign,.. he fell.. into a violent passion of love for a beautiful Jewish maid barely turned seventeen.

sensibleness (ˈsɛnsɪb(ə)lnɪs). [f. SENSIBLE *a.* + -NESS.]

†**1.** The quality or state of being sensible or capable of sensation; sensibility; sensitiveness.

1528 PAYNELL *Salerne's Regim.* R j b, Popie sede both taketh away the sensiblenes of the membres.. and prouoketh to slepe. **1597** A. M. tr. *Guillemeau's Fr. Chirurg.* 22/3 The yonge Chyrurgiane may knowe them by there sensiblenes, because they are verye dolorous and full of payne. **1656** W. MOUNTAGUE *Accompl. Woman* 124 Pain and sensiblenesse, are never in dead bodies. **17..** SHARP (J.), The sensibleness of the eye renders it subject to pain.

†**2.** Of speech: Intelligibility, impressiveness.

a **1586** SIDNEY *Apol. Poet.* (Arb.) 69 Because with a playne sensiblenes, they might win credit of popular eares.

†**3.** Tenderness of feeling, sensibility. *Obs.*

a **1631** DONNE *Serm.* lxxxv. (1649) II. 31 There lies a burden upon them too, to consider with a compassionate sensiblenesse, the grievances that oppresse the other part.

†**4.** The state or fact of being sensible or emotionally (esp. gratefully) conscious of something. Const. *of*; rarely with *clause*. *Obs.*

1605 A. WOTTON *Answ. late Popish Art.* Ded., All that remaines is by this, or some such like deed, to professe my sensiblenes of your great fauour. **1642** FULLER *Holy & Prof. St.* I. xii. 37 Blushing.. not arising from guiltinesse.. but.. from sensiblenesse of disgrace. *a* **1680** CHARNOCK *Attrib. God* (1834) I. 689 The fruit of these falls is.. a deeper sensibleness wherein their security lies. *a* **1708** BEVERIDGE *Thes. Theol.* (1711) II. 367 The first step to holiness and felicity, is sensibleness of our sin and misery.

†**5.** Perceptibility. *Obs.*

1653 H. MORE *Antid. Ath.* I. viii. (1712) 21 This absurdity cannot be excused from the sensibleness of Matter since the Atheist is forced to admit such things as fall not under Sense. **1784** J. BARRY *Lect. Art* v. (1848) 193 Bronze.. may, from the weight and sensibleness of its colour, do extremely well.

6. The quality of being sensible or of having good sense; intelligence, sound judgement.

1888 *Spectator* 15 Sept. 1246/2 That quality of sensibleness which has made him a valued member of Conservative Cabinets.

‖**sensiblerie** (sɑ̃sibləri). [Fr.]

= SENTIMENTALITY a.

1931 *Times Lit. Suppl.* 7 May 559/1 The sentiment is obviously genuine, and never falls into excesses of *sensiblerie*. **1960** *Twentieth Cent.* Aug. 169 A piece of long-drawn-out, commercial *sensiblerie*, with no real tragic bite. **1974** *Financial Times* 4 Apr. 32/1 A brotherhood utterly devoid of sentimentality or *sensiblerie*.

sensibly (ˈsɛnsɪblɪ), *adv.* Also 6 **sensybly, sensiblie, senciblie,** 6–7 **sencibly;** (uncontracted form: 7 **sensiblely.**). [f. SENSIBLE *a.* + -LY².]

1. a. In a manner perceptible to the senses; so far as can be perceived.

c **1425** *St. Mary of Oignies* I. x. in *Anglia* VIII. 146/38 So grete froste þat.. in þe holy chalys, while þe preste songe, wyne fros sensibly & sodeynly in to yce. **1541** R. COPLAND *Galyen's Terap.* 2 H ij, Some parte of the medycament wyll flowe by lytel & lytel in to yᵉ artere sensibly and manyfestly. **1588** SHAKS. *Tit. A.* IV. ii. 122 He is your brother Lords, sensibly fed Of that selfe blood that first gaue life to you. **1653** in Swayne *Churchw. Acc. Sarum* (1896) 228 The maine pillars did bulge out, and sensiblely shake. **1705** ADDISON *Italy, Ferrara* 114 From Venice to Ancona the Tide comes in very sensibly at its stated Periods. **1850** *Bohn's Hand-bk. Games* (1867) 561 If a ball is made to go to the brink of a pocket, and after sensibly standing still, should fall into it, the striker wins nothing. **1893** SIR R. BALL *Story of Sun* 36 Lines drawn from various points on the Earth to Pollux would all appear sensibly parallel.

b. In an appreciable degree.

1675–6 BOYLE in *Phil. Trans.* No. 122. 522 The two Ingredients were easily mingled, and grew not only sensibly but considerably hot [in the palm of his hand]. **1728** tr. *Newton's Treat. Syst. World* 123 Though those rays are not able sensibly to move the gross substances in our parts. **1762** LD. KAMES *Elem. Crit.* xviii. §4 (1774) II. 151 The pause also is sensibly affected by the position of the accent. *a* **1817** T. DWIGHT *Trav. New Eng.* (1823) IV. 358 At the end of two years, this currency, in consequence of enormous emissions, began sensibly to depreciate. **1880** GEIKIE *Phys. Geog.* iv. 278 The sea is said to be sensibly decreasing in size.

†**2. a.** With self-consciousness, consciously. **b.** Of feeling: Acutely, intensely. *Obs.*

1526 *Pilgr. Perf.* (W. de W. 1531) 288 b, And than he begynneth to loue sensybly: and than first he feleth that he loueth God. **1586** B. YOUNG *Guazzo's Civ. Conv.* IV. 176, I doe sensiblie feele all the superfluous humours (engendred by solitarinesse) consumed quite, and spent in mee. **1631** GOUGE *God's Arrows* III. §58. 296 No marvell then that they who.. rashly thrust themselves into warre, be made sensibly to feele the smart of their folly. **1678** BUNYAN *Pilgr.* I. (1900) 133 When he doth sensibly, and with heart-humiliation thus think, then hath he good thoughts of his own ways. **1719** DE FOE *Crusoe* I. (Globe) 114 It was now that I began sensibly to feel how much more happy this Life I now led was.. than the wicked.. Life I led all the past Part of my Days. **1805–6** CARY *Dante, Inf.* VI. 110 As each thing to more perfection grows, It feels more sensibly both good and pain.

†**3. a.** So as to be easily understood or to impress the feelings; clearly, strikingly. *Obs.*

1576 FLEMING *Panopl. Epist.* 226 Vnblameable affections, .. hath not their generation or issue, from the enticementes of Venerie, I meane (to speake more sensibly) from carnall pleasures. **1693** NORRIS *Pract. Disc.* (1722) IV. Pref. 2, I know not whether I have met with any thing that has struck me more Sensibly, or made a quicker Impression upon my Spirit than a certain Reflexion which [etc.]. *a* **1700** EVELYN *Diary* 20 Dec. 1673, But the description.. delighted me, so sensibly they spake of the excellent aire and climate in respect of our cloudy and splenetic country.

†**b.** So as to be keenly felt. *Obs.*

1655 J. JANE in *Nicholas Papers* (1892) II. 355 Never was the vanity of pretenders to wisdom and government more apparantly layed open to reproach.. nor the people required for their murmuringes more sensibly then ours have beene.

4. With good sense, intelligently; judiciously, reasonably.

1755 JOHNSON, *Sensibly*, in low language, judiciously, reasonably. **1828–32** in WEBSTER s.v., The man converses very sensibly on all common topics. **1898** G. B. SHAW *Candida* I. 103 Do you think that the things people make fools of themselves about are any less real and true than the things they behave sensibly about? *a* **1912** *Mod.* He behaved sensibly under the circumstances. **1932** D. L. SAYERS *Have his Carcase* i. 9 She was dressed sensibly in a short skirt and thin sweater. **1970** N. MARSH *When in Rome* iii. 51 They wore sensibly shady hats.

Comb. **1899** *Westm. Gaz.* 13 Jan. 3/2 A sensibly-written book, which will serve a useful purpose.

†ˈ**sensical,** *a. Obs. rare.* [f. SENSE *sb.* + -ICAL.] Sensible.

1797 S. J. PRATT *Family Secrets* in *Monthly Rev.* XXIII. 60 [Uses 'sensical' and 'sensate' for sensible]. **1839** J. ROGERS *Antipopopr.* I. iii. §1. 75 With sensical and thoughtful men.

sensifacient (ˌsɛnsɪˈfeɪʃ(ɪ)ənt), *a.* [f. L. *sens-us* SENSE *sb.* + -(I)FACIENT.] Producing sensation.

1879 HUXLEY *Sci. & Cult.* x. (1881) 257 The epithelium may be said to be receptive,.. and the sensorium sensifacient. **1899** *Allbutt's Syst. Med.* VI. 514 Sensifacient cells.

sensiferous (sɛnˈsɪfərəs), *a.* [f. L. *sens-us* SENSE *sb.* + -IFEROUS.] Conveying sensation.

1656 BLOUNT *Glossogr.* **1659** H. MORE *Immort. Soul* II. viii. (1713) 97 Besides, that the sensiferous impresses of motion through the eyes play under them. **1826** KIRBY & SP. *Entomol.* III. xxxiii. 356 Two jointed sensiferous organs. **1879** HUXLEY *Sci. & Cult.* x. (1881) 246 On Sensation and the Unity of Structure of sensiferous Organs.

sensific (sɛnˈsɪfɪk), *a.* (and *sb.*) [ad. late L. *sensificus*, f. L. *sens-us* SENSE *sb.*: see -IFIC.]

A. *adj.* Of nerves: Producing sensation.

1822 GOOD *Study Med.* III. 28 *marg.*, Hence sometimes a sensific power and sometimes a motory. **1835–6** *Todd's Cycl. Anat.* I. 800/2 Convulsion is not.. an affection.. of the sensific part of the nervous system.

B. *sb.* (or absol. use of adj.) Only in *pl.* = SIGNIFICS.

1896 [see SIGNIFICS].

sensifiˈcatory, *a.* [f. late L. *sensificāre* SENSIFY *v.*: see -ORY².] Producing sensation.

1879 HUXLEY *Sci. & Cult.* x. (1881) 268 Each consists of a receptive, a transmissive, and a sensificatory portion.

sensify (ˈsɛnsɪfaɪ), *v.* [ad. late L. *sensificāre*, f. *sens-us* SENSE *sb.*: see -IFY.] *trans.* To transform (physical changes) into sensation. Hence ˈ**sensiˌfying** *ppl. a.*

1678 J. BROWN *Disc. Wounds* 238 The Nerves are soon resolved and distended, the senses flagg, and the Sensifying Quality doth perish. **1881** W. M. WILLIAMS *Sci. in Short Chapters* (1882) 44 In such a world of intermediate activities the insect probably lives.. with his minute eye-like ear-bag sensifying material movements that lie between our world of sounds and our other far-distant worlds of heat and light.

sensigenous (sɛnˈsɪdʒɪnəs), *a.* [f. SENSE *sb.* + -(I)GEN + -OUS.] Producing sensation.

1874 HUXLEY in *Nature* 3 Sept. 365/2 The sensation which has passed away leaves behind molecules of the brain competent to its reproduction—'sensigenous molecules' so to speak. **1879** —— *Hume* ii. 73 The sensigenous object, and that masterful entity, the Ego.

sensile (ˈsɛnsɪl, -aɪl), *a.* [ad. L. *sensil-is* endowed with sensation, f. *sens-*, *sentīre* to feel: see -ILE.] Capable of perception, sentient.

1813 T. BUSBY *Lucretius* I. II. *Comm.* p. xxxv, Plato.. taught that sensible beings are formed from sensile atoms. *Ibid.* II. VI. 904 Others with stench the sensile nostrils teaze. **1843** WILKINSON tr. *Swedenborg's Anim. Kingd.* I. i. 41 Different organic series, muscular, glandular, and sensile.

sensillum (sɛnˈsɪləm). *Zool.* Pl. **sensilla.** Also **sensilla** (pl. -æ), **sensillium** (*rare*). [mod.L. (coined in Ger. by E. Haeckel in *Systematische Phylogenie* (1895) III. ii. 119), dim. of L. *sensus* perception.] A simple sensory receptor in invertebrates, esp. arthropods, consisting of a cell or small group of cells that is a modification of the cuticle or epidermis and is often hair- or rod-shaped.

1925 A. D. IMMS *Gen. Textbk. Entomol.* 65 The tactile sensillæ of insects are often distributed over the entire integument. **1935** R. E. SNODGRASS *Princ. Insect Morphol.* xvii. 525 The scolopophorous organs are usually compound sense organs, each consisting of a bundle of simple sensilla having a common point of attachment on the body wall. **1962** GORDON & LAVOIPIERRE *Entomol. for Students of Med.* xxxiv. 211 On the 9th tergite of both the male and female flea, there is a small pincushion-like structure (the pygidium or sensillium) which is believed to have a sensory function. **1962** *Science Survey* III. 281 The last main class of hearing organs in insects comprises the various hair sensillae, scattered all over the body. **1963** R. P. DALES *Annelids* vii. 143 The sense cells on these tentacles or cirri are commonly fusiform in shape with a sensilla or sensillae projecting through the cuticle. **1971** *Nature* 24 Dec. 477/1 Each campaniform sensillum [on a cockroach leg] functions through a single primary sense cell. **1973** *Jrnl. Invertebrate Path.* XXII. 409 (*caption*) Portion of another integumentary growth with apparent sensillium.

sensine, obs. variant of SENSYNE.

ˈ**sensing,** *vbl. sb.* [f. SENSE *v.* + -ING¹.] **1.** The action of SENSE *v.*

1647 tr. *Behmen's Clavis* §218 Wherein the Naturall will separateth it selfe in its Center, into a sensing. **1656–63** BP. W. LUCY *Observ. Hobbes* 37 When we have discerned things by our senses, and the act of sensing (pardon that word *sensing*, it is unusuall, yet significant) is done. **1659** HEYLIN *Certamen Epist.* 6 It is another subject (the sensing of the word Puritan) that I am speaking of. **1906** LAURIE *Synthetica* I. 18 The feeling of an object by a subject-being or entity and the re-flexion of it into its cosmic locus I call rudimentary sensing, or sensation.

2. *spec.* **a.** *U.S. Mil.* An observation of the point of impact of a shot with respect to the target.

1937 *Sun* (Baltimore) 16 Aug. 16/2 Transfers to the targets will be made by means of a high burst with shrapnel, the bursts being brought to a check point at a particular elevation and range by means of sensings from lateral observation points. **1944** H. F. Gregory *Anything Horse can Do* vii. 74 Conducting an artillery adjustment by communicating 'sensings' by changing the line of flight of the Autogiro. **1962** *Ordnance Techn. Terminol.* (U.S. Army Ordnance School, AD 660 112) 269/2 *Sensing*, the direction of a point of burst or impact, or centers of burst or impact with respect to the target; such as over, short, air or graze.

b. The action of an automatic device in detecting, observing, or measuring something. Freq. *attrib.*

1950 *Jrnl. Res. Nat. Bureau of Standards* (U.S.) XLV. 295/1 A sensing element in the gas stream normally attains a steady temperature below that of the gas itself, because of radiation and conduction from the sensing element. **1955** *Flight Test Man.* (Advisory Group on Aeronaut. Res. & Devel., NATO) I. IIA. x. 15/1 The collection methods of determining liquid water content below freezing..are essentially based upon the sensing of icing. **1962** F. I. Ordway et al. *Basic Astronautics* v. 185 (*caption*) Infrared vidicon tube... It could also be employed for horizon sensing. **1967** *Electronics* 6 Mar. 127/1 An infrared scanner will compete in the fast-developing market for thermal sensing and display devices. **1977** *Dædalus* Fall 38 All the rest of the electromagnetic spectrum became available to astronomers only when the development of sounding rockets and artificial satellites made it possible to send their sensing instruments above the atmosphere.

c. = *sense-finding* s.v. Sense *sb.* 30.

1961 C. H. Cotter *Princ. & Pract. Radio Direction Finding* ii. 36 The device provided to resolve the 180° ambiguity is known as a sensefinder, and the process of doing so is known as sensing. **1976** W. H. P. Canner *Air Navigation* vi. 139 Sensing refers to the resolution of the ambiguity in bearings.

sensism ('sɛnsɪz(ə)m). *rare.* [f. Sense *sb.* + -ism.] **a.** Devotion to the things of sense, sensuality. **b.** *Philos.* = Sensationalism.

1846 [see Sensationism 2]. **1857** W. Fleming *Voc. Philos.* 462 *Sensism*..is the doctrine that all our knowledge is derived originally from sense. *Ibid.* Sensism gives the single fact of sensation as sufficient to explain all mental phenomena. **1892** Lilly *Gt. Enigma* 74 Voluptuous sensism extracted from the purest idealism. **1903** W. Turner *Hist. Philos.* 268 The denial of the universal means sensism.

sensist ('sɛnsɪst). [f. Sense *sb.* + -ist.] = Sensationalist 1. Also *attrib.*

1874 Mivart in *Contemp. Rev.* Oct. 774 A wide divergence from the teaching of the last named writer has been introduced by his brother sensist, Mr. G. H. Lewes. *Ibid.* 786 The phenomena of Cosmical Evolution are presented by the sensist school in terms of matter and force. **1886** Lockhart *Rosmini* I. 102 Wily agents were spreading the pernicious tenets of the Sensists.

Hence **sen'sistic** *a.*

1882 T. Davidson in *Fortn. Rev.* July 18 A sensistic philosophy, which, by circumscribing the natural powers of the mind within the narrowest limits, left indefinite room for authority.

†**'sensitie.** *Obs. rare*⁻¹. [app. f. L. *sens-us* Sense *sb.* + -ity.] Sensation.

1613 Purchas *Pilgrimage* (1614) 180 Neither sensitie, facultie, nor appetite was amisse in him.

sensitive ('sɛnsɪtɪv), *a.* and *sb.* Forms: α. 5 sensitife, sensityf, 6 sensytyfe, sencitive, 7 sensetive, 5- sensitive. β. 6 censatyve, 6-8 sensative. [a. F. *sensitif, -ive* (13th c. in Hatz.-Darm.), ad. med.L. *sensitivus*, irreg. f. L. *sens-*, ppl. stem of *sentire* to feel. Cf. Sp., Pg., It. *sensitivo*. The β forms may possibly represent a med.L. **sensātīvus*, related to *sensātio*, but it is not evident that *sensitive* and *sensative* were regarded as distinct words.] A. *adj.*

1. a. Having the function of sensation or sensuous perception.

sensitive soul [med.L. *anima sensitiva*]: in scholastic philosophy, that one of the three kinds of 'soul' or of constituent parts of the soul which is concerned with sensation, and which is characteristic of animals; distinguished from the *vegetative soul*, which is common to animals with plants, and from the *intellective soul*, which in rational animals (men) is superadded to the two others. Similarly *sensitive virtue* [*virtus sensitiva*], the faculty of sensation.

α. *a* **1400-50** *Wars Alex.* 4381 Þe faire floryscht filds of floures & of herbys, Quare-of þe breth as of bawme blawis in oure noose, Þat ilk sensitife saule mast souorly delyte. *c* **1407** Lydg. *Reson & Sens.* 698 God..Hath yove and graunted vnto man..Twoo maners of knowlychynge... The first.. Called the vertu sensytif By which he feleth..Thinges.. Which to forn him be present. *c* **1449** Pecock *Repr.* I. xiv. 74 Tho same treuthis whiche outward sensityue wittis knowen. **1531** Elyot *Gov.* III. xxiv. (1880) II. 371 An other parte [*sc.* of the soull], wherin man doth participate with all other thynges lyuynge, which is called sensitife, by reason that therof the sensis do procede. **1577** tr. *Bullinger's Decades* IV. x. (1592) 755 For there is the soule vegetatiue which worketh in plants. There is the soule sensitiue which..giueth life to brute beastes. **1620** T. Granger *Div. Logike* 109 Seeing, hearing, &c. are acts of the sensitive powers. **1642** H. More *Song of Soul* II. i. II. xxv, That we term Soul sensitive, I'll call't form bestiall. **1653** —— *Antid. Ath.* I. viii. §13 (1712) 24 Corporeal Matter is the proper Object of the sensitive Faculty. *a* **1714** Abp. Sharp *Serm.* Wks. 1754 IV. 142 The seat of the one is in the intellectual reasonable nature; the seat of the other is in the sensitive. **1732** Pope *Ess. on Man* i. Argt, To possess any of the sensitive faculties in a higher degree, would render him miserable. **1769-90** Sir J. Reynolds *Disc.* vii. (1876) 421 All arts have means within them of applying themselves with success both to the intellectual and sensitive part of our natures. **1801** *Med. Jrnl.* V. 327 The sensitive power of the iris. *a* **1806** Bp. Horsley *Serm.* (1816) I. vii. 127 This spiritual sword of God's awful word..pierces to the very line of separation, as it were, of the sensitive and the intelligent principle. **1836** *Todd's Cycl. Anat.* III. 720 H/2 These are called sensitive nerves or nerves of common sensation. *a* **1881** Barratt *Phys. Metempiric* (1883) 22 We may reasonably infer that of which we might be sensible..by a hypothetical extension of our sensitive powers.

β. **1548** Vicary *Anat.* ii. (1888) 19 From the brayne commeth vij payre of Nerues sensatiues. **1594** Plat *Jewell-ho.* II. 16 Salt is no enemie either to the vegetatiue, or sensatiue natures. **1615** Crooke *Body of Man* 288 In sleepe the sensatiue faculties are all at rest. **1656-63** Bp. W. Lucy *Observ. Hobbes* 37 Yet there remains in the sensative memory that image, which represented the object at the first.

b. Of life, knowledge, perception (also formerly †of desires, feelings): Connected with the senses, sensuous. †Of objects: Perceptible by the senses.

α. **1530** Rastell *Purg.* I. vi, The beest which hath a lyfe sensytyve. **1536** Bellenden *Cron. Scot.* (1821) I. *Cosmogr.* Proheme 14 He that nold aganis his lustis strive But leiffis as beist of knawlege sensitive Eildis richt fast. **1608** D. T[uvill] *Ess. Pol. & Mor.* 4 Beeing for the most part led to iudge of matters onely by a Sensitiue apprehension they haue of them. **1633-55** Capel *Tentations* 11 Our sensitive love what follows the lower, and organical faculties of the soul. **1643** Milton *Divorce* I. ii. 6 The sensitive pleasing of the body. **1650** Baxter *Saints' R.* III. xi. (1662) 461 The sensitive sinfull appetite and passion may prevail with the Will. **1660** R. Coke *Justice Vind.* 7 The places of Scripture which testifie our Saviour's grief, sorrow, and fear: these passions being sensitive, do sufficiently convince that there was a sensual will in Christ. **1681-6** J. Scott *Chr. Life* (1747) III. 27 Hence it is that he so greedily prefers carnal before rational, and sensitive before spiritual Goods. **1690** Locke *Hum. Und.* IV. iii. §5 Sensitive Knowledge reaching no farther than the Existence of Things actually present to our Senses, is yet much narrower than either of the former. **1690** Norris *Beatitudes* (1694) I. 40 Once, indeed, 'tis said, that he rejoiced; but then it was not with an outward, sensitive and tumultuous Joy. **1707** *Curios. Husb. & Gard.* 296 When a Plant becomes an Animal, it..rises into a higher Station, by acquiring a Sensitive Life. *a* **1708** Beveridge *Priv. Th.* I. (1730) 104 By loving God, I do not understand that sensitive Affection I place upon material Objects. **1877** E. Caird *Philos. Kant* I. 174 Our sensitive perception of objects. **1889** Courtney *Mill* 129 Beliefs..gathered out of the sensitive experience of his forefathers.

β. **1743** N. Appleton *Serm.* 167 Our natural sensative Appetites and Desires.

†**c.** Of fever: Arising from sensation. *Obs.*

1794 E. Darwin *Zoon.* I. 391 Other new motions are then superadded, in consequence of sensation, which we shall call *febris sensitiva*, or sensitive fever. *Ibid.* 392 These sensitive fevers, like the irritative ones, resolve themselves into [etc.].

2. Of living beings: Endowed with the faculty of sensation. Formerly often: †'Having sense or perception, but not reason' (J., 1755).

α. **1555** Eden *Decades* (Arb.) 131 We wyll nowe therefore entreate of thynges sencitiue. **1584** R. Scot *Discov. Witchcr.* v. iv. (1886) 78 Our bodies are visible, sensitive, and passive. **1601** Holland *Pliny* XII. Pref. I. 356 The natures as well in generall, as particularly in parts, of all living and sensitive creatures within the compasse of our knowledge. **1726** Swift *Gulliver* IV. ii, As to those filthy Yahoos..I confess I never saw any sensitive being so detestable on all accounts. **1768** Pennant *Brit. Zool.* I. Pref. 5 Our fish,..our insects, and the various other sensitive productions of this kingdom. **1794** Paley *Evid.* Introd. (1800) I. 2 The Deity when he formed it consulted for the happiness of his sensitive creation. **1796** H. Hunter tr. *St.-Pierre's Stud. Nat.* (1799) II. 381 It is only for beings vegetative and sensitive that Nature has created the fossil kingdom.

β. **1509** Hawes *Past. Pleas.* xxxv. (Percy Soc.) 112 By these twayne every thyng hath growynge; Bothe vegitatyfe and censatyve also, And also intellectyve.

3. a. sensitive plant, †herb, †shrub, †tree, a shrub (*Mimosa pudica*, or *M. sensitiva*) possessing a high degree of irritability, causing the leaflets of the bipinnate leaves to fold together at the slightest touch (cf. humble-*plant*, sensible-*plant*); also applied with defining word to various plants possessing a similar quality, as **†bastard sensitive plant** (*Æschynomene americana*); **false sensitive plant** (*Æ. hispida*); **American sensitive plant** (*Cassia nictitans*), also called ***wild sensitive plant*** and ***sensitive pea*** (see Pea 3).

In the original use of this designation, the adj. belongs to sense 2 (not to sense 5); cf. Sensible *a.* 10.

1633 Johnson *Gerarde's Herbal* App. vii. 1599 This which I here call the sensitiue herb is..*Herba mimosa*, or the Mocking herbe. **1658** J. Jones *Ovid's Ibis* 45 Thus the sensitive tree if ye touch one leaf the whole tree will quake. **1659** R. Lovell *Herbal* 524 Sensitive plant, *Herba sensibilis*. **1666** J. Davies *Hist. Caribby Isl.* 64 A Sensitive-shrub valued at a very great rate. **1709** Swift & Addison *Tatler* No. 32 ¶2 She shrinks from the Touch like a Sensitive Plant. **1760** J. Lee *Introd. Bot.* App. 323 Plant, Bastard sensitive, *Æschynomene*. **1782** Cowper *Poet, Oyster, & Sensit. Plant* 22 When, cry the botanists—and stare—Did plants call'd sensitive grow there? **1820** Shelley *Sensit. Plant* 1 A Sensitive Plant in a garden grew. **1821** Barton *Flora N. Amer.* I. 102 *Æschynomene hispida.* False-Sensitive-Plant. **1845-50** Mrs. Lincoln *Lect. Bot.* 61 The American sensitive plant. **1871** Kingsley *At Last* xi, So away we went..through broad-leaved grasses, and the pink balls of the sensitive-plants.

fig. **1821** P. Egan *Boxiana* 1st Ser. III. 236 Martin went to work with both his hands so quickly, that his opponent's sensitive plant rolled about like a humming top, and he fell out of the ring covered with crimson. **1890** 'R. Boldrewood' *Col. Reformer* (1891) 139 Let but a single cloud darken the summer sky,..and the heart, that sensitive plant, shrinks instinctively at nature's warning. **1907** J. London *Let.* 27 Sept. (1966) 251 All 'sensitive plants' are ego-maniacs; they are colossally stuck upon themselves. **1926** Galsworthy *Silver Spoon* I. vi. 41 Well, sir, the Press is a sensitive plant. I'm afraid you might make it curl up. **1974** 'S. Woods' *Done to Death* 190 'So nice to be considered a sensitive plant,' said Emma.

b. sensitive brier, *Schrankia uncinata.* **sensitive fern,** *Onoclea sensibilis.*

1823 Crabb *Technol. Dict.*, Sensitive Fern. **1846-50** A. Wood *Class-bk. Bot.* 238 Sensitive Brier.

c. Of plants and their organs: Capable of responding to stimulation. Cf. 5.

1875 Darwin *Insectiv. Pl.* vii. 140 Some tentacles on the same leaf were more sensitive than others. **1880** C. & F. Darwin *Movem. Pl.* 191 A part or organ may be called sensitive, when its irritation excites movement in an adjoining part. **1882** Vines tr. *Sachs' Bot.* 729 The leaves of *Mimosa*..may again become sensitive when the temperature falls.

4. That feels quickly and acutely.

a. In physical sense, of a living being, an animal organ or tissue: Having quick or intense perception or sensation. Also (const. *to*), Readily and acutely affected with pain or pleasure by some particular influence.

1849 Lyell *2nd Vis. U.S.* II. 175 When people have recovered from the yellow fever, the skin, although in other respects as sensitive as ever, is no longer affected by a musquito bite. **1859** Dickens *T. Two Cities* I. v, Madame Defarge being sensitive to cold, was wrapped in fur. **1860** Tyndall *Glac.* I. v. 38 One effect of light upon the eye is to render it less sensitive. **1875** Jowett *Plato* (ed. 2) III. 587 The tongue is one of the most sensitive of organs.

b. With reference to mental feelings: Having quick and acute sensibilities; easily touched to emotion, impressionable; easily wounded by unkindness; occasionally, ready to take offence, 'touchy'. Const. *to*, rarely *of*.

1816 Scott *Old Mort.* xxxix, That mournful impression, ..which the sensitive mind usually receives from a return to the haunts of childhood. **1824** W. Irving *T. Trav.* I. 72 The scenes of blood which followed shocked his sensitive nature. **1838** Thirlwall *Greece* V. 215 They were the more sensitive to injuries and encroachments on their rights. **1849** Macaulay *Hist. Eng.* i. I. 84 His conscience, which, on occasions of little moment, was sufficiently sensitive. *a* **1859** *Ibid.* xxiv. V. 214 Torpid as Spain had become, there was still one point on which she was exquisitely sensitive. **1862** Grote *Hist. Greece* V. II. lx. 288 Citizens, full of impressibility—sensitive and demonstrative Greeks. **1871** R. H. Hutton *Theol. Ess.* i. (1888) 5 Sensitive to human emotions. **1878** Lecky *Eng. in 18th C.* II. vi. 163 A man of the most stainless and sensitive honour. **1888** H. S. Holland *Christ or Eccl.* p. vii, Every educated man must be sensitive of the strain laid by miracle upon..scientific.. methods of knowledge.

c. *spec.* Having the temperament that is receptive of hypnotic or other occult influences. Cf. B. 5.

1846 Gregory *Abstr. Reichenbach's Res. Magnetism* 2 Healthy sensitive subjects..experience no inconvenience from the approach of magnets.

5. *transf.* **a.** Readily altered or affected by some influence specified or implied. Const. *to*, *of*.

1828 Steuart *Planter's G.* (ed. 2) 506 Oaks and Beeches, the plants of all others the most sensitive of drought! **1853** W. Gregory *Inorg. Chem.* 254 Silver and all its compounds are very sensitive to sulphuretted hydrogen. **1897** Mary Kingsley *W. Africa* 689 Your life hangs on quinine, and.. it is most important to keep the system sensitive to it.

b. *Photogr.* Of paper or other prepared surface, of chemical substances, etc.: Susceptible to actinic influence.

1839 Fox Talbot in *Philos. Mag.* XIV. 204 When a sheet of this, which I shall call *Sensitive Paper*, is placed in a dark chamber. **1839** —— in *Rep. Brit. Assoc.* VIII. II. 3 A silver plate..covered with a stratum of iodide of silver, which is sensitive to light. **1846** Gregory *Abstr. Reichenbach's Res. Magnetism* 9 A very sensitive daguerreotype plate being prepared, was placed opposite to a magnet [etc.]. **1893** Hodges *Elem. Photogr.* (1907) 14 The sensitive plates, or films, are made to certain standard sizes. *Ibid.* 95 The paper is..very sensitive to all white light.

c. Of a scientific instrument of measurement: Indicating readily slight changes of condition, easily moved or affected by the external forces which it is constructed to detect or record.

1857 Miller *Elem. Chem., Org.* (1862) 157 Determining the specific gravity by means of a sensitive hydrometer. **1863** Tyndall *Heat* i. §8 (1870) 8 Had they..dipped sufficiently sensitive thermometers into the water..they would have found [etc.]. **1867** —— *Sound* vi. 243, I at one time intended to approach this subject of sensitive flames through a series of experiments, which [etc.]. **1872** Yeats *Techn. Hist. Comm.* 349 Balances are made sensitive to the fraction of a grain. **1873-81** Maxwell *Electr. & Magn.* II. 322 When the instrument is intended to indicate the existence of a feeble [electric] current, it is called a sensitive Galvanometer.

d. Of market-prices, stock, etc.: Having a tendency to fluctuate rapidly upon the publication of outside reports.

1866 Rogers *Agric. & Pr.* I. xxi. 548 Such an article would be extremely sensitive to demand. **1867** Latham

Black & White 12 We went also to the Gold Exchange, and gold happened to be 'very sensitive'..and would go up.

e. Of a drilling machine: designed to give the operator continuous and sensitive control over the pressure and rate of drilling.

1895 C. J. APPLEBY *Illustr. Handbk. Machinery* IV. 53 Six speed sensitive drilling machine..is capable of drilling holes up to ¾ in. diameter, and will swing 18 inches. **1942** [see *pillar drill* s.v. PILLAR *sb.* 12]. **1971** C. R. HINE *Machine Tools & Processes for Engineers* xi. 261 This machine is slightly heavier than the sensitive drill press.

f. Involved with or likely to affect national security. Also with reference to other issues: that must be treated with care; likely to give offence if mishandled.

1953 *Manch. Guardian Weekly* 7 May 2 People in 'sensitive' jobs or departments—that is in positions having access to top secret or policy information. **1968** *Globe & Mail* (Toronto) 17 Feb. 7/1 Under the policies of the Government of Canada no one can buy arms and ship them from Canada to any sensitive area, whether that be Vietnam or anywhere else. **1973** P. GEDDES *Ottawa Allegation* x. 138, I realise it's from a sensitive source, but could I see it for myself? **1977** T. HEALD *Just Desserts* iv. 68 Probe gently. We are in what is known as a sensitive area.

g. Of a mathematical, statistical, or physical quantity: largely or appreciably influenced by changes in some other quantity, the choice of method or model, etc. Const. *to*.

1955 [see ROBUST *a.* 4]. **1966** A. BATTERSBY *Math. in Managem.* ix. 231 The cost is not 'sensitive' to the batch size. **1968** FOX & MAYERS *Computing Methods for Scientists & Engineers* iii. 31 The results show that y_r is extremely sensitive, for large *r*, to small changes in the initial condition. **1979** G. E. P. BOX in Launer & Wilkinson *Robustness in Statistics* 211 How sensitive are inferences made about θ to these contemplated misspecifications of the model?

6. Music. ***sensitive note***: the leading note of a scale. Cf. SENSIBLE *a.* 10 b.

1867 MACFARREN *Harmony* (1892) 30 This 7th of the key is also frequently called the Sensitive-note. **1881** BROADHOUSE *Mus. Acoustics* 344 Modern harmony with..its constantly-present sensitive or leading note.

B. *sb.*

†**1.** A being that is capable of sensation. *Obs.*

c **1532** DU WES *Introd. Fr.* in *Palsgr.* 1053 Thynges created of God..ben elemented, vegetables and sensytyves, as ben all beestes. **1602** WARNER *Alb. Eng.* XIII. lxxvi. (1612) 316 The Sensitiues, as beastes, wormes, birdes, and fishes. **1651** BAXTER *Inf. Bapt.* 230 The Mediator God-man doth exercise part of his Authority..even among brutes, and sensitives that cannot know him. **1727** DE FOE *Hist. Appar.* iv. (1840) 28 In Mars..no vegetables or sensitives could subsist that we have any notion of, for want of Moisture.

†**2. a.** The faculty of sensation. *Obs.*

1603 HOLLAND *Plutarch's Mor.* 1042 Of necessitie both the sensitive must be divided and goe with the sensible, and also the imaginative with the imaginable. **1627** HAKEWELL *Apol.* (1630) 74 Not onely the reasonable soule of man, but the sensitive of the least gnat.

†**b.** That which is capable of feeling (something specified). *Obs.*

1744 AKENSIDE *Pleas. Imag.* II. 218 They rise to act their cruelties anew In my afflicted bosom, thus decreed The universal sensitive of pain, The wretched heir of evils not its own!

†**3.** *nonce-use.* One sensible of a favour. *Obs.*

1663 GERBIER *Counsel* b 8 b, An humble sensitive, Your Lordships Zealous and most humble Servant.

4. The Sensitive plant (see A. 3). [F. *la sensitive.*]

1707 *Curios. Husb. & Gard.* 87 The Sensitive..never opens its Leaves till some time after Sun-rising. **1893** STEVENSON *Isl. Nights' Entert., Beach of Falesá* iv, There are cocoa palms..and guavas and lots of sensitive.

fig. **1805** M. A. SHEE *Rhymes Art* 88 But arts, a tribe of sensitives, demand a hot-house culture.

5. *nonce-use.* One who is easily shocked.

1838 SOUTHEY *Doctor* V. 143 This I am told it was which alarmed the Literary Sensitives.

6. One sensitive to spiritualist or other occult influences, a medium.

1850 ASHBURNER tr. *Reichenbach's Dynamics, Magnetism,* etc. 333 The most remarkable individual of all the healthy sensitives, whose perceptions exceeded those even of many diseased observers, in strength, distinctness, and duration was..Josepha Zinkel. **1886** F. W. H. MYERS *Phantasms of Living* I. Introd. 63 Phenomena commonly attributed to 'spirits' (but many of which may perhaps be more safely ascribed to the automatic agency of the sensitive himself).

7. a. One in whom the sensitive faculty is highly developed. Also = SENSITIVIST.

1891 *Athenæum* 18 July 93/3 A new and active band of Dutch novelists who have thought it worth their while to take a fresh name—the Sensitives—the better to define their place in literature. **1907** J. LOBB *Talks with Dead* 59, I [Shakspere] was a man of extremes, a Sensitive, a term which embraces all the eccentricities of a soul tabernacled in clay. **1909** CHESTERTON *Thackeray* Introd. 31 He was a sublime emotional Englishman, who lived by atmosphere. He was a great sensitive.

b. *transf.* and *fig.*

1884 HAWEIS *Musical Mem.* iii. 94 New violins as a rule will take thicker strings than the fine old sensitives of the sixteenth or seventeenth centuries.

sensitively (ˈsɛnsɪtɪvlɪ), *adv.* [f. SENSITIVE *a.* + -LY².] In a sensitive manner.

†**1.** Feelingly, tenderly; with the emotions as distinguished from the intellect. *Obs.*

1644 HAMMOND *Pract. Catech.* I. iii. (1646) 33 The sensitive faculty..may expresse its selfe more sensitively toward that inferiour object then toward God. **1673** BAXTER *Let.* in *Acc. Sherlocke* ii. 170 And thus God may be sensitively, or passionately loved, and must be.

2. With reference to feeling: Acutely, intensely.

1833 T. HOOK *Parson's Dau.* II. x, He was sensitively alive to the force of ridicule. **1870** SPURGEON *Treas. Dav.* Ps. xliv. 1 To hear with the ears affects us more sensitively than to read with the eyes.

3. With delicate perception; also *transf.*

a **1881** ILLINGWORTH *Serm. College Chapel* 119 Never before..were the aspects and the processes of this natural world so curiously, sensitively, lovingly watched as now. **1881** HUXLEY in *Nature* 11 Aug. 346/1 A vast aggregate of molecular mechanisms,..sensitively adjusting themselves to every change in the surrounding world.

4. With pa. pple.: So as to be sensitive.

1897 MARY ALBERT *Diamond Shoe Buckles* 60 A delicate, sensitively-organized frame.

sensitiveness (ˈsɛnsɪtɪvnɪs). [-NESS.]

1. The power or capacity of sensation. Also, with reference to plants: Capacity of responding to stimulation.

1828 BALLANTYNE *Exam. Hum. Mind* 427 In regard to sensitiveness many of the lower animals surpass man. **1862** DARWIN *Orchids* vi. 212 She [Nature] has endowed these plants with, what must be called for want of a better term, sensitiveness. **1882** VINES tr. *Sachs' Bot.* 775 The sensitiveness of the leaves of Mimosa does not therefore depend on a change of growth caused by the irritation.

transf. **1848–9** CALHOUN *Wks.* (1874) IV. 284 Magic wires are stretching themselves in all directions over the earth, and when their mystic meshes shall have been..perfected, our globe itself will become endowed with sensitiveness.

2. Keen susceptibility to outward impressions, delicacy or keenness of feeling developed to an unusual or abnormal degree.

1825 SCOTT *Betrothed* viii, In slow and solid natures there is usually..a sensitiveness to the breach of petty observances. **1866** GEO. ELIOT *F. Holt* v, But the minister's sensitiveness gave another interpretation to the gaze which he divined rather than saw. **1886** *Manch. Exam.* 14 Jan. 5/3 The new French Agent at Cairo..seems to be gifted with great diplomatic sensitiveness. **1908** *Athenæum* 21 Nov. 637/3 The analysis of Beethoven's Ninth Symphony..shows vivid sensitiveness to musical impressions.

b. Morbid self-consciousness, touchiness.

1851 HELPS *Comp. Solit.* x. (1857) 176 At last even sensitive people learn to suffer less from sensitiveness. **1881** EMMA J. WORBOISE *Sissie* xv, Sensitiveness, *per se*, is too often nothing but wounded vanity.

3. The quality or state of being easily affected by or of readily indicating changes of condition; *Photogr.* susceptibility to actinic influence. See SENSITIVE *a.* 5, 5 b, 5 c.

1839 FOX TALBOT in *Rep. Brit. Assoc.* VIII. II. 5 The present degree of sensitiveness of the photogenic paper was stated to be as follows. **1857** *G. Bird's Urin. Depos.* (ed. 5) 387 Such is the sensitiveness of this test that five or six drops only of saccharine urine, diffused through water, is sufficient to show the effect. **1860** TYNDALL *Glac.* II. xx. 336 An extreme degree of sensitiveness has been ascribed to the glacier as regards the changes of temperature. **1885** *Sci. Amer.* 25 Apr. 262/3 A sensitive plate showing a reading of 25 will be regarded as having an extreme degree of sensitiveness.

sensitivism (ˈsɛnsɪtɪvɪz(ə)m). [f. SENSITIVE *a.* + -ISM.] The principles of the sensitivists.

1891 E. GOSSE *Introd. to Couperus' Footsteps of Fate* 14 For the peculiar quality which unites in one movement the varied elements of the school which I have attempted thus briefly to describe, the name Sensitivism has been invented by one of themselves, by Van Deyssel.

sensitivist (ˈsɛnsɪtɪvɪst). [f. SENSITIVE *a.* + -IST.] The designation of a school of novelists in Holland, who aim at combining in their methods the valuable qualities of impressionism and realism.

1891 E. GOSSE *Introd. to Couperus' Footsteps of Fate* 5 The Dutch Sensitivists. **1903** *Blackw. Mag.* Apr. 557/1 They would be realists, or naturalists, or sensitivists, or heaven knows what.

sensitivity (sɛnsɪˈtɪvɪtɪ). [f. SENSITIVE *a.* + -ITY. Cf. F. *sensitivité.*]

1. The quality of being sensitive, in various senses of the adj.

1803 W. TAYLOR in *Ann. Rev.* I. 401 An eloquent exuberance characterizes the style of our author, and a sensitivity of imagination which makes even the minutest phænomenon appear important to his attention. **1856** DOVE *Logic Chr. Faith* IV. ii. §5. 221 In the Vegetable World we behold the..germ of individual Sensitivity. **1880** BASTIAN *Brain* 57 Its sensitivity to such stimuli is..closely akin to the general organic irritability of protoplasm. **1882** *Athenæum* 25 Nov. 703/1 The number of grades between the weights that any person can distinguish has to be found by trial, and that number becomes the measure of the coarseness of his sensitivity. **1904** TITCHENER tr. *Wundt's Physiol. Psychol.* I. 265 We find..symptoms of abrogation or diminution of cutaneous sensitivity upon the uninjured side of the body.

2. The activity and experience of the senses.

1889 MIVART *Orig. Hum. Reas.* 75 Creatures whose whole being is entirely given up to sensitivity.

3. a. The degree to which a device, test, or procedure responds to small amounts of or slight changes in that to which it is designed to respond; the ratio of the response of a device to the stimulus causing it; = SENSITIVENESS 3.

1918 E. S. FERRY *Handbk. Physics Measurements* II. iv. 179 (*heading*) Determination of the sensitivity of a galvanometer. **1937** H. EAGLE *Lab. Diagnosis of Syphilis* vi. 117 The longer the incubation period, the greater was the sensitivity of the test. **1944** E. S. SMITH *Automatic Control Engin.* iii. 17 Sensitivity is merely the ratio effect/cause. The over-all sensitivity is equal to the product of all the component sensitivities of the instrument. **1955** *Sci. Amer.* Mar. 68/2 The three procedures represent an ascending scale of sensitivity, and a descending scale of specificity. **1973** *Nature* 7 Dec. 343/2 An unsuccessful search for gravitational radiation was reported about a year ago by Braginskii *et al.*, with detectors of comparable sensitivity to those of Weber.

b. *spec.* in *Radio,* (a measure of) the ability of a receiver or other part of a radio system to pick up or respond to weak radio signals.

1928 L. S. PALMER *Wireless Princ. & Pract.* ix. 305 Most poor rectifying contacts can be improved by either the application of a small potential difference or by the application of heat, but with some of these contacts the increased sensitivity persists after the removal of the potential difference or heat. **1931** MOYER & WOSTREL *Radio Handbk.* iii. 124 Many crystals do not have a uniform sensitivity over the entire surface. **1962** *Which?* Feb. 40/1 We tested the radios to see how well they would receive weak stations. Their ability to do this is called sensitivity. **1965** *Wireless World* Sept. 457/1 The sensitivity of an audio amplifier is nowadays (following the British Standard) often specified in terms of a 'sensitivity voltage', i.e. the e.m.f. applied in series with the stated source resistance, to the input terminals in order to obtain the rated output power or voltage. **1975** G. J. KING *Audio Handbk.* v. 111 Each channel of a two- or four-channel amplifier should be measured for sensitivity independently.

4. *Psychol.* Used *attrib.*, esp. in ***sensitivity group, training***, to denote training in small groups aimed at increasing a person's awareness of the behaviour, feelings, and motives of others and of himself. Cf. *T-group* s.v. T 7.

1954 *Personnel* XXX. 256/1 The suggested approach to leadership training combines these two features in order to focus sensitivity training on those interpersonal problems which intimately involve the members of the training group. **1964** M. ARGYLE *Psychol. & Social Probl.* x. 133 Many students could..benefit from sensitivity training, aimed at increasing the accuracy of perception of social situations. **1969** *Listener* 26 June 881/1 A sensitivity group of persons gets together in order to cultivate a heightened awareness of themselves and each other, in a sort of group therapy. **1971** *Harvest Years* Mar. 8/2 (*caption*) A few scenes from a sensitivity session. **1977** E. G. & N. C. BORMANN *Speech Communication* (ed. 2) i. 12 Sensitivity groups have been used to train management personnel..and to institute individual and organizational change.

†**sensiˌtivo-ˈrational**, *a. Obs. rare.* Sensitive and rational.

Wollaston (*Relig. Nat.* 1722) uses the mod.L. form *sensitivo-rationalis.*

1768–74 TUCKER *Lt. Nat.* (1834) I. 202 Man has been incompletely defined a rational animal; he is rather, to use Mr. Woolaston's words, sensitivo-rational. *Ibid.* II. 295 We are but sensitivo-rational creatures, having in our natures a spice of the angel and of the beast.

sensitization (sɛnsɪtaɪˈzeɪʃən). [f. SENSITIZE *v.* + -ATION.] **1.** The act or process of sensitizing.

1887 *Brit. Merc. Gaz.* 15 June 25/1 Experiments in sensitization of molecular masses of differential volumes, showing attraction, propulsion, and negation, will follow. **1904** *Brit. Med. Jrnl.* 10 Sept. 559/2 The view of Bordet and the French school generally, that the action of immune body is what they describe as a sensitization. **1916** [see SENSITIZIN]. **1947** *Ann. Rev. Microbiol.* I. 298 Very striking is the effect of mycobacteria on sensitization to some simple compounds such as picryl chloride and 2:4 dinitrochlorobenzene... When these are injected intraperitoneally a state of anaphylaxis alone ensues, while the use of mycobacteria produces in addition sensitization of the contact dermatitis type. **1969** *Daily Progress* (Charlottesville, Va.) 12 Jan. A2/4 It also brings its own problems of sensitization to the horse serum from which it is made.

2. *Psychol.* The fact or condition of responding in a sensitized or sensitive (as opp. to a repressed) manner, esp. to an emotional stimulus; the process of being sensitized to a particular stimulus.

1947 *Jrnl. Personality* XVI. 75 Such sensitization represents..the obverse of defense... We now find sensitization in the presence of 'dangerous' stimulus objects. **1959** *Ibid.* XXVII. 364 The opposite syndrome, composed of high Admission, low Denial, and high Anxiety scores describes the other end of the repression continuum, which has been labeled 'sensitization'. **1967** *Psychol. Reports* XX. 459 The word 'sensitization' is used because the purpose of the procedure is to build up an avoidance response to the undesirable stimulus. **1976** *Jrnl. Clin. Psychol.* XXXII. 321 Results were interpreted according to an approach-avoidance model of repression-sensitization.

sensitize (ˈsɛnsɪtaɪz), *v.* [f. SENSIT-IVE + -IZE.]

1. *trans.* (*Photogr.*) To render (a plate, film or paper) sensitive to the influence of light.

1856 R. F. BARNES *Dry Collodion Process* 31 The bath I employ for sensitizing dry plates. **1858** T. SUTTON *Dict. Photogr.* 12 Albumen..is not so sensitive as collodion..; but ..it will keep longer when sensitized. **1865** *J. Wylde's Circ. Sci.* I. 153/1 Nitrate of silver..is the salt usually employed to sensitise the paper. **1879** LEAKE *Photogr.* in *Cassell's Tech. Educ.* IV. 323/2 A plate should now be coated with collodion in the tent, and sensitised in the usual manner.

2. To make (a person) sensitive (in various senses of the adj.).

1880 WINGFIELD *In Her Majesty's Keeping* I. 70 Education, while it sensitises a man's fibre, is incapable of turning weakness into strength. **1978** *Dædalus* Spring 228 It is..reasonable to hope that the fraction of abuses, mistakes, surprises, and other alarming problems will drop as the professionals involved become more and more sensitized to the possibility of such problems.

3. *Physiol.* To render (an organ or organism) sensitive *to* the presence of some agent; *esp.* to render (the immune system) sensitive *to* the presence of antibody. Also *absol.*

1904 *Brit. Med. Jrnl.* 10 Sept. 559/2 These bacteria are previously sensitized by union with a substance existing in the plasma. **1909** *Jrnl. Amer. Med. Assoc.* 30 Oct. 1473/1 The substance which is produced in the corpus luteum and which sensitizes the mucosa of the uterus has a specific affinity to the uterine tissue. **1922** *Jrnl. Physiol.* LVI. 143 The presence of free CO_2 'sensitises' the nerve cells to H ions. **1947** *Ann. Rev. Microbiol.* I. 305 It would be of great interest to identify the fraction or fractions which exert the adjuvant effect of myco-bacteria and to know whether the effect could be produced without sensitizing to tuberculin. **1970** PASSMORE & ROBSON *Compan. Med. Stud.* II. xxii. 12/1 IgM antibodies are unable to sensitize tissues for anaphylactic reactions..although IgG and IgA molecules, are able to do so.

Hence **'sensitized** *ppl. a.*; **'sensitizing** *vbl. sb.* and *ppl. a.*

1861 *Photogr. News Alm.* in *J. Wylde's Circ. Sci.* (1865) I. 160/2 A thirty-five grain nitrate bath,..is the best sensitising solution. **1864** ROSCOE in *Reader* 24 Sept. 386/3 It was necessary to construct an apparatus in which photographic sensitized paper could be exposed to the sunlight for definite times. **1877** MALLOCK *New Republic* III. iii. II. 50 Culture is..the sensitising of the mental palate—the making it a good taster. **1886** LOWELL *Harvard Anniv.* Wks. 1890 VI. 139 It is not their antiquity, but its association with man, that endows them [*sc.* ancient buildings] with such sensitizing potency. **1909** *Jrnl. Amer. Med. Assoc.* 30 Oct. 1471/2, I have..been able to ascribe a definite function to the corpus luteum, namely, that of supplying a sensitizing substance to the uterus which prepares the latter to respond with the production of the maternal placenta, if an external stimulus of a mechanical nature is added. *Ibid.* 1472/1 We wished..to select the safest period for the egg to attach itself to a sensitized uterine mucosa. *Ibid.* 1473/1 This process of sensitizing enables the connective tissue of the uterine mucosa to proliferate periodically. **1941** *Nature* 26 July 116/1 The small, often-repeated doses of these drugs..provide a chance for the patient to become sensitized to the drug. **1947** *Ann. Rev. Microbiol.* I. 299 For the rapid production of allergic encephalitis in both the monkey and the guinea pig the presence of myco-bacteria in the sensitizing injection seems to be essential. **1978** *Price's Textbk. Practice of Med.* (ed. 12) IV. 381/1 The signs and symptoms of generalized anaphylaxis that may follow..the parenteral injection of foreign serum, protein, or drugs, or sometimes even insect bites or stings in a sensitized individual, include a marked fall in blood pressure [etc.].

sensitizer ('sɛnsɪtaɪzə(r)). [f. SENSITIZE *v.* + -ER[1].] **1.** *Photogr.* A substance or preparation used for sensitizing.

1873 G. DAWSON *Hardwich's Man. Photogr.* 132 To apply the Ammonio-nitrate Sensitizer, the paper should not be floated on it. **1889** *Anthony's Photogr. Bull.* II. 314 The addition to a sensitive film of certain coloring matters, which are known as optical sensitisers or selective sensitisers, renders the film sensitive to rays which would otherwise produce little or no photographic effect.

†**2.** *Immunol.* = SENSITIZIN. *Obs.*

1903 *Nature* 13 Aug. 360/2 The sensitizers of the tubercle bacillus. **1935** N. P. SHERWOOD *Immunol.* vi. 112 Anaphylactic sensitizers.—Many persons have considered these interesting antibodies as identical with the precipitins but more recently some doubt has been cast on this hypothesis.

3. *Psychol.* A person or thing that has a sensitizing effect; one who reacts by being sensitive to a stimulus (rather than repressing it).

1948 *Jrnl. Abnormal & Soc. Psychol.* XLIII. 151/2 Nature orientation acts as a sensitizer, lowering thresholds for acceptable stimulus objects. Let us call this mechanism selective sensitization. **1951** *Ibid.* XLVI. 557/1 Needs could act as sensitizers, lowering the recognition thresholds for need-related stimuli. **1972** S. R. MADDI *Personality Theories* v. 207 Psychiatric outpatients were.. classified on the basis of their therapeutic interviews and other clinical tests as either sensitizers or repressers. **1976** *Psychol. Rep.* XXXIX. 189 The death message resulted in significantly more.. anxiety than the neutral message for repressors as well as for sensitizers.

†**sensitizin** ('sɛnsɪtaɪzɪn). *Immunol. Obs.* [f. SENSITIZE *v.* + -IN[1].] A substance which confers sensitivity on a species of antibody.

1916 R. WEIL in *Jrnl. Immunol.* I. 1 In the following papers the term 'Anaphylactic antibody' has been replaced by the word 'Sensitizen'. This has the advantage of brevity. The word is formed on the analogy of the words precipitin and agglutinin, and carries its own significance—namely that substance which confers sensitization. **1920** *Ibid.* V. 319 The experiments furnish further evidence that precipitin and 'sensitizin' are identical.

sensitometer (sɛnsɪ'tɒmɪtə(r)). *Photogr.* [f. SENSIT-IVE + *-ometer*: see -METER.] An instrument for ascertaining the degree of sensitiveness of photographic plates, films, etc. Also *attrib.*

1880 *Brit. Jrnl. Photogr.* 3 Sept. 421/3 [Mr. Warnerke's] very useful 'sensitometer'. **1890** P. H. EMERSON *Naturalistic Photogr.* 159 The rapidity of plates can be measured by an instrument called a sensitometer. **1890** *Anthony's Photogr. Bull.* III. 372 The lower grades of dry plates, that is, those of low sensitometer power.

Hence **sensi'tometry**, the determination of the degree of sensitiveness.

1881 *Brit. Jrnl. Photogr.* 25 Feb. 97/1 Photographic literature during the last six months has contained very numerous articles on the question of sensitometry. **1907** SHEPPARD & MEES *Theory Photogr. Process* 276 Part III. The Sensitometry of Photographic Plates.

sensitometric (ˌsɛnsɪtəʊ'mɛtrɪk), *a. Photogr.* [f. SENSITOMETRY: cf. -METRIC.] Of or pertaining to sensitometry.

1881 *Brit. Jrnl. Photogr.* 25 Feb. 97/1 A committee was formed..to decide, if possible, the sensitometric question. **1949** *Electronic Engin.* XXI. 118/3 In such cases as motion picture processing where it is desirable to develop to constant gamma in the face of increasing exhaustion of developer, sensitometric strips are frequently included every few hundred feet so that the development may constantly be checked. **1967** E. CHAMBERS *Photolitho-Offset* vii. 85 The starting point of sensitometry requires an understanding of sensitometric principles, involving the sensitometric curve.

Hence **sensito'metrically** *adv.*

1891 *Photographic Jrnl.* XVI. 65 The raw emulsion was mixed with the silver salts of various dyes dissolved in alcoholic solution of ammonia and tested sensitometrically, as well as spectroscopically. **1969** *Amat. Photographer* 9 Apr. 67/1 The integrating method of enlarging photometry is perhaps more difficult to explain sensitometrically.

sensitory ('sɛnsɪtərɪ), *sb.* [f. L. *sens-, sentīre* to feel + *-it-* (after SENSITIVE) + -ORY[1].] = SENSORY *sb.*

1864 WEBSTER.

'sensitory, *a. rare*$^{-0}$. [Formed as prec. + -ORY[2].] = SENSORY *a.*

1887 *Cassell's Encycl. Dict.*

sensive ('sɛnsɪv), *a.* [a. OF. *sensif*, ad. Latin type **sensīvus*, f. *sens-, sentīre* to feel: see -IVE.]

1. Having the function of sensation or sensuous perception.

†*sensive soul* = sensible or sensitive soul: see those adjs.

1553 GRIMALDE *Cicero's Offices* Pref., Men of middle degree, like the sensiue soule shall attend to affaires and sciences more liberale. **1578** BANISTER *Hist. Man* VIII. 104 b, Galen sayth that for three principall endes Nature hath made such distribution of Nerues in the body. The first was to giue feelyng vnto the sensiue instrumentes. *a* **1586** SIDNEY *Arcadia* I. (1598) 82 Palmes doe reioyce to be ioynd by the match of a male to a female, And shall sensiue things be so sencelesse as to resist sence? **1612** CHAPMAN *Rev. Bussy d'Ambois* V. v. 134 Learnedst men hold that our sensive spirits A little time abide about the graues Of their deceased bodies. **1865** J. GROTE *Explor. Philos.* I. 13 The harmonizing together of our active powers, our sensive powers, and our various individual experience.

†**2.** Capable of sensation. *Obs.*

1598 B. JONSON *Ev. Man in Hum.* II. iii, The infection Which, as a subtle vapor, spreads it selfe, Confusedly, through euery sensiue part.

sensize ('sɛnsaɪz), *v.* [f. SENSE *sb.* + -IZE.] *trans.* To perceive by means of the senses. So **'sensized** *ppl. a.*

1846 J. D. MORELL *Hist. View Philos.* II. v. 86 'The world,' says Fichte, 'is the sensized material of our practical life.' **1862** *Sat. Rev.* 6 Sept. 284 What we sensise through the ear is simply the motion of the atmosphere.

sensor ('sɛnsɔː(r)), *a.* [irreg. shortened f. SENSORY, after *motor*.] = SENSORY.

1865 TYNDALL *Fragm. Sci.* (1879) I. xxi. 492 The transmission of intelligence through the sensor nerves. **1875** W. K. CLIFFORD *Lect.* (1879) II. 108 Various combinations of disturbances in the sensor tract are made to lead to the appropriate combinations of disturbances in the motor tract.

sensor ('sɛnsə(r)), *sb.* [f. the adj. or f. SENSE *v.* + -OR.] A device giving a signal for the detection or measurement of a physical property to which it responds.

1958 *New Scientist* 10 Apr. 22/2 The 'sensor' is a small cylinder enclosed in a bigger cylinder full of silicone fluid and set on bearings which allow it to turn. **1958** *Guided Missiles* (U.S. Dept. of the Air Force) vi. 273/1 Pickoffs include any of the devices that are used to transfer the energy received at the sensor to the following detecting and amplifying stage. **1963** *Ann. Reg. 1962* 401 Infra-red sensors designed to detect rocket launchings. **1969** *New Yorker* 12 Apr. 104/2 Inside his space suit, the astronaut has a number of sensors that report on the state of his health. **1975** *Sci. Amer.* July 108/2 A repellent acts in one way on the carbon dioxide sensor and in a different way on the moisture sensor. **1976** *Early Music* July 351/3 Its sensor passes over the object to be copied thousands of times in different directions, and passes this information to cutting heads. **1977** *Navy News* Aug. 32/1 Vast improvements in propulsion, sensor systems and weapons..have placed great demands on training facilities. **1980** *Sunday Express* 19 Oct. 27 Every Metro has brake pad wear sensors to tell you when to change the brake pads.

sensor, obs. form of CENSER *sb.*[1], CENSOR.

sensori- ('sɛnsərɪ), used as combining form of SENSOR or SENSORY, chiefly in **sensori-motor** *a.*, applied to nerves which are both sensory and motor; also to reflex actions which arise from stimulation of the organs of sense; also, that relates to activity involving both sensory and motor pathways; **sensori'neural** *a.*, applied to defective hearing that is due to a lesion of the inner ear or auditory nerve. Similarly ***sensori-digestive, -reflex, -volitional*** adjs.

1891 *Century Dict.* (citing A. S. Packard), *Sensoridigestive. **1855** BAIN *Senses & Int.* II. iv. §4 (1864) 263 This is the principle of *sensori-motor, or sensori-reflex actions. **1897** *Allbutt's Syst. Med.* III. 202 An ordinary sensorimotor nerve such as the sciatic. **1908** W. MCDOUGALL *Introd. Soc. Psychol.* ii. 29 An innate or inherited psycho-physical disposition, which..probably has the form of a compound system of sensori-motor arcs. **1932** S. ZUCKERMAN *Soc. Life Monkeys & Apes* ix. 147 The sensori-motor mechanisms of the primates differ from those of the lower mammals. **1977** *Language* LIII. 153 Piaget 1952 and Piaget and Inhelder 1971 view representation as an internalization of active sensori-motor imitation. [**1960** *Laryngoscope* LXX. 885 A sudden unilateral or bilateral sensory-neural (perceptive) hearing loss.] **1964** *Arch. Otolaryngol.* LXXX. 382/1 In this type of slowly progressive *sensorineural hearing loss the only finding is atrophy of the stria vascularis, the functional manifestation of which is hearing loss showing a flat audiometric curve. **1977** *Lancet* 12 Nov. 1003/2 Perforation of the round-window membrane was found in three children with severe sensorineural deafness. **1855** *Sensori-reflex [see *sensori-motor* above]. **1857** DUNGLISON *Med. Lex.*, **Sensori-volitional*, a term applied to nervous fibres which..are respectively concerned in sensation and volition.

sensorial (sɛn'sɔərɪəl), *a.* [f. SENSORI-UM or SENSORY + -AL[1].] **a.** Of or relating to the sensorium. Also, relating to sensation or sensory impressions. Hence **sen'sorially** *adv.*

1768 TUCKER *Lt. Nat.* I. I. iii. 56 If I can light upon any little hint which may do real service to somebody or other I care not thro' what channels it is conveyed; whether..by agitating the sensorial and motorial ether, or by beginning a succession of perceptions. **1799** SIR H. DAVY in Beddoes *Contrib. Phys. & Med. Knowl.* (1799) 41 The motion of light communicated to the nerve itself produces the sensorial affection. **1851** H. MAYO *Pop. Superst.* (ed. 2) 42 The most instructive case of sensorial illusions on record. **1890** W. JAMES *Princ. Psychol.* I. ii. 42 All of Munk's *birds* seemed totally blind (blind sensorially) after removal of the hemispheres by his operation. **1899** *Allbutt's Syst. Med.* VIII. 108 This may form part of a sensory and sensorial hemianæsthesia. **1935** *Jrnl. Compar. Psychol.* XX. 10 A stimulus, a..property of which was its membership in a series which was only in part sensorially present on any one trial. **1962** Y. MALKIEL in Householder & Saporta *Probl. Lexicogr.* 22 Multicolored plates..might be useful, especially to the sensorially perceptive etymologist.

†**b.** Pertaining to the brain as the centre of nervous energy; esp. in ***sensorial power***, vital energy proceeding from the brain to the rest of the system. *Obs.*

1794 E. DARWIN *Zoon.* I. 75 The sensorial power, or spirit of animation,..is perpetually renewed by the secretion or production of it in the brain and spinal marrow. **1822–29** *Good's Study Med.* (ed. 3) II. 292 The stream of nervous power, thus communicated by jets from the sensorial fountain. *Ibid.* IV. 501 The sensorial powers are those which are dependent on the sensorium or brain as their instrument or origin; and are three in number, the intellectual, the sensific, and the motory. **1833** *Cycl. Pract. Med.* II. 91/2 When there is a predisposition to epilepsy, a cause of either kind..may interrupt the equable transmission of the sensorial power by means of the nerves, and thus occasion a fit.

‖**senso'riolum.** *rare.* Pl. -ola. [mod.L. dim. of SENSORIUM.] A small sensorium: (*a*) (see quot. 1714); (*b*) a minute organ of sense.

1714 ADDISON *Spect.* No. 565 ⁋8 Brutes and Men have their *Sensoriola*, or little *Sensoriums*, by which they apprehend the Presence and perceive the Actions of a few Objects, that lie contiguous to them. **1843** WILKINSON tr. *Swedenborg's Anim. Kingd.* I. i. 37 That it shall have the power of..expanding and relaxing..its sensoriola or papillæ.

‖**sensorium** (sɛn'sɔərɪəm). Also 7–8 erron. cens-. [Late L. *sensōrium* (Boethius), f. *sens-*, ppl. stem of *sentīre* to feel: see -ORY.] The seat of sensation in the brain of man and other animals; the percipient centre to which sense-impressions are transmitted by the nerves. Also ***common sensorium*** (L. *sensorium commune*), †***first sensorium***. Formerly also used in a wider sense, for the brain as the organ of mind and the centre of nervous energy.

1647 H. MORE *Song of Soul* Notes 139/2 For there is first a tactuall conjunction as it were of the representative rayes of every thing, with our sensorium before we know the things themselves. **1664** POWER *Exp. Philos.* I. 69 Spontaneous motion is performed by continuation of the Animal Spirits, from the common Sensorium to the Muscle. *c* **1688** TRYON *Dreams* ii. (1695) 15 When the first Censorium (which is called the Organ of the common Sense) is bound and obstructed with a soporiferous vapour. **1737** PORTERFIELD in *Med. Ess. Edin.* (ed. 2) III. 219 Which Agitation is communicated to the *Sensorium*, or that Part of our Brain in which our Mind does principally reside. **1826** KIRBY & SP. *Entomol.* IV. I Sensation and perception are by the means of nerves and a common sensorium. **1872** DARWIN *Emotions* iv. 83 When the sensorium is strongly excited, the muscles of the body are generally thrown into violent action. **1879** CARPENTER *Mental Phys.* I. i. §13. 15 That we are not always conscious of the working of this Mechanism, is simply because our Sensorium is otherwise engaged.

b. Used playfully in non-technical writing (sometimes for 'brain' or 'mind').

1759 STERNE *Tr. Shandy* II. x, The ringing of the bell, and the rap upon the door, struck likewise strong upon the sensorium of my uncle Toby. **1814** SCOTT *Wav.* lxi, While these reflections passed like the stings of scorpions through

Waverley's sensorium. **1842** CAMPBELL *Pilgr. Glencoe* 469 An artery in his wise sensorium burst. **1908** E. V. LUCAS *Over Bemerton's* iii. (1909) 21 There was, as it were, a veil between them and my sensorium.

c. *fig.*

1714 ADDISON *Spect.* No. 565 ¶8 The noblest and most exalted Way of considering this infinite Space is that of Sir Isaac Newton, who calls it the *Sensorium* of the Godhead. *a* **1861** SIR F. PALGRAVE *Norm. & Eng.* III. 595 Rome became the common sensorium of Europe, and through Rome all the several portions of Latin Europe sympathized and felt with each other. **1867** MACGREGOR *Voy. Alone* (1868) 24 The tiller, that delicate and true sensorium of a boat.

sensory (ˈsɛnsərɪ), *sb.* [ad. L. *sensōrium*: see prec. and -ORY[1].]

†**1.** An organ of sense. *Obs.*

1626 BACON *Sylva* §255 Visibles, and Audibles doe.. languish and lessen by degrees, according to the Distance of the Obiects from the Sensories. **1692** BENTLEY *Boyle Lect.* v. 21 That we all have double Sensories, two Eyes, two Ears, two Nostrils, is an effectual Confutation of this Atheistical Sophism. **1714** DERHAM *Phys.-Theol.* IV. iii. (ed. 2) 123 The Bone.. serves.. as a substantial Guard to the Sensory [of the Ear].

fig. **1681** J. SCOTT *Chr. Life* I. iv. §4 (1684) 317 These heavenly Graces are the Palate by which the immortal Mind tastes.. its Heaven, the blessed Organs and Sensories by which it feels.. the Joys of the World to come.

2. = SENSORIUM. Also ***common*** or †***first sensory***.

1653 R. SANDERS *Physiogn.* 216 The irrigation of the brain, and of the first sensory, that is the obstruction of the common sense of the organs, indicates the Form. **1681** *Willis' Rem. Med. Wks.* Vocab., *Sensory*, the organ of feeling, or of discriminating by the senses; the common sensory or seat of such organ, placed in the brain. **1689** NORRIS *Reas. & Relig.* II. ii. 188 These Species are carried by the external Senses to the common Sensory. **1750** JOHNSON *Rambler* No. 78 ¶2 Uneasiness gives way by slow degrees, and is long before it quits its possession of the sensory. **1826** KIRBY & SP. *Entomol.* IV. xlv. 234 The agent between the common sensory and the sense is the consciousness or perception of the impression. **1822–29** *Good's Study Med.* (ed. 3) I. 195 The general bustle and hilarity.. break the sturdy chain of habit and association, and give leisure to the worn-out sensory to refresh itself. **1882** H. CALDERWOOD in *Schaff's Encycl. Relig. Knowl.* I. 36 Three distinct cognitive faculties—the sensory, the understanding, and the reason.

3. *Psychol.* A person in whom sensation supposedly dominates over action. *rare.*

1902, **1929** [see MOTOR *sb.* 2c].

sensory (ˈsɛnsərɪ), *a.* [ad. L. type *sensōrius*: see prec. and -ORY[2].] **1.** Belonging to sensation; carrying or transmitting sensation.

1749 HARTLEY *Observ. Man* I. 58 Sensory Vibrations. **1763** *Phil. Trans.* LIV. 184 These nerves are equally motory and sensory. **1799** SIR H. DAVY in Beddoes *Contrib. Phys. & Med. Knowl.* (1799) 21 The sensory organs. **1883** *Encycl. Brit.* XV. 279/1 The lower sensory ganglia, which receive all sensory impressions in the first instance. **1886** GURNEY, etc. *Phantasms of Living* I. 537 A dim and shadowy idea, when once it obtains a lodgment in the mind, may body itself forth as a sensory phantasm.

2. Special collocations: **sensory aphasia** *Path.*, aphasia evidenced by impaired speech, memory, writing, or reading which is due to cerebral defect or injury affecting comprehension or the ability to integrate incoming acoustic information, and freq. differentiated from incapacities deriving from motor defects; **sensory deprivation** *Psychol.*, the act or process whereby an organism is deprived of stimulation affecting one or more of the sense organs; the state or condition produced by such deprivation; **sensory-motor** *a.* = *sensori-motor a.* s.v. SENSORI-.

1884 *Brain* VI. 401 The author [*sc.* Wernicke] also makes good use of the phenomena of the different forms of aphasia, which he divides into motor, conductive, *sensory, and total aphasia. **1926** H. HEAD *Aphasia* I. II. iii. 202 'Sensory' aphasia, or amnesia, was divided into 'visual' and 'auditory'. **1959** *Psychol. Rev.* LXVI. 46/2 It is significant that with careful study of even a small number of patients, the traditional dichotomy between motor and sensory aphasia began to disappear. **1976** E. D. MYSAK *Path. Speech Syst.* iii. 85 Sensory aphasia [is reported] with tumors in the left parietal region. **1948** D. BAKAN *Investig. Effect of Sensory Deprivation on Stall Perception* i. 4 What is the effect of *sensory deprivation on the accuracy with which the pilot can detect the edge of the stall proper. **1961** S. COBB in P. Solomon et al. *Sensory Deprivation* p. xviii, The symptoms of the deprived child with 'atypical' and 'autistic' reactions are without doubt related to the phenomena seen in adults after experimental sensory deprivation. **1978** O'CONNOR & HERMELIN *Seeing & Hearing & Space & Time* v. 65 Sensory deprivation, especially of audition, appears to decrease duration. **1957** MENON & PATEL *Teaching of Eng. as Foreign Lang.* xi. 125 Spelling is a *sensory-motor habit acquired by motor responses to certain sensory stimuli.

Hence **ˈsensorily** *adv.*

1925 E. SITWELL *Poetry & Criticism* 20 Though it seems to us as though we heard them sensorily, yet the sound is unheard in reality. **1949** M. MEAD *Male & Female* i. 17 Needs.. for continuous contact with one sensorily identifiable human being throughout the first two years of life. **1954** *Essays in Criticism* IV. 313 Mill's attempt to define poetry as something not heard but *overheard*.. is successful .. in so far as it removes the sensorily ascertainable audience and replaces it with a mysterious audience.

sensour, obs. form of CENSOR, CENSURE.

sensour(e, senssar, obs. ff. CENSER *sb.*[1]

a **1400–50** *Wars Alex.* 1565 Sum with sensours.. Quare-of þe reke aromatike rase to þe welken. **1546** *Supplic. Poore Commons* 75 Sensoures, pixese, coopes. ? **1571** *Cov. Corpus Chr. Plays* App. II. 97 For mendyng of ij senssars.

sensse, variant of CENSE *sb.*[1] *Obs.*, incense.

c **1450** *Lay-Folks Mass-Bk.* E. 249 Gold, sensse, and myrre.

senssour, obs. form of CENSER *sb.*[1]

sensual (ˈsɛnsjuːəl, -ʃuːəl), *a.* and *sb.* Also 5–7 sensuall, 5 sensuel. [ad. late L. *sensuālis*, f. L. *sensu-s* SENSE *sb.*: see -AL[1]. Cf. F. *sensuel*, Sp., Pg. *sensual*, It. *sensuale.*] **A.** *adj.*

1. a. Of or pertaining to the senses or physical sensation; sensory. Now *rare.*

c **1450** *Mirour Saluacioun* 3346 So kept he the seints in helle with out payne sensuel felyng. *c* **1450** *Cov. Myst.* (Shaks. Soc.) 240 Thryes I tempte hym be ryth sotylle instawnce, Aftyr he fast fourty days ageyns sensual myth or reson. **1509** WATSON *Ship of Fools* i. (1517) A iij b, Where through I myghte lese my sensuall intellygence, for he that procureth too knowe ouermoche.. is in daunger for to be extraught from hymself [etc.]. *Ibid.* xviii. E iij b, It is impossyble y[t] his sensuall wyt may comprehende, and haue so many dyuers cogytacyons in an instaunte. **1526** *Pilgr. Perf.* (W. de W. 1531) 151 The beestes.. be made tame.. : that is to say, the sensuall powers of man or woman, whiche by synne euer rebelled.. be made obedyent to y[e] spiryte. **1597** HOOKER *Eccl. Pol.* I. xi. §4 Man doth seeke a triple perfection, first, a sensuall,.. then an intellectuall.. lastly a spirituall & diuine. **1604** T. WRIGHT *Passions* 229 Raging Mastives who, if they were loosed, one at another, they would fight till death, whereas in presence of the Bull.. they .. both, eyther by sensuall consent or naturall instinct, unite themselves in one to assault their common adversary. **1652** BENLOWES *Theoph.* IV. lxxiii, Let not dust blinde my sensual Eyes When as my spirits Energie transcends the skies. **1732** POPE *Ess. Man* I. 208 Far as Creation's ample range extends, The scale of sensual, mental pow'rs ascends. **1742** YOUNG *Nt. Th.* VII. 739 The wide stretcht realm of intellectual woe, Surpassing sensual far, is all our own. **1794** E. DARWIN *Zoon.* I. 11 Synonymous with the word idea, we shall sometimes use the words *sensual motion* in contradistinction to *muscular motion.* **1820** KEATS *Ode Grec. Urn* 13 Ye soft pipes, play on; Not to the sensual ear, but more endear'd, Pipe to the spirit ditties of no tone. **1846** I. WILLIAMS *Bapt., Voices of Dead*, But still the wall impassable Bars us around with sensual bond. **1881** WILLIAMSON in *Nature* 1 Sept. 414/1 The process of scientific investigation includes a great variety of operations, which may be considered under three headings, mental, sensual, and physical.

b. Perceptible by the senses. *rare.*

1529 MORE *Dyaloge* III. Wks. 243/2 Sometime as God, sometime as man,.. sometime as in y[e] persone of his sensuall parties of his own body, otherwhile in y[e] person of some particular part of his body mystical. **1774** GOLDSM. *Nat. Hist.* (1824) I. 245 A man born deaf must necessarily be dumb; and his whole sphere of knowledge must be bounded only by sensual objects. **1836** MRS. BROWNING *Poet's Vow* I. x, But, weights and shows of sensual things Too closely crossing him, On his soul's eyelid the pressure slid, And made its vision dim.

†**2.** Of living things: Endowed with the faculty of sensation (but not with reason). *Obs.*

1530 RASTELL *Bk. Purgat.* III. vii. 2 A soule sensytive whiche is in every brute sensuall best. **1696** TATE & BRADY *Ps.* xlix. 20 As like a sensual Beast he lives, So like a Beast he dies.

3. Of appetites and pleasures: Connected with the gratification of the senses. **a.** In neutral use: Sensuous, physical. Now *rare.*

1542 BOORDE *Dyetary* xii. (1870) 267 Clowtyd crayme.. is eaten more for a sensuall appetyde than for any good nowrysshement. **1618** WITHER *Motto, Nec curo* (1621) D 8 b, I care not for his loue. My dogge doth so; He loues, as farre as sensuall loue can go. **1650** BULWER *Anthropomet.* 239 Some unassayed sensual sweetnesse. **1740** CIBBER *Apol.* (1756) I. 303 This kind of entertainment [opera] being so entirely sensual, it had no possibility of getting the better of our reason but by its novelty. **1752** HUME *Polit. Disc.* ii. 37 No gratification, however sensual, can, of itself, be esteemed vicious. **1797** D. SIMPSON *Plea Relig* (1808) 190 The Gospel .. allows every sensual enjoyment that is consistent with the real good.. of man. **1834** MARRYAT *P. Simple* i, My father walked up and down the room with impatience, because he was kept from his dinner, and, like all orthodox divines, he was tenacious of the only sensual enjoyment permitted to his cloth.

b. In pejorative use, implying the notion of something base or vicious. Now often, Lewd, unchaste.

1477 *Rolls of Parlt.* VI. 191/1 Persones not dredyng God, .. but enclyned of sensuall appetite. *a* **1513** FABYAN *Chron.* v. cxxxii. (1811) 114 He was gyuen to all sensuall luste of his body. *a* **1541** WYATT in *Tottel's Misc.* (Arb.) 224 See thou kepe thee free From the foule yoke of sensuall bondage. **1634** MILTON *Comus* 77 They.. all their friends, and native home forget To roule with pleasure in a sensual stie. **1645** HAMMOND *Sins Weakn.* etc. §23. 13 From whence.. sinne is brought forth, that very consent of the will to the sensuall faculty, being formally sinne without, or before the acting of it. **1732** BERKELEY *Alciphr.* II. §17 Intervals of spleen; for relief of which he is driven into sensual excesses. **1850** ROBERTSON *Serm.* Ser. III. ix. (1853) 114 The sensual pleasure of the glutton.

4. Of persons, their dispositions, conduct, etc. **a.** Absorbed in the life of the senses; indifferent to intellectual and moral interests. In religious use: Destitute of spiritual life, worldly, irreligious. Now only in phr. ***the average sensual man*** (see AVERAGE *a.* 2 b).

1557 BIBLE (Genev.) *James* iii. 15 This wisdome is earthy, sensual [*so later versions*; Tindale, etc. *have* natural] and dyuelyshe. **1582** N. T. (Rhem.) *1 Cor.* ii. 14 The sensual [1611 naturall] man perceiueth not those things that are of the spirit of God. *Ibid., Jude* 19 These are they which segregate themselues, sensual, hauing not the Spirit. **1599** DAVIES *Nosce Teipsum* 95 As some sensuall spirits amongst vs.. Which hold the world to come, a faigned stage. **1656** EARL MONM. tr. *Boccalini's Advts. fr. Parnass.* I. v. 12 [He trusts] the Senat willingly with the revenge of any injury he can receive, when sensual men are very loath to remit the like into the hands of God. *a* **1676** HALE *Prim. Orig. Man.* IV. v. (1677) 333 Sensual Men are not willing to believe any thing whereby they have not a sufficient Evidence, as they think, to their Sense. **1677** GALE *Crt. Gentiles* IV. II. ii. 216 The brutish sensual World began to cal in question the very existence and providence of God. **1751** JOHNSON *Rambler* No. 178 ¶11 The gratifications of the palate; an entertainment so far removed from intellectual happiness, that scarcely the most shameless of the sensual herd have dared to defend it. **1882** M. ARNOLD *Irish Ess.* 230 But this whole drama.. may be best described as the theatre of the *homme sensuel moyen*, the average sensual man,.. whose city is Paris, and whose ideal is the free, gay, pleasurable life of Paris.

b. Excessively inclined to the gratification of the senses, voluptuous; often *spec.* with reference to sexual passion, lewd, unchaste. Of physiognomy or features: Indicative of a sensual disposition.

1530 PALSGR. 323/2 Sensuall gyven to vyce, *epicurien.* **1637** RALEIGH *Mahomet* 65 Don Roderigo.. began to repent him of his sensuall life. **1692** R. L'ESTRANGE *Fables* cxxvi. 118 These Wasps in a Hony-Pot are so many Sensual Men that are Plung'd in their Lusts and Pleasures. **1694** ATTERBURY *Serm.* (1726) I. 190 The Sensual Man is, of all Men living, the most improper for Enquiries after Truth. **1706** PHILLIPS (ed. Kersey), *Sensual*, Voluptuous, given to Pleasures, Carnal or Fleshly. **1712** STEELE *Spect.* No. 466 ¶5 Were any one to see Mariamne dance, let him be never so sensual a Brute, I defie him to entertain any Thoughts but of the highest Respect and Esteem towards her. **1876** GLADSTONE *Homeric Synchr.* 246 Homer has exhibited much repugnance to the sensual deity of Aphrodite. **1881** H. SMART *Race for Wife* i, By nature coarse and sensual in his habits. **1905** R. BAGOT *Passport* xxv. 268 The full mouth, with the sensual lips.

¶**c.** Misused for: Obstinately self-willed. *Obs.*

1524 WOLSEY in *St. Papers Hen. VIII*, IV. 198 The realme of Scotland, by taking sensuall and wilfull waies, shal soner chose to lyve in warre trouble inquietnes and adversite, than to florishe in joye [etc.]. **1538** *Ibid.* III. 36 His Lordshipp afterwarde despysid and maligned at the Kinges said Privaye Counsaile, following censuall and wilfull waies. **1539** EARL ORMOND *Ibid.* III. 150 My Lorde Deputie.. hath broght the successes of his sensuall apetittis and wilfull procedinges now to such pass and effect, that [etc.]. *a* **1548** HALL *Chron., Hen. VIII* 31 If any lawe or reason could have removed you from your sensuall opinions, ye have ben many and often tymes sufficientely aunswered to the same. **1584** BURGHLEY in Strype *Whitgift* App. III. (1718) 64, I favour no sensual & wilful Recusants.

5. a. Of opinions or ideas: Materialistic.

1656 JEANES *Mixt. Schol. Div.* 48 Austin told his friend Alipius, and Nebridius, that Epicurus his sensuall doctrine had with him carried away the garland from all Philosophers and Divines; unlesse [etc.]. **1830** D'ISRAELI *Chas. I*, III. xv. 329 Moses.. only accommodated such figurative expressions to the sensual comprehensions of his tribes. **1845** SARAH AUSTIN *Ranke's Hist. Ref.* VI. ix. III. 569 Views, at once transcendent and sensual, of the mission of a Messiah. **1871** ALABASTER *Wheel of Law* 67 He gives his own views of the common sensual idea of heaven.

b. *Philos.* = SENSATIONAL *a.* 2. *rare.*

1837–9 HALLAM *Lit. Eur.* III. iii. §94 The sensual and ideal schools of psychology.

†**B.** *sb. pl. Obs.*

1. a. The sensual faculties and appetites. **b.** The objects of sense.

a **1661** FULLER *Worthies, Hants* (1662) II. 8 His Intellectuals had such predominancy of his Sensuals, or rather Grace so ruled in both, that the Man in him being subordinate to the Christian, he lived a pattern of Piety. *a* **1676** HALE *Prim. Orig. Man.* IV. viii. (1677) 375 The objects, means, and occasions of our fears in relation to sensuals, are ever more and greater than the objects of our hopes.

2. Beings capable only of sensation, brutes.

1605 TIMME *Quersit.* Ded. 2 The souls of men and angels are reasonable;.. and the sensuals (as beasts and such like) not so. *a* **1644** QUARLES *Sol. Recant.* iii. 18 (1645) 14 Heav'n suffers mortals to be exercis'd In their own miseries, that they may see They'r not more happy then the sensuals bee.

sensualism (ˈsɛnʃuːəlɪz(ə)m). [f. SENSUAL *a.* + -ISM. Cf. F. *sensualisme* (1812 in sense 1).]

1. *Philos.* The doctrine that the senses are the sole source of knowledge; sensationalism.

1803 *Edin. Rev.* I. 264 The more inviting system of sensualism, in which all knowledge is supposed to consist of original impressions from without. **1832** LINBERG tr. *Cousin's Introd. Hist. Philos.* xii. 393, I define the Scotch philosophy, gentlemen, as an honorable protestation against the extravagances of the last consequences of sensualism. **1848** R. I. WILBERFORCE *Doctr. Incarnation* xiv. (1852) 401 The School of Locke replies that they [the premises of reason] owe their existence to the senses... That theory, which, matured by Locke's subtiler and more consistent disciple, Hume, may be called the system of sensualism.

2. Addiction to sensual indulgence.

1813 SHELLEY *Q. Mab* iv. 251 Is not thy youth A vain and feverish dream of sensualism? **1847** HELPS *Friends in C.* I. iv. 62 There is something quite military in the sensualism of the Romans—an 'arbiter bibendi' chosen [etc.]. **1906** CHARL. MANSFIELD *Girl & Gods* xv, The ruts and looseness on a face coarsened by sensualism.

3. Absorption in material interests.

1878 EMERSON *Misc. Papers, Fort. Republ.* Wks. (Bohn) III. 396 In this country..there is at present a great sensualism, a headlong devotion to trade.

sensualist ('sɛnʃuːəlɪst). [f. SENSUAL *a.* + -IST. Cf. F. *sensualiste* (1812 in sense 2).]

1. One whose disposition and conduct are sensual; one whose sole interests are in the things of sense; chiefly, one who is devoted to sensual pleasure, or given to vicious indulgence of the animal passions.

The various shades of meaning can hardly be distinguished in the early examples.

1662 HIBBERT *Body Divinity* I. 310 It is charged as a foul fault upon those sensualists that they had lived in pleasure. **1682** FLAVELL *Fear* ii. Wks. 1701 I. 577/1 As it is noted of those secure Sensualists, Amos vi. 3. They put far from them the evil Day. **1732** BERKELEY *Alciphr.* II. §16 Those pleasures which are highest in the esteem of sensualists. **1773** *Observ. State Poor* 64 It is not the fear of lothsome or excruciating disease, that will deter the sensualist or the epicure from the indulgences of their appetites. **1792** MARY WOLLSTONECR. *Rights Wom.* ii. 45 As blind obedience is ever sought for by power, tyrants and sensualists are in the right when they endeavour to keep women in the dark. **1831** CARLYLE *Sart. Res.* III. iii, Even for the basest Sensualist, what is Sense but the implement of Fantasy? **1871** BURR *Ad Fidem* ix. 176 The sty of the sensualist.

2. = SENSATIONALIST.

1852 WIGHT tr. *Cousin's Course Hist. Mod. Philos.* II. 138 On which side shall I rank myself, in this great battle of European philosophy in the eighteenth century? Shall I be a sensualist? **1856** FERRIER *Inst. Metaph.* x. vi. (ed. 2) 261 That school of philosophers who are called 'the sensualists'.

sensualistic (ˌsɛnʃuːə'lɪstɪk), *a.* [f. prec. + -IC.] Pertaining to sensualism in philosophy or art.

1852 WIGHT tr. *Cousin's Course Hist. Mod. Philos.* II. 49 The four great schools,..namely Platonic idealistic dogmatism, peripatetic sensualistic dogmatism, skepticism, and mysticism. *Ibid.* 87 Gassendi,..the scholar of the sensualistic school. **1854** H. ROGERS *Ess.* (1874) II. i. 38 Locke is the father of the whole sensualistic school of the eighteenth century. **1856** RUSKIN *Mod. Paint.* V. IX. ii. §13. 213 Sensualistic art, represented typically by that of Salvator.

sensuality (sɛnʃuː'ælɪtɪ). Forms: 4–6 **sensualite,** (4–5 **-litee, -lyte),** 4 **senswalyte,** 5 **sensewalite,** 5–6 **censualyte,** 6 **sensualytie, sensualitie,** 6– **sensuality.** [a. F. *sensualité,* ad. late L. *sensuālitās,* f. *sensuālis* SENSUAL *a.* Cf. Sp. *sensualidad,* It. *sensualità.*]

†**1.** The part of the nature of man that is concerned with the senses; chiefly, the animal instincts and appetites; the lower nature as distinguished from the reason; also *occas.* the faculty of sensation. *Obs.*

a **1340** HAMPOLE *Psalter* vi. 6 þe neþer party of my saule þat is cald þe sensualite. *Ibid.* xxx. 11 My saule þat is my sensualite. *c* **1386** CHAUCER *Pars. T.* 262 God sholde haue lordshipe ouer reson, and reson ouer sensualitee, and sensualitee ouer the body of man. *c* **1420** ? LYDG. *Assembly of Gods* 6 How that I myght make Reason & Sensualyte in oon to acorde. *c* **1440** HYLTON *Scala Perf.* (W. de W. 1494) II. xxviii, It shall be mortyfyed & pyned in the sensualyte eyther by dyuers syknes or by felable tourment of the fende. *c* **1450** tr. *De Imitatione* III. lviii. 136 Who euere kepe himself so under, þat sensualite obeye to reson, & reson to me in all þinges, he shal be a very victour of himself. *c* **1460** *Wisdom* 135 in *Macro Pl.* 40 þe on, sensualyte, Wyche ys clepyde þe flechly felynge. **1670** CRESSY 16 *Revelat. Div. Love* lvi. 145 That our sensuality by the vertue of Christs Passion, be brought up into the substance. **1828** *Blackw. Mag.* XXIII. 596 The grand arcanum of the learned gourmand is the proper sequence of the viands, and the skilful interception of the glass, by which his sensuality is piqued.

†**b.** *pl.* Physical necessities and appetites. *Obs.*

1697 C. LESLIE *Snake in Grass* (ed. 2) 152 Such a gross Conceit of the Resurrection, as if our Bodies shou'd be in the same frail condition as now, and addicted to Sensualities.

†**2.** The lower or animal nature regarded as a source of evil; the lusts of the flesh. Also *pl.*

1413 LYDG. *Pilgr. Sowle* (Caxton 1483) IV. xxviii. 73 This is the sensualite of men that draweth hym to synne and to bestly lustes. **1432–50** tr. *Higden* (Rolls) III. 349 An other dethe when the sawle..despisethe and refusethe the unlawefulle movenges and sensualites of the body. **1450–1530** *Myrr. Our Lady* 150 And that the reson desyreth, the sensualyte ageyne sayth. *c* **1470** HENRYSON *Mor. Fab.* v. (*Parl. Beasts*) xlviii, Thow may brek sensualiteis heid And fleschlie lust away fra the sall fle. **1509** BARCLAY *Shyp of Folys* (1874) I. 83 Suffre not your soules damned and lost to be By vayne lust and carnall sensualyte. **1621** T. WILLIAMSON tr. *Goulart's Wise Vieillard* 62 It pleaseth him to fortifie and strengthen vs, euen to ouercome ..sensualitie.

†**3.** The following of the lower nature in preference to the higher; absorption in the things of sense. *Obs.*

c **1407** LYDG. *Reson & Sens.* 678 This is the wey of Resoun ..But the tother..Ys..The wey of sensualyte, Which set his entente in al To thinges that be temporal. **1483** *Rolls of Parlt.* VI. 240/2 Lede by sensualite and concupiscence. **1548** *Act 2 & 3 Edw. VI,* c. 19 Preamble, Diverse.. turnynge their knowledge therein to satisfye their sensualitye. **1561** T. NORTON *Calvin's Inst.* III. vii. §1. 159 b, Wherby the mynd of man, voide from his own sensualitie of flesh, bendeth it selfe wholly to the will of Gods spirite.

¶**b.** Self-willed obstinacy. (Cf. SENSUAL *a.* 3 c.) *Obs.*

1536 R. COWLEY in *St. Papers Hen. VIII,* II. 370 Certain rynge leaders..applying moore to theire awne sensualities, singuler proffites, and affeccions, then to any good reason. **1538** LD. BUTLER *Ibid.* III. 95, I do take him to be..a man more mete to be governed, than to governe, for all his interprises be made upon his awne sensualitie, withowt thadvise..of thois that been put in trust by the Kingis Majestie. **1544** *Ibid.* 502 But..what for ther owne pryvate censualyte to ther olde ravyne and customes, no doubte bothe the saide McCharties..woll joyne with hym.

4. Excessive fondness for, or vicious indulgence in, the pleasures of the senses.

c **1450** *Cov. Myst.* (Shaks. Soc.) 244 And yf be sensualyte ..Synnyst dedly, thou xalt not therfore dyspeyre. **1594** NASHE *Unfort. Trav.* I 3 b, O (quoth he) long haue I liued sworne brothers in sensualitie with one Esdras of Granado: fiue hundred rapes and murders haue we committed betwixt vs. **1599** SHAKS. *Much Ado* IV. i. 62 Those pampred animalls, That rage in sauage sensualitie. **1603** HOLLAND *Plutarch's Mor.* 7 Loose and dissolute persons, abandoned to all sensualitie. **1685** R. BAXTER *Paraphr. N.T. 1 Tim.* v. 23 b, To use Wine, yea, much Wine or strong Drink for meer appetite, instead of a little for health, is sinful sensuality. **1692** R. L'ESTRANGE *Fables* ccxvii. 190 Here's a Reproof to Men of Sensuality and Pleasure. **1754** SHERLOCK *Disc.* (1759) I. xiv. 394 Sense produces no Sensuality, till it warms the Affections with the Pleasures of the World. **1771** SMOLLETT *Humph. Cl.* 6 May (1815) 70 He owns himself addicted to the delights of the stomach, and often jokes upon his own sensuality. **1779** JOHNSON *L.P., Pope* Wks. (1787) IV. 92 That he loved too well to eat, is certain; but that his sensuality shortened his life will not be hastily concluded. **1845** KITTO *Cycl. Bibl. Lit.* I. s.v. *Ecclesiastes,* Unrestrained merriment and giddy sensuality belong to those vanities which our author enumerates. **1879** FROUDE *Cæsar* ii. 16 The once hardy, abstemious mode of living degenerated into grossness and sensuality.

b. *pl.*

1477 EARL RIVERS (Caxton) *Dictes* 8 The ignorante men wol not abstyne them from their sensualitees. **1599** DAVIES *Nosce Teipsum* 100 Marre not her [*sc.* thy soul's] sense with Sensualities. **1803** *Med. & Phys. Jrnl.* IX. 321 Those capable of indulging in the pleasures and sensualities of a luxuriant table. **1817** COLERIDGE '*Blessed are ye that sow*' 66 *note,* Sensualities which both in sort and degree it would be libelling their Brother-beasts to call bestial.

†**c.** In innocent sense (as an oxymoron): A sensuous gratification or pleasure. *Obs.*

1604 T. WRIGHT *Passions* v. ii. 165 Euen..most devout men benefit their soules..with the sweetnesse of musicke.. with this sacred sensualitie and pleasant path which leadeth to the fountaine of spirituall comfort. **1900** *Westm. Gaz.* 1 Dec. 8/1 A Poet Laureate readily tolerated what he called 'the most innocent of sensualities' [snuff-taking].

5. *spec.* Lasciviousness, unchastity.

1463 ASHBY *Poems* i. 171 Yef thow tak a wyfe to thy freelte Ryght thoutfull thow art..Yef thow lyue aftyr censualyte, That ys acursyd and vnthryfty lyf. **1503** HAWES *Examp. Virt.* viii. 151 But best it is that he maryed be For to eschewe all yll censualyte. **1567** *Gude & Godlie B.* 197 Preistis..leif zour foule Sensualitie. *a* **1618** RALEIGH *Mahomet* (1637) 14 Taxing his sensualitie and drunkennesse. **1869** LECKY *Europ. Mor.* I. i. 150 Judging the sensuality of a nation by its statistics of illegitimate births. **1879** FROUDE *Cæsar* xii. 154 The gluttony, the drunkenness, and the viler forms of sensuality.

sensuali'zation. *rare.* [f. SENSUALIZE *v.* + -ATION.] The action of sensualizing.

1798 A. F. M. WILLICH *Elem. Crit. Philos.* 141 The sensualization of an idea of reason. **1800** W. TAYLOR in *Monthly Mag.* X. 505 Layers of affecting plainness, and affected sonorosity, of scholastic jargon, and oriental sensualization, succeed each other without blending. **1828** SOUTHEY in *Q. Rev.* XXXVIII. 202 A sort of intellectual sensualization.

sensualize ('sɛnʃuːəlaɪz), *v.* [f. SENSUAL *a.* + -IZE.]

1. *trans.* To render sensual. **a.** To imbue with sensual habits or dispositions; to inure to vicious indulgence.

a **1687** H. MORE *Lett.* (1694) 79 Nothing can more incrassate, and sensualize the Intellect, than such an Opinion. **1725** *Pope's Odyss.* I. *View Epic Poem* 10 Not to suffer ones self to be sensualiz'd by pleasures. **1860** PUSEY *Min. Proph.* 202 It is that luxury and ease which sensualize the soul, and make it dull, stupid, hard-hearted. **1868** F. E. PAGET *Lucretia* 302 It is no light crime to aid in sensualizing the character of a whole people.

b. To give a sensuous or materialistic character to.

1796 MORSE *Amer. Geog.* II. 570 The Indian bramins and parsees accuse the gaurs..of having sensualized those ideas [of a Supreme Being]. **1828** DE QUINCEY *Rhetoric* Wks. 1859 XI. 43 Milton is taxed with having too grossly sensualized his supernatural agents. **1833** LONGF. *Outre-Mer* Pr. Wks. 1886 I. 194 These representations have a tendency to sensualize and desecrate the character of holy things.

c. To explain by reference to sensation; to regard as originating from the senses.

1838 SIR W. HAMILTON in *Reid's Wks.* I. 128/2 *note,* Which, in place of sensualizing intellect, intellectualizes sense. **1877** E. CAIRD *Philos. Kant* II. xiii. 506 Locke sensualised the conception of the understanding.

d. To convert into or identify with something cognizable by the senses.

1884 [LAURIE] *Metaph. Nova & Vet.* 23 The percept thus becomes sensualized as an articulate sound. *Ibid.* 112, I have created my own difficulty by first sensualizing the dialectic percept, Cause.

2. *intr.* **a.** To live sensually.

1612 T. ADAMS *Gallant's Burden* 16 b, First, they visit the Tauerne,..then the Theater, and end in the Stewes... If they were Beasts, they could not better sensualize.

b. To entertain sensual notions.

1846 G. S. FABER *Lett. Tractar. Secess.* 176 The constant reproach of the sensualising Pagans was, that Christians had in their strange worship, neither altars nor sacrifices.

Hence **'sensualized** *ppl. a.*

1690 NORRIS *Beatitudes* vi. (1694) 167 A sensualized Soul would carry such Appetites with her thither for which she could find no suitable Objects. **1824** COLERIDGE *Aids Refl.* (1848) I. 33 Virtue may, possibly, add to the pleasure..a spiritual complacency, of which in your present sensualized state you can form no idea. **1829** *Blackw. Mag.* XXVI. 616 This was a lesson which our Lord sought to impress upon the degenerate and sensualized Jews of his day.

sensually ('sɛnʃuːəlɪ), *adv.* [f. SENSUAL *a.* + -LY[2].] In a sensual manner.

†**1.** In a manner perceptible to the senses. *Obs.*

1624 GATAKER *Transubst.* 109 That the very body of Christ in the Eucharist is broken with the Priest's hands.. not sacramentally only, but sensually. **1686** HORNECK *Crucif. Jesus* xi. 193 They cannot sensually but only in a sacramental, or representative way, be handled by the Priest.

2. With a view to the gratifying of the senses.

1630 MASSINGER *Picture* II. i, Succeeding times..would instruct Their fairest issue to meete sensually, Like other creatures. *c* **1655** A. SIDNEY in *19th Cent.* Jan. (1884) 59 An Angell loves spiritually;..a man that is composed of reason and sense, rationally and sensually both together.

3. With subservience to the senses or the lower nature; with undue indulgence of the physical appetites; lustfully, licentiously.

1576 FLEMING *Panopl. Epist.* 220 They shall neuer be wise or sober, so long as they be so sensually disposed. *a* **1618** RALEIGH *Mahomet* (1637) 51 He spared not sensually to follow in enticing and forcing mens wives and daughters.

Comb. **1662** H. MORE *Philos. Writ.* (1712) Pref. Gen. 8 For there is a sanctity even of Body and Complexion, which the sensually-minded do not so much as dream of.

†**'sensualness.** *Obs. rare.* [f. SENSUAL *a.* + -NESS.] = SENSUALITY.

1530 PALSGR. 269/1 Sensualnesse, *sensualité.* **1632** LITHGOW *Trav.* v. 219 Going beyond them in beastly sensualnesse, [they] become worse then bruite beasts.

sensuism ('sɛnʃuːɪz(ə)m). *Philos.* [f. L. *sensu-s* SENSE *sb.* + -ISM.]

1. = SENSATIONALISM 1, SENSUALISM 1.

1829 SIR W. HAMILTON *Discuss.* (1852) 2 Sensualism (or more correctly sensuism). **1872** *Contemp. Rev.* XX. 540 Sensationalism or sensuism, which would deny to all human knowledge the character of universality and necessity.

¶**2.** Tendency to indulge the sensuous imagination in religious meditation.

1878 GROSART in *H. More's Poems* Mem. Introd. 30/1, I suppose the meaning is that, unconsecrated by high personal devoutness, mysticism is apt to 'degenerate' into sensuism, if not sensualism.

sensuist ('sɛnʃuːɪst). *rare*[−0]. [f. L. *sensu-s* SENSE *sb.* + -IST.] = SENSUALIST 1.

1860 FARRAR *Orig. Lang.* 150 *note,* We consider this ['sensationalist'] on the whole a less objectionable term than 'sensualist' or 'sensuist'. **1887** in *Cassell's Encycl. Dict.*; and in later Dicts.

sensu'istic, *a. rare.* [f. L. *sensu-s* SENSE *sb.* + -ISTIC.] Inclined to sensuous indulgence.

1850 E. MONRO *Paroch. Work* 194 Their own nature being sensuistic, they readily give vigour to temptations.

sensu lato: see SENSU STRICTO.

sensum ('sɛnsəm). *Philos.* Pl. **sensa.** [L., sensed, that which is sensed, neut. pa. pple. of *sentīre* to discern by the senses, to perceive.] = SENSE-DATUM.

1868 A. BAIN *Senses & Intellect* (ed. 3) 376 In Sensation, we seem to have the sentient mind, and the thing felt— *sentiens* and *sensum.* **1920** S. ALEXANDER *Space, Time, & Deity* II. III. ii. 58 The non-mental external object which in this case is the *sensum* or *sensible.* **1923** C. D. BROAD *Sci. Thought* viii. 240 Such objects as y I am going to call Sensa. **1937** L. S. STEBBING *Philos. & Physicists* vi. 130 It is only because Russell and Joad *first* know that there are external objects that they are able to *infer* that there are private sensa. **1949** G. RYLE *Concept of Mind* vii. 213 The theory says that when a person has a visual sensation..his having this sensation consists in his finding or intuiting a sensum. **1967** *Encycl. Philos.* VII. 80/2 The essential point is that perceiving proper is the direct awareness of sensa. **1974** R. M. YOST in Carterette & Friedman *Handbk. Perception* I. ii. 33 One cannot locate a visual sensum in empty physical space without presupposing the Absolute Theory of Space.

sensuosity (sɛnʃuː'ɒsɪtɪ). *rare.* [f. SENSUOUS *a.*: see -OSITY.] The quality of being sensuous.

1755 BAILEY (ed. Scott), *Sensuosity,* sensitiveness. **1882** *Homiletic Monthly* Apr. 416 Much of what is called magnetism..and unction..in a speaker, is mere sensuosity.

sensuous ('sɛnʃuːəs, -sjuː-), *a.* [f. L. *sensu-s* SENSE *sb.* + -OUS.

Apparently invented by Milton, to avoid certain associations of the existing word *sensual,* and from him adopted by Coleridge; evidence of its use in the intervening period is wanting. Coleridge seems to have been mistaken in saying that it occurs in 'many others of our elder writers'.]

1. Of or pertaining to the senses; derived from, perceived by, or affecting the senses; concerned with sensation or sense-perception.

1641 MILTON *Reform.* I. 3 The Soule..finding the ease she had from her visible, and sensuous collegue the body in performance of Religious duties..shifted off from her selfe the labour of high soaring any more. **1644** —— *Educ.* 6 To which Poetry would be made subsequent, or indeed rather precedent, as being lesse suttle and fine, but more simple, sensuous, and passionate. **1814** COLERIDGE *Princ. Gen. Crit.* iii. in *Farley's Bristol Jrnl.* Aug., Thus, to express in one word what belongs to the senses, or the recipient and more passive faculty of the soul, I have reintroduced the word *sensuous*, used, among many others of our elder writers, by Milton. **1842** EMERSON *Lect., Transcend.* Wks. (Bohn) II. 279 The idealist.. does not deny the sensuous fact:.. but he will not see that alone. **1850** GROVE *Corr. Phys. Forces* (ed. 2) 15 Here the phenomena of motion are not made evident by the ordinary sensuous perception. **1850** TENNYSON *In Mem.* l, Be near me when the sensuous frame Is rack'd with pangs that conquer trust. **1856** R. A. VAUGHAN *Mystics* (1860) I. 225 Such men live in the outside of themselves —in the sensuous or intellectual nature. **1859** GULLICK & TIMBS *Paint.* 154 The external or sensuous qualities of art. *absol.* **1809-10** COLERIDGE *Friend* (1865) 96 The understanding, wherever it does not possess or use the reason, as another and inward eye, may be defined the conception of the sensuous.

b. Of words and their meanings, etc.: Relating to sensible objects. Of opinions, conceptions, etc.: Based on representations of sense, material.

1864 RAWLINSON *Anc. Mon., Assyria* viii. II. 277 Their religion.. was of a sensuous character. **1869** LECKY *Europ. Mor.* I. 142 The beginning of eloquence is pictorial sensuous and metaphorical. **1869** FARRAR *Fam. Speech* iv. (1873) 112 Languages very crude and sensuous in their character. **1871** BLACKIE *Four Phases Mor.* i. 132 The familiar and sensuous theology of Homer. **1874** SAYCE *Compar. Philol.* vi. 249 The oldest roots are of the most purely sensuous description.

c. Of pleasure: Received through the senses. Now often with some colouring from sense 3, implying a luxurious yielding up of oneself to passive enjoyment

1856 G. WILSON *Gateways Knowl.* (1859) 48 To be awaked from sleep by splendid music is to me the highest conceivable sensuous pleasure. **1862** MISS BRADDON *Lady Audley* vii, There is in the first taste of rustic life a kind of sensuous rapture scarcely to be described. **1877** BLACK *Green Past.* xxxvii. (1878) 295 It was something to gaze on with a placid and sensuous satisfaction. **1909** E. R. TENNANT in *Expositor* Aug. 123 That sensuous pleasure is a possibility is.. a thing to give God thanks for.

2. Devoted to the gratification of the senses. *rare.*

1859 I. TAYLOR *Logic in Theol.* 309 A sensuous or a frivolous life.

3. Readily affected by the senses; keenly alive to the pleasures of sensation; *occas.* of a poet or artist, moved by or appealing to the sensuous imagination. Also of physiognomy, etc. indicating a sensuous temperament.

In early use with favourable sense; now often with some notion of self-indulgent yielding to impressions or of a tendency to the sensual in imagination.

1870 EMERSON *Misc. Papers, Plutarch* Wks. (Bohn) III. 342 A poet in verse or prose must have a sensuous eye, but an intellectual co-perception. **1875** LOWELL *Spenser* Wks. 1890 IV. 317 A poet is innocently sensuous when his mind permeates and illumines his senses; when they muddy the mind, he becomes sensual. *a* **1876** G. DAWSON *Lect. Hamlet* (1888) 16 None can help having a certain admiration for sensuous nature when very beautiful... She [Ophelia] was the perfection of sensuousness. **1880** M. ARNOLD *Ess. Crit.* Ser. II. iv. (1895) 100 Keats as a poet is abundantly and enchantingly sensuous. **1895** RIDER HAGGARD *Heart of World* vii. (1899) 100 His mouth was cruel and sensuous. **1909** E. THOMAS *Jefferies* 122 His expression [was] sensuous, tender, 'silent and aware'.

¶**4.** In recent use sometimes of climate, surroundings, etc.: Conducive to a vague sense of physical enjoyment.

1878 JOAQUIN MILLER *Songs Italy* 51 How sensuous the night! how soft was the sound Of her voice on the night. **1878** H. S. WILSON *Alpine Ascents* 106 Their air and character [*sc.* those of the Italian lakes] are soft, sensuous, enervating.

sensuously ('sɛnʃuːəslɪ, -sjuː-), *adv.* [f. SENSUOUS *a.* + -LY².] In a sensuous manner.

1825 COLERIDGE *Aids Refl.* (1848) I. 326 To bring together every one of the sensible and ponderable stuffs or elements, that are sensuously perceived in the eye itself, or in the flesh itself. **1858** HAWTHORNE *Fr. & It. Note-bks.* I. 127 So warm and rich it is, so sensuously beautiful. **1877** E. CAIRD *Philos. Kant* II. viii. 357 The categories would have no use except in relation to a sensuously given manifold. **1886** SYMONDS *Renaiss. It., Cath. React.* (1898) VII. xi. 180 Venus.. takes that sensuously dreamy.. journey across the blue Mediterranean.

sensuousness ('sɛnʃuːəsnɪs, -sjuː-). [f. SENSUOUS *a.* + -NESS.] The quality of being sensuous.

1855 I. TAYLOR *Restor. Belief* (1856) 286 Easy, pleasure-loving sensuousness and sensuality. *a* **1876** [see SENSUOUS *a.* 3]. **1882-3** J. HARPER in *Schaff's Encycl. Relig. Knowl.* 1961 The sensuousness which distinguished the Old Dispensation from the New.

sensure, obs. form of CENSER *sb.*¹, CENSURE.

Sensurround ('sɛnsəraʊnd). Also **sensurround.** [Blend of SENSE *sb.* and SURROUND *v.*] The proprietary name of a special-effect technique whereby a cinema audience is apparently surrounded by low-frequency sound and air vibrations generated from the soundtrack of a film. Also *attrib.* and *transf.*

1974 *Newsweek* 2 Dec. 104/2 The quake under your seat is created by 'Sensurround', a system that hooks into the film's soundtrack and sets off low-level tremors at a cost of $500 a week to the theater owners. **1975** *New Yorker* 26 May 81/1 'But my dear,' said Mrs. Vreeland, her voice achieving in the small room much of the effect that Sensurround does in movie theaters, 'those wrapped heads are my *greatest achievement.*' *Ibid.* 82/2 'My *God,* Ferle,' said Mrs. Vreeland, employing her Sensurround voice. **1976** *Official Gaz.* (U.S. Patent Office) 6 Apr. 22/1 MCA Systems, Inc., Universal City, Calif.... *Sensurround* for electronic apparatus for generating special effects, including simulated earthquake effects, in motion picture theaters... First use Sept. 3, 1974. **1977** *Time* 11 July 51/3 *Rollercoaster* is the latest—and so far least—excuse to trot out Sensurround, that technology that is still in search of a character and, for that matter, a plot worthy of its woofers. **1980** *Spectator* 31 May 24/1 Every corner of the theatre is used to produce a sensurround, stereophonic effect, the noise and flashing all around us.

‖**sensu stricto** ('sɛnsuː 'strɪktəʊ). [L., lit. 'in the restricted meaning'.] Strictly speaking; in the narrow sense (of a term, esp. in the natural sciences). Opp. to **sensu lato** ('lɑːtəʊ) [L. *lātus* broad], in the broad sense. Cf. STRICTO SENSU.

1941 J. S. HUXLEY *Uniqueness of Man* xi. 240 Human biology is but an extension of biology *sensu stricto.* **1942** W. B. TURNBULL in *Bot. Rev.* VIII. 656 (*heading*) Algae (sensu lato). **1952** Sensu stricto [see *isochemical* adj. s.v. ISO- a.]. **1954** [see NEOCEREBELLUM]. **1959** A. R. CLAPHAM et al. *Excursion Flora Brit. Isles* 569 Sensu lato. In the broad sense. **1963** D. W. & E. E. HUMPHRIES tr. *Termier's Erosion & Sedimentation* xiv. 299 Griottes 'sensu stricto' composed of alternate beds of shale and limestones, irregularly corrugated. **1973** B. J. WILLIAMS *Evolution & Human Origins* xi. 176 In the material that follows I shall use the term Neandertal *sensu lato*, that is, in the broad sense. **1977** *Verbatim* Sept. 4/1 The trouble is caused not by length *sensu stricto* but by complexity.

sensyment, variant of SENSEMENT *Obs.*

sensyne, *adv. Sc. Obs.* Forms: 4 **senesyne**, 5-7 **sensyne**, 6-7 **sensyn**, 6-9 **sensine**. [f. SEN *prep.* + SYNE *adv.* Cf. the later SINSYNE.] Since then, from or after that time.

c **1375** *Sc. Leg. Saints* xviii. (*Egipciane*) 992 Quhat manere of clethinge had þou for to cleth þe sene syne? **1456** SIR G. HAYE *Law Arms* (S.T.S.) 38 He maid a citee, and callit it.. Saturne, that was callit sensyne Scitus. **1541** JAS. V in *St. Papers Hen. VIII*, V. 189 And inlikvise the innovationis maid sensyne. **1596** DALRYMPLE tr. *Leslie's Hist. Scot.* v. lxxiii. (S.T.S.) I. 281 Quha sen syn haue seruet sa faithfullie that cure,.. that [etc.]. **1638** in *Fasti Aberd.* (1854) 287 Ane new commission direct sen syn be his.. majestie. **1651** D. CALDERWOOD *Hist. Kirk* (1843) II. 337 Her Majestie,.. by diverse proclamations sensyne, hath expresslie forbiddin [etc.]. **1674** RAY *N.C. Words* 40 *Sensine*, Cumb. since then, Var. Dial. **1863-4** ATKINSON *Whitby Gloss.* s.v., It is now getting to look long sensine.

sensyr, obs. form of CENSER *sb.*¹

14.. *Nom.* in Wr.-Wülcker 720/43 *Hoc turibulum*, a sensyr.

†**sent**, *sb. Obs.* Also 5 **sente**. Aphetic form of ASSENT *sb.*

c **1350** *Will. Palerne* 1983 Þat þemperour ne schuld souche þa ȝhe at sent were. **1389** in *Eng. Gilds* (1870) 58 Be ye sent of alle ye breyeren and systers of yis gilde. *a* **1450** *Le Morte Arth.* 2278 Through the sente of All by-dene Ganne the kynge A lettre make.

†**sent**, *v. Obs.* Aphetic form of ASSENT *v.*

13.. *Gosp. Nicod.* 512 (Add. MS.) To þair consayle.. We will noȝt sent. *c* **1450** *St. Cuthbert* (Surtees) 5336 Þai prayde þair horse moght þar a byde; þe gude wyf sent þar to. **16..** *Eger & Grine* 38 in *Percy Fol. MS.* (1867) I. 355 They Ladye granted her good will, her father sented there soone till.

sent (sɛnt), *ppl. a.* [pa. pple. of SEND *v.*]

a. In senses of the vb. Also in comb. as HEAVEN-SENT.

1483 *Cath. Angl.* 330/1 Sent, *missus, destinatus.* **1667** MILTON *P.L.* IV. 852 The Sender not the sent. **1825** H. C. ROBINSON *Diary* Dec. (1967) 86 *Irving.* He is a highly gifted man; he is a sent man, but they who are sent sometimes go further than they ought.

b. *slang.* (See quot. 1940.)

1940 *Amer. Speech* Oct. 337/1 *To be sent*, to be completely satisfied and in a stupor from the drug. **1951** *Manch. Guardian* 21 June 5/1 The slang of jazz addicts, which is full of phrases like 'hepsters', getting 'high', being 'sent' and other euphemisms for the delirium induced by improvised solos on the cornet and slide trombone. **1958** *Spectator* 25 July 133/3 The girls wore thick eye-makeup and 'sent' expressions.

sent, obs. f. SCENT *sb.* and *v.*; obs. var. CENT².

sent(e, obs. forms of SAINT.

†'**sentement.** ? Short for PRESENTMENT.

c **1500** KENNEDY *Passion of Christ* 494 Na thing mycht cule þe hatrent of þair hert, Quhill be [? *read* he] to de to Pilat wes present, Quhilk be þe law wes justice in þat art, In caus of blude to schaw þe sentement. **1509** HAWES *Past. Pleas.* x. (Percy Soc.) 35 And if it [*sc.* the cause] be a lytle probable, From any maner stedfast argument, We ordre it for to be ryght stable, And than we never begyn our sentement, Recityng letters not convenient.

sentement, obs. form of SENTIMENT.

sentenar(e, obs. forms of CENTNER.

1615 in *Wedderburne's Compt Bk.*, etc. (S.H.S.) 263, 2 sentenar lead. *Ibid.*, 5 sentenare of lead.

sentence ('sɛntəns), *sb.* Also 4-5 **sentense**, 4-6 **sentens**, 5 **centence**, **centens(e**, **sentensce**. [a. F. *sentence* (12th c.) = Pr. *sentensa*, Sp. *sentencia*, Pg. *sentença*, It. *sentenza*, ad. L. *sententia* opinion, maxim, etc., irreg. (for **sentientia*) f. *sentīre* to feel, be of opinion.]

†**1.** Way of thinking, opinion. *Obs.*

1340 *Ayenb.* 69 Þer byeþ zome.. þet none guode techinge ne onderuongeþ ak alneway weryeþ hare sentense huet þet hit by. **1387-8** T. USK *Test. Love* III. ix. (Skeat) 6 The comune sentence of the people.. that every thing after destenee is ruled, false and wicked is to beleve. *c* **1400** *Rom. Rose* 5813 The baronage to councel wente; In many sentences they fille, And dyversly they seide hir wille. *c* **1412** HOCCLEVE *De Reg. Princ.* 364 Se how þat þe worþi prelacie, ..Endowyd of profound intelligence, Of al þis land werreyen þi sentence. **1534** MORE *Treat. Passion* Wks. 1329/2 Yet is it the most common sentence of al the old holye men. **1552** ABP. HAMILTON *Catech.* (1884) 4 Be ye perfite in ane mynd & in ane sentence. **1597** HOOKER *Eccl. Pol.* v. lxvii. §11 Touching the sentence of antiquitie in this cause. **1609** BIBLE (Douay) *Josh.* ix. 2 The Hetheite and Amorreite.. were gathered, to fight against Iosue and Israel with one minde, and one sentence.

2. a. The opinion pronounced by a person on some particular question, usually, one on which he is consulted or which is being deliberated upon.

1375 *Sc. Leg. Saints* iii. (*Andrew*) 1022 Þe bischope thocht, and all þe lafe, þe sentence ganand þat scho gafe. *c* **1386** CHAUCER *Melib.* ¶366, I wolde fayn knowe how that ye vnderstonde thilke wordes and what is youre sentence. **1422** YONGE tr. *Secreta Secret.* xxvi. 156 Ne yeue thow not lyghtly thy sentence. *c* **1470** HARDING *Chron.* CLXXVIII. ii, Emong theim selfes our lordes for hie prudence Of the bishop asked counsaill and sentence. **1535** COVERDALE *Acts* xv. 19 Wherfore my sentence is [Gr. ἐγὼ κρίνω], that [etc.]. **1583** BABINGTON *Commandm.* viii. (1590) 366 Olde Chaucer so long agoe set his sentence downe against this exercise. **1601** SHAKS. *All's Well* I. iii. 80 With that she.. gaue this sentence then, Among nine bad if one be good.. there's yet one good in ten. **1667** MILTON *P.L.* II. 51 My sentence is for open Warr: Of Wiles, More unexpert, I boast not. **1678** HOBBES *Decam. Physiolog.* x. 122 It were too bold to pronounce any sentence of its substance. **1725** POPE *Odyss.* III. 156 Thy Sire and I were one; nor vary'd aught In publick sentence, or in private thought.

b. *the four books* (or *the Book*) *of the Sentence(s*: the *Sententiarum libri quatuor*, a compilation of the opinions of the Fathers on questions of Christian doctrine, by Peter Lombard (12th c.), thence called ***the Master of the Sentences.***

1387 [see MASTER *sb.*¹ 13 b]. **1492** *Acta Domin. Conc.* (1839) 243/1 Ane buk contenand four bukis of þe sentence. **1563** MAN *Musculus' Commonpl.* 273 The Master of the Sentences did but gather together the opinions and Sentences of the Fathers. **1682** N. O. *Boileau's Lutrin* II. 10 This Baggage once in her mad Moods and Tenses Had Lombard read, the Master o' th' Sentences.

c. *the Reading of the Sentences*: the office of lecturing on the 'Books of Sentences' (see b), which was the special mark of the second of the three stages of the degree of Bachelor of Divinity in mediæval universities.

1691 WOOD *Ath. Oxon., Fasti* I. 745 Hieronim. Schlick, Count of Passan,.. was then admitted to the reading of the Sentences. **1885** LYTE *Univ. Oxf.* 107 The Dominicans [in 1313].. took exception to another recent statute of the University, which forbade any one to lecture on the text of the Bible who had not already lectured on the Sentences and taken the degree of Bachelor of Divinity.

3. An authoritative decision; a judgement pronounced by a tribunal. †**a.** *spec.* = sentence of excommunication.

c **1290** *S. Eng. Leg.* 133/932 ȝif ani man hond on ov set ich ov hote al-so þat ȝe þe sentence of holi churche for swuche violence ȝe do, And holdez vp holi churche riȝte þat ov is bi-take. **1297** R. GLOUC. (Rolls) 10370 He esste boc & candle þe sentence to do bliue. **1390** GOWER *Conf.* I. 259 This Pope.. Hath sent the bulle of his sentence With cursinge and with enterdit. *c* **1400** *Rule St. Benet* (Prose) xxiv. 21 Wylys sho is in sentence, sho ne sal noht be in cuuent, til it be amendid. *c* **1450** *Mirk's Festial* 281 As hit fell bysyde þe abbay of Lulsull by þre men þat hadden stolen an ox of þe abbot, and he had made a sentens þerfor. **1523** LD. BERNERS *Froiss.* I. cccxli. 536 Whiche of them yᵗ euer shulde breke this peace by any maner of wayes, shulde rynne in the sentence of the pope.

b. *gen.* The judgement or decision of a court in any civil or criminal cause. Now *rare* in popular use; still technically applied to the decisions of the ecclesiastical and admiralty courts.

c **1386** CHAUCER *Doctor's T.* 172 The Iuge answerde: Of this in his absence I may nat yeue diffynytyue sentence. **1446** in *Cov. Leet-bk.* 228 Declaracion of a centens yeuon for the priour & Couent of the Cathedrall churche of our Lady of Couentre ayeynest John Bredon. **1477** *Rolls of Parlt.* VI. 182/2 [The French king] by sentence judiciall dismyssed them and their pleggest oute of the seid Courte. **1535** COVERDALE *Isa.* v. 23 These gyue sentence with the vngodly for rewardes. **1550** *Reg. Privy Council Scot.* I. 97 My Lord Governour and Lordis of Secreit Counsale, efter lang reasoning upoun the allegeance forsaid be sentence interlocutor, fand that conforme to the lawis [etc.]. **1585** GREENE *Planetom.* Wks. (Grosart) V. 100 Sol, we haue agreed that your sensure shal stand for a sentence, and therefore I wil not inueigh against your verdict. **1590** SWINBURNE *Testaments* 9 These two sentences, haue these two contrary effects.., *the sentence interlocutorie*, may be reuoked at any time so longe as the principall cause dependeth vndecided. But the *sentence definitiue* cannot be reuoked. **1717** E. MILLER *Acc. Cambr.* 30 Tho' he prosecuted his Action with all the Vigour he could, it was about seven Years before it came to a Sentence, which was at last, in Favour of the Townsman. **1760-72** H. BROOKE *Fool of Qual.* (1809) III. 44 No civil or criminal sentence could take place, till the voice of the judge was affirmed by the court. **1817** SELWYN *Law Nisi Prius* (ed. 4) II. 946 By the sentence of a French court of admiralty it appeared, that the ship insured, 'warranted American', had been condemned as enemy's property. **1838** W. BELL *Dict. Law Scot.* s.v. *Decree*, A decree or decreet is the final judgment or sentence of a court, whereby the question at issue between the parties is decided. **1857** *Act 20 & 21 Vict.* c. 85 §16 A Sentence of Judicial Separation..may be obtained, either by the Husband or the Wife, on the ground of Adultery [etc.].

transf. **1702** *Eng. Theophrastus* 3 They cannot pass a just sentence upon the performances of their respective writers.

c. The judicial determination of the punishment to be inflicted on a convicted criminal. Hence, the punishment to which a criminal is sentenced. Also *transf.*

c **1340** HAMPOLE *Prose Tr.* 7 For-thy I had na stabyll purpos in gude, na perfite contrycyone, tharefore sentence of dampnacyone ffelle one me. *c* **1450** *Mirk's Festial* 245 þogh a woman by Goddys sentence bere hur childyr wyth so gret penance. **1588** SHAKS. *L.L.L.* I. i. 302 Sir I will pronounce your sentence: You shall fast a Weeke with Branne and water. **1604** —— *Oth.* I. iii. 119 If you do finde me foule, in her report, The Trust, the Office, I do hold of you, Not onely take away, but let your Sentence Euen fall vpon my life. **1662** *Tryal Sir H. Vane* 51 After that, out comes the Judgement or Sentence of Death against him. **1747** V. MATHIAS in Jesse *Selwyn & Contemp.* (1843) I. 118 I am now to desire you would contrive for to-morrow, that I may hear the Lord High Steward's speech, and sentence passed. **1769** BLACKSTONE *Comm.* IV. xxix. 373 When sentence of death, the most terrible and highest judgment in the laws of England, is pronounced. **1891** H. MATTHEWS in *Law Times* XCII. 96/1 A convict who gains by steady industry the maximum number of marks during each day of his sentence. **1893** LELAND *Mem.* I. 144 A noted murderer under sentence of death.

fig. **1715** DE FOE *Fam. Instruct.* I. i. (1841) I. 21 We are all under a sentence of death for the first Man's sin. **1842** KINGSLEY *Lett.* (1878) I. 61 Our sentence is to labour from the cradle to the grave. **1881** JOWETT *Thucyd.* I. 197 No one when venturing on a perilous enterprise ever yet passed a sentence of failure on himself.

†**d.** ***dark, hard sentence***: a difficult problem. (In Bible translations used to render Heb. *ḥīdāh*, Aram. *ăḥīdā* enigma, LXX πρόβλημα, Vulg. *propositio*.)

Cf. *hard sentence* (in sense 7) Chaucer *Astrol.* Prol. §1. **1535** COVERDALE *2 Chron.* ix. 1 The quene of rich Arabia ..came with a very greate tryne to Ierusalem..to proue Salomon with darke sentences. **1539** BIBLE (Great) *Ps.* lxxviii. 2, I wyll declare hard sentences of olde. **1563** SHUTE *Archit.* B iij, We can neither know or yet discusse the measures and harde sentences or questions of Symetrie.

4. a. A quoted saying of some eminent person, an apophthegm. Also, a pithy or pointed saying, an aphorism, maxim. *Obs.* exc. *Hist.*

In *Rhetoric* formerly used (after L. *sententia*) as the rendering of Gr. γνώμη GNOME[1].

c **1380** WYCLIF in *Sel. Eng. Wks.* II. 399 Crist seiþ to hise apostlis, ȝe shulen be blessid whanne men shulen curse you. .. And if þe Chirche were wel enformed of þis sentence.. men shulden not drede feyned cursingis. *c* **1386** CHAUCER *Man of Law's T.* 15 Herke what is the sentence of the wise: Bet is to dyen than haue Indigence. *c* **1420** *Pallad. on Husb.* I. 108 Now euery word and sentence is of cure. **1533** MORE *Answ. Poysoned Bks.* Wks. 1087/1 Then cometh there also on this part yᵉ saienges or sentences of yᵉ holy fathers. **1567** *Trial of Treas.* A iij, The wyse mans sentence. **1580** LYLY *Euphues* Wks. 1902 II. 158 Hungry stomackes are not to be fed with sayings against surfettings, nor thirst to be quenched with sentences against drunkennesse. **1593** SHAKS. *Lucr.* 244 Who feares a sentence or an old mans saw, Shall by a painted cloth be kept in awe. **1601** B. JONSON *Poet.* I. ii. 103 Thou speakest sentences, old Bias. **1657** J. SMITH *Myst. Rhet.* 244 Gnome is a figure when we bring in a sentence or such a remarkable saying of anothers to the same purpose with the Author. *a* **1679** HOBBES *Rhet.* (1840) 476 To hear a young man speak sentences, is ridiculous. **1727** POPE, etc. *Art of Sinking* xiii. 115 A poet or orator would have no more to do but to send to the particular traders in each kind,..to the apothegmatist for his sentences, &c. **1750** JOHNSON *Rambler* No. 79 ¶1 A Greek writer of sentences has laid down as a standing maxim, that he who believes not another on his oath, knows himself to be perjured. **1823** GILLIES tr. *Aristotle's Rhet.* II. xxi. 328 Sentences have great weight in discourse for two reasons. **1962** T. P. DUNNING in Davis & Wrenn *English & Medieval Studies* 178 That element of the *sentence* expressed by Pandarus in Book 1—Fortune as the way of the world—is here stated at some length by Criseyde.

b. In generalized use: Aphoristic speech, sententiousness. *Obs.* exc. *poet.*

c **1530** *Crt. of Love* 5, I write, as he that none intelligence Of metres hath, ne floures of sentence. **1649** MILTON *Eikon.* 32 A discourse full of sentence. **1917** T. S. ELIOT *Prufrock & Other Observations* 15 Politic, cautious, and meticulous; Full of high sentence, but a bit obtuse.

5. An indefinite portion of a discourse or writing; a 'passage'. Now only (with approach to sense 6), a short passage of Scripture in liturgical use.

c **1400** *Rule of St. Benet* (Prose) lv. 36 Þabbes sal ta yeme of þis sentence of þe dedis of þe apostils. *c* **1420** *Wars Alex.* (Prose) (E.E.T.S.) 46 Scho was riȝte sory and wrote a lettre vn-till hym þat contened this sentence [etc.]. **1549** *Bk. Com. Prayer, Communion,* Then shall folowe for the Offertory, one or mo, of these Sentences of holy scripture. **1557** NORTH *Gueuara's Diall Pr.* IV. Argt. (1568) 106 b, That man..that vouchsafeth not to spend one hower of the day to read a graue sentence of some good booke. **1611** COTGR., *Rubrique*, ..a special title or sentence of the Law written, or printed, in red. **1639** in *Brit. Mag.* (1834) VI. 379 For settyng up the sentences of Scripture in the church, o. 3. o. **1753** CHALLONER *Cath. Chr. Instr.* 94 After which he reads a short Sentence of Scripture.

6. a. A series of words in connected speech or writing, forming the grammatically complete expression of a single thought; in popular use often (= PERIOD *sb.* 10), such a portion of a composition or utterance as extends from one full stop to another. In *Grammar*, the verbal expression of a proposition, question, command, or request, containing normally a subject and a predicate (though either of these may be omitted by ellipsis).

In grammatical use, though not in popular language, a 'sentence' may consist of a single word, as in L. *algeo* 'I am cold', where the subject (= I) is expressed by the ending of the verb. English grammarians usually recognize three classes: simple sentences, complex sentences (which contain one or more subordinate clauses), and compound sentences (which have more than one subject or predicate).

1447 BOKENHAM *Seyntys, Agnes* 682 Fro sentence to sentence, I dar wele seyn, I hym haue folwyde euen by & by. **1526** *Pilgr. Perf.* (W. de W. 1531) 160 Euery lettre, syllable, worde, & sentence of his prayer & duty from the begynnynge to yᵉ ende. **1538** ELYOT *Dict., Tetracolon,* a sentence hauyng .iiii. membres. **1600** SHAKS. *A.Y.L.* III. ii. 144 At euerie sentence end; Will I Rosalinda write. **1631** in Rymer *Fœdera* XIX. 305 The Statute before mentioned, or any Clause, Sentence, Matter or Thing whatsoever therein conteyned. *a* **1653** BINNING *Princ. Chr. Relig.* Wks. (1735) 27 There is some hidden Secret that you must search for, that is inclosed within the Covering of Words and Sentences. **1712** ADDISON *Spect.* No. 550 ¶5, I have so well preserved my Taciturnity that I do not remember to have violated it with three Sentences in the space of almost two Years. **1728** CHAMBERS *Cycl.* s.v., Every Sentence comprehends at least Three Words. **1748** RICHARDSON *Clarissa* VII. 177, I would not lose a sentence that I could gain from lips so instructive. **1787** REID *Let. to Gregory* 26 Aug., In speech, the true natural unit is a sentence. **1819** SCOTT *Ivanhoe* iii, His displeasure was expressed in broken sentences. **1848** THACKERAY *Van. Fair* l, The combat, which we describe in a sentence or two, lasted for many weeks in poor Amelia's heart. **1870** JEVONS *Elem. Logic* vii. (1875) 61 What the logician calls a proposition the grammarian calls a sentence.

b. *Music.* A complete idea, usually consisting of two or four phrases.

1891 in *Century Dict.* **1893** SHEDLOCK tr. *Riemann's Dict. Mus.* s.v. *Phrase Signs,* The chief elements in Riemann's system are:..(3) The figures..showing period structure (2 for the point of stress of the first group of two measures;.. 8 for the point of stress of the whole sentence).

c. *Logic.* A correctly ordered series of signs or symbols that expresses a proposition in an artificial or logical language.

1937 A. SMEATON tr. *Carnap's Logical Syntax Lang.* I. 26 We have already surveyed all the possible ways of constructing sentences and numerical expressions in Language I. **1957** P. SUPPES *Introd. Logic* (1959) iii. 54 A sentence is a formula which has no free variables. **1976** EVANS & MCDOWELL *Truth & Meaning* p. viii, Conditions (1), (2), and (3) require that *L* be a logically perfect language, with sentences free from structural or lexical ambiguity.

†**7. a.** The thought or meaning expressed, as distinguished from the wording; the sense, substance, or gist (of a passage, a book, etc.). *Obs.*

a **1225** *Ancr. R.* 348 Nimeð nu god ȝeme, vor hit is almest Seint Beornardes sentence. **1340** HAMPOLE *Pr. Consc.* 9571 Þus may þis tretice, with þe sentence, Pryk and stirre a mans conscience. *c* **1380** WYCLIF *Wks.* (1880) 429 As lordis of englond han the bible in freynsch, so it were not aȝenus resoun þat þey hadden þe same sentense in Engliȝsch. *c* **1386** CHAUCER *Nun's Pr. T.* 345 *Mulier est hominis confusio*: Madame, the sentence of this latyn is, Womman is mannes Ioye and al his blis. *c* **1450** *Godstow Reg.* 27 The sentence of thys dede is, how John of synt John hathe grauntyd [etc.]. **1502** *Ord. Crysten Men* (W. de W. 1506) I. ii. 11 Or in othir langage or wordes betokenynge the same sentence. **1519** *Interl. Four Elem.* (Percy Soc.) 7 Perhappis in this matter muche eloquence Sholde make it tedyous or hurt the sentence. *a* **1555** LATIMER in Foxe *A. & M.* (1563) 1323/1 They..also added vnto his wordes, to alter his sentence. **1561** *Maitland Club Misc.* III. 284 He was sa far distant fra hyr he mycht not heyr the sentence of hyr word.

†**b.** ***in sentence***: = 'in substance'. Very common in Lydgate, often as a mere expletive. *Obs.*

c **1412** LYDG. *Reson & Sens.* 515 Thow hast wel sayed, For which I wil, in sentence, That thow yive me Audience. **1421** —— *Horse, Goose & Sheep* 9 in *Pol. Rel. & L. Poems* 15 Parties assemblid..Weren admitted to shewen in sentence, Ground of here quarell. *c* **1449** PECOCK *Repr.* III. viii. 322 And an other cronicler seith in sentence thus [etc.]. **1500–20** DUNBAR *Poems* xviii. 48 Gude James the Ferd..In sentens said full subtillie, 'Do weill', [etc.].

†**c.** In generalized use: Significance. *Obs.*

c **1386** CHAUCER *Prol.* 306 Noght o word spak he moore than was neede And that was..short and quyk and ful of hy sentence. **1402** *Repl. to J. Upland* in *Pol. Poems* (1859) II. 59 Now, Jak, to thi questions, nedes me moste answer, althouȝ thei wanten sentence and good thrift bothe. *c* **1430** LYDG. *Min. Poems* (Percy Soc.) 179 Problemys of olde likenesse and figures, Whiche proved been fructuous of sentence. **1563** FOXE *A. & M.* 828/2 To the xxviii. [article] he sayth as it lyeth it hath no sentence: nor he cannot vnderstande it. **1589** PUTTENHAM *Eng. Poesie* III. xxii. (Arb.) 262 Now if this disorder be in a whole clause which carieth more sentence then a word, it is then worst of all.

†**8.** Intelligence, insight, sound judgement. *Obs.*

c **1400** *Rule of St. Benet* (Prose) xxvii. 22 On alle maner sal þabbes entirmete hir Al maner of sentence at muster til hir sep. **1513** *Life Hen. V* (1911) 3, I have not enterprised the compilacion of this present volume vppon noe presumpcion of witt, sentence, or cunninge of my self. **1523** LD. BERNERS *Froiss.* I. cccxcix. 692 There Phylyppe Dartuell, by great sentence, shewed them fro poynt to poynt, the ryght that they thought they had in their quarell.

9. *attrib.* and *Comb.*, (sense 6) ***sentence-accent***, ***-building***, ***-completion***, ***-construction***, ***-form***, ***-formation***, ***-forming***, ***-formula***, ***-frame***, ***-intonation***, ***-making***, ***-meaning***, ***-melody***, ***-modifier***, ***-monger***, ***-pattern***, ***-rhythm***, ***-stress***, ***structure***, ***-type***; ***sentence-final***, ***-forming***, ***-initial*** (also ***-initially*** adv.), ***-modifying***, ***-opening*** adjs.; (sense 3) ***sentence-giving***; **sentence adverb** *Gram.*, an adverb used to qualify a complete sentence (see also quot. 1892); also **sentence adverbial**; **sentence-day**, the day of a trial in which the sentence is pronounced; **sentence diagram**, a schematic representation of the relationships between the constituent parts of a sentence; so **sentence diagramming**; **sentence-money**, **silver** *Scots Law* (see quot. 1747); **sentence-particle** *Gram.* (see quot. 1953); **sentence-token** *Logic* (see quot. 1936); **sentence-word**, a word that serves as a sentence.

1892 H. SWEET *New Eng. Gram.* I. 127 *Sentence-adverbs. The answer to the question *is he here?* can be either the affirmative *yes* or the negative *no*. It is evident that *yes* and *no* are sentence-modifying adverbs and at the same time sentence-words like come! John!, alas! **1916** E. A. SONNENSCHEIN *New Eng. Gram.* 33 Several..adverbs..may be used to qualify the sentence as a whole; when so used they are called sentence-adverbs. *Ibid.*, Some sentence-adverbs (especially 'too', 'else', 'only', 'even') may be used in such a way as to emphasize the word which stands next to them in the sentence. **1980** *Amer. Speech 1976* LI. 168 Among the adverbs were some that are often classed together as sentence adverbs: *luckily, wisely, foolishly, rightly.* **1964** KATZ & POSTAL *Integrated Theory of Linguistics Descriptions* iv. 95 The answers to yes-no questions are in fact *sentence adverbials, i.e., *yes, no,* and perhaps by extension *maybe, of course, certainly,* etc. **1921** H. E. PALMER *Princ. Lang.-Study* 22 Exercises exist which ensure accuracy in..*sentence-building. **1966** J. DERRICK *Teaching Eng. to Immigrants* v. 205 Other *sentence-completion exercises, in which there can be slightly more freedom of choice, can consist of 'half sentences' in which part or whole of the subject or predicate is missing and has to be filled in by the pupil. **1921** H. E. PALMER *Princ. Lang.-Study* iii. 58 The learner need know little about the sciences dealing with inflexions, *sentence-construction, or meanings. **1662** *Tryal Sir H. Vane* 51 Wednesday June 11. being the *Sentence-day. **1937** MOFFETT & JOHNSON *Basic Writing* 509 A *sentence diagram is merely a device by which the structure of a sentence can be..shown. *Ibid.* 632 (Index) *Sentence diagramming. **1977** *Language* LIII. 493/1 The syntax section is fully and competently developed... L compares phrase-structure trees to traditional sentence diagrams, with which many students will be familiar. **1959** *College Composition & Communication* May 91 The question of just what ends we hope to attain by the use of any system of sentence diagraming. **1949** *Sentence-final [see *intonationally* adv. s.v. INTONATION[1]]. **1978** *Language* LIV. 79 Lehmann observes that the interrogative in Japanese is marked by placing *ka* after verbs in sentence-final position. **1930** T. SASAKI *On Lang. of R. Bridges' Poetry* 92 The language of poetry is in not a few points similar to primitive language, which usually favours 'gegenständliches Denken', and therefore prefers attributive *sentence-form. **1965** *Language* XLI. 372 A form that differs from any elementary sentence-form of the language. **1935** G. K. ZIPF *Psycho-Biol. of Lang.* v. 185 They [*sc.* substantive and verb] are not a *sine qua non* of *sentence-formation. **1921** H. E. PALMER *Princ. Lang.-Study* 25 In choosing the units of our vocabulary we may be guided by..*sentence-forming utility. **1936** J. KANTOR *Objective Psychol. Gram.* III. xvii. 241 Those grammarians who call the verb a sentence-forming word, a phenomenon word, or an *Aussagewort*, also pay tribute to its action-referring character and save themselves from a too great stress of time. **1932** W. L. GRAFF *Lang.* I. iii. 132 Because it [*sc.* How do you do?] is itself a sentence, not merely sentence material, it may be termed a *sentence formula or a formular sentence. **1962** G. A. MILLER in *Amer. Psychologist* XVII. 756/1 One opinion is that we learn '*sentence frames' that we keep filed away in a sort of sentence-frame dictionary. The declarative, interrogative, affirmative, negative, active, passive, compound, complex, etc., sentence frames are all supposed to be learned separately and to have no intrinsic relation to one another. **1661** BLOUNT *Glossogr.* (ed. 2), *Judication*, ..*sentence-giving. **1964** *Language* XL. 6 Mere *sentence-initial position of *Wh* does not suffice to differentiate between inversion and noninversion. **1978** *Ibid.* LIV. 85 Sentence initial subjects in Japanese and English may be viewed as most distant from the verb. **1976** *Word 1971* XXVII. 302 This word is then placed *sentence-initially. **1934** J. J. HOGAN *Outl. Eng. Philol.* I. iv. 25 It [*sc.* the sentence] has a musical tune, *Sentence-Intonation. **1870** WHITNEY *Germ. Gramm.* Suppl. 3 The main peculiarities of German *sentence-making. **1945** *Mind* LIV. 366 The vital question 'how separate words.. can combine to yield *sentence-meanings' is dealt with very summarily. **1922** O. JESPERSEN *Language* I. iv. 97 The heightened interest in everything concerning 'accent' (stress and pitch) has also led to investigations of sentence-stress and *sentence-melody. **1928** H. POUTSMA *Gram. Late Mod. Eng.* (ed. 2) I. I. v. 320 The question whether an adverbial adjunct is a *sentence-modifier or a word-modifier, is of considerable importance. *Ibid.* i. 101 Weak *do* is used in connexion with *sentence-modifying *not*. **1747** *Acts of Sederunt* (1790) 397 Whereas Sheriffs and stewards have at present no other legal reward, for doing their duty, than *sentence-money, which is sort of poundage out of the sums decreed for. **1847** *Blackw. Mag.* July 46 Nor can he be simply transposed as many a decent *sentence-monger may. **1962** J. SÖDERLIND in F. Behre *Contrib. Eng. Syntax* 117 This is a bold type, found in *sentence-opening subject position. **1934** PRIEBSCH & COLLINSON *German Lang.* II. xi. 445 German has one Greek characteristic which makes it neater and fuller of expressive shades than English, viz. the use of *sentence-particles (*ja, doch*..etc.) and their cumulations (*ja doch*..etc.). **1953** *Trans. Philol. Soc. 1952* 6 The name 'sentence particle' (*satzpartikel*) was given by Kuhn to all unstressed and weak-stressed words which modify not one part of the sentence but the whole of it, and are therefore syntactically independent parts of the sentence. **1935** G. K. ZIPF *Psycho-Biol. of Lang.* v. 201 The question of equilibrium which lies at the root of the development of all *sentence-patterns. **1926** Fowler *Mod. Eng. Usage* 560/1 The separating adverb could have been placed outside the infinitive with little or in most cases no damage to the *sentence-rhythm. **1957** R. W. Zandvoort *Handbk. Eng. Gram.* vi. 239 The different word order..may be due to a desire for variety, as much as to the requirements of sentence-rhythm. **1641** *Sc. Acts Chas. I* (1870) V. 412/2 All *sentance silver tuelve pennyes of þe pund and other exactiones imposed wpoun sentances..to be pronounced by þe saidis Judges. **1884** H. Sweet in *13th Addr. Philol. Soc.* 93 *Sentence-stress, intonation, and, generally speaking, the higher phonetic analysis of our dialects, are almost ignored. **1872** Minto *Eng. Prose Lit.* Introd. 8 So defective were they in *sentence-structure, that [etc.]. **1936** *Jrnl. Philos.* XXXIII. 703 A **sentence-token* is a particular set of particular symbolic marks (of a sort, let us say, to represent a complete assertion). **1976** A. N. Prior *Doctrine of Propositions* i. 35 We may say at once that the dominant tendency in Logic is for the term 'proposition' to be used not for a 'sentence-token' but for a 'sentence-type'. **1933** L. Bloomfield *Language* x. 169 The use of the secondary phoneme [!] gives us the *sentence-type of exclamation. **1848** C. Bunsen in *Rep. Brit. Assoc. Advancem. Sci.* 282 The Egyptian root is not the unalterable particle, or rather *sentence-word, of the Chinese. **1889** Mivart *Orig. Hum. Reas.* 260 When used by a young child (or primitive man), sentence-words require to be supplemented by gesture-signs.

Hence **'sentencehood** [-hood], the condition of constituting a grammatically complete sentence.

1961 *Language Learning* XI. 175 These..are some of the requirements which one might reasonably set for an adequate theory of English 'sentencehood'. **1967** *Philos. Rev.* LXXVI. 151 In many sentences 'probable' can replace 'possible' without destroying sentencehood.

sentence ('sɛntəns), *v.* Also 7 **sentense**. [ad. F. *sentencier*, f. *sentence* sentence *sb.* Cf. med.L. *sententiāre*.]

†**1.** *intr.* To pass judgement. *Obs.*

c **1400** *Pilgr. Sowle* (Caxton 1483) iii. v. 53 Ye haue falsely sentenced ageyne the trewe parte by cause that he was poure and made nought your purs peysen so heuy. **1592** Warner *Alb. Eng.* viii. xxxix. (1612) 191 Like yoong Salomon, in sentencing betwixt Two mothers. **1624** Bedell *Lett.* x. 130 A Breue formed to sentence for the King. **1710** Norris *Chr. Prud.* iii. 127 A Habit of Sentencing, as I may call it, or Determining, particularly in those things which are not defined by any Law.

†**2.** *trans.* To adjudge, or apportion by legal decision. *Obs.*

1616 Chapman *Hesiod's Bk. Days* 9 The Day, when all litigious goods, Are iustly sentenc't, by the peoples voyces.

†**3.** To decree or order judicially. *Obs.*

1502 Arnolde *Chron.* (1811) 158 Therfore, we may noo more doo for that [it] is sentenced vpon that reame that this enemy hath to wynne it. *a* **1513** Fabyan *Chron.* vii. (1811) 351 Lastly it was sentencyd that the barons shuld restore all suche goodes, as they & theyre company had taken. **1607** Shaks. *Cor.* iii. iii. 22 Let them..Inforce the present execution Of what we chance to Sentence. **1613** Purchas *Pilgrimage* (1614) 387 One example of iustice is admirable, which he sentenced on the Gouernour of Casbin. **1652** Needham tr. *Selden's Mare Cl., Dom. Maris* 5 That Convention was onely instituted for the execution of such things as were formerly sentenced. **1660** *Trial Regic.* 71 But you may see by his sentencing what he did.

b. *transf.* (*nonce-use*).

1838 D. Jerrold *Men of Character* (1851) 30 'He had better keep his bed to-day?' asked Faddle benevolently. 'Yes, to-day', sentenced [Dr.] Saffron.

†**4.** To decide judicially. *Obs.*

1586 *Let. to Earle Leycester* 24 Forasmuch as she stood obstinately in the deniall of matter..most iustly sentenced against her. **1602** Fulbecke *1st Pt. Parall.* 5 As well these which are determinable by the Law of Nations, as these which are sentenced by the Ciuil Law and other Lawes. **1632** *Star Chamber Cases* (1886) 109 This cause came to be heard and sentenced this day. **1665** J. Webb *Stone-Heng* (1725) 160 The matter in Debate was by the parochial Assembly sentenced at first. **1681** *Heylin's De Jure Par. Episc.* Pref. 2 If..any Controversie arose touching Lands or Inheritance, they sentenced it.

†**5.** To declare judicially or authoritatively. Chiefly with complement. *Obs.*

a **1617** Bayne *On Eph.* (1658) 51 Justification doth sentence this of mee, that I am just before God. *a* **1619** Fotherby *Atheom.* (1622) Pref. 17 The Heathen Poet: who sentenceth all wicked, and licencious liuers, to bee no better, then a kinde of pragmaticall Atheists. **1625** Laud *Serm.* 19 June 18 They sinne against their owne conscience..by sentencing Good Euill, and Euill Good. **1662** Hibbert *Body Divinity* ii. 95 The clearness of his judgment..sentenceth the place venerable. **1680** H. More *Apocal. Apoc.* 211 An auspicious Title, signifying that they whose names were found there, should be sentenced worthy of eternal Life.

†**6.** To pass judgement on (a person or his actions, the merit of anything). *Obs.*

1597 Shaks. *2 Hen. IV*, v. ii. 98 After this cold considerance, sentence me. **1605** Verstegan *Dec. Intell.* Epist. 1, I know I..am lykest to receaue most controlement of such as are least able to sentence mee. **1642** Milton *Apol. Smect.* Wks. 1851 III. 251 His sufficiency must now be sentenc't, not by pondering the reason he shewes, but by calculating the yeares he brings. **1809** Malkin *Gil Blas* x. v. ¶4 Far from sentencing a piece on its first representation, we are jealous of its apparent merit while aided by scenic deception.

7. To pronounce sentence upon; to condemn *to* a punishment.

1592 Warner *Alb. Eng.* viii. xl. 175 He being then indighted, Was hardly found a Felon, and too stricktly sentenc'st so. **1607** Shaks. *Cor.* v. iv. 8 Our throats are sentenc'd, and stay vppon execution. **1634** Brereton *Trav.* (Chetham Soc.) 70 Slaves sentenced to the gallies. **1681** Flavel *Right. Man's Ref.* 179 Though they were sentenced to death, yea though they sentenced themselves. *a* **1700** Evelyn *Diary* 20 Dec. 1684, The offender was sentenc'd and repriev'd. *a* **1714** Abp. Sharp *Serm.* Wks. 1754 II. 94 A wretch,..being convicted of grievous crimes, and thereupon justly sentenced to suffer death for them. **1838** Thirlwall *Greece* xxxvii. V. 17 They sentenced Phœbidas to a fine of 10,000 drachmas. **1848** Dickens *Dombey* xxxiv, She was tried, and sentenced. **1849** Macaulay *Hist. Eng.* v. I. 566 He was hastily tried, convicted, and sentenced to be hanged.

transf. **1884** Browning *Family* 31 'Sole remedy is amputation'... His three sons heard their mother sentenced. **1895** Baring-Gould *Noémi* xxiv. (ed. 2) 339 Which had lighted up the face of the man sentenced to a living tomb.

8. In various nonce-uses: **a.** To put into sentences. Also *absol.* or *intr.* To compose sentences.

1623 Lisle *Ælfric on O. & N. Test.* To Rdr. 32 It would giue vs occasion either in wording or sentensing the principall parts thereof, to looke back a little into this outworne dialect. **1856** Ruskin *Mod. Paint.* III. iv. x. §22 Let a man have..a facility of rhyming or sentencing.

b. To influence by maxims. Also *to sentence it*: to speak in aphorisms.

1628 Feltham *Resolves* i. xciii. 272 Let me heare one wise man sentence it, rather then twenty Fooles, garrulous in their lengthened tattle. **1685** *Gracian's Courtier's Orac.* Pref., So it is as impossible by short documents to sentence them into their Wits and good Manners again.

Hence **sentenced** ('sɛntənst) *ppl. a.* Also **'sentencer**, one who sentences.

1589 Puttenham *Eng. Poesie* iii. xxiii. (Arb.) 270 He who can make the best and most differences of things by reasonable and wittie distinction is to be the fittest judge or sentencer of decencie. **1631** Heywood *2nd Pt. Fair Maid of West* v. L 4, The thief is found:..I beg That I may be his sentencer. ? *c* **1637** Cleveland *Elegy on Ben Jonson* 31 When thy maim'd Statue hath a Sentenc'd Face, And Looks that are the Horror of the Place. **1659** Gauden *Tears Ch.* iv. xxiii. 628 It becomes not me to sentence either the sentenced, or sentencers that adjudged him to death. **1801** Southey *Thalaba* iv. ix, Haruth and Maruth went, The chosen Sentencers. **1813** Byron *Corsair* iii. x, He had brooded lone O'er promised pangs to sentenced guilt fore-shown. **1890** *Athenæum* 10 May 603/3 A friend..convinces the Home Secretary that it was the dog, not the sentenced man, who pulled the trigger and shot the victim. **1902** *Westm. Gaz.* 7 Feb. 2/3 It is strange that the sight of a young fellow breaking down under his sentence should excite anyone, and particularly the sentencer, to such abuse.

sentenciall, obs. form of sentential *a.*

sentenel, obs. form of sentinel.

sentener, obs. form of centenier.

‖**sententia** (sɛn'tɛnʃɪə). Pl. -æ (erron. -a). [L.] = sentence *sb.* 4 a. Also in mod. use, a thought or reflection.

1917 E. E. Cummings *Let.* 5 May (1969) 19 The immemorially delightful sententia of a pocket-size sailor.. i.e. 'submarines pooh-pooh'. **1926** C. Connolly *Let.* 25 Dec. in *Romantic Friendship* (1975) 199, I sent you one diary for quotations and the other was for sententiae. **1933** R. Tuve *Seasons & Months* i. 43 The Seasons motif found new uses... It became a vehicle for 'sententia', folk proverbs which appealed to generations fed upon Hending and Alfred. **1960** *Times* 29 Sept. 15/5 Those platitudinous *sententiae* that pass for conversational small change. **1964** C. S. Lewis *Discarded Image* vii. 191 Chaucer begins with a *Sententia* or maxim in the *Parlement*. **1971** *English Studies* LII. 456 An attempt is made to trace the process by which the popular proverb attained equal status with the literary *sententia*.

sentential (sɛn'tɛnʃəl), *a.* [ad. L. *sententiāl-is* in the form of a sentence, f. *sententia*: see sentence *sb.* and -al[1].]

†**1.** Containing, or of the nature of, 'sentences' or 'maxims'. *Obs.*

a **1475** Ashby *Active Policy* 51 Right so though I haue not seien scripture Of many bookes right sentenciall [etc.]. **1582** T. Watson *Centurie of Love* lxxxix. (Arb.) 125 The two first staffes of this Sonnet are altogether sententiall, and euerie one verse of them is grownded vpon a diuerse reason and authoritie from the rest. **1645** Ussher *Body Div.* (1647) 13 Containing principally..holy sentences, (whence also they may be called Sententiall).

2. a. Pertaining to a sentence or series of words in syntactical connexion.

1646 Sir T. Browne *Pseud. Ep.* i. iv. 15 Verball expressions, or sententiall significations. **1775** T. Sheridan *Art of Reading* 142 Of the accentual speech I have mentioned two kinds; one verbal, the other sentential. **1776** Geddes *Prosp. New Transl. Bible* 127 My translation..is neither literal nor verbal; but, if I may use the term, strictly sentential. **1824** L. Murray *Eng. Gram.* (ed. 5) I. 379 There are two sorts of [poetical] pauses, one for sense and one for melody, perfectly distinct from each other. The former may be called sentential, the latter, harmonic pauses. The sentential pauses are those which are known to us by the name of stops. **1956** J. H. Greenberg in Saporta & Bastian *Psycholinguistics* (1961) 471/2 *Sentential meaning.* The meaning of a maximal linguistic structure (i.e., of a sentence). **1965** N. Chomsky *Aspects of Theory of Syntax* ii. 100 Nouns with sentential Complements (such as 'the *idea* that he might succeed'). **1978** *Studies in Eng. Lit.: Eng. Number* (Tokyo) 96 They are excluded either by Ross's 'rightward bounding constraint' and 'sentential subject constraint', or by Chomsky's 'subjacency condition'.

b. *Logic.* In collocations denoting logical operations relating to sentences or propositions; esp. as ***sentential calculus, connective, function***. Cf. propositional *a.* b.

1937 A. Smeaton tr. *Carnap's Logical Syntax of Lang.* iii. 91 Primitive sentences of the sentential calculus. *Ibid.* 138 Frege himself had already made a similar classification of all sentential functions into levels and kinds which also were arranged according to the kinds of their arguments. **1957** P. Suppes *Introd. Logic* iii. 43 We have developed the logic of the sentential connectives. **1966** *Math. Reviews* Jan. 7/1 The author presents a set of nine axiom schemes and two rules for the predicate calculus based on the infinite-valued sentential calculus of Lukasiewicz. **1976** G. Evans in Evans & McDowell *Truth & Meaning* viii. 215 Intuitionistic sentential connectives cannot be regarded as representing truth functions in any finite many-valued logic. **1976** A. R. Lacey *Dict. Philos.* 75 *x is red* can be called a propositional, statemental (rare) or sentential function, according as *blood is red* is regarded as a proposition, statement or sentence. Sentential functions are often called open sentences. The term *closed sentential function* is occasionally used of ordinary sentences.

3. Of the nature of a 'sentence' or final judicial decision. ? *Obs.*

a **1603** T. Cartwright *Confut. Rhem. N.T.* (1618) 121 The judgement of the Church doth not hinder the sententiall iudgement of our Sauiour. **1632** Lithgow *Trav.* x. 441 Seazing on their money be a sententiall forfeiture. **1677** Owen *Doctr. Justif.* iv. 186 No more is Justification the change of a person from inherent unrighteousness unto Righteousness, but a sentential Declaration of him to be Righteous. **1701** Beverley *Grand Apocal. Quest.* 9 After the Words going forth there is the Epoch of the 70 Weeks Fix'd; and in the Wise Provision of the Holy Spirit, we have an Explanation,..of the Words going forth by the Decree, or Sentential Word of the God of Israel.

4. *nonce-use.* Pertaining to opinion.

1792 D. Lloyd *Charact. Men*, etc. 22 Noisy discord and sentential strife.

sen'tentially, *adv.* *Obs.* or *rare.* Also 5–6 **sentencially**, **-yally**. [f. prec. (perh. not separately used until later) + -ly[2], after med.L. *sententiāliter*.]

1. By way of (judicial) sentence; judicially.

c **1400** *Pilgr. Sowle* (Caxton) ii. xliii. (1859) 50 To alle the remenaunt after, Iustice sentencyally seyd: goo, al ye condempned and foriuged to brenne withynne the fyre of Helle. **1447** Bokenham *Seyntys, Agnes* 262 Wherefore sentencyally I [the prefect] þe deuyse. *c* **1460** *Osney Reg.* 89, I axe þe saide Executours to þ[e] forsaide best..to þe saide church of Cudelynton and to my lordis aforsaide.. sentencially and diffinityfly to be condempned. **1544** Bale *Chron. Sir J. Oldcastle* 39 We sentencyallye and dyffynytyuely by this present wrytynge, iudge, declare and condemne the seyd syr Iohan Oldecastell..a most pernycyouse and detestable heretyque. **1673** Baxter *Let.* in *Answ. Dodwell* 83 Whether a man *de facto* have been drunk, ..it were hard judging sententially meerly on trust from others. **1681** Flavel *Meth. Grace* xxxii. 540 He is virtually condemned now, and will be sententially condemned in the judgment of the great day.

2. *rare.* In or by sentences.

1860 Worcester (citing *Coleridge*), *Sententially*, by means of sentences. In later Dicts.

sententiary (sɛn'tɛnʃɪərɪ), *sb.* (and *a.*) *Hist.* [f. med.L. *sententiāri-us* (see below), f. L. *sententia* sentence *sb.*: see -ary.]

A. *sb.* **a.** One who writes or utters sentences or aphorisms. **b.** A compiler of 'sentences' or opinions of doctors of the Church on theological questions. **c.** A commentator or lecturer on the Book of Sentences (see sentence *sb.* 2 b).

a **1603** T. Cartwright *Confut. Rhem. N.T.* (1618) 575 One of your owne, that lived about 170 yeares past, writing of your Sententiaries, alledgeth this place of the Apostle against them. **1629** H. Burton *Truth's Tri.* 2 Their school-diuinitie, as Gabriel Biel, one of their chiefe Sententiaries.. hath laid it downe. **1662** Hibbert *Body Divinity* i. 14 Using ..the Fathers, Scholasticks, Sententiaries, Canonists. **1817** Coleridge *'Blessed are ye!'* Introd. 14 The inspired poets, historians and sententiaries of the Jews. **1882–3** *Schaff's Encycl. Relig. Knowl.* III. 2490/1 The prevailing scholasticism [15th c.] and the method of the sententiaries.

¶ *erron.* A sententious discourse.

1843 Lytton *Last Bar.* ii. ii, It is easier to the warm heart of our cousin Warwick to preach sententiaries of sternness to his king, than to enforce the same by his own practice. *Ibid.* iii. vi, Though his sententiary as to nature and science lacked loyalty and respect.

B. *adj.* [*Mod.* as transl. of med.L. *sententiarius*.] ***Sententiary Bachelor***, a bachelor of the second order of theology in the Middle Ages, whose office was to lecture on the Sentences of Peter Lombard.

1889 in *Century Dict.* s.v. *Bachelor*.

So **sententi'arian**, †**sen'tentiarist** = prec. *sb.*

1677 Owen *Doctr. Justif.* Introd. 8 It is..to no purpose to handle the mysteries of the Gospel as if Holcot and Bricot, Thomas and Gabriel, with all the Sententiarists, Summists, and Quodlibetarians,..were to be raked out of their Graves to be our guides. **1882** Ogilvie, *Sententiarian.*

†**sen'tentiate**, *v.* *Obs. rare.* [f. med.L. *sententiāt-*, ppl. stem of *sententiāre*, f. L. *sententia*: see sentence *sb.* and -ate[3].] *trans.* To pronounce a judicial decision on, to adjudge or decide (a cause).

1593 Bilson *Govt. Christ's Ch.* 313 The fourth Councill of Carthage prohibiteth the bishop to heare and sententiate any mans cause without the presence of his Clergie. *a* **1693** *Urquhart's Rabelais* iii. xxxvii. 314 They very much doubted..if by any one part, or all of them together, it had been so judicially sententiated and awarded [*si plus iuridiquement eust esté par eux sententié*].

†**senˈtentiolist.** *Obs. rare*⁻¹. [f. L. *sententiol-a* a short aphorism, diminutive of *sententia* SENTENCE *sb.* + -IST.] A stickler for phrases.

1660 GAUDEN *Funeral Serm. Brounrig* 171 Not that he was such a Formalist, Verbalist, and Sententiolist, as could not endure any alteration of words, or phrases, or method, or manner of expressions in the Liturgie.

†**senˈtentioner.** *Obs. rare* [f. L. *sentent-ia* SENTENCE *sb.* + -ION[1] + -ER[1].] = SENTENTIARY *sb.*

1545 BALE *Image Both Ch.* I. vi. (1550) G iij b, Nothynge can be more euydent then this, specyally to them that hath red the tryflynge workes of the Sophisters, sentencyoners, schole doctoures, canonystes, and summystes. *Ibid.* ix. H ij, An infynyte table..of sentencyoners & summistes. **1581** J. BELL *Haddon's Answ. Osor.* 358 b, Wherein reygneth..For Evangelistes, cruell Canonistes, Copistes, Decretaries, Summularyes seditious Sententioners.

sententiosity (sɛntɛnʃɪˈɒsɪtɪ). *rare.* [f. L. *sententiōs-us* SENTENTIOUS + -ITY.] Sententiousness: also a sententious remark.

1646 SIR T. BROWNE *Pseud. Ep.* I. vi. 23 *Nosce teipsum* of Thales: *Nosce tempus* of Pittacus: *Nihil nimis* of Cleobulus; ..are but vulgar precepts in Morality, carrying with them nothing above the lyne, or beyond the extemporall sententiosity of common conceits with us. **1891** *Pall Mall Gaz.* 3 Feb. 7/1 A..dull compilation of sententiosities about the gross public and Byron and Shelley [etc.].

sententious (sɛnˈtɛnʃəs), *a.* Forms: 5 sentencyowse, 6 -cyous(e, -ci(o)us, sententius, -ouse, 6– sententious. [f. L. *sententiōsus* (Cicero), f. *sententia* SENTENCE *sb.*: see -OUS. Cf. F. *sentencieux*, OF. *sententieux* (13th c. in Hatz.-Darm.).]

†**1.** Full of meaning; also, of persons, full of intelligence or wisdom. *Obs.*

c **1440** *Promp. Parv.* 453/1 Sentencyowse, or full of sentence, *sententiosus.* **1503** HAWES *Examp. Virt.* Prol. 5 O vertuous Lydgat moche sentencyous. **1509** —— *Past. Pleas.* XIV. (Percy Soc.) 53 The boke of fame, whiche is sentencyous He [Chaucer] drewe hym selfe. **1513** DOUGLAS *Æneis* VI. Prol. 75 He is ane hie theolog sentencius. **1579** E. K. *Gloss. to Spenser's Sheph. Cal.* Nov. 83 This is a notable and sententious comparison. **1588** SHAKS. *L.L.L.* v. i. 3 Your reasons at dinner haue beene sharpe & sententious. **1622** PEACHAM *Compl. Gent.* vi. 43 Let your stile..bee..sententious, yea better furnished with sentences then words. **1648** CRASHAW *Delights of Muses* Wks. (1904) 135 Teares have Tongues, Sententious showers, o let them fall.

2. Of the nature of a 'sentence' or aphoristic saying.

1542 UDALL tr. *Erasmus* (*title*) Apophthegmes that is to saie, prompte, quicke, wittie and sentencious saiynges, of certain Emperours [etc.]. **1671** MILTON *P.R.* IV. 264 Brief sententious precepts. **1752** JOHNSON *Rambler* No. 205 ¶1 Sometimes [he] uttered grave reflections, and sententious maxims. **1841** D'ISRAELI *Amen. Lit.* (1867) 676 The depth of sentiment was contracted into sententious epigrams. **1908** *Q. Rev.* Apr. 341 Many sententious and quasi-proverbial lines are ascribed to him [Menander].

3. Of discourse, style, etc.: Abounding in pointed maxims, aphoristic. In recent use sometimes in bad sense, affectedly or pompously formal.

1509 HAWES *Past. Pleas.* VIII. (Percy Soc.) 29 To make of nought, reason sentencious, Clokynge a trouthe wyth colour tenebrous. **1579–80** NORTH *Plutarch, M. Cato* (1595) 373 His grace..in speaking..was pleasant and yet graue:..sententious, and yet familiar. **1624** GATAKER *Wife in Deed* 1 It hath this preeminence aboue most, if not all, the Bookes in the Bible; that many of them are Sententious, this consisteth all of Sentences. For what are Diuine Prouerbs, but select and choise Sentences. **1681** DINELEY *Jrnl.* in *Trans. Kilkenny Archæol. Soc.* Ser. II. II. 22 [The Irish language] is sharp and sententious, with quick apothegmes, and proper allusions. **1747** DODDRIDGE *Life Col. Gardiner* 175 [He] only replied, in his Sententious Manner, 'We have an Eternity to spend together'. **1770** LANGHORNE *Plutarch, Brutus* ¶4 In Greek he affected the sententious and laconic way [of speaking]. **1788** GIBBON *Decl. & F.* l. V. 187 Their wit [was] strong and sententious. **1782** MISS BURNEY *Cecilia* VI. i, The truth of this speech palliating its sententious absurdity, made Cecilia give up her faint attempt to soften him. **1833** MACAULAY *Ess., War Succ. Spain* ¶3 Lord Mahon is also a little too fond of uttering moral reflections in a style too sententious and oracular. **1850** W. IRVING *Mahomet* xxxix. (1853) 192 His ordinary discourse was grave and sententious. **1855** KINGSLEY *Westw. Ho!* ii, A long sententious letter, full of Latin quotations. **1858** G. MACDONALD *Phantastes* vii. (1878) 117 The sententious remarks of a pompous child. **1883** *Fortn. Rev.* Feb. 260 A person of gentlemanly bearing, small abilities, and sententious wisdom.

4. Of persons: Given to the utterance of maxims or pointed sayings. Now often in bad sense, addicted to pompous moralizing.

1598–9 B. JONSON *Case Altered* I. v. 289 Come, you are so sententious, my lord. **1600** SHAKS. *A.Y.L.* v. iv. 66 By my faith, he is very swift, and sententious. **1630** BRATHWAIT *Eng. Gentlem.* (1641) 5 This indifferencie towards fortune is excellently described by the sententious Seneca. **1700** CONGREVE *Way of World* II. v, Sententious Mirabell! Pr'ythee don't look with that violent and inflexible wise Face. **1732** BERKELEY *Alciphr.* ii. §7 Sallust was a sententious pedant. **1796** MME. D'ARBLAY *Camilla* V. 114 You grow so horrid sententious. **1823** SCOTT *Quentin D.* Introd., The Marquis de Hautlieu..was as short and sententious as French politeness permitted. **1880** MISS BRADDON *Just as I am* xxxvi, He was a sententious person.

†**5.** Of a symbol: Expressive of a whole sentence; opposed to *verbal*. *Obs.*

1586 FERNE *Blaz. Gentrie* 149 The matter whereof these armes do consist is the same that the auncient Hieroglyphiques weare with the Ægiptians, or the sententious Emblemes to the Greekes. **1701** GREW *Cosmol. Sacr.* II. vi. 68 The making of those Figures being tedious..put Men first upon contracting them..instead of Sententious Marks, to think of Verbal; such as the Chineses still retain.

†**6.** Of composition: Consisting of detached sentences. *Obs.*

1771 LUCKOMBE *Hist. Printing* 250 The first word of a new paragraph..is commonly put in Small Capitals... But this rule may be very well laid aside in matter which is too sententious and which would take up more Small Capitals than an ordinary..Fount could supply. *Ibid.* 386 Others are so sententious in their writing that they break off almost at every place that will admit of a Full-point.

senˈtentiously, *adv.* [f. prec. + -LY[2].]

†**1.** According to the sense; not word for word (of a translation). *Obs. rare*⁻¹.

c **1450** *Godstow Reg.* 26 A pore brodur and welwyller..hath purposed wyth goddys grace to make..fro latyn in-to englyssh, sentencyosly, as foloweth thys symple translacion.

2. In a sententious manner; tersely and pithily.

1481 CAXTON *Tulle of Old Age* I. (R. Suppl.), The sayd versis of the grete poete be of grete effect, purposed sentencyously in few wordis. **1513** BRADSHAW *St. Werburge* I. 3196 But as Salomon sayth sententiously, 'There may be no counseyll power ne prudence [etc.]'. **1622** PEACHAM *Compl. Gent.* x. 89 Iuvenal of Satyrists is the best, for..though he be sententiously tart, yet is his phrase cleare and open. **1716–17** BENTLEY *Serm.* xi. 372 Our Apostle concludes the whole with the words above, sententiously in way of Aphorism. **1862** GOULBURN *Pers. Relig.* 103 If the time which we can spare for such reading is short, books of thoughts, more or less sententiously expressed..will be found very serviceable. **1884** F. M. CRAWFORD *Rom. Singer* I. 31 'Who goes slowly goes surely', said the maestro sententiously.

sententiousness (sɛnˈtɛnʃəsnɪs). [f. SENTENTIOUS *a.* + -NESS.] The state or quality of being sententious.

1530 PALSGR. 269/1 *Sententiousnesse.* **1656** EARL MONM. tr. *Boccalini's Advts. fr. Parnass.* I. lxxxvi. 176 His brevity of succinct speaking, full of gravity, matter, sententiousness. **1725** BROOME *Notes to Pope's Odyss.* I. 41 The solemnity and sententiousness of this speech is taken notice of by Eustathius. **1828** D'ISRAELI *Chas. I,* I. iv. 80 The old King, with that pointed sententiousness he frequently used, said [etc.]. **1862** MISS BRADDON *Lady Audley* xxvii, 'When people make favourites, they are apt to be deceived by them', Miss Tonks answered, with icy sententiousness. **1870** MOZLEY *Univ. Serm.* iv. (1877) 94 The frigid sententiousness..of their utterance.

sentery, obs. form of SENTRY *sb.*[1]

†**senteur.** *Obs. rare*⁻¹. [a. F. *senteur* (14th c. in Hatz.-Darm.), f. *sent-ir* to smell + *-eur*: see SCENT *v.* and -OUR.] An odour or smell.

1601 HOLLAND *Pliny* XXVIII. xxviii. II. 314 Much seeking there is after his guts, for the pleasant senteurs and odors wherewith they be stuffed ful.

†**senthis.** *Obs. rare*⁻¹. ? Metathetic form of SITHENCE *adv.*

1501 DOUGLAS *Pal. Hon.* II. lvi, Senthis till me all veritie be kend, I repute better thus to mak ane end, Than ocht to say that suld heiraris engreif.

†**ˈsenticous,** *a. Obs. rare*⁻¹. [ad. L. *senticōsus*, f. *sentis* a thorn; see -OUS.] Prickly, thorny.

1657 TOMLINSON *Renou's Disp.* 338 It is a senticous shrub, low and hamated with many dark Prickles.

sentience (ˈsɛnʃɪəns). [f. SENTIENT *a.*: see -ENCE.] The condition or quality of being sentient, consciousness, susceptibility to sensation.

1839 POE *Fall House of Usher* Tales (1845) 74 This opinion [of Usher's], in its general form, was that of the sentience of all vegetable things. **1862** F. HALL *Hindu Philos. Syst.* 77 The Sānkhyas use them to prove, that the whole world, every constituent part of which is for an end, has for its author that which possesses no sentience,—nature. *a* **1881** A. BARRATT *Phys. Metempiric* (1883) 244 If physical *esse* is *intelligi*, and intelligence has been evolved from sentience, clearly physical objective existence has been produced by the ordinary impulse or inherent necessity of evolution.

sentiency (ˈsɛnʃɪənsɪ). [Formed as prec.; see -ENCY.] = prec.

a **1850** MRS. BROWNING *Isobel's Child* ix, All which broken sentiency And conclusion incomplete, Will gather and unite and climb To an immortality Good or evil. **1887** R. GARNETT *Life Carlyle* iv. 71 Reasoners who regard all phenomena as affections of their own sentiency. **1903** F. W. H. MYERS *Human Personality* II. 285 A universe in which even one being may have been summoned into a sentiency destined to inescapable pain.

sentient (ˈsɛnʃɪənt), *a.* and *sb.* [ad. L. *sentient-em*, pr. pple. of *sentīre* to feel.] **A.** *adj.*

1. That feels or is capable of feeling; having the power or function of sensation or of perception by the senses.

1632 GUILLIM *Heraldry* III. xxiv. (ed. 2) 250 Forasmuch as God would that the faculties both intelligent and sentient should predominate in the head [etc.]. *a* **1676** HALE *Prim. Orig. Man.* I. ii. (1677) 56 This acting of the sentient Phantasie is performed..by a presence of sense, as the Horse is under the sense of hunger, and that without any formal Syllogism presseth him to eat. **1733** CHEYNE *Eng. Malady* I. viii. §3 (1734) 71 The Nerves..propagate this Vibration..to the intelligent or sentient Principle in the Brain. **1846** GROTE *Greece* I. xiii. (1862) I. 197 [The legend] ascribes to the ship sentient powers. **1865** TYNDALL *Fragm. Sci.* (1879) I. ii. 73 Thus is sentient man acted on by Nature. **1879** LEWES *Probl. Life & Mind* Ser. III. I. 8 We can define it [the relation of Mind to Life] by analytically distinguishing certain functions as sentient from other functions as nutrient.

b. Conscious or percipient *of* something.

1815 SOUTHEY *Roderick* XVII. 45 Of all within Oblivious there he sate, sentient alone Of outward nature. **1844** MRS. BROWNING *Vis. Poets* xc, The poet's sight grew sentient Of a strange company around.

2. *Phys.* Of organs or tissues: Responsive to sensory stimuli.

1822–29 *Good's Study Med.* (ed. 3) IV. 290 The sentient fluid with which they [the papillæ of the tongue] are supplied. **1843** R. J. GRAVES *Syst. Clin. Med.* Introd. 14 In cases of tic douloureux we divide the sentient and not the motive nerves. **1878** M. FOSTER *Physiol.* III. i. 394 A stimulus being brought to bear on some sentient surface.

3. Characterized by the exercise of the senses.

1906 H. JONES in *Hibbert Jrnl.* Apr. 558 Sentient experience in short is reality, and what is not this, is not real.

B. a. *absol.* That which has sensation or feeling. **b.** *sb.* One who or something which has sensation.

1603 HOLLAND *Plutarch's Mor.* 1042 Intelligence is the motion of the intelligence about that which is stable..: but opinion is the mansion of the sentient about that which moveth. **1661** GLANVILL *Van. Dogm.* xxii. 220 Some extraordinary alterations in the Brain duplicate that which is but a single object to our undistemper'd Sentient. **1678** CUDWORTH *Intell. Syst.* I. i. §28. 34 They concluded, that all the Phænomena of Inanimate Bodies, and their various Transformations might be clearly resolved into these two things, Partly something that is Real..and partly something that is Phantastical in the Sentient. **1691** HOWE *Redeemer's Tears,* etc. (1846) 210 What can you think of that Spirit that feels every where? that is in the body a universal sentient? **1817** COLERIDGE *Biog. Lit.* (1907) I. viii. 90 How *being* can transform itself into a *knowing*, becomes conceivable on one only coindition; namely, if it can be shown that the *vis representativa*, or the Sentient, is itself a species of being. **1865** GROTE *Plato* I. i. 80 Particular modifications of atoms ..produced upon the sentient the impressions of different colours. **1886** F. W. H. MYERS *Phantasms Living* I. Introd. 71 The insentient has awoke..into sentiency; the sentient into the fuller consciousness of human minds.

Hence **ˈsentiently** *adv.*

1847 in WEBSTER.

sentiment (ˈsɛntɪmənt). Forms: α. 4 **sentment, centement,** 4–5 **sentemente,** 4–6 **sentement,** 5 **sentament;** β. 7– **sentiment.** [a. OF. *sentement* (12th c. in Hatz.-Darm.), ad. med.L. *sentimentum*, f. L. *sentīre* to feel; cf. Sp. *sentimiento*, Pg., It. *sentimento.*

In the 17th c. the word seems to have been re-introduced with the mod.Fr. spelling *sentiment* (1314 in Hatz.-Darm.).]

†**1.** Personal experience, one's own feeling. *Obs.*

c **1374** CHAUCER *Troilus* II. 13 For-whi to euery louere I me excuse That of no sentement I þis endite But out of latyn in my tunge it write. *c* **1385** —— *L.G.W.* 69 Ye loueres that kan make of sentement In this cas oght ye be diligent To forthren me sumwhat in my labour. *c* **1402** LYDG. *Compl. Bl. Knt.* 197 Right so fare I, that of no sentement Saye right naught..But as I herde..This man complayne with a pitous soun.

†**2.** Sensation, physical feeling. In later use, a knowledge due to vague sensation. *Obs.*

α. *c* **1374** CHAUCER *Troilus* IV. 1177 She cold was and withouten sentement.

β. **1660** SHARROCK *Vegetables* 42 The approach or sentiment of the coole and fresh aire. **1829** *Chapters Phys. Sci.* 334 While in turns it [*sc.* the hand] approaches nearer to or withdraws farther from this organ [*sc.* the eye], it teaches it to refer..to one place rather than to another, the impression that is produced on the retina, from the sentiment we have of every position of the hand.

†**3.** Sensible quality; in quot. = flavour. *Obs.*

c **1400** MAUNDEV. (1839) xviii. 189 And other Trees there ben also, that beren wyn of noble sentement.

†**4. a.** Intellectual or emotional perception. *Obs.*

c **1374** CHAUCER *Troilus* III. 43 Ye in my nakede herte sentement Inhelde and do me shewe of thi swetnesse.

†**b.** *pl.* ? Abilities. *Obs. rare*⁻¹.

c **1470** HARDING *Chron.* XXXIX. xvi, Bledud Gabred reigned, expert in song, And in all musike instrumentes Farre passyng was all other..Suche was his cunnyng and his sentementes, That for a god..Thei honoured hym.

†**5.** *in sentement* (Lydg.) = 'in sentence': see SENTENCE *sb.* 7 b. *Obs.*

1412–20 LYDG. *Chron. Troy* II. 1558 Whan þei were present, Ryȝt þus he seide, as in sentament [etc.]. **1426** —— *De Guil. Pilgr.* 1135 Transgressyoun ys..shortly, in sentement, Brekyng off a comaundement. *c* **1430** —— *Min. Poems* (Percy Soc.) 197, I dar conclude as to my feelyng, By confirmacioun as in sentement, Fewe men be stable heer in ther livyng.

6. a. What one feels with regard to something; mental attitude (of approval or disapproval, etc.); an opinion or view as to what is right or agreeable. Often *pl.* with collective sense.

1639 ROUSE *Heav. Univ.* vii. (1702) 99 Now there is an exact parallel to be drawn, betwixt one and the other, according to the sentiment of several of the Ancients. **1675** R. BURTHOGGE *Causa Dei* 38 We have not only Plato's Testimony, but..the common sentiment of all the World to Evince and Prove it. **1708** SWIFT *Abol. Chr.* Misc. (1711) 154, I shall handle it..with the utmost Deference to that great and profound Majority which is of another Sentiment. **1715** DE FOE *Fam. Instruct.* I. iv. (1841) I. 87 My sister Mary is quite of different sentiments from us all. **1773** EARL CARLISLE in Jesse *Selwyn & Contemp.* (1844) III. 61, I fear there will not be time to wait for your sentiments, but.. I think you will not disapprove of my taking this step. **1833** HT. MARTINEAU *Manch. Strike* iii. 27 What were his sentiments respecting the meeting? **1840** THIRLWALL *Greece* VII. 87 There needed..scarcely a voice to express the universal sentiment. **1848** DICKENS *Dombey* xxiv, Barnet, to say the truth, appeared to entertain an opposite sentiment on the subject. **1852** H. ROGERS *Ecl. Faith* (1853) 190 In one sentiment, indeed, you are pretty well agreed—that the Bible is to be discarded. **1875** JOWETT *Plato* (ed. 2) IV. 231 We are..not attempting to draw a precise line between his real sentiments and those..attributed to him.

b. In wider sense: An opinion, view (e.g. on a question of fact or scientific truth). ? *Obs.*

1675 BAXTER *Cath. Theol.* II. i. 17 Sure this is your own sentiment: For you deny not that God knoweth from eternity whether [etc.]. **1695** WOODWARD *Nat. Hist. Earth* Acc. Observ. 2 Proposing..to deliver my Sentiments on certain Heads of Natural History. **1760** DR. WALL in Jesse *Selwyn & Contemp.* (1843) I. 174 The duchess had too plainly explained her sentiments of Lady Coventry's condition. **1838** T. THOMSON *Chem. Org. Bodies* 951 His sentiments seem to have been implicitly adopted by his contemporaries.

†**c.** Phrase. ***in the same sentiments with, in sentiment with***: in agreement with, of the same mind as. *Obs.*

1741 MIDDLETON *Cicero* II. x. 458 He was in the same sentiments with Antony. **1777** A. ST. CLAIR in Sparks *Corr. Amer. Rev.* (1853) I. 402, I was fully in sentiment with them. **1797** WASHINGTON *Let.* Writ. 1892 XIII. 397, I am clearly in sentiment with you that [etc.].

d. ***them's my sentiments***: a colloq. expression of agreement or approval. (In quot. 1847, a declaration of belief.)

1847 THACKERAY *Van. Fair* (1848) xxi. 179 The sooner it is done the better, Mr. Osborne; them's my sentiments! **1886** J. BAILEY *Let.* 28 Nov. (1935) 26, I was delighted, as I could have said to every word: 'Them's my sentiments!' **1937** A. HUXLEY *Let.* 16 Feb. (1969) 414, I ought to have written long since to thank you for your Sunrise Poem, about which I felt strongly that them was my sentiments. **1940** 'B. M. BOWER' *Spirit of Range* xiv. 162 'I'm willing to be just a boneheaded cow-puncher.' 'Accent on the bone,' Pink murmured. 'Them's my sentiments, old socks.'

7. a. A mental feeling, an emotion. Now chiefly applied, and by psychologists sometimes restricted, to those feelings which involve an intellectual element or are concerned with ideal objects. In the 17–18th c. often *spec.* an amatory feeling or inclination.

1652 tr. *G. de Costes' Cleopatra* I. To Rdr., I can assure thee that he is better versed in the Sentiments of Love, then in his Breviary. **1663** S. PATRICK *Parab. Pilgr.* (1687) x. 57 This sight..gave him such a sentiment of joy, that [etc.]. **1728–46** THOMSON *Spring* 672 What melting sentiments of kindly care, On the new parents seize! **1749** SMOLLETT *Regic.* II. iv, When thy soft heart with kind compassion glows, Shall I the tender sentiment repress? **1771** —— *Humph. Cl.* 10 July (1815) 228 My uncle assured him he.. spoke from a sentiment of friendly regard to his interest. **1816** A. KNOX *Rem.* (1834) I. 52 The Church of England.. has manifested no sentiment with such unremitting intensity, as dread of..popery. **1817** CHALMERS *Astron. Disc.* i. (1852) 26 We should feel a sentiment of modesty at this just but humiliating representation. **1854** LOWELL *Keats* Wks. 1890 I. 226 Men who scrupulously practised the Ten Commandments as if there were never a *not* in any of them, felt every sentiment of their better nature outraged by the 'Lyrical Ballads'. **1872** SPENCER *Princ. Psychol.* (ed. 2) II. 578 The word Sentiments, as used in this and succeeding chapters, must be taken to comprehend those highest orders of Feelings which are entirely re-representative.

b. *Phrenology.* In *plural*, used as the name for the class of 'faculties' (including Veneration, Self-esteem, Benevolence, Wonder, etc.), which are concerned with emotion, and to which 'organs' are assigned at the top of the brain.

1815 SPURZHEIM *Physiogn. Syst.* III. ii. 275 The faculties which produce propensity, together with a peculiar feeling, and which I call sentiments. **1825** COMBE *Syst. Phrenol.* (ed. 2) 153 Genus II—Sentiments. This genus of faculties corresponds to the 'emotions' of the metaphysicians... Dr. Spurzheim has named these faculties Sentiments, because they produce a propensity to act, joined with an emotion or feeling of a certain kind.

8. a. A thought or reflection coloured by or proceeding from emotion.

1762 LD. KAMES *Elem. Crit.* xvi. (1774) I. 451 Every thought prompted by passion is termed a sentiment. **1848** THACKERAY *Van. Fair* lviii, This sentiment passed rapidly through William's mind, as he was holding Amelia's hand.

b. *esp.* An emotional thought expressed in literature or art; the feeling or meaning intended to be conveyed by a passage, as distinguished from the mode of expression.

1709 FELTON *Diss. Classics* (1718) 32 Their finest Expressions, and noblest Sentiments, are to be met with in these Transcribers. **1750** JOHNSON *Rambler* No. 37 ¶5 Either the sentiments must sink to the level of the speakers, or the speakers must be raised to the height of the sentiments. **1817** COLERIDGE *Biog. Lit.* (1907) II. 107 The sentiments and language are the poet's own. **1861** PALEY *Æschylus* (ed. 2) *Supplices* 970 *note*, In the next verse the δὲ connects the sentiment thus [etc.].

c. An epigrammatical expression of some striking or agreeable thought or wish, often of the nature of a proverb or in proverbial language, announced in the manner of a toast by a person proposing to drink with others in company.

1777 SHERIDAN *Sch. Scandal* III. iii, Come, Mr. Premium, I'll give you a sentiment; here's *Success to usury*! **1817** COLERIDGE *Biog. Lit.* (1907) II. 116 The speech from the convivial chair, announcing a toast or sentiment. **1842** MRS. KIRKLAND *Forest Life* I. 225 The 'sentiments' were drank at intervals in very innocent liquids.

9. In generalized use. **a.** Refined and tender emotion; exercise or manifestation of 'sensibility'; emotional reflection or meditation; appeal to the tender emotions in literature or art. Now chiefly in derisive use, conveying an imputation of either insincerity or mawkishness.

1768 STERNE *Sent. Journ.* I. 3 'Tis the monarch of a people ..so renown'd for sentiment and fine feelings, that I have to reason with. **1784** COWPER *Tiroc.* 539 New-fangled sentiment, the boasted grace Of those who never feel in the right place. **1883** STEVENSON *Silverado Sq.* 247 The tear of elegant sentiment permanently in his eye. **1888** BRYCE *Amer. Commw.* III. lxxx. 55 Nor do their moral and religious impulses remain in the soft haze of self-complacent sentiment.

attrib. **1747** CHESTERF. *Lett.* (1892) I. 75 Poets, romance or novel writers, and such sentiment-mongers.

b. Emotional regard to ideal considerations, as a principle of action or judgement.

1851 *Blackw. Mag.* July 20 A man in whose organization sentiment usurps too large a share for practical existence. **1878** MORLEY *Diderot* I. 177 Their metaphysic and psychology..were pregnant with humanistic sentiment. **1886** FROUDE *Oceana* 105 A nation with whom sentiment is nothing is on the way to cease to be a nation at all. **1908** R. BAGOT *A. Cuthbert* v. 45 Family sentiment is not everything.

†**10.** (See quot.) *Obs.*

1838 *Workwoman's Guide*, A necktie made of silk or velvet, and styled a sentiment.

sentimental (sɛntɪˈmɛntəl), *a.* [f. prec. + -AL[1].

The F. *sentimental*, according to Littré and Hatz.-Darm., is an adoption of the Eng. word as used by Sterne; so also G. *sentimental*.]

1. Of persons, their dispositions and actions: Characterized by sentiment. Originally in favourable sense: Characterized by or exhibiting refined and elevated feeling. In later use: Addicted to indulgence in superficial emotion; apt to be swayed by sentiment.

1749 LADY BRADSHAIGH in Mrs. Barbauld *Richardson's Corr.* (1804) IV. 282 What, in your opinion, is the meaning of the word *sentimental*, so much in vogue among the polite. .. Every thing clever and agreeable is comprehended in that word... I am frequently astonished to hear such a one is a *sentimental* man; we were a *sentimental* party; I have been taking a *sentimental* walk. **1752** H. WALPOLE *Let. to Mann* 27 July, I am still sentimental enough to flatter myself, that a man who could beg sixteen guineas, will not give them. **1763** FR. BROOKE *Hist. Lady J. Mandeville* (1820) 34 Your squires are an agreeable race of people, refined, sentimental, formed for the *belle passion*. **1823** SOUTHEY in *Q. Rev.* XXVIII. 517 Rousseau addressed himself to the sentimental classes, persons of ardent or morbid sensibility, who believe themselves to be composed of finer elements than the gross multitude. **1826** DISRAELI *Viv. Grey* v. xv, A soft sentimental whisper. **1827** SCOTT *Highl. Widow* v, Never satisfied with dropping a sentimental tear when there was room for the operation of effective charity. **1837** LANDOR *Imag. Conv., Steele & Addison* Wks. 1853 II. 152/2 Dear Addison! drunk, deliberate, moral, sentimental, foaming over with truth and virtue. **1862** MISS BRADDON *Lady Audley* xviii, You have no sentimental nonsense, no silly infatuation..to fear from me. **1865** DICKENS *Mut. Fr.* I. iv, I am not setting up to be sentimental about George Sampson.

b. *absol.* (with *the*). †Also (? *nonce-use*) as *sb.*, a sentimental person.

1784 *Unfort. Sensibility.* I. 39 Your dying sentimentals, who can..execute more mischief in a single hour, than [etc.]. **1849** G. CUPPLES *Green Hand* iv. (1856) 44 Come, come, old boy,..'twon't do for you to go to the sentimental, you know! **1908** R. BAGOT *A. Cuthbert* v. 48, I could hardly say more without approaching dangerously near to the sentimental.

†**c.** Arising from sentiment or refined æsthetic emotion. *Obs.*

1760–72 H. BROOKE *Fool of Qual.* (1809) III. 158 Music.. is but..a distant and faint echo of those sentimental and rapturous tunings. **1764** GOLDSM. *Hist. Eng. in Lett.* (1772) I. 41 They [i.e. the English in 7th cent.] were only incapable of sentimental pleasure.

2. Pertaining to sentiment. **a.** Arising from or determined by feeling rather than by reason.

1752 (*title*) Reflections on Sentimental Differences in Points of Faith. **1876** FREEMAN *Norm. Conq.* V. xxiv. 385 They might have a sentimental preference for the race to which they themselves belonged.

b. That is a matter of sentiment and not of material interests. Often in ***sentimental grievance***.

1891 *Weekly Notes* 200/1 The tenant for life..could override the sentimental interests of the remaindermen.

3. Of literary compositions (occas. of music or other art): Appealing to sentiment; expressive of the tender emotions, esp. those of love.

1762 LD. KAMES *Elem. Crit.* ii. (1774) I. 138 *note*, It is beyond the power of music to raise a passion or a sentiment: but it is in the power of music to raise emotions similar to what are raised by sentiments expressed in words pronounced with propriety and grace; and such music may justly be termed *sentimental*. **1779** SHERIDAN *Critic* I. i, A genteel comedy..written in a stile which they have lately tried to run down, the true sentimental, and nothing ridiculous in it. **1805** W. COOKE *Mem. Foote* I. 182 *Piety in Pattens*..was intended to ridicule a species of writing known under the name of *sentimental comedy*, which was then very much gaining ground upon the stage. **1877** A. W. WARD in *Encycl. Brit.* VII. 419/1 The sentimental drama of France and other countries. *Ibid.* 422/2 Yriarte and Jovellanos..produced a sentimental comedy in Diderot's manner.

sentimentalism (sɛntɪˈmɛntəlɪz(ə)m). [f. SENTIMENTAL *a.* + -ISM.]

1. The sentimental habit of mind; the disposition to attribute undue importance to sentimental considerations, or to be governed by sentiment in opposition to reason; the tendency to excessive indulgence in or insincere display of sentiment.

1817 BYRON *Beppo* li, How quickly would I..sell you, mix'd with western sentimentalism, Some samples of the finest Orientalism. **1837** CARLYLE *Fr. Rev.* I. II. iii, If we pierce through that rosepink vapour of Sentimentalism, Philanthropy, and Feasts of Morals. **1849** ROBERTSON *Serm.* Ser. I. x. (1866) 181 The sentimentalism of youth. **1873** MORLEY *Rousseau* xiv. II. 279 Such a faith is no rag of metaphysic floating in the sunshine of sentimentalism. **1888** BRYCE *Amer. Commw.* xciii. III. 303 Very few of the Reformers advocate woman's suffrage, apparently because they are opposed to sentimentalism.

2. An idea or expression indicative of sentimentality.

1833 FR. A. KEMBLE *Lett.* in *Rec. Girlhood* (1878) III. 170 My zeal for the cause of its people is an ignorant sentimentalism. **1865** CARLYLE *Fredk. Gt.* XXI. iii. IX. 299 What is to be done with that elegant inane creature, and his vaporous sentimentalisms. **1871** L. STEPHEN *Playgr. Eur.* ii. (1894) 39 It was of a piece with his [Rousseau's] other sentimentalisms. **1880** McCARTHY *Own Times* III. xli. 231 The..gushing sentimentalisms of a poet and a woman.

sentimentalist (sɛntɪˈmɛntəlɪst). [formed as prec. + -IST.] One who cultivates or affects sentimentality; one who holds sentimental doctrines.

1783 *Scots Trimmer* III. 27 Dean Milles, who is ravished with the beauties of Sterne, would, in all probability, have given the admirers of this charming sentimentalist a huge quarto, price only one guinea. **1784** R. BELL (*title*) Illuminations for legislators and for sentimentalists. **1793** W. ROBERTS *Looker-on* No. 63 (1794) II. 447 Let such as come under this latter description..not be confounded with ..those barren sentimentalists who love to refine upon sorrows without relieving them. **1821** HOOD *Sent. Journ.* Wks. 1862 I. 34 Some sentimentalists would have vented them upon the first dead dog or lame chicken they might meet with. **1858** J. H. NEWMAN *Hist. Sk.* III. IV. viii. 398 They were not dreamy sentimentalists to fall in love with melancholy winds. **1890** *Spectator* 15 Mar., The fixed notion that to help the rural poor you must injure the landlord, which is held by so many of the sentimentalists, makes it necessary to canvass all their schemes very closely.

attrib. *a* **1864** HAWTHORNE *Amer. Note-bks.* (1879) I. 29 A sighing, sentimentalist lover.

sentimentaˈlistic, *a. rare.* [f. SENTIMENTAL *a.* + -ISTIC.] Possessing sentimental characteristics; characterized by an exaggerated sentimentality.

1904 M. BEERBOHM *Let.* 13 Apr. (1964) 161 All this sounds very 'literary' and sentimentalistic, but it is real enough to me. **1912** E. POUND *Prolegomena* in *Poetry Rev.* Feb. 75 As for the nineteenth century,..I think we shall look back upon it as..a rather sentimentalistic, mannerish sort of a period.

sentimentality (ˌsɛntɪmɛnˈtælɪtɪ). [f. SENTIMENTAL *a.* + -ITY.] The quality of being sentimental; affectation of sensibility, exaggerated insistence upon the claims of sentiment.

1770 *Monthly Rev.* 181 In a fit of tenderness and sentimentality. **1774** WARTON *Hist. Eng. Poetry* I. xvii. 436 She [Chaucer's Prioress] has even the false pity and sentimentality of many modern ladies. **1813** BYRON *Jrnl.* 8 Dec. in *Sheridaniana* 229 Lord Holland told me a curious piece of sentimentality in Sheridan. **1859** GULLICK & TIMBS *Paint.* 158 The attainment of pure sentimentality in art. **1887** LOWELL *Old Eng. Dramat.* (1892) 128 His plays seem to me now to be chiefly remarkable for that filigree-work of sentiment which we call sentimentality.

b. *pl.* Sentimental notions.

1828 CARLYLE *Misc., Burns* (1840) I. 335 Here are..no hollow fantastic sentimentalities. **1847** *Fraser's Mag.* XXXVI. 525 Worn-out sentimentalities of the rose and nightingale. **1878** H. S. LEIGH *Town Garland* 205 The editors..They're all of them eager For sentimentalities put into rhyme.

sentiˌmentaliˈzation. [f. next + -ATION.] The action or process of sentimentalizing.

1839 *Q. Rev.* LXIV. 97 His implied negation of the inevitable results of evil training has a tendency to countenance their studied sentimentalization of the genus scamp. **1904** *Edin. Rev.* Oct. 315 A boyish poet woos her, offers her a love that shall be richer than her present mere sentimentalisation of conjugal duty.

sentimentalize (sɛntɪˈmɛntəlaɪz), *v.* [f. SENTIMENTAL *a.* + -IZE.]

1. a. *intr.* To indulge in sentimental thoughts or expressions. Also with *about*. Cf. SENTIMENTIZE *v.*

1788 W. COMBE *Orig. Lett. Sterne* 14 In the mean time we will philosophize and sentimentalize;—the last word is a bright invention of the moment in which it was written, for yours or Dr. Johnson's service. **1812** MAR. EDGEWORTH *Emilie de Coulanges* (1856) 201 They reproach and torment themselves, and refine and sentimentalize, till gratitude becomes burdensome. **1831** SOUTHEY in *Q. Rev.* XLV. 194

Here the historian of the conspiracy sentimentalizes. **1860** *Chamb. Jrnl.* XIV. 50 Coming out..to flirt and sentimentalise, and tease and love. **1902** R. BAGOT *Donna Diana* ii. 16 There is no novelty, no freshness, no mystery, for us—nothing, in short, to sentimentalize about.

b. quasi-*trans.* with *adv.*

1796 *Plain Sense* (ed. 2) II. 40 He will not find me so soon moralized and sentimentalized out of my rights as he found your sister.

2. *trans.* To make (a person, etc.) sentimental; to imbue (a person, work of art, etc.) with sentiment or sentimental qualities.

1821 *Examiner* 445/1 His leisure time he amuses..with cultivating his garden, and sentimentalizing it with inscriptions. **1832** MRS. STOWE *Let.* in *Life* (1889) III. 62 Coming away from New England has sentimentalised us all. **1874** SYMONDS *Sk. Italy & Greece* (1898) I. i. 12 Unrestrained indulgence in the pleasures of music..may tend to..sentimentalise the mind.

3. To turn into an object of sentiment.

1872 HOWELLS *Wedd. Journ.* (1892) 232 O yes.., sentimentalise him, do! Why don't you sentimentalise his helpless, overworked horse?

Hence **senti'mentalized** *ppl. a.*; **senti'mentalizing** *vbl. sb.* and *ppl. a.*

1789 E. SHERIDAN *Jrnl.* 20 Aug. (1960) viii. 184 Tickell marries Miss Lee next week and so ends his sentimentalising. **1856** KANE *Arctic Explor.* II. xix. 197, I.. whipped up my dogs so much after the manner of a sentimentalizing Christian, that our pagan Metek raised a prayer in their behalf. **1861** *Sat. Rev.* 22 June 650 Sentimentalizing with the Magdalen and swearing at the Papist are two forms of religious zeal already far too popular in England to need any additional stimulus. **1882** MISS BRADDON *Mt. Royal* I. iv. 105 He might stay at Mount-Royal for months sentimentalizing with Christabel.

sentimentalizer (sɛntɪˈmɛntəlaɪzə(r)). [-ER[1].] One who sentimentalizes.

1865 LOWELL *Thoreau* Wks. 1890 I. 373 We now and then detect under the surly and stoic garb something of the sophist and the sentimentalizer. **1801** *Harper's Mag.* July 279/1 A sentimentalizer of Bible stories.

sentimentally (sɛntɪˈmɛntəlɪ), *adv.* [f. SENTIMENTAL *a.* + -LY[2].]

1. With respect to sentiment.

1784 J. BARRY *Lect. Art* v. (1848) 187 An harmonious and sentimentally expressive chiaroscuro. **1821** LAMB *Elia* Ser. I. *Chapter on Ears*, I even think that sentimentally I am disposed to harmony. But organically I am incapable of a tune. **1884** J. TAIT *Mind in Matter* (1892) 282 The imprecatory Psalms may not supply singing of a sentimentally agreeable quality.

2. In a sentimental manner.

1815 JANE AUSTEN *Emma* I. viii, Elton may talk sentimentally but he will act rationally.

†**'sentimentize**, *v. nonce-wd.* [f. SENTIMENT + -IZE.] *intr.* ? = SENTIMENTALIZE *v.* I.

1753 RICHARDSON in Mrs. Barbauld *Corr.* (1804) II. 286, I am involved in sentimentizing:—very hard,..that I could not get myself excused from this task.

sentimentless (ˈsɛntɪməntlɪs), *a.* [f. SENTIMENT + -LESS.] Without sentiment.

1880 JESSIE FOTHERGILL *Wellfields* II. III. i. 146 Why is not genius created senseless, sexless, sentimentless? **1911** *Daily Express* 9 Nov. 5/7 'The War God' is extremely dramatic in its theme, which is the clash between the seer and the sentimentless man of affairs.

†**'sentinate**, *v. Obs. rare*⁻⁰. [f. late L. *sentīnāt-*, ppl. stem of *sentīnāre*, f. L. *sentina* bilge-water, sink; see -ATE[3].] (See quot.)

1623 COCKERAM II, To Pumpe water out of a ship. *Sentinate.*

†**'sentine.** *Obs. rare*⁻¹. [a. F. *sentine* or ad. L. *sentina* (see prec.).] A sink. In quot. *fig.*

1537 tr. *Latimer's Serm. Convoc.* ii. B vij b, Of the whiche al we..haue experience, the diuel to be a stynkyng sentine of all vices, a foule filthy chanel of al myscheues.

sentinel (ˈsɛntɪnəl), *sb.* Forms: 6–7 **centinell, sentinell, 6 centrinel, (centronel, centernell, centonell, sentonell, sentnell), 7 sentronell, sentenel, 6–9 centinel, 6– sentinel.** [a. F. *sentinelle* fem., sentinel, †watch-tower, ad. It. *sentinella* fem.; Sp. *centinela*, Pg. *sentinella*, are from It. or Fr.

No convincing etymology of the It. word has been proposed. The gender renders it probable that it originally denoted either the function of keeping watch (= sense 2), or a sentry-box, watch-tower, or the like. Cf. *spy, scout, guard*, the Fr. originals of which are all primarily fem.]

1. a. = SENTRY *sb.* 2. Phr. ***to stand sentinel*** (rarely pass. ***to be set sentinel***). †***forlorn sentinel***, = †***sentinel perdu, perdu sentinel***: see PERDU *a.* I.

[The phrases noted above are imitated from Fr.]

1579 DIGGES *Stratiot.* III. viii. 100 [The Scout Master] ought in placing of his night Watches or Sentinels, to vse great consideration. **1590** SPENSER *F.Q.* I. ix. 41 And he, that points the Centonell his roome, Doth license him depart at sound of morning droome. **1591** SHAKS. *1 Hen. VI*, II. i. 70, I was imploy'd..About relieuing of the Centinels. **1593** SUTCLIFFE *Pract. Laws of Arms* xxi. 228 No souldier appointed to stand sentinell, shall depart from the place, or sleepe in the place, vpon paine of death. **1598** YONG tr. *Montemayor's Diana* 120 The gate was opened to them out of hand by the Centrinels. **1598** BARRET *Theor. Warres* 106 Those which are set yet 30 pases farther, are to be single, which of some are improperly called forlorne Sentinels. **1639** *Laws & Ordin. War* 6 Whoever being set Sentinell by his Officer.., or other Service, shall be found drunk; shall dye for it. **1725** DE FOE *Voy. round World* (1840) 332 They went all to sleep,..without so much as a centinel placed for their guard. **1760** *Cautions & Adv. Officers of Army* 46 By making the Culprit do a double Duty, that is,..making him stand Centinel four Hours instead of two. **1784** *Cook's Third Voy.* II. III. vii. 114 John Harrison, a marine, who was sentinel at the observatory, deserted. **1814** SCOTT *Wav.* xlvi, The..officer..having sent out his night patrols, and posted his sentinels. **1832** W. IRVING *Alhambra* II. 179 'Who goes there?' said the centinel at the gate. **1855** MACAULAY *Hist. Eng.* xii. III. 191 The sentinels who paced the ramparts announced that the vanguard of the hostile army was in sight. **1861** *Two Cosmos* IV. i. II. 6 Cosmo is a great favourite with his regiment... The sentinels always present their arms to him as he passes. **1881** *Army Act* §6 Every person subject to military law who..Forces or strikes a soldier when acting as sentinel; or..Being a soldier acting as sentinel,..sleeps or is drunk on his post..shall..be liable to [etc.].

b. *transf.* and *fig.* One who or something which keeps guard like a military sentinel.

1590 SHAKS. *Mids. N.* II. ii. 26 *Fairy.* Hence away, now all is well; One aloofe, stand Centinell. *a* **1593** MARLOWE & NASHE *Dido* II. (1594) C 2 b, And in this groue..Ile lay Ascanius..: These milke white Doues shall be his Centronels. **1646** J. HALL *Horæ Vac.* 132 The mind having stood long centinell upon serious Thoughts, becomes.. sluggish. **1750** JOHNSON *Rambler* No. 3 ⁋4 A certain race of men..who stand as centinels in the avenues of fame. **1848** THACKERAY *Van. Fair* lv, Sir Pitt..had given orders not to be disturbed..—she slipped by the sentinel in livery. **1897** *Allbutt's Syst. Med.* III. 396 [Bad butter in pastry] thus escapes the very sense which was intended to act as a sentinel to the stomach. **1908** R. BAGOT *A. Cuthbert* v. 39 The grim cliff on which the castle stands sentinel over the North Sea.

†**c.** ***dark sentinel***: one employed to keep secret watch upon a person. ? *nonce-phrase.*

a **1635** NAUNTON *Fragm. Reg.* (Arb.) 36 But..why she should..permit him to go where and whither he listed, and onely on the security of a dark sentinell set over him, was.. beyond my apprehension.

†**2.** The occupation, duty or service of a sentinel; chiefly in ***to keep sentinel. in sentinel***, on guard as a sentinel. *Obs.*

1584 A. MUNDAY *Fidele & Fortunio* 640 in *Archiv Stud. neu. Spr.* CXXIII. 60 Being his turne as he said for to watch this night, And breaking vp sentinel when it began to be light. **1591** *Garrard's Art Warre* 1 Keeping sentinell in the night. **1597** BEARD *Theatre God's Judgem.* (1612) 287 The murderer being in sentinell, one of his owne fellowes vnawares shot him. **1603** HOLLAND *Plutarch's Mor.* 432 Those that kept the night sentinels. **1687** A. LOVELL tr. *Thevenot's Trav.* I. 23 In which Towers there are always some *Aadgemoglans* in Sentinel. *a* **1703** BURKITT *On N.T.* 1 Thess. v. 8 The soldiers that..kept centinel.

transf. and *fig.* **1612** BACON *Ess., Of Counsel* (Arb.) 322 Besides Councelles are not commonly so vnited, but that one keepeth Sentinell over another. *a* **1633** HERBERT *Priest to Temple* xviii. (1652) 73 The Parson in Sentinell.

†**3.** A military watch-tower for defence of a camp or the walls of a city. *Obs.*

1600 HOLLAND *Livy* XXV. 550 Many places were..smitten with lightning..and two watchmen in their Sentinels stricken starke dead. **1612–17** S. DANIEL *Hist. Eng.* 200 King Edward who had gotten to a winde-mill hill, beholding as from a Sentinell,..the countenance of the enemy. **1643** *Lancash. Valley of Achor* 21 The Enemy..fired an house neer the Sentinell. *Ibid.* 25 They fire Houses and Barnes without the sentinell... Thus they heated and smoaked our valiant souldiers from their Sentinell.

†**4.** (***private***) ***centinel***: a private soldier. *Obs.*

1710 STEELE *Tatler* No. 5 ⁋8 There were in the ranks of the company..one Unnion a corporal, and one Valentine a private centinel. **1741** in *Rep. Comm. Ho. Commons* II. 172 (Land Forces, etc.), 70 Grenadiers Coats and Breeches, at *1l. 8s.* 630 Centinels *ditto*, at *1l. 6s.* **1744–5–6** *Ibid.* II. 84, 87 Centinels [= 'Private Men']. **1762** GOLDSM. *Beau Nash* 80 He enlisted himself as a volunteer [in the Dutch army]. Here he underwent all the fatigues of a private centinel. **1797** *Monthly Mag.* III. 483 He..served as a private centinel under the duke of Marlborough, at..Blenheim. **1815** *Articles of War* xxi. 68 But Non-commissioned Officers may be discharged as Private Soldiers, and, by the order of the Colonel of the Regiment, or by the sentence of a Regimental Court-martial, be reduced to private Centinel. **1894** C. WALTON *Hist. Brit. Standing Army 1660 to 1700*, xxiii. 417 All soldiers..below the grade of lance-corporal were denominated Privates or more correctly private centinels or private soldiers.

5. *Naut.* (See quot.) Cf. SENTRY *sb.*[1] 5.

1904 W. HALL *Mod. Navigation* (1909) 73 The *Sentinel* is a device for signalling automatically that water of a certain depth has been reached. It is a lead towed behind the ship at a known depth, with gear fitted to it which completes an electric circuit on touching bottom. This circuit contains a bell on board the ship.

6. *attrib.* and *Comb.* **a.** appositive, quasi-*adj.* = acting or serving as a sentinel. **sentinel crab**, a crab of the Indian Ocean, *Podophthalmus vigil*; **sentinel pile** *Path.*, an external hæmorrhoid situated at the lower end of an anal fissure.

a **1658** LOVELACE *To Lucasta* 1 Like to the Sent'nel Stars, I watch all Night. **1863** WOOD *Illustr. Nat. Hist.* III. 586 The Sentinel-crab, so called from its extreme watchfulness [etc.]. **1867** AUGUSTA WILSON *Vashti* xxxiv, The two sentinel poplars that guarded the front. **1887** RUSKIN *Præterita* II. 396 The most noble view of Mont Blanc granted by any summit of his sentinel chains. **1910** *Practitioner* Apr. 520 It is probable that the fissure results from the tearing down of one of the anal valves, the free border of which eventually appears at the anus as a rounded œdematous tag—the so-called sentinel pile. **1974** R. M. KIRK et al. *Surgery* vi. 132 The oedematous skin at the lower end of the fissure protrudes as a 'sentinel' pile.

b. simple attrib., as ***sentinel duty***, †***-house***, †***posture***; ***sentinel-like, -wise*** advs.

1708 J. CHAMBERLAYNE *St. Gt. Brit.* I. II. xii. (1743) 107 They perform *centinel duty on foot. **1621** MOLLE *Camerar. Liv. Libr.* II. viii. 100 The..rampier of the Picts..at euerie miles end had a..tower.., and watch-towers or *sentinell-houses betweene. **1896** 'A. ST. AUBYN' *Bishop's Delusion* 54 The tall white lilies standing *sentinel-like on either side the garden path. **1625** MARKHAM *Souldiers Accid.* 24 Your *Sentinell Posture. **1642** J. CRUSO *Ord. Milit. Watches* 61 Every Sentinell must stand on his Sentinell posture.

sentinel (ˈsɛntɪnəl), *v.* [f. SENTINEL *sb.*]

1. *trans.* To stand guard over, to watch as a sentinel. *lit.* and *fig.*

1593 SHAKS. *Lucr.* 942 To wake the morne, and centinell the night. **1598** ROWLANDS *Betraying of Christ* 28 The watchfull bird that centinels the morne. **1629** FORD *Lover's Mel.* II. i. 27 All the powers That centinell iust Thrones, double their guards About your sacred Excellence. **1631** HEYWOOD *1st Pt. Fair Maid of West* I. 9 Wee'll centinel their safety: This place Ile guard. **1810** SCOTT *Lady of L.* I. xiv, And mountains, that like giants stand, To sentinel enchanted land. **1868** B. J. LOSSING *Hudson* 48 The winding road was..sentineled by lofty pines. **1894** CLARK RUSSELL *Good Ship Mohock* I. 138 The fellow on deck sentinelling the hatch let us see he was on guard.

†**2.** *intr.* To act as sentinel, stand sentinel, keep guard. *lit.* and *fig. Obs. rare.*

1593 NASHE *Christ's T.* 17 My vigilance shoulde haue sentineld for all your sleepes. **1610** G. FLETCHER *Christ's Vict.* I. xxii, And all the watchmen, that so nimbly runne, And centinel about the walled towers.

3. *trans.* To furnish with or as with a sentinel or with sentinels.

1656 S. H. *Golden Law* 33 The Lord Fairfax..wisely Sentinel'd and Perdu'd it to prevent Surprisals. **1820** SCOTT *Monast.* xxviii, They have sentinelled your door with armed men. **1864** *Daily Tel.* 1 Aug., A wide course had been prepared duly roped off and sentinelled with police. **1901** *Daily Chron.* 4 Oct. 7/1 Three passes led into our valley, and I gathered they were all well sentinelled.

4. To post as a sentinel.

1827 POLLOK *Course of Time* VII. (1869) 196 The light that fell From angel-chariots sentinelled on high. **1832** LONGF. *Native Land* 7 There dwells the soul..sentinelled in heaven. **1870** THORNBURY *Tour round Eng.* II. xx. 68 A statue of the builder sentinelled high up in an airy niche.

Hence **'sentinelled** *ppl. a.*

1852 H. SPENCER *Use & Beauty* Ess. 1891 II. 371 The mailed, moated, sentinelled security which was irksome to the nobles who needed it.

sentinelship (ˈsɛntɪnəlʃɪp). [f. SENTINEL *sb.* + -SHIP.] The office or duties of a sentinel.

1643 H. HEXHAM tr. *Laws Marshall Discipl. United Prov.* 3 If any souldier shalbe found sleeping on his centinelship, he shal..be punished with death. **1883** SPURGEON *Treas. Dav.* Ps. cxxxiv. (1886) VII. 144 Temple watching, night-sentinelship.

†**'senting,** *ppl. a. Obs. rare*⁻¹. [As if f. **sent* vb., a. L. *sentire* to perceive + -ING[2].] Sentient.

1572 J. JONES *Bathes Buckstone* Ep., Doing, being, growing, senting, and reasonable, as Microcosums.

senting, obs. f. SCENTING *vbl. sb.* and *ppl. a.*

sentisection (ˌsɛntɪˈsɛkʃən). [irreg. f. L. *sentīre* to feel + *sectiōn-em* SECTION.] The dissection of a living animal without an anæsthetic.

1889 in *Syd. Soc. Lex.* **1891** in *Century Dict.* (citing *B. G. Wilder*).

sentition (sɛnˈtɪʃən). *rare*⁻¹. [Badly f. L. *sentīre* to feel + -ITION.] (See quot.)

1865 J. GROTE *Treat. Moral Ideals* (1876) 30 Enjoyment.. is in the same sense the *summum bonum* as sentition or bare sensation is the *summum reale* or *summum verum.*

sentnell, sentonell, obs. forms of SENTINEL.

sentoku (ˈsɛntoku). [Jap.] Originally, a Chinese bronze produced during the era (1426–35) of Emperor Hsüan of the Ming Dynasty; later, a golden-yellow Japanese bronze vessel made after the Chinese fashion; the bronze itself.

1902 *Encycl. Brit.* XXIX. 722/2 A golden yellow bronze, called *sentoku.* **1904** E. DILLON *Porcelain* vi. 92 Hsuan-te (1425–35)... This period gave its name to the famous pale bronze so admired in later days by the Japanese... The name *Sentoku* that they give to it is the Japanese reading of the characters forming this emperor's name. **1931** *Illustr. London News* 15 Aug. 268/3 That..characteristic Japanese alloy, *sentoku*, a sort of yellow bronze which is very soft and resembles brass rather than bronze. **1968** G. SAVAGE *Conc. Hist. Bronzes* iv. 128 *Sentoku*, containing up to thirteen per cent of zinc, may have been used in the fifteenth century, and legend has it that vessels of this kind also contained gold.

sentorye, sentre, obs. ff. CENTAURY, CENTRE.

†**'sentre.** *Her. Obs.* [Perh. a spelling of CENTRE *sb.*] = PILE *sb.* 4.

1486 *Bk. St. Albans, Her.* b iv b, A Sentre in armys is called stakar of tentis [? *i.e.* a tent-stake]. *Ibid.* [see SENTRY *a.*].

†**sentrell.** *Sc. Obs.* ? Corrupt form of CENTNER.

1615 in *Wedderburne's Compt Bk.*, etc. (S.H.S.) 263 Ane schip..laitlie arryved from Danskyne..Conteining..3 quarteris sentrell of pewther..halff sentrell of pewtter perteining to Williame carmichaell.

sentrice, var. *centries* pl. of CENTRY *sb.*

1522 *Aberdeen Reg.* (1844) I. 105 Gelis Monro and his complecis tuk one hand to vphaue the sentrice of the brig to the samyn... In the said Gelis defalt, the said sentrice ar broking, spylt and away to the see haid.

sentronell, obs. form of SENTINEL.

sentry ('sɛntrı), *sb.*[1] Forms: 7 **sentrie**, (**centrie**, **-tree**, **sentery**), 7–8 **century**, 7–9 **centry**, 8– **sentry**. [Perh. a shortening or back-formation (apprehended as containing -RY *suffix*) from *centrinel* (1598), *centronel* (1594): see SENTINEL *sb.*]

†**1.** = SENTINEL *sb.* 3. *Obs.*

1611 COTGR., *Barbacane*,..some hold it also to be, a Sentrie, Scout-house, or hole. *Garite*,..also, a Sentrie, or little lodge for a Sentinell, built on high. *Guerite*.., also, a Sentrie, or Watch-tower. *Vedette*, a Sentrie, or Court of gard, placed without a fort, or campe. **1649** J. ROSWORM *Good Service Ill Rew.* in *Lanc. Tracts Civ. War* (Chetham Soc. 1844) 223, I advised him, that..he would immediately walk to the Deansgate, and from thence to the other Centuries, using his best encouragements to prop up their hearts against any dangers. **1653** COGAN tr. *Pinto's Trav.* xxx. (1663) 118 Instead of Bulwarks it hath Sentries or Watch-towers.

2. a. *Mil.* and *Naval.* An armed soldier or marine posted at a specified point to keep guard and to prevent the passing of an unauthorized person; spec. *Mil.*, each of the men of a military guard (see GUARD *sb.* 9) posted at regular intervals round an army in garrison or in the field to watch the enemy, prevent a surprise attack and challenge all comers. Phr. *to stand sentry.*

1632 J. HAYWARD tr. *Biondi's Eromena* 141 The great silence kept within, made them hold the enterprize for accomplished, there being neither Centrees, nor rounds to be seene. **1650** T. B. *Worcester's Apophth.* 53 The Lieutenant call'd upon the Centry to give fire. **1728** CHAMBERS *Cycl.* s.v. *Sentinel*, or *Sentry*, 'Tis not long since they said, To be on the Scout, in the same Sense as we now say, To stand Sentry. **1775** ADAIR *Amer. Ind.* 349 They appointed double centries over me. **1777** H. GATES in Sparks *Corr. Amer. Rev.* (1853) I. 437 The advanced sentries of my pickets are posted within shot. **1816** SINGER *Hist. Cards* 189 The other [soldier] with his arquebuss on his shoulder is standing centry. **1822** *Regul. & Ord. Army* 221 The Standing Orders..are to be distinctly read..after the Sentries first posted return to the Guard. **1838** LYTTON *Leila* I. i, The sentry at the gate saluted and admitted him. **1859** O. W. HOLMES *Boston Hill* 23, I hear their pacing sentry's tread. **1877** *Field Exerc. Infantry* 374 On the approach of any person, the Sentry will port Arms and call out, Halt! **1908** *King's Regul. & Ord. for Army* ¶937 The commander will visit his sentries at least twice by day and twice by night.

b. *transf.* and *fig.* One who or something which keeps guard like a military sentry.

1650 VAUGHAN *Silex Scint.* I. *Peace* Wks. (Grosart) I. 85 My soul, there is a countrie Far beyond the stars, Where stands a wingèd centrie All skilfull in the wars. **1670** SEDLEY in Medbourne *Tartuffe* Epil., Though Zeal stand Centry at the Gate of Sin, Yet all that have the Word pass freely in. **1710** STEELE *Tatler* No. 20 ¶4 She..got him a post upon a Stall in Wapping where he may be seen..as Centry to a Brandy-shop. **1746–7** HERVEY *Medit. & Contempl.* (1818) 224 His trusty dog, who, for a considerable time stood centry at the door,..snores with his master. **1901** *Speaker* 20 July 446/2 Wild geese..when on the feed throw out sentries which keep a strict look out.

3. The occupation, duty, or service of a sentry; also the watch kept by a sentry, esp. in *to keep sentry.*

1639 *Laws & Ordin. War* 9 Whosoever shall be convicted to have slept upon his Watch, Guard, or Centry..shall be put to death. **1643** SIR T. BROWNE *Relig. Med.* II. §12. 174 Thou whose nature cannot sleepe, On my temples centry keepe. **1667** MILTON *P.L.* II. 412 What evasion [can] bear him safe Through the strict Senteries and Stations thick Of Angels watching round? **1697** DRYDEN *Æneid* VI. 388 Here Toils, and Death, and Death's half-brother, Sleep, Forms terrible to view, their Centry keep. **1726** LEONI *Alberti's Archit.* I. 89 Your Soldiers..cannot be able to keep sufficient centry about it. **1835** in *Rep. Comm. Milit. Punishm.* (1836) 192 [Scale of Punishment] Dilatory on sentry (if slight) 1 extra sentry or drill. **1887** RIDER HAGGARD *Jess* xxxi, Some are on sentry.

†**4.** A military guard or watch. *Obs. rare*[−1].

1705 STANHOPE *Paraphr.* II. 587 The Pharisees.. obtained of Pilate to have..the Sepulchre watched by a strong Guard of Soldiers. This Centry would not suffer the Body to be conveyed out.

5. *Naut.* An apparatus in the form of an inverted wooden kite (towed from the stern of a vessel at a set depth), which is automatically released from its slings on striking the bottom and thus gives warning of the shoaling of the water by sounding a gong on board the vessel.

Invented by Mr. S. H. James, C.E., and adopted in the Royal Navy in 1889. Cf. SENTINEL *sb.* 5.

1894 S. T. S. LECKY *Wrinkles in Navig.* (ed. 9) 176 The Submarine Sentry.

6. *attrib.* and *Comb.*, as ***sentry bird, duty, place***; **sentry board**, 'a platform outside the gangway of a ship for a sentry to stand upon' (*Cent. Dict.* 1891); **sentry-fashion**, like a sentry; **sentry fish, lark** (see quots.); also SENTRY-BOX, SENTRY-GO.

1857 EMERSON *May-day* Poems (1883) 204 When pacing through the oaks he heard Sharp queries of the *sentry-bird. **1917** W. OWEN *Let.* 16 Jan. (1967) 428 Servants don't do *Sentry Duty. **1977** *Belfast Tel.* 28 Feb. 4/3 A soldier who shot dead a Derry man and injured two other people while on sentry duty in the city last May was jailed for five years. **1875** W. MCILWRAITH *Guide Wigtownsh.* 113 The [Custom-House] officer sauntered *sentry-fashion round and round his prize. **1664** HUBERT *Catal. Rarities* (1665) 25 A strange sort of Oyster, that is called the *Sentry fish for his nature; for it is fastned to the Rocks, and most commonly stands open to catch fish. **1869–73** T. R. JONES *Cassell's Bk. Birds* I. 208 The *Sentry Lark (*Macronyx capensis*) has received its name from the peculiar cry that it utters when disturbed, which sounds exactly like the *Qui vive!* employed as a challenge by French soldiers on guard. **1687** A. LOVELL tr. *Thevenot's Trav.* I. 116 The Tower of St. Nicholas..has.. a *Sentry-place at each Angle. **1809** MALKIN *Gil Blas* IX. vi. ¶1 The subject of my *sentry-watch could not be mistaken.

sentry ('sɛntrı), *sb.*[2] *Obs.* exc. *Comb.* in proper names. Also 6 **sentrie**, 7 **centrie**, **centori(e**, 8–9 **centry**, **sentry**. [A contracted form of the earlier *sentuarie*, *seintuarie*, *saintuarie*, variant forms of SANCTUARY influenced by the Fr. form *saintuaire*.] = SANCTUARY. Also *attrib.*

1590 NASHE *1st Pt. Pasquil's Apol.* C 4, He hath no way now to slyppe out of my handes, but to take sentrie in the Hospitall of Warwick. *c* **1600** *Rites of Durham* (Surtees) 59 Att y[e] easte end of the said Chapter howse..is a garth called y[e] centrie garth where all the priors & mounckes was buryed. **1774** W. GOSTLING *Walk about Canterb.* xi. 67 A wall..with a very ancient arch in it, corruptly called the centry gate as parting the cœmetery or burying place of the laity from that of the monks. **1781** *Gentl. Mag.* LI. 305/2 There is in most parishes of this county [Cornwall] a field (generally near the church-yard), which is commonly called the sentry (perhaps sanctuary). **1849** ROCK *Ch. of our Fathers* I. iv. 311 When Simeon the monk of Durham wrote. c. A.D. 1129, this latter cross stood in the centry-garth or cemetary of that cathedral. **1869** *N. & Q.* 4th Ser. III. 254 At Moreton Hampstead, co. Devon, is a large field adjoining the church; it is called the Sentry-field.

†'**sentry**, *a.* *Her.* *Obs.* [f. SENTRE + -Y.] = PILY *a.*

1486 *Bk. St. Albans, Her.* b iv b, The threde cootarmure restriall is calde in armys whan a cootarmure is sentry of dyuerse colowris to the poynt and whatt sentre mydyll in the point y[t] coloure is the felde. The blaseyr shall blase from y[t] colowre to the next colowre of the lefte side of the cootarmure and blase the colowre sentri. [**1889** ELVIN *Dict. Her.*, *Sentrie*, an old term for Piles.]

sentry ('sɛntrı), *v.* *rare.* [f. SENTRY *sb.*[1]]

a. *trans.* To guard as a sentry. **b.** *intr.* To perform the office of a sentry.

1820 J. S. KNOWLES *Virginius* V. II. 78 Though a legion Sentried that brothel, which he calls his palace, I'd tear her from him! **1873** W. S. MAYO *Never Again* xii, To where a postern, deep in shade, Is sentried only by the maid. **1900** *Daily News* 27 Sept. 5/1 Most of the prisoners are.. surrounded by a thick barbed wire fence, and sentried by the Gloucesters. **1910** T. HARDY in *Eng. Rev.* Apr. 1 The unslumbering sea, That sentrys up and down all night, all day, From cove to promontory.

c. *intr.* and *refl.* To place as a sentry; also *fig.*

1922 JOYCE *Ulysses* 221 Corny Kelleher..glanced..at a pine coffinlid sentried in a corner. **1979** G. SWARTHOUT *Skeletons* 155 John and Paul had sentried themselves before the bank door, barring my re-entry.

sentry-box. [f. SENTRY *sb.*[1] + BOX *sb.*[2] 13.] A small wooden structure in which a sentry may stand at his post in bad weather.

[**1716** GAY *Trivia* II. 176 The thoughtless Wits..Who 'gainst the Centry's Box discharge their Tea.] **1728** CHAMBERS *Cycl.*, *Centry Box*, a wooden Cell, or Lodge, made to shelter the Centry..from the Injuries of the Weather. **1753** HANWAY *Trav.* (1762) I. II. xv. 65 Sentry boxes are placed at certain distances. **1827** SYD. SMITH *Cath. Quest.* Wks. 1859 II. 127/1 What is really possessed of a country so subdued? four or five yards round a sentry-box, and no more. **1877** *Field Exerc. Infantry* 372 On the approach of the relief, a Sentry will place himself in front of his Sentry-box.

sentry-go. [Orig. a phrase of command; SENTRY (used vocatively) + GO *v.* (imperative).]

a. *int.* (See quot. 1867.) **b.** The patrol of a sentry; also, the duties of a sentry. Also *transf.*

1852–63 BURN *Techn. Dict.* II. (Eng.-Fr.), Sentry go! *en faction!* **1867** SMYTH *Sailor's Word-bk.*, *Sentry go!* The order to the new sentry to proceed to the relief of the previous one. **1880** *Daily Tel.* 23 Sept., The gallant fellows who were taking their turn at sentry-go on the other side of the Indus. **1884** ROBERTS in *19th Cent.* June 1059 Constant guard mounting, with its accompaniment of impaired health from 'sentry go'. **1886** STEVENSON *Treas. Isl.* xx, We'll have to do sentry-go. **1922** [see CAVE *int.*]. **1938** G. GREENE *Brighton Rock* I. i. 4 This was Hale's job to do sentry go, until a challenger released him, in every seaside town in turn.

Hence **sentry-going**, doing sentry-go.

1901 *Blackw. Mag.* Aug. 280/2 After his long term of hard labour at patrolling and sentry-going, as guardian of the line.

senttuary, sentuarie, obs. ff. SANCTUARY *sb.*[1]

†**senture.** *Obs. rare.* [a. F. *ceinture*: see CEINTURE.] A girdle.

a **1400–50** *Wars Alex.* 4963 þe kyng..him spoilis, Puttis of to þe selfe serke senture & othire. *c* **1400** *Beryn* 3925 A swerd I-shethid, with seynture I-fretid all with perelis.

sentwarie, -y, obs. ff. SANCTUARY *sb.*[1]

senty, obs. form of SEVENTY.

†**sentynode**, variant of CENTINODY.

1526 *Grete Herball* cccxlviii. (1529) T iv b.

senue, obs. form of SINEW *sb.*

Senufo (sə'nu:fəʊ). Also **Senoufo**, **Senufu**. [Akan.] A people of the Ivory Coast in western Africa; any of the sub-group of Gur (Niger-Congo) languages (or dialects) spoken by them. Also *attrib.* or as *adj.*

1911 F. W. H. MIGEOD *Languages of W. Afr.* I. i. 34 The Senufu..inhabit a big area of territory in the Ivory Coast hinterland. **1913** *Ibid.* II. xx. 317 Primeval languages not elsewhere classed:—*Berber*,..*Bisogo*,..*Senufo*. *Ibid.* xxi. 324 The Senufo group,..in the Ivory Coast lagoons. **1928** *Africa* I. 220 The best examples of this Western Sudanese art, in the work of the Bammana, Senoufo, Itabe and Mossi, show a strong preponderance of the tendency to cover with ornament. **1935** *Chambers's Encycl.* VIII. 609/1 The Siena or Senufo hold that a man's soul passes into the body of his totem-animal, and conversely the spirit of the dead animal enters a new-born child of the clan. **1969** MORGAN & PUGH *W. Afr.* I. i. 24 The Senoufo are a Voltaic community who have adopted many Manding and Akan customs. They live well to the south, in sub-Sudanic and sub-Guinean environments. **1972** *Times* 28 Nov. 24/5 (Advt.), A Senufo carved-wood mask. **1972** *Language* XLVIII. 848, 7a is given by..Sedlak for..Baule, Gbeya, Senufo-Senadi.

senurie, senurre, obs. forms of SEIGNIORY.

Senussi (sɛ'nu:sı). Also **Sanusi**, **Senoussi**, etc. [Arab. *sanūsī*, the name *Senussi* (see below).] (A member of) a Muslim religious fraternity founded in 1837 by Sidi Muhammad ibn Ali es-Senussi. Also *attrib.* or as *adj.*

1891 F. R. WINGATE *Mahdiism of Egyptian Sudan* i. 2 The Senussi branch of the Shadli school, so called from the Senus mountain in Algiers, dates its inception about 1837. **1899** A. S. WHITE *From Sphinx to Oracle* xii. 118 A man may become a Senussi without abandoning his Order. **1906** *Daily Chron.* 24 Apr. 7/6 The mysterious influence of the Senoussi. **1915** T. E. LAWRENCE *Let.* 22 Mar. (1938) 195 The Idrisi family, who are the Senussi and Assyr together. **1942** *R.A.F. Jrnl.* 27 June 15 The Senussi Arabs have a legend about the creation of the desert. **1949** E. E. EVANS-PRITCHARD *Sanusi of Cyrenaica* i. 8 The Sanusi have never shown themselves more hostile than other Muslims to Christians and Jews. **1959** *Listener* 15 Jan. 100/2 The Sanusi religious family, settled among the Bedouin tribes of Cyrenaica. **1978** A. MELVILLE-ROSS *Blindfold* xxi. 123 King Idris, with his strong pro-British leanings and strict Senussi code of honour.

Also **Se'nussian** *sb.* and *a.*; **Se'nuss(i)ism**, **Se'nussist** *a.* and *sb.*; **Se'nuss(i)ite** *sb.* and *a.*

1884 *Science* 14 Nov. 457 A Mussulman confraternity known as the Senousians. *Ibid.* 459 Five hundred camels.. ready at a moment's notice to convey to the interior the persons and property of the Senousian authorities. **1899** A. S. WHITE *From Sphinx to Oracle* xii. 114 Absolutism and occultness are the two most potent powers in Senussi-ism. **1900** *Daily News* 15 Jan. 6/4 The only great religious organization of Moslem Protestants in Northern Africa are the Senoussi-ites, and they are harmless. *Ibid.*, So far, owing to the secrecy observed by Senoussist emissaries, no direct evidence regarding the movement is obtainable. **1934** WEBSTER, Senusi... Also Senousi, Senussite. **1957** *Encycl. Brit.* XX. 331/2 The Darfur revolt of 1888–89..was nevertheless carried out in the name of the Senussites. *Ibid.* 332/2 In Cyrenaica Senussite resistance to the Italians was organized by Sheikh Rida. **1977** B. LUCAS tr. *De Foucauld's Lett. from Desert* vii. 139 Our Tuaregs remain calm despite the capture of Djanet by the Senoussists.

Senussia (sɛnu:'si:ə). Also **Senusiya**, etc. [Arab. *sanūsīya*.] The fraternity founded by es-Senussi.

1888 *Encycl. Brit.* XXIII. 575/2 The sectaries of Senúsíya are found in all parts of North Africa. **1891** F. R. WINGATE *Mahdiism Egyptian Sudan* i. 4 The Senussiyeh attacked the robbers. **1911** *Encycl. Brit.* XXIV. 649/1 Considerable diversity of opinion has prevailed among writers and travellers claiming knowledge of the *Senussia*. **1949** E. E. EVANS-PRITCHARD *Sanusi of Cyrenaica* i. 8 The Grand Sanusi had himself been a member of a succession of orders before he started his own and he allowed..members of other Orders to belong to the Sanusiya at the same time. **1974** *Encycl. Brit. Micropædia* VIII. 888/1 *Sanūsīyah*, also spelled *Sennusiya*, in a strict sense, a Muslim Ṣūfī (mystic) brotherhood established in 1837 by Sīdī Muhammad ibn 'Alī as-Sanūsī.

senvulle, obs. form of SINFUL *a.*

†**senvy.** *Obs.* Forms: 3 **senei**, 3–4, 6 **senevey**, 4 **senevei**, 4–5 **seneveye**, 4, 6 **senevy**, **synevey**, 4–7 **senvey**, 5 **senvyne**, **senefee**, **synewey**, 6 **senvye**, **synvy**, **sinvy**, 6–7 **senvie**, **seny**, 7 **seenie**, **seeny**, (**sceny**), 5–8 **senvy**. [a. OF. *seneve*, also *-vei*, *-vel*, *-vil* (mod.F. *sénevé*):—pop.L. **sinăpātium*, f. *sinăp-i* mustard.]

1. The mustard plant: see MUSTARD *sb.* 2.

c **1265** *Voc. Plants* in Wr.-Wülcker 554/9 *Sinapium*, [Fr.] *seneuel*, [? Eng.] senei. **1398** TREVISA *Barth. De P.R.* XVII. clv. (1495) 705 Senueye hyghte Sinapis..and though all the herbe in substaunce be kene and feruent: yet Bein louyth beste the floures of senuey. *c* **1440** *Promp. Parv.* 349/1 Mustard, or warlok, or se(n)vyne, herbe (MS. S. senwyn), *sinapis*. **1572** BOSSEWELL *Armorie* II. 76 b, Q. Beareth Argent and verte..6 leafes de Senuye d'Or. **1578** LYTE *Dodoens* V. lv. 618 There be two sortes of Senuie, the tame & the wilde, wherof also the tame or garden Senuie is of two sortes. *Ibid.* 619 The seconde kinde of tame Mustarde..whiche is the blacke Mustarde & common Senuy. **1584** COGAN *Haven Health* xxviii. 44 Senuie..bringeth foorth that seede whereof mustard is made. **1597** GERARDE *Herbal* II. ix. 190 The second kinde [of Mustard may be called] common Mustarde, or fielde Senuie. **1600** SURFLET *Country Farm* II. xxxvi. 244 Senuie or mustard delighteth in a fat ground. **1601** HOLLAND *Pliny* XX. xxii. II. 73 The hearbe Senvey, whereof there be three kinds. **1759** MILLS tr. *Duhamel's Husb.* II. ii. 267 The wheat seemed to have disappeared, to make room for a prodigious quantity of senvy, which looked extremely well.

2. = MUSTARD SEED 1.

1382 WYCLIF *Matt.* xiii. 31 The kyngdam of heuenes is like to a corn of seneuey. *Ibid.* xvii. 19 3if 3e shulen haue feith, as a corn of seneuey. *c* **1422** HOCCLEVE *Min. P.* 240 If yee haue as mochil feith as is the greyn of Senefee. *a* **1425** tr. *Arderne's Treat. Fistula*, etc. 85, I putte noȝt..in..ouer þe quantite of a corne of senvey. *c* **1440** *Pallad. on Husb.* III. 610 Senvy let sowe hit now. *c* **1440** *Gesta Rom.* 41 If ye haue feith, as moche as hath þe corn of synewey. **1505** *Will of Jerard* (Somerset Ho.), Beryng yerely to the heyre a pownd of Senvye. **1533** ELYOT *Cast. Helthe* (1539) 86 He that in suche wyse will vomite, let him eate hastyly..town-keris, rokat, synuy, or purslane. **1578** LYTE *Dodoens* v. lv. 619 The Mustarde, especially the seede which men cal Senuie, is hoate and dry, almost in the fourth degree. *a* **1618** *Rates Marchandises* M 4, Garble of Seny the pound ij.d.

3. *Comb.*: **senvy-seed** = MUSTARD SEED 1.

1298 in Rogers *Agric. & Pr.* II. 174/2 Seneueyseed. **13..** *Sloane MS.* 5 lf. 11/2 Sinapis, tam semen quam herba.. A(nglice) Seneuy sed. *c* **1440** *Pallad. on Husb.* viii. 149 A sester and a semycicle take Of senuey seed. *c* **1450** *ME. Med. Bk.* (Heinrich) 212 Seneueye seed. **1565** COOPER *Thesaurus, Sinapi*, senuie seede wherof mustarde is made. **1606** RIDER *Lat.-Eng. Dict., Sinape*,..seenie seed. **1607** TOPSELL *Four-f. Beasts* 518 White Sceny-seede..being put into broath.. will [etc.]. **1678** LITTLETON *Lat.-Eng. Dict., Sinape*,..seeny seed... *Eng.-Lat.*, Senvie seed.

†**ˈsenye.** *Obs.* Forms: 1 **seȝ(e)n, seng, seiȝn, seȝin,** 3 **seine,** 4 **seigne, seyne,** 5 **senge, synge;** *Vocabs.* 5 **seny(e, ceny, senny, sene;** 6 **senye;** *Sc.* 5 **seyne, senyhe, senȝe, seinye,** 6 **senȝie, seinȝe.** [App. of mixed origin: the OE. *seȝn* (ad. L. *signum* SIGN *sb.*) seems to have coalesced in early ME. with an aphetic form of *enseigne, asseigne,* ENSIGN *sb.*]

1. A military banner or standard = ENSIGN *sb.* 5.

Beowulf 2958 þa wæs æht boden Sweona leodum, seȝn Hiȝelace. *c* **900** tr. *Bæda's Hist.* III. ix. [xi.] (1890) 184 His seȝen, se wæs mid golde & mid godwebbe gefrætwad. *c* **1275** LAY. 9282 Nam he his seine and his scealdbripte. *c* **1330** R. BRUNNE *Chron. Wace* (Rolls) 5468 Waster non þat wolde hym feyne Whan þey sey þe kynges seigne. *Ibid.* 10024 Arthurr dide his folk abide, To arme þem, & til ordeyne Whylk schuld go, & wyþ whilk seyne.

2. A distinguishing mark, emblem, token. *in seyn that*, to signify *that*.

a **1000** *Cædmon's Gen.* 2370 Abraham..sette friðotacen.. on his selfes sunu, heht þæt seȝn weȝan heah ȝehwilcne, þe his hina wæs wæpnedcynnes. *a* **1375** *Joseph Arim.* 197 þis makeþ, quod þe wiht, þe marke of gold; And þis saues, quaþ þat wiht, þe seyne of seluer. ? *a* **1400** *Morte Arth.* 2055 He drissede in a derfe schelde,..With a dragone engowschede ..Deuorande a dolphyne..In seyne that oure soueraygne sulde be distroyede. *c* **1400** *Destr. Troy* 3108 Then Parys pertly proffert a seigne, For to telle his entent. *c* **1425** WYNTOUN *Orig. Cron.* v. iii. 433 (Cott.) A Roman..gat on þat seyne [*v.rr.* senyhe, senȝe] þat Brettownys bar; syne can he feyne Hym a Brettowne for to be. *c* **1440** *York Myst.* ix. 290 þus has god..Sette his senge [*sc.* the rainbow]..Vppe in þe Ayre of heght. *c* **1470** HENRYSON *Mor. Fab.* XI. (*Wolf & Sheep*) xvii, Ye gart me schute behind; Vpoun my hoichis the seinyeis may be sene. *c* **1470** HENRY *Wallace* IX. 170 The Rede Reiffar..Held out a gluff, in takyn off the trew. His men beheld, and weyll that senȝe knew.

3. A battle-cry, rallying cry = ENSIGN *sb.* 1.

1508 DUNBAR *Flyting* 139 Corrupt carioun, he sall I cry thy senȝie. *a* **1510** DOUGLAS *K. Hart* I. 222 Thai cryit on hicht thair seinȝe wounder lowde. **1535** STEWART *Cron. Scot.* (Rolls) II. 78 Syne loud on hicht he cryit hes his seinȝe, With that ane flicht of mony fleand ganȝe.

4. A book-marker.

c **1440** *Promp. Parv.* 453/1 Seny, of a boke, *indula*.

5. A token or tally used by innkeepers.

c **1440** *Promp. Parv.* 66/2 Ceny, or tokyn of an in or ostrye, *texera*. *Ibid.* 453/1 Senye, of an inne or ostrye, *texera*.

6. A signboard.

1569 *Reg. Privy Council Scot.* II. 33 Certane of the Baillies ..of Edinburgh..brak and kaist doun, senyeis of wyne, expres aganis all ordour, the said Cannongait being..evir in possessioun of selling of wyne.

senyeory, -our, obs. ff. SEIGNIORY, SEIGNIOR.

senyght(e, obs. forms of SENNIGHT.

senyhe, Sc. variant of SENYE *Obs.*

†**ˈsenyie.** *Sc. Obs.* Forms: 5 **senȝhe,** 6 **senȝe, sanȝe, seinȝie, seinze, seinye,** 6–7 **senȝie, senzie,** 8 **senyie,** (9 **senzie**). [App. an irregular alteration of SENE *sb.*[3], possibly due to association with *senyie* sign: see SENYE.] A deliberative meeting of clergy; a synod.

c **1425** WYNTOUN *Cron.* VI. i. 53 þis pape of Rome..Gert a senȝhe solempne be seyn. **1500-20** DUNBAR *Poems* xiv. 79 Off Sathanis senȝie syne sic ane vnsall menȝie. **1524** *Aberdeen Reg.* (1844) I. 107 Thai war informit that my lord of Aberdeen was nocht to cum afor the sanze. **1535** LYNDESAY *Satyre* 1967 Sir, I socht law thair..Bot I culd get nane at Sessioun nor Seinȝe. *a* **1572** KNOX *Hist. Reform.* Wks. (1846) I. 172 After the Pasche he came to Edinburgh, to hold the seinze, (as the Papistes terme thare unhappy assemblie of Baallis schaven sorte).

attrib. and *Comb.* **1683** G. MARTINE *Reliq. Divi Andreae* (1797) 40 And after the reformation, I find they met in the *senzie chamber. **1552** *Aberdeen Reg.* (1844) I. 280 That.. all sic sumpteous banketing be laid doun aluterlie except thre sobir and honest, viz., upoun the *senze day [etc.]. *a* **1578** LINDESAY (Pitscottie) *Chron. Scot.* (S.T.S.) II. 226 All maner of man havand entres to compeir vpone the seinzie day. **1819** W. TENNANT *Papistry Storm'd* (1827) 97 And terrour garr'd them loup pell-mell Frae *senzie-house, kirk, court and cell. **1596** J. MELVILL *Diary* (Wodrow Soc.) 330 In the *Seinzie ouk efter Pace.

senyor, -your(e, etc.: see SENIOR, SEIGNIOR.

senyster, senzie: see SINISTER, SENYIE.

‖**senza** (ˈsɛntsa), *prep. Mus.* [It.: see note s.v. SANS prep.] Without; in various phrases, as ***senza bassi*** without the basses, ***senza tempo*** in no definite time, etc.

1724 *Short Explic. Foreign Wds. in Mus. Bks., Senza*, without. This word is used in the following Manner. *Senza d'aria*, without the Air... *Senza Violino*, without the Violins [etc.]. **1740** GRASSINEAU *Mus. Dict., Senza*, signifies without, as *senza stromenti*—without instruments. **1762** STERNE *Tr. Shandy* VI. xi. 50 *Con l'arco* upon this;—*senza l'arco* upon that.—All I know is, that they are musical terms. **1945** A. HUXLEY *Time must have a Stop* ii. 16 Forbidden themes, repulsively fascinating, disgustingly attractive! Sebastian would embark on them with a quiet casualness —*pianissimo*, so to speak, and *senza espressione*. **1959** *Listener* 4 June 1001/3 Aubrey Brain played this *senza sord*.

seoc(k, seod, obs. ff. SICK, SEED.

seofe(n, seofeðe: see SEVEN, SEVENTH.

seogun: see SHOGUN.

seoile, variant of SOILE, seal (animal).

seok, seolk(e, -en: see SICK, SILK, -EN.

seollic, -ich(e, variant forms of SELLY *Obs.*

seoluer, seoly, obs. ff. SILVER, SEELY *a.*

seonne, seop, obs. forms of SIN, SHEEP.

seosynne, seotel: see SEASON, SETTLE *sb.*

seoððe, seoþþe, obs. forms of SITH.

seoudarie, obs. form of SUDARY.

seouwe, seow(e, obs. ff. SEW *v.*, SOW *v.*

seove, seoveniht: see SEVEN, SENNIGHT.

sep, obs. f. SHEEP.

sepage, var. SEEPAGE.

sepal (ˈsɛpəl). [ad. Fr. *sépale*, mod.L. *sepalum* (N. J. de Necker, *Phytologie philosophique*, 1790, p. 55, and *Corollarium ad Philosophiam botanicam Linnæi*, 1790, p. 18). Necker derives the word from Gr. σκέπη covering; as he refused to acknowledge the distinction between the calyx and the corolla (using the term *perigynanda* to comprise both), *sépale* (*sepalum*) in his use denotes the petals as well as what are now called 'sepals'.]

1. *Bot.* Each of the divisions or leaves of the calyx of a flower.

[**1821** GRAY *Nat. Arrangem. Brit. Pl.* I. 128 Sepales. Leaves, Sepala, Phylli, *Folioli calycini*. The distinct segments into which the calyx is divided.] **1829** LINDLEY *Synops. Brit. Flora* 7 Order 1. Ranunculaceæ *Juss.* Sepals 3-6. **1832** —— *Introd. Bot.* I. ii. 114 The sepals are generally longer than the corolla in æstivation..: during flowering they are mostly shorter. **1840** B. KINGDON tr. *De Candolle's Veg. Organogr.* II. III. ii. 48 Of the Calyx or Sepals. **1879** LUBBOCK *Sci. Lect.* i. 6 A common flower..consists, firstly of an outer envelope or calyx, sometimes tubular, sometimes consisting of separate leaves called sepals.

2. *Compar. Anat.* (See quot.)

1894 GOULD *Illustr. Dict. Med.* etc. *s.v.*, In the anatomy of the lower animals, certain thin, leaf-like organs are also called *sepals*.

Hence **ˈsepal(l)ed** *a.*, only in parasynthetic comb., as ***gamo-, two-sepalled***, etc., having one sepal, two sepals, etc.

1821 GRAY *Nat. Arrangem. Brit. Pl.* I. 124 Calyx... Composition. Gamo-sepaled, one-leafed... Two-sepaled, two-leaved... Many-sepaled. **1838** BARTON & CASTLE *Brit. Flora Med.* II. 465 *Sepalled*, having sepals. **1864** in WEBSTER, and in later Dicts.

sepaline (ˈsɛpəlɪn), *a.* [ad. mod.L. *sepalīn-us*, f. *sepal-um*: see SEPAL and -INE.] Of or belonging to the sepal of a flower.

1857 A. GRAY *First Less. Bot.* (1866) Gloss., *Sepaline*, relating to the sepals. **1870** HOOKER *Stud. Flora* 11 Aconitum..covered by the sepaline hood.

sepalody (ˈsɛpələʊdɪ). *Bot.* [ad. mod.L. **sepalōdium*, or f. mod.L. *sepal-um* SEPAL + -ODE[1] + -Y, after *phyllody*.] The reversion of the petals of a flower into sepals by inverse metamorphosis.

1887 *Cassell's Encycl. Dict.*

sepaloid (ˈsɛpəlɔɪd), *a. Bot.* [ad. mod.L. *sepaloid-eus*, f. *sepal-um*: see SEPAL and -OID.] Of the nature of or resembling a sepal.

1830 LINDLEY *Nat. Syst. Bot.* 135 Sepaloid petals. **1872** OLIVER *Elem. Bot.* II. 256 Observe..the sepaloid outer and petaloid inner perianth-leaves of Alisma.

separability (ˌsɛpərəˈbɪlɪtɪ). [f. SEPARABLE *a.* + -ITY.] The quality of being separable.

1640 BP. REYNOLDS *Passions* xxxiv. 418 Aristotle inferres the separability and independance of the understanding on the Body. **1742** tr. *Algarotti on Newton's Theory* II. 113 The Separability of the Rays is prejudicial to the Perfection of Telescopes. **1864** *Reader* 9 Apr. 459/1 This apparent separability between heat and light. **1890** *Spectator* 5 Apr. 463/2 The theory of the separability of the soul from the body.

separable (ˈsɛpərəb(ə)l), *a.* Also 5–7 **seperable.** [a. F. *séparable* (15th c.) or ad. L. *sēparābil-is*, f. *sēparāre*: see SEPARATE *v.* and -ABLE.]

1. Capable of being separated.

separable accident, quality: one which can be separated from its subject.

1393 LANGL. *P. Pl.* C. XIX. 193 Siþthen thei ben surlepes [*MS. G.* seperable]..thei han sondry names. **1532** TINDALE *Expos. Matt. v–vii.* Prol. (1550) 9 b, Though they [fayth, loue, and hope] be inseperable, yet they haue seperable and sondry offices. **1620** T. GRANGER *Div. Logike* 67 Common qualities, are separable, or inseparable. The former may be added or taken away from the subiect, without destruction thereof; as coldnesse from the water, whitenesse from paper. **1628** T. SPENCER *Logick* 64 Separable accidents. **1643** DIGGS *Unlawf. Taking Arms* iv. 93 That the Magistrate is separable from the man is evident. **1791** BURKE *App. Whigs* Wks. VI. 217 A true natural aristocracy is not a separate interest in the state, or separable from it. **1828** STARK *Elem. Nat. Hist.* II. 22 Shell..conical, separable into two parts. **1850** NEWMAN *Lect. Difficulties Anglicans* ix. 223 Catholics ..hold that faith and love,..faith and works, are simply separable, and ordinarily separated in fact.

b. *Gram.*

1773 BAYLY *Gram. Heb.* 14 The Cases are expressed either by entire Prepositions, called *separable*, or by a letter of the preposition prefixed to the noun, and called *inseparable*. **1815** S. LYON *Heb. Gram.* 61 Separable pronouns, signifying the agent. **1888** K. MEYER *Germ. Gram.* I. §246 Verbs compounded with separable prefixes.

†**2.** ? Capable of separating. *Obs. rare*[−1].

c **1600** SHAKS. *Sonn.* xxxvi. 6 In our two loues there is but one respect, Though in our liues a seperable spight.

Hence **ˈseparableness; ˈseparably** *adv.*

1628 COKE *On Litt.* 151 b, The Rent incident to the Reuersion separably, but the fealtie incident to the Reuersion inseparably. **1666** BOYLE *Orig. Formes & Qual.* To Rdr. b 5 b, The Separableness of Accidents from Subjects of Inhæsion. **1864** KINGSLEY *What, then, does Dr. Newman mean?* 33 The separableness of faith and works. **1906** *Tablet* 23 June 965 All idea of order or separableness among the elements of the spirit-life must be abandoned.

†**ˈseparalty,** altered form of SEVERALTY, after med.L. *sēparālis*: see SEVERAL *a.*

1567 in F. J. Baigent *Crondal Rec.* (1891) 167 That the said Deane and chapiter..shall..occupie and enjoye in separaltye..the grownde commonlie caulled the Great fleate ponde.

separate (ˈsɛpərət), *pa. pple.*, *a.*, and *sb.* Forms: 5–6 **seperat,** 5–7 **separat,** 6–8 **seperate,** 5– **separate.** [ad. L. *sēparāt-us*, pa. pple. of *sēparāre*: see SEPARATE *v.*]

†**A.** as *past pple.* Separated. *Obs.*

1432-50 tr. *Higden* (Rolls) I. 73 If hit were separate [L. *si separaretur*] in that maner from this worlde habitable. **1495** *Act 11 Hen. VII*, c. 34 Preamble, The same.. Hereditamentes shuld be..separat severed and disanexed from the Duchie of Cornwall. **1513** BRADSHAW *St. Werburge* II. 969 When all the officers departed were thens Supposynge the soule seperate from the body. **1555** PENDLETON in *Bonner's Homilies* 33 b, Those, that haue seperate from the catholyke church. **1646** R. BAILLIE *Anabaptism* (1647) 51 After they have separate from all other Churches. **1671** MILTON *Samson* 31 Why was my breeding order'd and prescrib'd As of a person separate to God. **1692** BENTLEY *Boyle Lect.* vii. 7 The Atoms or Particles which now constitute Heaven and Earth, being once separate and diffused in the Mundane Space,..could never [etc.].

B. *adj.*

1. a. Parted, divided, or withdrawn from others; disjoined, disconnected, detached, set or kept apart. Const. *from*.

1667 MILTON *P.L.* IX. 422 He sought them both, but wish'd his hap might find Eve separate. **1684** T. BURNET *Th. Earth* I. iv. 35 'Twere hard to conceive an eternal Watch, whose pieces were never separate one from another, nor ever in any other form. **1729** G. ADAMS tr. *Sophocles, Oedip. Colon.* II. 162 He died without Sepulchre, separate from any Man. **1796** WITHERING *Brit. Plants* (ed. 3) I. 80 Stamens and Pistils are said to be separate when they are found upon the same plant, but in different flowers. **1823** SCOTT *Quentin D.* xx, The moment in which I detect the least sign of treachery, thy head and body are three yards separate! **1846** BAXTER *Libr. Pract. Agric.* I. 29 Phosphorus..is never met with in a separate state, but always in combination with some other element. **1849** DICKENS *Barn. Rudge* ix, The footsteps appeared to have some object quite separate and disconnected from herself. **1850** TENNYSON *In Mem.* lxxxv. 66 A friendship..Which masters Time indeed, and is Eternal, separate from fears. **1865** LUBBOCK *Preh. Times* 41 Small separate plates of ice are formed.

b. Of persons, a dwelling, etc.: Withdrawn from society or intercourse; shut off from access. ***separate confinement***, the system of confining prisoners in separate cells.

1600 J. PORY tr. *Leo's Africa* III. 166 This castle..being separate from concourse of people, and a solitarie place fitte for a man to studie in. **1687** A. LOVELL tr. *Thevenot's Trav.* I. 24 The Women..are all lodged in a separate appartment together. **1697** DRYDEN *Æneid* VI. 954 Now, in a secret vale, the Trojan sees A sep'rate grove. **1815** SCOTT *Guy M.* lviii, See, here's the plan of my Bungalow, with all convenience for being separate and sulky when I please. **1819** SHELLEY *Cenci* V. ii. 191 Conduct these culprits each to separate cells. **1849** *Edin. Rev.* July 11 The tendency of prolonged separate confinement is to affect the mind. **1863** *Rep. Sel. Comm. Gaols* 13 Prisons..upon the separate system.

c. Of a soul: Not joined to a body, disembodied.

1653 H. More *Antid. Ath.* III. xiv. §1 (1712) 130 Separate Souls being ἰσάγγελοι, in a condition not unlike the Angels themselves. **1690** Locke *Hum. Und.* II. i. §15 Whatever Ideas the Mind can receive and contemplate without the help of the Body, it is reasonable to conclude, it can retain without the help of the Body too, or else the Soul, or any separate Spirit, will have but little advantage by thinking.

d. Parted or withdrawn from the Church.

1680 Stillingfl. *Mischief of Separation* 32 Nothing doth more alienate mens affections than withdrawing from each other into separate Congregations. **1686** J. Scott *Chr. Life* II. vii. Wks. 1718 I. 451 A Church that is separate from the Church Catholick.

2. a. Withdrawn or divided from something else so as to have an independent existence by itself.

separate establishment: see establishment 10 b.

a **1700** Evelyn *Diary* 18 July 1691, He..was..the sole industrious mover, that it should be made a separate parish. **1724** Waterland *Farther Vind. Chr. Div.* ii. 58 The prevailing Custom of Speech, which never gives the Name of Substances to any thing, but where the Substance is separate, or separable. **1827** Scott *Surg. Dau.* vii, He proceeded to enrol the troops into separate bodies. **1861** *Two Cosmos* v. iv. II. 156 He had ready for publication an Essay on the separate existence of Matter. **1887** Zincke *Hist. Wherstead* 188 If it is regarded disconnectedly and as a separate entity, it teaches little.

b. Belonging or peculiar to one, not common to or shared with the other or the others. In a hotel or boarding-house: ***separate table***. Also *spec.* of rooms, etc., to which each of a married couple retires separately.

separate maintenance: see maintenance 7 b.

1673 Temple *To Dk. Ormond* Wks. 1757 II. 235 This point can only be gained by a separate peace between us and Holland; for if the war should come to end in a general treaty [etc.]. **1706** Phillips (ed. Kersey), *Separate*, distinct, particular, different. **1711** Swift *Cond. Allies* (ed. 2) 86 Have not those two Realms their separate Maxims of Policy, which must operate in Times of Peace? **1756** *Old Maid* 21 Feb. 86, I have proposed separate beds, but he will never hear of it. **1771** *Junius Lett.* lix. 307 That each of them should act his separate part with honour and integrity to the public. **1815** Scott *Ld. of Isles* III. xxiv, 'Kind host', he said, 'our needs require A separate board and separate fire'. **1817** Jane Austen *Let.* 20 Feb. (1952) 480, I w^d recommend to her & Mr. D. the simple regimen of separate rooms. **1823** —— *Quentin D.* xxxvii, Each pressed forward upon his separate object. **1838** H. Martineau *Retrospect* I. 236 We.. had..a separate table, at Mrs. Peyton's boarding-house. **1840–1** De Quincey *Style* III. Wks. 1890 X. 203 One poem which..has a characteristic or separate beauty of its own. **1858** Ld. St. Leonards *Handy Bk. Prop. Law* xiii. 84 A married woman, although having separate estate, and living apart from her husband. **1872** Morley *Voltaire* i. 3 Luther and Calvin in their separate ways brought into splendid prominence their new ideas of moral order. **1910** *Bradshaw's Railway Guide* 1008 (Advt.), *White Lion*... Coffee Room (separate tables), Billiard Room. **1971** J. Fleming *Grim Death & Barrow Boys* xi. 161 A Private Hotel on the sea-front where they had dinner at night and separate tables. **1977** C. Storr *Tales from Psychiatrist's Couch* 36 She sleeps in a twin bed in London, but in the cottage we have separate rooms.

c. Considered or reckoned by itself (although mentioned as one of several); single, individual.

1840 Macaulay *Ess., Clive* ¶ 19 While the great body [of the empire], as a whole, was torpid and passive, every separate member began..to move with an energy all its own. **1851** Hawthorne *Ho. Sev. Gables* xvi, Just as there comes a warm sunbeam into every cottage window, so comes a love-beam of God's care and pity for every separate need. **1882** Vines tr. *Sachs' Bot.* 716 The metamorphoses of material proceed *pari passu* with the growth of the separate parts.

d. Distinct in occurrence or enumeration; not combined or put together.

1907 Hodges *Elem. Photogr.* (ed. 6) 161 Three separate baths of this strength.

e. Phr. ***separate but equal***, asserting the equality of races under racial segregation. *U.S.*

[**1776** T. Jefferson in *Dunlop's Pennsylvania Packet* 8 July 1/1 When in the course of human events, it becomes necessary for one People..to assume among the powers of the earth, the separate and equal station to which the laws of Nature and of Nature's God entitle them. **1890** *Louisiana Acts* CXI. 152 An Act..requiring all railway companies..to provide equal but separate accommodations for the white and colored races.] **1892** F. W. Gage *Negro Problem in U.S.* iii. 92 If railroad companies care to furnish separate but equal accommodations on equal terms to each race, no objection need be made. **1914** *U.S. Reports* (1915) CCXXXV. 160 It was not an infraction of the Fourteenth Amendment for a State to require separate, but equal, accommodations for the two races. **1948** *Time* 9 Feb. 75/1 In Missouri, where a 'separate but equal' law school has had its longest test. **1954** E. Warren in *U.S. Reports* CCCXLVII. 495 We conclude that in the field of public education the doctrine of 'separate but equal' has no place.

f. ***separate school*** Canad., a school receiving pupils from a racial or religious minority.

For detailed evidence and comment see *Dict. Canadianisms.*

1852 *Dundas Warden* (Canada West) 28 May 2/7 The law makes provision for Separate Schools, to meet an exigency —namely, the anticipated intrusion of the religious dogmas of a majority upon a minority. **1857** H. F. Douglass in *Ontario Hist.* (1963) June 88 Separate schools and churches are nuisances that should be abated as soon as possible, they are dark and hateful relics of Yankee Negrophobia. **1872** *Canadian Monthly* July 64/1 The Roman Catholics spoke frankly and sincerely for their separate schools, the New Brunswickers for their local liberties. **1911** *Daily Colonist* (Victoria, B.C.) 14 Apr. 5/2 Steps are being taken by the Roman Catholic authorities towards the establishment of separate schools in and near Vancouver. **1968** [see *junior high* (*school*) s.v. junior *a.* (*sb.*) 5]. **1976** *Globe & Mail* (Toronto) 16 Jan. 29/8 That meant I was Roman Catholic, ..that my oppressed and persecuted parents had to pay for my separate school education as well as the education of all the heathens in the public schools.

g. ***separate development***, the systematic development or regulation of a group or race by itself independently of other groups or races in a society; orig. and chiefly *S. Afr.*, = apartheid.

1955 *Summary Rep. Comm. Socio-Econ. Devel. Bantu Areas S. Afr.* III. xxv. 105/1 (*heading*) Objections to the policy of separate development. **1962** [see parallelism 2]. **1968** *Economist* 12 Oct. 17/1 A rigid, and openly acknowledged, form of 'separate development' operates there [*sc.* in Londonderry]. The most populous ward..is wholly Catholic..but skilful use of the 'property qualification' for local government elections [etc.]..ensure that these 12 councillors are Protestant Unionists. **1977** [see *plural democracy* s.v. plural *a.* (*sb.*) 2]. **1979** E. Norman *Christianity & World Order* v. 61 The Dutch Reformed Church does not teach white racial superiority, nor is Separate Development an attempt to institutionalize *racial discrimination*.

C. *sb.* (absol. or ellipt. uses of the adj.)

1. One who withdraws from the Church; a separatist.

1612 W. Sclater *Minister's Portion* 2 What ods is there betwixt this beggerly conclusion of those old beggers, and that of late separats, that make it Christs ordinance for Ministers to liue of their peoples voluntary contribution. **1647** Owen *Eshcol* (1648) 52 He that will not separate from world, and false-worship is a Separate from Christ. **1659** Gauden *Tears Ch.* I. ii. 41 Chusing rather to be a rank Separate, a meer Quaker, an arrant Seeker.

2. A member of an American Calvinistic Methodist sect of the 18th century, so called because organized into separate societies.

1882–3 *Schaff's Encycl. Relig. Knowl.* III. 2160.

3. *U.S.* An article or document issued separately; esp. a copy of an article reprinted from a magazine, volume of 'transactions', etc., for separate distribution.

1886 *Rep. of U.S. Sec. of Treasury* 405 (Cent.) It will be noticed that to the questions 16, 17, and 18, in the separate of January 18, 1886, no reply is given by the superintendent of the mint. **1892** *Athenæum* 12 Nov. 666/3 From time to time we receive odd 'separates' of papers published in the *Proceedings* of the United States National Museum. **1894** *Harvard Teachers' Assoc. Leaflet* No. 11. 4 The geographical report..might be reprinted in the annual report of the superintendent of public instruction, from which 'separates' could be struck off. **1897** *Nat. Science* Dec. 432 This 4to tract..cannot be a separate of the Mém. de l'Inst. paper.

4. *Math.* Any one of a set of partitions into which a partition of a number can be separated.

1888 MacMahon in *Amer. Jrnl. Math.* (1889) XI. 2 A partition is separated into separates by writing down a set of partitions, each separate partition in its own brackets, from left to right, so that when all the parts of these partitions are assembled in a single bracket, the partition which is separated is reproduced.

5. A period of separate confinement (see B. 1 b).

1862 *Cornh. Mag.* Nov. 640 Professional thieves..form a net-work..by..which all criminal knowledge circulates. In prison and out of it, in the lowly village lodging-house and ..'doing their separates' at Pentonville..they..spread criminal knowledge. **1904** A. Griffiths *50 Yrs. Publ. Service* xv. 193 There were penal servitude convicts of both sexes doing 'separates', the first probationary period of nine months, a modified form of solitary confinement.

6. *Geol.* Any of the fractions into which constituents of a soil or other material can be separated according to a property such as particle size or mineral composition. Cf. *soil separate* s.v. soil *sb.*[1] 10.

1909 A. G. McCall *Physical Properties of Soils* 84 The separates to be determined are as follows: Fine gravel 2·0–1·0 mm, Coarse sand 1·0–0·5,..Clay 0·005. **1924** F. E. Bear *Soil Managem.* vii. 56 In the Illinois soil survey, silt is defined as a separate the particles in which may vary from 0·03 to 0·001 millimeter in diameter. **1952** L. M. Thompson *Soils & Soil Fertility* ii. 10 The sand separate which occurs in an amount greater than any other separate is used to indicate the name; for example, fine sandy loam indicates a predominance of fine sand. **1977** *New Scientist* 21 Apr. 120/1 Isotopic abundance anomalies in mineral separates from meteorites.

7. *pl.* Articles of (esp. women's) dress which may be worn in various combinations and not only as parts of a matching outfit.

1945 *Britannica Bk. of Year* 276/2 These 'separates' were outfits of which the several parts could be inter-changed to form many combinations. **1948** *Sun* (Baltimore) 3 Apr. 3/7 (Advt.), Tropical separates... Of crisp tropical rayon suiting nicely tailored... You can either 'mix 'em or match 'em'. **1958** *TV Times* 20 June 15/2 She finds 'separates' ideal for her type of performance. **1964** *McCall's Sewing* i. 13/1 Separates are the answer to the schoolgirl's needs. Skirts, sweaters, jackets and blouses that can mix and match are perfect. **1979** *Sunday Star* (Toronto) 30 Sept. D2/2 She's learned the knack of putting her own looks together with separates. She's off to school one day in gray dress pants, hot pink sweater and pale pink tam.

8. A self-contained, free-standing component of a sound reproduction system. Usu. *pl.*

1974 *Times* 8 Apr. 12/1 Demand for all kinds of audio systems—'separates' and otherwise. **1977** *Gramophone* Apr. 1625/2 Akai showed, along with five new receivers, that it too was getting into a wide line of separates and speakers.

separate ('sɛpəreɪt), *v.* Also 6–8 seperate, 7 separat; *pa. t.* 6 *Sc.* seperat, 8 separate. [f. L. *sēparāt-*, ppl. stem of *sēparāre*, f. *sē-* (see se-) + *parāre* to make ready, prepare.]

I. Transitive senses.

1. a. To put apart, set asunder (two or more persons or things, or one *from* another); to disunite, disconnect, make a division between. Also with *out*.

1432–50 tr. *Higden* (Rolls) II. 249 [They] supposede that God wolde separate theyme that he myȝhte subiecte theym diuidede the rather to hym. **1526** Tindale *Rom.* viii. 35 Who shall seperate vs from goddes love? *a* **1568** Ascham *Scholem.* II. (Arb.) 113 And surelie the distance betwixt London and Lysbon, should not stoppe any kinde of frendlie dewtie..if the greatest matter of all did not in certeyne pointes separate our myndes. **1592** Shaks. *Rom. & Jul.* IV. v. 27 Life and these lips haue long bene seperated. **1606** —— *Tr. & Cr.* v. viii. 18 The dragon wing of night ore-spreds the earth And stickler-like the Armies seperates. **1633** Early Manch. *Al Mondo* (1636) 143 Naturall Death doth but separate the body from the soule: But spirituall Death separates the soule from God. **1667** Milton *P.L.* IX. 970 Rather then Death..Shall separate us, linkt in Love so deare. **1816** J. Smith *Panorama Sci. & Art* II. 279 Separate the wires, and the effect ceases. **1839** Lane *Arab. Nts.* I. 91 Being thus separated from my attendants, I lost my way. **1876** J. Parker *Paracl.* I. x. 158 What separates nation from nation so completely as ignorance of each other's speech? **1962** H. E. Beecheno *Introd. Bus. Stud.* xi. 93 For the mass of smaller businesses these functions must be separated out. **1980** V. Cunningham *Sp. Civil War Verse* 64 The various elements of his poetry can't be separated out like this.

b. *refl.*

1528 Tindale *Obed. Chr. Man* 42 They..have separated them selves from the laye men, countinge them viler then dogges. **1561** T. Hoby tr. *Castiglione's Courtyer* II. (1577) G viij, Hee ought to worke the matter wisely in seperating himselfe from the multitude. *a* **1600** Hooker *1st Serm. Jude* §11 (1614) 17 Men do separate themselues either by heresie, schisme, or apostasie. **1654** Bramhall *Just Vind.* ii. (1661) 9 If one part of the Universall Church do separate it self from another part,..not as it is a part of the Universal Church, but only so far as it is corrupted and degenerated. **1849** Macaulay *Hist. Eng.* ii. I. 173 To the Anglican Church he had always been strongly attached, and had repeatedly, where her interests were concerned, separated himself with regret from his dearest friends.

c. To put asunder in thought, to distinguish, treat as distinct. Also with *off*.

1651 Hobbes *Leviath.* II. xxx. 182 The good of the Soveraign and People, cannot be separated. **1793** Smeaton *Edystone L.* §315 When the elevation of the object becomes too small to be discerned, as separated from the luminous reflection. **1828** D'Israeli *Chas. I*, II. vi. 143 In modern history it seems to me always impossible to separate religion from politics. **1864** Bryce *Holy Rom. Emp.* vi. (1875) 85 Man had not yet learned to satisfy their consciences by separating the person from the office. **1894** H. Drummond *Ascent of Man* 12 It is as great a mistake..for the theologian to separate off the ship from the passengers as for the naturalist to separate off the passengers from the ship.

d. To discharge (a person) *from* the armed forces (*U.S. Mil.*); †to remove from employment.

1859 R. Thornton *Jrnl.* 25 June in E. C. Tabler *Zambezi Papers of Richard Thornton* (1963) I. 103 About 3 p.m. Dr. L. gave me an official letter separating me from the Expedition. **1888** *Civil Service* (U.S.) *Comm. 4th Rep.* 51 A statement of the number of persons who have been 'separated' from the classified service by removal, resignation, and death cannot be made. **1946** *Britannica Bk. of Year* 833/1 *Separate*, to discharge or release from active duty in the armed services. **1971** *Reader's Digest* (U.S. ed.) Oct. 13/1 This year one million veterans will be separated from the service.

2. To remove from conjugal cohabitation, esp. by a judicial decree. (Cf. separation 3.)

a **1540** Barnes *Wks.* (1573) 331/2 Commaundyng to forbydde priestes that had not yet maryed, for to marry. And those y^t had maried, to bee separated from their wyues. **1764** G. Williams in Jesse *Selwyn & Contemp.* (1843) I. 325 The Duke and Duchess of Grafton are separated, though the articles are not yet agreed upon between them. **1852** Thackeray *Esmond* I. xiii, My Lord Mohun was separated from his wife.

3. To keep apart or divide by an intervening space or barrier. Of the intervening medium: To part by lying between, to occupy the space or interval between.

1553 Eden *Treat. New Ind.* (Arb.) 32 Whether..nature.. had not so deuided and seperated the East from the West. **1585** T. Washington tr. *Nicholay's Voy.* II. xii. 47 The goulph of Ponthus..separateth Asia from Europe. **1600** J. Pory tr. *Leo's Africa* III. 208 It standeth so neere the mountaine last mentioned, that they are onely separated with the foresaid riuer. **1663** Gerbier *Counsel* e 6, Stables and even Kitchens ought to be separated from the main body of a Palace. **1727** [E. Dorrington] *Philip Quarll* (1816) 39 Climbing up the rock.., he found at the bottom of it a narrow lake, which separated it from the land. **1819** Scott *Ivanhoe* xliii, The younger race..had..broken down many of the barriers which separated for half a century the Norman victors from the vanquished Saxons. **1822** Parkinson *Outl. Oryctol.* 259 This shell has six turns, very projecting, deeply separated. **1849** Macaulay *Hist. Eng.* ii. I. 276 The ten centuries which separated the reign of Charlemagne from the reign of Napoleon. **1862** Stanley *Jew. Ch.* I. xiii. 303 The deep gulf which separates the two regions.

4. a. To set apart or segregate for a special purpose. Const. *for*, *to*, *unto*. (Chiefly in Biblical language.)

1526 TINDALE *Acts* xiii. 2 Seperat me Barnabas and Saul for the worke where vnto I have called them. 1611 BIBLE *Rom.* i. 1 Paul..separated vnto the Gospel of God. 1642 D. ROGERS *Naaman* 9 Who separated the Gentile and rejected the Iew? 1710 PRIDEAUX *Orig. Tithes* i. 12 Whoever of the ancient Patriarchs first separated a Tenth. 1785 PALEY *Mor. Philos.* v. vii. (1818) II. 92 Every trespass upon that reserve which public decency has established breaks down the fence by which the day is separated to the service of religion. 1798 M. CUTLER in *Life*, etc. (1888) II. 11 You are now, Sir, vested with power to ordain and separate others to the work of the ministry.

†**b.** To exclude, prohibit. *Obs. rare*$^{-1}$.

1644 MILTON *Areop.* (Arb.) 51 Lastly, who shall forbid and separat all idle resort, all evill company?

5. a. To remove or part (a substance) *from* another with which it is combined or mixed; esp. to do this by some technical process. Also with *out*.

1617 MORYSON *Itin.* III. 147 The Tinne and Leade is mingled with Silver, but so, as it doth not largely quit the cost of the labour in seperating or trying it. 1683 SOAME & DRYDEN *Boileau's Art Poet.* IV. 1090 From the fine gold I separate the allay. 1784 CULLEN tr. *Bergman's Phys. & Chem. Ess.* I. 221 The selenite may be still better separated from the iron, by boiling the dried residuum [etc.]. 1850 MCCOSH *Div. Govt.* II. ii. (1874) 205 It is in the furnace that the dross is separated. 1869 ROSCOE *Elem. Chem.* (1874) 198 Plants..are able slowly to separate out and assimilate the potash from these rocks and soils.

b. Of a gland: To secrete. Of a material substance: To give off or emit from itself. ? *Obs.*

1691 RAY *Creation* II. (1692) 33 There being Glandules on purpose to separate a humor for that purpose. 1796 MORSE *Amer. Geog.* I. 206 Furnished with glands, which separate a substance that has the smell of musk. 1805 SAUNDERS *Min. Waters* 286 Cheltenham water, when fresh drawn, appears tolerably clear... It becomes more turbid by standing, and separates air bubbles in a small quantity.

6. To divide into (two or more) parts. *rare.*

1581 J. HAMILTON *Cath. Tr.* 34 Moyses liftit vp his vand, and seperat the see. 1784 COWPER *Task* V. 196 As a shepherd separates his flock, These to the upland, to the valley those.

†**7.** *absol.* To make a division or severance. *Obs.*

1560 BIBLE (Geneva) *Isa.* lix. 2 Your iniquities haue separated betwene you and your God. *a*1653 BINNING *Princ. Chr. Relig.* Wks. (1735) 9 The Cloud of our Sins, that separates between God and us.

II. *intr.* (Cf. the reflexive use 1 b.)

8. a. Of a person: To quit the company or society of another or others; to go away, secede or withdraw *from* (esp. a church).

1684 BAXTER *Answ. Theol. Dial.* 19, I must not separate from every Kingdom, Church, or Family that is ill governed. 1711 *Countryman's Let. to Curate* 20 William Whittinghame one of those that Compiled the Francfort Liturgie, and separate with the rest to Geneva upon the Contest about the English Liturgie. 1815 SCOTT *Guy M.* xv, No, Miss Lucy Bertram, while I live I will not separate from you.

Indirect passive. 1595 F. JOHNSON (*title*) A Treatise of the Ministry of the Church of England. Wherein is handled this question, Whether it be to be separated from or joyned unto.

b. Of two or more persons: To quit each other's society or company; (of a company) to break up.

1690 LOCKE *Govt.* II. v. §39 When there was not room enough..for their Herds to feed together, they, by consent, ..separated, and inlarged their pasture. 1794 MRS. RADCLIFFE *Myst. Udolpho* iv, They separated at an early hour. 1861 WHYTE MELVILLE *Mkt. Harb.* xix, The conversation held between the latter and Mr. Sawyer.. before separating for the night. 1885 PATER *Marius* (1910) II. xx. 86 It was time for the company to separate.

c. To withdraw from conjugal cohabitation.

1686 tr. *Chardin's Trav. Persia* 332 The differences that happen between man and wife..and the Reasons that move 'em to separate. 1794 *Ann. Reg., Chron.* *11 The parties had separated the 24th of July, 1793, and no evidence had been produced to affect his client, but cohabitation since the separation. 1819 *Ibid.* (1820) 252 Is the prisoner your husband?.. Yes. I believe you separated from him for some time?—Yes.

9. a. Of a thing: To part (*from* something else); to be disunited or disjoined, to become detached; to draw apart or asunder.

1638 SIR T. HERBERT *Trav.* (ed. 2) 219 The bridge..has a plain and easie passage over 30 long boats, concatenated and made to separate at pleasure. 1739 S. SHARP *Oper. Surg.* Introd. 43 The Bullet makes an Eschar, which usually separates in a few days. 1774 GOLDSM. *Nat. Hist.* (1776) VI. 390 Swammerdam..was of opinion that the bones themselves separated from each other, and closed again. 1801 *Med. & Phys. Jrnl.* V. 222 The gangrene was separating. 1813 J. THOMSON *Lect. Inflam.* 549 The mortified parts separated, without assistance, from the sound parts. 1832 *John Bull* 13 Feb. 56/1 The roof of the nave has separated in one place from the wall.

b. Of a mineral or chemical substance: To be parted or disengaged from a mass or compound; to be drawn *out* from a solution in the form of crystals or as a precipitate.

1863 *Fownes' Chem.* (ed. 9) 486 The salt separates in minute needles. 1869 ROSCOE *Elem. Chem.* (1874) 211 On cooling, potassium nitrate separates out in crystals.

separated (ˈsɛpəreɪtɪd), *ppl. a.* [f. SEPARATE *v.* + -ED^{1}.] **1.** In senses of the verb: Set apart or asunder, disjoined, withdrawn, etc. Also *absol.*, esp. (orig. *U.S.*) in sense 'one who has withdrawn from a conjugal relationship but is not divorced' (chiefly *pl.*).

separated milk: milk from which the cream has been extracted by a separator.

1535 COVERDALE *Ezek.* xli. 13 The house..and the seperated buyldinge. 1597 A. M. tr. *Guillemeau's Fr. Chirurg.* 23/2 If the separated partes can not with ease be brought together. 1605 SHAKS. *Macb.* II. iii. 144 Our seperated fortune shall keepe vs both the safer. 1661 BOYLE *Scept. Chem.* IV. 255 The separated sulphurs or Chymical Oyles of things. *a*1676 HALE *Prim. Orig. Man.* IV. v. (1677) 333 The Sect of the Sadduces..denied..the Existence of Angels or separated Intelligences. *a*1715 BURNET *Own Time* (1766) I. 442 Every province is a separated state and has an entire sovereignty within itself. 1730 POPE *Let. to Gay* 11 Sept., I can't but look upon myself..as a separated spirit too from Courts and courtly fopperies. 1869 M. PATTISON *Serm.* (1885) 174 The Protestant or other separated communions. 1901 *Scotsman* 12 Apr. 5/4 To prevent the wholesale dilution of whole with separated milk. 1951 N. MITFORD *Blessing* II. v. 192 It's always like that with separated couples... Each one is trying to give the child a better time than the other. 1975 *Observer* (Colour Suppl.) 5 Jan. 7/2 Feiffer is 45, separated, has a daughter, lives in New York.

absol. 1700 T. BROWN tr. *Fresny's Amusem.* vii. Wks. 1709 III. I. 64 Widowhood..is much to be preferred before Separation; for the Separated are Savage Animals, uncapable of the prettiest Ties of Society. 1744 *Life & Adv. M. Bishop* 216 In the Morning all the separated got together again, to receive Orders. 1960 *Time* 17 Oct. 112/2 A collection of psychologizing short stories about young separateds. 1975 *Publishers Weekly* 27 Jan. 234/3 Explores the bisexual lifestyle through in-depth interviews with marrieds, singles and 'separateds'.

2. *Math.* (See quot. 1968.)

1956 J. M. H. OLMSTEAD *Intermediate Analysis* iii. 77 The set of rational numbers and the set of irrational numbers are disjoint, but are about as far from being separated as two disjoint sets of real numbers can be. 1964 T. O. MOORE *Elem. Gen. Topology* ii. 40 A space X is connected iff X is not the union of two separated sets. 1968 E. T. COPSON *Metric Spaces* v. 62 Two sets A and B in a metric space M are said to be separated if neither has a point in common with the closure of the other.

Hence **ˈseparatedly** *adv. rare.*

*a*1641 BP. MOUNTAGU *Acts & Mon.* (1642) 417 So no spirit did at all subsist, separatedly, subsisting alone, out or beside the body.

separately (ˈsɛpərətlɪ), *adv.* [-LY^{2}.] In a separate manner; singly, severally, apart.

1552 HULOET, Separatly, *separatim.* 1567 *Reg. Privy Council Scot.* I. 557 Togidder or separatlie as neid beis. 1612 BACON *Ess., Counsel* (Arb.) 324 It is of singuler vse to Princes, if they take the opinions of their Councell, both seperatly [1625 Seperately] and together. 1710 *Lond. Gaz.* No. 4736/4 Hannah the Wife of Richard Hamp..liveth separately from her said Husband. 1837 CARLYLE *Fr. Rev.* I. v. i, Two separate, perhaps separately-voting Orders. 1858 LD. ST. LEONARDS *Handy Bk. Prop. Law* xx. 155 If you leave to every one separately what you desire each to have. 1875 JOWETT *Plato* (ed. 2) I. 388 Other things which we need not separately enumerate.

ˈseparateness. [-NESS.] The quality, state, or fact of being separate.

1635-6 MEDE *Rev. God's House* (1638) 3 Sacred things, which continue their state of separatenesse and sanctitie. 1755 in JOHNSON. 1856 R. A. VAUGHAN *Mystics* (1860) II. XI. i. 219, I know men and women who pique themselves on their separateness from the world. 1879 GEO. ELIOT *Theo. Such* 355 The Jews were steadfast in their separateness, and through that separateness Christianity was born.

sepaˈratical, *a. rare.* [f. L. *sēparāt-* (see SEPARATE *v.*) + -IC (see -ATIC) + -AL^{1}.] Pertaining to separation in religion.

1846 WORCESTER (cites *T. Dwight*).

separating (ˈsɛpəreɪtɪŋ), *vbl. sb.* [f. SEPARATE *v.* + -ING^{1}.] The action of SEPARATE *v.*

*c*1550 CHEKE *Matt.* xxi. 44 *note*, This separating of chaf and dust awai from ye good corne is called in greek λικμᾶν. 1623 COCKERAM II, A Seperating of man and wife. *Diuorce.* 1644 MILTON *Divorce* I. x. (ed. 2) 26 By the separating of unmeet consorts. 1831 SCOTT *Ct. Robt.* xxii, If so, his meeting with his plighted bride, after so many years' absence, was but a delusive preface to their separating for ever.

attrib. 1641 FRENCH *Distill.* i. (1651) 34 Let the Oil that is drawn with the Water be separated with a..seperating Glass. 1855 D. K. CLARK *Railway Mach.* 153/2 Edwards' separating pipes..for disengaging the steam from the priming.

separating (ˈsɛpəreɪtɪŋ), *ppl. a.* [f. SEPARATE *v.* + -ING^{2}.] That separates, in various senses of the verb. † ***separating line*** = SEPARATRIX.

1694 HALLEY *Oughtred's Key Math.* 3 Decimal Parts are written in the same line with Integers; but are distinguished by a rectangular line; which is therefore called the Separating Line. 1850 MISS WARNER *Wide Wide World* xxxvi, She clasped Alice, as if she feared even then the separating hand. 1908 [MISS FOWLER] *Betw. Trent & Ancholme* 23 The low separating wall.

†**b.** = SEPARATIST *a.* (Cf. *dissenting.*) *Obs.*

1734 WATTS *Reliq. Juv.* (1789) 127 He attends the best of preachers in their separating meetings.

separation (sɛpəˈreɪʃən). Forms: 5-6 separacion, 6 -acyon, seperacion, 6-7 seperation, 6- separation. [a. OF. *separation, -acion*, F. *séparation* (= Pr. *separatio*, Sp. *separacion*, Pg. *separação*, It. *separazione*), ad. L. *sēparātiōn-em*, n. of action from *sēparāre*: see SEPARATE *v.*]

1. a. The action of separating or parting, of setting or keeping apart; the state of being separated or parted. † ***to make separation***, to make a severance or division.

1413 *Pilgr. Sowle* (Caxton 1483) IV. xix. 64 And so the tyme come that seperacion shold be made bitwene this swete appel and this Appeltre and so it felle to the erthe. 1526 *Pilgr. Perf.* (W. de W. 1531) 12 b, Saynt Austyn sayth, that the passage of ye chyldren of Israel from Egipt, signifyeth the separacyon of mannes soule from synne by..baptym. *c*1550 N. SMYTH tr. *Herodian* VI. 73 The Illirian nacions, dwellynge in a smale streyte,..doo onelye make seperacion betwene Italye, and Germanye. 1611 SHAKS. *Wint. T.* I. i. 28 Since their more mature Dignities, and Royall Necessities, made seperation of their Societie. 1650 JER. TAYLOR *Funeral Serm. C'tess Carbery* Wks. 1831 IV. 110 From whence it follows, that because the body casts fetters and restraints.. on the soul, that the soul is much freer in the state of separation. 1684 T. BURNET *Th. Earth* I. v. 63 The Chaos, when it was first set on work, ran all into divisions, and separations of one Element from another. 1788 GIBBON *Decl. & F.* l. V. 184 The separation of the Arabs from the rest of mankind, has accustomed them to confound the ideas of stranger and enemy. 1805 WORDSW. *Prelude* XIV. 346 The mind Learns..to keep In wholesome separation the two natures. 1841 MIALL in *Nonconf.* I. 2 The entire separation of Church and State is really their object. 1875 JOWETT *Plato* (ed. 2) V. 363 After the age of six years the time has arrived for the separation of the sexes. 1905 R. BAGOT *Passport* xxiv. 255 Nothing but a separation from her lover ..could accomplish this object.

b. *U.S.* Resignation or dismissal from employment, a university, etc.; discharge from the armed forces.

1779 T. JEFFERSON *Let.* 27 Mar. in *Writings* (1893) II. 179 The separation of these troops would be a breach of public faith. 1897 C. M. FLANDRAU *Harvard Episodes* 229 He would feel [sorrow] at what the official college gracefully terms the 'separation' of Billy from the University. 1923 J. D. HACKETT *Labor Terms* in *Managem. Engin.* May, *Separation*, the termination of employment, either voluntary or involuntary, at the instance of the employer or worker. 1955 *Univ. of Va. News Letter* 15 June 1/2 Just as births exceed deaths to yield an expanding population, so new entrants exceed separations through deaths and retirements to yield an expanding labor force. 1976 *Washington Post* 19 Apr. C15/10 (Advt.), Excellent opportunity in proposal writing for former surface Naval officer who completed 1 or 2 tours prior to separation.

c. ***separation of powers*** *Pol.*: the vesting of the legislative, executive, and judiciary powers of government in separate bodies.

[1748 MONTESQUIEU *De l'Esprit des Loix* I. XI. vi. 245 Il n'ya a point encore de Liberté, si la puissance de juger n'est pas séparée de la puissance législative & de l'exécutrice. 1788 A. HAMILTON et al. *Federalist* II. xlvii. 92 The Meaning of the Maxim, which requires a Separation of the Departments of Power, examined and ascertained.] 1896 A. L. LOWELL *Govts. & Parties in Continental Europe* I. i. 55 The Declaration of The Rights of Man proclaimed in 1789 that a community in which the separation of powers was not established had no constitution. 1921 J. BRYCE *Mod. Democracies* II. II. xxxix. 23 No official of the Federal Government is eligible to sit in Congress, no official of the Government of a State to sit in its legislature. This provision, a tribute to the famous doctrine of the Separation of Powers, was meant to prevent the Executive from controlling the Legislature. 1973 *N.Y. Times* 15 Aug. 36/1 President Nixon's attorneys..asserted that the constitutional separation of powers precluded the courts from commanding him to make those tapes available to a grand jury.

2. The action of separating oneself, withdrawing, or parting company. † ***to make separation***, to withdraw, go apart.

*c*1450 *Cov. Myst.* (Shaks. Soc.) 240 Whan the Soule from the body xal make Separacion. 1623 E. JESSOP *Discov. Err. Anabaptists* 85 Here we see..that a separation ought to be made from all kind of Idolatry and vnrighteousnes of the heathen. *a*1625 FLETCHER *Elder Bro.* III. v, Remove her where you will, I walk along still; For, like the light, we make no separation. 1686 J. SCOTT *Chr. Life* II. iii. Wks. 1718 I. 232 As separating into Parties..exposes the Separatists themselves to great Temptations to Atheism, so it doth those also who..stand engaged on neither Part of the Separation. 1848 THACKERAY *Van. Fair* xxiv, When a separation from those we love is imminent, [we] cannot rest until the parting be over. 1856 FROUDE *Hist. Eng.* (1858) I. iv. 356 It was the first active movement towards a separation from Rome. 1886 *Nat. Rev.* Mar. 83 With Mr. Parnell.. Separation is a means to an end.

3. Cessation of conjugal cohabitation, either by mutual consent of the parties or imposed by a judicial decree granted at the suit of one of them. ***judicial separation***: the name now given to the 'divorce *a mensa et thoro*' of the older English law: see DIVORCE *sb.* 1.

1600 J. CHAMBERLAIN *Lett.* (Camden) 98 But in conclusion the woman scaped better cheape then was looked for, having only sentence of separation *a mensâ et thoro.* 1613 SHAKS. *Hen. VIII*, II. i. 148 Did you not of late dayes heare A buzzing of a Separation Betweene the King and Katherine? 1700 T. BROWN tr. *Fresny's Amusem.* vii. Wks. 1709 III. I. 64 The usual Causes of Separation is assign'd as the Fault of the Wife. 1749 FIELDING *Tom Jones* XVIII. xi, In order to prevail with him..to consent to a separation from his wife. 1848 THACKERAY *Van. Fair* lxv, Wasn't there a scandal about their separation? 1857 *Act 20 & 21 Vict.* c. 85 §16 A Sentence of Judicial Separation (which shall have the Effect of a Divorce *à Mensâ et Thoro* under the existing Law ..) may be obtained, either by the Husband or the Wife, on the ground of Adultery [etc.].

†**4.** A sect of separatists or dissenters from *the* Church; esp. in the 17th cent., the body of Protestant nonconformists collectively. *Obs.*

1599 [H. Jacob] *title*, A short Treatise..Against the Reasons..of Maister Francis Johnson, with others of the Separation. **1608** Bernard *Chr. Advert.* 163 Positions.. maintained by some godlie Ministers of the Gospell against those of the Separation. **1610** B. Jonson *Alch.* iii. i, Such rebukes we of the Separation Must beare, with willing shoulders. **1623** E. Jessop *Discov. Err. Anabaptists* 80 Which is the best ordination and succession, the Church of Rome..hath..and which the separations doe contend for. **1710** S. Palmer *Proverbs* 141 This is both a court and a church-game, and the separation it self isn't free from it.

†**5.** A separated portion, a division. *Obs.*

1604 E. G[rimstone] *D'Acosta's Hist. Indies* vi. ii. 435 Every portion of these foure had thirteene separations which had all their signs or particular figures. **1785** Hutton in *Trans. Roy. Soc. Edin.* (1788) I. 246 By this means the separations of the stone diminish, in a progression from the centre towards the circumference.

6. The place where two or more objects separate or are divided from one another; a parting, line of division.

1615 Crooke *Body of Man* 435 In woemen they are diuided by a line, which separation the Greeks call λύσωμα.., in English we cal it the shed of the haire. **1839** W. Chambers *Tour Rhine* 47/1 We now come to the separation of the Maas and Waal branches of the river. **1851** Woodward *Mollusca* i. 48 In the *brachiopoda* the separation is horizontal.

7. Something that separates or effects a division or partition; an interval or break between two objects; a cause of separating. *rare.*

1715 Leoni *Palladio's Archit.* (1742) I. 68 The Walls, which make the separation of every Apartment. **1728** R. Morris *Anc. Archit.* 51 Some omit this Member, and have only the second Fascia, projected..beyond..the first, without any Separation. **1821** Rich *Journ. Persepolis* 25 Aug. in *Babylon & P.* (1839) 249 The separation or stop in the first [kind of Cuneiform inscription] is [an oblique wedge]. **1906** Belloc *Hills & Sea* 94 These dykes of the Fens are accursed things: they are the separation of friends and lovers.

†**8.** *Alchemy* and *Old Chem.* A process of analysis, extraction, or the like. ***water of separation*** (see quot. 1728). *Obs.*

1471 Ripley *Comp. Alch.* iii. ii. in Ashm. (1652) 139 And Separacyon ys callyd by Phylosophers dyffynycyon Of the sayd Elements tetraptatyve dyspersyon. **1626** Bacon *Sylva* §3 It seemeth Percolation..is a good kinde of Separation. *Ibid.* §798, I remember to haue heard..that a Fifteenth Part of Siluer, incorporate with Gold, will not be Recouered by any Water of Separation; Except you put a Greater Quantity of Siluer, to draw to it the Lesse; which..is the last Refuge in Separations. **1661** Boyle *Scept. Chem.* iv. 276 What Disparity there may be between the salts and sulphurs of Metals and other Minerals, I am not my self experienced enough in the separations and examens of them, to venture to determine. **1728** Chambers *Cycl.* II. 349/2 s.v. *Water*, A farther Use is in the making Separations of oily from saline Parts. *Ibid.* 351/2 *Water of Separation*, or *Depart*, is only *Aqua fortis*; thus called, because serving to separate Gold from Silver.

9. *Astr.* and *Astrol.* (See quot. 1819.)

1594 Davis *Seaman's Secr.* (1607) 6 Betweene the change and the full, it is called the Moone's separation from the Sunne. **1819** J. Wilson *Dict. Astrol.* 366 *Separation*, when two planets having been in partile configuration are beginning to separate. It is distinguished into simple and mutual.

10. *Med.* The process by which dead tissue becomes detached from the sound flesh.

1612 Woodall *Surg. Mate* Wks. (1653) 273 Separation is, whereby parts distracted are separated every one alike having his several being in himself. **1672** Wiseman *Treat. Wounds* ii. 14 It being a good Medicament to hasten separation of the Escars. **1800** *Med. & Phys. Jrnl.* III. 449, I know two or three cases where women have lost their lives by waiting too long for a spontaneous separation [*sc.* of the placenta]. **1801** *Ibid.* V. 80 No sloughing or separation took place, for the action of the absorbents was equal to the removal.

†**11.** *Navigation.* = departure 7 a. *Obs.*$^{-0}$

1704 J. Harris *Lex. Techn.* I, *Separation*, with some Writers of Navigation, is the same with what is more usually called, the *Departure*; that is, a Ships Difference of Longitude from any place, or from another Ship.

12. *Math.* The division of a partition into component partitions. Cf. separate *sb.* 4.

1888 MacMahon in *Proc. Lond. Math. Soc.* XIX. 243 It becomes necessary to consider the separation of such a partition into component partitions. *Ibid.* 254 In general, if there are θ separations of any partition and ϕ species of separation, there must be θ-ϕ syzygies between the θ separations.

13. *Horticulture.* (See quot.)

1891 L. H. Bailey *Nursery-bk.* (1896) 26 Separation, or the multiplication of plants by means of naturally detachable vegetative organs, is effected by means of bulbs, bulbels, bulb-scales, bulblets, corms, tubers, and sometimes by buds.

14. *Photogr.* and *Printing.* **a.** Each of three or more monochrome reproductions of a coloured picture, made in different colours in such a way that they combine to reproduce the full colour of the original.

1922 [see *colour separation* s.v. colour *sb.*[1] 19]. **1933** T. S. Barber *Art & Pract. Printing* IV. xiv. 163 The Three-colour Process requires three half-tones, made from photographic colour separations. **1967** Karch & Buber *Offset Processes* v. 170 In making the separation from a colored original or transparency, the circular glass halftone screen..is used. **1972** *Physics Bull.* Sept. 553/3 An original colour picture must first be processed to obtain four continuous tone 'separations', that is images on film which present the red, green and blue content of the original together with a 'key'.

b. The process of obtaining a set of monochrome reproductions of a coloured picture in each of which the tones correspond to the proportions of a particular colour in the original.

1924, 1930 [see *colour separation* s.v. colour *sb.*[1] 19]. **1931** F. R. Newens *Technique Colour Photogr.* iii. 25 This tri-pack gives extremely good colour separation. **1949** Melcher & Larrick *Printing & Promotion Handbk.* 48/2 Color separation is the technique by which the colors of the original art work..are sorted out so that all the reds appear in the red plate, the blue and the shades of blue in the blue plate, etc. *Ibid.* 49/1 Flat-color jobs present no problem... Full-color originals are more difficult. Here the printer may do his separations by the fake process method or by the process-color method. **1974** *Encycl. Brit. Macropædia* XIV. 304/2 In the direct method [of making colourplates], screen negatives are prepared directly from the copy through the colour-separation filters and a halftone screen.

15. *Physics* and *Aeronaut.* The separation of the boundary layer from the surface of a body moving relative to the surrounding fluid.

1926 H. Glauert *Elem. Aerofoil & Airscrew Theory* viii. 100 When two parallel layers of fluid are moving in the same direction with different velocities, the surface of separation is a vortex sheet. **1935** K. D. Wood *Techn. Aerodynamics* ii. 46 At zero lift, there is commonly a certain amount of separation under the nose of the airfoil. **1949** O. G. Sutton *Sci. of Flight* ii. 40 The air stream has found it difficult to turn the corner... In technical language the flow separates. We shall see later that separation is of immense importance in all problems of aerodynamics. **1978** D. Küchemann *Aerodynamic Design of Aircraft* ii. 37 The most important boundary-layer phenomenon is flow separation.

16. Distinction or difference between the signals carried by the two channels of a stereophonic system; a measure of this.

1960 Markell & Stanton *Installing Hi-Fi Systems* i. 11 The portion of the room in which the maximum stereo effect is heard is fairly limited, and complete separation between the sound signals at the ears of the listener is impossible in a practical situation. **1962** *Times* 5 July 15/6 In general quality the discs were still preferable although on the tapes the stereo 'separation' was more marked. **1974** Harvey & Bohlman *Stereo F.M. Radio Handbk.* vi. 129 Some adjustment over the degree of cross-coupling may be provided by a preset control..labelled separation. **1975** G. J. King *Audio Handbk.* viii. 185 For good stereo image placement the separation should not be less than 20 dB over the important part of the spectrum.

17. *attrib.*, as ***separation funnel, -scene***; **separation anxiety** *Psychol.*, anxiety provoked in a child by the threat or actuality of separation from its mother or mother substitute; also *transf.*; **separation factor** *Nucl. Engin.*, the ratio of the concentration of a particular isotope after a process of enrichment to the concentration before; also, the ratio of the concentrations in the two mixtures produced by the process; **separation negative**, a separation (sense 14 a above) in the form of a photographic negative; **separation-order**, an order of court for judicial separation (see 3); **separation plant**, an installation for the separation of isotopes of a chemical element; **separation point** *Physics* and *Aeronaut.*, a point on a surface at which boundary-layer separation begins.

1943 W. R. D. Fairbairn in *Brit. Jrnl. Med. Psychol.* XIX. 340/2 The problem of *separation-anxiety in the soldier is anticipated under a totalitarian regime by a previous exploitation of infantile dependence. **1973** J. Bowlby *Attachment & Loss* II. vi. 95 Despite Freud's increasing insistence on the key role of separation anxiety in neurosis, there has been marked reluctance to adopt his ideas. **1977** *Sunday Mail* (Brisbane) 23 Oct. 24/7 *Separation Anxiety*: The child fears the parent will abandon him. Newson and Newson showed that very many parents used this as a threat. **1945** H. D. Smyth *Gen. Acct. Devel. Atomic Energy Mil. Purposes* ix. 94 In nearly every process a high *separation factor means a low yield, a fact that calls for continual compromise. **1978** *Sci. Amer.* Aug. 31/3 A typical separation factor for an early machine was 1·25, which means that if the fraction of uranium 235 in the feed gas is 0·71 percent, as it is in natural uranium, the product contains ·794 uranium 235 and the waste contains ·635 percent. **1881** Tyndall *Floating Matter* iii. 171 A *separation-funnel' with a glass stopcock. **1931** F. R. Newens *Techniques Colour Photogr.* iii. 25 Although it is possible to produce the three-colour *separation negatives by a single exposure, either in a one-exposure tricolour camera, or by means of a film tri-pack.., neither method is at present readily available. **1957** P. Jenkins *Colour Separation Negatives* 30 A fundamental rule in separation-negative making is that any neutral (grey, white, or black) should be reproduced as an equal density on each of the three negatives. **1974** A. Sussman *Amateur Photographer's Handbk.* (ed. 8) xviii. 478 The problem of separation negatives, so far as the amateur is concerned, was overcome in 1935 when Eastman Kodak introduced Kodachrome film. **1887** *Cassell's Encycl. Dict.* s.v. *Separation*, A *separation order can also be granted in England by a magistrate on proof of cruelty. **1907** 'John Halsham' *Lonewood Corner* 74 The wife and her mangle presently get a separation-order. **1945** H. D. Smyth *Gen. Acct. Devel. Atomic Energy Mil. Purposes* viii. 84 The principal installations constructed at the Clinton Laboratory site were the pile and the *separation plant. **1974** *Encycl. Brit. Macropædia* XIII. 325/1 Groves arranged contracts for a gaseous diffusion separation plant, a plutonium production facility and a calutron pilot plant. **1946** A. W. Sherwood *Aerodynamics* vii. 101 If the velocity of flow over the sphere is increased, the local Reynolds number *Rl* for any point in the boundary layer is proportionally increased, with a maximum value at the *separation points. **1978** D. Küchemann *Aerodynamic Design of Aircraft* ii. 37 The flow lifts off the wall at a separation point where the skin friction becomes zero and the air flows backwards behind it. **1848** Thackeray *Van. Fair* lxvi, As for the *separation-scene from the child, while Becky was reciting it, Emmy retired altogether behind her pocket-handkerchief.

separationism (sɛpəˈreɪʃənɪz(ə)m). [-ism.] Advocacy of separation, or of a theory of separation.

1875 *Contemp. Rev.* XXV. 848 It may refer..to the separationism of Cerinthus, who maintained that the spiritual Being Christ descended on the man Jesus after the baptism. **1886** *Ch. Times* 7 May 347/2 The Ode of the Laureate, which was an emphatic protest against Separationism.

separationist (sɛpəˈreɪʃənɪst). [-ist.] One who advocates political separation or disruption. Also *attrib.* or quasi-*adj.*

1831 Ld. Holland *Let.* 3 Jan. in R. B. McDowell *Public Opinion in Ireland 1801–1846* (1952) vi. 143 Withdrawing from O'Connell and the separationists. **1882** *Q. Rev.* July 261 The moment that Mr. Gladstone succeeded to power, the Nationalists, the Separationists and all the rest of them saw that their opportunity had come. **1903** Conrad & Hueffer *Romance* ii. i. 48 El Demonio had, during the last two years, gutted a ship once a week, as if he wanted to help the Kingston Separationist papers.

separatism (ˈsɛpərətɪz(ə)m). [f. separate *a.* + -ism.] The disposition to separate or to be separate; advocacy of separation (esp. in regard to Church or State); the principles and practices of separatists.

1628 A. Leighton *App. Parlt.* 85 B. Whitgift wrote the quoted treatise..before seperatisme was hatched. **1641** Ld. Brooke *Eng. Episc.* ii. vii. 99 What is there then to be feared? Anabaptisme, Brownisme, Separatisme. **1831** Carlyle *Sart. Res.* iii. x, These people, animated with the zeal of a new Sect,..affect great purity and separatism. **1866** *Pall Mall Gaz.* 3 Dec. 5 The numerous accusations of separatism made against the Baltic provinces. **1876** Bancroft *Hist. U.S.* V. p. xxii, Confederation opposed by separatism. **1882** Farrar *Early Chr.* I. 512 The object of these developments was to enclose the Law in a hedge of separatism, out of which no Jew could break. **1957** P. Kemp *Mine were of Trouble* x. 190 Separatism and Anarchism were the strongest political forces in Catalonia. **1962** *Globe & Mail* (Toronto) 30 Jan. 4/1 Whoever is responsible..has done more for the advancement of separatism in this province [*sc.* Quebec] in 60 minutes than Dr. Chaput could in 60 years. **1971** *Daily Tel.* 19 July 7/4 The background that gave rise to Moslem separatism in British India, the emergence of the State of Pakistan, and the subsequent history. **1978** *Encounter* Feb. 12/2 Separatism is a problem in Quebec as well as in Scotland.

separatist (ˈsɛpərətɪst), *sb.* and *a.* [f. separate *a.* or *sb.* + -ist.] **A.** *sb.*

1. One who advocates ecclesiastical separation; one who belongs to a religious commmunity separated from the Church or from a particular church.

a. A member of any of the sects separated from the Church of England. In the 17th c. (hence in mod. use *Hist.*, with capital S) applied chiefly to the Independents and those who agreed with them in rejecting all ecclesiastical authority outside the individual congregation. In later use an occasional hostile designation for Protestant dissenters in general.

1608 Bernard *Chr. Advert.* 21 Disswasions from the way of the Separatists, as they haue principles by themselues, the grounds of their separation, commonly called Brownisme. **1620** Alured in Gutch *Coll. Cur.* (1781) I. 176 Some ignorant itching Separatists seek to find..an hole in our coat and church. **1632–3** Laud *Diary* 28 Feb., *Wks.* 1853 III. 217 Mr. Chancellor of London..brought me word how miserably I was slandered by some separatists. **1641** Ld. Brooke *Eng. Episc.* ii. vi. 90 The Church of England hath three maine Divisions; The Conformist, the Non-Conformist, and the Separatist. *Ibid.*, The Separist is subdivided too as they say into Separatist and Semi-Separatist. **1645** Pagitt *Heresiogr.* To Rdr. (ed. 2) D 2, The Brownists arrogate to themselves the name of Separatists, which well they may, being separated from their Mother Church, from all the Reformed Churches, and malitiously divided amongst themselves. *a* **1734** North *Exam.* ii. v. §65 (1740) 355 Do but observe what a persecuting Spirit, he bestows upon the Church of England, and the Members of it in general: when taken off the Papists, they diverted upon the Separatists. **1794** Mrs. Piozzi *Synonymy* II. 317 Between the open invasions of the Romanists on the one hand, and the undermining subtleties of Separatists on the other. **1843** Gladstone *Glean.* V. xcii. 79 The pious Separatists of our own Country. **1844** H. H. Wilson *Brit. India* ii. xii. II. 575 Congregations were formed under the direction of separatists. **1846** McCulloch *Acc. Brit. Empire* (1854) II. 279 They [Wesleyan methodists] ought more properly, perhaps, to be called separatists than dissenters. **1849** Macaulay *Hist. Eng.* i. I. 88 Every little congregation of separatists was tracked out and broken up. **1883** *Congregationalist* 829 The Separatists were the true ancestors of modern Congregationalists.

b. *gen.* A schismatic, sectarian; also a member of a congregation not belonging to any recognized denomination.

1641 Laud *Answ. to Ld. Say* Hist. etc. (1695) I. 501 The Name Separatist is a common Name to all Hereticks or Schismaticks, that separate for their Opinions sakes, either from the Catholick, or from any particular Orthodox Church. **1709** Stanhope *Paraphr.* IV. 236 Finding some Reproofs in his First Epistle ineffectual he threatens these

Separatists in his Second with the Censures of the Church. **1758** JORTIN *Erasmus* I. 255 To unite the Bohemian Separatists to the Church of Rome. **1793** *Statist. Acc. Scot.* V. 109 Of the whole inhabitants [of Scoonie], there are not above 150 separatists from the established church. **1796** MORSE *Amer. Geog.* I. 426 A small society of Separatists. **1856** R. A. VAUGHAN *Mystics* (1860) II. 321 Others were separatists from the religion established around them. **1860** J. CAIRNS *Mem. J. Brown* 169 The Relief Separatists, who arose twenty years after the Erskines.. arrived at this conviction much sooner than any parties in the Secession. **1882-3** *Schaff's Encycl. Relig. Knowl.* II. 999 The estates of Count Wittgenstein, the refuge of all separatists and mystics.

transf. **1859** ROSSE *Index of Dates, Shiites*, or Separatists, the name given to the Mohammedan sectaries, who venerate Ali as the rightful successor of the prophet.

c. Applied to those Wesleyan Methodists who in 1795-7 advocated separation from the Church of England.

1859 T. P. BUNTING *Life Jabez Bunting* I. vi. 87 The former class held strictly to Wesley's long and latest declaration, that his Preachers were mere Laymen.., while the Separatists either took the low ground of denying that the mere dispensation of the Sacraments implied any such assumption,..or [etc.].

d. *U.S.* A member of 'a communistic religious society (disbanded in 1898) of German Protestant peasants, who separated from the state church of Germany, emigrated, and settled at Zoar, Ohio, in 1817; also known as Zoarites and the Zoar community' (Webster, 1911).

1875 NORDHOFF *Commun. Soc. U.S.* 99 The Society of Separatists at Zoar.

e. ? Adopted as the designation of a particular sect.

1821 *Monthly Repos.* Apr. 254/2 House of Commons April 12... Mr. J. Smith presented a petition from a body of Christian people, dissenters from the Protestant Church, residing in London, who were denominated 'Separatists'.

f. A critic who ascribes the *Iliad* and the *Odyssey* or any portions of them to separate authors. Cf. SEPARATOR 1.

1903 A. PLATT *Iliad Bk. XVIII* p. xiv, Even among the ancients..there was a set of people called *χωρίζοντες* or Separatists, who held that the *Iliad* and *Odyssey* were by different authors. **1976** W. R. JOHNSON *Darkness Visible* 159 If I speak of things Homeric now as a separatist, now as a literal or oral unitarian, [etc.].

2. a. Often interpreted to mean: One who holds himself apart from others on the ground of superior piety. Hence used to render the etymological meaning of *Pharisee*.

1620 E. BLOUNT *Horæ Subsec.* 59 The Separatists, or Sanctified, as they terme themselves. **1624** T. GODWYN *Moses & Aaron* I. x. (1625) 44 We may English them [*sc.* the Pharisees] Separatists. **1627** FELTHAM *Resolves* II. xx. (1628) 18 If I liue vertuously, and with pietie, the World will hate mee, as a Separatist. **1629** DONNE *Serm.* xlix. (1640) 494 Both these, the present Sadduce, the carnall Atheist, and the present Pharisee, the Separatist. *a* **1652** BROME *Covent Gard.* IV. i, A great Separatist that is now writing a book against playing at Barlibreak, moulding of Cocklebread, and such like prophane exercises. **1661** SOUTH *Serm.* (1823) II. 336 So that the words amount to this, that St. Paul, before he was a Christian, was a rigid separatist. **1667** *Decay Chr. Piety* xiii. §1, I am not as this publican, was, we know, the voice of the proud Pharisee, whose very name signifies separation, and our modern separatists do but echo the same note. **1833** S. HOOLE *Disc.* xii. 150 The acknowledged offender on whom this self-congratulating separatist looks down with scorn and abhorrence. **1866** ANNIE HARWOOD tr. *De Pressensé's Jesus Christ* I. iii. 83 The pious party, henceforward designated by the name of Pharisees, or separatists.

†**b.** (See quot.) *Obs.*

1645 PAGITT *Heresiogr.* (ed. 2) 33 Separatists, a kind of Anabaptists so called, because they pretended to be separated from the world.

3. One who advocates political separation; applied, e.g. to the supporters of the secession of the Southern States from the United States in 1860-61, and (by opponents) to the advocates of Home Rule for Ireland.

1871 *Daily News* 21 Sept., The Reichsrath..declared that the Potocki Ministry was throwing itself too plainly into the arms of separatists. **1885** *Daily Tel.* 9 Sept. (Cassell), The Separatists know..that they have nothing to expect either from the Radical or the Whig section of the Liberal party. **1886** LD. R. CHURCHILL *Sp. at Manch.* 3 Mar., (1889) II. 23 Members of that party might be known as Unionists. Our opponents are the party of separation, and they may be known as 'Separatists'. **1886** *Pall Mall Gaz.* 16 Aug. 6/1 the majority of the Separatists—as the *Times* delights to call those who voted for the second reading [of the Home Rule Bill]. **1887** *Spectator* 2 July 888/2 'Separatist' simply describes what Unionists believe must be the outcome of Home-rule.

4. *nonce-use.* A causer of separation.

18.. M. ARNOLD (Webster 1911), Science has and will long have to be a divider and separatist, breaking arbitrary and fanciful connections.

B. *attrib.* (quasi-*adj.*) and *adj.* That is a separatist; pertaining to, consisting of, or characteristic of separatists. **a.** In ecclesiastical sense (see A. 1, 2).

1830 PUSEY *Hist. Enq.* II. 392 The same formularism.. will always much more appear in the smaller separatist parties.

b. In political sense (see A. 3).

1864 *Realm* 6 Apr. 1 The Hungarian regiments are composed of men..in no way interested in any revolutionary or separatist designs of the latter [Magyars]. **1869** RAWLINSON *Anc. Hist.* 168 The tendency of the Greek States, in spite of their separatist leanings. **1886** *Nat. Rev.* Mar. 83 The Separatist movement conducted by Mr. Parnell. **1887** CHAMBERLAIN *Sp.* 15 Apr. *Sp. Irish Question* (1890) 25 The organ of the Separatist party. **1901** *N. Amer. Rev.* Feb. 204 A man who saw that the future of the United States hinged on the one question, whether the national should prevail over the separatist principle.

separatistic (ˌsɛpərəˈtɪstɪk), *a.* [f. SEPARATIST + -IC.] Pertaining to or of the nature of separation. So †ˌ**separaˈtistical** *a.*

1610 R. BERNARD *Plain Evid.* 29 Mr. Smith a Separatisticall Erronist. **1830** PUSEY *Hist. Enq.* II. 292 Regulations intended only to check a fanatic or separatistic spirit. **1891** CHEYNE *Orig. Psalter* viii. 428 The growth of a mystic yet separatistic spiritual religion.

separative (ˈsɛpərətɪv), *a.* (*sb.*) [a. F. *séparatif* (16th c. in Hatz.-Darm.) or directly ad. late L. *sēparātīvus*, f. L. *sēparā-re*: see SEPARATE *v.* and -IVE.]

1. Tending to separate or to cause separation.

1592 TIMME *Ten Eng. Lepers* A 4 b, A Leprosie is..a fearefull, lothsome, contagious and separative maladie. **1645** RUTHERFORD *Trial & Tri. Faith* iii. 15 Grace is separative, and singleth out one of many. **1661** BOYLE *Scept. Chemist* I. 99 That..eminent Experiment of the Separative Virtue of extream Cold, that was made..in Nova Zembla. *a* **1774** GOLDSM. *Surv. Exp. Philos.* (1776) II. 364 We ought now.. to inquire how it comes that every object hath this separative power over the particles of light; how it imbibes one colour, while it copiously reflects another? **1821** LAMB *Elia* Ser. I. *Imperf. Sympathies*, The spirit of the synagogue is essentially separative. **1858** FROUDE *Hist. Eng.* IV. xviii. 55 The uniting influence was stronger than the separative. **1893** PULSFORD *Loyalty to Christ* II. 231 The fond, comfortable feeling..that we are better than others, is.. separative alike from God and man.

†**b.** *absol.* as *sb. Obs.*

1650 HUBBERT *Pill Formality* 88 It is such a separative, that it divorceth the pre-reputation of all thy actions.

2. *Gram.* †**a.** Applied to certain functions of the genitive (see quot.) **b.** Of conjunctions: Alternative, disjunctive.

1845 JELF *Gram. Grk. Lang.* §530 II. 156 Separative Genitive... All verbs expressing any notion of *removal, separation, departure, rising from*, may have a genitive of the point whence these began. **1888** KENNEDY *Revised Lat. Primer* (1900) §177 Co-ordinative Conjunctions are Connective:..Separative.

3. *Nat. Hist.* Of a mark or character: Affording ground for establishing a separate species or group.

1865 *Reader* 23 Dec. 716 This learned and popular author stands out firmly and solidly for an insurmountable, unsurpassable, separative distinction between man and brute.

Hence **ˈseparatively** *adv.*, **ˈseparativeness**.

1789 *Trifler* No. 41. 528 Individuals should separatively collect from observation and religion the art of life best calculated for their own real felicity. **1901** G. MATHESON in *Expositor* Aug. 107 To the mind of the Jew, the man who of all others emphasized the holiness of God, the distinctive feature of this holiness was its separativeness.

separator (ˈsɛpəreɪtə(r)). Also **separater**. [a. late L. *sēparātor*, agent-n. f. L. *sēparāre* to SEPARATE.]

1. One who or something which separates; *spec.* †one who separates from the Church, a separatist (common in the 17th c.); a critic who ascribes the Iliad and Odyssey to different authors (transl. of Gr. *χωρίζων*: see CHORIZONTES).

1607 *Scholast. Disc. agst. Antichrist* II. vi. 74 The scandal which the ceremonies giue to the Separators is greater then that which is giuen by images to Turks. **1608** BERNARD *Chr. Advert.* 48 *marg.*, The grieuous sinnes of the Separators. **1684** BAXTER *Twelve Argum.* §24. 42 Are these no Scandals? or not greater than offending or displeasing the dissenting Separators? **1842** EMERSON *Transcend.* Wks. (Bohn) II. 285 This retirement does not proceed from any whim on the part of these separators. **1860** BP. WILBERFORCE *Addr. Cand. Ordin.* 227 In such cases, the least offences are great separators, and..angry tempers need to be handled with the gentlest and most discerning touch. **1878** *Examiner* 2 Mar. 273/1 So Professor Jebb is a 'separater' and to a certain extent a follower of Wolf. **1890** *Illustr. Lond. News* 27 Dec. 810/2 The terminator of delights, the separator of companions, the desolator of abodes.

2. *pl.* The four teeth, two in each jaw, between the two central and the outer incisor-teeth of a horse. ? *Obs.*

1717 HOPE tr. *de Solleysel's Compl. Horseman.* **1726** *Dict. Rust.* (ed. 3) s.v. *Teeth*, The Middle-teeth or Separators (so called because they separate the Nippers from the Corner-teeth). **1808** *Compl. Grazier* (ed. 3) Introd. 20 When the horse is coming four years old he loses his four separaters or middle teeth.

3. An instrument or appliance for separating.

a. An apparatus for separating grain from refuse, or for separating the various sizes of grain.

1830 M. DONOVAN *Dom. Econ.* I. 347 After leaving the cooling floor the grain is let into the separator. **1880** J. W. HILL *Guide Agric. Implements* 5 Combined Double Aspirator, Separator, and Smutter. **1884** *Bath Herald* 27 Dec. 6/4 From the silos the wheat runs into a separator, which extracts the large and small refuse and dirt. *Ibid.*, In the purifying process the grain passes over a magnetic separator..which is sure to attract and hold fast..pieces of iron [etc.].

b. *Weaving.* = RAVE *sb.*[2] 3.

1831 G. R. PORTER *Silk Manuf.* 220 The instrument used for the purpose of guiding the threads of the warp and of spreading them regularly upon the yarn-roll is called a separator or ravel. **1842** [see RAVEL *sb.*[3]]. **1845** *Encycl. Metrop.* VIII. 734/1 In the beaming, the weaver sometimes employs a rude sort of instrument called a separator or ravel.

c. = *cream-separator* (see CREAM *sb.*[2] 7).

1884 [see *cream-separator*]. **1887** *Daily News* 20 May 6/5 A separator takes in the milk hot from the cow, whirls it round at a great speed, and in two minutes the cream flows out at one pipe and the milk at another.

d. A partition, a plate interposed between compartments, e.g. in a voltaic battery, a beehive, etc.

1881 T. W. COWAN *Bee Keepers Guide Bk.* viii. 43 Never use sections without separators. **1887** *Pall Mall Gaz.* 12 Aug. 10/2 The plates are zinc and carbon, the zinc being immersed in dilute sulphuric acid—the carbon in a solution of nitrate of soda. A porous separator keeps the liquids apart, save for diffusion through its pores. **1889** *Anthony's Photogr. Bull.* II. 51 These pieces of paper, or thin card, can be placed by the side of the slide, thus acting as a separater and preventing breakage when they are carried about.

e. *Telegraphy.* (See quot.)

1891 *Man. Instr. Army Telegr.* 86 Separators provide a simple means of doubling the capacity for work of a telegraph line, by providing on the same wire Morse and vibration circuits which are independent of each other.

f. A contrivance for separating water from steam.

1834 N. W. CUNDY *Inland Transit* 74 The purpose of the separator is to disengage or separate the water from the steam in which it is mechanically suspended. **1855** D. K. CLARK *Railway Mach.* 152/2 Edwards' Separator, for disengaging Priming. **1901** *Feilden's Mag.* IV. 415 A cylindrical water separator.

g. In various applications.

1881 RAYMOND *Mining Gloss.*, *Separator.* 1. A machine for separating, with the aid of water or air, materials of different specific gravity... 2. Any machine for separating materials, as the magnetic separator, for separating magnetite from its gangue. **1884** *Health Exhib. Catal.* 51/1 Automatic Rain-water Separators, to reject the foul and store the clean water from roofs. **1889** *Anthony's Photogr. Bull.* II. 312 The centrifugal separator..is an apparatus.. employed by manufacturers who want to separate relatively heavy matters suspended in a liquid.

4. *Math.*

1869 CAYLEY *Math. Papers* (1894) VII. 402 The parallel through S to a ray meets the sphere in two points, poles of a great circle which I call a 'separator'.

5. *attrib.*

1896 BRANNT *Anim. & Veg. Fats* II. 313 The oil..is, however, still mixed with some water, from which it is separated by means of a separator funnel. **1897** *Daily News* 23 Feb. 7/6 One of the engineers went to open the port bulkhead stop valve, when a separator pipe burst.

Hence **ˈseparatress**.

1630 *R. Johnson's Kingd. & Commw.* 117 The Severne, the separatresse of Wales and England.

separatory (ˈsɛpəreɪtərɪ), *sb.* ? *Obs.* [ad. mod.L. *sēparātōrium*, f. L. *sēparāre* to separate: see -ORY. Cf. F. *séparatoire.*] An instrument for separating; *spec.* in various uses (see quots.).

1656 BLOUNT *Glossogr.*, *Separatory*, the Chizel or Instrument, wherewith Chyrurgeons cut out the peeces of bones, left between the holes, which they bore with a Trepan. **1684** tr. *Bonet's Merc. Compit.* VIII. 296 Such especially is the Liver, the Colatory, Seive and Separatory of the Bile. **1706** PHILLIPS (ed. Kersey), *Separatory*... Also a Chymical Vessel for separating Oil from Water. **1791** G. WALLIS *Motherby's Med. Dict.* (ed. 3), A separatory... The name of an instrument for separating the pericranium from the cranium; also a chemical vessel for separating liquors. **1855** DUNGLISON *Med. Lex.* s.v., A Separatory..is a pharmaceutical vessel for separating fluids of different densities from each other.

ˈseparatory, *a.* [ad. mod.L. *sēparātōrius*, f. L. *sēparāre* to separate: see -ORY.] Having the function of separating.

1715 CHEYNE *Philos. Princ.* I. vi. (ed. 2) 298 The Lacteals are the emissary Vessels or separatory Ducts. **1896** BRANNT *Anim. & Veg. Fats* I. 14 The oldest method of determining the percentage of fat is by means of a separatory funnel.

‖**separatrix** (sɛpəˈreɪtrɪks). Pl. **separatrices** (-trɪsiːz). [late L., fem. agent-n. f. *sēparāre* to SEPARATE.

The feminine is in apposition with *līnea* line, understood.]

†**1. a.** The mark (originally **L**, later **|**), formerly used to separate the figures representing decimals from those representing integers; now superseded by the decimal point. **b.** (See quot. 1771). *Obs.*

1660 J. MOORE *Arith.* 11 But the best and most distinct way of distinguishing them [*sc.* Decimals] is by a rectangular line after the place of the unit, called Seperatrix. *Ibid.* 13 Therefore in writing of decimall parts let the seperatrix be always used. **1771** LUCKOMBE *Hist. Printing* 286 The Separatrix, or rule between the Numerator and Denominator [of fractions].

2. *Proof-correction.* (See quot.)

1892 A. OLDFIELD *Man. Typog.* iii, A wrong letter is noted by a stroke being drawn through and the proper letter written on the margin with a stroke after it. This stroke is placed after all corrections to keep the various marks separate. It is sometimes called the separatrix.

3. The line separating light and shade on a partly illuminated surface. Cf. TERMINATOR 2.

a **1912** In recent Dicts.

4. *Physics.* A boundary between regions having differing configurations of magnetic lines of force.

1956 *Proc. CERN Symp. High Energy Accelerators* I. 50/1 We see in fig. 3 the region of stability or 'bucket' within which particles execute stable phase oscillations... The bucket boundary, or separatrix is given by eq. (43). *Ibid.* 54/2 The region between the two separatrices. **1979** *Sci. Amer.* Aug. 44 (*caption*) The tokamak.. is equipped with a magnetic divertor, an arrangement in which a magnetic-field separatrix is employed to prevent impurity ions from entering the main plasma column.

†**separe**, *v. Obs.* Also 5–6 **sepayre**; 5 *pa. pple.* **sepered.** [a. F. *sépare-r* (14th c.), ad. L. *sēparāre*: see SEPARATE *v.* and SEVER.] To separate:

a. *trans.* (and *refl.*).

a **1450** *Knt. de la Tour* 181 And therfore, syth that God hath assembled them, no man mortal ouȝt not to separe them. **1484** CAXTON *Fables of Auian* xiv. (1889) 233 The lyon.. maade them to be separed eche one fro other. And whanne they were sepered, the lyon wente, and toke one of them. *c* **1489** —— *Blanchardyn* xxxv. 131 After dyuerse talkynke.. they sepayred hemsylf, & toke leue of eche other. **1509** WATSON *Ship of Fools* xxiv. (1517) F vij b, Whan that god shall separe the body from the soule. **1609** BIBLE (Douay) *3 Esdr.* iv. 17 Men cannot be separed from wemen.

b. *intr.*

c **1489** CAXTON *Sonnes of Aymon* xix. 441 Lordes, ye doo not well for to separe thus the one from the other. **1541** COPLAND *Guydon's Quest. Chirurg.* D ij, In some places the veynes do separe from the arteres. And the arteres be founde wtout veynes.

†'**separist.** *Obs. rare.* [f. SEPARE *v.* + -IST.] = SEPARATIST.

1616 R. C. *Times' Whistle* (1871) 15 Iove separat me from these Separists. **1641** LD. BROOKE *Eng. Episc.* II. vi. 90 The Separist is subdivided too, as they say, into Separatist and Semi-separatist. **1700** *Labour in Vain* in *Harl. Misc.* (1745) VI. 353 In contradiction to the present thought, My sole Opinion signifieth Nought; 'Tis over-rul'd, and I am surely cast, Which proves the Fate of Separists at last.

Hence †**sepa'ristic**, †**sepa'ristical** *adjs.* = SEPARATISTIC, -AL *adjs.*

1633 HEYWOOD *Eng. Trav.* Ep. Ded., If they haue beene vilefied of late by any Separisticall humorist. **1653** R. BAILLIE *Dissuas. Vind.* (1655) 15 A part of Mr. Robinson's Separistick congregation.

sepawn, sepayre, var. ff. SUPAWN, SEPARE *v.*

†**sepelible,** *a. Obs.*$^{-0}$ [ad. L. *sepelībilis*, f. *sepelīre* to bury: see -IBLE.] That may be buried.

1721 BAILEY, **1755** JOHNSON, *Sepilible* [sic].

†**sepelite,** *v. Obs. rare*$^{-1}$. [f. L. *sepelīt-*, rare ppl. stem of *sepelīre* to bury.] = SEPULT *v.*

1577 *Will of E. Prestwich* (Hulme, Manchester) 14 Oct., My body to be sepilited or buried within the Parish Church.

†**sepe'lition.** *Obs. rare*$^{-1}$. [ad. med.L. *sepelītio*, f. *sepelīre* to bury.] Burial.

1637 BP. HALL *Serm.* xxxi. Wks. 1808 V. 440 The other extreme is of them who do so over-honour the dead, that they abridge some parts of them of a due sepelition.

seperate, -ation, etc.: obs. ff. SEPARATE, etc.

sepetir (sɛpə'tɪə(r)). Also **sapetir.** [Mal.] A forest tree of the genus *Sindora* or *Pseudosindora*, belonging to the family Leguminosæ and native to south-east Asia; also, the hardwood timber produced by a tree of this kind.

[**1897** G. KING in *Jrnl. Asiatic Soc. Bengal* LXVI. II. 205 Mr. Curtis gives the Malay name of this [*Sindora intermedia* Baker] in Pangkor as '*Sapetir*'.] **1927** F. W. FOXWORTHY *Common Forest Trees Malay Peninsula* 91 It is doubtful if Sepetir produces more than one per cent of the timber in the forest. **1934** A. L. HOWARD *Man. Timbers of World* (ed. 2) 480 Sepetir... The colour of the wood is yellow-brown, with dark streaks. **1956** *Handbk. of Hardwoods* (Forest Prod. Res. Lab.) 210 Sepetir is the British Standard name for the timber of *Sindora* spp. and *Pseudosindora palustris.* **1971** *Country Life* 1 Apr. App. 42/2 A very rare.. occasional table.. the surfaces veneered in burnt walnut, rosewood, plane and sepetir (Malaya).

Sephadex ('sɛfədɛks). *Chem.* A proprietary term for a preparation of dextran used for the separation and purification of chemicals on the basis of molecular size.

1959 *Trade Marks Jrnl.* 16 Sept. 827/1 *Sephadex*... Polymers being chemical compounds for industrial use in the purification of chemical substances. Aktiebolaget Pharmacia.. Sweden.. 11th March 1959. **1970** [see DEXTRAN]. **1975** WILLIAMS & WILSON *Biologist's Guide to Princ. & Techniques Pract. Biochem.* iii. 79 Cellulose derivatives (and Sephadex materials) have been used successfully in this way. **1978** *Nature* 12 Oct. 565/2 It was reduced with sodium dithionite and then isolated in 0·01 M phosphate buffer (*p*H 7) by Sephadex chromatography.

‖**Sephardi** (sɪ'fɑːdiː). Pl. **Sephardim** (-diːm), **din** (-diːn). [mod.Heb. *sephardī*, f. *sephārād*, the name of a country mentioned only *Obad.* 20, and identified by the Rabbins with Spain.] A Spanish or Portuguese Jew, a Jew of Spanish or Portuguese descent. Also *attrib.* Hence **Se'phardic** *a.*, pertaining to the Sephardim.

1851 MAYHEW *Lond. Labour* II. 125 The Spanish and Portuguese Congregation of Jews, who are also called Sephardin. **1866** ENGEL *Nat. Mus.* 1 The synagogical hymns of the Sephardic Jews. **1892** ZANGWILL *Childr. Ghetto* I. 3 The pioneer colony of wealthy Sephardim, descendants of the Spanish crypto-Jews who had reached England viâ Holland. **1901** *Daily Chron.* 27 Dec. 4/4 The loans which Charles II., while in exile, received from Sephardi Jews at Amsterdam.

sephen ('sɛfɛn). Also **sephin.** [a. mod.L. *sephen* (specific name), a. Arab. *safan* shagreen.] A kind of sting-ray. Also *attrib.*

1854 BADHAM *Halieut.* 460 The Red Sea swarms with divers kinds of huge sharks and skate... The sephin is one of its own children. **1879** SIMMONDS *Commerc. Prod. Sea* 262 Galuchat or Sephen skin, from the back of the *Hypolophus Sephen* and *Trygon Sephen* Cloq. *Ibid.*, The best galuchat, or what we should call shagreen, is made from the skin of the sephen, which abounds in the Mediterranean Sea.

Sepher Torah, var. SEFER TORAH.

‖**sephiroth** ('sɛfɪrəʊθ), *pl.* Rarely in *sing.* **sephira.** [late Heb. *sephīrōth*, sing. *sephīrāh*, f. *sāphar* to number.] In the philosophy of the Cabbala, the ten hypostatized attributes or emanations by means of which the Infinite (*ēn sōph*) enters into relation with the finite.

1569 J. SANFORD tr. *Agrippa's Van. Artes* cii. 184 The Doctours of the Hebrewes say that this beast [the ass] is an example of fortitude.., and that his influence dependeth on *Sephiroth*, whiche is called *Hochma*, that is to say, wisdome. **1684** T. BURNET *Th. Earth* II. ix. 282 One Head in this Cabala was the doctrine of the Sephiroth. **1795** T. MAURICE *Hindostan* I. i. 72 Their [*sc.* the Rabbins] devout and rapturous expressions concerning the three great Sephiroth. **1847** SOANE *New Curios. Lit.* II. 76 This knowledge was in fact the original and proper Cabala, according to which.. a number of Sephiroths, Æons, or Emanations, flowed from God. **1855** SMEDLEY *Occult Sciences* 122 The seven names or sephira of the Hebrew Talmud. **1881** O'SHAUGHNESSY *Songs of Worker* 26 En Soph was manifest,.. but splendour covered Him; And circles of the Sephiroth tenfold, Vast and mysterious, intervening rolled. **1900** *New Century Rev.* VII. 376 In their totality these ten sephiroth represent and are called the *Primordial* or *Archetypal* man, *Adam* Kadmon... The seventh and eighth sephiroth, *Firmness* and *Splendour*, are the two legs... *Kingdom*, or *Shekinah*, the tenth sephira, represents the harmony of the whole archetypal man.

Hence **sephiric** (in recent Dicts.), **sephirot(h)ic** *adjs.*, pertaining to the sephiroth.

1873 LELAND *Egypt. Sketch-bk.* 210 Matter cabalistic, archetypal, sephirotic, metaphysical, ideal, and divine. **1900** *New Century Rev.* VII. 379 The following may be taken as the characteristic teaching of the Kabbalah:—.. 2. All that we perceive or know is of the sephirothic type.

sepia ('siːpɪə). Also 6–7 **sæpia,** 9 **seppia.** [a. L. *sēpia*, a. Gr. σηπία.

The Latin word gave It. *seppia*, F. *sèche*, Sp. *jibia*, Pg. *siba*; F. *sépia* in sense 2 is from It., as is prob. also the Eng. word in that sense.]

1. The cuttle-fish; now *rare* exc. *Zool.* a cuttle of the genus *Sepia* or family *Sepiidæ*; also, the genus itself.

1569 J. SANFORD tr. *Agrippa's Van. Artes* 10 b, They seeke in Aristotle an easines, they reproue his darkenes, and call him *Sepia* [*marg.* A fishe called a Cuttell]. **1589** *Pasquil's Ret.* C j b, They are the very Spawnes of the fish *Sæpia*, where the streame is cleere.. they vomit vp yncke to trouble the waters. **1607** WALKINGTON *Optic Glass* i. B, The Sepia's inkie humor. **1683** CAVE *Ecclesiastici* 333 Like the Fish Sepia, which being in danger to be taken by the Fisherman, throws out abundance of black Matter, which discolouring the Water all about, it safely escapes under that Covert. **1752** J. HILL *Hist. Anim.* 97 The body of the Sepia is of an oblong figure and depressed. **1771** PENNANT *Syn. Quadrup.* 242 They.. feed on lobsters, fish, *Sepiæ*, and shell fish. **1836** BUCKLAND *Geol. & Min.* xv. §2 (1837) I. 307 [The ink-bags] contain the fluid which the living sepia emits in the moment of alarm. **1839** T. BEALE *Nat. Hist. Sperm Whale* 58 The internal shell of the common sepia is large and broad. **1859–62** SIR J. RICHARDSON, etc. *Mus. Nat. Hist.* (1868) II. 315 The Common Sepia or Cuttle-fish (*Sepia officinalis*).

2. a. A pigment of a rich brown colour (used in monochrome water-colour painting) prepared from the inky secretion of the cuttle-fish; the colour of this pigment. Also called *Roman sepia.*

1821 CRAIG *Lect. Drawing*, etc. ii. 102 Water-colour sketches performed entirely in seppia, or bistre, or any brown colour. **1842** B'NESS BUNSEN in Hare *Life* (1879) II. ii. 46 Her outlines are in pen and sepia, like Flaxman's. **1861** HULME tr. *Moquin-Tandon* II. III. ii. 82 The pigment used in water colour painting and known as Roman Sepia. **1891** KIPLING *Light that Failed* viii, This shall be in sepia. It's a sweet material to work with.

b. The inky secretion itself. *rare.*

1886 *Globe* 27 Oct. (Cassell), Nobody who has not tasted the great cuttle-fish, his feelers cut up and stewed in the black ink or sepia which serves him, apparently, for blood, can imagine how good he is.

c. *ellipt.* A sepia drawing. [So Fr.]

1863 *Life in Normandy* I. 169 Will you shew the sepias to this gentleman?

3. In full *sepia bone*: Cuttle-bone, *esp.* as used in pharmacy, etc.; = SEPIUM.

1840 F. D. BENNETT *Narr. Whaling Voy.* II. App. 290 The interior of the back [of the Flying-Squid] contains an elastic horny rod, or substitute for the 'sepia bone' that occupies the same part in some other tribes of the cuttle-fish.

4. *attrib.* or as *adj.* **a.** = Of the colour of sepia; drawn in sepia. Also Comb., as *sepia-coloured, -eyed, -like, -tinted* adjs.; **sepia print** (see quot. 1940).

1827 HONE *Table Bk.* I. 445 A sepia drawing. **1849** C. BRONTE *Shirley* xi, Rich in crayon touches and sepia lights and shades. **1875** R. B. SHARPE *Catal. Striges Brit. Mus.* 154 The primary-coverts.. inclining to sepia-brown. **1892** W. E. WOODBURY *Encycl. Photogr.* 556 Black and sepia prints must not be washed together in the same dish. **1896** *Century Mag.* LI. 799/1 Dark-haired, sepia-eyed. **1899** CAGNEY tr. *von Jaksch's Clin. Diagn.* (ed. 4) 78 A sepia-like decomposition product. **1940** *Chambers's Techn. Dict.* 758/2 *Sepia print*.., a release print in which the image is dyed sepia instead of being left black. **1977** *Spare Rib* July 62/4 A marvellous collection of sepia prints showed women at work in the hospital's wards.

b. Of American Blacks: *euphem.* for 'black'. *U.S.*

1942 BERREY & VAN DEN BARK *Amer. Thes. Slang* §32/8 Negro color distinctions... *sepia.* **1944** H. L. MENCKEN in *Amer. Speech* XIX. 166 Some of them also use such terms as .. *sepia* to get away from the.. inaccurate *black*, and in 1944 there was a *Sepia* Miss America contest. **1947** S. LEWIS *Kingsblood Royal* xxiii. 138 A certain number of sepia merchants get rich on the rest of us chosen people.

sepiacean (siːpɪ'eɪʃən), *a.* and *sb. Zool.* [f. mod.L. *Sepiāceus*, f. SEPIA: see -ACEOUS.] Pertaining to, or a member of, the group *Sepiacea* of cuttle-fishes. Also **sepi'aceous** *a.*

1842 *Penny Cycl.* XXII. 360/2 The borders of the mantle or of the sac of the Sepiaceans. **1858** MAYNE *Expos. Lex.*, *Sepiaceus*.. a sepiaceous.

†'**sepian,** *a. Obs.*$^{-1}$ [f. SEPIA + -AN.] Inky.

1631 FULLER *David's Heinous Sin* xxxii, Sepian juice did sink Into his spongy paper.

sepic ('siːpɪk, 'sɛpɪk), *a. rare*$^{-0}$. [f. SEPIA + -IC.]

1879 WEBSTER Suppl., *Sepic*, pertaining to sepia; done in sepia, as a drawing.

Sepik ('sɛpɪk). [Native name.] The name of a river and district in Papua New Guinea, used *attrib.* of the peoples of the district and of their languages and artefacts.

1949 M. MEAD *Male & Female* viii. 178 The Sepik peoples—Iatmul, Tchambuk, and Mundugumor—make little of menstruation ceremonies. **1966** E. LINDALL *Time too Soon* (1967) xii. 120 We've got two Sepik policemen here. **1971** *Current Trends in Linguistics* VIII. 516 The first modern study of Sepik languages was that undertaken by Laycock. **1973** *Sunday Times* 10 June (Colour Suppl.) 42/1 Certain Protestants were notorious for destroying all native works of art, especially Sepik sculptures.

sepiment ('sɛpɪmənt). Now *rare* or *Obs.* [ad. L. *sēpiment-um*, f. *sēpīre* to hedge, f. *sēpes* hedge.] A hedge, fence, pale.

1656 BLOUNT *Glossogr.*, *Sepiment*, an hedge, pale, mound or inclosure. **1668** WILKINS *Real Char.* II. xi. §3. 279 Such things as are used for the fencing of Places; Sepiment, Wall, Pale, Fence, Enclosure, Fold, Mound. **1905** *Longman's Mag.* July 272 That hedge, its [an orchard's] southern sepiment.. is a huge mass of bramble.

†**b.** *transf.* and *fig.* Something that encloses or guards.

1660 WATERHOUSE *Arms & Arm.* 16 Making the sepiment of skyn which man is bounded with a symbol of his Mortality. **1678** *Lively Oracles* ii. §27 A farther testimony and sepiment to which, were the Samaritan, Chaldee, and Greek versions.

sepioid ('siːpɪɔɪd). *Zool.* [f. SEPIA + -OID.] A cuttle-fish of or related to the genus *Sepia.*

1857 AGASSIZ *Contrib. Nat. Hist. U.S.* I. 47 In the class of Cephalopoda, that of the Sepioids. **1893** *Proc. Boston Soc. Nat. Hist.* XXVI. 121 The sepioids may be convergent with belemnoids.

‖**sepiola** (sɪ'paɪələ). *Zool.* Also anglicized **sepiole** (cf. F. *sépiole*, Cuvier). [L., dim. of SEPIA.] The name of a genus of small cuttle-fishes.

[**1797** *Encycl. Brit.* (ed. 3) XVII. 282 The sepiola, or small cuttle, with a short body, rounded at the bottom.] **1835** KIRBY *Hab. & Inst. Anim.* II. xvii. 105 In some genera, as the poulpe and sepiole, besides eight shorter arms, there is a pair of very long ones. **1841** *Penny Cycl.* XXI. 255 Some [naked cephalopods] are of very large dimensions, and others—the *Sepiolæ* for instance—very small.

sepiolite ('siːpɪəlaɪt). *Geol.* [ad. G. *sepiolith* (Glocker 1847), f. Gr. σήπιον SEPIUM: see -LITE.] Meerschaum.

1854 DANA *Syst. Min.* (ed. 4) II. 277. **1875** DAWSON *Life's Dawn* v. 118 The great beds of sepiolite in the.. Tertiary strata of Europe.

sepiostaire (siːpɪə'stɛə(r)). *Zool.* Also in shortened form **sepiost.** [ad. F. *sépiostaire*, f. Gr. σηπία SEPIA + ὀστοῦν bone + *-aire* (cf. -ARY).] = CUTTLE-BONE.

1836 BUCKLAND *Geol. & Min.* II. 67 Sepia officinalis, shewing the position of the internal shell or sheath (Sepiostaire) within the dorsal portion of its sac. **1877** HUXLEY *Anat. Inv. Anim.* viii. 540 The sepiostaire or 'cuttle bone'.. is composed of a broad plate answering to the pen. **1888** ROLLESTON & JACKSON *Anim. Life* 458.

‖**sepium** ('siːpɪəm). Also in Gr. form **sepion.** [mod.L., a. Gr. σήπιον.] Cuttle-bone.

[**1752** *Chambers's Cycl.*, *Sepium, Sepiæ os,* or *testa*, cuttle-fish bone is a white.. testaceous substance.] **1835–6** *Todd's Cycl. Anat.* I. 546/1 The Sepium or Cuttle-bone is a well-known substance, and formerly figured in the Materia Medica as an antacid. **1895** A. H. COOKE *Molluscs* xiii. (Cambr. Nat. Hist.) 389 The sepion or 'cuttle-bone' runs the whole length and width of the body.

†**seplasiary.** *Obs.* [ad. late L. *sēplăsiārius*, f. *Sēplăsia*, name of a street in Capua where perfumers sold their wares.] A perfumer.

1650 CHARLETON *Paradoxes* 53 Sorcerers..destroy onely by poyson, which every common Seplasarie [*sic*] and petty Apothecary can imitate. **1651** BIGGS *New Disp.* ¶160 Distill'd out of herbs by the Seplasiaries or Apothecaries. **1658** PHILLIPS, *Seplasiary*, a compounder or seller of sweet ointments; also a nice effeminate man.

So †**seplasiator** *rare*$^{-0}$.

1656 BLOUNT *Glossogr.*, *Seplasiator*, he that makes sweet ointments.

sepoltur, obs. form of SEPULTURE.

sepometer (sɪˈpɒmɪtə(r)). [f. Gr. σήπ-ειν to rot + -(O)METER.] An instrument for detecting septic matter in the atmospheric air.

1876 RANSOME *Stethometry* App. 189 Dr. Angus Smith used his sepometer and the test of permanganate of potash to determine the quality of breathed air.

†**sepone**, *v. Obs. rare.* [ad. L. *sēpōnĕre*, f. *sē-* apart + *pōnĕre* to place.] To set apart.

1619 in *Fasti Aberd.* (1854) 276 The seponing of the sowme of fourtie pundis and uther casualties appointed for the mantenance of the edifice of the said universitie.

†**seˈpose**, *v. Obs.* [f. L. *sēposit-* (see next), reduced by analogy of POSE *v.*[1] and its compounds.]

1. *trans.* To set aside, dismiss from consideration.

1593 BILSON *Perpet. Govt.* vii. 79 If seposing a litle the names of men, wee examine the grounds of both interpretations. **1664** H. MORE *Myst. Iniq.* 90 The grand Points of the Christian Truth, which, that Parenthesis being seposed, do immediately follow.

2. To set apart or reserve.

c **1609** DONNE *Lett.* (1651) 111 God seposed a seventh of our time for his exterior worship. **1610** —— *Pseudo-martyr* 7 So is the treasure and crowne of Martyredome seposed for them, who take vp deuoutly the crosses of this life. *a* **1614** —— *Βιαθανατος* (1648) 147 Having purposely sepos'd the examples recorded in the Scriptures for our third part. **1626** —— *Serm.* xxi. (1640) 207 This is the harmony, this is the resurrection of a Christian,..that, he sepose some times, to think of nothing but God. **1641** H. L'ESTRANGE *God's Sabbath* 64 Gods seposing of a certain time for their.. Sanctification.

†**seˈposit**, *v. Obs.* [f. L. *sēposit-*, ppl. stem of *sēpōnĕre* SEPONE.] = prec. 1, 2.

1657 W. MORICE *Coena quasi Κοινὴ* Def. v. 62 Other things seposited for future discussion. *Ibid.* xv. 190 Such as were under penance, aswell as Catechumens,..such are still presupposed to be seposited from our discourse. **1661** FELTHAM *Lett.* in *Resolves*, etc. 67 Parents, and the nearest bloud must all for this be laid by and seposited.

†**sepoˈsition.** *Obs.* [ad. L. *sēpositiōnem*, n. of action f. *sēpōnĕre* SEPONE.] Setting aside.

1649 JER. TAYLOR *Gt. Exemp.* II. Disc. xi. 150 To this we must contend with prayer, with actuall dereliction & seposition of all our other affaires. **1656** BLOUNT *Glossogr.*

sepoy (ˈsiːpɔɪ, sɪˈpɔɪ), **sipahi** (sɪˈpɑːiː). *Anglo-Indian.* Forms: 7 seapy, 8 sepay, sipoy, cephoy, sea-poy, 8–9 seapoy, 8– sepoy. *β.* 8– sipahi, 9 sipahee. [ad. (prob. through Pg. *sipae*) Urdu = Pers. *sipāhī* horseman, soldier, f. *sipāh* army. Cf. F. *cipaye*. See also SPAHI.

In the following quot. the word is used in its orig. sense of 'horseman'.

1682 HEDGES *Diary* (Hakl. Soc.) I. 55, I went..to Ray Nundelall's to have had y^e^ Seapy, or Nabob's horseman, consigned to me.]

A native of India employed as a soldier under European, esp. British, discipline.

1717–18 in *Hedges' Diary* (Hakl. Soc.) II. p. ccclix, A Company of Sepoys with the Colours, Trumpets, and Countrey Musick. **1733** in G. W. Forrest *Sel. Lett. Bombay Secr.* (Home Ser.) II. 55 To make a thorough survey..of the island.., the number of the guns therein..and the number of fighting sepoys. *Ibid.* 57 That..the garrison of Seepoys shall become the subjects of the said Honble Company, and remain in their..service at the usual pay that is now paid to the garrison Seepoys of Bombay. **1757** J. H. GROSE *Voy. E. Indies* 62 Sepays, who have their proper officers, with the titles in the country-language, all however under the Orders of the English. **1761** *London Mag.* XXX. 184 A body of about 400 Europeans, with a train of artillery and 400 Seapoys. **1858** J. B. NORTON *Topics* 68 On the 22nd of January, 1857, Captain Wright, of the 70th Bengal native infantry, informed Major Bontien..of the unpleasant feeling among the sepoys in respect to the cartridges. **1878** WOLSELEY in *N. Amer. Rev.* CXXVII. 134 The dispatch of this handful of sepoys from Bombay to Malta.

β. **1798** JUSTAMOND tr. *Raynal's Hist. Philos.* I. 459 England has at present in India..54,000 sipahis well armed and disciplined. **1809** BROUGHTON *Lett. Mahratta Camp* iii. (1892) 25 Many of our Sipahees..have children whom they have..purchased in this manner. **1819** F. HAMILTON *Nepal* Index 362 Seapoy, properly Sipahi, in Nepal applied to irregular armed men employed in the police and revenue. **1850** *Chamb. Jrnl.* XIV. 344 The escort of sipahees.

b. *attrib.*, as *sepoy band*; **sepoy crab**, a species of crab found in the Indian and Pacific Oceans; **Sepoy Mutiny** or **Rebellion**, a revolt against British rule in India in 1857–8.

1763 in Jas. Long *Rec. Govt. Ft. William* (1869) 290 (Y.) Captains who command the Sepoy batallions. **1772** *Town & Country Mag.* 159 E'en wed a Seapoy chief and mend the breed. **1820** *Blackw. Mag.* VIII. 38 And guard with Sepoy band the peaceful vale. **1845** STOCQUELER *Handbk. Brit. India* (1854) 54 The fall of a European officer was invariably the signal for sepoy-faltering. **1857** W. SINCLAIR (*title*) The Sepoy Mutinies: their origin and their cure. **1857** *Househ. Words* 31 Jan. 105/1 Mr. Cuming frequently found sepoy-crabs on Lord Hood's Island in the Pacific.

seppande, variant of SHIPPEND, creator.

seppia, obs. variant of SEPIA.

‖**seppuku** (sɛˈpuːkuː). Also Seppuku, etc. [Jap., colloq. pronunc. of *setsu fuku*, f. Chinese *qiē* to cut (with a sword or knife) + *fù* belly.] = HARA-KIRI.

1871 A. B. MITFORD *Tales Old Japan* II. 193 Seppuku (*hara-kiri*) is the mode of suicide adopted amongst Samurai when they have no alternative but to die. **1890** B. H. CHAMBERLAIN *Things Japanese* 141 The Japanese word *harakiri*, so well-known all over the world, is but little used by the Japanese themselves. The Japanese almost always prefer to employ the synonym *seppuku*, which they consider more elegant because it is derived from the Chinese. **1923** J. STREET *Mysterious Japan* xvi. 198 At the sound of the guns he took his short sword and committed seppuku. **1947** R. BENEDICT *Chrysanthemum & Sword* x. 200 He could only come to terms with chu by killing himself according to the rules of seppuku. **1973** A. BROINOWSKI *Take one Ambassador* xi. 178 You would at once..kill yourself. By *seppuku*, slitting of the stomach.

seps (sɛps). [a. L. *sēps*, a. Gr. σήψ, f. σήπειν to make rotten.]

1. A very venomous serpent described by classical writers: see quots.

1562 TURNER *Herbal* II. 103 [Porcellayn] is..good agaynst the bytyng of a venemus beast, called seps. **1627** MAY *Lucan* IX. 829 The seps, whose bite Consumes the bones, dissolues the body quite. **1774** GOLDSM. *Nat. Hist.* IV. 126 The Seps, whose wound is very venomous, and causes the part affected to corrupt in a very short time. **1820** SHELLEY *Prometh. Unb.* III. i. 40 All my being, Like him whom the Numidian seps did thaw Into a dew with poison, is dissolved.

2. A lizard of the scincoid genus *Seps*, having a serpent-like body; a serpent-lizard.

[Cf. **1774** GOLDSM. *Nat. Hist.* VII. 157 The Chalcidian Lizard of Aldrovandus, very improperly called the Seps, by modern historians. This animal seems to make the shade that separates the lizard from the serpent race.]

1802 SHAW *Gen. Zool.* III. I. 252 Seps Lizard. *Ibid.*, The Seps is rather a small species. **1835** *Penny Cycl.* IV. 528/2 They [*sc.* Blind-worms] are, in short, as Cuvier observes, so to speak, Seps-lizards, without feet. **1873** MIVART *Elem. Anat.* 57 The little lizard *Seps*.

sepsine (ˈsɛpsɪn). [f. SEPS-IS + -INE[5].]

a. A poisonous crystalline substance obtained from decomposing yeast. **b.** A ptomaine of septic poison.

1880 FLINT *Princ. Med.* 83 Panum and other investigators have succeeded in isolating from decomposed fluids a substance..which, when injected..into the blood of animals, produces the symptoms of septicaemia. The name sepsin has been proposed for this substance. **1887** A. M. BROWN *Anim. Alkaloids* 2 In 1868, Bergmann and also Schmiedeberg obtained from the extracts of putrid beer a nitrogenous crystallizable substance which they called sepsine.

‖**sepsis** (ˈsɛpsɪs). [mod.L., a. Gr. σῆψις, f. σήπειν to rot.] Putrefaction, putrescence.

[**1858** MAYNE *Expos. Lex.*] **1876** tr. *Wagner's Gen. Pathol.* 348 True putrefaction, putrescence, sepsis. **1891** *Lancet* 16 May 1108/2 He believes that tuberculin increases the symptoms produced by sepsis.

sept (sɛpt), *sb.*[1] [ad. L. *sēptum*: see SEPTUM.]

1. An enclosure; an area marked off for a special purpose; a fold (*fig.*).

1548 in Strype *Eccl. Mem.* (1721) II. App. ZZZ. 403 Al the sept, scite, circuit and precincts of the college. *a* **1638** MEDE *Diatribæ* (1642) 47 And yet was not this abuse.. within those Septs of the Temple which the Jews accounted sacred. **1641** J. JACKSON *True Evang. T.* I. 28 What a ravenous beast he was, within the Sept of Christ. **1649** JER. TAYLOR *Gt. Exemp.* II. Ad. Sect. xi. 24 Jesus entred the Temple, and espyed a Mart kept in the holy Sept, A Faire upon holy ground. **1719** PRIDEAUX *Connect. O. & N.T.* II. II. (ed. 4) 96 No stranger should enter within the Sept of the temple. **1883** W. L. KERR *Abbey of Kilwinning* v. 72 While William, Abbot of Kylwynnyng, with his convent, were assembled in the Septs of the Abbey.

2. *Arch.* A dividing screen, railing, etc.

1821 BRITTON *Antiq. Canterbury* 61 [A chapel] inclosed with a double sept or rail of iron for fear of thieves. **1885** *Harper's Mag.* Apr. 761/1 The nave [is] divided from the aisles by an arched sept.

sept (sɛpt), *sb.*[2] Also 6 cepte, 6–7 septe, 7 cept, seapt. [prob. a var. of *sect*, which is used in the same sense in the 16th cent. (see SECT *sb.*[1] 7).

In OF. *septe* occurs in the 16th cent. as a by-form of *sette* (mod.F. *secte*):—L. *secta*; and It. *setta*, of the same origin, is found latinized as *septa* in mediæval documents. The spellings with *p* are perh. due to association with L. *sēptum* (see prec.).]

A division of a nation or tribe; a clan: orig. in reference to Ireland.

Occas. used by anthropologists (after Sir H. Maine, *Early Hist. Institutions*, 1875) for a clan consisting of those who are, or at least are believed to be, descendants of a common ancestor.

1517 in *10th Rep. Hist. MSS. Comm.* App. v. 399 No man ..shall..receve..enny of the Burkes, MacWilliams, the Kellies, nor no cepte elles. **1536** *St. Papers Hen. VIII*, II. 373 ThErle of Desmonde, and the Geraldines of his kyn and septe. **1568–9** *Act 11 Eliz.* in Bolton *Stat. Irel.* (1621) 321 The seapt of the Neyles. **1586** J. HOOKER *Hist. Irel.* in *Holinshed* II. 87/1 The sept of the Tooles. *a* **1628** F. GREVIL *Sidney* (1652) 21 The professors of every faculty would have striven no lesse for him than the Seaven Cities did to have Homer of their Sept. **1665** SIR T. HERBERT *Trav.* (1677) 135 The manner of living most usual amongst Hoords or Septs in Tartary. **1747** CARTE *Hist. England* I. 157 There was an infinite number of little tribes or Septs among the Cantabrians and Gallicians. **1814** SCOTT *Wav.* xvi, Chiefs.. whose word was accounted as a law by those of their own sept, or clan. **1847** GROTE *Greece* II. ix. III. 54 Amphion belonged to the gens or sept of the Bacchiadæ. **1868** MILL *Eng. & Irel.* 12 Before the Conquest, the Irish people knew nothing of absolute property in land. The land virtually belonged to the entire sept.

b. *transf.* A 'tribe' or class.

1610 B. RICH *Descr. Irel.* 37 There are other Septes or professions, namely of Bardes, which are in manner of Poets or Rythmers. **1679** PENN *Addr. Prot.* II. (1692) 138 'Tis of this great Order and Sept of Men only, that all Synods and Convocations are compounded. **1856** H. MILLER *Test. Rocks* xii. (1857) 493 The very curious relations that united into one great sept the prevailing members of the Oolitic flora.

septa-, erron. form of SEPTUA-.

‖**septæmia** (sɛpˈtiːmɪə). Also *U.S.* **septemia.** [mod.L., f. Gr. σηπτ-ός putrefying, putrefactive (f. σήπειν to rot) + αἷμα blood.] = SEPTICÆMIA.

1887 in *Cassell's Encycl. Dict.* **1888** *Daily News* 1 Dec. 2/6 The jury found that the deceased died from the effects of peritonitis and sceptœmia [*sic*] following inflammation.

septagon (ˈsɛptəgən), *a.* [ad. late L. *septagōnus*, hybrid f. L. *septem* seven + Gr. -γωνος -angled, -GON.] Heptagonal.

1756 AMORY *Buncle* (1770) I. 215 Making it [basalt] into pentagon, hexagon, and septagon columns. **1896** *Blackw. Mag.* Apr. 597 The rock itself..cut into septagon shape.

septal (ˈsɛptəl), *a.*[1] [f. SEPT-UM + -AL[1].]

1. Pertaining to, consisting of, or forming a septum or septa.

1839–47 *Todd's Cycl. Anat.* III. 732/2 The internal or septual [*sic*] branches [of the nose] are about twelve in number. **1851** RICHARDSON *Geol.* viii. 217 The body has no septal divisions. **1859** J. R. GREENE *Man. Anim. Kingd.*, *Protozoa* 22 Septa, each of which is perforated by one or more septal apertures, and in most cases indicated externally by a ridge or depression, called the septal line. **1881** MIVART *Cat* 76 The septal cartilage of the nose.

2. *Bot.* Growing in hedges.

1847 H. C. WATSON *Cybele Brit.* I. 66 The proposed series of terms run thus:—..Septal.—Plants of hedge-banks and hedge-rows. **1926** J. J. WALKER *Nat. Hist. Oxford Distr.* 114 *Cuscuta europæa* L. is very rare..; in Oxford it was associated with another septal species, *Humulus Lupulus* L.

3. *Archæol.* Designating a stone or slab forming a barrier between compartments in a burial chamber.

1910 T. H. BRUCE in J. A. Balfour *Book of Arran* 61 The chamber is divided by two septal slabs into three compartments. **1937** *Proc. Prehist. Soc.* New Ser. III. 167 The segmentation of the gallery is achieved by means of septal slabs, rather lower than the side slabs, and in the Irish cairns these septal slabs are set between pairs of vertical jamb stones. **1958** G. DANIEL *Megalith Builders Western Europe* ii. 44 This segmentation or septalisation may be done by jambs projecting from each side, or by transverse stones or septal stones... Septal stones sometimes reach..half-way up the height of a chamber.

septal (ˈsɛptəl), *a.*[2] [f. SEPT[2] + -AL[1].] Pertaining to a sept or clan.

1883 MCCARTHY *Outl. Irish Hist.* iii. 29 He had done much to Normanize the country by making large and wholly illegal grants of Septal territory to his followers.

†ˈ**septan**, *a.* [ad. mod.L. *septāna* (*febris*), tr. Gr. πυρετὸς ἑβδομαῖος (Galen), f. L. *sept-em* seven: see -AN.] Designating a fever of which the paroxysms recur every sixth (according to old reckoning, every seventh) day.

1657 *Expert Physician* 123 The Quintan, Sextan, Septan, and Nonan Feavers. **1747** tr. *Astruc's Fevers* 63 A septan, being really a quartan, of whose paroxysms none are perceptable, but those of every 7th day.

†**septangle.** *Obs.* [ad. late L. *septangulus*, f. *sept-em* seven + *angulus* ANGLE.] A heptagon.

1551 RECORDE *Pathw. Knowl.* I. Def., Septangles, whiche haue seuen angles. **1651** J. F[REAKE] *Agrippa's Occ. Philos.* 253 Triangle, quadrangle, sexangle, septangle, octangle and the rest. **1656** [see SEPTANGULAR].

So †**septangled** *a.* = next.

1706 PHILLIPS (ed. Kersey), *Septangle*, or *Septangled Figure.* **1709** V. MANDEY *Syst. Math., Arith.* (1729) 8 The Description of a Septangled form is impossible, and cannot be known by Human Minds.

septangular (sɛpˈtæŋgjʊlə(r)), *a.* [ad. mod.L. **septangulāris*, f. *septangulus* (see prec.).] Having seven angles, heptagonal.

1656 BLOUNT *Glossogr.*, *Septangular*, that hath seven corners, a Septangle. **1682** GREW *Anat. Pl.* III. I. i. 104 A great number of Vesicles: of which..some appear Pentangular, others..Septangular. **1819** TURTON *Conchol. Dict.* 92 *Murex septangularis.* Septangular Rock-shell. **1866** LOSSING *Hudson* (1868) 127 A line of defences in septangular form. **1902** W. L. NEWMAN *Politics of Aristotle* III. 556 Triangular and septangular harps.

Hence **sepˈtangularness.**

1730 BAILEY (folio), *Septangularness*, the having 7 Angles.

septanose (ˈsɛptənəʊz, -s). *Chem.* [a. G. *septanose* (Micheel & Suckfüll 1933, in *Ann. d.*

Chem. DII. 89), f. L. *sept-em* seven + *-anose* after FURANOSE, PYRANOSE.] A structure containing a seven-membered ring, adopted by some sugars; a sugar having this structure. Freq. *attrib.* Hence **'septanoside**, a glycoside in septanose form.

[**1933** *Chem. Abstr.* XXVII. 3453 An equil. mixt. of α- and β-2,3,4,5-tetraacetylgalactoseptanoses.] **1934** *Ibid.* XXVIII. 1025 For an approx. 1% soln. in 0·01 *N* HCl of the septanoside..the half-time value of hydrolysis at 95° is about 28 min. *Ibid.*, The 7-membered septanose ring is not strained. *Ibid.*, Some indication of a parallelism between the instability of the free sugars (furanoses, septanoses) and the ease of hydrolysis of their glucosides. **1948** R. J. McIlroy *Chem. of Polysaccharides* i. 4 A third type of ring, the seven membered or septanose structure has been prepared. This ring is comparable to the furanose ring in stability. It has not been obtained from natural sources. **1973** *Carbohydrate Res.* XXVIII. 75 It is found that the pseudorotation of the septanose ring and the dioxolane rings are correlated to the position of attachment of the latter rings to the central septanose ring. **1974** *Jrnl. Chem. Soc.: Chem. Commun.* 1010/1 Nitroethane condensed smoothly..with the hydrated dialdehyde (I) to give..the crystalline septanoside ..in 38% yield.

†**'septarchy.** *Obs. rare.* [f. L. *sept-em* seven + Gr. -αρχία sovereignty.] Sovereignty wielded by seven rulers; in quot. *fig.*

1630 J. Taylor (Water P.) *Bawd* Wks. II. 98/1 No man can deny Pride to bee another of the said Septarchy [i.e. the seven deadly sins].

septarian (sɛp'tɛərɪən), *a.* [f. SEPTARI-UM + -AN.] Of the form or character of septaria.

1867 *Ure's Dict. Arts* III. 631 A stratum of septarian stone, forming the Broad Bench on the coast of Dorsetshire, affords an excellent cement. **1882** Geikie *Text-bk. Geol.* IV. I. 488 Such septarian nodules..are abundant in many shales. **1884** H. G. Seeley *Phys. Geol. & Palæont.* 47 These concretions [*sc.* of phosphate of lime] rarely assume a septarian structure.

So **sep'tariate** *a.*; also **sep'tariiform** *a.*

1833-4 J. Phillips *Geol.* in *Encycl. Metrop.* (1845) VI. 621/1 Clay, 50 to 100 feet, with layers of nodules, often septariate. **1875** Dawson *Life's Dawn* iv. 91, I use the term 'septariiform' to denote the curdled appearance so often presented by the Laurentian serpentine.

‖**septarium** (sɛp'tɛərɪəm). *Geol.* Pl. **-aria** (-'ɛərɪə). [mod.L., f. L. *sēptum*: see SEPTUM and -ARIUM.]

1. A septal arrangement.

1785 Hutton in *Trans. Roy. Soc. Edinb.* (1788) I. 246 The form of these iron-stones is that of an oblate or much compressed sphere... In the circular or horizontal section, they present the most elegant septarium.

2. A nodule of argillaceous limestone, ironstone, or the like, of which the parts near the centre are cracked, the spaces between being filled with some mineral: formerly much used for cement. (Cf. *cement-stone*, *turtle-stone*.)

1791 E. Darwin *Bot. Gard.* I. Addit. Notes 39 The volcanic origin of these curious septaria. **1859** R. Hunt *Guide Mus. Pract. Geol.* (ed. 2) 32 Great quantities of cement stones are at present procured by dredging off the coast of Hampshire for the septaria which have been derived from the Barton clay. **1909** *Athenæum* 13 Mar. 314/3 The concretionary nodules of hard carbonate of lime, called 'septaria', which are found in the London clay.

septate ('sɛpteɪt), *a.* [ad. mod.L. *sēptātus* (in late L. = surrounded): see SEPTUM and -ATE².] Containing or divided by a septum or septa; partitioned.

1846 Dana *Zooph.* vii. (1848) 117 The cells..are transversely septate, rarely solid. **1871** W. A. Leighton *Lichen-flora* 9 Spores..simple or variously septate. **1884** Bower & Scott *De Bary's Phaner.* 139 These chambered or septate sacs. **1947** L. G. H. Huxley *Survey Princ. & Practice Wave Guides* ii. 39 The field configuration in the septate coaxial system is very similar..to the pattern of the principal wave on a coaxial transmission line.

So **'septated** *a.*

1877 Bennett *Thomé's Bot.* 366 It is comparatively rare for the wood-cells to become septated..by one, still more rare by several partition-walls. **1895** Dana *Man. Geol.* (ed. 4) 137 A piece of quartzyte..divided up, or septated, by the oxidation process.

septation (sɛp'teɪʃən). [f. SEPTUM + -ATION.] Division by a septum or septa.

1848 Lindley *Introd. Bot.* (ed. 4) II. 143 Filamentous matter multiplying itself by internal septation at the elongated apex. **1895** *Linn. Soc. Jrnl., Bot.* XXX. 442 The intercalary transverse septation of the articulations of certain branches of the creeping thallus.

sep'tato-, used as comb. f. mod.L. *sēptātus* SEPTATE.

1871 W. A. Leighton *Lichen-flora* 291 Paraphyses moderate, thicker at the fuscescent apices and there generally septato-articulate.

septcentenary (sɛptsɛn'tiːnərɪ). [f. L. *sept(em* seven + CENTENARY *sb.*, after *bicentenary*, etc.] A seven-hundredth anniversary.

1924 *Glasgow Herald* 21 Aug. 5/2 The present condition of Dornoch Cathedral, the septcentenary of which is to be celebrated on the 27th inst., presents a striking contrast to that of Elgin Cathedral. **1978** *Church Times* 29 Sept. 5/1 Septcentenary.—A programme of celebrations to mark the 700th anniversary of the establishment of a Christian church in Macclesfield is about to begin.

septectomy (sɛp'tɛktəmɪ). *Surg.* [f. SEPT(UM + -ECTOMY.] **a.** Resection of the nasal septum. *rare*⁻⁰.

1949 in *New Gould Med. Dict.* 922/2. **1961** in A. S. MacNalty *Brit. Med. Dict.* 1292/1.

b. Resection of the atrial septum; septostomy.

1972 *Lancet* 27 May 1140/1 Previous atrial septectomy or septostomy had been performed. **1977** *Ibid.* 18 June 1275/2 At the age of 4 weeks the pulmonary artery was banded,.. and atrial septectomy was performed.

septem-, L. *septem* seven, used in a few compounds, chiefly adjs. = SEPTI-¹ (which is more frequent): **septemde'cenary** [for *-decennary*], occurring once in 17 years; = SEPTENDECENNIAL. **'septemfid**, *Bot.* [L. *-fidus* cleft], divided into seven parts. **'septemfoil** [*-foil* as in CINQUEFOIL], an ornament of seven cusps or points. **septem'foliate**, *Bot.* [mod.L. *septemfoliātus*], having seven leaflets. **sep-tem'partite**, *Bot.*, divided nearly to the base into seven parts. **sep'tempedal** = SEPTIPEDAL. **sep'temvious** [L. *via* way] *nonce-wd.*, going seven different ways.

1843 Kirby & Sp. *Entomol.* (ed. 6) vi. I. 172 Their [*Cicada septemdecim*] *septemdecenary appearance. **1849** Balfour *Man. Bot.* § 148 [Simple leaves] may be..trifid, quinquefid, *septemfid, multifid. **1842** S. C. Hall *Ireland* II. 67 Having the space between the two arches filled by a rich cinque-foil, or rather *septem-foil. **1861** Bentley *Man. Bot.* 170 A leaf ..is septenate or septemfoliate, if there are seven [leaflets], as in the Horse-chestnut. **1847-54** Webster, **Septempartite*, divided nearly to the base into seven parts. **1656** Blount *Glossogr.*, **Septempedal*, of or belonging to seven feet, that is seven foot long. **1861** Reade *Cloister & H.* lxxiii, Officers of state ran *septemvious, seeking an ape to counteract the bloodthirsty tomfoolery of the human species.

September (sɛp'tɛmbə(r)). Also 3-6 **septembre**, 5 **semtembir**, **septembyr**. Abbreviated **Sep.**, **Sept.**, in 17th c. also **7ᵇʳ**. [a. L. *September* or its deriv. F. *septembre* (OF. *setembre*), f. *septem* seven, this month being the seventh of the old Roman year. The native OE. name was *hærfestmónað* HARVEST MONTH.] **a.** The ninth month of the year (according to the modern reckoning).

c **1050** [see OCTOBER]. *c* **1290** *S. Eng. Leg.* I. 12/392 Þe holie Rode was i-founde ase ȝe wutez, in May; He was anhauset in septembre sethþe on þe holie rode-daiȝ. **1338** R. Brunne *Chron.* (1810) 17 Þe ferþ day of Septembre, in þe he[r]uest tide. **1398** Trevisa *Barth. De P.R.* IX. xvii. (Bodl. MS.), The ixᵉ. moneþ hatte Septembre and haþ þat name for he is þe seuenþe moneþ after temporat rayne. *c* **1400** *Rule St. Benet* (Prose) 29 Til þe hali rodis dai in semtembir. **1500-20** Dunbar *Poems* lxv. 14 Without gud lyfe all in the self dois de As Mayis flouris dois in September dry. **1509** Hawes *Past. Pleas.* XXXI. (1555) T j b, Under our signet in our court ryall Of September the two and twenty day. **1600** Surflet *Country Farm* III. lxv. 581 The vttermost pilling of common walnuts..may be distilled in the moneth of September. **1628** *World Encomp. by Drake* 108 The 26 of Sept. **1676** C. Hatton *Corr.* (Camden) 129 Either this or another will be called to meet about 7ᵇʳ next. **1765** Earl Coventry in Jesse *Selwyn & Contemp.* (1843) I. 388. I think I shall reside here till the second week in September. **1853** A. R. Wallace *Amazon & Rio Negro* 201 On September 30th,..we again saw the opposite side of the river.

b. *personified* and *allusively*.

1596 Spenser *F.Q.* VII. vii. 38 Next him [*sc.* August], September marched eeke on foote. **16..** Middleton, etc. *Old Law* II. ii, *Simonides.* When dies thy husband? Is't not July next? *Eugenia.* Oh! you are too hot, sir: Pray cool yourself, and take September with you. **1712** Budgell *Spect.* No. 425 ¶3 September, who came next, seem'd in his Looks to promise a new Spring.

c. *attrib.*, as ***September day, dew, month***; **September massacres** *Fr. Hist.*, a mass killing of political prisoners in Paris on 2-6 September 1792; **September thorn** (see quot. 1832).

a **1425** *Cursor M.* 10998 (Trin.) Þenne bere she childe elizabeth In septembre moneth þe foure & twenty nyȝt. **1707** *Curios. Husb. & Gard.* 136 If you have any May-Dew, or September-Dew. **1805-6** Wordsworth *Prelude* (1959) x. 370, I thought of those September Massacres, Divided from me by a little month. **1832** J. Rennie *Butterfl. & Moths* 105 The September Thorn (*Geometra erosaria*, Stephens) appears in August and September in woods and parks. **1868** Morris *Earthly Par.* (1870) I. I. 10 It was a bright September afternoon. **1886** Ruskin *Præterita* II. 252 The September days were yet long enough for a sunset walk. **1905** Baroness Orczy *Scarlet Pimpernel* xi. 109 The news of the awful September massacres, and of the Reign of Terror and Anarchy. **1976** *Listener* 23-30 Dec. 817/1 There began to seem a fatal unsteadiness in the Revolution... There had been the atrocity of the September massacres.

Hence **Sep'tembered**, coloured with autumnal tints.

1866 Blackmore *Cradock Nowell* xxvi, His honest face was Septembered with many a vintage.

Sep'temberer. = SEPTEMBRIZER 1.

1837 Carlyle *Fr. Rev.* III. I. vi, The great Day of Judgement, when the Eternal..shall judge both Kings and Septemberers.

Sep'temberish, *a.* Also **Septembrish**. [f. SEPTEMBER + -ISH.] Pertaining to, like that of, September.

1851 Hawthorne in *Hawthorne & Wife* (1885) I. 425 A clear and beautiful sunset, with a brisk, Septembrish temperature. **1853** —— *Eng. Note-bks.* (1883) I. 437 A clear atmosphere, bright sunshine, and altogether a Septembrish feeling. **1886** E. S. Phelps *Burglars in Paradise* xi, These [*sc.* flowers] had a Septemberish look, as of a flower that was feeling bilious but would not own it.

†**Sep'tembral**, *a.* *Obs. rare*⁻¹. [ad. F. *septembral*, f. *septembre* SEPTEMBER: see -AL¹.] ***Septembral juice***, wine.

1653 Urquhart *Rabelais* II. i, The pure septembral juice [orig. *puree Septembrale*].

Septembrian (sɛp'tɛmbrɪən), *a.* and *sb. rare.* [f. SEPTEMBER + -IAN.]

A. *adj.* Belonging to September.

1800 Hurdis *Fav. Village* 18 Troops to the partridge at her ev'ning call Her scattered brood Septembrian.

B. *sb.* One who believes that our Lord was born in September.

1644 [E. Fisher] *Feast of Feasts* 25 No marvaile if these Septembrians oppose the tradition of Christs Church.

Septembrist (sɛp'tɛmbrɪst). [f. SEPTEMBER + -IST.] **a.** In Portugal, a supporter of the (successful) insurrection of September 1836 in favour of the restoration of the constitution of 1822. **b.** = SEPTEMBRIZER.

1840 *New Monthly Mag.* LIX. 439 Many individuals of importance..have joined the now dominant party, of the Septembrists [in Portugal]. **1844** *Fraser's Mag.* XXX. 320 Ho! St. Antoine, arouse thee now—ho! brave Septembrists all. **1885** *Encycl. Brit.* XIX. 553 (art. *Portugal*) It was now [1845] the turn of the radicals or Septembrists to have recourse to arms.

So **Sep'temb(e)rism**, the action or policy of the Septembrizers.

1837 Carlyle *Fr. Rev.* III. III. ix, A Citoyen Henriot, one whom some accuse of Septemberism, is made Generalissimo of the National Guard.

septembrize ('sɛptɛmbraɪz), *v.* orig. *Fr. Hist.* Also **-berize**. [ad. F. *septembriser*, f. *septembre* SEPTEMBER: see -IZE.] *trans.* and *intr.* To assassinate like the Septembrizers.

1793 *St. Papers* in *Ann. Reg.* 154 They kept them in the jails of Paris, to Septemberize them. **1794** tr. *Brissot's Addr. to Constituents* 46 They have gone the length of regretting with the Prussian Cloots, that they had not sufficiently septemberised. **1798** Jefferson *Let. to Jas. Madison* 26 Apr., The war hawks talk of septembrizing, deportation, and the examples for quelling sedition set by the French executive. **1819** W. Taylor in *Monthly Rev.* LXXXVIII. 537 The Abbé told me that he was to go..and visit one of the Septemberizing assassins.

Hence **septembri'zation**, action like that of the Septembrizers.

1802 Bentham *Panopt. Corr.* Wks. 1843 XI. 131 In my hearing he has defended Septembrization, and wished..to see it imitated here.

Septembrizer ('sɛptɛmbraɪzə(r)). Also **-ber-**. [ad. F. *septembriseur*, f. *septembriser* (see prec.).]

1. *Fr. Hist.* One who took part in or advocated the massacre of the political prisoners in Paris on September 2nd-5th, 1792. Also *transf.*, a bloodthirsty revolutionary.

1794 tr. *Brissot's Addr. to Constituents* 13 You will then see the Convention..confer the most honourable..missions upon these atrocious Septembrizers. **1820** *Scraps for Curious* 26, I saw at Meux a famous Septembrizer chop off the head of the curate of St. Nicholas. [**1866** *Spectator* 1 Dec. 1329 The wild thirst for blood which..turns decent, quiet citizens..into men like the Septembriseurs.]

2. = SEPTEMBRIST a.

1840 *New Monthly Mag.* LIX. 437 The revolutionary Septembrisers of the [Portuguese] ministry.

3. One who shoots partridges (in September): with allusion to sense 1.

1824 Byron *Juan* XVI. lxxx, Some deadly shots too, Septembrizers, seen Earliest to rise, and last to quit the search Of the poor partridge. **1834** *L. Hunt's London Jrnl.* No. 22. 171/2, I recollected the month, and thought how well its name was adapted to these Septembrizers of the birds.

septemfluous (sɛp'tɛmfluəs), *a.* [f. L. *septemflu-us* (f. *septem* seven + *fluĕre* to flow) + -OUS.] Flowing in seven streams.

1629 H. Burton *Truth's Tri.* 323 Aristotle..would desperately drowne himselfe in that septemfluous sea of Euripus. **1650** Fuller *Pisgah* IV. v. 81 Nothing being more famous in humane poetry and prose then this septemfluous river [Nile]. **1655** —— *Hist. Waltham-Abby* 5 The River Ley..which..seven times parteth from itself, whose septemfluous stream..is crossed again with so many bridges.

fig. *a* **1670** Hacket *Abp. Williams* I. (1692) 220 Doth salvation..depend upon your septemfluous sacraments?

septemia, U.S. spelling of SEPTÆMIA.

septemplicate. [f. L. *septem* seven + *-plicate* as in DUPLICATE, etc. Cf. L. *septemplex.*] One of seven copies of a document.

1805 Coleridge *Let. to D. Stuart* 20 Apr., The above is a duplicate, or rather a sex or septem-plicate of an order.

septemtryo(u)n, obs. forms of SEPTENTRION.

septemvir (sɛp'tɛmvə(r)). Pl. **septemviri** (-vɪraɪ). [L., sing. of *septemvirī*, f. *septem* seven

+ *virī* men.] One of a body of seven men associated in an office or commission.

a **1760** W. DUNCAN *Sel. Orat. Cicero* xvi. (1841) 355 Did you not desert him, when he put up for being a septemvir? **1841** BREWSTER *Martyrs Sci.* II. i. 132 John and Paul Hainzel, the one a septemvir, and the other the consul or burgomaster. **1883** *Sat. Rev.* 5 May 560/1 The scheme of Honours examinations..proposed by Professor Seeley and the other *septemviri* is simplicity itself.

† **sep'temviral,** *a. Obs. rare.* [f. prec. + -AL[1].] Pertaining to a septemvir.

1641 SIR S. D'EWES in Rushw. *Hist. Coll.* (1692) III. I. 314 The Septemviral Dignity and Suffrage he [the Duke of Bavaria] hath obtained by the Prince Elector's.. Misfortune.

septemvirate (sɛp'tɛmvɪrət). [ad. L. *septemvirātus*, f. *septemvir*: see SEPTEMVIR and -ATE[1].]

1. The office or dignity of a septemvir, government by septemviri.

1640 HOWELL *Dodona's Gr.* 72 This reason of State sounds well why the Septemvirate lets it continue there so long. *c* **1642** *Observ. his Majesty's late Answ.* 31 The whole kingdome is not to bee mastered..by the Traine Band,.. nor the maior part in Parliament by I know not what septemvirat. **1656** BLOUNT *Glossogr.*, *Septemvirate*, the authority of seven Officers in like power. **1756** NUGENT *Gr. Tour, Germany* II. 299 [At Nurenberg] The raising of forces or levying taxes, are usually referred to a select number of the council, stiled by way of eminence, the Septemvirate.

2. A group or set of seven men.

1781 T. DAVIES *Mem. Garrick* (ed. 3) II. 39 *note*, Swift, in his list of six great men, to whom no seventh (in his opinion) could be added, might have very safely made a septemvirate with Alfred. **1832–4** DE QUINCEY *Cæsars* Wks. 1859 X. 196 The legend of the Seven Sleepers, a septemvirate of Christian youths.

septenarian (sɛptɪ'nɛərɪən), *a.* [f. L. *septēnārius* SEPTENARY + -AN.]

† **1.** Used for SEPTENNARY.

1647 M. HUDSON *Div. Right Govt.* I. vi. 51 The septenarian madness of Nabuchad-nezzar, inflicted by God for destroying that septenarian work of Solomon (his holy Temple).

2. *Pros.* That is a septenarius.

1891 *Athenæum* 28 Feb. 275/1 Septenarian iambic lines.

So **septe'narious** *a. rare*$^{-0}$. = SEPTENARY *a.* 1.

1656 BLOUNT *Glossogr.*, *Septenarious*, of or belonging to seven, containing seven in number.

‖ **septenarius** (sɛptɪ'nɛərɪəs). *Pros.* Pl. -arii (-'ɛərɪaɪ). [L. *septēnārius*, f. *septēnī*, distributive of *septem* seven.] A line of seven feet, esp. the trochaic or iambic tetrameter catalectic.

1819 CAREY *Lat. Pros.* 273 The *Catalectic Trochaic Tetrameter* (called likewise *Quadratus*, *Octonarius*, and *Septenarius*) consists of seven feet..followed by a catalectic syllable... It is..only the Iambic Octonarius wanting the first syllable. **1872** KENNEDY tr. *Ten Brink's Hist. Eng. Lit.* 267 [In the southern English lives of saints] regular *septenarii* or tetrameters are more rarely found. **1894** *Gildersleeve's Lat. Gram.* §770 The strict Septenarius of the later poets keeps the odd feet pure. **1897** J. H. GRAY *Plautus' Trinummus* p. xxv, Trochaic septenarii.

septenary ('sɛptɪnərɪ, -iːnərɪ), *a.* and *sb.* Also 7 septyn-, 8 septin-. [ad. L. *septēnāri-us*, f. *septēnī*: see prec. and -ARY.] **A.** *adj.*

1. Pertaining or relating to the number seven; forming a group of seven. ***septenary number***, the number seven.

1601 [BP. W. BARLOW] *Defence* 118 If the force of this argument lie in the septenarie nvmber [of the sacraments]. **1641** H. L'ESTRANGE *God's Sabbath* 29 This septenary number gained Authority from the creation of the world, because the first works of God were made in six dayes, and the seventh was dedicated to rest as sacred. **1674** BOYLE *Excell. Theol.* II. iv. 167 To be able to reject the septenary number of the planets by the detection of the four satellites of Jupiter. **1694** MOTTEUX *Rabelais* IV. iv, Between whose Septenary Links [*chainons septenaires*],.. Rubies, Emeralds, and Unions were..set in. **1855** BAILEY *Mystic*, etc. 64 The septenary stars.

b. With reference to the division of time into periods based on the number seven, e.g. a week.

1646 SIR T. BROWNE *Pseud. Ep.* IV. iv. 212 This containeth but 27. dayes, and about 8. howres, which commeth short to compleat the septenary account. **1708** *Brit. Apollo* No. 75. 1/1 So is one in seven in a Constant Septinary return. **1745** R. JAMES *Med. Dict.*, *Septana*, a septinary Fever; that is, one which performs its Period in seven Days. **1848** R. W. HAMILTON *Horæ Sabb.* i. 16 That septenary notation of days which we call the week. **1866** J. G. MURPHY *Comm., Exodus* xvi. 23 Traces of the septenary division of time have been found among the Egyptians.

2. Consisting of seven lines. *nonce-use.*

1814 SOUTHEY in *Q. Rev.* XII. 69 Lydgate..preferred the septenary stanza.

B. *sb.* (Cf. HEBDOMAD, HEPTAD.)

1. The number seven.

1653 H. MORE *Conject. Cabbal.* 161 The Hebdomad or Septenary is a fit Symbole of God, as he is considered having finished these six days Creation. **1690** T. BURNET *Th. Earth* IV. iii. 148 Those constitutions of Moses that proceed so much upon a Septenary, or the number Seven.

2. A group or set of seven.

1594 *Mirr. Policy* (1599) 223 The seuen gifts of the Holy ghost, the seuen orders of the Church, seuen workes of mercy,..with sundry other septenaries. **1614** A. ROBERTS (*title*) A Sacred Septenarie, or the seven last wordes of our Sauiour Christ vttered vpon the Crosse. **1650** GELL *Serm.* 8 Aug. 15 The Septenary of Planets. **1652** URQUHART *Jewel* 231 The sacred septenary of the most highly-renowned men, for prudence and true wisdom. **1686** GOAD *Celest. Bodies* I. xv. 99 The Moon, which..runs from her Month to her Month by Septenaries. **1819** G. S. FABER *Dispens.* (1823) I. 258 A septenary of erratic living animals which are the seven Worlds or seven Planets. **1847** SOANE *New Curios. Lit.* I. 296 Philo Judæus..tells us that nature delights in a septenary; the planets, he says, are seven; the Bear is composed of seven stars [etc.].

3. A period of seven years (*occas.* weeks, days).

1577–86 HARRISON *England* I. ix, The time of the pentarchie indured likewise 49 yeares, or seauen septenaries. *a* **1639** WOTTON *Surv. Educ.* in *Reliq.* (1672) 78 Certain Periods, or Degrees of Change..every seven years; whereof the two first Septynaries..I will call the Obsequious Age. **1646** SIR T. BROWNE *Pseud. Ep.* IV. iv. 208 The dayes of men are usually cast up by septenaries. **1660** tr. *Amyraldus' Treat. conc. Relig.* III. v. 395 Septenaries of daies, or weeks, or months, or years, or ages? **1860** O. W. HOLMES *Elsie V.* xix, If Elsie could only outlive three septenaries, twenty-one years.

4. *Mus.* The seven notes of the diatonic scale.

1662 PLAYFORD *Introd. Skill Mus.* I. i. 2 By these Three Septenaries is distinguished three severall Parts, that the Scale is divided into. **1776** HAWKINS *Hist. Mus.* II. II. viii. 214 To shew the analogy between the seven planets and the chords included in the musical septenary. **1782** BURNEY *Hist. Mus.* II. 81 In completing the scale, or septenary.

5. *Pros.* = SEPTENARIUS.

Chiefly applied to the English metre represented, e.g. by the verse of the *Moral Ode* and the *Ormulum*.

1887 HORSTMANN *S. Eng. Leg.* Introd. p. ix, [MS. Egerton] generally shortens the lines from septenaries to Alexandrine verses, by omitting words [etc.]. **1891** J. C. PARSONS *Eng. Versif.* 80 A form..called the Septenary, with seven accents and fourteen syllables to the line.

septenate ('sɛptɪnət), *a. Bot.* [f. L. *septēnī* seven each + -ATE[2].] Growing in sevens, having seven divisions, heptamerous.

1830 LINDLEY *Nat. Syst. Bot.* 115 Leaves..compound, quinate or septenate. **1861** BENTLEY *Man. Bot.* 171 Septenate leaf of the Horse-chestnut.

ˌ**septende'cennial,** *a.* [f. L. *septendecim* seventeen, after *biennial*, *septennial*, etc.] Recurring every seventeen years.

1896 *Home Miss.* (N.Y.) Sept. 252 This splendid septendecennial..anniversary.

septen'decimal, *a.* [f. L. *septendecimus*, ordinal of *septendecim*.] Pertaining to the number seventeen. (In quot. used incorrectly for prec.)

1885 *Proc. Amer. Assoc. Adv. Sci.* XXXIV. 329 These insects [the periodical cicada] appear in fewer numbers at each septendecimal visit.

septennary (sɛp'tɛnərɪ), *a.* [f. L. *septenn-is* (f. *sept-em* seven + *annus* year) + -ARY.] Septennial.

1644 SIR E. DERING *Prop. Sacr.* Pref. e, They are elder then my septennary examination, which is confined between 1633, and 1640. **1655** FULLER *Ch. Hist.* II. x. §26 If Dunstan did septennary Penance, to expiate every mortall Sin. **1887** in *Westm. Gaz.* (1897) 6 Aug. 3/1 Whereas, by septennary revolutions, the Speakership of the Ports has now devolved upon us.

septennate (sɛp'tɛnət). [ad. F. *septennat*, f. L. *septenn-is* (see prec.) + *-at* = -ATE[1].] A period of seven years during which office is held, etc.

Orig. applied to the military dictatorship of Marshal MacMahon set up for seven years from 20 Nov. 1873.

1874 *Times* 13 Apr. 7/1 The Septennate [of Marshal MacMahon] and the Press. **1885** *Athenæum* 2 May 570/1 Lord Carnarvon passed under review the principal events which had marked his septennate. **1895** *Westm. Gaz.* 15 May 2/2 If this Bill fails or is withdrawn, a Conservative Septennate is as absolute a certainty as to-morrow's sunrise.

b. *German Hist.* A period of seven years during which the strength of the army is to remain fixed. Also *attrib.*

1885 LOWE *Bismarck* II. 401 *marg.*, The Military Septennate. **1887** *Pall Mall G.* 23 Feb. 11/2 Of the seats occupied by the members of this majority the Septennate party has already captured some thirty or forty by the displacement of former members. **1887** *Contemp. Rev.* LI. 592 The passing of the Septennate Bill will certainly make the French more inclined to pause before attacking Germany.

sep'tenniad. *rare.* [f. L. *septenni-um* (cf. next) + -AD.] A period of seven years.

1851 E. FITZGERALD *Euphranor* 50 And so I leave him at the end of his second septenniad.

septennial (sɛp'tɛnɪəl), *a.* [f. L. *septenni-um* SEPTENNIUM + -AL[1].]

1. Consisting of, or lasting, seven years.

Septennial Act (Eng. Hist.), an act of 1716 providing that 'all Parliaments shall and may respectively have Continuance for Seven Years, and no longer'. Hence allusive uses of *septennial*, as in quot. *a* 1832; cf. 1748 in sense 2.

1656 BLOUNT *Glossogr.*, *Septennial*, of seven years space. **1719** STEELE *Plebeian* No. 4 ad fin., Sitting out the remainder of the septennial term. **1759** SMOLLETT *Hist. Eng.* X. 42 (an. 1733) That a bill should be brought in for repealing the septennial act. **1772** *Junius Lett.* Ded. p. viii, Although the last session of a septennial parliament be usually employed in courting the favour of the people. *a* **1832** CRABBE *Posth. T.* xviii. *Boat Race* 6 When once enlisted upon either side, He must the rude septennial storm abide. **1881** *Nation* (N.Y.) XXXII. 384 The argument..may also be used in behalf of triennial or of septennial, or of decennial sessions.

2. Recurring every seven years.

1640 HOWELL *Dodona's Gr.* 23 Being dispensed withall for his septenniall visit. **1748** JOHNSON *Van. Hum. Wishes* 97 Our supple Tribes..ask no Questions but the Price of Votes; With Weekly Libels and Septennial Ale, Their Wish is full to riot and to rail. **1866** J. G. MURPHY *Comm., Exodus* xxiii. 10, 11 The septennial Sabbath thus bore a complete analogy to the hebdomadal. **1886** *Field* 30 Jan. 118/2 He was ready to accept a principle of septennial revaluations.

Hence **sep'tennialist**, one who is in favour of septennial parliaments; **septenni'ality**, the condition of being septennial.

1817 BENTHAM *Parl. Reform* Introd. 282 The reduction, of the at present established long term indicated by the word septenniality, to the dimensions of this short term. **1820** *Examiner* No. 612. 13/1 To Annual Parliaments the objections of the Septennialists are singularly weak. **1892** *Review of Rev.* V. 3/2 Balfour is too ardent a Septennialist to sanction a premature dissolution.

septennially (sɛp'tɛnɪəlɪ), *adv.* [f. SEPTENNIAL + -LY[2].] Every seven years.

1791 MACKINTOSH *Vind. Gallicæ* Wks. 1846 III. 117 A House of Lords, which..should..have a majority of its members septennially or triennially nominated by the King. **1829** GEN. P. THOMPSON *Exerc.* (1842) I. 134 It would be as much easier to take men's votes annually than septennially, as for a boy to comb his hair daily than once a week. **1846** MRS. GORE *Eng. Char.*, *Body-Coachman* I. 259 The fifteen guineas per annum were paid septennially.

† **sep'tennian,** *a. Obs. rare.* [Formed as SEPTENNIAL: see -AN.] Of seven years.

1716 M. DAVIES *Athen. Brit.* II. 355 Children, under the said Septennian Age.

‖ **septennium** (sɛp'tɛnɪəm). [L., f. *sept-em* seven + *annus* year.] A period of seven years.

1855 OGILVIE *Suppl.* **1868** M. PATTISON *Academ. Org.* v. 265 The septennium required for the arts degree.

† **sep'tennual.** *Obs.* [f. L. *septennis*, after *annual*.] A feast recurring every seven years.

1641 H. L'ESTRANGE *God's Sabbath* 58 The Law was read on the weekly Sabbath, as well as on the annuall of Tabernacles in the septennuall of Release.

septenous ('sɛptɪnəs), *a. Bot.* [Formed as SEPTENATE + -OUS.] = SEPTENATE.

1866 *Treas. Bot.*

† **septentrial,** *a. Obs.* [irreg. f. L. *septentrio* (see next) + -AL[1].] = SEPTENTRIONAL.

1549 in *Narr. Reform.* (Camden) 333 To calle up Baro, whom he taketh an orientalle or septentrialle spirit. **1622** DRAYTON *Poly-olb.* xx. 19 When Waveney in her way, on this Septentrial side..From Laphamford leads on her stream into the East. **1631** R. H. *Arraignm. Whole Creature* xii. §1. 171 Our Septentriall cold Countries.

Septentrion (sɛp'tɛntrɪən), *sb.* and *a. Obs.* exc. *arch.* Also 4–5 septem(p)trio(u)n, 4–6 -tryon. [ad. L. *septentriōn-*, sing. of *septentriōnēs*, orig. *septem triōnēs*, the seven stars of the constellation of the Great Bear, f. *septem* seven + *triōnes*, pl. of *trio* plough-ox. Cf. F. *septentrion*.] **A.** *sb.*

1. *pl.* (chiefly as Latin.) The constellation of the Great Bear, *occas.* the Little Bear.

1532 *Chaucer's Boethius* II. met. vi. Wks. fol. ccxlvi/2 This Nero gouerned by ceptre al the peoples that be vnder the colde sterris that highten the Septentrions [*MSS.* vii. tyryones, the seuene triones]. **1553** EDEN *Treat. Newe Ind.* (Arb.) 22 Ye seuen starres called *Septentriones* (being not farre from *Vrsa maior* called charles wayne). **1601** HOLLAND *Pliny* II. xxv. I. 16 That region of the skie which is under the North starre *Septentriones*. **1654** GAYTON *Pleas. Notes* IV. xxv. 286 What influence the septentriones had upon him.. is to be easily guess'd. **1715** tr. *Gregory's Astron.* (1726) I. 217 The Stars call'd the *Septem Triones*. **1859** LD. LYTTON *Wanderer* 21 Wild Desire; Which, hungering for the sources of the suns, Makes moan beyond the blue Septentrions.

2. The north; the northern region(s) of the earth or the heavens.

c **1386** CHAUCER *Monk's T.* 3657 He..This wyde world hadde in subieccioun Bothe Est and West North and Septemtrioun. *c* **1400** MAUNDEV. (1839) x. 117 In the Hed of that See of Galilee, toward the Septemtryon, is a strong Castelle. *c* **1440** *Pallad. on Husb.* I. 298 But from the cold Septemtrion decline, And from northwest ther chilling sonnys shine. **1503** *Kalender of Sheph.* (Sommer) H viij b, Drawyng towart the septentryon and other tymys towart the myd day. *c* **1511** *1st Eng. Bk. Amer.* (Arb.) Introd. 32/2 That other parte of Indien is aboute Septentryon. **1593** SHAKS. *3 Hen. VI*, I. iv. 136 Thou art as opposite to euery good, As the Antipodes are vnto vs, Or as the South to the Septentrion. **1652** J. WRIGHT tr. *Camus' Nat. Paradox* XII. 368 The Polonians have two powerfull..neighbours, the Moscovianns towards the Septentrion and the Turk in the Orientall part.

3. A northerner. *rare.*

1607 TOPSELL *Four-f. Beasts* 42 There is a constellation called the beare in the figure of seauen Starres like a Carte. .. The Septentrions call them *Triones*, that is yoked Oxen. **1854** LOWELL *Jrnl. Italy* Wks. 1890 I. 175 We graver-tempered and -mannered Septentrions.

B. *adj.* Northern; = next.

1632 LITHGOW *Trav.* VII. 318 The Sunne declining North-ward.., and warming..the Septentrion sides of these Cynthian mountaynes. **1671** MILTON *P.R.* IV. 31 A ridge of hills That screen'd the fruits of the earth and seats of men From cold Septentrion blasts. **1814** CARY *Dante, Purg.* XXXII. 98 And in their hands upheld those lights secure From blast septentrion and the gusty south. *a* **1849** H. COLERIDGE *Poems* (1850) II. 251 Their countless hosts Sped from their chill septentrion nursery.

septentrional (sɛpˈtɛntrɪənəl), *a.*, *sb.* Now *rare.* [ad. L. *septentriōnālis*, f. *septentrio* (see prec.). Cf. F. *septentrional* (14th c. in Hatz.-Darm.).]

A. *adj.* Belonging to the north, northern; formerly (of learning, etc.), pertaining to northern countries.

septentrional signs (Astron.), the first six signs of the zodiac.

c **1391** CHAUCER *Astrol.* II. §40 Than saw I wel that the body of Venus in hir latitude of degrees septemtrionals ascendid in the ende of the 8 degre fro the heved of Capricorne. *c* **1440** *Astron. Cal.* (MS. Ashm. 391), þis signe ys septentrional þ^t is of north partie. **1549** *Compl. Scot.* vi. 48 The pole artic, boreal, or septemtrional. *Ibid.* 52 The septemtrional tropic of cancer. **1557** H. BAKER *Rules Use Almanacs* C j b, When the sunne is in the signes septentrionalles. **1614** RALEIGH *Hist. World* I. 108 The body of Armenia standeth in fortie three degrees Septentrionall. *c* **1645** HOWELL *Lett.* (1650) I. 388 The Goths and other septentrional nations. **1705** HEARNE *Collect.* (O.H.S.) I. 52 The Catalogue of Septentrional MSS. **1718** HICKES & NELSON *J. Kettlewell* II. xxiv. 125 Dr. Marshall the.. reviver of Septentrional Learning in the University of Oxford. **1806** W. TAYLOR in *Ann. Rev.* IV. 562 The investigation of septentrional antiquities. **1835** SIR J. ROSS *Narr. 2nd Voy.* xvii. 270 What were the politics, gossipings, squabbles, friendships, or parties, in this septentrional city. **1848** *Fraser's Mag.* XXXVIII. 684 Disposed to dispute the septentrional hold of the country with its Austrian rival. **1887** PATER *Imag. Portraits* iv. 145 The Septentrional Apollo [Duke Carl of Rosenmold].

Hence †**septentrioˈnality**, northerliness (Bailey, 1730); †**sepˈtentrionally** *adv.*, in the direction of the north; †**sepˈtentrionate** *v. intr.*, to point to the north.

1646 SIR T. BROWNE *Pseud. Ep.* II. ii. 58 A directive or polary faculty, whereby conveniently they [*sc.* steel and iron] do septentrionate at one extreme, and Australize at another. *Ibid.* 62 If they [needles] be powerfully excited and equally let fall, they commonly sink down and break the water at that extream wherat they were septentrionally excited.

B. *sb.* = SEPTENTRION 2.

c **1400** MAUNDEV. (1839) xxiv. 255 Turquesten.. strecchethe him.. toward the Septentrionalle, to the Kyngdom of Chorasme.

sepˈtentrionaline. *Chem.* [f. L. *septentriōnālis* + -INE.] A crystalline alkaloid obtained from *Aconitum septentrionale.*

1897 *Jrnl. Chem. Soc.* LXXII. I. 303 Septentrionaline,.. which is a yellowish powder melting at 128·9°, acts as an anæsthetic.

septentriˈonic, *a. rare.* In quot. septem-. [f. L. *septentrio* SEPTENTRION + -IC.] Northern.

1844 *Fraser's Mag.* XXX. 318/2 The minstrelsie of our septemtrionic tubes was made applicable to classic themes.

So **septentriˈonical** *a. rare.*

1654 GAYTON *Pleas. Notes* IV. vi-vii. 203 The septentrionicall part of those Saxons.

septer(e, obs. forms of SCEPTRE *sb.*

septet(t, -ette (sɛpˈtɛt). *Mus.* Also (*italianized*) **septetto.** [a. G. *septet*, f. L. *septem*: see -ET[1], -ETTE.] **a.** A composition for seven voices or instruments.

1828 E. HOLMES *Ramble among Musicians of Germany* 263 He [*sc.* Hummel] was pleased to hear that a lady.. had repeatedly played in public his septett for the pianoforte. *a* **1837** (*title*) Beethoven's Grand Septett, Arranged for the Piano Forte, with Accompaniments of Flute, Violin, and Violoncello, by I. N. Hummel. **1841** tr. *Schindler's Beethoven* II. 380 Septett in E flat for Violin, Alto, Violoncello, Clarionet, Bassoon, Horn, and Double Bass. *Ibid.* 386 Trio.. (from the Septetto). **1863** *Reader* 1 Aug. 120/1 He is incapable of singing the duel septett (even transposed) without an effort so painful as to destroy the pleasure of the listener. **1872** KINGSLEY *Poems, Delectable Day* 17 The septette of Beethoven. **1909** *Blackw. Mag.* Apr. 488/1 The septette in 'Patience'.

b. *transf.* A set of seven.

1886 *Field* 9 Jan. 50/3 Another septette faced the starter for the inaptly named Thursday Hurdle Race. **1907** *Academy* 9 Mar. 230/1 A septette of water-colours by the late H. B. Brabazon.

septfoil (ˈsɛtfɔɪl). Also 6–7 set-. [ad. late L. *septifolium*, as if through OF.: see SEPTI-[1] and FOIL *sb.*[1], and cf. *cinquefoil.*]

1. The plant tormentil. Now *rare.*

1578 LYTE *Dodoens* I. lvii. 84 This herbe [sc. *Tormentilla*] is now called.. in English Setfoyle and Tormentill. **1607** TOPSELL *Four-f. Beasts* 616 For this disease the Sheap-heardes take no other thing but the Hearbe *Tormenti[ll]a*, or Set-foyle. **1764** *Museum Rust.* III. xiii. 56 Tormentil, or septfoil, grows wild on dry pastures and commons in most parts of England. **1812** CRABBE *Tales* x. 122 Here the dwarf sallows creep, the septfoil harsh. **1852** MORFIT *Tanning & Currying* (1853) 40 Certain annual plants—as the septfoil and bistort.

2. *Arch.* An ornament with seven cusps or points.

1849 [see SIXFOIL]. **1877** F. G. LEE *Gloss. Liturg. Terms.*

septi-[1], comb. form of L. *septem* seven, forming adjs. in L., several of which have analogues formed with *septem-*, as *septiceps*, *septichordis* (also *septemchordis*), *septicollis*, *septipēs* (also *septempedālis*); in English forming compounds for the most part adapted from or modelled on the L. compounds: **ˈseptichord,** seven-stringed. **ˈseptiˌcoloured,** of seven colours. **septiˈfarious** *rare*⁻⁰. [f. L. *septifariam* adv., in seven parts: see quots.] **septifluous** *rare*⁻⁰ = SEPTEMFLUOUS. **septiˈfolious** [L. *folium* leaf], having seven leaves. **ˈseptiˌfronted,** having seven foreheads. **septiˈlateral,** seven-sided. †**septimestre** [L. *septi-*, *septemmēstris*], seven months old. **ˈseptimontial** [L. *Septimontiālis*, f. *Septimontium* (*mont-*, *mons* mountain)], belonging to the feast held on the seven hills of Rome. **ˈseptipartite** = SEPTEMPARTITE. †**septipedal** [cf. SEPTEMPEDAL], seven feet in length. **ˈseptiregal,** of seven kings. **septiˈsyllable,** a word of seven syllables. **sepˈtivalent,** *Chem.*, combining with seven atoms of hydrogen or other univalent element or radical. **ˈseptizone** [L. *septizōnium*]: see quot.

1721 A. MALCOLM *Treat. Mus.* 522 A third Tetrachord was added to the *septichord Lyre. **1825** WATERTON *Wand. S. Amer.* IV. ii. 284, I was in hopes to have found the Grande Gobe Mouche of Buffon, and the *septicoloured Tangara. **1865** GROTE *Plato* I. i. 62 *note* x, A wheel painted with the seven prismatic colours and made to revolve rapidly, will look white, but it is still really septi-coloured. **1656** BLOUNT *Glossogr.*, **Septifarious*, of seven manner of fashions, sorts or ways. *a* **1860** A. GRAY (cited by Worcester), *Septifarious*, turned seven different ways. **1656** BLOUNT *Glossogr.*, **Septifluous.* See *Septemfluous.* **1721** BAILEY, **Septifolious Plants*, such as consist of 7 Leaves. *a* **1708** T. WARD *Eng. Ref.* IV. (1716) 363 With ten huge Horns on ev'ry Forhead, And with a *Septi-fronted Scull. **1658** SIR T. BROWNE *Pseud. Ep.* v. xxii. 331 Seven equicrural triangles.. whose bases are the seven sides of the *septilateral figure. **1834** H. AINSWORTH *Rookwood* III. iv, A septilateral figure. **1658** PHILLIPS, **Septimestre*, of seven moneths space. **1606** HOLLAND *Sueton.* 262 At the solemne *Septimontiall sacrifice, hee made a dole of Viands. **1808** G. S. FABER *View Prophecies* I. 124 Whether the division of the mystic Euphrates into seven streams denotes some *septipartite division of the Turkish empire. *a* **1878** SIR G. SCOTT *Lect. Archit.* (1879) II. 198 Sexpartite or septipartite vaulting. **1902** *Nature* 27 Nov. 80/2 If a line cutting the fourth portion in four real points be projected to infinity, the projection will be septipartite. **1606** BIRNIE *Kirk-Buriall* (1833) 3 To defraude the most landles liuer on life at lest of his *septipedall inheritance so equally proportioned to all by death. **1847** *Gentl. Mag.* July 45/2 Age has scarcely less likelihood of returning to childhood than Roman history of reverting to the Trojan origin and *septiregal succession. **1834** OSWALD (cited by Worcester), **Septisyllable.* **1872** WATTS *Dict. Chem.* VI. 243 Sodium also can act as a trivalent and as a *septivalent element. **1880** CLEMINSHAW *Wurtz' Atom. Theory* 229[Chlorine] is septivalent in perchloric acid. **1730** BAILEY (folo), **Septizone*, a Building girt with seven Rows of Columns.

septi-[2], comb. form of SEPTUM, as in SEPTIFEROUS, SEPTIFORM[2], SEPTIFRAGAL. (Cf. SEPTO-[2].)

septic (ˈsɛptɪk), *a.* and *sb.* Also 7 erron. sceptick. [ad. late L. *sēptic-us*, a. Gr. σηπτικός, f. σήπειν to putrefy.] **A.** *adj.* **1. a.** Putrefactive, putrefying; in mod. use, of disease, caused by the absorption of the products of putrefaction.

1605 TIMME *Quersit.* III. 160 Either septic putrifying, or caustic burning. **1684** tr. *Bonet's Merc. Compit.* VI. 211 Vitriol, according to Galen.. is of a corroding and sceptick quality. **1705** GREENHILL *Embalming* 272 After the nature of Septic and Escharotic Medicines, it corrodes and consumes the Flesh in a very short Time. **1752** PRINGLE *Obs. Dis. Army* III. vii. (1765) 337 The miasma or septic ferment.. being received into the blood. *Ibid.* App. p. xxxviii, It would seem that salt is subservient to digestion chiefly by its septic virtue, that is, by softening and resolving meats. **1806** *Med. & Phys. Jrnl.* XV. 79 If this matter is the sceptic [*sic*] principle, the foundation of all these chronic diseases. **1873** F. T. ROBERTS *Handbk. Med.* 92 The symptoms are of such a low type.. that they may be truly termed malignant. The terms 'putrid' or 'septic' are sometimes applied to fever under these circumstances. **1879** TYNDALL *Fragm. Sci.* (ed. 6) II. xiii. 334 The preventing of the wound from becoming a nidus for the propagation of septic bacteria. **1881** *Times* 25 Mar. 5 Illness has palpably been produced by the use, by paper-hangers, of size and paste undergoing or speedily entering on septic change.

†**b.** *septic acid*: nitric or nitrous acid. (Cf. SEPTON and SEPTOUS.) *Obs.*

1798 *Monthly Mag.* VI. 26 [Abstract of paper by Dr. S. L. Mitchill.] The azote, by the absorption of oxygen, is converted into nitrous oxide gas (septic acid), which is supposed to be the.. cause of infectious fever. **1800** S. L. MITCHILL in *Med. & Phys. Jrnl.* IV. 25 It is.. ordinarily impossible to procure one drop of pure and naked septic acid, by any decomposition of nitre.

2. *septic tank*, a tank (associated either with a sewage works or with a residence that is not connected to a main sewer) in which the solid portions of sewage are allowed to settle and accumulate and are purified by the action of anaerobic bacteria.

1902 *Encycl. Brit.* XXIX. 379/1 The 'septic tank-system' was devised by Cameron of Exeter in 1896. *Ibid.* XXXII. 526/1 At the present time the common cesspool is being resuscitated and improved under the name of a septic tank. **1909** *Chambers's Jrnl.* Feb. 87/1 The sewage system is of the latest character, with a septic tank. **1939** *Archit. Rev.* LXXXVI. 11/2 Bathrooms are installed on both ground and first floors, while other equipment includes an electric generating plant, a deep well with electric pump and septic tank. **1951** *Good Housek. Encycl.* 315/1 An adequate supply of good water at a safe distance from the septic tank. **1976** *Eastern Even. News* (Norwich) 13 Dec. 7/2 His septic tank did not work, and nor did most others in the village.

3. In trivial use: unpleasant, nasty, 'rotten'. *slang.*

1914 'I. HAY' *Knight on Wheels* xviii. 172 Philip enquired after Mr. Brett, and learned that that 'septic blighter' (Timothy's description) had retired from the position of Housemaster. **1932** S. GIBBONS *Cold Comfort Farm* xviii. 248 Rennett had had a pretty septic life. **1958** L. DURRELL *Balthazar* 248 What septic weather to-day! **1974** G. MITCHELL *Winking at Brim* vii. 62 Mummy and Daddy have had a row. Isn't it septic of them?

B. *sb.* †**1.** A septic or putrefactive substance. *Obs.*

1608 TOPSELL *Serpents* 218 The venome of the Salamander is reckoned among Septicks, or corroding things. **1684** tr. *Bonet's Merc. Compit.* III. 62 Septicks.. may not be applied to any Ulcer. **1756** C. LUCAS *Ess. Waters* I. 14 Acid of salt.. constitutes.. with regulus of antimony, a powerful septic. **1771** WATSON in *Phil. Trans.* LXI. 219 The proportion in which it acts as a septic.

2. *ellipt.* A septic tank. *Austral. colloq.*

1961 P. WHITE *Riders in Chariot* III. viii. 231 Rosetrees lived.. in a texture-brick home—city water, no sewerage, but their own septic. **1977** *Weekly Times* (Melbourne) 19 Jan. 65/2 (Advt.), Lovely new home.., 2 bathrooms, 2 septics and large living area.

‖**septicæmia** (sɛptɪˈsiːmɪə). Also *U.S.* **septicemia.** [mod.L., f. Gr. σηπτικ-ός SEPTIC + αἷμα blood: see -IA.] Septic poisoning.

1866 A. FLINT *Princ. Med.* 86 Putrid infection of the blood, or septicæmia. **1879** TYNDALL *Fragm. Sci.* (ed. 6) II. xiii. 335 Splenic fever was often overmastered by septicaemia. **1882** PLAYFAIR in *Standard* 17 Mar. 2/1 Puerperal septicæmia.

Hence **septiˈcæmic** *a.*

1873 T. H. GREEN *Introd. Pathol.* (ed. 2) 227 Those in which they [metastatic abscesses] occur being termed pyæmic, those in which they are absent, septicæmic. **1880** A. FLINT *Princ. Med.* 84 Good observers have failed to detect bacteria in septicæmic cases. **1896** *Allbutt's Syst. Med.* I. 597 Septicæmic patients.

ˈseptical, *a.* Now *rare* or *Obs.* [Formed as SEPTIC: see -ICAL.] = SEPTIC.

1646 SIR T. BROWNE *Pseud. Ep.* III. xiii. 139 There was no absurdity in Galen when as a Septicall medicine he commended the ashes of a Salamander. **1651** BIGGS *New Disp.* ⁋ 303 Their own septicall and escharoticall medicines. **1820** W. SCORESBY *Acc. Arctic Reg.* I. 343 Occasionally assailed by the septical influences of rain.

Hence **ˈseptically** *adv.*, so as to produce putrefaction.

1879 WEBSTER, *Suppl.*

septicidal (ˈsɛptɪsaɪdəl), *a. Bot.* [f. SEPTUM + L. *-cīdere*, comb. form of *cædĕre* to cut + -AL[1].] Applied to the form of dehiscence in which the pod splits through the dissepiments. Also to the capsule so divided. Hence **septiˈcidally** *adv.*, with septicidal dehiscence.

1819 LINDLEY tr. *Richard's Obs. Fruits & Seeds* 10 *note* The septicidal dehiscence of a plurilocular pericarp. **1830** —— *Nat. Syst. Bot.* 146 The plants called Sauvageæ.. have a septicidal dehiscence. **1857** HENFREY *Bot.* §247 Compound multilocular ovaries dehisce.. septicidally. **1870** HOOKER *Stud. Flora* 68 Hypericineæ.. Fruit a septicidal capsule. *Ibid.* 240 Capsule.. septicidally 2-valved.

septicine (ˈsɛptɪsaɪn). *Chem.* [ad. G. *septicin*: see SEPTIC and -INE.] (See quot.)

1876 *Jrnl. Chem. Soc., Abstr.* I. 405 Septicine, an Alkaloid formed during Putrefaction.

septicity (sɛpˈtɪsɪtɪ). [f. SEPTIC + -ITY, after F. *septicité.*] The quality or condition of being septic.

1828–32 in WEBSTER. **1893** *Brit. Med. Jrnl.* 10 June 1210 Septicity introduced brings disaster on your patient and discredit on yourself.

ˈseptico-, comb. form of Gr. σηπτικός SEPTIC.

1876 tr. *Wagner's Gen. Pathol.* 586 Pyæmia, Septico-pyæmia, is usually an acute disease, starting in a purulent or ichorous focus. **1911** WEBSTER, *Septico-pyæmic.*

‖**septier** (sɛtje). Also 6 ceptyer, 8–9 setier. [a. F. *septier*, var. *setier*, earlier *sestier*:—L. *sextārius*, f. *sextus* sixth.] A French measure of capacity for corn, etc.; a measure of land: see quots.

1514 in *Rutland Papers* (Camden) 26 In wyn iiij septiers. **1523** LD. BERNERS *Froiss.* I. cliii. 183 A ceptyer of whete was worthe at Parys viii. li. parisien, and a septier of otes at lx. s. of parays. **1588** ARCHDEACON tr. *True Discourse Army K. Spain* 69, 6320 septiers of Beanes and white Pease. **1633** GRIMESTON tr. *Polybius* VI. 202 A Septier of Wheate. *marg.* A Septier is two Mines, and a Mine two London bushels. **1674** JEAKE *Arith.* (1696) 114 A Septier of Land he saith is much about the Arpent. **1714** *Fr. Bk. Rates* 64 The Muid, Paris Measure, containing 12 Septiers, which makes 2 Tons. **1725** *Bradley's Fam. Dict.* s.v. *Hipocras*, Take three half Setiers of good Water boiled and cool'd, with half a Setier of good white Wine. **1776** ADAM SMITH *W.N.* I. xi. (1869) I. 211 The septier of wheat, a measure which contains a little more than four Winchester bushels. **1826** HENRY *Elem. Chem.* II. 631 The septier of Paris is 7736 French, or 9370·45 English, cubical inches. **1828** J. M. SPEARMAN *Brit. Gunner* (ed. 2) 423 The corn measure was the muid equal to 12 setiers, 48 mines, or 144 bushels... The wine measure was the muid of 36 setiers, 144 quarts, or 288 pints. **1831** J. DAVIES *Man. Mat. Med.* 27 Verre, or ½ setier (glass).

† **septiesm.** *Cards. Obs.* [a. OF. *septiesme* (mod.F. *septième*), ordinal of *sept* seven.] A sequence of seven.
1674 COTTON *Compl. Gamester* (1680) 59 The Elder acquaints you with his Sequences,..and they are Tierces, Quarts, Quints, Sixiesms, Septiesms, Huictiesms and Neufiesms. **1688** HOLME *Armoury* III. xvi. (Roxb.) 73/2 A Septeism, is a sequence of 7 cards.

septiferous (sɛp'tɪfərəs), *a.* [f. SEPTI-[2] + -FEROUS.] Having a septum or septa.
1821 W. P. C. BARTON *Flora N. Amer.* I. 113 Capsule.. 3-valved; valves septiferous in the middle. **1854** WOODWARD *Mollusca* 265 Beaks nearly terminal, septiferous internally.

septiform ('sɛptɪfɔːm), *a.*[1] [ad. late L. *septiformis*: see SEPTI-[1] and -FORM.] Sevenfold.
1728 in BAILEY. **1849** DIGBY *Compitum* II. 310 That they may acquire the septiform grace, to the exclusion of the seven sins. **1868** GLADSTONE *Juv. Mundi* xv. (1869) 532 The septiform system was apparently represented in the seven gates of Thebes. **1878** H. G. GUINNESS *Approaching End* Pref. (1880) p. viii, The epacts of the prophetic periods of Scripture form a remarkable septiform series.

septiform ('sɛptɪfɔːm), *a.*[2] [ad. mod.L. *septiformis* or F. *septiforme*: see SEPTI-[2] and -FORM.] Of the form or nature of a septum.
1826 KIRBY & SP. *Entomol.* xlvi. IV. 313 Septiform (*Septiformis*). When the Canthus forms an elevated ridge or septum. **1875** HUXLEY in *Encycl. Brit.* I. 131/1 A tendency to the development of septiform prominence is visible in the walls of the gastric passages of certain calcareous sponges.

septifragal (sɛp'tɪfrəgəl), *a. Bot.* [f. SEPTI-[2] + *frag-*, root of *frangĕre* to break + -AL[1].] Applied to the form of dehiscence in which the septa are separated from the valves.
1819 LINDLEY tr. *Richard's Obs. Fruits & Seeds* 10 It [*sc.* the valvular mode of dehiscence] is called septifragal when it bursts the external edge of the dissepiments, which are then divided from the valves. **1898** L. H. BAILEY *Less. with Plants* 265 Septifragal dehiscence..may occur in either loculicidal or septicidal pods.
Hence **sep'tifragally** *adv.*, with septifragal dehiscence.
1896 G. HENSLOW *Wild Flowers* 149 It [*sc.* the fruit] dehisces loculicidally (through the back) and septifragally (across the septa).

septile ('sɛptaɪl), *a.* [ad. mod.L. *septilis*: see SEPTUM and -ILE.] Pertaining to a septum or septa.
1866 *Treas. Bot.*

septillion (sɛp'tɪljən). *Arith.* [ad. F. *septillion* (16th cent.), f. L. *septem* seven, after *million.*] *orig.* The seventh power of a million, denoted by 1 followed by 42 cyphers. *U.S.* and now elsewhere, the eighth power of a thousand, denoted by 1 followed by 24 cyphers.
1690 LOCKE *Hum. Und.* II. xvi. §6 Septilions. **1870** [see OCTILLION]. **1875** GRINDON *Life* xxvi. 334 Thousands of plants consist of nothing more than a few such cells as in septillions make up an oak-tree. **1906** *Daily Chron.* 18 May 9/4 M. Inaudi subtracted correctly a sum of figures running into septillions—purely from memory.
Hence **sep'tillionth** *a.*, and *sb.* (in recent Dicts.).

septimal ('sɛptɪməl), *a.* [f. L. *septim-us* seventh + -AL[1].]
1. Of a numerical system: Based on the number 7.
1855 in OGILVIE Suppl. **1865** MILL *Comte* 195 The number seven..is to be made the basis of numeration, which is hereafter to be septimal instead of decimal.
2. *Mus.* Pertaining to a seventh.
1867 MACFARREN *Harmony* v. 161 There being then no sounded note with which the 7th forms a dissonance, in the absence of both the root and the 3rd of the chord, the 7th has no longer any of its septimal characteristics.

† **septima'narian.** *Obs.*[−0] [f. med.L. *septimānārius*, f. *septimāna* SEPTIMANE *sb.*] = HEBDOMADARY *sb.* Also † **septi'marian** [med.L. *septimārius*].
1661 BLOUNT *Glossogr.* (ed. 2), *Septimarians*, certain Officers in Monasteries, which were chosen every week. [Misprinted *Septinarian* in Bailey 1728, etc.] **1882** OGILVIE, *Septimanarian*, a monk on duty for a week in a monastery.

† **'septimane,** *sb. Obs. rare.* [ad. late L. *septimāna*, f. *septem* seven + *-āna*, fem. of *-ānus*, -AN, -ANE in a collective sense.] A week.
1603 HOLLAND *Plutarch's Mor.* Explan. Words, *Septimane*, A weeke or seven-night. **1694** J. SMITH *Doctr. Lord's Day* 52 The Eastern Nations..retained a true account of the order of days in the Septimane.
So **septimanal** *a.*, weekly.
1833 *Fraser's Mag.* VII. 706 Diurnal or septimanal literature.

† **septimane,** *a. Obs.*[−0] [ad. late L. *septimānus* (see prec.).] (See quot.)
1721 BAILEY, *Septimane*, of the order of 7, also belonging to a Week.

septime ('sɛptɪm). [ad. L. *septimus*, ordinal of *septem* seven.]
1. *Mus.* **a.** Proposed name for the octave. *rare*[−0]. **b.** [after G. *septime*] A seventh. (In recent Dicts.)
1763 *Ann. Reg., Misc.* 192 2 By dividing the musical notes into six, as nature directs, the unisound will fall on the seventh note, and should, for this reason, be called a septime, and not an octave.
2. *Fencing.* A parry: see quots.
1889 POLLOCK, etc. *Fencing* (Badm. Libr.) 46 To parry *septime*, bring the foil into septime by making it describe half a circle from right to left, passing under the adversary's blade or hand. *Ibid.* 77 From septime, to give the Bertrand riposte. **1897** *Encycl. Sport* I. 379/2 (Fencing) Septime: The hand opposite the right shoulder, the finger nails turned upwards, the arm half extended, elbow down, the blade horizontal, the point opposite the left shoulder.

septimole ('sɛptɪməʊl). *Mus.* [arbitrarily f. L. *septimus* seventh: cf. QUINTOLE.] A group of seven notes to be played in the time of four or six.
1854 SCHUBERTH *Mus. Handbk.* **1866** *Chamb. Encycl.* VIII. 618/2 When a note is divided into seven instead of four parts—for example, a minim into seven quavers, or a crotchet into seven semiquavers—the group is called a septimole.

septine ('sɛptɪn). [f. Gr. σηπτός, vbl. adj. f. σήπειν to rot: cf. SEPTIC and see -INE.] (See quot. 1875.) Hence '**septinous** *a.*
1875 B. W. RICHARDSON *Dis. Mod. Life* I. vi. 89, I succeeded in separating from the poisonous matter exuded from the peritoneal secretion of a patient labouring under surgical fever, a substance which would give a similar disease to an inferior animal... I named this substance 'septine'. **1877** *Times* 5 Oct. 4/5 [Dr. Richardson] classed the diseases produced by organic poisons as septinous instead of zymotic, he preferring the word septine for this poison.

septingen'tenary. [f. L. *septingentī* 700, after *centenary.*] A seven-hundredth anniversary.
1894 *Rochdale Times* May, St. Chad's church celebrating the 'septingentenary' of its birth-date.

Septinsular (sɛp'tɪnsjʊlə(r)), *a.* (*sb.*) [f. L. *septem* (see SEPTI-[1]) + *insula* island. Cf. the Fr. name *Sept-îles.*] ***Septinsular Republic***, etc.: the Ionian Islands. Also as *sb. pl.* the people of the Ionian Islands.
1809 *Ann. Reg.* Pref. p. iv, The restoration of the Government of the Septinsular Republic. **1859** *Times* 5 Dec. 10/6 The little Septinsular State which stands under the protection of Great Britain. **1889** *Athenæum* 6 July 20/3 A monograph of Andreas Hidromenos, 'The Struggle of the Septinsulars for National Unity'. **1898** MCCARTHY *Gladstone's Life* xvii. 190 The Senate of the Septinsular Commonwealth at Corfu.

septir, obs. form of SCEPTRE *sb.*

† **'septite.** *Chem. Obs.* [f. SEPT-OUS + -ITE.] A salt of septous acid; a nitrite or nitrate.
1799 S. L. MITCHILL in *Med. & Phys. Jrnl.* I. 47 These carbonates and septites of lime, pot-ash, and soda.

† **septleva.** *Obs.* Also **sept-et-le-va, sept and leva.** [Shortening of F. *sept-et-le-va*, lit. seven and the 'va', 'vade', or first stake.] At basset, seven times the amount of the first stake.
1701 FARQUHAR *Sir H. Wildair* II. ii, *Wild...* Who can resist the charms of Mattadors? *Lur.* Ay, Sir Harry; and then the *Sept le va, Quinze le Va, & Trante le Va!* **1706** MRS. CENTLIVRE *Basset-Table* IV. 50, I have only won a *Sept & Leva. Ibid.* 53 Do you think it possible to lose a *Trante & Leva*, a *Quinse-leva*,—and a *Sept-et-leva*,—and never turn once. **1709** SEYMOUR *Compl. Gamester* (1734) 115. **1716** POPE *Basset-Table* 14 in [Lady M. W. Montagu] *Crt. Poems* 2 As You by Love, so I by Fortune cross't; In One bad Deal, Three Septleva's have lost. **1756** H. WALPOLE *Let. H.S. Conway* 12 Feb., I am sorry she could not discover any wit in Mrs. Hussey's making a septleva.

septo-[1], comb. form of Gr. σηπτός (see SEPTON), as in: ˌ**septodiarrhœa**, septic diarrhœa (*Syd. Soc. Lex.* 1898); **septo'genic** *a.*, producing sepsis; '**septogerm**, a septic germ; **sep'tometer**, an instrument for the detection of organic impurities in the atmospheric air (*Syd. Soc. Lex.*).
1880 MACCORMAC *Antisept. Surg.* 104 There is a septogenic element in ordinary air. *Ibid.* 107 Experiment and clinical experience alike show that it will kill a certain proportion of septo-germs.

septo-[2], used as comb. form of SEPTUM, as in: **septoce'phalic** *a.* (see quot.); **septo'cephaly**, the condition of being septocephalic; **septo-ma'xillary**, applied to a small bone lying above the vomer in some birds and fishes; **sep'tometer**, an instrument for measuring the nasal septum; **sep'tostomy** *Surg.* [-STOMY], the surgical creation of a hole through the atrial septum; **sep'totomy** *Surg.* [-TOMY] = prec.
1878 BARTLEY tr. *Topinard's Anthrop.* I. v. 176 *Septocephalic, microcephalic, small skull. *Ibid.* Index, Septocephaly. **1874** W. K. PARKER in *Trans. Linnean Soc.* Ser. II. *Zool.* (1879) I. 8 The bones figured are what I at first called in the Reptile 'prævomers', and now call '*septo-maxillaries'. *Ibid.* 9 The main septo-maxillary piece. **1884** M. MACKENZIE *Dis. Throat & Nose* II. 435 An ingenious '*septometer' has been invented by Seiler, which serves to distinguish thickening [of the septum] from deviation when these affections occur separately. **1967** *Circulation* XXXVI. Suppl. 217/1 At the time of the diagnostic catheterization, atrial *septostomy is performed by the balloon-catheter technique. **1977** *Lancet* 18 June 1276/1 The arterial oxygen saturation was 34% and did not improve after balloon septostomy. **1966** *Jrnl. Amer. Med. Assoc.* 13 June 992/2 Early clinical trials on infants with TGV [i.e. transposition of the great vessels] indicate that the procedure is as effective in prolonging life as surgical *septotomy.

'septole. *Mus.* = SEPTIMOLE.
1854 SCHUBERTH *Mus. Handbk.*

† **septon** ('sɛptɒn). *Obs.* [mod.L., a. Gr. σηπτόν, neut. of σηπτός, vbl. adj. f. σήπειν to rot.
First in Fr. form *septone*, adopted by Brugnatelli, on the suggestion of Saltonstall, in *Annales de Chimie* (1798) XXIX. 181.]
A name for nitrogen, from its being regarded as the agent in putrefaction.
1798 *Monthly Mag.* July 26/1 The origin of the yellow fever is attributed by Dr. Mitchill to the putrefaction or spontaneous decomposition of such substances as contain much azote (according to Dr. Mitchill's Nomenclature *septon*). **1803** *Med. & Phys. Jrnl.* IX. 304 The gaseous oxyd of septon. **1834** *Good's Study Med.* (ed. 4) I. 712 The febrile miasm, and septon, or the elementary matter of putrescency, are the same thing.

Septoria (sɛp'tɔərɪə). Also **septoria.** [mod.L. (E. M. Fries *Novitiæ Floræ Suecicæ* (1819) v. 78, as *Septaria*; *Systema Orbis Vegetabilis* (1825) I. 119, as *Septoria*), f. L. *sept-um* SEPTUM + *-aria*, *-ōria.*] **a.** An imperfect fungus of the genus *Septoria*, which includes forms having spores borne in dark pycnidia and many of which cause disease in plants.
1891 *Bull. Torrey Bot. Club* XVIII. 372 The *Septoria* on celery is to all appearance non-septate. **1932** *Phytopathology* XXII. 795 Both Septorias were collected on celery from the Kalamazoo marshes. **1946** K. S. CHESTER *Nature & Prevention Cereal Rusts* x. 139 Later in the spring, when abundant foliage is available to both fungi, *Septoria* sometimes destroys the lower leaves while the leaf rust attacks the upper ones. **1972** R. GAIR et al. *Cereal Pests & Dis.* v. 128 In Scotland the common *Septoria* on barley is *S. avenae* f. sp. *triticea.*
b. One of several leaf spot diseases caused by a fungus of this kind. Also *attrib.*
1916 *Special Bull. Michigan Agric. Exper. Station* No. 77. 2 (*title*) The Septoria leaf spot disease of celery, or celery blight. **1920** *Bull. W. Australia Dept. Agric.* No. 69. 11 Septoria, or Dry Blight, is a fungus disease caused by one of three species of fungus. **1926** FAWCETT & LEE *Citrus Diseases & their Control* xviii. 478 (*caption*) Septoria spots on California lemon fruits. **1947** J. G. DICKINSON *Dis. Field Crops* xi. 217 Two Septoria blotches occur on wheat throughout the world. **1968** *Times* 16 Dec. 7/1 One disease, of which we had heard relatively little up to this year, seems to have had marked effects on the wheat crop. This was septoria, commonly known as glume blotch, although it also attacks seedlings and leaves earlier in the season. **1972** R. GAIR et al. *Cereal Pests & Dis.* vii. 154 Like other *Septoria* diseases, speckled blotch is favoured by wet and humid weather. **1976** E. SCARROW *N.Z. Vegetable Gardening Guide* 36 Brown spots appearing on the leaves of celery are due to a fungus disease called septoria, which is seed-borne.

septo(u)r, obs. forms of SCEPTRE *sb.*

† **'septous,** *a. Obs.* [f. SEPT-ON + -OUS.] ***septous acid***, nitrous (or nitric) acid.
1799 *Med. & Phys. Jrnl.* II. 184 Obtaining phosphoric acid from the bones of animals, by employing septous (nitrous) acid, which dissolved their lime.

† **sept psaumes.** *Obs.* Also **set sames.** [a. OF. *septpsaumes* (*sept* seven, *psaume* PSALM *sb.*).] The seven penitential psalms.
c **1300** *Beket* 1084 He..seide furst the set sames and siththe the letanye. *c* **1475** *Partenay* 1670 Thay sayd the sept psaulmes.

septre, obs. form of SCEPTRE *sb.*

'sept-ship. *rare.* [f. SEPT *sb.*[2]] Clanship.
1823 MOORE *Mem.* (1853) IV. 114 The spirit of sept-ship.

septuagenarian (ˌsɛptjʊədʒɪ'nɛərɪən), *a.* and *sb.* [f. L. *septuāgēnārius*, f. *septuāgēnī*, distributive of *septuāgintā* (see SEPTUAGINT).] **A.** *adj.*
1. Pertaining to the number seventy. *rare.*
1715 M. DAVIES *Athen. Brit.* I. 96 Unquestionably believ'd it [*sc.* the Septuagint] to have been perform'd by the same Septuagenarian and Binary number (for the Translators are reckon'd to have been 72 Elders of the Jews).
2. Seventy years old; characteristic of that age.
1793 tr. *Gresset's Ver-Vert* (ed. 2) 41 A sulky, sour, septagenarian [*sic*] maid Is made the keeper of the Renegade. **1883** *Brit. Q. Rev.* Oct. 441 Our septuagenarian premier.
B. *sb.* A person seventy years old.
1805 in *Spirit Publ. Jrnls.* IX. 1, I am an elderly man, verging now upon the glory of a septuagenarian. **1864** KNIGHT *Passages Work. Life* III. ii. 23 Landor..although.. a septuagenarian..was in the full vigour of his understanding.
Hence ˌ**septuage'narianism.**
1824 DIBDIN *Libr. Comp.* 532 In the plentitude of septuagenarianism.

septuagenary (ˌsɛptjʊəˈdʒiːnərɪ), *a.* and *sb.* Now *rare.* [ad. L. *septuāgēnārius* (see prec.). Cf. F. *septuagénaire.*] = prec.

1605 BACON *Adv. Learn.* I. 24 The same obiection.. Lucian maketh to Iupiter... And asketh whether they were become Septuagenarie, or whether the lawe..against old mens mariages had restrayned them. **1646** SIR T. BROWNE *Pseud. Ep.* III. ix. 125 Nor can the three hundred years of.. Nestor, overthrow the assertion of Moses, or afford a reasonable encouragement beyond his septuagenary determination. **1737** *Common Sense* I. 27, I have often observed Septuagenary great-grandmothers adorned, as they thought, with all the colours of the Rainbow. **1823** *Blackw. Mag.* XIII. 92, I was in appearance a middle-aged man, and in mind a septuagenary. **1850** *Fraser's Mag.* XLII. 2 The task would require..septuagenary years.

†**septuagene.** *Obs.* [Back-formation from prec.] A septuagenarian.

1656 J. WATTS *Scribe, Pharisee*, etc. Ep. Rdr. cj, A good way passed beyond a Septuagene.

Septuagesima (ˌsɛptjʊəˈdʒɛsɪmə). *Eccl.* Also β. 4–5 **Septuagesme**, 5 **-gesym**, 5–6 **-gesime**. [a. L. *septuāgēsima* (sc. *diēs*) fem. of *septuāgēsimus* seventieth, f. *septuāgintā* seventy; in early use through OF. *septuages(i)me.*

It has been conjectured that the analogy of the names *Quadragesima* and *Quinquagesima* suggested the unmeaning application of *Sexagesima* and *Septuagesima* to the two preceding Sundays. Another (less likely) conjecture is that *Septuagesima* means 'the seventieth day' before the octave of Easter. Both conjectures are in Alcuin (8th c.).]

1. In full *Septuagesima Sunday*: the third Sunday before Lent.

c **1380** WYCLIF *Sel. Wks.* II. 29 Wednesdai Gospel next after Septuagesme Sondai. *c* **1425** *Process. Nuns Chester* (1899) 4 This procession shalbe saide on Sonday & so forth from septuagesime to lenton. **1430** in Halliwell *Rara Mathem.* (1841) 92 þereby demyd I þat septuagesime sonday schal falle ȝe 28 day of..Januare. **1538** *Prymer in Englyshe* Cjb, Betwene Septuagesima and Easter thys psalme folowynge is sayde in steade of Te Deum. **1561** T. NORTON *Calvin's Inst.* IV. xix. 159b, There be no mariages celebrate, from Septuagesime to the vtas of Easter. **1753** CHALLONER *Cath. Chr. Instr.* 93 The Penitential Time between Septuagesima and Easter. **1860** NEALE *Comm. Ps.* I. 35 The Lauds of Septuagesima Sunday, as said in the Ambrosian Office. *a* **1866** —— *Notes on Div. Off.* (1877) 203 The custom of repeating it [*sc.* Alleluia] frequently on the Saturday before Septuagesima.

†**2.** The seventy days beginning with the third Sunday before Lent and ending with the Saturday in Easter week. Also *transf. Obs.*

†*Sunday in (the) S.* = *Dominica in Septuagesima*, i.e. Septuagesima Sunday.

1387 TREVISA *Higden* (Rolls) VIII. 223 He..lefte flesche [on] Monday and Wednesday, [and] also in Septuagesme [*v.r.* Septuagesima]. **1398** —— *Barth. De P.R.* IX. xxviii. (1495) 363 Septuagesme..stretchyth from the sondaye that hyghte Septuagesima..to the Saturday in Eester weke. *Ibid.* 364 Whan the Septuagesime of this lyfe is full ended, thenne we shall shyne in whyte in presence of thys lambe. *a* **1400** *Table of Lessons* in *Wyclif's Bible* IV. 685 The Sonday in Septuages. *c* **1450** *Mirk's Festial* 61 þys day is called Sonday yn þe Septagesim. **1483** CAXTON *Golden Legend* II. (1503) A viij b/2, In the saterdaye after ester, in whiche septuagesme is cumplete we synge dou[b]le Alleluya.

†**septuaˈgesimal**, *a. Obs. rare.* [f. L. *septuāgēsim-us* (see prec.) + -AL[1].] (See quot. 1656.)

In quot. 1646 (perh. Blount's source) the sense is 'limited to seventy years of life'; in quot. 1778 the word is misused for SEPTUAGENARIAN.

1646 SIR T. BROWNE *Pseud. Ep.* VI. vi. 298 In our abridged and septuagesimall ages, it is very rare and deserves a distich to behold the fourth generation. **1656** BLOUNT *Glossogr.*, *Septuagesimall*, pertaining to the number seventy, or Septuagesima Sunday. **1778** ELIZ. CARTER *Lett. to Mrs. Montagu* (1817) III. 145 (F. Hall) Your description of his septuagesimal gallantry would make one laugh.

Septuagint (ˈsɛptjʊədʒɪnt). [ad. L. *septuāgintā* seventy, f. weakened form of *septem* seven.]

†**1.** The 'seventy translators' of the Old Testament into Greek (see 2); = L. *septuaginta (interpretes)*, Gr. *οἱ Ο΄*. *Obs.*

[**1563** *Homilies* II. *Parell of Idol.* I. Eejb, Accordynge as the Septuaginta haue in theyr translation in Greke εἴδωλα. **1584** in D. Fenner *Def. Ministers* (1587) 44 Will you followe the *Septuaginta* in their whole translation?]

1589 COOPER *Admon.* 50 The translation..was.. according to the *Septuagint.* **1622** AILESBURY *Serm. 2nd June* 11 Which latter clause though it answer not the Originall; yet the Septuagint so translate it. *a* **1656** HALES *Golden Rem.* (1673) 84 The Septuagint, to make the sense more plain, do add another clause. **1684** T. BURNET *Th. Earth* II. vii. 251 The Septuagint, who render this word *Eden.*

†**b.** *pl.* in the same sense. *Obs.*

1577 HANMER *Anc. Eccl. Hist., Euseb.* V. viii. 84 The translation of the olde testament by the septuagintes. **1621** BP. MOUNTAGU *Diatribæ* 217 The Septuagints were no Grammarians, saith that bold bayard, Stenchius. **1653** GATAKER *Vind. Annot. Jer.* 36 Whether they..had studied upon the matter apart in their several cels, as the tale goes of the secluded Septuagints. **1656** BLOUNT *Glossogr.*

2. The Greek version of the Old Testament, which derives its name from the story that it was made by seventy-two Palestinian Jews at the request of Ptolemy Philadelphus (284–247 B.C.) and completed by them, in seclusion on the island of Pharos, in seventy-two days. (Denoted by LXX.)

The authority for the old story is the Letter of Aristeas to Philocrates, long known to be spurious, which purports to give contemporary evidence of the undertaking. The translation is now held to have been made by Egyptian Jews, independent of each other and living in different times.

1633 J. DONE (*title*) The Auncient History of the Septuagint. **1646** SIR T. BROWNE *Pseud. Ep.* VI. i. 278 As for the Septuagint, it is the first and most ancient Translation recorded. **1778** BP. LOWTH *Transl. Isaiah* Prelim. Diss. p. lxvi, The Greek Version, commonly called the Septuagint, or of the Seventy Interpreters. **1854** *Gentl. Mag.* Apr. 377/1 The severe condemnation which we have been compelled to pass on the Septuagints of the Christian Knowledge Society and the University of Oxford. **1887** *Bible* (R.V.) Pref., The Ancient Versions, the oldest of which, namely the Greek or Septuagint, was made, at least in part, some two centuries before the Christian era.

†**3.** *pl.* The 'seventy elders' of Israel. (*Exod.* xxiv. 1.) *Obs.*

1564 RASTELL *Confut. Jewel's Serm.* 137 He [*sc.* the pope] continueth in his supremacie, as a Moyses aboue the septuagintes.

4. A group of seventy.

1864 DE MORGAN in *Athenæum* 2 July 21 Not to mention the Iscariot which Leverrier and Adams calculated into existence, there is more than a septuagint of new planetoids. **1887** SIR W. HARCOURT in *Times* 29 Sept. 5/3 The Septuagint [of Liberal Unionists] still meets, I believe, at Devonshire House.

5. *attrib.* of sense 2.

1658 PHILLIPS s.v., The Septuagint translation of the Bible. **1684** T. BURNET *Th. Earth* I. iii. 24 If you follow the Septuagint Chronology. **1708** KERSEY s.v., The Septuagint or Septuagint-Bible. **1769** H. OWEN (*title*) An Enquiry into the present state of the Septuagint Version of the Old Testament. **1850** DONALDSON *New Cratylus* (ed. 2) §100. 151 The Septuagint translators.

ˌ**Septuaˈgintal**, *a.* [f. prec. + -AL[1].] Of or pertaining to the Septuagint.

1760 BYROM *Rem.* (1857) II. II. 618 The frequent Hebraisms that occur through the whole New Testament, and their Septuagintal style. **1854** *Gentl. Mag.* Apr. 377/1 In the third chapter of the Septuagintal Daniel. **1863** WESTCOTT in *W. Smith's Dict. Bible* s.v. *Vulgate* §19 The Septuagintal tradition was at length set aside. **1892** *Nation* LV. 482/2 Septuagintal text-criticism.

Hence **Septuaˈgintalist**, a student of or an authority upon the Septuagint.

1850 GRINFIELD *Apol. Septuagint* App. 177 Of all our Divines, Bishop Pearson, has proved himself the best Septuagintalist.

septual, erron. form of SEPTAL.

†ˈ**septuary**, *a.* and *sb. Obs.* [irreg. f. L. *septem* seven + -ARY, by association with *septuāgintā.*]

A. *adj.* Consisting of seven; septenary.

1604 T. WRIGHT *Clymact. Yeeres* 5 God hath appointed these Septuarie, and Nonarie yeeres as best seeming his wisdome and prouidence. *Ibid.* 8 In this septuarie number of our yeeres.

b. Of seven days.

1703 E. WARD *Lond. Spy* XVII. (1706) 403 After I had.. bestow'd two Pennyworth of Razorridge on the most Fertile part of my Face, whose Septuary Crop requir'd Mowing.

B. *sb.* A group of seven days.

1646 SIR T. BROWNE *Pseud. Ep.* IV. xii. 212 Months howsoever taken are not exactly divisible into septuaries or weeks.

septulate (ˈsɛptjʊlət), *a. Nat. Hist.* [ad. mod.L. *septulātus*: see next and -ATE[2].] Having a septulum or septula.

1864 WEBSTER.

‖**septulum** (ˈsɛptjʊləm). *Nat. Hist.* [mod.L., dim. of next.] A small or thin septum.

1826 KIRBY & SP. *Entomol.* xxxiii. III. 382 The *Septula*, the lesser ridges and partitions raised on the surfaces of the metaphragm. *Ibid.* xxxv. (1828) III. 584 The septula consist for the most part of the endosternum or internal sternum and its branches.

‖**septum** (ˈsɛptəm). Pl. **septa** (ˈsɛptə). [a. L. *sēptum, sæptum*, f. *sēpīre, sæpīre* to enclose, f. *sēpēs, sæpēs* hedge.] A partition; a dividing wall, membrane, layer, etc.; a dissepiment.

a. *gen.*

1733 TULL *Horse-Hoeing Husb.* xi. 125 When the Plants of the outer Row are too numerous on a shallow Mould, the Roots of these, which are always thickest near the Bottom of the Stems, make a *Septum* or Hedge betwixt the Roots of the middle..Row and the Interval. **1862** MILLER *Elem. Chem., Org.* (ed. 2) ii. §4. 114 It [*sc.* vegetable parchment] may be substituted for bladder as a septum, in electrolytic operations, with great advantage. **1871** 'STONEHENGE' *Brit. Sports* I. I. ii. §5. 38 Two pieces of stamped brass forming a strong septum in the cap. **1877** F. G. LEE *Gloss. Liturg. Terms*, *Septum*, a term used by certain seventeenth-century Anglican writers for the..rail, placed on each side of the entrance of the sanctuary, to support the communicants. *a* **1879** W. K. CLIFFORD *Lect.* I. 205 Hydrogen goes through a septum or wall of graphite four times as fast as oxygen does. **1883** F. DAY *Indian Fish* (Fish. Exhib. Publ.) 64 A hoop supporting a bag-like net..with a septum about 11 inches from mouth leading into the lower portion of the net.

b. *Anat.* e.g. the partition between the nostrils (*septum nasi*), the membrane separating the ventricles of the heart (*septum cordis*). ***septum lucidum*** or ***pellucidum***, a thin double layer of tissue forming a partition between the two lateral ventricles of the brain.

1698 W. COWPER *Anat. Humane Bodies* App., 7th Table, fig. 30, That part of the corpus callosum by Vieussens, call'd fornix vera, between which, and the fornix..is plac'd the septum lucidum. **1713** W. CHESELDEN *Anat. Human Body* III. xii. 135 Under the corpus callosum appear the two lateral or superior ventricles, which are divided into right and left by a very thin membrane named septum lucidum, which is extended between the corpus callosum and fornix. **1726** MONRO *Anat. Bones* 86 In some Sculls, besides the large osseus *Septum*, there are found in each *Sinus* several bony Pillars. **1733** *Winslow's Anat. Hum. Body* (1756) II. 243 The Falx, or great longitudinal Septum of the Dura Mater. **1781** PENNANT *Hist. Quadrup.* II. 530 The nostrils oval, and divided by a *septum*. **1803** C. BELL *Anat. Human Body* III. I. i. 15 Those septa, or, as they are called, processes of the dura mater, being extended across from the internal surface of the cranium, support the brain in the sudden motions of the body. **1807** R. MORRIS et al. *Edin. Med. & Physical Dict.* II, Septum lucidum, or Septum pellucidum. **1833** BREWSTER *Nat. Magic* iii. 312 Some of the party experienced sharp pains in the tips of their ears and in the septum of the nose. **1859** J. TOMES *Dental Surg.* 4 The septa, which divide into a series of cells that which at an earlier age was but a continuous groove. **1872** T. BRYANT *Pract. Surg.* 124, I have only removed one [*sc.* Polypus nasi] from the septum. **1880** GÜNTHER *Fishes* 66 In Notidanus, membranous septa.. cross the substance of the gelatinous notochord. **1883** MARTIN & MOALE *Verteb. Diss.* 128 The tendinous septum (*aponeurosis*) of the great pectoral muscle. **1899** F. H. GERRISH *Text-bk. Anat.* 362 The fascia sends inward to the femur two intermuscular septa, which partition the thigh into an anterior compartment and a posterior. **1942** F. A. METTLER *Neuroanatomy* iv. 97 Stretched between the copula, rostrum, genu and anterior half of the corpus callosum is a thin, vertically arranged membrane, the translucent septum (s. pellucidum). **1978** *Nature* 19 Jan. 209/1 Whether this input results in cellular discharge depends..on input through the second major afferent pathway to the hippocampus from the septum.

attrib. **1904** *Brit. Med. Jrnl.* 10 Sept. 606 Douglas's septum perforator and curved septum knife.

c. *Bot.* e.g. the division-wall of a cell, a partition in a compound ovary or spore.

1720 P. BLAIR *Bot. Ess.* ii. 54 The *Placentæ*..sometimes.. arise from an *Axis medius*,..fram'd by the Conjunction of the three Septa, which meet in the Center. **1830** LINDLEY *Nat. Syst. Bot.* 159 A fruit with the valves alternate with the septa. **1870** HOOKER *Stud. Flora* 85 Pod 2-valved, turgid or flat with a longitudinal septum. **1882** VINES *Sachs' Bot.* 259 The septum, at first simple, splits into two lamellæ.

d. *Geol.*

a **1728** WOODWARD *Nat. Hist. Fossils* I. (1729) I. 81 In those Bodies that are invested with a Crust, the Septa lessen and grow thinner as they approach the Crust. **1785** HUTTON in *Trans. Roy. Soc. Edinb.* (1788) I. 246 The septa have been formed by the uniform contraction of the internal parts of the stone. **1836** BUCKLAND *Geol. & Min.* xv. §4 (1837) I. 347 When these thin septa are converted into iron pyrites, their edges appear like golden filigrane work, meandering amid the pellucid spar. **1851** MANTELL *Petrifactions* iv. §6. 407 The dark partitions, or septa, are veins of spar.

e. *Zool.* e.g. one of the radiated plates of the cell of corals, one of the partitions of a chambered shell.

1815 S. BROOKES *Introd. Conchol.* 94 The septa transverse and perforated by a tube. **1846** DANA *Zooph.* (1848) 353 The transverse septa are sometimes seen to extend quite across the whole interior. **1861** J. R. GREENE *Man. Anim. Kingd., Cœlent.* 158 In..the *Aporosa* and *Perforata*,..septa, in sets of five or six, normally occur.

f. *Electronics.* A metal plate placed transversely across a waveguide and attached to the walls by conducting joints.

1947 L. G. H. HUXLEY *Survey Princ. & Practice of Wave Guides* ii. 39 The original electromagnetic field..transforms to that shown..where the magnetic loops are bent over so that their longitudinal portions run in opposite senses, one on each side of the septum. **1964** J. L. ALTMAN *Microwave Circuits* iii. 87 Symmetrical obstacles, such as irises, septa, and posts of various cross-sections and positions within the waveguide, are of great practical importance as matching elements..or as elements of waveguide filters and periodic structures.

†**sepˈtuncial**, *a. Obs.*$^{-0}$ [ad. late L. *septunciālis*, f. L. *sept-em* seven + *uncia* OUNCE[1].]

1656 BLOUNT *Glossogr.*, *Septuncial*, of seven ounces, or seven parts of the whole.

septuor (ˈsɛptjʊɔː(r)). [a. F. *septuor*, f. L. *septem*, after *quatuor* quartett.] = SEPTET.

1850 LONGF. *Life* (1891) II. 177 The first and longest a symphony..the last a Septuor, very beautiful. **1873** 'OUIDA' *Pascarel* I. 111 Phrase after phrase, chorus on chorus, solo and septuor, and recitative.

septuple (ˈsɛptju:p(ə)l), *a.* and *sb.* [ad. late L. *septuplus*, f. *septem* seven: see -PLE.] **A.** *adj.*

1. Sevenfold.

1834 *Tait's Mag.* I. 456 The 'quadruple' alliance will very soon be..a 'septuple' one. **1868** LOCKYER *Guillemin's Heavens* (ed. 3) 350, θ Orionis is a septuple star. **1882–3** SCHAFF in *Herzog's Encycl. Relig. Knowl.* I. 49 The septuple fulness of the Holy Spirit.

2. *Mus.* Having seven beats in a bar.

1884 *Grove's Dict. Mus.* IV. 120/1 There seems no reason why a Composer, visited by an inspiration in that direction, should not write an Air in Septuple Time, with seven beats in a bar.

B. *sb.* The seventh multiple.

1692 *Capt. Smith's Seaman's Gram.* II. xv. 123 The Cube of The Septuple thereof is 1·913. **1755** JOHNSON, *Septuple*, seven times as much. A technical term.

So ˈ**septuple** *v. trans.*, to multiply by 7, increase 7 times; ˌ**septupliˈcation**, multiplication by 7; †**septuply** *adv.*, sevenfold.

1615 T. ADAMS *Blacke Devill* 2 He that is quit of so bad a Guest, shall *septuple his owne woes by his re-entertainment. **1633** —— *Exp. 2 Peter* ii. 4 That furnace whose heate was septupled. **1833** HERSCHEL *Astron.* viii. 278

Let any one figure to himself the condition of our globe, were the sun to be septupled. **1674** JEAKE *Arith.* (1696) 25 *Septuplication, or to multiply by 7. **1654** VILVAIN *Theorem. Theol.* viii. 299 The Churches restauration, whos glory shal *septuply exceed the Suns splendor.

septuplet (ˈsɛptjʊplɛt). [f. L. *septuplus* (see prec.), after *triplet*, etc.]

1. = SEPTIMOLE.

1891 *Cent. Dict.*

2. One of seven offspring at a birth.

1898 *Syd. Soc. Lex.*

septur(e, obs. forms of SCEPTRE *sb.*

sepulchral (sɪˈpʌlkrəl), *a.* [ad. L. *sepulcrālis*, f. *sepulcr-um* SEPULCHRE *sb.*: see -AL[1]. Cf. F. *sépulcral*, Sp., Pg. *sepulcral*, It. *sepolcrale*, *sepulcrale*.]

1. Of or pertaining to burial or a place of burial. **a.** Pertaining to or serving as a sepulchre or tomb; forming part of a sepulchre, or its furniture; monumental.

sepulchral cone: a cone of baked clay found in some Egyptian tombs, intended to represent offerings of food.

*a***1631** DONNE *Poems, Ecstacie* 18 We like sepulchrall statues lay. **1645** MILTON *Passion* vii, Mine eye hath found that sad Sepulchral rock That was the Casket of Heav'ns richest store. **1728** POPE *Dunc.* I. 43 Sepulchral Lies, our holy walls to grace, And New-year Odes, and all the Grub-street race. **1740** GRAY *Let.* in *Poems* (1775) 85 A sepulchral marble at the villa Giustiniani. **1781** COWPER *Conversat.* 358 Old sepulchral urns. **1851** D. WILSON *Preh. Ann.* (1863) I. II. v. 423 The sepulchral-lamp, .. burning through long ages to light up the entombed ashes. **1904** BUDGE *3rd & 4th Egypt. Rooms Brit. Mus.* 107 A collection of baked clay 'cones', stamped with the names and titles of princes, chiefs, and officials who were buried in the necropolis of Thebes... The objects are commonly called sepulchral cones.

b. Pertaining to rights and customs connected with burial, funeral.

1615 CHAPMAN *Odyss.* III. 430 Thus hauing slaine him; a sepulchrall feast He made the Argiues. **1729** G. ADAMS tr. *Sophocles, Antig.* II. iv. II. 29 She .. copiously adorns the Carcase with sepulchral Libations. **1863** D. WILSON *Preh. Ann.* (ed. 2) I. iii. 76 The system of human sacrifices was not unknown among early Roman sepulchral rites.

†**c.** (See quot.) *Obs.*

1728 CHAMBERS *Cycl.* s.v., Sepulchral Hereticks, were thus call'd from their principal Error, which was, That by the Word *Hell*, whither the Scripture tells us Jesus Christ descended after his Death, they understood his Sepulcher.

2. *transf.* Suggestive of a sepulchre, appropriate to a tomb; dismal, gloomy, melancholy.

*a***1711** KEN *Hymnotheo* Poet. Wks. 1721 III. 73 Sepulchral Cypress, Lawrel, Pine, and Bays, Yew, and all Trees, whose Verdure ne're decays, Are planted in long Rows, where Mourners walk. **1796** SOUTHEY *Rudiger* xli, A deep sepulcral sound the cave Return'd. **1840** J. T. J. HEWLETT *P. Priggins* v, His laugh .. was a sepulchral oh! hah! which issued from his chest without any sympathetic movement of the muscles of his face. **1876** GEO. ELIOT *Dan. Der.* lxvii, The sepulchral Ezra.

†**3.** Like a tomb, serving to entomb. *Obs.*

1801 SOUTHEY *Thalaba* I. xxii, For this .. The silkworm of the East Spun her sepulchral egg. **1802** E. DARWIN *Orig. Soc.* IV. 61 With monstrous gape sepulchral whales devour Shoals at a gulp.

sepulchralize (sɪˈpʌlkrəlaɪz). [f. SEPULCHRAL *a.* + -IZE.] *trans.* 'To render sepulchral or solemn.'

1855 OGILVIE Suppl.

sepulchrally (sɪˈpʌlkrəlɪ), *adv.* [f. SEPULCHRAL *a.* + -LY[2].] In a sepulchral manner.

1819 H. BUSK *Banquet* III. 273 Where, it is said, sepulchrally they burn, Near some sarcophagus or sacred urn. **1898** *Westm. Gaz.* 20 Jan. 5/2 A current of sepulchrally icy air meets you inside.

Sepulchran (sɪˈpʌlkrən), *a.* [f. SEPULCHRE *sb.* + -AN.] ***Sepulchran nun***: a member of the Order of Canonesses Regular of the Holy Sepulchre; *pl.* the church of this order. Cf. SEPULCHRINE.

1844 A. P. DE LISLE in E. Purcell *Life* (1900) I. 130 Mr. and Mrs. Craven met us at Mass at the Sepulchran Nuns. **1857** G. OLIVER *Coll. Cath. Relig. Cornw.* 30 The English Sepulchran nuns had determined to emigrate from Liège.

sepulchre (ˈsɛpəlkə(r)), *sb.* Forms: 2–7 sepulcre, 4 sepulchur, 5 scepulcur, sepulkyr, 5–6 sepulcur(e, sepulker, 6 sepulcor, sepulcar, sepulcer, sepullcre, sepullcur, (sepulchree, sepulchrie, sepulcrye), 6–9 (now *U.S.*) sepulcher, 3– sepulchre. [a. OF. *sepulcre* (11th c. in Hatz.-Darm.), ad. L. *sepulcrum* (less correctly *sepulchrum*), f. root of L. *sepul-tus*, pa. pple. of *sepelīre* to bury; cf. Sp., Pg. *sepulcro*, It. *sepolcro*.]

1. A tomb or burial-place, a building, vault, or excavation, made for the interment of a human body. Now only *rhetorical* or *Hist.*

*c***1200** *Trin. Coll. Hom.* 101 Oðer is þat bitwenen his þrowenge and his ariste he lai on his sepulcre. *a***1225** *Ancr. R.* 170 Uor ȝe beoð mid Iesu Criste bitund ase ine sepulcre. *c***1290** *Holy Rood* 400 in *S. Eng. Leg.* 13 And þo he cam to Ierusalem of þe sepulchre he hadde doute þat ore louerd was on i-leid. **1340** HAMPOLE *Pr. Consc.* 5188 Þar es þe mount of calvery, And þe sepulcre of Crist fast þarby. *c***1386** CHAUCER *Wife's Prol.* 498 The sepulcre of hym Daryus Which that Appelles wroghte subtilly. *c***1440** *Gesta Rom.* xliv. 173 (Harl. MS.) As longe as eny bone is in the sepulcure of my husbonde. **1471** CAXTON *Recuyell* (Sommer) 402 The kyng gerion had brought vp that custome to make these sepulcres, for to haue remembrance of them that were vaylliant in armes. **1526** TINDALE *Luke* xi. 47 Wo be to you that bilde the sepulcres off the prophetes: for youre fathers kiled them. **1588** PARKE tr. *Mendoza's Hist. China* 43 Many instruments, which neuer haue playing till such time as the dead is put into the sepulcher. *c***1600** SHAKS. *Sonn.* lxviii, Before the goulden tresses of the dead, The right of sepulchers, were shorne away To liue a second life on second head. **1662** J. DAVIES tr. *Olearius' Voy. Ambass.* 321 Such as have gone on Pilgrimage to Mecca, to Mahomet's Sepulchre. *a***1701** MAUNDRELL *Journ. Jerus.* (1732) 14 We found there a multitude of Sepulchres hewn into the Rocks. **1756–7** tr. *Keysler's Trav.* (1760) I. 80 Under the choir of the church are the sepulchres of the old dukes of Bavaria. **1818** BYRON *Ch. Har.* IV. lxxix, The very sepulchres lie tenantless Of their heroic dwellers. **1883** R. W. DIXON *Mano* II. ii. 68 There was strange darkness cast o'er every street, And all was stiller than a sepulchre.

b. ***whited*** (†***painted***) ***sepulchre***: in biblical language, used fig. for a hypocrite, or one whose fair outward semblance conceals inward corruption.

[*c***1382** WYCLIF *Matt.* xxiii. 27 Woo to ȝou scribis and Pharisees, that ben lic to sepulcris maad whijt.] **1388** *Ibid.* Like to sepulcris whitid. [**1539** BIBLE (Great), painted sepulcres; **1582** *N. T.* (Rheims), whited sepulchres; so **1611**.] *c***1530** TINDALE *Prol. Rom.* (1538) W iv b, Christ .. calleth them ypocrytes, that is to saye, simulers and paynted sepulcres. **1782** V. KNOX *Ess.* xcvii. II. 61 Those varnished qualities, which, like whited sepulchres, are but a disguise for internal deformity. **1894** HALL CAINE *Manxman* 428 He was a sham,—a whited sepulchre.

c. *transf.* and *fig.*

1593 SHAKS. *3 Hen. VI* II. v. 115 My heart (sweet Boy) shall be thy Sepulcher, For from my heart, thine Image ne're shall go. **1627** J. TAYLOR (Water-P.) *Armado* C 3 b, Such beasts and birds of prey and rapine are commonly the liuing sepulchres of dead Horses. **1640** *Wand. Jew telling Fortunes* 38 He is a curse to Pasties; a tormenter of Poultry, a sepulchre to Lobsters. **1819** SHELLEY *Cenci* IV. i. 53, I will .. make his youth The sepulchre of hope, where evil thoughts Shall grow like weeds on a neglected tomb. **1845** DARWIN *Voy. Nat.* viii. (1879) 155 The whole area of the Pampas is one wide sepulchre of these extinct gigantic quadrupeds. **1881** JOWETT *Thucyd.* I. 122 The whole earth is the sepulchre of famous men.

2. ***the Holy*** (†***Saint***) ***Sepulchre*** (occas. ***the Sepulchre***): The cave in which Jesus Christ was buried outside the walls of Jerusalem; hence, the name for the group of buildings erected over the traditional site of this cave. Also in the title of some churches in other parts of the world erected in memory of this.

*c***1200** *Trin. Coll. Hom.* 21 And was his holie lichame leid in burieles in þe holie sepulcre þat men sechen giet in ierusalem. **1362** LANGL. *P. Pl.* A. VI. 17 Þis Folk fraynede him feire from whenne þat he coome? 'From Synay', he seide, 'and from the Sepulcre'. **1395** *E.E. Wills* (1882) 9 This was yeve and writen in the lordes In of Cherlton withoute Newgate, in the parosch of seynt sepulcre in the suburbe of london. *c***1400** MAUNDEV. (1839) vii. 79 The Chirche of the Sepulchre... The Chirche of Seynt Sepulchre. **1486** *Bk. St. Albans, Her.* b ij b, A knyght is made in .v. dyuerse placis In musturing in londe of werris. .. And at the sepulcur. **1660** F. BROOKE tr. *Le Blanc's Trav.* 13 As the holy Sepulcher at Ierusalem, is visited by Christians. **1825** SCOTT *Talism.* xi, Hewing with our swords the way to the Holy Sepulchre. **1898** A. H. THOMPSON *Camb. & Its Colleges* 301 Just opposite St. John's Chapel is the church of the Holy Sepulchre. *Ibid.* 303 St. Sepulchre's is one of those rare livings which are in the gift of the parishioners.

b. ***Knight of the*** (***Holy***) ***Sepulchre***: a member of a secular confraternity composed of those who were knighted in the crusades, esp. those knighted at the Holy Sepulchre itself.

Since 1342 the confraternity has existed only as a religious organization, having the Latin Patriarch of Jerusalem as its Grand-master.

1590 SEGAR *Bk. Honor* v. 59 Knights of the Sepulcher. **1617** MORYSON *Itin.* I. 235 [They] would make us Knights of the Sepulcher, so we would crave that honour. **1728** CHAMBERS *Cycl.* s.v. *Sepulchre*, To excite Rich and Noble Persons to visit the Holy Places, by giving them the Title of Knights of the Holy Sepulcher. **1873** LONGF. *Wayside Inn* III. *Landlord's Tale* 2 It was Sir Christopher Gardiner, Knight of the Holy Sepulchre.

3. a. *Antiq.* A permanent or temporary structure prepared in a church for the dramatic burial of the reserved Sacrament (sometimes also the Cross) upon Good Friday.

1389 in *Eng. Gilds* (1870) 48 On kandel of xvj. pound of waxe to brenne about þe sepulcre in þe fornseide Chirche of seynt Nicholas. **1426–7** *Rec. St. Mary at Hill* (1904) 63 First payd for the sepulcre for diuers naylis & wyres & glu, ix d ob. **1566** in Peacock *Eng. Ch. Furniture* (1866) 67 One sepulcre sold to Johnne orson and he hath made a presse therof to laie clothes therein. *a***1627** HAYWARD *Ann. Q. Eliz.* (Camden) 28 And not onely images, but rood-loftes, relickes, sepulchres, bookes [etc.] .. wer .. committed to the fire. **1739** BLOMFIELD *Norf.* (1805) II. 217 These sepulchres were erected alwayes (as I take it) on the north side of the chancel, near to the altar. **1791** J. TOWNSEND *Journ. Spain* (1792) III. 239 [At Valencia] In the sacristy, I saw a massive sepulchre of silver gilt, designed for the reception of the host on good Friday. **1836** PARKER *Gloss. Archit.* (1850) I. 421 At Bampton, Oxfordshire, is a singular example .. of a kind of double sepulchre, one over the other.

b. (See quot. 1753.)

1753 CHALLONER *Cath. Chr. Instr.* 220 The Place where the Blessed Sacrament is reserved in the Church in order for the Office of Good-Friday (on which Day there is no Consecration) is by the People called the Sepulchre, as representing by Anticipation the Burial of Christ. *a***1800** *Waterperry Chapel Reg.* in *Cath. Rec. Soc. Publ.* VII. 393 On Maundy Thursday Prayers in y[e] morning at 10 a clock after which y[e] Bd Sacrament is put into y[e] Sepulchre & y[e] Congregation, & Family wattch 2 by 2 till 10 a clock at night. **1853** DALE tr. *Baldeschi's Ceremonial* 187 A chapel of the sepulchre should be prepared. **1884** *Cath. Dict.* (1897) 445/2.

4. Interment, burial. *rare.*

1388 WYCLIF *Gen.* xxiii. 4 ȝyue ȝe to me riȝto of sepulcre [Vulg. *jus sepulcri*] with ȝou. **1601** SHAKS. *Twel. N.* III. iv. 262 His incensement at this moment is so implacable, that satisfaction can be none, but by pangs of death and sepulchre. **1706** PHILLIPS (ed. Kersey). **1871** NAPHEYS *Prevent. & Cure Dis.* I. xi. 331 Modes of sepulchre which have prevailed.

†**5.** App. some article of personal jewellery.

1567 SIR N. THROCKMORTON *Let. to Leicester* 30 Apr. (*MS. Magdalene Coll.*), I did remember you by Mr. Dier for sending your sepulchre as you told me by the way. Since your messenger had no better fortune in safe-carrying your token .. he has left no devices undone to recover your diamond. **1567** —— *Let. to Leicester* 10 May, Retain your adamant sepulchre until you have the condition better annexed.

6. *attrib.* and *Comb.* as †***sepulchre-door***; †(in sense 3) ***sepulchre-cloth***, ***-light***, ***-nails***; †**sepulchre-stone** (? cf. sense 5); †**sepulchre-table**, a sepulchral tablet; †**sepulchre-tree**, ? the beam or frame upon which the Easter sepulchre was placed.

1566 in Fowler *Hist. C.C.C.* (O.H.S.) 114 Item, a *sepulchre clothe of red and blewe braunched with golde. *c***1275** *Passion our Lord* 513 in *O.E. Misc.* 51 He hwelfde at þare *sepulchre-dure enne grete ston. **1505** *Cat. Anc. Deeds P.R.O.* (1906) V. 492 The *sepulcur lyghte in the seyd chyrche. **1546** in Throsby *Hist. & Antiq. Leicester* (1791) 246 Solde to Ryc[d]. Raynford the sepulchre light. **1494–5** *Rec. St. Mary at Hill* (1904) 214 Item, for the *sepulker nailes ob. **1489** *Will of Sandon* (Somerset Ho.), Lego ecclesie unum Agnus dei aureum cum lapide vulgariter dictum *Sepulcre stone. **1610** HOLLAND *Camden's Brit.* I. 236 [An inscription] in a grave or *Sepulcher-table [L. *in sepulchrali tabula*], betweene two little images. **1449** *Yatton Churchw. Acc.* (Som. Rec. Soc.) 90 For makyng of the *sepulkyr tre, xx[d].

sepulchre (ˈsɛpəlkə(r)), *v.* [f. SEPULCHRE *sb.*]

Formerly also stressed *seˈpulchre*.

1. *trans.* To place in a sepulchre; to bury.

16.. ROWLEY *Birth Merlin* v. i. (1662) G 3, A place .. Where Merlins Mother shall be sepulcher'd. **1649** J. TAYLOR (Water-P.) *Wand. West* 5 It is very probable that King Arthur (our English Worthy) was there sepulchred. **1791** COWPER *Iliad* XXIII. 103 My bones sepulchre not from thine apart. **1896** *Dublin Rev.* July 123 Had everyone been allowed .. to sepulchre their dead in the churches, there would very soon have been no space left.

b. *transf.* and *fig.*

1591 SHAKS. *Two Gent.* IV. ii. 118 Goe to thy Ladies graue and call hers [*sc.* her love] thence, Or at the least, in hers, sepulcher thine. **1616** B. JONSON *Epigr.* lxiv, Where merit is not sepulcher'd aliue. **1796** SOUTHEY *Lett. fr. Spain* (1799) 221 He may as well be buried in the Monastery as sepulchre himself in his chamber. **1856** MRS. BROWNING *Aur. Leigh* v. 1040 We are sepulchred alive in this close world.

2. To receive as in a sepulchre, to serve as a burial-place for.

1605 SHAKS. *Lear* II. iv. 134 If thou should'st not be glad, I would diuorce me from thy Mother Tombe, Sepulchring an Adultresse. **1634** MASSINGER *Very Woman* II. ii, That which was mortal of My dear Martino .. I know this mother earth hath sepulchred. **1813** BYRON *Corsair* I. i, When Ocean shrouds and sepulchres our dead. **1863** I. WILLIAMS *Baptistery* II. *Image*, xxii, Stillness and subterranean shade Her saints doth sepulchre. **1897** F. THOMPSON *New Poems* 187 O to that tomb be tender then, which bears Only the name of him it sepulchres!

†**ˈSepulcher.** *Obs. rare*[−1]. [f. SEPULCHRE *sb.* + -ER[2].] A member of the order of Knights of the Sepulchre.

1537 [COVERDALE] *Orig. & Sprynge of Sectes* 33 Sepulchrers order.

Sepulchrine (sɪˈpʌlkraɪn), *a.* (*sb.*) [f. SEPULCHRE *sb.* + -INE[1].] Used in the popular designation of the religious order of Canonesses Regular of the Holy Sepulchre. Also as *sb.*, a Sepulchrine nun.

*a***1800** in *Chron. St. Monica's, Louvain* (1904) I. 228 The Sepulchrine community with whom she dwelt. **1905** F. M. STEELE *Convents Gt. Brit.* 228 Another [daughter] was a Sepulchrine at Liège. *Ibid.*, A little volume preserved in the convent of the Sepulchrine nuns at Newhall.

†**ˈsepulchrize**, *v. Obs. rare.* [f. SEPULCHRE *sb.* + -IZE.] *trans.* To bury.

1595 T. EDWARDS *Cephalus & Procris*, etc. (Roxb.) 52 My wearied lims, Closse as I could to touch the Saint I couched, My bodie on the earth sepulchrizing him, That dying liu'd. **1632** LITHGOW *Trav.* VIII. 343 Thou in obliuion hast Sepulchrized here, Earths dearest life.

†**sepulchromany.** *nonce-wd.* [f. *sepulchro-*, SEPULCHRE + -MANIA.] 'Mania' relating to burial.

1606 BIRNIE *Kirk-Buriall* Ded., Brain-sicke superstitions, instanced especially in their manifold sepulchromany.

sepulchrous (sɪˈpʌlkrəs), *a. rare.* [f. SEPULCHRE *sb.* + -OUS.] Of the nature of a sepulchre.

1831 SCOTT *Ct. Robt.* vi, A perfume .. more suitable to sepulchrous chambers, than to the dwellings of men.

sepult (sɪˈpʌlt), *a.* [ad. L. *sepult-us*, pa. pple. of *sepelīre* to bury.] Buried.

1898 F. DAVIS *Silchester* 7 The sepult cities of the Romans are with us.

†**seˈpult**, *v. Obs.* [f. L. *sepult-*, ppl. stem of *sepelīre.*] *trans.* To bury.

1544 *Knaresb. Wills* (Surtees) I. 39 My bodie to be sepulted and buried. **1599** A. M. tr. *Gabelhouer's Bk. Physicke* 54/2 Occlude it then close together, and sepulte the same a cubite vnder grownde. **1657** TOMLINSON *Renou's Disp.* 342 The second..made of Holly-bark elixated, sepulted in mud, putrifyed.

fig. *a* **1548** HALL *Chron., Hen. IV* (1809) 6 And an hundred mo iniuries, whiche..he remitted and sepulted in obliuion.

†**ˈsepultary.** *Obs. rare*⁻¹. [f. L. *sepult-* (see SEPULT *v.*) + -ARY.] = SEPULTURE *sb.*

1581 PETTIE tr. *Guazzo's Civ. Conv.* I. (1586) 7 b, Leasure without learning, is a death & sepultarie [orig. *sepoltura*] of a liue man.

sepultural (sɪˈpʌltjʊərəl), *a.* [f. SEPULTURE *sb.* + -AL[1].] Of or pertaining to sepulture or burial.

1789 *J. Lewis's Mem. Dk. Glocester* 72 If the sepultural spot could be ascertained, he would erect a stately monument over it. **1821** *John Bull* 15 Jan. 40/1 No remains of sepultural enclosure were discernible. **1889** *Pop. Sci. Monthly* Mar. 697 A treatise on the funeral monuments and sepultural usages of the ancients.

sepulture (ˈsɛpəltjʊə(r)), *sb.* Forms: 4 *Sc.* sepultore, 5 supulture, sepulturre, sepoltur, 5–6 sepult(o)ur, 6 sepoltre, sepulter, 3– sepulture. [a. OF. *sepulture*, ad. L. *sepultūra* burial, f. *sepult-*, ppl. stem of *sepelīre* to bury; cf. Sp., Pg. *sepultura*, It. *sepoltura, sepultura.*]

1. Interment, burial.

1297 R. GLOUC. (Rolls) 3466 Wel aȝte þat be a wurþe stude wanne þer such sepulture ys. *c* **1315** SHOREHAM *Poems* (E.E.T.S.) 125 For þe offyce of hyre sepulture Was al an heuene gyse. *c* **1385** CHAUCER *L.G.W.* 2553 Myn body mote ȝe se..In the hauene of Athenys fletynge With-oute sepulture & berynge. *c* **1400** MAUNDEV. *Trav.* (1839) xxix. 243 The Erthe mynystrethe to us..oure Sepulture aftre oure Dethe. **1504** *Bury Wills* (Camden) 100 And I beqweth to the seid churche for my sepultur vj s. viij d. *c* **1586** C'TESS PEMBROKE *Ps.* LXXIX. ii, Their bodies killed With sepulture can no where meete. **1632** MASSINGER & FIELD *Fatal Dowry* II. i, He had rather dye aliue for debt Of the old man in prison, then he should Rob him of Sepulture. **1720** POPE *Iliad* XXII. 429 The common Rites of Sepulture bestow, To sooth a Father's and a Mother's woe. **1757** BURKE *Abridgm. Eng. Hist.* II. ii. Wks. 1812 V. 516 The monastery was always the place of sepulture for the greatest lords and kings. **1840** MACAULAY *Ess., Ranke* ¶51 Even the honours of sepulture were long withheld from his remains. **1902** 'FAIRLESS' *Roadmender* 30 Yesterday a funeral passed, from the workhouse at N——, a quaint sepulture without solemnities.

b. *transf.* and *fig.*

c **1386** CHAUCER *Pard. T.* 558 For dronkenesse is verray sepulture Of mannes wit and his discrecion. **1474** CAXTON *Chesse* I. iii. (1883) 15 Ydleness wyth oute ony ocupacion is sepulture of a many lyuyng. **1621** BACON in *Four C. Eng. Lett.* (1880) 43 For the house of Commons, I began my credit there, and now it must be the place of sepulture thereof. **1877** L. MORRIS *Epic Hades* II. 150 Tore thy limbs And left them to the Muses' sepulture.

2. A burial-place, grave, tomb: = SEPULCHRE *sb.* 1. Now only *arch.*

a **1375** *Cursor M.* 25614 (Fairf.) Squete ihesus..atte time of complin..þer was þou wondin laide in sepulture & noȝt fondin. **1387** TREVISA *Higden* (Rolls) V. 369 Þe place of pasture were i-torned to buriels and sepultures. *c* **1430** LYDG. *Min. Poems* (Percy Soc.) 142 Ther roos up oon out of his sepulture, Terrible of face. **1496** *Bury Wills* (Camden) 229 In the holy sepulture of the cherche yeerd of Seynt Marie. **1531** ELYOT *Gov.* II. vi, Marius..also caused Caius Cesar..to be violently drawen to the sepulture of one Varius ..and there to be dishonestly slayne. **1540** HEYWOOD *Four PP.* 14 At Hierusalem haue I bene Before Chrystes blessed sepulture. **1561** T. HOBY tr. *Castiglione's Courtyer* IV. (1577) T v, The manner was too reare about ones sepulture so many Obeliskes, as he that lay there buryed had slayne of his enimies. **1610** HOLLAND *Camden's Brit.* I. 593 A faire Abbay, the Sepulture in times past of..the Burnels. **1646** SIR T. BROWNE *Pseud. Ep.* I. vi. 23 She erected over their sepultures, a marble tombe of her owne. **1812** CARY *Dante, Purg.* v. 91 From Campaldino's field what force or chance Drew thee, that ne'er thy sepulture was known. **1868** STANLEY *Westm. Abb.* iii. 117 The Royal sepultures of Westminster were also remarkable from their connexion.. with the residence of the English Princes.

†**b.** *Holy Sepulture*: = SEPULCHRE *sb.* 2. *Obs.*

1525 LD. BERNERS *Froiss.* II. lxi. 204 All these wente to se and vysyte the holy sepulture.

†**c.** *transf.* and *fig. Obs.*

1463 ASHBY *Prisoner's Refl.* 344 Pryson properly ys a sepulture Of lyuyng men. **1622** MABBE tr. *Aleman's Guzman d' Alf.* II. 213 My money..was spent vpon Sepultures for dead bodies, on dead workes, and worldly vices.

†**3.** = SEPULCHRE *sb.* 3. *Obs.*

1485 *Acc. St. Marg. Southwark* in Feasey *Anc. Eng. H. Week Cerem.* (1897) 153 *Item.* ij blew Cortyns [to] draw afore the sepulture. **1494–5** *Acc. Ld. High Treas. Scot.* I. 228 Item, for the mending of the sepulture, the chapell dure, and Judas crois. **1553** *Rec. St. Mary at Hill* (1904) 51 Delyuered a stayned Cloth yat went about yᵉ Sepultere. **1557** *Churchw. Acc. St. Helens, Abingdon* (Nichols 1797) 141 To the sextin for watching the sepulter two nyghtes oo8.

attrib. **1527–8** *Rec. St. Mary at Hill* (1904) 343 Paid for an eln of fyne lynnyn cloth to amend the sepulture cloth wherat it was eiton with rattes.

sepulture (ˈsɛpəltjʊə(r)), *v.* [f. the sb.] *trans.* To bury, inter.

c **1489** CAXTON *Sonnes of Aymon* xxviii. 592 And after the sepulturynge of the holy corps, the brethern wente agen in to theyr countree. **1826** MRS. SHELLEY *Last Man* III. 146 Grave in which my heart lies sepultured, farewell for ever! **1897** F. THOMPSON *New Poems* 114 Thou gavest him his light, Though sepultured in night Beneath the dead bones of a perished world.

†**seˈpurture.** *Her. Obs.* (See quots.)

1688 HOLME *Armoury* II. 11/1 He beareth Sol, an Angel ..: Wings in Sepurture, Luna: Of some expenced:..If the Angels be sideways, and the Wings behind each other, they are termed Sepurture (or Expenced,) yet this..is not termed an Angel Sepurture; but an Angel kneeling, the Wings Sepurture. *Ibid.* 13/2 He beareth Or, a demy Angel in Sepurture, Gules... This is also termed a demy Angel, half faced, with Wings Sepurture, &c. *Ibid.* III. 156/2 He beareth Azure, an Angel, Wings Sepulture [*sic*], Argent. **1828–40** BERRY *Encycl. Her.* I, *Sepurture.* This ancient heraldic term is used in the same way as *endorsed*, as *wings sepurture*, or *endorsed*... *Sepurture disclosed* differs from the last, by merely showing more of the off wing. **1894** *Parker's Gloss. Her., Sepurture.*

seq. Pl. seqq. Also sq. Pl. sqq. Abbreviated forms in *sing.* of L. *sequens* the following, *sequente* and in what follows, *sequitur* it follows; in *pl.* of *sequentes, -tia* the following, *sequentibus* in the following places. Also, more fully, *et seq.*

1726 J. KER *Mem.* I. (1727) Index, Scotland, a View of their Affairs. 113, 131, & *seq.* **1753** *Chambers's Cycl.* Suppl. s.v. *Thistle, Tourn.* Inst. p. 440. seq. **1839** T. MITCHELL *Frogs of Aristoph.* Add. 414 See Creuz. Symb. iv. 108. sq. **1841** DONALDSON *Pindar, Nemea* vii. Introd. 235 The passage, which follows (v. 70, seqq.), is perhaps the most difficult. **1850** —— *New Cratylus* (ed. 2) §76. 111 *note*, See Grimm, *Gesch. der deutsch. Spr.* p. 824 sqq. **1885** GOODALE *Physiol. Bot.* 177 What has been already said about the structure of chlorophyll granules..(168 *et seq.*).

‖**sequa** (ˈsiːkwə). [perh. native W. Indian; cf. SEGRA.] (See quot. 1866.)

1866 *Treas. Bot.* 491/1 *Fevillea cordifolia* is the Sequa or Cacoon Antidote of Jamaica, where it is a common plant in shady woods. **1871** KINGSLEY *At Last* xiii, It has—like that curious flat gourd the Sequa—the property of keeping iron from rust.

†**seˈquaces,** *sb. pl. Obs.* [a. OF. *sequaces*, a. L. *sequācēs* pl. of *sequāx* that follows, a follower, f. *sequī* to follow.] Successors, followers.

1513 BRADSHAW *St. Werburge* Balade ii. 32 He hath..left it for holsome memoriall To all his sequaces. *a* **1660** *Contemp. Hist. Irel.* (Ir. Archæol. Soc.) II. 147 Why did this man, and those his sequaces, signe unto the former acts? *Ibid.* III. 43 Ormonde and his sequaces.

sequacious (sɪˈkweɪʃəs), *a.* [f. L. *sequāc-, sequāx* (see prec.) + -IOUS.]

1. Of a free agent or his attributes: Given to following another or others, esp. a leader. †Const. *to, of.*

1643 TRAPP *Comm. Gen.* vi. 20 See how sequacious these poor creatures are to God their Centurion. **1680** C. NESSE *Ch. Hist.* 30 How sequacious were they all to God..they all come at his call. **1687** DRYDEN *St. Cecilia's Day* vii, Orpheus cou'd lead the savage race, And Trees unrooted left their Place, Sequacious of the Lyre. **1766** BLACKSTONE *Comm.* II. 5 The frequent disappointments..induced them to gather together such animals as were of a more tame and sequacious nature. **1833** BP. HAMPDEN *Bampton Lect.* (1848) 73 We find individuals..like the Sophist of old, leading after them, by the charm of their voice, troops of sequacious hearers. **1885** G. ALLEN *Babylon* xi, Here..he could wander out into the woods alone (after he had shaken off the attentions of the too sequacious Almeda).

b. Given to slavish or unreasoning following of others (esp. in matters of thought or opinion). Common in the 17th c.

1653 GAUDEN *Hierasp.* To Rdr. (e), By seeming to.. admire their many new masters, and their rarer gifts; which make them worthy indeed of such soft and sequacious disciples. **1656** *Artif. Handsom.* 111 They make loud and fierce Declamations,..rather in a sequacious and credulous easinesse, than after the rate of any perswasive strictnesse. **1693** *Apol. Clergy Scot.* 32 A Momus, a poor sequacious Animal, that follows such as went before him. **1727–46** THOMSON *Summer* 1713 Those superstitious horrors that enslave The fond sequacious herd. **1842** W. HOWITT *Rur. & Dom. Life Germany* 202 The Germans..have thus acquired in matters of public opinion, a sequacious and yielding character. **1880** LADY EASTLAKE *Mrs. Grote* iv. 77 The sequacious deference to the Ministry of the day..filled us with painful reflections. **1885** M. PATTISON *Mem.* 208, I had been drawn into Tractarianism, not by the contagion of a sequacious zeal, but by the inner force of an inherited pietism. **1893** T. K. ABBOTT '*Do this*' etc. 5 Some passages of the LXX there are which have been referred to in the most sequacious manner by writer after writer.

†**2.** Of things: Readily yielding to traction; easily moulded to any required shape; ductile, pliable, flexible. *Obs.*

1640 BP. REYNOLDS *Passions* xxxi. 321 Of all Fire there is none so ductile, so sequacious and obsequious as this of Wrath. **1652** CULVERWEL *Disc. Lt. Nat.* I. vii. (1661) 47 Such falsities, as come disguis'd in a Syllogistical form, which by their sequacious windings, and gradual insinuations, twine about some weak understandings. **1657** TOMLINSON *Renou's Disp.* 716 The Salve..should be sequacious. **1661** G. RUST *Origen* 84 The inferiour spirit of the world..will not fail to bring her treasure into view when invited by congruous and sequacious dispositions of matter. **1673** GREW *Anat. Plants* (1682) 137 Convolvula's..wind..because their Parts are disposed so, as to render them more sequaceous to the external Motor. **1752** C. SMART *Hop-garden* II. 67 Now extract From the sequacious earth the pole.

3. Of musical notes, metrical feet: Following one another with unvarying regularity of order.

1795 COLERIDGE *Eolian Harp* 18 And now, its strings Boldlier swept, the long sequacious notes Over delicious surges sink and rise. **1864** D. W. THOMPSON *Daydreams Schoolm.* 243 That Hellenic speech..that rises and falls in Plato with the long sequacious music of an Æolian lute.

4. Of style or thought: Persisting in one continuous direction.

1828 DE QUINCEY *Rhet.* Wks. 1862 X. 41 Milton.. polonaises with a grand Castilian air, in paces too sequacious and processional. **1835** —— *Autobiog.* Wks. 1889 II. 69 The motions of his mind were slow, solemn, sequacious, like those of the planets.

Hence **seˈquaciously** *adv.*

1891 *Century Dict.* **1897** A. B. BRUCE in *Expositor's Grk. Test.* I. 148/1 *note*, One in a herd of swine might..begin to run wildly about, and be followed sequaciously by the whole flock.

sequaciousness (sɪˈkweɪʃəsnɪs). [f. SEQUACIOUS *a.* + -NESS.]

1. The state or condition of being sequacious.

1653 GAUDEN *Hierasp.* 69 Endless janglings..which would make Religion, a matter..of sequaciousness and feminine softness. **1656** *Artif. Handsom.* 181 It is time..to get beyond that servility and sequaciousnesse of conscience. **1851** DE QUINCEY *Ld. Carlisle on Pope* Wks. 1863 XII. 27 Pursuing them [*sc.* thoughts] through their unlinkings with the sequaciousness (pardon a Coleridgean word) that belongs to some process of creative nature. **1881** G. ALLEN *Evolutionist at Large* iii. 33 Another mountain trait in the stereotyped character of sheep is their well known sequaciousness.

†**2.** Ductility (of matter). *Obs.*

a **1676** HALE *Prim. Orig. Man.* IV. ii. (1677) 304 Although Almighty God be not bound or straitned in his Operation to the sequaciousness of the Matter.

sequacity (sɪˈkwæsɪtɪ). [ad. late L. *sequācitās*, f. *sequāc-* (see SEQUACIOUS) + -ITY.]

†**1.** Ductility, pliability (of matter). *Obs. rare*⁻¹.

1626 BACON *Sylva* §900 All Sperme, all Menstruous Substance,..haue euermore a Closenesse, Lentour and Sequacity.

2. Disposition or readiness to follow; lack of independence in action, judgement, thought, etc.

1654 WHITLOCK *Zootomia* 207 But this Liberty of Judgement..seemes allmost lost, either in Lazy, or blinde Sequacity of other mens Votes. **1838** SIR W. HAMILTON *Logic* App. (1866) II. 264 Another example of the passive sequacity of the logicians. They follow obediently in the footsteps of their great master. **1850** GROTE *Greece* II. lxii. VIII. 125 At best a tame and dumb sequacity to leaders whom they neither chose nor controled. **1876** BLACKMORE *Cripps* xxix, Against each good old-fashioned smoothness, and fine-fed sequacity, a rapid stir was now arising.

Sequanian (sɛˈkwɑːniːən), *a. Geol.* Also ‖**Sequanien.** [ad. F. *Séquanien*, f. L. *Sēquani* an ancient Celtic people of eastern Gaul: see -IAN.] Name of a substage of the Upper Jurassic in north-western Europe, below the Kimmeridgian; of or pertaining to this substage and the rocks that characterize it, and the geological age during which they were deposited.

1851 [see KIMMERIDGIAN *a.*]. **1881** *Q. Jrnl. Geol. Soc.* XXXVII. II. 571 De Loriol..wishes to call the Astartian and Corallian by one name, Sequanian. **1882** A. GEIKIE *Text-bk. Geol.* 797 *Corallien.* Some authors take the upper part of this group into a separate section under the name of Sequanien, largely developed in the east of France, where it consists of massive limestones sometimes 400 feet thick. **1903** *Ibid.* (ed. 4) II. 1156 The Oxfordian and Corallian divisions of the Jurassic system, or Callovian, Oxfordian, and Sequanian formations, are in general feebly represented in the Alpine region. **1970** R. J. SMALL *Study of Landforms* iv. 145 The widely out-cropping Bathonian dolomite has been carved into a multitude of minor karstic forms which are overlooked by gently rounded hills of Sequanian limestone.

sequar, variant of SIQUARE *Obs.*

sequel (ˈsiːkwəl), *sb.* Forms: 5–7 sequele, (5 sequely, 6 sequeale), 6–8 sequell, 6 sequeile, *north.* sequyle, 7 sequill, *Sc.* sequeill, 6– sequel. [a. OF. *sequelle* (mod.F. *séquelle*), ad. L. *sequēla* (*sequella*), f. *sequī* to follow.]

†**1.** A train of followers, band of adherents, following, suit; *rarely*, a follower. In *Feudal law*, the offspring, retinue, chattels, and appurtenances of a villein. *Obs.*

c **1420** LYDG. *Assembly of Gods* 871 These were her names: fyrst, Nygromansy, Geomansy, Magyk, and Glotony,.. Fysenamy also, and Pawmestry, And all her sequelys. **1432–50** tr. *Higden* (Rolls) II. 95 Whiche is callede otherwhile a sequele [L. *sequela*: *Trevisa* sewte] of natife men. *c* **1450** *Godstow Reg.* 559 The forsaid bondmen or natifs with all ther catallis sutis or sequelys. **1490** CAXTON *Eneydos* vi. 22 Thenne Eneas and all his sequele made theym redy for to ..leue the sayd countrey of Trase. **1491** —— *Vitas Patr.* (W. de W. 1495) II. 273/2 He had also a grete sequely & rowte of worldly & galaunt seruauntis. **1536** *St. Papers Hen. VIII*, II. 330 The great nombre of Irisshery, so being in exile, being togider with ther tenauntes and sequell. **1577** HARRISON *England* I. II. v. 164/2 The yeomanrie, of whom and their sequele, the labourers and artificers, I haue said somewhat euen now. **1591** Q. ELIZ. in *Lett. Eliz. & Jas.*

(Camden) 65 My lewde rebel, whose person and forse.. drawes few for sequel. **1611** SPEED *Hist. Gt. Brit.* IX. xii. §72 That eithers friends, adherents, and sequels, should be comprehended in the truce. *c* **1640** J. SMYTH *Lives Berkeleys* (1883) I. 190 His freeholders and villaines with their Sequells.

†**b.** *transf.* and *fig. Obs.*

1552 LATIMER *Serm. Lincolnsh.* i. (1584) 180 But nowe there be other dishes, which be sequels or hangynges on, wherewith the chiefe dishe is powdred. **1590** SOUTHWELL *M. Magd. Funerall Teares* Ded. 4 For passions being sequels of our nature, and allotted unto us, as the handmaids of reason. **1603** OWEN *Pembrokeshire* (1892) 114 These foure great Ilandes with their sequele.

c. *Scots Law.* (See quot. 1838.)

c **1609** *Inchaffray Charters* (S.H.S.) 171 The mylne of Dumfalleis mylnlandis astrictit multures and sequeillis thairof. **1701** in *Fasti Aberd.* (1854) 202 The milne of Balmad milne lands multures suckine sequells and knaveships thereof. **1754** ERSKINE *Princ. Sc. Law* (1809) 223 The sequels are the small quantities given to the servants, under the name of knaveship, bannock, and lock or gowpen. **1820** SCOTT *Monast.* xiii, Not one in the Halidome pays their multures more duly, sequels, arriage, and carriage. **1838** W. BELL *Dict. Law Scot.*, *Sequels*, in thirlage, are the small allowances of meal, or of manufactured victual, or of money composition, made to the servants at the dominant mill for their real or implied trouble in grinding the victual of the servient lands.

†**2.** Descendants, posterity; successors in inheritance. Also *pl. Obs.*

c **1440** *Alphabet of Tales* 199 And for þis, fro hensfurth, all his sequele at holdis þis same possession & knowis þerof, mon be punysshid. **1533** in Bolton *Stat. Irel.* (1621) 78 To pray.. for the prosperitie of the said Nicholas and his heyres and sequele. *a* **1547** SURREY in *Tottel's Misc.* (Arb.) 218 A goodly meane both to deterre from crime: And to her steppes our sequele to enflame. *a* **1548** HALL *Chron., Edw. IV* 212 b, Promising to beare his.. frendly favor to kyng Henry the sixte and his sequele. **1572** *Wills & Inv. N.C.* (Surtees) II. 387, I wyll that when these leases be expyred.. that thay or ther sequyles shall haue the same again.

fig. **1547** J. HARRISON *Exhort. Scottes* 230 All murders, robberies, spoyles, slaughters, and desolacions, beyng the sequele, and as it wer, yᵉ children of warre.

b. Law. ***sequels in estate***: (a person's) successors in a holding.

1889 *Daily News* 27 Nov. 7/3 The Bill will authorise Lord Tredegar and his sequels in estate, and trustees.. to exchange.. portions of the ballast land.. for [etc.].

3. That which follows as a result of an event or course of action; an after-consequence. ***in sequel to***, as a consequence of. †***by sequels***: by consecutive stages. *Obs.*

The sense has been rare since the 16th century; the occasional examples in 19th c. writers are akin to sense 6.

1477 EARL RIVERS (Caxton) *Dictes* 3 b, Suche tresor may nat by gadred wythoute the sequele be to hys daunger. *a* **1513** FABYAN *Chron.* IV. (1516) 23/2 Wherfore after punysshement done vpon some of his Enemyes, he ferynge yᵉ Sequell and Reuengement of the same laft that Countree. *a* **1530** HEYWOOD *Love* 1189 And he that lacketh any one of those three.. Deth must be sequell howe euer it be. *Ibid.* 1227 That my ioy by loue shall bryng deth in sequell. **1549** LATIMER *4th Serm. bef. Edw. VI*, M vij b, This gere came by Sequels... He by vnrepentaunce fel from euyll to worse, and from worse, to worste of al, til at the length he was made a spectacle to all the world. **1601** HOLLAND *Pliny* XXII. xxiii. II. 135 For I have seene the fearfull sequele of that experiment, in a man, who.. threw himselfe headlong from an high loft. **1651** HOBBES *Leviath.* I. iii. 10 The Future being but a fiction of the mind, applying the sequels of actions Past, to the actions that are Present. **1832** TENNYSON *Œnone* 151, I woo thee not with gifts. Sequel of guerdon could not alter me To fairer. **1883** FROUDE *Short Stud.* IV. iii. 270 He had assured himself that every phenomenon in the moral or material world was the sequel of a natural cause. **1895** W. MUNK *Life Halford* ii. 20 Cullen was still living and lecturing, though in sequel to age failing somewhat.

†**b.** Consequence, importance. *Obs.*

1588 *Marprel. Epist.* (Arb.) 26 The granting whereof.. would be.. newes of wofull sequell vnto the papists. **1591** G. FLETCHER *Russe Commw.* 82 b, There is no such affection.. betwixt the Pope & the Turke, as that he should banish a subiect for not obeying the Popes ordinance, specially in a matter of some sequele for the alteration of times within his owne countries. **1658** A. FOX tr. *Wurtz' Surg.* III. x. 247 The dressing is of as great sequel and concernment, as applyed medicines to Wounds.

†**c.** *concr.* Something developed from or produced by something else. *Obs.*

1669 W. SIMPSON *Hydrol. Chym.* 246 Whatever parts, or supposed simple Principles, any sort of Bodies are reducible into, they are but the sequels or after-products.. of those two real Principles, Water and Seed.

d. *Med.* = SEQUELA.

1897 *Allbutt's Syst. Med.* II. 237 The nervous sequels in mumps are not confined to cases which begin with such nervous symptoms. *Ibid.* III. 56 In many of these [cases] the lesions are rather of the nature of sequels.

†**4.** That which follows or is thought to follow as a logical consequence; an inference. *Obs.*

1565 JEWEL *Repl. Harding* (1611) 19 It is a very simple sequele, onely vpon remembrance of Christs Death to found the Masse. **1585** SANDYS *Serm.* viii. 133 The people pay tithes of that they haue, therefore there must needes be sufficient to maintaine them. If things were well ordered, this sequele were good. **1607** WALKINGTON *Opt. Glass* 20 So fareth it with the bodies and by sequele with the soules of men. **1622** MABBE tr. *Aleman's Guzman d'Alf.* I. 152 Doe they not.. make, I know not what vn-ioynted sequels, by which after one errour granted, they runne into a thousand. **1646** SIR T. BROWNE *Pseud. Ep.* I. xi. 44 These.. are scarce Rhetoricall sequells, concluding metaphors from realities. *a* **1658** LOVELACE *Poems, Adv. to Brother* vii, 'Tis a false sequel.. to suppose That, 'cause it is now ill, 'twill ere be so. **1689** PRIOR *Ep. to F. Shepherd* 39 Then he, by Sequel Logical, Writes best, who never thinks at all.

†**5.** Sequence, order of succession; also a number of things in succession, a series. *Obs.*

1599 SHAKS. *Hen. V*, v. ii. 361 The King hath graunted euery Article: His Daughter first; and in sequele, all. **1615** BP. ANDREWES *Serm.* (1629) 675 That second part is sett downe in a sequele of foure. *a* **1638** MEDE *Wks.* (1672) 581 The Apocalypse.. hath marks.. whereby the Order, Synchronism and Sequele of all the Visions therein contained may be found out and demonstrated. **1713** BENTLEY *Rem. Disc. Free-Thinking* I. (ed. 2) 18 Homer.. wrote a sequel of Songs and Rhapsodies, to be sung by himself for small earnings and good cheer. **1716** M. DAVIES *Athen. Brit.* III. 87 Molinet having got the Sequal or chaine of 400 Brass Medals of the Popes. **1771** LUCKOMBE *Hist. Printing* 15 Signatures.. at the bottom of the page, to shew the sequel of the sheets.

6. What happened or will happen afterwards; the ensuing course of affairs, subsequent train of events, issue, result, upshot. †***in sequel***, afterwards, subsequently, in the end. *Obs.*

1524 in Strype *Eccl. Mem.* I. I. iii. 50, I do tremble to remember the End of all these high and new Enterprizes. For oftentimes it hath been seen, that to a new Enterprize, there followeth a new Maner, and strange Sequel. **1567** FENTON *Trag. Disc.* 140 b, His prophecie also seamed fully verefyed in the sequeile of the licenceous lyuing of his new wif. **1579–80** NORTH *Plutarch, Artaxerxes* (1595) 1015 He could not haue deuised a fitter place.., as it fell out in sequell. **1599** SHAKS. *Much Ado* III. ii. 137 O plague right well preuented! so will you say, when you haue seene the sequele. **1666** in *10th Rep. Hist. MSS. Comm.* App. v. 24 By reason of some unlucky sequells of his first speedy coming into this kingdome.. hee is brought into a lower condition of fortune. **1667** MILTON *P.L.* x. 334 Hee, after Eve seduc't, unminded slunk Into the Wood fast by,.. To observe the sequel. **1711** in *10th Rep. Hist. MSS. Comm.* App. v. 176 Their lives are first taken away, and in sequel their estates. **1714** SWIFT *Pres. St. Aff.* (1741) 11 The October-Club which appeared so formidable at first.. proved in the Sequel to be the chief Support of those who suspected them. **1802** PALEY *Nat. Theol.* xx. 386 Uses which discover themselves in the sequel of the process. **1835** MARRYAT *J. Faithful* xxiv, Whether Captain Turnbull or I were right, remains to be proved in the sequel. **1876** J. PARKER *Paracl.* II. xviii. 295 We must await the sequel for a complete justification of this course.

†**b.** The remaining period (of the year, one's life).

1578 LYTE *Dodoens* VI. lxviii. 746 The Oke Apples.. forshewe the sequell of the yeere.. by the liuing thinges that are founde within them. **1586** MARLOWE *1st Pt. Tamburl.* v. i, That in the shortened sequel of my life I may pour forth my soul into thine arms. **1619** EARL SUFFOLK in *Fortescue Papers* (Camden) 80 And all the sequel of my lyfe after, lyue Your Majesties trwe subject and faithfull servaunt.

c. An age or period as following and influenced by (a former period).

1837 WHEWELL *Hist. Induct. Sci.* (1857) I. 10 When this step has been made.. there may generally be observed another period, which we may call the Sequel of the Epoch, during which the discovery has acquired a more perfect certainty. **1861** M. PATTISON *Ess.* (1889) I. 32 The nineteenth century is what it is as the sequel, not of the eighteenth century only, but of all the centuries that have preceded it.

7. The ensuing narrative, discourse, etc.; the following or remaining part of a narrative, etc.; that which follows as a continuation; esp. a literary work that, although complete in itself, forms a continuation of a preceding one.

a **1513** FABYAN *Chron.* I. Prol. (1533) 2 But of those dedes me lyste nat here to shewe For in the sequele they shall well appere. *a* **1548** HALL *Chron., Hen. IV* 1 b, What profite.. succeded in the realme of England by the union of the fornamed two noble families you shall apparantly perceive by the sequele of this.. history. **1591** SHAKS. *Two Gent.* II. i. 122 *Val.* I will write.. a thousand times as much: And yet —. *Sil.* A pretty period: well: I ghesse the sequell. **1644** VICARS *God in Mount* 147 Which.. proved a Babell, a hill of confusion to them in the issue, as you shall hear in the sequill. **1653** GATAKER *Vind. Annot. Jer.* 94 Wherein how they have either acquitted their Client, or acquighted themselvs, the sequele shal shew. **1689** LOCKE *Govt.* II. ii. §15 (1694) 176, I moreover affirm, That [etc.]; And I doubt not in the Sequel of this Discourse, to make it very clear. **1710** STEELE & ADDISON *Tatler* No. 253 ¶13 The Sequel of the Proceedings of this Day will be published on Tuesday next. **1740** CIBBER *Apol.* ix. 174 In *Love's Last Shift*, and in the Sequel of it, the *Relapse*. **1794** PALEY *Evid.* II. vii. (1817) 189, I will only observe, as a sequel of the argument, the remarkable similitude between the style of Saint John's Gospel, and of St. John's Epistle. **1858** E. A. BOND *Russia* (Hakl. Soc.) Introd. 1 The one [work] serves as a sequel to or complement of the other. **1862** STANLEY *Jew. Ch.* (1877) I. xv. 297 This story has an interest of its own.. independently of the grander narrative to which it is a close sequel. **1884** D. HUNTER tr. *Reuss's Hist. Canon* xiii. 244 We shall meet with it again more than once in the sequel of this history.

†**8.** *Phonetics.* (See quot.) *Obs. rare*⁻¹.

1706 LHUYD *Archæol. Brit.* 35/1 Sequels, or such Consonants as when they begin words, admit of none other immediately after them; tho they'l immediately follow. L,n,r.

†**'sequel**, *a. Obs. rare.* [f. SEQUEL *sb.*] That followed after, subsequent.

1632 LITHGOW *Trav.* VI. 293 The sequell morne, we marched through a fiery faced plaine. *Ibid.* x. 488 After this, their sequell answere being mortified, and I set at liberty.

†**'sequel**, *v. Obs. rare.* [f. SEQUEL *sb.*] *trans.* To follow. Hence †**'sequelled** *ppl. a.*

1594 *Zepheria* xl, If she shall attend what fortunes sequell'd The naufrage of my poor afflicted bark, Then tell [etc.]. **1805** in *Spirit Publ. Jrnls.* IX. 254 But ah! who can control his fate? My sequel'd tale I'll brief relate.

‖**sequela** (sɪˈkwiːlə). Pl. **sequelæ** (sɪˈkwiːliː). [L. *sequēla*: see SEQUEL *sb.*]

1. *Path.* A morbid affection occurring as the result of a previous disease. Chiefly *pl.*

c **1793** *Encycl. Brit.* (ed. 3) XI. 299/2 But.. these sequelæ of this disease are perhaps more readily overcome by country air. **1816** A. C. HUTCHISON *Pract. Obs. Surg.* (1826) 115, I had, recently, a case of the sequelæ of this malady. **1876** BRISTOWE *Th. & Pract. Med.* (1878) 529 The change .. is sometimes a sequela of myocarditis.

b. *transf.* A consequence.

1883 *Spectator* 28 Apr. (Stanf.), Those terrible sequelæ which interfere so deeply with human happiness. **1910** *Q. Rev.* Apr. 429 Ostentation and oppression on the part of the rich with the sequelæ of vice, crime and demoralisation.

2. A person's followers (cf. SEQUEL *sb.* 1). *rare.*

1858–9 MARSH *Eng. Lang.* xxx. (1860) 673 The long *e* in *there*, which Walker and his sequela make identical with *a* in *fate*.

†**se'quelarly**, *adv. Obs. rare*⁻¹. [f. L. *sequēla* SEQUEL *sb.* + -AR + -LY².] Subsequently.

1600 SIR J. DOWDALL in *Carew MSS.* (1869) 353 [The smoke of rebellion was first seen in.. Magweyre, next in Tyrone, and] sequelarly [in his confederates].

‖**sequelula** (sɪˈkwɛljʊlə). *nonce-wd.* [mod.L. dim. of *sequēla* SEQUELA.] A little sequel (sense 7) or continuation of a literary work.

1912 M. BEERBOHM *Christmas Garland* 61 (*title*) A sequelula to 'The Dynasts'. **1941** E. BLUNDEN *Thomas Hardy* 237 Soon after the completed publication of *The Dynasts*, a 'Sequelula' to it was delivered to the world.

sequenator (ˈsiːkwəneɪtə(r)). *Biochem.* [Irreg. f. SEQUEN(CE *v.* + -ATOR.] = SEQUENCER² 2.

1967 EDMAN & BEGG in *European Jrnl. Biochem.* I. 81/1 We propose the term 'sequenator' for an instrument which determines the sequence of an ordered linear polymer by repeating a chemical process. **1973** *MTP Internat. Rev. Sci., Org. Chem.* VI. 48 The operation of the sequenator relies on the insolubility of the protein during the extraction procedure and short peptide chains are too soluble to be successfully degraded. **1978** *Nature* 19 Jan. 281/2 The sequence of the first 44 residues of this peptide has been determined on a protein sequenator (unpublished results).

sequence (ˈsiːkwəns), *sb.* Also 4–6 **sequens.** [ad. late L. *sequentia*, f. *sequent-em*, pres. pple. of *sequī* to follow: see SEQUENT *a.* and -ENCE. Cf. OF. *sequence* (13th c. in Hatz.-Darm.), F. *séquence*, Sp. *secuencia*, Pg. *sequencia*, It. *seguenza*.

Orig. introduced (perh. through OF.) in the eccl. Latin sense (7 below). In this use *sequentia* was a transl. of eccl. Gr. ἀκολουθία, which denoted a neume or prolonged succession of notes sung on the last syllable of the Alleluia. When the Alleluia was adopted in the Western ritual, this neume was retained, but it became usual to sing it to a separate form of words, to which the name *sequentia* was transferred.

In its primary use the word first appears late in the 16th c.]

I. Succession, following.

1. a. The fact of following after or succeeding; the following of one thing after another in succession; an instance of this.

1593 SHAKS. *Rich. II*, II. i. 199 For how art thou a King But by faire sequence and succession? **1605** BACON *Adv. Learn.* I. ii. §2 For as in Man, the ripenesse of strength of the bodie and minde commeth much about an age..; So in States, Armes and Learning.. haue a concurrence or nere sequence in times. **1644** BULWER *Chirol.* 138 The ancient form of absolution.. may be also exhibited by one Hand laid in sequence of the other; or both conjoyned and held above the head. *a* **1656** BP. HALL *Serm.* Ps. cviii. 34 Wks. 1808 V. 240 What should I instance in that, whereof.. the whole world is full: the inevitable sequences of sin and punishment? **1833** CHALMERS *Const. Man* (1835) II. II. i. 143 The constancy of nature's Sequences. **1843** GROVE *Corr. Phys. Forces* (1846) 6 If.. we regard causation as invariable sequence, we can find no case in which a given antecedent is the only antecedent to a given sequent. **1843** MILL *Logic* I. v. §6. 139 Instead of Coexistence and Sequence, we shall sometimes say, for greater particularity, Order in Place, and Order in Time. **1862** SPENCER *First Princ.* II. iii. §47 (1867) 163 Relations of which the terms are not reversible become recognized as sequences proper; while relations of which the terms occur indifferently in both directions, become recognized as co-existences. **1866** G. MACDONALD *Ann. Q. Neighb.* xvi. (1878) 330 Now I must report another occurrence in regular sequence. **1884** [LAURIE] *Metaph. Nova & Vet.* 115 There are fixed in his associative memory certain sequences as always occurring.

†**b.** ***in sequence of***: in pursuance or consequence of. *Obs.*

a **1648** LD. HERBERT *Hen. VIII* (1649) 262 The Cardinall .. having read them, deliver'd immediatly the Great Seale; In sequence thereof, also submitting himself to the King. *Ibid.* 378 In sequence whereof, on the twelfth of March following.. the Bishop.. returned the Protestants this answer. *Ibid.* 394 France, where in sequence of a Protestation.. to attend the French King.. he resolved to march.

c. ***in sequence***: one after another.

1575 GASCOIGNE *Posies, Weeds* (1907) I. 463 Davids salutacions to Berzabe wherein are three sonets in sequence, written uppon this occation. **1588** SHAKS. *Tit. A.* IV. i. 37 *Ti.* Why lifts she vp her armes in sequence thus? *Mar.* I thinke she meanes that ther was more than one Confederate in the fact. **1638** R. BAKER tr. *Balzac's Lett.* (vol. II.) 113 Fortune hath robbed me of it, for feare I should.. have two pleasures in sequence. **1823** SOUTHEY *Hist. Penins. War* I. 20 The others were to be called upon in sequence. **1824** LANDOR *Imag. Conv., Johnson & Horne Tooke* Wks. 1853 I. 160/2 You will wonder at finding both a hexameter and pentameter, and in sequence.

2. a. Order of succession.

1586 A. DAY *Eng. Secretary* II. (1595) 4 Whereof the first in sequence which I will deliuer vnto you.. shall be in the state coniecturall. **1607** SHAKS. *Timon* v. i. 211 Tell Athens, in the sequence of degree, From high to low throughout. *a* **1631** DONNE *Lett.* (1651) 60, I doubt.. not that I writing in my dungeon of Michim without dating, have made the Chronologie and sequence of my Letters perplexed to you. **1657** SPARROW *Bk. Com. Prayer* (1661) 111 Wherein without any consideration of the sequence of time.. the holy Doctrine, Deeds and Miracles of our Lord are the chief matters of our meditations. **1833** CAROLINE BOWLES in Southey *Corr.* (1881) 277 Admiration, disappointment, and disgust has been, I think, the sequence of feeling with which I have read them. **1862** STANLEY *Jew. Ch.* (1877) I. xix. 364 Works.. arranged in chronological sequence. **1867** W. W. SMYTH *Coal & Coal-mining* 20 The annexed table exhibits the natural sequence where all the strata are developed. **1873** SPENCER *Stud. Sociol.* ii. 45 He asserts that there is a natural sequence among social actions. **1875** FORTNUM *Maiolica* iii. 24 The next example, two years later, in sequence of date.

b. *Gram.* Chiefly in ***sequence of tenses***, the manner in which the tense of a subordinate clause depends on that of the principal clause. Cf. CONSECUTION 2 b.

1848 J. T. WHITE *Xenophon's Anab.* I. viii. §15 (1872) Notes 72 What is in Latin the sequence of tenses is in Greek the sequence of moods. **1891** SONNENSCHEIN *Plautus' Rudens* 91 The sequence of tenses *hic dico.. qui adornaret ut faciat* is Plautine. **1892** L. KELLNER *Hist. Outl. Eng. Syntax* §371 Sequence of Tenses ('consecutio temporum'). Principal tenses depend on principal tenses; historical on historical.

c. *Biochem.* The order of the constituent nucleotides in a nucleic acid molecule or of the amino-acids in a polypeptide or protein molecule.

1959 *Arch. Biochem. & Biophysics* LXXXV. 290 The sequence of these trinucleotides was determined by digestion with semen monoesterase followed by snake venom diesterase with the resulting formation of a purine nucleoside, a purine nucletide (Pu), and a pyrimidine nucleotide (Py). **1965** *Science* 19 Mar. 1462/1 During protein synthesis, the amino acid sequence of the polypeptide chain is determined by the interaction of a messenger RNA with transfer RNA's specific for a given amino acid. **1970** *Biochem. Jrnl.* CXVIII. 831/1 The recent determination of partial sequences at the cohesive ends of DNA from bacteriophage λ.. is an excellent example of the application of repair reactions with DNA polymerase.. to nucleotide sequence studies. **1977** *Sci. Amer.* Dec. 55/1 The complete nucleotide sequence of the DNA of a small bacterial virus, $\phi X174$, has been established.

3. a. A continuous or connected series (of things).

In 16th c. examples there is sometimes an allusion to the specific sense 4.

1575 GASCOIGNE *Posies, Flowers* (1907) I. 85 Of such our patrone here, The viscont Mountacute, Hath many comely sequences, well sorted all in sute. *Ibid., Weeds* I. 463 In the beginning of the booke [he] wrote this sequence. **1589** *Pappe w. Hatchet* E iij, I haue manie sequences of Saints. **1605** BACON *Adv. Learn.* I. vii. §8. 35 b, In this sequence of sixe Princes, we doe see the blessed effects of Learning in soueraigntie. **1616** I. T. *A,B,C, of Armes* C 4, A perfect File is a sequence of men standing one behinde another. **1656** BLOUNT *Glossogr.*, *Sequences*, answering Verses, or Verses that answer one another sequentially; [**1661** adds] things that follow one another in order. *a* **1668** LASSELS *Voy. Italy* (1670) II. 183 This is one of the noblest palaces in Rome for.. the rare sequens of chambers, one going into the other. **1823** SCOTT *Peveril* xii, Then came a long sequence of reflections. **1829** CARLYLE *Voltaire* Misc. 1840 II. 102 Neither is that sequence which we love to speak of as 'a chain of causes', properly to be figured as a 'chain'. **1881** *Daily Tel.* 27 Dec. [The] orchestra struck up a sequence of patriotic and loyal airs.

b. *Mus.* (See quots.)

1752 tr. *Rameau's Treat. Mus.* 85 A Sequence, or Succession of Harmony, is nothing else but a Link or Chain of Keys and Governing-notes. **1838** G. F. GRAHAM *Mus. Comp.* 22/2 Sequences or chains of sevenths. **1867** MACFARREN *Harmony* (1892) 57 A Sequence, in the strict style, is the repetition of a melodic or harmonic progression at a higher or lower part of the scale, without a change of key.

c. *Math.* (*a*) A succession of natural numbers in order. *rare*.

1882 SYLVESTER in *Amer. Jrnl. Math.* V. 291.

(*b*) An endless succession of numerical quantities corresponding one to one with the natural numbers 1, 2, 3, etc., in order.

1910 SHEPPARD *Algebra* in *Encycl. Brit.* (ed. 11) I. 611/2.

(*c*) *spec.* (See quot.)

1911 G. B. MATHEWS *Number* in *Encycl. Brit.* (ed. 11) XIX. 850/1 A sequence is an unlimited succession of rational numbers $a_1, a_2, a_3 \ldots a_m, a_{m+1} \ldots$ (in order-type ω) the elements of which can be assigned by a definite rule, such that when any rational number ϵ, however small, has been fixed, it is possible to find an integer m, so that for *all* positive integral values of n the absolute value of $(a_{m+n} - a_m)$ is less than ϵ.

d. *Cinematogr.* and *Television.* A passage consisting of several shots unified about a single theme or event.

1929 *Morning Post* 24 May 12/7 Until recently, in all talking sequences, the actor has been compelled to be static. **1934** C. LAMBERT *Music Ho!* IV. 262 A famous sequence in the silent film *Mother*. **1941** B. SCHULBERG *What makes Sammy Run?* vi. 125 He stayed up.. reading one screen play after another... The plan was for him and Sammy to write alternate sequences. **1958** *Daily Mail* 19 July 8/8 Parody of a French film sequence set in a sleezy bistro. **1976** D. CLARK *Dread & Water* v. 105 He's got a movie shot of Silk climbing that mountain... The sequence is just one of Silk climbing.

e. *Geol.* (*a*) An ordered succession, esp. of strata in conformity.

1931 GREGORY & BARRETT *General Stratigr.* vi. 96 The fullest Russian sequence is in the Urals, where the Lower Devonian consists of marine slates, quartzites, and occasional limestones. **1975** A. E. RINGWOOD *Composition & Petrology of Earth's Mantle* vii. 243 In estimating the abundance of andesitic volcanism in Precambrian shield sequences, allowance should be made for the andesitic component of associated geosynclinal sediments.

(*b*) In various specific usages (see quots.)

1933 R. C. MOORE *Hist. Geol.* v. 54 No designation for the rocks of an era is in common use. The term 'sequence' will be used in this book. **1949** L. L. SLOSS et al. in *Mem. Geol. Soc. Amer.* No. 39. 110 The writers term the assemblages of strata separated by the above-described objective horizons 'sequences'. Sequences should be considered as rock units, assemblages of formations and groups. **1962** SILBERLING & ROBERTS in *Geol. Soc. Amer. Special Paper* No. 72. 6 A different kind of subdivision.. is required in northwestern Nevada for the upper Paleozoic and lower Mesozoic rocks. The subdivisions adopted are lithologically and geographically discrete units of major rank termed 'sequences' that are set apart from underlying or overlying sequences by unconformities.

4. a. *Cards.* A group of three or more cards of the same suit following in numerical order; a 'run'. Phrase, ***in sequence***. In *Poker*: see quot. 1882.

1575 GASCOIGNE *Posies* (1907) I. 392 Untill she had.. turned over and retossed every card in this sequence. **1656** BLOUNT *Glossogr.* s.v., A Sequence at Cards, is three of a sort that answer or follow one another, in number or degree. **1680** COTTON *Compl. Gamester* (ed. 2) 59 Picket... A Quart is a sequence of four Cards, a Quint of five, a Sixism of six, &c. These Sequences take their denomination from the highest Card in the Sequence. **1746** HOYLE *Whist* (ed. 6) 13 A Sequence of King, Queen, and Knave. **1784** COWPER *Task* I. 475 To divide and sort, Her mingled suits and sequences. **1816** SINGER *Hist. Cards* 239 If a king is played, and you have not the queen to form a sequence, you play the fool. **1868** PARDON *Card Player* 20 It is not necessary that the cards of a sequence should be played in consecutive order. **1869** BROWNING *Ring & Bk.* XI. 1601, I called king, Queen and knave in a sequence, and cards came, All three, three only! **1882** *Rules of Poker* 13 A Sequence Flush. Which is a sequence of five cards and *all* of the same suit. *Ibid.* 14 A Sequence. Which is all five cards not of the same suit but all in sequence. **1883** *Longm. Mag.* Sept. 499 All the cards in the hand being in sequence.

†**b.** 'A certaine game that standeth much on sequences' (Cotgr.). *Obs.*

1653 URQUHART *Rabelais* I. xxii, There he played.. At post and paire, or even and sequence.. At the sequences.

5. Something that follows. **a.** A logical consequence; also †an inference, conclusion.

1613 DAY *Dyall* viii. (1614) 207 Vpon which Confession if you please you may make these sequences: *First* what is the right and interest of Princes in matters Ecclesiasticall: *Secondly*, that [etc.]. **1861** J. G. HOLLAND *Less. Life* xi. 158 The logical sequence of disbelief in what Mr. Emerson calls a 'pistareen Providence' is a belief in pantheism or polytheism.

b. A subsequent event; sometimes contextually, a consequent event, a result.

1853 KANE *Grinnell Exp.* xxxvi. (1856) 325, I am, I fear, heterodox.. as to the direct action of remedies, and rarely allow myself to claim a sequence as a result. **1858** GEN. P. THOMPSON *Audi Alt.* III. 35 The Chinese felony and its Indian sequences. **1863** GEO. ELIOT *Romola* II. iv, A movement which was but a small sequence of her energetic resolution. **1872** YEATS *Growth Comm.* 9 Maritime commerce was the natural sequence to that along the courses of rivers.

†**c.** Event, end, issue, sequel. *Obs.*

1600 SURFLET *Country Farm* III. lxxxiii. 621 You must see to the ordering and continuing of your fire,.. euermore carefully looking vnto the sequence [orig. F. *l'euenement*] and successe of the worke. *a* **1648** LD. HERBERT *Hen. VIII* (1649) 402 They might afterwards repent their neglect of so great an offer, so it prov'd true, as by the sequence will appear.

6. The quality of being sequent; the fact of following as a logical inference or as a necessary result; orderly connexion between successive events or the successive parts of an argument or discourse; continuity, consecutiveness.

1828 CARLYLE *Goethe* Misc. 1840 I. 263 These two classes of works stand.. at first view, in strong contradiction, yet in truth, connected together by the strictest sequence. **1831** —— *Sart. Res.* I. iv, In this remarkable Volume, it is true, ..[there is] a certain show of outward method; but of true logical method and sequence there is too little. **1841** MYERS *Cath. Th.* III. xlviii. 180 A series of contemporaneous utterances,.. with no shape or sequence, no method or coherence. *a* **1854** H. REED *Lect. Eng. Hist.* ix. (1855) 282 As to the sequence, the connection of one with another, it is utter darkness. **1866** GEO. ELIOT *F. Holt* ix, With strange sequence to all that rapid tumult after a few moments' silence she said [etc.]. **1870** DICKENS *E. Drood* i, When any distinct word has been flung into the air, it has had no sense or sequence. **1876** FREEMAN *Norm. Conq.* V. xxiv. 378 Whatever we say of his premisses, his conclusions follow from them with a sequence which cannot be gainsayed. **1908** R. BAGOT *A. Cuthbert* xx. 249 No; every link was complete, every combination of circumstances crushing in its logical and cruel sequence.

II. 7. *Eccl.* **a.** A composition in rhythmical prose or accentual metre said or sung, in the Western Church, after the Alleluia and before the Gospel. Sometimes called a *prose*: see PROSE *sb.* 2.

1387 TREVISA *Higden* (Rolls) VII. 501 Þis is that Robart that made that sequence of the Holy Goost; Sancti spiritus assit nobis gratia. *a* **1400** *Leg. Rood.* App. 218 Þer clerkis synge her sequens. *c* **1430** LYDG. *Min. Poems* (E.E.T.S.) 15 That gloryous hevenly queene.. In whoos worshepe this sequence as I mene In hire feestys is songen. *c* **1440** *Alphabet of Tales* 77 When þai war att þe laste end of þe sequens & had songen þis vers; 'hunc diem gloriosum fecisti'. *c* **1449** [see PROSE *sb.* 2]. **1483** CAXTON *Gold. Leg.* 430/4 Duryng that tyme men saye noo sequence for the sequence sygnefyeth joye and consolacyon. **1513** BRADSHAW *St. Werburge* II. 1689 Playnly declaryng.. What.. excellence Our sauiour shewed for his spouse openly, As is rehersed at masse in her sequens. **1563** *Homilies* II. ii. *Agst. Peril of Idol.* III. (1623) 48 All our Legends, Hymnes, Sequenses, and Masses, did conteine Stories, Laudes, and Prayses of them [*sc.* the Saints]. **1725** J. LEWIS *Life Pecock* (1744) 158 The tropery.., a book of sequences. **1853** ROCK *Ch. of Fathers* III. II. xi. 21 This drawing out of the notation for the Alleluia, they called the 'sequence'... On all lower feast days the sequence, that is, the gradual Alleluia.. was sung. **18..** Alleluiatic sequence [see ALLELUIATIC *a.*]. **1881** LD. SELBORNE in *Encycl. Brit.* XII. 583/2 The 'Golden Sequence', 'Veni, sancte Spiritus' ('Holy Spirit, Lord of Light') is an early example of the transition of sequences from a simply rhythmical to a metrical form. **1903** C. E. OSBORNE *Life Dolling* xxiv. (1905) 229 The sequence was that usual at the burial of the dead in Western Christendom, the *Dies Iræ*.

†**b.** A sequencer or sequence-book. *Obs. rare*⁻¹.

1500 in Wordsw. & Littlehales *Old Service-bks.* (1904) 211 A boke of expownations and a sequens, both notyd.

c. ***sequence book***: a sequencer.

1862 BP. FORBES in *Ecclesiologist* XXIII. 35 The Sarum Tropers, or Sequence books.

III. 8. *attrib.* and *Comb.*, as **sequence control** *Computing*, a method of controlling the execution of distinct operations in a defined order; so **sequence-controlled** *ppl. a.*; **sequence dancing** (see quot. 1949); also **sequence dance**; **sequence date** *Archæol.*, a relative chronological date based upon comparison of a series of objects from an archæological site; hence **sequence dating**; **sequence shot** *Cinematogr.* (see quot. 1973); **sequence space** *Math.*, a space whose points are sequences.

1946 *Electr. Engin.* LXV. 387 (*caption*) Front view of calculator showing *sequence control mechanism.., which tells machine what to do and when to do it. **1962** Sequence control [see *control register* s.v. CONTROL *sb.* 5]. **1964** C. DENT *Quantity Surveying by Computer* iii. 24 Control is.. directed to address No. 2 in the memory store for its next instruction, and so on, in numerical sequence. This mode of operation is called 'Automatic Sequence Control'. **1946** *Ann. Computation Lab. Harvard Univ.* I. p. ix, In May 1944, the Staff of the Computation Project began operations with the Automatic *Sequence Controlled Calculator as an activity of the Bureau of Ships. **1950** W. W. STIFFLER *High-Speed Computing Devices* v. 63 An automatic sequence-controlled calculator is a computing machine into which such a [sequencing] mechanism is built. **1927** *Melody Maker* Sept. 865/2 They are to a great extent *sequence dances and based on what many consider to be old-fashioned steps and movements. **1978** *Abingdon Herald* 12 Jan. 1/9 The Wootton and Dry Sandford Sequence Dance Club. **1940** A. H. FRANKS *Ballroom Dancer's Handbk.* 109 *Sequence dancing really has no place in the art of modern ballroom dancing and such dances are regarded as novelties. **1949** A. CHUJOY *Dance Encycl.* 424/2 *Sequence Dancing*, a term used in England to describe those ballroom dances in which the steps have to be taken in a certain definite order, as a consequence of which all couples are always making the same movement at one time. **1980** *Radio Times* 29 Nov.–5 Dec. 86/3 This is Sequence Dancing... When one lady twirls 200 other ladies twirl. **1901** *Sequence date [see S.D. s.v. S 4 a]. **1920** W. M. F. PETRIE *Prehist. Egypt* ii. 4 For permanent reference the whole 900 graves, when placed in their most probable order or sequence, were divided in 51 equal sections, and these were numbered 30 to 80, and such numbers termed Sequence Dates, marked as S.D. **1923** T. E. PEET in *Cambr. Anc. Hist.* I. vi. 247 Petrie, at Diospolis Parva, invented the now famous system of 'Sequence Dating'. **1958** L. COTTRELL *Anvil of Civilisation* ii. 39 He [*sc.* Petrie] invented the system which we call 'sequence dating' which.. enables archaeologists to establish the *comparative* age of a site by the type of pottery found on it, even when it lies below the 'historical horizon'. **1973** S. HEATH in *Screen* Spring/Summer 114 A **sequence-shot*, a whole scene in one shot (e.g. *autonomous segment* 17 of *Adieu Philippine* showing Michel, the hero, and his friend Daniel working in the TV studio). **1974** M. TAYLOR tr. *Metz's Film Lang.* iii. 42 There was Jean Renoir with his many statements in favor of the sequence shot. **1940** H. S. ALLEN in *Proc. London Math. Soc.* XLVIII. 310 A set S of sequences containing the origin and such that for every x and y in S and every number r, $x + y$ and rx are in S is called a *sequence space. **1968** G. LUDWIG *Wave Mech.* I. iii. 37 The formulation of a matrix in diagonal form and the solution of the eigenvalue problem are therefore equivalent problems, the first being defined only in the sequence space.

sequence ('siːkwəns), *v.* [f. the sb.]

1. *trans.* To arrange in a definite sequence or order.

1954 *Computers & Automation* Dec. 20/2 *Sequence*,.. to select A if A is greater than or equal to B, and select B if A is less than B, or some variation of this operation. **1965** J. S. BRUNER in *Beyond Information Given* (1974) xxv. 442 We.. closed our eyes to the pedagogic problem of how to represent knowledge, how to sequence it in a form appropriate to young learners. **1974** M. B. BROWN *Economics of Imperialism* ix. 226 Countries can be sequenced as markets for different products according to their standards of consumption. **1976** *Daily Tel.* 12 Aug. 2/3 To get the maximum use out of Heathrow's two main runways aircraft are carefully 'sequenced' from the four reporting points that serve the airport.

2. *Biochem.* To ascertain the sequence of monomers in (a biological polymer such as a polypeptide or a nucleic acid).

1970 S. BLACKBURN *Protein Sequence Determination* xx. 274 The future should see the increasing use of methods able to sequence very large molecules. **1977** *Sci. Amer.* Dec. 67/2 Now that DNA can be sequenced readily and rapidly we can expect that in the next few years the precise composition of many DNA's will be established.

Hence **'sequenced** *ppl. a.*, **'sequencing** *vbl. sb.*

1961 P. Siegel *Understanding Digital Computers* xv. 329 A sequencing unit to be used with a drum memory and a two-address instruction is shown. **1970** *Nature* 14 Mar. 1026/2 Data.. on the patterns of change in amino-acid substitutions in all the completely sequenced proteins show anything but a random pattern of substitution. **1971** *Archivum Linguisticum* II. 139 The realization rules accept as input specific pairs of such feature-sets and render them as sequenced strings of morphemes which are, in surface structure, simple *NPs*. **1977** *Sci. Amer.* Dec. 56/2 The smallest DNA molecules, those of certain viruses, are perhaps 70 times longer than the 75-nucleotide transfer-RNA molecules that were the subject of early RNA sequencing.

sequencer[1] ('si:kwənsə(r)). Now *Hist.* [a. OF. *sequencier* (AF. **sequencer*), ad. L. *sequentiārius*: see SEQUENTIARY.] A book containing sequences.

1488 in *Archæologia* XLV. 118 A Primer and a Sequencer. **1904** Wordsw. & Littlehales *Old Service-bks.* Index, Sequentiale, Sequentiarius, a Sequencer, or Book of Sequences.

sequencer[2] ('si:kwənsə(r)). [f. SEQUENCE *sb.* + -ER[1].] **1. a.** (See quot.)

1954 *Computers & Automation* Dec. 21/1 *Sequencer*, in punch card machinery, a mechanism which will put items of information in sequence.

b. An apparatus for performing or initiating operations in the correct sequence; *spec.* one forming part of the control system of a computer.

1964 *New Scientist* 6 Feb. 319/1 A late decision to photograph the Moon in passing was defeated by a malfunction in the so-called central computer and sequencer. **1977** N. Freeling *Gadget* v. 222 We.. make an automatic sequencer which takes over the work of sending the signals. **1978** D. J. Kuck *Struct. Computers & Computations* I. iv. 282 The sequencer drives the entire machine through a specified sequence of events which carry out (indeed are) whatever the instruction is defined to do.

2. *Biochem.* An apparatus for determining the sequence of monomers in a biological polymer.

1971 *European Jrnl. Biochem.* XX. 89 Using the sequencer and unpurified reagents, it was possible to degrade entirely a 0·24 μmole sample of the 21 amino acid insulin A-chain (oxidized) and to analyze the products. **1977** *Sci. Amer.* Oct. 103/1 The exact positions at which the labeled amino acid appears are determined with the aid of an automatic machine called a sequencer, which chemically removes one amino acid at a time from the polypeptide chain beginning at the amino terminal (NH_2) end.

†**sequencery.** *Obs.*$^{-0}$ = SEQUENCER[1].

1483 *Cath. Angl.* 330/1 A Sequencery, *troporium.*

se'quenciar. *Hist.* [ad. med.L. *sequenciārius* (*sequentiārius*).] = SEQUENCER[1].

1904 Wordsw. & Littlehales *Old Service-bks.* 207 Then the name 'Troper' survived only as an alternate for the 'Sequenciar'.

sequency ('si:kwənsı). [ad. late L. *sequentia*: see SEQUENCE *sb.* and -ENCY.]

†**1.** = SEQUENCE *sb.* 7. *Obs.*

1641 R. B. K. *Parall. Liturgy with Mass-Book* 28 That famous sequency of Pentecost... In some of their sequencies.. are contained praises of the B. Virgin.

†**2.** The condition or fact of being sequent *to.*

1661 Glanvill *Van. Dogm.* iv. 40 The sole difficulties about the Will, its nature, and sequency to the Understanding, &c. have almost quite baffled inquiry.

†**3.** = SEQUENCE *sb.* 5 a. *Obs.*

1642 H. More *Song of Soul* II. iii. iv. xxxiv, Why was this world from all infinity Not made? saist thou: why? could it be so made? Say I. For well observe the sequency.

4. The quality of being sequent, or of following as a logical or natural consequence; connexion between successive events, or between the successive parts of an argument or discourse; consecutiveness.

1818 Coleridge in *Lit. Rem.* (1836) I. 231 The connexion of the parts with the sum total of the discourse is maintained by the sequency of the logic. **1826** E. Irving *Babylon* I. i. 48 Were it redeemed and set free from.. the sequency of cause and effect. **1857** J. W. Donaldson *Chr. Orthod.* 164 A want of sequency in the narrative of events. **1879** Meredith *Egoist* xxii, It was to suppose a sequency in the conduct of a variable damsel.

sequent ('si:kwənt), *a.* and *sb.* [a. OF. *sequent*, ad. L. *sequent-em*, pres. pple. of *sequī* to follow. Cf. Sp. *siguiente*, Pg. *seguinte*, *seqüente*, It. *seguente*, *sequente*.] **A.** *adj.*

1. That follows or comes after. †**a.** That one is about to say or mention; (the) following, ensuing. *Obs.*

a **1560** Rolland *Crt. Venus* I. 810 And scho in hand ane letter had quhairon Hir charge scho red, quhais tennour is sequent. **1607** Walter *Diary* (Camden) 15 There are extant books in print, the one by an eye-witness, to the sequent event. **1653** Ld. Brouncker tr. *Des Cartes' Compend. Mus.* 37 Such as are set in the Sequent Figure. **1821** *Rouge et Noir* 45 You'll find it in the sequent canto.

b. That succeeds or is subsequent in time or serial order. Now *rare.*

1601 Shaks. *All's Well* v. iii. 197 Of six preceding Ancestors, that Iemme Confer'd by testament to 'th sequent issue Hath it beene owed and worne. *a* **1643** Ld. Falkland, etc. *Infallibility* (1646) 191 Miracles.. creditably recorded from age to age, both in the Evangelists and other sequent Histories. *a* **1648** Ld. Herbert *Hen. VIII* (1649) 553 Priviledges.. of which Lodovicus Pius was in Possession, and all the sequent Kings. **1651** Cartwright *Cert. Relig.* I. 79 What primitive, or sequent Church ever taught.. such doctrine as this? **1667** Milton *P.L.* xii. 165 There he dies, and leaves his Race Growing into a Nation, and now grown Suspected to a sequent king. *a* **1763** Shenstone *Econ.* II. 256 Virtue then Requires the pruner's hand, the sequent stage It barely vegetates. **1867** Emerson *May-Day*, etc., Wks. (Bohn) III. 439 Nor sequent centuries could hit Orbit and sum of Shakspeare's wit. **1873** M. Collins *Squire Silchester* ix, The Rector.. enjoyed his sequent glass of port. **1887** Proctor *Chance & Luck* 133 From his sequent remarks it appears that he had very imperfect information.

c. That follows or moves in the train of another. *rare.*

1612 *Two Noble Kinsmen* I. ii. 65 Either I am The fore-horse in the Teame, or I am none That draw i'th sequent trace. **1805–6** Cary *Dante, Inf.* v. 98 The coast, where Po descends To rest in ocean with his sequent streams. **1874** Ruskin *Val D' Arno* (1886) 229 The treatment of light and shadow in the figures of the Christ and sequent angels.

2. That follows as a result or a logical conclusion. Const. *to, on, upon.*

1601 Shaks. *All's Well* II. ii. 56 Indeed your O Lord sir, is very sequent to your whipping. **1603** —— *Meas. for M.* v. i. 378 Immediate sentence then, and sequent death, Is all the grace I beg. **1605** —— *Lear* I. ii. 115 The sequent effects. **1796** G. L. Way tr. *Le Grand's Fabliaux* I. 52 Her son's arrest, and sequent punishment. **1853** *Zoologist* II. 3871 Some of the inferences drawn are not sequent on the premises. **1878** P. Bayne *Pur. Rev.* iii. 82 The strictly sequent corollary to the Puritan view of Antichrist.

3. Following one another in succession or in a series; successive.

1604 Shaks. *Oth.* I. ii. 41 The Gallies Haue sent a dozen sequent Messengers This very night, at one anothers heeles. **1870** Proctor *Other Worlds* xiii. 323 The never-ending chain of sequent events. **1877** E. R. Conder *Basis Faith* ii. 49 Every harmonious combination of events, sequent or coexistent. **1881** J. Sully *Illusions* 163 A very similar kind of unification takes place between sequent images under the form of transformation. **1884** [Laurie] *Metaph. Nova & Vet.* 115 The series of sequent movements which in a dog ends with the sensation of pain.

b. Characterized by continuous succession; forming an unbroken series or course; consecutive.

c **1600** Shaks. *Sonn.* lx, Like as the waues make towards the pibled shore, So.. our minuites.. In sequent toile all forwards do contend. **1688** Holme *Armoury* III. xix. (Roxb.) 188/2 A file, is a sequent number of men standing one behind an other. **1860** Reade *8th Commandm.* 318 A masterpiece of construction and arrangement, sequent, articulate, clear, pointed. **1872** Ruskin *Aratra Pentelici* 114 Perfectly arranged disposition of counted masses in a sequent order. **1875** Blackmore *Alice Lorraine* III. viii. 122 The sweet face, more and more lit up with sequent thought. **1898** Meredith *Odes Fr. Hist.* 58 Chamber to chamber of her sequent brain Gives answer.

4. That forms a sequel or continuation.

1833 I. Taylor *Fanat.* Pref. 4 The nearly connected and sequent subject.

B. *sb.*

†**1.** A follower, attendant. *Obs. rare*$^{-1}$.

1588 Shaks. *L.L.L.* iv. ii. 142 And here he hath framed a Letter to a sequent of the stranger Queenes.

†**2.** A unit of a sequence; esp. of playing-cards. Cf. SEQUENCE *sb.* 4. *Obs.*

1620 E. Blount *Horæ Subs.* 49 There bee others that delight in figures, and their words fall in, one after another like sequents. **1730** Swift *Game Traffic* Wks. 1743 VIII. 169 Dame Floyd looks out in grave suspence For pair-royals and sequents. **1734** Seymour *Compl. Gamester* I. (ed. 5) 93 (Picquet) Each is to examine what Cards he has in his Hands of the same Suit, which are Sequents.

†**3.** The following narrative; the subsequent course of events; the sequel. *Obs. rare*$^{-2}$.

1655 Terry *Voy. E. India* i. 36 A brave resolute man, as the sequent will demonstrate. *a* **1661** Fuller *Worthies, Linc.* (1662) II. 164 Elias de Trekingham, was born.. at a Village so called, as by the sequents will appear.

4. That which follows in order (of arrangement, time, etc.).

1833 W. Wirt in J. P. Kennedy *Life* (1872) II. xx. 353 [The 'De Senectute' is] infinitely superior, I think, to that 'De Amicitia' which.. follows it,—or even to the ..'Somnium Scipionis', usually the sequent of the two former. **1893** Fairbairn *Christ in Mod. Theol.* II. ii. §3. 55 The later [age] is the sequent in time but not in thought of the earlier.

5. That which follows naturally as a result; the consequent of an antecedent; also in ***logical sequent.***

1838 *Blackw. Mag.* XLIII. 200 Conscience, morality, and responsibility,.. may be shown to be based in consciousness, and necessary sequents thereof. **1841** Myers *Cath. Th.* IV. §5. 193 No human thought can deal with them ..as necessary antecedents or sequents in any logical deductions. **1884** [Laurie] *Metaph. Nova & Vet.* 119 The relation of antecedents and sequents. **1885** J. Martineau *Types Eth. Th.* (1889) I. 464 Assuming an interval between the two sequents (physical and mental) upon the molecular change. **1891** *Speaker* 2 May 528/1 Universal suffrage brought into France in 1789 its logical sequent; the right of the voter carried with it the duty of the defender.

sequential (sɪ'kwɛnʃəl), *a.* [f. late L. *sequentia* SEQUENCE *sb.*: see -AL[1].]

1. a. That follows as a sequel *to.* Of two or more things: Forming a sequence.

1854 *Chamb. Jrnl.* II. 82 A brief resumé of these thronging reminiscences must necessarily precede the telling of the story sequential to them. **1899** *Allbutt's Syst. Med.* VIII. 209 Mental action, though disorderly and not sequential to the question put. **1906** *Hibbert Jrnl.* Oct. 219 These two books, while not sequential, are closely related.

b. *Path.* Following as a secondary affection; occurring as a sequela to a previous disease.

1822–29 *Good's Study Med.* (ed. 3) V. 230 Sequential Labour.. Sequential, or after-pains as they are ordinarily called. **1904** *Brit. Med. Jrnl.* 10 Sept. 606 Inflammatory œdema is brought under the heading of phlegmonous laryngitis, primary and sequential.

c. Resultant, consequent.

1899 W. M. Davis in *Geog. Jrnl.* (R.G.S.) XIV. 487 'Initial' is therefore a term adapted to ideal rather than to actual cases, in treating which the term 'sequential' and its derivatives will be found more appropriate. **1900** J. Orr in *U.P. Mag.* Feb. 62/2 With these divisions of opinion on the nature of the Church are connected many sequential differences.

d. ***sequential induction*** (Biochem.): the formation in sequence of a group of related enzymes, consequent upon the induction of the first enzyme of the series (see quot. 1953).

1953 M. Cohn et al. in *Nature* 12 Dec. 1096/2 We.. propose the following terms and designations... The exposure of an organism to a single inducer which is also a substrate may result in the induction of a sequence of enzymes, since the metabolism of the primary, exogenous inducer gives rise to the formation of a succession of intermediary metabolites each of which in turn serves as an inducer for the enzyme which converts it into the next member of the metabolic chain. This phenomenon is termed 'sequential induction' (simultaneous or successive adaptation). **1968** H. Harris *Nucleus & Cytoplasm* vi. 118 We have glimpses of this kind of organization in the phenomenon of 'sequential induction' (induction *en chaîne*) of enzymes in bacteria. **1971** *Bacteriol. Rev.* XXXV. 89/2 A sequential induction is characterized by a shift in the chemical nature of the inducer.

2. a. That is characterized by the regular sequence of its parts; continuous.

1844 'A. Wallbridge' (*title*) The Sequential system of Musical Notation: a proposed new method of writing Music. Second edition. **1849** (*title*) The sequential book of church music. No. 1. **1862** S. Lucas *Secularia* 67 If the history of man has been in the main sequential. **1879** Carpenter *Mental Phys.* I. viii. 346 The complete engrossment of the consciousness by a particular series of Cerebral changes.. enables those changes to proceed with more sequential regularity. **1887** *Pall Mall Gaz.* 8 Nov. 4/2 There is in this country 'no sequential teaching'.

b. *Computers.* Of, pertaining to, or designating various aspects of a computer system and its control programming that operate or are utilized serially; ***sequential search***, a search through a data list or file that is carried out serially.

1951 *Proc. IRE* XXXIX. 276/2 *Sequential control*, the manner in which instructions to a digital computer are set up in sequence and are fed consecutively to the computer during the solution of a problem. **1964** T. W. McRae *Impact of Computers on Accounting* iii. 53 A computer.. carries out each of these operations in automatic sequence under the control of the computer programme. This particular characteristic is known as 'sequential processing'. **1965** *Information & Control* VIII. 159 (*heading*) Discrete sequential search. **1969** P. B. Jordain *Condensed Computer Encycl.* 447 Once written, a sequential file has to be read in the same order (or sometimes in the inverse order) in which it has been written. **1970** O. Dopping *Computers & Data Processing* x. 133 The magnetic tape can be called a sequential access memory, or serial access memory, because the records must be written and read in sequence. **1973** C. W. Gear *Introd. Computer Sci.* ii. 44 We refer to the set of input cards as a sequential data set because it is possible to read a card only after the preceding card has been read. **1979** J. E. Rowley *Mechanised In-House Information Syst.* i. 26 Any search must process the complete tape, from start to end, seeking matches between terms, i.e. a sequential search.

3. Pertaining to sequency of thought. *rare*$^{-1}$.

1853 Ruskin *Stones Ven.* III. ii. 38 God.. has given to the man whom he means for a student, the reflective, logical, sequential faculties.

4. *Mus.* Of the nature of a sequence.

1889 H. A. Harding *Analysis of Form* 5 A sequential passage leads to an inverted dominant pedal point. **1891** Prout *Counterpoint* (ed. 2) 100 The sequential character of the treble and tenor is maintained in the added alto part.

5. *Television.* **a.** Of or pertaining to the normal method of scanning a television image, in which all the lines are traversed in the same direction, with a rapid, blanked fly-back after each.

1940 *Chambers's Techn. Dict.* 759/1 *Sequential scanning*, scanning in which the spot traverses each line in the same direction, returning rapidly from the end of one line to the beginning of the next. **1942** *Electronics* Apr. 164/1 System 2 employs sequential scanning in order to eliminate interline flicker. **1966** G. H. Hotson *Television Receiver Theory* i. 5 A sequential raster.. would be set up by drawing 625 lines one under the other. **1967** H. A. Cole *Basic Television* iii. 26 Provided that the rate of sequential scanning is high enough, the eye can be successfully 'tricked', by reason of the persistence of its vision, into believing that a very rapidly renewed image on the viewing screen has in fact been there all the time.

b. Of, pertaining to, or designating various systems of colour television in which picture information for the primary colours is transmitted successively in quantities corresponding to a dot, line, or field. Cf. *dot-* (also *field-*, *line-*) *sequential system* s.v. DOT *sb.*[1] 5 f, FIELD *sb.* 21, LINE *sb.*[2] 32.

1947 *Electronics* Jan. 72/2 The sequential system is characterized by the fact that the transmitted signal contains information about one primary color only at any instant of time. **1951** *Proc. IRE* XXXIX. 1195/1 In the case of field-sequential or line-sequential presentation, step-wise switching from color to color is desired. In the case of dot-sequential presentation, sine-wave switching by circular deflection with uniform angular velocity is preferred. **1975** D. G. Fink *Electronics Engineers' Handbk.* xx. 12 The field sequential system employs a monochrome television camera, with a color-scanning disk mounting near the focal plane... The video signal derived from the camera tube thus consists of sequential color fields in the order that the primary light filters appear in front of the camera tube.

6. ***sequential circuit*** (Electronics), a logic circuit whose output depends on the order or timing of the inputs.

1954 D. A. Huffman in *Jrnl. Franklin Inst.* CCLVII. 165 In a circuit having secondary relays, the possibility of a 'memory' exists since the states of operation may not uniquely determine the output transmissions. A circuit having secondary relays will be called a sequential circuit. **1969** J. J. Sparkes *Transistor Switching* iv. 93 In combinational and sequential circuit diagrams it is usual to use special symbols. **1975** D. G. Fink *Electronics Engineers' Handbk.* xxiii. 41 In some cases problems exist in sequential circuits when a circuit action depends critically on which relay or logic element completes its operations first.

Hence **se'quentially** *adv.*; **se'quentialism** *rare* (see quot. 1848); **sequenti'ality**, the quality of being sequential.

1656 [see sequence *sb.* 3]. **1848** 'A. Wallbridge' *Council of Four* Advt., Sequentialism: The new Musical Reform. Preparing for publication, the third edition of the Sequential System of Musical Notation. **1855** *Fraser's Mag.* LI. 168 What common-place man.. has not dreams more lively and more sequentially evolved than this cento of wire-drawn reflections? **1883** *Harper's Mag.* LXVIII. 158 The story is remarkable for its fresh naturalness and sequentiality. **1891** Prout *Counterpoint* (ed. 2) 45 We may now employ the same figure—especially sequentially—for several bars.

sequentiary (sɪˈkwɛnʃərɪ). [ad. late L. *sequentiārius*, f. *sequentia* sequence *sb.*] = sequencer[1].

1500 *Ortus Vocab.*, *Troporium* [sic], a tropor a sequencyarye. **1857** *Ecclesiologist* XVIII. 205 An imperfect Sequentiary, apparently of the beginning of the fifteenth century. **1891** Mrs. Hernaman in *Newbery Ho. Mag.* July V. 20 Missals and Sequentiaries.

sequently (ˈsiːkwəntlɪ), *adv.* [f. sequent *a.* + -ly[2].] In sequent order.

1905 *Blackw. Mag.* Oct. 527/1 The whole of the events of the past few weeks flashed through his brain, clearly and sequently.

‖**'sequere me.** *Surg. Obs.* [L., lit. 'Follow me'.] The name of a flexible probe used in mediæval surgery.

a **1425** tr. *Arderne's Treat. Fistula*, etc. 8 Instrumentis þat perteneth to þe cure of þe fistule... Of whiche þe first is called 'Sequere me'—'follow me'. *Ibid.* 15, 22.

†**se'quest,** *v.*[1] *Obs. rare*[−1]. [Badly f. L. *sequī* to follow.] *trans.* To follow.

1567 Pikeryng *Horestes* 290 (Brandl), I thanke your grace, I shal sequest your gratius mind herin. *Ibid.* 807 So a wicked wight doth tourne Those that be good, and cause them eke his euell to sequest.

[**sequest,** *v.*[2] in some Dicts., is evolved from the misprints *sequested*, *sequesting*, for *sequestred*, *-tring*: see sequester *v.*]

†**se'quester,** *sb.*[1] *Obs.* Also 4 suquestre. [a. L. *sequester*; prob. f. *seques-, *sequos a position apart (whence *secus* adv., otherwise); the etymological sense of the word (which is primarily an adj.) would thus be 'standing apart'.] In *Civil Law*, a person with whom the parties in a suit deposit the thing contested until the case has been decided. Also, in wider sense, a mediator.

c **1380** *Antecrist* in Todd *Three Treat. Wyclif* (1851) 125 But take we heede to þe popes & cardinals boþe;.. & dekenes & officials & sequestris. *a* **1400** in *Eng. Gilds* (1870) 363 And þat no man ne legge in lond ne in tenement by-fore y-seyd, þe whyle þe suquestre ys þare set. **1555** Eden *Decades* (Arb.) 309 Kynge Iohn and pope Iulius dyed both in one day, wherby he [Basilius] lacked a conuenient sequester or solicitoure. **1592** West *1st Pt. Symbol.* §17 c, This doth take the possession from the parties in controuersie, and giueth the same to the Sequester or indifferent man, to thend he may deliuer the same to him that recouereth it. **1633** D. R[ogers] *Treat. Sacr.* i. 65 The Minister then is.. appointed as a Sequester betweene God and the Congregation.

†**se'quester,** *sb.*[2] *Obs.* [a. F. *séquestre*, ad. L. *sequestrum*, orig. neut. of *sequester* adj.: see prec.]

1. Sequestration, seclusion, isolation.

1604 Shaks. *Oth.* iii. iv. 40 This hand of yours requires A sequester from Liberty.

2. The office or court to which goods seized by an act of sequestration are taken.

1568 tr. *Gonsalvio's Sp. Inquis.* 59 b, All the goodes and merchandise which he brought with him.. were according to their common vsage seised and taken into the sequester.

3. *Path.* = sequestrum. [So in Fr.] ? *Obs.*

1831 South *Otto's Path. Anat.* ii. 146 A jelly-like mass gradually hardens and becomes ossified, surrounds, like a sheath,.. the necrotic bone, which is then called a sequester.

sequester (sɪˈkwɛstə(r)), *v.* Also 4–9 sequestre. [ad. late L. *sequestr-āre* to place in safe keeping, to remove, separate, f. L. *sequestr-*, *sequester*: see sequester *sb.*[1]

Cf. OF. *sequestrer* (14th c.), mod.F. *séquestrer*, Sp. *secuestrar*, Pg. *sequestrar*, It. *sequestrare*.]

1. *trans.* To set aside, separate. †**a.** To separate and reject; to eliminate; chiefly in immaterial sense, to set aside, dismiss from consideration.

c **1380** Wyclif *Sel. Wks.* III. 437 Sequestre we al mannes lawe, supposynge Crists ordynaunce. **1430–40** Lydg. *Bochas* iii. xviii. (1554) 90 b, Poetes.. should be quiet fro worldly mocion, And it sequester out of their remembraunce. **1537** *Inst. Chr. Man* O iij b, These be the wordes of Christe.. that we shulde sequester this care from us and seke for the kyngdome of god. **1625** Hart *Anat. Ur.* ii. i. 53 Thirdly, the great trouble.. nature hath in the expelling and sequestring such humours. **1661** Boyle *Scept. Chem.* iv. 259 They presume, that they can sequester the sulphur even of Minerals and Metalls.

†**b.** *Eccl.* To remove (a person) from the privileges of church-membership, to excommunicate.

1395 Purvey *Remonstr.* (1851) 29 He shal be sequestrid, or departid fro the chirche, til he knouleche his gilt and amende him. **14..** *Fothergill MS.* in Henderson *York Man.* (Surtees 1875) Pref. 16 We curse and descry and fro the boundes of all holy kyrke sequestre and depart all thos that this illys hase done [etc.]. **1579** Fulke *Heskins' Parl.* 146 It is to be.. prayed for, lest while any being sequestred, is separated from yᵉ body of Christe, he remaine farre from health. **1642** Jer. Taylor *Episc.* (1647) 223 If their Bishop have sequestred them from the holy Communion, they must not be suffered to communicate elsewhere.

†**c.** With religious signification: To set apart, consecrate to a particular service, to 'separate'. *Obs.*

1533 More *Answ. Poysoned Bk.* i. vi. (1534) 21 Hym hath god the father specyally sequestred and seuered and set asyde out of the nomber of all creatures. **1632** *Consecr. Chapel Merstham Hatch* in Legg. *17th cent. Consecr. Churches* (1911) 141 And after the ascention of our Saviour taught us by thy Apostles to distinguish [places] sequestred for religious exercises, from private houses. **1692** T. Watson *Body Divinity* 332 This Lord's Day is to be sequestred and set apart for Divine Worship. **1697** Burghope *Div. Worship* 147 Let him.. wholly sequester his soul to this work of religion.

†**d.** To remove from membership of a body, or from a public office or station. *Obs.*

1571 Hooker *Hist. Irel.* (1587) 128/2 in *Holinshed*, Euerie person of the parlement ought to keepe secret.. the secrets and things spoken and doone in the parlement house.. vpon paine to be sequestred out of the house. **1629** Maxwell *Herodian* 252 He tooke to wife.. Augusta, yet soone after diuorced her, and.. sequestred her to a priuate Life. **1667** Pepys *Diary* 3 Dec., The Court of Aldermen have sequestered him from their Court till he do bring in an account. **1761** Hume *Hist. Eng.* III. liv. 164 Immediately after Strafford was sequestered from parliament. **1827** Hallam *Const. Hist.* (1876) II. x. 165 Many had already been sequestered from their livings.

e. To seclude (a person, thing, or place) from general access or intercourse; to keep apart *from* society. Now *rare* or *Obs.* exc. in sequestered *ppl. a.*

c **1430** *Pilgr. Lyf Manhode* ii. xlvi. (1869) 93 For it is not in my powere to sequestre him longe from thee. **1497** Bp. Alcok *Mons Perfect.* B iij b, Herts sequestred from all carnall desyres. *c* **1550** N. Smyth *Herodian* vi. 73 Those which inhabite the Orient, are sequestred wyth great distaunce of lande, and Sea. **1588** Shaks. *Tit. A.* ii. iii. 75 Why are you sequestred from all your traine? **1604** E. G[rimstone] *D'Acosta's Hist. Indies* vi. xxvii. 489 They laboured and tooke paines to sequester their children from delights and liberties.. imploying them in honest and profitable exercises. *a* **1626** Bacon *War with Spain* (1629) 1, I had wholly sequestred my thoughts from ciuill affaires. **1698** South *Serm.* (1727) IV. 179 A Christian, in all Acts of Duty, ought to sequester his Mind from all Respect to an ensuing Reward. **1766** *Life of Quin* ii. 18 Cato.. being nine years sequestered in Mr. Addison's closet. **1805** Wordsw. *Prelude* ix. 116 Men Whom in the city, privilege of birth Sequestered from the rest.

refl. *c* **1450** tr. *De Imitatione* iii. xxxvi. (1893) 106 Fewe can fully sequestre & departe himself fro perissing creatures. *a* **1557** Mrs. M. Basset tr. *More's Treat. Passion* M.'s Wks. 1372/2 Sequestring themselfes from those wretched fetters that haue so long holden theim in sinne. **1583** Stubbes *Anat. Abus.* i. (1879) 93 It shalbe lawful for a man to sequester himself from his owne wife. **1603** Florio *Montaigne* i. xxxviii. 119 It is not enough for a man to have sequestred himselfe from the concourse of people... A man must sequester and recover himselfe from himselfe. **1657** *North's Plutarch* (1676) Add. Lives 34 He was resolved to sequester himself from the world. **1753** Richardson *Grandison* (1781) VI. 339 But why, Ladies,.. do you sequester yourselves from the company? **1834** De Quincey *Cæsars* Wks. 1859 X. 232 He sequestered himself from his subjects in the recesses of his palace. **1847** —— *Joan of Arc* ibid. III. 221 As surely as the wolf retires before cities, does the fairy sequester herself from the haunts of the licensed victualler.

f. To segregate, separate in thought from the surroundings.

1841 Emerson *Ess.* Ser. i. xii. 356 The virtue of art lies in detachment, in sequestering one object from the embarrassing variety.

2. To confiscate, appropriate, to take forcible possession of.

a **1513** Fabyan *Chron.* vii. (1811) 363 Than the commons of yᵉ cytie.. toke certayne of the aldermen, & caste theym in prysone, and sequestryd theyr goodes & dispoyled moche therof. **1534** Ld. Berners *Gold. Bk. M. Aurel.* (1546) L viij b, The gouernours.. commaunded all the saied shyppes to bee sequestred into theyr owne handes. **1621** Elsing *Debates Ho. Lords* (Camden) 21 His Majesty to be enfourmed that there is just grounde for his Majesty to sequestre the Seale, and then the L. Chancellor to come to the barre. **1640** in Rymer *Fœdera* (1735) XX. 429 We.. thereupon have been pleased to sequester the said Offices, into the Hands of Philip Burlamachy. **1644** Symonds *Diary* (Camden) 32 He is in rebellion and his estate sequestered. **1855** Milman *Lat. Chr.* ix. ii. (1864) V. 207 The German prelates were commanded.. to sequester the goods of all who had presumed to assist in the incarceration of an archbishop. **1887** *Pall Mall Gaz.* 2 June 7/2 The banker to-day sequestered some State property, which was sold by auction.

3. *Law.* **a.** To remove (property, etc.) from the possession of the owner temporarily; to seize and hold the effects of a debtor until the claims of creditors be satisfied; *Eccl.* to divert the income of a benefice to the payment of debts due from the incumbent, or for the purpose of making good dilapidations; to hold the income of a benefice during a vacancy for the benefit of the next incumbent.

1530 Palsgr. 709/1, I sequester, I put a thyng from the possessoure by the auctorite of a judge. **1538** Starkey *England* i. iv. 127 He hath.. the admynystratyon of intestate godys, by the reson wherof they be sequestryd from the profyt of al the frendys of hym wych so dyed intestate. **1647** Clarendon *Hist. Reb.* vii. §255 Both his Livings.. [were] sequester'd. **1731** Swift *Advant. Repeal. Test* Misc. 1735 V. 407 Every Bishop upon the Vacancy of a Church-Living, can sequester the Profits for the Use of the next Incumbent. **1790** Dallas *Amer. Law Rep.* I. 399 The profits of his property may be sequestered during war, but no forfeiture can take place. **1884** *Law Rep.* 25 *Chanc. Div.* 341 The Bishop.. was commanded to sequester the fruits and profits of the rectory.. until he should have levied the sum of £2285 13 4.

transf. and *fig.* **1678** Marvell *Growth Popery* Wks. 1872–5 IV. 251 But sequestring it [the Bible] only into such hands as were interested in the cheat, they had the opportunity to vitiate.. those Records by which the poor people hold their salvation. **1837** Bancroft *Hist. U.S.* II. 417 The liberties of New York were thus sequestered by a monarch [James II] who desired to imitate the despotism of France.

†**b.** To remove (property in dispute) from the possession of contending parties in a suit, until reference has been had to a third party as arbitrator or umpire. *Obs.*

1604 R. Cawdrey *Table Alph.* **1647** Fuller *Good Th. in Worse T.* To Rdr., For God and man beeing at ods, the difference was Sequestred or referred into Christs his hand to end and umpire it. **1656** Blount *Glossogr.*

c. To apply the process of sequestration to (a person); to sequestrate the estate or benefice of.

1681 Baxter *Apol. Nonconf. Min.* 80 The Vicar was sequestred by the Committee. **1709** Strype *Ann. Ref.* I. xxv. 253 Thomas Morrison, Rector of Henly upon Thames .. was sequestred. **1901** G. Douglas *Ho. Green Shutters* 328 Sandy.. was informing a bunch of unshaven bodies that the Gourlays were 'sequestered'.

†**d.** *intr.* (See quot.) *Obs.*

1704 J. Harris *Lex. Techn.* I, *Sequester*, is a Term used in the Civil Law for renouncing, as when a Widow comes into Court, and disclaims to have any thing to do, or to intermeddle with her Husband's Estate, who is Deceased; she is said to *Sequester*. **1706** Phillips (ed. Kersey).

†**4.** To withdraw into seclusion, to retire, keep apart. *Obs.*

1627 Sclater *Exp. 2 Thess.* (1629) 286 Is it our pride.. or what, that makes vs willingly sequester from such societie? **1644** Milton *Areop.* (Arb.) 51 To sequester out of the world into Atlantick and Eutopian polities.. will not mend our condition. **1838** *New Monthly Mag.* LIII. 541 Have you no hobby whereon you may whisk yourself away from this diurnal sphere, and so sequester from the real to the ideal?

5. *Chem.* To form a stable complex, esp. a chelate, with (an ion) so as effectively or actually to remove it from solution; to form a stable complex with (a biochemical molecule).

1934 R. E. Hall *U.S. Patent 1,956,515* 5/2 The water softening action of the sodium metaphosphate.. is rather to sequester or lock up the calcium in a but extremely slightly [*sic*] ionizable condition in a soluble sodium-calcium-metaphosphate complex molecule. **1953** *Sci. Amer.* June 70/2 The iron.. is tightly imprisoned and hidden away—'sequestered', in the poetic language of chelation technology—by EDTA's chelate rings. **1962** *Which?* Oct. 297/2 Instead of softening water by replacing the calcium and magnesium in hard water by sodium.. you can 'wrap up' the calcium and magnesium—sequester them—and so isolate them from the soap during washing. **1973** *Nature* 13 July 103/2 Insect yolk proteins.. are synthesized and secreted by the fat body, and are sequestered from the haemolymph by the developing oocytes. **1977** *Sci. Amer.* July 92/1 When the cations are sequestered in an organic cage molecule, the resulting complex is so stable that the 'backsliding' reaction is prevented.

Hence **se'questering** *vbl. sb.* and *ppl. a.*

1620 Shelton *Quix.* ii. xv. 91 And it might so be, that in this time of sequestring, he might forget all his vanities. **1653** Bulwer *Anthropomet.* 60 The sequestring variance of virile Nature. **1684** Baxter *Twelve Argum.* §16 They ordered the Sequestring of all Ministers that would not Fast and Pray. **1949** *Thorpe's Dict. Appl. Chem.* (ed. 4) IX. 512/2 The term 'sequestering' introduced by Hall Laboratories to designate the virtually complete elimination of Ca^{++} ions whilst retaining the calcium in solution in the form of a soluble complex. **1962** *Which?* Oct. 297/2 The best known sequestering agents for softening water in this way are the sodium metaphosphates. **1973** P. A. Allum *Politics & Society in Post-War Naples* ix. 316 Antonio Gava's manoeuvres to try to become Campanian Regional Chairman.. included the sequestering of a DC regional councillor in a trunk.

sequestered (sɪˈkwɛstəd), *ppl. a.* Also 7 sequestred. [f. SEQUESTER *v.* + -ED[1].]

†**1.** Separated; cut off from congenial surroundings. *Obs.*

1600 SHAKS. *A. Y. L.* II. i. 33 To the which place a poore sequestred Stag That from the Hunters, aime had tane a hurt, Did come to languish. **1766** [ANSTEY] *Bath Guide* ix. 2 To humbler Strains, ye Nine, descend And greet my poor sequester'd Friend. **1782** PRIESTLEY *Corrupt. Chr.* I. v. 413 [They] suffer some grief in their sequestered state.

b. Under sentence of sequestration; esp. *Eccl. Hist.* Of the dispossessed clergy under the Commonwealth: Deprived of a benefice.

a **1661** FULLER *Worthies, Gen.* xi. (1662) I. 37 Next I desire them to reflect upon aged sequestred Ministers; whom, with their charge, the (generally ill paid) fifth part will not maintain. **1663** COWLEY *Cutter Colman St.* v. xiii, Fifteen hundred pounds a year is no ill match for the daughter of a Sequestred Cavalier. **1673** R. HEAD *Canting Acad.* 79 He is a poor sequestred Parson. **1808** W. WILSON *Dissent. Churches* I. 366 At Cliff.. he succeeded Dr. Griffith Higges, the sequestered minister.

†**c.** Of estates, benefices, etc.: In sequestration.

1649 (*title*) Two Resolutions of Parliament respecting Tenants of Sequestred Estates. **1765–8** ERSKINE *Inst. Law Scot.* II. xii. §58 The rules by which a judicial factor on a sequestered estate ought to conduct himself.

†**d.** *Chem.* Separated, eliminated. *Obs.*

1661 BOYLE *Scept. Chem.* IV. 260 These sequestered substances.

2. Sheltered, retired, secluded.

1658 J. ROBINSON *Endoxa* Pref. 2 Neither my Genius, nor calling, will allow me a sequestred time, to dwell long upon any subject. **1750** GRAY *Elegy* 75 Along the cool sequester'd vale of life They kept the noiseless tenor of their way. **1773** COWPER *Ode to Peace* 17 And wilt thou quit the stream.. The grove and the sequester'd shed, To be a guest with them? **1818** SCOTT *Br. Lamm.* xxxv, To this sequestered spot Colonel Ashton had guided the stranger. **1878** H. S. LEIGH *Town Garland* 204 In a part of a suburb sequestered and gloomy I took up my quarters a twelvemonth ago.

b. Of persons: Retired, living a secluded life or in a quiet, unfrequented place.

1655 FULLER *Ch. Hist.* VI. i. §25 These Bonehomes,.. (the poorest of Orders) and Eremites, (the most sequestred of begging Fryers) had two.. Convents in England. **1783** WATSON *Philip III*, IV. (1793) I. 433 This imputation had often been cast upon the Morescoes, by speculative and sequestered men, who had no access to know the truth of their assertion. **1814** WORDSW. *Excurs.* v. 718 In powers of mind, In scale of culture, few among my flock Hold lower rank than this sequestered pair. **1834** DE QUINCEY *Cæsars* iv. Wks. 1890 VI. 323 The Emperor, himself a sacred and sequestered creature, might be supposed to enjoy the secret tutelage of the Supreme Deity.

transf. **1643** SIR T. BROWNE *Relig. Med.* II. §10 Those disordered motions, which accompany our sequestred imaginations. **1825** SCOTT *Betrothed* xxii, The household of the Lady Eveline.. was of a solemn and sequestered character, corresponding to her place of residence. **1868** BROWNING *Ring & Bk.* II. 989 Confess.. That, O Pompilia, thy sequestered eyes Had noticed.. More of the Canon, than that [etc.].

†**se'questerer.** *Obs. rare.* Also 6 sequestrer. [f. SEQUESTER *v.* + -ER[1].] = SEQUESTER *sb.*

14.. *Nom.* in Wr.-Wülcker 682/7 *Hic sequestarius*, a sequesterer. **1555** W. WATREMAN *Fardle Facions* II. i. 113 He that was the sequestrer of the couenante, becometh suretie for the parties.

†**se'questerment.** *Obs. rare.* [f. SEQUESTER *v.* + -MENT.] A private, secluded situation.

1778 *Saberna* 12 Seek out some lone sequesterment to dwell, Where spirit-shapes repair at dewy eve. **1835** J. P. KENNEDY *Horse Shoe Robinson* vii. (1860) 88 The sequesterment of the Dove Cote was not sufficient to shut out the noise nor the intrigues of the war.

†**se'questrable,** *a. Obs.* Also 7 sequesterable. [f. SEQUESTER *v.* + -ABLE.]

1. Capable of being sequestered, liable to sequestration.

1652–3 in *Royalist Comp. Papers, Lancs.* (1891) I. 185 Her sonne Henry at that tyme was.. noe way for his parte Seq[able], but hath ever bene a Protestant and a well wisher to the Parliament. **1656** in *Burton's Diary* (1828) I. 95 Persons not only sequestrable, but actually sequestered. **1807** W. TAYLOR in *Ann. Rev.* V. 200 Life-interests, such as entailed estates, church-livings and annuities, should be wholly sequestrable with less ceremony.

2. Separable.

1661 BOYLE *Scept. Chem., Physiol. Consid.* 34 Harts-Horn, and divers other Bodies.. that abound with not uneasily sequestrable Salt.

se'questral, *a.*[1] *nonce-wd.* [f. L. *sequestr-*, *sequester* adj. (see SEQUESTER) + -AL[1].] (See quot.)

1853 WHEWELL *Grotius* III. 365 Virgil calls a truce a sequestral peace [Grotius *quanquam Virgilius pacem sequestram dixit* (Æn. xi. 133)], which Servius, on the passage, explains as a temporary peace.

sequestral (sɪˈkwɛstrəl), *a.*[2] [f. SEQUESTR-UM + -AL[1].] Of or pertaining to a sequestrum.

1887 *Buck's Handbk. Med. Sci.* V. 128/1 Around the sequestral tube the bone has the involucral thickening.

sequestrant (sɪˈkwɛstrənt), *sb.* (*a.*) *Chem.* [ad. L. *sequestrānt-em*, pr. pple. of *sequestrāre* (see SEQUESTER *v.*).] A sequestering agent. Also *attrib.* or as *adj.*

1951 *Chem. Abstr.* XLV. 3756 (*heading*) Analytical applications of complexones (sequestrants). **1967** [see *lactobionic* adj. s.v. LACTO- 2]. **1972** *Sci. Amer.* Mar. 19/3 Sequestrants are added to food to bind trace metals and thus prevent any oxidative activity the metals in an ionized state might have on the food.

†**se'questrate,** *a. Obs.* Also 6–7 sequestrat. [ad. late L. *sequestrāt-us*, pa. pple. of *sequestrāre*: see SEQUESTER *v.* and -ATE[2].]

1. Separated, cut off *from.*

1482 *Monk of Evesham* (Arb.) 57 We came to a ful grete fylde, and as hyt semyd hyt was sette yn a lowe grownde sequestrate and departyd from al othir. **1502** ATKYNSON tr. *De Imitatione* I. i. (1893) 153 And who so may haue the iey of theire soule sequestrate in worldlye thynges, in this scripture of our lorde may fynde swete manna. **1600** W. WATSON *Decacordon* (1602) 48 Religious men.. wholy sequestrate from the world in body and mind. **1632** LITHGOW *Trav.* v. 194 Mount Libanus is sequestrate from the circum-iacent Regions.

b. Politically separate, independent.

1632 LITHGOW *Trav.* I. 25 The other sequestrate Tuscan iurisdiction, is the little comonwealth of Luca. *Ibid.* I. 39 This sequestrat Citty [Venice].

2. Sequestered, retired, secluded.

1632 LITHGOW *Trav.* VI. 297 Their dwellings being in sequestrate dennes. *Ibid.* VIII. 352 [They] made merry with vs in.. the best cheare their sequestrate cottage could afford. **1805** FORSYTH *Beauties Scot.* I. 342 It is.. easy, by planting their banks, to beautify.. a variety of sequestrate spots.

sequestrate (sɪˈkwɛstreɪt, ˈsiː-), *v.* Also 6–7 *Sc.* sequestrat. [f. late L. *sequestrāt-*, ppl. stem of *sequestrāre*: see SEQUESTER *v.* and -ATE[3].]

1. a. *trans.* To remove, put away; to seclude, keep away from general access or intercourse; to put in a place of concealment or confinement. = SEQUESTER *v.* 1. Now *rare.*

1513 DOUGLAS *Æneis* XI. iii. 76 Tuelf days of trewis thai band, to stanch debait, For to kepe pece and weris sequestrate. *c* **1555** HARPSFIELD *Divorce Hen. VIII* (1878) 199 A celestial spouse, from whom she shall never be sequestrated and divorced. **1582–8** *Hist. & Life Jas. VI* (1804) 54 We.. were compellit to sequestrat hir for a seasoun in preseoun. **1733** ARBUTHNOT *Ess. Effects Air* vii. 192 In general Contagions, more perish for want of Care and Necessaries, than by the Malignity of the Disease; they being, as it were, sequestrated from Mankind. **1831** SCOTT *Ct. Robt.* xxvi, My purpose went no farther than to sequestrate Alexius for a little time from the fatigues of empire. **1840** DE QUINCEY *Essenes* (1887) 260 A sect sequestrating themselves and locking up their doctrines as secrets.

b. *Physiol.* To render (a biochemical compound) metabolically unavailable without destroying it; to remove from the circulation.

1961 *Lancet* 29 July 258/1 The placenta, like the liver, can sequestrate and degrade insulin. **1977** *Proc. R. Soc. Med.* LXX. 521/1 They suggested that the increased titres might be due to failure of the cirrhotic liver to sequestrate gut-derived antigens, which then reached immunologically competent areas of the body.

2. *Law.* **a.** To divert the income of an estate or benefice, temporarily or permanently, from its owner into other hands. Cf. SEQUESTER *v.* 3.

1609 SKENE *Reg. Maj.* 63 Gif the patronage of anie kirk is sequestrat in the Kings hands, be reason of the contumacie of the patron [etc.]. **1804** WELLINGTON in Gurw. *Desp.* (1837) III. 26 It appears that half the revenue of the office.. has been lately sequestrated. **1839** W. O. MANNING *Law Nat.* IV. v. (1875) 189 A right to sequestrate the taxes. **1871** SMILES *Charac.* viii. (1876) 217 When.. all his worldly estate had been sequestrated.

b. = SEQUESTER *v.* 3 c. *Obs.* exc. *Hist.*

1546 J. HEYWOOD *Prov.* (1867) 14, I shall.. seperate All matters on both sydes, and than sequestrate Thone syde. **1650** W. DUNDAS *Let. to Cromwell* 9 Sept., When Ministers of the Gospel have been.. sequestrated.

†**c.** = SEQUESTER *v.* 3 b. *Obs.*

1656 BLOUNT *Glossogr.* **1761** HUME *Hist. Eng.* (1806) III. xlix. 778 To compromise all differences, it was agreed to sequestrate it [a fortress] into the hands of the infanta as a neutral person.

d. *Scots Law.* (*a*) To place (lands, belonging to a bankrupt, or of disputed ownership) in the hands of a judicial factor or trustee, for the prevention of waste, or in order that the income arising may be applied for the benefit of the creditors. (*b*) In modern use: To place (the property of a bankrupt) in the hands of a trustee to be divided among the creditors; hence *popularly*, to make (a person) bankrupt.

1726 [see SEQUESTRATED]. **1818** SCOTT *Hrt. Midl.* viii, The Deanses at Woodend!—I sequestrated them in the dear years, and now they are to flit, they'll starve. **1838** W. BELL *Dict. Law Scot.* s.v. *Sequestration*, The Court may, if they think proper, sequestrate the rents, and appoint a judicial factor. **1909** A. H. MILLAR *Forf. Estates Papers* (S.H.S.) Introd. 15 The creditors sequestrated many of the estates.

†**e.** *intr.* or *absol.* To perform an act of sequestration. *Obs. rare*[−1].

1765–8 ERSKINE *Inst. Law Scot.* II. xii. §56 The debtor's consent to sequestrate. **1818** SCOTT *Hrt. Midl.* i, Landlord sequestrates—creditors accept a composition.

3. *trans.* To confiscate. = SEQUESTER *v.* 2.

1640–1 *Kirkcudbr. Comm. Min. Bk.* (1855) 157 The whole goodes, geir, cornes, cattle, rentes and uthers perteining to thame, and now to the publict, are sequestrate and appryset to the use of the public. **1844** H. H. WILSON *Brit. India* II. 447 He did not long enjoy this accession to his resources, being shot as he sat in his court by a chief, whose Jagir he had sequestrated. **1860** MOTLEY *Netherl.* (1868) II. xv. 224 They found it convenient.. to sequestrate for their own private uses the property of the Catholic Church.

Hence **se'questrated** *ppl. a.*, in senses of the verb; also *rarely* † = SEQUESTERED.

1726 *Index Acts of Sederunt* s.v. *Factors*, That Factors upon sequestrated Estates, shall make and produce Rentals of the Estate. **1823** SCOTT *Quentin D.* Introd. *note*, An ancient sequestrated garden. **1865** *Good Words* VI. 143 Auctions and sales of sequestrated furniture.

sequestration (siːkwɛˈstreɪʃən). Forms: 4–5 sequestracoun, 5 sequestracyo(u)n, 5–6 sequestracion, 6 sequestratioun, 6– sequestration. [ad. late L. *sequestrātiōn-em*, f. L. *sequestrāre*: see SEQUESTER *v.* Cf. OF. *sequestration*, Sp. *secuestracion*, Pg. *sequestração*, It. *sequestrazione.*]

1. a. An act or the action of sequestering, banishment, exile; esp. *Eccl.*, a cutting off from the privileges of Church-membership, excommunication.

c **1400** *Apol. Loll.* 20 How þat we spek of curse oiþer it þat is dedly,.. or it þat is sequestracoun of þe iust man fro comyn. *a* **1450** in MYRC *Par. Pr.* (1902) 63 Alle þat brekuth or lettuth sequestracion of any prelatys, wit-oute here leue. **1581** BELL *Haddon's Answ. Osor.* 357 Ἀφορισμὸς. Sequestration. Whereby all offendours whatsoever, were excluded from the Sacraments. **1663** *Aron-bimnucha* 2 The gall and worm-wood of his exile, was, his sequestration from the Ark, the holy Ordinances and worship of his God. **1854** MILMAN *Lat. Chr.* III. vi. (1864) II. 89 The punishment of delinquents was sequestration from the oratory, the table, and the common meetings. **1898** *Syd. Soc. Lex.*, *Sequestration*,.. seclusion of infected persons or of lunatics.

b. *transf.* Separation, disjunction.

1567 FENTON *Trag. Disc.* ii. (1898) I. 112 The fatall sequestracion of our sowle and bodye. **1604** SHAKS. *Oth.* I. iii. 351 It was a violent Commencement in her, and thou shalt see an answerable Sequestration. **1666** BOYLE *Orig. Formes & Qual.* 266 This Antimony seem'd to have been a little refin'd by the sequestration of its unnecessary Sulphur. **1842** MRS. BROWNING *Grk. Chr. Poets* (1863) 177 Protesting .. against the sequestration of pauses.

†**c.** Setting apart, consecration. *Obs. rare.*

1654 WHITLOCK *Zootomia* 58 Professions, Sequestred by God, (and in that Sequestration confirmed by Policy,) for the good of Mankind. **1681** FLAVEL *Meth. Grace* xvi. 301 This blood.. was prepared by his voluntary sequestration, or sanctification of himself to this very use or purpose.

2. A state of being sequestered, separation, seclusion, retirement.

1565 in Strype *Ann. Ref.* (1709) I. xlvii. 476 To have some greater Restraint put upon the Lady Lenox and some harder Sequestration than she now hath. **1599** SHAKS. *Hen. V*, I. i. 58 And neuer noted in him any studie, Any retyrement, any sequestration, From open Haunts and Popularitie. **1628** FELTHAM *Resolves* I. xciv. 274 It is no other, but a place of retyring, and sequestration from the World. **1648–99** J. BEAUMONT *Psyche* XXIII. clxxvi. (1702) 354 Her Phylax tir'd with his long Sequestration From his dear Charge. **1791** BURKE *Corr.* (1844) III. 213 You observe that a sequestration from the connexions of society, makes the heart cold and unfeeling. **1835** WORDSW. *Death Charles Lamb* 121 O gift divine of quiet sequestration! **1863** COWDEN CLARKE *Shaks. Char.* xiv. 350 [She] had shown her enduring consciousness of the injuries she had sustained, by a sixteen years' sequestration of herself from his side.

fig. **1647** FULLER *Good Th. in Worse T.* To Rdr., I earnestly desire that in heaven both thou and I may ever bee under Sequestration in that Mediator for Gods glory.

3. *Law.* **a.** The appropriation of the income of a property in order to satisfy claims against the owner; esp. *Eccl.*, a writ diverting the income of a benefice to the advantage of the creditors of the incumbent.

1565 *Reg. Privy Council Scot.* I. 432 Arreistment and sequestratioun of the money foirsaid. *a* **1704** T. BROWN *Two Oxf. Scholars* Wks. 1730 I. 7 The Churchwardens tell me, that they have a sequestration upon my living.

b. *Eccl.* (See quot. 1641.)

1575–6 *Act 18 Eliz.* c. 11 §5 The Ordinary.. shall grante the Sequestracion of suche Proffites to suche Inhabitante.. w[th]in the Parrishe. **1641** *Termes de la Ley* 246 Sequestration .. is used also for the gathering of fruits and profits of a benefice voyd, unto the use of the next Incumbent. **1712** PRIDEAUX *Direct. Ch.-wardens* (ed. 4) 102 On a Suspension there must be a Sequestration for the serving of the Cure. **1827** HALLAM *Const. Hist.* iv. (1876) I. 180 They were in consequence suspended from their ministry, and their livings put in sequestration.

c. An order of court appointing the goods of a deceased person whose executor or executors have renounced probate, to be secured and administered; also, a writ of Chancery empowering commissioners or a sheriff to seize the property of the person against whom it is directed.

1591 *Wills & Inv. N.C.* (Surtees 1860) II. 199 For probate bondes and regestring 16s. 4d. For relapsinge of the sequestration 5s. 2d. **1641** *Termes de la Ley* 246 Sequestration.. is used also for the act of an Ordinary, when no man will medle with the goods and chattels of one deceased. **1768** BLACKSTONE *Comm.* III. xxvii. 444 If he eludes the search of the serjeant also, then a sequestration issues to seise all his personal estate, and the profits of his real. **1818** CRUISE *Digest* (ed. 2) II. 102 Sir John.. stood out all process of contempt to a sequestration. **1884** [see SEQUESTRATOR].

†**d.** The separation of a matter of controversy from the contending parties and its reference to an umpire or arbitrator. *Obs.*

1592 WEST *1st Pt. Symbol.* §17 A, The keeping of a thing litigious is called Sequestration, which is therefore defined, the deposition of a thing in controuersie.

e. Seizure of the possessions of a subject by the state; esp. the act of a belligerent power in seizing debts owing from its own subjects to the opposing power.

1568 tr. *Gonsalvio's Sp. Inquis.* 41b, They made Sequestration of the ship and goods, and caried the child to prison with the rest of his company. **1654** *(title)* An Ordinance for the better ordering and disposing the Estates under Sequestration. **1660** *(title)* An Act for Repeal of two Acts for Sequestrations. **1762–71** H. WALPOLE *Vertue's Anecd. Paint.* (1786) II. 279 He paid 545*l.* for his delinquency and sequestration. **1823** SCOTT *Peveril* i, His former delinquencies.. were severely punished by fine and sequestration. **1903** MORLEY *Gladstone* VIII. i. (1905) II. 248 The Cabinet.. considered the sequestration of the customs' dues at Smyrna to be practicable.

f. *Scots Law.* (See SEQUESTRATE *v.* 2 d.) *(a)* The placing of lands (belonging to a bankrupt, or of disputed ownership) under the control of a judicial factor or trustee. *(b)* In modern use: The placing of a bankrupt's estate in the hands of a trustee for division among the creditors.

1765–8 ERSKINE *Inst. Law Scot.* II. xii. §55 Sequestration of lands.. is a judicial act of the court of session, whereby the management of the subject sequestered is taken from the former possessor, and intrusted to the care of a factor or steward named by the court. **1838** W. BELL *Dict. Law Scot.* s.v. *Sequestration,* A petition praying for the sequestration of a land estate. **1870** *Standard* 16 Nov., The plaintiff, as the assignee of the Rev. J. Storie, who had become insolvent, brought this action to recover the total sum which had been paid to the defendant during the existence of the sequestration.

4. Seizure, confiscation.

1640 in Rymer *Fœdera* (1735) XX. 429 We.. have accordingly.. commanded our said Secretary to see the Sequestration [of the Office of Postmaster for foreign Parts, etc.] put in speedy Execution. **1694** *Milton's Lett. of State* 316 Upon this News, Antony and Manuel.. presently look'd upon the Goods as their own,.. covering this Fraud of theirs with a Sequestration of English Goods that soon after ensu'd. **1895** R. OLNEY in *Curr. Hist.* V. 197 To resent and to resist any sequestration of Venezuelan soil by Great Britain.

5. *Path.* (See quot.)

1898 *Syd. Soc. Lex.*, *Sequestration,* formation of a Sequestrum.

6. *Chem.* The action or state of being sequestered (sense 5).

1948 *Jrnl. Chem. Education* XXV. 483/1 In sequestration, the multivalent positive ion has practically disappeared from the solution without being evolved as a gas, removed as a precipitate or deposited as an element. **1959** R. L. SMITH *Sequestration of Metals* iii. 26 Sequestration is most usually achieved by chelation, even although chelation itself covers many phenomena which would not be considered sequestration. **1973** D. F. LONG tr. *Degrémont's Water Treatm. Handbk.* (ed. 4) ix. 293 The total sequestration of calcium requires about 50g of polyphosphate per degree TH.

7. *attrib.*

1648 *(title)* An additional Ordinance of Parliament for the better regulating and speedy bringing in the Sequestration Monies out of the Estates of Papists and Delinquents. **1816** G. J. BELL *Comm. Laws Scot.* (1826) II. 313 The proper manufacturing of the rude materials into a commodity, brings a person within the reach of the Sequestration Act. *Ibid.*, The provision which extends the Sequestration Law to manufacturers.

sequestrator ('siːkwɛstreɪtə(r)). [a. late L. *sequestrātor*, agent-n. f. L. *sequestrāre*: see SEQUESTRATE *v.*] One who sequestrates; a trustee or bailiff having control of property upon which there are claims by creditors. Also, a person named in a writ of sequestration as authorized to collect and administer the income of a sequestrated estate.

1646 T. EDWARDS *Gangrena* I. 62 Sequestratours, Collectours, Receivers. *a* **1658** CLEVELAND *Cl. Vind.* (1677) 99 The Committee-man hath a Side-man, or rather a Setter, hight a Sequestrator... He is the States Cormorant. *a* **1689** MRS. BEHN tr. *Cowley's Plants* VI. C.'s Wks. 1721 III. 453 The Warriour may a while his Spear forsake, But Sequestrators will no Respit take. **1712** PRIDEAUX *Direct. Ch.-wardens* (ed. 4) 102 The.. Church-wardens, or other Sequestrators, are to Account to him for.. the Profits. **1849** MACAULAY *Hist. Eng.* ii. I. 188 The Puritan, a conqueror, a ruler, a persecutor, a sequestrator, had been detested. **1884** CAVE in *Law Times Rep.* LI. 661/1 Persons who were named as sequestrators in a writ of sequestration against B.

b. *fig.* One who sets apart, a separator.

1654 WHITLOCK *Zootomia* 381 Even that first and worst Sequestratour, that sequestred man from his God, and so from his Happinesse.

†**seque'stratrix.** *Obs. rare*⁻¹. [a. L. **sequestrātrix*, fem. of *sequestrātor* SEQUESTRATOR.] A female sequestrator.

1657 H. PINNELL tr. *Paracelsus' Three Bks. Philos.* 9 Separation.. is the sequestratrix that gives to every thing its form and essence.

sequestrectomy (sɪkwɛ'strɛktəmɪ). *Surg.* [f. SEQUESTR(UM + -ECTOMY.] The surgical excision of a sequestrum or sequestra; = SEQUESTROTOMY.

1940 in *Chambers's Techn. Dict.* 759/1. **1954** E. L. FARQUHARSON *Textbk. Operative Surg.* v. 136 Sequestrectomy.—Small loose sequestra may be discovered only during an operation to improve drainage, and are then removed as part of the operation. **1963** R. WARREN *Surgery* xxxi. 1071/2 Sequestrectomy. Removal of sequestrum (or dead bone) is done primarily for osteomyelitis.

†**seque'stree.** *Obs.* [f. SEQUESTER *v.* + -EE.] = SEQUESTRATOR.

1611 COTGR., *Gardien de biens*, a Sequestree, or keeper of the goods of an indebted, or condemned person, seised by order of Law. **1765–8** ERSKINE *Inst. Law Scot.* III. i. §30 In which case a salary to the sequestree for his trouble is either expressed or implied. **1845** SARAH AUSTIN *Ranke's Hist. Ref.* III. 309 The elector of Saxony.. offered to place all the suppressed convents under sequestration; the sequestrees.. were to pledge themselves to the emperor to allow nothing to be abstracted from the property, till a council should decide on its application.

Sequestrene (sɪ'kwɛstriːn). Also **sequestrene.** [f. SEQUESTR(ATION + -ENE.] A proprietary term for preparations of ethylenediamine tetra-acetic acid and its salts used as sequestering agents; *spec.* one containing sequestered iron for use on iron-deficient soils.

1949 *Official Gaz.* (U.S. Patent Office) 8 Feb. 320/2 Alrose Chemical Co., Inc., Cranston, R.I... *Alro Sequestrene...* Claims use since Jan. 16, 1948. **1949** *Agric. Chemicals* IV. IV. 73/2 'Sequestrene', unlike the polyphospates, is compatible with cationic surface-active agents. **1951** *Proc. Soc. Exper. Biol. & Med.* LXXVI. 619/1 Four Sequestrenes are available at present, Sequestrene AA (the free acid), SNA 2 (di-sodium salt), SNA 3 (trisodium salt) and SNA 4 (tetrasodium salt). **1958** *Times* 4 Oct. 9/5 The green leaves become pale and chlorotic. There may be several reasons for this condition but nearly always application of sequestrene compound.. will effect a quick.. cure. **1965** *Listener* 1 July 25/3 Sequestrenes.. are now widely sold for application to plants suffering from an iron deficiency. **1977** *Vole* No. 1. 34/3 Rugosas.. may need sequestrene if there is an excess of lime.

sequestrotomy (siːkwɛ'strɒtəmɪ). *Surg.* [f. SEQUESTR-UM + Gr. -τομία a cutting.] The operation for the removal of a sequestrum.

1876 DUNGLISON *Med. Lex.*, *Sequestrotomy*, a hybrid term for the operation for necrosis. **1898** *Syd. Soc. Lex.*

‖**sequestrum** (sɪ'kwɛstrəm). *Path.* Pl. **sequestra.** [mod.L. use of L. *sequestrum* something separated, neut. of *sequester* adj.: see SEQUESTER *sb.*] A detached piece of bone lying within a cavity formed by necrosis. Also applied to a portion of skin separated by disease from the surrounding parts. Cf. SEQUESTER *sb.*² 3.

1831 SOUTH *Otto's Path. Anat.* II. 146 One or several holes ..which.. produce an outlet for the continually absorbed and diminished sequestrum. **1859** J. TOMES *Dental Surg.* 74 The teeth, whether permanent or temporary, implanted in the sequestrum, are usually lost. **1899** *Allbutt's Syst. Med.* VI. 584 A zone of ulceration, which leads to the gradual separation of a sequestrum of skin.

attrib. **1891** *Century Dict.*, Sequestrum forceps. **1895** *Catal. Surg. Instr.* 38.

sequill, obs. form of SEQUEL.

sequin ('siːkwɪn), *sb.* Also 8 **zequin.** See also CHEQUEEN, ZECCHIN. [a. F. *sequin*, ad. It. *zecchino*, f. *zecca* the mint (= Sp. *seca*), ad. Arab. *sikkaʰ* die for coining, whence SICCA¹.]

1. *Hist.* An Italian gold coin (originally Venetian); for its value, see quot. 1788. Also used as a name for a former Turkish coin, the sultanin.

1617 MORYSON *Itin.* I. 292 At Naples.. ten quatrines make one sequin. **1677** tr. *Tavernier's Grand Seignior's Seraglio* 14 The Scherif, otherwise called Sequin, or Sultanine. *a* **1701** MAUNDRELL *Journ. Jerus.* 6 Apr. (1810) 136 For which they pay the Turks a rent of one zequin a day. **1788** JEFFERSON *Writ.* (1859) II. 464 The government of Algiers demands of France sixty thousand sequins, or twenty-seven thousand pounds sterling. **1820** SHELLEY *Let.* Pr. Wks. (1888) II. 316, I bought the vases you saw for about twenty sequins less than Micale asked. **1870** DISRAELI *Lothair* lxxii, Velvet bags, one full of pearls, another of rubies, others of Venetian sequins. **1883** STEVENSON *Treas. Isl.* xxxiv, Moidores and sequins [etc.].

2. A small spangle used in the ornamentation of dresses, etc.

1882 *Daily News* 3 June 3/1 Never before, probably, have dress trimmings been more artistic than they are now. Sequins are the newest. **1891** *Leeds Merc.* 27 Apr. 4/7 The ..sleeves studded thickly over with tiny glittering silver sequins. **1909** 'VERNON LEE' in *Eng. Rev.* Feb. 454 Slave girls with stuff of striped silver about their loins and sequins at the end of their long hair.

3. *attrib.* and *Comb.*: (sense 1) ***sequin gold***; (sense 2) ***sequin-sewn, -weighted*** adjs.; †**sequin-hazard** = CHICKEN-HAZARD.

1837 DISRAELI *Venetia* v. viii, The gilding, although of two hundred years' duration, as bright.. [etc.]: *Sequin gold, as the Venetians tell you. **1825** T. HOOK *Sayings* Ser. II. *Man of Many Fr.* II. 8 If any body had a desire for a little *sequin hazard, there *were* such things as dice at hand. **1896** *Westm. Gaz.* 28 May 3/1 To much manipulate or trim embroidered and *sequin sewn fabrics were to defeat their charm. **1904** *Ibid.* 7 Jan. 3/2 An evening frock of black chiffon with wide insertion of *sequin-weighted lace.

sequin ('siːkwɪn), *v.* [f. SEQUIN *sb.*] *trans.* To ornament with sequins. Hence **'sequined** *ppl. a.* Also *fig.*

1894 *Daily News* 5 June 6/4 Sequinned net. *Ibid.* 22 June 6/7 The gold bonnet was sequinned in pink and green. **1905** MRS. C. N. WILLIAMSON *Castle of Shadows* v. 110 A tall woman in sequined black tulle. **1918** E. SITWELL *Clown's Houses* 8 Beside the sea, metallic-bright And sequined with the noisy light. **1969** 'E. LATHEN' *When in Greece* xiii. 140 The sea spread a sequined carpet.. below.

‖**sequitur** ('sɛkwɪtə(r)). [L. = it follows.] An inference or conclusion which follows from the premisses. Cf. NON SEQUITUR.

1836 J. M. GULLY *Magendie's Formul.* (ed. 2) 184 *note*, I do not see the sequitur in this sentence. **1837** BARHAM *Ingol. Leg., Spectre Tapp.*, Mr. Maguire.. looked as if he did not quite subscribe to the *sequitur*. **1863** COWDEN CLARKE *Shaks. Char.* ii. 57 What a reason to give for his being in a state of perdition!..—what a 'sequitur'!

Sequoia (sɪ'kwəʊɪə, sɪ'kwɔɪə). [mod.Latin (Endlicher, 1847); after *Sequoiah*, a Cherokee, who invented a syllabary for writing his native language.] A genus of large American coniferous trees belonging to the *Abietinæ*; a tree of this genus. Cf. REDWOOD *sb.* 2. Popularly often called *Wellingtonia*, the name given by Lindley, 1853.

1866 *Treas. Bot.*, *Sequoia* (including *Wellingtonia*). A genus of the Abietinæ tribe of *Coniferæ* from North-western America, closely allied to *Sciadopitys*. **1870** EMERSON *Soc. & Solit.*, *Farming* Wks. (Bohn) III. 60 The mammoth Sequoias rose to their enormous proportions. **1878** J. E. TAYLOR *Flowers* 61 The *Sequoias* (better known as *Wellingtonias*) of which there are now only two species. **1890** W. J. GORDON *Foundry* 123 There is the 'curly redwood', due to the sequoia taking a twist when young.

sequyle, obs. north. form of SEQUEL.